ENCYCLOPÆDIA BRITANNICA

The Encyclopædia Britannica
is published with the editorial advice and consultation
of the faculties of The University of Chicago
and of a committee of members of the faculties of Oxford, Cambridge
and London universities

*

"LET KNOWLEDGE GROW FROM MORE TO MORE
AND THUS BE HUMAN LIFE ENRICHED."

ENCYCLOPÆDIA BRITANNICA

A New Survey of Universal Knowledge

Volume 5

CAST-IRON to COLE

WILLIAM BENTON, Publisher

ENCYCLOPÆDIA BRITANNICA, INC.

CHICAGO · LONDON · TORONTO

FHB

PRINTED IN THE U.S.A.

FOUNDED  A.D. 1768

ENCYCLOPÆDIA BRITANNICA

Volume 5

CAST-IRON to COLE

CAST-IRON. It is said that cast-iron was first made in Sussex as early as the year 1350, but it was not until the end of the Tudor period that the practice of iron-founding was introduced into England from the continent of Europe where it had already been considerably developed. Although cast-iron and pig-iron have the same chemical composition, the expression cast-iron is generally applied to pig-iron which has been remelted in a crucible, or furnace, and cast into moulds.

Classification.—Cold- and hot-blast irons (*see* PIG-IRON) are divided, according to their content in phosphorus, into two main groups: (a) Hematite, and (b) Basic irons. The former contain only small percentages of this element, about .07%, while in the latter the phosphorus may reach as much as 3%. Each of these main groups is again subdivided into at least six grades, Nos. 1, 2, 3, foundry, forge and white irons. In passing along the series from "No. 1" to "white" the percentages of silicon and manganese gradually decrease, while those of combined carbon and sulphur increase. Hence it is possible, by mixing irons from different groups, to obtain cast-iron of almost any desired composition, due allowance being made for the changes which occur during remelting. Iron may be classified also according to (a) the method of manufacture; (b) the purpose for which it is intended; and (c) its composition. It was formerly graded by breaking the pig and examining the fracture, but this method has been largely superseded by chemical analysis.

(a) Method of Manufacture: (1) Coke Pig is smelted with coke; always with hot blast. (2) Charcoal Pig is smelted with charcoal, by hot or cold blast.

(b) Purpose for Which Intended: (3) Bessemer Pig. (4) Basic Open Hearth Pig. (5) Malleable Pig, for malleable cast-iron castings. (6) Foundry Pig. (7) Forge Pig is an inferior grade used for puddling and for some classes of foundry work.

(c) Chemical Composition: (8) Silicon Pig or High Silicon Pig. (9) Low Phosphorus Pig. (10) Special Low Phosphorus Pig. (11) Ferro-Alloys and Special Cast Irons (*e.g.*, ferro-manganese).

When pig-iron is melted under conditions which permit of the oxidation of the silicon, as in the cupola and reverberatory furnace, an iron which presents a greyish fracture when broken, and is quite soft and easy to machine, will, on continued remelting, ultimately become white and intensely hard. Conversely, by melting white iron with increasing quantities of siliceous pig-iron it is possible to convert the white into grey iron. These differences in appearance arise from changes in the condition of the carbon. Cast-iron contains upwards of 3.5% carbon, which in very grey iron is almost wholly in the graphitic state; this condition arises from the presence of large amounts of silicon, an element which has the property of decomposing carbide of iron (Fe_3C) into its constituents, iron and carbon. As the silicon is oxidized by remelting, more and more of the carbon combines with the iron, until ultimately, in white iron, carbon in the form of graphite is entirely absent. Manganese also is oxidized during remelting, while sulphur on the other hand is absorbed from the fuel.

Grades Commonly Used.—The following are examples of the grades in common use: for thin ornamental work, such as grates, stoves, hollow ware and other light castings, where in order to fill the mould great fluidity is required, a mixture of irons containing from 2.5% to 2.8% silicon and from 1.3% to 1.5% phosphorus is in common use; but in medium-sized castings and general work, where somewhat greater strength is required, iron containing a greater percentage of combined carbon and a reduced silicon content is necessary; and as strength rather than extreme fluidity is the main consideration, the phosphorus also may be reduced. For use in this connection, irons containing silicon from 2% to 2.25% and phosphorus from 1% to 1.3% are suitable. Where still greater strength is required, as in machinery castings, phosphorus and silicon are still further reduced, and a mixture of irons yielding an average content in silicon and phosphorus respectively of 1.15% to 1.2% and 0.4% to 0.6% is employed. In cases where castings have to resist wear, and have at the same time to machine with a highly polished surface, a very close grained iron is necessary, this condition being provided by an admixture of refined and cold-blast irons with an average silicon content of from 1% to 1.3%, and about 0.45% to 0.70% phosphorus. So far, only castings of the same physical properties throughout have been considered; for some classes of work, however, such as rolls used in the sheet metal industries and some types of car wheels, it is necessary to have an intensely hard surface and a soft interior in one and the same casting. This is obtained by taking advantage of the fact that given a suitable grade of iron, it is possible by rapid cooling to retain the carbon in the outside portion of the casting in the combined condition. This process is known as "chill casting" and the parts of the mould where the metal is to be hardened are made of iron instead of sand, so that, when the molten metal comes in contact with them heat is so rapidly extracted from it that the separation of graphite is prevented, and the carbon retained in the combined condition; while towards the centre of the casting, where the rate of cooling is not so rapid, decomposition of the cementite can take place, and in consequence the iron in this region is quite soft. In this class of work the selection of the pig-iron is of the greatest importance, slight differences in composition having very marked influences on the depth to which the hardening effect penetrates. Iron for chill casting should be low in phosphorus, and silicon also should not be too high, or the carbon will not remain in combination. About 1·5% of silicon is probably best, but opinion is not unanimous on this point.

Malleable Cast-Iron.—Ordinary cast-iron is melted readily and easily cast into any desired shape, but it has the disadvantage that castings so made are relatively weak and brittle. It is possible, however, by making use of the facility with which carbide of iron can be split up into its constituents, to make castings which are stronger than ordinary cast-iron ones, and yet possess a considerable degree of ductility, almost approaching wrought-iron in this respect, though unlike forgings of the latter metal they cannot be welded, except by the "bronze rod" process, and at a temperature below the melting point of iron. Castings made in this way are called "malleable cast-iron castings," or shortly "malleable castings." The process has been in use for many years, having been described by Reaumur in 1722. For the production of castings by this method a refined hematite pig-iron is used containing from 2·5% to 3·0% carbon and from 0·5% to 1·0% silicon (the lower figure for large, and the higher one for small castings), and having as little as possible of sulphur, phosphorus, and manganese. Sulphur is supposed to promote the formation of blow-holes, but it has been found that 0·25% may be present without ill effect. Silicon and manganese prevent the castings being converted; while an excess of phosphorus causes brittleness in the finished casting. The castings, when removed from the moulds, are extremely brittle, on account of the nature of the pig-iron used, and when broken present a white fracture; they are packed in boxes containing red hematite ore and then annealed for a period of four or five days at a temperature of 800° to 900° C. After this treatment they present a grey fracture and can be readily dressed with a file or chisel; they will also admit of a considerable amount of deformation without fracture. The process described is the one followed in Europe. In America, where the decomposition of the carbide of iron, not the direct oxidation of the carbon, is regarded as the chief essential in the process of conversion, the annealing of the castings is carried out in a slightly different manner. They are packed in boxes containing sand or clay with or without admixture of oxide, and annealed at a temperature rather lower than that used in European practice, viz., 700° to 800° C. By either method a malleable casting is obtained, but the products of each when broken present a very different appearance and are designated "white heart" and "black heart" castings respectively, terms which explain themselves.

Since about 1850 the use of cast-iron for structural purposes has been gradually superseded by steel, but so many other applications have been found for it, that it is still in considerable demand, as it is the cheapest form of commercial iron. Its tensile strength, though considerably less than that of steel, is ample for many purposes, while in compression its strength is greater than that of any other known metal.

See E. L. Rhead *The Principles and Practice of Ironfounding* (Manchester, 1910); T. Turner *The Metallurgy of Iron* (5th ed. 1918); W. H. Hatfield *Cast-iron in the Light of Recent Research* (2nd ed. 1918); H. A. Schwartz *American Malleable Cast Iron;* Richard Moldenke *The Principles of Iron Founding.* (T. BA.)

CASTLE, a small self-contained fortress, usually of the middle ages, though the term is sometimes used of prehistoric earthworks (*e.g.*, Hollingbury castle, Maiden castle), and sometimes of citadels (*e.g.*, the castles of Badajoz and Burgos) and small detached *forts d'arrêt* in modern times. It is also often applied to the principal mansion of a prince or nobleman, and in France (as *château*) to any country seat. Under its twofold aspect of a fortress and a residence, the mediaeval castle is inseparably connected with the subjects of fortification (*see* FORTIFICATION AND SIEGECRAFT) and architecture. For an account of Roman and pre-Roman *castella* in Britain *see* BRITAIN.

Mediaeval Castles.—The word "castle" (*castel*) was introduced into English shortly before the Norman Conquest to denote a type of fortress, then new to the country, brought in by the Norman knights summoned by Edward the Confessor to defend Herefordshire against the inroads of the Welsh. The essential feature of this type was a circular mound of earth surrounded by a dry ditch and flattened at the top. Around the crest of its summit was placed a timber palisade. This moated mound was styled in French *motte* (latinized *mota*). It is clearly depicted in the Bayeux tapestry, and was then familiar on the mainland of western Europe. A description of this earlier castle is given in the life of John, bishop of Terouanne (*Acta Sanctorum,* quoted by G. T. Clark, *Mediaeval Military Architecture*):—"The rich and the noble of that region being much given to feuds and bloodshed, fortify themselves . . . and by these strongholds subdue their equals and oppress their inferiors. They heap up a mound as high as they are able, and dig round it as broad a ditch as they can. . . . Round the summit of the mound they construct a palisade of timber to act as a wall. . . . Inside the palisade they erect a house, or rather a citadel, which looks down on the whole of the neighbourhood." St. John, bishop of Terouanne, died in 1130, but this castle of Merchem may be taken as typical of the practice of the 11th century. In addition to the mound, the citadel of the fortress, there was often appended to it a bailey or basecourt (*see* BAILEY), and sometimes two, of semilunar or horseshoe shape, so that the mound stood *à cheval* on the line of the enceinte. The rapidity and ease with which it was possible to construct castles of this type made them characteristic of the Conquest period in England. In later days a stone wall replaced the timber palisade and produced what is known as the shell-keep, as in the castles of Berkeley, Alnwick and Windsor.

The Normans introduced also two other types of castle, the one where they found a natural rock stronghold which only needed adaptation, as at Clifford, Ludlow, the Peak and Exeter, to produce a citadel; the other a wholly distinct type, the high rectangular tower of masonry, of which the Tower of London is the best-known example. This type belongs rather to the more settled conditions of the 12th century when speed was not a necessity, and in the first half of which the fine extant keeps of Hedingham and Rochester were erected. These towers were originally surrounded by palisades, usually on earthen ramparts, which were replaced later by stone walls. The whole fortress thus formed was styled a castle, but sometimes more precisely "tower and castle," the former being the citadel, and the latter the walled enclosure, thus preserving the meaning of the Roman *castellum.* Reliance was placed by the engineers of that time simply on the inherent strength of the structure, the walls of which defied the battering-ram, and could only be undermined at the cost of much time and labour, while the narrow apertures were constructed to exclude arrows or flaming brands.

Influence of the Crusades.—At this stage the crusades, and the consequent opportunities afforded to western engineers of studying the solid fortresses of the Byzantine empire, revolutionized the art of castle-building, which henceforward follows recognized principles. Many castles were built in the Holy Land by the crusaders of the 12th century, and it has been shown (Oman, *Art of War: the Middle Ages,* p. 529), that the designers realized, first, that a second line of defences should be built within the main enceinte, and a third line or keep inside the second line; and secondly, that a wall must be flanked by projecting towers. From the Byzantine engineers, through the crusaders, we derive, therefore, the cardinal principle of the mutual defence of all the parts of a fortress. The *donjon* of western Europe was regarded as the fortress, the outer walls as accessory defences; in the East each envelope was a fortress in itself, and the keep became merely the

KREMLIN, MOSCOW — CHATEAU OF COUCY — HELLENSTEIN, NEAR HEIDENHEIM — PLAN OF BERKELEY CASTLE, LATE NORMAN PERIOD — KRAK-DES-CHEVALIERS: PLAN — CHATEAU OF PIERREFONDS — WARWICK CASTLE — CHATEAU GAILLARD — CAERPHILLY CASTLE: PLAN — CASTLE OF ROOZENDAEL — CHATEAU DE MONTARGIS: PLAN

CHATEAUX OF COUCY, PIERREFONDS, GAILLARD, AND DE MONTARGIS FROM VIOLLET-LE-DUC, "DICTIONNAIRE RAISONNE DE L'ARCHITECTURE FRANÇAISE"; WARWICK CASTLE, BY COURTESY OF THE G. W. RAILWAY

last refuge of the garrison. Indeed, the keep, in several crusader castles, is no more than a tower, larger than the rest, built into the enceinte and serving for its flanking defence, while the fortress was made strongest on the most exposed front. The idea of the flanking towers soon penetrated to Europe, and Alnwick castle (1140–50) shows the influence of the new system. The finest of all castles of the middle ages was Richard Coeur de Lion's Château Gaillard (1197) on the Seine near Les Andeleys. Here the innermost ward was protected by an elaborate system of strong defences, which included a *tête-de-pont* covering the Seine bridge. The castle stood upon high ground and consisted of three distinct enceintes or wards besides the keep, which was in this case merely a strong tower forming part of the innermost ward. Round instead of rectangular towers gradually became more usual, the finest examples of their employment as keeps being at Conisborough in England and at Coucy in France. Against the feeble siege artillery of the 13th century a well built fortress was almost proof, but the mines and the battering ram were more formidable, and it was realized that corners in the stonework of the fortress were more vulnerable than a uniform curved surface. Château Gaillard fell to Philip Augustus in 1204 after a strenuous defence, and the success of the assailants was largely due to the skilful employment of mines. An angle of the noble keep of Rochester was undermined and brought down by John in 1215.

The Concentric Plan.—The next development was the extension of the principle of successive lines of defence to form what is called the "concentric" castle, in which each ward was placed wholly within another which enveloped it; places thus built on a flat site (*e.g.*, Caerphilly castle) became for the first time more formidable than strongholds perched upon hills such as Château Gaillard, where, although the more exposed parts possessed many successive lines of defence, at other points, for want of room, it was impossible to build more than one or, at most, two walls. In these cases, the fall of the inner ward by surprise, escalade or regular siege (as was sometimes feasible), entailed the fall of the whole castle. The adoption of the concentric system precluded any such mischance, and thus, even though siege-engines improved during the 13th and 14th centuries, the defence maintained itself superior to attack during the latter middle ages. Its final fall was due to the introduction of gunpowder. "In the 14th century the change begins, in the 15th it is fully developed, in the 16th the feudal fastness has become an anachronism."

Decline of Baronial Fortifications.—The general adoption of cannon placed in the hands of the central power, a force which ruined the baronial fortifications. The possessors of cannon were usually private individuals of the middle classes, from whom the prince hired the *matériel* and the workmen. A typical case will be found in the history of Brandenburg and Prussia (Carlyle, *Frederick the Great,* bk. iii.; ch. i.), the castle of Friesack, held by an intractable feudal noble, Dietrich von Quitzow, being reduced in two days by the elector Frederick I. with "Heavy Peg" (*Faule Grete*) and other guns (Feb. 1414). In England, the earl of Warwick in 1464 reduced the strong fortress of Bamborough in a week, and in Germany, Franz von Sickingen's stronghold of Landstuhl, formerly impregnable on its heights, was ruined in one day by the artillery of Philip of Hesse (1523). Heavy artillery was used for such work, of course, and against lighter natures, some castles and even fortified country-houses managed to make a stout stand as late as the Great Rebellion in England.

The castle thus ceases to be the fortress of small and ill-governing local magnates, and its later history is merged in that of modern fortification. But an interesting transitional type between the mediaeval stronghold and the modern fortress is found in the coast castles erected by Henry VIII., especially those at Deal, Sandown and Walmer (*c.* 1540). Walmer castle is still the official residence of the lord warden of the Cinque Ports. Viollet-le-Duc, in his *Annals of a Fortress* (English trans.), gives a full and interesting account of the repeated renovations of the fortress on his imaginary site in the valley of the Doubs, the construction by Charles the Bold of artillery towers at the angles of the castle, the protection of the masonry by earthen outworks and boulevards and, in the 17th century, the final service of the mediaeval walls and towers as a pure *enceinte de sûreté.* Here and there we find old castles serving as *forts d'arrêt* or block-houses in mountain passes and in some few cases, as at Dover, they formed the nucleus of purely military places of arms, but normally the castle falls into ruins, becomes a peaceful mansion, or is merged in the fortifications of the town which has grown up around it. In the *Annals of a Fortress* the site of the feudal castle is occupied by the citadel of the walled town. The baronial "castle" assumes *pari passu* the form of a mansion, retaining indeed some capacity for defence, but in the end losing all military characteristics save a few which survived as ornaments. Examples of such castellated mansions are seen in Wingfield Manor, Derbyshire, and Hurstmonceaux, Sussex, created in the 15th century. Many older castles which survived were altered to serve as residences. (C. F. A.)

Castles in English History.—Such strongholds as existed in England at the time of the Norman Conquest seem to have offered but little resistance to William the Conqueror, who, in order effectually to guard against invasions from without as well as to awe his newly-acquired subjects, immediately began to erect castles all over the kingdom, and likewise to repair and augment the old ones. Besides, as he had parcelled out the lands of the English amongst his followers, they, to protect themselves from the resentment of the despoiled natives, built strongholds and castles on their estates, and these were multiplied so rapidly during the troubled reign of King Stephen that the "adulterine" (*i.e.,* unauthorized) castles are said by one writer to have amounted to 1,115.

In the first instance, when the interest of the king and of his barons was identical, the former had only retained in his hands the castles in the chief towns of the shires, which were entrusted to his sheriffs or constables. But the great feudal revolts under the Conqueror and his sons showed how formidable an obstacle to the rule of the king was the existence of such fortresses in private hands, while the people hated them from the first for the oppressions connected with their erection and maintenance. It was, therefore, the settled policy of the Crown to strengthen the royal castles and increase their number, while jealously keeping in check those of the barons. But in the struggle between Stephen and the empress Maud for the crown, which became largely a war of sieges, the royal power was relaxed and there was an outburst of castle-building by the barons. These in many cases acted as petty sovereigns, and such was their tyranny that the native chronicler describes the castles as "filled with devils and evil men." These excesses paved the way for the pacification at the close of the reign, when it was provided that all unauthorized castles constructed during its course should be destroyed. Henry II., in spite of his power, was warned by the great revolt against him that he must still rely on castles, and the massive keeps of Newcastle and of Dover date from this period.

Under his sons the importance of the chief castles was recognized as so great that the struggle for their control was in the forefront of every contest. When Richard made vast grants at his accession to his brother John, he was careful to reserve the possession of certain castles, and when John rose against the king's minister, Longchamp, in 1191, the custody of castles was the chief point of dispute throughout their negotiations, and Lincoln was besieged on the king's behalf, as were Tickhill, Windsor and Marlborough subsequently, while the siege of Nottingham had to be completed by Richard himself on his arrival. To John, in turn, as king, the fall of Château Gaillard meant the loss of Rouen and of Normandy with it, and when he endeavoured to repudiate the newly-granted Great Charter, his first step was to prepare the royal castles against attack and make them his centres of resistance. The barons, who had begun their revolt by besieging the castle of Northampton, now assailed that of Oxford and seized Rochester castle. The king recovered Rochester after a severe struggle and captured Tonbridge, but thenceforth there was a war of sieges between John with his mercenaries and Louis of France with his Frenchmen and the barons, which was especially notable for the great defence of Dover castle by Hubert de Burgh against Louis. On the final triumph of the royal cause, after John's death, at the battle of Lincoln, the general pacification was accompanied by a fresh issue of the Great Charter in the autumn of 1217, in which the precedent of Stephen's reign was followed and a special clause inserted that all "adulterine" castles, namely those which had been constructed or rebuilt since the breaking out of war between John and the barons, should be immediately destroyed. And special stress was laid on this in the writs addressed to the sheriffs.

In 1223 Hubert de Burgh, as regent, demanded the surrender to the Crown of all royal castles not in official custody, and though he succeeded in this, Falkes de Breauté, John's mercenary, burst into revolt next year, and it cost a great national effort and a siege of nearly two months to reduce Bedford castle, which he had held. In the Barons' War (*q.v.*) castles again asserted their importance. The Provisions of Oxford included a list of the chief royal castles and of their appointed castellans with the oath that they were to take; but the alien favourites refused to make way for them till they were forcibly ejected. When war broke out it was Rochester castle that successfully held Simon de Montfort at bay in 1264, and in Pevensey castle that the fugitives from the rout of Lewes were able to defy his power. Finally, after his fall at Evesham, it was in Kenilworth castle that the remnant of his followers made their last stand, holding out nearly five months against all the forces of the Crown, till their provisions failed them at the close of 1266.

Thus for two centuries after the Norman Conquest castles had proved of primary consequence in English political struggles, revolts and warfare. And, although, when the country was again torn by civil strife, their military importance was of small account, the crown's historic jealousy of private fortification was still seen in the need to obtain the king's licence to "crenellate" (*i.e.,* embattle) the country mansion.

Bibliography.—J. A. Deville, *Histoire du Château-Gaillard* (1829), *Château d'Argues* (1839); E. E. Viollet-le-Duc, *Dictionnaire raisonnée, s.v.* "Architecture" and "Château" (1854); *Essay on the Military*

PHOTOGRAPHS, (1, 4, 7) EWING GALLOWAY, (2) THE GERMAN TOURIST INFORMATION BUREAU, (3) F. FRITH AND COMPANY, LTD., (5, 6) BURTON HOLMES, (7) ELMENDORFF

TYPES OF FEUDAL CASTLES

1. Alcazar at Segovia, built by Henry IV. of Castile (1454–74). This castle, placed for defence on a high, narrow plateau, served not only as the king's residence but also as the stronghold of the city walls. It is characteristic of the castle form which grew out of the combined military and residential requirements of the feudal period
2. The Bavarian royal castle of Neuschwanstein, although modern, accurately represents the type of castle building developed in the hills of Germany in the middle ages. It is a product of the German Romantic Movement, built for Ludwig II. to rival the castle of Wartburg, whose design it closely follows
3. Rochester castle, Kent, the great square keep, 120 feet high, all that remains of the original castle, which was probably built before 1126, by William de Corbeil, archbishop of Canterbury. (It belongs to the type of square Norman castle keep, illustrated also by the Tower of London)
4. Castella Coca, Spain, built soon after 1473. Like Alcazar at Segovia, it is one of a chain of fortifications built by the kingdom of Castile during the reconquest of Spain from the Moors. Its warm red brick walls and projecting turrets belong to the style called *Mudejar,* which was developed by Moorish workmen under Christian supervision. The battlements are of the Moorish type
5. Walls of the citadel of Carcassonne, dating from the 13th and early 14th centuries, as restored under the direction of Viollet-le-Duc in the middle of the 19th century. The restoration gives an idea of the original appearance of a great mediaeval castle, of which the high, unbroken, battlemented walls and projection towers, either square with battlements or round with conical roofs, are characteristic features
6. Castle of Vajda Hunyadi in Hungary, showing characteristics similar to castles in western Europe. The projection of the upper part of the towers—machicolation—enabled defenders to discharge missiles directly upon the attackers below. The buildings shown in this picture date chiefly from about 1400 with parts of the residence portion of a later date
7. Palace of the Prince of Monaco. 17th century castle as restored

PHOTOGRAPHS, (1) AEROFILMS LTD., (2) AEROFILMS LTD., FROM EWING GALLOWAY

TWO CASTLES OF GREAT BRITAIN

1. Windsor castle, a fortified spot since the early 11th century and a royal residence from the time of William the Conqueror. The round mound and ditch encircling the present round tower go back to the earliest building. In its present form, however, the castle dates largely from the time of Henry III., who built the first masonry structure (*c.* 1270), and Edward III., who almost entirely reconstructed it in 1344, as a meeting place for the Knights of the Garter. From that time on it has been continuously added to and improved—St. George's chapel, dating from 1473 to 1507; the Albert Memorial chapel, largely from 1501–03, (although the interior was much altered by Sir Gilbert Scott under Queen Victoria as a memorial to the prince consort) and the state apartments and residence quarters in the upper ward (to the right) from a reconstruction under George IV. and Queen Victoria, from designs by Sir Jeffrey Wyatville, who also increased the height of the old keep—the round tower near the centre. The oldest part of the existing castle is the round bell tower at the extreme left, with its high roof of French type, which dates from the time of Henry III. The greater part of the more recent construction having been built on foundations of older work, the whole presents an unusually vivid picture of what mediaeval castles of the largest type must have been in their prime
2. Carnarvon castle, Wales. Much smaller than Windsor, this also retains its ancient appearance. It was begun in 1283–84 by Edward I., from designs by his famous castle architect, Henry de Elreton, and was one of a chain of castles, including Conway and Beaumaris, intended for the pacification of the Welsh. Carnarvon was not completed until the reign of Edward II. Originally, a wall in the centre of the enclosed area divided it into two wards. The towers are of the British polygonal type. In France, at the time, round towers had become common. Despite the destruction of the interior residential buildings, Carnarvon castle is among the best preserved of those in the British Isles

Architecture of the Middle Ages, trans. M. Macdermott (1860); *Annals of a Fortress,* trans. B. Bucknall (1875); G. T. Clark, *Mediaeval Military Architecture in England,* 2 vol. (1884); C. W. C. Oman, *Art of War in the Middle Ages* (1885); J. H. Round, *Geoffrey de Mandeville* (1891); J. D. Mackenzie, *The Castles of England,* (1897); "English Castles," *Quarterly Review* (July 1894); G. Neilson, "The Motes in Norman Scotland," *Scottish Review,* lxiv (1898); W. St. John Hope, "English Castles of the 10th and 11th Centuries," *Archaeol. Journal,* lx (1902); "Castles of the Conquest," *Archeologia,* lviii (1902); E. S. Armitage, "Early Norman Castles of England," *Eng. Hist. Review,* xix (1904); "Anglo-Saxon Burhs and Early Norman Castles," *Scot. Soc. Ant. Proc.,* xxxiv (1900); "The Norman Origin of Irish Mottes," *The Antiquary* (Aug. and Sept. 1906); G. H. Orpen, "Motes and Norman Castles in Ireland," *Eng. Hist. Review,* xxi, xxii (1906–07). (J. H. R.)

CASTLEBAR, urban district and county town of Co. Mayo, Ireland, on the river and near the lough of same name. Pop. (1951) 5,288. The castle belonged to the De Burgh family but the town was founded in the reign of James I and received a charter in 1613. In 1641 the castle fell to the royalists. The town was held for a short period in 1798 by the French. Four miles northeast is a round tower 70 ft. high and 57 ft. in circumference. Trade is in linen goods and agricultural produce.

CASTLECONNELL, a village of Co. Limerick, Ireland, on the left bank of the Shannon, 18 mi. S.E. of Limerick on the Great Southern railway. There are remains of a castle from which the town took its name, which was the seat of the kings of Thomond. It was destroyed in 1690. Castleconnell is a centre for the salmon fishing of the lower Shannon. Pop. (1951) 244.

CASTLE DONINGTON, a town of northwest Leicestershire, Eng., 9¾ mi. S.E. of Derby by road. The population of the rural district in 1951 was 9,273 and of the parish (estimated) 2,967. The town lies on the flank of a hill overlooking the Trent valley. Hosiery, baskets and lace are the chief industries. Little remains of the castle, demolished by King John but rebuilt in 1278. The church of St. Edward is of Early English and later date. Donington hall is a castellated mansion standing in a park. The estate was once in the possession of Thomas Plantagenet, who sold it in 1594 to the earl of Huntingdon. In 1789 the then earl bequeathed it to the earl of Moira, who erected the present house in 1793.

CASTLE-DOUGLAS, a small burgh, Kirkcudbrightshire, Scot. Pop. (1951) 3,322. It lies at the north end of Carlingwark loch, about 8 mi. S.W. of Dumfries. It is the chief business centre of east Galloway and its sheep and cattle sales are the largest in the southwest of Scotland. Until 1765 it was only a village under the name of Causewayend, but the discovery of marl in the lake brought it prosperity and it was bought in 1792 by Sir William Douglas and renamed after him. On one of the islets in the loch is a crannog, or ancient lake dwelling. Threave castle, the Douglas stronghold (1369–1455) on an island in the Dee, was given to the National trust in 1948.

CASTLEFORD, an urban district in the West Riding of Yorkshire, Eng., 10 mi. S.E. of Leeds by road. Pop. (1951) 43,116. The district was considerably extended in 1938 and covers 6.8 sq.mi. There are collieries and large glass bottle and chemical works. It stands where Ermine street crosses the Aire river near its junction with the Calder and on the site of the Roman Legeolium. In 948 the name appeared as Ceasterford.

CASTLE GATE, a town in Carbon Co., Utah; 6,120 ft. above sea level; pop. (1950) 701. The name was taken from that of the gatelike passage in the canyon of Price river 1 mi. above the town. There projecting pinnacles of gray sandstone, 650–700 ft. high, close in on the valley, leaving only a narrow passage resembling a gateway in the walls of a ruined castle. The town is the home of one of the largest producing coal mines in the Book Cliffs field, originally opened by the Pleasant Valley Fuel Co. in 1888 and bought by Henry J. Kaiser interests in 1950.

CASTLE-GUARD, an arrangement under the feudal system, by which the duty of finding knights to guard royal castles was imposed on certain baronies and divided among their knights' fees. The greater barons provided for the guard of their castles by exacting a similar duty from their knights. In both cases the obligation was commuted very early for a fixed money payment, which, as "castle-guard rent," lasted down to modern times.

See J. H. Round, "Castle-Guard," in *Archaeological Journal,* vol. lix, and "Castleward and Coinage," in *The Commune of London* (1899); S. Painter, in *American Historical Review,* vol. xi, pp. 450–459 (1935); F. M. Stenton, *The First Century of English Feudalism,* pp. 190–215 (Oxford, 1932).

CASTLEMAINE, ROGER PALMER, EARL OF (1634–1705), first husband of the duchess of Cleveland (*see* CLEVELAND, BARBARA VILLIERS, DUCHESS OF), English diplomatist and author. He was an ardent Roman Catholic, who defended his coreligionists in several publications. He wrote on account in French of the war against Holland (1665–67) in which he had served. Denounced by Titus Oates as a Jesuit he was tried and acquitted, later serving James II as ambassador to Pope Innocent XI. After James II's flight, his Jacobite sympathies caused him to be suspected by the government, and his time was mainly spent either in prison or in exile.

Castlemaine died at Oswestry on July 21, 1705.

CASTLEMAINE, a town 70 mi. N.W. of Melbourne, Victoria, Australia. Pop. (1947) 5,809. Castlemaine's gold mines were among the first discovered in the colony. Slate and flagstone are quarried in the district, which is also an important wine and fruit-producing area. It is near the centre of the chief sheep belt of Australia.

CASTLE PINCKNEY NATIONAL MONUMENT, a tract of three and one-half acres in South Carolina, U.S., set apart in 1924 as a government reservation. It is the site of a fort which was erected in 1810 and had previously been occupied by a revolutionary fort.

CASTLEREAGH, VISCOUNT: *see* LONDONDERRY, ROBERT STEWART, 2ND MARQUESS OF.

CASTLE RISING, a small village of Norfolk, Eng., 4½ mi. N.E. of King's Lynn. The fine Norman keep stands within a 12-ac. enclosure, formed by artificial ramparts of earth, and a dike, which is crossed by an ancient bridge. The keep is square and massive, and the Norman carving, especially over the entrance, is very rich. The foundations of a small chapel were discovered outside the castle. The village of Castle Rising is the remnant of a town of no little importance. It is mentioned in Domesday Book and was later granted to William de Albini, whose son built the castle. It passed to Isabella, queen of Edward II, in 1332 but was exchanged for Brest castle by Richard II. It reverted to the crown in the 14th century and so remained until Henry VIII exchanged it for other lands with Thomas Howard, duke of Norfolk. A mayor is first mentioned in 1343 and a borough existed in the 15th century. A survey of 1589–90 declared that Castle Rising was an ancient borough by prescription. Castle Rising became a parliamentary borough in 1558, but was disfranchised in 1832, although a mayor was elected for special purposes until 1883. Its fairs and markets were formerly important. The church of St. Laurence is late Norman, with rich ornamentation; it shows traces of considerable alteration in the Early English period. The Bede house, founded in 1614 by Henry Howard, earl of Northampton, is an almshouse for old women. Its inhabitants still on occasion wear the high hats and red cloaks of Stuart times.

CASTLETON, a village of north Derbyshire, Eng., 17 mi. W. of Sheffield by road. Population (1949) 684. It lies about 600 ft. above sea level and is closely surrounded by limestone hills rising to heights of 1,400 to 1,700 ft. It is visited for its caves and mines—especially the Peak cavern, Treak Cliff cavern, the Speedwell mine and the Blue John mine and for Peveril castle, now a ruin, perched on a cliff above the village. Penetrating this cliff is the Peak cavern, which from the 16th century has served as a workshop, rent-free, to families making rope and twine. The strongly placed castle owes its fame to its site and to Sir Walter Scott's novel *Peveril of the Peak;* the fabric has been well repaired by the ministry of works. Before the Conquest the site was held by Gernebern and Hundinc, and early earthworks can still be traced. It was granted by William the Conqueror to William Peverel, who built the castle. In 1216 William Ferrers, earl of Derby, took it from the rebellious barons and was made governor by Henry III, who in 1223 granted a charter for a weekly market. In 1328 the castle was given to John of

Gaunt on his marriage with Blanche of Lancaster and thus became part of the duchy of Lancaster. Often used as a prison, it was almost impregnable in its day.

The church of St. Edmund at Castleton has a Norman chancel arch, old-fashioned box pews and a valuable collection of old books. The Speedwell mine, ¾ mi. W. of the village, offers the remarkable experience of a boat trip along a subterranean canal whose waters reappear in the village stream. Treak Cliff cavern has fine stalactitic formations, as also has the Blue John mine, the source of a beautiful fluorspar known as Blue John.

CASTLETOWN, the ancient capital of the Isle of Man (in Manx called *Balla Cashtal*), 8½ mi. S.W. of Douglas. Pop. (1951) 1,742. Area 2 sq.mi. A small tidal harbour is formed by the outflow of the Silverburn into Castletown bay. Castle Rushen, in the centre of the town, is said to have been founded in 947–960. The present building is essentially Norman, largely rebuilt in the 14th century and added onto in the 16th. Until the 18th century it was the residence of the lords of Man. The massive keep is square and is surrounded by an outer wall with towers and a moat. The council chamber and courthouse were built in 1644. Near the castle is the old House of Keys, where the Manx parliament met until the removal of the seat of government to Douglas in 1862. King William's college (endowed in 1668, founded in its present form in 1833) a mile N.E. of Castletown, is the principal school in the island. At Derbyhaven, adjoining Castletown, is the Ronaldsway airport.

CASTOR AND POLLUX, in Greek and Roman mythology the twin sons of Leda, and brothers of Helen and Clytaemnestra. They were also known as *Dioscuri* (Gr. "lads of Zeus"), for, according to later tradition, they were the children of Zeus and Leda, whose love the god had won under the form of a swan. In some versions Leda is represented as having brought forth two eggs, from one of which Castor and Pollux were born, from the other Helen. According to another account, Zeus was the father of Pollux and Helen, Tyndareus (king of Sparta) of Castor and Clytaemnestra. In Homer they are said to have been the children of Tyndareus and Leda, and Helen is said to have been the daughter of Leda by Zeus. The Dioscuri were specially reverenced among people of Dorian race, and were said to have reigned at Sparta, where also they were buried. They were the friends of sailors, appearing in the shape of St. Elmo's fire during storms. Later, they were confounded with the Cabeiri (*q.v.*).

CASTOREUM, an oily viscid gland secretion contained in two pairs of membranous sacs between the anus and external genitals of both the male and the female Russian and American beaver; known also as beaver musk. After drying, it comes into commerce as more or less solid masses, of brown colour and a strong, rather disagreeable odour, due to the presence of about 2% of an essential oil, in addition to which a number of odourless organic and inorganic substances have been isolated. It was formerly used medicinally as a stimulant in hysterical affections, but at present serves almost exclusively for blending perfumes, in the same way as musk and civet, usually in the form of an alcoholic extract.

CASTOR OIL, the fixed oil obtained from the seeds of the castor-oil plant or Palma Christi, *Ricinus communis,* family Euphorbiaceae. The plant is a native of tropical Africa, but is cultivated in most tropical and warmer temperate countries. Besides oil the seeds contain a powerful toxic substance (ricin) one of the phytotoxins to which an antiserum has been produced by immunological methods.

Much oil of excellent quality is obtained from India, Italy and California, U.S. The oil is obtained from the seeds by expression and decoction. One hundred pounds of good seeds may yield about five gallons of pure oil.

Castor oil is a viscid liquid, almost colourless when pure, with a slight odour, and a mild yet nauseous taste. Its specific gravity is 0.96 and it dissolves freely in alcohol, ether and glacial acetic acid. It contains palmitic and several other fatty acids, but the chief is ricinoleic acid which occurs in combination with glycerin. The ricinoleic acid is liberated by the gastric juices, and acts as a mild irritant to the gut. The dose is from one-half to one ounce. It acts in about five hours, increasing peristaltic and segmenting movements in the small intestine and allaying the normal antiperistalsis in the large bowel. It is useful for children and the aged, but must not be employed in cases of chronic constipation, which it only aggravates, while relieving the symptoms. It is also used as a lubricant especially in aeroplane motors.

CASTRATO, an adult male soprano who has been operated on in his youth to prevent his voice from changing in the ordinary way to the normal masculine pitch. In former days such singers were very numerous and included some of the most famous in the whole history of the art, such as Caffarelli, Velluti, Senesino and Farinelli, but thanks to improved public opinion the abominable practice to which they owed their existence has now been entirely abandoned. Evirati was another name for singers of this class.

CASTREN, MATTHIAS ALEXANDER (1813–1853), Finnish ethnologist and philologist, was born at Tervola, Kemi, Finland, on Dec. 2, 1813. In 1838 he joined a medical fellow-student, Dr. Ehrström, in a journey through Lapland. In the following year he travelled in Russian Karelia; and in 1841 he undertook, in company with Dr. Elias Lönnrot, a third journey, which extended as far as Obdorsk, and occupied three years. On his return he published his *Elementa grammatices Syrjaenae* and *Elementa grammatices Tscheremissae* (1844). He then undertook an exploration of the whole government of Siberia, which resulted in a vast addition to previous knowledge, but seriously affected his health. The first-fruits of his collections were published as *Versuch einer ostjakischen Sprachlehre* (St. Petersburg, 1849). In 1850 he published a treatise *De affixis personalibus linguarum Altaicarum,* and was appointed to the new chair of Finnish language and literature at Helsingfors, next year becoming chancellor of the university. He was engaged on a Samoyedic grammar when he died on May 7, 1853.

Five volumes of his collected works appeared from 1852 to 1858, containing respectively—(1) *Reseminnen från åren 1845–44;* (2) *Reseberättelser och bref åren 1845–49;* (3) *Föreläsningar i Finsk mythologi* (Germ. trans. by A. Schiefner, 1853); (4) *Ethnologiska föreläsningar öfver Altaiska folken;* and (5) *Smärre afhandlingar och akademiska dissertationer.*

CASTRENSIS, PAULUS, an Italian jurist of the 14th century. He studied under Baldus at Perugia, and was a fellow-pupil with Cardinal Zabarella. He was admitted to the degree of doctor of civil law in the University of Avignon, but it is uncertain when he first undertook the duties of a professor. A tradition, which has been handed down by Panzirolus, represents him as having taught law for a period of 57 years. He was professor at Vienna in 1390, at Avignon in 1394, and at Padua in 1429; and, at different periods, at Florence, at Bologna and at Perugia. He was for some time the vicar general of Cardinal Zabarella at Florence, and his eminence as a teacher of canon law may be inferred from the language of one of his pupils, who styles him "famosissimus juris utriusque monarca." His most complete treatise is his readings on the *Digest,* and it appears from a passage in his readings on the *Digestum Vetus* that he delivered them at a time when he had been actively engaged for 45 years as a teacher of civil law. His death is generally assigned to 1436, but it appears from an entry in a ms. of the *Digestum Vetus,* which is extant at Munich, made by the hand of one of his pupils who styles him "praeceptor meus," that he died on July 20, 1441.

CASTRES, a town of southwestern France, capital of an arrondissement in the department of Tarn, 29 mi. S.S.E. of Albi. Pop. (1946) 30,781. The busiest town of its department, it has been a cloth-working centre since the 14th century. It lies on both banks of the Agout, which is fringed by old houses with projecting upper storeys.

Castres grew up round a Benedictine abbey, probably founded in the 7th century. It was a place of considerable importance as early as the 12th century, and ranked as the second town of the Albigenses. During the Albigensian crusade it surrendered to Simon de Montfort: in 1356 it was raised to a countship by King John of France, and was united to the crown by Francis I in 1519. In the wars of the late 16th century the inhabitants sided with the Protestant party, fortified the town, and established an independent republic. They were brought to terms, however, by

Louis XIII, and forced to dismantle their fortifications; and the town was made the seat of the *chambre de l'édit,* for the investigation of the affairs of the Protestants, transferred (in 1679) to Castelnaudary. The bishopric of Castres, established by Pope John XXII in 1317, was abolished at the Revolution. The church and former cathedral of St. Benoît dates only from the 17th and 18th centuries. The *hôtel de ville,* which contains a museum with some fine paintings by Goya, occupies the former bishop's palace, designed by Jules Mansart in the 17th century; the Romanesque tower beside it is the only survival of the abbey. Of several old mansions the Renaissance hôtel de Nayrac is the most interesting. Castres has a subprefecture, tribunals of first instance and of commerce, a board of trade arbitrators and a chamber of commerce. Industries include, in addition to clothmaking, metalworking, tanning, turnery and the making of wooden shoes and furniture.

CASTRO, INEZ DE (d. 1355), mistress, and perhaps wife, of Peter I (Pedro), king of Portugal, called *Collo de Garza, i.e.,* "Heron's Neck," was born in Spanish Galicia, in the earlier years of the 14th century, daughter of Don Pedro Fernandez de Castro, and Dona Aldonça Soares de Villadares, a noble Portuguese lady. Educated at the semioriental provincial court of Juan Manuel, duke of Peñafiel, Inez grew up with Costança, the duke's daughter by a descendant of the royal house of Aragon, and her own cousin, who married in 1341 the infante Dom Pedro, son of Alphonso the Proud, king of Portugal. The young infanta and her cousin left Peñafiel and went to reside at Lisbon or at Coimbra, where Dom Pedro conceived that luckless passion for Inez which has immortalized them. Pedro's connection *par amours* with Inez would of itself have aroused no opposition. He might even have married her after the death of his wife in childbirth in 1345. According to his own assurance he did marry her in 1354. But by that time the rising power of the Castro family had created hatred among their rivals, both in Spain and Portugal. Alvaro Gonzales, Pedro Coelho and Diogo Lopes Pacheco persuaded the king, Alphonso, that his throne was in danger from an alliance between his son and the Castros, and urged the king to remove the danger by having Inez murdered. The old king went in secret to the palace at Coimbra, where Inez and the infante resided, accompanied by his three familiars, and by others who agreed with them. The beauty and tears of Inez disarmed his resolution, and he turned to leave her; but the men about him had gone too far to recede. Inez was stabbed to death and was buried immediately in the church of Santa Clara.

The infante had to be appeased by the concession of a large share in the government. The three murderers of Inez took refuge in Castile. In 1357, however, Alphonso died, and the infante was crowned king of Portugal. Peter the Cruel, his nephew, surrendered the murderers. Diogo Lopes escaped, but Coelho and Gonzales were executed, with horrible tortures, in the king's presence.

The story, not authenticated, of the exhumation and coronation of the corpse of Inez has often been told. It is said that to the dead body, crowned and robed in royal raiment and enthroned beside the king, the assembled nobles of Portugal paid homage as to their queen, swearing fealty on the withered hand of the corpse.

Inez was buried at Alcobaça, with extraordinary magnificence, in a tomb of white marble, surmounted by her crowned statue, destroyed by the French soldiery in 1810. From the brother of Inez, Alvaro Perez de Castro, the house of Portugal directly descended.

BIBLIOGRAPHY.—Fernão Lopes, *Chronica del Rey Dom Pedro* (1735); Camoens, *Os Lusiadas;* Antonio Ferreira, *Ines de Castro*—the first regular tragedy of the Renaissance after the *Sofonisba* of Trissino; Luis Velêz de Guevara, *Reinar despues de morir,* an admirable play; and Ferdinand Denis, *Chroniques chevaleresques de l'Espagne et du Portugal.*

CASTRO, JOÃO DE (1500–1548), called by Camoens *Castro Forte,* viceroy of the Portuguese Indies, the son of Alvaro de Castro, governor of Lisbon, served in north Africa between 1518 and 1538. In 1535 he accompanied the infante Dom Luis, son of Emanuel I, to the siege of Tunis. Returning to Lisbon, he received from the king the small commandership of São Pablo de Salvaterra. Soon after this he went with his uncle Garcia de Noronha to the Indies. On arrival at Goa he volunteered for the relief of Diu. Returning to Europe, he was given command in 1543 of a fleet to clear the European seas of pirates. In 1545 he was sent to the Indies with six sail. He defeated Mahmud king of Gujarat and the Adil Khan and relieved Diu, losing one of his sons in the battle. He then captured Broach, subdued Malacca, and in 1547 was appointed viceroy by João III. He died at Ormuz, in the arms of his friend St. Francis Xavier, on June 6, 1548. He was buried at Goa, and afterward taken home and buried in the convent of Bemfica.

BIBLIOGRAPHY.—Jacinto Freire de Andrade, *Vida de D. João de Castro* (1651), Eng. trans. by Sir Peter Wyche (1664); Diogo de Couto, *Decadas da Asia,* vi. The *Roteiros* or logbooks of Castro's voyages in the East (Lisbon, 1833, 1843 and 1872) are of great interest.

CASTROGIOVANNI (ENNA), a town and episcopal see (Arab., *Kasr-Yani,* corruption of *Castrum Ennae*), capital of the province of Enna, Sicily, 95 mi. by rail southeast of Palermo and 56 mi. west of Catania. It is situated in a strong strategic position, almost in the centre of the island, commanding a magnificent view of the interior. Pop. (1936) 21,261 (town); 23,817 (commune). Enna was one of the Sicel cities and the statement that it was colonized by Syracuse in 664 B.C. is improbable. It appears in history under Dionysius I of Syracuse, who after unsuccessful attempts finally acquired possession by treachery about 397 B.C. In 134–132 it was the headquarters of the slave revolt and was reduced only by treachery. Cicero speaks of it as a place of some importance, but in imperial times it seems to have been of little account. It was only by betrayal that the Saracens were able to take it in 859. In 1087 it fell into the hands of the Normans; and surviving fortifications are entirely mediaeval. The cathedral (1307) and a castle built by Frederick II of Aragon about 1300 are outstanding points of interest. There are no remains of the famous temple of Demeter, from which Verres, as Cicero tells us, removed the bronze statue of the goddess.

The lake of Pergusa where Persephone was carried off by Hades (Pluto, Dis), lies 4 mi. to the south.

Enna became a summer resort and established trade in sulphur and rock salt. It was the scene of heavy fighting in World War II.

CASTRO URDIALES, a port of northern Spain, province of Santander, on the Bay of Biscay and terminus of a branch railway connected with the Bilbao-Santander line. Pop. (1940) 6,181 (mun., 11,963).

Castro Urdiales is a modern town although its castle and parish church, on the rocky peninsula which protects the tiny bay, date from the middle ages when it was an important fishing port. Destroyed by the French in 1813, it was quickly rebuilt and increased rapidly in population and prosperity with the development of neighbouring iron mines and of railway communication, which took place after 1879. The port is naturally sheltered but an artificial harbour has been constructed. Iron ore is by far the greatest export, but fish, especially sardines in oil, and *chacolí* wine are also important.

CASTRO Y BELLVIS, GUILLÉN DE (1569–1631), Spanish dramatist, was a Valencian by birth, and early enjoyed a reputation as a man of letters. In 1591 he became a member of a local literary academy called the *Nocturnos.* At one time he was a captain of the coast guard, at another the protégé of Benavente, viceroy of Naples, who appointed him governor of Scigliano, near Naples. Castro was patronized by Osuna and Olivares, and was nominated a knight of the order of Santiago in 1623. He settled at Madrid in 1626, and died there on July 28, 1631, in such poverty that his funeral expenses were defrayed by charity. He probably made the acquaintance of Lope de Vega at the festivals (1620–22) held to commemorate the beatification and canonization of St. Isidore, the patron saint of Madrid. On the latter occasion Castro's *octavas* were awarded the first prize. Lope de Vega dedicated to him a celebrated play entitled *Las Almenas de Toro* (1619), and when Castro's *Comedias* were published in 1618–21 he dedicated the first volume to Lope de Vega's daughter. The drama that has made Castro's reputation is *Las Mocedades del Cid* (1599?), to the first part of which Corneille was largely indebted for the materials of his tragedy. The two parts of this play, like all those by Castro, have the genuine ring of the old romances; and, from their intense nationality, no less than for their primitive poetry and flowing versification, were among the most popular pieces of their day.

Castro's *Fuerza de la costumbre* is the source of *Love's Care,* a play ascribed to Fletcher. He is also the reputed author of *El Prodigio de los Montes,* from which Calderón derived *El Mágico prodigioso.*

His *Obras* were edited by E. J. Martínez (Madrid, 1925).

CASTRUCCIO CASTRACANI DEGLI ANTELMINELLI (1281–1328), duke of Lucca, born March 29, 1281, at Castruccio, near Lucca, was a noted *condottiere* and Ghibelline. He was exiled at an early age with his parents and others of their faction by the Guelphs, who were then in power. He served under Philip IV of France in Flanders, then with the Visconti in Lombardy, and in 1313 under the Ghibelline chief, Uguccione della Faggiuola, lord of Pisa, in central Italy. He assisted Uguccione in many enterprises, including the capture of Lucca (1314) and the victory over the Florentines at Montecatini (1315). An insurrection of the Lucchese led to the expulsion of Uguccione and his party, and Castruccio regained his freedom and position, and the Ghibelline triumph was assured. In 1316 he was elected lord of Lucca, and spent many years in incessant warfare against the Florentines.

He was at first the faithful adviser and stanch supporter of Frederick of Austria, who made him imperial vicar of Lucca in 1320. After the battle of Mühldorf he switched his allegiance to the emperor Louis the Bavarian, whom he served for several years. He defeated the Florentines at Altopascio in 1325, the year in which he was created duke of Lucca, Pistoja, Volterra and Luni by the emperor Louis the Bavarian. In 1327 he captured Pisa, of which he was made imperial vicar. But, subsequently, his relations with Louis seem to have grown less friendly and he was afterward excommunicated by the papal legate in the interests of the Guelphs. He died Sept. 3, 1328.

BIBLIOGRAPHY.—Niccolò Machiavelli's *Life of Castruccio* is a mere romance; it was translated into French, with notes, by Dreux de Radier in 1753. *See* F. Winkler, *Castruccio, Herzog von Lucca* (Berlin, 1897); Gino Capponi, *Storia di Firenze* and G. Sforza, *Castruccio Castracani degli Antelminelli in Lunigiana* (Modena, 1891); and S. de Sismondi *Histoire des républiques italiennes* (Brussels, 1838).

CASTRUM MINERVAE, an ancient town of the Sallentini in Calabria, 10 mi. south of Hydruntum (mod. Otranto), with an ancient temple of Minerva, said to have been founded by Idomeneus, who formed the tribe of the Sallentini from a mixture of Cretans, Illyrians and Italian Locrians. It is also said to have been the place where Aeneas first landed in Italy, the port of which he named *Portus Veneris.*

CAST STEEL: *see* CRUCIBLE CAST STEEL.

CASUAL LABOUR is a term used to denote discontinuous or irregular employment or, as a collective, the workers subject to such employment.

GREAT BRITAIN

Building.—The term casual labour is sometimes used to describe the employment conditions in such trades as building, which are frequently subject to large seasonal fluctuations. These fluctuations may be due directly to the climate: statistical inquiry has shown in various European countries a distinct correlation between the seasonal decline in employment in the industry during the winter months and the prevailing temperature during these months. Technological advances, however, considerably extended the possibilities of building construction in cold weather; and while in some respects the cost of winter building exceeds that of summer work, this may be offset by the benefits of eliminating seasonal fluctuations. Nevertheless, in the United Kingdom before 1939 there was a widespread reluctance on the part of prospective occupants to take a new house built at any other time than between April and September. Naturally this attitude disappeared in consequence of the housing shortage following World War II. Elsewhere leasing dates affect the period over which building tends to be spread. The matter is further discussed in the International Labour office report on *Seasonal Unemployment in the Construction Industry* (1951).

Port Labour.—The term casual worker is, however, more usually applied to the man whose employment normally, and not only periodically, consists of a succession of jobs of short duration, whose contract of engagement is by the day and even by the hour, and who, from the method by which he is engaged, may be uncertain in the morning whether work will be available in the afternoon. He was typified, particularly during the latter part of the 19th and the earlier part of the 20th centuries, by the casual labourer at the docks. It was in the dock industry and the ancillary transport trades that casualization was most extensive; it was here that the phenomenon was investigated at greatest length, and here that the biggest efforts toward decasualization were made.

The conditions governing labour in the London docks during the early years of the 20th century were succinctly described by William Henry Beveridge (afterward Lord Beveridge) in *Unemployment* (London, 1908). They may be taken as broadly applicable to the other large dock areas of Great Britain. The fundamental condition leading to the existence of casual labour in the docks was that the demand for labour was distributed among a multitude of different employers with little fluidity or co-operation between them. Two important features were the great irregularity of the arrival and departure of cargoes and the small extent to which machinery had at that time and even later been able to displace manual work. As a consequence of the irregularity of cargoes there were considerable daily or weekly variations in the amount of work to be done at any one centre of waterside employment. As a consequence of the dependence on manual labour the effects of this varying demand tended to be thrown mainly upon the labourers, whom, beyond certain limits, it was uneconomic to employ regularly, and who were taken on and put off at short notice as they were wanted or were not needed. Every distinct centre of waterside employment required for its smooth working to have immediately available a larger number of men than it could employ regularly or even adequately. From this it followed that each separate employer, in order to be able to call upon sufficient labour to satisfy his peak demand, tended to keep available a separate pool of potential labour; the aggregate of all these separate pools was much larger than would have been the case had there been complete co-operation and complete fluidity between the various centres of employment.

Each employer engaged his men as and where he could get them. What generally happened was that a number of men would assemble in a stated place at a stated time, and the employer's foreman would select workers from them, thus collecting a labour force sufficient to meet his firm's requirements for the next few hours. The formation of these separate pools of labour probably came about largely unconsciously. Men tended to return to a centre where they had previously been successful in getting work, and where they hoped they might be known, rather than to chance the hazards of going further afield. At the same time, however, some more or less deliberate measures appear to have been adopted by employers to keep the reserve together: thus work which might have been done always by the same men was sometimes given out in rotation so as to have enough men always in close attendance for emergencies. For example, a special committee on unskilled labour set up by the Charity Organization society (1908) reported that it was found at certain London wharves that the permanent staff averaged only 70% of the minimum numbers employed on the slackest days. The remaining 30% of constant work, together with the casual work, was distributed over a large reserve of irregular hands.

From the worker's point of view, the element of chance in securing employment was evidently the salient feature. The man seeking work in the first place had to forecast the probable demand for labour at the different centres within the docks without any adequate information. At any centre he chose he had to compete with a "struggling crowd," the great majority of whom were unknown to the employer or his agent who undertook the selection of workers. The effects of this irregular and unpredictable employment upon the individual were commented on by a number of sociologists at the end of the 19th and the early part of the 20th centuries. Speaking of casual labourers at the London docks in the 1880s, Beveridge says: "The knowledge that any man, whatever his experience, however bad his antecedents, might get a job at the Docks, attracted to their neighbourhood a perpetual stream of blackguards, weaklings and failures from every other occupation. The experience, soon made, that regular attendance was not necessary to secure selection on days when work happened to be plentiful and the daily alternations of hard exercise and idleness rapidly developed in those who came, if they had it not before, the greatest irregularity of habits and physical or moral incapacity for continuous exertion. The low physique and half-starved condition of many of the labourers made their work dear at 4*d.* an hour. The London dock casual was popularly regarded as 'the scum of the earth'; the system of dock employment was aptly described as, in effect, 'a gigantic system of outdoor relief.' All could get occasional shillings, few a decent living." (*Op. cit.*, 1930 ed. pp. 87–88, Longmans Green & Co. Limited.)

Decasualization Schemes.—Many attempts were made to introduce some measure of organization into this chaos. As a result partly of the strike of 1889, partly of the investigations of Charles Booth, the London and India Docks company initiated measures of decasualization during the 1890s and after, which included, first, the formation of registers or lists of workers to whom preference was normally given, and, second, the making of the whole of the company's dock area into a single labour market instead of a number of separate and distinct areas of employment. In the single labour market the required supplies of men were directed from a central office to the different work places. This scheme was extended when the Port of London authority was established in 1909.

During the first 30 years or so of the 20th century a number of other schemes were set up in various British ports. Thus in 1912 the port employers of Liverpool, the port-workers' trade union, the board of trade and the treasury co-operated to bring into existence the Liverpool dock scheme. Another scheme was set up in Bristol in 1916. The ministry of labour's Port Labour Inquiry committee, appointed in 1930, found 31 schemes which were at that time in operation in various ports. The report stated that by this date all major ports were involved with the exception of Glasgow and the Tyne and Wear ports, and that more than two-thirds of port transport workers were covered. The chief features of these schemes to promote decasualization were that: (1) they were all registration schemes—that is, that they involved the maintenance of a register of men who received preference in the selection of labour; (2) they were voluntary schemes, operating without any legal sanction, though generally with the assistance of the ministry of labour, which often provided secretarial or clerical help; (3) the majority of them were operated jointly by representatives of employers and of workers; (4) generally each scheme provided for the centralized engagement of labour, though it was stated that in some ports this was found to be impracticable; (5) no provision was made for guaranteed minimum income. The committee considered the question of labour wastage and recruitment—obviously an important feature of decasualization schemes—but reached no very definite conclusions. They found that the registration schemes had worked well and had brought into dock work a much better type of employee than was typical at the end of the 19th century; and they felt that registration was an essential preliminary to any decasualization scheme.

During World War II it became imperative to introduce a greater measure of organization into dock work, partly because of the general labour shortage, partly because of the effects of bombing and the need for greater flexibility of the labour force. Consequently, statutory port registration committees were set up early in the war; and under the Dock Labour (Essential Work) order, 1941, a National Dock Labour corporation, with local boards, was appointed. The order also empowered the minister to make dock labour schemes, the essential points of which were that all port workers were to be registered; that all workers, when not actually in employment, automatically entered a reserve pool and were deemed to be in the employment of the corporation; and that, when in the reserve pool, they had to report to a control point as required, and, if not allocated to jobs, received attendance money. Thus a system of guaranteed pay was a feature of these schemes.

Another phase in the process of dock labour decasualization began when, in 1946, the Dock Workers (Regulation of Employment) act was passed. This, with orders and a scheme made by the minister of labour under it in 1947, regulated the system of decasualization in Great Britain.

Provision was made for the setting up of a National Dock Labour board, which succeeded the corporation in June 1947 and became responsible for the administration of the scheme. In addition, local dock labour boards were to be set up in each port or group of ports; by the beginning of 1952 there were 25 such boards. The national board consists of a chairman and vice-chairman and not less than eight or more than ten other members, four of these other members representing dock employers and four dock workers. All the members of the board are appointed by the minister of labour after consultation with the National Joint Council for the Port Transport Industry. Local boards also consist of representatives of dock workers and of employers in equal numbers.

The chief functions of the national board are to maintain a labour force of a size suitable to current conditions, to maintain a register of employers and a register of workers and to provide for the training and welfare of dock workers. All these functions, except the first, are also functions of the local boards, and much of the work of the national board is in fact carried on through these local agencies.

Broadly speaking, only those persons whose names are on the board's register are eligible for employment in dock work. Every person whose name is on the register is required to attend at a call stand in his port at stated times, generally twice a day, for work. If none is available for him at any one of these "turns," he is entitled to "attendance money" at the rate of five shillings per turn. If he has attended a full week without obtaining work, his entitlement is increased so as to bring it up to a guaranteed week's wage, varying according to the age and medical category of the worker. The pay of those workers who have earned less in a week than the amount of the guaranteed wage is also made up to the minimum. If the worker does not report at the call stand and furnishes no adequate excuse he forfeits his claim to any payment for the week in question. Where conditions lead to a sudden temporary shortage of labour, the local board is empowered to open a temporary register until the abnormal shortage disappears. This provision, which would seem on the face of it to be contrary to the principle of decasualization, does not appear to have given rise to any great difficulties. The national board is also empowered to transfer labour from one port to another in order to equate supply and demand.

Attention was also given to the development of welfare services, including the provision of medical centres and canteens, the appointment of welfare officers, the promotion of educational activities and the supervision of benevolent funds.

The income of the national board is derived from a levy on the wage bills of the employers. This levy is equivalent to a percentage of the wage bill, the rate being fixed by the board from time to time. Out of this income the board pays attendance money and the amount necessary to make up each worker's pay to the guaranteed minimum. From it also come holiday pay, the employers' national insurance contributions and the expenses of maintaining welfare services.

The board is thus not in receipt of any public money. Moreover, although it was set up under the provisions of an act of parliament, it is not a department of government. Nor is it an employer. It may perhaps be described as the agent of the port employers, but it occupies a somewhat anomalous position which can give rise to difficult questions of practical politics.

Other European Countries and the Commonwealth.—In many other countries with large maritime interests decasualization schemes have been initiated. Such countries include Canada, Australia, New Zealand, India, France, the Netherlands, Belgium, Norway and Sweden. These schemes vary considerably in detail. It may be said, however, that they all include some method of limiting the number of dockers competing for work by granting to certain of them a priority right in the port concerned. In some of the countries mentioned above the scheme operates under statutory provision: thus in Australia the Stevedoring Industry board was established by an act of 1949 and has the duty of maintaining the labour supply and of organizing and controlling waterside workers. In others, decasualization regulations are included in the collective agreements between employers and unions, and the system is thus anchored to the principle of collective bargaining. The guarantee of a minimum income is embodied in such schemes as those of Australia, France and New Zealand, in which workers receive attendance money and (in New Zealand) a guaranteed minimum wage. Some further remarks on these schemes will be found in the International Labour office report on *Decasualisation of Dock Labour* (1949). (A. F. Ws.)

UNITED STATES

The term casual labour, whether applied to demand for labour or to the people who satisfy the demand, is used in the United States to describe irregular, short-time employment of a wide variety of types. It ranges from extra help for house cleaning, snow shovelling and the like, to short-time hirings on docks and in agriculture, lumbering, contracting and other industries. Many thousands pick up a precarious livelihood at such work. Caterers, hotels and restaurants and clubs, hire casual labour for waiting table and kitchen work at banquets and other social functions; advertisers, theatres, stores and many other businesses employ people for short periods to distribute advertising matter, help load or unload trucks or other equipment, deliver merchandise or do odd jobs. A multitude of small businesses such as wood sawyers, house builders, coal and ice companies and canneries often hire short-time help. Those enumerated are illustrations of the wide range of casual jobs in the business world in general.

The United States bureau of the census enumerates, as one classification, people who involuntarily work part time. They cannot get or cannot accept steady work. The census bureau stated (Sept. 20, 1951; *cf.* bibliography) that "a disproportionate part of the involuntary part-time workers are employed in private household work where work schedules are notably unsteady irrespective of the economic climate in general." This group includes cleaning women who work by the day, men who spade gardens, clean and install storm windows, rake leaves, and do similar odd jobs around the home. Every city and town and many rural communities have casual workers depending upon such employment. In total, they are a large number of people.

A clear distinction must be made between casual jobs, *i.e.*, jobs which create a demand for casual labourers, and casual labourers as such. Casual jobs are often accepted by people who are ordinarily in regular employment but who, during unemployment, seek casual work to tide themselves over a stringency. Casual labourers are people who consistently work irregularly. They depend for subsistence on picking up short jobs. They are often physically or psychologically incapable of steady employment. In a limited number of cases, they do casual work to supplement some other type of income. But in the large majority of cases, casual work is performed by casual labourers for whom it is their dependence for livelihood. These labourers are often deficient in work capacity; some are old or some physically deficient, or both. Most of them are below par physically and psychologically. They are a normal product of uncertain livelihood, too much unemployment, and often of demoralizing life experiences. Patterns of living which depend upon picking up odd jobs are seldom desirable socially or individually.

There is a twilight zone between mere part-time employment and casual employment. In individual cases it is frequently difficult to know whether to classify certain work as merely irregular or as casual. In agriculture, for instance, with its seasonal work, thousands of work opportunities of a definitely casual type arise. Harvesting of many crops which require much seasonal labour (such as picking fruit and berries, cultivating or harvesting green vegetables, working in the onion fields in Texas, or in the sugar beet fields in Colorado, Michigan and other states) also call for a large number of people hired for very short periods, either to replace hands who have quit or to step up the job to a faster pace for a short time.

The loading and unloading of ships has been for centuries an outstanding type of casual employment (*see* above). The unceasing hiring, laying off and new hiring of longshoremen for the loading or unloading of ships; the former unpredictability of the arrival times of ships; and the daily uncertainty about both the day's demands for labour and the number of men available, kept the dock situation in a constant state of flux. The ease with which unemployed men from other industries could come to the docks to pick up a few dollars intensified the competition for work, while the labour surplus ordinarily accumulated around the docks played into the employers' hands. Large numbers of longshoremen frequently found themselves on poor relief.

The unionization of U.S. longshoremen, particularly from the early 1930s onward, enabled the longshoremen to prevent easy access to longshore work by refusing to work with nonmembers or requiring nonmembers accepted for employment to have union permits, thus establishing union control over the labour supply. They established "dispatching halls" (hiring halls) in many ports, supervised by a joint committee of employer and union representatives or by the union. The hiring-hall system, which began at Seattle, Wash., in 1939, did much to change the casual labour situation on the docks to a regularized system of employment. The halls enabled the longshoremen to hold the dock work for those who made it their regular occupation and to divide the available work equitably among them. It insured the employers experienced men systematically dispatched to the boats as needed. The system did not work without frictions, disputes and delays in the handling of shipping, but it markedly diminished the casual character of longshore work.

The relatively full employment which prevailed in the years after 1941 did more than anything else to counteract casual employment. With industry, mining, transportation and agriculture all operating at a high level of productivity, there were more opportunities for workmen of less than maximum efficiency to get steady employment and a noticeable reduction in the proportion of casual workers in the industrial population.

BIBLIOGRAPHY.—The Governor's Committee to Survey the Agricultural Labor Resources of the San Joaquin Valley, *Agricultural Labor in the San Joaquin Valley: Final Report and Recommendations* (March 1951); Paul S. Taylor, "Perspective on Housing Migratory Agricultural Laborers," *Land Economics* (Aug. 1951); U.S. bureau of the census, *Current Population Reports: Labor Force,* Census Series P-50, No. 34 (Sept. 20, 1951); Joint Legislative Committee on Agriculture and Livestock Problems, *The Recruitment and Placement of Farm Laborers in California 1950,* (1951). (D. D. L.)

CASUALTIES, in military use, the losses of a force in war by death, wounds, sickness, desertion or any other cause (from Lat. *casus,* that which falls out). The duty of dealing with all casualties from wounds or sickness falls to the medical services, the personnel of which treats each case from the moment of its occurrence to the eventual recovery or death of the patient.

CASUAL WARD, the name given, under the British poor laws in force between 1834 and 1948, to a building for the purpose of giving temporary shelter to vagrants.

Under the poor law as reformed in 1834, the primary duty of boards of guardians was to relieve destitute persons within their districts. Gradually, however, it was extended to the administering of relief to vagrants, popularly called tramps and officially termed casual paupers. The casual ward was generally adjacent to the workhouse or poor law institution.

Any vagrant or unemployed person walking from place to place and seeking work usually obtained an order for the casual ward from the relieving officer or his assistant; vagrants were searched—usually perfunctorily—and deprived of money and tobacco, which were restored to them on discharge. They were given a bath on admission and a meal, usually sugarless cocoa and a piece of bread. For the night the clothes of the inmates were taken away (and sometimes disinfected) and a rough nightshirt provided. Sleeping accommodation on the floor or a truckle bed was provided either in cells or associated wards. In return for the food and lodging, tasks of wood sawing or chopping, digging, oakum picking or scrubbing floors were imposed, though in many of the wards the obligation was not too strictly enforced.

Poor Law Act, 1930.—After 1918 as a result of postwar conditions and industrial disputes the great increase in the numbers of wayfarers applying for assistance to the poor law guardians threw the system out of gear and, following the abolition of the boards of guardians by the Local Government act, 1929, and the transference of their functions to the county and borough councils, a reorganization was affected by the Poor Law act, 1930, supplemented by various orders. The provision of and admission to casual wards became the business of the public assistance committees of the councils, and joint vagrancy committees were established throughout the country to bring about a uniform system and effect economies in expenditure. The casual was admitted and supervised by trained officials, and ordinarily was not allowed to discharge himself before the second morning (excluding Sunday) following admission unless he had a current vacancy ticket given him by an employment exchange. (This was a card showing an appointment with a prospective employer, and entitled its owner to leave the casual ward immediately without detention.) His clothing was taken and cleaned if necessary; money and other articles were also taken from him and the cost of relief deducted before return; a day room and proper sleeping accommodation had to be provided, also a clean towel; and any case of infectious disease or mental illness had to be reported to the ministry by the medical officer, who had to visit the ward and examine every casual therein once a month.

National Assistance Act, 1948.—During World War II casual wards in England and Wales were closed. By the end of the war some had fallen into disrepair and some had been taken over permanently for other uses. Furthermore, between 1939 and 1945 the number of vagrants fell greatly; and though there appears to have been a steady increase in the years immediately after the war, the numbers, by the end of 1951, were apparently still far short of those in prewar years.

The 1948 act changed the administration of the casual wards. These, henceforward to be known as "reception centres," were placed under the National Assistance board. The great majority of the centres (which were fewer in number than the old casual wards) were housed in the identical buildings which had previously been used for such wards. Shortage of materials had made it impossible to erect new buildings, though it would have been preferable to do so. Again, although the responsibility for these centres was transferred to the National Assistance board, the act empowered it to make local authorities its agents in carrying out these duties; and this it ordinarily does.

The regimen of the English casual ward between 1931 and 1939, summarized above, was followed in reception centres; but while the standing principle of the prewar poor law administration in England and Wales had been to keep the vagrant moving, the major change made by the 1948 act was that vagrants should be encouraged to stay at the centres until some constructive action could be taken for their benefit. (A. F. Ws.)

CASUARIIDAE: *see* CASSOWARY.

CASUARINA, a genus of odd trees of the Casuarinaceae family containing about 35 species, chiefly Australian, but a few Indo-Malayan. The long whip-like green branches are longitudinally grooved and bear at the nodes whorls of small scale-leaves, the shoots resembling those of *Equisetum* (horse-tail). The flowers are unisexual. The staminate are born in spikes, each flower consisting of a central stamen which is surrounded by two scale-like perianth-leaves. The pistillate are borne in dense spherical heads; each flower stands in the axil of a bract and consists of two united carpels flanked by a pair of bracteoles; the long styles hang out beyond the bracts, and the one-chambered ovary contains two ovules. In the fruit the brateoles form two woody valves between which is a nutlet; the aggregate of fruits resembles small cones. Pollen is transferred by the wind to the long styles. The pollen-tube does not penetrate the ovule through the micropyle but enters at the opposite end—the chalaza (*see* ANGIOSPERMS). The wood is very hard, and several species are valuable timber trees. From a fancied resemblance of the wood to that of the oak these trees are known as "oaks," and the same species has different names in different parts such as "she-oak," "swamp-oak," "iron-wood" and "beef-wood." Several species are cultivated in the subtropical parts of the United States, especially the beef-wood (*C. equisetifolia*), which has become widely naturalized in Florida. *See* J. H. Maiden, *Useful Native Plants of Australia* (London and Sydney, 1889).

CASUISTRY was originally a term of disparagement. Coined in the first quarter of the 18th century from "casuist," perhaps by analogy with "sophistry," it expressed the contempt of emancipated "common sense" for all the labour and nicety of reasoning which the preceding century had expended on resolving cases of conscience. It afforded a vehicle also for the confused popular notion that casuistical activity was at once subversive of morality and an instrument of priestcraft. But in time, although the tendentious usage did not die (indeed it persists still in quarters where ratiocination in moral matters is suspect), the word grew respectable. It now signifies, like the French *casuistique,* that part of Christian moral theology which determines the morality of particular actions in particular circumstances, especially such as are apt to puzzle the conscience. The discovery that circumstances alter cases not being peculiar to Christianity, the name "casuistry" is given also to the application of any moral system, Christian or not, to concrete situations; but here in the main only casuistry as understood within the Roman Catholic and Anglican churches will be considered.

Moral theology may be described as the application of Christian dogma to human life. The scope of casuistry within this field is not, and probably cannot be, defined exactly. It is generally admitted that the casuist's concern is not with the rights and wrongs of actions considered in the abstract, but with the problems facing particular agents in particular situations; but opinions differ concerning the relation of his special function to general moral theology on the one hand and to the work of pastors, spiritual directors and confessors on the other. Most commonly he is represented as an expert consultant, who applies the "conclusions" of general moral theology to the diverse situations which confessors and others refer to him, in order to determine what moral obligations those situations present. On this view casuistry is the link between general moral theology, which is assumed to have finished its work when it has expounded the law of God more or less in abstraction from variable circumstances (though of course no formulation of the law is possible at all without reference to some circumstances), and the pastoral art, which enters intimately into the minds and situations of those whose consciences are actively engaged. Some would even further restrict casuistry to helping confessors in their judicial, as distinct from their advisory, capacity.

Although many casuists have accepted these limitations, it is doubtful whether casuistry can encompass its proper end under them. That end cannot be less than to enlighten puzzled consciences, that they may discern God's will and vocation in their actual situations. Therefore the casuist should not stop at determining strict moral obligation (though that is an essential part of his work), still less at helping the confessor to make ex post facto judgments with a view to absolution, but should focus whatever light his science affords for the direction of souls "in the ways of truth, so that they neither decline to the right hand nor to the left" (George Herbert, *A Priest to the Temple,* 1652). Since division of labour is necessary, the expert casuist will more often act as consultant than have immediate contact with those who need guidance. Indeed it is as a rule better that he should not be pastorally involved in the matters that he considers, for personal sympathy with hard cases and firsthand experience of the harm done by prevalent excesses can sway the judgment toward laxism or rigorism. But the smaller the degree of abstraction that underlies his resolutions, and the more fully he grasps the interior as well as the exterior circumstances of the agent, the more perfectly he fulfils his ministry.

Casuistry cannot attain its end, thus conceived, simply by

taking over "conclusions"—moral generalizations and axioms—from general moral theology and relating them to circumstances. Often the right resolution of a case requires direct reference to the fundamental mysteries of the Christian faith or fresh consideration of the God-given natures and ends of created beings. Whenever casuists cease to keep open their communications with ultimate theological truth and rely merely on ready-made generalizations and casuistical precedents, their science degenerates into a sort of moral case-law, unillumined by the Gospel. Moreover it is vital to recognize, in any estimate of the relation of casuistry to moral theology at large, that the resolution of particular cases, especially such as embody unprecedented circumstances, may throw new light on the moral law and so require that some "conclusion" of moral theology be reconsidered. It is thus that casuistry, adequately conceived, challenges the legalism which equates the law of God with current moral generalizations.

In every age the major part of the church's casuistical activity is exercised by word of mouth, often under the seal of the confessional, or in private correspondence. Published books are usually by-products of the principal work of casuists, many of whom—and among them the best—are content to write on souls alone. It follows that a literary history of casuistry can offer only a partial and to some extent a misleading view of the matter. Nevertheless it can be asserted that nothing that could be called a science emerged before the middle ages. Earlier casuistical reasoning, such as appears not only in the writings of the Fathers but in the New Testament itself (for instance, in I Corinthians), was necessarily occasional and unsystematic. Scientific casuistry could not establish itself until the 12th-century renaissance in western Christendom had made possible the articulation of theology, and the analysis of human action had so far progressed as to prevent confusion between the objective nature of an act, its purely circumstantial accompaniments and the subjective purpose of its agent. The fact that no comparable foundation was laid in the eastern church goes far to explain why scientific casuistry has been confined almost wholly to the western.

The rapid growth of the new science in the 13th century formed part of a striking development, largely Dominican in inspiration, of pastoral and penitential theology. The increasing importance of the sacrament of penance in the life of the church, to which the fourth Lateran council (1215), by its ruling on yearly confession to the parish priest, gave authoritative recognition, and the great expansion of canon law since the *Decretum* (between 1140 and 1150) of Franciscus Gratianus, had stimulated demand, both in the schools and in the confessional, for ampler and more systematic guidance than the old penitential books had ever afforded; and the need was met by a notable output of penitential and casuistical *summae,* among which the *Summa de casibus poenitentialibus* (between 1222 and 1230) of the eminent canonist St. Raymond of Peñafort and the *Summa confessorum* (between 1280 and 1298) of John of Freiburg were specially influential.

After sharing in the 15th-century lapse of theology into academic quibbling, casuistry again underwent, from the middle of the 16th century up to the middle of the 17th, remarkable development and expansion. The causes were various: theology, moral as well as dogmatic, forced by the controversies of the day to re-examine its foundations, was invigorated by renewed study of the great schoolmen, especially of St. Thomas Aquinas; contact with the New World and rapidly changing conditions of life brought fresh moral problems; and the intense activity of the new religious orders, especially the Society of Jesus, in the confessional and in spiritual direction both provided the casuist with material to work on and stimulated demand for casuistical literature.

Nor was it only in the Roman communion that casuistry flourished. In England at any rate "casuistical divinity" was very highly esteemed, by Puritans as well as by Anglicans, by laymen as well as by ecclesiastics.

Yet this, the great age of the casuist, in which he perfected his technique and demonstrated his concern with the whole of human life, was also the age in which he attracted the odium that gave the word "casuistry" its original meaning. The indignation against the Jesuits so bitingly voiced by the Jansenist Blaise Pascal in his *Provincial Letters* may be partly discounted, as springing from the rigoristic temper which feels that any qualification of moral precepts to suit circumstances undermines the absoluteness of the moral law; and the 18th-century dislike of casuistical divinity was due in the main to reaction against the epoch just past and to defects in the 18th-century mind. Nevertheless, when all is said, one has only to study, for instance, the work of Antonino Diana (1586–1663), whose *Resolutiones morales* were widely used, to see that, though Pascal overstated his case, he undoubtedly had a case to state. Confirmation of this may be found in the Anglican Jeremy Taylor's preface to his *Ductor Dubitantium* (1660).

While Taylor had no quarrel with casuistry as such, being a casuist himself, he was intensely critical of the casuistry of the Counter Reformation; and, even when his prejudices against Rome and against probabilism and his not altogether well-informed sympathy with Jansenism have been allowed for, the substance of his criticism remains.

It seems that the preoccupation with penance and the reliance on authorities which had been appropriate to the mediaeval situation were now having undesirable effects. First, the prime concern of many casuists being to assist the confessor (and the confessor as judge rather than as spiritual guide), their aim in writing was often nothing more exalted than to distribute the actions they considered under the three not very inspiring heads of "mortally sinful," "venially sinful" and "not sinful."

Within the terms of reference they had accepted this was probably inevitable, and in the hands of prudent confessors their work was doubtless put to good use. For in an age of earnest and skilful spiritual direction no less than of casuistry, when St. Francis de Sales (1567–1622) and many others taught the pursuit of perfection to Christians living in the world as well as to religious, priests cannot be presumed to have let their penitents believe that the resolutions of casuists marked the goal of Christian endeavour. Nevertheless the impression that casuistry offered a substandard was made, and persisted.

Secondly, the habit of relying too much on authorities—in other words, of judging opinions by the reputation of their authors as much as by their intrinsic reasonableness—caused the new and useful tool of probabilism to be abused. In itself probabilism (*q.v.*) means giving the benefit of the doubt. A man is doubtful whether, in the circumstances, he is bound by a certain obligation. Having canvassed the pros and cons, he finds substantial arguments (intrinsic probability) on both sides and has difficulty in deciding which way the balance inclines. Suppose, however, that he thinks there is rather more to be said in favour of the obligation than against it: is he then morally bound to fulfil it? The probabilist answers "No"; for as long as there is against the obligation a reasonable case which defies refutation, the obligation necessarily remains doubtful; and doubtful obligations cannot bind the conscience. Probabilism does not assert that it is "right" for the man not to fulfil the obligation: it merely says that, if he decides not to do so, he cannot, in view of the doubt, be accused of acting irresponsibly. But sometimes the agent is incapable of marshalling and evaluating the pros and cons. In such a case he may reasonably rely on extrinsic probability, that is, on the opinion of others who may be supposed to know what they are talking about; and if opinions differ, probabilism will again apply. Of course, if a man were found always taking the benefit of the doubt, we should begin to question his moral sincerity; but, granted conscientiousness, probabilism is a reasonable and prudent way of dealing with such problems. It is a different matter, however, when casuists, taking up probabilism too enthusiastically, consistently end their consideration of disputed questions by declaring two or more conflicting opinions probable; and the uncertainty which is spread by such practice is dangerously magnified if purely extrinsic probability is admitted, that is, if casuists, instead of carefully examining the Rev. Marcus Brutus' arguments, say in effect, "Brutus says so and so; and Brutus is an honourable man." But that is what many writers of the 16th and 17th centuries did, thus opening the door to laxity; for, as Jeremy Taylor remarked, casuists who too often conclude *alii aiunt, alii negant;*

BY COURTESY OF (1, 2, 3, 4, 6, 7, 8, 9, 10, 11, 12) NEW YORK ZOOLOGICAL SOCIETY, (5) FROM CHAMPION, "WITH A CAMERA IN TIGERLAND" (CHATTO AND WINDUS, LONDON; DOUBLEDAY, DORAN & CO., INC., NEW YORK)

MEMBERS OF THE CAT FAMILY FOUND IN AFRICA, ASIA AND AMERICA

1. Lion (*Panthera leo*), one of the two largest of the cat family, the other a tiger. It is found in Africa, Mesopotamia, Persia and India
2. The Bengal tiger (*Panthera tigris*), a fierce beast of prey which sometimes, especially in old age, becomes a man-eater
3. Lioness (*Panthera leo*), about a foot shorter than the adult male and generally considered more dangerous when attacked
4. Puma or mountain lion (Felis concolor), a large American cat extensively distributed from Canada to Patagonia. It is of a uniform colour
5. Tigress (*Panthera tigris*), somewhat smaller than the male but equally aggresive, especially when protecting her young
6. Leopard cat (Felis bengalensis), a small, savage wildcat of tropical Asia that feeds largely on game birds
7. Ocelot (Felis pardalis), an American forest cat ranging from Texas to Paraguay. Its fur is yellow or grey marked with spots
8. The red or bob-tail lynx (Lynx rufus), a North American species that ranges south to Mexico. Its reddish summer coat is less spotted
9. Jaguar (*Panthera onca*), the largest of American cats. It ranges from Texas to Patagonia and sometimes develops into a man-eater
10. Cheetah or Hunting Leopard (*Acinonyx jubata*), so called because it is used in the hunting of game. It is a native of Africa and Asia
11. The snow-leopard (*Panthera uncia*), an inhabitant of highland Central Asia. Its name is suggested by its grey spotted fur
12. Serval (*Felis serval*), an African wildcat that preys on small quadrupeds and is prized by the natives for its skin, which is a spotted yellow

CAT

BY COURTESY OF (3, 4) HELEN HILL SHAW, (8) GERTRUDE E. TAYLOR; PHOTOGRAPHS, (1, 2, 6, 7) THOMAS FALL COPR., (5, 9) THE KEYSTONE VIEW COMPANY, (10, 12) TOPICAL PRESS AGENCY, (11) W. G. BERRIDGE

DOMESTIC CATS

1. White Manx (tailless) cat, Champion Chelsea, "Villish Mona Veen"
2. Siamese cat, Champion "Simple"
3. Abyssinian (silver) male cat, owned by Mrs. Carew-Cox
4. Striped Manx cat
5. White Persian cat, "Morvich," owned by Mrs. J. H. Clark
6. Black Persian, Champion "Sally Girl"
7. Tabby cat
8. Red Tabby Persian cat
9. Blue Persian cat
10. Blotched domestic cat
11. The manul or Pallas's cat
12. Striped domestic cat

utrumque probabile ("Some say this, some that: both opinions probable") "entertain all interests, and comply with all persuasions, and send no one away unsatisfied."

It was the project of the English school of casuists—the Calvinists William Perkins (1558–1602) and his disciple William Ames (1576–1633), the Anglicans Joseph Hall (1574–1656), Robert Sanderson (1587–1663), Jeremy Taylor (1613–67) and John Sharp (1645–1714), and Richard Baxter (1615–91), who refused to conform in 1662—to purge casuistry of these blemishes: to banish the excesses of probabilism and make casuistical divinity a guide to holy living instead of merely the science of judgment on past sins, with a usefulness that would not be confined to the confessional. Although good work was done, the aim was not to be realized. The 18th century had no patience at all with the previous century's addiction to cases of conscience; and moral theology to all intents vanished from the Church of England for more than 100 years. Within Lutheranism it had already died. Indeed, if Karl Barth is right about the true nature of Protestantism, there is no room in it for a moral theology, let alone casuistry; and it is precisely the element in Emil Brunner's thought which Barth regards as Catholic and heterodox that enabled him to write *The Divine Imperative* (Eng. trans., London, 1937) and *Justice and the Social Order* (Eng. trans., London, 1945). It was therefore left to the Church of Rome to keep the torch of casuistry alight, albeit with a wavering and smoky flame, through a murky period, until the papal condemnation of laxist errors and the work of St. Alphonso Liguori (1696–1787) had prepared the way for better things.

The 19th-century revival in the Church of Rome produced some sound but on the whole uninspired manuals of moral theology, mostly with a casuistical turn; but the Anglican rediscovery of moral theology begat very little writing, the only work of casuistry worth mention being W. W. Webb's *The Cure of Souls* (New York, 1892). In the 20th century both Roman and Anglican writers came to pay considerable attention to contemporary sexual, matrimonial and medico-moral questions; and here an odd reversal is to be noted in that, while many Anglican conclusions (some of them obviously products of amateur casuistry) revived the *alii aiunt, alii negant; utrumque probabile* which Jeremy Taylor deplored, Roman casuistry grew if anything too rigid. By the middle of the century moral theology was engaged in re-examining its scriptural and dogmatic foundations, its methodology and aims and its relation to ascetics (*cf.* G. Gilleman, S.J., *Le Primat de la charité en théologie morale*, Louvain, 1952; and B. Olivier, O.P., and others, *Morale chrétienne et requêtes contemporaines,* Tournai, 1954). There were signs that reforms might ensue, the effect of which upon casuistry could not yet be foreseen.

BIBLIOGRAPHY.—For the literary history *see* T. J. Bouquillon, *Theologia moralis fundamentalis,* 3rd ed., pp. 71 ff. (Bruges, 1903). For a Roman Catholic view: *Dictionnaire de théologie catholique,* 3rd ed., *s.v.* "Cas de conscience" and "Casuistique" (1923). For an Anglican view: K. E. Kirk, *Conscience and Its Problems* (London, New York, 1927); also H. R. McAdoo, *The Structure of Caroline Moral Theology* (London, New York, 1949); and T. Wood, *English Casuistical Divinity During the Seventeenth Century* (London, 1952). For an account of casuistry in the less strict sense—a little marred by the intrusion of an individual moral philosophy: *Encyclopaedia of Religion and Ethics, s.v.* (London, 1910). For Stoic practice: Raymond Thamin, *Un problème moral dans l'antiquité* (Paris, 1884). For modern examples: E. J. Mahoney, *Questions and Answers,* part ii (London, 1949); F. L. Good and O. F. Kelly, *Marriage, Morals and Medical Ethics* (Dublin, 1952); and the *Cahiers Laënnec* (Paris, various dates) on medico-moral questions; also certain reports—commission appointed by the archbishop of Canterbury, *Artificial Human Insemination* (London, 1948); commission appointed by the archbishops of Canterbury and York, *The Church and the Atom* (London, 1948); Social and Industrial Commission of the Church Assembly, *Gambling: An Ethical Discussion* (London, 1950); Church of England Moral Welfare Council, *Human Sterilization* (London, undated). (G. B. B.)

CASUS BELLI, a situation said to justify a state in initiating war. The United Nations charter provided that warlike measures are permissible only if authorized by the Security council or the general assembly, or if necessary for "individual or collective self-defence" against "armed attack." (*See* ARBITRATION, INTERNATIONAL; WAR.) (Q. W.)

CAT, the name of the well-known domesticated animal *Felis catus,* but in a wider sense employed to denote all the more typical members of the family Felidae. The word "cat" is also applied to other objects, in all cases an application of the name of the animal. In mediaeval siegecraft the "cat" was a movable penthouse used to protect besiegers when approaching a wall or gateway.

"Cat" or "cat-head," in nautical usage, is the projecting beam on the bow of a ship used to clear the anchor from the sides of the vessel when weighed. The name is also used for a type of vessel, formerly used in the coal and timber trade in northeast England; it is still applied to a small rig of sailing boats. The instrument of punishment, generally called the "cat o' nine tails," consists of a handle of wood or rope, about 18 in. long, with nine knotted cords or thongs.

Origin of the Domestic Cat.—Although bones of cats were found in the dwellings of ancient cavemen, it is very probable that these cats were not domestic. About 3000 B.C. in Egypt, when agriculture had become well established, the Egyptians tamed the cat to protect their stores of grain. These animals proved so valuable that they were later considered to represent one of the gods, perhaps to give cats better protection. The wild species from which they were derived was the African wild cat (*Felis lybica*), one race of which occurred in Egypt. This is a gray cat with a slightly buffy cast, marked with blackish stripes and spots on the body and legs, the tail with a black tip and several rings, and the feet dusky. Its hair is short and the build and general proportions are like those of the common house cat. Modern domestic cats interbreed freely with the African wild cat.

From Egypt domestic cats spread slowly throughout the civilized world. In Europe they undoubtedly interbred with the European wild cat (*Felis silvestris*), a very closely related species with longer fur and tail. In the Egyptian wild cat the pads of the toes are wholly black, and the black extends up to the heel. In the European wild cat, on the other hand, the black is limited to a small round spot on the pads. In domestic cats with wild colouring the soles of the hind feet correspond in this particular with the Egyptian wild cat.

Two distinct types of so-called tabby cats are recognized. In one the pattern consists of narrow, vertical stripes and in the other of longitudinal or obliquely longitudinal stripes, which, on the sides of the body, tend to assume a spiral or whirl arrangement. One or other of these types is to be found in cats of almost all breeds, and there appear to be no intermediate stages. The striped type is the wild pattern of both European and African wild cats; but the origin of the blotched pattern was probably a mutation.

Tame cats from Egypt were imported into Italy at an early date by Phoenician traders and became established long before the Christian era. Their progeny spread over Europe, more or less crossed with the indigenous species. Remains of cats found in Roman villas at Silchester and Dursley are probably referable to the domesticated breed. The earliest record in Great Britain dates from about A.D. 936 when Howel Dda, prince of south central Wales, enacted a law for their protection.

There are fewer breeds of domestic cats than there are of dogs, and the differences are not so great as those shown in the various breeds of rabbits. Except in a very few cases there is no need to suppose crossing with other species to explain the peculiar characters of certain cats.

All animals are liable to show individual variation which can be selected and established in pure strains. Larger mutations occur rarely but are likely to make their appearance from time to time.

Breeds of Domestic Cats.—Apart from the division on the basis of their pattern, mentioned above, domestic cats are divided into short-haired and long-haired groups. The former resemble the wild cats of Europe and Africa, the long-haired types having developed in Persia and Afghanistan. Cats of both groups vary, on the one hand, toward melanism, black colouration like that seen in many wild species of cats, while on the other hand white cats are fairly common. A nearly white tiger and a similarly coloured cheeta have been reported, and an albino leopard is known, but albinism is very rare among all species of Felidae. Tortoise-shell cats are generally females with a mixed colour of black and yellow (and white); yellow or sandy cats are usually males. The genetic factors for red and black are thought to be situated in the sex chromosomes, which accounts for the peculiar inheritance of these colours.

There are two varieties of the long-haired cats, the Angora and the Persian. The former has a pointed head, long nose, and long, silky fur. The Persian (which may come from Afghanistan) has a rounded face and coarse fur; its tail is thickest near the tip. In the United States and parts of Europe the latter cat has replaced the Angora. These long-haired cats are often thought to have been derived from the manul (*Felis manul*) of the steppes of central Asia, but long-haired breeds of goats, rabbits and dogs indicate that it is not necessary to suppose such an unlikely ancestry.

The tailless or Manx cat, in which the tail may be represented merely by a tuft of hair without any bone, is common in the far east. In the Malay regions and Philippines normal long-tailed cats are rarely seen, and kink-tailed or short-tailed cats predominate. Whether the tailless cat reached the Isle of Man from elsewhere or whether it developed there as a sudden independent mutation is not known. The fur is usually longer and more lax than in ordinary cats. In New England and the middle Atlantic states they are often called "rabbit cats," and people suppose they are part rabbit, incredible as such a crossing would be. The cry is said to differ somewhat from that of tabby cats.

Among the domestic cats of India, spotted colouring, much like that of the Indian desert cat (*Felis constantina ornata*) is common. This cat is a close relative of the African wild cat, and crossing between it and domestic cats is quite possible.

The Abyssinian breed is characterized by lack of spots and stripes on the body, each hair being "ticked" like that of a wild rabbit (known to geneticists as agouti). The head and neck retain the typical markings of the African wild cat and the tail ends in a black tip. The colour is typically reddish brown. The fur is short, the ears relatively large and occasionally tipped with long hairs. Ordinary striped tabbies sometimes produce kittens with this type of colouration, and there is little question but that this breed originated entirely from the African wild cat, probably through the Egyptian cat.

By far the most remarkable of the domestic breeds is the Siamese cat. It was first imported into England in 1884 and reached the U.S. in 1895; it became popular and numerous in both countries. Siamese cats often have kinky tails and cross-eyes, defects which breeders have not been able to eliminate from the strain. The head is rather long and pointed, the body also elongate, the hair sleek and short, and the eyes blue. The general colour is cream or buffy, with the face, ears, paws and tail dark chocolate-coloured in a variety in which the eyes are yellow. The young are white. Temperature modifies the development of the colour, less blackish developing under warm conditions, while in cold the entire animal darkens more than normally. The Siamese type of colouration is known in rabbits and other animals, in which it is often called "Himalayan." In the several thousand years cats have been in Siam, the mutation undoubtedly appeared and was fixed by selection and careful breeding. After 1924, several strains of long-haired Siamese cats were produced scientifically by crossing with Persians and inbreeding.

Numerous clubs have been founded in Europe and North America to encourage the breeding of cats and to promote cat shows. Short-haired breeds are rather easy to manage, but the long-haired varieties need more care and when shedding are nuisances.

European Wild Cat.—The wild European species, *F. silvestris,* conforms closely in pattern to the striped phase of domestic tabby but is brownish gray or buffy. The hair of the tail is long, especially toward the tip, which gives a club shape to this member. The geographical range of the wild cat formerly included Great Britain, central and southern Europe, and portions of central Asia. It is now, however, much reduced in numbers and it is doubtful if it is found anywhere without at least a trace of the domestic form in its constitution. In Great Britain wild cats survive only in some Scottish forests. Remains of the wild cat occur in English caverns; in Ireland the wild species has apparently been unknown during the historic period.

The favourite haunts of the wild cat are mountain forests where rocks or cliffs are interspersed with trees. Crevices in the rocks or the hollow trunks of trees afford sites for the lairs, where the young (2 to 5) are produced and reared. The kittens, usually born in May, are at first blind, although furred. Wild cats are described as some of the most ferocious and untamable of all animals. How far this lends support to the view of the origin of our domestic breeds is uncertain. Hares, rabbits, field mice, water rats, rats, squirrels, moles, game birds, pigeons, and small birds form the chief food of the wild cat, while fawns of roe deer are sometimes killed.

BIBLIOGRAPHY.—St. George Mivart, *The Cat* (London, 1881); R. Lydekker, "Cats," in *Allen's Naturalists' Library* (1888); F. Hamilton, *The Wild Cat of Europe* (London, 1896); Frances Simpson, *The Book of the Cat* (London, 1903); E. H. Forbush, *The Domestic Cat* (Boston, 1916); E. B. Simmons, *Cats* (1935); E. B. H. Soame, *Cats, Long-Haired and Short* (1934); Carl Van Vechten, *Tiger in the House* (1920); Ida M. Mellen, *The Science and Mystery of the Cat* (New York, 1940). (J. E. HL.)

CATACLYSM, a great flood (Gr. κατακλυσμός, a deluge). In geology an overwhelming catastrophe producing sudden changes in the earth's surface; figuratively, any violent change that sweeps away the existing social or political order.

CATACOMBS. Tombs hewn in solid rock were used by the Etruscans as independent family burial places, grouped together. They often rise in the hillside by tiers or are on the same level branching off into streets and alleys. Their plan is for the most part that of a house and the walls are often covered with paintings in an archaic style in red and black. At Poggio Gaiella, near Chiusi, the ancient Clusium, is a cemetery with a sepulchral chamber containing a large hall about 25 ft. in diameter supported by a cylindrical rock pillar. Opening out of this and other chambers are low winding passages, just large enough for a man to creep through, and this tomb has been surmised to be that of Lars Porsena, king in his day of Etruria (*see* fig. 2).

In the days of the republic inhumation was general and the bodies of the Scipios and the Nasos were buried in still existing catacombs, the term applied by transference to subterranean excavations for the interment of the dead. Originally it designated the natural configuration—in hollows—of a district close to the Appian way (*see* ROME). In the vaults below the church of St. Sebastiano lay, according to tradition, the bodies of the apostles St. Peter and St. Paul for seven months until removed to the basilicas which bear their names. The place became an object of pilgrimage and its name κατακυμβας, "by the hollow," developed as a generic name for all burial places of the same kind.

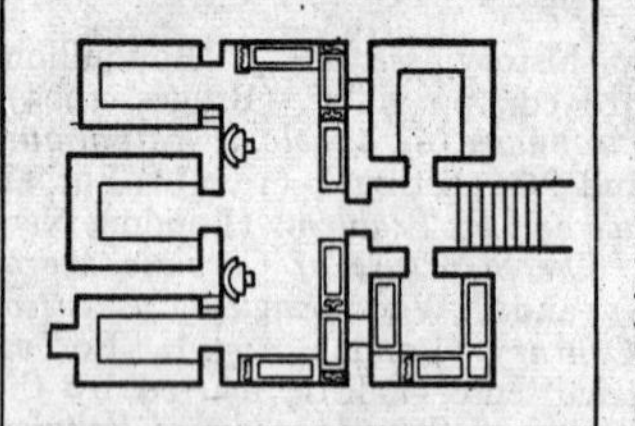

FROM DENNIS
FIG. 1.—PLAN OF ETRUSCAN TOMB AT CERVETRI

Rome is built upon a rock and the three strata named by geologists *tufa litoide, tufa granolare* and *pozzolana* have all been exploited. The *tufa litoide* is quarried as building stone. The catacombs of Rome—the most extensive known—are constructed in this stratum alone as it enabled the engineers to form vertical walls for the galleries in which the dead were placed and to work with comparative ease. The pozzolana used as an ingredient for mortar was worked from the lowest stratum so that in spite of old erroneous persistent beliefs the burial places are distinct from the pozzolana, excavated in different strata, though here and there starting from the same level. The catacombs form a vast labyrinth of narrow galleries usually from 3 to 4 ft. wide with small chambers at intervals, excavated at successive levels (fig. 1). The dead are buried in the galleries in long horizontal recesses in the walls, tier upon tier, even to 12 ranges. The galleries generally run in straight tiers, at the same level, in storeys (seven in one part of the cemetery of S. Calixtus), and intersect at various angles (*see* fig. 3). The graves (*loculi*) were usually parallel to

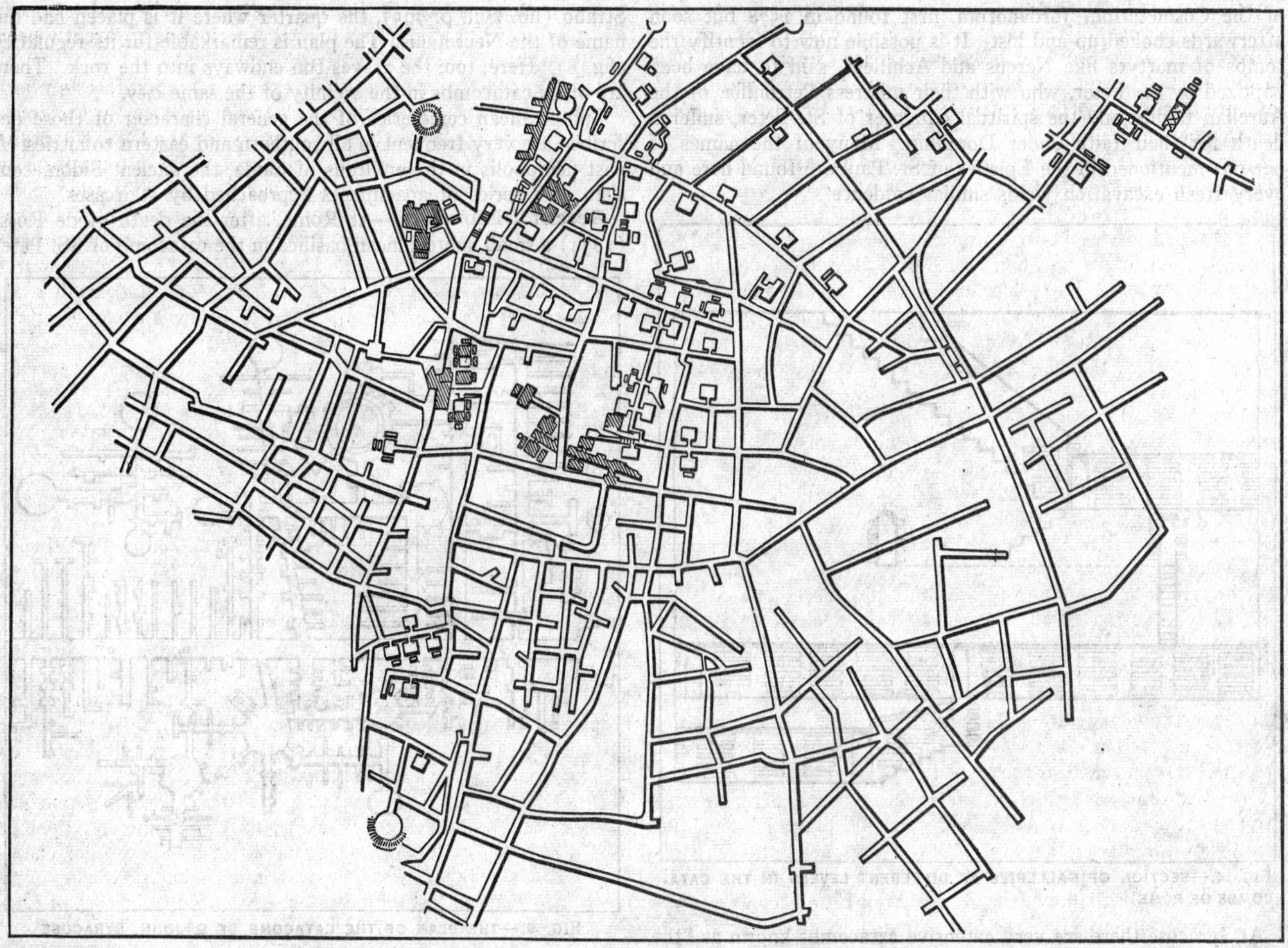

FROM MARTIGNY

FIG. 3.—PLAN OF PART OF THE CEMETERY OF S. AGNESE AT ROME

the gallery in Christian cemeteries, but in pagan areas the recess was usually at right angles. Some loculi held four or more bodies, most held one (fig. 5). They were carefully closed by slabs of marble or huge tiles cemented together. When an epitaph was set up, it was painted or engraved on these tiles. Table tombs and arched tombs are also found. Sarcophagi are rare. The family vaults—cubicula—were small apartments, usually rectangular, sometimes circular or polygonal, opening from the main corridors and frequently ranged regularly along the sides of the galleries. Loculi were cut for later burials in the same family area and the inscriptions and mural decorations were frequently damaged or destroyed. The funeral feast was celebrated by the family in its vault, both on the day of burial and on the anniversary. The Eucharist, the invariable accompaniment of funerals in the early Christian Church, was celebrated here, and in some of the catacombs are larger halls and connected suites of chapels which may have been constructed for congregational worship in the days of persecution (fig. 4). Baptisteries have been discovered. The catacombs were also used as places of refuge, for which they were admirably adapted, both by the intricacy of their design and by access through secret passages to sand quarries and the open country.

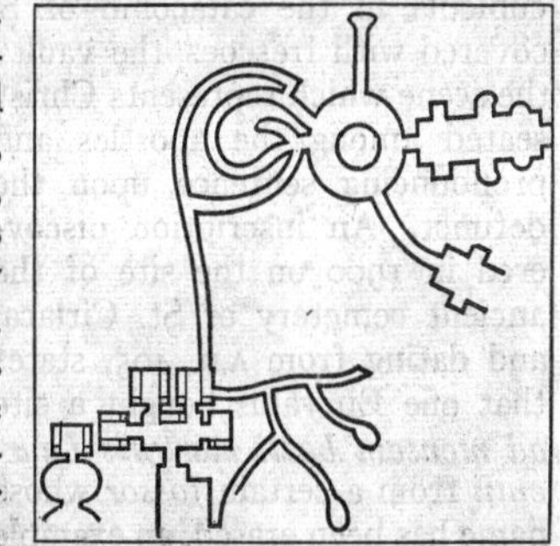

FROM DENNIS

FIG. 2.—PLAN OF A PORTION OF THE PRINCIPAL STOREY IN THE POGGIO GAIELLA CEMETERY

Almost without exception they had their origin in small burial areas, the property of private persons, and their great development was due to the spread of Christianity and the burial of the dead in this manner conformed to Roman usage. There was no reason for secrecy and since interment in rock-hewn tombs had been practised in Rome by Jewish settlers before the rise of the Christian Church, the practice may well have been popularly, perhaps correctly, associated with the Jewish population which contributed elements to the new religious order. At a later period the grave diggers seem to have acquired or to have established a kind of property in the catacombs and to make new graves recklessly destroyed the religious paintings on the walls. The major part of the catacombs belong to the 3rd and early part of the 4th centuries. By A.D. 354 when St. Jerome visited them, interment in them had become rare. By the time of Pope Damasus (A.D. 366–384) they had become the resort of pilgrims. They were adapted to this by the orders of the pope. The works of art were restored. The epitaphs were renewed. In this latter work he employed an engraver named Furius Philocalus whose work can be recognized at once.

As a result the improvements described have lessened the value of the catacombs as memorials of the religious art of the 2nd and 3rd centuries. Subterranean interment ceased with the sack of Rome by Alaric in A.D. 410. The catacombs shared in the destruction of Rome by the Goths in the 6th century and by the Lombards at a later date. Pope Paul I. and Pope Pascha I. found them in such decay and pollution that the holy relics they contained were translated elsewhere and the catacombs soon ceased to attract pilgrims. By degrees their existence was forgotten and they were discovered by chance in 1578 and have been studied, explored, investigated and described by scholars such as Baronius, Antonio Bosio (d. 1629), Marc Antonio Boldetti (*c.* 1720), Seroux d'Agincourt (1825) Raoul Rochette and most notably in recent times by Father Marchi of the Society of Jesus. Additions to our knowledge have been made by de Rossi and include the rediscovery near the catacomb of Priscilla, on the Via Salaria Nuova, of the Cosmeterium Jordanorum, first found in 1578 but soon afterwards choked up and lost. It is possible now to identify the tombs of martyrs like Nereus and Achilleus, said to have been baptized by St. Peter, who with their mistress Petronilla, of the Aurelian family and the spiritual daughter of St. Peter, suffered death for their faith under Domitian. Many of the names of persons mentioned in the Epistles of St. Paul are found here and every fresh excavation yields similar evidence.

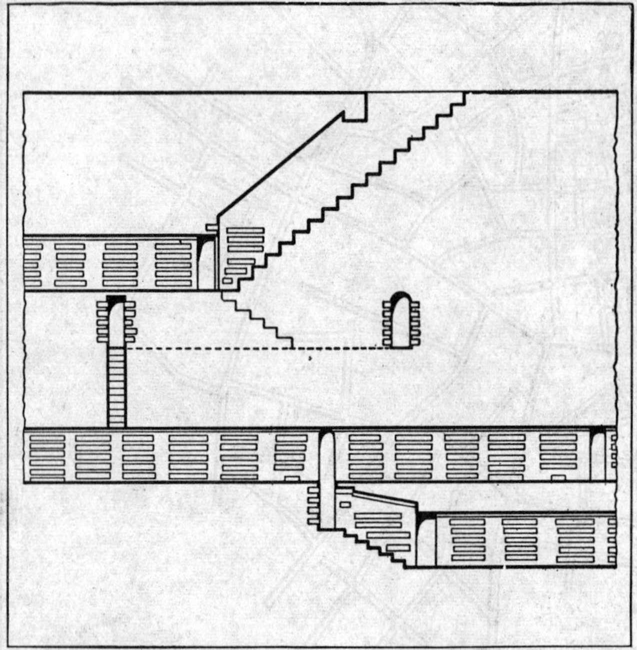

FIG. 4.—SECTION OF GALLERIES AT DIFFERENT LEVELS IN THE CATACOMBS OF ROME

At Syracuse there are very extensive catacombs known as "the Grottos of St. John." There is an entire underground city with several storeys of larger and smaller streets, squares and cross ways cut out of the rock; at the intersection of the cross ways are great circular halls of a bottle shape, like a glass-house furnace, lighted by air shafts. The galleries are generally very narrow, furnished on each side with arched tombs, and communicating with family sepulchral-chambers closed originally by doors, the marks of the hinges and staples being still visible. The walls are in many places coated with stucco adorned with frescoes including palms, doves, *labara* and other Christian symbols. This cemetery differs widely in arrangement from the Roman catacombs.

The catacombs at Malta are near the ancient capital of the island. The passages were all cut in a close-grained stone, and are very narrow, with arched ceilings, running very irregularly, and ramifying in all directions. The greater part of the tombs stand on either side of the galleries in square recesses (like the table-tombs of the Roman catacombs) and are rudely fashioned to imitate sarcophagi. The interments are not nearly so numerous as in other catacombs, nor are there any vestiges of painting, sculpture or inscriptions. At Taormina in Sicily is a Saracenic catacomb, also figured by Agincourt. The main corridor is 12 ft. wide, having three or more ranges of *loculi* on either side, running longitudinally into the rock, each originally closed by a stone bearing an inscription.

FROM DE ROSSI

FIG. 5.—LOCULI IN CATACOMBS OF ROME. GRAVES OF URBICA AND RUFINA

In Egypt we find a small Christian catacomb at Alexandria. The *loculi* here also are set endways to the passage. The walls are abundantly decorated with paintings, one of a liturgical character. But the most extensive catacombs at Alexandria are those of Egypto-Greek origin, from the largest of which, according to Strabo (lib. xvii. p. 795), the quarter where it is placed had the name of the Necropolis. The plan is remarkable for its regularity (fig. 8). Here, too, the graves run endways into the rock. There are other catacombs in the vicinity of the same city.

Subterranean cemeteries of the general character of those described are very frequent in all southern and eastern countries. A vast necropolis in the environs of Saida, the ancient Sidon, consists of a series of apartments approached by staircases.

Recent Discoveries.—At Rome, after the death of de Rossi (1894) a small subterranean basilica in the catacomb of SS. Peter and Marcellinus on the Via Labicana, with pious acclamations on the plaster similar to those in the Papal crypt in St. Calixtus was discovered in 1896. In the cemetery of Domitilla in 1897–1898 a fine double crypt with frescoes representing Christ seated between six male and female saints and an inscription relating to a new saint (Eulalius) in a cubiculum of the 3rd century was brought to light. In 1899–1900 were discovered two opposite cubicula in the catacomb of SS. Peter and Marcellinus, both covered with frescoes, the vault being in one case decorated with the scene which represents Christ seated among the apostles and pronouncing sentence upon the defunct. An inscription discovered in 1900 on the site of the ancient cemetery of St. Ciriaca, and dating from A.D. 405, states that one Euryalus bought a site *ad mensam beati martyris Laurentii* from a certain *fossor* whose name has been erased, an example of what was known as *memoriae damnatio*, or the blotting out of a name on account of some dishonourable action. In 1901–1902 excavations in the cemetery of Santa Priscilla, near the Cappella Greca, revealed a polygonal chamber which may have originally been the *nymphaeum* of the great villa of the Acilii Glabriones. It may have been used as a burial-place for martyrs, and as the sepulchral chapel of Pope Marcellinus, who died in A.D. 304 during the persecutions of Diocletian. In 1902, in that part of the Via Ardeatina which passes between the cemeteries of Calixtus and Domitilla, was discovered a crypt with frescoes and the sanctuary of a martyr; this, rather than a neighbouring crypt brought to light in 1897, may prove to be the sepulchral crypt of SS. Marcus and Marcellianus. In a cubiculum leading out of a gallery

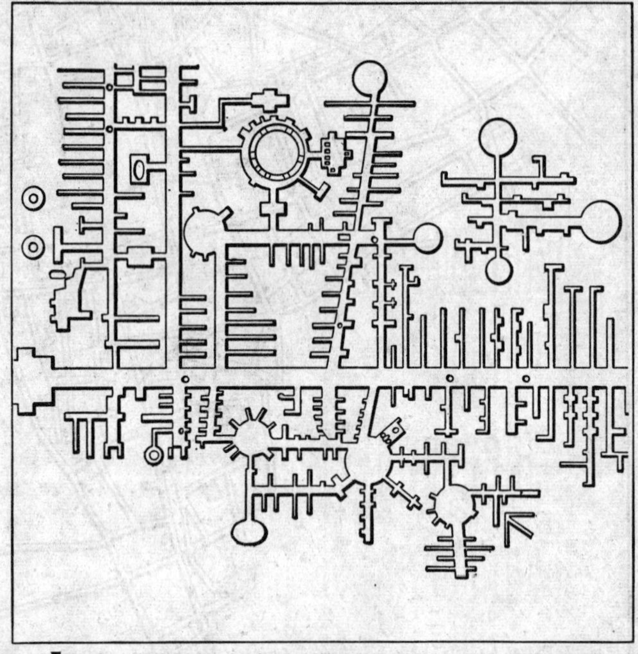

FIG. 6.—THE PLAN OF THE CATACOMB OF S. JOHN, SYRACUSE

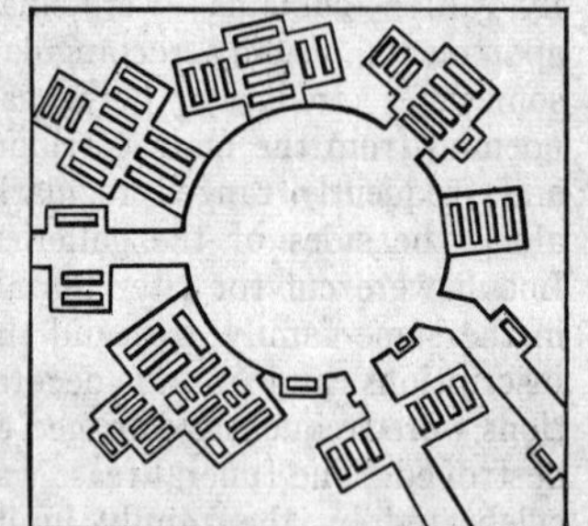

FIG. 7.—PLAN OF CIRCULAR HALL IN CATACOMBS OF S. JOHN, SYRACUSE

in the vicinity there was also discovered an interesting impression in plaster of an inscription of the mother of Pope Damasus, beginning:

Hic Damasi Mater Posvit Lavren (tia Membra).

In the same year building operations in the Via di Sant' Onofrio revealed the presence of catacombs beneath the foundations: examination of the *loculi* showed that no martyrs or illustrious persons were buried there. Work was also carried out at the catacomb of Albano (Marucchi *Nuovo Bull.*, 1902, pp. 89 ff.).

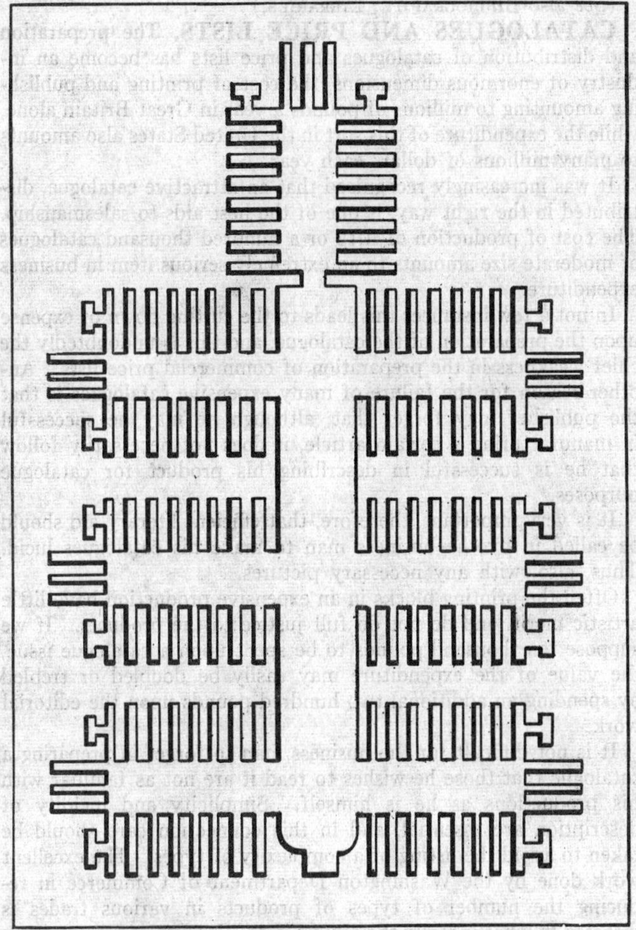

FIG. 8.—PLAN OF CATACOMB AT ALEXANDRIA

In 1903 a new cemetery with frescoes came to light on the Via Latina, considered by Marucchi to have belonged to a heretical sect. In the same year the Jewish cemetery on the Via Portuense, was rediscovered. The subterranean basilica of SS. Felix and Adauctus, discovered by Boldetti and afterwards choked up with ruins, was cleared again: the crypt, begun by Damasus and enlarged by Siricius, contains frescoes of the 6th–7th centuries. In the same year extensive catacombs were revealed on the site of Hadrumetum near Sousse in Tunisia.

In 1907–08 interesting discoveries were made in the South East of Sicily (P. Orsi, *Notizie degli Scavi*, 1908). The year 1911 witnessed the discovery of the remarkable *hypogeum* of Trebius Justus on the Via Latina, with frescoes showing gnostic influence (*Nuovo Bull.* 1911 and 1912). In 1912 a catacomb was found at Grottaferrata which has since been excavated by the Basilian monks. In 1915–1916 a *memoria* of SS. Peter and Paul was explored beneath the basilica of S. Sebastiano, *Ad catacumbas*, on the Appian way. *Graffiti* with invocations to these apostles, dating from the fourth century were discovered (Marucchi, *Nuovo Bullettino*, for 1916, 1917, 1919, 1920). In 1917 was found subterranean basilica of the first century, perhaps the work of a pagan *sodalitas* (g. Bagnani, *Journ. of Roman Studies*, 1919, p. 78). In 1919, not far from the Porta Maggiore and the ancient Via Labicana, a *hypogeum* with two frescoed chambers was discovered. The subjects were unusual; one, Christ instructing his sheep from a book recalled a passage in the inscriptions of Abercius in the Lateran; others were scenes from the story of Job diverging from those usual in the Catacombs; a group of 12 figures, perhaps apostles, including two recalling the traditional types of SS. Peter and Paul (Marucchi, *Nuovo Bull.* 1921). The year 1921 witnessed the rediscovery near the catacomb of Priscilla on the Via Salaria Nuova, of the *Coemeterium Jordanorum*, first found in 1578 but soon afterwards choked up and lost (Marucchi and Josi, *Nuovo Bull.* 1922).

BIBLIOGRAPHY.—The classical work on the catacombs of Rome is G. B. De Rossi's *Roma sotterranea*. The volume by Mgr. Wilpert, *Le Pitture delle catacombe romane* (Rome, 1903), in which all the important frescoes are reproduced in colours, is complementary to the *Roma sotterranea*. All new discoveries made by the *Commissione di archeologia sacra* are chronicled in the *Nuovo Bullettino de archeologia* the *Notizie degli scavi*.

For accounts of the catacombs *see*:—Armellini, *Gli Antichi Cimiteri cristiani di Roma e d'Italia* (Rome, 1893); O. Marucchi, *Le Catacombe romane* (Rome, 1903; also translated into French), *Manuale di epigrafia cristiana* (Milan, 1904); M. Besnier, *Les Catacombes de Rome* (Paris, 1909); F. X. Kraus (*Realencyklopädie* and *Geschichte der christlichen Kunst*) and Dom F. Cabrol's *Dictionnaire d'archéologie chrétienne et liturgie*, articles with bibliography, by H. Leclercq.

Among the older works are: Bosio, *Roma sotterranea*, Severano's edition (1632), and Aringhi's edition (1651); Boldetti, *Osservazioni sopra i cimiteri dei santi martiri* (Rome, 1720); Bottari, *Sculture e pitture sagre*, etc. (Rome, 1737–1754); Seroux d'Agincourt, *Histoire de l'art par les monuments* (Paris, 1823; German ed., 1840); G. Marchi, *Monumenti delle arti cristiane primitive* (Rome, 1844); Raoul Rochette, *Tableau des catacombes de Rome* (2nd ed., Paris, 1853); Perret, *Les Catacombes de Rome* (Paris, 1855)—a sumptuous folio work, but not always accurate; Roller, *Les Catacombes de Rome* (Paris, 1881); V. Schultze, *Die Katakomben* (Leipzig, 1882).

Works written in English are: Northcote and Brownlow, *Roma sotterranea* (London, 1869; based upon De Rossi); Wharton Marriott, *The Testimony of the Catacombs* (1870); J. H. Parker, *The Archaeology of Rome: the Catacombs;* Smith and Cheetham, *Dictionary of Christian Antiquities, s.v.* "Catacombs"; R. Lanciani, *Pagan and Christian Rome* (1892); W. Lowry, *Christian Art and Archaeology*, ch. ii. (1901; a useful introduction to the subject); H. Gee, "The Church in the Catacombs," in W. Lefroy's *Lectures in Ecclesiastical History* (1896); Th. Mommsen, in the *Contemporary Review* (May 1871).

The catacombs at Naples are described in C. F. Bellermann, *Über die ältesten christlichen Begräbnisstätten und besonders die Katakomben zu Neapel* (Hamburg, 1839); Armellini, as above and V. Schultze, *Die Katakomben von San Gennaro dei Poveri in Neapel* (Jena, 1877).

For the catacombs in Malta, A. A. Caruana, *Ancient Pagan Tombs and Christian Cemeteries in the Islands of Malta* (Malta, 1898), and A. Mayr, "Die altchristlichen Begräbnisstätten auf Malta," in *Römische Quartalschrift*, vol. xv. pp. 216 and 352 (Rome, 1901), and E. Becker, *Malta Sotterranea* (Strasbourg, 1913), may be consulted.

The fullest accounts of the Sicilian catacombs are given by J. Fuhrer, *Forschungen zur Sicilia sotterranea* (Munich, 1897); C. Barreca, *Le Catacombe di San Giovanni in Siracusa* (Syracuse, 1906); J. Fuhrer and V. Schultze, *Die altchristlichen Grabstätten Siziliens* (Berlin, 1907); and P. Orsi, *Per la Siracusa Sotterranea* (Catania, 1906).

A catacomb of the 5th century, discovered at Kertch in South Russia, is described by J. Kulakovsky in *Materials for Russian Archaeology* (St. Petersburg, 1896; a publication of the Russian Imperial Archaeological Commission), but it is written in Russian, as also is the account by V. Latyshev, in *Vizantieski Vremennik*, vol. vi. pp. 337 ff. (St. Petersburg, 1899).

The catacombs at Hadrumetum (Sousse) are described by A. F. Leynaud, *Les Catacombes d'Hadrumète, deuxième campagne de fouilles* (1904–1905). *See* also *Revue Tunisienne* (1905), p. 250.

For the catacombs of Alexandria, de Rossi in *Bull. di archeologia Cristiana* (Nov. 1864, Dec. 1865); Neroutsos Bey, *L'Ancienne Alexandrie.* (W. R. B.; O. M. D.)

CATAFALQUE, a word of unknown origin, occurring in various forms in many European languages, meaning a funeral scaffold or temporary stage; a movable structure of wood, sometimes richly decorated, erected temporarily at funeral ceremonies in a church to receive the coffin or effigy of the deceased; also an open hearse or funeral car.

CATALAN. It is generally assumed that Catalan was imported from Roussillon into Spain during Carolingian times; the contrary view has, however, been put forward, namely that Catalan originally developed in Spain and was introduced into Cerdagne and Roussillon by Catalan immigration. Whatever the truth may be, philologically Catalan is to be regarded as pertaining to the Provençal rather than to the Hispanic branch. Like Hispanic it changes L. *ū* into *u* and L. *au* into *o*, *cf.*, L. *mūrum*, Cat. *mur*, Hisp. *muro* (Prov. Fr. *mur*); L. *aurum*, Cat. and Hisp. *oro* (Prov. *aur*, Fr. *or*).

Unknown to Catalan, however, are the characteristically Hispanic diphthongizations of open *e* and open *o* in position; *cf.*, L. *terra*, Hisp. *tierra*, but Cat. *terra;* L. *fortem*, Hisp. *fuerte*, but Cat. *fort* (as in Prov. and Fr.). Moreover Catalan and Provençal both change proparoxytones into paroxytones, whereas in Hispanic the proparoxytones are preserved (*e.g.*, L. *anima*, Cat. and Prov. *alma, arma*).

Catalan survived in modern times in the major part of the department of the Pyrénées Orientales, in Andorra, at Alghero (Sardinia) whither it was brought by the Aragonese in the second quarter of the 14th century but where it steadily succumbed to the disruptive influence of Italian and Sardinian; in the provinces of Huesca, Saragossa, Ternel; in the greater part of the provinces of Castellon de la Plana and Alicante; in much of the province of Valencia; and in the Balearic Islands and Pithyusae, conquered by Jaime I of Aragon (1229–34).

Catalan embraces two groups, viz., (1) continental, subdivided into (*a*) oriental, (*b*) occidental, (*c*) Valencian, (*d*) Roussillonnais; (2) insular, subdivided into (*a*) dialects of the Balearic Islands and Pithyusae, (*b*) dialect of Alghero.

All these idioms present only minor phonetic differences. In the Balearic Islands *es, sa* constitute the definite article (as also in the subdialect of oriental Catalan termed for this reason, *salat*) instead of *el, la.*

The outstanding difference between the Catalan of Spain and that of Roussillon is that whereas the former is a real language with a flourishing literature the latter is a mere patois.

BIBLIOGRAPHY.—P. Fouché, *Chronique philologique des parlers provençaux anciens et modernes* (Bibl.) in *Revue de linguistique romane* T. II. (Janvier-Juin, 1926) p. 113–136; A. Griera, *Le domaine catalan* (*compte rendu rétrospectif jusqu'à 1924*) in *Revue de linguistique romane* T. I. (Janvier-Juin, 1925) p. 35–113. (L. B.)

CATALANI, ALFREDO (1854–1893), Italian composer, was born at Lucca, on June 19, 1854, and studied under the French composer, Emmanuel Bazin, at the Paris conservatoire and at the Milan conservatoire.

His well-known opera *La Wally*, first performed in 1892, was favourably received in Italy, and it was produced at the Metropolitan Opera house, New York city, in 1908–09. *Loreley* (Turin, 1890) was performed in Chicago, Ill., in 1918 and in New York city in 1921–22.

Catalani's other works include *La Falce*, his first dramatic work, produced in 1875; *Elda* (Turin, 1880), a four-act opera; *Dejanice* (Milan, 1883), also in four acts; *Ero e Leandro* (1885), a symphonic poem for orchestra; and *Edmea* (Milan, 1886), a three-act opera.

Catalani died in Milan on Aug. 7, 1893.

CATALANI, ANGELICA (1780–1849), Italian opera singer, was born at Sinigaglia, on May 10, 1780, and was the lucky possessor of one of the most remarkable soprano voices, of extraordinary compass and purity, ever known.

For nearly 30 years she sang at all the great opera houses, receiving very large fees.

At an early age she entered the Santa Lucia convent at Gubbio. After leaving the convent she had very successful engagements throughout Italy, first appearing in Venice at the age of 16.

She appeared at the Italian opera in Portugal in 1804 and later sang in Madrid and Paris, her reputation continuing to increase wherever she sang.

Her first appearance in London was at the King's theatre in 1806. She remained in England, a prima donna without a serious rival, for seven years.

Then she was given the management of the opera in Paris, but this resulted in financial failure because of the incapacity and extravagance of her husband, Captain Valabrègue—author of the historic remark, "ma femme et quatre ou cinq poupées voila tout ce qu'il faut"—whom she had married in 1806.

But her continental tours continued to be enormously successful until she retired in 1828.

She died of cholera in Paris on June 12, 1849.

CATALINA ISLAND: *see* SANTA CATALINA.

CATALOGUE, a list or enumeration, generally in alphabetical order, of persons, things, etc., and particularly of the contents of a museum or library.

A *catalogue raisonnée* is such a list classified according to subjects or on some other basis, usually with short explanations and notes.

(*See* also BIBLIOGRAPHY; LIBRARIES.)

CATALOGUES AND PRICE LISTS. The preparation and distribution of catalogues and price lists has become an industry of enormous dimensions, the cost of printing and publishing amounting to millions of pounds a year in Great Britain alone, while the expenditure of this sort in the United States also amounts to many millions of dollars each year.

It was increasingly recognized that an attractive catalogue, distributed in the right way, is one of the best aids to salesmanship. The cost of production of fifty or a hundred thousand catalogues of moderate size amounts to an extremely serious item in business expenditure.

In not a few instances this leads to the cutting down of expense upon the preparation of the catalogue, and this is undoubtedly the chief weakness in the preparation of commercial price lists. Another reason for the failure of many expensive catalogues is that the publisher may forget that, although he may be successful in manufacturing a certain article, it does not necessarily follow that he is successful in describing his product for catalogue purposes.

It is very important, therefore, that efficient literary aid should be called in by the business man to make his catalogues lucid. Thus, also, with any necessary pictures.

Often the printing blocks in an expensive production have little artistic merit, and do not do full justice to the products. If we suppose ten thousand pounds to be spent upon a catalogue issue, the value of the expenditure may easily be doubled or trebled by spending an additional two hundred pounds upon the editorial work.

It is not difficult for the business man to forget in preparing a catalogue that those he wishes to read it are not as familiar with his productions as he is himself. Simplicity and lucidity of description are essential, and in this connection care should be taken to avoid the listing of a complexity of types. The excellent work done by the Washington Department of Commerce in reducing the number of types of products in various trades is directed to what is really the same point. Variety, of course, there should be, but the types chosen for listing should be distinctly different, and the reasons for the differences very clearly stated.

If, for example, the catalogue offers a series of gas heaters and cookers, the types chosen should not only be essentially different, but the essential differences should be made quite clear to the reader. If the stove is a heating appliance, the kind of room for which it is suited, the kind of flue needed, the method of installation, and the cost of maintenance should all be demonstrated. When prices vary in a series, the reason for the differences should appear. Nothing is more confusing or stultifying in a catalogue than to be told on one page that Type A of a certain manufacture is the "best," or the "finest," when the very next page refers to another thing of the same sort priced at a much higher figure. What should be done is to show clearly that the article priced is good value at its price; good value for its particular purpose; good value to meet a particular need.

The Listing of "Extras."—Every endeavour should be made in drawing up a catalogue to offer each article ready for use, at a price covering the entire equipment necessary to put it into use. Thus, at one time it was the unfortunate practice of motor-car manufacturers to offer their machines at a certain price, and then to add a long list of extras necessary to fit out the machine ready for the road. This practice has, happily, been abandoned in the automobile industry, but it still obtains in many other trades. First, the buyer is offered the article at a certain price, but this price does not represent the thing ready for use or consumption; a number of extras are listed in a confusing way so that the real price of the article fit for use has to be worked out with more or less difficulty. The manufacturer of a machine-tool gains when he offers his product completely fitted with necessary safety-appliances; equally the manufacturer of a roofing felt is likely to increase his sales if his price list shows the material put into convenient rolls well packed, accompanied with the necessary amount of cement for the lapping of edges, and with purpose-made nails to fix it. The aim of every catalogue should be to offer the articles it lists ready for use.

The format of a catalogue is of great importance. The catalogue of a store should be divided into sections and well indexed. In the case of the small catalogue, or "folder," it is far better to concentrate upon one really good production at a time than to issue a sheaf of documents of different sizes which are only too likely to bewilder and irritate the would-be buyer. It is quite usual at trade exhibitions to be handed half a dozen differently shaped folders referring to a single object, instead of being given one handy, pocket-sized, beautifully printed, well-considered piece of printing.

An excellent aid to business in a catalogue, and one that is much appreciated by buyers, is the insertion of intelligent matter directly or indirectly relating to the articles offered. This may be illustrated by the case of a sports catalogue. The manufacturer of cricket-bats or tennis-rackets does well to include in his catalogue expert directions for the preservation of the articles sold, or hints on the laws of the game, or other interesting cognate matter. Again, the catalogue of a piano-player may well be accompanied by a lucid account of the invention, instructions for the care of the instrument, hints as to getting the best results from it, and so forth.

As to catalogues for the export market, it is an old complaint, and a just one, that their publishers too often fail to adapt them to the needs of the country to which they are supposed to appeal. If a catalogue is prepared for South America, for example, it is quite useless to prepare it in English; it should be translated into Spanish (or into Portuguese, if for Brazil) and weights and measures and prices expressed in their proper equivalents. Consular reports from foreign countries again and again dwell upon the neglect of these elementary measures for making an export catalogue useful.

CATALONIA (*Cataluña*), an autonomous region, and formerly a province of Spain, formerly also a principality of Aragon; bounded on the north by the Pyrenees, west by Aragon, south by Valencia, and east by the Mediterranean Sea. Population (1950) 3,240,313; area, 12,414 sq. miles. The triangular territory of Catalonia forms the north-east corner of the Iberian Peninsula. It was divided in 1833 into four provinces, Barcelona, Gerona, Lérida and Tarragona (*see* separate articles). The surface is much broken by southern spurs of the Pyrenees. Running south-west to north-east, and united on the north with one of the offsets of the Pyrenees, is the range of the Sierra Llena, which bisects Catalonia, and forms its central watershed. The principal rivers are the Ter, the Llobrégat and the Ebro (*q.v.*), which all run into the Mediterranean. The coast is in places difficult but has important harbours, *e.g.*, Barcelona and Tarragona. Cut off orographically on the south and west Catalonia has had more associations with south France than with the Douro or Guadalquivir basins, and the Catalan language differs considerably from Castilian Spanish and has affinities with Provençal. Catalonia was one of the first of the Roman possessions in Spain, forming the north-eastern portion of Hispania Tarraconensis. About 470 it was occupied by Alans and Goths. It was conquered by the Moors in 712, but these invaders were in turn dispossessed by the Spaniards and the troops of Charlemagne in 788. Catalonia was subsequently ruled by French counts, who soon made themselves independent of France. By the marriage of Count Raymond Berenger IV. of Barcelona with Petronilla of Aragon, Catalonia became annexed to Aragon but this union was frequently severed. In 1640, when Philip IV. attempted to deprive Catalonia of its rights and privileges, it gave itself up to Louis XIII. of France. It was restored to Spain in 1659, and was once more occupied by the French from 1694 to 1697. Under Philip V. Catalonia, in 1714, was deprived of its cortes and liberties. From 1808 to 1813 it was held by France. It was the scene of civil war in 1823, and of revolutionary operations in the Carlist wars. It supported the Loyalist cause in 1936–39. *See* also SPAIN and BARCELONA.

The average yearly temperature varies from 48° to 75°; the rainfall is about 21 in. with a maximum in the early fall months and a lower maximum in the spring. The dwarf-palm, orange, lime and olive grow in the warmer tracts; and on the higher grounds the thorn-apple, pomegranate, myrtle, esparto and heaths flourish. There is much woodland, but meadows and pastures are rare. Wheat, maize, millet, rye, flax, liquorice, vines and fruits of all sorts—especially nuts, almonds, oranges, figs and walnuts and chestnuts—are produced. Few cattle, but numbers of sheep, goats and swine are reared. Coastal fisheries are excellent. The wines are for the most part rough and strong, though good when matured. Catalonia was prominent in the wool industry early in the Middle Ages, and in modern times the extended use of water-power for textile manufacture made Barcelona an important industrial and commercial city. With the increase of irrigation the country around the city was developed as a wheat growing area.

CATALPA, a genus of trees belonging to the family Bignoniaceae and containing about 10 species in North America, the West Indies and China. The best known is the common catalpa (*C. bignonioides*), native to the southeastern United States, but often cultivated in parks and gardens, both in Europe and America. It is a stately tree with large, heart-shaped, pointed leaves and panicles of white, bell-shaped flowers streaked with yellow and brown-purple. The hardy catalpa (*C. speciosa*), with larger flowers, found in woods from Indiana to Missouri southward to Tennessee and Arkansas, has become naturalized elsewhere through cultivation, especially south of its native range.

CATALYSIS. Classically, the word catalysis means dissolution, destruction or ruin. J. J. Berzelius retained this meaning when, in 1836, he first applied the term to chemical reactions. He used it to describe the chemical decomposition of a substance hastened by a second substance (a catalyst) which did not enter into the composition of the product formed. With use, the original meaning of catalysis was lost. The term was applied to synthesis (constructive) as well as decomposition (destructive) reactions which are accelerated by a substance (the catalyst) not permanently changed in the process. Since the catalyst is not permanently changed, it may be used over and over again. A small amount of catalyst can thus effect the conversion of a large amount of the substance being changed. It is this property of catalysts which makes them so useful.

Catalysts may be gases, liquids and solids. They exert their catalytic effects on gases, liquids and solids to produce gases, liquids and solids. Although a few catalysts had been predicted for certain reactions, the science in mid-20th century had not progressed to the point where it was possible to predict generally a catalyst for a desired reaction. Catalysts for one reaction are often worthless for other reactions. Thus, catalysis bears some of the aspects of an art rather than a science in spite of the many facts known about catalysts and catalytic reactions.

PRACTICAL APPLICATIONS

Catalysis is of great social as well as technical and scientific importance. The average man rarely comes directly in contact with industrial catalysts and, therefore, does not realize what they do for him and how they affect the course of his life or even his death. The part played by catalysts in the production of fixed nitrogen (*see* NITROGEN, FIXATION OF) is a good example of such effects.

Fixed nitrogen is one of the essential ingredients of plant food and explosives. It is used in the form of ammonia (*q.v.*) or its derivatives, or as nitrates (*see* NITRIC ACID). Up until about 1915, fixed nitrogen was obtained from Chilean saltpetre, from a few saltpetre mines, from animal wastes and as a by-product of the coking of coal. At about this time, Fritz Haber and his co-workers produced synthetic ammonia by heating nitrogen and hydrogen, under high pressure, with a solid catalyst. Many different catalysts have been used. The early ones were osmium and ruthenium. These were expensive, and so cheaper catalysts were sought and found. Commercial plants employing this process have been installed in every industrial nation in the world.

Another catalytic reaction serves to complement the above reaction. Fixed nitrogen is needed in the form of nitrates as well as in the form of ammonia. Platinum catalysts were developed which catalyze the reaction between ammonia and the oxygen of the air, to form nitrogen dioxide which with water produces nitric acid. The over-all result is a high yield of nitric acid from the catalytic oxidation of ammonia.

These two catalytic reactions have made every nation independent, or potentially independent, of Chilean nitrate or other natural nitrate deposits. The result has been a decline in the price of fixed nitrogen, an increase in consumption and healthier plants for the farmer with better and more economical food for the average man.

These two catalytic reactions also have their sinister aspects, for, until the advent of the atomic bomb, fixed nitrogen was the backbone of both explosives (*q.v.*) and propellents. Thus, much of the destruction of World War I and World War II can be associated with these catalytic reactions, for the wars would have been quite different if both sides had had to depend on Chilean nitrates for their explosives.

Motor Fuels.—Aside from its application in the fixation of nitrogen, catalysis has other important social implications. A large part, if not most, of the aviation gasoline used by all nations taking part in World War II was made with the aid of catalysts. In the United States, the catalysts were used primarily for the conversion of petroleum (*q.v.*) into hydrocarbons of good antiknock quality. (1) Petroleum oils were catalytically cracked by means of synthetic silica-alumina or acid-treated clay (montmorillonite) catalysts. This process produced the "base" for the aviation gasoline, and it was responsible for a major part of the aviation gasoline produced. (2) Branched-chain paraffin hydrocarbons were synthesized by the so-called alkylation process, using sulphuric or hydrofluoric acid catalysts. Usually, isobutane and mixed butylenes were the raw materials for the process. These were produced by the catalytic as well as the thermal cracking of petroleum. The branched-chain paraffinic product was blended with the "base" from catalytic cracking. (3) Catalytic isomerization of paraffins was used to convert n-butane into isobutane and n-pentane into isopentane. Anhydrous aluminum chloride provided the essential catalytic material for all the commercial paraffin-isomerization processes. (4) Isopropylbenzene was produced from benzene and propylene by means of phosphoric acid catalysts. The isopropylbenzene was added to the gasoline to give extra power under take-off or combat conditions where fuel economy was not a consideration. The British catalytically produced *tert.*-butylbenzene from benzene and isobutylene and used it for similar purposes. (5) Propylene and butylene (*see* OLEFINE) were catalytically polymerized with the use of phosphoric and sulphuric acid catalysts (*see* POLYMERIZATION). The product was a mixture of branched-chain octenes. These were catalytically hydrogenated, with nickel or molybdenum catalysts to produce branched-chain octanes (*see* PARAFFIN HYDROCARBONS, CHEMISTRY OF) which were used in the same way alkylate was used. (6) Straight-run gasoline was converted to material suitable for use as aviation "base" by the hydroforming process. The major use of this process during World War II, however, was to produce synthetic toluene for manufacture of T.N.T. During the postwar period, vastly superior processes of this general type came into wide use for manufacture of motor gasoline and of synthetic benzene, toluene and xylenes.

The Germans, the Japanese and, to a certain extent, the British used catalytic processes to produce aviation fuels from coal. Two major processes were used. (1) A part of the coal was converted by means of heat, steam and catalysts into hydrogen. The hydrogen was caused to react catalytically with more of the coal at high pressures (*see* HYDROGENATION; PRESSURE CHEMISTRY) to produce liquid hydrocarbons which were used directly or further processed. (2) By means of heat, steam and catalysts, the coal was converted into a mixture of carbon monoxide and hydrogen. These were used in the Fischer-Tropsch process, with catalysts containing nickel or cobalt, to produce synthetic hydrocarbons. Since these hydrocarbons were mostly of the straight-chain variety, they had poor antiknock properties and required further treatment to make good aviation fuel. These Fischer-Tropsch processes also produced diesel fuels of excellent quality, waxes and raw materials for synthetic fats and soaps.

Other Applications.—Catalysts also play their subtle but essential role in the production of synthetic rubber. Most of the synthetic rubber produced in the United States has been made from butadiene (*q.v.*) and styrene which are produced with the use of the proper catalysts.

Sulphuric acid (*q.v.*), itself a catalyst for many reactions, is produced in huge quantities with the aid of vanadium oxide catalysts which serve in the oxidation of sulphur dioxide to sulphur trioxide.

Vanadium oxides, usually in combination with silver, are also used in the oxidation of naphthalene by air to phthalic anhydride (*q.v.*). The public sees phthalic anhydride only after it has been transformed by the chemist into synthetic resins (*q.v.*) or into synthetic dyestuffs (*see* DYES, SYNTHETIC).

Methyl alcohol is produced from carbon monoxide and hydrogen. Zinc oxide-chromium oxide combinations are catalysts for this process. By the addition of potassium carbonate to the catalyst, n-propyl, isobutyl and higher alcohols are also produced. By means of a copper catalyst, methyl alcohol is converted into formaldehyde. Formaldehyde reaches the public as such or after it has been converted into synthetic resins, such as the phenol-formaldehyde and urea-formaldehyde plastics.

Even our food has felt the influence of catalysts. A considerable portion of the solid fats used for shortening or for making margarine have been produced by the catalytic hydrogenation of oils with nickel as the catalyst. The catalyst is removed completely before the product is marketed. (*See* OILS, FATS AND WAXES.)

BIOCATALYSIS

Some of the most selective catalysts known, namely the enzymes (*q.v.*) occur in nature. Each enzyme usually has a single function and will not act as a catalyst in any other way. In digestive processes, for example, a number of catalytic reactions utilize this selective action of enzymes to convert food into the forms needed for use by the body.

It is entirely possible that some if not all of the vitamins (*q.v.*) and hormones (*q.v.*) are catalysts. They have the selective action that characterizes catalysts and, in most cases, a very small amount of substance can produce large effects.

FUNCTIONS OF CATALYSTS

A catalyst can increase the rate of a reaction but it cannot change the position of the final equilibrium reached in a true equilibrium reaction. In a simple reaction such as

$$SO_2 + \tfrac{1}{2}O_2 \longrightarrow SO_3$$

the catalyst merely hastens the reaction toward equilibrium. Reactions involving organic compounds may be more complicated in that several reactions are possible. Some catalysts are selective in that they can hasten one of the possible reactions toward equilibrium leaving the other possible reactions practically unaffected. For example, two common reactions of ethyl alcohol are:

$$C_2H_5OH \longrightarrow C_2H_4 + H_2O$$
$$C_2H_5OH \longrightarrow CH_3CHO + H_2.$$

The first one is catalyzed by gamma alumina, the second by copper, each to the practical exclusion of the other. In the absence of catalysts both reactions occur simultaneously but at a higher temperature than the catalytic reactions. It is the ability of catalysts to accelerate selectively one of several possible reactions which made catalysis so important in industrial organic chemistry.

THEORY

Catalysis may be divided into two broad branches depending on relations between the catalyst and the materials involved in the catalytic reaction. The branches are homogeneous catalysis and heterogeneous catalysis. In homogeneous catalysis there are no phase boundaries between the substances taking part in the reaction and the catalyst. Thus all reactions which involve only gases and which are catalyzed by a gaseous catalyst are homogeneous. The same is true for reactions involving mutually soluble liquids or dissolved solids when the catalyst is soluble in the mixture.

In heterogeneous catalysis there is a phase boundary between the catalyst and the substances reacting. The most common heterogeneous reactions are those involving solid catalysts with liquid or gaseous reactants.

Homogeneous Catalysis.—Suppose that a chemical reaction is occurring in the gaseous state, uninfluenced by the walls of the vessel. Suppose that an observer could follow the movement of all the individual atoms. He would notice persistent groupings of atoms (molecules) which move at velocities of the order of 1,000 m.p.h., colliding frequently with other molecules and emerging from the collision substantially unchanged. He would also notice that there are occasional collisions from which new molecules emerge, and perhaps that molecules occasionally fall apart in the absence of collisions. These events are called elementary reactions. (*See* REACTION KINETICS.) Types of elementary reactions include

$$\mathrm{A + B \longrightarrow C + D} \quad \text{(I)}$$
$$\mathrm{A + B \longrightarrow A + C} \quad \text{(II)}$$
$$\mathrm{A + B \longrightarrow C} \quad \text{(III)}$$
$$\mathrm{A \longrightarrow B + C} \quad \text{(IV)}$$
$$\mathrm{A + B + C \longrightarrow A + D} \quad \text{(V)}$$

It seemed reasonably certain in the 1950s that reactions of all these types actually occurred. Depending upon the reaction under study, the observer might note that only a single elementary reaction was occurring, or a number of different elementary reactions.

Such direct and detailed observations, of course, cannot be made. The objectives of reaction-rate theory, however, are to determine from the observable data what elementary reactions actually occur and what their rates are, and to interpret these rates in terms of interatomic forces and atomic dynamics.

Of the above elementary reactions, Types II and V are inherently catalytic reactions, since A emerges unchanged. Type V corresponds to the combination of free atoms, or simple radicals such as OH. In such cases, conservation of energy and momentum make it impossible for combination to occur without a third body to remove some of the energy. There is little specificity in the effectiveness of various third bodies, and Type V is a trivial and uninteresting example of catalysis. Likewise in the case of Type II, the examples known at mid-century were few and unimportant.

The noncatalytic reactions of Types I, III and IV may combine in many ways to produce a total reaction that represents catalysis. A simple illustration utilizing Type I reactions is

$$\mathrm{A + B \longrightarrow C + D}$$
$$\mathrm{C + E \longrightarrow B + F}$$

giving as the ultimate result

$$\mathrm{A + E \longrightarrow D + F}$$

catalyzed by B (or C). A specific example is

$$\begin{array}{l} \mathrm{O_3 + ClO_2 \longrightarrow ClO_3 + O_2} \\ \mathrm{ClO_3 + O_3 \longrightarrow ClO_2 + 2O_2} \\ \hline \mathrm{2O_3 \longrightarrow 3O_2} \end{array}$$

where the chlorine oxides are catalysts. In any complex mechanism of this character, it is more or less a matter of accident that the catalyst is regenerated. For this reason, there is little basis for distinguishing the theory of homogeneous gas phase catalysis from that of homogeneous gaseous reactions generally.

In solution, acids and bases are powerful catalysts for a wide variety of organic reactions. This special branch of the subject, in fact, has absorbed a predominant part of all the modern scientific work on homogeneous catalysis. The original concept of acid and base catalysis was that the effective catalysts were the hydrogen and hydroxyl ions. There are a number of important reactions, such as the hydrolysis of esters and the inversion of sucrose where the data available at mid-century were explicable on this basis. In general, however, it is necessary to invoke the modern definition of an acid (*see* ACIDS AND BASES) as a substance tending to lose a proton, and a base as one tending to gain a proton, and to recognize that all acids and bases may have catalytic activity.

The velocities of acid-base catalyzed reactions are strongly affected by the presence of neutral salts. It is customary to distinguish primary and secondary salt effects. The secondary salt effect occurs only in catalysis by weak electrolytes, and is caused by increased dissociation of the weak electrolyte caused by the presence of the neutral salt. This effect is purely thermodynamic in origin, and for sufficiently dilute solutions may be quantitatively predicted by the Debye-Hückel theory.

The primary salt effect, on the other hand, occurs with all acid-base catalysts of whatever strength. It is specific to the reaction, the catalyst and the added salt. The primary salt effect is usually positive (increase in reaction rate due to salt) but for basic catalysts is sometimes negative. The explanation current at mid-20th century for the primary salt effect is based on J. N. Bronsted's equation

$$k = k_0 \frac{f_A f_B}{f_X}$$

for the reaction rate constant k for the reaction

$$A + B \longrightarrow C + D$$

where f_A, f_B and f_X are the activity coefficients for A, B, and X, the assumed "critical complex" or intermediate compound, and k_0 is a constant. If this equation be granted, the calculation of primary salt effects then becomes a thermodynamic problem. Since definite information as to the critical complex, X, is limited to knowledge of its charge, this thermodynamic problem can be treated only approximately. The results, however, are consistent with experimental data on the primary salt effect.

The general picture of acid-base catalysis, from the standpoint of physical chemistry, is that the catalyst converts the reactant molecule to an ion by proton exchange, and that the ion then reacts. The interest of the organic chemist in the same phenomenon is largely that of interpreting the nature of the subsequent reactions. It is impossible to discuss the details here but it may be mentioned that reactions subject to acid-base catalysis include esterification, bromination, isomerization, molecular rearrangements, dehydration, alkylation and polymerization.

Heterogeneous Catalysis.—The best established examples of heterogeneous catalysis involve solid catalysts and liquid or gaseous reactants. It is almost universally true that massive materials have little or no catalytic activity, and that active catalysts are highly porous, and have total surface areas of 50-500 sq.mi./g. (5-50 ac./lb.).

There have been various theories with regard to the general nature of heterogeneous catalysis. In mid-20th century, however, there were few dissenters from the view that it involves a sequence of reactions in which the catalyst surface participates as an actual chemical reactant. The question whether the entire surface participates, or only a relatively few "active centres" such as edge or corner atoms in crystals, was in dispute.

Study of the adsorption of gases on catalyst surfaces reveals two types of adsorption (*q.v.*). The first type of adsorption is called physical or van der Waals' adsorption, since it is believed to be caused by intermolecular forces which do not disturb the existing valence bonds. The second type is called activated adsorption or chemisorption, since it is believed to represent the creation of new valence bonds. With few exceptions, heterogeneous catalysis depends on activated adsorption.

The rate of every heterogeneous reaction, therefore, depends in principle upon rates of adsorption, reaction and desorption. By reaction kinetic treatment of particular mechanisms it is possible to reproduce the major features of experimental rate data, namely that the reaction order is usually low and that retardation not only by the products but by some of the reactants is frequent. The quantitative value of such kinetic treatments is impaired by the practical necessity of using oversimplified models.

Negative Catalysis.—This term has been frequently, and rather loosely, applied to factors which decrease the rate of a reaction. On thermodynamic grounds a negative catalyst cannot produce an independently occurring reverse reaction. By definition, a negative catalyst cannot affect the reaction rate constant of any true elementary reaction. The only thing a negative catalyst can do, therefore, is to introduce additional elementary reactions, which may result in a lowered over-all reaction rate. This may be done either by stopping a reaction chain, or by destroying a catalyst. The latter effect is usually referred to as poisoning. Poisoning may be either permanent or temporary. From the practical standpoint, poisoning is usually objectionable, although there are a few cases in which selective poisoning is put to practical use. Substances which retard reactions by breaking chains are frequently called inhibitors. They are of major importance in preventing deterioration of gasoline, lubricants, rubber, fats, oils and other important commercial products. (*See* ANTIOXIDANTS.)

TECHNIQUE OF CATALYSIS

An outstanding feature of catalysis is the fact that chemical composition alone does not provide an adequate description of a catalyst. It has been seen that a large surface area is generally essential. It is common practice to use an inert material of large surface area as a "support" or "carrier." The active catalyst may be deposited on the support by chemical means. Commonly used supports include activated carbon, diatomaceous earth, pumice, silica gel and alumina. The use of supports is advantageous in some cases because a costly catalyst material such as platinum or silver is used more economically, and in other cases because greater stability is conferred on the catalyst.

Whether supports are used or not, the details of catalyst preparation exert major effects on the properties of the finished catalyst. Some of these effects may be correlated with such properties as crystal structure, crystal size, surface area and residual impurities, but many of them are as yet unexplained.

In many cases a catalyst can be improved by the addition of minor amounts of an additional component, which is not a catalyst by itself. Such a substance is called a "promoter." Sometimes a second promoter will still further enhance catalytic activity. In other cases a mixture of two catalytic materials will be more active than either alone; this effect is called "synergism." In still other cases a catalyst may be composed of two materials neither of which is active alone. Thus a catalyst composed of two materials may be a true two-component catalyst or a supported catalyst, or it may involve promotion or synergism.

It is possible to summarize only a few of the heterogeneous catalysts which have proved useful. For hydrogenations catalysts involving metallic nickel, iron, cobalt, platinum, palladium or copper, the oxides of copper, zinc or chromium, and the sulphides of molybdenum are common. For dehydrogenations the catalysts may involve: copper, platinum or palladium as metals, aluminum, magnesium, zinc, chromium and molybdenum as oxygen compounds, and nickel, molybdenum and tungsten as sulphur compounds. For oxidations the catalysts may involve: platinum and silver as metals, and vanadium, silver, copper and chromium as oxygen compounds. For dehydrations gamma alumina is by far the most largely used catalyst. Finally there is a group of apparently dissimilar "acid-acting" catalysts for Friedel-Crafts reactions and other reactions which involve carbonium ions. This group includes anhydrous aluminum chloride and bromide, boron fluoride, concentrated sulphuric and phosphoric acids, anhydrous hydrogen fluoride, and the silica-alumina type of catalyst used for catalytic cracking.

All known heterogeneous catalysts deteriorate with use. A common and perhaps universal cause of deterioration is loss of surface area by recrystallization. In some cases there is also an actual change in crystal type, such as from gamma alumina to alpha alumina. In addition, most catalysts are subject to "poisoning." Poisons are classed as temporary and permanent. Temporary poisons are adsorbed relatively weakly at reaction conditions, and these effects disappear more or less rapidly when the poisons are no longer present in the stream flowing to the catalyst. Permanent poisons are more strongly adsorbed, and their effects are not merely transient. Sulphur is a particularly common permanent poison for many metallic catalysts. An important "permanent" poison in some hydrocarbon reactions is a carbonaceous material of high molecular weight and of relatively low hydrogen content, which is formed as a minor reaction product. This material is produced in many high-temperature reactions, such as catalytic cracking and dehydrogenation. It is common industrial practice to "regenerate" the catalyst periodically by burning this "coke" under suitably controlled conditions. (C. L. T.; L. S. KL.)

CATAMARAN: *see* SHIP.

CATAMARCA, an Andean province of the Argentine republic, lying between 26° and 30° S. latitude and 65° and 69° 30′ W. longitude. It is bounded on the north by the province of Salta, east by the provinces of Tucumán and Santiago del Estero, south by the provinces of Córdoba and La Rioja and west by Chile, from which it is separated by the cordillera of the Andes. The area of Catamarca is approximately 45,829 sq.mi. Population (1947) 147,213. The chief city of the province is Catamarca (pop. [1947] 31,067), the capital, situated on a fertile tableland in the southeastern part of the province. Other important cities are Andalgalá, Tinogasta and Belén.

The region is in general mountainous, with many high peaks perpetually covered by snow. Between the numerous longitudinal ranges of mountains are tablelands and valleys, some of the latter being exceedingly fertile while others are completely barren and covered by sand. The climate varies with altitude but is for the most part warm and dry, the rainfall ranging from 8 to 15 in. in the west to 24 in. in the east. Water is one of the major problems in the province, and its scarcity greatly retarded the development of agriculture and grazing. The principal crops sown are alfalfa, maize and wheat. The principal minerals of the province that are exploited are wolfram, copper, mica, antimony, clay, asbestos and tin. Of these, and in direct response to markets created by World War II, wolfram and mica came to rank first in economic importance. Another industry that characterizes the region, carried on largely by women, is the hand weaving of fine ponchos and cloth from wool and vicuña. Olives are grown extensively.

Two railways, the former Central Córdoba and the Central Norte Argentino, merged in the national railway system, serve the southeastern part of the province. The latter line provides direct communication between the capital of the province and the federal capital, a distance of 895 mi. Highways are mostly in the eastern half of the province. (R. W. RD.; C. E. MC.)

CATAMARCA (*San Fernando de Catamarca*), capital of province of same name on Río del Valle de Catamarca, Argentina, 230 mi. (318 mi. by rail) N.N.W. of Córdoba. Pop. (1947 census) 31,067. The city stands in a narrow, picturesque valley at the foot of the Sierra de Ambato, 1,772 ft. above sea level. The valley is highly fertile, partially wooded, and produces fruit in abundance, wine and some cereals. In the city are flour mills and tanneries, and among its exports are leather, fruit, wine, flour and a curious embroidery for which the women of Catamarca have long been famous. There are several fine churches, which have been declared national monuments. The alameda is one of the most attractive in the Argentine republic, having a reservoir of 2 ac. surrounded by shrubbery and walks. Catamarca was founded in 1683 by Fernando de Mendoza because the town of Chacra, the former provincial capital had been found unhealthful. Previous to the selection of Chacra as the provincial capital, the seat of government was at San Juan de la Rivera de Londres, founded in 1558 and named after the capital of England by order of Philip II in honour of his marriage with Queen Mary. Catamara is one of the communities of the republic which most conserves the traditional spirit of the colonial and postindependence eras. (C. E. MC.)

CATANIA, a city and episcopal see of Sicily, the chief town of the province of Catania, on the east coast, 59 mi. S. of Messina by rail and 151 mi. S.E. of Palermo by rail (102 mi. direct). Pop. (1951) 297,531 (commune). The cathedral of S. Agatha, with relics of the saint, retains its three original Norman apses (1091), but is otherwise baroque and there are other good baroque churches and palaces. In the west the huge Benedictine abbey of S. Nicola (now suppressed) occupies about 21 ac. and contains the museum, a library, observatory, etc. This was the highest point of the ancient city, which lay almost entirely to the west of the modern Via Stesicorea Etuca, which runs for 3,000 yd. in a straight line toward the summit of Mt. Etna. The university, founded in 1444, has regained some of its former importance. To the south near the harbour is the massive Castel

Ursino, erected in 1232 by Frederick II. The Roman theatre (no Greek theatre has been found) has been superimposed upon the Greek building, some foundations of which, in calcareous stone, of which the seats are also made, still exist. It is 106 yd. in diameter, and is estimated to have accommodated 7,000 spectators. Close to it are the remains of the so-called Odeum, of similar plan to the theatre but without a stage, and to the north is the church of S. Maria Rotonda, originally a Roman domed structure, perhaps part of a bath. To the north, in the Piazza Stesicoro, is the amphitheatre, a considerable portion of which has been uncovered, including a part of the arcades of the exterior already excavated. The external diameters of the amphitheatre are 410 and 348 ft., while the corresponding diameters of the arena are 233 and 167 ft. It is thus the third largest Roman amphitheatre known, being surpassed only by that at Verona and the Colosseum. Remains of many other Roman buildings also exist beneath the modern town, among the best preserved of which may be noted the public baths (*Thermae Achilleae*) under the cathedral, and those under the church of S. Maria dell' Indirizzo. The number of baths is remarkable, and gives some idea of the luxury of the place in Roman times. The majority were excavated by Prince Ignazio Biscari (1719–86). Some monumental Roman tombs have also been found, and it is only from their position that we can infer the boundaries of the Roman city, for no remains of its walls exist.

Catania exports sulphur, pumice stone, asphalt, oranges and lemons, almonds, filberts, cereals, wine and oil. The harbour is a good one. There is an old harbour with an area of .03 sq.mi. and a new harbour of .16 sq. mi.; the combined length of quays is 2 mi. Sulphide of carbon is produced here; and there are large dyeworks.

The ancient Catina (Gr. *Katane*, Rom. *Catina*[1]) was founded in 729 B.C. by colonists from Naxos, perhaps on the site of an earlier Sicel settlement—the name is entirely un-Greek, and may be derived from *κάτινον*, which in the Sicel language, as *catinum* in Latin, meant a basin, and would thus describe the situation. Charondas, a citizen of Catina, is famous as its lawgiver, but his date and birthplace are alike uncertain; the fragments preserved of his laws show that they belong to a somewhat primitive period. The poet Stesichorus of Himera died here. Very little is heard of Catina in history until 476 B.C., when Hiero I. removed its inhabitants to Leontini, repeopled it with 5,000 Syracusans and 5,000 Peloponnesians, and changed its name to Aetna. In 461 B.C., however, with the help of Ducetius and the Syracusans, the former inhabitants recovered possession of their city and revived the old name. Catina was, however, an ally of Athens during the Syracusan expedition (415–413 B.C.), and served as the Athenian base of operations in the early part of the war. In 403 B.C. it was taken by Dionysius of Syracuse, who plundered the city, sold the inhabitants into slavery and replaced them with Campanian mercenaries. In the First Punic War it was one of the first cities of Sicily to be taken by the Romans (263 B.C.). In 123 B.C. there was an eruption of Etna so violent that the tithe on the territory of Catina payable to Rome was remitted for ten years. It appears to have flourished in the first century B.C., but to have suffered from the ravages of Sextus Pompeius. It became a Roman colony under Augustus, and it is from this period that the fertile plain, hitherto called the plain of Leontini, begins to be called the plain of Catina. It seems to have been at this time the most important city in the island, to judge from the language of Strabo and the number of inscriptions found there. In A.D. 251 a lava stream threatened the town and entered the amphitheatre, which in the time of Theodoric had fallen into ruins, as is clear from the fact that he permitted the use of its fallen stones for new buildings. It was occupied by Belisarius in 546, sacked by the Saracens in 902 and taken by the Normans. The latter founded the cathedral; but the town was almost entirely destroyed by earthquake in 1170, and devastated by Henry VI. in 1197. It became the usual residence of the Aragonese viceroys of the 13th and 14th centuries, and one of them, De Vego, reconstructed the fortifications in 1552. In 1669 an eruption of Etna partly filled up the harbour, but spared the town, which was, however, almost entirely destroyed by the earthquake of 1693. During World War II Catania was heavily bombed by Allied planes. Near Catania the Germans put up a stiff resistance against the British in the summer of 1943.

[1]This is the form vouched for by the inscriptions.

See A. Holm, *Catania Antica* (trans. G. Libertini) (Catania, 1925); F. de Roberto, *Catania* (Bergamo, Arti Grafiche, 1907).

CATANZARO, a town and episcopal see of Calabria, Italy, capital of the province of Catanzaro, 1,125 ft. above sea-level. Pop. (1936) 27,907 (town); 45,400 (commune). The station for the town (Catanzaro Sala) is on a branch connecting the two main lines along the east and west coasts of Calabria, 6 mi. N. by W. of Catanzaro Marina on the east coast, and 20 mi. E. of S. Eufemia Biforcazione, on the west coast line. The town enjoys a comparatively cool climate in summer, and commands fine views. Numerous wealthy families reside here. The town was bombed by the Allies in World War II.

CATAPHYLL, a botanical term denoting any rudimentary scalelike leaf which precedes the foliage leaves, as a bud scale, etc.

CATAPULT, a generic name for warlike engines of the crossbow type used by the ancients (Lat. *catapulta*, Gr. *καταπέλτης*). (*See* ENGINES OF WAR.) They are usually classed as (*a*) catapults and (*b*) ballistae (*λιθοβόλοι*). The former were smaller and were used with arrows for what is now called direct fire (*i.e.*, at low angles of elevation); the latter were large siege engines discharging heavy bolts or stones at a high angle of elevation, like the modern howitzer.

The essential parts of the catapult (see illustration) were the frame, the propelling gear, the trough (corresponding to the modern barrel) and the pedestal. The frame consisted of two horizontal beams forming top and bottom sills, and four strong upright bars mortised into them. The three open spaces or compartments resembling narrow windows, between these four uprights, carried the propelling and laying gear. The propelling gear occupied the two outer "windows." In each a thick skein of cord or sinews was fastened to the top and bottom sills and tightly twisted. The stiff wooden arms were inserted in the two skeins, and a specially strong bowstring joined the tips of these arms. In the middle compartment was the hinged fore-end of the trough, which was at right angles to the frame and at the back of it. The trough could be laid for elevation by a movable prop, the upper end of which was hinged to the trough, while the lower ran up and down a sort of trail fastened to the pedestal. The whole equipment was laid for "line" by turning the frame, and with it the trough, prop and trail by a pivot in the head of the pedestal. Sliding up and down in the trough was a block, fitted with a trigger mechanism, through which passed the middle of the bowstring. The pedestal was a strong and solid upright resting upon, and strutted to, a framework on the ground; its upper end, as mentioned above, took the pivot of the frame and the head of the trail.

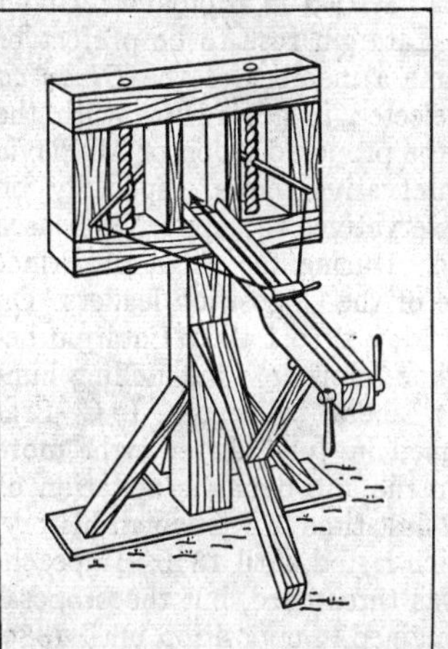

CATAPULT USED IN ANCIENT SIEGE WARFARE
This engine, capable of discharging a 26 in. arrow weighing ½ lb., had an effective range of 400 yards

On coming into action the machine was laid for direction and elevation. The block and with it the bowstring was next forced back against the resistance of the twisted skeins to the rear end of the trough, this being effected by a windlass attachment. The trigger being then pressed or struck with a hammer, the bowstring was released from the block, the stiff arms were violently brought back to the frame by the untwisting of the skeins, and the arrow was propelled through the centre "window" with great velocity. A small machine of the type described weighed about 85 lb., and sent a "three-span" (26in.) arrow weighing ½ lb. at an effective man-killing velocity somewhat over 400yds.

The ballista was considerably larger and more expensive than this. In Scipio's siege train, at the attack of New Carthage (Livy xxvi. 47, 5), the number of the ballistae was only one-sixth that of the catapults. In the ballista the rear end of the trough (which projected in front of the frame) always rested upon the ground, or rather was fixed to the framework of the pedestal—which was a heavy trestle construction—and the trough was thus restricted to the angle of elevation, giving the maximum range (45°). Even so, the range was not appreciably greater than that of a catapult, and in the case of the largest ballistae (90-pounder) it was much less. These enormous engines, which, once in position, could not be laid on any fresh target, were used for propelling beams and stones rather than for shooting arrows, that is, more for the destruction of material than for man-killing effect. The skeins that supplied the motive force of all these engines were made of the sinews of animals, twisted raw hide, horsehair rope, and, in at least one celebrated case, of women's hair. In 146 B.C., the authorities of Carthage, having surrendered their engines to the Romans in the vain hope of staying their advance, new ones were hurriedly constructed, and the women and virgins of the city cut off their hair to supply the needed skeins.

The modern implement known as a "catapult" is formed by a forked stick, to the forks of which are attached the ends of a piece of elastic. To the middle of this elastic a pocket is fitted to contain a bullet or small stone. In use the forked stick is held in the left hand and the pocket drawn back with the right. Aim is taken and, the pocket being released, the missile flies through the fork of the stick. Though classed as a toy, this weapon can do considerable execution among birds, etc., when skilfully used. The name of "catapult" has also been given to a bowling machine which is used for cricket practice.

CATARACT, a waterfall (Gr. καταρράκτης, a floodgate, or waterfall, something which rushes down). The earliest use in English is of a floodgate or portcullis, and this survives in the name of a disease of the eye (*see* EYE, DISEASES OF; OPHTHALMOLOGY). The term is also used of a device to regulate the strokes in certain types of steam-engine.

CATARGIU (or CATARGI), **LASCAR** (1823–1899), Rumanian statesman, belonged to an ancient Walachian family, one of whose members had been banished in the 17th century by Prince Matthew Bassaraba and had settled in Moldavia. Under Prince Gregory Ghica (1849–56) Catargiu rose to be prefect of police at Jassy. In 1857 he became a member of the *Divan ad hoc* of Moldavia, a commission elected in accordance with the treaty of Paris (1856) to vote on the proposed union of Moldavia and Walachia. His strongly conservative views, especially on agrarian reform, induced the Conservatives to support him as a candidate for the throne in 1859. During the reign of Prince Cuza (1859–66) Catargiu was one of the Opposition leaders. On the accession of Prince Charles in May 1866 Lascar Catargiu became president of the council (prime minister); but finding himself unable to co-operate with his Liberal colleagues, I. C. Bratianu and C. A. Rosetti, he resigned in July. After eight more ministerial changes, culminating in the anti-dynastic agitation of 1870–71, Catargiu formed, for the first time in Rumanian history, a stable Conservative cabinet, which lasted until 1876. Impeachment of himself and his cabinet was threatened, but the proposal was withdrawn in 1878, and he remained in opposition until 1889, when he formed a short-lived cabinet, taking the portfolio of the Interior. In the Florescu ministry of March 1891 he occupied the same position, and in Dec. he again became president of the council, retaining office until 1895. He died at Bucharest on April 11, 1899.

CATARRH, a term chiefly signifying mild inflammation of the mucous membrance of the respiratory passages, in popular language a "cold." It is the result of infection by a microorganism, especially *M. catarrhalis,* which may occasionally be a causative factor. Its pathogenic significance is slight.

The term catarrh is used in a wider sense to describe a similar pathological condition of any mucous surface in the body; *e.g.,* gastric catarrh, intestinal catarrh, etc. (*See* also ALIMENTARY SYSTEM, DISEASES OF THE; RESPIRATORY SYSTEM, DISEASES OF.)

CATARRHINE MONKEY, the term used (in contradistinction to Platyrrhine, *q.v.*) to describe those apes which have the nostrils approximated; the aperture pointing downward; and the intervening septum narrow. These are the distinguishing features of all the old world primates. (*See* PRIMATES.)

CATASTROPHE, in ancient Greek drama the change in the plot which leads up to the conclusion (Gr. καταστρέφειν, to overturn). Hence any sudden change, particularly of a disastrous nature, and, in earlier geological theories, a great convulsion of the earth's surface.

CATAWBA, the principal tribe of the eastern division of the Siouan stock of American Indians. The name is probably derived from the Choctaw *katápa,* meaning "divided" or "separated."

Formerly the dominant people of South Carolina, the Catawba also had divisions extending into North Carolina. In the 17th century the population was about 5,000, but by 1780 it had declined to about 500. By the beginning of the 20th century there were only about 60 members of the tribe.

The Catawba, who were at war with the Iroquois for a long time, furnished a valuable contingent to the South Carolina troops during the American Revolution. They retreated to Virginia upon the advance of British troops in 1870, but they later returned and occupied small towns on the Catawba river. They afterward leased their land and about 1841 sold all of it except one square mile to the state. At that time a number of them went to the territory of the Cherokee in western North Carolina, but they did not remain long with their former enemies and soon returned to South Carolina. A vocabulary of about 300 words, collected by Oscar M. Lieber, the geologist, in 1856, was published in *Collections of the South Carolina Historical Society,* vol. ii (1858).

See F. W. Hodge (ed.), *Handbook of the American Indians* (1912).

CATAWBA, an amber coloured, richly flavoured wine made from the light-red grape of the same name. The grape is a variety of the *Vitis labrusca,* a North American and Asiatic species, and takes its name from the Catawba river in North and South Carolina. In 1807 the grape was grown in Washington, D.C., but it was not until about 1823 that the name Catawba was given to it. It spread rapidly in New York, Ohio and Ontario and was extensively grown in the Finger lake section of New York. The vine is extremely prolific, the fruit being large and very sweet. The grapes are readily preserved, and their great use is partly accounted for by that fact. The wine is largely used as a base for champagne.

CATBALOGAN, a municipality (with administrative centre and 16 *barrios* or districts) and capital of the province and island of Samar, Philippine Islands. Pop. (1948) 26,839. It lies midway between the ports of Manila and Zamboanga and is a port of call for coastwise and other craft. Abacá (Manila hemp) is produced in the country tributary to the town and there are manufactures of woven fibres and mats which are also made from *tiking* (sedge). Most of these are exported. The fisheries are important. The vernacular is Samarino, a dialect of Bisayan. Of those inhabitants 6 to 19 inclusive, 21.6% attended school in 1939, and of those ten years old and over 37% were literate.

CATBIRD (*Dumetella carolinensis*), a North American bird of the thrasher family Mimidae, about 9 in. long, a summer visitor from the Gulf of Mexico, north to New Brunswick and Hudson Bay. Its plumage is slate-gray, with a black cap and tail and chestnut under tail coverts. It is noted for its beautiful song, with much of the charm of its close relative, the mocking-bird. The name expresses the mewing protest of the bird when angry. The catbird winters in the southern states, in Cuba and from Mexico to Panama. It is resident in Bermuda. In Australia, a name given to any one of several bowerbirds (*q.v.*), especially to *Ailuroedus crassirostris,* which builds no bower. The name comes from a catlike mewing.

CATBOAT, a small sailing-boat of the pleasure variety, having the mast stepped forward and carrying a single fore-and-aft mainsail set on a boom and gaff, known as a *cat rig.* They are also known as Una boats, and frequently carry a centre-board (*q.v.*).

CATCH, a form of concerted vocal music virtually indistinguishable from the round, save for the fact that it is always humorous in character. The catch had its greatest vogue in earlier centuries, when also the words to which it was sung were too often more jocose than refined. Particulars of various collections available occupy a column of small print in Grove. Of the innumerable catch and glee clubs which existed in England in former days one, known simply as the Catch Club, founded as long ago as 1761, still exists. (*See* also under Canon; Contrapuntal Forms; Glee; Rondel.)

CATCH-CROPS are rapidly growing crops that occupy the soil for short periods of time to absorb or "catch" nitrates that might otherwise be carried away in drainage waters. They are usually grown between the times of two principal crops or between the rows of another crop. Rye, oats and vetch are frequently used, but other crops and plants, including weeds, may serve as well. When the immature plants are plowed under, the nitrogen absorbed is returned to the soil where it can again be used to nourish other plants. Many gardeners and farmers have found that they can improve their production efficiency by giving attention to the use of catch-crops in their cropping systems.

In practice, however, the term catch-crops is often used with other meanings. Some regard them as quickly maturing crops grown between two principal crops for the purpose of keeping the land completely utilized. Defined in this way, catch-crops may occupy idle land for longer periods of time and include more species of plants than under the more restricted definition given above. The crops serving as catch-crops will be useful, not only for conserving nitrates, but also for soil protection, soil enrichment and as additional sources of feed for livestock.

Special crops planted between two principal crops for the purpose of protecting the soil against water and wind erosion are frequently called cover-crops. They may also function as catch-crops and as sources of organic matter for soil enrichment.

Crops planted between two principal crops, chiefly for the purpose of soil enrichment, are more accurately described as green manure crops. Legumes, because of their ability to obtain nitrogen from the atmosphere, are used more frequently for this purpose than non-legume crops. In the North American corn-belt, for instance, biennial sweet clover, a deep rooted legume, is widely used as a green manure crop. It is seeded in early spring in either fall- or spring-seeded grains and plowed under the following spring for corn. If conditions are favourable, as much as 100 lb. or more of atmospheric nitrogen and several tons of organic matter rich in nutrient minerals may be added to an acre of land. In addition to these benefits, the sweet clover or other green manure crops may also serve as catch and cover crops.

In view of the overlapping functions of catch, cover and green manure crops, it is difficult to use these classifications accurately. Some call all special crops planted between two principal crops catch-crops, while others use the designations that best express the major purposes for which the crops are grown. (F. C. Br.)

CATCHMENT AREAS. The term "catchment area" is used to describe the collecting area from which water would flow to a stream or river, the boundary of the area being determined by the ridge separating water flowing in opposite directions. The amount of water collected within the catchment area would depend on the extent of that area, the amount of rain which has fallen on the surface, and the proportion of that rainfall which has been lost by evaporation or absorption. The term "run-off" has been adopted to describe that portion of the rainfall which ultimately finds its way to the stream, and the ratio between the rainfall and the "run-off" varies widely, according to the climatic conditions. In England and Scotland the average annual rainfall varies from a little over 20 in. to 175 in., and the annual loss by evaporation from a land surface varies from about 10 to 18 in., being less in the north, increasing towards the south.

Evaporation.—The loss by evaporation depends on the hours of sunshine, the temperature, and the humidity of the atmosphere, and varies greatly during the different periods of the year as might naturally be expected. The following average figures for the period 1883–1900 illustrate the effect of these various factors on the proportion of the rainfall which flowed over Teddington weir from the Thames catchment area above that point.

	Average hours of sunshine.	Average temperature.	Average humidity.	Proportion of rainfall flowing over Teddington weir.
		Degrees.	Degrees.	Per cent.
Jan.–March	57·5	39·6	84·5	60·9
April–June	163·2	53	74·3	30
July–Sept.	159·8	60·2	75·7	12
Oct.–Dec.	46·1	41	86·5	28

The total annual loss by evaporation in Britain is less in regions of high rainfall than in areas of low rainfall, and the seasonal loss varies in a similar manner. The influence of climatic conditions on the evaporation is so marked, that in tropical countries the proportion of the rain which flows off the ground is small.

It has been held that forests tend to increase the discharge of a river by reducing evaporation, but such evidence as has been obtainable fails to support this view. Shade cast by the trees would reduce evaporation, but rain which would otherwise flow from the ground, is absorbed by the trees. Although forests have but little effect on the annual loss by evaporation, their presence has an influence in delaying the flow of water from the hillsides, and when a catchment area has been cleared of timber, floods tend to become more intense.

Evaporation from a water surface is greater than from a land surface, especially in tropical countries, and is a matter of importance when lakes occupy a considerable proportion of the catchment area.

Absorption.—The amount of rain falling on the surface which percolates downwards depends on the porosity of the surface soil and the nature of the underlying rock, whether impermeable, porous, or fissured.

When the surface is impermeable, there would be no loss by percolation.

When the surface is permeable but is underlain by impermeable rock, water percolates downwards till that rock is reached and then travels underground in the direction of the steepest inclination of the rock surface, which is generally towards the stream, water lost by percolation reappearing as springs. Such percolation has little influence on the annual run-off, but may have a marked effect on its variations throughout the year. Thick beds of permeable material, such as sand or gravel, absorb large volumes of water, acting as natural storage reservoirs. During periods of abundant rainfall the beds would become saturated, and during periods of dry weather water so absorbed would be gradually discharged, thus maintaining a considerable flow in the stream.

This point is of great importance when it is desired to utilize the water of a stream without constructing a storage reservoir to balance its fluctuations, as the quantity of water which could be taken during certain periods would be limited to the dry weather flow.

When the surface is permeable and is underlain with permeable or fissured rock, such as chalk, the entire rainfall on the catchment area might percolate downwards, reappearing in the form of springs issuing either within or without the limits of the catchment area.

In the former case there would be no surface flow above the point where the springs break out, and in the latter, the whole catchment area would be void of streams. (W. J. E. B.)

CATECHISM, a compendium of instruction (particularly of religious instruction) arranged in the form of questions and answers. The custom of catechizing was followed in the schools of Judaism and in the Early Church, where it helped to preserve the Gospel narrative. (*See* Catechumen.)

The catechism as we know it is intended primarily for children and uneducated persons. Its aim is to instruct, and it differs from a creed or confession in not being in the first instance an act of worship or a public profession of belief. The first regular catechisms seem to have grown out of the usual oral teaching of catechumens, and to have been compiled in the 8th and 9th centuries. They continued on through the Middle Ages to the 16th century. The original of all modern catechisms, because of its question and answer form, is the *Disputatio Puerorum Per Interrogationes Et Responsiones* (*Patr. Lat.*, CI, 1097–1144), of the 9th century. In the 12th century the *Elucidarium* of Honorius of Autun (*Patr. Lat.*, CLXXII, 1110–1176) and the *De Quinque Septenariis* of Hugh of St. Victor (*Patr. Lat.*, CLXXV, 405–414) were well known and had much influence on subsequent catechisms. Jean Gerson (1363–1429), chancellor of the University of Paris, took great interest in catechizing, taught children both at Paris and Lyons, and wrote among other catechetical works his *ABC des simples gens.* The first catechism printed in Germany was the *Christenspiegel* of Coelde, which first appeared in 1470, proved very popular and was in its 5th edition by 1514. But though catechisms had already been in use, the 16th century saw a tremendous increase in their number and importance, as ever-increasing facilities for printing were available and the age of the Reformation began. Both the new Protestant Churches and the Catholic Church strove zealously to instruct their members and to win new adherents.

In 1520 Luther had brought out a primer of religion dealing briefly with the Decalogue, the Creed and the Lord's Prayer; and other leaders had done something of the same kind. In 1529 all these efforts were superseded by Luther's Smaller Catechism meant for the people themselves and especially for children, and by his Larger Catechism intended for clergy and schoolmasters. These works did much to mould the character of the German people and powerfully influenced other compilations.

In 1537 John Calvin at Geneva published his catechism for children. It was called *Instruction and Confession of Faith for the use of the Church of Geneva* and explained the Decalogue, the Apostles' Creed, the Lord's Prayer and the Sacraments. It was the work of a man who knew little of the child mind, and, though it served as an admirable and transparent epitome of his famous *Institutes,* it was too long and too minute for the instruction of children. Calvin came to see this, and in 1542 drafted a new one which was much more suitable for teaching purposes. This was used in Geneva and in Scotland. The Reformed churches of the Palatinate, on the other hand, used the Heidelberg Catechism (1562–63), mainly the work of two of Calvin's disciples, Kaspar Olevianus and Zacharias Ursinus. This work is perhaps the most widely accepted symbol of the Calvinistic faith, and is noteworthy for its emphasis on the less controversial aspects of the Genevan theology. As revised by the synod of Dort in 1619, it became the standard of most of the Reformed churches of central Europe, and in time of the Dutch and German Reformed Churches of America.

Since 1648 the standard Presbyterian catechisms have been those compiled by the Westminster assembly, presented to parliament in 1647, and then authorized by the General Assembly of the Church of Scotland (July 1648) and by the Scottish parliament (Jan. 1649). The Larger Catechism is "for such as have made some proficiency in the knowledge of the Christian religion," but is too detailed and minute for memorizing, and has never received anything like the reception accorded to the Shorter Catechism, which is "for such as are of weaker capacity." The work was done by a committee presided over first by Herbert Palmer, master of Queens', Cambridge, and then by Anthony Tuckney, master of Emmanuel. The Shorter Catechism, after a brief introduction on the end, rule and essence of religion, is divided into two parts: I. The doctrines we are to believe (1) concerning the nature of God, (2) concerning the decrees of God and their execution. II. The duties we are to perform (1) in regard to the moral law, (2) in regard to the gospel—(*a*) inward duties, *i.e.,* faith and repentance, (*b*) outward duties as to the Word, the sacraments and prayer. It has 107 questions and answers, while that of the Anglican Church has but 24, grouping as it does the ten commandments and also the petitions of the Lord's Prayer, instead of dealing with them singly.

Though the Catholic Church had long been using catechisms, they were multiplied with new emphasis as the Church swung into the Counter Reformation. The most famous was that of the Jesuit Peter Canisius, first published in 1555. It went through 400 editions within 150 years. Another catechism which had a large circulation and greatly influenced later works was that of Bellarmine (1597); in France those of Auger (1563) and Bossuet (1687) were outstanding. The *Catechism of the Council of Trent,* completed in 1566, was never intended as an ordinary catechism. It was written for and addressed to parish priests, to serve as model and guide in their instructions and sermons to the people. The Catholic Church, because its unity of doctrine is otherwise so safeguarded, has never adopted any one official catechism for all its members. Each bishop is free to adapt his method of instruction to local conditions. Many bishops themselves, however, have desired a universal catechism; at the Vatican council (1870) the project was seriously discussed, with Bellarmine's catechism proposed as model. In more recent times well known catechisms have been the *Baltimore Catechism* (1885) in the United States, the *Penny Catechism* in England, and that of Deharbe (1847) in Germany. In the present century, pedagogical-catechetical congresses and periodicals (e.g., *Journal of Religious Instruction,* Joseph F. Wagner, N.Y.) have stimulated new methods, which methods in turn have produced new catechisms and aids. The classic survey of this period is *Où En Est L'Enseignement Religieux?* (Louvain, 1937), which lists and appraises the books and methods of the different countries.

Peter Mogilas, in 1643, composed the *Orthodox Confession of the Catholic and Apostolic Eastern Church.* This counteraction to the activities of the Jesuits and the Reformed Church was standardized by the synod of Jerusalem in 1672. A smaller catechism was drawn up by order of Peter the Great in 1723. The catechisms of Levshin Platon (1762) and V. D. Philaret (1839), each in his day metropolitan of Moscow, are bulky compilations which cannot be memorized, though there is a short introductory catechism, prefaced to Philaret's volume (Eng. trans. in Blackmore's *Doctrine of the Russian Church, 1845*).

The catechism of the Church of England is included in the Book of Common Prayer. It has two parts: (i) the baptismal covenant, the Creed, the Decalogue and the Lord's Prayer drawn up probably by Cranmer and Ridley in the time of Edward VI, and variously modified between then (1549) and 1661; (ii) the meaning of the two sacraments, written on the suggestion of James I at the Hampton Court conference in 1604 by John Overall, then dean of St. Paul's. This supplement to what had become known as the Shorter Catechism established its use as against the longer one, *King Edward VIth's Catechisme* which had been drawn up in 1553 by John Ponet, bishop of Winchester, and enlarged in 1570 by Alexander Nowell, Overall's predecessor as dean of St. Paul's. By the rubric of the Prayer Book and by the 59th canon of 1603, the clergy are enjoined to teach the catechism in church on Sundays and holidays after the second lesson at Evening Prayer. This custom, long fallen into disuse, has largely been revived during recent years, the children going to church for a special afternoon service of which catechizing is the chief feature. Compared with the thoroughness of most other catechisms this one seems scanty, but it has a better chance of being memorized, and its very simplicity has given it a firm hold on the inner life and conscience of devout members of the Anglican communion throughout the world.

Almost every Christian denomination has its catechism or catechisms. Besides those already enumerated there are two interesting joint productions. In 1898 the National Council of the Evangelical Free Churches in England and Wales published an *Evangelical Free Church Catechism,* representing directly or indirectly the beliefs of 60 or 70 millions of avowed Christians in all parts of the world, a striking example of inter-denominational unity. *The School Catechism* was issued in 1907 by a conference of members of the Reformed churches in Scotland, which met on the invitation of the Church of Scotland. In its compilation representatives of the Episcopal Church in Scotland co-operated, and the book, though "not designed to supersede the distinctive catechisms officially recognized by the several churches for the instruction of their own children," certainly "commends itself as suitable for use in schools where children of various churches are taught together."

During the 19th century in the United States the Sunday school was recognized by various Protestant denominations as the primary instrument for religious instruction. By the middle of the century the Bible was regarded as primary curriculum material, the catechism secondary, though still important.

See the *Encyclopaedia of Religion and Ethics, s.v.* (A. J. G.; X.)

CATECHU or CUTCH, an extract obtained from several plants (the derivation is from the Malay *Kachu*), its chief sources being the wood of two species of acacia (*A. catechu* and *A. suma*), both natives of India. This extract is known as black catechu. A similar extract, known in pharmacy as pale catechu (*Catechu pallidum*), and in general commerce as gambir, or *terra japonica,* is produced from the leaves of *Uncaria gambir* and *U. acida,* cinchonaceous plants growing in the East Indian archipelago. A third product to which the name catechu is also applied is obtained from the fruits of the areca or betel palm, *Areca catechu.* Ordinary black catechu is usually imported in three different forms. The first and best quality, known as Pegu catechu, is obtained in blocks externally covered with large leaves; the second and less pure variety is in masses, which have been moulded in sand; and the third consists of large cubes packed in coarse bags. The wood of the two species of *Acacia* yielding catechu is taken for the manufacture when the trees have attained a diameter of about one foot. The bark is stripped off and used for tanning and the trunk is split up into small fragments which are covered with water and boiled. When the extract has become sufficiently thick it is cast into the forms in which the catechu is found in commerce.

Catechu so prepared is a dark brown or, in mass, almost black substance, brittle, and having generally a shining lustre. It is astringent, with a sweetish taste. In cold water it disintegrates, and in boiling water, alcohol, acetic acid and strong caustic alkali it is completely dissolved. Chemically it consists of a mixture of a peculiar variety of tannin termed catechutannic acid with catechin or catechuic acid, and a brown substance due to the alteration of both these principles. Catechutannic acid is an amorphous body soluble in cold water, while catechin occurs in minute, white, silky, needle-shaped crystals which do not dissolve in cold water. A minute proportion of quercetin, a principle yielded by quercitron bark, has been obtained from catechu.

Gambir.—Gambir, which is similar in chemical composition to ordinary catechu, occurs in commerce in the form of cubes of about an inch in size with a pale brown or yellow colour and an even earthy fracture. For the preparation of this extract the plants above mentioned are stripped of their leaves and young twigs and these are boiled down in shallow pans. The juice is strained off, evaporated, and when sufficiently concentrated is cast into shallow boxes, where, as it hardens and dries, it is cut into small cubes. Gambir and catechu are extensively employed in dyeing and tanning. For dyeing they have been in use in India from the most remote period, but it was only during the 19th century that they were placed on the list of European dyeing substances. Catechu is fixed by oxidation of the colouring principle, catechin, on the cloth after dyeing or printing; and treated thus it yields a variety of durable tints of drabs, browns and olives with different mordants (*see* DYEING). The principal consumption of catechu occurs in the preparation of fibrous substances exposed to water, such as fishing lines and nets, and for colouring stout canvas used for covering boxes and portmanteaus under the name of tanned canvas. Gambir is used medicinally as an astringent, especially in the treatment of diarrhoea. It is no longer included in the United States *Pharmacopoeia.* In Great Britain, pale catechu is the official term.

CATECHUMEN, a technical term applied to a person receiving instruction in the Christian religion with a view to baptism (Gr. κατηχούμενος, one receiving instruction, from τηχεῖν, to teach orally). The catechumenate grew naturally out of Judaism, which as a missionary religion had to instruct recruits. These were admitted by circumcision and baptism, women by baptism only. Second-century practice in Palestine is described in *Yebamot* 47 a.b., "They acquaint him with some of the lighter and some of the weightier commandments. . . . As they show him the penalty of breaking commandments, so they show him the reward of keeping them. . . . If he accepts, they circumcise him forthwith . . . when he is healed they at once baptize him." The ordeal was clearly much lighter for women. For this and other reasons there was a considerable body of potential proselytes on for fringe of Judaism. They were known as "God-fearers"; if they shrank from circumcision themselves, they generally had the rite performed on their sons (G. F. Moore, *Judaism,* i, 323 ff.).

The Apostles are said to have instructed converts after baptism (Acts ii, 41–42); the earliest teaching was presumably an explanation of the Messianic prophecies in the Old Testament. On the gentile mission Paul's strongest appeal was made to the "God-fearers," who had been already won for monotheism and Jewish standards of morality, and for whom circumcision was no longer necessary. The word κατηχεῖν applied to Christian instruction, presumably both before and after baptism, occurs in the New Testament in Luke i, 4 (of Theophilus), Acts xviii, 25 (of Apollos—the exact meaning is disputed; *see* APOLLOS) and Gal. vi, 6 ("let him that is *taught* communicate with him that *teacheth* in all good things"). As the gentile element in the church preponderated, instruction became more definite. It was probably undertaken by the "teachers" (1 Cor. xii, 28). *The Teaching of the Twelve Apostles,* i–vi, is a manual of ethical teaching. The *Shepherd* of Hermas was widely used (Eus. *H. E.* III, iii, 6). Justin Martyr (*Apol.* i, 61) says converts are taught to pray for forgiveness before baptism.

In the 4th century, with the rise of heresy, detailed doctrinal teaching was given. Of those treatises which have survived, the most important are Cyril of Jerusalem's *Catechetical Lectures,* Gregory of Nyssa's *Catechetical Oration,* and Augustine's *De Rudibus Catechizandis.* By this time the postponement of baptism had become general; thus Constantine was not baptized till he was at the point of death. Accordingly a large proportion of Christians belonged to the catechumenate. Most of them were merely "adherents" of the church; others were under definite instruction for baptism. The preparation, preceded probably by a period of probation, generally coincided with the 40 days of Lent, the baptism taking place on Easter eve. The preparation consisted of (1) instruction in what must be renounced, (2) instruction in the faith, (3) exorcisms of evil spirits (*see* BAPTISM). All catechumens attended the first part of the Eucharistic service, known in the west as *Missa Catechumenorum,* after which they were "dismissed." As infant baptism became general, the catechumenate decayed. The baptismal rites now used are clearly adaptations of rites intended for the reception of adult catechumens. In the mission field the catechumenate has been revived and primitive conditions are repeated. Thus a polygamist will often be a lifelong "adherent" debarred from baptism by marriage difficulties of his own making. (W. K. L. C.)

CATEGORICAL, in common usage, means "unconditional" or "direct and explicit in statement"; also, "pertaining to a category."

1. *In Traditional Logic.*—The word is derived, as Petrus Hispanus tells us (in *Summulae Logicales, c.* 1245), from the Aristotelian κατηγορούμενον ("predicate") and thus means "predicative." (*See* LOGIC for an account of the traditional categorical propositions and categorical syllogism.)

2. *In Mathematics.*—A set of postulates is said to be categorical if every two models of the postulates are isomorphic. For example, in the case of Peano's postulates for arithmetic (*see* POSTULATE), a model is a system of meanings for the three primitive terms, "0", "number," "successor," which renders all the postulates true. That the postulates are categorical means that any two such models are isomorphic. *I.e.,* given two models, it is always possible to find a correspondence between the numbers of one model and the numbers of the other model, such that every number of either one of the models corresponds to a unique number in the other model, such that the 0 of one model corresponds to the 0 of the other model, and such that, if the numbers x, y of one model correspond to the numbers x', y' of the other model respectively, then y' is the successor of x' in the second model if and only if y is the successor of x in the first model. A categorical set of postulates thus determines uniquely the mathematical structure of a model, and in this sense no additional postulates are required (as distinguished from possible additional logical axioms [*see* AXIOM]). (Ao. C.)

3. *In Ethics.*—Kant introduced the term "categorical imperative" for a moral law that is unconditional or absolute, or whose validity or claim does not depend on any ulterior motive or end. According to Kant there is only one such categorical

imperative, which he formulates variously. One formula is: "Act only on such a maxim as you can will that it should become a universal law." This is purely formal, and expresses the condition of the rationality of conduct, rather than the condition of its morality. Another formula given by Kant is: "So act as to treat humanity, whether in your own person or in another, always as an end, and never as only a means." (*See* KANT, IMMANUEL and ETHICS, HISTORY OF.)

CATEGORICAL IMPERATIVE: *see* CATEGORICAL.

CATEGORY. The word "category" has come in unphilosophical contexts to mean much the same as "class," "type" or "kind." Recruits to the armed forces may be put into different categories, according to their physical qualities or according to their technical qualifications.

Originally the word belonged to Greek legal parlance, in which it meant "that of which a person is accused." Aristotle borrowed it for the special purposes of logical theory. In his use the Greek verb from which "category" derives meant "to predicate something of something"; *e.g.,* to assert of Socrates that he is a man, or is mortal, or is married to Xanthippe. Concentrating his attention upon simple assertions of the pattern "Socrates is such and such," Aristotle noticed that there are many important differences between the sorts of predicates that can be asserted of Socrates. To assert that Socrates is a man is to give a piece of information about Socrates of a radically different kind from that given by the assertion that Socrates is pale or that Socrates is older than Alcibiades. The first assertion tells us what Socrates is; the second tells us only what, at a particular moment, he is like in a particular respect; the third tells us only the result of a particular comparison between Socrates and Alcibiades. To put this point in another way, predicates like ". . . is a man" yield answers to the question "What is Socrates?"; predicates like ". . . is pale" yield answers to the question "What-like (*qualis*) is Socrates?"; predicates like ". . . in the market place" yield answers to the question "Where is Socrates?"; and so on. No answer to the question "Where is Socrates?" or "How big is Socrates?" is any answer to the question "What is Socrates?"; and no answer to the question "What is Socrates?" is any answer to the question "Where is Socrates?" or "What is Socrates now doing?" Predicates belong to different kinds or types; they yield answers to different questions.

Aristotle came to use the Greek word from which our noun "category" derives to signify not just predicate, but predicate *type.* "Man" and "monkey" are different predicates, but they are predicates of the same type or category. "Socrates is a man" is one answer, "Socrates is a monkey" is another, though false, answer to the question "What is Socrates?" Aristotle listed sometimes ten, sometimes fewer categories or predicate types and coined technical titles for them, some of which came direct from common Greek interrogative words like our "What?" and "How big?" The later latinization of Aristotelian logic originated our category titles like "quality," "quantity," "relation," "substance," "state" (or "condition") and others.

This distinction between kinds of predicate was required by Aristotle in order to resolve a number of logical paradoxes. For example, Socrates could, in the course of a short time, cease to be taller and come to be shorter than Alcibiades; so he is not at the later date what he was at the earlier date. Yet he does not cease to be a human being. How can he not be what he used to be (namely taller than Alcibiades) and still be what he used to be (namely a human being)? The answer is that a change of relation is not a change of sort. Similarly, Socrates who was pale yesterday may be flushed today, without his ceasing to be what he was yesterday, namely older than Alcibiades. A change of (colour) quality (of face) is not a change of (temporal) relation (between dates of birth). Aristotle also noticed the important point that the same word may be employed sometimes in one category and sometimes in another. We may describe a person, a regimen and a place as healthy, yet a place or a course of exercise cannot be well or unwell. To call a place or a regimen "healthy" is to say that it makes or causes people to be in good health. "Healthy" can mean "health-causing," or it can mean "health-enjoying," and the things that can be asserted or denied to be health-causing will or may be entirely different from the things, namely human beings and other living organisms, which can be asserted or denied to be in good health. A few words are category-pervasive. The notions of *being, one* and *good* appear, in different modifications, in every category. Such terms came later to be called "transcendentals."

Aristotle himself showed no particular veneration for his lists of sometimes ten, sometimes fewer predicate types. He did not attempt to prove that his lists were exhaustive or that they did not contain some redundancies. Piety induced some of his followers to assume that all conceivable predicates must be lodged in one or other of Aristotle's ten niches; considerations of economy have induced other thinkers to compress the list of irreducible predicate types to two or three. The categories of quality and relation have been held to exhaust the radical predicate types. More harm than good has been done by such economies.

There is however one traditional amplification of Aristotle's basic scheme which, whether or not it was intended by Aristotle himself, has proved important in philosophy and logical theory. The subject term of a proposition of the pattern "Socrates is a man" or "Socrates is elderly" cannot be classified with any of the possible predicates in such propositions. The name of a particular person or thing or event is not the name of a sort or a quality or a relation or a magnitude, etc. Socrates is of a sort, for he is a man; he has qualities, for he is white and wise; he is in relations, for he is married to Xanthippe; and so on. But he is not himself a sort, a quality, a relation or a magnitude, etc. The word "Socrates" could not yield the answer to any question of the form "Of what sort is this?", "Where is it?", "How big is it?" Instead, it has been held that a word like "Socrates" stands for a particular "substance," and "substance" has consequently been used as the title of a type of term which is not a predicate term, but a subject term. Various things can be asserted and denied of Socrates, but "Socrates" cannot be predicated, truly or falsely, of anything. It is not a possible predicate word. The idea that there may be various types of subject terms, as there are various types of predicates, has not been systematically developed—partly because the whole program of breaking all propositions alike down into subjects and predicates has come under effective criticism.

Kant converted the word "category" to a special use of his own, though he clearly believed that his scheme of ideas was closer to Aristotle's than it actually is. Kant was not interested in the different types of predicates predicable of a particular subject or substance, like Socrates. He was interested in the different types of judgment or proposition. In the three propositions "Socrates is mortal," "all men are mortal" and "some men are mortal," the predicates are not merely of the same type. They are the same predicate. But the three propositions differ from one another in another respect, that of what is sometimes called "logical form," in that the first is singular, being about one designated individual, the second is universal, being about every member of the class of men, while the third is particular, in being about some (at least one) undesignated members of the class of men. Socrates might be mortal without all men being mortal; Socrates could not be mortal without at least one member of the class of men being mortal, given that Socrates is a man. But some men might be mortal without Socrates being mortal; and we might know that all men are mortal without knowing that Socrates is mortal; since we might not know that Socrates was a man or even that there was anyone called "Socrates."

These differences of logical form are bound up with the implicational differences between the forces of "all . . . ," "some . . ." and "this . . ." (or "he" or "Socrates"). Other such differences are those hinging on the presence or absence of "not" (or some equivalent), the presence or absence of "if" or "or" (or their equivalents) and the presence or absence of "must" or "may" (or their equivalents). So, while Aristotle's list of categories derived from the study of the different types of predicates in simple, singular, affirmative propositions, Kant's doctrine starts from the consideration of the logically cardinal differences between simple and compound propositions, between affirmative and negative propositions, between universal, particular and singular propositions and between assertoric, apodictic and problematic propositions. Kant was not interested in the differences that had interested Aristotle.

For Aristotle, the notions of quality and quantity (or magnitude) were the types of such predicates as "white" or "sweet" and "six feet tall" or "three hundredweight" respectively. For Kant, differences of "quality" are, in the first instance, the differences between affirmative and negative propositions, and differences of "quantity" are the differences between universal, particular and singular propositions. For Aristotle, "being taller than" signifies a different relation from "being older than." For Kant, "if a metal is heated, it expands" expresses a different relation from that expressed by "this metal is expanding" or that expressed by "either today is Monday or today is Tuesday."

Kant, then, borrowed and transformed the Aristotelian title of "category" and some of the Aristotelian subtitles, like "quality," "quantity" and "relation." But he employed them to mark not just the differences between the logical structures of propositions, but something closely co-ordinated with them. Scientific knowledge, the sort of knowledge to which Isaac Newton had contributed so much, is expressed in systems of propositions or judgments. So too are metaphysical speculations. Propositions of both sorts would have to be of some logical form or other, either negative or affirmative; either universal or particular or singular; either categorical or hypothetical or disjunctive; either assertoric, apodictic or problematic.

But the propositions expressing knowledge of things in space and time embody these logical forms only in a specially restricted way, namely so as to be applicable to what human minds can perceive. The purely logical structure of subject-predicate belongs to any simple, singular, assertoric, affirmative proposition; but for a proposition of this structure to express empirical knowledge, it must assert that a spatiotemporal thing has at a given time a certain quality or is for a certain time in a certain state. The subject-predicate structure has, so to speak, to be geared down to the domain of perceivable things and happenings. Similarly, a proposition of natural science may be of the logical structure "if X, then Y"; but it cannot be merely of this structure. For it to apply to the actual world, it must assert a dependence of one temporal state of affairs from another; *i.e.*, a causal connection between events. Kant's categories are the ways in which the propositional structures extracted in logical theory function as the controlling principles of natural knowledge. The world disclosed by a Galileo or a Newton is a world of substances existing in space and time, changing and interacting according to causal laws. The questions that we put to nature are not whether there are substances existing, changing and interacting, but what substances there are and in what ways they change and interact.

At least a part of Kant's purpose was to explain the insolubility of certain speculative or metaphysical problems by showing that the very posing of these problems presupposed that the categories of, say, substance and causality apply as well to what is not as to what is empirical or phenomenal. He claimed to have proved, on the contrary, that the field of application of these and the other categories was as wide and only as wide as the field of what we human beings do or might perceive. There are and must be answers to our causal questions about empirically ascertainable events; there can be no answers to parallel questions about supposed states of affairs transcending human experiment and observation. Since Kant, the term "category" has tended to disappear from the technical parlance of philosophers and logicians. It has, perhaps, been so heavily loaded with disparate Aristotelian and Kantian connotations that philosophers and logicians have tried to find more noncommittal titles for their basic distinctions. The word "type" and the phrase "logical type," introduced by Bertrand Russell, have tended to displace the word "category," though it must not be supposed that either Aristotle's "category" or Kant's "category" is equivalent to Russell's "logical type."

One point needs further discussion. If we ask what Aristotle thought that his category-titles were titles of, no certain or unambiguous answer can be given. They were indeed titles for types of predicate, or, more broadly, types of "terms" (predicates *or* subjects) of simple, singular propositions. But to say this leaves open the question whether by "predicates" or, more broadly, "terms" we are referring (1) to the grammatical elements into which certain sorts of sentences are analyzed or (2) to things or entities for which such grammatical elements stand. Was Aristotle intending to classify certain classes of parts of speech, or was he intending to classify real things? Was he contributing to a branch of philology, or to the higher reaches of general taxonomy? Neither answer would be satisfactory; nor can either answer be safely fathered on to Aristotle.

Distinctions more or less akin to those which Aristotle drew are nowadays apt to be described not indeed as grammatical but as "semantic" distinctions—distinctions, that is, between kinds or modes of significance. We can and for certain purposes we need to exhibit the general way or ways in which, for example, what is meant by "or" (or *"ou"* or *"oder"*) differs from what is meant by "green" (or *"vert"* or *"grün"*). What is meant by the word "or" (or any equivalent expression) is clearly not a thing or a happening. So to specify its semantic function is not to put a thing or a happening into a species or a genus. On the other hand, to specify its semantic function is not just to say that "or" is an English conjunction, since what is being specified is not English as opposed to German or vice versa. On this view a category is a type of semantic function, neither a kind of linguistic expression nor yet a kind of thing or happening.

A child might be puzzled by the fact that while travellers can touch and photograph the North sea, travellers to the north pole can neither touch nor photograph it. It has to be explained to him not that the north pole differs from the North sea as an object, such as glass or air, differs from another object, such as wood or smoke, but rather that the expression "the north pole" and its equivalents do not have the same sort of meaning as the expression "the North sea" and its equivalents. "The North sea" is used to refer to a body of water in a certain place, whereas "the north pole" is used to refer to a certain place—*at* which there may indeed be now one ice hummock and now another. It is not itself an object. In short the expressions have different kinds of semantic function. Their meanings are of different logical types or of different categories. (G. R.)

CATENA, VINCENZO DI BIAGIO (*c.* 1480–1531), Venetian painter, formerly wrongly identified with Vincenzo dalle Destre of Treviso. In 1506 he and Giorgione were in partnership, as we learn from the inscription on the back of Giorgione's "Portrait of a Young Woman" in Vienna. He developed under the influence of Giovanni Bellini but there is no evidence that he ever worked in the Bellini studio. Characteristic early signed works are the "Virgin and Child with Saints and Donors" formerly in the Mond collection, the "Holy Family With a Saint" in Budapest, Hung., and the "Doge Leonardo Loredan Before the Virgin" in the Correr museum, Venice, It. The last two works are of about 1506, the time of Catena's documented association with Giorgione, and it is surprising to find that they are still entirely Bellinesque in character. A "Portrait of a Young Man" of this period is in the National gallery, London, Eng. The development of more advanced elements in his style may be traced in the "Virgin and Child with Saints and a Donor" at Liverpool, the "Holy Family with Saints and a Donor" in Berlin, Ger., and the "St. Jerome in His Study" (*c.* 1513) in London. The "Delivery of the Keys" in the Prado shows him under the influence of Palma Vecchio. A group of works showing Raphaelesque influence is often dated to his last years but may perhaps find better place in the period 1515–20. This influence first appears in the signed "Portrait of a Man" in Vienna and reaches its climax in the "Holy Family with St. Anne" at Dresden, Ger., which is based directly on a design from Raphael's studio. Giorgionesque and Titianesque influence flowers belatedly in the "Martyrdom of St. Christina" in the church of Sta. Maria Materdomini, Venice (1520). The successful fusion of the old and new in Venetian painting which this picture displays is Catena's particular achievement and characterizes the work of the last decade of his activity, culminating in the "Judith" of the Querini-Stampalia gallery, Venice, and the "Warrior Adoring the Infant Christ" in London. Characteristic late portraits are the "Giangiorgio Trissino" in the Louvre, Paris, "Venetian Senator" in New York city and the "Doge Andrea Gritti" (ascribed to Titian) in London.

BIBLIOGRAPHY.—G. Vasari, *Vite . . . etc.*, ed. by G. Milanesi, vol. iii, p. 643 (Florence, 1878–85); C. Ridolfi, *Le Maraviglie dell' arte . . . etc.*, ed. by D. von Hadeln, vol. i, p. 82 (Berlin, 1914–24); Thieme-Becker, *Künstlerlexikon*, vol. vi, p. 182 (Leipzig, 1912); Sir J. A. Crowe and G. B. Cavalcaselle, *History of Painting in North Italy*, ed. by T. Borenius, vol. i, p. 253 (London, 1912); B. Berenson, *Venetian Painting in America* (London, 1916); G. Robertson, *Vincenzo Catena* (Edinburgh, 1954). (G. H. RN.)

CATENARY: *see* CURVES, SPECIAL.

CATERAN, the band of fighting men of a Highland clan (Gaelic *ceathairine*, a collective word meaning peasantry); hence the term is applied to the Highland, and later to any, marauders or cattle lifters.

CATERHAM AND WARLINGHAM, an urban district (with Whyteleafe, Woldingham and Chaldon) in the E. Surrey parliamentary division, England, 18 mi. S. of London. Pop. (1951) 31,293. Area 12.9 sq.mi. In the North Downs, Caterham has grown since the opening of the railway in 1856 (electrified 1928) into a residential town with engineering, perfumery and other light industries. The depot of the brigade of guards is in the district.

CATESBY, ROBERT (1573–1605), English conspirator, son of Sir William Catesby of Lapworth, Warwick, prominent recusant, was born in 1573, and entered Gloucester hall (now Worcester college), Oxford, in 1586. In 1596 he was one of those arrested on suspicion during an illness of Queen Elizabeth I. In 1601 he took part in the rebellion of Essex, was wounded in the fight and imprisoned, but finally pardoned on the payment of an enormous fine. In 1602 he dispatched Thomas Winter and the Jesuit Tesimond *alias* Greenway to Spain to induce Philip III to organize an invasion of England, and in 1603, after James's accession, he was named as an accomplice in the "Bye plot." Exasperated by his personal misfortunes and by the repressive measures under which his co-religionists were suffering, he was now to be the chief instigator of the Gunpowder plot. The idea seems first to have entered his mind in May, 1603. About the middle of Jan. 1604 he imparted his scheme of blowing up the Parliament house to his cousin Thomas Winter, subsequently taking in Guy Fawkes and several other conspirators. But his determination not to allow warning to be given to the Roman Catholic peers was the actual cause of the failure of the plot. A fatal mistake had been made in imparting the secret to Francis Tresham, in order to secure his financial assistance; and there is little doubt that he was the author of the celebrated letter to his brother-in-law, Lord Monteagle, which betrayed the conspiracy to the government on Oct. 26. On receiving the news, Catesby exhibited extraordinary coolness; he refused to abandon the attempt, and his confidence was strengthened by Fawkes's report that nothing in the cellar had been touched or tampered with. After the discovery of the conspiracy Catesby fled with his fellow-plotters, taking refuge ultimately at Holbeche, Staffs., where on the night of Nov. 8 he was overtaken and killed. He had married Catherine, daughter of Thomas Leigh of Stoneleigh, Warwick, and left a son, Robert, who inherited that part of the family estate which had been settled on Catesby's mother and was untouched by the attainder. Robert is said to have married a daughter of Thomas Percy. (*See* also GUNPOWDER PLOT.)

CAT-FISH, the name generally given to the fishes of the suborder Siluroidea of the order Ostariophysi, in which the air-bladder is connected with the internal ear by a chain of ossicles, probably enabling the fishes to hear well. From the Cyprinoids (characins, carps and electric eels) the Siluroids are distinguished by having the body naked or armoured with bony plates, never normally scaled, and by a number of osteological characters: the air-bladder generally extends laterally so that on each side it is in contact with the skin above the pectoral fin. The name "cat-fish" has reference to the long barbels or feelers about the mouth, of which one pair supported by the maxillaries is always present; generally there are two pairs below the chin, and frequently another developed from the valves between the nostrils. Nearly all the Siluroids are fresh water fishes, but two families are secondarily marine, the Ariidae, found on the coasts and in estuaries of all tropical countries, and the Plotosidae of the Indo-Pacific. The group is a large and varied one, containing probably about 2,000 species belonging to 23 different families; most are omnivorous, feeding on almost any kind of animal or vegetable food, and acting as scavengers. The spines of the dorsal and pectoral fins, which are so generally present, are powerful weapons, capable of inflicting severe and sometimes poisonous wounds.

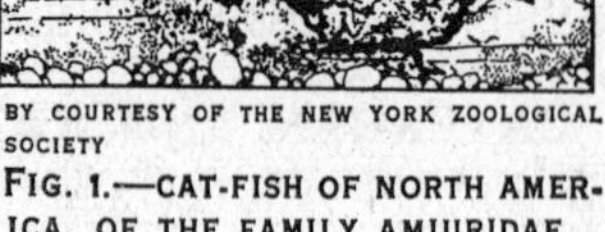

BY COURTESY OF THE NEW YORK ZOOLOGICAL SOCIETY

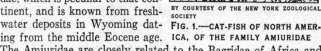

FIG. 1.—CAT-FISH OF NORTH AMERICA, OF THE FAMILY AMIURIDAE

The cat-fishes of North America belong to the family Amiuridae, which is peculiar to that continent, and is known from freshwater deposits in Wyoming dating from the middle Eocene age. The Amiuridae are closely related to the Bagridae of Africa and Asia, and like them and most Siluroids have a short dorsal fin, with a spine, followed by an adipose fin on the tail. The anterior rays of the pectoral fins are spinous. The head is rather flat, with the mouth terminal and moderately wide, and the jaws with bands of small teeth; there are eight barbels. There are about 25 species, some of which are small; *Amiurus lacustris* of the Great Lakes attains a weight of more than 150 lb. These fishes scoop out a nest in the mud, and the male parent guards the eggs, and later swims with the brood near the shore.

The European cat-fish (*Silurus glanis*), the "Wels" of the Germans, is said to reach a length of 10 ft. and a weight of 400 lb. It has a very long tail, beneath which is the long anal fin. Another species (*Parasilurus aristotelis*) occurs in Greece; the remaining Siluridae are Asiatic. In South and Central America are no less than nine families of Siluroids, all endemic. *Diplomyste* of Chile and Argentina, with toothed maxillary, is the most primitive living Siluroid, but other South American forms are highly specialized. Of the Aspredinidae, *Aspredo batrachus* is remarkable for the way in which the female carries the eggs on the abdomen; these sink into the soft spongy skin and a cup develops round each and then becomes stalked. The Trichomycteridae include *Stegophilus* and *Vandellia,* little slender naked fishes that live parasitically in the gill chambers of other fishes, and are said to enter the urethra of persons bathing, and by distending the short spines with which the gill-covers are armed, to cause inflammation or even death.

BY COURTESY OF THE NEW YORK ZOOLOGICAL SOCIETY

FIG. 2.—CAT-FISH OF THE GREAT LAKES, (AMIURUS LACUSTRIS)

The Loricariidae, with about 300 species, are mostly fishes that are covered by a long armour of five series of bony plates on each side, and have the lips expanded into a sucker by means of which they hold on to stones. They feed mainly on mud and algae and have a very long intestine that is coiled like a watch-spring. In some species there are pronounced sexual differences, the males having broader and blunter heads, margined with spines or bristles, or bearing branched tentacles on the snout. In the mountain streams of the Andes the Loricariidae are represented by small forms (*Cyclopium* or *Arges*) known as "prenadillas"; in these regions there are no carnivorous fishes to attack them and they are completely naked, having lost the bony armour that protects the lowland forms. A mining engineer who had diverted a stream in order to empty a pot-hole, observed a number of these fishes climb a precipice from the hole to the stream above it, obtaining alternate holds with the sucker and the rough surface of the pelvic fins; these were moved forward by the contraction of special muscles attached to the pelvic bones, while the sucker was holding. The Callichtyidae are another armoured family, but with only two rows of plates on each side of the body. Callichthys builds nests of grass, sometimes placed in a hole scooped out of the bank; both parents guard the nest. In the South American Doradidae, as in the similar but unrelated Mochochidae of Africa, the air-bladder is a sound-producing organ. *Doras* travels from one pond to another in the dry season, sometimes journeying all night. The Clariidae of Africa and Asia are also air-breathing fishes, provided with air-chambers above the gills; in *Clarias* special vascular tree-like organs nearly fill the chamber, but in *Saccobranchus* these are absent and the air-sac extends backwards for half the length of the fish. These are elongate, more or less eel-shaped fishes; in the dry season they burrow in the mud, but some species are said to leave their burrows at night and crawl about on land in search of food.

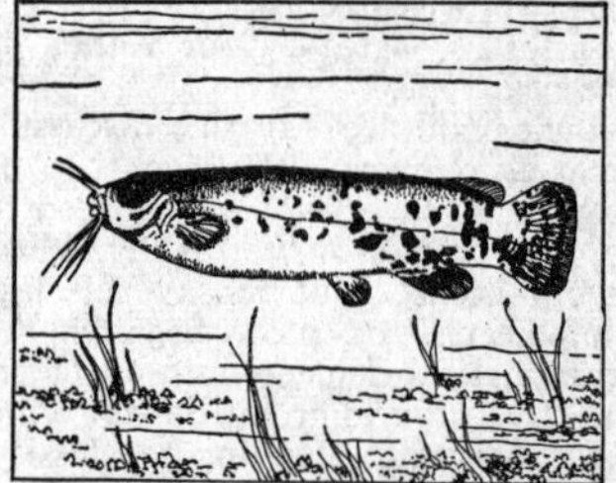

FROM JORDAN, "FISHES" (D. APPLETON)

FIG. 3.—CAT-FISH OF AFRICA, (MALOPTERURUS ELECTRICUS)

The African Amphiliidae and the Sisoridae of India have the lower surface of the head and abdomen flat and the paired fins horizontal, an adaptation to life in mountain torrents; in some genera the lips form a sucker similar to that of the Loricariidae. The electric cat-fish (*Malopterurus electricus*) is widely distributed in Africa. The skin is soft, and immediately beneath it lies the electric organ, formed of rhomboidal cells of a fine gelatinous substance, and differing from that of other fishes in being part of the tegumentary system, not derived from the muscles. Certain species of *Synodontis,* a genus common in the Nile, are white on the back and blackish beneath, a coloration connected with their habit of swimming belly upwards. The Ariidae, most of which live in salt water, are typical Siluroids in form and structure of the fins, whereas the other marine family, the Plotosidae, have a very long tail, with the long anal fin confluent with the caudal. In some species of *Arius* the eggs, few in number and as large as marbles, are carried about by the male in his mouth. *Bucklandium* from the lower Eocene (London clay) is an Ariid. (C. T. R.)

CATGUT, the name applied to cord of great toughness and tenacity prepared from the intestines of sheep, or occasionally from those of the horse, mule and ass. Those of the cat are not employed, and therefore it is supposed that the word is properly *kitgut, kit* meaning "fiddle," and that the present form has arisen through confusion with *kit*-cat. The substance is used for the strings of harps and violins, as well as other stringed musical instruments, for hanging the weights of clocks, for bow-strings, and for suturing wounds in surgery. To prepare it the intestines are cleaned, freed from fat, and steeped for some time in water, after which their external membrane is scraped off with a blunt knife. They are then steeped for some time in an alkaline lye, smoothed and equalized by drawing out, subjected to the antiseptic action of the fumes of burning sulphur, if necessary dyed, sorted into sizes, and twisted together into cords of various numbers of strands according to their uses. The best strings for musical instruments are imported from Italy ("Roman strings"), and it is found that lean and ill-fed animals yield the toughest gut.

CATHA, a shrub (*Catha edulis,* family Celastraceae) native to Arabia and to Africa from Abyssinia to the Cape. It is also cultivated, especially in Arabia, where it is called *khat, kat,* or *kasta.*

The Arabians make a kind of tea from the dried leaves and young shoots. These are also chewed extensively for their stimulant properties, which somewhat resemble those of coca.

CATHARS (Cathari or Catharists), a widespread heretical sect of the middle ages. This article relates to the Western Cathars, as they appear (1) in the Cathar Ritual written in Provençal and preserved in a 13th-century ms. in Lyons, published by Clédat, Paris, 1888; (2) in Bernard Gui's *Practica inquisitionis haereticae pravitatis,* edited by Canon C. Douais, Paris, 1886; and (3) in the *procès verbal* of the inquisitors' reports. Some are dualists, and believed that there are two gods or principles, one of good and the other of evil, both eternal; but as a rule they subordinated the evil to the good, and all were universalists in so far as they believed in the ultimate salvation of all men.

Their tenets were as follows:—The evil god, Satan, who inspired the malevolent parts of the Old Testament, is god and lord of this world, of the things that are seen and are temporal, and especially of the outward man which is decaying, of the earthen vessel, of the body of death, of the flesh which takes us captive under the law of sin and desire. This world is the only true purgatory and hell, being the antithesis of the world eternal, of the inward man renewed day by day, of Christ's kingdom which is not of this world. Men are the result of a primal war in heaven, when hosts of angels incited by Satan or Lucifer to revolt were driven out, and were imprisoned in terrestrial bodies created for them by the adversary.

How shall man escape from his prison-house of flesh, and undo the effects of his fall? For mere death brings no liberation, unless a man is become a new creation, a new Adam, as Christ was; unless he has received the gift of the spirit and become a vehicle of the Paraclete. If a man dies unreconciled to God through Christ, he must pass through another cycle of imprisonment in flesh; perhaps in a human, but with equal likelihood in an animal's body. For when after death the powers of the air throng around and persecute, the soul flees into the first lodging of clay that it finds. Christ was a life-giving spirit, and the *boni homines,* the "good men," as the Cathars called themselves, are his ambassadors. They alone have kept the spiritual baptism with fire which Christ instituted, and which has no connection with the water baptism of John; for the latter was an unregenerate soul, who failed to recognize the Christ, a Jew whose mode of baptism with water belongs to the fleeting outward world and is opposed to the kingdom of God.

The Cathars fell into two classes, corresponding to the Baptized and the Catechumens of the early church, namely, the Perfect, who had been "consoled," *i.e.,* had received the gift of the Paraclete; and the *credentes* or Believers. The Perfect formed the ordained priesthood and controlled the church; they received from the Believers unquestioning obedience, and as vessels of election in whom the Holy Spirit already dwelt, they were adored by the faithful, who were taught to prostrate themselves before them whenever they asked for their prayers. They alone were become adopted sons, and so able to use the Lord's Prayer, which begins, "Our Father, which art in heaven." The Perfect alone knew God and could address him in this prayer, the only one they used in their ceremonies. The mere *credens* could at best invoke the living saint, and ask him to pray for him.

All adherents of the sect seem to have kept three Lents in the year, as also to have fasted Mondays, Wednesdays and Fridays of each week; in these fasts a diet of bread and water was usual. But a *credens* under probation for initiation, which lasted at least one and often several years, fasted always. The life of a Perfect was so hard, and, thanks to the inquisitors, so fraught with danger, that most Believers deferred the rite until the death-bed, as in the early centuries many believers deferred baptism. The rule imposed complete chastity. The passages of the New Testament which seem to connive at the married relation were interpreted by the Cathars as spoken in regard of Christ and the church. The Perfect must also leave his father and mother. The family must be sacrificed to the divine kinship. He that loveth father or mother more than Christ is not worthy of him, nor he that loveth more his son or daughter. The Perfect takes up his cross and follows after Christ. He must abstain from all flesh diet except fish. He may not even eat cheese or eggs or milk, for they, like meat, are produced *per viam generationis seu coitus.* Everything that is sexually begotten is impure. Fish were supposed to be born in the water without sexual connection, and on the basis of this old physiological fallacy the Cathars framed their rule of fasting. And there was yet another reason why the Perfect should not eat animals, for a human soul might be imprisoned in its body. Nor might a Perfect or one in course of probation kill anything, for the Mosaic commandment applies to all life.

The central Cathar rite was *consolamentum,* or baptism with the spirit. The spirit received was the Paraclete, the Comforter, derived from God and sent by Christ, who said, "The Father is greater than I." Of a consubstantial Trinity the Cathars naturally had never heard. Infant baptism they rejected because it was unscriptural and because all baptism with water was an appanage of the Jewish demiurge Jehovah, and as such expressly rejected by Christ. The *consolamentum* removes original sin, undoes the effects of the primal fall, clothes upon us our habitation which is from heaven, restores to us the lost garment of immortality. A Consoled is an angel walking in the flesh, whom the thin screen of death alone separates from Christ and the beatific vision. The rite was appointed by Christ, and has been handed down from generation to generation by the *boni homines.*

In the case of a candidate for initiation the Perfect addresses the postulant by the name of Peter; and explains to him from Scripture the indwelling of the spirit in the Perfect, and his adoption as a son by God. The Lord's Prayer is then repeated by the postulant after the elder, who explains it clause by clause. Then came the Renunciation, primitive enough in form, but the postulant solemnly renounced, not Satan and his works and pomp, but the harlot church of the persecutors; he renounced the cross which its priests had signed on him by baptism and other magical rites. Next followed the spiritual baptism itself, consisting of imposition of hands, and holding the Gospel on the postulant's head. The elder begins a fresh allocution by citing Matt. xxviii. 19, Mark xvi. 15, 16, John iii. 3 (where the Cathars' text must originally have omitted in v. 5 the words "of water and," since their presence contradicts their argument). Acts ix. 17, 18, viii. 14–17, are then cited; also John xx. 21–23, Matt. xvi. 18, 19, Matt. xviii. 18–20, for the Perfect one receives in this rite power to bind and loose. The Perfect's vocation is then defined in terms of a strictly literal observance of the Commandments and the Sermon on the Mount. Asked if he will fulfil these demands, the postulant answers: "I have this will and determination. Pray God for me that he give me his strength." The next episode of the rite exactly reproduces the Roman *confiteor* as it stood in the 2nd century; "the postulant says: *'Parcite nobis.'* For all the sins I have committed, in word or thought or deed, I come for pardon to God and to the church and to you all.' And the Christians shall say: 'By God and by us and by the church may they be pardoned thee, and we pray God that he pardon you them.'"

There follows the act of "consoling." The elder takes the Gospel off the white cloth, where it has lain all through the ceremony, and places it on the postulant's head, and the other *boni homines* present place their right hands on his head; they shall say the *parcias* (spare), and thrice the "Let us adore the Father and Son and Holy Spirit," and then pray thus: "Holy Father, welcome thy servant in thy justice and send upon him thy grace and thy holy spirit." Then they repeat the "Let us adore," the Lord's Prayer, and read the Gospel (John i, 1–17). This was the vital part of the whole rite. The *credens* is now a Perfect one; the Perfect ones present give him the kiss of peace, and the rite is over.

The Cathar Eucharist was equally primitive, and is thus described by a contemporary writer in a 13th-century manuscript in the Milan library: "The Benediction of bread is thus performed by the Cathars. They all, men and women, go up to a table and standing up say the 'Our Father,' [as according to St. Gregory (*Ep.* ix, 12–26), was the custom of the apostles]. And he who is prior among them, at the close of the Lord's Prayer, shall take hold of the bread and say: 'Thanks be to the God of our Jesus Christ. May the Spirit be with us all.' And after that he breaks and distributes to all. And such bread is called bread blessed, although no one believes that out of it is made the body of Christ."

BIBLIOGRAPHY.—J. B. Mullinger, art. "Albigenses" in Hastings, *Encyclopaedia of Religion and Ethics,* vol. i; C. H. Haskins, "Robert le Bougre," *American Historical Review* (1902); F. C. Conybeare, *The Key of Truth* (Oxford, 1898); J. J. I. Döllinger, *Beiträge zur Sektengeschichte* (Munich, 1890); Jean Guiraud, *Questions d'histoire* (Paris, 1906); C. Douais, *Les Hérétiques du midi au XIIIe siècle* (Paris, 1891); L. Clédat, *Le Nouveau Testament, traduit au XIIIe siècle en langue provençale, suivi d'un rituel cathare* (Paris, 1887); C. Schmidt, *Histoire et doctrine de la secte des Cathares* (Paris, 1849).

CATHARSIS means purification. Since the time of Aristotle the term has been definitely associated with the question of the effects of tragedy on the spectators or on the actors. Aristotle maintained that tragedy and also certain kinds of music tend to purify the spectators and listeners by artistically exciting certain emotions which act as a kind of homeopathic relief from their own selfish passions. Goethe was of opinion that the catharsis affects the actors in the tragedy rather than the spectators or readers. Lessing, on the other hand, held that it affects the spectators and readers rather than the performers. Lessing also maintained that catharsis takes the form of a sublimation of the emotions or their conversion into virtuous dispositions.

BIBLIOGRAPHY.—Butcher, *Aristotle's Theory of Poetry* (1895); J. Bernays, *Zwei Abhandlunger über die Aristotelische Theorie des Dramas* (1880); G. E. Lessing, *Hamburgische Dramaturgie* (1769, etc.).

CATHARTIC, an agent used to relieve constipation. Aperients, laxatives, cathartics, eccoprotics, purgatives, physics, hydragogues and drastics, arranged in order of intensity, differ only in the degree to which they act. Cathartic action depends usually upon increased fluidity or bulk of the gut contents or upon irritation of the gut. Cathartics include: (1) saline cathartics such as sodium and magnesium sulphate, poorly absorbable salts that hold water in the gut by osmotic force; (2) bulk producers such as psyllium seeds and agar which take up water and swell, and bran which contains a high proportion of insoluble material; (3) emollients such as mineral oil which is poorly absorbed and coats the intestinal wall with an oily film, preventing the absorption of water; (4) irritant oils such as castor oil and croton oil; (5) anthracene derivatives such as senna, rhubarb, cascara and aloe which owe their activity to various polyhydroxyanthroquinones, present usually as glucosides; (6) the cathartic resins such as euphorbium, jalap, podophyllum, elaterium, gamboge and colocynth in which the active ingredient is usually a glucoresin; (7) miscellaneous irritants such as phenolphthalein and mercurous chloride (calomel).

Cathartics have been exploited by the patent-medicine industry probably more than any other group of drugs. Many cases of chronic constipation have resulted from their indiscriminate use. They should be taken only upon the advice of a physician since serious harm can result from an attempt to relieve gastrointestinal symptoms without knowing their cause.

CATHARTIDAE: *see* VULTURE.

CATHAY, the name by which China became known to mediaeval Europe. It is derived from Khitai, the name of the kingdom of Khitan Tatars (10th and 11th centuries A.D.) which, based on Manchuria (the northeastern gateway into China), included at times part of northern China as well and which toward its close had its capital at Yenking (Kublai Khan's Cambaluc, *q.v.,* and the modern Peking). The central Asian Tatars, in touch only with its northern territories, knew China by this name and the Russians through contact with them introduced it into Europe. The Russians and the peoples of central Asia still know China as Khitai or Kitai. Although in Marco Polo's time all China was under the control of the Great Khan, he limits Cathay to the country north of the Yangtze valley, calling southern China by the separate name of Mangi. The distinction was at that time a real one, since Mangi retained the old Sung culture practically undiluted while Cathay bore the impress of the Tatar conquest. In the 16th century, however, when European navigators reached far eastern waters via the Spice Islands it was Mangi which they knew as China (this name is thought to have been derived by neighbouring peoples from the Chin dynasty, 3rd century B.C., but is not found in the Chinese language); and Cathay was understood to lie away to the north of it and to be reached by a still undiscovered sea route. Hence ensued the search for the northwest and northeast passages from Europe. This dualism corresponds to the distinction apparent in Roman literature between the Seres—the Chinese as approached by the overland route—and the Sinae—the Chinese as approached by the sea route from the south. Only in the early 17th century was the identity of the country and of the people reached by the two routes appreciated.

CATHCART, the name of a family of Scottish, and from 1807 of British, peers, of whom the following are historically most important:

WILLIAM SCHAW CATHCART, 1ST EARL (1755–1843), was born at Petersham, Sept. 17, 1755. Leaving Eton in 1771, he went to St. Petersburg, where his father, the 9th Baron Cathcart (1721–76), was ambassador. He succeeded to the barony in 1776 and, having studied law at Dresden and Glasgow, was admitted to the Scottish faculty of advocates. In 1777 he joined the army and commanded troops in America, the Netherlands and Germany. He later served as commander in chief in Ireland (1803–05), and led the British expedition to Hanover (1805). In 1806 he was sent on a diplomatic mission to Russia and in 1807 commanded the land forces in the Copenhagen expedition. After the capture of Copenhagen he was created Viscount Cathcart of Cathcart and Baron Greenwich of Greenwich. He was promoted general in 1812. In July of the same year he was appointed ambassador and military commissioner in Russia, where he remained until 1820. He was created earl in 1814. He died at his estate near Glasgow, June 16, 1843.

CHARLES MURRAY CATHCART, 2ND EARL (1783–1859), eldest son of the above, succeeded to the title in 1843. He saw distinguished service in the Napoleonic wars and was commander in chief in Canada from 1846 to 1849. Cathcart's interest in science led to his discovery in 1841 of a new mineral which was named greenockite.

SIR GEORGE CATHCART (1794–1854), third surviving son of the 1st earl, served in the Napoleonic campaigns of 1812–15 and in 1846 became deputy lieutenant of the Tower of London. In 1852 he was made governor of the Cape, where he completed Sir Harry Smith's task of subduing the Kaffirs. In 1854 he returned to England and was sent to the Crimea in command of a division. He was killed at the battle of Inkerman.

CATHEDRAL (from Greek καθέδρα, Latin *cathedra,* chair or throne) is an adjective frequently used as a noun to mean a cathedral church (*ecclesia cathedralis*); that is, a church in which a bishop has his official seat (*sedes*) or throne.

Early Organization.—A cathedral church is not necessarily a large church, but from the 4th century was supposed to be in a town, not in a village. In Britain in the age of conversion this was not usually possible because there were practically no towns, but after the Norman conquest a number of English cathedrals were moved from villages to the most important town in the diocese. Occasionally two churches jointly share the distinction of containing the bishop's *cathedra* and are therefore said to be con-cathedral in relation to each other. Examples are in Ireland at Christ church and St. Patrick's, Dublin, and in England before the Reformation at Bath and Wells and at Coventry and Lichfield. Cathedral churches are of different degrees of dignity: the simple cathedral church of a diocesan bishop; the metropolitical church to which other diocesan cathedral churches of a province are suffragan; the primatial church under which are metropolitical churches and their provinces; patriarchal churches to which primatial, metropolitical and simple cathedral churches alike owe allegiance. The title "primate" was occasionally conferred on metropolitans of sees of dignity and importance, such as Canterbury, York and Rouen, whose cathedral churches remained simply metropolitical.

The bishop by canon law was pastor of his cathedral church, which was the mother church (*matrix ecclesia*) of his diocese or, as it was called in early times, parish (*parochia*), a word used later for the parishes into which the diocese was divided. His cathedral clergy, which included priests, deacons, subdeacons and clerks in minor orders, originally formed his *familia* or household and lived a communal life with him, sharing the common goods of the church and helping to serve its large parish. They were not usually monks, but their communities were often described as *monasteria,* a word which then had a less restricted meaning than it later acquired. Because of this, churches such as York and Lincoln, which never had monks attached to them, inherited the name minster or monastery. In time the common life was abandoned and the clergy lived in separate houses, but in the 8th and early 9th centuries the revival of the common life in a stricter form was advocated by reformers in the Carolingian empire, chiefly as a means of enforcing celibacy among cathedral clergy. The most famous and successful rule for cathedral clergy at this time was that of Bishop Chrodegang of Metz, written about 755. It was based largely on the Benedictine rule, but was less strict in requirements for individual poverty. At the council of Aix-la-Chapelle, 817, it was chosen as the basis for a widespread adoption of a common life at cathedral and collegiate churches throughout the empire. In England it was introduced at Canterbury for a short time about 813, and at several other cathedral churches in the 11th century, before the Norman conquest. The clergy who followed it were called canons or canonical clerks because they observed a definite rule or canon (from Greek κανών, rule).

Secular and Regular Cathedrals.—From the 10th century two increasingly divergent movements can be traced in the history of the organization of communities of canons. On the one hand, attempts to enforce the common life met with more resistance and, in times of invasions, with unrest and relaxation of ecclesiastical discipline, many cathedral canons acquired private property, lived in separate houses and divided a large part of the common estates and goods of their church into separate portions or prebends (provender) for themselves. Because of these separate possessions they were called "secular" canons. This division of common goods was recognized as permissible on the continent about the middle of the 11th century. However, this "secularizing" movement led, in the religious revival of the same period, to a renewed demand for clergy to live the communal apostolic life and, as a result, in the early 12th century many communities of canons adopted a strict form of common life under the rule of St. Augustine. They were called "regular" (from Latin *regula,* rule) or Augustinian canons, and their life soon became barely distinguishable from that of Benedictine monks. From this time cathedral churches were normally organized on either a regular or a secular basis. On the greater part of the continent the regular cathedrals of the middle ages were served by Augustinian or Premonstratensian canons, though in parts of Germany and in Denmark some were served by Benedictine monks. In England the 10th-century monastic revival had resulted in the introduction of Benedictine monks to serve three or four cathedrals, and in the ecclesiastical reorganization following the Norman conquest these were increased to nine—Canterbury, Winchester, Worcester, Rochester, Bath, Coventry, Ely, Norwich, Durham; that is, nearly half the total number of English mediaeval cathedrals. In Ireland at Downpatrick and in Sicily at Monreale, Benedictine cathedral chapters were also founded in the late 12th century under Anglo-Norman influence. England had only one Augustinian cathedral, Carlisle, founded in 1133. Christ church, Dublin, in Ireland and St. Andrews in Scotland were Augustinian, while Whithorn, the cathedral church of Galloway, was Premonstratensian. All the other mediaeval cathedrals of Britain gradually became secular in the period following the Norman conquest. A secular organization was first introduced at Salisbury, Lincoln, York and London about 1089–91, and later spread to Wells, Lichfield, Chichester, Hereford and Exeter in England and to Elgin (Moray), Glasgow and Aberdeen in Scotland.

Neither in the regular nor secular mediaeval cathedrals was the early intimate association of bishop and cathedral clergy maintained. With the end of the missionary period of conversion and with the formation of parishes, the cathedral church lost its parochial character, and the interests of its clergy became centred in its services and government, while the bishop was increasingly drawn away on diocesan duties or affairs of state. The cathedral chapters always kept certain links with their bishop and diocese. They continued to act as permanent trustees of episcopal property; their consent was necessary to episcopal acts which involved financial arrangements of the church and see; they sometimes exercised episcopal jurisdiction in a vacancy of a see and in 1215 were recognized as having the sole right to elect their bishop. But from the 11th or 12th century most cathedral chapters controlled their own property, which was separate from that of the bishop, and assumed, especially in northern France and England, the position of independent corporations, jealous of their rights and privileges. Mediaeval English bishops were often afraid to adventure themselves in their cathedral cities for fear of conflicts with their chapters. In the regular chapters the bishop was in the position of titular abbot, but attempts by him to act as abbot were quickly resented. The convent of regular canons or monks formed the chapter, of which the prior was head, and its constitution and way of life was ordered by the Benedictine or Augustinian rule.

The constitutions of the secular cathedral chapters showed greater variety. Their two main characteristics were separate prebendal incomes for the canons and a system of home government at the cathedral based on a varying number of dignitaries, who divided the administrative work between them and were supposed to be continuously resident. The prebends were of varying value, but many were sufficient to enable canons to be nonresident and do work at a distance from the cathedral in the rapidly expanding administrations of kings, popes, archbishops and bishops, in the growing schools of the 12th century and in the universities of the 13th century. Nonresidence was soon regarded as lawful, for a canonry, unlike a dignity, was without cure of souls. Nonresident canons, however, were forbidden to share in the chapter's common fund, which was kept for the residentiaries, who bore the "heat and burden of the day" at the cathedral. By the 14th century in England secular cathedral canons were usually fairly clearly divided into two groups, residentiaries and nonresidentiaries, and the residentiaries might form about a quarter of the full body of 21 to 54 canons. By the 16th and 17th centuries, because of the increase in the common fund and the reduction of the residentiaries to a small fixed number of five to nine, residence at these cathedrals had become a privilege to which nonresident prebendaries eagerly awaited election, and government was almost entirely vested in the small inner chapter of residentiaries.

In England the constitutions of the nine mediaeval secular cathedrals became in the course of the 12th, 13th and 14th centuries remarkably homogeneous. They have been described as four square, because they

EARLY ENGLISH GOTHIC
13TH CENTURY
SALISBURY, SOUTH AISLE

MODERN AMERICAN. COMPLETED EXTERIOR, ST. JOHN THE DIVINE, NEW YORK CITY
(CRAM AND FERGUSON, ARCHITECTS, FOR THE COMPLETION, 1910 ET SEQ)
(HEINS AND LAFARGE, ARCHITECTS, FOR OLDER PORTIONS, 1892 ET SEQ)

FRENCH GOTHIC
13TH–14TH CENTURIES
BEAUVAIS, THE CHOIR

CATHEDRAL OF ST. BASIL
MOSCOW, 1555–60
(BARMA AND POSTNIK, ARCHITECTS)

BYZANTINE, GREEK TYPE
11TH CENTURY
CATHEDRAL AT ATHENS

MODERN ENGLISH 1896 ONWARD
WESTMINSTER CATHEDRAL, LONDON
(J. F. BENTLEY, ARCHITECT)

SPANISH LATE GOTHIC AND RENAISSANCE
14TH-16TH CENTURIES
SEVILLE CATHEDRAL, SPAIN

FRENCH ROMANESQUE 12TH CENTURY
LA CATHEDRALE ST. PIERRE AT ANGOULEME
(RESTORED AND ALTERED, 19TH CENTURY)

O. T. Richard.

EXAMPLES OF CATHEDRAL ARCHITECTURE FROM THE 11TH TO THE 20TH CENTURY

Although a cathedral is usually large, a small building can serve, as in the case of the tiny cathedral at Athens. Salisbury and Beauvais cathedrals represent English and French phases of Gothic; that of Seville shows the Spanish late-Gothic-Renaissance transitional style; the curious St. Basil's cathedral, Moscow, combines Byzantine and Italian Renaissance features with Russian timber-church and tartar motifs and purely fanciful elements; and Westminster cathedral (Roman Catholic) and the cathedral of St. John the Divine are modern adaptations of Byzantine and Gothic precedents

were based on four great dignitaries who normally occupied the four terminal stalls in choir. The dean was president of the chapter and had cure of souls of all the cathedral clergy; the precentor was in charge of the music, liturgy and song school; the chancellor was the chapter's secretary and supervised the cathedral schools of grammar and theology; the treasurer guarded the church's treasures and provided lights and other material necessaries for the services. Under these were various deputies and officers, such as a subdean, succentor, vice-chancellor, grammar master, lecturer in theology, subtreasurer and sacrists, with masters or wardens of the fabric and common funds, some of whom were canons while others were vicars choral or chantry chaplains. Vicars choral were appointed from the 12th century not only by nonresident but also by residentiary canons, and corresponded to the *heuriers, matiniers* and demiprebendaries of some French chapters, whose chief duties were to sing the services. By the later middle ages they were in effect the working staffs of the cathedrals and formed minor self-governing corporations under the wealthy controlling corporation of the chapter.

English and Continental Development.—The English cathedral constitutions in their origins at the end of the 11th century can have been derived only from cathedrals of Normandy or northern France, where similar dignitaries then performed roughly similar functions, though their numbers, status and precedence still varied and were unfixed, and no one Norman cathedral provided an exact model. The remarkable similarity of the English constitutions of the later middle ages seems, however, to have been the result not merely of a common origin or imitation of a Norman model, but also of independent development in England in the 12th and 13th centuries and of the growing practice by English chapters of borrowing and adopting each others' customs, particularly those of Salisbury. On the continent there was far greater diversity in constitutions and titles, of which Chartres, with dignitaries in the 14th century, or Milan, with an archpriest at the head of the chapter, archdeacon and four *primicerii,* are particularly good examples. Generally it seems that the strong independent chapter with a dean as sole head under the bishop developed first in northern France about the 10th and 11th centuries. Elsewhere about this time there was often a division between the spiritual authority in the chapter, exercised usually by a dean in Germany and the Low Countries and by an archpriest in southern France and Italy, and the temporal authority of a provost or archdeacon, who administered the capitular estates. In Germany, Scandinavia and parts of eastern and southern France the provost often later emerged as sole head of the chapter, while in Italy about half the cathedrals came to have an archdeacon at their head.

In France most of the regular cathedral chapters were secularized about the time of the Reformation. In England Henry VIII dissolved the monastic cathedral chapters and, except for Bath and Coventry, refounded them as secular chapters under a dean with an organization suggested by that of English colleges of resident chantry priests in the later middle ages. These are called cathedrals of the New Foundation. He also founded six new cathedrals with similar constitutions in churches of dissolved monasteries at Bristol, Chester, Gloucester, Oxford, Peterborough and, for a time, Westminster. The nine mediaeval secular cathedrals, known as cathedrals of the Old Foundation, survived the Reformation with their constitutions practically unchanged; they underwent drastic changes and the loss of their prebendal estates by the Cathedrals act, 1840. Since 1836 3 ancient English collegiate churches, Ripon, Manchester and Southwell, and 18 parish churches (including the originally monastic churches of St. Albans and Southwark) have been converted into cathedrals of new dioceses, while new cathedrals have been built at Truro, Liverpool and Guildford.

BIBLIOGRAPHY.—Frances de Urrutigoyti, *De Ecclesiis Cathedralibus* (Venice, 1698); A. Barbosa, *Tractatus de Canonicis et Dignitatibus aliisque inferioribus Beneficiariis Cathedralium* (Lyons, 1700); L. Thomassin, *Vetus et nova Ecclesiae Disciplina* (Mainz, 1787); D. Bouix, "Tractatus de Capitulis" in *Institutiones Iuris canonici* (Paris, 1852); J. de Bordenave, *L'Estat des églises cathédrales* (Paris, 1643); L. d'Héricourt du Vatier, *Les Lois ecclésiastiques de France* (Paris, 1756); D. de Sainte Marthe and P. Piolin (eds.), *Gallia Christiana in Provincias ecclesiasticas distributa* (Paris, 1870, etc.); F. Ughelli, *Italia Sacra* (Venice, 1717–22); J. B. Daugaard, *Om de danske Klostre i Middelalderen* (Copenhagen, 1830); P. Hinschius, *Das Kirchenrecht der Katholiken und Protestanten in Deutschland,* vol. ii (Berlin, 1878); H. Bradshaw and C. Wordsworth, *Statutes of Lincoln Cathedral* (Cambridge, 1892–97); J. Dowden, *The Medieval Church in Scotland* (Glasgow, 1910); A. Hamilton Thompson, *Cathedral Churches of England* (London, 1925); K. Edwards, *The English Secular Cathedrals in the Middle Ages* (Manchester, 1949). (K. Es.)

Architecture.—The architectural history of the west European cathedral begins with the first large Christian basilicas—old St. Peter's and others—built in Rome soon after Constantine's edict of 323. The long colonnaded nave drew the worshipper's attention irresistibly to the eastern apse where stood the main altar and, behind that, the bishop's throne, later moved to a chancel between apse and nave. In the metropolitan churches, though not usually those of other cities, this eastward drive was checked by the intrusion of a large transverse space called *bema,* forerunner of the mediaeval transept and serving both to give room for ceremonial deployment before the altar and to withdraw the mystical focus of the church a little from the congregation. In later centuries this longitudinal and apsidal plan continued in use, with modifications, for many cathedrals and abbey churches (it is impossible to isolate the development of strictly "cathedral" buildings); the cathedral of S. Apollinare in Classe, Ravenna (534–539), was of this type, as was such a Carolingian abbey as Fulda (begun 802).

Hardly any of the typical features of the French High Gothic cathedral would have been possible without preliminary development in the Romanesque period (*c.* 1000–1200). Thus the cluster of apsidal chapels jutting from a passage or ambulatory laid round the main apse—chapels made necessary by increasing worship of saints and the growing custom of each canon saying Mass daily—is traceable at least to St. Martin at Tours of 997–1020; Durham had rib vaults, Nevers (Burgundy) a form of flying buttress and Autun (in the same province) pointed arcades almost half a century before the rebuilding of St. Denis abbey, 1137–44, as the first of the large true Gothic churches of the Île de France. But in the High Gothic cathedral these features developed rapidly: nave vaulting (rediscovered in early Romanesque times to replace the inflammable flat timber roof of the basilicas) was lightened and carried to ever greater heights; translucent glass displaced solid stone wall. The eastward drive of the Early Christian church was replaced by an upward drive: Romanesque Durham was 80 ft. high to the crown of its vaults; Notre Dame, Paris (1163–1208) reached 115 ft.; Beauvais (1272) 157 ft. (but after later partial collapse remains a truncated naveless folly).

By comparison the English mediaeval cathedral is of modest proportions, long and low; set within a cloistered precinct proclaiming its monastic or collegiate origin (viz., Canterbury), not jutting up directly from the street; entered through a quiet north porch rather than the spectacular western figure portals of the Île de France. English west fronts, however, often had an impressive program of sculpture, as at Wells, Exeter and elsewhere.

The imagination of the Renaissance humanist-architect was captured anew by the aesthetic possibilities of the "central" plan; of a cathedral centrally domed and symmetrically disposed north, south, east and west—a plan fairly common in earlier times (St. Sophia, Constantinople, and S. Vitale, Ravenna, in the 6th century; Aachen cathedral of the 9th; St. Mark's, Venice, in the 12th). Bramante and Michelangelo proposed completely symmetrical plans for the rebuilding of St. Peter's at the end of the 16th century, but the traditional needs of the church compelled Carlo Maderna to add a long western nave when he completed the cathedral after 1600. Sir Christopher Wren was faced with a similar difficulty and forced to a similar modification in the rebuilding of St. Paul's cathedral, London (1675–1710).

Neither the 19th century nor the modern architectural movement beginning in the 1880s produced a special cathedral style. Most architects freely adapted historical styles such as the Byzantine (Westminster cathedral, J. F. Bentley, 1896 *et seq.*) and Gothic (Liverpool, Sir G. G. Scott, 1903 *et seq.*, and the remodelled St. John the Divine, New York city, R. A. Cram and F. W. Ferguson, 1910 *et seq.*). However, in his designs for the new Coventry cathedral (approved 1951, modified 1952–53) B. Spence mainly rejected traditional architectural styles and used tent forms, facet vaulting and other new features. (*See* also BYZANTINE AND ROMANESQUE ARCHITECTURE; GOTHIC ARCHITECTURE; RELIGIOUS AND MEMORIAL ARCHITECTURE.)

BIBLIOGRAPHY.—N. Pevsner, *An Outline of European Architecture* (London, 1951); G. Grigson and M. Hürlimann, *English Cathedrals* (London, 1950); J. Borg and M. Hürlimann, *French Cathedrals* (London, 1951); J. P. Andrade, *Cathédrales d'Espagne* (Paris, 1952); P. Deschamps and Y. and E. R. Labande, *Sanctuaires d'Italie* (Paris, 1952); G. Dehio, *Geschichte der deutschen Kunst* (Berlin, 1921–31).

CATHELINEAU, JACQUES (1759–1793), French Vendean chieftain during the Revolution, was born on Jan. 5, 1759, at Tin-en-Manges, Maine-et-Loire. In the first years of the Revolution, Cathelineau listened to the exhortations of Catholic priests and royalist *émigrés* and joined the insurrection provoked by them against the revolutionary government. Collecting a band of peasants and smugglers, he took the château of Gallais, where he captured a cannon, christened by the Vendeans the "Missionary"; he then took the towns of Chemillé, Cholet, Vihiers and Chalonnes (March 1793). His companions committed atrocities which brought upon them terrible reprisals on the part of the Republicans. Meanwhile Cathelineau's troops increased, and he combined with the other Vendean chiefs, such as N. Stofflet and M. L. J. Gigot d'Elbée, taking the towns of Beaupréau, Fontenay and Saumur. The first successes of the Vendeans were a result of the fact that the Republicans had not expected an insurrection. When the resistance to the insurgents became more serious differences arose among their leaders. To avoid these rivalries, it is thought that Cathelineau was named generalissimo of the rebels, though his authority over the undisciplined troops was not increased by the new office. In 1793 all the Royalist forces tried to capture Nantes. Cathelineau entered the town in spite of the resistance of Gen. J. B. Clanclaux, but he was killed and the Vendean army broke up. Numerous relatives of Cathelineau also perished in the war of La Vendée. (*See* also CHOUANS; VENDÉE, WARS OF THE.)

See C. Port, "La Légende de Cathelineau," in *La Révolution française,* vol. xxiv (Paris, 1893); Abbé F. Charpentier, *Jacques Cathelineau, le Saint d'Anjou* (Paris, 1911).

CATHER, WILLA SIBERT (1873–1947), U.S. author, was born at Winchester, Va., and as a child of eight or nine was taken to a Nebraska ranch.

After her graduation from the University of Nebraska in 1895, she taught high school English, worked on the Pittsburgh *Leader* and travelled widely. Her first volume of stories, *The Troll Garden* (1905), led to an appointment as associate editor of *McClure's Magazine* (1906–12), which was then a vigorous periodical, a pioneer in the field of magazine journalism, less dignified than the old monthlies, but alive with the spirit of reform and direct appeal to an ever-increasing audience more interested in substance than in form. Miss Cather's first distinguished work in pure literature was *O Pioneers!* (1913), in which, on Sarah Orne Jewett's advice, she endeavoured to recapture "in memory, people and places" which she believed to be forgotten. With it she put herself in the forefront of those who had begun to realize the importance of pioneer life in America. *My Antonia* (1918) was another book with the same general background, which established her reputation as a novelist of unusual depth and power of beauty, who could see deep currents of emotion running in those Main Streets and prairies which Sinclair Lewis was to satirize for theii decline into dullness. In *One of Ours* (1922), she stepped aside, not altogether successfully, to tell a story of a western boy in World War I. This novel was awarded a Pulitzer prize. *The Song of the Lark* (1915) was another pioneer story; *A Lost Lady* (1923) was also told against a prairie background, but its simplicity of telling, its depth of tragedy and fineness of insight into the secret and the weakness of woman's charm far outweigh the interest of its local colour. In *The Professor's House* (1925), she began experiments with a new technique of story-telling, constructing her story of an intellectual's soul development according to the familiar methods of music. In *Death Comes for the Archbishop* (1927), she told in the form of a chronicle a simple and vivid story of two saints of the southwest. This, *A Lost Lady, Shadows on the Rock* (1931), and *Lucy Gayheart* (1935) are her best books. Her short stories in the collection *Youth and the Bright Medusa* (1920) escape the stereotyping that has devitalized so many U.S. short-story writers. Her first book was in verse, *April Twilights* (1903); her first novel, *Alexander's Bridge* (1912). Among the writers who in the early 20th century deepened and refined the study of American character, Willa Cather was perhaps pre-eminent. Her style is restrained, sometimes almost cold, but rising into passages of great beauty, and always in harmony with her subject. Her themes are broader and more human than Edith Wharton's; her analysis of human motives deeper than Booth Tarkington's; and she was perhaps closer to essential Americanism in its spiritual and emotional aspects than any other contemporary writer. She is not rich in humour, nor pointed in satire, and in this differed from her nearest contemporaries, but she came closest in U.S. literature of this period to the classic ideal of balance, insight, restraint. She died April 24, 1947, in New York city.

See articles on her work by T. K. Whipple in *Spokesmen: Modern Writers and American Life;* A. Porterfield, *Contemporary American Authors,* edited by J. C. Squire; Elizabeth S. Sergeant, *Fire Under the Andes* (1927). (H. S. C.)

CATHERINE, SAINT. The Roman hagiology contains seven saints of this name. 1. ST. CATHERINE OF ALEXANDRIA, virgin and martyr, whose day of commemoration recurs on Nov. 25. 2. ST. CATHERINE OF SIENA, 1347–80, Dominican tertiary whose feast is observed on April 30. 3. ST. CATHERINE OF SWEDEN, daughter of St. Bridget, who died abbess of Vadstena in 1381, and is commemorated on March 22. 4. ST. CATHERINE OF BOLOGNA, 1413–63, abbess of the Poor Clares in Bologna, canonized by Pope Clement XI, and mentioned in the Roman Martyrology on March 9. 5. ST. CATHERINE OF GENOA (1447–1510), who belonged to the noble family of Fieschi, devoted her life to the sick, especially during the plague at Genoa in 1497 and 1501. She was beatified by Clement X in 1675 and canonized by Clement XII in 1737, her feast being on July 22. *See* F. von Hügel, *The Mystical Element in Religion as studied in St. Catherine of Genoa,* 2nd ed. (1923). 6. ST. CATHERINE DE' RICCI, of Florence (1522–1590), became a Dominican nun at Prato. She was famous during her lifetime for the weekly ecstasy of the Passion, during which she experienced the sufferings of the Holy Virgin contemplating the Passion of her Son. She was canonized in 1746 by Benedict XIV, who fixed her festal day on Feb. 13. In Celtic and English martyrologies (Nov. 25) there is also commemorated St. Catherine Audley (*c.* 1400), a recluse of Ledbury, Hereford. Pius XI in 1930 canonized ST. CATHERINE TOMÀS (d. 1574), of Majorca.

Of the first two saints something more must be said. Of St. Catherine of Alexandria, history has little to tell. According to the legend recorded in the Roman martyrology, and in Simeon Metaphrastes, Catherine upbraided the Emperor Maximinus for his cruelties, and adjured him to give up the worship of false gods. The angry tyrant, unable to refute her arguments, sent for pagan scholars to argue with her, but they were discomfited. Catherine was then scourged and imprisoned. When the empress went to reason with her, Catherine converted her as well as the Roman general and his soldiers, who had accompanied her. Maximinus now ordered her to be broken on the wheel; but the wheel was shattered by her touch. The axe proved fatal, and the martyr's body was borne by angels to Mt. Sinai, where Justinian I. built the famous monastery in her honour. Another variation of the legend is that in which, having rejected many offers of marriage, she was taken to Heaven in vision and betrothed to Christ by the Virgin Mary.

Of these marvellous incidents very little, by the universal admission of Catholic scholars, has survived the test of modern criticism, though her actual existence is generally admitted. In the middle ages she was a most popular saint, her festival being, in certain dioceses of France, a holy day of obligation even as late as the 17th century. The wheel being her symbol, she was the patron saint of wheelwrights and mechanics, as well as the tutelary saint of nuns and maidens, and of philosophers.

St. Catherine of Siena, the youngest daughter of a dyer, was born on March 25, 1347. At an early age she began to practise asceticism and see visions, and when seven dedicated her virginity to Christ. In 1363 she became a Dominican tertiary, and renewed in her home the life of the anchorites in the desert. She resumed family life in 1366 when she began to tend the sick and the poor. Her peculiarities excited suspicion, and charges seem to have been brought against her by some of the Dominicans, to answer which she went to Florence in 1374, soon returning to Siena to tend the plague-stricken. At the invitation of the ruler of Pisa she visited that city in 1375 to arouse enthusiasm for the proposed crusade, and to prevent Pisa and Lucca joining the Tuscan league against the pope. Fra Raimondo relates that, after an ecstasy at Pisa, she told him she had received the *stigmata,* or imprint of the wounds of the crucified Christ, but by her prayer the marks were made invisible. In 1376, Catherine resolved to bring back Pope Gregory XI. from Avignon, attempting first by correspondence to reconcile Gregory and the Florentines, who had been placed under an interdict, and then going in person as the representative of the latter to Avignon. Gregory empowered her to treat for peace, but the Florentine ambassadors proved faithless. Catherine, however, was able to persuade the pope to return to Genoa and then to push on to Rome. There he found life very difficult, and in 1378 sent Catherine on an embassy to Florence, especially to the Guelph party. While she was urging the citizens to make peace with the pope there came the news of his death. During the troubles that ensued in Florence, Catherine nearly lost her life, and sorely regretted not winning her heart's desire, "the red rose of martyrdom." Peace was signed with the new pope, Urban VI., and Catherine, having accomplished her second great political task, went home to Siena. Thence on the outbreak of the schism Urban summoned her to Rome, where she quelled the revolt of the people and tried to win for Urban the support of Europe.

Under the great strain, she died on April 29, 1380, and was canonized by Pius II. in 1461.

Catherine lived on in her writings and disciples. Among the latter were her confessor and biographer, Fra Raimondo, later master-general of the Dominicans, William Flete, an ascetically-minded Cambridge man, Stephano Maconi, who became prior-general of the Carthusians, and the two secretaries, Neri di Landoccio and Francesco Malavolti. The last of her band of reformers, Tommaso Caffarini, died in 1434, but the work was taken up by Savonarola. Catherine's writings consist of: (1) a dialogue entitled, *The Book of Divine Doctrine, given in person by God the Father, speaking to the mind of the most glorious and holy virgin Catherine of Siena, and written down as she dictated it in the vulgar tongue, she being the while entranced, and actually hearing what God spoke in her.* The book has a significant place in the history of Italian literature. "In a language which is singularly poor in mystical works it stands with the *Divina Commedia* as one of the two supreme attempts to express the eternal in the symbolism of a day, to paint the union of the soul with the suprasensible while still imprisoned in the flesh." (2) The prayers (26 in all) which are mostly mystical outpourings. (3) Letters, nearly 400, addressed to kings, popes, cardinals, bishops, conventual bodies, political corporations and individuals. By their historical importance, their spiritual fragrance, their literary value, and their beautiful Tuscan vernacular, the letters put their author almost on a level with Petrarch.

AFTER A WOODCUT FROM "CATHARINA DA SIENA," 1500

ST. CATHERINE OF SIENA

BIBLIOGRAPHY.—*Acta Sanctorum* XII, pp. 861–986, contains the *Vita* of Fra Raimondo; *The Little Flowers of St. Catherine of Siena*, collected by Innocenzo Taurisano, tr. by Charlotte Dease, presents selections from the important sources, the *Vita*, the *Processus* (early testimonies of her followers), the *Miracoli*, the *Supplementum* and three of the saint's letters; *L'Opere*, ed. Girolamo Gigli (Rome 1866); J. Joergensen, *Life of St. Catherine of Siena* (1938); V. D. Scudder, *St. Catherine as seen in her Letters* (1905).

CATHERINE I. (1683–1727), empress of Russia, was the daughter of a Lithuanian peasant named Skavronsky, who died when she was a child. Martha Skavronskaya became a servant in the home of Pastor Glück, the Protestant superintendent of the Marienburg district, and married a Swedish dragoon called Johan. When the Swedes evacuated Marienburg, Martha became one of the prisoners of war of Marshal Sheremetev, who sold her to Prince Menshikov, at whose house, Peter the Great became her lover. After the birth of their first daughter Catherine, Martha was received into the Orthodox Church, when she was rechristened under the name of Catherine Alexeyevna, the tsarevich Alexius being her godfather. She received the title *Gosudaruinya* or sovereign (1710), and Peter, who had divorced the tsaritsa Eudoxia, married her in 1711. Henceforth the new tsaritsa was her husband's inseparable companion. She was with him during the campaign of the Pruth, and Peter always attributed the successful issue of that disastrous war to her courage and sang-froid. She was with him, too, during his earlier Caspian campaigns. He was devoted to her, and she was able to act as a buffer between the tsar and his advisers in his frequent accesses of rage.

By the *ukaz* of 1722 Catherine was proclaimed Peter's successor, to the exclusion of the grand-duke Peter, the only son of the tsarevich Alexius, and on May 7, 1724, was solemnly crowned empress-consort in the Uspensky cathedral at Moscow, on which occasion she wore a crown studded with no fewer than 2,564 precious stones, surmounted by a ruby, as large as a pigeon's egg, supporting a cross of brilliants. Within a few months of her coronation a dangerously familiar flirtation with her gentleman of the chamber, William Mons, caused some scandal. Mons was decapitated and his severed head, preserved in spirits, was placed in the apartments of the empress, but she attended Peter during his last illness, and closed his eyes when he died (Jan. 28, 1725). She was at once raised to the throne by the party of Prince Menshikov and Count Tolstoy with the support of the Guards.

The great administrative innovation of Catherine's reign was the establishment of the *Verkhovny Tainy Sovyet*, or supreme privy council. The executive power was thus concentrated in the hands of a few persons, mainly of the party of Reform (*ukaz* of Feb. 26, 1726). The foreign policy of Catherine I. was principally directed by the astute Andrei Ostermann. Russia now found herself opposed to England, chiefly because Catherine protected Charles Frederick, duke of Holstein, and George I. found that the Schleswig-Holstein question might be reopened to the detriment of his Hanoverian possessions. In the spring of 1726, an English squadron was sent to the Baltic and cast anchor before Reval. The empress protested, and the fleet was withdrawn, but on Aug. 6 Catherine acceded to the anti-English Austro-Spanish league. Catherine died on May 16, 1727. Though quite illiterate, she was an uncommonly shrewd, sensible and good-tempered woman. Her personal extravagance was a byword.

See the authorities referred to *s.v.* PETER I.

CATHERINE II. (1729–1796), empress of Russia, known as CATHERINE THE GREAT, was the daughter of Christian Augustus, prince of Anhalt-Zerbst, and his wife, Johanna Elizabeth of Holstein-Gottorp. She was born at Stettin on May 2, 1729. Her baptismal name was Sophia Augusta Frederica. In 1744 she was taken to Russia, to be affianced to the grand-duke Peter (afterwards Peter III.), the nephew of the empress Elizabeth, and her recognized heir. Frederick the Great favoured the alliance, his object being to strengthen the friendship between Prussia and Russia, to weaken the influence of Austria and to ruin the chancellor Bestuzhev, who was a known partisan of the Austrian alliance. The diplomatic intrigue failed, but Elizabeth took a strong liking to Sophia, and the marriage was finally decided on. On June 28, 1744, she was received into the Orthodox Church at Moscow, and was renamed Catherine Alexeyevna. On the 29th she was formally betrothed, and was married on Aug. 21, 1745 at St. Petersburg. Her married life was wretched. Peter was subnormal in physique and in mind, and his wife despised him. She was a clever and ambitious girl, and was determined that nothing should stand in the way of her ambitions. She accepted the conditions of her marriage because it was the means to power. During the 17 years of her life as grand-duchess she matured her mind and avoided a breach with Elizabeth. For ten years the marriage was barren, and the only reason for supposing that the future tsar Paul, who was born on Oct. 2, 1754, was the son of Peter, is the strong similarity of their characters. Catherine had many lovers. The scandalous chronicle of her life was the commonplace of all Europe. Her most trusted agents while she was still grand-duchess, and her chief ministers when she became empress, were also her lovers.

The Empress Elizabeth died on Jan. 5, 1762. The grand-duke succeeded without opposition as Peter III. He committed every possible folly, grovelled before Frederick the Great, insulted the Church, and threatened to divorce Catherine. She refrained from open opposition and acted with the political prudence which she had shown as grand-duchess. In July Peter foolishly retired with his Holsteiners to Oranienbaum, leaving his wife at St. Petersburg. On the 13th and 14th of that month, a "pronunciamiento" of the regiments of the guard removed him from the throne and made Catherine empress. She issued a manifesto in which she claimed to stand for the defence of Orthodoxy, and the glory of Russia. The guards were manipulated by the four Orlov brothers. The eldest, Gregory, was her recognized chief lover, and he was associated with his brother Alexis in the office of favourite. But the hatred felt for Peter III. was spontaneous, and Catherine had no need to do more than let it be known that she was prepared to profit by her husband's downfall. Peter was sent to a country house at Ropcha, where he died on July 17 in the course of a scuffle during dinner. His custodian, Alexis Orlov, said he could not remember what happened. Catherine in a second manifesto said she had accepted the throne for the good of the country and remarked that autocracy was a danger if the ruler lacked the requisite qualities.

Catherine the Great ruled Russia for 34 years. Although born a German princess she identified herself completely with the Russian people. She was in the truest sense the successor of Peter the Great. Her private life was the object of unceasing curiosity and interest among her contemporaries, and a mass of literature has grown up around the subject of her lovers and her relations with them. Catherine was never dominated by her lovers who were the instruments of her policy; it was she who governed Russia, not her favourites. Her main interests were intellectual and political, and her love affairs subsidiary. She was the disciple and friend of the Encyclopaedists, especially of Voltaire, the reading of whose works had first awakened her mind. She corresponded with him, with D'Alembert, and, more voluminously, with F. M. Grimm, who spent nearly a year at her court in 1777–78. Grimm reports that her conversation was even more brilliant than her letters. Catherine also corresponded at intervals with Frederick the Great and with Joseph II. Her letters are graceful and witty, and they show real political and diplomatic insight. She was determined to make Russian society as cultivated as the society of Paris and Berlin. At court she insisted on a high standard of decorum and of manners, she encouraged the nobles to travel, and fostered the love of French culture. She herself employed Grimm and others to collect works of art and antiquities for her, and practised sculpture and painting herself. She had a passion for reading, made a digest of Blackstone's *Commentaries* and found Buffon's *Histoire naturelle* light reading. Her enthusiasm for Russian history led her to begin to write a history of Russia from the earliest times, and she completed a play, having for its hero the legendary Oleg, which she said was an imitation of Shakespeare. Her comedies, proverbs, and tales are very numerous. To find time for all her activities she rose at five, made her own fire, and would sometimes work 15 hours a day. She seemed to have worked in bouts, taking long spells of work with intervals of relaxation. The new culture which she sought to impose on her court was not entirely superficial. She herself was kind and reasonable to her servants. She was not revengeful, and when she usurped the throne showed no hostility to her husband's advisers; nevertheless she had a fund of hardness, and showed little kindness to her son Paul.

Since Catherine was a disciple of the Encyclopaedists it was natural that she should start out with the definite intention of carrying out domestic reform in Russia, though by methods of the benevolent despotism fashionable in Europe in the period before the French Revolution shook the fabric of society. In fact she, a foreigner and usurper, had to depend for support on the nobility, whose privileges she vastly increased by relieving them of the duty of military service and giving them new powers over their serfs. She also increased their numbers by grants of Crown lands. Serfdom was not mitigated, but vastly increased under her rule. The terrible condition of the peasants led to one revolt after another in favour of one of the numerous pretenders, which culminated in the widespread rising on the Volga, the jacquerie led by Pugachev (1773–75). French culture among the landowners did not lead to any improvement in the handling of the peasants. This state of affairs was in startling contrast with the humanitarian tone of the *Instructions* which Catherine drew up for the grand commission which she summoned in Dec. 1766 to Moscow to advise on internal reform. The *Instructions,* based principally on the works of Montesquieu and Beccaria, were so radical that their circulation in France was forbidden. Very little came of the 18 months' work of the grand commission, except in the development of the organization of local government. With the outbreak of the French Revolution Catherine, like other European sovereigns, fell back on methods of repression. Radishchev, who wrote in his *Journey from St. Petersburg to Moscow* (1790) a truthful account of the condition of the peasants, was banished to Siberia, though the sentiments expressed were only those of Catherine's own *Instructions* of 1766. Catherine had some able assistants in her domestic administration, notably Sivers.

The foreign policy of her reign aimed at the expansion of Russia, and from that point of view was brilliantly successful. Catherine knew the limits to which she could safely go in the "russification" of frontier districts, and showed a certain liberality to the populations which she incorporated. She conducted her own foreign policy, and the galaxy of excellent soldiers and diplomats which she gathered round her carried out her instructions implicitly. She had the gift of discovering ability, and kept in the closest touch with all her servants. Among her generals were Alexander Galitsin, Rumyantsev, Peter Panin, Suvorov, and Potemkin. Suvorov was one of the greatest of Russian generals, but he never enjoyed quite the confidence she gave to Potemkin, whose military abilities were mediocre, but who was first her lover and then her close friend and correspondent. Her chief advisers and assistants in foreign business were Nikita Panin, Bezborodko, Repnin, Dmitri Galitsin and Vorontsoff. The story of the two shameless partitions of Poland and of the wars with Turkey which gave Russia the Crimea and free access to the Black sea for the products of the Ukraine is told under RUSSIA: *History.* It is sufficient to say here that the extension of Russian territory during her reign to the Niemen and the Dniester on the west, and to the Black sea on the south must be placed primarily to the account of Catherine's diplomacy and direction, well served as she was by her generals and her ministers.

She died on Nov. 10, 1796, of apoplexy.

The original sources for the history of her policy and her character are to be found in the publications of the Imperial Russian Historical Society, vols. i.–cix. (St. Petersburg), begun in 1867; her private and official correspondence will be found in vols. i., ii., iv., v., vi., vii., viii., ix., x., xiii., xiv., xv., xvii., xx., xxiii., xxxii., xxxiii., xxxvi., xlii., xliii., xlvii. xlviii., li., lvii., lxvii., lxviii., lxxxvii., xcvii., xcviii., cvii., cxv., cxviii. The *Memoires de l'imperatrice Catherine II., écrits par elle-même* (London 1859), with pref. by Alex. Herzen, bring her life up to the end of 1759, but were not begun until 1780. They must be used with caution, especially as regards her husband Peter III. *See* also A. Brückner, "Katharina die Zweite," in *Allgemeine Geschichte in Einzeldarstellungen* (Berlin 1883); O. Hoetzsch, "Catherine II.," in *Camb. Mod. Hist.* vol. vi., where a bibliography will be found. A complete bibliography was prepared by B. von Bilbassoff, *Katharina II., Kaiserin von Russland in Urteile der Weltliteratur* (Berlin, 1897). *See* also Princesse Lucien Murat, *La vie amoureuse de la grande Catherine* (1927); *Mémoires,* trs. by Katherine Anthony (1927); *Correspondence with Sir Charles Hanbury-Williams,* ed. and trans. by the Earl of Ilchester and Mrs. Langford-Brooke (1928).

CATHERINE DE MEDICI (1519–1589), queen of France, was born in Florence in 1519. She was a daughter of Lorenzo II. de Medici and a French princess, Madeleine de la Tour d'Auvergne. Having lost both her parents at an early age, Catherine was sent to a convent to be educated; and she was only 14 when she was married (1533) at Marseilles to the duke of Orleans, afterwards Henry II. It was her uncle, Pope Clement VII., who arranged the marriage with King Francis I., Henry's father, who was glad to strengthen his influence in the Italian peninsula. For ten years after her marriage she had no children. In consequence, a divorce began to be talked of at court. But Catherine had the happiness of bringing her husband grandchildren ere he died. During his reign (1547–59), Catherine lived a quiet and passive but observant life. Henry being completely under the influence of his mistress, Diane de Poitiers, she had little authority. In 1552, when the king left the kingdom for the campaign of Metz, she was nominated regent, but with very limited powers. This continued even after the accession of her son Francis II. Francis was under the spell of Mary Stuart, and she, little disposed to meddle with politics on her own account, was managed by her uncles, the cardinal of Lorraine and the duke of Guise. The queen-mother, however, soon grew weary of the domination of the Guises, and entered upon a course of secret opposition. On April 1, 1560, she placed in the chancellorship Michel de l'Hôpital (*q.v.*), who advocated the policy of conciliation.

On the death of Francis (Dec. 5, 1560), Catherine became regent during the minority of her second son, Charles IX. She was then 41 years old, but, although she was the mother of nine children, she was still very vigorous and active. She retained her influence for more than 20 years in the troubled period of the wars of religion. At first she listened to the moderate counsels of l'Hôpital in so far as to avoid siding definitely with either party. Like so many of the Italians of that time she looked upon statesmanship as a career in which finesse, lying and assassination were the most effective weapons. By habit a Catholic but above all things fond of power, she was determined to prevent the Protestants from getting the upper hand yet resolved not to allow them to be utterly crushed, in order to use them as a counterpoise to the Guises. This trimming policy met with little success; rage and suspicion so possessed men's minds that she could no longer control the opposing parties, and one civil war followed another to the end of her life.

In 1567, after the "Enterprise of Meaux," she dismissed l'Hôpital and joined the Catholic party. But, having failed to crush the Protestant rebellion by arms, she resumed in 1570 the policy of peace and negotiation. She conceived the project of marrying her favourite son, the duke of Anjou, to Queen Elizabeth of England, and her daughter Margaret to Henry of Navarre. To this end she became reconciled with the Protestants and allowed Comte Coligny to return to court and to re-enter the council. Of this step she quickly repented. Charles IX conceived a great affection for the admiral and showed signs of taking up an independent attitude. Catherine, thinking her influence menaced, sought to regain it, first by the murder of Coligny and, when that had failed, by the massacre of St. Bartholomew (*q.v.*). The chief responsibility for this crime, therefore, rests with Catherine; unlike the populace, she had not even the excuse of fanaticism. After the death of Charles in 1574, and the succession of Anjou under the name of Henry III, Catherine pursued her old policy of compromise and concessions; but as her influence is lost in that of her son, it is unnecessary to dwell upon it. She died on Jan. 5, 1589, a short time before the assassination of Henry, and the consequent extinction of the house of Valois.

In her taste for art and her love of magnificence and luxury, Catherine was a true Medici; in architecture especially she was well versed, and Philibert de l'Orme relates that she discussed with him the plan and decoration of her palace of the Tuileries. Catherine's policy provoked a crowd of pamphlets, the most celebrated being the *Discours merveilleux de la vie, actions et déportemens de la reine Catherine de Medicis,* in which Henri Estienne undoubtedly collaborated.

BIBLIOGRAPHY.—Hector de la Ferrière (ed.), *Lettres de Catherine de Medicis,* in *Collection de documents inédits sur l'histoire de France* (1880–1905); A. von Reumont, *Die Jugend Caterinas de Medici* (1854; French trans., A. Baschet, 1866); H. Bouchot, *Catherine de Medicis* (1899). For a more complete bibliography *see* Ernest Lavisse, *Histoire de France,* vol. v by H. Lemonnier, and vol. vi by J. H. Mariéjol (1904–05); *see* also E. Sichel, *Catherine de Medici and the French Reformation* (1905), *The Later Years of Catherine de Medici* (1908); J. H. Mariéjol, *Catherine de Medicis* (1920); L. Romier, *Le Royaume de Catherine de Medicis, etc.* (1921); P. Van Dyke, *Catherine de Medicis* (1923).

CATHERINE OF ARAGON (1485–1536), queen of Henry VIII of England, daughter of Ferdinand and Isabella of Spain, was born on Dec. 15, 1485. She left Spain in 1501 to marry Arthur, prince of Wales, eldest son of King Henry VII, and landed at Plymouth on Oct. 2. The wedding took place on Nov. 14 in London, and soon afterward Catherine accompanied her husband to Wales, where, in his 16th year, the prince died on April 2, 1502. On June 25, 1503, she was formally betrothed to the king's second son, Henry, now prince of Wales, and a papal dispensation for the alliance was obtained. The marriage, however, did not take place during the lifetime of Henry VII. Ferdinand endeavoured to cheat the English king of the marriage portion agreed upon, and Henry made use of the presence of the unmarried princess in England to extort new conditions and especially to urge the marriage of his daughter Mary to the archduke Charles, grandson of Ferdinand, and afterward Charles V. Catherine was thus from the first the unhappy victim of state politics. Writing to Ferdinand on March 9, 1509, she describes the state of poverty to which she was reduced and declares the king's unkindness impossible to be borne any longer.

Henry VIII married her on June 11, 1509. At first he showed himself an affectionate husband, and the alliance with Ferdinand was maintained against France. During Henry's invasion of France in 1513 she was made regent; she made the preparations for the Scottish expedition and was riding north to put herself at the head of the troops when the victory of Flodden Field ended the campaign. After Henry's return next year there was a breach with Ferdinand, and the king angrily reproached his wife; but she took occasion in 1520, during the visit of her nephew Charles V to England, to urge the policy of gaining his alliance rather than that of France. Immediately on his departure, on May 31, 1520, she accompanied the king to France, on the visit to Francis I, when the sovereigns met at the Field of the Cloth of Gold; but in 1522 war was declared against France and the emperor again welcomed to England. She is represented by Shakespeare as pleading in 1521 for the unfortunate duke of Buckingham. Between Jan. 1510 and Nov. 1518 Catherine gave birth to six children (including two princes), who were all stillborn or died in infancy except Mary, born in 1516, and opinion ascribed this series of disasters to the curse on incestuous unions. To avoid a fresh dispute concerning the succession and the revival of the civil war, a male heir to the throne was a pressing necessity. The question of the possible dissolution of the marriage occupied Henry's mind. It was doubtful whether the pope had the power to legalize his marriage with Catherine, his brother's betrothed, and the case for the desired divorce was therefore more hopeful.

Rumours, probably then unfounded, of an intended divorce had been heard abroad as early as 1524. But the creation in 1525 of the king's illegitimate son Henry, as duke of Richmond—the title borne by his grandfather Henry VII—and the precedence granted to him over all the peers as well as the princess Mary, together with the special honour paid at this time by the king to his own half-sister Mary, were the first real indications of the king's thoughts. In 1526 and perhaps earlier Thomas Wolsey had been making tentative inquiries at Rome on the subject. In May 1527 a collusive and secret suit was begun before the cardinal, who, as legate, summoned the king to defend himself from the charge of cohabitation with his brother's wife; but these proceedings were dropped. On June 22 Henry informed Catherine that they had been living in mortal sin and must separate. During Wolsey's absence in July at Paris, where he had been commissioned to discuss vaguely the divorce and Henry's marriage with Renée, daughter of Louis XII, Anne Boleyn (*q.v.*) is first heard of in connection with the king, his affection for her having, however, begun probably as early as 1523, and the cardinal on his return found her openly installed at the court. In October 1528 the pope issued a commission to Cardinal Campeggio and Wolsey to try the cause in England and bound himself not to revoke the case to Rome, confirming his promise by a secret decretal commission which, however, was destroyed by Campeggio. But the trial was a sham. Campeggio was forbidden to pronounce sentence without further reference to Rome, and was instructed to create delays, the pope assuring Charles V at the same time that the case should be ultimately revoked to Rome.

The object of all parties was now to persuade Catherine to enter a nunnery and thus relieve them of further embarrassment. While Henry's envoys were encouraged at Rome in believing that he might then make another marriage, Henry himself gave Catherine assurances that no other union would be contemplated in her lifetime. But Catherine with courage and dignity held fast to her rights, demanded a proper trial and appealed not only to the bull of dispensation, the validity of which was said to be vitiated by certain irregularities, but to a brief granted for the alliance by Pope Julius II. Henry declared the latter to be a forgery and endeavoured unsuccessfully to procure a declaration of its falsity from the pope. The court of the legates accordingly opened on May 31, 1529, the queen appearing before it on June 18 for the purpose of denying its jurisdiction. On the 21st both Henry and Catherine presented themselves before the tribunal, when the queen threw herself at Henry's feet and appealed for the last time to his sense of honour, recalling her own virtue and helplessness. Henry replied with kindness, showing that her wish for the revocation of the cause to Rome was unreasonable in view of the paramount influence then exercised by Charles V on the pope. Catherine nevertheless persisted in making appeal to Rome, and then withdrew. After her departure Henry, according to Cavendish, Wolsey's biographer, praised her virtues to the court. "She is, my lords, as true, as obedient, as conformable a wife as I could in my phantasy wish or desire. She hath all the virtues and qualities that ought to be in a woman of her dignity or in any other of baser estate." On her refusal to return, her plea was overruled and she was adjudged contumacious, while the sittings of the court continued in her absence. Subsequently the legates paid her a private visit of advice, but were unable to move her from her resolution. Finally, however, in July 1529, the case was, according to her wish, and as the result of the treaty of Barcelona and the pope's complete surrender to Charles V, revoked by the pope to Rome: a momentous act, which decided Henry's future attitude and occasioned the downfall of the whole papal authority in England. On March 7, 1530, Pope Clement issued a brief forbidding Henry to make a second marriage and ordering the restitution of Catherine to her rights till the cause was determined; while at the same time he professed to the French ambassador, the bishop of Tarbes, his pleasure should the marriage with Anne Boleyn have been already made, if only it were not by his authority (Cal. of State Papers, For. and Dom. iv, 6290). The same year Henry obtained opinions favourable to the divorce from the English, French and most of the Italian universities, but unfavourable answers from Germany, while a large number of English peers and ecclesiastics, including Wolsey and Archbishop Warham, joined in a memorial to the pope in support of Henry's cause.

Meanwhile, Catherine was still treated by Henry as his queen. On

May 31, 1531, she was visited by 30 privy councillors, who urged the trial of the case in England, but they met only with a firm refusal. On July 14 Henry left his wife at Windsor, removing himself to Woodstock, and never saw her again. In August she was ordered to reside at the Moor in Hertfordshire, and at the same time separated from the princess Mary, who was taken to Richmond. In October she again received a deputation of privy councillors and again refused to withdraw the case from Rome. In 1532 she sent the king a gold cup as a new year's gift, which the latter returned, and she was forbidden to hold any communication with him. Her cause found champions and sympathizers among the people, among the court preachers and in the house of commons, while Bishop Fisher had openly taken her part in the legatine trial. Subsequently Catherine was moved to Bishops Hatfield, while Henry and Anne Boleyn visited Francis I. Their marriage, anticipating any sentence of the nullity of the union with Catherine, took place after their return about Jan. 25, 1533. On May 10 Archbishop Cranmer opened his court and declared on the 23rd the nullity of Catherine's marriage and the validity of Anne's. On Aug. 10 the king caused proclamation to be made forbidding her the style of queen; but Catherine refused to yield the title for that of princess dowager. Not long afterward she was moved to Buckden in Huntingdonshire. There her household was considerably reduced, and she found herself hemmed in by spies and in fact a prisoner. A project for removing Catherine from Buckden to Somersham, in the isle of Ely, with a still narrower maintenance, was prevented by her resistance. The attempt in November to incriminate the queen in connection with Elizabeth Barton failed.

She passed her life now in religious devotions. On March 23, 1534, the pope pronounced her marriage valid, but by this time England had thrown off the papal jurisdiction, the parliament had transferred Catherine's jointure to Anne Boleyn, and the decree had no effect on Catherine's fortunes. She refused to swear to the new act of succession, which declared her marriage null and Anne's infant the heir to the throne, and soon afterward she was moved to Kimbolton, where she was well treated. On May 21 she was visited by the archbishop of York and Tunstall, bishop of Durham, who vainly threatened her with death if she persisted in her refusal. She was kept in strict seclusion, separated from Mary and from all outside communications, and in Dec. 1535 her health gave way. She died on Jan. 8, 1536, not without suspicions of poison, which, however, may be dismissed. She was buried by the king's order in Peterborough cathedral. Before her death she dictated a last letter to Henry, according to Polydore Vergil, expressing her forgiveness, begging his good offices for Mary and concluding with the astounding assurance—"I vow that mine eyes desire you above all things." The king himself affected no sorrow at her death and thanked God there was now no fear of war.

Catherine is described as "rather ugly than otherwise; of low stature and rather stout; very good and very religious; speaks Spanish, French, Flemish, English; more beloved by the islanders than any queen that has ever reigned." She was a woman of considerable education and culture, her scholarship and knowledge of the Bible being noted by Erasmus, who dedicated to her his book on *Christian Matrimony* in 1526. She endured her bitter and undeserved misfortunes with extraordinary courage and resolution, and at the same time with great womanly forbearance, of which a striking instance was the compassion shown by her for the fallen Wolsey.

Bibliography.—*See* the article in *Dict. of Nat. Biog.* by J. Gairdner, and those on Henry VIII and Wolsey, where the case is summed up adversely to Henry; and J. A. Froude, *The Divorce of Catherine of Aragon* (1891) where it is regarded from the contrary aspect; *Cambridge Modern History*, vol. ii (1903); A. F. Pollard, *Henry VIII* (1905); M. Hume, *The Wives of Henry VIII* (1905).

CATHERINE OF BRAGANZA (1638–1705), queen consort of Charles II of England, daughter of John IV of Portugal by Louisa de Gusman, daughter of the duke of Medina Sidonia, was born at Vila Viçosa, Port., on Nov. 25, 1638. She was a useful medium for contracting an alliance with England, and negotiations for a marriage, begun during the reign of Charles I, were renewed immediately after the Restoration. On June 23, 1661, in spite of Spanish and Dutch opposition, the marriage contract was signed, by which England secured Tangier and Bombay, valuable trading privileges, religious and commercial freedom in Portugal, and 2,000,000 Portuguese crowns (about £300,000), in return for military and naval support to be given to Portugal against Spain, and liberty of worship for Catherine; in May 1662 she reached England, and the marriage took place in London. Catherine had little personal charm, and Charles's preoccupation with his mistresses soon provoked a scene at court, where Catherine at first refused to receive the reigning favourite, Lady Castlemaine. Eventually, however, Catherine came to accept the position and showed considerable kindness to the king's mistresses and bastards. Charles, in return, generally treated her fairly kindly, but she always played a very secondary role at court. As the prospect of her bearing children diminished, schemes were set on foot to procure a divorce on various pretexts. As a Roman Catholic Catherine was attacked by the inventors of the Popish Plot; in 1678 the murder of Sir Edmund Berry Godfrey was ascribed to her servants, and Titus Oates accused her of a design to poison the king. On Nov. 24 Oates brought a charge of high treason against her, the commons passed an address for her removal from Whitehall, and it was only the king's protection that saved her from having to stand trial in June 1679. On Nov. 17 in the house of lords, the earl of Shaftesbury moved for a divorce, so that Charles might marry a Protestant, but the bill was opposed by the king and found little support among the peers. After the Oxford parliament Charles's influence revived and the queen's position was no more assailed.

During Charles's last illness in 1685 Catherine did much to assist his reconciliation with the Roman Catholic Church, and she exhibited great grief at his death. She afterward resided at Somerset house and at Hammersmith, where she had privately founded a convent. She interceded with great generosity, but ineffectually, for the duke of Monmouth the same year. On June 10, 1688, she was present at the birth of the prince of Wales and later gave evidence before the council that he was in fact Mary of Modena's child. She maintained at first good terms with William and Mary; but the practice of her religion aroused jealousies, while her establishment at Somerset house was said to be the home of cabals against the government; and in 1691 she settled for a short time at Euston. She left England finally in March 1692 and took up her residence at the palace of Bemposta, built by herself, near Lisbon, Port. In 1703 she supported the Methuen treaty, which cemented still further the alliance between Portugal and England, and in 1704 she was appointed regent of Portugal during the illness of her brother, King Pedro II, her administration being distinguished by several successes gained over the Spaniards. She died on Dec. 31, 1705, leaving her great wealth, the result of long hoarding, apart from charitable legacies, to King Pedro.

See L. C. Davidson, *Catherine of Braganza* (London, 1908); J. Mackay, *Catherine of Braganza* (London, Toronto, 1937).

CATHERINE OF VALOIS (1401–1437), queen of Henry V of England, daughter of Charles VI of France by Isabel of Bavaria, was born in Paris on Oct. 27, 1401. After negotiations for a marriage between Henry, prince of Wales, afterward Henry V, and each of her two elder sisters had broken down, Henry IV proposed that his son should marry Catherine in 1413, and Henry V renewed this proposal when he became king in March of the same year, demanding, however, a large dowry and the restoration of Normandy and other French territories. War broke out on the rejection of these demands, but finally, after the treaty of Troyes, Henry and Catherine were betrothed on May 21, 1420, and married at Troyes on June 2. Catherine was crowned in Westminster abbey in Feb. 1421, and gave birth to a son, afterward Henry VI, in the following December. In May 1422 she joined Henry in France, and after his death in the following August she returned to England. Her name now began to be coupled with that of Owen Tudor, a Welsh squire, and when in 1428 Humphrey, duke of Gloucester, secured the passing of an act to prevent her from marrying without the consent of the king and council, she seems already to have been married to Tudor. In 1436 Tudor was imprisoned, and Catherine retired to Bermondsey abbey, where she died on Jan. 3, 1437. By Tudor Catherine had three sons and a daughter; the eldest son, Edmund, created earl of Richmond in 1452, was the father of Henry VII.

See Agnes Strickland, *Lives of the Queens of England*, vol. iii, new ed. (London, 1851); J. H. Wylie and W. T. Waugh, *The Reign of Henry the Fifth*, 3 vol. (Cambridge, 1914–29).

CATHETUS, in architecture, the central circular form round which the volute or spiral of the Ionic or Composite order twists.

CATHODE, the conductor by which an electric current leaves an electrolyte (*q.v.*) or a discharge tube. It is also called the "negative" electrode. (*See* also Anode; Electricity, Conduction of: *Conduction in Liquids* and *Conduction in Gases.*)

CATHODE-RAY OSCILLOGRAPH. This instrument makes use of a sharply focused electron beam to display scientific data on a luminescent screen similar to that used in television. It is in a sense a modernization of the combination of a sensitive flame and rotating mirror described in 19th-century physics books.

As described in the article Radar, the vacuum tube ordinarily used focuses the electrons emitted from a hot cathode into a narrow beam which serves as a pointer. The beam passes between two pairs of metal plates and is deflected in a horizontal direction by an amount proportional to the electrical voltage across one pair of plates while it is deflected vertically by the second pair. If desired the intensity of the beam can be controlled by means of a third voltage placed on a metal mesh or grid near the cathode. After passing between the deflecting plates, the beam is allowed to impinge on a fluorescent screen which glows brightly at the point where the electrons hit it. The combination makes it possible to obtain a luminous graph relating the two applied voltages. Thus, if the deflecting voltages are simple harmonic waves whose periods are integrally related, the spot will trace out a pattern similar to the classical ones formed optically by the tuning forks of Jules Antoine Lissajous.

A typical application of the oscillograph is illustrated by the accompanying figure. In order to form this pattern the voltage across the horizontal deflecting plates was changed at a uniform rate for about one-thirtieth of a second, causing the spot to move from the left side of the screen to the right with constant velocity.

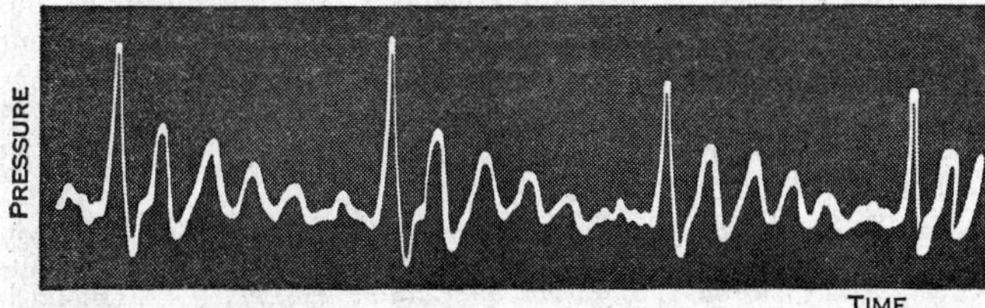

BY COURTESY OF DAVID BOGEN CO.

TIME VARIATION OF SOUND PRESSURE IN A SHORT *a*, AS IN "BRIT*a*NNICA" (FIRST *a*)

At the same time the letter *a* as in "Brit*a*nnica" was spoken into a microphone. The varying sound pressure at the microphone gave rise to a proportional voltage, and this after amplification was applied to the vertical plates resulting in a graph of the time variation of sound pressure.

Almost any graph can be plotted on the oscillograph by generating horizontal and vertical voltages proportional to the lengths, velocities or other quantities to be studied. The main power of the device comes from the extreme speed with which events can be recorded: trace speeds of 200 in. in one-millionth of a second have been utilized.

Many variations of the oscillograph tube have been made since the early one of Ferdinand Braun in 1897. Some for ultrafast measurements use patterns of microscopic dimensions; others for lecture purposes project the graphs on a movie screen. It has become perhaps the instrument most generally used by radio laboratories and also by radio repairmen. It finds increasing use in almost all branches of engineering and science.

(*See* also CATHODE RAYS; RADAR; TELEVISION.)

BIBLIOGRAPHY.—F. Braun, "Variable Current Apparatus," *Ann. d. Phys.*, 60:552–559 (1897); J. Zenneck, "Photographic Current Curves," *Ann. d. Phys.*, 69:838–853 (1899); J. J. Thomson, "Cathode Rays," *Philosophical Magazine*, series 5, vol. 44, p. 294 (Oct. 1897); L. E. Swedlund, "Cathode-Ray Tubes," in *Electrical Engineers Handbook*, ed. by H. Pender and K. McIlwain, 4th ed., 2:15–41 (New York, 1950; London, 1951). (L. B. A.)

CATHODE RAYS are the streams of negatively charged particles leaving the cathode in a discharge tube containing a gas at a low pressure (*see* ELECTRICITY, CONDUCTION OF: *Conduction in Gases*). The cathode rays consist of electrons (*see* ELECTRON, THE). Cathode rays have many applications, one of the chief being the excitation of X-rays by the impinging of swift electrons against a hard anticathode (*see* also COOLIDGE TUBE; X-RAYS, NATURE OF; SPECTROSCOPY, X-RAY). This bombardment, besides exciting X-rays, generates a considerable amount of heat and the anti-cathode can be used as a *cathode ray furnace* for melting small quantities of metal, etc. Forms of apparatus making use of the deflection of a beam of cathode rays by magnetic and electric fields are the *cathode ray oscillograph*, or cathode ray tube, which indicates the variation and values of an alternating current or voltage (*see* INSTRUMENTS, ELECTRICAL MEASURING), and the *cathode ray manometer*, in which a change of pressure is communicated to tourmaline crystals which become electrically charged (*see* ELECTRICITY) and produce an electric field which is measured by a cathode ray oscillograph.

CATHOLIC, derived from a Greek word meaning "universal" and used by ecclesiastical writers since the 2nd century to distinguish the church at large from local communities or heretical and schismatic sects. A notable exposition of the meaning of the term, as it had developed during the first three centuries, was given by Cyril of Jerusalem (348): the church is called catholic on the fourfold ground of its world-wide extension, its doctrinal completeness, its adaptation to the needs of men of every kind, and its moral and spiritual perfection (*Catech.*, xviii, 23). The theory that what has been universally taught or practised is true was first fully developed by St. Augustine in his controversy with the Donatists (393–420), but it received classic expression in a paragraph of St. Vincent of Lerin's *Commonitorium*, ii, 6 (434), from which the well-known formula, *quod ubique, quod semper, quod ab omnibus creditum est*, is derived. St. Vincent maintained—curiously enough apropos of an extreme Augustinian theory of grace—that the true faith was that which the church professed throughout the world in agreement with antiquity and the consensus of distinguished theological opinion in former generations (*cf. op. cit.*, ii, 3, 6, xx). Thus the term tended to acquire the sense of orthodox.

Some confusion in the history of the term has been inevitable as various groups, which have been condemned by Rome as heretical or schismatic, have not renounced their claim to the note of catholicity, so that in the modern world not only the Roman Catholic Church but also the Eastern Orthodox Church, the Anglican Church, and a variety of national churches and minor sects claim to be Catholic, if not the only true Catholic Church. From this point of view the meaning attached to the term "Catholic" and the claim to catholicity will be conditioned by the theory of the nature and constitution of the church accepted, being rigid and exclusive or tolerant and comprehensive as that is rigid or tolerant. The earlier theologians of the Anglican Church were primarily interested in proving the agreement of the Anglican theology with the teaching of the ante-Nicene Fathers, but with the Oxford movement a school of theologians arose who interpreted the catholicism of the Church of England in a much wider sense. A product of this school was the so-called "Branch theory" of the church, which maintained that the Anglican, Roman and Eastern Orthodox Churches were all branches of the one true Catholic Church, and that reunion could be achieved by concessions of these three divisions on controversial questions which divided them without affecting their catholic character. But this theory has been repeatedly condemned by Roman theologians. It has also failed to recommend itself to the Eastern Orthodox Church. (*See* also ORTHODOX EASTERN CHURCH.)

BIBLIOGRAPHY.—J. H. Newman, *Essays Critical and Historical*, (Essay x, "The Catholicity of the Anglican Church"); Ch. Gore, *Catholicism and Roman Catholicism* (1923); M. J. Congar, *Divided Christendom* (London, 1939). For further bibliographical data see *Christendom* (Chicago, 1935–), an oecumenical review published by the American Sections of the World Conference on Faith and Order.

CATHOLIC APOSTOLIC CHURCH, THE, a religious community often called "Irvingites," though neither actually founded nor anticipated by Edward Irving (*q.v.*). Irving's relation to this community was, according to its members, somewhat similar to that of John the Baptist to the early Christian Church, *i.e.* he was the forerunner and prophet of the coming dispensation, not the founder of a new sect; and indeed the only connection which Irving seems to have had with the existing organization of the Catholic Apostolic body was in "fostering spiritual persons who had been driven out of other congregations for the exercise of their spiritual gifts." Shortly after Irving's trial and deposition (1832), certain persons were, at some meetings held for prayer, designated as "called to be apostles of the Lord" by certain others claiming prophetic gifts. In the year 1835, six months after Irving's death, six others were similarly designated as "called" to complete the number of the "twelve," who were then formally "separated," by the pastors of the local congregations to which they belonged, to their higher office in the universal church on the 14th of July 1835. This separation is understood by the community not as "in any sense being a schism or separation from the one Catholic Church, but a separation to a special work of blessing and intercession on behalf of it." The "apostles" always held the supreme authority, though, as their number dwindled, "coadjutors" were appointed to assist the survivors, and to exercise the functions of the "apostolate." The last "apostle" died on the 3rd of February 1901.

For the service of the church a comprehensive book of liturgies and offices was provided by the "apostles." It dates from 1842 and is based on the Anglican, Roman and Greek liturgies. Lights, incense, vestments, holy water, chrism, and other adjuncts of worship are in constant use. The ceremonial in its completeness may be seen in the church in Gordon Square, London, and elsewhere. The community has always laid great stress on symbolism, and in the eucharist, while rejecting both transubstantiation and consubstantiation, holds strongly to a real (mystical) presence. It stresses also the "phenomena" of Christian experience and deems miracle and mystery to be of the essence of a spirit-filled church.

Each congregation is presided over by its "angel" or bishop (who ranks as angel-pastor in the Universal Church); under him are four-and-twenty priests, and with these are the deacons, seven of whom regulate the temporal affairs of the church—besides whom there are also "sub-deacons, acolytes, singers and door-keepers." The priesthood is supported by tithes.

See J. G. Simpson, art. "Irving and the Catholic Apostolic Church" in Hastings' *Encyclopaedia of Religion and Ethics;* and for further details of doctrines, ritual, etc., R. N. Bosworth, *Restoration of Apostles and Prophets, Readings on the Liturgy, The Church and Tabernacle* and *The Purpose of God in Creation and Redemption* (6th ed., 1888); G. Miller, *History and Doctrines of Irvingism* (1878).

CATHOLIC EMANCIPATION, the movement for the abolition of the penal laws against Catholics. (*See* ENGLISH HISTORY; IRELAND; ROMAN CATHOLIC CHURCH.)

CATHOLIC UNIVERSITY OF AMERICA, THE, an institution of higher education at Washington, D.C., founded at the third plenary council of Baltimore in 1884. The constitutions of the university were approved by Pope Leo XIII, and the graduate school of sacred sciences was opened Nov. 13, 1889. A school of philosophy and social sciences was inaugurated in 1895, followed by the school of law (1895) and the school of canon law (1923). A reorganization of the schools took place in 1930, when all courses in philosophy, letters and sciences, except technological, were grouped under the graduate school of arts and sciences and the college of arts and sciences. The technological courses were grouped under a school of engineering and architecture. Schools of social work, nursing education and social science were later added. In 1942 the university's teaching staff numbered 231. The enrolment was 2,027, of whom 1,029 were religious students and 998 lay students.

CATILINE (LUCIUS SERGIUS CATILINA) (*c.* 108–62 B.C.), a member of an ancient but impoverished patrician family of Rome. He was a supporter of Sulla, and during the proscription he was conspicuous for his greed and cruelty. He was guilty of at least one murder. In 77 he was a quaestor, in 68 praetor and in 67-66 governor of Africa. His impeachment for extortion having disqualified him as a candidate for the consulship, he formed a conspiracy, behind which, in all probability, were Crassus and Caesar. The new consuls were to be murdered on Jan. 1, but the plot—the execution of which was deferred till Feb. 5—failed. Soon after, Catiline was acquitted through bribery in the trial for extortion. His scheme widened. The city was to be fired; those who opposed the revolution were to be slain; all debts were to be cancelled; there was to be a proscription of wealthy citizens. Catiline intended to secure the consulship for 63 with C. Antonius as colleague, but Cicero got first place, and Catiline was defeated. C. Antonius, in whom Catiline hoped to find a supporter, was won over by his colleague Cicero. Before the next *comitia consularia* assembled, the orator had given so impressive a warning of impending danger that Catiline was once more rejected (63), and the consuls were invested with absolute authority. Catiline now resolved upon open war; preparations were set on foot throughout Italy, especially in Etruria, where revolt was raised by C. Manlius (or Mallius), one of Sulla's veterans. A plan to murder Cicero in his own house on the morning of Nov. 7 was frustrated. On the next day Cicero attacked Catiline so vigorously in the senate (in his first Catilinarian oration) that he fled to his army in Etruria. Next day Cicero awoke the terror of the people by a second oration delivered in the forum, in consequence of which Catiline and Manlius were declared public enemies, and the consul Antonius was despatched with an army against them. Meanwhile the conspirators in the city tried to induce some Gallic envoys who happened to be in Rome to join them. The plot was betrayed to Cicero, at whose instigation documentary evidence was obtained, implicating Lentulus and others. They were arrested, proved guilty and on Dec. 5 put to death in the underground dungeon on the slope of the Capitol. This act was afterwards attacked as a violation of the constitution, on the ground that the senate had no power of life and death over a Roman citizen. In the beginning of 62 Catiline saw his legions shut in between those of Metellus Celer and C. Antonius. Near Pistoria he was completely defeated by Antonius, and himself fell in the battle. It must not be forgotten that our authorities for this conspiracy were all members of the aristocratic party. Some of the incidents given as facts by Dio Cassius are absurdities; and Cicero paid more regard to the effect than to the truthfulness of an accusation. We find him at one time seeking a political union with Catiline; at another, declaiming against him as a murderer and profligate. Lastly, though Sallust's vivid narrative is consistent throughout, it is obvious that he cherished very bitter feelings against the democratic party. Nevertheless, we cannot regard Catiline as an honest enemy of the oligarchy, or as a disinterested champion of the provincials.

See E. S. Beesley, *Catiline, Clodius and Tiberius* (1878); E. von Stern, *Catilina und die Parteikampfe in Rom* 66–63 (1883); C. Thiaucourt, *Étude sur la conjuration de Catiline* (1887); J. E. Blondel, *Histoire économique de la conjuration de Catiline* (1893); Gaston Boissier, *La Conjuration de Catiline* (1905), and *Cicero and his Friends* (Eng. trans.); E. G. Hardy, "The Catilinarian Conspiracy—a re-study of the Evidence," *Journal of Roman Studies* (1917); W. H. Heitland, *The Roman Republic* (1923); T. Rice Holmes, *The Roman Republic* ch. IV., and part II. pp. 446–473 (1923); Tyrrell and Purser's ed. of Cicero's *Letters* (index vol. *s.v.* "Sergius Catilina").

CATINAT, NICHOLAS (1637–1712), marshal of France, was born on Sept. 1, 1637, in Paris, entered the Gardes Françaises at an early age, and distinguished himself at the siege of Lille in 1667. He served with great credit in the campaigns of 1676–78 in Flanders, was employed against the Vaudois in 1686, and after taking part in the siege of Philipsburg at the opening of the War of the League of Augsburg, he was appointed to command the French troops in the south-eastern theatre of war. In 1690 he conquered Savoy, and in 1691 Nice; the battle of Staffarda, won by him over the duke of Savoy in 1690, and that of Marsaglia in 1693, were among the greatest victories of the time. In 1696 Catinat forced the duke to make an alliance with France. He had in 1693 been made a marshal of France. At the beginning of the War of the Spanish Succession, Catinat was placed in charge of operations in Italy, but he was hampered by the orders of the court and the insufficiency of the forces for their task. He suffered a reverse at Carpi (1701) and was soon superseded by Villeroi, to whom he acted as second-in-command during the campaign of Chiari. He died at St. Gratien on Feb. 25, 1712.

CATION, a positively charged particle or ion which moves toward the negative electrode (cathode) during an electrolysis or an electrical discharge. The cation consists of a single atom or a group of atoms (radical) and bears a specific number of unit positive charges equal to its electrovalence. The silver ion (Ag^+) and the ammonium ion (NH_4^+) are both univalent cations while mercurous ion (Hg_2^{++}) and cupric ion (Cu^{++}) are bivalent cations. In solution the ion is usually in combination with a number of the solvent molecules. (*See* also ELECTRICITY; ELECTRICITY, CONDUCTION OF: *Conduction in Liquids;* ELECTROCHEMISTRY.)

(J. B. Ps.)

CATKIN or **AMENTUM,** a pendulous spike of simple flowers separated by bracts, found in many trees, as, for example, willow and poplar.

(*See* FLOWER.)

CATLETTSBURG, a residential city of northeastern Kentucky, U.S., on the Ohio river at the mouth of the Big Sandy, where Ohio, West Virginia and Kentucky meet; the county seat of Boyd county. It is on federal highway 60 and the Chesapeake and Ohio railway.

The population in 1950 was 4,750; it was 4,524 in 1940 by the federal census.

Oil refining and chemicals are the principal industries.

CATLIN, GEORGE (1796–1872), American ethnologist, was born at Wilkes-Barre (Pa.), in 1796. He was educated as a lawyer and practised in Philadelphia for two years; but art was his favourite pursuit, and forsaking the law he established himself at New York as a portrait painter. In 1832, realizing that the American Indians were dying out, he resolved to rescue their types and customs from oblivion. With this object he spent many years among the Indians in North and South America. He lived with them, acquired their languages, and studied very thoroughly their habits, customs and mode of life, making copious notes and many studies for paintings. In 1840 he came to Europe with his collection of paintings, most of which are now in the National museum, Washington, as the Catlin gallery; and in the following year he published the *Manners, Customs and Condition of the North American Indians* in two volumes, illustrated with 300 engravings. This was followed in 1844 by *The North American Portfolio,* containing 25 plates of hunting scenes and amusements in the Rocky mountains and the prairies of America, and in 1848 by *Eight Years' Travels and Residence in Europe.* In 1861 he published a curious little volume, in "manugraph," entitled *The Breath of Life,* on the advantage of keeping one's mouth habitually closed, especially during sleep; and in 1868 *Last Rambles amongst the Indians of the Rocky Mountains and the Andes.* He died in Jersey city (N.J.), on Dec. 22, 1872.

See W. H. Miner, *George Catlin* with an annotated bibl. (1901); also *My Life Among the Indians* (ed. by N. G. Humphreys, 1909).

CATO, DIONYSIUS, the supposed author of the *Dionysii Catonis Disticha de Moribus ad Filium.* In the middle ages the author of the *Disticha* was supposed to be Cato the elder, who wrote a *Carmen de Moribus,* but extracts from this in Aulus Gellius show that it was in prose. Nothing is really known of the author or date of the *Disticha;* it can only be assigned to the 3rd or 4th century A.D. It is a small collection of moral apophthegms, monotheistic in character, not specially Christian. The book had a great reputation in the middle ages, and was translated into many languages; it is frequently referred to by Chaucer, and in 1483 a translation was issued from Caxton's press at Westminster.

See editions by F. Hauthal (1869), with full account of mss. and early editions, and G. Némethy (1895), with critical notes; Eng. trans. by Chase (Madison, 1922); *see* also F. Zarncke, *Der deutsche Cato* (1852), a history of middle age German translations; J. Nehab, *Der altenglische Cato* (1879); E. Bischoff, *Prolegomena zum sogenannten Dionysius Cato* (1893), in which the name is discussed; F. Plessis, *Poésie latine* (1909), 663; for mediaeval translations and editions *see* Teuffel, *Hist. of Roman Lit.* § 398, 3.

CATO, MARCUS PORCIUS (95–46 B.C.), Roman philosopher, called *Uticensis.* On the death of his parents he was brought up in the house of his uncle, M. Livius Drusus. After serving in the ranks against Spartacus (72 B.C.) he acted as military tribune (67) in Macedonia. On his return he became quaestor, and showed so much zeal and integrity in the management of the public accounts that he obtained a provincial appointment in Asia, where he strengthened his reputation. He admired the discipline which Lucullus had enforced in his own eastern command, and supported his claims to a triumph, while he opposed the pretensions of Pompey. As tribune in 62 he prosecuted L. Licinius Murena, consul-elect, for bribery. Cato supported Cicero at the time of the conspiracy of Catiline and voted for the execution of the conspirators, thus incurring the resentment of Julius Caesar, who did his utmost to save them.

Cato was now regarded as one of the leaders of the senatorial nobility. He vainly opposed Caesar's candidature for the consulship in 59, and his attempt, in conjunction with Bibulus, to prevent the passing of Caesar's agrarian law proved unsuccessful. Yet he was still an obstacle of sufficient importance for the triumvirs to desire to get rid of him. At the instigation of Caesar he was sent with a mission to settle the affairs of Cyprus (58). On his return two years later he continued to struggle against the combined powers of the triumvirs in the city, and became involved in scenes of violence and riot. He obtained the praetorship in 54, and endeavoured to suppress bribery, in which all parties were equally interested. He failed to attain the consulship, and had made up his mind to retire from public life when the civil war broke out in 49. He realized that the sole chance for the free state lay in supporting Pompey, whom he had formerly opposed. At the outset of the war he was entrusted with the defence of Sicily, but finding it impossible to hold the island he joined Pompey at Dyrrhachium. He was not present at the battle of Pharsalus, and after the battle, when Pompey abandoned his party, Cato led a small remnant of their forces into Africa. After his famous march through the Libyan deserts, he shut himself up in Utica, and even after the decisive defeat at Thapsus (46), in spite of the wishes of his followers, he determined to keep the gates closed till he had sent off his adherents by sea. When the last of the transports had left the port he cheerfully dismissed his attendants, and soon afterwards stabbed himself.

He had been reading, we are told, in his last moments Plato's dialogue on the immortality of the soul, but his own philosophy had taught him to act upon a narrow sense of immediate duty without regard to the future. He conceived that he was placed in the world to play an active part, and when disabled from carrying out his principles, to retire gravely from it. He had lived for the free state, and it now seemed his duty to perish with it. In politics he was a typical doctrinaire, blind to the fact that his national ideal was an anachronism. The only composition by him which we possess is a letter to Cicero (*Ad. Fam.* xv. 5). The school of the Stoics, which took a leading part in the history of Rome under the earlier emperors, looked to him as its saint and patron. Immediately after his death Cato's character became the subject of discussion; Cicero's panegyric *Cato* was answered by Caesar in his *Anticato.* Brutus, dissatisfied with Cicero's work, produced another on the same subject; in Lucan Cato is represented as a model of virtue and disinterestedness.

See his *Life* by Plutarch; also C. W. Oman, *Seven Roman Statesmen of the Later Republic, Cato* . . . (1902); Mommsen, *Hist. of Rome* (Eng. trans.), bk. v. ch. v.; Gaston Boissier, *Cicero and his Friends* (Eng. trans., 1897); esp. pp. 277 foll.; Warde Fowler, *Social Life at Rome* (1909).

CATO, MARCUS PORCIUS (234–149 B.C.), Roman statesman, surnamed "The Censor" or "The Elder," was born at Tusculum of an ancient plebeian family. He was bred to agriculture, but, having attracted the notice of L. Valerius Flaccus, he was brought to Rome, and became successively quaestor (204), aedile (199), praetor (198), and consul (195). During his term of office he vainly opposed the repeal of the Lex Appia, to restrict extravagance on the part of women. Meanwhile he served in Africa, and took part in the campaign of Zama (202). He held a command in Sardinia and again in Spain, which he subdued with great cruelty, thereby gaining a triumph (194). In the year 191 he acted as military tribune in the war against Antiochus III. of Syria. If he was not personally engaged in the prosecution of the Scipios (Africanus and Asiaticus) for corruption, it was his spirit that animated the attack upon them. Cato's enmity dated from the African campaign when he quarrelled with Scipio for his lavish distribution of the spoil amongst the troops, and his general luxury and extravagance.

Cato opposed the spread of the new Hellenic culture which threatened to destroy ancient Roman simplicity. His purpose was shown most clearly in the discharge of the censorship; hence his title of "Censor." He revised with unsparing severity the lists of senators and knights, ejecting the men whom he judged unworthy, either on moral grounds or from want of means. The expulsion of L. Quinctius Flamininus for cruelty was an example of his rigid justice. His regulations against luxury were very stringent, and he supported the Lex Orchia (181) and Lex Voconia (169). He repaired the aqueducts, cleansed the sewers, prevented private persons drawing off public water for their own use, ordered the demolition of houses which encroached on the public way, and built the first basilica in the forum near the curia. He raised the amount paid by the publican for the right of farming the taxes, and at the same time diminished the contract prices for the construction of public works.

From the date of his censorship (184) to his death in 149, Cato held no public office, but continued to distinguish himself in the senate as the persistent opponent of the new ideas. Like many others he was shocked at the licence of the Bacchanalian mysteries; and he urged the dismissal of the philosophers (Carneades, Diogenes and Critolaus), who came as ambassadors from Athens, on account of the dangerous nature of their views. Almost his last public act was to urge his countrymen to the Third Punic War and the destruction of Carthage. In 157 he was one of the deputies sent to arbitrate between Carthage and Numidia and was so struck by Carthaginian prosperity that he was convinced that the security of Rome depended on the annihilation of Carthage.

From this time, in season and out of season, he kept repeating the cry: "Delenda est Carthago" ("Carthage must be destroyed").

Cato regarded the family as the germ of the State, and proved himself a hard husband, a strict father, a severe and cruel master. There was little difference apparently, in the esteem in which he held his wife and his slaves; his pride alone induced him to take a warmer interest in his sons. The Romans respected this behaviour as a traditional example of the old Roman manners (Livy xxxix. 40).

Cato was the first Latin prose writer of any importance, and the first author of a history of Rome in Latin. His treatise on agriculture (*De Agricultura* or *De Re Rustica*) is the only work by him that has been preserved. It contains a miscellaneous collection of rules of good husbandry, conveying much curious information on the domestic habits of the Romans of his age. His most important work *Origines,* in seven books, related the history of Rome from its earliest foundations to his own day. His speeches, of which 150 were collected, were chiefly directed against the young nobles of the day. He also wrote a set of maxims for the use of his son (*Praecepta ad Filium*) and some rules for everyday life in verse (*Carmen de Moribus*). The collection of proverbs in hexameter verse, extant under the name of Cato, probably belongs to the 4th century A.D. (*See* CATO, DIONYSIUS.)

BIBLIOGRAPHY.—There are lives of Cato by Cornelius Nepos, Plutarch and Aurelius Victor, and many particulars of his career and character are to be gathered from Livy and Cicero. *See* also G. Kurth *Caton l'ancien* (Bruges, 1872); F. Marcucci *Studio critico sulle Opere di Catōne il Maggiore* (1902). The best edition of the *De Agricultura* is by H. Keil (1884–91), of the fragments of the *Origines* by H. Peter (1883) in *Historicorum Romanorum Fragmenta,* of the fragments generally by H. Jordan (1860); *see* also J. Wordsworth *Fragments and Specimens of Early Latin* (1874); Mommsen *Hist. of Rome* (Eng. trans.) bk. iii. ch. xi. and xiv.; Warde Fowler *Social Life at Rome* (1909).

CATO, PUBLIUS VALERIUS, Roman poet and grammarian, was born about 100 B.C. He was the leader of the "new" school of poetry (*poetae novi,* as Cicero calls them). Its followers rejected the national epic and drama in favour of the artificial mythological epics and elegies of the Alexandrian school. The great influence of Cato is attested by the lines:—

Cato grammaticus, Latina Siren
Qui solus legit ac facit poetas.[1]

Our information regarding his life is derived from Suetonius (*De Grammaticis,* 11). He was a native of Cisalpine Gaul, and lost his property during the Sullan disturbances before he had attained his majority. He lived to a great age and during the latter part of his life was very poor. In addition to grammatical treatises, Cato wrote a number of poems, the best known of which were the *Lydia* and *Diana.* In the *Indignatio* (perhaps a short poem) he defended himself against the accusation that he was of servile birth. It is probable that he is the Cato mentioned as a critic of Lucilius in the lines by an unknown author prefixed to Horace, *Satires,* i. 10.

Among the minor poems attributed to Virgil is one called *Dirae* (or rather two, *Dirae* and *Lydia*). The *Dirae* consists of imprecations against the estate of which the writer has been deprived, and where he is obliged to leave his beloved Lydia; in the *Lydia,* on the other hand, the estate is envied as the possessor of his charmer. Joseph Justus Scaliger was the first to attribute the poem (divided into two by F. Jacobs) to Valerius Cato, on the ground that he had lost an estate and had written a *Lydia.* The balance of opinion is in favour of the *Dirae* being assigned to the beginning of the Augustan age, although O. Ribbeck supports the claims of Cato to the authorship. The best edition of these poems is by A. F. Näke (1847), with exhaustive commentary and excursuses; a clear account of the question will be found in M. Schanz's *Geschichte der römischen Literatur;* for the "new" school of poetry *see* Mommsen, *Hist. of Rome,* bk. v. ch. xii.; F. Plessis, *Poésie latine* (1909), 188.

CATS, JAKOB (1577–1660), Dutch poet and humorist, was born at Brouwershaven in Zeeland. He studied law at Leyden and at Orleans, and, returning to Holland, settled at The Hague, where he began to practise as an advocate. His pleading in defence of a wretched creature accused of witchcraft brought him many clients and some reputation. He had a serious love affair about this time, which was broken off on the very eve of marriage by his catching a tertian fever which defied all attempts at cure for some two years. For medical advice and change of air Cats went to England, where he consulted the highest authorities in vain. He returned to Zeeland to die, but was cured mysteriously by a strolling quack. He married in 1602 a lady of some property, Elisabeth von Valkenburg, and thenceforward lived at Grypskerke in Zeeland, where he devoted himself to farming and poetry. His best works are: *Emblemata* or *Minnebeelden* with *Maegdenplicht* (1618); *Spiegel van den ouden en nieuwen Tijt* (1627); *Houwelijck . . .* (1625); *Selfstrijt* (1620); *Ouderdom en Buytenleven op. Zorgh-Vliet* (1655); and *Gedachten op. slapelooze nachten* (1661). In 1621, on the expiration of the 12 years' truce with Spain, the breaking of the dykes drove him from his farm. He was made pensionary (stipendiary magistrate) of Middelburg; and two years afterwards of Dort. In 1627 Cats came to England on a mission to Charles I., who made him a knight. In 1636 he was made grand pensionary of Holland, and in 1648 keeper of the great seal; in 1651 he resigned his offices, but in 1657 he was sent a second time to England on what proved to be an unsuccessful mission to Cromwell. In the seclusion of his villa of Sorgvliet, near The Hague, he lived from this time till his death, occupied in the composition of his autobiography (*Eighty-two Years of My Life,* first printed at Leyden in 1734) and of his poems. He is still spoken of as "Father Cats" by his countrymen.

Cats was contemporary with Hooft and Vondel and other distinguished Dutch writers in the golden age of Dutch literature, but his Orangist and Calvinistic opinions separated him from the liberal school of Amsterdam poets. He was intimate with Constantin Huygens, whose political opinions were more nearly in agreement with his own. For an estimate of his poetry *see* DUTCH LANGUAGE AND LITERATURE. Hardly known outside Holland, among his own people for nearly two centuries his work enjoyed an enormous popularity.

See G. Derudder, *Un poète néerlandais: Cats, sa vie, son oeuvre* (Calais, 1898); G. Kalff, *Jakob Cats* (1902).

CAT'S-EYE, a name given to several distinct minerals, their common characteristic being that when cut with a convex surface they display a luminous band, like that seen by reflection in the eye of a cat. (1) Precious, oriental or chrysoberyl cat's-eye. This, the rarest of all, is a chatoyant variety of chrysoberyl (*q.v.*), showing in the finest stones a very sharply defined line of light. (2) Quartz cat's-eye. This is the common form of cat's-eye, in which the effect is due to the inclusion of parallel fibres of asbestos. It is obtained chiefly from Ceylon, but, though coming from the east, it is often called "occidental cats-eye"—a term intended simply to distinguish it from the finer oriental stone. It is readily distinguished by its inferior density, its specific gravity being only 2.65, while that of oriental cat's-eye is as high as 3.7. A greenish fibrous quartz, cut as cat's eye, occurs at Hof and some other localities in Bavaria. (3) Crocidolite cat's-eye, a beautiful golden brown mineral, with silky fibres, found in Griqualand West, and much used in recent years as an ornamental stone, sometimes under the name of "South African cat's-eye." It consists of fibrous quartz, coloured with oxide of iron, and results from the alteration of crocidolite (*see* ASBESTOS). (4) Corundum cat's-eye. In some asteriated corundum the star is imperfect and may be reduced to a luminous zone, producing an indistinct cat's-eye effect. (F. W. R.)

CATSKILL, a village of New York, U.S., on the west bank of the Hudson river, 35 mi. S. of Albany; the county seat of Greene county. It is on federal highway 9W, and is served by the West Shore branch of the New York Central railroad. Population (1950) 5,336; (1940) 5,429. Catskill is a summer resort, and is the gateway to the Catskill mountain region. Near by is the spot where Rip Van Winkle had his fabled sleep of 20 years. At Leeds, on the Mohican trail just northwest of the village, is a beautiful stone arch bridge of the 18th century. The bridge was reconstructed after an old design in 1939 by the highway department of the state. The first settler there was Derrick Teunis van Vechten, in 1680. The village was incorporated in 1806.

[1] "Cato, the grammarian, the Latin siren, who alone reads aloud the works and makes the reputation of poets."

CATSKILL MOUNTAINS, a group of moderate elevation pertaining to the Allegheny plateau and not included in the Appalachian system because they lack the internal structure and general parallelism of topographic features which characterize the Appalachian ranges. They are situated mainly in Greene and Ulster counties in the state of New York, with minor sections extending into Delaware and Schoharie counties. The Catskills rise to about the general height of the Highlands of Scotland or the Harz mountains of Germany, the group containing many summits above 3,000 ft. elevation and half a dozen approaching 4,000, Slide mountain (4,204 ft.) and Hunter mountain (4,025 ft.) being the only ones exceeding that figure.

The Catskills were not subject to the general folding which marked the elevation of the main ridges of the Appalachians. This gives the mountains the features of a carved plateau with scenery of a subdued type. There are, however, a number of rugged precipices on their outer faces and a number of deeply worn gorges called "cloves." Stony clove and Kaaterskill clove are picturesque gorges, the latter containing three cascades having a total fall of about 300 ft. The Devassego falls of the Schoharie are also strikingly picturesque. Some of the views which have become noted for their magnificent panorama are Pine Orchard ledge, where there is an unobstructed view of the mountain region of Massachusetts, Vermont and New Hampshire; Kaaterskill knob, North Mountain outlook, Sunset rock, Prospect rock, and others. The mountains are, as a whole, well wooded quite up to their summits—pine, spruce, oak, hickory, beech, maple, rhododendron and mountain laurel being common. The almost total absence of lakes is remarkable.

CATT, CARRIE LANE CHAPMAN (1859–1947), U.S. leader in the woman suffrage and peace movements, was born in Ripon, Wis., Jan. 9, 1859. She graduated from Iowa State college, Ames, in 1880. She married first Leo Chapman (1884; d. 1886), then George W. Catt (1890; d. 1905). In 1890 she had her first suffrage campaign experience under Susan B. Anthony in South Dakota.

Mrs. Catt reorganized the National American Woman Suffrage association on political district lines, 1909–15, so that in working for the vote women were trained for political action; she marshalled these seasoned campaigners, 1915–20, on a national scale to influence congress to submit the 19th amendment enfranchising women, and the state legislatures to ratify it. After bitter opposition in the senate, congress submitted the amendment in 1919, and it was ratified Aug. 26, 1920. Mrs. Catt reorganized the suffrage association, then 2,000,000 strong, as the National League of Women Voters, 1919–20.

In 1902 she founded the International Woman Suffrage alliance, which held its first congress in Berlin, 1904, and was its president until she retired at the congress in Rome, 1923. In 1911–12, accompanied by Aletta Jacobs of the Netherlands, she made a pioneer feminist voyage around the world.

In 1925 she enlisted the co-operation of 11 national women's organizations in the National Committee on the Cause and Cure of War, to start a campaign of education for U.S. participation in world organization for peace. Following World War II, she was vitally interested in the success of the United Nations, using her influence to have qualified women on certain commissions. She died on March 9, 1947.

Bibliography.—Mary Gray Peck, *Carrie Chapman Catt; a Biography* (1944); Susan B. Anthony and Ida H. Harper, *History of Woman Suffrage*, vol. 4, 5, 6 (1902–22). (M. G. P.)

CATTANEO, CARLO (1801–1869), Italian philosopher and republican, was the founder of the review *Il Politecnico.* He was the heart and soul of the Five Days of Milan (March 18–22, 1848), and bitterly opposed the hegemony of Piedmont in Italy. On the return of the Austrians he fled to Lugano, and there he wrote his *Storia della rivoluzione del 1848* and the *Archivio triennale delle cose d'Italia* (3 vol., 1850–55). An uncompromising opponent of Cavour, he steadfastly refused to stand for election to the Italian parliament owing to his inability to take the oath of allegiance to the monarchy.

See his *Opere edite ed inedite,* ed. by A. Bertani, 7 vol. (Florence, 1881–92), *Scritti politici ed epistolari,* ed. by G. Rosa and J. W. Mario (Florence, 1892) and *Scritti storici, letterari, etc.,* ed. by C. Romussi (Milan, 1898). *See* also A. and J. Mario, *Carlo Cattaneo* (Florence, 1884); E. Zanoni, *Carlo Cattaneo nella vita e nelle opere* (1898); G. Nolli, *La Filosofia di Carlo Cattaneo* (Crema, 1901); G. Salvemini, *Le più belle pagine di Carlo Cattaneo* (Milan, 1922).

CATTANEO, DANESE DI MICHELE (1509–1573), Italian sculptor, born at Colonnata, near Carrara, pupil of Jacopo Sansovino in Rome. It is said he was taken prisoner three times by the Imperialists during the "Sacco di Roma" in 1527. He fled to Florence, where he carved the marble bust of Alessandro de Medici; and then joined Sansovino in Venice. He was employed by his master on sculptures for the Libreria di San Marco and the Zecca. Among his works in Venice are the "Apollo" crowning the fountain in the Zecca; the "St. Jerome" in San Salvatore, the figures on the tombs of Leon Loredano in SS. Giovanni e Paolo, and of Andrea Badoer in the Scuola di S. Giovanni Battista. He also worked in Padua for the church of Sant' Antonio. The fine bust of Pietro Cardinal Bembo (1547) placed on the tomb in that church is by his hand. At Verona he built the tomb of Gian Fregoso in S. Anastasia with the help of his distinguished pupil Gerolamo Campagna. He returned to Padua in 1572, but death cut short his work on the reliefs for the Capella del Santo, which were completed by Campagna. Cattaneo was also a poet; his poems *Dell'amor di Marfisa* (1562) were praised by Torquato Tasso. His grandson Niccolo collected his writings.

CATTARO (Serbo-Croatian *Kotor*), a seaport of the former kingdom of Montenegro, Yugoslavia. Pop. (1931) 5,011. The town, which is Venetian in appearance, occupies a ledge between the Montenegrin mountains and the Bocche di Cattaro, a beautiful inlet of the Adriatic, which expands into five broad gulfs united by narrower channels, and forms one of the finest natural harbours in the world.

Cattaro is strongly fortified; on the seaward side Castelnuovo (Serbo-Croatian, *Erceg-novi*) guards the main entrance to the Bocche; on the landward side, long walls run from the town to the castle of San Giovanni far above, while the barren heights of the Krivosie, toward Montenegro, are crowned by small forts.

Cattaro is a Yugoslav city, divided almost equally between the Roman Catholic and the Orthodox creeds. It is the seat of a Roman Catholic bishop with a cathedral containing some beautiful marble sculptures, a collegiate church and several convents. There is a secondary school, a naval college, an interesting naval museum, and a forest school. Cattaro is famous for its lacemaking, and also does an extensive trade in cheese. It is the chief port for Montenegro and Cetinje. Castelnuovo, a picturesque town, rose around the citadel built in 1377 by a Bosnian king.

It has at various times been occupied by Turks, Venetians, Spaniards, Russians, French, English and Austrians. The Orthodox convent of St. Sava, standing amid beautiful gardens, was founded in the 16th century and contains many fine specimens of 17th-century silversmiths' work.

Rhizon, the modern port of Risano, from which a track leads into Montenegro, was a thriving "Illyrian" city as early as 229 B.C., and gave its name to the Bocche, then known as Rhizonicus Sinus. Rhizon submitted to Rome in 168 B.C. and about the same time Ascrivium, or Ascruvium, the modern Cattaro, is first mentioned as a neighbouring city. Justinian built a fortress above Ascrivium in A.D. 535, after expelling the Goths, and a second town probably grew up on the heights around it. The city was plundered by the Saracens in 840 and by the Bulgarians in 1102. In the next year it was ceded to Serbia by the Bulgarian tsar Samuel, but revolted, and only submitted in 1184 as a protected state. It was already an episcopal see, and in the 13th century Dominican and Franciscan monasteries were established to check the spread of Bogomilism. In the 14th century it was one of the capitals of the Serbian state of Diokitiya, and Stephen Dushan (1331–55) had his mint there, while its commerce, rivalling that of Ragusa, provoked the jealousy of Venice. After the downfall of Serbia in 1389, it was seized and abandoned by Venice and Hungary in turn, and finally passed under Venetian rule in 1420. It was besieged by the Turks in 1538 and 1657, visited by plague in 1572, and nearly destroyed by earthquakes in 1563 and 1667. In

1707 it passed to Austria; in 1805 it was assigned to Italy; in 1806 the Russians occupied it and Napoleon, to whom it had been ceded, took Ragusa in its stead. From 1807–13 it was united to the French empire; in the latter year, the Montenegrins aided by the British fleet held it for 5 months, and in 1814 it was restored by the Congress of Vienna to Austria, with whom it remained until 1918. During World War I the Montenegrins arrived before Cattaro, which was a centre of submarine activity. The Slav sailors mutinied in 1918 and many of them were shot or imprisoned. In 1918 it became part of Yugoslavia, but it was occupied in 1941 by Italy.

See G. Gelcich (Gelčić), *Memorie storiche sulle Bocche di Cattaro* (Zara, 1880).

CATTEGAT or **KATTEGAT** (Scand. "cat's-throat"), a strait forming part of the connection between the Baltic and the North seas. It lies north and south between Sweden and Denmark, and connects north with the Skaggerak and south through the Sound, Great Belt and Little Belt with the Baltic sea. Length about 150 mi., extreme breadth about 88 mi., area 9,840 sq.mi., mean depth not more than about 14 fathoms. (*See* BALTIC SEA.)

CATTELL, JAMES MCKEEN (1860–1944), U.S. psychologist and editor, born at Easton, Pa., May 25, 1860, A.B. Lafayette, 1880, Ph.D. Leipzig, 1886, is known for his researches and for the organization of co-operation in science. After lectureships at Pennsylvania, Bryn Mawr and Cambridge universities, he was professor of psychology at Pennsylvania, 1888–91, the first chair in psychology. He was professor at Columbia, 1891–1917. In 1929 he was elected president of the International Congress of Psychology. With James M. Baldwin, Cattell was editor of the *Psychological Review*, 1894–1904. He reorganized *Science* in 1894 and in 1900 it became the organ of the American Association for the Advancement of Science. In 1900 he took over *Popular Science Monthly*, later the *Science Monthly*. He also edited the *American Naturalist* and *School and Society*, 1915–39. Cattell was always interested in men of science and, in part as a tool in the study of development in science, he published (1906–39) *American Men of Science*. He organized the Psychological corporation in 1921 to promote psychological aid to industry and was long its president. Cattell died Jan. 20, 1944. (W. B. PY.)

CATTERMOLE, GEORGE (1800–1868), English painter, chiefly in water colours, was born at Dickleburgh, near Diss, Norfolk, in August 1800. At the age of 16 he began working as an architectural and topographical draughtsman. Cattermole was a painter of no inconsiderable gifts, with great facility in picturesque resource. He was also a book illustrator. At the Paris exhibition of 1855 he received one of the five first-class gold medals awarded to British painters. He died on July 24, 1868. Among his leading works are "The Murder of the Bishop of Liége" (15th century), "The Armourer Relating the Story of the Sword," "The Assassination of the Regent Murray by Hamilton of Bothwellhaugh," and (in oil) "A Terrible Secret."

CATTLE. The word "cattle," which etymologically merely denotes a form of property and is practically synonymous with "chattel," is by common usage a generic term for animals of the bovine race. The several animals that may be included under the term are usually divided into the following six groups: (1) buffaloes (India, Africa, etc.); (2) bison (Europe and North America); (3) the yak (Tibet, etc.); (4) the gaur, gayal and bantin (India and further India); (5) eastern and African domesticated cattle or zebu; and (6) western or European domesticated cattle. In addition to the two last-mentioned groups the India buffalo, yak, gayal and bantin have been domesticated. Apart from the buffaloes, which constitute a relatively primitive and rather distinct type, all the species enumerated are rather closely related. The buffaloes do not hybridize with the members of the other groups, but all the rest can be interbred without difficulty and the hybrids, or at least the female hybrids, are quite fertile. (*See* also AUROCHS; BANTIN; BISON; BOVIDAE; BUFFALO; GAUR; GAYAL; OX; YAK.)

The ox was one of the earliest of all animals to be domesticated for agricultural purposes. In western Europe there is no evidence of domestication in Palaeolithic times but there are plentiful remains in the Swiss lake dwellings and other deposits of Neolithic age. Domesticated cattle existed in Egypt about 3500 B.C., and possibly much earlier, while Babylonian remains have been assigned to still more remote ages.

In all likelihood the wild ancestors of European domesticated cattle belonged to one or more of the sub-species of the auroch or urus (*Bos primigenius*) which were widely distributed in Europe, western Asia and northern Africa in prehistoric times. However, the earliest known domesticated ox in Europe was a very small, slenderly built animal, with short horns, bearing all the marks of a prolonged existence under the care of man and contrasting very markedly with the contemporary wild urus. The conclusion has been drawn that the original domestication did not occur in western Europe; probably the little ox (*Bos longifrons* or *Bos brachyceros*), together with corresponding types of sheep and pig, was brought from Asia by Neolithic man in his migrations. Later, in the Bronze age particularly, a new and larger type of cattle, showing a closer resemblance to the European wild ox, made its appearance. Probably the *Bos longifrons* had been "graded up" by crossing with the wild type. The process was, however, not universal, and even today breeds like the Shetland, Jersey, Kerry and Brown Swiss show a marked resemblance to the Neolithic type.

Whether the zebu had a separate origin from the western ox is not known; some authorities seek to relate it with the bantin or gayal. In shape, colour, habits and even in voice, it presents many points of difference from western cattle; but the most striking of these, such as the presence of a hump, or the upward inclination of the horns, are not constant. There exist in Africa, Spain, China, etc., breeds which are intermediate between zebu and European cattle, but it is likely that some, at least, of these have arisen from crossing. The economic value of cattle arose from the docility of the males for draught and the aptitude of the females for supplying milk in excess of the requirements of their offspring. Ultimately they were utilized as food but this was in a sense secondary, and among some races their flesh was regarded, for religious or other reasons, as unfit for human consumption. The breeding and rearing of cattle for the primary purpose of supplying meat is a modern development.

Terminology.—In the terminology used to describe the sex and age of cattle, the male is first a "bull-calf" and if left intact becomes a "bull"; but if castrated he becomes a "steer" and in about two or three years grows to an "ox." The female is first a "heifer-calf," growing into a "heifer" and becoming after two or three years a "cow." A heifer is sometimes operated on to prevent breeding and is then a "spayed heifer." The age at which a steer becomes an ox and a heifer a cow is not clearly defined and the practice varies. Both in the male and female emasculation is practised because the animals are assumed to fatten more readily; in the case of bulls intended for use as working oxen the object of emasculation, as in the case of stallions, is to make them quieter and more tractable in work.

BREEDS

The exact definition of a "breed" of cattle is difficult, although the term is commonly used and in practice well understood. It may be said generally to connote a particular type of animal which has for a long period been bred only with those of the same, or closely similar, type, and has hereditary characteristics which are transmissible to its offspring. In every breed, however long established, instances of atavism may and do occur, but these are eliminated and do not affect its general purity. Breeds have been established by generations of cattle breeders aiming at the attainment and preservation of a particular type and working on the principle that "like begets like." It is only within very recent times that the laws of heredity founded on the researches of Mendel have been studied as a science. There are many old-established breeds on the continent as for example the Charolais and Normande of France, the Holsteins of Holland, the Campagna di Roma of Spain, and many others, but the British breeds are of particular interest because of their influence in building up the vast herds which furnish the supplies of beef on which other countries are largely dependent. (*See* BEEF.)

Beef Breeds.—*The Shorthorn.*—The Shorthorn is an example of improvement of beef cattle by selection within a breed. In the last quarter of the 18th century two brothers, Charles and Robert Colling, farming in Durham county, England, began to improve the local cattle of the Teeswater district of that county. Their efforts were supplemented by other constructive breeders, notably Thomas Bates and Thomas Booth in Yorkshire. As many cattle of this breed have been exported to other countries from Durham, they are often called by that name.

Shorthorns are distinguishable from other breeds by their colour markings. They may be solid red, red with white markings, white or roan. Roan colour is a mixture of red and white hairs. The Shorthorn is the only modern breed that has a roan colour, making this colouring an index of Shorthorn breeding. Colour, scale and blocky conformation are characteristics of the breed.

Shorthorns are to be found in practically every country of the world. They are numerous in North America, in South America, particularly in Argentina, in Europe, being the most popular breed in the British Isles, and are bred to some extent on the continent; in Australia they have long met with favour and have also been bred quite extensively in South Africa. In the United States, Shorthorns are most numerous in the corn belt states and have been used rather extensively in other areas for grading up native or scrub cattle.

The *Shorthorn Herdbook,* the first of its kind for cattle, was begun in 1822 by George Coates. It was published as a private compilation until 1876 when it was taken over by the Shorthorn society. The first U.S. *Shorthorn Herdbook,* which registers all types of Shorthorns except the Milking type in the United States, was published in 1846 and in 1867 the first Canadian *Shorthorn Herdbook* was begun.

Strains of Shorthorns have been selected for milk and butterfat production, as well as beef, and in the United States are called Milking Shorthorns; in Canada, Dual-Purpose Shorthorns; in England and Australia, Dairy Shorthorns. In England many herds of Shorthorn cattle still show the beef and milk combination developed by the early improvers of the breed. In the United States throughout large areas in the middle west as well as in parts of the New England states, Milking Shorthorns are popular.

The Polled Shorthorn, as the name implies, is a strain within the breed possessing all of the Shorthorn characteristics except horns. This strain of polled cattle was developed in the United States in the late 1880s and early 1890s through the use of naturally hornless registered Shorthorns found within the breed. While beef characteristics have been emphasized, many good milkers have been developed among Polled Shorthorns.

Lincolnshire Red Shorthorns are a specialized type of the original Shorthorn stock.

The Hereford.—The Hereford is the product of generations of intelligent breeding work on the part of landed proprietors and tenant farmers of the fertile valleys in the county of Hereford, England. The origin of the breed has been lost in obscurity but it is thought to have descended from the primitive cattle of the country. Herefordshire is noted for its luxuriant grasses, and in this district, for many generations, the Hereford was bred for beef and draught purposes. The characteristic colour, red with white face and white markings, has been fixed for only a comparatively short time. When the first herdbook was published in 1846, the editor grouped the breed into four classes: mottle faced; light gray; dark gray; and red with white faces. Twenty-five years later all the colours but the last had practically disappeared. The outstanding characteristics of the breed are uniformity of colour, early maturity and ability to thrive under adverse conditions.

Herefords were first introduced into the United States in 1817 by Henry Clay, who imported a young bull, a cow and a heifer to his home in Kentucky. In 1860 Herefords were introduced into Canada by F. W. Stone of Guelph, Ontario. In the range areas of North America, it has become the predominating breed from Canada on the north, to Mexico on the south. In Great Britain it is chiefly bred in Herefordshire and vicinity although herds of this breed are found in Scotland, Ireland and Wales. The Hereford has met with much success also under range conditions of Australia, New Zealand, Argentina, Uruguay and southern Brazil.

The first *Hereford Herdbook,* published in 1846 as a private enterprise, was taken over by the Hereford Cattle Breeders' Association of England in 1884. The American Hereford Cattle Breeders' association was organized in 1881, and in 1934 the official name was changed to American Hereford association.

In the United States there has been developed within the Hereford breed a strain without horns. This strain was developed by Warren Gammon of Iowa by selecting naturally hornless registered Herefords that differed from the standard Hereford only in the polled character. The number of Polled Herefords has increased very rapidly and herds are to be found throughout the United States. Polled Herefords have been exported to Canada, Mexico, South America, Hawaii, the Philippines and Australia. The American Polled Hereford Breeders' association is the national organization in the United States.

The Aberdeen Angus.—This breed of black, polled beef cattle, commonly called "doddies," originated in the county of Aberdeen, in Scotland. Its ancestry is obscure. The breed was improved and the present type of the cattle fixed early in the 19th century by a number of constructive breeders among whom Hugh Watson and William McCombie were the most famous.

The characteristic features of the breed are black colour, polled head, compact and low-set body, fine quality of flesh and high dressing percentage. The Aberdeen Angus is a beef breed of the highest rank and for years purebred or crossbred Angus steers have held high places of honour at the leading fat stock shows in Great Britain and in the United States. This breed was introduced into the United States in 1873 and after that date its influence spread widely in that and other countries. The first *Polled Herdbook* of Aberdeen Angus cattle was issued in Scotland in 1862. The American Aberdeen Angus Breeders' association was organized in 1883.

The Devon.—Devons are assumed to have descended from the smaller type of aboriginal cattle of Britain. Their neat, compact, symmetrical form and deep red colour—"rubies" as they are often called—make an attractive appearance in their native home in the hills of north Devon. For centuries they were bred primarily for draught purposes but early in the 19th century Francis Quartly, a north Devon breeder, is credited with having improved the breed for beef production. His herd became the chief source of supply of stock bulls for the entire district. John Tanner Davy continued the work of improvement and numerous famous Devons descended from his herd. A grandson, Colonel Davy, founded the *Devon Herdbook* in 1851 and brought the merits of the breed to the attention of other breeders. The first authentic record of registered Devons in America was a present of seven head of registered cattle of this breed sent to Robert Patterson of Baltimore by Thomas William Coke (later Earl of Leicester) of Holkham, England. Most of the early Devons in America descended from this shipment in 1817 and later shipments to the Patterson family. Because of its adaptability and hardiness the Devon breed has found favour in many other parts of the world—in New South Wales, South Africa, southern Brazil, Uruguay and the West Indies. The greatest number of Devons in the United States are found in New England.

In south Devon where the breed is also known as South Hams, the cattle are lighter coloured, larger, less active and also less symmetrical in conformation than the cattle of hilly north Devon. The South Devon is bred primarily for dairy purposes, producing a plentiful supply of milk of high quality, from which the well-known Devonshire cream is obtained.

The Galloway.—The beginnings of this breed of polled black cattle originating in Scotland are as obscure as the Aberdeen Angus. Although its native home is the ancient province or kingdom of Galloway in southwestern Scotland, it probably had a common origin with the Aberdeen Angus. The two breeds have much in common but the Galloway is to be distinguished from the Angus by its coat of curly black hair. The breed has never attained the prominence of other beef breeds but has been used quite extensively in producing "blue-gray" crossbred cattle, obtained by breeding white Shorthorn bulls to Galloway cows. The resulting crossbred animals produce unsurpassed and extremely popular beef carcasses. Organized effort to promote Galloway cattle first took place in 1862 in Scotland when the *Polled Herdbook* was begun. The first four volumes of this book included both Galloway and Aberdeen Angus cattle. In 1877 an independent Galloway Cattle society was formed which has been in existence ever since. The American Galloway Breeders' association was organized in 1882.

The Highland or West Highland.—The native home of this breed of cattle, sometimes called "Kyloes," is the upland region of western Scotland. Little is known of their early history though it is generally believed they are the aboriginal cattle in that district. A typical West Highland animal with wide spreading horns, long shaggy coat, sturdy frame, thick mane and heavy dewlap makes an impressive picture. The colour is variable, being yellow, red, black, brindle and a mixture of red and black with a tawny red predominating. No other breed of British ancestry equals the West Highland for hardiness and ability to thrive on scanty pasturage. Cattle of this breed are comparatively small and slow in maturing, but they make beef of fine grain and unsurpassed flavour. The breed is not distributed widely outside its native home although some exportations have been made to other countries.

The Longhorn.—The Longhorn breed of Britain is to be distinguished from longhorn cattle that were once numerous in the western range area of the United States. The latter were descended from cattle brought to America by the Spaniards and are now practically extinct. But a common characteristic of both is the excessive horn growth from which the name is derived. In England the Longhorn has been improved by selective mating. Shorthorns have largely displaced these cattle in almost every district, but a number of herds are still in existence.

The Sussex.—The Sussex breed, found in Sussex, Kent, Surrey and Hampshire, is descended from the original stock of the country and has probably undergone little change in outward appearance since the middle ages. The district in which it is bred has large areas of stiff, heavy soils, calling for great strength at the plow, a requirement for which oxen of this breed are admirably suited. The Sussex is a heavy muscular animal, dark red in colour and is valued as a good grazer where beef rather than milk is sought. It has not attained wide distribution and even in England is not widely bred outside of its own county.

The Red Poll.—The Red Poll breed represents a blending of the cattle which were common in Norfolk and Suffolk counties, England, for centuries. The horned, red, hardy Norfolk cattle were noted for their fleshing qualities while the larger-framed, hornless Suffolks were exceptionally good milkers. The merging of these two bloodlines about 1846 provided the foundation for the present breed. The aim of breeders has been to produce medium-sized, hardy, hornless cattle, red in colour, smooth and compact, and equally good as producers of beef and milk. The usefulness of the breed is now well known the world over. Exportations have been made to the United States, Canada, South Africa, Australia, New Zealand and South and Central America.

The Welsh.—The Welsh breed is black with fairly long horns. Until the beginning of the 20th century there were two types known as North and South Welsh, but they were amalgamated in 1904 when the Welsh Black Cattle society was formed and a common herdbook established. The cattle mature rather slowly but grow to a large size and furnish beef of high quality.

The Africander.—The Africander is widely distributed throughout the Union of South Africa. Although the origin of the breed is not definitely known, it probably goes back to the Indian (*Bos Indicus*) species and not to European (*Bos taurus*) cattle. The foundation of the breed was laid by the voortrekkers who valued their oxen above all other farm possessions. Before and after the Great Trek (1836) there existed a friendly rivalry among the farmers of South Africa to possess oxen that were uniform in conformation, shape of horns and colour markings, and that had hard, flinty feet and the straight easy action so desirable for trekking long distances.

The Africander has a hump over and slightly in front of the shoulders. This hump is more rounded, and blends more smoothly into the shoulder than that of zebu cattle. The colour may vary from dark to light red but dark red is preferred. After the days of the voortrekkers little attention was given to the development of milk production, but the Africander cow seldom fails to supply enough milk for her calf under the most adverse conditions. While the breed was developed primarily to produce trek oxen that would subsist entirely on the veld and survive droughts, later requirements have been for an early maturing, uniformly fleshed beef animal that maintains the hardiness of the earlier type. The Africander Cattle Breeders' society was formed in 1912 for the regulation and control of registrations of Africander cattle in the South African *Studbook*.

The first and only importation of Africander cattle into the United States was made in 1931 by the estate of Henrietta M. King (King ranch), Kingsville, Tex. The shipment consisted of 16 bulls and 13 cows and heifers.

Brahman (Zebu) Cattle.—The term Brahman has been selected by the United States department of agriculture as the name of all breeds of Indian cattle in the United States. In South America and in Europe these cattle are known as Zebus. Brahman cattle are characterized by a prominent hump above the shoulders, and an extreme development of loose, pendulous skin under the throat, on the dewlap, navel and the sheath of males. The rump is drooping. The head is long and narrow, ears are long and carried in a drooping manner, and horns differ widely according to sex and strain. The colour varies from shades of gray to black. Indian cattle, like those of Europe, vary in size, form and symmetry under the influence of local differences in climate, soil and available feed. In their native home, Indian cattle are used primarily for work and milk production. The vast majority of people of India are averse to killing them for food. Humped cattle of India were imported into the United States as early as 1849, but the importations that had the widest influence were made in 1906 and in 1924. These cattle were used in the gulf coast area of the United States for crossing with the improved breeds of beef cattle to produce a type adapted to the hot, humid conditions prevailing in that region.

The Santa Gertrudis.—This breed of cattle had its origin in the United States, having been developed by the King ranch in the state of Texas. It resulted from crossing Brahman bulls of about seven-eighths pure breeding, and purebred Shorthorn cows. Over a period of years, beginning in 1920, selective breeding was practised in which preference was given to red colour without sacrificing type and conformation. Santa Gertrudis cattle are, for the most part, solid red in colour with occasional small white markings, usually on the forehead or in the region of the flanks. They possess a slightly higher percentage of Shorthorn breeding than of Brahman.

The breed is named for one of the bulls that contributed much to its development. Santa Gertrudis cattle are the heaviest of the beef breeds when raised under similar conditions. They have great depth and length of body, with more loose skin about the neck, brisket and navel than the breeds of strictly British origin. They have proved to be highly adaptable to the gulf coast country where conditions are semitropical.

Dairy Breeds.—*The Holstein-Friesian.*—The Holstein-Friesian breed of cattle originated in north Holland and Friesland. Its chief characteristics are large size and black and white spotted markings, sharply defined rather than blended. These cattle are believed to have been selected for dairy qualities for about 2,000 years. They have long been widely distributed over the more fertile lowlands of continental Europe where they are valued highly for their milk-producing ability. However the milk has a relatively low butterfat content. When the Dutch colonized New York, they brought their cattle with them, but after the colony was ceded to the British crown and English settlers brought their own cattle, the Dutch cattle disappeared. The first exportation from Holland to the United States was in 1795, but the largest importations were made between the years 1879 and 1887. These cattle were registered in the *Holstein Herdbook* and the *Dutch*

Friesian Herdbook. In 1885 the two associations united in the Holstein-Friesian Association of America, the largest dairy breed association in the United States.

The breed is widely distributed although not so well adapted to rough, poor lands as some dairy breeds. Besides being well established in the lowland countries of western Europe in England, and throughout the United States, cattle of this breed are found in Canada, Australia, South America and South Africa.

The Jersey.—Within sight of the coast of Normandy in the English channel is a group of four small islands that have long been noted as the native home of two distinct breeds of dairy cattle—the Jersey and Guernsey. The Island of Jersey, the largest of the group, has an extremely mild climate and cattle can be outdoors most of the year. It is believed that the Jersey is descended from French cattle. Its colour is usually a shade of fawn or cream but darker shades are common. The fawn or cream has been attributed to the cattle of Normandy and the darker colour to those of Brittany. Jersey cattle are relatively small in size. The purity of the breed was recognized as early as in 1763, and in 1789 a law was passed prohibiting the importation of cattle into Jersey except for immediate slaughter. They have been introduced in large numbers into England, one of the earliest herds being formed in 1811. The first exportation to the United States was in 1850. The Jersey is adaptable to a wide range of conditions and its distribution is world-wide. Jersey milk is remarkably rich in butterfat, and for that reason animals of this breed are in demand for crossing with native stock to improve the quality of milk. The Royal Jersey Agricultural society, founded in 1833, assumed supervision of the breed on the Island of Jersey, while the English Jersey Cattle society, organized in the 1870s, became the registry association in Great Britain. The American Jersey Cattle club was organized in 1868, and under the supervision of this organization a register-of-merit system was established in 1903.

The Guernsey.—The Island of Guernsey, another of the Channel Islands, is the home of the Guernsey breed. Like the Jersey, this breed is thought to have descended from the cattle of near-by Normandy and Brittany. All of the cattle of the Channel Islands were at one time known as Alderneys. After laws had been enacted prohibiting the importation of cattle to the islands except for slaughter, the two distinct breeds—Jerseys and Guernseys—came to be recognized. Guernsey cattle are fawn coloured, marked with white, and are larger than their widely distributed sister breed, the Jersey. Guernseys are noted for the production of milk of a pronounced yellow colour. The first Guernseys were exported to the United States in 1830, but it was not until 1870 that the export business became extensive. Numbers of Guernsey cattle are to be found also in England, Australia and Canada. The Royal Guernsey Agricultural and Horticultural society supervises the breed on the Island of Guernsey, maintaining two herdbooks, one for general registration and the other for advanced registry. The American Guernsey Cattle club was organized in 1877 and supervises the advanced registry system and pedigree registration of Guernseys in the United States.

The Brown Swiss.—The native home of the Brown Swiss is Switzerland. The breed is probably one of the oldest in existence. While these cattle are classified as a dairy breed in the United States, they are often considered as a dual-purpose breed for they are heavier boned and thicker fleshed than the cattle of the Channel Islands breeds. The colour of the Brown Swiss varies from light brown or gray to a dark shade of these colours. Brown Swiss cows are good, persistent milkers, producing milk of average quality as compared with other breeds of dairy cattle.

This breed has found favour in Italy, Austria, Hungary, United States, Mexico and the South American countries. Brown Swiss were first introduced into the United States in 1869. The Brown Swiss Cattle Breeders' Association of America, organized in 1880, supervises the registration of pedigrees and the register of production of Brown Swiss cattle in the United States.

The Ayrshire.—The Ayrshire breed originated in the county of Ayr in southwestern Scotland in the latter part of the 18th century and is considered to be the only special dairy breed to have originated in the British Isles. Native cattle of the county from which the breed takes its name appear to have been improved by crossing with other breeds to develop a type that would meet local conditions. Further mating and selection moulded the breed into its present form. The Ayrshire has very distinctive horns, which are long and curve outward, upward and slightly backward. The body colour varies from almost pure white to nearly all cherry red or brown with any combination of colours. The beef qualities of the breed are of secondary importance but among dairy breeds the Ayrshire ranks high as a beef producer. The distribution of the Ayrshire is wide, and exportations have been made to many countries. The breed is strongly represented in Canada and the northeastern part of the United States and is found also on the continent of Europe, in South Africa, Australia, New Zealand, Puerto Rico, Mexico and Central America. The Ayrshire Breeders' Association of the United States of America has been instrumental in fostering herd testing and a system of selective registration for approved sires of the breed.

BIBLIOGRAPHY.—U.S. Department of Agriculture, *B.A.I. Twenty Seventh Annual Report* (1910); C. S. Plumb, *Types and Breeds of Farm Animals*, rev. ed. (1920); C. H. Eckles, *Dairy Cattle and Milk Production*, rev. by E. L. Anthony and L. S. Palmer (1942); A. H. Sanders, *The Cattle of the World, Their Place in the Human Scheme—Wild Types and Modern Breeds in Many Lands* (1926), *Shorthorn Cattle* (1918), *The Story of the Herefords* (1914); A. M. Bosman, *Cattle Farming in South Africa* (1932); W. H. Peters, *Livestock Production* (1942); M. Clawson, *Western Range Livestock Industry* (1950).

Pedigree Cattle Breeding.—Many breeds and subbreeds of cattle are distributed throughout the world. On the continent of Europe alone, between 40 and 50 distinct breeds are described by French and German writers. Great Britain is the home of 11 breeds which have been exported to the United States, and in addition as many more minor breeds of local importance are described by English writers. The art of breeding seems to have begun in England about 1770 as the result of the work of Robert Bakewell. Bakewell was not only a pioneer breeder but is reported to have kept records and notes on the progeny of his cattle in order to show the progress made. The activities of the Collings brothers in improving the Shorthorn breed rank next to those of Bakewell in livestock improvement. The work begun by these breeders spread over Great Britain and had a lasting influence on livestock improvement throughout the civilized world. As the fame of British cattle spread to other countries, a demand was created for these improved breeds. Cattle were exported to other countries to found new herds and to improve the native cattle. Practically all present-day pure breeds of farm animals became breeds before the practice of registration, issuing of pedigrees and publication of their respective herdbooks was begun.

The development of breed registry associations in the United States differs somewhat from that of Great Britain where herdbooks remained open, for a time at least, to all animals that met certain requirements as to breed characteristics. The British practice tended to broaden the base of the breed. Cattle breeders continue to direct their efforts toward further improvement of breeds. Individual excellence and pedigree are accepted as only a part of breed improvement, as the essential test of an animal's breeding ability is in the performance of its progeny. Nonselective testing and the use of progeny-tested animals for breed improvement have received increasing attention by constructive breeders. The herd test and advanced register, or record-of-merit testing introduced by breeders of dairy cattle, the get-of-sire class, and slaughter test of the progeny of beef breeds are all useful tools in determining the utility value of registered cattle.

Conflicts of opinion on the use of impartial ratings with pedigrees are usually based on whether the information gained by such measures has enough practical usefulness to be worth the cost. Animal breeding is still practised largely as an art, with greater emphasis placed on selection by observation than on any other procedure. The setting up of well-defined types by early breeders, followed by rigid selection of breeding stock, was the basis of present breeds. Most of the subsequent improvement in the common livestock of the world has been accomplished by the mating of purebred sires to common females. Even in this procedure best results are obtained when the females are selected with care and a high-quality registered sire is used. The effectiveness of this system of breeding is shown by the type of cattle found in the range area of the United States where most breeders have used registered bulls of the same breed for many generations. The result has been a uniform type of cattle in demand by feeders of the corn belt states. The mating of closely related animals has been highly successful in some cases and disastrous in others. Bakewell followed this practice, using animals of high merit, whereas Bates was not so successful. Twentieth-century breeders have followed this breeding practice only after using a sire so superior that a successor of equal or superior merit was difficult or impossible to find. Maintaining this standard of excellence by close breeding may also be possible when both parents are of high individual merit. Instances have occurred in which a new breed has been produced by crossing two or more well-established strains. In theory, the object of crossing two strains is to combine desirable characteristics possessed by each. Limiting factors are time and the expense of keeping the large numbers of animals necessary to fix the type. This system of breeding was followed in developing Polled Herefords, Polled Shorthorns, and the Santa Gertrudis breeds. A purebred sire has often been mated to purebred or high-grade females of another breed for the production of market animals. Crossing of two breeds generally produces offspring possessing greater vigour, ability to grow more rapidly, and ability to use feed somewhat more efficiently than either of the component purebred bloodlines.

After 1908 a number of co-operative dairy breeding associations were organized in the United States, the main purpose being to obtain for the members the services of registered proved sires at a reasonable cost. Another method of making extensive use of superior sires is by means of artificial insemination. Where artificial breeding associations were organized in the United States and trained technicians were available, this practice became a powerful medium of improving the masses of cattle of the country.

After 1900 there was growing appreciation of the value of scientific knowledge in breeding plans. A scientific approach to the study and practice of animal breeding has been made through the knowledge that the cell is the physical basis of inheritance and that all inheritance occurs in an orderly manner.

BIBLIOGRAPHY.—V. A. Rice, *The Breeding and Improvement of Farm Animals*, 4th ed. (1951); L. M. Winters, *Animal Breeding* (1948); J. L. Lush, *Animal Breeding Plans*, 3rd ed. (1945); John Hammond, *Farm Animals, Their Breeding, Growth and Inheritance* (1941).

Nutritive Requirements.—The feed consumed by cattle is used for a number of functions, depending to some extent on the purpose for which the animal is maintained. The larger part of the feed is required for normal body functions; the remainder is available for growth, fattening, reproduction and lactation. Sources of nutritive energy, protein, fat, minerals and vitamins are essential for the proper nutrition of cattle. Investigations of maintenance and production requirements have been of a highly technical nature and the results have provided feeding standards. As good pasture has a high content of protein, minerals and carotene, and is an economical source of nutritive elements, pasture improvement has received much attention in the United States. Pasture not only tends to maintain fertility in the herd, but also provides the cows with a surplus of various known and unknown nutritive essentials that can be stored in their bodies and thus ensure them against such deficiencies that might occur from the feeding of low-quality roughage during the winter. Experienced feeders have found that a liberal feeding of protein is necessary for high milk production, with a tendency to supply this element in the form of a vegetable protein from green leafy legumes. Vitamin and mineral requirements have also received considerable attention. The minerals most likely to be needed to supplement feeds are common salt, calcium, phosphorus, iodine and iron. Other minerals are sometimes required. Calcium and phosphorus requirements are closely associated, since the two elements are stored together in nearly fixed proportions in the bones and secreted together in nearly fixed proportions in the milk. If either element is deficient in the feed, both bone building and milk secretion are hindered. Phosphorus deficiency is a more common cause of nutritive trouble with cattle than calcium deficiency, since the soil in some parts of the world is deficient in phosphorus, and the forage of these areas is deficient in this element. Where cattle subsist almost entirely on the range it is practical and sometimes less expensive to supply phosphorus and perhaps other minerals from sources other than grain and forage crops.

As with minerals, vitamins are perhaps of greater concern in rations for growing and breeding stock than for fattening cattle. Vitamin A appears to be the one most likely to be deficient in feeds for dairy cows, or for steers fattened in areas where green leafy forage and yellow grain are limited. Newborn calves have no reserve of this element but it is supplied by colostrum. Carotene, the yellow pigment of the plant from which vitamin A is formed in the animal body, occurs in close association with the green colouring matter of pasture plants and other green forage. As a rule, the greener the colour of the hay, the greater the amount of carotene, but hay stored for long periods tends to lose much of its carotene though still retaining most of its colour. Cattle must have an adequate supply of vitamin D to enable them efficiently to assimilate and utilize the calcium and phosphorus in their feed. It is believed that farm animals of all types generally receive an adequate supply of this vitamin by exposure to the sun's rays, depending on the intensity of the sunlight and its concentration of ultraviolet rays. Knowledge of nutritional requirements of cattle is very rapidly changing and still incomplete, and must constantly be reappraised as newer knowledge is obtained. (*See* also FEEDING STUFFS AND LIVESTOCK FEEDING.)

BIBLIOGRAPHY.—F. B. Morrison and others, *Feeds and Feeding; a Handbook for the Student and Stockman*, 21st ed. (1948); L. A. Maynard, *Animal Nutrition*, 3rd ed. (1951); R. R. Snapp, *Beef Cattle; Their Feeding and Management in the Corn Belt States*, 3rd rev. ed. (1939).

Management, Care and Handling.—The management and care of beef and dairy cattle are highly specialized practices. In the United States, for example, the feeding of beef cattle in the corn belt states, the production of feeder and grass-fat cattle on the ranges of the west, and the production of milk in the dairy sections of the northeast and middle-western states, all require a high degree of skill with different equipment and management practices. The range area is composed of plains and mountainous areas useful for grazing purposes. Practical ranch operation commonly involves attention to deferred and selective grazing to maintain the supply of forage, selection and culling of the breeding herd, controlled breeding, a well-arranged water supply and the production of winter feed where necessary. All of these practices are conducive to good condition of the breeding herd and a satisfactory crop of vigorous calves capable of making good gains.

On a well-managed ranch, a relatively high percentage of the investment is in the livestock rather than equipment. The range may be fenced or not, depending on the type of ranch. Corrals are used where large numbers of cattle are handled. In connection with the corral, a chute for holding cattle while being branded or vaccinated is usually a desirable investment. Range cattle are branded as a means of identification. Brands are recorded by the owner in the state where the ranch is located. Rounding up cattle or working the range is a time of great activity, especially when fat cattle are to be shipped, the breeding herd shifted to winter range, and calves separated from their dams to be sold as feeders or held on the ranch. The winter range is usually a pasture or range that offers some natural protection from winter storms and provides grass or browse that is suitable for winter grazing. When necessary, maintenance rations of cheap roughages or small amounts of protein supplement are fed during the winter or early spring.

The fattening of beef cattle in the United States is closely related to the production of calves and yearlings in the range area. The most important feeding area is the corn belt states of the middle west where calves or yearlings from the western ranges are fattened in dry lots. These cattle are fed corn and hay in feed bunks with some silage, salt, and minerals. Most cattle feeders take it as a matter of course that cattle feeding cannot be made a successful enterprise without having hogs in the feed lot with the cattle. Inexpensive barns or sheds, feed racks and an adequate water supply are the most important items of equipment which with feed and labour go to make up the feeding operation.

While the production of feeder and grass-fat cattle in the range states is a highly specialized form of beef-cattle production in the United States, the maintenance of comparatively small breeding herds of registered cattle in many of the other states, as well as in the range area, requires a high degree of skill. Their care, management and breeding differ from those under which commercial range herds are handled. The registered cattle are produced primarily for breeding purposes and receive more attention and are fed more liberally as a rule than cattle produced primarily for slaughter. Breeding herds are made up of highly selected individuals conforming to the standards of the breed. Cows are bred to calve throughout the year, but most of the calves are born late in winter or early in the spring. During the summer months these calves run with their dams and may be fed grain in creeps while on pasture. Cows are usually maintained on pasture and roughage produced on the farm. Young cattle are given every opportunity to develop as considerable income is derived from the sale of young cattle, especially bulls, either at private sale or auction.

Dairy farming in the United States is usually distinct from the production of beef, but a certain amount of overlapping occurs. Approximately two-thirds of the dairy cows are cattle of specialized dairy breeds; the remainder consist of cattle of beef, dual-purpose, and mixed breeding. In commercial herds, replacements are commonly bought but some breeders grow their own replacements in order to improve production and lessen the danger of disease. Good cattle and modern methods of care and management are important elements in profitable dairying. Barns and equipment should be designed for producing and caring for milk efficiently and in a sanitary manner. The most common type of dairy barn in northern states is the two-story type with a loft for hay storage above the cows, whereas in the south where storage capacity is not so necessary, the one-story barn is more widely used. Practically every dairy farmer having a sufficient number of cattle to make the use of a silo profitable has one. Floors of dairy cattle barns are preferably of concrete, and the most common method of confining cows is with swinging stanchions. Water is often provided by means of automatic drinking fountains. Cows are milked twice daily, except in cases of advanced register or register of merit where three- and four-time milking may be practised. Milking machines are used successfully, especially where there is a labour shortage. On well-managed dairy farms each milking is weighed and butterfat tests are made at regular intervals. Most of the dairy breed associations have adopted herd-test plans under which all registered cows of the herd are tested. All these records are used as a part of the plan to show which cows are the most profitable. As feed is an important item in the cost of production, attention is given to the maintenance of pastures for summer feeding and the production of good-quality roughage for winter feeding. Good feeding, good breeding and the production of a sanitary product are the aims of the progressive dairyman.

BIBLIOGRAPHY.—R. R. Snapp, *Beef Cattle, Their Feeding and Management in the Corn Belt States*, 3rd rev. ed. (1939); C. H. Eckles, *Dairy Cattle and Milk Production*, rev. by E. L. Anthony and L. S. Palmer (1942); M. Clawson, *Western Range Livestock Industry* (1950).

CATTLE POPULATION AND WORLD TRADE

Estimates in round numbers of the cattle population of the world as averages for the years 1941–45 are shown in Table I.

Before the days of refrigeration as applied to transportation, most of the beef exports had been in the form of canned and cured meat. The first cargo of refrigerated beef was sent from the United States to England in 1874.

United States shipments of beef rose from 37,000,000 lb. in 1875–76 to 461,000,000 lb. in 1900–01. The marked expansion of beef exports from the United States from 1875 to 1900 was due in

TABLE I.—*Number of Cattle in Principal Countries and by Continents*
(Average 1941–45*)

Country	Number (Million head)	Country	Number (Million head)
North America, Central America and West Indies		U.S.S.R. (Europe and Asia)	47
United States	80	Africa	
Mexico	12	Union of South Africa	13
Canada	9	Madagascar	6
Cuba	5	Kenya	5
Other	5	Tanganyika	6
Estimated total	111	Anglo-Egyptian Sudan	3
South America		Other	41
Brazil	44	Estimated total	74
Argentina	33	Asia	
Colombia	11	India†	177
Uruguay	6	Pakistan†	32
Other	17	China‡	24
Estimated total	111	Turkey†	11
Europe		Thailand†	8
Germany (western)	12	Indonesia†	6
France	15	Burma†	5
Poland	10	Other	23
United Kingdom	9	Estimated total	286
Italy	8	Oceania	
Czechoslovakia	4	Australia	14
Yugoslavia†	4	New Zealand	5
Ireland	4	Estimated total	19
Rumania†	3	Estimated world total	745
Other†	28		
Estimated total	97		

Source: United States Department of Agriculture, agricultural statistics 1951. Compiled from official statistics of foreign governments, reports of the United States foreign service officers and other information.

*Average for 5 year period if available; otherwise for some year or years within or near.

†Buffaloes included.

‡Estimate for China includes China Proper (22 Provinces) Manchuria, Jehol and Sinkiang (Turkestan).

large measure to the settlement of new regions and the attendant expansion of livestock production in the United States and to the growing industrialization of Europe with the increasing demand for imported foodstuffs. But early in the 20th century an expanding domestic market, rapidly increasing competition from the southern hemisphere, and some expansion of livestock and meat production in northern and central Europe were responsible for a sharp decline in United States beef exports. By 1905 Argentina had surpassed the United States as an exporter of refrigerated beef and by 1914 United States exports of fresh beef had fallen to 6,000,000 lb. Exports of cured beef amounted to 23,000,000

TABLE II.—*World Trade in Cattle, 1929–50*
(In thousands of heads)

Imports				
Countries	Average 1929–33	Average 1934–38	Average 1939–43	Average 1946–50
United Kingdom	762	682	787	417
United States	203	361	764	400
Italy	182	101	27	125
Germany	153	156	...	227
U.S.S.R.	114	121	...	...
Austria	72	23	...	5
France	64	8	...	17
Greece	61	77	48	39
Chile	56	23	39	142
Japan	51	65	...	...
Czechoslovakia	46	0	...	12
Belgium	44	19	...	...
Argentina	41	1	...	...
Union of South Africa	31	54	107	173
British Malaya	28	27	17	7
Switzerland	13	9	2	27
Brazil	2	21	70	17

Exports				
Countries	Average 1929–33	Average 1934–38	Average 1939–43	Average 1946–50
Ireland	727	664	784	456
Denmark	145	128	163	146
Mexico	131	200	541	91
French West Africa	99	79	...	114
Hungary	96	76	75	...
Yugoslavia	96	61	...	12
Canada	93	197	293	305
Turkey†	88	76	29	32
Argentina	76	81	134	294
Rumania	76	49	30	...
Korea	50	67	28	...
France	43	7	...	35
Uruguay	33	66	119	2
China	30	33	...	...
Netherlands	25	3	...	15
Austria	18	8	...	4
United States	5	6	3	15

lb. in that year. From 1921 to the early 1950s imports of beef into the United States were larger than exports in most years.

From 1924 to 1950 the United Kingdom was by far the greatest importer of live cattle, buying mostly from Ireland as it had not permitted imports from the continent for decades. However, the economic war waged by the two countries between 1931 and 1938 greatly reduced the number imported. Central Europe was a second deficit region for cattle. German supplies came chiefly from Denmark. Austria and Czechoslovakia, Italy and Greece were largely supplied from Bulgaria, Hungary, Rumania and Yugoslavia. United States imports came mostly from Canada and Mexico. (A. C. Ck.)

DISEASES OF CATTLE

The greatest hazard in rearing cattle, practically everywhere, is disease. The most destructive diseases are caused by bacteria, protozoa and filterable viruses, but fungi, parasites, poisons, malnutrition and metabolic disturbances also exact heavy tolls.

Foot-and-mouth disease (*q.v.*), or aphthous fever, probably is the most widespread and contagious of all infectious maladies of animals. Cattle and other cloven-footed animals, including swine, sheep and goats, are susceptible. The most rigid quarantines and restrictions of movements of animals and animal products frequently fail to control the spread of the malady. In the U.S., the immediate slaughter of affected and exposed animals completely eradicated the infection on six occasions after 1900. This procedure has been followed in England and adopted from time to time in some countries on the European continent, but the proximity of areas in which the disease is established is a constant hazard. The disease is prevalent in most of Europe, Asia, Africa and South America but (in the early 1950s) had not occurred in the United States since 1929. In countries where the disease is enzootic or where infection recurs from adjoining infected countries, total eradication has been found economically unfeasible and measures to control the infection include prophylactic vaccination, using variations of the product originally developed by S. Schmidt of Denmark and O. Waldmann of Germany in the late 1930s. Some 60,000,000 vaccinations of cattle, goats, sheep and swine were applied by the Mexico-United States Commission for Eradication of Foot-and-Mouth Disease in Mexico, where after a five-year campaign, the disease was finally eradicated in Sept. 1952. Approximately 1,000,000 animals were destroyed in the cooperative program financed by both countries.

Rinderpest (*q.v.*), or cattle plague, a highly fatal, contagious, filterable-virus disease, was widespread in the 19th century practically all over the world but has not occurred in North America. Vigorous eradication measures were widely applied, and it remains only in Asiatic countries and parts of Africa. The disease is characterized chiefly by severe gastrointestinal involvement. Control in countries where the disease is enzootic involves quarantines and use of preventive vaccines prepared with chemically inactivated tissue or virus attenuated by propagation in other species—goat, rabbit, chicken embryo.

Contagious pleuropneumonia, or lung plague, was prevalent in many countries before the 20th century. By means of quarantines and slaughter of affected animals, the disease has been eradicated from Europe and North America. It persists in Asia, Australia, and parts of Africa.

Tuberculosis (*q.v.*) in cattle is a widespread, chronic, bacterial disease caused by an organism closely related to that of human tuberculosis. Almost all mammals, including man, are susceptible to bovine tuberculosis. Cattle are relatively insusceptible, however, to the human and avian types of the infection. The bovine infection may be readily transmitted by infected milk and milk products. Pasteurization is an effective safeguard. The disease may be successfully controlled by quarantines and repeated application of the tuberculin test. The test is accurate to a high degree even in mildly affected animals. The infected animals may be placed in quarantine, thus reducing spread of the disease, or they may be slaughtered at once. The latter procedure, with quarantines and disinfection of infected premises, has been followed in the United States. The extent of bovine tuberculosis, formerly averaging about 5% and much higher in some areas, has been reduced to less than 0.5% in all parts of the U.S. Repeated testing is necessary, however, as long as any infection remains.

Brucellosis (*q.v.*), or Bang's disease, which is characterized by abortion and sterility, is a problem wherever breeding operations are conducted. The infection, caused by *Brucella abortus*, is prevalent to a greater or lesser extent throughout the world. Diseased animals are detected by tests of the blood or milk. Control may be effected by segregation or destruction of affected animals, with appropriate quarantine measures, with or without the aid of preventive vaccine. The most widely used vaccine is prepared with the so-called strain 19 of *Brucella abortus* which is especially useful in immature cattle. Man frequently contracts the infection, referred to as undulant fever, from infected cattle, swine or goats.

Mastitis, or inflammation of the udder, rivals all bacterial infections of dairy cattle in the aggregate loss it causes. It occurs in acute and chronic forms. Death rarely results but the infection, which may be due to streptococci, staphylococci or other organisms, causes alteration and material reduction of the milk secretion. Since the development of the sulfonamides and other antibiotic agents such as penicillin and streptomycin, considerable success has been achieved in treatment. The disease may be controlled by segregation of infected animals, sanitation and careful milking practices.

Johne's disease, or paratuberculosis, is a chronic disease of cattle, which causes considerable loss in Great Britain, North America and other parts of the world. The causative organism, *Bacillus (Mycobacterium) paratuberculosis*, produces a chronic dysentery which results in progressive emaciation and death in many cases.

Two acute, fatal, bacterial diseases of cattle are anthrax and black quarter (blackleg). These occur in quite definitely defined districts in widely separated parts of the world. In these enzootic areas, vaccination with biological products prepared from the respective causative bacteria is generally effective in control. Anthrax may be acquired by other animals and also by man.

Bovines, like other ruminants, possess a complex stomach having four compartments, the largest of which, the rumen, or paunch, has a capacity of as much as 50 gal. This anatomical peculiarity is responsible for frequent digestive disturbances. Bloat and impaction are common. Cattle also frequently suffer from perforations of the stomach by foreign metallic objects which are commonly ingested with the feed and cause death if they penetrate the heart sac.

Calves, especially those of the dairy breeds, commonly develop fatal enteric disorders unless special care in feeding and sanitation is taken.

Dairy cows are prone to develop metabolic diseases. Milk fever, or parturient paresis, is the commonest of these. It occurs usually just after parturition and invariably results in death if treatment is not given. Another such disease is acetonaemia, or ketosis, in which there are acidosis, subnormal quantities of sugar in the blood and faulty fat metabolism, with excess formation of ketones in the body.

Cattle may be afflicted with other diseases, infectious and otherwise, which cause considerable losses. These include actinobacillosis and actinomycosis, both commonly referred to as lumpy jaw; cowpox, which is closely related to smallpox; epithelioma (cancer eye), hyperkeratosis; infectious keratitis (pink-eye); leptospirosis; leukemia; pasteurellosis (haemorrhagic septicaemia); rabies; rickets; and trypanosomiasis.

Bibliography.—F. Hutyra, J. Marek, and R. Manninger, *Special Pathology and Therapeutics of the Diseases of Domestic Animals*, ed. by J. R. Greig, J. R. Mohler and A. Eichhorn, 3 vol., 5th Eng. ed. (1947); U.S. Department of Agriculture Yearbook, "Keeping Livestock Healthy" (1942); W. A. Hagan and D. W. Bruner, *The Infectious Diseases of Domestic Animals* (1951). (M. S. Sn.)

Parasites of Cattle.—Parasites of cattle, belonging to such zoological groups as protozoa, worms and arthropods, cause extensive economic loss. Successful control measures generally consist in attacking the various parasites at vulnerable points in their life cycles.

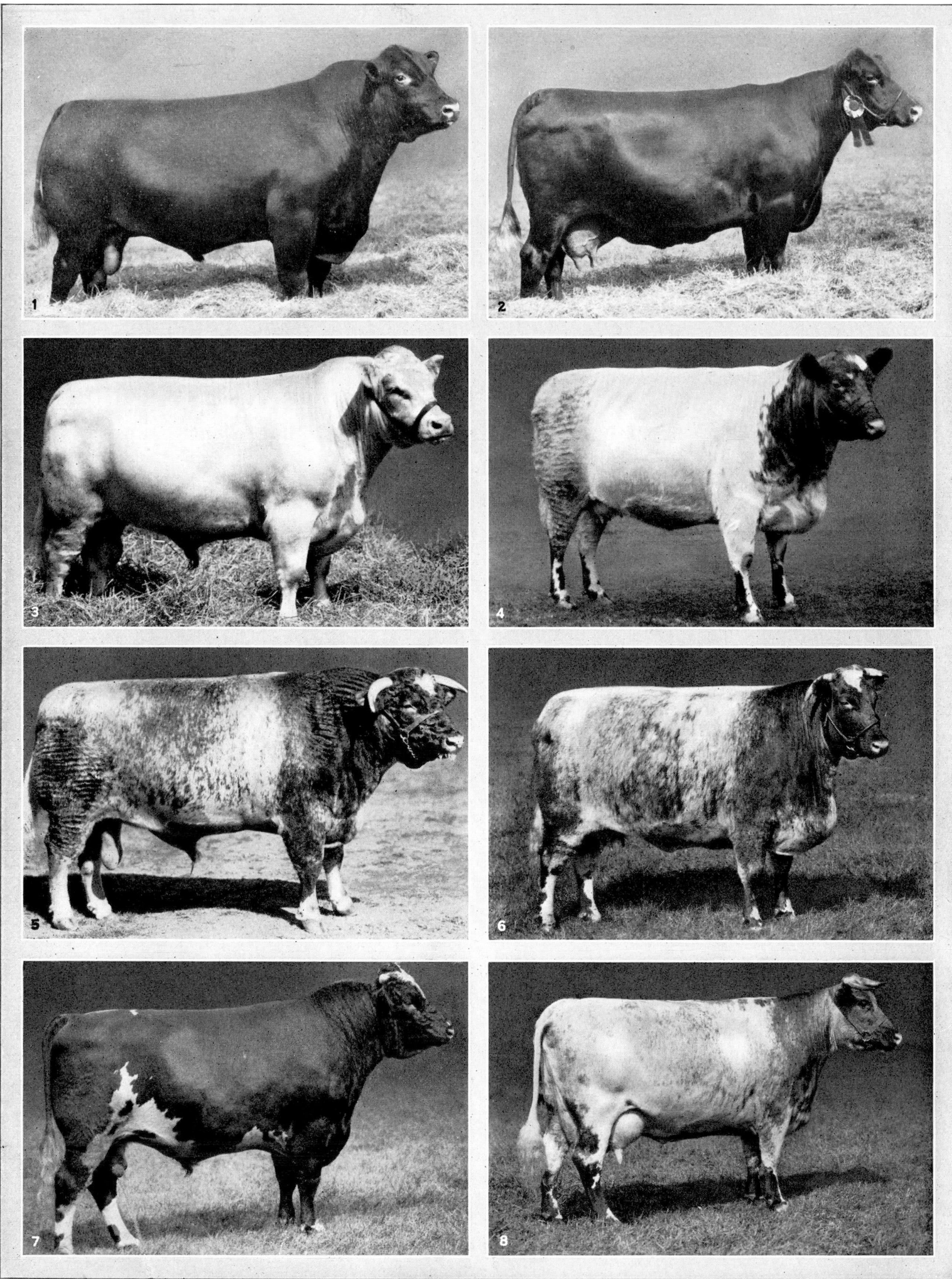

PHOTOGRAPHS, (1, 2, 3, 4, 7, 8) ROBERT F. HILDEBRAND, (5, 6) H. A. STROHMEYER, JR.

BREEDS OF CATTLE

1. Red poll bull
2. Red poll cow
3. Polled shorthorn bull
4. Polled shorthorn cow
5. Shorthorn bull
6. Shorthorn cow
7. Dairy shorthorn bull
8. Dairy shorthorn cow

CATTLE

PHOTOGRAPHS, (1, 2) U.S. DEPARTMENT OF AGRICULTURE, (3, 4, 5, 6, 7, 8) HILDEBRAND PICTURES, INC

BREEDS OF CATTLE

1. Aberdeen Angus bull
2. Aberdeen Angus cow
3. Galloway bull
4. Galloway cow
5. Hereford cow
6. Hereford bull
7. Highland bull
8. Highland cow

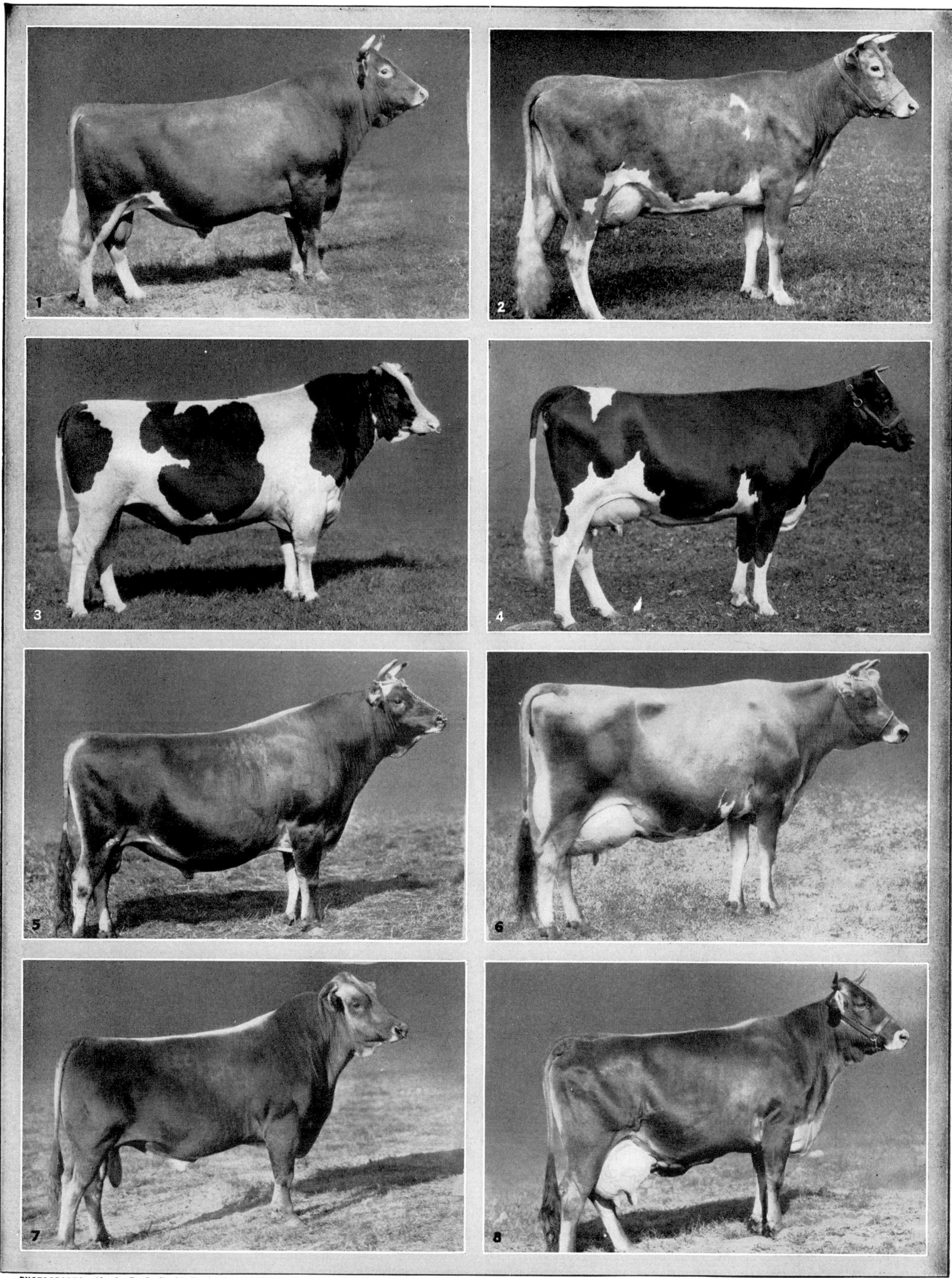

PHOTOGRAPHS, (1, 2, 5, 6, 7, 8) H. A. STROHMEYER, JR., (3, 4) ROBERT F. HILDEBRAND

BREEDS OF CATTLE

1. Guernsey bull
2. Guernsey cow
3. Holstein Friesian bull
4. Holstein Friesian cow
5. Jersey bull
6. Jersey cow
7. Brown Swiss bull
8. Brown Swiss cow

CATTLE

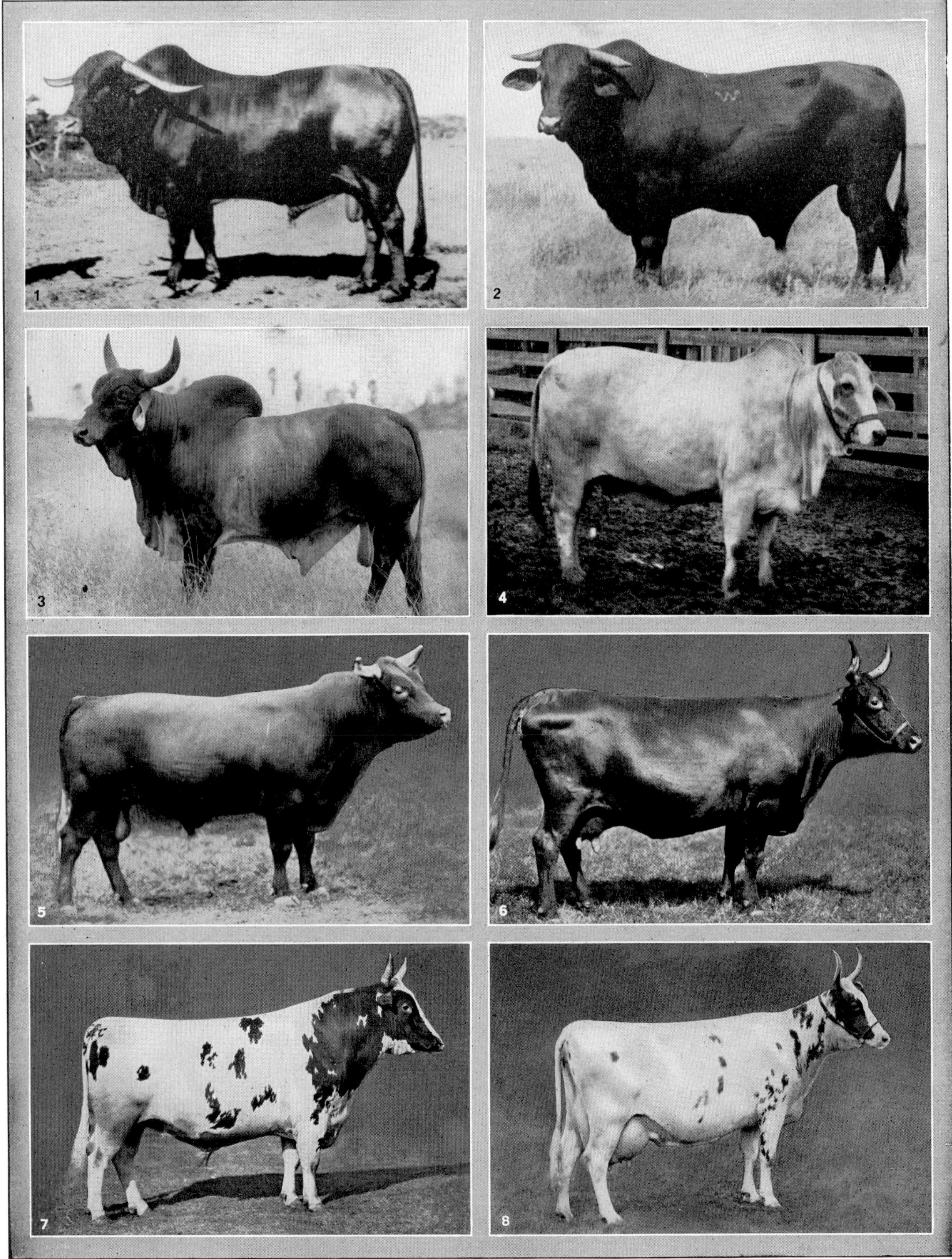

PHOTOGRAPHS (1, 2, 3, 4) U.S. DEPARTMENT OF AGRICULTURE, (5, 6) HILDEBRAND PICTURES, INC., (7, 8) H. A. STROHMEYER, JR.

BREEDS OF CATTLE

1. Africander bull
2. Santa Gertrudis bull
3. Brahman (zebu) bull
4. Brahman (zebu) cow
5. Devon bull
6. Devon cow
7. Ayrshire bull
8. Ayrshire cow

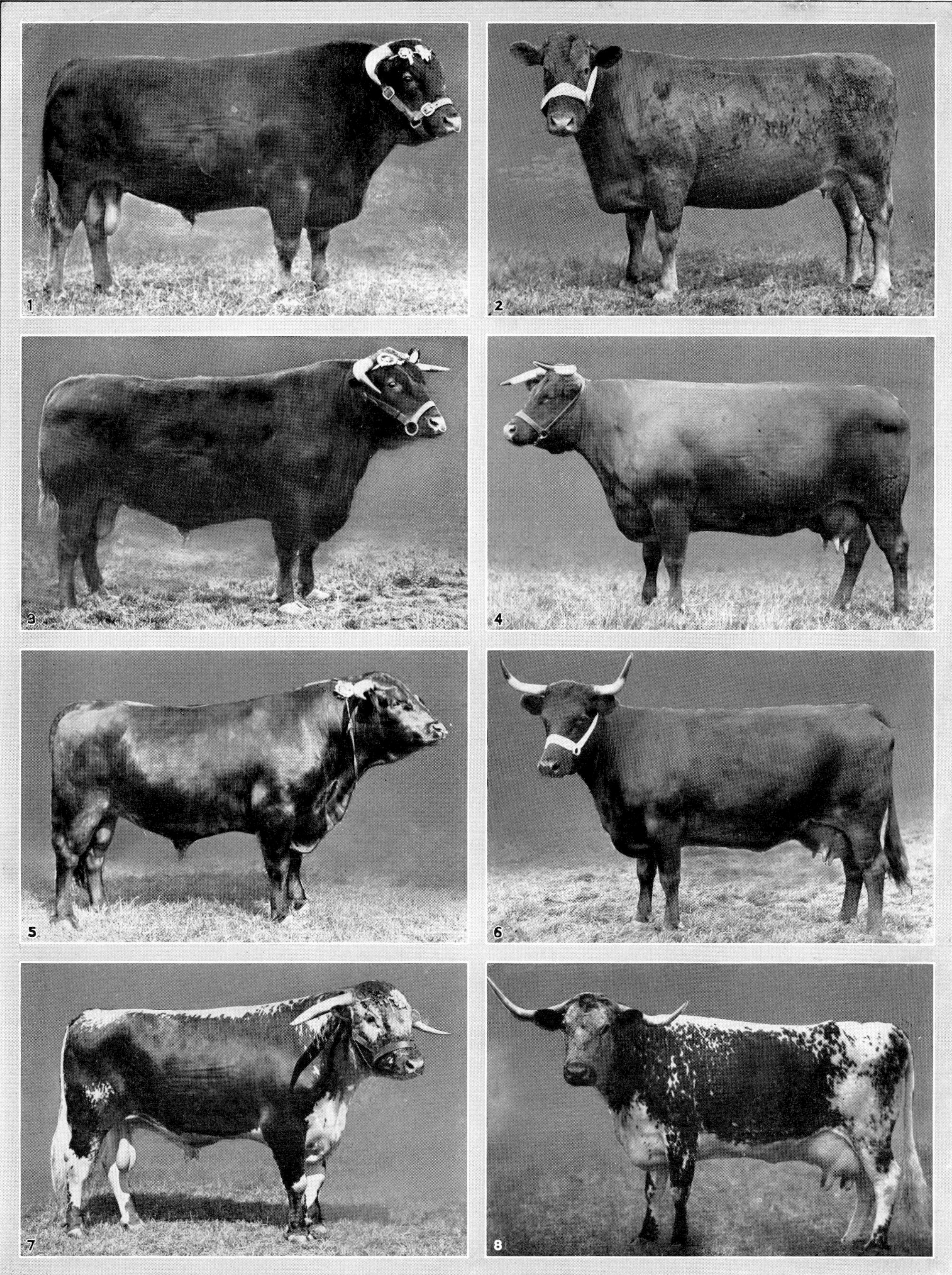

PHOTOGRAPHS, (1, 2, 3, 5, 7) SPORT AND GENERAL PRESS AGENCY, (4, 6, 8) "THE FARMER AND STOCKBREEDER"

BREEDS OF CATTLE

1. South Devon bull
2. South Devon cow
3. Sussex bull
4. Sussex cow
5. Welsh bull
6. Welsh black cow
7. Longhorn bull
8. Longhorn cow

The diseases caused by protozoa, or one-celled animals, are especially important in tropical and subtropical countries. Among the most destructive are piroplasmosis or tick fever, anaplasmosis, surra and nagana. All these diseases are caused by minute parasites that live in the red blood cells or in the blood stream, and are usually transmitted by blood-sucking arthropods such as ticks and flies; they are generally characterized by fever and destruction of the red cells. The monetary loss from these diseases is very great. However, by mid-20th century practically all of these losses had been eliminated in the United States through eradication of cattle ticks by systematic dipping of ticky cattle in standardized arsenical dips. Control of other protozoan blood diseases, especially those transmitted by flies, has been less satisfactory.

Other protozoan diseases of cattle are coccidiosis and venereal trichomoniasis. Coccidiosis is an intestinal disease characterized by bloody diarrhoea and emaciation. It is caused by sporozoan parasites that infect the inner lining of the intestine. The infection is largely in calves and is controlled by strict sanitation. Venereal trichomoniasis is caused by a small flagellate organism that is transmitted through coitus. Infection results in early abortion, sterility and other breeding difficulties.

The worm parasites are flukes, tapeworms and roundworms. The common liver fluke (*Fasciola hepatica*) lives in the bile ducts; it causes extensive damage to the liver and general unthriftiness of the infected animal. The complicated life history and control measures are the same as those discussed under diseases and parasites of sheep. (*See* SHEEP: *Parasites of Sheep.*)

Several species of tapeworms infest the digestive tract but these worms do not appear to cause extensive injury. The larval or bladderworm stage of the common tapeworm (*Taenia saginata*) of man occurs in the muscles and causes a condition known as "measly beef." Cattle acquire the infestation by swallowing the eggs while grazing on pastures that have been contaminated by excrement from tapeworm-infested persons.

Important roundworm parasites are lungworms, stomach worms and intestinal threadworms of which there are numerous species. All these worms are acquired by picking up the infective larvae while grazing. Roundworms cause unthriftiness, anaemia and digestive disturbances, especially diarrhoea. The injurious effects are most pronounced in calves and in animals under two years of age.

Sanitation, pasture rotation and avoidance of overstocking tend to control worm parasites. Medicinal treatment with anthelminthic drugs, especially phenothiazine, is of value in controlling stomach and intestinal roundworms.

The arthropod parasites include the ticks, mites, lice and flies. Aside from ticks and certain flies that transmit tick fever, anaplasmosis and other protozoan blood diseases, the most injurious arthropod parasites are the warble flies, *Hypoderma lineatum* and *H. bovis*. These flies lay their eggs on the legs of cattle. In a few days the eggs hatch and the young larvae penetrate the skin. They then migrate through the tissues of the body and eventually reach the back. Here the larvae or grubs, as they are sometimes called, complete their growth and produce swellings. The skin over each swelling becomes perforated and the holes so formed permit the larvae to breathe and to escape when they have completed their growth.

A somewhat similar fly larva (*Dermatobia hominis*), commonly referred to as nuche or gusano, infests cattle in Central and South America. The adult fly does not deposit its eggs directly on the skin as do the warble flies, but lays them on the bodies of mosquitoes and other bloodsucking insects. The eggs hatch and the larvae crawl onto the skin when the insect is feeding.

Hatching is stimulated by the warmth of the victim's body. Ox warbles may be controlled to some extent by manual extraction of the grubs or by the use of dusts, dips or washes containing insecticidal substances such as rotenone.

Other arthropods such as ticks, mites, lice and flies inflict considerable injury to animals by abstracting blood and causing irritation to the skin.

Such parasites living habitually on their hosts may be controlled by the use of insecticidal dips, washes or dusts; flies are best controlled by destruction of their breeding places.

BIBLIOGRAPHY.—*Diseases of Cattle,* U.S. Department of Agriculture, Washington (1942); "Keeping Livestock Healthy," *Yearbook,* U.S. Department of Agriculture, Washington (1942).

(E. W. PE.; X.)

CATULLUS, GAIUS VALERIUS (84?–54 B.C.), the greatest lyric poet of Rome. As regards his names and the dates of his birth and death, the most important external witness is that of Jerome, in the continuation of the Eusebian *Chronicle,* under the year 87 B.C., "Gaius Valerius Catullus, scriptor lyricus Veronae nascitur," and under 57 B.C., "Catullus xxx. aetatis anno Romae moritur." There is no controversy as to the gentile name, *Valerius.* Suetonius, in his *Life of Julius Caesar* (ch. 73), mentions the poet by the names "Valerium Catullum." Other persons who had the *cognomen* Catullus belonged to the Valerian gens, *e.g.* M. Valerius Catullus Messalinus, a *delator* in the reign of Domitian, mentioned in the fourth satire of Juvenal (l. 113).

Inscriptions show, further, that *Valerius* was a common name in the native province of Catullus, and belonged to other inhabitants of Verona besides the poet and his family (Schwabe, *Quaestiones Catullianae,* p. 27). Scholars have been divided in opinion as to whether his *praenomen* was *Gaius* or *Quintus,* and in the best MSS. the volume is called simply *Catulli Veronensis liber.* For *Gaius* we have the undoubted testimony, not only of Jerome, which rests on the much earlier authority of Seutonius, but also that of Apuleius. In support of *Quintus* a passage was quoted from the *Natural History* of Pliny (xxxvii. 6, 81). But the *praenomen* Q. is omitted in the best MSS., and in other passages of the same author the poet is spoken of as "Catullus Veronensis." The mistake may have arisen from confusion with Q. Catulus, the colleague of Marius in the Cimbric War, himself also the author of lyrical poems.

Internal evidence shows that certain poems were written two or three years after 57 B.C., the date of Catullus' death according to Jerome. Thus cxiii. was composed in 55 B.C., lv. either in that year or later, while xi., xxix., xlv. all appear to be written after Caesar's first invasion of Britain (55 B.C.). He is described by Ovid as "hedera juvenalia cinctus Tempora,"—a description somewhat more suitable to a man who dies in his thirtieth year than to one who dies three or four years later. Since no poem is certainly later than 54 B.C., it is best to retain Jerome's reckoning of Catullus' age as 30 years but to suppose him to have lived from 84 to 54 B.C.

Jerome's statement that Catullus was born at Verona is confirmed by other authorities. His father was important enough to act as Caesar's host, and it was probably at or near Verona that Caesar accepted the poet's apologies for the attacks on himself and Mamurra (xxix. and lvii.; *see* Suetonius *Jul.* 73); xciii. may represent Catullus' reply to earlier advances on Caesar's part. The poet's attitude was not due to republican sentiment, but the result of personal animosities. In xxix. he arraigns Pompey along with Caesar, and in xi. he recognizes the latter's greatness.

Catullus' complaints of poverty are not to be taken very seriously. He possessed a villa at Tibur as well as a retreat at Sirmio on Lake Garda, and the poems prove that he had the means to figure in the best society. Still his purse was often no doubt, as he says, "full of cobwebs" (xiii. 8).

On reaching manhood Catullus was sent to try his fortune at Rome. The premature death of his brother in Asia Minor seems to have recalled him to Verona (*cf.* lxviii.). In 57 B.C. he made a belated attempt at a public career by accompanying Memmius, the patron of Lucretius, to Bithynia, of which province Memmius had been appointed governor. His hopes of lining his purse at the expense of the provincials were not realized, and in the spring of 56 B.C. he left Nicaea (xlvi.) and returned to Italy, perhaps on his own yacht (*cf.* iv.); *en route* he visited his brother's tomb in the Troad (ci.). His delight at seeing Sirmio once more is charmingly expressed in xxxi. The poems show that his last years were divided between Verona and Rome. As a Transpadane, Catullus found many compatriots in the capital, and among them several representatives of the new movement in poetry led by Valerius Cato.

himself a native of Cisalpine Gaul. The poems reveal him on terms of intimate friendship with certain of the younger members of this circle; *e.g.*, Calvus (xiv., l., liii., xcvi.), Cinna (x., xcv., cxiii.), Cornificius (xxxviii.). He appears to have been acquainted with the two leading orators of the day—Cicero (xlix.), and Hortensius (lxv. and xcv.). Among friends of less eminence he counted a Caelius (lviii.) whom some identify with Cicero's protégé M. Caelius Rufus, thinking that lxix. and lxxvii. addressed to a Rufus, refer to the same man; this is possible, but in that case another Caelius must be meant in c., since Cicero's friend was not a native of Verona. Particularly dear to Catullus, but otherwise unknown to us, were two friends Veranius and Fabullus (ix., xii., xiii., xxviii., xlvii.), while in i. he dedicates his *libellus* to the biographer and historian Cornelius Nepos, who in after years left it on record that in his opinion Catullus and Lucretius were the two greatest poets of that period (Nepos, Life of Atticus xii., 4). Among Catullus' enemies the most furiously attacked in the poems—apart from Caesar and his lieutenant—are the pair Furius and Aurelius (xv., xvi., xxi., xxiii., xxiv., xxvi.), and one Gellius, who is the target of no fewer than seven epigrams. Other victims of his invective are Ravidus (xl.) and Rufus (*see* above), his rivals in love; a freedman Thallus (xxv.); a ridiculous fop Egnatius (xxxvii., xxxix.). To a false friend Alfenus he writes more in sorrow than in anger (xxx.). The most important influence in Catullus' life was that of his mistress Lesbia. Her real name was Clodia (Apuleius, *Apol.* 10); Catullus chose the pseudonym for its connection with Sappho (li., a translation of a famous ode of Sappho, was perhaps a first tribute to his mistress' charms). There can be little doubt that Clodia was the notorious sister of the demagogue, married in 63 B.C. to Q. Metellus Celer and suspected of responsibility for his death in 59 B.C. Cicero mentions her several times in his Letters, and has left a graphic picture of this dangerous beauty in the speech (*Pro Caelio*), in which he defended M. Caelius Rufus (*see* above), also one of her lovers, against the charge of having tried to poison her. Though Cicero writes as an advocate and Catullus as a lover, their descriptions are not inconsistent, and the final proof of identity is contained in lxxix., the *Lesbius* of which poem clearly covers a Clodius, not, however, the demagogue P. Clodius, but Sex. Clodius, a kinsman and associate of Publius, whom rumour represented as having relations with Clodia (Cicero, *De Dom.* 25) similar to those attributed to *Lesbius* by Catullus. A recent attempt to identify Lesbia with a younger sister and namesake of Metellus' wife, who married L. Lucullus and was divorced by him for alleged relations with her brother, appears unconvincing. Catullus was Clodia's lover during Metellus' lifetime (*cf.* lxxxiii.); the husband's death apparently brought other rivals on the scene, and Catullus' allegiance had been sorely tried before he left for Bithynia, but xi., the final renunciation, is subsequent to his return (*see* above). The data do not suffice to fix the course of the liaison more exactly.

Catullus' poetical activity began soon after his assumption of the *toga virilis* (*cf.* lxviii. 15–17); references in the poems suggest that he sometimes published his pieces separately or in small groups (*cf.* i. 4; xvi. 3.; xlii.; xliii. 7; liv. 6). Later (*cf.* i.) he formed a collection of his compositions and dedicated it to Cornelius Nepos, but it is a moot point what this *libellus* contained, whether it was identical with the present collection, and, if not, how the latter was formed. As arranged in the mss., the poems fall into three sections, viz., (1) i.–lx., shorter lyric pieces, (2) lxi.–lxviii., longer poems in a variety of metres, (3) lxix.–cxvi., elegiac epigrams. The hypothesis most in favour recently is that our present collection was formed in outline by Catullus himself before his death, and that afterwards his literary executors inserted in the groups so arranged sundry other material discovered among his remains, including unfinished pieces like xiva. and lx.

Though Catullus was an Italian of the Italians in character and temperament, it is impossible to appreciate his poetry correctly except in relation to Greek and more particularly Alexandrian poetry. Like that of the other *novi poetae,* his work has two aspects. On the one hand we have the shorter pieces in which any and every emotion of the moment finds instant expression, on the other the poems which earned Catullus the title of *doctus,* considerably longer than his *nugae* but short when compared with the Annales of a Volusius (xxxvi., xcv.). The poet's debt to Alexandrian models in these longer compositions, though hard to control to-day owing to the fragmentary survival of later Greek poetry, is universally admitted. Catullus himself declares lxvi. to be a translation from Callimachus (*cf.* lxv. 16); lxiv. is cast in the mould of a Hellenistic *epyllion;* lxviii., a mixture of the personal and narrative elegy, framed as a letter to a friend, also has Alexandrian forbears; lxii. adapts an epithalamium of Sappho after the manner of the later Greeks; even lxiii. (the *Attis*) which gives an impression of striking originality probably follows in the track of Callimachus or some other Alexandrian. The most original of these longer poems is probably lxi., the epithalamium for Manlius Torquatus and Vinia (or Iunia) Aurunculeia, since here Catullus has tried to fuse the native *versus Fescennini* with the Greek *hymenaeus;* it contains touches, *e.g.*, 216–220, marked by a tenderness unknown otherwise before Virgil. Even in the *nugae* Catullus' debt to Greece is greater than was realized till recently. Just as the life of the νεώτεροι with its interest centred on love and letters had been anticipated by that of the later Greeks (compare l. with the lines of Hedylus [*flor. circ.* 290 B.C.] preserved in Athenaeus xi. 473a; *see* also xxxv. and xxxviii.), so the forms, lyric παίγνιον and elegiac epigram, to express these emotions, had been fixed by the same predecessors. Hellenistic lyric only surviving in meagre fragments, Catullus' originality appears greater here than in his elegiacs which we can compare with the epigrams of the Greek Anthology, but metre (especially the scazon iambic and phalaecan hendecasyllabic), subject-matter, and often phrasing indicate his obligations. The poems on Lesbia's sparrow (ii. and iii.) and that on the yacht (iv.) had Hellenistic prototypes, and an Alexandrian element crops up even in such an ardent love-poem as vii. (*cf.* ll. 3–6). Nevertheless it is in these shorter pieces that Catullus is most Roman and most himself. The attacks on the smaller fry who had incurred his displeasure often revolt us to-day by their gratuitous obscenity, but the *iambi* on Caesar and his associates, which recall but far surpass in bitterness the popular lampoons current at the expense of the *imperator unicus,* were justly considered by their chief victim to have branded him with *perpetua stigmata.* On the other side the Lesbia cycle cannot be paralleled in ancient literature for sincerity of passion, passing through all the stages of joyous contentment, growing distrust, and wild despair to the poignant adieu of the disillusioned lover.

The best edition of Catullus is that by W. Kroll (Leipzig, 1923). The best English commentary is that by R. Ellis (2nd ed., 1889). Neither the current Oxford text (1904) nor the Teubner (1923) can be considered satisfactory. Volume vi. of the Loeb Classical Library (1912) contains a text and translation of Catullus along with Tibullus and the *Pervigilium Veneris.* The most recent translations into English are by Sir William Marris (1924) and F. A. Wright (n.d.). *See* also H. A. J. Munro, *Criticisms and Elucidations of Catullus* (2nd ed., 1905); K. P. Harrington, *Catullus and his Influence* (1923); Frank Tenney, *Catullus and Horace* (1928). (E. A. B.)

CATULUS, the name of a distinguished family of ancient Rome of the gens Lutatia. The following are its most important members:

1. GAIUS LUTATIUS CATULUS, Roman commander during the first Punic War, consul 242 B.C. With a fleet of 200 ships, he occupied the harbours of Lilybaeum and Drepanum. The Carthaginian relieving fleet was totally defeated off the Aegates Islands, March 10, 241, and Catulus shared in the triumph, though, owing to a wound, he took no part in the operations. (*See* PUNIC WARS: First, *ad fin.*)

2. QUINTUS LUTATIUS CATULUS, Roman general and consul with Marius in 102 B.C. In the war against the Cimbri and Teutoni (*qq.v.*) he was sent to hold the passage of the Alps, but was forced back over the Po (*see* MARIUS, GAIUS). In 101 the Cimbri were defeated on the Raudine plain, near Vercellae, by the united armies of Catulus and Marius. The chief honour being ascribed to Marius, Catulus became his bitter opponent. He sided with Sulla in the civil war, was included in the proscription list of 87, and committed suicide. He was distinguished as an orator and writer, and is said to have written the history of his consulship and the

Cimbrian War. Two epigrams by him have been preserved and are published in W. W. Merry's *Fragments of Roman Poetry* (Oxford, 1898, p. 173). *See* Plutarch, *Marius, Sulla;* Appian, *B.C.* i, 74; Vell. Pat. ii, 21; Florus iii, 21; Val. Max. vi, 3, ix, 13; Cicero, *De Oratore*, iii, 3, 8; *Brutus*, 35.

3. QUINTUS LUTATIUS CATULUS (*c.* 120–61 B.C.), son of the above, was a consistent supporter of the aristocracy. In 78 he was consul with Marcus Aemilius Lepidus, who proposed the overthrow of the Sullan constitution. Catulus vigorously opposed this, but Lepidus marched on Rome at the head of an army. He was defeated by Catulus and Pompey and fled to Sardinia. In 67 and 66 Catulus unsuccessfully opposed the Gabinian and Manilian laws, which conferred special powers upon Pompey. He consistently opposed Caesar, whom he tried to implicate in the Catilinarian conspiracy. Caesar, in return, accused him of embezzling public money during the reconstruction of the temple on the Capitol. Catulus's supporters rallied round him, and Caesar dropped the charge. Although not a man of great abilities, Catulus exercised considerable influence through his political consistency and his undoubted solicitude for the welfare of the state.

See Sallust, *Catilina*, 35, 49; Dio Cassius xxxvi. 13; Plutarch, *Crassus;* Suetonius, *Caesar*, 15.

CAUCA, a department of Colombia, on the Pacific coast. Area 11,660 sq.mi. Pop. (1938 census) 356,040; (1951 est.) 468,790. The Western Cordillera, traversing nearly its whole length from south to north, and the Central Cordillera, forming a part of its eastern frontier, give a very mountainous character to the region. It includes, besides, the fertile and healthful valley of the upper Cauca, and a part of the coastal plain. The region is rich in mines and valuable forests, but its inhabitants have made very little progress in agriculture because there are not adequate transportation facilities. Capital of department is Popayán, pop. (1947) 35,960.

CAUCASIAN AREA, NORTH. A natural area and former province in the Russian Soviet Federated Socialist Republic. Boundaries are: W., the Ukraine, the Sea of Azov and the Black sea; S., the Azerbaijan and Georgian republics; E., the Caspian sea; N., the Stalingrad and Voronezh regions. Area, 110,969 sq.mi. Pop. 8,324,788; urban 1,408,085, rural 6,916,703. The following are linked to it administratively: the Kabarda-Balkaria, North Ossetian, Checheno-Ingushetia and Daghestan autonomous republics, and the Adygei, Cherkess and Karachaev autonomous regions. Most of the area is a fertile plain, which has always been a zone of movement of peoples, owing to its situation between the Black sea and the Caspian, with the Caucasus on its southern flank. It formed a link between the Mediterranean civilizations which established trading colonies there, the Persian and Turkish empires of Asia Minor, the Tatar and Mongol steppe peoples, and the Russians from the northwest, all attracted by its fertility and its trading possibilities. In 1926 the varying elements in the population included Russians (Great Russians, Ukrainians and White Russians) 83.38%, Chechens, 2.72%, Ossetians 2.03%, Armenians 1.98%, Kabardians 1.85%, Greeks 1.14%, Germans 1.06%, Cherkess 1.03%, with Ingushes, Karachaevs, Jews, Poles, Kalmucks, Georgians, Tatars, Turks, Persians, Moldavians, Estonians, Czechs and Lesgians. In spite of these varied elements, the area has a certain economic unity: it is essentially an agricultural area undergoing a process of industrialization, and has an important export trade. In varying forms this export trade dates from a great antiquity. The west and southwest, with rich black earth soils, have intensive agriculture, market gardening and dairying, and a good net of communications; proximity of the Black sea and the Caucasus leads to increased rainfall and modification of summer heat and winter cold, abundance of streams and a longer vegetative period (*i.e.*, number of days with a temperature above 40° F.); in the Black sea area there are 275 days, and in Krasnodar, Maikop and Armavir 250, as against 200–210 days in the Donetz and Shakhtinsk areas. Towards the north and in the east the climatic influences are Continental, with drought conditions, and in the east the soils are chestnut-coloured (favourable to the growth of summer wheat in wet years), with about 10% saline and arid sands unfit for agriculture. The chief crops are summer wheat in the northern provinces, a hard variety in demand on the world market for flour and macaroni, etc., winter wheat in the wetter southwest districts, barley, maize, rye, millet and oats. Sunflower seed, providing food, oil, fuel and potash is increasingly cultivated in the Kuban area, as are crops new to the region such as cotton, soybeans, castor-oil plants and kenaf. Swampy tracts along the Kuban are being reclaimed and sown to rice, a crop also new to the region. There are vineyards in the Don, Black sea, Kuban and Terek areas: the Don wines are good, but the Kuban and Terek wine is sharp. Vineyards are being extended in the sandy areas along the Don. Tobacco is cultivated in the Kuban and Black sea regions. In the southwest Kuban and near the great cities and health resorts market gardening (especially of melons, pumpkins and potatoes) is prosperous. Agriculture suffered severely during World War I and was slowly recovering during the post-World War I years.

Cattle rearing is decreasing, and is mainly limited to the dry steppe and the hill pasture meadows. The stock of horses greatly diminished between 1914 and 1921. Horses are bred in Kuban and Kabardia and by the steppe nomads. In Kuban they are used as working animals. The gray Black sea cattle, related to the Ukrainian cattle, are the best working oxen, and are bred and used in the north and near Maikop. Dairy cattle (German) are in demand near the cities, while the Kalmucks breed the best cattle for meat. Formerly in the Stavropol steppe and the Salsk area there were 4,000,000 head of merino sheep, but they were catastrophically destroyed between 1914–21 and the number dropped to only 300,000 or 400,000. Goats are kept for milking, especially in the hill areas. Pig breeding recovered its pre-World War I level, especially in the Kuban and the maize zone of the foothills. Hens, geese, ducks and turkeys numbered 11,000,000 before World War II, and eggs, feathers, down and live and dead birds are exported (mainly to the home Russian markets). In Kuban, Terek and the foothills the long, warm summer and the flora favour beekeeping, and much good wax is exported.

The steppe and much of the plain is treeless, except near the streams and along the Don valley (oak and elm). On the foothills patches of mixed steppe and forest lead to the continuous beech, oak, hornbeam, ash, maple, lime and elm forest, above which are pines, birches and silver firs, with Alpine meadows higher still. The Black sea slopes yield yew and chestnut. The government is controlling timber felling on the foothills in view of the importance of tree growth in regulating the streams and in fixing the soil. In the higher regions much timber is neglected because of lack of labour and lack of transport. Of the timber, most goes to the treeless steppe, the markets of the near east and the Mediterranean. The silver fir is used in the home region for cellulose manufacture.

Fishing for bream, carp, herring, mackerel, sturgeon and anchovy is carried on in a primitive way, but suffers from lack of refrigerators and of quick transport. The mineral wealth consists of the Grozny and Maikop-Taman naphtha beds, the silver, lead and zinc ores of Alagir, south of Orjonikidze, lead ore on the upper Kuban, anthracite in the Shakhtinsk area and south of Batalpashinsk, and coal and iron ore on the north shore of Azov. Some of the mines are worked by peasant artels. The chief manufactures are foodstuffs (flour and fish, fruit and vegetable preserves) especially in the Kuban, naphtha refining at Grozny, Tuapse, Maikop (aviation benzine), cement at Novorossiysk, tobacco at Rostov, Krasnodar, Armavir and Orjonikidze, agricultural machinery at Rostov, Taganrog and Sylin, leather at Taganrog and Maikop, sugar near Armavir and in the Kuban. Maize products (brandy, starch and flour), textiles (wool, cotton, stockings, ropes), soap, potash, bricks, glass, tiles and paper are also manufactured and there are printing works at Rostov and other towns. Side by side with the factory industries go the koustar (peasant) industries and in the flour milling and oil pressing they produce 45% of the total. The chief towns in order of size of population in 1939 are: Rostov-on-Don 510,253; Krasnodar 203,946; Taganrog, Grozny, Shakhty, Orjonikidze (Vladikavkaz), Novorossiysk, Armavir, Maikop, Voroshilovsk, Pyatigorsk, all over 50,000; and Batalpashinsk, Millerop and Salsk.

These towns and their population are an indication of the

marked industrial development of the area, as is the fact that naphtha and not wheat is now the chief export. But agriculture is still, as in the past, the chief occupation of the area. In the internal life of the area it affects directly the welfare of four-fifths of the population and indirectly its development affects the remaining one-fifth, regulating markets, causing seasonal over-freightage of the transport network (railways, ports, elevators and refrigerators) and supplying the raw material for the factories and the food for the workers. The importance of the North Caucasian area in the economy of the U.S.S.R. as a source of supply of wheat and raw material is recognized by the government.

A canal was being constructed in 1944 to transfer part of the waters of the Kuban, which has an oversupply, to the Manich, a tributary of the lower Don. This canal was to irrigate 2,500,000 ac. of land. Eventually the Manich waterway will be extended to the Caspian sea, 390 mi. away. Its level will be maintained by a canal from the Terek which will also generate water power and irrigate a large expanse of steppe land.

CAUCASIAN LANGUAGES. This term is applied to the languages used on the Caucasian isthmus which do not belong to the Indo-German, or to the Semitic, or to the Turco-Mongolian family. They are divided into three groups—the *East Caucasian,* the *West Caucasian* and the *South Caucasian.* The East Caucasian group can be divided into eight branches: 1. The Chechen branch (the chief being the Chechen language of the middle course of the Terek and Daghestan); 2. Avaro-Andi (12 languages in West Daghestan, the chief being the Avar language); 3. Darghi (East Daghestan); 4. Samur (South Daghestan, the chief being the Kuri language, near Derbent); 5. Lakk or Kasi-Kumuk (Central Daghestan); 6. Artchi (one village in Central Daghestan); 7. Hinalugh (one village near the mountain Shah-Dag); and 8. Udi (two villages near the town Nukha). The West Caucasian languages have three branches: 1. Abhaz—region of Sukhum-Kale; 2. Ubykh—formerly dominant in the region of Sotchi, but now spoken only by a few families in Asia Minor; 3. Adyghe, with two dialects—Kabardi (in the so-called Kabarda, principal town Naltchik) and Kiakh or Cherkess (region of Kuban and the Caucasian shore of the Black sea). The South Caucasian languages are: 1. Georgian with its dialects; 2. Mingrelian and Laz; 3. Svanetian.

East Caucasian and West Caucasian are related and may be considered as two branches of the North Caucasian group. The relationship between this and the South Caucasian group has not, as yet, been scientifically proved, and in the present state of our knowledge the North Caucasian and South Caucasian groups must be considered as separate.

The North Caucasian languages are distinguished by an extraordinary abundance of *consonants,* which in Cherkess are 57 in number. Very characteristic of the phonetic system of North Caucasian languages are the lateral consonants, which convey the impression of combinations *kl, gl, thl;* then a great number of consonants of the type *k,* pronounced in the deep back part of the palate, etc. This superabundance of consonants is moderated in the East Caucasian group where consonants rarely come into contact with each other; but in West Caucasian languages the contact and combination of consonants occur very frequently, and the most complicated combinations, very difficult to pronounce, are admitted.

In the East Caucasian languages substantives are divided into classes or "genders"; their number varies in different languages (from two to six). In most cases, neither from the meaning of the word nor from any outward formal symptom is it possible to know to which class the substantive belongs. Very often the same substantive belongs in the singular to one class and in the plural to another. A consonant, specific for each group (*w, b, d, r, y*) is added as prefix, infix or suffix to the adjectives, verbs, pronouns, adverbs, etc., connected with the substantive. For example, the Avars say: *"Dow tchi wugo roqow"*—this man is in the house; *"Dob keto bugo roqob"*—this cat is in the house; *"Doy thladi Yigo roqoy"*—this wife is in the house. Substantives, adjectives and pronouns are declined; an extraordinary number of cases is used to express ideas that in other languages are expressed by a combination of words with prepositions. The Tabassaran language has 35 cases. The system of declension is based on the opposition of *Casus Agens* to *Casus Patiens.* The Casus Agens is used for the logical subject of transitive verbs, and Casus Patiens for the logical object of transitive and logical subject of intransitive verbs. The outward distinction between Casus Agens and Casus Patiens is expressed in a different way by different substantives. Thus, in the Kuri language *Lam*—"ass"—has Agens *Lamra* and *ghum*—"smoke"— has Agens *ghumadi.* All other cases are derived from the Agens by adding different endings. The plural is also formed differently from different substantives, so that the declension of substantives in East Caucasian languages is full of irregularities. The same is true of conjugation in most of these languages. The verbal root, *i.e.,* the invariable part of all verbal forms, consists mostly of one consonant. Before it are the prefixes, indicating the aspect of the verb (*i.e.,* whether the action is considered as a lasting process or as a concluded action) and the gender signs mentioned above agree with the Patiens of the sentence. After the root consonant come the elements, indicating time, mood and sometimes the person. There are many verbal forms and the difference of their meaning is often very subtle and difficult to define. The East Caucasian languages have therefore a complicated grammar with a great abundance and prodigality of forms. The same prodigality is found in the vocabulary; there are for instance special adverbs to indicate such notions as "five years ago," "four days later," etc.—these words having nothing in common with the corresponding numerals.

In the West Caucasian languages, declension is reduced to a minimum; the Adyghe and Ubykh languages have only three cases, the Abhaz has no declension at all. There are fewer verbal forms than in the East Caucasian languages. The vocabulary is poor, so that the simplest notions are expressed by compound words, *e.g.,* in Adyghe the beard is designated as "tail of the mouth," etc. The characteristic peculiarity of West Caucasian languages is a fondness for combining words. Notwithstanding these differences between East and West Caucasian languages, there are still important similarities in both these groups—viz., in the most elementary words, personal pronouns, numerals, simple verb roots, etc., so that there can be no doubt as to their relationship. There are also isolated similarities in the grammar, for instance the opposition of Casus Agens to Casus Patiens, traces of the different classes of substantives, etc.

The phonetic system of South Caucasian languages is simpler than that of the North Caucasian; there is a striking fondness for the agglomeration of consonants (*e.g.,* the Georgian, *mghwdl* is genit. for "priest"). There is only one gender. The declension is rich in case forms, but their formation is regular. The verb has a developed conjugation; the means of expressing personal forms through combination of certain prefixes and suffixes is complicated. In the South Caucasian languages the agreement of the verb with its subject and object varies with the tenses of the verb. In the present the subject is in the nominative and the object in the dative-accusative. In the Aorist the subject is in a special case (Agens?) and the object in the nominative, in the perfect the subject is in the dative and the object in the nominative.

Georgian alone has an ancient written literature, beginning with the 5th century A.D., and in recent years books and newspapers have begun to appear in other Caucasian languages.

BIBLIOGRAPHY.—Literature on North Caucasian languages is to be found in Meillet and Cohen's, *Les Langues du Monde* (Paris, 1924) and A. Dirr, *Einführung in das Studium der Kaukasischen Sprachen* (Leipzig, 1928). For *Georgian,* A. Dirr, *Theoretisch-praktische Grammatik der modernen Georgischen (Grusinischen) Sprache* (No. 81, Hartleben's *Kunst der Polyglottie* Series); F. N. Fink, *Die Haupttypen des Sprachbaues,* p. 132–149 (Leipzig, 1910). (N. S. T.)

CAUCASUS, a mountain range, stretching north-west to south-east from the Strait of Kerch (between the Black sea and Sea of Azov) to the Caspian sea, over 900m. long and varying from 30 to 140m. in width. In its general uniformity of direction, its comparatively narrow width, and its well-defined limits towards both south and north, it presents a closer analogy with the Pyrenees than with the Alps. The range, like the Pyrenees, maintains for considerable distances a high elevation, and is not cleft by natural passes, as in the Alps. In both ranges some of the highest summits stand on spurs of the main range, not on the main range itself, *e.g.,* Mts. Elbruz and Kasbek, Dykh-tau, Koshtan-tau, Janga-tau and Shkara. For purposes of description it is convenient to consider the range in four sections, a western, a middle with two subsections and an eastern.

Western Caucasus.—This section, extending from the Strait of Kerch to Mt. Elbruz in 42° 40′ E., is over 420m. long, and runs parallel to the north-east coast of the Black sea and only a short distance from it. Between the main range and the sea there intervene at least two parallel ranges separated by deep glens, and behind it a third subsidiary parallel range, likewise separated by a deep valley, and known as the Bokovoi Khrebet. All these ranges are crossed by numerous glens and gorges, and the rainfall being heavy and the exposure favourable, they are densely clothed with vegetation. Many of the spurs abut steeply upon the Black sea, so that this littoral region is very rugged and not readily accessible. The seaward flanking ranges run up to 4,000ft. and more, and in many places form cliffs which overhang the coast some 2,000–3,000ft., while the main range gradually ascends to 10,000–12,000ft. as it advances east, the principal peaks being Fisht (8,040ft.), Oshten (9,210ft.), Shuguz (10,640ft.), and Psysh (12,425ft.). The main range is built up of hard crystalline rocks, and the subsidiary chains are composed of softer strata (Cretaceous and Tertiary) which are more easily disintegrated. The snowline is about 9,000ft. on the loftiest summits, and east of Oshten the crest of the main range is capped with perpetual snow and carries many hanging glaciers, while larger glaciers creep down the principal valleys. The few passes lie at relatively great altitudes, so that although the northern versants of the various ranges all have a gentle slope, communication between the Black sea and the valley of the Kubañ, and the low steppe country beyond, is not easy. The more important passes, proceeding from west to east are Pshekh (5,435ft.), and Shetlib (6,060ft.), Pseashka (6,880ft.), Sanchar (7,990ft.); between the last-named and Elbruz are the passes of Marukh (11,500ft.), Klukhor (9,450ft.) and Nakhar (9,615ft.).

BY COURTESY OF NEAR EAST RELIEF

NATIVE OF THE CAUCASUS

Owing to topographical and climatic conditions the southern exposure fosters a luxuriant and abundant vegetation. The most distinguishing feature of the flora is the predominance of arborescent growths; forests cover 56% of the area and are not only dense but laced together with climbing and twining plants. The commonest species of trees are such as grow in central Europe, viz., ash, fir, pine, beech, acacia, maple, birch, box, chestnut, laurel, holm-oak, poplar, elm, lime, yew, elder, willow, oak. The common box is especially prevalent, but the preponderating species are *Coniferae,* including the Caucasian species *Pinus halepensis and P. insignis.* The commonest firs are *Abies nordmannia* and *A. orientalis.* There are two native oaks, *Quercus ponticus* and *Q. sessiliflora.* A great variety of shrubs grow on these slopes of the western Caucasus, chiefly the following species, several of which are indigenous—*Rhododendron ponticum, Azalea pontica, Aristotelia maqui, Agave americana, Cephalaria tatarica, Cotoneaster pyracantha, Citrus aurantium, Diospyros ebenum, Ficus carica, Illicium anisatum, Ligustrum caucasicum, Punica granatum, Philadelphus coronarius, Pyrus salicifolia, Rhus cotinus* and six species of *Viburnum.* A great variety of aquatic plants thrive excellently. The following purely Caucasian species also grow on the coast—five species of spearwort, three of saxifrage, *Aster caucasica, Dioscorea caucasica, Echinops raddeanus, Hedera colchica, Helleborus caucasica* and *Peucedanum caucasicum.* Here too are found magnolia, azalea, camellia, begonia and paulownia. Among the cultivated trees and shrubs the most valuable are the vine, peach, pomegranate, fig, olive (up to 1,500ft. above sea-level), chestnut, apricot, apple, pear, plum, cherry, melon, tea (on the coast between Sukhum-Kaleh and Batum), maize (yielding the staple food of the inhabitants), wheat (up to 6,000ft.), potatoes, peas, currants, cotton, rice, colza and tobacco. After the Russian conquest half a million of the inhabitants of this region being Mohammedans, and refusing to submit to the yoke of Christian Russia, emigrated into Turkish territory, and the country where they had lived remained for the most part unoccupied until after the beginning of the 20th century. The coast-line is remarkably regular, there being no deep bays and few seaports. The best accommodation that these latter afford consists of more or less open roadsteads, *e.g.,* Novorossiisk, Gelenjik, Anapa, Sukhum-Kaleh, Poti and Batum. Along the coast are summer bathing resorts similar to those of the south-east coast of the Crimea. The largest are Anapa, Gelenjik and Gagry.

Middle Caucasus: (*a*) **Western Half.**—This sub-section, having a length of 200m., reaches from Mt. Elbruz to Kasbek and the Pass of Darial. It contains the loftiest peaks of the whole range, of which those above 15,000ft. are:—Elbruz (west peak) 18,465ft. and (east peak) 18,345ft., Jaikyl 17,780ft., Dykh-tau 17,050ft., Shkara 17,040ft., Koshtan-tau 16,875ft., Janga-tau 16,660ft. (west peak) and 16,525ft. (east peak), Kasbek 16,545ft., Mishirghi-tau 16,410ft. (west peak) and 16,350ft. (east peak), Adish or Katuyn-tau 16,295ft., Gestola 15,940ft., Tetnuld 15,920ft., Gimarai-Khokh 15,670ft., Ushba 15,410ft. (south-west peak) and 15,400ft. (north-east peak), Ullu-auz 15,350ft., Adai-Khokh 15,275ft., Tikhtengen 15,135ft., Tiutiun-tau 15,115ft.

The crest of the main range runs at an altitude exceeding 10,000ft., but is surpassed in elevation by the secondary range to the north, the Bokovoi Khrebet. These ranges are connected by more than half a dozen short transverse spurs enclosing as many cirques. Besides the Bokovoi Khrebet several other short subsidiary ranges branch off from the main range at acute angles, with high glens between them. Down all these glens glacier streams descend, until they find an opportunity to pierce through the flanking ranges, which they do in deep gorges, and then race down the northern slopes of the mountains to enter the Terek or the Kubañ, or down the southern versant to join the Rion or the Kura. Amongst all these high glens there is a remarkable absence of lakes and waterfalls; nor are there down in the lower valleys, as one would expect in a region so extensively glaciated, any sheets of water corresponding to the Swiss lakes. In this section of the Caucasus the loftiest peaks do not as a rule rise on the main range, but in many cases on the short spurs that link it with the Bokovoi Khrebet and other subsidiary ranges.

Glaciers.—The snow-line runs at 9,500 to 10,000ft. on the northern face and 1,000ft. higher on the southern face. There are over 900 glaciers in this section, and although they often rival those of the Alps in size, they do not descend generally to such low altitudes. The best known are the Bezingi or Ullu, between Dykh-tau and Janga-tau, 10½m. long, and descending to 6,535ft. above sea-level; Leksyr, situated south of Adyr-su-bashi, 7½m. long, and its end at 5,690ft., the lowest point to which any glacier descends on the south side of the range; Tseya or Zea, descending 6m. from the Adai-khokh to 6,730ft.; Karagom, from the same mountain, 9½m. long, and reaching down to 5,790ft., the lowest on the northern side; Dyevdorak or Devdorak, from Kasbek, 2½m. long, its end at 7,530ft.; Khaldeh or Geresho 4¼m. long, from Shkara and Janga-tau; Tuyber from Tetnuld, 6½m. long, and reaching down to 6,565ft.; Tsanner or Zanner, the same length, but stopping short 240ft. higher, likewise given off by Tetnuld; while between that peak, Adish and Gestola originates the Adish or Lardkhat glacier, 5m. long and terminating at 7,450ft. The total area covered by glaciers in the central Caucasus is estimated at 625 to 650sq.m., the longest being the Maliev on Kasbek, 36m. long; but according to M. Rossikov several of the largest glaciers are retreating, the Tseya at the rate of something like 40–45ft. per annum.

Passes.—It is in this section that the mountain system is narrowest, and here (apart from the "gate" at Derbent close beside the Caspian) are the principal north to south communications, between south Russia and Armenia and Asia Minor. These are the passes of Darial and Mamison. Over the former, which lies immediately east of Kasbek, runs the Georgian military road (1811–64) from Vladikavkaz to Tiflis, cutting through the mountains by a beautiful gorge (8m. long), shut in by mountain walls nearly 6,000ft. high, and so narrow that there is only just room for the road and the river Terek side by side. The pass by which this road crosses the main range farther south is known as the Krestovaya Gora and lies 7,805ft. above sea-level. The Mamison pass, over which runs the Ossetic military road (made passable for vehicles in 1889) from the Terek (below Vladikavkaz) to Kutais in the valley of the Rion, skirting the eastern foot of the Adai-khokh, lies at an altitude of 9,270ft. and is situated a little south of the main range. Horses can traverse only the best of the other passes and only during a few weeks in summer. They range at altitudes of 9,000–12,500ft., and between the pass of Nakhar in the west and that of Mamison in the east there is not a pass below 10,000ft. The best known are Chiper (10,800–10,720ft.), Bassa (9,950ft.), Donguz-orun (10,490ft.), Becho (11,070ft.), Akh-su (12,465ft.), Bak (10,220ft.), Adyr-su (12,305ft.), Bezingi (10,090ft.), Shari-vizk (11,560ft.), Edena, Pasis-mta or Godivizk (11,270ft.), Shtulu-vizk (10,860ft.), Fytnargyn (11,130ft.), Bakh-fandak (9,570ft.), the two Karaul passes (11,680 and 11,270ft.) and Gurdzi-vizk (10,970ft.). The most frequented pass in Svanetia is that of Latpari (9,260ft.), situated in the first of the southern subsidiary ranges mentioned above, and thus connecting the valleys of the Ingur and the Tskhenis-Tskhali.

Flora.—In this section of the range again the southern slopes are clothed with vegetation of remarkable luxuriance and richness, more especially in the region of Svanetia (42°–43° E.). Here again the plants are bigger and the blossoms more abundant than in the Alps, forests of *Coniferae* predominate, and gigantic male ferns (*Aspidium filix-mas*), *Paris incompleta* (a member of the Trilliaceae), *Usnea* or tree-moss, box, holly (*Ilex aquifolium*), *Lilium monadelphum* and many of the herbaceous plants which flower in English gardens, grow here to an extraordinary size—monkshoods, *Cephalaria, Mulgedia* and groundsels. Other species are *Campanula, Pyrethrum,* aconite, *Cephaëlis,* speedwell, *Alchemilla sericea, Centaurea macrocephala, Primula grandis* and a species of primrose. Flowers of great beauty and abundance blossom up to 13,000ft. on the northern slope and on the southern slope ascend 2,000ft. higher. Walnuts grow up to an altitude of 5,400ft., the vine and mulberry to 3,250ft., the lime and ash to 4,000ft. The forests extend to the upper end of the limestone gorges. Above that the crystalline schists are bare of tree vegetation. The upper limit of arborescent vegetation is 7,000–7,500ft., of shrubs, *e.g.,* rhododendrons, 8,500ft., and of pasture-lands up to 9,000ft. The principal cultivated varieties of plants in this section are wheat, rye, oats, barley, beans, millet and tobacco.

Middle Caucasus: (*b*) **Eastern Part.**—In this sub-section, which stretches from Kasbek and the Darial gorge to the Baba-dagh in 48° 25′ E., a distance of 230m., the Caucasus attains its greatest breadth. For the whole distance the main range keeps an average elevation of 10,000ft., though the peaks are 2,000 to nearly 5,000ft. higher, the altitudes increasing towards the east. The glaciers decrease in the same proportion. Here the principal peaks, again found chiefly on the spurs and subsidiary ranges, are the Tsmiakom-khokh (13,570ft.), Shan-tau (14,530ft.), Kidenais-magali (13,840ft.), Zilga-khokh (12,645ft.), Zikari (12,565ft.), Choukhi (12,110ft.), Julti-dagh (12,430ft.), Alakhun-dagh (12,690ft.) and Maghi-dagh (12,445ft.). On the main range stand Borbalo (10,175ft.), Great Shavi-kildeh (12,325ft.), Murov (11,110ft.), Ansal (11,740ft.), Ginor-roso (11,120ft.), while farther east come Trfan-dagh (13,765ft.) and Bazardyuz or Kichen (14,727ft.). In the same direction, but again outside the main range, lie Shah-dagh (13,955ft.), Shalbuz (13,675ft.) and Malkamud (12,750ft.).

The most noteworthy feature of this section is the broad *highland region of Daghestan,* which flanks the main range on the north and sinks down to the Caspian sea (east), and to the valley of the Terek (north). On the north-west this rugged highland region is well defined by the transverse ridge of Andi, which to the east of Kasbek strikes off from the Caucasus range almost at right angles. The rest of the Daghestan region consists of a series of roughly parallel folds, of Jurassic age, ranging in altitudes from 7,500 up to 12,500ft., separated by deep river glens which cut it up into a number of arid, treeless plateaus. The most prominent of these tablelands is Bash-lam, which stretches east and west between the Chanti Argun and the Andian Koisu. Upon it rise the conspicuous peaks of Tebulos-mta (14,775ft.), Tugo-mta (13,795ft.), Komito-tavi or Kachu (14,010ft.), Donos-mta (13,560ft.), Diklos-mta (13,740ft.), Kvavlos-mta or Kolos-mta (13,080ft.), Motshekh-tsferi (13,140ft.) and Galavanas-tsferi (13,260ft.). Farther east is the Bogos tableland, stretching from south-south-west to east-north-east between the Andian Koisu and the Avarian Koisu and rising to over 13,400ft. in several peaks, *e.g.,* Antshovala (13,440ft.), Botshokh-meër (13,515ft.), Kosara-ku (13,420ft.) and Addala-shuogchol-meër (13,580ft.); and the Dyulty tableland reaching 12,400ft. between the Kara Koisu and the Kazikumukh Koisu. Névé and glaciers occur on some of these peaks, particularly on the slopes of Diklos-mta, where the glaciers descend to 7,700ft. (north) and to 8,350ft. (south). Here the passes are lower than those between Elbruz and Kasbek, though at appreciable heights, fully equal to those that lead up from the Black sea to the valley of the Kubañ in the western section of the range. The best known are the Krestovaya Gora (7,805ft.) on the Georgian military road south of Darial; Kodor (9,300ft.) and Sats-kheni, and Gudur (10,120ft.) and Salavat (9,280ft.), carrying the Akhty military road.

The *flora* of this section bears a general resemblance to that farther west. Ample details will be found in Dr. G. Radde's (1831–1903) monographs on Daghestan.

Eastern Caucasus.—This section of the Caucasus gradually dies away east of Baba-dagh (11,930ft.) towards the Caspian, terminating finally in the peninsula of Apsheron. It is, however, continued under the waters of the Caspian and reappears on its eastern side in the Kopet-dagh, which skirts the north-eastern frontier of Persia. In this section of the Caucasus no peak exceeds 9,000ft. in altitude and the crest of the main range retains no snow. The most frequented pass is Alty-agach (4,355ft.).

Between the northern and the southern sides of the range there is a great difference in climate, productions and scenery. In the south-western slopes and valleys where a heavy rainfall is combined with a warm temperature, magnificent forests clothe the mountain-sides and reach the waters of the Black sea. There the littoral from, say, Sukhum-kaleh to Batum, and the inland parts of the basin of the Rion, will bear comparison with any of the provinces of Italy in richness and variety of products. But farther inland, east of Tiflis, a great change becomes noticeable on the other side of the transverse ridge of the Suram or Meskes mountains. Arid upland plains and parched hillsides take the place of the rich verdure and luxuriant arborescent growth of Imeretia, Svanetia and Mingrelia, the districts which occupy the valleys of the Ingur and Rion and the tributaries of the latter. A very similar change likewise becomes noticeable in the higher regions of the Caucasus mountains north of the pass of Mamison. The valleys of the Rion and Ardon and of others that flow in the same direction, are almost wholly destitute of trees, but where the bare rock does not prevail, the mountain slopes are carpeted with grass. "Treeless valleys, bold rocks, slopes of forbidding steepness (even to eyes accustomed to those of the Alps), and stone-built villages, scarcely distinguishable from the neighbouring crags" (Freshfield). Austere and unattractive though those valleys are, the same epithets cannot be applied to the deep gorges by which in most cases the streams make their escape through the northern subsidiary range. These defiles are declared to be superior in grandeur to anything of the kind in the Alps. That of Darial (the Terek) is fairly well known, but those of the Cherek and the Urukh, farther west, are stated to be still more magnificent. Not only do the snow-clad ranges and the ice-panoplied peaks surpass the loftiest summits of the Alps in altitude; they also in many cases excel them in boldness and picturesqueness of outline, and equal the most difficult of them in steepness and relative inaccessibility.

Hydrography.—Nearly all the larger rivers of Caucasia have their sources in the central parts of the Caucasus range. The torrential streams of Mdzimta, Pzou, Bzyb and Kodor drain the country west of Elbruz. The Ingur, Tskhenis-Tskhali, Rion and its tributaries, *e.g.*, the Kvirila, are longer but also in part torrential; they drain the great glacier region between Elbruz and Kasbek. The Rion is the *Phasis* of the ancients and flows through the classic land of Colchis. The Lyakhva and Aragva, tributaries of the Kura, carry off the waters of the main range south of Kasbek, and other tributaries, such as the Yora and the Alazan, collect the surplus drainage of the main Caucasus range farther east. The other large river of this region, the Aras, has its sources, not in the Caucasus range, but on the Armenian highlands a long way south-west of Ararat. The rivers which go down northwards from the central Caucasus have longer courses than those on the south. The most important of these are the Kubañ and the Terek; most of the streams which have their sources among the central glaciers draining into the latter, *e.g.*, the Malka, Baksan, Chegem, Cherek, Urukh, Ardon. The Kuma, which alone pursues an independent course through the steppes, farther north than the Terek, has its sources, not in the main ranges of the Caucasus, but in a group of mountains near Pyatigorsk. Its waters become absorbed in the sands of the desert steppes before they reach the Caspian. Of the streams that carve into chequers the elevated plateau of Daghestan, four, known by the common name of the Koisu, unite to form the Sulak. The only other stream deserving of mention in this province is the Samur. Both rivers discharge their waters into the Caspian, as also does the Zumgail, a small stream which drains the eastern extremity of the Caucasus range.

Volcanic Evidences.—Ancient but now extinct volcanic centres occur frequently at the intersections of the main range with the transverse ranges; of these the most noteworthy are Elbruz and Kasbek. The town of Shemakha near the eastern end of the system was the scene of volcanic outbreaks as late as 1859, 1872 and 1902; while in the adjacent peninsula of Apsheron mud volcanoes exist in large numbers. All along the northern foot of the system hot mineral springs gush out at various places, such as Pyatigorsk, Zhelesnovodsk, Essentuki and Kislovodsk; and the series is continued along the north-eastern foot of the highlands of Daghestan, *e.g.*, Isti-su, Eskiendery, Akhta. Also similar evidences of volcanic activity characterize the northern border of the Armenian highlands on the southern side of the Rion-Kura depression, in the mountains of Ararat, Alagöz, Akmangan, Samsar, Godoreby, Great and Little Abull, and in the mineral springs of Borzhom, Abbas-tuman, Sleptzov, Mikhailovsk and Tiflis.

Geology.—The structure of the Caucasus is comparatively simple, and in the form of a fan. In the centre are crystalline rocks which disappear towards the east. Beneath them, on both sides, plunge the strongly folded Palaeozoic and Jurassic schists. On the north the folded beds are followed by a zone of Jurassic and Cretaceous beds which rapidly assume a gentle inclination towards the plain. On the south the corresponding zone is affected by numerous secondary folds which involve Upper Miocene deposits. In the east, the structure is somewhat modified. The crystalline band is lost. The northern Mesozoic zone is very much broader, and is thrown into simple folds like those of the Jura mountains. The Mesozoic zone is absent in the south, and the Palaeozoic zone sinks abruptly in a series of faulted steps to the plain of the Kura, beneath which no doubt the continuation of the Mesozoic zone is concealed.

The geological sequence begins with the granite and schists of the central zone, which extend from Fisht (west) to some distance beyond Kasbek (east). Then follow the Palaeozoic schists and slates. Fossils are extremely rare in these beds; *Buthotrephis* has long been known, and traces of *Calamites* and ferns, and in the west fossils which appear to indicate a Devonian age. Upon the Palaeozoic rest Mesozoic deposits (Lias to Upper Cretaceous). Different views exist as to the position of unconformities, but important ones occur at the base of the Tithonian (Upper Jurassic) and at the base of the Trias. In general the Upper Jurassic beds are much more calcareous on the north than they are on the south. The Mesozoic are followed by Tertiary deposits, which on the north are nearly horizontal but on the south are in part included in the folds—the Eocene and Miocene being folded, while later beds, though sometimes elevated, may not be affected by the folding. The final folding of the chain, proceeding from north-east, undoubtedly occurred at the end of the Miocene period. Folding also occurred probably during the Permian and again during the Upper Jurassic (direction south-west). Also the difference in character of the Jurassic beds on the two sides of the chain appears to indicate that a ridge existed in that period. The last phase in the history of the Caucasus was the growth of the great volcanoes of Elbruz and Kasbek, which stand upon the old rocks of the central zone, and by the outflow of sheets of lava upon the sides of the chain. The cones are composed largely of acid andesites, but many of the lavas are augite andesites and basalts. There seem to have been two periods of eruption, and as some of the lavas have flowed over Quaternary gravels, the latest outbursts must have been of very recent date.

Near the northern foot of the Caucasus, especially near the hot mineral springs of Pyatigorsk, a group of igneous rocks rises above the plain. They are laccolites of trachytic rock, and raised the Tertiary beds above them in the form of blisters. Subsequent denudation has removed the sedimentary covering and exposed the igneous core. Petroleum occurs in the Tertiary beds at both ends of the chain.

Bibliography.—The following is a selection of the more recent works. A. F. Mummery, *My climbs in the Alps and Caucasus* (1895); D. W. Freshfield, *Exploration of the Caucasus* (2nd ed., 1902, 2 vols.); H. Abich, *Aus Kaukasischen Ländern* (2 vols., 1896); C. von Hahn, *Kaukasische Reisen und Studien* (1896) and *Bilder aus dem Kaukasus* (1900); G. Merzbacher, *Aus den Hochregionen des Kaukasus* (2 vols., 1901); J. Mourier, *L'Art au Caucase* (new ed., 1912); E. A. Martel, *La Côte d'Azur russe* (1909); S. Graham, *A Vagabond in the Caucasus* (1911); A. Herbert, *Casuals in the Caucasus* (1912); M. Rikli, *Natur und Kulturbilden der Eiszeit im Kaukasus* (1914); M. Varandian, *La conflit arméno-géorgien et la guerre du Caucase* (1919); A. Dirr, *Caucasian folk-tales* (1925). The geology of the Caucasus is dealt with in E. Fournier, *Description géologique du Caucase central* (1896); F. Löwinson-Lessing, *Guide des Excursions du VIIe Congrès géol. internat.* (1897); and F. Oswald, *Notes on the Geological Map of the Caucasus* (1914). *A travers le Caucase* (1905) by E. Levier is especially valuable for botany and N. Y. Dinnik writes on the fauna in *Bull. Soc. Impériale des Naturalistes de Moscou* (1901). Much valuable information about the Caucasus is preserved in *Izvestia* and *Zapiski* of the Russian and Caucasian geographical societies. V. Dingelstedt has a number of papers on this region in the *Scottish Geographical Magazine* (1889–1904). A useful geological map is by F. Oswald (1914), scale of 1:1,000,000; and the Russian general staff have a good map on the scale of 1:210,000. (J. I. P.)

HISTORY

To the ancient Greeks Caucasia, and the mighty range which dominates it, were a region of mystery and romance. It was there that they placed the scene of the sufferings of Prometheus (*vide* Aeschylus, *Prometheus Vinctus*), and there, in the land of Colchis, which corresponds to the valley of the Rion, that they sent the Argonauts to fetch the golden fleece. Outside the domain of myth, the earliest connection of the Greeks with Caucasia would appear to have been through the maritime colonies, such as Dioscurias, which the Milesians founded on the Black sea coast in the 7th century B.C. For more than two thousand years the most powerful state in Caucasia was that of Georgia (*q.v.*). The southern portion of Transcaucasia fell during the 1st century B.C. under the sway of Armenia, and with that country passed under the dominion of Rome, and so eventually of the Eastern empire. During the 3rd century A.D. Georgia and Armenia were invaded and in great part occupied by the Khazars, and then for more than a thousand years the mountain fastnesses of this borderland between Europe and Asia were the refuge, or the resting-place, of successive waves of migration. The Huns and the Avars appeared in the 6th century, and the Mongols in the 13th. In the 10th century bands of Varangians or Russified Scandinavians sailed out of the Volga and coasted along the Caspian until they had doubled the Apsheron peninsula, when they landed and captured Barda, the chief town of Caucasian Albania.

But, apart from Georgia, historical interest in Caucasia centres in the long and persistent attempts which the Russians made to conquer it, and the heroic, though unavailing, resistance offered by the mountain races, more especially the Circassian and Lesghian tribes. Russian aggression began early in the 18th century, when Peter the Great, establishing his base at Astrakhan on the Volga, and using the Caspian for bringing up supplies and munitions of war, captured Derbent from the Persians in 1722, and Baku in 1723. But these conquests, with others made at the expense of Persia, were restored to the latter power after Peter's death, a dozen years later. At that period the Georgians were divided into various petty principalities, the chief of which were Imeretia and Georgia (Kharthlia), owing at times a more or less shadowy allegiance to the Ottoman sultan. In 1770, when at war with Turkey, the Russians crossed over the Caucasus and assisted the Imeretians to resist the Turks, and from the time of the ensuing peace of Kuchuk-kainarji the Georgian principalities looked to Russia as their protector against the Turks. In 1783 George XIII., prince of Georgia and Mingrelia, formally put himself under the suzerainty of Russia, and after his death Georgia was converted (1801) into a Russian province. The same fate overtook Imeretia nine years later. Meanwhile the Russians had also subdued the Ossetes (1802) and the Lesghian tribes (1803) of the middle Caucasus. By the peace of Gulistan in 1813 Persia ceded to Russia several districts in Eastern Caucasia, from Lenkoran northwards to Derbent. Nevertheless the mountain tribes were still independent, and their subjugation cost Russia a sustained effort of thirty years. At first the Russians were able to continue their policy of conquest and annexation without serious check. After acquiring the northern edge of the Armenian plateau, partly from Persia in 1828 and partly from Turkey in 1829, Russia in 1832 crushed a rising in Daghestan. The next seven years were occupied with the subjugation of the Abkhasians along the Black sea coast, and of other Circassian tribes in the west. Meanwhile Shamyl, a chief and religious leader of the Lesghians, had roused the Lesghian tribes farther east. His resistance was finally broken after 20 years of warfare by Prince Baryatinsky, who succeeded in capturing Shamyl's stronghold of Weden, and then in surrounding and capturing (1859) that chieftain himself on the inaccessible rocky platform of Gunib in the heart of Daghestan. But it was not until 1864 that the Russians finally stifled all opposition. Then followed a wholesale emigration of the Circassians, who sought an asylum in Turkish territory, leaving their native region almost uninhabited and desolate. During the Russo-Turkish War of 1877–78 the self-exiled Circassians and other Caucasian mountaineers, supported by a force of 14,000 Turks, made a determined attempt to wrest their native glens from the power of Russia; but, after suffering a severe defeat at the hands of General Alkhazov, the Turks withdrew, and were accompanied by some 30,000 Abkhasians, who settled in Asia Minor. A few months later the Lesghians in Daghestan, who had risen in revolt, were defeated and their country once more reduced to obedience. By the peace of Adrianople, Russia still further enlarged her Transcaucasian territories by the acquisition of the districts of Kars, Batum and Ardahan. After a peaceful period of a quarter of a century the Armenian subjects of Russia in Transcaucasia were filled with bitterness and discontent by the confiscation of the properties of their national (Gregorian) Church by the Russian treasury. Nor were their feelings more than half allayed by the arrangement which made their ecclesiastics salaried officers of the Russian state. This ferment of unrest, which was provoked in the years 1903–04, was exacerbated by the renewed outbreak of the century-long racial feud between the Tatars and the Armenians, at Baku and other places. Nearly the whole of the region between the Caucasus and the Perso-Turkish frontier on the south, from the Caspian sea on the one side to the Black sea on the other, was embroiled in a civil war of the most sanguinary and ruthless character, the inveterate racial animosities of the combatants being in both cases inflamed by religious fanaticism. An end was put to these disorders only by the mutual agreement of the two contestants in Sept. 1905.

The Revolution of 1905 in Russia aroused the desire for self-government that has never long been dormant in the Caucasus. The agrarian policy of the Tsarist Government added fuel to the fire of discontent, and the refusal to recognize their individual national languages was a further source of grievance to Armenians, Tatars and Georgians alike. Nevertheless the Russian Government ruthlessly pursued its repressive policy. On the outbreak of the World War in 1914, when they had learnt that Russia was the ally of France and Great Britain, the Caucasian nationalities eagerly responded to the call to arms. But even this action had no effect upon the Russian Government, and the governship of General Yudenitch was specially noteworthy for its severity. Hence the February Revolution of 1917 was hailed with joy throughout the Caucasus when the individual nationalities attempted to establish a Federal republic that should be governed by a Transcaucasian diet. But the failure of Kerensky's administration and the triumph of Bolshevism spelt failure for the Caucasian Republic also. The component states made a brief attempt to preserve their independence of Moscow under mildly socialistic forms of government, but the military strength of the Soviet soon overcame their resistance. First one and then another was overrun and conquered, and Soviet republics set up under the guidance of Moscow. Despite the maintenance by the Moscow Government of these republics in the Caucasus, the desire amongst some of the population for complete independence of the U.S.S.R. has not been extinguished.

CAUCASUS, CAMPAIGN IN THE. Though both Russian and Turk spoke of a "Caucasus front" and gave to their armies engaged on this front the designation "Caucasian" in World War I, the operations actually took place at a considerable distance from the Caucasus in the region covered by the historical term Armenia, a bleak, almost undeveloped area. In 1914, on the Russian side, railway communication ended at Sarikamis, about 40 mi. S.W. of Kars and 15 mi. from the frontier; on the Turkish side, 600 mi. of indifferent roads and tracks separated their armies operating in the Erzerum area from the railhead at Ankara.

The Turkish Plan.—The 3rd Turkish army had been assembling during Sept. and Oct. 1914 in the neighbourhood of Erzerum. It consisted of three army corps with the fighting strength of about 100,000 men. The plan evolved by Enver Pasha was a wide enveloping movement with Kars as the objective. This plan wholly ignored the absence of communications and the climatic conditions. The Russian attitude was, at the outset, purely defensive; two of the three regular corps, stationed in the Caucasus in peace, had been sent to the Austro-German front. Yet the Russians made the first advance, moving across the frontier on the road to Erzerum.

Enver arrived from Constantinople and assumed personal command of the 3rd army. He insisted, against the views of his German advisers, on putting into execution the ambitious plan he had conceived. Yet such fortitude and endurance did the poorly equipped and ill-fed Turkish troops display that they almost achieved the impossible. While the main Russian body was engaged with the 11th corps, the 9th corps appeared, in the last days of Dec. 1914, on the heights above Sarikamis, and the 10th corps on its left approached Kars. The Russian commander's nerve failed him at the crisis; and the situation was saved only by his chief of the staff, Gen. N. N. Yudenich. He collected forces for a counterattack, which resulted in the practical annihilation of the two Turkish turning corps, worn out and disorganized by their approach march; the 11th corps was then in its turn driven back. The losses of the Turkish 3rd army were about 85%. Enver at once handed over the command and returned to Constantinople.

During the whole of 1915 the fighting on the Caucasus front was of minor importance only, the main preoccupation lying elsewhere. The shattered 3rd army was gradually reconstituted under Mahmud Kiamil, and the Russians raised fresh units. But neither side was yet in shape for a serious offensive. In Sept. 1915 Grand Duke Nicholas took over command of the Caucasus front, an event which markedly enlarged the Russian effort in this theatre.

The Fall of Erzerum.—Once again an offensive on a large scale was made in the depth of winter. The grand duke wished to anticipate the arrival of Turkish reinforcements released by the British evacuation of Gallipoli. This enterprise was completely successful. The Russian capture of Erzerum (Feb. 16, 1916) was one of the finest feats of arms of World War I. The next Russian objective was Trebizond; its capture in April considerably simplified the supply problem. Meanwhile, the Turkish high command had decided on a counterstroke. It ordered the assembly of a new army, the 2nd, under Izzet Pasha, in the Mush-Kharput region, to attack the Russian flank and rear and recapture Erzerum. The plan was sound enough, but the assembly, begun in April, was not complete in July. The grand duke became aware of the Turkish intentions and anticipated their attack by a heavy blow at the 3rd army, and broke it. The Russians occupied Erzincan in July. The counterstroke of the 2nd army took place in August, giving the Russians time to transfer troops from their right wing to meet it. After some heavy fighting the 2nd army's effort was definitely held. It had gained little ground at a considerable sacrifice in men.

During the winter of 1916–17 no movements took place. The Turkish 2nd and 3rd armies (Mustafa Kemal and Vahib Pasha respectively), now combined under Izzet Pasha, suffered terrible privations. Nor were the Russians much better off.

Attempted Russo-British Co-operation.—In Dec. 1916 the British army in Mesopotamia, under Gen. Sir Frederick Maude, began the attacks on the Turks at Kut, which were to lead to the capture of Baghdad in March. It was agreed that the cavalry corps of Baratov from Persia and of Chernozubov from between lakes Urmia and Van should advance on Mosul and thus, in co-operation with Maude, end the Mesopotamian campaign. The grand duke adopted the plan wholeheartedly, and the Turks would not have been able to resist effectively. But weather conditions and the difficulty of organizing a line of supply through the mountains of the Persian border caused delay; then the Russian revolution broke out.

Collapse of the Russian Army.—Throughout the summer the Russian army lay inactive, gradually disintegrating. Yudenich, who had succeeded the grand duke, gave up the command in August and was succeeded by Przhevalsky. But the end was near. In December an armistice was concluded on the Caucasus front, and after the peace of Brest-Litovsk (March 3, 1918), the Turks occupied Batum on April 14 and Kars on the 26th. But the Turkish control of Transcaucasia was short-lived, for General Allenby's crushing victory in Palestine spelled the loss of the war for the Turks. (A. P. W.; X.)

CAUCHON, PIERRE, French ecclesiastic, was born near Reims and became bishop of Beauvais in 1420, after having been a leading master of the University of Paris and a civil servant to the Burgundian government. As a councillor to the duke of Bedford, he presided over the trial of Joan of Arc at Rouen, which constitutes his chief title to fame. He took care to conduct the trial according to inquisitorial procedure and to obtain from the Maid a confession which would save her life.

In 1432 he became bishop of Lisieux. He took part in the Council at Basel in 1435. Cauchon died in 1442 and was subsequently excommunicated by Calixtus III.

See A. Sarrazin, *Pierre Cauchon* (Paris, 1901); and works dealing with the trial of Joan of Arc (*q.v.*).

CAUCHY, AUGUSTIN LOUIS, Baron (1789–1857), French mathematician, was born in Paris, on Aug. 21, 1789, and died at Sceaux (Seine) on May 23, 1857. He studied at the École Polytechnique and the École des Ponts et Chaussées, and practised for some time as an engineer.

His health failed in 1813, and his father's friends, Lagrange and Laplace, persuaded him to devote himself entirely to mathematics. From 1816 onward he held three professorships in Paris, which he lost at the revolution of 1830, on declining to swear allegiance to Louis Philippe. A chair of mathematical physics was created for him at the University of Turin. He spent some time travelling with the duke of Bordeaux, grandson of Charles X, and in 1838 returned to France, resuming his chair at the École Polytechnique. Although acting only from the highest motives, Cauchy made himself objectionable to his colleagues by a self-righteous obstinacy and an aggressive religious bigotry.

The genius of Cauchy was promised in his simple solution of the problem of Apollonius (*i.e.,* to describe a circle touching three given circles) which he discovered in 1805, and in his generalization of Euler's theorem on polyhedra in 1811. More important is his memoir on wave propagation which obtained the *grand prix* of the Institut in 1816. His greatest contributions to mathematical science are characterized by the clear and rigorous methods which he introduced and are mainly embodied in his three great treatises, *Cours d'analyse de l'École Polytechnique* (1821); *Le Calcul infinitésimal* (1823); *Leçons sur les applications du calcul infinitésimal à la géométrie* (1826–28). He clarified the principles of the calculus by developing them with the aid of limits and continuity and was the first to prove Taylor's theorem rigorously, establishing his well-known form of the remainder. Thus the first phase of modern rigour, giving a satisfactory basis for the calculus, originated in Cauchy's lectures and researches of the 1820s in analysis. To the same period belongs his development of his (the first) version of the theory of functions of a complex variable, today indispensable in applied mathematics from physics to aeronautics. With equal originality, he made substantial contributions to the theory of numbers where, however, he went astray on Fermat's last theorem. He was one of the originators of the theory of permutation groups. In astronomy, he gave a shorter account than Leverrier's of the motion of Pallas. In mechanics, he made many researches, substituting the notion of the continuity of geometrical displacements for the principle of the continuity of matter. In optics, he developed the wave theory, and his name is associated with the simple dispersion formula. In elasticity, he originated the theory of stress, and his results are nearly as valuable as those of S. D. Poisson. His collected works, *Œuvres complètes d'Augustin Cauchy,* have been published in 27 volumes.

See C. A. Valson, *Le Baron Augustin Cauchy: sa vie et ses travaux* (1868).

CAUCUS, a political term used in the U.S. of a special form of party meeting, and in Great Britain of a system of party organization. The word originated in Boston, Mass., in the early part of the 18th century, when it was used as the name of a political club, the Caucus or Caucas club. There public matters were discussed and arrangements made for local elections and the choosing of candidates for offices. A contemporary reference to the club occurs in the diary of John Adams in 1763; but William Gordon (*History of the Independence of the United States of America* [1788]) speaks of the Caucus as having been in existence about 50 years before the time of writing (1774) and describes the methods used for securing the election of the candidates. The derivation of the word has been much disputed. The most plausible origin is an Algonquin word, *kaw-kaw-was,* meaning to talk, Indian words and names having been popular in America as titles for societies and clubs (*cf.* "Tammany"). In the United States "caucus" is used strictly of a meeting either of party managers or of duty voters, as for instance a "nominating caucus," for nominating candidates for office or for selecting delegates for a nominating convention. The caucus of the party in congress nominated the candidates for the offices of president and vice-president from 1800 till 1824, when the convention system was adopted. At the same time, the candidates for governor and lieutenant governor were nominated by the party members of the state legislatures in what was known as the legislative nominating caucus. Occasionally districts unrepresented in the legislature sent delegates to sit in with the members of the legislature when these nominations were made, and this was termed the mixed legislative nominating caucus. (*See* Primaries.)

The word is used in the United States to denote meetings of the members of a party in congress or in a legislature or a city council, to determine matters of party policy on proposed legislation or legislative offices. "Caucus" first came into use in Great Britain in 1878 in connection with the organization of the Liberal Association of Birmingham by Joseph Chamberlain and F. Schnadhorst on strict disciplinary lines, more particularly with a view to election management and the control of voters, which became the model for other Liberal associations throughout the country. It was to this supposed imitation of the U.S. political "machine" that Lord Beaconsfield gave the name "caucus," and the name came to be used, not in the U.S. sense of a meeting, but of a closely disciplined system of party organization, chiefly as a stock term of abuse applied by politicians of one party to the controlling organization of its opponents.

CAUDINE FORKS, the *furculae Caudinae*, narrow passes in the mountains near Caudium in Samnium (possibly near Forchia) where the Samnites defeated the Romans in 321 B.C. *See* ROME: *Ancient History;* and E. T. Salmon in *J. Rom. Studies,* p. 12 ff. (1929).

CAUL, a close-fitting woman's cap, especially one made of network worn in the 16th and 17th centuries; hence, the serous membranous covering to the heart, brain or the intestines, and particularly, a portion of the amnion, or bag of waters, which is sometimes found remaining round the head of a child after birth. To this, called in Scotland "sely how," holy or lucky hood, many superstitions have been attached; it was looked on as a sign of good luck, and when preserved, was kept as a protection against drowning.

CAULAINCOURT, ARMAND AUGUSTIN LOUIS, MARQUIS DE (1773–1827), later DUKE OF VICENZA, was born on Dec. 9, 1773. His father was the friend of Josephine de Beauharnais and of Talleyrand and, after Thermidor, was able to help his son who had, as a noble, been deprived of his captaincy by the Revolution and was a cavalry sergeant in 1794. J. B. A. Aubert-Dubayet took him to Constantinople in 1796–97. Jean Bernadotte gave him a regiment in 1799, which he led at Hohenlinden. He was a good soldier, but Talleyrand chose him for the mission in 1801 to St. Petersburg, where he made a lasting impression on Alexander I. On return in 1802 he was made aide-de-camp to Napoleon. A mission against royalist agents in 1804 involved him in the arrest of the duc d'Enghien, but he always resented the charge that he had been an accomplice in the crime. Having been grand equerry in the great campaigns, he went as ambassador to Russia in Nov. 1807 and struggled to maintain the alliance. He was made duke of Vicenza in June 1808. Recalled almost in disgrace in 1811, he made, at Wilno (Vilnius) in 1812, a memorable protest against the invasion, when Napoleon called him a "Russian." Yet he was Napoleon's sole companion in the sledge journey from Smorgoni in December. In 1813 he signed the armistice of Pläswitz in June, was plenipotentiary at Prague in August and replaced H. B. Maret as minister of foreign affairs in November. He was Napoleon's "man of peace" and has been charged with betraying him in order to secure it. After the congress of Châtillon (February-March 1814) he returned to Napoleon, negotiated with the tsar, concluded the treaty of April 10, 1814, and was with Napoleon in the grim week which followed. Minister again in the Hundred Days, he was saved from proscription by Alexander's intervention. In retirement he tried to clear his name in the Enghien case. He died of cancer on Feb. 19, 1827.

See his *Mémoires,* ed. by J. Hanoteau, 3 vol. (Paris, 1933; Eng. trans., London, 1950). (I. D. E.)

CAULICULUS, in architecture, a form like a stalk, crowned with leaves, but which grow scrolls, leaves or other stalks; especially in the Corinthian capital, and in the branching scroll or *rinceau.*

CAULIFLOWER: *see* CABBAGE.

CAULONIA (Καυλωνία), an ancient Greek city in Italy, in the country of the Bruttii, on the east coast of Calabria. It was the southernmost Achaean colony, established perhaps in the first half of the 7th century B.C. as an outpost of Croton, with a founder from Achaea in the Peloponnese. It was always a small city, but its copious and beautiful archaic coinage (from the second half of the 6th century B.C.) shows its importance. It took the side of Athens in the Peloponnesian War. Destroyed by Dionysius of Syracuse in 389 B.C. but soon afterward restored, it was captured by Campanian troops during the invasion of Pyrrhus and stood a siege (209 B.C.) in Hannibal's interest. After this it declined, and Strabo speaks of it as deserted. Excavations have revealed remains of the fortifications with towers of the Hellenistic period. Near the shore scanty remains of a large Doric temple (first half of 5th century B.C.) were found, and a small temple must have stood near the lighthouse; copious architectural terra cottas, with elements derived from the Ionic order, are associated with both. The excavated houses belong to a late period. The tombs date from the 6th to the 3rd centuries B.C. but are poor.

See P. Orsi in *Monumenti dei Lincei,* xxiii (Rome, 1914), 685 *ff.,* and xxix (1924), 409 *ff.*

CAUSALITY or **CAUSATION.** The word "cause" is derived from the Latin *causa,* the standard translation of the Greek αἴτιον and αἰτία. By the time it came into English, in the 13th century, the word already had a wide range of uses, some of them highly sophisticated, since it was a key term in science, philosophy and the law.

Sense I: Human Agency.—Both *causa* and its Greek equivalents were used in legal contexts to refer to the voluntary action of an agent for which he could be held responsible. The responsible person is the person whose action could have been otherwise and but for whose action the event under investigation would not have occurred. One can already detect here the idea of the point of application of a remedy, an idea which, as we shall see, is an important element in later uses.

Divorced from its association with the law courts, the word "cause" is used for any action which an agent performs in order to bring about an event or state of affairs (the effect), whether in nature or in another agent. Thus a man can cause a statue to be unveiled by pressing a button or cause another man to do something by offering him a bribe. In this sense (sense I), to cause an event to occur is to perform an action with the expectation and intention that the event will follow. The words "produce" and "bring about" are synonyms of "cause" and can be used either of the agent or of his action. We also have a vast number of more specialized verbs such as "hit," "kick," "lift" and "move" which may be said to express causal ideas.

When one man causes another to do something, the second man is, under some circumstances, said to act, not "of his own free will," but "under compulsion" or "under constraint." To have power over someone is to be able to constrain, compel or oblige him to do something. We shall see that the idea of compelling, like that of producing, plays a part in later senses of "cause."

In ordinary life we are often concerned to produce, prevent or counteract events and states of affairs, but our actions are limited to the movements of our own bodies. I can move my own foot; I cannot, in the same sense, move a stone; but I can cause a stone to move by kicking it. To bring about any change in natural objects, it is necessary for us to know what action that we can perform will be followed by the desired change. Thus I cannot, of my own volition, heat water; but I can put a kettle on the fire, and I know that, if I do this in suitable circumstances, the water will be heated. It is often the case that the same change can be brought about by any of a number of alternative actions. Thus I can light a room either by pressing a switch or by drawing back the curtains or by striking a match. Each of these actions is called a "sufficient condition" of producing light; and since, in practice, it is usually required to know only that an action will be *sufficient,* not that it is *necessary,* to produce the effect, the word "cause" usually means sufficient condition. It is important to notice that, when we use "cause" in this way, the effect must be very broadly conceived. The sort of light produced by pressing a switch is very different from that produced by striking a match. The more narrowly the effect is specified the fewer will be the possible alternative sufficient conditions. Beheading, shooting through the heart and administering a dose of arsenic are all ways of causing death; but if the condition of the corpse is specified more narrowly than by the word "dead," a number of these possible causes will be excluded.

A cause, in this sense, must clearly be prior in time to its effect. It need not be contiguous in space and time; but since we know from our everyday experience that the transmission of movement from one body to another only occurs when the bodies are in contact, common sense always assumes that cause and effect are linked by a continuous substance. By igniting one end of a fuse I can cause an explosion to occur several minutes later and several yards away; but only if the fuse is unbroken.

Sense II: Causes in Nature.—By a natural transition the word "cause" is also used (sense II) for a natural event that stands in the same relation to some other event or state of affairs as the action stood in sense I. Thus the explosion that I caused (sense I) by lighting the fuse could have been caused (sense II) by some sparks from a locomotive. For a reason to be given later, the ideas of "producing" and "compelling" which belong naturally to "cause" in sense I were retained for "cause" in sense II. A cause (sense II) was thought to be, not merely the sufficient condition of its effect, but something which had the power to produce it.

A great part of our early education consists in the discovery of causes in these two senses. Thus, in order to achieve our most elementary aims, it is necessary for us to know that fire burns, that food nourishes and that bodily injury causes pain. The idea of cause has its roots in purposive activity and is employed in the first instance when we are concerned to produce or to prevent something. To discover the cause of something is to discover what has to be altered by our own activity in order to produce or to prevent that thing; but once the word "cause" comes to be applied to natural events, the notion of altering the course of events tends to be dropped. "Cause" is then used in a nonpractical, purely diagnostic way in cases where we have no interest in altering events or power to alter them. Thus we can speak of the cause of an eclipse or of an earthquake. The connecting link between the practical and the purely diagnostic uses is the idea of "sufficient condition." To discover the cause of an event is to discover something among its temporal antecedents such that, if it had not been present, the event would not have occurred.

Cause in the Practical Sciences.—The concept of cause is widely employed in the practical sciences, such as medicine and engineering. For in these sciences we are largely interested either in bringing about a certain state of affairs (*e.g.*, building a bridge) or in locating the sufficient condition of a state of affairs with a view to its removal (*e.g.*, discovering the cause of a disease or of the breakdown of a machine). The procedure of a practical scientist differs from that of an ordinary intelligent man only in that he needs to be more careful and accurate in his diagnosis of causes and in that he is assisted in his diagnosis by being able to draw on a large fund of theoretical science (*e.g.*, physiology or mechanics).

From this it has been concluded that all science is the search for causes. This conception has been popular with philosophers such as Francis Bacon and J. S. Mill, who regarded science primarily as a means of acquiring power over nature. But to conclude that the statements of theoretical science must be fundamentally causal in form is to make the error of introducing into theoretical science a concept which has its roots in practical activity and which always bears the mark of its origin. Causal explanations necessarily (from the meaning of the word) spotlight a particular event or state of affairs and explain it in terms of temporally prior sufficient conditions; but theoretical sciences are not limited to this mode of explanation and have in fact tended to discard it in favour of other modes. (*See* below, *Historical Development*.)

Sense III: Cause as Explanation.—The word "cause" has also a wider use (sense III) in which it is equivalent to "explanation," whether or not the explanation is causal in senses I or II. Thus the word "because" can be used to introduce any type of answer to a question beginning "Why?" In this sense a cause need not be an action or event, but may be a state of affairs, a trait of character or, indeed, anything such that, if it were not present, the effect would not occur. Thus a husband's jealousy might be the cause of the breakdown of a marriage and the weakness of a link in a chain the cause of the chain's breaking. In the latter case the weakness of the link is not thought to be the sole cause; for, in calling it the cause, we do not intend to imply that no other conditions were necessary. We know that many factors must be present in the antecedent other than that called "the cause"; for example, the weak link would not have broken if no strain had been put on it. For this reason Mill thought that the selection of one factor as cause from a total set of antecedents was arbitrary.

There is, however, always a reason for our choice. We single out, as cause, that factor which it is possible or convenient for us to alter in order to produce or to prevent the effect. The breaking point of a chain is a function both of the strength of its weakest link and of the load put on it; consequently we can prevent the weak link's breaking again either by replacing it by a stronger one or by refraining from subjecting it to such heavy loads. We select the weakness of the link or the weight of the load as cause according to the remedy which it is most desirable to apply. Similarly, mosquitoes are said to cause malaria, although, for malaria to occur, there must be human bodies as well as mosquitoes; but it would be impolitic to try to abolish malaria by eliminating the human race. In this sense of "cause" alternative explanations do not exclude each other; any number of them can be true, and the cause will be relative to the interests and abilities of the investigator.

Historical Development.—The connection between the three senses seems probably to lie in the historical fact that, when the serious investigation of nature began in the 6th century B.C., it was customary to couch all explanations of natural events in anthropomorphic terms. The pattern of explanation appropriate to human action, which already contained the idea of cause (sense I), was thought applicable to natural phenomena; and, this being so, it was inevitable that the idea of cause (sense II) should retain the anthropomorphic elements of producing and compelling. The idea that a cause (sense II) is an agent which has the power to produce its effect or to compel it to occur bedevilled philosophical and scientific accounts of causation until the matter was clarified by David Hume (*see* below, *Hume's Criticism*) in the 18th century.

Cause from Aristotle to Copernicus.—For Aristotle all science was the search for causes (*i.e.*, explanations). His "four causes," which provided the framework of explanation until the 16th century, were four general types of answer to the question, "Why is something what it is?" Two of these causes, the material and the formal, we should regard as pertaining to the description of a thing rather than to a causal explanation of it. The material cause is the matter or "potential" from which the thing is made; the formal cause is, literally, the shape or, metaphorically, the structure or organizing principle which distinguishes it from other bits of the same matter (*see* FORM). Thus the material cause of a statue is a piece of bronze, the formal cause its human shape. A mathematical formula, for example the equation of a circle in Cartesian geometry, would be a formal cause.

Aristotle's efficient and final causes, on the other hand, correspond more closely to our uses of "cause." The efficient cause is the agent (*e.g.*, the sculptor) who brings the thing into being or imposes the form on the matter; the final cause is the purpose for which the thing is produced. That the whole scheme is anthropomorphic is shown both by the presence of the idea of "producing" in efficient cause and also by the fact that the final cause was thought to be, in the last resort, the only complete and satisfactory explanation of why a thing is what it is. The underlying idea is that everything does what it does because it is trying to achieve its purpose. In particular, all motion is explained as being due to a thing's attempt to come to rest at its natural resting place.

Cause in Renaissance Science.—In the period from Copernicus to Sir Isaac Newton the concept of causation underwent a change that may be described as the progressive elimination of the anthropomorphic elements in the Aristotelian conception. Two main strands can be detected in this change: (1) the attempt to refine the concept of cause (sense II) in such a way as to make it suitable for the purposes of theoretical science (*see* below, *The Refined Concept*); and (2) the transition from explanations in terms of efficient causes to explanations in terms of law.

Although the Aristotelian conception of explanation dominated the middle ages, a minority of mathematically minded scientists continued to follow the tradition of Pythagoras and Plato. According to this tradition, to explain a phenomenon is to discover the laws which it obeys. The astronomer Ptolemy, in the 2nd century A.D., maintained that it was legitimate to interpret the facts of planetary motion by means of any mathematical scheme which would "save the phenomena"; and Copernicus' heliocentric theory was accepted in the first instance, not because it was experimentally verified, but because it saved the phenomena with greater mathematical elegance than did its rivals. The 15th and 16th centuries witnessed a great revival of Platonism; Johann Kepler equated "causes" with "reasons" and regarded the cause of planetary motion as a set of laws from which the observed movements of the planets can be deduced. This view introduces the idea of necessity into that of causation, first in an anthropomorphic sense as the necessity by which objects are compelled to obey God's laws and secondly as the logical necessity which relates premisses to conclusions.

The transition from explanations in terms of efficient causes to explanations in terms of law was largely the work of Galileo. From the point of view of an analysis of causation the importance of his work is threefold. In the first place, he undermined Aristotelian explanations of why things move as they do by showing in a series of experiments that they do not move in the ways which the explanations presuppose. This discredited the whole enterprise of explaining phenomena in terms of final causes and thereby opened the way for other types of explanation. Secondly, the substitution of exact description for explanation (or, as it is sometimes put, of the question "How?" for the question "Why?") led eventually to a conception of science in which all explanation just *is* description. A phenomenon is now said to be explained when the regularity which it exemplifies is able to be incorporated into a system of laws, for example, by being shown to be a logical consequence of those laws. In this way Kepler's laws of planetary motion, which are compendious ways of describing the movements of the known planets, are said to be explained when they are shown to follow from Newton's general laws of motion when constants are substituted for the variables in Newton's laws. Thirdly, Galileo and his contemporaries limited their descriptions to those aspects of phenomena that can be measured, and the spectacular success of physics resulted in its being taken as a model for all the theoretical sciences. Hence scientific explanation came to be thought of as the discovery of functional correlations between variables, a conception from which the idea of efficient cause has disappeared.

Cause in Newton's Philosophy.—The full implications of this revolution in theoretical science were not, however, appreciated at the time. In Newtonian physics, the concept of efficient cause, with its attendant idea of "production" and the contrast between "caused" and "free," still survives as an anomalous element. In the first law of motion, "free motion" is said to be uniform motion in a straight line, and forces are introduced as the causes of deviation from free motion. All observed motions can be analyzed into two components, a free component (inertia) and a component due to a force acting. The second law states that the force acting on a body is always proportional to the product of its mass and acceleration; but Newton never regarded the word "force" just as a name for this product. As a natural scientist he eschewed speculation into the nature of forces, thinking it sufficient for scientific purposes that we should be able to calculate and observe their effects. But he always regarded a force as an unknown somewhat which is the efficient cause of observed motion.

In a modern statement of Newtonian mechanics this conception of forces as efficient causes disappears, what remains being a set of differential equations correlating the total state of an isolated system at any one time with its total state at any other time. An example will help to make this clear. Consider a moving billiard ball striking another which is at rest. From the point of view of common sense the movement of the first ball up to the moment of impact is one event (the cause) and the movements of the two balls after impact is another, complex event (the effect). From the standpoint of classical mechanics, however, the system is not divided into two events. It is considered as a single system in which there is at every time the same quantity of momentum. From the equations of motion of the system together with a specification of the position and velocity of each body in it at any given time, we can calculate (if we disregard disturbing factors such as friction) the position and velocity of each body in the system at any other time. Since the laws of mechanics are reversible in respect of time, the division of the system into an earlier and a later phase is irrelevant.

These two explanations do not conflict with one another and it would be a mistake to say that, if the explanation furnished by classical mechanics is true, the common sense explanation must be false. The concept of cause reappears naturally in any practical or diagnostic application of the laws of mechanics. For, if I want to impart a given velocity to the second ball, the laws of mechanics enable me to calculate the momentum that must be introduced into the system by the movement of my arm. Similarly, if I want to explain why the second ball moved as it did, I can calculate by means of the laws of mechanics the velocity with which a ball of known mass must have struck it.

The Refined Concept of Cause.—We must now return to the attempt to refine the concept of cause (sense II) for the purposes of theoretical science. It is this attempt that gives rise to most of the traditional philosophical problems about causation. These problems are mainly due (1) to a confusion between cause in sense II and cause in sense III whereby some philosophers have been led to suppose that all explanations of natural phenomena must be causal in sense II; and (2) to the retention of the elements of "producing" and "compelling" from sense I. Hobbes defined a cause as "the aggregate of all the accidents both of the agents how many so ever they be, and of the patient, put together; which when they are all supposed to be present, it cannot be understood but that the effect is produced at the same instant: and if any one of them be wanting, it cannot be understood but that the effect is not produced." The word "accident" is here used in a technical sense in which it is roughly equivalent to "quality."

This concept of cause resembles the unrefined concept (sense II) in that causal statements are made in qualitative, not quantitative, terms and in that it retains the idea of "producing." It differs, however, from the unrefined concept in many important ways. The causal relation is said to be logically necessary: the cause is a necessary as well as a sufficient condition of the effect, and cause and effect are contemporaneous. These ill-assorted elements cannot in fact be comprised within a single concept and it is not difficult to deduce absurdities from a concept so composed.

We have already seen that a cause in sense II is necessarily prior to its effect in time and that it is one element singled out from the total antecedent of the effect, the selection being relative to the interests and abilities of the investigator. We have also seen that the effect had to be more or less vaguely specified. In the refined concept both cause and effect must be precisely specified and the cause is the total necessary and sufficient condition. It now follows that cause and effect must be instantaneous events and must be contemporaneous with each other. For, if the cause has duration, however short, it cannot in its earlier phases be sufficient to produce its effect, since the effect does not occur. The total antecedent only becomes sufficient at the instant the effect occurs: at any prior time the supposed cause is not sufficient to produce the effect, and it follows that cause and effect must be contemporaneous. If this is so, the cause of the cause must be contemporaneous with it; so all causes and effects will be contemporaneous.

From argument such as this some philosophers have tried to prove the unreality of time and change; but all such arguments are illegitimate in that they depend on employing a concept of cause that contains self-contradictory elements. We cannot employ both the idea of producing and the idea of a total set of necessary and sufficient conditions in the same concept, since the idea of producing is essentially that of an action which, supervening on a given set of conditions, is followed by an event which would not have occurred if the action had not supervened, while the idea of a total set of necessary and sufficient conditions requires cause and effect to be contemporaneous.

Hume's Criticism of the Concept of Cause.—The full implications of the revolution in physics outlined above were first appreciated by David Hume, who showed in the first place that the relation of cause and effect is neither logically necessary nor observable in a single instance. It is not logically necessary since we can conceive of an event's being preceded by any other event whatsoever, and what we can conceive could (logically) occur. If in fact an event of a certain type is always preceded by the same other type of event, we only know this from experience.

Equally, the relation is not observable in a single instance since all that we observe in an instance is a succession of events; we do not observe in the earlier event that "power" or "agency" which is essential to the concept of cause. And if we cannot observe this in a single instance we cannot observe it in any number of instances. Nevertheless, Hume knew that when we call something a cause we intend to assert more than temporal priority and contiguity in time and place. The third element, which he called "necessary connection," had been thought to lie in the "efficacy" or "productive power" of the cause. But Hume saw that, divorced from their associations with human action, words such as "efficacy," "agency," "power" and "production" are mere synonyms for the necessary connection that they are supposed to explain. Finally Hume came to the view that for an assertion of causality we require, besides contiguity and succession, only that the succession should have been repeated many times without any contrary instance; and he held that the idea of necessary connection was the determination of the mind to pass from the idea of the cause to that of the effect. An assertion of cause is an expression of confident expectation based on habit.

As a contribution to the problem of induction Hume's analysis was of the greatest importance; but as an explanation of the idea of necessary connection it seems inadequate. Hume failed to notice that this idea is really that of logical necessity transported from its proper place in a deductive system to an improper place in causal (sense II) explanations. When we say that the planets "must" move as they do, we do not mean that they are compelled to do so by efficient causes; we mean that the description of their observed motions follows logically from the laws of motion that we have adopted. The planets must move as they do, *if* Newton's laws are true and if the observations from which their movements are predicted were correct.

Following Hume, J. S. Mill defined the cause of a phenomenon as "the antecedent or concurrence of antecedents on which it is invariably and unconditionally consequent." The word "unconditionally" reintroduces the confusions inherent in the refined concept of cause. Since Mill was mainly interested in the social sciences, his theory represents a trend away from explanations in terms of mathematically formulated laws toward the older view of causation as a relation between events qualitatively described. His canons of induction require the analysis of complex events into factors and the discovery, by observation and experiment, of those factors which are invariably and unconditionally present when a certain phenomenon occurs and absent when it does not occur. Such an analysis, however, cannot be exhaustive without introducing the absurdities involved in the concept of an unconditional cause. Mill's canons of induction are useful in ordinary life and in the practical sciences, in fact wherever we are operating with the concept of cause (sense II) and do not attempt to refine it by requiring the cause to be necessary, sufficient and unconditional.

The Present State of the Question.—The notion of efficient cause survives in our ordinary language in such words as "produce," "bring about," "make," "due to," "result of" and "consequence of" and in the host of more specialized causal verbs. When the subject of these verbs is an inanimate thing the anthropomorphic element is a mere linguistic survival and does not (for most people) express anything present in thought: the cause is simply thought of as a sufficient condition discovered to be sufficient by experience. In ordinary life we are not troubled by the logical problem of induction; that is to say, we do not stop to ask why the fact that a succession of events has been observed to occur many times should justify our expectation that it will occur again. The examination of this problem is beyond the scope of this article. (*See* INDUCTION.)

In the sciences, explanations are mostly of the type known as "hypothetico-deductive," according to which observation suggests a generalization or law from which consequences can be deduced. The consequences can then be verified or falsified by controlled experiment or, where this is impossible, by observation. In the theoretical sciences, generalizations and laws usually take the form of functional correlations between variables, and the idea of efficient cause does not appear. Any set of laws which saves the phenomena is considered legitimate; but since a given set of phenomena can be saved by any of an infinite number of alternative sets of laws it is necessary to provide criteria for choosing one set rather than another. The usual criteria are mathematical simplicity (which is largely a matter of taste), comprehensiveness and predictive fruitfulness. The concept of efficient cause still appears within this framework in those sciences which depend largely on qualitative analysis and, especially, in the practical sciences.

BIBLIOGRAPHY.—D. Hume, *Treatise of Human Nature,* book i (London, 1739); J. S. Mill, *System of Logic,* book iii (London, 1843; 9th rev. ed., 1875); K. Pearson, *Grammar of Science* (London, 1911); Bertrand Russell, *Mysticism and Logic* (London, New York, 1918); E. A. Burtt, *Metaphysical Foundations of Modern Physical Science* (London, New York, 1925); R. G. Collingwood, *Essay on Metaphysics* (Oxford, New York, 1940); V. F. Lenzen, *Causality in Natural Science* (Springfield, 1953; Oxford, 1954). (P. H. N.-S.)

CAUSE AND EFFECT: *see* CAUSALITY OR CAUSATION.

CAUSEWAY. A path on a raised dam or mound across marshes or low-lying ground; the word is also used of old paved highways, such as the Roman military roads. "Causey" is still used dialectically in England for a paved or cobbled footpath. The word is properly "causey-way," from *causey,* a mound or dam which is derived, through the Norman-French *caucie* (*cf.* modern *chaussée*), from the late Latin *via calciata,* a road stamped firm with the feet (*calcare,* to tread).

CAUSSES, a natural region in the south of the central plateau of France, chiefly in the departments of Lozère and Aveyron, west of the curving Cevennes and south of the Lot valley. This vast plateau of Jurassic limestone, sloping westward, is divided into several sections by deep-cut river channels. These smaller plateaus, barren and deserted, are called the *Causses* from *cau,* the local form of the French *chaux* (*i.e.,* lime). The most typical is the Causse Méjan, south of the Tarn between Florac and Millau, a sterile sparsely peopled tableland lying between 3,000 and 4,000 ft. above sea level. To the north lies the Causse de Sauveterre prolonged westward by the Causse de Sévérac. Those of Quercy, Gramat and Rouergue are lower and less arid. Drainage features such as underground streams, fissures and potholes (*avens*) are characteristic. The inhabitants (Caussenards) cultivate rye and potatoes where possible but subsist for the most part on the sheep from whose milk Roquefort cheese is made. Similar dry limestone areas elsewhere are designated under the cognate German *Karst* or Italian *Carso* (*qq.v.*).

CAUSSIN DE PERCEVAL, ARMAND PIERRE (1795–1871), French orientalist, was born in Paris and died there during the siege.

After extended travels in Asia Minor, he succeeded his father Jean Jacques (1759–1835) as professor of Arabic at the Collège de France.

His works include a useful *Grammaire arabe vulgaire* (4th ed., 1858), and an enlarged edition of Élie Bocthor's *Dictionnaire français-arabe* (3rd ed., 1864); but his great reputation rests on his *Essai sur l'histoire des Arabes avant l'Islamisme, pendant l'époque de Mahomet,* 3 vol. (1847–49), in which the native traditions as to the early history of the Arabs, down to the death of Mohammed and the complete subjection of all the tribes to Islam, are set forth with much learning and lucidity.

CAUSTIC. That which burns (Gr. καυστικός, burning). In *surgery,* the term given to substances which destroy living tissues and so inhibit the action of organic poisons, as in bites, malignant disease and gangrenous processes. Such caustic substances include silver nitrate (lunar caustic), potassium and sodium hydrates (the caustic alkalis) (*see* ALKALI), zinc chloride, an acid solution of mercuric nitrate, and pure carbolic acid (phenol).

In *mathematics,* the "caustic surfaces" of a given surface are the envelopes of the normals to the surface, or the loci of its centres of curvature.

In *optics* (geometrical optics) the term "caustic" is applied to the envelope of luminous rays after reflection or refraction. In the first case the envelope is termed a cata-caustic, in the second a dia-caustic. Cata-caustics are to be observed as bright curves when light is allowed to fall on a polished cylindrical surface as a napkin ring or a curved polished riband of steel placed on a table. By varying the curvature of the riband of steel or moving the source of light a variety of patterns can be obtained. The investigation of caustics, based as it is on the assumption of the law of the rectilinear propagation of light and the validity of the experimental laws of reflection and refraction, is essentially of a geometrical nature, and as such attracted the attention of mathematicians of the 17th and succeeding centuries, more notably John Bernoulli, G. F. de l'Hopital, E. W. Tschirnhausen and Louis Carre.

See Arthur Cayley, *Memoirs on Caustics* in Phil. Trans. for 1857 and 1867.

CAUSTIC SODA (sodium hydroxide, NaOH) is a solid, white, deliquescent chemical compound much used as an intermediate material in the production of many chemicals. It is generally made by one of two methods, either through exchange of base by the causticizing of soda-ash (Na_2CO_3) with hydrated lime or directly, through the action of an electric current upon a solution of common salt (NaCl). The latter newer process is tending to supersede the former, especially where cheap electric power is available or where a ready market for chlorine and hydrogen, by-products of the electrolytic process, exists. Because of its large production, caustic soda is classed as a "heavy chemical." It is used as an alkaline reagent, in the manufacture of soap, sodium salts, rayon, paper, medicines, textile products, in petroleum and vegetable oil refining, in tanning and in the synthesis of many organic compounds such as indigo, alizarin, resorcin, formates and oxalates.

CAUTERETS, a watering place of southwestern France in the department of Hautes-Pyrénées, 20 mi. S.W. of Lourdes by rail. Pop. (1946) 1,012. It lies in the beautiful valley of the Gave de Cauterets, and is well known for its thermal springs, and as a station for winter sports. About 50,000 visitors are attracted annually. The 22 springs produce copious supplies of sulphuretted water and serve nine *établissements*. Their temperature varies between 75° and 137°. Cauterets is a centre for excursions, the Monné (8,937 ft.), the Cabaliros (7,651 ft.), the Pic de Chabarrou (9,550 ft.), the Vignemale (10,820 ft.), and other summits being in its neighbourhood. The properties of the waters have been known at least since the 10th century. They became famous in the 16th century when Marguerite de Valois composed the "Heptameron," on the model of Boccaccio's "Decameron," while visiting the spa with her court.

CAUTÍN, a province of southern Chile, bounded north by Malleco and Arauco, east by Argentina, south by Valdivia, and west by the Pacific. Area 6,707 sq.mi.; pop. (1952 census) 365,072, including many European immigrants, principally Germans. Cautín lies within the temperate rain forest region of the south, its chief products are timber, cattle, grain and apples. The state railway from Santiago to Puerto Montt crosses the province from north to south; branch lines to such places as Cherquenco, Cunco, Tolten and Carahue provide good rail service to most parts of the province. Two partially navigable rivers cross the province from east to west, the Tolten and the Cautín, the lower reaches of the latter being known as the Río Imperial. The province once formed part of the territory occupied by the Araucanian Indians, and Temuco, the capital of the province, long remained the centre of greatest concentration of these people. Temuco, a city of 51,497 inhabitants in 1952, is on the Río Cautín. It is an important rail centre, market town, and gateway to the famous lake district of south Chile.

CAUTLEY, SIR PROBY THOMAS (1802–1871), English engineer and palaeontologist, was born in Suffolk in 1802. After several years' service in the Bengal artillery, which he joined in 1819, he was engaged on the reconstruction of the Doab canal. He had charge of the completed canal for 12 years (1831–43). In 1840 he reported on the proposed Ganges canal, for the irrigation of the country between the rivers Ganges, Hindan, and Jumna. This project was sanctioned in 1841, but work was not begun until 1843, and even then Cautley found himself hampered in its execution by the opposition of Lord Ellenborough. For want of competent help he had to do the drudgery of surveying and levelling himself, for some time. From 1845 to 1848 he was in England because of ill-health, and on his return to India he was appointed director of canals in the North-West Frontier Province. After the Ganges canal was opened in 1854 he spent some time in England, and from 1858 to 1868 he occupied a seat on the council of India. He died at Sydenham, near London, on Jan. 25, 1871. Cautley was a distinguished palaeontologist and contributed numerous memoirs, some written in collaboration with Hugh Falconer, to the *Proceedings* of the Bengal Asiatic society and the Geological Society of London on the geology and fossil remains of the Sivalik hills.

CAUVERY (Kaveri), a river of southern India. Rising in Coorg, high amid the Western Ghats, in 12° 25′ N. lat. and 75° 34′ E. long., it flows generally southeast across the plateau of Mysore, and finally enters the Bay of Bengal through two principal mouths in Tanjore district. Its length is 472 mi. Its course in Coorg is tortuous, and its bed generally rocky with high banks covered with luxuriant vegetation. On entering Mysore it passes through a narrow gorge, then widens to a breadth of 300 to 400 yd. The bed is too rocky for navigation. In its course through Mysore the channel is interrupted by a number of anicuts or dams for irrigation. In Mysore the Cauvery forms the two islands of Seringapatam and Sivasamudram, which vie in sanctity with Srirangam Island lower down in Trichinopoly district. Around Sivasamudram Island are the celebrated falls of the Cauvery, where the river branches into two channels, each making a descent of about 320 ft. After entering Madras state, the Cauvery forms the boundary between the Coimbatore and Salem districts, until it reaches Trichinopoly district. Sweeping past the historic rock of Trichinopoly, it again breaks at Srirangam Island into two channels, which enclose between them the delta of Tanjore, the garden of southern India. The northern and larger channel is called the Coleroon (Kolidam). On the seaward side of the delta are the open roadsteads of Negapatam and Karikal. The only navigation on any part of its course is carried on in basket-work boats.

There is an extensive irrigation system in the delta. The Grand anicut (or weir), built in the 2nd century where the Cauvery divides into two channels, feeds the deltaic irrigation system of Tanjore. A second anicut across the Coleroon (1836–38) was necessary to save the old system from the disaster of silting, but it also added to the irrigated area. The Mettur project, a dam and canal more than 200 mi. from the sea, was completed in 1938. It improved the water supply to more than 1,000,000 ac. already irrigated, added another 300,000 ac. and provided 50,000 kw. of electric power, thus creating an important industrial area. The Cauvery falls, under an older power scheme, provide electricity to Mysore and Bangalore and the Kolar gold mines.

The Cauvery is known to devout Hindus as Dakshini Ganga, or the Ganges of the south, and its entire course is holy ground. (T. Her)

CAVA DEI TIRRENI, a town and episcopal see of Campania, Italy, in the province of Salerno, 6 mi. N.W. by rail from the town of Salerno. Pop. (1951), commune, 39,086. It lies fairly high in a richly cultivated valley, surrounded by wooded hills, and is a favourite resort. A mile to the southwest is the village of Corpo di Cava (1,970 ft.), with the Benedictine abbey of La Trinità della Cava, founded in 1025 by St. Alferius. The church and the greater part of the buildings were entirely modernized in 1796. The old Gothic cloisters are preserved. The archives, now national property, include documents and manuscripts of great value.

M. Morcaldi, *Codex Diplomaticus Cavensis* (1873–93) published many important documents relating to the abbey.

CAVAEDIUM, in architecture, a synonym for atrium (*q.v.*), the central hall or court of a Roman house. Vitruvius lists five types: (1) The Tuscanicum. This, the most common type, was without columns, the hole in the roof being supported by the framing of the roof timbers. (2) The Tetrastylon, in which four columns supported the roof at the corners of its opening. (3) The Corinthian, in which more than four columns are employed, so that the cavaedium becomes, in essence, a peristyle (*q.v.*). (4) The Displuviatum, where the roof sloped down, away from the opening, instead of toward it. (5) The Testudinatum, in which the entire area was covered by a continuous roof.

CAVAGNARI, SIR PIERRE LOUIS NAPOLEON (1841–1879), British military administrator, the son of a French general by his marriage with an Irish lady, was born at Stenay,

Meuse, on July 4, 1841. He obtained naturalization as an Englishman, and entered the military service of the East India Company. He served through the Oudh campaign against the mutineers in 1858 and 1859. In 1861 he was appointed an assistant commissioner in the Punjab, and in 1877 became deputy commissioner of Peshawar and took part in several expeditions against the hill tribes. In 1878 he was attached to the staff of the British mission to Kabul, which the Afghans refused to allow to proceed. In May 1879, after the death of the amir Shere Ali, Cavagnari negotiated and signed the treaty of Gandamak with his successor, Yakub Khan. By this the Afghans agreed to admit a British resident at Kabul, and Cavagnari was appointed. He took up his residence in July, and for a time all seemed to go well, but on Sept. 3 Cavagnari and the other European members of the mission were massacred in a sudden rising of mutinous Afghan troops. (*See* AFGHANISTAN.)

CAVAIGNAC, LOUIS EUGÈNE (1802–1857), French general, born in Paris on Oct. 15, 1802, belonged to a family famous in French revolutionary annals. He was the son of JEAN-BAPTISTE CAVAIGNAC (1762–1829), who was a member of the Convention, and acted as its commissioner in the repression of the opponents of the Revolution in various parts of France. At the Restoration he was proscribed as a regicide. Jean-Baptiste's brother, JACQUES MARIE, VICOMTE CAVAIGNAC (1773–1855), was one of Napoleon's generals and commanded the cavalry of the 11th Corps in the retreat from Moscow (1812). GODEFROY CAVAIGNAC (1801–1845), elder brother of Louis Eugène, took part in the Parisian risings of Oct. 1830, 1832 and 1834, and was one of the founders of the Société des Droits de l'Homme. Very highly esteemed for his chivalrous character among the republicans, he was probably personally both the most estimable and able of the old guard of republicans. His reputation was largely, if not wholly, responsible later for the advancement of Louis Eugène, who entered the army.

In 1831 Louis Eugène was removed from active duty in consequence of his declared republicanism, but in 1832 he was recalled to the service and sent to Algeria, where he held a series of commands during the next 16 years. In 1848, the revolutionary Government promoted him governor-general. He refused the post of minister of war because the Government would not fall in with his plan to occupy Paris by troops. Like L. A. Thiers, Cavaignac conceived the idea of drawing the "red republicans" of Paris out into open insurrection, in order that they might be crushed and the domination of the moderates secured. After the National Assembly had eliminated the Socialist members Louis Blanc and Albert (*qq.v.*) from the Government, Cavaignac was made minister of war. The revolt on which he had calculated broke out on June 22, 1848 (*see* NATIONAL WORKSHOPS). Cavaignac withdrew his troops from the affected parts of Paris, till, in his opinion, the revolt had gained sufficient head. He took advantage of the general panic, further, to insist on the resignation of the Government and the granting of dictatorial powers to himself, which was agreed on June 25. His attack on the Parisian rebels, who were exclusively working class, led to the bloodiest and most obstinate conflict that had up till then occurred in Paris; at its end, in his victory on the 26th, Cavaignac permitted, in accordance with his plan, the severest reprisals which decimated the ranks of the Socialists and broke their power.

Both he and his adversaries expected that after laying down his dictatorship he would be elected president. But they had not allowed for the magic of the name of "Louis Napoleon Bonaparte"; a "landslide" of peasant and proletarian votes gave 5,434,226 to the future Napoleon III. and only 1,448,107 to Cavaignac. The disappointed general went into opposition and at the time of the *coup d'état* (Dec. 2, 1851) was even imprisoned for a short while. After his release he abandoned politics and died in retirement on Oct. 28, 1857.

See Louis Menard, *Prologue d'une Révolution* (reprinted 1904); Ch. Schmidt, *Les Journées de juin 1848* (1926); P. de la Gorce, *Histoire de la 2de République* (1914); G. Renard, *La République de 1848* (1900–8); R. W. Postgate, *Revolution from 1789 to 1906* (1920, full bibliog.).

His son, JACQUES MARIE EUGÈNE GODEFROI CAVAIGNAC (1853–1905), French politician, was born in Paris on May 21, 1853. He served as a civil engineer in Angoulême until 1881, when he became master of requests in the Council of State. In 1882 he was elected deputy for Saint-Calais (Sarthe) in the republican interest. In 1885–86 he was under-secretary for war in the Henri Brisson Ministry, and he served in the cabinet of Émile Loubet (1892) as minister of marine and of the colonies. He had exchanged his moderate republicanism for radical views before he became war minister in the cabinet of Léon Bourgeois (1895–96). He was again minister of war in the Brisson cabinet in July 1898, when he read in the chamber a document which definitely incriminated Capt. Alfred Dreyfus. On Aug. 30, however, he stated that this had been discovered to be a forgery by Col. Henry, but he refused to concur with his colleagues in a revision of the Dreyfus prosecution, which was the logical outcome of his own exposure of the forgery. Resigning his portfolio, he joined the Nationalist group in the chamber, and became an energetic supporter of the Ligue de la Patrie Française. In 1899 Cavaignac was an unsuccessful candidate for the presidency of the republic. He died at his country-seat near Flée (Sarthe) on Sept. 25, 1905. He wrote an important book on the *Formation de la Prusse contemporaine* (1891–98), dealing with the events of 1806–13.

See J. M. Cavaignac, *Les deux généraux Cavaignac* (1897); A. Deschamps, *Les deux généraux Cavaignac* (1898); W. Arnoulim, *L'Action clericale en France, Les Cavaignacs devant l'histoire* (1905).

CAVAILLON, a town of south-eastern France in the department of Vaucluse, 20 mi. S.E. of Avignon. Pop. (1936), 8,452. It lies at the southern foot of Mount St. Jacques on the right bank of the Durance above its confluence with the Coulon. To the south of the present town lay the Roman *Cabellio,* a place of some note in territory of the Cavares. Since mediaeval times the town has for the most part followed the fortunes of the Comtat Venaissin, in which it was included. Till the Revolution it was the see of a bishop, and had a large number of monastic establishments. The church of St. Véran is a fine example of 12th century Provençal architecture, with a cloister adjoining. The town is the centre of a rich and well-irrigated plain, which produces fruits and early vegetables. Silk-worms are reared, and silk is an important article of trade. The preparation of preserved vegetables and fruits, distilling and the manufacture of straw hats and leather are carried on.

CAVALCANTI, GUIDO (*c.* 1250–1300), Italian poet and philosopher, was the son of a philosopher whom Dante, in the *Inferno*, condemns to torment among the epicureans and atheists; but he himself was a friend of the poet. By marriage with Beatrice, daughter of Farinata Uberti, he became head of the Ghibellines. He was banished to Sarzana, where he caught a fever, of which he died. Cavalcanti has left a number of love sonnets and canzoni, in honor of a French lady, whom he calls Mandetta. His complete poetical works are contained in Giunti's collection (Florence, 1527; Venice, 1531–32).

The most famous of his sonnets and canzoni are translated by D. G. Rossetti in his *Dante and his Circle* (1874).

CAVALCASELLE, GIOVANNI BATTISTA (1820–1897), Italian writer on art, was born at Legnago on Jan. 22, 1820. He became a student at the Academia delle Belle Arti in Venice, and from early youth studied the art treasures of Italy. His relations sent him to Padua, hoping that he might become an engineer, but in 1844 he returned to his artistic studies. He visited the cities of Tuscany, and then set out to see the masterpieces of Italian art in foreign countries. During a stay in Germany in 1846 and 1847 he made the acquaintance of Joseph Archer Crowe in a post carriage between Hamm and Minden. The two young men felt drawn to each other and met again in Berlin, where they studied together some pictures in the museum. On his return to Venice Cavalcaselle took an active part in the revolution of 1848 against the Austrian rule. He was arrested by Austrian gendarmes and narrowly escaped being shot. He then joined the forces of Garibaldi and was taken prisoner by the French in 1849. He arrived in a miserable plight in Paris, where by good fortune he again met Crowe, and with his help came to

London. The two friends occupied rooms together and worked on a history of early Flemish painters, published in 1857. In the same year Cavalcaselle returned to Italy. In 1864 Crowe and Cavalcaselle published their great work, *New History of Italian Painting,* which was followed by the *History of Painting in North Italy.* Other joint works were *Titian* (1876) and *Raphael* (1883). Cavalcaselle's independent writings are of less importance: *Sul più autentico ritratto di Dante* (1865); *Sulla conservazione dei Monumenti ed oggetti di belle arti; Sulle riforme dell' insegnamento academico* (1875).

Cavalcaselle was for some time secretary to the great art critic and collector, Giovanni Morelli, and his travelling companion when Morelli compiled the inventory of the works of art in the Marca d'Ancona for the Italian Government. Towards the end of his life Cavalcaselle held office as ispettore di belle arti in the Ministry of Education in Rome. He died on Oct. 31, 1897.

Crowe and Cavalcaselle's histories of Italian art are standard works, and have recently been re-edited by Langton Douglas and Tancred Borenius.

CAVALIER, JEAN (1681–1740), the famous chief of the Camisards (*q.v.*), was born at Mas Roux, near Anduze (Gard), on Nov. 28, 1681. His father, an illiterate peasant, had been compelled by persecution to become a Roman Catholic along with his family, but his mother brought him up secretly in the Protestant faith. Threatened with prosecution for his religious opinions he went to Geneva, where he passed the year 1701; he returned to the Cévennes on the eve of the rebellion of the Camisards, who by the murder of the Abbé du Chayla at Pont-de-Monvert on the night of July 24, 1702, raised the standard of revolt. Some months later he became their leader. He showed an extraordinary genius for war. Within a period of two years he was to hold in check Count Maurice de Broglie and Marshal Montrevel, and to carry on one of the most terrible partisan wars in French history.

He maintained the most severe discipline. Each battle increased the terror of his name. On Christmas day, 1702, he dared to hold a religious assembly at the very gates of Alais, and put to flight the local militia which came forth to attack him. At Vagnas, on Feb. 10, 1703, he routed the royal troops, but, defeated in his turn, he was compelled to find safety in flight. But he reappeared, was again defeated at Tour de Bellot (April 30), and again recovered himself, recruits flocking to him to fill up the places of the slain. Cavalier boldly carried the war into the plain, made terrible reprisals, and threatened even Nîmes itself. On April 16, 1704, he encountered Marshal Montrevel himself at the bridge of Nages, with 1,000 men against 5,000, and, though defeated after a desperate conflict, he made a successful retreat. Cavalier was induced to attend a conference at Pont d'Avène near Alais on May 11, 1704, and on May 16, he made submission at Nîmes. Louis XIV. gave him a commission as colonel, which Villars presented to him personally, and a pension of 1,200 livres. At the same time the king authorized the formation of a Camisard regiment for service in Spain under his command.

Before leaving the Cévennes for the last time he went to Alais and to Ribaute, followed by an immense concourse of people. But Cavalier had not been able to obtain liberty of conscience, and his Camisards almost to a man broke forth in wrath against him, reproaching him for what they described as his treacherous desertion. On June 21, 1704, with a hundred Camisards who were still faithful to him, he departed from Nîmes and came to Neu-Brisach (Alsace), where he was to be quartered. From Dijon he went on to Paris, where Louis XIV. gave him audience and heard his explanation of the revolt of the Cévennes. Returning to Dijon, fearing to be imprisoned in the fortress of Neu-Brisach, he escaped with his troop near Montbéliard and took refuge at Lausanne. But he was too much of a soldier to abandon the career of arms. He offered his services to the duke of Savoy, and with his Camisards made war in the Val d'Aosta. After the peace he crossed to England, where he formed a regiment of refugees which took part in the Spanish expedition under the earl of Peterborough and Sir Cloudesley Shovel in May, 1705. At the battle of Almansa the Camisards found themselves opposed to a French regiment, and without firing the two bodies rushed one upon the other. "I fought," Cavalier wrote on July 10, "as long as a man stood beside me and until numbers overpowered me, losing also an immense quantity of blood from a dozen wounds which I received." Marshal Berwick never spoke of this tragic event without visible emotion.

On his return to England a small pension was given him. He settled at Dublin, where he published *Memoirs of the Wars of the Cévennes under Col. Cavalier,* written in French and translated into English with a dedication to Lord Carteret (1726). He was made general on Oct. 27, 1735, and on May 25, 1738, was appointed lieutenant-governor of Jersey. He was promoted major-general in July, 1739, and died in the following year.

See N. A. F. Puaux, *Vie de Jean Cavalier* (1868); David C. A. Agnew, *Protestant Exiles from France,* ii. 54–66 (1871); Charvey, *Jean Cavalier: nouveaux documents inédits* (1884). Eugène Sue popularized the name of the Camisard chief in *Jean Cavalier ou les fanatiques des Cévennes* (1840). A new edition of Cavalier's *Mémoires sur la guerre des Cévennes* was published by F. Puaux in 1918.

CAVALIER, a horseman, particularly a horse-soldier or one of gentle birth, trained in knightly exercises. The word is taken through the French from the Late Lat. *caballarius,* a horseman. *Chevalier,* the French word of parallel descent, means "knight," and is chiefly used in English for a member of certain foreign military or other orders, particularly of the Legion of Honour. Cavalier in English was early applied in a contemptuous sense to an overbearing swashbuckler. Originally used as a term of reproach, it was soon adopted as a title of honour by the supporters of Charles I. in the Great Rebellion, who applied Roundhead to their opponents, and at the Restoration the court party preserved the name, which survived till the rise of the term Tory (*see* WHIG AND TORY). The term "cavalier," in fortification, means a work of great command constructed in the interior of a fort, bastion or other defence, so as to fire over the main parapet without interfering with its firing. A greater volume of fire can thus be obtained, but the great height of the cavalier makes it an easy target for a besieger's guns.

CAVALIERI, BONAVENTURA (1598–1647), Italian mathematician, was born at Milan; his name also occurs in the forms Cavallieri, Cavaglieri, Cavalerius, and de Cavalerüs. He became a Jesuit at an early age and later was inspired to study mathematics by reading a copy of Euclid. On the recommendation of his Order he was made a professor at Bologna in 1629; the post, which he held until he died, was renewed periodically. In 1635 Cavalieri wrote *Geometria indivisibilium continuorum nova quadam ratione promota,* in which he first stated his principle of indivisibles. The form of the principle was unsatisfactory and was attacked by Guldin. In reply to this attack Cavalieri wrote *Exercitationes geometricae sex* (1647), stating the principle in the more satisfactory form in which it was used by 17th century mathematicians. This work also contained the first rigorous proof of Guldin's theorem relating to the volume of a solid of revolution. The theorem had occurred in the writings of Pappus and had been used in an unsatisfactory fashion by Kepler. Using the principle of indivisibles as a sort of integral calculus, Cavalieri solved a number of problems proposed by Kepler. Other books by Cavalieri are: *Lo specchio ustorio ovvero trattato delle settioni coniche* (1632), *Directorium generale uranometricum, in quo trigonometriae logarithmicae fundamenta ac regula demonstrantur* (1632) and *Trigonometria plana et sphaerica* (1643). Cavalieri died at Bologna on Dec. 3, 1647.

The life of Cavalieri has been written by P. Frisi (Milan, 1776), and by F. Predari (Milan, 1843).

CAVALIERI, EMILIO DEL (1550?–1599?), Italian composer, was born in Rome about 1550 of a noble family and became one of the famous Florentine group of musical reformers —Peri, Rinuccini, Caccini and the rest—who had such an important influence on the subsequent developments of the art.

Cavalieri's style is more facile than that of Peri and Caccini, but he is inferior to them in depth of musical expression. He is, however, important as having been the first to apply the new monodic style to sacred music, and as the founder of the Roman school of the 17th century which included Domenico Mazzocchi, Giacomo Carissimi and Alessandro Scarlatti.

CAVALLI, FRANCESCO (1602–1676), an early Italian operatic composer of note, was born at Crema in 1602. His real name was Pietro Francesco Caletti-Bruni, but he is better known by that of Cavalli, the name of his patron, a Venetian nobleman. He became a singer at St. Mark's in Venice in 1617, second organist in 1639, first organist in 1665 and in 1668 *maestro di cappella.* He is, however, chiefly important for his operas, 27 of which are still extant, most of them being preserved in the library of St. Mark's at Venice.

Claudio Monteverdi had found opera a musico-literary experiment, and left it a magnificent dramatic spectacle.

Cavalli succeeded in making it a popular entertainment. He reduced Monteverdi's extravagant orchestra to more practical limits, introduced melodious arias into his music and popular types into his libretti. His operas have all the characteristic exaggerations and absurdities of the 17th century, but they have also a remarkably strong sense of dramatic effect as well as a great musical facility and a grotesque humour which was characteristic of Italian grand opera down to the death of Alessandro Scarlatti.

CAVALLINI, PIETRO (*c.* 1259–1344), Italian painter, born in Rome, was taught painting and mosaic by Giotto di Bondone while employed at Rome; it is believed that he assisted his master in the mosaic of the Navicella or ship of St. Peter, in the porch of the church of that saint. He also studied under the Cosmati. Luigi Lanzi describes him as an adept in both arts, and mentions with approbation his grand fresco of a crucifixion at Assisi, still in tolerable preservation; he was, moreover, versed in architecture and in sculpture.

According to George Vertue, it is highly probable that Cavallini executed, in 1279, the mosaics and other ornaments of the tomb of Edward the Confessor in Westminster abbey. Cavallini would thus be the Petrus Civis Romanus whose name is inscribed on the shrine; but a comparison of dates invalidates this surmise.

He died in 1344 at the age of 85. Some important works by Cavallini in the church of Santa Cecilia in Trastevere, Rome, were discovered early in the 20th century.

CAVALLOTTI, FELICE (1842–1898), Italian politician, poet and dramatic author, was born in Milan. In 1860 and 1866 he fought with the Garibaldian corps, but he first attained notoriety by his antimonarchical lampoons in the *Gazzetta di Milano* and the *Gazzetta Roas* between 1866 and 1872. Elected to parliament in 1872, his turbulent eloquence secured for him the leadership of the extreme left in 1886 on Agostino Bertani's death. His advocacy of democratic reform made him the most popular man of his day next to Francesco Crispi, against whom he waged an unceasing and bitter campaign. He was killed in a duel with Count Macola.

See A. de Mohr, *Felice Cavallotti: La Vita e le opere* (Milan, 1899).

CAVALRY, known in most armies after World War II as armoured cavalry, constitutes one of the major ground combat arms of a military force and is the element the main duties of which are to furnish full terrestrial information of the enemy while screening the movements of its own army; to pursue and demoralize a defeated enemy; at all times to threaten and intercept his communications (lines of supply and command); in battle to strike suddenly and swiftly at weakened points, turn exposed flanks or force or exploit a penetration or breakthrough. While it could fight dismounted, cavalry originally was considered as an arm which fought on horseback, using the horse's mobility in manoeuvring and his impetus in charging.

By the middle of the 16th century the term cavalry was applied to mounted men of all kinds employed for combatant purposes. Cavalry missions have always required a high degree of mobility, and during the early part of the 20th century, in order to accomplish assigned tasks, the arm adopted fast-moving armoured vehicles. Cavalry operating entirely in armoured fighting vehicles became known as "mechanized cavalry" and subsequently as "armoured cavalry." The weapons of the armoured cavalry are tanks, self-propelled guns and howitzers, automatic weapons, mortars, rocket launchers, rifles, pistols, bayonets and grenades.

The U.S. army organization act of 1950 eliminated cavalry as a branch and provided for an armour branch, "a continuation of the cavalry."

History of Cavalry Tactics.—The two most primitive types of soldier are the foot soldier and the horse soldier, the first being characteristic of early European warfare, and the second of early Asiatic warfare, since in southern Europe (that is, in the countries south and west of the Danube and the Rhine) few suitable breeds of war horses existed—hence the poverty of Roman cavalry and of early Grecian cavalry. When infantry met infantry, battles were decided by numbers or armament or discipline; and when cavalry met cavalry, as in Scythia, battles were seldom decided at all, degenerating as they normally did into skirmishes, forays and scattered pursuits. In hilly country, such as most of Greece, cavalry were normally impotent to attack infantry, as is exemplified in the Graeco-Persian Wars (490–479 B.C.); while in open plain land, so frequently found in Asia Minor, they could destroy infantry by besieging them in the field, as happened to Crassus, at Carrhae in 53 B.C. The truth of the matter is that the two arms were complementary, each providing the other with powers not inherent in either separately. Infantry in an advance were useless unless their rear services were protected, and so also were cavalry in the advance, unless the positions won by them could be held so that their forward movement might not be interrupted.

The art of an advance through a hostile country has always pivoted on the power of pushing forward a secure and movable base in order to develop from it offensive power. Once infantry and cavalry were combined, the first formed the movable base, and the second provided the offensive power. The function of cavalry in any armed force was to fill that requirement of a balanced army which demands a fighting ground element superior to the main element—infantry—in mobility near and on the battlefield, and possessing in common with that arm the ability to engage in offensive and defensive fighting, whether independently or in conjunction with other arms.

When the advance merged into the attack, three targets would present themselves; namely, the enemy's infantry, his cavalry and his baggage train. If the third could be seized and held, the severest possible blow could be dealt the enemy's organization; consequently the supply services would be well protected by the battle front. Infantry could oppose infantry frontally, but if attacked in flank, or rear, by infantry or cavalry, they were taken at a tremendous disadvantage. Throughout history flank protection was furnished by cavalry. The infantry front may then be pictured as a slowly moving wall behind which were assembled the supply services, and on the flanks of which were hinged two cavalry wings, which, like doors, could swing forward and backward, "flapping" away any hostile force which might attempt to raid the baggage train, or attack the infantry in the rear. In battle, the first problem was, therefore, the destruction of one or both of the hostile cavalry wings, for when once the opposing infantry wall was bereft of its swinging doors, not only did its flanks become attackable, but also its rear. If, meanwhile, its front could be so firmly held that it was unable to change front, a cavalry attack on its flanks, or rear, was likely to prove decisive. In brief, the object of infantry was to provide a base of operations for cavalry; and the power of cavalry was to be sought, first in ability to overcome their like, and second in being able to develop a sufficiency of speed so as to circumvent an infantry front, and attack it in the rear before it could face about, which, in the case of an organized army, was an extremely difficult and dangerous operation; impossible if the front was firmly held.

Early Cavalry.—During the early classical age tactical organization was based on the nature of the country rather than on any idea of weapon co-operation or combination between the arms. Thus, in Sparta there was practically no cavalry, while in Scythia mounted bowmen alone existed. Nevertheless, as soon as the Asiatic horsemen came into contact with European foot soldiers, as took place in the 5th century B.C., the problem of tactical co-operation, namely, how to equip, arm and manoeuvre a body of men so that offensive power may be developed from a protective base, was thrust to the fore. This problem was solved by Philip of Macedon, and proved out by his son Alexander the Great.

The backbone of Philip's army was the phalanx, or infantry mass. Armed with the Sarissa, a pike from 18 to 21ft. long, it formed an impenetrable hedge of spears to cavalry attack, though it offered a somewhat vulnerable target to archers both mounted and on foot. To protect it from these, numbers of lightly armed infantry were attached to it, their duty being very similar to that of the British light infantry during the Peninsular War in Spain at the beginning of the 19th century. Recognizing the strong protective and resisting power which the phalanx possessed, Philip was one of the first among the ancients to grasp the fact that stability of organization alone is insufficient to guarantee the act of disruption being followed up by the act of annihilation. The phalanx could not pursue without breaking its formation, it was not armed for the pursuit, and in the pursuit, the pursued almost invariably moves faster than the pursuer, whether both be on foot or mounted. To render the act of annihilation possible, Philip added to the phalanx a superb force of cavalry in the proportion of one trooper to every six heavy foot soldiers. This cavalry he organized in three bodies: Heavy armoured cavalry for the charge, his Companion cavalry being the most notable corps; light cavalry, or Hussars, for reconnaissance and outpost work, and Dragoons who could fight on foot or on horseback. His heavy cavalry doctrine was profoundly simple—horse and rider combined were used as a "projectile" against the enemy once he was held by the phalanx, when the object of his cavalry became the annihilation of all resistance. The tactics which his son developed from this organization were equally simple, and astonishingly effective. Advancing in parallel order to his enemy, he obliqued his right, bringing it forward, and while his centre, protected on its left by the left cavalry wing, held the enemy to his ground, he delivered a series of terrific punches at his opponent's centre, or left, with a view to penetrate or envelop. At the battles of the Granicus (334 B.C.), Issus (333 B.C.), and Gaugamela (331 B.C.) his Companion cavalry decided the day, and at the battle of the Hydaspes (326 B.C.) his cavalry so completely dislocated the Indian Army that his phalanx was able to disrupt it.

Cavalry as the Decisive Arm: 327 B.C.-Adrianople, A.D. 378.—From the days of Alexander onwards, cavalry, on account of their mobility, became the decisive arm. Hannibal's use of cavalry was superb, as the battles of the Trebbia (218 B.C.) and of Cannae (216 B.C.) testify. In both of these the Carthaginian cavalry completely dislocated the Roman legions by a rear attack. In the Roman armies the lack of good cavalry proved their ruin, and it was not until such a force was raised and trained by Scipio Africanus that the Carthaginians were eventually defeated at the battle of Ilipa (205 B.C.), and annihilated at that of Zama (202 B.C.). At Ilipa Scipio beat Hasdrubal by a double envelopment carried out by infantry and cavalry, and at Zama he smashed Hannibal by holding him in front with infantry and striking him in rear with cavalry.

During the days of Julius Caesar, the most serious defeat sustained by the Romans was that of Crassus at the hands of Surena, the Parthian general, whose entire force was composed of mounted archers and heavy cavalry. The Parthians, adopting an improved form of Scythian tactics, won a decisive victory; of the 40,000 Romans who crossed the Euphrates 20,000 were killed and 10,000 made prisoners. The Parthian success was due to the inability of the Romans to develop offensive power from a moving base. Their organization did not enable them to ward off shock and envelopment, while that of their enemy did permit of them enveloping and charging; for in this battle their heavy cavalry provided the necessary stability for the attack of their mounted bowmen and the distraction effected by this attack enabled the heavy cavalry of the Parthians to dislocate and disrupt the Roman legions.

From the battle of Pharsalus (48 B.C.) the legion learned for a space how to hold its own against cavalry, mainly by employing cavalry. Under Diocletian (A.D. 245–313) cavalry rose from one-tenth to one-third of the infantry, and numbered some 160,000; but this great mass of horse was withdrawn from the infantry, and by being formed into a frontier guard lost its offensive spirit. Meanwhile a steady decline took place in the infantry, mercenaries were enlisted, discipline was relaxed, pay increased and armour discarded because of its weight. Of the latter Vegetius wrote: ". . . to avoid fatigue, they allow themselves to be butchered shamefully like cattle." This separation of infantry and cavalry was the main tactical cause of the decline of Rome's military power. The unsupported Roman cavalry, trained as frontier police and for protective duties, were no match for the fierce barbarian horsemen who were now distracting the empire. From the first irruption of the Goths, in the year 248, the Roman cavalry were steadily increased until by the reign of Constantine (288–337) cavalry composed the principal part of the Roman armies; but all in vain. At Adrianople in 378, three Roman legions sent against the Visigoths were overwhelmed and practically annihilated. The Gothic horsemen, *having perfected a new-fangled stirrup,* rode and fought with a vigour and deadliness new to the mounted warrior. Caught massed under a blazing sun, the Roman flank was struck relentlessly by the Gothic horse, and again the dislocation of the Romans, which heralded their disruption, was effected by a cavalry rear attack. The Emperor Valens lost his life, and 40,000 legionnaires perished. From that day cavalry was to become the predominant arm for a thousand years, while the infantry deteriorated into a mere auxiliary.

Cavalry the Predominant Arm: Chalons, 451-Agincourt, 1415.—Fifty-two years after Adrianople, Roman arms at Tricameron won a decisive victory over the Vandals in Africa purely by cavalry. Belisarius had found so little use for his infantry that he mounted them to serve as dragoons. In Europe, however, the hardy and warlike barbarian tribes, fighting chiefly on horseback, soon flooded the Roman provinces. By 410 A.D., the Goths under Alaric captured Rome, and the "mistress of the world" was handed over to the licentious fury of the Huns. The barbarian advance culminated in the battle of Chalons (451) where Attila, after uniting Germany and Scythia, was met and defeated by Aetius and Theodoric. This was the last victory won by Imperial Rome in the West; the dark ages descended upon western Europe, and in the conduct of war that area entered the epoch of the iron-clad lancer.

From the days of Justinian (483–565) to those of the fourth Crusade, which resulted in the sack of Constantinople (1204), highly organized armies comprising well-equipped heavy and light cavalry were maintained by the Eastern empire. In the West, however, military art virtually disappeared, and as principalities took form and feudalism was established the common folk were virtually prohibited from taking part in the "noble" trade of war, which was carried on by raiding and pillaging barons. As the military caste of this period was based on wealth, and as western Europe was largely roadless, cavalry remained the predominant arm, and sought perfection not through improved tactics, or organization, but through armour. By the opening of the 9th century the old military organization of Rome had been replaced by comparatively small bands of mailed knights followed by a mob of retainers who pillaged the countryside and so acted as "administrative units." In England, in the Low Countries and in Switzerland, infantry were still maintained, but were so ill-equipped that when confronted by cavalry in open, or even semi-open, country they were forced to seek protection behind palisades, as was the case with the Saxons at Hastings (1066). Under Charlemagne the mail-clad knight was reaching his zenith, and, as is always the case when the peak of supremacy is topped, decline follows. To the knight of the middle ages the protective base of his offensive power was no longer afforded by the infantry mass, but by the armour he wore, his mobility being provided by his horse. As long as he was not met by equally well mounted and armoured antagonists this combination of mobility and protection proved tactically irresistible, yet seldom did it lead to profitable strategical results. But as soon as he was, it became neutralized, and with neutralization, tactics as an art utterly deteriorated and were replaced by mob fighting.

This self-contained protective power of cavalry is most noticeable during the Crusades, for in spite of the low discipline of the

Christian knights and their very rudimentary knowledge of tactics, normally their casualties were remarkably small. At the battle of Hazarth (1125), Baldwin lost only 24 men, while the Turkish losses amounted to 2,000; at Jaffa (1191) two Crusaders were killed on one side and 700 Turks on the other. The Crusaders, however, lost large numbers of horses, and as the rabble of beggars and vagrants who accompanied them were useless as infantry (further, the code of chivalry did not sanction their use), at times it became necessary for knights to fight on foot, or to abstain from fighting altogether. This involuntary change in tactics led to the Crusaders rediscovering the value of the protective infantry base as a mobile fortress from which the mounted knights could sally forth. In 1248, St. Louis of France adopted this change intentionally. Near Damietta he landed his knights and drew them up on foot in order of battle to cover his disembarkation. The interesting point to note in these operations is that the action of these knights foreshadowed the approaching revival of infantry: "They formed up in serried ranks, placed their bucklers upright in the sand before them, and resting their long lances on the top of their shields, presented an impenetrable array of steel points, before which the Muslim horse fell back in confusion." One of the military influences of the Crusades was the weakening of feudalism through the rise of a commercial class made rich by buying up the knights' lands. This class was concentrated in the cities, and as early as 1057 Pavia and Milan raised armies of their own, largely composed of infantry.

Another result of increasing prosperity was the reintroduction of plate armour, which though it rendered the knight on foot practically invulnerable to infantry attack, when mounted, more and more did it sacrifice his mobility to protection. This seriously influenced the value of the dismounted base, for armour had become so heavy that the dismounted knight was unable to move far on foot. At the battle of Tagliacozzo (1268), Conradin's Ghibelline knights were so heavily armoured that Charles of Anjou's cavalry, after having exhausted them by repeated charges, rolled them out of their saddles by seizing them by their shoulders.

With signs of cavalry power diminishing in the West, there appeared in the East the very essence of power by the mounted warrior. In the latter part of the 12th century there arose on the plains of Mongolia the most formidable cavalry warrior of human annals—Genghis Khan. Utilizing the horsemanship and spirit of conflict which permeated the character of his people, he created vast organized mounted hordes which swept the entire northern and eastern areas of Asia. It is alleged that a mounted force of 700,000 men, held together by a discipline of unyielding iron, rode to his will. Death was the penalty for turning back during action without an order or for neglecting to pick up equipment dropped by a front-file man. From a penetrating native perception, the Khan conceived the powers of co-ordinated and disciplined cavalry. Vigilant and ceaseless training perfected a standard for tactical measures. "A man of my bodyguard," Genghis Khan had announced, "is superior to a regimental commander of another division." The tactical skill of the Mongols had been developed in the stress of war. They had learned to keep track of an enemy's movements while concealing their own. In manoeuvre for battle they had learned not to depend on commands given by a voice which often cannot be heard in the uproar of moving mounted men. Regiments signalled their movements by raising black or white flags during the day and by a similar use of coloured lanterns at night. Other signals were given by the use of whistling arrows, which emitted sound through a hollow pierced head. They hid their formations at times behind a drifting smoke screen. The Mongol horde, unlike the Crusade, formed a movement of deadly intensity by virtue of its disciplined co-ordination and cohesion towards a common end. Followed by immense trains of wagons and great herds of cattle, they could exist for years off the country invaded. They crossed rivers on ice or in leathern boats. They fought mainly with arrows, avoiding close struggle, and strove to destroy their enemies from afar with projectile weapons. There was a fluidity and flexibility in their movements found wanting in the fixed, cumbersome ranks of European forces.

After the death of the great Khan, 150,000 Mongols under the able Sabutai, in 1235, marched towards the setting sun and threatened to flood the whole of Europe. In the next six years this enormous horde had marched one-fourth the distance around the globe. Sabutai swept through present day Russia and on to the plains of Hungary and Poland. Eastern Europe, from the Carpathians to the Baltic, fell under his domain. Although victorious in their fierce battle with the Poles at Wahlstall in April 1241, the strength of the invading Mongols had been so taxed that they turned back to the East. The leaders of western Europe learned little concerning the capacity of highly mobile cavalry in great numbers presented to them by the Mongolian mounted men.

Meanwhile, in western Europe progress in the construction of the bow and the crossbow was another reason for increasing the thickness of armour. At the siege of Abergavenny, in 1182, it is recorded that the Welsh arrows could penetrate an oak door four inches thick. No chain mail could withstand such a blow, consequently plate armour was worn over the mail shirt. As armour increased in weight natural obstacles began to play a decisive part on the battlefield. When ground could not be crossed on horseback it had to be crossed on foot, and the knight deprived of his horse lost much of his tactical value, consequently an able enemy sought every means in his power to compel him to dismount. One of these means was choice of ground, another, archery; for horse armour never proved satisfactory.

At the battle of Dupplin Muir (1332), Baliol and Beaumont did not beat the earl of Mar by reckless charges, but by skillful weapon co-operation. The majority of their knights were dismounted and formed into a phalanx, the flanks of which were protected by archers, while 40 mounted knights were kept in reserve. The earl of Mar charged the phalanx which remained unshaken; his knights, immobilized by the archers on the flanks, were routed by Baliol's mounted squadron. This battle is the birth of a new era in tactics—the tactics of bow, pike and lance combined. It formed the mould in which all the English operations of the Hundred Years' War were cast, a war which proved disastrous to the gallant but insubordinate French chivalry, as the battles of Crécy (1346), Poitiers (1356), and Agincourt (1415) testify. The cavalry difficulty throughout was the armouring of the horse. At Crécy (where gunpowder was first introduced) the horse proved the weak link in the French organization, for of the next great battle, namely Poitiers, John le Bel wrote of the French knights: "All fought on foot, through fear that, as at the battle of Crécy, the archers would kill their horses." Meanwhile in Switzerland infantry armed with pike and halberd, and fighting in phalangeal order, were taking toll of German and Austrian cavalry; and in Bohemia, Ziska by employing wagons in laager created movable fortresses known as the Wagenburg (wagon fort) against which his enemy's cavalry shattered themselves in vain. As wealth increased, mercenaries once again came to the fore, and being professional soldiers whose pay as well as whose lives depended on their art, tactics once again began to assume a coherent form, especially under the English commander-in-chief of Pope Urban V, Sir John Hawkwood, who may be considered the first great general of modern times. From the battle of Poitiers onwards cavalry fell into a rapid decline; the French knights learned nothing, and as the bow and pike destroyed them a new weapon arose in the crude bombards of the 14th century, which was destined to revolutionize the whole art of war, to reduce cavalry to the position they held in the days of the Scythians, and to advance infantry to the heyday of the Spartan phalanx. At the battle of Formigny (1450), three small culverins threw the English archers into disorder, and at Morat (1476) Charles the Bold of Burgundy was defeated by the Swiss who made good use of 6,000 hand guns.

Cavalry in the Age of Gunpowder.—For 1,000 years cavalry had sought to solve the problem of mobility through protection by armour. This being no longer possible, because armour could be penetrated by the bullet, after much trial and error a solution was sought through fire-power (the very cause of its obsolescence), that is to say, by combining cavalry with the other arms. In 1494, Charles VIII of France entered Rome, and in the words of Machiavelli: "He conquered Italy with a piece of chalk."

Arming a tenth of his infantry with the escopette, a species of arquebus, and accompanied by 140 heavy cannon and a number of small pieces, nothing could resist him, and so all he had to do was to chalk off areas on the map to which he wished to go, and there he went.

As armour grew lighter the knight exchanged his lance for the petronel, a type of hand cannon, in order to fire on infantry in place of charging them. This form of attack was first used by the French at the battle of Cerisoles, in 1544, and proved effective because the attack could be prolonged indefinitely, and against such organized Scythian tactics the infantry were powerless until the arquebus was improved, when cavalry became more immobile than ever. Soon the petronel was replaced by the arquebus-à-rouet, and a little later on by the wheel-lock pistol, which was first used by the German cavalry at the battle of St. Quentin, in 1557.

The lance now vanished, and attempts were made to develop cavalry mobility by mixing squadrons with infantry units. As early as the battle of Pavia (1525), the Marquis of Pescara had adopted this organization, and though in a clumsy way it linked fire-power and shock, the mobility of cavalry was so limited by the pace of the infantry that the cavalry attack was reduced to a walk. Twenty-five years after this battle, Marshal de Brissac mounted a number of his infantrymen on horseback, and the era of the modern Dragoon, or mounted infantryman, was initiated.

During the Thirty Years' War (1618–48) the employment of cavalry increased, cavalry mobility being sought not through their own fire power but through that of infantry, and especially artillery. Supported by artillery, Gustavus Adolphus' cavalry rode forward, fired their pistols and charged home with the sword. At Breitenfeld (1631) and at Lutzen (1632) his cavalry played the decisive part. In England he was emulated by Cromwell—the battle of Grantham (1643) was decided by the sword, so was Marston Moor (1644), and so was Naseby (1645). In France the reversion to shock tactics was no whit behind-hand: Turenne favoured the *arme blanche,* and issued instructions to his cavalry to use the sword alone. The impetuous Condé did likewise, and so also Marshal Luxembourg at Leuze, in 1691. In Germany, however, Montecuculi still favoured fire-arms for cavalry; he considered the lance useless, and looked upon the horses of his Dragoons solely as a means of conveyance.

This change is significant and cannot alone be attributed to the genius of such cavalry leaders as Pappenheim and Gustavus. The underlying reason for it is probably to be found in the universal adoption of the matchlock, and the consequent reduction of the pikemen. The matchlock was a slow-loading and unreliable weapon, especially in rainy weather when infantry are apt to be surprised in mist or fog. It was on such occasions as these that cavalry frequently proved themselves the decisive arm, up to the adoption of the percussion cap in 1839. A notable instance of this was the battle of Eylau (1807). During the 18th century the idea of the shock continued to grow. Marlborough used cavalry in mass. Blenheim (1704) was decided by cavalry, and so was Malplaquet (1708). In these battles are to be discovered the germ of the superb cavalry actions of Ziethen and Seydlitz, which characterized the Seven Years' War (1756–63). Charles XII of Sweden carried the shock to its extreme. He prohibited the use of armour, raced over Europe, rode to death two horses while reviewing a regiment, and met an impetuous end at Pultowa (1709). Marshal Saxe, in a reasoned degree, emulated him.

Under Frederick the Great, cavalry once again reached its zenith, and out of 22 of his battles at least 15 were won by the cavalry arm working in close co-operation with gun and musket. In his regulations for cavalry Frederick wrote: "They will move off at a fast trot and charge at the gallop, being careful to be well closed together. His Majesty will guarantee that the enemy will be beaten every time they are charged in this way." The exploits of Seydlitz and Ziethen proved that Frederick was not wrong. Rosbach (1757) was a great cavalry victory, and so, in a lesser degree, was Zorndorf (1758). The secret of Frederick's success lay not only in the artillery preparation which heralded the charge, nor in his system of attack, but in the training of his troopers.

The war of the American Revolution (1775–81) provides no example of outstanding cavalry work, nor do the French Revolutionary Wars, except for the brilliant charge of the English 15th Hussars at Villers-en-Couché (1794), where some 300 British and Austrian cavalry charged and routed 10,000 French infantry and cavalry, driving them into Cambrai with a loss of 1,200 men. The slowing down of the shock first became perceptible in Bonaparte's campaign in Egypt, when the world-famed Mameluke cavalry failed to make any real impression on his infantry squares. At Mount Tabor (1799) 6,000 French infantry under Kléber gained a decisive victory over 30,000 Turks and Mamelukes. From this battle onwards to the World War of 1914–18 the declining power of cavalry remains constant.

Napoleon relied on all arms, but particularly on fire power, and in spite of the many cavalry charges executed during his wars, his cavalry were pre-eminently a strategic force for observation and protection, and a tactical force for pursuit. With his strategic employment of cavalry, no commander was ever more completely informed at all times of the movements and composition of the hostile army than was Napoleon. His earlier manoeuvres, conceived after a careful synchronization of time and space factors, were made practical by skillfully led cavalry. Far-flung columns, well in advance of his main armies, not only kept him posted of hostile movements but were influential in manoeuvring an enemy into an area of Napoleon's own selection. Once contact was gained by main bodies, cavalry invariably were withdrawn to flanks or to the rear in reserve. While mounted charges were executed, they were made at that period in battle when the enemy was shattered by fire and the keen discernment of Napoleon foresaw conclusive results. From the flanks and rear his cavalry were able to deliver the decisive thrust or spring in pursuit of a routed enemy, which meant destruction rather than an orderly retirement and the ability to fight again after reconcentration and reorganization. At Eylau (1807) Napoleonic cavalry, encountering the Russian Cossacks, were confronted for the first time by a mobile element of their own quality; pursuit proved impossible, and strategic reconnaissance ineffective. In the Emperor's subsequent campaigns of 1812–13–14, superior enemy cavalry nullified any real fruits of victory, and in the retreat from Moscow were responsible mainly for the gradual disintegration of the Grand Army. The freedom of manoeuvre, the basis of Napoleon's success, had been reversed.

The Napoleonic wars were followed by 40 years of profound military coma. In 1823, Capt. John Norton, of the 34th English Regiment, invented the cylindro-conoidal bullet. He received no encouragement, for the duke of Wellington considered that the Brown Bess could not be bettered, yet Norton's bullet was the greatest military invention since the flint-lock. In 1853, Capt. Minié, of the French army, invented a similar projectile. In England, Sir William Napier opposed its adoption as he considered that it would destroy the infantry spirit by turning infantry into "long range assassins." It was, however, adopted; it had a range of 1,000yd., and it sealed the doom of the cavalry charge. The war in Crimea (1854–55) taught soldiers nothing new regarding cavalry except to emphasize its misuse by ill-informed commanders of combined arms and to demonstrate the gallantry and spirit of the arm. The battle of Balaclava gave to the world only the famed epic of "The Charge of the Light Brigade" and evidence of the courage, discipline and combative will to close with an enemy characteristic of the British mounted warrior. (*See* BALACLAVA.) (J. F. C. F.; J. K. H.; X.)

The Mounted Rifleman.—In the next war, the American Civil War (1861–65), a pronounced transition in cavalry tactics took form. The evolution of its tactics switched radically from the accepted European tenets of that day. The Confederate states, largely rural and agricultural, were able to create promptly a considerable cavalry to be used in strictly cavalry roles. The Union, largely of urban population, organized cavalry at a slower pace and employed it, initially, on the futile assignments of outpost, convoy, messenger and other associated activities. Employing cavalry in large units, Lee, in Virginia, was able to reap the benefit of decisive victories during the first two years of the war; his own intentions were always screened from the enemy, while their movements and dispositions habitually were known to him. By May 1862, the Union, finally awake, assembled 10,000 horses into a cavalry corps. At Chancellorsville this formidable cavalry force was dispatched southward on a useless raid. Lee's cavalry, under James Stuart, discovering an open flank on the Union right, skilfully screened the movement of Thomas ("Stonewall") Jackson's corps, which launched a powerful surprise attack resulting in one of the most complete victories of Confederate arms. By 1863 cavalry tactics on both sides had become concerned principally with dismounted action and proved so effective that the mounted charge was a rarity thereafter. The eventual defeat of Lee was made possible in part through the able employment of a highly mobile cavalry and infantry force under Philip Sheridan. Repeated attacks against the Confederate lines of supply effected their dislocation by depriving them of a protected base. Increased powers of weapon fire had forced a new development of the cavalry dragoon or mounted rifleman—not to be confused with mounted infantry, which utilizes horses only as transportation and habitually fights dismounted; the mounted rifleman is trained and equipped to fight either dismounted or mounted. The revolver, introduced in this war, had proven a formidable cavalry weapon.

The wars which followed in Europe in 1866 and 1870 were marked by a complete disregard of the cavalry lessons learned from the American Civil War. The Austro-Prussian War (1866) saw 56,000 cavalrymen still armed with the lance and sabre charging in the face of the breech-loading needle gun and the Minié rifle. The Franco-German War (1870–71) saw 96,000 cavalry take the field similarly equipped. Their tactics called only for mounted action. French cavalry had learned nothing since Waterloo. The Germans were bold and pushful, using their cavalry strategically with considerable effect in order to cover their own movements while discovering those of the enemy. The massed charge was attempted. Jean A. Margueritte failed; Adalbert von Bredow succeeded, but at terrific cost. His was the last successful massed boot-to-boot cavalry charge in military history.

In South Africa (1899–1902) the Boers, accepting the lessons of the American Civil War, fought with large numbers of mounted riflemen who moved hither and yon, came and went, attacked and retired almost at will. The British faced this type of action initially with a force in which infantry predominated and included a few cavalry regiments armed with swords or lances and depending mainly on these weapons for combat. Not until British mounted elements were reorganized on a dragoon basis were the British able to conquer a people immeasurably their inferior in numbers and resources.

In the Russo-Japanese War (1904–05) cavalry action of little consequence occurred. The outstanding note was the absence of the lance and sword, which were nowhere seen. In combat, the rifle was supreme; any thought of reliance on the sword was banished. The few achievements of Russian cavalry in this war came through the effect of fire action. Little use was made of the cavalry masses of Alexei Kuropatkin organized and equipped on the European model of massed action. Japanese cavalry, with few exceptions, carried out their performances with the carbine and usually in close touch with their own infantry.

World War I.—During World War I, little use was made of the potential power of cavalry available to both sides. The limitations which the bullet placed on cavalry movement begot the trench; for had cavalry been able to move, the construction of entrenched fronts would have been all but impossible. On the western front, ten German cavalry divisions (approximately 70,000) faced ten French and one British cavalry divisions. The tool was there for the appearance of a master of the art of war capable of visualizing the power and capabilities of a numerous cavalry on missions of inspired and skillful design. There was need for mounted riflemen, not the European cavalry of that day relying principally on the sword and lance in mounted action. The French cavalry were split into useless detachments, and the only sizable force, under Sordet, was marched futilely over the whole of southern Belgium and northern France; his operations availed nothing. The single British cavalry division, operating collectively as a unit, rendered invaluable assistance to the main forces by employing ground fire to delay the German advance south of Mons until reorganization behind them was effected. While their grand plan conceived a powerful enveloping thrust southward through northwestern France, the Germans made little use of the potential power of their cavalry to aid that operation. The bulk of their mounted forces was scattered over the fronts of several field armies rather than assembled for a decisive effort.

On the eastern front, Russia produced initially 24 cavalry divisions (approximately 200,000 horsemen), but like the leaders of ancient Rome, the Russian commanders expended the potential power of this force by scattering it along an entire frontier. The armies of Alexander Samsonov and Paul Rennenkampf invaded East Prussia with forces totalling 400,000 combined arms to meet the most crushing defeat of the war at Tannenberg. The decisive victory of the Germans was made possible largely by the success of a single German cavalry division in delaying the army of Rennenkampf. Later, Russia increased its cavalry to 54 divisions; but with military leaders unable to cope with the requirements of massed co-ordination, this vast force accomplished little. It was, indeed, the indirect cause of breaking down the transportation system of the country by the requirements of forage.

Cavalry achievements in this war reached their highest plane in Palestine under Edmund Allenby, an outstanding commander of mobile troops. At Armageddon, Sept. 1918, Allenby faced a strong Turkish army with a superior force of combined arms including three cavalry divisions and bombardment aviation. Crushing the enemy right, he dispatched his cavalry, not against the hostile flank, but against the rear. Fleeing Turkish elements crowded into the ravines and defiles which characterized the terrain. Halted and confused by combat aviation, they were annihilated when struck by the charging cavalry columns. The lesson of Armageddon lay not so much in the prowess of ground mobility as in the example of the formidable power of such forces when supported by fire from the air—a dreadful warning of the devastating type of future war. The transcendent lesson from this war was an exemplification of the need of essential supporting fires for all cavalry action—again, fire power and movement.

Four years of stabilized warfare on the continent of Europe had contributed little to the concept of offensive manoeuvre predicated on fire power and movement. Industrial civilization had furnished new potentialities to the power of weapon fires by development of automatic arms and the co-ordinated concentrative effect of massed artillery. Advancement in automotive vehicles afforded new concepts in factors of time and space. Combat aviation gave new reaches to radii of action and means of fire support. Armoured divisions were developed between World Wars I and II which included all supporting arms needed in modern warfare: infantry, artillery, signal, engineers, etc. These divisions were organized for missions requiring independent action, using great mobility and fire power.

World War II.—From the earliest stages of World War II, there emerged military leaders who had developed as an art of war the co-ordinated employment of mass machines on the ground and in the air. The Germans had conceived the effective means of creating fire power from a moving base for the support of highly mobile combat elements through close tactical air support. They produced a fire effect so devastating as to dislocate all hostile defenses and permit freedom of movement for a mobile mass. Under this rain of fire from the air the newer heavy cavalry breached hostile positions by the power of shock. The lighter cavalry, with amazing powers of mobility, rushed forward through the breaches to spread fanlike in devastating attacks upon the nerve and supply centres in the rear. Once in the open the sustained drive of this new cavalry continued under the protective power of their own self-contained fire. Mobility reached great heights. Poland as a first-class power was crushed in the space of days. The highly publicized static defenses of the French Maginot line were passed, and the streamlined power of the German offensive quickly overran western Europe. There were few if any battles of mass tanks on the European continent up to this time but in Africa on the Libyan, with a wide expanse of terrain, a new theory was developed. Armed forces fought each other with as many as 500 tanks employed on each side. Mobility, surprise and shock were the deciding factors.

In the summer of 1944 the Allied Powers invaded the Normandy coast and launched a successful attack by a team of combined arms with each arm playing its major role. There were infantry, armoured divisions, separate tank battalions, all supported by tactical and strategic air. The operation began with one of the largest air-support missions of the entire war; 2,500 supporting aircraft flew over St. Lô, Fr., to saturate an area 6,000 yd. wide by 3,000 yd. deep. This was followed by close fighter support over advancing armoured columns. In this operation, the infantry divisions, with separate tank battalions in support, made the initial hole in the German lines and held the shoulders of the penetration, while the armoured divisions, using their speed, shock and mobility, splintered the enemy defenses and drove more than 400 mi. into the rear of the enemy's lines. Six weeks later the Allied armies, stopped by a lack of supplies, were at the German border.

Sixteen U.S. armoured divisions successfully applied the principles of fire, movement and shock action to help defeat the axis in World War II. Under Gen. George S. Patton, Jr., many of these units fought their way from Normandy to the Rhine and the Danube, overcoming the last of the famed German panzers in the west. At the same time other elements were pushing up the rugged Italian peninsula and through southeastern France to join their comrades beyond the Alps. With them in this effort were separate mechanized cavalry units which had been designed and equipped primarily for reconnaissance missions, and a large number of separate tank battalions. The reconnaissance units were called upon to perform a great variety of combat missions and spent only a small part of their time on reconnaissance.

It was generally acknowledged after World War II that the tank had become the decisive weapon of the ground force combat team. Military leaders recognized the strategic and tactical importance of armour and its characteristic mobility, massed fire power and terrific shock action.

Bibliography.—G. T. Denison, *History of Cavalry From the Earliest Times, With Lessons for the Future,* 2nd ed. (1913); Niccolò Machiavelli, *Arte della Guerra* (1520); Wallhausen, *Art militaire à cheval* (1621); Gabriel Daniel, *Histoire de la milice française* (1721); Melfort, *Traité sur la cavalerie* (1776); Brack, *Avant-postes de cavalerie legère* (1831); Roemer, *Cavalry: Its History, Management and Uses in War* (1863); Sir Evelyn Wood, *Cavalry in the Waterloo Campaign* (1895); F. N. Maude, *Cavalry: Its Past and Future* (1903); Prince Kraft zu Hohenlohe-Ingelfingen, *Letters on Cavalry* (1880), *Conversations on Cavalry* (1892); E. Nolan, *Cavalry, Its History and Tactics* (1855); C. von Schmidt, *Instruction for the Training, Employment and Leading of Cavalry* (1881); V. Verdy du Vernois, *The Cavalry Division* (1873); Sir Evelyn Wood, *Achievements of Cavalry* (1893); Canitz, *Histoire des exploits et des vicissitudes de la cavalerie prussienne dans les campagnes de Frederic II* (1849); Foucart, *La Cavalerie pendant la campagne de Prusse* (1880); Bernhardi, *Cavalry in Future Wars* (1906); Pelet Narbonne, *Cavalry on Service* (1906); *A Brief Record of the Advance of the Egyptian Expeditionary Force, Under the Command of Gen. Sir Edmund H. H. Allenby, G.C.B., G.C.M.G.* (1919); R. M. P. Preston, *The Desert Mounted Corps* (1921); Gen. M. von Poseck, *The German Cavalry, 1914* (1923); William A. Mitchell, *Outline of the World's Military History* (1931); J. F. C. Fuller, *Decisive Battles* (1940); T. R. Phillips (ed.), *Roots of Strategy* (1940); Roger Shaw, *One Hundred and Seventy-five Battles by Land, Sea, and Air* (1937); Jomini, *Art of War* (1862); U.S. Cavalry School, *Cavalry Combat* (1937); Matthew F. Steele, *American Campaigns,* 2 vol., rev.; Harold Lamb, *March of the Barbarians* (1940); H. M. Cole, *United States Army in World War II: European Theater of Operations, Lorraine Campaign* (1950); Mildred H. Gillie, *Forging the Thunderbolt* (1947). (J. K. H.; C. W. He.)

CAVAN, one of the three counties of the old province of Ulster which are part of the Republic of Ireland. It is bounded north by Fermanagh and Monaghan, east by Monaghan and Meath, south by Meath, Westmeath and Longford and west by Longford and Leitrim. Pop. (1951) 66,377. Area 730 sq.mi.

In the northwest, County Cavan is occupied by hills of Millstone Grit, forming a wild country of mountains and bogs and rising to 2,188 ft. in the Cuilcagh. There occurs the Shannon Pot, source of the Shannon river. Farther east, approaching the county town of the same name, there is an extensive low-lying area of drift-covered Carboniferous limestone, resulting in undulating land. This region is one of the classic examples of drumlin topography, the innumerable low boulder-clay hills giving rise to a most complex drainage pattern consisting of a multiplicity of lakes known as Lough Oughter. The drainage system centres finally on the river Erne, which bisects the county from south to north. Many other lakes are scattered over the county, the largest being Lough Gowna, Lough Sheelin and Lough Ramor, all on or near the southern boundary. The eastern part of the county is developed on Silurian and Ordovician rocks, while near Kingscourt, in the extreme east, occurs an outlier of Triassic beds, downfaulted among the older Palaeozoics. Extensive deposits of gypsum have been located in this Triassic outlier, and an important manufacture of plaster and wallboard, capable of supplying all Irish needs and providing an export trade also, was developed after World War II.

The soil is generally a stiff clay, cold and watery, but capable of much improvement by drainage. In those districts not well adapted for tillage, the ground is peculiarly favourable for trees. The woods were at one time considerable, and the timber found in the bogs is of large dimensions. The farms are generally small, though in the higher lands there are larger grazing farms. Oats and potatoes are the principal crops; cattle rearing is the main occupation of the people. Flax, once of some importance, is almost neglected. The bleaching of linen and the distillation of whisky are both carried on to a small extent.

The town of Cavan was for centuries the seat of the O'Reillys, rulers of East Breifne (the western part of the county). In 1579 Cavan was made shire ground as part of Connaught, and in 1584 it was formed into a county of Ulster.

Some few remains of antiquity exist in the shape of cairns, raths and the ruins of small castles, chief among the latter being the 13th-century O'Reilly fortress, Cloughoughter castle, which stands on an island (an ancient crannog) of Lough Oughter. It was taken by the Cromwellians in 1653 and has been in ruins ever since. Three miles from the town of Cavan is Kilmore, which has a Protestant cathedral (1858–60) containing a Romanesque doorway brought from the abbey of Trinity Island in Lough Oughter. The see of Kilmore or Tir Briuin (Breffni) dates from before 1136, but in 1839 Ardagh was added to it and in 1841 Elphin was united to Kilmore and Ardagh to form the see of Kilmore and Elphin and Ardagh. The seat of the Roman Catholic bishop of Kilmore is at Cavan. County Cavan returns four members to the *dail eireann.* (D. G.)

CAVAN, an urban district and county town of County Cavan, Ire., 85½ mi. N.W. of Dublin by railway. Pop. (1951) 3,555. A Franciscan friary, founded in 1300 by Giolla O'Reilly, formerly existed there and was the burial place of O'Reilly of Breifne (d. 1491) and of Owen Roe O'Neill (d. 1649). On Tullymongan hill was the principal residence of the O'Reillys. The town was burned in 1690 by the Enniskilleners under Wolseley when they defeated James II's troops under the duke of Berwick. The town has some linen trade. It is the seat of the Roman Catholic diocese of Kilmore, which includes parts of counties Leitrim, Fermanagh, Meath and Sligo, and its modern Romanesque cathedral was completed in 1941.

CAVANILLES, ANTONIO JOSÉ (1745–1804), Spanish botanist, was born in Valencia on Jan. 16, 1745. In 1801 he became director of the botanic gardens at Madrid, where he died on May 4, 1804. In 1785–86 he published *Monadelphiae Classis Dissertationes X,* and in 1791 he began to issue *Icones et descriptiones plantarum Hispaniae.*

CAVATINA, originally a short song of simple character, without a second strain or any repetition of the air. It is now frequently applied to a simple melodious air, as distinguished from a brilliant aria, recitative, etc.

CAVAZZOLA (Cavazzuola), the usual appellation of Paolo Morando (*c.* 1486–1522), Italian painter. He was first trained under Francesco Morone, but his first dated work, the "Madonna Cagnola" (1508; Villa Gazzada near Varese), shows the Venetian characteristics acquired from his more notable master, F. Bonsignori; these were fully developed in his "Madonna" of 1514 (Berlin). Later, he was influenced by Raphael.

BY COURTESY OF (3) ATCHISON, TOPEKA AND SANTA FE RAILWAY, (4, 6) LURAY CAVERNS CORPORATION, (5) THE WESTINGHOUSE LAMP COMPANY; PHOTOGRAPHS, (1) KEYSTONE VIEW CO., (7, 8) PUBLISHERS PHOTO SERVICE, (2, 9) EWING GALLOWAY

FAMOUS CAVES THROUGHOUT THE WORLD

1. The Giants' hall. Carlsbad Caverns, national park, New Mexico. Series of connected caverns, probably largest in world
2. Great Onyx cave, near Mammoth cave, Kentucky
3. Carlsbad cave, national monument, New Mexico. The king's throne room
4. Caverns of Luray, Virginia, Leidy column, in the blanket room
5. Shenandoah caverns, Virginia. "The Castle of Cardross"
6. Caverns of Luray, Virginia. Helen's Shawl
7. Black Hills, South Dakota. Wind cave
8. Syracuse, Sicily. The Ear of Dionysius
9. Indian Chamber cave, Jenolan, N.S.W., Australia. The Orient cave

In his earlier pictures the figures are frontal and rather flat; later they are turned a little and more definitely modelled. His works can be identified by vivid, hard colour, a strong interest in small birds and other naturalistic details, over-careful drawing of eyes and the depiction of a finger of one hand in a pointing gesture. These features can be seen in the "Isabella d'Este" (*c.* 1514), apparently the only surviving painted likeness of the great noblewoman. Cavazzola's other works include the "Passion" polyptych, finished in 1517 (Verona); "St. Roch" (left wing of an altarpiece, 1518) and "Virgin and Child," both in the National gallery, London; and his last dated work, the "Vision of the Madonna" altarpiece (1522, Verona). According to G. Vasari, in aspiring to greatness he undermined his health. He worked mainly in his native Verona, dying there on Aug. 13, 1522.

See A. Aleardi, *Paulo Morando* (Verona, 1853).

CAVE, EDWARD (1691–1754), English printer, was born at Newton, Warwickshire, Feb. 27, 1691, and died Jan. 10, 1754. He entered the grammar school at Rugby, where his father was a cobbler, but was involved in pranks which cost him the headmaster's favour and the hope of proceeding to the university. After many vicissitudes he became apprentice to a London printer and was sent to Norwich to conduct a printing house and weekly paper. While engaged in printing and journalism, he obtained employment in the post office (1723) and presently a clerkship of franks, retiring only in 1745. He meanwhile undertook the exchange of news between London and provincial papers. In 1728 he was implicated with others in a charge of breach of privilege. In 1731 he bought a printing house and set up a press at St. John's Gate, Clerkenwell, and launched the *Gentleman's Magazine* (*see* PERIODICAL), of which he remained proprietor during his lifetime, editing it under the pseudonym of Sylvanus Urban, Gent. This, the first magazine, offered extracts and abridgments from the contemporary press, "with some other matters of Use or Amusement that will be communicated to us." In 1732 he began to issue from surreptitious and often scanty reports accounts of the debates in both houses of parliament, and in 1738 was censured for printing the king's answer to an address before it had been announced by the speaker. Thenceforth the debates appeared as those of the "senate of Great Lilliput." In 1747 he was reprimanded for publishing an account of the trial of Lord Lovat and discontinued the reports, beginning afresh with brief accounts of transactions in parliament in 1752.

From Cave Samuel Johnson got his earliest regular literary employment, on these debates and in other writing and editing. Cave was, moreover, concerned in the publication of several of Johnson's works besides those which appeared (in whole or in part) in the magazine: notably, *London,* the *Life of Savage, Irene* and the *Rambler.* On his death, Johnson wrote a sympathetic obituary notice.

See John Nichols, *Literary Anecdotes of the Eighteenth Century,* vol. v (London, 1812) and *Introduction to General Index of the Gentleman's Magazine* (London, 1821); C. L. Carson, *The First Magazine* (Providence, R.I., 1938); B. B. Hoover, *Samuel Johnson's Parliamentary Reporting* (Berkeley, Calif., 1953). (M. M. Ls.)

CAVE, a cavity in rock large enough for human entrance and traverse. Cavern is nearly synonymous, but generally means a large cave or a large connected group of caves. A rock shelter is a cave whose mouth is the largest cross section of the cavity and whose roof has adequate projection out over the floor. Collapse of part of the cave roof to make a hole completely through to the surface constitutes one common type of sinkhole, a cave without a roof.

Origin.—Caves may originate with the making of the rock which encloses them or they may be secondary to the rock making. To the first group belong caves in congealed lava flows, made generally by freezing of the surface of the lava stream while the deeper portion remains liquid and continues to flow. Failure of supply under these conditions may allow the fluid lava to drain out and leave a linear hollow tube perhaps tens of feet in diameter.

Most caves belong to the second group, having been made by removal of material after the enclosing rock was made. Some of these occur along exposed coasts where mechanical erosion occurs under vigorous wave attack. These sea caves are not limited to any particular kind of rock and they lack marked linearity and subterranean extent. Rock shelters commonly are the result of crumbling and falling away of weak rock on a hillside beneath stronger rock which forms the roof.

Limestone and Dolomite Caves.—These rocks contain the largest caves and the largest number of caves of the earth's surface. They are all secondary, having been made by the solvent action of circulating ground water. These calcareous rocks, slightly soluble in pure water, are more rapidly attacked if the water has brought organic acid or carbon dioxide down from the surface in it. The circulation occurs chiefly along the usually horizontal bedding planes and the commonly vertical joint cracks, the water moving under gravity to lower levels and to eventual escape as springs and seepages. The sides of these primitive passages are attacked and the dissolved material removed; thus enlargement results. From perhaps a multitude of such early water routes, integration of the subterranean water system proceeds by greater enlargement of more favourably located routes and abandonment of less favoured ones.

Limestone and dolomite caves have been discovered in well drillings below the water table (upper level of saturated rock) and therefore completely filled with water. Some caves are enterable in dry weather only, being completely filled during the rainy seasons. Many are traversable at all times, although they carry perennial streams on their floors. Some lack streams entirely, but possess shapes and wall sculptures that indubitably are of solutional origin.

The question therefore arises as to whether caves in calcareous rock (1) have been made in large measure by solutional and abrasional stream work on the floor while only air occupied the upper part of the cave, and thus have been deepened and perhaps widened in the manner by which surface streams enlarge

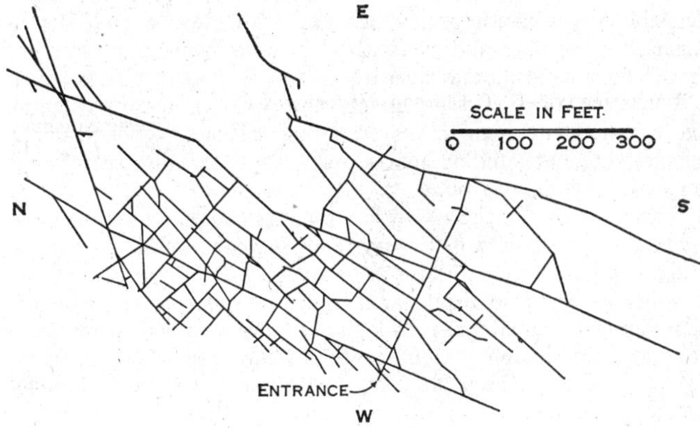

PLAN OF MARK TWAIN CAVE, HANNIBAL, MO.

An outstanding example of a cave system in which the ground plan was determined entirely by vertical joints and in which development occurred almost wholly below an earlier, higher water table

their valleys or (2) have been made at some earlier time when the water table was higher in the rock, the cave being completely filled at the time. Lowering of the water table occurs in any region as the surface streams deepen their valleys and thus provide lower exits for seepages and springs. Thus, by this second view, enterable limestone and dolomite caves, with streams on their floors, are going through a second episode in their development. They are still water routes, but their enlargement now is occurring only in the basal portions.

The many caves possessing solutional shapes on their ceilings seem to require, for their origin, a tube-full flow, like that of a water main. The ground plan of many caves suggests the street system of a city, a multitude of narrow, linear, intersecting passages having been developed along two or more sets of nearly vertical joints in the rock. This lack of integration into one main water course with tributary courses argues strongly for origin in the saturated zone below the water table.

There are many horizontally extended caves under hills whose catch of rainfall never could have provided the ground-water flow recorded and whose directional control of any ground-water circulation does not fit the cave pattern. Such caves must be older than the hills and valleys of the region and are therefore judged to be products of the second method of origin.

A limestone or dolomite cave therefore is, or once was, a subterranean water course, its length far greater than its width or height. During a large part of its development it functioned like a pipe line, the flow occurring under hydrostatic conditions. After lowering of the water table, the cave became more like a roofed valley, with a free surface stream on its floor for a time, perhaps to the present.

Secondary Deposits.—Most enterable caves have ceased to grow larger; instead, they are suffering decrease in size from the secondary deposition of calcium carbonate in the form of travertine and stalagmites on the floor, draperies and curtains on the walls, and stalactites on the ceiling. The deposited material has been obtained from the roof rock by downward percolating rain water since air came to occupy the cave. To these secondary growths caves owe much of their beauty and most of their interest to the average visitor. Forms of the deposits are extraordinarily varied, chiefly in vertical dimensions, and fancy sees in them an almost unbelievable range of resemblances to forms already in the beholder's experience. The usual pure white of the calcium carbonate may be mottled and shaded with delicate hues of red, yellow and gray. Translucency may characterize some of the deposits and lend added charm.

Primitive Shelter.—Primitive man in all lands has utilized the natural shelter provided by caves, the rock shelter type having been his favourite. His tools, weapons, ornaments, hearths, the bones of his kills, even his wall pictographs and paintings have provided archaeologists with so much information that "cave man" has become a popular term for our early ancestors (*see* ARCHAEOLOGY: *Old World Archaeology*). Ice Age (Pleistocene) extinct carnivores—cave bear, cave lion, cave hyena—also used available caves south of the ice sheets of Europe and North America as refuges and dens, their remains being preserved in earthy floor deposits and beneath secondary floors of travertine.

Romance of Caves.—Legends and written history include many stories involving caves as heroes' refuges, robbers' dens, savages' holdouts, hiding places for conspirators or patriots or persecuted religious groups.

Every country in the world has commercialized caves, opened, lighted, paved where necessary and provided with stairways, bridges and even elevators for the convenience of sightseers. The lure of underground exploration of "wild caves" has produced many groups of amateur speleologists, popularly called spelunkers. (*See* also articles on various caves, such as COLOSSAL CAVERN; FINGAL'S CAVE; JACOBS' CAVERN; KENT'S CAVERN; LURAY CAVERN; MAMMOTH CAVE; POSTOJNA; WYANDOTTE CAVE; etc.)

BIBLIOGRAPHY.—W. M. Davis, "Origin of Limestone Caverns," *Bulletin of the Geological Society of America*, vol. xli, pp. 475–628 (1930); J. H. Bretz, "Vadose and Phreatic Features of Limestone Caverns," *Journal of Geology*, vol. l, pp. 675–871 (1942); W. M. McGill, *Caverns of Virginia*, bulletin 35, Virginia Geological Survey (1935); R. W. Stone, *Pennsylvania Caves*, bulletin G3, Pennsylvania Geological Survey (Harrisburg, Pa., 1932); W. E. Davies, *Caverns of West Virginia*, vol. xix, West Virginia Geological Survey (1949). (J. H. Bz.)

CAVEA, a term applied to the rows of spectators' seats in Greek and Roman theatres and in Roman amphitheatres; also, less commonly, to the cells for wild beasts underneath the arena.

CAVEAT, in law, a notice given by the party interested (caveator) to the proper officer of a court of justice to prevent the taking of a certain step without warning. It is entered in connection with dealings in land registered in the land registry, with the grant of marriage licences, to prevent the issuing of a lunacy commission, to stay the probate of a will, letters of administration, etc. "Caveat" is also a term used in United States patent law (*see* PATENTS).

CAVEAT EMPTOR, a Latin phrase meaning literally "Let the buyer beware." It represents a legal rule in the purchase and sale of personal property that the buyer purchases at his own risk in the absence of an express warranty, or unless the law implies a seller's warranty, or there is found to have been fraud in the transaction. (*See* SALE OF GOODS.)

CAVELL, EDITH LOUISA (1865–1915), British nurse, was born Dec. 4, 1865, at Swardeston, Norfolk. She entered the London hospital as a probationer in 1895. In 1907 she was appointed the first matron of the Berkendael Medical institute, Brussels, which became a Red Cross hospital on the outbreak of World War I. From November 1914 to July 1915 wounded and derelict English and French soldiers were hidden from the Germans by Prince Reginald de Croy at his château near Mons, thence conveyed to the houses of Edith Cavell and others in Brussels, and furnished by them with money to reach the Dutch frontier, with the aid of guides obtained through Philippe Baucq. On Aug. 5, 1915, Edith Cavell was arrested and imprisoned. She admitted having sheltered and helped to convey to the frontier about 200 English, French and Belgians. A court-martial was held (Oct. 7 and 8), and a Belgian lawyer, Sadi Kirschen, defended Edith Cavell. On Oct. 9 she and Philippe Baucq were sentenced to death with three others who were afterward reprieved. Despite efforts to obtain a reprieve in which Brand Whitlock, the U.S. minister at Brussels, was active, Miss Cavell and Baucq were shot on Oct. 12. Miss Cavell, who had tended many wounded German soldiers with devoted care, faced the firing squad with a dignity which moved the world. To the British chaplain who administered a final sacrament, she made the remark, "Patriotism is not enough," which at once became as historic as Nelson's utterance at Trafalgar. On May 15, 1919, her body was removed to Norwich cathedral, after a memorial service in Westminster abbey. A memorial statue stands opposite the National Portrait gallery, London.

BIBLIOGRAPHY.—Ambroise Got (ed.), *The Case of Miss Cavell From the Unpublished Documents of the Trial* (1920); Sadi Kirschen, *Devant les conseils de guerre allemands* (1919); *Correspondence With the United States Ambassador Respecting the Execution of Miss Cavell at Brussels*, cd. 8013, H.M.S.O. (1915).

CAVENDISH, GEORGE (1500–1562?), the biographer of Cardinal Wolsey, was the elder son of Thomas Cavendish, clerk of the pipe in the exchequer. About 1527 he entered the service of Cardinal Wolsey as a gentleman-usher, and for the next three years he was in the closest personal attendance on the great man. It is plain that he enjoyed Wolsey's closest confidence to the end, for after the cardinal's death George Cavendish was called before the privy council and closely examined as to Wolsey's latest acts and words. Many years passed before his biography was composed. At length, in 1557, he wrote it out in its final form. It was impossible to publish it in the author's lifetime, but it was widely circulated in manuscript. The book was first printed in 1641 in a garbled text under the title of *The Negotiations of Thomas Wolsey*. The genuine text, from contemporary manuscripts, was first published in 1810. Until that time it was believed that the book was the composition of George Cavendish's younger brother William, the founder of Chatsworth, who also was attached to Wolsey; but Joseph Hunter, in a tract called *Who Wrote Cavendish's Life of Wolsey?* (1814), proved the claim of George. The book is the sole authentic record of a multitude of events highly important in a particularly interesting section of the history of England. Its biographical excellence was first emphasized by Bishop Mandell Creighton, who insisted that Cavendish was the earliest of the great English biographers and an individual writer of particular charm and originality.

See the edition of the *Life* published by S. W. Singer in 1815, which was reprinted, with a biographical introduction, by Henry Morley in the Universal Library Series (1885). *See* also Francis Bickley, *The Cavendish Family* (1911).

CAVENDISH, HENRY (1731–1810), English chemist and physicist, elder son of Lord Charles Cavendish, brother of the 3rd duke of Devonshire, and Lady Anne Grey, daughter of the duke of Kent, was born at Nice on Oct. 10, 1731. He was sent to school at Hackney in 1742, and in 1749 entered Peterhouse, Cambridge, which he left in 1753 without taking a degree. He appears to have spent some time in Paris with his brother Frederick during the following years, and apparently occupied himself in the study of mathematics and physics. Until he was about 40 he seems to have enjoyed a moderate allowance from his father

(d. 1783), but in the latter part of his life an aunt left him a fortune which, together with his patrimony, made him one of the richest men of his time. It was commonly said that he was the richest of the philosophers and the most philosophical of the rich.

Cavendish lived principally at Clapham Common, but he had also a town house in Bloomsbury which is now marked with a tablet. His library was in a house in Dean street, Soho; and there he used to attend on appointed days to lend books to men who were properly vouched for. He was a regular attendant at the meetings of the Royal society, of which he became a fellow in 1760, and he dined every Thursday with the club composed of its members. Otherwise, he had little intercourse with society; indeed, his chief object in life seems to have been to avoid the attention of his fellows. With his relatives he had little communication, and even Lord George Cavendish, his second cousin, whom he made his principal heir, he saw only for a few minutes once a year. His dinner was ordered daily by a note placed on the hall table, and his women servants were instructed to keep out of his sight on pain of dismissal. In person he was tall and rather thin; his dress was old-fashioned and singularly uniform, and was inclined to be shabby about the times when the precisely arranged visits of his tailor were due. He had a slight hesitation in his speech, and his air of timidity and reserve was almost ludicrous. He never married. He died at Clapham on Feb. 24, 1810, leaving funded property worth £700,000, and a landed estate of £8,000 a year, together with canal and other property, and £50,000 at his bankers'. He was buried in the family vault at All Saints' church, Derby. In 1927 this church became the cathedral church of the new diocese of Derby, and it was decided to erect a monument there to Henry Cavendish.

Cavendish's scientific work was wide in its range. He took for his motto, "Everything is ordered by measure, number and weight." The papers he himself published form an incomplete record of his researches, since many of the results he obtained became generally known only years after his death; yet the Institute of France in 1803 chose him as one of its eight foreign associates. His first communication to the Royal society, a chemical paper on "Factitious Airs" (*Philosophical Transactions*, 1766), consisted of three parts, a fourth part remaining unpublished until 1839, when it was communicated to the British association by Canon W. Vernon Harcourt. This paper dealt mostly with "inflammable air" (hydrogen), which he was the first to recognize as a distinct substance, and "fixed air" (carbon dioxide). He determined the specific gravity of these gases with reference to common air, investigated the extent to which they are absorbed by various liquids and noted that the air produced by fermentation and putrefaction has properties identical with those of fixed air obtained from marble. He introduced new refinements into his experiments, such as the use of drying agents and the correction of the volume of a gas for temperature and pressure. In the following year he published a paper on the analysis of one of the London pump waters (from Rathbone place, Oxford street), which is closely connected with the memoirs referred to above, since it shows that the calcareous matter in that water is held in solution by the "fixed air" present and can be precipitated by lime. In 1783 he described observations he had made to determine whether or not the atmosphere is constant in composition; after testing the air on nearly 60 different days in 1781 he could find, after 400 determinations in the proportion of oxygen, no difference of which he could be sure, nor could he detect any sensible variation at different places. Two papers on "Experiments on Air," printed in the *Philosophical Transactions* for 1784 and 1785, contain his great discoveries of the compound nature of water and the composition of nitric acid. Starting from an experiment, narrated by Joseph Priestley, in which John Warltire fired a mixture of common air and hydrogen by electricity, with the result that there was a diminution of volume and a deposition of moisture, Cavendish burned about two parts of hydrogen with five of common air and noticed that the only liquid product was water. In another experiment he fired by electric spark a mixture of hydrogen and oxygen in a glass globe, similar to the apparatus now called "Cavendish's eudiometer," and again obtained water. Proceeding with these experiments he found that the resulting water contained nitric acid. In the second of the two papers he gives an account of the methods by which the composition of nitric acid was discovered. He observed also that a small fraction, about $\frac{1}{120}$, of the "phlogisticated air" of the atmosphere differed from the rest. In this residue he doubtless had a sample of the inert gas argon, which was only recognized as a distinct entity more than 100 years later by J. W. Rayleigh and Sir William Ramsay (*qq.v.*). In the meantime, many able chemists, including such masters as J. L. Gay-Lussac and R. W. von Bunsen, had made "complete" analyses of atmospheric air. It may be noted that, while Cavendish adhered to the phlogistic doctrine, he did not hold it with anything like the tenacity that characterized Priestley. Thus, in his 1784 paper on "Experiments on Air," he remarks that not only the experiments he is describing but also "most other phenomena of nature seem explicable as well, or nearly as well," upon the Lavoisierian view; but he did not accept it and continued to use the language of the phlogistic theory. Experiments on arsenic, published for the first time in 1921, showed that Cavendish had investigated the properties of arsenic acid about ten years before K. W. Scheele. He showed that arsenic oxide contained less phlogiston (*i.e.*, more oxygen) than arsenious oxide, which in turn contained less than free arsenic.

Cavendish's work on electricity, with the exception of two papers containing relatively unimportant matter, remained in the possession of the Devonshire family until 1879, when the papers were edited by James Clerk Maxwell as the *Electrical Researches of the Hon. Henry Cavendish.* This work shows that Cavendish had anticipated the researches of C. A. Coulomb, Michael Faraday and others. He investigated the capacity of condensers and constructed a series of condensers with which he measured the capacity of various pieces of apparatus using the "inch of electricity" as the unit of capacity. He discovered specific inductive capacity and measured this quantity; he showed that electric charges are confined to the surface of a conductor and that the inverse square law of force between charges holds to within 2%. Cavendish introduced the idea of potential under the name of "degree of electrification" in a paper published in 1771 under the title "Attempt to Explain Some of the Principal Phenomena of Electricity by Means of an Elastic Fluid." He investigated the power of different substances to conduct electrostatic discharges (*Phil. Trans.*, 1775) and completed an inquiry which amounted to an anticipation of Ohm's law.

Cavendish took up the study of heat, and had he published his results promptly he might have anticipated Joseph Black (*q.v.*) as the discoverer of latent heat and of specific heat. He published a paper on the freezing point of mercury in 1783, and in this paper he expressed doubt of the fluid theory of heat. He regarded heat as a manifestation of internal motion of the smallest particles, whereas Black considered it to be material in nature.

Cavendish's last great achievement was his series of experiments to determine the destiny of the earth (*Phil. Trans.*, 1798). The apparatus he employed was devised by John Michell, though Cavendish had the most important parts reconstructed to his own designs. The figure he gives for the specific gravity of the earth is 5.48, but in fact the mean of the 29 results he records works out at 5.448. Other publications of his later years dealt with the height of an aurora seen in 1784 (*Phil. Trans.*, 1790), the civil year of the Hindus (*ibid.*, 1792), and an improved method of graduating astronomical instruments (*ibid.*, 1809). Cavendish also had a taste for geology and made several tours in England for the purpose of gratifying it.

A *Life* by George Wilson (1818–59), printed for the Cavendish society in 1851, contains an account of his writings, both published and unpublished, together with a critical inquiry into the claims of all the alleged discoverers of the composition of water. Some of his instruments are preserved in the Royal institution, London, and his name is commemorated in the Cavendish Physical laboratory at Cambridge, which was built by the 7th duke of Devonshire.

The remainder of Cavendish's papers was placed at the disposition of the Royal society by the duke of Devonshire. In 1921 the previously published work, together with a number of unpublished experiments, appeared under the title *The Scientific Papers of the Honourable Henry Cavendish, F.R.S.; Vol. I, The Electrical Researches,* revised with preface and notes by Sir J. Larmor; *Vol. II, Chemical and Dynamical,* edited by Sir Thomas Edward Thorpe, with additions by Charles Chree and others.

BIBLIOGRAPHY.—H. Brougham, *Lives of the Philosophers of the Time of George III* (1855); B. Jaffe, essay in his *Crucibles* (New York, London, 1930); E. Roberts, *Famous Chemists* (1911); T. E. Thorpe, *Essays in Historical Chemistry* (1894); G. Lockemann, essay in *Das Buch der grossen Chemiker* (1929).

CAVENDISH or CANDISH, **THOMAS** (1555?–1592), the third circumnavigator of the globe, was born in Trimley St. Martin, Suffolk, and educated at Corpus Christi college, Cambridge. In 1585 he accompanied Sir Richard Grenville to America. Soon returning to England, he undertook an elaborate imitation of Drake's great voyage. On July 21, 1586, he sailed from Plymouth with 123 men in three vessels, only one of which (the "Desire," of 140 tons) returned. By way of Sierra Leone, the Cape Verde Islands and Cabo Frio in Brazil, he coasted down to Patagonia (where he discovered "Port Desire," his only important contribution to knowledge), and passing through the Straits of Magellan fell upon the Spanish settlements and shipping on the west coast of South and Central America and of Mexico. Among his captures was the treasure galleon the "Great St. Anne," which he seized off Cape St. Lucas, the southern extremity of California (Nov. 14, 1587). After this success he struck across the Pacific for home, touching at the Ladrones, Philippines, Moluccas and

Java. He rounded the Cape of Good Hope, and arrived at Plymouth on Sept. 9–10, 1588, having circumnavigated the globe in two years and 50 days. It is said that his sailors were clothed in silk, his sails were damask and his topmast covered with cloth of gold. Yet by 1591 he was again in difficulties, and planned a fresh American and Pacific venture. John Davis (*q.v.*) accompanied him, but the voyage (undertaken with five vessels) was an utter failure. He died and was buried at sea, on the way home, May 20, 1592.

Bibliography.—Richard Hakluyt, *Principal Navigations,* (1) edition of 1589, p. 809 (N.H.'s narrative of the voyage of 1586–88); (2) edition of 1599–1600, vol. iii, pp. 803–825 (Francis Pretty's narrative of the same); (3) edition of 1599–1600, vol. iii, pp. 251–253 (on the venture of 1585); (4) edition of 1599–1600, vol. iii, pp. 845–852 (John Lane's narrative of the last voyage, of 1591–1592); also *Stationers' Registers* (Arber), vol. ii, pp. 505–509; the Molyneux Globe of 1592, in the library of the Middle Temple, London, and the Ballads in *Biog. Brit.,* vol. i, p. 1196; E. S. Payne, *Voyages of the Elizabethan Seamen to America,* 2 vol. (1893–1900).

CAVENDISH, SIR WILLIAM (*c.* 1505–1557), founder of the English noble house of Cavendish, was the younger brother of George Cavendish (*q.v.*). His father, Thomas, was a descendant of Sir John Cavendish, the judge, who in 1381 was murdered by Jack Straw's insurgent peasants at Bury St. Edmunds. Of William's education nothing seems known, but in 1530 he was appointed one of the commissioners for visiting monasteries; he worked directly under Thomas Cromwell, whom he calls "master," and to whom many of his extant letters are addressed. In 1541 he was auditor of the court of augmentations, in 1546 treasurer of the king's chamber, and was knighted and sworn of the privy council. Under Edward VI and Mary he continued in favour at court; during the latter's reign he partially conformed, but on the occasion of the war with France he with other Derbyshire gentlemen refused the loan of £100 demanded by the queen. He died in 1557. Cavendish acquired large properties from the spoils of the monasteries, but in accordance with the wish of his third wife, Elizabeth, he sold them to purchase land in Derbyshire. This wife was the celebrated "building Bess of Hardwick," daughter of John Hardwicke of Hardwicke, Derbyshire; she completed the original building of Chatsworth house,—begun in 1553 by her husband,—of which nothing now remains. Her fourth husband was George Talbot, 6th earl of Shrewsbury. By her Cavendish had six children; an elder son who died without issue; William, who in 1618 was created earl of Devonshire; Charles, whose son William became 1st duke of Newcastle; Frances, who married Sir Henry Pierpont and was the ancestress of the dukes of Kingston; Elizabeth, who married Charles Stuart, earl of Lennox, and was the mother of Arabella Stuart; and Mary, who married Gilbert Talbot, 7th earl of Shrewsbury.

CAVETTO, in architecture, any projecting moulding (*q.v.*) with a concave profile of single curvature.

CAVIARE or Caviar, the roe of various species of *Acipenser* or sturgeon prepared, in several qualities, as an article of food. The word is common to most European languages and supposed to be of Turk or Tatar origin, but the Turk word *khavyah* is probably derived from the Italian *caviala;* the word does not appear in Russian.

The best caviare, which can only be made in winter and is difficult to preserve, is the loosely granulated, almost liquid kind, known in Russia as *ikra.* It is prepared by beating the ovaries and straining through a sieve to clear the eggs of the membranes, fibres and fatty matter; it is then salted with from 4% to 6% of salt. The difficulty of preparation and of transport made it a table delicacy in western Europe, where it has been known since the 16th century, as is evidenced by Hamlet's "His play . . . pleased not the million, 'twas caviare to the general."

Caviare is eaten either as an hors d'oeuvre, particularly in Russia and northern Europe, with kümmel or other liqueurs, or as a savoury, or as a flavouring to other dishes. The coarser quality, in Russia known as *pajusnaya* (from *pajus,* the adherent skin of the ovaries), is more strongly salted in brine and is pressed into a more solid form than the *ikra;* it is then packed in small barrels or hermetically sealed tins. This forms a staple article of food in eastern Europe and Russia, where the best forms of caviare are still made. The greater quantity of the coarser kinds are exported from Astrakhan, the centre of the trade. Large amounts are made each year for export in America and also in Germany, Norway and Sweden. The roe of tunny and mullet pickled in brine and vinegar, is used, under the name of "botargo," along the Mediterranean littoral and in the Levant.

CAVIGLIA, ENRICO (1862–1945), Italian soldier, was born at Finale Marina (Genoa) on May 4, 1862. After Italy's entry into World War I he was promoted to major general and commanded the Bari brigade. In June 1916 he took over the 29th division and later was promoted lieutenant general. In July 1917 he was given command of the 24th corps, which broke through the Austrian lines on the Bainsizza plateau. In June 1918 he was chosen to command the 8th army, which played an important part in the final victory of Vittorio Veneto. From January to June 1919 Caviglia was minister of war, and as such became a senator. In November of the same year he was promoted army general. In Jan. 1920 he took over the command in Venezia Giulia. His task was difficult, since the discipline of the troops had been severely shaken by the example of Gabriele d'Annunzio's Fiume raid. He restored discipline, and ultimately (Dec. 1920) did not hesitate to use force in driving D'Annunzio from Fiume. In 1926 he was made a marshal. He died March 22, 1945.

CAVITE, a municipality and capital of the province of Cavite, Luzon, Philippines, on a forked tongue of land in Manila bay, 8 mi. S. of Manila. Pop. (1948) 35,052.

A native town was already in existence there when the Spaniards arrived and took possession after their occupation of Manila. The Dutch bombarded Cavite in 1647 and it was long a revolutionary centre. In 1872 a military insurrection broke out and in 1896 there was an execution of 13 of the insurgents to whom a monument was erected by their Filipino sympathizers in 1906. The home of Emilio Aguinaldo, the insurrection leader against both Spain and the United States, was the adjoining municipality of Cavite Viejo.

On May 1, 1898, Commodore George Dewey of the United States navy commanded a naval force which overcame the Spanish fleet and captured the town. From 1898 until 1941 it was the chief naval base and coaling station of the U.S. fleet in Asiatic waters, the coaling docks being at Sangley point in the north end of the municipality. But on Dec. 7 it was attacked by Japanese forces, who held it until 1945, when the base was recaptured by the U.S. After the Philippines became independent, provisions were made to allow the U.S. to continue to hold it for certain limited activities.

The surrounding region, of volcanic origin, is fertile and produces Manila hemp, rice, sugar, copra, cacao, coffee and corn. There are convenient transportation connections with Manila. The U.S. navy established a radio station and arsenal, and remains of Spanish fortifications were still visible in modern times.

CAVOUR, CAMILLO BENSO, Count of (1810–1861), Italian statesman, was born at Turin on Aug. 1, 1810. Being a younger son (his brother Gustavo was the eldest), Cavour was destined for the army, and became an engineer officer. He soon developed strongly marked Liberal tendencies and an uncompromising dislike for absolutism and clericalism, which made him a suspect in the eyes of the police and of the reactionaries. After the accession to the throne of Charles Albert, whom he always distrusted, he resigned his commission (1831). During the next few years he devoted himself to the study of political and social problems, to foreign travel and to acquiring a thorough knowledge of practical agriculture. Cavour's political ideas were greatly influenced by the July revolution of 1830 in France, which proved that a historic monarchy was not incompatible with Liberal principles, and he became more than ever convinced of the benefits of a constitutional monarchy as opposed both to despotism and to republicanism. He applied his knowledge of agriculture to the management of his father's estate at Leri, which he greatly improved, he founded the Piedmontese Agricultural society and took the lead in promoting the introduction of steam navigation, railways and factories into the country. Thus his mind gradually evolved, and he began to dream dreams of a united Italy free of foreign influence. In 1847 the psychological moment seemed to have arrived, for the new pope, Pius IX., showed Liberal tendencies and seemed ready to lead all the forces of Italian patriotism against the Austrian domination. Cavour, although he realized that a really Liberal pope was an impossibility, saw the importance of the movement and the necessity of profiting by it. He founded a newspaper at Turin called *Il Risorgimento,* which advocated the ideas of constitutional reform. In Jan. 1848 the revolution first broke out in Sicily, and Cavour, in a speech before a delegation of journalists, declared that the king must take a decided line and grant his people a constitution. Charles Albert, after much hesitation, was induced to grant a charter of liberties (Feb. 8, 1848). Cavour continued his journalistic activity, and his articles in the *Risorgimento* came to exercise great influence both on the king and on public opinion. When the news of the revolt of the Milanese against the Austrians reached Turin on March 19, Cavour advocated war against Austria. His article in the *Risorgimento* made such an impression that it put an end to the king's vacillations, and a few days after its appearance war was declared (March 25).

During the war elections were held in Piedmont. Cavour was returned in June, and he took his seat in parliament on the right as a Conservative. He was not a good speaker, but he gradually developed a strong argumentative power, and he rose at times to the highest level of an eloquence which was never rhetorical. After the dissolution in Jan. 1849, Cavour was not re-elected. The new parliament had to discuss, in the first instance, the all-important question of whether the campaign should be continued now that the armistice was about to expire. The king decided on a last desperate throw, and recommenced hostilities. On March 23 the Piedmontese were totally defeated at Novara, a disaster which was followed immediately by the abdication of Charles Albert in favour of his son Victor Emmanuel II. The new king was obliged to conclude peace with Austria and the Italian revolution was crushed, but Cavour did not despair. There were fresh elections in July, and this time Cavour was returned. His speech on March 7, 1850, in which he said that, "Piedmont, gathering to itself all the living forces of Italy, would be soon in a position to lead our mother-country to the high destinies to which she is called," struck the first note of encouragement after the dark days of the preceding year. He supported the ministry of which Massimo d'Azeglio was president in its work of reform and restoration, and in October of the same year, on the death of Santa Rosa, he himself was appointed minister of agriculture, industry and commerce. In 1851 he also assumed the portfolio of finance, and devoted himself to the task of reorganizing the Piedmontese finances. By far the ablest man in the cabinet, he soon came to dominate it, but as a result of a quarrel with d'Azeglio he resigned; he made use of his freedom to visit England and France again, in order to sound public opinion on the Italian question. In London he found the leaders of both parties friendly. At this time Sir James Hudson was appointed British minister at Turin, where he became the intimate friend of Cavour and gave him valuable assistance. In Paris, Cavour had a long interview with Prince Louis Napoleon, then president of the republic, and also met several Italian exiles in France.

On Cavour's return he found a new cabinet crisis, and was invited to form a ministry. By Nov. 4, he was prime minister. He devoted the first years of his premiership to developing the economic resources of the country; but in preparing it for greater destinies, he had to meet the heavy expenditure by increased taxation. Cavour's first international difficulty was with Austria; after the abortive rising at Milan in Feb. 1853, the Austrian Government, in addition to other measures of repression, confiscated the estates of those Lombards who had become naturalized Piedmontese, although they had nothing to do with the outbreak. Cavour took a strong line on this question, and on Austria's refusal to withdraw the obnoxious decree, he recalled the Piedmontese minister from Vienna. Then followed the Crimean War, in which Cavour first showed his extraordinary political insight and diplomatic genius. In spite of many difficulties and opposition from both extreme Conservatives and Radicals, he negotiated Piedmontese participation in the campaign as a means of bringing the Italian question before the Great Powers. General Dabormida, the minister of foreign affairs, disapproved of this policy and resigned. The vacant portfolio was offered to d'Azeglio, who refused it; whereupon Cavour assumed it himself. On the same day (Jan. 10, 1855) the treaty with France and England was signed, and shortly afterwards 15,000 Piedmontese troops under General La Marmora were despatched to the Crimea.

Events at first seemed to justify the fears of Cavour's opponents. Cholera attacked the Piedmontese soldiers, who for a long time had no occasion to distinguish themselves in action; public opinion became despondent and began to blame Cavour, and even he himself lost heart. Then came the news of the battle of the Tchernaya, fought and won by the Italians, which turned sadness and doubt into jubilation. Joy was felt throughout Italy, especially at Milan, where the victory was the first sign of daylight amid the gloom caused by the return of the Austrians. On the summoning of the Congress of Paris at the conclusion of the war, Cavour represented Piedmont. After much discussion, and in spite of the opposition of Austria, who as mediator occupied a predominant position, Cavour obtained that Piedmont should be treated as one of the Great Powers. By his marvellous diplomatic skill, far superior to that of his colleagues, he first succeeded in isolating Austria, secondly in indirectly compromising Napoleon in the Italian question, and thirdly in getting the wretched conditions of Italy discussed by the representatives of the Great Powers. It was now manifest that the liberation of Italy was personified in him. Cavour's chief measure of internal reform during this period was a bill for suppressing all monastic orders unconnected with education, preaching or charity; this aroused strong opposition and led to the minister's resignation. But he was soon recalled, for the country could not do without him, and the bill was passed (May 29, 1855).

Cavour now saw that war with Austria was merely a question of time, and he began to establish connections with the revolutionaries of all parts of Italy. He continued to strengthen Piedmont's military resources, but he well knew that Piedmont could not defeat Austria single-handed. He would have preferred an alliance with Great Britain, who would never demand territorial compensation; but although British sympathies were with Italy, the British Government was keenly anxious to avoid war. From Napoleon more was to be hoped, for the emperor still preserved some of his revolutionary instincts, while the insecurity of his situation at home made him eager to gain popularity by winning military glory abroad; but he still hesitated, and Cavour devoted the whole of his ability to overcoming his doubts. In spite of the Orsini outrage, an "accidental" meeting between Napoleon and Cavour was arranged and took place at Plombières in July, and although no definite treaty was signed the basis of an agreement was laid, whereby France and Piedmont were to declare war against Austria with the object of expelling her from Italy, and a north Italian State was to be formed; in exchange for this help France was to receive Savoy and possibly Nice. A marriage was to be arranged between Prince Jerome Bonaparte and Princess Clothilde, Victor Emmanuel's daughter. But the emperor still hesitated, and Cavour saw that the only way to overcome the many obstacles in his path was to force Austria's hand. Then there was the danger lest an Italy freed by French arms should be overwhelmed under French predominance; for this reason Cavour was determined to secure the co-operation of volunteers from other parts of Italy, and that the war should be accompanied by a series of risings against Austria and the local despots.

The moment war was seen to be imminent, parties of Italians of all classes, especially Lombards, poured into Piedmont to enlist in the army. Cavour also had a secret interview with Garibaldi, with whom he arranged to organize volunteer corps so that the army should be not merely that of Piedmont, but of all Italy. Every day the situation grew more critical, and on Jan. 10, 1859 the king in his speech from the throne pronounced the memorable words "that he could not remain deaf to the cry of pain (*il grido di dolore*) that reached him from all parts of Italy" —words which, although actually suggested by Napoleon, rang like a trumpet-call throughout the land. In the meanwhile the marriage negotiations were concluded, and during the emperor's visit to Turin a military convention was signed between the two States, and Savoy and Nice were promised to France as a reward for the expulsion of the Austrians from Italy. But Napoleon, ever hesitating, jumped at the Russian proposal to settle the Italian question by means of his own favourite expedient, a congress. To this Austria agreed on condition that Piedmont should disarm and should be excluded from the congress; England supported the scheme, but desired that all the Italian States should be represented. Cavour was in despair at the turn events were taking but decided at last reluctantly to accept the proposal, lest Piedmont should be abandoned by all, while he clung to the hope that Austria would reject it. On April 19, the Austrian emperor, on the advice of the military party, did reject it; and on the 23rd, to Cavour's inexpressible joy, Austria sent an ultimatum demanding the disarmament of Piedmont. Cavour replied that his Government had agreed to the congress proposed by the Powers and that it had nothing more to say. On quitting the chamber that day he said to a friend: "I am leaving the last sitting of the last Piedmontese parliament"—the next would represent united Italy. France now allied herself definitely with Piedmont, and England, delighted at Cavour's acquiescence became wholly friendly to the Italian cause. A few days later Austria declared war.

As La Marmora now took the chief command of the army Cavour added the ministry of war to the others he already held. His activity at this time was astounding, for he was virtually dictator and controlled single-handed nearly all the chief offices of the State. The French and Piedmontese forces defeated the Austrians in several battles, and the people rose in arms at Parma, Modena, Florence and Bologna; the local princes were expelled and provisional governments set up. Cavour sent special commissioners to take charge of the various provinces in Victor Emmanuel's name. But these events, together with Prussia's menacing attitude, began to alarm Napoleon, who, after Solferino, concluded an armistice with Austria at Villafranca on July 8, without previously informing Cavour. When Cavour heard of it he was thunderstruck; he immediately interviewed the king at Monzambano, and in violent, almost disrespectful language implored him not to make peace until Venice was free. But Victor Emmanuel saw that nothing was to be gained by a refusal, and much against his own inclination, signed the peace preliminaries at Villafranca, adding the phrase, "pour ce qui me concerne," which meant that he was not responsible for what the people of other parts of Italy might do (July 12). Lombardy was to be ceded to Piedmont, Venetia to remain Austrian, the deposed princes to be reinstated, and the pope made president of an Italian confederation.

The cabinet resigned the next day, and Cavour privately advised the revolutionists of central Italy to resist the return of the princes, by force if necessary. Palmerston, who had meanwhile succeeded Malmesbury as foreign minister, informed France and Austria that Great Britain would never tolerate their armed intervention in favour of the central Italian despots. On Nov. 10, peace was signed at Zürich, and on the fall of the Rattazzi-La Marmora cabinet the king, in spite of the quarrel at Monzambano, asked Cavour to take office again. Napoleon still refused to consent to the union of Tuscany with Piedmont, but Cavour saw that Napoleon might be ready to deal; although the bargain of the preceding year had not been exactly fulfilled, as the Austrians were still in Venice, he again brought forward the question of Nice and Savoy. On March 24, the treaty was signed, and the emperor's opposition to the annexation of central Italy withdrawn. On April 2, the parliament representing Piedmont, the duchies of Parma and Modena, Tuscany and Romagna, met, and Cavour had the difficult and ungrateful task of explaining the cession of Nice and Savoy. In spite of some opposition, the agreement was ratified by a large majority.

The situation in the kingdom of Naples was now becoming critical, and Cavour had to follow a somewhat double-faced policy, on the one hand negotiating with the Bourbon king (Francis II.), suggesting a division of Italy between him and Victor Emmanuel, and on the other secretly backing up the revolutionary agitation. Having now learnt that Garibaldi was planning an expedition to Sicily with his volunteers, he decided not to oppose its departure; on May 5, it sailed from Quarto near Genoa. Garibaldi with his immortal Thousand landed at Marsala, and the whole rotten fabric of the Bourbon Government collapsed. He crossed over to the mainland, and entered Naples in triumph. But Cavour feared, that, although Garibaldi himself had always loyally acted in the king of Italy's name, the republicans around him might lead him to commit some imprudence and plunge the country into anarchy, and that Garibaldi might invade the papal States, which would have led to further international complications. But the pope had made considerable armaments; his forces, consisting largely of brigands and foreigners under the French general Lamoricière, maintained a menacing attitude on the frontier; Cavour decided on the momentous step of annexing the papal States with the exception of the Roman province. The Italian forces crossed the frontier from Romagna on Sept. 11, and were everywhere received with open arms by the people; Ancona was taken, Lamoricière was defeated and captured at the battle of Castelfidardo, and on the 20th King Victor marched into the Neapolitan kingdom. On Oct. 1, Garibaldi defeated the Neapolitan troops on the Volturno, and Gaeta alone, where King Francis of Naples had retired, still held out.

Cavour had to use all his tact to restrain Garibaldi from marching on Rome and at the same time not to appear ungrateful. He refused to act despotically, and summoned parliament to vote on the annexation, which it did on the 11th. Two days later Garibaldi magnanimously gave in to the nation's will and handed his conquests over to King Victor as a free gift. Gaeta surrendered on Feb. 13, and King Francis retired to Rome. Parliament was dissolved once more; the new chamber showed an overwhelming majority in favour of Cavour, and Victor Emmanuel was proclaimed king of Italy.

The last question with which Cavour had to deal was that of Rome. In October he declared in parliament that Rome must be the capital of Italy, for no other city was recognized as such by the whole country, and in Jan. 1861 a resolution to that effect was passed. But owing to Napoleon's attitude he had to proceed warily, and made no attempt for the present to carry out the nation's wishes. At the same time he was anxious that the Church should preserve the fullest liberty, and he believed in the principle of "a free Church in a free State." The long strain of these last years had been almost unbearable, and at last began to tell; the negotiations with Garibaldi were particularly trying, for while the great statesman wished to treat the hero and his volunteers generously, he could not permit all the Garibaldian officers to be received into the regular army with the same ranks they held in the volunteer forces. This question, together with that of Nice, led to a painful scene in the chamber between the two men, although they were formally reconciled a few days later. For some time past Cavour had been unwell and irritable, and the scene with Garibaldi undoubtedly hastened his end. A fever set in, and after a short illness he passed away on June 6, 1861. He was buried on his ancestral estate of Santena.

The death of Cavour was a terrible loss to Italy; there remained many problems to be solved in which his genius and personality were urgently needed. But the great work had been carried to such a point that lesser men might now complete the structure. He is undoubtedly the greatest figure of the *Risorgimento,* and although other men and other forces co-operated in the movement, it was Cavour who organized it and skilfully conducted the negotiations necessary to overcome all, apparently insuperable, obstacles. (L. V.)

BIBLIOGRAPHY.—C. Benso di Cavour, *Opere politico-economiche* (Cuneo, 1855) and *Discorsi parlamentari* (Turin, 1863–72); W. de la Rive, *Le Comte de Cavour* (1862), the work of a contemporary and intimate friend; H. von Treitschke, "Cavour" in his *Historische und politische Aufsätze* (Leipzig, 1871); G. Massari, *Il Conte di Cavour* (Turin, 1873); L. Chiala, *Lettere edite ed inedite del Conte di Cavour* (Turin, 1883–87); D. Zanichelli, *Gli Scritti del Conte di Cavour* (Bologna, 1892), and *Cavour* (Florence, 1905); G. Buzzaconi, *Bibliografia Cavouriana* (Turin, 1898); Countess E. Martinengo Cesaresco, *Cavour* (London, 1898), an excellent little monograph; F. X. Krauss, *Cavour* (Mainz, 1902); E. Artom, *L'Opere politica del Sena-*

tore Isacco Artom nel Risorgimento Italiano (Bologna, 1905), a biography of Cavour's devoted private secretary, containing new material; W. R. Thayer, *Life and Times of Cavour* (1911); F. Ruffeni, *La Giovinezza del Conte di Cavour* (1912); P. Orsi, *Cavour and the Making of Modern Italy* (new ed. 1926); G. M. Paléologue, *Cavour* (1926); *Il Carteggio Cavour-Nigra, 1858–61* (Bologna, 1926).

CAVOUR (anc. *Caburrum* or *Forum Vibii*), a village of Piedmont, Italy, in the province of Turin, 32 mi. S.W. by rail and steam tram (via Pinerolo) from the town of Turin. Pop. 1,547 (town); 6,244 (commune). It lies on the north side of a huge isolated mass of granite (the Rocca di Cavour) which rises from the plain. On the summit was the Roman village. The town gave its name to the Benso family of Chieri, who were raised to the marquisate in 1771, and of which the statesman Cavour was a member.

CAVY, the name of several South American rodents of the family Caviidae (*see* RODENTIA); originally it was confined to the domesticated guinea pig and its allies of the genus *Cavia.* (The word "guinea" here may be a corruption of "Guiana" but more probably it means "foreign.") The true cavies are small, self-coloured animals, with short, rounded ears and no tail. They are partly diurnal and live in burrows. The diet is vegetarian and their cries are faint squeaks and grunts. Unlike the prolific guinea pig, which begins to breed at two months old and may be the parent of several hundred individuals in a year, the wild cavies breed only once a year, producing one or two young at a time. These are born in a very advanced stage of development and begin to feed themselves the following day.

Cavies are widely distributed in South America. The original of the domestic race is *C. cutleri* of Peru. *C. niata* is found at great elevations in the Andes. The restless cavy of Brazil is *C. pamparum.* The Patagonian cavy or mara (*Dolichotis australis*) resembles a hare in shape and habits, but lives in a burrow. Fossil species of this genus, of which there is a second smaller type in Argentina, have been found in Brazil and the Argentine.

CAWDOR, village and civil parish, Nairnshire, Scotland. Pop. (1931) 767. The village is situated 5 mi. S.S.W. of Nairn and 3 mi. from Gollanfield Junction on the L.M.S.R. In the vicinity is a large distillery. The castle was the scene, according to the tradition which Shakespeare has perpetuated, of the murder of King Duncan by Macbeth, thane of Cawdor (or Calder), in 1040. Since the oldest part of the structure dates from 1454, however, and seemingly had no predecessor, the tradition has no foundation in fact. The building stands on the rocky bank of Cawdor burn, a right-bank tributary of the Nairn. The massive keep with small turrets is the original portion of the castle, and to it were added, in the 17th century, the modern buildings forming two sides of a square. It is the seat of Earl Cawdor. Kilravock (pronounced *Kilrawk*) castle, 1½ mi. W. of Cawdor, commands the left bank of the Nairn. Its keep dates from 1460, and the later buildings belong to the 17th century. It has been continuously tenanted by the Roses, who settled at Kilravock in 1293, after which date son succeeded father in direct descent. Queen Mary was received at the castle in 1562, and Prince Charles Edward was entertained four days before the battle of Culloden. The gardens are beautiful.

CAWNPORE, a city and district of British India in the Allahabad division of the United Provinces. The city is situated on the south bank of the Ganges, 40 m. south-west of Lucknow, and formed from early times a frontier outpost of the people of Oudh and Bengal against their northern neighbours. Clive selected it, on account of its commanding position, as the cantonment for the brigade of troops lent him by the nawab of Oudh. In 1801, when the Ceded Provinces were acquired by the East India Company, it became the chief British frontier station, but by the time of the Mutiny the frontier had left it behind, and it was denuded of troops. It is now again a military station of some importance, and a very large railway centre. But its industrial development has been unique in northern India. Starting with a government harness factory, the manufacture of leather goods in every form has attained the position of a first-class industry. There are also large cotton-mills, a woollen manufactory with a world-wide reputation and a number of engineering and other minor industries. Extensive city improvements have been launched in order to keep pace with the sanitary requirements of the growing labour force. On the outskirts of the city is a fine agricultural college and demonstration farm. The population of the city and cantonment in 1941 was 487,324.

The name of Cawnpore is indelibly connected with the blackest episode in the history of the Indian Mutiny—the massacre here in July 1857 of hundreds of women and children by the Nana Sahib. The entrenchment, where General Sir H. M. Wheeler with his small band of soldiers and the European and Eurasian residents were exposed for 21 days to the fire of the mutineers, is merely a bare field. About three-quarters of a mile away, on the banks of the river Ganges, is the Massacre Ghat. A grassy road between banks 10 to 12 ft. high leads down to the river, and it was among the trees on these banks that the murderers concealed themselves and shot down the little garrison as soon as they were embarked in the boats which were to take them to safety. On the Ghat itself, or temple steps down to the water, some 600 helpless people were slain, in spite of a promise of safe conduct from the Nana. The remaining 200 victims, who had escaped the bullets of the siege and survived the butchery of the river bank, were massacred afterwards and cast down the famous well of Cawnpore, which is now marked by a memorial and surrounded by gardens. The memorial is crowned by the figure of an angel in white marble, and on the wall of the well itself is the following inscription:

> Sacred to the perpetual Memory of a great company of Christian people, chiefly Women and Children, who near this spot were cruelly murdered by the followers of the rebel Nana Dhundu Pant, of Bithur, and cast, the dying with the dead, into the well below, on the xvth day of July, MDCCCLVII.

The DISTRICT OF CAWNPORE is situated between the Ganges and Jumna rivers, and is a portion of the well-watered and fertile tract known as the Doab, the total area being 2,372 sq.mi. The general inclination of the country is from north to south. Besides the two great rivers, the principal streams are the Arand or Rhind, the Kavan or Singar, the Isan and the Pandu. The district is watered by four branches of the Ganges canal. The population in 1941 was 1,556,247.

CAXTON, WILLIAM (*c.* 1422–1491), the first English printer, was born somewhere in the Weald of Kent. The name, which was apparently pronounced Cauxton, is identical with Causton, the name of a manor in the parish of Hadlow. The date of Caxton's birth was arbitrarily fixed in 1748 by Oldys as 1412. Blades, however, inferred that in 1438, when he was apprenticed to Robert Large, he would not have been more than 16 years of age. Robert Large was a rich silk mercer who became lord mayor of London in 1439, and the fact of Caxton's apprenticeship to him argues that Caxton's own parents were in a good position. When Large died in 1441, Caxton was probably sent direct to Bruges, then the central foreign market of the Anglo-Flemish trade, for he presently entered business there on his own account. In 1450 his name appears in the Bruges records as standing joint surety for the sum of £100; and in 1463 he was acting governor of the company of Merchant Adventurers in the Low Countries. This association, sometimes known as the "English Nation," was dominated by the Mercers' Company, to the livery of which Caxton had been formally admitted in London in 1453. In 1464 he was appointed to negotiate with Philip, duke of Burgundy, the renewal of a treaty concerning the wool trade, which was about to expire. These attempts failed, but he was again employed in a similar but successful mission in Oct. 1468 to the new duke, Charles the Bold, who had just married Princess Margaret of York, sister of Edward IV. The last mention of Caxton in the capacity of governor of the "English Nation" is on Aug. 13, 1469, and it was probably about that time that he entered the household of the duchess Margaret, possibly in the position of commercial adviser.

He had already begun his translation of the popular mediaeval romance of Troy, *The Recuyell of the Historyes of Troye,* from the French of Raoul le Fèvre; and, after laying it aside for some time, he resumed it at the wish of the duchess Margaret, to whom the ms. was presented. From July 1471 until after Midsummer 1472 Caxton was in Cologne, and it was there, as his disciple

Wynkyn de Worde tells us, that he learned the art of printing. On his return to Bruges, he set up a press, in partnership with Colard Mansion, and there his *Recuyell* was printed in 1474 or 1475. His second book, *The Game and Playe of Chesse,* from the *Liber de ludo scacchorum* of Jacobus de Cessolis through the French of Jehan de Vignay, was finished in 1474, and printed in 1476; the last book printed by Mansion and Caxton at Bruges was the *Quatre derrenieres choses,* an anonymous treatise usually known as *De quattuor novissimis.*

BY COURTESY OF THE JOHN RYLANDS LIBRARY
CAXTON'S DEVICE, CONSISTING OF HIS INITIALS AND TRADE MARK, FOUND IN 11 OF HIS 102 BOOKS AND BROADSIDES. IT IS 5½"x4½"

Then Caxton returned to England and established himself, at Michaelmas, 1476, in the almonry at Westminster at the sign of the Red Pale. The first known piece of printing issued from the Caxton press in England is an *Indulgence* printed by Caxton and issued by Abbot Sant on Dec. 13, 1476, which was discovered in the Record Office in 1928 by Mr. S. C. Ratcliffe. The first dated book printed in England was Lord Rivers' translation (revised by Caxton) of *The Dictes and sayenges of the phylosophers* (1477) (*see* BLACK LETTER). The date, Nov. 18, 1477, is given in the colophon to the copy in the John Rylands Library, Manchester, the only one which possesses the colophon. From this time until his death Caxton was busy writing and printing. His services to English literature, apart from his work as a printer (*see* TYPOGRAPHY), are very considerable. His most important original work is an eighth book added to the *Polychronicon* (vol. viii. in the Rolls Series edition) of Ralph Higden. Caxton revised and printed John of Trevisa's work, and brought down the narrative himself from 1358 to 1460, using as his authorities *Fasciculus temporum,* a popular work in the 15th century, and an unknown *Aureus de universo.* He printed Chaucer's *Canterbury Tales* (1478? and 1483), *Troilus and Creseide* (1483?), the *House of Fame* (1483?), and the translation of Boethius (1478?); Gower's *Confessio Amantis* (1483), and many poems of Lydgate. His press

Et sic est finis.

Thus endeth this book of the dyctes and notable wyse sayenges of the phylosophers late translated and drawen
out of frenshe into our englisshe tonge by my forsaide lord
Therle of Ryuers and lord Skales and by hys coman-
dement sette in forme and emprynted in this manere as
ye maye here in this booke see Whiche was fynisshed the
xviij day of the moneth of Nouembre & the seuententh
yere of the regne of kyng Edward the fourth.

BY COURTESY OF THE JOHN RYLANDS LIBRARY, MANCHESTER
COLOPHON TO CAXTON'S "DICTES AND SAYENGES OF THE PHYLOSOPHERS" (1477), THE FIRST BOOK PRINTED IN ENGLAND TO BEAR A DATE
The colophon, an inscription placed at the end of a book in early times, contained information now usually found on the title page

was, however, not worked for purely literary ends, but was a commercial speculation. For the many service-books which he printed there was no doubt a sure sale, and he met the taste of the upper classes by the tales of chivalry which issued regularly from his press. He printed Malory's *Morte d'Arthur,* and himself translated from the French the *Boke of Histories of Jason* (1477?), *The Historye of Reynart the Foxe* (from the Dutch, 1481 and 1489?), *Godfrey of Boloyne* or *The Siege and Conqueste of Jherusalem* (1481), *The Lyf of Charles the Grete* (1485), *The Knyght Parys and the Fayr Vyenne* (1485), *Blanchardyn and Eglantine* (1489?), *The Foure Sonnes of Aymon* (1489?); also the *Morale Proverbs* (1478), and the *Fayttes of Armes and of Chyualrye* (1489) of Christine de Pisan. The most ambitious production of his press was perhaps his version of the *Golden Legend,* the translation of which he finished in Nov. 1483. It is based on the lives of the saints as given in the 13th century *Legenda aurea* of Jacobus de Voragine, but Caxton chiefly used existing French and English versions for his compilation. The book is illustrated by 70 woodcuts, and Caxton says he was only encouraged to persevere in his laborious and expensive task by the liberality of William, earl of Arundel. The idleness which he so often deprecates in his prefaces was no vice of his, for in addition to his voluminous translations his output as a printer was over 18,000 pages, and he published 96 separate works or editions of works, with apparently little skilled assistance.

The different founts of type used by Caxton are illustrated by Blades and Duff, and there is an excellent selection of Caxtons in the British Museum and in the University library at Cambridge. His books have no title-pages, and from 1487 onwards are usually adorned with a curious device, consisting of the letters W.C. separated by a trade mark, with an elaborate border above and below. The flourishes on the trade mark have been fancifully interpreted as S.C. for Sancta Colonia, implying that Caxton learnt his art at Cologne, and the whole mark has been read as 74, for 1474, the date of his first printed book. This device was subsequently adopted with small alterations by his successor at the Westminster press, Wynkyn de Worde. The first of his books containing woodcut illustrations was his *Myrrour of the World* (1481), translated from Vincent de Beauvais, but he had used a woodcut initial letter in his broadside *Indulgence* printed in 1476.

No record of Caxton's marriage or of the birth of his children has been found, but Gerard Croppe was separated from his wife Elizabeth, daughter of William Caxton, before 1496, when Croppe made certain claims in connection with his father-in-law's will.

BIBLIOGRAPHY.—Earlier biographies of Caxton were superseded by the work of William Blades, whose *Life and Typography of William Caxton* (1861–63) remains the standard authority. It contains a bibliography of each of the works issued from Caxton's press. For later discoveries *see* E. Gordon Duff, *William Caxton* (1905) and H. R. Plomer, *William Caxton* (1925). Many of Caxton's translations are available in modern reprints.

CAYAPAS, a tribe of South American Indians, belonging to the Barbacoan (*q.v.*) linguistic stock or sub-stock. Their habitat is the lower Cayapas river and adjacent coasts in northern Ecuador. Traditionally they formerly lived in the upland region about Quito, moving to the coast a short time before the first appearance of Europeans.

They became much mixed with Negroes, and relatively little of their original culture survives.

See S. A. Barrett, "The Cayapa Indians of Ecuador" (Museum of the American Indian, *Indian Notes and Monographs,* no. 40. New York, 1925).

CAYENNE, capital of French Guiana, is a port standing at the northwestern end of the "isle of Cayenne" formed by the estuaries of the Cayenne and the Mahoury rivers. Its plan is that of a rectangle lying along the sea-front. Its streets, built on a rectangular pattern, are lined by brick or wooden houses of one or two stories. The church of the Holy Saviour and the Jesuits' house are of some antiquity; and there are other interesting buildings, including the Préfecture, around the Place d'Armes. To the west, Mont Cépérou and the Fort Saint-Michel dominate the harbour.

Suitably purified water is available at the rate of 5,000 cu.m. per day. Fever is kept down by draining the marshes and by spraying DDT.

The sea wind mitigates the heat, and the climate, though humid, is healthful. Population (1946) 10,961.

The harbour is liable to be silted up, and there is a bar at the entrance, allowing only 3.80 m. of draught at high tide. There is a metal wharf, but big ships unload at Larivot (a few kilometres distant) or at the Îles du Salut. Once a month a ship goes between Cayenne and Fort de France (Martinique), and aircraft of the New York-Buenos Aires line land four times a week at the aerodrome.

An avenue running along the sea-front joins Cayenne to the suburbs of Chaton and Montabo, where are the buildings of the Institut Français d'Amérique Tropicale and the Institut Pasteur. (For history, *see* GUIANA.) (HU. DE.)

CAYENNE PEPPER (*Guinea Pepper, Spanish Pepper, Chilly*), a preparation from the dried fruit of various species of *Capsicum,* a genus of the family Solanaceae. The true peppers are members of a totally distinct family, Piperaceae. The fruits of *Capsicum* have a strong, pungent flavour. The capsicums bear a greenish-white flower, with a star-shaped corolla and five anthers standing up in the centre of the flower like a tube, through which projects the slender style. The podlike fruit consists of an envelope at first fleshy and afterwards leathery, within which are the spongy pulp and several seeds. The plants are herbaceous or shrubby; the leaves are entire, and alternate, or in pairs near one another; the flowers are solitary and do not arise in the leaf-axils. There are about 30 species, natives of Central and South America. In the United States chief production is in Louisiana and South Carolina. The output is about 1,000,000 lb. dried. The principal source of cayenne pepper is *C. annuum,* the spur or goat pepper, a dwarf shrub, a native of South America, but commonly cultivated in the East Indies. It produces a small, narrow, bright red pod, having very pungent properties.

Chillies, the dried fruit of capsicums, are used to make chilly-vinegar, as well as for pickles. Cayenne pepper is manufactured from the ripe fruits, which are dried, ground, mixed with wheat flour and made into cakes with yeast; the cakes are baked till hard, like biscuit, and then ground and sifted.

Chillies have been in use from time immemorial; they are eaten in great quantity by the people of Guiana and other warm countries and in Europe are consumed both as a spice and as medicine.

CAYEY, an interior town of Puerto Rico. Pop. (1950) 18,402, an increase of 227% over 1940. The population of the municipal district in 1950 was 36,634.

The altitude is 1,400 ft.; average temperature about 71° F. Cayey, one of the most healthful towns of the island, is on the military highway built by Spain diagonally across the island from San Juan on the Atlantic ocean to Ponce on the Caribbean sea. One of the branches of this highway extends to Guayama and another to Salinas, both on the Caribbean.

Because of its healthful climate the Spanish rulers established a military post there; the Americans succeeding them used it as a U.S. army post.

The town is the centre of a region where tobacco and coffee of superior quality are produced, and has many warehouses and factories.

CAYLEY, ARTHUR (1821–1895), English mathematician, was born at Richmond, Surrey, on Aug. 16, 1821. He entered Trinity college, Cambridge, as a pensioner, became a scholar in May 1840, senior wrangler, first Smith's prizeman and fellow of Trinity in 1842 and a major fellow in 1845. In 1846, he entered at Lincoln's Inn, and became a pupil of the conveyancer Mr. Christie. While practising law he met J. J. Sylvester, and the two spent much time profitably discussing mathematics. He was called to the bar in 1849, and remained at the bar till he was elected to the new Sadlerian chair of pure mathematics at Cambridge in 1863, when he married Susan, daughter of Robert Moline of Greenwich. He held this chair till his death, on Jan. 26, 1895. His 800 mathematical papers, published in 13 large quarto volumes by the Cambridge University press, treat of nearly every subject of pure mathematics, and of theoretical dynamics and spherical and physical astronomy. He was as much a geometrician as an analyst. Of special mention are his ten memoirs on quantics in which he developed the theory of algebraic invariants (1854–78), his creation of the theory of matrices, his researches on the theory of groups, his memoir on abstract geometry, the geometry of *n*-dimensional space, a subject which he created, his introduction to geometry of the "absolute," his researches on the higher singularities of curves and surfaces, the classification of cubic curves, additions to the theories of rational transformation and correspondence, the theory of the twenty-seven lines that lie on a cubic surface, the theory of elliptic functions, the attraction of ellipsoids, and the British association reports, 1857 and 1862, on recent progress in general and special theoretical dynamics, and on the secular acceleration of the moon's mean motion. Competent judges have compared him with Leonhard Euler for his range, analytical power and introduction of new and fertile theories. He received nearly every academic distinction that can be conferred upon a man of science. His nature was noble and generous, and the universal appreciation of this fact gave him great influence in his university. His recreations were the Victorian classics, water-colour sketching and architecture. His portrait, by Lowes Dickinson, was placed in the hall of Trinity college in 1874, and his bust, by Henry Wiles, in the library of the same college in 1888.

CAYLUS, ANNE CLAUDE, COMTE DE, Marquis d'Esternay, baron de Bransac (1692–1765), French archaeologist and man of letters, was born in Paris. His mother, the comtesse de Caylus (1673–1729), was a cousin of Mme. de Maintenon, who brought her up like her own daughter. She wrote valuable memoirs of the court of Louis XIV entitled *Souvenirs;* these were edited by Voltaire (1770) and by many later editors, notably by Ch. Asselineau (1860). Caylus was on active service with the French army from 1709–14. After the Peace of Rastadt he travelled in Italy, Greece, the East, England and Germany. He became an active member of the Academy of Painting and Sculpture and of the Academy of Inscriptions. Among his works are *Recueil d'antiquités égyptiennes, étrusques, grecques, romaines et gauloises* (7 vol. 1752–67), *Numismata Aurea Imperatorum Romanorum,* and a *Mémoire* (1755) on the method of encaustic painting with wax mentioned by Pliny, which he claimed to have rediscovered. Caylus was himself an admirable engraver; he also caused engravings to be made of Bartoli's copies from ancient pictures. He encouraged young artists, but his patronage was somewhat capricious. Diderot expressed this fact in an epigram in his *Salon* of 1765: "La mort nous a délivrés du plus cruel des amateurs." The Comte de Caylus had quite another side to his character.

He had a thorough acquaintance with the gayest and most disreputable sides of Parisian life, and left a number of more or less witty stories dealing with it. These were collected (Amsterdam, 1787) as his *Oeuvres badines complètes.* The best of them is the *Histoire de M. Guillaume, cocher* (*c.* 1730).

CAYMAN (or CAIMAN), the name applied to the broad-snouted crocodilians of South America. The black cayman (*Melanosuchus niger*) of the Amazon is a large species, reaching 16 ft. in length. Other smaller species (*Caiman* spp.) are extremely abundant in tropical America. (*See* CROCODILIAN.) (K. P. S.)

CAYMAN ISLANDS, three low-lying islands in the West Indies, Grand Cayman, Little Cayman and Cayman Brac, are between 79° 44′ and 81° 27′ W. and 19° 15′ and 19° 45′ N., a dependency of Jamaica, which lies 110–156 mi. E.S.E. Grand Cayman, a flat rock-bound island protected by coral reefs, is approximately 20 mi. long and 8 mi. broad at a maximum. It has two towns, Georgetown and Boddentown. Little Cayman and Cayman Brac are both about 60 mi. N.E. of Grand Cayman. While the soil is shallow and not infertile, commerce is dependent almost exclusively on the various marine industries. The thatch palm *Thrinax argentea* is used for the manufacture of thatch rope for export to Jamaica, but the main industry is the catching of turtles, sharks and sponges. The export of phosphate, coconuts and sisal has ceased. Local mahogany is used to build yachts and schooners.

The government is administered by a commissioner, and the laws passed by the local legislature are subject to the assent of the governor of Jamaica. Pop. (census 1943) 6,670. Land area 93 sq.mi.

The islands were discovered by Columbus, who named them Tortugas, from the turtles with which the surrounding seas abound. They were never occupied by the Spaniards and were colonized from Jamaica by the British.

CAYUGA AND SENECA CANAL: *see* NEW YORK STATE BARGE CANAL SYSTEM.

CAYUSE, an Indian tribe (of the Waiilatpuan linguistic family), that formerly inhabited northeastern Oregon and part of Washington and was noted for its horses and warlike character.

They were closely allied with the Wallawalla and Nez Percés tribes, and there was a great deal of intermarriage, particularly with the latter tribe. The Cayuse signed the treaty of 1855 establishing the Umatilla reservation, where they then lived. The tribe's population was officially given as 404 in 1904, but no Cayuse of pure blood was found on the reservation at the beginning of the 20th century.

Marcus Whitman, who had established a mission near the present city of Walla Walla, Wash., in 1838, his wife and 12 others were massacred in an attack by the Cayuse in 1847. The Indians blamed Whitman, who was a doctor, for the large number of deaths caused by disease. Volunteer troops carried on a prolonged, indecisive campaign against the tribe until five Indians, who confessed to the murders, were voluntarily surrendered in 1850.

In the western states of the United States the term cayuse refers to an Indian pony. In *Three Thousand Miles Through the Rocky Mountains* (1869), A. K. McClure used the word in this sense in his remark that "Twice our kiyuse broke nearly out of the harnass. . . . The kiyuse is never perfectly tamed."

CAYUVAVAN, a linguistic stock of South American Indians comprising but a single tribe. The validity of this stock is doubtful. The Cayuvavas formerly lived in northern Bolivia on and west of the Mamore river for some 60 mi. above its confluence with the Guaporé. The surviving remnants are now mainly settled at the mission of Exaltacion de Santa Cruz. The Indians of this group were sedentary agriculturists, and known as the best canoemen of the region. They appear to have retained little of their old culture and, like many of the tribes of this area, are very little known.

See A. D'Orbigny, *L'Homme Americain* (Paris, 1839).

CAZALÈS, JACQUES ANTOINE MARIE DE (1758–1805), French orator and politician, was born at Grenade in Languedoc, of a family of the lower nobility. Before 1789 he was a cavalry officer, but in that year was returned as deputy to the states general. In the Constituent Assembly he belonged to the section of moderate royalists who sought to set up a constitution on the English model, and his speeches in favour of retaining the right of war and peace in the king's hands and on the organization of the judiciary gained the applause even of his opponents. After the insurrection of Aug. 10, 1792, which led to the downfall of royalty, Cazalès emigrated. He fought in the army of the *émigrés* against revolutionary France, lived in Switzerland and in England, and did not return to France until 1803. He died on Nov. 24, 1805. His son, Edmond de Cazalès, wrote philosophical and religious studies.

See *Discours de Cazalès*, ed. by Chare (1821), with an introduction; F. A. Aulard, *Les Orateurs de la Constituante* (2nd ed., 1905).

CAZALIS, HENRI (1840–1909), French poet and man of letters, was born at Cormeilles-en-Parisis (Seine-et-Oise). He wrote under the pseudonyms of Jean Caselli and Jean Lahor. His oriental habits of thought earned for him the title of the "Hindou du Parnasse contemporain."

His works include: *Chants populaires de l'Italie* (1865); *Vita tristis, Réveries fantastiques, Romances sans musique* (1865); *Le Livre du néant* (1872); *Henry Regnault, sa vie et son oeuvre* (1872); *L'Illusion* (1875–93); *Melancholia* (1878); *Cantique des cantiques* (1885); *Les Quatrains d'Al-Gazali* (1896); *William Morris* (1897). *See* P. Bourget in *Anthologie des poètes fr. du XIX.e siècle* (1887–88); J. Lemaître, *Les Contemporains* (1889); E. Faguet in *Revue bleue* (Oct. 1893).

CAZEMBE, the name of an African kingdom which was situated south of Lake Mweru and north of Lake Bangweulu, between 9° and 11° S. In 1894 it was divided between Northern Rhodesia and Belgian Congo. The Cazembe kingdom was named after Muata Cazembe, the hereditary name of its ruler. It was founded by the Baluba, who formed a powerful state in the Kasai region. Muata Yamvo, the Baluba ruler, desiring to control the salt deposits of the Bangweulu, conquered the area early in the 17th century. Baluba formed the aristocracy of the conquered country, and a Baluba was appointed ruler with the title Muata Cazembe. Although autonomous in its political affairs, Cazembe remained nominally dependent on the Baluba state until 1875. Economically, the country was well developed on account of its ivory trade monopoly with Arabs and Portuguese on the east coast. Also, the copper mines of Katanga were an important source of wealth. (Under European control the Katanga copper mines developed into large industries which in 1953 supplied about one-sixth of the world's production.) About 1875 the Baluba dynasty was overthrown by Msiri, an east African adventurer of the Nyamwezi tribe, who conquered Cazembe and the adjacent areas. After Msiri's death the kingdom disintegrated rapidly. Cazembe was first visited in 1796 by Manoel Caetano Pereira, a Portuguese merchant; F. J. M. de Lacerda visited Cazembe in 1798 and David Livingstone in 1868. The Cazembe dynasty still survives in the paramount chieftaincy of the Balunda tribe in the Kawambwa district of Northern Rhodesia, where the present Cazembe is a descendant of the ancient kings.

See Brohez, "Ethnographie katangaise," *Bulletin, Société Belge de Geographie* (Brussels, 1909); R. F. Burton (ed.), *The Lands of the Cazembe* (London, 1873). (H. A. Wr.; X.)

CAZIN, JEAN CHARLES (1841–1901), French painter, was born at Samer, Pas-de-Calais, May 25, 1841, and died at Le Lavandou, Var, March 27, 1901. He studied in Paris and at Tours and in 1871 was persuaded by Alphonse Legros (*q.v.*) to go to England. There he made designs for the Fulham pottery and, more important, came under the sway of the Pre-Raphaelites, whose influence shows in his earlier religious pictures, such as "Hagar and Ishmael" (1880, Luxembourg).

Later he turned to idealistic landscape with subordinate figures, in the general tradition of J. F. Millet and of J. B. C. Corot (*e.g.*, "Souvenir de fête" [1881, Petit Palais, Paris] and "Journée faite" [1888, Lyons]).

See L. Bénédite, *J.-C. Cazin* (Paris, 1901).

CAZOTTE, JACQUES (1719–1792), French author, was born at Dijon. He was educated by the Jesuits, and at 27 obtained a public office at Martinique, returning to Paris in 1760 with the rank of commissioner-general. The most famous of his works is the *Diable amoureux* (1772), a tale with a Spanish setting in which the hero raises the devil. About 1775 Cazotte embraced the views of the Illuminati, declaring himself possessed of the power of prophecy. It was upon this fact that La Harpe based his famous *jeu d'esprit,* in which he represents Cazotte as prophesying the most minute events of the Revolution. On the discovery of some fantastic letters in Aug. 1792, Cazotte was arrested; and though he escaped for a time through the heroism of his daughter he was executed on Sept. 25.

Other works by Cazotte are *Les Mille et une fadaises* (1742; Eng. trans. 1927); and a prose epic *Ollivier* (1762). The only complete edition is the *Oeuvres badines et morales, historiques et philosophiques de Jacques Cazotte* (1816–17), though more than one collection appeared during his lifetime. An edition de luxe of the *Diable amoureux* was edited (1878) by A. J. Pons, and a selection of Cazotte's *Contes,* edited (1880) by Octave Uzanne, is included in the series of *Petits Conteurs du XVIIIe siècle*. The best notice of Cazotte is in the *Illuminés* (1852) of Gérard de Nerval.

CAZUNGO: *see* ANGOLA.

"C" BATTERY is an electric battery, used in radio circuits. It is connected between the cathode or negative electrode and the grid of a vacuum tube and supplies a direct voltage to the grid.

CEANOTHUS, a showy genus of North American shrubs and woody vines of the buckthorn family (Rhamnaceae), comprising more than 50 species found chiefly in the Pacific coast region, 30 of which are native to California. The small white or blue flowers are borne in handsome dense panicles or umbels. Several are grown as garden plants. Only two species occur east of the Rocky mountains—the New Jersey tea (*C. americanus*), so called because its leaves were used as tea during the American Revolution, and *C. ovatus*. The genus attains its maximum development in the foothills and mountains of California, often constituting a considerable part of the chaparral. Noteworthy representatives are the California lilac and the Oregon tea-tree (*qq.v.*).

See M. Van Rensselaer and H. E. McMinn, *Ceanothus,* xii, 1–308, illus. (1942).

CEARÁ, a northern maritime State of Brazil, bounded north by the Atlantic, east by the Atlantic and the States of Rio Grande do Norte and Paraíba, south by Pernambuco, and west by Piauí, and having an area of 57,371 sq. miles. It lies partly upon the northeast slope of the great Brazilian plateau, and partly upon the sandy coastal plain. Its surface is a succession of great terraces, facing north and northeast, formed by the denudation of the ancient sandstone plateau which once covered this part of the continent; the terraces are seamed by watercourses, and their valleys broken by hills and ranges of highlands, usually described as mountain ranges, but in fact only the remains of the ancient plateau, capped with horizontal strata of sandstone and having a remarkably uniform altitude of 2,000 to 2,400 ft. The flat top of such a range is called a *chapada* or *taboleiro,* and its width in places is from 32 to 56 mi.

The boundary line with Piauí follows one of these ranges, the Serra Ibiapaba, which unites with another range on the southern boundary of the state known as the Serra do Araripe. Another range, or escarpment, crosses the state from east to west, but is broken into two principal divisions, each having several local names. These ranges are not continuous, the breaking down of the ancient plateau having been irregular and uneven. The higher ranges intercept considerable moisture from the southeast trade winds, and their flanks and valleys are covered with forest, but the plateaus are either thinly wooded or open campo. These upland forests are of a scrubby character and are called *caatingas.*

The sandy, coastal plain, with a width of 12 to 18 mi., is nearly bare of vegetation; behind there is a more elevated region with broken surfaces and sandy soil which is amenable to cultivation and produces fruit, cotton and most tropical products when conditions are favourable. The rivers of the state are small and, with one or two exceptions, become completely dry in the dry season. The largest is the Jaguaribe, which flows entirely across the state in a northeast direction with an estimated length of 210 to 465 mi. The year is divided into a rainy and dry season, the rains generally beginning in October and lasting until December. The soil of the interior is thin and porous and does not retain moisture; consequently the long, dry season turns this part of the country into a barren waste, relieved only by vegetation along the river courses and mountain ranges and by the hardy, widely distributed carnauba palm (*Copernicia cerifera*), which in places forms groves of considerable extent. Sometimes the rains fail altogether, and then a drought (*sêca*) ensues, causing famine and pestilence throughout the entire region. The most destructive droughts recorded were those of 1711, 1723, 1777–78, 1790, 1825, 1844–45 and 1877–79, the last-mentioned destroying nearly all the livestock in the state and causing through starvation and pestilence the deaths of nearly 500,000 persons—more than half the population—while thousands more were obliged to emigrate to other states.

There are two lines of railway running inland from the coast: the Baturité line from Fortaleza to Crato, in the southern part of the state, and to Patos in the state of Paraíba; and the Sobral line from Camocim to Crateús, about 210 mi. The railways were built by the national government after the drought of 1877–79 to give work to the starving refugees. Great dams are also being constructed and extensive irrigation systems laid out.

Only a very small percentage of the population, which numbered 2,735,702 (1950 census), is of European origin, the large majority being mestizos. There are few Negroes.

The state of Ceará became a bishopric of the Roman Catholic Church in 1853, the bishop having his residence at Fortaleza. The state is represented in the national congress by 3 senators and 17 deputies. The capital, Fortaleza, sometimes called Ceará, is the principal commercial centre and shipping port. Its population was 213,604 and that of the *município* was 280,084 in 1950. The principal towns are Aracati, Baturité, Acaraú, Crato, Maranguape and Sobral.

The territory of Ceará included three of the *capitanias* originally granted by the Portuguese crown in 1534. The first attempts to settle the territory failed, and the earliest Portuguese settlement was made near the mouth of the Rio Camocim in 1604. The French were already established on the coast, with their headquarters at St. Louis, now Maranhão. Ceará was occupied by the Dutch from 1637 to 1654, and became a dependency of Pernambuco in 1680; this relationship lasted until 1799, when the *capitania* of Ceará was made independent. The *capitania* became a province in 1822 under Dom Pedro I. A revolution followed in 1824, the president of the province was deposed 15 days after his arrival, and a republic was proclaimed. Internal dissensions broke out, the new president was assassinated, and after a brief reign of terror the province resumed its allegiance to the empire. Ceará was one of the first provinces of Brazil to abolish slavery.

Bibliography.—Rodolpho Theophilo, *Historia da Secca do Ceará, 1877 a 1880* (Fortaleza, 1883); Elizabeth Agassiz and Louis Agassiz, *A Journey in Brazil* (Boston, 1869); George Gardiner, *Travels in the Interior of Brazil* (1846); C. F. Hartt, *Geology and Physical Geography of Brazil* (Boston, 1870); H. H. Smith, *Brazil: The Amazon and the Coast* (1879); Pierre Denis, *Brazil* (New York and London, 1911); I. W. McConnell, "Irrigation in Brazil," *Bull. Pan-Am. Union,* vol. liii, pp. 688–706 (1924); R. C. Mossman, "The Climate of São Paulo and Ceará," *Quart. Jour.,* Roy. Met. Soc., vol. xlv, pp. 53–63, 69–79; F. W. Friese, "The Drought Region of Northeastern Brazil," *Geogr. Rev.,* vol. xxviii, pp. 363–78 (1938). (R. d'E.; X.)

CEAWLIN (d. 593), king of the West Saxons, included, in the *Anglo-Saxon Chronicle,* among the "Bretwaldas" or specially powerful kings, succeeded his father Cynric in 560. He took Silchester, and moving eastward Ceawlin and his brother Cutha defeated the forces of Aethelberht, king of Kent, at the battle of Wibbandun in 568. In 577 he led the West Saxons from Winchester towards the Severn valley; gained a victory over three British kings, Conmail, Condidan and Farinmail, at Deorham and added the district round Gloucester, Bath and Cirencester to his kingdom, thus isolating the Britons of Cornwall from those of Wales. A further advance was begun in 583. Uriconium, a town near the Wrekin, and Pengwyrn, the modern Shrewsbury, were destroyed, but Ceawlin was defeated by the Britons at Fethanleag or Faddiley, near Nantwich, and his progress was effectually checked. Internal strife among the West Saxons followed. In 591 Ceawlin lost the western part of his kingdom; in 592 he was defeated by his nephew, Ceolric, at Wanborough, driven from Wessex and was killed in 593.

See *Two of the Saxon Chronicles,* ed. by C. Plummer (Oxford, 1892); E. Guest, *Origines Celticae,* vol. ii (1883).

CEBES, the name of two Greek philosophers. (1) Cebes of Cyzicus, mentioned in Athenaeus (iv, 156 d), seems to have been a Stoic, who lived during the reign of Marcus Aurelius. Some would attribute to him the *Tabula Cebetis* (*see* below), but as that work was well known in the time of Lucian, it is probably to be placed earlier. (2) Cebes of Thebes, a disciple of Socrates and Philolaus. He is one of the speakers in the *Phaedo* of Plato, in which he is represented as an earnest seeker after virtue and truth, keen in argument and cautious in decision. Three dialogues, the Ἑβδόμη, the Φρύνιχος and the Πίναξ or *Tabula,* are ascribed to him by Suidas and Diogenes Laërtius. The two former are lost, and most scholars deny the authenticity of the *Tabula* on the ground of material and verbal anachronisms. They attribute it either to Cebes of Cyzicus (above) or to an anonymous author, of the 1st century a.d., who assumed the character of Cebes of Thebes. In the form of an interpretation of an allegorical picture in the temple of Cronus at Athens or Thebes, it develops the Platonic theory of pre-existence, and shows that true education consists in the formation of character.

The *Tabula* has been translated both into European languages and into Arabic (the latter published with the Greek text and Lat. trans. by Salmasius in 1640); Eng. trans. by H. E. Seebohm (Chipping Camden, 1906). It is usually printed together with Epictetus. Separate eds. by S. S. Jerram (with intro. and notes, 1878), C. Prächter (1893) and many others. *See* Zeller's *History of Greek Philosophy;* F. Klopfer, *De Cebetis Tabula* (1818–22); C. Prächter, *Cebetis Tabula quanam aetate conscripta esse videatur* (1885); R. T. Clark, *Characters of Theophrastus, etc.* (1909).

CEBU (Bisayan Sugbu), the second of the 21 chartered Philippine cities in rank of population, 167,411 in 1948 (an increase of 101,909 since 1918) is in the island province of Cebu, of which it is the capital and is on the east coast.

Cebu is one of the most historic points in the Philippines. A native village had long existed on the site of the present city when Magellan, commander of the first world encircling expedition, landed there on April 7, 1521. Opposite the site lies

Mactan Island (whose northwest shore forms the harbour's outer rim) where he met the native chief, Sicatuan, where each sealed a truce compact with his own blood and where, despite the compact, the great navigator lost his life. The image of Santo Niño (the Holy Child), now housed in the Augustinian church, is said to date from that period. The next distinguished foreign visitor was Miguel López de Legazpi, who arrived with some Augustinian friars, including Urdaneta, in 1565; and for the ensuing six years Cebu was the capital of whatever portion of the Philippines the Spaniards ruled. That distinction ceased with Legazpi's removal to what is now Manila; but Cebu has continued to be an important centre for the Bisayas, rivalled by Iloilo alone, which the former has now far outstripped. Toward the end of the 18th century the Roman Catholic cathedral was completed. Cebuanos took a prominent part in the insurrections against both Spain and the United States; but Cebu has profited immensely by the American occupation and its wide streets, motor roads, modern buildings and public school system are but a few of the results.

Cebu was open to foreign trade in 1863. It had long been a port of entry and its harbour is amply protected from the typhoons and baguios to which the region is subject. The city is also the principal one on the railway which skirts the province's eastern coast. An extensive maritime trade is carried on with Manila and Leyte, Bohol and the Negros provinces, Mindanao and elsewhere. The chief exports are abacá (Manila hemp), tobacco, sugar and copra. Manufactures of pottery, fabrics, sugar sacks and salt are carried on.

Cebu is a Roman Catholic Episcopal see and 137,555 of its adherents were reported from there in 1939. The bishop's palace, though small, is noted for its interior decorations. There were also reported from Cebu 2,971 members of the Independent Filipino Church, 2,139 Protestants, 1,262 Buddhists and several thousand of other, or no religious affiliation. Cebuano, the local Bisayan, is the vernacular. There is a provincial high school together with grade and parochial schools, a branch of the Philippine library and a meteorological station.

CECCO D'ASCOLI (1257–1327), the popular name of FRANCESCO DEGLI STABILI, a famous Italian encyclopaedist and poet—Cecco being the diminutive of Francesco, and Ascoli, in the marshes of Ancona, the place of his birth. In 1322 he was made professor of astrology at Bologna university, but, having written a commentary on the sphere of John de Sacrobosco (pub. Venice, 1518), in which he propounded daring theories concerning the agency of demons, he got into difficulties with the clerical party. He betook himself to Florence, where his attack on the *Commedia* of Dante, and the *Canzone d' Amore* of Guido Cavalcanti sealed his fate. He was burned at Florence in 1327.

His *Acerba* (from *acervus*), an encyclopaedic poem (best ed. Venice, 1510), consists of four books in *sesta rima,* treating in order of astronomy and meteorology, of stellar influences, of physiognomy, of the vices and virtues of minerals, of the love of animals, of moral, physical and theological problems.

See G. Castelli, *La Vita e le Opere di C. d'Ascoli* (Bologna, 1892), and C. Lozzi, *C. d'Ascoli* (1904).

CECIL, the name of a famous English family. This house, whose two branches hold each a marquessate, had a great statesman and administrator to establish and enrich it. The first Lord Burghley's many inquiries concerning the origin of his family created for it more than one splendid and improbable genealogy, although his grandfather is the first ascertained ancestor. In the latter half of the 15th century a family of yeomen or small gentry with the surname of Seyceld, whose descendants were accepted by Lord Burghley as his kinsmen, lived on their lands at Allt yr Ynys in Walterstone, a Herefordshire parish on the Welsh marches. Of the will of Richard ap Philip Seyceld of Allt yr Ynys, made in 1508, one David ap Richard Seyceld, apparently his younger son, was overseer. This David seems identical with David Cyssell, Scisseld or Cecill, a yeoman admitted in 1494 to the freedom of Stamford in Lincolnshire. At Stamford he prospered, being three times mayor and three times member of parliament for the borough, and he served as sheriff of Northamptonshire in 1532–33. Remaining in the service of Henry VIII. he was advanced to be yeoman of the chamber and sergeant-at-arms, being rewarded with several profitable leases and offices. By his first marriage David Cecil left at his death in 1536 a son and heir, Richard Cecil, who enjoyed a place at court as yeoman of the king's wardrobe under Henry VIII. and Edward VI. A gentleman of the privy chamber and sometime sheriff of Rutland, Richard Cecil had his share at the distribution of abbey lands, St. Michael's priory in Stamford being among the grants made to him. William Cecil, only son of Richard, was born, by his own account, in 1520, at Bourne in Lincolnshire. He advanced himself first in the service of the protector Somerset, after whose fall, his great abilities being necessary to the council, he was made a secretary of state and sworn of the privy council. In 1571 he was created Lord Burghley, and from 1572, when he was given the Garter, he was lord high treasurer and principal minister to Queen Elizabeth. By his first wife, Mary Cheke, sister of the scholar Sir John Cheke, tutor to Edward VI., he was father to Thomas, first earl of Exeter. By a second wife, Mildred Cooke, the most learned lady of her time, he had an only surviving son, Robert Cecil, ancestor of the house of Salisbury.

Created earl of Exeter by James I., the second Lord Burghley was more soldier than statesman, and from his death to the present day the elder line of the Cecils has taken small part in public affairs. William Cecil, 2nd earl of Exeter, took as his first wife the Lady Roos, daughter and heir of the 3rd earl of Rutland of the Manners family. The son of this marriage inherited the barony of Roos as heir general, and died as a Roman Catholic at Naples in 1618 leaving no issue. A third son of the 1st earl was Edward Cecil, a somewhat incompetent military commander, created in 1625 Lord Cecil of Putney and Viscount Wimbledon, titles that died with him in 1638, although he was thrice married. In 1801 a marquessate was given to the 10th earl of Exeter, the story of whose marriage with Sarah Hoggins, daughter of a Shropshire husbandman, has been refined by Tennyson into the romance of "The Lord of Burleigh." This elder line is still seated at Burghley, the great mansion built by their ancestor, the first lord.

The younger or Hatfield line was founded by Robert Cecil, the only surviving son of the great Burghley's second marriage. As a secretary of State he followed in his father's steps, and on the death of Elizabeth he may be said to have secured the accession of King James, who created him Lord Cecil of Essendine (1603), Viscount Cranborne (1604), and earl of Salisbury (1605). Forced by the king to exchange his house of Theobalds for Hatfield, he died in 1612, worn out with incessant labour, before he could inhabit the house which he built upon his new Hertfordshire estate. Of Burghley and his son Salisbury, "great ministers of state in the eyes of Christendom," Clarendon writes that "their wisdom and virtues died with them." The 2nd earl of Salisbury, "a man of no words, except in hunting and hawking," was at first remarked for his obsequiousness to the court party, but taking no part in the Civil War came at last to sit in the Protector's parliament. After the Restoration, Pepys saw him, old and discredited, at Hatfield, and notes him as "my simple Lord Salisbury." The 7th earl was created marquess of Salisbury in 1789.

Hatfield House, a great Jacobean mansion which has suffered much from restoration and rebuilding, contains in its library the famous series of state papers which passed through the hands of Burghley and his son Salisbury, invaluable sources for the history of their period. (O. B.)

(*See* also, EXETER, EARL, MARQUESS AND DUKE OF; members of the Cecil family separately mentioned are: BURGHLEY, WILLIAM CECIL; SALISBURY, ROBERT ARTHUR TALBOT GASCOGNE-CECIL, 3RD MARQUESS OF; SALISBURY, ROBERT CECIL, 1ST EARL OF; CECIL, HUGH RICHARD; CECIL OF CHELWOOD, 1ST VISCOUNT).

CECIL, HUGH RICHARD (BARON QUICKSWOOD) (1869–), English politician, youngest son of the 3rd Marquess of Salisbury, the prime minister, was born on Oct. 14, 1869, and was educated at Eton and University college, Oxford, where he obtained a first class in modern history in 1891, and was elected a fellow of Hertford college. He became one of his father's secretaries. He sat in the House of Commons as a Unionist for Greenwich (1895–1906), and for Oxford university from 1910 onward. He took a keen interest in church matters and was remarkable in debate for his oratorical powers and the loftiness of his ideals. In the stormy debates on the Balfour Education bill of 1902 he maintained that the only possible basis of general agreement was that every child should be brought up in the belief of its parents. He and Winston Churchill gathered round them, in the early years of the 20th century, a small group of young and able Conservative members, whose independent proceedings attracted some attention. He took a decided part in resisting tariff reform, and had no seat in the House between 1906 and 1910. He threw himself immediately and with passion into the struggle over the proposed curtailment of the powers of the House of Lords, and was active in resistance to the Parliament bill.

During the World War he joined the Flying Corps; he also served as a member of the commission that enquired into the Mesopotamia expedition. After the war he took a less active part in politics, but generally found himself in agreement with his brother, Lord Robert (later Lord Cecil of Chelwood), in adopting a more independent attitude toward the Coalition Government. With him, too, he supported the Enabling bill, and he became a prominent member of the Church Assembly set up in accordance with its provisions. In the conflict which arose over the Prayer Book Measure in 1928 he gave energetic support to the new proposals, both inside and out of the House of Commons. In 1936 he was appointed Provost of Eton, and resigned from parliament. He was created baron in 1941.

CECIL OF CHELWOOD, EDGAR ALGERNON ROBERT CECIL, 1ST VISCOUNT (1864–), British statesman, known before his elevation to the peerage as Lord Robert Cecil, third son of the third Marquess of Salisbury, was born on Sept. 14, 1864. He was educated at Eton and University college, Oxford, and was a prominent speaker at the Oxford Union. Lord Robert acted as one of his father's private secretaries from 1886 to 1888. He was called to the bar at the Inner Temple in 1887, and appeared in many important cases. He took silk in 1900.

In 1906 he entered parliament as Conservative member for East Marylebone, and he was one of the principal critics of Birrell's abortive education bill of that year. On many questions he took a heterodox position from the party point of view. In particular he dissociated himself from the tariff reform policy of Chamberlain, and thereby with Parliament from 1910 to 1911, when he was returned at a by-election for the Hitchin division of Herts, retaining this seat until his elevation to the peerage in 1923. He immediately resumed his old place as a powerful, though independent critic of Liberal policy, especially of the disestablishment of the church in Wales. He was one of the best friends of the women suffragists, and expressed the strongest disapprobation of the violent measures taken against them, though he did not palliate the offences against law and order of the extreme militants. Ultimately, after women had been granted the suffrage, he had the satisfaction of carrying a resolution "to amend the law with respect to the capacity of women to sit in Parliament" (Oct. 21, 1918).

Lord Robert was in office throughout the World War from the time that the Unionists associated themselves with the Government in May 1915 till the Armistice. As under-secretary for foreign affairs, then as minister of blockade and lastly as assistant secretary of State for foreign affairs, he was mainly concerned with the vital question of blockade. Lord Robert resigned at the general election of 1918 on the ground that he could not support the decision of the coalition Ministry to treat Welsh disestablishment as a *fait accompli.* Though no longer a minister of the crown, he nevertheless went over to Paris in 1919, where he served as chairman of the Supreme Economic Council, and played one of the principal parts, together with President Wilson and Gen. Smuts, in drafting the Covenant. After the peace he advocated increasingly full co-operation in the work of the League of Nations. In 1920 he attended the first Assembly of the League in Geneva as a representative of South Africa. In Parliament he steadily drifted into opposition to the coalition Ministry, and, though he did not form part of Bonar Law's Unionist Ministry in 1922, he joined Baldwin's first cabinet in May 1923 as Lord Privy Seal. He was raised to the peerage in Dec. 1923. He returned to office in Baldwin's second cabinet, in Nov. 1924, as chancellor of the duchy of Lancaster, and on several occasions acted as deputy for the foreign secretary, Sir Austen Chamberlain, on the Council of the League of Nations. As the principal British representative on the Disarmament Commission at Geneva in 1926–27 he found that his instructions necessitated a policy not in complete accordance with his convictions, and in 1927 he resigned his place in the Baldwin administration. President (1919–45) of the League of Nations Union, Lord Cecil remained, in face of the effects upon European and world affairs of German and Italian policy, uncompromisingly loyal to the League covenant. In 1937 he was awarded the Nobel peace prize.

CECILIA, SAINT (d. *c.* 176), patron saint of music and of the blind, is commemorated on Nov. 22. She was supposed to have been a noble Roman who with her husband and converts suffered martyrdom (*c.* 230), under the emperor Alexander Severus, but the researches of de Rossi (*Roma Sotteranea* ii. 147) confirm the statement of Fortunatus, bishop of Poitiers (d. 600), that she perished in Sicily under Marcus Aurelius (*c.* 176). The 4th century church at Rome in her honour was rebuilt by Pope Paschal I. (*c.* 820) and again in 1599. Cecilia, whose musical fame rests on a passing notice in her legend that she praised God by instrumental and vocal music, has inspired many a masterpiece in art, including the Raphael at Bologna, the Rubens in Berlin, the Domenichino in Paris, and in literature she is commemorated by Chaucer's "Seconde Nonnes Tale" and by Dryden's famous ode, set to music by Handel in 1736 and later by Sir Hubert Parry (1889).

Another St. Cecilia, who suffered in Africa in the persecution of Diocletian (303–304), is commemorated on Feb. 11.

U. Chevalier, *Répertoire des sources historiques* (1905), i. 826 f.

CECROPIA, in botany, a genus of trees (family Moraceae), native of tropical America. They are of rapid growth, affording a light wood used for making floats. *C. peltata* is the trumpet tree, so-called from the use of its hollow stems by the Uaupé Indians as a musical instrument. It is a tree reaching about 50ft. in height with a large spreading head, and deeply lobed leaves 12in. or more in diameter. The hollows of the stems and branches are inhabited by ants, which it has been claimed in return for the shelter thus afforded, and food in the form of succulent growths on the base of the leaf-stalks, repel the attacks of leaf-cutting ants which would otherwise strip the tree of its leaves. This is an instance of "myrmecophily," *i.e.,* a living together for mutual benefit of the ants and the plant.

CECROPS, traditionally the first king of Attica (Pausanias ix. 33). He was said to have divided the inhabitants into 12 communities, to have instituted the laws of marriage and property and a new form of worship. The introduction of bloodless sacrifice, the burial of the dead and the invention of writing were also attributed to him. He is said to have acted as umpire during the dispute of Poseidon and Athena for the possession of Attica. As one of the *autochthones* (*q.v.*) of Attica, Cecrops is represented as human in the upper part of his body, while the lower part is shaped like a dragon. Miss J. E. Harrison (in *Classical Review,* Jan. 1895) endeavours to show that Cecrops is the husband of Athena, identical with the snake-like Zeus Soter or Sosipolis, and the father of Erechtheus-Erichthonius.

CEDAR, a name applied to several coniferous trees (*see* Gymnosperms), and a few broad-leaved species.

Cedrus libani, the far-famed Cedar of Lebanon, is a tree which because of its beauty and stateliness has always been a favourite with poets and painters. It is frequently mentioned in the Scriptures as a symbol of power, prosperity and longevity. It grows to a height of from 50 to 80 ft. and at an elevation of about 6,000 ft. above sea-level. The bole of young trees is straight and upright and one or two leading branches usually rise above the rest. As the tree increases in size, however, the upper branches become mingled together to form a clump-headed crown. Numerous lateral ramifying branches spread, tier upon tier, in a horizontal direction from the main trunk and cover a compass of ground the diameter of which is often greater than the height of the tree. The branchlets of the cedar assume the same orientation as the branches, and the foliage is very dense. The tree is evergreen; new leaves are developed every spring, but their fall is gradual. In shape the leaves are straight, tapering, cylindrical and pointed, about 1 in. long, dark green and borne in spirally arranged tufts of about 30. The male and female flowers grow on the same tree but on separate branches. The cones, borne on the upper side of the branches, are flattened at the ends and are 4 to 5 in. in length and 2 in. wide; they require two years to mature and while growing exude much resin. The scales are closely pressed to one another, reddish in colour, and at maturity fall away from the central axis. The seeds are provided with a long membranous wing. The root system is large and ramifying. This cedar, which flourishes best on sandy, loamy soils, appears in great numbers on Mt. Lebanon, chiefly on the western slopes, where it usually occurs in groves, some of which contain several thousand trees. There are also large forests on the higher slopes of the Taurus and Anti-Taurus mountains. The wood is fragrant, though not so strongly scented as that of the juniper or red cedar of America. It is generally reddish-brown, light and of a coarse grain and spongy texture, easy to work, but liable to shrink and warp.

Mountain-grown wood is harder, stronger, more durable and exhibits greater dimensional stability.

The Cedar of Lebanon is cultivated in Europe for ornament only. It thrives well in parks and gardens, but the young plants are unable to withstand great variations of temperature. The term *Eres* (cedar) of Scripture does not apply strictly to one kind of plant: the "cedars" for masts, mentioned in Ezek. xxvii. 5, must have been pine trees. Drawers of cedar or chips of the wood are now employed to protect furs and woollen stuffs from injury by moths. Cedar wood, however, is said to be injurious to natural history objects and to instruments placed in cabinets made of it, because the resinous matter in the wood acts as a corrosive.

The genus *Cedrus* contains two other closely allied species, namely, *C. deodara*, the deodar, or "god tree" of the Himalayas, and *C. atlantica*, the Atlas cedar of the Atlas range in north Africa.

The deodar forms forests on the mountains of Afghanistan, north Baluchistan and the northwest Himalayas at elevations of from 5,500 to 12,000 ft.; it may develop a clear bole of from 60 to 70 ft. under the crown. The wood is close-grained, long-fibred, scented and highly resinous and resists the action of water. The foliage is of a paler green, the leaves are slenderer and longer and the twigs are thinner than those of *C. libani*. The tree is employed for a variety of useful purposes, especially in building. It is cultivated in England and in California as an ornamental plant.

C. atlantica has shorter and denser leaves than *C. libani;* the leaves are glaucous, sometimes of a silvery whiteness, and the cones smaller than in the other two forms. Growth is somewhat more rapid than that of the ordinary cedar, but the tree produces a similar timber. It is found at altitudes of from 4,000 to 6,000 ft.

The name cedar is applied to species of several other genera of conifers, including *Juniperus, Thuja, Libocedrus, Chamaecyparis* and *Cupressus. Libocedrus decurrens,* of western North America, is known in the United States as incense cedar. *Chamaecyparis lawsoniana* is the Port Orford white cedar, a native of Oregon and California. The Bermuda cedar (*Juniperus bermudiana*) and the eastern red cedar (*J. virginiana*) are used in joinery and in the manufacture of pencils. Another species, the Atlantic white cedar (*Chamaecyparis thyoides*), is found in swamps along the southern coastal plains. The Spanish cedar is *Juniperus thurifera,* a native of the western Mediterranean region. Another species, *J. oxycedrus,* common in the Mediterranean region, forms a shrub or low tree with spreading branches and short, stiff, prickly leaves. A species of cypress, *Cupressus lusitanica,* naturalized in the neighbourhood of Cintra, is known as the Cedar of Goa. The genus *Widdringtonia* of tropical and South Africa is also known locally as cedar. The Japanese cedar (*Cryptomeria japonica*) is more closely related to the bald cypress. The family Meliaceae (which is entirely distinct from the conifers) includes, along with the mahoganies and other valuable timber trees, the Jamaica and the Australian red cedars, *Cedrela odorata* and *C. toona,* respectively. (E. S. Hr.)

CEDAR-BIRD or **CEDAR WAXWING:** *see* WAXWING.

CEDAR CITY, a city of Iron county, Utah, in the southwestern part of the state, at an elevation of 5,840 ft.; on federal highway 91, and the terminus of a branch line of the Union Pacific railway, constructed in 1923. The population was 6,172 in 1950 by the federal census. It is the largest city within a radius of 200 mi.; is surrounded by vast expanses of grazing country and potential agricultural land, with some 50,000ac. in irrigated farms, and by great deposits of iron, coal and gypsum; and is the gateway to the Zion National park, Bryce canyon, the north rim of the Grand canyon, Kaibab forest and Cedar Breaks. A Branch of the State agricultural college is situated here. In 1849 an exploring party sent out by Brigham Young discovered the beds of iron ore which gave the county its name. A volunteer company established a colony at Parowan, the county seat, in 1851. Cedar City was settled in 1851, and became the centre of the iron industry of that period, sending 12,500 lb. of pig-iron to Salt Lake City in the next eight years, besides manufacturing many articles of iron. With the development of rail transportation from the east the industry languished. In 1923 mining was begun on a large scale around Iron Springs, 10m. W. of Cedar City, and the present production (by stripping methods) is about 250,000 tons a year, averaging 53% in iron content.

CEDAR CREEK, a small branch of the North Fork of the Shenandoah river, Virginia (U.S.A.). It is known in American history as the scene of a memorable battle, which took place on Oct. 19, 1864, between the Union army under Gen. Sheridan and the Confederates under Gen. Early. (*See* SHENANDOAH VALLEY CAMPAIGNS.)

CEDAR FALLS, a city of Black Hawk county, Iowa, U.S.A., on the Cedar river, 100 mi. W. of Dubuque. It is on federal highways 20 and 218, and is served by the Rock Island, the Illinois Central, the Chicago Great Western and the Waterloo, Cedar Falls and Northern railways. The population in 1950 (federal census) was 14,336. More than 50 creameries are within a radius of 30 mi. The city is adjacent to the Josh Higgins state parkway. It utilizes its water power for sundry manufactures. It is the seat of the State Teachers college (established in 1876 as a normal school), which has a resident enrolment of more than 2,000.

Settlement began there in 1847. The town was laid out in 1851, and chartered as a city in 1865.

CEDAR RAPIDS, a city of Linn county, Iowa, U.S.A., on the Cedar river, in the east-central part of the state. It is on federal highways 30, 218 and 151; and is served by the Chicago, Milwaukee, St. Paul and Pacific, the Chicago and North Western, the Rock Island, the Illinois Central, the Cedar Rapids and Iowa City, the Waterloo, Cedar Falls and Northern railways and United Air Lines. The population was 72,149 in 1950; 62,120 in 1940; 56,097 in 1930; 45,566 in 1920 and 25,656 in 1900 by the federal census. The rapids in the river supply abundant water power, and the city ranks second in the state as a manufacturing centre, with an aggregate factory output valued at $200,000,000.

The leading products are cereals, corn products, meat packing, road building and mining machinery, farm hardware, ice cream machinery, radio transmitters, poultry and stock food, and milling. There is "Quaker Oats," the largest single unit cereal mill in the world. The city has an extensive jobbing business in all staple lines, and is the distributing centre for a rich agricultural district. Bank deposits in 1950 amounted to $120,622,869.

The city has an air of substantial prosperity. Its principal streets are 80 to 100 ft. wide, well paved and shaded. The assessed valuation of property in 1950 was $117,879,852. There are 23 fine parks, in one of which (Hawkeye Downs) an annual rodeo show is held.

One Bohemian periodical and one Swedish, with a substantial circulation, are published there. Coe college, a co-educational Presbyterian institution, which grew out of the Cedar Rapids Collegiate institute (1851), was chartered under its present name and opened in 1881. It has an enrolment of 800.

Cedar Rapids was settled in 1838; incorporated in 1856; and adopted a commission form of government in 1908.

CEDARTOWN, a city of Georgia, U.S., 62 mi. W.N.W. of Atlanta, served by the Central of Georgia and the Seaboard Air Line railways; the county seat of Polk county. Pop. (1950) 9,470.

There are important mineral deposits in the vicinity, especially of iron, manganese, marble and slate. Diesel railroad shops, cotton, and woollen mills, a tire cord fabric factory, etc., were established there.

The Big spring, on the ancient meeting ground of former Cherokee Indian inhabitants, flows at a rate of more than 5,000,000 gal. of pure water daily, and gives the city its entire supply of water. Cedartown was incorporated as a city in 1898.

CÉDULA, the Spanish form of the English word "schedule," of which *cedule* is an obsolete variant; in modern financial usage it refers more specifically to certain securities issued by the South American governments.

CEFALÙ (anc. CEPHALOEDIUM), a seaport and episcopal see of the province of Palermo, Sicily, 42 mi. E. of Palermo by rail. Pop. (1951) 11,813 (commune). The ancient town is named from the headland (Gr. Κεφαλή, head) upon which it stood (1,233 ft.); its fortifications extended to the shore, on the side where the modern town now is, in the form of two long walls protecting the port.

There are remains of a wall of massive rectangular blocks of stone at the modern Porta Garibaldi on the south.

It does not appear in history before 396 B.C., and seems to have owed its importance mainly to its naturally strong position. A small ancient building in good polygonal work (a style of construction very rare in Sicily) consists of a passage on each side of which a chamber opens. The doorways are of finely cut stone and of Greek type. On the summit of the promontory are extensive remains of a Saracenic castle.

The new town was founded at the foot of the mountain, by the shore, by Roger II in 1131, and the cathedral was begun in the same year. The exterior is largely decorated with interlacing pointed arches; the windows also are pointed. On each side of the façade is a massive tower of four stories. The roundheaded Norman portal is worthy of note. The interior was restored in 1559, though the pointed arches of the nave, borne by ancient granite columns, are still visible. The only mosaics preserved are those of the apse and the last bay of the choir; they are remarkably fine specimens of the art of the period (1148) and were carefully restored in 1859–62. Fine cloisters, coeval with the cathedral, adjoin it.

CEHEGÍN, a town of southeastern Spain, in the province of Murcia, on the right bank of the Arcos river, a small tributary of the Segura. Pop. (1950) (mun. 15,830). Cehegín is the market for local wine, olive oil and hemp and for marble and a little iron from the neighbouring hills.

Some of the older houses, the parish church and the convent of San Francisco, which contains still legible Roman inscriptions, are built of stone from the ruins of Begastri, a Roman colony which stood on an adjacent hill.

The name Cehegín is sometimes associated with that of the Zenaga, Senhaja or Senajeh, a North African tribe which invaded Spain in the 11th century.

CEILING, the overhead surface or surfaces covering a room; the underside of a floor or a roof; often used as a surface built to hide the floor and roof construction; the term is also employed, technically, for any finished boarding or sheathing and especially for a type of narrow, thin board, tongued and grooved, with a moulding on the edge.

Ceilings, in the larger sense of the word, have been favourite places for decoration from the earliest times, by painting the flat surface, as in the case of Egyptian tombs; by emphasizing the structural members of roof or floor, as in the beamed ceilings of the period of Francis I in France or the ceilings of Italian mediaeval churches (*e.g.*, S. Miniato at Florence); by treating it as a field for an over-all pattern of relief (*e.g.*, the earlier rooms of Hampton Court palace near London).

Of Greek ceilings little is known, except for some of marble, over temple porticoes, decorated with small, sunk panels or coffers, with moulded edges, and the field further decorated in polychrome. Roman ceilings were rich with relief and painting, as is evidenced by the vault soffits of Pompeian baths. Italian Renaissance architects found in similar examples inspiration for much of their most charming painted and relief decoration in stucco, and Robert Adam's 18th-century designs for ceilings ornamented with ovals, fans, hanging garlands, delicate scrolls and little painted panels have the same origin. The general Gothic tendency to use structural elements decoratively led to the rich development of the beamed ceiling, in which large cross girders support smaller floor beams at right angles to them, beams and girders being richly chamfered and moulded and often painted in bright colours (the Palazzo Davanzati in Florence contains numerous late 14th-century examples).

In the Renaissance, ceiling design was developed to its highest pitch of originality and variety. Three types were elaborated. The first is the coffered ceiling, in the complex design of which the Italian Renaissance architects far outdid their Roman prototypes. Circular, square, octagonal and L-shaped coffers, with their edges richly carved and the field of each coffer decorated with a rosette, abound. Occasionally pendants are found at the intersections (the Hall of the Two Hundred in the Palazzo Vecchio at Florence and various rooms of the ducal palace at Mantua are good examples). The second type consists of ceilings wholly or partly vaulted, often with arched intersections, with painted bands bringing out the architectural design and with pictures filling the remainder of the space, as in the loggia of the Farnesina villa in Rome, decorated by Raphael and Giulio Romano. In the baroque period, fantastic figures in heavy relief, scrolls, cartouches and garlands were also used to decorate ceilings of this type; *e.g.*, the Pitti palace, Florence; many French ceilings of the Louis XIV style are similar. In the third type, particularly characteristic of Venice (*e.g.*, the doge's palace), the ceiling became one large framed picture.

The early Renaissance saw in England another interesting development, that of plaster ceilings covered with an intricate pattern of intersecting curved lines, ornamented with foliage, grotesque animals and heraldic devices, and frequently accented by repeated large pendants; *e.g.*, Bramall hall; Hatfield house, London; Knowle; Sizergh. Later, the skilful English plaster workers were trained into a more classic vein, largely through the influence of Inigo Jones, who developed a type with large and deeply recessed panels, bold mouldings and bands of high-relief foliage and fruit, which remained fashionable for about a century after 1650.

In modern work the general tendency is toward simplified ceilings. Rich colour decoration is, however, sometimes found, especially in public buildings; an example in the United States is the Nebraska state capitol, designed by B. G. Goodhue, with ceilings by Hildreth Méière. (T. F. H.)

For the term "ceiling" as used in the science of the weather, *see* CLOUD and METEOROLOGY.

CELAENAE, an ancient city of Phrygia, situated on the great trade route to the east. It was the starting point of the march of Cyrus (401 B.C.) with the 10,000 against Artaxerxes. Its acropolis long held out against Alexander in 333 and surrendered to him at last by arrangement. Antigonus made it the capital of his kingdom; Antiochus of Syria, the son of Seleucus, refounded it on a more open site as Apameia (*q.v.*). West of the acropolis were the palace of Xerxes and the agora, in or near which is the cavern whence the Marsyas, one of the sources of the Maeander, issues.

See G. Weber, *Dineir-Celènes* (1892).

CELANDINE (*Chelidonium majus*), a common British plant, a member of the poppy family (Papaveraceae), an erect branched herb from 1 to 2 ft. high with a yellow juice, much-divided leaves and yellow flowers nearly an inch across, succeeded by a narrow, thin pod opening by a pair of fine valves, separating upward. The plant grows in waste places and hedgerows, and is probably an escape from cultivation. It has become widely naturalized in eastern North America, in open grounds, roadsides and in woods from Maine to Ontario and Illinois southward to North Carolina. The lesser celandine is a species of *Ranunculus* (*R. Ficaria*), a small low-growing herb with smooth heart-shaped leaves and bright yellow flowers about an inch across, borne each on a stout stalk springing from a leaf-axil. It flowers in early spring, in pastures and waste-places. It is sparingly introduced into the United States from Massachusetts to Maryland.

CELANO, a town of the Abruzzi, Italy, province of Aquila, 73 mi. E. of Rome by rail. Pop. (1951) 12,686 (commune). It is on a hill above the Lago Fucino, and is dominated by a square castle, with round towers at the angles, erected in its present form in 1451. It contains three churches with 13th century façades in the style of those of Aquila. The origin of the town goes back to Lombard times, but it was destroyed in 1223, and rebuilt on a different site in 1227. It was damaged by the earthquake of 1915. It was the birthplace of Thomas of Celano, author of the *Dies Irae,* and biographer of S. Francis and S. Clara.

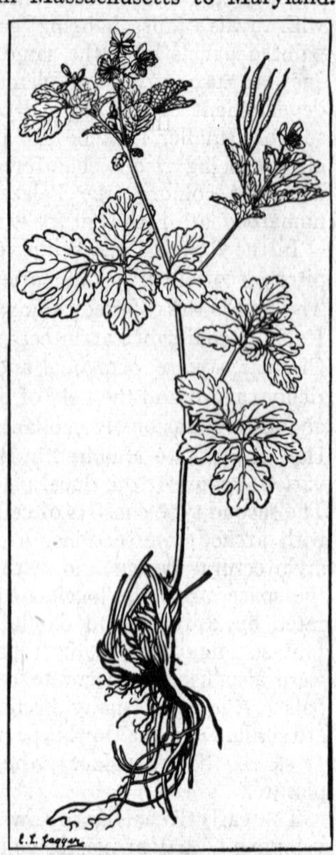

GREATER CELANDINE, A YELLOW FLOWERED PLANT OF TEMPERATE REGIONS, SOMETIMES USED IN MEDICINE

CELEBES, one of the four great Sunda Islands in Indonesia. It extends from 1° 45′ N. to 5° 37′ S. and from 118° 49′ E. to 125° 5′ E. From the backbone of the island, which runs north and south, three long peninsulas project north-east, east and south-east, respectively, the first being much the longest. These peninsulas form great gulfs—on the eastern side, from north to south they are: the Gulfs of Tomini, or Gorontalo, Tolo and Boni, the first being the largest. Thus the island is of very curious shape, and its length, 800 mi., and coastline, 2,000 mi., are quite disproportionate to its breadth, which averages between 36 and 120 mi., and at one point narrows to 18 mi. As a result, no place in Celebes is as far as 70 mi. from the sea. Celebes is situated in a very deep sea, between Borneo, west, which is in a shallow sea, on a shelf off the continent of Asia, and New Guinea, east, also in a shallow sea, and on a shelf projecting from Australia. The coast is dangerously fringed by drying coral reefs with many shoals and banks. The whole island is mountainous. Two parallel ranges run from north to south in the main central mass, and a northern extension of this traverses the entire northern arm of Celebes to Menado. From these ranges a single range projects north-eastwards to the extreme end of the eastern arm of the island, and two parallel ranges run, in a south-easterly direction, throughout the greater part of the south-eastern arm. The great central ranges (with Kamboeno, 9,678 ft., centre, and Piek van Bonthain, 9,419 ft., south) throw out large spurs, which dominate the central and western parts of Celebes. In the extreme north-east (Mt. Klabat, 6,545 ft.) and south the mountains are volcanic, some in the former region being active, while solfataras and hot springs are found in Minahasa. Wide rift valleys between the mountain ranges contain several lakes—in the north (Minahasa), Tondano, 2,000 ft. above sea level, 9 mi. long and 3½ mi. wide, (Gorontalo), Limboto, Batudaka, and Bolano Sawu, in the central nucleus, Lake Lindu, further south, in the same rift, Tempe and Sidenreng (monsoon lakes), and east of these, extending into the south-eastern arm, the principal lakes of the island—Poso, Matana and Towuti. They are very deep, Matana having been sounded to 1,500 ft. and Poso to 1,000 ft.

The rivers of Celebes are short and unimportant, for waterfalls and rapids are frequent; their mouths are obstructed by bars, and there is very little coastal plain, save at the head of the Gulf of Boni and near Macassar and among mangrove-swamps of the north coast of the Gulf of Tomini. The Jenemeja, which flows into the Gulf of Boni, is wide and navigable for some distance from its mouth, the Poso, which enters the Gulf of Tomini, is also wide and navigable, for very small craft, to Paluasi, the Sadang, entering the Gulf of Mandar, on the south-west coast, has many affluents, and is navigable by *sampans,* the Lasolo, south-east, admits steamers for 16 miles from its mouth; the rivers of Gorontalo are very small. The best natural harbours are Menado bay, Amurang bay, Kwandang bay, and Dondo bay, on the north coast; Tambu bay, Pare Pare bay, and Palu bay (Donggala), on the west coast; Gorontalo and Poso, in the Gulf of Tomini, with the Gulf of Poh, which penetrates eastward for 22 miles; the bays of Tomori, Kendari, and Staring, in the Gulf of Tolo, and the bays of Mengkoka, Palopo, Usu (Luwu), and Sopang, in the Gulf of Boni. Off the west coast is the Spermunde archipelago, a number of low islands surrounded by coral reefs; off the south coast, Saleyer; at the end of the south-eastern peninsula are several islands, of which the most important are Kabaena, Muna, Wowoni, and Buton (*q.v.*). They are separated from the peninsula by the straits of Tioro and Wowoni, both dangerous. The Banggai or Peling islands lie off the eastern extremity of Celebes, and though they belong politically to Ternate, geographically they resemble Celebes. In the Gulf of Tomini are the Schildpad islands, extending for nearly 80 miles east and west, the chief of them Talata Koh, Togian and Batu Daka, the Sangihe (Sangir) islands (*q.v.*), form the north-east extension of Celebes towards Mindanao, in the Philippines, which is continued by the Talaua group, north-east of these. With the adjacent islands, the area of Celebes is estimated at 77,855 sq.mi. and without them—72,986 sq.mi. The population of Celebes and the islands under its government, included in the residency of Menado, was, in 1930, 4,231,906.

Its situation between the two shelves of the Asian and Australian continents makes the geology of Celebes specially interesting. The broad central block is a complex of igneous rocks, with granite, gneiss, diorite and amphibolite characters, pierced in places by later eruptives, mostly Tertiary. This block is enclosed around its base by Cretaceous rocks, overlaid by Tertiaries and recent alluvial deposits towards the coasts. In the south-east corner of the block there is a broad band of pre-Tertiary tuffs, fringed occasionally by coral limestone. The northern part of the Gulf of Boni is widely bordered by Pleistocene and alluvial deposits, resting in the north-east upon late Tertiaries: a band of old plutonic rocks stretches from near Paloppo across the Gulf of Boni and the south-east peninsula to the Gulf of Tolo.

The meridional ridge of Celebes has an axis of crystalline schist, tourmaline quartzite, and glaucophane schist, penetrated and overlaid by andesite and basalt, flanked by tuffs, overlaid by late Tertiary *Orbitoides* limestone. The southern extension from the central block shows late Tertiary limestone, raised in parts, to a height of more than 3,000ft. and portions of the Archaean foundation are revealed. East of the central block is a faulted and depressed area of crystalline schists and metamorphosed shales, with gneiss and metamorphic limestones. The south-eastern and eastern peninsulas are, in the main, a broken crustal block with plutonic rocks. Metamorphics run southwards along the Gulf of Boni inland, a series of Pleistocene to recent rocks passes near to north of Muna island, with no Tertiaries except a small patch on Buton island. Around Mengkoka bay is a fringe of coral limestone, which borders Kabaena, covers more than two-thirds of Muna, all except the centre of Buton, and all of Wowoni, and the small islands north of it. There are indications of Jurassic rocks south of Lake Matana and metamorphics re-appear in Peling island. The north-eastern peninsula has northern and southern belts. The northern belt consists mostly of sedimentary rocks, Cretaceous or Tertiary, some altered by metamorphism. This belt runs parallel with the coast, and is separated by a parallel fault line from the southern belt, which consists of granites, gneisses, schists and intrusives, with Archaean schists and altered rocks, caught in faults: the valleys are filled with recent deposits.

Older rocks, Cretaceous and Tertiary, are preserved in occasional east and west bands, and in places near the south coast there are fringes of coral limestone. Minahasa is volcanic, and differs structurally from any other portion of Celebes.

The climate of Celebes is hot but is tempered by sea winds, which reach every part. Mean temperature ranges between 86° and 72°, with absolute extremes of 94° and 66°; it falls to below 50° at high altitudes on the mountains. At Palu, on the west coast, rainfall averages only 20.92 in., as compared with 116.11 at Macassar, while Menado and Gorontalo, both in the northeastern peninsula, average 106.48 in. and only 47.45 respectively. Macassar averages 132 rainy days annually; Palu only 77.

In the matter of fauna Celebes is the poorest island in the archipelago in the number of its species, yet among these it has animal forms which have no close allies in any other part of the world except in three of the neighbouring islands—Bachian, Buru and Sulu. Most interesting of these are the babirusa or pig deer, so named by the Malays from its long and slender legs and curved tusks, resembling horns; the black crested baboon (*Cynopithecus nigrescens*), akin to the African baboon; and the anoa, or dwarf buffalo, hunted extensively by the natives for its flesh. There are peculiar varieties of other indigenous animals, including five squirrels, a pig, a deer, two wood rats and two marsupials. Celebes has a number of peculiar species of parrots, woodpeckers, hawks, cuckoos, hornbills, starlings, flycatchers and pigeons; the brush turkey is found there. Crocodiles are common, there are snakes of various kinds, and many peculiar species of beetles and butterflies, while there is a distinct cleavage between the freshwater fishes of Borneo and Celebes. Although it has species which belong neither to the one nor to the other, the fauna of Celebes is more Asiatic than Australian, and the island is established as a transitional region between the oriental and Australian zoological regions. It is one of the oldest parts of the archipelago.

Much of Celebes is still covered with forest, especially around the Gulf of Tolo where it is almost primaeval and practically without tracks or clearings. The vegetation grows on the sides of precipitous and almost vertical mountain slopes, and the scenery is exceedingly varied and picturesque. "Nowhere in the archipelago," wrote A. R. Wallace, "have I seen such gorges, chasms and precipices as abound in the district of Maros; in many parts there are vertical or even over-hanging precipices five or six hundred feet high, yet completely clothed with a tapestry of vegetation." The rift valleys are extremely fertile, and there are extensive plateaus at varying heights where there is rich pastureland. The flora shows many resemblances to that of the Philippines, is more Indian in character in the west of the island and more Australian in the east, and while the trees of the lower slopes of the mountains differ strongly from those of Java and are smaller, the alpine flora is very similar. There are many kinds of palms—fanleaf, rattan, sago, *Arenga saccharifera,* which gives fibre for ropes, juice for sugar and a beverage known as sagueir; bamboo, breadfruit, tamarind and coconut trees flourish. Staple food crops grown are rice (mostly sawah) and maize; sugar cane, tobacco and vegetables are also raised. The chief commodity for export is copra, followed by corn, coffee, nutmegs, rubber and kapok; copal, damar and rattan are collected, also cattle horns and hides, for export. Fishing for turtles and mother-of-pearl is carried on extensively, and there is a trade in ebony, sandalwood and timber of other kinds. *Kayulara* and *Kolaka,* two kinds of timber almost impervious to attacks of the pileworm, are found in Celebes, and there is teak on the island of Muna. Gold occurs in Menado, and mines have been established there; nickel has been found and exploitation started in 1937. Iron, copper and lead exist and, in south Celebes, a little coal.

In Minahasa there are 105 people to the square mile, in other parts of Menado only 30 and, in the rest of the island and dependencies, 37. The coasts are generally well populated; there are large stretches of mountainous territory entirely uninhabited. There are at least six quite different native peoples of Celebes—the Toala, Toraja, Buginese, Macassars, Minahasese and Gorontalese. The first-named are found scattered all over the island, sometimes living in communities among other peoples, the result of having been enslaved by them originally. It is thought that they represent the true aborigines of Celebes. They are short and dark and have wavy or curly hair, a broad, flat nose, prominent mouth and receding chin. They are quite undeveloped and uncivilized, shy jungle dwellers, partly nomadic but quiet good-tempered people, and with a distinct language of their own. The Toraja are a collection of tribes, living in central, southeast and east Celebes. Living in isolated groups, in a very thinly populated country, they differ very much in development. Of Malayo-Polynesian stock, and divided into highland and lowland people, in some parts they intermingled with the Toala; in others they came under a Buginese and Macassarese civilizing influence. They are pagan (with an increasing Mohammedan element, however), are gradually giving up their fortified villages, in very inaccessible positions, for neat little settlements of houses standing each in its own garden, and they are becoming reconciled to the government's prohibition of head-hunting and of divination by spear throwing, but they are unclean and short-lived. The mountain peoples are more strongly built than those of the plains, with more prominent cheekbones, thinner lips and smaller eyes. Both have large mouths, thick lips and, usually, a broad nose, skin varying from light to dark brown and smooth, black hair, worn long. The women work harder than the men. Courteous and good-tempered when their confidence has been gained, they are agriculturists with only a few industries such as plaiting, pottery, wood carving and ironworking. Bark clothing is worn in remote districts, and Malayan style cotton garments where there is contact with more advanced cultures; many ornaments are worn and teeth are filed. Society is organized on the family basis, and the tribe is an extension of the family, a man choosing a wife from another branch of his own family. There are no social distinctions or tribal chiefs and woman has, comparatively, a high position among the Toraja, being able to choose her own husband. They collect forest produce and grow rice, possess their own language, with many dialects, and Christian schools have been well received by them. The Buginese and Macassars, probably of Toraja descent, came into touch with Hindu culture in southern Celebes, their home, and later were converted to Islam. They are now all Mohammedans, but with traces of Hinduism and paganism. Well built, fairly light skinned and energetic, they are very keen traders, proud, passionate and vindictive, devoted to feasting, gambling and cockfighting. As shipbuilders and seafarers they are unsurpassed in the archipelago; their excellent prahus are to be found everywhere in Malayan seas.

Society is both endogamic and exogamic, with survivals of a matriarchate, but Mohammedan law and customs are displacing all others. Both peoples are abstemious, feed chiefly on rice, maize and fish, eating buffalo flesh on festive occasions only; clothing is Malayan in style. They are extremely industrious, but their industries are not in a high state of development. Weaving is one of the chief, cotton sarongs of fine material being exported in large numbers from Mandar. Plaited goods of superior quality are made in Boni, gold- and silversmiths are mostly in Macassar, Gowa, Mandar and Boni, ironworkers in Luwu, Laiwui and Mandar, while shipbuilders flourish in Pambauwang, the Bira regency and elsewhere. Forest produce is collected, buffaloes, cattle and horses are kept, hunting and fishing are indulged in, for pleasure and as a means of livelihood, and their sea-carrying trade thrived in spite of steamship competition. A peculiar written alphabet, shared by Buginese and Macassars, is used also by some of the tribes of northern Celebes and by people of Sumbawa. The Macassar language and Buginese, to which it is nearly allied, belong to the Malayo-Javanese group. Arabic letters are being used for religious literature, and books in Arabic are read. There is a slight native literature, historical, legal, epistolary, and poetical. The Buginese and Macassars, like other groups in Celebes and throughout the archipelago, began to adopt Malay as a lingua franca and were encouraged therein by Dutch authority. The Minahasese are quite distinct in type from the other inhabitants of Celebes, they are closely related to the people of the islands of Siau and Sangi, and are probably part of an immigrant race from the north which settled there, and in the Philippines, of partly Caucasian type. They have a very light skin (some of the women have red cheeks and lips), lighter than any other race in the Archipelago, high nose, prominent lips, eyes widely separated, stiff, short, black hair and pleasant features, and they are tall and strong. Like the Maoris, a few generations back they were a savage, warlike race, constantly engaged in raids and head-hunting. European influence has completely eliminated this, and today the Minahasese are Christian, live in European style (each village has its church and school), are cleanly, sober and industrious, make good soldiers, being used extensively in the Dutch Colonial army and police, and compete successfully with Amboinese and Eurasians as clerks, schoolmasters, etc. They have a native tongue, but Malay and Dutch are superseding it. Their territory proper is in the extreme north and northeast, cultivation (coffee, coco-nuts and spices are grown largely), is in the European style, and their numbers do not exceed 300,000. The Gorontalese, who live in the west and south of the northeastern peninsula, are of the Toraja family, not related to the Minahasese, and largely Mohammedan, a short, smooth-haired, and rather light-skinned people, with a marked difference between the people of the coast and inland. They are agriculturists (rice, maize, coco-nuts and tobacco are grown), forest products collected, and weaving and plaiting are carried on, some of the finest materials in Celebes being produced.

They are neither strong nor very industrious; preponderance of women has encouraged extensive polygamy. In numbers they are estimated at about 223,000. Pagan (inland) and Mohammedan coastal tribes live on Banggai and Peleng.

For administrative purposes Celebes is divided into two separate divisions—the residency of Celebes, with dependencies (southeastern, southern peninsulas and islands, and the west coast), and the residency of Menado (the northeastern peninsula and the coast of the Gulf of Tomini—including the Banggai Islands).

The population of Celebes and dependencies is 3,093,251, composed of 4,537 Europeans and Eurasians, 25,497 foreign Asiatics, including Chinese and Arabs, and 3,063,217 natives. The population is much larger on the coasts than inland. The chief port and trade centre and the seat of the resident is Macassar (*q.v.*), with a population of 84,855 (3,447 Europeans included). All the other towns of any importance of Celebes, quite small in comparison with Macassar, are on the coast; for communications hardly exist inland, although the whole country is under direct Dutch rule, with some modification in a few districts of Menado and in the two small states of Luwu and Wajo, where the "short declaration" applies. Authority is enforced by officials on tour and just suffices to pave the way for civilization. Bonthain, on the south coast, is a small port and trade centre (population 6,711); such, also, are Pare Pare, Mamudyu and Madyene on the west coast. On the Gulf of Boni are Kajang, Palima, Desu Bay, Palopo and Kolaka, and on the east coast and Gulf of Tolo—Kendari, Salabanka, Bunku, Koloneday and Luwuk, and on the southern shore of the Gulf of Tomini—Pagimana, Bunta, Posso and Parigi. Some of these places are very small, but all are ordinarily ports of call for ships of the Royal Packet Navigation company and trade centres, zones of collection for great tracts of the hinterland. The residency of Menado has a population of 1,138,655, including 3,146 Europeans and Eurasians, and 25,123 foreign Asiatics. The chief port and centre of administration is Menado, in the extreme northeast, on Menado bay, with a population of 27,544. Unlike the rest of Celebes, Menado has centres of population inland, on plateaus among the mountains, and of these Tondano (2,000 ft.), near the lake and river of the same name, is the chief, with a population of 15,007. It has a cool, refreshing climate, and, situated amid beautiful mountain scenery, is quite a health resort. A pretty little town near by is Tomohon, a few hundred feet higher, which has a training school for native girls and a training college for native preachers, and a wireless station. Gorontalo, on the south coast of the peninsula, is a very important port and trade centre. It has an excellent harbour, with a magnificent approach, mountain ridges, thickly clad with vegetation running down to the shore, on either side of the narrow Gorontalo bay. (Lake Limboto is not far distant.) It has a population of 15,603, does a busy trade in copra, coffee and other products, and, like Menado, is in direct touch with ports in Java, Singapore and other large ports. Small ports on the north coast are Amurang, on the bay of that name, and with a safe anchorage in all weathers, Kwandang, on Kwandang bay, having ruins of an old fort, and Palehleh, a centre for the gold-mining district, near by; on the southeast coast are Kema, Buna and Jikol; on the west coast lies the port of Donggala (pop. 3,821), the seat of an assistant resident. Service was suspended some years ago on a short tramway (28.7 mi. long), from Macassar to Takalar. Sea transport provides the principal, and in most parts, the only means of communication, though motor roads exist in Menado and southern Celebes. Macassar has cable communication with Java, Menado with Borneo, and Gorontalo with Ternate (Moluccas); there is a telegraph line between Amurang and Menado; and Macassar, Menado and Gorontalo have telephone systems. Imports and exports were respectively, in 1939, for Menado 3,280,000 and 5,176,000 guilders, and for Celebes and dependencies 16,028,000 and 17,057,000 guilders.

The Portuguese appear to have discovered and established some influence in Celebes in 1512 when they were monopolizing the spice trade of the Moluccas. The sultan of Macassar, as head of the state of Gowa (southwestern Celebes) favoured the Portuguese and the English, who later attempted to get a footing in Celebes. This annoyed the Dutch, who defeated the sultan early in the 17th century, though the Portuguese helped him. In 1607 a Dutch settlement at Macassar began to establish a firm trade footing in southern Celebes. The Dutch then used the sultan to check the power of Ternate in the Moluccas, and with their friendship he was able to subdue Boni, a rival state in southeast Celebes, and to hold Luwu, but he grew too powerful, and the Dutch (1654) conquered the island of Tidore in spite of a Macassarese fleet. War with Gowa, interrupted only by indecisive treaties, lasted till 1667, when the Dutch Admiral Speelman crushed Gowa and the Macassarese, with help from Boni, and imposed the Bongay treaty. Gowa abandoned all claims to supremacy, surrendered lands to the Dutch East India company, left to it trade monopoly, and fell into decay. Boni's growth in power led the Dutch later to protect the independence of Gowa but the Dutch used their Buginese allies of Boni in the early wars in Java, and during the British occupation of Java, Raffles had to send an expedition to Celebes against the unruly Buginese in Boni. When Dutch power in Java was restored, a Dutch expedition had to be sent to Boni; but it was not until 1848 that Boni submitted to the Bongay treaty in a revised form. The treaty was not kept and a second expedition, in 1859, made Boni a fief of the Netherlands government, while part of its territory was ceded to the Dutch. The last prince, La Pawowoni Kraeng Segeri, refused in 1905 to pay certain dues and interfered with other states, and he was banished, and Boni then lost its independence completely. About the same time Gowa interfered in another part of Celebes. The Dutch sent troops and in 1911, Gowa, too, was incorporated in Dutch territory. The state of Luwu signed the Bongay treaty in 1667, but it was not until after the Boni War, in 1861, that the Dutch succeeded in establishing any real influence there and there was some trouble in 1886 over the refusal of Luwu to pay a fine for the murder of some shipwrecked sailors on its coast; but in 1905 it agreed to abide by the "short declaration," which then was also applied to the state of Wajo, likewise a signatory of the Bongay treaty, but which had at times been in open revolt, often in trouble with Boni, and had experienced serious internal disorder as recently as 1902. Menado was first colonized by the Spaniards, on the northern coast, and settlers were attracted from neighbouring islands. The sultan of Ternate also claimed suzerainty over it, and fairly early in the 17th century the Dutch entered into relations with the natives of the country to protect them from both Spaniards and Ternate. In 1657 the present capital and fort were built, at Menado, and a trade agreement was signed for the delivery of a certain amount of ironwood annually. In 1677 the Sangi and Talaua islands, and later, certain small kingdoms on the north coast, were placed under the rule of the Dutch governor of Ternate, and from that time onwards Dutch influence expanded, until the conquest of the East Indies by the Japanese during World War II. Japan landed troops at the northern tip of the Celebes Jan. 11, 1942, and within a month controlled most of the island except the remote interior areas.

BIBLIOGRAPHY.—A. R. Wallace, *The Malay Archipelago* (1890); P. and F. Sarasin, *Reisen in Celebes* (Wiesbaden, 1905); F. Sarasin, *Versuch einer Anthropologie der Insel Celebes* (Wiesbaden, 1906); Handbook of the Netherlands East Indies Department of Agriculture, Industry and Commerce, Buitenzorg. (E. E. L.; X.)

CELERY (*Apium graveolens*), a biennial plant (fam. Umbelliferae) which, in its wild state, occurs in England by the sides of ditches and in marshy places, especially near the sea, producing a furrowed stalk and compound leaves with wedge-shaped leaflets, the whole plant having a coarse, rank taste and a peculiar smell. It is also widely distributed in the north temperate region of the old world. By improvement through breeding and selection and blanching, the stalks lose their acrid qualities and assume the mild sweetish aromatic taste peculiar to celery as a salad plant. A large number of varieties are cultivated by gardeners, which are ranged under three classes, green, white and red—the improved green varieties being generally the best flavoured and most crisp and tender. Red varieties are little known in the United States. Both blanched and green it is stewed and used in soups. In the south of Europe celery is much used in its natural condition. In the United States approximately 590,000 tons annually were grown commercially in 1940 and 1941. It was grown most extensively in California, Florida, Michigan and New York, in the order named, at that time.

Celeriac, or turnip-rooted celery (*Apium graveolens,* var. rapaceum), is a variety cultivated more for its roots than for the stalks, although both are edible. It is chiefly grown in northern Europe. (V. R. B.)

CÉLESTE, MADAME (1815–1882), French dancer and actress, was born in Paris on Aug. 16, 1815. As a little girl she was a pupil in the ballet class at the Opéra, and made her début at the Bowery theatre, New York city, at 15. In England in 1837 she gave up dancing, and appeared as an actress. In 1844 she joined Benjamin Webster in the management of the Adelphi, and afterwards took the sole management of the Lyceum till 1861. She retired in 1870. She died in Paris on Feb. 12, 1882.

CELESTIAL MECHANICS is the branch of astronomy that deals with the mathematical theory of the motions of celestial bodies. The foundation was laid by Sir Isaac Newton by the publication in 1687 of his *Philosophiae Naturalis Principia Mathematica,* usually referred to as the *Principia.* Here he published the three laws of motion which express the principles of mechanics, consolidating progress begun with the pioneer work of Galileo Galilei earlier in the 17th century. Newton also formulated the universal law of gravitation which states that any two particles of mass in the universe attract each other with a force that varies directly as the product of the masses and inversely as the square of the distance between them. These foundations permit the statement of a problem in celestial mechanics in the form of a set of equations of motion, ordinary differential equations of the second order. A proper understanding of the subject requires knowledge of this branch of mathematics.

An important triumph of Newton's was that Kepler's three laws of planetary motion, which had been derived empirically by Johann Kepler, were obtained as a consequence of the law of gravitation in conjunction with the laws of motion, applied to the problem of two bodies (*see* ORBIT, in which basic technical terms used in this article are defined). The next in order of difficulty is the case in which three bodies are considered, the famous problem of three bodies. The solar system, consisting of the sun and nine known principal planets, all but three surrounded by one or more satellites, constitutes a problem of many bodies. The significant circumstance that the mass of the sun is about 1,000 times that of the most massive planet, Jupiter, makes the sun's gravitational attraction far outweigh the mutual attractions of the planets. This suggests a process of successive approximations that has become the standard procedure in the mathematical theory of planetary motion, the deviations from elliptic motion being called the perturbations. In the case of the moon's motion the earth produces the principal attraction. Notwithstanding the very great mass of the sun, the effect of the sun's attraction is a small fraction of that of the earth owing to the close proximity of the latter. However, in the case of some satellites the perturbations produced by the sun's attraction may reach very sizable amounts. The mutual attractions of the component stars in triple and quadruple systems of stars suggest other interesting problems in celestial mechanics. In all known cases the configuration is always similar to that of the sun-earth-moon system, and methods similar to those employed in the study of satellite motion may be used. In part because of observational difficulties this field is not as far advanced as the study of motions in the solar system.

During the 18th century powerful analytical methods, made possible by the development of differential and integral calculus, were applied to the problems of celestial mechanics. These methods were generally successful in accounting for the observed motions of bodies in the solar system, and for more than 200 years this success built up a high degree of confidence in Newtonian mechanics and Newton's law of gravitation. This attitude was well expressed by J. H. Poincaré who wrote, in 1892, that ". . . the ultimate aim of celestial mechanics is to solve the great problem of knowing whether Newton's law alone explains all astronomical phenomena." On account of the necessary introduction of the theory of relativity the statement would require modification.

Relativity Effects.—It is now recognized that the Newtonian laws of motion and law of gravitation are approximations to the true laws governing the motions of celestial bodies (*see* RELATIVITY). It has been found, however, that the relativity effects, *i.e.,* the deviations from the motions derived on the basis of the classical Newtonian theory, are exceedingly small in all astronomical problems. In the motion of the perihelion of the innermost planet, Mercury, and in a very few other cases, they are large enough to be revealed by the most precise observations. A comparison between observations and theory, in which the perturbations are properly taken into account, confirms the excess of the motion of the perihelion in the amount of 43 seconds of arc per century, as required by the theory of relativity. This is one of the most convincing observational proofs of the theory of relativity. The effect diminishes rapidly for planets at a greater distance from the sun. In the case of the earth the relativity advance of the perihelion is about 4 seconds of arc per century, just large enough to be confirmed by the observations. On account of the smallness of the relativity effects in problems in celestial mechanics the justified procedure is to continue the use of the equations of motion following from the classical theory, and to apply the small relativity corrections, if at all necessary, in a minor adjustment of the results.

Gravitational Attraction of Finite Bodies.—The Newtonian law of gravitation is stated for particles, not for bodies of finite extent. It was shown by Newton that bodies the masses of which are arranged with perfect spherical symmetry attract each other in accordance with the law of gravitation as if the masses were concentrated in the centres of the respective spheres. It is found that the effect of nonsphericity diminishes rapidly with the distance between the bodies. Hence in the solar system in which the principal bodies are all nearly spherical and the distances, as a rule, large compared with the dimensions of the bodies, it is in many cases permissible to treat the planets and satellites as point-masses. Some interesting exceptions exist: the innermost satellite of Jupiter's system revolves in an orbit the radius of which is only $2\frac{1}{2}$ times the radius of the planet. Owing to its rapid rotation the planet is flattened, and its gravitational attraction differs appreciably from that of a spherical body of the same mass. The principal effect upon the motion of the satellite is an advance of the perijove and a backward motion of the node, both at the rate of $2\frac{1}{2}$ revolutions a year. The innermost satellite of Saturn shows a similar effect with a rate of one revolution a year. These are extraordinary cases; in most satellite orbits the resulting effect is small.

Other Branches of the Subject.—A related branch of celestial mechanics is the gravitational theory of rotating liquid or gaseous masses with applications to the earth and the other larger planets. Astrophysical applications to close double stars have become increasingly important (*see* GEODESY and PRECESSION OF THE EQUINOXES). Newton explained the ocean tides as caused by the gravitational attraction of the moon and the sun. Sir George Howard Darwin, in addition to developing modern methods of tidal analysis and tidal prediction, also treated the cosmogonic aspect of tidal theory in his work on the development of the earth-moon system (*see* TIDES).

The various subjects described are recognized branches of celestial mechanics, which may be understood to embrace all of gravitational astronomy. The central problem, however, remains that of the mutual attractions among three or more bodies, each treated as a point-mass. There are two distinct approaches to the subject. The astronomer is forced to use methods that lead to a practical solution, even if they have the defect that the representation of the motion is valid for a limited interval of time only. The mathematician insists on using only processes of unquestionable validity, and is not primarily concerned with the astronomical requirements. Both points of view are meritorious, and each has had effects upon the development of the other.

Planetary Theory.—An important method for the treatment of planetary perturbations was introduced by Joseph Louis Lagrange (1736–1813). In an elliptic orbit the six orbital elements have constant values, completely determined by the three co-ordinates and the three components of the velocity at any time. Since the attractions by other planets cause a planet to follow a path differing from a fixed ellipse, the elements of its orbit so determined will necessarily vary with the time. Hence one may describe the "perturbed" orbit of a planet by giving the elements as functions of the time. Lagrange's method provides a process for deriving analytical expressions for the derivatives of the varying elements. These expressions are rigorous, but their integration requires the introduction of a process of successive approximations. The ordinary procedure gives rise to the presence of terms proportional to the time, in addition to periodic terms, in the final expressions for the elements. The terms proportional to the time, t, are called secular terms. Their presence raises such questions as whether the eccentricity of a planetary orbit may increase indefinitely, endangering the stability of the planetary system. Such a conclusion would be very superficial. The terms obtained in further approximations, having higher powers of t as factor, will modify the terms obtained in the earlier approximations in a manner that cannot be foreseen without appropriate mathematical analysis.

The integration of the periodic terms introduces divisors of the form $kn+k'n'$, in which n, n' are the mean motions of the two planets, and k, k' integers, both positive and negative. In the mean longitude the squares of these divisors occur. Whatever the mean motions, there will always be linear combinations $kn+k'n'$, small compared with either of the mean motions, n or n'. Such small divisors cause large coefficients in long-period terms, with the principal effect in the mean longitude. The motions of the planets Jupiter and Saturn furnish one of the most interesting illustrations of the effects of small divisors. The annual motions of the two planets are very nearly in ratio 5 to 2, which produces a long-period term with period of about 900 years. The amplitude of the perturbation in the mean longitude is 1,196 seconds of arc in Jupiter and 2,908 seconds of arc in Saturn. These are "the great inequalities" in the motions of these planets the cause of which was discovered by Laplace in 1786. The small divisors in celestial mechanics are related to the more general problem of resonance in mechanical systems.

A more direct approach to the solution of the perturbation problem is that in which the perturbations in the co-ordinates are obtained directly. Among the methods of this type that were employed with success may be mentioned those of Pierre Simon de Laplace and of Simon Newcomb. The apparent advantages are largely cancelled, however, in cases of planetary motion in which large perturbations due to small divisors are an important feature. In such cases a method in which the mean longitude is obtained has decided advantages. By an ingenious procedure, P. A. Hansen succeeded in deriving a method that combines the advantages of the two solutions of the perturbation problem. This method has been tested in numerous applications, and was chosen by G. W. Hill for his theory of Jupiter and Saturn, the most difficult problem among the principal planets.

An accomplishment that demonstrated strikingly the power of the theory of planetary motions was the discovery of the planet Neptune in 1846. Its presence and location in the sky had been predicted with astonishing accuracy by J. C. Adams and by U. J. J. Leverrier from deviations in the motion of the planet Uranus (*see* NEPTUNE). Attempts were made to discover planets beyond Neptune by a similar procedure, but the discovery of Pluto at the Lowell observatory in 1930 must be ascribed to perseverance in systematic search rather than accuracy of prediction by mathematical theory.

Secular Variations.—Planetary theories of the types described are entirely satisfactory for the immediate purposes of astronomy; the construction of tables that represent the motion of a planet for a limited time, say, a few thousand years. For questions concerning the stability of the solar system or, generally, its configuration in the very distant past and future such representations of planetary motion are insufficient. The question arose whether the secular terms occurring in planetary theories could be avoided. Lagrange obtained a solution in which he ignored the periodic terms. Retaining only the terms of the lowest power in the elements he obtained for the variation of the elements two sets of linear differential equations with constant coefficients, the eccentricity and perihelion appearing in one set, the inclination and node in the other. For the principal planets of the solar system, excluding Pluto, these equations have been solved in closed trigonometric form. In a solution of this type one obtains for the eccentricity and perihelion of each planet expressions containing eight trigonometric terms, the separate terms constituting oscillations with periods ranging from 57,000 years to 2,100,000 years. Similar expressions are obtained for the elements defining the positions of the orbital planes in space. These results give at least some indication of the long-period fluctuations in the elements of the planetary orbits. They should, however, be applied with caution. Further approximations present the same difficulty of small divisors as is met in the case of the periodic perturbations of the ordinary planetary theory. A still outstanding problem is the inclusion of Pluto in the solution of the secular variations. This will require a novel approach since the ordinary procedure leads to divergent developments.

The asteroids or minor planets furnish a rich field of application of the processes of celestial mechanics. The existence of the gaps in the ring of asteroids leads to the difficult theory of resonance in planetary motion. The application of the theory of secular variations led K. Hirayama to the discovery of five families of minor planets. He concluded that the members of each family must be fragments of a larger parent body. F. L. Whipple established a similar relationship between the orbit of Encke's comet and the orbits of certain meteors determined from trails on photographic plates obtained at the Harvard observatory (*see* MINOR PLANETS).

Satellite Motion.—A common feature of all satellite problems is that the motion proceeds at a much more rapid rate than among planetary orbits. In the moon's motion the line of apsides goes through a revolution in about nine years, the node in 19 years. These periods should be compared with the periods of tens or hundreds of thousands of years that affect the motions of the perihelia and nodes of planetary orbits. Consequently, in a satellite theory one cannot permit the appearance of the time in the coefficients of perturbation terms in the manner in which they are tolerated in planetary theories. One must aim at expressions free from this defect. The most complete solution of a satellite problem is the lunar theory (*see* MOON). Elaborate investigations have also been devoted to the satellite systems of Jupiter and Saturn. These systems present cases of resonance that are among the more interesting problems of celestial mechanics.

Modern Methods.—From the time of Lagrange until the present mathematical astronomers have made attempts to introduce the more perfect methods used in the lunar theory into the problem of planetary motion. A method similar to that used by Charles Eugène Delaunay in the lunar theory has been applied to planetary problems, but its application to the entire system of principal planets would be exceedingly laborious.

G. W. Hill opened up a new approach to problems in celestial mechanics by his use of a periodic orbit as a first approximation to the lunar theory. This subject was very fully investigated by J. H. Poincaré, whose work has led to a clearer understanding of the mathematical questions involved. Principally because of his work it is now recognized that, from a mathematical point of view, even such perfect developments as the lunar theories by Delaunay and by Brown leave something to be desired.

On account of the analytical difficulty of many problems in celestial mechanics investigators have resorted to the method of numerical integration. The method is used extensively for calculating the motions of asteroids and comets, and also in mathematical researches in the problem of three bodies.

The General Problem of Three Bodies.—This problem possesses ten known integrals, all of an algebraic character. Such an integral is a function of the co-ordinates and momenta of the three bodies that remains constant throughout the motion. The original equations of the problem form a system of the 18th order, nine differential equations of the second order. With the aid of the ten integrals, the "elimination of the nodes" and the elimination of the time the system may be reduced to one of the sixth order. This reduction was actually made by Lagrange and improved by later authors by the use of the canonical form of the equations. The reduction of the problem of three bodies with the aid of known integrals suggested that, if additional integrals were discovered, the problem might be further reduced and even completely solved. All such attempts failed; finally H. Bruns, in 1887, proved that no further algebraic integrals of the three-body problem exist. Soon afterward Poincaré proved that no further integrals uniform with respect to the elliptic elements exist. This result is of the greatest importance since it proves that the developments in trigonometric series used in the astronomical methods cannot converge for all values of the constants within a finite range. It does not exclude such a representation in the case of particular orbits; obvious examples are furnished by the periodic solutions and by the particular solutions which were first studied by Lagrange (*see* TROJAN PLANETS).

The simplified problem in which one of the three bodies has negligible mass and moves in the orbital plane of the two massive bodies, which are supposed to move in circular orbits, is the so-called restricted problem. The system of equations is one of the fourth order with one known integral, the Jacobian integral. Let $1-m$ and m be the masses of the finite bodies; r, r_1, r_2, the distances of the infinitesimal mass from the centre of the mass and the two bodies respectively, and V the velocity of the infinitesimal mass in a co-ordinate system the origin of which is at the centre of mass, and which rotates uniformly with the period of revolution of the finite masses. The Jacobian integral, if the units of time and distance are conveniently chosen, is then

$$r^2 + \frac{2(1-m)}{r_1} + \frac{2m}{r_2} = V^2 + C,$$

C being an arbitrary constant. By putting $V^2=0$ one obtains a single family of curves with C as parameter. These "curves of zero velocity" may be looked upon as barriers in the sense that an orbit for which the constant of the Jacobian integral equals C' can never cross any of these curves of zero velocity for which C' exceeds C. The curves of zero velocity were first introduced by Hill with application to the moon's motion and have figured prominently in more recent studies of the restricted problem.

A totally different approach to the solution of the problem of three bodies was made by using developments in powers of a variable related to the time. If applied to the original equations the method fails owing to the singularities of the differential equations that correspond to collisions. These singularities may be removed by suitable changes of variables, a procedure known as regularization. The first significant step in this direction was made by P. Painlevé. In 1912 K. F. Sundmann obtained a solution for the general problem of three bodies that can be expanded as power series which are convergent, but not uniformly so, for all values of the time. This result is of great theoretical interest, although its actual application to astronomical problems is excluded by practical difficulties. Moreover, the form of the solution does not reveal the character of the orbits.

In the restricted problem, the use of the Jacobian integral permits the elimination of one of the velocity components. Hence the motion can be represented completely by a trajectory in a three-dimensional phase space comparable with a streamline in a noncompressible fluid. This approach permits an attack upon problems that were not accessible by other methods. The earlier developments are due to Poincaré; important advances were made by G. D. Birkhoff, especially on questions concerning the probability that a trajectory returns to the same small region in space.

BIBLIOGRAPHY.—An elementary exposition of the principles of celestial mechanics is found in Russell, Dugan and Stewart, *Astronomy*, vol. i, chap. x (1926). Introductory treatises are: F. R. Moulton, *Introduction to Celestial Mechanics*, 2nd. ed. (1914); H. C. Plummer, *An Introductory Treatise on Dynamical Astronomy* (1918). The standard treatise covering developments through the 19th century is F. Tisserand, *Traité de Mécanique Céleste*, 4 vols. (1889–96). Excellent chapters on the mathematical aspects of the problem of three bodies are contained in E. T. Whittaker, *A Treatise on the Analytical Dynamics of Particles and Rigid Bodies*, 4th. ed. (1937). Other important works for specialists are: J. H. Poincaré, *Les Méthodes Nouvelles de la Mécanique Céleste*, 3 vols. (1892–99); E. W. Brown, *An Introductory Treatise on the Lunar Theory* (1896); J. H. Poincaré, *Leçons de Mécanique Céleste*, 3 vols. (1905–10); *Enc. der Math. Wiss.*, vol. vi, 2A, 2B, (1905–34); G. W. Hill, *Collected Math. Works*, 4 vols. (1905–07); G. D. Birkhoff, *Dynamical Systems* (Amer. Math. Soc. Colloquium Publ., vol. ix, 1927); A. Wintner, *The Analytical Foundations of Celestial Mechanics* (1941). (D. BR.)

CELESTIAL SPHERE, the imaginary sphere of indefinite radius on which the positions of the fixed stars are defined by their directions relative to an observer at its centre. The earth's axis meets the celestial sphere in two points, the *celestial poles*. (*See* ASTRONOMY: *Observational Astronomy*.)

CELESTINA, LA, the popular alternative title attached from 1519 (or earlier) to the anonymous *Comedia de Calisto y Melibea*, a Spanish novel in dialogue which was celebrated throughout Europe during the 16th century. The authorship of the *Celestina* and the date of its composition are doubtful. An anonymous prefatory letter in the editions subsequent to 1501 attributes the book to Juan de Mena or Rodrigo Cota, but this ascription is universally rejected. The prevailing opinion is that the author of the 21 acts was Fernando de Rojas, apparently a Spanish Jew resident at the Puebla de Montalban in the province of Toledo; R. Foulché-Delbosc, however, maintains that the original 16 acts are by an unknown writer who had no part in the five supplementary acts. Some scholars give 1483 as the date of composition; others hold that the book was written in 1497. These questions are still unsettled. The *Celestina* excels all earlier Spanish works in tragic force, in impressive conception, and in the realistic rendering of characters drawn from all classes of society. It passed through innumerable editions in Spain, and was the first Spanish book to find acceptance throughout western Europe. A Latin version by Caspar Barth was issued under the title of *Pornoboscodidascalus latinus* (1624) with all the critical apparatus of a recognized classic. James Mabbe's English rendering (1631) is one of the best translations ever published. The original edition of 1499 has been reprinted by R. Foulché-Delbosc in the *Bibliotheca Hispanica*, vol. xii (1902).

BIBLIOGRAPHY.—M. Menéndez y Pelayo's introduction to the *Celestina* (Vigo, 1899–1900); R. Foulché-Delbosc, "Observations sur la Célestine" in the *Revue hispanique*, vol. vii, pp. 28–80 (1900) and vol. ix, pp. 171–199 (1902); and K. Haebler, "Bemerkungen zur Celestina," in the *Revue hispanique*, vol. ix, pp. 139–170 (1902).

CELESTINE (CAELESTINUS), the name of five popes:

CELESTINE I (Saint), pope from 422 to 432. After his triumph over the dissensions caused by the faction of Eulalius (*see* BONIFACE I) his episcopate was peaceful. He instructed Cyril, bishop of Alexandria, to inquire into the doctrines of Nestorius. To extirpate Pelagianism, he sent to Britain a deacon, Palladius, at whose instigation St. Germanus of Auxerre followed to inculcate orthodoxy among the clergy of Britain. Celestine also commissioned Palladius to preach the gospel in Ireland which was beginning to rally to Christianity. Celestine was the first pope who is known to have taken a direct interest in Britain and Ireland. (X.)

CELESTINE II (Guido di Castello), pope from 1143 to 1144, came of obscure Umbrian parentage. He was able and learned, and studied under Peter Abélard, whom he held in lasting admiration. Made cardinal deacon in 1127, he was pope from Sept. 26, 1143, to March 8, 1144.

He removed the interdict which Innocent II had employed against Louis VII of France.

CELESTINE III (Giacinto Bobone), pope from 1191 to 1198, once cardinal deacon of Santa Maria in Cosmedin, became pope on March 30, 1191. Henry VI of Germany forced the pontiff to crown him emperor and three years later took possession of the Norman kingdom of Sicily; he refused tribute and the oath of allegiance, and even appointed bishops subject to his own jurisdiction; moreover, he gave his brother in fief the estates which had belonged to the countess Matilda of Tuscany. Celestine dared not excommunicate him.

He played throughout a temporizing policy, refusing even to take decisive action when the emperor imprisoned Richard Coeur de Lion as he was returning from the crusade. Richard had been set free before the dilatory pope put Leopold of Austria, his original captor, under the ban.

Celestine died on Jan. 8, 1198.

CELESTINE IV (Godfrey Castiglione), pope in 1241, nephew of Urban III (1185–87), was archpriest and chancellor at Milan, before he joined the Cistercians. In 1227 Gregory IX created him cardinal priest, and in 1239 cardinal bishop of Sabina. Elected to succeed Gregory on Oct. 25, 1241, he died on Nov. 10 before consecration.

CELESTINE V (St. Peter Celestine or Peter of Morrone), pope in 1294, was born of poor parents at Isernia about 1215, and adopted an eremitical way of life on Monte Morrone. He attracted other ascetics whom he organized into a congregation which was later called the Celestines (*q.v.*). They were incorporated by Urban IV into the Benedictine order (1263). His *Opuscula* (Naples, 1640) are probably not genuine.

A fight between the Colonna and the Orsini, as well as dissensions among the cardinals, prevented a papal election for more than two years after the death of Nicholas IV. Finally, Celestine was elected on July 5, 1294.

Apocalyptic notions then current doubtless aided his election, for Joachim of Floris and his school looked to monasticism to deliver the church and the world. Multitudes came to Celestine's coronation and he began his reign the idol of visionaries, of extremists and of the populace. But the pope was in the power of Charles II of Naples, and became his tool against Aragon. When he wished to abdicate, Benedetto Gaetano, destined to succeed him as Boniface VIII, removed all scruples against this unheard of procedure by finding a precedent in the case of Clement I. Celestine abdicated on Dec. 13, 1294, and died in a monastic cell in the castle of Fumone on May 19, 1296. He was canonized as St. Peter Celestine by Clement V in 1313.

BIBLIOGRAPHY.—H. Finke, *Aus den Tagen Bonifaz VIII* (Münster, 1902); Antinori, *Celestino V ed il sesto centenario della sua incoronazione* (Aquila, 1894); H. K. Mann, *Lives of the Popes,* vol. xvii and xviii (London, St. Louis, 1931–32). (C. H. LE.)

CELESTINE or CELESTITE, a name applied to native strontium sulphate ($SrSO_4$), having been suggested by the celestial blue colour which it occasionally presents. It is usually colourless, or a delicate shade of blue. It crystallizes in the orthorhombic system, being isomorphous with barytes (*see* BARITE). The cleavage is a perfect parallel to the basal pinacoid, and a less marked parallel to the prism. Although celestine much resembles barytes in its physical properties, having for example the same hardness (3), it is less dense, its specific gravity being 3.9. It is less abundant than barytes, but is, however, much more soluble.

Celestine occurs in the Triassic rocks of Britain, especially in veins and geodes in the Keuper marl in the neighbourhood of Bristol. At Wickwar and Yate in Gloucestershire it is worked for industrial purposes. Colourless crystals of great beauty occur in association with calcite and native sulphur in the sulphur deposits of Sicily, as at Girgenti. Very large tabular crystals are found in limestone on Strontian island in Lake Erie; and a blue fibrous variety from near Frankstown, Blair county, Pa., is notable as having been the original celestine on which the species was founded by A. G. Werner in 1798.

Celestine is much used for the preparation of strontium hydrate, which is employed in refining beetroot sugar. (F. W. R.)

CELESTINES, a religious order founded about 1260 by Peter of Morrone, afterwards Pope Celestine V. (1294). It was an attempt to unite the eremitical and cenobitical modes of life. Peter's first disciples lived as hermits on Mount Majella in the Abruzzi. The Benedictine rule was taken as the basis of the life, but was supplemented by regulations notably increasing the austerities practised. The form of government was borrowed largely from those prevailing in the mendicant orders. Indeed, though the Celestines are reckoned as a branch of the Benedictines, there is little in common between them. During the founder's lifetime the order spread rapidly, and eventually there were about 150 monasteries in Italy, and others in France, Bohemia and the Netherlands. The French houses formed a separate congregation, the head-house being in Paris. The French Revolution and those of the 19th century destroyed their houses, and the Celestine order seems no longer to exist.

See Helyot, *Histoire des ordres religieux* (1792), vi. c. 23; Max Heimbucher, *Orden und Kongregationen* (1896), i. § 22, p. 134; the art. "Cölestiner" in Wetzer und Welte, *Kirchenlexicon* (ed. 2), Herzog-Hauck, *Realencyklopädie* (ed. 3) and *Catholic Encyclopaedia,* vol. xvi. pp. 19, 20.

CELIBACY, the state of being unmarried. In the original Latin (*caelibatus,* from *caelebs,* unmarried) it meant merely the fact of being unmarried, but was later restricted almost entirely to the perpetual renunciation of marriage, especially for religious motives. Celibacy was a practice of various religions even in pre-Christian times, as exemplified in the Roman vestal virgins and in Buddhist monasticism. Judaism frowned on celibacy, and considered childlessness a reproach, for it banished the hope of begetting the Messiah. But marriage was rejected by the majority of the Jewish sect of Essenes, which arose about two centuries before Christ, probably from Persian-Babylonian influences during the captivity and from contact with Hellenism through the Greek language.

Christ commended celibacy for the sake of the kingdom of heaven (Matt. xix, 12), but did not prescribe it; and St. Paul praised virginity as better than marriage (I Cor. vii; 7, 32–40). Celibacy was a common practice among the early Christians, who were inspired by the example of Christ, the virtues of self-control and self-denial, and the freedom from family cares which would leave greater liberty for prayer, contemplation and apostolic activity, and would win the confidence and respect of the people. The practice was not confined to the clergy, but it became by church law an obligation for those who wished to embrace the clerical state.

Origins of Clerical Celibacy.—The majority of scholars agree that the law of clerical celibacy was not of apostolic origin. St. Paul recommended celibacy, but he also wrote that a bishop should be a man of one wife (I Tim. iii, 2; Titus i, 6). This was generally understood to exclude from bishoprics, not unmarried men, but rather men who had married more than once, at least after their baptism. A few contemporaries of St. John Chrysostom found in these texts a command that a bishop should have a wife, and this interpretation was revived in the 16th century by the Protestant reformers.

While no strict law of celibacy existed during the first three centuries of Christianity, its practice was in honour among the clergy from the time of the apostles. Tertullian admired the number of celibate clergy and Origen contrasted the spiritual fatherhood of the priests of the New Testament with the carnal paternity of the Levites of the Old Law. At the same time, according to Clement of Alexandria, the church approved of clergymen who had married; if they used their marriage rights without sin, they would be saved by having children. When a law of celibacy was proposed in the ecumenical council of Nicaea in 325, Paphnutius, a celibate Egyptian bishop, objected that nothing should be added to the ancient tradition which opposed marriage after ordination, but did not prohibit wedded life for those who married before ordination. The council accepted this advice and contented itself with the provision that the clergy should not have in their houses unmarried women other than near relatives.[1]

Celibacy in the Oriental Church.—The law of clerical celibacy developed during and after the 4th century, more stringently in the west than in the east. The practice of celibacy was esteemed in the eastern church, but was not universal. The council of Ancyra in 314 allowed a candidate for the diaconate to state his choice of celibacy or marriage, and bound him accordingly. A few years later the council of Gangra condemned any disdain for the ministry of married priests. The bishops, however, practised continence even when married, and this custom gradually passed into church law, for which Justinian established civil sanctions. The discipline of the oriental church was finally fixed in the council of Trullo in 692. Absolute continence was prescribed for bishops; if they had been married they could not be consecrated unless their wives would enter monasteries. Ordained priests, deacons, and subdeacons could not marry, but they were free to retain wives they had taken before ordination.[2] This law has remained substantially the same in the eastern churches, but the practice has been to select bishops only from the unmarried priests.

Many of the eastern churches that have reunited with the Roman see have also accepted the stricter Roman discipline, but the retention of the old oriental practice has been tolerated in some of them.

The Early Latin Church.—After the beginning of the 4th century the custom of clerical celibacy gradually evolved into a legal obligation in the western church. The council of Elvira (Grenada) about the year 300 prescribed continence for bishops, priests and deacons.[3] This was merely a provincial council local to a part of Spain, but it has been prominent in the history of celibacy since it established the earliest recorded legislation on this subject. The same discipline was decreed in 386 by the church in Rome, and Pope Siricius set about making it universal in the Latin church. By letters to Spain and Africa he notified the bishops of the ruling, and prescribed penalties for violations.[4] A few years later Pope Innocent I wrote to the bishops of Rouen (404) and Toulouse (405) in the same vein. Councils in Carthage in 390 and 401 prohibited matrimonial intercourse of priests and deacons. At about the same time councils in Toledo and Turin barred advancement in orders if deacons or priests failed to observe continence with their wives. French councils demanded a promise of perpetual chastity from candidates for the diaconate. The church in England and Ireland also followed the continental law. Pope St. Leo I (440–461) restated the law of celibacy and included subdeacons among its subjects.[5]

The law met with opposition and St. Jerome knew of more than 300 married bishops. Other writers and many epitaphs of the clergy recorded clerical marriages as late as the 6th century. Time was required for the law to be universally accepted, but it was clear and definite after the 6th century except for subdeacons, for whom it became general in the 9th century.

Since married men received orders and undertook the obligation of celibacy, their wives were to be treated as sisters thereafter, and were called deaconess, priestess and episcopess. The wife of a priest or deacon remained mistress of his house, but a bishop's wife was to live in a separate home, and measures of vigilance were prescribed for them. But the proximity of the married couple was a source of danger, and violations of the law were not rare, although it was generally well observed during the Merovingian period, and many of the clergy were unmarried.

In the 8th century violations of the law became more frequent especially when Charles Martel began to distribute benefices to men who were more interested in the income than in the duties of a cleric. There was chaos in the Frankish church, as St. Boniface reported to Pope Zachary, but the saint succeeded in effecting a great reform there. In Spain King Witiza went so far as to abrogate the law of celibacy. With the advent of the Carlovingians better discipline was restored. Various councils renewed the old canons and Charlemagne sanctioned the traditional church law. But after the break-up of his empire the laws of both church and state were largely disregarded. During the 10th and most of the 11th centuries the laxity of the clergy made clerical marriages quite numerous. In many places the abuse was so rampant that marriage tended to become the normal state of the clergy with no stigma attached to it. The term "concubinage" was applied to these unions, but not in its strict sense, for the church had not yet made holy orders an impediment to valid wedlock. Some clerics did keep mistresses, but others contracted true marriages, either secretly, or even openly, as Pope Leo VII deplored in a letter to the Gauls and Germans.

In the middle of the 10th century the bishop of Augsburg was St. Ulric to whom an extant letter in favour of sacerdotal marriage has been attributed. Dr. Henry C. Lea in his *History of Sacerdotal Celibacy* vouched for its authenticity, but no careful scholar after the middle of the 19th century would disagree with August Potthast's evaluation in his bibliography of mediaeval history. He catalogues the letter under the heading, "Pseudo-Udalricus" as a fabrication of about 1075, a century after Ulric's death in 973, and a period of sharp controversy between the papacy and the empire.[6]

Reforms of Gregory VII.—In the 11th century the church began to re-establish the old canons, but the long-standing abuse was not repressed without a struggle. It took the exhortation of the most virtuous among the clergy and the drastic legislation of the greatest of the popes to bring about a reform. Severe laws and penalties were enforced, not only against the incontinent clergy, but also against their illegal partners. Some of the clergy who were liberated serfs took free women to wife in order to have children who would be free and inherit their property according to the civil law. Hence Benedict VIII, in the synod of Pavia about 1022, decreed the children of the clergy to be serfs of the church, and Henry II incorporated this into the law of the empire.

Leo IX in the Lateran synod of 1049 enslaved the concubines of the Roman clergy to the Lateran palace. Various synods in England and France allowed the rural clergy to keep the wives they had taken, but forbade future clerical marriage.

St. Peter Damien and Hildebrand were strong supporters and advisers of the popes of this period, and when Hildebrand became Pope Gregory VII in 1073, he made strenuous efforts to restore the ancient discipline. Many clerics believed that contrary custom had abrogated the law and made their marriages blameless, so when Gregory's legates instructed the German hierarchy to enforce celibacy, some of the clergy threatened to give up their ministry rather than their wives, saying that the pope might get angels to take their places. Similar disturbances occurred in France, but Gregory was not to be turned from his purpose. He took the unprecedented and dangerous step of subjecting the clergy to the judgment of the laity. He wrote several letters exhorting princes and people to refuse, and even to hinder by force, the ministrations of priests who were tainted with incontinence.[7] The temporary harm of such a measure was justified by the permanent gain effected, for the efforts of Gregory and his immediate successors brought about the desired reform. One of the principal causes of clerical incontinence was removed by the eventual settlement of the conflict over lay investitures. Finally the first and second ecumenical councils of the Lateran

[1]Socrates, *Hist. eccl.*, I I, c. XI; *Concilium Nicaenum*, can. 3; Mansi, *Concilia*, vol. 2, col. 670.
[2]*Concilium Trullanum*, can. 6, 12, 13, 48; Mansi, *Concilia*, vol. 11, col. 944–948, 965.
[3]*Concilium Eliberitanum*, can. 33; *ibid.*, vol. 2, col. 11.
[4]*Epist. ad Himerium; Epist. ad Afros.*
[5]St. Leo I, *Epistle XIV*, c. IV.

[6]Lea, *History of Sacerdotal Celibacy*, vol. I, p. 171; *see* Thurston, "A Saint Averse to Celibacy," *The Month*, vol. III (1908) pp. 311–315.
[7]*Cf.* Gregorius VII ad Germanos, Mansi, *Concilia*, vol. 20, col. 625.

(1123 and 1139) removed the possibility of clerical marriage after ordination to the subdiaconate by making this and higher orders an impediment to valid marriage.[1] After these decrees the unlawful unions of clerics were mere concubinage. These steps led to a general observance of the law so that in the 13th century concubinage was the rare exception among the clergy.

A new decline set in during the 14th and 15th centuries and various princes and churchmen proposed the adoption of the practice of the oriental church. The question was raised, without result, in the councils of Vienne (1311–12), Constance (1414–18) and Basel (1431–49). Some priests claimed special dispensations from the law of celibacy and even used forged papal documents to prove their claim.

In the 16th century Martin Luther and other Protestant leaders attacked clerical celibacy, and as Protestantism progressed, some Roman Catholics thought a relaxation of the law might help to restore unity in the church.

Modern Roman Discipline.—The great reforming council of Trent, after long discussion, retained the earlier laws, including the Lateran decree that holy orders nullify an attempt to marry, and defined as an article of faith the church's power so to legislate.[2] The observance of the law was greatly forwarded by founding seminaries in which the candidates were trained in virtue while being instructed in preparation for ordination.

After Trent, at the request of Ferdinand I and Maximillian II, Pope Pius IV for a time considered permitting clerical marriage in Germany, but the question was shelved and the law of Trent remained the settled legislation of the church. It was incorporated into the 1918 *Codex Juris Canonici* in canons 132, 987 and 1072.

Dispensations have sometimes been granted to subdeacons and deacons who returned to lay status, but to priests very rarely and only in view of the common welfare. General dispensations were given in England to the clergy who had embraced Anglicanism and married, but who wished to return to Rome under Mary Tudor; and to the small section of the French clergy who had unfrocked themselves and married in fear of the Terror.

The church never absolutely prohibited the ordination of married men, but to protect the rights of their wives the practice arose of refusing ordination unless the wife freely vowed perpetual chastity. This was the law in the 14th century.[3] The 1918 code of canon law prohibited ordination of a married man without the very rarely granted dispensation of the Holy See.

There has been occasional laxity since the council of Trent, and in the early 19th century there was German agitation for a mitigation of the law, but in general the celibacy of the Roman Catholic clergy has won respect and influence in and outside their church.

The practice of celibacy was revived in the Church of England during the latter part of the 19th century by some monastic institutions which also made foundations in America.

Bibliography.—Among the best treatments of celibacy are F. X. Funk, "Cölibat und Priesterehe," in his *Kirchengeschichtliche Abhandlungen und Untersuchungen*, 1897, vol. I, pp. 69-120; and E. Vacandard, "Célibat," in *Dictionnaire de Théologie Catholique*, 1923, vol. II, part 2, col. 2068–2088. A good historical and archaeological treatment of the first eight centuries is found in H. Leclercq, "Célibat," in *Dictionnaire d'Archéologie Chrétienne et de Liturgie*, 1925, vol. II, part 2, col. 2802–2831, where a complete bibliography also is found. A good English treatment with detailed discussion of celibacy in England is Herbert Thurston's "Celibacy of the Clergy," in *The Catholic Encyclopedia*, vol. III, pp. 481–488. The best known opponent of clerical celibacy is Henry C. Lea, *History of Sacerdotal Celibacy in the Christian Church*, 1907, but he has been charged with superficial and biased scholarship by Roman Catholic scholars and some others. Disaffection was expressed by Johann and Augustin Theiner in *Einführung der erzwungenen Ehelosigkeit*, 1828, which was prohibited by the Holy See and afterward repudiated by Augustin Theiner.

(H. R. W.)

CELINA, an incorporated village in western Ohio, U.S.A., on Grand lake (or Lake St. Marys); the county seat of Mercer county. It is served by the Cincinnati Northern and the Nickel Plate railways. Pop. (1950) 5,703 by the federal census. Celina is a summer resort, the commercial centre of a farming region and an important furniture-manufacturing town. Stearic acid, printed and metal products are also manufactured. The village was settled in 1834 and incorporated in 1885. Grand lake is an artificial lake, 9 mi. long by 3 mi. wide, built to feed the old Miami and Erie canal.

CELL, originally a small detached room in a building (Lat. *cella*, a small room), particularly a small monastic house (*see* Abbey).

Also used for the small sleeping apartments of the monks, or the small dwelling of a hermit. This use still survives in the small separate chambers in a prison (*q.v.*). The word also denotes various small compartments which build up a compound structure, such as honeycomb, etc.

In electricity a cell may be defined as a system which produces electromotive force by chemical action.

For voltaic, dry and concentration cells *see* Battery; for gas cell *see* Hydrogen Ions; for standard cell *see* Instruments, Electrical.

In biology the term cell denotes microscopic structural elements which form the bulk of the tissues of animals and plants of visible dimensions. The precise meaning of the term cell in biological literature is set forth in the article Cytology (*q.v.*). When the term came into usage in biology, it referred to the smallest units of structure that the microscope could reveal in the animal or plant body. First used by Robert Hooke (1665) for the minute cavities of cork, a tissue which he described as made up of "little boxes or cells," it is a survival from the microscopic descriptions of plant structure made by 17th century botanists, and as such is really a misnomer, for tissues of animals rarely display the honeycomb-like appearance of pith, cork, etc., when examined microscopically. To-day the cell is recognized to be a complex, consisting of a number of well-defined structures (*nucleus, mitochondria,* etc.) so that it is no longer possible to define the cell as the ultimate structural unit of living matter. On the other hand, it is a physiological unit. It is the delimitation of this characteristic complex of microscopically visible units by a boundary which possesses the physical property of differential permeability to different kinds of molecules that characterizes the individual cell, which has thus come to be regarded as a unit of physiological activity of a certain order. The fact that the respective contributions of the maternal and paternal parents to the physical constitution of the offspring are derived in each case from a single cell of the parent-body has revolutionized the study of heredity; and has stimulated a considerable body of research which makes it possible to-day to envisage the structural basis of hereditary transmission and the determination of sex.

Thus the Cell Doctrine, *i.e.*, the recognition of the cell originally as the structural unit of the body and later as a unit of physiological activity, has exerted its influence on every department of biological thought since the doctrine was formulated by M. J. Schleiden and Theodor Schwann in 1839.

(L. T. H.)

A DUNCAN PHYFE CELLARET OF THE 19TH CENTURY, MOUNTED WITH CLAW FEET

CELLA, in architecture, the Latin name corresponding to the Greek *naos*, used for the enclosed room or sanctuary of a Greek or Roman temple or any building of similar plan.

CELLARET (*i.e.*, little cellar), strictly that portion of a sideboard which is used for holding bottles and decanters. Sometimes it is a drawer, divided into compartments lined with zinc, and sometimes a cupboard, but still an integral part of the sideboard. In the latter part of the 18th century, when the sideboard was in process of evolution from a side table with drawers into the large and important piece of furniture which it eventually be-

[1] *Conc. Lateranense* I, can. 21; *ibid.*, II, can. 7; *see Decretum Gratiani*, dist. XXVII, c. 8; *ibid.*, *causa* XXVII, q. 1, c. 40.

[2] *Concilium Tridentinum*, sess. XXIV, can. 4 and 9; Mansi, *Concilia*, vol. 33, col. 150–151.

[3] See *Corpus iuris canonici, cap. unic., tit. 6, de voto et voti redemptione, in Extravag. Ioannis XXII.*

came, the cellaret was a detached receptacle. It was most commonly of mahogany or rosewood, many-sided or even octagonal, and occasionally oval, bound with broad bands of brass and lined with zinc partitions to hold the ice for cooling wine. Sometimes a tap was fixed in the lower part for drawing off the water from the melted ice. Cellarets were usually placed under the sideboard, and were, as a rule, handsome and well-proportioned; but as the artistic impulse which created the great 18th-century English school of furniture died away, their form grew debased, and under the influence of the British Empire fashion, which drew its inspiration from a bastard classicism, they assumed the shape of sarcophagi incongruously mounted with lions' heads and claw feet. Hepplewhite called them *gardes du vin;* they are now nearly always known as "wine-coolers."

CELLE, a town of Germany, in the district of Hanover, Lower Saxony, on the left bank of the navigable Aller, near its junction with the Fuse and the Lachte, 23 mi. N.E. of Hanover. Pop. (1950) 59,667. Founded in 1292, the town was the residence of the dukes of Lüneburg-Celle, a cadet branch of the ducal house of Brunswick, from the 14th century until 1705. The most interesting building is the former ducal palace, begun in 1485 in Late Gothic style, but with extensive Renaissance additions of the late 17th century. There are manufactures of biscuits, umbrellas, leather, sugar, dyes and paper, and trade is carried on in wax and timber. Celle is the seat of the court of appeal from the superior courts of Aurich, Detmold, Göttingen, Hanover, Hildesheim, Lüneburg, Osnabrück, Stade and Verden.

CELLIER, ALFRED (1844–1891), English composer of light operas of which one, "Dorothy," enjoyed prodigious popularity, running from Sept. 25, 1886, till April 1889. "The Mountebanks," to a libretto by W. S. Gilbert, was also very successful.

CELLINI, BENVENUTO (1500–1571), Italian artist, metal worker and sculptor, born in Florence on Nov. 1, 1500. His father was a musician and artificer of musical instruments, who married Maria Lisabetta Granacci, and 18 years elapsed before they had any children. Benvenuto (meaning "welcome") was the third child. The father destined him for his own profession and tried to thwart his inclination for design and metal work. At 15, however, he was apprenticed to a goldsmith, Antonio di Sandro, named Marcone. He had already attracted some notice in Florence when, being implicated in a brawl, he was banished to Siena where he worked for Francesco Castoro, a goldsmith. He visited Bologna and Pisa, and returned to Florence before he went to Rome in 1519. To this period belong a silver casket, some silver candlesticks, a vase for the bishop of Salamanca, and the gold medallion of "Leda and the Swan"—the head and torso of Leda cut in hard stone—executed for Gonfaloniere Gabbrello Cesarino, which is now in the Vienna museum. In the attack upon Rome (1527) by the constable de Bourbon, the bravery of Cellini proved of signal service to Pope Clement VII.; if we may believe his own accounts, his was the hand which shot the Bourbon dead, and he afterwards killed Philibert, prince of Orange. His exploits paved the way for a reconciliation with the Florentine magistrates and his return to Florence. Here he worked on medals, the most famous of which are "Hercules and the Nemean Lion," in gold repoussé work, and "Atlas supporting the Sphere," in chased gold. From Florence he went to the court of the duke of Mantua, and thence again to Rome, where he was employed in the working of jewellery and the execution of dies for private medals and for the papal mint. Here, in 1529, he avenged a brother's death by slaying the slayer; soon afterwards he had to flee to Naples to shelter himself from the consequences of an affray with a notary, Ser Benedetto, whom he wounded, but on the accession of Paul III. he was reinstated. The plots of Pierluigi Farnese, a natural son of Paul III., led to his retreat from Rome to Florence and Venice, and once more he was restored with greater honour than before.

On returning from a visit to the court of Francis I., being now aged 37, he was imprisoned for some time on a charge (apparently false) of having embezzled during the war the gems of the pontifical tiara. At last, however, he was released at the intercession of Pierluigi's wife, and more especially of the Cardinal d'Este of Ferrara. For a while after this he worked at the court of Francis I. at Fontainebleau and in Paris. But the enmity of the duchesse d'Etampes and the intrigues of the king's favourites led him, after about five years of laborious and sumptuous work, to retire in 1545 in disgust to Florence. During the war with Siena, Cellini was appointed to strengthen the defences of his native city. In 1565 he married Piera de Salvadore Parigi. He died in Florence on Feb. 13, 1571, and was buried in the church of the Annunziata.

Besides the works in gold and silver which have been mentioned, Cellini executed several pieces of sculpture. The most distinguished is the bronze group of "Perseus holding the head of Medusa," now in the Loggia dei Lanzi at Florence, one of the most typical monuments of the Italian Renaissance.

Not less characteristic of its splendidly gifted and barbarically untameable author are his autobiographical memoirs begun in Florence in 1558—a production of the utmost energy, directness, and racy animation, setting forth one of the most singular careers in all the annals of fine art. His amours and hatreds, his passions and delights, his love of the sumptuous and the exquisite in art, his self-applause and self-assertion, make this one of the most singular and fascinating books in existence. The original manuscript is at the Laurenziana in Florence. Cellini also wrote treatises on the goldsmith's art, on sculpture, and on design (translated by C. R. Ashbee, 1899).

Among his works of art, many of which have perished, were a colossal Mars for a fountain at Fontainebleau and the bronzes of the doorway, coins for the papal and Florentine states, a Jupiter in silver of life size, and a bronze bust of Bindo Altoviti. His other works in existence to-day are the celebrated salt-cellar made for Francis I. at Vienna; a medallion of Clement VII. in commemoration of the peace between the Christian princes, 1530, signed with the artist's name; a medal of Francis I. with his portrait, also signed; and a medal of Cardinal Pietro Bembo. Cellini, while employed at the papal mint at Rome during the papacy of Clement VII. and later of Paul III., executed the dies of several coins and medals, some of which still survive. He also executed in 1535 for Alessandro de' Medici, first duke of Florence, a 40-soldi piece, with a bust of the duke on one side and standing figures of the saints Cosmo and Damian on the other.

The important works which have perished include the uncompleted chalice intended for Clement VII.; a gold cover for a prayer-book as a gift from Pope Paul III. to Charles V.; large silver statues of Jupiter, Vulcan, and Mars, wrought for Francis I. during his sojourn in Paris; a bust of Julius Caesar; and a silver cup for the cardinal of Ferrara. The magnificent gold "button," or morse, made by Cellini for the cope of Clement VII., appears to have been sacrificed by Pius VI., in furnishing the indemnity of 30,000,000 francs demanded by Napoleon in 1797. Fortunately there are in the print room of the British Museum three water-colour drawings of this splendid morse done by F. Bertoli in the first half of the 18th century.

BIBLIOGRAPHY.—Cellini's autobiography was published by O. Bacci (1900). English translations by J. A. Symonds, Thomas Roscoe, A. Macdonnell and R. H. Cust. Bolzenthal, *Skizzen zur Kunstgeschichte der modernen Medaillen-Arbeit 1429–1840* (1840); J. Friedländer, *Die italienischen Schaumunzen des 15en Jahrhunderts* (1880–82); A. Armand, *Les médailleurs italiens des 15e et 16e siècles* (1883–87); Eugène Plon, *Cellini, orfèvre, médailleur, etc.* (1883); A. Heiss, *Les médailleurs florentins* (1887); E. Babelon, *La gravure en pierres fines* (1894); N. Rondot, *Les médailleurs lyonnais* (Mâcon, 1897); L. Dimier, *Cellini à la cour de France* (1898); Dr. Julius Cahn, *Medaillen und Plaketten der Sammlung W. P. Metzler* (Frankfort-on-Main, 1898); Molinier, *Les Plaquettes;* I. B. Supino, *Il Medagliere Mediceo nel R. Museo Nazionale di Firenze* (Florence, 1899); T. Longueville, *Cellini, His Times and Contemporaries* (1899); *L'Arte di Benvenuto Cellini* (Florence, 1901); C. von Fabriczy, *Medaillen der italienischen Renaissance* (Leipzig); L. Forrer, *Biographical Dictionary of Medallists, etc.* (1904).

CELLOPHANE, a thin film of regenerated cellulose, usually clear and transparent, used primarily as a flexible packaging material. While the word "cellophane" is a trade mark in England, France, Canada and many other countries, in the United States it became, by court decision, a generic term.

In 1892 the English chemists C. F. Cross, E. J. Bevan and C. Beadle discovered viscose, a solution of cellulose treated with caustic soda and carbon disulphide. Six years later C. H. Stearn was granted a British patent for producing films from viscose. It was not until 1911, however, that J. E. Brandenberger, a Swiss, designed a machine for continuous production of a strong, transparent film. Brandenberger coined the term "cellophane" by combining "cellulose" and "diaphane," the French word for "transparent."

World War I delayed large-scale development. In 1920 a French company, La Cellophane, was formed, and a cellophane plant was built at Bezons, near Paris. Three years later E. I. du Pont de Nemours & Company acquired rights from La Cellophane to manufacture the product in the United States and produced the first U.S.-made cellophane at Buffalo, N.Y., in 1924.

By the 1950s, U.S. production, which was less than 500,000 lb. in 1924, was estimated at more than 250,000,000 lb. annually and was believed to account for well over half the world's supply, although no precise production figures were published.

Several factors contributed importantly to cellophane's growth. Moistureproof cellophane, invented in 1927 by W. H. Charch and K. E. Prindle, gave the film new usefulness as a protective wrap for foods. By the 1950s about 90% of the U.S. production was moistureproof, and about 70% of the total went to the food industry. More than 50 varieties of cellophane had been developed. Basically, the film is transparent, odour resistant, tough, grease-proof and gas impermeable. It can be made in various thicknesses and colours. By applying special coatings, it can be made moistureproof, partially moistureproof, and heat-sealing.

Cellophane manufacture starts with steeping of sheets of wood pulp in caustic soda to form alkali cellulose. After removal of excess liquids, the sheets are shredded, aged to control molecular weight, and discharged into steel drums known as barattes. Carbon disulphide is added to the slowly rotating barattes, forming sodium cellulose xanthate. The xanthate is dissolved in another caustic solution to form viscose.

Carefully ripened viscose is piped to the casting machine, where it is extruded through a metal slit into an acid bath in which it coagulates to a film and is regenerated into cellulose. Driven rolls carry the film through a further series of baths where it is washed and bleached, and softening materials are added. The film then enters the dryer, passing over heated rolls and through circulating hot air. Finally, it is wound up in mill rolls, which may weigh as much as 950 lb. and contain up to 5 mi. of film.

If the cellophane is to be coated, the film is led through a coating bath, over doctor knives or rolls to remove excess coating and to distribute the coating evenly, and then through drying and humidifying chambers.

Finished mill rolls are commonly slit to widths required for use on automatic packaging machinery, though some are unwound on large drums to be cut and trimmed to sheet form for use in handwrapping operations.

Bibliography.—G. C. Inskeep and P. Van Horn, "Cellophane Production," *Industrial and Engineering Chemistry,* 44:2511 (Nov. 1952); L. L. Leach, "Cellophane," *Encyclopedia of Chemical Technology,* 3:280 (1949). (J. L. Bl.)

CELLULOID, the first synthetic plastic material, also known as xylonite or artificial ivory. The invention of celluloid in 1870 in the U.S. is commonly ascribed to J. W. Hyatt and I. S. Hyatt, who first realized the necessity of working cellulose nitrate, camphor and alcohol under heat and pressure. Their efforts were based upon earlier investigations by A. Parkes and D. Spill in Great Britain. In the U.S., "Celluloid" is a trade name. Celluloid is a homogeneous colloidal dispersion of cellulose nitrate and camphor. Its commercial importance persists because of its good properties: resilience; high tensile strength (up to 12,000 lb. per square inch); toughness; a density of 1.40; high lustre; low cost; uniformity; resistance to water, oils and dilute acids; ready workability; and the great variety of colours, from transparent crystal and pastel shades through bizarre mottles and pearls, in which it can be fabricated.

Since it is based upon a nitrate ester of cellulose, a long-chain polymer, Celluloid is thermoplastic in character. It can be worked in moulds at 200° to 220° F., and it becomes brittle at −70° F. At room temperatures it may be sawed, drilled, turned, planed, buffed and polished. Direct sunlight, or storage above 120° F. will discolour it, and decomposition sets in above 365° F. The flammability is best controlled by the use of it in articles of thick cross section, or as a sheath covering other materials which dissipate heat more rapidly.

Although both Celluloid and smokeless powder are made from cellulose nitrate, the degree of nitration for the plastic is much lower than for the propellant, hence the relative safety of the former. Celluloid of the best quality requires nitrated cellulose from purified, bleached cotton linters. These are nitrated with agitation in chrome steel pots with a large excess of concentrated nitric acid in the presence of sulphuric acid. The nitrated fibres are freed from excess acid in centrifuges, and further purified and washed. The wet fibres are then pressed, and the water is displaced with alcohol.

A homogeneous paste is then made by mixing the fibres with more alcohol and camphor in a chrome-lined vacuum kneader. Excess solvent is evaporated; the paste is passed through heavy hydraulic strainers and then milled on heated rolls to mix in colour and fillers, to remove solvent and to form slabs. The slabs are trimmed, fitted in heavy steel baking chases provided with heating channels and pressed; the colloid is thereby compacted into cakes while heated at 190° to 220° F. The mass is cooled, sliced into sheets, seasoned to remove residual solvent and polished. Slabs from the rolls may be extruded into rods or tubes of varied cross section, through a die fed by a screw or hydraulic press.

The great diversity in designs made from Celluloid is accomplished by assembling varicoloured blocks in layers and columns in the baking chase, by incorporating orienting pigments and pearl essences in the roll mass and by mechanically twisting and working the stock before extrusion.

Grades, Fabrication and Uses of Celluloid.—Two main grades of Celluloid were available at mid-20th century. The softer, with 30% to 32% camphor, is extruded to make hammer heads for beating aluminum sheet for aircraft, and oil-resistant handles for screw drivers and chisels. The harder common variety, containing 23% camphor, is used in sheet, rods and tubes. Sheeting, available in thicknesses ranging from 0.005 to 0.250 in., may be cut into blanks, heated and moulded under pressures up to 2,000 lb. per square inch. Thin sheets when warm may be drawn, swaged or blown into doll heads, floating toys and ping-pong balls. Sheeting or thin tubing provides a scuff- and mar-resistant sheathing for wooden shoe heels, toilet seats and bus and trolley stanchions.

The plastic, softened in hot water, is stretched over the form and cooled in place. Piano keys, dresser sets, cutlery handles, dental plates, spectacle frames, accumulator boxes, ammunition components, toothbrushes, drawing curves and cut combs are also made from sheet. Button forms, ornaments, dice, etc., may be cut or formed from rods. Celluloid tubing forms the basis of most fountain pens because of dimensional stability, and resistance to ink and handling. Much tubing is used in Great Britain for the bodies and handles of bicycle pumps.

Although much research had been directed toward a better plasticizer than camphor for Celluloid, nothing really superior had been found by the 1950s. Ortho-nitrodiphenyl, the closest approach, has more colour and odour. Camphor and cellulose nitrate form a weak association complex (J. R. Katz, J. C. Derksen *et al., Z. Phys. Chem.* A, 1930) and give a material which has greater tensile strength than the cellulose nitrate itself. Synthetic camphor makes as good a Celluloid as natural camphor. A small amount of aromatic phosphate replaces camphor in a few special applications, but the thousands of patented processes directed to the flameproofing of Celluloid by admixture of bromate, phosphate or chloride compounds and salts produce inferior materials.

Although less flammable synthetic polymers have replaced Celluloid in such markets as safety glass and telephone mouthpieces, it was still widely used at mid-20th century for its excellent physical properties. Manufacture was carried out in Austria, Belgium, France, Germany, Great Britain, Japan, U.S.S.R., Switzerland and the U.S.

Bibliography.—*Plastics Catalog* (1939–45); R. Houwink, *Elasticity, Plasticity and Structure of Matter* (1937); E. Ott, *Cellulose and Cellulose Derivatives* (1943). (W. E. Gr.)

CELLULOSE is the chief constituent of the cell walls of higher plants and comprises at least one-third of all the vegetable matter in the world. It is, therefore, the most abundant of all naturally occurring organic compounds. Cellulose has also been found in the lower species of the vegetable kingdom, such as mosses and ferns, algae and fungi and bacteria. Its occurrence in one representative of the animal kingdom—the marine organisms of the class of Tunicata—has also been reported.

In its natural state, cellulose is accompanied by other materials whose nature and amount vary from plant to plant. Technically, the name cellulose is applied to the products obtained by subjecting vegetable matter to certain purification processes which remove most of the noncellulosic materials. Celluloses from different sources differ in their content of noncellulosic compounds, in the molecular weight of the cellulose and in their fibre structure. The alpha-cellulose content of a cellulose pulp, *i.e.*, the portion insoluble in 17.5% sodium hydroxide at 20° C., serves as a rough measure of its purity. No simple, specific test is available for the identification of cellulose. The formation of cellobiose octaacetate on treatment with a mixture of acetic anhydride and sulphuric acid has been used to demonstrate the presence of cellulose. Cellulose yields characteristic X-ray diffraction patterns which will provide adequate identification. Its density, as determined on kier-boiled cotton, is 1.58; mercerized and regenerated cellulose rayons have densities ranging from 1.53 to 1.55.

Despite its wide distribution in nature, most of the cellulose used industrially is obtained from wood and cotton. The composition of wood varies widely with the species. Cellulose is the chief constituent and is present in amounts up to about 50% on an oven-dry basis. Wood also contains appreciable quantities of lignin and polysaccharides other than cellulose in addition to minor amounts of resins, gums, proteins and inorganic matter.

Cellulose (wood pulp) is prepared from wood by removal of the noncellulosic constituents. The following pulping processes are the ones most widely used: (1) the sulphite process, which employs a solution of calcium bisulphite and sulphur dioxide; (2) the soda process, in which a sodium hydroxide solution is used; and (3) the sulphate process, in which pulping is effected by a solution of sodium hydroxide and sodium sulphide; a modern modification of this process involves an acid hydrolysis of the wood prior to the conventional treatment. (The sulphate process was so named because sodium sulphate is the raw material used for the production of the sodium sulphide.) Most of the so-called dissolving wood pulps used in the manufacture of cellulose derivatives are prepared by the sulphite process. As ordinarily prepared, these sulphite pulps contain 88% to 90% alpha-cellulose; alkaline purification treatments are used to obtain pulps with higher alpha-cellulose contents. Increasing amounts of dissolving wood pulp are also being made by the modified sulphate process mentioned above.

Cotton is the purest naturally occurring form of cellulose. Raw cotton contains, on an oven-dry basis, less than 10% of noncellulosic impurities which include proteins, fats and waxes, pectic substances, carbohydrates and inorganic compounds. Chemical cotton for the manufacture of cellulose derivatives is prepared from cotton linters, which are the short fibres removed from cotton seeds after the long fibres have been taken off by ginning for use in textiles.

The cotton linters are purified by pressure digestion at 130° to 180° C. with a solution containing 2% to 5% sodium hydroxide and by a subsequent bleaching to remove colour bodies. Chemical cotton contains about 99% alpha-cellulose.

The viscosity of cellulose, or, more precisely, the viscosity of a solution of cellulose at some definite concentration, is an important property by which the product is characterized for industrial use. Aqueous solutions of cuprammonium hydroxide and of cupri-ethylenediamine hydroxide are the commonest cellulose solvents used for the viscosity determination; cellulose concentrations less than 5% are usually employed. The viscosity is determined at a definite temperature by measuring either the efflux time of the solution in a capillary viscometer, or the time required for a glass or metal sphere to fall through a given depth of solution in a tube of prescribed size. The viscosity determinations are empirical, and the conditions of test must, therefore, be defined exactly in reporting viscosity values.

The moisture content of cellulose, which has an important effect on its chemical behaviour and on its mechanical and electrical properties, rises or drops with increase or decrease in the relative humidity of the atmosphere. The moisture content reached on desorption is higher than that reached on adsorption and varies somewhat with the source and purity, and with the treatment. Thus, for a bleached surgical cotton, the moisture content varies from about 4.6% at 30% relative humidity to about 7.9% at 60% relative humidity; the corresponding figures for a bleached sulphite pulp are 5.6% and 9.5%. High-temperature drying reduces the ability of cellulose fibres to absorb moisture whereas mercerization causes a marked increase in moisture sorption.

Chemical Constitution.—Elementary analysis of the purest available form of cellulose, obtained by purification of cotton, shows that it is composed of 44.4% carbon, 6.2% hydrogen and 49.4% oxygen. These figures correspond to the theoretical composition of a hexose anhydride with the formula $C_6H_{10}O_5$. The hexose anhydride is identified as anhydroglucose (specifically anhydroglucopyranose) by the fact that hydrolysis of cellulose gives an almost quantitative yield (more than 95%) of glucose.

Each anhydroglucose unit contains three alcoholic hydroxyl groups, two secondary and one primary, which can be esterified or etherified. Considerable evidence is available to show that the molecular weight of cellulose is much greater than that of a single anhydroglucose unit. Controlled hydrolysis of cellulose has yielded cellobiose, cellotriaose, cellotetraose and cellopentaose, which contain two, three, four and five anhydroglucose units, respectively. These and other observations prove clearly that cellulose molecules are made up of many anhydroglucose units linked together by primary beta-glucosidic linkages as shown in the formula in Fig. 1.

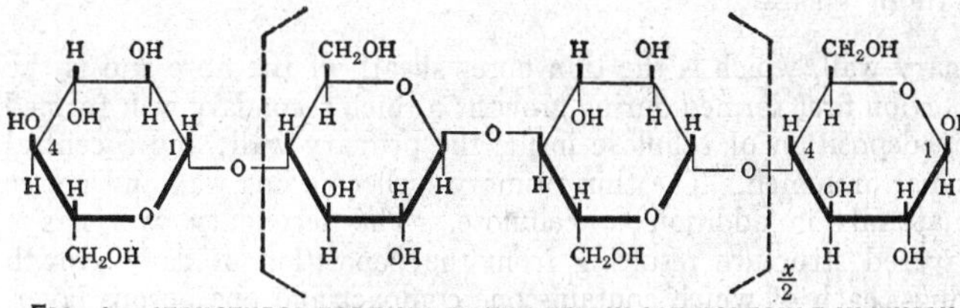

FIG. 1.—STRUCTURAL FORMULA OF THE CELLULOSE MOLECULE IN WHICH $x + 2$ REPRESENTS THE NUMBER OF GLUCOSE ANHYDRIDE UNITS IN THE MOLECULE

In the Fig. 1 formula, the glucose unit at the extreme right has a potential aldehyde group at position 1, whereas the other terminal glucose unit contains an extra free hydroxyl group at position 4. The potential aldehyde group cannot be detected readily in cellulose of high molecular weight; however, even cellulose whose molecular weight has been reduced somewhat by acid hydrolysis exhibits an aldehydic reducing action. In celluloses which have been treated with oxidizing agents, the aldehyde group has usually been converted to a carboxyl group.

Conclusive evidence has been accumulated to show not only that cellulose has an extremely high molecular weight but also that all the molecules in any sample of the substance are not of the same molecular weight. The evidence for this nonuniformity with respect to molecular weight includes the results of fractional solution and fractional precipitation experiments. Molecular-weight determinations on unfractionated samples of cellulose or its derivatives will, therefore, yield only average values. The usual cryoscopic and ebullioscopic methods are unsuitable for determining large molecular weights. The viscosity method is the simplest and most useful method of molecular-weight determination. It depends on the relation between the molecular weight of a sample of cellulose (or of a cellulose derivative) and the viscosity of a dilute solution of the material. The viscosity method is not an absolute one and must be standardized against the osmotic-pressure, light-scattering or ultracentrifuge method. Some typical molecular weights based on viscosity measurements are given in the accompanying table:

	Molecular weight (average)	Number of anhydroglucose units per molecule
Native cellulose	More than 570,000	More than 3,500
Chemical cotton	100,000–500,000	600–3,000
Wood pulps	100,000–210,000	600–1,300
Commercial regenerated celluloses	30,000– 90,000	200– 600
Commercial nitrocelluloses	45,000–875,000	175–3,500
Commercial cellulose acetates	45,000–100,000	175– 360

Fibre Structure.—Microscopic examination of the gross structure of native cellulose fibres reveals that, although they have diverse structural patterns, they also have some general structural similarities (Fig. 2). The cotton fibre is composed of a pri-

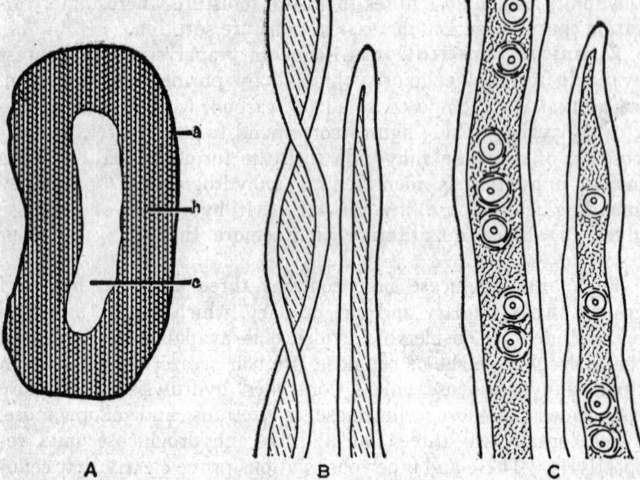

BY COURTESY OF HERCULES POWDER COMPANY, INC.

FIG. 2.—CROSS SECTION (A) OF A COTTON FIBRE SHOWING (a) PRIMARY WALL, (b) SECONDARY WALL AND (c) CENTRAL CANAL. COTTON FIBRES (B) AND WOOD TRACHEIDS (C) SHOW MIDDLE PORTION AND TIP OF FIBRES

mary wall, which is the thin outer sheath of the fibre and is the portion first formed during growth; a thick secondary wall formed by deposition of cellulose inside the primary wall; and a central canal or lumen. The thin primary wall contains wax and pectic materials in addition to cellulose. The secondary wall has a layered structure resulting from the deposition of daily growth rings, each of which contains one compact and one porous layer. Although woods contain a wide variety of cells, the tracheid fibres (Fig. 2, C) are of chief interest since they constitute most of the fibres in commercial wood pulps. In wood, the fibres are separated from each other by layers of an intercellular substance known as the middle lamella and consisting chiefly of lignin. The fibre proper contains a primary and a secondary wall (both composed largely of cellulose) and a lumen. Investigations with the electron microscope show that the cell walls of all native cellulose fibres are made up of small fibrous elements known as fibrils, whose width may be as small as 0.000001 in.

X-ray examination of cellulose fibres yields diffraction patterns which show that they are made up, to a large extent, of crystalline cellulose. At least two general types of crystal structure have been observed—native and hydrate. With the exception of the cellulose in the marine alga *Halicystis* which has the hydrate structure, all naturally occurring fibres have the native structure. The hydrate structure occurs in mercerized fibres and in cellulose regenerated from solution or from a derivative.

The X-ray diffraction patterns of native fibres indicate that their crystallinity is discontinuous and that each fibre is an aggregate of small crystalline areas (crystallites or micelles) and amorphous, intercrystalline areas. It is believed that cellulose chains crystallize in such a way that the crystalline regularity is interrupted by irregular regions which behave as amorphous matter toward X-rays and also toward the penetration of swelling and dispersing agents; there is probably a continuous transition between crystalline and amorphous areas of such nature that an individual cellulose chain may pass through several regions of complete order and complete disorder.

Cellulose Degradation.—In the degradation of cellulose, chemical changes occur which result in a reduction of the chain length of the cellulose molecules and, hence, in a weakening of the fibre structure. In some cases, cellulose is deliberately degraded to bring about a desired reduction in the viscosity of the cellulose and of the derivatives made from it. In the hydrolytic degradation which is catalyzed by hydrogen ions (*i.e.*, aqueous solutions of acids), cleavage of 1:4 beta-glucosidic linkages between anhydroglucose units occurs with the formation of two new terminal glucose units. One of these is characterized by the presence of a reducing hemiacetal group, the other by an extra hydroxyl group. If the hydrolysis is carried to completion, the cellulose is converted almost quantitatively to glucose. If only partial hydrolysis takes place, degraded products are obtained to which the name hydrocellulose has been given. A wide variety of hydrocelluloses can be prepared. Their properties are determined by the conditions of the hydrolytic treatment. In general, degradation of cellulose by acids is accompanied by a decrease in viscosity and in tensile strength; by an increase in reducing power and in solubility in aqueous alkalies.

Cellulose can be degraded by oxidizing agents under a wide variety of conditions, and consequently oxycelluloses of widely varying properties can be obtained. Oxidation is of importance in certain commercial operations, such as bleaching, and the reaction of cellulose with oxygen in the presence of alkali in the preparation of viscose and cellulose ethers. In general, oxycelluloses of the reducing type are formed with neutral or acid oxidizing media, whereas alkaline media yield the acidic type of oxycellulose. The exact nature of the chemical changes produced by oxidation is not known, but it appears that three points in the cellulose molecule may be attacked: (1) the aldehydic end groups may be oxidized to carboxyl groups; (2) the primary alcohol groups may be oxidized to aldehyde or carboxyl groups; thus, oxidation with nitrogen dioxide results largely in the conversion of the primary alcohol groups to carboxyls; (3) the 2,3-glycol group in the anhydroglucose unit may be converted to ketone, aldehyde or carboxyl groups. Oxidation with periodic acid causes cleavage at the 2,3-position and formation of aldehyde groups. The action of oxidizing agents other than nitrogen dioxide and periodic acid is much less specific and probably results in attack on different groups in the cellulose molecule. Some types of oxidation do not result in direct scission of the chain molecules but decrease the chemical stability of some of the linkages in the molecule toward alkalies.

Degradation of cellulose takes place on heating, the extent of degradation depending on the temperature and duration of heating. Above 140° C., reducing groups are formed and viscosity decreases slowly. In general, heating lowers the tensile strength of cotton and regenerated cellulose fibres. The degradation by heat is slower in the absence of oxygen. Drastic destruction occurs on heating at relatively high temperatures. Destructive distillation in vacuum yields beta-glucosan, carbon monoxide, carbon dioxide, water and small amounts of gaseous hydrocarbons. Of the derivatives, cellulose acetate seems to possess the best heat stability and nitrocellulose the poorest. Cellulose suffers loss in fibre strength and viscosity on exposure to light. This degradation is accelerated by oxygen, certain metallic catalysts and some dyes; other dyes seem to exert an inhibiting effect. Degradation by light is influenced by temperature and moisture.

A variety of bacteria, fungi and protozoa causes decomposition of cellulose with the ultimate production of carbon dioxide and water. The ability of ruminants, horses and insects to digest cellulose is believed to be caused by the presence in their intestines of cellulose-decomposing bacteria and fungi.

Derivatives.—In the preparation of cellulose derivatives the hydroxyl groups are replaced by substituent groups. The degree of substitution is customarily designated by the average number of hydroxyl units replaced per anhydroglucose unit. Thus, a derivative in which all the hydroxyl groups have been substituted is said to have the maximum substitution of 3.0. If analysis shows that, on the average, 2.5 hydroxyl groups have reacted, the product has a substitution of 2.5. Each molecule contains hundreds of hydroxyl groups and practically all of these are replaced when fully substituted derivatives are prepared; *e.g.*, cellulose triacetate, trimethyl cellulose. However, most of the derivatives which have attained industrial importance are not fully substituted and contain appreciable amounts of free hydroxyl groups. The chance for reaction of any hydroxyl group is affected by its position in the anhydroglucose unit, by the presence of neighbouring hydroxyl groups and by the position in the fibre structure of the molecule to which it is attached. The rate of reaction of cellulose fibres is determined by the rate of diffusion of reagent to the individual hydroxyl groups. Diffusion is rapid in the amorphous areas of fibres and relatively slow in the crystalline areas. Swelling of the fibres will accelerate diffusion and, hence, the rate of reaction. If swelling takes place uniformly throughout each fibre, the reaction will proceed uniformly. These factors are usually of importance in the preparation of uniform derivatives with substitution less than 3.0.

Uniform substitution in all cellulose molecules is obtained directly when reaction takes place in solution, as in the case of etherification of cellulose dissolved in an aqueous solution of a quaternary ammonium base; any effect caused by fibre structure is eliminated and the distribution of ether groups along the molecule is determined by the relative reactivities of the hydroxyls and by chance. As would be expected in a homogeneous reaction of this type, the primary hydroxyls are more reactive than the secondary hydroxyls.

Nitration of cellulose is unique in that uniform reaction takes place even though fibre structure is retained throughout the reaction. This behaviour is caused by the fact that nitration is an equilibrium reaction which is apparently unaffected by fibre structure, and that the extent of nitration is determined by the composition of the nitrating acid. Cellulose formate is the only other common derivative whose preparation involves an equilibrium reaction; in this case, however, the product dissolves in the esterification reagent. The partially substituted organic acid esters which are of industrial importance (*e.g.*, cellulose acetate) are prepared by first esterifying completely in a medium in which the product dissolves and then uniformly removing some of the substituent groups by hydrolysis while the cellulose ester is in solution. It will be apparent from the foregoing discussion that derivatives with substitution less than 3.0 are not mixtures of cellulose and stoichiometric compounds having substitution of 1, 2 or 3. This view is supported by numerous fractionation experiments on commercial derivatives, in which it was found that the substitution of the individual fractions fell within a comparatively narrow range.

In the preparation of derivatives, substituent groups are introduced into the cellulose molecule; these produce marked changes in physical properties and thereby determine the industrial usefulness of the derivatives. This effect on properties is determined both by the nature of the substituent group and by the degree of substitution. The mechanical and other physical properties of cellulose and cellulose derivatives are affected by their average molecular weight. If their molecular weight is too low, they yield plastics with poor strength or lose their ability to form films or fibres. An increase in molecular weight above the lower limit causes a marked improvement in the strength of plastics, films and fibres. There is also an upper limit beyond which further increase in molecular weight causes only slight improvement in strength. The physical properties are also affected by molecular-weight distribution, that is, by the relative numbers and sizes of the molecules that make up the average value. In particular, the presence of relatively small molecules of cellulose or cellulose derivatives exerts a harmful effect on their strength properties.

In industrial operations, the viscosity of derivatives is used as a measure of molecular weight. The viscosity is controlled by selecting cellulose of a given viscosity for the starting material, by regulating the conditions of the reaction and, in some cases, by appropriate aftertreatment of the cellulose derivative. As in the case of cellulose itself, the viscosity of derivatives is determined on a solution of standard concentration by the capillary viscometer or falling-sphere methods.

Cellulose Esters.—Cellulose nitrate, which is usually referred to as nitrocellulose, is the only ester of cellulose and an inorganic acid which is produced commercially. It is prepared by nitrating cellulose with a mixture of nitric acid, sulphuric acid and water. After removal of most of the acid mixture, the fibrous nitrocellulose is given a series of washing treatments to remove last traces of acid and so obtain a product of good stability. The extent of nitration, which is usually designated by the nitrogen content, and the other properties of nitrocellulose are determined to a large extent by the composition of the nitration reagent and the other reaction conditions. For many purposes, the viscosity of nitrocellulose may be controlled by selecting cellulose of the proper viscosity and by regulating the reaction conditions. In the manufacture of low-viscosity nitrocelluloses for use in lacquers, the product is usually given a special treatment after nitration to reduce the viscosity to the desired level. In the best method for the reduction of viscosity, an aqueous suspension of nitrocellulose is heated under pressure in a continuous digester. Cellulose trinitrate (14.14% N) is not produced commercially because it is difficult to prepare and has limited solubility in common solvents. Nitrocelluloses containing 12.5% to 13.5% nitrogen (substitution 2.4–2.8) are used in explosives; those containing about 12% nitrogen (substitution 2.2) are used in lacquers, photographic film and cement, and celluloid plastics and special lacquers are made with nitrocelluloses containing about 11% nitrogen (substitution 2.0). Cellulose sulphates have been made on a semicommercial scale. Cellulose phosphates have also been prepared but are of only academic interest. The use of sulphuric acid in the reagent mixtures used to nitrate and acetylate cellulose results in the introduction of a small amount of sulphate groups into nitrocellulose and cellulose acetate. Because these sulphate groups exert an adverse effect on the stability of these products, special treatments are used to eliminate sulphate groups and to counteract the effect of any traces that are not removed.

The esters of cellulose with organic acids may be prepared by treating cellulose with the appropriate acid, acid anhydride or acid chloride. Literally hundreds of such esters had been prepared by the 1950s, but only a few of them had attained technical importance. Formic acid is the only organic acid which will effect appreciable esterification of cellulose by direct reaction with it. Cellulose formate has not been used commercially because of its poor resistance to hydrolysis. Cellulose acetate, the most important of the cellulose organic acid esters, is prepared by treating cellulose with more than three moles of acetic anhydride in a suitable solvent such as acetic acid or methylene chloride, in the presence of a catalyst such as sulphuric acid. The product of this reaction is primary cellulose acetate, which approximates cellulose triacetate in substitution (acetyl content, 44.8%). Because of its high melting point, its solubility in only a few solvents and its lack of flexibility, cellulose triacetate has attained only limited use; *e.g.*, in fields where its high moisture resistance is important. By adding to the homogeneous primary acetate reaction mixture an excess of water over that required to decompose unreacted acetic anhydride, the reaction is reversed and acetyl groups are uniformly removed by hydrolysis; the hydrolysis reaction is stopped at the desired point by the addition of a base to neutralize the catalyst. The cellulose acetate is precipitated from solution by the addition of water, and then given a series of washing treatments to remove last traces of acid and thereby ensure good stability. In this way products are obtained with acetyl contents ranging down to about 37% acetyl (substitution about 2.2) and which are soluble in acetone and other solvents. These cellulose acetates find wide use in the manufacture of rayon, plastics and photographic film. Mixed cellulose esters, such as cellulose acetate propionate and cellulose acetate butyrate, attained industrial importance because of their great moisture resistance and wider compatibility with plasticizers than ordinary cellulose acetates. These mixed esters are prepared by esterifying cellulose with mixtures of the appropriate acid anhydrides.

Cellulose xanthate is an important derivative of cellulose which has only a transitory existence in the process of preparing viscose rayon and cellulose film. In the first step in the process, cellulose is treated with a solution of 18% sodium hydroxide to form so-called alkali or soda cellulose. After removal of the excess sodium hydroxide solution, the alkali cellulose is allowed to stand in contact with air (aging) to reduce viscosity to a desired level. The alkali cellulose is then treated with carbon disulphide to form cellulose xanthate. In commercial practice, slightly more than one xanthate group is introduced for each two anhydroglucose units in the cellulose molecule. The cellulose xanthate is dissolved in 6% sodium hydroxide solution to yield the solution commonly known as viscose, which is then ripened to effect partial decomposition of the cellulose xanthate and to improve its coagulation properties. The ripened viscose is extruded continuously in the form of threads or films into an acid precipitating bath; the regenerated cellulose is then suitably washed and dried.

Cellulose Ethers.—The cellulose ethers which have attained industrial importance include ethyl cellulose, methyl cellulose, carboxymethyl cellulose, hydroxyethyl cellulose and benzyl cellulose. In most cases, these ethers are prepared commercially by the interaction of cellulose and the halide or sulphate of the appropriate alcohol in the presence of an alkali, usually sodium hydroxide. Presumably, alkali cellulose is formed as an intermediate product. The extent of etherification is determined by the reaction temperature and the relative proportions of cellulose, alkali, etherifying agent and water in the reaction mixture. Commercially, the methyl, carboxymethyl and hydroxyethyl ethers are produced only in the low-substitution types which are soluble in water or in dilute solutions of an alkali. The preparation of the hydroxyethyl ether is unique in that it may be carried out by treatment of alkali cellulose either with ethylene chlorohydrin or with ethylene oxide. Carboxymethyl cellulose is prepared by treating alkali cellulose with sodium chloroacetate. Carboxymethyl cellulose will dissolve completely in water if some or all of its carboxyl groups are neutralized by NaOH, KOH or NH_4OH. All of the ethyl and benzyl ethers of cellulose produced commercially are of the types which are soluble in organic solvents; *i.e.*, with substitution more than 2.0. Ethyl cellulose possesses good resistance to acids and alkalies, high flexibility at low temperature, good electrical properties, solubility in a wide range of solvents and ready compatibility with many resins and plasticizers. These properties have won for ethyl cellulose wide use in protective coatings and plastics. Benzyl cellulose has not attained wide use because of its poor stability on exposure to light or to the action of oxygen at elevated temperatures.

Cellulose Addition Compounds.—Cellulose has the ability to form addition compounds with a variety of reagents. Although some investigators believe that the formation of alkali cellulose is a physical process, others believe that the mode of reaction of alkali cellulose in etherification indicates that it is a compound of the alcoholate type. (A true alkoxide, sodium cellulosate, is formed when cellulose is treated with a solution of sodium or sodamide in liquid ammonia.) However, the most widely accepted view is that alkali cellulose is an addition compound of the type $(C_6H_{10}O_5)_x.(NaOH)_y$. The results of X-ray analysis indicate that cellulose may form several different addition compounds with alkali, the compositions of which are determined by the type of cellulose used, the alkali concentration and the temperature. Treatment with aqueous solutions of alkalies (usually sodium hydroxide) has two important practical applications: (1) the modification of the physical and chemical properties of fibres, as in mercerization; and (2) the preparation of alkali cellulose as an intermediate in the manufacture of viscose and cellulose ethers. The ability of aqueous solutions of cuprammonium hydroxide and of strong acids to dissolve cellulose seems to depend on the formation of addition compounds. So-called cuprammonium rayon is prepared by extruding a cuprammonium hydroxide solution of cellulose in the form of filaments into an acid precipitating bath where the cellulose is regenerated.

Uses of Cellulose and Derivatives.—The mere mention of such products as rayon, cellophane, plastics and lacquers suffices to recall the enormous development which took place after 1920 in industries based on cellulose and its derivatives. However, the principal industrial applications of cellulose and its derivatives are so numerous and varied that they can be only summarized here:

Purified Natural Cellulose Fibres

Textiles.—Cotton is the natural fibre most widely used; flax and ramie are used to a much smaller extent.

Paper.—Purified fibres for papermaking are obtained from wood, grasses and straws, seed hairs (cotton rags and cotton linters) and bast fibres (flax).

Miscellaneous.—Vulcanized fibre, plastics fillers, filtering media and surgical cotton.

Regenerated Cellulose and Cellulose Derivatives

Lacquers.—Nitrocellulose lacquers are used for spray-coating automobiles, aeroplanes and furniture; and for dip-coating hardware, brush handles and other mass production items. Cellulose acetate propionate and cellulose acetate butyrate are used in clear metal finishes for outdoor use. Ethyl cellulose is used in coatings for ignition cables in automobile and aeroplane motors and other coatings requiring flexibility at low temperatures.

Plastics.—Nitrocellulose plastics (celluloid) have the best combination of physical properties, apart from heat sensitivity and flammability, of all the thermoplastic materials; large volume uses are spectacles frames and sanitary supplies. Cellulose acetate is used widely in making plastics by injection moulding and where flame resistance is important; *e.g.*, in motor housings and electric light ornaments. Cellulose acetate butyrate plastics are used where water resistance and dimensional stability are important; *e.g.*, in steering wheels and various types of piping. Ethyl cellulose plastics are tough over the widest range of temperature and are used in hammer heads and flashlights.

Rayon.—Viscose rayon, cellulose acetate rayon and cuprammonium rayon.

Films and Foils.—Nitrocellulose is used in commercial motion-picture film, X-ray film and microfilm for duplication of records, etc. Cellulose acetate propionate and cellulose acetate butyrate films are used where high dimensional stability is required; *e.g.*, aerial mapping. Thin sheets of regenerated cellulose (cellophane), cellulose acetate and ethyl cellulose are used for merchandise packaging. Regenerated cellulose is made from nitrocellulose for the production of sausage casings.

Textiles.—Artificial leather is made by coating cotton fabrics with solutions containing nitrocellulose and other ingredients. Aircraft fabric coatings may contain nitrocellulose, high-substitution cellulose acetate, cellulose acetate butyrate or cellulose acetate propionate. Flexible finishes on garment and upholstery leathers are produced with nitrocellulose lacquer emulsions. Hydroxyethyl cellulose and sodium carboxymethyl cellulose are used in textile sizes. Sodium carboxymethyl cellulose is also used as a detergent aid in textile washing.

Coated Paper and Cellophane.—Lacquer coatings containing nitrocellulose or other cellulose derivatives improve the grease and oil resistance, washability and electrical properties of paper. The moistureproof coating on cellophane contains nitrocellulose and a small amount of wax. Paper disks coated with ethyl cellulose are used for sound recording in the home. Methyl cellulose is used to greaseproof paper. Sodium carboxymethyl cellulose is used in special papers because it improves fibre bonding.

Adhesives.—Cellulose derivatives are used in a wide variety of special adhesives.

Explosives.—Nitrocellulose is a minor ingredient in blasting gelatin and the major ingredient in smokeless powders, including rocket powder.

Thickening Agents and Protective Colloids.—Methyl cellulose and sodium carboxymethyl cellulose are used to increase the viscosity of certain food products, textile finishes and printing pastes, latex dispersions and paints.

BIBLIOGRAPHY.—Charles Dorée, *Methods of Cellulose Chemistry* (1947); Emil Heuser, *The Chemistry of Cellulose* (1944); J. T. Marsh and F. C. Wood, *An Introduction to the Chemistry of Cellulose* (1945); K. H. Meyer, *Natural and Synthetic High Polymers* (1950); Emil Ott (ed.), *Cellulose and Cellulose Derivatives* (1943; revised edition in preparation); R. G. Siu, *Microbial Decomposition of Cellulose* (1951); Louis E. Wise (ed.), *Wood Chemistry* (1944). (EM. O.)

CELSIUS, ANDERS (1701–1744), Swedish astronomer, was born on Nov. 27, 1701, in Uppsala, where he was professor of astronomy (1730–44). At Nuremberg he published in 1733 a collection of 316 observations of the aurora borealis made by himself and others 1716–32. In Paris he advocated the measurement of an arc of the meridian in Lapland, and took part, in 1736, in the expedition organized for the purpose by the French academy. Six years later he described the centigrade thermometer in a paper read before the Swedish Academy of Sciences (*see* THERMOMETRY). Celsius died at Uppsala on April 25, 1744. He wrote: *Nova Methodus distantiam solis a terra determinandi* (1730); *De Observationibus pro figura telluris determinanda* (1738); besides many less important works. The centigrade thermometer is often called the Celsius thermometer, as other thermometers are named after Gabriel Fahrenheit and René de Réaumur.

See W. Ostwald's *Klassiker der exacten Wissenschaften,* no. 57 (Leipzig, 1904), where Celsius's memoir on the thermometric scale is given in German with critical and biographical notes.

CELSIUS SCALE: *see* THERMOMETRY.

CELSUS (*c.* A.D. 178), an eclectic Platonist and opponent of Christianity known mainly through the reputation of his work, *The True Word* (or *Account; ἀληθὴς λόγος*), brought to light in 248 by Origen who in his *Against Celsus* quotes, paraphrases and reproduces about nine-tenths of it. On internal evidence the work seems to be of Alexandrian origin and to date between 176–180.

Its attack on Christianity is opened by a rehearsal of Jewish taunts levelled at the Christians. Jesus was the natural son of Mary and Joseph. He did not convince even His own countrymen. His companions as well as His poverty were inconsistent with divine dignity. The Incarnation is absurd, for God stands in no special relation to man as against animals. Christ's miracles, like His resurrection, were inventions of His disciples. The Christians lack unity among themselves and their teachers have no power over educated men. Their doctrine comes from Plato and the Stoics, especially their belief in the future life and the spirituality of God. Their resurrection of the body is a corruption of the doctrine of transmigration and ignores the fact that matter is evil. Celsus ends his work by inviting the Christians to join the religion of the majority, to become good citizens, to give thanks to the powers of nature and to abandon the idea of establishing the universal rule of their doctrines. His work, which shows the strength of the church in his day, is conspicuous for its lack of bitterness against the Christians, its recognition of the abuses of paganism, and its knowledge of the Old Testament and the Synoptic Gospels and also of the gnostic writings. Echoes of it are found in Tertullian and Marcus Minucius Felix (*see* MINUCIUS FELIX, MARCUS), but it lay forgotten until Origen gave it new life.

Celsus was not a professed philosopher but a man of the world whose religion was the empire. His keen mind combined an intimate knowledge and appreciation of the various national religions and mythologies with many genuine moral convictions as well as a sceptical tendency. For him, philosophy alone could impart some notion of the Father of the universe, a notion which the elect soul must develop.

BIBLIOGRAPHY.—*The True Word* is contained in Origen's work *Against Celsus,* published in Migne, *Patrol. Graec. xi.* The text has been reconstructed and trans. into German by T. Keim, *Celsus Wahres Wort* (1873). *See* also J. Patrick, *The Apology of Origen* (1829); L. Rougier, *Celse* (Paris, 1925); F. S. Muth, *Der Kampf des heidnischen Philosophen Celsus gegen das Christentum* (Mainz, 1899); A. Harnack *Gesch. der altchristlichen Lit. I;* and Herzog, *Realencyclopädie.*

CELT or KELT, the generic name of an ancient people, the bulk of whom inhabited the central and western parts of Europe. (For the sense of a primitive stone tool, *see* the separate article, CELT.) Much confusion has arisen from the inaccurate use of the terms Celt and Celtic. It is the practice to speak of rather short and dark-complexioned Celtic-speaking people of France, Great Britain and Ireland as Celts, although the ancient writers seem to have applied the term Celt chiefly to folk of great stature and with fair hair and blue or gray eyes.

The ancient writers regarded as homogeneous all the fair-haired peoples dwelling north of the Alps, the Greeks terming them all *Keltoi.* Physically they fall into two loosely-divided groups, which shade off into each other. The first of these is restricted to northwestern Europe, having its chief seat in Scandinavia. It is distinguished by a long head, a long face, a narrow aquiline nose, blue eyes, very light hair and great stature. Those are the peoples usually termed Nordic. The other group is marked by a round head, a broad face, a nose often rather broad and heavy, hazel-gray eyes, light chestnut hair; they are thick-set and of medium height. This race is often termed Celtic or Alpine from the fact of its occurrence all along the great mountain chain from southwest France, in Savoy, in Switzerland, the Po valley and Tirol, as well as in Auvergne, Brittany, Normandy, Burgundy, the Ardennes and the Vosges. It thus stands geographically and in physical features between the Nordic type of Scandinavian and the so-called Mediterranean race with its long head, long face, its rather broad nose, dark brown or black hair, dark eyes and slender form, and medium height. In the Alps and the Danube valley some of the Celts or their forefathers had dwelt from the Stone Age. But it was during the development of the La Tène culture that the Celts attained their maximum power, and it was the La Tène period (500 B.C.–A.D 1) that witnessed the tremendous and remarkable expansion of these people from their homeland in central Europe. Much of their power has been ascribed to great skill in metallurgy, especially in regard to the working of the native iron resources.

The beginning of the 3rd century B.C. was the period of the greatest Celtic movement, but the expansion had no doubt begun long before that period. One of the earliest advances was directed against the Mediterranean coast of France, and at much the same time other bands of the Celts spread southward into Spain, penetrating into that country as far south as Gades (Cadiz), some tribes (*e.g.,* Turdentani and Turduli) forming permanent settlements and being still powerful there in Roman times; and in northern central Spain, from the mixture of Celts with the native Iberians, the population henceforward was called Celtiberian. About this time also took place a great invasion of Italy; Segovisus and Bellovisus, the nephews of Ambigatus, led armies through Switzerland, and over the Brenner and by the Maritime Alps, respectively (Livy, v, 34). The tribes who sent some of their numbers to invade Italy and settle there were the Bituriges, Arverni, Senones, Aedui, Ambarri, Carnuti and Aulerci.

Certain material remains found in north Italy (*e.g.,* at Sesto Calende) may belong to this invasion. The next great wave of Celts recorded swept down on north Italy shortly before 400 B.C. These invaders broke up the Etruscan power in a few years, and even occupied Rome after the disaster on the Allia (390 B.C.). Bought off by gold they withdrew from Rome, but they continued to hold a great part of northern Italy, extending as far south as Sena Gallica (*Sinigaglia*), and henceforward they were a standing source of danger to Rome, especially in the Samnite Wars, until at last they were either subdued or expelled (*e.g.,* the Boii from the plains of the Po). At the same time as the invasion of Italy they had made fresh descents into the Danube valley and the upper Balkan, and perhaps may have pushed into southern Russia, but at this time they never made their way into Greece, though the Athenian ladies copied the style of hair and dress of the Cimbrian women. About 280 B.C. the Celts gathered a great host at the head of the Adriatic, and accompanied by the Illyrian tribe of Autariatae, they overthrew the Macedonians, overran Thessaly, and invaded Phocis in order to sack Delphi, but they were finally repulsed, chiefly by the efforts of the Aetolians (279 B.C.). The remnant of those who returned from Greece joined that part of their army which had remained in Thrace, and marched for the Hellespont. There some of their number settled near Byzantium, having conquered the native Thracians, and made Tyle their capital. The Byzantines had to pay them a yearly tribute of 80 talents until, on the death of the Gallic king Cavarus (some time after 220 B.C.), they were annihilated by the Thracians. The main body of the Gauls who had marched to the Hellespont crossed it under the leadership of Leonnorius and Lutarius. Straightway they overran the greater part of Asia Minor, and laid under tribute all west of Taurus, even the Seleucid kings. At last Attalus, king of Pergamum, defeated them in a series of battles commemorated on the Pergamene sculptures, and thereafter they were confined to a strip of land in the interior of Asia Minor, the Galatia of history. Their three tribes—Trocmi, Tolistobogians and Tectosages—submitted to Rome (189 B.C.), but they remained autonomous till the death of their king Amyntas, when Augustus erected Galatia into a province. Their descendants were probably St. Paul's "foolish Galatians" (*see* GALATIA). Nor was it only toward the south and the Hellespont that the Celtic tide ever set. They passed eastward to the Danube mouth and into southern Russia, as far as the Sea of Azov, mingling with the Scythians, as is proved by the name Celtoscyths. Mithridates VI of Pontus seems to have negotiated with them to gain their aid against Rome, and Bituitus, a Gallic mercenary, was with him at his death.

The Celts moved westward likewise and two divisions of them reached the British Isles, namely the Brythons and the Goidels. The Brythons crossed the channel and established themselves in England and Wales but the Goidels, probably in the 4th century B.C., passed directly from the mouth of the Loire to Ireland where they quickly became a ruling caste. At a much later period there were settlements of Goidels from Ireland on the western fringe of England, Wales and Scotland. The Celtic invasions of the British Isles are in all probability to be correlated with the advent of the La Tène culture (though this is a disputed point), and it is thought to be unlikely that the invaders came over in large migrating hordes that displaced the older population. It is more probable that the new Celtic strain was quickly merged in the native races and that the principal result of the invasion was that the Celtic overlords imposed the Celtic language on the indigenous folk.

BIBLIOGRAPHY.—Ridgeway, *Early Age of Greece*, vol. i, and *Oldest Irish Epic;* Ripley, *The Races of Europe;* Sergi, *The Mediterranean Race;* Eoin MacNeill, *Phases of Irish History;* T. D. Kendrick, *The Druids.*

CELT, as once used by the British and French archaeologists, described the hatchets, adzes or chisels of chipped or shaped stone used by primitive man. The word is variously derived from the Welsh *cellt,* a flintstone (the material of which the weapons are chiefly made, though celts of basalt felstone and jade are found), from being supposed to be the implement peculiar to the Celtic peoples; or, more probably, from a Low Latin word *celtis,* a chisel. The term is somewhat loosely applied to metal as well as stone axeheads. In general form, stone celts approach an oval in section, with sides more or less straight and one end broader and sharper than the other. In length they vary from about 2 to as much as 16 in. Some were fixed in wooden handles, and in the later stone adzes, holes are sometimes found pierced to receive the handles.

The term celt has been largely superseded by axe, though it is by no means certain that all celts were axes. Some, such as the larger ones of ground stone, may well have been used in agriculture for moving the soil. Many were doubtless mounted as adzes, particularly those of the shoe-last type (*Schuhlastenbeil*), which have a very wide European distribution from the Balkans to Scandinavia.

Bronze celts are found in Europe, in Siberia, Burma (the Shan States) and China. They are flat, flanged, winged and socketed. An intermediate form is called palstave; and it has been suggested that the socketed celt was derived from the palstave by a natural transition, the invention being attributed to the people of the Lausitz culture of Germany. It is equally possible that the socketed celt was suggested by the beating over of the wings of the winged celt of Switzerland and Bavaria. Both explanations may be correct. The socket itself had been independently invented in England in the early Bronze Age, where it was applied to the spearhead.

In the west of England the country folks believe that the weapons fell originally from the sky as thunderbolts, and that the water in which they are boiled is a specific for rheumatism. In the north and in Scotland they are safeguards against cattle diseases. In Brittany a stone celt is thrown into a well to purify the water. In Sweden they are regarded as a protection against lightning. In Norway the belief is that, if they are genuine thunderbolts, a thread tied round them when placed on hot coals will not burn but will become moist. In Germany, Spain and Italy, the same beliefs prevailed. In Japan the stones are accounted of medicinal value, while in Burma and Assam they are regarded as thunderbolts and as infallible specifics for ophthalmia. In Africa they are the weapons of the Thunder God. In India and among the Greeks the hatchet appears to have had a sacred importance, doubtlessly derived from the universal superstitious awe with which these weapons of prehistoric man were regarded.

BIBLIOGRAPHY.—Sir J. Evans, *Ancient Stone Implements, Weapons and Ornaments of Great Britain* (1897); Lord Avebury, *Prehistoric Times* (1865–1900), *Origin of Civilization* (1870); E. B. Tylor, *Anthropology* (1881), *Primitive Culture,* 7th ed. (1924). For the history of polished stone axes up to the 17th century *see* Marcel Baudouin and Lionel Bonnemère in the *Bulletin de la Société d'Anthropologie de Paris* (April-May, 1905).

CELTES, KONRAD (1459–1508), German humanist and Latin poet, was born at Wipfeld, near Schweinfurt. After studying at Heidelberg, Celtes led the wandering life of a scholar of the Renaissance, teaching in various universities and everywhere establishing learned societies on the model of the academy of Pomponius Laetus at Rome. Among these was the *Sodalitas litteraria Rhenana* or *Celtica* at Mainz (1491). In 1486 he published his first book, *Ars versificandi et carminum,* which gained him the honour of being crowned as the first poet laureate of Germany, the ceremony being performed by the emperor Frederick III at the diet of Nuermberg in 1487. In 1497 he was appointed by the emperor Maximilian I to the post of professor of poetry and rhetoric at Vienna, and in 1502 was made head of the new Collegium Poetarum et Mathematicorum, with the right of conferring the laureateship. He did much to introduce system into the methods of teaching, to purify the Latin of learned intercourse, and to further the study of the classics, especially the Greek. But he was more than a mere classicist of the Renaissance. He was keenly interested in history and topography, especially in that of his native country. It was he who first unearthed (in the convent of St. Emmeran at Regensburg) the Latin poems of the nun Hrosvitha of Gandersheim, of which he published an edition (Nuermberg, 1501). He also published an historical poem, *Ligurinus sive de rebus gestis Frederici primi imperatoris libri x* (Augsburg, 1507), and the map of the Roman empire known as the *Tabula Peutingeriana* (after Konrad Peutinger, to whom he left it). He projected a great work on Germany; but of this only the *Germania generalis* and an historical work in prose, *De origine, situ, moribus et institutis Nurimbergae libellus,* appeared. As a writer of Latin verse Celtes far surpassed any of his predecessors. His epigrams, edited by Hartfelder, were published at Berlin in 1881. His editions of the classics are now, of course, out of date.

For a full list of Celtes's works *see* Engelbert Klüpfel, *De vita et scriptis Conradi Celtis* (Freiburg, 1827); Johann Aschbach, *Die früheren Wanderjahre des Conrad Celtes* (1869); Hartmann, *Konrad Celtes in Nürnberg* (Nuermberg, 1889).

CELTIBERIA, a term used by Greek and Roman writers to denote sometimes the whole northeast of Spain, and sometimes the northeast part of the central plateau. The latter was the correct use. The Celtiberi were the most warlike people in Spain and for a long time offered a stubborn resistance to the Romans. They served both Carthaginians and Romans as mercenaries, and Livy (xxiv, 49), states that they were the first mercenaries in the Roman army. In 179 B.C. the whole country was subdued by T. Sempronius Gracchus, who by his generous treatment of the vanquished gained their esteem and affection. In 153 they again revolted and were not finally overcome until the capture of Numantia by Scipio the younger (133 B.C.). After the fall of Numantia, and still more after the death of Sertorius (72 B.C.), the Celtiberians became gradually romanized, and town life grew up among their valleys. Clunia, for instance, became a Roman municipality, and ruins of its walls, gates and theatre testify to its civilization; Bilbilis (Bambola), another municipality, was the birthplace of Martial.

The Celtiberians may have been descendants of Celtic immigrants from Gaul into Iberia (Spain), or a mixed race of Celts and Spaniards (Iberians); that a strong Celtic element existed in Spain is proved both by numerous traditions and by the more trustworthy evidence of place names.

Their country was rough and unfruitful as a whole (barley, however, was cultivated), being chiefly used for the pasture of sheep. Its inhabitants either led a nomadic life or occupied small villages; large towns were few. Their infantry and cavalry were both excellent. They carried double-edged swords and short daggers for use hand to hand; their defensive armour was a light Gallic shield, or a round wicker buckler, and greaves of felt around their legs. They wore brazen helmets with purple crests, and rough-haired black cloaks, in which they slept on the bare ground. They were said to offer sacrifice to a nameless god at the time of the full moon, when all the household danced together before the doors of the houses.

Although cruel to their enemies, they were hospitable to strangers. They ate meat of all kinds, and drank a kind of mead.

E. Hübner's article in Pauly-Wissowa's *Realencyklopädie*, iii (1886–93), collects all the ancient references.

CELTIC LANGUAGES. The Celtic languages form one group of the Indo-European family of languages, intermediate between the Italic and Teutonic groups, but distinguished from these and other branches of the family by certain well-marked characteristics, the most notable of which are the loss of initial and inter-vocalic *p*, and the change of Indo-European *ē* to *ī*, the Indo-European labialized velar *gv* is represented by *b*, while the medial aspirates *bh, dh, gh* result in simple voiced stops. Indo-European sonants *r* and *l* become *ri, li*. The initial mutations which are so characteristic of the living languages arose after the Romans had left Britain. The Celtic languages and the Italic dialects stand in a close relationship to one another. The features common to both Celtic and Italic are: (1) the genative singular ending *-ī* of masculine and neuter stems in *o;* (2) verbal nouns in *-tion;* (3) the *b-* future; (4) the passive formation in *-r*.

The various Celtic dialects are: (1) Gaulish; (2) Goidelic, including Irish, Scottish Gaelic, and Manx; (3) Brythonic, including Welsh, Breton, and Cornish. Gaulish and Brythonic change the Indo-European labialized velar guttural *qu* to *p*, while the Goidelic dialects retain the *qu*, which later gives up the labial element and becomes *k*. (*See* Cornish Language; Gaelic Language; Indo-Europeans; Manx Language and Literature; Welsh Language and Literature.)

Bibliography.—Windisch's article "Keltische Sprachen" in Ersch und Gruber's *Allgemeine Encyklopädie der Wissenschaften und Künste*, and V. Tourneur, *Esquisse d'une histoire des études celtiques*, vol. ii with full bibliography (Liége, 1905); Zeuss's *Grammatica Celtica* as revised by Ebel; a comparative grammar of the Celtic dialects by H. Pedersen (Göttingen, 1908); H. Zimmer, "Die Kelt. Litteraturen" in *Die Kultur d. Gegenwart* (Berlin and Leipzig, 1909); Whitley Stokes and A. Bezzenberger, *Wortschatz der keltischen spracheinheit* (Göttingen, 1894); A. Meillet and M. Cohen, *Les Langues du Monde* (1924).

CELTIC LITERATURE: *see* Breton Literature; Cornish Language; Irish Literature; Scottish Literature; Welsh Language and Literature.

CELTIUM is the name given by G. Urbain and A. Dauvillier to the element of atomic number 72, for which the former obtained some evidence from X-ray spectra in 1911. Their claim to have discovered this element was, however, disputed by D. Coster and G. Hevesy (1923) who named it *Hafnium*, under which heading it is described. Of the resulting polemical papers only a few are suggested for reference.

Bibliography.—D. Coster and G. Hevesy, *Nature*, 111:79, 252, 462 (1923); G. Urbain and/or A. Dauvillier, *ibid.*, p. 218, *Comptes rendus*, 176:676 (1923); *Chemistry and Industry*, 42:764 (1923).

CEMBAL D'AMORE or Cembal D'Amour, a keyboard instrument invented by the famous organ and clavièr maker Gottfried Silbermann, who was later so prominently identified with the earlier pianofortes. It was a kind of clavichord with strings of double the usual length, and its other mechanism modified to correspond, but it was not a success.

CEMBALO or Cimbalo, the Italian names for a dulcimer (*cf.* cymbal); whence, in due course, clavicembalo for a pianoforte, otherwise a keyed dulcimer. Hence, too, the frequent use of the word cembalo in earlier days in the case of pianoforte music; as used in such cases it was merely a contraction of clavicembalo. (*See* Dulcimer.)

CEMENT. The word cement apparently was first used of a mixture of broken stone, tiles, etc., with some binding material, and later it was used of a material capable of adhering to, and uniting into a cohesive mass, portions of substances not in themselves adhesive. The use of cementing material dates from very early days, and it is probable that adhesive clay was one of the first materials used for uniting stones, etc. Bitumen probably was also used for the same purpose, while the use of burned gypsum, and also lime, dates back to the time of the Egyptians.

In its widest sense the word cement includes an infinite variety of materials, and ranges from the clay used to bind stones and other materials together to form the natives' huts in tropical countries, or the clay in the sand used by small boys to make sand models, up to the modern rapid hardening cements which are capable of binding three times their own weight of sand together in such a way that, at the end of 24 hr., they will stand a compression of several thousand pounds per square inch. It also includes those materials which join individual crystals together to form masses of rock, etc., such as the cementitious material which joins the grains of sand together in a sandstone, and ultimately merges into glues, solders and adhesives in general, between which there is no sharply defined line of demarcation.

In its more restricted sense, particularly if it is unqualified and used in connection with building and engineering, the word practically always means portland cement, as this is by far the most important cement used at the present time, the world's output amounting to millions of tons per annum. A fairly full description of this cement is therefore justified, and a brief description of other cements will be given toward the end of this article.

Portland Cement.—Portland cement is made by burning a mixture of calcareous and argillaceous material to clinkering temperature, and grinding the resulting clinker. The mixture may be a natural one (such as the marls) or an artificial one (such as chalk or limestone) for the calcareous material, and clay or shale for the argillaceous material. The binding qualities of modern cements are very considerable, and it is possible to make good concrete from properly graded sand and ballast with the use of 1 part of cement to 12, or more, parts of aggregate; but as it is not always possible in practice to obtain a thorough distribution of cement throughout the mass, it is customary to use a larger proportion of cement; *e.g.*, 1:3:5 parts of cement, sand and gravel; and for a better quality concrete, 1 part of cement to 2 or 3 parts of sand, and 3 or 4 parts of gravel. A good cement mortar can be made from 1 part of cement to 4 or 5 parts of clean sharp sand, free from clay. If the mixture is too rich (*e.g.*, equal parts of sand and cement) there is danger of cracks due to shrinkage, and apart from this the extra strength gained by using a greater proportion of cement than 1 to 3 of sand is so small that the additional cost is not justified.

History.—Very little definite information about the preparation and uses of cement can be found before the 18th century. Various districts gained reputations for the special qualities of their lime cements, such as the power of setting hard under water, but the reasons for these special qualities were not known until the last century. John Smeaton was one of the first to make any serious attempt to grapple with the question of the cause of the varying hydraulic properties of different lime cements. In 1756, while engaged on the construction of the Eddystone lighthouse, he made a series of experiments to find the best cement capable of hardening under water. The result of these experiments revealed the fact that the best hydraulic limes were made from limestone containing an appreciable quantity of clay. This led to a number of investigators carrying out experiments. In 1796 Parker invented his Roman cement, which was made by "reducing to powder certain burned stones or argillaceous productions called 'noddles' of clay." This cement "will set . . . in 10 or 20 minutes either in or out of water." The raw materials for Roman cement were burned to just short of the vitrifying temperature, whereas for hydraulic lime the raw materials were heated to a much lower temperature, which was just sufficient to decompose the calcium carbonate. This was a distinct advance, as the overburned or vitrified pieces of lime had formerly been picked out and rejected as being useless for mortar.

Vicat, in 1813, made a series of experiments on the effect of adding different clays in varying proportions to slaked lime, and then burning the mixture. The success of these experiments led other investigators to try artificial mixtures of clay and calcareous materials and in 1822 Frost brought out his British cement, which was soon followed by Joseph Aspdin (1824) with portland cement. Both of these, however, were hydraulic limes, in that the mixtures were only calcined and not clinkered. Aspdin was apparently the first to use the word portland to define a particular type of cement, although Smeaton, over half a century earlier, had said that cement made from these materials would "equal the best merchantable Portland stone in solidity and durability." His portland cement was, of course, quite different from modern portland cement, but nevertheless the colour and properties of concrete made from this cement were somewhat similar to Portland stone.

By this time (1820–30) works were springing up in various parts of the country where the raw materials were suitable; Parker's Roman cement was manufactured at Northfleet, Kent; British cement was made by Frost at Swanscombe; and the Aspdins were making portland cement at Wakefield and Gateshead. This portland cement, as mentioned above, was more of the nature of hydraulic lime; but about 1845 I. C. Johnson, who was then manager of Messrs. White & Sons' works at Swanscombe, Kent, produced a cement of the modern portland cement type, by burning the raw materials "with unusually strong heat until the mass was nearly vitrified," and this clinker, when finely ground, made a cement which was far in advance of the ordinary type produced at that time.

During the next few years many works started making true portland cement, both in Britain and in other countries. In France, Dupont and Demarle were delivering fairly large quantities of portland cement in 1850 from their works at Boulogne-sur-Mer and the demand continued to grow. Naturally with such a demand, and with such scanty knowledge as to the special requirements necessary for ensuring the production of good sound cement, a large quantity of inferior material came on to the market, and failures resulting from this gave the cement a doubtful reputation. Investigations for improving the quality of cement continued with moderate results. Grant's tests, in 1865, show an average tensile strength of 353.2 lb. for $2\frac{1}{4}$ sq.in. ($1\frac{1}{2}$ in. × $1\frac{1}{2}$ in.) cement and sand briquettes (1:1) at seven days (157 lb. per sq.in.), while in 1878 a tensile strength of 500 lb. ($2\frac{1}{4}$-in. briquettes), *i.e.,* 222 lb. per sq.in., was specified for briquettes made from 6 parts of cement to 10 parts of sharp sand. This may be compared with modern rapid-hardening cement, which, with 1 part of cement to 3 parts of standard sand, has a tensile strength of more than 500 lb., and sometimes more than 600 lb. per sq.in. after 24 hr.

Manufacture.—When cement was first made from stone noddles, as in Parker's method, the stone was placed in a bottle kiln or dome kiln ordinarily used for burning lime. When at a later date artificial mixtures of chalk and argillaceous materials were used, it was found that the best and most intimate mixtures were made by beating clay and chalk into a thin slip or slurry with water. This slurry was then allowed to stand in large settling tanks, or backs, until the material had settled, and the water was drawn off and the deposit dried and burned. The time taken for the settling and drying of the raw materials was so great that efforts were made to improve the kiln (which, of course, could only be fed with dry material) by utilizing the waste heat for drying the slurry. One of the first of these was the chamber kiln of I. C. Johnson, which consisted of a long horizontal chamber connected with the top of the ordinary kiln, so that the hot gases from the latter had to pass through the chamber on the way to the chimney stack. The liquid slurry, either from the backs or direct from the washmill, was placed on the floor of the chamber and was effectively dried by the hot gases passing over it, providing the layer of slurry was not too thick. The chamber had to be of considerable length in order to provide floor space to dry sufficient slurry for a full charge of the kiln, and improvements in the direction of shortening this were made by Batchelor and others, by providing two or three floors one above the other. Coke was used for burning the raw materials and ranged from 8 to 9 cwt. per ton of clinker. In 1870 Goreham patented his method of grinding his slurry with burr stones, thereby producing a better slurry and containing only 40%–42% of water, a proportion much less than was usual at that time, which, of course, facilitated drying. The construction of the bottle kiln, even in its improved form, the chamber kiln, necessitated intermittent firing, as each charge of fuel and dried slurry had to be built up by hand. Experiments with the object of doing away with this costly intermittent method led to the development of shaft kilns, with continuous burning of the raw material. The shaft kiln, as its name implies, consists of a vertical shaft, the top of which leads into a chimney. A few feet from the ground level removable bars are fixed across the shaft. On to these bars is placed a layer of coke, then alternate layers of dried slurry and coke until the kiln is filled. The coke at the bottom is fired, and this burns the raw material above it, while the hot gases pass through and heat the layers above. As the coke burns away the cement clinker drops on to the bars and heats the incoming air, while the burning zone rises to about half way up the shaft. The partly cooled clinker on the bars is removed from time to time and fresh layers of dried slurry and coke are put in on top. The process thus becomes continuous, and the loss of time in waiting for the kiln to heat up and cool down, together with the resultant loss of heat, which is unavoidable with the chamber kiln, is entirely overcome in the shaft kiln. Modifications of the shaft kiln were patented by Dietszch, Stein, Schneider and others, and the different types became known by the names of the patentees. The next improvement was the use of forced draught instead of natural induced draught from the chimneys, and tests on a standard Schneider kiln showed an increase in output from the normal 70 tons per week to 150 tons per week when using mechanical draught.

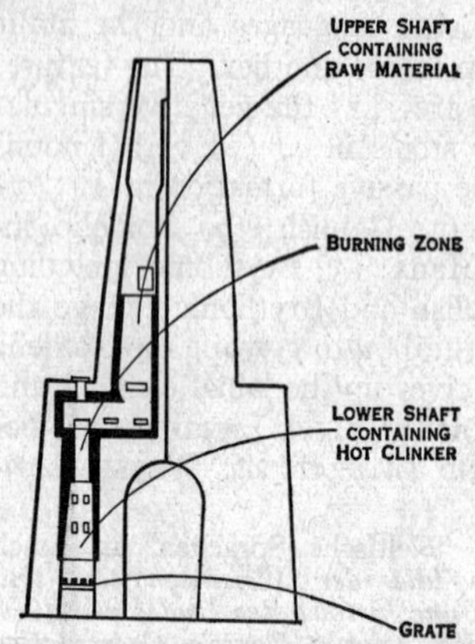

FIG. 1.—DIETSZCH SHAFT KILN

Fresh layers of coke and slurry are added from the top as soon as the coke at the bottom is burned away, thus keeping the burning process continuous

One of the weaknesses of the shaft kiln—or a fixed kiln—is the difficulty of ensuring even burning of the clinker, some of it being underburned while other portions were heavily clinkered, and various mechanical improvements have been made in the grate with the object of keeping the whole of the material in the kiln on the move by the continuous withdrawal of the clinker. The improvements in the shaft kiln reduced the quantity of fuel required from 70% to 80% of the weight of good clinker produced by the old kiln to 20% to 30% (dried slurry being used in both cases). This economy of fuel and the small amount of handling required, together with low capital cost, render the shaft kiln method suitable for use where the small output does not justify the cost of the rotary kiln.

Other methods of preventing the waste of heat resulting from the heating up and cooling of the old type of kiln were investigated. One of the most successful was the Hoffman ring kiln, which consisted of a number of kilns arranged in a ring around a central chimney. The flues from the kilns are so arranged that air, which is heated by being drawn through clinker which is cooling, is used for burning the fuel in the next kiln or two, and the hot gases are drawn through the other kilns to heat the raw materials before passing into the main flue. These ring kilns are very economical of fuel but require skilled hands for charging, and the labour costs are high.

Another method, which laid the foundations for the modern rotary kiln process, was devised by Thomas Russell Crampton, who in 1877 patented a method for burning "portland and other cements in revolving furnaces heated by the gases resulting from the combustion of coal or carbonaceous material" or "by the combustion of air and powdered carbonaceous material."

In 1885 Frederick Ransome patented a method of burning dry powdered materials in a rotating cylinder by means of which he hoped to obtain the finished product from the kiln in a powder form sufficiently fine for use without further grinding, evidently overlooking the fact that clinkering is an essential process in the manufacture of true portland cement. He also stated that the raw material might be fed in either at the chimney end of the kiln or at the firing end, which suggests that he had not appre-

INITIAL STAGES IN MANUFACTURE OF CEMENT

Top left: Blasting rock at the quarry
Top right: Power shovel loading rocks into truck for trip to the mill
Centre left: Rocks being delivered to the preliminary crusher
Centre right: Crushed rock being emptied into storage bins by a travelling crane. Clinker, gypsum and crushed limestone are stored
Bottom left: Revolving cylinder of armour plate containing various sized steel balls which pulverize rock to proper size
Bottom right: Slurry classifier from which overflow is sent to storage tanks. Coarse particles are returned to mill for further grinding

CEMENT

BY COURTESY OF PORTLAND CEMENT ASSOCIATION

FURTHER STAGES IN CEMENT MANUFACTURE

Top left: Slurry storage tanks
Top right: Twin kilns in which slurry is burned
Centre left: Control panel for a portland cement kiln
Centre right: Belt conveyor transporting clinker from storage to finish mill
Bottom left: Packaging finished portland cement in self-sealing bags
Bottom right: General view of a portland cement manufacturing plant

Analyses of Typical Materials

	Chalk	Limestone	Blue Lias limestone	Marl	Gault clay	Clay	Shale
	%	%	%	%	%	%	%
Silica (SiO_2)	5.94	1.16	12.66	13.10	37.68	58.78	60.20
Alumina (Al_2O_3)	1.46	0.33	3.92	3.98	14.92	18.42	19.42
Ferric oxide (Fe_2O_3)	1.20	0.08	1.50	1.72	6.28	7.60	8.24
Lime (CaO)	50.68	54.82	43.26	44.58	17.84	0.52	0.40
Magnesia (MgO)	0.51	0.28	1.30	0.48	1.61	1.90	1.46
Sulphuric anhydride (SO_3)	Trace	Trace	0.39	Trace	0.69	Trace	Trace
Carbonic anhydride (CO_2), combined water (H_2O) and alkalies	40.21	43.33	36.97	36.14	20.99	12.78	10.28
	100.00	100.00	100.00	100.00	100.00	100.00	100.00

ciated the full value of feeding the kiln at the end opposite to that used for burning the fuel. Further improvements were effected by F. W. S. Stokes who in 1888 patented a method of drying the slurry by passing the hot gases from the rotating kiln through a revolving drum on to the outside of which the slurry was fed. He also used another revolving drum for cooling the clinker, utilizing the waste heat for heating the air supplied to the fuel in the kiln. In 1895 and 1896 E. H. Hurry and H. J. Seaman obtained various patents for improvements in cooling the clinker, arrangements for using powdered coal with an air blast for burning, etc., and various other developments have been made with the rotary kiln, until it has very nearly displaced all others where a large output of portland cement clinker is required. Among the first rotary kilns erected was that at Arlesey (1887). This was 26 ft. long and 5 ft. in diameter, and forms an interesting comparison with those now in common use, which are 200 to 300 ft. long, and 8½ ft. to 12½ ft. in diameter.

Modern practice is to grind a mixture of suitable calcareous and argillaceous materials, either wet or dry, in such proportions as will give the correct composition to the finished cement. The wet ground material is pumped, in the form of a slurry containing about 40% water, into a series of large mixing tanks having a capacity of 1,000 to 2,000 tons of slurry, and from these it is pumped into the kiln. The dry ground raw material is carried by a conveyor to the storage bins, and from the bins it is fed into the kiln after having been damped to prevent too much dust being blown up the chimney. The raw material, either in the form of slurry or damp meal, enters the kiln at the top end close to the chimney and meets the oncoming hot gases. As the kiln revolves the raw materials fall down toward the clinkering zone, having been first dried by the hot gases, and then having the carbon dioxide driven off from the calcareous materials. In the clinkering zone, where the heat is maintained by the combustion of powdered coal carried in by a blast of air, the lime of the calcareous materials combines with the silica and alumina of the argillaceous materials, and at this stage they partially fuse or clinker together, an action which is facilitated by the alkalies and iron oxide, etc., in the materials. The partially fused product or cement clinker passes from the lower end of the kiln to the cooler, where it parts with some of its heat to the air going to the kiln. The clinker, with the addition of a little gypsum or water to regulate the setting time, is then ground in ball and tube mills to such a fineness that the finished product—portland cement—leaves a residue of less than 10%, usually 1% to 3%, on a sieve having 32,400 meshes to the square inch.

The raw materials consist of argillaceous or alumina and silica bearing materials and calcareous materials, the former including clay, shale, slate, etc., and some forms of slag, and the latter including chalk, limestone, marine shells, etc., while many materials such as marls, gault clays, cement rock, etc., contain natural mixtures of both the calcareous and argillaceous constituents.

The method of obtaining the raw materials will depend on whether they are hard or soft. With soft materials, such as clay, marl and soft chalk, a steam digger or scraper is used. After the overburden or top refuse material has been removed, a face is opened up in the material. The steam digger is brought up to this face, and the teeth of the digger bite into the material, and, on being lifted upward, break or cut away lumps which fall into the bucket. The bucket, which holds from ½ to 3 cu.yd. or more, is swung around and emptied into a truck which is then taken to the washmill. For very soft materials, such as mud or clay under water, a dredging machine—a form of chain bucket excavator—is used. For hard materials, such as limestone, etc., the rock is blasted with an explosive such as gelignite, which will break it into pieces sufficiently small for the crusher to take. If the pieces are too large they are very difficult to handle or break again, and it is in regulating the position and depth of the bore-holes, and the size of the charge, that the good quarry foreman shows his skill in obtaining the greatest quantity of loose rock of the right size with the least cost. The broken rock lying at the base of the quarry is picked up by a power shovel or a grab, taking up 3 cu.yd. or more at a time, put into trucks and taken to the mills.

Grinding Raw Materials.—The methods used depend on whether the materials are soft or hard. Soft materials are usually washed down with water until they form a slurry of the consistence of cream, containing about 40% water. The trucks of marl or chalk and clay are tipped into a washmill, which consists of a large circular tank of concrete about 14 ft. or more in diameter, with baffles and slotted screens (⅛ in. to $\frac{3}{16}$ in. slots) let into the sides. Water is allowed to run into the mill and a number of harrows suspended on chains from radial arms from the centre of the mill are caused to revolve at a rapid rate. These harrows break up the large pieces of chalk, etc., and by dashing the raw materials, suspended in the water, against the screens and baffles, break up the clay and chalk into such fine particles that about 98% will pass through a sieve having 180 meshes to the linear inch. If, owing to the presence of coarse particles of sand, etc., the slurry is too coarse, it may be necessary to finish it off in a tube mill. In the U.S. the 200-mesh sieve is commonly used.

Hard materials are first put through a crusher which may be of the jaw type, in which the stone is fed in between two steel jaws set at an angle, one of which moves backward and forward with a rocking motion, or through a gyratory crusher, in which the gyratory motion of a central jaw causes a crushing action against an outer jaw, or through some other form of crusher suitable for large stone. The crushed stone is fed into smaller crushers which may be one of the above types, or a hammer mill in which rods with hinged hammer heads are allowed to swing around rapidly and break the stone against stationary bars on the outer edge of the mill, or if the material is sufficiently soft it may be fed into crushing rolls.

From this fine crushing the small stone is taken by a conveyor to the tube mills, and then to the kiln. The process differs according to whether the dry process or the wet process is used. In the dry process the limestone and shale, etc., are fed into the mills from the weighing machines or feed tables (which regulate the quantity) in such proportions as will give a finished product of the correct composition. The mills may be of various types. In the ball and tube mill, separate or combined, steel balls falling over each other in a revolving cylinder have a pounding or hammering action on the particles of stone between the balls. In the centrifugal type of mill a heavy mass of steel is caused to revolve rapidly, and centrifugal force causes it to press against a stationary ring and exerts both a crushing and grinding action on the stone between the revolving weight and the ring. In the Fuller mill the revolving weights are large steel balls, in the Griffin mills they are large pestles, while in mills of the Hercules, Huntingdon, Sturtevant and Kent types they consist of movable or swinging rolls.

The finely ground raw meal from the mills is passed into the storage bin, from which it is fed into the kiln, after being damped if necessary. From this point the treatment is the same as the wet process. The advantage of the dry process is a saving of fuel, and of water, if the water supply is limited. Also, where waste-heat boilers are installed, more heat is available for power generation. For a long time it was generally believed that dry raw materials could not be mixed sufficiently well to ensure even composition, but since the introduction of compressed air devices for conveying these materials (cement pumps), and the floating of the materials in storage bins by use of compressed air, a state of practical fluidity is obtained which results in dry blending as thorough as can be accomplished by the wet process.

In the wet process the limestone and shale from the feed tables, or weighing machines, are fed into the ball mill and then the tube mill, or into a compound mill where the two are combined, and the requisite quantity of water added at the same time. The normal slurry coming from the mills contains about 40% water, and leaves less than 2% residue on a sieve having 180 meshes to the linear inch, but as it occasionally contains coarse particles which have passed through the mills, it is customary to put the slurry through a separator, usually of a centrifugal type, which rejects all the coarse particles. The slurry from the sump of the washmill, in the case of soft materials, the tube mill in the case of hard materials, or the separator, is pumped to the mixers, which are large tanks capable of holding 1,000 to 2,000 tons of slurry. These mixers serve three purposes: (1) they allow corrections to be made in the composition of the slurry, (2) they overcome any temporary variation in the composition by dispersing it and mixing it with the large bulk, and (3) they give efficient storage, allowing the grinding plant to be shut down over the week end (and at night, if required) while the kiln continues to run. To prevent settlement in the tanks the slurry is continuously kept on the move.

This is done either mechanically by rotating arms with paddles, or by the release of compressed air in the bottom of the tank, which bubbles up through the slurry.

Until comparatively recently cement manufacturers obtained slurry mixtures entirely by blending natural raw materials. In 1934 a process of flotation, long employed in the concentration of ore, was adapted to the connection or benefication of limestones. In fine grinding rocks they are largely broken down into their mineralogical constituents such as calcite, quartz, mica, etc. By employing the principles of froth flotation the calcite can be floated off, so that a slurry containing originally perhaps only 40% calcium carbonate (lime material) can be concentrated to 75%. Similarly, excesses of silica, alumina, iron oxide, magnesium-bearing minerals such as mica, etc., may be separated and used, or discarded. The flotation process applied to cement raw materials has greatly widened possibilities of cement manufacture from rock deposits previously rejected. It also makes possible manufacture of various kinds of portland cement—that is cements adapted for special purposes such as low heat of hydration, sulphate resisting, etc.

From the mixers the slurry is pumped to a small tank at the top end of the kiln, from which it is fed into the kiln at such rate as the burner thinks necessary. The usual method of doing this is by a spoon feed, the revolving spoons dipping into the tank and delivering the slurry into the kiln. Occasionally the feed is regulated by a variable orifice leading into a delivery pipe. Whichever of these two methods is used, it is the regular practice to keep the tank at constant level by overpumping and allowing the excess of slurry to run back to the mixer through an overflow pipe. Other methods, such as the spray feed and dewatering the slurry by means of vacuum filters, have been tried with some success.

Burning.—The most essential part of the manufacture of portland cement is the complete chemical combination of certain constituents; viz., silica, alumina and lime. The other constituents, particularly the iron oxide and alkalies, play their part but are subsidiary to the three main constituents. These readily combine at a high temperature, but at this temperature it is difficult to get the kiln lining to stand up, and therefore every means should be taken which will assist the chemical combination to take place at a somewhat lower temperature, and also prevent any excessive attack on the lining bricks. Fine grinding plays an important part in meeting the first of these two requirements, and the second is met by obtaining a coating of a more fusible slurry to adhere to the lining brick, and thus protect them.

The kiln itself consists of a cylindrical shell made of steel plates lined with fire bricks for nearly the whole of its length. The length varies from 150 ft. to 350 ft. or more, and the diameter from 8 ft. to 14 ft., usually with an enlarged diameter at the firing zone, so that the clinker may be allowed to soak at the high temperature. The kiln itself is carried on three to six tires, according to its length, and is driven by a gear ring usually fixed a little below the middle of the kiln. The expansion of the kiln is considerable, and therefore the tires and gear ring are not riveted directly on to the kiln, lest they be fractured, but are fixed to metal bands riveted at one end to the kiln, and are also supported by guide blocks. As the kiln is set at an angle usually of 1 in 25, the tendency of the kiln to slide down while revolving is counteracted by having the faces of the tires and the supporting rollers set at an angle. As a further precaution check rollers are fixed so that should the kiln slip down a little these rollers come into action on the side of the tires and stop the kiln from slipping off the supporting rollers. At the upper end, where the slurry or damp meal is fed in, the kiln passes into the dust chamber through a joint which is reasonably tight to prevent loss of draught, and the hot gases, having deposited a large portion of the dust, are led into the chimney.

Before the chimney, flues are sometimes installed leading under boilers where steam is generated for turbine-generator units which furnish sufficient power to operate the plant. Near cities and towns plants are frequently equipped with dust collectors, either mechanical or of electrical precipitation type. Otherwise dust losses may amount to 5% or more of the kiln output; and neighbours object to dust. The lower end of the kiln is fitted with a large adjustable hood, on rails, which allows access to the interior for relining, etc. The white hot clinker falls through an opening in the bottom of the hood into a clinker cooler. The old method of cooling was to allow the clinker to roll through a refractory-lined cylinder, similar to the kiln but smaller, open at the lower end. Later installations used air-quenching devices, usually an enclosed slowly moving grate, through which a blast of cold air was blown. It is quite generally believed, in the United States at least, that quickly cooled clinker is superior. The kiln is fired through a pipe opening, usually in the centre of the hood, with a mixture of pulverized coal, natural gas or oil, and air. This primary air is heated by being passed over or through the clinker. Secondary air to complete combustion is admitted through openings in or around the hood. Modern installations use heated primary air to dry the coal in the pulverizer as well as inject it into the kiln. Burning formerly depended largely on the judgment of the attendant (the burner) but indicating and recording instruments permit accurate control, and in the newest installations instrumental control of kiln speed, draft, and feed practically eliminate the personal equation of the burner.

Clinker Grinding.—The clinker as it comes from the kiln is in a fairly stable condition, and may be stored for months in the open if necessary without any appreciable deterioration. This, however, represents so much locked up capital, and it is therefore customary to grind the clinker soon after it is made. Very fresh clinker appears to be a little tougher than clinker which has been allowed to stand a week or two, and this sometimes affects the power required for grinding. The clinker from modern kilns is usually small enough to be fed directly into a ball mill or a high-speed mill, but if it is too large it is passed through a crusher first. As it is usually necessary to add a definite proportion of gypsum to the clinker in order to regulate the setting time of the cement, both the clinker and gypsum are passed over feed tables before being mixed and fed into the mills. The feed tables are simple devices for regulating the quantity of any material passing over them in a given time and consist of a revolving table, fixed scrapers and a vertical feed pipe, with an adjustable collar, just above the centre of the feed table. The material falls in a heap in the centre of the table, and as it revolves a portion of the material is guided by the scrapers away from the heap to the edge of the table, from which it falls on to a conveyor and is taken to the mills. The heap in the centre is at once replenished from the feed pipe, and the size of the heap, and therefore the quantity removed by the scraper, is regulated by the height of the adjustable collar of the feed pipe above the table.

The mills used for grinding the clinker are of the same types as those described for the grinding of the raw materials. The type most frequently used for clinker grinding in modern plant in Britain is the compound mill, which is usually 7 or 8 ft. in diameter and 30 to 40 ft. long.

The fineness of portland cement was formerly universally specified as percentages passing very fine mesh testing sieves, but there is a tendency to drop sieve sizes and specify specific surface area, which is the calculated surface area in square centimetres per gram.

Storing and Packing.—Finished cement from the grinding mills is conveyed to storage bins or silos by belt conveyors, screw conveyors, bucket elevators, or in recent installations by a screw conveyor-compressed air device known as a cement pump, which delivers through piping a steady flow of cement suspended in or made fluid by air. Storage bins are generally cylindrical reinforced-concrete silos, holding 12,000 to 15,000 bbl. (2,500 to 3,000 tons) each. Storage was originally considered desirable to season the cement. This is no longer essential with a properly made cement, but storage of as much as one-fourth to one-half the annual capacity of the plant is desirable in order to provide continuous and economic operation. Moreover, large purchasers demand that the cement be held and tested before shipment, and some tests require 30 days' time.

The cement is withdrawn from the silos by screw conveyors or cement pumps and conveyed to small bins serving packing machines, or is conveyed directly to spouts or pipes for bulk shipment in specially designed railway cars, barges and motor trucks. Most of the cement is packed in cotton or paper valve bags, which in the United States hold 94 lb. net, or approximately 1 cu.ft. of cement. The tops of the bags or sacks are tied or sealed before filling and a turned-in corner, or valve, on the bottom provides the opening for slipping the bag over the spout of the bag-packing machine. These machines utilize the principle that cement flows freely when the proper amount of compressed air is injected into the feeding device. A single operator can manipulate three to four loading spouts. The flow of cement into the bags is automatically cut off when the proper weight is reached, the material in the bag closes the corner valve, and the bag drops off to a belt conveyor below. The empty bags must be slipped over the filling spout by the operator. In one type of machine this is the only manual part of the operation. Cotton bags are returned to the cement manufacturer (a discount being allowed on the purchase price for their return), and are reused many times.

Cement for export is often packed in wooden barrels or steel containers, which stand on scales while being filled. Originally all cement was shipped in barrels, the standard U.S. barrel holding 376 lb. net. Four bags therefore are equivalent to one barrel. The fact that the trade marks or brands of the older cement companies are circular designs is because they were intended to be used on barrel heads.

Layout of Works.—For the purpose of economy and efficiency, considerable care must be exercised in the layout of the works, so that the raw materials and coal are delivered at the places where they are to be used, and the clinker and cement stores are in the proper position for the minimum handling of these materials.

Analysis and Tests.—Drafting specifications to insure quality of portland cement is complicated because qualities most desired are physical—workability, strength, durability, impermeability and density in the mortar and concrete made with cement—and these may be obtained with cements of various chemical compositions. After years of argument, the Cement committee of the American Society for Testing Materials by 1939 had reduced its specifications to simple form covering only the following factors: (1) chemical limits; (2) soundness; (3) time of setting; (4) tensile strength; (5) packaging and marking; (6) storage; (7) inspection; (8) rejection; (9) methods of testing.

The chemical limits are that the cement shall show on testing amounts not greater than indicated with the respective tolerances in the following table:

	Limits (%)	*Tolerances* (%)
Loss on ignition	4.00	0.25
Insoluble residue	0.85	0.15
Sulphuric anhydride (SiO_3) . . .	2.00	0.10
Magnesia (MgO)	5.00	0.40

The A.S.T.M. soundness test consists of subjecting a pat of neat cement (cement mixed with water) to five hours' steaming. The pat must not distort, crack, check or disintegrate. A soundness test used by U.S. cement manufacturers in their own laboratories for control purposes, and one included in many specifications, consists of subjecting 1-in. square bars of neat cement, usually 10 in. long, to an autoclave test with steam at 350 lb. pressure for three hours. The bar should not disintegrate, or expand in length more than 1% (although no limit has been fixed). Elsewhere than in the United States the Le Chatelier test is widely used, wherein the expansion of neat cement moulded in a small brass cylinder, after immersion in boiling water for three hours, is measured. The chief causes of unsoundness of cement are assumed to be free, dead-burned, uncombined lime and magnesia which remain unhydrated for a long time at ordinary temperatures.

Time of setting as determined by a Vicat needle must not be less than 45 min., or by a Gillmore needle 60 min. In this test the penetration of a weighted needle during the setting period is the criterion. The final set must be attained within ten hours.

The strengths of mortar specimens made of 1 part of cement and 3 parts of standard sand, according to the A.S.T.M. specifications for standard portland cement, must equal or exceed the following:

Age in days	Storage of specimen	Tensile strength Lb. per sq. in.
7	{1 day in moist air 6 days in water	275
28	{1 day in moist air 27 days in water	350

For high early strength portland cement the following:

Age in days	Storage of specimen	Option No. 1 Tensile strength P.S.I.	Option No. 2 Compressive strength P.S.I.
1	1 day in moist air	275	1,300
3	{1 day in moist air 2 days in water	375	3,000

This was not considered necessary in the A.S.T.M. specifications for several years prior to 1940. In that year new specifications were adopted covering five types of portland cement, with requirements for fineness varying from minimums 1,600 sq.cm. per gram to 1,800. While the A.S.T.M. specifications do not designate these five varieties of portland cement by other names than type I, type II, etc., they conform closely to the five varieties defined by the U.S. bureau of reclamation in the table on page 110A, except that the order is different: Type I is so-called standard cement; type II, modified; type III, high early strength; type IV, low heat of hydration; type V, sulphate resisting. Modern cements are ground to sizes measured in microns rather than openings of the finest wire sieves, yet specifications requiring from 92% to 98% to pass a 200-mesh sieve (200 meshes to the linear inch, or openings of 74 microns on a side) are common—in some instances to insure that a small percentage be retained on the sieve and the cement be not too finely ground. Many specifications define required fineness in terms of specific surface area per gram, as 1,700 sq.cm. (calculated on the assumption that the particles are spheres). This estimation is made by use of an instrument known as a turbidimeter, which determines the turbidity of a suspension of cement in some nonreactive liquid medium, such as kerosene, by measuring the intensity of light penetrating the suspension. Determination of the approximate percentages of the various sizes of particles is also made by use of an elutriator using either a liquid or air medium.

Composition.—The essential chemical components of portland cement are the oxides of calcium, silicon, aluminum and iron—CaO, SiO_2, Al_2O_3, Fe_2O_3. As a result of adding gypsum to control the setting time SO_3, sulphuric anhydride, is also present. Other constituents such as magnesium oxide (MgO) and compounds of sodium and potassium are usually present in small amounts. Chemical analyses are made in terms of these oxides, although they do not exist in unhydrated cement as simple oxides but are in complicated combinations brought about by partial melting, forming liquid and solid solutions and subsequent cooling to phase equilibrium, depending not only on the proportions of the various oxides but on the temperatures of the melt and of that of the freezing or crystallization. It is therefore possible to obtain cements with quite different characteristics from the same proportions of the essential oxides. The chemical analysis of a typical portland cement is given by F. M. Lea and C. H. Desch as follows:

Lime, CaO	64.10%
Silica, SiO_2	22.90%
Alumina, Al_2O_3	4.50%
Iron oxide, Fe_2O_3	3.11%
Magnesia, MgO	0.79%
Rutile, TiO_2	0.24%
Sodium oxide, Na_2O	0.54%
Potassium oxide, K_2O	0.64%
Sulphuric anhydride, SO_3	2.37%
Loss on ignition by difference	0.81%

From this analysis it is possible, by certain assumptions, to calculate the probable compound composition in the quaternary system $CaO.Al_2O_3.SiO_2.Fe_2O_3$ as

$4CaO.Al_2O_3.Fe_2O_3$	9.5%	$3CaO.SiO_2$	42.0%
$3CaO.Al_2O_3$	6.7%	$2CaO.SiO_2$	34.0%

The two latter, tricalcium silicate and dicalcium silicate, are the most essential and useful. Their actual identification can be made only by microscopic or X-ray analysis.

Uses of Portland Cement.—The demand for portland cement for use in structural work continues to grow, and, in addition to this, portland cement is being used for an increasing variety of purposes (*see* CONCRETE), which can only be briefly mentioned. Concrete, sometimes reinforced with iron or steel, is being used for all big structural buildings, engineering works, harbours, docks, ships, piers, bridges, piles, general building, artificial stone, roads (both foundation and surface), water towers, natatoria, lakes, etc., and the facility with which the concrete can be placed in any position and the fact that local stone and sand can frequently be used to the extent of 5 to 10 parts to 1 of cement are very important points with regard to cost of labour and carriage, as compared with that of stone. Concrete is also used for smaller articles such as telegraph poles, railway signal posts, sleepers, fencing posts, monuments, tombstones, coffins, troughs of various kinds, tiles, bricks, pipes (spun and moulded), paving blocks, manhole covers, etc. Very considerable developments have also been made in the use of cement for ornamental work, including not only that required for buildings, but sculptural work of all description, both large and small; and by the introduction of various aggregates, excellent substitutes for different ornamental stones have been made, frequently having improved weathering properties. Portland cement is particularly useful where there is much repetition of ornamental work; *e.g.*, for the capitals of pillars, tracery, etc. In the case of stone each piece must be carved separately, whereas a few moulds will be sufficient for a large number of blocks of cement concrete.

Theory of Setting.—The reason for the setting and hardening of portland cement continues to afford abundance of scope for fascinating research work. The comparatively simple ternary system of the lime-silica-alumina group becomes very complicated through thermal changes which are very dependent on the temperature from which the clinker is cooled, and also on the rate of cooling. Moreover, the balance of solution of the various constituents is modified by the different impurities included in the clinker. In addition to this there is some evidence that the constituents of the cement itself tend to acquire a more stable condition on storage. The investigation of the setting and hardening of cement is still more difficult. The simple hydration theory of earlier days has, on closer investigation, resolved itself into an extremely complex system which includes an infinite number of partially hydrated compounds, together with the formation of new compounds. A large amount of research work has been carried out on fairly pure preparations of the various silicates and aluminates of lime with good results; but their value is restricted because very different and complex action takes place when they are mixed, which accounts for the widely differing results obtained by the most recent research. Some of the above compounds have helped in the identification of some of the constituents in set cement (*e.g.*, small hexagonal plate crystals of tricalcium aluminate, fine needle crystals of monocalcium silicate, colloidal masses of monocalcium silicate, large hexagonal crystals of calcium hydrate, etc.), and apparently the colloidal monocalcium silicate plays a large part in the hardening of the cement. Thus the two schools of theorists—the crystalline and colloidal—are being brought together. Although no final conclusions have been reached, the general results of these investigations have been valuable and have resulted in a very marked improvement in the quality of portland cement.

OTHER CEMENTS

Rapid-Hardening Cements.—The demand for speed in construction during recent years has resulted in the development of the aluminous type cements—those high in alumina. They differ from portland cements in the proportions of lime, silica, and alumina; the lime varying from 36.5% to 44%, the silica from 4.5% to 9.5%, and the alumina from 36.5% to 44%. Since impure bauxite is the source of the alumina there is usually a considerable percentage of iron present as Fe_2O_3, sometimes as much as 14%. Such cements develop tensile strengths in 1:3 mortar briquettes of more than 500 p.s.i. in one day, or as much as ordinary portland cement briquettes in 28 days. Concrete made with these cements is more resistant to the action of sea water and sulphate waters than that made with ordinary portland cement. It also has refractory properties. It hydrates with the release of much more heat than portland cement, and for that reason is not suitable for mass concrete under ordinary conditions. It has been used quite successfully for winter concrete construction because its heat of hydration delays freezing and because it hardens so rapidly. Aluminous cements, like portland cement, are made in rotary kilns and also in electric furnaces. The melting or slagging in the formation of the clinker is carried farther than in the manufacture of portland cement, and it costs much more to produce.

The success of aluminous cements led to development of portland cements that also harden rapidly—known in the United States, where most of this development has taken place, as high early strength portland cements. With these it is possible to obtain one-day strengths comparable to those of aluminous cements. They differ from standard portland cement in having a higher tricalcium silicate ($3CaO.SiO_2$) content and are usually more finely ground. They also develop more heat of hydration than desirable for mass concrete.

Low-Heat Cements.—To avoid so far as possible cracks in great masses of concrete, which are caused by temperature changes during the hardening and curing period, a low heat of hydration portland cement has been developed. It was first used on a large scale for the construction of the Hoover dam on the Colorado river by the U.S. bureau of reclamation. These low-heat cements are characterized by high percentages of dicalcium silicate ($2Ca.SiO_2$) and tetracalcium alumino ferrite ($4CaO.Al_2O_3.Fe_2O_3$) and low percentages of tricalcium silicate ($3Ca.SiO_2$) and tricalcium aluminate ($3CaO.Al_2O_3$). While the actual criterion is low heat of hydration, which can be accurately determined by a special type of calorimeter, specifications used by the United States government aim to secure the desired quality through chemical limitations, which require a high percentage of silica, low lime and both alumina and iron oxide low or present in such prescribed ratios that the calculated $3CaO.Al_2O_3$ shall be low (6% to 8%).

For similar massive concrete structures a modified portland cement has been developed and is extensively used by the United States government. The compound composition of modified cement is characterized by low tricalcium aluminate ($3CaO.Al_2O_3$) and high tetracalcium alumino ferrite ($4CaO.Al_2O_3.Fe_2O_3$) with the percentages of tricalcium silicate ($3Ca.SiO_2$) and dicalcium silicate ($2CaO.SiO_2$) approximately the same as in standard portland cement. The hydration of tricalcium aluminate is the cause of most of the undesired heat and the object is to combine the alumina in the less active tetracalcium alumino ferrite, although it is known that this component has little value as a cementing material.

Sulphate-Resisting Cements.—For concrete structures in regions exposed to alkali soils and waters it has been found that ordinary portland cements often proved unsatisfactory. Two types of cement have been developed to provide more resistant concrete. A portland cement designed for this purpose is unusually high in tricalcium silicate ($3CaO.SiO_2$) and dicalcium silicate ($2CaO.SiO_2$) and unusually low in tricalcium aluminate ($3CaO.Al_2O_3$) and tetracalcium alumino ferrite ($4CaO.Al_2O_3.Fe_2O_3$), the sum of these two being less than for any other type of cement. It is difficult to manufacture because it is low in fluxing agents (alumina and iron). The second type of cement designed for sulphate resistance is portland-pozzolana. In the manufacture of these, portland cement and a pozzolana, natural or artificial, are intimately mixed or ground together. A pozzolana is defined as a siliceous material which will react with lime in the presence of water at ordinary temperatures. Obviously, there are various degrees of pozzolanic activity. This type of cement has been much more extensively made and used in Europe than in the United States.

A comparison of the compound compositions of these cements (omitting the portland-pozzolana) is given in the following table (from the *Concrete Manual*, U.S. bureau of reclamation), in which tricalcium silicate ($3CaO.SiO_2$) is designated, as is common in cement literature, as C_3S; dicalcium silicate ($2CaO.SiO_2$) as C_2S; tricalcium aluminate ($3CaO.Al_2O_3$) as C_3A; tetracalcium alumino ferrite ($4CaO.Al_2O_3.Fe_2O_3$) as C_4AF:

Type of Cement		Compound Composition (Percentages)							Ignition loss
		C_3S	C_2S	C_3A	C_4AF	$CaSO_4$	Free CaO	MgO	
High early strength portland	Max.	70	38	17	10	4.6	4.2	4.8	2.7
	Min.	34	0	7	6	2.2	0.1	1.0	1.1
	Average	56	15	12	8	3.9	1.3	2.6	1.9
Standard portland	Max.	54	43	14	10	3.3	1.5	3.8	2.3
	Min.	29	22	9	6	2.2	0.0	0.7	0.6
	Average	43	31	12	8	2.8	0.8	2.4	1.2
Modified portland	Max.	50	46	9	18	3.3	1.8	4.4	2.0
	Min.	29	22	3	10	1.9	0.1	1.5	0.5
	Average	43	30	6	13	2.9	0.6	3.0	1.0
Sulphate-resisting portland	Max.	55	49	6	9	3.1	0.6	2.3	1.2
	Min.	35	27	4	5	2.7	0.1	0.7	0.8
	Average	43	40	5	7	2.9	0.4	1.6	1.0
Low-heat portland	Max.	33	61	8	18	4.0	0.9	4.1	1.9
	Min.	10	41	3	6	2.5	0.0	1.0	0.0
	Average	21	51	6	14	3.2	0.3	2.7	1.1

White Cements.—White portland cements are of approximately the same composition as standard portland cements except that the iron oxide content is very low, and special care must be taken in processing to avoid contamination which would discolour the product. Cryolite and fluorspar are frequently used as fluxing agents. Suitable raw materials are quite scarce.

Portland Blast-Furnace Cement.—A type of cement made largely in Germany (Eisenportland) is a mixture of portland cement clinker and granulated slag ground to the required fineness. It is a pozzolana cement, as understood in the United States. A similar cement, although not a true portland, is made of a mixture of hydrated lime and granulated slag.

Masonry Cements.—A great variety of cements for brick and stone masonry have been developed to overcome the harsh-working handicap of ordinary portland cement mortars. They consist of mixtures of portland cement with one or more of the following: hydrated lime, granulated slag, pulverized limestone, colloidal clay, diatomaceous earth or other finely divided form of silica, calcium stearate, paraffin, etc. The various ingredients and their proportions are often kept secret or are patented and they are frequently described as patent mortar cements.

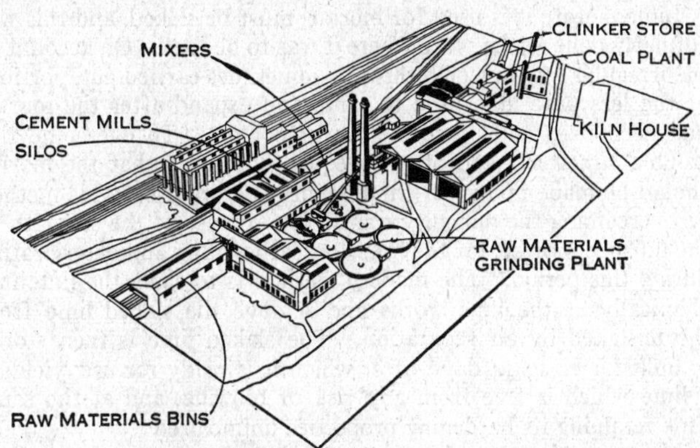

FIG. 2.—DIAGRAM OF LAYOUT OF A WET PROCESS CEMENT PLANT
The raw materials are ground to a slurry which is then pumped into the mixers and from there to the rotating kiln. In passing through the kiln it becomes dried, then decarbonated and finally, in the burning zone, clinkered. The white hot clinker passes through coolers, heating the air for the kilns, and when cool, is ground in tube mills

Natural Cements.—In the United States the rapid development of the portland cement industry was caused in large measure by discovery of large deposits of natural cement rock. The Lehigh valley is a notable example. These argillaceous limestones contain the necessary minerals for portland cement manufacture in approximately the correct proportions. Later refinements in manufacture have made it necessary in some cases to add to the mix small quantities of higher grade limestones or to concentrate the calcium carbonate in the original stone by flotation. For many years cements made from these limestones in vertical shaft kilns, like lime, were used, and are still used to some extent, as natural cements, without attempting to simulate portland cement.

Lime Cements.—These include various grades, from the pure "fat" white lime through the gray limes to the hydraulic limes which have already been referred to under portland cement. White lime consists of oxide of calcium, or, in its slaked form, hydrate of calcium. It is prepared by calcining calcium carbonate (chalk or limestone) until all the carbonic anhydride has been driven off and only the oxide is left. This oxide (quicklime) has great affinity for water, with which it combines readily, forming calcium hydrate, or slaked lime. This action is exothermic (*i.e.*, gives out heat) and is very vigorous unless it is properly controlled. The dry slaked lime occupies two or three times the volume of the original quicklime, according to the method by which it is slaked. Gray lime is an impure form of white lime, and according to the quantity and nature of the impurities, its properties vary between white lime and hydraulic lime. The latter differs from white or gray lime in that, owing to the amount of argillaceous material contained in it, the lime slakes comparatively slowly, and when used for making mortar is capable of hardening under water.

Lime, probably on account of its long history, is frequently made in the simplest form of kiln, the bottle kiln, which is extremely extravagant with both coal and labour, particularly if white lime is being produced as this must be kept free from the ash of the fuel. Various other kilns, such as those described under portland cement, are also used, but the rotary kiln is in very general use for limestone burning, fired either with producer gas or with pulverized coal, and lime is obtained from this kiln with great economy of labour and fuel provided the raw material is sufficiently pure. Another great advantage of this kiln is that it will take "smalls"; *i.e.*, material which is so small that it would choke a stationary kiln, and therefore has to be rejected. On the other hand a rotary kiln is not suitable for burning large lumps of chalk or limestone, and as there is a certain demand for large lumps of lime (probably because of the uncertain quality of the fine stuff in the earlier days), it is still necessary to use fixed kilns if this demand is to be met.

Lime, before it is used for mortar, must be slaked, and this was formerly done at the place where it was to be used. On account of the irregular way in which this was sometimes carried out, portions of the less pure lime used to slake and expand after the mortar had been used and cause the work to blow. To overcome this trouble, architects and others frequently specify that the mortar should be made up two or three months before use. This method of overcoming the difficulty was at the expense of the strength of the finished mortar, for the lime was carbonating and deteriorating during this period. The modern method is to slake the lime mechanically at the lime works and remove the slaked lime from the unslaked by air separation. The slaked lime is then stored in bulk for 10 to 14 days, after which it is ready for use, yielding a lime which is free from any risk of blowing, and at the same time retaining its hardening properties unimpaired.

Mortar made from white lime and the purer forms of gray lime works very easily under the trowel, and if necessary, can be floated off to a very smooth surface for facing walls, etc., and on account of this property the white lime is frequently spoken of as "fat" lime because it is supposed to suggest the smoothness of butter. Experiments have been made to improve the lime for mortar purposes, etc., by the addition of various substances to the water used for slaking, or to the slaked lime.

The setting of white lime and gray lime is largely due to drying out, and to a small extent calcium hydrate recrystallization. The hardening appears to be almost entirely due to the lime combining with the carbon dioxide in the air and forming calcium carbonate, although this is sometimes assisted by a slight pozzolanic effect of the silica in the sand or other material used with the lime. In hydraulic lime the setting and hardening properties are due to a combination of the above with that of those constituents which are similar to portland cement. For most purposes portland cement has taken the place of hydraulic lime; but there are still certain conditions where the latter is preferable to the former, particularly for embedding large steel sections, where the hardening effect should not take place until the steel has finally settled into position.

Selenitic Cement.—The addition of 5% to 10% of plaster of Paris to lime increases the hardening properties of the latter by 50% to 100%, and this mixture is sometimes known as selenitic cement.

Pozzolanic Cement.—Lime, in the presence of water, readily combines with silica in the active state and forms a calcium silicate similar to that in portland cement. Various natural and artificial materials, such as pozzolana, trass, kieselguhr, pumice, tufa, santorin earth, granulated slag, etc., contain active silica, and where the cost is low they make a useful addition to lime mortar. To obtain the best effect the granulated slag, or other material, should be ground with the lime until both materials are in a fine state of division and intimately mixed.

When properly made, pozzolanic cements will attain a strength approaching that of portland cement; but frequently the material is simply mixed with the lime, and the bulk of the pozzolanic material acts as an aggregate instead of an active constituent of the cement.

Calcium Sulphate Cements.—This class includes all those cements which primarily depend on the hydration of calcium sulphate for their setting and hardening properties and includes plaster of Paris, Keene's cement, Parian cement, etc. The raw material is gypsum (*q.v.*), which may be almost chemically pure, in which case it is suitable for Keene's cement and other special brands, or may contain a small quantity of foreign matter, when it is suitable for ordinary plaster of Paris. The mode of preparation is to calcine the gypsum at a comparatively low temperature, viz., about 205° C. for plaster of Paris, at which temperature the gypsum loses three-fourths of its combined water, and at about 500° C. for the Keene's cement class, when the whole of the combined water is driven off. At a higher temperature the gypsum becomes "dead burned" and will then only hydrate very slowly, or in some cases not at all. The gypsum for plaster of Paris is usually calcined either in ovens or in kettles, and for Keene's cement in kilns, where the ash of the fuel can be kept away from the finished product. These methods are inferior in economy to the rotary kiln, and this type of kiln will probably be the method of the future as, if fired with producer gas, the product is not contaminated with ash. The setting of plaster of Paris depends on the fact that when $2CaSO_4.H_2O$ is treated with water it dissolves, forming a super-saturated solution of $CaSO_4.2H_2O$. The excess held temporarily in solution is then deposited in crystals of $CaSO_4.2H_2O$. In the light of this knowledge the mode of setting of plaster of Paris becomes clear. The plaster is mixed with a quantity of water sufficient to make it into a smooth paste; this quantity of water is quite insufficient to dissolve the whole of it, but it dissolves a small part and gives a super-saturated solution of $CaSO_4.2H_2O$. In a few minutes the surplus hydrated calcium sulphate is deposited from the solution and the water is capable again of dissolving $2CaSO_4.H_2O$, which in turn is fully hydrated and deposited as $CaSO_4.2H_2O$. The process goes on until a relatively small quantity of water has by instalments dissolved and hydrated the $2CaSO_4.H_2O$, and has deposited $CaSO_4.H_2O$ in felted crystals forming a solid mass well cemented together. The setting is rapid, occupying only a few minutes, and is accompanied by a considerable expansion of the mass. There is reason to suppose that the change described takes place in two stages, the gypsum first forming orthorhombic crystals and then crystallizing in the monosymmetric system. Gypsum thus crystallized in its normal monosymmetric form is more stable under ordinary conditions than the orthorhombic form. Correlatively, in its process of dehydration to form plaster of Paris, monosymmetric gypsum is converted into the orthorhombic form before it begins to be dehydrated.

The essential difference between the setting of Keene's cement and that of plaster of Paris is that the former takes place much more slowly, occupying hours instead of minutes, and the considerable heating and expansion which characterize the setting of plaster of Paris are much less marked.

It is the practice in Great Britain to burn pure gypsum at a low temperature so as to convert it into the hydrate $2CaSO_4.H_2O$, to soak the lumps in a solution of alum or of aluminium sulphate, and to recalcine them at about 500° C. Instead of alum various other salts—borax, cream of tartar, potassium carbonate, etc.—may be used. On grinding the recalcined lumps they give Keene's cement, Parian cement, Keating's cement, etc. The quantity of these materials is so small that analyses of Keene's cement show it to be almost pure anhydrous calcium sulphate and make it difficult to explain what, if any, influence these minute amounts of alum and the like can exert on the setting of the cement.

These cements form excellent decorative plasters on account of their clean white colour and the sharpness of the castings made from them, this latter quality being due to their expansion when setting. Keene's cement is especially adaptable for surfaces where a hard polished finish is required. All cements having calcium sulphate as their base are suitable only for indoor work because of their solubility in water.

Oxychloride Cements.—In 1853 Sorel discovered that zinc chloride solution, when mixed with zinc oxide, formed a very hard cement, and later he found that magnesium chloride, magnesia and various other metallic oxides and chlorides did the same, an oxychloride being formed in each case. Of these the most important is the magnesia oxychloride, commonly known as Sorel cement, and on account of its great strength and unusual binding properties it is used for such widely different purposes as uniting carborundum for grindstones, where great strength and rigidity are required, and binding wood sawdust together to form monolithic floors which have a certain amount of spring in them. It is also used for making artificial marble and other ornamental stone, and if cast on glass which has been waxed to prevent adhesion the material, on removal of the glass, will have a highly glazed surface.

The magnesia, which should be freshly calcined and ground, is mixed with several times its volume of carborundum, wood sawdust, sand or other material, and is then moistened with a solution of magnesium chloride having a density of 25°–30° Baume, and thoroughly mixed so that each grain of material is covered with the magnesia oxychloride. The plastic mass is then put into moulds, or placed in position and floated off.

The speed of setting and hardening is dependent on the freshness of the magnesia and the strength of the solution of the magnesium chloride, and when the right strength has been found for any particular batch of materials this should be rigidly adhered to for the work.

Adhesive Cements.—Mixtures of animal, mineral and vegetable substances are employed in great variety in the arts for making joints, mending broken china, etc. A strong cement for alabaster and marble, which sets in a day, may be prepared by mixing 12 parts of portland cement, 8 of fine sand and 1 of infusorial earth, and making them into a thick paste with silicate of soda; the object to be cemented need not be heated. Casein, with some solvent, usually an alkali, forms the basis of many waterproof cements and cold-water glues. For stone, marble and earthenware a strong cement, insoluble in water, can be made as follows: skimmed-milk cheese is boiled in water till of a gluey consistency, washed, kneaded well in cold water, and incorporated with quicklime; the composition is warmed for use. A similar cement is a mixture of dried fresh curd with one-tenth of its weight of quicklime and a little camphor; it is made into a paste with water when employed. A cement for Derbyshire spar and china, etc., is composed of 7 parts of rosin and 1 of wax, with a little plaster of Paris; a small quantity only should be applied to the surfaces to be united, for, as a general rule, the thinner the stratum of cement the more powerful its action. Quicklime mixed with white of egg, hardened Canada balsam, and thick copal or mastic varnish are also used for cementing broken china, which should be warmed before their application. For small articles, shellac dissolved in spirits of wine is a very convenient cement.

Cements such as marine glue are solutions of shellac, India rubber, or asphaltum in benzine or naphtha. For use with wood which is exposed to moisture, as in the case of wooden cisterns, a mixture may be made of 4 parts of linseed oil, boiled with litharge, and 8 parts of melted glue; other strong cements for the same purpose are prepared by softening gelatine in cold water and dissolving it by heat in linseed oil, or by mixing glue with one-fourth of its weight of turpentine, or with a little bichromate of potash. Mahogany cement, for filling up cracks in wood, consists of 4 parts of beeswax, 1 of Indian red, and yellow ochre to give colour. Cutler's cement, used for fixing knife blades in their hafts, is made of equal parts of brick dust and rosin, melted, or of 4 parts of rosin with 1 each of beeswax and brick dust. For covering bottle corks a mixture of pitch, brick dust and rosin is employed. A cheap cement, sometimes used to fix iron rails in stonework, is melted brimstone, or brimstone and brick dust. For pipe-joints a mixture of iron turnings, sulphur and sal ammoniac, moistened with water, is employed. Japanese cement, for uniting surfaces of paper, is made by mixing rice flour with water and boiling it. Jewellers' or Armenian cement consists of isinglass with mastic and gum ammoniac dissolved in spirit. Gold and silver chasers keep their work firm by means of a cement of pitch and rosin, a little tallow and brick dust to thicken. Temporary cement, for lathe work, such as the polishing and grinding of jewellery and optical glasses, is compounded thus: rosin, 4 oz., whitening previously made red hot, 4 oz., wax, ¼ oz.

Bibliography.—F. M. Lea and C. H. Desch, *The Chemistry of Cement and Concrete* (1935); D. B. Butler, *Portland Cement*, 3rd ed. (1913); B. Blount, W. H. Woodcock and H. J. Gillett, *Cement* (1920); E. A. Dancaster, *Limes and Cements*, 2nd ed. (1920); E. C. Eckel, *Cements, Limes and Plasters*, 3rd ed. (1928); A. C. Davis, *Portland Cement* (1934), *A Hundred Years of Portland Cement* (1924); G. R. Redgrave and C. Spackman, *Calcareous Cements*, 3rd ed. (1924); R. W. Lesley, J. B. Loker and G. S. Bartlett, *History of Portland Cement in the United States* (1925); R. W. Meade, *Portland Cement* (1938); H. L. Childe, *Manufacture and Uses of Concrete Products and Cast Stone* (1927); Cement Marketing Co., *Everyday Uses of Cement*, 4th ed. (London, 1921; rev. ed., 1928). See also *Concrete and Constructional Engineering* (London); *Rock Products, Cement and Engineering News; Le Ciment* (Paris); and various publications of the Building Research Station, London; the Mineral Industry, New York; the National Bureau of Standards, Washington, D.C.

(W. H. Wo.; N. C. R.)

CEMENTATION, a metallurgical term which describes processes by which one substance is, by exposure to great heat in a furnace, caused to interpenetrate and change the character of another. Although a high temperature is employed, the process is not one of melting materials together, but of combining them through contact at a temperature which is below their melting points. Thus, in the manufacture of blister steel by cementation, a rod of iron becomes steel because exposed at a temperature of about 1,000° C. to carbon which penetrates its substance. (*See* Blister Steel; Iron and Steel.)

CEMENT ROCK. A cement rock is an argillaceous (clayey) limestone whose composition is such that it may be used for the manufacture of cement without the addition of other earth materials or with the addition of only relatively small amounts of such materials. Some cement rocks contain the mineral quartz as silt or sand particles along with their argillaceous component. The principal carbonate in cement rocks employed for portland cement manufacture is calcium carbonate; magnesium carbonate must be low, in accordance with the usual specifications for Portland cement raw materials. High-calcium limestone, clay or shale may be blended with the cement rock to modify its composition. Rock used for making natural cement, sometimes referred to as a natural-cement rock, is of similar character to that mentioned above but the allowable amount of magnesium carbonate is flexible. Both dolomitic and calcitic argillaceous limestones have been used as natural-cement rocks.

Bibliography.—W. M. Myers, *Industrial Minerals and Rocks*, 2nd ed. (1949); R. H. Bogue, *The Chemistry of Portland Cement* (1947); Edwin C. Eckel, *Cements, Limes and Plasters* (1928). (J. E. Lr.)

CEMETERY, literally a sleeping place, the name applied by the early Christians to the places set apart for the burial of their dead. These were generally extramural and unconnected with churches, the practice of interment in churches or churchyards being unknown in the first centuries of the Christian era. The term cemetery has, therefore, been appropriately applied in modern times to the burial grounds, generally extramural, which have been substituted for the overcrowded churchyards of populous parishes both urban and rural (*see* Burial).

From 1840 to 1855 attention was repeatedly called to the insanitary condition of the London churchyards by the press and by parliamentary committees, the first of which reported in 1843. The vaults under the pavements of the churches and the small spaces of open ground surrounding them were crammed with coffins. In many of the buildings the air was so tainted with the products of corruption as to be a direct and palpable source of disease and death to those who frequented them.

In the churchyards coffins were placed tier above tier in the graves until they were within a few feet (or sometimes even a few inches) of the surface, and the level of the ground was often raised to that of the lower windows of the church.

To make room for fresh interments the sextons had recourse to the surreptitious removal of bones and partially decayed remains, and in some cases the contents of the graves were systematically transferred to pits adjacent to the site, the grave diggers appropriating the coffin-plates, handles and nails to be sold as waste metal.

The neighbourhood of the churchyards was always unhealthy, the air being vitiated by the gaseous emanations from the graves, and the water, wherever it was obtained from wells, containing organic matter, the source of which could not be mistaken.

In all the large towns the evil prevailed in a greater or less degree. In London, however, because of the immense population and the consequent mortality, it forced itself more readily upon public attention; and after more than one partial measure of relief had been passed the churchyards were, with a few exceptions, finally closed by the act of 1855.

The cemeteries, which occupy a large extent of ground north, south, east and west became henceforth the burial-places of the metropolis. Several London cemeteries had been established by private enterprise before the passing of the Burial Act of 1855 (Kensal Green cemetery dates from 1832), but that enactment forms the epoch from which the general development of cemeteries in Great Britain and Ireland began. Burial within the limits of cities and towns is now almost everywhere abolished,

BY COURTESY OF THOMAS F. LEE

COMMUNAL VAULTS, GUATEMALA

In these concrete walls with rows of receptacles for coffins, the remains of the dead are left intact so long as rent is paid. On failure to pay the rent, the bones are removed and buried in a common heap, and the "pigeon hole" is rented again

and where it is still in use it is surrounded by such safeguards as make it practically innocuous. The increasing practice of cremation (*q.v.*) has assisted in the movement for disposing of the dead in more sanitary conditions; and the practice of burying the dead in more open coffins, and abandoning the old system of family graves, has had considerable effect.

In England a cemetery is either the property of a private company incorporated by Act of Parliament or of a local authority and is subject to the Cemeteries Clauses Act 1847, the Public Health Act, 1875 and the Public Health (Interments) Act, 1879. By S. 33 of the Burial Act, 1852, a burial board under such conditions as it thinks proper may sell the exclusive right of burial, either in perpetuity, or for a limited period, in grave spaces; the right of constructing any vault or place of burial with the exclusive right of burial therein in perpetuity, or for a limited period; and also the right of erecting and placing any monument, gravestone, tablet or monumental inscription. By S. 38 the general management, regulation and control of a burial ground is vested in the burial board. Regulations are made by the Minister of Health and Rules may be made by the board. By S. 44 of the Cemeteries Clauses Act 1847 the grant of the right of burial, whether in perpetuity or for a limited time, becomes the personal estate of the grantee. Under such a grant there is implied the right to visit the grave, and to plant shrubs and plants and to keep the surface in order, and if there is a monument, head or curb stones to keep them in repair (see *Ashby* v. *Harris* [1868] L.R. 3 C.P. 523). This case was discussed, but not overruled in *McGough* v. *Lancaster Burial Board* (1888) 21 Q.B. D. 323 where, in consequence of a rule of the board, made prior to the grant, prohibiting the placing of glass shades on graves, it was held that the grant of burial in a grave space to the plaintiff did not include a right to place a glass shade on his grave. Although a burial board cannot sell the freehold of a grave space, the property in a vault, tomb, monument, headstone, curb or any other erection remains in the person who erected them. See *Spooner* v. *Brewster* (1825) 3 Bing. 136 and *Sims* v. *The London Necropolis Co.* (1885) 1 T.L.R. 584; but *see* also *Hoskyns Abrahall* v. *Paignton U.D.C.* (1928) 2 Ch. (*See* J. B. Little, *Law of Burial*, 1902.)

UNITED STATES

In the United States cemeteries were the final outgrowth of individual burial places on the farms or near the homes of the earliest settlers. Later the burial place was connected with the church, which custom is not entirely obsolete. Prominent men were buried beneath the church building for a long time during the 17th and 18th centuries, but the crowded conditions together with the fact that the practice was recognized as unsanitary caused it to be abandoned. In villages and small towns the church "graveyards" grew into disrepute many years ago because of the neglect they were subjected to. There was no provision for care of such burial places, except the slight attention a sexton would give, and disorder resulted. Detached cemeteries have been in use in the United States since 1831 when Mt. Auburn was established in Boston. Philadelphia soon after set up some notable large burial places and Greenwood in New York had its beginning in 1840. From 1860 churchyard burials have gradually been discontinued until to-day they are but exceptions to the rule of beautiful community cemeteries. From single burial plots on private property, to church graveyards, to cemeteries and now to "memorial parks" has been a notable transition.

During the days when cemeteries were maintained by and in connection with the church, members and their families were entitled to a burial site. No expense was attached to the burial except the cost of opening the grave. No funds were available for upkeep which accounts for the deterioration of the property, and the ultimate abandoning of that type. In the cemeteries of to-day lots are sold by the city or village, if owned by such a body, or by the association, which has charge. A definite fee is charged for perpetual care and a charge is made for opening the grave and

BY COURTESY OF THE PORTLAND CEMENT ASSOCIATION

ENTRANCE TO VALHALLA MEMORIAL PARK IN BURBANK, CALIFORNIA

other duties performed by the sexton or superintendent. Generally speaking cemeteries are supposed to be maintained with no idea of profit, and that holds good in a great majority of places.

Some churches have their own cemeteries, though not in connection with the church, notably the Catholic church. The Jews have many beautiful burial sites, and now and then one comes across a cemetery maintained by one or another of the Protestant societies. Throughout the country there are many beautiful cemeteries maintained by the Masonic or other fraternities for their own members and members of their families. There are many

PHOTOGRAPHS, (1, 4) PUBLISHERS PHOTO SERVICE, (2, 6) UNDERWOOD AND UNDERWOOD, (3, 5) BURTON HOLMES FROM EWING GALLOWAY

CEMETERIES IN THE EAST AND WEST

1. Palestine, Jewish cemetery in the Garden of Gethsemane, valley of Jehoshaphat, showing tombs of S. James, Absalom and Zachariah in the foreground
2. Amphitheatre at Arlington National Cemetery, Washington, D.C., showing soldiers' graves in the background
3. Cemetery in Matsue, Japan
4. Indian graves in southern Chile
5. Talma's tomb in the Père Lachaise cemetery, Paris
6. Graveyard of the Ages, in Canton, southern China

State and national cemeteries in the United States provided by statute, given over to the burial of departed army and navy men, and men connected with State institutions, usually attached to soldiers' homes or army posts.

CENACLE, the term applied to the eating-room of a Roman house in which the supper (*cena*) or latest meal was taken. It was sometimes placed in an upper storey. The Last Supper in the New Testament was taken in the cenacle, in the "large upper room" cited in St. Mark (xiv. 15) and St. Luke (xxii. 12).

CENCI, BEATRICE (chĕn′chē) (1577–1599), a Roman woman, famous for her tragic history, was born on Feb. 6, 1577, in the Cenci palace in Rome. She was the daughter, by his first wife, of Francesco Cenci (1549–1598), a vicious man of great wealth. He was tried in 1594 for sodomy, but was released on payment of a fine of 100,000 scudi. Cenci had 12 children by his first wife; his second wife, Lucrezia Petroni, a widow with three daughters, brought him no children. He was embroiled with his sons and after the trial he decided to remove his wife Lucrezia, with Beatrice, to La Petrella, a lonely castle on the road to Naples which he obtained from Marzio Colonna. There in 1595 he shut up his wife and daughter in the upper rooms of the castle, and there he visited them from time to time treating them, especially Beatrice, with great brutality. There is no evidence for the charge of attempted incest with his daughter, but the details of life at La Petrella, as given in the subsequent trial, were revolting, and might well have given colour to the accusation. Beatrice seems to have found refuge in a liaison with the keeper of the castle, Olimpio Calvetti. At intervals the two younger Cenci children, Bernardo and Paolo, visited La Petrella. Olimpio was expelled by Colonna from the castle at the demand of Francesco Cenci, who does not, however, seem to have known of his relations with Beatrice. At length, Beatrice, with her stepmother and with her brother Giacomo and Bernardo, decided to secure the murder of their father. He was killed in his bed (Sept. 9, 1598) by Olimpio and a hired assassin named Marzio.

Information having been communicated to Rome, the whole of the Cenci family were arrested early in 1599. Lucrezia, Giacomo and Bernardo confessed the crime; and Beatrice, who at first denied everything, even under torture, also ended by confessing. Great efforts were made to obtain mercy for the accused, but the pope (Clement VIII.) refused to grant a pardon; on Sept. 11, 1599, Beatrice and Lucrezia were beheaded, and Giacomo, after having been tortured with red-hot pincers, was killed with a mace, drawn and quartered. Bernardo's penalty, on account of his youth, was commuted to perpetual imprisonment, and after a year's confinement he was pardoned. The property of the family was confiscated. There is a study by Guido Reni or Guercino in the Palazzo Barberini said to represent Beatrice, but it is unlikely that Reni saw her.

The history of the Cenci family has been the subject of poems, dramas and novels. Shelley found in it material for his great tragedy. The most famous of the novels is F. D. Guerrazzi's *Beatrice Cenci* (Milan, 1872). The first attempt to deal with the subject on documentary evidence is A. Bertolotti's *Francesco Cenci e la sua famiglia* (2nd ed., Florence, 1879), containing a number of interesting documents which place the events in their true light; *cf.* Labruzzi's article in the *Nuova Antologia,* 1879, vol. xiv., and another in the *Edinburgh Review,* Jan. 1879. *See* also C. Ricci, *Beatrice Cenci,* 2 vols. (1923), where new documents and new information are to be found.

CENOBITES, monks who lived together in a convent or community under a rule and a superior—in contrast to hermits or anchorets who live in isolation (from Gr. κοινός, *common,* and βίος, *life*). *See* MONASTICISM.

CENOMANI (Kĕn-ŏ-mah′nē), a branch of the Aulerci in Gallia Celtica, whose territory corresponded generally to Maine (department of Sarthe). Their chief town was Vindinum, afterwards Civitas Cenomanorum (whence Le Mans). They assisted Vercingetorix in the great rising (52 B.C.) with a force of 5,000 men. Under Augustus they formed a *civitas stipendiaria* (tributary community) of Gallia Lugdunensis. About 400 B.C., under the leadership of Elitovius (Livy v. 35), a large number of the Cenomani crossed into Italy, drove the Etruscans southwards, and occupied their territory. The limits of their territory are not clearly defined, but were probably the Adige on the east, the Addua on the west and the Padus (Po) on the south. Their chief towns were Brixia (Brescia) and Verona. They assisted the Romans in the Gallic war (225 B.C.), when the Boii and Insubres took up arms against Rome, and during the war against Hannibal. They joined in the revolt of the Gauls under Hamilcar (200), but after they had been defeated by the consul Gaius Cornelius (197) they finally submitted. In 49 B.C., with the rest of Gallia Transpadana, they acquired the rights of citizenship.

BIBLIOGRAPHY.—A. Desjardins, *Géographie historique de la Gaule romaine,* ii. (1876–93); Arbois de Jubainville, *Les Premiers Habitants de l'Europe* (1889–94); article and authorities in *La Grande Encyclopédie;* C. Hülsen in Pauly-Wissowa's *Realencyklopädie,* iii. pt. 2 (1899); full ancient authorities in A. Holder, *Alt-celtischer Sprachschatz,* i. (1896).

CENOTAPH, a monument or tablet to the memory of a person whose body is buried elsewhere (Gr. κενός, empty, τάφος tomb). The custom arose from the erection of monuments to those whose bodies could not be recovered, as in the case of drowning. The term is often used of the monuments raised in many places in memory of those who perished on the field in the World War, especially of the cenotaph in Whitehall, London, the scene of an annual memorial service on the anniversary of Armistice Day (*q.v.*).

CENSOR. I. *In ancient Rome,* the title of the two Roman officials who presided over the census (from Lat. *censere,* assess, estimate), the registration of individual citizens for the purpose of determining the duties which they owed to the community. This idea of "discretionary power" was never entirely lost; although it came to be intimately associated with the appreciation of morals. The censorship was the Roman manifestation of the state control of conduct.

The office was instituted in 443 B.C. to relieve the consuls of the duties of registration. The election always took place in the *Comitia Centuriata* (*see* COMITIA). The censorship, although lacking the imperium, was one of the higher magistracies, and was regarded as the crown of a political career. It was an irresponsible office; and the only limitations on its powers were the restriction of tenure to a year and a half, and the restraint imposed on each censor by the fact that no act of his was valid without the assent of his colleague.

The original functions of the censors were (1) the registration of citizens in the state-divisions, such as tribes and centuries; (2) the taxation of such citizens based on an estimate of their property; (3) the right of exclusion from public functions on moral grounds, known as the *regimen morum;* (4) the solemn act of purification (*lustrum*) which closed the census. Two other functions were subsequently added: (5) the selection of the senate (*lectio senatus, see* SENATE), and (6) certain financial duties such as the leasing of the contracts for tax-collecting and for the repair of public buildings. The census involved a detailed examination of the citizen body as represented by the heads of families. In connection with this review the censors published their edicts stating the moral rules they intended to enforce. Disqualification might be the result of offences in private relations or in public life. Certain kinds of employment (*e.g.,* acting) caused a stigma. *Infamia,* the general name for the penalties inflicted by the censors, varied in degree. A senator might lose his seat, a citizen his place in tribe and century, and so his vote. All disabilities inflicted by one pair of censors might be removed by their successors.

The censorship lasted as long as the republic; and it was only suspended, not abolished, during the principate. Although the *princeps* exercised censorial functions he was seldom censor. Yet the office itself was held by Claudius and Vespasian. Domitian assumed the title of life censor, but he was not followed.

BIBLIOGRAPHY.—Mommsen, *Römisches Staatsrecht* (1887), ii., 331, *et seq.;* A. H. J. Greenidge, *Roman Public Life* (1901); J. E. Sandys, *Companion to Latin Studies* (1921), with useful bibliography; W. E. Heitland, *Roman Republic* (1923).

II. In modern times the word "censor" is used generally for one who exercises supervision over the conduct of other persons. In the Universities of Oxford and Cambridge it is the title of the supervisor of those students who are not attached to a college, hall or hostel. In Oxford the censor is nominated by the vice-chancellor and the proctors, and holds office for five years; in Cambridge he is similarly appointed, and holds office for life. The censors of the Royal College of Physicians are the officials who grant licences.

Council of Censors, in American constitutional history, was the name given to a council provided by the constitution of Pennsylvania from 1776 to 1790, and by the constitution of Vermont from 1777 to 1870. Under both constitutions the council of censors was elected once in seven years, for the purpose of enquiring into the working of the governmental departments, the conduct of the state officers, and the working of the laws, and as to whether the constitution had been violated in any particular. The Vermont council of censors, limited in number to thirteen, had power, if they thought the constitution required amending in any particular, to call a convention for the purpose. A convention summoned by the council in 1870 amended the constitution by abolishing the censors.

For the censorship of the press, *see* PRESS LAWS; for the censorship of plays, LORD CHAMBERLAIN.

CENSORINUS, Roman grammarian and writer, flourished during the 3rd century A.D. He was the author of a lost work *De Accentibus* and of an extant treatise *De Die Natali,* written in 238, dedicated to his patron as a birthday gift and dealing with the natural history of man, the influence of the stars and genii, music, religious rites, astronomy and the doctrines of the Greek philosophers. The second part deals with chronological and mathematical questions and has been useful in determining the principal epochs of ancient history. The chief authorities used were Varro and Suetonius. Some scholars hold that the work is practically an adaptation of the lost *Pratum* of Suetonius. The fragments of a work *De Natali Institutione* are not by Censorinus.

The only good edition with commentary is still that of H. Lindenbrog (1614); the most recent critical editions are by O. Jahn (1845), F. Hultsch (1867), and J. Cholodniak (1889). There is an English translation of the *De Die Natali* (the first 11 chapters being omitted), with notes by W. Maude (1900).

CENSORSHIP. The censors in ancient Rome were the magistrates who drew up the register or census of the citizens and had the supervision of public morals (*see* CENSOR). Their functions in numbering the people have given us the English word "census"; and from their other activities the word "censorship" is derived.

Censorship in modern practice may be defined as action taken by the governing authority to examine letters and other communications and also the text of proposed books, stage plays and the like in order to prevent any publication which would be contrary to the public interest or inconvenient or displeasing to that governing authority.

Religious censorship has at times been attempted by several sections of Christianity. The Roman Catholic Church in particular worked out a complete system, *pari passu* with the secular censorships of national states: the *Index Librorum Prohibitorum* (*q.v.*) is published by papal authority as a catalogue of printed publications prohibited to Catholics on doctrinal or moral grounds. In modern times, however, it has been found impossible for the Congregation of the Index to keep pace with the output of the printing presses of the world; but there exist general rules which the particular prohibitions of the Index are intended only to supplement.

GREAT BRITAIN

Press Censorship.—There is a popular idea among Englishmen that the freedom of the press is one of their birthrights and that their ancestors always fought fiercely for it. The statute book, however, shows that this idea is not wholly correct.

From the time of the general introduction of printing, at the end of the 15th century, until the year 1695 there was a rigorous censorship of the press in England; and it was a criminal offense to publish any printed matter without first obtaining a licence to do so. Control was exercised by the Star Chamber and then by ordinances of the Long parliament, till in 1662 parliament passed the Licensing act (for the censorship of the press), which was renewed from time to time.

When the Licensing act was due for a further renewal in 1695, parliament had no intention of abolishing the control of the press. But the licensers (as the press censors were called) had been continually in dispute with the press; and evasions and complaints indicated that the administration of the censorship was defective. The house of commons appointed a select committee to report on ways and means to improve the censorship and to make it more effective. By what appears to have been an entirely fortuitous circumstance, the Licensing act was allowed to lapse before the select committee had reported; and it was never renewed. During World Wars I and II in the 20th century a measure of censorship was necessary for reasons of national security; but otherwise there was no censorship of the press in England after 1695. In Scotland the censorship of the press lingered on until the 18th century; and the Statute for the Licensing of the Press was not formally repealed until 1907. In Ireland also, before the union with Great Britain in 1800, there were Irish acts of parliament for the control of the press; but these were repealed.

In the United Kingdom the press is thus free to publish what it pleases, except that a few modern statutes prohibit the publication of certain particular items, for instance the details of divorce proceedings; and the publication of seditious, blasphemous, obscene or libellous matter is subject to the ordinary consequences of the law.

In the Irish Free State a Censorship of Publications board was set up in 1929, with power to prohibit any publications containing indecent or obscene matter and also any publications advocating birth control; and members of the public are entitled to complain about books or periodicals containing matter which they consider ought to be prohibited. In its report for the year 1947, however, the board said: "The Board noted with surprise and disappointment that a number of complaints concerned books which had been prohibited, sometimes for a long period. These complaints covered books obtained from bookshops in Dublin and elsewhere, and from circulating libraries in various parts of the country. The Board, while being aware of the difficulty of securing a complete enforcement of its decisions, is left in consequence with the uncomfortable feeling that much of its work is at present being done in vain."

Stage Play Censorship.—From its early beginnings in the 16th century the English theatre was placed under royal control; and in spite of many determined attempts to abolish it, the censorship of stage plays continued to survive under the direction of the lord chamberlain, one of the high officers of the royal household, to whom it was first assigned by the Licensing act, 1737.

The present powers of the lord chamberlain are defined by the Theatres act, 1843, and include the power to forbid the acting of any stage play whenever he is of the opinion that "it is fitting for the preservation of good manners, decorum, or of the public peace to do so"; moreover, for the purpose of this censorship, a stage play means any entertainment on the stage of a dramatic character. This statute, which applies to the whole of Great Britain, makes it a criminal offense to act a stage play not submitted to the examiner appointed by the lord chamberlain. Ireland was never regarded as falling within the lord chamberlain's jurisdiction; the drama there has always been regulated by special legislation.

In 1865 a petition was presented by 21 dramatic authors of note for the abolition of the lord chamberlain's censorship, but a select committee of both houses of parliament recommended no change. In 1907, after much intermediate agitation had taken place, 71 authors (including J. M. Barrie, Thomas Hardy, George Bernard Shaw and Algernon Charles Swinburne) joined in a letter to the *Times* (London) and their language did not err on the side of mildness. In consequence another select committee was appointed. Its report, published in 1909, recommended that "it should be optional to submit a play for licence, and legal to perform an unlicensed play whether it had been submitted or not"; but the report was not followed by legislative action. In 1949 a private member's bill for the repeal of the censorship of plays was introduced in the house of commons, and its second reading was carried by 76 votes to 37; it did not however succeed in reaching the statute book.

Pragmatically regarded, the lord chamberlain's censorship may be said on the whole to have justified itself. Playwrights have opposed it strongly because they resent what they consider the examiner's arbitrary interference with the free expression of their art; theatrical managers on the other hand have been strong in their support of it because, without the lord chamberlain's licence, the successful run of an expensively produced play might be jeopardized by the activities of local councils and common informers.

Film Censorship.—The censorship of films is exercised by the British Board of Film Censors, a private body which has no constitutional or statutory authority. The board was set up in 1912 by the film industry itself to regulate the industry's own standards of morals and propriety.

The official influence of the British Board of Film Censors on films shown to the public had its origin in the fact that films are made of highly inflammable material. This led to the passing of the Cinematograph act, 1909, which, in order to ensure the public's safety from fire, made it a criminal offense throughout the United Kingdom to exhibit films to the public except in buildings inspected and licensed by the local county council. It was later established, as the result of various decisions of the high court, that the terms of the statute gave the county council power not only to see that there were adequate means of escape in cases of fire but also to impose all sorts of other conditions, in respect of the licensed buildings, such as the banning of particular films (whether inflammable or not) and the prohibition of Sunday opening; and it became the almost universal practice for the county council's licence to be granted on condition that no film be shown unless it has been certified for public exhibition by the British Board of Film Censors. All these arrangements arose out of the provisions of the Cinematograph act, 1909. The Cinematograph act, 1952, widened the power of film censorship in the United Kingdom and extended it to noninflammable films.

In the republic of Ireland, films are censored by the official censor of films, appointed by the ministry of home affairs.

Television and Broadcasting Censorship.—As stated above, a drama is subject to the censorship of the lord chamberlain if it is acted on the stage and (in effect) to that of the British Board of Film Censors if it is shown in a cinema. The same drama shown on a television screen would not be subject to censorship, except, of course, that television is under the control of the British Broadcasting corporation.

Broadcasting and television in the United Kingdom constitute a government monopoly, for which the postmaster general is responsible to parliament, and the monopoly is operated by the B.B.C. under licence from the postmaster general. This enables the governors of the B.B.C. to censor anything which is broadcast or televised; but the ultimate power (not exercised in peacetime) lies with the postmaster general, who may require the corporation to refrain from sending out any particular item.

Postal and Telegraph Censorship.—Posts and telegraphs in the United Kingdom are a government monopoly; and the crown has the power, recognized and preserved by section 56 of the Post Office act, 1908, to detain and open any postal packet. This power is not exercised in peacetime except to prevent obvious breaches of the law, such as the sending of obscene matter through the post. In wartime it enables the government to impose a complete censorship on all incoming and outgoing mail. The government has similar powers under the Telegraph acts over all forms of telecommunication. (T. S. Pe.)

Wartime Censorship.—In 1544 a royal proclamation of Henry VIII ordered, under pain of imprisonment, that all books containing news of his majesty's army in Scotland should be brought in and burned, doubtless because the published account of the campaign was displeasing to the king. But it was not until the Crimean War that the need was seen for preventing the publication of news because of its value to the enemy. Lord Raglan, the commander of the British forces at Sevastopol, complained that a war correspondent's dispatch, published in the *Times* of Oct. 23, 1854, had given away invaluable details to the Russians; and a circular letter was consequently sent by the war office warning newspaper editors of the danger in publishing dispatches from their correspondents at the front and urging them to expunge such parts of the dispatches "as they might consider calculated to furnish valuable information to the enemy."

No actual British censorship of the press was set up until World War I. But already in 1913 the admiralty and the war office had in anticipation reached an agreement with the press to set up the joint Admiralty, War Office and Press committee; and the press undertook to respect the warnings (or "D. notices" as they were called) issued by the committee and accordingly "to withhold from publication information the exclusion of which from the papers appeared to the department concerned to be desirable in the national interest." On the outbreak of war in 1914 an official press bureau was set up, the functions of which were: (1) to issue official communiqués and thus to supply the press with "a steady stream of trustworthy information" about the war; and (2) to censor the items which the newspapers submitted of their own accord for censorship in fulfilment of the arrangements made between the government and the press.

The censorship of the press was on a voluntary basis throughout; and, as the government had no peacetime powers of control over it, the only sanction which lay behind the censorship was that of the wartime Defence of the Realm regulations, which made it an offense to publish "without lawful authority" any military information or any information directly or indirectly useful to the enemy. Information which had been passed for publication after submission to censorship by the official press bureau was information published with lawful authority; and the imprimatur of the official press bureau accordingly relieved the editor of a newspaper from liability under the Defence of the Realm regulations. Nevertheless the regulations of 1914 created an absolute prohibition on the publication of military information unless it had been passed by the official press bureau; and in 1918 the editor of the *London Morning Post* was prosecuted and convicted for publishing information in contravention of the regulations, although it was proved in his defense that it was already known to the Germans.

On the outbreak of World War II in 1939, defense regulations made similar provisions, subject however to the new and important condition that no person was to be found guilty of a contravention if he proved that the publication was not likely to prejudice the defense of the realm or the efficient prosecution of the war. Not only therefore did the imprimatur of the censorship relieve an editor from liability; but he could, at his own risk, publish also with impunity information stopped by the censorship, if he could later convince a magistrate that the safety of the realm or the efficient prosecution of the war had not been prejudiced. In spite of this freedom and notwithstanding the enormous volume of news published there were between 1939 and 1945 only four prosecutions for infringement of the censorship regulations. Security in these matters rested not on the defense regulations but on the agreement with the press of 1913: under this editors voluntarily undertook to respect the "defense notices" issued by the press censorship division of the ministry of information. Even in wartime the United Kingdom never knew the system adopted in so many other countries, whereby the whole of a book or a newspaper had to be submitted for the government's approval before it was printed.

Broadcasting, Film and Postal Censorship.—World War II was the first war in which news was broadcast and in which there was extensive publication of news by the medium of newsreels in cinemas; and, in the interests of national security, both these means of communicating information were submitted to the same censorship at the ministry of information as that applied to printed matter.

In World War I the "postal censorship" and the "cable censorship" were two branches of the war office; in World War II a separate department, the "postal and telegraph censorship," was set up.

During both world wars the censorship of letters and telecommunications was a vast network designed to defeat the enemy's attempts to extract information from behind the lines: it necessitated a strict examination of any suspect documents which might convey, by the use of codes, ciphers, special inks or any other devices, messages intended for the enemy. As a result many enemy agents were apprehended and channels of communication closed. Communications obtained from enemy agents were in many cases altered so as to convey false information and then allowed to proceed. In addition letters and telegrams destined for countries contiguous to the enemy's were censored if they contained details of air raids or other information likely to be useful, although the senders may not have meant to help the enemy.

In both world wars the censorship of press mail and press telegrams was undertaken by the press censors and not by the postal and telegraph censors. (G. P. T.)

THE UNITED STATES

Preventive censorship, or the examination before publication of some form of communication (book or periodical, theatrical presentation, motion picture or radio broadcast) by an official licensing agency with power to approve, change or suppress the offering, has not been a characteristic American method of controlling the public mind or morals. Freedom of communication has generally been limited by postpublication prosecutions under laws proscribing certain communications as dangerous to public order, public morals or the security of the state. The threat of punishment and at times extraordinary extensions of judicial or administrative prerogatives constitute a punitive censorship that through fear enforces silence or breeds conformity.

Censorship in the American Colonies.—Preventive censorships have existed from colonial days to the present. The first printing press (Cambridge, 1638) was licensed by the Massachusetts theocracy. Religious books were censored until 1695, and after that special manuscripts were submitted to authority. The crown governors acted as licensers, and from 1686 to 1730 were instructed in their charters that "no book, pamphlet or other matter be printed without your especial leave and consent." The first newspaper, *Publick Occurrences Both Forreign and Domestick,* Boston, 1690, was suppressed after one issue. "Published by Authority" appeared on newspapers until about 1725. Since, prepublication censorship has existed only in wartime. The trial of John Peter Zenger, publisher of the *New York Journal,* in 1734, ended one kind of postpublication control by establishing the right of the jury to determine not only the fact of publication, but whether the words constituted a libel. The judge had hitherto claimed this dangerous prerogative. Since 1776 the state constitutions have almost universally guaranteed freedom of the press. In 1791 the 1st amendment to the constitution of the United States declared: "Congress shall make no law . . . abridging the freedom of speech or of the press." This ended all censorship. The courts agreed with the narrow dictum of Blackstone: "The liberty of the press consists in laying no previous restraints upon publications, and not in freedom from censure for criminal matter when published." (*Patterson* v. *Colorado,* 205 United States 454, 1907). But liberals, showing that precensorship had ended by 1730, have claimed that the 1st amendment must also protect free expression against "abridging" by police powers, after publication. After World War I the supreme court set up two great new safeguards of liberty. (1) In 1919 the court declared that the test of punishable words is whether their nature and the circumstances of their use "create a clear and present danger that they will bring about the substantive evils Congress has a right to prevent." (*Schenck* v. *United States,* 249 United States 47). The dangerous and outworn test of some remote "bad tendency" was by-passed. (2) In 1925, and subsequently, the court declared that the liberties of the 1st amendment were secured to the citizen against infringement by the states. The principle that James Madison had failed to get into the Bill of Rights, the justices wrote in: "We may and do assume that freedom of speech and the press are among the fundamental personal rights and liberties protected by the due process clause of the Fourteenth Amendment." (*Gitlow* v. *New York,* 268 United States 652).

Military Censorship.—War has generally re-established some principle of censorship. During the flurry with France in 1798, the Federalist party passed the Sedition act, which provided punishments for publications, oral or printed, that reflected on the government, promoted sedition or resistance to law. About ten persons, chiefly Republican editors, were convicted. The issue defeated the Federalists in 1800, and the law lapsed, without interpretation by the supreme court. Pres. Thomas Jefferson released every person under punishment or prosecution. During the Civil War (1861–65) the postmaster general barred from the mails several Northern periodicals opposed to the war. Certain editors were imprisoned on the mere order of the secretary of state or of war. Newspaper offices in Missouri, Chicago and New York city were actually seized by troops, and issues of papers suppressed. Certain correspondents had to submit articles to the military for approval. Telegraphic dispatches were censored in Washington. In Colorado, 1904, and West Virginia, 1912, state militia under so-called martial law arrested editors, or suppressed and censored labour papers during strikes. In World War I the press established a voluntary censorship. Informal control was exercised through a governmental instrument, the Committee on Public Information. The newspapers, press associations and other organizations co-operated to prevent the disclosure of military or naval information, or matter calculated to weaken public morale. Strict military censorship was applied to news from correspondents with the U.S. forces abroad. Foreign language periodicals in the United States were regulated by the Trading with the Enemy act (United States Compiled Statutes, 1918, 3,115½ j.) and had to file English translations. The department of justice declared, however, that the constitutional right of free speech existed in war as in peace.

In World War II the army and navy enforced compulsory censorship in areas under their control. The press criticized some rulings as unreasonable or discriminatory. On Dec. 19, 1941, Pres. Franklin D. Roosevelt (under the First War Powers act) established the Office of Censorship, with Byron Price as director, to meet two needs. (1) It exercised a compulsory security censorship, with penalties, on communications each way between the United States and foreign countries, especially by mail, cable or radio. Domestic publications were previewed for adaptation for export, sometimes even as to opinion content. Correspondents complained that nonmilitary news dispatches critical of U.S. policy on internal race or labour controversies were held up to avoid unfavourable repercussions abroad. Such controls were gradually relaxed. (2) The office set up a voluntary self-censorship by the domestic press and radio, based on Codes of Wartime Practices for each medium (Jan. 15, 1942, with later revisions), listing the kinds of information that could aid the enemy. These included, for example, troop movements, weather news, some advertising and reports on uranium production and covered unforeseen risks of messages via open microphones and request programs. The industry associations of both media co-operated; editors approved especially the speedy expert advice and clarification on individual problems from the office. No penalties were provided, no restraints on advocacy or political debate were imposed. Potential sanctions did exist—possible imposition of statutory censorship, control of news gathering, public report of violations—but were not invoked. The censorship worked because of the patriotic resolve of all interests not to aid the enemy and not to curtail freedom of opinion.

The Postal Censorship.—The so-called "postal censorship" is based on the power of the postmaster general to deny the second-class mailing privilege to publications that contain matter forbidden by certain federal statutes. The idea was born in 1835 when southern representatives in congress tried to pass a law forbidding federal postmasters from distributing "incendiary" matter advocating the abolition of Negro slavery in states that had banned such agitation. The law failed of passage, but in fact southern postmasters never delivered abolitionist papers. In the Civil War, a congressional committee upheld the postmaster general's power to bar recalcitrant northern journals from the mails. In 1868 lottery information was forbidden the mails by law, and in 1873 the famous "Comstock law" against obscene matter and contraceptive information was passed. This produced many prosecutions and punishments. Later, matter furthering frauds or the sale of alcoholic liquors or advocating criminal anarchy was proscribed by statutes. The final extension came during World War I when title XII of the Espionage act of June 15, 1917, made nonmailable any matter violating these specifications in title I:

(i) making false statements or reports with intent to interfere with the operations or success of the armed forces of the United States; (ii) wilfully causing or trying to cause insubordination, disloyalty, mutiny, or refusal of duty in the armed forces; (iii) wilfully obstructing the recruiting or enlistment services of the United States.

Heavy penalties (fine or imprisonment) were to be imposed on those attempting to use the mails for these purposes. The Sedition act, May 16, 1918, added nine other specifications, such as obstructing the sale of United States bonds; publishing language intended to cause scorn or contempt for the government, constitution, flag or uniform; urging curtailment of the production of war needs. The postmaster general could act on "evidence satisfactory to him." Under these acts, the mailing privilege was denied to one or more issues of two Socialist dailies, to many Socialist and radical magazines and even journals of liberal opinion. Periodicals had their second-class privilege absolutely suspended. Books and pamphlets were barred. More than 100 publications were interfered with to some degree—the widest interference with the press in the nation's history.

The courts have always held that these statutes do not limit freedom of the press, usually denying review of such bans, as they are held legitimate exercises of an executive function. The post office avoids the position of a censor by refusing to define objectionable matter in advance. The liberal view holds that since the government enjoys a postal monopoly, the publication denied this preferential rate (granted publications to encourage the dissemination of knowledge) cannot compete with those enjoying the privilege.

Censorship of Motion Pictures.—The federal government under the interstate commerce power, forbade the importation or transportation of prize fight films and lewd or obscene films. (Penal code, section 245, revision of June 5, 1920.) Few cases arose under these statutes. Proposals to establish a board of censors in the office of education were defeated. Preventive censorships continued to exist in Pennsylvania (1911), Ohio (1913), Kansas (1914), Maryland, Virginia and New York. Boards of appointed "well-qualified" persons, receiving salaries, preview all films for public exhibition and may ban an entire film, delete scenes or words, or prescribe revision. The supreme court held such censorships constitutional. Since certain of the large states with censorships are important sources of revenue, the producers edit all films to conform to their codes, and thus six states influence the character of the films offered in all the states. Since 1935 the Catholic Legion of Decency has had considerable influence on the character of film offerings through its regularly published listings of approved and disapproved films. The producers set up a voluntary self-censorship under a strict code. Certain municipalities control motion pictures through police powers, especially through licensing ordinances for exhibitions. Cases arose on films dealing with birth phenomena and those viewed as inflammatory of race, religious or international controversy.

Censorship of Radio Broadcasting.—The Federal Communications commission, created by public law 416, June 19, 1934, was empowered to license public broadcasting stations to use wave channels and time periods as "public interest, convenience, or necessity requires" (section 303). Its censorship powers were explicitly limited to prohibiting profane or obscene language and to enforcing equal rights for legal candidates for public office. It intervened in cases of alleged obscenity or profanity and to correct advertising abuses. Its acts revealed no political motives. Liberals declared the commission exercised an indirect censorship, since station owners, required to secure renewal of licences at short intervals, would conform to the program standards implied by the commission's acts or utterances. Liberals opposed as legally unwarranted the commission's order (May 1939) that shortwave broadcasts "reflect the culture of the United States and international good will." As for the stations, they scrutinize materials before broadcasting them, at times censor offerings and even bar speakers. Labour and Socialist organizations charged that these precautions, defensible as preventives of libelous or scandalous utterances, sometimes limited their air freedom. The self-regulatory code adopted by the National Association of Broadcasters (1939) set high standards for the handling of controversial issues and religion with fairness and freedom.

Censorship of Plays and Books.—No formal censorship of the theatre has ever existed in the United States. Interference has been by local prosecutors or the police, who have, on complaint, viewed exhibitions and sometimes ordered them withdrawn or amended, or instituted proceedings against both producers and actors that have in certain cases resulted in fines or jail sentences. The New York statute (1927) included matter dealing with sex perversions under obscenity. The suspension of the licences of theatres offering alleged immoral burlesque shows revealed the commissioner as a potential censor.

Interferences with the distribution of books and periodicals have been under the postal law, the customs law (later providing for judicial review) and local morality ordinances. Liberal court decisions have limited the activities of the New York Vice society against alleged pornographic publications that in the past had suppressed books of admitted literary worth. In Boston, the Watch and Ward society, by agreement with the prosecutor, listed books for the sale of which booksellers might be prosecuted. Later the police established their own censorship under which a number of volumes were proscribed, although many were sold everywhere else in the United States.

Bibliography.—Zechariah Chafee, Jr., *Free Speech in The United States* (1941), and *Government and Mass Communications* (1947); Leon Whipple, *The Story of Civil Liberty in the United States* (1927); Morris Ernst and A. Lindey, *The Censor Marches On* (1940); *A Free and Responsible Press* (1947); publications on radio and the movies, from the Commission on Freedom of the Press. (L. R. W.)

CENSUS. In modern usage, primarily denotes the periodical survey of the number and condition of the people—more fully described as "census of population" where necessary to distinguish it from the census of production, census of agriculture and similar institutions.

History.—Numberings of the people and national stocktakings are known to have been conducted from very ancient times. The Old Testament records the enumeration at the Exodus of the fighting strength of the Children of Israel and of the non-military Levites, and the famous enumeration of fighting men, conducted by Joab at the command of David, on which the divine wrath was visited. Records survive of a complete cadastral survey and census of Babylonia comprising agriculture, stock and produce, which appears to have been carried out for fiscal purposes in the third millennium B.C., and in the Persian empire, in China and in Egypt similar surveys are known to have taken place for the assessment of fiscal, military or labour liabilities. A most notable example was the Roman census, from which the modern institution derives its name: under this system the members and property of every family were enumerated quinquennially for the purpose of determining their civil status and corresponding liabilities. Dating from pre-republican Rome, the Roman census was extended by Augustus in 5 B.C. to the Roman empire and thus covered the whole of the civilized world of those times. The Roman census perished in the wreck of the Roman empire. Feudalism may have rendered the revival of census-taking, even when practicable, less necessary; and superstition may have contributed to its abeyance. The Christian Church remembered the punishment of Israel; and even in the British House of Commons in 1753 it was possible for the fear to be expressed that a numbering of the people would be followed by "some great public misfortune or epidemical distemper." It is, of course natural that objections to taxation or military service should assume the cloak of religious scruple; but there must have been more than this. It is impossible not to infer that in the Old Testament story and in the purificatory sacrifice concluding the Roman census folk-memory lingered of a primitive *taboo*. And these speculations receive interesting support from the announcement, in connection with the Kenya census of 1926, that the authorities anticipated trouble with certain tribes among whom there was a strict *taboo* against counting either themselves, their wives or their cattle.

Thus, apart from undertakings such as Charlemagne's Breviary and the English Domesday Book (an inquest upon geld assessments) there was a long interval in census history until the mid-17th century, when a periodical census of the modern type was instituted in La Nouvelle France (Quebec) and Acadie (Nova Scotia). Enumerations of population took place in several of the German States from 1742 onwards, in Sweden in 1748, Denmark in 1769 and Spain in 1787. In Great Britain, after proposals had been made and defeated in 1753, the census was definitely established in 1801. From these and similar beginnings in other countries the institution of the census rapidly gained a permanent place in the organization of nearly all modern States, the most recent convert being Turkey in 1927. It will be seen that the precursors of the modern census were almost wholly executive operations discharging essential functions of government such as military recruitment and taxation. But in the long interval which preceded the revival these functions cut for themselves other channels of administration; and when inquests and surveys upon a national scale were again resumed it was with a very different object, viz., to supply knowledge for the guidance of public policy and to "substitute certainty for conjecture" upon the vexed questions of fact which are vital to political action and foresight.

CONCEPTION AND EVOLUTION OF MODERN CENSUS

The census, as now conceived, has two main objects. It provides an instantaneous picture of the community—a cross-section of the body-politic exhibiting its constitution at the point of time when it is made. It thus affords knowledge of numbers and conditions which is valid for the particular point of time and, with approximations, for adjacent periods. But all things are subject to change; and knowledge of the force and direction of changes in the community are even more important than the facts at any given date. A single sounding will disclose what depth of water is below the keel; but not without repeated soundings is it known whether the water is shoaling, and how rapidly. Hence in the modern census each enumeration is conceived not only as a source of static knowledge but as an item in a consecutive series. From the succession of these alone can be ascertained and measured those great drifts and currents in the national life which, whether deemed good or evil, whether resistible or irresistible, must at least be known and reckoned with.

House to House Visitation.—The first among the questions upon which certainty was deemed requisite was the number of the population. Such a numbering entails a house-to-house visitation coupled with enquiries of the inmates. This process (primitive, but not to be bettered) affords opportunities, on the one hand, and imports limitations on the other, which have substantially determined the scope and evolution of census-taking. In the first place, the itinerary may be planned so as to group the dwellings visited according to any designed arrangement of boundaries: thus information obtained respecting the population of each areal group may be separately recorded and becomes available, not only as a component part of the national total, but also by itself, or as a component part of larger areal units, for the purpose of exhibiting the local distribution of that total. Further, the need to ensure that no dwelling is omitted leads to a record being made of all premises on the itinerary. It is but a step to include particulars of each dwelling, *e.g.,* whether inhabited or vacant, and the number of its rooms, thus affording, in combination with other material, statistics as to housing conditions, overcrowding, etc. The convenience of obtaining particulars from one spokesman on behalf of each family or household leads to a system of household returns which themselves afford a count of such families. But the germ of the fertile elaboration of census enquiries is to be found in the fact that the information is obtained by direct enquiry of the persons concerned, thus permitting of the inclusion of every subject on which the individual can reasonably be expected to state his own position and that of his dependants. Age may be asked and given: the relationship and marital status of persons comprised in the household group can be described. Birthplace and nationality may be stated. A further group of personal particulars has furnished a great body of statistical material relative to occupation and industry. Every occupied person can state his job in terms which permit of precise occupational classification. And in addition to stating that he is, for example, a crane-driver, he can add that he is employed by a firm of brewers, thus enabling himself to be classed to the industry which he serves. Other enquiries are regularly included where the conditions render them suitable, such as religion, language spoken and literacy. Comparatively complicated enquiries may be included such as the "fertility of marriage" enquiry in English, French, Netherlands, Spanish and Norwegian censuses (date of marriage: number of deceased and number and ages of living children of the marriage).

The Personal Aspect.—The common element in all these enquiries is that they are personal. It has been suggested that the whole field of statistics can be viewed as concerned with either *personnel* or with *material:* this is not an entirely watertight division, but it accurately represents an important difference between the main points of view from which statistical information is sought and studied. The census as an instrument for the collection of information is predominantly concerned with aspects of *personnel,* and covers the major portion of that province. It is unable to elucidate any subject except as an attribute of the individual man or woman. The inclusion of agricultural statistics in some countries is an apparent exception: but such enquiries may be in a sense an extension of the record of dwellings. The homestead is visited; it is noted that so many acres of arable, etc., are annexed and that there is stock of a certain kind and number. This is consistent with the census procedure, which must locate as it counts: it cannot deal with wealth which is everywhere and nowhere. Subjects such as exports and imports are clearly out of the picture. But there are some limitations in the field of personal attributes. The enquiry must be capable of being simply put and answered. Intrinsically there is nothing to prevent the use of the census to ascertain the distribution of the national wealth or income; but the preparation of a statement in the form necessary to furnish the answer upon a uniform basis would be beyond the power of most individuals. If all particulars needed for the calculation were asked they would need a census schedule to themselves; and if the final figure alone were to be given there would be no security that it was properly arrived at. An enquiry of all wage-earners as to the rate of pay received (as in the Spanish census) would not be subject to the same objection.

Difficulty of Verification.—But in many countries another general limitation would apply. Census returns cannot be verified, in view of the magnitude of the operations; and it is useless to make any enquiry respecting which individuals may have any conscious motive, real or fancied, for suppressing or distorting the facts. Hence information which in the popular apprehension might be used by the authorities for enforcing individual liabilities, such as taxation, cannot profitably be asked; and truthful information upon subjects, such as illegitimacy, which are felt to be delicate is often unobtainable owing to a fear of it becoming public. These considerations have tended to emphasize the character of the modern census as a source of abstract statistical information only. Whatever expectations may have been formed in the early days of the census revival as to its incidental utility for executive purposes, census administrators have had to choose between making it an effective instrument for the collection of statistics only and making the worst of both worlds. Another minor limitation applies to the doubtful ability of the individual to give reliable answers to enquiries as to infirmities such as blindness, deafness, etc. Even if no bias due to prejudice arises, the terms employed are unavoidably indefinite; and the conditions themselves cannot be properly assessed save by trained medical judgment. It is becoming recognized that the census can afford little assistance of value in this sphere.

Advantages.—Within limitations the census has the peculiar and enormous advantage that all the varied attributes which it records are related to the individual to whom they jointly belong. Hence every type and class of information obtained can be presented in combination with every other type and class. If it be assumed, for the sake of illustration, that the collection of occupational data is omitted from the census and separately organized by means of returns from employers, information might still be forthcoming of the number of metal spinners, while the census would continue to state the number of men aged 49. But between the two sets of figures there would be a gulf; it would be impossible to obtain the number of metal spinners aged 49. Given, however, the inclusion of both enquiries in the census any combination of these and other results is possible; and a census enquiry, as distinct from one separately promoted, not only affords the desired information but adds a fuller and richer significance to all those which it supplements.

Utility of Census.—And as the scope of the census has expanded, so the sphere of its utility has been enlarged. It still discharges its original function as an intelligence service of the government by which it is promoted in both legislation and administration. Estimates cannot be framed, for example, of the money provision requisite in future for the payment of old age pensions, or of the school provision needed for the rising generation, without the help of census material. Social insurance schemes equally rely upon such material for their actuarial foundation. Electoral redistribution must be largely based upon population distribution; in South Africa constituencies are rearranged on the results of each census. Census statistics are the common tools and material of the business of government in ways too numerous to detail; but they are equally indispensable to the direction of State policy. In matters of defence the most pacific nation cannot afford not to know where it stands and whither it is tending. Questions of unemployment cannot begin to be considered without a knowledge of the industrial disposition of the people. Policy respecting migration still depends upon a recognition of the forces of population pressure which have so often changed the face of history. Knowledge of all these facts, even where not directly contributing to the solution of the problems of statecraft or state-policy, nevertheless forms a background against which they must be viewed. And for the public service in its widest significance the census provides material for research and study, helping to define and clarify the issues on the great questions to which there is as yet no agreed answer, and which, so far from having been admitted within the sphere of government responsibility, are but vaguely stirring in the conscience of the community. Not among the least of the services of the census is that which it renders to statistical method whereby, for example, mortality data may be converted into mortality rates, thus eliminating variables and reducing to a comparable basis a wealth of material which for many purposes would otherwise be useless.

CENSUS METHOD AND PRACTICE

Within the essential framework of the census system—house-to-house visitation coupled with enquiries—diversities in national practice are for the most part of little moment. But in one case, at any rate, a question of method is also a question of principle. Populations are represented in some countries *de jure,* in others *de facto.* A *de facto* enumeration, following the principle of the instantaneous picture, allocates individuals to the areas in which they are physically found at the census date, regardless of their usual residences. A *de jure* distribution, on the other hand, is that which assigns the population to the respective areas of usual residence. Where populations are immobile, one set of figures serves both purposes: but in most industrially developed countries there is much, and increasing, population movement. It is usual in *de facto* enumerations to select a census date which so far as possible avoids population movement and on which *de facto* thus approximates to *de jure*: otherwise a *de facto* distribution is apt to be fortuitous and meaningless. But *de jure* as a norm is not valid for all purposes. What, after all, is the population of Blackpool? The number of its permanent winter residents, or its doubled or tripled complement of the holiday season upon whom so much of its existence and conditions depends? The great daily migrations between home and workplace raise a similar question: what, it may again be asked, is the population of the City of London—the 13,000 night residents, or the 400,000 who spend there a third of the most active portion of their lives? The truth is, of course, that there is no one answer: the purpose to be served determines the choice. But it will be clear, at any rate, that the meaning of the term "population" admits of some refinements.

Typical Systems.—The following outline will afford an indication of the scope and salient features of a few typical census systems. The English census has been hitherto decennial, though quinquennial powers are now available. The return is made by the householder, the enumeration being *de facto*. The schedule included the name, relationship to householder, age, sex, marital condition, orphanhood, birthplace, nationality, school attendance, occupation, industry, industrial status (whether employer, employee or working on own account), place of work, and number and ages of living children and stepchildren under 16.

France.—In France the census is quinquennial: a skeleton household return is made by the householder, supplemented by a separate return by each member. The former includes absent members and distinguishes temporary residents, thus providing for a *de jure* distribution. The individual schedule required name, sex, date and place of birth, nationality, marital condition, date of marriage, number of deceased and number and ages of living children of the marriage, usual residence (if temporarily present), literacy, and principal and secondary occupations, together with particulars of principal industry, industrial status, number of employees, or if employee, whether unemployed.

Italy.—In Italy the regular census is decennial: the return, which is made by the householder, includes particulars as in France for a *de jure* distribution. The schedule required the name, father's name (and whether alive or dead), relationship to householder, sex, date and place of birth, marital condition, literacy, principal and secondary occupations, whether owning property (distinguishing land and buildings), and nationality.

Germany.—Germany afforded an interesting example of a quinquennial census of alternately greater and lesser scope. The schedule comprised name, relationship to householder, sex, date of birth and marital status, with the distinctions requisite to provide a *de jure* distribution.

In 1925 these enquiries were supplemented by religion, nationality, mother tongue, last residence before World War I, principal and secondary occupations and industry and industrial status. The return is made by the householder.

Population Registers.—As seen in the foregoing examples, the frequency of the census series is usually decennial or quinquennial: the latter is generally deemed desirable on statistical grounds, but the census is an expensive and laborious undertaking. The attractive prospect has at times been indulged of the creation of population registers, containing in respect of each individual the particulars usually elucidated by the census, and accurately maintained, as a mirror of the people and of the passing phases of their lives, by reports of all changes in the personnel or in the particulars recorded about them. Given such registers, it has been urged, a census of the written records could be taken at any time, however frequent, to ascertain the current position regarding all or any of the recorded particulars without the labour and expense of the census visitation. The prospect, though attractive, is hardly realizable. Were it the case that all the requisite information is already available through one channel or another, nothing would be needed but their complete co-ordination for the maintenance of the registers. But in all countries there are great gaps in the essential information which could not be filled without a revolution in national habits or administrative machinery. Maintenance of the occupational and industrial record, for example, would involve a duty to notify change of occupation or employment in the case of every individual. Maintenance of accurate particulars as to local distribution would involve an obligation to report every change of address.

Population registers with a limited scope exist in some countries, such as The Netherlands, Belgium and Sweden; and many systems of public supervision require the registration of residence, arrival and departure. But such countries do not dispense with a census, and it seems doubtful whether removals are notified with sufficient completeness for statistical purposes. It will be clear that in Great Britain, at any rate, and in other countries similarly situated, the proposition would impose upon every individual a host of new obligations which though trifling in themselves would not be discharged without legal enforcement, and which, for want of sympathy with their purpose, would appear meaningless and oppressive. Such a system even if practicable would not be less laborious and costly than the census: it would be rigid, moreover, and lacking the valuable capacity of the census proper to experiment in new methods and new fields of enquiry on each successive occasion.

But while the census remains indispensable, the essential element of value in such proposals is well recognized, viz., the coordination of all continuously available demographic material, such as that of vital registration, with the periodical census results. The census population of a given date may be corrected by allowance for births and deaths over any subsequent period to show the population at a later date as modified by net natural increase or decrease. Allowance for the remaining factor of migration is necessary to complete the adjustment; and, given adequate records of migration, a population figure may thus be constructed which is as correct and authoritative as any census product. The process could be carried into further detail were the migration records fully complementary to the registration data. But if inadequate for the construction of fully authentic intercensal statistics, the supplementary sources are invaluable in the framing of estimates to bridge the intercensal gap. Vital registration is closely related to the census both in subject-matter and through their association for joint or mutual service; and cannot be ignored in any study of the census system.

See the articles POPULATION; BIRTH RATE; DEATH RATE and MARRIAGE RATE; *see* also official census publications of the respective national governments, and the United Nations, *Monthly Bulletin of Statistics* and *Demographic Yearbook*. (S. P. V.; X.)

UNITED STATES

The federal census, which began in 1790 and has been taken every ten years since under a mandate contained in the U.S. constitution, was the outgrowth of a controversy in the convention which prepared the document. Representatives of the smaller states as a rule claimed that the vote, and so the influence, of the states in the proposed government should be equal. Representatives of the larger states as a rule claimed that their greater population and wealth were entitled to recognition. The controversy ended in the creation of a bicameral legislature in the lower branch of which the claim of the larger states found recognition, while in the upper, the senate, each state had two votes. In the house of representatives seats were to be distributed in proportion to the population, and the convention, foreseeing rapid changes of population, ordained an enumeration of the inhabitants and a redistribution or reapportionment of seats in the house of representatives every ten years.

The provision of the constitution on the subject is as follows:

Representatives and direct taxes shall be apportioned among the several states which may be included within this Union according to their respective numbers, which shall be determined by adding to the whole number of free persons, including those bound to service for a term of years and excluding Indians not taxed, three-fifths of all other persons. The actual enumeration shall be made within three years after the first meeting of the Congress of the United States, and within every subsequent term of ten years, in such manner as they shall by law direct.

In 1790 the population was reported classed as slaves and free, the free classed as white and others, the free whites as males and females, and the free white males as under or above 16 years of age. In 1800 and 1810 the same classification was preserved, except that five age groups instead of two were given for free white males and the same five were applied also to free white females. In connection with the census of 1810 an attempt was made to gather certain industrial statistics showing "the number, nature, extent, situation and value of the arts and manufactures of the United States." In 1820 a sixth age class was introduced for free white males, an age classification of four periods was applied to the free coloured and the slaves of each sex, and the number of aliens and of persons engaged in agriculture, in manufactures and in commerce was called for. The inquiry into industrial statistics begun in 1810 was also repeated and extended. In 1830, 13 age classes were employed for free whites of each sex, and six for the free coloured and the slaves of each sex.

The law under which the census of 1840 was taken provided for the collection of statistics on agriculture, manufacturing, mining, commerce and education, as well as on population—representing a tendency to make the census overinclusive which persisted through 1880.

The census of 1850 employed six schedules: for free inhabitants, for slaves, for deaths during the preceding year, for agriculture, for manufactures and for social statistics. The last asked for returns regarding valuation, taxation, educational and religious statistics, pauperism, crime and the prevailing rates of wages in each municipal division. It was also the first U.S. census to give a line of the schedule to each person, death or establishment enumerated, and thus to make the returns in the individual form indispensable for a detailed classification and compilation. The results of this census were tabulated with care and skill, and a preliminary analysis gave the salient results and in some cases compared them with European figures.

The census of 1860 followed the model of its predecessor with slight changes. When the time for the next census approached it was felt that new legislation was needed, and a committee of the house of representatives, with James A. Garfield, afterward president of the United States, at its head, made a careful and thorough study of the situation and reported an excellent bill, which passed the house, but was defeated by untoward influences in the senate. In consequence the census of 1870 was taken with the outgrown machinery established 20 years earlier, a law characterized by Francis A. Walker, the superintendent of the census, who administered it, as "clumsy, antiquated and barbarous." It suffered also from the fact that large parts of the country had not recovered from the ruin wrought by four years of civil war. In consequence this census marks the lowest ebb of U.S. census work. The accuracy of the results is generally denied by competent experts. The serious errors were of omission, probably confined in the main to the southern states, and especially frequent among the Negroes.

After 1870 the development of census work in the United States was steady and rapid. The law which had been prepared by the house committee for the census of 1870 furnished a basis for greatly improved legislation in 1879, under which the census of 1880 was taken. By this law the census office for the first time was allowed to call into existence and to control an adequate local staff of supervisors and enumerators. The scope of the work was so extended as to make the 22 quarto volumes of the tenth census almost an encyclopaedia, not only of the population, but also of the products and resources of the United States. Probably no other census in the world has ever covered so wide a range of subjects, and perhaps none except that of India and the succeeding U.S. census has extended through so many volumes. The topics usually contained in a census suffered from the great addition of other and less pertinent matter, and the reputation of the work was unfavourably affected by the length of time required to prepare and publish the volumes (the last ones not appearing until near the end of the decade), the original underestimate of the cost of the work, which made frequent supplementary appropriations necessary, the resignation of the superintendent, Francis A. Walker, in 1882, and the disability and death of his successor, Charles W. Seaton. The 11th census was taken under a law almost identical with that of the 10th, and extended through 25 large volumes, presenting a work almost as encyclopaedic, but much more distinctively statistical.

SCOPE OF CENSUS NARROWED

Competent discussion between 1890 and 1900 fastened on this point, and under the law of 1899 the scope of the census of 1900 was greatly narrowed. This was secured not by abandoning any of the numerous inquiries which had overloaded the two preceding censuses, but by dividing them into major and minor groups, the major group embracing those inquiries, population, vital statistics, agriculture and manufactures, for making which enumerators were needed in the field; the minor group embracing those which could be conducted by correspondence supplemented to a slight degree, if necessary, by field agents at strategic points. The law required the completion of the major inquiries in three years (the two preceding censuses had taken more than twice as long to finish) and postponed the minor inquiries until the major group was completed. The new law thus foreshadowed, but did not establish, an office functioning without interruption, and as a natural consequence of it, in 1902 the bureau of the census was made permanent. This important and salutary change was maintained in subsequent legislation.

In no field of census work has it been more beneficial than in that of vital statistics. The registration of births and deaths is under the jurisdiction of the states, only 11 of which had registration systems in 1900 adequate to meet the requirements for admission to the death registration area which was set up at that time. Model registration laws were formulated, however, and these were adopted and put into effect year by year in additional states until, in 1933, all the states were included in both death and birth registration areas, giving a complete coverage of the United States. Statistics of deaths and births compiled from state records are published by the bureau of the census in its annual volumes entitled, respectively, *Mortality Statistics* and *Birth, Stillbirth, and Infant Mortality Statistics.* Statistics of marriage and divorce were collected for the years from 1867 to 1906, for 1916 and for 1922 to 1932—the latter appearing in a series of annual reports. These reports were resumed on an annual basis beginning with 1940.

The census of 1910 was the first decennial census taken under the permanent census bureau. This census covered four subjects, namely, population, agriculture, manufactures and mines and quarries, many of the other subjects included in earlier decennial censuses having been taken care of either by annual reports, as in the case of vital statistics, or by inquiries conducted between the decennial census years, as in the case of the statistics of religious bodies and of benevolent and corrective institutions. The most significant additions to the list of questions asked on the 1910 population schedule, as compared with that of 1900, were mother tongue and ability to speak English, with special reference to the foreign-born; and for the gainful workers, industry as well as occupation, and unemployment. The data on gainful workers were tabulated by occupation in combination with industry, though only a limited publication was made, by reason of insufficiency of funds at the close of the census period. For a similar reason the unemployment data were not published at all. A new basis of distinction between urban and rural population, in which all incorporated places having 2,500 inhabitants or more were counted as urban (a definition which was used through 1940) was set up; and many details were added to the tabulations published for counties and the smaller cities.

The population census of 1920 was patterned closely after that of 1910, except for the omission of questions on unemployment and the introduction into the general tabulations of a new category, namely the farm population, that is the population living on farms. (Dwellings or homes had been classified as farm and nonfarm in earlier censuses, from 1890, but no extended use had been made of this subdivision, nor any tabulations of population classified as farm and nonfarm.)

In order to expedite the publication of the new census data, the text in the main reports of this census was limited to such descriptive and explanatory matter as was required for the understanding of the figures. These reports were supplemented by more detailed analysis of important topics in a series of 12 monographs, which appeared at intervals during the decade.

In 1930 one significant question, namely, the value or rent of the home, was added to the population schedule; and there was a separate schedule on unemployment, going into this subject in far more detail than ever before. The 1930 reports were published, like those of 1920, with little analytical text. There were, however, many added details in the 1930 tabulations, including a tabulation of gainful workers by counties, increased age data for counties and the smaller cities, a brief classification of the population of townships and an entire volume devoted to statistics of families, in addition to two volumes on unemployment. The classification of the population as farm and nonfarm, introduced in a limited way in 1920, was carried much further in the form of an almost universal subdivision of the rural population into rural farm and rural nonfarm. Bulletins containing the final census counts for states, counties, townships or districts and incorporated places were published for all states before the end of the census year, 1930, these forming an advance showing of the data which later appeared as vol. 1 of the census reports. A second series, presenting much tabulated detail, and a series on unemployment were published before the end of 1931, followed closely by a series on occupations and a new series on families.

An important innovation in 1940 was the census of housing, which was taken in close connection with the census of population and in which were incorporated certain items previously a part of the population census reports, in particular, tenure and value or rent of home and mortgage debt. This census covered also various items descriptive of housing units, including exterior material, year built, type of structure and state of repair. There were also questions with regard to such facilities as plumbing equipment; water supply; and heating, lighting and refrigeration equipment. Some items from the housing census are published for the larger cities by blocks, this being the first instance in which census statistics have been published for such small areas. A new feature in the 1940 population census itself was the provision for asking a part of the questions with respect to 1 person in 20 rather than for the entire population, thus providing a 5% random sample as a basis for the tabulation of statistics. This device was introduced primarily to take care of additional questions for which there was no space on the main schedule. The sample questions included usual occupation (in distinction from present occupation), veteran status, social security registration, mother tongue, place of birth of parents and a group of questions on fertility. These additional questions were asked of those persons whose names fell on certain numbered lines of the main schedule. Brief preliminary cards containing the basic items of colour, sex, age and work status were also punched from these selected lines and tabulated many months in advance of the date on which these important characteristics of the population could have been obtained from the complete tabulation. New questions contained on the main population schedule included one on highest grade of school completed (which replaced the old question on illiteracy) and a question on place of residence in 1935, which formed the basis for the first direct statistics of population migration. The section on work status provided the basis for a count not only of persons seeking work but also of those employed on emergency work projects, as well as of those employed in private industry or on regular government work. Persons not in the labour force were for the first time classified into significant categories, such as housewives, students, persons unable to work, etc.; and there were supplementary questions on extent of unemployment, number of weeks worked in 1939 and amount of wage or salary income during 1939. Extensive and very significant reports on fertility in 1940 and 1910 were published, based partly on questions on the number of children ever born to each ever-married woman, in the sample section of the 1940 census schedule, and partly on similar questions on the 1910 schedule.

The 1950 census was in most respects similar to that of 1940. The sample was increased to 20%, in order to provide usable data for smaller areas; the question on mother tongue was omitted, and of course that on emergency employment, since there were no persons in that status in 1950; the data on migration were obtained through a question on residence one year prior to the census (rather than five years earlier, as in 1940); and the questions on income were expanded to include total income from all sources, that is, not only wage and salary income (as in 1940) but also income from one's own business or farm, and income from "all other sources." The questions on education, migration and income were transferred to the 20% sample section of the schedule, along with several of the less important housing items.

There were two significant changes in definition. First, the urban area was expanded to include not only incorporated places of 2,500 or more, as in 1940 and earlier, but also: (1) the thickly settled suburban area or "urban fringe" around each city of 50,000 or more; and (2) various unincorporated places of 2,500 or more—some of which had been arbitrarily included in 1940, however, under special rule.

The newly defined urban population exceeded what would have been classified as urban under the 1940 definition by about 8,000,000 or about 9%.

The farm population classification, on the other hand, was somewhat reduced, by excluding from the count considerable numbers of households which, while occupying dwellings nominally located on a farm, paid cash rent for these dwellings. The justification for this change was that, once a house and a plot of ground were rented out for strictly residential purposes, the plot of ground ceased to be a part of a farm. (A farm had long been defined as a piece of land which is farmed, that is, used for the production of crops or livestock products.)

The later and more accurately defined farm population was smaller by about 2,000,000 than what had been expected under the old definition.

The federal census has long made periodic reports on agriculture and manufactures. In 1925 a mid-decade census of agriculture was introduced, somewhat limited in scope. A census of manufactures formed a part of the decennial inquiry down to 1940, with additional inquiries within the decade, sometimes quinquennial and sometimes biennial. Censuses of "distribution" or "business" were taken in 1930 and 1940. Legislation enacted in 1948 provided that a census of manufactures and a census of business (including service activities as well as wholesale and retail trade) be taken in 1954 and every five years thereafter. The dates were specifically set outside the decennial census periods, so as to distribute the work load of the census bureau more evenly over the decade. (W. F. W.; L. E. T.)

CENSUS OF AGRICULTURE: *see* AGRICULTURE: *Agricultural Statistics.*

CENSUS OF PRODUCTION: *see* PRODUCTION, CENSUS OF.

CENT. A small copper or bronze coin. In the United States and Canada, it is the one-hundredth part of a dollar, approximately equivalent to a British halfpenny. In Holland the guilder is divided into one hundred cents.

CENTAUREA, a genus of the family Compositae, containing about 500 species, almost all natives of the Old World, with the principal centre in the Mediterranean region. The plants are herbs with entire or cut, often spiny-toothed, leaves and ovoid or globose involucres surrounding a showy head of tubular, oblique or two-lipped florets, the outer of which are usually large and neuter, the inner bisexual. Four species are native in Great Britain. *C. nigra* is the knapweed, common in meadows and pastureland; *C. cyanus* is the bluebottle or cornflower, well-known as a weed, much grown as a garden annual and the national floral emblem of Germany; *C. calcitrapa* is the star-thistle, a rare plant with rose-purple flower-heads enveloped by involucral bracts which end in a long, stiff spine.

In eastern North America, in addition to the species mentioned, the brown knapweed (*C. jacea*), the scabious knapweed (*C. scabiosa*), the Tirol knapweed (*C. vochinensis*), the spotted knapweed (*C. maculosa*), the yellow star-thistle (*C. solstitialis*) and the rayless centaury (*C. melitensis*) are more or less extensively naturalized. On the Pacific coast *C. melitensis,* there known as Napa thistle, is a troublesome weed, especially in California, as is also *C. solstitialis;* less pernicious are the star-thistle, the bluebottle and the Turkistan thistle (*C. repens*). The only native North American species, the basket-flower or American star-thistle (*C. americana*) is a robust annual 2 ft. to 6 ft. high, with very showy rose-coloured or purplish flower-heads, 3 in. to 5 in. across. It is found in dry plains from Missouri to Louisiana, and westward to Arizona and Mexico, and is also grown as an ornamental plant.

The best-known garden plants are a dusty miller (*C. cineraria*), the bluebottle (*C. cyanus*), the sweet sultan (*C. moschata*) and the mountain bluet (*C. montana*).

CENTAURS (Gr. κένταυροι), in Greek mythology, a race of beings part horse, part man, dwelling in the mountains of Thessaly and Arcadia. The centaurs are usually said to be the offspring of Ixion and Nephele. They are best known for their fight with the Lapithae, caused by their attempt to carry off Deidameia on the day of her marriage to Peirithous, king of the Lapithae, himself the son of Ixion. In later times they are often represented drawing the car of Dionysus, or bound and ridden by Eros, in allusion to their drunken and amorous habits. Their general character is that of wild, lawless and inhospitable beings, the slaves of their animal passions, with the exception of Pholus and Cheiron.

They are variously explained by a fancied resemblance to the shapes of clouds, or as spirits of the rushing mountain torrents or winds, etc. Perhaps the likeliest suggestion is that they are a distorted recollection of some savage tribe, reputed by its neighbours to be composed of monsters. Like the defeat of the Titans by Zeus, the contests with the Centaurs typified the struggle between civilization and barbarism. In early art they were represented as human beings in front, with the body and hind legs of a horse attached to the back; later, they were men only as far as the waist.

See Roscher's *Lexikon, s.v. Kentauren;* P. V. Baur, *Centaurs in Ancient Art* (Berlin, 1912); G. Dumezil, *Le Proleme des Centaures* (Paris, 1929).

CENTAURUS (the "Centaur"), in astronomy, a southern constellation (invisible in northern lands) rich in bright stars and globular clusters. The two stars α, β are known as the southern Pointers since they point to the Southern Cross. One of these, α Centauri, is the third brightest star in the sky, and it is found to be our nearest neighbour; the distance is 4 light years (parallax $=0.75''$). It is a double star of which the brighter component is almost a replica of the sun, having nearly the same brightness and mass but slightly lower surface temperature; there is also a third widely separated faint companion called Proxima Centauri, because it is slightly nearer to us than the main star.

The constellation also contains ω Centauri which is the finest example of a globular star-cluster; it is probably the nearest object of this class, but the distance is no less than 20,000 light years.

Photographs of it show more than 6,000 stars within a circle of $20'$ diameter, but the number must be much greater. (A. S. E.)

CENTAURY, any herb of the genus *Centaurium* family Gentianaceae; also, especially in America, the milkwort (*Polygala paucifolia*). The common centaury of Europe, *C. confertum,* occurs in dry pastures and on sandy coasts in Great Britain and is often cultivated for ornament.

The centaury presents many varieties, differing in length of stem, degree of branching, width and shape of leaves, and laxity or closeness of the inflorescence.

CENTENARY, the celebration of an event after a hundred years. The word "centennial" (from Lat. *centum,* a hundred, and *annus,* a year), though usually an adjective as in "the Centennial State," the name given to Colorado on its admission to statehood in 1876, is also used as a synonym of centenary.

CENTERING, a term applied to the erection of temporary woodwork to support arches, etc., while they are setting. Thus, in the case of an arch, the carpenter forms a "turning-piece" shaped to take the bricks or masonry, and properly tied and braced. This is strutted in position, when the arch is completed by the bricklayer or mason. As soon as the work is set, the centering is carefully removed, which is called "striking the centering." The same method is used in building brick sewers. The origin of the word "centering" is obvious from the primary use in centred arches, but the same term is applied to the use of scaffold-boards to support concrete floors while they are setting hard. (*See* CARPENTRY.)

CENTERVILLE, a city of south central Iowa, U.S., 88 mi. S.E. of Des Moines; county seat of Appanoose county, served by the Burlington, the Rock Island and the Southern Iowa (freight; electric) railways. The altitude is 1,013 ft. Pop. (1950) 7,606. Large quantities of coal are mined in the vicinity. Quarrying of limestone, stock raising and dairying, ironworks, a soybean mill and creameries are among the industries. In 1846 the town was platted as Chaldea, later called Senterville and finally changed to Centerville by the legislature. It was chartered as a city in 1870. The town was, at one time, an important ferry terminal for the Chariton river.

A junior college was established there in 1930 and provides normal school training and liberal arts courses; a football stadium and a large park near the centre of the city provide recreational facilities.

CENTERVILLE, a town in southwestern Pennsylvania, U.S. It is situated in Washington county about 26 mi. S. of Pittsburgh and about 5 mi. W. of the Monongahela river, on federal highway 40.

The altitude is 1,160 ft. Pop. (1950) 5,874; (1940) 6,317 by the federal census.

The town derives its chief income from farming and mining. It is administered by a mayor-council government. The town, which is incorporated, was laid out as a pike town in 1821 although the first settlers established themselves within the borough as early as 1766. Its name derived from its relative position between Washington and Uniontown.

The deep narrow valley of the near-by Monongahela river is the most conspicuous topographical feature in the rolling, hilly country which comprises Washington county. The area is one of the earliest to be explored west of the Allegheny mountains and it is rich in historical sites.

The earliest settlers in the region were chiefly of Scotch-Irish and German descent, coming there from eastern Pennsylvania, Virginia and Maryland.

CENTIGRADE SCALE: *see* THERMOMETRY.

CENTIME. The one-hundredth part of a franc, the monetary unit of France, Belgium, and Switzerland, is termed a *centime.* It is from Lat. *centum,* hundred. In Italy the hundredth part of the *lira* is called a *centesimo;* in Spain the hundredth part of the *peseta* is called a *centimo.*

CENTIPEDE, an animal with a distinct head, one pair of feelers (antennae) and a long segmented body, each typical segment of which is provided with a single pair of walking legs. The centipedes form in the phylum Arthropoda (*q.v.*), the distinct class Chilopoda in which well defined subdivisions may be made as follows:—

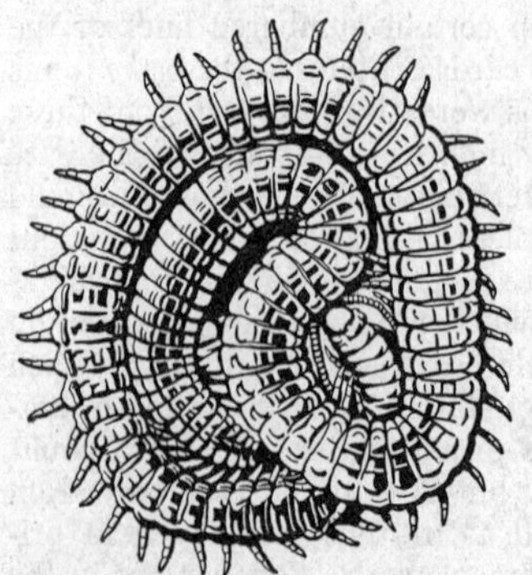

BY COURTESY OF HUGH MAIN

FIG. 1.—A TYPICAL MEMBER OF THE GEOPHILOMORPHA (ORYA BARBARICA), ONE OF THE LUMINOUS CENTIPEDES

First subclass Epimorpha, in which the young leave the egg with the full number of body segments and walking legs.

This subclass comprises two orders:—

(*i.*) Geophilomorpha (containing ten families) with *Geophilus* as the typical genus, and

(*ii.*) Scolopendromorpha (containing two families), *Scolopendra* being the typical genus.

Second subclass Anamorpha, in which the young leave the egg with seven pairs of legs. Afterward there are periods of growth each of which is followed by a change of skin, resulting in an increase in the number of pairs of limbs until the adult condition is reached. In this subclass, also, there are two orders:—

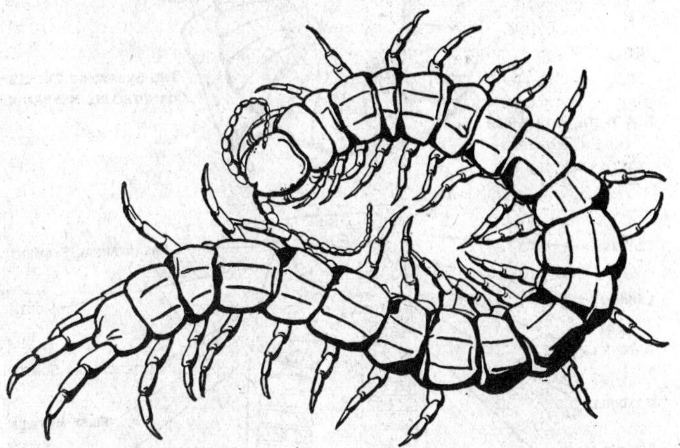

BY COURTESY OF HUGH MAIN
FIG. 2.—SCOLOPENDRA MORSITANS A TYPICAL MEMBER OF THE SCOLOPENDROMORPHA

(*i.*) Lithobiomorpha (containing three families). *Lithobius* is the typical genus, and

(*ii.*) Scutigeromorpha (consisting of one family), with the genus *Scutigera* as type.

The head of the centipede (*see* fig. 6) bears a pair of many-jointed antennae. Three pairs of mouth appendages are present, the mandibles, first maxillae and second maxillae. Right and left first maxillae are fused to form a kind of lower lip to the mouth. The second maxillae, which lie behind the first, are but slightly modified walking legs, in which some of the constituent leg segments are still easily recognizable. But though their bases meet in the mid-line, the second maxillae do not form a lower lip to the mouth, for this is formed by the first maxillae. There is therefore nothing comparable with the labium of insects.

The head, body and limbs are invested with cuticle which remains flexible wherever movement of the parts is necessary, and elsewhere is thickened by a deposition of horny chitin. In a typical limb-bearing segment consisting of a roof, a floor and side walls, the cuticle covering these is reinforced to form definite protecting and supporting plates or sclerites, differently arranged in different forms. Except at the joints the cuticle of the limbs is similarly hardened.

The last three segments of the body (called pregenital, genital and anal segments) are without walking legs.

AFTER VERHOEFF, IN BRONN, "KLASSEN UND ORDNUNGEN DES TIER-REICHS" (WINTER)
FIG. 3.—A TYPICAL MEMBER OF THE LITHOBIOMORPHA, THE COMMON CENTIPEDE OF EUROPEAN FIELDS AND GARDENS

Eyes occur in most Lithobiomorpha, all Scutigeromorpha and in all Scolopendromorpha except one family (Cryptopidae). They are absent in Geophilomorpha. A simple eye (ocellus) or a group of separate ocelli is usual but in Scutigeromorpha the external lenses of the group of units fuse into a single faceted lens.

On each side of the head in *Lithobius* a sense organ (organ of Tömösvary) of unknown function occurs; it consists of a group of cells below the chitin associated with an external hollow near the antenna. The frontal organ of *Lithobius* and *Scolopendra* consists of a group of deep-seated nerve cells behind each eye—its use is unknown.

The digestive tube is simple; it receives, in front, the products of the salivary glands and, further back, those of the excretory (Malpighian) tubules. Its opening is in the anal segment.

The main nerve cord lies below the gut and ends in front in a nerve mass (the suboesophageal ganglion) united with the supra-oesophageal ganglion or "brain," which lies above the front of the gut, by a pair of stout nerve cords.

Breathing is by air tubes or tracheae which open at the sides of the body except in the Scutigeromorpha in which the openings are in the middle line of the back.

BY COURTESY OF HUGH MAIN
FIG. 4.—A TYPICAL MEMBER OF THE SCUTIGEROMORPHA (SCUTIGERA), THE HOUSE CENTIPEDE

The heart, which lies above the gut, is a simple tube and the blood circulation is in the direction usual in invertebrates—forward dorsally and backward ventrally.

The reproductive system, which lies above the gut, varies in different centipedes. In the male the number of testes ranges from 1 to 24. In the adult female the ovary is always unpaired. The reproductive system opens in the genital segment.

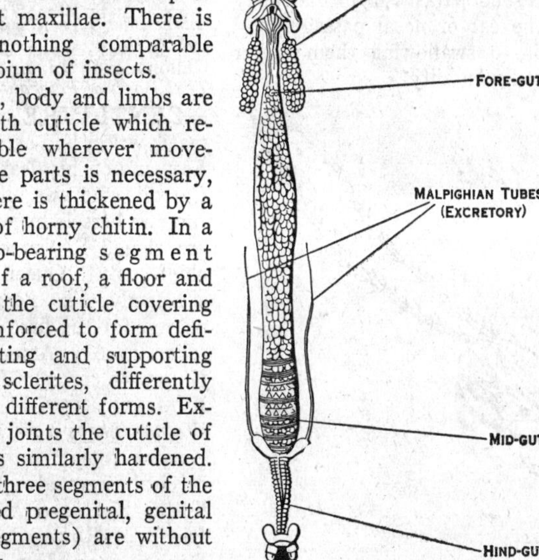

AFTER VERHOEFF, IN BRONN, "KLASSEN UND ORDNUNGEN DES TIER-REICHS" (WINTER)
FIG. 5.—DIGESTIVE TRACT OF A CENTIPEDE (LITHOBIUS FORFICATUS)

Owing to the retiring habits of centipedes comparatively little is known about their reproduction. Although the satisfactory observation of copulation has never been recorded, on anatomical grounds it is believed to take place. In the Anamorpha the female after laying each egg carries it about between the specialized claws at the hinder end of her body and eventually, when it has been smeared with a secretion or earth, or both, lays it down where its covering is sufficient protection against enemies.

The eggs of Epimorpha are laid in an open nest and the female guards them faithfully until hatching takes place.

The egg is rich in yolk; this serves as food for the developing centipede which grows from a special area in the lower part of the egg. An examination of the developing animal when the process has been some time in progress may reveal the beginnings of the various head segments and of the walking limbs. When the animal at length leaves the egg its form varies as already indicated, according to the order to which it belongs.

Centipedes as a class have a world-wide distribution. Fossil centipedes occur in amber of Oligocene age but all older remains tentatively referred to the class Chilopoda are problematical.

Many Geophilomorpha have the power to give light, but as these animals are blind the property is perhaps accidental. The light is produced by the simultaneous discharge upon the lower surface of the body of two kinds of glands, which occur in the floor of the body segments. When the two fluids mix outside the body a light is produced.

When the gardener hunting for slugs at night sees *Lithobius* carrying off a small slug and shaking it as a terrier shakes a rat he rightly assumes that the centipede is his friend; but *Lithobius* may kill and eat beneficial insects as well. Geophilomorpha are certainly carnivorous at times, but one species (*Haplophilus subterraneus*) has been known to damage growing celery, lettuce and onions, and other species are likely to be similarly injurious at times.

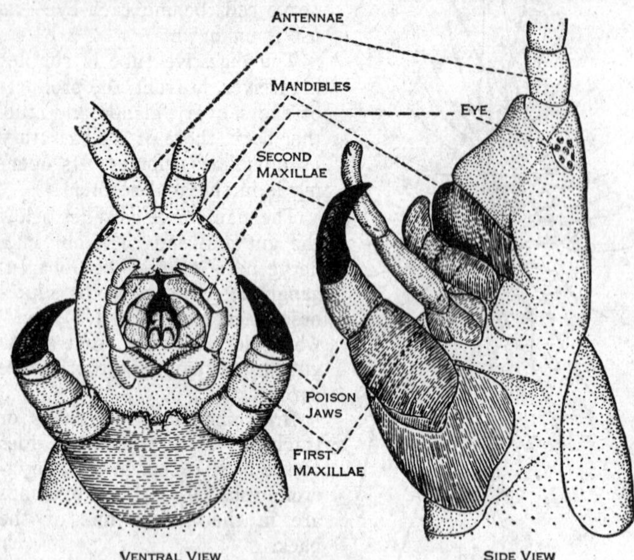

FIG. 6.—HEAD OF CENTIPEDE (SCOLOPENDRA)

The painful bite of large centipedes may on occasion cause danger to life. "The part bitten should be bathed in a solution of ammonia—about 1 in 5" (Hirst). Pseudoparasitism in man may be due to accidental invasion of the ear or nasal passages and adjacent sinuses by Chilopoda; or to swallowing them either accidentally or in a state of impaired mentality.

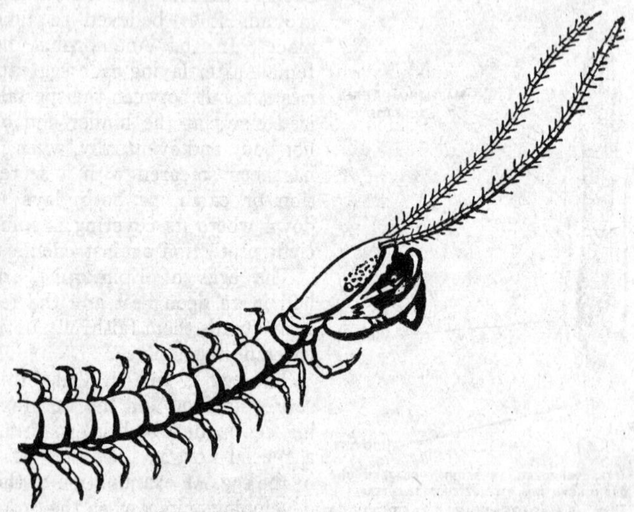

FIG. 7.—LITHOBIUS EATING A SLUG

Brief mention of centipedes is made by early writers (Aristotle, Pliny, Aelian). Oviedo, the companion of Columbus, describes the occurrence of centipedes in the island of Santo Domingo, where he was supervisor of gold smeltings, and mentions the bright light emitted by some of them.

The literature in English is very scattered—most of the best modern accounts are in German.

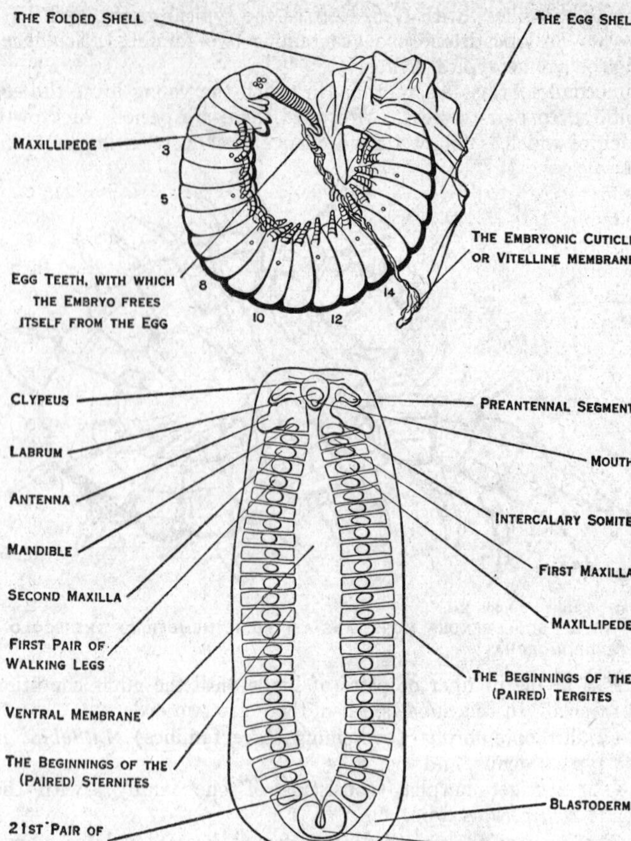

FIG. 8.—DEVELOPMENT OF A CENTIPEDE (SCOLOPENDRA CINGULATA)
Above, the embryo in the act of leaving the egg. The front part of the egg shell is already removed, and the back part thrown into folds. The embryonic cuticle is still attached to the end of the antennae. The numbers indicate leg-bearing somites. Below, developing embryo

See F. G. Sinclair, "Myriapods" in *Cambridge Natural History,* vol. 5 (1895); K. W. Verhoeff, "Chilopoda" in Bronn's *Klassen und Ordnungen des Tier-Reichs;* K. Graf v. Attems, "Chilopoda" in *Handbuch der Zoologie,* vol. 4 (1926); S. G. and H. K. Brade-Birks, "Luminous Chilopoda" in *Annals and Magazine of Natural History* (1920); Zittel's *Text Book of Palaeontology* (edit. Eastman, 1913). (S. G. B.-B.; X.)

CENTLIVRE, SUSANNA (*c.* 1667–1723), English dramatic writer and actress, married at 16 the nephew of Sir Stephen Fox, and on his death within a year she married an officer named Carroll, who was killed in a duel. Left in poverty, she began to support herself by writing for the stage. Some of her early plays are signed S. Carroll. In 1706 she married Joseph Centlivre, chief cook to Queen Anne, who survived her. Her first play was a tragedy, *The Perjured Husband* (1700), and she herself appeared for the first time at Bath in her comedy *Love at a Venture* (1706). Among her most successful comedies are: *The Gamester* (1705); *The Busy Body* (1709); *A Bold Stroke for a Wife* (1718); *The Basset-table* (1706); and *The Wonder! a Woman keeps a Secret* (1714), in which, as the jealous husband, Garrick found one of his best parts. Her plots, verging on the farcical, were always ingenious and amusing, and the dialogue fluent. She never seems to have acted in London, but she was a friend of Rowe, Farquhar and Steele. Mrs. Centlivre died on Dec. 1, 1723. Her dramatic works were published, with a biography, in 1761 (reprinted 1872).

BIBLIOGRAPHY.—W. J. Jerrold, *Five Queer Women* (1929).

CENTO, a town of Emilia, Italy, province of Ferrara, 18 mi. S.E. direct from the town of Ferrara, 50 ft. above sea level; it is reached by road (6 mi. to the west) from the station of S. Pietro in Casale, 15 mi. S.W. by W. of Ferrara, and also by a steam tramway (18 mi. N.) from Bologna to Pieve di Cento, on the opposite bank of the Reno. Pop. (1936) 5,677 (town); 22,371 (commune). It was the birthplace of the painter Giovanni Francesco Barbieri (Guercino).

CENTO, a composition made up by collecting passages from various works. The Byzantine Greeks manufactured several out of the poems of Homer, among which may be mentioned the life of Christ by the famous empress Eudoxia, and a version of the biblical history of Eden and the Fall. The Romans of the later empire and the monks of the middle ages were fond of constructing poems out of the verse of Virgil. Such were the *Cento Nuptialis* of Ausonius, the sketch of biblical history which was compiled in the 4th century by Proba Falconia, wife of a Roman proconsul, and the hymns in honour of St. Quirinus taken from Virgil and Horace by Metellus, a monk of Tegernsee, in the latter half of the 12th century. Specimens may be found in the work of Aldus Manutius (Venice, 1504; Frankfurt, 1541, 1544). In 1535 Laelius Capitulus produced from Virgil an attack upon the dissolute lives of the monks; in 1536 there appeared at Venice a *Petrarca Spirituale;* and in 1634 Alexander Ross (a Scotsman and one of the chaplains of Charles I) published a *Virgilius Evangelizans, seu Historia Domini nostri Jesu Christi Virgilianis verbis et versibus descripta.*

CENTRAL AMERICA, the major isthmus lying between North America and South America and extending from the Isthmus of Tehuantepec, in Mexico, through the Isthmus of Panamá to Colombia. This geographical region includes the Mexican states of Yucatán, Campeche, Tabasco and Chiapas and the territory of Quintana Roo; the republics of Guatemala, Honduras, El Salvador, Nicaragua, Costa Rica and Panamá; and the crown colony of British Honduras, which is claimed also by Guatemala and is known to Spanish-speaking peoples as Belize. The approximate over-all extent of Central America is thus from 7° to 21° 30′ N. lat. and from 77° (due south of Washington, D.C.) to 94° (due south of Beaumont, Tex.) W. long., or roughly 1,150 statute mi. east and west by 1,000 mi. north and south. The total area is approximately 300,000 sq.mi. and the population is more than 11,100,000 (1950 census figures and reliable estimates), of which 92,487 sq.mi. and 2,339,030 inhabitants are in the five above-mentioned Mexican states and territory.

Central America trends mainly northwest and southeast, as seen in its southwestern margin, the gently sinuous and occasionally indented Pacific coast line, roughly paralleling the volcano-studded mountain backbone, which is visible from the shore at most points. The eastern and northern coasts border the Gulf of Mexico and the Caribbean sea and are characterized by more extensive lowlands and lower mountains than the Pacific side; also by long, straight steplike north-south and east-west segments in the northern portion. The low-lying Yucatán peninsula extends northward, from the flat Guatemalan Petén department and British Honduras, as the major anomaly in the isthmus, and presents the principal barrier separating the Gulf of Mexico from the Caribbean sea. Only the narrow Yucatán channel between the northeastern tip of the peninsula (Cape Catoche) and the western tip of Cuba connects these two mediterranean bodies of water.

The term "Middle America" is sometimes used as a synonym for Central America, but more often regional geographers include all of Mexico, Central America and the West Indies in Middle America as distinguished from North America and South America.

Because of their history of former political unity and sporadic efforts at restoring a union, the countries of the early 19th-century Central American federation (Guatemala, Honduras, El Salvador, Nicaragua and Costa Rica) are frequently referred to as the Five Republics of Central America. Not until the beginning of the 20th-century (1903) did Panamá begin its independent political life, as it formerly was a narrow, isthmian extension of western Colombia.

Certain physical, historical and cultural similarities lend validity to the regional concept of Central America, most of which was geologically related, was occupied by the ancient Maya Indians and was embraced in the Spanish colonial *audiencia,* or judicial district, of Guatemala.

GEOLOGY AND PHYSIOGRAPHY

Central America geologically is one of the most complex regions in the world, and much of it is little known. In many ways it resembles an enormous island, being in reality a double peninsula, since it is attached at both ends: in Mexico, at the Tehuantepec constriction, and in Panamá, where it joins South America. Many of its peculiar characteristics may be explained by this peninsular nature. Northwestern Central America probably was insular during parts of the Palaeozoic era, and was linked to the Greater Antilles, though separated from North and South America by narrow straits.

The oldest-known geologic formations in the area are Palaeozoic, usually designated as pre-Permian, since no rocks of proved age older than Permian have been found. Most so-called Carboniferous rocks are of early and middle Permian age, and Pre-Cambrian or Archaean formations may be no older than middle Palaeozoic.

The original nuclear core of Central America, typified by granite and metamorphic sedimentary rocks, embraces parts of the present political areas of Chiapas, Guatemala, Honduras, British Honduras and Nicaragua. The date of this ancient formation is uncertain, but it was probably Pre-Cambrian. Sections of the primordial nucleus, which trend in great east-west arcs (the Antillean or Caribbean mountain system, as distinguished from the Andean system), have been continuously above the sea since early geological time, and the region appears to have been originally a westward continuation of the Greater Antilles (Cuba, Jamaica, Haiti and Puerto Rico). It was broken apart and the West Indian segment separated into islands by faulting during various periods of geologic history, especially in late Cenozoic (Pliocene-Pleistocene). Probably there was a westward extension of the core land of Central America to Baja California in Cretaceous time. Marginal to the old nucleus on the north, a large area sank, starting in the middle Jurassic period, as the Gulf of Mexico began to form. Later deposits (mostly Pliocene and Quaternary) were re-uplifted as the nonfolded marine mantle formations of Tabasco, Campeche and Yucatán, in Mexican Central America, and the contiguous states of Oaxaca and Veracruz, continuing across the Isthmus of Tehuantepec into the main region of Mexico. Ranges of younger volcanoes, striking essentially northwest-southeast, overlie and largely bury the east-west basement Antillean mountains.

Southeast of the nuclear, ancient Central American land mass lies a distinct geologic region, including present-day Panamá, Costa Rica and southern Nicaragua. Largely of volcanic origin, the narrow Costa Rica-Panamá isthmus, barely 40 mi. wide at the Panama Canal, is geologically recent, having emerged as land only in the middle Miocene period. Then a great submarine ridge was arched up more than 12,000 ft. above the ocean floor, and from the late Miocene through the Pleistocene period intrusive mountains were uplifted upon the crest of the ridge, from western Panamá to southern Nicaragua, terminating in a period of intense and explosive volcanic activity. It was through the eruptions of volcanoes that the great ridge was built up above sea level. Though the Panamá isthmus has the east-west striking S-curve typical of the Antillean system, the trend becomes more nearly northwest-southeast as western Panamá near the Costa Rican border merges with the Pacific volcanic ranges.

Marine Portals and Land Bridges.—Previously, except for a brief land-bridge period from late Cretaceous to middle Eocene, a wide portal had been open through the Panamá-Costa Rica area, with intermingling of Atlantic and Pacific waters. Easterly winds probably forced some movement of water from the Caribbean into the Pacific as a part of the North Equatorial current; hence, it is unlikely that any Gulf stream existed. Brazilian land reptiles, though related to those of Africa and India, were quite distinct from those of North America. Marine molluscs, horn corals, echinids, decapods and sea pens migrated through the portal from the Pacific to the Caribbean. Marine faunas on the two coasts of Central America are closely related as a result of the Panamá and (Pliocene) Tehuantepec portals.

The end of the middle Miocene period saw the beginning of the narrow Panamá land bridge which has continued to the present time. Interchange of marine waters, flora and fauna ceased when the portal closed, and intermigration of animals and plants, interrupted since the Eocene period, was resumed, first between South America and Central America-West Indies, then (Pliocene to present), after the closing of the Tehauntepec portal, between South America and North America. Several orders of mammals, including some marsupials and primates, probably crossed the Cretaceous-Eocene land bridge from North America to South America, and four orders definitely crossed the later Pliocene-Pleistocene bridge. These included the carnivores (*e.g.*, dog, cat), proboscideans (*e.g.*, mastodon), artiodactyls (*e.g.*, deer, pig) and perissodactyls (*e.g.*, tapir).

The Tehuantepec portal was also important in Central American geologic history, having been open during upper Miocene and lower Pliocene and possibly during Eocene times. These past interoceanic straits gave Central America its insular state in middle geologic ages and are reflected today in the narrow isthmuses at either end, which now give the region its peninsular character. Changes in climates as well as in fauna and flora must have resulted from these revolutionary geologic events.

The three narrowest lowland sections of the isthmus, Tehuantepec, the lakes of Nicaragua, and Panamá, were long considered for various canal projects before the Panama Canal was constructed (1904–14).

NORTHWESTERN CENTRAL AMERICA

Highlands.—Surface rock formations in the Central American highlands include widespread marine sediments, especially beds of shales, limestones, sandstones and conglomerates. Many of these were laid down during Permian and Cretaceous ages, and, though fossils occur, the record is incomplete, in part because fossil collections are inadequate. In northwestern Central America these deposits largely cover the ancient crystalline core, and in turn they are overlain, especially near the Pacific coast, by extensive and often immensely deep younger volcanic materials.

Ancient Mountains of Nuclear Central America.—The principal mountains of the oldest periods of folding and faulting, which were late Permian and an undetermined age prior to that, include the Sierra Madre of southern Chiapas, striking northwest-southeast; the Sierra de Chuacús and Sierra de las Minas of south central Guatemala, the former striking almost east-west, the latter east-northeast and west-southwest; and the Sierra de la Grita, del Espíritu Santo and de Omoa in Honduras, roughly parallel in strike with Chuacús, just across the international boundary and beyond the Río Motagua in Guatemala. These folded mountains of ancient crystalline and sedimentary rocks form a nearly symmetrical shallow crescentic arc that is convex to the south. A northern outlier is seen in the core of the Cockscomb horst (up-faulted block) mountains of south central British Honduras, the highest point of which is more than 3,600 ft. In the middle highland region of Guatemala, which is the type area for nuclear Central America, the landscape is characteristically one of steep relief, with deep parallel valleys between high ridges (summits mostly between 8,000 and 10,000 ft.) having sharply dissected flanks where streams flow through barrancas (gullies and canyons).

Other ancient mountains having pre-Permian granites, gneisses and schists and east-west strike are to be seen in Honduras, especially the northern third, and in northern Nicaragua. The mountains are separated into short, steep and rugged ranges with fault basins in between, and though there is little order in the intricately dissected highlands, a northern and a somewhat higher southern system of cordilleras may be discerned. The highest point is 9,400 ft., in the Cerros de Celaque, but most of the many summits are under 8,000 ft. Honduras as a whole is the most mountainous country of Central America, having extremely narrow and limited coastal and interior plains. The highlands of northwestern, interior Nicaragua are similar in height and ruggedness to those of Honduras, though of undetermined age.

Highlands of Middle and Recent Geologic Time.—Except for the most recent and currently active volcanoes along the Pacific side, which have buried the older strata to the north and east, the highlands of northwestern Central America were uplifted to their present high elevations during Mesozoic and Cenozoic (especially Pliocene), "mediaeval" and "recent" geologic time, respectively.

The plateau of San Cristobal, or Mesa Central, in Chiapas consists of nearly horizontal Cretaceous beds which were enormously up-faulted during the Pliocene period, and it towers above the Río Grijalva valley. Contiguous with this highland, across the border in west central Guatemala, the Altos Cuchumatanes horst stands as one of the most impressive nonvolcanic mountain areas in the whole region. The east-west southward-facing front of this great limestone block rises to a high point of more than 13,000 ft., higher than all the great volcanoes to the south except Tajumulco (13,814 ft.). It presents a nearly straight 40-mi. east-west wall more than 10,000 ft. in elevation above sea level and with relief heights above the Río Negro from 3,000 to 5,000 ft. This is the dominant single relief block in all the highlands of Central America. The lofty summits are smoothly rolling, with sinkholes characteristic of karst topography in limestone areas, but around the margins of the massif profound canyons drop away to breathtaking depths. Following the crescentic arc farther eastward through the Alta Verapaz, the Pliocene orogeny is manifested in other features of step and block faulting, mostly minor as to relief except for the hill lands south of the Cockscomb mountains of British Honduras. This is the same great faulting series that separated Cuba from Yucatán and broke apart the islands of the Greater Antilles.

Major Structural Depressions.—Enormous troughs caused by faulting and folding are prominent relief features in northern Central America, notably the central depression of Chiapas, a great graben (down-faulted block) through which flows the Río Grijalva and where the capital city, Tuxtla Gutiérrez, is situated. This depression lies between and parallel to the Sierra Madre and the Mesa Central. The east-flowing Río Negro and the west-flowing Salegua of Guatemala follow structural valleys having the great scarp of the Cuchumatanes as a north wall. The Motagua and Polochic rivers drain northeastward and eastward through deep, ancient furrows, ultimately reaching the Caribbean. Lago de Izabal (Golfo Dulce) lies at the foot of the Polochic valley. The great Honduras depression, or Plain of Comayagua, is a graben, but its strike is anomalous in that it trends north-south, transverse to the Antillean mountain structure. More than 40 mi. long and having widths up to 15 mi., this trough is one of the major fault zones of Central America and is continued northward by the Río Humuya valley and southward by the Goascoran. Many of the rivers of southern Honduras flow through deep box canyons cut in lava beds, and this incision by drainage accentuates structural lines.

Recent Volcanoes.—The most prominent and striking feature of the mountains of Central America is the file of conical peaks, nearly all of them recent volcanoes, at or near the Pacific from Tacana, on the southern Mexico-Guatemala border, to Chiriquí, an outlier just across the Costa Rican boundary in Panamá. Only in southeastern Costa Rica and Panamá is the volcanic chain widely broken. These volcanoes, more than 100 large and 150 minor ones in all, trend in overlapping arcs, roughly northwest-southeast. They are geologically young (possibly pre-Miocene in places, definitely Pliocene to Recent) and form a mantle resting upon the older east-west ranges which they cross diagonally. The older volcanic lavas and ash beds, some of them having great thickness, form a broader base upon which the recently and presently active volcanoes rest.

Two distinct series of volcanic mountains, trending in gentle minor convex arcs toward the Pacific, may be traced as follows: one from Chiapas through Guatemala and El Salvador, and another through Nicaragua and Costa Rica into Panamá. Each series has a length of approximately 350 mi. (excluding Chiriquí because of its isolation from the others), with the two merging in the region of the Gulf of Fonseca.

The northwestern or Guatemalan (as distinguished from Costa Rican) series is the larger and more important, with a base of volcanic deposits extending the full length of the zone, from about 40 mi. N.W. of Tacana volcano, an average of 40 mi. wide in the western portion and 60 mi. in the eastern, where it covers nearly all of El Salvador. In Chiapas and Guatemala the crest of the older volcanic mantle forms the continental divide, with the recent volcanoes to the southwest and parallel with it and, roughly, with the Pacific coast. The numerous short, steep streams flowing to the Pacific follow antecedent courses, resulting in enormous gaps between the volcanoes and deep dissection of the loose volcanic detritus. Some cones are simple and well formed, as Tacana and Tajumulco (the highest peak in Central America, 13,814 ft.) at the western extremity of the Guatemalan group, and other smaller ones at the east. The central volcanoes tend to have multiple peaks, such as Santiaguito-Santa María, Atitlán-Tolimán and Fuego-Acatenango. In all such cases the coastward vent is the younger, the first-named of each of the above pairs. Fuego has been intermittently active for centuries, Santiaguito only for a few years but with rapid, continued growth. The blocking of openings by lava, especially andesitic, which is highly viscous and hardens rapidly, causes lateral explosions and the birth of new basal cones, as was the case with Santa María in 1902. Most of the western Guatemalan lava and ash is light-coloured andesitic, becoming darker and more basaltic toward El Salvador.

Consequently, in the latter border zone, wide fields of dark lava with lower, shield-type volcanoes present a markedly different landscape from the towering cones of the west. Izalco, in El Salvador, has been one of the most active vents in Central America during its short life.

Extensive deposits of volcanic ash, mostly light buff-coloured, from earlier eruptions, filled a number of highland valleys near the headwaters of streams, forming highly fertile basins that have had a long history of intensive settlement and cultivation. One of the most noteworthy of these is the basin of Quezaltenango, second city of Guatemala, situated in the upper Samalá basin at an elevation of nearly 8,000 ft. From San Juan Ostuncalco to Totonicapán this nearly level, open bolson is more than 22 mi. long.

Volcanism has disturbed the drainage with resultant formation of a number of lakes, some of them spectacularly beautiful, such as Atitlán, in a collapse basin (*caldera*) that is partly volcano dammed, and Amatitlán, wholly dammed, in Guatemala; and Coatepeque, Ilopango and others in volcanic depressions in El Salvador.

Earthquakes.—A broad Pacific belt, southeastward to Panamá, is subject to frequent and violent seismic activity characteristic of such highly unstable volcanic areas, some earthquakes being caused by eruptive activity, others by faulting. A number of cities have thus been destroyed, notably Antigua Guatemala in 1773 and modern Guatemala city in 1917–18. Ash eruptions may cover wide areas, as spectacularly illustrated by the tremendous explosion of Coseguina (Nicaragua), which spread ash dust more than 500 mi.

Lowlands.—The gently sloping Pacific coastal plain, attaining a maximum width of about 35 mi., is composed mostly of Quaternary volcanic alluvium, reflecting in its sharply convex curve toward the Pacific the great volume of ejecta which has been blown from the vents, then much of it carried westward by the easterly trade winds and reworked by streams. In El Salvador and Nicaragua the coastal plain narrows.

By far the most extensive lowlands of Central America are to be found in the extreme north. The great plain of the Petén, in Guatemala, at the base of the predominantly limestone peninsula of Yucatán, is almost all less than 1,000 ft. in elevation. The Mesozoic and Cenozoic sedimentary beds are largely horizontal. The descent to these northern lowlands is by steps as a result of block faulting along the strike during the Pliocene period. The marine beds of Tabasco, Campeche, Yucatán and Quintana Roo, as in northern British Honduras and the Petén, are so low and horizontal that there is little stream development—almost none on the outer peninsula. The Usumacinta, the only large river, is marginal to the Petén, at the foot of the Chiapas highlands. Sinkholes (*cenotes*) are numerous, the result of limestone solution, in a karst area, and it is here that water is obtained by the inhabitants, who must also depend upon windmills and catchment basins. Swamps and marshes are extensive, especially in Tabasco. Large beds of little-weathered sea shells attest to the recency of the emergence of this area. The deposits themselves are of Cenozoic age, Eocene through Pleistocene. The present width of the peninsula dates to late Pleistocene uplift, and the straight coastal lines are fault features, the largest being the east coast of the peninsula, more than 400 mi. long. Late Pleistocene subsidences along the north and west coasts of the Yucatán peninsula have caused certain marine invasions, most notable of which is the Laguna de Terminos in Campeche.

The second largest lowland plain of northern Central America is that of eastern Honduras (essentially the disputed area, claimed also by Nicaragua) and the eastern portion of Nicaragua, almost half the area of the older, northern province, about 100 mi. wide in the area of the upper Tuma river. Most of the larger rivers of Nicaragua and Honduras cross this lowland, notably the Coco, along the disputed Honduras border, and the Patuca, in the disputed zone. The igneous basement rocks of the lowlands are covered mostly by undisturbed, nearly horizontal marine Pleistocene beds and Recent alluvial deposits. In places, granites are exposed. Except for these two large lowland areas, and a few limited river valleys, this coastal plain of Nicaragua, Honduras and El Salvador is extremely narrow.

SOUTHEASTERN CENTRAL AMERICA

The distinct geologic province of southeastern Central America includes the long, narrow, S-shaped Isthmus of Panamá and Costa Rica and the low Nicaraguan lakes trough and coastal volcanic range. The present land bridge between North and South America is of geologically recent origin (late Miocene). Prior to the formation of the isthmus, a large, deep marine portal had been open, from Eocene to late Miocene, permitting free circulation of water between the Atlantic and Pacific oceans. The flow was mostly westward, under the influence of easterly winds that drive the North Equatorial current. The isthmus at the narrowest point, near the Panama Canal, is about 40 mi. wide, and at the widest part, at the Nicoya peninsula, it is more than 150 mi. wide. The growth of this connecting link was by volcanic action, mainly in Eocene time, forming a ridge upon an elongated submarine arch. Basaltic and especially andesitic volcanic materials are overlain by early Cenozoic marine beds. Intrusive mountains were uplifted in upper Miocene-Pliocene, and through later Pliocene and Pleistocene were further built up by numerous highly active volcanoes of the explosive type. Chiriquí, at 11,410 ft. elevation, stands atop the isthmian ridge about 24,000 ft. above the ocean floor on either side.

Panamá.—The topography of Panamá is irregular and broken, more hilly lowland than mountainous, with most of its area under 1,500 ft. elevation. The highest points, a number of them over 7,000 ft., are in the west, along the igneous Serranía de Tabasará, and culminating in Chiriquí volcano. The lower Serranía del Darién forms the eastern backbone along the Caribbean. Though primarily volcanic, some sedimentaries, especially limestones, shales and sandstones of the early Cenozoic, prior to the Miocene and later uplifts, cover the igneous rocks. This is best seen in the east, near the Colombian border. The limited Tertiary marine beds of Panamá are thinner and less folded than those of Costa Rica. Folding parallels the coast and often is asymmetric, with steeper slopes toward the Caribbean, especially notable in Darién. A number of north-south thrust faults cut across central Panamá and seemingly have locally affected relief and drainage. There is no longer any active volcanism in Panamá.

Costa Rica.—The Costa Rican highlands extend from southeast to northwest, the full length of the country, in a diagonal trend that brings them nearer the Pacific side, especially in the north. Three distinct, contiguous cordilleras, having roughly parallel strikes but different arc trends and a central break in continuity, may readily be traced: the Cordillera de Guanacaste, or Volcanic range, in the northwest, with six major volcanoes between 4,500 and 6,200 ft. high; the Cordillera Central, just north of the centre and with nearly east-west strike and four large volcanoes, the highest being intermittently active Turrialba at 12,300 ft.; and the Cordillera de Talamanca, the largest and highest of the three ranges, which is continued in Panamá to a point near Chiriquí volcano. Between the latter two chains, and near the convergence of the three, is the sedimentary Candelaria highland, the economic, cultural and political as well as the approximate geographical centre of Costa Rica. San José, the capital city, has a favourable situation there that in many ways is parallel to that of Guatemala city. Both are near the continental divide, are just under 4,000 and 5,000 ft. elevation, respectively, in highlands near volcanoes, nearer the Pacific coast than the Atlantic and served by coast-to-coast rail connections. From the Candelaria divide two major rivers flow in opposite directions—the Río Grande de Pirris, west-southwestward to the Pacific at the Gulf of Nicoya, and the Reventazón, northeastward to the Caribbean sea. The railroad follows these valleys, with terminals at the ports of Limón on the Caribbean and Puntarenas on the Pacific.

The highest point in Costa Rica is not a volcano. It is Cerro Chirripó Grande, 12,588 ft., summit of a large area of the Talamanca range almost 10,000 ft. in elevation, the only Costa Rican area of its size having such elevation. It is almost comparable in elevation and extent with the Cuchumatanes highlands in Guatemala, and it has even greater relief height (7,000 ft. in four miles).

Great transverse ridges extending coastward in both directions from Chirripó Grande serve as effective barriers to movement along the Pacific and Caribbean lowlands. The Pacific flanking ridge merges with a coast range that parallels the southern third of the Costa Rican Pacific plain, and between it and the Talamanca range is the General highland. These two elevated areas are made up of deep-seated crystalline rocks, both light and dark types, and were formed by thrust faulting. The Caribbean coastal lowlands are much wider than the Pacific lowlands and continue into Nicaragua, across the San Juan valley and in the lowland lakes (Managua and Nicaragua) trough. The Pacific coastal lowland is limited to a very few miles in width except at the bases of the large peninsulas of Nicoya, Osa and Burica. There is much swampland along the lower river valleys of both coasts.

Nicaragua.—The southwest Nicaraguan coastal volcanoes form a continuation of the Costa Rican Volcanic range and belong geologically to the Costa Rican mountain arc, which meets the Guatemalan arc somewhere near the Gulf of Fonseca. At present-day San Juan plain, the wide lowland gap between the highlands of Costa Rica and Nicaragua, there was an ocean portal open between late Oligocene and middle Miocene times, judging from marine deposits and especially West Indian type *Orbitoides* fossils found west of Lake Nicaragua. Late Miocene-Pliocene elevation of a narrow isthmus across the present San Juan valley resulted in the formation of a large embayment, in place of the present lakes region, extending from the Gulf of Fonseca to the Gulf of Papagayo, with the ancient Nicaraguan highlands forming the Pacific bay shore line. This narrow east-coastal land bridge was eroded by streams flowing away toward the Pacific and Caribbean from the low continental divide. At the same time (Oligocene-early Miocene) the line of volcanoes of Nicaragua began to form, and, with their renewed activity in Recent time, continuing to the present, they built up a nearly straight barrier, which broadened as the volcanoes grew and ultimately filled in most of the bay, leaving lakes Managua and Nicaragua (the latter more than 100 mi. by 40 mi.) as the only remnant water surfaces, now fresh. Three volcanic cones arose on two islands above the surface of Lake Nicaragua, and one in Lake Managua, with four others bordering it, including active Momotombo. The drainage divide shifted to the Pacific range, and the lake waters freshened and began to flow the long way out to the Caribbean through the San Juan river. This low trough cutting diagonally across Nicaragua is the locus of most of the economic, cultural and political life of the country, with the capital city, Managua, and Granada situated in the interlakes area, and the second city, León, just off on the Pacific coastal margin. Great interest has been shown in this low trough, most of it under 350 ft. elevation, as the site of a projected interocean canal. It was seriously considered for the crossing before the Panama Canal was built, and, afterward, as an alternate route.

CLIMATES AND WEATHER TYPES

Temperatures.—Locally, throughout Central America, as in certain other parts of tropical Latin America, climates are usually classified into three simple vertical groups: *tierra caliente,* hot land; *tierra templada,* temperate land; and *tierra fria,* or cold land. This corresponds with and probably stems from the old division of the earth into torrid, temperate and frigid zones dating back to the ancient Greeks. It is difficult to fix any limits to these "climates," which are altitudinally conditioned thermal zones. The "hot land" is, of course, the lowest in elevation above sea level. Citing western Guatemala as a typical illustration, this is approximately from 26° C. (78.8° F.) mean annual temperature at sea level to 22° C. (71.6° F.) at 1,000 m. (about 3,280 ft.) above mean sea level. The temperate belt extends upward from this point to about 1,900 m. (6,233 ft.), where the annual temperature is normally about 17° C. (62.6° F.). Above that, in the upper mountains and valleys, is the "cold land," culminating with about 5° C. (41° F.) at the summit of Tajumulco volcano (13,814 ft. or 4,211 m.), the highest point in Central America. Temperatures, hence also altitudinal zone lines, are slightly higher in the countries to the southeast. Any temperature limits can be set arbitrarily, but for world comparisons the Köppen "tropical" and "mesothermal" (temperate) types, with the coldest months warmer and cooler, respectively, than 18° C. (64.4° F.), are valid in Central America. The Köppen tropical-mesothermal isotherm (equal-temperature line) follows about the 1,450-m. (4,756-ft.) isohyps or contour line, which is just in the centre of the "temperate" zone of local usage.

By far the greater part of Central America has tropical climatic conditions, the terminal isthmuses, the narrow Pacific coastal lowlands and the broader Gulf and Caribbean coastal plains, as well as the entire Yucatán peninsula into the Petén of Guatemala, all being warm to hot the year around. Cooler, temperate conditions are limited to the higher mountain and intermountain basin and plateau areas.

Rainfall.—Rainfall, which has far greater seasonal variability than temperature, is not taken into account in the local climate classification. It is, however, the basis for the seasonal distinctions, "summer" being the dry season, with its clear skies, warm sun and pleasant weather, and "winter" being the more dismal rainy season, when cloudy skies actually may reduce daytime temperature maxima to points below those of summer. It must be borne in mind that local summer is climatologically winter, for the sun during that season (November through April) is highest south of the equator most of the time. Conversely, local winter is climatological summer, the rainy season, May through October, with maxima in June and September. This seasonal rainfall regime is characteristic of the Pacific lowlands south to Panamá, the Isthmus of Tehuantepec and most of the Yucatán peninsula, which have the Köppen tropical savanna climate. Highland regions nearer the Pacific coast, as in Chiapas, southwestern Guatemala and El Salvador, have the cooler phase of the summer-rain, winter-dry type. Toward the southeast the dry season is shorter, as the total annual rainfall for the region as a whole tends to increase. San José, Costa Rica, has five months of dry season (December-April), and Balboa, Canal Zone, has only three months, January to March inclusive, as compared with the six dry months of similarly situated stations in northwestern Central America.

The Pacific coast is in general drier than opposite points on the Caribbean, from British Honduras southeastward. East coastal Nicaragua is especially rainy, Greytown (San Juan del Norte) having recorded an annual average of more than 260 in. Similarly, highlands toward the Carribean side have rainfall distributed more evenly through the year, as seen as far interior as the Alta Verapaz (Cobán area) of Guatemala. Rainfall is concentrated along windward sides of mountain ranges, especially along the coastal volcanic chains. The southern Guatemala coffee belt is delimited by this, and the premium grades depend upon the cooler highland temperatures. Annual precipitation there ranges between 400 and 550 cm. (160 and 220 in.), according to exposure, in altitudes between 700 and 1,400 m. (about 2,300 and 4,600 ft.). The dry season is also reduced there, to three or four months (December-March). Deep valleys are generally much drier than adjacent highland areas. This is evident not only in the east-west structural valleys of Guatemala, where rain shadow conditions exist with respect to both northerly and southerly rain-bearing winds, but also in such north-south troughs as the Honduras depression.

The driest major area in Central America is the low northern tip of the Yucatán peninsula, where Progreso registers 19 in. In the hot tropics, where evaporation is always high, this amount of rainfall usually means almost desert conditions. There it is drier steppe (Köppen). Southeastern Guatemala is perhaps the next largest of the drier areas, though it exhibits less extreme aridity than north Yucatán. The greater rainfall of the north (Caribbean) coasts as compared with the south (Pacific), except for Yucatán, can be seen in comparing the annual rainfall of Colón, at the north end of the Panama Canal, more than 127 in., with Balboa Heights, at the south end of the Panama Canal about 40 mi. away, with 69 in. Colón has two slightly drier months in winter (February-March).

Weather.—Diurnal ranges of temperature generally exceed annual ranges in Central America, as elsewhere in the tropics. In highland Guatemala, for example, daily variations of 15° C. (27° F.) are common in the dry season, while the annual range is less than 5° C. (9° F.).. The prevailing winds in most of the region are northeasterly (between east-northeast and north-northeast), characteristic of the northern hemisphere trade winds, especially strong in the winter half-year. "Northers," strong, gusty north winds which may blow for several days, occur in northern Central America, into El Salvador, the effects of anticyclonic fronts of cold polar air masses that roll across North America in winter. They bring exceedingly clear skies, even in the afternoon. Because of the narrowness and dominantly marine nature of the isthmus of Central America, land-and-sea breezes are well developed. There, in the tropics, daytime heating of land surfaces, especially in the mountains, is intense, creating low pressure and onshore winds. These oppose the trades and, in the dry months of the Pacific region, result only in cloudiness from mid-morning to shortly after dark. In the rainy season, when the sun is nearly overhead at noon, or is even to the north, the trades are weakened and southerly winds with greater intensity bring rain. Hail is rare, usually coming in March and April in the high northern mountains. At night, as the land cools, especially in the highlands, the land breeze sets in. In winter on the south coast, as it strengthens the trades, the sky is swept clear, usually before midnight except at the height of the rainy season. Then cloudy nights may occur, and continuous rain night and day for several days. Mountain fog above 5,000 or 6,000 ft. is common at such times, as it is in afternoons throughout most of the year. On the north coast, as in Honduras, the northerly sea breeze joins forces with the northeast trades, which are strongest in winter, so that there is actually a winter maximum of rainfall in certain sections (La Ceiba to Puerto Castilla, for example). Rain throughout most of Central America comes usually in the form of intense tropical thunderstorms, from late morning to evening in normal rainy-season weather or at any time of day during *temporales,* or stormy wet spells. At such times relative humidity is constantly high. Hurricanes occasionally strike the northern Caribbean coast, from late July to early October. Belize especially has suffered the effects of these outer-tropical storms, and great destruction has been caused by them in the banana area around Puerto Barrios, Guatemala, but away from these coasts the effects of such storms is slight.

NATURAL VEGETATION AND SOILS

Because of the great range of climatic and edaphic conditions and the crossroads situation of the isthmus, the flora of Central America is extraordinarily diversified, containing thousands of species of many types of plants. Furthermore, the natural vegetation has been much altered by cultivation. For these reasons, it is extremely difficult to generalize regarding the vegetative cover. Certain broad generalizations may be made, however.

Tropical Rain Forest.—The most extensive single vegetation type is that of the tropical rain forest, found mostly near north and east coasts and slopes near these coasts. It consists of tall, spreading broad-leaved trees, with lower-storied trees underneath and a fairly clear sunless floor where only shade-tolerant herbaceous plants and shrubs can grow. The external aspect of these forests is similar to that of other rain forests of the world, as in the Amazon and Congo valleys and in parts of the East Indies.

Common among the taller trees are meliaceous (including mahogany), lauraceous and sapotaceous genera, *Ceiba, Ficus* and many others, and among the lower plants, *Inga, Carica, Cecropia,* palms and tree ferns. Great serpentine climbing vines and slender, rubbery hanging ones, such epiphytes as orchids and bromeliads, and long-leaf ferns add to the luxuriance of this forest. In vines as in trees, textures range from very soft to very hard. One fleshy vine contains potable water for those who recognize it. The numerous species of trees tend to be scattered, rather than occurring in pure stands as they do in the less benign high-latitude climates. Thus, in lumbering for mahogany or balsa, or tapping the latex for rubber or chicle, each tree must be sought out individually in the forest. This is lonely, difficult and costly work.

Though soils, except for alluvial bottom lands, tend to be only of superficial fertility, with shallow humus leaf mould underlain by leached and sometimes cemented subsoils, these forest areas are often cleared for agriculture even by primitive natives. They kill trees by girdling, cutting only through the cambium layer of dicotyledonous types and burning the dead trunks. Much of the lighter, regrown rain forest, especially in the old Maya area of the Yucatán peninsula, has been affected thus by human occupancy.

Great areas of rain forest have been cleared for plantation agriculture, primarily for bananas, secondarily for coffee, cacao, abacá and other crops. Corn, beans and such annual staples will grow throughout the year. This clearing has been most extensive in the rain forests of the eastern and northern (Caribbean) coast, in isolated areas from Guatemala to Panamá. There the rain forest reaches its widest extent, covering most of the eastern half of Nicaragua. It narrows along the north coast of Honduras, broadening again across the base of the Yucatán peninsula, into Campeche and westward through Tabasco, to the Isthmus of Tehuantepec. Along the middle slopes of the Pacific coastal highlands, mainly between 3,000 and 4,500 ft., as in the coffee belt of Guatemala, a monsoon forest that resembles a rain forest occurs, but with the tree ferns and epiphytic luxuriance of the cloud forest.

Park-Savanna, Deciduous Woodland and Gallery Forests.—Almost the entire Pacific lowland is characterized by open park land, with deciduous trees interspersed by tall savanna grasses and sedges, except where gallery forests border the innumerable streams. Scattered out over the more open interstream areas are occasional giant trees such as the ceibas, with wide, spreading crowns high above the ground, and many smaller trees which become seared and brown or even bare during the long, dusty dry season (generally November through April). Because of the open, grassy patches and drier climate, this coast has been especially important for cattle raising since shortly after the conquest. With the onset of the rains in April and May, the landscape becomes green and bright with flowers, and corn, beans, cotton, cassava and other crops begin to grow. In moist, marshy areas such broad grasses as calathea abound, and corn can be grown throughout the year, with a crop in three or four months at any season, and with better results than on the excessively wet Caribbean coast.

Mangrove, Outercoastal Swamps.—Groves of giant corozo or cohune palm grow in the outer Pacific lowlands, and fan palms, mangrove (*Rhizophora mangle* especially) and other swamp plants are found along the shore and the brackish lagoons of both the Pacific and the Caribbean. Soils along the outer coast that during the rainy season become impassable clay mires dry with deep, gaping cracks and uneven blocks and may be almost impassable in the dry season as well. The volcanic soils of the upper Pacific coast and piedmont are usually excellent for crops, particularly coffee and rubber.

Cactus, Thornbush, Scrub, Subxerophytic.—Thornbush, cactus and scrubby trees dominate the vegetation of the northern tip of the Yucatán peninsula, corresponding somewhat with the state of that name, where henequen cultivation for fibre is the principal occupation. Eastern Guatemala has similar vegetation, especially around Zacapa and the deep Río Motagua depression; it continues into El Salvador and covers also other deep interior Guatemalan valleys, the central depression of Chiapas and the Honduras depression. Where drought is extreme, tall cactus forms such as species of *Cereus* and *Opuntia* are dominant; thornbush genera, including acacias and mimosas, and species of *Crescentia,* a scrubby tree useful for its calabash fruit with a receptacle shell, are also found.

Mixed Coniferous-Hardwood Forests.—On most of the mountains and plateaus of middle elevation (4,500–7,500 ft.) of northwestern Central America (Chiapas, Guatemala, Honduras, El Salvador and northern Nicaragua) the forest is mixed coniferous (especially pines) and hardwoods (notably oaks, *Quercus*) and often rather open than dense. This is frequently the result of clearing for agriculture, which is especially important in the major areas of human settlement. Maize has the greatest acreage of crops locally consumed, and coffee among the export products. In the high valleys, where it is somewhat drier, agaves are important for fibre. Exposed seaward slopes between 4,500 and 7,000 ft. in Guatemala and El Salvador are covered in places with cloud forest, most luxuriant growths, wet and green and often covered with epiphytes. There the tree ferns are at their best.

Temperate flora from Nicaragua northward seems to have more elements which originated in North America, whereas south of Nicaragua more can be traced to the Andes of northern South America. As in geology, the major dividing line is Nicaragua-Costa Rica. South of Nicaragua, too, the pines diminish in importance, but oaks are well represented in the Costa Rican highlands.

Alpine Bunch Grass, Conifers, Meadows.—In the highest mountain areas, above about 8,000 ft., coarse, giant bunch grass, somewhat larger than the common types of the Andean altiplanos of northern South America, is common. In highland Guatemala it is widely used for roof thatch. Cypress trees, junipers and pines grow on the higher ridges and summits, often in almost pure stands at elevations above about 10,000 ft. There also, where summits are smooth and rolling as on the high Cuchumatanes, alpine meadows of short grasses and low flowering plants of many colours are typical. Sheep raising is the principal occupation, as it is too high for most agriculture, even wheat and potatoes. Besides the cold, which excludes some crops, the deep surface layers of raw humus, in places approaching peat, are unfavourable to cultivation. Mountain fogs are frequent during the day, but it is less rainy than at lower elevations.

ARCHAEOLOGY AND HISTORY

PRECONQUEST PERIOD

Northwestern Central America: Maya.—In the extreme northwestern part of Central America, especially Guatemala, Chiapas, British Honduras and the northern Yucatán peninsula, one of the most elaborate Indian civilizations of the American continents flourished for centuries before the arrival of the Spanish conquerors. This was the Maya civilization, whose extraordinary sculptures on stone, made without metal tools, and whose high attainments in mathematics, astronomy, the domestication and development of many important cultivated plants, including varieties of corn and beans, attest to their outstanding advancements in arts and sciences. For their religion and social organization they were likewise remarkable. They invented a vertical enumeration by position and a calendar more accurate than that used in the world today.

The story of the Maya and their contemporary eastern neighbours (in the present-day Honduras-Guatemala border zone) of different linguistic stock, the Chorotega, can be pieced together from archaeological remains preserving their writings in stone. The hieroglyphs have been little deciphered except for dates. Prior "archaic" cultures are obscure, but it is evident from their remains, buried under great ash and lava deposits, that they were basket and pottery makers for an undetermined period through centuries far antedating the Christian era. At Uaxactun archaeologists have discovered a sequence which shows that the Maya civilization, with its elaborate architecture and brilliant ceramic art and sculpture, developed from the "archaic" pottery makers.

The Maya pushed the Chorotega northward into Chiapas, Mexico, and southeastward into the Pacific coastal areas of El Salvador, Honduras, Nicaragua and Costa Rica early in the Christian era. The ultimate origin of the new world Indian populations is, in the opinion of most anthropologists and archaeologists, western Asia. From there they migrated into the new world via the Bering straits during periods when geologic and climatic factors made this feasible. The Maya civilization represents one of the major accomplishments of the descendants of these immigrants. There is reason to believe that there were close connections between the Maya of Petén and Chiapas and groups occupying the Isthmus of Tehuantepec. It was expected that research and excavation being conducted in that region would clarify whether this was the ancestral home of the Maya or whether it was occupied by a closely allied civilization. Maya tradition held only that they came from Tula, in eastern Mexico.

As builders of great stone temples, probably indicative of large centres of population but not necessarily so (dwelling sites have rarely left recognizable traces), the Maya started in the central part of their later territory, in the Petén and Chiapas regions, along and near the great water highway the Río Usumacinta. The population there today is the sparsest in all Central America, and the great temples of Tikal, Uaxactun, Yaxchilán and Palenque were buried under a covering of rain forest, virtually forgotten by the outside world until near the middle of the 19th century. Their classic period began there about the beginning of the 4th century A.D., according to most accepted calculations. Somewhere between the 6th and 8th centuries they reached their highest development, having spread southward to Honduras, where Copán still retains their well-preserved works of art, northward into all of Yucatán and westward into most of Chiapas. Between the 8th and 10th centuries, according to their dated monuments, they seem to have declined. This decline is related to the increasing population, impoverishment of farm land and resulting social tensions which were not resolved until what many authorities consider was a major breakdown in the Maya classic period civilization. During the 10th and 11th centuries a renaissance period of Maya civilization occurred along the northern edge of the Yucatán peninsula. This occurred under the political and military influence of the Toltecs, who amalgamated with and changed the ceremonial and religious emphasis of Maya civilization. The great cities of Uxmal, Chichen-Itzá and Mayapán, which became the dominant Mayan league, were the result of the blending of the artistic and sacred aspects of Maya civilization with the military emphasis and secular organization of the Toltecs.

This New Empire, as the renaissance period is usually called, in turn had declined by the 14th century and was decadent when the Spaniards arrived to hasten its final downfall. In the Guatemalan highlands from the 11th century until the Spanish conquest, the Maya also flourished, notably in the principal city-states of the Cakchiquels and Quichés, who were warring among themselves and with their neighbours. There, as in Yucatán and elsewhere, this civil strife worked in favour of the invading Spaniards.

Mexican Influence.—Mexican influence on the Maya, through the Toltecs, culturally, and the later Aztecs, militarily, was marked. This is seen today archaeologically in such features as the ball courts and linguistically in the Pipil (Nahuatl or Aztec) speech among the peoples along the Pacific coastal areas from Chiapas to Panamá. These Pipils are thought to have reached Central America originally as merchants and Aztec mercenaries. They made extended trade voyages for Soconusco cacao, quetzal feathers from the Guatemala highlands, shellfish purple from the Gulf of Nicoya and other special products of Central America which were much in demand in Mexico. The Aztecs borrowed many cultural traits from the Maya, including the calendar and the feathered serpent god (Maya, Kukulcan; Aztec, Quetzalcoatl), which provided some of the best-known motifs for their sculpture. The Maya renaissance bore somewhat the relationship to the Aztecs that the Hellenistic Greek period did to the Romans. Why the Maya declined is not known, but exhaustion of shallow forest soils and encroachment, after forest burnings, by grasses, difficult to work without the plow and draught animals (both lacking in the new world), must have contributed in large measure.

Archaeologists have differed greatly in their interpretations of Mayan dates. Preliminary evidence from radiation analysis made at the Institute for Nuclear Studies of The University of Chicago seems to support Herbert J. Spinden's dating. His historical outline of the Maya, showing comparative dates, is as shown in Table I.

TABLE I.—*Maya Periods According to Spinden*

Period	Date, A.D.	Date, Maya calendar
Protohistoric period	before 160	9-0-0-0-0
Calendar and hieroglyphic system developed		
First definitely known date	47	
Early period	160–358	9-0-0-0-0 to 9-10-0-0-0
Great southern cities began to develop; *e.g.*, Tikal	214	
Some of even earlier-style carvings		
Middle period	358–455	9-10-0-0-0 to 9-15-0-0-0
Beautiful works of art of great simplicity		
Great period	455–600	
Brilliant growth of great cities; *e.g.*, Quiriguá, Yaxchilán, Palenque		
Great advances in astronomy and architecture		
Termination caused by civil war, social decay		
Transition period	600–960	
Shift of emphasis to north, probably central Yucatán		
Almost no pictorial sculpture		
Period of Mayapán league	960–1195	
Revival of architecture in northern Yucatán		
League of three cities (Uxmal, Chichen-Itzá, Mayapán) and other cities		
Period of Mexican influence	1195–1442	
Toltec supremacy and influence (brief, prior to middle 14th century)		
Modern period	1442 to present	
Many warring factors		
Abandonment of cities		
Itzás founded Tayasal on an island in Lake Petén (site of modern Flores); there preserved Maya culture in isolation until 1696		

Robert Wauchope outlines the sequence of Maya periods as follows: (1) preagricultural; (2) basic agricultural; (3) formative (village and urban forms and protoclassic); (4) classic (early and late); (5) readjustment (Mexican period); (6) militaristic; (7) Spanish conquest. (F. W. McB.; J. B–J.)

Southeastern Central America.—The southeastern limit of Maya-Mexican influence is indefinite, but it seems to be somewhere in southern Nicaragua. The Chorotega reached Costa Rica, as seen in the linguistic island on the Nicoya peninsula, and islands of Nahuatlan speech are scattered through Costa Rica to western Panamá, but these are isolated exotics. In pre-Columbian cultures, as in so many other respects, the Nicaragua-Costa Rica lowlands are at the approximate border zone, which is overlapping and confused. Some monolithic sculptures of the Maya-Mexican type have been found on islands in the large Nicaraguan lakes. Southeastward from north central Costa Rica, Chibchan and other South American ethnological and archaeological elements predominate. Talamancan pottery design techniques from the Costa Rica-Panamá border region resemble those of Colombia, Ecuador and Peru, and the gold huacos, cast and hammered as in Colombia, are almost indistinguishable from Colombian work. Evidences of Pacific coastal trade contacts between southeastern Central American peoples and the Inca of the Peruvian coast were observed by the first Spanish explorers.

SPANISH CONQUEST AND COLONIAL PERIOD

Gold-hunting expeditions of the Spaniards, exploring southward from their base in Santo Domingo, brought them first to the coast of Central America at Panamá, or Darien, as the narrowest portion of the isthmus was called, about the beginning of the 16th century. Alonso de Ojeda may have visited the north coast in 1499, but it is known that Rodrigo de Bastidas sighted the eastern section while scouting from the Gulf of Venezuela in 1501, and Columbus on his fourth voyage, following the coast from Honduras, probably went as far east as Puerto Bello, which he is said to have named. He entered several small bays for shelter, and many historians contend that he was seeking a passage to the orient. His reactions to Indians wearing gold ornaments, especially notable near Veragua, the Spaniards' acquisition of the gold by "barter" and their constant query as to the source of the gold fail to support the "eastern passage" idea. It was hope for gold which led the Spaniards eastward instead of westward from Honduras.

Spanish Penetration From the Southeast.—Spanish settlement on the mainland began on the east coast of the Gulf of Urabá, separating the isthmus from South America, where a short-lived colony was founded in 1509. This gulf became the dividing point between Castilla del Oro (Golden Castille), extending northwestward to Cape Gracias a Dios and including the coasts of modern Nicaragua, Costa Rica and Panamá, and Nueva Andalucia, extending northeastward to Cape de la Vela, being essentially the present coast of Colombia. The regional term which included both these colonies was Tierra Firme (Mainland). The colony was relocated in 1510 at the mouth of the Atrato river, was called Santa María de la Antigua del Darien, the first real settlement and first city (1515) founded by Europeans on the new world mainland, and an important base of exploration and exploitation. It became notorious for its unhealthfulness and fatal fevers, including malaria and yellow fever, but gold dust, trinkets and some pearls came in from the west, and the Spanish push was in that direction. Thus the Pacific, previously well known for pearls, was "discovered" officially by Vasco Nuñez de Balboa in 1513, in the name of the king. Pedro Arias de Avila (better known as Pedrarias Davila), who was sent to replace Balboa and later had him beheaded, united Castilla del Oro and Nueva Andalucia as Castilla Aurifica, extending from Cape de la Vela to Veragua. His search for gold, which occurred in some abundance in Veragua province east of the young volcanic mountains, was characteristically ruthless, and the native Indian inhabitants were almost wiped out within a few years. Many new diseases, brought by the white man, ravaged the Indians there as elsewhere and aided the conquest.

In 1519, the year Hernan Cortes began the conquest of Mexico, Pedrarias founded the city of Panamá (just east of its present site), which attracted most of the inhabitants of Antigua (Urabá colony). The last of those who remained in the older city were massacred by Indians, and in 1524 the town was destroyed and thenceforth abandoned. Panamá grew rapidly and was made a city by royal decree in 1521. The Pacific coast had the advantages of a drier, more healthful climate and relative safety from pirates, who had to march overland from the Caribbean (Francis Drake, Henry Morgan and others later raided Panamá nevertheless). Panamá was the exploration base for the development of Central America from the east, and, even more important, the mandatory gateway to Peru. All the great riches from that wealthy South American colony of Spain had to pass through Panamá. The first Caribbean port for the transisthmian portage that anticipated the Panama Canal was Nombre de Dios, important during most of the 16th century. It had a good harbour and an easy overland route to Panamá, almost due south of it. But it suffered heavily from piracy, gales and diseases, and was a miserable post that teemed with life only when the silver fleets came in. Later in the century, the port of transshipment was shifted a little westward to Puerto Bello, but it became just as bad, though it remained active through the colonial period. Panamá flourished as a great and wealthy city, and in 1753 was made an *audiencia* or seat of colonial Spanish government. Negroes were brought in as pearl divers and slaves to replace the Indians, so that the city became the largest single slave market in Spanish America, and the composition of the population became increasingly black. Here as elsewhere along the drier Pacific coast, cattle became especially important in the open savannahs and woodlands.

Having explored and scratched off the superficial wealth of all Panamá by 1522, Pedrarias moved to greener pastures, this time in Nicaragua, where some scouting had been conducted for several years. In this northwestward shift the Spaniards by-passed Costa Rica, attracted by the gold-bearing sands of Nicaragua. Also in the latter country, in the great lakes depression, two large Indian towns, the largest yet encountered, occupied the sites where Managua, on Lake Managua, and Granada, on Lake Nicaragua, later grew. These were outpost settlements of the old Maya-Toltec-Aztec town-builder complex, and as they were far removed from Panamá the Indians were not completely wiped out. The plundering was good, but it had attracted another group of plunderers from the north, men sent out by Cortes from Mexico. These stopped Pedrarias' forces, and civil strife ensued in western Nicaragua. The villa of León was established as a frontier fortress to hold Cortes' men in check. For many years the Gulf of Fonseca region was the scene of much conflict and hatred.

Costa Rica was not settled by Europeans until after the middle of the 16th century, when settlement was begun by Franciscan missionaries, notably those of Talamanca. Lay Spaniards came in gradually, and the theme of settlement was agricultural rather than mineral. During the Spanish colonial period it was one of the spots of thinnest colonization. Cartago, which began as a religious centre, was the chief town until the early 18th century, when this distinction passed to San José.

Spanish Penetration From the Northwest.—Penetration and settlement of Central America from Mexico, in the northwest, was nearly contemporaneous with that from Panamá in the southeast. Pedro de Alvarado, capable lieutenant of Cortes, was sent out from Mexico to undertake the conquest of Guatemala. This was another chapter in the Spanish story of small bands of men who overcame enormous odds by daring and by the elements of terror and surprise injected with the first sight of mounted men with firearms. Strategy, the use of enemy factions as allies, and cruelty, for which Alvarado became almost as well known as Pedrarias, all contributed, as did the new diseases which accompanied and even preceded the Spaniards. There is evidence that influenza was among the pandemic maladies which they introduced to a people with no immunity.

Alvarado crossed the Isthmus of Tehuantepec in 1522, following the Pacific coastal lowlands through Soconusco, Chiapas, famous for cacao, money of the Mayas and Aztecs and drink of the nobility. There were many large towns and colonies of Maya-speaking Indians along the volcanic piedmont. The Pipil, a Nahuatl-speaking group that pushed southeastward from Mexico on trade journeys, especially for cacao, had established small colonies, and Alvarado was accompanied by Aztec mercenaries, who were responsible for the naming of so many places in Guatemala by Mexican names which supplanted the Maya. The major and decisive battle between Spaniards and Guatemalan Indians took place on the highland plain of Quezaltenango, where the pre-Columbian Quiché city of Xelajú was situated. Vastly outnumbered, the Europeans defeated the Quiché-speaking hordes and marched on across the mountains to establish the first capital of Guatemala in 1524.

The Indians were driven mercilessly in a mad and futile search for gold in this land of so much volcanic and limestone cover; but, probably because of relatively inaccessible mountain retreats, many thousands were able to survive. Today their descendants form the largest Indian concentration in Central America and one of those least modified by outside influences. In a larger measure than elsewhere, they were able to resist much of the modification wrought by the Spanish land-grant systems (*repartimiento*), where great tracts and the inhabitants on them were given by the crown to loyal and influential subjects for their personal use and the "protection" of peons; and to withstand also the effects of the church practice of the *reducción*, whereby native peoples were brought from their scattered settlements into compact, nucleated ones more easily controlled by the missions. Lowland and piedmont Guatemala provided the Spaniards with cacao, cochineal, indigo, sarsaparilla and many other valuable products. El Salvador, with its low elevations and extensive tropical climatic areas, was especially important for these items. Consequently, there was great destruction of the Indians, and El Salvador is largely a mestizo country today. These areal terms are used in their modern sense, for in colonial times the captaincy general of Guatemala included all of Central America except Panamá, which exercised jurisdiction over most of the Spanish colonial provinces from Nicaragua through South America.

Honduras, which had been claimed for Spain first by Columbus in 1502, was later the field of activity of Cristobal de Olid, Cortes' captain who was sent by water in 1522 to establish a colony and to block the expansion of Pedrarias. His expedition, which set up its base at Trujillo, was contemporaneous with the overland conquest of Guatemala by Alvarado and was successful in blocking Panamá. But his revolt and treachery made life difficult for Cortes, who was forced to undertake a most arduous punitive expedition. Puerto Cortés, which he founded, still bears his name. Underlain by old crystalline rocks, Honduras was rich in minerals and provided much placer gold. After intensive exploitation, especially about the middle of the 16th century, this was largely exhausted. Honduras had five villas during most of the 16th century, more than any of the present Central American republics (Guatemala had one). These were Trujillo, Gracias a Dios, Comayagua, the old capital, and the important gold camps of Olancho and Naca. Many Negroes were brought in to work the placers. Cattle raising was of great importance and more lasting then mining.

Chiapas was also of some importance for placer mining, but was especially noted for horses, mules, cattle and other livestock. Like Guatemala in most respects, it was entered and colonized from that country.

Yucatán, which had been a stepping stone in the conquest of Mexico, held no mineral wealth or other attraction for exploitation, and it was not until after 1550 that the Spaniards attempted to colonize it. Unsuited to production of indigo or cochineal, it was at first a cattle region. Mérida, the capital, was a bishop's seat and active missionary base. Sisal, the old port, later gave its name to the fibre, locally called henequen.

As cattle raising was concentrated in the drier regions of the Pacific and northern Yucatán, so forestry yielded greatest returns in the wet tropics. Timber, dyewoods, medicinal products, gums and flavouring extracts were rich products from the rain forests of the base of the Yucatán peninsula along the Caribbean coast to Panamá. The British imported Negroes from Jamaica and other islands in the West Indies to work in the forests, as they had earlier brought in Carib Indians. Both stocks are still prominent along the Caribbean coast, and the Mosquito Indians are more Negroid than Indian. The Lacandon Indians of Petén and Chiapas, last survivors of Maya speech, show strong Negroid traits.

The political fragmentation of the centrifugal, particularistic European colonies and their vassals, physical differentiation of peoples and the locations of towns were largely determined by the end of the colonial period.

PERIOD OF INDEPENDENCE

All of Central America was included in the captaincy general, or military government, of Guatemala during the early colonial period. It formed a part of the viceroyalty of Mexico, then called New Spain, but its captains general reported directly to the Spanish crown. The *real audiencia* (Spanish judicial seat) of Guatemala, established in 1570, did not include Panamá, which had its own *audiencia* (as a part of New Andalucia and, after 1718, the viceroyalty of New Granada), and thenceforth the captaincy general of Guatemala included all of Central America except Panamá.

The colonial province of Guatemala declared its independence from Spain, which in its decadent state was unable to maintain its colonial empire, in 1821, as New Granada had in 1819. Mexico also ended three centuries of Spanish domination and became independent in 1821, after more than ten years of fighting. The short-lived Mexican empire of Agustín de Iturbide assumed jurisdiction over Guatemala, as it then was defined, from 1822 to 1823, when autonomy was returned to the Central American province with the downfall of Iturbide. The Republic of the United States of Central America (or Central American Union) was then formed. This was dissolved in 1839, and the five constituent states of

Guatemala, El Salvador, Honduras, Nicaragua and Costa Rica, which corresponded roughly to colonial departments of the captaincy general of Guatemala, became independent republics. Panamá formed a part of Colombia until 1903. Except for British Honduras, all of Central America is made up of republics or parts of republics. "His Majesty's Settlement in the Bay of Honduras," which owes its origin, in 1638, to its strategic position adjacent to the Spanish Main and to rich forest products, is still a British crown colony, though it is claimed by Guatemala and appears as a dependency on all Guatemalan maps. (*See* also CLAYTON-BULWER TREATY.)

Agricultural Revolution.—The colonial economic picture largely prevailed until the great development of coffeegrowing began about the middle of the 19th century and Central America went into the world agricultural export market. This was surprisingly late, in view of the enormous popularity of the European coffeehouses during the 17th and 18th centuries, going back to about 1650 in London. Though the world's supply of coffee had come from Yemen, in Arabia, until the end of the 17th century, the Dutch had sent the plant to Surinam in 1718, Martinique received it in 1720, and Haiti became the world's principal producer during the second half of the 18th century. That it had reached Central America by this time is evident in a casual mention of coffee, in a manuscript dated 1783, as a minor plant in the cacao lands of Soconusco, Chiapas. It was little consumed, however, at that time, and the Spaniards did not have a tradition of large-scale agricultural production for export.

Guatemala, one of the chief Central American producers, did not begin large coffee plantings until between 1855 and 1860, when the south slopes of the Pacific coastal volcanoes, with their deep ash soils and monsoon climate, were found to be ideal. The Chiapas coffee region is in the same type of environment. Costa Rica, with similar natural advantages on a smaller scale in the highlands near San José, started major production about the same time (1850), though it had begun exporting in 1825 and coffee was its chief export crop in 1829. Earliest country to produce for export, by the middle of the 20th century it trailed the top two, with less than one-third the production of Guatemala and of El Salvador, the leader despite a late start (1870). German settlers pioneered coffeegrowing in Guatemala, Chiapas and El Salvador, as did the English in Costa Rica. Nicaraguan coffee production is usually about equal to that of Costa Rica, but the other republics are minor producers.

The quality of coffee is an expression of elevation, the highest grade coming from the highest land. In Guatemala it is even officially graded by the altitude of the plantation on which it grows, the upper limit being nearly 6,000 ft. An aristocratic economic and social system grew up with the plantation, especially in Guatemala. Cacao, cochineal and indigo, formerly grown in small plots, were almost entirely replaced there by coffee, based on large landholdings. In El Salvador, a mestizo country with few Indians, the plantations were smaller, with indigo maintaining a considerable importance, and there was less concentration of wealth within a population minority.

Central America and Colombia produce a large percentage of the world's high-grade blending coffee, which must be grown at fairly high altitude, under taller shade trees, with the ground carefully cleared.

Bananas were next in the 19th-century development of plantation agriculture. Though some types of this fruit were known in Central America before the Spaniards arrived, the banana of commerce is reported to have originated in India and to have reached Santo Domingo, West Indies, via the Canary Islands, in 1519. The chief banana-producing countries at mid-20th century were Honduras, Panamá, Guatemala and Costa Rica. Nicaragua's production was cut seriously by the Panamá disease (banana wilt), which was a special hazard in the Caribbean rain forest region.

Late in the 19th century, Yucatán began to develop its important binder-twine industry based on large-scale production of sisal, or henequen, fibre. This was an outgrowth of the needs of the small-grain industry in the United States for twine to tie up the harvested shocks. A highly aristocratic system developed in the state of Yucatán, in the dry, northern portion of the peninsula, which came to provide half the world supply of this twine.

In the rain forest areas of the base of the Yucatán peninsula, especially the Petén department of Guatemala, the tapping of chicle became important as the chief supply of chewing gum, exported mainly to the United States.

ECONOMIC PATTERNS AND FUNCTIONS OF CENTRAL AMERICA

AGRICULTURE

The economy of Central America, like that of most of the American tropics, is based almost exclusively upon agriculture, as pointed out above. Production of food crops for local consumption and of export crops for foreign markets employs the vast majority of the region's labour force and accounts for almost all the foreign trade. In the early 1950s more than three-fourths of the gainfully employed population worked in agriculture, and more than 90% of the exports from the various countries were made up of agricultural commodities.

This basic economy, however, is not uniform either in structure or in function. There is considerable variation in agricultural techniques, in crops produced, in the disposal of these crops and in numerous other facets of production. A simple breakdown of the over-all agricultural economy reveals at least two broad types. These are subsistence food crop tillage and commercial agriculture characterized by export crops such as coffee and bananas.

Subsistence Tillage.—Subsistence crop tillage is for the most part a carry-over from the preconquest period. Its principal products are corn, beans, potatoes, rice and other food crops which are the staples of the local diet. Production is concentrated upon small farms (generally less than ten acres) or upon labourers' provision grounds on large estates. The crops are largely consumed by the farm family, and if there is a surplus it is sold in the markets of near-by towns.

In terms of total land under cultivation, the number of people affected and the bulk of agricultural production, this type of agriculture is probably the most important in Central America. It is the mainstay of the small landholder and the landless tenant and is particularly important in areas such as southwest Guatemala, the lake region of Nicaragua, central Costa Rica, El Salvador and eastern Panamá where rural population densities are high. Since subsistence tillage is of little significance in the export economy of the region, however, the tendency has been to relegate it to a position of less importance than commercial farming.

Commercial Agriculture.—In turn, commercial agriculture may be divided into two types: one developed and controlled largely by local interests and another by foreign interests. The former type is the basic commercial economy of the local populace. Its traditional and by far its most important crop is coffee. However, efforts to improve and diversify agriculture gave emphasis to other export crops such as cane sugar, cotton, sesame and henequen. In addition, food crops for domestic consumption, such as corn, wheat and fruits, are also characteristic of many of the coffee farms, locally called *fincas*.

Ownership within this domestic commercial economy is for the most part in the hands of well-to-do native families. With the possible exception of Guatemala, foreign investment in the coffee economy has been relatively small. In Guatemala prior to World War II, Germans owned or controlled from 30% to 40% of the country's coffee plantations. In 1942, however, the government took these plantations over, and they were placed under the administration of the Central Bank of Guatemala.

Production within this type of agriculture hinges upon the hacienda system, with large, privately owned farms worked by a labour force of Indians and mestizos. In Guatemala, for example, 80% of the 1950 coffee crop was produced on 1,500 large farms employing 426,000 labourers. Because of the climatic requirements of coffee and associated crops, this type of economy tends to concentrate on the lower slopes of the tropical highlands. The portion of this zone, popularly called the *tierra templada,* that is best for coffee lies approximately between 3,000 and 6,000 ft. above sea level.

The commercial plantation economy developed by foreign capital in Central America is largely a phenomenon of the banana industry. From a meagre beginning in the 1870s, U.S. capital and initiative, led by the United Fruit company, developed a vast economic structure with investments running into hundreds of millions of dollars. The enterprise called for acquiring and clearing thousands of acres of thinly occupied jungle lowlands; the construction of roads, wharves and other transportation facilities; the purchase of a vast fleet of ships; the improvement of sanitation and numerous other undertakings. Reports indicate that by the middle of the 20th century the United Fruit company alone owned almost 400,000 ac. of land, operated or owned more than 1,000 mi. of railways and had millions of dollars tied up in buildings, equipment, livestock and other property in the region.

At first the banana plantations were located primarily on the more humid Caribbean coast. The attacks of the Panamá disease, hurricane damage and other obstacles, however, necessitated a large-scale shift (starting about 1935) to the less humid Pacific coastal area, where production must depend upon irrigation, often from overhead, as at Tiquisate, Guatemala. Much of the land on the Caribbean side which no longer produced bananas was put to producing cacao, palm oil, abacá (Manila hemp) and other cash crops.

To the commercial agriculture associated with bananas the countries of Central America have contributed the land and part of the labour. In turn, they have received such benefits as improved sanitation and transportation, the construction of schools, the clearance of large tracts of jungle lowlands and considerable income from taxes. In most respects, however, this commercial agriculture is little more than a foreign enterprise lightly grafted to the economic framework of the region. It must be kept in mind that the capital, the administrative and technical skills, the machinery and the markets are all foreign and, consequently, the lion's share of the profits also goes to foreign investors.

SUBSIDIARY ECONOMIC ACTIVITIES

In addition to the basic agricultural economy, there are a number of subsidiary occupations which play roles of varying importance within the economic structure of Central America. Chief among these are grazing, mining, lumbering and manufacturing.

Compared with coffee and bananas, grazing is a relatively old economy in Central America. It dates back to the early colonial period, and in terms of land utilization, quality of stock and disposal of products it has changed little through the years. Primary emphasis has been on cattle of unimproved breed, low in beef yields and quality but high in resistance to ticks and other environmental handicaps of the region. Stock raising has always been concentrated on the less humid Pacific savannah lands, but some stock raising is to be found in all sectors. Feeding is almost exclusively on the range or natural pasture basis, and markets are generally local. Honduras, Nicaragua and Panamá have developed a significant export trade in cattle with neighbouring countries, but, because of the scarcity of meat-processing facilities, cattle are driven or transported to markets on the hoof. Efforts were being made to improve both the meat and dairy industries by importing high-bred animals from the United States in the period following World War II.

Mining dates back to the conquistadors, but, unlike Mexico, Central America has achieved only small importance in this activity. Gold and silver have been and still are by far the most important minerals produced in the region. These metals figure among the exports of all the political units but are of particular significance only in Honduras and Nicaragua, where old crystalline rocks are less covered by later sedimentary and volcanic beds. Numerous other minerals such as copper, iron, nickel and mercury have been discovered. Exploitation of these minerals is limited, however, because of difficulties of transportation and lack of capital and machinery.

Lumbering, like mining, also figures in the economy of the entire region. In spite of this, the forest resources have been only slightly developed. Primitive logging methods, poor transportation and other obstacles have kept the extensive tropical hardwood forests in practically virgin state. Mahogany is the chief export, but other tropical woods such as balsam, brazilwood, rosewood and ebony are of some significance. Lumbering has been developed on both the Caribbean and Pacific sides of the region, but the more luxuriant forests of the Caribbean have been more extensively exploited. In British Honduras lumbering surpasses even agriculture in importance.

Manufacturing industries, although showing a tendency to increase since World War II, are still small-scale and undeveloped. Lack of capital and skilled labour and poor transportation have limited manufacturing to the processing of certain agricultural products and the production of a few consumer goods for the local market, such as beverages, shoes, soap, ceramics, matches, cement and cigarettes. Many of the manufactures are still in the primitive handicraft stage, and all are associated with small plants, a small number of workmen, limited capital and total reliance upon the local market. Only in a few places, as in the Indian region of western Guatemala, has a significant tourist trade in weaving and other handicrafts been developed.

COMMERCE

The commerce of Central America shows two outstanding characteristics: first, export goods made up primarily of unfinished raw materials and imports of finished goods; and, second, a strong reliance upon the United States both as a source of imports and market for exports, representing usually more than two-thirds in each case. The commerce of the region showed considerable increase in the years following World War II, with an annual average of about $450,000,000, of which roughly 60% represented imports and 40% exports. For the region as a whole the chief items of export are bananas, coffee, gold, fibres and lumber. The imports lean heavily on textiles, machinery, petroleum products, chemicals and foodstuffs. In addition to the United States, other countries that figure significantly in Central American trade are Canada, Great Britain, Mexico and the Netherlands Antilles (Curaçao.)

FOREIGN INVESTMENTS IN CENTRAL AMERICA

Paucity of local capital, the reluctance of native investors to enter new enterprises and the significant exploitable resources of Central America made the region an important focus for foreign investments. Most of the economic development which took place after the latter half of the 19th century had to rely upon foreign capital either directly invested by foreign-owned corporations or loaned to local governments to finance improvements. For example, of the three major railway systems developed in Costa Rica, the Pacific railway (San José to Puntarenas) is owned by the government but was built largely with funds borrowed abroad; the second line (San José to Limón) is owned and operated by the Northern Railway company, a British concern; and the third line serving the Pacific coast is owned by the United Fruit company, a United States concern.

Much of the early foreign capital which entered Central America was British and German. The increasing interest of United States corporations in the region, however, placed the United States far above the British and other foreign investors. The Germans largely lost out as a result of World War II. In the early 1950s United States capital represented usually between 75% and 100% of all foreign investments in all the units of Central America except British Honduras.

Foreign investment in the region has concentrated primarily upon commercial agriculture, public utilities, transportation and, to a lesser degree, mining and lumbering. For example, of the more than $110,000,000 of foreign capital invested in Guatemala in 1948, it is estimated that 95% was in agriculture, public utilities and transportation. Approximately the same percentage applied to Costa Rica and Honduras.

Among the outstanding foreign corporations with heavy investments in Central America are the United Fruit company, the International Railways of Central America, the American and Foreign

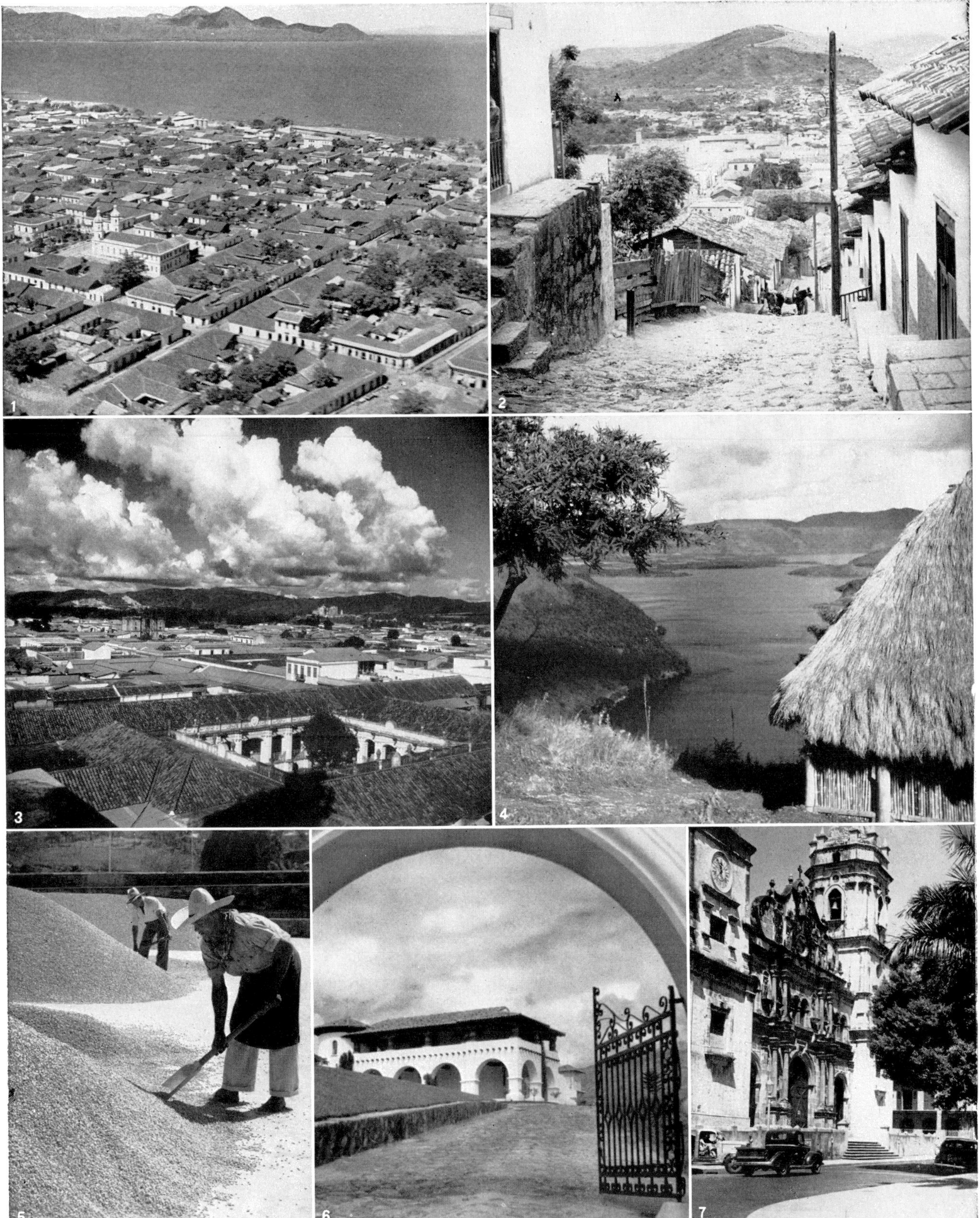

PHOTOGRAPHS, (1, 2, 4, 6, 7) PAUL'S PHOTOS, (3) EWING GALLOWAY, (5) PIX

URBAN AND COUNTRY SCENES IN CENTRAL AMERICA

1. Air view of Managua, capital of Nicaragua, on the southern shore of Lake Managua. In the left centre is the main cathedral with its double towers
2. A typical street in Tegucigalpa, Honduras, with the gutter in the centre instead of along the sides
3. Panoramic view of Guatemala City, Guatemala
4. Overlooking Lake Amatitlan, 17 mi. from Guatemala City
5. Workmen drying and ripening coffee beans in Costa Rica
6. Residence on a coffee *finca* (plantation) on the outskirts of San Salvador, El Salvador. In the coffee-picking season, the larger *fincas* may hire as many as 2,000 men
7. The main cathedral in Panama City

Power company, the New York and Honduras Rosario Mining company and the Northern Railway company. Private individuals with direct investments or with government bonds represent various nationalities, but chief among them are Americans, British and French. In addition to corporations and private individuals, some capital for improvement has been made available to local governments by private banks, particularly those of the United States.

There has been a considerable change in policy on the part of Central American governments toward foreign investment. The "free hand" which foreign capital was given in the late 19th and early 20th centuries has been sharply regulated. As a result, further large-scale influx of foreign capital is being discouraged. The economy of the region continues to be plagued by problems stemming from political instability and a thick crust of traditionalism and from frictions inherent in a society sharply divided by race, class and culture.

COMMUNICATIONS

Transcontinental railroads cross the Isthmus of Tehuantepec, eastern Guatemala, central Costa Rica and Panamá (Canal Zone). A standard-gauge line in Mexico meets a narrow-gauge at the Guatemala border on the Pacific coast, and the Guatemalan line (International Railways of Central America) has a branch to El Salvador from Zacapa. Otherwise, railroads are short and limited to individual countries, connecting parts of more populous areas and crop lands, as banana plantations. Honduras has no rail connection between Tegucigalpa, the capital, and the coast. Roads and highways, though covering more of the countries than railroads, are still limited and inadequate. Only major roads are paved, as a rule, and these are narrow. Extensive areas are thinly populated because of rain forest or unhealthful conditions or rough terrain. Though this limits the demand for roads, the building of transportation lines would tend to fill in the population of many sections.

The Pan-American highway, long under construction, was by the mid-1950s still incomplete. Though Mexico had finished its part to the Guatemalan border, it reached this point in the highlands where the Guatemala section had to cross the immense Cuchumatanes mountains in order to connect. There was a gap of 25 mi. An alternate route crossed Guatemala from Tapachula, Mex., to El Salvador, which had paved all but 21 mi. of all-weather road to the Honduras border. El Salvador has one of the best highway systems in Central America. Honduras had completed its part of the highway, unpaved, but all-weather. Tegucigalpa, the only capital not on the route, was connected by an all-weather road. The Nicaraguan segment was complete and more than half paved, the rest all-weather. In Costa Rica, the first 79 mi. in from the Nicaraguan border was virtually impassable. A similar stretch in southeastern Costa Rica had yet to be constructed, and the first 15 mi. into Panamá as well. From a point about 38 mi. E. of Panamá city, no road existed to connect the isthmus with South America.

Most of the countries have government-owned telephone and telegraph systems connecting the principal towns.

POPULATION COMPOSITION AND DISTRIBUTION

The major concentrations of population in Central America are in the southwestern highlands of Guatemala, the north coast and interior valleys of Honduras, interior El Salvador, the Nicaraguan Pacific lowlands, the central highlands of Costa Rica and the Pacific lowlands of Panamá, with areas of lesser density along the north coast of Yucatán, the Chiapas depression, central Guatemala, the Pacific piedmont of Chiapas and Guatemala and northeast coastal Nicaragua. The largest single concentration is in southwestern Guatemala, but El Salvador has the highest national density (about 140 per square mile).

More than one-half the total population lives on the narrow Pacific slope, which is probably not more than one-fifth the total land area. This slope is higher and drier and consequently much more healthful. The areas of sparsest population are the low Yucatán peninsula, except for the north coast, and the large interior forests of eastern Honduras and Nicaragua, Costa Rica and Panamá. In these same Caribbean lowland areas, extending up through British Honduras, is most of the Negro population, latest arrivals in Central America by way of the West Indies. These have intermarried with the scattered hunting tribes of Indians who inhabit parts of the same region, notably the Mosquito, Paya and Carib. The Negro-Indian cross is called zambo. The Indians of the Caribbean coast depend upon agriculture in temporary forest clearings, with cassava as their chief staple, and upon hunting and fishing. Negroes provide most of the labour for plantation and shipping operations.

White descendants of the Spanish colonial settlers, with admixtures of other European stocks and usually a heavy infusion of native Indian and some Negro blood, especially in the Caribbean lowlands, make up the principal element of the population of Central America as a whole. There is great variation among the individual countries. Costa Rica has the largest population of pure European stock, mostly Spanish mixed with some English and German, concentrated on the central plateau and the Pacific slopes. There are barely more than 1,000 Indians. More than half the inhabitants of the Caribbean lowlands are Negroes, most of them from the West Indies. El Salvador is a mestizo country, with almost no Indians. The largest Indian populations are in Yucatán, Chiapas and Guatemala. In the latter two areas, these people live mostly in the highlands, where there has been much physical and cultural blending with descendants of the early Spaniards. The distinction between the two groups is cultural rather than physical. A native non-Indian of predominantly European culture traits is called a Ladino, which is usually, though not necessarily, synonymous with mestizo. A person of "pure" Indian blood, by adopting a predominance of traits derived from Europe, may become a Ladino. Latin-American censuses, following the lead set by Mexico in 1930, supplemented racial characteristics by cultural in enumerating the various elements in the population.

TABLE II.—*Political Divisions of Central America**

Country	Area (in sq.mi.)	Population	Capital	Population
Mexico	92,487	2,339,030	...	...
Yucatán	14,868	515,256	Mérida	155,899
Campeche	19,670	121,411	Campeche	31,374
Tabasco	9,782	351,106	Villa Hermosa	33,588
Chiapas	28,729	903,200	Tuxtla Gutiérrez	28,262
Quintana Roo	19,438	26,996	Chetumal	7,247
Central American Republics	199,976	8,674,735	...	...
Guatemala	42,042	2,787,030	Guatemala	293,998
Honduras	43,277	1,368,605	Tegucigalpa	72,385
El Salvador	13,176	1,855,917	San Salvador	161,951
Nicaragua	53,668	1,057,023	Managua	109,352
Costa Rica	19,238	800,875	San José	86,909
Panamá	28,575	805,285	Panamá	127,874
Dependent areas	9,228	119,714		
British Honduras	8,866	66,892†	Belize	21,886‡
Canal Zone	362	52,822	(Balboa, chief town)	4,162
Grand totals	301,691	11,133,479		

*All population figures 1950 census unless otherwise indicated.
†1950 estimate. ‡1946 census.

The highland Guatemala-Chiapas Indians are among the most distinctive and colourful people in the world. They speak about 20 different dialects, most of them of the Maya linguistic stock, showing extraordinary local variations. In dress, economic pursuits and religious customs they are equally varied. Their basic agriculture is highly developed, mostly originating in that of their pre-Columbian ancestors. The ancient Maya developed an important series of domesticated plants, including varieties of maize, the principal staple crop, lima and kidney beans and probably types of squashes, avocados, chilies and many other useful plants. These have been variously borrowed and distributed throughout the world since the conquest. Many old world crops were adopted in turn by the central American natives. Wheat is extensively grown in the higher mountains, but tropical wheat is usually low in gluten. Rice and sugar, coffee and bananas and many temperate fruits and vegetables have filled important economic roles among low and middle altitude exotics.

The sheep of the highlands, the cattle of the drier areas—in fact, all livestock except turkeys and Muscovy ducks—came to Central America from the old world.

The Indians commonly specialize to a marked degree, both in agricultural products and in supplementary handicrafts. Of the latter, weaving is outstanding, having been developed to a high point of technical perfection, artistic beauty and originality. One specialty, that of fashioning and decorating tree-calabash receptacles, is limited to a single locality in Guatemala.

Such specialization has inevitably led to a vigorous development of local and intersectional trade and teeming weekly markets, economic nerve centres that have never-ending colour and variety, both as to products and their human vendors and consumers.

Religious festivals, combining a veneer of Roman Catholicism over an impenetrable substratum of pagan rites, likewise stimulate periodic fairs, and the combination produces an unspoiled pageantry that is rarely equalled anywhere in the world.

These Indians have no tribal organization nor any cultural differences based upon language. The *municipios,* the smallest civil administrative divisions, similar to townships, are the cultural units, within which intermarriage (usually by common law) and the rites of religious brotherhoods are practised and costumes, economic pursuits and other cultural traits may be nearly uniform. These tend to differ sharply from one another, even among small adjacent *municipios,* especially those which are isolated by rugged, mountainous terrain, as in the vicinity of Lake Atitlán, Guatemala.

BIBLIOGRAPHY.—*Geology and Physiography:* Charles Schuchert, *Historical Geology of the Antillean-Caribbean Region* (1935), the most comprehensive geological study, includes extensive bibliographies subdivided by regions, of special value in palaeontology and palaeogeography; Oscar Schmieder, *Geografía de América,* Spanish trans. by P. R. Hendrichs Pérez, contains a useful section on Central America with a full bibliography.

Climates and Weather Types: Karl T. Sapper, *Klimakunde von Mittelamerika,* vol. ii, part H, in *Handbuch der Klimatologie,* ed. by Wladimir Köppen and Rudolf Geiger (1932), contains the most complete statistical summary, description, cartographic delineation (small-scale) and bibliography of the climates of Central America; Robert De C. Ward and Charles F. Brooks, *Climates of North America,* vol. ii, part J, sec. 1, *Handbuch der Klimatologie* (1936), contains a chapter on Mexico, including climatological data, descriptions, maps and bibliography for Mexican Central America; F. Webster McBryde, "Studies in Guatemalan Meteorology," *Bulletin of the American Meteorological Society,* in two parts (June and December 1942), contains microclimatological analysis and description, especially of weather and seasons, station data and large-scale climatic map, of a typical area in Pacific Central America.

Natural Vegetation and Soils: Frans Verdoorn (ed.), *Plants and Plant Science in Latin America* (1945), contains an especially wide selection of articles on natural and cultivated plants, vegetation, notes on forestry, conservation, botanical institutions and collections, geology, climatology and soils, with many detailed topical bibliographies; Paul C. Standley, in *Trees and Shrubs of Mexico* (1920-26), *Flora of Costa Rica* (1937-38), *Flora of Guatemala* (with Julian A. Steyermark) (1946–) and other volumes dealing with the flora of most of the countries of Central America, provides the basic references of great bibliographic as well as taxonomic and descriptive value.

Archaeology and History: Preconquest Period: H. J. Spinden, *Ancient Civilizations of Mexico and Central America,* 3rd ed. (1928), is of special value in Maya chronology; among the earlier works of permanent value concerning the Maya and related cultures are T. A. Joyce, *Mexican Archaeology* (1914), *Central American and West Indian Archaeology* (1916) and *Maya and Mexican Art* (1927); *The Maya and Their Neighbors* (A. M. Tozzer memorial volume, by a number of authors) (1940) contains a series of articles on Central American cultures by contemporary specialists, with bibliographies; Sylvanus G. Morley, *The Ancient Maya* (1946), is a comprehensive study of the Maya, with extensive bibliography; J. H. Steward, (ed.), *Handbook of South American Indians,* vol. iv (1948), contains a number of articles on Central American archaeology.

Spanish Conquest and Colonial Period: G. Fernández de Oviedo y Valdés, *Historia general y natural de las Indias* (1851–55), is the earliest full account of the conquest period and is of special value as a basic reference; Bernal Díaz del Castillo, *History of the Conquest of New Spain* (1917), is one of the most important first-hand accounts of the conquest of Mexico; Frans Blom, *Conquest of Yucatan* (1936), excellent on this phase of the conquest, includes a valuable bibliography; Ricardo Fernández Guardia, *History of the Discovery and Conquest of Costa Rica,* Eng. trans. by H. W. Van Dyke (1913), and C. L. G. Anderson, *Old Panama and Castilla del Oro* (1911), cover the conquest of southeastern Central America, the latter with a full bibliography.

Period of Independence: John L. Stephens, *Incidents of Travel in Central America, Chiapas, and Yucatán* (1841), and E. G. Squier, *The States of Central America* (1858), give good accounts of early and middle 19th-century Central America; H. H. Bancroft, *History of Central America* (1883–90), is a comprehensive basic work, of special bibliographic value; Joseph B. Bishop, *The Panama Gateway* (1913), M. W. Williams, *Anglo-American Isthmian Diplomacy, 1815–1915* (1916), and Miles P. DuVal, *Cadiz to Cathay: The Story of the Long Struggle for a Waterway Across the American Isthmus* (1940), are three references that deal with the transisthmian transportation problem.

Economic, Demographic and Geographical Publications: Few recent studies deal with Central America as a whole, so it is necessary here to list mainly books on individual countries: Chester L. Jones, *Caribbean Interests of the United States* (1916), D. G. Munro, *The Five Republics of Central America* (1916), and Preston James, *Latin America,* rev. ed. (1950), contain general data and bibliographies. For individual countries, *see* Erna Fergusson, *Guatemala* (1937); Chester L. Jones, *Guatemala, Past and Present* (1940); F. W. McBryde, *Sololá* (1933) and *Cultural and Historical Geography of Southwest Guatemala* (1947), especially for economic and cultural data on modern Indians and ethnobotany of the principal Indian region of Central America; Sol Tax, *Penny Capitalism: A Guatemalan Indian Economy* (1953); W. Vogt, *The Population of El Salvador and Its Natural Resources* (1946); W. S. Stokes, *Honduras: An Area Study in Government* (1950); Chester L. Jones, *Costa Rica and Civilization in the Caribbean* (1935); J. B. Biesanz and M. Biesanz, *Costa Rican Life* (1944); W. Vogt, *The Population of Costa Rica and Its Natural Resources* (1946); W. D. McCain, *The United States and the Republic of Panama* (1937).

(F. W. McB.)

CENTRAL AND NORTH AMERICAN LANGUAGES. The population of aboriginal America north of Mexico (about 1,150,000), at the time of the discovery of America by Columbus, spoke an astonishing number of languages, most of which are still spoken, though in many cases by only a bare handful of individuals. Certain of them, like Sioux and Navaho, are still flourishing languages.

They consist of a number of distinct stocks, which differ fundamentally from each other in vocabulary, phonetics and grammatical form. Some of these stocks, such as Algonkin, Siouan and Athabaskan, consist of a large number of distinct languages; others seem to be limited to a small number of languages or dialects or even to a single language. The so-called "Powell classification" of languages north of Mexico recognizes no less than 55 of these "stocks" (*see* the revised map of 1915 issued by the Bureau of American Ethnology), excluding Arawak, a South American stock originally represented in the West Indies and perhaps also on the southwestern coast of Florida.

The distribution of these 55 stocks is uneven; 37 of them are either entirely or largely in territory draining into the Pacific, and 22 of these have a coast line on the Pacific. Only 7 linguistic stocks had an Atlantic coast line. Besides the Pacific coast, in the lower Mississippi and Gulf coast, languages of 10 stocks were spoken (apart from Arawak). The most widely distributed stocks are: *Eskimoan,* which includes Eskimo dialects ranging from east Greenland west to southern Alaska and East Cape, Siberia, as well as the Aleut of Alaska Peninsula and the Aleutian Islands; *Algonkian,* which embraces a large number of languages spoken along the Atlantic coast from eastern Quebec and Cape Breton Island south to the coast of North Carolina, in the interior of Labrador, in the northern part of the drainage of the St. Lawrence, in the country of the three upper Great Lakes and the upper Mississippi, and west into the plains of the Saskatchewan and the upper Missouri; *Iroquoian,* which consists of languages originally spoken in three disconnected areas—the region of Lakes Erie and Ontario and the St. Lawrence, eastern Virginia and North Carolina, and the southern Alleghany country (Cherokee); *Muskogian* (including Natchez), which occupies the Gulf region from the mouth of the Mississippi east into Florida and Georgia and north into Tennessee and Kentucky; *Siouan,* divided into four geographically distinct groups—an eastern group in Virginia and North and South Carolina, a small southern contingent (Biloxi) in southern Mississippi, the main group in the valley of the Missouri (eastern Montana and Saskatchewan southeast through Arkansas), and a colony of the main group (Winnebago) in the region of Green Bay, Wisconsin; *Caddoan,* spoken in the southern Plains (from Nebraska south into Texas and Louisiana) and in an isolated enclave (Arikara) along the Missouri in North and South Dakota; *Shoshonean,* which occupies the greater part of the Great Basin area and contiguous territory in southern California and the southwestern Plains (Texas), also, disconnected from this vast stretch, three mesas in the Pueblo region of northern Arizona (Hopi); *Athabaskan,* divided into three geographically distinct groups of languages—Northern (the valleys of the Mackenzie and Yukon, from just short of Hudson's Bay west to Cook Inlet, Alaska, and from Great Bear Lake and the Mackenzie delta south to the headwaters of the Saskatchewan), Pacific (two disconnected areas, one in southwestern Oregon and northwestern California, the other a little south of this in California), and Southern (large parts of Arizona and New Mexico, with adjoining regions of Utah, Texas and Mexico)—besides isolated enclaves in southern British Columbia, Washington and northern Oregon; and *Salishan,* in southern British Columbia, most of Washington, and northern Idaho and Montana, with two isolated offshoots, one (Bella Coola) to the north on the British Columbia coast, the other (Tillamook) to the south in northwestern Oregon.

The remaining 46 stocks, according to Powell's classification, in alphabetical order, are: *Atakapa* (Gulf coast of Louisiana and Texas); *Beothuk* (Newfoundland; extinct); *Chimakuan* (northwestern Washington); *Chimariko* (northwestern California);

Chinook (lower Columbia river, in Washington and Oregon); *Chitimacha* (southern Louisiana); *Chumash* (southwestern California); *Coahuiltecan* (lower Rio Grande, in Texas and Mexico); *Coos* (Oregon coast); *Costanoan* (western California south of San Francisco Bay); *Esselen* (southwestern California; extinct); *Haida* (Queen Charlotte Islands and part of southern Alaska); *Kalapuya* (northwestern Oregon); *Karankawa* (Texas coast); *Karok* (northwestern California); *Keres* (certain Rio Grande pueblos, New Mexico); *Kiowa* (southern Plains, in Kansas, Colorado, Oklahoma, and Texas); *Kootenay* (upper Columbia river, in British Columbia and adjoining parts of Idaho and Montana); *Lutuami,* consisting of Klamath and Modoc (southern Oregon and northeastern California); *Maidu* (eastern part of Sacramento valley, California); *Miwok* (central California); *Piman* or Sonoran (southern Arizona and south into Mexico as far as the state of Jalisco); *Pomo* (western California north of San Francisco Bay); *Sahaptin* (middle Columbia River valley, in Washington, Oregon and Idaho); *Salinan* (southwestern California); *Shastan* or Shasta-Achomawi (northern California and southern Oregon); *Takelma* (southwestern Oregon); *Tanoan* (certain pueblos in New Mexico, Arizona, and originally also in Chihuahua, Mexico); *Timuqua* (Florida; extinct); *Tlingit* (southern Alaska); *Tonkawa* (Texas); *Tsimshian* (western British Columbia); *Tunica* (Mississippi River, in Louisiana and Mississippi); *Waiilatpuan,* consisting of Molala and Cayuse (northern Oregon); *Wakashan,* consisting of Kwakiutl and Nootka (coast of British Columbia); *Washo* (western Nevada and eastern California); *Wintun* (north central California); *Wiyot* (northwestern California); *Yakonan* (Oregon coast); *Yana* (northern California); *Yokuts* (south-central California); *Yuchi* (Savannah river, in Georgia and South Carolina); *Yuki* (western California); *Yuman* (lower Colorado River valley, in Arizona, southern California and south into all or most of lower California); *Yurok* (northwestern California); *Zuñi* (pueblo of New Mexico). To these was later added, as distinct from Yakonan, *Siuslaw* (Oregon Coast).

This complex classification of native languages in North America is very probably only a first approximation to the historic truth. There are clearly far-reaching resemblances in both structure and vocabulary among linguistic stocks classified by Powell as genetically distinct. Certain resemblances in vocabulary and phonetics are undoubtedly due to borrowing of one language from another, but the more deep-lying resemblances, such as can be demonstrated, for instance, for Shoshonean, Piman, and Nahuatl (Mexico) or for Athabaskan and Tlingit, must be due to a common origin now greatly obscured by the operation of phonetic laws, grammatical developments and losses, analogical disturbances, and borrowing of elements from alien sources.

It is impossible to say at present what is the irreducible number of linguistic stocks that should be recognized for America north of Mexico, as scientific comparative work on these difficult languages is still in its infancy. The following reductions of linguistic stocks which have been proposed may be looked upon as either probable or very possible: 1, *Wiyot* and *Yurok,* to which may have to be added Algonkian (of which Beothuk may be a very divergent member); 2, *Iroquoian* and *Caddoan;* 3, *Uto-Aztekan,* consisting of Shoshonean, Piman and Nahuatl; 4, *Athabaskan* and *Tlingit,* with *Haida* as a more distant relative; 5, *Mosan,* consisting of Salish, Chimakuan and Wakashan; 6, *Atakapa, Tunica* and *Chitimacha;* 7, *Coahuiltecan, Tonkawa* and *Karankawa;* 8, *Kiowa* and *Tanoan;* 9, *Takelma, Kalapuya* and *Coos-Siuslaw-Yakonan;* 10, *Sahaptin, Waiilatpuan* and *Lutuami;* 11, a large group known as *Hokan,* consisting of Karok, Chimariko, Shastan, Yana, Pomo, Washo, Esselen, Yuman, Salinan, Chumash, and in Mexico, Seri and Chontal; 12, *Penutian,* consisting of Miwok-Costanoan, Yokuts, Maidu and Wintun.

A more far-reaching scheme than Powell's, suggestive but not demonstrable in all its features at the present time, is Sapir's.

These linguistic classifications, shown in the next column, do not correspond at all closely to the racial or sub-racial lines that have been drawn for North America, nor to the culture areas into which the tribes have been grouped by ethnographers. Thus, the Athabaskan stock counts among its tribes representatives of four of the major culture areas of the continent: Plateau-Mackenzie area, southern outlier of West Coast area, Plains area and Southwestern area.

Proposed Classification of American Indian Languages North of Mexico (and Certain Languages of Mexico and Central America)

I. *Eskimo-Aleut*

II. *Algonkin-Wakashan*

- 1. Algonkin-Ritwan
  - (1) Algonkin
  - (2) Beothuk (?)
  - (3) Ritwan
    - (a) Wiyot
    - (b) Yurok
- 2. Kootenay
- 3. Mosan (Wakashan-Salish)
  - (1) Wakashan (Kwakiutl-Nootka)
  - (2) Chimakuan
  - (3) Salish

III. *Nadene*

- 1. Haida
- 2. Continental Nadene
  - (1) Tlingit
  - (2) Athabaskan

IV. *Penutian*

- 1. Californian Penutian
  - (1) Miwok-Costanoan
  - (2) Yokuts
  - (3) Maidu
  - (4) Wintun
- 2. Oregon Penutian
  - (1) Takelma
  - (2) Coast Oregon Penutian
    - (a) Coos
    - (b) Siuslaw
    - (c) Yakonan
  - (3) Kalapuya
- 3. Chinook
- 4. Tsimshian
- 5. Plateau Penutian
  - (1) Sahaptin
  - (2) Waiilatpuan (Molala-Cayuse)
  - (3) Lutuami (Klamath-Modoc)
- 6. Mexican Penutian
  - (1) Mixe-Zoque
  - (2) Huave

V. *Hokan-Siouan*

- 1. Hokan-Coahuiltecan
  - A. Hokan
    - (1) Northern Hokan
      - (a) Karok, Chimariko, Shasta-Achomawi
      - (b) Yana
      - (c) Pomo
    - (2) Washo
    - (3) Esselen-Yuman
      - (a) Esselen
      - (b) Yuman
    - (4) Salinan-Seri
      - (a) Salinan
      - (b) Chumash
      - (c) Seri
    - (5) Tequistlatecan (Chontal)
  - B. Subtiaba-Tlappanec
  - C. Coahuiltecan
    - (1) Tonkawa
    - (2) Coahuilteco
      - (a) Coahuilteco proper
      - (b) Cotoname
      - (c) Comecrudo
    - (3) Karankawa
- 2. Yuki
- 3. Keres
- 4. Tunican
  - (1) Tunica-Atakapa
  - (2) Chitimacha
- 5. Iroquois-Caddoan
  - (1) Iroquoian
  - (2) Caddoan
- 6. Eastern group
  - (1) Siouan-Yuchi
    - (a) Siouan
    - (b) Yuchi
  - (2) Natchez-Muskogian
    - (a) Natchez
    - (b) Muskogian
    - (c) Timucua (?)

VI. *Aztec-Tanoan*

- 1. Uto-Aztekan
  - (1) Nahuatl
  - (2) Piman
  - (3) Shoshonean
- 2. Tanoan-Kiowa
  - (1) Tanoan
  - (2) Kiowa
- 3. Zuñi (?)

The aboriginal languages of North America differ from each other in both phonetic and morphological respects. Some are polysynthetic (or "holophrastic") in structure, such as Algonkian, Yana, Kwakiutl-Nootka, or Eskimo. Others, like Takelma and Yokuts, are of an inflective cast and may be compared, for structural outlines, to Latin or Greek; still others, like Coos, while inflective, have been reduced to the relatively analytic status of such a language as English; agglutinative languages of moderate complexity, comparable to Turkish, are common, say Shoshonean or Sahaptin.

The term "polysynthetic" indicates that the language is far more than ordinarily synthetic in form, that the word embodies many more or less concrete notions that would in most languages be indicated by the grouping of independent words in the sentence. The Yana word *yābanaumawildjigummaha'nigi* "let us, each one (of us), move indeed to the west across (the creek)!" is "polysynthetic" in structure. It consists of elements of three types—a nuclear element or "stem," *yā-* "several people move"; formal elements of mode (*-ha-*, hortatory) and person (*-nigi* "we"); and elements of a modifying sort which cannot occur independently but which nevertheless express ideas that would ordinarily be rendered by independent words (*-banauma-* "everybody," *-wil-* "across," *-dji-* "to the west," *-gumma-* "indeed"). Such constructions are not uncommon in native America but are by no means universal.

Phonetically these languages differ enormously. Some, like Pawnee (Caddoan stock), have a simple consonantal structure, others make all manner of fine consonantal discriminations and possess many strange types of consonants, such as voiceless *l*-sounds, "glottalized" consonants, and velar *k*-sounds, that are infrequent elsewhere. Kutchin, an Athabaskan language of Alaska, possesses no less than 55 consonantal "phonemes," distinct consonantal elements of the total phonetic pattern. A considerable number of the native languages of North America are pitch languages, *i.e.*, they use pitch differences in otherwise similar syllables to make lexical or grammatical distinctions. Such languages are Tlingit, Athabaskan (certain dialects of this group have lost pitch as an inherently necessary element of language), Takelma, Shasta-Achomawi, Yuman, Tanoan. Navaho may serve as an example of such a pitch language. Every syllable in its words is definitely high or low in pitch, or, less frequently, has a falling or rising tone. Thus, *bini'* means "his nostril" if the two syllables have a high tone, "his face" if they have a low tone, and "at his waist, centre" if the first syllable is low and the second high; *yāzīd* means "you pour it (sandy mass) down" if the first syllable is low and the second high, but "I have poured it down" if both are low.

The six major linguistic groups of Sapir's scheme may be characterized as follows:

I. The *Eskimo-Aleut* languages are "polysynthetic" and inflective; use suffixes only, never prefixes, reduplication, inner stem modification, or compounding of independent stems; have a great elaboration of the formal aspect of verb structure, particularly as regards mode and person; and make a fundamental distinction between the transitive and intransitive verb, to which corresponds the nominal case distinction of agentive-genitive and absolutive (or objective).

II. The *Algonkin-Wakashan* languages, too, are "polysynthetic" and, especially as regards Algonkian, inflective; make use of suffixes, to a much less extent, particularly in Algonkian and Ritwan, of prefixes; have important inner stem modifications, including reduplication; have a weak development of case; and illustrate to a marked degree the process of building up noun and verb themes by suffixing to stems local, instrumental, adverbial, and concretely verbalizing elements.

III. The *Nadene* languages, probably the most specialized of all, are tone languages and, while presenting a superficially "polysynthetic" aspect, are built up, fundamentally, of monosyllabic elements of prevailingly nominal significance which have fixed order with reference to each other and combine into morphologically loose "words"; emphasize voice and "aspect" rather than tense; make a fundamental distinction between active and static verb forms; make abundant use of postpositions after both nouns and verb forms; and compound nominal stems freely. The radical element of these languages is probably always nominal in force and the verb is typically a derivative of a nominal base, which need not be found as such.

IV. The *Penutian* languages are far less cumbersome in structure than the preceding three but are more tightly knit, presenting many analogies to the Indo-European languages; make use of suffixes of formal, rather than concrete, significance; show many types of inner stem change; and possess true nominal cases, for the most part. Chinook seems to have developed a secondary "polysynthetic" form on the basis of a broken down form of Penutian; while Tsimshian and Maidu have probably been considerably influenced by contact with Mosan and with Shoshonean and Hokan respectively.

V. The *Hokan-Siouan* languages are prevailingly agglutinative; tend to use prefixes rather than suffixes for the more formal elements, particularly the pronominal elements of the verb; distinguish active and static verbs; and make free use of compounding of stems and of nominal incorporation.

VI. The *Aztec-Tanoan* languages are moderately "polysynthetic"; suffix many elements of formal significance; make a sharp formal distinction between noun and verb; make free use of reduplication, compounding of stems and nominal incorporation; and possess many postpositions. Pronominal elements, in some cases nouns, have different forms for subject and object but the subject is not differentiated, as in types I. and IV., for intransitive and transitive constructions. (E. Sa.)

Bibliography.—J. W. Powell, "Indian Linguistic Families of America north of Mexico," Bureau of Ethnology, 7th *Annual Report*, pp. 1–142 (Washington, 1891); Franz Boas, "Handbook of American Indian Languages," Bureau of American Ethnology, *Bull. 40* (pt. 1, 1911; pt. 2, 1922); P. Rivet, "Langues de l'Amérique du Nord," pp. 607–628 of A. Meillet et M. Cohen, *"Les Langues du Monde* (Paris, 1924).

Mexican and Central American Languages.—The classification of the native languages of Middle America is not in quite so advanced a stage as is that of the many languages spoken north of Mexico. The languages are, some of them, spoken by large populations, numbering millions, as in the case of Nahuatl (or Mexican) and the Maya of Yucatan; others are confined to very small groups, like the Subtiaba-Tlappanec of Nicaragua and Guerrero, or are extinct, as is Waïcuri in Lower California. Nahuatl, Maya (with Quiche, Kekchi, and Cakchiquel, which belong to the Mayan stock), and Zapotec were great culture languages which had developed ideographic methods of writing.

The languages of Middle America may be conveniently grouped into three main sets: A., southern outliers of stocks located chiefly north of Mexico; B., stocks spoken only in Mexico and Central America, so far as is known at present; C., northern outliers of South American stocks. It is quite probable that relationships will eventually be discovered between some of the languages of group B and languages lying further north.

To group A belong three distinct stocks: *Uto-Aztekan,* with two subdivisions, *Sonoran* (or *Piman*), spoken in a large number of dialects in northern Mexico, and *Nahuatl* (or *Aztek*), spoken in central Mexico and in a number of isolated southern enclaves —the Pacific coast of Oaxaca (Pochutla), three disconnected areas in Salvador and Guatemala (Pipil), two areas in Nicaragua and one in Costa Rica (Nicarao), and the Chiriqui region of Costa Rica (Sigua), of which dialects Nicarao and Sigua are now extinct—with *Cuitlateco* of Michoacan as a doubtful member of the stock; *Hokan-Coahuiltecan,* represented by *Hokan* proper, which includes Seri (coast of Sonora), Yuman (in Lower California), and Tequistlateco or Chontal (coast of Oaxaca), by *Coahuiltecan* (Pakawan), of the lower Rio Grande, and by *Subtiaba-Tlappanec,* which is spoken in two small areas in Guerrero, one in Salvador, and one in Nicaragua; and *Athabaskan* (Apache tribes of Chihuahua and Coahuila).

The Middle American languages proper (group B) may, with reservations, be classified into 15 linguistic stocks, which in alphabetic order, are: *Chinantec* (Oaxaca and western Vera Cruz); *Janambre* (Tamaulipas; extinct); *Jicaque* (northern Honduras); *Lenca* (Honduras and Salvador); *Mayan* (Yucatan and neighboring states of southern Mexico, British Honduras, western Honduras, and Guatemala), with an aberrant dialect group, *Huastec,* in the northeastern coast region of Mexico (Vera Cruz, San Luis Potosi, Tamaulipas); *Miskito-Sumo-Matagalpa,* consisting of three distinct language groups: *Miskito* (coast of Nicaragua and Honduras), *Sumo-Ulua* (eastern Nicaragua and southern Honduras), and *Matagalpa* (Nicaragua; a small enclave, Cacaopera, in Salvador); *Mixe-Zoque-Huave,* spoken in four disconnected groups, *Mixe-Zoque* (Oaxaca, Vera Cruz, Chiapas, and Tabasco), *Tapachultec* (southeastern Chiapas; extinct), *Aguacatec* (Guatemala, extinct), and *Huave* (coast of Oaxaca); *Mixtec-Zapotec,* a group of languages that some consider as composed of four independent stocks: *Mixtec* (Guerrero, Puebla, and western Oaxaca), *Amusgo* (Guerrero and Oaxaca), *Zapotec* (Oaxaca), and *Cuicatec* (northern Oaxaca); *Olive* (Tamaulipas; extinct); *Otomian,* consisting of three distinct groups: *Otomi* (large part of central Mexico), *Mazatec* (Guerrero,

Puebla, Oaxaca; includes *Trique* and *Chocho*), and the geographically distant *Chiapanec-Mangue* (*Chiapanec* in Chiapas; *Mangue* and related languages in three disconnected areas in Nicaragua and Costa Rica); *Paya* (Honduras); *Tarascan* (Michoacan); *Totonac* (Hidalgo, Puebla, and coast of Vera Cruz); *Waïcuri* (southern part of Lower California; extinct); *Xinca* (southeastern Guatemala).

The outliers from South America are two: *Carib* (coast of Honduras and British Honduras; transferred in post-Columbian times from the Antilles); *Chibchan* (Costa Rica and Panama). In the West Indies two South American stocks were represented, *Carib* and *Arawak,* the latter constituting an older stream which had overrun the Greater Antilles and penetrated into Florida.

As to the languages of group B, some connect Chinantec, Mixtec-Zapotec, and Otomian in one great linguistic stock, *Mixtec-Zapotec-Otomi.* Both Xinca and Lenca (also Paya and Jicaque?) may be remote southern outliers of the Penutian languages of North America. Waïcuri may have been related to Yuman. It is by no means unlikely that such important Middle American stocks as Mayan, Totonac, and Tarascan may also belong to certain of the larger stock groupings that have been suggested for North America; *e.g.,* Maya may fit into the Hokan-Siouan framework, Tarascan into Aztek-Tanoan.

Middle America, in spite of its special cultural position, is distinctly a part of the whole North American linguistic complex and is connected with North America by innumerable threads. On the other hand, there seems to be a much sharper line of linguistic division, distributionally speaking, between Middle and South America. This line is approximately at the boundary between Nicaragua and Costa Rica; allowances being made for Nahuatl and Otomian enclaves in Costa Rica and for an Arawak colony in Florida, we may say that Costa Rica, Panama, and the West Indies belong linguistically to South America. The Chibchan, Arawak, and Carib stocks of the southern continent were obviously diffusing northward at the time of the Conquest, but evidence seems to indicate that for Mexico and Central America as a whole the ethnic and linguistic movement was from north to south. Middle America may be looked upon as a great pocket for the reception of a number of distinct southward-moving peoples and the linguistic evidence is sure to throw much light in the future on the ethnic and culture streams which traversed these regions.

Two linguistic groups seem to stand out as archaically Middle American: Miskito-Sumo-Matagalpa, in Central America, and Mixtec-Zapotec-Otomi, with its center of gravity in southern Mexico. The latter of these sent offshoots that reached as far south as Costa Rica. The Penutian languages, centered in Oregon and California, must early have extended far to the south, as they seem to be represented in Mexico and Central America by Mixe-Zoque, Huave, Xinca, and Lenca. These southern offshoots are now cut from their northern cognate languages by a vast number of intrusive languages, *e.g.,* Hokan and Aztek-Tanoan. The Mayan languages, apparently of Hokan-Siouan type, may have drifted south at about an equally early date. Presumably later than the Penutian and Mayan movements into Middle America is the Hokan-Coahuiltecan stream, represented by at least three distinct groups—Coahuiltecan (N.E. Mexico), Subtiaba-Tlappanec (Guerrero, Nicaragua), and a relatively late stream of Hokan languages proper (Yuman; Seri; and Chontal in Oaxaca). Not too early must have been the Uto-Aztekan movement to the south, consisting of an advance guard of Nahuatl-speaking tribes, a rear guard of Sonoran-speaking tribes (Cora, Huichol, Tarahumare, Tepehuane). The Nahuatl language eventually pushed south as far as Costa Rica. Last of all, the Apache dialects of Chihuahua brought into Mexico the southernmost outpost of the Nadene group of languages, which extend north nearly to the Arctic. (E. Sa.)

Bibliography.—C. Thomas and J. R. Swanton, "Indian Languages of Mexico and Central America and their Geographical Distribution," Bureau of American Ethnology, *Bull. 44* (Washington, 1911); W. Lehmann, *Zentral-Amerika,* I. Theil, "Die Sprachen Zentral-Amerikas" (Berlin, 1920); P. Rivet, "Langues de l'Amérique Centrale," pp. 629–638 of A. Meillet et M. Cohen, *Less Langues du Monde* (Paris, 1924).

CENTRAL BANK. Central banks are institutions charged with the function of regulating the supply, cost and use of money with a view to promoting national and international economic stability and welfare. They differ from other banking institutions in that they are vested with the public interest and are not operated primarily as profit-making business enterprises.

Evolution.—Modern central banks are the outcome of a long evolution. Originally many of them were established for the purpose of serving the state by extending loans and of providing currency of uniform value in adequate amount for the needs of the country. They became the principal, in many countries the only, issuers of paper money. In modern times the principal function of central banks is regulation of the supply and use of money in the service of commerce and industry, but in times of emergency, such as war, they become in the main instruments for facilitating government finance.

Heavy reliance on central banks for government financing during World War I and the inflationary excesses which subsequently developed led to a movement for strict limitation of government borrowing from central banks, but the necessities of World War II largely subordinated such limitations. In wartime the central bank, as all other institutions, must support the government's war needs and its stabilizing function becomes secondary to this purpose.

During the 1920s and 1930s most countries went through booms and depressions caused largely by nonmonetary factors and not traceable to variations in the supply or cost of money. The viewpoint gradually developed that a central bank is but one of many public agencies which must act in concert if the purpose of establishing and maintaining a stable and expanding volume of national income and a rising level of economic wellbeing is to be achieved.

Older institutions have nothing in their charters indicative of the broad modern concept of central bank functions, but in practice it has been widely recognized. In charters of more recently established central banks, such as the Bank of Canada, it is explicitly stated.

Functions.—With these broad objectives as their goal, central banks have the following principal functions and authorities: (1) creation of money by issuing notes and by creating bankers' balances which through custom or law must be held by commercial banks as reserves in an amount proportionate to their liabilities; (2) influencing the volume, cost and use of money by expanding and contracting bankers' cash, or reserves. This the central bank accomplishes by establishing and varying the rate at which it will make advances or discounts on the initiative of commercial banks or the market; by purchasing or selling on its own initiative such securities as government obligations and acceptances (or bills), and, in some countries, principally the United States, by increasing or decreasing the ratio of reserves to deposits that commercial banks are required to hold. (3) In addition to these general influences on the use of money, some central banks have the power to influence specific uses of money. For example, in the United States the Federal Reserve board of governors has authority to prescribe margins for stock market loans, and also (on an emergency war basis) to regulate certain types of consumer credit. In some countries limited selective regulation of the use of money is undertaken by varying the rate at which paper originating from different types of transactions will be discounted by the central bank. Central banks (4) serve as fiscal agents of the government; (5) perform numerous services for the banking system, among which the most important is check clearance; (6) serve as correspondents of central banks of other countries; and (7) supervise banks with a view to enforcing compliance with banking laws and maintenance of sound banking conditions. This function is performed by central banks of different countries in different ways. In England, for example, which has a highly centralized branch banking system, the central bank performs this function largely through its informal but potent influence on the management of the joint-stock banks. In the United States, where the vast majority of more than 14,000 banks are independent, responsibility for bank supervision is vested in the central bank by law; it is, however, shared with certain other government agencies.

Banks of Issue.—Most central banks hold a monopoly of note issue, which in the case of some older institutions was acquired by gradual absorption or extinction of rival issues. In modern times the notes of new central banks may be launched while the circulation of older currency, issued by banks or government treasuries, continues temporarily or permanently.

Up to the end of 1944, national governments of the following countries had granted a monopoly of issue to their central banks: *Europe:* France, Belgium, the Netherlands, Switzerland, Norway, Sweden, Denmark, Finland, Estonia, Latvia, Lithuania, Spain, Portugal, Italy, Hungary, Poland, Czechoslovakia, Bulgaria, Rumania, Yugoslavia, Greece, Albania; *Middle East:* Turkey, Egypt, Iran; *Far East and Oceania:* China (monopoly to Central Bank of China, 1942), Japan, Australia, New Zealand; *Africa:* Union of South Africa; *North and Central America:* Mexico, Costa Rica, Nicaragua, Guatemala, El Salvador; *South America:* Argentina, Bolivia, Chile, Colombia, Ecuador, Peru, Paraguay (1943), Venezuela (1939).

Colonial central banks or banks of issue exist in some French, Belgian, Dutch, Portuguese and Japanese colonies. In 1944 the Caisse Centrale de la France d'Outre-Mer (formerly "Caisse Centrale de la France Libre") was authorized to function as a central bank of a unique type, directing the credit policy of colonial banks of issue in Free French territory.

Some leading central banks do not (1945) have a monopoly of note issue. Note circulation of the 12 Federal Reserve banks of the United States, Dec. 31, 1944, amounted to $21,482,000,000 while other paper currency (silver certificates of the U.S. treasury and other note issues of the government) amounted to $2,615,000,000, only part of which was to be retired.

The Bank of England has a monopoly of note issue for England and Wales but eight Scottish banks have fixed quotas totalling £2,676,350 and quotas of six banks in Northern Ireland totalled £2,197,792 (approved by treasury up to Dec. 23, 1944). Issues exceeding these quotas must be covered by gold or other legal tender. After the opening of the Bank of Canada in 1935, chartered bank notes were being reduced by schedule and were eventually to be taken over by the central bank. A similar situation existed in Eire after the Central Bank of Ireland was established in 1942. In British India, government notes circulate with those of the reserve bank. Currency of the State Bank of the U.S.S.R. serves only as bank or deposit currency. The circulating medium, besides coin, is rouble notes of the state treasury. Germany's note circulation (1944) included, besides Reichsbank notes, the notes of the Deutsche Rentenbank, the issue of which was extended by decrees of 1930 and 1939.

During World War II the axis powers set up in several occupied countries new banks of issue or central banks whose notes were designed to supersede the national currency. Disposal of these superimposed currencies, as well as of the military currency circulated by Germany and Japan in occupied countries and by the allies in liberated countries, presented a complicated postwar problem.

Relation to the State.—Relation of the central bank to the state, more particularly to the fiscal authority, varies from country to country, but in general the central bank has responsibility for the volume and cost of money, while the fiscal authority has responsibility for meeting government expenses through taxation and borrowing. It is generally believed that, since the two functions and responsibilities are distinct and may at times indicate different courses of action, the public good is served best by keeping them in separate institutions. It is increasingly recognized, however, that while the central bank has the obligation to formulate its policies in accordance with its own judgment and in ordinary times should have a large measure of autonomy, in times of national emergency the will of the fiscal authority must prevail. At such times the central bank must function chiefly as an adviser, the degree of its influence depending on the confidence which it commands with other branches of the government and the general public.

In some countries the central bank is owned in whole or in part by the state, in others it is privately owned. Private ownership of central banks, however, is in effect merely a contribution of private capital to a public institution operated for a public purpose.

Economic Intelligence.—Enlargement of the objectives which the central bank must aim to achieve has resulted in increasing emphasis on the maintenance of effective economic intelligence services at central banks. The interrelationships of economic forces make it necessary for the policy-making authorities of central banks to keep abreast of all important economic developments, domestic and foreign, with a view to enabling them not only to determine their own policies in the light of all available facts and analyses, but also to be in a position to give sound counsel to other public bodies that formulate other phases of the nation's interrelated economic policies.

(*See* BANCA D'ITALIA; BANKING; BANK OF ENGLAND; BANQUE DE FRANCE; MONEY.)

BIBLIOGRAPHY.—Annual reports and other publications of central banks; M. H. de Kock, *Central Banking* (1939); Staff members, Board of Governors, Federal Reserve System, *Banking Studies* (1941); Sir John Clapham, *The Bank of England* (1944). (E. A. GR.)

CENTRAL ELECTRICITY BOARD. A British body corporate appointed by the minister of transport under the terms of the Electricity (Supply) Acts, 1926 and 1935, to organize and control the generation of electricity throughout Great Britain. This it has effected by means of the "grid" system (*see* ELECTRICITY SUPPLY: COMMERCIAL ASPECTS) which, constructed at a cost of some £30,000,000, at the end of 1938 comprised 4,378 mi. of transmission lines and 304 switching and transforming stations with an aggregate transforming capacity of 10,422,000 kva., and during the year had an output of 24,376,000,000 units compared with the 4,016 units sold in the same area in 1925. The board consists of a chairman and seven members; the first chairman, Sir Andrew Duncan, was succeeded in 1935 by Sir Archibald Page, the former chief engineer and manager. The board has borrowing powers up to £60,000,000. Annual reports and statements of accounts are published.

Before the passing of the 1926 act there were over 500 unconnected generating stations in Great Britain, 32 of which supplied half the power; by means of the act much of the capital extravagance entailed by this lack of co-ordination was eliminated, the general level of the cost of production was lowered, and the availability of electricity throughout the country increased; the larger and more efficient generating stations became "selected stations" and were interconnected by the grid with each other and with the systems of authorized undertakers not owning selected stations, and great economies were effected by the use of the more efficient stations for the long-hour or base load and the restriction of the use of the less efficient stations to the short-hour or peak load, many of these latter being completely closed during the summer months. The output of all selected stations is purchased by the board and is sold by them to the distributing authorities, including the owners of the stations themselves, at a tariff fixed by the board and approved by the Electricity Commissioners; authorized undertakers have the right to demand supplies from the board, and under the 1935 act the board is empowered to supply electricity to railway companies for traction purposes, which it now does in the case of the Southern railway.

At the end of 1938 the selected stations numbered 137 with a total installed capacity of 8,264,160 kw. (as against 3,096,000 kw. in 1925), and the board controlled in addition 35 nonselected stations, the operation of the whole 171 being so controlled that only 30 ran for the full year. Of the 560 distributing undertakings 217 were supplied directly and a further 300 indirectly by the board, which in 1938 produced 97.2% of the electricity consumption of the country.

The offices of the board are in Trafalgar Buildings, Charing Cross, London.

CENTRAL FALLS, a city of Providence county, Rhode Island, U.S.A., on the Blackstone river, 5 mi. N. of Providence; served by the New York, New Haven and Hartford railroad. The population in 1950 was 23,550; in 1940 it was 25,248 by federal census. The river furnishes water power for large manufacturing industries (chiefly cotton mills). A settlement was made there about 1763.

About 1780 a chocolate mill was erected, and until 1827 the town was called Chocolateville. It was incorporated as the Central Falls Fire District of Smithfield in 1847, and in 1896 was chartered as a city.

CENTRALIA, a city of southern Illinois, U.S., about 60 mi. E. of Saint Louis, in Marion and Clinton counties. It is on federal highway 51 and state highway 161, and is served by the Illinois Central, Burlington, Southern and the Missouri-Illinois railways. The population in 1950 was 13,863.

Centralia is in a fertile fruit-growing and dairying region, and there are coal mines and oil wells in the vicinity. The city has a large wholesale trade. Two of the railroads have division repair shops there, and there are several other manufacturing industries.

Centralia was founded in 1853 by the Illinois Central Railroad company, and was chartered as a city in 1859.

CENTRALIA, a city of Lewis county, Washington, U.S., on the Pacific highway, about halfway between Seattle and Portland. It is served by four transcontinental railways: the Chicago, Milwaukee, St. Paul and Pacific; the Great Northern; the Northern Pacific and the Union Pacific. The population was 8,657 in 1950, and was 7,414 in 1940 by the federal census. Chehalis, the county seat, lies 4 mi. S., and between the two cities are the southwestern Washington fairgrounds. Centralia has saw and shingle mills, furniture and concrete culvert factories and railroad shops, and gloves, shoes, knit goods and bakery supplies are produced. In Borst park, 1½ mi. W. of the city, is a blockhouse built by the early settlers as a stronghold against the Indians. Centralia is situated on the Cochrain Donation claim. It was laid out by George Washington, a former Negro of Cochrain, who became the owner of the land on the death of his master in 1852, and at first it was called Washington's Addition. Later it was known for a few years as Skookumchuck Station, and then as Centerville, until the present name was adopted in 1887. In 1914 a commission form of government was adopted. The municipal water and power system is operated by the city. Once dependent upon lumber industry, the main industries are now railroading and retail trade.

CENTRAL INDIA, the name given by the British to a collection of Indian states which formed a separate agency until India's independence. Central India must not be confused with the Central Provinces. It consisted of two large detached tracts of country which, with Jhansi as a pivot, spread outward east and west into the peninsula, reaching northward to within about 30 mi. of Agra and southward to the valley of the Nerbudda and the Vindhya and Satpura ranges. On the north and northeast it was bounded by the United Provinces; on the west and southwest by Rajputana and part of the Bombay Presidency; on the south and east by the Central Provinces and Chota Nagpur; the Jhansi district of the United Provinces and the Saugor district of the Central Provinces separated the two tracts.

Before the removal of Gwalior from the agency in 1921 Central India could be roughly described as an enormous triangle with the Nerbudda and Son rivers forming its hypotenuse, and having for one side the valley of the Ganges and for the other the Chambal river and the Chittor hills. The Central India agency, therefore, was not a compact administration but a collection of states varying in area, revenue and population, and in their relationship to the paramount power. All, however, were subject to the political control of the resident, or agent to the governor general, who had his headquarters at Indore. According to the 1941 census the total area of the agency was 52,047 sq.mi. and the total population 7,506,427.

History.—In the 7th century B.C. northern India and part of the Deccan were divided into 16 principalities, the 16 *Mahajanapadas* of the Buddhist *Anguttara Nikāya.* Two of the more important of these kingdoms, Avanti with its capital at Ujjain and Vatsa, of which the chief town was Kausambhi, roughly corresponded to the territories included in the Central India agency. These two kingdoms were later incorporated into the vast Maurya empire of Chandragupta and Asoka.

From the Junagadh rock inscription it may be inferred that in the 2nd century A.D. Rudradaman, the greatest of the western satraps, ruled over Avanti, that is, eastern and western Malwa. Both Avanti and Vatsa were included in the Gupta empire under Chandragupta II (*c.* 385–*c.* 413). Although the extent of Harsha's dominions in the first half of the 7th century is a matter of controversy, modern opinion inclines to the view that they embraced these two areas. In the 9th century Central India formed a bone of contention between the Gurjara-Pratiharas of Kanauj and the Rashtrakutas of the Deccan. The evidence is conflicting as both sides boast of their victories, but it appears to have been an indecisive conflict with the Nerbudda as a fluctuating frontier. It was not until the early 13th century that the Moslem invaders began to penetrate into Central India.

In 1234, Iltutmish, the sultan of Delhi, entered Malwa and captured Bhilsa and Ujjain. With the decline of Tughlak power toward the end of the next century, Central India no longer acknowledged the suzerainty of Delhi and was divided into independent kingdoms, the most important of which was the Moslem kingdom of Malwa. Malwa's independence came to an end in 1562 when it was conquered by Akbar. It remained a province of the Mogul empire until the decline of Mogul power in the first half of the 18th century, when Central India was overrun by the Marathas who had rebelled against the central government of Delhi. Central India was dominated by the Maratha *peshwas* until the third battle of Panipat (1761), after which it was split up among the Maratha generals, the most important of whom were Sindhia of Gwalior and Holkar of Indore.

The marquess Wellesley was the first governor general to feel that it was impossible to live in amity with the Marathas and that the time had come for the British to stand forth as the paramount power. He therefore declared war on their chiefs but was recalled before he was able completely to crush their power. His immediate successors adopted a policy of nonintervention with the result that Central India became a prey to anarchy and was continually ravaged by plundering bands of Pindaris and Pathans whom the Marathas were powerless to control. It was left for the marquess of Hastings to complete the work of Wellesley; and, by 1818, these robber bands and their protectors, the Marathas, had been crushed. As a result of this campaign the British became the paramount power in India south of Sind and the Punjab. The settlement and pacification of Central India after this campaign was the work of Sir John Malcolm. Between 1830 and 1835 the Thugs who infested this area were suppressed by Capt. (afterward Sir) William Sleeman. Apart from disturbances during the Mutiny of 1857 Central India under British rule enjoyed unbroken peace.

The term Central India was officially applied at first to Malwa alone; but in 1854 Bundelkhand and Baghelkhand were added to Malwa to form the Central India agency, and Sir Robert Hamilton was appointed agent to the governor general. In 1901, for administrative purposes, it was divided into the following eight units, two of which were classed as residencies and six as agencies: (1) Gwalior residency (Gwalior state and 11 small states and estates); (2) Indore residency (Indore state and 2 estates); (3) Baghelkhand agency (Rewa state and 11 minor states and estates); (4) Bhopal agency (Bhopal state and 21 minor states and estates); (5) Bhopawar agency (Dhar and Barwani states and 20 minor states and estates); (6) Bundelkhand agency (Datia, Orchha, Samthar, Charkhari, Chhattarpur and Panna states and 17 minor states and estates); (7) Indore agency (Dewas Senior and Dewas Junior and 4 estates); (8) Malwa agency (Jaora and Ratlam states and 12 estates).

The chief administrative changes after 1901 were: (1) the abolition of the Indore agency in 1907 and its amalgamation with the Malwa agency; (2) the removal of Gwalior from the agency in 1921; (3) the amalgamation in 1931 of the Baghelkhand and Bundelkhand agencies.

After the achievement of Indian independence the Central India agency was divided into two separate administrations: Madhya Bharat (*q.v.;* the united state of Gwalior, Indore and Malwa);

and Vindhya Pradesh (which includes the 25 states of Baghelkhand, and Bundelkhand, of which Rewa is the largest). Bhopal (*q.v.*) was detached to form a separate entity.

Bibliography.—*Administration Reports* (Indore, 1866 ff.); J. C. Grant Duff, *A History of the Mahrattas*, 2 vol. (London, 1921); J. Malcolm, *A Memoir of Central India*, 2 vol. (London, 1823); H. T. Prinsep, *History of the Transactions in India, During the Administration of the Marquis of Hastings*, 2 vol. (London, 1825); and R. Sinh, *Malwa in Transition* (Bombay, 1936). (C. C. D.)

CENTRAL PROVINCES AND BERAR, a former province of British India and (from 1947 to 1950) of the dominion of India; from Jan. 26, 1950, a "part A" (governor's) state of the republic of India under the name of Madhya Pradesh. The Central Provinces of India were formed in 1862, and were augmented in 1903 by the Hyderabad assigned districts of Berar, which in 1902 had been leased in perpetuity to the British government by the nizam, at an annual rent of 25 lakhs of rupees. In 1905 most of the Sambalpur district and five Oriya-speaking states were transferred to Bengal, and five Hindi-speaking states from Chota Nagpur received in exchange. The province, therefore, now consisted of the four divisions of Jubbulpore, Nagpur, Chhattisgarh and Berar, which were divided into the 19 districts of Saugor, Jubbulpore, Mandla, Hoshangabad, Nimar, Betul, Chhindwara, Wardha, Nagpur, Chanda, Bhandara, Balaghat, Raipur, Bilaspur, Drug, Amraoti, Akola, Buldana and Yeotmal. The state capital is Nagpur, but from April to July the seat of government is at Pachmarhi. The province was enlarged in 1948 by the incorporation of the feudatory princely states of Bastar, Changbhakar, Chhuikhadan, Jashpur, Kanker, Kawardha, Khairagarh, Korea, Makrai, Nandgaon, Raigarh, Sakti, Sarangarh, Surguja and Udaipur, so increasing the area by more than 38,000 sq.mi. and the population by more than 4,000,000. Total area of Madhya Pradesh (1951) 130,272 sq.mi.; total population (1951 census) 21,247,533.

South of the Vindhyan plateau are the Nerbudda valley districts extending from Jubbulpore on the east to north Nimar on the west. South of these again is the great Satpura range of hills and plateaus upon which are situated the four plateau districts of Betul, Chhindwara, Seoni and Mandla and the uplands of Balaghat. South of the Satpuras are the three great plains of Berar, Nagpur and Chhattisgarh, all bounded by hills on the south, Chhattisgarh being divided from the rest of the state by the Maikal range.

The state is bounded on the east by the states of Behar and Orissa, on the southeast by Madras, on the south by Hyderabad, on the west by Bombay, Madhya Bharat (formerly western districts of the Central India agency) and Bhopal, and on the north by Vindhya Pradesh (former eastern Central India) and Uttar Pradesh (former United Provinces).

Only the two Vindhyan districts drain into the Gangetic plain. The waters of the rest of the northern districts and west Berar are carried by the Nerbudda and the Tapti, fed by their many tributaries rising in the Satpuras, into the Arabian sea. South Berar and the Nagpur division drain southeastward into the Godavari, the principal rivers being the Wainganga, the Wardha, the Painganga and their numerous tributaries. The eastern and southeastern portion, Chhattisgarh, is drained by the Mahanadi to the Bay of Bengal. Except for short reaches none of these rivers is navigable throughout the year.

Climate.—In climate the Vindhyan and Satpura districts are comparatively temperate; the Nerbudda valley is not, and the three great plains south of the Satpuras have the temperature of the Deccan, the heat from March to the middle of June being excessive, but very dry. The three northern tracts enjoy a pleasant cold season; in the three southern ones the cold is limited to occasional snaps, and the season is cool rather than cold. But, except in the extreme south of Chanda and the tracts nearest Bengal where the rains produce an exceedingly steamy atmosphere, the state has the advantage of a reasonably cool, rainy season, since both the cyclonic storms from the Bay of Bengal and the steady current of the southwest monsoon from the Arabian sea bring it moisture-laden clouds. The rainfall varies in the west from 25 to 30 in., and in the east from 50 to 60 in The monsoon period is divided between early rains, often deficient; middle rains, seldom failing completely; and late rains, premature cessation of which frequently causes severe losses. In 1896 the late rains failed completely, and in 1899 all three periods were failures. These caused the most extensive famines in the history of the province since it had come under British rule. (R. H. C.; B. R. P.)

HISTORY

The two territories forming the greater part of the present state have a somewhat different history. The history of Berar is mainly the history of the Deccan, to which it geographically belongs. The Central Provinces were known to the races of the north as the "Forests of the South," inhabited by Rakshas or demons, but ancient Rajput dynasties penetrated to the more open parts of the country, and of these the famous Hai Hai Bansi dynasty ruled Chhattisgarh for many centuries until conquered by the Bhonslas in 1741.

The Gonds.—The rest of the Central Provinces were known as Gondwana, the kingdom of the Gonds, who held the wildest parts of the country. The oldest Gond kingdom was that of Chanda in the south, to which a history of about 800 years is sometimes attributed. In the north was the kingdom of Garha-Mandla, from which sprang the two subkingdoms of Deogarh in Chhindwara and Kherla in Betul. This last was overthrown by Hoshang Shah of Malwa, the founder of Hoshangabad. The Gond kings, who must have established their rule over older Rajput dynasties, were fond of describing themselves as Rajgonds, and of claiming a Rajput origin.

One of these Gond kings named Sangramsha, said to have been the 47th of the Garha-Mandla house, in 1480 extended his dominion over the Nerbudda valley and the Vindhyan districts. Sangramsha lived until 1530, but a successor of his, Chandrasha, was forced to cede these territories to the Moguls in 1570. Though these Garha-Mandla chiefs owed a nominal allegiance to the Mogul emperor they maintained a virtual independence until the weakening of the Mogul power let in the predatory forces of the Marathas and (in the north) the Bundela chiefs. The Garha-Mandla raj was finally overthrown by the Peshwa in 1780.

The Gond rajah of Deogarh had paid a visit of homage to Delhi, and was so impressed with what he saw there, that he became a Mohammedan, adopting the name of Bakht Buland and establishing a new capital at Nagpur. He was himself an enlightened chief, but one of his grandsons, quarrelling over the succession, invited Raghoji Bhonsla from Berar to help him against his brother.

The Marathas.—Raghoji with his Marathas accomplished this mission and returned to his own territory, but later he established himself at Nagpur. Raghoji I sprung from a peasant family in Satara, was a great leader, and by 1751 had conquered the territories of Nagpur, Chanda and Chhattisgarh. He defied the Peshwa, raided Bengal, and extended his sovereignty over Orissa. He died in 1755 and his son Janoji was forced to submit to the Peshwa, but the next rajah, Mudhoji, and, after him, Raghoji II, acquired by purchase the northern territories as well, and the Nagpur state thereafter comprised the whole of the Central Provinces, Orissa and some of the Chota Nagpur states. By joining Sindia against the British in 1803, and as the result of Wellesley's victories of Assaye and Argaon, Raghoji lost Cuttack, Sambalpur and part of Berar. His successor, Mudhoji (known as Appa Sahib), by a treacherous attack on the British in 1818, was forced to cede the whole of the northern districts. Appa Sahib was allowed to hold the Nagpur territory, but on his further treachery being discovered he fled, and an infant grandson of Raghoji II was recognized as rajah by the British government. During his minority the Nagpur territories were administered by the British resident until 1840. The raja Raghoji III died in 1853 without male issue, and Lord Dalhousie declared the Nagpur state an escheat.

Central Provinces Under British Rule.—The northern territories ceded in 1818 and known as the Saugor Nerbudda territories were administered as part of the province of Agra. When the Nagpur territories escheated in 1853, they were administered by a commissioner as the Nagpur province. In 1861 they were amalgamated with the northern territories and became the Central Provinces. In 1903, Berar was added to the charge of the chief commissioner. In 1905, on the partition of Bengal, the Sambalpur district and the Oriya states adjacent to it were transferred to Bengal in exchange for five Hindi-speaking states of Chota Nagpur.

The first chief commissioner was the energetic Sir Richard Temple. His successor, Sir John Morris, governed the province for over 15 years, after which came a rapid succession of chief commissioners. The pioneer work of Sir Richard Temple and Sir John Morris, aided by a commission consisting mainly of military officers, provided the province with several important trunk roads and with a land settlement on the zamindari system. The Tenancy act of 1883 gave the tenantry of the province a degree of security in their holdings which no other zamindari province in India enjoyed to a like extent. The land settlements then made were afterward twice revised under a system which will always be associated with the name of Sir Bampfylde Fuller.

The first railway was opened in 1870, and the railway system of the present day extends to nearly 2,000 mi. The two trunk railways between Bombay and Calcutta pass through the north and south of the province respectively. The Marathi-speaking districts in the south and west are more advanced than the Hindi-speaking districts of the north and east.

There were serious setbacks; disastrous famines occurred in 1867, 1897 and 1900, while there were serious crop failures in 1907, 1913, 1918, and 1920, which would have produced similar results but for the vastly improved protection afforded by the increased credit and prosperity of the people. Plague has also taken its toll of the large towns, the worst epidemics known having been in 1903 and 1909. The influenza outbreak of 1918–19 accounted for about 950,000 deaths.

Following the implementation of the Government of India act, 1935, the province was constituted autonomous on April 1, 1937, and in that year came under the rule of a popularly elected Congress party ministry.

History of Berar.—The fertile plain of Berar (the ancient Vidharba) had a chequered history. It was under the sway of the various dynasties that ruled southern India until the Mohammedan invasion at the end of the 13th century, when it formed a province of the Bahmani dynasty, but about 1490 a rebellious governor, Imadul-Mulk, declared his independence and established a kingdom, which was again wrested from his descendants in 1572 by the Ahmednagar king. It was ceded by him to the Moguls in 1595, when his own capital was besieged by them, and the emperor Akbar's sons governed it together with Ahmednagar and Khandesh until Akbar's death in 1605. It then came under the rule of Malik Ambar the Abyssinian. On his death in 1626, the emperor Shah Jehan once more annexed it.

Toward the end of the 17th century, when Mogul power was waning, Berar began to be overrun by the Marathas, who won from Delhi their claim to blackmail (*chunth*). In 1724 Nizam Asaf Jah, establishing the independent line of nizams of Hyderabad, laid claim to Berar. This claim was disputed by the Bhonsla rajahs, and for about 50 years the inhabitants were harried and ground down by this conflict of authorities. This was ended by Wellesley's victories of Assaye and Argaon in 1803, when the country west of the Wardha river was ceded to the nizam.

Pindari and Bhil raiders, and also the exactions of their disputing rulers, harried the people. The nizam pledged the revenues as security for loans taken by him, the result being further exactions from the tax farmers to whom the revenues had been assigned. The British at last intervened in 1853, and a treaty was made with the nizam by which these territories came under British administration under the title of the Hyderabad assigned districts. On the subject of boundaries this treaty was again revised in 1860, and it was agreed that the British government should administer Berar in trust for the nizam, to whom was given the balance of the revenues after the cost of the Hyderabad contingent and of the administration of these districts had been met. Lord Curzon later concluded a fresh treaty with the nizam whereby the latter agreed to give a perpetual lease of these districts to the British government in return for an annual payment of 25 lakhs of rupees.

The six districts of Berar were reduced to four and a commissioner's division attached to the Central Provinces, but the sovereign rights of the nizam continued. By an agreement dated Oct. 24, 1936, the king-emperor reaffirmed the nizam's sovereignty over Berar, and the nizam agreed to Berar and the Central Provinces being administered together as one province.

Berar, after centuries of harassment, became a peaceful and prosperous subprovince, made wealthy by the cotton crop and cotton industry, and cultivated by as prosperous a tenantry as could be found anywhere in India outside the most highly irrigated tracts. The revenue settlements of Berar are ryotwari, namely, made with the peasantry direct.

The system follows generally that of the adjacent districts of Bombay, and village headmen in Berar perform, for a percentage remuneration on the revenue they collect, duties which in the Central Provinces proper were assigned to the malguzars, or village proprietors. After the institution of the republic the Madhya Pradesh legislature passed measures to extend the ryotwari system to the whole state. (R. H. C.; C. C. D.)

POPULATION

Nearly one-fifth of the people are of aboriginal and old Dravidian races, Gonds being the most numerous. Most of the rest are immigrants, mainly Hindus, who entered either in very ancient days or else intermittently (notably when the Moguls conquered the Deccan and exercised suzerainty over the Gond chiefs). Many of these came from Malwa, some from Hindustan, but with the entry of the Marathas on the scene in the 18th century, a large influx of Marathi-speaking people poured in from the west. On the fringes along the east and south there are Oriya and Telugu immigrants. Moslems numbering about 3.6% of the population are to be found mainly in the towns, being descendants of settlers who clustered around Mogul posts and certain seats of government, or such special cities as Burhanpur and Ellichpur. Individual Moslem families occupied land in the interior, but while only 12.45% of the total population is urban about 40% of the Moslems live in the towns.

With such heterogeneous elements and origins, there are great diversities of language. There are ten major languages, with many separate dialects of the same. Hindi is spoken by 56% of the population, Marathi by 31% and Gondi by 7%. About 200,000 people are returned as speaking many minor languages.

The first regular census was taken in the Central Provinces in 1872, in Berar a few years earlier. The figures of that census may be taken as representing the high-water mark of development before railways entered the province. The contrast provided by the 1941 census is notable.

	Population 1872	Population 1941 census
C. P.—British districts.	7,723,535	13,208,718
Berar	2,227,654	3,604,866
Feudatory states	928,195	4,064,000
	10,879,384	20,877,584

This increase was shown in spite of a decrease during the decade 1891–1901 caused by the great famines and the first ravages of plague, and virtual stagnation in the decade 1911–1921 which included World War I, two serious crop failures, and the great influenza scourge of 1918–19.

The state made strides educationally. Colleges and high schools and subsidiary institutions multiplied in numbers, and there is a teaching and affiliating university with headquarters at Nagpur, founded in 1923, and another centred upon Saugor, founded in 1946. In the 40 years between 1881 and 1921 literacy among males increased from 51 to 103 per thousand, and among females from 1 to 8 per thousand; in 1941 the coresponding figures were 196 per thousand and 48 per thousand. In 1921, 84 per 10,000, or under 1% of the males could read English, but only 9 per 10,000 females, or under 1 per thousand; by 1941, 161 per 10,000 males and 24 per 10,000 females could read English. Great efforts were made to extend medical relief in hospitals and dispensaries, better knowledge of hygiene and child welfare. The public revenue reflected the general advancement; in 1926–27 it was 534 lakhs of rupees, and in 1947–48 it was 1,224 lakhs.

ECONOMICS

The trade of the country increased greatly, the value of the rail-borne traffic being about 60 crores of rupees annually. The bulk of the exports are cotton, wheat, rice, oil seeds and other agricultural produce, but coal and manganese are now important items. Coal is unfortunately of too poor a quality to be of any use for metallurgical purposes. There are coal fields in Narsinghpur, Chanda and Wun (Berar), and in the Pench valley in Chhindwara (*q.v.*). It is used in cotton mills and factories and to some extent on the railways. The manganese deposits in Nagpur, Bhandara, Balaghat and Chhindwara are being vigorously worked and about 500,000 tons a year are produced. There are plentiful bauxite deposits in Jubbulpore and Balaghat awaiting exploitation. Iron ore is found in many districts, but worked only by indigenous methods in small charcoal furnaces. There are large deposits of excellent ore in Chanda, but for want of coking coal it is practically untouched. There is also valuable limestone in many places, notably near Katni, where lime and cement works are important industries.

There were 1,217 factories of all kinds in the Central Provinces and Berar in 1945, together employing more than 110,000 persons. However, outside the cotton industry the gun-carriage factory in Jubbulpore and the government and railway workshops, organized manufacturing industries are confined mostly to small concerns scattered about in various districts, but the motor trade and electrical installations are increasing. Rural and small hand industries include hand weaving, the manufacture of brass and copper utensils, pottery, shoes, baskets, bamboo matting, carpentry and smithy work, but the larger colonies of handicraftsmen have suffered from the competition of machine-made goods, both local and imported. In the mass, however, cottage and hand industries still have a large output. They depend on agricultural prosperity and suffer with agriculture from the effects of bad seasons.

Agriculture.—A line drawn from Katni in the north to Chanda in the south roughly divides the agriculture of the country. East of that line the principal crop is rice, and the rainfall is heavy. West of it, there are two sections—the northern in which wheat, gram and cold-weather crops are the most important; the southern in which cotton and *jawari* or great millet (sorghum) are the important staples. The Nerbudda valley and the Vindhyan districts are the large wheat-producing areas; Nimar, Berar and Nagpur (west), mainly composed of Deccan trap, are the great cotton and *jawari* tracts; but while cotton and *jawari* are quite insignificant in the rice country, and rice is insignificant west of the line of division described, practically every district in the state contains some heavy black soil areas which produce wheat and cold-weather crops. This variety of soil and cropping affords a certain degree of insurance against capricious rainfall. There are nearly 6,000,000 ac. of rice, 3,500,000 ac. of wheat, 4,750,000 ac. of *jawari* millet and 3,250,000 ac. of cotton. Besides these, there are large areas under oil seeds—linseed, sesamum and niger being the most important. There are pulses and peas of many kinds, and in the hills and light soils, small millet (*kodo* and *kutki*), the staple food of the aboriginal tribes.

In Berar the system of land revenue settlement is the ryotwari system, on the Bombay model. In the Central Provinces proper the proprietary system of Agra formerly prevailed, but the Central Provinces tenant enjoyed by law and tradition a degree of protection greater than in any proprietary province, and with this security against arbitrary ejectment and arbitrary enhancement of rent, he thrived in spite of fluctuations caused by bad seasons and resulting debts. In 1951, however, the Madhya Pradesh legislative assembly enacted measures extending the ryotwari system to the former Central Provinces divisions. Much was accomplished by the creation and expansion of the agricultural department from small beginnings to a well-regulated service with experimental seed and demonstration farms, model cattle farms, scientific research and education to improve the yields and better the lot of the cultivator, while co-operative banks and societies spread all over the country, affording cheaper credit than the moneylender would offer.

In the rice districts there are numerous irrigation works made by the people themselves, though few of these can stand against protracted drought. Government irrigation works only began to be undertaken after the report of the irrigation commission in 1903; important irrigation works, including the Wainganga, Tandula, Mahanadi, Kharung and Maniari canals, were later undertaken at a cost of more than 7 crores of rupees. By the 1950s these protected 500,000 ac. from the effects of drought. There were still several large projects under construction and investigation, principally in the Bilaspur district, which had been somewhat neglected in this respect. The area of government reserved forests in 1948–49 was 19,414 sq.mi.; there were also about 9,000 sq.mi. of private woods. On the absorption of the feudatory states into the province 7,455 sq.mi. of reserved forests and 10,464 sq.mi. of other forests were added. There are valuable sal (*Shorea robusta*) forests in the northeast, and teak (*Tektona grandis*) in almost every district, though teak of fine girth is limited to a few well-known reserves. There are many miscellaneous kinds of timber, bamboos and minor produce of commercial value, while there are edible fruits and roots with which the forest tribes supplement their food supply. The mohua tree (*Bassia latifolia*) has a flower which is edible, and from which country liquor is distilled, as well as a nut from which oil is extracted. The government forests yielded in 1947–48 a revenue of about 152 lakhs of rupees.

Communications.—Before the railways, there was a burst of activity in the construction of some important trunk roads, some of which were allowed to fall into disrepair when the trunk lines of railways were built. A branch of the East Indian railway from Allahabad to Jubbulpore was the first railway constructed in the province in 1870, while the G.I.P., bifurcating at Bhusawal, in Khandesh, sent one line to meet the East Indian at Jubbulpore, and a second branch through Berar to Nagpur. It was 20 years before the Bengal-Nagpur railway, absorbing a state metre-gauge line from Nagpur to the borders of Chhattisgarh (opened in 1881) made a second connection between Bombay and Calcutta via Nagpur and Bilaspur, from which place a branch went over the Ghats and across Rewa state to join the East Indian at Katni. The Indian Midland railway, afterward amalgamated with the G.I.P., made a fresh connection from Itarsi in Hoshangabad, via Bhopal, Gwalior and Jhansi, with Agra and Delhi, and a branch from Bina, through Saugor and Damoh, connecting with Katni followed a few years later. The turn of the century saw the next development by the Bengal-Nagpur railway of narrow-gauge lines (2 ft. 6 in.) across the Satpuras from Gondia in Bhandara to Jubbulpore, with branches to Seoni, Chhindwara and Mandla on the Satpura plateau. This was followed by a line from Gondia southwestward to Chanda, where it met an extension of the Warora Coal railway to the new coal field at Ballaspur, a few miles south of Chanda. Connections on the same narrow gauge with this branch to Nagpur and on to Chhindwara followed. A further broad-gauge connection between Nagpur and Itarsi was completed in 1926, crossing the Satpura district of Betul with a branch into the Chhindwara coal field.

Two links were constructed to complete direct broad-gauge connections between southern India and the north, one from Warangal to Chanda, and the other from Vizianagram on the east coast to Raipur. One more link on the metre gauge was required to join the Hyderabad-Godaveri railway at Hingoli with the Rajputana-Mulwa railway at Khandwa, via Basim and Akola. With this addition, the network of railways in Madhya Pradesh state would be completed, representing a length of 2,800 mi. inside the state. In 1946 there were 2,594 mi. of railway (1,741 mi. broad gauge and 853 narrow and metre gauge). There are also feeder lines in the cotton country of Berar and Wardha, controlled by private companies; by the 1950s only a few feeder lines remained to be constructed. In 1946 there were about 18,600 mi. of roads, 5,750 mi. were metalled, 3,100 unmetalled and 9,750 rough forest roads and cart tracks; however, with the great increases of motor traffic which had begun to penetrate even the remoter areas, there was still an enormous scope for road construction.

(R. H. C.; B. R. P.)

Bibliography.—*Administrative Reports of the Central Provinces and Berar* (Nagpur, monthly); Bishop E. Chatterton, *Story of Gondwana* (London, 1916); R. V. Russell, *Tribes and Castes of the Central Provinces of India,* 4 vol. (London, 1916); W. V. Grigson, *The Maria Gonds of Bastar* (1938); H. V. H. Elwin, *The Baiga* (London, 1939); W. Ruben, *Eisenschmiede und Dämonen in Indien* (Leyden, 1939 ff.).

CENTRAL SCHOOLS. The English central school grew out of the top end of the public elementary school. It had had similar predecessors. Within a few years after the passing of the Elementary Education act, 1870, which established the English national system, some of the larger and more enterprising school boards began to provide schools, centrally situated to serve relatively large districts, which offered more advanced instruction to elementary school children who had successfully completed the work of the normal school. These schools were variously called higher board, higher central, higher elementary or, more often, higher grade schools.

The Cockerton judgment of 1901, which ruled that a school board had no legal right to use its funds to provide education other than elementary in an elementary school, put an end to this movement, and most of the higher grade schools were absorbed into the statutory system of secondary education established by the Education act, 1902. But again, within a few years some of the local education authorities (which had replaced the school boards in 1902) began to experiment with the provision of separate schools for the abler among the older elementary school pupils. By about 1905 the London County council had established at least one central school, and Manchester was making similar experiments. It was from this movement that the central school proper developed.

In 1911 the London County council established a system of central schools throughout its area. Its declared purpose was to prepare boys and girls for immediate employment on leaving school, and its essential features were (1) entry at 11–12 years, from elementary schools; (2) a 4-year course; *i.e.*, one extending a year beyond the minimum leaving age; (3) a technical or commercial bias (or both) to the curriculum. Entry was either by recommendation of an inspector or head teacher or, more usually, by examination; places being offered to pupils who narrowly failed to gain entry to the council's secondary schools.

In 1912 Manchester established six district central schools on similar lines, and after World War I many other local authorities followed suit. Not all were so selective of pupils as London and Manchester. During the 1920s three types of central schools developed: (1) those in which pupils were selected, usually by examination, at the entry age of 11; (2) those to which children of 11 years and over were admitted on the request of their parents, supported by the recommendation of their head teacher; (3) those into which all the children in a given district who did not enter secondary school were collected. The first type was known as the selective central school, and the third type as the nonselective.

Nonselective central schools normally gave a general post-primary education which often included a considerable amount of practical work in art and handcrafts. Selective central schools tended increasingly during the first two years to give a general education, including usually one foreign language, and thereafter one or more courses with a definite bias, engineering being the most usual for boys and domestic science for girls. Some schools, however, emulated the recognized secondary (grammar) schools, providing an academic curriculum and presenting pupils for the school certificate examination.

In 1926 the consultative committee of the board of education, in their report on *The Education of the Adolescent* (the Hadow report), recommended that both selective and nonselective central schools should have secondary status, under the name of modern schools. This recommendation was not adopted, but in accordance with another recommendation local authorities began to reorganize their elementary schools into junior and senior schools with separate premises; and this, with other causes, tended to sharpen the distinction between the selective and nonselective schools, the latter frequently being called senior schools and tending to depart farther from the traditional academic curriculum, whereas the selective schools tended to become more academic.

The central school disappeared from the English educational system on the passing of the Education act, 1944, when all post-primary schools received secondary status. (H. C. D.)

CENTREBOARD or DROP KEEL, a drop board or iron plate employed in the smaller kind of sailing boats in place of a fixed keel; it is housed in a trunk or casing so as to be capable of being lowered through the boat's bottom when required to give stability, or to prevent making leeway in a wind, and can be hoisted in shallow water or when running before the wind.

CENTRIFUGE is commonly defined as a machine using centrifugal force for separating materials of different densities, but has the broader connotation of any machine designed for the specific purpose of subjecting materials to a sustained centrifugal force. Being of essentially the same nature as gravitational force, centrifugal force can be employed to accelerate or greatly accentuate many processes otherwise dependent on the comparatively meagre attraction of gravity. Apparently this fact was early recognized, for it is known that centrifugal machines were used in the 10th century A.D. for extracting tung oil.

Centrifugal Force.—As enunciated by Sir Isaac Newton in his famous laws of force and motion, a freely moving body tends to travel in a straight line, and if directed along a curved path, it will exert a force against the directing or restraining object in its continual effort to "fly off" onto a straight tangent course. For example, it is a familiar observation that an object revolving in a circle exerts a force away from the centre of rotation. Also, there is general appreciation of the fact that the amount of this force can be increased by increasing either the angular velocity of rotation (S), the mass of the object (M) or the radius (R) of the circle through which the object moves. Perhaps not so generally appreciated is the fact that whereas the centrifugal force is directly proportional to the radius and to the mass, it is, as examination of the formula below will show, proportional to the square of the angular velocity. For example, doubling the number of revolutions per minute will increase the centrifugal force by a factor of 4 (equals 2 times 2); increasing the speed by a factor of 10 will increase the force by a factor of 100 (equals 10 times 10). The actual amount of centrifugal force (F), expressed in dynes (1 gram of force = 980 dynes), is given by:

$$F = \frac{\pi^2 S^2 MR}{900}$$

where S is in revolutions per minute, M is in grams and R is in centimetres.

In order that a clearer concept of the amount of centrifugal force acting on an object may be provided, the force is often compared directly with the weight (pull of gravity) of the object and the amount of force is stated as so many "times gravity" or so many "g's." For example, an object revolving at the rate of 600 r.p.m. in a circle having a radius of 10 cm. (equivalent to 3.94 in.) generates a centrifugal force which is 41 times gravity. Through the use of special research apparatus, forces greater than 5,000,000 times gravity have been produced by spinning small metal rotors of about pea size at speeds exceeding 1,000,000 r.p.m.

The rotating element of a centrifuge is usually driven about a fixed axis by an electric motor, or by an air turbine in some high-speed machines, and is variously known as a rotor, rotator, bowl, drum or centrifugal. For the minimizing of vibration and strain on the shaft and bearings, it is essential that a loaded rotor be well balanced; *i.e.*, that the total mass be so distributed about the axis of rotation that the resultant of all the elemental forces is zero. If the bearings are suited to high speeds and if ample power is available to overcome the frictional resistance of the bearings and the surrounding air, the only limitation to the speed of a well-balanced rotor is the strength against rupture of the material from which it is made. For example, a 15-cm. (6-in. diameter) duralumin rotor used in certain biological studies and designed especially for high speeds has a limiting speed for routine operation of about 60,000 r.p.m. In a rotor of given design, the maximum angular velocity obtainable before rupture is to a close approximation inversely proportional to the rotor's diameter. Thus, a small rotor having only one-half the diameter of a larger one can be as safely rotated at twice the angular velocity and with the production at the periphery of twice the centrifugal force.

Effect on Liquids.—Of special importance is the centrifugal behaviour of liquids, particularly those in which is suspended solid particulate matter of small size or globules of an immiscible fluid; *e.g.*, the suspended particles in a water-oil emulsion. The net force acting on any portion of the liquid is the vector resultant of both the centrifugal force and the force of gravity. However, in general the force of gravity is so small in comparison with the centrifugal force generated during operation that its effect may be neglected in the present discussion of principles. In the centrifugal field of force, the liquid tries to distribute itself as far as possible from the axis of rotation, filling the outer portions of the container and forming a free surface which is everywhere equidistant from the axis and hence cylindrical in shape.

Any suspended particles which are more dense than the suspending liquid tend to migrate toward the periphery, while any having a lower specific gravity move toward the surface. The rapidity with which this migration proceeds is dependent on the intensity of the centrifugal force, the difference between the density of the particle and that of the suspending liquid, the viscosity of the liquid, the size and shape of the particle and to some extent the concentration of the particles and the degree to which they are electrically charged. The net motivating force exerted on the particle is the difference between the centrifugal force acting on it and the opposing buoyancy of the liquid, the buoyancy being equivalent to the centrifugal force acting on the volume of liquid displaced by the particle. In a steady state of migration, this net motivating force must be equal to the viscous drag of the liquid. For spherical, electrically neutral particles in dilute suspensions this resistance has been shown by G. G. Stokes to be given by the following relationship:

$$f = 6 \pi \eta r s$$

where f is the resistance in dynes, η is the viscosity in poises, r is the radius of the particle in centimetres and s is the speed of migration in centimetres per second. Equating the expressions for the resistive and the net motivating forces and solving for s, one finds that the rate of movement is proportional to the square of the particle's radius:

$$s = \frac{\pi^2 S^2 R (\delta - \rho) r^2}{4050 \eta}$$

where δ and ρ are the densities of the particle and the suspending fluid respectively. Thus, all other things being equal, a particle having a diameter 10 times that of a given particle will require only 1/100 as much average centrifugal force to move a given distance in a given time. The table, though somewhat oversimplified for the sake of clarity, gives some idea of actual requirements for particles of various sizes, the assumption being made that no remixing occurs within the fluids. Actually, remixing is a definite problem in the centrifugation of small particles at high speeds and is discussed in the next section.

From the foregoing discussion, it is clear that a practically complete separation of the suspending medium and the suspended phase can be produced if the centrifugation is allowed to continue until all particles have collected against the outer wall of the rotor. It should also be noted that a partial separation of two groups of suspended particles of different size can be effected by allowing centrifugation to continue only long enough for all of the larger particles to be completely packed into the sediment, since then many of the small particles will still be suspended in the fluid. If purification of the larger, as well as the smaller particles is desired, the supernatant fluid can be drawn off and the sediment resuspended in some suitable liquid and subsequently centrifuged again to effect further separation. This process may be repeated any number of times.

Industrial Centrifuges.—There are numerous industrial applications of centrifugal force. Thick-walled metal pipe and tubing are cast by pouring the molten metal into cylindrical moulds which are then rotated while the metal sets into the solid state. Perforated rotating drums or baskets are used for extracting fluids from various natural products after crushing, for throwing off the excess water from washed clothes and for retaining sugar crystals while the liquor in which the crystallization took place is drained off under the action of centrifugal force. However, the greatest advantage of the centrifugal method is realized in fractionating fine suspensions of solid or liquid material. The cream separator is a familiar example. Though variously modified to suit the particular application, most machines employed for such purposes are of the continuous-flow type, as illustrated by (A) in the figure. The bowl or rotor, generally cylindrical in shape, is provided with a central opening to permit the continuous introduction of liquid during operation, and with one or more exit ports from which the centrifuged fluid can overflow and be thrown into collectors.

In the simplest type of machine, only one exit port is provided for the supernatant fluid, the sedimented particles being collected in the precipitated form after the rotation has been stopped. In other machines two overflow passages are used, one being at the level of the supernatant fluid and the other leading from the peripheral section of the fluid to an exit port located at a slightly greater radial distance than the overflow for the supernatant fluid. With this arrangement both a "light" fraction (supernatant) and a "heavy" fraction (of increased density because of increased concentration of heavier material or loss of lighter material) of fluid can be continually collected, the flow being kept sufficiently rapid to prevent complete sedimentation of the particles if they are of such a nature as to pack easily into a semisolid sediment.

In many cases, centrifugal bowls are provided with a series of laminations, usually conical in shape and known as separators. Subdividing the fluid into thin layers generally has the effect of speeding up the separating process by reducing the distance through which a particle has to move before its effective removal from the main body of fluid. As soon as a particle reaches the wall of a separator, it can collect with other particles into larger groups that will slide along the wall into the heavy fraction at the periphery, or toward the surface if the particles are of low density. Such an arrangement also minimizes stirring and remixing as the fluid flows through the centrifuge.

Laboratory Centrifuges.—Centrifuges are used extensively in biological and chemical laboratories for the clarification of fluids and for the concentration and purification of various biological and chemical agents.

Most laboratory centrifuges are of the swinging-bucket type (B in figure) or, for work at higher speeds especially, of the inclined-tube type (C in figure).

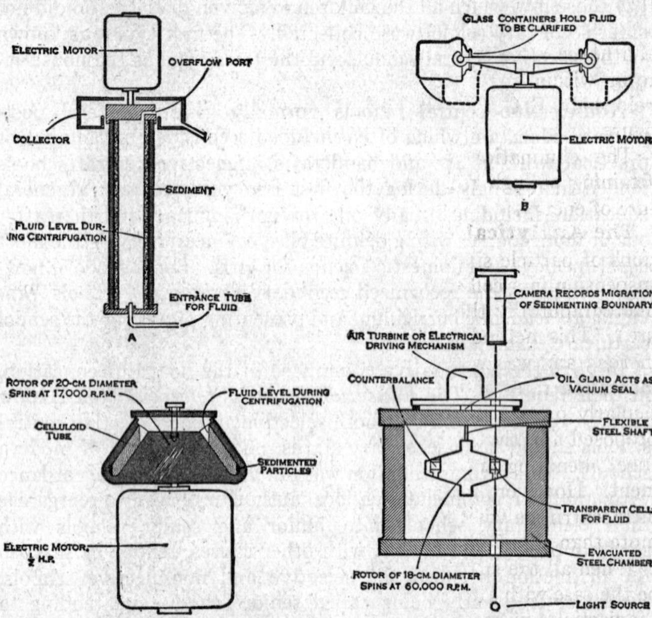

PRIMARY CENTRIFUGAL METHODS: (A) INDUSTRIAL CENTRIFUGE OF CONTINUOUS FLOW TYPE; (B) LOW-SPEED LABORATORY CENTRIFUGE WITH SWINGING BUCKETS; (C) LABORATORY CENTRIFUGE WITH INCLINED TUBES; (D) OPTICAL ULTRACENTRIFUGE FOR MEASUREMENT OF SEDIMENTATION RATES AND DETERMINATION OF PARTICLE SIZES

Submicroscopic disease agents such as influenza virus, smallpox virus, yellow fever virus and the virus of infantile paralysis are nearly always obtained in the presence of considerable extraneous material of both larger and smaller particle size. They might be found in the excreta, blood or other body fluids of an animal, or they might be recovered from ground extracts of certain tissues such as those of the brain or the lungs. Through the process of differential centrifugation already described, these biological agents can be partially purified for further study or for practical purposes such as the manufacture of vaccines.

Laboratory centrifuges of proper design may be used not only for preparative purposes but for semiquantitative investigation as well. As a matter of fact, such a study in various degrees of refinement is usually a preliminary step in selecting appropriate rotational speeds and centrifugation times for a desired purification procedure. If excessive convective disturbances and remixing within the fluid can be avoided, the approximate size of the sedimenting particles can be computed by determining the minimum time required at a given speed for a definite amount of sedimentation and applying the previously discussed formula for spherical particles. The method depends on the sampling of the centrifuged column of fluid at various levels and the determination, by specific biological, physical, or chemical tests, of the amount of the respective agent present in each sample. In less quantitative work, almost all of the supernatant fluid may be drawn off into one sample and compared with the sediment after resuspension in fresh fluid.

Two practical difficulties often limit the efficiency of the sedimentation process and make quantitative determinations of sedimentation rate uncertain if not impossible. One involves the remixing caused by the tendency of the fluid to continue revolving as the centrifuge is decelerated to rest. The other involves convection currents caused by slight differences in the temperature of the liquid at different levels, and it is most serious with small particles which require long periods of centrifugation. Since convection is essentially a buoyancy phenomenon, its intensity is stepped up almost directly in proportion to the amount of centrifugal force, and hence convection can be caused by extremely small temperature differences, such as might arise from the difference in the amount of frictional air resistance suffered by a rotor at its periphery and at its centre.

The first difficulty can largely be avoided by using small centrifuge containers and by packing the particles under study into a semisolid sediment before stopping the centrifuge. Air resistance, and hence almost all convection, can be avoided by spinning the rotor within an evacuated chamber according to a method developed by E. G. Pickels and J. W. Beams, illustrated by (D) in the figure.

The elimination of air resistance also makes possible the attaining of high rotational speeds with relatively little expenditure of energy.

The Analytical Ultracentrifuge.—More precise determinations of particle size and weight can be made by centrifuging the suspension in a cell fitted with transparent windows and recording photographically the progress of the sedimentation (*see* D in figure). This method was first used by T. Svedberg and J. B. Nichols in 1923 and was widely applied thereafter to determine the sedimentation rates and sizes of many submicroscopic particles, particularly protein molecules and viruses. Svedberg and H. Rinde proposed for the first optical centrifuge the name "ultracentrifuge," denoting an instrument suitable for quantitative measurement. However, it became general practice to associate the term ultracentrifuge with any type of centrifuge operating at speeds of more than about 20,000 r.p.m.

When all the suspended particles are of the same size, as might be the case with a solution of haemoglobin molecules, for example, the particles within any elemental zone of fluid, and hence within the same field of force, will migrate through the liquid at the same rate. Thus, the particles originally at the inner surface of the fluid will form a "rear line of march," or moving boundary, which demarcates the supernatant fluid and the sedimenting solute. It is by photographic recording of the continually changing position of this boundary at repeated intervals that precise determinations of sedimentation rate are made. From the sedimentation rate, in turn, the size or molecular weight of the particles can be determined if the shape factor is eliminated by a measurement of the diffusion constant. If particle groups of differing size are present, each group will form a separate boundary which sediments at a rate characteristic of the particle size. From a study of such multiple boundaries, the composition (from the standpoint of size) of the suspended matter in various biological fluids can be determined and reinvestigated following various treatments.

Migrating boundaries may be detected either through the absorption of visible or ultra-violet light by the sedimenting particles or through the refraction of transmitted light occasioned by the concentration gradient existing at the boundary. The first ultracentrifuges to operate at more than 50,000 r.p.m. were driven by an oil turbine about a horizontal axis in a hydrogen atmosphere at reduced pressure. As illustrated in the figure, most ultracentrifugal rotors are spun in an evacuated chamber about a vertical axis, and power is supplied by an air turbine or a special electric motor. For supporting the load at high speeds with a minimum of frictional resistance, successful use has been made of air bearings, magnetic bearings and mechanical bearings of novel design.

The rotor is connected to the driving mechanism through a flexible steel shaft, about ⅛ in. in diameter, which permits a limited degree of self-balancing.

Following World War II, electrically-driven ultracentrifuges operating at speeds up to 60,000 r.p.m. became available for both analytical and preparative purposes in biochemical and other research laboratories. The serum proteins and other naturally-occurring macromolecules were subjected to extensive study. Through refinements the analytical method was made applicable in certain cases even to small molecules of simple chemical structure. This was accomplished through a layering of clear solvent above the solution during acceleration of the ultracentrifuge. An initially sharp sedimentation boundary was thus formed away from the meniscus and its rate measured in spite of the slow sedimentation and rapid diffusion, which otherwise would prevent the formation of a measurable boundary by such small particles.

*Sedimentation of Spherical Particles Suspended in Aqueous Media**

Assumed diameter of particle, in cm. (1 cm.=0.39 in.)	Examples of particles in size range of same order	Average centrifugal force necessary to produce sedimentation of 1 cm. in 10 min., expressed as number times gravity	Approx. no. of r.p.m. required, assuming average distance of liquid from axis of rotation to be 10 cm.
1/1,000 . . .	Red blood cells	1.8	120
1/10,000 . . .	Typhus rickettsia	180	1,200
1/100,000 . . .	Influenza virus	18,000	12,000
1/1,000,000 . .	Protein molecules	1,800,000	120,000†

*Assuming viscosity equal to that of water, specific gravity of medium equal to 1 and the average specific gravity of particles equal to 1.3 (order of magnitude for many biological materials).

†Because of the limited strength of materials, speeds above approximately 50,000 r.p.m. are not feasible with rotors of the assumed size. At this speed, an hour or more would be required to produce the indicated sedimentation of animal proteins.

See T. Svedberg and K. O. Pedersen, *The Ultracentrifuge* (1940); E. G. Pickels, "Ultracentrifugation," *Methods in Medical Research* (1952). (E. G. P.)

CENTUMVIRI, an ancient court of civil jurisdiction at Rome. The word is derived from *centum,* hundred, and *vir,* man. The antiquity of the court is attested by the symbol and formula used in its procedure, the lance (*hasta*) as the sign of true ownership, the oath (*sacramentum*), the ancient formula for recovery of property or assertion of liberty. Its concern was with matters of debt and of the property of which account was taken at the census. The *centumviri* were never regarded as magistrates, but as *judices,* and as such would be appointed for a fixed term of service by the magistrate, probably by the *praetor urbanus.* But in Cicero's time they were elected by the *Comitia Tributa.* They then numbered 105. Their original number is uncertain. It was increased by Augustus and in Pliny's time had reached 180. The office was probably open in quite early times to both patricians and plebeians.

Bibliography.—A. H. J. Greenidge, *Legal Procedure of Cicero's Time,* pp. 40 ff., 58 ff., 182 ff., 264 (1901); J. E. Sandys, *Companion to Latin Studies,* with useful bibliography (1921).

CENTURION (Lat. *centurio*), in the ancient Roman army, an officer in command of a *centuria,* originally a body of a hundred infantry, later the sixtieth part of the normal legion. There were, therefore, in the legion 60 centurions, who, though theoretically subordinate to the six military tribunes, were the actual working officers of the legion. For the most part the centurions were promoted from the ranks: they were arranged in a complicated order of seniority; the senior centurion of the legion (*primus pilus*) was an officer of very high importance. Besides commanding the centuries of the legion, centurions were "seconded" for various kinds of special service; *e.g.,* for staff employment, the command of auxiliaries. (*See* Roman Army.)

See also J. E. Sandys, *Companion to Latin Studies,* sec. 752 (1921).

CENTURIPE, a town of Sicily, province of Catania, 2,380 ft. above sea level, 7 mi. N. of the railway station of Catenanuova-

Centuripe, which is 28 mi. W. from Catania. It was formerly called Centorbi (anc. Κεντόριπα) or Centuripae. Pop. (1936) 9,255 (town); 10,802 (commune). Thucydides called it a Sicel city; it allied itself with Athens against Syracuse, and remained independent (apart from Agathocles' domination) till the first Punic War. Cicero, perhaps exaggerating, called it the largest and richest city in Sicily, with 10,000 inhabitants cultivating a large territory. It appears to have suffered much in the war against Sextus Pompeius, and not to have regained its former prosperity under the empire. Frederick II. partly destroyed it in 1233, and its ruin was completed by Charles of Anjou. Considerable remains of buildings, including Hellenistic houses with wall paintings, thermal establishments and cisterns, and a number of substruction walls on the steep slopes, mostly of the Roman period, still exist; Hellenistic *terra-cottas* and finely painted vases, both of local manufacture, have been discovered, and a large number of tombs have been excavated. It is surrounded by deep ravines, due to erosion.

See G. Libertini, *Centuripe* (Catania, 1926).

CENTURY, the name for a unit (*centuria*) in the Roman army, originally amounting to 100 men, and for one of the divisions into which the Roman people was separated for voting purposes (*see* COMITIA). The word is applied more particularly to a period of 100 years. The "century-plant" is a name given to the agave (*q.v.*), or American aloe, from the supposition that it flowers once only in every 100 years.

CEOS, an island in the Aegean sea (Gr. Κέως mod. ZEA or KEA), 14 mi. off the coast of Attica, in the group of the Cyclades and the eparchy of Syra. Its greatest length is about 15 mi. and its breadth about 8 mi. Mount Elias in the centre is 1,864 ft. high. Among its productions are lemons, citrons, olives, wine, honey and valonia. There were formerly four towns in the island: Iulis, about 3 mi. from the northwest shore, represented by the town of Kea, Coressia, the harbour of Iulis, Carthaea, in the southeast, at S'tais Polais village; and Poieëssa, in the southwest. Iulis was the birthplace of the lyric poets Simonides and Bacchylides, the philosophers Prodicus and Ariston and the physician Erasistratus. From its excellent code, the title of Cean Laws passed into a proverb. One of them forbade a citizen to protract his life beyond 60 years. Ceos fought on the Greek side at Artemisium and Salamis; joined the Delian league, and also the Athenian alliance in 377 B.C.; revolted in 363–362, but was reduced again. Athens then assumed monopoly of the ruddle, or red earth, the most valuable product of the island. Ceos was divided in A.D. 1207 among four Italian adventurers; was included in the duchy of Naxos in 1537; passed under Turkish rule in 1566 and thence into the Greek kingdom; in 1941 it was occupied by German troops. Silver coins of Carthaea and Coressia date from the 6th century B.C. *See* Pridik, *De Cei Insulae rebus* (1892).

CEPHALIC INDEX, the percentage of breadth to length in any skull. The longer diameter of a skull, the antero-posterior diameter, is taken as 100; if the shorter or transverse diameter exceeds 80 the skull is broad (brachycephalic), if between 80 and 75 it is mesaticephalic, and if below 75 dolichocephalic (*see* RACES OF MANKIND).

CEPHALONIA, largest of the Ionian Islands on the west of the Greek mainland (Ital. *Cefalonia;* ancient and modern official Greek *Kephallenia,* Κεφαλληνία). Pop. (1951) 47,369. Its length is 31 mi. and its breadth varies from about 20 mi. in the southern portion to less than 3 mi. in the promontory opposite Ithaca. The whole island is mountainous, the main range running from northwest to southeast. The ancient Mt. Aenos, now Elato or Monte Negro (5,315 ft.), frequently has snow for several months. There are few permanent streams except the Rakli, and springs are likely to fail in dry summers. In the west a gulf runs up from the south, a distance of about 7 mi.; on its east side is the chief town Argostoli (*q.v.*) (Argostolion), and on its west the rival city of Lexourion. About a mile west of Argostoli, a stream of sea water running into a chasm in the shore is made to operate "sea mills." About 5 mi. from Argostoli is the Venetian castle of St. George. The ruins of Crane are close to Argostoli, those of Pale to Lexourion. On the other side of the island the remains of Same are on the bay of the same name, those of Proni, or Pronni, farther south above the vale of Rakli. All these have impressive walls, Cyclopean and Hellenic. Near the village of Scala is a nameless site with Roman baths and tessellated pavements, a brick temple and rock tombs. The inhabitants of Cephalonia have always been industrious in the construction of cultivation terraces. But only a small proportion of the soil is under cultivation, and the grain production meagre. The chief crop is the currant, in which Cephalonia surpasses Zante. The fruit is smaller than that of the Morea, and has a peculiar flavour; it ordinarily finds a market in the Netherlands, Belgium and Germany. The grape vine also is grown, for wine. The olive crop is of importance, and cotton is grown in the low grounds. Manufactures are few: lace from aloe fibre, Turkey carpets and basket work in the villages; and boatbuilding at both the principal towns. Of all the seven "Ionian Islands" Cephalonia and Zante (*q.v.*) are most purely Greek.

History.—In the Homeric poems the Cephallenes are subjects of Ulysses, but Cephallenia is not mentioned: probably it is represented by Same (*see,* however, under ITHACA). In the Persian War the island took but little part; in the Peloponnesian it sided with the Athenians. The town of Pale supported the Aetolian cause and was vainly besieged by Philip V. of Macedon in 218 B.C. In 189 B.C. all the cities surrendered to the Romans, but Same afterwards revolted, and was reduced only after a siege of four months. The island was presented by Hadrian to Athens, but it appears again later as "free and autonomous." After the division of the Roman empire, it was attached to Byzantium till 1082, when it was captured by Robert Guiscard, who died, however, during the revolt of 1085. In 1204 it was assigned to Gaius, prince of Tarentum, who accepted the protection of Venice in 1215; and after 1225 it was held with Santa Maura and Zante by the Tocco family at Naples. Formally made over to Venice in 1350 by the prince of Tarentum, it fell to the Turks from 1479 to 1500, but Venice held it again till the fall of the republic.

For some time it was administered for the French government, but in 1809 it was taken by the British. Under vigorous governors, like Major de Bosset (1809–13) and Sir Charles Napier (1818–1827), the island advanced in material prosperity, but was several times the scene of political disturbances. It retained longer than the sister islands traces of feudal influence exerted by the landed proprietors, but has been gradually becoming more democratic. Under the Venetians it was divided into eight districts, and an elaborate system of police was in force; after its annexation to Greece it was broken up into twenty demarchies, each with its separate jurisdiction and revenues, and the police system was abolished. In 1941 it was occupied by Italy.

BIBLIOGRAPHY.—A special treatise on the antiquities of Cephalonia was written by Petrus Maurocenus. *See* Holland's *Travels* (1815); Ansted's *Ionian Islands* (1863); Viscount Kirkwall's *Four Years in Ionian Islands* (1864); Wiebel's *Die Insel Kephalonia;* parliamentary papers. Riemann, *Recherches archéologiques sur les Iles Ioniennes* (Paris, 1879–1880); Partsch, *Kephallenia und Ithaka* (1890); Pauly-Wissowa *s.v., see* also CORFU; IONIAN ISLANDS.

CEPHALOPODA, a group of highly organized invertebrate animals of exclusively marine distribution constituting a class of the phylum Mollusca. Some 150 genera of living cephalopods are known, of which the octopus, the squid and the cuttlefish (*qq.v.*) are the most familiar representatives. The extinct forms, however, outnumber the living, the class having attained very great diversity in late Palaeozoic and Mesozoic times. Of extinct cephalopods the Ammonites (*q.v.*) and Belemnites are the most familiar examples.

The Cephalopoda agree with the rest of the Mollusca in general structure and appear to have the closest affinity with the Gastropoda (snails, periwinkles, limpets, etc.). They have a more or less elongate body (visceral mass) covered by a "mantle." The latter secretes a shell and encloses a cavity in which the gills are suspended. The alimentary canal is furnished with the characteristic molluscan rasping tongue or radula. These animals differ from the rest of the Mollusca primarily in that the head and foot are approximated, so that the mouth is situated in the middle of the foot, and the edges of the latter are drawn out into a number of appendages (arms and tentacles). The area just above the edge of the foot, from which the epipodium of the Gastropoda is developed, is produced to form a peculiar organ of locomotion, the funnel. The majority of living cephalopods possess fins and their shell is in a reduced or degenerate condition, a tendency apparent in many fossil forms. In short the leading feature of cephalopod organization and the dominating theme of their evolution is the development of organs that subserve a vigorous aggressive mode of life unhampered by the heavy calcareous shell that is carried by their more sedentary and inactive relatives. Nevertheless the living *Nautilus* (*q.v.*) and many forms now extinct retain the shell in a complete condition.

FROM WILLEY, "ZOOLOGICAL RESULTS" (QUARTERLY JOURNAL OF MICROSCOPICAL SCIENCE)
FIG. 1.—NAUTILUS POMPILIUS (ABOUT 1/12 NATURAL SIZE)

For invertebrate animals the Cephalopoda attain a large average size and the genus *Architeuthis* (giant squids) are actually the largest living invertebrates, the Atlantic species *Architeuthis princeps* attaining a total length of 52ft. (inclusive of the tentacles). The shell of the fossil ammonite (*Pachydiscus seppenradensis*) from Westphalia (Cretaceous) measures 6ft. 8in. in diameter and is the largest shelled mollusc. Though not such a flourishing group as they were in secondary times, the Cephalopoda are still one of the dominating groups of marine animals. They are the principal prey of whales and other marine carnivora and the relentless enemies of Crustacea and small fishes. The bizarre appearance of Cephalopoda, their sinister eyes and the secretive habits of some of the shore-living forms have made them a subject of legend among imaginative peoples. Modern authors have not hesitated to exaggerate the horrors of the attack of a giant squid or octopus; and Denis de Montfort and Victor Hugo have invested them with a melodramatic violence that has taken root in popular fancy. Nor is this reputation for ferocity unmerited, as far as attacks on human subjects are concerned.

Classification.—In the past decade the classification of the Cephalopoda has undergone a considerable amount of revision principally owing to the work of Naef and other German zoologists. The following is the scheme drawn up by Grimpe (1922):

Class. Cephalopoda.
- Sub class 1. Protocephalopoda.
  - Order 1. Nautiloidea.
  - Order 2. Ammonoidea.
- Sub class 2. Metacephalopoda.
  - Order 1. Octopoda.
    - Sub order 1. Cirrata.
    - Sub order 2. Palaeoctopoda.
    - Sub order 3. Incirrata.
  - Order 2. Decapoda.
    - Sub order 1. Sepioidea.
    - Sub order 2. Teuthoidea.
    - Sub order 3. Belemnoidea.

It will be seen that this scheme recognizes the fundamental distinction proposed by Owen, which separates *Nautilus* and its allies from the octopods, squids and cuttlefish. This distinction is without doubt sound, for it rests on the fact that, within the limits of our knowledge, the *Nautilus* has a more primitive organization than the rest of the Cephalopoda. It has a wholly external coiled shell, four gills and kidneys, and other features which we are justly entitled to regard as primitive. It must, however, be recognized that we can deal only with the shell of the extinct nautiloids and the ammonites and we do not know if the rest of their organization was like that of *Nautilus*. It is a fair inference, however, that the living and fossil nautiloids and the ammonoids are a natural group. Grimpe's scheme differs herein from the older classification in raising the main sub-divisions to the status of sub-classes and in thus emphasizing their distinctness as is done in the case of the streptoneurous and euthyneurous gastropods. This is an advantage and may be safely adopted.

The classification of the Dibranchia proposed by Naef and Grimpe involves a more fundamental change. In its primary division into Octopoda and Decapoda it follows traditional lines. In its secondary division of these groups, however, it departs from the latter for reasons which appear to us well-founded. Among the Octopoda the fossil *Palaeoctopus* merits recognition as representing a separate sub-order. It is, however, in the reorganization of the Decapoda that the new scheme has most to recommend it. The recognition of the three sub-orders Sepioidea, Teuthoidea and Belemnoidea has the advantage of taking into account our knowledge of the phylogeny of the order, and marking the three great tendencies that can be recognized in the evolution of the decapod shell. The older "Oigopsida" are, as far as nearly all their living representatives are concerned, preserved intact. But the Belemnite-like fossil forms are quite reasonably abstracted from them and placed in a separate sub-order. The older "Myopsida," which contained forms with radically dissimilar shells, such as *Sepia* and *Loligo,* are resolved into two sections, one of which (*Sepia, Sepiola, Spirula* and certain extinct forms) is elevated to sub-ordinal rank (the *Sepioidea*), while the other (*Loligo,* etc.) is treated as a section of the Teuthoidea along with the Oigopsida (as above restricted). It may be reasonably objected that this has the effect of placing forms such as *Sepiola* which, like *Loligo,* have a chitinous, non-calcified shell in a different sub-order from *Loligo* and the Oigopsida, and of disregarding certain points of similarity between the *Loliginidae* and *Sepiidae*. Nevertheless it is held that in spite of this fact, *Sepiola* and its allies are more closely allied anatomically to *Spirula,* which has the distinction of being the only living dibranch with a coiled and partly external calcareous shell, than to *Loligo* and the Oigopsida, and that phylogenetically they can thus be attached to the sepioid stock. Concerning the affinities of *Spirula,* a good deal of controversy has taken place. It seems best to accept Chun's view that it is a sepioid form, as the reasons set forth at length by him in his study of this interesting genus (*Wissenschaftliche Ergebnisse der Deutschen Tiefsee Expedn.* Bd. 18, 1915) are sufficiently convincing.

BY COURTESY OF F. M. DUNCAN
FIG. 2.—AN OCTOPUS RESTING ON THE SEA BOTTOM (ABOUT 1/10 NATURAL SIZE)

Anatomy and Physiology.—In fig. 3 is given a diagram illustrating the structure of a cephalopod. Though schematic, this diagram gives a very fair idea of the organization of such forms as the common cuttlefish, squid and octopus. The view has been widely accepted that in the Cephalopoda the surface of the foot has become very much shortened as compared with that of other molluscs, the length of the body being reduced, while its height is increased. This modification of what we may assume to be the original plan of molluscan organization is held to have been brought about by the foot shifting forwards until it became involved in the head, its edges growing round and encircling the mouth. It will be seen in the section on Development that this process is actually indicated in the embryo, so that on this, as well as other grounds, we may regard the current view as to how the cephalopod organization was attained as substantially accurate. As to which surface of a cephalopod should be called anterior and which posterior we are on sound morphological ground if we regard the head and foot as ventral and the mantle-cavity as posterior. Nevertheless in many cephalopods, which move about by swimming, the long axis of the body becomes horizontal, like that of a fish, and the anterior surface might be more appropriately termed "upper" or "dorsal" and the posterior surface "under" or "ventral."

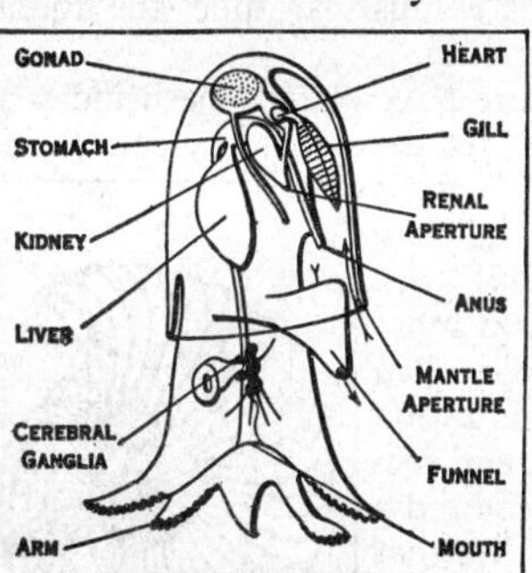

FROM LANKESTER, "TREATISE ON ZOOLOGY" (BLACK)
FIG. 3.—DIAGRAM ILLUSTRATING THE STRUCTURE OF A CEPHALOPOD

The viscera of our typical cephalopod are covered by a dome-shaped or elongated sheath of skin, the mantle, which is in close contact with the body anteriorly, but posteriorly is free and encloses the mantle cavity, into which the gills project and the anus, kidneys and reproductive system open.

Below the visceral mass are the head and foot which together continue the main mass of the body. On the posterior side of this head-foot (cephalo-pedal mass) is a muscular tube, the funnel. The circlet of arms encircles the mouth.

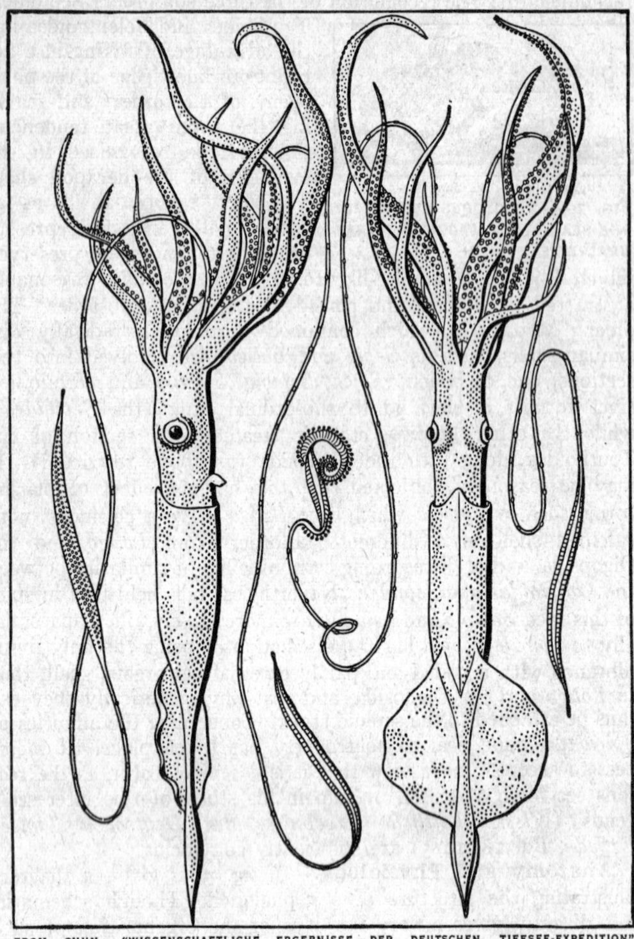

FROM CHUN, "WISSENSCHAFTLICHE ERGEBNISSE DER DEUTSCHEN TIEFSEE-EXPEDITION" (FISCHER)

FIG. 4.—CHIROTEUTHIS IMPERATOR (ABOUT ¼ NATURAL SIZE)

The main divergences of structure have already been indicated in the section on classification; but, for the sake of rendering clear the importance of some of the details which follow, it is necessary to recall two important facts, first that *Nautilus* with its external coiled shell represents a more primitive and less specialized type than do the Dibranchia, a grade of organization seen in many anatomical features, and secondly that the Dibranchia have acquired a more active and vigorous mode of life that has led to certain marked departures in structure and function from the type represented by *Nautilus* and (we may assume) the ammonites. Lastly among the Dibranchia themselves certain important habitudinal divergences are established, and hand in hand with these we must note structural and physiological adaptations, *e.g.*, to a life permanently spent in the great depths of the sea, to a permanent floating life or to a more active and aggressive existence near the surface. The details of cephalopod anatomy and physiology may be studied in any good zoological textbook or in divers special papers and monographs. The following account attempts to eliminate detail and to present the main structural and physiological features of the class in relation to the mode of life of the animals concerned.

FROM "GUIDE TO FOSSIL INVERTEBRATES" (BRITISH MUSEUM)

FIG. 5.—A TRIASSIC AMMONITE. TRACHYCERAS AON (ABOUT ¾ NATURAL SIZE)

External Anatomy and General Organization.—The nautiloids and ammonites were in all probability mainly shallow-water animals living near the bottom. They relied for protection on a calcareous external shell and their speed of movement was probably inconsiderable. The modern *Nautilus* represents this mode of life pretty closely. The Dibranchia, are as we have seen, on the whole more active, and swimming or floating has become their characteristic mode of locomotion. Accordingly we notice the following features in their external organizations: (1) The mantle, which in the majority of molluscs and in the Tetrabranchia has a passive role and merely contains the viscera and secretes the shell, has become involved in the mechanism of locomotion. It has lost or almost entirely lost the rigid shell and has become highly muscular. Its expansion and contraction promote a locomotor water-current by drawing water into the mantle cavity and expelling it through the funnel. The rapid ejection of this jet of water enables the animal to execute rapid retrograde movements. As a means of sealing the mantle aperture while the locomotor jet is under compression, there is developed an "adhesive apparatus," a cartilaginous stud or ridge on each side of the edge of the mantle and a pair of corresponding sockets on the head into which the studs or ridges fit so that the mantle edge is locked to the head. (2) The funnel in *Nautilus* is represented by two muscular folds which meet in the middle line. In the Dibranchia these folds are completely fused up and form a complete tube. (3) Additional locomotor appendages in the shape of fins are developed from the sides of the mantle. These may become very large and no doubt assist in balancing the animal. (4) In accordance with their active, mainly reptorial mode of life, the circumoral appendages, which are many and feebly developed in *Nautilus,* are fewer in number in the Dibranchia, but more muscular and provided with suckers which in the Decapoda are furnished with horny, often toothed rims. In certain forms the teeth of the suckers are modified as large and formidable hooks. Two of the arms are specially modified in the Decapoda for the capture of prey.

FROM "GUIDE TO FOSSIL INVERTEBRATES" (BRITISH MUSEUM)

FIG. 6.—UNCOILED CRETACEOUS AMMONITES (ABOUT ¾ NATURAL SIZE)

Upper, *Crioceras emericianum.* Lower, *Heteroceras emericianum*

Internal Anatomy.—(1) *Internal supporting structures.* All the Cephalopoda have an internal cartilaginous covering of the main ganglia of the nervous system. In the Dibranchia this is more complete than it is in *Nautilus.* It encircles the ganglia and constitutes a kind of skull. Besides this structure the greater mobility of the Dibranchia is secured by other skeletal supports of the muscles which are found at the base of the fins, in the "neck," gills and arms of various forms. (2) *Viscera.* The alimentary system of the Cephalopoda consists of a muscular *buccal* mass furnished with a pair of jaws (mandibles) and a rasping tongue (radula), oesophagus, salivary glands, stomach, coecum, liver and intestine. Efficient mastication is secured by the

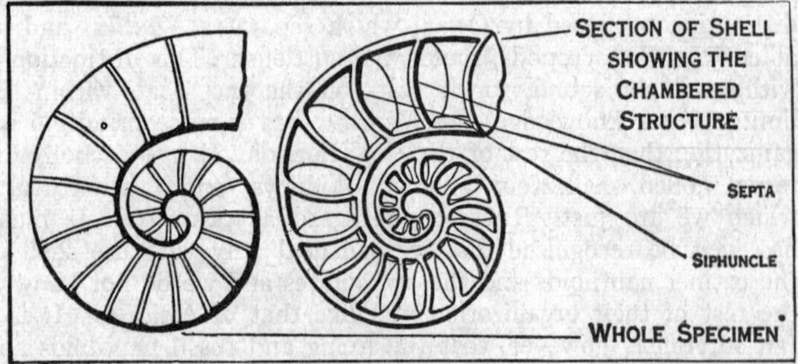

FROM "GUIDE TO MOLLUSCA" (BRITISH MUSEUM)

FIG. 7.—SPIRULA PERONII (ABOUT ½ NATURAL SIZE)

powerful mandibles and sharp-pointed teeth of the radula. In the Octopoda the oesophagus is expanded to form a crop and in the Cirrata, possibly in relation to the special diet of these mainly deep-sea animals, which seem to feed on bottom débris, the radula is frequently degenerate or absent and there is a "second stomach," a capacious dilatation of the intestine. In the Dibranchia the pancreatic element of the liver is partly separated from the latter. Nearly all the members of this subclass have a diverticulum of the intestine situated near the anus in which is secreted a dark fluid ("sepia" or "ink"). This can be forcibly discharged, and the dark cloud thus formed in the water serves as a means of escape from enemies. (*See* section *Distribution and Natural History.*) This so-called ink-sac is absent in *Nautilus* and in certain deep-sea Octopoda.

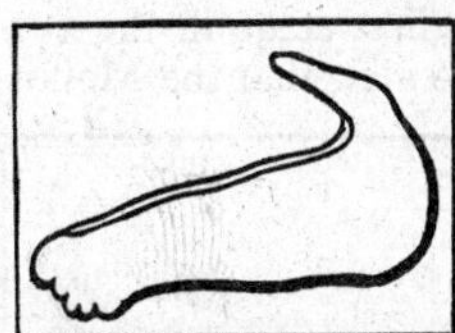

FROM ROBSON, "ANNALS AND MAGAZINE OF NATURAL HISTORY" (TAYLOR & FRANCIS)
FIG. 8.—ARM-HOOK OF MESONYCHOTEUTHIS HAMILTONI (HIGHLY MAGNIFIED)

Circulatory and Respiratory System.—These systems are very highly developed in the Cephalopoda. Unlike the rest of the Mollusca the blood is conveyed to and from the tissues in vessels instead of mainly through a system of diffuse cavities (*lacunae*), though the vascular system of *Nautilus* is partly lacunar. The process of circulation and oxygenation is more concentrated in the Dibranchia, which have only two cardiac auricles and two gills instead of four auricles and four gills as in *Nautilus.* The mechanism of respiration is likewise more efficient in the Dibranchia, the rhythmical contractions and expansion of the mantle musculature procuring a very effective circulation of water over the gills. The latter are feather-like in general plan, *i.e.,* they consist of a central axis with side-branches disposed down each side of it. There are as many as 40 filaments a side in some Dibranchia; but in the Octopoda they are less numerous, and in abyssal forms (*e.g.,* the Cirroteuthidae) they are very much reduced in number and length.

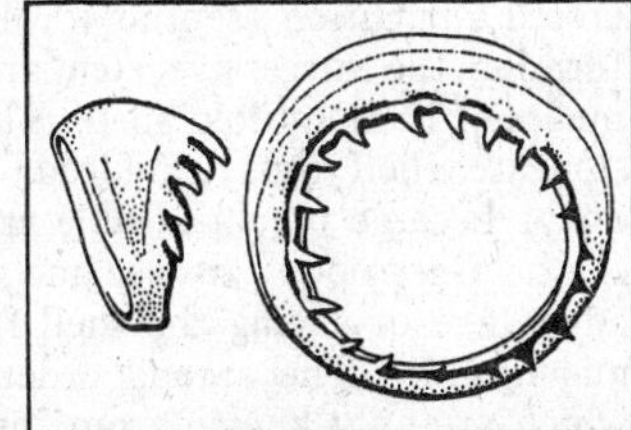

FROM JATTA, "CEFALOPODI" IN "FAUNA UND FLORA DES GOLFES VON NEAPEL" (STAZIONE ZOOLOGICA DI NAPOLI)
FIG. 9.—TWO VIEWS OF THE HORNY RINGS OF SUCKERS OF TODARODES SAGITTATUS
Note the sharp teeth on the rims

Renal Organs.—The excretion of nitrogenous waste is carried out exclusively by the kidneys; the liver, which in certain other molluscs has an excretory as well as digestive role, does not participate in this function. There are four kidneys in *Nautilus* and two in the Dibranchia.

Nervous System.—The chief ganglionic centres of the Cephalopoda are concentrated in the head and are very closely approximated. Such intimate union is not usually found in other molluscs, but is nevertheless seen in certain Gastropoda. This condensation of the central nervous system is seen in *Nautilus* and is carried still further in certain Dibranchia. Features indicative of functional specialization are found in the latter, *e.g.,* in some of the Teuthoidea the cerebral centres are subdivided and the pedal ganglia are likewise divided into brachial and epipodial elements which innervate the arms and funnel respectively. The sense-organs of the Cephalopoda are eyes, rhinophores (olfactory organs), statocysts (organs for the nervous regulation of balance) and tactile structures. The eyes of *Nautilus* are of a more primitive construction than those of the Dibranchia in that they have no retractive lens and the optic cavity is open to the exterior. In the Dibranchia the eyes are very complex and approach those of the Vertebrata in efficiency.

FROM LANKESTER, "TREATISE ON ZOOLOGY" (BLACK)
FIG. 10.—ROW OF TEETH IN RADULA OF AN OCTOPUS (HIGHLY MAGNIFIED)

Reproductive System.—The sexes are separate in the Cephalopoda. No instances of hermaphroditism or of sex-change such as are found in other molluscs have so far been reported in this class. Sexual dimorphism is of fairly regular occurrence; but it is usually expressed in slight differences of size and the proportion of various parts. In the pelagic Argonautidae (Octopoda) the male is very much smaller than the female, and in the cuttlefish (*Doratosepion confusa*) the males are distinguished by the possession of long tail-like prolongations of the fins. In nearly all cephalopods the males are in addition distinguished by the modification of one or more of the appendages as an organ of copulation. The male reproductive system is on the whole a little more complex than the female, chiefly in relation to the method of copulation. The spermatozoa are transferred by the male to the female in long tubes (spermatophores) which are formed in a special sac (Needham's organ) on the course of the male *vas deferens.* These tubes are deposited either in the neighbourhood of the mouth of the female (*Nautilus; Sepia, Loligo* and other Teuthoidea) or in the mantle-cavity (Octopoda; certain Teuthoidea) by means of the copulatory organ (hectocotylus [Dibranchia]: spadix [*Nautilus*]). The latter is a simple spoon-like modification of one of the arms in the Octopoda. In the Decapoda a great diversity of modifications is found which may involve more than one arm. Similarly in *Nautilus* an accessory copulatory organ (*antispadix*) is found. It has recently been suggested that some of the peculiar modifications found in the Decapoda enable the copulatory arm or arms to be used as an organ of stimulation.

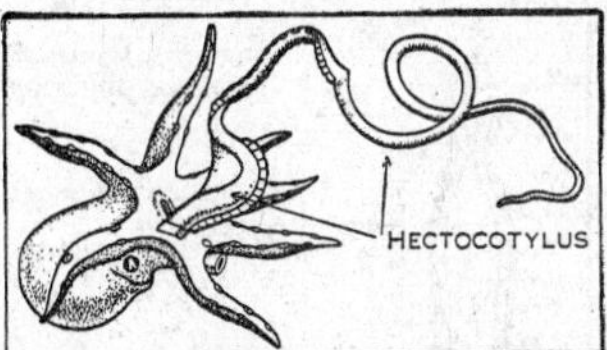

PEGGY COLLINGS AFTER H. MUELLER, 1852
FIG. 11. — MALE OF ARGONAUTA ARGO SHOWING HECTOCOTYLUS; (ABOUT NATURAL SIZE)

Colour Change and Luminescence.—Besides the permanent colour of the skin, the Dibranchia possess a cutaneous system of contractile cells (chromatophores) containing pigment which can be expanded or contracted so as to exhibit or conceal the pigment either of all the cells simultaneously or only of those containing a certain pigment. The circumstances in which these changes are brought about are discussed in the section on *Distribution and Natural History.*

In certain Decapoda, principally those which live at great depths, special light-organs are developed in various regions of the mantle, arms and head. These organs are not found in *Nautilus* and the Octopoda (except in *Melanoteuthis lucens*).

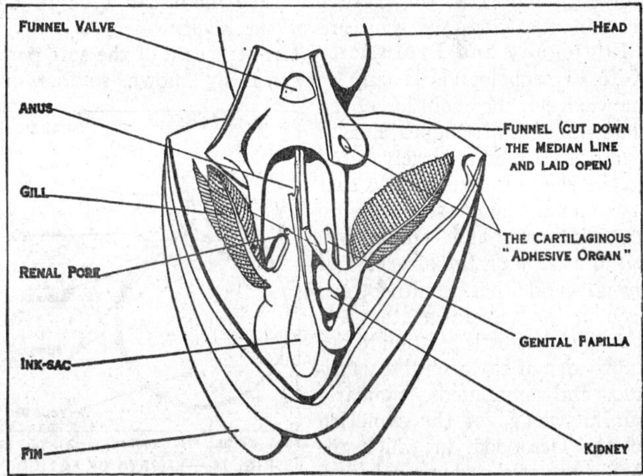

FROM LANKESTER, "TREATISE ON ZOOLOGY" (BLACK)
FIG. 12.—THE MANTLE CAVITY OF A CUTTLEFISH (SEPIA) OPENED IN ORDER TO DISPLAY ITS CONTENTS

They are only sparsely found in the littoral *Sepiidae* and *Loliginidae;* but a special type of light-organ said to produce the peculiar phenomenon of "bacterial light" has been described in certain species of *Sepiola* and *Loligo* (Meyer: Pierantoni: Robson).

Development.—The development of *Nautilus* is unfortunately not yet known, so that if any clues to the phylogeny of the cephalopods may be obtainable from the embryology of their most primitive living representative, they are still withheld from us. The eggs of all cephalopods are provided with a remarkable amount of yolk so that, unlike that of the rest of the Mollusca, the segmentation is incomplete and restricted to one end of the egg. The embryo is likewise localized at that end and the ectoderm appears stretched out over one extremity of a large mass of yolk. Later on, a sheet of cells is developed below the ectoderm, commencing from that edge of the ectoderm at which the anus is subsequently developed; and after this, cells migrating inwards from the ectoderm give rise to the mesendoderm. The development of the various organs need not occupy us; but it is necessary to point out that the mouth in the early stage of development is not surrounded by the arm-rudiments. The latter arise as outgrowths of the lateral and posterior edges of the primordial embryonic area. These outgrowths pass forwards during later development until they reach and encircle the mouth. The funnel arises as a paired outgrowth of the same area, a condition which is retained in the adult *Nautilus,* while in the Dibranchia the two portions fuse together in the median line. The development of the Cephalopoda varies somewhat after the germ layers have been developed, according as to whether there is a yolk-sac or not. The embryo of *Sepia, Loligo* and *Octopus* is provided with a yolk-sac which may become partly internal; while in certain Decapoda presumed to be archaic there is less yolk and the yolk-sac is practically absent ("Oigopsid embryo" of Grenacher). Nevertheless, although we may regard the latter mode of development as less specialized than that of the heavily yolked egg, *e.g.,* of *Sepia,* there is no certain indication in the development of any known cephalopod of those larval phases that characterize the development of other Mollusca. The embryological history of the members of the Cephalopoda reveals as much specialization and differentiation from the more primitive molluscan type of development as does the structure of the adult.

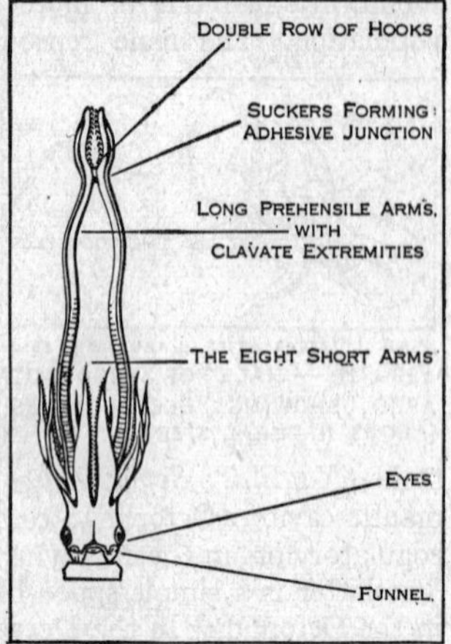

FROM TODD, "ENCYCLOPAEDIA OF ANATOMY" (LONGMANS, GREEN, & CO.)
FIG. 13.—ARMS AND TENTACLES OF A LARGE SQUID, ONYCHOTEUTHIS

Phylogeny and Evolution.—The structure of the soft parts of fossil cephalopods is only very scantily known, so that our knowledge of the evolution of the class since its first appearance in Cambrian times is largely based on the shell. It thus follows that our main division of the class into Tetrabranchia and Dibranchia, based as it is on the structure of the gills and other primitive traits seen in the visceral anatomy of *Nautilus,* has little relation to our knowledge of the primitive nautiloids and ammonoids. Similarly our knowledge of the evolution of the Octopoda, in which the shell is vestigial and non-calcified, is rather compromised by the absence of verifiable fossil remains.

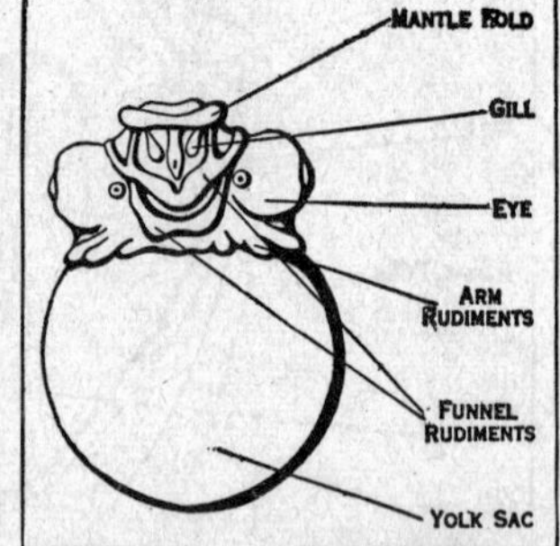

FROM MEYER, "TINTENFISCHE" (KLINKHARDT)
FIG. 14.—EMBRYO OF LOLIGO

In order to understand the evolutionary history of the Cephalopoda as revealed by the geological record, it is necessary to allude to the shell of *Nautilus,* which, by reason of its general organization, is regarded as the most primitive living cephalopod. This shell is coiled and subdivided into a number of closed chambers, the last of which is occupied by the animal. Throughout the system of chambers runs a median tube, the siphuncle. The earliest forms which we can recognize as cephalopods are found in Cambrian rocks. In *Orthoceras* (fig. 17) we see the unmistakable chambered shell and median siphuncle of the nautiloid. The shell is, however, straight, not coiled. At a later stage we find the shell becoming coiled like that of a true *Nautilus.* This is well seen in the Silurian *Ophidioceras.* In Triassic rocks are found remains closely resembling our modern *Nautilus;* but the latter did not actually appear until the early Tertiary.

This short sketch gives us a clue to the first stage in the evolution of the Cephalopoda. If we accept the view that the Mollusca are a homogeneous group, it is reasonable to suppose that the primitive Mollusca from which the Cephalopoda sprang were provided with a simple cap-like shell not unlike that of a limpet. What circumstances of adaptation or internal momentum dictated the lines on which cephalopod evolution should proceed are not known; but the first result was an elongation of the shell achieved by the deposition of lime salts around the edge of the primitive cap-like shell as the animal progressively shifted its position away from the apex. At each successive growth-period the back of the visceral mass secreted a partition (septum), thus forming the successive compartments of the nautiloid shell. The elongate shell thus produced, which we see in *Orthoceras,* no doubt became unmanageable and liable to injury. As in the case of the Gastropoda, it became coiled, which had the mechanical advantage of saving the shell from accident and making it more manageable. The second order of tetrabranchs, the ammonites, which are only known from fossil forms, was a very large group and the plentiful remains of their shells at certain horizons has provided material for special studies of evolutionary phenomena at once fascinating and baffling. The ammonites are ranked as Tetrabranchia on conchological grounds; but we do not know in fact whether they possessed the anatomical structure of the nautiloids. They differed essentially from the true nautiloids in having a marginal siphon and a persistent embryonic whorl at the apex of the shell (protoconch). It is customary to derive them from Devonian forms with straight shells, such as *Bactrites,* though in fact *Bactrites* itself has certain nautiloid traits. Coiled ammonites appear in the upper Devonian (*Goniatites*), and thereafter follow a great variety of forms. They are distinguished by tendencies towards uncoiling and great complexity of the sutures (line of junction between the septa and the main shell-wall) which illustrate remarkable phenomena of growth (mostly modifications of the principle of Recapitulation). Some lineages (or evolutionary strains) illustrate retrogressive evolution, the later members of such series reacquiring traits seen in earlier stages of the series. These retrogressive stages are especially noticeable in the Cretaceous period, at the end of which the ammonites became extinct. It is not yet safe to say that this group as a whole ran a straight course through increasing complexity to a climax from which they passed to senescence and ultimate decay. It is tempting to read such a plain evolutionary theme into their story; but it seems more likely that as Swynnerton suggests, they were cut off when still a flourishing group by a great secular "revolution" of climate and earth-change, rather than by the exhaustion of their own evolutionary momentum. The history of the dibranchiate Cephalopoda is dominated by one main evolutionary theme. Our modern squids, cuttlefish and octopods are distinguished from the nautiloid forms by the possession of an internal and partly degenerate shell. In one form alone (*Spirula*) the shell is still partly external. The position and state of the shell in the

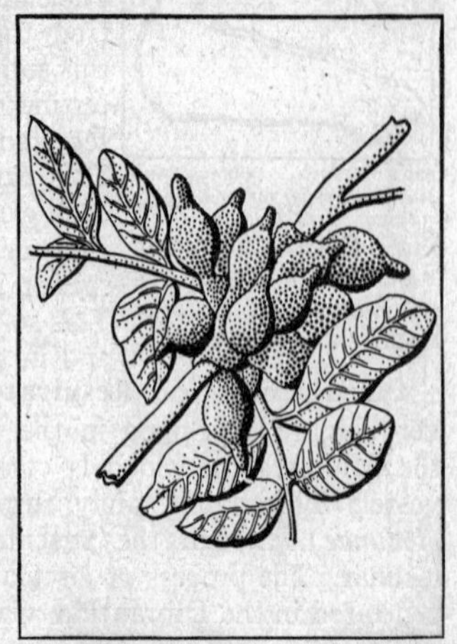
FROM JATTA, "CEFALOPODI" IN "FAUNA UND FLORA DES GOLFES VON NEAPEL" (STAZIONE ZOOLOGICA DI NAPOLI)
FIG. 15.—EGGS OF THE COMMON CUTTLEFISH, SEPIA OFFICINALIS

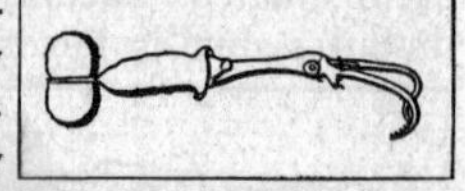
FROM ROBSON, "ANNALS AND MAGAZINE OF NATURAL HISTORY" (TAYLOR & FRANCIS)
FIG 16.—LARVA OF CHIROTEUTHIS ("DOVATOPSIS" STAGE)

PAINTED FOR THE ENCYCLOPÆDIA BRITANNICA BY HELEN DAMROSCH TEE-VAN FROM SPECIMENS IN THE AMERICAN MUSEUM OF NATURAL HISTORY

CUTTLEFISH, OCTOPUSES AND SQUIDS OF THE MEDITERRANEAN

1. Squid (*Todarodes sagittatus*)
2. Common squid (*Loligo vulgaris*)
3. Octopus (*Rossia macrosoma*)
4. Squid (*Loligo marmorae*) discharging the ink which squids eject as a screen against their enemies
5. Paper nautilus (*Argonauta argo*)
6. Octopus (*Scaeurgus tetracirrus*)
7. Octopus (*Ocythoe tuberculata*)
8. Common cuttlefish (*Sepia officinalis*)
9. *Sepiola aurantiaca*
10. Eggs of cuttlefish (*Sepia officinalis*)
11. Common octopus (*Octopus vulgaris*)

Dibranchia is due to the progressive overgrowth of the shell by the mantle and the formation around the shell of a secondary sheath, the various parts of which eventually become larger than the shell itself. The loss of the true shell probably went hand in hand with the gradual acquisition of an active swimming habit, in which the protection of a rigid outer covering was replaced by greater mobility entailing the development of

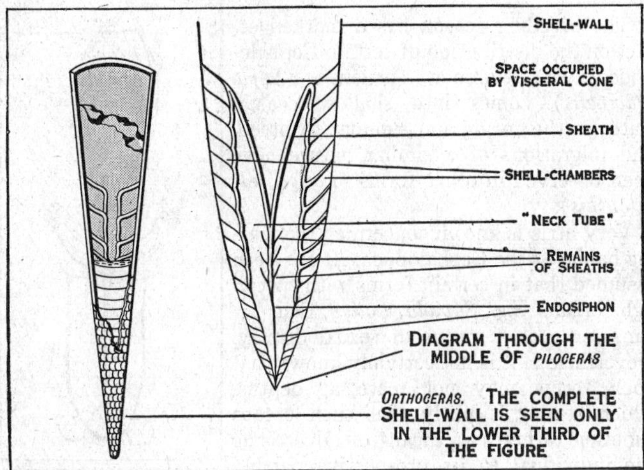

FROM "GUIDE TO FOSSIL INVERTEBRATES" (BRITISH MUSEUM)

FIG. 17.—DIAGRAM OF SECTIONS THROUGH THE SHELL OF PALAEOZOIC NAUTILOIDEA, SHOWING THE CHAMBERED STRUCTURE

stronger pallial muscles. At the same time the acquisition of a fresh orientation probably entailed a readjustment of the centre of gravity of the animal, the heavy, more or less terminal shell being incompatible with rapid movement in a horizontal position. Of forms which connect the Dibranchia with the Tetrabranchia we have no direct evidence. According to Naef we may distinguish certain orthoceratid nautiloids which show an approach to the oldest Dibranchia; but it is not until Triassic times that we meet in *Aulacoceras* unmistakable evidence of the modification of the shell. This tendency is seen at its best in the Belemnites. It consists primarily in the enclosure of the apex of the shell in an external calcified sheath, the guard, and the development of an accessory plate, the pro-ostracum, at the anterior end of the shell. The forms which exhibit these modifications were undoubtedly dibranchiates, as they possessed the characteristic ink-sac and hooks on their suckers. The belemnites gave rise to several lines of descent. In one of these the guard is reduced and the original shell (phragmocone) is coiled (*Spirulirostra*). Further reduction of the guard and more extensive coiling of the phragmocone produced the shell of the modern *Spirula*. In another line the guard is similarly reduced, and the extension of the phragmoconal septa as closely set and numerous layers up the surface of the pro-ostracum led through the *Belosepia* to the modern cuttlefish. The modern Teuthoidea (*Loliginidae* and "Oigopsida") are distinguished by the loss of phragmocone and guard and the persistence of the pro-ostracum as a horny "pen." These forms appear in the Jurassic and are probably developed from belemnite-like ancestors. Of living Teuthoidea *Ommastrephes* preserves a trace of the phragmocone.

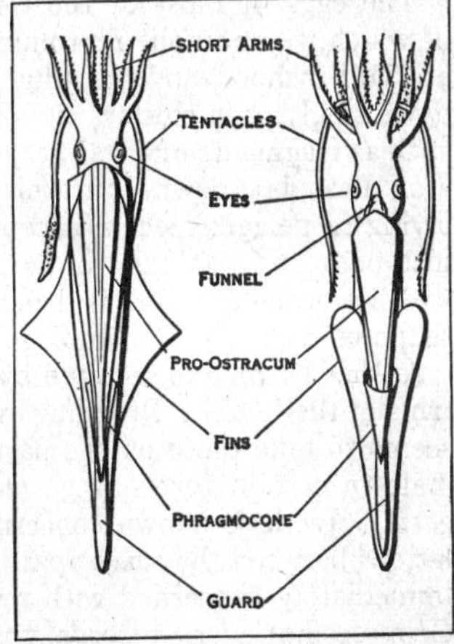

FROM "GUIDE TO FOSSIL INVERTEBRATES" (BRITISH MUSEUM)

FIG. 18.—RESTORATION OF THE ANIMAL AND SHELL OF A BELEMNITE

Left, dorsal view; right, ventral view

Owing to the great reduction of the shell in living Octopoda, in which it persists as fine cartilaginous "stylets" or as somewhat better-developed fin-supports (Cirrata), the stylets, or fin-supports, are usually regarded as vestiges of the shell; but it is possible that this interpretation is wrong. We have no knowledge of the ancestry of this group. The structure of *Palaeoctopus newboldi* from the Cretaceous of Syria affords no clue to the early stages of octopod evolution. This form combines cirromorph and octopod characters; but in general it appears to be more octopus-like. Of the modern Octopoda it is likely that the Cirrata, in spite of much specialization in relation to the abyssal habit, are an older group than the true octopods. As far as the rudiment of the shell is concerned such forms as *Cirroteuthis mülleri* and *Vampyroteuthis* are more primitive than *Octopus, Eledone* and the *Argonautidae*.

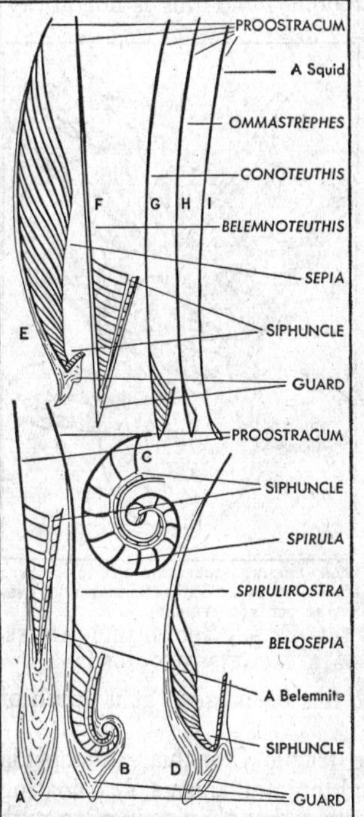

FROM "GUIDE TO FOSSIL INVERTEBRATES" (BRITISH MUSEUM)

FIG. 19.—THE BELEMNITE AND ITS DESCENDANTS. SECTIONS THROUGH THE MIDDLE OF THE SHELL

Distribution and Natural History.—The Cephalopoda are exclusively marine animals. No authentic records are available of their occupation of fresh or brackish water. Although they are occasionally carried into estuaries, they do not tolerate water of reduced salinity. In this respect they are comparable with the Amphineura and Scaphopoda among other Mollusca and with the Echinoderma and Brachiopoda. It is interesting, but rather fruitless to speculate as to why so highly organized and dominant a group has never, as far as we know, accommodated itself to fresh water. The fact that there are many littoral species further emphasizes this exclusiveness. One record is known to the author of an octopod being found living at the mouth of a fresh water stream (Hoyle, 1907), and it is interesting to note that certain species have penetrated into those areas of the Suez canal which have a *higher* salinity than that of normal sea water. No differences have so far been recorded in the numerical frequency of the cephalopods of those parts of the ocean which have a relatively low salinity (*e.g.*, under 34 per mille, as in Arctic and Antarctic waters), and those with an average or high salinity (35 per mille and upwards). In areas of extremely low salinity, such as the Baltic sea, cephalopods are very sparsely represented.

Concerning the horizontal (geographical) distribution of cephalopods, as far as it can be dissociated from the vertical distribution (*see* later), little need be said. Many genera and some species are, in the light of modern taxonomy, cosmopolitan in their distribution. Thus the small oigopsids *Cranchia scabra* and *Pyrgopsis pacificus* are found in the Atlantic, Indian and Pacific oceans, though they do not pass into high latitudes. The common European *Octopus vulgaris* and *O. macropus* have, on unimpeachable authority, been recorded from the Far East. On the whole the distribution of the species and some of the genera is very much the same as in other great groups of marine animals, *i.e.*, it is in general determined by the great oceanic "divides." Thus the Canaries current cuts off a north-east Atlantic fauna from an equatorial and south Atlantic one at about latitude 18°N., and the great "divide" off Cape Agulhas (South Africa) separates Atlantic and Indo-Pacific faunas. Nevertheless, these barriers (due to marked changes in salinity and temperature) seem to be by no means rigid in their effects. Several Mediterranean species are found in the south Atlantic and certain species are common to the Atlantic and Indo-Pacific regions; so that the species can only be grouped into faunas in a very broad fashion. Other qualifications have also to be made. In the first place it is very likely that many species which occur at the surface, *e.g.*, in the cold

Benguela current of the south-east Atlantic may be found in deeper water in the Indian ocean, so that the Agulhas "divide" may be only effective at the surface and have a limiting effect only on those Cephalopoda which cannot descend to great depths. Secondly, the identification of species from contrasted areas should depend on a very exact taxonomy, and this is not always easy in practice, as the condition and number of specimens collected is not always satisfactory. It will be convenient to consider vertical distribution at the same time as the general mode of life of these animals. *Nautilus* seems to keep near the bottom in the neighbourhood of islands and reefs and has been obtained at a depth of 300 fathoms. It comes into shallow water quite frequently; but Dr. A. Willey believes it breeds in very deep water. The larger Decapoda spend their life swimming at various depths. Some are strictly littoral such as *Sepia* and *Loligo.* Most of the Teuthoidea are pelagic, *i.e.,* they live in the open sea far from land, and some of them have a very considerable vertical distribution. *Chiroteuthis lacertosa* has been taken at a depth of 2,949 fathoms.

FROM JOUBIN, "RÉSULTATS DES CAMPAGNES SCIENTIFIQUES DU PRINCE ALBERT 1er" (INSTITUT OCÉANOGRAPHIQUE)

FIG. 20.—CIRROTEUTHIS UMBELLATA, AN ABYSSAL OCTOPOD

In the adult stage the small and fragile Cranchias (Oigopsida consuta) are to be reckoned as planktonic organisms, *i.e.,* floating more or less at the mercy of currents rather than swimming with or against the latter. The Octopoda mainly dwell on or near the bottom either crawling on the latter or swimming a short distance off it. Some of them, however, *e.g., Eledonella* and *Cirroteuthis,* are not confined to the bottom and are found in mid-water at very considerable depths. Although the large family of the Octopodidae mainly inhabits shallow water, the Octopoda as a whole contain a very large nucleus of deep water forms (one species of *Eledonella* has been taken in 2,900 fathoms), which display well marked adaptations to life in abyssal conditions.

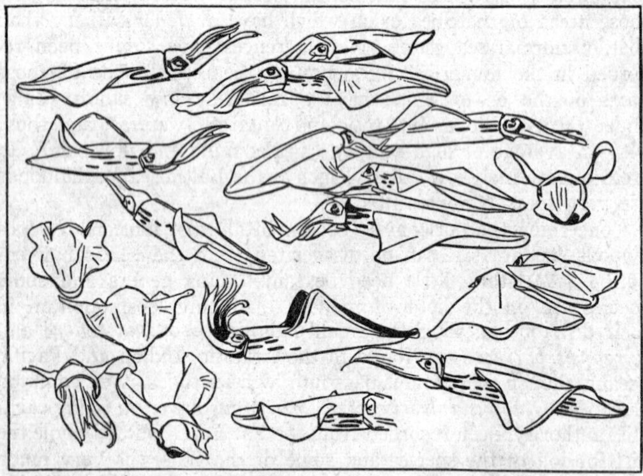

FROM MEHEUT, "ÉTUDE DE LA MER" (LEVY)

FIG. 21.—SQUIDS OF VARIOUS SPECIES SWIMMING

Alcide d'Orbigny in his account of the Mollusca of South America, asserted that the Cephalopoda are in general "sociable," *i.e.,* gregarious, and this statement is certainly true of *Nautilus* which were always found together in droves by the native divers employed by Dr. A. Willey, who observed its habits in New Guinea, etc. Nevertheless, Jatta, who made a special study of the Mediterranean forms, was of the opinion that only certain pelagic forms are thus gregarious (*e.g., Todarodes, Ocythöe*). We should avoid concluding that the coincidence of a large number of individuals necessarily implies either a sociable instinct or a desire for the protection afforded by a community, as it may be due to the accidental coincidence of large numbers of individuals ("population maximum") in somewhat restricted breeding or feeding grounds. Nevertheless, Verrill has adduced evidence that the shoaling of young *Loligo pealei* off the coast of New England is not thus accidental.

The breeding season has a marked effect on the distribution of certain Cephalopoda. The common cuttlefish (*Sepia officinalis*) comes into shallow coastal water in the spring and summer to breed, and migrations of a similar nature have been observed in other forms (*Loligo, Alloteuthis*).

Very little is known concerning the mating habits of the Cephalopoda. It has been assumed that in certain forms with special light organs, *e.g., Sepiola, Loligo,* their organs serve as a means of sexual display. Nevertheless, it is not certainly known that such forms may not mate at depths, which render it likely that such organs function rather as a means of advertising the individual to its prospective partner than as an incitement to coitus. The actual process of coitus has been studied by several naturalists (Racovitza, Drew, Levy, etc.); but, while we know the general lines on which it takes place, the details and particularly those relating to the use of the hectocotylus are not very well known (see *Reproductive System*). Nor again are we informed as to the bionomic significance of some of the more remarkable cases of sexual dimorphism among these animals, *e.g.,* of the highly elongate and fringed arms of *Sepia burnupi* and *lorigera* (Massy, Wülker) and the still more remarkable dimorphism in *Doratosepion confusa* (Massy and Robson, Robson and Carleton).

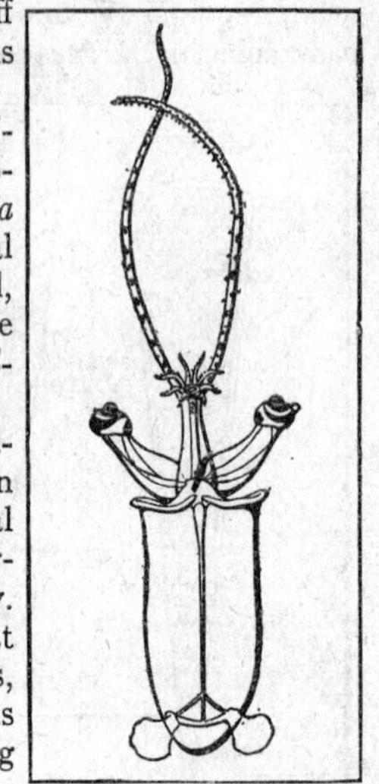

FROM CHUN, "WISSENSCHAFTLICHE ERGEBNISSE DER DEUTSCHEN TIEFSEE-EXPEDITION" (FISCHER)

FIG. 22.—BATHOTHAUMA LYROMMA

The eggs of most of the Cephalopoda, of which we know the reproductive habits, are laid inshore, and are usually fastened down singly or in clusters on bottom débris such as fragments of coral, stems of plants, etc. Less is known concerning the egg-laying of pelagic species, except in special instances such as that of *Argonauta,* in which a brood chamber is developed in the shape of a shell (not homologous with the true shell) which is secreted by the dorsal arms of the female. Brooding over the eggs seems to take place on the part of the female in certain forms (*e.g., Octopus vulgaris*). Little is known concerning the relations between the sexes apart from those immediately concerned with reproduction. Grimpe, however, records that in captivity *Sepia officinalis* is strictly monogamous though capable of reproduction.

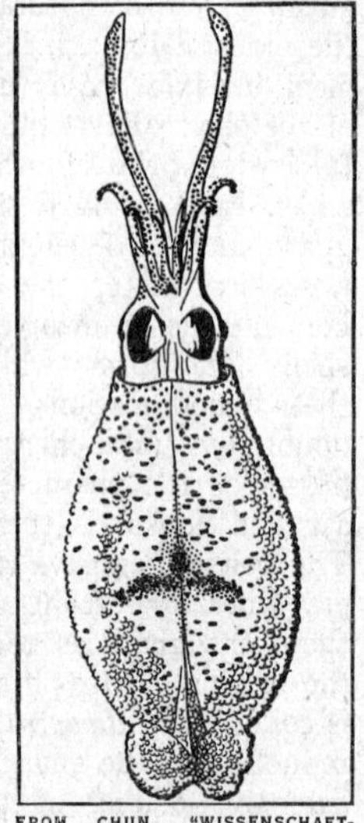

FROM CHUN, "WISSENSCHAFTLICHE ERGEBNISSE DER DEUTSCHEN TIEFSEE-EXPEDITION" (FISCHER)

FIG. 23.—CRANCHIA SCABRA

The majority of living Cephalopoda are carnivorous and live principally on Crustacea. Small fishes and other molluscs, however, often form part of their diet and there is some evidence that in nature certain species are cannibals. In the Channel Isles *Octopus vulgaris* partly subsists on the ormer (*Haliotis*) and has been made responsible (though on insufficient evidence) for a marked decrease in the numbers of that mollusc. The Cirrata whose reduced musculature and radula indicate a loss of activity and of masticatory power probably feed on bottom-débris or minute plankton. The latter in the shape of copepods, pteropods, etc., are probably the food of the smaller pelagic Decapoda. The Cephalopoda are in their turn preyed upon by whales, porpoises,

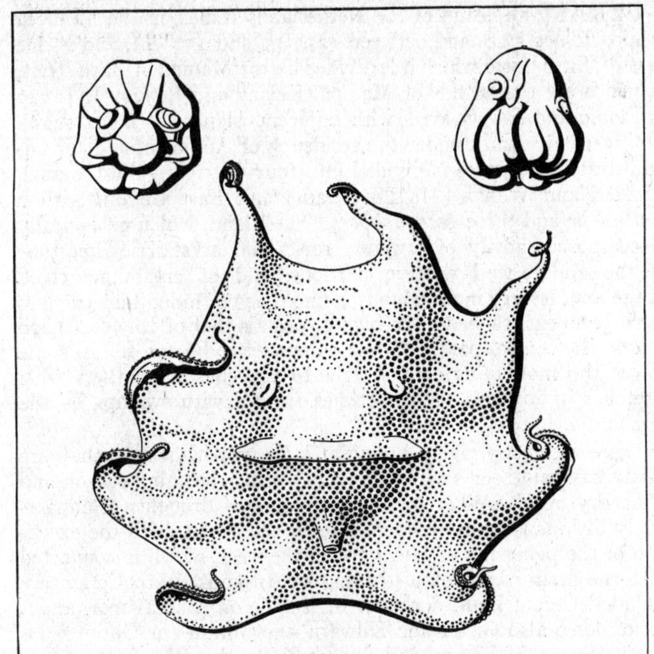

FROM CHUN, "WISSENSCHAFTLICHE ERGEBNISSE DER DEUTSCHEN TIEFSEE-EXPEDITION" (FISCHER)

FIG. 24.—TWO HIGHLY MODIFIED OCTOPODS
Two upper figures, *Opisthoteuthis medusoides;* lower, *Opisthoteuthis extensa*

dolphins, seals and sea birds. The stomachs of whales are often found to contain fragments of Cephalopoda (mandibles and sucker rings), and it is held that the waxlike substance known as ambergris, which is used in perfumery and is found floating at sea or drifted ashore, is composed largely of cephalopod tissue voided by whales. It is not to be doubted that large squids maintain a desperate struggle with any whale that may attack them, as specimens of the latter are sometimes taken with the marks of sucker rings imprinted in their skin.

The colour changes produced in the skin of most cephalopods by the contraction and expansion of the chromatophores have been variously interpreted as affording protective or obliterative coloration or as an expression of certain emotions. It is likely that both these effects are secured by this means. The common octopus has been observed to assume a very close mimetic resemblance to the colour of its background. On the other hand observations have been made on colour changes in *Sepiola atlantica* which seemed to be the reverse of protective, as judged by the human eye. The chief means of avoiding capture is, however, provided by the "ink" which is expelled from the ink sac when the animal is attacked. It was originally thought that the ink formed a kind of "smoke screen" behind or in which the animal was hidden from its enemy. Later observations, however, tended to suggest that the jet of ink, when shot out, remains as a definitely shaped object in the water and serves as a "dummy" to engage the attention of the enemy, while the cephalopod, changing its colour so that it is almost transparent, darts off in another direction. Whether this explanation is applicable to all cases is uncertain; and in any case it is uncertain why, if many cephalopods can assume something approaching protective transparency, it should be necessary to add to the means of concealment. The matter is plainly in need of further investigation. The Cephalopoda as a whole are not distinguished by individual eccentricities of behaviour. It is worth while, however, to mention three interesting cases: (1) many pelagic squids and cuttlefishes keep very near the surface when swimming, and one of them, "the flying squid," *Ommastrephes bartrami,* often shoots out of the water in rough weather and has been several times carried by its leaps on to the decks of ships; (2) the male of the pelagic octopod *Ocythoe* is often found inhabiting the discarded case of the Tunicate *Salpa,* a habit in which it resembles the Crustacean *Phronima;* (3) Syun'iti Sasaki described a remarkable habit and structural modification in the small cuttlefish *Idiosepius paradoxus.* The latter, which is found in Japanese waters, is often found adhering to seaweeds by means of a rudimentary sucker developed in the dorsal region of the mantle. No instances of parasitism and only one doubtful case of commensalism were recorded among these animals.

Economic Uses.—The Cephalopoda are of considerable value to man, principally as a direct source of food. They also constitute a large part of the diet of certain animals, such as whales and seals, which are of economic importance and in certain parts of the world they are regularly caught on a large scale as bait for certain valuable food fishes. Squids, cuttlefishes and octopods are eaten by man in many parts of the world. Information concerning the people who regularly eat these animals is by no means complete as yet. The "Anglo-Saxon" people (possibly the "Nordics" generally) do not as a rule eat them, even when a regular supply is available. They are largely consumed by south European (Mediterranean) peoples and in India, Indochina, Malaysia, China, Japan and the Pacific islands. Concerning the littoral natives of Africa and central South America no certain information is available. In the Mediterranean region cephalopods have been eaten since early times. They are either fried or boiled for the table; but in the east, *e.g.,* Indochina and south India, they are also sun-dried for human consumption. In Japan the squid fishery attains a very great importance and in one year more than 77,161 short tons of squid were landed (Imperial Japanese government statistics). *Ommastrephes sloanei* is the chief form taken in these fisheries. The bait fisheries of south India are a very important local activity and in North America the cod fishermen rely largely on various squids for baiting their lines. The only other important material obtained from cephalopods is "cuttlebone" (the internal shell of the *Sepiidae*). The uses of this article are described in the article CUTTLEFISH. Among primitive peoples and in ancient times in Europe various parts of cephalopods have been used in magical operations and in medicine. Cuttlebone has been used in the treatment of leprosy and for various disorders of the heart.

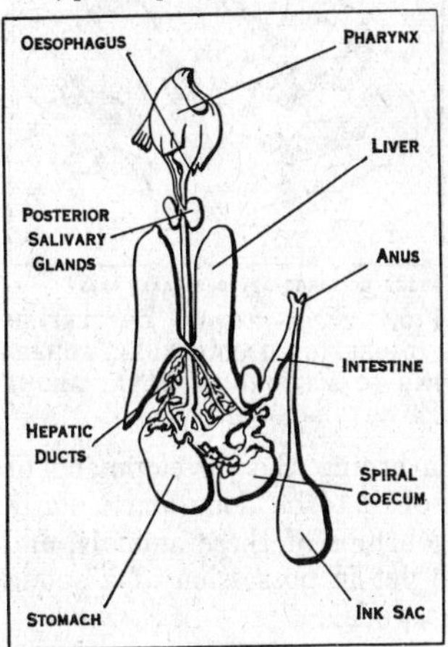

FROM MEYER, "TINTENFISCHE" (KLINKHARDT)

FIG. 25.—ALIMENTARY SYSTEM OF A CUTTLEFISH (SEPIA)

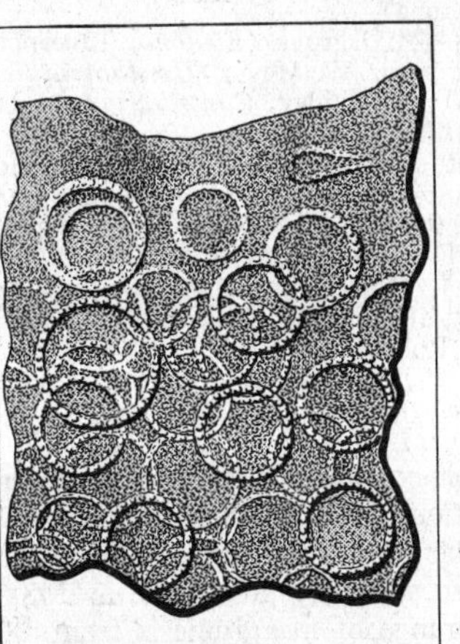

FROM MURRAY & HJORT, "DEPTHS OF THE OCEAN" (MACMILLAN & CO.)

FIG. 26.—SKIN OF WHALE SCARRED BY THE SUCKERS OF ARCHITEUTHIS
Note the marks of the sucker teeth on the circumference of each ring

Historical.—The study of the Cephalopoda was initiated by Aristotle who devoted much attention to the group. The modern investigation of their morphology may be dated from Cuvier, who gave them the name by which they are now known. H. de Blainville (1777–1850) and Alcide d'Orbigny (1802–57) laid the foundation of the systematic study of the group, the great monograph *Mémoire sur les Céphalopodes Acétabulifères* of D'Orbigny being a landmark in systematic zoology. This work includes descriptions of fossil forms as well as of living species. R. Owen contributed substantially to the knowledge of the morphology of the class, particularly by his *Memoir on the Pearly Nautilus* (1832). A. Kölliker may be said to have founded the embryological study of cephalopods (1843) and Alpheus Hyatt (1868) led the way in early palaeontological studies of these animals. The rarer pelagic and deep sea forms were only obtained slowly and, although the Cirrata were known as early as 1836 (Eschricht), it was not until toward the end of the last century that the "Challenger" expedition and the researches of W. Hoyle and A. E. Verrill obtained the first substantial contribution to our knowledge of these forms. Since then, C. Chun, I. Steenstrup, A. Appelöf, G. Pfeffer, L. Joubin, A. Naef, S. S. Berry, G. Grimpe, M. Sasaki and A. Massy have contributed to our knowledge of the living forms, while L. Branco, J. Foord and G. C. Crick, S. Buckman and R. Abel have organized the study of fossil forms. Particular mention must be made of the work of Naef, who subjected the living and fossil forms to a synthetic treatment. Apart from our lack of information concerning the development of *Nautilus* there still remains much work to be done, particularly on the habits and oecological relationships of these animals, and it is to be doubted whether we are yet in possession of a sound systematic arrangement of the Decapoda.

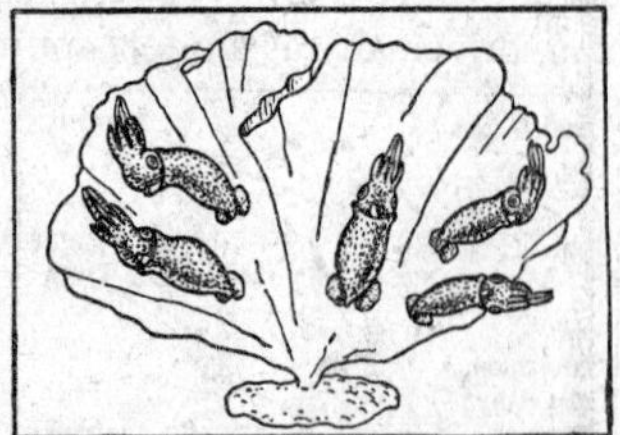

PEGGY COLLINGS AFTER SASAKI, 1923

FIG. 27. — PYGMY CUTTLEFISH (IDIOSEPIUS PARADOXUS) ADHERING TO A FROND OF ULVA; ABOUT ½ NATURAL SIZE

BIBLIOGRAPHY.—A. General Treatises.—P. Pelseneer, "Mollusca" in Lankester's *Treatise on Zoology* (1905); W. Meyer, "Tintenfische" (1913); A. Naef, *Fauna e Flora del Golfo di Napoli* (Monogr., xxxv., 1921–23); J. Thiele, "Mollusca" in Kükenthal and Krumbach's *Handbuch der Zoologie* (1926). All these contain bibliographies.

B. Systematic.—W. Hoyle, "A Catalogue of Recent Cephalopoda," *Proc. R. Phys. Soc. Edinburgh* (1889–1907); Naef, *op. cit.;* G. Pfeffer, "Cephalopoden" in *Ergebn. Plankton Expedn.* (Bd. ii, F., 1912); G. Grimpe, *Sitzber. Naturf Ges. Leipzig* (ix, 1922); G. C. Robson, *A Monograph of Recent Cephalopoda,* vol. 1 (1929), vol. 2 (1932).

C. Distributional.—Mediterranean: A. Naef, *op. cit.* (Bibl.). Atlantic: G. Pfeffer, *op. cit.* (Bibl.); L. Joubin, *Res. camp. Sci. Albert I* (Monaco), *passim.* Atlantic and Indian Oceans: C. Chun, *Wiss. Ergebn. Deutsche Tiefsee Expedn.* (Bd. xviii, 1910, 1915). South Africa: G. Robson, *Proc. Zool. Soc. London* (1924). Indian Ocean: A. Massy, *Rec. Indian Museum* (1916). Pacific: S. S. Berry, *Bull. Bureau Fisheries* (xxx, xxxii, 1910, 1912).

D. Monographs of special forms.—A. Isgrove (*Eledone*) Liverpool Mar. Bio. Comm. Memoir No. xxiii, 1909. W. Meyer (*Opisthoteuthis*), *Zeitschr. Wiss. Zoologie* (85, 1906). A. Willey, *Contribution to the Natural History of the Pearly Nautilus* (1902).

E. Special Subjects (Important general papers published since 1905).—(a) Deep-sea forms: Chun, *op. cit.;* Joubin, *op. cit.;* Robson, *Proc. Zool. Soc. London* (1926). (b) Luminescence: Berry, *Biolog. Bulletin,* 2 parts, 1920 (Bibl.); U. Pierantoni, *Pub. Staz. Zool. Napoli* (2, 1918). (c) Breeding Habits: J. Drew, *Journ. Morphology* (22, 1911); A. Levy, *Zool. Anzeigr.* (39, 1912). (d) Hectocotylus: Hoyle, *Rept. Brit. Assocn.*, p. 520 (1907); Robson, *Proc. Malac. Soc. London* (1926). (e) *Spirula:* Chun, *op. cit.;* Joubin, *op. cit.* (1920). (f) Palaeontology: R. Abel, *Paläobiologie der Cephalopoden* (1915); Naef, *Die Fossilen Tintenfische* (1922). (G. C. R.; X.)

CEPHEUS, in Greek mythology, the father of Andromeda (*q.v.*); in astronomy, a constellation of the northern hemisphere. The star δ Cephei is the type star of a class of variables called Cepheids (*see* STAR). It was discovered by Goodricke in 1785. The period is 5·37 days and the range of magnitude is from 3·6 to 4·2. The star β Cephei is also a famous Cepheid variable; although its range of brightness is only 0·05 mag. its variability was detected by Professor Paul Guthnick of Berlin University by photoelectric measurements.

CEPHISODOTUS, the name of a near relative, and of the son of, Praxiteles, both sculptors like himself. The former must have flourished about 400 B.C. A noted work of his was Peace bearing the infant Wealth, of which a copy exists at Munich. Peace is a Madonna-like figure of a somewhat conservative type. He made certain statues for the city of Megalopolis, founded in 370 B.C. (*See* H. Stuart Jones, *Ancient Writers on Greek Sculpture* § 182–185 [1895].) Of the work of the younger Cephisodotus we have no remains; he flourished in the latter part of the 4th century B.C., and was noted for portraits of Menander, of the orator Lycurgus, and others. (*See* J. Overbeck, *Antike Schriftquellen,* p. 255.)

CERAM, an island of the Netherlands Indies, in the Molucca group. It lies 3° S. and between 127° 45′ and 131° E., and is due east of Buru, from which it is divided by the Manipa or Buru strait, in which are the islands of Manipa, Kelang and Boano. It is 216 mi. long, and has an area, with adjacent islands, of 6,621 sq.mi. Politically, it comes under the residency of Amboina, and for administrative purposes is divided into four districts—West Ceram, Amahai and Wahai (Middle Ceram) and East Ceram, with a *controleur* and three *gezaghebbers.* The island, which geologically is composed mostly of eruptive rocks and crystalline limestone in the middle and western portions, and of crystalline chalk in the east, is very mountainous, a fine range of mountains traversing it from east to west. The highest peak is that of Binaya (9,600 ft.), in the central part, and four others exceed 6,000 ft. In some places the mountains extend right to the coast; in others wide stretches of lowland are sometimes fringed with swamps by the seashore.

There are many rivers, running to the north mostly; they are partly navigable for small craft only during the rainy season and often dry up altogether during the period of drought. Comparatively little is known of the interior of the island, with the exception of the peninsula of Hoalmoal in the west, which is connected with the main island by a low, narrow isthmus. With Ceram are included Ceram Laut, a cluster of islands on a coral reef, about 20 mi. long, also Gisser and Kilwaru, the Goram (or Gorong) Islands (Suruaki, Goram and Manawoka), the Watubela group, and the Teor Isles, all of which lie southeast of Ceram.

The larger islands are of Tertiary (Miocene) formation, and the others of recent coral. None has hills of over 1,000 ft. and most are thickly wooded, while Suruaki has extensive swamps. Many of the Watubela islands have rugged hills covered with coconut palms, and some of the Teor group are entirely waterless, owing to the nature of their coral rock.

Ceram is covered with dense tropical forests, which provide excellent timber (ironwood is general) and yield a variety of forest products, including cajeput oil, damar and wild nutmeg, and in the swamps of the coast and valleys the sago palm thrives abundantly. Both the flora and the fauna of the island lack variety and characteristic specimens; of a forest in the centre A. R. Wallace wrote: "I have never been in a forest so utterly desert of animal life as this appeared to be." The cassowary is the outstanding feature of the fauna, which includes deer, cuscus, pig, shrews, cockatoos, lories, hornbills and birds of paradise, and there are many species of fish in the rivers. The climate is hot and moist, the rainfall being a heavy one, and earthquakes occur. Ceram had in 1930 a population of 95,636, largely in coastal regions and composed mostly of immigrants from Java, Macassar, Ternate and other parts of the archipelago. The people are partly Christian and partly Mohammedan. The Christians live mainly in the west (the Mohammedans in the southeast) and dress and live in the style of the Christian Amboinese, to whom they are nearly related. Fishing and agriculture are the chief pursuits. Most of the tropical fruits of Malaya are grown, also rice, maize, sugar cane, tobacco and coconuts; sago flour is produced and cajeput oil distilled. Trade in these products is in the hands of Chinese, Arabs and Macassars, but there are also some coconut, spice and other plantations under European supervision and copra is the chief article of export. There is a small oil field near Bula Bay (east coast), producing 117,946 tons of crude oil in 1939. The people of the coasts are semi-civilized; not so those of the interior, who are of a mixed Malay-Papuan stock; the practice of head-hunting, however, is becoming a thing of the past. They are largely pagan in religion, wear little in the way of clothing, live in houses built on piles and use as weapons the bow and arrow, *parang* and lance. They are hunters and fishers, and collect forest products, keep pigs and dogs, have a patriarchal social system and a form of marriage sometimes endogamic, sometimes exogamic. Women have a good position among them and are well treated, and, especially among the mountain folk, morality is high. Weaving is known in some parts, and weapons and plaited goods are manufactured. China plates and dishes are considered objects of the highest value, and the people like long ceremonial feasts. There is a secret society among the people of the west, the *Kakihan,* the main object seeming to be maintenance of old customs in the face of foreign influence, but it has also a strong religious significance, initiation being a form of death and resurrection ritual; and the people generally are divided into the two divisions of *Pata-siwa* (the Ternate party) and *Pata-lima* (the Tidore party). The Ceramese are a strong and muscular people, cheerful and honest, but inclined to be very excitable, and extremely independent. The natives of the middle and east are far more peaceful in their ways than those of the west, but civilization is making headway among all, as the result of increasing trade facilities and the provision of schools in many districts, maintained by the Dutch government, with Amboinese headmasters. Amahai, in the south (centre), has a good harbour. Other ports of call are Piru (west), Wahai (north), Tehoru (south) and Bula Bay (east); roads are nonexistent. There is an airfield at Bula Bay. Ceramese, a language without either script or literature (yet the people sing songs of former ages which have been handed down orally), is divided into thirty-five different dialects, and is nearly related to the indigenous language of Amboina. Malay is used commonly on the coasts. The people of the Ceram Laut Islands (pop. 6,000), Gisser and Kilwaru are Mohammedan. They are fishers, build boats, weave sarongs, manufacture knives and live in quite well-built wooden houses, in tidy villages, generally by the seashore. Gisser, with Kilwaru, is a trade centre for the region of southeastern Ceram and the islands and is a port of call for vessels of the Royal Packet Navigation Co.

The population of the Goram Islands, which are more fertile than those of Ceram Laut, is also about 6,000, and Mohammedan, the people being fishers and traders and the women good weavers. The Watubela islanders are Mohammedan also; they produce scarcely anything beyond copra, which they trade for the products they lack. Boano has a population of 1,300, Christian and Mohammedan, and an infertile soil, which drives its people to seek a livelihood on neighbouring islands, and Manipa has nearly 1,000 inhabitants, who grow a good deal of sago.

In the mid-17th century a fort established at Cambello extended Dutch influence, with help from Ternate, which claimed suzerainty. The power of Amboina later helped the Dutch to acquire the whole island in spite of trouble when they destroyed clove plantations in order to uphold Amboina's monopoly. Later still, there were expeditions against the natives of the interior, but after 1910 all was quiet. During World War II, Ceram was occupied by the Japanese in Feb. 1942.

Bibliography.—A. R. Wallace, *The Malay Archipelago* (1890).

(E. E. L.; X.)

CERAMICS or **KERAMICS,** a general term for the history and art of making pottery. (*See* Pottery and Porcelain.)

CERARGYRITE, the name usually applied by mineralogists to naturally-occurring silver chloride, though sometimes taken to include the bromide and iodide as well, or mixtures of them. It crystallizes rarely in the cubic system, but usually forms horn-like masses, known to miners as horn-silver. It is very soft, being easily cut with a knife, and usually of a dirty grey or yellowish colour. It is an important ore of silver, occurring in considerable quantity in the oxidation zone of silver lodes in dry climates, such as Chile, Peru, and Broken Hill in New South Wales, where the surface waters are rich in chlorides, bromides and iodides.

(R. H. Ra.)

CERATOSAURUS, an extinct carnivorous dinosaur whose remains are found in the Upper Jurassic of Colorado. Like its relatives Allosaurus (*q.v.*) and Tyrannosaurus (*see* Dinosauria), it was bipedal in progression. The single species, *C. nasicornis,* reached a length of 20 ft. and, as its name implies, was distinguished by a small horn on the nose. (*See* Reptiles.)

CERBERUS, in Greek mythology, the dog who guarded the entrance to the lower world. According to Hesiod (*Theog.,* 311), he was a 50-headed monster, the offspring of Typhon and Echidna. He was variously represented with one, two or (usually) three heads, often with the tail of a snake or with snakes growing from his head or twined round his body. One of the tasks imposed upon Hercules was to fetch Cerberus from below to the upper world, a favourite subject of ancient vase paintings.

CERCIDIPHYLLUM, a genus of plants of the Trochodendraceae family. *C. japonicum,* the katsura tree, native to Japan, is a hardy, ornamental, shrubby tree of pyramidal habit, almost fastigiate when young, with handsome light green foliage, purplish when unfolding and turning bright yellow or partially scarlet in autumn. Commonly there are several trunks, usually 20–30 ft. in height, but sometimes attaining 100 ft.

C. japonicum var. *sinense,* from western China, usually consists of a single trunk which may exceed 100 ft. It is the largest of all broad-leaved trees known from China; the trunk is often free of branches for nearly 50 ft. above the ground and may attain a girth of 25 ft. or even more. (J. M. Bl.)

CERDIC (d. 534), founder of the West Saxon kingdom, is described as an ealdorman who in 495 landed with his son Cynric in Hampshire, where he was attacked at once by the Britons, under Natanleod. Nothing more is heard of him until 508, when he defeated the Britons with great slaughter. Strengthened by fresh arrivals of Saxons, he gained another victory in 519 at Certicesford, the modern Charford, and in this year took the title of king. Turning westward, Cerdic appears to have been defeated by the Britons in 520 at Badbury or Mount Badon, in Dorset, and in 527 yet another fight with the Britons is recorded. His last work was the conquest of the Isle of Wight (530), probably in the interest of some Jutish allies.

See E. Guest, *Origines Celticae* (1883); Bede, *Historiae ecclesiasticae gentis Anglorum libri,* v, ed. C. Plummer (Oxford, 1896); Gildas, *De excidio Britanniae,* ed. Th. Mommsen (1898); Nennius, *Historia Brittonum,* ed., Th. Mommsen (1898); *Anglo-Saxon Chronicle,* edited by C. Plummer (Oxford, 1892–99).

CERDONIANS, a Gnostic sect, founded by Cerdo, a Syrian, who came to Rome about 137, but concerning whose history little is known. Most of what the Fathers narrate of Cerdo's tenets has probably been transferred to him from his famous pupil Marcion, like whom he is said to have rejected the Old Testament and the New, except part of Luke's Gospel and of Paul's Epistles. (*See* Marcion and the Marcionite Churches; also Gnosticism.)

CEREALIS (Cerialis), **PETILLIUS** (1st century a.d.), Roman general, a relative of the Emperor Vespasian. In a.d. 61 he was in Britain as legate of the ninth legion, which was overwhelmed by the Britons. In the civil war of 69 he supported Vespasian, and in 70, after holding the consulship, he put down the revolt of Civilis (*q.v.*). In 71, as governor of Britain, where he had as a subordinate the famous Agricola, he defeated the powerful Brigantes. Tacitus says that he was a bold soldier rather than a careful general.

See Tacitus, *Annals,* xiv, 32; *Histories,* iii, 59, 78; iv, 71, 75, 86; v, 21; *Agricola,* 8, 17. *See* also B. Henderson, *Civil War and Rebellion in the Roman Empire* (1908).

CEREALS. Cereals are those members of the grass family which have edible starchy seeds. Rice, wheat, rye, barley, oats, maize (known as corn in the Americas), sorghum and some of the millets are the common cereals. All are summer or winter annuals and are grown primarily for the seed which is used for human food or as feed for livestock.

Cereals have provided the basis on which the civilizations of the world have been developed. When ancient man discovered these plants which provided a source of food and learned how to grow them, roving bands were transformed into settled communities. The growing of these crops required much less of primitive man's time to provide the necessary food for himself and family and feed for his animals, thus leaving time to develop the arts and sciences which distinguish civilized man from the savage. Cereal grains now as in ancient times provide more food with a smaller expenditure of effort than any other crops. Because of their low moisture content they are easily stored and transported. Grain storehouses have been found in the excavated ruins of many ancient cities: wheat and barley in those in Mesopotamia, Egypt, Greece and Rome, and maize in the ruins and caves of the Mayas, Aztecs, Incas and other Indian peoples of the western hemisphere.

Wheat, rice and rye are grown primarily for human food, while maize, barley, oats and sorghum are grown mostly for livestock feed although in some countries even these are important food crops. Because they can be easily shipped without loss or deterioration in quality and are grown in some countries in great excess of local needs, wheat and rice are shipped in large quantities into countries which do not produce enough starchy foods to meet their domestic needs. On the other hand a large part of the maize, barley, oats and sorghum, especially in the English-speaking nations, is fed to livestock on the farms where it is grown and is sent to markets in the form of meat, dairy and poultry products. During World War II a large amount of wheat and maize was used in the United States to produce alcohol for the manufacture of munitions and synthetic rubber.

Wheat is the aristocrat of cereals and is grown on a larger world acreage than any other crop. It is adapted to a wider range of climatic conditions than any other crop with the possible exception of barley. However the important wheat-growing regions of the world are confined to the temperate zones where the annual rainfall is between about 13 and 35 inches. Barley, oats and rye are grown in much the same areas except that winter wheat and rye are grown extensively in some areas where barley and oats will not survive when fall-sown and when spring-sown will not yield as well as winter wheat.

Because rye will survive more severe winters and will produce larger yields of grain on soils of low fertility than other cereals, it is the main food grain in certain regions of Europe and Asia. Oats are grown most extensively in the corn belt of North America because they fit so well into rotations with corn and clover, and in the cooler regions of Europe.

Rice is the principal cereal grown in the warmer humid areas of the temperate zone and in the tropics where water for irrigation is available and the land is of suitable topography and soil type for flooding. The crop is submerged in four to eight inches of water most of the time from seeding to maturity. It responds with high yields to the intensive methods of production practised in the densely populated areas of the orient where it forms the chief article of food.

Corn is grown mainly in the temperate zones in regions having a rainfall above eight inches for the three summer months or where the land is irrigated as in Egypt. Unknown outside the Americas before being taken to Europe by Columbus, it is now one of the principal crops in the Danube basin and in other regions of the old world.

Sorghum is a very important crop in parts of Africa, Asia and the southern great plains of the United States where it is too hot and dry for corn to be grown successfully.

Wheat, barley, oats, rye and rice are known also as the small grains. They are grown in close drills and are not cultivated during the growing season. Maize and sorghum are grown in rows about 42 inches apart and are cultivated during the growing season to control weeds. The coarse stalks and leaves of maize and sorghum either with or without the ears and heads are often fed to livestock as occasionally, also, are the finer-stemmed millet and oats. More often the small grains and millet are cut for hay before they are mature. Sometimes the small grains are used for fall, winter or spring pasture.

In the major cereal-growing regions of the world such as the prairies and plains of the United States and Canada, the grain belt of Australia, the pampas of Argentina and the Ukraine of Russia, preparation of the land, seeding and harvesting of the crop are done very efficiently by machinery which has been developed during the last hundred years. For example, it is estimated that in 1830 about 58 hours of man labour were required to grow, harvest, thresh and clean an acre of wheat yielding 20 bushels while with the machines in common use in 1940 only 3 man-hours of labour were required.

Like man, each of the cereal crops is subject to destructive diseases and also to drought and other adverse weather conditions which have caused great losses to growers and have sometimes resulted in famines. The ancient Greeks and Romans had special gods for cereal crops and held festivals to prevail upon them to protect the growing crops from rusts and smuts and to bring forth a good harvest. During the last 40 years scientists have devised methods for controlling many of these diseases and have developed improved varieties which are highly resistant to many of these diseases as well as to adverse weather conditions. Improved cultural practices and better varieties are adding hundreds of millions of bushels to cereal production each year. (*See* also BARLEY; MAIZE; MILLET; OATS; RICE; RYE; SORGHUM; WHEAT.)

(B. B. B.)

Cereals in Diet.—The dietary properties of the entire seed of wheat, rice, barley, rye, maize, oat and millet resemble each other in most respects. They are all deficient in calcium and vitamin A (except yellow maize), and the biological value of their protein moiety is lower than that of the proteins of milk, meats and eggs. When any one of these cereals is supplemented with calcium, vitamin A and a source of proteins of animal origin, it is rendered complete nutritionally.

Under the chronic conditions of scarcity of foods which prevailed generally in most parts of the world before the invention of modern farm machinery from 1840 on, cereals remained the most important food crop, although the yields were low because of inferiority of varieties and poor cultivation technique throughout Europe. With the development of modern machinery and improved selection through plant breeding, wheat production has been enormously increased. The price range of cereal products is small as compared with prices of the more expensive foods such as meats, milk, eggs, fruits and vegetables other than the potato. Bread grains and potatoes are the cheapest foods. Whenever economic conditions prevail which lower the incomes of families or increase the cost of foods, the tendency has been for people to subsist more largely on bread and potatoes. Since the potato is not constituted so as to make good the deficiencies of cereals, such dietaries as are largely derived from these sources are nutritionally inadequate. Much malnutrition in Europe and elsewhere in recent decades has been due to this cause.

Before the year 1879 the milling of wheat was done in the same manner as in the days of Moses, viz., between millstones. This precluded production of flour more refined than could be achieved by sifting out the coarser particles. With the invention of the roller mill, the wheat berry could be separated into more than 20 mill streams, each of different composition. Especially important from the nutritional standpoint is the removal of the germ and the outer layers of the wheat, which are, with the exception of the outermost or bran layer, the most nutritious parts of the grain. Modern white flour is essentially free from fat, which in whole meal grows rancid on long storage. It contains only the protein moiety of the grain which has the lowest nutritive value. In addition, most of the vitamins and mineral elements, except phosphorus and potassium, are milled out and go into stock feed. Modern white flour is milled for commercial expediency rather than in the interest of the people's health. Because of the hazards of marketing a more highly nutritious flour for breadmaking, it is clear that there is much to justify modern milling processes from the economic point of view. As a World War II measure Canada introduced a long extraction wheat flour known as Canada Approved Flour, which represented about 85% of the wheat berry as compared with ordinary flour which is refined to the least nutritious 70% of the wheat. Later, England adopted the practice of manufacture of a similar flour. Such flour is superior to ordinary white flour in nutritive value, being superior in vitamin and mineral nutrient values and in the quality of its proteins. In the interest of health it would be advisable to adopt such flour to the maximum extent to which commercial transport and storage of flour permit.

The practice of improving the quality of commercially baked bread by the use of skim milk instead of water in preparing the bread mix became general in the United States after World War I. As much as six per cent of nonfat milk solids in bread improves greatly the nutritive value of the loaf by compensating for all of the nutritive deficiencies of white flour except iron. Four to six per cent milk bread becomes stale less rapidly than does bread made without milk, crumbs less on cutting, and otherwise makes a highly desirable bread. This method of improving bread has become popular with bakers.

With the development of the synthetic production of several of the vitamins and consequent lowering of their cost, a movement was started to "enrich" bread made from white flour by the addition of thiamin, riboflavin, niacin and iron, with calcium and phosphorus additions optional. While it is true that such "enrichment" of a white flour bread may safeguard the health of people whose dietaries are of low quality, it is not clear that it is a wise policy to pay for the inclusion of these vitamins and iron in the diets of good to high quality which, there are good reasons for believing, represent those of a large majority of the people. An excess of vitamins has not been shown to be of benefit.

It is a wise policy to promote the manufacture of bread of the highest possible nutritive value. It would seem desirable nutritionally to include small percentages of wheat germ, corn (maize) germ, dried brewers' yeast, rice polishings, as well as the maximum amount of nonfat milk solids, in commercial bread formulae. Such a policy would go far toward justifying the milling of highly refined flour of good keeping quality. At the same time the nutritionally superior parts of the grain which have hitherto been used largely for animal feeding would be used to improve human nutrition.

Maize meal (corn meal) and corn grits are widely used as human foods, especially in the southern United States, in parts of Italy, Rumania, Egypt and elsewhere. Since maize contains about one-fifth as much niacin as does wheat, pellagra, which is due to niacin deficiency, has been common only where corn is extensively used as a bread grain or as corn-meal mush (polenta). The milling of maize by modern machinery produces a meal for human consumption which is as much depleted in nutrients as is white flour. Barley and rye are extensively used as human food only in areas where wheat does not yield well. These cereals are profitable agricultural crops in the thin sandy soils of northern Europe (rye) and in regions too hot and dry or too wet and cold for wheat. There are varieties of barley which yield a harvest under conditions too extreme for wheat production. Where rye and barley are used as bread grains they are not milled and refined as is wheat but are employed as essentially whole meal products. Oats, which are prepared for human consumption as rolled oats and oatmeal, are the only cereal marketed solely as a whole grain product. Machinery for their degermination has not been perfected.

Where wheat or other cereals are marketed for use as breakfast cereals, it is advisable to provide products which represent the entire seed because of their superior food values.

Rice is second only to wheat in the quantity grown and used as human food. Being the one cereal which grows in swampy land, it forms the principal food of many millions of people in the warmer and wetter areas of the world. The flavour of whole rice is generally less relished than is that of polished rice. Polishing is desirable from the same commercial standpoint as is the refining of white flour. Both products keep well. Polishing removes the bran and aleurone layers from the surface of the kernel and also the germ. Polished rice closely resembles white patent wheat flour in dietary properties. Attempts have been made, and some progress achieved, in the distribution of "undermilled" rice and steamed rice. The former product contains some of the outer layers (silverskin) of the grain, and some germ. In the preparation of steamed rice the grain is steeped in water warm enough to facilitate permeation of the grain and gelatinization of the surface starch. These processes which serve to retain the thiamin content of rice have been promoted as a means of preventing the disease beri-beri which afflicts people whose diet is too largely derived from polished rice.

Sorghums, and also the seeds of several grasses popularly known as millets, are among the hardiest of the cereals in withstanding drought. They are extensively employed as human food in semiarid regions throughout the world. They are the least palatable of the cereals and are eaten from necessity rather than from choice. The use of these seed grains is most common in the U.S.S.R., northern Asia and Africa.

Because of great improvements in cereals through plant breeding, the use of appropriate machinery for the preparation of the soil, for planting, cultivation, harvesting and threshing of cereals, their production has been enormously increased within the past hundred years. They are our least expensive and most important foods as sources of calories, thiamin and protein, notwithstanding the latter is of rather poor quality as compared with foods of animal origin. Because of their dietary deficiencies, especially when refined derivatives of cereals are eaten, the ideal way to use cereals in the diet is in menus in which occur liberal amounts of milk and milk products, meats, eggs, fish, poultry, together with appropriate amounts of green and yellow vegetables and some fresh vegetable foods suitable for eating in the uncooked state for their antiscorbutic properties. The fact is well established that none of our common foods is complete nutritionally when eaten as the sole source of nutriment. The keynote to successful nutrition is the proper selection of foods, each deficient in one or more respects, but so constituted as to supplement each other's shortcomings and to make collectively a complete diet. (*See* also BREAD AND BREAD MANUFACTURE; FLOUR AND FLOUR MANUFACTURE.)

BIBLIOGRAPHY.—J. Russell Smith, *The World's Food Resources* (1919); McCollum, Orent-Keiles and Day, *The Newer Knowledge of Nutrition* (1939); H. C. Sherman, *The Chemistry of Food and Nutrition* (1941). (E. V. M.)

CEREBELLUM: *see* BRAIN; also EQUILIBRIUM, ANIMAL.

CEREMONIAL. In the military sense the prescribed drill and formations for certain specific occasions such as parades, reviews, guard duty, funerals, trooping the colours and lining streets, as distinct from drill applicable to field exercises.

CERES, goddess of the growth of food plants, worshipped, alone or with the god Cerus, over a considerable part of Italy. (Oscan *Keri—;* probably connected with *cre-are, cre-sco;?* "creatress"). Her cult was early overlaid by that of Demeter, who was widely worshipped in Sicily and Magna Graecia, *cf.* DEMETER. On the advice of the Sibylline Books, a cult of Ceres Liber and Libera was introduced into Rome in 496 B.C., to check a famine. Liber and Libera seem to represent the *Iakchos* and *Kore* of the Eleusinian cult. The ritual of this worship was largely if not wholly Greek. The temple, which was built on the Aventine in 493 B.C., and was of Etruscan shape but decorated by Greek artists, became a centre of plebeian activities, religious and political. Ceres was regarded as the patroness of the corn trade, which seems to have been early in plebeian hands. The chief festivals of this cult were:

(1) *Ludi Ceriales,* introduced before 202 B.C., and ultimately lasting from April 12–19;

(2) an annual festival, instituted before 217 B.C., celebrated in secret by the women and apparently dealing with the union of *Kore* and *Hades;*

(3) from 191 B.C. on, a fast (*ieiunium Cereris*), held every five years, but later every year on Oct. 4. All these are on Greek lines.

See Wissowa, *Religion und Kultus* (2nd ed.), pp. 192 *et seq.*, 297 *et seq.*

CERIGNOLA, a town of Apulia, Italy, in the province of Foggia, 26 mi. S.E. by rail from the town of Foggia. Pop. (1936) 37,163 (town); 39,540 (commune). It was rebuilt after a great earthquake in 1731. It has a considerable agricultural trade and also trade in merino and mattress wool. In 1503 the Spaniards under Gonzalo de Cordoba defeated the French under the duc de Nemours below the town—a victory which made the kingdom of Naples into a Spanish province in Italy. Cerignola lies on the Via Traiana between Herdoniae and Canusium.

CERIGOTTO, called locally Lius (anc. *Aegilia* or *Ogylos;* mod. official Gr. *Antikythera*), an island of Greece, between Cythera (Cerigo) and Crete, about 20 mi. from each. The inhabitants are mainly Cretan refugees, and in favourable seasons export wheat. It was long a resort of pirates. Close to its coast in 1900 an ancient ship was discovered, laden with bronze and marble statues. Cerigotto was occupied by Germany in 1941.

CERINTHUS (*c.* A.D. 100), a Christian heretic, known to St. John. Hippolytus (*Haer.* vii, 33) credits him with an Egyptian training, but there can be no truth in the notice given by Epiphanius (*Haer.* xxviii, 4) that Cerinthus had led the Judaizing opposition against Paul at Jerusalem.

According to Irenaeus (*Adv. haeres.*, I, 26, 1), Cerinthus taught that the world had been made by angels, from one of whom, the god of the Jews, the Israelites had received this imperfect law. The only New Testament writing which he accepted was a mutilated Gospel of Matthew. Jesus was the offspring of Joseph and Mary, and on Him at the baptism descended the Christ, the divine power, revealing the unknown Father, and endowing Him with miraculous power. This Christ left Jesus before the Passion and the resurrection. According to Philastrius and St. Epiphanius, Cerinthus admitted circumcision and the observance of the Sabbath. Gaius, the priest (*c.* 200), and Dionysius of Alexandria (*q.v.*) accused him of a crude form of Chiliasm. Cerinthus is a blend of judaizing Christian and Gnostic.

CERIUM (symbol Ce, atomic number 58, atomic weight 140.13) is the commonest metallic element of the rare-earth group and was discovered in 1803 by Martin Heinrich Klaproth and independently by Jons Jakob Berzelius and Wilhelm Hisinger; Berzelius named the element after the asteroid Ceres, discovered in 1801. The element is not really scarce in the earth's crust. Several investigators have estimated its abundance as being greater than that of tin, silver, mercury or tungsten. The metal has four stable isotopes: Ce^{136} (less than 0.2%), Ce^{138} (less than 0.3%), Ce^{140} (88.5%) and Ce^{142} (approximately 11%); radioactive isotopes are found among the fission products of thorium, uranium and plutonium. (*See* ISOTOPES; RADIOACTIVITY, ARTIFICIAL.) It occurs most abundantly in the minerals monazite, cerite, allanite and bastnasite, accompanied by other members of the rare-earth group. The latter mineral is found in extensive deposits in the western United States. The metal is formed by electrolysis of the anhydrous fused halides or by thermo-reduction with the alkali metals or with the alkaline-earth metals. It has an iron-gray colour and a hardness similar to that of tin or silver. The metal is slowly oxidized in air and reacts with boiling water, liberating hydrogen. Malleable and ductile, it possesses good thermal conductivity with a fairly high latent heat of fusion and melts at approximately 804° C. It combines readily with the halogens, is soluble in dilute acids and readily forms a hydride and a nitride. At room temperatures the metal is reported to exist in two allotropic forms. The α form (hexagonal close-packed, $a=3.65$ A [Angstrom unit $=10^{-8}$ cm.], $c=5.96$ A) has a calculated density $=6.78$ g. per cubic centimetre; the β or common form (cubic close-packed, $a=5.172$ A) has a calculated density $=6.731$ g. per cubic centimetre. A condensed cubic form exists at liquid air temperatures and has a density about 18% greater than the above. Undoubtedly other crystalline forms exist at high temperatures.

Cerium is a powerful reducing agent and, in the form of wire, burns brilliantly when heated. Since cerium is the only member of the rare-earth group which forms a higher series of compounds (other than the oxide), such as CeX_4, it is the most easily purified member of the group. These compounds upon hydrolysis form precipitates of basic salts practically free from the other rare earths. The purification is easily accomplished by carefully boiling a solution of the mixed nitrates and potassium bromate, with the gradual addition of ground marble to keep down the resulting acidity. The precipitated basic nitrate is washed with a 1% solution of nitric acid and may be further purified by repeating the process. A number of other methods were developed for separating cerium from the other rare earths based on the fact that it can be oxidized to the tetravalent state, in which it differs in properties from the other rare earths not so oxidized. Some promising procedures were found by which the tetravalent cerium salts are removed by solvent extraction.

Ceric oxide (CeO_2) is commonly formed when the cerium salts of the volatile acids are roasted in air. The pure oxide is a nearly white powder which is insoluble in nitric and hydrochloric acids but is soluble in sulphuric acid. The corresponding ceric salts, such as $Ce(SO_4)_2$, possess a yellow or orange-red colour; they are diamagnetic or at most show only a slight residual paramagnetism. The cerous salts, such as $Ce_2(SO_4)_3$, are more stable, are colourless, show no sharp-lined absorption spectra in the visible or ultra-violet regions and are paramagnetic.

Cerium has several practical uses. The tetravalent salts are employed as oxidizing agents in analytical chemistry and as therapeutic agents. Cerium nitrate finds application in the manufacture of Welsbach gas mantles and in the ceramic and textile industries. It is an ingredient of carbon-impregnated arcs used by the motion-picture industry. Cerium metal is used in metallurgy to form alloys, the commonest being misch metal. This alloy is usually manufactured directly from the crude rare earths and contains approximately 45% to 50% cerium, 22% to 25% lanthanum, 15% to 17% neodymium, 8% to 10% praseodymium, terbium, yttrium and samarium, 0 to 5% iron and 0.1% to 0.3% silicon. Since the properties of the other rare-earth metals are similar to those of cerium, this alloy is generally used in place of crude cerium. Misch metal and metallic cerium are good reducing agents and oxidize rapidly. These metals are employed as active deoxidizers or "getters" in the iron industry and are well known as scavengers and purifiers in various types of foundry melts. They have also found considerable application in the light metal industry, since they tend to give sound castings of aluminum and magnesium when present in small amounts. They are employed in pyrophoric flints and are valuable as a constituent of the "getters" used in the manufacture of vacuum tubes and similar equipment. Cerium oxide is used as an opacifier in the making of porcelain coatings for signs. It is also employed as an abrasive in polishing glass, for which purpose it has properties superior to those of rouge. (*See* RARE EARTHS.) (F. H. SP.)

CERNUSCHI, HENRI (1821–1896), Italian politician and economist, was born at Milan. He played a part in the revolutionary movement and was compelled to leave Italy in 1850. He then settled in France, where he made a large fortune. Cernuschi is best known as an ardent champion of bimetallism, and the word itself is commonly supposed to have originated with him—at least in its English form it is first found in his *Silver Vindicated* (1876).

Among his other works may be mentioned *Mécanique de l'échange* (1861); *Le Bimétallisme en Angleterre* (1879); *Le Grand procès de l'Union latine* (1884); *Illusion des sociétés coopératives* (1886).

CEROGRAPHY, the art of painting in wax; from the Gr. κηρός, wax, and γράφειν, to write. (*See* ENCAUSTIC PAINTING.) It is also the name of a wax process employed in printing in which engraved sheets of wax are used after they have been electrotyped.

CERRO GORDO. A mountain pass, 60 mi. N.W. of Veracruz, Mex., along the National highway from the coast to the capital of Mexico.

Here Gen. Winfield Scott in his advance to Mexico City during the war between the United States and Mexico (1846–48) met his first determined resistance. Brig. Gen. D. E. Twiggs's leading column was stopped by the river ravine on his left, fire from the emplaced Mexican artillery on the centre heights, and rugged terrain on his right (April 12, 1847).

After Scott arrived (April 14) several later-prominent officers, among them Capt. Robert E. Lee, were sent out on reconnaissance. Lee located a trail leading to the rear of the left flank of the Mexican army but was forced to hide in their midst behind a fallen log for several hours before he could return. As the result of this reconnaissance, General Scott made plans to divide his troops and concentrate a major attack by using the natural barrier of the rough country to hide his sweep around the Mexican left. A simultaneous frontal advance was also to be made.

His force numbered about 8,500 as against approximately 12,000 Mexicans under Gen. Antonio Lopez de Santa Anna. On April 17 Twiggs, guided by Lee, advanced and occupied the prominent hill La Atalaya according to plan. Instead of waiting to attack at the same time with Gen. James Shields's brigade, which had a longer distance to march, Twiggs's impetuously advancing troops prematurely attempted to capture the commanding position El Telégrafo, beyond La Atalaya, but were repulsed. Shields's brigade, with artillery, came into position during the evening through a hampering rain. The next morning, April 18, the attack on El Telégrafo was renewed, and cheering troops under Col. W. S. Harney fought their way up the slope, capturing the crest by hand-to-hand fighting. The parallel seizure of the Spur by Col. Bennet Riley's troops and the emergence of Shields's brigade into the open near Santa Anna's main camp caused the Mexican army, afraid of being cut off, to flee.

The planned frontal attack was made by Brig. Gen. G. J. Pillow against the emplaced batteries on the three ridges immediately in front of the American army; it was unsuccessful.

The Mexican loss was 40 cannon, 4,000 muskets, about 4,000 prisoners and about 1,100 casualties. The American loss is given as 63 killed and 353 wounded.

BIBLIOGRAPHY.—J. H. Smith, *The War With Mexico*, vol. ii (New York, 1919); A. H. Bill, *Rehearsal for Conflict* (New York, 1947); R. S. Henry, *The Story of the Mexican War* (Indianapolis, 1950).

(G. J. S.)

CERTALDO, a town of Tuscany, It., in the province of Florence, 35 mi. S.S.W. by rail and 18 mi. direct from the town of Florence. Pop. (1951) 12,089 (commune). It was the home of the family of Giovanni Boccaccio, who died and was buried there in 1375. His house of brick was restored in 1823. A statue of him was erected in the principal square in 1875. The Palazzo Pretorio, or del Vicariato, the residence of the Florentine governors, restored to its original condition, has a picturesque façade and court.

CERTHIIDAE: *see* TREE-CREEPER.

CERTIFICATE OF DEPOSIT, a written receipt from a bank acknowledging the deposit therein of a certain sum of money. Under such certificate, money may be deposited either on a demand basis or a time basis, but in either case it cannot be drawn against by cheque. To withdraw funds deposited under a certificate of deposit it is necessary to present the certificate itself, properly endorsed.

In the United States certificates of deposit are negotiable when properly endorsed and are usually acceptable as security for loans. (*See* WARRANT.)

CERTIFIED CHEQUE, a cheque regularly drawn against a depositor's account in a bank but having stamped or written on the face the word "certified" or "accepted," or the phrase "good when properly indorsed," or "good through clearing house," or some other expression commonly used, and the signature of a bank official, usually a cashier or paying teller, qualified to make certifications. The certification is the bank's guarantee that the signature of the drawer is genuine and that there are and will be sufficient funds, to his credit to pay the cheque. A certified cheque becomes an obligation of the bank itself instead of merely an order upon the bank by the drawer. Immediately upon the certification of a cheque, the amount certified is set aside from the drawer's account specially for the purpose of paying the cheque; and other cheques which may be presented ahead of that certified will not be allowed to withdraw the funds so segregated. The advantage of the certified cheque is that it will not be refused payment on the ground of "no funds," or "not sufficient funds."

A cheque may be certified at the request of either the drawer or a holder. If certified at the request of a holder, however, both the drawer and the indorsers, if any, are released from obligation and the holder must look for payment to the bank alone, and the bank is absolutely liable unless the cheque was "raised," either before or after the certification. When a bank certifies a cheque at the request of the drawer, the latter is not released from liability, and if the bank should fail before the cheque is presented for payment, the holder will have recourse against the drawer.

(J. H. B.)

CERTIFIED PUBLIC ACCOUNTANT, a U.S. designation the use of which is restricted by state law to accountants who have met the legal requirements of the state or states in which they seek recognition. In addition to meeting certain educational and professional demands, candidates must also submit to written examinations in the subjects prescribed. Upon fulfilling the conditions of the particular state, the accountant receives a certificate which entitles him to use the expression "certified public accountant" after his name, or the abbreviation, C.P.A.

There are no regulations, either state or federal, which prohibit an accountant who has not received a certificate from engaging in professional practice, but certain assignments which are made by courts of law can be handled only by certified public accountants; without this certificate, accountants are finding it increasingly difficult to gain a footing in the profession. (*See* ACCOUNTING.)

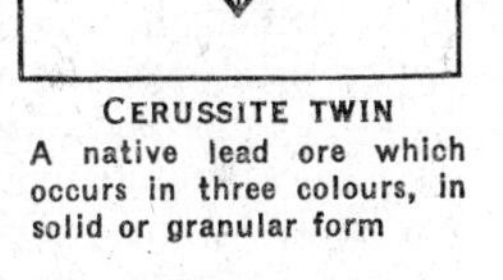

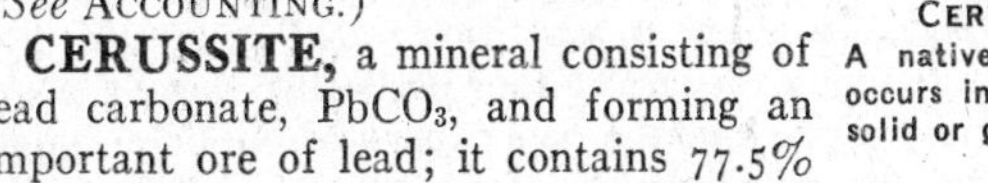

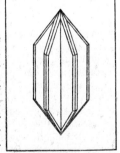

CERUSSITE TWIN
A native lead ore which occurs in three colours, in solid or granular form

CERUSSITE, a mineral consisting of lead carbonate, $PbCO_3$, and forming an important ore of lead; it contains 77.5% of the metal. The name is derived from the Latin *cerussa,* "white lead." It crystallizes in the orthorhombic system, and often forms pseudo-hexagonal twins like those of aragonite, with which it is isomorphous. It also occurs in compact granular or fibrous forms. It is usually colourless or white, sometimes grey or greenish, and is usually more or less transparent: some well-formed crystals have a brilliant lustre. Its hardness is 3–3.5 and density 6.5. It effervesces with dilute nitric acid. Cerussite occurs in large quantities in the upper oxidized portions of lead deposits. (CL. F.)

CERUTTI, GIUSEPPE (1738–1792), French author and politician, was born at Turin. He taught at the Jesuit college at Lyons and wrote an *Apologie* (1762) for his order. His *Mémoire pour le peuple français* (1788) advocates the claims of the *tiers état.* He was a member of the legislative assembly and a friend of Mirabeau, whose funeral oration he pronounced. He, with Rabaut Saint-Étienne and Grouvelle, founded the weekly sheet *La Feuille villageoise,* addressed to the villages of France to inform them of the progress of the Revolution.

On the *Mémoire pour le peuple français, see* F. A. Aulard in *La Révolution française,* tom. xv. (1888).

CERVANTES SAAVEDRA, MIGUEL DE (1547–1616), Spanish novelist, playwright and poet, was born at Alcalá de Henares. He was the second son of Rodrigo de Cervantes, an apothecary and surgeon, and Leonor de Cortinas. The exact date of Cervantes' birth is not recorded; he was baptized on Oct. 9, 1547, in the church of Santa María la Mayor at Alcalá. There are indications that Rodrigo de Cervantes resided at Valladolid in 1554, at Madrid in 1561, at Seville in 1564–65, and at Madrid from 1566 onwards. It may be assumed that his family accompanied him, and it seems likely that either at Valladolid or at Madrid Cervantes saw the famous actor, manager and dramatist, Lope de Rueda, of whose performances he speaks enthusiastically in the preface to his plays. In 1569 a Madrid schoolmaster, Juan López de Hoyos, issued a work commemorative of Philip II's third wife, Isabel de Valois, who had died on Oct. 3, 1568. This volume, entitled *Hystoria y relación verdadera de la enfermedad, felicissimo tránsito, y sumptuosas exequias fúnebres de la Sereníssima Reyna de España Doña Isabel de Valoys, nuestra Señora,* contains six contributions by Cervantes: a sonnet, four redondillas, and an elegy. López de Hoyos introduced Cervantes as "our dear and beloved pupil," and the elegy was dedicated to Cardinal Espinosa "in the name of the whole school." It has been inferred that Cervantes was educated by López de Hoyos, but this conclusion is untenable, for López de Hoyos' school was not opened till 1567. On Oct. 13, 1568 Giulio Acquaviva reached Madrid charged with a special mission to Philip II; he left for Rome on Dec. 2, and Cervantes is supposed to have accompanied him. This conjecture is based solely on a passage in the dedication of the *Galatea,* where the writer speaks of having been "camarero to Cardinal Acquaviva at Rome." There is, however, no reason to think that Cervantes met Acquaviva in Madrid; the probability is that he enlisted as a supernumerary towards the end of 1568, that he served in Italy, and there entered the household of Acquaviva, who had been raised to the cardinalate on May 17, 1570. All that is known with certainty is that Cervantes was in Rome at the end of 1569, for on Dec. 22 of that year the fact was recorded in an official information lodged by Rodrigo de Cervantes with a view to proving his son's legitimacy and untainted Christian descent.

There is evidence, more or less, that he enlisted in the regular army in 1570; in 1571 he was serving as a private in the company commanded by Captain Diego de Urbina which formed part of Miguel de Moncada's famous regiment, and on Sept. 16 he sailed from Messina on board the "Marquesa," which formed part of the armada under Don John of Austria. At the battle of Lepanto (Oct. 7, 1571) the "Marquesa" was in the thickest of the conflict. As the fleet came into action Cervantes lay below, ill with fever; but, despite the remonstrances of his comrades he vehemently insisted on rising to take his share in the fighting and was posted with 12 men under him in a boat by the galley's side. He received three gunshot wounds, two in the chest, and one which permanently maimed his left hand—"for the greater glory of the right," in his own phrase. On Oct. 30, the fleet returned to Messina, where Cervantes went into hospital, and during his convalescence received grants-in-aid amounting to 82 ducats. On April 29, 1572 he was transferred to Captain Manuel Ponce de León's company in Lope de Figueroa's regiment; he shared in the indecisive naval engagement off Navarino on Oct. 7, 1572, in the capture of Tunis on Oct. 10, 1573, and in the unsuccessful expedition to relieve the Goletta in the autumn of 1574. The rest of his military service was spent in garrison at Palermo and Naples, and shortly after the arrival of Don John at Naples on June 18, 1575, Cervantes was granted leave to return to Spain; he received a recommendatory letter from Don John to Philip II., and a similar testimonial from the duke de Sessa, viceroy of Sicily. Armed with these credentials, Cervantes embarked on the "Sol" to push his claim for promotion in Spain.

On Sept. 26, 1575, near Les Trois Maries off the coast of Marseilles, the "Sol" and its companion ships the "Mendoza" and the "Higuera" encountered a squadron of Barbary corsairs under Arnaut Mami; Cervantes, his brother Rodrigo and other Spaniards were captured, and were taken as prisoners to Algiers. Cervantes became the slave of a Greek renegade named Dali Mami, and, as the letters found on him were taken to prove that he was a man of importance in a position to pay a high ransom, he was put under special surveillance. In 1576 he induced a Moor to guide him and other Christian captives to Oran; the Moor deserted them on the road, the baffled fugitives returned to Algiers, and Cervantes was treated with additional severity. In the spring of 1577 two priests of the Order of Mercy arrived in Algiers with a sum of 300 crowns entrusted to them by Cervantes' parents; the amount was insufficient to free him, and was spent in ransoming his brother Rodrigo. Cervantes made another attempt to escape in Sept. 1577, but was betrayed by the renegade whose services he had enlisted. On being brought before Hassan Pasha, the viceroy of Algiers, he took the blame on himself, and was threatened with death; struck, however, by the heroic bearing of the prisoner, Hassan remitted the sentence, and bought Cervantes from Dali Mami for 500 crowns. In 1577 the captive addressed to the Spanish secretary of State, Mateo Vázquez, a versified letter suggesting that an expedition should be fitted out to seize Algiers; the project, though practicable, was not entertained. In 1578 Cervantes was sentenced to 2,000 strokes for sending a letter begging help from Martín de Córdoba, governor of Oran; the punishment was not, however, inflicted on him. Meanwhile his family were not idle. In March, 1578 his father presented a petition to the king setting forth Cervantes' services; the duke de Sessa repeated his testimony to the captive's merits; in the spring of 1579 Cervantes' mother applied for leave to export 2,000 ducats' worth of goods from Valencia to Algiers, and on July 31, 1579 she gave the Trinitarian monks, Juan Gil and Antón de la Bella, a sum of 250 ducats to be applied to her son's ransom. On his side Cervantes was indefatigable, and towards the end of 1579 he arranged to secure a frigate; but the plot was revealed to Hassan by Juan Blanco de Paz, a Dominican monk, who appears to have conceived an unaccountable hatred of Cervantes. Once more the conspirator's life was spared by Hassan, who, it is recorded, declared that "so long as he had the maimed Spaniard in safe keeping, his Christians, ships and city were secure." On May 29, 1580 the two Trinitarians arrived in Algiers: they were barely in time, for Hassan's term of office was drawing to a close, and the arrangement of any ransom was a slow process, involving much patient bargaining. Hassan refused to accept less than 500 gold ducats for his slave; the available funds fell short of this amount, and the balance was collected from the Christian traders of Algiers. Cervantes was already embarked for Constantinople when the money was paid on Sept. 19, 1580. The first use that he made of his liberty was to cause affidavits of his proceedings at Algiers to be drawn up; he sailed for Spain towards the end of October, landed at Denia in November, and made his way to Madrid. He signed an information before a notary in that city on Dec. 18, 1580.

PATIO OF CERVANTES' HOUSE

These dates prove that he cannot, as is often alleged, have served under Alva in the Portuguese campaign of 1580: that campaign ended with the battle of Alcántara on Aug. 25, 1580. It seems certain, however, that he visited Portugal soon after his return from Algiers, and in May 1581, he was sent from Thomar on a mission to Oran. Construed literally, a formal statement of his services, signed by Cervantes on May 21, 1590 makes it appear that he served in the Azores campaigns of 1582–83; but the wording of the document is involved, the claims of Cervantes are confused with those of his brother Rodrigo (who was promoted ensign at the Azores), and on the whole it is doubtful if he took part in either of the expeditions under Santa Cruz. In any case, the stories of his residence in Portugal, and of his love affairs with a noble Portuguese lady, who bore him a daughter, are simple inventions. From 1582–83 to 1587 Cervantes seems to have written copiously for the stage, and in the Adjunta al Parnaso he mentions several of his plays as "worthy of praise"; these were *El Trato de Argel, La Numancia, La Gran Turquesa, La Batalla naval, La Jerusalén, La Amaranta ó la de Mayo, El Bosque amoroso, La Unica y Bizarra Arsinda*—"and many others which I do not remember, but that which I most prize and pique myself on was and is, one called *La Confusa,* which, with all respect to as many sword-and-cloak plays as have been staged up to the present, may take a prominent place as being good among the best." Of these only *El Trato de Argel* and *La Numancia* have survived, and, though *La Numancia* contains many fine rhetorical passages, both plays go to prove that the author's genius was not essentially dramatic. In Feb. 1584 he obtained a licence to print a pastoral novel entitled *Primera parte de la Galatea,* the copyright of which he sold on June 14, to Blas de Robles, a bookseller at Alcalá de Henares, for 1,336 *reales*. On Dec. 12 he married Catalina de Palacios Salazar y Vozmediano of Esquivias, 18 years his junior. The *Galatea* was published in the spring of 1585. It was only twice reprinted—once at Lisbon (1590), and once at Paris (1611)—during the author's lifetime; but it won him a measure of repute; it was his favourite among his books, and during the 30 years that remained to him he repeatedly announced the second part which is promised conditionally in the text. However, it is not greatly to be regretted that the continuation was never published, though the *Galatea* is interesting as the first deliberate bid for fame on the part of a great genius. It is an exercise in the pseudo-classic literature introduced into Italy by Sannazaro, and transplanted to Spain by the Portuguese Montemõr; and, ingenious or eloquent as the Renaissance prose-pastoral may be, its innate artificiality stifles Cervantes' rich and glowing realism. He himself recognized its defects; with all his weakness for the *Galatea,* he ruefully allows that "it proposes something and concludes nothing." Its comparative failure was a serious matter for Cervantes who had no other resource but his pen; his plays were probably less successful than his account of them would imply, and at any rate play-writing was not at this time a lucrative occupation in Spain. No doubt the death of his father on June 13, 1585, increased the burden of Cervantes' responsibilities; and the dowry of his wife, as appears from a document dated Aug. 9, 1586, consisted of nothing more valuable than five vines, an orchard, some household furniture, four beehives, 45 hens and chickens, one cock and a crucible.

It had become evident that Cervantes could not gain his bread by literature, and in 1587 he went to Seville to seek employment in connection with the provisioning of the Invincible Armada. He was placed under the orders of Antonio de Guevara, and before Feb. 24 was excommunicated for excessive zeal in collecting wheat at Ecija. During the next few months he was engaged in gathering stores at Seville and the adjacent district, and after the defeat of the Armada he was retained as commissary to the galleys. Tired of the drudgery, and without any prospect of advancement, on May 21, 1590 Cervantes drew up a petition to the king, recording his services and applying for one of four posts then vacant in the American colonies; a place in the department of public accounts in New Granada, the governorship of Soconusco in Guatemala, the position of auditor to the galleys at Cartagena, or that of *corregidor* in the city of La Paz. The petition was referred to the Council of the Indies, and was annotated with the words: "Let him look for something nearer home." In Nov. 1590 he was in such straits that he borrowed money to buy himself a suit of clothes, and in Aug. 1592 his sureties were called upon to make good a deficiency of 795 *reales* in his accounts. His thoughts turned to literature once more, and on Sept. 5, 1592, he signed a contract with Rodrigo Osorio undertaking to write six plays at 50 ducats each, no payment to be made unless Osorio considered that each of these pieces was "one of the best ever produced in Spain." Nothing came of this agreement, and it appears that, between the date of signing it and Sept. 19, Cervantes was imprisoned (for reasons unknown to us) at Castro del Río. He was speedily released, and continued to perquisition as before in Andalusía; but his literary ambitions were not dead, and in May 1595 he won the first prize (three silver spoons) at a poetical tourney held in honour of St. Hyacinth at Saragossa. Shortly afterwards Cervantes found himself in difficulties with the exchequer officials. He entrusted a sum of 7,400 *reales* to a merchant named Simón Freire de Lima with instructions to pay the amount into the treasury at Madrid; the agent became bankrupt and absconded, leaving Cervantes responsible for the deficit. By some means the money was raised, and the debt was liquidated on Jan. 21, 1597. But Cervantes' position was shaken, and his unbusinesslike habits lent themselves to misinterpretation. On Sept. 6, 1597 he was ordered to find sureties that he would present himself at Madrid within 20 days, and there submit to the exchequer vouchers for all official moneys collected by him in Granada and elsewhere. No such sureties being available, he was committed to Seville gaol, but was released on Dec. 1, on condition that he complied with the original order of the court within 30 days. He was apparently unable to find bail, was dismissed from the public service, and sank into extreme poverty. During a momentary absence from Seville in Feb. 1599, he was again summoned to Madrid by the treasury, but does not appear to have obeyed; it is only too likely that he had not the money to pay for the journey. There is some reason to think that he was imprisoned at Seville in 1602, but nothing positive is known of his existence between 1600 and Feb. 8, 1603: at the latter date he seems to have been at Valladolid, to which city Philip III. had removed the court in 1601.

Since the publication of the *Galatea* in 1585 Cervantes' contributions to literature had been limited to occasional poems. In 1591 he published a ballad in Andrés de Villalta's *Flor de varios y nuevos romances;* in 1595 he composed a poem, already mentioned, to celebrate the canonization of St. Hyacinth; in 1596 he wrote a sonnet ridiculing Medina Sidonia's tardy entry into Cadiz after the English invaders had retired, and in the same year his sonnet lauding Santa Cruz was printed in Cristóbal Mosquera de Figueroa's *Comentario en breve compendio de disciplina militar;* to 1597 is assigned a sonnet (the authenticity of which is disputed) commemorative of the poet Herrera; in 1598 he wrote two sonnets and a copy of quintillas on the death of Philip II.; and in 1602 a complimentary sonnet from his pen appeared in the second edition of Lope de Vega's *Dragontea.* Curiously enough, it is by Lope de Vega that *Don Quixote* is first mentioned. Writing to an unknown correspondent (apparently a physician) on Aug. 14, 1604, Lope de Vega says that "no poet is as bad as Cervantes, nor so foolish as to praise *Don Quixote,*" and he goes on to speak of his own plays as being odious to Cervantes. It is obvious that the two men had quarrelled since 1602, and that Lope de Vega smarted under the satire of himself and his works in Cervantes' forthcoming book; *Don Quixote* may have been circulated in manuscript, or may even have been printed before the official licence was granted on Sept. 26, 1604. It was published early in 1605, and was dedicated to the seventh duke de Béjar in phrases largely borrowed from the dedication in Herrera's edition (1580) of Garcilaso de la Vega, and from Francisco de Medina's preface to that work.

The mention of Bernardo de la Vega's *Pastor de Iberia* shows that the sixth chapter of *Don Quixote* cannot have been written before 1591. In the prologue Cervantes describes his masterpiece as being "just what might be begotten in a gaol"; on the strength of this passage, it has been thought that he conceived the story, and perhaps began writing it, during one of his terms of imprisonment at Seville between 1597 and 1602. Within a few weeks of its publication at Madrid, three pirated editions of *Don Quixote* were issued at Lisbon; a second authorized edition, imperfectly revised, was hurried out at Madrid; and another reprint appeared at Valencia with an *aprobacíon* dated July 18, 1605. With the exception of Alemán's *Guzmán de Alfarache,* no Spanish book of the period was more successful. Modern criticism is prone to regard *Don Quixote* as a symbolic, didactic or controversial work intended to bring about radical reforms in Church and State. Such interpretations did not occur to Cervantes' contemporaries, nor to Cervantes himself. There is no reason for rejecting his plain statement that his main object was to ridicule the romances of chivalry, which in their latest developments had become a tissue of tiresome absurdities. It seems clear that his first intention was merely to parody these extravagances in a short story; but as he proceeded the immense possibilities of the subject became more evident to him, and he ended by expanding his work into a brilliant panorama of Spanish society as it existed during the 16th century. Nobles, knights, poets, courtly gentlemen, priests, traders, farmers, barbers, muleteers, scullions and convicts; accomplished ladies, impassioned damsels, Moorish beauties, simple-hearted country girls and kindly kitchen-wenches of questionable morals—all these are presented with the genial fidelity which comes of sympathetic insight. The immediate vogue of *Don Quixote* was due chiefly to its variety of incident, to its wealth of comedy bordering on farce, and perhaps also to its keen thrusts at eminent contemporaries; its reticent pathos, its large humanity, and its penetrating criticism of life were less speedily appreciated.

Meanwhile on April 12, 1605, Cervantes authorized his publisher to proceed against the Lisbon booksellers who threatened to introduce their piratical reprints into Castile. By June the citizens of Valladolid already regarded Don Quixote and Sancho Panza as proverbial types. Practically nothing is known of Cervantes' life between 1605 and 1608. A *Relación* of the festivities held to celebrate the birth of Philip IV., and a certain *Carta á don Diego Astudillo Carrillo* have been erroneously ascribed to him; during these three years he apparently wrote nothing beyond three sonnets, and one of these is of doubtful authenticity. The depositions of the Valladolid enquiry show that he was living in poverty five months after the appearance of *Don Quixote,* and the fact that he borrowed 450 *reales* from his publisher before Nov. 1607 would convey the idea that his position improved slowly, if at all. But it is difficult to reconcile this view of his circumstances with the details concerning his illegitimate daughter revealed in documents recently discovered. Isabel de Saavedra was stated to be a spinster when arrested at Valladolid in June, 1605; the settlement of her marriage with Luis de Molina in 1608 describes her as the widow of Diego Sanz, as the mother of a daughter eight months old, and as owning house-property of some value. These particulars are perplexing, and the situation is further complicated by the publication of a deed in which Cervantes declares that he himself is the real owner of this house property, and that his daughter has merely a life-interest in it. This claim may be regarded as a legal fiction; it cannot easily be reconciled with Cervantes' statement towards the end of his life, that he was dependent on the bounty of the count de Lemos and of Bernardo de Sandoval, cardinal-archbishop of Toledo. In 1609 he joined the newly founded confraternity of the Slaves of the Most Blessed Sacrament; in 1610 Lemos was appointed viceroy of Naples, and Cervantes was keenly disappointed at not being chosen to accompany his patron. In 1611 he joined the Academia Selvaje, and there appears to have renewed his former friendly relations with Lope de Vega; in 1613 he dedicated his *Novelas exemplares* to the count de Lemos, and disposed of his rights for 1,600 *reales* and 24 copies of the book. The 12 tales in this volume, some of them written very much later than others, are of unequal merit, but they contain some of the writer's best work, and the two picaresque stories—*Rinconete y Cortadillo* and the *Coloquio de los perros*—are superb examples of their kind, and would alone entitle Cervantes to take rank with the greatest masters of Spanish prose. In 1614 he published the *Viage del Parnaso,* a burlesque poem suggested by the *Viaggio in Parnaso* (1582) of the Perugian poet Cesare Caporali. It contains some interesting autobiographical passages, much flattery of contemporary poetasters, and a few happy satirical touches; but, though it is Cervantes' most serious bid for fame as a poet, it has seldom been reprinted, and would probably have been forgotten but for an admirably humorous postscript in prose which is worthy of the author at his best. In the preface to his *Ocho comedias y ocho entremeses nuevos* (1615) he good-humouredly admits that his dramatic works found no favour with managers, and, when this collection was first reprinted (1749), the editor advanced the fantastic theory that the *comedias* were deliberate exercises in absurdity, intended to parody the popular dramas of the day. This view cannot be maintained, but a sharp distinction must be drawn between the eight set plays and the eight interludes; with one or two exceptions, the *comedias* or set plays are unsuccessful experiments in Lope de Vega's manner, while the *entremeses* or interludes, particularly those in prose, are models of spontaneous gaiety and ingenious wit.

In the preface to the *Novelas exemplares* Cervantes had announced the speedy appearance of the sequel to *Don Quixote* which he had vaguely promised at the end of the first part. He was at work on the 59th chapter of his continuation when he learned that he had been anticipated by Alonso Fernandez de Avellaneda of Tordesillas, whose *Segundo tomo del ingenioso hidalgo don Quixote de la Mancha* was published at Tarragona in 1614. On the assumption that Fernandez de Avellaneda is a pseudonym, this spurious sequel has been ascribed to the king's confessor, Luis de Aliaga, to Cervantes' old enemy, Blanco de Paz, to his old friend, Bartolomé Leonardo de Argensola, to the three great dramatists, Lope de Vega, Tirso de Molina and Ruiz de Alarcón, to Alonso Fernandez, to Juan José Martí, to Alfonso Lamberto, to Luis de Granada, and probably to others. Some of these attributions are manifestly absurd (for example, Luis de Granada died 17 years before the first part of *Don Quixote* was published) and all of them are improbable conjectures; if Avellaneda be not the real name of the author, his identity is still undiscovered. His book is not devoid of literary talent and robust humour, and possibly he began it under the impression that Cervantes was no more likely to finish *Don Quixote* than to finish the *Galatea*. He should, however, have abandoned his project on reading the announcement in the preface to the *Novelas exemplares;* what he actually did was to disgrace himself by writing an insolent preface taunting Cervantes with his physical defects, his moral infirmities, his age, loneliness and experiences in gaol. He was too intelligent to imagine that his continuation could hold its own against the authentic sequel, and malignantly avowed his intention of being first in the field and so spoiling Cervantes' market. It is quite possible that *Don Quixote* might have been left incomplete but for this insulting intrusion; Cervantes was a leisurely writer and was, as he states, engaged on *El Engaño á los ojos*, *Las Semanas del Jardín* and *El Famoso Bernardo*, none of which has been preserved. Avellaneda forced him to concentrate his attention on his masterpiece, and the authentic second part of *Don Quixote* appeared towards the end of 1615. The last 14 chapters are damaged by undignified denunciations of Avellaneda; but, apart from this, the second part of *Don Quixote* is an improvement on the first. The humour is more subtle and mature; the style is of more even excellence; and the characters of the bachelor and of the physician, Pedro Recio de Agüero, are presented with a more vivid effect than any of the secondary characters in the first part. Cervantes had clearly profited by the criticism of those who objected to "the countless cudgellings inflicted on Señor Don Quixote," and to the irrelevant interpolation of extraneous stories in the text. Don Quixote moves through the second part with unruffled dignity; Sancho Panza loses something of his rustic cunning, but he gains in wit, sense and manners. The original conception is unchanged in essentials, but it is more logically developed, and there is a notable progress in construction. Cervantes had grown to love his knight and squire, and he understood his own creations better than at the outset; more completely master of his craft, he wrote his sequel with the unfaltering confidence of a renowned artist bent on sustaining his reputation.

The first part of *Don Quixote* had been reprinted at Madrid in 1608; it had been produced at Brussels in 1607 and 1611, and at Milan in 1610; it had been translated into English in 1612 and into French in 1614. Cervantes was celebrated in and out of Spain, but his celebrity had not brought him wealth. The members of the French special embassy, sent to Madrid in Feb. 1615, under the Commandeur de Sillery, heard with amazement that the author of the *Galatea*, the *Novelas exemplares* and *Don Quixote* was "old, a soldier, a gentleman and poor." He now worked assiduously at *Los Trabajos de Persiles y Sigismunda,* which, as he had jocosely prophesied in the preface to the second part of *Don Quixote,* would be "either the worst or the best book ever written in our tongue." It is the most carefully written of his prose works, and the least animated or attractive of them; signs of fatigue and of waning powers are unmistakably visible. On April 18, 1616, Cervantes received the sacrament of extreme unction; next day he wrote the dedication of *Persiles y Sigismunda* to the count de Lemos—the most moving and gallant of farewells. He died at Madrid in the Calle del León on April 23; he was borne from his house "with his face uncovered," according to the rule of the Tertiaries of St. Francis, and on April 24 was buried in the church attached to the convent of the Trinitarian nuns in the Calle de Cantarranas. There he rests (the story of his remains being removed in 1633 to the Calle del Humilladero has no foundation in fact) but the exact position of his grave is unknown. Early in 1617 *Persiles y Sigismunda* was published, and passed through eight editions within two years; but the interest in it soon died away, and it was not reprinted between 1625 and 1719. Cervantes' wife died without issue on Oct. 31, 1626; his natural daughter, who survived both the child of her first marriage and her second husband, died on Sept. 20, 1652. Cervantes is represented solely by his works. The *Novelas exemplares* alone would give him the foremost place among Spanish novelists; *Don Quixote* entitles him to rank with the greatest writers of all time: "children turn its leaves, young people read it, grown men understand it, old folk praise it." It has outlived all changes of literary taste, and is even more popular to-day than it was three centuries ago.

BIBLIOGRAPHY.—L. Rius *Bibliografía crítica de las obras de Miguel de Cervantes Saavedra* (1895–1905); *Obras completas*, ed. R. Academia Esp. (1917–23); ed. R. Schevill and A. Bonilla-San Martín (1914–23); *Complete Works* (Glasgow, 1901–06)—ed. James Fitzmaurice-Kelly; *Don Quijote* (Madrid, 1916–17), ed. F. Rodríguez Marín; *Don Quixote* (London, 1898–99), ed. James Fitzmaurice-Kelly and John Ormsby; *Novelas ejemplares*, ed. F. Rodríguez Marín (1914–17); *Entremeses*, ed. E. Cotarelo y Mori (1911).—*See:* A. Morel-Fatio *L'Espagne de Don Quichotte* in *Études sur l'Espagne* (1895, 2me serie); R. Foulché-Delbosc *Étude sur "La tia fingida,"* in the *Revue hispanique* (1899), vol. vi. pp. 256–306; Julián Apraiz *Estudio histórico-crítico sobre las Novelas ejemplares de Cervantes* (1901); Francisco A. de Icaza *Las Novelas ejemplares de Cervantes* (1901); Francisco Rodríguez Marín *El Loaysa de "El Celoso Extremeño"* (Sevilla, 1901); P. Groussac *Une Énigme littéraire; le Don Quichotte d'Avellaneda* (1903); Alonso Fernández de Avellaneda *El ingenioso hidalgo Don Quixote de la Mancha* (Barcelona, 1905)—ed. M. Menéndez y Pelayo; J. Cejador y Frauca *La Lengua de Cervantes* (1905–06); C. Pérez Pastor *Documentos Cervantinos hasta ahora inéditos* (1897–1902); J. Fitzmaurice-Kelly *Miguel de Cervantes Saavedra, A Memoir* (1913); F. Rodríguez Marín *Nuevos documentos cervantinos hasta ahora inéditos* (1914); J. Fitzmaurice-Kelly *Cervantes and Shakespeare* (1916); R. Schevill *Cervantes* (1919); Miguel de Unamuno *The Life of Don Quixote and Sancho* (1914; Eng. trans., 1927). (J. F.-K.)

CERVERA, PASCUAL CERVERA Y TOPETE (1839–1909), Spanish admiral, was born at Medina Sidonia. As a sublieutenant he took part in the naval operations on the coast of Morocco during the campaign of 1859–60. Then he was engaged in operations in the Sulu Islands and the Philippines, and afterwards on the West Indian station during the first Cuban War (1868–78), returning to Spain in 1873 to serve on the Basque coast against the Carlists. He distinguished himself in defending the Carraca arsenal near Cadiz against the Federals in 1873. He became minister of marine in 1892, in a cabinet presided over by Sagasta, but he withdrew from the cabinet when he found that his colleagues, from political motives, declined to support his reforms and, on the other hand, unwisely cut down the naval estimates. When in 1898 the Spanish-American War (*q.v.*) broke out, he was chosen to command a squadron composed of four first-class cruisers, which was totally destroyed by the superior forces of the enemy. After the war, Cervera and his captains were honourably acquitted by the supreme naval and military court of the realm. In 1901 he became vice-admiral, in 1902 chief of staff of the Spanish navy, and in 1903 was made life senator.

See A. Risco, *Apuntes Biograficos del Cervera y Topete* (Toledo, 1920).

CESAREVICH (better Tsesarevich), the title until 1917 of the heir-apparent to the Russian throne. The full official title was *Nasliednik Tsarevich; i.e.,* "heir of Caesar," and in Russian the heir to the throne was commonly called simply *Nasliednik,* the word *Tsarevich* never being used alone. *Tsarevich* means any son of the emperor. The Cesarewitch handicap race at Newmarket, founded in 1839, was named after the prince, afterwards Alexander II. of Russia, who paid a state visit to England that year.

CESARI, GIUSEPPE (1568?–1640), called Il Cavaliere d'Arpino, also Il Giuseppino, Italian painter, born in Rome. His father was a native of Arpino. Cesari ranks as the head of the so-called "Idealists" of his period, as opposed to the "Naturalists," of whom Michelangelo da Caravaggio was the leader. Lanzi stigmatized Cesari as not less the corrupter of taste in painting than Marino was in poetry. The defects of drawing and perspective in his work may be seen in his frescoes in the Capitol at Rome, which occupied him at intervals during 40 years. He died in Rome in 1640. His brother Bernardino assisted in many of his works.

CESAROTTI, MELCHIORE (1730–1808), Italian poet, was born on May 15, 1730, at Padua, where he held the chair of rhetoric, and in 1768 the professorship of Greek and Hebrew. Cesarotti is best known as the author of an admirable translation (2 vols., 1763) of Ossian, which raised up many imitators of the Ossianic style. He also produced a number of prose works on aesthetics. He died at Padua on Nov. 3, 1808.

See the complete edition of his works (42 vols., Pisa, 1800–13); G. F. Barbieri, *Memoirs* (Padua, 1810); L. Alemanni, *Un Filosofo delle lettere* (Turin, 1894).

CESENA (anc. Caesena), a town and episcopal see of Emilia, Italy, province of Forlì, 12m. S.E. by rail from the town of Forlì, on the line between Bologna and Rimini, 144ft. above sea-level. Pop. (1936) 20,043 (town); 61,314 (commune). The town is at the foot of the Apennines, and is crowned by a mediaeval fortress (Rocca). The fine early Renaissance library was built for Domenico Malatesta in 1452 by Matteo Nuti, and its internal arrangements, with the original desks to which the books are still chained, are well preserved. It also contains a picture gallery. There are some fine palaces in the town. On the hill to the south-east the handsome church of S. Maria del Monte, after the style of Bramante, has carved stalls of the 16th century. The ancient Caesena was a station on the Via Aemilia and a fortress in the wars of Theodoric and Narses. In 1357 it was unsuccessfully defended by the wife of Francesco Ordelaffi, lord of Forlì, against the papal troops under Albornoz. In 1377 it was sacked by Cardinal Robert of Geneva (afterwards Clement VII., antipope). It was then held by the Malatesta of Rimini until 1465, when it came under the dominion of the Church. Both Pius VI. (1717) and Pius VII. (1742) were born at Cesena.

CESNOLA, LUIGI PALMA DI (1832–1904), Italian-American soldier and archaeologist, was born at Rivarolo, near Turin, Italy, on July 29, 1832, of an ancient but impoverished family. Educated for a military career, he served with distinction against Austria (1848–49) and in the Crimean war, and going to New York in 1860, founded there a training school for army officers. He fought in the American Civil War as colonel of a New York cavalry regiment, received mention for bravery in several encounters, was wounded and imprisoned, and after the war was brevetted brigadier-general. Renouncing his Italian titles, he received a presidential appointment as U.S. consul to Cyprus (1865–77), where he made extensive excavations of ancient pottery at Larnaca and Salinos, and verified and surveyed the sites of Paphos, Soli and Pali. In 1872 the New York Metropolitan Museum purchased his collection, which became the nucleus for subsequent extensive acquisitions. In 1879 he was appointed director of the museum, a post which he filled until his death, and in which he displayed foresight and energy. The authority of his restorations was questioned in an article in the *New York Herald* (Aug. 1880), but the question, on being referred to a special committee, was decided in his favour. In 1897 he received a Congressional medal of honour for conspicuous military services. He died in New York on Nov. 21, 1904. He is the author of *Cyprus, Its Ancient Cities, Tombs, and Temples* (1877), and of a *Descriptive Atlas of the Cesnola Collection of Cypriote Antiquities* (1884–86). His brother, Alessandro Palma di Cesnola, born in 1839, conducted excavations at Paphos (where he was U.S. vice-consul) and Salamis, on behalf of the British Government. These are described in *Salaminia* (1882). (*See* Cyprus.)

For the Cesnola controversy, *see* D. D. Cobham's *Attempt at a Bibliography of Cyprus* (4th ed., 1900). (W. B. P.)

CESPEDES (in Ital. Cedaspe), **PABLO DE** (1538–1608), Spanish poet, painter, sculptor and architect, was born at Cordova and educated at Alcalá de Henares, where he studied theology and oriental languages. On leaving the university he went to Rome, where he became the pupil and friend of Federigo Zuccaro, under whose direction he studied particularly the works of Raphael and Michelangelo. In 1560, while he was yet in Rome, proceedings were taken against him by the Inquisition at Valladolid, but they were dropped. He returned to Spain a little before 1577 and received a prebend of the cathedral at Cordova, where he resided till his death. Cristobal de Vera, Juan de Peñalosa and Zambrano were among his pupils. His best picture is a "Last Supper" at Cordova, but there are good examples of his work at Seville and at Madrid. Cespedes was author of several opuscules in prose on subjects connected with his profession. His poem on "The Art of Painting," partly preserved by Pacheco, is esteemed the best didactic verse in Spanish. It contains a glowing eulogy of Michelangelo. The few remaining fragments were first printed by Pacheco in his treatise *Del arte de la pintura,* in 1649.

CÉSPEDES Y MENESES, GONZALO DE (1585?–1638), Spanish novelist, was born at Madrid, and published his celebrated romance, the *Poema trágico del Español Gerardo, y desengaño del amor lascivo* in 1615–17. His treatment of political questions in the *Historia apologética en los sucesos del reyno de Aragón, y su ciudad de Zaragoza, años de 91 y 92* (1622), having led to the confiscation of the book, Céspedes took up his residence at Saragossa and Lisbon. While in exile he issued a collection of short stories entitled *Historias peregrinas y exemplares* (1623), and wrote the first part of his *Historia de Felipe IV.* (1631), a fulsome eulogy which was rewarded by the post of official historiographer to the Spanish king. Céspedes died on Jan. 27, 1638. His novels, though written in an affected style, display considerable imagination and insight into character. The *Poema trágico* was utilized by Fletcher in *The Spanish Curate* and *The Maid of the Mill.*

The *Historias peregrinas* had been reprinted (1906) with a valuable introduction by Sr. Cotarelo y Mori.

CESS, a term formerly more particularly applied to local taxation, in which sense it still is used in Ireland; otherwise it has been superseded by "rate." In India it is applied, with the qualifying word prefixed, to any taxation, such as "irrigation-cess" and the like, and in Scotland to the land-tax. The word is a shortened form of "assess"; and the spelling is due to a mistaken connection with "census."

CESSIO BONORUM, in Roman law, a voluntary surrender of goods by a debtor to his creditors. It did not amount to a discharge unless the property ceded was sufficient for the purpose, but it secured the debtor from personal arrest. The creditors sold the goods in satisfaction, *pro tanto,* of their claims. The procedure of *cessio bonorum* avoided infamy, and the debtor, though his after-acquired property might be proceeded against, could not be deprived of the bare necessaries of life. The main features of the Roman law of *cessio bonorum* were adopted in Scots law, and also in the French and several other legal systems. In England it exists under the internal regulations of certain commercial bodies, such as the recognized Stock Exchanges. In Scotland the process of *cessio bonorum* was abolished by the Bankruptcy (Scotland) act, 1913. (*See* further, BANKRUPTCY.)

CESTI, MARC'ANTONIO (1618–1669), Italian musical composer, was born at Florence (or according to some authorities at Arezzo) in 1618. He was a pupil of Carissimi, and is known principally as a composer of operas, notable for the pure and delicate style of their airs, the most celebrated of which were *La Dori* (Venice, 1663) and *Il Pomo d' Oro* (Vienna, 1666–67).

CESTIUS, LUCIUS, surnamed PIUS, Latin rhetorician, was a native of Smyrna, a Greek by birth. According to Jerome, he was teaching Latin at Rome in the year 13 B.C. As an orator in the schools he enjoyed a great reputation. As a public orator, on the other hand, he was a failure. Specimens of his declamations will be found in the works of Seneca the rhetorician.

See Seneca, *Controv.*, ix, 3, 12; J. Brzoska, in Pauly-Wissowa's *Realencyklopädie*, iii, 2 (1899) and *Suasoriae*, vii, 13 (for anecdotes).

CESTODA: *see* TAPEWORMS.

CESTUI, CESTUY: *see* TRUST AND TRUSTEES.

CETACEA, an order of mammals (from the Gr. κῆτος, a whale), divisible into three suborders: Archaeoceti, exclusively fossil; Mystacoceti, whalebone whales; and Odontoceti, toothed whales, comprising sperm whales, bottle-nosed whales and dolphins. The term "whale" does not indicate a natural division of the order, and it is used here to mean any member of the Cetacea, irrespective of size. The lengths of these animals are mostly between 4 and 100 ft. Their ancestors were probably land mammals, whose structure has been modified in many respects to adapt them for life in the water, from birth to death. Whales are warm-blooded, breathing air by lungs, without scales in their skin, with hands of the five-fingered type, with skeleton, brain, heart and blood vessels mammalian in structure, reproducing like other mammals and nourishing their young with milk; in all these respects differing essentially from fishes, to which they have a merely superficial resemblance. Certain species swim habitually in large schools. A few live entirely in fresh water. The majority are marine, some frequenting the coasts, but others oceanic, rarely approaching land. Many undertake extensive migrations and have a wide distribution. Whales have been known to follow a ship for several consecutive days, and Racovitza has used this as an argument for the view that they do not sleep.

External Form (fig. 1).—Whales swim mainly by the tail, which is produced into two horizontal flukes, not supported by any part of the skeleton, and are thus easily distinguished from fishes, in which the tail is vertical. A dorsal fin, similarly without skeleton, is generally present. The mouth has immovable lips. The fore limbs (flippers) have the form of paddles and are used

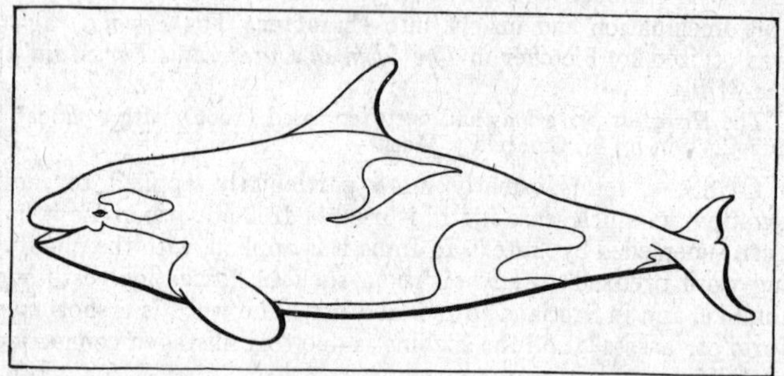

AFTER LUTKEN

FIG. 1.—KILLER (GRAMPUS ORCA), THE LARGEST OF THE DOLPHINS

principally for maintaining the balance of the body and for steering. External hind limbs are wanting. The neck is short and rarely distinguishable in the living animal. The nostrils (blowholes) have been shifted to the upper side of the head, at some distance from the tip of the snout or beak (except in the sperm whale). The part in front of the blowhole may resemble a forehead, but it really belongs to the beak. Eyes are well developed, but there are no external ears and the outer opening of the ear is minute. The skin is smooth, hairs being usually absent in the adult, except as occasional vestiges. The vent is at the root of the tail, behind the reproductive opening, on either side of which, in the female, is a groove containing a teat. The umbilicus (navel) is often visible farther forward, especially in young individuals.

Other Distinguishing Characters.—The brain case is short and lofty; the nasal canals pass nearly vertically downward in front of it, and the facial part is prolonged horizontally forward as a rostrum. The auditory bones are highly modified; the tympanics are shell-like and loosely attached to the skull. The neck vertebrae are of the typical mammalian number (seven), short, often fusing with one another; the second, if free, has no prominent odontoid process, the structure on which the head turns in other mammals. The lumbar and caudal vertebrae are freely movable, the interlocking processes of their upper arches disappearing from the thorax backward. The ribs are very movable on the vertebrae and sternum (breastbone). The clavicles (collarbones) are wanting. The flippers show no external division into hand, forearm and upper arm and are without definite joints at the elbow and wrist. They contain the typical mammalian bones, but the finger joints (phalanges) are more numerous in some of the digits than in other mammals. Digits are five or four without nails. The pelvis is represented by a small curved bone on each side, embedded in the flesh near the reproductive opening; it does not articulate with the vertebral column, which has no fused sacral vertebrae. In right whales and the sperm whale each half may carry a small bony or cartilaginous vestigial hind limb. The brain is large, its cerebral hemispheres much convoluted. Olfactory organs are almost absent, the nasal passages being functionally continuous with the larynx. The diaphragm is very oblique, and the stomach has several distinct chambers. The main arteries and veins break up into plexuses of vessels known as *retia mirabilia*. The kidneys are lobulated. The male organ is usually completely retracted, thus not interrupting the smooth contour of the body. The testes are within the abdomen, the uterus bicornuate, the placenta diffuse.

Respiration.—A large whale usually rises to breathe every 5–10 minutes, but the interval may be at least 45 minutes. The blowholes (fig. 2) are either two longitudinal slits (whalebone whales) or a single crescentic slit (toothed whales). On reaching the surface, the whale exposes and opens its nostrils, which are closed during submergence, and discharges the exhausted air from its lungs. This is done with considerable force, often producing an audible sound, and the animal is said to blow. The moist air projected upward is visible from a long distance, in the case of the larger whales, as a column containing particles of condensed water (the spout) formerly regarded as a fountain of water ejected from the head. Expiration is followed immediately by inspiration, and the whale then sinks horizontally. It repeats these actions several times, rising to the surface on each occasion without exposing much more than the part of its head which carries the blowholes. When it has thus thoroughly changed the air in its lungs, it rises in a different manner. The back is strongly arched and much of it becomes visible. The back fin, if present, appears to be situated on a rotating wheel, rising from behind, reaching the summit of the arched back and descending into the water in front. The whale then leaves the surface and is said to sound. The maximum depth of its dive has been supposed to be at least 100 fathoms. The right whales, humpback and sperm whale (but not the rorquals) usually throw their tails above the surface as they sound; and at other times, like many of the dolphins, they leap completely clear of the water. Differences in these respects, and in the form and direction of the spout, enable whalers to distinguish species.

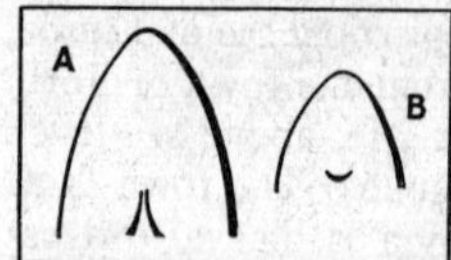

FIG. 2.—BLOWHOLES, FROM ABOVE
A. Whalebone whale
B. Dolphin

The horizontal position of the tail flukes facilitates rising to the surface and returning to the depths, movements of vital importance to the Cetacea. Another effective adaptation to aquatic life is the course taken by the air in passing to the lungs. The larynx and epiglottis form a tube passing through the pharynx into the lower end of the nasal passages (fig. 3). Here it is grasped by the soft palate, and the blowholes thus become continuous with the windpipe and lungs, the mouth being used solely for feeding—as in recently born marsupials, but not as in other adult mammals, which can breathe through either the nose or the mouth.

Prolonged submergence involves other demands on the respiratory organs. The thoracic cavity of the Cetacea is unusually extensible, and thus provides for a corresponding expansion of the lungs, depending on the loose attachments of the ribs and the

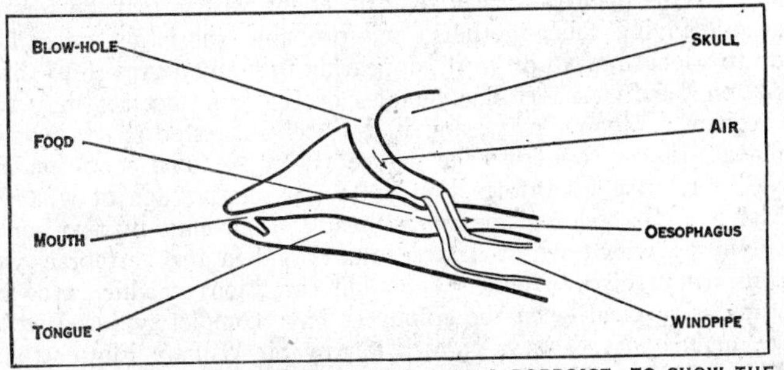

FIG. 3.—MEDIAN SECTION OF THE HEAD OF A PORPOISE, TO SHOW THE COURSE TAKEN BY AIR AND BY THE FOOD

considerable projection of the oblique diaphragm into the cavity of the contracted thorax. Whales have a larger amount of blood, in proportion to their size, than other mammals, and this involves an increased capacity for carrying oxygen to the tissues by means of haemoglobin, the red colouring matter. The very deep red colour of the muscles seems to imply that these structures also hold a specially large quantity of oxygen. The characteristic retia mirabilia are further adaptations. In the common porpoise, for instance, the upper and lateral parts of the thorax are covered by an elaborate arterial rete mirabile, lying just outside its lining membrane. Branches of this plexus extend upwards into the neural canal of the vertebral column, an arrangement which ensures an adequate supply of oxygen to the spinal cord and brain. Although physiological evidence cannot be quoted, the retia mirabilia probably act as reservoirs, the arterial portions containing a large supply of oxygen, the amount of which may largely influence the duration of submergence. The venous portions probably hold exhausted blood, which would otherwise circulate too freely. The principal danger to which a diver is exposed is the liberation of gas-bubbles into his blood, due to diminishing water-pressure, if the ascent to the surface is too rapid. The retia may perhaps have the function of retaining bubbles and of preventing their access to the general circulation.

Hair.—Whales maintain a constant high temperature, not very different from that of man. A hairy coat has been discarded, as a means of avoiding the loss of heat, in favour of blubber; but a few vestigial hairs may occur—an unmistakable sign of the origin of Cetacea from land mammals. In *Inia* numerous scattered hairs occur on the beak. Whalebone whales have hairs, in *Rhachianectes* up to 40 mm. long, on parts of the head and lower jaw; and in dolphins a few long hairs are found on the beak, before birth.

Skin and Colour.—The outer, horny layer of the epidermis is thin and readily separates from the body after death. The deeper layer is nearly always pigmented in certain parts, which then appear black, or varying shades of gray, brown or blue. The commonest type of colouration is dark above and white below, the relative extent of these regions varying with the species, the white area sometimes increasing with age. Many dolphins have a black streak extending from the eye to the flipper, perhaps representing the lower limit of the ancestral dark region. Some whales are completely black or white. In certain cases the normal white is replaced by a bright yellow colour. A. G. Bennett found that in Antarctic rorquals this is due to an external film composed of an enormous number of diatoms. These unicellular algae were found all over the skin, but were not conspicuous on the dark parts. In the common porpoise and its allies the skin of the edge of the dorsal fin or flippers bears a series of small, horny tubercles, which have been considered by some authors to indicate an affinity to Edentate mammals, a conclusion not universally accepted. The deeper part of the skin (dermis) is usually inconspicuous, but is better developed in the Delphinapterinae. The white whale, belonging to this subfamily, has a thick epidermis and a rather thinner dermis, and its skin has been used commercially as "porpoise leather."

Blubber.—This characteristic part of a cetacean is formed of tough fibrous tissue enclosing an enormous amount of oil. It invests every part of the whale, but is thicker in certain regions, for instance near the dorsal fin. In the sperm whale the maximum thickness is as much as 14 in., and in the Greenland whale 20 inches. In the latter, according to Scoresby, 4 tuns of blubber, by volume, yield 3 tuns of oil. In a whale of 70 tons the blubber weighs about 30 tons, and 2 tuns of oil may be extracted from each of the gigantic lower lips. The blubber of the rorquals now hunted is thinner, and in the smaller dolphins it does not much exceed one inch. Although specially important in retaining heat, the insulating properties of this layer probably afford protection against an excess of warmth in tropical waters. Blubber is little developed in newly born whales, and perhaps for this reason the parent resorts to warmer water to give birth to her young. It varies in condition at different times, a whale being often lean on its first arrival in polar seas, where the blubber improves in quality owing to the large amount of food found in those waters. The stomachs of whales captured in temperate latitudes are sometimes empty, and blubber is probably a reserve material which can be drawn on when food is scarce. It may further help materially to prevent the crushing of the tissues, during a deep dive, by the enormous pressure of the superjacent water.

Food.—Dolphins typically eat fishes, to which diet they are adapted by their teeth, generally numerous and uniformly conical; but cuttlefish also may be eaten. The stomach of a species of *Sotalia* has been found to contain vegetable matter. The Killer is exceptional in eating marine mammals and birds, in addition to fishes. The sperm whale and the bottle-nosed whales (Ziphiidae) are mainly dependent on cuttlefish, some of which must be obtained at considerable depths; but these also take occasional fishes. A diet of cuttlefish is often associated with a reduction of the number of teeth, in certain dolphins, the sperm whale and the Ziphiidae.

Whalebone.—The whalebone whales feed exclusively on plankton (*q.v.*), including fishes. They obtain food by means of a whalebone sieve, and the adequacy of the method may be estimated by the fact that two tons of plankton have been taken from the stomach of a blue whale. Plankton is specially abundant in the cold waters of both polar regions, and whales visit them to profit by this plenty.

Whalebone or baleen is derived from the skin lining the mouth and has nothing to do with true bone. The sieve is composed of

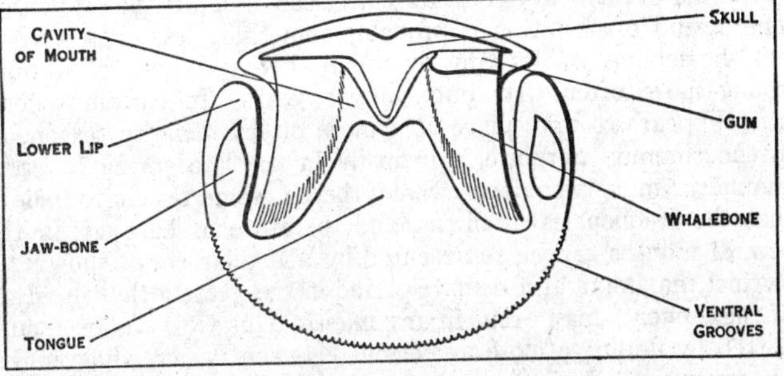

FIG. 4.—TRANSVERSE SECTION OF A RORQUAL'S HEAD TO SHOW WHALEBONE

two sides, each running longitudinally along the entire length of the outermost part of the palate, and being continuous with its fellow at the front of the beak. A side consists of as many as 300–400 transversely placed, flexible, and horny blades, embedded at their base in a substance known as the gum, and with a short interval between each two. The blades are longest and widest at the middle of the series and progressively smaller towards both ends, where they become very short. Seen from the front or back, an isolated blade appears roughly triangular (fig. 4), the shortest side embedded in the gum, the outer border straight, and the inner border slightly convex. On the inner aspect of each principal blade is a transverse row of a few very short blades; and all the blades are produced into long hairlike structures, composed of the same substance as the whalebone itself. Owing to the presence of these hairs, the sieve, seen from its inner side, resembles a door-mat or the fleece of a sheep. Between the two sieves lies the tongue, which is of immense size, in contrast with the much smaller tongue of the toothed whales.

The two halves of the lower jaw are greatly arched outwards, the mouth being thus enormous. The blades are bent backwards by the closure of the mouth, recovering a vertical position, by their own elasticity, as it opens. The great lower lip overlaps the outer edges of the blades, and the water must thus escape from the mouth through the chinks between these structures. The whale feeds, after sounding, by swimming through a shoal of plankton with its mouth open. Water enters at the front end; and, before it leaves, the food has been strained off by the hairy fringes of the baleen plates. The mouth is then closed, the tongue having no doubt helped to force out the water, while licking the food off the sieve. The characters of the baleen afford one of the most convenient ways of distinguishing species of whalebone whales. The blades are longest in the Greenland whale, where they may reach the astonishing length of 15 feet.

Sense Organs.—The olfactory organs are greatly reduced, and it is doubtful whether whales have the sense of smell. The nasal passages, however, are of vital importance, since they serve as the sole method of admitting air to the lungs. The eyes are small, with arrangements for withstanding water pressure. W. Scoresby stated that vision is acute in the Greenland whale, which is dull of hearing in the air, but is readily alarmed by even a slight splashing in the water. The external auditory passage is narrow and opens by a minute hole on the head, not far behind the eye. In whalebone whales it is blocked by a large mass of wax, several inches in length, and it cannot be of much service in hearing. It is believed that vibrations in the water reach the ear through sacs given off by the Eustachian tubes or through the bones and other tissues of the head. The tympanic bones are dense and conchlike, well developed and attached to the periotic by two slender pedicles. There can be little doubt that the auditory organs are of real importance.

Breeding.—The Cetacea are in all respects typically mammalian in their reproduction. The young is nourished in the uterus by a placenta, and is not born until it has attained a form essentially that of the adult, sometimes exceeding one-third the length of the mother. In the common porpoise ($5\frac{1}{2}$ ft.) the newly born young is about 2 ft. long, and in the largest whalebone whales at least 20 feet. A single young is typically produced, but twins occur and 7 foetuses have been found in a blue whale. The period of gestation is probably something less than a year, but whalebone whales are commonly believed not to produce young more often than once in two years. In certain species birth appears to take place at a more or less definite season, as in the common porpoise, principally in the late spring or early summer. Among whalebone whales there is some reason to believe that the frequencies of births, and therefore of pairings, in the several months can be represented by a regular curve showing a distinct maximum at a definite period in the year; although either of these events may occur in any month. This view has been supported by finding a close agreement between the breeding curves of northern and southern races of the same species, with the significant difference that the maxima are about six months apart, corresponding with the difference in seasons between the two hemispheres. Tropical species, such as the sperm whale, perhaps have no definite breeding period.

Migrations.—The principal movements of many whales are largely connected with the two functions of feeding and reproduction. The humpback, for instance, appears in large numbers in sub-antarctic waters in the spring (October) and remains there till the summer. As the season advances it becomes less numerous, but it is found off the south and west African coasts at the time that would be expected on the assumption that it is moving northwards. At the height of the southern winter it is found even as far north as the equator, and it travels southwards again as the spring returns. It is probable that this species, like others, seeks warmer water in which to bring forth its young and that pairing takes place at about the same time. Its journey to the far south is for the purpose of feeding.

Growth and Age.—Little can be said of the duration of life in whales; and statements that large individuals must be of great age may be dismissed as unproven. Young whales may be found accompanying their mothers, and probably subsisting on milk, up to a length of 40 or 50 ft., appearing to imply a growth to that size in the first year. The females of the same species may be pregnant at about 60 ft.; and it has been suggested that a whale reaches the reproductive age very early in life. The condition of the skeleton gives information as to the relative age of whales. Many of the bones of mammals grow at their ends by two bony epiphyses, which are at first separable and in the vertebrae are conspicuous discs of bone. The adult condition, at which growth stops, is reached when the epiphyses have completely fused with the main bones. It was pointed out by Sir William Flower that fusion begins at the two ends of the vertebral column; the cervical and caudal vertebrae commencing the process, which gradually extends from both ends towards the middle. This obviously gives some information as to the relative age of adolescent individuals, but it leaves untouched the question of the duration of life.

Species Hunted.—The whaling industry (*see* WHALE FISHERIES) has been mainly based on about nine species, of which all but the sperm whale are whalebone whales. The Basques hunted the Atlantic right whale (*Eubalaena glacialis*) at an early date, and the industry was specially flourishing in the 12th and 13th centuries. The arctic fishery began about 1611 and was based on the Greenland whale (*Balaena mysticetus*). The hunting of the sperm whale (*Physeter catodon*) began about a century later; and the southern right whale (*Eubalaena australis*) was captured in large numbers by some of the vessels subsequently engaged in this industry. The Pacific gray whale (*Rhachianectes glaucus*) was taken in considerable numbers on the coast of California before the middle of the 19th century. Modern whaling depends mainly on two species of rorqual, the great blue whale (*Sibbaldus musculus*) and the fin whale (*Balaenoptera physalus*) though the sei whale (*B. borealis*) is not unimportant in certain localities. The humpback (*Megaptera nodosa*) has at times been the most important constituent of the catch of modern whalers, who in one or two localities take a few specimens of Bryde's whale (*Balaenoptera brydei*). The following, of less importance commercially than the great whales, have also been systematically captured by whalers or fishermen at various times:—the narwhal (*Monodon monoceros*), the white whale (*Delphinapterus leucas*), the pilot whale (*Globicephala ventricosa*), the bottle-nosed whale (*Hyperoodon rostratus*), the common porpoise (*Phocoena phocoena*), and others of the smaller dolphins.

History gives a melancholy record of the results of intensive whaling. The Atlantic right whale is no longer to be found on the Biscay coast, and, though it made some recovery during the 19th century, it was believed at one time to have become extinct. The southern right whale, once extremely common on the coasts of South Africa and Kerguelen, and in other localities, is occasionally represented in whaling returns by a very few specimens. The Greenland whale disappeared successively from the bays of Spitsbergen, the Greenland sea, Davis straits and the region of Bering straits. There is no indication of the reappearance of these animals off Spitsbergen or Jan Mayen, where they were formerly present "in immense numbers"; and, though a few probably linger in some of the old localities, the Greenland trade is dead. The Pacific gray whale was nearly exterminated off the coast of California, and was thought to be extinct. It has recently reappeared in small numbers, and a few are being taken by the Japanese in their own waters. The capture of humpbacks has seriously declined. In 1844 the United States alone had 315 vessels employed in the chase of the sperm whale, but one fishing ground after another had to be abandoned. Sperm whales are still taken at whaling stations, off the coasts of Natal and the British Isles and in the Straits of Gibraltar, but the large fleets formerly engaged in the chase of these animals have ceased to exist. Of the important species, the blue whale, the fin whale, the humpback, the sei whale and the sperm whale alone survive in considerable numbers; and the disappearance of the first two would involve the extinction of the greater part of the industry.

The invention of an improved harpoon gun in 1865 gave a new impetus to whaling, and this has culminated in the extraordinary success of operations in the dependencies of the Falkland Islands and Ross sea. The reintroduction of pelagic whaling, by methods far more efficient than those formerly practised, has resulted in new dangers to the whales.

The facts are ominous, and history is likely to repeat itself unless adequate steps can be taken in time. Experience has shown that whales do not readily come back to an old locality, even when they have been free from pursuit for many years. The number of whales recently taken in sub-antarctic waters has several times exceeded 30,000 in a single season, and in 1937–38 it was more than 46,000. History gives no justification for the belief that whaling can continue indefinitely at this rate, and the necessity of controlling the industry is urgent.

Commercial Products.—Whalebone, the most valuable product of the Greenland whale, was at one time worth £2,000 a ton. That of the rorquals is shorter and of inferior quality. Oil is produced by all Cetacea, but the sperm oil of the sperm whale and Ziphioids differs in constitution from the train oil or whale oil of other whales. Spermaceti and ambergris are products of the sperm whale. Guano and other materials are obtained by grinding the dried flesh and bones of large whales. Meat of good quality is available from nearly all Cetacea. The flesh of dolphins was formerly esteemed a delicacy; and it had the advantage, in Roman Catholic countries, of being considered fish which could be eaten on fast days. The common porpoise was formerly hunted on a large scale for its meat. Ivory is obtained from the tusk of the narwhal and from the teeth of the sperm whale. Leather can be prepared from the skin of the white whale.

CLASSIFICATION

Suborder 1.—ARCHAEOCETI. The *Basilosauridae, Dorudontidae* and *Protocetidae* of the Eocene and Oligocene, constituting this group, are believed to have been derived from the Creodonta, the primitive fossil members of the Carnivora; but Gregory thinks that they may have descended from Insectivora of the type represented by *Pantolestes*. Their skull characters are intermediate between those of their supposed ancestors and those of recent Cetacea in the position of the nostrils, the relations of the maxillae and the dentition, which consists of 3 incisors, 1 canine, 4 premolars, and 3–2 molars on either side of each jaw. The first 4 or 5 teeth are conical and single-rooted, and the other teeth are double-rooted, with serrated crowns. A milk dentition is found.

The recent Cetacea have no milk teeth, and there is no differentiation into incisors, canines and molars. The *Squalodontidae* (Oligocene to Pliocene), included in the Odontoceti, are believed to have descended from the Archaeocetes and to have given rise to some at least of the recent toothed whales. The origin of the Mystacoceti is uncertain.

Suborder 2.—MYSTACOCETI, whalebone whales. Whalebone present; teeth wanting in the adult, numerous and vestigial in the embryo; lower jaw large, its halves curved outwards (fig. 5, B) and loosely united in front; blowholes two longitudinal slits (fig. 2, A); skull symmetrical, the nasal bones relatively well developed, maxillae not covering the orbital plates of the frontals; first pair of ribs alone joining the sternum, which consists of one piece. The females are slightly larger than the males.

Family 1.—*Rhachianectidae,* with *Rhachianectes glaucus,* Pacific gray whale (fig. L, p. 170; 45 ft.). Head small, less than one-quarter the total length; dorsal fin wanting; flippers 4-fingered. R. C. Andrews considers *Rhachianectes* the most primitive of the Mystacoceti, in view of the occurrence of long hairs scattered over the entire head and lower jaw, the short and relatively few baleen blades, the free neck vertebrae, the large pelvis, and other characters. The lower side of the throat region has two or three grooves. *Rhachianectes* prefers shallow water, swimming even in the surf and occurs in the North Pacific, from California northwards to the Arctic ocean and off Japan and Korea.

Family 2.—*Balaenidae.* Skull much arched; baleen long and narrow; ventral grooves wanting; neck vertebrae fused.

Neobalaena marginata, pygmy whale (20 ft.), is doubtfully placed in this family. It differs from the right whales in its small head, about one-fifth the total length, in its less arched rostrum, in having a dorsal fin and in its 4-fingered flippers. It is known from New Zealand and Australia.

Balaena and *Eubalaena,* right whales. Dorsal fin wanting; flippers broad, with 5 fingers; head one-quarter to one-third the total length.

Balaena mysticetus, Greenland whale (fig. A, p. 170; 60 ft.). Head enormous, one-third the total length; rostrum greatly arched, providing room for exceptionally long baleen, up to 15 feet. Arctic, circumpolar, and formerly abundant off Spitsbergen, both sides of Greenland and the North Pacific to Beaufort sea, but reduced by whaling to the verge of extinction.

Eubalaena glacialis, Atlantic right whale or Biscay whale (fig. B, p. 170), about the same size, but differing from *B. mysticetus* in its less arched head, its shorter baleen (up to 9 ft.) and the shape of its lower lip. It was formerly common in the Bay of Biscay and it has been recorded from the Mediterranean. It has been hunted, in recent years, off Iceland, Norway and the British Isles. It visits the eastern United States, its northern range in the Atlantic coinciding nearly with the southern limit of the Greenland whale; but, like other right whales, it avoids the tropics.

Eubalaena australis, southern right whale. Resembling *E. glacialis,* but found off Australia, Kerguelen and other parts of the southern sea, where 193,522 were killed by American whalers in 1804–17. A few are still taken off South Georgia, the South Shetlands and the African coasts. The *Eubalaena,* hunted in Japan, may be a distinct species.

Family 3.—*Balaenopteridae,* rorquals and humpback. Rostrum less arched than in Balaenidae, baleen blades shorter and broader; dorsal fin present; skin covering the throat with numerous, conspicuous, longitudinal grooves; flippers narrow; neck vertebrae free. At least 90% of the whales now hunted belong to this family.

Balaenoptera and *Sibbaldus,* rorquals. Body relatively slender; dorsal fin well marked; flippers small, narrow and pointed.

Sibbaldus musculus, blue whale or Sibbald's rorqual (fig. F. p. 170; at least 100 ft.) is the largest of all animals and the most important in the estimation of modern whalers. Colour nearly uniformly bluish-gray above and below, including both surfaces of the tail-flukes; baleen jet black, with black fringes. Cosmopolitan, on the assumption that (as in others of the family) the northern and southern races belong to the same species, from polar to temperate seas, occasionally reaching the equator. Food, small Crustacea (Euphausians, etc.).

Balaenoptera physalus, fin whale or razorback (fig. G, p. 170; up to at least 80 ft., in the south). Dark above and pure white below, including the lower surface of the tail-flukes. Baleen with alternate, vertical stripes of slate colour and yellow or white, the fringes similarly light in colour, the anterior 3 or 4 ft. of the right series nearly always completely white; lower jaw white on the right side, dark on the left, but the asymmetry of colour of baleen and skin may be reversed. Food, small Crustacea and fishes. This whale is captured in large numbers at most of the whaling stations. Its distribution is as wide as that of the blue whale, but it is rarely found in the tropics. It is common on both sides of the Atlantic, and it enters the Mediterranean. A few are stranded annually on the British coasts.

B. borealis, sei whale or Rudolphi's rorqual (fig. H, p. 170; 52 ft.). White and dark parts not so sharply delimited as in the fin whale; lower surface of tail-flukes bluish-gray; baleen black, its fringes white, silky and curling. Temperate parts of all the oceans, not wandering so near the poles as the two preceding species. Food, Crustacea, less often fishes.

B. brydei, Bryde's whale. Nearly as large as the sei whale, from which it differs in having straight hairs on its baleen blades, and

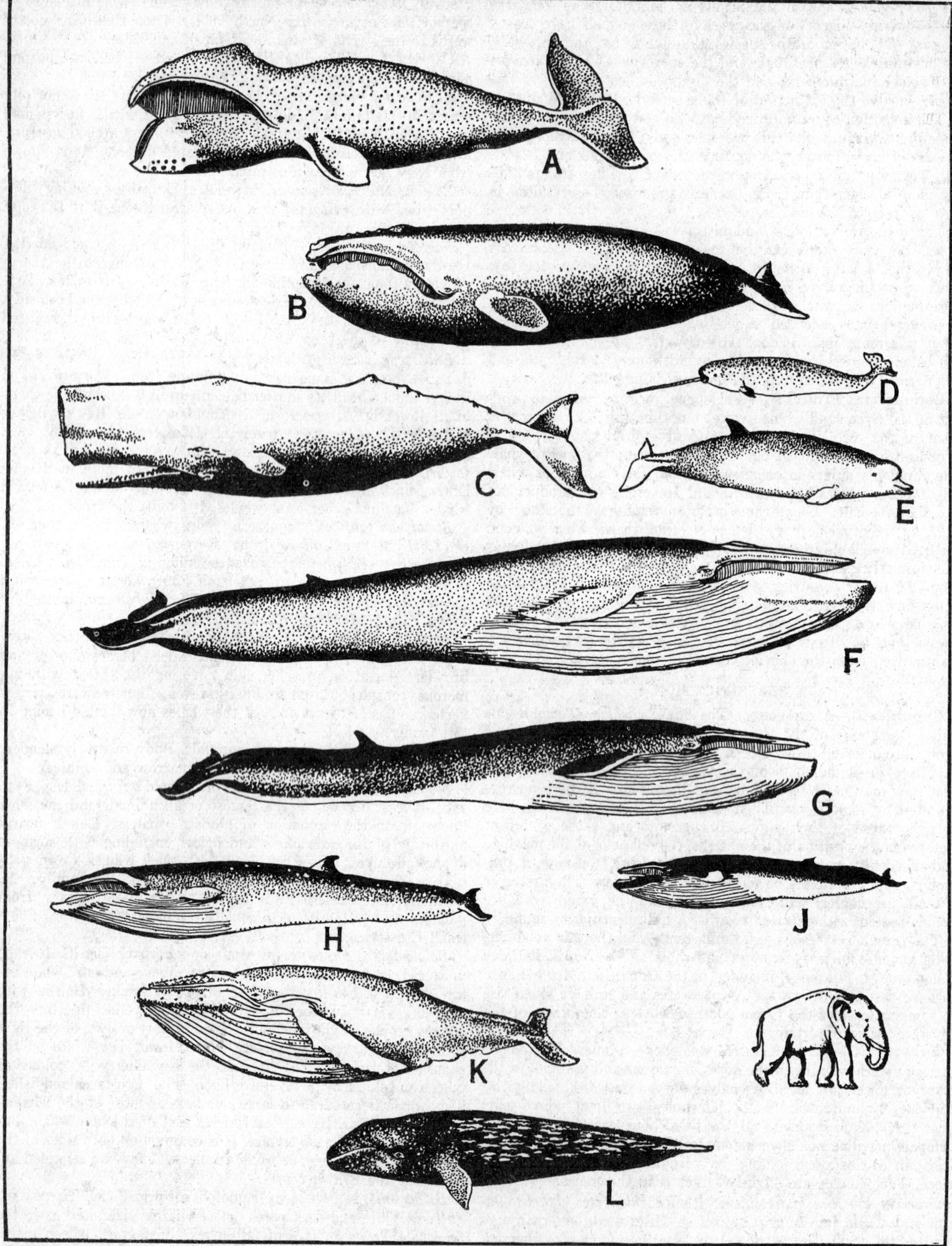

FROM (B) ALLEN, "WHALEBONE WHALES OF NEW ENGLAND," (C) SCAMMON, "MARINE MAMMALS OF N.W. AMERICA," (E) "NATUURKUNDIGE VERHANDELINGEN," (F, G, J, K) "CHRISTIANIA VIDENSKAPSSELSKAPS FORHANDLINGEN," (H, L) ANDREWS, "MEMOIRS OF THE AMERICAN MUSEUM OF NATURAL HISTORY"

VARIOUS TYPES OF WHALES

A, Greenland whale (after Scoresby). B, Atlantic right whale. C, sperm whale. D, narwhal (after Scoresby). E, bottle-nosed whale (after Vrolik). F, blue whale (after Sars). G, fin whale (after Sars). H, sei whale. J, lesser rorqual (after Sars). K, humpback whale (after Sars). L, Pacific grey whale (African Elephant, "Jumbo," 11 feet high, reproduced to same scale)

in its food, which consists principally of fishes. South and West Africa, apparently reaching the West Indies.

B. acutorostrata, lesser rorqual (fig. J, p. 170; 33 ft.). Coloration as in the fin whale (without asymmetry of colour); a conspicuous white area on the outer side of the flipper. Baleen and its fringes all white or yellowish. Food, largely fishes, but also Crustacea. Temperate and polar latitudes of both hemispheres, including the British and both North American coasts, but not hunted.

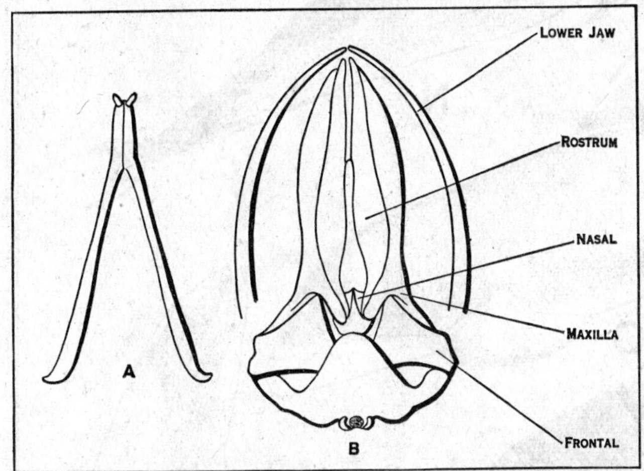

AFTER ESCHRICHT AND REINHARDT

FIG. 5.—A. LOWER JAW OF TOOTHED WHALE (ZIPHIUS, MALE); B. SKULL OF WHALEBONE WHALE (MEGAPTERA) FROM ABOVE

Megaptera nodosa, humpback (fig. K, p. 170; 52 ft.). Body thick, dorsal fin evanescent; flippers enormously long, nearly one-third the total length. Colour variable, sometimes nearly all black, but with varying amounts of white in other individuals; flippers sometimes pure white; baleen and its fringes black. Food, fishes and Crustacea. Cosmopolitan, from the Arctic to the Antarctic ocean, and more frequenting warm water than the rorquals. The humpback was almost the only species hunted at the commencement of the great antarctic whaling enterprise, beginning 1905, and was almost equally important on the African coasts. The numbers frequenting the whaling localities have greatly diminished.

Suborder 3.—ODONTOCETI, toothed whales. Teeth present throughout life; whalebone wanting; lower jaw more or less triangular (fig. 5, A), the front part often narrow, the two halves firmly united; blowhole single (fig. 2, B); skull asymmetrical, nasals reduced, maxillae covering the orbital plates of the frontals; several pairs of ribs joining the sternum, which consists, in the young at least, of several pieces.

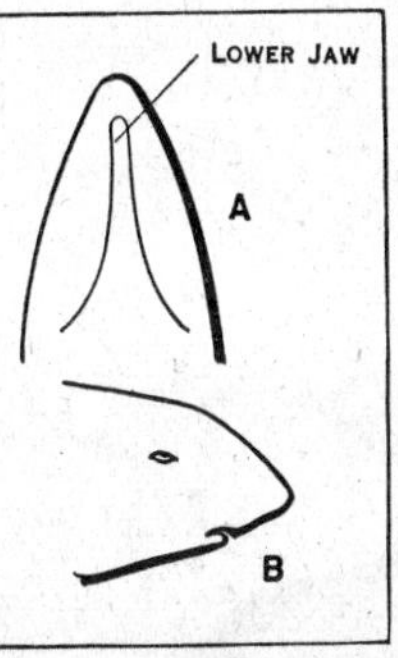

AFTER ESCHRICHT AND REINHARDT

FIG. 6.—WHALE HEADS A. HEAD OF A SPERM WHALE FROM BELOW; B. HEAD OF A KOGIA WHALE FROM THE SIDE

Family 1.—*Physeteridae,* sperm whales. Teeth numerous in lower jaw, vestigial or absent in upper jaw in recent forms.

Physeter catodon, sperm whale (fig. C, p. 170; 63 ft.). Size gigantic; head immense, about one-third the total length; snout enormous, truncated, extended beyond the narrow, ventrally situated mouth (fig. 6, A); lower teeth 20–26 on each side, of great size, up to 4 lb. in weight, conical; about 8 pairs of smaller, often malformed, upper teeth; left nasal passage alone developed, the single blowhole curved, on the upper, left side of the snout, near its front end; dorsal fin reduced to a low hump, continued as a ridge towards the tail; colour black or brown all over, sometimes marked with white, especially in aged individuals. Male up to 63 ft., female not often exceeding 35 feet. The sperm whale occurs in all tropical waters, but stragglers, nearly always old males, reach both polar seas. It is polygamous, a school of females being accompanied by one or two large males. The sperm oil produced by this species is everywhere mixed with spermaceti, most of which is obtained from a receptacle, the case, occupying much of the snout, to the right of the single nasal passage, and capable of containing nearly 500 gal. of mixed oil and spermaceti. The sperm whale dives to a great depth, in pursuit of cuttlefish, its main food, though it also eats fishes. The case is supposed, by its buoyancy, to support the gigantic skull and to facilitate a rapid return to the surface. Ambergris is a morbid concretion of the intestine, commanding a high price.

Kogia, lesser sperm whale (about 10 ft.) resembles *Physeter* in general characters, except for the blowhole, which is located on top of the head, the single nasal passage, and the presence of a spermaceti organ; but the head (fig. 6, B) is relatively much smaller. Lower teeth, about 12 on each side, long, delicate, and curved; upper teeth wanting. Indian ocean and coasts of Australia, and recorded from eastern North America, Brittany and Holland.

Family 2.—*Ziphiidae,* beaked whales. Allied to the *Physeteridae* and producing sperm oil, but teeth much more reduced. A pair of longitudinal grooves in the throat region (fig. 9, A–C). Dorsal fin behind the middle of the body; tail (fig. 7, A) not notched at the junction of the flukes, flippers small; functional teeth (fig. 8, A, B) 1–2 pairs in the lower jaw, generally below the gum in females; minute vestiges of teeth may occur in either jaw. Food, cuttlefish. The rostrum becomes consolidated into a hard, bony mass in *Ziphius* and *Mesoplodon,* and these fragments are found in British late Tertiary deposits.

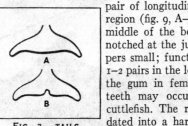

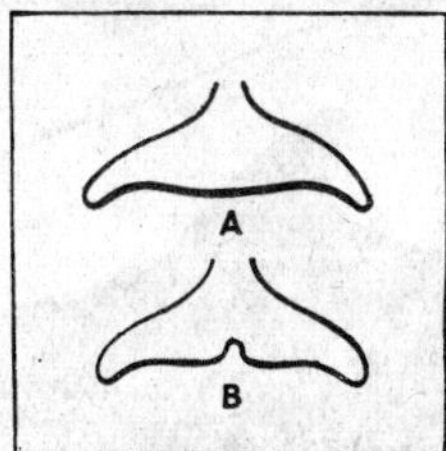

FIG. 7.—TAILS
A. Tail of Ziphioid
B. Tail of dolphin

Berardius has 2 pairs of large teeth at the front end of the lower jaw (fig. 8, A). *B. bairdi* (40 ft.), North Pacific, is the largest Ziphioid. *B. arnuxi,* New Zealand, Argentina, not uncommon in antarctic waters.

Ziphius cavirostris, Cuvier's whale (26 ft.) has one pair of teeth at the tip of the lower jaw, much more massive in males (fig. 5, A) than in females, in which they remain beneath the gum. Cosmopolitan, and not uncommon at certain times along the British coasts.

Hyperoodon rostratus, bottle-nosed whale (fig. E, p. 170; male, 31 ft.; female, 25 ft.). Teeth small, one pair (occasionally two pairs) at the tip of the lower jaw, alike in both sexes, remaining concealed till a late period, but then piercing the gum, at least in old males. Distinguished from *Ziphius* by a large bony crest on the upper side of each maxilla. With increasing age these crests become immense in the male, producing a notable alteration in the head, the forehead (fig. 9, B) becoming enormous and truncated. Common in the North Atlantic, where it has been extensively hunted to the north of Scotland; and frequently stranded on the British coasts, though rare in the eastern United States. *H. planifrons,* Australia, New Zealand and Argentina.

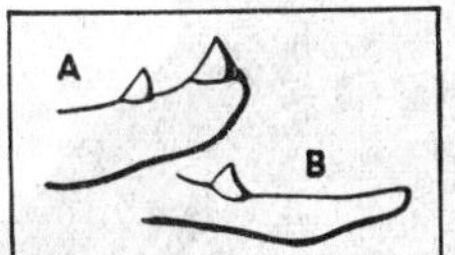

FIG. 8.—FRONT ENDS OF LOWER JAWS
A. Berardius
B. Mesoplodon bidens

Mesoplodon (fig. 9, C). Teeth, one pair (fig. 8, B), smaller in females and usually remaining beneath the gum, typically near the angle of the mouth, but in three species at the tip of the jaw. Of these, *M. mirus* has been stranded on the Irish coast; and *M. pacificus,* described in 1926 from a Queensland skull, appears to be about 25 ft. long, and would therefore be the largest *Mesoplodon. M. bidens,* Sowerby's whale (15 ft.), has its teeth in the typical position (fig. 8, B). Up to 1914 nearly half the records were British strandings, the others being from the Baltic to the eastern United States. *M. layardi,* of South Africa, Australia and New Zealand, has an extraordinary modification of its teeth, which curve over the beak, nearly meeting and preventing the mouth being opened to more than a small extent. *Mesoplodon* is oceanic, like other Ziphioids; but its species (about ten) appear to have a relatively restricted distribution.

Family 3.—*Platanistidae.* Inhabiting rivers or estuaries. Neck vertebrae larger than usual, not fused; pterygoid bones completely covering palatine bones on ventral aspect of skull; outer borders of maxillaries prolonged into incurved fanlike structures that largely roof over the facial depression; beak slender; flippers

BY COURTESY OF (M, O) THE TRUSTEES OF THE BRITISH MUSEUM; (N, Q) FROM "TRANSACTIONS," 1880 (ZOOLOGICAL SOCIETY OF LONDON); (P) LUTKEN, "VIDENSK SELSK, SKRIFTER" (DET KONGELIGE DANSKE VIDENSKABERNES SELSKAB, COPENHAGEN); (R, S) W. H. FLOWER IN "TRANSACTIONS" (ZOOLOGICAL SOCIETY OF LONDON); (U) R. COLLETT, "NORGES PATTEDYR" (H. ASCHEHOUG & CO., OSLO)

COMMON PORPOISE, WHITE WHALE AND TYPES OF DOLPHINS

M, Common Porpoise (after Harmer). N, Common Dolphin (after Flower). O, White-beaked Dolphin (after Harmer). P. Steno rostratus. Q, Commerson's Dolphin (after Harmer). R, Bottle-nosed Dolphin. S, Risso's Dolphin. T, Susu (after Anderson). U, White Whale

large and broad, with few phalanges. Food, fishes, captured by probing the mud with the long, narrow jaws, which have numerous teeth; as well as Crustacea and probably other small animals.

Platanista gangetica, Susu (fig. T, p. 172; 8 ft.). Blind; dorsal fin reduced; remarkable, large bony crests at the base of the rostrum. Teeth about 30 on either side of each jaw. Ganges, Indus and Brahmaputra, nearly to their head waters.

Family 4.—*Iniidae.* Inhabiting rivers and fresh-water lakes. Neck vertebrae large, not fused; pterygoid bones not completely covering palatine bones on ventral aspect of skull; maxillary with a more or less fenestrated process projecting backward freely below level of orbit; beak elongated; flippers large and broad. Food, mainly fishes.

Lipotes vexillifer (8 ft.), with a reduced dorsal fin, is whitish all over, its upper jaw curved upwards. Teeth about 32. Tung Ting lake, about 600 mi. from the mouth of the Yangtze Kiang river.

Inia geoffrensis (8 ft.), also with a reduced dorsal fin. The beak is covered with numerous short hairs, a primitive feature. Teeth, 26–32. Amazon river, from near its head waters.

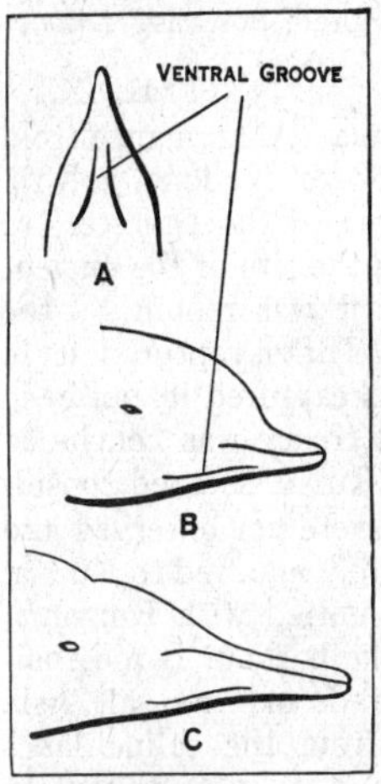

FIG. 9.—HEADS OF ZIPHIOIDS
A. Hyperoodon, young, from below
B. Hyperoodon, side view
C. Mesoplodon bidens, adult female

Family 5.—*Delphinidae,* dolphins (fig. 1) and porpoises. Dorsal fin present or absent; Tail (fig. 7, B) with a notch at the junction of the flukes.

Subfamily A.—*Delphininae.* Dorsal fin present, except as noted below. Fore flippers generally pointed and sickle-shaped. Neck vertebrae mostly fused with one another. Teeth (except *Gramphidelphis*) in both jaws, usually numerous. The numbers recorded below (on either side of each jaw) do not include the reduced teeth commonly found at the front end on both jaws below the gum. Alisphenoid not overspread by pterygoid and no external reduplication of pterygoid.

Delphinus delphis, common dolphin (fig. N, p. 172; 8 ft.). Beak about 5 in. long in middle line, separated from rest of head by a distinct groove (fig. 10, A), a character obvious in representations of this animal on Greek coins and elsewhere. Mainly black above and white below, the sides with longitudinal streaks of white, brown, yellow or gray. Palate of skull with two deep, longitudinal grooves. Teeth 40–50, diameter 3–3.5 millimetres. The "dolphins," which pursue flying fish and change colour when dying, are fishes (*Coryphaena*), not to be confused with the cetacean. Cosmopolitan, common in the Atlantic and Mediterranean, frequently stranded on the British coasts, but rarely on the east side of England. Food, fishes and cuttlefish. The stomach of a Mediterranean specimen was found by Dr. J. Schmidt to contain 15,191 otoliths (ear bones), indicating the recent consumption of more than 7,500 small fishes.

Stenella, with many species, often spotted or with longitudinal dark lines on the sides, is oceanic. Beak and teeth as in *Delphinus,* but palate of skull not grooved.

Lissodelphis peronii. Black and white, sharply delimited, the white including the flippers and continued past the mouth to the upper side of the "forehead." Dorsal fin wanting. Teeth as in *Delphinus.* Southern seas, with one record from New Guinea.

Lagenorhynchus. Beak short, usually distinct (fig. 10, B); sides generally with oblique light areas; upper and lower keels of root of tail strongly marked; vertebrae numerous, about 73–92. The two following British species, also found in eastern United States, reach 9 ft., the beak 2 in. long in the middle line:—*L. albirostris,* white-beaked dolphin (fig. O, p. 172); upper lip white; teeth 22–25, diameter 7 millimetres.—*L. acutus,* white-sided dolphin; upper lip black; very distinct light areas on the sides; teeth 30–34, diameter 4 millimetres. Other species in Indian, Pacific and Southern oceans.

Cephalorhynchus (fig. Q, p. 172). Small dolphins, about the size of the common porpoise, from southern seas, usually conspicuously coloured and without sharply marked beak. Teeth 25–31, small.

Steno rostratus (fig. P, p. 172; $8\frac{1}{2}$ ft.). Mainly dark, spotted with white; beak long, distinct; teeth 20–27, large, with slightly rugose crowns. Atlantic, Pacific and Indian oceans.

Sotalia. Resembling *Steno,* but teeth more numerous (up to 35), with smooth crowns. Species of *Sotalia* occur in fresh water in China (colour, milky white) and the Amazon. *S. tëuszii,* from the Cameroons, has been found to contain leaves, mangrove fruits, and grass in its stomach. Other species, from the tropical parts of the Indian and Atlantic oceans.

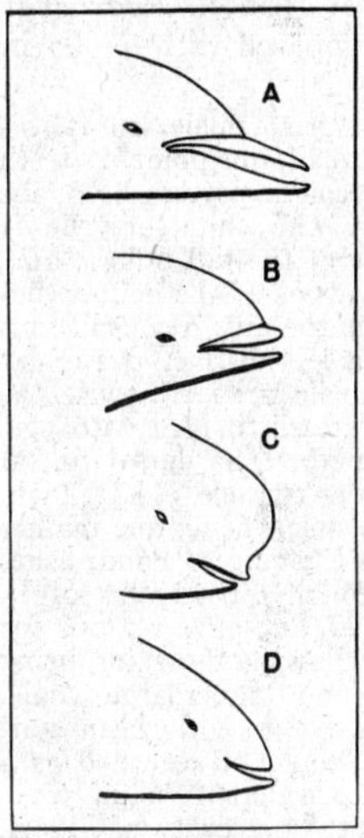

FIG. 10.—DOLPHIN HEADS
A. Delphinus
B. Lagenorhynchus
C. Globicephala
D. Phocoena

Tursiops. Beak rather longer than in *Lagenorhynchus,* teeth larger. *T. truncatus,* bottle-nosed dolphin (fig. R, p. 172; 10–11 ft.), is common in British seas and off the eastern United States. Dark above and white below; teeth 20–23, large, diameter 8.5–10 millimetres. Other species from the Mediterranean, Red sea, North Pacific, Australia and New Zealand. The natives of Moreton bay, Queensland, are said to co-operate with schools of dolphins (probably *Tursiops*) in beach fishing, the dolphins driving the fishes ashore and being rewarded for their assistance by fishes offered on the points of spears.

Gramphidelphis griseus, Risso's dolphin (fig. S, p. 172; 11 ft.). Nearly uniformly grayish; beak wanting, forehead prominent; flippers long; teeth completely absent in upper jaw (except for rare vestiges); lower teeth, 2–7, confined to the front end of the jaw, large, diameter 14 millimetres. Apparently cosmopolitan, reaching Britain and the eastern United States. "Pelorus Jack," an individual which was well known in New Zealand, a few years ago, from its habit of accompanying steamers in Pelorus sound, is believed to have belonged to this species.

Globicephala. Forehead greatly swollen and prominent (fig. 10, C); flippers specially long. *G. ventricosa,* pilot whale, blackfish or caa'ing whale (28 ft.) is black all over. Teeth 7–11, large, diameter 10–11 mm., at the front end of the jaws. Large schools have frequently been driven ashore, 1,540 individuals having been killed in two hours, in 1845, at the Shetland Islands. It is known that 117,456 individuals were captured at the Faeroe Islands between 1584 and 1883. Both sides of the Atlantic and in the Pacific, Indian ocean and southern seas.

Pseudorca crassidens, false killer (19 ft.). Teeth 8–10, almost as large as those of the killer; black all over, flippers narrow. Originally described by Owen from a subfossil skeleton from the Lincolnshire fens. Two skeletons have recently been found in the Cambridgeshire fens. A school of more than 100 specimens was stranded in the Bay of Kiel in 1861, and a school of about 150 on the east coast of Scotland in 1927. It is said to occur in large parties off New Zealand and Tasmania, and it has been recorded from India, Queensland, both sides of North America and Argentina.

Orcella brevirostris (7 ft.). Head as in *Gramphidelphis,* dorsal fin low; rostrum of skull very short; teeth 12–14, small. Ascends the Irrawaddy river, Burma, to 900 miles from the sea, and occurs in the Bay of Bengal, and off Singapore and Borneo.

Phocoena and the two following have teeth with an expanded, spade-shaped crown, differing from the conical teeth of other dolphins. *P. phocoena,* common porpoise (fig. M, p. 172; $5\frac{1}{2}$ ft.), is black above and white below, with some variation. Head short, without beak (fig. 10, D), dorsal fin triangular, commonly with small, horny tubercles on its front edge. Male reproductive opening unusually far forward, below the dorsal fin; teeth 22–26. The porpoise was formerly much in request as an article of diet, and there were important fisheries off Normandy and at the entrance to the Baltic. It frequents coasts and often ascends rivers. It is specially characteristic of the Atlantic coasts, on both sides, and it reaches the Azores. The porpoise of the Black sea and eastern Mediterranean has been considered distinct. Other species from South America.

Neomeris. Resembles *Phocoena* in having skin tubercles, but has no dorsal fin. Teeth 16–21. India and Japan (marine); Tung Ting lake and other parts of the Yangtze Kiang, hundreds of miles from the sea.

Phocoenoides, with two species from the North Pacific, also has skin tubercles. Teeth 19–22, much smaller than in *Phocoena;* vertebrae specially numerous, 95–98, as compared with 64–67 in *Phocoena phocoena.*

Grampus orca, killer or grampus (male 31 ft.; female, 16 ft.).—Beak wanting; dorsal fin large; flippers very broad, not pointed; teeth exceptionally large and strong, diameter 2 in.; colour-pattern bold, the black and light parts sharply delimited (fig. 1). The white (or yellow) extends over the lower jaw and the lower side of the tail flukes; and, just behind the dorsal fin, is produced backwards as a lobe defined below by a tongue of black passing forwards from the tail; a conspicuous white area, above and behind the eye; and a less distinct triangular mark behind and below the dorsal fin. The male is nearly twice the length of the female and all its fins increase greatly in size with age, to an extent disproportionate to the body length. The dorsal fin, at first recurved as in the female, becomes an erect triangle 5½ ft. high. The flippers reach a size of 6x4 ft., their enlargement being due mainly to the inordinate growth of the cartilage of the phalanges. Food, fishes and marine mammals and birds. Eschricht found the remains of 13 porpoises and 14 seals in the stomach of a killer, and gave reasons for believing that seals are flayed after being swallowed, the skins being then disgorged. The story that killers combine to attack a large whale, forcing its mouth open and eating the tongue, has recently been confirmed by R. C. Andrews. Although a killer should be regarded as a dangerous animal there seems to be little evidence that it willingly attacks man. The motive for a combined assault, by a party of killers, on an ice floe, as recorded in *Scott's Last Voyage,* may have been the capture of the dogs (mistaken for seals), and not of the man. *G. orca,* if all killers belong to one species, is cosmopolitan, extending from pole to pole, though it is apparently not often found in the tropics. It is not uncommon in British and American waters.

Feresa. Relatively little is known regarding this porpoise.

Subfamily B.—*Stenodelphinae.* Dorsal fin present; neck vertebrae free; flippers broad and bluntly rounded distally; beak slender. Teeth, 58–62 on either side of upper and lower jaws, of normal delphine type. Alisphenoid overspread by pterygoid; external and internal reduplications of pterygoid large.

Stenodelphis (or *Pontoporia*) *blainvillii* (5 ft.). Dorsal fin well developed; jaws long and delicate; teeth 50–60. La Plata estuary.

Subfamily C.—*Monodontinae.* No dorsal fin; neck vertebrae free; flippers broad. Teeth tusklike in manner of growth, reduced to one or two forward projecting tusks. Alisphenoid not overspread by pterygoid; no external reduplication of pterygoid.

Monodon monoceros, narwhal (fig. D, p. 170; 15–20 ft.). Adult grayish-white, with leopardlike spots, sometimes whitish when old; young unspotted; teeth unlike those of any other animal, reduced (except for vestiges in the foetus) to a single upper pair. In females these remain concealed in the bone, but the left one exceptionally develops as in the male. The right tooth of the male remains similarly concealed, but the left tooth, the horn of the traditional Unicorn, grows spirally to an enormous length, up to 9 ft., 4½ in., projecting forwards from the upper lip. In rare cases the asymmetry may be reversed, the right tooth becoming the tusk; or the animal has two tusks, about equally developed. One or two "bidental" specimens have been recorded as female, but further evidence on the sex is required. Arctic, rarely reaching Britain. Large numbers of narwhals are killed by the Eskimos in certain parts of Greenland, where the males protrude their tusks through holes in the ice when they rise to breathe.

Subfamily D.—*Delphinapterinae.* Dorsal fin wanting; neck vertebrae free; flippers broad; dermis of skin more developed than usual. Teeth tusklike in manner of growth; not more than ten teeth on either side of upper jaws, and eight in lower jaws. Alisphenoid overspread by pterygoids; reduplications of pterygoids small. Food, mainly cuttlefish, but also fishes.

Delphinapterus leucas, white whale or Beluga (fig. U, p. 172; 18 ft.). Adult pure white all over, young dark brown-gray; teeth 8–10, diameter 20 millimetres. Arctic and circumpolar, reaching the St. Lawrence and (rarely) the British coast. Formerly hunted on a large scale.

BIBLIOGRAPHY.—*General works.* F. E. Beddard, *A Book of Whales* (1900); J. T. Jenkins, *History of the Whale Fisheries* (1921); K. A. von Zittel, *Text-book of Palaeontology,* vol. iii (1925); H. Winge, "Interrelationships of Cetacea," *Smithson. Misc. Coll.* lxxii, No. 8 (1921); G. S. Miller, Jr., "The Telescoping of the Cetacean Skull," *Smithson. Misc. Coll.,* lxxvi, No. 5 (1923); *Whaling.*—W. Scoresby, *Account of the Arctic Regions* (Edinburgh, 1820); R. C. Andrews, *Whale Hunting with Gun and Camera* (1916); *Rep. Interdepartmental Comm. Dependencies of Falkland Islands,* 1920, Stationery Office, Cmd. 657; S. Risting, *Av Hvalfangstens Historie* (History of Whaling) (Oslo, 1922). *Special works.*—F. W. True, "Whalebone Whales of W. North Atlantic," *Smithson. Contr.* xxxiii (1904); G. M. Allen, "Whalebone Whales of New England," *Mem. Bost. Soc. Nat. Hist.,* viii, No. 2, p. 105 (Boston, Mass., 1916); R. C. Andrews, "California Grey Whale," *Mem. Amer. Mus. Nat. Hist.,* N.S., i, part 5, p. 227 (1914), and "Sei Whale," *ibid.;* part 6, p. 289 (1916); F. W. True, "Review of the Delphinidae," *Bull. U.S. Nat. Mus.,* No. 36 (1889); S. F. Harmer, *British Cetacea Stranded 1913–1926,* Brit. Mus. Nat. Hist. (1927); R. Collett, *Norges Pattedyr* (Norwegian Mammals), p. 543 (Oslo, 1911–12); E. J. Slijper, *Die cetaceen vergleichend-anatomisch und systematisch; ein beitrag zur vergleichenden anatomie des blutgefäss-, nerven- und muskelsystems, sowie des rumpfskelettes der säugetiere, mit studien über die theorie des aussterbens und der foetalisation* (The Hague, 1936); R. Kellogg, "The History of Whales—Their Adaptation to Life in the Water," *Quart. Rev. Biol.,* vol. 3, no. 1, pp. 29–76, no. 2, pp. 174–208 (1928); *idem, A Review of the Archaeoceti,* Carnegie Inst., Washington, publ. 482, pp. xv–366 (1936); *idem,* "Adaptation of Structure to Function in Whales," Carnegie Inst., Washington, publ. 501, pp. 649–82 (1938); *idem,* "Whales, Giants of the Sea," *Nat. Geog. Mag.,* vol. 77, no. 1, pp. 35–90 (1940); N. A. Mackintosh and J. F. G. Wheeler, "Southern Blue and Fin whales," *Discovery Reports,* Cambridge, vol. 1, pp. 257–540 (1929); L. Harrison Matthews, "The Humpback Whale, Megaptera nodosa," *Discovery Reports,* Cambridge, vol. 17, pp. 7–92 (1937); *idem,* "The Sperm Whale, Physeter catodon," *Discovery Reports,* Cambridge, vol. 17, pp. 93–168 (1938); *idem,* "The Sei Whale, Balaenoptera borealis," *Discovery Reports,* Cambridge, vol. 17, pp. 183–290 (1938).

(S. F. H.; X.)

CETATEA ALBA, a town of Rumania (Akkerman, in old Slav, *Byelgorod, i.e.,* white town) in lat. 46° 12′ N., long. 30° 19′ E., on the right bank of the estuary (liman) of the Dniester, 12 mi. from the Black sea. The town stands on the site of the ancient Milesian colony of Tyras. Centuries later it was rebuilt by the Genoese and named Mauro Castro. The Turks captured it in 1484. In 1770, 1774 and 1806 the Russians captured it, but each time returned it to the Turks. In 1826 a treaty was concluded there between Russia and the Porte, when Russia secured considerable advantages: the terms of the treaty were not observed and war broke out in 1828. In 1881 it was definitely annexed to Russia, but in March 1918, when Bessarabia was united with Rumania, Cetatea Alba became a Rumanian town. The harbour is too shallow to admit large vessels, but there is a trade in wine, salt, fish, wool and tallow. The salt is obtained from the saline lakes (limans) in the neighbourhood. The town and its suburbs contain beautiful gardens and vineyards. It is surrounded by ramparts and commanded by a citadel. Pop. (1930) 33,495. Rumania ceded the town, with Bessarabia, to the U.S.S.R. in June 1940, but regained it in 1941 during the German invasion of the soviet union.

CETHEGUS, the name of a Roman patrician family of the Cornelian gens. Two individuals are of some importance:—

(1) MARCUS CORNELIUS CETHEGUS, pontifex maximus and curule aedile, 213 B.C. In 211, as praetor, he had charge of Apulia; later, he was sent to Sicily, where he proved a successful administrator. In 209 he was censor, and in 204 consul. In 203 he was proconsul in Upper Italy, where, in conjunction with the praetor P. Quintilius Varus, he defeated Mago, Hannibal's brother, in Insubrian territory, and obliged him to leave Italy. He died in 196. He had a great reputation as an orator, and is characterized by Ennius as "the quintessence of persuasiveness" (*suadae medulla*). Horace (*Ars Poët.* 50; *Epistles,* ii, 2. 117) calls him an authority on the use of Latin words.

See Livy xxv, 2; 41, xxvii, 11, xxix, 11, xxx, 18.

(2) GAIUS CORNELIUS CETHEGUS, the boldest of Catiline's associates, joined the conspiracy in the hope of getting his debts cancelled. When Catiline left Rome in 63 B.C., Cethegus remained behind as leader of the conspirators with P. Lentulus Sura. He undertook to murder Cicero and other prominent men, but was hampered by the dilatoriness of Sura. He was condemned to death, and executed, with Sura and others, on the night of Dec. 5.

See Sallust, *Catilina,* 46–55; Cicero, *In Cat.* iii, 5–7; Appian, *Bell. Civ.* ii, 2–5; *see* also CATILINE.

CETINA, GUTIERRE DE (1518?–1572?), Spanish poet and soldier, was born at Seville. He served under Charles V in Italy and Germany, but retired from the army in 1545 to settle in Seville. Soon afterwards, however, he sailed for Mexico, where he spent most of the rest of his life. He was killed in a street brawl in Los Angeles. A follower of Boscan and Garcilaso de la Vega, Cetina adopted the doctrines of the Italian school and, under the name of Vandalio, wrote an extensive series of poems in the newly introduced metres; his sonnets are remarkable for elegance of form, but his other productions are mostly adaptations from Petrarch, Ariosto and Ludovico Dolce. His works have been well edited by Joaquín Hazañas y la Rúa (Seville, 1895).

See A. M. Withers, ***The Sources of the Poetry of Gutierre de Cetina,*** etc. (1923).

CETINJE (Serbian, *Tsetinye*), capital of former kingdom of Montenegro, Yugoslavia, in a narrow plain deep in the limestone mountains, 2,068 ft. above the sea. Pop. (1931) 6,367. On one peak stands the white dynastic tomb erected by its last ruler, and on another the old bell tower formerly used for the heads of Turks. The country is bare and stony, with cultivated rich red soil in rock crevices. Winter snow and spring and autumn floods make communications difficult. Cetinje contains two parallel streets of whitewashed cottages, connected by smaller ones; the church (1478) of a fortified monastery, visited by pilgrims to the tomb of Peter I (1782–1830); the old palace, the residence of the late King Nicholas and his heir; the court of appeal; a school; barracks; a seminary for priests and teachers, established by the tsar Alexander II (1855–81); a library and reading room; a theatre; a museum; a hospital; a bank, and a war memorial. The girls' school founded by the tsaritsa Marie was closed in 1913. Near the old palace stood the celebrated plane tree beneath which Prince Nicholas gave audience until the end of the 19th century. Near the modern palace, in a glass house, guarded by a sentry, is a contour map of the country, some 60 ft. long, on which every fort, town, village, road and stream is depicted. A zigzag highway, a triumph of engineering, winds through the mountain passes between Cetinje and Cattaro, passing the impregnable Mt. Lovčen. Here Peter II (1830–51), the poet ruler, is buried. He introduced a prison and a printing press, but the latter was soon melted down for bullets. There is little trade, though mineral waters are manufactured. Cetinje owes its origin to Ivan the Black, who was forced in 1484 to withdraw from Zhabliak, his former capital. In 1941, with the dismemberment of Yugoslavia, the town and the whole of Montenegro came under Italian control.

CETTE (SÈTE), a seaport of southern France in the department of Hérault, 18 mi. S.W. of Montpellier, at the junction of the P.L.M. and Midi railways. Pop. (1936) 35,306. After Marseille it is the principal commercial port on the south coast of France. The port was created in 1666 by the agency of Colbert, minister of Louis XIV, and according to the plans of Vauban; toward the end of the 17th century its development was aided by the opening of the Canal du Midi. The older part of Cette occupies the foot and slope of the isolated Mont St. Clair (590 ft.), situated on a tongue of land between the Mediterranean and the lagoon of Thau. This well-built quarter is bounded on the east by the Canal de Cette, which leads from the lagoon of Thau to the Old Basin and the outer harbour. Across the canal lie the newer quarters, which chiefly occupy two islands separated from each other by a wet dock and bounded on the east by the Canal Maritime, parallel to the Canal de Cette. A lateral canal unites the northern ends of the two main canals. A huge breakwater protects the entrance to the harbour, which is one of the safest in France. The outer port and the Old Basin (the fishing harbour) are enclosed by a mole to the south and by a jetty to the east. Behind the outer port lies an inner basin which communicates with the Canal Maritime. The entire area of the harbour, including the canals, is 111 acres with a quayage length of more than 8,000 yards. The public institutions of Cette include tribunals of commerce and of maritime commerce, councils of arbitration in commercial and fishing affairs, an exchange and chamber of commerce. Cette is much resorted to for sea bathing. The town is connected with Lyons by the canal from the Rhône to Cette, and with Bordeaux by the Canal du Midi. The shipping trade is carried on with South America, the chief ports of the Mediterranean, and especially with Spain. The chief exports are wines, brandy and chemical products; the chief imports are coal, timber, petroleum and chemical substances. Small craft are employed in the sardine, tunny, cod and other fisheries. Shellfish are obtained from the lagoon of Thau. There are factories for the pickling of sardines, for the manufacture of liqueurs and casks, and for the treatment of sulphur, phosphates and nitrate of soda. The Schneider company of Creusot also have metallurgical works at Cette, and there are wire-making establishments.

CETUS ("The Whale"), in astronomy, a constellation of the southern hemisphere, fabled by the Greeks to be the monster sent by Neptune to devour Andromeda, but which was slain by Perseus. It contains the long-period variable star Mira Ceti (*o* Ceti), which was the first star recognized to be variable (by Fabricius in 1596). It usually ranges from the ninth to the third magnitude in about 340 days; but this kind of variation is always rather irregular. It has recently been found to have a companion distant rather less than a second of arc. The companion was first suspected from spectroscopic observations; when looked for visually it was easily seen, but it is difficult to understand why it had escaped notice in a star which was so continually studied. The companion is itself a very interesting star, possessing an unusual type of spectrum with bright lines. (A. S. E.)

CETYWAYO (d. 1884), king of the Zulus, was the eldest son of King Umpande or Panda and a nephew of the two previous kings, Dingaan and Chaka. Cetywayo was a young man when in 1840 his father was placed on the throne by the aid of the Natal Boers; and three years later Natal became a British colony. Cetywayo had inherited much of the military talent of his uncle Chaka, the organizer of the Zulu military system, and chafed under his father's peaceful policy towards his British and Boer neighbours. Suspecting Panda of favouring a younger son, Umbulazi, as his successor, Cetywayo made war on his brother, whom he defeated and slew at a great battle on the banks of the Tugela in Dec. 1856. In the following year, at an assembly of the Zulus, the management of the affairs of the nation was entrusted to Cetywayo, though the old chief kept the title of king. Cetywayo was, however, suspicious of the Natal government, which afforded protection to two of his brothers. The feeling of distrust was removed in 1861 by a visit from Theophilus Shepstone, secretary for native affairs in Natal, who induced Panda to proclaim Cetywayo publicly as the future king. Friendly relations were then maintained between the Zulus and Natal for many years. In 1872 Panda died and Cetywayo was declared king, Aug. 1873, in the presence of Shepstone, to whom he made promises to live at peace with his neighbours and to govern his people more humanely. These promises were not kept. Cetywayo's attitude became menacing; he allowed a minor chief to make raids into the Transvaal, and seized natives within the Natal border.

Sir Bartle Frere, who became high commissioner of South Africa in March 1877, was convinced that the Kafir revolt of that year on the eastern border of Cape Colony was part of a design or desire "for a general and simultaneous rising of Kafirdom against white civilization"; and in Dec. 1878 Frere sent the Zulu king an ultimatum, which, while awarding him the territory he claimed from the Boers, required him to make reparation for the outrages committed within the British borders, to receive a British resident, to disband his regiments, and to allow his young men to marry without the necessity of having first "washed their spears." Cetywayo, who had found a defender in Bishop Colenso, vouchsafed no reply, and Lord Chelmsford entered Zululand, at the head of 13,000 troops, on Jan. 11, 1879, to enforce the British demands. After the initial disaster of Isandhlwana and the defense of Rorke's Drift the Zulus were utterly routed at Ulundi (July 4). Cetywayo became a fugitive, but was captured on Aug. 28. His kingdom was divided among 13 chiefs and he himself taken to Capetown, whence he was brought to London in Aug. 1882. While he was in England the Gladstone government decided upon his restoration. Restoration, however, proved to refer only to a portion of his old kingdom. Even there one of his kinsmen and chief enemies, Usibepu, was allowed to retain the territory allotted to him in 1879. Cetywayo was reinstalled on Jan. 29, 1883, by Shepstone, but his enemies, headed by Usibepu, attacked him within a week, and after a struggle of nearly a year's duration he was defeated and his kraal destroyed. He then took refuge in the native reserve, where he died at Ekowe, on Feb. 8, 1884.

His son Dinizulu was exiled to St. Helena (1889–98), and was then allowed to return home and become a chief. He was arrested in Dec. 1907 for alleged complicity in a Zulu revolt, and in Nov. 1908 was tried before a special court. His defense was undertaken by Mr. W. P. Schreiner. The charge of treason was not proved, but he was convicted of harbouring rebels and sentenced to four years' imprisonment.

The Life of Sir Bartle Frere, by John Martineau, vol. ii, ch. 18 to 21, contains much information concerning Cetywayo.

CEUTA (Arabic SEBTA), a Spanish military and convict station and seaport on the north coast of Morocco, in 35° 54′ N., 5° 18′ W. Pop. (census, 1945) 60,353. It is situated on a promontory connected with the mainland by a narrow isthmus, and marking the southeastern end of the Straits of Gibraltar, which between Ceuta and Gibraltar have a width of 14 miles. The promontory terminates in a bold headland, the Montagne des Singes, with seven peaks, of which the highest, the Monte del Hacko—the ancient Ablya, one of the "Pillars of Hercules"—rises 636 ft. above the sea.

Ceuta occupies in part the site of a Carthaginian colony, which was succeeded by a Roman colony said to have been called *Ad Septem Fratres* and also *Exilissa* or *Lissa Civitas.* From the Romans the town passed to the Vandals and afterward to Byzantium, the emperor Justinian restoring its fortifications in 535. In 618 the town, then known as Septon, fell into the hands of the Visigoths. It was the last stronghold in North Africa which held out against the Arabs. At that date (A.D. 711) the governor was Count Julian, who, to avenge a family wrong, invited the Arabs to conquer Spain. The Arabs called the town Cibta or Sebta, hence the Spanish form, Ceuta. It was repeatedly captured by rival Berber and Spanish-Moorish dynasties but became, nevertheless, an important industrial and commercial city, being noted for its brassware and its trade in ivory, gold and slaves. It is said to have been the first place in the west where a paper manufactory was established. In 1415 the town was captured by the Portuguese. It passed to Spain in 1580 on the subjugation of Portugal by Philip II, and was definitely assigned to the Spanish crown by the Treaty of Lisbon in 1688. The town has been several times unsuccessfully besieged by the Moors, one siege, under Mulai Ismail, lasting 26 years (1694–1720). In 1810, with the consent of Spain, it was occupied by British troops, but was restored to Spain at the close of the Napoleonic Wars. Its territory was enlarged after the war between Spain and Morocco in 1860.

Ceuta consists of two quarters, the old town, covering the low ground of the isthmus, and the modern town, built on the hills forming the north and west faces of the peninsula. Between the old and new quarters, and on the north side of the isthmus, lies the port. The fortifications date from the Portuguese occupation. For civil purposes Ceuta is attached to the province of Cadiz. It is a free port. Trade increased markedly during World War II.

CEVA, TOMASSO (1648–1736), Italian mathematician, was born at Milan on Dec. 20, 1648. He taught mathematics at the Jesuit college in Milan, and was a member of the order. While at the Brera college he co-operated with Saccheri in a number of mathematical researches. In 1678 Ceva published some work containing the theorem which is known by his name and which deals with the concurrency of straight lines through the vertices of a triangle. He died at Milan on Feb. 3, 1736.

CEVA, a town of Piedmont, Italy, province of Cuneo, 33 mi. E. by rail from the town of Cuneo, on the line to Savona, 1,270 ft. above sea level. Pop. (1951) 5,567 (commune). The mediaeval fortress (defending the confines of Piedmont toward Liguria) was destroyed by the French in 1800, after cession to them in 1796. Cevan cheese (*caseus cebanus*) was famous in Roman times. A branch railway runs from Ceva through Garessio, with its marble quarries, to Ormea (2,398 ft.), 22 mi. to the south through the upper valley of the Tanaro. From Ormea a road runs south to (31 mi.) Oneglia on the Ligurian coast.

CÉVENNES, a mountain range of southern France, forming the south and east fringe of the Plateau Central and part of the watershed between Atlantic and Mediterranean basins. It consists of a narrow ridge some 320 mi. long, with numerous lofty plateaux and secondary ranges branching from it. The northern division, nowhere over 3,320 ft., is called the mountains of Charollais, Beaujolais and Lyonnais, from the Col de Longpendu (west of Châlon-sur-Saône) in a southerly direction to the Col de Gier. The central Cévennes, comprising the volcanic chain of Vivarais, incline southwest and extend as far as the Lozère group. The northern portion of this chain forms the Boutières range. Farther south it includes the Gerbier des Joncs (5,089 ft.), the Mont de Mézenc (5,750 ft.), the culminating point of the entire range, and the Tanargue group. South of Mont Lozère, where the Pic Finiels reaches 5,584 ft., lies the range strictly called the Cévennes. This region stretches south to include the Aigoual and Espérou groups. Under various local names (the Garrigues, the mountains of Espinouse and Lacaune) and with numerous offshoots, the range extends southwest and then west to the Montagne Noire. In the south, the Cévennes separate the barren region of the Causses from sunny Languedoc, where olive, vine and mulberry flourish. Northward the contrast between the two slopes is less striking.

The Cévennes proper are a folded belt of Palaeozoic rocks along the southeast border of the central plateau of France. Concealed in part by later deposits, these folds extend from Castelnaudary to near Valence, where they sink suddenly beneath the Tertiary and recent deposits of the Rhône valley. Rocks from Cambrian to Carboniferous are included in the folded belt, and the gneiss and schist which form so much of the chain consist, in part at least, of metamorphosed Cambrian beds. The structure is complicated by extensive overthrusting from the southeast. The principal folding is of Hercynian age. Permian and later beds lie unconformably upon the denuded folds, and in the space between the Montagne Noire and the Cévennes proper the folded belt is buried beneath the horizontal Jurassic strata of the Causses. Folding was renewed along the southeast margin at the close of the Eocene period. The Secondary and Tertiary beds of Languedoc were crushed against the central plateau and were frequently overfolded, but the ancient Palaeozoic chain acted as part of the unyielding massif, and the folding did not extend beyond its foot.

The Cévennes form the watershed between the basins of the Loire and the Garonne to the west and those of the Saône and Rhône to the east. In the south the Orb, the Hérault and the Vidourle flow directly into the Gulf of Lyons; farther north, the Gard, the Cèze and the Ardèche flow to the Rhône. The Vivarais mountains and the northern Cévennes approach the right banks of the Rhone and Saône closely, and short torrents flow down to those rivers; on the west side the streams are tributaries of the Loire, which rises at the foot of Mont Mézenc. A short distance to the south on the same side are the sources of the Allier and Lot. The waters of the northwestern slope of the southern Cévennes drain into the Tarn. In the Lozère group and the southern Cévennes generally, is good summer pasturage for huge flocks. Silkworm-rearing and the cultivation of peaches, chestnuts and other fruits are also carried on. In the Vivarais cattle are reared, while on the slopes of the Beaujolais are flourishing vineyards.

CEYLON, a large island in the Indian ocean and a self-governing member of the Commonwealth of Nations. It is 272 mi. long and 140 mi. wide at its broadest part and has an area of 25,332 sq.mi., about half the size of England. It lies between 5° 55′ and 9° 50′ N. and between 79° 42′ and 81° 52′ E., and is situated southeast of Cape Cormorin in India, from which it is separated by the 30-mi.-wide Palk strait.

Physical Features.—Except for a few rocky promontories, such as at Trincomalee, the low coast of Ceylon is subject to erosion, although a coral reef a few hundred yards out to sea prevents serious damage. The coast is beset on the northwest by shoals and rocks, and the island of Mannar (Manaar), which forms an integral part of Ceylon, is almost joined to the Indian mainland by a chain of sandy islets known as Adam's Bridge, just north of which a daily ferry service runs from Talaimannar to Dhanushkodi on the Indian coast. The west coast, from Puttalam southward, and the whole of the south coast are fringed by coconut palms which grow to the water's edge; but the east coast is more rugged and, except along a short stretch north and south of Bat-

PHOTOGRAPHS, (1, 3, 4, 5) WERNER COHNITZ-PIX, (2) DEANE DICKASON FROM EWING GALLOWAY

THE CITIES OF CEYLON

1. Dutch church in the fortified town of Jaffna built in 1705, during the Netherlands occupation
2. Clock tower and lighthouse in the "Fort" or business quarter of Colombo, the capital
3. An elaborate mosque in Colombo
4. Rickshas and motor cars go side by side on the streets of Colombo
5. Gateway of the ancient fort in Galle, a seaport on the south coast

CEYLON

PHOTOGRAPHS, (1, 2) FRITZ HENLE, (3-6) WERNER COHNITZ-PIX

NATIVE OCCUPATIONS IN CEYLON

1. An outrigger fishing canoe drawn up on the beach
2. Ox-drawn carts in Ceylon
3. Labourers unloading coconuts on a plantation
4. Villagers filling a water cart from a well
5. Sinhalese and Taniel rubber tappers reporting for work on a rubber plantation
6. Loading crates of tea for export at the docks of Colombo

ticaloa, the palms of the south and west are replaced by scrub jungle starting at high-water mark. Round the northern and northwestern end of the island palmyra palms grow on the low shores and, where cultivation is absent, scrub jungle is found. Deep water is usually available close to the reef, though there are a few dangerous rocks well known to navigators.

The centre of the broad southern end of Ceylon consists of a mountain massif, covering about 4,000 sq.mi. and known as Up Country, in contrast with the Low Country or surrounding coastal plain from which, about 45 to 60 mi. inland, rise the foothills. This massif intercepts the rains of both monsoons, or periods of more or less constant wind, bringing rain from the southwest during the period April to September, and from the northeast from October to March. Thus April to September constitutes the wet season in the southwest and the dry season in the northeast, whereas conversely October to March is the dry season in the southwest and the wet season in the northeast.

Although the two monsoons form the main feature in the Ceylon climate, the factors of total annual rainfall and elevation above sea level also have the effect of creating a wet and a dry zone, quite distinct from the monsoons or seasons. As a result of these phenomena the mountains, with the western plain, comprise the wet zone, where the annual rainfall in places reaches 200 in., and the vegetation, both cultivated and natural, differs entirely from that of the northern and eastern plains, which form the dry zone, with an average rainfall of less than 50 in. a year.

Among the 150 mountains, ranging in height from 3,000 to 7,400 ft., the most famous, because of its religious associations, is Adam's Peak (7,360 ft.), but the highest summit is Pidurutalagala (8,274 ft.) near the highland health resort of Nuwara Eliya (6,000 ft.), where the temperature is cool, with frost at night in December and January, but no snow or natural ice.

R. H. BASSETT, C.M.G., C.B.E.
THE TISSAMAHARAMA DAGOBA. DAGOBAS ARE HEMISPHERICAL STRUCTURES BUILT WITH BRICKS, AND USUALLY CONTAIN A RELIC OF THE LORD BUDDHA, OR OF A BUDDHIST SAINT

The climate of the Low Country is hot, particularly from March to May, the average mean temperature ranging from 79° to 82° F., combined with a high degree of humidity in the wet zone. The length of the day does not vary more than an hour at any season because of the proximity of Ceylon to the equator. Colombo is situated in 79° 50′ 45″ E., and the day is further advanced there than at Greenwich by 5 hr. 19 min. 23 sec.

The largest river in Ceylon, the Mahaveli, draining the eastern slopes of the mountains, falls into the sea near Trincomalee after a 206-mi. course which, like that of all rivers in Ceylon, is navigable by small boats only in its lower reaches because of rapids upstream. The next largest river is the Malwatte (104 mi.) or Aruvi (Tamil), which reaches the west coast at Arippu, just south of Mannar. No other river in Ceylon is 100 mi. long, but the Deduru, Kelani and Kalu, all of considerable size, drain the western slopes, with the Walawe and Gin flowing to the south.

Flora.—The species of plants in Ceylon number between 3,000 and 4,000. Their distribution varies a great deal according to the rainfall. Equatorial rain forest is predominant in the hill country, except where it has been replaced by tea or rubber, and xerophytic jungle and scrub in the dry parts of the east and north. There are open tracts of grassland called *patanas* in the drier areas of the hill country, and in the lowlands to the east are some regions of richer grassland.

Round the coast the mangrove grows on muddy shores, screw pines (*Pandanus ceylanicus* and *P. tectorius*) where it is sandy, coconuts and other palms along the southwest and south coasts and palmyra palms in the north. The forests of the wet zone grow much higher than in the dry and produce certain valuable woods such as *nedum* and calamander. Among the many beautiful varieties of flowering trees are the flame tree, tulip tree, golden shower (*Cassia fistula*), *Datura fastuosa* and *Amherstia nobilis*. At the high elevations orchids flourish, in particular the Wesak orchid (*Dendrobium MacCarthiae*), and the trees become lower and flat-topped with rhododendrons much in evidence. In the dry zone there is much low scrub jungle and, farther inland, forests with valuable timber such as satinwood, ebony and milla.

Beside the Low Country jungle streams huge kumbuk trees grow, while everywhere there are climbing plants and epiphytes of many kinds, among them the brilliant orange-red *Gloriosa superba*. The jak tree, euphorbias, cacti, guava and castor oil are among the plants found almost all over the island. On pools and abandoned tanks East Indian lotus (*Nelumbo nucifera*) is often seen. Colombo is famous for its flowering trees, and in March and April Ceylon is prolific in flowers of all kinds, including almost all those grown in English gardens. Up Country gardens produce many English vegetables. The herbaceous plants of the dry zone belong largely to the families Leguminoseae, Acanthaceae and Scrophulariaceae.

Fauna.—The density of highly civilized population round Colombo in the southwest makes it easy to forget that two-thirds of Ceylon is under thick jungle, inhabited principally by wild animals which, however, find it increasingly difficult to survive in spite of the protection afforded by the game department and the society for the protection of fauna.

The most interesting and important animal in Ceylon is the elephant, a subspecies of the Indian form, seldom developing tusks, which, after it has been domesticated, is largely used for haulage of timber where there are no roads and for handling heavy weights in construction work. Elephants, adorned with sumptuous cloths and trappings, also play a prominent part in religious processions, carrying the sacred Buddhist relics. Though much scarcer than when the island was still almost uncleared of jungle, there are still a number of herds of wild elephants in the forests from which recruits to the ranks of domestic elephants are taken. The herd is shepherded into a kraal or stockade by means of a gradually enveloping drive, carried out by hundreds of men over a period of several weeks. Once inside the stockade the wild elephants are noosed by the hind legs and tied to trees, an operation requiring both skill and courage. The recruit, after his excitement has subsided, is then led away by two tame elephants, from whom he soon learns his duties and becomes a useful work animal.

The small domestic cattle are hardy and are capable of drawing heavy loads in single- or double-yoked carts, but they are usually rather underfed because of lack of good pasture and therefore are neither good milk producers nor fat for eating.

The water buffalo (*Bubalus bubalis*) is common, both tame and, in the more distant jungles, wild. Domestic buffaloes are used to plow rice fields and to tread out grain, but otherwise lead a semiwild life, except for a small number kept in dairies.

Ceylon possesses four kinds of deer: the sambar or "Ceylon elk" (*Cervus unicolor*); the spotted deer (*Axis axis*); the barking deer (*Muntiacus muntjak*); and the hog deer (*Axis porcinus*), now almost extinct in Ceylon. A little chevrotain, the mouse deer (*Tragulus meminna*), is common. There are no antelopes.

Three species of monkeys are found: the small brown toque monkey (*Macaca sinica*), which abounds, and two langurs known as *wanduru* (*Presbytis senex* and *P. entellus*). The only other member of the primates is the little slender loris (*Loris tardigradus*), which creeps about the trees at night eating fruit and catching small birds and insects while they are asleep. Twenty-seven Chiroptera have been identified, among them the large fruit-eating bat, the Indian flying fox (*Pteropus giganteus*). This bat roosts in noisy, quarrelsome colonies, hanging upside down all day in tall trees. At evening these huge bats fly in long procession to mango gardens and fig trees, where they do considerable damage.

Lions and tigers are not found in Ceylon, but the leopard is common, as also are smaller wild cats, such as the fishing cat, polecat and civets of various species. The only dangerous carnivore is the sloth bear (*Melursus ursinus*), which, when surprised, attacks on sight. It is common in the wilder jungles, where Sinhalese bearing marks of its savagery are not infrequently met.

Otters are not rare in the hills; wild pigs are abundant and the ubiquitous jackal is familiar to children in the role of "Nariya," a clever, likable rascal corresponding to Br'er Fox. There are several species of mongooses and squirrels, including the flying squirrels, which, by means of the skin stretched between their legs and tails, can glide down from a height for a considerable distance. The tree rat is found in gardens and houses all over the island, having become as urban as a London wood pigeon. The brown rat and the bandicoot rat, which grows up to two feet long, are common everywhere. House mice abound, as do shrews, usually called in English "muskrats" because of their smell, although their Tamil name means "gloomy face." The porcupine (*Hystrix indica*) damages young rubber trees, and hares provide considerable sport, even in semiurban areas. The only representative of the Edentata is the scaly anteater or pangolin (*Manis crassicaudata*), which, being entirely nocturnal, is seldom seen.

About 372 species of birds are recorded, approximately 120 of which are winter migrants from Asia and 50 others occasional visitors. Of the remaining 200 residents, about 60 species are endemic. Among these indigenous species the most noteworthy are the Ceylon jungle fowl (*Gallus lafayetti*), the blue magpie (*Cissa ornata*), the yellow-eared bulbul (*Kelaartia penicillata*), the grayheaded babbler (*Turdoides cinereifrons*), the red-faced malkoha (*Phoenicophaes pyrrhocephalus*), the green-billed coucal (*Centropus chlororhynchus*) and Legge's flowerpecker (*Acmonorhynchus vincens*). The avifauna of the south includes most endemic species and shows a close affinity to that of the Travancore hills, while the birds of the dry, flat north are more like those of the Carnatic. Bulbuls, babblers, barbets, kingfishers, cuckoos and crows are ubiquitous, while thrushes, flycatchers, chats, drongos, mynahs, sunbirds, parakeets, woodpeckers, hawks and owls are all well represented. Pigeons of several kinds and game birds are common, the latter including peafowl, jungle fowl, numerous kinds of duck, partridge and snipe. The large artificial lakes, known as "tanks," in the dry zone are frequented by herons, storks, flamingoes, egrets, spoonbills and waders in thousands, especially in the nesting season, when the bushes and trees at the water's edge are white with birds. Terns are the most numerous sea fowl, gulls being only winter visitors.

The only kinds of poisonous snakes that need be feared are the cobra (*Naja naja*), the tic-polonga or Russell's viper (*Vipera russelli*) and one or two species of krait. Other venomous kinds are either very slightly so or else are very rare. The rock or Indian python (*Python molurus*) is common in jungles, and rat snakes, grass snakes and green whip snakes are frequently encountered. The hamadryad does not live in a wild state in Ceylon.

Two species of crocodile occur, the marsh crocodile or mugger (*Crocodilus palustris*) in the lakes, and the larger estuarine crocodile (*C. porosus*) in the rivers and estuaries. Both species were shot for their hides and became rare until, in 1945, they were protected by legislation, with the result that they thereafter became plentiful again. The talagoya, or common Indian monitor (*Varanus bengalensis*), and its larger relative the aquatic kabaragoya (*V. salvator*) are similarly protected and are therefore numerous. The handsome starred tortoise (*Testudo elegans*) is common, and the neighbouring seas are inhabited by several species of turtle. From the shell of the hawksbill turtle the famous tortoise-shell ware is made.

The commonest lizards are several species of the genus *Calotes*, which are erroneously called chameleons from their habit of changing colour from green and gray to red. One species (*Calotes versicolor*) is often called the bloodsucker. There are also several true chameleons and many small skinks and geckos; the latter frequent houses. Thirty-seven species of frogs and toads are recorded.

The dugong occurs in the shallow seas of the northwest, where it comes to feed upon a seaweed that grows there. It is now rare, being taken for its food value, and has been brought under legislative protection, but in the past, when it was far more plentiful, it gave rise to the mermaid legend, as a result of the female's habit of sitting almost upright in the water nursing her young one in her flippers. Sharks are common all round the island.

Of the fresh-water fish the most useful are the catfish, or lula, and the gurami; the latter is an imported species, some of which escaped from a pond in Peradeniya botanical gardens during a flood and were found multiplying profusely in the Mahaveli river several years later. The species is being distributed all over the island by the fisheries department. In Nuwara Eliya district the streams contain rainbow trout established and stocked by the fishing club. The most popular sea fish for eating is the seer, but the blood fishes, though less in demand, are much more plentiful.

The teeming invertebrate life includes ants of various kinds, termites which destroy wood, bees, hornets, butterflies and moths (some of which are brilliantly coloured and whose wing span may be anything from six inches to a fraction of an inch), many kinds of flies, spiders including the tarantula, mosquitoes, leeches on land and in water, scorpions and many others. (R. H. Bt.)

HISTORY

The island of Ceylon was known to Brahmanical literature under the name of Lanka; to the Greeks and Romans as Taprobane; to the Mohammedan seamen and merchants, who for so long had a monopoly of the sea-borne trade of the Indian ocean, as Serendib, which it has been suggested is a corruption of the Sanskrit Sinhaladvipa; and to the Portuguese as Zeylan, from which is derived its modern name. The presumed aboriginal inhabitants of the island were the people today called Veddas, a few of whom still occupy certain rock shelters in the Eastern province of the island. A careful and scientific examination of these people was made in 1910 by Brenda Seligman and C. G. Seligman. Though their language is said to have certain Indian affinities, they seem ethnologically to be related to the rather lightly coloured, wavy-haired race which is found surviving as somewhat the higher of the two principal aboriginal races in many parts of southeastern Asia. The Veddas are probably related to the Semang or Pangan of the Malay peninsula and to the Andaman islanders. Of the latter race, however, no trace has ever been found in Ceylon. The Veddas are regarded by the Sinhalese as of *goigama*—viz., husbandman–caste.

The great Hindu epic, the *Ramayana*, tells of the conquest of the greater part of the island by the hero Rama, who, with his army, crossed Adam's Bridge (*q.v.*) by the aid of the monkey god Hanuman and his host, the object of his invasion being, as in the case of Menelaus, the recovery of his wife, Sita, who had been abducted by Rawana, king of Lanka. The invaders would appear to have penetrated deep into the heart of the massif which occupies the centre of the southern portion of Ceylon. Unlike most oriental countries, Ceylon can boast a written history of considerable antiquity, the Mahavamsa. This chronicle tells of the landing of Vijaya, the first Sinhalese king, in 483 B.C., accompanied by a small band of Aryan-speaking followers who must, it is thought, have sailed from some point on the northern or northeastern shores of the Bay of Bengal, since the greater part of southern India has, from time immemorial, been inhabited by people of Dravidian stock. Vijaya married a local princess—quite possibly a Vedda—and is said to have become the king of all Ceylon. It is noteworthy that, until the Sinhalese had been driven from the flat plains north of Dambulla by successive invaders from southern India, they appear never to have attempted to populate at all densely the forest, which of old covered the hills and valleys of the central massif and the rich, moist areas in the plains immediately surrounding it. Instead, they established themselves throughout the vast, flat, arid country to the north of Dambulla, which extends to Puttalam on the west, to Kalkuda, about 20 mi. N.N.W. of Batticaloa on the east, northward to Point Pedro in the Jaffna peninsula, and northwest to Talaimannar. This country (Pihiti was its ancient name) they rendered capable of supporting a considerable population by the construction of one of the most elaborate irrigation systems ever attempted by mankind. It may, however, safely be concluded that Ceylon is more thickly populated than it has been at any previous period of its history.

The Sinhalese kings had long been established at Anuradhapura, though their earliest capial was at Raja-Ratta, when in 246 B.C. the island was visited by Mahinda, a Buddhist priest and a son of Asoka, who is piously believed to have reached Mihintale from his father's capital, Magadha, accompanied by a few disciples, by levitation. A branch of the sacred Bo tree, seated beneath the shade of which Gautama attained to Buddhahood, was imported from Magadha and planted at Anuradhapura. Tradition tells that Gautama himself visited Ceylon, in the course of his ministrations, on three occasions, the last descent being on Adam's Peak (*q.v.*). Though he is said personally to have undertaken the instruction of the people, there is nothing to show that Buddhism became established in Ceylon before the 3rd century B.C. From that time onward, however, up to the present time, it has been the religion to which the vast majority of Sinhalese adhere. Buddhism is essentially a tolerant, nonproselytizing philosophical system, and as it spread Buddhist temples and monasteries were established in all parts of Ceylon. In the course of time, too, the Buddhist Church acquired ownership of much of the most fertile land, donated to it by the kings or by wealthy individuals. Buddhism became the state religion of Kandy, the king of which was head of the church. The word Mahavamsa means *The Genealogy of the Great,* and, as was to be expected, the priestly chroniclers, who wrote in Pali, a tongue not understood by the people, had nothing to say about them. They tell also with apparent fidelity the long, tangled story of successive murderous strivings for the throne and of the frequent invasions of northern and central Ceylon by princes and armies of southern India, one of which led to the usurpation of the throne of Anuradhapura for a period by the Tamil Elala, who was slain by the Sinhalese kingly and saintly hero Dutegemunu (*c.* 190 B.C.). The ruins of Anuradhapura as we know them today (they were buried in jungle and completely deserted and neglected until about 1845) are interesting but disappointing in that it is not easy to reconstruct from them any very vivid picture of the city in its prime. The upper structures were of timber, and all have long ago perished, leaving only the foundations for the instruction of archaeologists. The massive *dagobas*—the pyramidal structures which are veritable hills laboriously constructed of small sun-dried bricks—and some of the buildings of Polonnaruwa are in a somewhat better state of repair. Both these ancient capitals, which had for centuries been completely deserted and surrendered to the jungle by the Sinhalese, have become under British rule places of monthly pilgrimage to which hundreds of thousands of pious Buddhists annually resort. A great deal of archaeological and epigraphical work was done under government auspices by the archaeological department established by Sir William Gregory (1872–77). But the history of Ceylon under its Sinhalese kings is mainly a chronicle of royal crimes, virtues and delinquencies; of the long-drawn-out struggle with invading princes and armies from southern India; and of internecine strife between the Sinhalese kings of Pihiti (viz., northern Ceylon) and the chiefs of Rohuna and Maya-Ratta, the two districts or provinces into which the then sparsely populated southern portion of the island was divided. The last great revival of the glory of Sinhalese monarchy took place under Prakrama Bahu, who was crowned king of Pihiti in 1153 at Polannaruwa, and in 1155 king of all Lanka, after successful war against Rohuna. His reign is lovingly styled the "Golden Age of Lanka" by the past-praising Sinhalese of today; but his wars, his invasion of Pegu in Burma and of the Pandyan country in southern India, his enormous activity as a builder of nonremunerative works, such as his palace with its reputed 4,000 apartments, dancing halls, *dagobas,* monasteries and temples, as well as his construction and restoration of innumerable irrigation tanks, must have imposed an almost unendurable strain upon the energies of his subjects. Fanatically religious, he lavished land and treasure upon the priesthood, who repaid him by giving him in the Mahavamsa a superhumanly excellent character; he persecuted ruthlessly heretical Buddhist sects, which by the hierarchy was also accounted to him for righteousness; he endowed Brahmans, in a fine but hardly consistent spirit of religious toleration; and, in imitation of Asoka, he imposed vegetarianism upon his overwrought people and punished with great severity the taking of animal life either in the water or on the land. The people must have been reduced in large numbers to a condition indistinguishable from slavery, and it is certain that this great monarch did much to ruin his country economically by his improvidence. Ceylon, or more properly Pihiti, had been conquered and annexed by Indian princes on several occasions, but in 1408, in revenge for an insult offered to an envoy, a Chinese army invaded the island and carried King Vijaya Bahu IV into captivity. For 30 years Ceylon remained tributary to China.

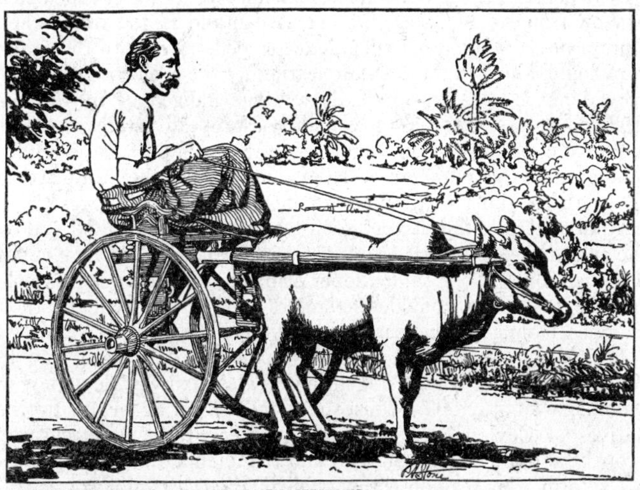

BY COURTESY OF THE CANADIAN PACIFIC STEAMSHIPS

RACING BULLOCK CART IN CEYLON DRIVEN BY A NATIVE DRESSED IN LOCAL MALE FASHION. HE WEARS A SKIRT AND A COMB

Ceylon was first visited by the Portuguese when Francisco de Almeida landed there in 1505. He found an island divided into seven kingdoms, each ruled by its separate monarch and each frequently at odds with one or more of its neighbours. In 1517 a fort was erected at Colombo by orders of the viceroy at Goa, with the permission of the king of Cotta; and from this time onward until the end of the 16th century the Portuguese were constantly at war with one or another of the native kingdoms. It is claimed that, when attacking and conquering Jaffna (Jaffnapatam) they obtained possession of the Tooth relic, and, in spite of the enormous ransom offered for it, publicly burned it in the market place at Goa in obedience to the archbishop, who would not suffer the viceroy to make money out of the sale of what he accounted an idol. By the Sinhalese priesthood, who still possess a Tooth relic the shrine of which is at Kandy, it is asserted that the object captured at Jaffna was a false tooth. The Portuguese won a firm foothold on the western littoral, and they succeeded in converting the bulk of the *karawa* or fisher-caste Sinhalese to Christianity. Conversions upon a considerable scale, but almost invariably among the lower-caste sections of the population, were similarly effected in other parts of the island; as estimated in 1946, Christians numbered 603,235 or nearly 10% of the total population of Ceylon, most of them being Roman Catholics. The proselytizing fervour and cynical rapacity of the Portuguese won for them hosts of enemies among the natives of all ranks, while their inherited traditional hatred for the Moors—by which term they described all Mohammedans—rendered them peculiarly odious to the latter, whose trade and shipping monopolies they had destroyed. The French, the Dutch and the British, when in turn they set the bull of Alexander VI at defiance and forced their way into the Indian ocean, were accordingly welcomed as deliverers by the people of the east generally; and the trading centres the Portuguese had established in the beginning with such dauntless courage, where they had exploited and persecuted the native populations so ruthlessly, fell before the Dutch and the British, fighting often in alliance with native potentates.

The Dutch captain Joris Spilberg landed on the east coast of Ceylon in 1602 and was welcomed by the king of Kandy, who besought him to help in the ejection of the hated Portuguese. No action of importance was taken, however, until 1638–39, when a Dutch expedition attacked and destroyed the Portuguese forts on the east coast. In 1644 Negombo, which had once before been unsuccessfully attacked, fell to the Dutch; and in 1656 and 1658 Colombo and Jaffna were successively captured. The Dutch thus became masters of practically the whole of the maritime provinces of Ceylon, the kingdom of Kandy alone retaining its independence. The Dutch forthwith set about the task of the methodical and efficient administration of the country in a fashion never attempted by the Portuguese. They taxed the people heavily, but the land registers which they instituted have endured to this day, as also has Roman-Dutch law, many of the provisions of which are now deeply ingrained in the traditions of the Low Country Sinhalese peasantry and landholders. They also undertook public works upon a considerable scale and built excellent houses for their own accommodation, public offices, law courts and churches, many of

THE TEMPLE OF THE SACRED TOOTH AT KANDY, CEYLON

The tooth in this temple is said to have belonged to the Buddha, although the Portuguese claim to have captured the original tooth during their suzerainty over Ceylon (1517–1600), and to have burned it in the market-place of Goa

which still survive; the roads which they made opened up the interior and greatly stimulated the trade of the island. Tolerant to Buddhism, Hinduism and Mohammedanism, they persecuted the Catholics persistently, but the religion which had been acquired by thousands of Sinhalese and by the Ceylon-born Tamils of Jaffna and Mannar was too deeply rooted in the peoples' hearts for its extirpation to be possible. Throughout the Dutch period Kandy maintained its independence.

The British, who had dispatched an embassy to the king of Kandy from Madras as early as 1762 without result, after various naval skirmishes in the neighbourhood of Trincomalee and Batticaloa, sent a well-equipped force against the Dutch in Ceylon in 1795, met with only a feeble resistance and in less than a year had obtained possession of the island. The Dutch rule had lasted for about 140 years, a period equal to that of Portuguese domination; but while the latter left Ceylon more distracted and no more developed than they had found it on their arrival, the Dutch administration, if somewhat harsh and unimaginative, worked genuine and permanent improvement in almost every branch of the social and economic life of the people. The Dutch practice, followed by them for so long in almost all their overseas possessions, of taking over oppressive local systems of taxation, which had been endurable only because evasion was so common, and thereafter applying them with ruthless efficiency made their rule highly unpopular; and even today the Burghers, who are the descendants of the former Dutch rulers and settlers, are far from being loved by the Sinhalese. These Ceylonese Dutchmen, though many of their families have dilutions of oriental blood in their veins, have retained their national character, their sturdy self-esteem, their traditions and high ideals of probity and conduct in a very remarkable degree. Over a long period they had a practical monopoly of the clerical work in most public departments and held most positions of trust in public departments and commercial houses.

At first Ceylon was administered from Madras, but an attempt to apply the Madras revenue system and the employment of a host of Malabar collectors led to a rebellion. The treaty of Amiens (1802) formally ceded Ceylon to Great Britain and it became a British crown colony; the following year Kandy was invaded and occupied. The garrison was shortly afterward treacherously massacred after it had been induced to lay down its arms. It was not till 1815, however, that the Kandyan chiefs (with some of whom at an earlier period Gov. Frederick North, later earl of Guilford, had carried on discreditable intrigues against their king) invoked the aid of the British to rid themselves of this tyrant of Malabar stock whose cruelties had surpassed endurance. The Kandyan kingdom was thus voluntarily handed over to the British crown, which guaranteed its people civil and religious liberty and the maintenance of their ancient customs. An insurrection which broke out shortly after was easily suppressed, and the second treaty (1818) which followed it did not materially alter in any respect the status of the Kandyan chiefs and people vis-à-vis the crown. The pacification and opening up of the mountain country by the construction of roads led immediately to a great incursion of Low Country Sinhalese, Mohammedan and Hindu traders and European coffee planters. These latter penetrated into the virgin forest and, aided in the task of clearing by the Sinhalese villagers, carved out estates for themselves. The indigenous inhabitants declined to work for a wage on the European estates, save as artisans, etc., and it was found necessary to import as voluntary immigrants large numbers of Tamil coolies from the arid districts of southern India. Attempts to introduce cinchona were only partially successful, but very soon tea began to be planted and by the end of the century it was covering a far larger area than coffee had ever done. Then came rubber planting, an enterprise in which, for the first time, Sinhalese planters took an active part, their energies having in the past been confined to the cultivation of coffee, which ended in disaster, to some cocoa planting and to coconut planting. Large fortunes were also made by Ceylonese in plumbago mining. The consequent acquisition of wealth by the natives of Ceylon, and especially by men of the *karawa* caste, brought about a social upheaval and led to an agitation for political reform, the real object of which (though stimulus was imparted to it by the Morley-Minto reforms in British India) was to break the monopoly which the highest-caste *goigama* aristocracy had till then enjoyed of representing Sinhalese interests in the legislative council. During the agitation that preceded the granting of these claims, ill feeling based on caste prejudice, on the angry passions which such prejudice aroused and on racial animosity began for the first time to become vocal in Ceylon. The first scheme of reform was worked out in 1909 by Col. Seely, then undersecretary of state for the colonies, and accepted by Gov. Sir Henry McCallum, in spite of the protests of his executive councillors and the obvious inapplicability of Seely's scheme as originally framed by him to local circumstances. The first election of a representative of the educated Ceylonese was fought purely on caste lines, a high-caste Tamil being chosen with the aid of the high-caste Sinhalese vote, caste prejudice thus proving to be a stronger passion than racial bias. A state of growing unrest was thus created, and this was increased by the outbreak of World War I. A religious fracas at Gampola in 1915 between the Buddhists and Mohammedans resulted in riots which were quelled only after imposition of martial law, but in spite of this Ceylon emerged from the war comparatively unscathed.

The political problems in Ceylon were rendered particularly difficult of solution because of the very heterogeneous population. The Low Country Sinhalese, more sophisticated than the Kandyans, were spread throughout the Kandyan provinces and claimed, as Buddhists, a share in the management of Kandyan temporalities. The Kandyans, on the other hand, viewing penetration of their country by Low Country Sinhalese with dislike, remembered that these folk aided the Portuguese, the Dutch and the British in their several attacks on the Kandyan kingdom. Therefore they regarded any system of government that placed the supreme power in the hands of a majority with acute apprehension. These feelings were in some degree shared by the Ceylonese Tamils, though in their case it was they who invaded the country occupied by the Low Country Sinhalese. The Burghers were still more apprehensive; while the Europeans, who represented huge financial interests, alike in the world of commerce and in agricultural enterprise, were only 0.18% of the total population of the island.

The Low Country Sinhalese and Tamils formed in 1919 the Ceylon National Congress, but the latter withdrew in 1921 because, fearing Sinhalese predominance, they insisted that any change in the constitution should make provision for communal electorates. Meanwhile, in 1920 the composition of the legislative council was altered to 14 official and 23 unofficial members, and by another change in 1924 that body comprised 36 unofficial members (3 of whom were Europeans and the majority of whom were elected) and 12 official. At the same time three unofficial Ceylonese (two Sinhalese and one Tamil) and one European had been added to the executive council. Responsibility for the good administration of the island continued, none the less, to be vested solely in the governor, who was unable to discharge it save by the good will of the unofficial majority in the legislative council or by the exercise of his power of veto, which could easily be countered by a refusal to vote supply. Because of the resulting impasse, the working of the constitution was investigated during 1927–28 by the Donoughmore commission, and as outcome of that body's recommendations a new constitution came into force in 1931. Both the legislative and the executive councils were dissolved, and their place was taken by a state council having legislative and also executive functions. The new council consisted of 3 official members, 50 elected members and not more than 8 members nominated by the governor. The three official members ex officio were the chief secretary, legal secretary and financial secretary (formerly known, respectively, as the colonial secretary, attorney general and treasurer); while they could take part in debates they could not vote, and thus there was no longer an official minority. All elected members were elected on a territorial basis (the franchise being very wide), communal representation being abolished. The members of a new council proceeded by secret ballot to divide their total number (excluding the three officials, known as officers of state) into seven executive committees to administer seven of the ten groups into which the government departments were divided; each of the remaining three groups was supervised by an officer of state. Each executive committee elected a chairman, and these seven chairmen, termed ministers, and the three officers of state constituted a board of ministers; the three officials, who had no vote, served in an advisory capacity, the most important function of the board being the preparation of the annual estimates of revenue and expenditure.

In World War II it became necessary for Ceylon not only to grow many of the foodstuffs hitherto imported but vastly to increase its exports. As a producer of tea it ranked second only to India, and after Japanese occupation of the Malayan territories the island became the British empire's principal source of plantation rubber. In 1942 Ceylon was placed under the control of a British admiral, who left administration to the civil authorities until such time as the threat of Japanese attack might compel him to intervene. The British cabinet undertook to grant the colony full responsible internal government after conclusion of hostilities. The Soulbury commission of 1944–45 recommended further constitutional advance, and in May 1946 a new constitution was promulgated under which the executive committees of the Donoughmore constitution were replaced by cabinet government under the leadership of a prime minister. Agitation for full dominion status continued and resulted in the Ceylon Independence act of 1947. On Feb. 4, 1948, Ceylon became a dominion of the British Commonwealth. Don Stephen Senanayake had become prime minister in Sept. 1947 and continued as such until his death on March 22, 1952. He was succeeded by his son, Dudley Senanayake, who however resigned because of ill-health on Oct. 12, 1953, when Sir John Kotelawala succeeded him. On July 17, 1954, in succession to Lord Soulbury, Sir Oliver Goonetilleke became the first Ceylonese governor general.

(W. B. Pn.; C. C. D.)

In the mid-1950s Ceylon's external policy appeared to be shaped by a more-or-less positive anticommunism, in contrast with India's "noninvolvement"; by a sympathy toward the west somewhat greater than that shown by her neighbours; and by a certain apprehension of Indian domination. On Jan. 10, 1955, however, the resolutions committee of the government parliamentary group recommended that Ceylon should become a republic in May 1956.

SOCIAL AND ECONOMIC CONDITIONS

People.—The population of Ceylon at the time of the 1953 census was 8,098,637. Ceylon nationals as a whole are known as Ceylonese, a national name including not only the two principal groups (*i.e.*, Sinhalese and Ceylon Tamils) but also Ceylon Moors, who are the descendants of seafaring Arab merchants; Malays, the remnant of the Ceylon Malay regiments; Burghers, descendants of the Dutch; Eurasians; a few Portuguese; and a small number of naturalized Europeans, Indians and other nationalities. The Sinhalese themselves are of two main types, Low Country Sinhalese, who inhabit the plains, and Kandyans from the mountains. The Veddas or aboriginals are almost extinct as a pure race, but there are a number of half Veddas and quarter Veddas, intermixed with Sinhalese. The numerical strength of the various groups in Ceylon in 1953 is given in the table.

Group	Number	Group	Number
Low Country Sinhalese	3,464,126	Other Ceylonese*	20,678
Kandyan Sinhalese	2,157,206	Indians†	984,327
Ceylon Tamils	908,705	Pakistanis	5,749
Ceylon Moors	468,146	Europeans	5,886
Burghers	43,916	Other non-Ceylonese	11,162
Malays	28,736		

*Incl. Veddas (2,361 in 1946), Eurasians and naturalized Europeans and Indians.
†Mainly Tamils.

Towns.—For administration Ceylon is divided into nine provinces, with the most populous area in the west, around the capital, Colombo (423,481 in 1953), where the port handles 2,000,000 tons of cargo a year. Colombo harbour is artificially constructed by a concrete breakwater enclosing the roadstead. It was being modernized in the 1950s, and Queen Elizabeth II opened the first alongside quay when her ship the "Gothic" berthed there in 1954. The business quarter is close to the harbour in the areas occupied by the ancient fort, of which few traces except the name remain, and in the adjoining *pettah*, or bazaar. The wealthier residential sector is in the part of the town used by the Dutch as cinnamon gardens and is still known by that name.

The next largest cities are Jaffna (77,218 in 1953), in the Northern (Tamil) province, with a small port, and Dehiwala-Mt. Lavinia (80,086), on the fringe of Colombo. Then come Kandy (57,539), the capital of the Central province, famous for the Temple of the Tooth, and Moratuwa (58,160) and Kotte (53,862), both in the Western province. Trincomalee (28,236) is a naval base with one of the finest and largest natural landlocked harbours in the world. Galle (55,874), in the south, is a small natural harbour for ships of the freighter class, which, until overshadowed by the building of Colombo harbour at the end of the 19th century, was the main port of Ceylon.

Religion.—The Sinhalese are mainly Buddhists, both in religion and culture, and the Tamils are principally Hindus, with a culture akin to that of India. Moors and Malays are Moslems; with their exception a considerable proportion of all groups are Christians. Distribution of religions in 1953 was as follows: Buddhists 5,217,143; Hindus 1,614,004; Christians 714,874; Moslems 541,812. Religion plays a large part in Ceylonese life; the public holidays, 22 in all, are based on festivals, and pilgrimages feature prominently both in business and pleasure. The most famous pilgrimage is the ascent of Adam's Peak (*q.v.*), which takes place in March and April, during which months the peak can be clearly seen from the sea to the southwest. This periodical distant and mysterious view of the mountain, in the centuries before accurate surveys of its height and position had been made, caused it to become an object of awe and legend to passing mariners. At sunrise the huge shadow of the mountain, thrown upon the mist in the valleys, can be seen from the summit, with its tip on the coast 60 mi. to the west, one of the most impressive sights in the world.

Another goal of pilgrims and tourists is the Temple of the Tooth in Kandy, wherein is enshrined the Sacred Tooth relic of the Lord Buddha. The Perahera, or annual torchlit temple procession, in which 100 gorgeously caparisoned elephants and hundreds of dancers take part, draws thousands of devotees and sightseers.

At Anuradhapura is the famous 2,000-year-old Bo tree, an offshoot of the tree under which Buddha meditated. This tree has the oldest authenticated history of any tree in the world.

Education.—Education was made free in 1945. It is based on the English system, from the village primary school through junior, senior and central schools to the university; the last is located on a site of great beauty near the famous botanical gardens at Peradeniya outside Kandy. Most villages have their own schools, either in the village itself or within a mile or two of it, and 57.8% of the population is literate, a high percentage compared with other Asian countries. The main languages are Sinhalese and Tamil, but 6.3% of the people can read and write English, while a much larger proportion can speak it.

Constitution.—Under the constitution, framed by the Soulbury commission and promulgated in 1946, there was established a house of representatives consisting of 101 members, 95 elected by universal franchise, including women, and a maximum of 6 nominated by the governor general if he is satisfied that any important interest is not otherwise represented. There is also an upper house or senate consisting of 30 members, of whom 15 are elected by the house of representatives and 15 appointed by the governor general. A number of ministers, headed by the prime minister, form the cabinet. Labour legislation provides for compulsory employment of a percentage of Ceylonese labour, workmen's compensation, maternity benefits and wage boards for several trades. Trade unionism strengthened after independence.

Agriculture.—The principal occupation of the inhabitants of Ceylon is agriculture. The most important crops are rice, for local consumption only; coconuts for local consumption and export of the oil; tea, mainly for export, although the large home demand is also met; and rubber, entirely for export. Other crops are cacao, cinnamon, cardamom, citronella, tobacco, pepper, palmyra, areca nuts and oil seeds such as sesame. Vegetables for local use are grown in profusion, and English varieties of vegetables grow well on the hills.

Rice, known as paddy before it is milled, is grown by Ceylonese on lands supplied with water through a large and efficient irrigation system of extensive artificial reservoirs or "tanks," originally built by the Sinhalese kings many centuries ago and restored by the British government. Except in government farms and in the agricultural "colonies" organized below the restored tanks, agricultural methods are still primitive, and fields are cultivated with an old-fashioned plow drawn by buffaloes. Mechanization is handicapped by the small size of the individual rice fields and the difficulty of reaching them with motor vehicles, but modern techniques such as transplating are practised.

The coconut tree is, next to rice, the most valuable crop, providing food, drink, oil for cooking and burning, rope, cattle food, timber and thatch, while all nuts not required for internal use find a lucrative market abroad in the form of copra and oil. About 1,800,000,000 nuts are produced annually on about 1,000,000 ac. of which more than four-fifths consists of village smallholdings and gardens.

Tea is grown mainly in the hills, on estates opened by British companies after the failure of the coffee crop, due to a pest in the 1870s. The annual export of tea from Ceylon is more than 300,000,000 lb. The majority of the labourers on tea estates are Tamils from India, but every year a larger number of Ceylonese are taking to the work and replacing the immigrants.

Rubber, introduced into Ceylon from South America in 1876, is grown principally on estates in the low country, but there are a number of village smallholdings. The annual export from Ceylon is about 220,000,000 lb.

Industry.—Ceylon is so largely agricultural that industry has developed slowly, being confined to a hydroelectric scheme, rice milling, coconut oil production and goods manufactured from other coconut oil products; but, with the coming of independence in 1947, industrial development became an important government policy. By 1952 the first stage of the hydroelectric scheme had been completed; in the north a cement factory had been set up and, in the south, a plywood factory was functioning, while factories for the manufacture of paper, vegetable oil products, glass, ceramics and DDT were completed in 1955. In May 1955 the government approved a six-year Rs. 2,100,000,000 (£161,000,000) economic development program.

Ceylon fisheries are the subject of active scientific development, and trawling is successfully conducted on the Wadge bank, off Cape Cormorin. Pearl fishing is a lucrative industry, but intermittent because of the vagaries of the oysters, which do not always select Ceylon waters for their residence.

The minerals of economic importance are plumbago or graphite, gem stones, ilmenite, iron, monazite, thorianite and mica. Plumbago is found in veins in the western part of the island, and gems, the most valuable of which are sapphires and other varieties of corundum, occur in river gravels, washed down from the southwest flank of the mountain mass. The gem industry, one of Ceylon's most romantic features, has been practised for centuries by digging pits 30 ft. deep, down to the gem gravel. This, when washed in a basket, reveals, beside sapphires, cinnamon rubies, cat's-eyes, zircons and most of the semiprecious stones. The principal area for gems is around Ratnapura, "Gem City."

There is a vast deposit of ilmenite on the shore at Pulmoddai, north of Trincomalee, and about 6,000,000 tons of good-quality surface iron are available in the southwest.

Transport.—Transport in Ceylon is well developed in the tea, rubber and coconut areas but, although there were about 14,000 mi. of motorable roads in 1955, the jungles of the north and east are sparsely traversed. The bullock cart is still universally used, but buses and lorries serve every part of the country, however isolated, and the railway (896 mi. in 1955, all 5 ft. 6 in. gauge, except 87 mi. 2 ft. 6 in. gauge) reaches all but the southeastern district with a frequent service. There is daily air service from Colombo to Jaffna, and to Trichinopoly in India.

Economy and Finance.—As the prosperity of Ceylon depends so greatly on its three main exportable agricultural products (*i.e.*, tea, rubber and coconuts), its economy, though prosperous, has to be regarded as precarious. Great efforts were therefore being made by the 1950s to establish a greater measure of self-sufficiency, by the construction of major social development works, such as the huge Gal-oya all-purpose dam, large irrigation works and new factories. Figures for foreign trade in 1954 were: imports Rs. 1,397,000,000; exports Rs. 1,809,000,000. The main sources of imports were: U.K. 21%; India 14%; Burma 9%; U.S. and Canada 4%. Main destinations of exports were: U.K. 29%; India and Burma 25%; U.S. and Canada 11%.

The unit rate of income tax in 1950 was 9½%, but only 1 person in every 260 at that time fell within the taxable scope. The

1950–51 budget showed revenue as Rs. 794,000,000 and expenditure as Rs. 704,000,000; the 1951–52 budget estimate was revenue Rs. 896,000,000 and expenditure Rs. 886,000,000. The monetary unit is the rupee with an exchange rate in 1952 of Rs. 13.13 to the pound sterling and Rs. 4.775 to $1 U.S.

BIBLIOGRAPHY.—L. A. Mills, *Ceylon Under British Rule, 1795–1932* (1933); D. M. Hussey, *Ceylon and World History,* 3 vol. (Colombo, 1938); C. W. B. Elliott, *The Real Ceylon* (Colombo, 1938); H. W. Codrington, *A Short History of Ceylon* (London, 1939); Lord Holden, *Ceylon* (1939); W. T. Keble, *Ceylon, Beaten Track* (Colombo, 1940); P. E. Pieris, *Ceylon and the Hollanders, 1658–1796* (Colombo, 1930); Sir William Ivor Jennings, *The Constitution of Ceylon,* 2nd ed. (1951); R. H. Bassett, *Romantic Ceylon* (Colombo, 1937).

(R. H. BT.; X.)

CÉZANNE, PAUL (1839–1906), French painter, was born at Aix, the ancient capital town of Provence, on Jan. 19, 1839.. His father was a banker. Paul was educated at the *lycée* of the town, where he formed an intimate friendship with Émile Zola, the novelist. The two boys were both inspired by a love of the classics, particularly of Virgil, through whom, perhaps, Cézanne realized the beauty of his native country. Both decided to consecrate themselves to art. Zola settled down early to a literary career in Paris, but Cézanne endeavoured to comply with his father's wish that he should carry on the family bank. After two unsuccessful attempts the father allowed Paul to settle in Paris and attend the art school. He arrived there in 1863.

Cézanne became known as one of the most extreme of the young revolutionary painters, the bitterest in his denunciation of official art and of Ingres who, then in his old age, was regarded as the head of the reactionaries. In this way he became acquainted with the group of painters who encircled Manet, and who afterwards became known as the impressionists. But Cézanne's work in his early years shows no sign of this frequentation. At this period he was most influenced by Delacroix and by the Baroque painters whom Delacroix studied, by Rubens and Tintoretto. His ambition was to create grandiose compositions of a purely imaginative description, expressive of his own internal moods, using either violently dramatic themes—"Les Assassins," "L'Autopsie," "Lazare" —or lyrical motives—"Le Jugement de Paris," "Déjeuners sur l'herbe." He also painted a series of portraits in which dramatic and psychological effects were undertoned. In these the influence of Courbet is evident. They are painted with broad strokes, the palette-knife ploughing up and planting down an exceedingly thick and dense impasto. In all these early works the colour is reduced to a few simple notes in which black, white and earth reds and yellows predominate. The tension of Cézanne's imaginative life shows itself in the tumultuous vehemence of these early compositions. He trusts to his inner convictions with a blind and reckless courage which was unfortunately not supported by the gifts necessary to make such an imagery plausible, or to give verisimilitude to the contorted poses of his Tintorettesque nudes. His outlook on nature seems to have been confined for the most part to the search for motives of chiaroscuro suitable to the dramatic effects of his imaginative designs. He showed at this stage nothing of the curiosity about natural effects of colour which distinguished the impressionist group. He was, in fact, far more concerned with expressing the exaltation of his own feelings, inspired by literature or imaginative brooding, than with the phenomena of the visible world. A few still-lifes of this period show, however, how much greater his native endowment was in this direction than in the one he was consciously pursuing; but even in these the dramatic evocations of the thing seen are what chiefly interested him.

During the years 1872–73 a great change came over Cézanne. He spent the summers of these years at Auvers-sur-Oise in the company of Camille Pissarro, who was one of the impressionists. Pissarro was some years older than Cézanne and had already discovered his personal style and perfected a methodical and precise technique adapted to it. Cézanne, who had hitherto trusted to the inspiration of his imaginative ideas for his daring, but rather fortuitous technique, here for the first time underwent a methodical course of training. He learned for the first time to look on nature with a curious and contemplative gaze, and he learned a precise and methodical technical process, by which to record the results thus obtained. Above all, the whole world of "atmospheric" colour was thus revealed to him. Certain pictures painted by Cézanne in these years approximate very nearly to Pissarro's work, but they show Cézanne's greater power of organizing form, and the greater profundity of the conceptions which his contemplation of natural appearance provoked in his intensely passionate nature. For these years, then, Cézanne may be counted an impressionist.

But Cézanne's response to appearances gave him a notion of design more vigorously constructed, and evocative of far deeper feelings, than any that the impressionists envisaged. To them the weft of colour which nature revealed to their specialized visual sense was all that mattered; out of that each artist could choose unconsciously those harmonies which specially appealed to him. But Cézanne always believed in some underlying reality of a more permanent kind, more consonant with the deeper instincts of human nature. The impressionist vision was both too casual and too imperfectly organized for him. It missed part of the truth which the older masters had apprehended. Cézanne summed up his own attitude by saying that his ambition was to do Poussin over again after nature, *i.e.,* to incorporate into a clearly organized formal unity, like Poussin's, the vision of natural appearance as enriched by impressionist researches. From this point Cézanne's personal vision and his personal expression of it were established. Such changes as his style underwent in the succeeding decades were only gradual modifications of what he had established once for all. The essentials of that style were due, as we have seen, to the special use he made of the impressionist vision. They were based upon the most rigorous construction of the design by means of the interplay of clearly articulated planes. But the movement of these planes, their salience and recession, was interpreted quite as much by changes in local colour as by the definition of form by light and shade. A characteristic of Cézanne's completely realized manner is the extreme simplicity of the approach, the fact that objects are presented in full frontal aspect. In nearly all his portraits the sitter is placed nearly in the centre of the canvas, the head and body being seen nearly in full face. In the landscapes a similar treatment is found; objects are extended in planes parallel to the picture plane, and frequently the main mass will be centrally placed. Such extreme symmetrical simplicity of approach takes us back to the practice of the Italian Primitives. It is violently opposed to the principles of Baroque composition as followed by most of Cézanne's predecessors and by himself in his early period.

Such an exaggeratedly simple disposition would probably strike us as crude and uninteresting if it were not that within the volumes which he places before us in this elementary fashion, his analysis of changes of surface and plastic movement is pushed to an extraordinary degree, and this is accompanied by innumerable slight modulations of colour, so that the whole surface takes on something of the infinity of natural appearance. This practice he developed with ever-increasing power. In the '70s and early '80s, the almost laborious scrutiny of infinitesimal colour changes led him to load the canvas with repeated layers of colour, though without ever losing purity and intensity. Later on he was able to get the same multiplicity of surface with thinner layers of colour. Together with this he tended also to simplify the colour changes, adopting even a regular principle of colour sequences to express movements away from the highest relief of any given volume. All this was strictly in keeping with his philosophical conception of the aim of painting. In everything he did he sought a synthesis in which the most rigorously logical plastic structure should be combined with the utmost liveliness of surface; that is to say, he sought, without losing the infinitude of natural appearance, to give to it an intelligibility and a logical coherence which it lacks. This, no doubt, is more or less the problem of all painting; what distinguishes Cézanne is his endeavour to attain this synthesis when each of the opposite terms is at its highest pitch.

To the last decade of the 19th century belong some of his most celebrated works: the portrait of Geffroy, which is perhaps unequalled in modern art for the completeness of its realization, the complexity and assurance of its harmonies; several versions of a composition of men seated at a café table and playing cards, in which the primitive simplicity of the arrangement gives an elemental grandeur to the forms; and a series of landscapes in which the pyramidal mass of Mt. Ste. Victoire dominates the design. Even to the end of his life, Cézanne always cherished the hope of creating imaginative and "poetical" designs of nude figures in landscape, after the manner of some of Giorgione's and Titian's pictures. But in this he was hampered by his extreme reluctance to draw from the nude model, and most of these grandiose attempts remain failures.

At the very end of his life there seems to have been a kind of recrudescence in Cézanne of the romantic tendencies of his youth. His paintings became richer, more intense and vivid in colour, more agitated in rhythm, more vehement in accent; they also departed more and more from the careful analysis of natural appearance of the middle period, as though his long apprenticeship to nature had ceased and he felt free to follow unhesitatingly his instinctive feeling. The middle and end of Cézanne's life was passed in great seclusion at Aix, with occasional visits to Paris. In the 1880s and 1890s his very name had become almost unknown in the larger art circles of Paris, though he never lacked a few enthusiastic admirers. Gradually his fame began to circulate among the more intelligent artists, and in 1904 a retrospective exhibition of his works in the Autumn Salon revealed to the public the existence of this almost unknown genius. It was the only foretaste of his posthumous fame which he experienced. He died Oct. 23, 1906.

BIBLIOGRAPHY.—G. Coquiot, *Cézanne* (1919); J. Gasquet, *Cézanne* (1921); G. Rivière, *Le Maître Paul Cézanne* (1923); A. Vollard, *Paul Cézanne,* trans. H. L. van Doren (1924); J. Meier-Graefe, *Cézanne,* trans. J. Holroyd-Reece (1927); R. Fry, *Cézanne* (1927).

(R. FR.)

C.G.S. SYSTEM, a system of units which takes as a basis the centimetre, the gram and the second. (*See* PHYSICAL UNITS and ABSOLUTE UNITS.)

CHABAZITE, a mineral species belonging to the group of zeolites. It occurs as white to flesh-red crystals which vary from transparent to translucent and have a vitreous lustre. The crystals are rhombohedral, and the predominating form is often a rhombohedron with interfacial angles of 85° 14′; they therefore closely resemble cubes in appearance, and the mineral was in fact early (in 1772) described as a cubic zeolite. A characteristic feature is the twinning, the crystals being in many cases interpenetration twins with the corners of small crystals in twinned position projecting from the faces of the main crystal. A flat lenticular form of crystal is also common, this variety being known as phacolite (from φακός, a lentil). The hardness is $4\frac{1}{2}$, and the specific gravity 2.08–2.16.

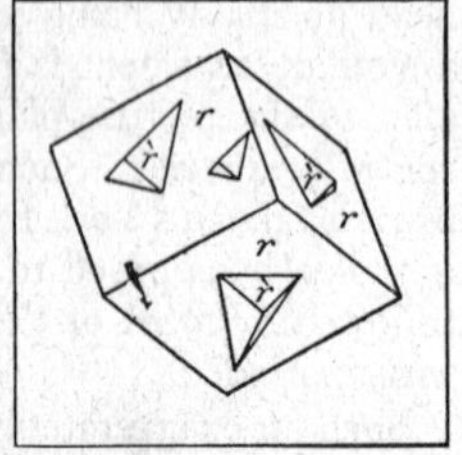

TWINNED CRYSTAL OF CHABAZITE
Interpenetrating rhombohedra (nearly cubic in form) are especially characteristic of this mineral

Chemically, chabazite is a complex hydrated calcium and sodium silicate. The composition is, however, variable, and is best expressed as an isomorphous mixture of the molecules $(Ca,Na_2)Al_2Si_4O_{12}+4H_2O$ and $(Ca,Na_2)Al_2(Si_3O_8)_2+8H_2O$, which are analogous to the feldspars. Most analyses correspond with a formula midway between these extremes, namely $(Ca,Na_2)Al_2(SiO_3)_4+6H_2O$. Chabazite occurs with other zeolites in the amygdaloidal cavities of basaltic rocks; occasionally it has been found in gneisses and schists. Gmelinite is another species of zeolite which may be mentioned here, since it is closely related to chabazite. It forms large flesh-red crystals usually of hexagonal habit, and was early known as soda-chabazite, it having the composition of chabazite, but with sodium predominating over calcium $(Na_2.Ca)\ Al_2(SiO_3)_4+6H_2O$. (L. J. S.)

CHABLIS, a town of north central France, in the department of Yonne, on the left bank of the Serein, 14 mi. E. of Auxerre by road. Pop. (1946) 1,786. Its church of St. Martin belongs to the end of the 12th century. The town gives its name to a well-known white wine (*see* BURGUNDY WINES).

CHABOT, FRANÇOIS (1757–1794), French revolutionary, born at St. Geniez, near Aveyron, had been a Franciscan friar before the Revolution, and after the civil constitution of the clergy continued to act as "constitutional" priest. Then he was elected to the legislative assembly, sitting at the extreme left, and forming with C. Bazire and Merlin de Thionville the "Cordelier trio." Re-elected to the convention he voted for the death of Louis XVI, and opposed the proposal to prosecute the authors of the massacre of September. Compromised in the falsification of a decree suppressing the India company and in a plot to bribe certain members of the convention, especially Fabre d'Eglantine and C. Bazire, he was condemned by the Revolutionary tribunal and executed on April 5, 1794.

See *François Chabot . . . à ses concitoyens, . . . pluviose, an II, Mémoire apologetique, . . .* etc. ed. A. Mathiez (1914); J. M. J. A. de Bonald, *François Chabot, membre de la Convention* (1908).

CHABOT, PHILIPPE DE, SEIGNEUR DE BRION, COUNT OF CHARNY AND BUZANÇAIS (1492?–1543), admiral of France. The Chabot family was one of the oldest and most powerful in Poitou. Philippe was a cadet of the Jarnac branch. He was a companion of Francis I as a child, and on that king's accession received many honours and estates. After the battle of Pavia he was made admiral of France and governor of Burgundy (1526), and shared with Anne de Montmorency the direction of affairs. He was at the height of his power in 1535, and commanded the army for the invasion of the states of the duke of Savoy; but in the campaigns of 1536 and 1537 he was eclipsed by Montmorency, and his influence began to wane. He was accused by his enemies of peculation, and condemned on Feb. 10, 1541, to a fine of 1,500,000 livres, to banishment, and to the confiscation of his estates. Through the good offices of Madam d'Étampes he obtained the king's pardon (March 1541) and was reinstated, while Montmorency was disgraced. He died on June 1, 1543.

CHABRIAS (4th century B.C.), Athenian general. In 388 B.C. he defeated the Spartans of Aegina and commanded the fleet sent to assist Evagoras, king of Cyprus, against the Persians. In 378, when Athens joined Thebes against Sparta, he defeated Agesilaus near Thebes. On this occasion he invented a manoeuvre, which consisted in receiving a charge on the left knee, with shields resting on the ground and spears pointed against the enemy. In 376 he defeated the Spartan fleet off Naxos, but, when he might have destroyed the enemy, remembering Arginusae (*q.v.*), he delayed to pick up his dead. Later, when the Athenians joined the Spartans, he repulsed Epaminondas before Corinth. In 366, together with Callistratus, he was accused of treachery in advising the surrender of Oropus to the Thebans. He was acquitted, and soon after he accepted a command under Tachos, king of Egypt, who had revolted against Persia. On the outbreak of the Social War (357) he joined Chares in the command of the Athenian fleet. He lost his life in an attack on the island of Chios, probably in the same year. *See* also DELIAN LEAGUE.

See Cornelius Nepos, *Chabrias;* Xenophon, *Hellenica,* v, 1–4; Diod. Sic. xv, 29–34; *Cambridge Ancient History,* vol. vi (1927) chapters iii, vi and viii (with useful bibliography).

CHABRIER, ALEXIS EMMANUEL (1841–1894), French composer, was born at Ambert, Puy de Dôme, on Jan. 18, 1841, and first attracted general attention in 1883 by his brilliant orchestral rhapsody entitled *España,* the themes of which he had jotted down when travelling in Spain. His opera *Gwendoline,* produced at Brussels on April 10, 1886, was successful too and still more so its successor, of a lighter type, *Le Roi malgré lui,* which was brought out in Paris at the Opéra Comique.

CHACMA, the Cape baboon, *Papio comatus,* inhabiting the mountains of South Africa as far north as the Zambezi. The size of an English mastiff, this powerful baboon is blackish-gray in colour with a tinge of green due to the yellow rings on the hairs. Unlike most of its tribe, it is a good climber. It is destructive to crops.

CHACO, a territory of northern Argentina, part of a large district known as the Gran Chaco, bounded north by the territory of Formosa, east by Paraguay and Corrientes, south by Santa Fé and west by Santiago del Estero and Salta. It became the province of President Perón in 1950, with a constitution of a type not previously known in Argentina—the corporate state. It is rich in timber (more than 70 varieties of hardwoods), and sugar, cotton and other products are profitably cultivated on its plains. The capital is Resistencia. The Bermejo river forms its northern boundary and the Paraguay and Paraná rivers its eastern. Pop. (1947) 430,555; area, 38,468 sq.mi. (C. E. Mc.)

Northern Chaco had long been the subject of dispute between Bolivia and Paraguay. Armed clashes over its possession began in 1928 and gradually developed into open war. All efforts of other states and the League of Nations to mediate were unavailing. And the belligerents continued their bloody struggle in spite of a seeming bankruptcy on both sides. Paraguay, on the whole, proved the more successful in arms. Finally a truce was arranged on June 12, 1935. Under the arbitral award of 1938, Paraguay received most of the disputed area.

CHACO CANYON, a tract of about 20,000 ac. in north-western New Mexico, U.S.A., set apart in 1907 as a national monument. It contains the most remarkable architectural remains of prehistoric North America and has yielded a rich collection of objects illustrative of a vanished civilization. The buildings, which sometimes attained a height of at least four storys, show a variety of methods in stone construction. Several are of enormous size, Pueblo Bonito, the largest, measuring 667 ft. by 315 ft.; a wall still standing rises to 48 feet. This building, like most of the others, constituted a veritable village and contained 800 rooms and 32 *kivas,* or large ceremonial halls. Chetro-Kettle and Peñasco Blanco are similar structures, while other ruins show that the private house also was in use.

CHACONNE, a slow dance, introduced into Spain by the Moors, now obsolete. It resembled the Passacaglia. The word is used also of the music composed for this dance—a slow, stately movement in $\frac{3}{4}$ time. Such a movement was often introduced into a sonata, and formed the conventional finale to an opera or ballet until the time of Gluck. The most famous of all chaconnes is that of Bach for violin unaccompanied—a colossal example which is generally played as an independent piece, though it is actually a movement in one of his violin sonatas (No. 4).

CHAD (Ceadda), **SAINT** (d. 672), brother of Cedd, whom he succeeded as abbot at Lastingham, was consecrated bishop of the Northumbrians by Wine, the West Saxon bishop, at the request of Oswy in 664. On the return of Wilfrid from France, where he had been sent to be consecrated to the same see, a dispute arose, which was settled by Theodore in favour of Wilfrid. Chad thereupon retired to Lastingham, whence with the permission of Oswy he was summoned by Wulfhere of Mercia to succeed his bishop Jaruman (d. 667). Chad built a monastery at Barrow in Lincolnshire and fixed his see at Lichfield.

See Bede's *Hist. Eccl.;* Eddius, *Vita Wilfridi,* xiv., xv., ed. J. Raine, Rolls series (1879).

CHAD, a lake of northern Central Africa lying between 12° 50′ and 14° 10′ N. and 13° and 15° E. It lies about 800 ft. above the sea in the borderland between the Sudan and the Sahara. The lake has greatly shrunken since it was first seen by Europeans; this is attributed to the progressive desiccation of the region. Thus a town which in 1850 was on the southern margin of the lake was in 1905 over 20m. from it. But as the west shore is perfectly flat, a slight rise in the water causes the inundation of a considerable area, a fact to be remembered in considering the estimates made as to the size of the lake. In any case the Chad is but the remnant of what in recent geological times was a very much larger sheet of water spreading south, north cast and east of its present limits. A considerable area lying to the north-east is below the level of the lake. Around the north-west and north shores is a continuous chain of gently sloping sand-hills covered with bush. In the east, the country of Kanem, the desiccation has been most marked. Along this coast is a continuous chain of islands running from north-west to south-east. They are generally low, being composed of sand and clay, and lie from 5 to 20m. from the shore, which throughout its eastern side nowhere faces open water. Two principal groups of islands are distinguished, the Kuri archipelago in the south, and the Buduma in the north. The inhabitants of Buduma were noted pirates until reduced to order by the French. The coastline is, in general, undefined and marshy, and broken into numerous bays and peninsulas. It is also, especially on the east, lined by lagoons which communicate with the lake by intricate channels, while across the middle of the lake are numerous mud-banks, marshes, islands and dense growths of aqueous plants. Another stretch of marsh usually cuts off the northernmost part of the lake from the central sections. The open water varies in depth from 3ft. in the north-west to over 20 in the south. Fed by the Shari and other rivers, the lake has no outlet. The flood water brought down by the Shari in December and January causes the lake to rise to a maximum of 24ft., the water spreading over low-lying ground, left dry again in May or June. But after several seasons of heavy rainfall the waters have remained for years beyond their low-water level. Nevertheless the loss by evaporation (estimated in the dry season to be 10in. a month) and percolation is believed to exceed the amount of water received.

The southern basin of Chad is described under the Shari, which empties its waters into the lake about the middle of the southern shore, forming a delta of considerable extent. Beyond the south-east corner of the lake is a channel or depression known as the Soro or Bahr-el-Ghazal (not to be confounded with the Bahr-el-Ghazal affluent of the Nile). This channel goes north-north-east and some 250m. from the lake reaches its lowest point, 500ft. below Chad, in what is known as the Kiri lake (now dry). The remarkable levels led to the supposition of a connection between the basins of the Chad and the Nile. The French explorer, Jean Tilho, in his 1912–17 expedition showed that this was not the case and that the Chad is a closed basin. The Soro depression continues north-east some distance beyond Kiri. Then in the valleys between the Tibesti and Ennedi mountains the ground gradually rises and forms the watershed between Nile and Chad. In this direction, however, Chad at one time extended to the foothills of Tibesti and Borku. Besides the Shari, the Yedseram and Ulge enter the Chad on the south. The only other important affluent of the Chad is the Waube or Yo (otherwise the Komadugu Yobe), which rises near Kano, and flowing eastward enters the lake on its western side 40m. N. of Kuka.

Lake Chad is supposed to have been known by report to Ptolemy, and is identified by some writers with the Kura lake of the middle ages. It was first seen by white men in 1823 when it was reached by way of Tripoli by Walter Oudney, Hugh Clapperton and Dixon Denham. By them the lake was named Waterloo. In 1850 James Richardson, accompanied by Heinrich Barth and Adolf Overweg, reached the lake, also via Tripoli, and Overweg was the first European to navigate its waters (1851). The lake was visited by Eduard Vogel (1855) and by Gustav Nachtigal (1870), the last-named investigating its hydrography in some detail. Owing to an exaggerated belief in its economic importance there was during the partition of Africa a "race" for Lake Chad; in 1890–93 its shores were divided by treaty between Great Britain, France and Germany. The first of these nations to make good its footing in the region was France. A small steamer, brought from the Congo by Emile Gentil, was in 1897 launched on the Shari, and, reaching the Chad, navigated the southern part of the lake. A British force under Col. T. L. N. Morland visited the western or Bornu side of the lake at the beginning of 1902, and in May of the same year the Germans reached Chad from the Cameroons. In 1902–03 French officers under Col. Destenave made detailed surveys of the south-eastern and eastern shores and the adjacent islands. In 1905 Boyd Alexander, a British officer, found that the lake then contained few stretches of open water. Later travellers found a good deal of open water; the extent of the water varying from year to year. One of the ancient trade routes across the Sahara from Tripoli to Kuka in Bornu strikes the lake at its north-west corner, but this has lost much of its former importance. As one of the results of the World War, that part of the lake region which was German passed (1919) under French mandate.

See the works of Denham, Clapperton, Barth and Nachtigal cited in the biographical notices: Jean Tilho in *La Géographie* (March, 1906); and the *Geog. Journal,* vol. lvi. (1920); Boyd Alexander, *From the Niger to the Nile,* vol. i. (1907); A. Chevalier, *Mission Chari-Lac Tchad 1902–1904* (1908); E. Lenfant, *La Grande Route du Tchad* (1905); H. Freydenberg, *Étude sur le Tchad et le bassin du Chari*

(1908); P. H. Lamb, "Notes on a visit to Lake Chad" in *Geog. Journal* (Dec. 1921).

CHADDERTON, an urban district of Lancashire, England on the river Irk, 1 mi. W. of Oldham. Pop. (est. 1938), 30,270. Area, 4.71 sq.mi. It is a textile town, with some metalworking.

CHADERTON, LAURENCE (?1536–1640), Puritan divine, was born at Lees Hall, Oldham, Lancashire, was educated at Christ's college, Cambridge, and on the foundation of Emmanuel college in 1584, Sir Walter Mildmay, the founder, chose Chaderton for the first master. Chaderton was one of the four divines appointed to represent the Puritans at the Hampton Court conference; and he was also one of the translators of the Bible. He provided for 12 fellows and more than 40 scholars in Emmanuel college. Fearing that he might have a successor who held Arminian doctrines, he resigned the mastership in favour of John Preston. He died on Nov. 13, 1640, at the age of about 103, preserving his bodily and mental faculties to the end.

Chaderton published a sermon preached at St. Paul's Cross about 1580, and a treatise *On Justification* at Leyden. Other theological works remain in manuscript.

CHADRON, a city of northwestern Nebraska, U.S., in the heart of the Pine Ridge country, at an altitude of 3,370 ft.; the county seat of Dawes county. It is on federal highway 20 and the Chicago and North Western railway. The population was 4,645 in 1950, and was 4,262 in 1940 by the federal census. Pine-clad buttes give the city a delightful setting, and the Black hills of South Dakota are visible in the distance.

Chadron is the trade centre of a fine cattle and farming region, a division point on the railway, which maintains a roundhouse and machine shops there, and the seat of a state teachers' college (established 1911), which has an enrolment of more than 1,200. Four miles west is an emergency landing field and a weather station. The Pine Ridge Indian reservation (in South Dakota) is 35 mi. north, and 8 mi. south is a state park. Chadron was settled in 1885 and incorporated in 1886.

CHADWICK, SIR EDWIN (1800–1890), English sanitary reformer, was born at Longsight, near Manchester, Jan. 24, 1800, and was educated for the bar. His essays in the *Westminster Review* introduced him to the notice of Jeremy Bentham, who engaged him as a literary assistant. In 1832 he was employed by the royal commission on the poor laws as an investigator, and in 1833 he was made a full member of that body. In conjunction with Nassau W. Senior he drafted the report of 1834 which procured the passing of the new poor law. His special contribution was the institution of the union as the area of administration. In 1834 he was appointed secretary to the poor law commissioners. His relations with his official chiefs became much strained, and the disagreement led among other causes, to the dissolution of the poor law commission in 1846. Chadwick's chief contribution to political controversy was his constant advocacy of entrusting certain departments of local affairs to trained and selected experts, instead of to representatives elected on the principle of local self-government. His report on "The Sanitary Condition of the Labouring Population" (1842) is a valuable historical document. He was a commissioner of the board of health for improving the water supply, drainage and cleansing of great towns, from its establishment in 1848 to its abolition in 1854. He was made K.C.B. in 1889. He died at East Sheen, Surrey, on July 6, 1890.

See Haven Emerson, "Public Health Diagnosis," *Journal of Preventive Medicine,* vol. i, pp. 401–427 (1927).

CHADWICK, SIR JAMES (1891–), British physicist, was born in Manchester on Oct. 20, 1891. He was educated at the universities of Manchester and Cambridge, and at Charlottenburg institution in Berlin, where he studied under Hans Geiger. In 1921 he was made a fellow of Gonville and Caius college, Cambridge, and two years later became assistant director of radioactive research at the Cavendish laboratory, Cambridge. Chadwick received the 1935 Nobel award in physics for his discovery of the neutron. He was knighted in 1945 and became master of Gonville and Caius college in 1948. His writings include *Radiations from Radioactive Substances* (with E. Rutherford and C. D. Ellis [1930]).

CHAEREMON, Athenian dramatist of the first half of the 4th century B.C. Aristotle (*Rhetoric,* iii. 12) says his works were intended for reading, not for representation. According to Suidas, he wrote comedy as well as tragedy, and the title of his *Achilles, Slayer of Thersites* suggests that it was a satyric drama. His *Centaurus* is described by Aristotle (*Poet.* i. 12) as a rhapsody in all kinds of metres. The fragments of Chaeremon are correct in form and have an easy rhythm, but are marred by a florid style. It is not agreed whether he is the author of three epigrams in the Greek Anthology (Palatine vii. 469, 720, 721) which bear his name.

See H. Bartsch, *De Chaeremone Poëta tragico* (1843); fragments in A. Nauck, *Fragmenta Tragicorum Graecorum.*

CHAEREMON, of Alexandria (1st century A.D.) Stoic philosopher and grammarian. He was superintendent of part of the Alexandrian library and belonged to the higher ranks of the priesthood. In A.D. 49 he was summoned to Rome, with Alexander of Aegae, to become tutor to the youthful Nero. He was the author of a *History of Egypt;* of works on *Comets, Egyptian Astrology,* and *Hieroglyphics;* and of a treatise on *Expletive Conjunctions.* Chaeremon was the chief of the party which explained the Egyptian religious system as an allegory of the worship of nature. He can hardly be identical with the Chaeremon who accompanied (*c.* 26 B.C.; Strabo xvii. p. 806) Aelius Gallus, praefect of Egypt, on a journey into the interior.

Fragments in C. Müller, *Fragmenta Historicorum Graecorum,* iii. 495–499.

CHAERONEIA, an ancient town of Boeotia, about 7m. W. of Orchomenus. It may be the Homeric Arne. The site is partly occupied by the village of Kapraena; the ancient citadel was known as the Petrachus, and there is a theatre cut in the rock. Until the 4th century B.C. it was a dependency of Orchomenus. Its importance lay in its strategic position, the last serious obstacle to an invader of central Greece from the north. Two great battles were fought on this site in antiquity. In 338 B.C. Philip II. of Macedon defeated a confederation of Greek States (*see* below). In 86 B.C. the Roman general L. Cornelius Sulla defeated the army of Mithridates VI., king of Pontus, near Chaeroneia. Numerical superiority was neutralized by judicious choice of ground and the steadiness of the legionaries. Chaeroneia was the birthplace of Plutarch, who returned to his native town in old age, and was long held in honour. Pausanias (ix. 40) mentions the divine honours accorded at Chaeroneia to the sceptre of Agamemnon. (*Iliad,* ii. 101.) A colossal seated lion a little to the south-east of the site marks the grave of the Boeotians who fell fighting against Philip. This lion was found broken to pieces; the tradition that it was blown up by Odysseus Androutsos is incorrect (*see* Murray, *Handbook for Greece,* ed. 5. 1884, p. 409). It was re-erected in 1905.

BIBLIOGRAPHY.—Thucydides iv. 76; Diodorus xvi. 85–86; Plutarch, *Alexander,* ch. 9; *Sulla,* chs. 16–19; Appian, *Mithridatica,* chs. 42–45; W. M. Leake, *Travels in Northern Greece* (London, 1835), ii. 112–117, 192–201; B. V. Head, *Historia Numorum* (Oxford, 1887), p. 292; J. Kromayer, *Antike Schlachtfelder in Griechenland* (Berlin, 1903), pp. 127–195; G. Sotiriades in *Athen. Mitteil.* 1903, pp. 301 ff.; 1905, p. 120; 1906, p. 396; 'Εφημ. 'Αρχαιολ., 1908, p. 65.

CHAERONEIA, BATTLE OF, 338 B.C. This is of great historial importance as the victory by which Philip II (*q.v.*) definitely established the Macedonian supremacy in Greece. In military history, however, too little is known of its details to give it marked significance. Philip's path into Boeotia was barred by the allied Athenians and Thebans both at the western route from Cytinium to Amphissa and the eastern pass of Parapotamii from Elateia to Chaeroneia. Philip first placed himself at Elateia; then, by a ruse of withdrawal, put the defenders of the western route still more off their guard and, moving from Cytinium by night, debouched into western Boeotia at Amphissa. He was thus on the rear of but at a distance from the defenders of the eastern pass, who thereupon fell back from Parapotamii. But instead of passing eastwards through hilly country which would have aided the resistance, he switched his army back to Elateia, moved unopposed through the pass of Parapotamii and descended upon the enemy's main army at Chaeroneia. Philip placed his 18-year old son, Alexander, in charge of the left wing, where his best troops faced the redoubtable Thebans and after a bitter struggle gained the upper hand. Meanwhile he had retired his right wing elastically before the onset of the Athenians until he had drawn them on to low ground while he had retired on to a rising slope. Then, suddenly he launched a counterstroke and disrupted the Athenians. Both the victorious Macedonian wings now converged inwards upon the allied centre and crushed it between them. With the overthrow of the Theban army and the annihilation of the famous "Sacred Band" the sceptre of military as well as of political supremacy passed to the "new model" army of Macedonia that Philip had created. (*See* also MANTINEIA; GRANICUS, BATTLE OF THE; ALEXANDER III.)

CHAETOGNATHA, a small group of transparent and for the most part pelagic organisms, whose position is very isolated. There are eight genera and 38 species; the best-known genus is *Sagitta* with 27 species. These animals exist in extraordinary quantities, so that under certain conditions the surface of the sea seems almost stiff with the incredible multitude of organisms which pervade it. Rough seas cause them to drop into deeper water. Deep-sea forms also occur, but the group is essentially pelagic. The Chaetognatha form part of the diet of pelagic fishes. They are very voracious, readily devouring herring fry as big as themselves.

As a rule the body is 1 to 3 cm. in length, though some species are larger, by 4 or 5 mm. in breadth, and is shaped something like a torpedo with side flanges and a slightly swollen, rounded head. It can be divided into three regions—(i.) head, (ii.) trunk, and (iii.) tail, separated from one another by two transverse septa. The almost spherical head is covered by a hood which can be retracted; it bears upon its side a number of sickle-shaped, chitinous hooks and rows of low spines. A pair of eyes lie dorsally. The trunk contains a spacious body-cavity filled during the breeding season by the swollen ovaries, and the same is true of the tail, substituting testes for ovaries.

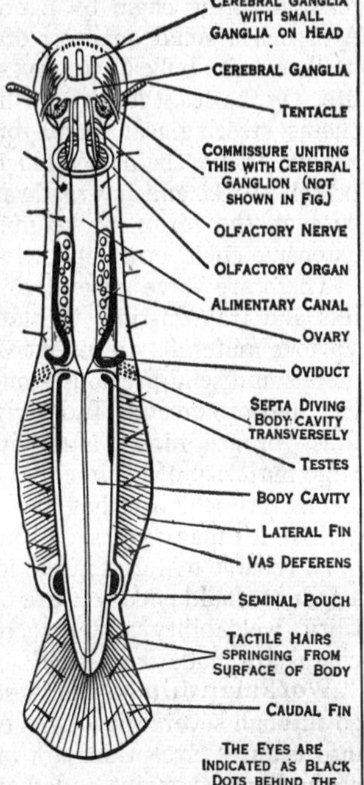

CHAETOGNATHA, "ARROW-WORM," A GROUP OF TRANSPARENT ORGANISMS WHICH EXIST IN GREAT QUANTITIES NEAR THE SURFACE OF THE OPEN SEA

The skin consists of a transparent cuticle secreted by the underlying ectoderm; beneath this is a basement membrane; and then a layer of longitudinal muscle fibres which are limited inside by a layer of peritoneal cells. The muscles are striated and arranged in four quadrants. Along each side of the body stretches a horizontal fin and a similar flange surrounds the tail.

The mouth opens on to the ventral surface of the head. It leads into a straight alimentary canal whose walls consist of a layer of ciliated cells, ensheathed in a thin layer of peritoneal cells. There is no armature, and there are no glands, and the whole tract can be divided only into an oesophagus and an intestine. A median mesentery running dorsoventrally supports the alimentary canal and is continued behind it into the tail, thus dividing the body cavity into two lateral halves.

There are no specialized circulatory, respiratory or excretory organs. The nervous system consists of a cerebral ganglion in the head, and a ventral ganglion in the trunk, with lateral commissures uniting these ganglia on each side. There is a minute but extensive nervous plexus all over the body.

Chaetognatha are hermaphrodite. The ovaries are attached to the side walls of the trunk region; between them and the body wall lie the two oviducts whose inner and anterior end is closed, their outer ends opening one on each side of the anus, where the trunk joins the tail. This oviduct fits closely over a second duct, the receptaculum seminis, which the spermatozoa enter, passing through the walls and finally reaching the ripe ovum. Temporary oviducts are formed at each oviposition. A number of ova ripen simultaneously. The two testes lie in the tail and the spermatozoa pass out through short vasa deferentia with internal ciliated funnels.

With hardly an exception the transparent eggs are laid into the sea and float on its surface. The development is direct and there is no larval stage. As in some insects, the cells destined to form the reproductive organs are very early apparent.

The great bulk of the group is pelagic, as the transparent nature of all their tissues indicates. They move by flexing their bodies. The Chaetognatha appear to have no close relatives, and probably arose from the primitive *Procoelomate* stock in very ancient times. Recently Meek has attempted to show that they are related to the vertebrates.

(*See* also PLANKTON.)

See G. T. Burfield, "Sagitta" (*L.M.B.C Memoirs,* xxviii. (1927); Meek, *Proc. Zool. Soc.* (Lond. 1928).

CHAETOPODA, originally a zoological class, including all the Annelida (*q.v.*), except the Echiurida (*q.v.*). F. E. Beddard used the term to cover the classes Archiannelida, Polychaeta, Oligochaeta, Hirudinea (leeches) and Myzostomida. Parker and Haswell (*Textbook of Zoology*) use the term to include only the Polychaeta and Oligochaeta. The characteristic feature of Chaetopoda is the possession of bristles (*setae*). The term is now obsolete.

CHAFER, a word used in modern speech to distinguish the beetles of the family Scarabaeidae, and more especially those species which feed on leaves in the adult state. For the characters of the Scarabaeidae, *see* COLEOPTERA.

This family includes a large number of beetles, some of which feed on dung and others on vegetable tissues.

The cockchafers and their near allies belong to the subfamily Melolonthinae, and the rose-chafers to the Cetoniinae; in both the beetles eat leaves, and their grubs spend a long life underground devouring roots.

In Europe the Melolonthines that are usually noted as injurious are the two species of cockchafer (*Melolontha melolontha* and *M. hippocastani*), large heavy beetles with black pubescent prothorax, brown elytra and an elongated pointed tail-process; the summer-chafer (*Amphimallon solstitialis*), a smaller pale brown chafer.

In the United States, Melolonthines of the genus *Phyllophaga* (popularly known as "May beetles" or "June beetles") may do considerable damage to strawberries, corn (maize), wheat and grass crops.

The most important species is probably *Phyllophaga rugosa,* which frequently is very destructive to corn.

The larvae of the chafers are heavy, soft-skinned grubs, with hard brown heads provided with powerful mandibles, three pairs of well-developed legs, and a swollen abdomen. As they grow, they become strongly flexed towards the ventral surface, and lie curled up in their earthen cells, feeding on roots. The larval life lasts several years, and in hard frosts the grubs go deep down away from the surface.

Pupation takes place in the autumn, and though the perfect insect emerges from the cuticle very soon afterwards, it remains in its underground cell until the ensuing summer. After pairing, the female crawls down into the soil to lay her eggs. The grubs of chafers, when turned up by the plow, are greedily devoured by poultry, pigs and various wild birds.

CHAFF, the husks left after threshing grain (A.S. *ceaf,* allied to O.H.Ger. *cheva,* a husk or pod); also hay and straw chopped fine as food for cattle; hence, the worthless part of anything. The colloquial phrase, to chaff, meaning to make fun of a person, is derived from this word, or from "to chafe," meaning to irritate.

CHAFFARINAS or **ZAFFARINES,** a group of islands owned by Spain, 2½ mi. north of Cabo del Agua, in Morocco. Pop. *c.* 345, mainly soldiers of a garrison stationed there. The islands, which were the *Tresinsulae* of the Romans and the *Zafrān* of the Arabs, were occupied by Spain in 1848. Construction of breakwaters between the islands of Isabella II and El Rey were undertaken; one dike was destroyed by storm in 1914. The largest island, Del Congreso, is rocky and hilly.

CHAFFCUTTER: *see* PROCESSING MACHINERY.

CHAFFEE, ADNA ROMANZA (1842–1914), United States soldier, born April 14, 1842, in Orwell, Ohio. He enlisted in the 6th cavalry regiment July 22, 1861, and was a member of that regiment for 25 years. The 6th cavalry was with the Army of the Potomac through most of the Civil War. Chaffee was commissioned 2nd lieutenant in May 1863, was wounded and taken prisoner at Gettysburg, refused to be paroled and was abandoned with other wounded. On Feb. 22, 1865, he was made 1st lieutenant. After the war the 6th cavalry was sent to Texas, and in 1867 Chaffee resigned, planning to enter private business. He was persuaded to change his mind, was restored to his rank, and served in the southwest until the Spanish-American War broke out, rising to the rank of lieutenant colonel. He served in the Spanish-American War, and at its conclusion was made chief of staff of the military governor of Cuba until May 1900. He became a colonel in May 1899. Chaffee commanded the U.S. troops in China during the Boxer uprising, and was military governor of the Philippine Islands July 1901–Sept. 1902. In 1904 he was promoted to lieutenant general and detailed as chief of staff. He retired Feb. 1, 1906, and died in Los Angeles, Calif., Nov. 1, 1914.

CHAFFINCH, a bird (*Fringilla coelebs*), belonging to the family Fringillidae (*see* FINCH), distinguished, in the male sex, by the deep grayish blue of its crown feathers, the yellowish green of its rump, two conspicuous bars of white on the wing coverts, and the reddish brown passing into vinous red of the throat and breast. The female is drab, but shows the same white markings as the male; the young males resemble the females until after the first autumn moult. The chaffinch breeds early, and its song may be heard in February. It builds its nest on trees and bushes, preferring those overgrown with lichens. The nest is composed of moss and wool, lined with grass and feathers. It lays four or five eggs of a pale bluish buff, streaked and spotted with purplish red. In spring the chaffinch is destructive to early flowers, and to young radishes and turnips; in summer it feeds on insects and their larvae, while in autumn and winter its food consists of grain and other seeds. On the continent of Europe the chaffinch is a favourite songbird. In winter chaffinches form small flocks, often composed solely of males. The continental chaffinch (*F. c. coelebs*) ranges generally over Europe to tree-limit in the north, wintering southward. The British chaffinch (*F. c. gengleri*) is a breeding resident. Allied races are found in northwest Africa, Canaries, Madeira and Azores. (G. F. Ss.)

CHAGRES, a village of the Republic of Panamá, on the Atlantic coast of the Isthmus, at the mouth of the Chagres river, and about 8 mi. W. of Colón. It has a harbour from 10 to 12 ft. deep, which is difficult to enter, however, on account of bars at its mouth. The port was discovered by Columbus in 1502, and was opened for traffic with Panamá, on the Pacific coast, by way of the Chagres river, in the 16th century. With the decline of Porto Bello in the 18th century Chagres became the chief Atlantic port of the Isthmus, and was at the height of its importance during the rush of gold-hunters across the Isthmus to California in 1849 and the years following. With the completion of the Panamá railway in 1855, however, travel was diverted to Colón, and Chagres soon became a village of miserable huts, with no evidence of its former importance. On a high rock at the mouth of the river stands the castle of Lorenzo, which was destroyed by Sir Henry Morgan when he captured the town in 1671, but was rebuilt soon afterwards by the Spaniards. Chagres was again captured in 1740 by British forces under Admiral Edward Vernon.

CHAIN-GANG, an American method of handling convicts, working principally on State road construction, stone quarrying and bridge building in the States of Virginia, North Carolina, Georgia, Florida and Alabama. The convicts are generally housed in temporary buildings of rough construction with inadequate sanitary arrangements, and are more or less isolated. In Virginia and Alabama the buildings are of a portable type, similar in construction to an army barrack. In some instances in Georgia a steel wagon cage is used. These cages are about 18 ft. long and 10 ft. wide and sometimes house as many as 18 men, sleeping in triple-decked bunks. The housing conditions differ in the several States, Alabama having by far the best conditions. In all of the camps except Alabama some method of chaining the men who are not trusties is in use. The most common method is the use of the "bull-chain," 4 ft. long, weighing about 3 lb., which is attached to a heavy iron cuff riveted around the right ankle. In going to and from work and during the time the convicts are confined in their quarters, the end of the bull-chain is attached to a long master chain which keeps all of the convicts leashed together. Sometimes, especially in the case of men who have attempted to or who have escaped and been returned, step-chains are used in addition to the bull-chain. These are attached by the use of leg irons, to both ankles, and are from 15 in. to 22 in. in length. Harsh methods of punishment prevail, ranging from solitary confinement on diminished rations to whipping, and, in Georgia, to the use of antiquated stocks and sweat-boxes. While, due to the long outdoor season, the labour of chain-gangs affords a great saving in the cost of road construction and is valuable in the prevention of idleness on the part of prisoners, the chaining of the men cannot help but have a definite demoralizing effect. In addition to the State chain-gangs there are in many localities similar county chain-gangs. (W. B. Co.)

CHAIN MANUFACTURE is the fabrication of a series of links, usually of metal, which are joined together by one of several methods. A chain provides a flexible loop or a connection between objects. The metal of the link is sometimes twisted to form a knot, or welded to strengthen the connection. Many methods of manufacturing chain by hand and machinery are now in vogue. Although a small quantity of chain is used for holding prisoners in check, the bulk of it serves man in various phases of his daily life. On the sea it is used for huge ship anchor chains, deck lashing chains, steering gear chains, buoy chains, etc. Railways use safety chains, brake chains, conductor's valve chains, etc. For motor travel on wet and icy roadways, anti-skid chains are used. Likewise on the farm, in the mine, the forest, the shop or on any extensive engineering operation, usage is found for chain.

There are three general classifications of chain: welded, weldless and transmission, the latter being literally a weldless style. Various materials are used in the manufacture of chain. Precious metals and semi-precious stones are formed into chains for jewellery and ornaments. Industrial chains are made from iron, steel, brass, bronze, nickel, aluminium and other metals or alloys. The large majority of commercial chain is made from wrought iron or steel. Wrought iron has had preference among fire-welded chain makers for many years. Wrought iron is generally regarded as the most reliable material in the manufacture of chains for uses where a failure would endanger life or property. It has considerable ductility, weldability and rust resistance. However, many reliable chains are made from steel.

Workmanship.—Hand and machine-made chain links usually go through several processes before they are ready for assembling into chains. Exceptions are in the instances of links used in cast chain, knotted chains and chain made directly from the solid bar. These processes vary widely in the different types of chain. In hand-made chain, the first operation consists of cutting the bar into short sections to a predetermined length, governed by the size of the link to be made. This short section is flattened, usually called "scarfed," at each end and then bent into a U shape. The scarfed ends are then brought to a welding temperature, threaded through the last finished link, and the weld completed by hammering. To give the welded end a finished appearance, concave tools, called "dollies," are sometimes placed over the weld and by additional hammering on the dollies, the weld is smoothed and shaped. The heating material for the chain maker's furnace is either coke, oil or gas.

By the use of machines some of these operations in this method are eliminated and others made easier. Bars or rods of metal are wound by machine into oval coils and single convolutions of the coils are cut on an angle of about 45°, thus furnishing single-scarfed links ready for placing in the furnace to be heated. When the scarfed ends are at a welding temperature, the link is removed from the fire, threaded into the last completed link and the weld completed. Completion of the weld is accomplished with the aid of a hand hammer which is used to close the scarfed ends of the link together with a few blows. From this point the weld is completed in a power hammer, equipped with dies which fit over the welded end of the link. These hammers are operated by foot power, direct drive or indirect drive from some remote source of power. Chains made by this method have a slight twist in them. This twist is caused by the coiling operation. When the chain is for uses where this twist would be objectionable the twist is removed in a power hammer having especially designed dies, which straighten each link immediately after it is welded.

Electric Welded Chain.—This is the latest development in welded chain manufacture. A large part of the world's tonnage of small welded chain is now made by this method. Sizes up to $\frac{3}{4}$ in. diameter are commercially made in large quantities. Any of the larger sizes can be electrically welded but manufacturing costs in 1928 were too high. Three types of electric welds are in general use at the present time—the butt weld, the half-butt weld and the flash weld. All of these are of the resistance type, in which the electric current, passing through the material and across the butted ends of the link, produces sufficient heat to raise the metal to the welding or fusing temperature. A later development in electric chain welding is called "percussion welding," but it is not being used commercially. In this latter method, an electrically charged condenser is discharged across the butted ends of a chain link.

Links for electric welding are prepared differently than for fire welding. In the electric method, coils of wire or rods are passed through a chain-forming machine, which automatically straightens the wire, cuts the required length, threads the wire into the last completed link and forms the link, making a continuous chain ready for the welding machine. This butted chain is passed through a chain-welding machine which welds the links. Some welding machines weld alternate links and others consecutive links. They are automatic with one operator attending many machines, or semi-automatic, requiring the services of an operator for each machine. In the electric-weld process the weld is usually made at the side of the link. In the fire-weld process the weld is usually at the end of the link, the exception being certain very large sizes which are sometimes made with the weld at the side. Some electric-welded chain is made with weld at the end of the link, but this is the exception, rather than the rule. In the upset-welding method the links are welded at a relatively low temperature and the butted ends pressed together by a relatively low pressure. This type of weld is characterized by the extruded metal at the weld, forming a bulge which is seldom trimmed off. The semi-upset welding method is similar to the full-upset, with the exception that when the weld is about to be completed a die is placed over one-half the diameter of the material at the butted portion. This die prevents the metal from being forced to the outer side of the link.

Flash welding is also of the resistance type. It is distinguished by a small amount of metal extruded at the butted ends when the pressure is applied to form the weld. Because of the pressure and closeness of the electrodes, this excess metal, sometimes called the "flash," takes the shape of a flattened ring, differing in this respect from the bulge of the upset-weld. The "flash" is trimmed off close to the diameter of the material, leaving a smooth weld which, when polished, defies detection.

Welded chain is used largely in the straight link variety; however, some use is also made of twisted links. This type has the links twisted so that each link will be in approximately the same plane and therefore lie flat. In the fire-weld method each link is twisted as completed, but in the electric process the completed chain is passed through a machine which automatically twists the links. Other chains which have the same general shape as the welded chains, yet are not welded, include cast chains, which are made by casting metal in properly shaped molds, and solid link chains, made by stamping a solid cuneiform bar into the shape of stiff chain and twisting the individual links apart to make it flexible. The result is a solid, link chain having the appearance of a welded chain.

Anchor Chain.—For ship anchors is used a chain with links having a bar, called a stud, across the inside width of each link. This is called "stud-link" chain and in marine circles is referred to as a chain cable. Both the forming and welding operations are similar to the open link fire-welded chain. After the open link is completed, the stud, concave at each end, is inserted in the link and the sides pressed together. A relatively small amount of stud-link chain is made by a steam hammer process in which the link bars are upset; *i.e.*, balled on the end and scarfed by machines. The scarfed ends are heated and the weld completed on a steam hammer. In cast steel chain the stud is cast at the same time as the balance of the link and becomes a solid part of the link. Studs used in wrought iron chain are either castings or drop forgings. There are several reasons for putting the stud in this type of chain. It prevents the chain from fouling, adds weight to the link and prevents the link from deforming at a relatively low load. It does not increase the tensile strength of the chain, as is generally supposed.

Weldless Chain.—The term "weldless chain" covers a wide range of styles and broadly includes knotted chains, stamped link chains, transmission chains, bead chains, malleable chains, etc. Knotted chains bear a close relationship to the welded chain because they were developed, as a low-priced product, to replace small sizes of welded chain. They are practically all made upon automatic machines which fabricate the chain by straightening the wire, cutting, threading and tying, a single machine making the complete chain from the coil of wire to the finished product. There are about a dozen different styles of these chains in general use. Other forms of weldless wire chains contain no knot and consist simply of twisted wires hooked together—such as jack chain and ladder chain. Stamped link chain such as sash chain and transmission chain require at least two operations in their manufacture. The first operation blanks the links and the second, either automatic or by hand, assembles them. Bead or ball chain, commonly used in electric light fixtures, consists of a series of hollow balls joined by solid bars, the latter having a ball or cross-pipe formed at its ends. This chain is also made entirely by automatic machines. Jewellery chain in an almost endless variety is made from precious metals and used chiefly for ornament. Such chains are often made with oddly shaped links and with combinations of differently shaped links. Those made automatically bear somewhat of a uniform construction throughout their length, while other designs formed and ornamented by hand, vary in details with almost every link.

Finishes used on chain include practically every known finish for which there is a demand. Many chains are sold in their natural finish, as they come from the forge or machine. Some are polished highly by tumbling in sawdust, sand or leather scraps. Protective coatings, such as asphaltum, zinc, tin and lacquer are frequently used. Various colours of paints, powders and japans are used on chains for ornamental purposes, such as chandelier chain. Still others are plated with copper, brass, chromium, cadmium, nickel and other metals or alloys. At present, Cradley Heath, in the Black Country of England, is the centre of heavy-chain manufacture, while York, Pennsylvania, U.S.A., is the centre of small-chain manufacture. (H. M. B.)

Testing.—After welded chain is made it should be given a "proof test" and each link examined for exterior defects. The purpose of this test is to determine if there are any hidden defects which would render the chain unsafe for its rated working load. Any load which is higher than the rated working load yet lower than the elastic limit of the chain link is suitable for this proof test. Railroads, testing bureaus, large users of chain, etc., have specifications giving definite loads to which the various sizes and grades of chain must be tested by the manufacturer. For many years it has been customary to proof test welded chain to a load equal to one-half of the average ultimate tensile strength. Many chain manufacturers continue to follow this practice. Some chain authorities feel that such a load is injurious to the chain links especially when applied to iron chains. They recommend as a substitute a load about 25% higher than the working load. The statutory proof load required by the British board of trade applying to close-link chain for use on British ships is: proof load to be $12d^2$ tons, where d is the diameter in inches of the iron in the link. For stud-link chain the proof load is 50% higher than for the open-link chain although the tensile strength is practically the same. Knotted types of chain are not proof tested. There are no standard dimensions for chain links. Link dimensions vary with different manufacturers. Well proportioned links can be designed by making the outside dimensions $4\frac{1}{2}$ by $3\frac{1}{4}$ times the diameter of the material, for close-link chain and 6 by 3·6 times for stud-link chains. These dimensions can be varied.

Destruction Tests.—To determine what ultimate tensile strength may be expected from a finished chain a section several feet long should be tested to destruction. Toughness and ductility of the iron from which the links are made should be given greater consideration than merely high tensile strength when selecting a chain for use where a reliable chain is required. Chain with a high tensile strength is often brittle and will break without warning whereas a chain made from a ductile material will stretch considerably before breaking. Toughness and ductility can best be determined by observing the structure of the break and by the relative amount of reduction in area and the elongation at the point of fracture. These features should be determined in a straight bar of the material from which the links are to be made. Total stretch of a chain before breaking is of little value in determining the toughness and ductility of the material because the elongation of the chain is governed primarily by the shape of the links and not by the composition of the material.

Permissible Loading.—Maximum working loads for chains should be based upon the proof test and should never be higher than the rated working loads suggested by the manufacturer of the chain, individual specifications or testing bureau for the size and grade of chain being considered. Working loads are always given to be used when the chain is lifting in a vertical position. It should be noted (*see* table) that the working load of a chain

Working Loads of Sling Chains When Used at Angles
Wrought Iron Open Link Chain

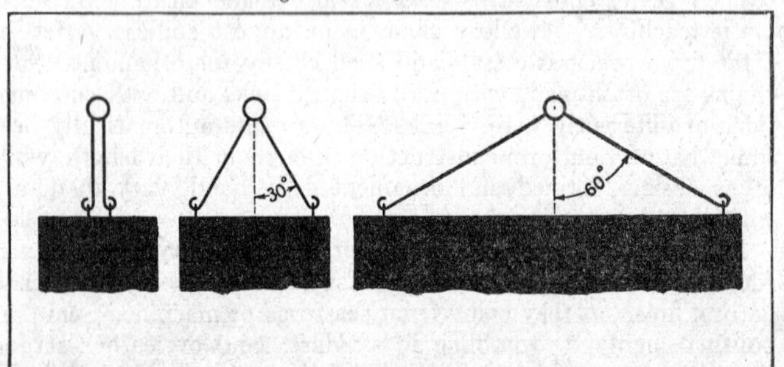

Size chain, inches	Maximum working load for each branch of sling when used for vertical lift. In lbs.	Maximum working load for each branch of sling when used at angle of 30° from vertical. In lbs.	Maximum working load for each branch of sling when used at angle of 60° from vertical. In lbs.
$\frac{1}{4}$ . .	1,100	950	550
$\frac{3}{8}$ . .	2,700	2,350	1,350
$\frac{1}{2}$ . .	4,500	3,900	2,250
$\frac{5}{8}$ . .	6,900	6,000	3,450
$\frac{3}{4}$ . .	10,100	8,750	5,050
$\frac{7}{8}$ . .	14,000	12,000	7,000
1 . .	18,600	16,000	9,300
$1\frac{1}{4}$ . .	28,800	25,000	14,400
$1\frac{1}{2}$ . .	40,800	35,000	20,400
$1\frac{3}{4}$ . .	52,500	45,500	26,250
2 . .	66,600	57,500	33,300

when lifting at any angle to the vertical line is always lower than for the vertical lift. When lifting at an angle of 60° to the direction of pull, as with a double sling chain, the working load is only one-half of the working load for the same chain when used for vertical lifting. (H. M. B.; W. L. Gn.)

CHAIN-SHOT, two large bullets or half-bullets fastened together by a chain; formerly used in naval engagements to cut rigging, etc., and sometimes in land battles as a short-range projectile.

CHAIN STORE. The chain store system of merchandising (known in Great Britain as "multiple shops") is largely an American phenomenon. Although chain stores operate extensively in most countries and despite the fact that the chain idea of distribution was practised on a limited scale in China as early as 200 B.C. and in Japan from as early as 1643, chain stores had their real development and growth, as methods of store operation, in the U.S. during the 20th century. Chain store methods spread into the operations of virtually all types of retail establishments until, by the 1950s, they were responsible for approximately 30% of the total retail volume in the United States.

Definition of a Chain.—Marketing associations, the Federal Trade commission and the census of American business differed substantially in their definitions of chains, chiefly on the basis of the nature of merchandise handled and the number of stores operated. In the more common sense, however, retail chain stores are considered to be any system of two or more centrally owned retail stores dealing in substantially similar lines of goods. This definition recognizes three characteristics which must exist before a retail business can be classified as a chain—two or more units, central ownership and basically similar lines of merchandise. Although many chain stores are both centrally owned and operated, central or uniform operation is not a requisite characteristic of a chain store system. In many important chains the store units, though centrally owned and carrying substantially the same lines of goods, are largely individually operated and adapted to the needs and characteristics of the particular markets they serve.

An interesting aspect of this definition is that the various units must carry substantially the same lines of merchandise. This does not mean that they must carry identical lines but rather that the nature of their merchandise must be basically similar. Thus, if two or more stores, centrally owned, handled entirely different types of goods, despite their common ownership these stores could not centralize or pool their buying, exchange strategic merchandising information and in other ways enjoy the advantages of genuine chain store operation. For these reasons, this type of central retail ownership is not considered to be a chain-operated system.

Development in the United States.—The first chain store system in America probably developed with the Hudson's Bay company and its series of trading posts established in Canada prior to 1750. In the United States, the chain store idea was first put into effect by the Great Atlantic and Pacific Tea company in 1858. This company added its second store the following year. Park and Tilford became a chain in 1860, and the F. W. Woolworth company began this type of operation in the variety field in 1879. By 1900, it is estimated, there were about 700 such operations in the United States.

As late as 1920, however, U.S. chain stores were responsible for only about 4% of the total retail trade of the nation. From 1920 to 1930 the system had a spectacular growth. By 1926 it was responsible for approximately 9% of estimated retail sales; by 1930 this percentage had risen to more than 20%. From 1930 to 1933, despite adverse economic conditions, chain stores continued their growth. In 1931 chains were responsible for 21.7% of the total retail trade. In 1933 they produced approximately 25% of the nation's total retail volume. From 1933 to 1939, however, the growth was substantially arrested. The biggest factor obstructing their growth during this period was the extensive enactment of anti-chain store legislation. The rapid rise of the chains had aroused serious concern on the part of local independent retailers. Furthermore, because the chains buy largely directly from manufacturers or producers, circumventing the wholesaler, much of the wholesale trade joined independent retail businesses in their efforts to stop growth of the chains. These two groups exerted a powerful influence on local and national legislative bodies, with the result that restrictive laws were introduced and passed. Some observers then concluded that chain stores had reached their maximum activity and were in the process of decline. Although the growth had been considerably slackened, it was recognized that this method of retail operation had made an outstanding contribution to distribution. In 1944 chains, while operating fewer units, produced 27% of total retail sales. In 1948 the percentage was 29.6% and was produced in 162,655 units whose sales volume totalled $38,691,321,000.

Operating Characteristics.—The explanation of the growing and continued success of the chains lies in their peculiar and economically sound methods of operation. Some of the important characteristics of operation which give them distinct advantages in the field of distribution are as follows:

Large-Scale Buying.—By pooling the merchandise needs of a number of stores, the chains are characteristically in a position to engage in large-scale buying. This buying ability gives them many advantages in the selection of sources, in the establishment of merchandise standards and specifications, in obtaining volume prices and in the maintenance of secure sources of supply.

Direct Buying.—Because of the size of the orders they place, they are usually able to buy directly from producers and manufacturers and thereby cut costs and reduce merchandise delivering time.

Standardized Lines.—Most chain stores concentrate on the handling of standardized lines of staple merchandise. Although some merchandise fashion goods and other specialty items successfully, the broad chain store development has been in staple goods which have had more or less wide universal demand in the territory served by the company. This merchandising policy has helped to reduce markdowns, to increase turnover and to operate at lower costs.

Standardized Operating Methods.—As chains add additional units, they are in an advantageous position to experiment with operating procedures and methods. Out of these experiments they develop efficient merchandising and operating techniques which may become standardized throughout the system.

Selected Locations.—Chain store owners have been particularly conscious of the importance of proper location in the success of their businesses. Partly because of their ability to analyze the value of a particular site and partly because of financial ability to buy the locations they want, chain stores often occupy the best retail sites. Some chains, however, because of the nature of the merchandise they handle and the consumer acceptance they enjoy, do not need central locations. These stores have been extremely successful in moving away from central shopping districts and establishing separate shopping areas of their own.

Distributed Risks.—Through the operation of many units, chain stores are able to distribute and balance co-operatively merchandising and operating risks.

Although almost every type of retail store may be chain operated, the system has been most successful in the merchandising of such lines as variety merchandise, shoes, automobile accessories, dairy products, groceries and meats, cigars and tobacco, drugs, paint and glass, newspapers and magazines and women's ready-to-wear clothing. In all these lines more than 25% of retail sales are made through chains.

(O. P. R.)

Great Britain.—There are two main types of chain store in Great Britain, the multiple shop and the "variety" chain store, both of which developed in the second half of the 19th century. By 1900 there were important multiple tea dealers, grocers and provision merchants, chemists, news agents and tobacconists. Examples of the variety chain stores were the Penny Bazaars which flourished at the end of the 19th century; Marks and Spencer, first opened in 1887; and Woolworth, which spread from the United States to England in 1910.

In 1950, according to the first census of distribution, retail firms (other than co-operative societies) with ten or more establishments (branches) handled retail sales to the value of £1,156,000,000; that is, 23% of a total of £4,923,000,000 handled by all retail shops. More than 80% of the trade of the multiples was handled by firms with 25 or more branches. The share of multiples with ten or more branches in the principal divisions of retail trade was: 34% in chemists' goods, 33% in clothing, 25% in hardware, 25% in books and stationery, 23% in furniture, 22% in groceries, 18% in other food retailing, 12% in confectionery, tobacco and newspapers and 9% in jewellery, sports goods and fancy goods. Variety stores were almost exclusively of the multiple type.

Most multiple organizations developed from small retailing beginnings. In a few trades (*e.g.*, in footwear) some manufacturers set up their own chains of retail shops. In others some multiples extended their operations by going into manufacturing. The "tied house" system of the brewing industry is a form of retailing which has some but not all of the typical characteristics of multiple store control and management.

The growth of multiple trading in the 20th century became an important competitive force in retailing, affecting the small-scale independent shopkeepers, the department stores and the co-operative societies. In Great Britain, unlike some other European countries and the United States, no government measures have ever been introduced to control the growth or to handicap the operation of multiple firms. There has been no discriminatory taxation. In 1937 an unsuccessful attempt was made to introduce a private bill in parliament to restrict the activities and growth of multiples.

(B. S. Y.)

CHAIR, a movable seat, usually with four legs and for a single person, the most varied and familiar article of domestic furniture. (In Mid. Eng. *chaere,* through O.Fr. *chaëre* or *chaiere,* from Lat. *cathedra,* later *caledra,* Gr. *καθδέρα* seat, *cf.* "cathedral"; the modern Fr. form *chaise,* a chair, has been adopted in English with a particular meaning as a form of carriage; *chaire* in French is still used of a professorial or ecclesiastical "chair," or *cathedra.*) The chair is of extreme antiquity, although for many centuries and indeed for thousands of years it was an appanage of state and dignity rather than an article of ordinary use. "The chair" is still extensively used as an emblem of authority. It was not until the 16th century that it became common anywhere. The chest, the bench and the stool were until then the ordinary seats of everyday life, and the number of chairs which have survived from an earlier date is exceedingly limited; most of such examples are of ecclesiastical or seigneurial origin.

Ancient Chairs.—In ancient Egypt they were of great richness and splendour. Fashioned of ebony and ivory, or of carved and gilded wood, they were covered with costly stuffs and supported upon representations of the legs of beasts of the chase or the figures of captives. The earliest monuments of Nineveh represent a chair without a back but with carved legs ending in lions' claws or bulls' hoofs; others are supported by figures in the nature of caryatides or by animals. The earliest known form of Greek chair, going back to five or six centuries before Christ, had a back but stood straight up, front and back. On the frieze of the Parthenon Zeus occupies a square seat with a bar-back and thick turned legs; it is ornamented with winged sphinxes and the feet of beasts. The characteristic Roman chairs were of marble, also adorned with sphinxes; the curule chair was originally very similar in form to the modern folding chair, but eventually received a good deal of ornament.

The most famous of the very few chairs which have come down from a remote antiquity is the reputed chair of St. Peter in St. Peter's at Rome. The wooden portions are much decayed, but it would appear to be Byzantine work of the 6th century, and to be really an ancient *sedia gestatoria.* It has ivory carvings representing the labours of Hercules. A few pieces of an earlier oaken chair have been let in; the existing one, Gregorovius says, is of acacia wood. The legend that this was the curule chair of the senator Pudens is necessarily apocryphal. It is not, as is popularly supposed, enclosed in Bernini's bronze chair, but is kept under triple lock and exhibited only once in a century.

"DAGOBERT CHAIR," OF CAST BRONZE AND PROBABLY MORE THAN 1,000 YEARS OLD

Byzantium, like Greece and Rome, affected the curule form of chair, and in addition to lions' heads and winged figures of Victory and dolphin-shaped arms used also the lyre-back which has been made familiar by the pseudo-classical revival of the end of the 18th century. The chair of Maximian in the cathedral of Ravenna is believed to date from the middle of the 6th century. It is of marble, round, with a high back, and is carved in high relief with figures of saints and scenes from the Gospels—the Annunciation, the Adoration of the Magi, the flight into Egypt, and the baptism of Christ. The smaller spaces are filled with carvings of animals, birds, flowers and foliated ornament. Another very ancient seat is the so-called "Chair of Dagobert" in the Louvre. It is of cast bronze, sharpened with the chisel and partially gilt; it is of the curule or faldstool type and supported upon legs terminating in the heads and feet of animals. The seat, which was probably of leather, has disappeared. Its attribution depends entirely upon the statement of Suger, abbot of St. Denis in the 12th century, who added a back and arms. Its age has been much discussed, but Viollet-le-Duc dated it to early Merovingian times.

BY COURTESY OF THE METROPOLITAN MUSEUM OF ART

SPANISH ARMCHAIR OF THE 17TH CENTURY, HEAVY IN CONSTRUCTION AND ELABORATELY CARVED

To the same generic type belongs the famous abbots' chair of Glastonbury; such chairs might readily be taken to pieces when their owners travelled. The *faldisternium* in time acquired arms and a back, while retaining its folding shape. The most famous, as well as the most ancient, English chair is that made at the end of the 13th century for Edward I., in which most subsequent monarchs have been crowned. It is of an architectural type and of oak, and was covered with gilded *gesso* which long since disappeared.

Transition.—Passing from these historic examples we find the chair monopolized by the ruler, lay or ecclesiastical, to a comparatively late date. As the seat of authority it stood at the head of the lord's table, on his dais, by the side of his bed. The seigneurial chair, commoner in France and the Netherlands than in England, is a very interesting type, approximating in many respects to the episcopal or abbatial throne or stall. It early acquired a very high back and sometimes had a canopy. Arms were invariable, and the lower part was closed in with panelled or carved front and sides—the seat, indeed, was often hinged and sometimes closed with a key. That we are still said to sit "in" an arm-chair and "on" other kinds of chairs is a reminiscence of the time when the lord or seigneur sat "in his chair." These throne-like seats were always architectural in character, and as Gothic feeling waned took the distinctive characteristics of Renaissance work. It was owing in great measure to the Renaissance that the chair ceased to be an appanage of state, and became the customary companion of whomsoever could afford to buy it. Once the idea of privilege faded the chair speedily came into general use, and almost at once began to reflect the fashions of the hour. No other piece of furniture has ever been so close an index to sumptuary changes. It has varied in size, shape and sturdiness with the fashion of women's dress as well as men's. Thus the chair which was not, even with its arms purposely suppressed, too ample during the several reigns of some form or other of hoops and farthingale, became monstrous when these protuberances disappeared. Again, the costly laced coats of the dandy of the 18th and early 19th centuries were so threatened by the ordinary form of seat that a "conversation chair" was devised, which enabled the buck and the ruffler to sit with his face to the back, his valuable tails hanging unimpeded over the front. The early chair almost invariably had arms, and it was not until towards the close of the 16th century that the smaller form grew common.

The 17th Century.—The majority of the chairs of all countries until the middle of the 17th century were of oak without upholstery, and when it became customary to cushion them, leather was sometimes employed; subsequently velvet and silk were extensively used, and at a later period cheaper and often more durable materials. Leather was not infrequently used even for the costly and elaborate chairs of the faldstool form—occasionally sheathed in thin plates of silver—which Venice sent all over Europe. To this day, indeed, leather is one of the most frequently employed materials for chair covering. The outstanding characteristic of most chairs until the middle of the 17th century was massiveness and solidity. Being usually made of oak, they were of considerable weight, and it was not until the introduction of the handsome Louis XIII. chairs with cane backs and seats that either weight or solidity was reduced. Although English furniture derives so extensively from foreign and especially French and Italian models, the earlier forms of English chairs owed but little to exotic influences.

This was especially the case down to the end of the Tudor period, after which France began to set her mark upon the British chair. The squat variety, with heavy and sombre back, carved like a piece of panelling, gave place to a taller, more slender, and more elegant form, in which the framework only was carved, and attempts were made at ornament in new directions. The stretcher especially offered opportunities which were not lost upon the cabinet-makers of the Restoration. From a mere uncompromising cross-bar intended to strengthen the construction, it blossomed into an elaborate scroll-work or an exceedingly graceful semicircular ornament connecting all four legs, with a vase-shaped knob in the centre. The arms and legs of chairs of this period were scrolled, the splats of the back often showing a rich arrangement of spirals and scrolls. This most decorative of all types appears to have been popularized in England by the cavaliers who had been in exile with Charles II. and had become familiar with it in the north-western parts of the European Continent.

During the reign of William and Mary these charming forms degenerated into something much stiffer and more rectangular, with a solid, more or less fiddle-shaped splat and a cabriole leg with pad feet. The more ornamental examples had cane seats and ill-proportioned cane backs. From these forms was gradually developed the Chippendale chair, with its elaborately interlaced back, its graceful arms and square or cabriole legs, the latter terminating in the claw and ball or the pad foot. Hepplewhite, Sheraton and Adam all aimed at lightening the chair, which, even in the master hands of Chippendale, remained comparatively heavy. The endeavour succeeded, and the modern chair is everywhere comparatively slight. Chippendale and Hepplewhite between them determined what appears to be the final form of the chair, for since their time practically no new type has lasted, and in its main characteristics the chair of the 20th century is the direct derivative of that of the later 18th.

The 18th century was, indeed, the golden age of the chair, especially in France and England, between which there was considerable give and take of ideas. Diderot could not refrain from writing of them in his *Encyclopédie*. The typical Louis Seize chair, oval-backed and ample of seat, with descending arms and round-reeded legs, covered in Beauvais or some such gay tapestry woven with Boucher or Watteau-like scenes, is a very gracious object, in which the period reached its high-water mark. The Empire brought in squat and squabby shapes, comfortable enough no doubt, but entirely destitute of inspiration. English Empire chairs were often heavier and more sombre than those of French design. Thenceforward the chair in all countries ceased to attract the artist. The *art nouveau* school has occasionally produced something of not unpleasing simplicity; but more often its efforts have been frankly ugly or even grotesque. There have been practically no novelties. So much, indeed, is the present indebted to the past in this matter that even the revolving chair, now so

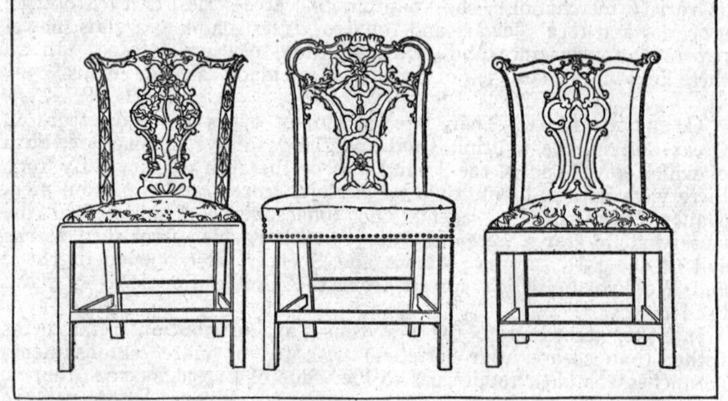

FROM ELLWOOD, "FURNITURE AND DECORATION"

CHIPPENDALE CHAIRS, WHICH IN THE 18TH CENTURY REPLACED THE HEAVIER MODELS OF TRADITION

CHAIRS OF THE 15TH TO THE 18TH CENTURY

1. Italian Renaissance armchair
2. Spanish Renaissance armchair
3. Italian "Dante" chair, 16th century
4. Italian Renaissance armchair
5. Louis XV. armchair. Gilded wood
6. Louis XVI. armchair
7. Chinese Chippendale, 1775–80
8. Hepplewhite chair, 1780–85
9. Chippendale ladder back, 1760–70

familiar in offices, has a pedigree of something like four centuries (*see* also INTERIOR DECORATION). (J. P.-B.)

CHAISE, a light two- or four-wheeled carriage with a movable hood or "calash" (the French for "chair," through a transference from a "sedan-chair" to a wheeled vehicle). The "post-chaise" was the fast-travelling carriage of the 18th and early 19th centuries. It was closed and four-wheeled for two or four horses and with the driver riding postillion.

CHAITANYA, Indian mystic, was born in 1485 at Navidvip, Bengal (died *c.* 1534). He was educated at the pathsala, or primary school of Navidvip and at eight years of age entered the Sanskrit tol. At an early age he became proficient in Sanskrit grammar and rhetoric. He initiated a popular religious movement within the Vaishnava faith (a cult of Vishnu). Chaitanya emphasized the path of bhakti (of devotion and direct relation to God) in contrast to the priestcraft and religious convention of the day. The Chaitanya Vaishnavas are a distinct religious sect in India to-day and the sankirton (chorus singing accompanied by drums and cymbals), emphasized and developed by Chaitanya, still forms the centre of its religious rites.

CHAKMA, a tribe in India, of mixed origin, probably the descendants of prisoners taken by the Arakanese from the Mogul armies who were provided with Magh, Mon or Arakanese wives. It migrated from the southern portion of the Chittagong coastal plain towards the end of the 18th century and is now settled on the middle reaches of the Karnaphuli and its tributaries in the Chittagong Hills tracts. The language is a dialect of Bengali, but the old script, now falling into disuse, is closely allied to the ancient Khmer script. The men dress in Bengali style, but the women wear a distinctive long blue skirt with a red border, and after puberty a strip of silk over the breasts. The religion is Animism, with a thin veneer of Buddhism. The dead are burned on the banks of streams. The tribe is divided into patrilineal endogamous clans, but the power of the heads of the separate clans has in course of time been absorbed by one family, the head of whom is known as the Chakma chief. Despite strong and prolonged Bengali influence the underlying culture is Burmese or Mon. Only of recent years is shifting cultivation being gradually abandoned for plough cultivation. The houses are flimsily built on piles and the villages are invariably on the banks of streams.

See T. H. Lewin, *Hill Tracts of Chittagong and Dwellers Therein* (Calcutta, 1869); G. A. Grierson, *Linguistic Survey of India,* vol. v., part 9. (J. P. M.)

CHAKRATA, a small mountain cantonment in the Dehra Dun district of the United Provinces of India, on the range of hills overlooking the valleys of the Jumna and the Tons, at an elevation of 7,000 ft.

CHALCEDON, more correctly **CALCHEDON,** an ancient maritime town of Bithynia, in Asia Minor, almost directly opposite Byzantium, south of Scutari. It was a Megarian colony founded on a site so obviously inferior to that which was within view on the opposite shore, that it received from the oracle the name of "the City of the Blind." In its early history it shared the fortunes of Byzantium, vacillated long between the Lacedaemonian and the Athenian interests, and was at last bequeathed to the Romans by Attalus III. of Pergamum (133 B.C.). It was partly destroyed by Mithridates, but recovered during the Empire, and in A.D. 451 was the seat of the Fourth General Council. It fell under the repeated attacks of the barbarian hordes who crossed over after having ravaged Byzantium, and furnished an encampment to the Persians under Chosroes, *c.* 616–626. The Turks used it as a quarry for building materials for Constantinople. To the south are the ruins of Panteichion, where Belisarius is said to have lived in retirement.

See J. von Hammer, *Constantinopolis* (Pesth, 1822); Murray's *Handbook for Constantinople* (London, 1900).

CHALCEDON, COUNCIL OF, the fourth oecumenical council of the Catholic Church, was held in 451, its occasion being the Eutychian heresy and the notorious "Robber Synod" (*see* EUTYCHES and EPHESUS, COUNCILS OF), which called forth vigorous protests both in the East and West, and a loud demand for a new general council, a demand that was ignored by the Eutychian Theodosius II., but speedily granted by his successor, Marcian. In response to the imperial summons, 500 to 600 bishops, all Eastern, except the Roman legates and two Africans, assembled in Chalcedon on Oct. 8, 451. The bishop of Rome claimed for his legates the right to preside, and insisted that any act that failed to receive their approval would be invalid. The first session was tumultuous; party feeling ran high, and scurrilous epithets were bandied to and fro. The acts of the Robber Synod were examined; fraud, violence and coercion were charged against it; its entire proceedings were annulled, and, at the third session, its leader, Dioscurus, was deposed and degraded. The emperor requested a declaration of the true faith; but the sentiment of the council was opposed to a new symbol. It contented itself with reaffirming the Nicene and Constantinopolitan creeds and the Ephesine formula of 431, and accepting, only after examination, the Christological statement contained in the *Epistola Dogmatica* of Leo I. (*q.v.*) to Flavianus. Thus the council rejected both Nestorianism and Eutychianism, and stood upon the doctrine that Christ had two natures, each perfect in itself and each distinct from the other, yet perfectly united in one person, who was at once both God and man. With this statement, which was formally subscribed in the presence of the emperor, the development of the Christological doctrine was completed, but not in a manner to obviate further controversy (*see* MONOPHYSITES and MONOTHELITES).

The remaining sessions were occupied with matters of discipline, episcopal jurisdiction, organization of diocese and parish, occupations of the clergy and the like; and confirmed the third canon of the second oecumenical council, which accorded to Constantinople equal privileges (ἴσα πρεσβεῖα) with Rome, and the second rank among the patriarchates, and, in addition, granted to Constantinople patriarchal jurisdiction over Pontus, Asia and Thrace. The Roman legates, who were absent (designedly?) when this famous (xxviii.) canon was adopted, protested against it, but in vain, the imperial commissioners deciding in favour of its regularity and validity. Leo I., although he recognized the council as oecumenical and confirmed its doctrinal decrees, rejected canon xxviii. on the ground that it contravened the 6th canon of Nicaea and infringed the rights of Alexandria and Antioch. In what proportion zeal for the ancient canons and the rights of others, and jealous fear of encroachment upon his own jurisdiction, were mixed in the motives of Leo, it would be interesting to know. The canon was universally received in the East (*see* CONSTANTINOPLE, COUNCILS OF).

The emperor Marcian approved the doctrinal decrees of the council and enjoined silence in regard to theological questions. Eutyches and Dioscurus and their followers were deposed and banished.

See Hefele, *Church Councils* (2nd ed.) ii. pp. 394–578 (Eng. trans., iii. pp. 268–464); also bibliographies in Herzog-Hauck, *Realencyklopädie,* 3rd ed., *s.v.,* "Eutyches" (by Loofs) and *s.v.* "Nestorianer" (by Kessler); and the general histories of Christian Doctrine.

CHALCEDONY or **CALCEDONY,** a variety of native silica occurring in concretionary, mammillated or stalactitic forms of waxy lustre and a great variety of colours—usually bluish white, grey, yellow or brown. It has a compact fibrous structure and a fine splintery fracture. Its relation to quartz has been the subject of a long controversy; one theory supposed it to be a mixture of quartz and opal, while the other held that it was a mineral distinct from quartz. Chalcedony fibres are usually, though not invariably, uniaxial and positive, but differ from quartz in that the optic axis is perpendicular to the length. Further, the refractive indices, double refraction, specific gravity and hardness are all slightly less for chalcedony than for quartz. The fine structure of the two minerals must, however, be very similar for their X-ray powder-photographs are identical. This result, which favours the view that chalcedony is a mixture of quartz and opal, is further supported by optical considerations; for by assigning reasonable values to the density, refractive index and amount of the opal supposed to be present, it is possible to account for all the characters of chalcedony.

Chalcedony occurs in veins and amygdules of volcanic rocks

together with zeolites and other hydrated silicates. It is deposited from residual magmatic solutions as well as being entirely secondary. In this mode of occurrence it is a common mineral in many volcanic fields, as in the basalts of northern Ireland, the Faroe Islands, Iceland, the Deccan (India). Chalcedonic pseudomorphs after other minerals often give rise to very interesting specimens. The name "enhydros" is given to hollow nodules of chalcedony containing water and an air bubble which is visible through the semitransparent wall. In all ages chalcedony has been the stone most used by the gem engraver, and many coloured varieties, described under special headings, are still cut and polished as ornamental stones. (*See* AGATE; BLOODSTONE OR HELIOTROPE; CARNELIAN OR CORNELIAN; CHRYSOPRASE; MOCHA STONE; ONYX.) (W. A. W.)

CHALCIS or KHALKIS, the chief town of the island of Euboea, Greece, is on the strait of the Euripus at its narrowest point. Pop. (1951) 23,768. Ancient Chalcis was peopled by Ionians, and early developed industrial and colonizing activity. In the 7th and 8th centuries it founded 30 townships on the peninsula of Chalcidice, and several important cities in Sicily (*q.v.*). Its metalwork, purple and pottery found markets among these settlements, and were distributed widely in the ships of its allies Corinth and Samos. In the so-called Lelantine War, Chalcis won from its neighbour and rival Eretria the best agricultural district of Euboea and became the chief city of the island. But its prosperity was broken by disastrous wars with the Athenians, and it became a member of both the Delian Leagues. In the Hellenistic period it was one of the fortresses by which Macedon controlled Greece. Antiochus III of Syria (192) and Mithradates VI of Pontus (88) used it as a base for invading Greece. Under Roman rule Chalcis retained some commercial prosperity; after the 6th century A.D. it again served to protect central Greece against northern invaders. From 1209 it was under Venetian control; in 1470 it passed to the Ottoman Turks, who made it the seat of a pasha. In 1688 it was successfully held against Venetian attack. The modern town has considerable export trade and railway connection with Athens and Peiraeus (1904). The old walled Castro, toward the Euripus, is inhabited by Jewish and Turkish families; the modern suburb outside it, by Greeks. A part of the Castro was destroyed by the earthquake of 1894; part, the famous "Black Bridge," which gave its mediaeval name "Negroponte" to Euboea, has been replaced by a modern swing bridge in the widening of the Euripus. The church of St. Paraskeve, once the chief church of the Venetians, dates from the Byzantine period, though many of its details are Western. The Turkish mosque was turned into a guardhouse.

BIBLIOGRAPHY.—Strabo vii, fr. II, x, p. 447; Herodotus v, 77; Thucydides i, 15; *Corpus Inscr. Atticarum,* iv (1) 27a, iv (2) 10, iv (2) p. 22; W. M. Leake, *Travels in Northern Greece* (London, 1835), ii, 254–270; E. Curtius in *Hermes,* x (1876), p. 220 *sqq.;* A. Holm, *Lange Fehde* (Berlin, 1884); H. Dondorff, *De Rebus Chalcidensium* (Göttingen, 1869); for coinage, B. V. Head, *Historia Numorum* (Oxford, 1887), pp. 303–305.

CHALCOCITE, a mineral consisting of cuprous sulphide (Cu_2S), crystallizing in the orthorhombic system. It is known also as copper glance, redruthite and vitreous copper. The crystals have the form of six-sided tables or prisms which are usually twinned, with the result that they simulate hexagonal symmetry. The mineral more often occurs as compact masses, which are sometimes of considerable extent. The colour is dark lead gray with a metallic lustre, but this is never very bright, since the material is readily altered, becoming black and dull on exposure to light. The mineral is soft (H.$=2\frac{1}{2}$) and sectile; specific gravity 5.7. It has a hexagonal polymorph not known to occur in nature.

Next to chalcopyrite, chalcocite is the most important ore of copper, and is perhaps the most characteristic mineral of the zone of secondary enrichment. It seems probable however that at some localities, *e.g.,* Butte, Mont., it is of primary origin. The best crystals are from St. Just, St. Ives and Redruth in Cornwall, and from Bristol in Connecticut. (CL. F.)

CHALCONDYLES (or CHALCOCONDYLAS), **LAONICUS,** the only Athenian Byzantine writer. He wrote a history, in ten books, of the period from 1298–1463, describing the fall of the Greek empire and the rise of the Ottoman Turks, down to the conquest of the Venetians and Mathias, king of Hungary, by Mohammed II. The capture of Constantinople he rightly regarded as an event of far-reaching importance. The work incidentally gives an interesting sketch of the civilization of England, France and Germany, whose assistance the Greeks sought against the Turks. Chalcondyles' chronology is defective, and his use of the old Greek place names causes confusion.

Editio princeps, ed. J. B. Baumbach (1615); In Bonn *Corpus Scriptorum Hist. Byz.* ed. I. Bekker (1843); Migne, *Patrologia Graeca,* clix. There is a French translation by Blaise de Vigenère (1577, later ed. by Artus Thomas with valuable illustrations on Turkish matters); *see* also F. Gregorovius, *Geschichte der Stadt Athen im Mittelalter,* ii (1889); Gibbon, *Decline and Fall,* ch. 66; C. Krumbacher, *Geschichte der byzantinischen Literatur* (1897). There is a biographical sketch of Laonicus and his brother in Greek by Antonius Calosynas, a physician of Toledo, who lived in the latter part of the 16th century (*see* C. Hopf, *Chroniques gréco-romanes,* 1873).

His brother, DEMETRIUS CHALCONDYLES (1424–1511), was born in Athens. In 1477 he went to Italy, where Cardinal Bessarion became his patron. He became famous as a teacher of Greek and the Platonic philosophy; in 1463 he was made professor at Padua, and in 1479 was summoned by Lorenzo de' Medici to Florence. In 1492 he removed to Milan, where he died in 1511. He was associated with Marsilius Ficinus, Angelus Politianus and Theodorus Gaza, in the revival of letters in the western world. One of his pupils at Florence was the famous John Reuchlin. Demetrius Chalcondyles published the editio princeps of Homer (1488), Isocrates (1493) and Suidas (1499), and a Greek grammar (*Erotemata*) in the form of question and answer.

BIBLIOGRAPHY.—H. Hody, *De Graecis illustribus* (1742); C. Hopf, *Chroniques gréco-romanes* (1873); E. Legrand, *Bibliographie hellénique,* i (1885).

CHALCOPYRITE or **COPPER-PYRITES,** a copper iron sulphide ($CuFeS_2$), an important ore of copper.

Chalcopyrite crystallizes in the scalenohedral class of the tetragonal system, but the form is so nearly cubic that it was not recognized as tetragonal until accurate measurements were made in 1822. Crystals are usually tetrahedral in aspect but frequently twinned, and they are often complex and difficult to decipher. The fracture is conchoidal, and the material is brittle. Hardness 4; specific gravity 4.2. The colour is brass-yellow, and the lustre metallic; the streak, or colour of the powder, is greenish-black. The mineral is especially liable to surface alteration, tarnishing with beautiful iridescent colours; a blue colour usually predominates, probably due to the alteration of the chalcopyrite to covellite (CuS). It is commonly found massive, granular to compact.

Chalcopyrite may be readily distinguished from pyrite (or iron pyrites), which it somewhat resembles in appearance, by its deeper colour and lower degree of hardness: the former is easily scratched by a knife, while the latter can only be scratched with difficulty or not at all. Chalcopyrite is decomposed by nitric acid with separation of sulphur and formation of a green solution; ammonia added in excess to this solution changes the green colour to deep blue and precipitates red ferric hydroxide.

The chemical formula $CuFeS_2$ corresponds with the percentage composition Cu$=34.5$, Fe$=30.5$, S$=35.0$. However, analyses usually show the presence of more iron, due to the intimate admixture of pyrite. Traces of gold, silver, selenium or thallium are sometimes present, and the mineral is sometimes worked as an ore of gold or silver, which may be present in solid solution.

Chalcopyrite is of wide distribution and is the commonest of the ores of copper. Extensive deposits are mined in the United States, particularly at Butte, Mont., and in Namaqualand, South Africa. Well-crystallized specimens are met with at many localities; for example, formerly at Wheal Towan in the St. Agnes district of Cornwall, Eng., at Freiberg in Saxony, Ger., and Joplin, Mo. (L. J. S.; CL. F.)

CHALDAEA (CHALDEA). "Chaldaea" and "Chaldaeans" are frequently used in the Old Testament as equivalents for "Babylonia" and "Babylonians." Chaldaea was really the name of a country, used in two senses. It was first applied to the extreme southern district, whose ancient capital was the city of *Bit*

Yakīn, the chief seat of the renowned Chaldaean rebel Merodach-baladan, who harassed the Assyrian kings Sargon and Sennacherib. It is not as yet possible to fix the exact boundaries of the original home of the Chaldaeans, but it may be regarded as having been the long stretch of alluvial land situated at the then separate mouths of the Tigris and Euphrates, which rivers now combine to flow into the Persian Gulf in the waters of the majestic *Shatt el-ʿArab.*

The name "Chaldaea," however, soon came to have a more extensive application. In the days of the Assyrian king Adad-nirāri III. (811–782 B.C.), the term *mat Kaldū* covered practically all Babylonia. Furthermore, Merodach-baladan was called by Sargon II. (722–705 B.C.) "king of the land of the Chaldaeans" and "king of the land of Bīt Yakīn" after the old capital city; but there is no satisfactory evidence that Merodach-baladan had the right to the title "Babylonian." The racial distinction between the Chaldaeans and the Babylonians proper seems to have existed until a much later date. That they differed from the Arabs and Aramaeans appear to follow from the distinction made by Sennacherib (705–681 B.C.) between the Chaldaeans and these races. Later, during the period covering the fall of Assyria and the rise of the Neo-Babylonian empire, the term *mat Kaldū* was not only applied to all Babylonia, but also embraced the territory of certain foreign nations who were later included by Ezekiel (xxiii. 23) under the expression "Chaldaeans."

The Chaldaeans probably first came from Arabia, the supposed original home of the Semitic races, at a very early date along the coast of the Persian Gulf and settled in the neighbourhood of Ur ("Ur of the Chaldees," Gen. xi. 28), whence they began a series of encroachments, partly by warfare and partly by immigration, against the other Semitic Babylonians. These aggressions after many centuries ended in the Chaldaean supremacy of Nabopolassar and his successors (from *c.* 625), although there is no positive proof that Nabopolassar was purely Chaldaean in blood. The sudden rise of the later Babylonian empire under Nebuchadnezzar, the son of Nabopolassar, must have tended to produce so thorough an amalgamation of the Chaldaeans and Babylonians, who had theretofore been considered as two kindred branches of the same original Semite stock, that in the course of time no perceptible differences existed between them. The language of these Chaldaeans differed in no way from the ordinary Semitic Babylonian idiom which was practically identical with that of Assyria. Consequently, the term "Chaldaean" came quite naturally to be used in later days as synonymous with "Babylonian," and through a misunderstanding the term *Chaldee* (*q.v.*) was subsequently applied to the Aramaic language.

The derivation of the name "Chaldaean" is uncertain. It is probably connected with the Semitic stem *kasādu* (conquer), in which case *Kaldi-Kašdi,* with the well-known interchange of *l* and *š,* would mean "conquerors." It is also possible that *Kašdu-Kaldū* is connected with the proper name Chesed, who is represented as having been the nephew of Abraham (Gen. xxii. 22). But there is no connection between the Black sea people called "Chaldaeans" by Xenophon (*Anab.* vii. 25) and the Chaldaeans of Babylonia. (For *Chaldians see* URARTU.)

In Daniel, the term "Chaldaeans" commonly means "astrologers, astronomers," as it also does in the classical authors (Herodotus, Strabo, Diodorus, etc.). In Daniel i. 4, by the expression "tongue of the Chaldaeans," the writer evidently meant the language in which the celebrated Babylonian works on astrology and divination were composed. It is now known that the literary idiom of the Babylonian wise men was the non-Semitic Sumerian; but it is not probable that the late author of *Daniel* (*q.v.*) was aware of this fact. The word "Chaldaean" is applied as a race-name to the Babylonians (Dan. iii. 8, v. 30, ix. 1); but the expression is used oftener, either as a name for some special class of magicians, or as a term for magicians in general (ix. 1). The transfer of the name of the people to a special class can perhaps be explained. When in later times "Chaldaean" and "Babylonian" became practically synonymous, the term "Chaldaean" lived on in the secondary restricted sense of "wise men." The early *Kaldi* had seized and held from very ancient times the region of old Sumer, which was the centre of the primitive non-Semitic culture. It seems extremely probable that these Chaldaean Semites were so strongly influenced by the foreign civilization as to adopt it eventually as their own. Then, as the Chaldaeans soon became the dominant people, the priestly caste of that region developed into a Chaldaean institution. It is reasonable to conjecture that southern Babylonia, the home of the old culture, supplied Babylon and other important cities with priests, who from their descent were correctly called "Chaldaeans." This name in later times, owing to the racial amalgamation of the Chaldaeans and Babylonians, lost its former national force, and became, as it occurs in Daniel, a distinctive appellation of the Babylonian priestly class. *Kalū* (priest) in Babylonian, which has no etymological connection with *Kaldū,* may have contributed paronomastically towards the popular use of the term "Chaldaeans" for the Babylonian magi. (*See* also ASTROLOGY.)

See BABYLONIA AND ASSYRIA and the commentaries on the book of Daniel. (J. D. PR.)

CHALDEE, a term formerly applied to the Aramaic portions of the biblical books of Ezra and Daniel or to the vernacular paraphrases of the Old Testament (*see* TARGUM), on the assumption that the language was that of Chaldaea (*q.v.*). But the cuneiform inscriptions show that the language of the Chaldaeans was Assyrian; and it is now known that the substitution of Aramaic for Hebrew as the vernacular of Palestine took place very gradually. The dialect wrongly called "Chaldee" is really the language of the South-Western Arameans, who were the immediate neighbours of the Jews. *See* SEMITIC LANGUAGES.

CHALDER or **CHALDRON,** an old dry measure of capacity, usually called chalder in Scotland and chaldron in England. In Scotland the chalder was equivalent to 16 bolls (*q.v.*) of corn, and was used in computing the stipends of parish ministers, but, like the chaldron, it varied according to the locality and the commodity measured. As a measure for lime and coal, the chalder and the chaldron vary from 32 bushels upwards, and are in general equivalent in weight to about 25½ cwt.

CHALET, a term applied to the timber houses of Switzerland, the Bavarian Alps, Tirol and the French Alps. The chalet is distinguished above all by the frank and interesting manner in which it makes use of its material, wood. The timber used is generally in heavy planks, from 3 to 6in. thick, and carefully framed together somewhat in the manner of a log-house. Side walls, generally low, often project beyond the ends, forming porches or loggias, closed at the ends. Upper floors, almost universally, project over the storeys below, with all sorts of fantastic

BY COURTESY OF BURTON HOLMES

CHARACTERISTIC CHALET IN THE TIROL

and interesting bracket treatments. Balconies across the front are common and are frequently enriched with carved railings. Windows are small and hung as casements. In general, roofs are of low pitch and project enormously, both at the eaves and at the gable ends, which are occasionally snubbed with a small triangle of sloping roof at the top. The roof surfaces are covered with large wood shingles, slabs of slate or stone; in the wilder districts planks are often laid over the roof covering and weighted with boulders to prevent damage from heavy gales. In plan, the chalet tends towards the square; frequently, not only the house proper, but stables and storage barns are included under one enormous roof. Many local peculiarities of detail exist. (*See* HOUSE.)

CHALIAPIN, FYODOR IVANOVICH (1873–1938), (shạhl-yah'pēn) Russian bass singer, born at Kazan, on Feb. 1, 1873. His early career was a varied and adventurous one; he was by turns porter, shoemaker, hunter and street sweeper. He received his first musical training as a choirboy at Kazan, but his serious studies as a singer were made under Oussatov at Tiflis, where he made his first appearance in opera in 1892 in *A Life for the Tsar.* He then sang in 1894 at the Summer theatre, St. Petersburg (Leningrad), and later at the Imperial opera house. After visiting Milan he took important parts in the Mamantoff opera company, and at a private opera house in Moscow in 1896. In 1913, during the Russian opera season organized by Sir Thomas Beecham at Drury Lane, London, he appeared in *Boris Godunov, Ivan the Terrible,* and *La Khovantchina.* His superb bass voice and remarkable dramatic powers took his audience by storm, and he had a similar success in *Prince Igor.* During the World War and afterwards, until 1921, he remained in Russia. His first appearance outside Russia after the war was at the Albert Hall, London, in 1921. He visited America in 1908; his second tour there was in 1922–23. Among his most famous parts may be named those of Ivan the Terrible in Rimsky-Korsakov's *Maid of Pskof*; Salieri in *Mozart and Salieri;* Leporello in *Don Giovanni;* Don Basilio in the *Barber of Seville;* and Mephisto in *Mefistofele.*

See his *Pages from my Life* (1927).

CHALICE, the cup used in the celebration of the Eucharist (*q.v.*). For the various forms which the chalice so used has taken, *see* DRINKING VESSELS. The ancient custom of mixing water with wine in the Eucharistic service, practised from early times in both Eastern (except the Armenian) and Western Churches, is known as that of the "mixed chalice." The practice has been generally discontinued since the Reformation in the English Church, but is not illegal if it is not done ceremonially (*Martin* v. *Mackonochie,* 1868, L.R. 2 P.C. 365; *Read* v. *Bp. of Lincoln,* 1892, A.C. 664).

CHALIER, MARIE JOSEPH (1747–1793), French revolutionary, became a partner in a business firm at Lyons for which he travelled in the Levant, in Italy, Spain and Portugal. He became the orator and leader of the Jacobins of Lyons, and induced the other revolutionary clubs and the commune of the city to arrest a great number of Royalists in the night of Feb. 5, 1793. The mayor, supported by the national guard, opposed this project. Chalier demanded of the Convention the establishment of a revolutionary tribunal and the levy of a revolutionary army at Lyons. The Convention refused, and the anti-revolutionary party, encouraged by this refusal, took action. On May 29–30, 1793, the sections rose; the Jacobins were dispossessed of the municipality and Chalier arrested. On July 15, in spite of the order of the Convention, he was brought before the criminal tribunal of the Rhone-et-Loire, condemned to death, and guillotined the next day.

See N. Wahl, "Étude sur Chalier," in *Revue historique,* t. xxxiv.; and *Les Premières Années de la Révolution à Lyon* (1894).

CHALK is a white or greyish, loosely coherent kind of limestone rock, composed almost entirely of the calcareous remains of minute marine organisms (foraminifera, cocoliths, etc.) and fragments of shells. The purest kinds contain up to 99% of calcium carbonate in the form of the mineral calcite. Silica is always present in small amounts as the mineral opal, representing the remains of other minute marine organisms and sponge spicules. Minute grains of quartz, felspar, zircon, rutile and other minerals are also present. With the admixture of clayey material there may be an insensible gradation from pure chalk to chalk-marl. Not only may there be considerable variation in the composition of chalk (phosphatic, glauconitic, etc.) but there may also be wide variations in the colour (snow-white, grey, etc.) and the texture of the material. It may be soft, incoherent and porous or quite hard and crystalline.

The uses of chalk are numerous; for example, as a writing material in the form of white and coloured crayons, for the manufacture of quicklime, mortar, Portland cement (*see* CEMENT), plaster and as a fertilizer.

Whiting is prepared by grinding chalk and collecting the finer sediments from water; this is used for polishing, making putty and many other purposes. Under the name of "paris white," chalk is used in the manufacture of india-rubber goods, oilcloth, wallpaper, etc. The harder kinds are extensively used as a building stone.

Large quantities of chalk are quarried in England in Kent, Surrey, Sussex, Cambridgeshire, Lincolnshire and Hampshire, Kent being by far the most important.

In the United States there are extensive beds of chalk in Kansas, Arkansas and Texas.

CHALKHILL, JOHN (fl. 1600?), English poet. Two songs by him are included in Izaak Walton's *Compleat Angler,* and in 1683 appeared "Thealma and Clearchus. A Pastoral History in smooth and easie Verse. Written long since by John Chalkhill, Esq., an Acquaintant and Friend of Edmund Spencer," together with a preface written five years earlier by Walton. Another poem, "Alcilia, Philoparthens Loving Follie" (1595, reprinted in vol. x. of the *Jahrbuch des deutschen Shakespeare-Vereins*), was at one time attributed to him. Nothing further is known of the poet, but a person of his name occurs as one of the coroners for Middlesex in the later years of Queen Elizabeth's reign. Professor Saintsbury, who included *Thealma and Clearchus* in vol. ii. of his *Minor Poets of the Caroline Period* (Oxford, 1906), points out a marked resemblance between his work and that of William Chamberlayne.

CHALKING THE DOOR, a former Scottish custom of tenant eviction within burgh. The law was that "a burgh officer, in presence of witnesses, chalks the most patent door 40 days before Whit Sunday, having made out an execution of 'chalking,' in which his name must be inserted, and which must be subscribed by himself and two witnesses." This ceremony proceeded simply on the verbal order of the proprietor. The Removal Terms (Scotland) Act 1886 introduced, as optional to "chalking," the procedure of giving notice to remove by registered letter posted to the last known address of the tenant. The Sheriff Courts (Scotland) Act 1907 requires written notice of removal to be given to the tenant as a prerequisite of ejection, and "chalking the door" is now an obsolete practice.

CHALLEMEL-LACOUR, PAUL AMAND (1827–1896), French statesman, was born at Avranches on May 19, 1827. Educated at the École Normale Supérieure, he became professor of philosophy at Pau and at Limoges, but was obliged to leave France after the coup d'état of 1851. He settled in Zürich, where he became professor of French literature in 1856. Three years later the amnesty permitted his return to France. Appointed by the government of national defence prefect of the Rhone in 1870, he suppressed the communard rising at Lyons directed by Bakunin. He became a deputy to the National Assembly in 1872, and in 1876 a member of the Senate. Though Challemel-Lacour sat at first on the extreme Left, he modified his opinions as time went on, and towards the close of his career was a foremost representative of moderate republicanism. He was French ambassador at Berne (1879), London (1880), minister of foreign affairs in the Jules Ferry cabinet (for some months in 1883), vice-president of the Senate (1890), president of the Senate (1893). His close and reasoned eloquence made him one of the most conspicuous members of the Senate. He died in Paris on Oct. 26, 1896.

See *Oeuvres oratoires de Challemel-Lacour* (1897) and *Études et réflexions d'un Pessimiste* (1901), edited by J. Reinach. *See* also H. Defasse, *Challemel-Lacour.*

CHALLENGE: *see* DUEL.

"CHALLENGER" EXPEDITION. The scientific results of several short expeditions between 1860 and 1870 encouraged the commissioning of a vessel for a prolonged cruise for oceanic exploration. H.M.S. "Challenger," a wooden corvette of 2,306 tons, under Captain (afterwards Sir) George Nares with a scientific staff under Prof. (afterwards Sir) C. Wyville Thomson as director, was sent out in Dec. 1872. The staff included John

Murray (afterwards Sir) and H. N. Moseley, biologists; Dr. von Willemoes-Suhm, Commander Tizard and J. Y. Buchanan, chemist and geologist. The Atlantic was crossed several times. From Cape Town south-east and east the ship visited the various islands between 45° and 50° S., reached Kerguelen island in Jan. 1874, and proceeded south about the meridian of 80° east. She was the first steamship to cross the Antarctic Circle; early in March she made for Melbourne. Thence the route led by New Zealand, the Fiji islands, Torres strait, the Banda sea, and the China sea to Hongkong. The western Pacific was then explored northward to Yokohama, after which the "Challenger" struck across the ocean by Honolulu and Tahiti to Valparaiso. She then coasted south, penetrated the Straits of Magellan, touched at Montevideo, recrossed the Atlantic by Ascension and the Azores, and reached Sheerness in May 1876. The *"Challenger" Report* was issued in 50 volumes (London, 1880–95), mainly under Sir John Murray, who succeeded Wyville Thomson in 1882.

See also Lord G. Campbell, *Log Letters from the "Challenger"* (1876); W. J. J. Spry, *Cruise of H. M. S. "Challenger"* (1876); Sir C. Wyville Thomson, *Voyage of the "Challenger," The Atlantic, Preliminary Account of General Results* (1877); J. J. Wild, *At Anchor; Narrative of Experiences afloat and ashore during the Voyage of H.M.S. "Challenger"* (1878); H. N. Moseley, *Notes by a Naturalist on the "Challenger"* (1879).

CHALLIS, a light, all-wool fabric of almost gossamer texture used for women's dressing gowns and children's suits and dresses. Challis is distinguished from all the other muslin-delaine weaves, of which class it is a member, by the tiny romantic designs in which it is printed. These designs are mostly of 18th and 19th century inspiration and show conventionalized versions of dots, rose-buds, violets and other flowers.

CHALLONER, RICHARD (1691–1781), English Roman Catholic prelate, was born at Lewes, Sussex, on Sept. 29, 1691, and educated at the English college at Douai, where he was ordained a priest in 1716, took his degrees in divinity, and was appointed professor in that faculty. In 1730 he was sent to London. The controversial treatises which he published in rapid succession attracted much attention, particularly his *Catholic Christian Instructed* (1737), with its witty reply to Dr. Conyers Middleton's *Letters from Rome, showing an Exact Conformity between Popery and Paganism.* In 1741 Challoner was raised to the episcopal dignity at Hammersmith and nominated coadjutor with right of succession to Bishop Benjamin Petre, vicar-apostolic of the London district, whom he succeeded in 1758. He died on Jan. 12, 1781. Bishop Challoner was the author of numerous controversial and devotional works, including the *Garden of the Soul* (1740?), one of the most popular manuals of devotion. He re-edited the Douai Bible (1749–1750), correcting the obsolete language and orthography. Of his historical works the most valuable is his *Memoirs of Missionary Priests and other Catholicks of both Sexes who suffered Death or Imprisonment in England on account of their Religion, from the year 1577 till the end of the reign of Charles II.* (1741, latest ed., 1924) intended as an antidote to Foxe's martyrology. He also published anonymously, in 1745 *Britannia Sancta,* or lives of the British saints, now superseded by that of Alban Butler.

See E. H. Burton, *Life and Times of Bishop Challoner* (1909).

CHALMERS, ALEXANDER (1759–1834), Scottish writer, was born in Aberdeen on March 29, 1759, and died in London on Dec. 19, 1834. He was educated as a doctor, but gave up this profession for journalism, and he was for some time editor of the *Morning Herald.* Besides editions of the works of Shakespeare, Beattie, Fielding, Johnson, Warton, Pope, Gibbon and Bolingbroke, he published *A General Biographical Dictionary* in 32 vols. (1812–17); a *Glossary to Shakespeare* (1797); an edition of Steeven's *Shakespeare* (1809); and the *British Essayists,* beginning with the *Tatler* and ending with the *Observer,* with biographical and historical prefaces and a general index.

CHALMERS, GEORGE (1742–1825), Scottish antiquarian and political writer, was born at Fochabers, Moray, and emigrated to Maryland in 1763, where he practised as a lawyer until the outbreak of the war of American Independence, when he returned to England. In 1786 he was appointed chief clerk to the privy council, an office which he held until his death in London May 31 1825.

Of some 30 works which he wrote the most important are *Political Annals of the present United Colonies from their Settlement to the Peace of 1763* (1780), drawn from the American State papers, and *Caledonia, An Account, Historical and Topographical, of North Britain* (1807–24). Neither of these is complete. Of the *Political Annals* only one volume was published, bringing the history down to 1688; and *Caledonia* covers only the southern counties of Scotland.

Chalmers wrote biographical sketches of Defoe, Allan Ramsay, Sir David Lyndsay, and others, prefixed to their collected works, and a *Life of Mary Queen of Scots* (1818). He engaged in many literary and historical controversies with Malone, Steevens, Dr. Jamieson, and others.

CHALMERS, GEORGE PAUL (1836–1878), Scottish portrait and landscape painter, was born at Montrose and studied at Edinburgh. The best of his works are "The End of the Harvest" (1873), "Running Water" (1875), and "The Legend" (in the National Gallery, Edinburgh). He became an associate (1867) and a full member (1871) of the Royal Scottish Academy.

CHALMERS, JAMES (1841–1901), Scottish missionary to New Guinea, was born at Ardrishaig in Argyll. He was appointed to Rarotonga in the South Pacific in 1866. After ten years' service he was transferred to New Guinea. Chalmers did much to open up the island, and, with his colleague W. G. Lawes, gave valuable aid in the British annexation of the south-east coast of the island. On April 8, 1901, in company with a brother missionary, Oliver Tomkins, he was killed by cannibals at Goaribari island. R. L. Stevenson has left on record his high appreciation of Chalmers's character and work.

See his *Autobiography and Letters* (1902).

CHALMERS, THOMAS (1780–1847), Scottish divine, was born at Anstruther, Fifeshire, on March 17, 1780. In 1799 he was licensed by the St. Andrews presbytery. After further study at Edinburgh he became assistant to the professor of mathematics at St. Andrews, and was ordained as minister of Kilmany, Fifeshire. In 1808 he published an *Inquiry into the Extent and Stability of National Resources,* a contribution to the discussion created by Bonaparte's commercial policy. His article on "Christianity" in the *Edinburgh Encyclopaedia* enhanced his reputation as an author. In 1815 he became minister of the Tron church, Glasgow, and his repute as a preacher spread throughout the United Kingdom. A series of sermons on the relation between discoveries of astronomy and the Christian revelation was published in Jan. 1817, and within a year nine editions and 20,000 copies were in circulation. When he visited London Wilberforce wrote, "all the world is wild about Dr. Chalmers."

In Sept. 1819 he became minister of the church and parish of St. John where he was singularly successful in dealing with the problem of poverty. When he undertook the management of the parish its poor cost the city £1,400 per annum, and in four years, the expenditure was reduced to £280 per annum. In 1823, after eight years of work at high pressure he was glad to accept the chair of moral philosophy at St. Andrews, the seventh academic offer made to him during the eight years spent in Glasgow. In Nov. 1828 he was transferred to the chair of theology in Edinburgh.

In 1826 he published a third volume of the *Christian and Civic Economy of Large Towns,* a continuation of work begun at St. John's, Glasgow. In 1832 he published a *Political Economy,* and in 1833 appeared his Bridgwater treatise on *The Adaptation of External Nature to the Moral and Intellectual Constitution of Man.* In 1834 he became leader of the evangelical section of the Scottish Church in the general assembly. In 1841 the movement which ended in the Disruption was rapidly culminating, and Dr. Chalmers found himself at the head of the party which stood for the principle that "no minister shall be intruded into any parish contrary to the will of the congregation." Cases of conflict between the Church and the civil power arose in Auchterarder, Dunkeld and Marnoch; and when the courts made it clear that the Church, in their opinion, held its temporalities on condition of rendering such obedience as the courts required, the Church appealed to the Government for relief. In Jan. 1843 the Government put a final and peremptory negative on the Church's claims for spiritual independence. On May 18, 1843, 470 clergymen withdrew from the general assembly and constituted themselves the Free Church of Scotland, with Dr. Chalmers as moderator. He had prepared a sustentation fund scheme for the support of the seceding ministers, and this was at once put into successful operation. He himself became principal of the newly founded Free Church college, Edinburgh. On May 30, 1847 immediately after his return from the House of Commons, where he had given evidence as to the refusal of sites for Free Churches, by Scottish landowners, he was found dead in bed.

Dr. Chalmers' writings are a valuable source for argument and illustration on the question of Establishment. They run to 38 volumes concerned with theology, devotional practice and social economy. The most important of them is his *Institutes of Theology* written in his later years at the Free Church college.

BIBLIOGRAPHY.—W. Hanna *Memoirs* (Edinburgh, 1849–52); *Correspondence* (1853); and *Lives* by E. B. Ramsay (3rd ed. 1867); D. Fraser (1881); Mrs. Oliphant (1893) and W. G. Blaikie (1896).

CHALONER, SIR THOMAS, the elder (1521–1565), English diplomatist and poet, the son of Roger Chaloner, a mercer of London, was educated at Oxford and Cambridge. In 1540 he went as secretary to Sir Henry Knyvett to the court of Charles V, whom he accompanied in his expedition to Algiers in 1541. In 1547 Chaloner served in the expedition to Scotland, and was knighted after the battle of Pinkie, by the protector Somerset. He was a witness against Bishop Bonner, in 1549, and against Stephen Gardiner, bishop of Winchester, in 1551. He was sent on missions to Scotland in 1551, 1552 and 1555–56; on an embassy to France in 1553; and under Elizabeth was resident ambassador in the Netherlands (1558–60) and Spain (1561–64). He returned home in 1564, and died at Clerkenwell on Oct. 14, 1565.

Chaloner's most important works are "How King Richard the Second was for his evil governance deposed" printed in the first, 1559, edition of William Baldwin's *Mirror for Magistrates,* best ed. by Lily B. Campbell (Cambridge, 1938); *De Rep. Anglorum instauranda libri decem,* published by W. Mallim (1579); and *The Praise of Folly, Moriae encomium . . . by Erasmus . . . Englished by Sir Thomas Chaloner, Knight* (1549; ed. Janet E. Ashbee, London, 1901).

CHÂLONS-SUR-MARNE, a town of northeastern France, capital of the department of Marne, 107 mi. E. of Paris on the main line of the Eastern railway to Nancy and 25 mi. S.E. of Reims. Pop. (1946) 31,120. The town proper is bordered on the west by the lateral canal of the Marne and is traversed by branches of the canal and by small streams.

Châlons-sur-Marne occupies the site of the chief town of the Catalauni and, on the plain between it and Troyes, Attila was defeated by the Romans in 451. In the 10th and following centuries it attained great prosperity under its bishops, who were ecclesiastical peers of France. In 1214 the militia of Châlons served at the battle of Bouvines; and in the 15th century the citizens twice repulsed the English from their walls. In the 16th century the town sided with Henry IV., king of France, who in 1589 transferred thither the parliament of Paris, which shortly afterwards burnt the bulls of Gregory XIV. and Clement VIII. The camp of Châlons, about 16 m. N. of the town, was established in 1856 by Napoleon III. and is a training-centre for troops. Châlons was occupied by the Germans in August, 1914, and was retaken by Foch in September, 1914. The cathedral of St. Étienne (chiefly 13th century) has a 17th century west façade. There are stained-glass windows of the 13th century in the north transept. Notre-Dame, of the 12th and 13th centuries, is conspicuous for its four Romanesque towers, two flanking the apse, two flanking the principal façade. The churches of St. Alpin, St. Jean and St. Loup date from various periods between the 11th and 17th centuries. The hôtel-de-ville (1771), the prefecture (1759–1764), the college, once a Jesuit establishment, and a training college which occupies the Augustinian abbey of Toussaints (16th and 17th centuries), are noteworthy civil buildings. The houses are generally ill-built, but some old mansions remain. The town is the seat of a bishop and a prefect, has tribunals of first instance and of commerce, a chamber of commerce, a board of trade-arbitrators, a museum and a library. The principal industry is brewing, which is carried on in the suburb of Marne. Galleries hewn in a limestone hill are used as store-houses for beer. The preparation of champagne, the manufacture of boots, brushes, wire-goods and wall-paper also occupy many hands. There is trade in cereals. (X.)

Battle of Châlons.—The battle of the Catalaunian Plains, "fierce, manifold, huge, stubborn, without its like in the history of times past" (Priscus), was fought between Attila and the Roman Aëtius in 451 A.D.

The Huns had crossed the Danube in the first quarter of the fifth century. Uldin, their leader was driven back by the soldiers of Byzantium; but by 424 the Byzantine court was paying the Huns a tribute of 350lb. of gold. Some ten years later Attila, nephew of a king who had brought the Huns to some rough unity of predatory purpose, became joint ruler with his brother. Attila, a typical Kalmuck in appearance, thereupon began a career of plunder. In another ten years he had forced the eastern empire to multiply sixfold the annual tribute. In six more years he had become lord of the lands north of the middle and lower Danube, and wasted the northern Balkan country. He forbade his Huns and Germans subject to him to take service in the imperial armies. The western Roman armies had long ceased to find their soldiers from within the frontiers; therefore Attila could cut off one of the main supplies of men.

Aëtius had been no enemy of the Huns, and had used them to make an end of the Burgundian kingdom about Worms (whence the Nibelungenlied). In 450 a good soldier, Marcian, became emperor of the East, and refused to pay the Hunnic tribute. A few months earlier a discontented Roman princess had given Attila a pretext for turning to that quarter of the world which he had not yet plundered. Justa Gratia Honoria, sister of the emperor Valentinian III. had plotted with a lover to take the throne. The plot was discovered; Honoria was married to a respectable and harmless senator. Honoria boldly sent to Attila for help, with her ring to show from what quarter the message came. Attila took the ring to mean that Honoria would be his wife. The time was good for using this claim; Gaiseric, king of the Vandals, fearing an attack from the Visigoths in southwest Gaul, had asked for Attila's alliance.

In 451 Attila led into Gaul a host of Huns, Alans and tributary Germans. Two parties were disputing the kingship of the Franks on the Rhine; one group joined the Huns, and thereby decided Attila's route. On April 7 this host plundered Metz, and thence moved slowly towards Orleans. Aëtius had not crossed the Alps in time to hold the Rhine; nor could he do much without Visigothic help. The fall of Orleans would leave the way open across the Loire to the Visigothic lands; therefore the Visigoths listened to Aëtius' messengers. An army of Romans (that is, of Romanized Germans) and Visigoths marched to save Orleans. Legends of the prowess of a Christian bishop (the legend of St. Geneviève is of the same time) have clouded over the history of the attack upon Orleans. But the town was on the point of falling when Aëtius and Theodoric, the Visigothic king, forced the Huns to retire.

Attila took the road northwards to Troyes and collected his forces on the plains well fitted for his cavalry. Chalons has been named as the chosen battlefield; but the *campi Catalaunici* include most of Champagne. The best chroniclers speak of a certain "Mauriac place." There was a Moirey west of Troyes, and there is a Méry-sur-Seine where bones, weapons and gold ornaments have been found. Here, about sixteen miles north-west of Troyes, some scholars think must be the "Mauriac place" and the tomb of Theodoric. On the night before the battle those Franks who favoured Aëtius broke through to him after a slaughter of 15,000 men. Before the day began Attila took the voice of his augurs; the Huns would be beaten (a likely prophecy about a retreating tribal host), but the enemy leader would fall. Attila could get another army; the empire had not another Aëtius, nor would anyone else be likely to keep together the Visigoths and Romans. By delaying until 3 P.M. Attila planned to secure his retreat in the darkness. The chroniclers say that on one side the field sloped towards a slight hill; for this hill the armies fought. In the place of honour on the Roman right were the Visigoths; on the left Aëtius, and with him as a hostage, Thorismund son of Theodoric; in the centre, enclosed by more trusted troops were the Alan auxiliaries of the Romans. Aëtius hoped that the Huns might try to drive in this centre, for Attila kept in the midst of his Huns, and set the Ostrogoths and Gepidae on the left, and on his right the lesser German allies. Here was the decision. Aëtius seized the hill; his Alans were forced back, but now he could take the Huns on one flank, while on the other the Visigoths attacked. Thus the victory in this last great battle of western Roman power was won by the tactics which Hannibal had used at Cannae.

The Huns expected another attack, since in the immense slaughter Theodoric had been killed but Aëtius was alive. Attila, within his ring of wagons, prepared for death; but Aëtius feared a camp of desperate men whose strength was in their archery. Nor was he willing to secure in Gaul a Visigothic predominance against which the Huns might yet be his allies. He persuaded Thorismund to hasten to Toulouse, lest his brothers should take his inheritance. Attila escaped to ravage Italy in 452, and to die, or be murdered in a drunken sleep in 453. Was this battle of the "Mauriac place," one of the world's decisive battles? The Huns showed nothing of the fruitfulness of the Germanic peoples who came within the Empire, and their power could scarcely have survived for long the death of a king who was as rare as a Saladin among the Kurds. A son of Attila and Honoria might have been another Aëtius, if Attila's other sons had not put him to death; but the coming of the Huns was only an episode before the greater confusion of the dark ages, before the victory of Charles Martel, and the splendour and dominion of Charlemagne.

(E. L. W.)

CHALON-SUR-SAÔNE, an industrial town of east-central France, capital of an arrondissement in the department of Saône-et-Loire, 81 mi. N. of Lyons by the P.L.M. railway. Pop. (1946) 32,683. It is a well-built town, with fine quays, situated on the right bank of the Saône at its junction with the Canal du Centre. A 15th century bridge with 18th century obelisks, leads to the suburb of St. Laurent on an island in the river. Chalon-sur-Saône is identified with the ancient *Cabillonum,* an important town of the Aedui. It was chosen in the 6th century by Gontram, king of Burgundy, as his capital. The bishopric, founded in the 4th century, was suppressed at the Revolution. In feudal times Chalon was the capital of a countship. In 1237 it was given in exchange for other fiefs in the Jura by Jean le Sage, whose descendants nevertheless retained the title. Hugh IV, duke of Burgundy, the other party to the exchange, gave the citizens a communal charter in 1256. The town resisted a division of the Austrian army in 1814.

The church of St. Vincent, once the cathedral, dates mainly from the 12th to the 15th centuries, and has a choir in the 13th century Burgundian style. The old bishop's palace dates from the 15th century. The church of St. Pierre, with two lofty steeples, is late 17th century. Chalon preserves remains of its ancient ramparts and a number of old houses. It is the seat of a sub-prefect and a court of assizes, and has tribunals of first instance and commerce and a chamber of commerce. Chalon ranks next to Le Creusot among the manufacturing towns of Burgundy. Its position at the junction of the Canal du Centre and the Saône, and as a railway centre for Lyons, Paris, Dole, Lons-le-Saunier and Roanne, brings it a large transit trade. The founding and working of copper and iron are its main industries; the large engineering works of Petite-Creusot, a branch of those of Le Creusot, construct bridges, tug-boats etc., and there are chemical works, straw-hat factories, oil-works and tile-works. It is a busy corn-market and trades widely in wine, grain and timber.

CHALUKYA, the name of an Indian dynasty which ruled in the Deccan from A.D. 550 to 750, and again from 973 to 1190. The Chalukyas claimed to be Rajputs from the north. The dynasty was founded by a chief named Pulakesin I, who mastered the town of Vatapi (now Bādāmī, in the Bijapur district) about 550. His sons extended their principality east and west; but the founder of the Chalukya greatness was his grandson Pulakesin II, who succeeded in 608 and established as his viceroy in Vengi (609) his brother Kubja Vishnuvardhana, who in 615 declared his independence and established the dynasty of Eastern Chalukyas, which lasted till 1070. In 620 Pulakesin defeated Harsha (*q.v.*), the powerful overlord of northern India, and established the Nerbudda as the boundary between the South and North. He also defeated in turn the Chola, Pandya and Kerala kings, and by 630 was beyond dispute the most powerful sovereign in the Deccan. In 655 the Chalukya power was restored by Pulakesin's son Vikramaditya I.; but the struggle with the Pallavas continued until, in 740, Vikramaditya II. destroyed the Pallava capital. In 750 Vikramaditya's son, Kirtivarman Chalukya, was overthrown by the Rashtrakutas.

In 973, Taila or Tailapa II. (d. 995), a scion of the royal Chalukya race, succeeded in overthrowing the Rashtrakuta king Kakka II. He was the founder of the dynasty known as the Chalukyas of Kalyani. About A.D. 1000 a formidable invasion by the Chola king Rajaraja the Great was defeated, and in 1052 Somesvara I., or Ahamavalla (d. 1068), the founder of Kalyani, defeated and slew the Chola Rajadhiraja. The reign of Vikramaditya VI., or Vikramanka, which lasted from 1076 to 1126, formed another period of Chalukya greatness. In 1156 the commander-in-chief Bijjala (or Vijjana) Kalachurya revolted, and he and his sons held the kingdom till 1183, when Somesvara IV Chalukya recovered part of his patrimony, only to succumb, *c.* 1190, to the Yadavas of Devagiri and the Hoysalas of Dorasamudra. Henceforth the Chalukya rajas ranked only as petty chiefs.

BIBLIOGRAPHY.—J. F. Fleet, *Dynasties of the Kanarese Districts* (Bombay, 1896); R. G. Bhandarker, "Early History of the Deccan," *Bombay Gazetteer,* vol. i, part ii (1896); Vincent A. Smith, *Early History of India,* ed. by S. M. Edwardes (Oxford, 1924); D. C. Ganguly, *The Eastern Cālukyas* (Benares, 1937).

CHALUMEAU is a word having several different musical meanings (from Lat. *calamus,* a reed). Thus it is the name of an obsolete wind instrument, with a single beating reed, of the clarinet type; and also of a later instrument, with a double reed, which developed into the oboe. It is used also for the deepest notes of the clarinet and further, in its German form of Schalmey or Schalmei, for the chanter of the bag-pipe and for an old kind of organ stop of chalumeau-like quality.

CHALYBÄUS, HEINRICH MORITZ (1796–1862), German philosopher, was born at Pfaffroda in Saxony. He lectured at Dresden on the history of German philosophy, and in 1839 became professor in Kiel university. His first published work *Historische Entwickelung der spekulativen Philosophie von Kant bis Hegel* (1837, Eng. tr. 1854), still ranks among the best expositions of 19th century German thought. His chief works are *Entwurf eines Systems der Wissenschaftslehre* (Kiel, 1846) and *System der spekulativen Ethik* (1850).

See Überweg, *Grundriss der Gesch. der Philosophie,* Bd. iv. (1923).

CHALYBITE: *see* SIDERITE.

CHAM, a Muslim tribe of Indo-China, rather dark skinned with Oceanic affinities, practising circumcision but with strong traces of Hinduism, phallic worship and animism surviving in their beliefs and customs. Thus they believe in a plurality of souls, eighteen of which are mortal, attached to each individual, and associate the departure of the soul at death with the flight of a bird. They bury their dead close to their best rice fields, and have a series of ceremonies depending on the operations of the agricultural year; the reaping of the rice crop must be initiated by a woman. In the family the matrilineal system is still followed. Children are given opprobrious names, probably to obviate the malice of the spirits. Speech is tabu when collecting the valuable "eagle wood" (*aquilaria agallocha*), and invulnerability is procured by anointing the body with human bile. The Cham are fond of regattas and boat races, and play chess using canoes instead of bishops. The language of the tribe is connected with Cambodian and with Oceanic tongues and, like the dolichocephaly of its speakers, and their customs, suggests an Indonesian basis for the tribe.

See Baudesson, *Indo-China and its Primitive People* (1919); Leuba, *Les Chams et leur Art* (1923).

CHAMBA, a municipality, *tehsil* (administrative subdivision) and district in Himachal Pradesh, northern India. Chamba town (pop., 1951, 6,858) is situated above the Ravi gorge.

CHAMBA TEHSIL (area 1,429 sq.mi.) had a population in 1951 of 75,970.

CHAMBA DISTRICT (area 3,135 sq.mi.; pop., 1951, 176,050) corresponds almost exactly with the former princely state of that name. The state was founded in the 6th century: it was sometimes subject to Kashmir and later to the Mogul empire, but was always in practice autonomous. It was brought under British influence and declared independent of Kashmir in 1846; and was controlled under British paramountcy through the Punjab agency (Lahore residency). On April 15, 1948, it was merged with Himachal Pradesh, forming that state's isolated northwestern tract. The district is wholly mountainous, reaching above the snowline in east, north and centre.

CHAMBER, THE KING'S, the *camera regis,* was, in the later middle ages, an important financial office. In origin it was the king's bedroom, with cupboards and chests for clothes and valuables. The servants in charge of this room, the king's chamberlains as they were called (*see* CHAMBERLAIN), were in such close touch with the king that they were often consulted and employed by him on matters not strictly within their province. Thus, the king's chamber was, from the beginning, something more than mere sleeping quarters. It was an office where the king attended to private and public business alike, the greater part of which related to finance, and a storehouse for jewels, money and archives. From it, the first department to grow up within the royal household (*q.v.*), there sprang many mediaeval and modern ministries of state. Not only in England but throughout western Europe kings and magnates had their chamber, the *chambre des comptes* of the kings of France and the *camera apostolica* of the popes being cases in point.

In England the reconstruction following on the Norman Conquest provided the monarchy with a regular income from taxation, the collection and administration of which threw upon the chamber so much extra work that it became concerned primarily with finance. A hierarchy of clerical and lay officials came into being to assist the original staff. But, whereas in Europe generally, for example in the papacy and in France, the *camera curiae,* the chamber of the court, was the sole treasury of the state, in England by the 12th century, the king's chamber had developed a branch to deal with the finances of the kingdom as opposed to the more personal finances of the king. This was the exchequer (*q.v.*), the first department of the household to become a public office. It soon superseded the chamber, which then found itself once more a simple domestic and court office, although certain moneys continued to be paid to it rather than to the exchequer. The activities of the chamber were curtailed still further in the 13th century by the growth of a second offshoot, the king's wardrobe (*see* WARDROBES), by which it was ultimately replaced as the chief financial and administrative office of the household. Yet the chamber persisted, responsible to the king alone and overlapping the jurisdiction of both exchequer and wardrobe. Though its former power had been whittled down to authority over only the intimate financial needs of the king, there were several attempts to give it a foremost position in administration. Some of them, especially those of Edward II, Edward III and Henry VII, achieved considerable success.

Faced by a hostile baronage which sometimes dominated the chief public offices and interfered in the government of the royal household, Edward II turned to the chamber to secure independence of aristocracy, parliament and exchequer. To finance it adequately he allotted to it the management and income of certain lands which fell into his hands. The forfeited estates of the Templars (*q.v.*) were the first large block of lands to be brought under the authority of the chamber (1309). In 1322 the confiscation of the possessions of certain rebellious magnates, known as the "contrariants," put into Edward's power many more lands, which were soon reserved to the chamber, although only for a few months. The chamber staff was increased to discharge the duties involved in the care of an estate, and the secret seal fostered by Edward II in opposition to the privy seal (*see* SEALS: *Small*), which the barons strove to control, was entrusted to it. In the schemes of the younger Hugh Despenser, made king's chamberlain in 1322, the chamber played a leading part, but its progress was checked by Edward II's deposition, and its lands transferred to the exchequer.

In 1332 Edward III revived the chamber on the lines indicated by Despenser, and gradually placed a large number of lands at its disposal. A special seal, the griffin (*see* SEALS: *Small*), was set up for their service and the regular staff was again augmented. Edward III's need, however, differed from that of his father. Instead of an alienated baronage to contend with, Edward III had a foreign enemy, France, against whom all parties were united. Consequently he had less inducement to cultivate the chamber for purely prerogative purposes. His chamber seems to have met little unfriendly criticism, and, in the first phase of the Hundred Years' War, had a fair opportunity of proving its worth. During the early campaigns, its chief officers took a conspicuous share in administration at home as well as with the armies abroad. But the estate upon which it largely relied disappointed expectations, most of the proceeds being swallowed up by the costs of its administration. Without considerable funds the chamber was crippled. In 1355–56, therefore, the estate was given up, and for it an annual sum of 10,000 marks (£6,666, 13*s.* 4*d.*) payable by the exchequer, was substituted. This, the *certum* (fixed amount), was supplemented, as before the estate revenue had been, by casual receipts from the exchequer and elsewhere. Although the chamber was still answerable only to the king, its utility as an instrument of prerogative was diminished by this close dependence upon the exchequer. A further limitation was its total lack of skilfully devised, well-tried machinery to enforce its authority, for the griffin seal and the organization set up to administer the lands disappeared along with the estate. If, for the rest of Edward III's reign, the chamber occupied a recognized, amply endowed place in the administration, it was definitely subordinated to the exchequer. It was the royal privy purse, and a means whereby the king's will could be communicated to other departments, but little more.

On the accession of Richard II, a child with few personal expenses, the king's chamber suffered a natural relapse. When, in 1380, it was restored to something of its old dignity, the policy of 1355–56 was adopted, and a yearly allowance was granted to it, first from the customs, then, two years later, from the exchequer. On this *certum,* at most not more than two-thirds of that enjoyed under Edward III, the chamber was mainly dependent to the end of the 14th century, though in some years large casual payments were received. Such an office was valueless to a despotically minded king, and Richard II seems never to have thought of making it a chief instrument of his prerogative. Yet chamber officials figured prominently among his confidants, and it was in his reign that the office of king's secretary (*see* SECRETARY OF STATE) assumed definite shape, the final result being the withdrawal from the chamber of the secretary and his seal, the signet (*see* SEALS: *Small*), the successor to the secret seal.

Of chamber history in the greater part of the 15th century little is known, but the office lived on. Then, in the restoration of financial stability after the Wars of the Roses (*q.v.*), Henry VII advanced it to a position of supreme importance. Although he began to put the exchequer into working order, he wanted some less rigid, less elaborate machinery to supply him at once with the steady income necessary to strengthen government and throne. Like Edward II and Edward III he had recourse to the chamber as the most suitable instrument and one that was, besides, entirely in his control. Forfeited estates and crown lands were once again reserved to it, and other moneys were paid to it instead of to the exchequer. A new staff grew up, and to the daily labours of the regenerated office the king gave constant oversight. Unlike the Edwards, Henry was able to make the chamber effective, for, although he too diverted to the chamber revenues ordinarily paid and accounted for to the exchequer, and imposed upon it functions technically belonging to the exchequer, the exchequer's extreme weakness, due to civil war, prevented remonstrance from that quarter.

Soon after the death of Henry VII., however, the exchequer, grown stronger, tried to insist that issues formerly paid to it, and accounts customarily rendered to it for audit, should still follow those rules, and not go to the chamber. In reply to this claim Henry VIII. induced parliament to recognize his father's system. Thus the chamber, already possessing wider influence than in the 14th century, seemed well on the way to recapturing its original position in the State. But Henry VIII., hard-working as he was, attended less to the routine of government than Henry VII., and the exchequer slowly deprived the chamber of all its newly given power. When the exchequer had recovered from the effects of the Wars of the Roses, not even Henry VIII. himself could maintain for the chamber the supremacy won under the guidance of Henry VII. Yet it was not until Mary's reign that the exchequer regained its traditional status, and then it was an exchequer changed at heart. From the end of the 13th century the chamber's rise and fall was chiefly determined by the weakness or strength of the exchequer. By taking over the best the chamber had to offer, the exchequer rendered it harmless for all time. There was no subsequent attempt to revive the work of that department, and only a memory of past glory is preserved in the office of the modern lord chamberlain (*q.v.*).

Bibliography.—T. F. Tout, *The Place of the Reign of Edward II. in English History* (1914, bibl.); A. P. Newton, "The King's Chamber, under the Early Tudors," *English Historical Review*, xxxii (1917); T. F. Tout, *Chapters in the Administrative History of Mediaeval England* (vols.i–vi. 1920–33) (D. M. B.)

CHAMBERLAIN, ARTHUR NEVILLE (1869–1940), British politician, was born March 18, 1869, the son of Joseph Chamberlain by his second wife. Educated at Rugby and Mason college, Birmingham, he was successful in business in Birmingham and was lord mayor in 1915–16.

After serving on the central board of control of the liquor traffic and as director of national service during World War I., he became M.P. for the Ladywood division of Birmingham in 1918, was postmaster general from Oct. 1922 to March 1923, and then minister of health.

In Aug. 1923 he was made chancellor of the exchequer, but the government fell before he could present a budget. Again health minister in 1924, he carried out useful pension, housing and pure-food reforms. In 1931 he again became chancellor of the exchequer, retaining office until he succeeded Baldwin as prime minister in May 1937.

During his premiership, Chamberlain had to face a profound crisis in Europe, and to meet the growing might of nazi Germany. His aim was to ward off the danger of war by acquiescing in what he considered to be reasonable German demands, and this policy of appeasement reached its climax in the Munich agreement of Sept. 30, 1938, and the joint Anglo-German declaration of intention not to war on each other.

Chamberlain held that "peace in our time" was assured by this agreement, and as such augury it was hailed by his country. But Hitler's abrogation of the Munich agreement six months later with the complete absorption of Czechoslovakia proved these hopes to be illusory. Chamberlain then declared that Britain would oppose further nazi aggression by force and gave a guarantee of assistance to Poland (March 31, 1939). It was never clear how this guarantee could be made effective, however, for during the summer of 1939 the government failed to come to an agreement with Russia, the only power which could materially have helped Poland. After the Russo-German agreement of Aug. 1939, the German attack on Poland forced Chamberlain to declare war on Germany on Sept. 3, 1939.

Though essentially a peacetime leader, Chamberlain remained prime minister during the period of the "phoney" war, but the military debacle in Norway and the German attack on the Low Countries and France forced him to resign on May 10, 1940, in favour of Winston Churchill (*q.v.*). He was appointed lord president of the council and remained in the cabinet until Oct. 3, when he resigned this office and the leadership of the Conservative party because of ill-health. On Nov. 9, 1940, he died, a disillusioned man who had seen destroyed all his hopes of maintaining peace in Europe. (C. M. Cl.)

CHAMBERLAIN, SIR (JOSEPH) AUSTEN (1863–1937), the eldest son of Joseph Chamberlain (*q.v.*) and of his first wife, Harriet Kenrick, was born at Birmingham on Oct. 16, 1863. He was educated at Rugby and Trinity College, Cambridge, and afterwards studied in Paris and Berlin. During the early stages of the Home Rule controversy he acted as his father's private secretary, and in 1892 was returned unopposed as M.P. for East Worcestershire. This seat he held until 1914, when, on his father's death, he succeeded him as a member for West Birmingham. "I was born in Birmingham," he said when he was given the freedom of that city in 1926. "I was bred in Birmingham; Birmingham is in my blood and in my bones, and wherever I go and whatever I am, I shall remain a Birmingham man."

His maiden speech drew from Gladstone the famous compliment, uttered in his father's presence, that it was one which must have been "dear and refreshing to a father's heart." After a short apprenticeship as a private member, he was a civil lord of the Admiralty (1895–1900), financial secretary to the Treasury (1900–2) and postmaster-general (1902). This rapid promotion was not due merely to the towering influence of his father, during the days of his great colonial secretaryship. Though the son's powers were of a solid rather than of a showy order, his administrative ability and his cogency in debate steadily developed with opportunity. His command of clear statement was exceptional; and he could be unexpectedly formidable in defence. In 1903 he was promoted to the chancellorship of the Exchequer. He ardently espoused his father's fiscal policy of tariff reform, nor did he slacken in its advocacy when Joseph Chamberlain left the Balfour administration in order to prosecute, with less embarrassment to the prime minister, his unofficial campaign. Unfriendly critics suggested at the time that the son's promotion to the second post in the Government was made in the hope of continuing his father's activities within reasonable bounds and preventing the threatened rupture in the party. This is not an adequate view. The father outside the Cabinet, like the son inside it, wished not to rupture their party but to convert it as a whole to the new doctrine of closer Imperial economic union and tariff-defence at home against foreign protection. Austen Chamberlain remained at the exchequer till the Unionist *débâcle* at the polls in 1906 and there acquired the reputation of being a departmentalist of the best Victorian type—safe, cautious, hard-working, and signally loyal to his associates. This loyalty was unflinching and more than once self-sacrificial.

During the long Liberal domination from 1906 to the World War Austen Chamberlain consolidated his position as a Unionist leader and gained the high esteem of all parties. He suffered, however, a great disappointment when Balfour, faced by the discontent and revolt of the rank and file, resigned his leadership of the Unionist party in 1911. Austen Chamberlain's claims to the succession were well supported. But a slightly stronger section favoured the claims of Walter Long, and as neither would yield to the other, both honourably agreed to the election of Bonar Law.

When the first Coalition Government was formed, in 1915, Austen Chamberlain entered Asquith's Cabinet as secretary of state for India, and held this post until 1917, when he resigned in consequence of the Government's decision to submit to a judicial investigation the charges and criticisms embodied in the report of the Mesopotamia commission. In his view the public interest and his personal honour alike required his resignation, though not one of the charges referred to him. The official responsibilities for the "horrible break-down" of the hospital arrangements during the first advance on Baghdad were incurred without his personal knowledge. His insistence on resignation was over-scrupulous, but showed that his views of what principle and loyalty demand were stricter than the normal. He did not long remain out of office. In April 1918 he became a member of the War Cabinet and after the Armistice returned to the chancellorship of the Exchequer in succession to Bonar Law. His guiding principle during the next two years was to strengthen British credit and pay off debt, and to that end he called upon the taxpayer to make unprecedentedly heavy sacrifices, especially in respect of income tax, super-tax and excess profits duty. At the Treasury in a very British way he preserved an iron tradition of fiscal integrity.

In 1921 Bonar Law's failing health caused his withdrawal from active politics. Austen Chamberlain stepped into the vacant leadership of the House of Commons amid general acclamation. The post carried with it the virtual promise of the leadership of the Conservative party, ten years after the frustration of that chance in 1911. But the restraints and compromises of coalition had already begun to be irksome to many Conservatives, who distrusted the direction in which the Liberal prime minister of the Coalition was leading them. Austen Chamberlain, as lord privy seal and leader of the House, found that his staunch loyalty to his chief was bringing him into disfavour with many of the Conservative rank and file. The complaint was that he did not stand up to Lloyd George with sufficient firmness and that he sacrificed too many Conservative principles. This feeling was sharply intensified when Austen Chamberlain took a leading part at the end of 1921 in the startling settlement with Sinn Fein and the establishment of the Irish Free State. He pleaded boldly and eloquently for this "act of faith." He had been, indeed, the first to suggest to the prime minister that a choice had to be made between negotiations with the rebels and a thorough reconquest of Ireland.

Most of the Conservative party accepted the treaty with reluctance and with forebodings. Party confidence in Austen Chamberlain was further weakened by his steady refusal to listen to suggestions that fidelity to Conservative principles required him to lead his party out of Coalition bondage into party independence and freedom. His view, shared by his principal Conservative colleagues in the Lloyd George administration, was that Coalition was still necessary to deal with the difficult problems of the post-War period and not less to obviate the dangers of a socialist government, which, without co-operation between the two older parties, could not in their view long be averted. When, therefore, the discontented Conservative Diehards carried their revolt to success, and at the Carlton Club meeting on Oct. 19, 1922, offered the leadership to Bonar Law—who accepted it—Austen Chamberlain once more saw the ruin of his highest chances in politics. He and those of his colleagues who shared his views and quitted office with Lloyd George, naturally had no place in Bonar Law's Cabinet. He remained a private member during Baldwin's first administration and during the short period of the succeeding Labour Government. The dissensions in the Conservative party were gradually healed. When Baldwin formed his second administration, at the end of 1924, the post of foreign secretary was accepted by Austen Chamberlain. Then began a new stage of his career. Thirteen days after he entered on his duties at the Foreign Office (*i.e.*, on Nov. 20, 1924) Sir Lee Stack, governor general of the Sudan and Sirdar of the Egyptian army, was murdered in Cairo. The resultant situation was handled by Austen Chamberlain with a promptness and firmness that prevented further trouble, and at once established his own prestige as foreign secretary. Without delay he applied himself, at the beginning of 1925, to the remarkable diplomacy which produced the Locarno treaties. That diplomacy was pursued throughout the year, and it was mainly due to his moral earnestness and determination (for the sceptics abounded) that the treaties were initialled at Locarno on Oct. 16, 1925, Austen Chamberlain's birthday. For the nature of those treaties *see* LOCARNO, PACT OF. For the part he had played in this big step towards post-War reconciliation in Europe, Chamberlain received the Garter on Nov. 30, 1925 and the Nobel prize for peace in the same year (jointly with Charles G. Dawes). He increased the general pacific tendency in Europe by making the League of Nations a first consideration of his policy, himself attending all the meetings of the Council and Assembly. Germany's entry into the League in September 1926 was an event for which he personally was entitled to much credit. In 1927 his policy in the Chinese crisis was both conciliatory and strong. A military force was sent out to safeguard against possible attack and anarchy the great commercial community of Shanghai, but Great Britain also was the first in the field with proposals for large and increasing concessions to Chinese nationalism.

In May 1927 he reluctantly broke off relations with Russia after the Arcos raid, when it became clear that Bolshevism was violating normal diplomatic rules both in China and Britain. In the summer he initiated discussions with Sarwat Pasha for an Anglo-Egyptian treaty of alliance. A nine months' effort was thwarted early in 1928 by Cairo's repudiation of Sarwat and the emergence of Nahas Pasha as his successor. The failure of the three-Power naval conference at Geneva in July was not directly his responsibility. During the winter of 1927–28 and up to the summer of 1928 his general policy was concerned with a consideration of Kellogg's proposal for a Peace Pact, which he supported with some reserves as to interpretation, though wholly endorsing its principle. The Pact was duly signed in August. In the autumn of 1928 illness forced him to take a long sea voyage through the Panama Canal to California and thence through Canada homewards. His health had been rapidly restored, but in his absence the Foreign Office was widely attacked for its effort—wrapped in needless mystery—to concert with France joint suggestions to America on the subject of naval limitation. Public criticism made an end of this method, for which the Admiralty and the Cabinet generally were mainly responsible. Sir Austen died Mar. 16, 1937.

BIBLIOGRAPHY.—George Glasgow, *From Dawes to Locarno* (1925); A. J. Toynbee, C. A. Macartney and others, *Survey of International Affairs* (1926); Sir A. Chamberlain, *Peace in Our Time:* addresses on Europe and the Empire (1928).

CHAMBERLAIN, CHARLES JOSEPH (1863–1943), U.S. plant morphologist and cytologist, was born near Sullivan, Ohio on Feb. 23, 1863 and educated at Oberlin college, graduating in 1888. Most of his life he was connected with the University of Chicago, from which he obtained the degree of Ph.D. in 1897 and Sci.D. in 1923. He became instructor in 1901, spent one year in Bonn, Germany where he worked in the laboratory of Prof. Eduard Strasburger, and after his return, was appointed assistant professor in 1907, associate professor in 1911 and was professor of plant morphology and cytology from 1915 until his retirement in 1931. He was fundamental in organizing botanical laboratories and was in charge of them from the beginning. His interest in morphology and life history of cycads caused him to make many exploring trips which resulted in the assembling of the most extensive and complete collection of living cycads in the greenhouses of the university. He visited Mexico in 1904, 1906, 1908 and 1910 and made a long journey in 1911–12 to New Zealand and Australia, returning through South Africa. In 1914 and 1922 he collected in Cuba. He died on Feb. 5, 1943.

His publications include *Morphology of Spermatophytes* (1901); *Morphology of Angiosperms* (1903) *and Morphology of Gymnosperms* (1910, ed. 2, 1917) all in collaboration with J. M. Coulter; among his other works are *Methods in Plant Histology* (1901, ed. 5, 1932) and *Gymnosperms, Structure and Evolution* (1935).

See *Bot. Gaz.*, vol. civ (1943) and *Chronica Botanica*, vol. vii (1943).

CHAMBERLAIN, JOSEPH (1836–1914), British statesman, third son of Joseph Chamberlain, master of the Cordwainers' Company, was born at Camberwell Grove, London, on July 8, 1836. His father carried on the family business of boot and shoe manufacture, and was a Unitarian in religion and a Liberal in politics. Young Joseph Chamberlain was educated at Canonbury (1845–50), and at University college school, London (1850–52). After two years in his father's office in London, he was sent to Birmingham to represent his father's interest in the firm of Nettlefold, screw manufacturers. Nettlefold and Chamberlain employed new inventions and new methods of attracting customers. After years of success Chamberlain himself, with daring but sure ability amalgamated rival firms so as to reduce competition. In 1874 he was able to retire with an ample fortune. Taking a more and more important part in the municipal and political life of Birmingham, in 1868 when the Birmingham Liberal Association was reorganized, he became one of its leading members. In 1869 he was elected chairman of the executive council of the new National Education League. He took an active part in education, started classes for his workmen, and himself taught history, French and arithmetic in a Unitarian Sunday school. In 1869 he was elected a member of the town council. He married in 1868 his first wife's cousin, Florence Kendrick (d. 1875).

In 1870 he was elected a member of the first school board for Birmingham; and for the next six years, and especially after 1873, when he became leader of a majority and chairman, he actively championed the Nonconformist opposition to denominationalism. He was then regarded as a republican—the term signifying rather that he held advanced Radical opinions, which were construed by average men in the light of the current political developments in France, than that he really favoured republican institutions for Britain. His programme was "free Church, free land, free schools, free labour." At the general election of 1874 he stood as a parliamentary candidate for Sheffield, but without success. Between 1869 and 1873 he worked in the Birmingham town council for the realization of the projects of municipal reform preached by Dawson, Dr. Dale and Bunce (of the "Birmingham Post"). In 1873 his party obtained a majority, and he was elected mayor, an office he retained by re-election until June 1876. As mayor he had to receive the prince and princess of Wales on their visit in June 1874, an occasion which excited some curiosity because of his reputation as a republican; but the behaviour of the Radical mayor satisfied the requirements alike of *The Times* and of *Punch*.

Birmingham.—The period of his mayoralty was important for Birmingham itself, and the stupendous energy which Chamberlain brought to bear on evil conditions in Birmingham had repercussions in every municipality in the country. The conference of local sanitary authorities summoned by him in 1874 and held in Jan. 1875 was the beginning of the modern movement for better and healthier organization of town life. In Birmingham he carried through the municipalization of the supply of gas and water, and the improvement scheme by which slums were cleared away and 40 acres laid out in new streets and open spaces. New municipal buildings were erected, Highgate park was opened for recreation, and the free library and art gallery were developed. The prosperity of modern Birmingham dates from 1875 and 1876, when these admirably administered reforms were initiated, and by his share in them Chamberlain became not only one of its most popular citizens but also a man of mark outside. An orator of a practical but consummate type, cool and hard-hitting, his spare figure, incisive features and single eye-glass soon made him a favourite subject for the caricaturist; and in later life his aggressiveness made his actions and speeches the object of more controversy than was the lot of any other politician of his time. In private life his loyalty to his friends, and his "genius for friendship" (as John Morley said) made a curious contrast to his capacity for arousing the bitterest political hostility. It may be added here that the interest taken by him in Birmingham remained undiminished during his life, and he was the founder of Birmingham university (1900), of which he became chancellor.

In 1876 Dixon resigned his seat in parliament, and Chamberlain was returned for Birmingham in his place unopposed, as John Bright's colleague. He made his maiden speech in the House of Commons on Aug. 4, 1876, on Lord Sandon's education bill. At this period, too, he paid much attention to the question of licensing reform, and in 1876 he examined the Gothenburg system in Sweden, and advocated a solution of the problem in England on similar lines. During 1877 the new federation of Liberal associations, which became known as the "Caucus," was started under Chamberlain's influence in Birmingham, the results of which were clearly shown in the general election of 1880.

After the general election of 1880 the Liberal party numbered 349 against 243 Conservatives and 60 Irish Nationalists. Gladstone was compelled to recognize the services of the Radicals in the election by the inclusion of Dilke and Chamberlain, who were sworn allies, in the new ministry. They had resolved together that one of them must be in the cabinet. The prime minister had not contemplated the admission of either, and was determined not to have both. Chamberlain, willing to give the preference to Dilke, was himself chosen as president of the Board of Trade. Dilke became under-secretary for foreign affairs but, at the end of 1882, he too entered the cabinet as president of the Local Government Board, and the alliance between the two rising ministers was more powerful than ever. The position of the Radicals in the 1880–85 Government was extremely difficult. Gladstone naturally turned rather to his old friends, Granville and Spencer, and had little personal sympathy with the new men. Dilke and Chamberlain stood for more far-reaching social reforms at home than their elder colleagues, and on foreign affairs there were many difficulties. In Egypt Chamberlain demanded more vigorous measures after the massacre at Alexandria (1882), yet insisted that the Government must not be tied to the bondholders' interest, but must give legitimate effect to Egyptian nationalist aspirations. Again in Feb. 1884 he would have given instructions to Baring to arrange for the relief of the Sudan garrisons, but no steps were taken, and, when at last a much more elaborate expedition than that at first urged by Chamberlain was sent, it was too late to avoid the tragedy of Gordon.

Irish Policy.—But the deepest fissure was on Irish policy. Chamberlain hated coercion, and held a positive view of Irish affairs. He made a personal effort in 1882 to heal the Irish sore. On the understanding that he would be disavowed if he failed, he was authorized to negotiate with Parnell and succeeded. The result was the "Kilmainham treaty." Parnell, on May 2, 1882, was released from Kilmainham gaol, having agreed to advise the cessation of outrages and the payment of rent, while Gladstone's ministry was to relax its coercive administration. Thereupon, W. E. Forster, the Irish secretary, resigned. His successor, the blameless Lord Frederick Cavendish, was immediately murdered in Phoenix park. This tragedy darkened the whole aspect of Irish affairs. Chamberlain, conspicuously marked out for the post of danger, was prepared to face the risk, but was not appointed. He refused to allow the tragedy to divert him from a definitely remedial policy. Eventually in 1885, after indirect negotiation through Capt. O'Shea with Parnell, he placed before the cabinet a scheme for Irish government on lines of semi-Home Rule without weakening, however, the imperial connection. A "central council," or national elective board was to be set up in Dublin, and Parnell was to forego obstruction to a bill which would reduce coercion to a minimum. The Irish bishops were thought to favour the plan. When these proposals for devolution came before the cabinet (May 9) all the peers, except Granville, voted against them; of the commoners only Hartington opposed them. Proposals for a Coercion bill and a land purchase bill were then put forward. Dilke and Chamberlain resigned, the latter being definitely opposed to land purchase unaccompanied by local autonomy. But the resignations did not take effect before the Government was defeated on the budget (June 8).

Both before and after the defeat Chamberlain associated himself with what was known as the "unauthorized programme," *i.e.*, free education, small holdings for agricultural labourers, graduated taxation and local government. In June 1885 he made a speech at Birmingham, treating the reforms just mentioned as the "ransom" that property must pay to society for the security it enjoys. In October Chamberlain defined his ideas to Gladstone. They were that local authorities must have the right of appropriation for public purposes, that a radical readjustment of taxation was necessary, and that ministers must be free to advocate free education, even if some of their colleagues opposed it. At the general election of Nov. 1885 Chamberlain was returned for West Birmingham. The Liberal strength in the nation generally was, however, reduced to 335 members, though the Radical section held their own; and the Irish vote became necessary to Gladstone if he was to command a majority. Chamberlain still had an open mind on the Irish question. He foresaw that between Home Rule and separation there was but a step, and in a letter written on Dec. 26 he went so far as to discuss a federalist scheme for the British Isles with five separate parliaments. In December it was stated that Gladstone intended to propose Home Rule for Ireland, and when the new parliament met in Jan. 1886 Lord Salisbury's ministry was defeated on the address, on an amendment moved by Chamberlain's Birmingham henchman, Jesse Collings, embodying the "three acres and a cow" of the Radical programme. Lord Hartington (afterwards duke of Devonshire) and some other Liberals, declined to join Gladstone in view of the altered attitude he was adopting towards Ireland. But Chamberlain—stipulating for liberty of judgment on the prime minister's Irish policy when embodied in definite legislative shape—entered the cabinet as president of the Local Government Board (with Jesse Collings as parliamentary secretary). On March 15, 1886, he resigned, explaining in the House of Commons (April 8), that while he had always been in favour of the largest extension of local government to Ireland consistent with the integrity of the empire and the supremacy of the imperial parliament, and had therefore joined Gladstone when he believed that agreement might be possible, he was unable to recognize that the scheme communicated by Gladstone to his colleagues maintained those conditions. At the same time he was not irreconcilable, and invited Gladstone even then to modify the bill so as to remove the objections of Radical dissentients. This indecisive attitude did not last long, and the split in the party rapidly widened. At Birmingham Chamberlain was supported by the local "Two Thousand," but deserted by the national "Caucus" of the Liberal party and by its organizer, his own former lieutenant, Schnadhorst. In May the Radicals who followed Bright and Chamberlain, and the Whigs who took their cue from Lord Hartington, decided to vote against the second reading of the Home Rule bill, instead of allowing it to be taken and then pressing for modifications in committee, and on June 7 the bill was defeated by 343 to 313, 94 Liberal Unionists—as they were generally called—voting against the Government. Chamberlain was the object of the bitterest attacks from the Gladstonians for his share in this result; and open war was proclaimed by the Home Rulers against the "dissentient Liberals"—the description used by Gladstone. The general election, however, returned to Parliament 316 Conservatives, 78 Liberal Unionists, and only 276 Gladstonians and Nationalists, Birmingham returning seven Unionist members. When the House met in August, it was decided by the Liberal Unionists, under Hartington's leadership, that their policy henceforth was essentially to put in the Tories and to keep Gladstone out. The old Liberal feeling still prevailing among them was too strong, however, for their leaders to take office in a coalition ministry. For them as a whole it was enough to be able to tie down the Conservative Government to such measures as were not offensive to Liberal Unionist principles; but Chamberlain from the first was determined to impose on that Government a progressive policy in British social questions as the price of his indispensable support on the Irish question. It still seemed possible, moreover, that the Gladstonians might be brought to modify their Home Rule proposals, and in Jan. 1887 a Round Table conference, suggested by Chamberlain, was held between him and Sir G. Trevelyan for the Liberal Unionists, with Sir William Harcourt, John Morley and Lord Herschell for the Gladstonians, but no *rapprochement* was effected.

Reform.—The influence of his views upon the domestic legislation of the Government was bringing about a more complete union in the Unionist party, and destroying the old lines of political cleavage. Before 1892 Chamberlain had the satisfaction of seeing Lord Salisbury's ministry pass such important acts, from a progressive standpoint, as those dealing with coal mines regulation, allotments, county councils, housing of the working classes, free education and agricultural holdings, besides Irish legislation like the Ashbourne Act, the Land Act of 1891, and the Light Railways and Congested District acts.

In Oct. 1887, Chamberlain, Sir L. Sackville West and Sir Charles Tupper were selected by the Government as British plenipotentiaries to discuss with the United States the Canadian fisheries dispute, and a treaty was signed by them at Washington on February 15, 1888. The Senate, however, refused to ratify it; but a protocol provided for a *modus vivendi* giving American fishing vessels similar advantages to those contemplated in the treaty. This arrangement, prolonged from year to year, proved to be a real settlement. Chamberlain returned home in March, his already strong feelings of friendliness to the United States much strengthened. This sentiment was reinforced in Nov. 1888, by his marriage with his third wife, Miss Endicott, daughter of the United States secretary of war in President Cleveland's first administration.

At the general election of 1892 Chamberlain was again returned, with an increased majority, for West Birmingham, but the Unionist party as a whole was narrowly defeated; the Irish Nationalist vote again held the balance in the House of Commons and, with a small and precarious majority, Gladstone returned to office, pledged to Home Rule for Ireland. On Feb. 13, 1893, that wonderful veteran, now in his 84th year, introduced his second Home Rule bill, which was read a third time on Sept. 1. During the 82 days' discussion in the House of Commons Chamberlain was its most acute, ceaseless, unsparing critic, and he moved public opinion outside the House. His chief contribution to the discussions during the later stages of the Gladstone and Rosebery ministries was in connection with Asquith's abortive Employers' Liability bill, when he foreshadowed the broader method of "compensation for accidents," afterwards carried out, in favour of the working classes by the act of 1897. Outside parliament he was busy formulating proposals for old age pensions, which had a prominent place in the Unionist programme of 1895. After his visit to America in 1889 he was developing the imperialist outlook which profoundly modified his future activity.

South Africa.—In 1895 he became secretary of State for the colonies in Lord Salisbury's ministry. His influence in the Unionist cabinet was soon visible in the Workmen's Compensation act and other measures. This act, though in formal charge of the home secretary, was universally and rightly associated with Chamberlain. Another less important "social" measure, which formed part of the Chamberlain programme, was the Small Houses Acquisition Act of 1899; but the problem of old age pensions was less easily solved. This subject had been handed over in 1893 to a royal commission, and further discussed by a select committee in 1899 and a departmental committee in 1900, but both of these threw cold water on the schemes laid before them.

From New Year 1896 (the date of the Jameson Raid) onwards South Africa demanded the chief attention of the colonial secretary (*see* SOUTH AFRICA, and for details TRANSVAAL). In his negotiations with President Kruger one masterful temperament was pitted against another. Chamberlain had a very difficult part to play in a situation dominated by suspicion on both sides. While he firmly insisted on the rights of Great Britain and of British subjects in the Transvaal, he was the continual object of Radical criticism at home. Attempts were even made to ascribe financial motives to Chamberlain's actions, and the political atmosphere was thick with suspicion and scandal. The report of the Commons committee (July 1897) definitely acquitted both Chamberlain and the Colonial Office of any privity in the Jameson Raid, but Chamberlain's detractors continued to assert the contrary. Opposition hostility reached such a pitch that in 1899 there was hardly an act of the cabinet during the negotiations with President Kruger which was not attributed to the personal malignity and unscrupulousness of the colonial secretary. In fact he gave ample scope to the man on the spot, Sir Alfred (Lord) Milner, whom he had sent out as high commissioner in 1897. The Bloemfontein Conference of 1899 was a serious attempt to secure amicable agreement; but its failure did not deter Chamberlain from making repeated efforts to ensure peace. In the Transvaal the original Boer burghers had become an armed minority, determined at all costs to maintain its racial ascendancy. Since the opening of the gold mines, the unenfranchised outlanders, chiefly British, had become the majority of the adult inhabitants and supplied most of the revenue. Their plight was one of "taxation without representation." Chamberlain offered as part of a general settlement of the franchise and other outstanding questions, to give complete guarantees against any attack on the independence of the republic. But President Kruger's ultimatum demanded, in effect, the military withdrawal and political abdication of Britain in South Africa, and the Boer War began. It lasted for over 2½ years before the two Dutch republics formally surrendered. Throughout this period, Chamberlain was the mainstay of British public opinion when nearly all the world was hostile. The elections of 1900 (when he was again returned, unopposed, for West Birmingham) turned upon the individuality of a single minister more than any since the days of Gladstone's ascendancy, and Chamberlain, never conspicuous for inclination to turn his other cheek to the smiter, was not slow to return the blows with interest.

Apart from South Africa, his most important work at this time was the successful passing of the Australian Commonwealth Act (1900), when both tact and firmness were needed to settle certain differences between the imperial Government and the colonial delegates.

Chamberlain's tenure of the office of colonial secretary between 1895 and 1900 must always be regarded as a turning-point in the history of the relations between the British colonies and the mother country. In spirit he was an imperial federationist even before his separation from Gladstone. From 1887 onwards he worked for a *rapprochement* of the different parts of the empire for purposes of defence and commerce. In 1895 he struck a new note of constructive statesmanship, basing itself on the economic necessities of a world-wide empire. Not the least of the anxieties of the Colonial Office during this period was the situation in the West Indies, where the cane-sugar industry was being steadily undermined by the European bounties given to exports of Continental beet, and though the Government restricted themselves to attempts at removing the bounties by negotiation and to measures for palliating the worst effects in the West Indies, Chamberlain made no secret of his repudiation of the Cobden club view that retaliation would be contrary to the doctrines of free trade. He set to work to educate public opinion at home into understanding that the responsibilities of the mother country are not merely to be construed according to the selfish interests of a nation of consumers. As regards foreign affairs, Chamberlain more than once (particularly at Birmingham, May 13, 1898, and at Leicester, Nov. 30, 1899) indicated his leanings towards a closer understanding between the British empire, the United States and Germany. The unusually outspoken and pointed expression, however, of his disinclination to submit to Muscovite duplicity or to "pin-pricks" or "unmannerliness" from France was widely criticized. For three years from the spring of 1898 to 1901 he worked strenuously in secret for an Anglo-German alliance. He was convinced that this project was the chief key to the peace of the world. The Kaiser and Bülow hoped rather by keeping free hands to become arbiters of the world.

Boer War.—During the progress of the Boer War from 1899 to 1902, Chamberlain, as colonial secretary, naturally played only a subordinate part during the carrying out of the military operations. But in parliament and on the platform he was more than ever supreme—the chief animating influence of the British empire. He was the hero of the one side, just as he was the bugbear of the other. On Feb. 13, 1902, he was presented with an address in a gold casket by the corporation of the city of London, and entertained at luncheon at the Mansion House, an honour not unconnected with the strong feeling recently aroused by his firm reply (at Birmingham, Jan. 11) to disparaging remarks made by the German chancellor in the Reichstag (Jan. 8). Against offensive allegations abroad Chamberlain had defended the British army in South Africa, and declared its conduct to be as good as that of the Germans in 1870–71. The way in which England's difficulties called forth colonial assistance intensified his imperialism. More and more the problems of empire engrossed him, and a new enthusiasm for imperial projects arose in the Unionist party under his inspiration. No English statesman probably—except Peel—has ever been, at different times in his career, so able an advocate of apparently contradictory policies, and his opponents baited him with quotations from his earlier speeches. He replied in effect that to flinch from adopting new methods and even new opinions in face of totally changed circumstances, is either practical folly or moral cowardice.

The settlement after the war was full of difficulties, financial and others, in South Africa. When Arthur Balfour succeeded Lord Salisbury as prime minister in July 1902, Chamberlain agreed to serve loyally under him, and the friendship between the two leaders was indeed one of the most marked features of the political situation. In Nov. 1902 Chamberlain, bent upon a conciliatory settlement with the Boers, went out to South Africa. He travelled from place to place (Dec. 26–Feb. 25), arranged with the leading Transvaal financiers that in return for support from the British Government in raising a Transvaal loan they would guarantee a large proportion of a Transvaal debt of £30,000,000 which, by so much, should repay the British Treasury the cost of the war, and when he returned in March 1903, satisfaction was general in the country over the success of his mission. But meantime two things had happened. He desired above all things imperial union. At the Imperial Conference of 1902 the attitude of the overseas premiers had shown that the only way to the beginnings of a closer political union of the whole empire was on lines of mutually preferential commerce, deviating from the strict traditional doctrines of "free trade"—that is of equally free imports for all products, whether of foreign or British—imperial origin. But at home—while he was still in South Africa—some of his colleagues had gone a long way, behind the scenes, to destroy one of the very factors on which the practical scheme for imperial commercial federation seemed to hinge. In the budget of 1902 a duty of a shilling a quarter on imported corn had been reintroduced. This small tax was regarded as only a registration duty. Even by free-trade ministers like Gladstone it had been left up to 1869 untouched, and its removal by Robert Lowe (Lord Sherbrooke) had since then been widely regarded as a piece of economic pedantry. The more advanced imperialists, as well as the more old-fashioned protectionists (like Lord Chaplin) who formed a small but integral part of the Conservative body, had looked forward to this tax being converted into a differential one between foreign and colonial corn, so as to introduce a scheme of colonial preference. The latter principle would be introduced even by a remission of sixpence in favour of grain grown "under the flag" overseas. Ritchie, the chancellor of the exchequer, having a surplus in prospect and taxation to take off, persuaded the cabinet to abolish the corn-duty altogether. Chamberlain himself had proposed only to take it off as regards colonial, but not foreign corn—thus inaugurating a preferential system—and when he left for South Africa he did not imagine that this principle was in danger. But in his absence, a majority of the cabinet supported Ritchie. To those who had hoped so to handle the tax as to make it a lever for a gradual change in the established fiscal system, the total abolition was a bitter blow. At once there began, though not at first openly, a split between the more rigid free-traders—advocates of cheap food and free imports—and those who desired to use the opportunities of a tariff, of however moderate a kind, for attaining national and imperial and not merely revenue advantages. This idea had for some time been forming in Chamberlain's mind, and now took full possession of it. For the moment he remained in the cabinet, but the seed of dissension was sown. The first public intimation of his views was given in an epoch-marking speech to his constituents at Birmingham (May 15, 1903), when he outlined a plan for raising more money by a rearranged tariff, partly to obtain a preferential system for the empire and partly to produce funds for social reform at home. On May 28 in the House of Commons he spoke on the same subject, and declared "if you are to give a preference to the colonies, you must put a tax on food." Putting the necessity of food-taxes in the forefront was injudicious; but imperialist conviction and enthusiasm were more conspicuous than electioneering prudence in the launching of Chamberlain's new scheme. His courage was heroic; his tactics fell short of the old unfailing mastery of manoeuvre.

Tariff Reform.—Chamberlain argued that since 1870 certain other countries (Germany and the United States), with protective tariffs, had increased their trade in much larger proportion, while English trade had been chiefly maintained by the increased business done with British colonies. A scientific enquiry into the facts was needed. For a time the demand merely for enquiry, and the production of figures, gave no sufficient occasion for dissension among Unionists, even when, like Sir M. Hicks Beach, they were convinced free-importers on purely economic as well as political grounds. Balfour, as premier, managed to hold his colleagues and party together by taking the line that particular opinions on economic subjects should not be made a test of party loyalty. The Tariff Reform League was founded in order to further Chamberlain's policy, holding its inaugural meeting on July 21; and it began to take an active part in issuing leaflets and in work at by-elections.

Meanwhile, the death of Lord Salisbury (Aug. 22) removed a weighty figure from the councils of the Unionist party. The cabinet met several times at the beginning of September, and the question of their attitude towards the fiscal problem became acute. The public had its first intimation of impending events in the appearance on Sept. 16 of Balfour's *Economic Notes on Insular Free Trade,* which had been previously circulated as a cabinet memorandum. The next day appeared the Board of Trade Fiscal Blue-Book, and on the 18th conflicting resignations were announced—not only of the more rigid free-traders in the cabinet, Ritchie and Lord George Hamilton, but also of Chamberlain himself for the opposite reason. His exit from the British Government after eight years of office was an event discussed with interest throughout the world.

Letters in cordial terms were published, which had passed between Chamberlain (Sept. 9) and Balfour (Sept. 16). Chamberlain pointed out that he was committed to a preferential scheme involving new duties on food, and could not remain in the Government without prejudice while it was excluded from the party programme; remaining loyal to Balfour and his general objects, he could best promote this course from outside, and he suggested that the Government might confine its policy to the "assertion of our freedom in the caste of all commercial relations with foreign countries." Balfour, while reluctantly admitting the necessity of Chamberlain's taking a freer hand, expressed his agreement in the desirability of a closer fiscal union with the colonies, but questioned the immediate practicability of any scheme; he was willing to adopt fiscal reform so far as it covered retaliatory duties, but thought that the exclusion of taxation of food from the party programme was in existing circumstances necessary, so long as public opinion was not ripe.

The tariff reform movement itself was now outside the purely official programme, and Chamberlain (backed by a majority of the Unionist members) threw himself with impetuous ardour into a crusade on its behalf, while at the same time supporting Balfour in parliament, and leaving it to him to decide as to the policy of going to the country when the time should be ripe. On Oct. 6 he opened his campaign with a speech at Glasgow. Analysing the trade statistics as between 1872 and 1902, he insisted that British progress involved a relative decline compared with that of protectionist foreign countries like Germany and the United States; Great Britain exported less and less of manufactured goods, and imported more and more; the exports to foreign countries had decreased, and it was only the increased exports to the colonies that maintained the British position. This was the outcome of the working of a one-sided free-trade system. Now was the time for consolidating British trade relations with the colonies. A further increase of £26,000,000 a year in the trade with the colonies might be obtained by a preferential tariff, and this meant additional employment at home for 166,000 workmen, or subsistence for a population of a far larger number. His positive proposals were: (1) no tax on raw materials; (2) a small tax on food other than colonial, *e.g.,* two shillings a quarter on foreign corn but excepting maize, and 5% on meat and dairy produce excluding bacon; (3) a 10% general tariff on imported manufactured goods. To meet any increased cost of living, he proposed to reduce the duties on tea, sugar and other articles of general consumption.

Colonial Preference.—"The colonies," he said, "are prepared to meet us; in return for a very moderate preference, they will give us a substantial advantage in their markets." This speech was the type of others which followed quickly during the year. At Greenock next day he emphasized the necessity of retaliating against foreign tariffs. The practice of "dumping" must be met; if foreign goods were brought into England to undersell British manufacturers, either the Fair Wages clause and the Factory Acts and the Compensation Act would have to be repealed, or the workmen would have to take lower wages, or lose their work, "Agriculture has been practically destroyed, sugar has gone, silk has gone, iron is threatened, wool is threatened, cotton will go! How long are you going to stand it?" In all his speeches he managed to point his argument by application to local industries. On Jan. 18, 1904, Chamberlain ended his series of speeches by a meeting at the Guildhall, in the city of London, the key-note being his exhortation to his audience to "think imperially."

Chamberlain needed a rest, and was away in Italy and Egypt from March to May, 1904, and again in November. He made three important speeches at Welbeck (Aug. 4), at Luton (Oct. 5), and at Limehouse (Dec. 15), but he had nothing substantial to add to his case. The Russo-Japanese War in Manchuria distracted popular attention from his campaign.

In Jan. 1905 some correspondence was published between Chamberlain and the duke of Devonshire, dating from the previous October, as to difficulties arising from the central Liberal-Unionist organization subsidizing local associations which had adopted the programme of tariff reform. The duke objected to this departure from neutrality, and suggested that it was becoming "impossible with any advantage to maintain under existing circumstances the existence of the Liberal-Unionist organization." Chamberlain retorted that this was a matter for a general meeting of delegates to decide; if the duke was out-voted he might resign his presidency; for his own part he was prepared to allow the local associations to be subsidized impartially, so long as they supported the Government, but he was not prepared for the violent disruption, which the duke apparently contemplated, of an association so necessary to the success of the Unionist cause. The duke was in a difficult position as president of the organization, since most of the local associations supported Chamberlain; and he replied that the differences between them were vital, and he would not be responsible for dividing the association into sections, but would rather resign. Chamberlain then called a general meeting on his own responsibility in February, when a new constitution was proposed; and in May, at the annual meeting of the Liberal-Unionist council, the free-food Unionists, being in a minority, retired, and the association was reorganized under Chamberlain's auspices, Lord Lansdowne and Lord Selborne (both of them cabinet ministers) becoming vice-presidents. On July 14 the reconstituted Liberal-Unionist organization held a great demonstration in the Albert hall, and Chamberlain's success in ousting the duke of Devonshire and the other free-trade members of the old Liberal-Unionist party, and imposing his own fiscal policy upon the Liberal-Unionist caucus, was now complete.

In reply to Balfour's appeal for the sinking of differences (Newcastle, Nov. 14), Chamberlain insisted at Bristol (Nov. 21) on the adoption of his fiscal policy; and Balfour resigned on Dec. 4 on the ground that he no longer retained the confidence of the party. At the crushing Unionist defeat in the general election which followed in Jan. 1906, Chamberlain was triumphantly returned for West Birmingham, and all the divisions of Birmingham returned Chamberlainite members. This, by contrast with the national disaster to the Unionist party as a whole, was one of the astonishing features of all British electoral history.

But he had no desire to set himself up as leader in Balfour's place, and after private negotiations with the ex-prime minister, a common platform was arranged between them, on which Balfour—for whom a seat was found in the City of London—should continue to lead the remnant of the party. The "Valentine's Day" formula was given in a letter from Balfour of Feb. 14 which admitted the necessity of making fiscal reform the first plank in the Unionist platform, and accepted a general tariff on manufactured goods and a small duty on foreign corn as "not in principle objectionable."

It may be left to future historians to attempt a considered judgment on the English tariff reform movement, and on Chamberlain's responsibility for the Unionist *débâcle* of 1906. But while his enemies taunted him with having twice wrecked his party—first the Radical party under Gladstone, and secondly the Unionist party under Balfour—no well-informed critic doubted his sincerity, or failed to recognize that in leaving the cabinet and embarking on his fiscal campaign he showed real devotion to an idea. In championing the cause of imperial fiscal union, by means involving the abandonment of a system of taxation which had become part of British orthodoxy, he followed the guidance of a profound conviction that the stability of the empire and the very existence of the hegemony of the United Kingdom depended upon the conversion of public opinion to a revision of the current economic doctrine. For the second time he had staked an already established position on his refusal to compromise with his convictions on a question which appeared to him of vital and immediate importance.

Mr. Chamberlain's own activity in the political field was cut short in the middle of the session of 1906. His 70th birthday was celebrated in Birmingham with immense enthusiasm shared in spirit by the bulk of the Unionist party in Great Britain and by idealists of imperialism throughout the British dominions. His fatigue before this apotheosis was extreme. Immediately afterwards he had a stroke of paralysis. He never spoke in public again. Though, for some time, his adherents hoped that he might return to the House of Commons, he was quite incapacitated for any public work. At the general election of Jan. 1910 Chamberlain was returned unopposed for West Birmingham again. His last sad appearance in the House was in the February following when, while few members were present, the formality of signing the roll was performed for him by his eldest son.

He died at his house, Highbury, Birmingham, on July 2, 1914. His last speech had been made on July 9, 1906. In that speech he uttered words which may fairly be given as his political testament: "The union of the Empire," he said, "must be preceded and accompanied by a better understanding, by a better sympathy. To secure that is the highest object of statesmanship now at the beginning of the 20th century; and if these were the last words that I were permitted to utter to you, I would rejoice to utter them in your presence, and with your approval. I know that the fruition of our hopes is certain. I hope I may live to congratulate you upon our common triumph; but in any case I have faith in the people. I trust in the good sense, the intelligence and the patriotism of the majority, the vast majority, of my countrymen."

Joseph Chamberlain had a singularly happy home life, and during his long illness had the devoted attention of Mrs. Chamberlain. Both his sons, Joseph Austen and Arthur Neville, rose to high position amongst statesmen, and are separately noticed.

See H. W. Lucy, *Speeches of Joseph Chamberlain, with a sketch of his life* (1885); *Speeches on Home Rule and the Irish Question 1881–87* (1887); *Foreign and Colonial Speeches* (1897); *Imperial Union and Tariff Reform, 15 May–Nov. 4, 1903* (2nd ed. 1910); C. W. Boyd, *Mr. Chamberlain's Speeches* (2 vols., 1914). The authorized *Life* of Chamberlain, by J. L. Garvin, is in preparation. The existing biographies were written during Chamberlain's lifetime by N. M. Marris (1900), S. H. Jeyes (1903), Louis Creswick (4 vols., 1904), Alexander Mackintosh (1906) and by Viscount Milner, J. Spender, Sir Henry Lucy and others (pub. 1912). Much information, including letters and reports of conversations, is to be found in biographies of his contemporaries, notably in those of Gladstone, the duke of Devonshire, Granville, Goschen and Harcourt, which will be found noted under those heads. For the South African period *see* the despatches published in the parliamentary papers series, Accounts and Papers (Colonies and British Possessions, South Africa), for the years in question, and *The "Times" History of the War in South Africa* (edit. L. C. S. Amery, vol. i. and vi. 1900–09); and for the suggested *rapprochement* with Germany at the turn of the century, E. Fischer, *Holstein's grosses Nein; Die deutschenglischen Bündnisverhandlungen von, 1898–1901* (1925); H. von Eckhardstein, *Lebens erinnerungen und politische Denkwürdigkeiten* (Leipzig, 1919, etc.); Erich Brandenburg, *Von Bismarck zum Weltkriege* (1924, trans. by A. E. Adams, 1927); *Die Grossepolitik der Europäischen Kabinette, 1871–1914;* and F. Meinecke, *Geschichte des Deutsch Englischen Bündnissproblems, 1890–1901* (1927).

CHAMBERLAIN, SIR NEVILLE BOWLES (1820–1902), British field-marshal, was born at Rio de Janeiro Jan. 10, 1820, the son of Henry Chamberlain, consul-general and chargé d'affaires in Brazil. He entered the East India Company's army in 1837 and served in the first Afghan war (1839–42), in the Gwalior campaign of 1843, and in the Punjab campaign of 1848–49. After that date, promotion was rapid, and he commanded several expeditions against the tribes on the northwest frontier. During the Indian mutiny he became adjutant general of the Indian army and, for his services at the siege of Delhi and elsewhere, was rewarded with a series of honours. He gained more honours after the Umbeyla campaign in 1863. Chamberlain was made lieutenant general in 1872 and appointed G.C.S.I. in 1873 and G.C.B. in 1875. From 1876 to 1881 he was commander in chief of the Madras army. In 1879 he was sent on a mission to Sher Ali, whose refusal to allow him to enter Afghanistan precipitated the outbreak of the second Afghan war. Chamberlain agreed with Lord Lytton that the British government should take steps to show its resentment at a "gross and unprovoked insult," but he did not approve of the policy of disintegration of Afghanistan adopted by Lytton after the second occupation of Kabul. He disapproved of the retention of Kandahar in 1880, recognizing the difficulty involved in maintaining additional outposts. He returned to England in 1881 and received the rank of field marshal in 1900. He died at Lordswood, near Southampton, Feb. 18, 1902.

See W. H. Page and A. H. Mason, *Record of the Expeditions against the North-West Frontier Tribes* (London, 1884); G. W. Forrest, *Life of Chamberlain* (1909).

CHAMBERLAIN, etymologically, and also to a large extent historically, an officer charged with the superintendence of domestic affairs. Such were the chamberlains of monasteries or cathedrals, who had charge of the finances, gave notice of chapter meetings, and provided the materials necessary for the services. In these cases, as in that of the apostolic chamberlain of the Roman see, the title was borrowed from the usage of the courts of the western secular princes. A royal chamberlain is now a court official whose function is in general to attend on the person of the sovereign and to regulate the etiquette of the palace. He is the representative of the mediaeval *camberlanus, cambellanus* or *cubicularius,* whose office was modelled on that of the *praefectus sacri cubiculi* or *cubicularius* of the Roman emperors. But at the outset there was another class of chamberlains, the *camerarii, i.e.,* high officials charged with the administration of the royal treasury (*camera*). The *camerarius* of the Carolingian emperors was the equivalent of the *hordere* or *thesaurarius* (treasurer) of the Anglo-Saxon kings; he develops into the *Erzkämmerer* (*archicamerarius*) of the Holy Roman Empire, an office held by the margraves of Brandenburg, and the *grand chambrier* of France, who held his *chamberie* as a fief. Similarly in England after the Norman conquest the *hordere* becomes the chamberlain. This office was of great importance. Before the Conquest the *hordere* had been, with the marshal, the principal officer of the king's court; and under the Norman sovereigns his functions were manifold. As he had charge of the administration of the royal household, his office was of financial importance, for a portion of the royal revenue was paid, not into the exchequer, but in *camera regis.* In time the office became hereditary and titular, but the complexity of the duties necessitated a division of the work, and the office was split up into three: the hereditary and sinecure office of *magister camerarius* or lord great chamberlain (*q.v.*) the more important domestic office of *camerarius regis,* king's chamberlain or lord chamberlain (*q.v.*) and the chamberlains (*camerarii*) of the exchequer, two in number, who were originally representatives of the chamberlain at the exchequer, and afterwards in conjunction with the treasurer presided over that department. In 1826 the last of these officials died, when by an act passed 44 years earlier they disappeared.

In France the office of *grand chambrier* was early overshadowed by the *chamberlains* (*cubicularii, cambellani,* but sometimes also *camerarii*), officials in close personal attendance on the king, men at first of low rank, but of great and ever-increasing influence. As the office of *grand chambrier,* held by great feudal nobles seldom at court, became more and more honorary, the chamberlains grew in power, in numbers, and in rank, until, in the 13th century, one of them emerges as a great officer of State, the *chambellan de France* or *grand chambellan* (also *magister cambellanorum, mestre chamberlenc*), who at times shares with the *grand chambrier* the revenues derived from certain trades in the city of Paris. The honorary office of *grand chambrier* survived till the time of Henry II., who was himself the last to hold it before his accession; that of *grand chambellan,* which in its turn soon became purely honorary, survived till the Revolution. Among the prerogatives of the *grand chambellan,* which survived to the last, was the right to hand the king his shirt at the ceremonial levee. The offices of *grand chambellan, premier chambellan,* and *chambellan* were revived by Napoleon, continued under the Restoration, abolished by Louis Philippe, and again restored by Napoleon III.

In the papal Curia the apostolic chamberlain (*camerarius*) is at the head of the treasury (*camera thesauraria*) and, in the days of the temporal power, not only administered the papal finances but possessed an extensive civil and criminal jurisdiction. During a vacancy of the Holy See he is at the head of the administration of the Roman Church. The office dates from the 11th century, when it superseded that of archdeacon of the Roman Church, and the close personal relations of the *camerarius* with the pope, together with the fact that he is the official guardian of the ceremonial vestments and treasures, point to the fact that he is also the representative of the former *vestararius* and *vice-dominus*, whose functions were merged in the new office.

In England the modern representatives of the *cubicularii* are the gentlemen and grooms of the bed-chamber; in Germany were the *Kammerherr* (*Kämmerer*, from *camerarius*, in Bavaria and Austria) and *Kammerjunker*. The insignia of their office is a gold key attached to their coats behind.

Many corporations appoint a chamberlain. The chamberlain of the corporation of the city of London, who is treasurer of the corporation, admits persons to the freedom of the city, and, in the chamberlain's court, of which he and the vice-chamberlain are judges, exercises concurrent jurisdiction with the police court in determining disputes between masters and apprentices. Formerly nominated by the crown, since 1688 he has been elected annually by the liverymen. He has a salary of £2,000 a year. Similarly in Germany the administration of the finances of a city is called the *Kämmerei* and the official in charge of it the *Kämmerer*.

See Lord Chamberlain; Lord Great Chamberlain; Household, Royal; Du Cange, *Glossarium*, s. "Camerarius" and "Cambellanus"; Père Anselme, *Hist. généalogique et chronologique de la maison royale de France, etc.* (3rd ed. 1726–33); A. Luchaire, *Manuel des institutions françaises* (1892); W. R. Anson, *Law and Custom of the Constitution* (1896); Hinschius, *Kirchenrecht*, i. 405 (1869).

CHAMBERLAYNE, WILLIAM (1619–1679), English poet, died on July 11, 1679. Nothing is known of his history except that he practised as a physician at Shaftesbury in Dorsetshire, and fought on the Royalist side at the second battle of Newbury. His works are: *Pharonnida* (1659), a verse romance in five books; *Love's Victory* (1658), a tragi-comedy, acted under another title in 1678 at the Theatre Royal; *England's Jubilee* (1660), a poem in honour of the Restoration. A prose version of *Pharonnida*, entitled *Eromena* or *The Noble Stranger*, appeared in 1683. Southey speaks of him as "a poet to whom I am indebted for many hours of delight." *Pharonnida* was reprinted by S. W. Singer in 1820, and again in 1905 by Prof. G. Saintsbury in *Minor Poets of the Caroline Period* (vol. i.). The poem is loose in construction, but contains some passages of great beauty.

CHAMBERLIN, THOMAS CHROWDER (1843–1928), American educator and geologist, was born at Mattoon, Ill., on Sept. 25, 1843. He graduated at Beloit college in 1866 (A.B.) and returned to the college in 1873 as professor of geology, serving also as assistant State geologist of Wisconsin until 1876, when he was made chief geologist of the Wisconsin Geological Survey (1876–82). From 1882 to 1887 he served as U.S. geologist in charge of the glacial division; from 1887 to 1892, as president of the University of Wisconsin; from 1892 to 1919, as head of the geological department of the University of Chicago, retiring as professor emeritus in 1919. He studied glaciers in Switzerland in 1878 and in Greenland in 1894, as geologist to the Peary relief expedition. His principal scientific work in later years has been the study of fundamental problems in geology particularly as related to the origin and growth of the earth, the developing of the planetesimal hypothesis of the planets, planetoids and satellites; and the chondrulitic hypothesis of the origin of chondrulites, comets and meteorites. He died in Chicago, Nov. 15, 1928.

His chief publications are *Geology of Wisconsin* (1879–82); *Reports of the Glacial division U.S. Geol. Survey* (1882–87); a three-volume treatise on geology (with R. D. Salisbury, 1906); reports on researches on certain fundamental problems in geology to the Carnegie Institution of Washington, *Year Books* 2 to 27; *The Tidal and Other Problems* (1909), "Diastrophism and the Formative Processes," numerous articles in the *Journal of Geology*, vol. xxi. (1913–21); *The Origin of the Earth* (1916); *The Two Solar Families, The Sun's Children* (1928).

CHAMBER MUSIC, a term obviously denoting music for performance in a room of a private house, has acquired the special meaning of large works in the sonata style for a group of individual instruments; although it may be borne in mind that in the early 18th century vocal cantatas for solo voices were at least as important as purely instrumental compositions.

One feature of immaturity is common to all the chamber music, vocal and instrumental, between and including Corelli and Bach; namely, that the harmonic background is left to the harpsichord player to extemporize from the indications given by a figured bass (*q.v.*). Even works with elaborate obligato harpsichord parts, have passages which presuppose this extempore element. Only the concerted music of the French clavecinists Couperin and Rameau consistently leaves nothing undetermined.

Works with Continuo.—The forms of chamber music are those of music at large, and it has no independent history. But it is very definite in the principles which determine its texture; and the element of the figured bass or continuo puts the earlier chamber music into an altogether different category from the art which arose with Haydn. As is shown in the articles Instrumentation, Music and Sonata Forms, the sonata-style of Haydn and Mozart irrevocably brought the dramatic element into music; but in addition to this, it brought alike into chamber music and orchestral music a fundamental principle that all players in an instrumental combination should between them provide their own harmonic background without the aid of a continuo part.

The disappearance of the continuo in later chamber music marks the realization of the central classical idea of the style, according to which there is no part in the ensemble left either indeterminate or in permanent subordination.

With its disappearance must also disappear the conception of the ensemble as a group of treble instruments over a firm bass, requiring a middle mass of harmony on an altogether remoter plane to hold them together. The middle part must be on the same plane as the others, and all must be as ready to provide the background as to carry on the main lines. There were no string quartets in the continuo period; and, what is more significant, the viola parts in the orchestra of Bach and Handel are, except when accompanying a choral fugue, neither interesting in themselves nor sufficient to fill up the gap between violins and bass. Their function is to reinforce the continuo without going a step out of their way to make the harmony always complete.

Haydn's first Quartets.—Rightly understood and performed, the result is perfectly mature; but it is worlds away from the crudest of Haydn's first quartets which, written before the death of Handel, show the criterion of self-sufficiency firmly established, so that there is no room for a continuo. The first string quartets are not clearly distinguished from orchestral music; wind parts have been discovered for Haydn's op. 1, No. 5 and op. 2, No. 3, and Haydn throughout his life remained capable of occasionally forgetting that his quartet-violoncello was not supported by a double-bass. But few processes in the history of music are more fascinating than the steady emergence of Haydn's quartet-style from the matrix of orchestral habit. In the quartets of op. 9 which he afterwards wished to regard as the beginning of his work, the four string parts are equally necessary and equally alive. They are not equally prominent; because the criterion is not polyphony but self-sufficiency for the purposes of this kind of music; and in this kind of music the normal place for melody is on the top.

In the very important six quartets, op. 20, Haydn discovers the character of the violoncello as something more than a bass to the violins—you can hear him discover it in the fourth bar of op. 20, No. 1; and with this discovery all possibility of the use of a double-bass vanishes, though miscalculations occur in the latest quartets. Had Haydn been a great violoncellist his first quartets might have been as luxurious as the quintets of Boccherini (*q.v.*), and he might have dallied longer in the bypaths of a style which tries to give each instrument in turn its display of solo-work. But Haydn's line of progress is steady and direct, and no document in the history of music is more important than his op. 20, with its three fugues (which secure autonomy and equality of parts by a return to the old polyphony), its passages of turn-about solo, its experiments in rich and special effects, and, most important of all, its achievements in quite normal quartet-writing such as pervades the remaining forty-odd quartets which end with his pathetic last fragment, op. 103.

Haydn's pianoforte trios also cover his whole career but they show, from first to last, no effort to achieve more than pianoforte sonatas with string accompaniment.

Mozart.—Mozart was an inveterate polyphonist by the time he was 12 years old, and the character of the viola, unnoticed by Haydn in his ripest quartets, is imaginatively realized in quartets written by Mozart at the age of 17. The point is not that the viola takes part in a more polyphonic style (though Mozart's early quartets are full of contrapuntal and canonic forms) but that the composer's imagination is attentive to the tone of the instrument in every note he writes for it.

Mozart's pianoforte trios, which are very insufficiently appreciated by historians and players, are perfect examples of independence of parts, no less than the two great pianoforte quartets (which should have been six but that the publisher cried off his bargain because of their difficulty) and the quintet for pianoforte and wind instruments. The set of six great string quartets (avowedly inspired by and affectionately dedicated to Haydn) contains some of the profoundest music outside Beethoven; and of the four remaining quartets, the last three, written for the King of Prussia, who was a good violoncellist, gave his majesty a grateful and prominent part and showed that Mozart's wit was able to maintain the full greatness of his style even when he was restricted to a lighter vein of sentiment.

His string quintets are as great as the quartets. Mozart prefers a second viola as the fifth member; and the only case where he suggested a second violoncello was by way of substitute for the horn in a little quintet for the curious combination of one violin, two violas, violoncello and horn. The combination of wind instruments with strings is a special problem the mention of which brings us back to reconsider the central idea of chamber music as now realized by Haydn and Mozart.

Vocal music has here dropped below the horizon. The human voice inevitably thrusts all instruments into the background; and we are now at the stage where the forces engaged in chamber music must be on planes sufficiently near to combine in one mental focus. A slight divergence of plane will give the mind pleasures analogous to those of stereoscopic vision. For example, the greatest masters of chamber music with pianoforte take pleasure in supporting heavy but incomplete pianoforte chords by the low notes of the violoncello: a procedure puzzling to self-centred pianoforte virtuosos, and never risked by composers who have not attained a pure style. Again, the clarinet, in the wonderful quintets by Mozart (A major) and Brahms (B minor) does not and is not intended to blend with the strings, but it nowhere gives a more intense pleasure than where it behaves as an inner part exactly like the others. These works belong to the highest regions of the art.

Wind and Other Combinations.—The flute blends with nothing; even among other wind instruments it is like water-colour among oils. It accordingly plays a part in witty little works, such as Beethoven's serenade for flute, violin and viola (twice imitated by Reger), and Mozart's two quartets with strings. The oboe, once not much less important in continuo chamber music than the flute (Handel confessed to "writing like a devil for it" when he was a boy) requires other wind instruments to relieve the ear of its plaintive tone, though Mozart wrote a pretty little quartet for it with strings, and Beethoven achieved a remarkable *tour-de-force* in an early trio for two oboes and cor anglais. But the further consideration of wind instruments brings us again to the borderland regions of chamber music. What are the smallest forces that can make a coherent combination for chamber music; and at what point do the forces become too large to cohere?

The pianoforte, even when treated in Mozart's hard-pencil line-drawing style, provides a central mass of complete harmony that can absorb shocks and combine (*pace* the virtuoso player) with anything. The question begins to be interesting when we deal with the strings alone. Duets for two violins are obviously a *tour-de-force,* since their bass can never go below a contralto G. This *tour-de-force* is executed on a large scale with a mastery and euphony beyond praise by Spohr. Mozart, coming to the rescue of Michael Haydn, who was prevented by illness from completing a set of six commissioned by the archbishop of Salzburg, wrote two for violin and viola, which profit greatly by the extra lower fifth and which are written with great zest and a reckless disregard (justified by personal knowledge) of the chance that the archbishop might detect their difference from the dutiful efforts of brother Michael.

Trios for two violins and any kind of bass but the viola, are ominously suggestive of a return to, or non-emergence from, the continuo method; and indeed it may be doubted whether any Italian composer before Cherubini (*q.v.*) ever did quite emerge therefrom. Trios for violin, viola and violoncello are a very different matter. They represent the problem of the string quartet intensified into a *tour-de-force.* Mozart's great example, the divertimento in E flat, is in all its six movements on a scale and a plane of thought that its title vainly belies. It inspired Beethoven to one of his biggest early works, the Trio op. 3; and the success of this encouraged Beethoven to write the three string Trios op. 9, of which the first, in G major, and the third, in C minor, are bolder in conception and execution than even the largest of the six string quartets, op. 18, and not less sonorous than any string quartet written before or since.

The string quartet represents the normal apparatus for a chamber music work of homogeneous tone. String quintets are usually produced in Mozart's way by doubling the viola. Doubling the violoncello, as in Schubert's great C major quintet, produces a very rich tone and sets the first violoncello free to soar into the cantabile region without (as in other quintets and in quartets) depriving the ensemble of a deep bass. Sextets, for two violins, two violas and two violoncellos, are represented in the two great works of Brahms. Octets for strings show signs of clotting into an orchestral style. Spohr hit upon the device of dividing the eight into antiphonal quartets; and his four double quartets are much nearer to the true style of chamber music than his string quartets, where his lower parts have the simplicity of early Haydn while the first violin plays a concerto above them. Mendelssohn in the wonderful octet which he wrote at the age of 16, does not find Spohr's simple antiphonal scheme worth the trouble of specially grouping the players when he can use 255 different combinations of the eight without enquiring how they are seated.

As for the semi-orchestral borderland of septets and octets in which several wind instruments join and a double-bass adds depth without any normal capacity to rise into cantabile or solo work, this borderland (inhabited by Beethoven's septet, Schubert's octet and many glorious serenades and divertimenti of Mozart) has a fascinating aesthetic of its own. Wind instruments by themselves are happiest in pairs, as their tones contrast too sharply otherwise to blend at all, though Reicha, who composed regularly for two hours before breakfast every morning, ground out over 100 quintets for flute, oboe, clarinet, horn and bassoon, all admirably euphonious, if they are up to the sample passages quoted by him in his treatise on composition. It is unreasonable to blame Mozart's glorious serenade for 13 wind instruments for sounding like a military band; we ought rather to wish that a military band could sound like a Mozart serenade.

Modern Tendencies.—Nothing remains to be said about chamber music, classical or modern, apart from the general tendencies of the art. The exclusive prevalence of sonata form in the classics is a result of the fact that when several persons assemble to play together they prefer to make the most of their opportunity. Smaller works are liable to be overlooked; how otherwise can we account for the fact that most musicians do not realize the existence of three quiet minutes of the most delicate writing in Beethoven's third manner, the quintet-fugue op. 137? A spirited capriccio and a pretty fugue by Mendelssohn have dropped out of sight for no other reason, while the andante and scherzo published with them and Schubert's allegro in C minor have roused interest as fragments of full-sized works.

In modern times the sonata form no longer obstructs the view of other possibilities. Mr. W. W. Cobbett's prize competitions stimulated English composers to the production of fantasies in terse continuous-movement forms. Less important are the numerous experiments in the use of the human voice without words in an otherwise instrumental scheme. Nature responds cattishly to the pitchfork. Saint-Saëns has a charming manner which puts the trumpet on its best behaviour in his amusing septet. The trombone and side-drums in the chamber music of Stravinsky will do well enough in a very smart house-party where all the conversation is carried on in an esoteric family slang and the guests are expected to enjoy booby-traps. Very different is the outlook of some of our younger masters such as Hindemith, Jarnach, and others whose renunciation of beauty is in itself a youthfully romantic gesture, and is accompanied by endless pains in securing adequate performance. The work of masterly performers can indeed alone save the new ideas from being swamped in a universal dullness which no external smartness can long distinguish from that commemorated in the Dunciad.

(D. F. T.)

CHAMBER ORCHESTRA, a small orchestra of some 20 or 30 players suited to the performance of works of the smaller and lighter order.

CHAMBERS, EPHRAIM (d. 1740), English encyclopaedist, was born at Kendal, Westmorland, and apprenticed to a globe-maker in London. The first edition of his *Universal Dictionary of Arts and Sciences* appeared by subscription in 1728, in two vols., fol., dedicated to the king. The *Encyclopédie* of Diderot and d'Alembert owed its inception to a French translation of Chambers's work. In addition to the *Cyclopaedia*, Chambers wrote for the *Literary Magazine* (1735–36), and translated the *History and Memoirs of the Royal Academy of Sciences at Paris* (1742), and the *Practice of Perspective* from the French of Jean Dubreuil. He died on May 15, 1740.

CHAMBERS, GEORGE (1803–1840), English marine painter, born at Whitby, Yorkshire, was the son of a seaman, and for several years he pursued his father's calling. He then took lessons from a drawing-master, and found a ready sale for small and cheap pictures of shipping. Coming to London, he was employed by Thomas Horner to assist in painting the great panorama of London for the Colosseum (the exhibition building in Regent's park, demolished *c.* 1860). His best works represent naval battles. Two of these—the "Bombardment of Algiers in 1816," and the "Capture of Porto Bello"—are in Greenwich hospital. He died on Oct. 28, 1840.

A *Life*, by John Watkins, was published in 1841.

CHAMBERS, ROBERT (1802–1871), Scottish author and publisher, was born at Peebles on July 10, 1802. A small circulating library in the town, and a copy of the *Encyclopædia Britannica* which his father had purchased, furnished the boy with stores of reading of which he eagerly availed himself. Long afterwards he wrote of his early years—"Books, not playthings, filled my hands in childhood. At 12 I was deep, not only in poetry and fiction, but in encyclopaedias." The family removed to Edinburgh in 1813, and in 1818 Robert began business at 16 as a bookstall-keeper in Leith Walk. In 1819 his elder brother William had begun a similar business, and the two eventually united as partners in the publishing firm of W. and R. Chambers. Robert Chambers was an enthusiast for the history and antiquities of Edinburgh, and his *Traditions of Edinburgh* (1824), secured for him the personal friendship of Sir Walter Scott. A *History of the Rebellions in Scotland from 1638 to 1745* (1828), and numerous other works followed.

At the beginning of 1832 William Chambers started a weekly publication under the title of *Chambers's Edinburgh Journal* (known since 1854 as *Chambers's Journal of Literature, Science and Arts*), which speedily attained a large circulation.

Among the numerous works of which Robert was in whole or in part the author, the *Biographical Dictionary of Eminent Scotsmen* (Glasgow, 1832–35), the *Cyclopaedia of English Literature* (1844), the *Life and Works of Robert Burns* (1851), *Ancient Sea Margins* (1848), the *Domestic Annals of Scotland* (1859–61) and the *Book of Days* (1862–64) were the most important. *Chambers's Encyclopaedia* (1859–68), with Dr. Andrew Findlater as editor, was carried out under the superintendence of the brothers (*see* ENCYCLOPAEDIA).

As a geologist, Robert Chambers published *Tracings of the North of Europe* (1851) and *Tracings in Iceland and the Faröe Islands* (1856). His knowledge of geology was one of the principal grounds on which the authorship of the *Vestiges of the Natural History of Creation* (1843–46) was eventually assigned to him. The *Book of Days*, a miscellany of popular antiquities, was his last publication. He died at St. Andrews on March 17, 1871.

His brother, WILLIAM CHAMBERS (1800–83), the financial genius of the publishing firm, was born at Peebles, on April 16, 1800. He laid the city of Edinburgh under the greatest obligations by his public spirit and munificence. As lord provost he procured the passing in 1867 of the Improvement Act, which led to the reconstruction of a great part of the Old Town, and at a later date he proposed and carried out, largely at his own expense, the restoration of the noble and then neglected church of St. Giles, making it in a sense "the Westminster Abbey of Scotland." This service was fitly acknowledged by the offer of a baronetcy, which he did not live to receive, dying on May 20, 1883, three days before the reopening of the church. He was the author of a history of St. Giles, of a memoir of himself and his brother (1872), and of many other useful publications. On his death in 1883 Robert Chambers (1832–88), son of Robert Chambers, succeeded as head of the firm, and edited the *Journal* until his death. His eldest son, Charles Edward Stuart Chambers (b. 1859), became editor of the *Journal* and chairman of W. & R. Chambers, Ltd.

See also *Memoir of Robert Chambers, with Autobiographic Reminiscences of William Chambers* (1872), the 13th ed. of which (1884) has a supplementary chapter; Alexander Ireland's preface to the 12th ed. (1884) of the *Vestiges of Creation;* the *Story of a Long and Busy Life* (1884), by William Chambers; and some discriminating appreciation in James Payn's *Some Literary Recollections* (1884), chapter v. The *Select Writings of Robert Chambers* were published in seven vols. in 1847, and a complete list of the works of the brothers is added to *A Catalogue of Some of the Rarer Books . . . in the Collection of C. E. S. Chambers* (Edinburgh, 1891).

CHAMBERS, SIR WILLIAM (1726–1796), British architect, was the grandson of a rich merchant who had financed the armies of Charles XII., but was paid in base money, and whose son remained in Sweden many years endeavouring to obtain redress. In 1728 the latter returned to England and settled at Ripon, where William, who was born in Stockholm, was educated. At the age of 16 he became supercargo to the Swedish East India Company, and, voyaging to Canton, made drawings of Chinese architecture, furniture and costume which served as basis for his *Designs for Chinese Buildings,* etc. (1757). Two years later he quitted the sea to study architecture seriously, and spent a long time in Italy, devoting special attention to the buildings of classical and Renaissance architects. He also studied under Clérisseau in Paris, with whom, and with the sculptor Wilton, he lived at Rome. In 1755 he returned to England where his first important commission was a villa for Lord Bessborough at Roehampton, but he made his reputation by the grounds he laid out and the buildings he designed at Kew, among them being the pagoda in the gardens, between 1757 and 1762 for Augusta, princess dowager of Wales. He published (1759) a *Treatise on Civil Architecture* and in 1772 a *Dissertation on Oriental Gardening,* which attempted to prove the inferiority of European to Chinese landscape gardening. As a furniture designer and internal decorator he is credited with the creation of that "Chinese Style" which was for a time furiously popular, although Thomas Chippendale (*q.v.*) had published designs in that manner at a somewhat earlier date. He became architect to the king and queen, comptroller of his majesty's works, and afterwards surveyor-general. In 1775 he was appointed architect of Somerset House, his greatest monument, at a salary of £2,000 a year. He also designed town mansions for Earl Gower at Whitehall and Lord Melbourne in Piccadilly, built Charlemont House, Dublin, and Duddingston House, near Edinburgh. He designed the market house at Worcester, was employed by the earl of Pembroke at Wilton, by the duke of Marlborough at Blenheim, and by the duke of Bedford in Bloomsbury. Although his practice was mainly classic, he made Gothic additions to Milton Abbey in Dorset. Sir William numbered among his friends Dr. Johnson, Goldsmith, Sir Joshua Reynolds, David Garrick and Dr. Burney.

CHAMBERS, in law, the rooms of counsel or of judges or judicial officers who deal with questions of practice and other matters not of sufficient importance to be dealt with in court. It is doubtful at what period the practice of exercising jurisdiction "in chambers" commenced in England; there is no statutory sanction before 1821, though the custom can be traced back to the 17th century. An Act of 1821 provided for sittings in chambers in vacation, and an Act of 1822 empowered the sovereign to call upon the judges by warrant to sit in chambers on as many days in vacation as should seem fit, while the Law Terms Act, 1830, defined the jurisdiction to be exercised at chambers. The Judges' Chambers Act, 1867, was the first Act, however, to lay down proper regulations for chamber work, and the Judicature Act, 1873, preserved that jurisdiction and gave power to increase it as might be directed or authorized by rules of court to be thereafter made. (*See* PRACTICE AND PROCEDURE.)

CHAMBERSBURG, a borough of Franklin county, Pennsylvania, U.S.A., on an elevated site in the broad and fertile Cumberland valley, 52 mi. S.W. of Harrisburg; it is on federal highways 11 and 30, and is served by the Pennsylvania and the Western Maryland railways. Pop. (1950) 17,205. It is the county seat and has large grain elevators, food processing plants and various other industries.

Wilson college, a Presbyterian institution for women, chartered in 1869, is there. Chambersburg was founded in 1730 by Benjamin Chambers. He built a stone fort after Gen. Edward Braddock's defeat (1755) and surrounded it with a stockade as a defense against the Indians. At Chambersburg Gen. Robert E. Lee massed his troops for his attack on Gettysburg. On July 30, 1864, a large part of the borough was burned by Confederates. The birthplace of Pres. James Buchanan is near by, and 10 mi. E. is Caledonia State Forest reserve.

CHAMBERS OF COMMERCE: *see* TRADE ORGANIZATION.

CHAMBER SYMPHONY, a musical composition written for a small orchestra exceeding in numbers the largest of the ordinary chamber music combinations (octet or nonet) but not approaching those of a full orchestra, and confined usually to a single instrument in each class. Such a work is Franz Schreker's Kammersymphonie for 23 solo instruments; another has been written by Schönberg.

CHAMBÉRY, a city of France, capital of the department of Savoie, pleasantly situated on the Leisse, in a fertile valley among the Alps, 79 mi. by rail S.S.W. of Geneva. Pop. (1946) 29,975. It was formerly capital of the duchy of Savoy, and remains, with its quiet narrow streets and its girdle of boulevards, a typical old provincial capital of France. The neighbouring country is dotted with summer resorts, and the town is a favourite centre for excursions. Chambéry grew up around a castle of the counts of Savoy, who resided there in the 13th, 14th and 15th centuries. A Roman station (Lemincum) in the vicinity has given its name to the rock of Lémenc, which overlooks the town on the north. Between 1536 and 1713 Chambéry was several times occupied by the French; in 1742 it was captured by a Franco-Spanish army; and in 1792 it was occupied by the Republican forces, and became the capital of the department of Mont Blanc. Restored to the house of Savoy by the treaties of Vienna and Paris, it was again surrendered to France in 1860.

The principal buildings are the cathedral, dating from the 14th and 15th centuries; the Hôtel-Dieu, founded in 1647, and the castle, a modern building serving as the prefecture, with only a great square tower belonging to the original structure; Chambéry is the seat of an archbishop (raised from a bishopric in 1817) and of a superior tribunal. It has long been famous as a regional culture-centre, and possesses an academy (1819) and several learned societies. Local benefactions have profited greatly from the fortune of General Boigne (1751–1830), amassed in India. Among the manufactures are silk-gauze, lace, leather and hats; there are also aluminium-works.

CHAMBORD, HENRI CHARLES FERDINAND MARIE DIEUDONNE, COMTE DE (1820–1883), the "King Henry V." of the French legitimists, was born in Paris on Sept. 29, 1820, son of the duc de Berry, the elder son of the comte d'Artois (afterwards Charles X.), and princess Caroline Ferdinande Louise of Naples. Born seven months after the assassination of his father, he was hailed as the "enfant du miracle," and was made the subject of one of Lamartine's most famous poems. He was created duc de Bordeaux, and in 1821, as the result of a subscription organized by the Government, received the château of Chambord. His education was inspired by detestation of the French Revolution and its principles. After the revolution of July, Charles X. vainly endeavoured to save the Bourbon cause by abdicating in his favour and proclaiming him king under the title of Henry V. (Aug. 2, 1830). The comte de Chambord accompanied his grandfather into exile, and resided successively at Holyrood, Prague and Görz. The death of his grandfather, Charles X., in 1836, and his uncle, the duc d'Angoulême, in 1844, left him the last male representative of the elder branch of the Bourbon family; and his marriage with the archduchess Maria Theresa, eldest daughter of the duke of Modena (Nov. 7, 1846), remained without issue. The title to the throne thus passed to the comte de Paris, as representative of the Orleans branch of the house of Bourbon, and the history of the comte de Chambord's life is largely an account of the efforts made to unite the Royalist party by effecting a reconciliation between the two princes.

Though he continued to hold an informal court, both on his travels and at his castle of Frohsdorf, near Vienna, yet he allowed the revolution of 1848 and the *coup d'état* of 1851 to pass without any decisive assertion of his claims. It was the Italian war of 1859, with its menace to the pope's independence, that roused him at last to activity, thus making common cause with the Church. The Royalists now began an active campaign against the Empire. On Dec. 9, 1866, Chambord addressed a manifesto to Gen. Saint-Priest, in which he declared the cause of the pope to be that of society and liberty, and held out promises of retrenchment, civil and religious liberty "and above all honesty." Again, on Sept. 4, 1870, after the fall of the Empire, he invited Frenchmen to accept a Government "whose basis was right and whose principle was honesty," and promised to drive the enemy from French soil. Fortune favoured him. The elections placed the Republican party in a minority in the National Assembly; the abrogation of the law of exile against the royal family permitted him to return to his castle of Chambord; and it was thence that on July 5, 1871, he issued a proclamation, in which for the first time he publicly posed as king, and declared that he would never abandon the white standard of the Bourbons, "the flag of Henry IV., Francis I., and Joan of Arc," for the tricolour of the Revolution. He again quitted France, and answered the attempts to make him renounce his claims in favour of the comte de Paris by the declaration (Jan. 25, 1872) that he would never abdicate. A constitutional programme, signed by some 280 members of the National Assembly was presented for his acceptance, but without result. The fall of Thiers in May 1873, however, offered an opportunity to the Royalists by which they hastened to profit. The comte de Paris and the prince de Joinville journeyed to Frohsdorf, and were formally reconciled with the head of the family (Aug. 5). The Royalists were united, the premier (the duc de Broglie) an open adherent, the president (MacMahon) a benevolent neutral. MM. Lucien Brun and Chesnelong were sent to interview the comte de Chambord at Salzburg, and obtain the definite assurances that alone were wanting. They returned with the news that he accepted the principles of the French Revolution and the tricolour flag. But a letter to Chesnelong, dated Salzburg, Oct. 27, declared that he had been misunderstood: he would give no guarantees; he would not inaugurate his reign by an act of weakness, nor become "le roi légitime de la Révolution." "Je suis le pilote nécessaire," he added, "le seul capable de conduire le navire au port, parce que j'ai mission et autorité pour cela." A last effort was made in the national assembly in June 1874 by the duc de la Rochefoucauld-Bisaccia, who formally moved the restoration of the monarchy. The comte de Chambord on July 2 issued a fresh manifesto, which added nothing to his former declarations. The motion was rejected by 272 to 79, and on Feb. 25, 1875, the assembly definitely adopted the republic as the national form of government. The count died at Frohsdorf on Aug. 24, 1883.

See *Manifestes et programmes politiques de M. le comte de Chambord, 1848–73* (1873), and *Correspondance de la famille royale et principalement de Mgr. le comte de Chambord avec le comte de Bouillé* (1884). Of the literature relating to him, mention may be made of *Henri V. et la monarchie traditionnelle* (1871); *Le Comte de Chambord étudié dans ses voyages et sa correspondance* (1880); H. de Pène, *Henri de France* (1885).

CHAMBORD, a village of central France, in the department of Loir-et-Cher, on the left bank of the Cosson, 10 mi. E. by N. of Blois. Pop. (1936) 165. The village stands in the park of Chambord, which is enclosed by a wall 22 mi. in circumference. The celebrated château (*see* ARCHITECTURE) forms a parallelogram flanked at the angles by round towers and enclosing a square block of buildings, the façade of which forms the centre of the main front. There is a chapel of the 16th century and a famous double staircase. The château was originally a hunting-lodge of the counts of Blois, the rebuilding of which was begun by Francis I in 1526, and completed under Henry II. It was the residence of several succeeding monarchs, and under Louis XIV considerable alterations were made. In the same reign Molière's *Monsieur de Pourceaugnac* and *Le Bourgeois gentilhomme* were performed here for the first time. Stanislas of Poland lived at Chambord, which was bestowed by his son-in-law, Louis XV, upon Marshal Saxe. It was given by Napoleon to Marshal Berthier, from whose widow it was purchased by subscription in 1821, and presented to the duc de Bordeaux, who assumed the title of comte de Chambord. On his death it came by bequest to the family of Parma. The estate was sequestrated in 1914.

CHAMBRE ARDENTE, the term for an extraordinary court of justice in France, mainly held for the trials of heretics (Fr. "burning chamber"). These courts were originated by the Cardinal of Lorraine, the first of them meeting in 1535 under Francis I. The *Chambre Ardente* co-operated with an inquisitorial tribunal also established by Francis I, the duty of which was to discover cases of heresy and hand them over for final judgment to the *Chambre Ardente*. The court was abolished in 1682.

See N. Weiss, *La Chambre Ardente* (Paris, 1889).

CHAMELEON, the common name of members of one of the most remarkable of the families of lizards, Chameleontidae. Because of the similar ability to change colour, the same name is misapplied to American lizards of the genus *Anolis* (Iguanidae). The great majority of chameleons are referable to the genus *Chamaeleo* (containing about 70 species), the remaining genera, *Rhampholeon, Leandria* and *Brookesia,* containing only a few dwarfed forms. The group is found in Africa and Madagascar, Arabia, southern India and Ceylon. The grasping feet are formed by the fusion of the digits into two opposable bundles, the two outer digits being opposed to the three inner on the forelimb and vice versa on the hindlimb, and, like the prehensile tail, are correlated with climbing habits. The eyes are large and independently movable, but the eyelids are fused into one circular fold which leaves only the pupil visible; the eyes can also, unlike those of other reptiles, be focussed upon one spot, giving the binocular vision necessary for the nice appreciation of distances required in the use of the tongue. This organ is very large, club-shaped and provided with a sticky secretion at its tip; the basal portion is narrow and composed of very elastic fibres, which, when the tongue is not in use, are telescoped over the elongated copular piece of the hyoid, which acts as a support. By means of its muscular mechanism the tongue can be shot out to a remarkable distance, somewhat exceeding the length of the body; the elasticity of the basal fibres assists in its rapid withdrawal. It is by means of this extraordinary mechanism that the chameleon secures its prey; flies and other insects are deliberately stalked until within range, then out shoots the tongue and the victim is withdrawn adhering to its sticky tip.

The ability of chameleons to change colour is proverbial, but their powers are usually exaggerated and are quite equalled by those of some other lizards. Change of colour is partly reflex in response to emotional stimuli and partly controlled through the eye; changes in the intensity of light, change of temperature and emotion produce marked and characteristic changes, but there is little direct response to the colour of the environment. The normal colour of the common chameleon may be gray-green with innumerable small dark specks and with rows of pale-brown patches on the sides of the body; in the dark at normal temperatures the colour fades to a cream-colour with irregular yellow spots, but exposure to hot sunlight causes the whole animal to darken until it may be uniformly dull black. High temperatures without direct sunlight usually produce greens and low temperatures dull grays; excitement and fright bring paler shades with brown patches and yellow spots, while anger causes the lighter areas to darken.

THE TRUE CHAMELEONS. ABOVE: THE COMMON CHAMELEON OF THE MEDITERRANEAN REGION. BELOW: THREE DIVERSE TYPES OF AFRICAN CHAMELEONS

Propagation is in most cases by means of eggs; these are small, oval, white in colour and provided with a tough parchmentlike shell. They are buried by the mother and left to be incubated by the heat of the sun. A few species, *e.g.,* the dwarf chameleon of South Africa (*C. pumilus*), retain the eggs within the body until they hatch, so that the young are born alive.

An extraordinary feature of the group is a tendency toward the production of excrescences on the head. Many species have the occiput produced backwards into a pointed casque and this may assume extraordinary dimensions; but the most remarkable developments are the horns of some of the tropical African and Malagasy species. In different forms there may be one, two, three or four horns or a single, flexible, dermal flap on the tip of the snout; in some species these appendages occur only on the male but in others they are present on both sexes.

(D. M. S. W.; X.)

CHAMFER, CHAMPFER or **CHAUMFER,** an architectural term for the cutting off of the edges of the corners of a beam, post or other similar form, and also the slanting surface so produced. Chamfers are frequently hollowed or moulded. When the chamfer does not run the full length of the member that it decorates, the shoulder, diagonal cut or moulding against which it stops is known as a stop chamfer.

CHAMFORT, SEBASTIEN ROCH NICOLAS (1741–1794), French wit and man of letters, was born at a little village near Clermont in Auvergne, the son of a grocer named Nicolas. Educated as a free scholar at the Collège des Grassins, he lived from hand to mouth in Paris mainly on the hospitality of people who were only too glad to give him board and lodging in exchange for the pleasure of the conversation for which he was famous. Thus Mme. Helvétius entertained him at Sèvres for some years. He had a great success with his comedies *La Jeune Indienne* (1764) and *Le Marchand de Smyrne* (1770). In 1775, while taking the waters at Barèges, he met the duchesse de Grammont, sister of Choiseul, through whose influence he was introduced at court. In 1776 his poor tragedy *Mustapha et Zeangir* was played at Fontainebleau before Louis XVI and Marie Antoinette; the king gave him a further pension of 1,200 livres, and the prince de Condé made him his secretary. But he was a Bohemian naturally and by habit, and the restraints of the court irked him. In 1781 he was elected to the Academy; in 1784, through the influence of Calonne, he became secretary to the king's sister, Mme. Elizabeth, and in 1786 he received a pension of 2,000 livres from the royal treasury. He was thus once more attached to the court, and made himself friends in spite of the reach and tendency of his unalterable irony; but he quitted it for ever after an unfortunate and mysterious love affair, and was received into the house of M. de Vaudreuil. Here in 1783 he had met Mirabeau, with whom he remained to the last on terms of intimate friendship.

The outbreak of the Revolution made a profound change in Chamfort's life. Theoretically he had long been a republican, and he now devoted all his small fortune to the revolutionary propaganda. Until Aug. 31, 1791, he was secretary of the Jacobin club; he entered the Bastille among the first of the storming party. He worked for the *Mercure de France,* collaborated with Ginguené in the *Feuille villageoise,* and drew up for Talleyrand his *Adresse au peuple français.*

With the reign of Marat and Robespierre, however, his uncompromising Jacobinism grew critical, and with the fall of the Girondins his political life came to an end. But he could not restrain the tongue that had made him famous; he no more spared the Convention than he had spared the court. He was imprisoned for a short time, and released; but he had determined to prefer death to a repetition of confinement, and when he was again threatened with arrest he attempted suicide with pistol and with poniard, dictating to those who came to arrest him the well-known declaration: *"Moi, Sebastien-Roch-Nicolas Chamfort, déclare avoir voulu mourir en homme libre plutôt que d'être reconduit en esclave dans une maison d'arrêt,"* which he signed in a firm hand and in his own blood. He lingered on until April 13, 1794 in charge of a gendarme. To the Abbé Sieyès Chamfort had given fortune in the title of a pamphlet (*"Qu'est-ce que le Tiers-État? Tout. Qu'a-t-il? Rien"*), and to Sieyès did Chamfort retail his supreme sarcasm, the famous *"Je m'en vais enfin de ce monde où il faut que le coeur se brise ou se bronze."* The maker of constitutions followed the dead wit to the grave.

The writings of Chamfort, which include comedies, political articles, literary criticisms, portraits, letters and verses, are colourless and uninteresting. His genius was in conversation. His *Maximes et Pensées* are, after those of La Rochefoucauld, the most brilliant and suggestive sayings of the 18th century. The aphorisms of Chamfort, less systematic and psychologically less important than those of La Rochefoucauld, are as significant in their violence and iconoclastic spirit of the period of storm and preparation that gave them birth as the *Réflexions* in their exquisite restraint and elaborate subtlety are characteristic of the tranquil elegance of their epoch; and they have the advantage in richness of colour, in picturesqueness of phrase, in passion, in audacity. Sainte-Beuve compares them to "well-minted coins that retain their value," and to keen arrows that *arrivent brusquement et sifflent encore.*

The *Oeuvres complètes de Nicolas Chamfort* appeared at Paris, 5 vols. (1824–25), selections one vol. (1852), with a biographical and critical preface by Arsène Houssaye and *Oeuvres choisies,* with a preface and notes by M. de Lescure (1879). *See* also Sainte-Beuve, *Causeries du Lundi;* M. Pellisson, *Chamfort, étude sur sa vie* (1895).

CHAMFRON or **CHANFRIN.** A horse's forehead, more particularly the piece of armour which covered the front of a barded horse.

CHAMIER, FREDERICK (1796–1870), English novelist, was the son of an Anglo-Indian official, and served in the navy from 1809 to 1856. Captain Chamier wrote several popular sea-stories, including *The Life of a Sailor* (1832), *Ben Brace* (1836), *The Arethusa* (1837), *Jack Adams* (1838), *Tom Bowling* (1841), and *Jack Malcolm's Log* (1846). He also edited and brought down to 1827 James's *Naval History* (1837).

CHAMILLART, MICHEL (1652–1721), French statesman, minister of Louis XIV. In 1690 he was made intendant of finances, and on Sept. 5, 1699, the king appointed him controller-general of finances, and on Jan. 7, 1700, minister of war. From the first Chamillart's position was a difficult one. The deficit amounted to more than 53 million livres, and the credit of the state was almost exhausted. In Oct. 1706 he showed the king that the debts immediately due amounted to 288 millions, and that the deficit already foreseen for 1707 was 160 millions. In Oct. 1707 he saw with consternation that the revenue for 1708 was already entirely eaten up by anticipation, so that neither money nor credit remained for 1708. In these conditions Chamillart resigned his office of controller-general. Public opinion attributed to him the ruin of the country, though he had tried in 1700 to improve the condition of commerce by the creation of a council of commerce. As secretary of state for war he had to place in the field the army for the War of the Spanish Succession, and to reorganize it three times, after the great defeats of 1704, 1706 and 1708. With an empty treasury he succeeded only in part, and he frankly warned the king that the enemy would soon be able to dictate the terms of peace. He resigned office in 1709, and died on April 14, 1721.

See G. Esnault, *Michel Chamillart, contrôleur général et secrétaire d'état de la guerre, correspondance et papiers inédits* (1885); A. de Boislisle *Correspondance des contrôleurs généraux* (vol. ii., 1883); M. Langlois, *Louis XIV. et la cour. D'après trois témoins nouveaux: Bélise Beauvillier, Chamillart.* (1926).

CHAMINADE, CÉCILE (1861–1944), French composer, was born in Paris on Aug. 8, 1861. She studied in Paris, her musical talent being shown at the age of eight by the writing of some church music which attracted Bizet's attention; and at eighteen she came out in public as a pianist. Her own compositions, both songs (in large numbers) and instrumental pieces, are melodious and effective and have enjoyed great popularity.

CHAMISE (*Adenostoma fasciculatum*). A North American shrub of the rose family (Rosaceae), called also chamiso, found in the chaparral belt on foothills and mountain slopes in California, ranging up to 5,000 ft. altitude. It grows from 2 ft. to 10 ft. high, with shreddy brown bark; slender twiggy branches; resinous, narrow leaves in bundles or fascicles, and small white flowers in panicled clusters. Chamise is the most abundant and characteristic small shrub of the higher foothills west of the Sierra Nevada, where, between the lower foothills and the yellow pine belt, it often forms a distinct zone called chamisal. (*See* CHAPARRAL.)

CHAMISSO, ADELBERT VON (LOUIS CHARLES ADELAIDE DE) (1781–1838), German poet and botanist, was born at the château of Boncourt in Champagne, the ancestral seat of his family. Driven from France by the revolution, his parents settled in Berlin, where in 1796 young Chamisso obtained the post of page-in-waiting to the queen, and in 1798 entered a Prussian infantry regiment as ensign. In close collaboration with Varnhagen von Ense, he founded in 1803 the *Berliner Musenalmanach,* in which his first verses appeared. Although the enterprise was a failure, it brought him to the notice of literary celebrities. He left the army in 1808, and in 1810 joined the charmed circle of Mme. de Staël, following her in her exile to Coppet in Switzerland. In 1813 he wrote the prose narrative *Peter Schlemihl,* the man who sold his shadow. The most famous of all his works, it has been translated into most European languages (English by W. Howitt). In 1815 Chamisso was appointed botanist to the Russian ship "Rurik," which Otto von Kotzebue commanded on a scientific voyage round the world. He published his diary (*Tagebuch*) of this expedition in 1821. In 1818 he became custodian of the botanical gardens in Berlin. From 1829 he brought out the *Deutsche Musenalmanach,* in which his later poems were mainly published. He died on Aug. 21, 1838.

As a scientist Chamisso wrote *Bemerkungen und Ansichten,* and *Übersicht der nutzbarsten und schädlichsten Gewächse in Norddeutschland* (1829). His *Frauenliebe und -leben* (1830), a cycle of lyrical poems, which was set to music by Schumann, were particularly famous. Noteworthy are also *Schloss Boncourt* and *Salas y Gomez.* In the lyrical expression of the domestic emotions he displays a fine felicity, and he knew how to treat with true feeling a tale of love or vengeance. *Die Löwenbraut* may be taken as a sample of his weird and powerful simplicity; and *Vergeltung* is remarkable for a pitiless precision of treatment.

The first collected edition of Chamisso's works was edited by J. E. Hitzig (6 vols., 1836; 6th ed., 1874); there are also excellent editions by M. Koch (1883) and O. F. Walzel (1892). On Chamisso's life *see* J. E. Hitzig, "Leben und Briefe von Adelbert von Chamisso" (in the *Gesammelte Werke*); K. Fulda, *Chamisso und seine Zeit* (1881); G. Hofmeister, *Adelbert von Chamisso* (1884); and E. du Bois-Reymond, *Adelbert von Chamisso als Naturforscher* (1889).

CHAMKANNI, a small tribe of Ghoria Khel Pathans in Kurram, Afghanistan.

CHAMOIS, the Franco-Swiss name of a hollow-horned ruminant known in German as *Gemse* or *Gemsbok;* scientifically, *Rupicapra rupicapra.* It is the only species in the genus, though every European range possesses a local race. It is the type of the tribe *Rupicaprini,* which includes several goatlike genera (*see* BOVIDAE). About the size of a roebuck, with a short tail, it is distinguished by the vertical, backwardly directed horns in both sexes, though these are larger in the male. Though differing in the shade of their hair, all the various races have black and white face markings and a black tail and dorsal stripe. The alpine race is chestnut brown in summer, lighter and grayer in winter. A thick underfur is developed in the cold weather.

BY COURTESY OF E. L. SANBORN AND THE NEW YORK ZOOLOGICAL SOCIETY

CHAMOIS, A GOAT ANTELOPE

Chamois live in small herds, but the old males join these only during the rutting season (October), when they engage in fierce contests with each other. The period of gestation is 20 weeks, and the usual number of offspring is one. In summer the animals ascend to the snow line, being exceeded in the loftiness of their haunts only by the ibex. In winter they descend to wooded regions. Chamois hunting is a favourite sport of the Swiss and Tirolese and of amateurs from all countries. As a result of this, the chamois has become rare in many of its old haunts, but it is now preserved in the Swiss National park in the Engadine. Exceedingly wary and astonishingly agile, the animal is very difficult of approach. It feeds in summer on mountain herbs and flowers, in winter on the young shoots of the pine.

The skin is very soft and is made into the original "shammy" leather, though this is also made from the skins of other animals. The flesh is prized as venison. During the 20th century the chamois was successfully introduced from Austria into New Zealand.

CHAMOMILE or CAMOMILE FLOWERS, the flower heads of *Anthemis nobilis* (family Compositae), a herb indigenous to western Europe. It is cultivated for medicinal purposes in Surrey, at several places in Saxony and in France and Belgium, that grown in England being much more valuable than any of the other chamomiles. In the wild plant the florets of the ray are ligulate and white and contain pistils only, those of the disk being tubular and yellow; but under cultivation the whole of the florets tend to become ligulate and white, in which state the flower heads are said to be double.

The flower heads have a warm aromatic odour, which is characteristic of the entire plant, and a very bitter taste. In addition to a bitter extractive principle, they yield a volatile liquid, which on its first extraction is of a pale blue colour, but becomes a yellowish brown on exposure to light. It has the characteristic odour of the flowers and consists of a mixture of butyl and amyl angelates and valerates. Chamomile is used in medicine in the form of its volatile oil.

Wild chamomile is *Matricaria chamomilla,* a weed common in waste and cultivated ground especially in the southern counties of England. It has somewhat the appearance of true chamomile, but a fainter scent.

CHAMONIX-MONT-BLANC, a well-known alpine tourist resort, in the department of Haute-Savoie, southeast France. Pop. (1946) 3,642.

The valley of Chamonix runs from northeast to southwest and is watered by the Arve, which rises in the Mer de Glace. On the southeast towers the snowclad chain of Mont Blanc, and on the northwest the rugged chain of the Brévent and of the Aiguilles Rouges.

Chamonix (3,416 ft.) is the best starting point for the exploration of the glaciers of the Mont Blanc chain, as well as for the ascent of Mont Blanc itself. It is connected with Geneva by a railway (55 mi.).

The valley is first heard of about 1091, when it was granted by the count of the Genevois to the great Benedictine house of St. Michel de la Cluse, near Turin, which, by the early 13th century, had established a priory there. In 1786 the inhabitants bought their freedom from the canons of Sallanches, to whom the priory had been transferred in 1519. In 1530 the count of the Genevois granted the privilege of holding two fairs a year. The tourist industry dates from the 18th century, but its development is modern.

The first party to publish (1744) an account of its visit was that of R. Pococke, W. Windham and other Englishmen who visited the Mer de Glace in 1741.

CHAMPAGNE, an ancient province of France, bounded north by Liège and Luxembourg; east by Lorraine; south by Burgundy; and west by Picardy and Ile de France. It forms the modern departments of Ardennes, Marne, Aube and Haute Marne, with part of Aisne, Seine-et-Marne, Yonne and Meuse. Its name is derived from the immense plains near Reims, Châlons and Troyes. The province was constituted by joining to the countship of Champagne the ecclesiastical duchies of Reims and Langres and the ecclesiastical countship of Châlons. From 1152 to 1234 the countship of Champagne reckoned among its dependencies the countship of Blois and Chartres, of which Touraine was a fief, and the countship of Sancerre and various scattered fiefs in the Bourbonnais and in Burgundy. The countships of Troyes and Meaux were also absorbed into this amalgamation of territories which became known as the "countship of Champagne and Brie." (*See* TROYES.) (A. Lo.)

The counts of Champagne were descendants of Odo I (Odo II of Blois; *see* BLOIS, COUNTSHIP OF), who acquired the title in 1019 or 1020. The most famous of these counts were Theobald or Thibaut II (1125–52), already count of Blois (as Theobald IV) and Meaux, one of the most powerful barons of his time; Henry I the Liberal (1152–81; son-in-law of Louis VII of France), who went on the crusade in 1178 and was taken prisoner by the Turks; Henry II (1181–97), who, reaching the Holy Land in 1190, married Isabella, widow of Conrad, marquis of Montferrat, and became king of Jerusalem; and, most famous of all, Theobald IV (*see* THIBAUT [1201–53], son of Theobald III [1197–1201] and Blanche of Navarre). Theobald IV took part in the expedition of Louis VIII of France against the Albigenses (1226), came into prominence in the first years of St. Louis's reign, succeeded to the throne of Navarre as Theobald I on the death of his maternal uncle Sancho VII (1234) and went on an expedition to the Holy Land in 1239–40. He acquired moreover a reputation as a *poète courtois.* Theobald V (II of Navarre; 1254–70) married Isabella, daughter of St. Louis, and died on his return from the eighth crusade after its failure in Tunis. Henry III (I of Navarre), his brother and successor, died in 1274, leaving an only daughter, Joan of Navarre, who married the heir presumptive to the throne of France, Philip the Fair, in 1284 and became queen of France, dying in 1305. At that time the countship passed to her son, Louis le Hutin, who joined it to the crown on his accession as Louis X in 1314.

The great celebrity of Champagne, in the middle ages, lay in its fairs, particularly in the 12th and 13th centuries. At the crossing of the roads from Flanders, Germany, Italy and Provence, Champagne was indeed a convenient meeting place for foreigners. Drapers from the north, wool merchants from England, importers of alum, dyes and spices from the Mediterranean ports, dealers in linen and in furs from Germany and leather sellers from Spain and Africa could easily meet there and bargain together. The great fairs lasted 49 days each and were six in number: one at Lagny, one at Bar-sur-Aube, two at Provins and two at Troyes. Each fair opened with a week devoted to the receiving of merchandise; four weeks then were spent in selling and the last fortnight in the settling of accounts. For this purpose, clearances and transfers of funds came more and more to be used between customers; and thus the fairs became regular banking centres and clearinghouses, where people not connected with business might also do their transactions (*see* BANKING).

These fairs had a special legislation; and special magistrates called "masters of the fairs" had control of the police there. Thanks to the fairs, Champagne, rather a poor region at first because of the nature of its soil, became rich; and this accounts both for the opulence of its towns (particularly under Henry the Liberal and Theobald IV) and for the emancipation of the cities as well as for more violent movements (*communes*) that took place early.

From the beginning of the 14th century, the superiority of Italian shipping and commercial methods brought about the cities' decline.

In the 16th century Champagne played a prominent part, from a military viewpoint, as a frontier province against the territories of the Spanish Habsburgs and was seriously shaken by the wars of religion.

BIBLIOGRAPHY.—R. Crozet, *Histoire de Champagne* (Paris, 1933); Elizabeth Chapin, *Les Villes de foires de Champagne des origines au début du XIVe siècle* (Paris, 1937); R. Gandilhon, *Histoire de Champagne, bibliographie champenoise, publications des années 1920 à 1945* (Dijon, 1947). (M. PAC.)

CHAMPAGNE, BATTLES IN. This was the name commonly if vaguely given to a number of long drawn-out offensives on the western front in World War I. Among the principal ones the first was the French attack east of Reims on Sept. 25, 1915, an outline of which will be found in the article on WORLD WAR I.

The simultaneous British offensive at Loos (*q.v.*), north of Lens, was intended to be subsidiary to this, as was also a lesser French offensive south of Lens. Still more important in scale and design was the French offensive west of Reims in April 1917, frequently called the Nivelle offensive. The failure of this ambitious plan for a swift and decisive break-through culminated in mutinies which seriously endangered the fighting efficiency of the French army; only after some months was its morale restored by the sympathetic and prudent leadership of Gen. Pétain.

The Autumn Offensive, 1915.—During the summer of 1915 local attacks had been carried out in the Vosges and Argonne, while preparations were being made for operations on a large scale in Champagne and for a powerful diversion in Artois. The objective in Champagne was the rupture of the German front from Bazancourt to Challerange, so as to outflank their positions to the north of Reims and in the Argonne. It was hoped thus to roll up the eastern part of the German front. Under the direction of Gen. de Castelnau the attack was made by the II. Army (Pétain) with the right of the IV. Army (de Langle de Cary) and the left of the III. Army (Humbert), a total of 35 divisions, or at least 420 battalions, against the German III. Army (Einem), which had at first only 70 battalions, later reinforced to 192. However, the secret of the future offensive was so badly kept that as early as Aug. 15 a German order had foreseen it. The artillery preparation began on Sept. 22, and at 9:15 A.M. on Sept. 25 the assault was launched and penetrated along almost the whole front to a depth of from 2,000 to 4,000yd. reaching even the second position in one sector. But the German command, foreshadowing the method of elastic defence which became famous in 1918, had withdrawn the guns and allowed the lightly held first position to act as a shock-absorber. Progress then became slow and costly.

On Sept. 28 and 29 a part of the second position was carried to the west of Le Mesnil and Navarin farm and a break through was made in a narrow section, but the Germans quickly closed the gap. The French cavalry corps had to retire on the 28th to the rear lines without having been engaged. On the 30th a general order announced the end of the operations with the capture of 25,000 prisoners and 150 guns. Nevertheless, abortive attacks continued until Oct. 8. The Champagne offensive cost the French 80,000 killed and missing and 100,000 sick and wounded. The results were not in due proportion to this sacrifice, mainly because the attacks had lacked the characteristics of surprise, rapidity and continuity, and had been continued too long.

French Offensive on the Aisne, 1917.—The strategical and political controversies which preceded the opening of the allies' offensive campaign of 1917 are dealt with in the article on WORLD WAR I. On the Aisne, the French offensive was to extend from Vailly to Reims. Gen. Pétain, consulted by Nivelle on the proposed action, criticized it freely and refused the leadership, which was entrusted to Gen. Michelet. The V. Army (Masel), which had held this front since 1914, closed on its right to make room for the VI. Army (Mangin), while the X. Army (Duchêne) was in reserve. Nivelle had decided on a rapid attack which aimed at carrying the positions and all the artillery zone at the first assault. This resembled the method twice employed at Verdun. No one raised any serious objection, but Nivelle foretold an immediate exploitation of the success by the X. Army, which should carry it as far to the north as possible. Michelet estimated that the whole operation might be accomplished the first day, or at latest on the morning of the second. He indicated as objectives the foot of the heights to the north of the Ailette, the plain of Laon, and the east of Brimont fort. The only objection was raised by Mangin, who called attention particularly to the importance of good atmospheric conditions. This did not modify Nivelle's wishes, and Michelet exaggerated them by giving such detailed orders that no initiative was left to the army commanders.

The preparation for the offensive was in full swing when the German retreat to the Hindenburg line began. Nivelle's plan had to be modified, the Oise-Somme attack lost all interest and that upon the Aisne alone remained. Mangin called attention to the fact that the retirement had left a right-angled salient about the Laffaux mill and that an attack to the north would be able to take the Chemin des Dames in reverse. The commander-in-chief admitted this and two divisions were devoted to this local operation. In addition it was decided that the IV. Army (Anthoine) should attack the Massif de Moronvilliers, east of Reims. On top of this a political incident led to the retirement of Gen. Lyautey, Minister of War. He was replaced by M. Painlevé, who was hostile to Nivelle's plans. This weakened the confidence of the commander-in-chief's subordinates, and Nivelle went so far as to offer his resignation, which was refused.

The British share of the offensive began on April 9 before Arras. The operations on the Aisne should have begun on April 12, but were put off, first to the 14th, then to the 16th on account of the bad weather. The front of attack measured 25 miles. The VI. Army (Mangin) operated on nearly 10m. with 17 divisions plus a cavalry division and a territorial division, 1,669 guns, of which 823 were heavy or large; the V. Army (Masel) had a nearly similar strength but with 1,967 guns (1,107 heavy or large). The artillery preparation commenced on April 5 and continued until the 15th on account of the postponement of the attack. It sufficed, but its duration permitted the Germans to make suitable dispositions and there was no surprise. On the morning of April 16 the Allies carried the first German line on the whole front. The right and centre of the V. Army gained a depth of 1½ to 2m., but on the left a tank attack, badly conducted, failed with heavy losses and the infantry rapidly came to a standstill on the plateau of Craonne. The right of the VI. Army took the position of Hurtebise and pushed as far as the Ailette, but further east the fighting was desperate and the gain insignificant. In the centre progress was more satisfactory, though difficult. On the left, the commencement was good, but the advance quickly became wild, and at certain points it was practically negligible.

To sum up, although some good results had been obtained the hoped for success had not been won. Badly informed, Nivelle imagined that on the 17th he ought to stop the northern advance of the VI. Army and push the V. Army towards the north-east. This order became delayed, so on the 17th Mangin continued his attacks, notably in the centre, where he made a marked advance on the front Braye en Laonnois-Ostel. The situation having changed Mangin ordered a vigorous pursuit, in spite of the stopping order. Slow progress was made towards the Chemin des Dames. On the same date (17th) the IV. Army (Anthoine) had made good progress in the Massif de Moronvilliers. Between the 16th and 20th the French captured 21,000 prisoners and 183 guns, and advanced some 5m. on the Aisne front of 7½m. width. Of the 52 German divisions in reserve available on April 1 only 16 remained unengaged. This result was less than had been hoped, but it was nevertheless appreciable and certainly superior to those of preceding offensives.

Unhappily the morale behind the front line was rapidly declining, the losses being greatly exaggerated. Nevertheless, Nivelle continued his operations. The X. Army took up its position on the plateau de Craonne, between the V. and VI. Armies, but on April 27 Michelet wrote that he had not strength enough for a general offensive toward the north and that he proposed to limit himself to local attacks. Nivelle accepted this solution. These operations, rendered more difficult by the unfortunate intervention of politicians, produced very poor results. The IV. Army on May 4 captured the Craonne plateau, and Laffaux mill was carried on the 5th. For several months, however, the X. Army could only with difficulty hold on to the crest of the Chemin des Dames. The French had lost from April 16 to 25, 15,000 dead, 60,000 wounded and 20,500 missing. Nevertheless, all the 52 reserve German divisions of April 1 had been employed by May 4, and quiet sectors had been robbed to reinforce the Aisne line. Up to May 25, 99 German divisions had already appeared on the front attacked, of which 11 had appeared twice. This expenditure was triple that before Verdun in ten months.

(B. E. P.; C. M. E. M.)

CHAMPAGNE WINES. Champagne is a pale gold or straw-coloured table wine which has been made naturally effervescent through a second fermentation in a bottle or other closed container. It is the best-known of all sparkling wines (*see* WINE), having been developed to perfection through centuries in the former province in France from which it gets its name.

In France, but not normally elsewhere, the name Champagne is restricted to wine obtained from grapes grown in hillside vineyards within a rough triangle connecting Reims, Epernay and Châlons-sur-Marne. White table wines of a number of these vineyards, usually from Pinot noir, Chardonnay and Pinot blanc grape varieties, are blended together to combine their differing characteristics. To the blend are added a special Champagne yeast, and some sugar, either alone or in a syrup with aged wine. In the resulting fermentation carbon dioxide gas seeks to escape; but, blocked by the closed container, it becomes fixed in the wine, to reveal itself in the form of tiny, pungent bubbles, when the bottle is opened for use.

Either of two types of closed containers may be used to encase the fermenting Champagne. In the older, classic method, bottles able to withstand pressures of as much as 100 lb. per sq.in. are employed. Thick corks, held by steel clamps called agraffes, block the necks. The filled bottles are stacked horizontally in tiers and left so for a period of months, until the second fermentation completes itself.

Unwanted sediment is created during the fermentation, and, to remove this, workers place the bottles in racks, necks downward. Each day for months they lift each bottle slightly, twist and partly turn it. The repeated action, called "riddling," shifts the sediment along the glass until it comes to rest on the cork. At this point the bottle's neck is immersed in a freezing solution; the clamp is then released and the gas pressure forces out the cork and a small quantity of frozen wine, containing the sediment. This process is known as "disgorging."

Quickly, before much of the Champagne can be lost, a little sweet liqueur is added, the bottle is strongly corked, the cork is wired on, and, except for final aging, the effervescent wine is ready for use. The amount of liqueur added determines the degree of sweetness of the Champagne. A Champagne may be almost completely dry of sugar ("brut"), semi-dry (usually labelled "extra-dry," "dry" or "sec") or sweet ("doux").

The second, and faster and less expensive, way of producing Champagne is by the "bulk" process. In this, the wine has its second fermentation in large glass-lined tanks which may hold 50 or even 1,000 gallons. From these, after fermentation, the wine is transferred, under pressure, directly into bottles; the sediment is left behind in the tank or removed by a filter.

Outside of France, wines produced in the manner and possessed of the characteristics of Champagne may be sold under that label qualified with the name of the place of origin. When the "bulk" process has been used the governments of some countries, including the U.S., require that fact to be stated. (*See* WINE.)

BIBLIOGRAPHY.—André L. Simon, *The Supply, the Care and the Sale of Wine* (1923), *Champagne* (1934); H. Warner Allen, *The Wines of France* (1924); C. Moreau-Bérillon, *Au pays du Champagne, Le vignoble, Le vin* (1913); Frank Schoonmaker and Tom Marvel, *The Complete Wine Book* (1934); Wine Advisory Board, San Francisco, *Wine Handbook Series*, vol. ii (1943). (H. A. Cw.)

CHAMPAGNY, JEAN BAPTISTE NOMPERE DE, DUC DE CADORE (1756–1834), French politician, was born at Roanne on Aug. 4, 1756, and entered the navy in 1774. He fought through the war in America and resigned in 1787. Elected deputy by the *noblesse* of Forez to the states-general in 1789, he went over to the third estate on June 21 and collaborated in the work of the Constituent Assembly, especially occupying himself with the reorganization of the navy. He remained in private life from 1791–99, when Napoleon named him member of the council of state. From July 1801 to Aug. 1804 he was ambassador of France at Vienna and directed the incessant negotiations between the two courts. As minister of the interior (1804–7) he proved an administrator of the first order. In Aug. 1807 he succeeded Talleyrand as minister for foreign affairs. He directed the annexation of the Papal states in April 1808, worked to secure the abdication of Charles IV. of Spain in May 1808, negotiated the peace of Vienna (1809) and the marriage of Napoleon. In April 1811 a quarrel with the emperor led to his retirement. In 1814, after the abdication, the empress sent him on a fruitless mission to the emperor of Austria. Then he went over to the Bourbons. During the Hundred Days he again joined Napoleon. This led to his exclusion by Louis XVIII., but in 1819 he recovered his dignity of peer. He died in Paris on July 3, 1834. Three of his sons achieved distinction. François (1804–1882) wrote a history of the Roman empire, in three parts—(1) *Les Césars* (1841–43, 4 vols.); (2) *Les Antonins* (1863, 3 vols.); (3) *Les Césars du III siècle* (1870, 3 vols.). Napoleon (1806–1872) published a *Traité de la police municipale* in 4 vols. (1844–61), and was a deputy in the Corps Législatif from 1852–70. Jérome Paul (1809–86) was also deputy in the Corps Législatif from 1853–70, and was made honorary chamberlain in 1859. He worked on the official publication of the correspondence of Napoleon I.

CHAMPAIGN, a city of Champaign county, Illinois, U.S.A., in a rich agricultural region, 125 mi. S. by W. of Chicago. It is on federal highways 45 and 150; is served by the Big Four, the Illinois Central, the Wabash and the Illinois Traction railways; and has a commercial airport. The population in 1950 was 39,397. Champaign and Urbana, adjoining it on the east, form practically one city, with common public utilities and civic enterprises. The only separate institutions are the post offices and the city governments. Champaign has the greater part of the business and industrial activities, which include railroad repair shops and manufactures of heavy castings, soybean oil and feed, bleachers, gloves, concrete measuring devices, impact registers, caps and gowns. The campus of the University of Illinois (*q.v.*) lies partly in Champaign.

At Rantoul, 14 mi. N., is Chanute field, a flying field of the U.S. army air corps. Champaign was founded in 1855 and incorporated as a city in 1860.

CHAMPAIGNE, PHILIPPE DE (1602–1674), Belgian painter of the French school, was born at Brussels of a poor family. He was a pupil of J. Fouquières; and, going to Paris in 1621, was employed by N. Du Chesne to paint with Nicholas Poussin in the palace of the Luxembourg. His best works are to be found at Vincennes, and in the church of the Carmelites at Paris, where is his celebrated Crucifix, a signal perspective success, on one of the vaultings. After the death of Du Chesne, Philippe became first painter to the Queen of France, and ultimately rector of the Academy of Paris. As his age advanced and his health failed, he retired to Port Royal, where he had a daughter cloistered as a nun, of whom (along with Catherine Agnès Arnauld) he painted a picture highly remarkable for its solid, unaffected truth. This, indeed, is the general character of his work—grave reality, without special elevation or depth of character or charm of warm or stately colour. He produced an immense number of paintings, religious and other subjects as well as portraits, dispersed over various parts of France and now over the galleries of Europe.

Philippe died on Aug. 12, 1674.

CHAMPARAN, a district of India, in the Tirhut division of Bihar, occupying the northwest corner of Bihar, between the two rivers Gandak and Baghmati and the Nepal hills. It has an area of 3,553 sq.mi., and a population (1941) of 2,397,569.

The district is a vast level, except in the north and northwest, where outliers of the Himalayas, known as the Sumeswar and Dun ranges, extend for about 15 mi. into the alluvial plain. The former hills rise to a height of 2,884 ft. at Fort Sumeswar; at their eastern extremity is the Bhikna Thori pass into Nepal. The two ranges, which have an area of about 364 sq.mi., contain stretches of forest and jungle. Elsewhere the land is closely cultivated and teems with an active agricultural population. The principal rivers are the Gandak, navigable all the year round, the Burh Gandak, Lelbagi, Dhanauti and Baghmati. Old beds of rivers intersect Champaran, and one of these forms a chain of lakes which occupies an area of 139 sq.mi. in the centre of the district.

Champaran was the chief seat of indigo planting in Bihar before the decline of that industry. There are a number of salpetre refineries.

The district suffered severely from drought in 1866 and 1874, and again in 1897. As a protection against crop failures the Tribini and Dhaka canals were constructed. The former derives its supply from the Gandak river at Tribini immediately below the Nepal frontier and irrigates a tract in the north of the district. The latter is a minor work taking off from the river Lalbukaya and irrigating several thousand acres in the east. A considerable trade is conducted with Nepal.

Sugauli, a small military station, was the scene of a massacre during the Mutiny; it was there that the Nepalese treaty of 1815 was signed. Three of the sandstone pillars with pillar edicts which Asoka erected to mark the stages of his journey into Nepal are found in this district at the following places: Lauriya Nandangarh, Lauriya Araraj and Rampurisa.

CHAMPEAUX, WILLIAM OF (*c.* 1070–1121), French scholastic, was born at Champeaux near Melun. After studying under Anselm of Laon and Roscelin, he taught in the cathedral school of Paris, where he opposed Roscelin and had Abélard as a pupil.

In 1103 he became a canon of Notre Dame but in 1108 retired to the abbey of St. Victor, where he resumed his lectures. He afterward became bishop of Châlons-sur-Marne, and took part in the dispute concerning investitures as a supporter of Calixtus II. His theological works are the *De Eucharistia* (inserted by Jean Mabillon in his edition of the works of St. Bernard) and the *De Origine Animae* (in E. Martène's *Anecd. nov.*, vol. v, 1717), in which he upholds the theory of creatianism (that a soul is specially created for each human being).

In his *De Generibus et Speciebus* (printed by V. Cousin in *Ouvrages inédits d'Abélard,* 1836), William shows himself an excessive realist by declaring that the universal is the whole reality of the individual, but in his later *Sententiae* (extracts published in G. Lefèvre, *Les variations de G. de Champeaux,* Lille, 1898), he adopts a moderate realism.

For his views and controversies with Abélard *see* ABÉLARD; SCHOLASTICISM.

See Lefèvre, *op. cit.;* Hurtault, "Théologie de G. de Champeaux," in *Rev. de sc. eccl. et sc. cath.* (1908–09); E. Michaud, *G. de Champeaux et les écoles de Paris au XIIe siècle,* 2nd ed. (Paris, 1868); Ueberweg, *Grundriss der Gesch. der Phil.,* Teil ii (Berlin, 1928).

CHAMPERICO, a Pacific port of Guatemala, Central America, 28 mi. by the International Railways of Central America from Retalhuleu. Pop. (1950) 982. Exports are chiefly coffee. The harbour is an open roadstead, ships being served by lighter.

CHAMPERTY, in common law, a bargain between a plaintiff or defendant in a cause and another person, to divide the land (*campum partiri*) or other subject matter of the action in the event of success, in consideration of that person carrying on or defending the suit partly or wholly at his own expense. It is a misdemeanour punishable by fine or imprisonment. It differs only from maintenance, in that the recompense for the service which has been given is always part of the matter in action, or some profit growing out of it. Such an agreement is illegal and void.

It is not, however, illegal to charge the subject matter of an action in order to obtain the means of prosecuting or defending it.

CHAMPION, in the judicial combats of the middle ages the substitute for a party to the suit disabled from bearing arms or specially exempt from the duty to do so. Hence the word has come to be applied to any one who "champions," or contends on behalf of, any person or cause.

In the laws of the Lombards (lib. ii, tit. 56, sections 38, 39), those who by reason of youth, age or infirmity could not bear arms were allowed to nominate champions, and the same provision was made in the case of women (lib. i, tit. 3, section 6; tit. 16, section 2). This was practically the rule laid down in all subsequent legislation on the subject.

The clergy, as individuals or corporations, were represented by champions; in the case of bishops and abbots this function was part of the duties of the *advocatus* (*see* ADVOCATE). Du Cange gives instances of mercenary champions who were regarded as "infamous persons," and sometimes, in case of defeat, were condemned to lose hand or foot. Sometimes championships were "serjeanties"; *i.e.,* rendered service to lords, churches or cities in consideration of the grant of certain fiefs or annual money payments.

The office of "king's champion" (*campio regis*) is peculiar to England. His function was to ride, clad in complete armour, on his right the high constable, on his left the earl marshal, into Westminster hall during the coronation banquet and challenge to single combat anyone who should dispute the king's right to reign. The challenge was thrice repeated by the herald, at the entrance to the hall, in the centre and at the foot of the dais. On picking up his gauntlet for the third time, the champion was pledged by the king in a gilt-covered cup, which was then presented to him as his fee by the king. If he had had occasion to fight, and had been victorious, his fee would have been the armour he wore and the horse he rode, the second best in the royal stables; but no such occasion ever arose. This ceremonial was last performed at the coronation of George IV.

The office of king's champion is of great antiquity, but of the actual exercise of the office the earliest record dates from the coronation of Richard II. On this occasion the champion, Sir John Dymoke, appeared at the door of the abbey immediately after the coronation mass, but was peremptorily told to go away and return later; moreover, in his bill presented to the court of claims, he stated that the champion was to ride in the procession before the service, and make his challenge to all the world. This seems to show that the ceremony, as might be expected, was originally performed before the king's coronation, when it would have had some significance. The manor of Scrivelsby is held in grand serjeanty by the service of acting as the king's champion, although the service became obsolete with the coronation banquet.

BIBLIOGRAPHY.—Du Cange, *Glossarium, s.v.* "Campio"; L. G. Wickham Legg, *English Coronation Records* (1901); J. H. T. Perkins, *The Coronation Book* (1902).

CHAMPIONNET, JEAN ETIENNE (1762–1800), French general, born at Valence, enlisted in the army at an early age and served in the great siege of Gibraltar. In May 1793 he was charged with the suppression of the disturbances in the Jura, which he quelled without bloodshed. Under Pichegru he took part in the Rhine campaign of that year as a brigade commander and at Weissenburg and in the Palatinate won the warm commendation of Hoche. He commanded the left wing of the French armies on the Rhine, between Neuwied and Düsseldorf, and took part in the expeditions to the Lahn and the Main. In 1798 Championnet was named commander-in-chief of the "army of Rome," which was protecting the infant Roman republic against the Neapolitan court and the British fleet. The Austrian general Mack had a tenfold superiority in numbers, but Championnet captured Naples itself and there set up the Parthenopean republic. But his intense earnestness and intolerance of opposition soon embroiled him with the civilians, and the general was recalled in disgrace. The following year, however, saw him again in the field as commander-in-chief of the "army of the Alps." The campaign which followed was uniformly unsuccessful, and, worn out by the unequal struggle, Championnet died at Antibes, on Jan. 9, 1800.

See A.R.C. de St. Albin, *Championnet, ou les Campagnes de Hollande, de Rome et de Naples* (1860); M. Faure, *Souvenirs du Général Championnet* (1904).

CHAMPLAIN, SAMUEL DE (1567–1635), French explorer, colonial pioneer and first governor of French Canada, was born at Brouage on the Bay of Biscay. His father was a sea captain, and the boy was early skilled in seamanship and navigation. He entered the army of Henry IV., and served in Brittany. When the army of the League was disbanded he accompanied his uncle, who had charge of the ships in which the Spanish allies were conveyed home, and on reaching Cadiz secured (1599) the command of one of the vessels about to make an expedition to the West Indies. He was gone over two years, visiting all the principal ports and pushing inland from Vera Cruz to the city of Mexico. The ms. account of his adventures, *Bref Discours des Choses plus remarquables que Samuel Champlain de Brouage a recognues aux Indes Occidentales,* is in the library at Dieppe. It was not published in French until 1870, although an English translation was printed by the Hakluyt Society in 1859. It contains a suggestion of a Panama canal, "by which the voyage to the south sea would be shortened by more than 1,500 leagues." In 1603 Champlain made his first voyage to Canada, being sent out by Aymar de Clermont, on whom the king had bestowed a patent. Champlain at once established friendly relations with the Indians and explored the St. Lawrence to the rapids above Montreal. On his return he published *Des sauvages, ou voyage de Samuel Champlain de Brouage fait en la France Nouvelle.* During his absence de Clermont had died, and his privileges and fur trade monopolies were conferred upon Pierre du Guast, Sieur de Monts (1560–*c.* 1630). With him, in 1604, Champlain was engaged in exploring the coast as far south as Cape Cod, in seeking a site for a new settlement, and in making surveys and charts. They first settled on an island near the mouth of the St. Croix river, and then at Port Royal—now Annapolis, Nova Scotia.

Meanwhile the Basques and Bretons got de Monts' patent revoked, and Champlain returned to Europe. When, however, in modified form, the patent was re-granted to his patron, Champlain induced him to abandon Acadia and establish a settlement on the St. Lawrence. Champlain was placed in command of one of the two vessels sent out. He was to explore and colonize, while the other vessel traded, to pay for the expedition. Champlain fixed on the site of Quebec and founded the first white settlement there in July 1608, giving it its present name. In the spring he joined a war party of Algonquins and Hurons, discovered the great lake that bears his name, and, near the present Ticonderoga, took part in the victory which they obtained over the Iroquois. The Iroquois naturally turned first to the Dutch and then to the English for allies. Champlain then returned to France, but in 1611 was back in Canada, and established a trading post at Mont Royal. He was subsequently appointed lieutenant-general in New France.

In 1613 Champlain again crossed the Atlantic and endeavoured to confirm Nicolas de Vignau's alleged discovery of a short route to the ocean by the Ottawa river, a great lake at its source, and another river flowing north therefrom. That year he got as far as Allumette Island in the Ottawa, but two years later, with a "Great War Party" of Indians, he crossed Lake Nipissing and the eastern ends of Lakes Huron and Ontario, and attacked an Onondaga fortified town a few miles south of Lake Oneida. This was the end of his wanderings. He now devoted himself to the growth and strengthening of Quebec. Every year he went to France with this end in view. He was one of the 100 associates of the Company of New France, created by Richelieu to reform abuses and take over all his country's interests in the new world. But in 1629 Quebec was forced to surrender to the English. Champlain was taken to England a prisoner, but when Canada was restored to the French he returned (1633) to his post, where he died. He had married in 1610, Hélène Boullé, then but 12 years old. She did not leave France for Canada, however, until ten years later. After his death she became a nun.

Champlain's works in six vols. were published under the patronage of the University of Laval in 1870. There is a careful trans. of *Champlain's Voyages,* by A. N. and E. G. Bourne (1906) in the "Trailmaker" series ed. by Prof. J. B. McMaster. *See* F. Parkman, *Pioneers of France in the New World* (1865); J. Winsor, *Cartier to Frontenac* (1894); G. Gravier, *Vie de S. Champlain* (1900); N. E. Dionne, *Champlain* (1905); R. Flenly, *S. Champlain* (Toronto, 1924).

CHAMPLAIN, LAKE. This lake is chiefly in the United States, between the States of New York and Vermont, but extends about 6m. into the Province of Quebec, Canada. It is about 125m. long, covers an area of about 600sq.m., varies in width from ¼m. to 12m. and in depth from 100ft. to a maximum of about 400 feet. It drains into the St. Lawrence through the Richelieu river. Lake Champlain receives the waters of Lake George through a small stream containing rapids and falls. It receives the drainage from many other streams, all of them small. The most important ports on the lake are Burlington, Vt., Rouses Point, Plattsburg and Port Henry, New York. Plattsburg Barracks, a beautiful army post, is located on its shores at the city of the same name. It was at this post that the first experiment in training young men for the citizens army was tried out by Gen. Leonard Wood in 1915. The experience here gained was of great value during the World War when speed and efficiency were so essential. Since the World War, many young men of New York and other nearby States have been trained here in the Citizens Military Training Camps and in the Reserve Officers Training Corps.

Lake Champlain is a link in the international water line of communication between the Hudson river and the lower St. Lawrence. The total commerce passing the narrows of the lower end of the lake in 1926 was 115,000 tons. The through traffic consists principally of southbound lumber and pulp-wood and northbound coal. Local traffic is comparatively unimportant. The route from the St. Lawrence south is via the Richelieu river, with the St. Ours lock and dam in its lower course and the Chambly canal in its upper reach. This canal has 9 locks with total lift of 74 feet. The locks have the following dimensions: length, 118ft. (110ft. available); width, 22½ft.; depth on sills, 7ft. (reduced at low water to 6½ft.). The width of the canal is 36ft. at the bottom and 60ft. at the water surface. The "Champlain canal" connects Lake Champlain, at Whitehall, with the Hudson river at Waterford, New York. There are 12 locks with total lockage of 182 feet. The summit level is at elevation 140 and is supplied with water from the headwaters of the Hudson.

With the Green mountains on the east and the Adirondacks on the west, the scenery is rugged and beautiful. Many islands dot the northern portion of the lake. It was discovered in 1609 by the French explorer and soldier Samuel de Champlain, from whom the lake takes its name. During the early period of settlement of the North American continent Lake Champlain was the gateway between French Canada and the English colonies. It played an important part in all the wars in which the people to the north and south of it were on opposite sides. It is rich in the history and traditions of these early days. Champlain, with an expedition of about 80 friendly Montagues Indians, defeated the Iroquois on its shores in 1609. Thus began the long struggle between the French and the Five Nations.

In 1731 the French built a fort at Crown Point and in 1755 another at Ticonderoga; both were important strategic points in the French and Indian War as well as in the American Revolution. They controlled the easiest and most natural route between

Canada and New York. During the Seven Years' War (French and Indian) English and colonial expeditions twice failed to capture Crown Point. It was finally occupied by Amherst in 1759. Early in the American Revolution it was captured by a detachment of Ethan Allen's Green Mountain Boys. Ft. Ticonderoga was the scene of the severe repulse administered to Gen. Abercrombie by Gen. Montcalm in 1758. Later on it was captured by Amherst. At the beginning of the Revolution it was captured in a surprise attack by Capt. Ethan Allen. When asked by the British commander, Capt. La Place, by what authority the surrender of the fort was demanded, Capt. Allen made his historic reply, "In the name of the great Jehovah and the continental congress." During the subsequent years of the war the fort changed hands several times. On Oct. 11, 1776, the first battle between an American and a British fleet, the battle of Valcour island, was fought on the lake. Benedict Arnold, the American commander, with a decidedly inferior force, inflicted severe damage on the enemy and then during the night escaped. Although overtaken two days later he again, after a fight of a few hours, made a successful retreat saving all his men.

At the beginning of the War of 1812 the American naval force on the lake, though very small, was superior to that of the British, but on June 3, 1813, the British captured two American sloops in the narrow channel at the northern end and gained supremacy. Both sides now began to build and equip vessels for a decisive contest. By May 1814, the Americans had regained supremacy, and four months later a British land force of 11,000 men under Sir George Prevost and a naval force of 16 vessels of about 2,402 tons with 937 men and 92 guns under Capt. George Downie confronted an American land force of 1,500 men under Brigadier General Alexander Macomb, strongly entrenched at Plattsburg, and an American naval force in Plattsburg bay of 14 vessels of about 2,244 tons with 882 men and 86 guns under Commodore Thomas MacDonough (1783–1825). The naval battle occurred on the morning of Sept. 11, 1814. Although the weight of the metal thrown by the guns of MacDonough's American fleet was greater than that of the British fleet, the latter had more guns of long range. Knowing that in a battle in the open lake he would be at a disadvantage, MacDonough anchored his fleet in such a way as to force Downie to pass between him and the land and to prevent him from anchoring his fleet out of range of the American guns. Downie was killed early in the fight, and the British fleet was soon driven out of action or surrendered. The American loss was 52 killed and 58 wounded, and the British loss was 57 killed and 92 wounded. The land forces engaged in desultory fighting but no decisive action occurred. As the lake was entirely in the control of the Americans, Prevost was forced to retreat during the night of Sept. 12–13, leaving his sick and wounded behind. The British gave up further efforts to invade New York.

See B. C. Butler, *Lake George and Lake Champlain* (Albany, N.Y., 1868); Francis Parkman, *Montcalm and Wolfe* (Boston, 1884) and *Historie Handbook of the Northern Tour* (Boston, 1885); F. W. Halsey, "The Historical Significance of the Hudson and Champlain Valley," *N.Y. State Hist. Assoc. Proc.*, vol. ix., pp. 227–236 (Albany, 1910); and E. T. Gillispie, "The War Path," ib., vol. x., pp. 139–155 (Albany, 1911). (E. JA.)

CHAMPLAIN CANAL: *see* NEW YORK STATE BARGE CANAL SYSTEM.

CHAMPMESLÉ, MARIE (1642–1698), née DESMARES, French actress, was born in Rouen and made her first appearance on the stage at Rouen with Charles Chevillet (1645–1701), who called himself sieur de Champmeslé, and they were married in 1666. By 1669 they were playing in Paris at the Théâtre du Marais. The next year, as Hermione in Racine's *Andromaque*, she had a great success at the Hôtel de Bourgogne. Her intimacy with Racine dates from then. Some of his finest tragedies were written for her, but her repertoire was not confined to them, and many an indifferent play—like Thomas Corpeille's *Ariane* and *Comte d'Essex*—owed its success to "her natural manner of acting and her pathetic rendering of the hapless heroine." *Phèdre* was the climax of her triumphs, and when she and her husband deserted the Hôtel de Bourgogne (*see* BÉJART *ad fin.*), it was selected to open the Comédie Française on Aug. 26, 1680. There, with Mme. Guérin as the leading comedy actress, she played the great tragic love parts for more than 30 years, dying on May 15, 1698. La Fontaine dedicated to her his novel *Belphégor*, and Boileau immortalized her in verse.

Her brother, the actor NICOLAS DESMARES (*c.* 1650–1714), began as a member of a subsidized company at Copenhagen. After 1685 he played peasant parts with great success at the Comédie Française. His daughter, to whom Christian V. and his queen stood sponsors, CHRISTINE ANTOINETTE CHARLOTTE DESMARES (1682–1753), was a fine actress in both tragedy and soubrette parts. She made her début at the Comédie Française in 1699, in La Grange Chancel's *Oreste et Pylade*, and was at once received as *sociétaire*. She retired in 1721.

CHAMPOLLION, JEAN FRANÇOIS (1790–1832), French Egyptologist, called LE JEUNE to distinguish him from Champollion-Figeac (*q.v.*), his elder brother, was born at Figeac, in the department of Lot, on Dec. 23, 1790. At the age of 16 he read before the academy of Grenoble a paper in which he maintained that the Coptic was the ancient language of Egypt. He soon after removed to Paris. In 1809 he was made professor of history in the Lyceum of Grenoble. His first decipherment of hieroglyphics dates from 1821. In 1824 he was sent by Charles X. to visit the Egyptian antiquities in the museums of Italy; and on his return was appointed director of the Egyptian museum at the Louvre. In 1828 he was commissioned to conduct a scientific expedition to Egypt in company with Rosellini. In March 1831 he received the chair of Egyptian antiquities, which had been created specially for him, in the Collège de France. He was engaged with Rosellini in publishing the results of their Egyptian researches when he died at Paris (1832). Champollion is now universally acknowledged to have been the founder of Egyptology.

He wrote *L'Égypte, sous les Pharaons* (2 vols. 8vo. 1814); *Sur l'écriture hiératique* (1821); *Sur l'écriture démotique; Précis du système hiéroglyphique, etc.* (1824); *Panthéon égyptien, ou collection des personnages mythologiques de l'ancienne Égypte* (incomplete); *Monumens de l'Égypte et de la Nubie considérés par rapport à l'histoire, la religion, etc.; Grammaire égyptienne* (1836), and *Dictionnaire égyptienne* (1841), edited by his brother; *Analyse méthodique du texte démotique de Rosette; Aperçu des résultats historiques de la découverte de l'alphabet hiéroglyphique* (1827); *Mémoires sur les signes employés par les Égyptiens dans leurs trois systèmes graphiques à la notation des principales divisions du temps; Lettres écrites d'Égypte et de Nubie* (1833). Champollion also wrote several letters on Egyptian subjects, addressed at different periods to the duc de Blacas and others.

See H. Hartleben, *Champollion, sein Leben und sein Werk,* 2 vol. (1906); *Lettres de Champollion le Jeune* (1909).

CHAMPOLLION-FIGEAC, JACQUES JOSEPH (1778–1867), French archaeologist, elder brother of Jean François Champollion, was born at Figeac in the department of Lot, on Oct. 5, 1778. He became keeper of manuscripts at the Bibliothèque Nationale in Paris, and professor of palaeography at the École des Chartes. In 1849 he became librarian of the palace of Fontainebleau. His works include, *Nouvelles recherches sur les patois ou idiomes vulgaires de la France* (1809), *Annales de Lagides* (1819) and *Chartes latines sur papyrus du VIe siècle de l'ère chrétienne.* His son AIMÉ (1812–1894) became his assistant at the Bibliothèque Nationale, and in addition to a number of historical works wrote a biographical and bibliographical study of his family in *Les Deux Champollion* (Grenoble, 1887).

CHANCE, an accident or event, a phenomenon which has no apparent or discoverable cause; hence an event which has not been expected, a piece of good or bad fortune. From the popular idea that anything of which no assignable cause is known has therefore no cause, chance was regarded as having a substantial objective existence, being itself the source of such uncaused phenomena. For the philosophic theories relating to this subject *see* ACCIDENTALISM.

"Chance," in the theory of probability, is used in two ways. In the stricter or mathematical usage, it is synonymous with probability, *i.e.*, if a particular event may occur in n ways in an aggregate of p events, then the "chance" of the particular event occurring is given by the fraction n/p. In the second usage, the "chance" is regarded as the ratio of the number of ways which a particular event may occur to the number of ways in which it may not occur; mathematically expressed, this chance is $n/(p-n)$. This is more usually called Odds (*see* PROBABILITY). In the English law relating to gaming and wagering a distinction is drawn between games of chance and games of skill (*see* GAMBLING AND BETTING).

CHANCEL, strictly, that part of a church close to the altar and separated from the nave (*q.v.*) by cancelli or screens. This

LOOKING DOWN OVER THE CHOIR INTO THE CHANCEL OF THE SALAMANCA CATHEDRAL, SPAIN. THE ALTAR IS SEEN IN THE CENTRE BACKGROUND

space, originally known as the space *inter cancellos,* or *locus altaris cancellis septus,* came itself to be called the chancel. Later the word came to include the whole of that part of the church occupied by altars, communion tables and all the officiating clergy and singers, *i.e.,* the presbytery (*q.v.*), the chancel proper and the choir (*q.v.*). In some cases the word is used synonymously with choir.

In basilican churches, the chancel is set apart only by a low railing; *e.g.,* S. Clemente, Rome. Such divisions correspond more to the altar, communion or sanctuary rail of a modern church than to the developed mediaeval chancel screen. In the highly organized mediaeval church, the chancel is clearly differentiated from the nave by the raising of the floor level, and by the chancel or rood screen (*see* JUBÉ). This screen is frequently continued on each side, behind the choir stalls, and around the east end of the cathedrals of sanctuary, as in Paris, Bourges and Amiens. At the side, such screens form the back of the choir stalls. The chancel screen in front of the altar is sometimes only a low parapet, sometimes a light, openwork structure of wood or metal, but often, especially in the large cathedrals and abbeys of England, a massive and solid stone structure, frequently carrying the organ. In collegiate and monastic churches, these screens thus completely separated the spaces reserved for services for the members of the clerical community from the spaces for popular services, for which a second altar was usually set up to the west of the screen, as formerly in Westminster Abbey.

Chancel sizes vary enormously. On the European continent they usually extend from the east end to the crossing, as in many modern churches, but in abbey churches, and generally in English mediaeval churches, they comprise also several bays of the nave. In the churches of Paris the chancel is relatively small. The chancel screen becomes more open and its main function is to support a crucifixion group; it is, therefore, primarily a rood screen. In small churches the chancel is sometimes lower and narrower than the nave.

CHANCELLOR, RICHARD (d. 1556), English seaman, is said to have been brought up by the father of Sir Philip Sidney. Nothing is known of his own family except that he had two sons. In 1553 Sir Hugh Willoughby fitted out an expedition in search of the North-East passage to China, of which Chancellor was appointed pilot general. It was arranged that the expedition should meet at Vardö, but because of unfavourable weather Chancellor's was the only one of the seven ships which arrived. He therefore went on alone into the White sea, and thence overland to Moscow. There the emperor showed him great hospitality and gave him a letter for the king of England giving very favourable conditions for English trade. Chancellor rejoined his ship in the summer of 1554, and went back to England after having, by his successful negotiations, laid the foundations of English trade with Russia. The Muscovy company was established as a result. In 1555 Chancellor left England again for Moscow, which he reached in November. He lost his life in a wreck on the return voyage, on Nov. 10, 1556, off Pitsligo on the coast of Aberdeenshire.

See R. Hakluyt, *Principal Navigations . . . of the English Nation,* 1st ed. (London, 1589)

CHANCELLOR, an official title used by most of the peoples whose civilization has arisen directly or indirectly out of the Roman empire. It stands for very various duties, and is borne by officers of various degrees of dignity. The original chancellors were the *cancellarii* of Roman courts of justice, ushers who sat at the *cancelli* or lattice work screens of a "basilica" or law court, which separated the judge and counsel from the audience (*see* CHANCEL). In the later Eastern empire the *cancellarii* were promoted at first to notarial duties. The barbarian kingdoms which arose on the ruin of the empire in the West copied more or less intelligently the Roman model in all their judicial and financial administration. Under the Frankish kings of the Merovingian dynasty the *cancellarii* were subordinates of the great officer of state called the *referendarius,* the predecessor of the modern chancellor. The office became established under the form *archi-cancellarius,* or chief of the *cancellarii.* Stubbs says that the Carolingian chancellor was the royal notary and the arch-chancellor keeper of the royal seal. His functions would naturally be discharged by a cleric in times when book learning was mainly confined to the clergy. From the reign of Louis the Pious the post was held by a bishop. By an equally natural process he became the chief secretary of the king and of the queen, who also had her chancellor. Such an office would develop on the judicial as well as the administrative side. Appeals and petitions of aggrieved persons would pass through the chancellor's hands, as well as the political correspondence of the king. Great officers and corporations also had occasion to employ an agent to do secretarial, notarial and judicial work for them, and called him by the convenient name of chancellor.

The Chancellor in England.—The model of the Carolingian court was followed by the mediaeval states of Western Europe. In England the office of chancellor dates back to the reign of Edward the Confessor, the first English king to use the Norman practice of sealing instead of signing documents. The chancellor was originally, and long continued to be, an ecclesiastic, who combined the functions of the most dignified of the royal chaplains, the king's secretary in secular matters, and keeper of the royal seal. From the first, then, though at the outset overshadowed by that of the justiciar, the office of chancellor was one of great influence. As chaplain the chancellor was keeper of the king's conscience; as secretary he enjoyed the royal confidence in secular affairs; as keeper of the seal he was necessary to all formal expressions of the royal will. By him and his staff of chaplains the whole secretarial work of the royal household was conducted, the accounts were kept under the justiciar and treasurer, writs were drawn up and sealed, and the royal correspondence was carried on. He was, in fact, as Stubbs put it, a sort of secretary of state for all departments. "This is he," wrote John of Salisbury (d. 1180), "who cancels (*cancellat*) the evil laws of the realm, and makes equitable (*aequa*) the commands of a pious prince," a curious anticipation of the chancellor's later equitable jurisdiction. Under Henry II, indeed, the chancellor was already employed in judicial work, either in attendance on the king or in provincial visitations; though the peculiar jurisdiction of the chancery was of later growth. By this time, however, the chancellor was "great alike in Curia and Exchequer"; he was *secundus a rege, i.e.,* took precedence immediately after the justiciar, and nothing was done either in the Curia or the exchequer without his consent. So great was his office that William Fitz Stephen, the biographer of Becket, tells us that it was not purchasable (*emenda non est*), a statement which requires modification, since it was in fact more than once sold under Henry I., Stephen, Richard and John (Stubbs, *Const. Hist.* i. pp. 384–497; Gneist, *Const. Hist. of England,* p. 219), an evil precedent which was, however, not long followed.

The judicial duties of the chancellor grew out of the fact that all petitions addressed to the king passed through his hands. The number and variety of these became so great that in 1280, under Edward I., an ordinance was issued directing the chancellor and the justices to deal with the greater number of them; those which involved the use of the great seal being specially referred to the chancellor. The chancellor and justices were to determine which of them were "so great, and of grace, that the chancellor and others would not despatch them without the king," and these the chancellor and other chief ministers were to carry in person to the king (Stubbs ii. 263, and note, and p. 268). At this period the chancellor, though employed in equity, had ministerial functions only; but when, in the reign of Edward III., the chancellor ceased to follow the court his tribunal acquired a more definite character, and petitions for grace and favour began to be addressed primarily to him, instead of being merely examined and passed on by him to the king; and in the 22nd year of this reign matters which were of grace were definitely committed to the chancellor for decision. This is the starting-point of the equitable jurisdiction of the chancellor, whence developed that immense body of rules, supplementing the deficiencies or modifying the harshness of the common law, which is known as Equity (*q.v.*).

The Chancellor in Parliament.—The position of the chancellor as speaker or prolocutor of the House of Lords dates from the time when the ministers of the royal Curia formed *ex officio* a part of the *commune concilium* and parliament. The chancellor originally attended with the other officials, and he continued to attend *ex officio* after they had ceased to do so. If he chanced to be a bishop, he was summoned regularly *qua* bishop; otherwise he attended without summons. When not a peer the chancellor had no place in parliament except as chancellor, and the act of 31 Henry VIII. cap. 10 (1539) laid down that, if not a peer, he had "no interest to give any assent or dissent in the House." Yet Sir Robert Bourchier (d. 1349), the first lay chancellor, had protested in 1341 against the first statute of 15 Edward III. (on trial by peers, etc.), on the ground that it had not received his assent and was contrary to the laws of the realm. From the time, however, of William, Lord Cowper (first lord high chancellor of Great Britain in 1705, created Baron Cowper in 1706), all chancellors have been made peers on their elevation to the woolsack. Sometimes the custody of the great seal has been transferred from the chancellor to a special official, the lord keeper of the great seal (*see* LORD KEEPER OF THE GREAT SEAL); this was notably the case under Queen Elizabeth (*cf.* the French *garde des sceaux,* below). Sometimes it is put into commission, being affixed by lords commissioners of the great seal. By the Catholic Emancipation Act of 1829 it was enacted that none of these offices could be held by a Roman Catholic (*see* further under LORD HIGH CHANCELLOR). The office of lord chancellor of Ireland and that of chancellor of Scotland (who ceased to be appointed after the Act of Union 1707) followed the same lines.

Chancellor of the Exchequer.—The title of chancellor, without the predicates "high" or "lord," is also applied in Great Britain to a number of other officials and functionaries. Of these the most important is the chancellor of the Exchequer, an office which originated in the separation of the chancery from the Exchequer in the reign of Henry III. (1216–72). His duties consisted originally in the custody and employment of the seal of the Exchequer, in the keeping of a counter-roll to check the roll kept by the treasurer, and in the discharge of certain judicial functions in the exchequer of account. So long as the treasury board was in active working the chancellorship of the Exchequer was an office of small importance, and even during a great part of the 19th century was not necessarily a cabinet office, unless held in conjunction with that of first lord of the Treasury. At the present time the chancellor of the Exchequer is minister of finance, and therefore always of cabinet rank (*see* EXCHEQUER).

Chancellor of the Duchy.—The chancellor of the duchy of Lancaster is the representative of the crown in the management of its lands and the control of its courts in the duchy of Lancaster, the property of which is scattered over several counties. These lands and privileges, though their inheritance has always been vested in the king and his heirs, have always been kept distinct from the hereditary revenues of the sovereign, whose palatine rights as duke of Lancaster were distinct from his rights as king. The Judicature Act of 1873 left only the chancery court of the duchy, but the chancellor can appoint and dismiss the county court judges within the limits of the duchy; he is responsible also for the land revenues of the duchy, which are the private property of the sovereign, and keeps the seal of the duchy. As the judicial and estate work is done by subordinate officials, the office is usually given to a minister whose assistance is necessary to a government, but who for one reason or another cannot undertake the duties of an important department. John Bright described him as the maid-of-all-work of the cabinet.

Ecclesiastical Chancellors.—The chancellor of a diocese is the official who presides over the bishop's court and exercises jurisdiction in his name. This use of the word is comparatively modern, and, though employed in acts of parliament, is not mentioned in the commission, having apparently been adopted on the analogy of the like title in the State. The chancellor was originally the keeper of the archbishop's or bishop's seals; but the office, as now understood, includes two other offices distinguished in the commission by the titles of vicar-general and official principal (*see* ECCLESIASTICAL JURISDICTION). The chancellor of a diocese must be distinguished from the chancellor of a cathedral, whose office is the same as that of the ancient *scholasticus* (*see* CATHEDRAL).

Academic, etc.—The chancellor of an order of knighthood discharges notarial duties and keeps the seal. The chancellor of a university is an official of mediaeval origin. The appointment was originally made by the popes, and the office from the first was one of great dignity and originally of great power. The chancellor was, as he remains, the head of the university; he had the general superintendence of its studies and of its discipline, could make and unmake laws, try and punish offences, appoint to professorial chairs and admit students to the various degrees. In England the chancellorship of the universities is conferred on noblemen or statesmen of distinction, whose principal function is to look after the general interests of the university, especially in its relations with the government. The chancellor is represented in the university by a vice-chancellor, who performs the administrative and judicial functions of the office. In the United States the heads of certain educational establishments have the title of chancellor. In Scotland, the foreman of a jury is called its chancellor. In the United States the chancellors are judges of the chancery courts of the states, *e.g.,* Delaware and New Jersey, where these courts are still maintained as distinct from the courts of common law. In other states, *e.g.,* New York since 1847, the title has been abolished, and there is no federal chancellor.

In diplomacy generally the chancellor of an embassy or legation is an official attached to the suite of an ambassador or minister. He performs the functions of a secretary, archivist, notary and the like, and is at the head of the chancery, or chancellery, of the mission. The functions of this office are the transcribing and registering of official despatches and other documents, and generally the transaction of all the minor business, *e.g.,* marriages, passports and the like, connected with the duties of a diplomatic agent towards his nationals in a foreign country.

France.—The country in which the office of chancellor followed most closely the same lines as in England is France. He had become a great officer under the Carolingians, and he grew still greater under the Capetian sovereigns. The great chancellor, *summus cancellarius* or *archi-cancellarius,* was a dignitary who had indeed little real power. The post was commonly filled by the archbishop of Reims, or the bishop of Paris. The *cancellarius,* who formed part of the royal court and administration, was officially known as the *sub-cancellarius* in relation to the *summus cancellarius,* but as *proto-cancellarius* in regard to his subordinate *cancellarii.* He was a very great officer, an ecclesiastic who was the chief of the king's chaplains or king's clerks, who administered all ecclesiastical affairs; he had judicial powers, and from the 12th century had the general control of foreign affairs. The chancellor in fact became so great that the Capetian kings, who did not forget the mayor of the palace, grew afraid of him. Few of the early ecclesiastical chancellors failed to come into collision with the king, or parted with him on good terms. Philip Augustus suspended the chancellorship throughout the whole of his reign, and appointed a keeper of the seals (*garde les sceaux*). The office was revived under Louis VIII., but the ecclesiastical chancellorship was finally suppressed in 1227. The kings of the 13th century employed only keepers of the seal. Under the reign of Philip IV. le Bel, lay chancellors were first appointed. From the reign of Charles V. to that of Louis XI. the French *chancelier* was elected by the royal council. In the 16th century he became irremovable, a distinction more honourable than effective, for though the king could not dismiss him from office he could, and on some occasions did, deprive him of the right to exercise his functions, and entrusted them to a keeper of the seal. The *chancelier* from the 13th century downwards was the head of the law, and performed the duties which are now entrusted to the minister of justice. His office was abolished by the Revolution. The smaller *chanceliers* of the provincial *parlements* and royal courts disappeared at the same time. But when Napoleon was organizing the empire he created an arch-chancellor, an office which was imitated rather from the *Erz-Kanzler* of the Holy Roman empire than from the old French *chancelier.* At the Restoration the office of chancellor of France was restored, the chancellor being president of the House of Peers, but it was finally abolished at the revolution of 1848. The administration of the Legion of Honour is presided over by a *grand chancelier,* who is a grand cross of the order, and who advises the head of the state in matters concerning the order. The title of *chancelier* continues also to be used in France for the large class of officials who discharge notarial duties in some public offices, in embassies and consulates. They draw up diplomas and prepare all formal documents, and have charge of the registration and preservation of the archives.

Spain.—In Spain the office of chancellor, *canciller,* was introduced by Alphonso VII. (1126–57), who adopted it from the court of his cousins of the Capetian dynasty of France. The *canciller* did not in Spain go beyond the king's notary. The chancellor of the privy seal, *canciller del sello de la puridad* (literally the secret seal), was the king's secretary, and sealed all papers other than diplomas and charters. The office was abolished in 1496, and its functions were transferred to the royal secretaries. The *cancelario* was the chancellor of a university. *The canciller* succeeded the *maesescuela* or *scholasticus* of a church or monastery. *Canciller mayor de Castilla* is an honorary title of the archbishops of Toledo. The *gran canciller de las Indias,* high chancellor of the Indies, held the seal used for the American dominions of Spain, and presided at the council in the absence of the president. The office disappeared with the loss of Spain's empire in America.

Italy, Germany, etc.—In central and northern Europe, and in Italy, the office had different fortunes. In southern Italy, where Naples and Sicily were feudally organized, the chancellors of the Norman kings, who followed Anglo-Norman precedents very closely, and, at least in Sicily, employed Englishmen, were such officers as were known in the West. The similarity is somewhat concealed by the fact that these sovereigns also adopted names and offices from the imperial court at Constantinople. Their chancellor was officially known as Protonotary and Logothete, and their example was followed by the German princes of the Hohenstaufen family, who acquired the kingdoms of Naples and Sicily. The papal or apostolic chancery is dealt with in the article on the Curia Romana (q.v.).

The title of arch-chancellor (*Erz-Kanzler*) was borne by three great ecclesiastical dignitaries of the Holy Roman empire. The archbishop of Mainz was arch-chancellor for Germany. The archbishop of Cologne held the dignity for Italy, and the archbishop of Trier for Gaul and the kingdom of Arles. The second and third of these dignities became purely formal with the decline of the empire in the 13th century. But the arch-chancellorship of Germany remained to some extent a reality till the empire was finally dissolved in 1806. The office continued to be attached to the archbishopric of Mainz, which was an electorate. Karl von Dalberg, the last holder of the office, and the first prince primate of the Confederation of the Rhine, continued to act in show at least as chancellor of that body, and was after a fashion the predecessor of the *Bundeskanzler,* or chancellor of the North German Confederation. The duties imposed on the imperial chancery by the very complicated constitution of the empire were, however, discharged by a vice-chancellor attached to the court of the emperor. The abbot of Fulda was chancellor to the empress.

The house of Austria in their hereditary dominions, and in those of their possessions which they treated as hereditary, even where the sovereignty was in theory elective, made a large and peculiar use of the title chancellor. The officers so called were of course distinct from the arch-chancellor and vice-chancellor of the empire, although the imperial crown became in practice hereditary in the house of Habsburg. In the family states their administration was, to use a phrase familiar to the French, "polysynodic." As it was when fully developed, and as it remained until the March revolution of 1848, it was conducted through boards presided over by a chancellor. There were three aulic chancellorships for the internal affairs of their dominions, "a united aulic chancellorship for all parts of the empire (*i.e.,* of Austria, not the Holy Roman) not belonging to Hungary or Transylvania, and a separate chancellorship for each of those last-mentioned provinces" (Hartig, *Genesis of the Revolution in Austria*). There were also a house, a court, and a state chancellor for the business of the imperial household and foreign affairs, who were not, however, the presidents of a board. These "aulic" (*i.e.,* court) officers were in fact secretaries of the sovereign, and administrative or political rather than judicial in character, though the boards over which they presided controlled judicial as well as administrative affairs. In the case of such statesmen as Kaunitz and Metternich, who were house, court and state chancellors as well as "united aulic" chancellors, the combination of offices made them in practice prime ministers, or rather lieutenants-general, of the sovereign.

In the modern German empire the *Reichskanzler* was the immediate successor of the *Bundeskanzler,* or chancellor of the North German Confederation (*Bund*). But the *Bundeskanzler,* who bore no sort of resemblance save in name to the *Erz-Kanzler* of the old empire, was in a position not perhaps actually like that of Prince Kaunitz, but capable of becoming much the same thing. When the German empire was established in 1871 Prince Bismarck, who was *Bundeskanzler* and became *Reichskanzler,* took care that his position should be as like as possible to that of Prince Kaunitz or Prince Metternich. The constitution of the German empire is separately dealt with, but it may be pointed out here that the *Reichskanzler* was the federal minister of the empire, the chief of the federal officials, and a great political officer, who directed the foreign affairs, and superintended the internal affairs, of the empire.

In these German states the title of chancellor is also given as in France to government and diplomatic officials who do notarial duties and have charge of archives. The title of chancellor has naturally been widely used in the German and Scandinavian States, and in Russia since the reign of Peter the Great. It has there, as elsewhere, wavered between being a political and a judicial office. Frederick the Great of Prussia created a *Gross-Kanzler* for judicial duties in 1746. But there was in Prussia a state chancellorship on the Austrian model. It was allowed to lapse on the death of Hardenberg in 1822. The Prussian chancellor after his time was one of the four court ministries (*Hofämter*) of the Prussian monarchy.

BIBLIOGRAPHY.—K. F. Stumpf, *Die Reichs Kanzler* (Innsbruck, 1865–73); P. Hinschius, *Kirchenrecht* (1869); Du Cange, *Glossarium*, *s.v.* "Cancellarius"; W. Stubbs, *Const. Hist. of England* (1874–78); G. Seeliger, *Erzkanzler und Reichskanzleien* (*ib.*, 1889); Rudolph Gneist, *Hist. of the English Constitution* (Eng. trans., 1891); A. Luchaire, *Manuel des institutions françaises* (1892); L. O. Pike, *Const. Hist. of the House of Lords* (1894); Sir R. J. Phillimore, *Eccles. Law* (1895); P. Pradier-Fodéré, *Cours de droit diplomatique*, ii. 542 (1899); Sir W. R. Anson, *The Law and Custom of the Constitution*, vol. ii. part i. (1907).

CHANCELLORSVILLE, a village of Spottsylvania county, Virginia, U.S.A., situated almost midway between Washington and Richmond. It was the central point of one of the greatest battles of the Civil War, fought on May 2 and 3, 1863, between the Union army of the Potomac under Maj.-gen. Hooker, and the Confederate army of Northern Virginia under Gen. Lee. (*See* AMERICAN CIVIL WAR, and WILDERNESS.) Gen. "Stonewall" Jackson was mortally wounded in this battle.

CHANCE-MEDLEY, an accident of a mixed character, an old term in English law for a form of homicide arising out of a sudden affray or quarrel. This term is not in use in the United States. Manslaughter in one of its various degrees would embrace such a homicide, under U.S. law.

CHANCERY. In English law, the court of the lord chancellor is called the court of chancery. It was consolidated in 1873, along with the other superior courts in the supreme court of judicature. Its origin is noticed in the article CHANCELLOR.

The jurisdiction of the court falls into three clearly marked divisions: a miscellaneous jurisdiction, a common law jurisdiction and, most important, jurisdiction in equity. Of the miscellaneous jurisdiction the most important surviving branches are the jurisdiction in bankruptcy and that in lunacy. Originally, however, the miscellaneous jurisdiction of the chancellor included such diverse matters as the power to punish the misdemeanours of sheriffs and the punishment of those receiving children into an order of friars without the consent of their parents. The common law jurisdiction was never very important: it included the power of holding pleas upon the writ of *scire facias* (*q.v.*) and the jurisdiction possessed by all the superior courts of trying personal actions brought for and against its own officers. Such jurisdiction had largely fallen into desuetude by the end of the 16th century.

The equitable jurisdiction of the court originated in the power which the chancellor assumed in the middle ages of modifying a strict and formal legal system on moral grounds. The distinction between law and the equity which gradually modifies it is one which is common to many legal systems. In England, because the remedies which the common law courts could give were early limited by the forms of writs available, men turned to the chancellor for equity and the two systems came to be administered by wholly independent tribunals whose decisions were frequently in conflict. (*See* EQUITY.) The early jurisdiction of the court of chancery was from its nature extremely vague. As late as the 17th century John Selden said of it: "Equity is a roguish thing. For law we have a measure ..... equity is according to the conscience of him that is Chancellor and as that is larger or narrower so is equity. Tis all one as if they should make the standard for the measure a chancellor's foot." In fact, however, by the beginning of the 17th century it is possible to discern certain general principles in the exercise of the court's jurisdiction. Thus, it had begun to give to the *cestui que* trust (*see* TRUST AND TRUSTEES) that protection against the legal owner of his property which enabled landowners to evade the technicalities of the feudal system, and it was using the injunction to restrain the immoral or fraudulent exercise of legal rights. The early 17th century was the principal turning point in the history of the court, for the common lawyers were seeking to prohibit the chancery from interfering with common law rights. James I resolved the conflict between the two jurisdictions in favour of chancery by ordering that "our Chancellor and Keeper of the Great Seal for the time being shall not hereinafter desist to give unto our subjects, upon their several complaints, now or hereafter to be made, such relief in equity (notwithstanding any proceedings at the common law against them) as shall stand with the merit and justice of their cause, and with the former ancient and continued practice and proceeding of our Chancery." From this time onward, although the conflict did not die down until the end of the century, the court gradually developed jurisdiction co-ordinate with that of the common law courts and on settled principles and, in the 18th and 19th centuries, it came to follow precedent as strictly as they. The principal distinction between the two systems was that whereas the rules of common law were supposed to have been established since time immemorial, those of equity could in almost every case be traced to the chancellor who invented them.

In the 19th century the jurisdiction of chancery, now clearly defined, was frequently classified by its relationship to the common law as exclusive, concurrent or auxiliary. Exclusive was its jurisdiction over the forms of property which it recognized, such as trusts and powers, the separate estate of married women and the mortgagor's equity of redemption, and in such matters as the administration of the estates of deceased persons, partnerships and the guardianship of infants. It had concurrent jurisdiction where it gave remedies such as specific performance of contracts and injunctions which the common law did not give. Its jurisdiction was said to be auxiliary where it supplemented the otherwise inadequate machinery of the courts by means of subpoena and discovery. (*See* PRACTICE AND PROCEDURE.)

The existence of two sets of tribunals of co-ordinate jurisdiction had manifest inconveniences and the delays and injustices which resulted from it had, by the early 19th century, become a public scandal. Various attempts, more or less successful, were made to remedy this during the century, and these culminated in the great Judicature act of 1873. Section 24 of this act (repealed and replaced by the Judicature act, 1925, section 37 [1]) enacted that in every civil cause or matter commenced in the high court of justice, law and equity should be administered by the high court of justice and the court of appeal respectively, according to the rules therein contained, which provided for giving effect in all cases to "equitable rights and other matters of equity." The 44th section of the act of 1925 declared the law to be administered in England on certain points, and ordained that "generally in all matters not hereinbefore particularly mentioned in which there is any conflict or variance between the rules of equity and the rules of common law with reference to the same matter, the rules of equity shall prevail." The 56th section specifically assigned certain matters to the chancery division, including those noticed above as having been within the peculiar jurisdiction of the old court of chancery.

The chancery division originally consisted of the lord chancellor as president and the master of the rolls and the vice-chancellors. The master of the rolls was also a member of the new court of appeal, but Sir George Jessel, who held office when the new system came into force, regularly sat as a judge of first instance until 1881, when, by an act of that year (s.2) the master of the rolls became a member of the court of appeal only. By the middle of the 20th century, the chancery division consisted of the lord chancellor and six puisne judges, who were divided into groups of three. To these groups were respectively assigned matters within the peculiar jurisdiction of the division.

In the United States chancery is generally used as a synonym of equity. Chancery courts are equity courts in a few jurisdictions where such courts are separately maintained. For the diplomatic sense of chancery (chancellery) *see* CHANCELLOR and DIPLOMATIC.

(W. P. G.)

CHAN CHAN or GRAN CHIMU, a ruined and deserted pre-Inca city on the coast of Peru, situated some 300 mi. north of Lima and approximately 2 mi. north of Trujillo, in the department of La Libertad. It was once the capital of a populous, powerful and relatively advanced civilization variously known as the Chimu, Yunga or Mochica, whose influence extended from the department of Lambeyeque southward to Ancón, not far from Lima.

The city itself covers a considerable area, and from a careful survey and estimate must have had a population of at least 250,000 at the height of its glory. It consists of a group of separate walled cities, each surrounded by massive walls from 30 to 40 ft. high, from 8 to 12 ft. in thickness at the base and from 1 to 3 ft. at the top; the walls, as well as the houses, so-called palaces, temples and other structures are constructed of adobe bricks, plastered over in most cases with a smooth coat of adobe. No stone and apparently little or no wood entered into the buildings.

Owing to a dry and comparatively rainless climate with no great extremes of temperature the ruins, which under other conditions would surely have disappeared, are in a remarkable state of preservation.

The Chimu.—Whence the population came no one can say. We do know, however, from skeletal remains that are found in great abundance in the burying-grounds about and in the ruins, that they were totally unlike any of the other pre-Columbian peoples of South America, the characteristic that distinguished them being that they were a broad-skulled or brachycephalic race while the Quichuas and Aymaras, Andean tribes who formed the Inca confederation, were respectively a mesaticephalic (or normal) and a dolichocephalic (or long-skulled) people. In this peculiarity the Chimu were more closely allied to the Mayas of the Yucatan peninsula, Southern Mexico, Guatemala and Honduras than any other people of the Western Hemisphere. This lends colour to the theory that they were an off-shoot of the Mayas that broke away from the original stock in remote times and made their way to the coast of Peru where they established and built up the civilization of which we are here treating.

When they settled on these shores is equally hazy. Certain it is that if they drifted here by sea they must have come in comparatively small numbers. On the other hand, if they migrated by land—which seems less probable—they must, at the rate primitive people and people without any fixed objective migrate, have been centuries in building up the civilization of which we find remains to-day, so that it is quite probable that their advent on the coast of Peru may have been about the time of the beginning of the Christian era.

We know their fate somewhat more definitely from legends and accounts related by the Incas upon the arrival of the Spaniards. From these we learn that for a century, more or less, a bitter war was waged between the Inca confederation or Andean tribes and the coastal peoples, the Chimu in the north and the Nazca in the south. Many and fierce are the struggles recorded and the Incas eventually defeated the coastal tribes at their great fortress of Paramonga, near Supe, not far from Huacho on the Peruvian coast north of Lima. This fortress remains to this day and is in a remarkable state of preservation. Having been defeated at Paramonga the Chimu retired behind the walls of their capital, Chan Chan, and were here starved into submission by the besieging Incas. Whether the Chimu were wholly exterminated by their enemies or whether, as was the Inca custom with conquered tribes, they were broken up and distributed in small numbers throughout the empire, we do not know. Certain it is, however, that when the Spaniards came there were no evident remains of the Chimu save their ruined and deserted cities, remains of their irrigation systems and other like traces. This extermination of the coastal peoples has been reckoned to have taken place some 130 or 140 years before the coming of the Spaniards, which would put it in the neighbourhood of the year A.D. 1400.

Remains.—From a study of the ruins we know that Chan Chan was the seat of a great empire whose extent was the entire coast from Lambeyeque on the north to about Ancón on the south. We also know that these were a people who lived mainly by agricultural pursuits. In the vicinity of Chan Chan itself, in the valley of the Chicama, Moche, Viru and other Andean streams, there are evidences of truly remarkable systems of irrigation and certain signs that agriculture was carried on to a considerably greater extent in those ancient times than it is to-day. Fishing also formed an important part of their life and conventionalized figures of fishes and maritime birds form the principal motifs in their mural and other decorations.

That they were highly developed in the arts is likewise patent. They knew the art of mining, smelting and working such metals as gold, silver and copper, though none of the other metals have been found in the ruins. Metal utensils, ornaments and other objects are still found in and about Chan Chan, as are also the remains of an ancient smelter, with considerable quantities of slag. The Chimu were also expert potters; examples of their work are to be found in many museums. Strange to note, there are three known strata of pottery, that in the lowest being of the finest quality, while the top stratum is the poorest, indicating that the art degenerated. From their pottery much of their life and habits may be reconstructed. Wood, as has been noted, appears to play very little part in their arts. This is probably because of the indigenous trees, the willow was too soft and perishable for practical use and the algarroba too hard to be worked. Hence wood was used but little, if at all, except in the making of idols, musical instruments and small objects.

Save for a few small settlements, notably at Huanchaco and at Moche, in the vicinity of Trujillo, where the inhabitants show traces of brachycephalism, the ruined cities, irrigation works, fortresses and the like, as well as all traces of these peoples, have disappeared. (O. Ho.)

CHANCRE is a term formerly used loosely, to designate any sore or ulcer, especially one of a corroding nature or venereal origin. It is now applied almost exclusively to the primary lesion of syphilis, which used to be called a hard, indurated or Hunterian chancre. It appears at the site of inoculation in from one to seven weeks after exposure, and is most commonly found on the external genitals, but sometimes on the lip, tongue and other parts. A small, hard, translucent swelling appears at the infected spot, becomes gradually larger (up to one inch), and often breaks in the centre leaving a shallow ulcer. This lesion is the chancre and represents the first reaction of body tissues to the causative agent, *Treponema pallidum*. Diagnosis is established by finding the organism in scrapings from the ulcer. (*See* VENEREAL DISEASES.)

CHANDA. The southernmost District of the Central Provinces of British India.

Chanda Town is the old capital of an ancient Gond dynasty, situated near the confluence of the Erai and Wardha rivers. It once had a much larger population for there are now waste and cultivated fields inside the stone walls, which have a circumference of five and a half miles, whilst the modern suburbs of the town have grown up outside the city walls, and in the jungles which hem in the city on two sides there are many traces of old habitations. The town is noted for its silk woven fabrics, ornamental slippers and other minor industries of the same kind. Outside one of the gates is held an annual fair attended by 100,000 people. After a great decline from its ancient status as a Gond capital, it has begun to revive with the construction of roads and railway communications, and its population was (1941) 35,730 as compared with 16,000 in 1872.

District of Chanda.—The District of Chanda is one of the largest districts in the Central Provinces, having an area of 9,205 sq.mi., but the twenty Zamindari estates which it contains account for 4,000 sq.mi. of wild and thinly populated country, while government forest reserves cover no less than 2,700 sq.mi., and include valuable teak and other timber, and large bamboo jungles. Coal of a poor quality is found in the extreme west at Ballarpur and Ghugus, while iron ore of high grade is found in the eastern part of the District.

Except in the north-west and on the borders of the Wardha and Nagpur Districts, where cotton and wheat are both grown and there are large areas under juar (sorghum), rice and the small millets are the principal crops. Numbers of irrigation tanks have been constructed by the people to water rice and sugar-cane, to which the Government has added a number of storage reservoirs of some magnitude.

Many useful roads have been made since the great famines, and Chanda town is now connected with Wardha on the G.I.P. railway via Warora (where the colliery is now worked out), and by narrow gauge lines with Nagpur and Gondia in the Bhandara district.

It is a most picturesque part of the country, with varied scenery, wooded hills and interesting archaeological remains, old temples and forts, notably at Chanda itself, Bhandak, Markandi and Wairagarh, but the climate is unpleasantly hot, the forests malarious, and the people unprogressive. Several languages are spoken.

The Marathi of the north-west gives way to Telugu in the south and to Hindi (Chhattisgarhi) in the north-east. In all the wilder tracts aboriginal races predominate, and Gondi and other tribal dialects are common, as in the neighbouring Bastar state. The total population of the district in 1941 was 873,284. In the famine decade (1891–1901) there was a sharp decrease, and there was also a setback in population in the decade 1911–21 as a result of an epidemic of influenza.

CHANDAUSI, a town of India in the Moradabad district of Uttar Pradesh; an important junction (for Aligarh) on the Oudh and Rohilkand railway. Pop. (1941) 28,763. It exports cotton, hemp, sugar and stone.

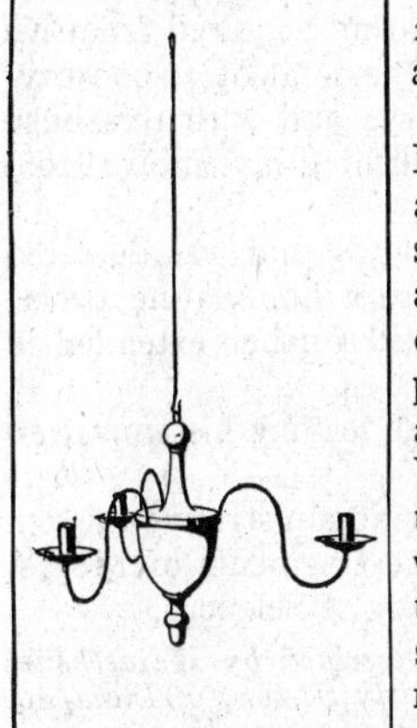

BY COURTESY OF THE PENNSYLVANIA MUSEUM

AMERICAN BRASS CHANDELIER, 18TH CENTURY

CHAND BARDAI (*c.* A.D. 1200), Hindu poet, a native of Lahore, who lived at the court of Prithiraj, the last Hindu sovereign of Delhi. His *Prithiraj Rasau,* a poem of some 100,000 stanzas, chronicling his master's deeds and the contemporary history of his part of India, is valuable as the earliest monument of the Western Hindi language, and the first of the long series of bardic chronicles for which Rajputana is celebrated. It is written in ballad form, and portions of it are still sung by itinerant bards throughout north-western India and Rajputana.

See J. Tod, *Annals and Antiquities of Rajast'han* (2 vols., 1829–1832).

CHANDELIER, a frame of metal, wood, crystal, glass or china, suspended from the roof or ceiling for the purpose of holding lights. The word is French, but the appliance has lost its original significance of a candle-holder, the chandelier being now chiefly used for gas and electric lighting. Clusters of hanging lights were in use as early as the 14th century, and appear originally to have been almost invariably of wood. They were, however, so speedily ruined by grease that metal was gradually substituted, and fine and comparatively early examples in beaten iron, brass, copper and even silver are still extant. Throughout the 17th century the hanging candle-holder of brass or bronze was common throughout northern Europe, as innumerable pictures and engravings testify. In the great periods of the art of decoration in France many magnificent chandeliers were made by Boulle, and at a later date by Gouthière and Thomire and others among the extraordinarily clever *fondeurs-ciseleurs* of the second half of the 18th century. The chandelier in rock crystal and its imitations had come in at least a hundred years before their day, and continued in favour to the middle of the 19th century, or even somewhat later. It reached at last the most extreme elaboration of banality, with ropes of pendants and hanging faceted drops often called lustres. When many lights were burning in one of these chandeliers an effect of splendour was produced that was not out of place in a ballroom, but the ordinary household varieties were extremely ugly and inartistic. The more purely domestic chandelier usually carries from two to six lights. The present use of electricity and the modern ideas of interior lighting have pushed into the background the elaborate specimens of the past few centuries and substituted the simpler designs with smaller clusters of lights.

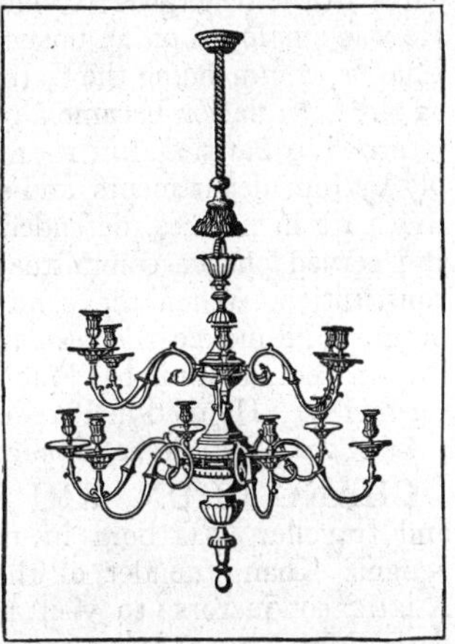

BY COURTESY OF THE METROPOLITAN MUSEUM OF ART

ENGLISH CHANDELIER BY ADAMS, ILLUSTRATIVE OF THE MORE ELABORATE MODELS OF THE LATTER PART OF THE 18TH CENTURY

(*See* also LIGHTING AND ARTIFICIAL ILLUMINATION; INTERIOR DECORATION.)

CHANDERNAGORE or **CHANDARNAGAR,** a former French settlement in India, with a small adjoining territory, situated on the right bank of the river Hugli, 20m. above Calcutta. Area 3 sq.mi.; pop. (1941) 38,284. Chandernagore has played an important part in the European history of Bengal. It became a permanent French settlement in 1688, but did not rise to any importance till the time of Dupleix, during whose administration the town was transformed and became the focus for a considerable maritime trade.

In 1757 Chandernagore was bombarded by an English fleet under Admiral Watson and captured. On peace being established the town was restored to the French in 1763.

When hostilities afterward broke out in 1794, the English again took possession of the town and held it till 1816, when it was a second time given up to the French. Following a plebescite in 1949 Chandernagore was incorporated into India (1950) and became part of Hooghly district, West Bengal (1954).

BY COURTESY OF THE METROPOLITAN MUSEUM OF ART

MODERN ELECTRIC CHANDELIER WITH FROSTED GLOBES AND SILVERED METAL

CHANDLER, RICHARD (1738–1810), British antiquary, was born at Elson in Hampshire. In 1759 he published fragments from the Greek minor poets, with notes (*Elegiaca Graeca*); and in 1763 a fine edition of the Arundelian marbles, *Marmora Oxoniensia,* with a Latin translation, and suggestions for supplying the lacunae. He was sent by the Dilettanti Society with Revett, an architect, and Pars, a painter, to explore the antiquities of Ionia and Greece (1763–66); and the result of their work was the two magnificent folios of Ionian antiquities published in 1769. Other works by Chandler were *Inscriptiones Antiquae pleraeque nondum editae* (1774); *Travels in Asia Minor* (1775); *Travels in Greece* (1776); *History of Ilium* (1803); in which he asserted the accuracy of Homer's geography. His *Life of Bishop Waynflete,* lord high chancellor to Henry VI., appeared in 1811.

A complete edition (with notes by Revett) of the *Travels in Asia Minor and Greece* was published by R. Churton (1825), with an "Account of the Author."

CHANDLER, SAMUEL (1693–1766), English Nonconformist divine, was born in 1693 at Hungerford, Berkshire. He took a leading part in the deist controversies of the time, and discussed with some of the bishops the possibility of an act of comprehension. From 1716–26 he preached at Peckham, and for 40 years he was pastor of a meeting-house in Old Jewry. He died on May 8, 1766, leaving four vols. of sermons (1768), and a paraphrase of the Epistles to the Galatians and Ephesians (1777), several works on the evidence of Christianity, and various pamphlets against Roman Catholicism.

CHANDLER, ZACHARIAH (1813–1879), American politician, was born at Bedford, N.H., on Dec. 10, 1813. In 1833 he removed to Detroit, Mich., where he became a prosperous dry-goods merchant. He took a prominent part as a Whig in politics, and, impelled by his strong anti-slavery views, actively furthered the work of the "underground railroad," of which Detroit was one of the principal "transfer" points. He was one of the organizers in Michigan of the Republican Party, and in 1857 succeeded Lewis Cass in the U.S. Senate, serving until 1875. Throughout the Civil War he allied himself with the most radical of the Republican faction in opposition to President Lincoln's policy, and subsequently became one of the bitterest opponents of President Johnson's plan of reconstruction. From Oct. 1875, to March 1877, he was secretary of the interior in the cabinet of President Grant. In Feb. 1879, he was re-elected to the Senate.

He died at Chicago, Ill., on Nov. 1, 1879. By his extraordinary force of character he exercised a wide personal influence during his lifetime, but failed to stamp his personality upon any measure or policy of lasting importance.

CHANDOS, BARONS AND DUKES OF. The English title of Chandos began as a barony in 1554, and was continued in the family of Brydges (becoming a dukedom in 1719) till 1789. In 1822 the dukedom was revived in connection with that of Buckingham.

JOHN BRYDGES, 1st Baron Chandos (*c.* 1490–1557), a son of Sir Giles Brydges, or Bruges (d. 1511), was a prominent figure at the English court during the reigns of Henry VIII., Edward VI. and Mary. He took part in suppressing the rebellion of Sir Thomas Wyat in 1554, and as lieutenant of the Tower of London during the earlier part of Mary's reign, had the custody, not only of Lady Jane Grey and of Wyat, but for a short time of the princess Elizabeth. He was created Baron Chandos of Sudeley in 1554, one of his ancestors, Alice, being a grand-daughter of Sir Thomas Chandos (d. 1375), and he died in March 1557. The three succeeding barons, direct descendants of the 1st baron, were all members of parliament and persons of some importance. Grey, 5th Baron Chandos (*c.* 1580–1621), lord-lieutenant of Gloucestershire, was called the "king of the Cotswolds," owing to his generosity and his magnificent style of living at his residence, Sudeley Castle. His elder son George, 6th Baron Chandos (1620–1655), was a supporter of Charles I. during his struggle with Parliament. After the death of his brother William in 1676 the barony came to a kinsman, Sir James Brydges, Bart. (1642–1714), who was English ambassador to Constantinople from 1680–1685.

JAMES BRYDGES, 1st duke of Chandos (1673–1744), son and heir of the last-named, had been member of parliament for Hereford from 1698 to 1714, and, three days after his father's death, was created Viscount Wilton and earl of Carnarvon. For eight years, from 1705 to 1713, during the War of the Spanish Succession, he was paymaster-general of the forces abroad, and in this capacity he amassed great wealth. In 1719 he was created marquess of Carnarvon and duke of Chandos. The duke is chiefly remembered on account of his connection with Handel and with Pope. He built a magnificent house at Canons near Edgware in Middlesex. For over two years Handel, employed by Chandos, lived at Canons, where he composed his oratorio *Esther*. Pope, who in his *Moral Essays (Epistle to the Earl of Burlington)* doubtless described Canons under the guise of "Timon's Villa," referred to the duke in the line, "Thus gracious Chandos is belov'd at sight"; but Swift, less complimentary, called him "a great complier with every court." After his death on Aug. 9, 1744, Canons was pulled down. He was succeeded by his son Henry, 2nd duke (1708–1771), and grandson James, 3rd duke (1731–1789). The third duke's only daughter, Anna Elizabeth, who became Baroness Kinloss on her father's death, was married in 1796 to Richard Grenville, afterwards marquess of Buckingham; and in 1822 this nobleman was created duke of Buckingham and Chandos (*see* BUCKINGHAM, EARLS, MARQUESSES AND DUKES OF).

See G. E. C(okayne), *Complete Peerage* (1887–98); and J. R. Robinson, *The Princely Chandos, i.e.,* the 1st duke (1893).

CHANDOS, SIR JOHN (d. 1370), English soldier, fought at the siege of Cambrai (1337), at Crécy in 1346, and at Poitiers, where he saved the life of the Black Prince. For these services Edward III. gave him the lands of the viscount of Saint Sauveur in Cotentin, and appointed him lieutenant in France, and vice-chamberlain of the royal household in 1360. In 1362 he was made constable of Guienne, and defeated Charles de Blois at Auray in 1364. Chandos accompanied the Black Prince on his expedition in 1367, to restore Pedro the Cruel to the throne of Castile, and won the victory of Navaret over Bertrand du Guesclin. Appointed seneschal of Poitou in 1369, he was mortally wounded in an encounter with the French at the bridge of Lussac near Poitiers, and died on the day after the battle, Jan. 1, 1370.

CHANDRAGUPTA MAURYA (reigned 321–296 B.C.), known to the Greeks as Sandracottus, founder of the Maurya empire and first paramount ruler of India, was the son of a king of Magadha by a woman of humble origin, whose caste he took and whose name, Mura, is said to have been the origin of that of Maurya assumed by his dynasty. As a youth he was driven into exile by his kinsman, the reigning king of Magadha. In the course of his wanderings he met Alexander the Great, and, according to Plutarch (*Alexander,* cap. 62), encouraged him to invade the Ganges kingdom. On the death of Alexander he attacked the Macedonian garrisons and conquered the Punjab. He next attacked Magadha, dethroned and slew the king, and established himself on the throne (321). The great army acquired from his predecessor he increased until it reached the total of 30,000 cavalry, 9,000 elephants and 600,000 infantry; and with this huge force he overran all northern India, establishing his empire from the Arabian sea to the Bay of Bengal.

Seleucus I Nicator crossed the Indus in 305, but was defeated by Chandragupta and forced eventually to a humiliating peace, by which the empire of the latter was still further extended in the north.

About six years later Chandragupta died, leaving his empire to his son Bindusura.

An excellent account of the court and administrative system of Chandragupta has been preserved in the fragments of Megasthenes, who came to Pataliputra as the envoy of Seleucus.

See J. W. MacCrindle, *Ancient India as Described by Megasthenes and Arrian* (Calcutta, 1877); V. A. Smith, *Early History of India,* ed. S. M. Edwardes (Oxford, 1924); also the article INDIA: *History.*

CHANGARNIER, NICOLAS ANNE THÉODULE (1793–1877), French general, was born at Autun on April 26, 1793. Educated at St. Cyr, he served for a short time in the bodyguard of Louis XVIII., and entered the line as a lieutenant in January 1815. In 1830 he entered the Royal Guard and was sent to Algeria, where he served with great distinction until 1848, and had just succeeded Gen. Cavaignac as governor of the colony when he was recalled to command the National Guard. An avowed enemy of republican institutions, he at first upheld the power of the president; but in January 1851 he opposed Louis Napoleon's policy, was deprived of his double command, and at the *coup d'état* in December was arrested and sent to Mazas until his banishment from France by the decree of Jan. 9, 1852. He returned to France after the general amnesty. In 1870 he was present with the headquarters, and afterwards with Bazaine in Metz. He was employed on an unsuccessful mission to Prince Frederick Charles, commanding the German army which besieged Metz, and on the capitulation became a prisoner of war. At the armistice he returned to Paris, and in 1871 was elected to the National Assembly by four departments, and sat for the Somme. He took an active part in politics, defended the conduct of Marshal Bazaine, and served on the committee which elaborated the monarchical constitution. When the comte de Chambord refused the compromise, he moved the resolution to extend the executive power for ten years to Marshal MacMahon. He was elected a life senator in 1875. He died in Paris on Feb. 14, 1877.

See Comte d'Antioche, *Changarnier* (1891).

CHANG CHUN, KIU (1148–1227), Chinese Taoist sage and traveller, was born in 1148. In 1219 he was invited by Jenghiz Khan, founder of the Mongol empire and greatest of Asiatic conquerors, to visit him. Jenghiz' letter of invitation, dated May 15, 1219 (by present reckoning), has been preserved, and is among the curiosities of history; here the terrible warrior appears as a meek disciple of wisdom, modest and simple, almost Socratic in his self-examination, alive to many of the deepest truths of life and government. Chang Chun obeyed this summons; and leaving his home in Shantung (Feb. 1220), journeyed first to Peking. Learning that Jenghiz had gone far west upon fresh conquests, the sage stayed the winter in Peking. In February 1221 he started again and crossed eastern Mongolia to the camp of Jenghiz' brother Ujughen, near Lake Bör or Buyur in the upper basin of the Kerulun-Amur. Thence he travelled south-westward up the Kerulun, crossed the Karakorum region in north-central Mongolia, and so came to the Chinese Altai, probably passing near the present Uliassutai. After traversing the Altai he visited Bishbalig (modern Urumtsi), and moved along the north side of the Tian Shan range to lake Sairam, Almalig (or Kulja), and the rich valley of the Ili. We then trace him to the Chu, over this river to Talas and the Tashkent region, and over the Jaxartes (or Syr Daria) to Samarkand, where he halted for some months. Finally, through the "Iron Gates" of Termit, over the Oxus, and by way of Balkh and northern Afghanistan, Chang Chun reached Jenghiz' camp near the Hindu Kush. Returning home he followed much the same course as on his outward route: certain deviations, however, occur, such as a visit to Kuku Khoto. He was back in Peking by the end of January 1224. From the narrative of his expedition (the *Si yu ki,* written by his pupil and companion Li Chi Ch'ang) we derive some of the most faithful and vivid pictures ever drawn of nature and man between the Great Wall of China and Kabul, between the Aral and the Yellow sea. We may particularly notice the sketches of the Mongols, and of the people of Samarkand and its neighbourhood; the account of the fertility and products of the latter region, as of the Ili valley, at or near Almalig-Kulja; and the description of various great mountain ranges, peaks and defiles, such as the Chinese Altai, the Tian Shan, Mt. Bogdo-ola (?) and the Iron Gates of Termit. There is, moreover, a noteworthy reference to a land apparently identical with the uppermost valley of the Yenisei. After his return Chang Chun lived at Peking till his death on July 23, 1227. By order of Jenghiz some of the former imperial garden-grounds were made over to him for the foundation of a Taoist monastery.

BIBLIOGRAPHY.—*See* E. Bretschneider, *Mediaeval Researches from Eastern Asiatic Sources,* vol. i, pp. 35–108, where a complete translation of *Si yu Ki: Travels to the West of K'iu Ch'ang Ch'un* is given, with a valuable commentary; C. R. Beazley, *Dawn of Modern Geography,* iii, 539. (C. R. B.)

CHANGE, the substitution of one thing for another, hence any alteration or variation, so applied to the moon's passing from one phase to another. The use of the word for a place of commercial business has usually been taken to be a shortened form of "exchange" (*see* EXCHANGE, FOREIGN). "Change" is particularly used of coins of lower denomination given in substitution for those of larger denomination or for a note, cheque, etc., and also for the balance of a sum paid larger than that which is due. A further application is that in bell ringing, of the variations in order in which a peal of bells may be rung (*see* BELL).

CHANGELING, the term used of a child substituted or changed for another. It was formerly believed that infants were sometimes stolen from their cradles by the fairies before christening, so that in the highlands of Scotland babies were strictly watched till then. Any specially peevish or weakly baby was regarded as a changeling. The belief is referred to by William Shakespeare, Edmund Spenser and other authors.

See Pennant, *Tour in Scotland,* p. 257 (1796); W. Wirt Sikes, *British Goblins* (1880).

CHANGE OF LIFE. The period of life occurring naturally in women when the reproduction function ceases. It occurs artificially in women when the ovaries are removed.

Analogous changes occur in men at a later period in life also associated with alterations in reproductive capacity. (*See* MENOPAUSE; CLIMACTERIC.)

CHANGOAN, a tribe or small group of tribes of South American Indians, forming an independent linguistic stock. The Changos occupied the arid coast of the desert of Atacama in northern Chile. They are an almost dwarfish fisherfolk of very simple culture, and are now nearly extinct, except in the vicinity of Cobija. The Changos depended largely on shellfish for food. They wore little clothing, and had huts of poles and thatch. Their dead were buried at length instead of flexed.

See E. Boman, *Antiquités de la Région Andéenne de la République Argentine et du Désert d'Atacama* (Paris, 1908).

CHANGRA or CANKIRI (anc. *Gangra;* called also till the time of Caracalla, *Germanicopolis,* after the emperor Claudius), the chief town of a vilayet of the same name in Turkey, situated in a rich, well-watered valley; altitude 2,500 ft. The ground is impregnated with salt and the town is unhealthful. Pop. (1950) 14,161. Gangra, the capital of the Paphlagonian kingdom of Deiotarus Philadelphus, son of Castor, was taken into the Roman province of Galatia on his death in 6–5 B.C. The earlier town was built on the hill behind the modern city, on which are the ruins of a late fortress; while the Roman city occupied the site of the modern. In Christian times Gangra was the metropolitan see of Paphlagonia.

Synod of Gangra.—Conjectures as to the date of this synod vary from 341 to 376. The synodal letter states that 21 bishops assembled to take action concerning Eustathius (of Sebaste?) and his followers, who contemned marriage, disparaged the offices of the church, held conventicles of their own, wore a peculiar dress, denounced riches, and affected especial sanctity. The synod condemned the Eustathian practices. The 20 canons of Gangra were declared oecumenical by the Council of Chalcedon, 451.

See Mansi ii, pp. 1095–1122; Hardouin i, pp. 530–540; Hefele, 2nd ed., i, pp. 777 *sqq.* (Eng. trans., ii, pp. 325 *sqq.*).

CHANG TSO-LIN (1873–1928), Chinese military leader, born in the province of Fengtien. Of humble origin and without education, he was successively a swineherd, a menial in the Catholic mission at Newchwang and a labourer on the Peking-Mukden railway. Later he abandoned regular employment and rose to prominence in 1904 as a leader of *Hunghutse,* or Manchurian brigands, when he and his band became irregular allies of Japan during the Russo-Japanese War. After the Treaty of Portsmouth, under Japanese advice, he submitted to the Chinese government, and he and his following were incorporated in the Chinese army. He received quick promotion, and attained command of a division. In 1913 he was appointed *Tutuh,* later *Tuchun* (both terms denoting military governor) of Fengtien.

Chang Tso-lin faithfully served the young republic of China, and opposed both Yuan Shih-k'ai's monarchical aspirations in 1916 and Chang Hsün's attempted restoration of the imperial dynasty in 1917. In 1918 he was appointed inspector-general of the three eastern provinces, *i.e.,* of Manchuria, and, while civil government slowly weakened, his military control became absolute. He adopted the course, unusual in China, of punctually paying, feeding and disciplining his troops, and by this means he became a dominant factor in the unstable politics of the country. In civil life his activities were boundless: mining, farming, stock breeding, banking, railway construction, in these and many other forms of industrial enterprise, his hand was felt.

During the concluding 12 years of his life, while maintaining autocratic control of Manchuria, he made four descents upon Peking, actuated on each occasion by the desire to set up a stable form of government for the country. In 1920, when, during the halting and incapable presidency of Hsu Shih-chang, the government fell under the control of the reactionary militarists known as the Anfu party, he drove their leaders into retirement, and, in co-operation with Ts'ao Kun, the *Tuchun* of Chihli, made an attempt to form an administration. Their efforts were fruitless, and in 1921 he again came to Peking and installed a cabinet under Liang Shih-yi. Upon this occasion he was defeated by General Wu Pei-fu and driven back to Manchuria, whereupon he declared the independence of the three eastern provinces. His third incursion took place in 1924, when large forces under Wu Pei-fu assembled near the Great Wall to repel the Manchurian invasion. Owing to the treacherous defection of Fêng Yu-hsiang, who withdrew to Peking and "declared for peace," Wu Pei-fu's forces collapsed, and Chang's army pressed forward, eventually occupying Shantung, Anhwei and Kiang-su. In the latter part of this year he was occupied in suppressing the revolt of one of his lieutenants, by name Kuo Sung-ling, whom he defeated outside Mukden and executed. His final coming to Peking was in Dec. 1926, when he once more announced his intention to reorganize the government. In June 1927, he formed a cabinet consisting entirely of his own adherents, with Pan Fu as premier, he himself, under the title of generalissimo, becoming president. He watched from Peking the victorious Southern Nationalist army reach the Yangtze, and their further advance in 1928 to Peking. His troops, after some show of defending the capital, received orders to stop further opposition, and Chang himself left for Mukden by train on June 3. Before he reached his destination the train was bombed and he succumbed to injuries received.

Soft-voiced and of delicate constitution, suave yet resolute, Chang Tso-lin would have been an admirable viceroy under the

Empress Dowager's régime. It was the only system of government he understood, and his failure to bring about union and a stable government is evidence of how far removed he was *au fond* from realizing the strides which the country had made in acquiring race-consciousness and a political sense. His administrative achievements in Manchuria, and his friendliness towards foreigners, are among his claims to be styled a Chinese patriot.

(W. E. L.)

CHANNEL FERRY, the first type of cross-channel ferry between England and France was designed to meet the urgent need to supply the British armies in France and Belgium during World War I. An inland water transport section of the royal engineers was formed in 1914 to make use of the waterways behind the lines and a similar organization (later known as the Directorate of Inland Waterways and Docks, R.E.) was set up in England. A cross-channel barge route was started from Richborough, in Kent, to Calais, where the barges continued up the canals to Vendroux, Audruicq, Zeneghem and other points. The 255 steel barges so employed, each carrying about 200 tons of stores, ammunition, etc., were towed across the chanel by tugs, of which 67 were available, and provided a reliable service; no barge was ever reported lost on the channel crossing.

However, this method did not suffice for all needs and was, from 1917 to 1918, supplemented by three specially built train ferries which sailed from Richborough to Calais and Dunkirk, and from Southampton to Dieppe. Railway vehicles were propelled into the ferry at the stern, the two entry tracks spreading into four tracks on the deck of the vessel itself; the capacity in terms of four-wheeled freight cars was 54 per ferry. Rail-mounted guns and locomotives could be carried on the two centre tracks. About 1,000 locomotives were thus dispatched from Richborough to Audruicq shops, almost ready for instant service.

Nearly all these locomotives were returned to England in 1919 by these same train ferries, together with passenger coaches which had been employed on ambulance trains or leave and demobilization trains in France, Belgium, Germany and Italy. In 1919 the train ferries were adjusted to take motor vehicles instead of freight cars, if required.

At the ports, vehicles were loaded or unloaded by means of movable aprons, which could be raised or lowered to overcome small tidal differences in level. Because of the range of channel tides, amounting to 25 ft., the aprons at Calais and Dunkirk had to be within enclosed water areas, the levels being protected by locks.

After World War I the ferry services were discontinued but, after a few special voyages carrying British-built rolling stock for export to the continent, they were acquired by Great Eastern Train Ferries, Ltd., and placed in service between Harwich and Zeebrugge, where suitable aprons (in effect, hinged lifting bridges) were constructed for loading and unloading purposes. The tidal range at Harwich is only 12½ ft. and, therefore, the necessity of passing through locks was obviated at that port. This service was inaugurated in April 1924 and required the close co-operation of the London and North Eastern railway. The service acquired traffic in vegetables, cheese, eggs, fruit, machinery, silk and rolling stock.

In conjunction with Great Eastern Train Ferries was the Anglo-Belge Ferry Boat company, which owned many of the freight cars employed on the train ferry service. Later the three former wartime train ferries, operating between Harwich and Zeebrugge, became part of the London and North Eastern railway fleet.

Further train ferry developments across the channel were delayed by the possible building of a channel tunnel, but that project was turned down by the British government in 1930.

The Harwich-Zeebrugge freight service permitted traffic to move without transhipment between all parts of England, Scotland and Wales and any station served by the standard gauge railways of continental Europe, stretching from Narvik to Sicily and from the Spanish frontier to Istanbul. Its success led the Southern railway to start in Oct. 1936, in conjunction with the then Nord railway of France, a train ferry service from Dover to Dunkirk. Three vessels, with a gross tonnage of 2,989 each, were specially built in Great Britain, the "Twickenham Ferry," the "Hampton Ferry," and the "Shepperton Ferry"; they were designed to carry passenger coaches and sleeping cars as well as freight cars across the English channel.

Difficulties were experienced in the construction of the train ferry dock at Dover, because of faults in the chalk formation, but on completion a night ferry service for passengers was started between London (Victoria) and Paris (Nord), as well as other services for freight traffic.

As a consequence of World War II, the London and North Eastern railway train ferry fleet was reduced, but the two fleets, Harwich-Zeebrugge and Dover-Dunkirk, received new vessels in replacement. Though subject to restrictions on international trade, traffic tended to increase after World War II and the night ferry passenger service between London and Paris proved exceedingly popular. The Harwich route continued to cater for freight traffic only.

Train ferry services occur other than across the English channel and the North sea. One of the most famous examples is the train ferry service across the Great Belt, operated by the Danish State railways. This carries diesel trains, sleeping cars and passenger coaches on the Stockholm-Paris and other services, while jointly with the Swedish State railways a route is operated between Malmö and Copenhagen. Before World War II there was a joint German-Swedish service between Sassnitz and Trelleborg, while a Danish service ran between Gjedser and Warnemunde, but these routes were diverted after 1946. Another European instance is the train ferry operated by the Italian State railways from the toe of Italy to Sicily, on which fine motor vessels were placed in service after 1946.

Japanese National railways have long operated some train ferry routes between the several islands. The Canadian National railways operate a train ferry service to Prince Edward Island. Others occur on Lake Michigan, where freight cars are carried by train ferries of the Grand Trunk Western (Canadian National railways) and of the Pere Marquette (Chesapeake & Ohio railway) from ports in Michigan, such as Grand Haven and Ludington, to Milwaukee, Manitowoc and Kewaunee in Wisconsin.

Train ferries ply between Cuba and certain east coast and gulf ports in the United States and railway equipment is ferried across such great harbours as San Francisco and New York.

(C. E. R. S.)

CHANNEL ISLANDS (French *Iles Normandes*), an archipelago in the English channel, the only part of the ancient duchy of Normandy still attached to the English crown. It lies from 50 to 100 mi. south of Weymouth in the bay formed by the west coast of Normandy and the north coast of Brittany. There are four principal islands: Jersey, 44⅞ sq.mi., pop. (1951 census) 57,296; Guernsey, 24½ sq.mi., pop. 43,547; Alderney, 3 sq.mi., pop. 1,321; and Sark, 2 sq.mi., pop. 563. St. Helier is the chief town of Jersey, St. Peter Port of Guernsey and St. Anne of Alderney. Planes fly regularly from London, Southampton, Bristol and Cardiff to Guernsey and Jersey; ships sail daily from Weymouth or Southampton. Jersey is in regular communication by air and sea with Guernsey, Dinard and St. Malo; Guernsey by air and sea with Jersey and Alderney, by air with Dinard and by sea with Sark.

The four main islands, JERSEY, GUERNSEY, ALDERNEY and SARK are each described in separate articles.

Lesser Islands.—Besides the main islands there are innumerable islets in the group. To the north lie the Casquets, where in 1744 1,100 men perished when H.M.S. "Victory" was wrecked, and where many lives were lost in 1899 when the mail boat "Stella" went down. The lighthouse keepers are the only inhabitants.

Ortac and Burhou are uninhabited; a large colony of gannets has taken possession of the former.

Lihou (38 ac.), off the west coast of Guernsey, was the site of the once famous church of Notre Dame de Lihou, served by the monks of Mont St. Michel. This was so sacred a spot that, when Peter Heylyn wrote 100 years after the Reformation, passing fishermen still lowered their sails in salute, though only the steeple remained. This steeple was blown up in 1793 lest it should give cover to invaders.

Between Guernsey and Sark, 3 mi. from the former, is Herm (320 ac.), with 36 inhabitants at the 1951 census. In 1155 Henry II gave the island to the abbey of St. Helier, which established a small daughter house (*cenobiolum*) there with a church dedicated to St. Tugual. In 1440 Franciscans built a friary. John Leland's map of 1540 has the note: "Once a cell of Canons Regular, now Franciscans." When the Reformation overtook the islands, Herm became for a time the last refuge of the Roman Catholics. Later the governors of Guernsey used it as a game preserve. Philip Dumaresq wrote in 1685: "The Governor keeps deer there, having a lodge for a keeper, where formerly stood a convent, the ruins whereof are yet seen." In the 19th century it was let to private tenants, one of whom, the German zoologist, Prince von Blücher, acclimatized wallabies there; World War I ended his tenancy.

In 1946 the States of Guernsey bought the island for use as a resort for Guernsey. By some freak of the tide a shell beach half a mile long has been formed, on which about 200 varieties of shells have been found.

South of Herm is Jethou (44 ac.), a round islet about half a mile in diameter. Richard, duke of Normandy, granted it to his shipmaster Restald, who became a monk of Mont St. Michel and bequeathed it to his abbey; but the only income the abbey ever derived from it came from wreckage. An assize roll of 1309 reported: "There hath rarely lived there any man." But in 1951 there were 13 inhabitants. Botanically Jethou is interesting as the home of a white pimpernel and a yellow forget-me-not said to be peculiar to the island.

West of Sark and separated only by a channel 70 yd. wide is Brecqhou (74 ac.). Before World War II it was a favourite picnicking place with only one farmhouse on it; then a mansion was built there with gardeners' cottages, etc., and the whole island became private property.

Northeast of Jersey lie the Ecrehou Islands and south of Jersey the Minquiers Islands, two long reefs of rocks. At low tide the Minquiers reef is larger than Jersey, but at high tide only one peak, the Maîtresse Ile, is large enough for habitation. On the Ecrehou three islets, Marmoutier, Blanche Ile and Maître Ile, have houses on them. Sovereignty over the Ecrehou and Minquiers Islands was for more than 300 years a matter of dispute between France and England. In Dec. 1951, the question was referred to the International Court of Justice.

Further south Les Roches Douvres with their lighthouse and the 15 islets of Chausey with their one farm, lighthouse, church and two hotels, and their floating population of lobster trappers (the great granite quarries that were once the staple industry have gone bankrupt) form part of the Channel Islands geologically; but apart from one brief interval they have always been under French rule.

PHYSIOGRAPHY

The Channel Islands are summits of a partially submerged portion of the Armorican massif and fall topographically into four groups. The northerly group comprises Alderney, Burhou, Ortac, the Casquets and other islets which lie due west of Cap de la Hague. The westerly includes Guernsey, Herm, Jethou, Sark and several islets; the Little Russel strait separates Guernsey from Herm, the Great Russel strait separates Herm from Sark. A third group, separated from the second by La Déroute strait, includes Jersey and the Ecrehou Islands. A fourth consists of the Minquiers Islands and the Iles Chausey.

A fall in sea level to the 30-fathom line would connect all the islands with the Cotentin peninsula of Normandy. In postglacial times with a rising temperature the sea has gradually risen, successively cutting off islands and groups of islands. Jersey probably remained connected with the continent till the Bronze Age.

Geology.—Geologically the islands are related to the Cotentin peninsula and Brittany. Metamorphic rocks, almost certainly pre-Cambrian, cover large areas. Much of Sark consists of hornblende, schist and associated gneiss. Granite and diorite gneisses form southern Guernsey, the Paternosters, Dirouilles, the Ecrehou Islands, the Chaussée des Boeufs and the Minquiers Islands. Mudstones and fine sandstones (greywackes), probably pre-Cambrian (Fr. *Briovérien*), form much of Jersey and a minute patch of southwest Guernsey. In east Jersey these rocks are overlaid by massive volcanic flows, probably pre-Cambrian (Uriconian), consisting of andesite followed by rhyolite, which shows exceptionally fine spherulite structures. East and southeast Alderney and the reefs north and northwest of the island consist of Lower Cambrian sandstone (the *grès pourpré* of Normandy). The northeast corner of Jersey consists of an unusually coarse and massive conglomerate, probably Permian. In north Guernsey and north and west Alderney gabbros and diorites are dominant. Similar rocks also occur in southeast Jersey and around Sorel point. In all cases granite intrusions have followed, giving rise by mixing to a variety of hybrid diorites.

Granites without associated diorites and gabbros form the north and southwest parts of Sark, the west of Brecqhou, all Herm and Jethou, extensive tracts of northwest and southwest Jersey and all the Chausey group. The plutonic rocks of Alderney are pre-Cambrian; most of those of Jersey and those of the Chausey Islands probably carboniferous, but except in Alderney there is no clear evidence of age. All the rocks so far described, especially the metamorphic and plutonic series, are cut by numerous intrusive dykes of dolerite and mica-lamprophyre and, in west Alderney and southeast Jersey, of granite-porphyry. Raised beaches occur at about 25 ft., 60 ft. and 120 ft. above the modern sea level. They are overlaid by head or stony clay and by brick earth or loess of Pleistocene age. More recent deposits of peat, alluvium and blown sand, with relics of Neolithic and later human occupation, form the low-lying coastal areas. Peat and forest beds found down to low-tide mark are evidence of a sea level lower than at present.

Flora.—The two main factors affecting the flora of the Channel Islands are the lack of chalk and limestone and the warm climate. About 700 species of wild flowers have been identified, mostly belonging to the Lusitanian element. Many flowers bloom in December and introduced plants such as *Erigeron mucronatus* from Mexico and the *Nerine sarniensis* from South Africa flourish.

In the 17th century bulbs of the latter, now called the Guernsey Lily, having at Cape Town been taken on board a ship returning home from Japan, were washed ashore at Guernsey when the ship was wrecked near the Channel Islands. Several Mediterranean species, such as *Echium plantagineum* and *Linaria pelisseriana* in Jersey and the grass *Milium scabrum* in Guernsey, are not found in the British Isles proper.

Jersey became an island at a much later date than Guernsey and so it has a larger and more varied flora (about 50 more species of flowering plants); for example the wood anemone and cross-leaved heath are found in Jersey but not in Guernsey. After the last Ice Age the land sank and when it rose again forest spread from southern Europe. Guernsey and its near-by islands were some of the high places in this forest that were cut off when the land sank once more. There are no woods left in any of the islands because of intense cultivation, but analysis of pollen from Jersey peat shows that oak, ash, birch, lime, wych-elm, beech, pine, cedar, hazel and alder are all indigenous species. Other trees spread to Jersey later. Ferns, mosses, fungi and lichens are abundant; a form of the European quillwort, *Isoetes hystrix,* is found in Guernsey and Alderney but nowhere else in the United Kingdom.

Fauna.—Some animals found in Jersey never reached the Guernsey group because, as explained above, the former became an island so much later. The fauna is continental rather than British in character. The Guernsey vole belongs to the older fauna; the bank vole is confined to Jersey and is its commonest mammal. Probably late arrivals, the mole is found only in Jersey and Alderney, and the squirrel only in Jersey. The stoat occurs in Guernsey and Jersey but there are no weasels. All the islands have hedgehogs, mice, rats, rabbits and continental types of shrews.

The Jersey shrew, a variety of the British shrewmouse, is found only in Jersey.

Among the commonest birds are jays and magpies. Woodland and small species are not well represented. Barn owls, peregrines, gannets, storm petrels and many more breed in the islands. Winter visitors include the short-eared owl, snow bunting and water rail as well as thousands of waders, swans, geese and ducks that feed on grass wrack along the shores. The oyster catcher, Kentish plover and mallard stay to breed. Many migrants pass through in spring and autumn. The corn crake, once common, is only a summer visitor.

Pheasants and partridges have been shot to extinction in Guernsey and Jersey.

Porpoises and dolphins are plentiful around the coasts while the ormer, not found in the British Isles proper, occurs on all the shores.

The common toad and palmated newt, the green lizard, wall lizard and slowworm, and the grass snake are indigenous to Jersey. There are no poisonous snakes. The frog, *Rana dabmatina,* not found in Great Britain, Ireland or northern France, occurs in Jersey, Guernsey, Alderney and Sark. Of insects, one of the ant lions, a group not represented elsewhere in the United Kingdom, inhabits the Channel Islands.

HISTORY

The early history of the islands is obscure. About 100,000 B.C. Neanderthal men were living in caves in Jersey, which was then joined to the continent. Iberian settlers about 2000 B.C. left flint implements everywhere, great chamber tombs (dolmens) in Jersey, Guernsey and Alderney, and two impressive statues of their goddess mother in Guernsey. Next came the Gauls; then the Romans added the islands to their empire. Coins show that for more than 500 years their money circulated, but only in Alderney has any trace of Roman buildings been found. Several of the early Breton saints are said to have visited the islands, the best-authenticated stories being those of St. Samson's mission to Guernsey (*c.* A.D. 530) and St. Magloire's foundation of a monastery in Sark (*c.* 568).

History proper begins when Rollo the Viking established the duchy of Normandy. In A.D. 933 William Longsword, the second duke, annexed the whole archipelago and for the next 270 years it was ruled from Rouen. William of Normandy's conquest of England made no difference to this. The islands' seat of government was not moved to Westminster but remained in Rouen.

But in 1204, when the king of France conquered continental Normandy, some new form of government had to be evolved. The islands were never incorporated with England. "The King of England hath nothing in these islands," said the assize roll of 1331, "except his status as Duke." So gradually a home rule constitution came into being.

A document ascribed to King John was long regarded by the islanders as their "magna carta," but modern criticism leaves little doubt that it is not genuine. But each island possessed judges, known as *jurats,* elected by the larger landowners (*optimates*)—12 each for Jersey and Guernsey, 6 each for Alderney and Sark. This is an institution peculiar to the islands, of which the origin is unknown. These *jurats* assumed control and issued ordinances, the breach of which they were able as judges to punish. The king in his capacity as duke appointed a warden to represent him; and later, when wardens were often absentees, two bailiffs were installed as their lieutenants, one for Jersey, the other for the rest of the group. The bailiffs, who at first were servants of the warden, in the 14th century became the king's bailiffs, representatives of the crown.

Lying as they did within sight of ships passing down the English channel, the islands were constantly raided. In the 9th century the Vikings began to plunder them and continued to do so for 100 years. Robert Wace, the Jersey poet, wrote of the devastation "En Auremen (Alderney), en Guernesi,/ En Sairc, en Erim (Herm), en Gersi." After their separation from Normandy the incursions were resumed. After a French raid in 1294 a Jersey petition reported that "Men and women were killed to the number of 1,500. The houses were burnt and the corn; so the people have nothing to eat." In 1336 David Bruce, when driven from his Scottish throne, "attacked Guernsey and Jersey inhumanly, committing arson, murder, and divers other atrocities." In 1339 another Jersey petition said: "The island hath been destroyed and burnt three times this year." This continued till 1484 when a bull of Pope Sixtus IV brought relief. Having learned with horror, he said, that miscreants were wont to land, burn houses and goods, carry off crops and cattle and murder the inhabitants, he pronounced "sentence of eternal damnation with confiscation of goods" on all who should commit such crimes in the islands "or within sight of them as far as human eye shall reach."

This secured the islands the unusual privilege of neutrality, which even survived the Reformation, for when Elizabeth I confirmed the prerogatives of Jersey she wrote: "One is that in time of war merchants of all nations can without impediment frequent the islands to escape storms or for purposes of trade, and depart without molestation, and remain in safety as long as the island is in sight."

The Reformation reached the islands from France and won a rapid victory. The church became fervently Calvinist with the Presbyterian form of government and Presbyterian ordination. Under Mary an unsuccessful attempt was made to restore Catholicism, but the martyrdom of three women in Guernsey, one of whom gave birth in the fire to a child, confirmed the people yet more firmly in their Protestant faith.

In 1620 James I forced Jersey to accept Anglicanism, but Presbyterianism survived in Guernsey till 1660 and in Sark till 1674. The islands before the Reformation formed part of the diocese of Coutances, but later they were placed under the bishops of Winchester.

During the Civil Wars their Puritan views led most of the islanders to support the parliament. In Guernsey the royalist lieutenant governor was besieged for nine years in Castle Cornet. In Jersey at first the same thing happened. Sir Phillippe de Carteret, the lieutenant governor, was besieged in Elizabeth castle and died there; but his nephew, Sir George Carteret, recovered the island for the king and held it with an iron hand till 1651, when he too had to surrender.

William of Orange abolished the neutrality of the islands in 1689, and during the war of 1778–83 there were two unsuccessful attacks on Jersey, in 1779 and 1781. The second, under Baron de Rullecourt, is famous for the victory over the invaders achieved through the bravery of the young Major Francis Peirson, who however fell when the French were on the point of surrender. During the revolutionary period in France the islands were the home of many refugees. In the 18th century various attempts were made to introduce the English customhouse system, but these proved practically a failure, and the islands throve on smuggling and privateering down to the Napoleonic wars.

The 19th century brought some prosperity from maritime commerce so long as wooden sailing ships were in general use. Later, intensive cultivation for export to English markets caused unprecedented development. The encouragement of the tourist traffic was a contributing factor.

During World War I the islands suffered little, but in World War II, when France surrendered, their defense became impossible and the government offered to evacuate the inhabitants. The response of the islands varied. In Alderney the entire population embarked. Of Guernsey's 43,000 inhabitants 23,000 departed. In Jersey 41,000 remained and only 10,000 left. The Germans occupied all the islands on June 30–July 1, 1940, and fortified them with attendant destruction and deportations, to be "the mailed fist of the Western Wall." Following the German surrender in Europe, the islands were relieved by British forces on May 9, 1945.

Language.—From the 9th to the 19th centuries everyone in the islands spoke French. Debates in the states (the insular legislature), pleadings in the courts and sermons in the churches were in French, while the countryfolk spoke, as some still do, a dialect of Old Norman French. But the steady inflow of English residents made English so dominant that French became almost a foreign language. In Alderney, where English soldiers and harbour builders outnumbered the natives, French had succumbed by the middle of the 19th century. The other islands gradually followed suit. In 1900 Jersey allowed English to be spoken in the states. French ceased to be the official language in Guernsey in 1946.

GOVERNMENT AND ADMINISTRATION

Constitution.—After the upheaval of World War II the islands could not settle down to the *status quo ante.* A demand arose for reforms, and the privy council sent a commission to advise the local authorities. From these discussions a new constitution emerged for each island, but much of the old framework survived. The lieutenant governors still represent the queen and are the channels of communication between the local government and the crown. The bailiffs retain their duties as chief justices, prime ministers and speakers. The states lost none of their powers, though they were purged of nonelected members. In Jersey they consist of elected senators, *connétables,* and deputies; in Guernsey of *conseillers,* elected by an intermediate body called the States of Election, people's deputies, representatives of the *douzaines* (parish councils), and representatives of Alderney. In each island the *jurats* were relegated to their original duties as judges, and in Guernsey the *connétables* too lost their seats in the states. But Jersey retained its *centeniers* and *vingteniers;* Guernsey its sheriff with his sword and gold chain and its *douzeniers;* Sark its *sénéschal* and *prévot.*

In Alderney, however, the restoration of its old status as a semi-independent political unit proved impracticable, and for financial and administrative work it was amalgamated with Guernsey.

Law.—The laws of the islands differ in certain details. The law of inheritance for example is different in Jersey and Guernsey and Sark. Guernsey has no trial by jury, though it has long been the practice in criminal cases in Jersey. But in each island the legal system is based on the 13th-century *Grand Coutumier de Normandie.* One example of these old Norman customs is the *Clameur de Haro.* If an islander finds someone interfering with his property, he has only to cry "Haro, haro, haro! A l'aide mon prince! On me fait tort" and the aggressor has to desist till the court has decided the case. The English law courts have no authority in the islands. Appeals from decisions of the local courts are made to the queen in council; however, during 1952 legal provisions were made for an insular court of appeal for the whole group.

Feudal Relics.—The Normans brought the feudal system with them and divided the islands into fiefs. Each *seigneur* had his seigneurial court and some their own gallows. Most of these powers have long disappeared but a few survive. In Jersey, if a landowner dies without a direct heir, the *seigneur* claims for a year and a day the income of his estate; the *seigneurs* of St. Ouen's and La Motte still license taverners. In Sark the dame receives a tithe of all crops grown and one-thirteenth of the price whenever land is sold. No one but she may keep pigeons or a female dog.

Defense.—The militia, which played so large a part in the past in the defense of all the islands, in which for more than 500 years every man from 16 to 60 had to serve, became unsuitable for modern warfare. After World War II the problem of the islands' military training came under discussion. In May 1952 Guernsey rejected conscription on the grounds that in any case enough volunteers came forward; in the same year Jersey tabled a measure to introduce two years' compulsory service followed by three years in the reserve. The enactment of this measure was strongly opposed, especially by the farmers.

ECONOMICS

Industry.—The islanders have been very versatile in adopting new industries when one has begun to fail. When vast shoals of cod were discovered off Newfoundland in the 16th century, fishing fleets from the islands crossed the Atlantic, and the operation of fleets in this way continued for 300 years. In 1872 the Jersey boats alone numbered more than 400.

From Elizabeth I's time knitting woollen "guernseys," "jerseys" and stockings became a major occupation. In 1685 Dumaresq declared that "At least half the people in Jersey depend upon the manufacture of stockings" and in Alderney "they adict themselves to the manufacture of knit waistcoats, whereby they neglect fishing."

About this time Guernsey was exporting 4,000 pairs of stockings weekly.

During the American and Napoleonic Wars much wealth was won by privateering, and a roaring trade was done with English smugglers, who loaded their ships with tobacco and spirits to be furtively landed in England. And, till wooden ships went out of use, shipbuilding yards in Jersey and Guernsey were constantly busy.

But the basic industry has always been agriculture. There is, however, a difference between the islands. Guernsey's high ground is in the south, so the island slopes toward the north; Jersey slopes southward. This southerly tilt enables Jersey to grow most of its crops in the open, whereas there are many acres of hothouses in Guernsey.

Jersey growers concentrate mainly on early potatoes and tomatoes. The chief exports of Guernsey are tomatoes, flowers and grapes. In addition each island is famous for its pedigreed cattle. Jersey and Guernsey cows (the breeds are not identical) fetch high prices in England and the United States, and even in New Zealand.

Coinage.—Jersey and Guernsey each has a copper coinage of its own. Up to 1830 they used French *livres tournois, sous* and *liards,* but in that year Guernsey issued coins of 1 *double,* 4 *doubles,* and 8 *doubles,* the 1 *double* being the equivalent of the French *liard* and the 8 *doubles* of the English penny. The bailiwick of Guernsey has its own £1 and 10 *s.* notes.

In 1834 Jersey adopted the English system of pounds, shillings and pence, and in 1841 it too put into circulation its own pence, halfpence and farthings, however, to equate the new currency with the old, the farthing was regarded as worth two *liards,* and that made the penny only worth $\frac{1}{13}$th of a shilling, which remained its value till 1877, when its inscription was changed to "$\frac{1}{12}$th of a shilling."

BIBLIOGRAPHY.—T. D. Kendrick, *Archaeology of the Channel Islands;* vol. i, *Guernsey* (London, 1928); J. Hawkes, *ibid.;* vol. ii, *Jersey* (Jersey, 1937); G. R. Balleine, *The Bailiwick of Jersey* (London, 1951); C. P. Le Huray, *The Bailiwick of Guernsey* (London, 1952); E. F. Carey, *The Channel Islands* (London, 1904); G. Dupont, *Histoire du Cotentin et ses Iles* (Caen, 1885); J. H. Le Patourel, *Medieval Administration of the Channel Islands* (Oxford, 1937); G. Dury, *The Channel Islands* (Land Utilization Survey, London, 1950); P. Vercel, *Trois Pots de Fleurs* (Paris, 1947); A. J. Eagleston, *The Channel Islands Under Tudor Government* (Cambridge, 1949); R. M. Lockley, *The Charm of the Channel Islands* (London, 1950); R. Dobson, *Birds of the Channel Islands* (London, 1952). (G. R. B.)

CHANNELL, SIR WILLIAM FRY (1804–1873), British jurist, was born on Aug. 31, 1804. His education was fragmentary, but he was an avid reader in his youth and prepared for a legal career, being called to the bar in 1827. In 1840 he was made a sergeant of the court of common pleas, and in 1857 he was appointed to the court of exchequer, being knighted that same year. Illness forced his retirement from the bench in Jan. 1873, and he could not accept formal appointment as a member of the privy council. Shortly thereafter, on Feb. 26, 1873, he died in London.

CHANNEL TUNNEL (ENGLISH CHANNEL). A tunnel under the English channel was first proposed by a French engineer, Thomé de Gamond (1807–75), who submitted a scheme for it to Napoleon III in 1856. He was joined in his work by the British engineers, Isambard Brunel, Joseph Lock and Robert Stephenson, and later by Sir John Hawkshaw. The proposal was seriously considered by the railway companies on both sides of the channel, and a convention with the French government to regulate it was signed in 1875. Then the bitter rivalry of the South Eastern and the Chatham and Dover railway companies created difficulties and the scheme became a political question. W. E. Gladstone was a keen supporter, as were John Bright, Lord Lansdowne and Lord Salisbury, while Joseph Chamberlain and the war office opposed. The subject was referred to a joint select committee of the commons, which considered many reports by

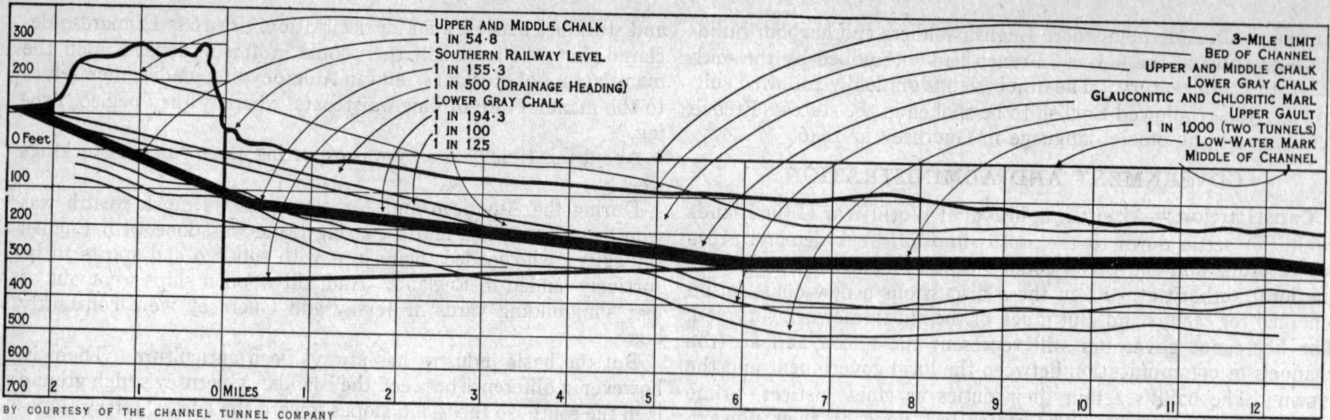

Fig. 1.—English half, showing section of tunnel from behind Dover cliffs to mid-channel. The tunnel would include two tubes in the impermeable gray chalk, and drainage heading with shaft on the shore, where the water would be pumped up into the sea

generals favouring the scheme and a memorandum by Lord Wolseley strongly resisting it. The committee decided against the proposal by 6 to 4, Lord Lansdowne, the chairman, voting for it. Thereafter succeeding British governments all opposed the scheme.

After Louis Blériot had flown the channel in 1909, a Channel

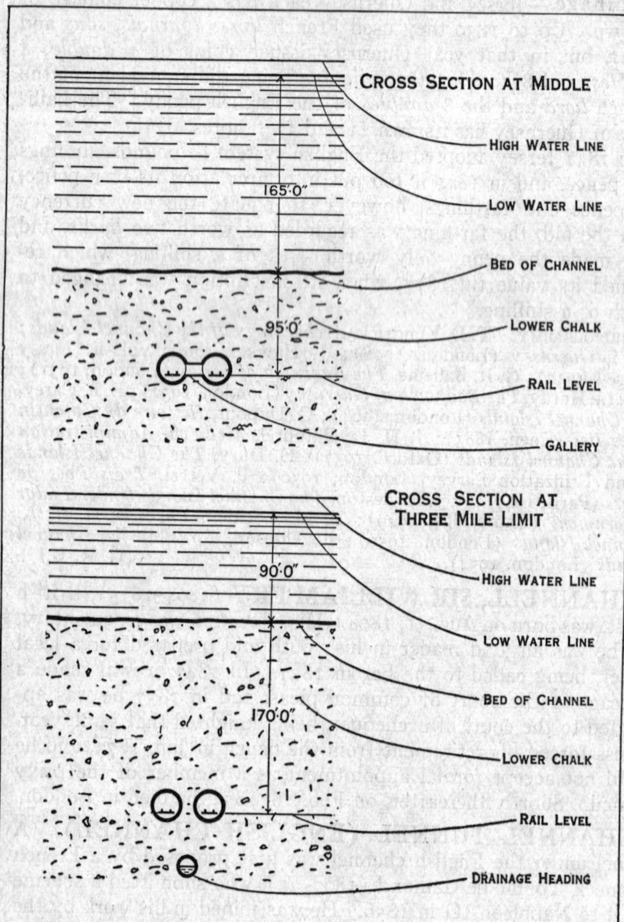

Fig. 2.—Cross sections of the proposed channel tunnel

Tunnel committee was formed in the house of commons, under the chairmanship of Sir Arthur Fell, which ultimately numbered more than 400 members of parliament. The Labour party joined en masse and Herbert Asquith promised to have inquiries made. World War I broke out and nothing could be done. After the war David Lloyd George promised to make more inquiries. Andrew Bonar Law and Stanley Baldwin did nothing. James Ramsay MacDonald, in July 1924, offered to consult all the living ex-prime ministers. The five met and rejected the scheme, although a two to one majority of M.P.'s supported it.

So the Channel tunnel scheme was shelved again but the idea did not die.

The French Channel Tunnel company had received a concession from their government and could resume work at any time but the English Channel Tunnel company could do nothing further without an act of parliament, to which no British government had yet consented by the mid-1950s.

It is a great project, comparable only with the Suez and Panama canals, but its story has reflected little credit on any but the engineers who perfected the scheme.

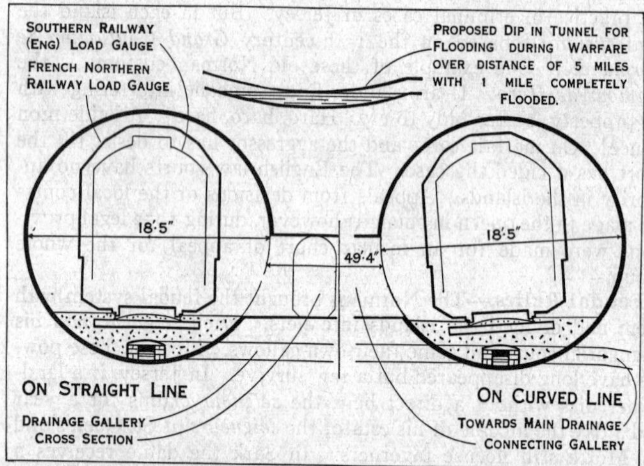

Fig. 3.—Details of the proposed twin channel tunnel, showing connecting gallery and drainage heading, also difference in the size of English and continental rolling stock

The proposals involve a double tunnel more than 30 mi. long, of which more than 20 mi. would be under the open sea. Two tunnels would be driven about 50 ft. apart, each about 20 ft. in diameter, and the two connected by frequent cross galleries. The tunnel would run from near Wissant in France, between Boulogne and Calais to behind the Shakespeare cliffs in England between Dover and Folkestone.

Drainage would be effected by a smaller 10-ft.-diameter tunnel at a lower level than the railway tunnels and discharging into shafts on each side of the channel from which the seepage would be pumped up into the sea. The tunnels, which would be steel lined, would be driven throughout in the bed of gray chalk which extends under the channel and outcrops on both sides. Two exploratory headings, each $1\frac{1}{4}$ mi. long, were driven from Sangatte near Calais and from the shore under Shakespeare cliff where the old works can be seen from the Folkestone to Dover railway. Although these headings are unlined, the percolation of water into them has been negligible.

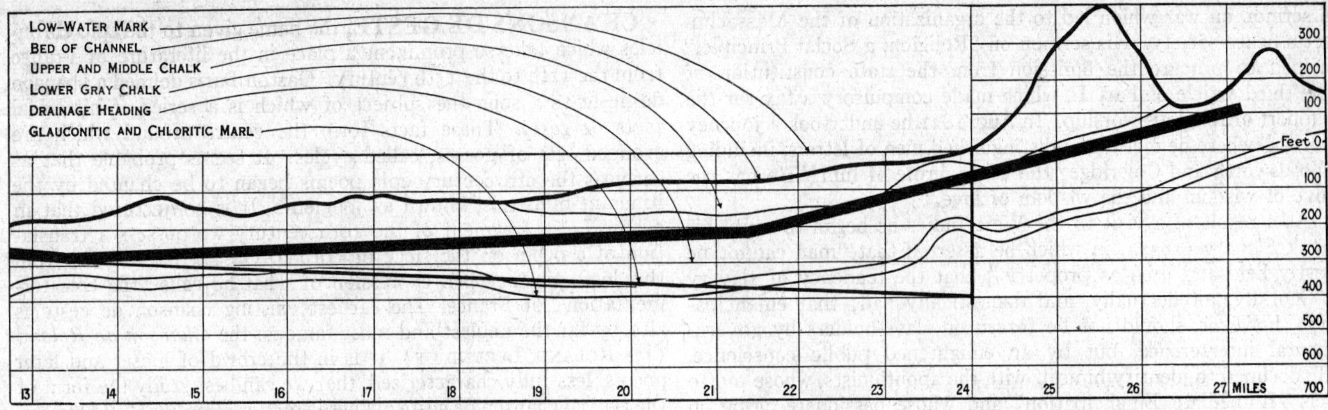

BY COURTESY OF THE CHANNEL TUNNEL COMPANY

FIG. 4.—LONGITUDINAL SECTION OF FRENCH HALF, SHOWING LEVEL OF TUNNEL FROM MID-CHANNEL TO THE MOUTH OF THE TUNNEL IN FRANCE, BEHIND CAP BLANC NEZ, BETWEEN CALAIS AND BOULOGNE, WITH DRAINAGE HEADING AND SHAFT FOR PUMPS ON SEASHORE NEAR SANGATTE

The cost of the scheme was estimated before World War II at about £25,000,000 to £30,000,000, but engineering costs increased greatly afterward. Also against the scheme has been the great increase in air transport, as this has, to some extent served the purpose for which the tunnel was designed. Nevertheless the conception of the channel tunnel remains unquestionably one of the greatest engineering proposals in the world. The scheme was reconsidered during the early days of World War II, but not proceeded with as the period of construction would have been too great to make it practicable as a war measure.

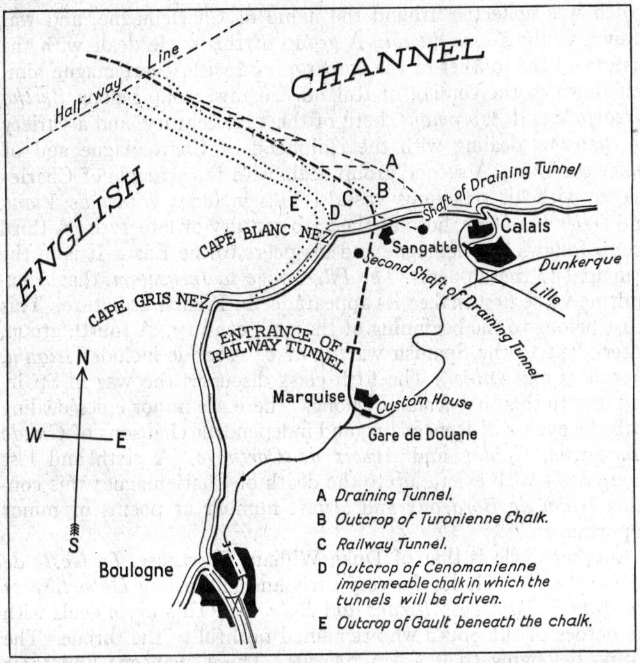

BY COURTESY OF M. LE TROCQUER

FIG. 5.—PLAN OF THE FRENCH PORTION OF PROPOSED CHANNEL TUNNEL, SHOWING POSITION OF CUSTOM HOUSE, JUNCTION WITH THE NORTHERN RAILWAY OF FRANCE, AND THE ROUTE OF THE TUNNEL TO MID-CHANNEL

BIBLIOGRAPHY.—Joint Select Committee, Report and Evidence, *Blue Book*, 47 (1883); Albert Sartiaux, *Le Tunnel sous-marin* (Lille, 1907); Nord railway of France, *Revue des Deux Mondes* (Oct. 1913); Arthur Fell, "Channel Tunnel," paper read to Royal Society of Arts (London, 1913); Lord Sydenham of Combe, *Military Aspect of the Tunnel* (London, 1914); Winston S. Churchill, article in *Weekly Dispatch* (London, July 27, 1924); Yves le Trocquer, "Engineering Features of Channel Tunnel," paper read to Institute of Structural Engineers (London, May 6, 1927); Channel Tunnel Committee, *Report* (H.M.S.O., London, 1930).

(A. F.; W. Hw.)

CHANNING, EDWARD TYRRELL (1790–1856), U.S. editor, was born at Newport, R.I., on Dec. 12, 1790, the brother of William Ellery and Walter Channing (*qq.v.*). He studied at Harvard university and was admitted to the bar in 1813. His interests lay rather in journalism, however, and in May 1818 he became editor of the young *North American Review,* remaining in this post until Oct. 1819, when he became professor of rhetoric at Harvard. At Harvard he wrote little, but his influence as a teacher was great; among his students was Edward Everett Hale. Channing retired from the Harvard faculty at the age of 60 and died Feb. 8, 1856, at Cambridge, Mass.

CHANNING, WALTER (1786–1876), U.S. physician, was born at Newport, R.I., the brother of William Ellery and Edward Tyrrell Channing (*qq.v.*). He studied at Harvard university and at the medical school of the University of Pennsylvania, Philadelphia, Pa., where he received his M.D. in 1809. He then studied medicine in Europe before returning to Boston, Mass., in 1812 to set up practice as an obstetrician.

Three years later he was appointed first professor of obstetrics at Harvard, where later he was dean of the medical school (1819–47). In 1847 he first used ether as an anaesthetic in deliveries, and in the next year reported its successful employment in more than 500 labour cases.

Channing was one of the founders of the Boston Lying-In hospital in 1832 and was a co-editor of the *Boston Medical and Surgical Journal.* From 1822 to 1825 he was librarian of the Massachusetts Medical society, and from 1828 to 1840 acted as treasurer of the society.

CHANNING, WILLIAM ELLERY (1780–1842), American divine and philanthropist, was born in Newport, R.I., April 7, 1780. Channing seemed to have inherited from his father sweetness of temper and warmth of affection, and from his mother that strong moral discernment and straightforward rectitude of purpose and action which formed striking features of his character.

He prepared for college in New London under the care of his uncle, the Rev. Henry Channing, to this period tracing the beginning of his spiritual life, and in 1794 entered Harvard college. In his college vacations he taught at Lancaster, Mass., and in term time he stinted himself in food to save time for study—an experiment which produced acute dyspepsia.

Nevertheless, he felt that he got little good from his college course.

After graduating in 1798, he lived at Richmond as tutor in the family of David Meade Randolph, U.S. marshal for Virginia. He returned "a thin and pallid invalid," to spend a year and a half in Newport, which had always delighted him by its beauty, and in 1802 went to Cambridge as regent (or general proctor) in Harvard; in the autumn of 1802 he began to preach. On June 1, 1803, he was ordained pastor of the Federal street Congregational church in Boston.

Channing did not become known as "the apostle of Unitarianism" until after his sermon preached at the ordination of the Rev. Jared Sparks in 1819 and the publication of his articles in *The Christian Disciple,* "Objections to Unitarian Christianity Considered" and "The Moral Argument Against Calvinism." He took a keen interest in all public questions; and in 1816 he preached a sermon on war which led to the organization of the Massachusetts peace society. His sermon on "Religion, a Social Principle," helped to procure the omission from the state constitution of the third article of Part I., which made compulsory a tax for the support of religious worship. In Aug. 1821 he undertook a journey abroad, where he met many distinguished men of letters, including Wordsworth and Coleridge; the latter wrote of him, "He has the love of wisdom and the wisdom of love."

As a result of a visit to the West Indies he began to write his book *Slavery* (1835), in which he asserted that "man cannot be justly held and used as property"; that the tendency of slavery is morally, intellectually, and domestically bad; that emancipation, however, should not be forced on slave-holders by governmental interference, but by an enlightened public conscience. He declined to identify himself with the abolitionists, whose motto was "Immediate Emancipation" and whose passionate agitation he thought unsuited to the work they were attempting. In 1837 he published *Thoughts on the Evils of a Spirit of Conquest, and on Slavery: A Letter on the Annexation of Texas to the United States,* addressed to Henry Clay—arguing that the Texan revolt from Mexican rule was largely the work of land-speculators, and of those who resolved "to throw Texas open to slave-holders and slaves"—and warning of its serious consequences. Channing's pamphlet *Emancipation* (1840) dealt with the success of emancipation in the West Indies, as related in Joseph John Gurney's *Familiar Letters to Henry Clay of Kentucky* (1840). In 1842 he published *The Duty of the Free States; or Remarks Suggested by the Case of the Creole,* a careful analysis of the letter of complaint from the American to the British government, and a defence of the position taken by the British government. On Aug. 1, 1842, he delivered at Lenox (Mass.) an address celebrating the anniversary of emancipation in the British West Indies. Two months later, Oct. 2, 1842, he died at Bennington, Vermont.

Physically, Channing was short and slight; his eyes were unnaturally large; his voice wonderfully clear. He was not a great pastor, and lacked social tact, but by the few who knew him well he was almost worshipped. His sermons were noted for their rare simplicity and gracefulness of style. To the name "Unitarian" Channing objected strongly, thinking "unity" as abstract a word as "trinity" and as little expressing the close fatherly relation of God to man. It is to be noted that he strongly objected to the growth of "Unitarian orthodoxy" and its increasing narrowness. Channing believed in historic Christianity and in the story of the resurrection, "a fact which comes to me with a certainty I find in few ancient histories," although he held that the Scriptures were not inspired but merely records of inspiration. In the controversies into which he was forced he continually displayed the greatest breadth and catholicity of view. The differences in New England churches he considered were largely verbal, and he said that "would Trinitarians tell us what they mean, their system would generally be found little else than a mystical form of the Unitarian doctrine." His opposition to Calvinism was so great, however, that even in 1812 he declared "existence a curse" if Calvinism be true. Possibly his boldest and most elaborate defence of Unitarianism was his sermon on *Unitarianism most favourable to Piety,* preached in 1826, and the election sermon of 1830 was his greatest plea for spiritual and intellectual freedom.

Channing's reputation as an author was probably based largely on his publication in *The Christian Examiner* of *Remarks on the Character and Writings of John Milton* (1826), *Remarks on the Life and Character of Napoleon Bonaparte* (1827–28), and an *Essay on the Character and Writings of Fénelon* (1829). An *Essay on Self-Culture* introduced Franklin lectures delivered in Boston in 1838. Channing was an intimate friend of Horace Mann, and his views on the education of children are stated by Elizabeth Palmer Peabody to have anticipated those of Froebel. His *Complete Works* have appeared in various editions since 1841.

See the *Memoir* by W. H. Channing (1848); Elizabeth P. Peabody, *Reminiscences of the Rev. William Ellery Channing, D.D.* (1880), intimate but inexact; J. W. Chadwick, *William Ellery Channing, Minister of Religion* (1903); W. M. Salter, "Channing as a Social Reformer," *Unitarian Review* (March 1888); and C. W. Eliot, *Four American Leaders* (1906).

CHANSONS DE GESTE, the name given to the epic chronicles which take so prominent a place in the literature of France from the 11th to the 15th century. Gaston Paris defined a chanson de geste as a song the subject of which is a series of historical facts or *gesta.* These facts form the centre around which are grouped sets of poems, called cycles. It seems probable that as early as the 9th century epic poems began to be chanted by the itinerant minstrels, known as jongleurs. It is conjectured that in a base Latin fragment of the 10th century we possess a translation of a poem on the siege of Girona. Gaston Paris dates from this lost epic the open expression of what he calls "the epic fermentation" of France. The earliest existing chanson de geste is also by far the noblest and most famous, the *Chanson de Roland* (*see* ROLAND, LEGEND OF). It is in the crowd of looser and later poems, less fully characterized, that we can best study the form of the typical chanson de geste. These epics were national and historical; their anonymous writers composed them spontaneously, to a common model, with little regard to the artificial niceties of style. The earlier examples are monotonous, primitive and superficial. Two great merits, however, all the best of these poems possess, force and lucidity; they are full of Gallic pride, they breathe the spirit of an indomitable warlike energy. All their figures belong to the same social order of things, and all illustrate the same fighting aristocracy. The moving principle is that of chivalry, and what is presented is, invariably, the life of a mediaeval soldier.

Perhaps the most important cycle of chansons de geste was that which was collected around the name of Charlemagne, and was known as the *Geste du roi.* A group of this cycle dealt with the history of the mother of the emperor, and with Charlemagne himself down to the coming of Roland. To this group belong *Bertha Greatfoot* and *Aspremont,* both of the 12th century, and a variety of chansons dealing with the childhood of Charlemagne and of Ogier the Dane. A second group deals with the struggle of Charlemagne with his rebellious vassals. This includes *Girart de Viane* and *Ogier the Dane,* both of the 13th century or late 12th. A third group follows Charlemagne and his peers to the East. It is in the principal of these poems, *The Pilgrimage to Jerusalem,* that Alexandrine verse first makes its appearance in French literature. This must belong to the beginning of the 12th century. A fourth group, antecedent to the Spanish war, is of *c.* 1200; it includes *Aiquin, Fierabras* and *Otinel.* The fifth class discusses the war in Spain, and it is to this that *Roland* belongs; there are minor epics dealing with the events of Roncevaux, and independent chansons of *Gui de Bourgogne, Gaidon* and *Anseïs de Carthage.* A sixth and last group deals with events up to the death of Charlemagne; this contains *Huon de Bordeaux* and a vast number of poems of minor importance.

Another cycle is that of Duke William Shortnose, *La Geste de Guillaume.* It includes the very early and interesting *Departure of the Aimeri Children, Aliscans* and *Rainoart.* This cycle deals with the heroes of the South who remained faithful to the throne. The poems belonging to it are numerous. These chansons find their direct opposites in those which form the great cycle of *La Geste de Doon de Mayence,* sometimes called "la faulse geste," because it deals with the feats of the traitors, of the rebellious family of Ganelon. This is the geste of the Northmen, always hostile to the Carlovingian dynasty. It comprises some of the most famous of the chansons, in particular *Parise la duchesse* and *The Four Sons of Aymon.* Several of its sections are the production of a known poet, Raimbert of Paris. From this triple division of the main body of the chansons are excluded certain poems of minor importance.

All the best of the early chansons de geste are written in ten-syllable verse, divided into stanzas or *laisses* of different length, united by a single assonance. Rhyme came in with the 13th century, and had the effect in languid bards of weakening the narrative; the sing-song of it led at last to the abandonment of verse in favour of plain historical prose.

See G. Paris, *Histoire poétique de Charlemagne* (1865) and *La Littérature française au moyen âge* (1890); P. Meyer, *Recherches sur l'épopée française* (1867); A. Longnon, *Les Quatre Fils Aimon,* etc. (1879); L. Gautier, *Les Epopées françaises* (4 vols., 1878–94)

CHANT, the name given to the tunes used in the English Church since the Reformation for the psalms and canticles (Fr. *chant,* from Lat. *cantare,* to sing). For the chant or *cantus firmus* of the Roman Church *see* PLAINSONG. In the English chant each section consists of a reciting note of indefinite length, followed by a phrase in regular time called a "mediation." Chants are "single," if written for one verse only, "double," if for two. "Quadruple" chants for four verses have also been written.

CHANTABUN or CHANDABURI, a town on the east side of the Gulf of Siam, Thailand, in 102° 6′ E., 12° 38′ N. Chantabun changvad (district) has an area of 2,301 sq.mi., and a pop. (1937) of 100,938, divided among Thai, Cambodians, Chinese and minor races. It lies about 12 mi. from the sea on a river navigable for small craft. Rice is the leading crop, but the 1,300 ac. of pepper produce three-fourths of the country's 200-ton annual output. There is trade in rubies, sapphires, cardamoms and rosewood. As part of the nationwide road-building program inaugurated about 1935, Chantabun was connected with Bangkok by a 209-mi. all-weather highway. An extension leads to Trat, close to the Indo-China frontier. In 1905 it was made headquarters of a high commissioner of a circle. Circles were abolished in 1932. Roman Catholic missionaries have been active since the 17th century, and converts are numerous.

CHANTADA, a city of northwestern Spain, in Lugo province, on the left bank of the Rio de Chantada, a small right-hand tributary of the river Miño, and on the main road from Lugo to Orense. Pop. (1940) 1,552 (mun., 15,127). Chantada is the chief town of the fertile region between the Miño and the heights of El Faro. Despite the lack of railway communication, it has a thriving trade in grain, flax, potatoes and dairy produce.

CHANTAL, JANE FRANCES, BARONESS DE (1572–1641), French saint and founder of the Order of the Visitation, was born Jan. 28, 1572, at Dijon, the daughter of the president of the *parlement* of Burgundy. At the age of 20 she married Baron de Chantal, but on his death, four years later, resolved to devote herself to the religious life. In 1604 she met St. Francis de Sales, and her four children being provided for, she went to Annecy where she founded the Congregation of the Visitation in June 1610. She was canonized in 1767, her feast being observed Aug. 21.

See F. M. de Chaugy, *Ste. J. F. de Chantal,* 8 vols. (1874–79); H. Bremond, *Sainte Chantal* (1912); and *The Spirit of St. J. F. de Chantal as shown in her Letters* (1922).

CHANTARELLE, an edible fungus, known botanically as *Cantharellus cibarius* (family, Agaricaceae) found in woods in summer. It is golden yellow, somewhat inversely conical in shape and about 2 in. broad and high. The cap is flattened above with a central depression and a thick-lobed irregular margin. Running down into the stem from the cap are a number of shallow thick gills. The substance of the fungus is dry and opaque with a peculiar smell suggesting ripe apricots or plums. The flesh is whitish tinged with yellow. The chantarelle is sold in the markets of Europe, where it forms a regular article of food, but seems little known in Great Britain; it is common in coniferous woods in northeastern United States and Canada. Before being cooked they should be allowed to dry, and then thrown into boiling water.

Care should be taken to distinguish the true chantarelle from the false Chantarelle (*C. aurantiacus*), a closely related species which is suspected of having caused poisoning. The latter species is more orange in colour, with thinner, broader and closer gills.

CHANTAVOINE, HENRI (1850–1918), French man of letters, was born at Montpellier on Aug. 6, 1850, and died at Galuire (Rhône) on Aug. 15, 1918. He was associated with the *Nouvelle Revue* from its foundation in 1879, and he joined the *Journal des débats* in 1884. His poems include *Poèmes sincères* (1877), *Satires contemporaines* (1881), *Ad memoriam* (1884), *Au fil des jours* (1889).

CHANTILLY, a town of northern France, in the department of Oise, 25 mi. N. of Paris on the Northern railway to St. Quentin. Pop. (1936) 5,054. It is situated to the north of the forest of Chantilly and is one of the favourite Parisian resorts. Its name was long associated with the manufacture, now decayed, of lace and blonde; it is still more celebrated for its château and its park (laid out originally in the 17th century), and as the scene of the annual races of the French Jockey Club. The château consists of the palace built from 1876 to 1885 and of an older portion adjoining it known as the châtelet. In the reign of Charles VI. the lordship belonged to Pierre d'Orgemont, chancellor of France. In 1484 it passed to the house of Montmorency, and in 1632 to the house of Condé. Louis II., prince de Condé, enjoyed here the society of La Bruyère, Racine, Molière, La Fontaine, Boileau and others. The stables close to the racecourse were built from 1719 to 1735 by the duke of Bourbon. The grand château was destroyed about the time of the Revolution, but the châtelet still remains one of the finest specimens of Renaissance architecture in France. The château d'Enghien, facing the entrance to the grand château, was built in 1770 as a guest-house. In 1830 the estate passed into the hands of Henri, duc d'Aumale, fourth son of Louis Philippe. In 1852 the house of Orléans was declared incapable of possessing property in France, and Chantilly was accordingly sold by auction, but passed back into the hands of the duc d'Aumale who built the palace, on the foundations of the grand château. He installed in the châtelet a valuable library and a collection of paintings. In 1886 he gave the park and château with its collections to the Institute of France in trust for the nation, reserving to himself only a life interest.

CHANTREY, SIR FRANCIS LEGATT (1781–1841), English sculptor, was born on April 7, 1781, at Norton, near Sheffield. After receiving lessons in carving and painting, Chantrey went to try his fortune in Dublin and Edinburgh, and finally (1802) in London. He exhibited pictures at the Academy for some years from 1804, but from 1807 onwards devoted himself mainly to sculpture. His first imaginative work in sculpture was the model of the head of Satan, which was exhibited at the Royal Academy in 1808. He afterwards executed for Greenwich hospital four colossal busts of the admirals Duncan, Howe, Vincent and Nelson; and the next bust which he executed, that of Horne Tooke, procured him commissions to the extent of £12,000. He received many honours, was elected R.A. in 1818, and received a knighthood in 1835. He died suddenly on Nov. 25, 1841.

His principal works are the statues of Washington in the State House at Boston, U.S.A.; of George III. in the Guildhall, London; of George IV. at Brighton; of Pitt in Hanover Square, London; of James Watt in Westminster Abbey; of Canning in Liverpool; of Lord President Blair and Lord Melville in Edinburgh. Of his equestrian statues the most famous are those of Sir Thomas Munro in Calcutta and the duke of Wellington in front of the London Exchange. But the finest of Chantrey's works are his busts and his delineations of children. The figures of two children asleep in each other's arms, which form a monumental design in Lichfield cathedral, have always been admired for beauty, simplicity and grace. Allan Cunningham and Weekes were his chief assistants, and were indeed the active executants of many works that pass under Chantrey's name. *See* A. J. Raymond, *Life and work of Sir Francis Chantrey* (1904); for his will *see* CHANTREY BEQUEST.

CHANTREY BEQUEST. By the will dated Dec. 31, 1840, Sir Francis Chantrey (*q.v.*), left his whole residuary personal estate after the decease or on the second marriage of his widow (less certain specified annuities and bequests) in trust for the president and trustees of the Royal Academy (or in the event of the dissolution of the Royal Academy, to such society as might take its place), the income to be devoted to the encouragement of British fine art in painting and sculpture only, by "the purchase of works of fine art of the highest merit . . . that can be obtained." The funds might be allowed to accumulate for not more than five years; works by British or foreign artists might be acquired, so long as such works were entirely executed in Great Britain. The prices were to be "liberal," and no sympathy for an artist or his family was to influence the selection or the purchase of works, which were to be acquired solely on the ground of intrinsic merit. No commission or orders might be given: the works must be finished before purchase. An annual sum of £300 and £50 was to be paid to the president of the Royal Academy and the secretary respectively, for the discharge of their duties in carrying out the provisions of the will.

Lady Chantrey died in 1875, and two years later the fund became available for the purchase of paintings and sculptures. The capital sum amounted to £105,000. Galleries in the Victoria and Albert Museum at South Kensington were at first used, until in 1898 the Royal Academy arranged with the Treasury for the transference of the collection to the National Gallery of British Art, which had been erected by Sir Henry Tate at Millbank.

A growing discontent with the interpretation by the Royal Academy of the terms of the will found forcible expression in the press in 1903, and a debate in the House of Lords led to the appointment of a select committee of that House (June to Aug. 1904). Its report made recommendations with a view to the prevention of certain former errors of administration, but dismissed other charges against the Academy. A memorandum was issued by the Royal Academy (Feb. 1905) disagreeing with certain recommendations, but allowing others.

See *The Administration of the Chantrey Bequest,* by D. S. MacColl (1904), a highly controversial publication; *Chantrey and His Bequest,* by Arthur Fish, a complete illustrated record of the purchases, etc. (1904); *The Royal Academy, its Uses and Abuses,* by H. J. Laidlay (1898), controversial; *Report from the Select Committee of the House of Lords on the Chantrey Trust; together with the Proceedings of the Committee, Minutes of Evidence and Appendix* (1904).

CHANT ROYAL, one of the fixed forms of verse invented by the ingenuity of the poets of mediaeval France. It is composed of five verses, identical in arrangement, of 10 or 11 lines each, and an envoi of 5, 6 or 7 lines. All the verses are written on the five rhymes in the first verse, the entire poem, therefore, consisting of 60 lines or more, in the course of which five rhymes are repeated. It has been conjectured that the chant royal is an extended ballade, or a ballade conceived upon a larger scale; but which form preceded the other appears to be uncertain. On this point Henri de Croï, who wrote about these forms of verse in his *Art et science de rhétorique* (1493), throws no light. He dwells, however, on the great dignity of what he calls the "Champt Royal," and says that those who defy with success the ardour of its rules deserve crowns and garlands for their pains. Étienne Pasquier (1529–1615) points out that the chant royal, by its length and rigidity, is better fitted than the ballade for solemn and pompous themes. In early French literature, the most admired chants royaux are those of Clément Marot; his *Chant royal chrestien,* with its refrain

Santé au corps, et Paradis à l'âme,

was celebrated. Théodore de Banville defines the chant royal as essentially belonging to ages of faith, when its subjects could be either the exploits of a hero of royal race or the processional splendours of religion. La Fontaine was the latest of the French poets to attempt the chant royal, until it was resuscitated in modern times.

This species of poem was unknown in English mediaeval literature and was only introduced into Great Britain in the last quarter of the 19th century. The earliest chant royal in English was that published by Edmund Gosse in 1877, "The Praise of Dionysus."

In the middle ages the chant royal was largely used for the praise of the Virgin Mary. Eustache Deschamps (1340–1410) distinguishes these Marian chants royaux, which were called "serventois," by the absence of an envoi. These poems are first mentioned by Rutebeuf, a *trouvère* of the 13th century. The chant royal is practically unknown outside French and English literature.

CHANTRY, a small chapel in or adjoining a church, endowed for maintaining priests to chant masses for the soul of the founder or of some one named by him. It generally contained the founder's tomb and had an entrance from the outside for the chantry priest. The word is applied either to the endowment funds or to the chapel itself.

CHANUTE, a city of Neosho county, Kansas, U.S.A., 120 mi. S.S.W. of Kansas City, near the Neosho river. It is on federal highways 59, 169 and state highways 39 and 57. It is served by the Missouri-Kansas-Texas and the Santa Fe railways. Pop. (1950) 10,241. Chanute is in the midcontinent oil and gas field and is surrounded by a farming and fruit-growing country. Shale and clay are found near by. Chanute is headquarters of a division of the Atchison, Topeka and Santa Fe railway system. The principal industries are: refineries, railway shops; brick, tile, cement and oil-field machinery manufactures; dress, broom, mattress and boiler factories; and machine and tank shops.

Four towns—New Chicago, Tioga, Chicago Junction and Alliance—founded here about 1870, were consolidated in 1872, and named after Octave Chanute (b. 1832), civil engineer and aeronautist, who was the engineer of the railway then under construction. Natural gas and oil were discovered in 1899.

CHANZY, ANTOINE EUGÈNE ALFRED (1823–1883), French general, was born at Nouart (Ardennes) on March 18, 1823. The son of a cavalry officer, he was educated at the naval school at Brest, but enlisted in the artillery, and was commissioned in the Zouaves in 1843. Although he acquired an excellent professional reputation during war service in Algeria and in Lombardy, he was in bad odour at the War Office on account of suspected contributions to the press, and at the outbreak of the Franco-German War was refused a brigade command. After the revolution, however, the government of national defence gave him command of the XVI. Corps of the army of the Loire. (For the operations of the Orleans campaign which followed, *see* FRANCO-GERMAN WAR.) After the second battle of Orleans and the separation of the two wings of the French army, Chanzy was appointed to command that in the west, designated the second army of the Loire. He displayed conspicuous moral courage in the fighting from Beaugency to the Loire, in his retreat to Le Mans, and in retiring to Laval behind the Mayenne. He was made a grand officer of the Legion of Honour, and was elected to the National Assembly. At the beginning of the commune, Chanzy, then at Paris, fell into the hands of the insurgents, by whom he was liberated on giving his parole not to serve against them A ransom of £40,000 was also paid by the Government for him In 1872 he became a member of the committee of defence and commander of the VII. Army Corps, and in 1873 was appointed governor of Algeria, where he remained for six years. In 1875 he was elected a life senator, in 1878 received the grand cross of the Legion of Honour, and in 1879, without his consent, was nominated for the presidency of the republic, receiving a third of the total votes. For two years he was ambassador at St. Petersburg (Leningrad). He died suddenly, while commanding the VI. Army Corps at Châlons-sur-Marne, on Jan. 4, 1883, and his remains received a state funeral. He was the author of *La Deuxième Armée de la Loire* (1872).

See J. M. Villefranche, *Historie du Général Chanzy* (1890).

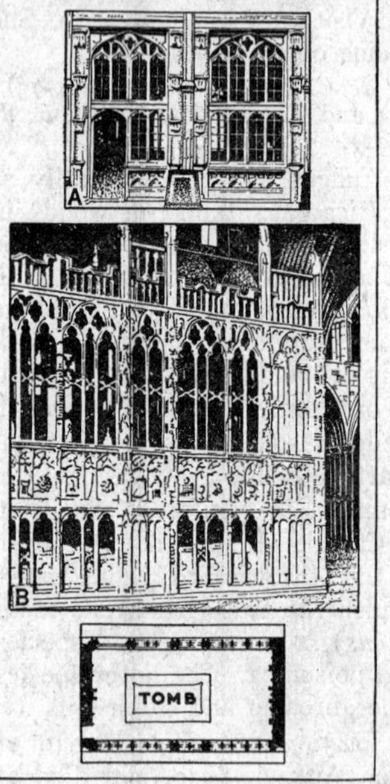

BY COURTESY OF SIMPSON, "HISTORY OF ARCHITECTURAL DEVELOPMENT" (LONGMANS, GREEN & CO.); GARDNER, "A GUIDE TO ENGLISH GOTHIC ARCHITECTURE" (CAMBRIDGE UNIVERSITY PRESS); SIR BANISTER FLETCHER, "HISTORY OF ARCHITECTURE ON THE COMPARATIVE METHOD," EIGHTH ED. (1928) BATSFORD

A, CHANTRY TOMB, CHRIST CHURCH, HAMPSHIRE (c. 1530). B, TOMB OF PRINCE ARTHUR, WORCESTER CATHEDRAL (c. 1505)

CHAOS, in the Hesiodic theogony, the infinite empty space which existed before all things (*Theog.* 116, 123). It is not, however, a mere vacuum, being filled with clouds and darkness; from it proceed Erebus and Nyx (Night), whose children are Aether (upper air) and Hemera (Day). In the Orphic cosmogony the origin of all goes back to Chronos, the personification of time, who produces Aether and Chaos. In the Aristophanic parody (*Birds,* 691) the winged Eros in conjunction with gloomy Chaos brings forth the race of birds. The later Roman conception (Ovid, *Metam.* i. 7) makes Chaos the original crude, shapeless mass, into which the architect of the world introduces order and harmony, and from which individual forms are created. When contrasted with cosmos (the orderly universe) the word has various meanings:—the space between heaven and earth; the underworld and its ruler; the immeasurable darkness; the indefinite in space and time. In modern usage "chaos" denotes a state of disorder and confusion.

CHAPACURAN, a tribe or small group of tribes of South American Indians, regarded on rather slender evidence as constituting an independent linguistic stock. The stock, which comprises the Ites, Pawumwas and other smaller tribes in addition to the Chapacuras, seems to have occupied the whole of the basin of the Rio Blanco in north-eastern Bolivia, together with the Guaporé from the mouth of the Blanco to its confluence with the Mamore, as well as the eastern tributaries of the Guaporé between 12° and 13° S. Lat. The Chapacuras themselves lived on the Rio Blanco and about lake Chitiopa. They were a peaceful, sedentary agricultural folk, whose culture was generally similar to that of the Chiquitos (*q.v.*). The Pawumwas go almost naked, and use the blow-gun with poisoned darts.

See G. de Crequi-Montfort and P. Rivet, *Linguistique Bolivienne; La famille linguistique Capakura* (*J. Soc. Americanistes de Paris* [n.s.], vol. x., pp. 119–173); J. D. Haseman, *Some notes on the Pawumwa Indians* (*American Anthropologist* [n.s.], vol. xiv., pp. 333–350).

CHAPAIS, SIR (JOSEPH AMABLE) THOMAS (1858–1946), Canadian lawyer, statesman and historian, was born at St. Denis-de-la-Bouteillerie, Quebec, on March 23, 1858, son of Senator J. C. Chapais, one of the "Fathers of Confederation." Chapais was educated at St. Anne's college, Laval university, and was called to the Quebec bar in 1879. In March 1892 he was called to the legislative council of Quebec, was a minister without portfolio in the Taillon government, and was elected leader of the government in the executive council (Jan. 1893); speaker of the legislative council (April 1895); president of the executive council (May 1896), and minister of colonization and mines (Jan. 1897). He retired from office in May 1897. From 1884 to 1901 Chapais edited *Le Courrier du Canada* of Quebec. In 1907 he was appointed professor at Laval university. He published several works on history and law, including *Cours d'Histoire du Canada, 1760–1814* (8 vols., 1919–35). On Dec. 31, 1919, he was called to the senate of Canada. He was knighted in 1935. He died at St. Denis, Que., on July 15, 1946.

CHAPARRAL, a mixed forest formation of low hard-leaved, stunted trees and shrubs resulting from short, wet, cool winters and long, arid, hot summers. The word is believed to have been derived from *chaparro*, the Spanish name for live oak. Chaparral grows slowly and shrubs 25 years old will usually average not more than 2 or 3 in. in diameter and 5 or 6 ft. in height. This type of forest growth occurs chiefly in southern California in the United States, along the coast of Chile, in Europe and Asia along the Mediterranean and as far east as Turkistan, in Africa near the Cape of Good Hope and on the southern and southwestern coasts of Australia and Tasmania. Its chief economic value lies in its ability to conserve water supply, which it accomplishes below the surface through its root system and above the surface by breaking the force of hot winds and shading the ground to prevent evaporation.

Of the 150 different species of woody plants believed to exist in the chaparral of Southern California 20 dominant types—among them chamise, manzanita, ceanothus, sumac, sage-brush, scrub oak and buckthorn (*qq.v.*)—represent 90% of the growth. In former times the Indians used the nuts, berries and seeds of several of the varieties for food. Some species were once in demand as fuel supply and others are still used for fencing. The bee industry flourishes in the chaparral region, several profusely flowering shrubs, as the black sage, being excellent honey plants. It is estimated that there are 5,500,000 acres of chaparral in the United States. Chaparral formations protect the upper watersheds of the coastal streams in California for a distance of about 450 miles.

CHAPBOOK, the comparatively modern name applied by booksellers and bibliophiles to the little stitched tracts written for the common people and formerly circulated in England, Scotland and the American colonies by itinerant dealers or chapmen, consisting chiefly of vulgarized versions of popular stories, such as *Tom Thumb, Jack the Giant Killer, Mother Shipton,* and *Reynard the Fox*—travels, biographies and religious treatises. Few of the older chapbooks exist. Samuel Pepys collected some of the best and had them bound into small quarto volumes which he called *Vulgaria;* also four volumes of a smaller size, which he lettered *Penny Witticisms, Penny Merriments, Penny Compliments* and *Penny Godlinesses.* The early chapbooks were the direct descendants of the black letter tracts of Wynkyn de Worde. It was in France that the printing-press first began to supply reading for the common people. At the end of the 15th century there was a large popular literature of farces, tales in verse and prose, satires, almanacs, etc., stitched together so as to contain a few leaves, and circulated by itinerant booksellers, known as colporteurs. Most early English chapbooks are adaptations or translations of these French originals, and were introduced into England early in the 16th century. The chapbooks of the 17th century present us with valuable illustrations of the manners of the time; one of the best known is that containing the story of Dick Whittington. In France literature of this kind has been the object of close and systematic study, and *L'Histoire des livres populaires ou de la littérature du colportage* by Charles Nisard (1854) goes deeply into the subject. Amongst English books may be mentioned *Notices of Fugitive Tracts and Chapbooks,* by J. O. Halliwell-Phillipps (1849); *Chapbooks of the 18th Century,* by John Ashton (1882), and some reprints by the Villon Society in 1885.

CHAPE, a cover or metal plate, such as the cap upon the needle in the compass, also the transverse guard of a sword which protects the hand (Fr. *chape,* a hood, cope or sheath); also, a support or catch to attach one thing to another, as the hook on a belt to which the sword is fastened; and the tip of a fox's brush.

CHAPEL, a place of religious worship, either a subordinate division of a church, or a separate building distinguished from a church by the special conditions of its foundation or use. *Capella,* the diminutive of *cappa,* a cloak, was the name given to the shrine in which the cloak (*cappa brevior*) of St. Martin was kept and carried about by the Frankish kings on their journeys, when oaths were taken on it. This peculiar use was transferred to any sanctuary containing relics, the priest of which was called *capellanus* or chaplain. By a further extension, the word was identified with all places of worship which were not mother churches (*ecclesiae matrices*), so as to include a large number of miscellaneous foundations. Most nearly akin to the original meaning is the application of the term to the oratories attached to royal residences. Thus the Sainte Chapelle, the palace chapel at Paris, consecrated in 1248, was built by St. Louis to enshrine the relic of the Crown of Thorns, ransomed by him from the Venetians, who held it in pawn from John of Brienne, the Latin emperor of the East. In the next century, chapels were founded by princes of the French royal house at Bourges, Riom and elsewhere for which the same title was adopted. Such chapels royal were usually founded as collegiate establishments, like Edward III.'s chapels of St. Stephen at Westminster and St. George at Windsor. Collegiate chapels were also founded by prelates and noblemen in connection with their castles and manor-houses, such as the chapel of St. Mary and the Holy Angels at the gate of the palace at York, founded by Archbishop Roger (1154–81), and that of St. Elizabeth before the gate of Wolvesey Castle at Winchester, founded by Bishop John of Pontoise (1282–1304).

The chapel of the castle or manor-house, however, was generally served by a single domestic chaplain. For oratories in connection with private houses an episcopal licence was required, so as to safeguard the rights of the churches in whose parishes they were established. Though frequently within the house itself, they were also erected as separate buildings, and some, which served as churches for the lord of the manor and his tenants, acquired the status of free chapels, which implied exemption from parochial and archidiaconal, and occasionally, though not always, from episcopal jurisdiction. Certain churches, in the patronage of the Crown or owing their foundation to the king, were regarded as royal free chapels and free chapels on manors probably originated in the grant of special privileges to their owners by the Crown. In time, such free chapels, governed by rectors, sometimes lost their peculiar character and were reckoned as parish churches; but, where the status of a free chapel remained, their incumbents were held to be without cure of souls.

Parish Chapels.—More numerous, however, than free chapels were the chapels in outlying hamlets of large parishes, maintained by the inhabitants and served daily, or on certain days in the week, by chaplains provided at the expense of the parochial incumbent. Some of these, which, as time went on, acquired rights of baptism and burial, were parochial chapels; others, merely chantry chapels in small villages, without such rights, were, properly speaking, chapels of ease. The origin of such foundations was usually the difficulty experienced by the inhabitants in attending the mother church in bad weather, when the streams were swollen and the roads impassable. In Leicestershire, early in the thirteenth century, there were more than a hundred of these dependent chapels in about two hundred parishes, and the proportion elsewhere was not very different.

Subordinate Buildings.—The idea of a chapel as a subordinate or dependent building is implied by its use for the areas appropriated to the minor altars within or projecting from the walls of a church. The services held in these were called chantries (*cantariae*), and, by a transference of ideas to which there are many parallels in mediaeval usage, the chapels themselves were often known as chantries. Of the use of chapel to signify the oratory of a private establishment, the most familar examples are the chapels of colleges at Oxford and Cambridge. Similarly the places of worship in hospitals, almshouses, etc., are called chapels, as well as those which, like chapels of cemeteries, are generally restricted to some special use. Proprietary chapels, founded in London and other English towns during the eighteenth and early nineteenth centuries, were established, with a licence for divine service, by private individuals or groups of trustees. The growth of Nonconformity, however, gave the word a particular application to dissenting places of worship. In Ireland the term has clung persistently to those of the Roman Church, a survival of an old use which in England was derived from the chapels or religious establishments maintained by Henrietta Maria and other Roman Catholic queens. But, apart from this, the modern tendency is to abandon the employment of the word for special classes of religious building, and to give the title church to all indiscriminately.

There are many instances in mediaeval wills and inventories of the application of the term chapel to sets of vestments and altar furniture, as constituting the necessary fittings of a private oratory. Another transference of the sense occasionally found is from the chapel itself to the collective members of the foundation.

(A. H. T.)

CHAPEL. In the printing trade, the name of the fellowship of compositors (and, nowadays, of all crafts) in a printing works. The president is termed the "father of the chapel." In the United States he is called "the chairman." The name chapel is used not only of the fellowship itself but of the meetings which it holds. At these meetings, the chapel discusses such things as the general welfare of the body, the conditions of work, relations with employers, and trade union matters.

The accepted version of the origin of the use of the word chapel in this connection is that it is derived from the fact that Caxton first set up his press in or near Westminster Abbey. Writing in 1716, Myles Davies, in his *Athenae Britannicae* says, "William Caxton first practis'd Printing in the Abbey of Westminster, A.D. 1471, thence a Printing-Room came to be call'd a Chappell amongst our Printers." Another explanation is offered by Joseph Moxon, who in his *Mechanick Exercises* (1683) says, "Every Printing-house is by the Custom of Time out of mind, called a Chappel: and all the Workmen that belong to it are Members of the Chappel: and the oldest Freeman is Father of the Chappel. I suppose this stile was originally conferred upon it by the courtesie of some great Churchman, or men (doubtless when Chappels were in more veneration than of late years they have been here in England), who for the Books of Divinity that proceeded from a Printing-house gave it the Reverend Title of Chappel."

CHAPELAIN, JEAN (1595–1674), French poet and man of letters, was born in Paris and spent 17 years in the service of M. de la Trousse, grand provost of France. He was employed by Cardinal Richelieu in the organization of the Académie Française. In 1632, in a conversation with the cardinal, he had laid down the canon of the unities of time and space which should govern the drama. The unities had already been advocated by Jules-César Scaliger (*Art poétique*, 1561), and by the abbé d'Aubignac (*Pratique du théâtre*, 1657), but the doctrine appears to have been unfamiliar to Richelieu, who invited Chapelain to draw up *Les Sentiments de l'Académie sur "le Cid,"* in which deviation from the rule is denounced. His great reputation seemed to be enhanced by the success of the first 12 cantos of his epic *La Pucelle* (1656), on which he had been at work for 20 years, but it was shattered by Gilles Boileau in his early satires, and the remaining cantos of the epic remained unprinted until 1882, when they were edited by H. Herluison. Chapelain drew up the statutes of the academy, and laid down the rules for the great grammar and dictionary to be produced.

In 1663 Chapelain was employed by Jean-Baptiste Colbert to draw up a list of men of letters with observations for use by the crown in the distribution of honours and pensions.

Bibliography.—There is a very favourable estimate of Chapelain's merits as a critic in George Saintsbury's *A History of Criticism*, ii, 256–261, 3 vol. (1900–04). An analysis of *La Pucelle* is given in pp. 23–79 of Robert Southey's *Joan of Arc* (1796). *See* also *Les Lettres de Jean Chapelain* (edit. P. Tanuzey de Larroque, 1880–83); *Lettres inédites . . . à P. D. Huet* (1658–73, edit. L. G. Pellissier, 1894); Julien Duchesne, *Les Poèmes épiques du XVIIe siècle* (1870); the abbé A. Fabre, *Les Ennemis de Chapelain* (1888), *Chapelain et nos deux premières académies* (1890); A. Muehlan, *Jean Chapelain* (1893); George Collas, *Jean Chapelain* (1912). *See* further the edition of Chapelain's critical work, *Jean Chapelain, opuscules critiques*, published with an introduction by Alfred C. Hunter in 1936, and the University of Minnesota edition of *Les Sentiments de l'Académie française sur "le Cid"* (1916).

CHAPEL-EN-LE-FRITH, an old market town in Derbyshire, Eng., 5¾ mi. N. of Buxton by road. Pop. (1950) 6,010. The manufacture of brake and clutch linings is important. The site was formerly part of the royal forest (or *frith*) of the Peak. The church of St. Thomas of Canterbury dates from the 13th century and the Ford hall from the 15th.

CHAPEL HILL, a town of Orange county, North Carolina, U.S., on a high ridge 28 mi. N.W. of Raleigh, in a dairying, tobacco and cotton-growing district. It is on federal highways 15 and 501; served by the Southern railway. Pop. (1950) 9,169. It is the seat of the University of North Carolina, which occupies a beautiful campus of 106 ac. and owns adjoining tracts of 1,500 ac.

CHAPELLE ARDENTE, the chapel or room in which the corpse of a sovereign or other exalted personage lies in state pending the funeral service. The name is in allusion to the many candles lighted round the catafalque. This custom is first chronicled as occurring at the obsequies of Dagobert I (602–638).

CHAPERON, originally a cap or hood (Fr. *chape*) worn by nobles and Knights of the Garter in full dress, and after the 16th century by middle-aged ladies. In the 19th century the word was used of a married or elderly lady (*cf.* "duenna") escorting or protecting a young and unmarried girl in public places and in society.

CHAPLAIN, originally, according to Du Cange (*Gloss. med. et inf. Lat.*), the custodian of the cloak (*cappa* or *capella*) of St. Martin of Tours, which was preserved as a relic by the French kings, and carried with the army in wartime, when it was kept in a tent known itself as *capella* (Fr. *chapelain;* M. Lat. *capellanus*). It is also suggested that the *capella* was the tent-like canopy erected by the French kings over the altar for soldiers in the field, without special reference to St. Martin. However this may be, the name *capellanus* was generally applied to custodians of sacred relics preserved in royal chapels, etc.; and the office gradually extended its scope, *capellani* acquiring spiritual jurisdiction and increasing in number, so that an arch-chaplain was appointed as their head, who from the time of Charlemagne was a high prelate, and who became an important personage in the realm. In France the arch-chaplain was grand-almoner, and both in France and in the Holy Roman Empire was also high chancellor of the realm. The office was abolished in France in 1789, revived by Pius IX. in 1857, and again abolished on the fall of the Second Empire. The word chaplain now signifies a clergyman attached to the household of a sovereign or his representatives (ambassadors, judges, etc.), or of a bishop or nobleman, or private individual having a chapel in his house, to the army or navy, or to institutions (*e.g.* parliament, colleges, cemeteries, prisons). As chaplain he has no parochial duties, but in some cases a parish priest is also appointed to a chaplaincy; *e.g.* an Anglican bishop often appoints beneficed clergymen as his examining chaplains. The British sovereign has 36 "Chaplains in Ordinary," who officiate in rotation, as well as "Honorary Chaplains" and "Domestic Chaplains." There are also royal chaplains in Scotland. The Indian civil service appoints a number of chaplains of the Church of England and the Church of Scotland, who are subject to the same conditions as other civil servants. Chaplains are also appointed under the Foreign Office to embassies, consulates, etc. Workhouse chaplains are appointed by overseers and guardians on the direction of the Ministry of Health. Prison chaplains are appointed by the home secretary.

In the British army there are two kinds of chaplains, permanent and occasional. The former, described as Chaplains to the Forces, hold commissions, serving throughout the empire except in India; they number about 100, and include a Chaplain-General who ranks as a major-general, and four classes of subordinate chaplains who rank respectively as colonels, lieutenant-colonels, majors and captains. Special chaplains (Acting Chaplains for Temporary Service) may be appointed by a secretary of state. Permanent chaplains may be Church of England, Roman Catholic or Presbyterian; Wesleyans (if they prefer not to accept commissions) may be appointed Acting Chaplains. In the navy, every large ship in commission has a chaplain; at the head of the naval chaplains is the Chaplain of the Fleet. But the ecclesiastical superior of all Roman Catholic chaplains in both army and navy is the archbishop of Westminster, by decree of Propaganda (1906). In 1909 a Chaplains' Department of the Territorial Force was formed, having no denominational restriction.

In France, military and naval chaplaincies were abolished on the separation of Church and State. In the army of the United States of America the establishment of chaplains was fixed in 1904 by Congress at 57 (15 with the rank of major), 12 for the artillery corps and one each for the cavalry and infantry regiments. There is no distinction of sect. In the U.S. navy the chaplains number 24, 13 ranking as lieutenants, seven as commanders, four as captains.

The Roman Catholic Church also recognizes a class of beneficed chaplains, supported out of "pious foundations" for the specific duty of saying, or arranging for, certain masses, or taking part in certain services. These chaplains are classified as follows:—*Ecclesiastical,* if the foundation has been recognized officially as a benefice; *Lay,* if this recognition has not been obtained; *Mercenary,* if the benefaction has been entrusted to a layman to procure the desired celebration (such trustees are sometimes called "Lay Chaplains"); *Collative,* if it is provided that a bishop shall erect the foundation into a benefice.

Other classes of chaplains are:—(1) *Parochial* or *Auxiliary Chaplains,* appointed to assist a parish priest (usually by the bishop, but sometimes by the parish priest, as allowed by the Council of Trent); (2) *Chaplains of Convents,* appointed by a bishop: these must be men of mature age, should not be regulars if secular priests can be obtained, and are not generally appointed for life; (3) *Pontifical Chaplains,* some of whom (known as Private Chaplains) assist the pontiff in the celebration of Mass; others attached directly to the pope are honorary private chaplains who occasionally assist the private chaplains, private clerics of the chapel, common chaplains and supernumerary chaplains. The common chaplains were instituted by Alexander VII., and in 1907 were definitely allowed the title "Monsignore"—pertaining also to cardinals, archbishops, and bishops—by Pius X.

CHAPLIN, CHARLES SPENCER (1889-), cinema actor, was born April 16, 1889, of English parentage, and passed his childhood in London. At an early age he appeared on the music-hall stage with his father and his brother Sydney, taking small parts in vaudeville. After a short experience on the legitimate stage, he re-entered vaudeville in London as a member of the Fred Karno company. In 1910 he went to the United States as leading comedian in a Karno production, *A Night in an English Music Hall.* He attracted the attention of Joseph M. Schenck, and on the latter's suggestion he was engaged by Mack Sennett to make films with the Keystone Comedy Company at Hollywood, California. In 1918 he formed his own company, and he produced a series of films which placed him in the front rank of artists. Among the more successful of his later releases were: *A Dog's Life* (1918), *Shoulder Arms* (1918), *The Kid* (1921), *The Idle Class* (1921), *The Gold Rush* (1925), and *The Circus* (1926). In all of these he was the central figure. In 1931, he produced and acted in *City Lights,* in 1936 *Modern Times,* in 1940 *The Great Dictator* and in 1947 *Monsieur Verdoux.*

CHAPLIN, HENRY CHAPLIN, 1st Viscount (1840–1923), English statesman, son of the Rev. Henry Chaplin, of Blankney, Lincolnshire, was born Dec. 22, 1840, and died May 29, 1923. He was educated at Harrow and Christ Church, Oxford. Entering parliament in 1868, he sat as Conservative member, first for Mid-Lincolnshire (1868–1906), and then for Wimbledon. As the typical English country gentleman, the "Squire of Blankney" was one of the leaders of the agricultural interest. He was chancellor of the duchy of Lancaster (1885–86) and president of the new Board of Agriculture (1889–92); as president of the Local Government Board (1895–1900) he was responsible for the Agricultural Rates Act of 1896, and he was a member of Mr. Chamberlain's Tariff Commission. During the Coalition government of 1915, Chaplin was the leader of the nominal opposition until his elevation to the peerage in 1916.

See E. Stewart, *Henry Chaplin* (1926).

CHAPMAN, FRANK MICHLER (1864–1945), American ornithologist, born at Englewood, N.J., June 12, 1864, had no formal education beyond academy. He joined the staff of the American Museum of Natural History, New York city, as assistant in 1887, served as assistant curator (1888–1901) and associate curator (1901–08) of ornithology and mammalogy, and as curator of ornithology (1908–42) until his retirement. He died in New York city on Nov. 15, 1945. He originated the habitat bird groups and seasonal bird exhibits; and, beginning in 1887, travelled widely, collecting and photographing the birds of temperate and tropical America. He did pioneer work to popularize bird study, publishing his widely used *Handbook of Birds of Eastern North America* (1895), *The Warblers of North America* (1907), and a dozen other popular books. His technical papers covered life histories, geographical distribution, and systematic relationships of American birds, after 1911 dealing largely with the origin of Andean bird life and resulting in volumes on *The Distribution of Bird Life in Colombia* (1917), *Birds of the Urubamba Valley, Peru* (1921), and *The Distribution of Bird-Life in Ecuador* (1926). His field adventures are well presented in his *Camps and Cruises of an Ornithologist* (1908) and *Autobiography of a Bird-Lover* (1933). He was founder and editor (1898–35) of *Bird-Lore* magazine, president of the American Ornithologists union (1911–14), and vice-president of the Explorers club (1910–18). He was awarded the first Linnean medal (1912), the first Elliot medal (1918) of the National Academy of Sciences, the Roosevelt medal (1928) and the Burroughs medal (1929). Brown university, Providence, R.I., awarded him the Sc.D. degree in 1913. (G. F. Ss.)

CHAPMAN, GEORGE (1559–1634), English poet and dramatist, translator of Homer, was born near Hitchin. There is no record of his university career, though Anthony Wood (*Athen. Oxon.* ii. 575) claims that he spent some time in Oxford. He had become a play-writer in London, and had published some poems when he appeared in Henslowe's *Diary* on Feb. 12, 1596, as the author of the *Blind Beggar of Alexandria.* Thenceforward his name repeatedly appears in connection with payments for various plays until 1599, after which date he appears to have written masques for the Children of the Chapel (afterwards of the Revels) in the intervals of working on the translation of Homer. In 1598 he had completed Marlowe's poem, *Hero and Leander.* Apparently he was imprisoned for a short time for his share in the play *Eastward Ho,* which gave offence to James I by certain quips against the Scots. He was encouraged in his translation of Homer by Prince Henry, to whom he was server in ordinary, but on the prince's death in 1612 Chapman lost his appointment and the promise of a life pension made by the prince was not fulfilled. He found a new patron in Robert Carr, earl of Somerset, to whom the two folio volumes *The Whole Works of Homer, Prince of Poets, in his Iliads and Odysses* (1615) are dedicated. *The Crowne of all Homer's Workes, Batrachomyomachia, or the Battaile of Frogs and Mise. His Hymns and Epigrams* appeared in 1624. The poet died on May 12, 1634.

Chapman enjoyed the friendship and admiration of his great contemporaries. John Webster in the preface to his *White Devil* praised his "full and heightened style," and Ben Jonson told Drummond of Hawthornden that Fletcher and Chapman "were loved of him." But the good relations with Jonson were apparently interrupted later. It was suggested by William Minto, who has been followed by later writers, that Chapman was the "rival poet" of Shakespeare's sonnets. Sir E. K. Chambers, however, thinks that the assumption would be more plausible if any relation between the earl of Southampton and Chapman, earlier than a stray dedication shared with others in 1609, could be established.

Chapman's *Homer* gives him a high place in English literature. Swinburne, in the criticism contributed to an earlier edition of the *Encyclopædia Britannica,* gave an admirable and considered judgment of the work. "The objections," he said, "which a just and adequate judgment may bring against Chapman's master-work, his translation of Homer, may be summed up in three epithets: it is romantic, laborious, Elizabethan. The qualities implied by these epithets are the reverse of those which should distinguish a translator of Homer; but setting this apart, and considering the poems as in the main original works, the superstructure of a romantic poet on the submerged foundations of Greek verse, no praise can be too warm or high for the power, the freshness, the indefatigable strength and inextinguishable fire which animate this exalted work."

On the great qualities of his tragedies and comedies Swinburne wrote: "The most notable examples of his tragic work are comprised in the series of plays taken, and adapted sometimes with singular licence, from the records of such parts of French history as lie between the reign of Francis I. and the reign of Henry IV., ranging in date of subject from the trial and death of Admiral Chabot to the treason and execution of Marshal Biron. The two plays bearing as epigraph the name of that famous soldier and conspirator are a storehouse of lofty thought and splendid verse, with scarcely a flash or sparkle of dramatic action. The one play of Chapman's whose popularity on the stage survived the Restoration is *Bussy d'Ambois* (d'Amboise)—a tragedy not lacking in violence of action or emotion, and abounding even more in sweet and sublime interludes than in crabbed and bombastic passages. His rarest jewels of thought and verse detachable from the context lie embedded in the tragedy of *Caesar and Pompey,* whence the finest of them were first extracted by the unerring and unequalled critical genius of Charles Lamb. In most of his tragedies the lofty and labouring spirit of Chapman may be said rather to shine fitfully through parts than steadily to pervade the whole; they show nobly altogether as they stand, but even better by help of excerpts and selections. But the excellence of his best comedies can only be appreciated by a student who reads them fairly and fearlessly through, and, having made some small deductions on the score of occasional pedantry and occasional indecency, finds in *All Fools, Monsieur d'Olive, The Gentleman Usher,* and *The Widow's Tears* a wealth and vigour of humorous invention, a tender and earnest grace of romantic poetry, which may atone alike for these passing blemishes and for the lack of such clear-cut perfection of character and such dramatic progression of interest as we find only in the yet higher poets of the English heroic age."

The list of the principal plays of George Chapman is as follows: *The Blinde Begger of Alexandria . . .* (acted 1596, printed 1598), a popular comedy; *An Humerous dayes Myrth* (May 1597; printed 1599); *Al Fooles, A Comedy* (1599, if it may be taken as identical with a play entered by Henslowe as "The World runs on wheels," printed 1605); *The Gentleman Usher* (*c.* 1601, pr. 1606), a comedy; *Monsieur d'Olive* (1604, pr. 1606), one of his most amusing and successful comedies; *Eastward Ho* (1605), written in conjunction with Ben Jonson and John Marston, an excellent comedy of city life; *Bussy d'Ambois, A Tragedie* (1604, pr. 1607, 1608, 1616, 1641, etc.), the scene of which is laid in the court of Henry III.; *The Revenge of Bussy d'Ambois, a Tragedie* (pr. 1613, but probably written much earlier); *The Conspiracie, And Tragedie of Charles Duke of Byron, Marshall of France . . . in two plays* (1608; pr. 1608 and 1625), severely cut after its first performance, which provoked a lively protest from the French ambassador; *May-Day, A witty Comedie* (pr. 1611, but probably acted as early as 1601); *The Widdowes Teares. A Comedie* (pr. 1612; produced perhaps as early as 1605); *Caesar and Pompey* (pr. 1631), written, says Chapman in the dedication, "long since," but never staged.

In *The Tragedie of Chabot Admirall of France* (*c.* 1613; pr. 1639) he collaborated with James Shirley, and in *Eastward Ho* (1605, pr. 1605), with Jonson and Marston. *The memorable Masque of the two Honourable Houses or Inns of Court,* was performed at court in 1613 in honour of the marriage of the Princess Elizabeth.

The standard edition of Chapman is the *Works,* edited by R. H. Shepherd (1874–75), the third volume of which contains an "Essay on the Poetical and Dramatic Works of George Chapman," by Swinburne, printed separately in 1875. The selection of his plays (1895) for the Mermaid Series is edited by W. L. Phelps. The edition by T. M. Parrott (1910–14) includes *Alphonsus, Emperor of Germany,* and other plays sometimes attributed to Chapman. For the sources of the plays *see* Emil Koeppel, "Quellen Studien zu den Dramen George Chapman's, Philip Massinger's und John Ford's," in *Quellen und Forschungen zur Sprach und Kulturgeschichte* (vol. 82, Strassburg, 1897). The suggestion of W. Minto (see *Characteristics of the English Poets,* 1885) that Chapman was the "rival poet" of Shakespeare's sonnets is amplified in A. Acheson's *Shakespeare and the Rival Poet* (1903). For the relations between Shakespeare and Chapman, *see* also J. M. Robertson, *Shakespeare and Chapman* (1917).

For other criticisms of his translation of Homer *see* Matthew Arnold, *Lectures on translating Homer* (1861), and Dr. A. Lohff, *George Chapman's Ilias-Übersetzung* (1903).

CHAPMAN, JOHN ("Johnny Appleseed") (1774–1845), American frontier nurseryman and folk character, was born in Leominster, Mass., Sept. 26, 1774. Little is known of him until he appeared in western Pennsylvania shortly before 1800. According to tradition, he had planted by 1801 a chain of seedling apple nurseries in advance of the settlements from the Allegheny to central Ohio. He spent about 25 years in north-central Ohio. Here the "Johnny Appleseed" stories largely originated, springing not only from his business, but from his eccentricities of manners and dress, Swedenborgian religious views, extreme kindness to wild animals, great generosity and unusual exploits of courage and endurance. By 1828 his nurserying reached northwestern Ohio and Indiana.

From 1834 Chapman operated around Fort Wayne, Ind., where he died in March 1845.

The folktales portray him on a spiritual mission preparing the wilderness for the westward movement. He has become the patron saint of American orcharding, floriculture and conservation. Late extension of the early oral tradition has been largely literary—stimulated notably by Henry Howe's *Historical Collections of Ohio* (1847, 1889), an article by W. D. Haley in *Harper's* Nov. 1871, and later imaginative treatments such as those by Eleanor Atkinson, Vachel Lindsay, Newell Dwight Hillis and Walt Disney.

BIBLIOGRAPHY.—Allen County-Fort Wayne Historical Society, *Johnny Appleseed Source Book* (1949); Harlan Hatcher and others, *Johnny Appleseed: A Voice in the Wilderness,* (1945); Robert Price, *John Chapman: A Bibliography of Johnny Appleseed in American History, Literature and Folklore* (1944), and articles in *New England Quarterly* (Sept. 1939 and Sept. 1944); Florence E. Wheeler, "John Chapman's Line of Descent from Edward Chapman of Ipswich," *Ohio Archaelogical and Historical Quarterly* (Jan. 1939). (RT. P.)

CHAPMAN, one who buys or sells, a trader or dealer, especially an itinerant pedlar. The word "chap," now a slang term, meant originally a customer. The word chapman is from Mid. Eng. *cheap,* to barter, from which we get the name of the famous London thoroughfare "Cheapside."

CHAPONE, HESTER (1727–1801), English essayist, daughter of Thomas Mulso, a country gentleman, was born at Twywell, Northamptonshire, on Oct. 27, 1727. At the age of nine she wrote a romance entitled *The Loves of Amoret and Melissa.* While on a visit to Canterbury she met the learned Mrs. Elizabeth Carter, and then became one of the little court of women who gathered at North End, Fulham, around Samuel Richardson, and in Miss Susannah Highmore's sketch of the novelist reading *Sir Charles Grandison* to his friends Miss Mulso is the central figure. In 1760 Miss Mulso, with her father's reluctant consent, married the attorney, John Chapone, who had been befriended by Richardson. Her husband died within a year of her marriage. Her best known work, *Letters on the Improvement of the Mind* (1772) brought her numerous requests from distinguished persons to undertake the education of their children. She died on Dec. 25, 1801.

See *The Posthumous Works of Mrs. Chapone, containing her correspondence with Mr. Richardson; a series of letters to Mrs. Elizabeth Carter . . . together with an account of her life and character drawn up by her own family,* 4 vol. (1807).

CHAPPE, CLAUDE (1763–1805), French engineer, was born at Brûlon (Sarthe) in 1763. With his brother, Ignace (1760–1829), he was the inventor of an optical telegraph widely used in France until it was superseded by the electric telegraph. His device consisted of an upright post, on the top of which was fastened a transverse bar, while at the ends of the latter two smaller arms moved on pivots. The position of these bars represented words or letters; and by means of machines placed at such intervals that each was distinctly visible from the next, messages could be conveyed through 50 leagues in a quarter of an hour. The machine was adopted by the legislative assembly in 1792, and in the following year Chappe was appointed *ingénieur-télégraphe;* but the originality of his invention was so much questioned that he was seized with melancholia and (it is said) committed suicide at Paris on Jan. 23, 1805.

CHAPPELL, WILLIAM (1809–1888), English writer on music, a member of the London musical firm of Chappell and Co., was born on Nov. 20, 1809, eldest son of Samuel Chappell (d. 1834), who founded the business. William Chappell deserves remembrance for having started the Musical Antiquarian society in 1840 and for his *Popular Music of the Olden Time* (1855–59)—an expansion of a collection of "national English airs" made by him in 1838–40.

The modern revival of interest in English folk songs owed much to this work, which was later re-edited by H. E. Wooldridge (1893). William's brother, Thomas Patey Chappell (d. 1902), introduced in 1859 the Monday and Saturday Popular concerts at St. James's hall, which were successfully managed by a younger brother, S. Arthur Chappell, till they came to an end toward the close of the 19th century.

CHAPTER HOUSE, the chamber in which the chapter or heads of the monastic bodies (*see* ABBEY; CATHEDRAL) assemble to transact business. They are of various forms; some are oblong apartments, as Canterbury, Exeter, Chester, Gloucester, etc.; some octagonal, as Salisbury, Westminster, Wells, York, etc. That at Worcester is circular; most are vaulted internally and polygonal externally, and some, as Salisbury, Wells, Lincoln, Worcester, etc., depend on a single slight vaulting shaft for the support of the massive vaulting. They are often provided with a vestibule, as at Westminster, Lincoln and Salisbury and are almost exclusively English. On the continent of Europe the chapter house is universally rectangular and frequently of great size and dignity.

In the United States the word chapter house refers almost invariably to the campus meeting or residence halls of the members of the collegiate Greek-letter societies—fraternities or sororities with names chosen from various combinations of the Greek alphabet, as Delta Theta Psi, Sigma Alpha, etc.

CHAPU, HENRI (1833–1891), French sculptor and medallist, born in Le Mée (Seine et Marne) on Sept. 29, 1833. He studied at the École des Beaux-Arts under Pradier and Duret and, having gained the Prix-de-Rome in 1855, spent five years in Rome. He was famous as a portrait medallist, and he executed many portrait busts and monuments; his statuary representing allegorical and mythological figures is sincere in feeling and poetical in conception.

His first success was attained by a figure of "Mercury" (1861, Luxembourg museum, Paris); then followed "The Sower" (1865); the "Nymph Clythia" (1866, Dijon museum). His fame was established by his statue of "Jeanne d'Arc" (1870, Luxembourg museum), representing her as a simple peasant kneeling in prayer. In 1872 Chapu undertook the monument to Henri Regnault with the fine figure of "Jeunesse" in the courtyard of the École des Beaux-Arts. In 1877 he sculptured the tomb of the Contesse Agoult (Daniel Stern) at Père Lachaise, and in 1887 he completed the monument to the archbishop Dupanloup. Among his portrait work may be mentioned Leon Bonnat (1864); Alexandre Dumas (1876); the bronze of J. E. Schneiders (1878) at Le Creuzot; the monument to the Galignani brothers (1888), representing them in modern costume, which was then an innovation and excited much comment, and the bust of Alexandra, Princess of Wales. The monument to Flaubert, with an allegorical figure of "Truth," is his last important work. Chapu died in Paris on April 21, 1891. The museums of Rouen and Bayonne contain a number of his drawings.

See O. Fidère, *Chapu, sa vie et son oeuvre* (1894).

CHAPU, a port of China on the north shore of Hangchow bay (30° 39′ N., 121° 6′ E.). It is built on a series of low hills and was long an outport of Hangchow. Chapu was the only harbour at Hangchow bay near Shanghai (50 mi.). At Chapu the Japanese succeeded in landing, in Nov. 1937, on the flank of the Chinese armies retreating from Shanghai.

CHAPULTEPEC, ancient seat of the Montezumas, situated in the west quarter of the city of Mexico.

On its rocky heights stands the summer palace of the president of the republic, in which is housed also the National Military school. At the base of this rising ground which commands the surrounding country is located a famous grove of cypresses estimated to be some thousand years old. Upon this whole critical position was fought the last actual battle of the war between Mexico and the United States (1846–48). Maj. Gen. Winfield Scott after the disaster of El Molino del Rey found that he had available about 7,000 badly shaken United States troops, far from their base and in the heart of a hostile country. Opposing him General Antonio Lopez de Santa Anna, the president of the republic, controlled at least twice that number. The natural and artificial strength of the palace, its proximity to the U.S. goal and its meaning relative to governmental power made its possession by the contending forces of the greatest moment. After several days of reconnaissance, feints and preparations, Scott decided that this stronghold between him and the capital must be taken.

On Sept. 12, 1847, an all-day bombardment of the buildings, surrounding forts and redoubts convinced him of the necessity of an assault. During the following night both the U.S. and Mexican batteries and positions were strengthened and Scott's plans for an attack in front and reverse were crystallized. Maj. Gen. J. A. Quitman's troops were directed to advance to the rear of the palace by way of the Tacubaya road, whereas Maj. Gen. G. J. Pillow's division was given the task of striking the front by way of El Molino del Rey and the cypress grove. From early dawn on Sept. 13 until 8 A.M.—about two hours and a half—the U.S. guns hurled solid shot, grape, canister and shells at the barriers of stone and mortar. At the end of that time the infantry went forward to the assault, the main blow being delivered by regular troops upon the Mexican points of vantage in the cypress grove. Lieut. "Stonewall" Jackson, later of Civil War fame, handled on his own initiative a section of John B. Magruder's field battery in such a manner as to cut off the northern retreat of the Mexican fugitives. The major portion of Scott's forces went forward doggedly under severe fire. Officers on both sides became casualties to a disproportionate degree. When the United States troops finally reached the ditch they found there no ladders with which to scale the parapets. Although Brig. Gen. P. F. Smith gallantly led a turning movement toward the rear of the palace, he was met by such a galling fire that his losses, including the wounded Lieut. James Longstreet, were sufficient to stop him.

The suspense and curtailment of enthusiasm among Scott's troops as they crouched behind any available cover, while waiting for the implements that would enable them to go over the top of the barrier, lent serious apprehensions as to the success of the U.S. effort. When, after about 20 min., the ladders arrived, the previous restiveness reacted upon the men in the form of ardour to proceed. They swarmed over the parapets with such impetus that in a very few minutes of sharp hand-to-hand fighting Chapultepec was in their hands. Since its capture was but a means to an end, and the exploitation of the success involved the seizure of the city of Mexico itself, it was necessary to move onward immediately. Quitman set out over the Belen causeway toward the capital. After overwhelming a field redan in his front he came upon decided opposition at the gate which was protected by a formidable citadel beyond. Quitman's ammunition having been exhausted and all his staff officers having been killed or wounded, his position was not fortunate.

To check Mexican reinforcements, Scott sent Brigadier General Worth's brigade, together with some smaller units, along the Verónica causeway. Finding his advance likewise blocked by heavy fire, Worth sent Col. John Garland's force through the fields to outflank the San Cosme gate which lay about a mile north of Quitman's troops. By crawling through mud, forcing their way through houses and using such cover as was available, in small bodies they reached the rear of the position. During this procedure, Lieut. U. S. Grant had a mountain howitzer dragged through the mud and mounted upon the roof of a building. About six o'clock in the evening Worth forced an entrance into the city proper, and shortly activities ceased for the night. Though the capital was not yet under U.S. control, General Santa Anna chose to retire with his forces to Guadalupe Hidalgo. Next morning when Scott was ready to renew hostilities, the city of Mexico was unexpectedly surrendered.

BIBLIOGRAPHY.—Justin H. Smith, *The War with Mexico,* vol. I (1919); George B. McClellan, *The Mexican War Diary* (1917); C. M. Wilcox, *History of the Mexican War* (1892); W. A. Ganoe, *The History of the United States Army* (1924); Original Correspondence and Reports in Old Files Section, Adjutant General's Office, Washington, D.C. (W. A. G.)

CHAR, the name given to fishes of the genus *Salvelinus,* which differs from *Salmo* (salmon and trout) in having the vomerine teeth present only on the head of the bone, which is raised and has a boat-shaped depression behind it. *Salvelinus alpinus* of the Arctic ocean is a marine fish that enters rivers to breed and may form fresh-water colonies, especially in lakes. It is represented by many isolated colonies in lakes that it entered in glacial times, far to the south of its present range in the sea, in Scandinavia and the Alps, in Scotland, Ireland and the Lake District of England and in North America. Many of these lacustrine forms differ considerably from the northern migratory char and have been described as distinct species; they are more or less similar to trout but have smaller scales and are generally beautifully coloured—bluish or olive above, often with bright orange spots on the sides; the belly varies from pink to scarlet, the coloration being most intense in the breeding males. The migratory fish are silvery, with the spots inconspicuous. *Salvelinus fontinalis,* the brook trout of eastern North America, is mainly a river fish, distinguished by the blackish mottling of the back and the dorsal and caudal fins; sea-run individuals (the Canadian "salmon trout") are plain silvery. *Cristivomer namaycush,* the Great Lake trout of North America, is a grayish fish with dark markings on the dorsal and caudal fins; it is distinguished from other char by the widely forked caudal fin; it reaches a weight of 100 lb. (C. T. R.)

CHARABANC, a large form of wagonette-like vehicle for passengers, with benched seats arranged in rows, looking forward, commonly used for large parties, as public conveyances or for excursions. The word is French for benched carriage; in the English motor trade the term "motor coach" is preferred.

CHARACTER. To ask what character is, reveals the confusion of ordinary thought about it. Instincts, habits, impulses, desires, emotions, sentiments all belong to it. But what relation do they bear to one another? What is the part of character that has to be controlled and what is its controlling part? Whence come those things that are called "principles" of conduct, and "ideals," and the multitude of "qualities of character"—courage, steadfastness, sincerity, tolerance, generosity, patience and honesty and their opposites? We do not know. The first general problem of the psychology of character is therefore to transform the chaos of the ordinary conception of it into one in which the parts of character are seen to bear a clear and intelligible relation to the whole. There are certain common but useful antitheses: "character and intelligence"; "character and circumstances"; "character and conduct." Conduct is the expression of character; only actions that are in some degree under voluntary control are included in conduct. Reflex actions are not included in conduct; instinctive actions are. Character is the driving force; intelligence guides it to its destination; together they sum up the human mind and are inseparable in it.

Stages of Character.—These may be classed under three heads, which roughly correspond to three levels of mental development: (1) the instinctive; (2) the emotional; (3) the level of sentiment; and again roughly these three are represented in (1) the life of the animal; (2) the life of the child and (3) the life of the adult human being. The first is the most perfect in organization; but also the most rigid, in which intelligence has the least formative influence. The second is the most helpless and marks the transition from a lower to a higher form of organization, for which the guidance of the adult mind is indispensable. The third is the most plastic and comprehensive; but its organization is never completed. In it reflection, reason and self-control have their full opportunities; yet it is the region of folly and error, with which we can hardly charge the animals; of mistaken valuations followed by disillusions; of progress and decadence; of constancy and infidelity. It has never been understood.

The Human Instincts.—Animal instincts are inherited dispositions having specific patterns of behaviour for the attainment of their ends. An impulse felt in consciousness precedes their operation; attention accompanies it and serves to adapt the pattern of behaviour to the actual situation. Human instincts have lost these patterns except in the case of simple instincts, as sucking, shrinking and clinging; in others the child must learn by experience to acquire new means to replace the old. The end for an animal is perceived—a hole or cover; the end for man may be conceived—a secret thought. In this sense, as instinctive impulses defined by their ends, we can enumerate the most important human instincts. They are flight and pursuit, concealment and display, domination and submission, attraction and repulsion, destruction and construction, crying for protection and giving protection, curiosity and search and the food and sex instincts. The ends are only proximate ones, assumed to have been selected first for their biological utility; but in man they are also indispensable to the ends which he invents—wealth, power, fame, well-being, happiness, perfection.

The instincts sometimes act independently of emotion, finding in their own impulses when unchecked the force to attain their ends; but (1) when their impulses are obstructed they tend to arouse anger or fear; (2) when they attain their ends, joy or satisfaction; (3) when they fail completely, sorrow or despair. The emotions never act independently of instincts and tend to organize in their systems all that subserve their ends. Hence, we find concealment not only in fear, but in the anger of revenge; in shame; in envy; in sorrow; in the joy of children's games. This seems to be the relation between instincts and emotions.

Difference Between Instinct and Emotion.—An instinct advancing to its end unchecked does not need to arouse emotion. In itself it is unlike emotion; it is most like habit. Both instinct and habit are orderly and stable, showing so little variability in action that we forecast the course of it. Emotion unrestrained is unstable and disorderly; its actions often surprise us. We follow our strong habits often without recognizing them; they are calm and unobtrusive; we can not help recognizing our strong emotions. Hence it is, when emotion and instinct are conjoined, the second as it comes into operation tends to calm the first. It is the moments before action, we remark, that are so tense. For the force which emotion brings is for the needs of a certain situation. It should not therefore persist for long; and if it does, it tends to become pathological, as we see in the case of our morbid fears.

Besides these differences between instincts and emotions there are those based on the nature of their systems. Emotion is potentially more complex. Concealment is only one of many instincts organized in fear which may choose this instinct or any other better adapted to the actual situation: flight, shrinking or clutching or shrieks for protection. From the time of Bain it has been recognized that strong emotion is accompanied by a diffused nervous disturbance, and this may render emotion more adaptable to a changing situation; whereas when an instinct is unchecked, and following out the normal course of its behaviour, the nervous discharge tends to be restricted to those channels which sustain this behaviour. Here the intervention of emotion would be not only superfluous but harmful. The value of emotion lies in these two points of difference from instinct: (1) the force which it brings to deal with a given situation and (2) its potentially more complex and adaptable system. It is indispensable to the sentiments, and without it there could neither be love nor hate. All great changes of character are initiated by emotion.

The Stage of the Sentiments.—That which has to exercise control must have a wider outlook than that which is to be controlled; but unless it moves us its warnings are ineffectual. It must move us by some other influence than emotion. Self-control comes from a higher system than emotion and one that by its comprehensiveness more adequately represents the self. Love and hate, the chief sentiments, have this comprehensiveness. They are that governing part of character to which we have referred; and all the part which has to be governed is beneath them, under their authority. Love obtains its great organizing desires directed to its unchanging ends of union, happiness and well-being of the loved object, reciprocity of love and the desire to be happy in the love of the object. But in hate these ends are reversed: not preservation and union, but destruction and separation; not happiness and well-being, but misery and the worst possible state of the object, and yet withal, the desire to be happy in the separation, misery and destruction of the object.

In these great desires love and hate find the principles of their self-control—not in their emotions.

Repression.—Repression is an extreme form of the self-control of sentiments. For if some of our emotions have to be regulated as being either too strong or too weak, others which are judged to be harmful in view of their ends have to be repressed. Such repression of things within the mind corresponds most nearly to "destruction" of things without us. We would destroy some things in our character if we could; but we can only repress them, which means to exclude them from consciousness and prevent as far as possible their return to it.

Conscience.—There is another sentiment distinct from both love and hate, which, like them, often undergoes repressions. The uniqueness of conscience makes it difficult to interpret, for there is a particular conscience belonging to all love of which its ideals are a part. This is partial to the loved object. It is the repository of that part of the moral beliefs of the community in which the individual has been instructed and which he has adopted through authority and suggestion. It is therefore apt to differ from one person to another. But when it is a living force of character, it grows with a man's experience of life and through the illusions and disappointments of love. These impress certain ideals and duties upon his mind differently from hearsay, however often repeated. They become the most vital part of his conscience, being there freed from the partiality to which love at first confined them. And as the ideals of love are much the same in its different varieties, the most general and important duties come to be impressed, sooner or later, on most men.

Thus is shown in merest outline how the parts of character are related to one another and the whole—how the instincts, habits, emotions and desires function in the sentiments of man, and there represent the unity of his character. Yet how incompletely they represent it. The potentials of his character transcend for better and worse everything that he has drawn from them to build up his actual loves and hates, and remain a perpetual enigma to him. The word is also applied to symbols of notation; letters of the alphabet, and, more particularly to ideographs; in such phrases as "the characters of the Chinese language number nearly 50,000." By extension of the philosophical meaning a "character" has almost become synonymous with "reputation." Still further development of this idea is found in the description of a person as "a character" ("an odd or eccentric person").

BIBLIOGRAPHY.—A. Bain, *The Study of Character* (1861); A. F. Shand, *Foundations of Character* (1914); A. A. Robaek, *The Psychology of Character* (1927); Theophrastus' *Characters*, contains the oldest extant sketches of types of character. (A. F. S.)

CHARADE, a kind of riddle, probably invented in France during the 18th century, in which a word of two or more syllables is divined by guessing and combining into one word (the answer) the different syllables, each of which is described, as an independent word, by the giver of the charade. Charades may be either in prose or in verse. Of poetic charades those by W. Mackworth Praed are well known and excellent examples, while the following is a good specimen in prose. "My *first* is company; my *second* shuns company; my *third* collects company; and my *whole* amuses company." The solution is *Co-nun-drum.* The most popular form of this amusement is the acted charade, in which the meaning of the different syllables is acted out on the stage, the audience being left to guess each syllable and thus, combining the meaning of all the syllables, the whole word. A brilliant description of the acted charade is given in Thackeray's *Vanity Fair.*

In many circles of the London "intelligentsia" the charade became, by 1900, such a hobby that elaborate presentations were made, planned weeks in advance and with expensive or hard to acquire costumes and properties comparable to those used in amateur theatricals. Such elaborate charades continued to be produced in the 20th century, though simplification induced by World War I became the custom.

In the United States the charade in somewhat different form was resurgent in the 1930s and 1940s. It was called "The Game." Whatever group assembled was divided into two teams. Each team designated one member of the opposing team to personify a quotation, a person living or dead, a phrase or an idea, in such manner that his teammates might guess the subject. The designated actor was not permitted to use his voice in any way or to indicate any inanimate object in the room for the guidance of his teammates. The object of the actor was to assist his teammates in guessing the subject in the shortest possible time. A timekeeper determined the team which had arrived at the proper answer in the shorter time and thus had won the contest.

CHARADRIIDAE: *see* LAPWING; PLOVER; TURNSTONE.

CHARADRIIFORMES, an order of birds, most members of which are shore birds, gulls and auks. The young are active and down-clad at hatching.

(*See* AUKS; AVOCET; CURLEW; GULL; ORNITHOLOGY; PHALAROPE; PLOVER; SANDPIPER; SHEATHBILL; SNIPE; TERN; WOODCOCK.)

CHARCOAL. Charcoal is the residue obtained when a carbonaceous material of animal or vegetable origin is partially burned or heated in the absence of air. It is essentially an impure form of carbon (*q.v.*) produced by the unit process of pyrolysis or decomposition by heat, often called "destructive distillation" when, as in this case, the material is decomposed into volatile and nonvolatile fractions. Coke (*q.v.*) is manufactured by the application of a similar process to bituminous coal and may be regarded as a special form of charcoal.

Various charcoals are given names which identify them with the materials from which they are derived: wood charcoal, blood charcoal, etc. Bone charcoal contains only about 12% carbon and consists principally of calcium phosphate and carbonate.

Wood Charcoal.—This material was produced for many centuries by stacking wood into heaps which were partially covered with earth to limit the access of air; the heaps were fired and the charcoal recovered but all by-products were wasted.

This process has been almost completely replaced by those using by-product ovens. In the older of these, cordwood is loaded into large steel buggies which run on standard rails. They are rolled into ovens heated by the combustion of coal, natural gas or the gas and tar formed during the carbonization. In the newer Stafford process dry wood in the form of relatively small pieces preheated to 300° F. is charged continuously into large cylindrical retorts. Once started, the process maintains itself by the heat liberated in the decomposition reactions.

The vapours from either of these processes are cooled to condense tar and pyroligneous liquor which form separate layers. The aqueous layer is redistilled to remove soluble tar. In the older recovery processes acetic acid was obtained by neutralizing the pyroligneous acid with lime, evaporating to dryness and liberating the acetic acid from its calcium salt by means of sulphuric acid. In 1945 this process was used in only a few small plants, the others having adopted more economical operations depending upon rectification and selective solvent extraction.

The products obtained from the distillation of hardwood are given by R. S. McBride as follows in per cent by weight: charcoal 25.2, methanol 1.9, acetic acid 2.9, tar and oil 5.0, gas 18.3, water, etc., 46.7. The gas from the process consists mainly of carbon dioxide 53%, carbon monoxide 27% and methane 15%.

After the production of acetone by fermentation (1915) and later from propylene, its manufacture by destructive distillation of calcium acetate was abandoned. The commercial synthesis of methanol from carbon monoxide and hydrogen and the advent of cheap acetic acid made from acetylene or ethyl alcohol caused the prices of the principal by-products of the charcoal industry to decrease considerably. As a result, in 1940 only 9% of the methanol was made by wood distillation and the large additional demand for methanol from which to produce the formaldehyde required for plastics and explosives needed in World War II was met by still greater expansion of the synthetic methanol industry.

Wood distillation may be expected to continue on a stable basis but by mid-century and after it supplied a diminishing fraction of the total market for all of its principal by-products with the exception of wood tar. The demand for charcoal is thus the factor which determines the magnitude of the wood distillation industry. In fact, interest has revived in charcoal processes in which the by-products are burned because of their low value. The chief use for charcoal is as a blast-furnace fuel although coke is much more commonly employed. Where natural or artificial gas or cheap electricity is not readily available charcoal is employed as a household cooking fuel, its clean flame and great ability to radiate heat recommending it particularly for broiling. Charcoal is employed for miscellaneous metallurgical purposes such as case hardening (*q.v.*), in the manufacture of black powder and as a starting material for chemical synthesis. Carbon disulphide, important in the production of carbon tetrachloride (fire-extinguisher fluid and dry-cleaning agent) and of rayon and rubber accelerators, is made by the action of sulphur on charcoal. Sodium cyanide, important in the metallurgy of gold and silver, as a poison and in the manufacture of plastics, is made by passing ammonia over a mixture of sodium and charcoal.

Activated Charcoal.—The ability of charcoal to deodorize air and decolorize solutions has long been known. These effects occur through the phenomenon of adsorption (*q.v.*) by which charcoal, in common with other solids of large internal area, attracts and holds on the surface of its pores various materials which while there sometimes undergo chemical change. Since charcoal adsorbs oxygen from the air, organic materials simultaneously adsorbed may be oxidized while held on the charcoal surface. Polymerization and hydrolysis frequently occur. Before 1900, R. von Ostrejko made the important discovery that the adsorptive power of charcoal may be strongly enhanced by partial oxidation at a bright red temperature in a current of steam or carbon dioxide. A similar effect is obtained by the action of oxygen (air) at much lower temperatures (300–450° C.) but this reaction is exothermic and thus harder to control. The subjection of charcoal to the action of a limited air supply in the temperature range 800–1,000° C. results in excellent activation; the chemical attack on the charcoal in this case is primarily by carbon dioxide formed in the reaction between carbon monoxide and inwardly diffusing oxygen. The product of such processes is called activated charcoal or active carbon.

Another method of obtaining active charcoal is to carbonize organic material by heating it in the presence of certain solutions such as aqueous zinc chloride or phosphoric acid which exert a dissolving action upon the organic matter and a catalytic effect upon its pyrolysis. A higher yield of charcoal is obtained than in ordinary destructive distillation and the original cell structure, which is reproduced in ordinary charcoal with the utmost fidelity, may disappear completely, the resulting product having a black, glassy fracture. After the impregnated charcoal has cooled, it is extracted with water and acid to remove foreign materials and then dried.

During World War I, N. K. Chaney discovered that lignite, bituminous or anthracite coal may serve as an economical source of excellent activated charcoal if it is carefully carbonized and subjected to steam activation. Chlorinated coal behaves particularly well but requires a binder such as wood tar followed by recarbonization to form pellets which are mechanically strong.

Active carbon is manufactured for three principal purposes: (1) gas masks; (2) decolorization; and (3) water purification. The advent of chemical warfare in World War I sharply emphasized the value of activated carbon in a respirator or gas mask. Removal of toxic vapours must be remarkably complete since a concentration of a few parts per million of such gases as phosgene may result fatally. Of all materials tried only active charcoal was satisfactory and by the end of the war the soldiers of all belligerent countries were wearing respirators containing it. The Allies employed partial oxidation processes and nut shells and hardwood were the principal sources of the charcoals employed. Germany used a zinc-chloride process operated on pine wood.

After World War I active carbons were employed for the removal of gasoline vapours from natural gas and for solvent recovery in connection with such processes as the manufacture of artificial leather, pyroxylin window shades and metal lacquering where large quantities of relatively expensive solvents are evaporated. By 1930 the charcoal gasoline recovery process was almost entirely obsolete but installations employing active carbon were later used increasingly for solvent recovery where their slightly greater initial and operating costs were compensated for by their high efficiency, particularly where the material recovered was expensive or occurred at low concentration.

Bone charcoal towers were first used for decolorizing sugar solutions in 1815. Vegetable decolorizing carbons threatened to displace them after their commercial introduction around 1910 because only one-thirtieth the quantity of material is required and there is a consequent saving in time, fuel, wash water, building space and investment in equipment. Plants employing activated carbon can operate efficiently on a much smaller scale than those using bone char and hence are often built adjacent to the raw sugar mills to produce "plantation white" sugar. Sugar refineries with bone char towers already installed, however, have little incentive to change over to vegetable decolorizing carbons.

Where highly acidic solutions are decolorized, bone black is unsuitable because of its high ash content. Here decolorizing carbons replaced older forms of charcoal.

A still later application of active carbon is in the elimination of the objectionable odour of city water which contains chlorophenols formed by the action of chlorine (introduced to kill bacteria) upon traces of phenols present in the water. Relatively small quantities of activated carbon, introduced as a powder and removed by filtration or present as a bed of granular material through which the water trickles, will render the water palatable. The same may be said for colours and odours produced by algae growing in reservoirs.

Bibliography.—Charles Letnam Mantell, *Industrial Carbon* (1928); R. Norris Shreve, *Chemical Process Industries* (1945); Clifford Cook Furnas (ed.), *Rogers' Manual of Industrial Chemistry*, 6th ed. (1942); Oskar Kausch, *Die aktive Kohle* (1928). (H. B. Hs.)

CHARCOT, JEAN BAPTISTE ETIENNE AUGUSTE (1867–1936), the son of the French physician Jean M. Charcot (*q.v.*), was educated as a physician but became best known as an explorer. Born at Neuilly-sur-Seine in 1867, Jean Baptiste Charcot, who studied at the École Alsacienne, was an intern at the Hospital of Paris from 1890 to 1894 and was also connected with the Pasteur institute, 1890–93. He was chief of the clinic of the faculty of medicine at Paris from 1896 to 1898.

Charcot commanded an expedition to the antarctic in the "Français," 1903–05, exploring the western side of Graham Land to 67° S. In 1908, in command of the "Pourquoi Pas?," he returned to the antarctic and spent the winter of 1909 on Petermann Island (65° S.). Further explorations south and west were made the following summer. Charcot Land, which he named after his father, was discovered, and a number of contributions to scientific research resulted from the voyage. He later did research on and made explorations to the arctic, and in 1921 he studied Rockall Island, a North Atlantic British possession.

On Sept. 16, 1936, the "Pourquoi Pas?" was wrecked off the western coast of Iceland, and 39 men, including Charcot and a number of other scientists, were lost at sea.

In addition to *Atrophie musculaire progressive* and various other works on medicine, he published *Le Français au Pôle Sud* (1906); *Le "Pourquoi Pas?" dans Antarctique* (1911; Eng. trans. 1912); *Autour du Pôle Sud*, 2 vol. (1912); and *Christophe Colomb vu par un marin* (1928).

CHARCOT, JEAN MARTIN (1825–1893), French physician, was born in Paris on Nov. 29, 1825. In 1853 he took his M.D. at Paris, and three years later was appointed physician of the Central Hospital bureau. In 1860 he became professor of pathological anatomy in the medical faculty of Paris, and in 1862 began his connection with the Salpêtrière, where he created the great neurological clinic. As regards hysteria, which he defined as a psychosis superinduced by ideation, he threw the sexual theory into disrepute and studied the disease in relation to hypnotism. In muscular atrophy he differentiated between the ordinary wasting and the rarer amyothropic lateral sclerosis (1874) and described with Pierre Marie the progressive neural or peroneal type (1886). He differentiated the essential lesions of locomotor ataxia and described both the gastric crisis and the joint affections (Charcot's disease). He separated multiple sclerosis from paralysis agitans. In diseases of the brain, the most notable contributions were his articles on cerebral localization, the studies of aphasia and the discovery of the miliary aneurisms and their importance in cerebral haemorrhage. Charcot greatly promoted the study of medicine in art (see *Nouvelle Iconographie de la Salpêtrière,* 1888). He died on Aug. 16, 1893.

His best known works are *Leçons sur les maladies du système nerveux,* 5 vol. (1872–93) and *Leçons du mardi à la Salpêtrière,* 2 vol. (1889–90).

See F. Garrison, *Hist. of Medicine;* W. Osler in *Johns Hopkins Hospital Bulletin* (1893); F. H. Mackay and Emilie Legrand, "Jean Martin Charcot, 1825–1893," *Arch. Neurol. and Psychiat.*, 34:390–400 (1935).

CHARD, JOHN ROUSE MERRIOTT (1847–1897), British soldier, was born at Boxhill, near Plymouth, on Dec. 21, 1847, and in 1868 entered the royal engineers. In 1878 Lieut. Chard was ordered to South Africa to take part in the Zulu War, and was stationed at the small post of Rorke's Drift to protect the bridges across the Buffalo river and some sick men and stores. There, with Lieut. Gonville Bromhead (1856–91) and 80 men of the 2nd 24th foot, he heard, on Jan. 22, 1879, of the disaster of Isandhlwana from some fugitives who had escaped the slaughter. Believing that the victorious Zulus would attempt to cross into Natal, they prepared, hastily, to hold the Drift until help came. They barricaded and loopholed the old church and hospital and improvised defenses from wagons, bags of Indian corn, etc.

Early in the afternoon they were attacked by more than 3,000 Zulus, who, after hours of desperate hand-to-hand fighting, carried the outer defenses, an inner low wall of biscuit boxes and the hospital, room by room. The garrison then retired to the stone kraal, and repulsed attack after attack through the night.

The next morning relieving forces appeared and the enemy retired. The spirited defense of Rorke's Drift saved Natal from a Zulu invasion. The gallantry of Chard and Bromhead was rewarded with the Victoria Cross and immediate promotion to the rank of captain and brevet major. On Chard's return to England he became a popular hero. From 1893 to 1896 he commanded the royal engineers at Singapore, and in 1897 he was made a colonel. He died the same year at Hatch-Beauchamp, near Taunton, on Nov. 1.

CHARD, a market town and municipal borough in Somersetshire, England, 16 mi. S.S.E. of Taunton by road. Pop. (1951) 5,218. Area 1.6 sq.mi. It lies on a hillside close to the Devon and Dorset borders and the runnels by the sides of the main street are said to flow, one south to the English channel, the other north to the Bristol channel. Industries include agricultural machinery, surgical supplies, lace, shirts and collars and dairy produce. The town takes its name from Cerdic who founded the kingdom of Wessex, and appears as Cedre in the Domesday Book. The bishop of Bath held Chard in 1086 and in 1234 his successor granted the first charter which was confirmed in 1253 (when a Monday market and a fair on July 25 were granted), 1280 and 1285. The corporation seal dates from 1570. The town was incorporated by grant of Charles I in 1642 and Charles II gave a charter in 1683 (when two more fair days were added). The cruciform parish church of St. Mary the Virgin is Perpendicular of the 15th century. The grammar school was founded in 1671 when William Symes gave his house for the purpose. Another Tudor house is the court house of the manor which contains the room where Judge Jeffreys condemned to death 12 natives of Chard for taking part in the Monmouth rebellion.

CHARD or Swiss Chard, a name given to the edible leaf beet (*Beta vulgaris* var. *cicla*), a variety of the beet (*q.v.*) in which the leaves and leafstalks, instead of the roots, have become greatly developed. The plant is a biennial with somewhat branched and thickened but not fleshy roots and large leaves borne on stalks sometimes 2 ft. long and 1 in. to 3 in. wide. It is grown for the tender leaves and leafstalks; the former are boiled and served like spinach, the latter, like asparagus. Swiss chard is popular as a home-garden potherb because of its ease of culture, productiveness and tolerance to moderately hot weather. It furnishes an abundance of greens after the weather becomes too warm for growing spinach and other early greens.

CHARDIN, JEAN SIMÉON (1699–1779), French *genre* painter, the son of Jean Chardin, master carpenter, was born in Paris on Nov. 2, 1699, and died Dec. 6, 1779. He became famous for his still-life pictures and domestic interiors, which are well represented at the Louvre, and for figure painting, as in his *Le Bénédicité* (1740) and is one of the great French colourists.

See A. Dayot, *J. B. Siméon Chardin* (1905); H. E. A. Furst, *Chardin* (1911); E. Pilon, *Chardin* (1911).

CHARDIN, SIR JOHN (1643–1713), French traveller, was born in Paris in 1643. His father, a wealthy jeweller, gave him an excellent education and trained him in his own art; but instead of settling down in the ordinary routine of the craft he set out in company with a Lyons merchant named Raisin in 1665 for Persia and India, partly on business and partly to gratify his own inclinations.

After a highly successful journey, during which he had received the patronage of Shah Abbas II of Persia, he returned to France in 1670, and there published in the following year *Récit du Couronnement du roi de Perse Soliman III.*

He set out again for Persia in Aug. 1671. The second journey was much more adventurous than the first for, instead of going directly to his destination, he passed by Smyrna, Constantinople, the Crimea, Caucasia, Mingrelia and Georgia. He did not reach Ispahan until June 1673. After four years spent in researches throughout Persia, he again visited India, and returned to Europe by the Cape of Good Hope in 1677. The persecution of Protestants in France led him, in 1681, to settle in London, where he was appointed jeweller to the court and was knighted by Charles II.

In 1683 he was sent to Holland as representative of the English East India company, and in 1686 he published the first part of his narrative, *The Travels of Sir John Chardin into Persia and the East Indies,* etc. (London).

Sir John died in London in 1713 and was buried in Westminster Abbey.

BIBLIOGRAPHY.—The complete account of Chardin's travels appeared at Amsterdam in 1711, under the title of *Journal du voyage du chevalier Chardin*. The Persian portion is to be found in vol. ii of Harris' *Collection* (1705), and extracts are reprinted by Pinkerton in vol. ix. The best complete reprint is by Langlès (1811).

CHARENTE, an inland department of southwestern France, comprehending the ancient province of Angoumois and small portions of Saintonge, Poitou, Marche, Limousin and Périgord. It is bounded north by the departments of Deux-Sèvres and Vienne, east by those of Haute Vienne and Dordogne, south by Dordogne and Charente-Maritime and west by Charente-Maritime. Area 2,306 sq.mi. Pop. (1946) 311,137. The Confolentais (known also as the *Terres Froides*) in the northeast is a region of granitic rocks which may be considered as a western extension of the Massif Central. There some parts exceed 1,000 ft. in height and the whole provides good upland pasture for cattle. The remainder of the department, known as the Terres Chaudes, consists of Jurassic, Cretaceous and Tertiary deposits and provides rich arable land. Cereals and potatoes are the principal crops and chestnuts, walnuts and cider apples the chief fruits. The Terre Champagne is noted for its vines, much of the wine produced being distilled into brandy named after the town of Cognac. A large area drains to the Charente river, the chief affluents of which, in this section, are the Tardoire, the Touvre and the Né. The Confolentais is watered by the Vienne, a tributary of the Loire, while the district of Barbezieux, noted for its poultry farming, belongs almost wholly to the basin of the Gironde. Charente has stone quarries, peat workings and beds of clay which supply brick and tileworks and earthenware manufactories. There is a large foundry of naval guns at Ruelle. Flour mills and leatherworks are numerous. Angoulême is a paper-making centre and manufactures gunpowder. Coal, salt and timber are prominent imports. Exports include paper, brandy, stone and agricultural products. The department is served chiefly by the Orléans and Ouest-État railways, and the Charente is navigable below Angoulême. Charente is divided into the three *arrondissements* of Angoulême, Cognac and Confolens (29 cantons, 424 communes). It belongs to the region of the 12th army corps, to the province of the archbishop of Bordeaux and to the *académie* (educational division) of Poitiers. Its court of appeal is at Bordeaux. Angoulême (*q.v.*) is the capital, and Cognac, Confolens, Jarnac (*qq.v.*) and La Rochefoucauld are other towns. The department abounds in churches of Romanesque architecture, of which those of Bassac, St. Amant-de-Boixe (portions of which are Gothic), Plassac and Gensac-la-Pallue may be mentioned. There are remains of a Gothic abbey church at La Couronne, and Roman remains at St. Cybardeaux, Brossac and Chassenon (where are ruins of the Gallo-Roman town of Cassinomagus).

CHARENTE-MARITIME, a maritime department of southwestern France, comprehending the old provinces of Saintonge and Aunis and a small portion of Poitou, and including the islands of Ré, Oléron, Aix and Madame. Area, 2,792 sq.mi. Pop. (1946) 416,187. It is bounded north by Vendée, northeast by Deux-Sèvres, east by Charente, southeast by Dordogne, southwest by Gironde and the estuary of the Gironde and west by the Bay of Biscay. The department is low lying and consists of Jurassic, Cretaceous, Tertiary and Quaternary deposits which run in a northwesterly direction. This trend can be traced also in many sections of the coast and in the islands of Oléron and Ré. Post-Pleistocene submergence has resulted in the formation of many inlets and estuaries, particularly the Gironde, and there are several good harbours, the chief of which are La Rochelle and Rochefort. The latter has developed at the expense of Tonnay-Charente which is too high up the river to cope with modern shipping. Oysters and mussels are bred in the neighbourhood of La Rochelle and Marennes and there are many fishing villages. Royan, on the north shore of the Gironde, is a much-frequented watering place. The chief crops are wheat, oats, maize, barley and potatoes. Horse and cattle raising is carried on and dairying is prosperous. A considerable quantity of wine, most of which is distilled into brandy, is produced. The department has a few peat-workings, and produces freestone, lime and cement; the salt marshes of the coast are important. Shipbuilding, iron founding, machine construction and the making of glass, pottery, bricks and earthenware are also carried on. The railways traversing the department belong to the Ouest-État system, except one section of the Paris-Bordeaux line belonging to the Orléans company. Internal communication is facilitated by the navigable reaches of the Charente, the Sèvre Niortaise, the Boutonne, the Seudre and the Gironde and by the canals of the coast. There are five *arrondissements* (40 cantons, 483 communes), cognominal with the towns of La Rochelle, Rochefort, Saintes, Saint-Jean-d'Angély and Jonzac. The department forms the diocese of La Rochelle, and is attached to the 18th military region, and in educational matters to the *académie* of Poitiers. Its court of appeal is at Poitiers. La Rochelle, Saint-Jean-d'Angély, Rochefort and Saintes are the principal towns. Surgères and Aulnay possess fine Romanesque churches. Pons has a château of the 15th and 16th centuries and a keep of the 12th century.

CHARENTON-LE-PONT, a town of northern France in the department of Seine, situated on the right bank of the Marne at its confluence with the Seine. Pop. (1946) 21,457. *Le Pont* refers to the stone bridge of ten arches which crosses the Marne and unites the town with Alfortville, well known for its veterinary school founded in 1766. In the 16th and 17th centuries Charenton was the scene of the ecclesiastical councils of the Protestant party, which had its principal church in the town. At the neighbouring St. Maurice is the well known Hospice de Charenton. Charenton has a port on the Canal de St. Maurice, besides the Marne, and carries on boatbuilding and the manufacture of tiles and porcelain.

CHARES, of Lindus in Rhodes, a sculptor pupil of Lysippus, who fashioned for the Rhodians a colossal bronze statue of the sun god, the cost of which was defrayed by selling the warlike engines left by Demetrius Poliorcetes after the siege in 303 B.C. (Pliny, *Nat. Hist.* xxxiv, 41). The colossus was seventy cubits (105 ft.) in height. The notion that it bestrode the harbour is absurd. It was thrown down by an earthquake after 56 years.

See E. A. Gardner, *Handbook of Greek Sculpture* (1915), par. 61.

CHARES, of Mytilene, a Greek belonging to the suite of Alexander the Great, to whom he was appointed court marshal. He wrote a history of Alexander in ten books, dealing mainly with the private life of the king. The fragments are chiefly preserved in Athenaeus.

See *Scriptores Rerum Alexandri* (pp. 114–20) in the Didot edition of Arrian.

CHARES, Athenian general, is first heard of in 366 B.C. as assisting the Phliasians, who had been attacked by Argos and Sicyon. In 361 he visited Corcyra, where he helped the oligarchs to expel the democrats, a policy which led to the subsequent defection of the island from Athens.

In 357 Chares was appointed to the command in the Social War, together with Chabrias, after whose death before Chios he was associated with Iphicrates and Timotheus. (For the naval battle in the Hellespont, *see* TIMOTHEUS.) Chares, having successfully thrown the blame for the defeat on his colleagues, was left sole commander; but, receiving no supplies from Athens, he joined the rebellious satrap Artabazus.

A complaint from the Persian king, who threatened to send 300 ships to the assistance of the confederates, led to the conclusion of peace (355) between Athens and its rebellious allies and to the recall of Chares.

In 349 he was sent to the assistance of Olynthus against Philip II of Macedon, but he returned without having effected anything. In the following year, when he reached Olynthus, he found it already in the hands of Philip.

In 340 he was appointed to the command of a force sent to aid Byzantium against Philip, but the inhabitants, remembering his former plunderings and extortions, refused to receive him. In 338 he was defeated by Philip at Amphissa, and was one of the commanders at the disastrous battle of Chaeroneia (*see* CHAERONEIA, BATTLE OF). Lysicles, one of his colleagues, was condemned to death, while Chares does not seem to have been even accused.

After the conquest of Thebes by Alexander (335), Chares is said to have been one of the Athenian orators and generals whose surrender was demanded. Two years later he was living at Sigeum, for Arrian (*Anabasis* i, 12) states that he went from there to pay his respects to Alexander. In 332 he entered the service of Darius and took over the command of a Persian force in Mytilene, but he capitulated on the approach of a Macedonian fleet on condition of being allowed to retire unmolested.

He is last heard of at Taenarum, and is supposed to have died at Sigeum. Although boastful and vainglorious, Chares was not lacking in personal courage and was among the best Athenian generals of his time. At the best, however, he was "hardly more than an ordinary leader of mercenaries" (A. Holm). He openly boasted of his profligacy, was exceedingly avaricious and his bad faith became proverbial.

See Diod. Sic. xv, 75, 95, xvi, 7, 21, 22, 85–88; Plutarch, *Phocion,* 14; Theopompus, *ap.* Athenaeum, xii, p. 532; *Cambridge Ancient History,* vol. vi (1927), ch. viii and ix (with useful bibliography).

CHARGE, a load (Late Lat. *carricare,* to load in a *carrus* or wagon); *cf.* "cargo," "charger," a large dish. The word is used also for the powder and shot to load a firearm, the accumulation of electricity in a battery, the necessary quantity of dynamite or other explosive in blasting and a device borne on an escutcheon in heraldry. "Charge" can mean a burden, and so a care or duty laid upon one, as in the instructions given by a judge to a jury or by a bishop to the clergy of his diocese. In the sense of a pecuniary burden the word is applied to the price of goods, to an encumbrance on property and the expense of running a business. Further uses of the word are of an attack by cavalry, by a bull or elephant or by a football player; "charger," originally a horse ridden in a charge, now means a horse ridden by an officer, whether of infantry or cavalry.

CHARGÉ D'AFFAIRES: *see* AMBASSADOR; DIPLOMACY.

CHARGER, a riding horse allotted to a military officer for war; any mechanism adapted for charging, as for placing explosives in boreholes for blasting, and that used in loading a magazine rifle or a machine gun, etc.; a large shallow dish.

CHARGING ORDER: *see* PRACTICE AND PROCEDURE.

CHARIBERT (d. 567), king of the Franks, was the son of Clotaire I. On Clotaire's death in 561 his estates were divided between his sons, Charibert receiving Paris as his capital, together with Rouen, Tours, Poitiers, Limoges, Bordeaux and Toulouse. Besides his wife, Ingoberga, he had unions with Merofleda, a wool carder's daughter, and Theodogilda, the daughter of a neatherd. He was one of the most dissolute of the Merovingian kings.

(C. PF.)

CHARIDEMUS, of Oreus in Euboea, Greek mercenary leader. He fought under the Athenian general Iphicrates against Amphipolis *c.* 367 B.C. but later joined Cotys, king of Thrace, against Athens. Soon afterward he fell into the hands of the Athenians and accepted the offer of Timotheus to re-enter their service. He was given Athenian citizenship. Having been dismissed by Timotheus (362) he joined the revolted satraps Memnon and Mentor in Asia. In 360 he was elected a *strategos.* After more service under the Athenians, he again joined Cotys, on whose murder (359) he was appointed guardian to his youthful son Cersobleptes. In 357, on the arrival of Chares with considerable forces, the Chersonese was restored to Athens. The supporters of Charidemus represented this as due to his efforts; and, in spite of the opposition of Demosthenes, he was honoured with a golden crown and it was resolved that this person should be inviolable. In 351 he commanded the Athenian forces in the Thracian Chersonese against Philip II of Macedon, and in 349 he superseded Chares as commander in the Olynthian War. He achieved little success, but made himself detested and was in turn replaced by Chares. After Chaeroneia the war party would have entrusted Charidemus with a command but the peace party secured the appointment of Phocion. He was one of those whose surrender was demanded by Alexander after the destruction of Thebes, but escaped with banishment. He fled to Darius III of Persia, who received him with distinction. But, having expressed his dissatisfaction with the preparations made by the king just before the battle of Issus (333), he was put to death.

Demosthenes, *Contra Aristocratem,* is the chief source, the other evidence is collected in A. Schäfer, *Demosthenes und seine Zeit,* 2nd ed. (Leipzig, 1885).

CHARING CROSS, the locality about the west end of the Strand and the north end of Whitehall, London, in the city of Westminster. Here Edward I erected the last of the series of crosses in memory of his queen Eleanor (d. 1290). The derivation from Edward's "dear queen" (*chère reine*) is apocryphal. The cross was destroyed in 1647, and in 1675 an equestrian statue of Charles I by Hubert LeSueur was erected at the top of Whitehall, where several regicides had been executed, at the place where the cross stood. The modern cross (1863) stands within the forecourt of Charing Cross railway station. Formerly an important terminus for the continent, the station is now mostly concerned with trains serving southern England. The name (Cyrring in 1000) may refer to the neighbouring sharp bend in the river Thames.

CHARIOT. In antiquity, a car used in battle, for the chase, in public processions and in games. The Greek chariot had two wheels and was made to be drawn by two horses; if a third, or more commonly, two reserve horses were added, they were attached on each side of the main pair by a single trace fastened to the front of the chariot, as may be seen on two prize vases in the British Museum from the Panathenaic games at Athens. On the monuments there is no other sign of traces, from the want of which wheeling round must have been difficult. Immediately on the axle (ἄξων, *axis*), without springs of any kind, rested the basket or body (δίφρος) of the chariot, which consisted of a floor to stand on and a semicircular guard round the front about half the height of the driver. It was entirely open at the back, so that the combatant might readily leap to the ground and up again as was necessary. There was no seat, and generally only room for the combatant and his charioteer to stand in. The pole (ῥυμός, *temo*) was probably attached to the middle of the axle, though it appears to spring from the front of the basket; at the end of the pole was the yoke (ζυγόν, *jugum*), which consisted of two small saddles fitting the necks of the horses and fastened by broad bands round the chest. Besides this the harness of each horse consisted of a bridle and a pair of reins, mostly the same as in use now, made of leather and ornamented with studs of ivory or metal. The reins were passed through rings attached to the collar bands or yoke, and were long enough to be tied round the waist of the charioteer in case of his having to defend himself. The wheels and body of

FROM DAREMBERG ET SAGLIO, "DICTIONNAIRE DES ANTIQUITÉS"

A GREEK CHARIOT (REPRODUCED FROM THE MELOS VASE)

the chariot were usually of wood, strengthened in places with bronze or iron; the wheels had four to eight spokes and tires of bronze or iron. This description applies generally to the chariots of all the nations of antiquity.

Chariot Mountings.—The chariots of the Egyptians and Assyrians, with whom the bow was the principal arm of attack, were richly mounted with quivers full of arrows, while those of the Greeks, whose characteristic weapon was the spear, were plain except as regards mere decoration. Among the Persians, again, and more remarkably among the ancient Britons, there was

FROM THE "JOURNAL OF HELLENIC STUDIES"

TYPES OF CHARIOTS USED BY THREE NATIONS OF ANTIQUITY

1. Light Greek chariot equipped with four-spoked wheels (from a vase)
2. Roman chariot of the type driven in triumphal processions (from a medal of the emperor Trajan)
3. Irish chariot used in battle. Closed in the back and open in front, this model is the reverse of those employed by the Greeks, Romans and Assyrians

a class of chariot having the wheels mounted with sharp, sickle-shaped blades, which cut to pieces whatever came in their way. This was probably an invention of the Persians; Cyrus the younger employed these chariots in large numbers. Among the Greeks and Romans, on the other hand, the chariot had passed out of use in war before historical times and was retained only for races in the public games, or for processions, without undergoing any alteration apparently, its form continuing to correspond with the description of Homer, though it was lighter in build, having to carry only the charioteer. On two Panathenaic prize vases in the British Museum are figures of racing *bigae,* in which, contrary to the description given above, the driver is seated with his feet resting on a board hanging down in front close to the legs of his horses. The *biga* itself consists of a seat resting on the axle, with a

FROM DAREMBERG ET SAGLIO, "DICTIONNAIRE DES ANTIQUITÉS"

ASSYRIAN CHARIOT CARRYING BOWMEN

rail at each side to protect the driver from the wheels. The chariot was unsuited to the uneven soil of Greece and Italy, and it is not improbable that these nations had brought it with them as part of their original habits from their former seats in the east. The Jews used "iron" chariots apparently strengthened by metal.

The chief authorities are J. C. Ginzrot, *Die Wagen und Fahrwerke der Grieche und Römer* (1817); C. F. Grashof, *Über das Fuhrwerk bei Homer und Hesiod* (1846); W. Leaf in *Journal of Hellenic Studies,* v; E. Buchholz, *Die homerischen Realien* (1871–85); W. Helbig, *Das homerische Epos aus den Denkmälern erlautert* (1884), and the article "Currus" in Daremberg and Saglio, *Dictionnaire des Antiquités.*

CHARISIUS, FLAVIUS SOSIPATER, Latin grammarian, flourished about the middle of the 4th century A.D. He was probably an African by birth, summoned to Constantinople to take the place of Euanthius, a learned commentator on Terence. The *Ars Grammatica* of Charisius, part of which is still extant, is valuable as containing excerpts from the earlier writers on grammar, who are in many cases mentioned by name—Q. Remmius Palaemon, C. Julius Romanus, Cominianus.

The best edition is by H. Keil, *Grammatici Latini, i* (1857); *see* also article by G. Götz in Pauly-Wissowa's *Realencyklopädie,* iii, 2 (1899); Teuffel-Schwabe, *Hist. of Roman Literature* (Eng. trans.), par. 419, 1, 2; Fröhde, in *Jahr. f. Philol.,* 18 suppl., 567–672 (1892). New edition by Barwick in Teubner series (1925).

CHARITON, of Aphrodisias, in Caria, the author of a Greek romance entitled *The Loves of Chaereas and Callirrhoë,* probably flourished in the 4th century A.D. The action of the story, which is to a certain extent historical, takes place during the time of the Peloponnesian War.

Editions by J. P. D'Orville (1783), G. A. Hirschig (1856) and R. Hercher (1859); there is an (anonymous) English trans. (1764); *see* also E. Rohde, *Der griechische Roman* (1900).

CHARITON, a city of southern Iowa, U.S., 53 mi. S.E. of Des Moines; the county seat of Lucas county. It is on federal highway 34, and is served by the Burlington and Rock Island railways. The population by 1950 federal census was 5,320. Coal is mined in the vicinity, and the city has a creamery, broom factory, men's work clothing factory and a heavy iron fabrication works. It was settled about 1850.

CHARITY. The word "charity" has a wide range of meanings. It denotes the impulse to give friendship, love, aid and service. It represents, too, both a personal and a social endeavour to ameliorate the conditions which prevail in society. It stands also for a specific association or institution designed to promote some form of social service, usually the relief of the poor.

Most of the words used in Greek, Roman or Hebrew literature to signify good will are primarily words expressive of the affections, of the relations existing between parents and children or between husband and wife, such as ἀγάπη, *amor, amicitia*. *Caritas* or charity, on the other hand, had a somewhat different meaning and referred rather to the relation of the individual to those outside his family; in the first instance *caritas* signified a high price, thus dearness. It was not dissimilar in meaning to the word χάρις, which also had a commercial sense but signified as well gratitude, grace, kindness. In English ecclesiastical documents it was spelled *charitas*. In the Authorized Version of the New Testament, ἀγάπη is translated "charity," and it was used by St. Paul as a translation of the Hebrew word *hesed,* which in the same version of the Old Testament is translated "mercy"; *e.g.,* "I desired mercy and not sacrifice." Almsgiving, *sedaquah,* is translated in the Septuagint by the word ἐλεημοσύνη and in the Authorized Version by the word "righteousness"; it represents the deed which is done or the gift which is made under a sense of religious obligation.

Charity therefore has no necessary relation to relief or alms. Although as a matter of fact it has largely concerned itself with the help of the class usually called the poor and with problems of distress, it is also closely allied to the sense of obligation to one's fellow men as a whole and to the view that society, acting through its appropriate organs, has a collective duty to ensure the well-being of all its members.

Early History of Charity.—To speak broadly, among simpler peoples the family unit was also the agency for sustaining those of its members who fell into distress. Thus the patriarchal family held together successive generations in one community which provided a special niche for old people, the sick and disabled, widows and orphans. With the growth of cities, this form of social organization was dislocated and new methods became necessary. Sometimes, therefore, the state provided charitable aid: thus in Egypt the pharaoh and his appointed agents gave shelter to the poor and distributed bread and clothing. It was believed that charity and good works would assist the soul to attain salvation after death.

In ancient India charity was active from early times. It was promoted by the teachings of the Buddha; and the Buddhist emperor Asoka, according to one of his inscriptions, provided medical facilities throughout his realm and caused wells to be dug and trees to be planted for the enjoyment of man and beast. The infirmaries of Buddhist monasteries sometimes took patients in from outside. In Ceylon, Buddhist monks used to study medicine in order to practise it in a charitable capacity.

In China, houses of refuge for sick people existed at any rate from the introduction of Buddhism in the beginning of the Christian era. The emperor Kublai Khan in 1271 initiated a wide program of relief and social reform including the setting up of nursing establishments.

In China, however, as in many other countries, much benevolent and charitable work was also, from early times, undertaken by private agencies such as guilds and craft associations. It is typical that these paid attention not only to the material needs of the sick and infirm but also to their spiritual needs and to the religious proprieties: thus much importance was attached to the burial of deceased members in a fitting manner.

Early Greek society as mirrored in the *Odyssey* and in Hesiod's works is centred in the clan family and the phratry. Every one outside these units was a stranger: the man who had no brotherhood and was subject to no law, who had no hearth and no family, was suspect. Generally, however, the wayfarer could find food and water and shelter at the houses of the well-to-do, or he could share the hospitality of the peasants. The man who was a wayfarer and beggar almost by profession was not unknown. A system of almsgiving was recognized as a duty.

In the later Greek state, society consisted of citizens and slaves, the slaves enabling the citizens to have leisure for education, war and government. The slaves formed the greater part of the population and were permanently dependent on members of the civic class, so that the only poverty was that of the poor citizens cared for in the first instance by members of the clan family. Public policy and charity alike required that the poverty of citizens should be relieved and citizenhood preserved. In Attica the citizens were aided in various ways; *e.g.,* by legal enactments for release from debts, by emigration, by a free supply of corn, by poor relief for the infirm and by relief for the children of those fallen in war, not to speak of voluntary public service and gifts from individuals.

Three constituents of Roman life were important in their bearing on the subject of this article: the family, the plebs and slavery. The plebs, who were the clients of the great patrician families, gradually became impoverished, and slavery increased *pari passu.* The clan family in early Rome was the dominant political factor. In its development it became unsocial, and the stronger clan families crushed the weaker. The ager publicus, which belonged to the state and had in the early days been distributed to citizens without property, came more and more into the hands of the rich families, and other measures had to be taken to enable the poorer and now impoverished citizens to live. A kind of poor relief in the shape of cheap or free distribution of corn was instituted: the *annona civica.* The right to relief was dependent on the right of citizenship: it was hereditary and passed from father to son.

It was thus in the nature of a continuous endowed charity affecting not one family or group of families but the whole population. Later, for reasons of economy, it became an imperative necessity to restrict the civic bounty to as few persons as possible, and severe penalties were exacted for misappropriation. Those who received it did so as a statutory right, and no labour was required in return. The institution may be regarded less as charity than as public relief designed to allay discontent.

The *sportula* represented the charity of the patron to his clients and of the head of the clan family to those who attended at his house. During the empire particularly, leading citizens displayed munificence and benevolence in other ways: thus when new cities sprang up in the 1st and 2nd centuries A.D. rich citizens gave freely for education, municipal games, etc. Some of their gifts took the form of sums of money or land for the creation and upkeep of religious or charitable institutions.

Guilds were widespread in the Roman and Hellenistic world and these conducted charitable relief for such members as had fallen upon misfortune; they cared for orphans, made loans to the needy, met the funeral expenses of members and helped widows.

Jewish ethical thought recognized from the beginning that the poor had rights and that the rich had duties. This was exemplified in injunctions such as that for the remission of debts every 7th or sabbatic year and every 50th or jubilee year; and in those governing the right of the poor to glean in the fields, the distribution of largess at weddings and at funerals and the giving of alms. Ideal and practice were continued in later Jewish history, partly because of the need for solidarity.

From the period of the fall of the Jewish state, the charity overseer was part of the recognized institutional system of every community. Numerous voluntary associations existed for the care of the indigent and unfortunate. Every ghetto had its lodging house for indigent strangers. It was laid down in the codes that a town without its proper charity organizations was no proper residence for a self-respecting Jew. It was expected of the mediaeval Jew that he should devote a tithe of his income at the very least to philanthropic objects.

Early Christianity.—In early Christian teaching charity was also given a prominent place, as a consequence of the precepts of Jesus Christ, particularly of the great commandments of St. Matthew's Gospel: "Thou shalt love the Lord thy God," "Thou shalt love thy neighbour as thyself" and "all things whatsoever ye would that men should do to you, do ye even so to them." Private liberality was encouraged; but Christianity instituted, apparently from the first, a church fund and associated charity closely with the cult and officials of the church. Gifts were brought every week or month to the service and entrusted to the president, by whom they were laid on the Lord's table and so consecrated to God. The recipient thus obtained them from the hand of God. The love feasts or agapae must also be mentioned among methods of maintenance: these were common meals, to which each contributed as he was able, the poor thus getting food and drink. The duty of distributing these gifts was entrusted to the deacons. The church attached particular importance to the support of widows and orphans, the sick, infirm, poor, disabled and prisoners.

After about the middle of the 4th century, both the need for charity and the means of supplying it increased. The earlier congregational method was replaced by a diocesan one: every church in a city or district was subordinated to the bishop for this purpose. He worked through his steward and could now call upon greatly increased funds. The emperor Constantine I in 321 authorized the church to receive legacies, and after this date considerable property was accumulated for the endowment of charities. As a result of these gifts numerous institutions were opened to cater for various classes of the needy or unfortunate. These included xenodochia or hostels for travellers and institutions for babies, orphans, old people, the blind and other classes. Non-Christians as well as Christians were admitted. St. Basil the Great in 370 founded a number of institutions in Caesarea for the relief of travellers, children, widows, old people, lepers, cripples and the sick. The first Christian hospital in Rome was founded toward the end of the 4th century.

In this period developed the doctrine that saw the value of charity to lie in its effect not so much on the recipient as on the giver: thus St. John Chrysostom says, "If there were no poor the greater part of your sins would not be removed; they are the healers of your wounds."

Early Islam.—Proof of the philanthropic spirit actuating the rulers and nobility of Islam is afforded by their foundation of hospitals, one of the glories of Arabic civilization. In the year 707 the caliph Al-Walid I founded at Damascus the first Arab hospital. Harun al-Rashid founded another at Baghdad in 792. The great hospital opened in Cairo in 1283 by the sultan Kala'un foreshadowed many later developments. It had special wards for dysentery cases, feverish patients, ophthalmic cases, the injured and convalescents; an organized medical service with male and female nurses; storerooms, kitchens, a dispensary, an herb garden, a library, lecture rooms and common rooms for the doctors. Storytellers and musicians were employed to amuse the patients. "I have founded this institution," wrote the sultan, "for kings and servants, for amirs and common soldiers, for rich and poor, for free and bond, for men and women alike." Indigent patients received five pieces of gold on their discharge. Famous doctors—including some Christians and Jews—attended the inpatients and also made domiciliary visits, distributing food and medicines.

The Christian Middle Ages.—At the time of Charlemagne (742?–814) the system of relief was mainly parochial and consisted principally of assistance in the home. But after that time the institutional method appears to have predominated, and the monastery or hospital in one form or another gradually encroached on the parish. Alms were distributed at the doors of churches, monasteries and wealthy houses.

In addition, large number of hospitals were set up in Christendom during the middle ages: more than 750 had been founded in England alone by 1540. Hospitals were originally places of hospitality for the needy, including travellers and the old as well as the sick; they were the ancestors of the modern almshouse as well as of the hospital. Notable English foundations were St. Bartholomew's, London, which in its early days received both the sick poor and foundling children, and St. Thomas's hospital, founded by Peter, bishop of Winchester, in 1215.

A special type of hospital was the lazar house. The first known leper hospital was founded in western Armenia between 260 and 270. Over the next 13 centuries many such institutions were established for the reception of the victims of leprosy and the diseases often mistaken for it. These might be provided by the municipal authority but were sometimes endowed by charitable individuals, the diocese or religious orders.

Domiciliary charity, which had declined after the time of Charlemagne, took on a new importance from the 12th or 13th centuries with the rise of the Franciscans and the formation of various lay orders such as the Beghards and the Alexians or Cellites who cared for the sick, the insane and young people in moral danger.

Franciscan friars also set up the first *monti di pietà* in Orvieto and Perugia (15th century).

Besides the charitable efforts of religious bodies, municipal authorities took an increasing share in promoting the welfare of their inhabitants. This naturally happened first in the countries where town life was early important: in Italy, for example, in the 9th century. By about the 13th century at the latest every urban parish in what is now Belgium had its *table du Saint Esprit* or *table des pauvres,* which was the relieving office of those times. The *chambre des pauvres* administered several parishes simultaneously, and *maîtres des pauvres,* the representatives of the *table* or *chambre,* were elected by notables. Mendicancy was controlled: only children, apprentices, old people, cripples and women with dependent children were allowed to beg. Pilgrims excepted, it was still necessary for applicants for relief to be resident in the parish.

Other secular organizations with charitable activities were the merchant and craft guilds which rose to importance in the later middle ages.

The monastic system of relief began to break down a considerable time before the Reformation. The methods of charity practised by the monasteries had been indiscriminate, and their almsgiving had tended less to the relief of honest poverty than to the fostering of a class of professional beggars. As Thomas Fuller said: "The Abbeys did but maintain the poor which they made." Furthermore, the property of the hospices had often been diverted from its intended use and the hospitality of monasteries or hospices placed at the service of rich men rather than devoted to the benefit of the poor. Ecclesiastical councils and the popes themselves tried to put a stop to such abuses by threatening the administrators of hospices with heavy penalties. In 1311 the council of Vienne forbade the transformation of charitable institutions into clerical benefices and condemned the "administrators of xenodochia, lazarettos, hospices and hospitals who unfeelingly refuse to carry out founders' wishes and shamefully consume the revenues of these establishments." This edict was to be renewed by the council of Trent. In France from the time of Louis XII a series of ordinances of a similar tenor sought to reorganize the administration of such institutions and to take them out of the control of religious bodies.

The same tendencies toward decay had been found in England as in continental countries, and the suppression of the monasteries under Henry VIII and Edward VI did not destroy a system of relief that had previously been working effectively, but merely rendered more apparent the amount of pauperism that had previously existed. It is probable, however, that pauperism was increased by other factors operating at the time, such as the enclosure movement.

16th–19th Centuries.—Under Henry VIII and Edward VI the property of hospitals and guilds was in many cases confiscated. The old systems of charitable relief, for what they were worth, having thus been largely interrupted, new organizations had to be created. The only effective means of raising money for the support of the poor was, it seemed, a compulsory tax, and the administration of statutory relief naturally devolved on the central government. The principle of poor law relief from a compulsory tax having been adopted, it was enacted (1572–73) that the aged and infirm should be cared for by a new authority, the overseers of the poor; and in 1601 two more acts were passed, that for the relief of the poor (43 Eliz. 2) and that for the furtherance and protection of endowed charities (*see* below). Thus the poor were given a statutory minimum of relief which, it was expected, would be supplemented by voluntary benevolence. The poor law was philanthropic in its origin; but the philanthropy later disappeared, and the object of the law appeared to be more and more to relieve the burden of poor rates.

The history of charity from the middle of the 16th century is a history of the remedying of deficiencies in statutory provision partly by supplementing it and partly by educating the public conscience so as to extend it. It is also a history of the discovery and investigation of new needs.

Thus poor relief was centralized and regulated in several continental cities by ordinances of the 15th and 16th centuries. Their methods however seem to have been largely palliative. A more rational method of approaching the problem was proposed by the Spanish humanist Juan Luis Vives in his book *De Subventione pauperum* (1526): this included the co-ordination of charitable activities, a census of the indigent population, detailed inquiries into individual cases and the application of measures suited to each set of circumstances and aiming at permanent rehabilitation. It had no immediate results, however. Examples of voluntary enterprise supplementing official work included an early employment exchange opened in Paris in 1630 by Théophraste Renaudot and "friendly visiting" among the poor, instituted by the preacher Thomas Chalmers (1819), by Daniel von der Heydt, author of the Elberfeld poor relief system, *q.v.* (1852), and by A. F. Ozanam, founder of the Société de Saint Vincent de Paul (1833), among others. Soup kitchens for the poor were provided by Benjamin Thompson, Count Rumford, in Bavaria around the end of the 18th century. But in general the picture until at any rate the middle of the 19th century is one of a large number of separate and often jealous organizations for the relief of the poor, pursuing many useful and some less useful lines of activity, but lacking any real knowledge of the extent and causes of poverty.

The later history of the relief of the sick exhibits also a progressively keener perception of differing needs leading to increased specialization of services. In the 17th century a clearer distinction began to be drawn between institutions where treatment was provided and those where shelter was given to the aged and the poor, but it was not until the 18th that hospitals really began to concentrate upon acute cases. At this time both the planning of hospitals and medical and nursing treatment were exceedingly rudimentary, and a long period of energetic work by devoted voluntary workers such as Claude-Humbert Piarron de Chamousset, Sir John Pringle, John Howard and Florence Nightingale was necessary to improve them. At the same time new needs were successively discovered and provided for. Medical dispensaries were set up in France in the 17th century. In London 53 well-known doctors in 1696 each subscribed £10 for the creation of a free dispensary where they offered their services. Specialized hospitals for tuberculosis, cancer, diseases of the eye and diseases of the ear and throat began to be set up in the 18th and early 19th centuries. The broadening conception of medical treatment also led, in the latter part of the 19th century, to the development of "hospital social services": in 1895 the first lady almoner was appointed at the Royal Free hospital, London; in the same year a similar post was created at the Charity hospital, Berlin; and nine years later a post-hospital relief service was organized in New York city.

Relief of the blind by alms and by shelter had existed in ancient times; but again, efforts to assist them to develop their capacities and to live as far as possible normal lives were not made until relatively late. In 1749 Denis Diderot suggested that the blind could be taught to read and write by touch. A satisfactory alphabet, however, was not achieved until the time of Louis Braille (1829). Subsequently much attention has been given to the matter of training and placing blind people. Work for the deaf, for children, for old people and for other dependent or disabled classes has followed a similar course of a more and more discriminating study of needs and of ways to meet these needs on the part of a succession of public-spirited men and women.

These forms of charity concentrated chiefly on the individual. But charitable effort also concerned itself with the improvement of the environment—with better housing, town planning and the preservation of the beauties of the countryside for the benefit of the mass of the people. In England, movements to improve the housing of the poor were largely a 19th-century phenomenon: the prince consort was president of an association founded in 1844 to provide workingmen's dwellings; and in the 1860s the Peabody trust, set up for the same purpose, was followed by others. In an allied sphere of work, Octavia Hill in the 1860s invented the vocation of housing manager and exercised a remarkable educative and social influence upon her tenants. After these efforts to improve housing the wider principle began to be recalled that the improvement of the environment must take into account not only individual houses but also the town as a whole and the countryside around it.

Much charitable work in the early 19th century was carried on by individuals and societies having little connection with one another. Around the middle of the century, however, it began more and more to be felt that this lack of system led to waste of effort. Societies worked without adequate knowledge of what others were doing and without any proper examination of the circumstances of applicants. As a consequence of this feeling, a number of co-ordinating and organizing societies were set up in various parts of Europe. One of the first and best known of these was the Charity Organisation society, London, formed in 1869, at first called the Society for Organizing Charitable Relief and Repressing Mendicity. The aims of this body were avowedly to prevent the continuance of indiscriminate relief giving and the consequent pauperization of the recipients. Its methods included careful inquiries into every case, the submission of written reports by the social workers concerned and the careful discussion of facts with a view to discovering the causes of distress and planning their removal. In its early days the society incurred, rightly or wrongly, a considerable amount of antagonism from the working classes on account of its alleged harsh and unsympathetic attitude. At the same time there is no doubt that it played an important part in the investigation of the causes of poverty and associated ills and in the development of casework and other social techniques. It was also one of the first to emphasize the necessity of training for charitable work. It started training courses for social workers in 1893, an example which was followed by many other bodies throughout the world. Further advances in the systematization and effectiveness of charitable work were made during the later 19th century: thus the first large-scale survey of poverty conducted on precise methods was begun in London in 1889 by Charles Booth and was the forerunner of a host of others in many countries which were of immense value in focusing charitable effort.

The State and Voluntary Effort.—Public social service is, it will have been seen, not a new thing; what was perhaps characteristic of the 20th century was the view that it is the function of the state as the appropriate organ of society to take systematic measures to ensure adequate minimum standards and adequate social opportunities for all its members. To do so became possible partly through the increased knowledge accumulated as a result of the work referred to above.

Nevertheless, voluntary effort for social service continued to play an extremely important part in the 20th century. In Great Britain, social service bodies wholly or mainly independent of government control existed in astonishing variety—their numbers and, therefore, the aggregate of their funds being virtually impossible to determine accurately. The same richness of voluntary effort is found in many other countries: for example in Italy and in France, where their vigour is assisted by a widespread distrust of centralized bureaucracy; in Denmark, where voluntary effort is responsible for most residential institutions for children, for most day centres, such as kindergartens, and also for many institutions for the special care and rehabilitation of the handicapped; and in the Netherlands, where, as it is a principle to make use of voluntary organizations wherever possible, the public agencies supplement voluntary ones.

After World War II the future of voluntary charitable effort in Great Britain appeared somewhat uncertain. The state took over a good deal which formerly was the province of private philanthropy. Moreover, costs rose steeply, and taxation and financial stringency led to a diminution of income from donations and subscriptions. Indeed, many voluntary social service bodies were drawing an appreciable proportion of their income from central or local government sources in the form of grants-in-aid, payments for services and the like. In this way the position and the work of voluntary associations became more closely linked than before with those of public social services. This change in position and function was assisted by legislation that made it either mandatory or permissive for public departments to make use of voluntary bodies in carrying out certain duties in the field of social welfare, such as, for example, the youth service. It was thus often difficult to say where official action ended and voluntary service began.

Charitable Endowments.—The existence of endowed charities in early and mediaeval times was referred to above. After the dissolution of the monasteries and the seizure of funds of guilds and chantries in England, the Statute of Charitable Uses (43 Eliz. 4 [1601]) was passed to provide for reform of abuses and encourage further charitable gifts. Many trusts were founded in the 17th and 18th centuries, but, consequent upon widespread maladministration by trustees, a movement for reform began in the early 19th century. In 1835 a select committee was appointed; resulting from its recommendations, an act of 1853 set up the Charity commission, which had and still had in the early 1950s the duty of watching over charitable trusts. Its powers and duties included those of inquiry into the affairs of a charity, in connection with which it could require the production of accounts; control over dealings in real estate; removal of trustees (subject to conditions); and the preparation of schemes, under certain conditions, where it appeared that the original objects of a trust could not be fulfilled. (*See* CHARITY COMMISSIONERS FOR ENGLAND AND WALES.) *See* also CASUAL WARD; PENSIONS; POOR LAW; RELIEF; SOCIAL SECURITY.

BIBLIOGRAPHY.—L. Lallemand, *Histoire de la charité* (Paris, 1902–12); Various authors, articles on charity in J. Hastings, *Encyclopaedia of Religion and Ethics,* vol. iii (Edinburgh, 1910); E. Westermarck, *Origin and Development of the Moral Ideas,* 2nd ed., esp. ch. xxiii (London, 1917); Sir C. Loch, *Charity and Social Life* (London, 1910); R. Sand, *The Advance to Social Medicine* (1952); M. Rostovtzeff, *Social and Economic History of the Roman Empire* (Oxford, 1926); A. Harnack, *The Mission and Expansion of Christianity in the First Three Centuries,* Eng. trans., 2 vol., 2nd ed., esp. book ii, ch. iv (London, 1908); S. W. Baron, *A Social and Religious History of the Jews,* 3 vol. (1937); C. Roth, *The Jewish Contribution to Civilisation* (London, 1938); Sir W. Ashley, *English Economic History,* 2 vol., esp. book ii, ch. v (London, 1919–20); B. Kirkman Gray, *A History of English Philanthropy* (London, 1905); M. Simey, *Charitable Effort in Liverpool in the Nineteenth Century* (Liverpool, 1951); H. Bosanquet, *Social Work in London, 1865 to 1912: a History of the Charity Organisation Society* (London, 1914); E. Hodder, *The Life and Work of the Seventh Earl of Shaftesbury, K.G.,* 2 vol. (London, 1886); E. H. C. Moberly Bell, *Octavia Hill* (London, 1942); Lord Beveridge, *Voluntary Action* (London, 1948); A. C. F. Bourdillon (ed.), *Voluntary Social Services* (London, 1945); H. A. Mess, *Voluntary Social Services Since 1918* (London, 1948); Sir A. Hobhouse, *The Dead Hand: Addresses on the Subject of Endowments and Settlements of Property* (London, 1880); Family Welfare Association, *Annual Charities Register and Digest* (London); United Nations, Department of Social Affairs, *Methods of Social Welfare Administration* (1950). (A. F. Ws.)

UNITED STATES

The history of charity in the United States, as elsewhere, is one of many social, religious and economic theories, influences and endeavours, all of which left their imprint on both popular and educated thought. The universal principles of Christian doctrine which were a fusion of the Jewish and Graeco-Roman philosophies obtained.

The structure of charity organization in the United States had its origin largely in the English system; the American poor laws followed English legislation and practice until about the early 19th century. Most of the states even in the second half of the 20th century continued to cling to many of the old Elizabethan poor law principles in philosophy and practice. The principle of settlement or legal residence as a requirement for receiving assistance still prevailed generally. States had fluctuated in their adherence to the old English principle of relative responsibility, but on the whole it still had public acceptance. There had never been any question of the moral or ethical responsibility to support needy close relatives, but in practice the attempt to enforce this as a legal obligation had been filled with heartaches, damaged familial relationships, costly judicial procedures and withal very little money resulting from court action for the support of the dependent relative.

The English poor law principle of "less eligibility" also continued to permeate popular belief regarding charity and public assistance in the United States—that is, the recipient of charity should not receive in assistance more than an amount the lowest paid worker can earn. Inherent in this principle is the fear that the individual would prefer to receive charity rather than to work. This attitude had prevailed especially with reference to the unemployed, able-bodied man.

Yet, experience both in the United States and England had disproved this theory. Experience had shown that assistance which does not allow the recipient and his family to function as self-respecting members of the community tends to pauperize rather than the contrary. Likewise, when assistance is given in a positive way the recipient is in a better position to become a self-supporting and self-respecting person.

In the development of U.S. public charitable activity until about the middle of the 19th century, there was an almost complete disregard of the effect of charity on the beneficiary. Charity of this early period was largely motivated by communal purposes or class interests as contrasted with the personal concern and gratification of early ecclesiastical charities.

The growing private charitable activities of this period did not differ much from those of the various governmental bodies since they, too, were nourished by the mounting wealth of the industrial middle class. The addition to charitable theory and practice of a genuine interest in the individual recipient and of the recognition of his rights as a person did not come until near the close of the 19th century.

Individuals such as Joseph Tuckerman, Thomas Eddy, Samuel Gridley Howe, Dorothea Dix and Charles Loring Brace made important contributions to this new and important concept of charity. Early antecedents of modern family service societies likewise contributed. From the early 1840s until about 1877 these societies played major roles in the giving of relief and in charitable reform. They worked for the breakdown of the old traditional concept of the poor as a class apart from the rest of the population. They protested against indiscriminate giving of charity and attempted to devise methods of preventing it. They worked toward the development of the scientific method in the administration of charity. Some of the recommendations of the early societies were quite in advance of the times. They proposed to divide the cities into small districts, each district to have two or three volunteer visitors who were to call on the poor in their own homes, thereby having close contact with and first-hand knowledge of the applicant and later the recipient. Some of the societies proposed to promote life insurance and savings banks, to prohibit street begging and to establish houses of employment for those who could not find work. They devised a plan whereby all spontaneous charity could flow into one channel for distribution. Many of the early attempts failed, however, because they lost purpose and direction as they gave more attention to agitating for temperance rather than charitable reform, thus tending to confuse moral objectives with the relief of physical want.

Efforts at charitable reform continued, however, and in 1877 the Charity Organization Societies movement started. Its objectives included co-operation between all charitable agencies in a local community; full and accurate knowledge of individuals receiving service; adequate and prompt relief; employment for all able and willing to work; establishment of relations of personal interest and sympathy between the poor and the well-to-do; and collection and dissemination of knowledge about administration of charity. The study of causes of individual failure to adjust to family or to the social environment led the Charity Organization societies to the realization that help must come from persons who had studied social sciences and the available knowledge of human relations. This realization hastened the transition from a service by volunteer friendly visitors to one carried on more and more by salaried workers with professional training.

Types.—By the second half of the 20th century the charitable activities of individuals varied greatly in the United States. To many people, charity was little more than a series of miscellaneous activities described vaguely as doing good or as helping people—giving clothing or baskets of food to the poor at Christmas, providing free medical and dental care for the sick poor and clothing and recreation for poor children. Others might not give food, clothing or money directly to the beneficiary but rather give their personal contributions to a social agency which in turn served the needy person. Others, as members of a church, might contribute to the operation of a charitable institution maintained by the church. Clubs or other social organizations might sponsor entertainments to raise money for various charitable purposes. While the philosophy inherent in public assistance was not fundamentally the same as the traditional concept of private charity, public relief was still popularly confused with charity. The scope of charity had undergone many changes with regard to potential beneficiaries, and the types of benefits had reflected the changing social standards of the communities. To some individuals, the giving of charity may involve a real personal feeling of responsibility with an attempt to understand and meet the needs of those who receive charity regardless of the form it takes or the way in which it is administered. Modern social work practice indicated that those who are most understanding of the emotional and psychological needs of people and the problems involved in receiving charity are willing to have social agencies with professionally trained staffs give the service and financial assistance to the recipient. The individual donor may implement his own charitable impulses not only by giving money to the agency but by such voluntary activity as serving on committees of the social agency.

By mid-20th century in the United States, individuals only rarely sought out the beneficiaries of their own charitable acts. To organize charity is to give to it an ordered nature and definite purpose and to associate members of the community together for the purpose. Private charitable giving for welfare purposes in the United States is largely channeled through the community chest or some similar agency which is organized to collect voluntary contributions through a single annual campaign. Through some such organization as the Council of Social Agencies, welfare and health services are co-ordinated to prevent duplication and overlapping of services.

Religious Charities.—The profession of the Roman Catholic faith obligates the communicant to works of charity. The basic Catholic theory for social service is stimulated in every phase of the church organization. The world-wide structure of the church permits universal teaching regarding charity to be brought to every individual member of the church. Each parish, diocese and province recognizes the corporate responsibility for social service. The standards of modern scientific social work are accepted in general by Catholic social work up to the beginning of the supernatural element, which is always regarded as superior and implies the highest kind of inspiration and aspiration for the services to others.

The title Catholic Charities is usually used to designate the federation of the Catholic social services in a diocese. This is the official agency of the bishop which plans, directs and coordinates all charitable activities in the diocese. It is customary to delegate the actual administration of the Catholic Charities to a priest trained in social work.

Jewish social work has its origins in biblical injunctions and practice. While these practices were modified to meet changing needs, the old traditions persisted. The scope and structure of Jewish social work is determined largely by the character of the Jewish population and by the community in which they live; there is no hierarchy as in Catholic social work and the local agency is autonomous and fully independent. In earlier days, Jewish agencies took pride in taking care of their own, but later they accepted the belief that most of the needs of people must be met by public welfare and that the main function of Jewish social work is to supplement governmental services. In many ways the basic core of Jewish social service is the following statement from the Talmud: "The noblest charity is to prevent a man from accepting charity and the best alms are to enable a man to dispense with alms."

Protestant churches also offer a variety of social services, but their basic theological teaching is that members should support, financially and morally, not only their own church agencies, but also those of the general community which are nonsectarian in nature. The organized social services of the Protestant churches are manifestations, in varying degrees, of the following religious motives: Christian charity and the personal concern of the church for its own people; the evangelistic hope that the religious life of the individual given service will be strengthened; and a widely humanitarian and democratic concern for the welfare of people and the general improvement of society and the concept of good works.

Child and Family Welfare.—There are many areas in which organized U.S. private social work functions, but in general, they may all be classified either as: (1) child welfare services; or (2) services to families and adults. The great concern over the welfare of children was expressed in the several White House conferences called by different presidents of the United States. The first conference in 1909 was chiefly concerned with the problems of neglected, dependent and handicapped children. Out of that conference came the United States children's bureau, established to study the needs of children and to set standards for children's services. Thereafter, White House conferences were called every ten years by the president, each one studying children's needs from increasingly broad perspectives. In 1950, for example, more than 5,000 adults and youths gathered in Washington, D.C., to consider the needs of children in the United States and territories. Two documents, the Children's charter in 1930, and the Pledge to Children in 1950, represented the philosophy of a nation toward its children.

Services to families and individuals comprise the second large area of U.S. welfare. As stated earlier, the antecedents of the private family welfare agency in the United States played an important role historically in meeting the needs of people and in the organization of charity. As the need for better trained workers became apparent, training courses for staff workers were organized by some of the larger societies. In 1898 the New York City Community Organization society inaugurated the New York School of Philanthropy, first professional school of social work. The modern family service agency is a highly specialized treatment agency offering its services on a selective basis to families with problems of emotional and personality adjustments rather than mainly financial needs.

Bibliography.—United States Library of Congress, Division of Bibliography, brief list of references on the *Historical Development of Charity and Social Work;* William J. Kerby, *The Social Mission of Charity* (1944); Frank D. Watson, *The Charity Organization Movement in the United States* (1922); Amos G. Warner, Stuart A. Queen and Ernest B. Harper, *American Charities and Social Work* (1930); Ephraim Frisch, *An Historical Survey of Jewish Philanthropy* (1924); F. Emerson Andrews, *Philanthropic Giving* (1950); Edward C. Jenkins, *Philanthropy in America* (1950); Gordon Hamilton, *The Theory and Practice of Social Case Work,* 2nd ed. (1951); Charlotte Towle, *Common Human Needs* (1952); American Association of Social Workers, *Social Work Year Book* (biennial); Helen Leland Witmer, *Social Work; an Analysis of a Social Institution* (1942); Herbert Hewitt Stroup, *Social Work: an Introduction to the Field* (1948); Frank J. Bruno, *Trends in Social Work as Reflected in the Proceedings of the National Conference of Social Work, 1874–1946* (1948); *Proceedings of the National Conference of Social Work* (annual).

(M. C. Bl.; C. E. Me.)

CHARITY COMMISSIONERS FOR ENGLAND AND WALES. As a result of the reports of a committee of the house of commons appointed in 1816 on the motion of Henry (afterward Lord) Brougham, four successive statutory commissions were appointed between 1818 and 1835, the fourth expiring on July 1, 1837. The reports of these commissions are known as the Parliamentary Reports of the Former Commissioners for Inquiring Concerning Charities. They form the main source of information about charities then in existence. There followed many attempts to pass legislation to give effect to the suggestions made by the members of the fourth commission in their final general report and by a select committee of the house of commons appointed in 1835 to examine the reports of the statutory commissions so far as then published. In 1853 the first Charitable Trusts act was passed, which established the Board of Charity Commissioners for England and Wales.

Under the 1853 act and the Charitable Trusts Amendment act

1855, the functions of the charity commissioners were: (1) to inquire into the administration of charities; (2) to give advice to trustees of charities; (3) to assist trustees in developing the property and in executing the trusts of charities by supplementing their powers where defective; (4) to control the action of the trustees of charities in dealing with the corpus of endowments, the commissioners' consent being required to sales, mortgages and long leases of land; (5) to control the taking of legal proceedings on behalf of charities, so as to prevent unnecessary litigation and its attendant cost; (6) to secure the rendering of annual accounts. Later, various statutes conferred additional functions on the commissioners.

The object of the Charitable Trusts acts, 1853 to 1939, was to secure the better administration of endowed charities. The acts accordingly provided for control of dealings with capital endowments, required the rendering by trustees of annual accounts, gave the charity commissioners wide powers of inquiry and provided means of vesting property, appointing and removing trustees and remodelling trusts without resort to expensive legal proceedings. The charity commissioners were not themselves empowered, however, to administer or manage charitable trusts. Educational charities were made subject to the jurisdiction of the minister of education.

The Official Trustee of Charity Lands, a corporation sole, was constituted to hold charity lands which might be vested in him by a court of competent jurisdiction or by an order of the charity commissioners. The Official Trustees of Charitable Funds, who are incorporated, were constituted to hold stocks, shares securities and monies belonging to charities. On Dec. 31, 1952, they held a total of £119,707,852. These were holding trustees only and could not enter into the administration or management of any charity.

CHARIVARI, a French term of uncertain origin, but probably onomatopoeic, for a mock serenade, "rough music," made by beating on kettles, fire irons, tea trays or tin pans. The charivari was anciently in France a regular wedding custom, all bridal couples being thus serenaded. Later it was reserved for ill-assorted and unpopular marriages and as a mockery for all who were unpopular. At the beginning of the 17th century, wedding charivaris were forbidden by the council of Tours, but the custom still lingers in rural districts. The French of Louisiana and Canada introduced the charivari into America, where it became known under the corrupted name of "shivaree."

CHARKHARI, a town in southern Uttar Pradesh, India, 40 mi. W. of Banda. The population in 1941 was 12,638.

Ghee and cloth fabrics are produced there.

Charkhari was the capital of the former Indian state of the same name in the Bundelkhand agency of Central India. The state, which was surrounded on all sides by other states of Central India except near the town of Charkhari, where it met the former United Provinces, was founded by Bijai Bahadur, a *sanad* being granted him in 1804 and another in 1811.

In 1948 the state of Charkhari became part of the new state of Vindhya Pradesh, and two years later a detached part was merged with a district of Uttar Pradesh.

CHARLATAN, originally one who "patters" to a crowd to sell his wares (Ital. *ciarlatano,* from *ciarlare,* to chatter), like a "cheap-jack" or "quack" doctor—"quack" being similarly derived from the noise made by a duck; so an impostor who pretends to have some special skill or knowledge.

CHARLEMAGNE LEGENDS. Innumerable legends soon gathered round the memory of the great emperor. He was represented as a warrior performing superhuman feats, as a ruler dispensing perfect justice, and even as a martyr suffering for the faith. It was confidently believed towards the close of the 10th century that he had made a pilgrimage to Jerusalem; and, as in the case of many other great rulers, it was reported that he was only sleeping to awake in the hour of his country's need. The legendary Charlemagne and his warriors were endowed with the great deeds of earlier kings and heroes of the Frankish kingdom, for the romancers were not troubled by considerations of chronology. National traditions extending over centuries were grouped round Charlemagne, his father Pippin, and his son Louis. The history of Charles Martel especially was absorbed in the Charlemagne legend. But if Charles's name was associated with the heroism of his predecessors he was credited with equal readiness with the weaknesses of his successors. In the histories of the wars with his vassals he is often little more than a tyrannical dotard, who is made to submit to gross insult. This picture of affairs is drawn from later times, and the sympathies of the poet are generally with the rebels against the monarchy.

Charlemagne's wars in Italy, Spain and Saxony formed part of the common epic material, and there are references to his wars against the Slavs; but especially he remained in the popular mind as the great champion of Christianity against the creed of Mohammed. In 1164 Charles was canonized; yet this gave him no real claim to saintship, but his festival was observed in some places until comparatively recent times. Charlemagne was endowed with the good and bad qualities of the epic king, and as in the case of Agamemnon and Arthur, his exploits paled beside those of his chief warriors. These were not originally known as the peers famous in later Carolingian romance. The peers numbered 12 most probably by analogy with the 12 Apostles. The lists of them are very various, but all include the names of Roland and Oliver. The chief heroes who fought Charlemagne's battles were Roland; Ganelon, afterwards the traitor; Turpin, the fighting archbishop of Reims; Duke Naimes of Bavaria, the wise counsellor who is always on the side of justice; Ogier the Dane, the hero of a whole series of romances; and Guillaume of Toulouse, the defender of Narbonne.

The defeat of Roncesvalles, which so deeply impressed the popular mind, has not a corresponding importance in real history. But it chanced to find as its exponent a poet whose genius established in the *Chanson de Roland* (*see* ROLAND, LEGEND OF) a model for his successors, and definitely fixed the type of later heroic poems. The other early *chansons* to which reference is made in *Roland* are *Aspremont, Enfances Ogier, Guiteclin, Balan,* relating to Charlemagne's wars in Italy and Saxony. *Basin* or *Carl et Elégast* (preserved in Dutch and Icelandic), the *Pèlerinage de Charlemagne* and *Le Couronnement Looys* also belong to the heroic period. The purely fictitious and romantic tales added to the personal history of Charlemagne and his warriors in the 13th century are inferior in manner, and belong to the decadence of romance. The old tales, very much distorted in the 15th century prose versions, were to undergo still further degradation in 18th century compilations.

According to *Berte aus grans piés,* in the 13th century *remaniement* of the Brabantine *trouvère* Adenet le Roi, Charlemagne was the son of Pippin and of Berte, the daughter of Flore and Blanchefleur, king and queen of Hungary. *Mainet* (12th century) and the kindred poems in German and Italian relate the *enfances* (youthful exploits) of Charlemagne. He delivered Rome from the besieging Saracens, and returned to France in triumph. But his wife Galienne, daughter of Galafre, whom he had converted to the Christian faith, died on her way to rejoin him. Charlemagne then made an expedition to Italy (*Enfances Ogier* in the Venetian *Charlemagne,* and the first part of the *Chevalerie Ogier de Dannemarche* by Raimbert of Paris, 12th century) to raise the siege of Rome, which was besieged by the Saracen emir Corsuble. *Aspremont* (12th century) describes a fictitious campaign against the Saracen King Agolant in Calabria, and is chiefly devoted to the *enfances* of Roland. The wars of Charlemagne with his vassals are described in *Girart de Roussillon, Renaut de Montauban, Huon de Bordeaux,* and in the latter part of the *Chevalerie Ogier,* which belong properly to the cycle connected with Doon of Mayence.

The legend of the pilgrimage of Charlemagne to the Holy Sepulchre probably originated in a desire to authenticate the relics in the abbey of Saint Denis, supposed to have been brought to Aix by Charlemagne, and is preserved in a 12th-century romance, *Le Pèlerinage de Charlemagne.* The legend of the conquest of Armorica is preserved in *Aiquin* (12th century). *La destruction de Rome* is a 13th-century version of the older *chanson* of the emir Balan, who collected an army in Spain and sailed to Rome. The defenders were overpowered and the city destroyed before the advent of Charlemagne, who, however, avenged the disaster by a great battle in Spain. The romance of *Fierabras* (13th century) was one of the most popular in the 15th century, and by later additions came to have pretensions to be a complete history of Charlemagne. *Otinel* (13th century) is also pure fiction. *L'Entrée en Espagne,* preserved in a 14th-century Italian compilation, relates the beginning of the Spanish War, the siege of Pampeluna, and the legendary combat of Roland with Ferragus. Charlemagne's march on Saragossa, and the capture of Huesca, Barcelona and Girone, gave rise to *La Prise de Pampelune* (14th century, based on a lost *chanson*); and *Gui de Bourgogne* (12th century) tells how the children of the barons, after appointing Guy as king of France, set out to find and rescue their fathers, who are represented as having been fighting in Spain for 27 years. The *Chanson de Roland* relates the historic defeat of Roncesvalles on Aug. 15, 778, and forms the very crown of the whole Carolingian legend. The two 13th-century romances, *Gaidon* and *Anseis de Carthage,* contain a purely fictitious account of the end of the war in Spain, and of the establishment of a Frankish kingdom under the rule of Anseis. Charlemagne was recalled from Spain by the news of the outbreak of the Saxons. The contest between Charlemagne and Widukind (*Guiteclin*) offered abundant epic material. Unfortunately the original *Guiteclin* is lost, but the legend is preserved in *Les Saisnes* (*c.* 1300) of Jehan Bodel, which is largely occupied by the loves of Baudouin and Sibille, the wife of Guiteclin. The adventures of Blanchefleur, wife of Charlemagne, form a variation of the common tale of the innocent wife falsely accused, and are told in *Macaire* and in the extant fragments of *La Reine Sibille* (14th century). After the conquest of the Saracens and the Saxons, the defeat of the Northmen, and the suppression of the feudal revolts, the emperor abdicated in favour of his son Louis (*Le Couronnement Looys,* 12th century). Charles's harangue to his son is in the best tradition of epic romance. The memory of Roncesvalles haunts him on his death-bed, and at the moment of death he has a vision of Roland.

The mythic element is practically lacking in the French legends, but in Germany some part of the Odin myth was associated with Charles's name. The constellation of the Great Bear, generally associated with Odin, is Karlswagen in German, and Charles's Wain in English. There were mediaeval chroniclers who did not fear to assert that Charles rose from the dead to take part in the Crusades. In the ms. *Annales S. Stephani Frisingenses* (15th century), which formerly belonged to the abbey of Weihenstephan, and is now at Munich, the childhood of Charlemagne is practically the same as that of many mythic heroes. This work, generally known as the chronicle of Weihenstephan, gives among other legends a curious history of the emperor's passion for a dead woman, caused by a charm given to Charles by a serpent to whom he had rendered justice. The charm was finally dropped into a well at Aix, which thenceforward became Charles's favourite residence. The story of Roland's birth from the union of Charles with his sister Gilles, also found in German and Scandinavian versions, has abundant parallels in mythology, and was probably transferred from mythology to Charlemagne.

The Latin chronicle, wrongly ascribed to Turpin (Tilpinus), bishop of Reims from 753 to 800, was in reality composed by a Frenchman between 1140 and 1150. Alberic Trium Fontium, a monk of the Cistercian monastery of Trois Fontanes in the diocese of Châlons, embodied much poetical fiction in his chronicle (*c.* 1249). A large section of the *Chronique rimée* (*c.* 1243) of Philippe Mousket is devoted to Charlemagne's exploits. At the beginning of the 14th century Girard of Amiens made a dull compilation known as *Charlemagne* from the *chansons de gests,* authentic history and the pseudo-Turpin. *La Conqueste que fit le grand roi Charlemaigne es Espaignes* (pr. 1486) is the same work as the prose compilation of *Fierabras* (pr. 1478), and Caxton's *Lyf of Charles the Grete* (1485).

The Charlemagne legend was fully developed in Italy, where it was to have later a great poetic development at the hands of Boiardo, Ariosto and Tasso. There are two important Italian compilations, ms. XIII. of the library of St. Mark, Venice (*c.* 1200), and the *Reali di Francia* (*c.* 1400) of a Florentine writer, Andrea da Barberino (b. 1370), edited by G. Vandelli (Bologna, 1892). The six books of this work are rivalled in importance by the ten branches of the Norse *Karlamagnus saga,* written under the reign of Haakon V. This forms a consecutive legendary history of Charles, and is apparently based on earlier versions of the French Charlemagne poems than those which we possess. It thus furnishes a guide to the older forms of stories, and moreover preserves the substance of others which have not survived in their French form. A popular abridgement, the *Keiser Karl Magnus Krönike* (pr. Malmö, 1534), drawn up in Danish, serves in some cases to complete the earlier work. The 2,000 lines of the German *Kaiserchronik* on the history of Charlemagne belong to the first half of the 12th century, and were perhaps the work of Conrad, the poet of the *Ruolantes Liet.* The German poet known as the Stricker used the same sources as the author of the chronicle of Weihenstephan for his *Karl* (*c.* 1230). The earliest important Spanish version was the *Chronica Hispaniae* (*c.* 1284) of Rodrigo de Toledo.

The French and Norman-French *chansons* circulated as freely in England as in France, and it was therefore not until the period of decadence that English versions were made. The English metrical romances of Charlemagne are:—*Rowlandes Song* (15th century); *The Taill of Rauf Coilyear* (*c.* 1475, pr. by R. Lekpreuik, St. Andrews, 1472), apparently original; *Sir Ferumbras* (*c.* 1380) and the *Sowdone of Babylone* (*c.* 1400) from an early version of *Fierabras;* a fragmentary *Roland and Vernagu* (Ferragus); two versions of *Otuel* (Otinel); and a *Sege of Melayne* (*c.* 1390), forming a prologue to Otinel unknown in French.

For the historical Charlemagne *see* CHARLES THE GREAT.

BIBLIOGRAPHY.—The most important works on the Charlemagne cycle of romance are J. Bédier, *Les légendes épiques* (4 vol., 1908–13) and *La Chanson de Roland* (1927), and for the German legend, vol. iii. of H. F. Massmann's ed. of the *Kaiserchronik* (Quedlinburg, 1849–54). *The English Charlemagne Romances* were edited (extra series) for the Early Eng. Text Soc. by Sidney J. Herrtage, Emil Hausknecht, Octavia Richardson and Sidney Lee (1879–81), the romance of *Duke Huon of Bordeaux* containing a general account of the cycle by Sidney Lee; the *Karlamagnussaga,* by C. R. Unger (Christiania, 1860), *see* also G. Paris in *Bibl. de l'Ecole des Chartes* (1864–65). For individual *chansons see* L. Gautier, *Les Épopées françaises* (new ed. 1919 etc.) and J. Bédier, *op. cit.,* to which the following should be added: A. Thomas, *L'Entrée d'Espagne* (Société des Anciens Textes Français, 1913); L. Brandin, *La Chanson d'Aspremont* (1923–24), and *Sir Otuel,* ed. S. J. Herrtage (*E.E.T.S.,* 1880). For the Carolingian romances relating to Roland, *see* ROLAND, LEGEND OF; *Les Saisnes,* ed. F. Michel (1839); *The Sege of Melaine,* introductory to *Otinel,* preserved in English only (ed. *E.E.T.S.,* 1880); *Simon de Pouille,* analysis in *Epop. fr.* (iii. pp. 346 *seq.*); *Voyage de C. à Jérusalem,* ed. E. Koschwitz (Heilbronn, 1879). For the chronicle of the Pseudo-Turpin, *see* an edition by Castets (Paris, 1881) for the "Société des langues romanes," and J. Bédier in *Légendes epiques,* t. iii. The Spanish versions of Carolingian legends are studied by Milà y Fontanals, *De la poesia heroico-popular castellana* (Barcelona, 1874). (L. B.)

CHARLEMONT, JAMES CAULFEILD, 1ST EARL OF (1728–1799), Irish statesman, son of the third viscount Charlemont, was born in Dublin on Aug. 18, 1728, and succeeded his father as fourth viscount in 1734. Lord Charlemont is historically interesting for his political connection with Flood and Grattan. For various early services in Ireland he was made an earl in 1763, but he disregarded court favours and cordially joined Grattan in 1780 in the assertion of Irish independence, being chosen commander-in-chief of the volunteer force. He was president of the volunteer convention in Dublin in November 1783, and was a strong opponent of the proposals for the Union. Lord Charlemont was a cultivated man, with liberal and artistic tastes, and his house was a centre of literary society in Dublin. He died on Aug. 4, 1799.

See F. Hardy, *Memoirs of the political and private life of James Caulfeild, Earl of Charlemont* (1810; 2nd ed., 1812); *Original Letters, principally from Lord Charlemont, . . . Edmund Burke, . . . etc.* (1820).

CHARLEROI (CAROLUS REX), a town in the province of Hainaut, Belgium. Pop. (1939) 28,183. It was founded in 1666 on the site of a village called Charnoy, by the Spanish governor Roderigo, and named after his sovereign Charles II. of Spain. Charleroi is the centre of the chief coalfield of Belgium, with important metallurgical and glass industries. It is connected by canal with Brussels, and from its position on the Sambre communicates by water with France. It was ceded soon after its foundation to France by the treaty of Aix-la-Chapelle, and Vauban fortified it. During the French occupation the town was considerably extended, and its fortifications strengthened to resist the attacks of William of Orange. In 1794 Charleroi again fell into the hands of the French, and it was dismantled by them. In 1816 it was re-fortified under Wellington's direction, but was finally dismantled in 1859. Parts of the old ramparts are left near the railway station. The battle of Charleroi (Aug. 22–23, 1914) was fought between German and French troops. In World War II, Charleroi was occupied by the Germans soon after the fall of Namur in May 1940.

CHARLEROI, a borough of Washington county, Pennsylvania, U.S.A., on the Monongahela river, 29 mi. S. of Pittsburgh; served by the Pennsylvania railroad. The population in 1950 was 9,864 and was 10,784 in 1940 by the federal census. It is in the "Pittsburgh" coal field, and has important manufactures of glass products (Corning Glass works). Charleroi was founded in 1890 and named for Charleroi, Belgium, whence some of the city's early glassworkers emigrated.

CHARLES, a masculine proper name (Fr. *Charles;* Span. *Carlos;* Ital. *Carlo;* Ger. *Karl*), meaning originally "man." It has been borne by many European sovereigns and princes.

CHARLES (1525–1574), cardinal of Lorraine, French statesman, was the second son of Claude of Lorraine, duke of Guise, and brother of Francis, duke of Guise. He was archbishop of Reims in 1538 and cardinal in 1547. At first he was called the cardinal of Guise, but in 1550, on the death of his uncle John, cardinal of Lorraine, he in his turn took the style of cardinal of Lorraine. A master of intrigue, he was, like all the Guises, ambitious and devoid of scruples. With his brother, Duke Francis, the cardinal was all-powerful during the reigns of Henry II. and Francis II.; in 1558 and 1559 he was one of the negotiators of the treaty of Cateau-Cambrésis; he persecuted the reformers pitilessly and helped to provoke the crisis of the wars of religion. The death of Francis II. deprived him of power, but he remained one of the principal leaders of the Catholic party. In 1561, at the Colloquy of Poissy, he was commissioned to reply to Theodore Beza (*q.v.*). In 1562 at the Council of Trent, he at first defended the rights of the Gallican Church against the pretensions of the pope; but after the assassination of his brother he approached the court of Rome, and on his return to France he endeavoured, in vain, to obtain the promulgation of the decrees of the council (1564). In 1567, when the Protestants took up arms, he held for some time the first place in the king's council, but Catherine de' Medici soon grew weary of his arrogance and in 1570 he had to leave the court. He endeavoured to regain favour by negotiating at Rome the dispensation for the marriage of Henry of Navarre with Margaret of Valois (1572). He died on Dec. 26, 1574, at the beginning of the reign of Henry III.

A large amount of correspondence is preserved in the Bibliothèque Nationale. *See* also J. J. Guillemin, *Le Cardinal de Lorraine* (1847); René de Bouillé, *Histoire des ducs de Guise* (1849); H. Forneron, *Les Guises et leur époque* (1877); H. N. Williams, *The Brood of False Lorraine* (1918).

CHARLES, ST., called The Good (le Bon), or The Dane (*c.* 1084–1127), count of Flanders, was the only son of St. Canute or Knut IV., king of Denmark, by Adela, daughter of Robert the Frisian, count of Flanders. On the assassination of Canute in 1086, his widow fled to Flanders, with her son. Charles was brought up by his mother and grandfather, Robert the Frisian, on whose death he did great services to his uncle, Robert II., and his cousin, Baldwin VII., counts of Flanders. Baldwin died of a wound in 1119, and, having no issue, left his countship by will to Charles the Dane. Charles had to fight for his heritage, but he soon won, and secured his position by his clemency. He devoted himself to the welfare of his subjects, and exerted himself in the cause of Christianity, both by his bounty and by his example. He well deserved the surname of *Le Bon.* He refused the crown of Jerusalem on the death of Baldwin, and in 1125 nomination as a candidate for the imperial crown in succession to Henry V. He was murdered while praying in the church of St. Donatian at Bruges on March 2, 1127, because, by throwing open granaries there in a famine, he had broken the merchants' monopoly.

See J. Perneel, *Histoire du Règne de Charles le Bon, précédé d'un résumé de l'histoire de Flandres* (Brussels, 1830), and *Charles le Bon, Comte de Flandre* (Lille, 1853).

CHARLES THE GREAT (Charlemagne), king of the Franks and emperor, born April 2, 742 or 743, was the eldest son of Pepin III. by Berta (Bertrada), daughter of Charibert of Laon. At that date the Franks were governed by Pepin and his brother Carloman, who ruled as mayors of the palace under a fainéant Merovingian king. By the abdication of Carloman, in 747, Pepin became sole ruler, as his father Charles Martel had been. In 751 Pepin deposed the last Merovingian (Childeric III.) and himself assumed the Frankish crown, with the approbation of Pope Zacharias. In 754 Pope Stephen II. visited Pepin at Paris and anointed him as king, together with his two sons, Charles and Carloman. Between these two the kingdom was equally divided by Pepin on his death-bed (768), Charles receiving Austrasia, Neustria and western Aquitaine. This arrangement was displeasing to his junior, who perhaps claimed the whole inheritance on the ground that he was born after their father's coronation (751). In 769 Charles suppressed an Aquitanian rising, led by the aged Duke Hunold, and received the submission of Lupus, duke of Gascony, although Carloman declined to give any assistance. In 770 Charles married the daughter of Desiderius, king of the Lombards, probably to strengthen the influence which Pepin III. had acquired in Italian politics. But in 771 he repudiated the Lombard princess and married Hildegarde, a Suabian lady, who became the mother of his three legitimate sons, Charles, Pepin and Lewis. Desiderius naturally resented the slight put upon his daughter and seized the first opportunity of revenge. This presented itself in 771, when King Carloman died and Charles, in accordance with Frankish law, appropriated the vacant kingdom to the exclusion of his brother's infant sons. Their mother, Queen Gerberga, fled with them to the court of Desiderius, who announced his intention of supporting their claims and vainly urged the pope to crown them (772). Hadrian, who had lately succeeded Stephen II., endangered the safety of the papal States by refusing this demand, since Charles was preoccupied with his first Saxon campaign, and Desiderius plundered and conquered at his will in central Italy. But in the autumn of 772 Charles gave ear to Hadrian's appeal for help, and demanded satisfaction from the Lombards for himself and for the pope. Since Desiderius was defiant, the Frankish host was summoned to meet at Geneva in May 773. From Geneva the main army, led by Charles himself, marched over the Mt. Cenis to Susa, where it encountered the Lombard army, under Desiderius, holding a fortified position, and was brought to a halt. Meanwhile a second Frankish army, which had crossed the Great St. Bernard, threatened the communications of the Lombards, who as soon as they perceived their danger fell back in haste, some to Pavia and others to Verona. Verona surrendered to the Franks in the winter of 773–774, and here the nephews of Charles fell into his hands. Their fate is uncertain, but they troubled him no more. Pavia was reduced, after a long blockade, in the following summer. Desiderius, who was found there, ended his days as a monk at Corbie on the Somme. After the fall of Pavia Charles took the title of king of the Lombards. Frankish garrisons and Frankish officials were established at Pavia and in other cities of the kingdom. But some of the Lombard dukes in north and central Italy were allowed to remain in office as vassals of the conqueror. The ducal house of Benevento remained *de facto* independent, though in 788 the reigning duke agreed to pay an annual tribute, to date his charters by the regnal years of Charles, and to inscribe the name of Charles upon his coinage. Charles abstained from meddling with the Greek possessions in south Italy—Calabria, Apulia, Naples, Salerno, Amalfi. But later in his reign he acquired the Greek provinces of Venetia, Istria and Dalmatia. His relations with the papacy were defined during a visit which he paid to Rome at the Easter feast of 774. He was then acclaimed as Patrician of the Romans, and he confirmed the so-called Donation of 754 by which his father had guaranteed to the papacy its ancient and lawful possessions in Italy. The text of the Donation only survives in a corrupt and interpolated copy. It cannot have been precisely worded since Hadrian and Charles, who were otherwise good friends, differed sharply about its interpretation. As Patrician, Charles claimed the right of hearing appeals from the Roman law-courts, and he exacted an oath of allegiance from the Romans when Hadrian's successor was elected, though he did not interfere with the election. In 800 he presided over the tribunal before which Leo III. purged himself of various accusations. But it was Lewis the Pious who first established (in 824) the right of the emperor to supervise the temporal administration of the pope through an envoy permanently residing in Rome.

From 774 to 799 Charles was at war with the Saxons, a heathen race whose lands lay east of the Rhine and north of Hesse and Thuringia. Though troublesome neighbours of the Franks they had become tributaries of Pepin III. in 758, and the Frankish annalists do not explain the first Saxon war of Charles (in 772) by reference to any provocation that he had received. Their paganism may have been their chief offence; the chief event of the campaign was the destruction of the sacred pillar Irminsul, together with its grove and temple. The Saxons retaliated by raiding Hesse while Charles was absent in Italy, and on his return, in 775, he opened a war of conquest which was only completed in the 14th campaign. There was no cohesion between the Saxon tribes, and they were much inferior to the Franks in military science and equipment. But their country had strong natural defences (the hills and forests of the Teutoburger Wald and the Harz country, the Weser and the Elbe with their tributary streams) which made it difficult for the Franks to invade rapidly or to retreat with impunity. The Frankish host was only available in the summer months, and it was difficult to find garrisons for conquered districts. The Saxons usually offered submission when they were attacked in force, and rebelled again when Charles withdrew his forces. He did not make his difficulties lighter when he insisted that those who submitted should accept baptism. His chief opponent was the Westphalian chieftain Widukind who, in 778, raided the east bank of the Rhine up to Coblenz, and, in 782, destroyed a Frankish punitive force in Saxony. The second of these exploits was atrociously revenged in the massacre of Verden, where Charles put to the sword no less than 4,500 Saxon captives in one day. In 785 Widukind submitted upon terms and was baptized, after Charles had wintered in Saxony, and had harried the land continuously for some months. After this year the chief centres of resistance were the marshes on the left bank of the lower Elbe and Nordalbingia (Schleswig). To these districts Charles applied in 799 and 804 a policy of deportations, transplanting combatants and non-combatants alike to other parts of his empire. He legislated for the conquered lands on more than one occasion. His *Capitulatio de Partibus Saxoniae* (probably of 785) denounces penalties of the severest kind against idolators and those who wrong churches or ecclesiastics; it also obliges the whole population to pay tithes to the Church. His *Capitulare Saxonicum* (797), issued after consultation with representatives of the Saxons, modifies in some respects the customary law of the race, to make it conformable with Frankish law. The customary law itself is recorded in his *Lex Saxonum,* of uncertain date. Charles founded in Saxony the bishoprics of Munster, Minden, Osnabrück, Paderborn and Bremen. He appointed Saxon nobles as his counts, and required them to hold law-courts in the Frankish manner. He directed the clergy to report to himself those counts who perverted the course of justice. In or before 797 he began to send his *missi dominici* to perambulate in Saxony. No public assembly of the Saxons was lawful unless convoked by these officials. Under this system Saxony was tranquil after 804. In the ninth century the Saxons, while retaining much of their primitive law and culture, became fervently Christian and thoroughly reconciled to Frankish rule.

Bavaria was annexed by Charles more easily and earlier than Saxony. Tassilo, the last Bavarian duke of the Agilolfing line received the duchy in 748 from the hands of Pepin III., to whom he took the oath of fealty; but he persistently absented himself from the annual assembly, and took no part in the campaigns of Pepin or of Charles. Under pressure he renewed his fealty in 781 and 787. But on the second occasion he only took the oath when the Frankish host was on the march to invade Bavaria, and in 788 he was indicted before the assembly for conspiring with the Avars. His life was spared, but he was relegated to a monastery, and Bavaria was divided between Frankish counts. In the 9th century the Bavarians were the chief support of the East Frankish monarchy and Regensburg was the chief residence of Lewis the German. As the master of Bavaria Charles came into collision with the Avars, who had been settled in the Hungarian steppes since 568. In 791 he harried their western lands, between the rivers Enns and Raab. The fortified camp (Ring) of the Avar Khan was sacked in 795 by the Margrave Eric of Friuli, and totally destroyed by Pepin, the second son of Charles in 796. After this disaster the Avars sent to Aachen certain of their chiefs who made peace and accepted baptism. Bishop Arno of Salzburg was commissioned by Charles to convert the Avar nation, and in 805 the Khan, finding himself hard pressed by the Slavs, became a Christian and placed himself under the emperor's protection.

More celebrated, but historically less important, than this easterly expansion of Frankish power is the campaigning with which Charles and his lieutenants harassed the Arabs of northern Spain. In 778 Charles himself commanded an expedition against Saragossa. It was a failure, since he did not receive the support which he had expected from some rebellious emirs. As he was retreating through the Pyrenees his rear-guard was destroyed, not by the Arabs, but by the Christian Basques of Pampeluna, whom he had exasperated by destroying the walls of that city. Einhard the biographer of Charles, treats this disaster as insignificant; but the fate of Roland, the Warden of the Breton march, who fell at Roncevaux with other famous warriors (Aug. 15, 778), passed into legend and song. To repair his relations with the Spanish Christians Charles took their side in the Adoptianist controversy, when they indicted the archbishop of Toledo as a heretic. He desired to create a Frankish march on the south slope of the Pyrenees, as an outwork for the defence of Narbonne and Septimania; and in this object he succeeded. In 801 Barcelona was captured by his son Lewis with the help of Count William of Toulouse, a hero whose name, like that of Roland, lives in mediaeval epic. In 807 Pampeluna accepted the protection of Charles and became the second bastion of the "Spanish Mark," which effectively defended both the western and the eastern passes of the Pyrenees.

Only thrice between 774 and 779 did Charles revisit Italy. In each case his primary object was to tighten his hold upon the Lombard kingdom. In 775 he crushed a Lombard rebellion in which the dukes of Friuli, Chiusi and Spoleto were supported by their compatriot, the independent ruler of Benevento; Rotgaud of Friuli lost his duchy, and Hildebrand of Spoleto, who had placed himself under the Pope's protection in 773, was forced to become a royal vassal. In 780 and in 787 Charles crossed the Alps to assert his supremacy over Benevento, an object, which, as already noted, he did not completely realize. During the second of these three visits he induced Pope Hadrian to crown his sons Pepin and Lewis as kings of Italy and Aquitaine. The Teutonic lands he reserved for himself and for his eldest son and namesake. These arrangements suggest that Italian affairs did not occupy the first place in his thoughts and calculations; and it is significant that, even after his imperial coronation, he held to the plan of 780. In this same year, while still in Italy he accepted the suggestion of the Empress Irene that his eldest daughter Rotrude should marry Irene's son and ward, the young Constantine VI. But Charles repudiated this arrangement in 787, probably because Irene and her son in that year induced the Seventh Council of Nicaea to restore image worship in the Greek Church, and called upon the Latin Church to imitate a policy which Charles and the Frankish clergy regarded as superstitious and absurd. Pope Hadrian, whose legates were present at the Council of Nicaea, agreed with its decision, but his wishes were ignored by the king. In 794 Charles held a council of the Frankish Church at Frankfurt to refute the worshippers of images. It was attended by Papal envoys and representatives of the Italian, Spanish, and English clergy. The arguments on which Charles and his advisers relied are set forth in the *Libri Carolini,* four tracts composed in the years 789–791 by the king's orders, and published in his name. It is uncertain whether Charles was inspired by religious zeal or by a desire to discredit the Greek empire. The *Libri Carolini* expressly dispute the right of Constantine VI. to be regarded as the lawful heir of the *Imperium Romanum;* but there is no other evidence to suggest that Charles at this time coveted the imperial dignity. Perhaps the long struggle for the extirpation of Saxon idolatry was responsible for the vigour with which he and the Frankish Church pursued this controversy. There was no irremediable rupture of relations with the Greek empire; for in 798 Irene sent ambassadors to Aachen to inform Charles that Constantine VI. had been deposed and that she had been acknowledged as her son's successor. Among the Frankish clergy it appears to have been the accepted view that Constantine was infamously treated and that a woman was incapable of holding the empire. There is nothing to suggest that Irene's ambassadors were discourteously received. But in 800 Charles allowed himself to be crowned as emperor at Rome by Pope Leo III.

The secret history of this coronation, and the motives of those who counselled it, can only be conjectured. Leo III., the successor of Hadrian, was freely elected by the Roman clergy and people in 795. Charles readily acknowledged the validity of the election, but until 799 we hear of no further correspondence between the papal and the Frankish courts. In 799 a Roman faction, who accused Leo of adultery and perjury, endeavoured to get rid of him. Brutally assaulted in the streets of Rome, he narrowly escaped the loss of tongue and eyes and was confined in a Roman monastery; but his attendants succeeded in conveying him to the Duke of Spoleto for protection. Leo's character was unfavourably judged by some of the Frankish clergy; for which reason Charles declined to reinstate him until the accusations of his enemies were disproved. In July 799 Leo was brought to the king at Paderborn, ostensibly as an honoured guest, and remained there for some days. He was finally sent back to Rome, escorted by a commission of archbishops, bishops and counts, who held a judicial enquiry and reported that nothing had been proved against the Pope. In Nov. 800 the king appeared at Rome, and spent more than three weeks in reviewing the situation. His chief difficulty, we are told, was still to decide how he would deal with the pope. No accuser dared to state a case against Leo, but it is evident that he was not generally popular in Rome. At last, on Dec. 23, Leo cleared himself in St. Peter's church, taking a solemn oath upon the Gospels, that he was innocent. On Christmas Day, after celebrating mass in the same church, he crowned Charles as emperor in the presence of the Roman people who were evidently not taken by surprise, since they acclaimed Charles in the set form of words which was used to welcome a patrician. Two theologians of the emperor, Anghilbert and Alcuin prophesied obscurely (in prose and verse) the imperial coronation some months before it actually occurred. Charles may have hesitated to run the risk of a war with Constantinople; but the biographer's statement, that he was crowned unawares and against his will, is not convincing.

Once crowned, he showed himself ready and eager to come to some arrangement with Constantinople. In 801 he made an offer of marriage to Irene, but she was deposed shortly after his envoys arrived at the Greek court. They were well treated by her successor Nicephorus I., who made counter-proposals for an honourable peace between West and East. Charles responded amicably and proposed a boundary line which would have given him Venetia, and the coast towns of Istria and Dalmatia. But Nicephorus preferred to fight for these newly lost provinces, and there ensued a naval war in the Adriatic, conducted on the Frankish side by King Pepin. After the death of Pepin (July 8, 810) Charles hurriedly offered peace, with the surrender of all his claims to the disputed territories. The offer was accepted by Michael Rhangabé, who succeeded Nicephorus in 811; and in 812 Greek envoys came to Aachen and saluted the emperor of the West as *Basileus,* thus acknowledging the equality of the two empires. In view of these facts it cannot reasonably be contended that Charles regarded the Roman empire as indivisible.

In 806 Charles, in accordance with Frankish custom, drew up a scheme for the partition of his realms between his three legitimate sons. It provided that each son should be absolute in his own sphere, and did not designate a successor to the empire. But in 813, when peace had been made with Constantinople, and Charles the Young and Pepin were dead, he nominated Lewis the Pious as his consort and successor in the empire, at the same time assigning Italy to Bernhard the son of Pepin. Charles thus asserted the hereditary character of the empire. It is remarkable that the coronation of Lewis took place, not at Rome, but at Aachen, and that Charles himself placed the crown upon his son's head, as if with the intention of showing to the world that the pope had no voice in the disposal of the empire. Next to the Greeks the Danes were the chief enemies with whom Charles had to deal in his last years. A Danish kingdom was already in existence, and it menaced his north-eastern frontier; Danish pirates were already harrying the British Isles. In 809 Charles built a fort at Itzehoe to protect the right bank of the Elbe. In 811 and 812 he concluded treaties with Danish kings. But he relied especially upon his North sea fleet which was based upon Boulogne, and built in his shipyards at Ghent. He ordered that ships should be found for defence of all ports and navigable rivers on his northern coasts. He also maintained patrols in the Mediterranean from Narbonne to the mouth of the Tiber, to guard against the descents of Arab pirates, but the danger from this side did not engage his personal attention. By capitularies of 802 and 811 he made naval service obligatory on all the inhabitants of maritime provinces, even upon the magnates. It was no fault of his that the Franks failed to create a strong naval power against the evil days that were in sight.

The reign of Charles witnessed a revival of arts and letters in Francia. Illuminators, goldsmiths, workers in ivory and metal reached a high degree of skill, although the higher arts were still neglected, and the emperor's chapel at Aachen was adorned with pillars and bronze portals fetched from Rome and Ravenna. Among the Frankish clergy scholarship was encouraged in the reign of Pepin, by the king himself and by the Englishman Boniface, archbishop of Mainz. Charles stimulated the clergy to further efforts. He himself studied Latin grammar with Peter of Pisa, rhetoric and dialectic and astronomy with Alcuin of York, and he listened with attention while his clerks read to him works of history or St. Augustine's *De Civitate Dei.* The effect of classical studies, upon Charles himself and his advisers, is revealed in his legislation which is more grammatically and intelligently composed than those of his predecessors. He aspired to emulate the legislators of Constantinople. Though he never attempted to make a code, he revised the laws of the Salian and Ripuarian Franks, and caused those of the Saxons, Thuringians and Frisians to be written down. His Capitularies, which were binding on his subjects without respect of race, supply a remarkable conspectus of Frankish institutions. In these texts we can study the duties of his counts and *missi,* the functions of the local law courts and assemblies, the law of vassalage, the rights of exempted estates (*immunitates*), the composition of the national host; the *Capitulare de Villis* even supplies full information concerning the management of the royal demesnes. The credit for the details of this legislation is due to the arch-chaplain and the clerks of the royal chaplain, ecclesiastics who were trained in seminaries of the Carlovingian renaissance. By his *Admonitio Generalis* (789) Charles required that every bishop should test the theological education of his priests, and that reading schools should be everywhere established. For a select minority a higher type of education was provided in cathedral schools, such as those of Orleans and Lyons, and in such monastic schools as those of Tours, Corbie, St. Riquier, Metz and St. Wandrille. The Palace school, a Merovingian institution, was reorganized by Alcuin in the years 782–796. In it were educated the emperor's children, the sons of great nobles and also some ecclesiastics who afterwards did much to promote the new studies, as for example Adalhard of Corbie and Anghilbert of St. Riquier. The Palace school declined after the death of Charles, but the new cathedral and monastic schools produced a remarkable race of literati. To the libraries founded in connection with such schools we are indebted for the oldest extant manuscripts of Caesar, Sallust, Lucretius, Tacitus and Suetonius, and many of the works of Cicero. In the emperor's lifetime, and with his encouragement, the text of the Latin Vulgate was restored to a purer form by Alcuin and other scholars. One of these recensions not the work of Alcuin, was officially recommended to the Frankish bishops by the encyclical *De Emendatione Librorum* (*c.* 787). The scholars whom Charles patronized are well remembered as excellent grammarians. In their hands Latin became once more a polished and flexible medium of literary expression. The thoughts which they expressed in copious prose and verse are often banal pleasantries or insipid exhortations. Alcuin's letters, a few topical poems by Alcuin and Theodulf of Orleans, and the biography of Charles by Einhard, one of the royal clerks, are the cream of this Carolingian literature.

At Aachen he built a palace (of which no trace is left) and a chapel which, with many alterations and restorations, is incorporated in the existing cathedral. He commenced to build another palace at Ingelheim near Mainz, which was the great bridge-head for his armies, and a third at Nymwegen (near the Saxon border) of which the chapel, consecrated by Leo III., is the only relic. For three years, 792–794, he settled at Regensburg, the old Bavarian capital, but this step was taken for political and military reasons. At Aachen he was in his homeland. The forests of the neighbourhood gave him good hunting; with his sons and his nobles and his bodyguards he bathed and swam in the hot springs which still feed the *Kaiserbad.* In his dress, as in his pastimes, he affected the old Frankish mode, and he disdained elaborate banquets, preferring a simple, heavy meal at which the staple dish was broiled venison, served to him on the spit by his huntsmen. When business of State was in hand he was prompt, methodical and labourious. He prided himself on the magnificent furniture of his chapel and on the decorum with which its services were celebrated. He kept to the end his interest in scholarship and in theology, and left a large library of manuscripts. But his private life was lax in one respect. Though a devoted husband to three of his four wives, he had illegitimate offspring by five mistresses. His court was dissolute and the conduct of his daughters caused grave scandals.

Charles died on Jan. 28, 814, after four years of failing health, from an attack of pleurisy. He was buried in the chapel at Aachen, probably in the antique sarcophagus which is preserved there; this at all events is the coffin in which his bones were found in 1165, when they were disinterred by Frederick Barbarossa.

Bibliography.—Eginhardus (Einhard), *Vita Kardi Imperatoris* (1883), in G. H. Pertz, *Scriptores Rerum Germanicarum* (1839 etc.); *Capitularia Regum Francorum* (1881), in *Monumenta Germaniae historica* Gesellschaft für ältere deutsche Geschichtkunde (ed. by A. Boretius. Hanover and Berlin, 1877 etc.); *Annales Regni Francorum* (ed. by F. Kurze 1895) in the Octavo series of Pertz's *Scriptores.* Among mod. works: S. Abel, *Jahrbücher des Fränkischen Reiches unter Karl dem. Grossen* (1888), in *Jahrbücher der deutschen Geschichte.* Herausgegeben durch die historische Commission bei der königl. Academie der Wissenschaft (Berlin and Leipzig, 1862, etc.); T. Hodgkin, *Charles the Great* (1897), in Foreign Statesmen (ed. by J. B. Bury, 1896, etc.), and *Italy and Her Invaders* vol. viii. (2nd ed. 1892–99); H. W. C. Davis, *Charlemagne, Charles the Great, The Hero of Two Nations* (1900); Charles Edward Russell, *Charlemagne, First of the Moderns* (1930). (H. W. C. D.)

CHARLES II.,[1] called The Bald (823–877), Roman emperor and king of the West Franks, the son of the emperor Louis the Pious, was born in 823. The death of the emperor in 840 was the signal for the outbreak of war between his sons. Charles allied himself with his brother Louis the German to resist the pretensions of the emperor Lothair, and the two allies conquered him in the bloody victory of Fontenoy-en-Puisaye (June 25, 841). In the following year the two brothers confirmed their alliance by the celebrated oaths of Strasbourg (*see* France: *History*). The war was brought to an end by the treaty of Verdun (Aug. 843), which gave to Charles the Bald the kingdom of the western Franks, which practically corresponded with what is now France, as far as the Meuse, the Saône and the Rhone, with the addition of the Spanish March as far as the Ebro. The first years of his reign up to the death of Lothair I. (855) were comparatively peaceful, and during them was continued the system of "confraternal government" of the sons of Louis the Pious, who had various meetings with one another, at Coblenz (848), at Meersen (851), and at Attigny (854). In 858 Louis the German invaded the kingdom of Charles. In 860 he in his turn tried to seize the kingdom of his nephew, Charles of Provence, but met with a repulse. On the death of Lothair II. in 869 he tried to seize his dominions, but by the treaty of Meersen (870) was compelled to share them with Louis the German. Besides this, Charles had to struggle against the incessant rebellions in Aquitaine, against the Bretons, who inflicted on the king the defeats of Ballon (845) and Juvardeil (851), and especially against the Normans, who devastated the country in the north of Gaul, the valleys of the Seine and Loire, and even up to the borders of Aquitaine. Charles led various expeditions against the invaders, and tried to put a barrier in their way by having fortified bridges built over all the rivers. In 875, after the death of the emperor Louis II., Charles the Bald, supported by Pope John VIII., descended into Italy, receiving the royal crown at Pavia and the imperial crown at Rome. But Louis the German revenged himself for Charles's success by invading and devastating his dominions. Charles was recalled to Gaul, and after the death of Louis the German (Aug. 28, 876), in his turn made an attempt to seize his kingdom, but at Andernach met with a shameful defeat (Oct. 8, 876). In the meantime, John VIII., who was menaced by the Saracens, was continually urging him to come to Italy, and Charles again crossed the Alps. At the same time Carloman, son of Louis the German, entered northern Italy. Charles started on his way back to Gaul, and died while crossing the pass of the Mont Cenis, Oct. 5 or 6, 877. He was succeeded by his son Louis the Stammerer.

Bibliography.—The most important authority for the history of Charles's reign is represented by the *Annales Bertiniani,* which were the work of Prudentius, bishop of Troyes, up to 861, then up to 882 of the celebrated Hincmar, archbishop of Reims. This prince's charters are to be found published in the collections of the *Académie des Inscriptions,* by M. M. Prou. The most complete history of the reign is found in E. Dümmler, *Geschichte des ostfränkischen Reiches* (3 vols., Leipzig, 1887–88). *See* also J. Calmette, *La Diplomatie carolingienne du traité de Verdun à la mort le Charles le Chauve* (Paris, 1901), and F. Lot, "Une Année du règne de Charles le Chauve," in *Le Moyen-Âge* (1902), pp. 393–438; F. Lot and L. Halphen, *Le Règne de Charles le Chauve* (1909); M. Jusselin, *La Chancellerie de Charles le Chauve d'après les notes tironiennes* (1922).

CHARLES III., The Fat (832–888), Roman emperor and king of the West Franks, was the youngest of the three sons of Louis the German, and received from his father the kingdom of Swabia (Alamannia). After the death of his two brothers in succession, Carloman (880) and Louis the Young (882), he inherited the whole of his father's dominions. He was crowned emperor at Rome by Pope John VIII. (Feb. 881). On his return to Germany he led an expedition against the Norsemen of Friesland, but instead of engaging with them he preferred to make terms and paid them tribute. In 880 the death of Carloman brought into his possession the west Frankish realm, and in 885 he got rid of his rival Hugh of Alsace, an illegitimate son of Lothair II. In spite of six expeditions into Italy, he did not succeed in pacifying the country, nor in delivering it from the Saracens. He was equally unfortunate in Gaul and in Germany against the Norsemen, who in 886–887 besieged Paris. The emperor appeared before the city with a large army (Oct. 886), but contented himself by buying the retreat of the invaders at the price of a heavy ransom, and his permission for them to ravage Burgundy without his interfering. On his return to Alamannia the general discontent showed itself openly and a conspiracy was formed against him. He was deposed by an assembly which met at Frankfürt or at Tribur (Nov. 887), and died in poverty at Neidingen on the Danube (Jan. 18, 888).

See E. Dümmler, *Geschichte des Ostfränkischen Reiches,* vol. iii. (Leipzig, 1888); W. Stubbs, *Germany in the Early Middle Ages,* edit. A. Hassall, ch. iv. (1908).

CHARLES IV. (1316–1378), Roman emperor and king of Bohemia, the eldest son of John of Luxemburg, king of Bohemia,

[1]For Charles I., Roman emperor, *see* Charles the Great; *cf.* under Charles I. of France below.

and Elizabeth, sister of Wenceslas III., was born at Prague on May 14, 1316, and in 1323 went to the court of his uncle, Charles IV., king of France, where he remained for seven years. He married Blanche, sister of King Philip VI., the successor of Charles IV. In 1333 he was made margrave of Moravia. Three years later he undertook the government of Tirol on behalf of his brother John Henry, and was soon actively concerned in a struggle for the possession of this country. In consequence of an alliance between his father and Pope Clement VI., the relentless enemy of the emperor Louis IV., Charles was chosen German king in opposition to Louis by some of the princes at Rense on July 11, 1346. Confirming the papacy in the possession of wide territories, he promised to annul the acts of Louis against Clement, to take no part in Italian affairs, and to defend and protect the church. In 1346 he fought at Crécy, where his father was killed. As king of Bohemia he returned to Germany, and after being crowned German king at Bonn on Nov. 26, 1346, prepared to attack Louis. After the death of the emperor in October 1347 Charles was soon the undisputed ruler of Germany.

In 1350 the king was visited at Prague by Cola di Rienzi, who urged him to go to Italy, where the poet Petrarch and the citizens of Florence also implored his presence. Charles kept Rienzi in prison for a year, and then handed him over to Clement at Avignon. Four years later, however, he crossed the Alps without an army, received the Lombard crown at Milan on Jan. 6, 1355, and was crowned emperor at Rome by a cardinal on April 5. On his return Charles was occupied with the administration of Germany, then just recovering from the Black Death, and in 1356 he promulgated the Golden Bull (*q.v.*) to regulate the election of the king. He was unremitting in his efforts to secure other territories and to strengthen the Bohemian monarchy. To this end he purchased part of the upper Palatinate of the Rhine in 1353, and in 1367 annexed Lower Lusatia to Bohemia and bought numerous estates in various parts of Germany. On the death in 1363 of Meinhard, duke of Upper Bavaria and count of Tirol, Upper Bavaria was claimed by the sons of the emperor Louis IV., and Tirol by Rudolph IV., duke of Austria. Both claims were admitted by Charles on the understanding that if these families died out both territories should pass to the house of Luxemburg. About the same time he was promised the succession to the margravate of Brandenburg, which he actually obtained for his son Wenceslas in 1373. He also gained a considerable portion of Silesian territory, partly by inheritance through his third wife, Anna, daughter of Henry II., duke of Schweidnitz. In 1365 Charles visited Pope Urban V. at Avignon and undertook to escort him to Rome; and on the same occasion was crowned king of Burgundy, or Arles, at Arles on June 4, 1365. During his later years the emperor took little part in German affairs beyond securing the election of his son Wenceslas as king of the Romans in 1376, and negotiating a peace between the Swabian league and some nobles in 1378. After dividing his lands between his three sons, he died on Nov. 29, 1378, at Prague, where he was buried.

Charles, who according to the emperor Maximilian I. was the step-father of the empire, but the father of Bohemia, brought the latter country to a high state of prosperity. In 1348 he founded the university of Prague, and afterwards made this city the seat of an archbishop. He was an accomplished diplomatist, possessed a penetrating intellect, and was capable of much trickery in order to gain his ends. He was superstitious and peace-loving, had few personal wants, and is described as a round-shouldered man of medium height, with black hair and beard, and sallow cheeks.

His autobiography, the "Vita Caroli IV.," which deals with events down to the year 1346, and various other documents relating to his life and times, are published in the *Fontes rerum Germanicarum*, Band I., edited by J. F. Böhmer (Leipzig, 1885). For other documents relating to the time see *Die Regesten des Kaiserreichs unter Kaiser Karl IV.*, edited by J. F. Böhmer and A. Huber (Innsbruck, 1889); *Acta Karoli IV. imperatoris inedita* (Innsbruck, 1891); E. Werunsky, *Excerpta ex registris Clementis VI. et Innocentii VI.* (Innsbruck, 1885). *See* also E. Werunsky, *Geschichte Kaiser Karls IV. und seiner Zeit* (Innsbruck, 1880–92); H. Friedjung, *Kaiser Karl IV. und sein Antheil am geistigen Leben seiner Zeit* (Vienna, 1876); A. Gottlob, *Karls IV. private und politische Beziehungen zu Frankreich* (Innsbruck, 1883); O. Winckelmann, *Die Beziehungen Kaiser Karls IV. zum Königreich Arelat* (Strasbourg, 1882); K. Palm, "Zu Karls IV. Politik gegen Baiern," in the *Forschungen zur deutschen Geschichte*, Band xv. (Göttingen, 1862–66); Th. Lindner, "Karl IV. und die Wittelsbacher," and S. Stienherz, "Die Beziehungen Ludwigs I. von Ungarn zu Karl IV.," and "Karl IV. und die österreichischen Freiheitsbriefe," in the *Mittheilungen des Instituts für österreichische Geschichtsforschung* (Innsbruck, 1880); G. G. Walsh, *The Emperor Charles IV.* (1924).

CHARLES V. (1500–1558), Roman emperor and (as Charles I.) king of Spain, was born in Ghent on Feb. 20, 1500. His parents were Philip of Burgundy and Joanna, third child of Ferdinand and Isabella. Philip died in 1506, and Charles succeeded to his Netherland possessions and the county of Burgundy (Franche Comté). His grandfather, the emperor Maximilian, as regent, appointed his daughter Margaret vice-regent, and under her strenuous guardianship Charles lived in the Netherlands until the estates declared him of age in 1515. In Castile, Ferdinand, king of Aragon, acted as regent for his daughter Joanna, whose intellect was already clouded. On Jan. 23, 1516, Ferdinand died. Charles's visit to Spain was delayed until the autumn of 1517, and only in 1518 was he formally recognized as king conjointly with his mother, firstly by the cortes of Castile and then by those of Aragon. Joanna lived to the very eve of her son's abdication, so that he was only for some months technically sole king of Spain. During this Spanish visit Maximilian died, and Charles succeeded to the inheritance of the Habsburgs, to which was shortly added the duchy of Württemberg. Maximilian had also intended that he should succeed as emperor. In spite of the formidable rivalry of Francis I. and the opposition of Pope Leo X., pecuniary corruption and national feeling combined to secure his election in 1519. Charles hurriedly left Spain, and after a visit to Henry VIII. and his aunt Catherine was crowned at Aix on Oct. 23, 1520.

The difficulty of Charles's reign consists in the complexity of interests caused by the unnatural aggregate of distinct territories and races. The Crown of Castile brought with it the two recently conquered kingdoms of Navarre and Granada, together with the new colonies in America and scattered possessions in northern Africa. That of Aragon comprised the three distinct States of Aragon, Valencia and Catalonia, and in addition the kingdoms of Naples, Sicily and Sardinia, each with a separate character and constitution of its own. No less than eight independent cortes or parliaments existed in this Spanish-Italian group, adding greatly to the intricacy of government. In the Netherland provinces again the tie was almost purely personal; there existed only the rudiments of a central administration and a common representative system, while the county of Burgundy had a history apart. Much the same was true of the Habsburg group of States, but Charles soon freed himself from direct responsibility for their government by making them over, together with Württemberg, to his brother Ferdinand. The empire entailed serious liabilities on its ruler without furnishing any reliable assets; only through the cumbrous machinery of the diet could Charles tap the military and financial resources of Germany. His problem here was complicated by the growth of Lutheranism, which he had to face at his very first diet in 1521. In addition to such administrative difficulties Charles had inherited a quarrel with France, to which the rivalry of Francis I. for the Empire gave a personal character. Almost equally formidable was the advance of Sultan Suleiman up the Danube, and the union of the Turkish naval power with that of the Barbary States of northern Africa. Against Lutheran Germany the Catholic emperor might hope to rely upon the pope, and against France on England. But the attitude of the popes was almost uniformly disagreeable, while from Henry VIII. and Edward VI. Charles met with more unpleasantness than favour.

The difficulty of Charles himself is also that of the historian and reader of his reign. It is probably more instructive to treat it according to the emperor's several problems than in strict chronological order. Yet an attempt to distinguish the several periods of his career may serve as a useful introduction. The two best dividing lines are, perhaps, the coronation as emperor at Bologna in 1530, and the peace of Crépy in 1544. Until his visit to Italy (1529) Charles remained in the background of the European stage, except for his momentous meeting with Luther at the diet of Worms (1521). This meeting in itself forms a subdivision. Previously to this, during his nominal rule in the Netherlands, his visit to Spain and his candidature for the Empire, he seemed, as it was said, spell-bound under the ferule of his minister Chièvres. Almost every report represented him as colourless, reserved and weak. His dependence on his Flemish counsellors provoked the rising in Castile, the feebleness of his government the social war in Aragon. The religious question first gave him a living interest, and at this moment Chièvres died. Aleander, the papal nuncio at Worms, now recognized that public opinion had been wrong in its estimate of Charles. Never again was he under tutelage. The necessity, however, of residence in Spain prevented his taking a personal part in the great fight with Francis I. for Italy. He could claim no credit for the capture of his rival at Pavia. When his army sacked Rome and held Pope Clement VII. prisoner, he could not have known where this army was. And when later the French overran Naples, and all but deprived him of his hold on Italy, he had to instruct his generals that they must shift for themselves. The world had become afraid of him, but knew little of his character. In the second main division of his career Charles changed all this. No monarch until Napoleon was so widely seen in Europe and in Africa. At the head of his army Charles forced the Turks backwards down the Danube (1532). He personally conquered Tunis (1535), and was only prevented by "act of God" from winning Algiers (1541). The invasion of Provence in 1536 was headed by the emperor. In person he crushed the rebellion of Ghent (1540). In his last war with Francis (1542–44) he journeyed from Spain to the Netherlands, brought the rebellious duke of Cleves to his knees, and was within easy reach of Paris when he made the peace of Crépy (1544). In Germany, meanwhile, from the diet of Augsburg (1530) onwards, he had presided at the diets or conferences, which, as he hoped, would effect the reunion of the Church.

Peace with France and the Turk and a short spell of friendliness with Pope Paul III. enabled Charles at last to devote his whole energies to the healing of religious schism. Conciliation proving impossible, he led the army which received the submission of the Lutheran States, and then captured the elector of Saxony at Mühlberg, after which the other leader, Philip of Hesse, capitulated. The Armed Diet of 1548 was the high-water mark of Charles's power. Here, in defiance of the pope, he published the Interim which was meant to reconcile the Lutherans with the Church, and the so-called Reform which was to amend its abuses. During the next four years, owing to ill-health and loss of insight, his power was ebbing. In 1552 he was flying over the Brenner from Maurice of Saxony, a princeling whose fortunes he had made. Once again the old complications had arisen. His old enemy's son, Henry II., had attacked him indirectly in Piedmont and Parma, and then directly in Germany in alliance with Maurice. Once more the Turk was moving in the Danube and in the western Mediterranean. The humiliation of his flight gave Charles new spirit, and he once more led an army through Germany against the French, only to be checked by the duke of Guise's defence of Metz. Henceforth the waves of his fortune plashed to and fro until his abdication without much ostensible loss or gain.

Charles's Policy.—Charles had abundance of good sense, but little creative genius, and he was by nature conservative. Consequently he never sought to impose any new or common principles of administration on his several States. He took them as he found them, and at most, as in the Netherlands, improved upon what he found. So also in dealing with rival powers his policy may be called opportunist. He was indeed accused by his enemies of emulating Charlemagne, of aiming at universal empire. Historians have frequently repeated this charge. Charles himself in later life laughingly denied the imputation, and facts are in favour of his denial. When Francis I. was in his power he made no attempt to dismember France, in spite of his pledges to his allies Henry VIII. and the duke of Bourbon. He did, indeed, demand the duchy of Burgundy, because he believed this to have been unrighteously stolen by Louis XI from his grandmother when a helpless girl. The claim was not pressed, and at the height of his fortunes in 1548 he advised his son never to surrender it, but also never to make it a cause of war. When Clement VII. was his prisoner he was vehemently urged to overthrow the temporal power, to restore imperial dominion in Italy, at least to make the papacy harmless for the future. In reply he restored his enemy to the whole of his dominions, even reimposing him by force on the Florentine republic. To the end of his life his conscience was sensitive as to Ferdinand's expulsion of the house of Albret from Spanish Navarre, though this was essential to the safety of Spain. Though always at war he was essentially a lover of peace, and all his wars were virtually defensive. "Not greedy of territory," wrote Marcantonio Contarini in 1536, "but most greedy of peace and quiet." For peace he made sacrifices which angered his hot-headed brother Ferdinand. He would not aid in expelling the sultan's puppet Zapolya from Ferdinand's kingdom of Hungary, and he suffered the restoration of the ruffianly duke of Württemberg, to the grave prejudice of German Catholicism. In spite of his protests, Henry VIII. with impunity ill-treated his aunt Catherine, and the feeble Government of Edward VI. bullied his cousin Mary, who had been his fiancée. No serious efforts were made to restore his brother-in-law, Christian II., to the throne of Denmark, and he advised his son Philip to make friends with the usurper. After the defeat of the Lutheran Powers in 1547 he did not gain a palm's breadth of territory for himself. He resisted Ferdinand's claim for Württemberg, which the duke had deserved to forfeit; he disliked his acceptance of the voluntary surrender of the city of Constance; he would not have it said that he had gone to war for the benefit of the house of Habsburg.

On the other hand, Charles V.'s policy was not merely negative. He enlarged upon the old Habsburg practice of marriage as a means of alliance of influence. Previously to his election as emperor, his sister Isabella was married to Christian II. of Denmark, and the marriages of Mary and Ferdinand with the king of Hungary and his sister had been arranged. Before he was 20 Charles himself had been engaged some ten times with a view to political combinations. Naturally, therefore, he regarded his near relations as diplomatic assets. The federative system was equally familiar; Germany, the Netherlands, and even Spain, were in a measure federations. Combining these two principles, he would within his more immediate spheres of influence strengthen existing federations by intermarriage, while he hoped that the same means would convert the jarring Powers of Europe into a happy family. He made it a condition of the Treaty of Madrid (1526) that Francis I. should marry his sister Eleanor, Manuel of Portugal's widow, in the hope, not that she would be an ally or a spy within the enemy's camp, but an instrument of peace. His son's marriage with Mary Tudor would not only salve the rubs with England, but give such absolute security to the Netherlands that France would shrink from war. The personal union of all the Iberian kingdoms under a single ruler had long been an aim of Spanish statecraft. So Charles had married his sister Eleanor, much against her will, to the old king Manuel, and then his sister Catherine to his successor. The empress was a Portuguese infanta, and Philip's first wife was another. It is thus small wonder that, within a quarter of a century of Charles's death, Philip became king of Portugal.

In the wars with Francis I. Italy was the stake. In spite of his success Charles for long made no direct conquests. He would convert the peninsula into a federation mainly matrimonial. Savoy, the important buffer state, was detached from France by the marriage of the somewhat feeble duke to Charles's capable and devoted sister-in-law, Beatrice of Portugal. Milan, conquered from France, was granted to Francesco Sforza, heir of the old dynasty, and even after his treason was restored to him. In the vain hope of offspring Charles sacrificed his niece, Christina of Denmark, to the valetudinarian duke. In the long negotiations for a Habsburg-Valois dynasty which followed Francesco's death, Charles was probably sincere. He insisted that his daughter or niece should marry the third rather than the second son of Francis I., in order, apart from other reasons, to run less risk of the duchy falling under French dominion. The final investiture of Philip was forced upon him, and does not represent his saner policy. The Medici of Florence, the Gonzaga of Mantua, the papal house of Farnese, were all attached by Habsburg marriages. The republics of Genoa and Siena were drawn into the circle through the agency of their chief noble families, the Doria and Piccolomini; while Charles behaved with scrupulous moderation towards Venice in spite of her active hostility before and after the League of Cognac. Occasional acts of violence there were, such as the participation in the murder of Pierluigi Farnese, and the measures which provoked the rebellion of Siena. These were due to the difficulty of controlling the imperial agents from a distance, and in part to the faults of the victim prince and republic. On the whole, the loose federation of viceroyalties and principalities harmonized with Italian interests and traditions. The alternative was not Italian independence, but French domination. At any rate, Charles's structure was so durable that the French met with no real success in Italy until the 18th century.

Germany offered a fine field for a creative intellect, since the evils of her disintegration stood confessed. On the other hand, princes and towns were so jealous of an increase of central authority that Charles, at least until his victory over the League of Schmalkalden, had little effective power. Owing to his wars with French and Turks he was rarely in Germany, and his visits were very short. His problem was infinitely complicated by the union of Lutheranism and princely independence. He fell back on the old policy of Maximilian, and strove to create a party by personal alliances and intermarriage. In this he met with some success. The friendship of the electors of Brandenburg, whether Catholic or Protestant, was unbroken. In the war of Schmalkalden half the Protestant princes were on Charles's side or friendly neutrals. At the critical moment which preceded this, the lately rebellious duke of Cleves and the heir of Bavaria were secured through the agency of two of Ferdinand's invaluable daughters. The relations, indeed, between the two old enemies, Austria and Bavaria, were permanently improved. The elector palatine, whose love affairs with his sister Eleanor Charles as a boy had roughly broken, received in compensation a Danish niece. Her sister, widow of Francesco Sforza, was utilized to gain a hold upon the French dynasty which ruled Lorraine. More than once there were proposals for winning the hostile house of Saxony by matrimonial means. After his victory over the League of Schmalkalden, Charles perhaps had really a chance of making the imperial power a reality. But he lacked either courage or imagination, contenting himself with proposals for voluntary association on the lines of the defunct Swabian League, and dropping even these when public opinion was against them. Now, too, he made his great mistake in attempting to foist Philip upon the Empire as Ferdinand's successor. Gossip reported that Ferdinand himself was to be set aside, and careless historians have given currency to this. Such an idea was impossible. Charles wished Philip to succeed Ferdinand, while he ultimately conceded that Ferdinand's son Maximilian should follow Philip, and even in his lifetime exercise the practical power in Germany. This scheme irritated Ferdinand and his popular and ambitious son at the critical moment when it was essential that the Habsburgs should hold together against princely malcontents. Philip was imprudently introduced to Germany, which had also just received a foretaste of the unpleasant characteristics of Spanish troops. Yet the person rather than the policy was, perhaps, at fault. It was natural that the quasi-hereditary succession should revert to the elder line. France proved her recuperative power by the occupation of Savoy and of Metz, Toul and Verdun, the military keys of Lorraine. The separation of the Empire and Spain left two weakened Powers not always at accord, and neither of them permanently able to cope on equal terms with France. Nevertheless, this scheme did contribute in no small measure to the failure of Charles in Germany. The main cause was, of course, the religious schism, but his treatment of this requires separate consideration.

The characteristics of Charles's government, its mingled conservatism and adaptability, are best seen in Spain and the Netherlands, with which he was in closer personal contact than with Italy and Germany. In Spain, when once he knew the country, he never repeated the mistakes which on his first visit caused the rising of the communes. The cortes of Castile were regularly summoned, and though he would allow no encroachment on the Crown's prerogatives, he was equally scrupulous in respecting their constitutional rights. Indirectly, Crown influence increased owing to the greater control which had gradually been exercised over the composition of the municipal councils, which often returned the deputies for the cortes. Charles was throughout nervous as to the power and wealth of the greater nobles. They rather than the Crown had conquered the communes, and in the past they rather than the towns had been the enemies of monarchy. In the cortes of 1538 Charles came into collision with the nobles as a class. They usually attended only on ceremonial occasions, since they were exempted from direct taxation, which was the main function of the cortes. Now, however, they were summoned because Charles was bent upon a scheme of indirect taxation which would have affected all classes. They offered an uncompromising opposition, and Charles somewhat angrily dismissed them, nor did he ever summon them again.

Charles was well served by his ministers, whom he very rarely changed. After the death of the Piedmontese Gattinara he relied mainly on Nicolas Perrenot de Granvella for Netherland and German affairs, and on Francisco de los Cobos for Spanish, while the younger Granvella was being trained. From 1520–55 these were the only ministers of high importance. Above all, Charles never had a court favourite, and the only women who exercised any influence were his natural advisers, his wife, his aunt Margaret and his sister Mary. In all these ladies he was peculiarly fortunate.

The reign of Charles was in America the age of conquest and organization. Upon his accession the settlements upon the mainland were insignificant; by 1556 conquest was practically complete, and civil and ecclesiastical government firmly established. Actual expansion was the work of great adventurers starting on their own impulse from the older colonies. To Charles fell the task of encouraging such ventures, of controlling the conquerors, of settling the relations between colonists and natives, which involved those between the colonists and the missionary colonial Church. He must arrest de-population, provide for the labour market, regulate oceanic trade, and check military preponderance by civil and ecclesiastical organization. In America Charles took an unceasing interest; he had a boundless belief in its possibilities, and a determination to safeguard the interests of the Crown. Cortes, Pedro de Alvarado and the brothers Pizarro were brought into close personal communication with him. If he bestowed on Cortes the confidence which the loyal conqueror deserved, he showed the sternest determination in crushing the rebellious and autonomous instincts of Almagro and the Pizarros. But for this, Peru and Chile must have become independent almost as soon as they were conquered. Throughout he strove to protect the natives, to prevent actual slavery, and the consequent raids upon the natives. If in many respects he failed, yet the organization of Spanish America and the survival of the native races were perhaps the most permanent results of his reign. It is a proof of the complexity of his interests that the march of the Turk upon Vienna and of the French on Naples delayed until the following reign the foundation of Spain's eastern empire. Charles carefully organized the expedition of Magellan, which sailed for the Moluccas and discovered the Philippines. Unfortunately, his straits for money in 1529 compelled him to mortgage to Portugal his disputed claim to the Moluccas, and the Philippines consequently dropped out of sight.

If in the administration of Spain Charles did little more than mark time, in the Netherlands advance was rapid. Of the seven northern provinces he added five, containing more than half the area of the later United Provinces. In the south he freed Flanders and Artois from French suzerainty, annexed Tournai and Cambrai, and closed the natural line of French advance through the great bishopric of Liège by a line of fortresses across its western frontier. Much was done to convert the aggregate of jarring provinces into a harmonious unity by means of common principles of law and finance, and by the creation of a national army. While every province had its own assembly, there were at Charles's accession only the rudiments of estates-general for the Netherlands at large. At the close of the reign the common parliamentary system was in full swing, and was fast converting the loosely knit provinces into a State.

In the Netherlands Charles showed none of the jealousy with which he regarded the Spanish nobles. He encouraged the growth of large estates through primogeniture; he gave the nobles the provincial governorships, the great court offices, the command of the professional cavalry. In the Order of the Golden Fleece and the long established presence of the court at Brussels, he possessed advantages which he lacked in Spain. The nobility were utilized as a link between the court and the provinces. Very different was it with the Church. By far the greater part of the Netherlands fell under foreign sees, which were peculiarly liable to papal exactions and to the intrigues of rival Powers. Thus the usual conflict between civil and ecclesiastical jurisdiction was peculiarly acute. To remedy this dualism of authority and the consequent moral and religious abuses, Charles early designed the creation of a national diocesan system, and this was a cherished project throughout his life. The papacy unfortunately thwarted him, and the scheme, which under Charles would have been carried with national assent and created a national Church-system, took the appearance under Philip of alien domination. If in Germany Charles was emperor, he was in the Netherlands territorial prince, and thus his interests might easily be at disaccord with those of the Empire. Consequently, just as he had shaken off French suzerainty from Flanders and Artois, so he loosened the tie of the other provinces to Germany. In 1548 they were declared free and sovereign principalities not subject to imperial laws, and all the territories were incorporated in the Burgundian circle. It was, indeed, agreed that they should contribute to imperial taxation, and in return receive imperial protection. But this soon became a dead letter, and the Netherlands were really severed from the Empire, save for the nominal feudal tie in the case of some provinces.

Charles's Religious Aims.—Charles V. is, in the eyes of many, the very picture of a Catholic zealot. Popular opinion is probably based in the main upon the letters written from Yuste in 1558, when two hot-beds of heresy had been discovered in Spain herself, and on the contemporary codicil to his will. Charles was not then the responsible authority. There is a long step between a violent letter and a violent act. Few men would care to have their lives judged by letters written in the last extremities of gout. Less pardonable was the earlier persecution of the Valencian Moriscoes in 1525–26. The edict of persecution was cruel and unnecessary, and all expert opinion in Valencia was against it. It was not, however, actually enforced until after the victory of Pavia. It seems likely that Charles in a fit of religious exaltation regarded the persecution as a sacrificial thank-offering for his miraculous preservation. Henceforth the reign was marked by extreme leniency. Spain enjoyed a long lull in the activity of her Inquisition. At Naples in 1547 a rumour that the Spanish Inquisition was to be introduced to check the growth of heresy in influential quarters produced a dangerous revolt. The briefs were, however, issued by Paul III., no friend of Charles, and when a Neapolitan deputation visited the emperor he disclaimed any intention of making innovations. Of a different type to all the above was the persecution in the Netherlands. Here it was deliberate, chronic, and on an ascending scale. In the Netherlands the heretics were his immediate subjects, and as in every other State, Catholic or Lutheran, they must conform to their prince's religion. But there was more than this. After the suppression of the German peasant revolt in 1525 many of the refugees found shelter in the teeming Netherland cities, and heresy took the form, not of Lutheranism, but of Anabaptism, which was believed to be perilous to society and the State. The Government put down Anabaptism, as a modern Government might stamp out anarchism. The edicts were, indeed, directed against heresy in general, and were as harsh as they could be—at least on paper. Yet when Charles was assured that they were embarrassing foreign trade he let it be understood that they should not affect the foreign mercantile communities. Prudential considerations proved frequently a drag upon religious zeal.

The relations of Charles to heresy must be judged in the main by his treatment of German Lutheranism. Here he had to deal with organized Churches protected by their princes, supported by revenues filched from his own Church and stiffened by formulae as rigid as those of Catholicism. The length and stubbornness of the conflict will serve to show that Charles's religious conservatism had a measure of elasticity, that he was not a bigot and nothing more. The two more obvious courses towards the restoration of Catholic unity were force and reconciliation, in other words, a religious war or a general council. Neither of these was a simple remedy. The latter was impossible without papal concurrence, inoperative without the assistance of the European Powers, and merely irritant without the adhesion of the Lutherans. It was most improbable that the papacy, the Powers and the Lutherans would combine in a measure so palpably advantageous to the emperor. Force was hopeless save in the absence of war with France and the Turk, and of papal hostility in Italian territorial politics. Charles must obtain subsidies from ecclesiastical sources, and the support of all German Catholics, especially of the traditional rival, Bavaria. Even so the Protestants would probably be the stronger, and therefore they must be divided by utilizing any religious split, any class distinction, any personal or traditional dislikes, or else by bribery. Force and reconciliation seeming equally difficult; could an alternative be found in toleration? The experiment might take the form either of individual toleration, or of toleration for the Lutheran States. The former would be equally objectionable to Lutheran and Catholic princes as loosening their grip upon their subjects. Territorial toleration might seem equally obnoxious to the emperor, for its recognition would strengthen the anti-imperial particularism so closely associated with Lutheranism. If Charles could find no permanent specific, he must apply a provisional palliative. It was absolutely necessary to patch, if not to cure, because Germany must be pulled together to resist French and Turks. Such palliatives were two—suspension and comprehension. Suspension deferred the execution of penalties incurred by heresy, either for a term of years, or until a council should decide. Thus it recognized the divorce of the two religions, but limited it by time. Comprehension instead of recognizing the divorce would strive to conceal the breach. It was a domestic remedy, German and national, not European and papal. To become permanent it must receive the sanction of pope and council, for the Roman emperor could not set up a Church of Germany. Yet the formula adopted might conceivably be found to fall within the four corners of the faith, and so obviate the necessity alike of force or council. Such were the conditions of the emperor's task, and such the methods which he actually pursued. He would advance now on one line, now on another, now on two or three concurrently, but he never definitely abandoned any. This fusion of obstinacy and versatility was a marked feature of his character.

Suspension was of course often accidental and involuntary. The two chief stages of Lutheran growth naturally corresponded with the periods, each of nine years, when Charles was absent. Deliberate suspension was usually a consequence of the failure of comprehension. Thus at Augsburg in 1530 the wide gulf between the Lutheran confession and the Catholic confutation led to the definite suspensive treaty granted to the Lutherans at Nuremberg (1532). Charles dared not employ the alternative of force, because he needed their aid for the Turkish war. In 1541, after a series of religious conferences, he personally presented a compromise in the so-called Book of Regensburg, which was rejected by both parties. He then proposed that the articles agreed upon should be compulsory, while on others toleration should be exercised until a national council should decide. Never before nor after did he go so far upon the path of toleration, or so nearly accept a national settlement. He was then burning to set sail for Algiers. His last formal suspensive measure was that of Spires (Speyer) in 1544, when he was marching against Francis.

He promised a free and general council to be held in Germany, and, as a preparation, a national religious congress. The Lutherans were privately assured that a measure of comprehension should be concluded with or without papal approval. Meanwhile all edicts against heresy were suspended. No wonder that Charles afterwards confessed that he could scarcely reconcile these concessions with his conscience, but he won Lutheran aid for his campaign. The peace of Crépy gave all the conditions required for the employment of force. He had peace with French and Turk, he won the active support of the pope, he had deeply divided the Lutherans and reconciled Bavaria. Finding that the Lutherans would not accept the council summoned by the pope to Trent, he resorted to force, and force succeeded. At the Armed Diet of 1548 reunion seemed within reach. But Paul III. in direct opposition to Charles's wish had withdrawn the council from Trent to Bologna. Charles could not force Lutherans to submit to a council which he did not himself recognize, and he could not bring himself to national schism. Thus, falling back upon his old palliatives, he issued the Interim and the accompanying Reform of the Clergy, pending a final settlement by a satisfactory general council. These measures pleased neither party, and Charles at the very height of his power had failed. He was conscious of failure, and made few attempts even to enforce the Interim. Henceforward political complications gathered round him anew. The only remedy was toleration in some form, independent of the papacy and limitless in time. To this Charles could never assent. His ideal was shattered, but it was a great ideal, and the patience, the moderation, even at times the adroitness with which he had striven towards it, proved him to be no bigot.

Abdication and Death.—The idea of abdication had long been present with Charles, and in 1555 he acted upon it. To Ferdinand he gave his full authority as emperor, although at his brother's earnest request formal abdication was delayed until 1558. In the Hall of the Golden Fleece at Brussels on Oct. 25, 1555, he formally resigned to Philip the sovereignty of his beloved Netherlands. Turning from his son to the representatives of the estates he said: "Gentlemen, you must not be astonished if, old and feeble as I am in all my members, and also from the love I bear you, I shed some tears." In the Netherlands at least the love was reciprocal, and tears were infectious among the thousand deputies who listened to their sovereign's last speech. On Jan. 16, 1556, Charles resigned his Spanish kingdoms and that of Sicily, and shortly afterwards his county of Burgundy. On Sept. 17 he sailed from Flushing on the last of his many voyages, an English fleet from Portland bearing him company down the channel. In Feb. 1557 he was installed in the home which he had chosen at Yuste in Estremadura.

The excellent books which have been written upon the emperor's retirement have inspired an interest out of all proportion to its real significance. His little house was attached to the monastery, but was not within it. He was neither an ascetic nor a recluse. Gastronomic indiscretions still entailed their inevitable penalties. Society was not confined to interchange of civilities with the brethren. His relations, his chief friends, his official historians, all found their way to Yuste. Couriers brought news of Philip's war and peace with Pope Paul IV., of the victories of Saint Quentin and Gravelines, of the French capture of Calais, of the danger of Oran. As head of the family he intervened in the delicate relations with the closely allied house of Portugal; he even negotiated with the house of Navarre for reparation for the wrong done by his grandfather Ferdinand, which appeared to weigh upon his conscience. Above all he was shocked by the discovery that Spain, his own court, and his very chapel were infected with heresy. His violent letters to his son and daughter recommending immediate persecution, his profession of regret at having kept his word when Luther was in his power, have weighed too heavily on his reputation. The feverish phrases of religious exaltation due to broken health and unnatural retirement cannot balance the deliberate humanity and honour of wholesome manhood. Apart from such occasional moments of excitement, the emperor's last years passed tranquilly enough. At first he would shoot pigeons in the monastery woods, and till his last illness tended his garden and his animal pets, or watched the operations of Torriani, maker of clocks and mechanical toys. After an illness of three weeks the call came in the early hours of the Feast of St. Matthew, who, as his chaplain said, had for Christ's sake forsaken wealth even as Charles had forsaken empire. The dying man clasped his wife's crucifix to his breast till his fingers lost their hold. The archbishop held it before his eyes, and with the cry of "*Ay Jesus!*" died, in the words of his faithful squire, D. Luis de Quijada, "the chief of men that had ever been or would ever be." Posterity need not agree, but no great man can boast a more honest panegyric.

In character Charles stands high among contemporary princes. It consists of pairs of contrasts, but the better side is usually stronger than the worse. Steadfast honesty of purpose was occasionally warped by self-interest, or rather he was apt to think that his own course must needs be that of righteousness. Self-control would give way, but very rarely, to squalls of passion. Obstinacy and irresolution were fairly balanced, the former generally bearing upon ends, the latter upon means. His own ideals were constant, but he could gradually assimilate the views of others, and could bend to argument and circumstance; yet even here he had a habit of harking back to earlier schemes which he had seemed to have definitely abandoned. As a soldier he must rank very high. It was said that his being emperor lost to Spain the best light horseman of her army. At every crisis he was admirably cool, setting a truly royal example to his men. His mettle was displayed when he was attacked on the burning sands of Tunis, when his troops were driven in panic from Algiers, when in spite of physical suffering he forded the Elbe at Mühlberg, and when he was bombarded by the vastly superior Lutheran artillery under the walls of Ingolstadt. When blamed for exposing himself on this last occasion, "I could not help it," he apologized; "we were short of hands, I could not set a bad example." Nevertheless he was by nature timid. Just before this very action he had a fit of trembling, and he was afraid of mice and spiders. The force of his example was not confined to the field. Melanchthon wrote from Augsburg in 1530 that he was a model of continence, temperance and moderation, that the old domestic discipline was now only preserved in the imperial household. He tenderly loved his wife, whom he had married for pecuniary and diplomatic reasons. Of his two well-known illegitimate children, Margaret was born before he married, and Don John long after his wife's death, but he felt this latter to be a child of shame. His sobriety was frequently contrasted with the universal drunkenness of the German and Flemish nobles, which he earnestly condemned. But on his appetite he could place no control, in spite of the ruinous effects of his gluttony upon his health. In dress, in his household, and in his stable he was simple and economical. He loved children, flowers, animals and birds. Professional jesters amused him, and he was not above a joke himself. Maps and mechanical inventions greatly interested him, and in later life he became fond of reading. He takes his place indeed among authors, for he dictated the commentaries on his own career. Of music he possessed a really fine knowledge, and his high appreciation of Titian proves the purity of his feeling for art. The little collection of books and pictures which he carried to Yuste is an index of his tastes. Charles was undeniably plain. He confessed that he was by nature ugly, but that as artists usually painted him uglier than he was strangers on seeing him were agreeably disappointed. The protruding lower jaw and the thin pale face were redeemed by the fine open brow and the bright speaking eyes. He was, moreover, well made, and in youth had an incomparable leg. Above all no man could doubt his dignity; Charles was every inch an emperor. (E. Ar.)

Bibliography.—*Memoirs* written by Charles in 1550, and treating somewhat fully of the years 1543–48; W. Robertson, *History of the Emperor Charles V.* (many editions), an English classic, which needs supplementing by later authorities; *Commentaires de Charles-quint*, ed. Baron Kervyn de Lettenhove (Brussels, 1862); G. de Leva, *Storia documentata di Carlo V. in correlazione all' Italia* (5 vols., Venice, 1862–94), a general history of the reign, though with special reference to its Italian aspects, and extending to 1552; article by L. P. Gachard in *Biographie nationale*, vol. iii. (1872), an excellent compressed account; F. A. Mignet, *Rivalité de François I. et de*

Charles-quint (2 vols., 1875); H. Baumgarten, *Geschichte Karls V.* (3 vols., Stuttgart, 1885–93), very full but extending only to 1539; E. Armstrong, *The Emperor Charles V.* (2 vols., 1902), to which reference may be made for monographs and collections of documents bearing on the reign. The life of Charles V. at Yuste may be studied in L. P. Gachard's *Retraite et mort de Charles-quint au monastère de Yuste* (Brussels, 1854–55), and in Sir W. Stirling-Maxwell's *The Cloister Life of the Emperor Charles V.* (4 editions from 1852); also in W. H. Prescott's edition of Robertson's *History* (1857). *See* also F. Harting, *Karl V. und die deutsche Reichstände von 1546 bis 1555* (1910); P. Mexia, *Historia de Carlos Quinto* (1918); P. Kalhoff, *Die Kaiserwahl Friedrichs IV. und Karl V.* (1925); M. Rosi, *Il Primato di Carlo V.* (1925).

CHARLES VI. (1685–1740), Roman emperor, was born on Oct. 1, 1685, at Vienna. He was the second son of the emperor Leopold I. by his third marriage with Eleanore, daughter of Philip William of Neuburg, elector palatine of the Rhine. When the Spanish branch of the house of Habsburg became extinct in 1700, he was put forward as the lawful heir in opposition to Philip V., the Bourbon to whom the Spanish dominions had been left by the will of Charles II. of Spain. He was proclaimed at Vienna on Sept. 19, 1703, and made his way to Spain by the Low Countries, England and Lisbon, remaining in Spain till 1711, mostly in Catalonia, where the Habsburg party was strong. Although he had a certain tenacity of purpose he displayed none of the qualities required in a prince who had to gain his throne by the sword (*See* SPANISH SUCCESSION, WAR OF). In 1708 he was married at Barcelona to Elizabeth Christina of Brunswick-Wolfenbüttel (1691–1750), a Lutheran princess who was persuaded to accept Roman Catholicism. On the death of his elder brother Joseph I. on April 17, 1711, Charles inherited the hereditary possessions of the house of Habsburg and their claims on the Empire. The death of Joseph without male issue had been foreseen, and Charles had at one time been prepared to give up Spain and the Indies on condition that he was allowed to retain Naples, Sicily and the Milanese. But when the case arose his natural obstinacy led him to declare that he would not think of surrendering any of the rights of his family. It was with great difficulty that he was persuaded to leave Spain, months after the death of his brother (on Sept. 27, 1711). Only the emphatic refusal of the European powers to tolerate the reconstruction of the empire of Charles V. forced him to give a sullen submission to necessity. He abandoned Spain and was crowned emperor in December 1711, but for a long time he would not recognize Philip V. Charles showed an enlightened, though not always successful, interest in the commercial prosperity of his subjects, but from the date of his return to Germany till his death his ruling passion was to secure his inheritance against dismemberment. As early as 1713 he had begun to prepare the "Pragmatic Sanction" which was to regulate the succession, and it became the object of his policy to obtain the recognition of his daughter Maria Theresa as his heiress. His last days were embittered by a disastrous war with Turkey, in which he lost almost all he had gained by the peace of Passarowitz. He died at Vienna on Oct. 20, 1740, and with him expired the male line of his house.

For the personal character of Charles VI. *see* A. von Arneth, *Geschichte Maria Theresias* (Vienna, 1863–79). Dr. Franz Krones, R. v. Marchland, *Grundriss der österreichischen Geschichte* (Vienna, 1882), gives a very copious bibliography. *See* also J. Ziekursch, *Die Kaiserwahl Karls VI.* (1902).

CHARLES VII. (1697–1745), Roman emperor, known also as Charles Albert, elector of Bavaria, was the son of the elector Maximilian Emanuel and his second wife, Theresa Cunigunda, daughter of John Sobieski, king of Poland. He was born on Aug. 6, 1697. His father having taken the side of Louis XIV. of France in the War of the Spanish Succession (*q.v.*), Bavaria was occupied by the allies. Charles and his brother Clement, afterwards archbishop of Cologne, were carried prisoners to Vienna, and were educated by the Jesuits under the name of the counts of Wittelsbach. When his father was restored to his electorate Charles was released, and in 1717 he led the Bavarian contingent of the imperial army which served under Prince Eugene against the Turks, and is said to have distinguished himself at Belgrade. On Sept. 25, 1722, he was betrothed to Maria Amelia, the younger of the two orphan daughters of the emperor Joseph I. Her uncle Charles VI. insisted that the Bavarian house should recognize the Pragmatic Sanction which established his daughter Maria Theresa as heiress of the Habsburg dominions. They did so, but with secret protests and mental reservations of their rights, which were designed to render the recognition valueless. The electors of Bavaria had claims on the possessions of the Habsburgs under the will of the emperor Ferdinand I., who died in 1564.

Charles succeeded his father on Feb. 26, 1726. His policy was to keep on good terms with the emperor while slipping out of his obligation to accept the Pragmatic Sanction and intriguing to secure French support for his claims whenever Charles VI. should die. These claims were advanced immediately after the death of Charles VI. on Oct. 20, 1740. Charles Albert now entered into the league against Maria Theresa, to the great misfortune of himself and his subjects. By the help of her enemies he was elected emperor in opposition to her husband Francis, grand duke of Tuscany, on Jan. 24, 1742, under the title of Charles VII. and was crowned at Frankfurt-am-Main on Feb. 12. But as his army had been neglected, he was utterly unable to resist the Austrian troops. While he was being crowned his hereditary dominions in Bavaria were being overrun. During the War of the Austrian Succession (*q.v.*) he was a mere puppet in the hands of the anti-Austrian coalition, and was often in want of mere necessities. In the changes of the war he was able to re-enter his capital, Munich, in 1743, but had immediately afterwards to take flight again. He was restored by Frederick the Great in Oct. 1744, but died worn out at Munich on Jan. 20, 1745.

See A. von Arneth, *Geschichte Maria Theresias* (Vienna, 1863–79), and P. T. Heigel, *Der österreichische Erbfolgestreit und die Kaiserwahl Karls VII.* (Munich, 1877).

CHARLES I. (1887–1922), emperor of Austria and king of Hungary, born Aug. 17, 1887, in Persenbeug, in Lower Austria, was the son of the archduke Otto (1865–1906), and Princess Maria Josepha of Saxony (1867–1944). The death of his father in 1906 and the renunciation by his uncle, the archduke Francis Ferdinand, on his marriage with the countess Chotek (1900) of any right of succession for the children of this union, made him heir-presumptive to his great-uncle, the emperor, Francis Joseph. In Oct. 1911 he married the princess Zita of Bourbon-Parma. Of this marriage there were several sons and daughters, the eldest of whom, Otto, was born in 1912. Charles' relations with the emperor were not intimate, and those with Francis Ferdinand not cordial. After the death of Francis Ferdinand the old emperor took steps to initiate him in affairs of State; but these studies were interrupted almost immediately by the outbreak of the World War. After a period at headquarters at Teschen, Charles commanded the 20th Corps in the offensive of 1916 against Italy, later commanding an army on the eastern front.

Charles as Emperor.—On Nov. 21, 1916, he succeeded to the throne, at a period of extreme difficulty, which he hoped to meet by making a complete change in the leading military and political posts in the monarchy. The changes, however, usually proved unfortunate. Charles himself was an amiable man of excellent intentions, but his abilities were mediocre and his preparatory training inadequate. He lacked calmness and endurance, and was prone to headlong, precipitate actions. He was powerfully influenced by his immediate entourage—his wife and mother-in-law—while distrusting all other advisers. But he was most bitterly—and justly—reproached for insincerity. Not merely his enemies, but his allies, particularly German statesmen and the emperor William, soon felt that they could not trust his word; a sentiment shared by the peoples of the Danubian monarchy.

On Charles' accession the Constitution in Austria was still suspended. In May 1917 he summoned parliament once more, but the concessions Charles now made to the Slavonic nationalities remained fruitless, merely alienating the majority of the German Austrians, while his concessions to the Magyars in Hungary similarly irritated the conservatives of Vienna and the non-Magyars of Hungary, without checking the separatist movement. He was equally unfortunate in his peace proposals. While refusing the idea of a separate peace for Austria, he endeavoured to persuade

Germany to buy a general peace by territorial concessions in the west. But the negotiations opened by Count Czernin only bred ill-will, which culminated on the publication of the so-called "Sixtus letter" of March 24, 1917. Charles' belated effort to convert Austria into a Federal State on national lines (Oct. 16, 1918) was rendered futile by the failure to apply it to Hungary; and Charles was obliged to renounce participation in the Government of Austria on Nov. 11, 1918, and of Hungary two days later. (*See* HABSBURG.) After the proclamation of the Austrian republic, Charles retired to his castle of Eckartsau; thence he went, the Austrian Government having demanded his departure, on March 24, 1919, to Switzerland, where he stayed first at Schloss Gstaad and later at Prangins. His attempt at the end of March 1921 to secure his restoration as king of Hungary failed owing to the attitude of the regent, Horthy, and other leading Hungarians and the unanimous opposition of the Succession States and the Entente.

Charles returned to Switzerland, where a provisional prolongation of his residence was accorded him subject to certain conditions. In Oct. 1921, however, he made a surprise air flight with his wife from Switzerland to the Burgenland, where he was joined by a small force of armed Royalists, at whose head he marched on Budapest. But the Allied Powers, as well as the "Little Entente," made it clear that a *coup d'état* would not be tolerated, and there was a strong rally at Budapest to the side of the Horthy Government. The Royalists were met near Budapest and defeated, Charles and Zita being themselves arrested at Tihany.

On instructions from the Powers, the definite deposition of Charles and renunciation of his claims to the throne were insisted upon, and he and his wife were handed over to the custody of the Allies for internment. Refused the right of asylum by Switzerland, on the ground that he had not adhered to the conditions agreed upon, and accorded a reception by Portugal alone, he was conveyed upon the English ship "Cardiff" to Funchal, Madeira. Here he lived in straitened circumstances until his death on April 1, 1922.

BIBLIOGRAPHY.—Karl Werkmann, *Der Tote auf Madeira* (1923); Aladar von Boroviczeny, *Der König und sein Reichverweser* (1924); R. Fester, *Kaiser Karl und der Wendepunkt des Weltkrieges* (1925).

CHARLES I (1600–1649), king of Great Britain and Ireland, the second son of James I and Anne of Denmark, was born on Nov. 19, 1600. At his baptism he was created duke of Albany, and on Jan. 16, 1605 duke of York. He was a backward child, so weak that he could scarcely walk and very slow in beginning to talk, but he grew stronger, became a good horseman and walker, though an impediment hampered his speech all his life. In 1612, by the death of his elder brother Henry, he became heir apparent, and was created prince of Wales on Nov. 3, 1616. In 1618 he fell under the influence of the duke of Buckingham, who had already established an ascendancy over the king and dominated the royal councils. The prince felt keenly his sister Elizabeth's humiliation when her husband, Frederick V, was driven from the throne of Bohemia at the beginning of the Thirty Years' War, and was soon to lose his hereditary electorate the Palatinate. The prince shared his father's belief that to save and, after 1622, to recover the Palatinate an alliance with Spain was necessary. Negotiations for a marriage between Charles and the Infanta Maria had been proceeding since 1614. In 1623 the prince and the favourite, Buckingham, thought to remove all obstacles by a visit to Madrid. Travelling incognito, they arrived at the Spanish capital in March. Charles promised to repeal the penal laws against Roman Catholics within three years, but on the restitution of the Palatinate, now conquered by Spanish armies, he was adamant. When he found that the Spanish would not help Frederick, he and Buckingham angrily returned home. The incident illustrates Charles's devotion to dynastic interests, a most important factor in his foreign policy. It also reveals his strange indifference to wider issues, including the fate of Protestantism in Europe and the sentiments of his future subjects. The enthusiastic welcome he received on his arrival without a Spanish bride proved how unpopular the marriage would have been. Charles immediately pressed for war with Spain to avenge his treatment there and to help his sister. A parliament was summoned in Feb. 1624 and applauded the end of negotiations with Spain. In his blind zeal Charles urged the commons to impeach the earl of Middlesex, the only councillor who resisted a breach with Spain. He found that members would welcome a naval war with Spain and an alliance with the Dutch but not, as he and Buckingham wanted, a war in Germany. There was another difference. Englishmen had disliked the Spanish match because they realized that concessions to Catholics would be inevitable, but Charles was now seeking a French bride and to gain her would be obliged to relax the penal laws. Although parliament voted only the modest sum of £300,000, Charles persuaded his father to prepare for a continental war. The treaty with the Dutch promising English pay for 6,000 soldiers was signed in June 1624, a force under a soldier of fortune, Ernst von Mansfeld, was assembled to recover the Palatinate, and Christian IV of Denmark was promised £30,000 a month as the price of armed intervention in Germany. These engagements plus a war with Spain would require additional grants from parliament of £1,000,000. At this point James I died (March 27, 1625) and Charles became king in name as he had practically been in fact since his return from Madrid.

Charles was married by proxy in Paris to Henrietta Maria, daughter of Henry IV, among the articles of the marriage treaty being a pledge that English Catholics should enjoy freedom of worship. Buckingham went to France to bring the bride home but failed to induce Louis XIII and Richelieu to adopt his grandiose schemes to attack the Spanish Netherlands. Politically the marriage had lost its charm before the young bride of fifteen joined her husband in June. Soon her attempts to insist that the marriage articles should be honoured caused much friction and led Charles to send her French attendants home. Not until after Buckingham's assassination did she exercise much influence. Meanwhile the relation of Charles with his subjects rapidly became worse. His first parliament granted him only about a seventh of the money he required and, when it began to hint that Buckingham was too powerful, he promptly dissolved it.

Before Charles's second parliament met, the expedition against Cádiz had failed disastrously. Probably a more poorly equipped fleet and army never left the English shores, but Charles would not listen to a word of complaint against Buckingham, who was mainly to blame. When the commons attacked the favourite the king assumed responsibility for his acts and emphasized that he was "the man whom the king delighteth to honour." Even after Charles had warned "that parliaments are altogether in my power for their calling, sitting and dissolution; therefore, as I find the fruits of them good or evil they are to continue, or not to be," the commons persisted and impeached Buckingham. To save him Charles put an end to the session. No money had been granted so the king exacted nearly £300,000 by a forced loan, yet he failed to remit the subsidies promised to his allies on the continent. Consequently in 1626, Ernst von Mansfeld and Christian IV, their unpaid soldiers deserting or falling sick daily, were both defeated and the way to north Germany was open to the Catholic forces. Just at the moment when the fortunes of continental Protestantism were at their lowest ebb Charles involved England in a war with France, thus destroying any hope that Louis XIII might check the Imperialists' progress. He supported the Huguenots at La Rochelle, posing as a Protestant champion in the wrong place. A more rational cause of the war was the dispute over maritime rights. Charles had permitted the seizure of French ships bound to the Spanish Netherlands and allowed the sale of their cargoes before the prize courts had condemned them. In 1627 Buckingham led an expedition to the Isle of Rhè opposite La Rochelle. He could not capture a fort on the isle and had to sail home after heavy losses. The need of money obliged Charles to call his third parliament, but he found it determined to render grievances before voting any supplies. When he refused to submit to any statutory curtailment of his prerogative, parliament leaders adapted a method individuals had used in the past when desirous of bringing an action against the crown. The Petition of Right (1628) requested the king not to: (1) compel any man to make "any gift, loan, benevolence, tax or such like charge" without consent of parliament; (2) imprison a free man without specifying the cause; (3) billet soldiers upon private citizens against their will; and (4) use martial law in time of peace. The royal assent was reluctantly given only after a threat to impeach Buckingham. The duke's assassination (Aug. 23, 1628) removed a constant source of friction between king and parliament, but now an even more enduring subject of dispute came to the fore. The foreign policy of the preceding decade and the king's evident preference for Arminian divines (*see* ARMINIUS, JACOBUS) made many suspect that he was not at heart a sound Protestant. Also the Arminian clergy in their sermons and writings magnified the royal prerogative and defended the theory of the divine right of kings. When, therefore, Charles heard the commons were preparing a remonstrance against his ecclesiastical policy, he dissolved parliament, but before they dispersed some of the members forcibly held the speaker in his chair while they passed resolutions denouncing as an enemy to his country whoever introduced innovations in religion, sought to introduce popery or Arminianism or unorthodox opinions or advised the levying of tonnage and poundage or paid these duties. These resolutions combined political and religious grievances and created the union of the constitutionalists and Puritans which was in the 1640s to form the parliamentarian party.

At the end of the first civil war the royalist historian, the earl of Clarendon, wrote that "no man can shew me a source from whence these waters of bitterness we now taste have more probably flowed, than from the unseasonable, unskilful, and precipitate dissolution of parliaments." Yet the king returned from dismissing parliament in high spirits as if relieved of a heavy yoke. In a declaration he promised to maintain the true religion and the just rights of his subjects. He meant what he said, but of truth and justice he intended to be the judge. A firm believer in the divine right of kings, Charles especially stressed that kings were answerable to God alone, and possible misgovernment was a matter between them and their Maker. A good subject would obey the Lord's anointed without question. Criticism *ipso facto* branded the critic as both disloyal and sinful. Because parliaments had disputed the royal prerogative they must cease to be. Such were the king's resolutions when he began the eleven years of unparliamentary government (1629–40). He saw he could not afford an adventurous foreign policy and signed a peace with France in 1629 and with Spain the next year. Apart from some futile efforts to recover the Palatinate, among them being attempted alliances with Spain (1631 and 1634) one item of which was the partition of the United Provinces, Charles had no foreign policy. He did nothing to uphold continental Protestantism or the balance of power. To increase the revenue he had recourse not to direct taxation but to all kinds of obsolete levies. Owners of property of a certain value were fined for not seeking patents of knighthood. Possessors of large estates learned that their land had once formed part of a royal forest and they had either to surrender it or redeem it at a high price. A commission of depopulation found that many landlords had demolished houses to make enclosures and compelled them to restore the land to commoners and to rebuild the cottages. Measures of this nature, though in some cases perfectly just, raised powerful enemies for the king.

The most lucrative finance measure was ship money. In 1634 writs were issued to seaports specifying the sums needed for the ships each was to furnish the royal navy. From 1635 to 1639 writs were also addressed to inland counties on the ground they all were equally concerned with the defense of the realm. When men saw that the king thus was adding about £200,000 to his revenues they began to dispute the legality of ship money. In 1638 the judges decided seven to five in the famous case of the crown versus John Hampden that the king could take what measures he thought necessary for national safety. One judge pronounced that *rex* was *lex,* and another that acts to restrain the king from commanding the services and goods of his subjects were voided. These pronouncements alarmed all Englishmen who had been brought up to believe that what concerned all should be approved by all. More and more declined to pay ship money so that the amount not collected rose from 20% to 80% during 1638 and 1639. Charles's ecclesiastical policy also created widespread discontent. Like all the Stuarts he detested Presbyterianism and its organization. He also repudiated the doctrine of predestination. In contradiction to its theory of the two kingdoms, lay and spiritual, in the former the king being the head, but in the latter only a member, he claimed supremacy in all matters ecclesiastical and civil. He and William Laud viewed the Church of England as a branch of the primitive Catholic church before the introduction of Romish errors. They wished to return to what they felt was historic Christianity and they regretted aspects of the Reformation. They detested the participation of laymen in any decision respecting doctrine or discipline whether as members of parliament in England or of the general assembly in Scotland. They believed in unity of church and state and dissent from the one implied disaffection in the other. Their ideal was a strict uniformity of worship even in what they regarded as "things indifferent." Their efforts to improve the stipends of the clergy which had failed to keep pace with the rising cost of living and to repair the fabric of churches, too often neglected since the Reformation, were commendable. But the new emphasis on ritual and sacerdotalism was repugnant to many who suspected a drift Romeward. This suspicion was confirmed or appeared to be confirmed by the reception at court of papal agents and by the Queen's favour to her coreligionists. The leniency showed to Catholics was in striking contrast to the severity to Puritans like Prynne, Burton, and Bastwick. All attacked episcopacy and denied its divine origin. In their eyes, as one of them wrote, the church was as full of ceremonies as a dog of fleas. Unfair as many of their attacks were, vulgar as much of their abuse was, the attitude of the crowds that witnessed their sufferings in the pillory or cheered them on their way to their distant jails left little doubt that they and not the prelates represented the common man. Charles seems to have expected that the peace and plenty England enjoyed during most of the 1630s would reconcile his subjects to his authoritarian rule. A model of his form of government could be seen in Ireland. There Thomas Wentworth had enhanced the royal power so that, he boasted, Charles was as absolute as any king in the world. All the people had to do with their government was to obey the king and trust to his fatherly love and not worry about their imaginary liberty.

In Scotland Presbyterianism had been established by the nobles and middle classes combined. James had split the coalition and was able to curb the ministers by imposing episcopacy. Charles, less wise, in the first year of his reign alienated the nobles by the act of revocation which reclaimed for the church and crown all lands alienated since 1542. He also annoyed the Scottish peers in the same way as the English by appointing ecclesiastics to important state positions, but open resistance did not begin until 1637 when the attempts to use a new service book in Edinburgh led to a famous riot. Opposition to this prayer book was largely composed of two elements, patriotism and Presbyterianism, or hatred of England and hatred of Rome. When Charles heard of the tumults his first comment was, "I mean to be obeyed." His initial refusal to contemplate any concessions usually led in the end to greater surrenders than an early compliance would have required. Charles soon found he had aroused a nation to arms. Scots of every degree signed the National Covenant to resist always the recent ecclesiastical innovations and at the same time support their king in defense of the true religion and their laws and liberties. Charles allowed a general assembly to meet but tried to dissolve it when he recognized its intentions. It continued to sit and swept away the prayer book and episcopacy. Charles hoped to restore his authority by force. He called upon the nobility to serve at their own expense and summoned the militia from the northern counties. Men of all degrees served so unwillingly that Charles saw he could not make headway against the enthusiastic army of the Covenant. He was obliged to sign the treaty of Berwick (June 1639) permitting all ecclesiastical questions to be settled by a general assembly and all civil matters by parliament. All the measures taken during more than half a century to magnify the royal authority and to depress the presbytery were discarded. Rather than endure this rebuff the king determined to summon a parliament in England to gain supplies to renew the war against the Scots. When the Short parliament met in April 1640 members were asked to proceed immediately to pass a money bill but John Pym, who now led the opposition to the king, spoke of grievances. When the king professed that after money had been granted he would be willing to consider complaints, the commons fixed a day to debate troubles in Scotland. Thereupon Charles once again dissolved parliament. He committed one of the greatest blunders of his reign because this parliament would probably have been content with moderate, not revolutionary, changes in the government. He was equally at fault in promulgating the canons of 1640 which contained among other articles obnoxious to Puritans, the command to every minister to read each quarter a statement that kings were of divine origin and given by God a supreme power over all persons, and that to bear arms against the king was to resist power ordained of God and so incur damnation. Charles soon discovered that his subjects did not accept this definition of their duties. To punish the Scots, he now called upon the militia of the southern counties but the only time they encountered the Scots they gave way to disgraceful panic, leaving Northumberland and Durham open to their enemies. Charles was constrained to open negotiations but found the Scots would agree to an armistice only on condition that they should continue to occupy the north counties and be paid £850 a day. They were looking forward to a settlement with an English parliament rather than with the king. Charles had no option but to summon a parliament. Unless it met and granted supplies his forces in Yorkshire would disband and the Scottish army could march unopposed to London, where it was likely to be welcomed. Thus when it met on Nov. 3, 1640 the Long parliament had in effect an army in its pay, a situation lasting until the following August when the treaty with the Scots was completed. Thus the king dared not dismiss this parliament as he had four others. Charles had so few supporters that he could not save his advisers from imprisonment or exile, or, in the case of the earl of Strafford (the former Wentworth), execution. He promised Strafford three weeks before the end that he should not suffer in life, honour or fortune. But the royal intervention did more harm than good and an obscure army plot which included an attempt to put the Tower of London into loyal hands was fatal. Charles, feeling that his wife's life was not safe from the armed mob that surrounded the palace shouting for justice, gave way. Strafford had urged the king not to let him be a hindrance to reconciliation between king and parliament. When he heard that the Bill of Attainder had been signed he is said to have exclaimed, "put not your trust in princes." Charles regretted his consent all his life and regarded his own death as an expiation for the sacrifice of his faithful servant. He is not known to have expressed any sorrow that he was largely responsible for the general apprehension that Strafford was too dangerous a man to let live.

During the first year of the Long parliament the king could not oppose measures to abolish prerogative courts like the Star Chamber and High commission and declare unlawful the financial expedients used during the 1630s. He even consented to acts to ensure that parliament meet every third year and that it could not be dissolved without its own consent. Pym and his adherents had established the reign of law so far as statutes could achieve it. They had effectively curbed the royal power but had not provided a substitute to rule the country. The constitution in 1641 may be likened to an old locomotive which parliament had equipped with powerful brakes but left the engine unrepaired.

In Aug. 1641 Charles paid a second visit to Scotland. His gracious reception induced the belief that the Scots would maintain and place at his command some of the army now returning from north England. He also thought that he could bribe his bitterest opponents by promises of preferment to office and promotions in the peerage. He was disappointed in both respects. The Scottish army was disbanded, and the earl of Argyll, though created a marquis, and other covenanting leaders could not be bought. Instead, they insisted that officers of state must be acceptable to parliament. While the king was failing to form a Scottish party to intervene in England he was ordering his agents in Ireland to try to secure the support of Irish Catholics by vague offers of toleration. It was highly improbable that Charles ever seriously pondered the question whether Scottish Presbyterians and Irish Catholics could be combined to coerce his English subjects. That he never seemed to have considered his policy in all its bearings was a permanent weakness. Instead he passed from one intrigue to another without seeing that the ultimate result would be general distrust. During his absence from London parliament passed the first of the many ordinances it was to issue without the royal assent hitherto regarded as essential to give a bill the force of law.

When after a month's recess the Long parliament reopened in Oct. 1641 the king was in a stronger position. He had taken into his councils Edward Hyde, later earl of Clarendon, who formed a party of constitutional royalists. The text for the many state papers he wrote for the king he borrowed from a speech of Pym's, "the law is that which puts the difference betwixt good and evil, betwixt justice and injustice." He sought to prove that the king was now the guardian of the constitution against the innovations of parliamentary leaders animated by selfish ambition. He urged the king to take his stand on the known laws of the land and await a reaction in his favour. The opponents of episcopacy at first demanded the punishment of obnoxious bishops like Laud but were now demanding the abolition of the order. This assault was likely to rally many defenders and split assailants who were not agreed on what to substitute for the Anglican church. The king unfortunately for himself lacked the firmness and patience to follow Hyde's policy for long. He was always intriguing to regain the powers he had surrendered.

Towards the end of 1641 two events of great significance to Charles I occurred: the Irish Rebellion and the passage of the Grand Remonstrance. On Oct. 23 the native Irish with some Anglo-Irish Catholics rose against the English and Scots who had dispossessed them of their land and outlawed their religion. They slaughtered several thousand Protestants. Very exaggerated news of the massacre reached England and Charles's opponents depicted the dangers to Protestants in the most lurid colours. The need for an army to put down the rebellion raised the question whether king or parliament should control it. The commons required that the king should employ only ministers approved by parliament, otherwise they would entrust the reconquest of Ireland to those in whom they had confidence. This was the most revolutionary step hitherto taken. At the same time the commons debated the Grand Remonstrance, which was an appeal to the country in the form of a partisan statement of the grievances already redressed and of the evils still to be cured. Its passage by 11 votes only showed that nearly half the commons were now royalists. Once again Charles threw away his chances. His attempt to arrest the five members in the house of commons (Jan. 4, 1642) lost him most of the ground he had regained. Had the parliamentarians shown moderation during the next six months the king must have submitted to their demands, but their Nineteen Propositions (June 2) sought to reduce him to a mere titular sovereign and left the church to be reformed by the Puritans. They voted that the cost of raising an army should be borne by malignants or those who had not actively assisted the parliament. The result was that many in this vague category who might otherwise have remained neutral took up arms for the king.

The civil wars are described under the separate article GREAT REBELLION and are here included only for the king's actions. He proved himself a good strategist but a poor tactician. He realized that London was the heart of the parliamentary cause but was unable to co-ordinate his different armies to attack it. However, the material resources at parliament's command were much superior to his especially after the Solemn League and Covenant (Sept. 1643) had brought a Scottish army into England. The new model army formed early in 1645 ended the first civil war in a year. During and after the war various negotiations between king and parliament produced no results. The king could never put himself in the position of a national leader. All concessions he regarded as temporary, wrested from him by rebels. He told his wife in 1646 with reference to the establishment of Presbyterianism for three years that he did so in order to "lay a ground for a perfect recovery of that (the Anglican church), which, to abandon, were directly against my conscience, and, I am confident, destructive to monarchy." Unfortunately for his reputation his conscience did not prevent his returning evasive, his enemies thought deceitful, answers to all overtures for peace. He fancied that sooner or later quarrels between parliament, the army and the Scots would make him arbitrator of their differences. Therefore, he tried to spin out time until his enemies were at each others' throats, but he exhausted their patience so that the Scots to whom he had delivered himself in May 1646 surrendered him to the English parliament in January. In June 1647 Cornet Joyce under Oliver Cromwell's orders carried off the king and brought him into the army's custody. Charles escaped to the Isle of Wight and in Dec. 1647 signed with the Scottish commissioners the Engagement for the establishment of Presbyterianism for three years and the suppression of the sectaries. Thus the union between Presbyterians and royalists was formed which was ultimately to lead to the Restoration. Its immediate results were the victory of the army over its enemies and its determination to bring the king to trial. After some 140 M.P.'s had been expelled from parliament by Pride's purge (Dec. 1648), the remnant appointed commissioners to form a court. The king declined to acknowledge its authority, whereupon the sentence was passed that he should be beheaded as a tyrant and public enemy to his people. On the scaffold (Jan. 30, 1649) he submitted to his fate with a quiet dignity. He said that he "did not believe the happiness of people lay in sharing government, subject and sovereign being clean different." This persistent denial of a subject's constitutional rights was a main cause of his failure. His support of the Anglican church probably commended itself to the majority of Englishmen though they disliked the Laudian principles so dear to the king.

Charles's private life was most exemplary. He was an affectionate husband and father, devout in his religion and regular in his habits. He looked every inch a king. He had a genuine interest in painting, especially of the Italian school, and so far as his limited resources allowed was a great collector and patron of the arts. Immediately after his death appeared *Eikon Basilike* which was thought to be at the time the king's own account of his sufferings, though it is now known to have been written by John Gauden, perhaps after consultation with the king or examination of some of his papers. It earned for him his reputation as a martyred king.

He was survived by his wife (*see* HENRIETTA MARIA), his sons Charles, James (*see* CHARLES II and JAMES II), and Henry, duke of Gloucester (1639–60), and his daughters Mary (1631–60), who married William II of Orange, Elizabeth (1635–50), and Henrietta (1644–70) who married Philip, duke of Orleans.

BIBLIOGRAPHY.—The public life of Charles I is part of the history of Great Britain and sources and later works for it can be found in *Bibliography of British History, Stuart Period, 1603–1714,* ed., G. Davies (Oxford, 1928) or in the bibliographies appended to such histories as G. M. Trevelyan, *England under the Stuarts* (New York, 1904); F. C. Montague, *The History of England From the Accession of James I to the Restoration, 1603–1660* (New York, 1907); G. Davies, *The Early Stuarts, 1603–1660* (Oxford, 1937). Two works by S. R. Gardiner are indispensable: *History of England,* 10 vol. (1884) and *Great Civil War, 1642–1649,* 4 vol. (New York, 1893). The proclamations, declarations, etc., issued by the king or in his name can be found in many collections such as *Reliquiae sacrae Carolinae* (1649), *Basilika: The Workes of King Charles* (1662) or *Letters, Speeches, and Proclamations of King Charles I,* ed., Sir Charles Petrie (London, 1935). Those written by Edward Hyde (later Earl of Clarendon) are printed in his *History of the Great Rebellion,* 6 vol. (Oxford, 1888), which, together with his *Life,* 2 vol. (1857), has interesting comments on the king and his policy. The king's private correspondence is not large, but his character is well illustrated in *Charles I in 1646: Letters of King Charles the First,* ed., John Bruce, (1856). The best biographies are by F. M. G. Higham, *Charles I* (London, 1932) and E. C. Wingfield-Stratford, *Charles King of England 1600–1637* (London, 1949), *King Charles and King Pym 1637–1643,* (London, 1949) and *King Charles the Martyr 1643–1649* (London, 1950). Sir John Skelton, *Charles I* (1898) has many illustrations. Studies of special topics include J. G. Muddiman, *The Trial of King Charles the First* (1928), Gordon Albion, *Charles I and the Court of Rome* (Louvrain, Belg.; London, 1935), G. M. Young, *Charles I and Cromwell* (London, 1935); H. P. Cooke, *Charles I and His Earlier Parliaments* (London, 1939), and F. F. Madan, ed., *A New Bibliography of the Eikon Basilike of King Charles the First* (London, 1950). For Charles as a patron of art and a collector *see* Francis Henry Taylor, *The Taste of Angels* (Boston; Toronto, 1948), and *The Burlington Magazine,* Jan. 1949. (G. Ds.)

CHARLES II (1630–1685), king of Great Britain and Ireland, 2nd son of Charles I and Henrietta Maria, was born on May 29, 1630. In 1638 the duke of Newcastle was appointed as his governor, but his education was interrupted by the Civil War. In 1645 Charles I sent him into the west of England, where his council included, among others, Sir Edward Hyde. In March 1646 the royalist defeats drove him to the Scilly Isles and later to Jersey, and in July he joined his mother in Paris. He remained there under her control for two years, and continued his studies, Thomas Hobbes being his tutor for mathematics.

In 1648 Charles cruised with some English ships off the mouth of the Thames, but effected nothing and retired to Holland. In Jan. 1649 he sent a blank sheet of paper, bearing his signature, to parliament, for the insertion of any terms which would save his father's life. After Charles I's execution on Jan. 30, 1649, he was proclaimed king in Scotland and parts of Ireland and in the Channel Islands. He went to Jersey in September, but was obliged to retire to Breda (Feb. 1650), and from that place he came to terms with the Scots, accepting the Covenant and abandoning the earl of Montrose, whom he had encouraged to attempt another royalist rising in Scotland. He landed in Scotland on June 23, 1650, after pledging himself to Presbyterianism in both Scotland and England. An attempt to escape from the Covenanters, known as "the Start," failed, and on Jan. 1, 1651, Charles was crowned as king of Scots at Scone. Oliver Cromwell's advance forced him to march into England and on Sept. 3 Cromwell defeated him at Worcester. Charles showed great courage in the battle, and after an amazing series of adventures, including his concealment in the "royal oak" at Boscobel, sailed from Brighton for France on Oct. 15.

His advisers were henceforward the royalists, Hyde, duke of Ormonde, and, from 1654, Sir Edward Nicholas. Plots for risings in England and Scotland and for Cromwell's assassination failed. In 1654 Cromwell's negotiations with France drove Charles to Germany, but after Cromwell's alliance with France he made a treaty with Spain (April 1656) and resided at Bruges or Brussels. His chief source of income was a Spanish pension; and he was very poor. Cromwell's death did not immediately alter his position and in 1659 he went to Fuenterrabia, where the peace of the Pyrenees was being negotiated between France and Spain, to ask for military aid. This journey and a royalist rising in England just before it were alike fruitless.

Events in England brought about the Restoration, which the royalists alone could not have accomplished. By the end of 1659 a return to the old constitution was the only escape from the alternatives of military government or anarchy. George Monck (duke of Albemarle) advanced with an armed force from Scotland; by recalling the secluded members of the Long parliament, power was transferred from the Independents to the Presbyterians. A "free" parliament was summoned to meet in April 1660 while Monck opened negotiations with Charles, who, following his advice, issued the Declaration of Breda April 4. Largely the work of Hyde, it promised a general amnesty and liberty of conscience and to the army full arrears of pay, leaving the final settlement in each case to parliament; it also promised that all questions about the transfers of lands during the past years of revolutions should be determined in parliament. The Convention parliament, in which the secular peers again sat, accepted the declaration and Charles was proclaimed king on May 8. On May 25 he landed at Dover, where he was met by Monck, and on May 29, amid universal rejoicing, arrived at Whitehall.

The agreement of Charles and Monck in leaving the settlement to parliament meant that the Restoration was a restoration of parliamentary government, not of personal monarchy. Charles was not a conqueror and had no armed force of his own, while during the last 20 years almost all classes in England had acquired a permanent interest in politics. The administration could not be carried on without the help of men who had already been employed by the revolutionary governments and the new council included faithful royalists and former rebels.

The willing co-operation of the Convention and the unbounded loyalty of its successor in its earlier years encouraged Charles to entrust many matters to parliament. The Restoration dissolved the legislative union with Scotland and Ireland, and led to the re-establishment of their separate parliaments. In Scotland the return of the old order was complete, and brought back episcopacy and repression; in Ireland the Cromwellian settlement was firmly established and was upheld by English opinion.

Hyde, created earl of Clarendon, was still Charles's chief adviser, and directed the work of reconstruction in England. All the acts of the revolutionary governments since 1642 were held to be invalid; judicial proceedings since that date were confirmed by a special act. The Navigation act of 1651 was re-enacted; the abolition of feudal incidents (the abolition of tenure by knight service, of the feudal dues attaching to it, and of the court of wards and its local agents which dealt with them) completed in 1646, was maintained by a new act. The Indemnity bill led to disputes between Charles and parliament, Charles desiring lenity. Thirteen regicides and young Sir Henry Vane were executed; 25 regicides, John Lambert and Sir Arthur Hesilrige were imprisoned for life; otherwise the amnesty was complete. Crown and church lands, and other lands sequestered by the revolutionary governments, reverted to their former owners, but royalists who had sold part of their lands to meet the fines inflicted on them received no compensation. By means of special taxes the army was paid off by Feb. 1661 though, as a result of the alarm caused by Thomas Venner's rising, Charles was able to retain Monck's regiment of infantry, known henceforward as the Coldstream guards, and a cavalry regiment, the Blues. By 1685, mainly by the return of regiments from Dunkirk and Tangier, this force was increased by five regiments of foot and one of dragoons. The government's income was fixed at £1,200,000, but the sources allocated did not produce that amount, and the government was involved from the start in pecuniary difficulties for which it was not responsible.

The restoration of the church was slower. Charles was pledged to toleration, and plans for comprehension were put forward. The Convention was dissolved in Dec. 1660 without settling anything, and the Savoy conference between Anglicans and Presbyterians, proved sterile. Charles was crowned on April 23, 1661, and a new parliament met on May 8; as it sat until 1679 it is called the Long Parliament of the Restoration, and sometimes the Cavalier or the Pensionary parliament. It contained at the start, and until by-elections gradually changed its character, an overwhelming royalist and Anglican majority, and Charles and the earl of Clarendon could not restrain it on religious questions. The bishops returned to the upper house on Nov. 20, 1661. On May 19, 1662, the Act of Uniformity was passed, enjoining the use of the Book of Common Prayer, which had been specially revised, and included new services of Jan. 30 and May 29 (the dates of the execution of Charles I and the Restoration); as a result about 1,200 of the clergy, who refused to conform, left their livings on St. Bartholomew's day (Aug. 24); another 800 had already been ejected. The Presbyterians had hitherto tried to gain control of the national church while remaining within it. Now those among them who did not conform were driven to take up a position definitely outside it and, together with the various independent sects, came to be known as Nonconformists or Dissenters. Charles tried to relieve them and the Roman Catholics by a declaration of indulgence issued on Dec. 26, 1662, but it was opposed by Clarendon and by parliament; and a series of acts was passed, including the Conventicle and Five Mile acts, forbidding the Nonconformists their special forms of worship; it is unjustly called the Clarendon code. The Corporation act (1661) drove the Nonconformists from power in the boroughs; the Licensing act (1662), establishing a censorship, and the repeal of the 1641 Triennial act and the passing of a new act, requiring triennial parliaments but providing no machinery for enforcing this requirement if the king failed to observe it, completed the reconstruction of the constitution.

Charles's foreign policy was largely a continuation of Cromwell's, although based on material rather than on religious considerations. Peace was made with Spain, but Jamaica and Dunkirk were retained, and Charles, when he married the Portuguese Catherine of Braganza in 1662, pledged himself to give Portugal military support in its struggle with Spain. The marriage, which brought Bombay and Tangier to England as parts of Catherine's dowry, drew England closer to France; the two countries were further connected by the marriage of Charles's sister, Henrietta Anne, to the duke of Orleans and by the sale of Dunkirk to France. Dunkirk was a costly possession and Charles had neither the money nor the troops to hold it effectively. In 1664 English commercial expansion and minor political differences led to war with the Dutch, formally declared in Feb. 1665. The struggle was indecisive, but England was weakened by the Great Plague in 1665, and the Fire of London in 1666. Financial exhaustion led to negotiations, and in 1667 the Dutch, by burning the English ships in the Medway, enforced the conclusion of the peace of Breda. Both sides kept their conquests, England obtaining New York and New Jersey. Parliament demanded a sacrifice and attacked Clarendon. Charles was annoyed by his opposition to toleration and tired of his lectures on his private misconduct; to the delight of the courtiers and the younger politicians he allowed him to be exiled.

Free from tutelage, Charles determined to follow his own policy. He was very short of money, disliked parliamentary control and believed that he could escape from his difficulties by an alliance with the Catholics and the Dissenters at home and the French abroad; his desire for toleration and his personal inclination toward Catholicism, increased by his knowledge of the attitude of his brother James, duke of York, alike recommended this policy. He also wanted to revenge himself on the Dutch for his humiliation at Chatham. Henceforward he never gave complete confidence to any minister. He now employed Sir Thomas Clifford and the earl of Arlington but allowed the duke of Buckingham some show of power. These three with Lord Ashley and the earl of Lauderdale, formed the notorious Cabal, so-called because the first letters of their names formed that word. It was not a ministry in the modern sense, there being no common policy or joint responsibility. Charles hoped to attain his ends by the support of Louis XIV, who, engaged in promoting his queen's claims to the Spanish succession, was prepared to buy the alliance or the neutrality of England.

The Triple Alliance, formed in 1668 between England, Holland and Sweden, appeared for a time to threaten Louis's projects. It was extremely popular in England, but Charles excused his share in it to Louis, whom it infuriated against the Dutch. In 1669 Charles declared to the French ambassador his desire to be reconciled to Rome, and through the duchess of Orleans negotiated with Louis the secret treaty of Dover, signed on May 22, 1670. Charles was to declare himself a Catholic when the time seemed ripe; in view of possible disturbances Louis was to pay him rather more than £150,000 and to provide 6,000 men; thereafter France and England were to join in a war against the Dutch. (*See* Dover, Treaty of.) Only Clifford and Arlington among the ministers signed this treaty; in Dec. 1670 the whole Cabal signed a feigned treaty, which omitted the conversion clauses. Charles was easily led to postpone them; what importance he attached to them cannot be determined. In 1671 Louis sent Louise de Kéroualle, later duchess of Portsmouth, to England to become Charles's mistress.

The war against the Dutch began in 1672; at the same time, to win support, Charles issued the Declaration of Indulgence, suspending the penal laws, and postponed all payments of assignations on the revenue; this was the "Stop of the Exchequer," affecting the London bankers. The war, although it established British commercial and naval supremacy, was unpopular. In 1673 parliament forced Charles to cancel the Declaration of Indulgence and to pass the Test act, which drove Catholics, including Clifford and James, from office. In 1674 Charles was obliged to make peace with the Dutch.

The earl of Danby (Sir Thomas Osborne, later duke of Leeds) succeeded the Cabal. His policy, based on the alliance of church and crown, was calculated to detach from the opposition the loyalists driven to it by hatred of the Cabal; by patronage and corruption he increased their number and formed a strong "Court party" in parliament. Ashley, now earl of Shaftesbury, led the opposition "Country party" to which the by-elections furnished recruits. It was generally predominant, but French subsidies enabled Charles to resist it. Danby was obliged to concur in this, but tried to direct foreign policy along more popular lines, and in Nov. 1677 brought about the marriage of James's daughter, Mary, with William of Orange (afterward William III and Mary II). Charles turned against Louis who, not without bribery, persuaded the Country party to refuse supplies for the army and then made the Peace of Nijmegen with the Dutch.

Hatred of the Cabal and distrust of Charles had prepared the way for Titus Oates, who, in Aug. 1678 denounced an intended rising of the Catholics. This, the "popish plot," was almost entirely fictitious, as Charles readily discovered, but it received apparent confirmation from Edward Coleman's letters and the death of Sir Edmund Berry Godfrey (*q.v.*). Shaftesbury promoted the ensuing general panic. Charles let the agitation take its course, intervening only when Oates accused the queen; between 1678 and 1681 some 35 victims were executed, although Charles knew most of them to be innocent of the charges brought against them. He now realized the importance of the unhesitating support of the church. He dissolved parliament in Jan. 1679 to save Danby from impeachment, after the revelation by Montague of that minister's acquiescence in the financial dealings with Louis XIV. The Licensing act lapsed immediately, resulting in a flood of pamphlets and newspapers. James was sent abroad; an experimental reform of the council failed; the new parliament had to be dissolved within a few months. The exclusion of James from the succession to the throne was now proposed; his place was to be taken by the duke of Monmouth, Charles's eldest illegitimate son. A new parliament met in Oct. 1680; the Exclusion bill passed the commons, but was defeated in the lords by the genius of George Savile, marquess of Halifax. The commons refused to consider the alternative plan, which Charles was prepared to accept, of limiting the powers of a Catholic successor. In March 1681 a new parliament met at Oxford, where the London mob could not dominate it, but as the Exclusion bill was introduced immediately, it was dissolved after sitting for one week only. Henceforward Charles governed without parliaments.

It was at this time that the terms Whig and Tory emerged as party names for the supporters and opponents of the Exclusion bill. Charles began to attack the Whigs and had their leader, Shaftesbury, indicted for high treason, but the London grand jury threw out the charge. A writ of *quo warranto* brought against London compelled it to surrender its charter, whereupon a general attack was made on the municipal charters throughout the kingdom. The new charters gave the Tories control over the appointment of municipal officers and the return of the borough members. James returned to England. Some of the defeated Whigs formed the Rye House plot in 1683; its discovery led to the execution of Lord William Russell, earl of Essex, and Algernon Sidney. The Tory reaction had now reached its climax, but Charles was not yet prepared to face another parliament. As a result shortage of income compelled him, in spite of subsidies from Louis XIV, to abandon Tangier (1683) and to allow the navy to decay; meanwhile he could only watch the increase of French power, including the seizure of Strasbourg. He may have been considering a change of policy when he was taken seriously ill on Feb. 2, 1685. He made a profession of the Catholic faith, received the sacrament and died on Feb. 6.

In appearance Charles was tall and dark; besides numerous portraits there is a wax effigy, taken from the corpse, in Westminster abbey. He was active, walked rapidly and was an excellent horseman; he loved all outdoor sports, but was happiest at sea. He was a keen patron of the turf and rode well. He had an excellent constitution, was careful about his diet and rarely drank to excess. His manners were excellent; he was affable and easy, but too good-natured to be able to refuse requests. His wit was more suitable for a private gentleman than for a king, but was free from malice. His fits of anger were rare and brief. His memory was excellent. His gaiety, good nature and freedom from pretense made him generally popular. His notorious lasciviousness contained no "seraphic" element; he accepted the mistresses chosen for him. The sums he spent on them did not seriously embarrass his finances, but made it difficult for him to ask parliament for money for other purposes.

He had no legitimate children; the most important of his many illegitimate children were: by Lucy Walter, James Scott, duke of Monmouth and Buccleuch (1649–1685); by Lady Castlemaine (later duchess of Cleveland), Charles, Henry and George Fitzroy, dukes of Southampton, Grafton and Northumberland; by the duchess of Portsmouth, Charles Lennox, duke of Richmond; by Nell Gwyn, Charles Beauclerk, duke of St. Albans; by Catherine Peg, Charles FitzCharles, earl of Plymouth.

Charles once said that "he was no atheist, but he could not think God would make a man miserable only for taking a little pleasure out of the way." He inclined toward Roman Catholicism, partly on political grounds, but Halifax, perhaps reflecting Charles's own view, thought that creed most compatible with his lax morality. The date of his change of belief is uncertain, but he was not reconciled to Rome until his deathbed, and attended Anglican services regularly during his life. He was a good judge of sermons and did not object to remonstrances so long as he was not expected to reform and they were in good taste. His desire for toleration was based not on principle, but on indifference and good nature and the memory of his promises. Charles was interested in science, had his own laboratory, and gave the Royal society its charter. He encouraged applied science especially when it concerned navigation; his knowledge of naval architecture was praised by Samuel Pepys, but was considered by most contemporaries to be greater than his rank permitted. He patronized the theatre and enjoyed the lighter forms of literature.

The reign was politically sterile because Charles's achievements were undone and his foreign policy reversed by the revolution of 1688; but the transfer of power from the crown to the house of commons went on steadily during the existence of the Long Parliament of the Restoration. It was a time of administrative progress, notably in the navy and in the treasury system, and between 1660 and 1688 the administration of the old colonial empire reached its highest point of efficiency. Charles himself contributed by his interest in naval, commercial and colonial expansion, but sacrificed these objects too easily to his personal and dynastic policy. Attempts to vindicate the latter have not been wholly successful, for much of his conduct admits no justification. He was too lazy and fond of pleasure to apply himself steadily to business, but energetic on occasion and always intelligent. Charles Halifax notes his powers of dissimulation. He was unwilling to face prolonged opposition, being determined "not to go on his travels again." He was selfish and callous but not vindictive. During the reign there was great material and intellectual progress and some improvement in manners.

Writers who denounce the morals of the age rely too much on Pepys and Philibert Gramont. The tendency has been to judge the country at large by Charles's characteristics, and to dwell on his vices without considering his gifts. Closer study modified many of the older verdicts.

Bibliography.—O. Airy, *Charles II* (London, 1904); A. Bryant, *King Charles II* (London, 1931); D. Ogg, *England in the Reign of Charles II*, 2 vol. (Oxford, 1934); G. N. Clark, *The Later Stuarts, 1660–1714*, (Oxford, 1934). (X.; R. B. Wm.)

CHARLES I AND II, kings of France. By the French, Charles the Great, Roman emperor and king of the Franks, is reckoned the first of the series of French kings named Charles (*see* Charles the Great).

Similarly the emperor Charles II the Bald (*q.v.*) is reckoned as Charles II of France. In some enumerations the emperor Charles III the Fat (*q.v.*) is reckoned as Charles II of France, Charlemagne not being included in the list and Charles the Bald being styled Charles I.

CHARLES III, The Simple (879–929), king of France, was a posthumous son of Louis the Stammerer and of his second wife Adelaide. On the deposition of Charles the Fat in 887 he was excluded from the throne because of his youth; but during the reign of Odo, who had succeeded Charles, he gained the recognition of a certain number of notables and was crowned at Reims by Archbishop Fulk (*q.v.*) on Jan. 28, 893. He now got some support from the emperor Arnulf; and Odo ceded part of Neustria to him. When Odo died (Jan. 1, 898), he obtained possession of the whole kingdom. His most important act was the treaty of Saint Clair-sur-Epte with the Normans in 911. Some of them were baptized; the kernel of the duchy of Normandy (*q.v.*) was ceded to them; but the story of the marriage of their chief Rollo with the king's sister Gisela, related by the chronicler Dudo of Saint Quentin, is very doubtful. The same year Charles, on the invitation of the barons, took possession of the kingdom of Lotharingia. But the Neustrian barons, jealous of the growth of the royal authority and discontented with the favour shown by the king to his counsellor Hagano, rebelled and in 922 elected Robert, brother of King Odo, in place of Charles. Robert was killed in the battle of Soissons (923), but the victory remained with his party, who elected Rudolph, duke of Burgundy, king. In his extremity Charles trusted himself to Herbert, count of Vermandois, who deceived him and imprisoned him at Château-Thierry and afterward at Péronne, where he died on Oct. 7, 929. In 907 he had married Frederona, sister of Bovo, bishop of Châlons. After her death he married Eadgifu (Odgiva), daughter of Edward the Elder, king of the English, who was the mother of Louis IV.

See A. Eckel, *Charles le Simple* (Paris, 1899).

CHARLES IV (1294–1328), king of France, called THE FAIR, third and youngest son of Philip IV, received La Marche from his father as an appanage in 1311 (it was raised to the rank of *comté-pairie* in 1316). When his brother Philip V died on Jan. 2, 1322, leaving one daughter and a widow with child (another daughter), Charles acted on the precedent established by Philip in 1316 and took the crown without difficulty, leaving to his two nieces only their mother's dowry, the county of Burgundy.

The most important fact of his reign was the renewal of war with England. In 1323 Charles ordered the building of a castle at Saint Sardos, a small village of Agenais, depending on the priory of Sarlat, his direct vassal, with which he had concluded a treaty of *pariage*. The seneschal of Guienne thought this a usurpation of his English master's rights, stormed the town and hanged a number of Charles's officers. Thereupon, on July 1, 1324, Charles pronounced the confiscation of Aquitaine and Ponthieu, alleging also that Edward II had made no homage.

A French army occupied all Aquitaine, except Bordeaux, Bayonne and Saint Sever. In March 1325 Edward sent his wife Isabella (Charles's sister) to Paris to negotiate; and, as Edward did not wish to go to France to do homage, she obtained (Sept. 1325) that Aquitaine and Ponthieu should go to her son Edward, who would make homage. But Charles claimed to keep Agenais and La Réole, and Edward II rejected the arrangement. Aquitaine and Ponthieu were again confiscated, and the overthrow of Edward II prevented any English resistance. On March 31, 1327, Isabella, now regent of England, signed a treaty by which her son recovered his fief, less Agenais and Bazadais.

This renewal of the war made serious financial difficulties for Charles, who had to put civil offices up for auction, to increase duties on trade and to make the salaries of the magistrates dependent on the exaction of heavy fines.

On the pretext of a crusade to free Armenia from the Turks, he obtained from the pope a tithe levied on the clergy, which he kept for his own use. As his predecessors had done, he confiscated the property of the Lombard bankers. He summoned a number of assemblies to obtain support for these measures and to try again to reform the coinage, but they were held only locally, in *bailliages* and *sénéchaussées*. In 1326, he was satisfied with a meeting of prelates and barons in Meaux, which accepted the principle of a subsidy for the war.

Charles died at Vincennes on Feb. 1, 1328. He had been married three times, first to Blanche of Burgundy, who in May 1314 was convicted of adultery, then to Mary of Luxembourg (d. 1324) and thirdly to Joan of Évreux. He left one daughter by Mary; and his widow was with child.

See R. Fawtier, *L'Europe occidentale de 1270 à 1328* (Paris, 1940); J. Viard, ed., *Journaux du trésor de Charles IV le Bel* (Paris, 1917). (F. CT.)

CHARLES V (1337–1380), king of France, called THE WISE, was born at the château of Vincennes, on Jan. 21, 1337, the son of John II and Bona of Luxembourg. In 1349 he became dauphin of the Viennois by purchase from Humbert II and in 1355 he was created duke of Normandy. After the battle of Poitiers (1356) where his father was taken prisoner by the English, he arranged for the government of Normandy and proceeded to Paris, where he took the title of lieutenant of the kingdom. During the years of John II's imprisonment in England, Charles assumed the government of France. He summoned the states general of northern France (*Langue d'Oïl*) to Paris in Oct. 1356 to obtain men and money to carry on the war. But under the leadership of Étienne Marcel, provost of the Parisian merchants and president of the third estate, and Robert le Coq, bishop of Laon, president of the clergy and a partisan of Charles II of Navarre, the states refused any aid except on conditions which Charles declined to accept. They demanded the dismissal of a number of the royal ministers; the establishment of a commission elected from the three estates to regulate the dauphin's administration and of another board to act as council of war; also the release of Charles of Navarre, who had been imprisoned by King John. The estates of Languedoc, summoned to Toulouse, also made protests against misgovernment, but they agreed to raise a war levy on terms to which the dauphin acceded. Charles sought the alliance of his uncle, the emperor Charles IV, to whom he did homage at Metz as dauphin of the Viennois, and he was also made imperial vicar of Dauphiné, thus acknowledging the imperial jurisdiction. But he gained small material advantage from these proceedings. The states general were again convoked in Feb. 1357. Their demands were more moderate than in the preceding year, but they nominated members to replace certain obnoxious persons on the royal council and demanded the right to assemble without the royal summons and certain administrative reforms. In return they promised to raise and finance an army of 30,000 men, but the money—a tithe levied on the annual revenues of the clergy and nobility—voted for this object was not to pass through the dauphin's hands. Charles had to yield and issued an ordinance of reform (March 3), but the agreement was annulled by letters from King John, who announced at the same time the conclusion of a two years' truce. Charles had tried to escape from the power of the reformers by leaving Paris, but he returned for a new meeting of the estates in the autumn of 1357.

Meanwhile, Charles of Navarre had been released by his partisans and, allying himself with Étienne Marcel, had become a popular hero in Paris. The dauphin was obliged to receive him and to undergo an apparent reconciliation. In Paris Marcel was supreme. He forced his way into the dauphin's palace (Feb. 22, 1358), and Charles's servants, Jean de Conflans, marshal of Champagne, and Robert de Clermont, marshal of Normandy, were murdered before his eyes. Charles was powerless against Marcel, who compelled him to take the title of regent to prevent the possibility of further intervention from King John. But he fled from Paris on March 28, obtained from the provincial assemblies the money refused him by the states general and blockaded the capital by the seizure of Meaux and Montereau. Charles of Navarre, now in league with the English and master of lower Normandy and of the approaches to Paris, returned to the immediate neighbourhood of the city, and Marcel found himself driven to avowed cooperation with the dauphin's enemies, the English and the Navarrese. In defiance of a recent ordinance prohibiting provincial assemblies, Charles presided over the estates of Picardy and Artois and then over those of Champagne. The states general of 1358 summoned to Compiègne instead of Paris, granted a large aid.

The condition of northern France was rendered more desperate by the outbreak (May–June 1358) of the peasant revolt known as the Jacquerie, which was repressed with a ferocity far exceeding the excesses of the rebels. Within the walls of Paris, Jean Maillart had formed a royalist party; Marcel was assassinated (July 31, 1358), and the dauphin entered Paris two days later. A reaction in Charles's favour had set in, and the estates of 1359 supported him in repudiating the treaty of London (1359), which King John had signed in anxiety for his personal freedom, and voted money unconditionally for the continuation of the war.

From this time the estates were only once convoked by Charles, who thenceforward professed to summon the assembly of notables or provincial bodies. Charles of Navarre was induced to end his war with the regent. But Edward III landed at Calais in October; and a great part of the country was exposed to depredations from the English troops. In the scarcity of money Charles had recourse to the debasement of the coinage, which suffered no less than 22 variations in the two years before the treaty of Brétigny. This disastrous financial expedient was made good later, the coinage being established on a firm basis during the 16 years of Charles's reign in accordance with the principles of Nicolas Oresme. On the conclusion of peace, King John was restored to France, but being unable to raise his ransom, he returned in 1364 to England, where he died in April, leaving the crown to Charles, who was crowned at Reims on May 19.

The new king found an able servant in Bertrand du Guesclin, who won a victory over the Navarrese troops at Cocherel and took prisoner their best general, Jean de Grailly, captal de Buch. The establishment of Charles's brother, Philip the Bold, in the duchy of Burgundy, though it constituted in the event a serious menace to the monarchy, put an end to the king of Navarre's ambitions in that direction. A treaty of peace between the two kings was signed in 1365, by which Charles of Navarre gave up Mantes, Meulan and the county of Longueville in exchange for Montpellier. Negotiations were renewed in 1370, and Charles of Navarre did homage for his French possessions, though he was then considering a new alliance with Edward III. Du Guesclin undertook to free France from the depredations of the "free companies," mercenary soldiers put out of employment by the cessation of the war. An attempt to send them on a crusade against the Turks failed, and Du Guesclin led them to Spain to put Henry of Trastamara on the throne of Castile. By the marriage of Philip the Bold with Margaret of Flanders, Charles detached the Flemings from the English alliance. Then as soon as he had restored something like order in the internal affairs of the kingdom, he provoked a quarrel with the English.

The text of the treaty of Brétigny presented technical difficulties of which Charles availed himself. The English power in Guienne was weakened by the disastrous Spanish expedition of the Black Prince, Edward, prince of Wales, whom Charles summoned before the *parlement* of Paris in Jan. 1369 to answer the charges preferred against him by his subjects, thus expressly repudiating the English sovereignty in Guienne. The Black Prince failed to obey. War was renewed at once on the Gascon frontier. Between 1371 and 1373 Poitou and Saintonge were reconquered by Du Guesclin, and soon the English had to abandon all their territory north of the Garonne. John IV of Brittany (Jean de Montfort) had won his duchy with English help by the defeat of Charles of Blois, the French nominee, at Auray in 1364. His sympathies remained English, and he was obliged to take refuge in England (1373) and later in Flanders, while the English only retained a footing in two or three coast towns. Charles restrained his armies from fighting an uneven pitched battle with the English; they contented themselves with defensive and guerrilla tactics. The towns were defended, and the English left to do as they would in the countryside. There they could not maintain themselves; they gradually retreated until in 1380 only Bayonne, Bordeaux, Brest, Cherbourg and Calais were still in English hands.

Charles alleged in 1378 that he had proof of Charles of Navarre's treasonable designs. He seized the Norman towns held by the Navarrese, while Henry of Trastamara invaded Navarre. The conditions of peace that he imposed rendered his lifelong enemy at last powerless. A premature attempt to annex the duchy of Brittany to the royal domain failed. Charles summoned the duke to Paris in 1378 and on his nonappearance committed one of his rare errors of policy by confiscating his duchy. But the Bretons rose to defend their independence and recalled their duke. The matter was still unsettled when Charles, whose health had always been delicate, died at Vincennes on Sept. 16, 1380. His wife, Joan of Bourbon, had died in 1378, and the succession devolved on their elder son Charles, a boy of 12. Their younger son was Louis, later duke of Orléans.

Personally Charles was no soldier. He owed the signal successes of his reign partly to his skilful choice of advisers and administrators, to his chancellors Jean and Guillaume de Dormans and Pierre d'Orgemont, to Hugues Aubriot, provost of Paris, Bureau de la Rivière and others; partly to a singular coolness and subtlety in the exercise of a not overscrupulous diplomacy, which made him a dangerous enemy. He had learned prudence and self-restraint in the troubled times of the regency, and did not lose his moderation in success. He modelled his private life on that of his predecessor St. Louis, but was no fanatic in religion, for he refused his support to the violent methods of the Inquisition in southern France and allowed the Jews to return to the country, at the same time confirming their privileges. His support of the schismatic pope Clement VII at Avignon although apparently sincere, was a major political blunder.

Charles V was a student of astrology, medicine, law and philosophy and collected a large and valuable library at the Louvre, which became the nucleus of the great Bibliothèque Royale. He gathered round him a group of distinguished writers and thinkers, among whom were Raoul de Presles, Philippe de Mézières, Nicolas Oresme and others. The ideas of these men were applied by him to the practical work of administration, though he confined himself chiefly to the consolidation and improvement of existing institutions. The power of the nobility was lessened by restrictions which, without prohibiting private wars, made them practically impossible. The feudal fortresses were regularly inspected by the central authority, many of them were demolished on the pretext that they might serve as vantage points for the English invaders, and the nobles themselves became in many cases paid officers of the king. The feudal nobility was further weakened by the accession to the *noblesse* of many townsmen. The indirect taxes imposed in 1360 to provide for the ransom of his father and the direct taxes decreed for the war against the companies in 1363 were levied throughout his reign.

The system of royal commissioners for the collection of the revenues took shape, with *élus* in the districts and a board of "general councillors" at the head. Charles's military reforms were intended to restore discipline and to provide for the regular pay of the soldiers and for the levying of archers from among the peasantry. After 1372 he established a strong navy, which under Jean de Vienne threatened the English coast between 1377 and 1380. A special reserve fund was instituted for financing the war, and taxation became heavier, since Charles set no limits to the gratification of his tastes in the collection of jewels, precious objects and books or of his love of building, examples of which are the renovation of the Louvre and the erection of the palace of Saint Paul in Paris. Charles, in spite of his merits, was not popular, and revolts of discontented taxpayers, especially in the south, broke out during the last months of his reign.

BIBLIOGRAPHY.—Jean Froissart, *Chronicles of England, France, Spain, etc.*, Eng. trans. by Lord Berners, ed. by W. P. Ker (London, 1901); *Grandes chroniques de France*, 4 vol., ed. by R. Delachenal (Paris, 1910–20); Christine de Pisan, *Le Livre des faits et bonnes moeurs du sage roy Charles V*, ed. by S. Solente, 2 vol. (Paris, 1936–40); L. V. Delisle, *Mandements et actes divers de Charles V* (Paris, 1874); J. J. Champollion-Figeac, *Lettres de rois . . . depuis Louis VII jusqu'à Henri IV*, pp. 167 ff., vol. ii (Paris, 1839); the anonymous *Songe du vergier* or *Somnium viridarii*, written in 1376, and giving the political ideas of Charles V and his advisers; R. Delachenal, *Histoire de Charles V*, 5 vol. (1908–31).

CHARLES VI (1368–1422), king of France, son of Charles V and Joan of Bourbon, was born in Paris on Dec. 3, 1368. He received the appanage of Dauphiné at his birth and was thus the first of the princes of France to bear the title of dauphin from infancy. Charles V entrusted his education to Philippe de Mézières and fixed his majority at 14. He succeeded to the throne in 1380 at the age of 12, and the government was divided between his paternal uncles, Louis, duke of Anjou, John, duke of Berry, Philip the Bold, duke of Burgundy, and his mother's brother, Louis II, duke of Bourbon. Considerable discontent existed in the south of France at the time of the death of Charles V, and when the duke of Anjou reimposed certain taxes which the late king had remitted at the end of his reign there were revolts at Puy and Montpellier. Paris, Rouen, the cities of Flanders, with Amiens, Orléans, Reims and other French towns, also rose (1382) in revolt against taxation. Charles VI marched to the help of the count of Flanders against the insurgents headed by Philip van Artevelde and gained a complete victory at Roosebeke (Nov. 27, 1382). Strengthened by this success the king, on his return to Paris in the following January, exacted vengeance on the citizens by fines, executions and the suppression of the privileges of the city. The help sent by the English to the Flemish cities resulted in a second Flemish campaign. In 1385 Jean de Vienne made an unsuccessful descent on the Scottish coast, and Charles equipped a fleet at Sluys for the invasion of England; but a series of delays ended in the destruction of the ships by the English.

In 1385 Charles married Isabella (*q.v.;* otherwise Elizabeth, or Isabeau), daughter of Stephen II, duke of Bavaria. Three years later, with the help of his brother, Louis, duke of Touraine (later duke of Orléans), he threw off the tutelage of his uncles, whom he replaced by Bureau de la Rivière and others among his father's counsellors, nicknamed by the royal princes the *marmousets* because of their humble origin. Two years later he deprived the duke of Berry of the government of Languedoc. The opening years of Charles VI's effective rule promised well, but excess in gaiety of all kinds undermined his constitution, and in Aug. 1392 he had an attack of madness at Le Mans, when on his way to Brittany to force from John V the surrender of his cousin Pierre de Craon, who had tried to assassinate the constable Olivier de Clisson in the streets of Paris. Other attacks followed, and it became evident that Charles was unable permanently to sustain the royal authority. Clisson, Bureau de la Rivière, Jean Le Mercier and the other *marmousets* were driven from office, and the royal dukes regained their power. The rivalries between the most powerful of these (the duke of Burgundy, who during the king's attacks of madness practically ruled the country, and the duke of Orléans) were a constant menace to order.

In 1396 peace with England seemed assured by the marriage of Richard II with Charles's daughter Isabella, but the Lancastrian revolution of 1399 destroyed the diplomatic advantages gained by this union. In France the country was disturbed by the papal schism. At an assembly of the clergy held in Paris in 1398 it was resolved to refuse to recognize the authority of Benedict XIII, who succeeded Clement VII as schismatic pope at Avignon. The question became a party one; Benedict was supported by Louis of Orléans, while Philip the Bold and Paris university opposed him. Obedience to Benedict's authority was resumed in 1403, only to be withdrawn again in 1408, when the king declared himself the guardian and protector of the French church, which was indeed for a time self-governing. Edicts further extending the royal power in ecclesiastical affairs were even issued in 1418, after the schism was at an end.

The king's intelligence became yearly feebler, and in 1404 on the death of Philip the Bold the influence of the duke of Orléans increased. Queen Isabella, who had generally supported the Burgundian party, was now practically separated from her husband and was replaced by a young Burgundian lady, Odette de Champdivers. Isabella was freely accused of intrigue with the duke of Orléans. The relations between John the Fearless of Burgundy and the duke of Orléans became more embittered, and on Nov. 23, 1407, Orléans was murdered in the streets of Paris at the instigation of his rival. In vain did the king, in his rare moments of sanity, try to reconcile the factions by the peace of Chartres in 1409. The young duke Charles of Orléans formed alliances with the dukes of Berry, Bourbon and Brittany and others constituting the party known as the Armagnacs (*see* ARMAGNAC) against the Burgundians, who had gained the upper hand in the royal council. In 1411 John the Fearless contracted an alliance with Henry IV of England, and civil war began in the autumn, but in 1412 the Armagnacs in their turn sought English aid and, by promising the sovereignty of Aquitaine to the English king, gave John the opportunity of posing as defender of France. In Paris the Burgundians were hand in hand with the corporation of the butchers, who were the leaders of the Parisian populace. The malcontents, who took their name from one of their number, Simon Caboche, penetrated into the palace of the dauphin Louis and demanded the surrender of the unpopular members of his household. A royal ordinance, promising reforms in administration, was promulgated on May 27, 1413, and some of the royal advisers were executed. The king and the dauphin, powerless in the hands of Duke John and the Parisians, appealed secretly to the Armagnac princes, who entered Paris in September. As a result the ordinance extracted by the Cabochiens was rescinded, and many of the insurgents were banished from the city.

In the next year Henry V of England, after concluding an alliance with Burgundy, resumed the pretensions of Edward III to the crown of France, and in 1415 followed the disastrous battle of Agincourt. The two elder sons of Charles VI, the dauphin Louis, duke of Guienne, and John, duke of Touraine, died in 1415 and 1417, and Charles, count of Ponthieu, became heir apparent. Paris was governed by Bernard of Armagnac, constable of France, who expelled all suspected of Burgundian sympathies and treated Paris like a conquered city. Queen Isabella was imprisoned at Tours, but escaped to Burgundy. The capture of Paris by the Burgundians on May 29, 1418, was followed by a series of horrible massacres of the Armagnacs; and in July, Duke John and Isabella, who assumed the title of regent, entered Paris. Meanwhile Henry V had completed the conquest of Normandy. The murder of John the Fearless in 1419 under the eyes of the dauphin Charles threw the Burgundians definitely into the arms of the English, and his successor Philip the Good, in concert with Queen Isabella, concluded (1420) the treaty of Troyes with Henry V, who became regent of France. Charles VI had long been of no account in the government, and the state of neglect in which he existed at Senlis induced Henry V to undertake the reorganization of his household. He went to Paris in Sept. 1422 and died on Oct. 21.

BIBLIOGRAPHY.—The chief authorities for the reign of Charles VI are: *Chronica Caroli VI,* written by a monk of Saint Denis, commissioned officially to write the history of his time, ed. by L. F. Bellaguet with a French trans. 6 vol. (1839–52); Jean Juvénal des Ursins, *Chronique de Charles VI,* printed by D. Godefroy in *Histoire de Charles VI* (Paris, 1653), chiefly an abridgment of the monk of St. Denis's narrative; a fragment of the *Grandes Chroniques de Saint Denis* covering the years 1381–83 ed. J. Pichon (1864); correspondence printed by J. J. Champollion-Figeac in *Lettres de rois,* vol. ii (Paris, 1839); Société de l'Histoire de France, *Choix de pièces inédites rel. au règne de Charles VI,* 2 vol. ed. by L. Douët d'Arcq (Paris, 1863–64); J. Froissart, *Chroniques;* Enguerrand de Monstrelet, *Chroniques,* covering the first half of the 15th century, Eng. trans., 4 vol. (1809); *Chronique des quatre premiers Valois,* by an unknown author, ed. S. Luce (Paris, 1862). *See* also A. Coville, in E. Lavisse, *Histoire de France,* iv, 267 ff. (Paris, 1902); E. Petit, "Séjours de Charles VI" *Bull. du com. des travaux hist.* (Paris, 1893); L. Mirot, *Les Insurrections urbaines au début du règne de Charles VI* (Paris, 1906); M. Thibault, *Isabeau de Bavière, reine de France: la jeunesse* (Paris, 1903); F. D. S. Darwin, *Louis d'Orléans* (London, 1936); J. d'Avout, *La Querelle des Armagnacs et des Bourguignons* (Paris, 1943).

CHARLES VII (1403–1461), king of France, fifth son of Charles VI and Isabella of Bavaria, was born in Paris on Feb. 22, 1403. The count of Ponthieu, as he was called in his boyhood, was betrothed in 1413 to Mary of Anjou, daughter of Louis II, duke of Anjou and king of Sicily, and spent the next two years at the Angevin court. He received the duchy of Touraine in 1416 and became dauphin (on his brother John's death) and lieutenant-general of the kingdom in 1417 and regent in Dec. 1418; but his authority in northern France was paralyzed in 1419 by the murder of John the Fearless, duke of Burgundy, in his presence at Montereau. Although the deed was apparently not premeditated, as the English and Burgundians declared, it ruined Charles's cause for the time. He was disinherited by the treaty of Troyes in 1420 and at the time of his father's death in 1422 had retired to Méhun-sur-Yèvre, near Bourges, which had been the nominal seat of government since 1418. He was recognized as king in Touraine, Berry and Poitou, in Languedoc and other provinces of southern France; but the English power in the north was presently increased by the provinces of Champagne and Maine, as the result of the victories of Cravant (1423) and Verneuil (1424). The Armagnac administrators who had been driven out of Paris by the duke of Bedford gathered round the young king, nicknamed the "king of Bourges"; but he was weak in body and mind and was under the domination of Jean Louvet and Tanguy du Chastel, the instigators of the murder of John the Fearless, and other discredited partisans. The power of these favourites was shaken by the influence of the queen's mother, Yolande of Aragon, duchess of Anjou. She sought the alliance of John V, duke of Brittany, who, however, vacillated throughout his life between the English and French alliance, concerned chiefly to maintain the independence of his duchy. His brother, Arthur of Brittany, earl of Richmond (comte de Richemont), was reconciled with the king and became constable in 1425, with the avowed intention of making peace between Charles and the duke of Burgundy. Richemont caused the assassination of Charles's favourites Pierre de Giac and Le Camus de Beaulieu and imposed one of his own choosing, Georges de la Trémoïlle, an adventurer who rapidly usurped the constable's power. For five years (1427–32) a private war between these two exhausted the Armagnac forces, and central France returned to anarchy.

Meanwhile Bedford had established settled government throughout the north of France, and in 1428 he advanced to the siege of Orléans. For the movement which was to lead to the deliverance of France from the English invaders, *see* JOAN OF ARC. The siege of Orléans was raised by her efforts on May 8, 1429, and two months later Charles VII was crowned at Reims. But the court put every difficulty in the way of her military career, and received the news of her capture before Compiègne (1430) with indifference. No measures were taken for her deliverance or her ransom, and Normandy and the Ile de France remained in English hands. Fifteen years of anarchy and civil war intervened before peace was restored. The duke of Bedford died in 1435, and in the same year Philip the Good of Burgundy concluded a treaty with Charles at Arras, after fruitless negotiations for an English treaty. From this time Charles's policy was strengthened. La Trémoïlle had been assassinated in 1433 by the constable's orders, with the connivance of Yolande of Aragon. For his former favourites were substituted energetic advisers, his brother-in-law Charles of Anjou, Dunois (the famous bastard of Orléans), Pierre de Brézé, Richemont and others. Richemont entered Paris on April 13, 1436, and in the next five years the finance of the country was restored. Charles himself commanded the troops who captured Pontoise in 1441 and made a successful expedition in the south in 1442. Meanwhile the *Ecorcheurs* plundered the kingdom; the princes of the blood and the great nobles made a formidable league against the crown in 1440 which included Charles I, duke of Bourbon, John II, duke of Alençon, John IV of Armagnac, and the dauphin, afterward Louis XI. The revolt broke out in Poitou in 1440 and was known as the Praguerie. Charles repressed the rising and finally brought over the rebel nobles individually by considerable concessions. In 1444 a truce was concluded with England at Tours, and Charles proceeded to organize a regular army, consisting of cavalry from the nobility (grouped in companies and paid by the king) and of plebeian infantry (the *francs archers*). The central authority was gradually made effective.

Charles collected the *taille* and the *aides* without summoning the estates; and he weakened the *parlement* of Paris and extended the scope of the royal justice by creating *parlements* at Toulouse and at Bordeaux and by maintaining the Normandy exchequer in office. The bailiffs were inspected by commissaries. Insurrections in Normandy and domestic troubles weakened the English in France. The conquest of Normandy was completed by the battle of Formigny (April 15, 1450). Guienne was conquered in 1451 by Dunois, but not subdued, and another expedition was necessary in 1453, when Talbot was defeated and slain at Castillon. Meanwhile in 1450 Charles had resolved on the rehabilitation of Joan of Arc. This was granted in 1456 by the Holy See. The only foothold retained by the English on French ground was Calais. The change which made Charles take an active part in public affairs is said to have been largely due to the influence of Agnes Sorel, who became his mistress in 1444 and died in 1450. Pierre de Brézé, who had had a large share in the repression of the Praguerie, obtained through her a dominating influence over the king. Charles and René of Anjou retired from court, and the greater part of the members of the king's council were drawn from the bourgeois classes, for example Jacques Coeur (*q.v.*). These men revived economic life; ruined peasants were given tax relief, corporations reorganized, the Lyons fairs reestablished, and the coinage restored. It was by the zeal of these councillors that Charles obtained the surname of "The Well-Served."

Charles continued his father's general policy in church matters. He desired to preserve as far as possible the liberties of the Gallican church. With the council of Constance (1414–18) the Great Schism was practically healed. Charles, while careful to protest against its renewal, supported the anti-papal contentions of the French members of the council of Basel (1431–49), and in 1438 he promulgated the Pragmatic Sanction at Bourges, by which the patronage of ecclesiastical benefices was removed from the Holy See, while certain interventions of the royal power were admitted. Bishops and abbots were to be elected, in accordance with ancient custom, by their clergy. After the English had evacuated French territory Charles still had to cope with feudal revolt and with the hostility of the dauphin, who was in open revolt in 1446 and for the next ten years ruled like an independent sovereign in Dauphiné. He took refuge in 1457 with Charles's most formidable enemy, Philip of Burgundy. Charles VII nevertheless found means to prevent Philip from attaining his ambitions in Lorraine and in Germany. But the dauphin succeeded in embarrassing his father's policy at home and abroad, and had his own party in the court.

Charles VII died at Mehun-sur-Yèvre on July 22, 1461. He believed that he was poisoned by his son, who cannot, however, be accused of anything more than an eager expectation of his death.

BIBLIOGRAPHY.—A. Vallet de Viriville, *Histoire de Charles VII roi de France, et de son époque (1403–1461)*, 3 vol. (Paris, 1862–65); G. du Fresne de Beaucourt, *Histoire de Charles VII*, 6 vol. (Paris, 1881–91); N. Valois, *Histoire de la Pragmatique Sanction de Bourges sous Charles VII* (Paris, 1906); G. Dodu, "Le Roi de Bourges," *Revue Historique*, vol. clxix (Paris, 1928); J. d'Avout, *La Querelle des Armagnacs et des Bourguignons* (Paris, 1943); P. Champion and P. de Thoisy, *Bourgogne, France et Angleterre au traité de Troyes, Jean de Thoisy, évêque de Tournai, membre du Conseil du Roi* (Paris, 1943); E. Perroy, *La Guerre de Cent Ans* (Paris, 1945). For a contemporary narrative *see* the *Histoire de Charles VII*, by Thomas Basin, bishop of Lisieux and member of the royal council, ed. by C. Samaran, 2 vol. (Paris, 1933–45).

CHARLES VIII (1470–1498), king of France, was the only son of Louis XI. On the death of Louis in 1483 Charles, a lad of 13, was incapable of governing. Until 1492 he abandoned the government to his sister Anne of Beaujeu, who defended the royal authority against the claims of the states general (1484) and against the blundering agitation known as "la guerre folle." Anne negotiated Charles's marriage with Anne of Brittany in 1491 and thus connected the dukedom with the French crown. Charles, however, dreamed of glory.

Urged by his favourite, Étienne de Vesc, he threw off the yoke of the Beaujeus and their policy. He proposed at first to claim the rights of the house of Anjou, to which Louis XI had succeeded, on the kingdom of Naples and to use this as a steppingstone to Constantinople and to his own coronation as emperor of the east. He sacrificed everything to this policy, signed disastrous treaties with England and Aragon to keep his hands free, and set out in 1494. On May 12, 1495, he entered Naples in great pomp, clothed in the imperial insignia. A general coalition, the League of Venice, was formed against him, however, and he was forced to return to France. He was preparing a fresh expedition when he died as the result of an accident at Amboise on April 8, 1498.

See J. S. C. Bridge, *A History of France from the Death of Louis XI* 2 vol. (Oxford, 1921–24); H. F. Delaborde, *Expédition de Charles VIII en Italie* (Paris, 1888).

CHARLES IX (1550–1574), king of France, was born at Saint Germain-en-Laye, on June 27, 1550, the second son of Henry II and of Catherine de Medici. He became king, under his mother's regency, in 1560, on the death of his brother Francis II. Charles seems to have had some promising qualities as a young man, but his health was poor. Stricken with tuberculosis (as were other members of his family) and subject to hallucinations, with a tendency to mental derangement from his childhood, he finally ruined his constitution by strenuous exercise and undue indulgence in hunting. Proclaimed of age on Aug. 17, 1563, he submitted docilely to his mother's continued authority. To strengthen the prestige of the crown, she took him on a two years' tour of his kingdom; but he really cared little for the business of government, in which he intervened only spasmodically. In 1570 he was married to Elizabeth of Austria, daughter of the Holy Roman emperor Maximilian II. Meanwhile, however, his brother the duke of Anjou (later Henry III of France) had won victories over the Huguenots at Jarnac and at Moncontour, which aroused Charles's jealousy. When Gaspard de Coligny (*q.v.*) came to court, Charles at first received him warmly and seemed to favour his plan for intervention against the Spaniards in the Low Countries. Then Catherine, anxious to avert the dangers of so rash an undertaking, prevailed on him to abandon Coligny: the massacre of St. Bartholomew's day (1572) was the result. This led to a renewal of civil war, during which there could be no question of enterprises in the Low Countries, whatever Charles's ambitions. Moreover, as his health grew worse, his character changed, to become melancholy and morose. He died on May 30, 1574, leaving a bastard son, Charles, count of Auvergne and later duke of Angoulême, by his mistress Marie Touchet. A pupil of the great Jacques Amyot, the king had had a sincere love of literature, writing poems and a work on hunting, *Traité de la chasse royale* (published 1625; new ed. 1858), as well as making himself the patron of the Pléïade and of Jean Antoine de Baïf's academy.

Bibliography.—L. Batiffol, *Le Siècle de la Renaissance* (Paris, 1909; Eng. trans., London, 1916); L. Romier, *Catholiques et Huguenots à la cour de Charles IX* (Paris, 1924); J. Vienot, *Histoire de la Réforme française* (Paris, 1926); the "Collection Clio," *Le XVIe Siècle* (Paris. 1950); and works cited under Catherine de Medici. H. Hauser, *La Prépondérance espagnole* (Paris, 1933), vol. ix in the series *Peuples et civilisations,* gives a bibliography.

CHARLES X (1757–1836), king of France from 1824 to 1830, was the fourth child of the dauphin Louis, son of Louis XV and of Marie Josephe of Saxony. He was known before his accession as Charles Philippe, count of Artois. At the age of 16 he married Marie Thérèse of Savoy, sister-in-law of his brother, the count of Provence (Louis XVIII). His youth was passed in scandalous dissipation, which drew upon himself and his coterie the detestation of the people of Paris.

Although lacking military tastes, he joined the French army at the siege of Gibraltar in 1772, merely for distraction. In a few years he had incurred a debt of 56,000,000 fr., a burden assumed by the impoverished state. Prior to the Revolution he took only a minor part in politics, but when it broke out he soon became, with the queen, the chief of the reactionary party at court.

In July 1789 he left France, became leader of the *émigrés* and visited several courts of Europe in the royalist interest.

After the execution of Louis XVI, he received from his brother, the count of Provence, the title of lieutenant general of the realm and, on the death of Louis XVII, that of monsieur.

In 1795 he attempted to aid the royalist rising of La Vendée, landing at the island of Yeu. But he refused to advance farther and to put himself resolutely at the head of his party, although warmly acclaimed by it. Courage failing him, he returned to England, settling first in London, then in Holyrood palace at Edinburgh and afterward at Hartwell. He remained at Hartwell until 1813, returning to France in Feb. 1814 and entering Paris in April, in the track of the Allies. During the reign of his brother, Louis XVIII, he was the leader of the Ultraroyalists, the party of extreme reaction. On succeeding to the throne in Sept. 1824 he won a passing popularity. But his coronation at Reims, with all the gorgeous ceremonial of the old regime, proclaimed his intention of ruling as the most Christian king, by divine right.

It was soon apparent that the weight of the crown would be consistently thrown into the scale of the reactionary forces. The *émigrés* were awarded a milliard as compensation for their confiscated lands; and Gallicans and Liberals alike were offended by measures which threw increased power into the hands of the Jesuits and Ultramontanes. In a few months there were disquieting signs of the growing unpopularity of the king. The royal princesses were insulted in the streets; and on April 29, 1825, Charles, when reviewing the national guard, was met with cries from the ranks of "Down with the ministers!" His reply was, next day, a decree disbanding the citizen army. In 1829 Charles consented unwillingly to try a policy of compromise. Villèle's successor was the vicomte de Martignac, who took Decazes for his model; and in the speech from the throne Charles declared that the happiness of France depended on "the sincere union of the royal authority with the liberties consecrated by the charter."

But Charles had none of the patience and common sense which had enabled Louis XVIII to play with decency the part of a constitutional king. "I would rather hew wood," he exclaimed, "than be a king under the conditions of the king of England"; and when the Liberal opposition obstructed all the measures proposed by a ministry not selected from the parliamentary majority, he lost patience. "I told you," he said, "that there was no coming to terms with these men." Martignac was dismissed; and Prince Jules de Polignac, the very incarnation of clericalism and reaction, was called to the helm of state.

A formidable agitation sprang up, which only served to make the king more obstinate. In opening the session of 1830 he declared that he would "find the power" to overcome the obstacles placed in his path by "culpable manoeuvres." The reply of the chambers was a protest against "the unjust distrust of the sentiment and reason of France"; whereupon they were first prorogued, and on May 16 dissolved. The result of the new elections was a large increase in the opposition; and Charles, on the advice of his ministers, determined on a virtual suspension of the constitution. On July 26 were issued the famous "four ordinances" which were the immediate cause of the revolution.

With singular fatuity Charles had taken no precautions in view of a violent outbreak. Marshal Marmont, who commanded the scattered troops in Paris, had received no orders, beyond a jesting command from the duke of Angoulême to place them under arms "as some windows might be broken." At the beginning of the revolution Charles was at St. Cloud, whence on the news of the fighting he withdrew first to Versailles and then to Rambouillet.

So little did he understand the seriousness of the situation that, when the laconic message "All is over!" was brought to him, he believed that the insurrection had been suppressed.

On realizing that the revolutionaries had been successful he abdicated in favour of his grandson, the duke of Bordeaux (comte de Chambord), and appointed Louis Philippe, duke of Orléans, lieutenant general of the kingdom (July 30). But, on the news of Louis Philippe's acceptance of the crown, he gave up and began a dignified retreat to the sea coast, followed by his suite and surrounded by the infantry, cavalry and artillery of the guard. Beyond sending a corps of observation to follow his movements, the new government did nothing to arrest his escape.

At Maintenon Charles took leave of the bulk of his troops and, proceeding with an escort of about 1,200 men to Cherbourg, took ship there for England on Aug. 16.

For a time he returned to Holyrood palace at Edinburgh, which was again placed at his disposal. He died at Göritz, where he had gone for his health, on Nov. 6, 1836. The best that can be said of Charles X is that, if he did not know how to rule, he knew how to cease to rule. The dignity of his exit was more worthy of the ancient splendour of the royal house of France than the theatrical humility of Louis Philippe's entrance.

Charles, however, was an impossible monarch for the 19th century or perhaps for any other century. He was, it has been said, a typical Bourbon, unable either to learn or to forget, and the closing years of his life he spent in religious austerities, intended to expiate not his failure to grasp a great opportunity but the comparatively venial excesses of his youth. This, at any rate, represents the general verdict of history. It is interesting, however, to note that the liberal-minded and shrewd critic of men, King Leopold I of the Belgians, formed a different estimate.

In a letter of Nov. 18, 1836, addressed to Princess (afterward Queen) Victoria, Leopold wrote: "History will state that Louis XVIII was a most liberal monarch, reigning with great mildness and justice to his end, but that his brother, from his despotic and harsh disposition, upset all the other had done, and lost the throne. Louis XVIII was a clever, hard-hearted man, shackled by no principle, very proud and false. Charles X an honest man, a kind friend, an honourable master, sincere in his opinions, and inclined to do everything that is right. That teaches us what we ought to believe in history as it is compiled according to ostensible events and results known to the generality of people."

See Alphonse de Lamartine, *Hist. de la restauration* (1851–52); Louis Blanc, *Hist. de dix ans, 1830–1840* (1842–44); G.I. de Montbel, *Dernière Époque de l'hist. de Charles X.*, 5th ed. (1840); Théodore Anne, *Mémoires, souvenirs, et anecdotes sur l'intérieur du palais de Charles X. et les évènements de 1815 à 1830* (1831); *Journal de Saint-Cloud à Cherbourg;* P. Védrenne, *Vie de Charles X.* (1879); Petit, *Charles X.* (1886); P. L. F. Villeneuve, *Charles X. et Louis XIX. en exil Mémoires inédits* (1889); Imbert de Saint-Amand, *La Cour de Charles X.* (1892).

CHARLES I. (1288–1342), king of Hungary, the son of Charles Martell of Naples, and Clemencia, daughter of the emperor Rudolph, was known as Charles Robert before his enthronement as king of Hungary in 1309. He claimed the Hungarian Crown, as the grandson of Stephen V., under the banner of the pope, and was crowned at Esztergom after the death of the last Arpad, Andrew III. (1301), but was forced the same year to surrender the Crown to Wenceslaus II. of Bohemia (1289–1306), who in 1305 transferred his rights to Duke Otto of Bavaria. Duke Otto was taken prisoner by the Hungarians and Charles was enthroned at Budapest on June 15, 1309, though his installation was not regarded as valid till he was crowned with the sacred crown (which was recovered from the robber barons) at Székesfehérvár on Aug. 27, 1310. After three years of warfare Charles at length put down all the elements of rapine and disorder at Rozgony (June 15, 1312). His foreign policy aimed at the aggrandizement of his family, but Hungary also benefited greatly from it. His most successful achievement was the union with Poland for mutual defence against the Habsburgs and the Czechs, which was accomplished by the Convention of Trencsén (1335), confirmed the same year at the brilliant Congress of Visegrád, where all the princes of Central Europe met to compose their differences. The result of the congress was a combined attack by the Magyars and the Poles upon the emperor Louis and his ally Albert of Austria, which was decided in Charles's favour in 1337. Charles wished to unite the kingdoms of Hungary and Naples under his eldest son Louis, but was frustrated by Venice and the pope, who feared that Hungary might become the dominant Adriatic Power. He was, however, compensated for this disappointment by his compact (1339) with his ally and brother-in-law, Casimir of Poland, whereby it was agreed that Louis should succeed to the throne of Poland on the death of the childless Casimir. Charles was a statesman of the first rank, who not only raised Hungary once more to the rank of a great Power, but enriched and civilized her. In character he was pious, courtly and valiant, popular alike with the nobility and the middle classes, whose increasing welfare he did so much to promote, and much beloved by the clergy. His court was famous throughout Europe as a school of chivalry.

Three sons, Louis, Andrew and Stephen survived him. He died on July 16, 1342, and was laid beside the high altar at Székesfehérvár, the ancient burial place of the Arpads.

See Béla Kerékgyartó, *The Hungarian Royal Court under the House of Anjou* (Hung.) (Budapest, 1881); *Rationes Collectorum Pontif. in Hungaria* (Budapest, 1887); *Diplomas of the Angevin Period,* edit. Imre Nagy (Hung. and Lat.) vols. i.–iii. (Budapest, 1878, etc.).

CHARLES I. (1226–1285), king of Naples and Sicily and count of Anjou, was the seventh child of Louis VIII. of France and Blanche of Castile. Louis died a few months after Charles's birth and was succeeded by his son Louis IX. (St. Louis), and on the death in 1232 of the third son, John, count of Anjou and Maine, those fiefs were conferred on Charles. In 1246 he married Beatrice, daughter and heiress of Raymond Bérenger V., the last count of Provence, and after defeating James I. of Aragon and other rivals with the help of his brother, the French king, he took possession of his new county. In 1248 he accompanied Louis in the crusade to Egypt, but on the defeat of the Crusaders he was taken prisoner with his brother. Shortly afterwards he was ransomed, and returned to Provence in 1250. Charles's ambition aimed at wider fields, and he extended his influence by the subjugation of Marseille in 1257, and two years later several communes of Piedmont recognized his suzerainty. In 1262 Pope Urban IV. determined to destroy the power of the Hohenstaufen in Italy, and offered the kingdoms of Naples and Sicily, in consideration of a yearly tribute, to Charles of Anjou. After long negotiations he accepted the Sicilian and Neapolitan crowns, and in 1264 he sent a first expedition of Provençals to Italy; he also collected a large army and navy in Provence and France with the help of King Louis, and by an alliance with the cities of Lombardy was able to send part of his force overland. Pope Clement IV. confirmed the Sicilian agreement on conditions even more favourable to Charles, who sailed in 1265, and conferred on the expedition all the privileges of a crusade. After narrowly escaping capture by Manfred's fleet he reached Rome safely, where he was crowned king of the Two Sicilies. The land army arrived soon afterwards, and on Feb. 26, 1266, Charles encountered his rival Manfred the bastard of the emperor Frederick II., at Benevento (*q.v.*), where after a hard-fought battle Manfred was defeated and killed, and the whole kingdom was soon in Charles's possession. Then Conradin, Frederick's grandson and last legitimate descendant of the Hohenstaufen, came into Italy, where he found many partisans among the Ghibellines of Lombardy and Tuscany, and among Manfred's former adherents in the south. He was totally defeated by Charles at Tagliacozzo (Aug. 23, 1268); taken prisoner, he was tried as a rebel and executed at Naples.

Charles was now one of the most powerful sovereigns of Europe, for besides ruling over Provence and Anjou and the kingdom of the Two Sicilies, he was imperial vicar of Tuscany, lord of many cities of Lombardy and Piedmont, and as the pope's favourite practically arbiter of the papal states, especially during the interregnum between the death of Clement IV. (1268) and the election of Gregory X. (1272). In 1272 he took part with Louis IX. in a crusade to north Africa. The election of Rudolph of Habsburg as German king, and that of Nicholas III. to the Holy See (1277), diminished Charles's power, for the new pope set himself to compose the difference between Guelphs and Ghibellines in the Italian cities, but at his death Charles secured the election of his henchman Martin IV. (1281), who recommenced persecuting the Ghibellines. But the cruelty of the French rulers of Sicily provoked in 1282 the rebellion known as the Sicilian Vespers (*see* VESPERS, SICILIAN). Charles determined to subjugate the island and sailed with his fleet for Messina. The city held out until Peter III. of Aragon arrived in Sicily, and a Sicilian-Catalan fleet under the Calabrese admiral, Roger de Lauria, completely destroyed that of Charles. In May 1284 Roger de Lauria appeared before Naples and destroyed another Angevin fleet commanded by Charles's son, who was taken prisoner. Charles came to Naples with a new fleet from Provence, and was preparing to invade Sicily again, when he died at Foggia on Jan. 7, 1285. An extremely able soldier and a skilful statesman, his inordinate ambition and his cruelty created enemies on all sides, and led to the collapse of the edifice of dominion which he had raised.

CHARLES II. (1250–1309), king of Naples and Sicily, son of Charles I., had been captured by Ruggiero di Lauria in the naval battle at Naples in 1284, and when his father died he was still a prisoner in the hands of Peter of Aragon. In 1288 Charles was liberated on the understanding that he was to retain Naples alone, Sicily being left to the Aragonese, and to induce his cousin Charles of Valois to renounce the kingdom of Aragon given to him by Pope Martin IV. He went to Rieti, where the new pope Nicholas IV. immediately absolved him from all the conditions he had sworn to observe, crowned him king of the Two Sicilies (1289), and excommunicated Alphonso, while Charles of Valois, in alliance with Castile, prepared to take possession of Aragon. Alphonso III., the Aragonese king, being hard pressed, had to promise to withdraw the troops he had sent to help his brother James in Sicily, to renounce all rights over the island, and pay a tribute to the Holy See. But Alphonso died childless in 1291 before the treaty could be carried out, and James took possession of Aragon, leaving the government of Sicily to the third brother Frederick. The new pope Boniface VIII., elected in 1294 at Naples under the auspices of King Charles, mediated between the latter and James, and a most dishonourable treaty was signed. An attempt was made to bribe Frederick into consenting to the arrangement, but being backed up by his people he refused, and was afterward crowned king of Sicily. The ensuing war was fought with great fury and peace was not made until 1302 at Caltabellotta, Charles II giving up all rights to Sicily and agreeing to the marriage of his daughter Leonora to King Frederick; the treaty was ratified by the pope in 1303. Charles died in Aug. 1309, and was succeeded by his son Robert.

BIBLIOGRAPHY.—A. de Saint-Priest, *Histoire de la conquête de Naples par Charles d'Anjou,* 4 vol. (1847–49); S. de Sismondi, in *Histoire des républiques italiennes,* vol. ii. (Brussels, 1838), gives a good general sketch; R. Sternfeld, *Karl von Anjou als Graf von Provence* (1888); Charles's connection with north Italy is dealt with in Merkel's *La Dominazione di Carlo d'Angiò in Piemonte e in Lombardia* (Turin, 1891), while the R. Deputazione di Storia Patria Toscana has recently published a *Codice diplomatico delle relazioni di Carlo d'Angiò con la Toscano;* Durrien, *Archives angevines de Naples* (Toulouse, 1866–1867). M. Amari's *La Guerra del Vespro Siciliano,* 8th ed. (Florence, 1876) is a valuable history, but is prejudiced and should be compared with L. Cadier, *Essai sur l'administration du royaume de Sicile sous Charles I et Charles II d'Anjou* (1891, *Bibl. des écoles françaises d'Athènes et de Rome,* fasc. 59), which contains many documents.

CHARLES II (1332–1387), called THE BAD, king of Navarre and count of Évreux, was a son of Joan of France, queen of Navarre, by her marriage with Philip, count of Évreux. He succeeded his mother in 1349 and married Joan, daughter of John II of France, in 1352. Trouble soon arose between John II and his son-in-law. The promised dowry had not been paid, and the county of Angoulême, formerly belonging to Joan of France was then in the possession of John's favourite, the constable Charles of La Cerda. In Jan. 1354 the constable was assassinated, and John was forced to make a treaty at Mantes and to compensate Charles for the loss of Angoulême by a large grant of lands, chiefly in Normandy. In Normandy, Charles was partly responsible for some unrest and was seized by the French king at Rouen in April 1356, remaining in captivity until Nov. 1357, after John became a prisoner in England. Charles was then considered by Étienne Marcel and his party as a suitable rival to the dauphin (afterward King Charles V). Peace was made, but the dauphin's failure to restore to Charles his confiscated estates led again to war, quickly followed by a new treaty, after which Charles took part in suppressing the peasant rising known as the *Jacquerie.*

However, in June 1358, he returned to Paris and became captain-general of the city, which was soon besieged by the dauphin. Charles left Paris just before the murder of Marcel in July and continued his alternate policy of war and peace, until the conclusion of the treaty of Brétigny in May 1360 deprived him of the alliance of the English and compelled him to make peace with King John. When the duchy of Burgundy became vacant in Nov. 1361, Charles made an unsuccessful claim for it.

In July 1362, he invaded Aragon in alliance with Peter the Cruel, king of Castile, but he soon deserted his new ally for Peter IV, king of Aragon. In turn he made treaties of alliance with the kings of Castile and Aragon and with Edward of England. Then in 1371 he returned to the allegiance of Charles V of France. He was accused in 1378 of attempting to poison the king of France and other prominent persons and of other crimes; his French estates were seized (except Cherbourg which he sold to the English). After the death of Charles V, in 1380, the king of Navarre did not interfere in the internal affairs of France. His lands in France were handed over to his eldest son Charles, who governed them with the consent of the new king, Charles VI. Charles died on Jan. 1, 1387, and was succeeded by his son Charles; one of his daughters, Joan, dowager duchess of Brittany, became the wife of Henry IV of England.

BIBLIOGRAPHY.—D. F. Secousse, *Mémoires pour servir à l'histoire de Charles II roi de Navarre* (Paris, 1755–58); Jean Froissart, *Chroniques,* ed. by S. Luce and G. Raynaud, 11 vol. (Paris, 1869–99); Edmond Meyer, *Charles II roi de Navarre et la Normandie au XIVe siècle* (Paris, 1898); R. Delachenal, *Premières négociations de Charles le Mauvais avec les Anglais* (Paris, 1900), *Histoire de Charles V,* 5 vol. (Paris, 1908–31).

CHARLES III (1361–1425), called THE NOBLE, king of Navarre and count of Évreux, was the eldest son of Charles II the Bad (*q.v.*) and was married in 1375 to Eleanor, daughter of Henry II, king of Castile. Charles became king of Navarre in 1387, and in contrast to his father's reign his was a period of peace and order. He regained Cherbourg (which had been handed over by Charles II to Richard II of England) in 1393 and exchanged it for certain other lands in France in 1403. He was created duke of Nemours and made a peer of France.

Charles died at Olite on Sept. 8, 1425. After the death of his two sons in 1402 the king secured his kingdom for his daughter Blanche (d. 1441), who took for her second husband John (afterward John II, king of Aragon); and the cortes of Navarre swore to recognize Charles (*q.v.*), prince of Viana, her son by this marriage, as king after his mother's death.

CHARLES I (KARL EITEL; in Rum. CAROL; 1839–1914), first king of Rumania, was born on April 20, 1839, the second son of Prince Charles Antony of Hohenzollern-Sigmaringen, head of the South German and Catholic branch of the Hohenzollerns, who had acted as minister-president of Prussia immediately before Bismarck. His mother was the daughter of the grand duke Charles of Baden and of Stéphanie de Beauharnais. Educated at Dresden and at Bonn, he became an officer in the Prussian army and served against Denmark in 1864. The leaders of the newly united principalities of Moldavia and Walachia, balked of their original desire for a foreign prince, looked abroad again after the overthrow of Alexander John Cuza and, failing Philip of Flanders, offered the throne to Charles, with the tacit approval of Napoleon III. By a plebiscite held in Rumania on April 20, 1866, Charles was almost unanimously elected prince; he had to be smuggled into the country because of the hostility of Russia, Austria and Turkey, but rapidly gained general recognition. Given wide powers under the constitution of July 11, 1866, he showed great tact in dealing with the struggles between the Liberal and Conservative parties, and his administrative, economic and military reforms earned him deep respect at home and abroad.

In 1869 he married Elizabeth (*q.v.*), daughter of Prince Hermann of Wied and a Lutheran; he had already undertaken to educate his children in the Orthodox faith, despite papal disapproval. The sympathy of Rumanians with France in the Franco-German War led to a wave of hostility against the German prince, which, coinciding with a railway scandal, led him to offer abdication. With difficulty persuaded to remain, Charles was later to win great popularity when he led a Rumanian and Russian contingent to victory at Plevna in the Russo-Turkish War of 1877–78. As a consequence of his vigorous action, Rumania secured recognition from the powers of its complete independence of Turkey in 1880 and was proclaimed a kingdom on March 26, 1881, Charles and his consort being crowned on May 22. As king, Charles proved most successful in home policy, greatly improving the financial and military position of his country. He and the queen, who became known as a poetess under the name of Carmen Sylva, gave special encouragement to the fine arts. In foreign policy Charles remained true to Germany, signing a secret treaty with the Central Powers in 1883; the failure of Rumania, still Francophile, to implement that treaty in Aug. 1914 broke him down. On Oct. 10, 1914, he died in his palace at Sinaia. As the only child of Charles's marriage, a daughter, had died in 1874, the succession was settled on his brother's son, who became Ferdinand I of Rumania.

See the official biography, *Aus dem Leben König Karls von Rumänien,* 4 vol. (Stuttgart, 1894–1900), with abridged Eng. trans. (London and New York, 1899); also D. A. Sturdza, *Charles Ier roi de Roumanie: chronique, actes, documents,* 2 vol. (Bucharest, 1899–1904). (B. BR.)

CHARLES II (1661–1700), king of Spain, the son of Philip IV by his second marriage with Maria, daughter of the emperor Ferdinand III, was born on Nov. 11, 1661. Weak, indolent and almost imbecile from his birth, Charles was brought up under the tutelage of his Austrian mother, who was later exiled from court by the younger Don John of Austria, a natural son of Philip IV. In 1679, Charles married Maria Louisa of Orleans, thereby satisfying French interests, which were still more advanced by his acceptance of the treaty of Ratisbon, June 1684. On the death of the French princess in the stifling atmosphere of the Spanish court, Charles married Maria Ana of Neuberg in

1689, and Austrian interests were again promoted. Always decrepit in mind and body, the king, driven wild by the conflict between his wish to transmit his inheritance to "the illustrious house of Austria," his own kin, and the belief instilled into him by the partisans of the French claimant that only the power of Louis XIV. could avert the dismemberment of the empire, was at last reduced to an abject condition. Under pressure from the cardinal archbishop of Toledo, Portocarrero, he finally made a will in favour of Philip, duke of Anjou, grandson of Louis XIV., thereby ending the inglorious line of the Spanish Habsburgs. He died on Nov. 1, 1700.

See M. de Villars, *Lettres* (1868); P. de Villars, *Mémoires de la Cour d'Espagne* (1893); G. Maura Gamaza, *Carlos II. y su Corte,* 2 vols. (1915). (For a genealogical table of the Spanish Habsburgs, *see* HABSBURG.)

CHARLES III. (1716–1788), king of Spain, born on Jan. 20, 1716, was the first son of the second marriage of Philip V. with Elizabeth Farnese of Parma. In 1732 he was sent to rule as duke of Parma by right of his mother, and two years later, 1734, made himself master of Naples and Sicily and began there the work of internal reform which he afterwards continued in Spain. On the death of his half-brother Ferdinand VI. he became king of Spain and resigned the Two Sicilies to his third son, Ferdinand.

As king of Spain his foreign policy was disastrous. His strong family feeling and his detestation of England, which was unchecked after the death of his wife, Maria Amelia, daughter of Frederick Augustus II. of Saxony, in 1760, led him into the Family Compact with France. Spain was entangled in the close of the Seven Years' War, to her great loss. In 1779 he was, somewhat reluctantly, led to join France and the American insurgents against England. His internal government was on the whole beneficial to the country. He improved sanitation, suppressed lawlessness, encouraged trade and industry, and constructed roads and canals. Although a sincere Roman Catholic, he consented to the expulsion of the Jesuits from Spain, reduced the number of idle clergy, and rendered the Inquisition ineffectual. When he died on Dec. 14, 1788, Charles, the greatest of the Spanish Bourbons, left the reputation of an enlightened monarch.

BIBLIOGRAPHY.—*See* M. Danvila y Collado, *Reign of Charles III.* (6 vols.), in the *Historia General de España de la Real Academia de la Historia* (1892, etc.); J. Addison, *Charles the Third of Spain* (1900); F. Rousseau, *Règne de Charles III. d'Espagne* (1907).

CHARLES IV. (1748–1819), king of Spain, second son of Charles III. and his wife Maria Amelia of Saxony, was born on Nov. 11, 1748. The elder brother was set aside as imbecile and epileptic. Charles married Maria Luisa of Parma, his first cousin, who, on his succession to the throne in 1788, directed affairs with the assistance of her lover Godoy (*q.v.*). The king was too slothful to have more than a passive part in the direction of his own Government. If he ever understood that his kingdom was treated as a mere dependence by France, he consoled himself with a belief in his divine right and the sanctity of his person. When he was told that his son Ferdinand was appealing to Napoleon against Godoy, he took the side of the favourite, and when the populace rose at Aranjuez in 1808 he abdicated to save the minister. He took refuge in France, and being imprisoned with his son he was with difficulty restrained from assaulting him. Finally he abdicated in favour of Napoleon and died at Rome on Jan. 20, 1819.

See General Gomez de Arteche (*Historia del Reinado de Carlos IV.*) in the *Historia General de España de la Real Academia de la Historia* (1892, etc.); A. Savine, *L'Abdication de Bayonne.* (1908).

CHARLES IX. (1550–1611), king of Sweden, the youngest son of Gustavus Vasa and Margareto Lejonhufrud, was born on Oct. 4, 1550. By his father's will he received the duchy of Södermanland (Sudermania) in 1560. In 1568 he and his brother John led the rebellion against Eric XIV., but when John became king, as John III., the relations between the two brothers were strained. Duke Charles was the centre of the opposition to John's attempts to romanize Sweden on the one hand, and he resisted all the king's efforts to restrict his authority as duke of Södermanland on the other, though in 1587 he was obliged to resign his claim to autonomy within his own duchy. The religious question came to a crisis on the death of John III. in 1592, when his eldest son, Sigismund, a devoted Catholic who was already king of Poland, succeeded to the throne of Sweden. Duke Charles came forward as the champion of the Protestant majority, who were alarmed lest Sigismund should attempt to re-catholicize Sweden; it was with his assent that they held the famous Synod or "Uppsala-möte" Feb. 1593, which proclaimed Sweden's adherence to the Augsburg Confession; and when Sigismund arrived in Sweden Charles, who had governed jointly with the Estates during his absence, backed by an army, compelled him, before he could be crowned, to guarantee to maintain the Uppsala convention, thereby recognizing that Sweden was essentially a Protestant state. In Aug. 1594 when Sigismund left for Poland, Charles was left in control of affairs, and in 1595 he was elected regent by the *Riksdag* of Söderköping. He ruled firmly, almost despotically. Roman Catholicism was suppressed. In May 1595 the peace of Teusin was concluded with Russia, who recognized Sweden's title to Narva and Estonia. By 1597 however, the country was in a state of civil war. Charles had quarrelled with the council over their refusal to make war on Finland, whose ruler, Klas Fleming, refused to recognize Charles's authority as opposed to that of Sigismund. Sigismund forbade the summoning of the *Riksdag* which supported Charles, and authorized the council to govern alone, but Charles summoned the *Riksdag* when the council was not sitting, and persuaded it to give him all the powers of government. He then sailed to Finland and captured Åbo. Sigismund landed at Kalmar in Sweden with an army, in July 1598, but though large numbers of the nobles flocked to his standards he was regarded as a heretic by the majority of the Swedish nation. Charles defeated him at Stångebro on Sept. 25, 1598, after which he fled for aid to Poland, though he had promised to disband his forces and to abide by the decision of the Estates. He was formally deposed by the *Riksdag* in 1599, and on Feb. 24, 1600, the diet of Linköping declared that he and his posterity had forfeited the Swedish throne, and passing over duke John, the second son of John III., a youth of ten, recognized Duke Charles as king under the title of Charles IX.

Charles proceeded to conquer Finland, and to take cruel vengeance on the nobles who had opposed him. He did not, however, style himself king until March 6, 1604, after Duke John had formally renounced his claim, and was not crowned until March 15, 1607. His short reign was a period of uninterrupted warfare. In the long war with Poland (1600–60), begun in his reign, he was on the whole unsuccessful, his severest defeat being at Kirkholm (Sept. 1605) (*see* CHODKIEWICZ, JAN KAROL). Sweden and Poland also supported rival claimants to the tsardom in Russia. In 1610 Charles, who had concluded an alliance with the tsar Basil against Sigismund in 1609 and who aimed at obtaining the county of Keksholm for Sweden, sent an army under Jakob de la Gardie (*q.v.*) to Moscow. After his defeat by the Polish general, Zolkievski, at Klutsjino (June, 1610) and the collapse of Basil, de la Gardie seized Keksholm and Novgorod in 1611. In the same year Christian IV. (*q.v.*) of Denmark declared war on Sweden, partly as a result of Charles's pretensions to Lapland, and his veto on trade with Riga and Kurland and his foundation of the city of Göteborg (Gothenburg), partly from an ambition to conquer Sweden. Christian besieged Kalmar (whence the name "Kalmar War," given to this war). In July, 1611, Charles IX. fought an indecisive battle near that city, and on the 28th the castle of Kalmar was surrendered treacherously. Old and worn out, Charles died on Oct. 30, leaving his son, Gustavus Adolphus, to carry on war with Denmark and Russia. As a ruler Charles IX. is the link between his great father Gustavus Vasa and his still greater son. He consolidated the work of Gustavus Vasa, the creation of a great Protestant state: he prepared the way for the erection of the Protestant empire of Gustavus Adolphus. By his first wife Marie, daughter of the elector palatine Louis VI., he had six children, of whom only one daughter, Catherine, survived; by his second wife, Christina, daughter of Adolphus, duke of Holstein-Gottorp, he had five children, including Gustavus Adolphus and Charles Philip, duke of Finland.

See *Sveriges Historia,* vol. iii. (1878); R. N. Bain, *Scandinavia* (1905); *see* also SWEDEN: *History.* (R. N. B.; X.)

CHARLES X. (Charles Gustavus) (1622–1660), king of Sweden, son of John Casimir, count palatine of Zweibrücken, and Catherine, sister of Gustavus Adolphus, was born at Nyköping Castle on Nov. 8, 1622. He learnt the art of war under the great Lennart Torstensson, being present at the second battle of Breitenfeld and at Jankowitz. From 1646 to 1648 he frequented the Swedish court. It was supposed that he would marry the queen regnant, Christina, and to compensate her cousin for a broken half-promise she declared him (1649) her successor, despite the opposition of the senate headed by Axel Oxenstjerna. In 1648 he was appointed generalissimo of the Swedish forces in Germany, and acted as Swedish plenipotentiary at the executive congress of Nuremberg, assembled (1650) to execute the details of the peace of Westphalia. As the recognized heir to the throne, his position on his return to Sweden was a difficult one, in view of the unpopularity of the queen. Charles, therefore, wisely withdrew to the isle of Öland till the abdication of Christina (June 5, 1654) called him to the throne.

The beginning of his reign was devoted to the healing of domestic discords and in preparation for a new policy of conquest. He contracted a political marriage (Oct. 24, 1654) with Hedwig Leonora, the daughter of Frederick III., duke of Holstein-Gottorp, by way of securing a future ally against Denmark. The two great pressing national questions, war and the restitution of the alienated crown lands, were considered at the *Riksdag* which assembled at Stockholm in March 1655. The war question was decided in three days by a secret committee presided over by the king, who easily persuaded the delegates that a war with Poland was necessary and might prove very advantageous; but the consideration of the question of the subsidies due to the crown for military purposes was postponed to the following *Riksdag* (*see* Sweden: *History*). On July 15 Charles quitted Sweden to engage in his Polish adventure. By the time war was declared he had at his disposal 50,000 men and 50 warships. Hostilities had already begun with the occupation of Dünaburg (Dvinsk) in Polish Livonia by the Swedes (July 1, 1655), and the Polish army encamped among the marshes of the Netze concluded a convention (July 25) whereby the palatinates of Posen and Kalisz placed themselves under the protection of the Swedish king. The Swedes then entered Warsaw without opposition and occupied the whole of Great Poland. The Polish king, John Casimir, fled to Silesia. Meanwhile Charles pressed on towards Cracow, which was captured after a two months' siege. The fall of Cracow extinguished the last hope of the boldest Pole; but before the end of the year an extraordinary reaction began in Poland itself. On Oct. 18 the Swedes invested the fortress-monastery of Czestochowa, but the place was heroically defended; and after a seventy days' siege the besiegers were compelled to retire with great loss.

This astounding success elicited an outburst of popular enthusiasm which gave the war a national and religious character. The tactlessness of Charles, the rapacity of his generals, the barbarity of his mercenaries, his refusal to legalize his position by summoning the Polish diet, his negotiations for the partition of the very state he affected to befriend, awoke the long slumbering public spirit of the country. In the beginning of 1656 John Casimir returned from exile and the Polish army was reorganized and increased. By this time Charles had discovered that it was easier to defeat the Poles than to conquer Poland. His chief object, the conquest of Prussia, was still unaccomplished, and a new foe arose in the elector of Brandenburg, alarmed by the ambition of the Swedish king. Charles forced the elector, indeed, at the point of the sword to become his ally and vassal (treaty of Königsberg, Jan. 17, 1656); but the Polish national rising now imperatively demanded his presence in the south. For weeks he scoured the interminable snow-covered plains of Poland in pursuit of the Polish guerillas, penetrating as far south as Jaroslav in Galicia, by which time he had lost two-thirds of his 15,000 men with no apparent result. His retreat from Jaroslav to Warsaw, with the fragments of his host, amidst three converging armies, in a marshy forest region, intersected in every direction by well-guarded rivers, was one of his most brilliant achievements. But his necessities were overwhelming. On June 21 Warsaw was retaken by the Poles, and four days later Charles was obliged to purchase the assistance of Frederick William by the treaty of Marienburg. On July 18–20 the combined Swedes and Brandenburgers, 18,000 strong, after a three days' battle, defeated John Casimir's army of 50,000 at Warsaw and reoccupied the Polish capital; but this brilliant feat of arms was altogether useless, and when the suspicious attitude of Frederick William compelled the Swedish king at last to open negotiations with the Poles, they refused the terms offered, the war was resumed, and Charles concluded an offensive and defensive alliance with the elector of Brandenburg (treaty of Labiau, Nov. 20) whereby it was agreed that Frederick William and his heirs should henceforth possess the full sovereignty of East Prussia. In the meantime the hostile Dutch dominated Danzig, and the tsar started a campaign against the Swedish Baltic provinces.

The alliance of the elector had now become indispensable on almost any terms. So serious, indeed, were the difficulties of Charles X. in Poland, in spite of the assistance of the elector and of George Rákóczy II., prince of Transylvania, that it was with extreme satisfaction that he received the tidings of the Danish declaration of war (June 1, 1657) which enabled him honourably to emerge from the inglorious Polish imbroglio. He had learnt from Torstensson that Denmark was most vulnerable if attacked from the south, and, imitating the strategy of his master, he fell upon her with a velocity which paralyzed resistance. At the end of June 1657, at the head of 6,000 seasoned veterans, he executed a rapid march from the interior of Poland to Stettin, and reached the borders of Holstein on July 18. The Danish army at once dispersed and the duchy of Bremen was recovered by the Swedes, who in the early autumn swarmed over Jutland and firmly established themselves in the duchies. But the fortress of Fredriksodde (Fredericia) on the Little Belt held Charles's little army at bay from mid-August to mid-October, while the fleet of Denmark, after a stubborn two days' battle, compelled the Swedish fleet to abandon its projected attack on the Danish islands. In July an offensive and defensive alliance was concluded between Denmark and Poland. The elector of Brandenburg joined the league against Sweden, and compelled Charles to accept the proffered mediation of Cromwell and Mazarin. The negotiations foundered, however, upon the refusal of Sweden to refer the points in dispute to a general peace-congress, and Charles was still further encouraged by the capture of Fredriksodde (Oct. 23–24). In the middle of December 1657 began the great frost which was to be so fatal to Denmark. On Jan. 28, 1658, Charles X. arrived at Haderslev (Hadersleben) in South Jutland, when it was estimated that in a couple of days the ice of the Little Belt would be firm enough to bear even the passage of a mail-clad host to the island of Fünen. Early in the morning of Jan. 30 the Swedish king gave the order to start, the horsemen dismounting where the ice was weakest, and cautiously leading their horses as far apart as possible, when they swung into their saddles again, closed their ranks and made a dash for the shore. The whole of Fünen was won with the loss of only two companies of cavalry, which disappeared under the ice while fighting with the Danish left wing. Charles, with his eyes fixed steadily on Copenhagen, resolved to cross the frozen Great Belt also. After some hesitation, he accepted the advice of his chief engineer officer Erik Dahlberg, who acted as pioneer throughout, and chose the more circuitous route from Svendborg, by the islands of Langeland, Laaland and Falstër, in preference to the direct route from Nyborg to Korsør, which would have been across a broad, almost uninterrupted expanse of ice. On the night of Feb. 5 the transit began, the cavalry leading the way through the snow-covered ice, which quickly thawed beneath the horses' hoofs so that the infantry which followed after had to wade through half an ell of sludge, fearing every moment lest the rotting ice should break beneath their feet. At three o'clock in the afternoon, Dahlberg leading the way, the army reached Grimsted in Laaland without losing a man. On Feb. 8 Charles reached Falster. On the 11th he stood safely on the soil of Sjaelland (Zealand). The medal struck to commemorate "the glorious transit of the Baltic Sea" bore the haughty inscription: *Natura hoc debuit uni.*

The crushing effect of this unheard-of achievement on the Danish Government found expression in the treaties of Taastrup (Feb. 18) and Roskilde (Feb. 26, 1658), whereby Denmark sacrificed nearly half her territory to save the rest (*see* DENMARK: *History*). But even this was not enough for the conqueror. Military ambition and greed of conquest moved Charles X. to what, divested of all its pomp and circumstance, was an outrageous act of political brigandage. At a council held at Gottorp (July 7), Charles X. resolved, without any warning, in defiance of all international equity, to let loose his veterans upon Denmark a second time. For the details of this second struggle, with the concomitant diplomatic intervention of the western powers, who were determined to prevent the closing of the Sound, *see* FREDERICK III., king of Denmark, and DENMARK: *History*. Only after great hesitation would Charles X. consent to reopen negotiations with Denmark direct, at the same time proposing to exercise pressure upon the enemy by a simultaneous winter campaign in Norway. Such an enterprise necessitated fresh subsidies from his already impoverished people, and obliged him in December 1659 to cross over to Sweden to meet the estates, whom he had summoned to Gothenburg. The lower estates murmured at the imposition of fresh burdens; and Charles had need of all his adroitness to persuade them that his demands were reasonable and necessary. At the very beginning of the *Riksdag*, in January 1660, it was noticed that the king was ill; but he spared himself as little in the council-chamber as in the battle-field, till death suddenly overtook him on the night of Feb. 12–13, 1660, in his thirty-eighth year.

See M. Veibull, *Sveriges Storhedstid* (Stockholm, 1881); F. F. Carlson, *Sveriges Historia under Konungarne af Pfalziska Huset* (Stockholm, 1883–85); E. Haumant, *La Guerre du nord et la paix d'Oliva* (1893); G. Jones, *The Diplomatic Relations between Cromwell and Charles X.* (Lincoln, Nebraska, 1897); R. Nisbet Bain, *Scandinavia* (1905); J. Levin-Carlklum, *Karl II. Gustav* (Stockholm, 1912); H. Rosengren, *Karl II. Gustaf före tronkestigingen* (Uppsala, 1913); J. Stefánsson, *Denmark and Sweden* (1916)

CHARLES XI. (1655–1697), king of Sweden, the only son of Charles X. and Hedwig Leonora of Holstein-Gottorp, was born in the palace at Stockholm on Nov. 24, 1655. His father, who died when the child was in his fourth year, appointed a regency of five great ministers of state with the queen as president. For the history of the regency, of the settlement of the Danish and Russian loans, and the later humiliating dependence on France (*see* SWEDEN: *History*). The young king's education was neglected. When he attained his majority, he was ignorant of the very rudiments of state-craft and almost illiterate. It was the disaster of the Scanian war which first called forth his sterling qualities and hardened him into a premature manhood.

In 1675 the Brandenburgers, Pomeranians and Danes had overrun Pomerania and Bremen, and the Danes were preparing to invade Sweden itself. Amidst universal anarchy, the young king, barely twenty years of age, inexperienced, ill-served, snatching at every expedient, worked day and night in his newly-formed camp in Scania (Skåne) to arm the nation for its mortal struggle. The Danes launched invasion from three directions in 1676. The victory of Fyllebro (Aug. 17, 1676), when Charles and his commander-in-chief S. G. Helmfeld routed a Danish division, was the first Swedish success, and on Dec. 4, on the tableland of Helgonabäck, near Lund, the young Swedish monarch defeated Christian V. of Denmark, who also commanded his army in person. After a ferocious contest, the Danes were practically annihilated. The battle of Lund was, relatively to the number engaged, one of the bloodiest engagements of modern times. More than half the combatants (8,357, of whom 3,000 were Swedes) actually perished on the battle-field. All the Swedish commanders, notably John Gyllenstierna, showed remarkable ability, but the chief glory of the day indisputably belongs to Charles XI. This great victory restored to the Swedes their self-confidence and prestige. In the following year, Charles with 9,000 men routed 12,000 Danes near Landskrona (July 15, 1678). This proved to be the last pitched battle of the war, the Danes never again venturing to attack their once more invincible enemy in the open field. In Germany, the Swedes, faced by the Great Elector, lost ground. In 1679 Louis XIV. dictated the terms of a general pacification, and Charles XI., who bitterly resented "the insufferable tutelage" of the French king, acquiesced in a peace which at least left his empire practically intact. Both Christian V. of Denmark and Frederick William, the Great Elector, were forced to restore their conquests (*see* SWEDEN: *History*). Good understanding between Denmark and Sweden followed the peace of Lund, and there relations were cemented by the marriage of Charles with Ulrica Leonora, sister of Christian V. Charles devoted the rest of his life to the gigantic task of rehabilitating Sweden by means of a *reduktion,* or recovery of alienated crown lands, a process which involved the examination of every title deed in the kingdom, and resulted in the complete readjustment of the finances. But vast as it was, the *reduktion* represents only a tithe of Charles XI.'s immense activity. Finance, commerce, the national armaments by sea and land, judicial procedure, church government, education, even art and science—everything, in short—emerged recast from his shaping hand. For the strengthening in his reign of the power of the crown, which left Sweden practically an absolute monarchy (*see* SWEDEN: *History*). Charles XI. died on April 5, 1697, in his forty-first year. He had seven children, of whom only three survived him, a son Charles, and two daughters, Hedwig Sophia, duchess of Holstein, and Ulrica Leonora, who ultimately succeeded her brother on the Swedish throne.

After Gustavus Vasa and Gustavus Adolphus, Charles XI. was, perhaps, the greatest of all the kings of Sweden. His modest, homespun figure has indeed been unduly eclipsed by the brilliant and colossal shapes of his heroic father and his meteoric son; yet in reality Charles XI. is far worthier of admiration than either Charles X. or Charles XII. He was in an eminent degree a great master-builder. He found Sweden in ruins, and devoted his whole life to laying the solid foundations of a new order of things which, in its essential features, has endured to the present day.

See Martin Veibull, *Sveriges Storhedstid* (Stockholm, 1881); Frederick Ferdinand Carlson, *Sveriges Historia under Konungarne af Pfalziska Huset* (Stockholm, 1883–1885); Robert Nisbet Bain, *Scandinavia* (Cambridge, 1905); O. Sjögren, *Karl den Elfte och Svenska Folket* (Stockholm, 1897); S. Jacobsen, *Den nordiske Kriegs Krönicke,* 1675–1679 (Copenhagen, 1897); J. A. de Mesmes d'Avaux, *Négociations du comte d'Avaux,* 1693, 1697, 1698 (Utrecht, 1882, etc.).

CHARLES XII. (1682–1718), king of Sweden, the only surviving son of Charles XI. and Ulrica Leonora, daughter of Frederick III. of Denmark, was born on June 17, 1682. He was carefully educated by excellent tutors under the watchful eyes of his parents. Charles XI. personally supervised his son's physical training. He was taught to ride before he was four and at eight he was quite at home in his saddle.

As he grew older his father took him on all his rounds, reviewing troops, inspecting studs, foundries, dockyards and granaries. Thus the lad was gradually initiated into all the *minutiae* of administration. The influence of Charles XI. over his son was, indeed, far greater than is commonly supposed, and it accounts for much in Charles XII.'s character which is otherwise inexplicable, for instance his precocious reserve and taciturnity, his dislike of everything French, and his inordinate contempt for purely diplomatic methods. On the whole, his early training was admirable; but the young prince was not allowed the opportunity of gradually gaining experience under his guardians. At the *Riksdag* assembled at Stockholm in 1697, the estates, jealous of the influence of the regents, offered full sovereignty to the young monarch, the senate acquiesced, and, after some hesitation, Charles at last declared that he could not resist the urgent appeal of his subjects and would take over the government of the realm "in God's name." The subsequent coronation was marked by portentous novelties, the most significant of which was the king's omission to take the usual coronation oath, which omission was interpreted to mean that he considered himself under no obligation to his subjects. The general opinion of the young king was, however, still favourable. His conduct was evidently regulated by strict principle and not by mere caprice. His intense application to affairs is noted by the English minister, John Robinson (1650–1723).

The coalition formed against Sweden by Johann Reinhold

Patkul, which resulted in the outbreak of the Great Northern War (1699), abruptly put an end to Charles XII.'s political apprenticeship, and forced the sword into his hand. The young king resolved to attack Denmark the nearest of his three enemies—Denmark, Poland and Russia—first. The timidity of the Danish admiral Ulrik C. Gyldenlöve, and the daring of Charles, who forced his nervous and protesting admiral to attempt the passage of the eastern channel of the Sound, the dangerous *flinterend,* hitherto reputed to be unnavigable, enabled the Swedish king to effect a landing at Humleback in Sjaelland (Zealand), a few miles north of Copenhagen (Aug. 4, 1700). He now hoped to accomplish what his grandfather, fifty years before, had vainly attempted —the destruction of the Danish-Norwegian monarchy by capturing its capital. But for once prudential considerations prevailed, and the short and bloodless war was terminated by the peace of Traventhal (Aug. 18), whereby Frederick IV. conceded full sovereignty to Charles's ally and kinsman the duke of Gottorp, besides paying him an indemnity of 200,000 rix-dollars and solemnly engaging to commit no hostilities against Sweden in future. From Sjaelland Charles now hastened to Livonia with 8,000 men. On Oct. 6 he had reached Pernau, with the intention of first relieving Riga, but, hearing that Narva was in great straits, he decided to turn northwards against the tsar. He set out for Narva on Nov. 13 against the advice of all his generals, who feared the effect on untried troops of a week's march through a wasted land, along boggy roads guarded by no fewer than three formidable passes which a little engineering skill could easily have made impregnable. Fortunately, the first two passes were unoccupied; and the third, Pyhäjoggi, was captured by Charles, who with 400 horsemen put 6,000 Russian cavalry to flight. On Nov. 19 the little army reached Lagena, a village about 9m. from Narva, whence it signalled its approach to the beleaguered fortress, and early on the following morning it advanced in battle array. The attack on the Russian fortified camp began at two o'clock in the afternoon, in the midst of a violent snowstorm; and by nightfall the whole position was in the hands of the Swedes: the Russian army was annihilated. The triumph was as cheap as it was crushing; it cost Charles less than 2,000 men.

After Narva, Charles XII. stood at the parting of ways. His best advisers urged him to turn all his forces against the panic-stricken Muscovites; to go into winter quarters amongst them and live at their expense; to fan into a flame the smouldering discontent caused by the reforms of Peter the Great; and so disable Russia for some time to come. But Charles was determined to punish the treachery of Augustus of Poland (*see* POLAND: *History*). It is easy from the vantage-point of two centuries to criticize Charles XII. for neglecting the Russians to pursue the Saxons; but at the beginning of the 18th century his decision was natural enough. The real question was, which of the two foes was the more dangerous, and Charles had many reasons to think the civilized and martial Saxons far more formidable than the imbecile Muscovites. Charles also rightly felt that he could never trust the treacherous Augustus to remain quiet, even if he made peace with him. To leave such a foe in his rear, while he plunged into the heart of Russia would have been hazardous indeed. From this point of view Charles's whole Polish policy, which has been blamed so long and so loudly—the policy of placing a nominee of his own on the Polish throne—takes quite another complexion: it was a policy not of overvaulting ambition, but of prudential self-defence.

First, however, Charles cleared Livonia of the invader (July 1701), subsequently occupying the duchy of Courland and converting it into a Swedish governor-generalship. In Jan. 1702 Charles established himself at Bielowice in Lithuania, and, after issuing a proclamation declaring that "the elector of Saxony" had forfeited the Polish crown, set out for Warsaw, which he reached on May 14. The cardinal-primate was then sent for and commanded to summon a diet, for the purpose of deposing Augustus. A fortnight later Charles quitted Warsaw, to seek the elector; on July 2 routed the combined Poles and Saxons at Klissow; and three weeks later, captured the fortress of Cracow by an act of almost fabulous audacity. Thus, within four months of the opening of the campaign, the Polish capital and the coronation city were both in the possession of the Swedes. After Klissow, Augustus made every effort to put an end to the war, but Charles would not even consider his offers. By this time, too, he had conceived a passion for the perils and adventures of warfare. His character was hardening, and he deliberately adopted the most barbarous expedients for converting the Augustan Poles to his views.

The campaign of 1703 was remarkable for Charles's victory at Pultusk (April 21) and the long siege of Thorn, which occupied him eight months but cost him only 50 men. On July 2, 1704, with the assistance of a bribing fund, Charles's ambassador at Warsaw, Count Arvid Bernhard Horn, succeeded in forcing through the election of Charles's candidate to the Polish throne, Stanislaus Leszczynski, who could not be crowned however till Sept. 24, 1705, by which time the Saxons had again been defeated at Punitz. From the autumn of 1705 to the spring of 1706, Charles was occupied in pursuing the Russian auxiliary army under Ogilvie through the forests of Lithuania. On Aug. 5, he recrossed the Vistula and established himself in Saxony, where his presence in the heart of Europe at the very crisis of the war of the Spanish Succession, fluttered all the western diplomats. The allies, in particular, at once suspected that Louis XIV. had bought the Swedes. Marlborough was forthwith sent from the Hague to the castle of Altranstädt near Leipzig, where Charles had fixed his headquarters, "to endeavour to penetrate the designs" of the king of Sweden. He soon convinced himself that western Europe had nothing to fear from Charles, and that no bribes were necessary to turn the Swedish arms from Germany to Russia. Five months later (Sept. 1707) Augustus was forced to sign the peace of Altranstädt, whereby he resigned the Polish throne and renounced every anti-Swedish alliance. Charles's departure from Saxony was delayed for twelve months by a quarrel with the emperor. The court of Vienna had treated the Silesian Protestants with tyrannical severity, in direct contravention of the treaty of Osnabrück, of which Sweden was one of the guarantors; and Charles demanded summary and complete restitution so dictatorially that the emperor prepared for war. But the allies interfered in Charles's favour, lest he might be tempted to aid France, and induced the emperor to satisfy all the Swedish king's demands, the maritime Powers at the same time agreeing to guarantee the provisions of the peace of Altranstädt.

Nothing now prevented Charles from turning his victorious arms against the tsar; and on Aug. 13, 1707, he evacuated Saxony at the head of the largest host he ever commanded, consisting of 24,000 horse and 20,000 foot. Delayed during the autumn months in Poland by the tardy arrival of reinforcements from Pomerania, it was not till Nov. 1707 that Charles was able to take the field. On New Year's Day 1708 he crossed the Vistula, though the ice was in a dangerous condition. On July 4, 1708 he cut in two the line of the Russian army, 6m. long, which barred his progress on the Wabis, near Holowczyn, and compelled it to retreat. The victory of Holowczyn, memorable besides as the last pitched battle won by Charles XII., opened up the way to the Dnieper. The Swedish army now began to suffer severely, bread and fodder running short. The Russians slowly retired before the invader, burning and destroying everything in his path. On Dec. 20 it was plain to Charles himself that Moscow was inaccessible. But the idea of a retreat was intolerable to him, so he determined to march southwards instead of northwards as suggested by his generals, and join his forces with those of the hetman of the Dnieperian Cossacks, Ivan Mazepa, who had 100,000 horsemen and a fresh and fruitful land at his disposal. Short of falling back upon Livonia, it was the best plan adoptable in the circumstances, but it was rendered abortive by Peter's destruction of Mazepa's capital Baturin, so that when Mazepa joined Charles at Horki, on Nov. 8, 1708, it was as a ruined man with little more than 1,300 personal attendants (*see* MAZEPA-KOLEDINSKY, IVAN STEPANOVICH). More serious was the destruction of the relief army which Levenhaupt was bringing to Charles from Livonia, and which, hampered by hundreds of loaded wagons, was overtaken and almost destroyed at Lyesna after a two days' battle against fourfold odds (October). The very elements now began to fight against the perishing but still unconquered host. The winter of 1708 was the severest that Europe had known for a century. By Nov. 1 firewood would not ignite in the open air, and the soldiers warmed themselves over big bonfires of straw. By the time the army reached the little Ukranian fortress of Hadjacz in January 1709, wine and spirits froze into solid masses of ice; birds on the wing fell dead.

Never had Charles XII. seemed so superhuman as during these awful days. It is not too much to say that his imperturbable equanimity, his serene *bonhomie* kept the host together. The frost broke at the end of Feb. 1709, and then the spring floods put an end to all active operations till May, when Charles began the siege of the fortress of Poltava, which he wished to make a base for subsequent operations while awaiting reinforcements from Sweden and Poland. On June 7 a bullet wound put Charles *hors de combat,* whereupon Peter threw the greater part of his forces over the river Vorskla, which separated the two armies (June 19–25). On June 26 Charles held a council of war, at which it was resolved to attack the Russians in their entrenchments on the following day. The Swedes joyfully accepted the chances of battle and, advancing with irresistible *élan,* were, at first, successful on both wings. Then one or two tactical blunders were committed; and the tsar, taking courage, enveloped the little band in a vast semicircle bristling with the most modern guns, which fired five times to the Swedes' once, and swept away the guards before they could draw their swords. The Swedish infantry was well nigh annihilated, while the 14,000 cavalry, exhausted and demoralized, surrendered two days later at Perevolochna on Dnieper. Charles himself with 1,500 horsemen took refuge in Turkish territory.

For the first time in his life Charles was now obliged to have recourse to diplomacy; and his pen proved almost as formidable as his sword. He procured the dismissal of four Russophil grand-viziers in succession, and between 1710 and 1712 induced the Porte to declare war against the tsar three times. But after Nov. 1712 the Porte had no more money to spare; and, the tsar making a show of submission, the sultan began to regard Charles as a troublesome guest. On Feb. 1, 1713 he was attacked by the Turks in his camp at Bender, and made prisoner. Charles lingered on in Turkey 15 months longer, in the hope of obtaining a cavalry escort sufficiently strong to enable him to restore his credit in Poland. Disappointed of this last hope, and moved by the despairing appeals of his sister Ulrica and the senate to return to Sweden while there was still a Sweden to return to, he quitted Demotika on Sept. 20, 1714, and attended by a single squire arrived unexpectedly at midnight, on Nov. 11, at Stralsund.

For the historical events of the following years *see* SWEDEN: *History.* Here it need only be said that Sweden, during the course of the Great Northern War, had innumerable opportunities of obtaining an honourable and even advantageous peace, but they all foundered on the dogged refusal of Charles to consent to the smallest concession to his despoilers. Even now he would listen to no offers of compromise, and after defending Stralsund with desperate courage till it was a mere rubbish heap, returned to Sweden after an absence of 14 years. Here he collected another army of 20,000 men, with which he so strongly entrenched himself on the Scanian coast in 1716 that his combined enemies shrank from attacking him, whereupon he assumed the offensive by attacking Norway in 1717, and again in 1718, in order to conquer sufficient territory to enable him to extort better terms from his enemies. It was during this second adventure that he met his death. On Dec. 11, when the Swedish approaches had come within 280 paces of the fortress of Fredriksten, which the Swedes were closely besieging, Charles looked over the parapet of the foremost trench, and was shot through the head.

(R. N. B.)

BIBLIOGRAPHY.—Charles XII., *Die eigenhändigen Briefe König Karls XII.* (1894); M. Weibull, *Sveriges Storhedstid* (1881); F. F. Carlson, *Sveriges Historia under Konungarne af Pfalziska Huset* (1883–85); Oscar II., *Några bidrag till Sveriges Krigshistoria åren 1711–1713* (1892); D. Krmann, "Historia ablegationis D. Krmann ad regem Sueciae Carolum XII.," in *Monumenta Hungariae Historica* vol. 33, 34 (Budapest, 1894); R. N. Bain, *Charles XII. and the Collapse of the Swedish Empire* (1895); *Bidrag til den Store Nordiske Krigs Historie* (official publ. Copenhagen, 1899–1900); G. Syveton, *Louis XIV. et Charles XII.* (1900); C. Hallendorff, *Karl XII. i Ukraina* (1915); N. Herlitz, *Studier över Carl XII.'s Politik 1703–04* (1916); R. Fåhraens, *Karl XI. och Karl XII.* in "Sverige's Historia" Series (1921); Ballagi Aladár, *XII. Károly és a svédek Atvonulási Magyarországon* (Budapest, 1922); A. Munthe, *Karl XII. och den Ryska Sjömakten* (1924); E. Godley, *Charles XII. of Sweden* (1928).

CHARLES XIII. (1748–1818), king of Sweden and Norway, the second son of Adolphus Frederick, king of Sweden, and Louisa Ulrica, sister of Frederick the Great, was born at Stockholm on Oct. 7, 1748. In 1772 he co-operated in the revolutionary plans of his brother Gustavus III. (*q.v.*). During the Russo-Swedish War of 1788 he served as admiral of the fleet at the battles of Hogland (June 17, 1788) and Öland (July 26, 1789). On the death of Gustavus III., Charles, now duke of Sudermania, acted as regent of Sweden till 1796; but the real ruler of the country was Gustaf Adolf Reuterholm (*q.v.*). These four years may be briefly described as alternations of fantastic Jacobinism and ruthless despotism. On the accession of Gustavus IV. (Nov. 1796), the duke became a mere cipher in politics till March 13, 1809, when those who had dethroned Gustavus IV. appointed him regent, and finally elected him king. But by this time he was prematurely decrepit, and Bernadotte (*see* CHARLES XIV JOHN) took over the government as soon as he landed in Sweden (1810). By the union of 1814 Charles became the first king of Sweden and Norway. He married his cousin Hedwig Elizabeth Charlotte of Holstein-Gottorp (1759–1818), but their only child died in infancy (1798). Charles XIII., who for eight years had been king only in title, died on Feb. 5, 1818.

See *Sveriges Historia* vol. v. (1884); *Drottning Hedwig Charlottes Dagbokshandteckningar* (1898); Robert Nisbet Bain, *Gustavus III. and his Contemporaries* (1895); *ib. Scandinavia* (1905).

CHARLES XIV JOHN (CARL JOHAN; BERNADOTTE) (1763–1844), king of Sweden and Norway, born at Pau in the French province of Béarn, Jan. 26, 1763, was the son of Henri Bernadotte (1711–1780), an *avocat,* and Jeanne St. Jean (1725–1809). Several of the ancestors on each side had been weavers. The family name of Deu Pouey had been changed to Bernadotte in the early 17th century (after the name of a house taken over from the distaff side). He was baptized Jean, known as Jean Baptiste, and later added the name Jules; his regular signature was merely "J. Bernadotte." Of his childhood and youth it is known only that he was repeatedly ill, and that he probably attended a Benedictine school in Pau for at least a short period.

In 1780, five months after his father's death, Bernadotte enlisted in the army of Louis XVI, in the Royal-la-Marine regiment. In varied service he became successively grenadier, corporal, sergeant, quartermaster, sergeant major, and early in 1790 adjutant, the highest rank among noncommissioned officers. The Revolution created difficulties within the army and between army and citizenry, but Bernadotte stood staunchly for maintenance of authority and judicial processes—once leading a group of under-officers in defense of their colonel in a disagreement with revolutionary civil authorities. Soon legislation opened the way for non-nobles to become officers, and early in 1792 Bernadotte was elected a lieutenant (the commission was dated as of Nov. 6, 1791). He was attached to the 36th regiment and went into action along the Rhine with Adam Custine. In the defeat of May 17, 1793, a panic was begun when a group of volunteers fired on their own cavalry; Bernadotte sprang into the midst of the chaos, and with a fiery speech restored order and reorganized the battalion for the fight. Here he was at his best, in one of those fine gestures of self-forgetfulness to be repeated again and again in the crises of campaigns to come. He went through all the ranks, becoming captain in 1793, and in 1794 passing from lieutenant colonel to colonel, on to brigadier general and general of division (Oct. 22). He served in the army of the Sambre and Meuse with General Jean Baptiste Kléber (1794–95), and distinguished himself for his ability to inspire troops in desperate situations. In 1796 he campaigned in north Germany. Here, as in the Low Countries, he was marked as one of the disciplinarians of the army, trying to save the population from plundering by soldiery and winning an unusual degree of respect from the inhabitants.

In 1797 came the first meeting between Bernadotte and Napoleon, when the general from the army of the Rhine led 20,000 troops to reinforce General Bonaparte in Italy. Both were proud and ambitious, but the Corsican was cool, unscrupulous, eager only for power; Bernadotte showed the characteristics of his Gascon forebears—vain, emotional, loyal, eager chiefly for glory. The two spectacular leaders seemed to sense rivalry and cross-purposes from the first, and the soldiers in their armies were none too friendly; the "citizens' army" of Bonaparte nicknamed the newcomers the "gentlemen" because of their superior smartness and discipline. Nevertheless, at the passage of the Tagliamento and the taking of Gradisca, Bernadotte and his proud division from the Rhine distinguished themselves for valour. After the campaign Bernadotte began a serious reading program, probably roused to do so by Bonaparte's superior knowledge of military science and history.

Though he was next slated to succeed Bonaparte in command of the army of Italy, both Bernadotte and the Austrians were shocked when he was named ambassador to Vienna. He was hardly a proper symbol of diplomatic reconciliation and he had no experience to fit him for the post. From January to April 1798 he did his soldier's best, but the mission ended on April 14 after a Viennese mob rioted against the embassy because of the hanging out of the tricolour.

Back in Paris the general and ambassador was free to enjoy for a time the delights of the salons of Mme. de Staël and Mme. Récamier, where he met the leading political and literary figures of the day. He also renewed acquaintance with the "pretty girl from Marseilles with the gay smile"—Désirée Clary—former fiancée of Joseph Bonaparte, of Napoleon and of Leonard Duphot. Her sister Julie had married Joseph Bonaparte, so that when Bernadotte married Désirée, Aug. 17, 1798, he came into the fringes of the Bonaparte clan.

In the fall of 1798 Bernadotte commanded the army of Mayence and arranged peace with Hesse-Darmstadt. He rejected the offer of command over the army of Italy because he considered the troops insufficient—as events proved them to be. He likewise refused the offer from Paul Barras to lead a *coup d'état* to force reconstitution of the Directory. In July 1799 the directors made him minister of war at a critical point in the fortunes of France. For ten weeks he applied his restless energy to problems of organization, recruiting and supply, but his growing fame and his constitutional scruples irritated Emmanuel-Joseph Sieyès, who engineered his removal. Bernadotte was thus out of office when Bonaparte returned from Egypt. Bonaparte asked his old colleague to join in his coup, but Bernadotte refused, promising only that he would take no initiative in opposition. On the success of the coup d'état of the 18th Brumaire, Bernadotte and Désirée went into brief hiding. He had been the most probable leader of the forces wishing to defend the Directory, but had passed up the chance to act by refusing to assume responsibility. Bernadotte was soon reconciled to the new regime, and from 1800 to 1810 was closely associated with the empire building of Napoleon, active in campaigns and administration, but repeatedly suspect because of his independent attitude and his connections with the opponents of the emperor. Bonaparte "absorbed" the Gascon general, as he did many of the potential opposition, by giving him position and prestige in the new regime.

Bernadotte became a councillor of state, and commander of the army of the west. He expected to defend Brittany from an attack by England, but found his job to be largely suppression of rebellion. Upon returning to Paris in the winter of 1801 he retired to Plombières because of suspicion directed against him on account of the Rennes plot. He was one of two or three generals most likely to be raised to high power if anything happened to Bonaparte; his unwillingness to co-operate in the Brumaire coup was well known; inevitably his name was discussed in connection with each successive plot against first consul or emperor. No evidence has been found to link him with any real plot, though it is clear that he would have favoured constitutional legislative action to limit the power of the first consul or even to overthrow him. Bonaparte was angry and suspicious and in Jan. 1803, in order to get Bernadotte out of the country, appointed him minister to the United States. While waiting to sail Bernadotte got wind of approaching war between France and England, so returned to Paris for an active military post. War was delayed and Bernadotte remained inactive in Paris for a year. Then Napoleon made himself emperor and Bernadotte declared full loyalty to him, having decided that nothing else was possible. He was named one of the 18 marshals of France (May 19, 1804) and early in June left for his new post as governor of Hanover. Here he was both military commander and civil administrative officer; in the combined capacity he showed executive skill and an ability to win the affection and respect of the citizenry. He showered privileges on the University of Göttingen and attempted in tax policy to ease the load of the poor and transfer the burden to the wealthy, including nobility and church. Here he began also to accumulate his small fortune, with "gifts" of 300,000 francs from Hanover and 200,000 francs from Bremen.

In 1805 the war with Austria became active and Bernadotte was ordered in August to lead his forces to Würzburg. He was given command of the I corps, including the Bavarian army. Difficulties with roads and boats and the inefficiency of the Bavarian forces delayed his march toward Vienna and brought reproaches from the emperor. Extraordinary marches brought the I corps to Austerlitz, where it occupied the centre. It played a relatively small role in the battle, partly because its cavalry had been transferred to Murat just before the battle. Bernadotte was annoyed, but Napoleon seemed pleased with him on this occasion. The next task given him (Feb. 19, 1806) was the occupation of Ansbach.

In accord with the imperial policy of naming outstanding generals to the new nobility, Bernadotte was made prince of Ponte Corvo, June 5, 1806. Ponte Corvo was an enclave of 5,600 inhabitants within the territory of the kingdom of Naples.

In October 1806 Bernadotte commanded a strengthened I corps of 15,000 to 21,000 men, including a French division under Pierre Dupont de L'Étang. Bernadotte did not participate actively in the conflicts at Jena or Auerstadt, and was blamed by Napoleon for not being where he should have been. Real responsibility for his absence rests upon Napoleon's unawareness of the Prussian position and upon the vagueness and indirectness of the orders of Marshal Louis Berthier, chief of staff. This in turn may have been caused by Berthier's personal antagonism to Bernadotte. After the battle Napoleon needed a scapegoat and used Bernadotte for the purpose. That he had no fundamental complaint is evidenced by the enlarged responsibility given to Bernadotte two months later—command over three corps which made up the left wing in the Polish campaign. In the meantime Bernadotte showed unusual energy and skill in the pursuit of the Prussians, especially at Halle and in the attack on Lübeck (where some 1,000 Swedish prisoners were taken, and tactful handling of whom was to pay dividends later). By tactics of speed and daring Bernadotte led his troops to a victory over the Russians at Mohrungen (Jan. 25, 1807), but missed the action at Eylau because of the capture of his orders. On June 5 he was wounded by a shot in the neck, and this kept him from the battle of Friedland.

On July 14, 1807, Bernadotte was named governor of the occupied Hanseatic cities. Again he was both administrator and commander, and asssumed the position of a viceroy. Soon he was scheduled to lead a combination of German, French and Spanish troops in an attack on Sweden. The emperor, who may not have intended the threat seriously, required a peculiar distribution of the troops. The total result was that the Spanish contingent deserted en masse and was carried off by English ships (Aug. 1808). The expedition against Sweden was abandoned, and French military power was once more directed against Austria. Bernadotte was ill at the beginning of the campaign with his recurrent blood-spitting. Further difficulties with Chief of Staff Louis Alexandre Berthier, and the inclusion in his IX corps of the ill-prepared Saxon allies combined with his illness to make him beg for release from service. Napoleon disregarded these appeals and Bernadotte organized his forces and proceeded with the campaign, commanding mostly allied troops, with few French. In the decisive battle at Wagram, Dupas' division was withdrawn without Bernadotte's knowledge and the marshal found himself with depleted strength at the centre of the Austrian attack; in killed, wounded and missing he lost one-third of his soldiers and was forced to retire from the town of Wagram. As compensation for his bitterness and disappointment he issued on July 8, 1809, a bombastic order of the day exaggeratedly praising the skill and courage of the Saxon forces. Shortly before the battle he had stretched his authority to accede to an armistice for the Swedes. On July 10, perhaps partly as a penalty for these acts, the IX corps was dissolved, and Bernadotte was allowed to return to Paris "for reasons of health" but obviously in deep disfavour.

Bernadotte was therefore in Paris when word arrived (July 29, 1809) of the threatening British invasion at Walcheren. He offered his services, but the ministers, not clear as to his status, hesitated to put him in command. A despatch from Napoleon then ordered them to send Bernadotte if he was at hand. It is clear evidence of the emperor's confidence in the ability of the marshal despite their recent differences. Bernadotte went north immediately and ably organized the defense, though disease rather than force of arms proved the undoing of the British expedition. When the danger had disappeared and Bernadotte returned to Paris late in September political suspicions still surrounded him, and the minister of war tried to force him to go at once to a health resort—or presumably anywhere far from Paris. Bernadotte insisted on his right to live where he pleased, but yielded to an order to go to the emperor's headquarters in Vienna, where he remained Oct. 9–21, 1809. He then returned to Paris.

In the midst of this shadow and uncertainty came the dramatic call to a new life as crown prince and heir to the throne of Sweden. In 1809 Sweden had lost Finland to Russia; a palace revolution had overthrown King Gustav IV Adolf, and put on the throne the aged, childless Charles XIII, with the Danish Christian August as elected crown prince. In June 1810 the prince suddenly died, and Sweden, at the nadir of her fortunes, was forced again to seek a man to pilot the state and to be ready to succeed the ruler. It was natural to seek at least the advice of the master of Europe, then at the pinnacle of his power. Hence a delegation was despatched to Napoleon, but the emperor's peculiar reluctance to exert influence in this affair soon placed the initiative in the wholly unauthorized hands of baron Otto Mörner. Mörner was a young Swedish patriot who knew of Bernadotte's military career, his administration of Hanover and the Hansa towns, and his charitable treatment of Swedish prisoners. He contacted the marshal-prince and aroused his interest, then gained support from a few other Swedes in Paris. On his return to Sweden the government arrested him, but the fire had been lighted. The delegates to the special *Riksdag* in Örebro were influenced by the prince's military reputation and by the knowledge that his fortune would bolster the feeble Swedish *Riksbank*. Previous candidates were abandoned at the eleventh hour, and on Aug. 21, 1810, Bernadotte was elected crown prince. On Oct. 20 he accepted the Lutheran faith and landed in Sweden, there to establish the only enduring dynasty of the Napoleonic regime. Continuity in Sweden was maintained by his adoption as son by Charles XIII, and both king and queen were quickly charmed by the new heir, who took the name of Carl Johan (Charles John). The crown prince at once assumed actual leadership of the government and acted officially as regent during the prolonged illnesses of the king.

Foreign policy was of necessity the chief concern of Bernadotte's first years in Sweden. The majority of the people hoped for the reconquest of Finland and expected this to come by alliance with France. But a small group in the government looked instead to an annexation of Norway. Bernadotte himself, with vision undistorted by hereditary hatred of Russia, felt that any attempt to wrest Finland from the vast empire to the east would but perpetuate war and lead to the complete ruin of Sweden. Norway seemed to him a natural geographic and cultural unit with Sweden; he therefore bent every energy to make the Swedes forget Finland and build a peninsular Scandinavian state. He was guided also by three convictions: a belief in the inevitability of Napoleon's collapse; the idea that Sweden's economy demanded close ties with Great Britain and the smashing of the continental system; his personal need to achieve something for Sweden which would establish him and his family in power. Napoleon tried to deprive his ex-marshal of any opportunity to reorient Swedish policy, and on the heels of Bernadotte's departure sent a demand that Sweden declare war on Britain; Swedish Pomerania must cease to serve as a leak in the "continental system." In Nov. 1810 Sweden had no choice, but she declared war with her fingers crossed and fought it with her hands folded, in a tacit understanding with the English that there would be no shooting. Napoleonic annoyance at this state of affairs led at last to the sudden French occupation of Swedish Pomerania in Jan. 1812.

This attack on Swedish territory was all that was needed to disillusion the Francophile Swedes and win approval for Bernadotte's policy. Immediately negotiations began with Alexander of Russia for an alliance against Napoleon. This was concluded in April 1812, and in August Bernadotte and Alexander met in cordial conference at Åbo (Turku), Finland. Alexander pledged to send 35,000 men to help Bernadotte conquer Norway from Denmark, and Bernadotte pledged that as soon as this aim was accomplished he would lead an army to the continent to aid Russia against Napoleon. Russia at the least won the friendship of its age-old enemy at a critical moment, and Sweden won the first ally for her major political shift. Through the coming months, while the French were staggering back from the disaster of the Moscow campaign, Bernadotte tried to gain other allies. His services were so eagerly desired that Britain (March 1813) and Prussia (April 1813) signed the clauses hateful to them guaranteeing Sweden possession of Norway, and Britain granted a generous subsidy. Austria held aloof. The allies then brought combined pressure on Bernadotte to forego his right to get Norway at once and aid in the great campaign against Napoleon. Bernadotte agreed, and an extra war with Denmark was thus postponed. But the crown prince came to distrust the good faith of his allies, and antagonisms grew.

Bernadotte landed 30,000 men at Stralsund in May 1813, but withheld them from action because the promised Russian and Prussian troops had not yet been sent him. Russia and Prussia made a ten weeks' armistice with Napoleon on June 4 and all action was delayed. In the interim misunderstandings were alleviated, and at the general conference at Trachenberg in July Bernadotte mapped out what came to be the basic plan of campaign which led to Leipzig. The foreign contingents were given to Carl Johan, who became commander of all the forces in north Germany, the right wing of the sweeping semicircular offensive. Fighting was resumed on Aug. 17, 1813, and on Aug. 23 he disposed his forces for the defeat of Oudinot at Grossbeeren, Germany. The Prussians bore the brunt of battle and blamed Bernadotte for sparing his Swedes—which he frankly did. He considered the war in north Germany a primarily Prussian concern; he did not share the desire of the Germans to exterminate all Frenchmen; and he felt the need to save his Swedes for the war with Denmark—he therefore would not waste them. Hence at the battle of Dennewitz, Sept. 6, there was the same skilful and successful disposition of troops, and the Prussians again did the lion's share of fighting.

Gradually now the armies converged toward Leipzig, where on Oct. 16–19 was fought the decisive Battle of the Nations. Here again, though his preliminary movements were above reproach, he showed a reluctance to come to direct grips with the French. Obviously he could not afford to risk an allied defeat, yet he hoped that the other armies could accomplish the common object. Though he was not present the first day of the battle, his artillery took a prominent part on the second day (the 18th) and the Swedish infantry joined battle on the 19th.

After the battle at Leipzig Bernadotte decided that French defeat was assured and that he had better collect on the unrealized promises of his allies. On Oct. 29 he turned his armies north and in a rapid but unspectacular campaign forced Denmark to sue for peace. In the treaty of Kiel (Jan. 14, 1814) King Frederick VI of Denmark signed over Norway to the Swedish crown (the transfer did not include the overseas possessions). Swedish control was far from being established in Norway, but the insistence and threats of the allies could be no longer disregarded—Bernadotte had to move toward France.

Nevertheless, the army of the north got only to the Netherlands, and Bernadotte's headquarters were long in Liége. He seemed to move with leaden feet while the Austrians, the Russians and the eager Prussians battered Napoleon into abdication. Natural hesitancy to invade his homeland was heightened in Bernadotte's case by an irresistible ambition: to become king or "protector" in France on the overthrow of the emperor. The tsar encouraged the idea and friends such as Mme. de Stäel and Benjamin Constant urged it; ten years earlier he had been a logical choice for leadership by the opposition—why not now? He failed to realize how completely he was alienated from the French people. He failed to appreciate also that the victorious allies would not tolerate another military man at the head of the French state. Furthermore, he would not risk his comfortable position in Sweden by a bold stroke which might leave him with nothing. Hence his dream faded into thin air, and his brief visit to Paris after the armistice was far from glorious.

Difficulties in the north recalled him to duty. The Norwegians refused to recognize the treaty of Kiel: the king of Denmark was also king of Norway, but he had no right to transfer sovereignty. Some Norwegians desired union with Sweden, but most preferred to attempt independence. An assembly drew up the constitution of Eidsvold (May 17, 1814) and chose the Danish *Statholder* Christian Frederick as king. Bernadotte blamed Danish intrigue for the Norwegian opposition but hastened north determined to conquer the country directly.

With the reluctant but unwavering support of his allies he conducted an efficient and almost bloodless campaign. On Aug. 14 the Norwegians signed the convention of Moss and within the next few weeks arrangements were worked out which preserved the essential liberal principles of the Eidsvold constitution, the only real change being that which required that the king be the king of Sweden. At a time when military force could have established, temporarily at least, any regime it wished, it is significant that Bernadotte insisted on a humane and decidedly democratic settlement. Future conflicts of authority and opinion between parliament and king and between Norway and Sweden were often severe, but obviously 1814 definitely set Norway on the road to the complete independence which it realized in 1905. From the standpoint of Bernadotte and the Swedes much had been accomplished: retirement from Pomerania and from Finland took Sweden out of two areas of conflict; the connection with Norway prevented that land from being used again by Denmark as a place from which to attack Sweden in the back. The long era of peace in the north from 1814 to 1940 is in itself evidence of the farsightedness of Bernadotte's "policy of 1812."

The 30 years following 1814 were fruitful ones for Bernadotte and for the kingdoms of Sweden and Norway, though they brought the inevitable tensions of a changing social, economic and political life. Bernadotte's ties with his old homeland were gradually cut. Prince Oscar, Bernadotte's only child (born 1799), had come to Sweden with his mother in 1811 (January) and was reared as a Swede. Désirée, however, had returned to Paris and did not come to Sweden to stay until 1823, on the occasion of Prince Oscar's betrothal and marriage (to Princess Josephine, daughter of Eugene de Beauharnais, granddaughter of the king of Bavaria). Through this marriage and its issue the Bernadotte dynasty was destined to continue in Sweden, long-lived and prolific. Though actually the most influential figure in the state from 1810 on, Bernadotte did not acquire the royal title until Feb. 5, 1818, upon the death of Charles XIII.

Having achieved the great goal of his foreign policy, the aim of Bernadotte after 1814 was to retain his position. During the period of the Congress of Vienna there were those who thought that the parvenu prince should be sacrificed to the principle of legitimacy. Prince Clemens W. N. Lothar von Metternich, Louis XVIII, and later Charles X of France were hostile, and the sons of the deposed Gustav IV Adolf were potential troublemakers. But the friendship of Tsars Alexander and Nicholas, and the support of the British government, both based upon recognition of Bernadotte's services and the legality of his position, left his status undisturbed. During the "Hundred Days" of 1815 Bernadotte watched events with keen interest, but avoided involvement.

The dispute with Denmark over the debt settlement and the conflict with Russia over the Norwegian-Russian frontier were arranged by compromise, and relations with Russia were maintained on a basis of mutual respect—plus watchfulness. Toward Britain the former French marshal changed his attitude when he changed his responsibilities, for he recognized the vital importance to Sweden and Norway of British trade and of the British navy.

A man trained for the battlefield and habituated to command inevitably had some difficulties adjusting himself to the procedure of councils and parliaments. His republican ideals and his common sense had many times to check his autocratic tendencies and his feeling that he alone was right. His failure to learn Swedish made his work more difficult and his mind more suspicious. He wanted to control things himself. Hence he tried to strengthen the merely suspensive veto he had over the legislation of the Norwegian *Storting,* and he exercised a conservative influence in Sweden. Yet when the opposition was really strong he knew how to yield or to compromise. His experience, his knowledge and his magnetic personal charm gave him a power in the state far outweighing that of any of the statesmen of the north in his day; his conscientious attention to the duties of kingship gave him a real mastery over the affairs of state, and won him the admiration and love of the common people.

Norway resented the method by which union had been achieved, and bitter internal controversies arose over questions like payment of the national debt, the celebration of May 17 (the Eidsvold constitution) and the abolition of the nobility. On Norway's responsibility to pay the agreed share of the Danish debt Bernadotte was adamant and even threatened the use of the military to force submission. On the questions of May 17 and the abolition of the nobility he yielded with fear and ill grace to the will of the Norwegian people. Again and again in such cases he would defy and threaten, then adapt himself to necessity. His impulsive gasconades led many both then and since to think of him as emotionally unstable. But always, though bold in talk, he was cautious and farsighted in action. Through royal yielding to pressures which were really strong the democratic processes and forces steadily matured.

Bernadotte was keenly interested in the welfare of the people as a whole and provided a stimulating though paternalistic leadership. He encouraged the founding of the Academy of Agriculture in 1811, was largely responsible for the rebuilding of the great library at the University of Uppsala, and for the spread of popular education. When he first went north he feared that "cognac would be the ruin of the Swedish people" and in the 1830s was able to give strong support to Per Wieselgren and the temperance movement. He likewise promoted medical education and the physical education program of P. H. Ling. National finance was one of his primary interests and he vigorously supported such projects as Platen's famous Göta canal.

Opposition to the king's autocratic methods and dominating position in Swedish life led to demands for his abdication in the late 1830s, and to some republican agitation. But he rode out the storm in Sweden as he had already done in Norway, and at the jubilee in 1843 his peoples were united in sincere expressions of admiration and gratitude to the "grand old man" of the north. When he died, aged 81, March 8, 1844, he left two kingdoms vastly stronger, more prosperous and more populous than in 1810, and a new dynasty firmly entrenched.

Bibliography.—B. Sarrans, Jeune, *Histoire de Bernadotte, Charles XIV Jean* (2 vol., Paris, 1845); B. von Schinkel (ed. by C. W. Bergman and S. J. Boëthius), *Minnen ur Sveriges nyare historia* (12 vol. plus 3, Stockholm and Uppsala, 1855–93); Yngvar Nielsen, *Carl Johan som han virkelig var* (Christiania [Oslo], 1897); J. E. Sars, *Norges politiske historia* (Christiania, 1899); C. Schefer, *Bernadotte roi* (1899); Léonce Pingaud, *Bernadotte, Napoleon et les Bourbons 1797–1844* (Paris, 1901); *Correspondance inédite de l'Empereur Alexandre et de Bernadotte pendant l'année 1812* (1909); Sir Dunbar Plunkett Barton, *Bernadotte, the First Phase* (1914), *Bernadotte and Napoleon 1763–1810* (1921), *Bernadotte, Prince and King* (1925), and *The Amazing Career of Bernadotte* (1929); S. Clason, *Karl XIII och Karl XIV Johan* (vol. XI of *Sveriges Historia,* Stockholm, 1923); F. W. Morén, *Kring 1812 års politik* (Stockholm, 1927); Franklin D. Scott, *Bernadotte and the Fall of Napoleon* (1935); T. T. Höjer, *Carl XIV Johan, den franska tiden* (first of a three volume definitive biography, Stockholm, 1939). (F. D. S.)

CHARLES XV. (1826–1872), king of Sweden and Norway, eldest son of Oscar I., king of Sweden and Norway, and Josephine Beauharnais of Leuchtenberg, was born on May 3, 1826. On June 19, 1850, he married Louisa, daughter of Prince Frederick of the Netherlands. He became regent on Sept. 25, 1857, and king on the death of his father (July 8, 1859). His reign was remarkable for its manifold and far-reaching reforms. Sweden's existing communal law (1862), ecclesiastical law (1863) and criminal law (1864) were enacted. Charles XV. also materially assisted De Geer (*q.v.*) to carry through his memorable reform of the diet in 1865. Charles was a warm advocate of "pan-Scandinavianism" and the political solidarity of the three northern kingdoms, and his enthusiasm led him to give half promises of help to Denmark on the eve of the war of 1864. In view, however, of the unpreparedness of the Swedish army and the absence of support from any of the powers, Charles was forced to observe a strict neutrality. He died at Malmö on Sept. 18, 1872. Charles XV. enjoyed an unusual degree of popularity in both his kingdoms. He was an amateur painter and his *Dikter* show him to have been a true poet. He left one child, a daughter, Louisa Josephina Eugenia, who in 1869 married the crown prince Frederick of Denmark.

See C. Bååth-Holmberg, *Carl XV., som enskild man, konung och konstnär* (Stockholm, 1891); Yngvar Nielsen, *Det norske og svenske Kongehus fra 1818* (Christiania [Oslo], 1883).

CHARLES (Karl Alexander) (1712–1780), prince of Lorraine, the youngest son of Leopold, duke of Lorraine, and grandson of Charles V., duke of Lorraine (*see* p. 289), was born at Lunéville on Dec. 12, 1712. After his elder brother Francis, the duke, had exchanged Lorraine for Tuscany and married Maria Theresa, Charles became an Austrian officer, and he served in the campaigns of 1737 and 1738 against the Turks. At the outbreak of the Silesian wars in 1740 (*see* Austrian Succession, War of the), the queen made her brother-in-law a field marshal, and in 1742 Charles encountered Frederick the Great for the first time at the battle of Chotusitz (May 17). He conducted the successful campaign of 1743 against the French and Bavarians. He married, Jan. 1744, Marianne of Austria (died in 1744), sister of Maria Theresa, who made them jointly governors-general of the Austrian Netherlands. When the war broke out afresh, Charles, at the head of the Austrian army on the Rhine, crossed that river, but on Frederick's resumption of the Silesian war he hurried to Bohemia, whence, aided by the advice of the veteran field marshal Traun, he quickly expelled the Prussians. He took the field again in 1745 in Silesia, but this time without the advice of Traun, and he was twice severely defeated by Frederick, at Hohenfriedberg and at Soor. Subsequently, as commander-in-chief in the Low Countries he received, at Roucoux, a heavy defeat at the hands of Marshal Saxe. His government of the Austrian Netherlands during the peace of 1749–56 was marked by many reforms. After the first reverses of the Seven Years' War (*q.v.*), Maria Theresa called Charles again to the supreme command in the field. The campaign of 1757 opened with Frederick's great victory of Prague, and Prince Charles was shut up with his army in that fortress. In the victory of the relieving army under Daun at Kolin Charles had no part, but he won the battle of Breslau, and great enthusiasm was displayed in Austria over the victory, which seemed to be the final blow to Frederick. But soon afterwards the king of Prussia routed the French at Rossbach, and, swiftly returning to Silesia, he inflicted on Charles the complete and crushing defeat of Leuthen (Dec. 5, 1757). A mere remnant of the Austrian army reassembled after the pursuit, and Charles was relieved of his command. For a year thereafter Prince Charles acted as a military adviser at

Vienna, he then returned to Brussels, where he continued to govern till his death on July 4, 1780, at the castle of Tervueren.

See L. Percy, *Charles de Lorraine et la cour de Bruxelles sous le règne de Marie Thérèse* (1903).

CHARLES (1421–1461), prince of Viana, sometimes called Charles IV., king of Navarre, was the son of John, afterwards John II., king of Aragon, by his marriage with Blanche, daughter of Charles III. of Navarre. Both his grandfather Charles and his mother, who ruled over Navarre, had bequeathed this kingdom to Charles, whose right had also been recognized by the Cortes; but when Blanche died in 1441 her husband John seized the government. The ill-feeling between father and son was increased when in 1447 John took for his second wife Joanna Henriquez, a Castilian princess, who bore him a son, afterwards Ferdinand I., king of Spain. When Joanna began to interfere in the internal affairs of Navarre civil war broke out; and in 1452 Charles, although aided by John II., king of Castile, was taken prisoner. Released upon promising not to take the kingly title until after his father's death, the prince, again unsuccessful in an appeal to arms, took refuge in Italy with Alphonso V., king of Aragon, Naples and Sicily. In 1458 Alphonso died and John became king of Aragon, while Charles was offered Naples and Sicily. He declined these proposals, and having been reconciled with his father returned to Navarre in 1459. Aspiring to marry a Castilian princess, he was thrown into prison by his father; the Catalans rose in his favour, and John was obliged to yield. Charles was recognized as perpetual governor of Catalonia and heir to the kingdom, but he died on Sept. 23, 1461. Charles was a cultured prince; he translated the *Ethics* of Aristotle into Spanish (Saragossa, 1509) and wrote a chronicle of the kings of Navarre, *Crónica de los reyes de Navarra,* an edition of which, edited by J. Yangues y Miranda, was published at Pampeluna (1843).

See G. Desdevises du Dézert, *Carlos d'Aragon* (Paris, 1889).

CHARLES [KARL LUDWIG] (1771–1847), archduke of Austria and duke of Teschen, third son of the emperor Leopold II., was born at Florence (his father being then grand-duke of Tuscany) on Sept. 5, 1771. His youth was spent in Tuscany, at Vienna and in the Austrian Netherlands, where he began his career of military service in the war of the French Revolution. He commanded a brigade at Jemappes, and in the campaign of 1793 distinguished himself at the action of Aldenhoven and the battle of Neerwinden. In this year he became *Statthalter* in Belgium and received the army rank of lieutenant field marshal, which promotion was soon followed by that to *Feldzeugmeister* (master of ordnance). In the remainder of the war in the Low Countries he held high commands, and he was present at Fleurus. In 1795 he served on the Rhine, and in the following year was entrusted with the chief control of all the Austrian forces on that river. His conduct of the operations against Jourdan and Moreau in 1796 marked him out at once as one of the greatest generals in Europe. At first falling back carefully and avoiding a decision, he finally marched away, leaving a mere screen in front of Moreau; falling upon Jourdan he beat him in the battles of Amberg and Würzburg, and drove him over the Rhine with great loss. He then turned upon Moreau's army, which he defeated and forced out of Germany. For this campaign, one of the most brilliant in modern history, *see* FRENCH REVOLUTIONARY WARS. In 1797 he was sent to arrest the victorious march of Gen. Bonaparte in Italy, and he conducted the retreat of the over-matched Austrians with the highest skill. In the campaign of 1799 he was once more opposed to Jourdan, whom he defeated in the battles of Osterach and Stokach, following up his success by invading Switzerland and defeating Masséna in the (first) battle of Zürich, after which he re-entered Germany and drove the French once more over the Rhine. Ill-health, however, forced him to retire to Bohemia, whence he was soon recalled to undertake the task of checking Moreau's advance on Vienna. The result of the battle of Hohenlinden had, however, foredoomed the attempt, and the archduke had to make the armistice of Steyer. His popularity was now such that the diet of Ratisbon, which met in 1802, resolved to erect a statue in his honour and to give him the title of saviour of his country; but Charles refused both distinctions.

In the short and disastrous war of 1805 the archduke Charles commanded what was intended to be the main army, in Italy, but events made Germany the decisive theatre of operations, and the defeats sustained on the Danube neutralized the success obtained by the archduke over Masséna in the desperately fought battle of Caldiero. With the conclusion of peace began his active work of army reorganization, which was first tested on the field in 1809. As generalissimo of the army he had been made field marshal some years before. As president of the Council of War, and supported by the prestige of being the only general who had proved capable of defeating the French, he promptly initiated a far-reaching scheme of reform, which replaced the obsolete methods of the 18th century, the chief characteristics of the new order being the adoption of the "nation in arms" principle and of the French war organization and tactics. The new army was surprised in the process of transition by the war of 1809, of which Charles was commander in chief; yet even so it proved a far more formidable opponent than the old, and, against the now heterogeneous army which Napoleon controlled (*see* NAPOLEONIC CAMPAIGNS) it succumbed only after a desperate struggle. Its initial successes were neutralized by the reverses of Abensberg, Landshut and Eckmühl; but, after the evacuation of Vienna, the archduke won the great battle of Aspern-Essling (*q.v.*) and soon afterwards fought the still more desperate battle of Wagram (*q.v.*), at the close of which the Austrians were defeated but not routed; they had inflicted upon Napoleon a loss of over 50,000 men in the two battles. At the end of the campaign the archduke gave up all his military offices, and spent the rest of his life in retirement, except a short time in 1815, when he was governor of Mainz. In 1822 he succeeded to the duchy of Saxe-Teschen. The archduke Charles married, in 1815, Princess Henrietta of Nassau-Weilburg (d. 1829). He had four sons, the eldest of whom, the archduke Albert (*q.v.*) became one of the most celebrated generals in Europe, and two daughters, the elder of whom became queen of Naples. He died at Vienna on April 30, 1847.

The caution which the archduke preached so earnestly in his strategical works, he displayed in practice only when the situation seemed to demand it, though his education certainly prejudiced him in favour of the defensive at all costs. He was at the same time capable of forming and executing the most daring offensive strategy, and his tactical skill in the handling of troops, whether in wide turning movements, as at Würzburg and Zürich, or in masses, as at Aspern and Wagram, was certainly equal to that of any leader of his time, Napoleon only excepted. The campaign of 1796 is considered almost faultless. That he sustained defeat in 1809 was due in part to the great numerical superiority of the French and their allies, and in part to the condition of his newly reorganized troops. His six weeks' inaction after the victory of Aspern is, however, open to unfavourable criticism. As a military writer, his position in the evolution of the art of war is very important, and his doctrines had naturally the greatest weight. Nevertheless they cannot but be considered as antiquated even in 1806. Caution and the importance of "strategic points" are the chief features of his system. The rigidity of his geographical strategy may be gathered from the direction that "this principle is *never* to be departed from." Again and again he repeats the advice that nothing should be hazarded unless one's army is *completely* secure, a rule which he himself neglected with such brilliant results in 1796. In his tactical writings the same spirit is conspicuous. His reserve in battle is designed to "cover a retreat." The baneful influence of these principles was shown in the maintenance of Königgrätz-Josefstadt in 1866 as a "strategic point," which was preferred to the defeat of the separated Prussian armies; in the strange plans produced in Vienna for the campaign of 1859, and in the "almost unintelligible" battle of Montebello in the same year. The theory and the practice of the archduke Charles form one of the most curious contrasts in military history. In the one he is often unreal, in the other he displayed, besides great skill, a vivid activity which made him for long the most formidable opponent of Napoleon.

His writings were edited by the archduke Albert and his brother the archduke William in the *Ausgewählte Schriften seiner Kgl. Hoheit Erzh. Karl v. Österreich* (1862; reprinted 1893, Vienna and Leipzig), which includes the *Grundsätze der Kriegskunst für die Generäle* (1806), *Grundsätze der Strategie erläutert durch die Darstellung des Feldzugs 1796* (1814), *Gesch. des Feldzugs von 1799* (1819)—the two latter invaluable contributions to the history of the war, and papers "on the higher art of war," etc. *See*, besides the histories of the period, F. J. A. Schneidawind, *Karl, Erzherzog v. Österr. und die österr. Armee* (Vienna, 1840) and *Das Buch vom Erzh. Karl* (1848); Ed. Duller, *Erzh. Karl von Österr.* (1845–47); H. von Zeissberg, *Erzh. Karl von Österr.* (Vienna, 1893); C. von Binder-Krieglstein, *Geist und Stoff im Kriege* (Vienna, 1893); M. E. von Angeli, *Erzherzog Karl als Feldherr und Heere-organisator,* 5 vol. (Vienna and Leipzig, 1896–97); R. V. Caemmerer, *Development of Strategical Science,* Eng. trans. by Karl von Donat, ch. iv (1905).

CHARLES (*c.* 1319–1364), duke of Brittany, known as CHARLES OF BLOIS and CHARLES OF CHÂTILLON, was the son of Guy of Châtillon, count of Blois (d. 1342), and of Margaret of Valois, sister of Philip VI of France. In 1337 Charles married Joan the Lame of Penthièvre (d. 1384), daughter of Guy of Brittany, count of Penthièvre (d. 1331), and thus acquired a right to the succession of the duchy of Brittany. On the death of John III, duke of Brittany, in April 1341, his brother John, count of Montfort l'Amaury, and his niece Joan, wife of Charles of Blois, disputed the succession. Charles of Blois, sustained by Philip VI, captured John of Montfort, who was supported by King Edward III, at Nantes, besieged his wife Joan of Flanders at Hennebont and took Quimper and Guérande (1344). But next year his partisans were defeated at Cadoret, and in June 1347 Charles was himself wounded and taken prisoner at La Roche-Derrien. He was not liberated until 1356, when he continued the war against the young John of Montfort and perished in the battle of Auray, on Sept. 29, 1364. In his lifetime he had been held a saint and a thaumaturge by the people; and his grave and relics were venerated, and his cult developed. In 1904 his beatification was proclaimed by the Holy See.

See Monuments du procès de canonisation du bienheureux Charles de Blois, duc de Bretagne, 1320–64 (Saint-Brieux, 1921).

CHARLES, called THE BOLD or LE TÉMÉRAIRE (1433–1477), duke of Burgundy, succeeded his father, Philip the Good, in 1467, after taking his place during his last illness (April 12, 1465, to June 15, 1467); before this, his title was count of Charolais. Born at Dijon, French by his paternal ancestry, brought up in the French manner as a friend of the dauphin (afterward Louis XI of France) and married successively to his French cousins Catherine (d. 1446), daughter of Charles VII of France, and Isabella (d. 1465), daughter of Charles I of Bourbon, Charles did not become hostile to the French crown until he took over the government of his duchy. Then it pleased him to remember the foreign origins of Isabella of Portugal, his mother, who was John of Gaunt's granddaughter, and of his third wife, whom he was to marry in 1468, Margaret of York, a sister of Edward IV of England. Throughout his reign, Charles aimed at making the Burgundian territories independent of France.

Charles was almost entirely successful until 1474. He succeeded in extending his possessions, in organizing them as a state and in freeing them from the French crown. Much annoyed by Louis XI's repurchase of the towns on the Somme which had been temporarily ceded to Philip the Good by the treaty of Arras (1435), he entered upon his lifelong struggle against Louis and became one of the principal leaders of the League of the Public Weal. After the battle of Montlhéry (July 16, 1465), he forced Louis to restore to him the towns on the Somme and to promise him the hand of his daughter Catherine of France, as his third wife, with Champagne as dowry. But when Louis encouraged Dinant in its revolt against Burgundy, Charles sacked it (1466); and the Liégeois, whom the French were continually inciting to revolt, were defeated in battle and deprived of their liberties after the death of Philip the Good (1467). Louis now tried negotiations with Charles at Péronne (Oct. 1468). There, in the course of the discussions, Charles was informed of a fresh revolt of the Liégeois, secretly fomented by Louis. Looking on Louis as a traitor, Charles nevertheless treated with him but at the same time forced him to assist in quelling the revolt; the town was destroyed and the inhabitants were massacred. The truce was not lasting. Louis cited Charles to appear before the *parlement* of Paris and seized some of the towns on the Somme. The duke retaliated by invading Normandy and the Île-de-France, ravaged the country as far as Rouen, but failed in an attack on Beauvais (1471–72). He decided to wait, before renewing his attempt, for the conclusion of an alliance with Edward IV and for the solution of the problem relative to the eastern border of his states.

Charles wished to extend his territories as far as the Rhine and to make them into a single unit by acquiring the lands between Burgundy, Luxembourg and the Netherlands. He lost no opportunity: he purchased the county of Ferrette, the landgraviate of Alsace and some other towns from the archduke Sigismund of Austria in 1469; he compelled the old duke Arnold of Gelderland to transfer his estates to him in 1473; and he set nominees of his own in certain other places and wished to do the same at Cologne, where he intended to install a garrison as it was both an important centre of trade and an imperial electorate (1469–74). To achieve his territorial aims, it only remained for him to subdue the Swiss cantons and to get Lorraine from René II (René of Vaudémont).

Meanwhile Charles had been reorganizing his army and the administration of his territories. Statutes promulgated at Thionville (1473) instituted companies of four squadrons, at his expense, and made rules for discipline and tactics; Charles also had many excellent guns cast. He hired mercenaries and took many Italian *condottieri* into his service. Intending to centralize the government, he created by statute a single *chambre des comptes,* a *chambre du trésor* to survey the administration of the domain and a *chambre des généraux* to control the collection of taxes. He exacted very heavy taxes indeed from the *états-généraux,* which became a regular institution in his territories. Moreover, he established the *grand conseil* at Malines, with jurisdiction to supersede that of the *parlement* of Paris, which he no longer recognized.

It remained for Charles to acquire a royal title. For a short time he entertained designs on the imperial crown; but this he renounced. On the other hand, he believed that he had persuaded the emperor Frederick III, in the course of conversations at Trèves (Trier), to agree to crown him king. The royal insignia were ready and the ceremony arranged, when Frederick precipitately fled by night (Sept. 1473). He probably was suspicious of the ambitious Charles.

In less than three years, Charles's dream vanished. The crown had slipped through his fingers. He was obliged to give up his plan of taking the little town of Neuss, which he had unsuccessfully besieged for ten months (July 1474 to June 1475), from the citizens of Cologne. Moreover, the treaty of Picquigny (Aug. 29, 1475) concluded by Edward IV and Louis XI made certain the defection of his English ally. Attacked by René of Lorraine and his allies, Charles took Nancy in Nov. 1475; but in March and in June 1476, he was defeated by the Swiss, at Grandson and at Morat (*see* SWITZERLAND: *History*). Next October he lost Nancy. Then, on Jan. 5, 1477, a further battle was fought outside Nancy, and Charles himself was killed; his mutilated body was discovered some days later.

The fragility of his achievement is proved by its rapid disintegration during the minority of Mary, his daughter by Isabella of Bourbon. Yet Charles the Bold was not merely a belated representative of the chivalrous spirit; he was a man of wide knowledge and culture, already a prince of the Renaissance. His haste, his lack of adaptability and his obstinacy lost him much more than did his visionary approach and his boldness.

BIBLIOGRAPHY.—Olivier de la Marche, *Mémoires,* ed. by H. Beaune and J. d'Arbaumont (Paris, 1883); Philippe de Commynes, *Mémoires,* ed. by Mlle. Dupont (Paris, 1840–47), by B. de Mandrot (Paris, 1901–03) or by J. Calmette and G. Durville (Paris, 1924–25); also R. Putnam, *Charles the Bold* (London, 1908); A. C. P. Haggard, *Louis XI and Charles the Bold* (London, 1913); H. Pirenne, *Histoire de Belgique,* vol. ii, 5th ed. (Brussels, 1929); J. Faussemagne, *L'Apanage ducal de Bourgogne dans ses rapports avec la monarchie française* (Lyons, 1937); J. Bartier, *Charles le Téméraire* (Brussels, 1944); M. Mätzenauer, *Studien zur Politik Karls des Kühnen bis 1474* (Zurich, 1946).

(MI. M.)

CHARLES (953–*c.* 992), duke of Lower Lorraine, was a younger son of the Frankish king Louis IV and thus a member of the Carolingian family. He received the duchy of Lower Lorraine from the emperor Otto II in 977; and he aided Otto in his struggle with King Lothair, with whom however he became reconciled after Otto's death. On the death of his nephew Louis V (987), Charles made an effort to secure the Frankish crown. Hugh Capet, however, was the successful candidate, and war broke out. Charles had gained some successes and had captured Reims (989), when in 991 he was treacherously seized by Adalberon (*q.v.*), bishop of Laon, and handed over to Hugh. Imprisoned with his wife and his younger children at Orléans, Charles did not long survive his humiliation. His eldest son Otto, duke of Lower Lorraine, died *c.* 1012.

See F. Lot, *Les derniers Carolingiens* (Paris, 1891).

CHARLES II (d. 1431), duke of Lorraine, called THE BOLD, is sometimes referred to as Charles I. A son of Duke John I, he succeeded his father in 1390; but he neglected his duchy and passed his life in warfare. He died on Jan. 25, 1431, leaving two daughters, one of whom, Isabella (d. 1453) married René I of Anjou (1409–80), king of Naples, who succeeded his father-in-law as duke of Lorraine.

CHARLES III (1543–1608), called THE GREAT, duke of Lorraine, was a son of Duke Francis I (d. 1545) and a descendant of René of Anjou. Born at Nancy on Feb. 18, 1543, he was brought up at the court of Henry II of France, marrying Henry's daughter Claude in 1559. He took part in the wars of religion in France and was a member of the Holy league. The duke, who was an excellent ruler of Lorraine, died at Nancy on May 14, 1608. He had three sons: Henry (d. 1624) and Francis (d. 1632), who became in turn dukes of Lorraine, and Charles (d. 1607), bishop of Metz and Strasbourg.

CHARLES IV (1604–1675), duke of Lorraine and Bar, born at Nancy on April 5, 1604, became duke in 1624 by right of his wife Nicole, his uncle Henry II's daughter and heiress, whom he had married in 1621. As, however, both he and his father, Francis of Vaudémont, wished to abolish the female right of succession to the duchy, Francis was proclaimed to be Henry's rightful successor in Nov. 1625; then he abdicated in Charles's favour after a few days' reign. To counter French interventions in the affairs of Lorraine, Charles in 1627 began negotiations with England against France, while at the same time supporting the Holy Roman emperor against the Swedes (*see* THIRTY YEARS' WAR); and from 1629 he took up the cause of Gaston of Orléans against Louis XIII. Subdued by the French in 1632 (treaty of Liverdun, June 26) and again in 1633 (when he had to cede Nancy), Charles abdicated on Jan. 19, 1634, in favour of his brother, Cardinal Nicolas Francis (who left the church and married Nicole's sister Claude), and entered the imperial service; Charles was banished from the kingdom of France. He took part in the battle of Nordlingen and in successive campaigns along the French eastern frontier. The treaty of Saint Germain (March 29, 1641) restored Lorraine and Bar to him, shorn of several towns and fortresses; but as he proved treacherous again, the duchies were again occupied and declared neutral (June 1644). Returning then to the imperial service, Charles transferred himself to the Spanish after the peace of Westphalia, from which he was excluded. In 1652 he made two incursions into France on behalf of the Fronde (*q.v.*), but in 1654 the Spaniards arrested him for intriguing with Cardinal Mazarin. Imprisoned at Antwerp and Toledo till the treaty of the Pyrenees (1659), he recovered his duchies by the treaty of Vincennes (Feb. 28, 1661) and then arranged to sell them to Louis XIV by the treaty of Montmartre (Feb. 6, 1662), which was however annulled by the treaty of Noméy (Aug. 31, 1663). French troops overran Lorraine yet again in 1670, and Charles was severely defeated by Marshal Turenne at Sinzheim in 1674. In 1675, however, he defeated François de Créquy at Konzer Brücke (Aug. 11) and captured him at Trier (Sept. 6); but on Sept. 18 he died in a village near Birkenfeld. Charles Henry of Vaudémont (1649–1723) was his bastard son by Béatrix de Cusance.

A brave and skilful soldier, Charles was an impolitic statesman, missing good opportunities and paying always a heavy price to redeem his acts of rashness.

BIBLIOGRAPHY.—R. Parisot, *Histoire de Lorraine,* vol. ii (Paris, 1922); F. des Robert, *Campagnes de Charles IV . . . 1638–48,* 2 vol. (Paris, 1883–88), *Charles IV et Mazarin* (Nancy, 1899).

CHARLES V (1643–1690), duke of Lorraine and Bar, was born in Vienna on April 3, 1643, the son of Charles IV's brother Nicolas Francis. Emperor Leopold I gave him a regiment in 1664, and he distinguished himself at the battle of Saint Gotthard. He was a candidate for the Polish crown in 1668–69 and again, when the French were occupying Lorraine, in 1674. Recognized by all save France as his uncle's heir in 1675, he was never to possess his duchies. Promoted field marshal by the emperor in 1675, he took Philippsburg in 1676. He married Eleonora Maria, dowager queen of Poland and the emperor's sister, in 1678. The peace of Nijmegen offered him his duchies under conditions that he rejected. In 1683, with a weak imperial army, he opposed the Turkish advance on Vienna. Two months after the Turks had invested the city, John Sobieski's Poles and the Bavarian and Saxon contingents arrived to reinforce Charles, and on Sept. 12 the Christians routed the enemy and raised the siege. Advancing into Hungary, Charles besieged Buda (1684), stormed Neuhäusel (1685), finally took Buda (1686) and, in Aug. 1687, won the great victory of Mohács. Transferred to the Rhine for the War of the Grand Alliance, Charles took Mainz and Bonn in 1689 but died suddenly at Wels on April 18, 1690. As well as the military genius that made him one of Louis XIV's most respected adversaries, he had qualities of statesmanship; but these he could not exert for the benefit of his duchies. At the peace of Ryswick (1697) Lorraine and Bar were assigned to his son Leopold Joseph Charles (1679–1729).

CHARLES II (CHARLES LOUIS DE BOURBON) (1799–1883), duke of Parma, succeeded his mother, Maria Louisa in the duchy of Lucca in 1824. He introduced economy into the administration, increased the schools, and in 1832 became a Protestant. In 1842 he returned to the Catholic Church and made Thomas Ward, an English groom, his prime minister, a man not without ability and tact. In 1847 he declared himself hostile to the reforms introduced by Pius IX. The Lucchesi demanded the constitution of 1805, promised them by the treaty of Vienna, and a national guard, but the duke, in spite of the warnings of Ward, refused all concessions. A few weeks later he sold his life interest in the duchy to Tuscany. On Oct. 17 Maria Louisa of Austria, duchess of Parma, died, and Charles Louis succeeded to her throne by the terms of the Florence treaty, assuming the style of Charles II. His administration of Parma was characterized by ruinous finance, debts, disorder and increased taxation, and he concluded an offensive and defensive alliance with Austria. After the outbreak of the revolution in 1848, he abdicated in April and left Parma in the hands of a provisional government, whereupon the people voted for union with Piedmont. Later Charles II issued an edict from Weistropp annulling the acts of the provisional government.

In May 1849 Charles confirmed his abdication, and was succeeded by his son CHARLES III (1823–54), who, protected by Austrian troops, placed Parma under martial law, inflicted heavy penalties on the members of the late provisional government, closed the university and instituted a regular policy of persecution. A violent ruler, a drunkard and a libertine, he was assassinated on March 26, 1854. At his death his widow, Louisa (1819–64), sister of the comte de Chambord, became regent during the minority of his son Robert (1848–1907), who was dispossessed when the duchy was annexed to the kingdom of Sardinia in 1860.

CHARLES (1270–1325), count of Valois, of Anjou and of Maine, third son of Philip III, king of France, was born on March 12, 1270. He received in appanage the four lordships of Crépy, La Ferté-Milon, Pierrefonds and Béthisy, which together formed the countship of Valois. A handsome man, a brilliant and generous knight, but an ambitious and needy prince, he was a pretender to many crowns and had the strange destiny to be "son of a king, brother of a king, uncle of three kings, father of a king, but never a king." In 1284 Martin IV, having excommunicated Peter III, king of Aragon, offered his kingdom to Charles; but the campaign in Catalonia, by which Philip III attempted to conquer it for his son, was a disaster, and Philip died on his return. In 1290 Charles married Margaret, daughter of Charles II of Naples, and renounced his pretensions to Aragon in return for the counties of Anjou and Maine; his brother, Philip IV, gave him Alençon and Perche. Asked by Boniface VIII for his aid against the Ghibellines, Charles went to Italy in 1301, entered Florence and helped Charles of Naples to reconquer Calabria and Apulia from the house of Aragon, but failed in Sicily. Having married (1301) Catherine de Courtenay, a granddaughter of the eastern emperor Baldwin II, he tried to assert his rights to Byzantium. In 1308, on the death of Albert of Austria, he was a candidate for the western empire, with Philip IV's support; but Pope Clement V quashed his candidature in favour of Henry of Luxemburg. Despite these failures, Charles was a loyal servant of the French kings, particularly in war; he commanded their armies in Guienne (1295 and 1324) and in Flanders (1297, 1299, 1300, 1303, 1314, 1315); in 1300 he took Douai, Béthune and Dam and received the submission of Guy of Dampierre; and in 1304 he helped Philip IV win the battle of Mons-en-Pévèle. Under Louis X he headed the party of feudal reaction and was the main instrument of Enguerrand de Marigny's ruin. In 1316, at Louis's death, he tried unsuccessfully to be made regent. He died at Le Perray (Seine-et-Oise) on Dec. 16, 1325. He had been married three times and had 14 children. His eldest son, Philip, became king of France in 1328, the first of the royal house of Valois.

See Joseph Petit, *Charles de Valois* (Paris, 1900).

CHARLES, ELIZABETH (1828–1896), English author, was born at Tavistock on Jan. 2 1828, the daughter of John Rundle, M.P., and died at Hampstead on March 28 1896. In 1851 she married Andrew Paton Charles. Her best known book, *The Chronicles of the Schönberg-Cotta Family,* was published in 1862, and was translated into most of the European languages, into Arabic, and into many Indian dialects. Mrs. Charles wrote in all some 50 books, the majority of a semi-religious character.

CHARLES, JACQUES ALEXANDRE CÉSAR (1746–1823), French mathematician and physicist, was born at Beaugency, Loiret, on Nov. 12, 1746. From being a clerk in the ministry of finance, he turned to scientific pursuits, and became one of the most acute of physical researchers and inventors. He was the first, in 1783, to employ hydrogen for the inflation of balloons (*see* BALLOON), and about 1787 he anticipated Gay Lussac's law of the dilatation of gases with heat, which on that account is sometimes known by his name. He improved the Gravesand heliostat and the aerometer of Fahrenheit and invented a "thermometric hydrometer," a "goniometer by reflection" and many other ingenious physical devices. In 1785 he was elected to the Academy of Sciences, and subsequently he became professor of physics at the Conservatoire des Arts et Métiers. He died in Paris on April 7, 1823. His published papers are chiefly concerned with mathematical topics.

CHARLES, THOMAS (1755–1814), Welsh Nonconformist divine, was born at Longmoor, Carmarthenshire, on Oct. 14, 1755, and educated at Jesus college, Oxford, for the Church. He was ordained priest in 1782, and held some curacies in Somersetshire, but he resigned these in 1783 and returned to Wales. He had fallen under the influence of the Welsh revivalists before he went to Oxford, and had Methodist connections. He found no pulpit open to him in the Church in Wales, and joined the Calvinistic Methodists in 1784.

He had already begun to provide classes for poor children in Bala; he now held the classes in the chapel, and gradually began the system of Welsh Circulating Schools, on the model devised by Griffith Jones (d. 1761). By 1794 he had 20 travelling masters at work. In 1785 he had become the agent of the Sunday School Society in Wales; he secured supplies of Welsh Bibles from the S.P.C.K. and in 1801 alone nearly 3,000 were distributed. In 1802 he went to London to place Welsh requirements before the Religious Tract Society, and put his case so well that his friends decided to found a society for the publication and distribution of the Scriptures. This was the origin of the British and Foreign Bible Society. He stimulated similar educational movements in Ireland and Scotland. In 1810 he led the movement for the establishing of a regular ordained ministry in the Calvinistic Methodist connection, and, this work accomplished, returned to his task of fostering auxiliary Bible societies. He died on Oct. 5, 1814. Charles compiled the *Geiriadur Ysgrythyrol,* a biblical dictionary (4 vols. 1805–08), which has passed through many editions; he drew up the first definite constitution of the Welsh Methodists, and wrote many Welsh tracts. The first Welsh biography of Charles appeared in 1816. *See* W. Hughes, *Life and Letters of Thomas Charles* (Rhyl 1881), in which some of Charles's minor writings are reprinted.

CHARLES ALBERT (CARLO ALBERTO) (1798–1849), king of Sardinia (Piedmont), son of Prince Charles of Savoy-Carignano and Princess Albertine of Saxe-Courland, was born on Oct. 12, 1798, a few days before the French occupied Piedmont and forced his cousin, King Charles Emmanuel, to take refuge in Sardinia. In 1802 King Charles Emmanuel abdicated in favour of his brother, Victor Emmanuel I. On the fall of Napoleon in 1814 the Piedmontese court returned to Turin, and the king was anxious to secure the succession for Charles Albert, knowing that Austria meditated excluding him from it in favour of an Austrian archduke. He was summoned to Turin, given tutors to instruct him in legitimist principles, and on Oct. 1, 1817, married the archduchess Maria Theresa of Tuscany, who, on March 14, 1820, gave birth to Victor Emmanuel, afterwards king of Italy.

The Piedmontese government at this time was most reactionary, and had made a clean sweep of all French institutions. But there were strong Italian nationalists and anti-Austrian tendencies among the younger nobles and army officers, and the Carbonari and other revolutionary societies had made much progress. Their hopes centred in the young Carignano, whose agreeable manners had endeared him to all, and who had many friends among the Liberals and Carbonari. Early in 1820 a revolutionary movement was set on foot. Charles Albert no doubt was aware of this, but he never actually became a Carbonaro, and was surprised and startled when after the outbreak of the Neapolitan revolution of 1820 some of the leading conspirators in the Piedmontese army informed him that a military rising was ready and that they counted on his help (March 2, 1821). He induced them to delay the outbreak and informed the king, requesting him, however, not to punish anyone. On the 10th the garrison of Alessandria mutinied, and two days later Turin was in the hands of the insurgents, the people demanding the Spanish constitution. The king at once abdicated and appointed Charles Albert regent. The latter, pressed by the revolutionists and abandoned by his ministers, granted the constitution and sent to inform Charles Felix, who was now king, of the occurrence. Charles Felix, who was then at Modena, repudiated the regent's acts, accepted Austrian military assistance, with which the rising was easily quelled, and exiled Charles Albert to Florence. The young prince found himself the most unpopular man in Italy, for while the Liberals looked on him as a traitor, to the king and the Conservatives he was a dangerous revolutionist. At the Congress of Verona (1822) the Austrian chancellor, Prince Metternich, tried to induce Charles Felix to set aside Charles Albert's rights of succession. But the king was piqued by Austria's interference, and as both the grand-duke of Tuscany and the duke of Wellington supported him, Charles Albert's claims were respected. But it was not until he had signed a secret undertaking binding himself, as soon as he ascended the throne, to place himself under the tutelage of a council composed of the higher clergy and the knights of the Annunziata, and to maintain the existing forms of the monarchy (D. Berti, *Cesare Alfieri,* xi. 77, Rome, 1871), that he was allowed to return to Turin and forgiven.

On the death of Charles Felix (April 27, 1831) Charles Albert succeeded; he inherited a kingdom without an army, with an empty treasury, a chaotic administration and mediaeval laws. His first task was to set his house in order; he reorganized the finances, created the army, and started Piedmont on a path which, if not liberalism, was at least progress. In 1833 a conspiracy of the *Giovane Italia* society, organized by Mazzini, was discovered, and a number of its members punished with ruthless severity. The election in 1846 of Pius IX., who appeared to be a Liberal and an

Italian patriot to some extent, reconciled the king to the Liberal movement, for it accorded with his religious views. On Oct. 30 he issued a decree granting wide reforms, and when risings broke out in other parts of Italy early in 1848, and further liberties were demanded, he was at last induced to grant the constitution (Feb. 8).

When the news of the Milanese revolt against the Austrians reached Turin (March 19) public opinion demanded that the Piedmontese should succour their struggling brothers; and after some hesitation the king declared war. But much time had been wasted and many precious opportunities lost. With an army of 60,000 Piedmontese troops and 30,000 men from other parts of Italy the king took the field, and after defeating the Austrians at Pastrengo on April 30, and at Goito on May 30, where he was himself slightly wounded, more time was wasted in useless operations. Radetzky, the Austrian general, having received reinforcements, drove the centre of the extended Italian line back across the Mincio (July 23), and in the two days' fighting at Custozza (July 24–25) the Piedmontese were beaten, forced to retreat and to ask for an armistice. The revolutionary movement throughout Italy was breaking down, but Charles Albert felt that while he possessed an army he could not abandon the Lombards and Venetians, and determined to stake all on a last chance. On March 12, 1849, he denounced the armistice and took the field again with an army of 80,000 men. He gave the chief command to the Polish general Chrzanowski, but he was completely out-generalled and defeated at La Bicocca near Novara on the 23rd. The Piedmontese fought with great bravery, and the unhappy king sought death in vain. After the battle he asked terms of Radetzky, who demanded the occupation by Austria of a large part of Piedmont, and the heir to the throne as a hostage. Thereupon, feeling himself to be the obstacle to better conditions, Charles Albert abdicated in favour of his son Victor Emmanuel. That same night he departed alone and made his way to Oporto, where he retired into a monastery and died on July 28, 1849.

Charles Albert was not a man of first-rate ability; he was of a hopelessly vacillating character. Devout and mystical to an almost morbid degree, hating revolution and distrusting Liberalism, he was a confirmed pessimist, yet he had many noble qualities: he was brave to the verge of foolhardiness, devoted to his country, and ready to risk his crown to free Italy from the foreigner. To him the people of Italy owe a great debt, for if he failed in his object he at least materialized the idea of the Risorgimento in a practical shape, and the charges which the Republicans and demagogues brought against him were monstrously unjust.

Bibliography.—Besides the general works on modern Italy, *see* the Marquis Costa de Beauregard's interesting volumes *La Jeunesse du roi Charles Albert* (1899) and *Novare et Oporto* (1890), based on the king's letters and the journal of Sylvain Costa, his faithful equerry, though the author's views are those of an old-fashioned Savoyard who dislikes the idea of Italian unity; Ernesto Masi's *Il Segreto del Re Carlo Alberto* (Bologna, 1891) is a very illuminating essay; Domenico Perrero, *Gli Ultimi Reali di Savoia* (Turin, 1889); L. Cappelletti, *Storia di Carlo Alberto* (1891); Nicomede Bianchi, *Storia della diplomazia europea in Italia* (8 vols., Turin, 1865, etc.), a most important work of a general character, and the same author's *Scritti e lettere di Carlo Alberto* (1879) and his *Storia della monarchia piemontese* (Turin, 1877); Count S. della Margherita, *Memorandum storico-politico* (Turin, 1851); A. Luzio, *Carlo Alberto e Giuseppe Mazzini* (1923); he also edited *Le Lettere di Carlo Alberto al Car. Luigi Bianco di Barbania* (Turin, 1924); A. di Saluzzo, *Carlo Alberto della restaurazione all' avvenimento al trono* (1926).

CHARLES AUGUSTUS (Karl August) (1757–1828), grand-duke of Saxe-Weimar, friend and patron of Goethe, was the son of Constantine, duke of Saxe-Weimar-Eisenach, and Anna Amalia of Brunswick. Educated under the regency of his mother —his father died in 1757—Charles Augustus assumed the reins of government in 1775, in which year he married Princess Louise of Hesse-Darmstadt. In the affairs of Germany and of Europe his character gave him an influence out of all proportion to his position as a sovereign prince. He had early faced the problem presented by the decay of the empire, and began to work for the unity of Germany. The plans of the emperor Joseph II., which threatened to absorb a great part of Germany into the heterogeneous Habsburg monarchy, threw him into the arms of Prussia, and he was the prime mover in the establishment of the league of princes (*Fürstenbund*) in 1785, by which, under the leadership of Frederick the Great, Joseph's intrigues were frustrated. He was, however, under no illusion as to the power of Austria, and he wisely refused the offer of the Hungarian crown, made to him in 1787 by Prussia at the instance of the Magyar malcontents, with the dry remark that he had no desire to be another "Winter King." In 1788 he took service in the Prussian army as major-general in active command of a regiment. As such he was present, with Goethe, at the cannonade of Valmy in 1792, and in 1794 at the siege of Mainz and the battles of Pirmasenz (Sept. 14) and Kaiserslautern (Oct. 28–30). After this, dissatisfied with the attitude of the Powers, he resigned; but rejoined on the accession of his friend King Frederick William III. to the Prussian throne. The disastrous campaign of Jena (1806) followed; on Oct. 14, the day after the battle, Weimar was sacked; and Charles Augustus, to prevent the confiscation of his territories, was forced to join the Confederation of the Rhine. From this time till after the Moscow campaign of 1812 his contingent fought under the French flag in all Napoleon's wars. In 1813, however, he joined the Grand Alliance, and at the beginning of 1814 took the command of a corps of 30,000 men operating in the Netherlands.

At the Congress of Vienna Charles Augustus was present in person and protested vainly against the narrow policy of the Powers in confining their debates to the "rights of the princes" to the exclusion of the "rights of the people." His services in the war of liberation were rewarded with an extension of territory and the title of grand-duke. He was the first of the German princes to grant a liberal constitution to his state under Article XIII. of the Act of Confederation (May 5, 1816); and his concession of full liberty to the press made Weimar for a while the focus of journalistic agitation against the existing order. Metternich dubbed him contemptuously "der grosse Bursche" for his patronage of the "revolutionary" Burschenschaften; and the celebrated "festival" held at the Wartburg by his permission in 1818 brought down upon him the wrath of the Great Powers. Charles Augustus was compelled to yield to the remonstrances of Prussia, Austria and Russia; the liberty of the press was again restricted in the grand-duchy, but, thanks to the good understanding between the grand-duke and his people, the régime of the Carlsbad Decrees pressed less heavily upon Weimar than upon other German States.

Charles Augustus died on June 14, 1828, and left two sons; Charles Frederick (d. 1853), by whom he was succeeded, and Bernhard, duke of Saxe-Weimar (1792–1862), who distinguished himself as commander of the Dutch troops in the Belgian campaign of 1830, and from 1847 to 1850 held the command of the forces in the Dutch East Indies. Bernhard's son, William Augustus Edward, known as Prince Edward of Saxe-Weimar (1823–1902), entered the British army, served with much distinction in the Crimean War, and became colonel of the 1st Life Guards and a field-marshal; in 1851 he contracted a morganatic marriage with Lady Augusta Gordon-Lennox (d. 1904), daughter of the 5th duke of Richmond and Gordon, who in Germany received the title of countess of Dornburg, but was granted the rank of princess in Great Britain by royal decree in 1866.

Bibliography.—Karl August's Correspondence with Goethe was published in 2 vols. at Weimar in 1863. *See* F. X. Wegele, *Karl August, Grossherzog von Sachsen-Weimar* (Leipzig, 1850); W. Wachsmuth, *Herzog Karl August und Goethe* (Leipzig, 1911); W. Bode, *Karl August von Weimar, Jugendjahre* (1913); H. von Egloffstein, *Karl August während des Krieges von 1813* (1913) and *Karl August auf dem Wiener Kongress* (Jena, 1915).

CHARLES D'ORLÉANS: *see* Orléans, Charles, Duke of.

CHARLES EDWARD (Charles Edward Louis Philip Casimir Stuart) (1720–1788), English prince, called the "Young Pretender" and also the "Young Chevalier," was born at Rome on Dec. 31, 1720. He was the grandson of King James II. of England and elder son of James, the "Old Pretender," by whom (as James III.) he was created at his birth prince of Wales, the title he bore among the English Jacobites during his father's lifetime. The young prince was educated at his father's miniature court in Rome, with James Murray, Jacobite earl of Dunbar, for his governor, and under various tutors, amongst whom were the learned Chevalier Ramsay, Sir Thomas Sheridan and the abbé Légoux. He learned the English, French and Italian languages, but his extant letters in English are singularly ill-spelt and illiterate. In 1734 he accompanied his cousin, the duke of Liria, afterwards duke of Berwick, on his expedition in aid of Don Carlos, and the boy of 13 shared with credit the dangers of the successful siege of Gaeta.

The Old Pretender calculated upon foreign aid in his attempts to restore the monarchy of the Stuarts; and the idea of rebellion unassisted by invasion or by support of any kind from abroad, was Charles Edward's own. Jacobite hopes mainly rested in France, and the warm sympathy which Cardinal Tencin, who had succeeded Fleury as French minister, felt for the Old Pretender resulted in a definite scheme for an invasion of England to be timed simultaneously with a prearranged Scottish rebellion. Charles was secretly despatched to Paris in January, 1744. A squadron under Admiral Roquefeuil sailed (Feb. 6) from Brest. Transports for 7,000 troops, to be led by Marshal Saxe, accompanied by the young prince, were in readiness to set sail for England. Meanwhile a strong English fleet appeared in the Downs, and a series of storms provided a probably welcome excuse to the French government for the cancellation of Marshal Saxe's orders. Louis declined to surrender Charles, but no official hospitality was offered him, and he lived in retirement. Charles Edward had made at Rome the acquaintance of Lord Elcho and of John Murray of Broughton; Murray visited him in Paris, and was told that he would come to Scotland in the summer of 1745, even though he came alone. His friends in Scotland saw no chance of success, and messengers, who do not seem to have reached him, were sent expressly to inform him. On July 13, 1745, he sailed from Nantes for Scotland on board the small brig "La Doutelle," which was accompanied by a war frigate, the "Elisabeth," provided by an Irishman at Dunkirk and laden with arms and ammunition. The latter fell in (July 20) with an English man-of-war, the "Lion," and had to return to France; Charles escaped during the engagement, and arrived on Aug. 3 off Erisca, a little island of the Hebrides. Receiving, however, but a cool reception from Macdonald of Boisdale, he set sail again and arrived at the Bay of Loch-na-nuagh on the west coast of Inverness-shire.

The Macdonalds of Clanranald and Kinloch Moidart, along with other chieftains, attempted in vain to dissuade him from the rashness of an unaided rising, but Lochiel and other chieftains, although they had sought to dissuade Charles from coming at all, now called out the clans. On Aug. 19, in the valley of Glenfinnan, the standard of James III. and VIII. was raised. Within a week about 2,000 men, mainly from the Macdonald clan, had joined him. Sir John Cope left Stirling for Inverness on Aug. 20 with 25 companies of foot, leaving the road to the south open to Charles. In the beginning of September the Jacobite army, reinforced by some accessions, notably by Lord George Murray, entered Perth. Crossing the Forth unopposed at the Fords of Frew and passing through Stirling and Linlithgow, he arrived within a few miles of Edinburgh, and on Sept. 16 a body of his skirmishers defeated the dragoons of Colonel Gardiner in what was known as the "Canter of Coltbrig." A few of Cameron's Highlanders having on the following morning, by a happy ruse, forced their way through the Canongate, Charles entered the city at noon. On the 18th he publicly proclaimed James VIII. of Scotland at the Market Cross and occupied Holyrood.

Cope had by this time brought his disappointed forces by sea to Dunbar. On the 20th Charles met and defeated him at Prestonpans, and returned to prosecute the siege of Edinburgh Castle, which, however, he raised on Gen. Guest's threatening to lay the city in ruins. He still hoped for French assistance definitely promised on Oct. 24 by secret treaty. In the beginning of November Charles left Edinburgh to invade England. He was at the head of at least 5,000 men; but the ranks were gradually thinned by the desertion of Highlanders, whose tradition had led them to consider war merely as a raid. Having passed through Kelso, on Nov. 9 he laid siege to Carlisle which capitulated in a week. Manchester provided the prince with 150 recruits under Francis Towneley. On Dec. 4 he had reached Derby. Charles's officers were under no illusions about the strength of English resistance, but hoped that the advance might lead to intervention from France. When they found that the English counties did not rise they advised retreat. Two armies under English leadership were now in the field against Charles, one under Marshal Wade, whom he had evaded by entering England by the west, and the other under William, duke of Cumberland, who had returned from the Continent. On Dec. 6 Charles began his retreat northward. Closely pursued by Cumberland, he marched by way of Carlisle across the border, and at last stopped to invest Stirling Castle. At Falkirk, on Jan. 17, 1746, he defeated Gen. Hawley, who had marched from Edinburgh to intercept his retreat. The Jacobite army had been strengthened by Gordons, Mackintoshes and others, but the accessions were counter-balanced by desertions. A fortnight later, however, Charles raised the siege of Stirling, and after a weary march rested his troops at Inverness. Having taken Forts George and Augustus, and after varying success against the supporters of the government in the north, he at last prepared to face the duke of Cumberland, who had passed the early spring at Aberdeen. On April 8 the duke marched thence to meet Charles, whose little army, exhausted with a futile night march, half-starving, and broken by desertion, was completely worsted at Culloden on April 16, 1746.

This decisive defeat sealed the fate of Charles Edward and the house of Stuart. Hunted hither and thither Charles, upon whose head a reward of £30,000 had a year before been set, was for over five months relentlessly pursued by the troops and spies of the government. Disguised in female attire and aided by a passport obtained by the devoted Flora MacDonald, he passed through Skye, and towards the end of July took refuge in the cave of Coiraghoth in the Braes of Glenmoriston. In August he joined Lochiel and Cluny Macpherson, with whom he remained in hiding until the arrival of two French ships at Loch-na-nuagh, enabled him to sail for France. He reached Roscoff, near Morlaix, on Sept. 29, 1746. He remained in France for two years, but the Treaty of Aix-la-Chapelle entailed his expulsion from France. After his brother Henry's acceptance of a cardinal's hat in July 1747, he broke off communication with his father in Rome (who had approved the step), nor did he ever see him again. The enmity of the British government to Charles Edward made peace with France an impossibility so long as she continued to harbour the young prince. A condition of the Treaty of Aix-la-Chapelle, concluded in October 1748, was that every member of the house of Stuart should be expelled from the French dominions. Charles declared, he would not be bound by its provisions. But his indignation and persistent refusal to leave France were met at last with force; he was apprehended, imprisoned for a week at Vincennes, and on Dec. 17 conducted to the French border. He lingered at Avignon; but Pope Benedict XIV., alarmed by the threat of a bombardment of Civita Vecchia, advised the prince to withdraw. Charles quietly disappeared. For years Europe watched for him in vain. It is now established, almost with certainty, that he returned to the neighbourhood of Paris. In 1750 and again, it is thought, in 1754, he was in London, hatching futile plots and risking his safety for his hopeless cause, and even abjuring the Roman Catholic faith in order to further his political interests.

During the next ten years of his life Charles Edward's illicit connection with Miss Clementina Walkinshaw (d. 1802), whom he had first met at Bannockburn House while conducting the siege of Stirling, his imperious fretful temper, his drunken habits and debauched life, could no longer be concealed. He wandered over Europe in disguise, alienating his friends and crushing the hopes of his party; and in 1766, on returning to Rome at the death of his father, he was treated by Pope Clement XIII. with coldness, and his title as heir to the British throne was openly repudiated by all the great Catholic powers. It was probably through the influence of the French court, still intriguing against England, that the marriage between Charles (now self-styled count of Albany) and Princess Louise of Stolberg was arranged in 1772. The union proved childless and unhappy, and in 1780 the countess fled for refuge from her husband's drunken violence to a convent in Florence. Later, the countess of Albany (*q.v.*) threw herself on the protection of her brother-in-law Henry, Cardinal York, at Rome, and a formal separation was arranged in 1784. Charles, lonely, ill, and evidently near death, now summoned to Florence his natural daughter, Charlotte Stuart, the child of Clementina Walkinshaw, born at Liége in October 1753 and hitherto neglected by the prince. Charlotte Stuart, who was declared legitimate and created duchess of Albany, tended her father for the remaining years of his life. She contrived to reconcile the two Stuart brothers, so that in 1785 Charles returned to Rome, where he died in the old Palazzo Muti on Jan. 30, 1788. He was buried in his brother's cathedral church at Frascati, but in 1807 his remains were removed to the *Grotte Vaticane* of St. Peter's. His daughter Charlotte died unmarried at Bologna in November, 1789.

See A. C. Ewald, *Life and Times of Charles Stuart, the Young Pretender* (2 vols. 1875); C. S. Terry, *Life of the Young Pretender, and The Rising of 1745; with Bibliography of Jacobite History 1689–1788* (Scott. Hist. fr. Contemp. Writers, iii.) (1900); Earl Stanhope, *History of England* (1836) and *Decline of the Last Stuarts* (1854); Bishop R. Forbes, *The Lyon in Mourning* (1895–96); Andrew Lang, *Pickle, the Spy* (1897), and *Prince Charles Edward* (1900); R. Chambers, *History of the Rebellion in Scotland.*

CHARLES EMMANUEL I. (CARLO EMANUELE) (1562–1630), duke of Savoy, succeeded his father, Emmanuel Philibert, in 1580. His three chief objects were the conquest of Geneva, of Saluzzo and of Monferrato. Saluzzo he succeeded in wresting from France in 1588. In 1590 he sent an expedition to Provence in the interests of the Catholic League, and followed it himself later, but the peace of 1593, by which Henry of Navarre was recognized as king of France, put an end to his ambitions. In the war between France and Spain Charles sided with the latter, with varying success. Finally, by the Peace of Lyons (1601), he gave up all territories beyond the Rhône, but his possession of Saluzzo was confirmed. His attempt to capture Geneva by treachery and with the help of Spain (the famous *escalade*) in 1602 failed completely. On the death in 1612 of Duke Francesco Gonzaga of Mantua, who was lord of Monferrato, Charles Emmanuel made a successful *coup de main* on that district. This arrayed the Venetians, Tuscany, the Empire and Spain against him, and he was obliged to relinquish his conquest. The terms of the peace of 1618 left him more or less in the *status quo ante.* In 1628 he was in alliance with Spain in the war against France and the French invaded the duchy. The duke fought desperately, but was taken ill at Savigliano and died in 1630. He was succeeded by his son Victor Amedeo I., while his third son Tommaso founded the line of Savoy-Carignano from which the present royal house of Italy is descended.

See E. Ricotti, *Storia della monarchia piemontese,* vols. iii. and iv. (Florence, 1865); T. Raulich, *Storia di Carlo Emanuele I.* (Milan, 1896–1902); G. Curti, *Carlo Emanuele I. secondo; più recenti studii* (Milan, 1894).

CHARLES MARTEL, "The Hammer," (*c.* 688–741), Frankish ruler, son of Pippin II., mayor of the palace, and Chalpaïda. Charles was baptized by St. Rigobert, bishop of Reims. At the death of his father in 714, Pippin's widow Plectrude claimed the government in Austrasia and Neustria in the name of her grandchildren, and had Charles thrown into prison. But the Neustrians threw off the Austrasian yoke and entered into an offensive alliance with the Frisians and Saxons. In the general anarchy Charles succeeded in escaping, defeated the Neustrians at Amblève, south of Liége, in 716, and at Vincy, near Cambrai, in 717, and forced them to come to terms. In Austrasia he wrested the power from Plectrude, and took the title of mayor of the palace, thus prejudicing the interests of his nephews. According to the Frankish custom he proclaimed a king in Austrasia in the person of the young Clotaire IV., but in reality Charles was the sole master—the entry in the annals for the year 717 being "Carolus regnare coepit." Once in possession of Austrasia, Charles sought to extend his dominion over Neustria also. In 719 he defeated Ragenfrid, the Neustrian mayor of the palace, at Soissons, and forced him to retreat to Angers. Ragenfrid died in 731, and from that time Charles had no competitor in the western kingdom. He obliged the inhabitants of Burgundy to submit, and disposed of the Burgundian bishoprics and countships to his *leudes.* In Aquitaine Duke Odo (Eudes) exercised independent authority, but in 719 Charles forced him to recognize the suzerainty of northern France, at least nominally. After the alliance between Charles and Odo on the field of Poitiers, the mayor of the palace left Aquitaine to Odo's son Hunald, who paid homage to him. Besides establishing a certain unity in Gaul, Charles saved it from a very great peril. In 711 the Arabs had conquered Spain. In 720 they crossed the Pyrenees, seized Narbonensis, a dependency of the kingdom of the Visigoths, and advanced on Gaul. By his able policy Odo succeeded in arresting their progress for some years; but a new vali, 'Abd-ar-Rahmān, a member of an extremely fanatical sect, resumed the attack, reached Poitiers, and advanced on Tours, the holy town of Gaul. In Oct. 732 (just 100 years after the death of Mohammed) Charles gained a brilliant victory over 'Abd-ar-Rahmān, who was called back to Africa by the revolts of the Berbers and had to give up the struggle. This was the last of the great Arab invasions of Europe. After his victory Charles took the offensive, and endeavoured to wrest Narbonensis from the Muslims. Although he was not successful in his attempt to recover Narbonne (737), he destroyed the fortresses of Agde, Béziers and Maguelonne, and set fire to the amphitheatre at Nîmes. He subdued also the Germanic tribes; annexed Frisia, where Christianity was beginning to make progress; put an end to the duchy of Alemannia; intervened in the internal affairs of the dukes of Bavaria; made expeditions into Saxony; and in 738 compelled some of the Saxon tribes to pay him tribute. He also gave St. Boniface a safe conduct for his missions in Thuringia, Alemannia and Bavaria.

During the government of Charles Martel important changes appear to have been made in the internal administration. Under him began the great assemblies of nobles known as the *champs de Mars.* To attach his *leudes* Charles had to give them church lands as *precarium,* and this had a very great influence in the development of the feudal system. It was from the *precarium,* or ecclesiastical benefice, that the feudal fief originated. Vassalage, too, acquired a greater consistency at this period, and its rules began to crystallize. Under Charles occurred the first attempt at reconciliation between the papacy and the Franks. Pope Gregory III., menaced by the Lombards, invoked the aid of Charles (739), sent him a deputation with the keys of the Holy Sepulchre and the chains of St. Peter, and offered to break with the emperor and Constantinople, and to give Charles the Roman consulate (*ut a partibus imperatoris recederet et Romanum consulatum Carolo sanciret*). This proposal, though unsuccessful, was the starting point of a new papal policy. Since the death of Theuderich IV. in 737 there had been no king of the Franks. In 741 Charles divided the kingdom between his two sons, as though he were himself master of the realm. To the elder, Carloman, he gave Austrasia, Alemannia and Thuringia, with suzerainty over Bavaria; the younger, Pippin, received Neustria, Burgundy and Provence. Shortly after this division of the kingdom Charles died at Quierzy on Oct. 22, 741, and was buried at St. Denis. The characters of Charles Martel and his grandson Charlemagne offer many striking points of resemblance. Both were men of courage and activity, and the two men are often confused in the *chansons de geste.*

See T. Breysig, *Jahrbücher d. fränk. Reichs 714–741; die Zeit Karl Martells* (Leipzig, 1869); A. Beugnot, "Sur la spoliation des biens du clergé attribuée à Charles Martel," in the *Mém. de l'Acad. des Inscr. et Belles-Lettres,* xix. (1853); U. Chevalier, *Bio-bibliographie* (2nd ed. 1904). **(C. Pf.)**

CHARLES CITY, a city of northern Iowa, U.S.A., on Cedar river; the county seat of Floyd county. It is on federal highways 18 and 218 and served by the Chicago, Milwaukee, St. Paul and Pacific, Illinois Central, and Charles City Western railways. The population in 1930 federal census was 8,039; in 1940, 8,681; in 1950, 10,277.

It is in a rich agricultural region; has abundant water power; manufactures tractors, office equipment and other articles; and has extensive nurseries, specializing in evergreens and roses.

The city was founded in 1850 and incorporated in 1860.

CHARLESTON, a city of eastern Illinois, U.S., on the Nickel Plate and the Big Four railways, 45 mi. W. of Terre Haute, Ind.; the county seat of Coles county. Pop. (1950) 9,146; (1940) 8,197. It has broom and shoe factories and railroad shops. The Eastern Illinois State Teachers college, established in 1895, has an enrolment of about 1,500. In the vicinity are the Lincoln Log Cabin State park and the Fox Ridge State park. Charleston was made the county seat in 1831 and was incorporated in 1839. One of the Lincoln-Douglas debates was held there in 1858.

CHARLESTON, oldest city of South Carolina, U.S., is an important South Atlantic seaport, an industrial area and an all-year resort, on a narrow peninsula between the Cooper and Ashley rivers, at the head of the bay (Charleston harbour) formed by their confluence, 7½ mi. from the ocean bar. It is the county seat of Charleston county, headquarters of the customs district of South Carolina, headquarters of the 6th naval district, official state port and headquarters of the South Carolina Ports authority. Charleston is on federal highways 17, 701, 52, 176 and 78; and is served by the Atlantic Coast Line, the Seaboard Air Line and the Southern railways, by Eastern, National, Delta and Southern air lines; also by a number of coastwise, intercoastal and foreign steamship lines.

The population in the 1950 federal census was 68,243 and that of Charleston county, constituting the Charleston metropolitan area, was 159,838. The city, whose city limits had not been extended in more than 100 years, has a total land area of only 5.12 sq.mi., of which 4.5 is usable; the highest elevation above datum plane is 16 ft.; the waterfront area within the city limits extends for nine miles.

On islands in the harbour are Fort Sumter and Castle Pinckney, both national monuments. At the southwest corner of the city, on the Ashley river, are the Atlantic fleet naval minecraft base headquarters. North of the city, on the west bank of the Cooper river, is the Charleston naval base and naval shipyard, with lengthy docks, ship repair facilities and destroyer building ways. Still farther north (10.4 mi. above the custom house) are the vast port terminals. Also in this vicinity is a U.S. ordnance depot.

The spacious harbour, almost landlocked, protected by two converging stone jetties (15,443 and 19,104 ft. long), accommodates vessels with a draught of 30 ft. Inbound traffic consists principally of petroleum products, Egyptian long-staple cotton, materials for fertilizer manufacture and sugar; outbound traffic, of cotton and cotton goods from the Carolinas and Georgia, coal from West Virginia and Virginia, crossties, treated and untreated lumber, petroleum products and peanuts. Trade with foreign countries in 1950 amounted to 953,047 tons. Customs revenues at the end of the fiscal year July 2, 1950, totalled $2,522,039. Charleston is an important centre for the distribution of oil and has several large fertilizer plants. Following World War II its industrial development and growth were substantial, with more than 50 new industries having been established by 1951, the majority at the northern end of the peninsula well outside the city limits. Among the leading manufactures are wood pulp and allied products, woven asbestos, pressure creosoted timber, cigars, men's shirts, optical products, furniture, steel products and ironwork. The city is a bunkering and repair station for both commercial and naval vessels; a market for the agricultural products (notably vegetables, cotton and tobacco) and the pine and hardwoods of the state, and for the fresh and canned oysters, crabs, shrimp and fish caught off the coast.

Charleston has a unique charm and beauty. At the lower end of the peninsula is the Battery, or White Point gardens, planted with live oaks and palmettos. Beach resorts (Isle of Palms, Sullivan's Island and Folly beach) are developed on outlying islands which formerly (until 1718) were the haunts of pirates.

The Magnolia gardens, up the Ashley river, are a monument to the exquisite taste and poetic imagination of the Rev. John Grimké Drayton, who created them when in the 1840s his physician ordered him to lead an outdoor life. At Middleton Place, farther up the river, one wing of the great Tudor mansion still stands, and there are gardens which had renown in England in the 18th century. Other noted garden estates are Cypress Gardens, Runnymede, Pierates Cruze and Mateeba. Among the many educational institutions of the city are the College of Charleston, founded in 1770, chartered in 1785 and taken over by the city in 1837 (the first municipal college in the country); the Medical College of the State of South Carolina, a state institution founded in 1823; and the Citadel, The Military College of South Carolina, created by the legislature in 1842. The Charleston library was founded in 1748; the museum in 1773.

The first English settlement in South Carolina, named after the reigning king, was made at Albemarle point on the west bank of the Ashley in 1670; but in 1672 a new town was begun on the present site, and the seat of government was moved to it in 1680. It soon became the largest and wealthiest settlement south of Philadelphia, Pa.; the brilliant social and cultural centre of the province and later of the state; the home of the Pinckneys, the Rutledges, the Gadsdens, the Laurenses and many other notable families. Magnificent estates were developed in the surrounding country. The port shipped one specialty after another—rice, indigo, tobacco, lumber, cotton—before entering on its present phase as a more general cargo port. Charleston was the capital of the state until 1790. Until 1783 it was governed by ordinances passed by the legislature and enforced partly by provincial officials and partly by the churchwardens. The city charter of 1783, with many amendments, is still in force.

Charleston was attacked by a combined fleet of Spanish and French in 1706; withstood attacks from the British in 1776 and in 1779, but in 1780 was captured from the land side by Sir Henry Clinton and became the base of operations in the Carolinas, remaining under military rule until Dec. 14, 1782. It was the centre of the nullification movement of 1832–33. The bombardment and capture of Ft. Sumter (April 12–13, 1861) by the South Carolinians marked the beginning of the Civil War. From 1862 to 1865 Charleston was almost continually under siege by the Federal naval and military forces, and on Feb. 17, 1865, the Confederates evacuated the city, after burning large stores of cotton and other supplies to keep them from coming into possession of the enemy. Charleston was devastated by hurricanes in 1699, in 1752 and in 1854; by epidemic in 1699 and in 1854; by fire in 1740; and by an earthquake on Aug. 31, 1886, which damaged 90% of the buildings.

BIBLIOGRAPHY.—William A. Courtenay, *Charleston, S.C.* (1884); Albert Simons and Samuel Lapham, Jr., *Charleston, South Carolina,* including sketches of many of the historic buildings (1927); Robert Molloy, *Charleston, a Gracious Heritage* (1947); William Oliver Stevens, *Charleston, Historic City of Gardens* (1939); S. G. Stoney, *Charleston, Azaleas and Old Bricks* (1939).

CHARLESTON, the capital of West Virginia, U.S., on the Kanawha river at the mouth of the Elk, southwest of the centre of the state; the county seat of Kanawha county. It is on U.S. highways 21, 35, 60, 119; and is served by the Baltimore and Ohio, Chesapeake and Ohio, New York Central and Virginian railways and by American, Eastern, Capital and Piedmont air lines. There is inland waterway transportation to the Gulf of Mexico. The population in 1950 was 73,501; in 1940 it was 67,914 by the federal census. The city is an important industrial area for the production of natural resources (coal, oil, natural gas, salt brines, limestone, lumber, clays) and manufacture of base chemicals (nylon basic salt, Vinylite and polyethylene resins, antifreezes), glass, farm implements, brick and tile and synthetic rubber. There is a U.S. naval ordnance plant for production of armour plate, naval guns and projectiles. Manufacturing and natural-resource-production investments were estimated in excess of $600,000,000 in 1950. Charleston's assessed valuation of property in 1950 was $161,784,100. An outstanding capitol was completed there in 1933 to replace the one built in 1880.

Charleston was settled soon after the American Revolution and was incorporated in 1794. It was on the route of migration to the Ohio valley and became a transfer and shipping centre. Daniel Boone and Simon Kenton, noted frontiersmen, operated in the Charleston area and Boone represented Charleston in the Virginia assembly, 1790–91. In 1870, when Charleston was chartered as a city, the population was only 3,162. Charleston remained the capital of the state from 1870 excepting for the decade 1875–85, when the capital was Wheeling.

CHARLESTOWN, formerly a separate city of Middlesex county, Mass., U.S., but since 1874 a part of the city of Boston, with which it had long before been in many respects practically one. It is situated on a small peninsula on Boston harbour, between the mouths of the Mystic and Charles rivers; the first bridge across the Charles, built in 1786, connected Charlestown and Boston. A large and important United States navy yard (1800), and the Massachusetts state prison (1805) are there; the old burying ground contains the grave of John Harvard and that of Thomas Beecher, the first American member of the famous Beecher family; and there is a soldiers' and sailors' monument (1872), designed by Martin Milmore. Charlestown was founded in 1628 or 1629, being the oldest part of Boston, and soon rose into importance; it was organized as a township in 1630, and was chartered as a city in 1847. Within its limits was fought, on June 17, 1775, the battle of Bunker Hill (*q.v.*), when Charlestown was almost completely destroyed by the British. The Bunker Hill monument commemorates the battle. The original territory of the township was very large, and from parts of it were formed Woburn (1642), Malden (1649), Stoneham (1725) and Somerville (1842); other parts were annexed to Cambridge, to Medford and to Arlington. S. F. B. Morse, the inventor of the electric telegraph, was born there; and Charlestown was the home of Samuel Dexter (1761–1816), an eminent lawyer, secretary of war in the cabinet of Pres. John Adams, and of Oliver Holden (1765–1831), a composer of hymn tunes, including "Coronation."

BIBLIOGRAPHY.—R. Frothingham, *History of Charlestown* (1845), covering 1629–1775; J. F. Hunnewell, *A Century of Town Life . . . 1775–1887* (1888); Timothy T. Sawyer, *Old Charlestown* (1902); and H. H. Sprague, *The Founding of Charlestown by the Spragues* (1910).

CHARLET, NICOLAS TOUSSAINT (1792–1845), French designer and painter, more especially of military subjects, was born in Paris on Dec. 20, 1792, and died there on Oct. 30, 1845. The son of a dragoon in the Republican army, he was educated at the Lycée Napoléon, and served in the national guard in 1814. In 1816 Charlet entered the atelier of Antoine Gros, and soon began issuing the first of those lithographed designs of subjects drawn from the Napoleonic wars which eventually brought him renown. Lithographs (about 2,000 altogether), water colours, sepia drawings, numerous oil sketches and a few etchings followed one another rapidly, and he exhibited some large canvases. His best work was the "Episode in the Retreat from Russia," exhibited in the salon of 1836.

See De La Combe, *Charlet, sa vie, ses oeuvres* (1856).

CHARLEVILLE, a town of northeastern France, in the department of Ardennes, 50 mi. N.E. of Reims. Pop. (1946) 20,193. Charleville is situated within a bend of the Meuse on its left bank, opposite Mézières, with which it is united by a suspension bridge. The town was founded in 1606 by Charles III (Gonzaga), duke of Nevers, afterward duke of Mantua, and is laid out on a definite plan. The Place Ducale is a large square surrounded by old houses. On the right bank of the Meuse is Mont Olympe, with the ruins of a fortress dismantled under Louis XIV. Charleville, which shares with Mézières the administrative institutions of the department of Ardennes, has tribunals of first instance and of commerce, a chamber of commerce and a board of trade-arbitrators. Its chief industries are metal founding, the manufacture of iron goods and the making of bricks. Brushes and clay pipes are also made.

CHARLEVOIX, PIERRE FRANÇOIS XAVIER DE (1682–1761), French Jesuit traveller and historian, was born at St. Quentin, Fr., on Oct. 29, 1682. At 16 he entered the Society of Jesus; and at 23 was sent to Canada, where he remained for four years as professor at Quebec, Que. In 1720–22, under orders from the regent, he visited North America for the second time, and went along the Great Lakes and down the Mississippi. He died at La Flèche, Fr., on Feb. 1, 1761.

Among his works are: *Histoire de l'isle espagnole ou de Saint Domingue* (1730), based on manuscript memoirs of P. Jean-Baptiste le Pers and original sources; *Histoire de Paraguay* (1756); *Vie de la Mère Marie de l'incarnation, institutrice et première supérieure des Urselines de la Nouvelle France* (1724); *Histoire et description générale de la Nouvelle France* (1744; in English 1761; tr. J. G. Shea, 1866–72), a work of capital importance for Canadian history.

CHARLEVOIX, a city of Michigan, U.S., on Lake Michigan, with Lake Charlevoix on its eastern boundary and Round lake harbour in the centre of the town; a port of entry and the county seat of Charlevoix county. It is on federal highway 31 and state highway 66, and is served by the Chesapeake and Ohio railway, buses and lake steamers.

The population in 1950 was 2,664. The summer population is more than 10,000. Charlevoix is one of the most popular summer resorts of the state, and has a considerable fishing industry. It was platted as a village in 1866, and was incorporated as a city in 1905.

CHARLOTTE (1840–1927), empress of Mexico, only daughter of Leopold I, king of Belgium, and Louise, princess of Orleans, was born at Laeken, near Brussels, on June 7, 1840. She married in 1857 the archduke Maximilian of Austria, and went with him to Mexico in 1864, when he accepted the Mexican crown. When it became evident in 1866 that Maximilian's position was untenable, she was sent by her husband to Europe to implore the assistance of Napoleon III, who had decided to withdraw the French troops from Mexico. In this mission she failed, and foreseeing a catastrophe (Maximilian was shot in 1867) she went out of her mind (Sept. 1866). Charlotte was placed by her family under care in a Belgian château and survived until Jan. 19, 1927. (*See* also MAXIMILIAN.)

See Count Corti, *Maximilian und Carlotta von Mexico,* 2 vol. (1924).

CHARLOTTE, a city of Michigan, U.S., 18 mi. S.W. of Lansing; on federal highway 27, and served by the Grand Trunk and the Michigan Central railways; the county seat of Eaton county. The population in 1950 was 6,589; in 1940 it was 5,544. It has varied manufacturing industries, including radio and television, and is the trade centre of a rich agricultural and dairying region, which raises large quantities of beans.

CHARLOTTE, a city in southern North Carolina, U.S., 175 mi. S.W. of Raleigh; the county seat of Mecklenburg county. It is on federal highways 21, 29 and 74; and is served by the Southern, the Norfolk and Southern, the Piedmont and Northern Electric and the Seaboard Air Line railways; also by Capital and Eastern air lines. The population in 1950 was 133,219, and in 1940 it was 100,899 by the federal census. Cotton, corn, wheat and truck crops are grown in the vicinity. Charlotte is at the heart of the hydroelectric development and the textile industry of the southern Piedmont. Many northern manufacturers of machinery, dyestuffs and other items needed for the equipment of cotton mills have branches there, and it is a distributing point for automobiles and their accessories. Bank clearings for 1949 amounted to $3,981,298,386. The assessed valuation of property in 1949, was $200,000,000. Within the city limits are large textile mills and knitting mills. The output of the Charlotte factories includes approximately 200 diversified products. Printing and publishing is an important industry.

Charlotte is the seat of Queens college for women, originally chartered by the colonial legislature in 1771; and of the Johnson C. Smith university for Negroes (formerly Biddle university), founded in 1867. The city was settled about 1750, and incorporated in 1768. It has a commission form of government with mayor, city manager and seven councilmen. A monument in front of the courthouse commemorates the signing of the Mecklenburg Declaration of Independence in May 1775. For a brief period in 1780 the city was occupied by Lord Cornwallis, who nicknamed it "the hornets' nest." Later it became the principal base of Gen. Nathanael Greene's operations. Andrew Jackson and James K. Polk were born near by, and on April 10, 1865, Jefferson Davis convened his cabinet there for its last meeting.

"CHARLOTTE DUNDAS," the name given by her inventor to the first practical steamship. William Symington, in 1802, built the tug "Charlotte Dundas," a paddle-wheel steamer, and successfully tried her on the Forth and Clyde canal; the name was a compliment to the family of Lord Dundas, who suggested the experiment, and the boat was built for the Forth and Clyde Canal Company. The motive-power employed was a double-acting condensing engine constructed by James Watt. The engine was fixed horizontally and actuated the crank of a stern-shaft which carried the paddle-wheel. The "Charlotte Dundas" managed to tow two vessels with a burden of 140 tons, in the teeth of a strong

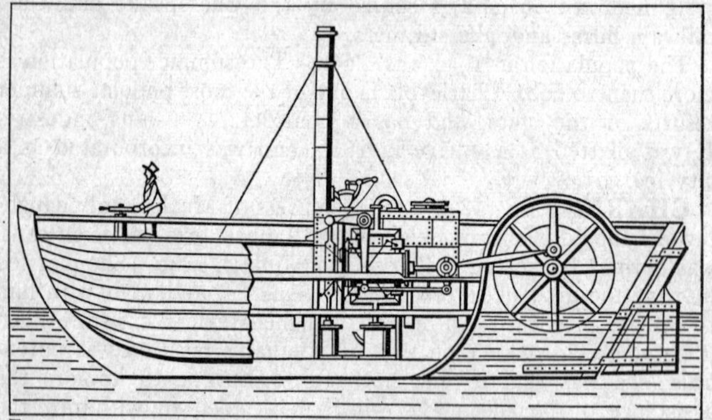

THE "CHARLOTTE DUNDAS," THE FIRST PRACTICAL STEAMBOAT, BUILT IN 1802 BY WILLIAM SYMINGTON AND DRIVEN BY AN ENGINE SUPPLIED BY JAMES WATT

wind, at the rate of 3½m. an hour. Five years later, the American Robert Fulton, who had witnessed the "Charlotte Dundas" experiment, built the famous "Clermont" on the River Hudson.

CHARLOTTENBURG, a town incorporated in the Greater Berlin scheme of 1912 (which came into full operation in 1920), in the *Land* of Prussia, on the river Spree; its earlier name was Lietzenburg. The central part of the town is connected with Berlin by an avenue, the Charlottenburger Chaussée. The Schloss, built in 1696 for the electress Sophie Charlotte, queen of the elector Frederick, after whom the town was named, contains a collection of antiquities and paintings. In Charlottenburg is the Physikalisch-technische Reichsanstalt, a state institution for the carrying out of scientific experiments and measurements, and for testing instruments of precision, materials, etc. In addition to the famous royal porcelain manufactory, there are many industries, notably iron-works, grouped along the banks of the Spree.

CHARLOTTESVILLE, a city in the beautiful Piedmont region of Virginia, U.S., on the Rivanna river, 70 mi. W.N.W. of Richmond; the county seat of Albemarle county, but administratively independent of it. It is served by the Chesapeake and Ohio and the Southern railways. The population in 1950 was 25,969, and in 1940, 19,400, by federal census. It is the seat of the University of Virginia and the trade centre of an agricultural district noted for its fine apples and peaches. There are a law-book publishing house, woollen mill, silk mill, dress shirt and underwear plants and pen and pencil factory.

On a hill three miles east, visible from all parts of the city, is Monticello, the home of Thomas Jefferson from 1770 until his death, now a national memorial. The house was planned by Jefferson and built under his supervision. It is one of the most interesting examples of colonial architecture. His grave is on the estate. Two miles beyond Monticello is Ash Lawn, home of James Monroe. Mirador, the girlhood home of Lady Astor, is about 20 mi. west of the city. The site of Charlottesville was a part of the Castle Hill estate of Thomas Walker (1715–94). The town (named after Queen Charlotte) was incorporated in 1762. In 1888 it was chartered as a city, independent of the county. It has a commission manager form of government. In 1779–80 about 4,000 of Gen. John Burgoyne's troops, surrendered under the convention of Saratoga, were quartered there. In June 1781 Sir Banastre Tarleton raided the town and vicinity, destroying the public records and nearly capturing Jefferson. Jefferson owed his escape to the warning brought by a young Virginian soldier, Jack Jouett, who rode 40 mi. across rough country through the night to outstrip Tarleton, after accidently getting a clue to his plans through conversation overheard at a tavern.

CHARLOTTETOWN, the capital of the province of Prince Edward Island, Can., situated in Queen's county, on Hillsborough river. Pop. (1951) 15,887. It has a good harbour, and the river is navigable by large vessels for several miles. The export trade of the island centres there, and the city has regular communication by steamer with the chief U.S. and Canadian ports, is served by the Canadian National railways through a ferry service and has a large terminal airport.

Besides the government buildings and the courthouse, it contains the Prince of Wales college, supported by the province, the Roman Catholic college of St. Dunstan's and a normal school. Among its manufactures are woollen goods, lumber, canned goods and foundry products; its fisheries are extensive and important. The town was founded in 1750 by the French under the name of Port la Joie, but under British rule it changed its name in honour of the queen of George III.

CHARM, an incantation, verses sung with supposed magical results, hence anything possessing powers of bringing good luck or averting evil, particularly articles worn with that purpose, such as an amulet. It is thus used of small trinkets attached to bracelets or chains. The word is also used, figuratively, of fascinating qualities of feature, voice or character. It is derived through the Fr. from the Lat. *carmen,* a song.

CHARMES, FRANCIS (1848–1916), French journalist and politician, was born at Aurillac, Cantal, on April 21, 1848. He was educated at Aurillac and at the lycées of Clermont-Ferrand and Poitiers. He was editor of the *Journal des Débats* from 1872 to 1880, and from 1889 to 1907. During the interval he served in the political department of the Foreign office. He sat in the chamber of deputies from 1881 to 1885 and from 1889 to 1898, and in 1900 became a senator. Charmes is, however, best known for his connection with the *Revue des Deux Mondes.* In 1893 he began his famous political writings in the *Revue,* and in 1907 became its editor. His literary and political articles were one of the features of French literary history during the last years of the 19th century. He died in Paris on Jan. 4, 1916.

CHARMEUSE. In textiles, the proprietary name for a silk dress fabric of light and delicate texture suitable for gowns, party wraps, and such like garments for purely dress purposes, and for which strength and durability are not essential qualities. This fabric has a rich and more lustrous appearance on the face side than on the reverse side, which latter is of a more subdued lustre. This difference in lustre results from the particular weave structure of the fabric, and the difference between the character, counts and number of warp and weft threads employed. A typical example of charmeuse consists of a very light texture developed by the 12-end warp-face satin weave, and produced from a grenadine organzine warp, and a two-ply pure schappe silk weft, or else crêpe de Chine twist for the warp, and schappe silk for the weft. Charmeuse is also sometimes developed by employing the warp-face satin weave in combination with a light voile foundation texture. This is produced by introducing two picks of fine and hard-twisted weft alternately with two picks of schappe silk weft. In this structure the fine picks of weft interweave with the warp threads in the plain weave order, that is, under and over successive warp threads, thereby serving to reinforce the satin weave texture which would otherwise be very weak and flimsy. After weaving, the fabric is piece-dyed and finished with the characteristic soft finish to which it owes its good draping qualities. (H. N.)

CHARNAY (CLAUDE JOSEPH), DÉSIRÉ (1828–1915), French traveller and archaeologist, was born in Fleurie (Rhône), studied at the Lycée Charlemagne, and in 1850 became a teacher in New Orleans, Louisiana. He travelled in Mexico under a commission from the French ministry of education, in 1857–61; in Madagascar in 1863; in South America, particularly Chile and Argentina, in 1875; and in Java and Australia in 1878. In 1880–83 he again visited the ruined cities of Mexico. Pierre Lorillard of New York contributed to defray the expense of this expedition, and Charnay named a great ruined city near the Guatemalan boundary line Ville Lorillard in his honour. Charnay went to Yucatan in 1886. His works include: *Le Mexique, souvenirs et impressions de voyage* (1863) and *Les Anciennes Villes* *du Nouveau Monde* (1885; Eng. trans. 1887). He elaborated a theory of Toltec migrations and considered the prehistoric Mexican to be of Asiatic origin, because of observed similarities to Japanese architecture, Chinese decoration, Malaysian language and Cambodian dress, etc.

See *Recueil de Voyages*, etc., vol. xix (1903).

CHARNEL HOUSE, a place for the storage of human bones, specifically that rendered necessary by the fact that many crowded mediaeval cemeteries were used again and again, so that each new burial unearthed the bones of people long dead. Charnel houses were sometimes situated in church crypts, and sometimes as separate buildings in the churchyards; chantry chapels were occasionally added.

CHARNOCK, JOB (d. 1693), English founder of Calcutta, went to India in 1655 or 1656 and soon joined the East India company's service. He was stationed at Cossimbazar and then at Patna. In 1686 he became chief agent at Hugli. Besieged there by the Mogul viceroy of Bengal, he put the company's goods and servants on board his light vessels and dropped down the river 27 mi. to the village of Sutanati, a place well chosen for the purpose of defense, which occupied the site of what is now Calcutta. It was only, however, at the third attempt that Charnock finally settled down at this spot, and the selection of Calcutta as the capital of India was entirely due to his stubborn resolution.

See N. N. Raye, *The Annals of the Early English Settlement in Bihar* (Calcutta, 1927).

CHARNOCK or CHERNOCK, **ROBERT** (*c.* 1663–1696), English conspirator, was educated at Magdalen college, Oxford, becoming a fellow of his college and a Roman Catholic priest. When in 1687 the dispute arose between James II and the fellows of Magdalen over the election of a president, Charnock favoured the first royal nominee, Anthony Farmer, and also the succeeding one, Samuel Parker, bishop of Oxford. Almost alone among the fellows he was not driven out in Nov. 1687, and he became dean and then vice-president of the college under the new regime, but was expelled in Oct. 1688. Residing at the court of the Stuarts in France, or conspiring in England, Charnock and Sir George Barclay appear to have been implicated in the attempt to kill William III near Turnham Green, in Feb. 1696. Barclay escaped, but Charnock was arrested, was tried and found guilty and was hanged on March 18, 1696.

CHARNOCKITE, in petrology a series of igneous rocks (originally described by Sir T. H. Holland) from Madras presidency, southern India, and forming a well-defined petrographic province of Archaean age. The name is derived from that of the founder of Calcutta, Job Charnock, whose tombstone is made of a typical member of the series. The series includes a wide range of rock types from ultrabasic pyroxenites through intermediate types—norites and quartz-hypersthene-diorites—to acid pyroxene-granites. The term charnockite is often specifically reserved for the acid hypersthene-granite. One of the distinguishing features of the series is the recurrence in many members of a strongly pleochroic red-to-green hypersthene. The typical members of the series, however, show other peculiar mineralogical features; namely, the development of *schiller* structures, from the presence of minute plate- or rod-shaped enclosures disposed parallel to definite crystallographic planes or axes. The optical effect of these enclosures is seen in the blue opalescence of the quartz, the milky shimmer of the feldspar and the bronzelike lustre of the rhombic pyroxene. Myrmekitic, microperthitic and antiperthitic structures are common in the feldspars. In the soda-lime feldspars there is a striking tendency to absence of the usual twinning lamellae. The members of the charnockite series frequently show a banded or gneissic structure, now usually interpreted as a flow banding, the result of movement during the epoch of crystallization. Chemically, the series is distinctly subalkaline, with a dominance of iron oxides over magnesia and lime.

The mineralogical characters of the charnockite series, particularly the occurrence of pyroxene in the acid members and the nature of the constituent microperthite, have been ascribed to consolidation from relatively dry magmas: the investigators of some provinces (Adelie Land, Uganda) have, however, interpreted the series as igneous rocks which have acquired their special characters by recrystallization in deep-seated metamorphism.

The various members are of widespread distribution and great petrological importance. In southern India they occur in the Nilgiri hills, the Shevaroys and the western Ghats, extending southward to Cape Comorin and reappearing in Ceylon. They occur in the Archaean shield of Western and South Australia and in Adelie and Enderby Lands, Antarctica. Similar rocks are known from the Ivory coast of west Africa, the eastern part of Ellesmere Land; from the Cortlandt series near Peekskill, N.Y.; and they recur at other localities in the eastern United States and Canada. The most noteworthy occurrences in the northern hemisphere are in southwestern and western Norway, at Egersund and Soggendal, and over a large area in the Bergen and Jotunheimen districts. The majority of the known occurrences of the charnockite series are of Archaean age, but it is probable that the anorthosite-charnockite series of the Bergen-Jotunheimen districts is of lower Palaeozoic (Caledonian) age. (C. E. T.)

CHARNWOOD FOREST, an upland tract in north Leicestershire (*q.v.*), England, southwest of Loughborough. Much of it is barren, though there are extensive tracts of woodland. More than 6,000 ac. are at a height exceeding 600 ft.; the loftiest point, Bardon Hill, is 912 ft.

CHAROLLES, a town of east central France, capital of an arrondissement in the department of Saône-et-Loire, at the confluence of the Semence and Arconce, 39 mi. W.N.W. of Mâcon. Pop. (1946) 2,852.

Charolles was the capital of Charolais, which from the early 14th century gave the title of count to its possessors. The ruins of their castle are on a hill near the town. In 1327 the countship passed by marriage to the house of Armagnac, and in 1390 it was sold to Philip of Burgundy. After the death of Charles the Bold it was seized by Louis XI of France, but in 1493 it was ceded by Charles VIII to Maximilian of Austria. Ultimately passing to the Spanish kings, its possession became disputed, until in 1684 it was assigned to Louis, prince de Condé, a creditor of the king of Spain. It was united to the French crown in 1771. There are stone quarries in the vicinity; the town is also the centre for trade in the famous breed of Charolais cattle.

CHARON, in Greek mythology, the son of Erebus and Nyx (Night). It was his duty to ferry over the Styx and Acheron those souls of the deceased who had duly received the rites of burial, in payment for which service he received an obol, which was placed in the mouth of the corpse. He is probably a product of popular belief, not mentioned in Homer or Hesiod. He is represented as a morose and grisly old man. In Etruscan he is called Charun, and appears as a death demon, armed with a hammer. Finally he came to be regarded as the image of death and the world below. As such he survives in the Charos, or Charontas, of the modern Greeks.

See the classical dictionaries, especially W. H. Roscher's *Lexikon, s.v.*

CHARONDAS, a celebrated lawgiver of Catina in Sicily. His date is uncertain. Some make him a pupil of Pythagoras (*c.* 580–504 B.C.); but all that can be said is that he was earlier than Anaxilaus of Regium (494–476), who abolished his laws, previously in used at Regium. His laws, originally written in verse, were adopted by the other Chalcidic colonies in Sicily and Italy. According to Aristotle there was nothing special about these laws, except that Charondas introduced actions for perjury; but he speaks highly of the precision with which they were drawn up (*Politics*, ii, 12). The legal fragments attributed to him by Stobaeus and Diodorus are of late (neo-Pythagorean) origin.

See Bentley, *On Phalaris,* which (according to B. Niese, *s.v.* in Pauly, *Realencyklopädie*) contains the best account of Charondas; A. Holm, *Geschichte Siciliens,* i; F. D. Gerlach, *Zaleukos, Charondas, und Pythagoras* (1858); also GREEK LAW.

CHARPENTIER, FRANÇOIS (1620–1702), French archaeologist and man of letters, was born in Paris. In his *Excellence de la langue française* (1683) he anticipated Charles Perrault in the famous academical dispute concerning the relative merit of the ancients and moderns. He is credited with a share in the production of the magnificent series of medals that commemorate the principal events of the age of Louis XIV.

CHARRIÈRE, ISABELLE DE (1740–1805), Swiss author, was Dutch by birth, her maiden name being Van Tuyll van Seeroskerken van Zuylen. She married in 1771 her brother's tutor, St. Hyacinthe de Charrière, and settled with him at

Colombier, near Lausanne. Her *Lettres neuchâteloises* (Amsterdam, 1784) offer a simple and attractive picture of French manners. This, with *Caliste, ou lettres écrites de Lausanne* (2 vols. Geneva, 1785–88), was analysed and highly praised by Sainte-Beuve in his *Portraits de femmes* and in vol. iii. of his *Portraits littéraires*. She wrote a number of other novels, and some political tracts; but is perhaps best remembered by her liaison with Benjamin Constant (*q.v.*) between 1787 and 1796.

Her letters to Constant were printed in the *Revue suisse* (April 1844), her *Lettres-Mémoires* by E H. Gaullieur in the same review in 1857, and all the available material is utilized in a monograph on her and her work by P. Godet, the editor of her *Oeuvres complètes* (3 vols. 1907–09), in his *Madame de Charrière et ses amis* (2 vols., Geneva, 1906).

CHARRON, PIERRE (1541–1603), French philosopher, was born in Paris. He entered the Church, and was appointed preacher in ordinary to Marguerite, wife of Henry IV. of Navarre. At Bordeaux he met Montaigne, whose intimate friend he became.

In 1594 Charron published (at first anonymously, afterwards under the name of "Benoit Vaillant, Advocate of the Holy Faith," and also, in 1594, in his own name) *Les Trois Vérités*, in which he seeks to prove that there is a God and a true religion, that the true religion is the Christian, and that the true Church is the Roman Catholic. It is chiefly an answer to the famous Protestant work entitled *Le Traité de l'Église* by Du Plessis Mornay. It was followed in 1600 by *Discours chrestiens*, a book of very eloquent sermons. In 1601 Charron published at Bordeaux the famous *De la sagesse*, a complete popular system of moral philosophy. Usually it is coupled with the Essays of Montaigne, to which the author is under very extensive obligations in it. Charron suddenly stood forth as the representative of the most complete intellectual scepticism. The *De la sagesse* brought upon its author the most violent attacks. It received, however, the warm support of Henry IV. and of the president Pierre Jeannin (1540–1622).

Charron's psychology is sensationalist. With sense all our knowledge commences. The soul, located in the ventricles of the brain, is affected by the temperament of the individual; the dry temperament brings intelligence; the moist, memory; the hot, imagination. The immortality of the soul is the most universal of beliefs, but the most feebly supported by reason. As to man's power of attaining truth, he plainly declares that none of our faculties enable us to distinguish truth from error. On a pessimistic view of human nature Charron founded a moral system that may be summarized as follows: Man comes into the world to endure; let him endure then, and that in silence. Our compassion should be like that of God, who succours the suffering without sharing in their pain. Avoid vulgar errors; cherish universal sympathy. Let no passion or attachment become too powerful for restraint. Follow the customs and laws which surround you. Morality has no connection with religion. Reason is the ultimate criterion.

Charron holds that all religions grow from small beginnings and increase by popular contagion; all teach that God is to be appeased by prayers, presents, vows, but especially, and most irrationally, by human suffering. Each is said by its devotees to have been given by inspiration. In fact, however, a man is a Christian, Jew, or Mohammedan, before he knows he is a man. But while he openly declares religion to be "strange to common sense," the practical result at which Charron arrives is that one is not to sit in judgment on his faith, but to be "simple and obedient," and to allow himself to be led by public authority. Another rule is to avoid superstition, which he defines as the belief that God is like a hard judge, and that therefore He must be flattered and importuned, and won over by pain and sacrifice. True piety is the knowledge of God and of one's self, the latter knowledge being necessary to the former. It leads to spiritual worship; for external ceremony is merely for our advantage, not for His glory. Charron is thus the founder of modern secularism. His political views are neither original nor independent. He pours scorn on the common herd, declares the sovereign to be the source of law, and asserts that popular freedom is dangerous.

A summary and defence of the *Sagesse* appeared in 1606. In 1607 Michel de la Rochemaillet prefixed to an edition of the *Sagesse* a Life. His complete works, with this Life, were published in 1635. An excellent abridgment of the *Sagesse* is given in Tennemann's *Philosophie*, vol. ix.; an edition with notes by A. Duval appeared in 1824.

See H. T. Buckle, *Intro. to History of Civilization in England*, vol. ii. p. 19 (1869); Abbé Lezat, *De la prédication sous Henri IV*. (1871); Liebscher, *Charron u. sein Werk, De la sagesse* (Leipzig, 1890); J. Owen, *Skeptics of the French Renaissance* (1893); W. E. H. Lecky, *Rationalism in Europe* (new ed. 1910); J. B. Sabrié, *De l'humanisme au rationalisme, Pierre Charron* (1913); J. M. Robertson, *A Short History of Free Thought*, vol. i. p. 480 (3rd. ed. 1915).

CHARRUA, an almost extinct tribe of South American Indians, wild and warlike, formerly ranging over Uruguay and part of southern Brazil. They were dark and heavily built, fought on horses and used the bolas or weighted lasso.

CHART. A chart is a marine map intended specially for the use of the seaman, to assist him to navigate seas and oceans, to sail from port to port and by its means to ascertain the position of a ship with reference to the land, the direction in which to steer, the distance to sail and the dangers to avoid. The water area on charts is studded with numerous small figures; these are the soundings, indicating in fathoms or in feet or in a combination of the two (as shown in the title of the chart) at mean low water spring tides the depth of water at any particular position. Charts show the nature of the sea bottom, the irregularity in its character and give information of the greatest importance to the mariner. No matter how well the land may be surveyed a chart is practically valueless unless soundings are shown.

The British admiralty charts are compiled, drawn and published by the hydrographic department. This department as established under Earl Spencer by an Order in Council in 1795 consisted of the hydrographer, one assistant and one draughtsman. The first hydrographer was Alexander Dalrymple, a gentleman in the East India Company's service; on his supersession in 1808 the office of hydrographer was filled by Captain Thomas Hurd, R.N., and has since been held by officers of the Royal Navy, amongst whom may be mentioned Admirals Sir Edward Parry, Sir Francis Beaufort and Sir William Wharton. At the present time, 1928, the department consists of the hydrographer, 15 naval assistants, 23 chief cartographers, and cartographers, 57 draughtsmen and 38 clerical staff, apart from the numerous engravers, printers, etc., who are employed in the final stages of preparing the work for publication.

Charts prepared by the hydrographic department and published by order of the Lords Commissioners of the Admiralty are compiled from the labours of British naval officers employed in the surveying service, also from surveys made by the Royal Australian Navy, Royal Indian Marine, South African Naval Service and contributions from officers of the Royal navy and mercantile marine. Generally speaking each maritime nation is considered to be responsible for the charting of its own coastal waters and those of its dependencies; the majority of these have efficient and well-organized hydrographic offices, carry out their own surveys and publish charts for the use of seamen. There is a free interchange of hydrographic information as between nations and foreign government charts are utilized and incorporated in various charts and publications produced by the British Admiralty, acknowledgment of the source of the information being made in the title of the chart. Admiralty charts, which are published with the view of meeting the wants of the seaman in all parts of the world, may be classed under five heads, viz., ocean, general, coastal, harbour and physical charts; they are constructed on either mercator or gnomonic projection according to scale and locality. After preparation at the hydrographic department they are engraved on copper plates which thereafter become the original printing medium and which are in constant correction due to the absolute necessity that the latest information should be available.

The depth of the sea is obtained by sounding line, wire or by sonic methods; all soundings are reduced to mean low water spring tides. The times and heights of the tides with the direction and the velocity of the tidal streams are also ascertained. The original surveys drawn by the surveyors afloat are forwarded to the Admiralty and form the basis of the published charts. The ocean and general charts are compiled and drawn at the hydrographic

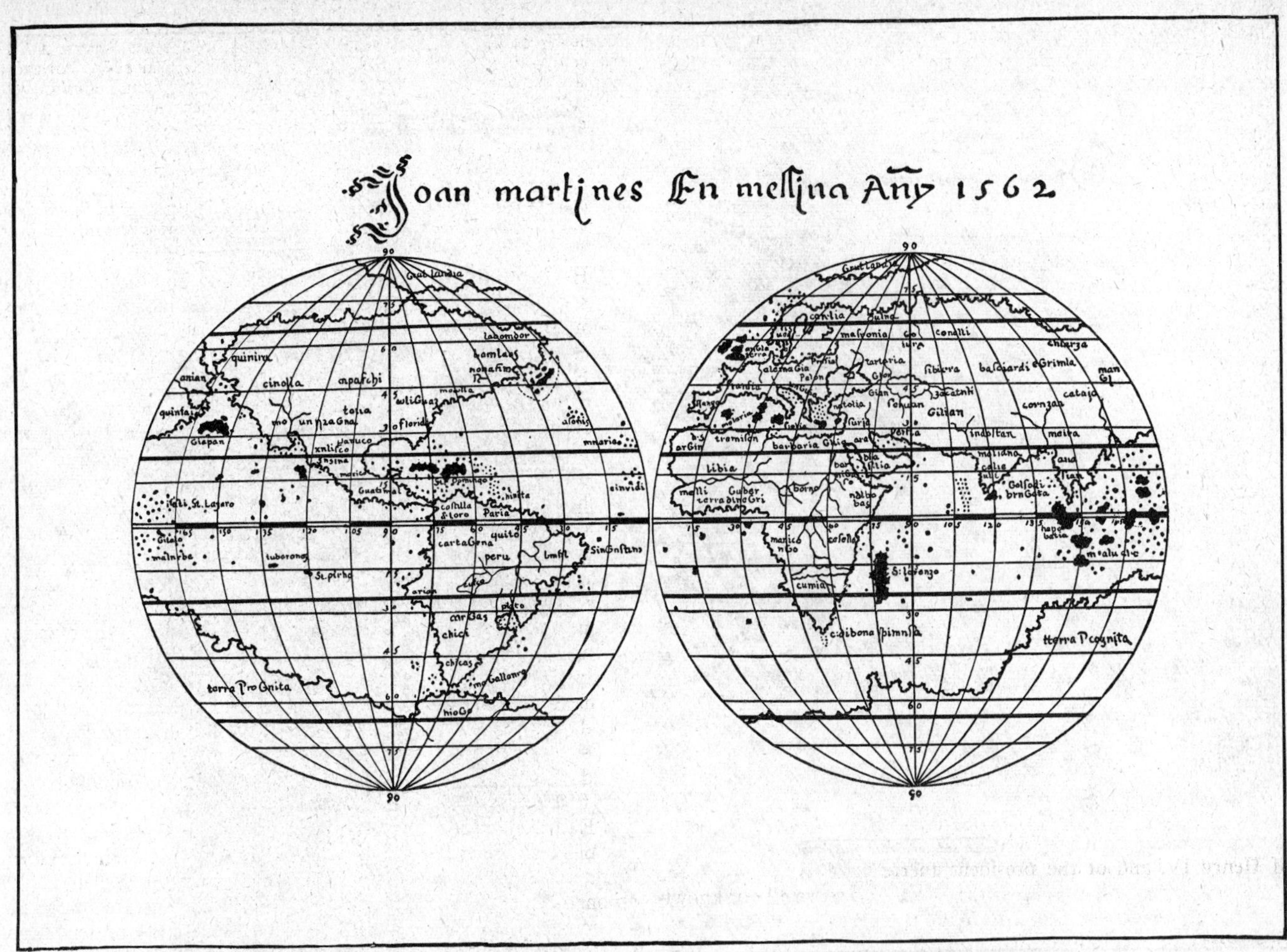

BY COURTESY OF THE HISPANIC SOCIETY OF AMERICA

THE WORLD IN TWO HEMISPHERES, FROM THE ATLAS OF 7 CHARTS BY MARTINES OF MESSINA (1562), SHOWING THE EXTENT OF MARITIME DISCOVERY AT THAT DATE. THE AUSTRALIAN CONTINENT WAS STILL "TERRA INCOGNITA."

department; original documents, existing charts, latest surveys and maps have all to be consulted and their compilation requires experience and judgment, for the compiler has to decide what to omit, what to insert, and to arrange the necessary work in such a manner that full information is given to the seaman. A very slight error may lead to great disaster and every symbol on the chart must be delineated with great care. No pains are spared in the effort to lay before the public the labours of the hydrographic surveyors and explorers not only of England, but of all the maritime world, to reduce their various styles into a comprehensive system and to furnish the seaman with a guide of which he may take full advantage. Certain abbreviations are used on charts and are fully described in a special publication.

There are still enormous areas which are unsurveyed or not surveyed in sufficient detail for modern requirements. Charts of these localities are usually drawn in hairline so that the experienced seaman sees at a glance that caution is necessary. The charts issued to the public are correct at the time of publication and are kept corrected for newly reported dangers, changes in character or position of lights and buoys, recent publications of foreign governments, etc., this information being supplied gratis to the public in the Admiralty notices to mariners which are published weekly. Charts are supplemented by the "sailing directions" covering the whole of the navigable portion of the globe, tide tables, light lists, the Admiralty list of wireless time signals, the nautical almanac, distance tables, ocean passages of the world, in which is included information regarding winds and currents, etc.

NAUTICAL SURVEYING

Naval hydrographic surveying has since the termination of the war in 1918 steadily progressed in adopting the latest methods and instruments which have become available to the surveyor ashore and afloat. It is not often realized that the hydrographic surveyor has to combine the work of the land surveyor with his own.

Instruments.—The following are the principal instruments required for use in the field and it should be noted that various scientific inventions of great benefit to the surveyor, and of which full advantage has already been taken, were designed and perfected during the World War, 1914–18.

Theodolites (*q.v.*) in current use (1928) are 4 in., 5 in. and 6 in. The majority of these are micrometer theodolites reading to 10 seconds. The use of the theodolite for astronomical and tacheometer work is now universal.

Sextants for observing with stand and artificial horizon are still supplied and improvements in this instrument have been adopted; amalgamated troughs consisting of gold-covered plates on which a thin film of mercury is floated have superseded the old artificial horizon consisting of a mercury bath; the new pattern is far less sensitive to earth tremors. This instrument for work on shore is now to a great extent superseded by other more precise and compact instruments.

Astrolabe à prisme, a very precise instrument, is one of these. It is used for finding position and enables altitudes of any stars at the altitude of 45° or 60° to be observed. The latest form of astrolabe enables observations of stars to be easily and accurately made as follows with the 60° instrument—one step of $7\frac{1}{2}'$ on either side of 60°, that is 3 observations of $59° 52\frac{1}{2}'$, 60°, $60° 07\frac{1}{2}'$ can be taken of one star. With the 45° instrument—four steps of 5′ on either side of 45°, that is 11 observations of 44° 35′, 44° 40′, 44° 45′, 44° 50′, 44° 55′, 45°, 45° 05′, 45° 10′, 45° 15′, 45° 20′, 45° 25′—can be taken of one star. The great advantage of this instrument is that with one setting up of the instrument and without a number of necessary readjustments, as in a theodolite, both time and latitude can be determined, provided of

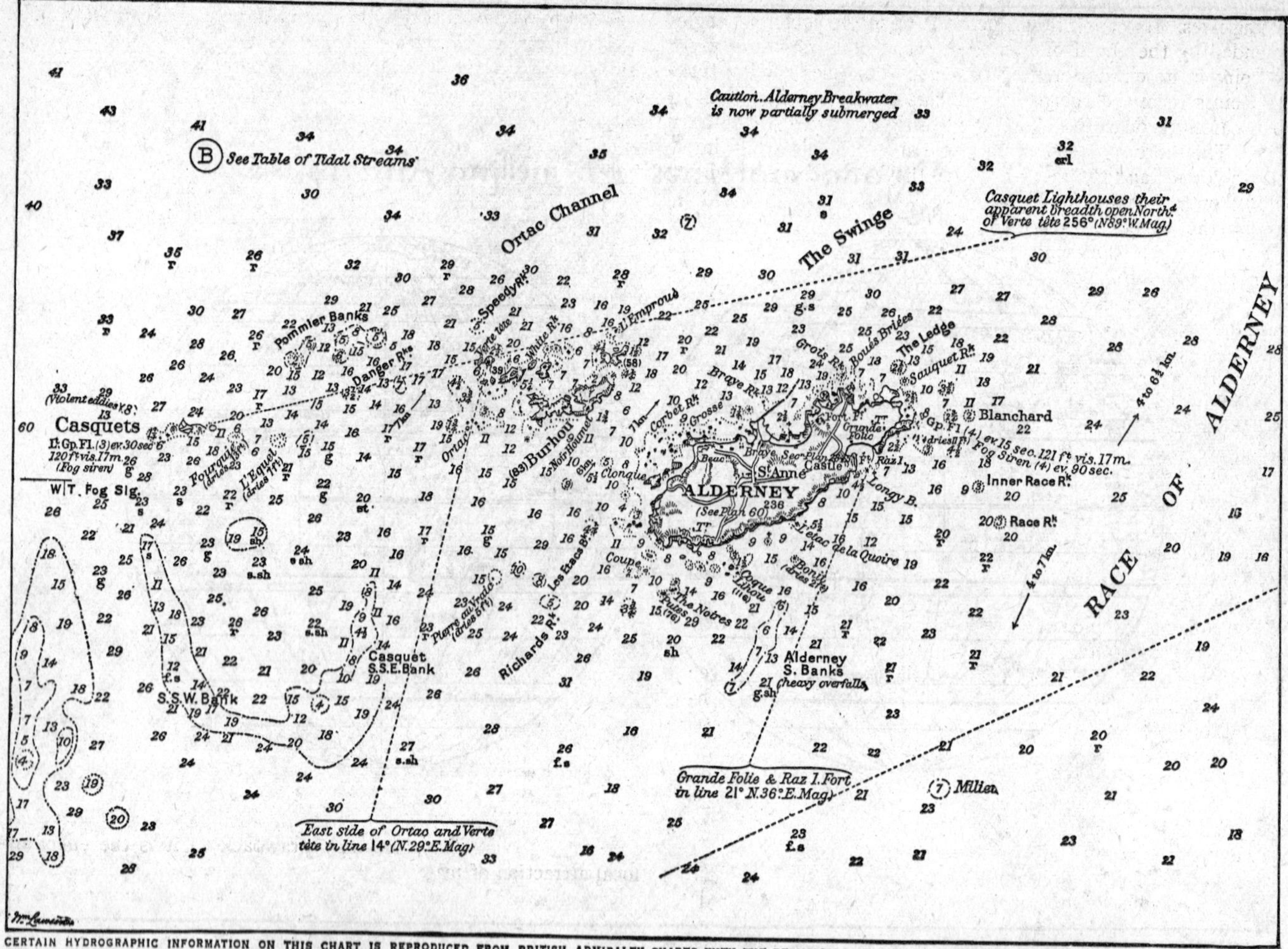

CERTAIN HYDROGRAPHIC INFORMATION ON THIS CHART IS REPRODUCED FROM BRITISH ADMIRALTY CHARTS WITH THE PERMISSION OF THE CONTROLLER OF H.M. STATIONERY OFFICE, AND OF THE HYDROGRAPHER OF THE NAVY, WHO ARE IN NO WAY RESPONSIBLE, HOWEVER, FOR THIS CHART

PORTION OF A CHART OF THE CHANNEL ISLANDS, SHOWING THE ISLAND OF ALDERNEY AND THE DANGEROUS ROCKS KNOWN AS THE CASQUETS. THE FIGURES GIVE SOUNDINGS IN FATHOMS

course that the best and latest method of obtaining error of the time used (*i.e.*, wireless time signals) is adopted.

When it is found necessary to measure bases the hydrographic surveyor uses the 500 ft. steel measuring tape and is provided with the Kew standardization certificate. In surveying abroad where no local triangulation exists, the accurate measurement of a base is recognized as a most important step, second only to a satisfactory base extension. Tacheometers and tacheometer staves marked according to the Admiralty pattern are used for measuring distances up to over 2,000 ft. where extreme accuracy is not necessary. One-metre base range-finders are useful in measuring short bases for plans of harbours, etc., when time or circumstances do not permit of a more accurate method.

Sounding Sextants differ from ordinary sextants in being lighter and handier; the arc which is of brass is cut to minutes, reading to large angles of as much as 140° and fitted with a telescope of high power.

Station Pointer is in constant use for all kinds of plotting: it enables the observer's position to be fixed by two angles between three objects suitably placed, the centre of the instrument indicating the observer's position when set and applied to the plotting sheet.

Sun Signals for reflecting the rays of the sun to distance stations for the purpose of obtaining accurate angles and measurements. The most convenient form is Galton's Sun Signal, which is easy to operate, compact and portable.

In addition *pocket aneroid barometers* for topographical purposes, *prismatic compasses, patent logs, Lucas sounding machines,* both large and small, James's *submarine sentry, tacheometer staves,* etc., are also required. For chart room use *graduated brass scales, steel straight edges, beam compasses* of various lengths, *rectangular protractors, circular brass protractors, mathematical drawing instruments, weights, drawing boards* and *paper* are required.

MARKS AND BEACONS

Every survey must have fixed objects which are first plotted on the sheets, technically known as "points." Natural marks of all kinds are utilized, but these must be supplemented by whitewash marks, cairns, flags, etc. On low coasts and islets flag staffs upwards of 100 ft. high made of several spars lashed together must sometimes be erected in order to get the necessary range of vision. A fixed beacon can be erected in shallow water by constructing a tripod of spars about 45 ft. long. The heads of two of them are lashed together and the heels kept open at a fixed distance by a plank nailed at about 5 ft. above the heels of the spars. These are taken out by three boats and the third tripod leg lashed in position on the boats, the heel in the opposite direction to the other two. The first two legs, weighted, are let go together; using the third leg as a prop, the tripod is hauled into position and secured by guys and by additional weights. A vertical pole with bamboo and flag, the heel being weighted, is lashed to the fork.

Floating Beacons.—These as a rule are specially constructed to carry a flag 12 to 16 ft. square on a bamboo from 30 to 35 ft. long. The beacon is secured to an anchor by means of chain or wire moorings and is visible under good conditions for a distance of about 10 miles. A beacon has been moored by sounding wire in depths of 3,000 fathoms with a weight of 100 lb.

Fixing.—In nautical surveying a thorough knowledge of the principles involved in a station-pointer fix is essential. The method of fixing by two angles between three fixed points is generally known as the "two-circle method," but there are really three circles involved. The "station-pointer" is the instrument used for plotting fixes. Its construction depends upon the fact that angles subtended by the chord of a segment of a circle measured from any point in its circumference are equal. The lines joining three fixed points form the chords of segments of three circles, each of which passes through the observer's position and two of the fixed points. The more rectangular the angle at which the circles intersect each other, and the more sensitive they are, the better will be the fix; one condition is useless without the other. A circle is "sensitive" when the angle between the two objects responds readily to any small movement of the observer towards or away from the centre of the circle passing through the observer's position and the objects. This is most markedly the case when one object is very close to the observer and the other very distant, but not so when *both* objects are distant. In the accompanying diagrams A, B, C are the objects, and X the observer. Fig. 1 shows the circle passing through C, B and X, cutting the circle ABX at a good angle, and therefore fixing X independently of the circle CAX, which is less sensitive, but being nearly tangential they give no cut with each other. The third cuts both at right angles; it is, however, far less sensitive, and for that reason if the right and left hand objects are both distant the fix must be bad. In such a case as this, because the angles CBX, BXA are both so sensitive, and the accuracy of the fix depends on the precision with which the angle CXA is measured, that angle should be observed direct, together with one of the other angles composing it. Fig. 3 represents a case where the points are badly disposed, approaching the condition known as "on the circle," passing through the three points. All three circles cut one another at such a fine angle as to give a very poor fix. The centre of the station-pointer could be moved considerably without materially affecting the coincidence of the legs with the three points. To avoid a bad fix the following rules are safe.

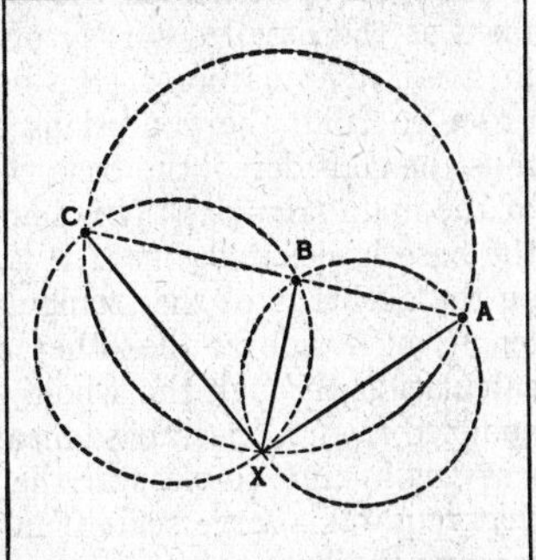

FIG. 1

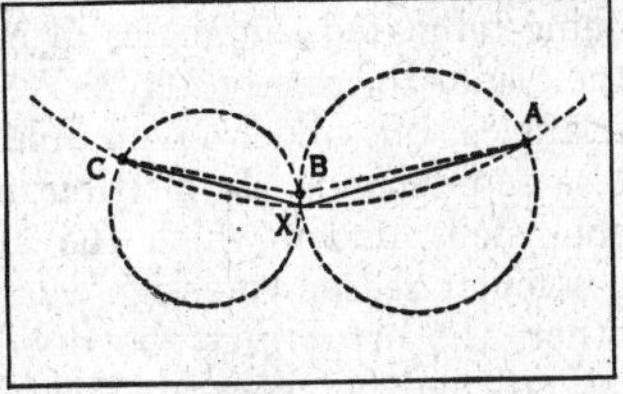

FIG. 2

Choose objects disposed as follows: (a) One outside object distant and the other two near, the angle between the two near objects being not less than 30° or more than 140°. The amount of the angle between the middle and distant object is immaterial. (b) The three objects nearly in a straight line, the angle between any two being not less than 30°. (c) The observer's position being inside the triangle formed by the objects.

A fix on the line of two points in transit, with an angle to a third point, becomes more sensitive as the distance between the transit points increases relatively to the distance between the front transit point and the observer; the more nearly the angle to the third point approaches a right angle, and the nearer it is situated to the observer, the better the fix. If the third point is at a long distance, small errors either of observation or plotting will affect the result considerably.

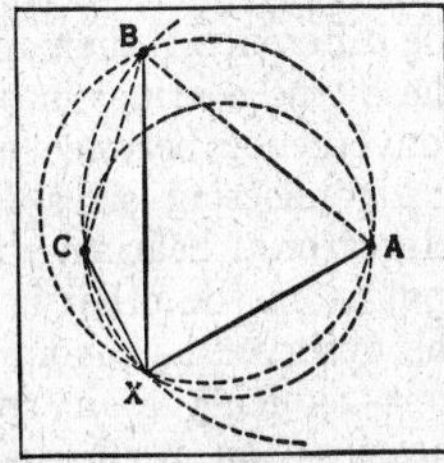

FIG. 3

Tracing-paper answers exactly the same purpose as the station-pointer. The angles are laid off from a centre representing the position, and the lines brought to pass through the points as before. This has often to be used, as when points are close together on a small scale the central part of the station-pointer will often hide them and prevent the use of the instrument. The use of tracing-paper permits any number of angles to different points to be laid down on it, which under certain conditions of fixing is sometimes an advantage.

Bases.—Marine surveys are founded upon triangulation and measured bases of some description, yet when plotted irregularly the system of triangles is not always apparent. The triangulation ranges from the rough triangle of a running survey to the carefully formed triangles of detailed surveys. The measured base for an extended survey is provisional only, the scale resting ultimately mainly upon the astronomical position observed as its extremes. In the case of a plan the base is absolute. The main triangulation establishes a series of points known as main stations, from which and to which angles are taken to fix other stations. A sufficiency of secondary stations enables the detail of the chart to be filled in between them. The points embracing the area to be worked on, having been plotted, are transferred to field boards, upon which the detail of the work in the field is plotted; when complete the work is traced and re-transferred to the plotting sheet, which is then inked in as the finished chart, and is graduated on the gnomonic projection on the astronomical positions of two points situated near opposite corners of the chart.

The kind of base ordinarily used is one measured by a steel tape of 100 or 500 ft. length on flat ground of convenient length, between two points visible from one another and so situated that a triangulation can be extended from them to embrace other points in the survey. The error of the steel tape is noted before leaving the ship, and again on returning, by comparing its length with a standard. The correction so found, also corrections for temperature, sag, etc., are applied to obtain the final result. A masthead angle base is at times useful for small plans, etc., when circumstances do not permit of a base being measured on shore. The height of the masthead to the water line being known the simple calculation necessary to obtain the distance is easily computed.

Astronomical Base.—The difference of latitude between two stations visible from each other and nearly in the same meridian, combined with their true bearings, gives an excellent base for an extended triangulation; the only drawback to it is the effect of local attraction of masses of land in the vicinity on the pendulum, or, in other words, on the mercury in the artificial horizon. The base stations should be as far apart as possible, in order to minimize the effect of any error in the astronomical observations. The observation spots would not necessarily be actually at the base stations, which would probably be situated on summits at some little distance in order to command distant views. In such cases each observation spot would be connected with its corresponding base station by a subsidiary triangulation, a short base being measured for the purpose. If possible, the observation spots should be east or west of the mountain station from which the true bearings are observed.

If the base stations A and B are so situated that by reason of distance or of high land intervening they are invisible from one another, but both visible from some main station C between them, when the main triangulation is completed, the ratio of the sides AC, BC can be determined. From this ratio and the observed angle ACB, the angles ABC, BAC can be found. The true bearing of the lines AC or BC being known, the true bearing of the base stations A and B can be deduced.

Extension of Base.—A base of any description is seldom long enough to plot from directly, and in order to diminish errors of plotting it is necessary to begin on the longest side possible so as to work inwards. A short base measured on flat ground will give a better result than a longer one measured over inequalities, provided that the triangulation is carefully extended by means of judiciously selected triangles, great care being taken to plumb the centre of each station. To facilitate the extension of the base in as few triangles as possible, the base should be placed so that there are two stations, one on each side of it, subtending angles at them of from 30° to 40°, the distances between which, on being calculated in the triangles of the quadrilateral so formed, will constitute the first extension of the base. Similarly, two other stations placed one on each side of the last two will form another quadrilateral, giving a yet longer side, and so on.

Main Triangulation.—The angles to be used in the main triangulation scheme must be very carefully observed and the theodolite placed exactly over the centre of the station. Main angles are usually repeated several times by resetting the vernier at intervals equidistant along the arc, in order to eliminate instrumental errors as well as errors of observation. The selection of an object suitable for a zero is important. It should, if possible, be another main station at some distance, but not so far or so high as to be easily obscured, well defined, and likely to be permanent. Angles to secondary stations should be repeated. Rough sketches from all stations with angles are of great assistance in identifying objects from different points of view.

False Station.—When the theodolite cannot for any reason be placed over the centre of a station, if the distance be measured and the theodolite reading of it be noted, the observed angles may be reduced to what they would be at the centre of the station. False stations have frequently to be made in practice; a simple rule to meet all cases is of great assistance to avoid the possibility of error in applying the correction with its proper sign It may very easily be found as follows.

Rule.—Put down the theodolite reading which it is required to correct (increased if necessary by 360°), and from it subtract the theodolite reading of the centre of the station. Call this remainder θ. With θ as a "course" and the number of feet from the theodolite to the station as a "distance," enter the traverse table and take out the greater increment if θ lies between 45° and 135°, or between 225° and 315°, and the lesser increment for other angles. The accompanying diagram (fig. 4) will assist the memory. Refer this increment to the "table of subtended angles by various lengths at different distances" (using the distance of the object observed) and find the corresponding correction in arc, which mark + or − according as θ is under or over 180°. Apply this correction to the observed theodolite angle. A "table of subtended angles" is unnecessary if the formula

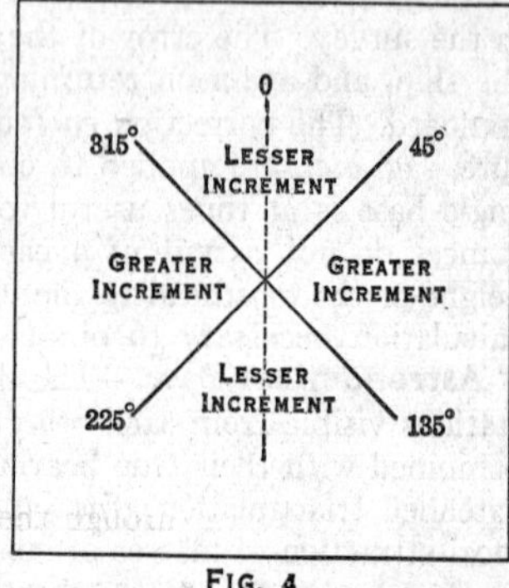

FIG. 4

$$\text{Angle in seconds} = \frac{\text{Number of feet subtended} \times 34}{\text{Distance of object in sea miles}}$$

be used instead.

The difference of the reciprocal true bearings between two stations is called the "convergency." The formula for calculating it is: Conv. in minutes = dist. in sea miles × sin. Merc. bearing × tan. mid. lat. Whenever true bearings are used in triangulation, the effect of convergency must be considered and applied. In north latitudes the southerly bearing is the greater of the two, and in south latitudes the northerly bearing. The Mercatorial bearing between two stations is the mean of their reciprocal true bearings.

Triangulated Coast Survey.—After a preliminary run over the ground to note suitable positions for stations on prominent headlands, islands and summits not too far back from the coast, and, if no former survey exists, to make at the same time a rough plot of them by compass and patent log, a scheme must be formed for the main triangulation with the object of enclosing the whole survey in as few triangles as possible, regard being paid to the limit of vision of each station due to its height, to the existing meteorological conditions, to the limitations imposed by higher land intervening, and to its accessibility. The triangles decided upon should be well-conditioned, taking care not to introduce an angle of less than 30° to 35°, which is only permissible when the two longer sides of such a triangle are of nearly equal length, and when the determination of this length does not depend on the short side. In open country the selection of stations is a comparatively easy matter, but in country densely wooded the time occupied by a triangulation is largely governed by the judicious selection of stations quickly reached, sufficiently elevated to command distant views, and situated on summits capable of being readily cleared of trees in the required directions, an all-round view being, of course, desirable though not always attainable. The positions of secondary stations will also generally be decided upon during the preliminary reconnaissance. The object of these stations is to break up the large primary triangles into triangles of smaller size, dividing up the distances between the primary stations into suitable lengths; they are selected with a view to greater accessibility than the latter, and should therefore usually be near the coast and at no great elevation. Upon angles from these will depend the position of the coastline marks, to be erected and fixed as the detailed survey of each section of the coast is taken in hand. The nature of the base to be used, and its position in order to fulfil the conditions specified under the head of *Bases* must be considered, the base when extended forming a side of one of the main triangles. It is immaterial at what part of the survey the base is situated, but if it is near one end, a satisfactory check on the accuracy of the triangulation is obtained by comparing the length of a side at the other extreme of the survey, derived by calculation through the whole system of triangles with its length deduced from a check base measured in its vicinity. It is generally a saving of time to measure the base at some anchorage or harbour that requires a large scale plan. The triangulation involved in extending the base to connect it with the main triangulation scheme can thus be utilized for both purposes, and while it is being calculated and plotted the survey of the plan can be proceeded with. The bearings are observed at both ends of the survey and at other selected stations and the results subsequently compared. Astronomical observations for latitude and longitude are obtained at observation spots near the extremes of the survey and are connected with the primary triangulation; they are usually disposed at intervals of from 100 to 150 m., and thus errors due to a triangulation carried out with theodolites of moderate diameter do not accumulate to any serious extent.

Calculating the Triangulation.—The triangles as observed being tabulated the angles of each triangle are corrected to bring their sum to exactly 180°. We must expect to find errors in the triangles, but under favourable conditions they will only amount to a few seconds. In distributing the errors we must consider the conditions under which the angles were observed; failing any particular reason to assign a larger error to one angle than to another, the error must be divided equally. The various quadrilaterals and polygons are then adjusted to make the whole triangulation as rigid as possible and bring the whole network into agreement. The length of base being determined, the sides of all the triangles involved are calculated by the ordinary rules of trigonometry. Starting from the true bearing observed at one end of the survey, the bearing of the side of each triangle that forms the immediate line of junction from one to the other is found by applying the angles necessary for the purpose in the respective triangles, not forgetting to apply the convergency between each pair of stations when reversing the bearings. The bearing of the final side is then compared with the bearing obtained by direct observation at that end of the survey. The difference is principally due to accumulated errors in the triangulation; half of the difference is then applied to the bearing of each side. Convert these true bearings into Mercatorial bearings by applying half the convergency between each pair of stations. With the lengths of the connecting sides found from the measured base and their Mercatorial bearing, the Mercatorial bearing of one observation spot from the other is found by middle latitude sailing. Taking the observed astronomical positions of the observation spots and first reducing their true difference longitude to departure, as measured on a spheriod from the formula

$$\text{Dep.} = \text{T.D. long.} \frac{\text{No. ft. in 1 m. of long.}}{\text{No. ft. in 1 m. of lat.}}$$

then with the d. lat. and dep. the Mercatorial true bearing and distance between the observation spots is calculated by middle latitude sailing, and compared with that by triangulation and measured base. To adjust any discrepancy, it is necessary to consider the probable error of the observation for latitude and meridian distance; within those limits the astronomical positions may safely be altered in order to harmonize the results; it is more important to bring the bearings into close agreement than the distance. From the amended astronomical position the Mercatorial true bearings and distance between them are re-calculated. The difference between this Mercatorial bearing and that found from the triangulation and measured base must be applied to the bearing of each side to get the final corrected bearings, and to the logarithm of each side of the triangulation as originally calculated must be added or subtracted the difference between the logarithms of the distance of the amended positions of the observation spots and the same distance by triangulation.

Calculating Intermediate Astronomical Positions.—The latitude and longitude of any intermediate main station may now be calculated from the finally corrected Mercatorial true bearings and lengths of sides. The difference longitude so found is what it would be if measured on a true sphere, whereas we require it as measured on a spheroid, which is slightly less. The correction $=\text{d. long.}\ \frac{\cos^2 \text{mid. lat.}}{150}$ must therefore be subtracted; or the true difference longitude may be found direct from the formula $\text{Dep.}\ \frac{\text{No. ft. in 1 m. of lat.}}{\text{No. ft. in 1 m. of long.}}$. From the foregoing it is seen that in a triangulation for hydrographical purposes both the bearings of the sides and their lengths ultimately depend almost entirely upon the astronomical observations at the extremes of the survey; the observed true bearings and measured base are consequently more in the nature of checks than anything else. It is obvious, therefore, that the nearer together the observation spots, the greater effect will a given error in the astronomical positions have upon the length and direction of the sides of the triangulation, and in such cases the bearings as actually observed must not be altered to any large extent when a trifling change in the astronomical positions might perhaps effect the required harmony. For the reasons given under *Astronomical Base,* high land near observation spots may cause very false results, which may often account for discrepancies when situated on opposite sides of a mountainous country.

Plotting.—Great care is requisite in projecting on paper the points of a survey. The paper should be allowed to stretch and shrink as it pleases until it comes to a stand, being exposed to the air for four or five hours daily, and finally well flattened out by being placed on a table with drawing boards placed over it heavily weighted. If the triangulation and co-ordinates have been calculated beforehand throughout, it is more advantageous to plot by co-ordinates or distances rather than by chords. The main stations are thus got down in less time and with less trouble, but these are only a small proportion of the points to be plotted, and if chords or distances are used long lines must be ruled between the stations as zeros for plotting other points by chords. In ruling these lines care must be taken to draw them exactly through the centre of the pricks denoting the stations, but, however, carefully drawn, there is liability to slight error in any line projected to a point lying beyond the distance of the stations between which the zero line is drawn. In plotting by distances, therefore, all points that will subsequently have to be plotted by chords should lie well within the area covered by the main triangulation. Three distances must be measured to obtain an intersection of the arcs cutting each other at a sufficiently broad angle; the plotting of the main stations once begun must be completed before distortion of the paper can occur from change in the humidity of the atmosphere. Plotting, whether by distance or by chords, must be begun on as long a side as possible, so as to plot inwards, or with decreasing distances. In plotting by chords it is important to remember in the selection of lines of reference (or zero lines), that that should be preferred which makes the smallest angle with the line to be projected from it, and of the angular points those nearest to the object to be projected from them.

Irregular Methods of Plotting.—In surveys for the ordinary purposes of navigation, it may happen that a regular system of triangulation cannot be carried out; the judicious use of the ship in such cases is often essential, and with proper care excellent results may be obtained. A few examples will best illustrate some of the methods used, but circumstances vary in every survey. Fixing a position by means of the "back-angle" is one of the most ordinary expedients. Angles having been observed at A, to the station B, and certain other fixed points of the survey, C and D for instance; if A is shot up from B, at which station angles to the same fixed points have been observed, then it is not necessary to visit those points to fix A. For instance, in the triangle ABC, two of the angles have been observed, and therefore the third angle at C is known (the three angles of a triangle being equal to 180°), and it is called the "calculated or back-angle from C." A necessary condition is that the receiving angle at A, between any two lines (direct or calculated), must give a good cut; also the points from which the "back-angles" are calculated should not be situated at too great distances from A, relatively to the distance between A and B. A station may be plotted by laying down the line to it from one station, and then placing on tracing-paper a number of the angles taken at it, including the angle to the station from which it has been observed. If the points to which angles are taken are well situated, a good position is then obtained. Sometimes the main stations must be carried on with a point plotted by only two angles. An effort must be made to check this subsequently by getting an "angle back" from stations dependent upon it to some old well-fixed point; failing this, two stations being plotted with two angles, pricking one and laying down the line to the other will afford a check. A well-defined mountain peak, far inland and never visited, when once it is well fixed is often invaluable in carrying on an irregular triangulation, as it may remain visible when all other original points of the survey have disappeared, and "back-angles" from it may be continually obtained, or it may be used for plotting on true bearing lines of it. In plotting the true bearing of such a peak, the convergency must be found and applied to get the reversed bearing, which is then laid down from a meridian drawn through it; of the reversed bearing of any other line already drawn through the peak being known, it may simply be laid down with that as a zero. A rough position of the spot from which the true bearing was taken must be assumed in order to calculate the convergency. Fig. 5 will illustrate the foregoing remarks. A and B are astronomical observation spots at the extremes of a survey, from both of which the high inaccessible peak C is visible. D, E, F are intermediate stations; A and D, D and E, E and F, F and B being respectively visible from each other. G is visible from A and D, and C is visible from all stations. The latitudes of A and B and meridian distance between them being determined, and the true bearing of C being observed from both observation spots, angles are observed at all the stations. Calculating the spheroidal correction from the formula, correction $=\text{d. long.}\ \frac{\cos^2 \text{mid. lat.}}{150}$ and adding it to the true (or chronometric) d. long. between A and B to obtain the spherical d. long.; with this spherical d. long. and the d. lat., the Mercatorial true bearing and distance is found by middle latitude sailing (which is an equally correct but shorter method than by spherical trigonometry, and may be safely used when dealing with the distances usual between observation spots in nautical surveys). The convergency is also calculated, and the true bearing of A from B and B from A are thus determined. In the plane triangle ABC the angle A is the difference between the calculated bearing of B and the observed bearing of C from A. The distance AB having been calculated, the side AC is found. Laying down AC on the paper on the required scale, D is plotted on its direct shot from A, and on the angle back from C, calculated in the triangle ACD. G is plotted on the direct shots from A and D, and on the angle back from C, calculated either in the triangle ACG or GCD.

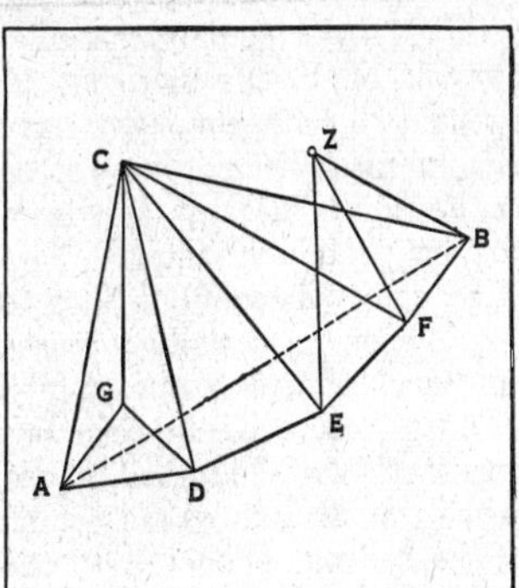

FIG. 5.

The perfect intersection of the three lines at G assures these four points being correct. E, F and B are plotted in a similar manner. The points depend on calculated angles, and except for the first four points we have no check, either on the accuracy of the angles observed in the field or on the plotting. Another well-defined object in such a position, for instance as Z, visible from three or more stations, would afford the necessary check, if lines laid off to it from as many stations as possible gave a good intersection. If no such point, however, exists a certain degree of check on the angles observed is derived by applying the sum of all the calculated angles at C to the true bearing of A from C (found by reversing observed bearing of C from A with convergency applied), which will give the bearing of B from C. Reverse this bearing with convergency applied, and compare it with the observed bearing of C from B. If the discrepancy is but small, it will be a strong presumption in favour of the substantial accuracy of the work. If the calculated true bearing of B from A be now laid down, it is very unlikely that the line will pass through B, but this is due to the discrepancy which must always be expected between astronomical positions and triangulation. If some of the stations between A and B require to be placed somewhat closely to one another, it may be desirable to obtain fresh true bearings of C instead of carrying on the original bearing by means of the calculated angle. In all cases of irregular plotting the ship is very useful, especially if she is moored taut without the swivel, and angles are observed from the bow. Floating beacons also assist an irregular triangulation.

Sketch Surveys.—Surveys of various degrees of accuracy are included among sketch surveys. The roughest description is the running survey, when the work is done by the ship steaming along the coast, fixing points, and sketching in the coast-line by bearings and angles, relying for her position upon her courses and distances as registered by patent log, necessarily regardless of the effect of wind and current and errors of steering. At the other extreme comes the modified running survey, which in point of practical accuracy falls little short of that attained by irregular triangulation. Some of these modifications will be briefly noticed. A running survey of a coast-line between two harbours, that have been surveyed independently and astronomically fixed, may often be carried out by fixing the ship on the points already laid down on the harbour surveys and shooting up prominent intermediate natural objects, assisted by theodolite angles. Theodolite lines to the ship and floating beacons suitably placed, materially increase the value of any such work. A sketch survey of a coast upon which it is impossible to land may be carried out by dropping beacons at intervals of about 8 m., well out from the land and placed abreast prominent natural objects called the "breastmarks," which must be capable of recognition from the beacons anchored off the next "breastmark" on either side. The distance between the beacons is found by running a patent log both ways, noting the time occupied by each run; if the current has remained constant, a tolerably good result can be obtained. At the first beacon, angles are observed between the second beacon and the two "breastmarks," and "intermediate" mark, and any other natural object which will serve as "points." At the second beacon, angles are observed between the first beacon and the same objects as before. Plotting on the line of the two beacons as a base, all the points observed can be pricked in on two shots. At a position about midway between the beacons, simultaneous angles are observed to all the points and laid off on tracing-paper, which will afford the necessary check, and the foundation is thus laid for filling in the detail of coast-line, topography, and soundings off this particular stretch of coast. Each section of coast is complete in itself on its own base; the weak point lies in the junction of the different sections, as the patent log bases will not agree precisely, and the scales of adjacent sections are liable to be slightly different. This is obviated, as far as possible, by fixing on the points of one section and shooting up those of another, which will check any great irregularity of scale creeping in. The bearing is preserved by getting occasional true bearing lines at the beacons of the most distant point visible. In all cases of using angles from the ship under weigh, several assistants are necessary, so that the principal angles may be taken simultaneously, the remainder being connected immediately afterwards with zeros involving the smallest possible error due to the ship not being absolutely stationary, these zeros being included amongst the primary angles. When close to a beacon, if its bearing is noted and the distance in feet obtained from its elevation, the angles are readily reduced to the beacon itself. Astronomical positions by twilight stars keep a check upon the work.

Sketch Surveys by Compass Bearings and Vertical Angles.—In the case of an island culminating in a high, well-defined summit visible from all directions, a useful and accurate method is to steam round it at a sufficient distance to obtain a true horizon, stopping to make as many stations as may be desirable, and fixing by compass bearing of the summit and its vertical angle. The height is roughly obtained by shooting in the summit, from two positions on a patent log whilst approaching it. With this approximate height and Lecky's vertical danger angle tables, each station may be plotted on its bearing of the summit. From these stations the island is shot in by angles between its tangents and the summit, and angles to any other natural features, plotting the work as we go on any convenient scale which must be considered only as provisional. On completing the circuit of the island, the true scale is found by measuring the total distance in inches on the plotting sheet from the first to the last station, and dividing it by the distance in miles between them as shown by patent log. The final height of the summit bears to the rough height used in plotting the direct proportion of the provisional scale to the true scale. This method may be utilized for the sketch survey of a coast where there are well-defined peaks of sufficient height at convenient intervals, and would be superior to an ordinary running survey. From positions of the ship fixed by bearings and elevation of one peak, another farther along the coast is shot in and its height determined; this second peak is then used in its turn to fix a third, and so on. Lecky's tables will show what effect an error of say 1′ in altitude will produce for any given height and distance, and the limits of distance must depend upon this consideration.

Surveys of Banks out of Sight of Land.—On striking shoal soundings unexpectedly, the ship may either be anchored at once and the shoal sounded by boats starring round her, using compass and masthead angle; or if the shoal is of large extent and may be prudently crossed in the ship, it is a good plan to get two beacons laid down on a bearing from one another and patent log distance of 4 or 5 m. With another beacon (or mark-boat, carrying a large black flag on a bamboo 30 ft. high) fixed on this base, forming an equilateral triangle, and the ship anchored as a fourth point, soundings may be carried out by the boats fixing by station-pointer. The ship's position is determined by observations of twilight stars.

Coastlining.—In a detailed survey the coast is sketched in by walking along it, fixing and plotting at intervals. Fixed marks along the shore afford a check on the minor coast-line fixes. When impracticable to fix in the ordinary way subtense methods are used. Greater accuracy is obtained if the work is plotted on the field board at once; this is not always possible but the angles being registered and sketches made of the intervening coast the work may be plotted afterwards. It is with the high water line that the coast-liner is chiefly concerned, delineating its character according to the accepted symbols. The sounder is responsible for the position of the dry line at low water. Heights of cliffs, rocks, islets, etc., must be inserted either from measurement or from the formula,

$$\text{Height in feet} = \frac{\text{Angle of elevation in seconds} \times \text{distance in miles}}{34},$$

and details of topography near the coast, including roads, houses and enclosures must be shown. Rocks above water or on which the sea breaks should be fixed. Coast-line may be sketched from a boat off shore by fixing and shooting up natural objects from selected positions.

Soundings.—The most important feature of a chart is the sounding, and the more complete this is the better is the survey.

Small scale surveys are apt to be misleading; such a survey may appear closely sounded but in reality it sometimes fails to disclose indications of shoal water. Sounding may be commenced as soon as sufficient points are plotted; but off an intricate coast it is better to get the coast-line in first. Lines of soundings are run by the boats perpendicular to the coast, at a distance apart governed by the scale; five lines to the inch is about as close as can be run without overcrowding. The distance apart will vary with the depth of water and the nature of the coast; for instance a rocky coast with shallow water off it will need closer examination than a steep coast. The prolongation of a point under water will require special care to ensure the fathom lines being correct. When soundings begin to decrease to seaward intermediate lines or lines crossing those previously run should be obtained. If possible lines of soundings should be run on transits; these may generally be picked up by fixing when on the required line, noting the angle on the protractor between the line and some fixed mark on the field board, then placing the angle on the sextant and noting what objects intersect at that angle. On large scale surveys it may be necessary to place transit marks in the required positions. The boat is fixed by two angles, with an occasional third angle as a check; the distance between the fixes is dependent upon the scale of the chart and the rapidity with which the depth alters; the 3, 6 and 10 fathom lines should always be fixed, allowing roughly for the tidal reduction. The nature of the bottom must be taken every few casts and recorded. It is best to plot each fix on the sounding board at once, joining the fixes by straight lines and numbering them for identification. The tidal reduction being obtained, the reduced soundings corrected for any lead line error are written in the field-book in red underneath each sounding as originally noted; they are then placed in their proper position on the board between the fixes. Suspicious ground should be closely examined; a small buoy anchored on the shoal is useful to guide the boat while trying for the least depth. Sweeping for a reported pinnacle rock should be resorted to when sounding fails to discover it. Local information from fishermen and others is often of value. Up to depths of about 15 fathoms the hand lead-line is used from the boats, but beyond that depth the Lucas machine for wire effects a great saving of time and labour. The deeper soundings of a survey are usually obtained from the ship, but steamboats with wire sounding machines often assist very materially. By the aid of a steam winch, a 100-lb. lead is hove forward to the end of the lower boom rigged out, from which it is dropped by reversing the winch, soundings of 50 fathoms may be picked up from the sounding platform aft, whilst going at a speed of 5 to 6 knots. In deeper water it is quicker to stop the ship and sound from aft with the wire sounding machine. In running lines of soundings on and off shore, it is essential to be able to fix as far from the land as possible. Angles will be taken from aloft for this purpose, and floating beacons dropped in selected positions will be of assistance. A single fixed point on the land used in conjunction with two beacons suitably placed will give an admirable fix.

Echo Sounding.—This method of obtaining the depth is likely to prove of increasing value as time goes on and its efficiency becomes known. The principle is that an electric impulse is transmitted from the bottom of a ship, strikes the bed of the ocean and is reflected as an echo which is received by a hydrophone. The sound waves are sent out at fixed intervals and the echo is heard in telephone receivers connected with the hydrophone. The velocity of sound in water being known the depth can be calculated provided the time interval is accurately measured. A hand wheel, working a depth scale and connected with the telephonic gear is manipulated until echoes are heard in the receiver; the depth can then be read off the circular scale.

The Admiralty echo sounding apparatus shallow water type is designed to register depths of from 3 to 120 fathoms; for greater depths a modified form of echo gear is utilized. The saving of time is particularly noticeable where great depths are being obtained, the echo gear giving a result in a few seconds, whereas with a wire sounding machine the operation is a lengthy proceeding often occupying more than an hour. The disadvantage of echo sounding is that it is impossible to determine the nature of the bottom by this means and where a survey is in progress this must be obtained with the lead.

Vigias.[1]—A certain percentage of *vigias* which are reported and placed on the charts eventually turn out to have no existence, but before it is possible to expunge them the area has to be examined. Submarine banks rising from great depths necessarily stand on bases many square miles in area. Of recent years our knowledge of the angle of slope that may be expected to occur at different depths has been much extended. From depths upwards of 2,000 fathoms the slope is so gradual that a bank could hardly approach the surface in less than 7 m. from such a sounding; therefore anywhere within an area of at least 150 sq.m. all round a bank rising from these depths, a sounding must show some decided indications of a rise in the bottom. Under such circumstances, soundings at intervals of 7 m., and run in parallel lines 7 m. apart, enclosing areas of only 50 sq.m. between any four adjacent soundings, should clear up the ground and lead to the discovery of any shoal. As the depth decreases the angle of slope rapidly increases, and a shoal might occur within three-quarters of a mile or even half a mile of such a sounding as 500 fathoms. An appreciation of these facts will indicate the distance apart at which it is proper to obtain soundings. Contour lines will show in which direction to prosecute the search. When once a decided indication is found, it is not difficult to follow it up by paying attention to the contour lines as developed by successive soundings. Discoloured water, ripplings, fish jumping or birds hovering about may assist in locating a shoal, but the submarine sentry towed at a depth of 40 fathoms is here most valuable, and may save hours of hunting. Reports being more liable to errors of longitude than of latitude, a greater margin is necessary in that direction. Long parallel lines east and west are preferable, but the necessity of turning the ship more or less head to wind at every sounding makes it desirable to run the lines with the wind abeam, which tends to disturb the dead reckoning least. The current should be allowed for in shaping the course to preserve the parallelism of the lines, but the less frequently the course is altered the better. A good position should be obtained at morning and evening twilight by pairs of stars on opposite bearings, the lines of position of one pair cutting those of another pair nearly at right angles. The dead reckoning should be checked by lines of position from observations of the sun about every two hours throughout the day, preferably whilst a sounding is being obtained and the ship stationary.

Tides.—The datum for reduction of soundings is mean low-water springs, the level of which is referred to a permanent bench mark in order that future surveys may be reduced to the same datum level. Whilst sounding is going on the height of the water above this level is observed by a tide gauge. The time of high-water at full and change, called the "establishment," and the heights to which spring and neap tides respectively rise above the datum are also required. It is seldom that a sufficiently long series of observations can be obtained for their discussion by harmonic analysis, and therefore the graphical method is preferred. A good portable automatic tide gauge suitable for all requirements is much to be desired.

Tidal streams and surface currents are observed from the ship or boats at anchor by means of a current log. An alternative method is to follow a drifting buoy fixing the position at intervals. Tidal streams often run for some hours after high or low water by the shore; it is important to determine whether the change of stream occurs at a regular time of the tide.

Undercurrents are also of importance. A deep-sea current meter devised (1876) by Lieutenant Pillsbury, U.S.N., has been used with success on many occasions, notably in the investigation of the Gulf Stream. More recent developments of deep-sea current meters are the Ekman, Jacobsen, Sverdrup, Woolaston and Carruthers instruments. The instrument is lowered to the required depth and brought into action by a messenger, travelling down the supporting line and operating a lever which sets the instrument

[1]Spanish word meaning "look-out," used of marks on the chart signifying obstruction to navigation.

free, or some similar contrivance. On the completion of the necessary interval the meter is locked whilst still below the surface, hauled up and examined. The time during which the instrument has been working at the required depth is known and the direction and strength of the current can be determined from the mechanical arrangements.

Topography.—Generally speaking the topographical features should be delineated as far back as the skyline viewed from seaward, in order to assist the navigator to recognize the land. Summits of hills, conspicuous spurs, cliffs, etc., are fixed and their heights determined by theodolite elevations or depressions to and from positions where the height above the water is known. The shape is delineated by contour lines sketched by eye, assisted by an aneroid barometer. In wooded country much of the topography may have to be determined from the ship; sketches from different positions at anchor with the necessary angles to fix the features give a fair idea of the general lie of the country.

Latitudes.—Circum-meridian altitudes of stars observed by sextant in the artificial horizon is one of the methods adopted for observations for latitudes. Arranged in pairs of nearly the same altitude north and south of zenith, the mean of each pair give a result from which instrumental and personal errors and errors due to atmospheric conditions are eliminated. The mean of several such pairs should have a probable error of not more than $\pm 1''$. The observations of each star should be confined to within 5 or 6 minutes on either side of the meridian. Two stars selected to "pair" should pass the meridian within an hour of each other, and should not differ in altitude more than 2° or 3°. Artificial horizon roof error is eliminated by always keeping the same end of the roof towards the observer; when observing a single object, as the sun, the roof must be reversed when half way through the observations. The observations are reduced to the meridian by Raper's method. When pairs of stars are not observed, circum-meridian altitudes of the sun may be resorted to, but being observed on one side of the zenith only, none of the errors to which all observations are liable can be eliminated.

Chronometer Errors.—Equal altitudes of sun or stars by sextant and artificial horizon are employed to obtain chronometer errors. Six sets of eleven observations, A.M. and P.M., observing both limbs of the sun, should give a result which, under favourable conditions of latitude and declination, may be expected to vary less than two-tenths of a second from the normal personal equation of the observer. Stars give equally good results. In high latitudes sextant observations diminish in value owing to the slower movement in altitude. In the case of the sun all the chronometers are compared with the "standard" at apparent noon; the comparisons with the chronometer used for the observations on each occasion of landing and returning to the ship are worked up to noon. In the case of stars, the chronometer comparisons on leaving and again on returning are worked up to an intermediate time. A convenient system, which retains the advantage of the equal altitude method, whilst avoiding the necessity of waiting some hours for the P.M. observation, is to observe two stars at equal altitudes on opposite sides of the meridian, and, combining the observations, treat them as relating to an imaginary star having the mean right ascension and mean declination of the two stars selected, which should have nearly the same declination and should differ from 4^h to 8^h in R.A.

Meridian Distances.—The error of chronometer on mean time of place being obtained, the local time is transferred from one observation spot to another by the ship carrying usually eight box chronometers. The best results are found by using travelling rates, which are deduced from the difference of the errors found on leaving an observation spot and returning to it; from this difference is eliminated that portion which may have accumulated during an interval between two determinations of error at the other, or any intermediate, observation spot. A travelling rate may also be obtained from observations at two places, the meridian distance between which is known; this rate may then be used for the meridian distance between places observed during the passage. Failing travelling rates, the mean of the harbour rates at either end must be used. The same observer, using the same instrument, must be employed throughout the observations of a meridian distance.

If the telegraph is available, it should be used. The error on local time at each end of the wire is obtained, and a number of telegraphic signals are exchanged between the observers, an equal number being transmitted and received at either end. The local time of sending a signal from one place being known and the local time of its reception being noted, the difference is the meridian distance. The retardation due to the time occupied by the current in travelling along the wire is eliminated by sending signals in both directions. The relative personal equation of the observers at either end, both in their observations for time, and also in receiving and transmitting signals, is eliminated by changing ends and repeating the operations. If this is impracticable, the personal equations should be determined and applied to the results. Chronometers keeping solar time at one end of the wire, and sidereal time at the other end, materially increase the accuracy with which signals can be exchanged, for the same reason that comparisons between sidereal clocks at an observatory are made through the medium of a solar clock. Time by means of the sextant can be so readily obtained, and within such small limits of error, by skilled observers, that in hydrographic surveys it is often employed; but if transit instruments are available, and sufficient time can be devoted to erecting them properly, the value of the work is greatly enhanced.

True Bearings are obtained on shore by observing with theodolite the horizontal angle between the object selected as the zero and the sun, taking the latter in each quadrant as defined by the cross-wires of the telescope. The altitude may be read on the vertical arc of the theodolite; except in high latitudes, where a second observer with sextant and artificial horizon are necessary, unless the precise errors of the chronometers are known, when the time can be obtained by carrying a pocket chronometer to the station. The sun should be near the prime vertical and at a low altitude; the theodolite must be very carefully levelled, especially in the position with the telescope pointing towards the sun. To eliminate instrumental errors the observations should be repeated with vernier set at intervals equidistant along the arc, and A.M. and P.M. observations should be taken at about equal altitudes.

At sea true bearings are obtained by measuring with a sextant the angle between the sun and some distant well-defined object making an angle of from 100° to 120° and observing the altitude of the sun at the same time, together with that of the terrestrial object. The sun's altitude should be low to get the best results, and both limbs should be observed. The sun's true bearing is calculated from its altitude, the latitude and its declination; the horizontal angle is applied to obtain the true bearing of the zero. On shore the theodolite gives the horizontal angle direct, but with sextant observations it must be deduced from the angular distance and the elevation.

See Wharton and Field, *Hydrographical Surveying* (1920); C. F. Close, *Textbook of Hydrographical Surveying* (1925); John Ball and H. Knox Shaw, *The Handbook of the Prismatic Astrolabe,* Egyptian Government, Cairo Government Press (1919); *Echo Sounding,* H. M. Stationery Office (1926); R. M. Abraham, *Surveying Instruments,* London. (J. A. ED.)

CHARTER, a written instrument, contract, or convention by which grants of property or of rights and privileges are confirmed and held. The use of the word for any written document is obsolete in England, but is preserved in France, *e.g.,* the École des Chartes at Paris. In feudal times charters of privileges were granted, not only by the Crown, but by mesne lords both lay and ecclesiastical, as well to communities, such as boroughs, gilds and religious foundations, as to individuals. In modern usage grants by charter have become all but obsolete, though in England this form is still used in the incorporation by the Crown of certain public bodies (*see* CHARTERED COMPANIES).

The grant of the Great Charter by King John in 1215 (*see* MAGNA CARTA), which guaranteed the preservation of English liberties, led to a special association of the word with constitutional privileges, and so in modern times it has been applied to constitutions granted by sovereigns to their subjects, in contradistinction to those based on "the will of the people." Such was the Charter (*Charte*) granted by Louis XVIII. to France in 1814. In Portugal the constitution granted by Dom Pedro in 1826 was called by the French party the "Charter," while that devised by the Cortes in 1821 was known as the "Constitution." Magna Carta also suggested to the English radicals in 1838 the name "People's Charter," which they gave to their published programme of reforms (*see* CHARTISM). This association of the idea of liberty with the word charter led to its figurative use in the sense of freedom or licence.

The common colloquialism "to charter," in the sense of to take, or hire, is derived from the special use of "to charter" as to hire (a ship) by charter-party.

CHARTERED ACCOUNTANT: *see* ACCOUNTING.

CHARTERED COMPANIES. A chartered company is a corporation enjoying certain rights and privileges, and bound by certain obligations under a special charter granted to it by the sovereign authority of the State, such charter defining and limiting those rights, privileges and obligations, and the localities in which they are to be exercised. Such companies existed in early times, but have undergone changes and modifications in accordance with the developments which have taken place in the economic history of the States where they have existed. In Great Britain the first charters for foreign trade were granted, not to English companies but to branches of the Hanseatic League (*q v.*), and it was not till 1598 that England was finally relieved from the presence of a foreign chartered company. In that year Queen Elizabeth closed the steel-yard where Teutons had been established for 700 years.

Of all early English chartered companies, the "Merchant Adventurers" conducted its operations the most widely. Itself a development of very early trading gilds, at the height of its prosperity it employed as many as 50,000 persons in the Netherlands. In the reign of Elizabeth British trade with the Netherlands, reached, in one year, 12,000,000 ducats, and in that of James I. the company's yearly commerce with Germany and the Netherlands was as much as £1,000,000. Hamburg afterwards was its principal depot, and it became known as the "Hamburg company." Here it maintained itself until as late as 1808, when the company was at last dissolved. In the "Merchant Adventurers'" enterprises is to be seen the germ of the trading companies which had so remarkable a development in the 16th and 17th centuries. These old regulated trade gilds passed gradually into joint-stock associations, which were capable of far greater extension in both the number of members and the amount of stock, each member being only accountable for the amount of his own stock, and being able to transfer it at will to any other person.

The discovery of the New World, and the opening out of fresh trading routes to the Indies, gave an extraordinary impulse to shipping, commerce and industrial enterprise throughout western Europe. The English, French and Dutch Governments were ready to assist trade by the granting of charters to trading associations. The Baltic trade had already been the sphere of activities of an English company, since Henry IV. founded one by charter in 1404; and Elizabeth revived this "Eastland company" in 1579. To the "Russia company," which received its first charter in 1553, Great Britain owed its first intercourse with Russia and a direct trade with the Levant and Persia. Later, the Turkey company was founded, which in 1592, after amalgamation with the Venice company, took the name of the Levant company. Like the Muscovy company it was still trading in the 18th century. Both the Russia and Turkey companies had an important effect upon British relations with those empires. They maintained British influence in those countries, and even paid the expenses of the embassies which were sent out by the English Government to their courts.

The chartered companies which were formed during this period for trade with the Indies and the New World have had a more wide-reaching influence in history. The East India company (*q.v.*) is dealt with elsewhere. Charters were given to companies trading to Guiana and the Canaries, but none of these enjoyed a very long or prosperous existence, principally owing to the difficulties caused by foreign competition. It is when we turn to North America that the importance of the chartered company, as a colonizing rather than a trading agency, is seen in its full development. The "Hudson's Bay company," which still exists as a commercial concern, is dealt with under its own heading, but many of the 13 British North American colonies were in their inception chartered companies very much in the modern acceptation of the term. The history of these companies will be found under the heading of the different colonies of which they were the origin. It is necessary, however, to bear in mind that two classes of charters are to be found in force among the early American colonies: (1) Those granted to private individuals or to trading associations, which were often useful when the colony was first founded, but which were later withdrawn when the country had become settled and was looking forward to commercial expansion. The colonies were then brought under the direct control of the Crown, and their trade subject only to regulation by the Government. Thus the Virginia company lost their charter in 1624. The substitution of royal and later of parliamentary control for that of the company was an important factor in the growth of the Navigation Acts. (2) The second class of charters were those granted to the settlers themselves as a guarantee of their system of government. This, for example, was the effect of the charter granted to Massachusetts. In the later 17th century, however, the cancellation or amendment of the charters, and the growth of legislative assemblies tended to produce a uniformity of colonial practice, irrespective of the original character of the colony.

Chartered companies continued to be formed for the development of new trade, *e.g.*, the Royal African company in 1662 and the South Sea company in 1711.

In France and Holland, no less than in England, the institution of chartered companies became a settled principle of the Governments of those countries during the whole of the period in question. In France from 1599 to 1789, more than 70 of such companies came into existence, but after 1770, when the great *Compagnie des Indes orientales* went into liquidation, they were almost abandoned, and finally perished in the general sweeping away of privileges which followed on the outbreak of the Revolution. The monopoly rights granted to such companies were in accordance with the views generally accepted at the time, although there were many critics even in the 17th century. There were serious difficulties in the way of private trade owing to the large capital required to maintain factories and the necessity for their supervision. It was only the need for capital which induced statesmen like Colbert to countenance them, and Montesquieu took the same view (*Esprit des lois*, t. xx.c. 10). John de Witt's view was that such companies were not useful for colonization properly so called, because they wanted quick returns to pay their dividends. So, even in France and Holland, opinion was by no means settled as to their utility. In England historic protests were made against such monopolies, but the chartered companies were less exclusive in England than in either France or Holland. French commercial companies were more privileged, exclusive and artificial than those in Holland and England. Those of Holland may be said to have been national enterprises. French companies were more fettered than their rivals by the royal power and had less initiative of their own, and therefore had less chance of surviving.

During the last 20 years of the 19th century there was a great revival of the system of chartered companies in Great Britain. It was a feature of the general growth of interest in colonial expansion and commercial development which had made itself felt almost universally among European nations. But the modern companies were not like those of the 16th and 17th centuries; they were not monopolists, and were more definitely subject to the control of the Home Government. The charters, in fact, prohibited any monopoly of trade, and prescribed a State control which is their distinguishing feature. It is to be exercised in almost all directions in which the companies may come into contact with matters political; it is inevitable in all disputes of the companies with foreign Powers and is extended over all decrees of the company regarding the administration of its territories, the treatment of natives and mining regulations. In all cases of dispute between the companies and the natives the secretary of State is *ex officio* the judge, and to the secretary of State (in the case of the British South Africa company) the accounts of administration had to be submitted for approbation. The British character of the company is insisted upon in each case in the charter which calls it into life. The Crown always retains complete control over the company by reserving to itself the power of revoking the charter in case of the neglect of the stipulations. Special clauses were inserted in the charters of the British East Africa and South Africa companies enabling the Government to forfeit their charters if they did not promote the objects alleged as reasons for demanding a charter.

The chartered company of these days is therefore very strongly fixed within limits imposed by law on its political action. As a whole, however, very remarkable results have been achieved. This may be attributed in no small degree to the personality of the men who have had the supreme direction at home and abroad, and who have, by their social position and personal qualities, acquired the confidence of the public. With the exception of the Royal Niger company, it would be incorrect to say that they have been financially successful, but in the domain of Government generally it may be said that they have added vast territories to the British empire (in Africa about 1,700,000 sq.m.), and in these territories they have acted as a civilizing force. They have made roads, opened facilities for trade, enforced peace and laid, at all events, the foundation of settled administration; while anti-slavery and anti-alcohol campaigns have been carried on, the latter certainly being against the immediate pecuniary interests of the companies themselves. The occupation of Uganda certainly, and of the Nigerian territory and Rhodesia probably, will prove to have been rather for the benefit of posterity than of the companies which effected it. In the two cases where the companies have been bought out by the State, they have had no compensation for much that they have expended.

One common characteristic is to be noted in the histories of the old chartered companies and the new. In both periods the company has been used by the English Government as a useful instrument of colonial expansion, but in both periods only for temporary uses. When the colony is settled, or Government established, the State takes the lead. This is well illustrated by the history of the slow decline of the independence of the East India company in the 18th century and of the British South Africa company in the 20th. Both these companies are distinguished for their length of days, but both had to submit to the gradual penetration of State control.

See also BORNEO, NIGERIA, RHODESIA, etc. For the share of the chartered company in the development of the modern trading company, *see* COMPANY.

BIBLIOGRAPHY.—Bonnassieux, *Les Grandes Compagnies de commerce* (1892); Chailly-Bert, *Les Compagnies de colonisation sous l'ancien régime* (1898); Cawston and Keane, *The Early Chartered Companies* (1896); W. Cunningham, *A History of British Industry and Commerce* (1890, 1892); D. Hannay, *The Great Chartered Companies* (1926); J. Scott Keltie, *The Partition of Africa* (1895); Leroy-Beaulieu, *De la colonisation chez les peuples modernes* (1898); *Les Nouvelles Sociétés anglosaxonnes* (1897); Sir C. P. Lucas, *Beginnings of English Overseas Enterprise* (1917); W. MacDonald, *Select Charters illustrative of American History, 1606–1775* (New York, 1899); B. P. Poore, *Federal and State Constitutions,* etc. (Washington, 1877; a more complete collection of American colonial charters); H. L. Osgood, *American Colonies in the 17th Cent.* (1904–07); W. R. Scott, *Joint Stock Companies to 1720* (1910, etc.); Carton de Wiart, *Les Grandes Compagnies coloniales anglaises au 19me siècle* (1899); J. A. Williamson, *Maritime Enterprise, 1485–1558* (1913); "Compagnies de Charte," "Colonies," "Privilege," in *Nouveau Dictionnaire d'économie politique* (1892); and "Companies, Chartered," in *Encyclopaedia of the Laws of England,* edit. A. Wood Renton (1907–09).

CHARTERHOUSE, a corruption of the French *maison chartreuse,* a religious house of the Carthusians (*q.v.*). The name is found in various places in England (*e.g.,* Charterhouse-on-Mendip, Charterhouse Hinton) where the Carthusians were established, but is most familiarly applied to the Charterhouse, London. Near the old city wall, west of the modern thoroughfare of Aldersgate, a Carthusian monastery was founded in 1371 by Sir Walter de Manny. After its dissolution in 1535, the property was occupied for a time by Queen Elizabeth (in 1558) and by James I. In May 1611 the Charterhouse came into the hands of Thomas Sutton (1532–1611) of Snaith, Lincolnshire, who later settled in London. In 1611, the year of his death, he endowed a hospital on the site of the Charterhouse, calling it the hospital of King James and in his will he bequeathed money to maintain a chapel, hospital (almshouse) and school. The will was hotly contested but upheld in court, and the foundation was finally constituted to afford a home for 80 male pensioners and to educate 40 boys.

The school developed, and now ranks as a public school. In 1872 it was removed to new buildings near Godalming in Surrey. The pensioners still occupy the picturesque buildings of mellowed red brick, which include a panelled chapel, in which is the founder's tomb, the fine dining hall—rebuilt by the monks about 1520—the old library and the great staircase. Many of the buildings were ruined in World War II. Of the hall, the chimney piece and some woodwork survive. The master's house and adjacent buildings were burned out, but the chapel was unharmed. The hall (1872) of Merchant Taylors' school was also burned out.

CHARTER-PARTY: *see* AFFREIGHTMENT.

CHARTIER, ALAIN (*c.* 1392–*c.* 1430), French poet and political writer, was born at Bayeux about 1392. His eldest brother, Guillaume, became bishop of Paris; and Thomas became notary to the king. Jean Chartier, a monk of St. Denis, whose history of Charles VII. is printed in vol. iii. of *Les Grands Chroniques de Saint-Denis* (1477), was not, as is sometimes stated, also a brother of the poet. Alain studied, as his elder brother had done, at the University of Paris. His earliest poem is the *Livre des quatre dames,* written after the battle of Agincourt. This was followed by the *Débat du réveille-matin, La Belle Dame sans merci* and others. He was attached to the dauphin, afterwards Charles VII., acting in the triple capacity of clerk, notary and financial secretary. In 1422 he wrote the famous *Quadrilogue-invectif.* The interlocutors in this dialogue are France herself and the three orders of the State. Chartier lays bare the abuses of the feudal army and the sufferings of the peasants. He rendered an immense service to his country by maintaining that the cause of France, though desperate to all appearance, was not yet lost if the contending factions could lay aside their differences in the face of the common enemy. In 1424 Chartier was sent on an embassy to Germany, and three years later he accompanied to Scotland the mission sent to negotiate the marriage of Margaret of Scotland, then not four years old, with the dauphin, afterwards Louis XI. In 1429 he wrote the *Livre d'espérance,* which contains a fierce attack on the nobility and clergy. He was the author of a diatribe on the courtiers of Charles VII., entitled *Le Curial,* translated into English (*Here followeth the copy of a lettre whyche maistre A. Charetier wrote to his brother*) by Caxton about 1484. The story of the famous kiss bestowed by Margaret of Scotland on *la précieuse bouche de laquelle sont issus et sortis tant de bons mots et vertueuses paroles* is mythical, for Margaret did not come to France till 1436, after the poet's death. Jean de Masles, who annotated a portion of his verse, has recorded how the pages and young gentlemen of that epoch were required daily to learn by heart passages of his *Bréviaire des nobles.* John Lydgate studied him affectionately. *La Belle Dame sans merci* was translated into English by Sir Richard Ros about 1640, with an introduction of his own; and Clément Marot and Octavien de Saint-Gelais, writing 50 years after his death, find many fair words for the old poet, their master and predecessor.

See Mancel, *Alain Chartier, étude bibliographique et littéraire,* 8vo (1849); D. Delaunay's *Étude sur Alain Chartier* (1876), with considerable extracts from his writings, and G. Joret-Desclosières, *Alain Chartier* (4th ed., 1899). His works were edited by A. Duchesne (Paris, 1617).

CHARTISM, the name of a revolutionary democratic agitation in Great Britain which came into prominence in 1838 and disappeared after 1850.

The "People's Charter" was the name given to a bill containing the famous six points—equal electoral areas, universal suffrage, payment of members, no property qualifications, vote by ballot, and annual parliaments—all but the last of which have since been secured. These points, which from 1768 had been, partially at least, the common property of all radical agitation, were first collected into one petition on Feb. 18 1837, by the London Workingmen's Association, founded by William Lovett, as a result of the great disappointment of the Reform Bill of 1832, which enfranchised only the middle class. These six points were drafted into a bill known as the Charter by Lovett, with possibly some assistance from Francis Place, which was published on May 8 1838; and the formal constitution of the Chartist movement is commonly dated from a great meeting held on Aug. 8 on Newhall Hill at which the Charter was approved.

The ultimate aims of the movement were economic—"social equality" or, in the phrase of G. J. Harney's *London Democrat,* (April 27 1839) "that all shall have a good house to live in with a garden back or front, just as the occupier likes; good clothing to keep him warm and to make him look respectable, and plenty of good food and drink to make him look and *feel* happy." The Chartists were not unanimous about the means of securing this social equality, but a provisional agreement on universal suffrage as the necessary first step provided the basis of the movement. The London Workingmen's Association, which launched the campaign by sending out "missionaries" all over Great Britain, consisted of skilled workers mostly above the poverty line: not so the supporters to whom they appealed. The factory workers, colliers and handloom workers of the North and Midlands, who became the chief adherents of Chartism, were passing through a period of extreme misery and degradation, which was not at this time mitigated by any effectively administered Factory Act (except one which limited, in some cases, the working hours of certain children to 12). Two Tory factory reformers, Richard Oastler and the Rev. J. R. Stephens, were, moreover, conducting, in an exceedingly violent manner, a campaign against the provisions of the Poor Law of 1834, which aimed at making poor relief more unpleasant than the most unpleasant means of gaining a livelihood outside. Oastler and Stephens, whose campaign in several areas succeeded in postponing its application, threw their weight into the Chartist movement, and over the whole of the Northern area torchlight meetings were held at night on the moors, in which armed insurrection was freely advocated. Scotland, and the west of England, which was evangelized by Henry Vincent, the most eloquent Chartist orator, were the moderate areas: the Welsh miners were the most revolutionary. Feargus O'Connor (*q.v.*), an Irish squire who had formerly (1832–35) been one of O'Connell's "tail" in Parliament, became rapidly the most popular leader, and rarely made a speech without alluding to physical force.

The new Chartist plan of campaign was, however, provided by a banker, Thos. Attwood, M.P. for Birmingham, who trusted that a Charter parliament would adopt his views on currency. He proposed the election, by the disfranchised, of an anti-Parliament to be called the Convention which would sit as a rival to the House of Commons and present a petition, signed by the mass of the working class, for the enactment of the Charter as the law of the land. If the Commons refused, the Convention would then call a general strike (the "Sacred Month"). This exhilarating programme was enthusiastically taken up; the petition was signed by 1,280,000 people and the members of the Convention, elected by public meetings, held their first sitting in London on Feb. 4 1839. The Convention was at the beginning controlled by the "moral force men" headed by Lovett, but it was not able to prevent frequent violent conflicts with the police (in which the Chartists were not uncommonly victorious) and the moderates entirely lost control when on July 12 the Commons, after long delays, rejected the petition. Post-dated orders for the General Strike were forthwith issued, amid great excitement. Only a few days had passed, however, when the Convention realized that it had behind it no organization and no preparations, and in consequence somewhat ignominiously cancelled the orders on July 22.

What the "moral force men" would not do, others were prepared to attempt. During the Convention a secret military organization had been formed, directed by a committee of five: its plans were completed at a private conference held in the autumn at Heckmondwike. The signal for the insurrection was to be given by the capture of Newport (Mon.) and the release of Vincent from Monmouth Castle. The other centres of revolt appear to have been in Lancashire and Yorkshire. The attack on Newport was led by the ex-mayor and J.P., John Frost, on the morning of Nov. 4. It was to have been in three columns, but owing to mismanagement the columns failed to unite at Risca and Frost attacked alone with about 3,000 men armed with rifles and mandrils (collier's picks). Warning had been given and the Chartists walked into a trap in the square outside the Westgate hotel. They were defeated after a very brief struggle, leaving a considerable number (the figures are disputed) of killed and wounded. The leaders, Frost, Jones and Williams, were sentenced to death, afterwards mitigated to transportation. The police also rounded up nearly every other Chartist leader of importance, and secured sentences of one or two years' imprisonment.

On the release of the leaders in 1840 and 1841 renewed quarrels broke out between the "physical force men" led by O'Connor and his assistant on the *Northern Star,* G. J. Harney, and the "moral force men" led by Lovett and Bronterre O'Brien. The latter considered that the working class had not sufficient strength to achieve reform alone and should now invite the aid of sympathetic middle-class groupings: O'Connor and his allies declared that the middle-class reformers, responsible for the deception of 1832, were also the worst oppressors of the operatives in the factories and mines. O'Connor, with the assistance of his journal the *Star,* which secured a hitherto unparalleled circulation, carried the day and drove the other section out of the movement. His popularity became enormous, due to his hard work, his hatred of the middle class and his remarkable invective, of which the following is a specimen: "You—I was just coming to you when I was describing the materials of which our spurious aristocracy is composed. You, gentlemen, belong to the big-bellied, little-brained, numskull aristocracy. How dare you hiss me, you contemptible set of platterfaced, amphibious politicians?" A national organization, technically illegal, called the National Charter Association, was founded, which gave some coherence to the movement. It secured the allegiance of a number of trade union branches and promoted a second petition which received the startling number of 3,315,752 signatures. The year 1842, when this was presented, marks the high water-mark of Chartism. After its rejection on May 2, the Chartist executive turned an existing small strike at Ashton into a general strike for the Charter (Aug. 12). They brought out Lancashire, Cheshire, the Potteries and several other industrial districts; the strikers marching from town to town knocking the plugs out of the boilers where resistance was offered (hence the name Plug Riots). Owing to inadequate communications, the strike spread slowly, but trades as far north as Aberdeen had decided to come out, when, his nerve failing, O'Connor suddenly declared the strike was a plot of the Anti-Corn Law League. This action broke up the strike which ended almost at once in defeat. Thereafter Chartism entered into a period of decline, in which interest was chiefly directed to a financially unsound scheme for settling Chartists on the land as smallholders, by means of a National Land Company directed by O'Connor. One settlement only (O'Connorville, 1847, Herringsgate, Bucks) was opened. Enthusiasm was revived in 1847 by the election of O'Connor as M.P. for Nottingham, and in 1848 by the sensational series of revolutions on the continent. Fired by the hope of similar victories, O'Connor promoted a petition, which he said had 6,000,000 signatures, and arranged for the calling of a "National Assembly." The petition was to be presented by a procession of Chartists marching from Kennington Common to the House of Commons on April 10 1848. Believing this to be the day fixed for the revolution, the Government garrisoned London so heavily that the procession was abandoned. The petition, further, was announced by the Government to contain under 2,000,000 signatures, and it was also discovered that the Land Company was bankrupt. Under the influence of this series of fiascos, O'Connor became distracted in his mind: his successor, Ernest Jones, endeavoured in vain to revive the legal movement which by about 1854 may be regarded as extinct. The illegal revolutionary organization prepared an insurrection for Whit-Monday 1848, later adjourned to Aug. 15, but as it was carefully watched and, indeed, partly directed by police informers, its effort was suppressed without difficulty.

The disappearance of Chartism was due not so much to the folly of its leaders as to the increasing comfort of the working class in the period of prosperity following on the Corn Law Repeal (1846), and the enforcement of the factory reforms secured by Lord Shaftesbury (*q.v.*). Working-class interest henceforward was diverted to the co-operative movement and the new craft trade unions, of which the most famous, the Amalgamated Society of Engineers, was founded in 1851.

BIBLIOGRAPHY.—There are two *Histories of the Chartist Movement,* both unfinished, by Mark Hovell (1917) and Julius West (1920). *See* also M. Beer, *History of British Socialism* 2 vols. (1919, 1920). For original authorities *see* R. W. Postgate, *Revolution from 1789 to 1906* (1920); R. G. Gammage, *History of Chartism* (1854); W. Lovett, *Life and Struggles of William Lovett* (republished 1920); *Trial of John Frost under a special Commission of Oyer and Terminer* (1840); Francis Place's mss. (Brit. Mus., Add mss. 27,819–21), and the file of the *Northern Star.* (R. W. P.)

CHARTRES, a city of north-western France, capital of the department of Eure-et-Loir, 55 m. south-west of Paris on the railway to Le Mans. Pop. (1936) 26,747. Chartres is on the left bank of the Eure, on a hill crowned by its famous cathedral, the spires of which are a landmark on the plain of Beauce, "the granary of France." The Eure, which divides into three branches, is crossed by several bridges, some ancient, and is fringed by remains of fortifications, notably the Porte Guillaume (14th century) flanked by towers. The steep, narrow streets of the old town contrast with the boulevards which encircle it and divide it from the suburbs. The cathedral of Notre-Dame (*see* ARCHITECTURE: *Gothic Architecture;* STAINED GLASS; SCULPTURE), was founded by Bishop Fulbert (11th century) on the site of a church which had been destroyed by fire. In 1194 another fire made new building necessary and the present church was finished by 1240; there have been minor additions and alterations since that time. A fire in 1836 destroyed the upper woodwork. The statuary of the portals, the stained glass of the 13th century, and the choir-screen of the Renaissance are all unique. The south spire, the Clocher Vieux (351 ft. high), dates from the 12th century; the Clocher Neuf (377 ft.) was not completed till the 16th century. The cathedral is 440 ft. long, its choir measures 150 ft. across, and the vaulting is 121 ft. high. The abbey church of St. Pierre, chiefly 13th century, contains fine stained glass and twelve representations of the apostles in enamel (1547) by Léonard Limosin. St. Martin-au-Val is a 12th century church. The hôtel de ville (17th century) contains a museum and library, an older hôtel de ville is of the 13th century, and there are mediaeval and Renaissance houses.

Chartres was one of the principal towns of the Carnutes, and by the Romans was called *Autricum,* from the river *Autura* (Eure), and afterwards *civitas Carnutum.* It was burnt by the Normans in 858, and unsuccessfully besieged by them in 911. It was in English hands 1417–32. It was attacked unsuccessfully by the Protestants in 1568, and was taken in 1591 by Henry IV., who was crowned there three years afterwards. It was seized by the Germans on Oct. 21, 1870, and used as a centre of operations. During the middle ages it gave its name to a countship held by the counts of Blois and Champagne and afterwards by the house of Châtillon, a member of which in 1286 sold it to the crown. It was raised to the rank of a duchy in 1528 by Francis I.

The town is the seat of a bishop, a prefecture, a court of assizes, and has tribunals of first instance and of commerce and a chamber of commerce. It is a market-town for Beauce. Game-pies of Chartres are well known, and industries include flour milling, timber sawing, brewing, distilling, iron founding, leather manufacture, dyeing, and the manufacture of stained glass, billiard requisites, hosiery, machinery, etc.

See M. T. Bulteau, *Monographie de la cathédrale de Chartres* (1887). A. Plerval, *Chartres, sa cathédrale, ses monuments* (1896); H. J. L. J Massé, *Chartres: its Cathedral and Churches* (1900); E. Houvet, *Cathédrale de Chartres* (1922).

CHARTREUSE. A celebrated liqueur, green and yellow, with a distinctive flavouring of angelica root. It is made at La Grande Chartreuse, the old Carthusian monastery near Grenoble. The Carthusian order of monks was founded by Saint Bruno of Cologne in 1084. In 1607 the Maréchal d'Estrées gave to the Carthusian Fathers the recipe of the elixir. It was supposed to be concocted from a distillation of herbs, culled on the slopes of the Dauphiné valley, and the finest brandy. In 1757 Brother Gérôme Maubec, "a very clever apothecary," perfected the formula, the secret of which, however, was never divulged nor discovered by analysis. Although in the Revolution of 1793 the Carthusians were despoiled of their property, they retained the secrets of their formula. In 1816 they were allowed to return to their monastery, but in 1901 were in trouble again owing to the decree for the expulsion of the religious orders from France. They locked themselves in their monastery, but were eventually expelled and their distillery at Fourvoire was sold, including their trade-mark. The monks emigrated to Farneta, near Lucca, in Italy, and later acquired a distillery at Tarragona in Spain, taking their famous recipe with them. Meantime, the new French owners of the monastery near Grenoble began to sell an imitation liqueur under the original trade-mark. Thereupon the monks adopted *Les Pères Chartreux* as their new trade-mark and registered it in many countries. In London, the high court of justice decided that the French "Chartreuse" could not lawfully be sold in the United Kingdom as being the monks' product. This decision was qualified by the fact that certain stocks of the original liqueur remained in existence and it was ruled that these might be sold lawfully. If bottles are merely labelled "Chartreuse" it is certain that the liqueur was made by the monks before their expulsion from France. The only guarantee of their origin is the printer's name, Alier, on the label, but stocks bearing this label were virtually exhausted by 1944. In 1938 the Carthusian monks were allowed to return to their property at Grenoble and the distillation of the liqueur was being revived there. (J. V. M.; F. W. D.)

CHARTREUSE, LA GRANDE, the mother house of the order of Carthusian monks (*see* CARTHUSIANS). It is situated in the French department of the Isère, about 12½ m. N. of Grenoble, at a height of 3,205 ft. above the sea, in the heart of a group of limestone mountains, and not far from the source of the Guiers Mort. The original settlement here was founded by St. Bruno in 1084, and derived its name from the small village to the southeast, formerly known as Cartusia, and now as St. Pierre de Chartreuse. The first convent on the present site was built between 1132 and 1137, but the actual buildings date only from about 1676, the older ones often having been burned. One of the most famous of the early Carthusian monks was St. Hugh of Lincoln, who lived here from 1160 to 1181, when he went to England as prior of the first Carthusian house at Witham, Somerset; in 1181 he became bishop of Lincoln, and before his death in 1200 had built the angel choir and other portions of the cathedral there.

The monks were expelled in 1792, but were allowed to return in 1816, when they had to pay rent for the use of the buildings and the forests around. They were again expelled in 1903, and were dispersed in various houses in England, at Pinerolo (Italy) and at Tarragona (Spain). The high roofs of dark slate, the cross-surmounted turrets and the lofty clock-tower are the chief features of the buildings of the convent, which are not very striking. Women were formerly lodged in the old infirmary, close to the main gate, which is now a hotel. Within the conventual buildings are four halls formerly used for the reception of the priors of various branch houses in France, Italy, Burgundy and Germany. The very plain and unadorned chapel dates from the 15th century, but the cloisters, around which cluster the 36 small houses for the fully professed monks, are of later date. The library contained before the Revolution a very fine collection of books and mss., most of them now in the town library at Grenoble.

CHARWOMAN. A word of interesting origin, meaning one who is hired to do occasional household work. "Char" or "chare," which forms the first part of the word, is common, in many forms, to Teutonic languages, meaning a "turn," and, in this original sense, is seen in "ajar," properly "on char," of a door "on the turn" in the act of closing. It is thus applied to a "turn of work," an odd job, and is so used, in the form "chore," in the United States, and in dialects of the south-west of England.

CHASE, SALMON PORTLAND (1808–1873), American statesman and jurist, was born in Cornish, N.H., on Jan. 13, 1808. His father died in 1817, and the son passed several years (1820–24) in Ohio with his uncle, Bishop Philander Chase (1775–1852), the foremost pioneer of the Protestant Episcopal Church in the West. He graduated at Dartmouth college in 1826, and after studying law under William Wirt, attorney-general of the United States, in Washington, D.C., was admitted to the bar in 1829, and removed to Cincinnati, O., in 1830. Here he soon gained a position of prominence at the bar.

At a time when public opinion in Cincinnati was largely dominated by Southern business connections, Chase, influenced probably by James G. Birney, associated himself after about 1836 with the anti-slavery movement, and became recognized as the leader of the political reformers as opposed to the Garrisonian abolitionists. To the cause he freely gave his services as a lawyer, and was particularly conspicuous as counsel for fugitive slaves seized in Ohio for rendition to slavery under the Fugitive Slave law of 1793—indeed, he came to be known as the "attorney-general of fugitive slaves." His argument (1847) in the famous Van Zandt case before the United States Supreme Court attracted particular attention, though in this as in other cases of the kind the judgment was against him. In brief he contended that slavery was "local, not national," that it could exist only by virtue of positive State law, that the Federal Government was not empowered by the Constitution to create slavery anywhere, and that "when a slave leaves the jurisdiction of a State he ceases to be a slave, because he continues to be a man and leaves behind him the law which made him a slave."

In 1841 he abandoned the Whig Party, with which he had previously been affiliated, and for seven years was the undisputed leader of the Liberty Party in Ohio; he was remarkably skilful in drafting platforms and addresses, and it was he who prepared the national Liberty platform of 1843 and the Liberty address of 1845. Realizing in time that a third-party movement could not succeed, he took the lead during the campaign of 1848 in combining the Liberty Party with the Barnburners or Van Buren Democrats of New York to form the Free-Soilers. He drafted the famous Free-Soil platform, and it was largely through his influence that Van Buren was nominated for the presidency. His object, however, was not to establish a permanent new party organization, but to bring pressure to bear upon Northern Democrats to force them to adopt a policy opposed to the further extension of slavery.

In 1849 he was elected to the United States Senate as the result of a coalition between the Democrats and a small group of Free-Soilers in the State legislature; and for some years thereafter, except in 1852, when he rejoined the Free-Soilers, he classed himself as an Independent Democrat, though he was out of harmony with the leaders of the Democratic Party. During his service in the Senate (1849–55) he was pre-eminently the champion of anti-slavery in that body, and no one spoke more ably than he did against the Compromise Measures of 1850 and the Kansas-Nebraska bill of 1854. The Kansas-Nebraska legislation, and the subsequent troubles in Kansas, having convinced him of the futility of trying to influence the Democrats, he assumed the leadership in the North-west of the movement to form a new party to oppose the extension of slavery. The "Appeal of the Independent Democrats in Congress to the People of the United States," written by Chase and Giddings, and published in the New York *Times* of Jan. 24, 1854, may be regarded as the earliest draft of the Republican Party creed. He was the first Republican governor of Ohio, serving from 1855 to 1859.

Although, with the exception of Seward, he was the most prominent Republican in the country, and had done more against slavery than any other Republican, he failed to secure the nomination for the presidency in 1860, partly because his views on the question of protection were not orthodox from a Republican point of view, and partly because the old line Whig element could not forgive his coalition with the Democrats in the senatorial campaign of 1849; his uncompromising and conspicuous anti-slavery record, too, was against him from the point of view of "availability." As secretary of the Treasury in President Lincoln's cabinet in 1861–64, during the first three years of the Civil War, he rendered services of the greatest value. That period of crisis witnessed two great changes in American financial policy, the establishment of a national banking system and the issue of a legal tender paper currency. The former was Chase's own particular measure. He suggested the idea, worked out all of the important principles and many of the details, and induced Congress to accept them. The success of that system alone warrants his being placed in the first rank of American financiers. It not only secured an immediate market for Government bonds, but it also provided a stable uniform national currency.

Perhaps Chase's chief defect as a statesman was an insatiable desire for supreme office. It was partly this ambition, and also temperamental differences from the president, which led him to retire from the cabinet in June 1864. A few months later (Dec. 6, 1864) he was appointed chief justice of the United States Supreme Court to succeed Judge Taney, a position which he held until his death. Toward the end of his life he gradually drifted back toward his old Democratic position, and made an unsuccessful effort to secure the nomination of the Democratic Party for the presidency in 1872. He died in New York city on May 7, 1873. Chase was one of the ablest political leaders of the Civil War period, and deserves to be placed in the front rank of American statesmen.

The standard biography is A. B. Hart's *Salmon Portland Chase* in the "American Statesmen Series" (1899). Less philosophical, but containing a greater wealth of detail, is J. W. Shuckers' *Life and Public Services of Salmon Portland Chase* (1874). R. B. Warden's *Account of the Private Life and Public Services of Salmon Portland Chase* (Cincinnati, 1874) deals more fully with Chase's private life. *See* also Floyd Pershing Gates, *Salmon P. Chase and the Independent Democrats* (1918); and Arthur M. Schlesinger, *Salmon Portland Chase, Undergraduate and Pedagogue* (1919).

CHASE, SAMUEL (1741–1811), American jurist, was born in Somerset county (Md.), April 17, 1741. He was admitted to the bar at Annapolis in 1761, and for more than 20 years was a member of the Maryland legislature. He took an active part in the resistance to the Stamp Act, and from 1774 to 1778 and 1784 to 1785 was a member of the Continental Congress. He did much to persuade Maryland to advocate a formal separation of the 13 colonies from Great Britain, and signed the Declaration of Independence on Aug. 2, 1776. In 1791 he became chief judge of the Maryland general court, but resigned in 1796 to become associate justice of the U.S. Supreme Court. Because of his activities on behalf of the Federalist party, the House of Representatives adopted a resolution of impeachment in March, 1804, and on Dec. 7, 1804, the House managers, chief among whom were John Randolph, Joseph H. Nicholson (1770–1817), and Caesar A. Rodney (1772–1824), laid their articles of impeachment before the Senate. The trial, which lasted from Jan. 2 to March 1, 1805, ensued on an indictment of eight articles, dealing with his conduct in the Fries and Callender trials, with his treatment of a Delaware grand jury, and (in article viii.) with his making "highly indecent, extra-judicial" reflections upon the national administration. On only three articles was there a majority against Judge Chase, the largest, on article viii., being four short of the necessary two-thirds to convict.

"The case," says Henry Adams, "proved impeachment to be an impracticable thing for partisan purposes, and it decided the permanence of those lines of constitutional development which were a reflection of the common law." Judge Chase resumed his seat on the bench, and occupied it until his death, June 19, 1811.

See *The Trial of Samuel Chase* (2 vols., Washington, 1805), reported by Samuel H. Smith and Thomas Lloyd; an article in *The American Law Review,* vol. xxxiii. (St. Louis, 1899); and Henry Adams's *History of the United States,* vol. ii. (1889). *See* also J. H. Hazelton, *The Declaration of Independence* (1906); and *The Maryland Signers of the Declaration of Independence* (Baltimore, 1912).

CHASE, WILLIAM MERRITT (1849–1916), American painter, was born at Franklin, Ind., on Nov. 1, 1849. He was a pupil of B. F. Hays in Indianapolis, of J. O. Eaton in New York and of A. Wagner and Piloty in Munich. In New York he established a school of his own, after having taught with success for some years at the Art Students' League. A worker in all mediums—oils, water-colour, pastel and etching—painting with distinction the figure, landscape and still life, he is perhaps best known by his portraits, his sitters numbering some of the most important men and women of his time.

Chase won many honours at home and abroad, became a member of the National Academy of Design, New York, and for ten years was president of the Society of American Artists. In 1912 he was awarded the Proctor Prize by the National Academy of Design for his "Portrait of Mrs. H." At the Panama Pacific Exposition (1915) a special room was assigned to his works. Among his most important canvases are "Ready for the Ride" (Union League Club, N.Y.), "The Apprentice," "Court Jester," and portraits of the painters, Whistler and Duveneck; of General Webb and of Peter Cooper.

See J. Walker McSpadden, *Famous Painters of America* (1916).

CHASE. (1) The pursuit of wild animals for food or sport (Fr. *chasse,* Lat. *capere,* to take), and so the pursuit of anything. (*See* Hunting.) The word was also applied to park land reserved for the breeding and hunting of wild animals; *cf.* various place-names in England, as Cannock Chase. It is also a term for a stroke in tennis. (*See* Lawn Tennis and Tennis.) (2) An enclosure (Fr. *châsse,* Lat. *capsa,* a box), such as the muzzle-end of a gun in front of the trunnions, or, in typography (*q.v.*) the frame enclosing the page of type. (*See* Printing.)

CHASE NATIONAL BANK, THE, of the city of New York was founded on Sept. 12, 1877. Its first published balance sheet (Dec. 27, 1877) showed total resources of $1,042,009.25. The statement for March 30, 1940, showed total resources of $3,-345,528,389.43; common capital stock of $100,270,000.00 and surplus and undivided profits of $136,486,918.24. On the same date, the bank had 35 branches in greater New York, and branches in London, Havana, San Juan, Panama, Colon, Cristobal and Balboa. An affiliate, The Chase Bank (organized under the Edge Act), had branches in Paris, Shanghai, Hongkong and Tientsin. The Chase National Bank occupies a prominent position in the field of both domestic and foreign commercial banking, acts as New York correspondent for thousands of other banks in the United States and abroad, and maintains a large trust department.

Principal executive officers in 1940 were Winthrop W. Aldrich, chairman, board of directors, and H. Donald Campbell, president. Mergers with three other large New York banks and a number of smaller institutions were consummated between 1921 and 1931, as follows:

Nov. 23, 1921, Metropolitan Bank; April 12, 1926, Mechanics & Metals National Bank; Dec. 28, 1927, Mutual Bank; Jan. 26, 1929, Garfield National Bank; Aug. 24, 1929, National Park Bank; June 2, 1930, Equitable Trust Company and Interstate Trust Company; Dec. 19, 1931, American Express Bank & Trust Co.

CHASING, the art of producing figures and ornamental patterns, either raised or indented, on metallic surfaces by means of steel tools or punches. (*See* Silversmiths' and Goldsmiths' Work.) The chaser first outlines the pattern on the surface he is to ornament, after which, if the work requires bold or high embossments, this is blocked out by a process called "snarling." The snarling iron is a long iron tool turned up at the end, and made so that when securely fastened in a vice the upturned end can reach and press against any portion of the interior of the vase or object to be chased. The part to be raised being held firmly against the upturned point of the snarling iron, the workman gives the shoulder or opposite end a sharp blow which raises the surface of the metal held against the tool. When the blocking out from the interior is finished, the object to be chased is filled with molten pitch, which is allowed to harden. It is then fastened to a sandbag, and with hammer and a multitude of small punches of different outline the details of the pattern (lined, smooth or "mat") are worked out. Embossing and stamping from steel dies and rolled ornaments have taken the place of chased ornamentations in the cheaper kinds of plated works. (*See* Embossing.)

CHASLES, MICHEL (1793–1880), French mathematician, was born on Nov. 15, 1793, at Epernon. He was educated at Paris, and engaged in business, which he later gave up for the study of mathematics. Chasles was made professor of geodesy and mechanics at the Polytechnic school and later professor of higher geometry at the Sorbonne. He and Steiner independently elaborated modern projective geometry, but the interchange of scientific ideas was so poor that the former did not know of the work of the latter. Chasles used his "method of characteristics" and his "principle of correspondence" to solve many problems; the solutions were published in a series of papers in *Comptes Rendus.* The problem of the attraction of an ellipsoid on an external point was solved by him in 1846. Many of his original memoirs were later published in the *Journal de l'École Polytechnique.* Chasles wrote two text-books, *Higher Geometry* (1852) and *Conic Sections* (1865). His *Aperçu historique sur l'origine et la développement des méthodes en géometrie* (1837) is a standard work, the subject being continued in *Rapport sur le progrès de la géometrie* (1870). Chasles died in Paris on Dec. 18, 1880.

CHASLES, PHILARÈTE (1798–1873), French critic and man of letters, was born at Mainvilliers (Eure et Loir). His father, P. J. M. Chasles (1754–1826), was a member of the Convention, and brought up his son according to the principles of Rousseau's *Émile.* Philarète, after a régime of outdoor life, followed by some years of classical study, was apprenticed to a printer. He contributed to the *Revue des deux mondes,* until he had a violent quarrel, terminating in a lawsuit, with François Buloz, who won his case. He became librarian of the Bibliothèque Mazarine, and from 1841 was professor of comparative literature at the Collège de France. During his active life he produced some 50 volumes of literary history and criticism and of social history.

Among his best critical works is *Dix-huitième Siècle en Angleterre . . .* (1846), one of a series of 20 vols. of *Études de littérature comparée* (1846–75), which he called later *Trente ans de critique.* An account of his strenuous boyhood is given in his *Maison de mon père.* His *Mémoires* (1876–77) did not fulfil the expectations based on his brilliant talk.

CHASSÉ, a gliding step in dancing, so called since one foot is brought up behind, or chases, the other. The *chassé croisé* is a double variety of the step.

CHASSELOUP-LAUBAT, FRANÇOIS, Marquis de (1754–1833), French general and military engineer, was born at St. Sernin (Lower Charente), and entered the French engineers in 1774. In 1791 he was promoted captain, and his ability was recognized in the campaigns of 1792. After serving as chief engineer at the siege of Mainz (1796), he was sent to Italy, where he conducted the first siege of Mantua, and afterwards to the new Rhine frontier of France. He was chief of engineers in the army of Italy in 1799, and Napoleon's engineer general in 1800; and he was afterwards employed in reconstructing the defences of the famous Quadrilateral in northern Italy (1801–05). His *chef-d'oeuvre* was the great fortress of Alessandria on the Tanaro. Chasseloup served in Napoleon's campaign of 1806–07, directing the sieges of Colberg, Danzig and Stralsund; and again in 1809, in Italy. Soon after his last campaign, in Russia (1812), he retired from active service, and was made a peer of France and a knight of St. Louis by Louis XVIII. He voted in the chamber of peers against the condemnation of Marshal Ney. In politics he belonged to the constitutional party.

As an engineer Chasseloup was an adherent, though of advanced views, of the old bastioned system. His front was applied to Alessandria, as has been stated, and contains many elaborations of the bastion trace, with, in particular, masked flanks in the tenaille, which served as extra flanks of the bastions. The bastion itself was carefully and minutely retrenched. The ordinary ravelin he replaced by a heavy casemated caponier after the example of Montalembert, and, like Bousmard's, his own ravelin was a large and powerful work pushed out beyond the glacis.

Chasseloup's only published works were, *Correspondance d'un général français avec un général autrichien.* (1801; republ. 1803 or 1809 as *Correspondance de deux généraux . . .*) and *Extraits de Mémoires sur quelques parties de l'artillerie et de fortifications* (Milan, 1805; republ. 1811 as *Essais sur quelques parties . . .*). The most important of his papers are in ms. in the Depôt of Fortifications, Paris.

CHASSEPOT, officially "fusil modèle 1866," a military breech-loading rifle, famous as the arm of the French forces in the Franco-German War of 1870–71. It was called after its inventor, Antoine Alphonse Chassepot (1833–1905), who had previously constructed a series of experimental forms of breech-loader, and it became the French service weapon in 1866. In the following year it made its first appearance on the battlefield at Mentana, where it inflicted severe losses upon Garibaldi's troops. In the war of 1870 it proved very greatly superior to the German needle-gun. The breech was closed by a bolt very similar to those of more modern rifles, and amongst the technical features of interest were the method of obturation and the retention of the paper cartridge. It was sighted to 1,312yd. (1,200 metres).

CHASSÉRIAU, THÉODORE (1819–1856), French painter, was born in the Antilles on Sept. 20, 1819, and died in Paris on Oct. 8, 1856. He studied under Ingres at Paris and at Rome, subsequently falling under the influence of Paul Delaroche. In his short life he produced little. There are decorative paintings by him in the church of St. Méry and the Salle des Comptes in the Palais d'Orsay, and some characteristic lithographs, imaginative in character and original in execution, which link him with the artists of the '70s and '80s rather than with his contemporaries or predecessors.

CHASSEURS, light infantry or cavalry regiments in the French army (from Fr. *chasser,* to hunt). The first light infantry (*chasseurs à pied*) units were raised in 1743, and by 1794 their number had increased to 21 battalions. The name then disappeared until 1840, but by 1870 they had again increased to their original figure, and by the outbreak of World War I to 30 battalions, of which 12 were known as *Chasseurs Alpins.* They were specially equipped and trained for mountain warfare.

Under the French army organization at mid-20th century these 30 battalions of *chasseurs* were formed as independent units for administrative purposes, but were grouped into demibrigades of three battalions for war. They were distinguished from line infantry by their dark blue uniforms. During the period just prior to World War II a few battalions of *chasseurs* were integrated into armoured divisions as motorized infantry. The French army after that war included a number of battalions of *chasseurs,* of which several were alpine or motorized.

The light cavalry (*chasseurs à cheval*) regiments were first instituted in 1779. They performed notable service in the European campaigns of the Second Empire. At the close of World War I they were represented by five regiments of *Chasseurs d'Afrique* originally recruited for service in Algeria. The peace and war organization of these *Chasseurs d'Afrique* regiments corresponded in general to that of a line cavalry unit. Between World Wars I and II and during the latter war the number of these regiments increased progressively, and they were transformed into armoured units.

The only unit of mounted *Chasseurs d'Afrique* still in existence in 1951 was a squadron stationed at Senlis, France.

(C. W. He.)

CHASTELARD, PIERRE DE BOCSOZEL DE (1540–1563), French poet, was born in Dauphiné, a scion of the house of Bayard. His name is inseparably connected with Mary, Queen of Scots. From the service of the Constable Montmorency, Chastelard, then a page, passed to the household of Marshal Damville, whom he accompanied on his journey to Scotland in escort of Mary (1561). He returned to Paris in the marshal's train, but left for Scotland again shortly afterwards, bearing letters of recommendation to Mary from his old protector, Montmorency, and the *Regrets* addressed to the ex-queen of France by Pierre Ronsard, his master in the art of song. He undertook to transmit to the poet the service of plate with which Mary rewarded him. But he had fallen in love with the queen, who is said to have encouraged his passion. The young man hid himself under her bed, where he was discovered by her maids of honour. Mary pardoned the offence, but Chastelard was so rash as again to violate her privacy. He was discovered a second time, seized, sentenced and hanged the next morning. He met his fate valiantly and consistently, reading, on his way to the scaffold, his master's noble *Hymne de la mort,* and turning at the instant of doom towards the palace of Holyrood, to address to his unseen mistress the famous farewell—"Adieu, la plus belle et la plus cruelle princesse du monde." This at least is the version of the *Vie des dames illustres* of Brantôme.

CHASTELLAIN, GEORGES (*c.* 1415–1475), Burgundian poet and chronicler, was a native of Alost, in Flanders. He saw active service in the Anglo-French Wars and elsewhere. In 1434 he received a gift from Philip the Good, duke of Burgundy, for his military service. After the peace of Arras (1435) he abandoned soldiering for diplomacy. The next ten years were spent in France, where he was connected with Georges de la Trémoille, and afterwards entered the household of Pierre de Brézé, at that time seneschal of Poitou, by whom he was employed on missions to the duke of Burgundy, in an attempt to establish better relations between Charles VII. and the duke. On the further breach between the two princes, Chastellain left the French service to enter Philip's household, and in 1457 he became a member of the ducal council. He was continually employed on diplomatic errands until 1455, when he was made Burgundian historiographer. He worked at his *Chronique,* with occasional interruptions in his retreat to fulfil missions in France, or to visit the Burgundian court. He was assisted, from about 1463 onwards, by his disciple and continuator, Jean Molinet, whose rhetorical and redundant style may be fairly traced in some passages of the *Chronique.* Chastellain died at Valenciennes on Feb. 13 (according to the treasury accounts), or on March 20 (according to his epitaph), 1475. Only about one-third of the whole *Chronique,* which extended from 1419 to 1474, is extant.

Among his contemporaries Chastellain acquired a reputation by his poems and occasional pieces. He was no mere annalist, but proposed to fuse and shape his vast material to his own conclusions, in accordance with his political experience. The most interesting feature of his work is the skill with which he pictures the leading figures of his time.

The known extant fragments of Chastellain's *Chronique* with his other works were edited by Kervyn de Lettenhove for the Brussels Academy in 1863–66 (Brussels) as *Oeuvres de Georges Chastellain.* This edition includes three volumes of minor pieces of considerable interest, especially *Le Temple de Boccace,* dedicated to Margaret of Anjou, and the *Déprécation* for Pierre Brézé, imprisoned by Louis XI. The attribution to Chastellain is in some cases erroneous, notably in the case of the *Livre des faits de Jacques de Lalaing,* which is probably the work of Lefèbvre de Saint-Remi, herald of the Golden Fleece. In the allegorical *Oultré d'amour* it has been thought a real romance between Brézé and a lady of the royal house is concealed.

See A. Molinier, *Les Sources de l'histoire de France;* notices by Kervyn de Lettenhove prefixed to the *Oeuvres* and in the *Biographie nationale de Belgique;* and Kenneth Urwin, *Georges Çhastellain: la vie, les oeuvres* (Paris, 1937).

CHASUBLE, a liturgical vestment of the Catholic Church, being the outermost garment worn by bishops and priests when celebrating the Mass. The word is derived, through the French, from the Latin *casula,* a little house or hut. Since the chasuble (or *planeta,* as it is also called in the Roman Missal) is only used at the Mass, or rarely for functions intimately connected with the sacrament of the altar, it may be regarded as the Mass vestment *par excellence.* According to the prevailing model in the Roman Catholic Church it is a scapular-like cloak, with a hole in the middle for the head, falling down over breast and back, and leaving the arms uncovered at the sides. Its shape and size, however, differ considerably in various countries (*see* fig.), while some churches—*e.g.,* those of certain monastic orders—have retained or reverted to the earlier "Gothic" forms to be described later. According to the decisions of the Congregation of Rites, chasubles must not be of linen, cotton or woollen stuffs, but of silk; though a mixture of wool (or linen and cotton) and silk is allowed if the silk completely cover the other material on the outer side.

The chasuble, like the kindred vestments in the Eastern Churches, is derived from the Roman *paenula* or *planeta,* a cloak worn by all classes and both sexes in the Graeco-Roman world (*see* VESTMENTS).

At the Reformation the chasuble was rejected with the other vestments by the more extreme Protestants. Its use, however, survived in the Lutheran churches; and though in those of Germany it is no longer worn, it still forms part of the liturgical costume of the Scandinavian Evangelical churches. In the Church of England, though it was prescribed alternatively with the cope in the first prayer-Book of Edward VI., it was ultimately discarded with the other "Mass vestments." (*See* VESTMENTS.)

Form.—The chasuble was originally a tent-like robe which fell in loose folds below the knee of the wearer. Its inconvenience, however, was obvious, and a process of cutting away at the sides began, which continued until the tent-shaped chasuble of the 12th century had developed in the 16th into the present scapular-like vestment. This process was, moreover, hastened by the substitution of costly and elaborately embroidered materials for the simple stuffs of which the vestment had originally been composed: for, as it became heavier and stiffer, it had to be made smaller.

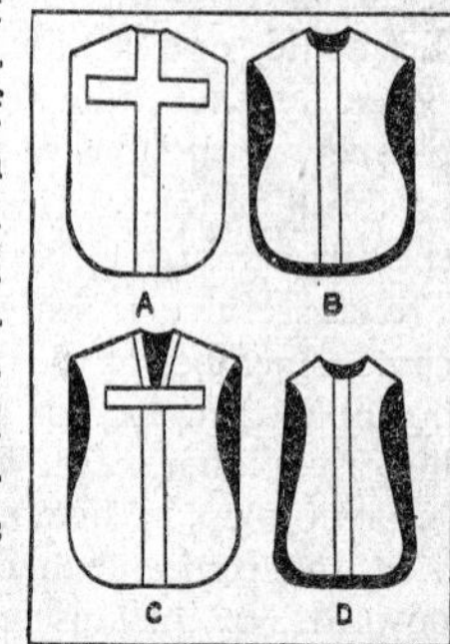

FROM BRAUN, "DIE LITURGISCHE GEWANDUNG IM OCCIDENT UND ORIENT" (HERDER, FREIBURG IM BREISGAU)

COMPARATIVE SIZES AND SHAPES OF CHASUBLES AS NOW IN USE IN VARIOUS COUNTRIES (A & B) GERMAN, (C) ROMAN, (D) SPANISH

Decoration.—Chasubles were until the 10th century generally quite plain, and even at the close of this century, when the custom of decorating the chasuble with orphreys had become common, there was no definite rule as to their disposition. From this time onward, the embroidery became ever more and more elaborate, and the orphreys were broadened to allow of their being decorated with figures. About the middle of the 13th century, the cross with horizontal arms begins to appear on the back of the vestment, and by the 15th this had become the most usual form. Sometimes the back of the chasuble has no cross, but only a vertical orphrey, and in this case the front, besides the vertical stripe, has a horizontal orphrey just below the neck opening. This latter is the type used in the local Roman Church, which has been adopted in certain dioceses in South Germany and Switzerland, and of late years in the Roman Catholic churches in England, *e.g.*, Westminster cathedral.

The earlier decoration of the forked cross, *i.e.*, a vertical orphrey with two arms turned upwards over the shoulders, was commonly retained in England and has thus been largely adopted by the "Anglo-Catholic" clergy in modern times. Father Braun gives proof that this decoration was not even originally conceived as a cross at all, citing early instances of its having been worn by laymen and even by non-Christians. It was not until the 13th century that the symbolical meaning of the cross began to be elaborated, and this was accentuated from the 14th century onward by the custom of adding to it the figure of the crucified Christ and other symbols of the Passion. This, however, did not represent any definite rule; and the orphreys of chasubles were decorated with a great variety of pictorial subjects. The local Roman Church, true to its ancient traditions, adhered to the simpler forms. The modern Roman chasuble, besides the conventional arabesque pattern, is decorated, according to rule, with the arms of the archbishop and his see.

The Eastern Church.—The original equivalent of the chasuble is the phelonion, from the Lat. *paenula.* It is a vestment of the type of the Western bell chasuble; but, instead of being cut away at the sides, it is either gathered up or cut short in front. In the Armenian, Syrian, Chaldaean and Coptic rites it is cope-shaped. The phelonion is not in the East so specifically a eucharistic vestment as in the West, but is worn at other solemn functions besides the liturgy, *e.g.*, marriages, processions. The Greek and Greek Melchite metropolitans now wear the *sakkos* instead of the phelonion; and in the Russian, Ruthenian, Bulgarian and Italo-Greek churches this vestment has superseded the phelonion in the case of all bishops (*see* DALMATIC and VESTMENTS).

See J. BRAUN, S. J., *Die liturgische Gewandung* (1907), pp. 149–247, Dom H. Leclerq, in Cabrol, *Dict. d'Archéol. Chrét. et de Liturgie,* and the bibliography to the article VESTMENTS.

CHATALJA LINES, a fortified position 25m. W. of and covering Constantinople, extending from the Black sea at Karaburnu to the Sea of Marmara at Buyuk Chekmedje. They form a very strong position, covered in part by lakes and marshes, and commanding all the country to the west. They were first constructed during the Russo-Turkish war of 1877–78, but were not at that time the scene of fighting. During the Balkan war of 1912, however, they afforded a secure refuge to the Turkish armies defeated in the open field by the Bulgarians, and when the latter attacked them in mid-November of that year, with insufficient artillery preparation, they were repulsed with heavy loss. In the World War the lines were once more reconditioned in expectation of an Allied attack on Constantinople.

CHÂTEAU, the French word for castle (*q.v.*). The development of the castle in the 15th and 16th centuries into houses arranged rather for residence than defence led to a corresponding widening of the meaning of the term *château,* which came to be applied to any seigniorial residence and so generally to all country houses of any pretensions (*cf.* the Germ. *Schloss*). The French distinguish the fortified from the residential type by describing the former as the *château fort,* the latter as the *château de plaisance.* The development of the one into the other is admirably illustrated by the *châteaux* scattered along the Loire. Of these, Langeais, still in perfect preservation, is a fine type of the *château fort,* with its 10th century keep and 13th century walls. Amboise (1490), Blois (1500–40), Chambord (begun 1526), Chenonceaux (1515–60), Azay-le-Rideau (1521), may be taken as typical examples of the *château de plaisance* of the transition period, all retaining some of the architectural characteristics of the mediaeval castle In English the word *château* is often used to translate foreign words, *e.g.*, *Schloss,* meaning country house or mansion.

See RENAISSANCE ARCHITECTURE. For the Loire *châteaux see* Theodore Andrea Cook, *Old Touraine* (1892). (T. F. H.)

CHATEAUBRIAND, FRANÇOIS RENÉ, VICOMTE DE (1768–1848), French author, youngest son of René Auguste de Chateaubriand, comte de Combourg, was born at St. Malo on Sept. 4, 1768. He was a brilliant representative of the reaction against the ideas of the French Revolution, and the most conspicuous figure in French literature during the First Empire. His naturally poetical temperament was fostered in childhood by picturesque influences, the mysterious reserve of his morose father, the ardent piety of his mother, the traditions of his ancient family, the legends and antiquated customs of the sequestered Breton district, above all, the vagueness and solemnity of the neighbouring ocean. His closest friend was his sister Lucille,[1] a passionate-hearted girl, divided between her devotion to him and to religion. François received his education at Dol and Rennes. From Rennes he proceeded to the College of Dinan, to prepare for the priesthood, but decided, after a year's holiday at the family château of Combourg (1786) to enter the army. In 1788 he received the tonsure in order to enter the order of the Knights of Malta. In Paris (1787–89) he met La Harpe, Évariste Parny, "Pindare" Lebrun, Nicolas Chamfort, Pierre Louis Ginguené, and others, of whom he has left portraits in his memoirs. In 1791 he departed for America to take part in a romantic scheme for the discovery of the North-West Passage. The passage was not found or even attempted, but the adventurer returned from his seven months' stay in America enriched with new ideas and new imagery. In 1792 he married Mlle. Céleste Buisson de Lavigne, a girl of 17, who brought him a small fortune. He then joined the *émigrés,* and after many vicissitudes reached London, where he lived in great poverty.

From his English exile (1794–99) dates the *Natchez* (first printed in his *Oeuvres complètes,* 1826–31), a prose epic portraying the life of the Red Indians. Two brilliant episodes originally designed for this work, *Atala* and *René,* are famous. Chateaubriand's first publication, however, was the *Essai historique, politique et moral sur les révolutions* . . . (London, 1797), which the author subsequently retracted, but did not suppress. In this volume he appears as a mediator between royalist and revolution-

[1]Her *Oeuvres* were edited in 1879, with a memoir, by Anatole France.

ary ideas, a free-thinker in religion, and a disciple of Rousseau. A great change in his views was, however, at hand, induced, if we accept his own statement, by a letter from his sister Julie (Mme. de Farcy), telling him of the grief his views had caused his mother, who had died soon after her release from the Conciergerie in the same year. His brother had perished on the scaffold in April 1794, and both his sisters, Lucile and Julie, and his wife had been imprisoned at Rennes. Mme. de Farcy did not long survive her imprisonment.

On Chateaubriand's return to France in 1800 the *Génie du christianisme* was already in an advanced state. Chateaubriand's favourite resort in Paris was the salon of Pauline de Beaumont, who was to fill a great place in his life, and gave him some help in the preparation of his book. *Atala, ou les amours de deux sauvages dans le désert,* used as an episode in the *Génie du christianisme,* appeared separately in 1801 and immediately made his reputation. Alike in its merits and defects the piece is a more emphatic and highly coloured *Paul et Virginie*. The *Génie du christianisme, ou beautés de la religion chrétienne,* appeared in 1802, upon the eve of Napoleon's re-establishment of the Catholic religion in France. No coincidence could have been more opportune, and Chateaubriand esteemed himself the counterpart of Napoleon in the intellectual order. The work is not to be judged by its apologetics, but as a masterpiece of literary art. Its influence in French literature was immense. The *Éloa* of Alfred de Vigny, the *Harmonies* of Lamartine and even the *Légende des siècles* of Victor Hugo may be said to have been inspired by the *Génie du christianisme.* At the moment of publication it admirably subserved the statecraft of Napoleon, and Talleyrand in 1803 appointed the writer *attaché* to the French legation at Rome, whither he was followed by Mme. de Beaumont, who died there.

When his insubordinate and intriguing spirit compelled his recall he was transferred as envoy to the canton of the Valais. The murder of the duke of Enghien (March 21, 1804) took place before he took up this appointment. Chateaubriand immediately resigned his post. In 1807 he offended Napoleon by an article in the *Mercure de France* (July 4), containing allusions to Nero which were rightly taken to refer to the emperor. The *Mercure,* of which he had become proprietor, was temporarily suppressed, and was in the next year amalgamated with the *Décade*. In 1806, he had made a pilgrimage to Jerusalem, undertaken in quest of new imagery. He returned by way of Tunis, Carthage, Cadiz and Granada. At Granada he met Mme. de Mouchy, and the place and the meeting apparently suggested the romantic tale of *Le Dernier Abencérage,* which, for political reasons, remained unprinted until the publication of the *Oeuvres complètes* (1826–31). The journey also produced *L'Itinéraire de Paris à Jérusalem . . .* (3 vols., 1811), and inspired his prose epic, *Les Martyrs, ou le triomphe de la religion chrétienne* (2 vols., 1809). *René* had appeared in 1802 as an episode of the *Génie du christianisme,* and a separate unauthorized edition appeared at Leipzig. The tale forms a connecting link in European literature between *Werther* and *Childe Harold;* it paints the misery of a morbid and dissatisfied soul. Chateaubriand betrayed amazing egotism in describing his sister Lucile in the Amélie of the story, and much is obviously descriptive of his own early surroundings. With *Les Natchez* his career as an imaginative writer is closed. In 1831 he published his *Études ou discours historiques . . .* (4 vols.) dealing with the fall of the Roman empire.

Chateaubriand's vanity and ambition made him dangerous and untrustworthy as a political associate. He was forbidden to deliver the address he had prepared (1811) for his reception to the Academy on M. J. Chénier on account of the bitter allusions to Napoleon contained in it. From this date until 1814 Chateaubriand lived in seclusion at the Vallée-aux-loups, an estate he had bought in 1807 at Aulnay. His pamphlet *De Bonaparte, des Bourbons, et de la nécessité de se rallier à nos princes légitimes,* appeared on March 31, 1814, the day of the entrance of the allies into Paris. Louis XVIII. declared that it had been worth a hundred thousand men to him. Chateaubriand, as minister of the interior, accompanied him to Ghent during the Hundred Days, and for a time associated himself with the excesses of the royalist reaction. But he rapidly drifted into liberalism and opposition, and was disgraced in Sept. 1816 for his pamphlet *De la monarchie selon la charte*. He had to sell his library and his house of the Vallée-aux-loups.

After the fall of his opponent, the duc Decazes, Chateaubriand obtained the Berlin embassy (1821), from which he was transferred to London (1822), and he also acted as French plenipotentiary at the Congress of Verona (1822). He here made himself mainly responsible for the iniquitous invasion of Spain. He was foreign minister for a brief period, and then, after another interlude of effective pamphleteering in opposition, accepted the embassy to Rome in 1827, under the Martignac administration, but resigned it at Prince Polignac's accession to office.

During the first half of Louis Philippe's reign he wrote a *Mémoire sur la captivité de madame la duchesse de Berry* (1833) and other legitimist pamphlets; but as the prospect of his again performing a conspicuous part diminished, he relapsed into an attitude of complete discouragement. His *Congrès de Vérone* (1838), *Vie de Rancé* (1844), and his translation of Milton, *Le Paradis perdu de Milton* (1836), belong to the writings of these later days. He died on July 4, 1848, affectionately tended by his old friend Madame Récamier, herself deprived of sight. For the last 15 years of his life he had been engaged on his *Mémoires,* and his chief distraction had been his daily visit to Madame Récamier, at whose house he met the European celebrities. He was buried in the Grand Bé, an islet in the bay of St. Malo. Shortly after his death appeared his celebrated *Mémoires d'outre-tombe* (12 vols., 1849–50). These memoirs undoubtedly reveal his vanity, his egotism, the frequent hollowness of his professed convictions, and his incapacity for sincere attachment, except, perhaps, in the case of Madame Récamier. Though the book must be read with the greatest caution where others are concerned, it is perhaps now the most read of all his works.

Chateaubriand is chiefly significant as marking the transition from the old classical to the modern romantic school. The fertility of ideas, vehemence of expression and luxury of natural description, which he shares with the romanticists, are controlled by a discipline learnt in the school of their predecessors. His palette, always brilliant, is never gaudy; he is not merely a painter but an artist. He is a master of epigrammatic and incisive sayings. Perhaps, however, the most truly characteristic feature of his genius is the peculiar magical touch which Matthew Arnold indicated as a note of Celtic extraction, which supplies an element of sincerity to Chateaubriand's declamation. Egotism was his master-passion. He is a signal instance of the compatibility of genuine poetic emotion, of sympathy with the grander aspects both of man and nature, and of munificence in pecuniary matters, with absorption in self and general sterility of heart.

Bibliography.—The *Oeuvres complètes* of Chateaubriand were printed in 28 vols., 1826–31; in 20 vols., 1829–31; and in many later editions, notably in 1858–61, in 20 vols., with an introductory study by Sainte-Beuve. The principal authority for Chateaubriand's biography is the *Mémoires d'outre-tombe* (1849–50), of which there is an English translation, *The Memoirs of . . . Chateaubriand* (6 vols., 1902), by A. Teixeira de Mattos, based on the edition (4 vols., 1899–1901) of Edmond Biré. This work should be supplemented by the *Souvenirs et correspondances tirés des papiers de Mme. Recamier* (2 vols., 1859, ed. Mme. Ch. Lenormant). *See* also Comte de Marcellus, *Chateaubriand et son temps* (1859); the same editor's *Souvenirs diplomatiques; correspondance intime de Chateaubriand* (1858); C. A. Sainte-Beuve, *Chateaubriand et son groupe littéraire sous l'empire* (2 vols., 1861, new and revised ed., 3 vols., 1872); other articles by Sainte-Beuve, who was in this case a somewhat prejudiced critic, in the *Portraits contemporains,* vols. i. and ii.; *Causeries du lundi,* vols. i., ii. and x.; *Nouveaux Lundis,* vol. iii.; *Premiers Lundis,* vol. iii.; A. Vinet, *Études sur la litt. française au XIXe siècle* (1849); M. de Lescure, *Chateaubriand* (1892) in the *Grands écrivains français;* Émile Faguet, *Études littéraires sur le XIXe siècle* (1887); and *Essai d'une bio-bibliographie de Chateaubriand et de sa famille* (Vannes, 1896), by René Kerviler. Joseph Bédier, in *Études critiques* (1903), deals with the American writings, and there is an admirable criticism of the *Génie du christianisme* in F. Brunetière's *Hist. de la litt. française* vol. iv. (1917). Some correspondence with Sainte-Beuve was edited by Louis Thomas in 1904, and some letters to Mme. de Staël appeared in the *Revue des deux mondes* (Oct. 1903).

CHÂTEAUBRIANT, a town of western France, capital of an arrondissement in the department of Loire-Inférieure, on the left bank of the Chère, 40 mi. N.N.E. of Nantes by rail. Pop. (1954) 9,284.

It takes its name from a castle founded in the 11th century by Briant, count of Penthièvre, remains of which still exist though it was shattered in 1488. The new castle, begun in 1524 by Jean de Laval, and famous in history as the residence of Françoise de Foix, mistress of Francis I, has a beautiful colonnade running at right angles to the main building. It was presented to the department by the duc d'Aumale in 1852. The interesting Romanesque church is dedicated to St. Jean de Béré. Châteaubriant is the seat of a subprefect and has a tribunal of first instance. It is a big agricultural centre with an important cattle market. Plows and agricultural machinery are made.

CHÂTEAU-D'OEX, resort, Switzerland, 20 mi. from Montreux, in the Sarine valley, 3,152 ft. above sea level, below the northwest end of the Bernese Oberland. Pop. (1950) 3,381. The castle was replaced by a church and the village has many attractive chalets scattered on the hillside, which are enriched with pine woods. The village is much frequented both in summer and in winter, and sports of both seasons are well developed.

CHÂTEAUDUN, a town of north central France, capital of an *arrondissement* in the department of Eure-et-Loir, 28 mi. S.S.W. of Chartres. Pop. (1954) 9,687. It stands on high ground near the left bank of the Loir. The streets radiate from a central square, the town being replanned after fires in 1723 and 1870.

Châteaudun (*Castrodunum*), a tourist centre, was the capital of the countship of Dunois in the middle ages. The castle was founded in the 10th century, rebuilt by Jean Dunois, bastard of Orléans, in the 15th century and entirely restored after 1946. It contains some ancient tapestries, and in the chapel are valuable statues. The 12th-century church of La Madeleine belonged to an abbey, the buildings of which are occupied by the law courts and hospital. The ruined chapel of Nôtre-Dame and the churches of St. Valérian and St. Jean are mediaeval. The museum contains a unique collection of 4,000 birds, another of Egyptian objects and a library of 52,000 volumes. In 1954 a college was being built. Since 1936 agriculture has largely given place to industry, and rubber, optical instruments, machine tools and telephones are made. There is also a military air base. (H. J.-R. B.)

CHÂTEAU-GONTIER, a town of western France and chief town of the *arrondissement* of Laval, department of Mayenne, on the Mayenne, 18 mi. S. by E. of Laval. Pop. (1954) 6,729. Château-Gontier owes its origin and its name to a castle erected in the first half of the 11th century by Gontier, the steward of Fulk Nerra of Anjou, on the site of a monastery belonging to the monks of St. Aubin d'Angers. The church of St. Jean dates from the 11th century. The town suffered severely during the wars of the League. In 1793 it was occupied by the Vendeans. It is one of the biggest agricultural centres of western France, and its fairs and markets are especially important for white geese and poultry. (At. E. D.)

CHÂTEAU-RENAULT, FRANÇOIS LOUIS DE ROUSSELET, Marquis de (1637–1716), French admiral, entered the army in 1658, but in 1661 was transferred to the navy. His early services were mostly performed in cruises against the Barbary pirates; he distinguished himself in the expedition under the duc de Beaufort (1664) and in that of 1672. When war broke out between England and France in 1689, he was in command at Brest and was chosen to carry the troops and stores sent by the French king to the aid of James II in Ireland. Although he was watched by Admiral Herbert (Lord Torrington, *q.v.*), with whom he fought an indecisive action in Bantry bay, he executed his mission with success. Château-Renault commanded a squadron under Tourville at the battle of Beachy Head in 1690. He was with Tourville in the attack on the Smyrna convoy in 1693. On the death of Tourville in 1701 he was named to the vacant post of vice-admiral of France.

On the outbreak of the War of the Spanish Succession, he was charged with the protection of the Spanish galleons which were to bring the treasure from America. These, with his fleet of French and Spanish warships, he brought to anchor in Vigo bay on Sept. 22 (Sept. 11, Old Style), 1702; but official obstacles delayed the landing of the cargo, and order for the transport of the bullion inland to Lugo by the Galician militia had only just arrived when, on Oct. 22, the superior Anglo-Dutch fleet under Sir George Rooke, on its way back from the unsuccessful enterprise against Cadiz, appeared outside the bay. Next day the enemy broke Château-Renault's boom across the harbour, burned or captured the warships and the galleons after a savage engagement, landed troops and seized an enormous quantity of the merchandise. Louis XIV considered Château-Renault free from blame, but the Spanish government declined to give him the rank of grandee, which was to have been the reward for bringing the bullion home. He was however made a marshal of France in 1703 and lieutenant-general of Brittany in 1704. In 1708, on the death of his nephew, he inherited the marquisate of Château-Renault. On Nov. 15, 1716, he died in Paris.

Bibliography.—J. J. R. Calmon-Maison, *Le Maréchal de Château-Renault* (Paris, 1903); Léon Guérin, *Les Marins illustres de la France* (Paris, 1861), *Histoire maritime de la France . . . jusqu'à la paix de Nimègue,* vol. iii, iv (Paris, 1863); for the English view in the controversy on Bantry bay, Beachy Head and Vigo, *see* W. M. Clowes, *The Royal Navy*, vol. ii (London, 1898).

CHÂTEAUROUX, MARIE ANNE DE MAILLY-NESLE, Duchesse de (1717–1744), mistress of Louis XV of France, was the fifth daughter of Louis de Mailly, marquis de Nesle. She was married in 1734 to the marquis de La Tournelle, who died in 1740. Her eldest sister, Louise Julie, comtesse de Mailly (1710–51), had been succeeded as the king's mistress by the next eldest, Pauline Félicité, marquise de Vintimille (1712–41). After the latter's death, Madame de La Tournelle, backed by the duc de Richelieu, took her place, despite the dismay of Cardinal Fleury and the opposition of the comte de Maurepas: her price included the definitive dismissal of Madame de Mailly from court (1742) and the title of duchesse de Châteauroux for herself (1743). She incited Louis to look for military glory and received a letter of thanks from Frederick II of Prussia for her part in negotiating the alliance of 1744. Louis allowed her to join him with the army at Metz, dismissed her under pressure from the church during his illness there, but recalled her to court on his recovery. She died, suddenly, on Dec. 8, 1744.

See E. and J. de Goncourt, *La Duchesse de Châteauroux et ses soeurs,* new ed. (Paris, 1889); also the *Histoire de Madame de Châteauroux tirée des mémoires de la duchesse de Brancas* (Paris, 1919).

CHÂTEAUROUX, a town of central France, capital of the department of Indre, situated on the left bank of the Indre, 88 mi. S. of Orléans on the main line of the Paris-Toulouse railway. Pop. (1954) 36,420. The old town, close to the river, forms a nucleus around which a newer and more extensive quarter, bordered by boulevards, has grown up; the suburbs of St. Christophe and Déols lie on the right bank of the river. Châteauroux owes its name and origin to the castle founded about the middle of the 10th century by Raoul, prince of Déols, which later passed to Henry II of England, falling eventually to the Condé family (1612). The present Château-Raoul dates from the 14th and 15th centuries. The old Église des Cordeliers (13th century) and St. Martial are the finest monuments. The Napoleon museum, an 18th-century house, contains a library with the oldest extant manuscript of the *Chanson de Roland* and the Bréviaire Parisien manuscript of the 15th century. Châteauroux is the seat of a prefect and of a court of assizes. It has tribunals of first instance and of commerce and a board of trade arbitrators and a chamber of commerce. Textiles and machinery are manufactured, and there is a state tobacco factory. (Y. E.)

CHÂTEAU-THIERRY, a town of northern France, in the department of Aisne, 59 mi. E.N.E. of Paris on the Eastern railway to Nancy. Pop. (1946) 7,661. Château-Thierry is built on rising ground on the right bank of the Marne, over which a fine stone bridge was built, connecting it with the suburb of Marne. On the top of a hill are the ruins of a castle, said to have been built by Charles Martel for the Frankish king, Thierry IV, whence the name of the town. The chief relic is a gateway flanked by massive round towers, known as the Porte Saint-Pierre. A belfry of the 15th century and the church of St. Crépin (Crispin) of the same period are of some interest.

Château-Thierry was formerly the capital of the district of Brie Pouilleuse, and received the title of duchy from Charles IX in 1566. It was captured by the English in 1421, by Charles V in 1544, and sacked by the Spanish in 1591. During the wars of the Fronde it was pillaged in 1652; and in the campaign of 1814 it suffered severely, under Blücher, the Russo-Prussian forces being beaten by Napoleon in the neighbourhood. It was the farthest point reached by the Germans in their offensive of May 27, 1918. The 2nd and 3rd divisions of the American Expeditionary force were sent to the Marne in the Château-Thierry region to assist the hard-pressed French forces. At Château-Thierry itself a U.S. machine-gun battalion took part in the successful defense of the river crossing, while to the west of the town the 2nd division, under Gen. Omar Bundy, fought the fiercely contested engagement of Belleau Wood.

(*See* German Offensive, 1918; Marne, Second Battle of the.)

La Fontaine was born in the town in 1621. His house is still preserved in the street that bears his name.

The distinctive industry is the manufacture of mathematical and musical instruments. There is trade in the white wine of the neighbourhood, and in agricultural products. Gypsum, millstone and paving stone are quarried in the vicinity.

CHÂTELAIN, in France originally merely the equivalent of the English castellan, *i.e.,* the commander of a castle. With the growth of the feudal system, however, the title gained in France a special significance which it never acquired in England, as implying the jurisdiction of which the castle became the centre.

The *châtelain* was originally, in Carolingian times, an official of the count; with the development of feudalism the office became a fief, and so ultimately hereditary. In this as in other respects the *châtelain* was the equivalent of the viscount (*q.v.*); sometimes the two titles were combined, but more usually in those provinces where there were *châtelains* there were no viscounts, and vice versa.

The title *châtelain* continued also to be applied to the inferior officer, or *concierge châtelain,* who was merely a castellan in the English sense. The power and status of *châtelains* necessarily varied greatly at different periods and places; occasionally they were great nobles with an extensive jurisdiction, as in the Low Countries.

The *châtellenie* (*castellania*), or jurisdiction of the *châtelain,* as a territorial division for certain judicial and administrative purposes, survived the disappearance of the title and office of the *châtelain* in France, and continued till the Revolution.

See Achille Luchaire, *Manuel des institutions françaises* (1892); Du Cange, *Glossarium, s.* "Castellanus."

CHATELAINE, the mistress of a castle. From the custom of a chatelaine of carrying the keys of the castle suspended from her girdle, the word was applied in the late 19th century to the collection of short chains, worn by ladies, to which keys, penknife, needlecase, scissors, etc., were attached.

CHÂTELET, EMILIE DE BRETEUIL, Marquise du (1706–1749), French mathematician and physicist, daughter of Louis Nicholas le Tonnelier, Baron de Breteuil, was born in Paris on Dec. 17, 1706. Her father gave her a solid classical training, and she added knowledge of English and Italian. She was also an accomplished musician. When she was 19 she married the marquis Florent du Châtelet and they had three children. Although she participated in the social life of the Regency, she became a serious student of metaphysics, physics and chemistry. While studying with Samuel Koenig she wrote *Institutions de physique* (1740), an exposition of the philosophy of Gottfried Leibnitz. She was the first to translate Isaac Newton's *Principia Mathematica* into French. Her translation, prefaced by Voltaire, was published in 1756 after her death under the direction of Alexis Clairault.

Both because of her scientific writings and her long close relationship with Voltaire, to whom she was introduced about 1733, Émilie du Châtelet won renown. She and Voltaire spent the next 15 years together, living most of the time at Cirey, the château of the Du Châtelets in Champagne. The residence served as a quiet haven for their studies and as a refuge from the Paris police who were often on the trail of Voltaire. On those occasions when he ran into trouble with the authorities, she exerted considerable power at court to extricate him.

Her scientific training enabled her to render Voltaire invaluable assistance and to stimulate his interest in science and in metaphysics. After Madame du Châtelet had protested against the conventional type of written history, which she called "nothing but an old almanac," Voltaire composed his *Essai sur les moeurs et l'esprit des nations,* which, with its emphasis on the social and intellectual forces that had shaped history, marked a departure in historical writing.

Even after Émilie du Châtelet had transferred her affections to the poet Jean de Saint-Lambert, she and Voltaire remained close friends. They were visiting at the court of Stanislas of Poland in Lunéville when she died on Sept. 10, 1749, in childbirth.

Other works by Madame du Châtelet include *Réponse à la lettre de Mairan sur la question des forces vives* (Brussels, 1741); *Doutes sur les religions* (Paris, 1792); *Réflexions sur le bonheur* (Paris, 1796); and M. Asse (ed.) *Lettres* (Paris, no date).

Bibliography.—Frank Hamel, *An Eighteenth Century Marquise, a Study of Emilie du Châtelet and Her Times* (London, 1910); Richard Aldington, *Voltaire* (1925); Georg Brandes, *Voltaire* (1930); Margaret S. Libby, *The Attitude of Voltaire to Magic and the Sciences* (1935); A. Maurel, *The Romance of Madame du Châtelet and Voltaire* (1931); and Ira Wade, *Voltaire and Madame du Châtelet, an Essay on the Intellectual Activity at Cirey* (1941), which emphasizes Madame du Châtelet's work on Biblical criticism.

CHÂTELET, the word used in France for a building designed for the defense of an outwork or gate, sometimes of great strength, but distinguished from the *château,* or castle proper, in being purely defensive and not residential (from Med. Lat. *castella*).

In Paris, before the Revolution, this word was applied both to a particular building and to the jurisdiction of which it was the seat. This building had been first a castle defending the approach to the Cité. Tradition traced its existence back to Roman times, and in the 18th century one of the rooms in the great tower was still called *Caesar's room.* The jurisdiction was that of the provostship (prévôté) and viscountship of Paris, which was of feudal origin, probably going back to the counts of Paris.

It was not till the time of St. Louis that, with the appointment of Étienne Boileau, the provostship of Paris became a public office no longer put up to sale (*prévôté en garde*). When the *baillis* (*see* Bailiff and Bailie) were created, the provost of Paris discharged the functions of a *bailli,* in which capacity he heard appeals from the seigniorial and inferior judges of the city and its neighbourhood, keeping, however, his title of provost. When under Henry II certain *bailliages* became presidial jurisdictions (*présidiaux*), *i.e.,* received the right of judging without appeal, the Châtelet was made a presidial court. Finally, various tribunals peculiar to the city of Paris, *i.e.,* courts exercising jurisdictions outside the common law or corresponding to certain *cours d'exception* which existed in the provinces, were united with the Châtelet, of which they became divisions (*chambres*). Thus the lieutenant general of the police made it the seat of his jurisdiction, and the provost of the Île de France, who had the same criminal jurisdiction as the provosts of the marshals of France in other provinces, sat there also. As to the *personnel* of the Châtelet, it was originally the same as in the *bailliages,* except that after the 14th century it had some special officials, the auditors and the examiners of inquests. Like the *baillis,* the provost had lieutenants who were deputies for him, and in addition gradually acquired a considerable body of *ex officio* councillors. This last staff, however, was not yet in existence at the end of the 14th century, for it is not mentioned in the *Registre criminel du Châtelet* (1389–92).

In 1674 the whole *personnel* was doubled at the time when the new Châtelet was established side by side with the old, the two being soon after amalgamated. On the eve of the Revolution it comprised, besides the provost whose office had become honorary, the *lieutenant civil* who presided over the *chambre de prévôté au parc civil* or court of first instance; the *lieutenant criminel,* who presided over the criminal court; two *lieutenants particuliers,* who presided in turn over the *chambre du présidial* or court of appeal; a *juge auditeur;* 64 councillors (*conseillers*); the *procureur du roi,* four *avocats du roi,* and eight *substituts, i.e.* deputies of the *procureur* (*see* PROCURATOR), beside a host of minor officials. Under the Revolution the Constituent Assembly em-

THE CHÂTELET, PARIS, ORIGINALLY A FORTRESS, LATER A PRISON AND COURTHOUSE, AS IT LOOKED BEFORE ITS DESTRUCTION IN 1802

powered the Châtelet to try cases of *lèse-nation.* It was before this court that was opened the inquiry following on the events of Oct. 5 and 6, 1789 (Louis' removal to Paris). It was suppressed by the law of Aug. 16, 1790, together with the other tribunals of the *ancien régime.* The site of the building still bears the name of Châtelet. (J. P. E.; X.)

CHÂTELLERAULT, a town of western France, capital of an arrondissement in the department of Vienne, 19 mi. N.N.E. of Poitiers on the Orleans railway. Pop. (1946) 22,809. It is situated on the right bank of the Vienne and is connected with the suburb of Châteauneuf by a stone bridge of the 16th and 17th centuries. Châtellerault (or Châtelherault: *Castellum Airaldi*) derives its name from a fortress built in the 10th century by Airaud, viscount of its territory. In 1515 it was made a duchy in favour of François de Bourbon, but was soon reunited to the crown. In 1548 it was bestowed on James Hamilton, 2nd earl of Arran (*see* HAMILTON). The manufacture of cutlery dates from the 14th century and is carried on in villages along the banks of the Clain. The most important industrial establishment is the national small-arms factory, established in 1819.

CHATHAM, WILLIAM PITT, 1ST EARL OF (1708–1778), was born at Golden square, Westminster, on Nov. 15, 1708. His father was Robert, son of the famous Governor Pitt of Madras; his mother Harriet Villiers, daughter of Viscountess Grandison. He was the fourth child of a family of seven, most of whom showed signs of mental instability. He was educated in the classics at Eton and Trinity college, Oxford. At Eton he made friends with many who later became his political associates, and especially with George Lyttelton, Henry Fielding, Charles Pratt and Charles Hanbury Williams. He left Oxford after only one year, partly because of the persistent gout from which he already suffered, and spent some months studying law at the University of Utrecht. A large number of deaths among the influential members of his family when he was still only 20 left his career uncertain, but his steps were guided toward politics by the marriage, in 1728, of his brother to Christian Lyttelton, sister of his school friend George Lyttelton. Through the Lytteltons the Pitts became connected with the widely ramified clan of the Temples and Grenvilles, one of the most powerful groups in the land-owning oligarchy which, under the Hanoverian monarchs, virtually governed Britain. The leader of the group, Viscount Cobham, wielded great wealth and patronage and it was through his gift that William, in 1731, was appointed a cornet in the king's own regiment of horse, which later became the 1st dragoon guards. This commission brought him an income of £150 a year and an introduction to court and public life.

In 1735 he entered the house of commons as member for Old Sarum, one of his brother's pocket boroughs, which later became the most notorious example of all pocket boroughs. He belonged inevitably to the group of "Cobham's cubs," the connection of family friends and place hunters whom Cobham was mobilizing to oppose the ministry of Sir Robert Walpole. Calling themselves "patriots," they joined with discontented Whigs like Lord Carteret and William Pulteney and Hanoverian Tories like Sir William Wyndham to rally the opposition forces behind the prince of Wales, Frederick Louis. At a time when a regular standing opposition in parliament was generally regarded as factious and even traitorous, since ministers were the king's ministers, it became common for political groups opposed to the government to seek respectability by alliance with the heir to the throne. Since it was normal for Hanoverian monarchs to be in a state of violent hostility with their eldest sons, royal power was habitually divided against itself. Politicians excluded from office looked to "the rising sun," and the prince of Wales used both his own patronage and the hopes of future office to unite them against his father and his father's ministers. At this time Viscount Bolingbroke was especially active in his efforts to form in this way a solid opposition to Walpole. So Pitt entered parliament at a crucial stage of party development. His maiden speech provoked reprisals from Walpole, who deprived him of his military commission in an effort to "muzzle this terrible cornet of horse."

In 1737 the prince of Wales made him a groom of the bedchamber with a salary of £400 a year. Despite his status as a relatively poor dependent of a powerful Whig clan, and as a pensioner of the prince of Wales, Pitt already showed some appreciation of that independence of mind and that appeal to popular support which were to gain him unique personal prestige in English political life. His talents as an orator had become clear. His exploitation of the position of patriotic martyr, by driving around the southern counties after his dismissal by Walpole, showed a readiness to appeal to public opinion outside parliament, as well as his lively sense of the histrionic. He repeatedly referred to the "voice of England," which had to be sought outside parliament because parliament was so packed with place men and sinecurists. He claimed to speak for the commercial interests and even the colonists oversea, both scarcely represented in the commons. Although the member for Old Sarum could hardly claim directly to represent such interests, he more and more put forward arguments that would logically deny the whole system of oligarchical control over the electorate and over parliament. If he was a Whig he was, par excellence, a wayward Whig, using in the cause of opposition arguments which carried far beyond the close oligarchy enjoyed by the Whig families.

When Walpole at last fell from power in 1742 he was replaced by a ministry which included his old colleagues the duke of Newcastle and Lord Hardwicke, with Carteret as secretary of state. Pulteney was silenced by a peerage. The "boy patriots," of whom Pitt was by now the acknowledged parliamentary leader, were still excluded from power. They were left with no option but to oppose Carteret even more vehemently than they had attacked Walpole.

From 1741 to 1748 Great Britain was engaged in the complex diplomacy and strategy of the War of the Austrian Succession. The chief menace to British security was Bourbon power in Europe, and the aim of British policy was therefore to diminish French power in every way possible. Pitt differed from Carteret more about means than about ends. George II and Carteret saw the issue as primarily a continental one and aimed at a coalition of German states, led by Britain and Hanover, to support Maria Theresa of Austria in her struggle against France. Pitt insisted that Great Britain should concentrate on attacking France where it was most vulnerable and where British naval power brought the greatest advantage—that is, in France's colonial possessions, which obstructed British enterprise and expansion in America and India. He accordingly attacked, in a series of great speeches, the government's policy of continental alliances and subsidies and exploited the unpopularity of the royal connection with Hanover. Carteret was condemned as "a Hanover troop minister," and as "an infamous minister who seems to have renounced the name of an Englishman." It was possible to be a "patriot" in a new and additional sense, and to appeal to every sort of national and popular prejudice.

When Carteret was forced to resign in 1744 Newcastle and his brother, Henry Pelham, took office. They wanted to include Pitt but George II had been so offended by Pitt's attacks on Hanover that he refused to accept him. During the Jacobite rising of 1745 Pitt gained new stature as the one statesman of effectiveness and vigour; and the rising was itself a further argument against the continental policy of the king. In Feb. 1746 the king agreed to appoint Pitt joint vice-treasurer of Ireland at £3,000 a year, and two months later he became paymaster general of the forces. His first ten years in parliament had been spent in opposition and he had earned a formidable reputation as a *frondeur*. His acceptance of the paymastership, which was notoriously the richest plum of place hunters, at first caused bewilderment and recriminations, even from his friends. It seemed that the "patriot" had been bought by the government. But it gave Pitt a further opportunity to earn a unique reputation for honesty and disinterestedness. He renounced for himself all the rich perquisites of the office except its official salary of more than £4,000. He also introduced many useful reforms in the administration of the office and dramatically regained his reputation for both scrupulous honesty and efficiency. He held the office for nine years and left it still a poor man.

But a legacy of £10,000 from the old duchess of Marlborough enabled him to indulge in more lavish expenditure and generosity. He spent a good deal on landscape gardening and bought South lodge at Enfield. In 1754 he married Hester Grenville and thereafter found, in a supremely happy home life, a new source of strength and escape from his somewhat solitary existence. In policy he supported the Pelhams' alliance with Hanover, but tried to strengthen British naval power as the chief weapon of both offense and defense. When Henry Pelham died, in 1754, Pitt hoped to become leader of the house of commons. The duke of Newcastle, jealous of Pitt's abilities and distrustful of his only serious rival, Henry Fox, manoeuvred into office a colourless nonentity, Sir Thomas Robinson. Pitt and Fox joined in baiting and ridiculing Robinson, but when he was driven to resign it was Fox whom Newcastle took in as secretary of state. Pitt transferred his attacks to the Newcastle-Fox combination, likening it to "the conflux at Lyons of the Rhône and the Saône: this a feeble, languid stream, and, though languid, of no depth—the other a boisterous and overbearing torrent—but they meet at last." The jibe cost him the pay office, from which he was dismissed in 1755.

The outbreak of the Seven Years' War gave Pitt his supreme opportunity for statesmanship. It began with heavy losses and considerable confusion of policy. The popular demand for Pitt became irresistible, and he declared "I know that I can save this country and that no one else can." In Nov. 1756 he formed a ministry which excluded Newcastle, with the duke of Devonshire as its nominal head. In June 1757 Newcastle returned to office on the understanding that he should control all the patronage and leave Pitt to conduct the war. It proved to be an admirable division of labour.

Pitt determined that it should be in every sense a national war and a war at sea. He got rid of the German mercenaries who had been sent over to resist invasion and revived the militia, which he made into a serviceable defense force. He re-equipped and reorganized the navy. He sought to unite all parties and public opinion behind a coherent and intelligible war policy. He seized upon America and India as the main objects of British strategy. He sent his main expeditions to America, to ensure the conquest of Canada; and supported the East India company and their "heaven-born general" Robert Clive in their struggle against the French East India company. He also subsidized and reinforced the armies of Frederick the Great of Prussia, so as to engage the main French armies on the continent, while he used naval power to harrass the French on their own coasts, in the West Indies and in Africa. He chose good generals and admirals—James Wolfe, Jeffrey Amherst, and Edward Boscawen, Edward Hawke, Charles Saunders, George Pocock, Charles Watson—and he inspired them with a new spirit of dash and enterprise. Against so resolute and concerted a policy the Bourbon powers even in alliance could not avail. At the treaty of Paris in 1763 Great Britain remained supreme in North America and India, held Minorca as a Mediterranean base and gained territory in Africa and the West Indies. Pitt had given Britain a new empire as well as preserving and consolidating the old.

But before the war ended Pitt had been forced to resign. In 1760 George III came to the throne resolved, as was his chief adviser Bute, to end the war as speedily as possible. When Pitt failed to persuade his colleagues to forestall Spain's entry into hostilities by an immediate declaration of war he resigned, in Oct. 1761. He had tended to concentrate the whole conduct of government into his own hands and had worked with a furious energy. His haughty and aloof manner, which alienated so many of his colleagues, and his high-handed treatment of affairs, rendered tolerable only so long as he was proved right, had earned him respect and admiration but little friendship. When his resignation was accompanied by the grant of a peerage to Hester and an annuity of £3,000 a year for himself, there was again an outburst of abuse and scurrility. Just as when he had accepted the pay office, this acceptance of a peerage and a pension seemed to be the result of a political bargain and a sordid anticlimax to so brilliant a career. As rewards for his immense services they were meagre enough; but it is some measure of the unique repute for high-minded disinterestedness which he had won that his acceptance of such rewards should provoke so much bitter disillusionment. His effigy was burned in the City, and Hester was reviled as Lady Cheat'em.

He attacked the terms of the treaty of Paris as an inadequate recognition of Great Britain's world-wide successes. The intense unpopularity of Bute and Pitt's role as champion of national rights soon restored his popular appeal. But his career as a war minister was now over. He had delivered 115 speeches since he had entered parliament and more than half of them had been concerned with war or preparations for war. As a supremely successful secretary of state during the Seven Years' War he had combined colonial and naval operations with containing operations in Europe, and had shown that they were not alternative theories of strategy but were complementary. The rest of his political career was devoted to attempting a similar reconciliation of principles: of imperial power with constitutional liberty.

When Bute resigned in April 1763, he was succeeded by George Grenville. Pitt's attacks on his administration completed the breach between the two brothers-in-law. He condemned the action taken by the ministry against John Wilkes, for his attack on the king's speech in no. 45 of the *North Briton*, and opposed Grenville's Stamp act. He took no active part in politics between 1764 and 1766, and was now becoming subject to the recurrent fits of manic-depressive insanity which were to cloud the rest of his life. In 1765 he was left, by Sir William Pynsent, the estate of Burton Pynsent in Somerset, worth more than £3,000 a year. In Jan. 1766 he re-entered the stage with a passionate appeal for imperial liberty. Of the American colonists, who had resisted the Stamp act, he proclaimed, "as subjects they are entitled to the common right of representation, and cannot be bound to pay taxes without their consent." He supported and defended their resistance and demanded the complete repeal of the Stamp act. This was done, but replaced by a Declaratory act maintaining the right of taxation. Grenville's successors, the Rockinghams, found their position equally untenable and in July 1766 the king asked Pitt to form a ministry drawn from all sections of the house.

The idea of an all-party ministry had long haunted English politics. Parties were regarded as factions and the unit of parliamentary politics was not party but aristocratic group connection. Every ministry was a combination of several such groups and the groups excluded tended to form an opposition until some of them, at least, were offered places. While the notion of a regularly formed opposition was viewed with much distrust, it was natural to seek strength for government in a "broad-bottomed" or all-party administration. Pitt had propounded the view that a ministry should be formed on the principle of "measures and not men": that is, that ministers should be appointed for their abilities and policies, and not because of their group connections. This has often been assumed to mean agreement with the aims of George III, who in his efforts to recover for the crown the use of royal patronage, which the first two Georges had allowed to fall into the hands of the Whig oligarchy, was seeking a ministry similarly united on principles rather than on group affiliations. But Pitt's interests were different. He was not concerned to attack the system of group connections, but rather to insert himself, alongside the oligarchic leaders, as an individual who should be indispensable to any effective administration. He played, by instinct and temperament, something of a lone hand in politics. His main principle was that the king's government must be carried on, and what he wanted was strong, coherent and efficient administration. In 1763 he told the king that "it cannot be carried on without the great families who have supported the Revolution Government, and other great persons of whose abilities and integrity the public have had experience, and who have weight and credit in the nation." He repeatedly showed that he had no wish to destroy the oligarchic groups, but was perfectly willing to collaborate with them so long as they would acknowledge his own unique position and influence. Accordingly, his ministry of 1766 included Henry Conway and Lord Northington from the previous ministry, Lord Camden, Lord Grafton and Lord Shelburne who were his own followers, and Lord North and Charles Townshend. It could have worked well only if Pitt himself had remained in active control over it. But he accepted an earldom and took the almost sinecure post of lord privy seal. The "great commoner" retired to the lords, and fell ill for another two years. The luckless duke of Grafton was left in nominal control of the government just when the disturbances in America and in Middlesex, over the Wilkes elections case, were reaching their climax.

The new ministry was probably doomed to failure from the start. Its members held contrary views about America, and had little harmony of temperament or purpose. It is doubtful if even Chatham could have made them into a team; certainly the indolent Grafton could not. Engulfed in a black fit of insanity, Chatham withdrew completely and, in 1768, resigned office. His own chancellor of the exchequer, Townshend, imposed a series of duties on the American colonists which brought in little revenue but caused widespread discontent. He appeared in the lords in 1770 to launch a savage attack on the ministry, and on the house of commons for its surrender to the wishes of the king in the Middlesex elections, when it not only expelled Wilkes but illegally declared the defeated candidate, H. L. Luttrell, elected. He supported the City in its protests against the government and demanded a dissolution to get rid of a subservient commons. He even proposed a measure of parliamentary reform to strengthen the county representation as against the boroughs, the "rotten parts" of the constitution. In the following year he pressed for triennial, instead of septennial, elections, as a method of bringing the commons more closely into touch with public opinion in the country. His early "radical" propensities came more into the open.

During the last ten years of his life, 1768–78, he acquired a group of followers of his own, including Grafton, Shelburne, Camden and Isaac Barré. In parliamentary action he was driven to rely more upon this group and less upon his own eloquence and popularity. Instead of being able, in Burke's words, "to keep hovering in air, over all parties, and to souse down where the prey may prove best," he was driven into active alliance with the Rockingham group. He was forced into the normal Whig procedure of negotiating group alliances and in his deliberate disruption of the Grafton ministry in 1770 he acted little differently from the ordinary party man in opposition. The end of his career showed that there was little permanent place, in 18th century politics, for one who claimed to depend primarily upon a personal reputation for ability and disinterestedness. In the end he, like the king himself, found that he had to come down into the arena and deal with politicians and group connections on their own ground.

His last years were clouded by illness and only on rare occasions did he emerge from seclusion to appeal for a more generous and understanding treatment of America. Yet he broke with the Whig groups when they were prepared to recognize the independence of the 13 colonies and when the Americans had allied with Britain's traditional enemy, France. His last speech in the lords was a protest against any diminution of an empire based on freedom. In 1775 he hurriedly introduced a bill designed to suspend repressive measures in Boston, maintain the legislative authority of parliament over the colonies, and yet use the Continental congress established at Philadelphia as a body for assessing the monetary contributions of each colony. The bill was summarily rejected, but is the best indication of how Chatham would have handled the American problem.

After 1771 it was his practice to emerge only occasionally, as the elder statesman, to promote or attack individual measures, but not to attempt, as in 1770, to overthrow the ministry as a whole. He spent most of these years enjoying the life of a country gentleman, or in gloomy seclusion as an invalid. He died at Hayes, Middlesex, on May 11, 1778, and was buried in Westminster abbey.

Chatham remains a brilliant and dominant yet enigmatic figure in 18th century history. Even the fragmentary reports of his speeches which survive endorse his contemporary reputation as one of the greatest orators that England has ever known. As a war minister he combined immense breadth of vision with brilliant executive ability. As a statesman, he raised British power and prestige to great heights, and added large territories to Britain's overseas possessions. As a man he was a model of devotion to his family as well as of unstinted public service. But his genius was erratic, his political behaviour at times factious and at variance with his professed principles. The penalty of his eminence was a certain isolation. He had the defects of spiritual pride and haughtiness, which were perhaps the natural counterparts to his great talents.

His role in the development of the English party system is ambiguous. He did not seek to destroy the system of aristocratic patronage and group connection in politics, yet he in effect did much to undermine their power and to introduce into parliamentary life the force of public opinion. By his sustained and vigorous opposition to ministers such as Walpole, Carteret, Fox, Bute, Grenville and Grafton, he established a powerful tradition of the merits and rights of an organized opposition in parliament; yet this development seemed to be denied by his support for the idea of an all-party administration based on "measures and not men." He had a less profound insight than his contemporary, Edmund Burke, into the basic implications of a constitutional parliamentary system. He remains, none the less, one of the greatest geniuses of statecraft in British history.

Bibliography.—Basil Williams, *The Life of William Pitt, Earl of Chatham*, 2 vol. (London, 1913); William Cuthbert Brian Tunstall, *William Pitt, Earl of Chatham* (London, 1938); Lord Rosebery, *Chatham, His Early Life and Connections* (London, 1910); Frederic Harrison, *Chatham* (London, 1905); A. von Ruville, *William Pitt, Earl of Chatham*, trans. H. J. Chaytor, 3 vol. (1907); D. Winstanley, *Personal and Party Government* (Cambridge, 1910) and *Lord Chatham and the Whig Opposition* (Cambridge, 1912). The chief published sources are: W. S. Taylor and J. H. Pringle (ed.), *Correspondence of William Pitt, Earl of Chatham*, 4 vol. (London, 1838–40); G. S. Kimball (ed.), *Correspondence of William Pitt When Secretary of State*, 2 vol. (1906). (D. Tn.)

CHATHAM, an incorporated town and port of entry in Northumberland county, New Brunswick, Canada, with good harbour on the Miramichi river, 24 mi. from its mouth and on the Canadian National railway. Pop. (1951) 5,223. The town contains a Roman Catholic pro-cathedral. The chief industries are saw mills, pulp mills and fish curing plants. Ships load millions of feet of lumber annually for foreign markets. (C. Cy.)

CHATHAM, a city and port of entry of Ontario, Canada, and the capital of Kent county, 64 mi. S.W. of London and 11 mi. N. of Lake Erie, on the Thames river and the Canadian National, Canadian Pacific, Chesapeake and Ohio, and Wabash railways. Pop. (1951) 21,218. It has steamboat connection with Detroit and the cities on Lakes Huron and Erie. It is situated in a rich agricultural and fruit-growing district, and carries on a large export trade. It contains canneries, planing and flour mills, manufactories of fanning mills, binder-twine, woven-wire goods, engines and auto parts, and a large beet sugar factory. (C. Cy.)

CHATHAM, a port and municipal borough in the parliamentary division of Rochester and Chatham, Kent, Eng., on the right bank of the river Medway 10 mi. above its confluence with the Thames, and about 30 mi. E.S.E. of London by road. Pop. (1951) 46,940. Area 6.8 sq.mi. Though a distinct borough, it is coterminous with Rochester on the west and forms, with it and Gillingham on the east, one large conurbation of which Chatham is the principal shopping, commercial and entertainment centre. Industries include flour mills, timber works, etc., but by far the biggest employer is the royal naval dockyard.

Chatham (*Ceteham, Chetham*) belonged at the time of Domesday to Odo, bishop of Bayeux. It later formed a suburb of Rochester, but Henry VIII and Elizabeth I established dockyards and an arsenal. The dockyard was altered and improved by Charles I and Charles II and became the chief naval station of England. In 1708 an act was passed for extending the fortifications of Chatham, and the town grew around the dockyard.

The royal naval dockyard is situated to the north of the town, on a point, partly of reclaimed marsh, beyond which the sharply curving river widens from about 400 yd. to its broad tidal estuary. The dockyard covers more than 500 ac. and has a river frontage of more than 3 mi. It is equipped both for building and repairing naval vessels of all kinds. There is a church in the dockyard, and near at hand are the royal naval, royal marine and royal engineers' barracks. Chatham has a number of striking memorials to members of the services in various campaigns. A series of open spaces on the hill east of the town are known as the "Chatham lines." On this hill a number of forts were erected to defend the port during the Napoleonic wars; conspicuous on the heights is the royal naval war memorial. Just below Fort Amherst is the town hall. Fort Pitt was adapted to house a girls' technical school. The High street is formed by part of the ancient Watling street connecting Canterbury and London.

St. Mary's church occupies a site in similar use since Saxon times. Norman and Early English features from the old church, which was destroyed by fire, are incorporated in the present 18th century building (thoroughly restored in 1903). The church contains a memorial to Stephen Borough (d. 1584) who in 1553 discovered the northern passage to Archangel. Near the railway station is a monument to Thomas Waghorn (d. 1850), a Chatham man who founded the overland route to India. St. Bartholomew's chapel, originally attached to the hospital for lepers founded by Gundulph, bishop of Rochester in 1078, is partly Norman. The hospital still has connections with Rochester cathedral. The Hospital of Sir John Hawkins, knight, in Chatham, for ex-seamen and ex-shipwrights of Chatham and Sheerness dockyards, was founded in 1592 by Sir John Hawkins and rebuilt in the middle of the 18th century. The fund called the Chatham Chest, originated by Hawkins and Drake in 1588, was incorporated with Greenwich hospital in 1802.

Charles Dickens and his family lived from 1817 to 1821 in a house at Ordnance terrace, where his father worked in the navy pay office, and Chatham people were the originals of certain characters in *Sketches by Boz* and *David Copperfield*.

Chatham was constituted a parliamentary borough by the Reform bill of 1832. In 1918 the municipal boroughs of Chatham, Gillingham and Rochester combined to return two members to parliament. The town, with the suburb of Luton, was incorporated in 1890.

CHATHAM ISLANDS, a small group of islands in the Pacific ocean forming part of New Zealand, 450 mi. due E. of Lyttleton, in South Island, in about 44° S., 177° W. It consists of three islands, a large one called Whairikauri, or Chatham Island, a small one, Rangihaute, or Pitt Island, and a third, Rangatira, or South-East Island. There are also several rocky islets. Whairikauri, of which the highest point reaches about 1,000 ft., is remarkable for the number of small lakes it contains. Its form is irregular, being about 38 mi. in length and 25 mi. in extreme breadth, with an area of 321 sq. miles. The geological structure (mainly volcanic rocks with schists and Tertiary limestone) indicates that the islands were once part of New Zealand. In general, the soil is extremely fertile, and where it is naturally drained a rich vegetation of fern and flax occurs. On the southwestern side is Petre bay, on which, at the mouth of the river Mantagu, is Waitangi, the main settlement.

The islands were discovered in 1791 by Lieutenant W. R. Broughton (1762–1821) who gave them the name of Chatham after the earl of Chatham. He called the natives Morioris or Maiorioris. In 1831 they were conquered by 800 Maori who were landed from a European vessel. The natives were almost exterminated, and disease killed off most of the remainder. Their language was akin to that of the Maori of New Zealand, though they differed from them physically. Cattle and sheep are bred. At one period whalers visiting these seas used to call at the Chathams for supplies. The chief exports are wool and fishery products, particularly frozen fish. The area of the group is 372 sq.mi. In 1945 the population on all islands totalled only 505 (290 Europeans and 215 Maori). The 1951 total was 471.

There are no indigenous mammals; the reptiles belong to New Zealand species. The birds—the largest factor in the fauna—have become very greatly reduced through the introduction of cats, dogs and pigs, as well as by constant destruction. The larger bell-bird is now scarce, the fruit-pigeon and the two endemic rails are extinct. The fossil avian forms are very important, especially from the point of view of the geographical distribution of species and the survival of the older forms in these remote corners. There have been discovered the remains of a species of swan belonging to the South American genus *Chenopis,* and of the tuatara (*Hatteria*) lizard, the unique species of an ancient family now surviving only in New Zealand. One of the finest of the endemic flowering plants of the group is the boraginaceous "Chatham Island lily" (*Myositidium nobile*), and a gigantic forget-me-not, growing on the shores. Dracophyllums, leucopogous, and arborescent ragworts are characteristic forms in the vegetation.

CHÂTILLON-SUR-SEINE, a town of eastern France, in the department of Côte-d'Or, on the Eastern and P.L.M. railways, 67 mi. N.N.W. of Dijon. Pop. (1946), 4,109. It is situated on the upper Seine, which is here joined by the Douix, the source of which is much visited. Châtillon, an old feudal town, anciently consisted of two parts, Chaumont, belonging to the duchy of Burgundy, and Bourg, ruled by the bishop of Langres; they did not coalesce till the end of the 16th century. It was taken by the English in 1360 and by Louis XI in 1475, during his struggle with Charles the Bold. Châtillon was one of the first cities to adhere to the League, but suffered severely from the oppression of its garrisons and governors. It is associated with the abortive conference of 1814 between the representatives of Napoleon and the Allies. The ruined 13th century castle of the dukes of Burgundy lies above the town. Near by stands the church of St. Vorles, begun in the 10th century, but with many additions; it contains a sculptured Holy Sepulchre of the 16th century and a number of frescoes. Marshal Marmont, duke of Ragusa was born at Châtillon in 1774, and built a château here. Its industries include iron-founding and the manufacture of agricultural machinery.

CHATSWORTH, the principal seat of the dukes of Devonshire, in the parish of Edensor, Derbyshire. Chatsworth house stands close to the left bank of the River Derwent, 2¾ mi. E.N.E. of Bakewell. The park is more than 11 mi. in circumference. The house is built around a large open courtyard which has a fountain in the centre. The gardens are adorned with sculptures by Gabriel Cibber and its fountains are said to be surpassed only by those at Versailles. The house contains a library and art collection which includes works by Reynolds, Holbein, Dürer, Memlinc, Murillo, Dolci, Veronese, Titian, Michelangelo, Leonardo da Vinci and Correggio, and sculptures by Canova, Bertel Thorwaldsen, Chantrey and R. J. Wyatt. Beyond the river, and immediately opposite the house, is the model village of Edensor: of Saxon origin, it was almost entirely rebuilt by the 6th duke. The parish church, built by Sir Gilbert Scott to replace a much older building, contains a brass in memory of John Beaton, confidential servant to Mary queen of Scots.

Chatsworth (*Chetesworde, Chattesworth,* "Ceatt's homestead") took its name from Ceatt, one of its Saxon owners. It was entrusted by William the Conqueror to the custody of William Peverel. It afterward belonged for many generations to the family of Leech, and was purchased in the reign of Elizabeth I by Sir William Cavendish, husband of the famous Bess of Hardwick. In 1553 he began to build Chatsworth house, which was completed, after his death, by his widow, later countess of Shrewsbury. Here Mary queen of Scots spent several years of her imprisonment under the care of the earl of Shrewsbury. During the Civil War, Chatsworth was occupied as a fortress by both parties and subsequently pulled down. The present house was designed by William Talman for the 4th earl (created 1st duke in 1694). Although a marble slab in the Great hall states that it was begun in 1688, work was already in progress in 1687. The long north wing was added (1820–27) by Sir Jeffry Wyatville for the 6th duke who also extended the east side (1827–34) and rebuilt the interior of the south wing.

CHATTANOOGA, a city of Tennessee, U.S., on the Tennessee river, at the southern boundary of the state adjoining Georgia; county seat of Hamilton county. It is at the intersection of federal highways 11, 27, 41 and 64.

It is served by the following railroads: Southern, Nashville, Chattanooga and St. Louis, the Central of Georgia and the Tennessee, Alabama and Georgia. By air it is served by Capital, Delta, and Eastern air lines. The Tennessee river is navigable all year round, and river steamers and barges supplement the city's transportation requirements. The land area of the incorporated city is 27.4 sq.mi. The population by the 1950 federal census was 130,333; in 1940 it was 128,163.

Chattanooga is the geographic centre and largest city of the Tennessee Valley authority's development program.

The mile-long $36,000,000 Chickamauga dam is in the northern outskirts of the city; the Watts Bar dam and Hales Bar dam are near by. Manufacturing is the principal industry. Chief among the city's industrial products are: textiles, farm implements, steam boilers, gas, coal and electric stoves and ranges, plumbing supplies, machinery, bathtubs, soil pipe, structural steel, furniture, chemicals, paper, glass bottles, ceramic products, beverages, medicines, cement, candy and electrically treated iron ore. Its educational institutions include: University of Chattanooga (coeducational); two private military schools for boys, Baylor school and McCallie school; one private school for girls, Girls' Preparatory school; and two private grammar-kindergarten schools, Bright school and Wert school; Chattanooga College of Law; Cadek Conservatory of Music; and Tennessee Temple college (Baptist theological).

Signal mountain and Lookout mountain, on the northern and southern outskirts, respectively, of Chattanooga have units of the national military park which offer unusual views of the Tennessee river, Chattanooga and surrounding country. Ascending Lookout mountain is a steep incline railway. Inside Lookout mountain is a cave which contains a natural waterfall 145 ft. high; atop the mountain are unusual rock formations and fine gardens. Lake Chickamauga, a 59-mile-long body of water formed on the Tennessee river by the Chickamauga dam, is a centre for yachting, swimming and fishing. On exhibition in the Union Station is "The General," an old locomotive that was captured by Northern troops in the Civil War and, after a running battle, was recaptured by the Confederates.

A large municipal auditorium, built as a memorial to men of Chattanooga who served in World War I, houses all types of indoor performances.

The beginning of Chattanooga dates from the establishment of a trading post on the Tennessee river by Timothy Meigs and John Ross. Meigs soon died and the trading post, located near what is now downtown Chattanooga, became known as Ross' Landing. In 1834 Ross, who was a Cherokee chief, also built a home about 6 mi. from the landing in what is now Rossville, Ga.; this home is still standing. In 1817 missionaries had established their first mission in the Cherokee nation about 5 mi. east of Ross' Landing and in 1818 the mission was named Brainerd mission in honour of David Brainerd, a missionary among New England Indians. It was incorporated as Chattanooga in 1851, and received a city charter in 1866. In 1911 it adopted a commission form of government. In 1860 the population was 2,545; in 1880, 12,892; in 1900, 30,154. The iron industry was well established even before the development of hydroelectric power, because of the proximity of coal-fields and iron mines. The city and its environs were the scene of important engagements in the Civil War, notably the battles of Chickamauga, on Sept. 19–20, 1863; and of Missionary Ridge and Lookout mountain ("the battle above the clouds"), on Nov. 24–25, 1863. The national cemetery in the city contains 14,248 graves (5,059 marked "unknown"), and there is also a Confederate cemetery. Chickamauga and Chattanooga national military park (8,146.33 ac.) in Tennessee and Georgia was established in 1890. In both the Spanish-American War and World War I it was used for the mobilization and training of troops. Chickamauga battlefield is dotted with more than 2,000 monuments, and many others are scattered over Missionary Ridge, Lookout mountain, Signal mountain and other historic spots. Ft. Oglethorpe, just north of the battlefield, is a regimental cavalry post.

Battle of Chattanooga.—From late September to Nov. 24, 1863, the Army of the Cumberland was invested in Chattanooga by the Confederates, whose position lay along Missionary Ridge from its north end toward Rossville, whence their entrenchments extended westward to Lookout mountain, which dominates the whole ground, the Tennessee running directly beneath it. Thus Rosecrans was confined to a semicircle of low ground around Chattanooga itself, and his supplies had to make a long and difficult detour from Bridgeport, the main road being under fire

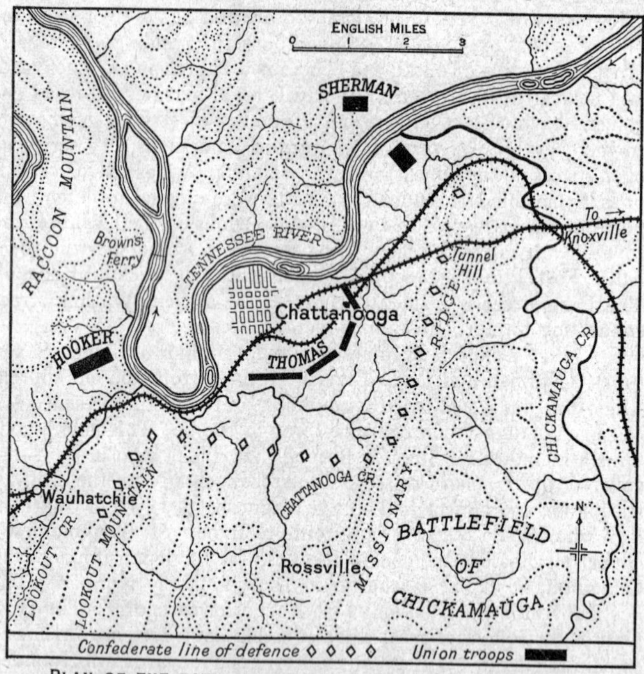

PLAN OF THE BATTLE OF CHATTANOOGA, NOV. 23–25, 1863

from the Confederate position on Lookout and in the Wauhatchie valley adjacent. Bragg indeed expected that Rosecrans would be starved into retreat. But the Federals once more, and this time on a far larger scale, concentrated in the face of the enemy. The XI and XII corps from Virginia, under Hooker, were transferred by rail to reinforce Rosecrans; other troops were called up from the Mississippi, and on Oct. 16 the Federal government reconstituted the western armies under the supreme command of General Grant. The XV corps of the Army of the Tennessee, under Sherman, was on the march from the Mississippi. Hooker's troops had already arrived when Grant reached Chattanooga on Oct. 23. The Army of the Cumberland was now under Thomas, Rosecrans having been recalled. The first action was fought at Brown's Ferry in the Wauhatchie valley, where Hooker executed with complete precision a plan for the revictualling of Chattanooga, established himself near Wauhatchie on the 28th, and repulsed a determined attack on the same night. But Sherman was still far distant, and the Federal forces at Knoxville, against which a large detachment of Bragg's army under Longstreet was now sent, were in grave danger. Grant waited for Sherman's four divisions, but prepared everything for battle in the meantime. His plan was that Thomas, in the Chattanooga lines, should contain the Confederate centre on Missionary Ridge, while Hooker on the right, at Wauhatchie, was to attack Lookout mountain, and Sherman, farther up the river, was to carry out the decisive attack against Bragg's extreme right wing at the end of Missionary Ridge. The last marches of the XV corps were delayed by stormy weather, Bragg reinforced Longstreet, and telegraphic communication between Grant and the Federals at Knoxville had already ceased. But Grant would not move forward without Sherman, and the battle of Chattanooga was fought more than two months after Chickamauga. On Nov. 23 a forward move of Thomas's army, intended as a demonstration, developed into a serious and successful action, whereby the first line of the Confederate centre was driven in for some distance. Bragg was now much weakened by successive detachments having been sent to Knoxville, and on the 24th the real battle began. Sherman's corps was gradually brought over the river near the mouth of Chickamauga creek and formed up on the east side.

The attack began at 1 P.M. and was locally a complete success. The heights attacked were in Sherman's hands, and fortified against counter-attack, before nightfall. Hooker in the meanwhile had fought the "Battle above the Clouds" on the steep face of Lookout mountain, and though opposed by an equal force of Confederates, had completely driven the enemy from the mountain. The 24th then had been a day of success for the Federals, and the decisive attack of the three armies in concert was to take place on the 25th. But the maps deceived Grant and Sherman as they had previously deceived Rosecrans. Sherman had captured, not the north point of Missionary Ridge, but a detached hill, and a new and more serious action had to be fought for the possession of Tunnel Hill, where Bragg's right now lay strongly entrenched. The Confederates used every effort to hold the position and all Sherman's efforts were made in vain. Hooker, who was moving on Rossville, had not progressed far, and Bragg was still free to reinforce his right. Grant therefore directed Thomas to move forward on the centre to relieve the pressure on Sherman. The Army of the Cumberland was, after all, to strike the decisive blow. About 3.30 P.M. the centre advanced on the Confederate's trenches at the foot of Missionary Ridge. These were carried at the first rush, and the troops were ordered to lie down and await orders. Then occurred one of the most dramatic episodes of the war. Suddenly, and without orders either from Grant or the officers at the front, the whole line of the Army of the Cumberland rose and rushed up the ridge. Two successive lines of entrenchments were carried at once. In a short time the crest was stormed, and after a last attempt at resistance the enemy's centre fled in the wildest confusion. The pursuit was pressed home by the divisional generals, notably by Sheridan. Hooker now advanced in earnest on Rossville, and by nightfall the whole Confederate army, except the troops on Tunnel Hill, was retreating in disorder. These too were withdrawn in the night, and the victory of the Federals was complete. Bragg lost 8,684 men killed, wounded and prisoners out of perhaps 34,000 men engaged; Grant, with 60,000 men, lost about 6,000.

CHATTEL, a term used in English law as equivalent to "personal property," that is, property which, on the death of the owner, devolves on his executor or administrator to be distributed (unless disposed of by will) among the next of kin according to the Statutes of Distributions. Chattels are divided into *chattels real* and *chattels personal.* Chattels real are those interests in land for which no "real action" (*see* PRACTICE AND PROCEDURE) lies; estates which are less than freehold (estates for years, at will, or by sufferance) are chattels real. Chattels personal are such things as belong immediately to the person of the owner, and for which, if they are injuriously withheld from him, he has no remedy other than by a personal action. Chattels personal are divided into *choses in possession* and *choses in action* (*see* CHOSE).

CHATTEL MORTGAGE, a transaction by which an owner of personal property transfers the property to a creditor for the purpose of securing payment of the debt. The chattel mortgage differs from a pledge in that the latter requires transfer of possession and control of the goods to the creditor, whereas in the typical chattel mortgage full possession and use of the goods remain in the mortgagor. And precisely here lie both the great economic advantage and the social danger of the device. For, having possession, use and control, the mortgagor retains the economic use of goods which he is vastly better able to utilize than is his lender; indeed, out of such use he may realize the wherewithal to pay off the very debt secured by the mortgage. So in the case of a chattel mortgage on crops to be sown or grown, the advances of the country banker are intended to finance the growing of those crops, and will normally be repaid out of its sale. And so with live stock mortgages and mortgages on the equipment of a factory, of a small plant, etc. On the other hand, the continued and unrestricted possession of the goods by the mortgagor is likely to mislead his other creditors, present or prospective, into the belief that his assets are greater than they are; and in the event of trouble, the mortgagee's prior claim, if sustained, may come in to cut them off from any possibility of realizing their debts. Out of this double need has arisen legislation in all American States except Pennsylvania (which does not recognize the chattel mortgage) limiting the validity of the transaction unless the mortgagee takes possession, or unless the mortgage instrument is filed for public information in some prescribed public office. But the details of the legislation are amazingly diverse. In some States the filing is required to be in the county where the mortgagor resides; in others, in that where the goods are located, in still others, in both. In some States possession or filing must occur at once, to be effective; in others, within a fixed period, such as ten days; in still others it is effective as soon as it occurs, whenever that may be. Everywhere, persons purchasing the goods from the mortgagor in possession take free of the mortgage if it has not been filed, and if they are ignorant of it. Everywhere, some of the mortgagor's creditors can disregard the mortgage, if it remains unfiled; but the precise classes of creditors protected vary widely. It may be safely stated, however, that a mortgagee who does not comply with the statute nowhere acquires a satisfactory security.

The requirements of form are equally diverse. The form of apparently outright bill of sale (*q.v.*) is permissible, but not widely used, to evidence chattel mortgages in the United States. In States where no form is required, save a paper signed by the mortgagor, the object is to allow business to be done simply and quickly. But some States attempt to avoid fraudulent practices of mortgagees by requiring the mortgagor to receive, and give a receipt for, a copy of the mortgage; the purpose is to make fraudulent alteration easy to detect. Others fear dishonest practices of mortgagors, and require witnesses or formal acknowledgment to make the document valid. Here the attempt is, in part, to prevent the mortgagor from later denying that he gave the mortgage. Others require, in addition, affidavits by the mortgagor, or by the mortgagee, or by both, that the debt secured is in truth owed, and the transaction *bona fide.* This last requirement arises out of the apparently not uncommon practice of debtors—especially merchants—when approaching insolvency, of creating fictitious debts to their friends, and attempting to divert their assets by colourable mortgages to secure such debts. And because of a similar fear of creditors being misled, a mortgage on a merchant's floating stock in trade has been hedged about by the courts with so many restrictions as to make it worthless as a continuing security to-day. That chattel mortgages are regarded—at least where merchants are the mortgagors—as signs of serious financial difficulty, sufficient to cause suspension of credit, is partly due to this fact, partly to their evil odour because of much attempted fraudulent use, and partly to the fact that in open-credit selling the sellers properly insist on the stock of goods continuing unencumbered: they have supplied the goods; they do not want those same goods to be diverted to paying debts to others.

Almost everywhere a chattel mortgage is good between mortgagor and mortgagee, despite non-compliance with such formalities or with the filing provisions of the local statute. The mortgagee can take possession and foreclose on default in payment of the debt, or in any other of the terms of the transaction—common requirements being that the mortgagor shall keep the goods on the premises, shall not attempt to sell them, nor suffer attachment of the goods by other creditors, and so on. The risk of loss by fire or theft lies, always, on the mortgagor; and often, too, he is required by the mortgage to keep the goods insured for the mortgagee's benefit.

Chattel mortgages are in wide use. Crop mortgages are a major basis for financing current farm operations throughout the country. The same is true of live stock raising; save that here the mortgages are commonly taken in the first instance by specialized mortgage companies rather than by banks or local merchants. The wide-spread instalment selling business makes considerable use of the device, though more of the conditional sale (*see* INSTALMENT PURCHASE). In the shape of mortgages on articles of personal use such as automobiles, and on household furniture, chattel mortgages underlie many of the small consumption loans of needy borrowers—often with serious abuses. And they are becoming increasingly important in corporate mortgage-bond issues, since a mortgage on plant is obviously seriously impaired unless it can be made to cover the plant's equipment as well. In this last field serious discrepancy is beginning to be felt between the real estate portion of the security, as to which recording, once effected, is good forever, and the chattel portion, as to which periodical refiling is necessary. Finally, the chattel mortgage, in the peculiar form of the trust receipt, is used in the financing of imports, and of the sale of automobiles. In this form—an exception carved by the courts out of general statutes—it is good as against the mortgagor's creditors irrespective of filing or possession; but not as against purchasers without notice.

In the United States the chattel mortgage takes the place of the bill of sale, the latter term being there applied to a signed document describing goods and evidencing their sale, which a seller gives to a buyer who for some reason requires evidence of his ownership. Of late years the prevalence of automobile thefts has led generally to legislation requiring a bill of sale to be made out in the case of sales of second hand cars, and filed with the licensing authorities of the State. (K. N. L.)

See L. A. Jones, *Chattel Mortgages* (Indianapolis, 1908); *Hubbell's Legal Directory* (annual); Karl T. Frederick (1922), 22 *Col. L. Rev.*, 395, 546; C. Eliot, *The Farmer's Campaign for Credit* (N.Y., 1927).

CHATTERER, the general name applied to the members of two families of birds. The South American chatterers are the Cotingidae, woodland birds, feeding mainly on fruit; the best known are the cocks of the rock, umbrella and bellbirds (*qq.v.*). Chatterer was once inappropriately applied to the waxwing (*q.v.*), originally wrongly placed in a genus of jays, *Garrulus,* which was rendered *chatterer* in an early book on ornithology.

CHATTERIS, urban district and market town in the Isle of Ely, Cambridgeshire, England, 25½ mi. N. by W. of Cambridge by the L.N.E.R. Pop. (1938) 5,085. Area 21 sq.mi. St. Peter's church is principally Decorated. Parts remain of a Benedictine convent founded in the 10th century and rebuilt after fire in the early 14th.

To the north runs the great Forty-foot Drain, also called Vermuyden's, after the Dutch engineer, whose name is associated with the fen drainage works of the mid 17th century.

CHATTERJI, BANKIM CHANDRA (BANKIMACHANDRA CHATTOPADHYAYĀ) (1838–1894), Indian novelist, was born in the district of the Twenty-four Parganas in Bengal on June 27, 1838, and was by caste a Brahman. He was educated at the Hugli college, at the Presidency college in Calcutta, and at Calcutta university, where he was the first to take the degree of B.A. (1858). He entered the Indian civil service, and served as deputy magistrate in various districts of Bengal, his official services being recognized, on his retirement in 1891, by the title of rai bahadur and the C.I.E. He died April 8, 1894. Bankim Chandra was the greatest novelist of India during the 19th century, whether judged by the amount and quality of his writings, or by the influence which they have continued to exercise. He created in India a school of fiction on the European model. His novels include *Durges-Nandini, Kapala-Kundala, Mrinalini,* and *Bisha-Brikkha.* His outstanding work however is the *Ananda Math,* a story of the Sannyasi rebellion of 1772. The rebels gained a crushing victory over the British and Mohammedan forces. This success was, however, not followed up as a mysterious "physician," speaking as a divinely-inspired prophet, advised Satyananda to abandon further resistance, as, for the time, British rule was the only alternative to Mohammedan oppression. This book contains the famous song *Bande Mataram.*

Although the *Bande Mataram* was not used during Chatterji's life time as a party war-cry, it became, during the agitation which followed the partition of Bengal, the recognized patriotic song of the revolutionary party. The words *Bande Mataram,* "Hail to thee; Mother" are usually held to be an invocation to Kali, the goddess of death and destruction. The Sanyassi rebels are represented as having erected, in addition to the dark image of Kali "The Mother who has been," a *white* marble statue of the "Mother that shall be": the poet sings the praise of the "Mother"

> as Lachmi bowered in the flower
> that in the water grows,

but he also praises her as "Durga, bearing ten weapons." Other passages, too, are susceptible of revolutionary interpretation. Whatever Chatterji's original intention (it is sometimes held that it is merely an invocation of the Motherland) the story of the Sanyassis, the ingenious language and its stirring air, the *Mallar-Kawali-Tal,* all have a strong appeal to the Hindu mind and the *Bande Mataram* has become a powerful influence in political agitation and the accepted hymn of the extremist party.

In his earlier years Bankim Chandra served his apprenticeship in literature under Ishwar Chandra Gupta, the chief poet and satirist of Bengal during the earlier half of the 19th century. Bankim Chandra's friend and colleague, Dina Bandhu Mitra, was virtually the founder of the modern Bengali drama. Among the younger men who venerated Bankim Chandra, and benefited by his example and advice, may be mentioned two distinguished poets, Nabin Chandra Sen and Rabindranath Tagore.

CHATTERTON, THOMAS (1752–1770), English poet, was born at Bristol on Nov. 20, 1752, three months after the death of his father, who had been master of the Pile street free school, at Bristol. In 1760 Chatterton was sent to the Colston free school where he stayed for eight years. But this Bristol blue-coat school had little share in the education of its marvellous pupil. The office of sexton at the church St. Mary Redcliffe had been held for nearly two centuries by the Chatterton family, and under the guidance of his uncle, the child found his favourite haunt in the beautiful old church, deriving a fresh interest, when he was able to read, in certain quaint old chests, where parchment deeds, old as the Wars of the Roses, lay unheeded and forgotten. In 1763 a beautiful cross of curious workmanship, which had adorned the churchyard of St. Mary Redcliffe for upwards of three centuries, was destroyed by a churchwarden, and the boy sent to the local journal on Jan. 7, 1764, a clever satire on the parish vandal. His delight was to lock himself in a little attic, where, with books, cherished parchments, saved from the loot of the muniment room of St. Mary Redcliffe, and drawing materials, he lived in thought with his 15th century heroes and heroines. The first of his literary mystifications, the duologue of "Elinoure and Juga," was written before he was twelve years old, and he showed it to the usher at Colston's hospital, T. Phillips, as the work of a 15th century poet.

His "Rowleian" jargon appears to have been chiefly the result of the study of John Kersey's *Dictionarium Anglo-Britannicum,* and Prof. W. W. Skeat seems to think his knowledge even of Chaucer was very slight. He had already conceived the romance of Thomas Rowley, an imaginary monk of the 15th century, and lived for the most part in an ideal world of his own, in that elder time when Edward IV. was England's king, and Master William Canynge—familiar to him among the recumbent effigies in Redcliffe church—still ruled in Bristol's civic chair. Canynge is represented as an enlightened patron of literature, and Rowley's dramatic interludes were written for performance at his house. In order to escape a marriage urged by the king, Canynge retired to the college of Westbury in Gloucestershire, where he enjoyed the society of Rowley, and eventually became dean of the institution. The literary masquerade which thus constituted the life-dream of the boy was wrought out by him in fragments of prose and verse into a coherent romance, until the credulous scholars and antiquaries of his day were persuaded into the belief that there had lain in the parish chest of Redcliffe church for upwards of three centuries, a collection of mss. of rare merit, the work of Thomas Rowley, an unknown priest of Bristol in the days of Henry VI., and his poet laureate, John Lydgate.

Among the Bristol patrons of Chatterton were two pewterers, George Catcott and his partner Henry Burgum. Catcott was one of the most zealous believers in Rowley, and continued to collect his reputed writings long after the death of their real author. On Burgum, who had risen in life by his own exertions, the blue-coat boy palmed off the de Bergham pedigree, and other equally apocryphal evidences of the pewterer's descent from an ancestry old as the Norman Conquest. The de Bergham quartering, blazoned on a piece of parchment doubtless recovered from the Redcliffe muniment chest, was itself supposed to have lain for centuries in that ancient depository. The pedigree was professedly collected by Chatterton from original records, including "The Rowley mss." The pedigree still exists in Chatterton's own handwriting, copied into a book in which he had previously transcribed portions of antique verse, under the title of "Poems by Thomas Rowley, priest of St. John's, in the city of Bristol"; and in one of these, "The Tournament," Syrr Johan de Berghamme plays a conspicuous part. The ennobled pewterer rewarded Chatterton with five shillings, and was satirized for this valuation of a noble pedigree in some of Chatterton's latest verse.

On July 1, 1767, Chatterton was transferred to the office of John Lambert, attorney, to whom he was bound apprentice as a clerk. There he found leisure for his own favourite pursuits. An ancient stone bridge on the Avon, built in the reign of Henry II., had been displaced by a new bridge opened in 1768. Shortly afterwards the editor of *Felix Farley's Journal* received from a correspondent, signing himself *Dunelmus Bristoliensis*, a "description of the mayor's first passing over the old bridge," professedly derived from an ancient ms. The original manuscript is now preserved in the British Museum, along with other Chatterton mss., most of which were ultimately incorporated by William Barrett in his *History and Antiquities of the city of Bristol*, published nearly 20 years after the poet's death. It was at this time that the definite story made its appearance—over which critics and antiquaries wrangled for nearly a century—of numerous ancient poems and other mss. taken by the elder Chatterton from a coffer in the muniment room of Redcliffe church, and transcribed, and so rescued from oblivion, by his son. The pieces include the "Bristowe Tragedie, or the Dethe of Syr Charles Bawdin," a ballad celebrating the death of the Lancastrian knight, Charles Baldwin; "Ælla," a "Tragycal Enterlude," as Chatterton styles it, but in reality a dramatic poem of sustained power; "Goddwyn," a dramatic fragment; "Tournament," "Battle of Hastings," "The Parliament of Sprites," "Balade of Charitie," with numerous shorter pieces, forming altogether a volume of poetry, the rare merit of which is indisputable, wholly apart from the fact that it was the production of a mere boy.

In Dec., 1768, in his seventeenth year, he wrote to Dodsley, the London publisher, offering to procure for him "copies of several ancient poems, and an interlude, perhaps the oldest dramatic piece extant, wrote by one Rowley, a priest in Bristol, who lived in the reigns of Henry VI. and Edward IV." To this letter, as well as to another letter enclosing an extract from the tragedy of "Ælla," no answer appears to have been returned. Chatterton then bethought him of Horace Walpole, who not only indulged in a mediaeval renaissance of his own, but was the reputed author of a spurious antique in the *Castle of Otranto.* He wrote to him offering him a document entitled "The Ryse of Peyncteyne yn Englande, wroten by T. Rowleie, 1469, for Mastre Canynge," accompanied by notes which included specimens of Rowley's poetry. To this Walpole replied with courteous acknowledgments. He characterized the verses as "wonderful for their harmony and spirit," and added, "Give me leave to ask you where Rowley's poems are to be had? I should not be sorry to print them; or at least a specimen of them, if they have never been printed." Chatterton replied, enclosing additional specimens of antique verse, and telling Walpole that he was the son of a poor widow, and clerk to an attorney, and he hinted a wish that he might help him to some more congenial occupation. Walpole's manner underwent an abrupt change. The specimens of verse had been submitted to his friends, Gray and Mason, and pronounced modern. He now coldly advised the boy to stick to the attorney's office, and "when he should have made a fortune," he might betake himself to more favourite studies. Chatterton had to write three times before he recovered his mss. Walpole has been loaded with more than his just share of responsibility for the fate of the unhappy poet, of whom he admitted when too late, "I do not believe there ever existed so masterly a genius."

Chatterton now began to contribute to the *Town and County Magazine* and other London periodicals. Assuming the vein of Junius—then in the full blaze of his triumph—he turned his pen against the duke of Grafton, the earl of Bute, and the princess of Wales. He had just despatched one of his political diatribes to the *Middlesex Journal,* when he sat down on Easter Eve, April 17, 1770, and penned his "Last Will and Testament," a strange satirical compound of jest and earnest, in which he intimated his intention of putting an end to his life the following evening. Among his satirical bequests, such as his "humility" to the Rev. Mr. Camplin, his "religion" to Dean Barton, and his "modesty" along with his "prosody and grammar" to Mr. Burgum, he leaves "to Bristol all his spirit and disinterestedness, parcels of goods unknown on its quay since the days of Canynge and Rowley." In more genuine earnestness he recalls the name of Michael Clayfield, a friend to whom he owed intelligent sympathy. The will was probably purposely prepared in order to frighten his master into letting him go. Lambert cancelled his indentures, his friends made him up a purse, and on the 25th or 26th of the month he arrived in London.

Chatterton was already known to the readers of the *Middlesex Journal* as a rival of Junius, under the *nom de plume* of Decimus. He had also been a contributor to Hamilton's *Town and County Magazine,* and speedily found access to the *Freeholder's Magazine,* another political miscellany strong for Wilkes and liberty. Wilkes himself had noted his trenchant style, "and expressed a desire to know the author"; and Lord Mayor Beckford graciously acknowledged a political address of his, and greeted him "as politely as a citizen could." But of actual money he received little. He was extremely abstemious, but his diligence was great, and his versatility wonderful. He could assume the style of Junius or Smollett, reproduce the satiric bitterness of Churchhill, parody Macpherson's Ossian, or write in the manner of Pope, or with the polished grace of Gray and Collins. He wrote political letters, eclogues, lyrics, operas and satires, both in prose and verse. In June, 1770—after Chatterton had been some nine weeks in London—he removed from Shoreditch, where he had hitherto lodged with a relative, to an attic in Brook street, Holborn, where, for the first time, he enjoyed uninterrupted solitude. The romance of his earlier years revived, and he transcribed from an imaginary parchment of the old priest Rowley his "Excelente Balade of Charitie." This fine poem, perversely disguised in archaic language, he sent to the editor of the *Town and County Magazine,* and had it rejected.

The high hopes of the sanguine boy had begun to fade. He had not yet completed his second month in London, and already failure and starvation stared him in the face. The note of his actual receipts, found in his pocket-book after his death, shows that Hamilton, Fell and other editors who had been so liberal in flattery had paid him at the rate of a shilling for an article, and somewhat less than eightpence each for his songs; while much which had been accepted was held in reserve, and still unpaid for. The beginning of a new month revealed to him the indefinite postponement of the publication and payment of his work. He had wished, according to his foster-mother, to study medicine with Barrett; in his desperation he now reverted to this, and wrote to Barrett for a letter to help him to an opening as a surgeon's assistant on board an African trader. He appealed also to Mr. Catcott to forward his plan, but in vain. On Aug. 24, 1770, he retired for the last time to his attic in Brook street, carrying with him the arsenic which he there drank, after tearing into fragments whatever literary remains were at hand.

He was only seventeen years and nine months old; but the best of his numerous productions, both in prose and verse, require no allowance to be made for the immature years of their author. He pictures Lydgate, the monk of Bury St. Edmund's, challenging Rowley to a trial at versemaking, and under cover of this fiction, produces his "Songe of Ælla," a piece of rare lyrical beauty, worthy of comparison with any antique or modern production of its class. Again, in his "Tragedy of Goddwyn," of which only a fragment has been preserved, the "Ode to Liberty," with which it abruptly closes, may claim a place among the finest martial lyrics in the language. The death of Chatterton attracted little notice at the time; for the few who then entertained any appreciative estimate of the Rowley poems regarded him as their mere transcriber. He was interred in a burying-ground attached to Shoe Lane Workhouse. A monument has since been erected to his memory in Redcliffe churchyard, Bristol, with the appropriate inscription, borrowed from his "Will," and so supplied by the poet's own pen—"To the memory of Thomas Chatterton. Reader! judge not. If thou art a Christian, believe that he shall be judged by a Superior Power. To that Power only is he now answerable."

Bibliography.—*Poems supposed to have been written at Bristol by Thomas Rowley and others, in the Fifteenth Century* (1777) was edited by Thomas Tyrwhitt; Thomas Warton, in his *History of English Poetry* (1778); vol. ii., section viii., gives Rowley a place among the 15th century poets; but neither of these critics believed in the antiquity of the poems. In 1782 a new edition of Rowley's poems appeared, with a "Commentary, in which the antiquity of them is considered and defended," by Jeremiah Milles, dean of Exeter. The controversy which raged round the Rowley poems is discussed in A. Kippis *Biographia Britannica* (vol. iv., 1789), where there is a detailed account by G. Gregory of Chatterton's life (pp. 573–619). This was reprinted in the edition (1803) of Chatterton's *Works* by R. Southey and J. Cottle, published for the benefit of the poet's sister. The neglected condition of the study of earlier English in the 18th century alone accounts for the temporary success of Chatterton's mystification. It has long been agreed that Chatterton was solely responsible for the Rowley Poems, but the language and style are analysed in confirmation of this view by Prof. W. W. Skeat in an introductory essay prefaced to vol. ii. of *The Poetical Works of Thomas Chatterton* (1871) in the "Aldine Edition of the British Poets." This, which is the most convenient edition, also contains a memoir of the poet by Edward Bell. The spelling of the Rowley poems is there modernized, and many of the archaic words are replaced by modern equivalents provided in many cases from Chatterton's own notes, the theory being that Chatterton usually composed in modern English, and inserted his peculiar words and his complicated orthography afterwards. *See* also H. B. Forman, *Thomas Chatterton and his latest Editor* (1874). The Chatterton mss., originally in the possession of William Barrett of Bristol, were left by his heir to the British Museum in 1800. Others are preserved in the Bristol library.

Chatterton's genius and his tragic death are commemorated by Shelley in *Adonais*, by Wordsworth in "Resolution and Independence," by Coleridge in "A Monody on the Death of Chatterton," by D. G. Rossetti in "Five English Poets"; John Keats inscribed *Endymion* "to the memory of Thomas Chatterton." Alfred de Vigny's drama of *Chatterton* gives an altogether fictitious account of the poet. Sir Herbert Croft, in his *Love and Madness,* interpolated a long and valuable account of Chatterton, giving many of the poet's letters, and much information obtained from his family and friends (pp. 125–244, letter li.). There is a valuable collection of "Chattertoniana" in the British Museum, consisting of separate works by Chatterton, newspaper cuttings, articles, dealing with the Rowley controversy and other subjects, with ms. notes by Joseph Haslewood, and several autograph letters. F. A. Hyatt and W. Bazeley, *Chattertoniana* (Gloucester, 1914), a catalogue of printed matter.

Among biographies of Chatterton may be mentioned Daniel Wilson, *Chatterton: A Biographical Study* (1869); D. Masson, *Chatterton: A Biography* (1899); Helene Richter, "Thomas Chatterton" (1900), in *Wiener Beitrage zur engl. Philologie;* C. E. Russell, *Chatterton,* (1909); J. H. Ingram, *The True Chatterton* (1910); Sir E. Clarke, *New Lights on Chatterton* (1916), a paper read before the Bibliographical Society, London.

CHATTI, an ancient German tribe inhabiting the upper reaches of the rivers Weser, Eder, Fulda and Werra, a district approximately corresponding to Hesse-Cassel, though probably somewhat more extensive. They frequently came into conflict with the Romans during the early years of the 1st century A.D. Eventually they formed a portion of the Franks and were incorporated in the kingdom of Clovis at the beginning of the 6th century.

See Tacitus, *Annals,* i., ii., xi., xii. and xiii.; *Germania,* 30–31.

CHAUCER, GEOFFREY (1340?–1400), English poet, was born, about 1340, of a family which had been settled in London for at least two generations, but probably came from the eastern counties. His father, John Chaucer, lived at one time in Cordwainer street, the quarter of the shoemakers, with which the name Chaucer (a French form of the Latin *Calcearius*) connects the family. But John Chaucer, his father Robert, and a stepfather Richard, were vintners, and Robert and John held offices connected with the customs on wine. Geoffrey was probably born at Thames street, where his father is found living somewhat later, with a wife, Agnes, niece of Hamo de Compton, probably the poet's mother. In 1357 Geoffrey is found, apparently as a lad, in the service of Elizabeth, countess of Ulster, wife of Lionel, duke of Clarence. In 1359 he went to the war in France and is heard of at Retters, *i.e.,* Rethel, near Reims, and as being taken prisoner. The king contributed £16 to his ransom and it is probable that after his return he was for some time at the Inner Temple, where, at a considerable cost, an education was given likely to help suitable men for civil employment under the Crown. By June 20, 1367, he had been long enough in the king's service to be granted a pension of 20 marks, probably in connection with his marriage with a Philippa, one of two daughters of Sir Payne Roet, who in the previous September had been granted a pension of ten marks for her services to the queen as one of her *domicellae.* Philippa's sister, Katherine, after the death of her husband, Sir Hugh de Swynford, in 1372, became governess to John of Gaunt's children, and subsequently his mistress, and (in 1396) his wife. The marriage with Philippa thus helps to account for the favour subsequently shown to Chaucer by John of Gaunt.

In the grant of his pension Chaucer is called "dilectus vallectus noster," our beloved yeoman; before the end of 1368 he had risen to one of the king's esquires. In September of the following year John of Gaunt's wife, the duchess Blanche, died at the age of 29, and Chaucer wrote in her honour *The Book of the Duchesse,* a poem of 1,334 lines in octosyllabic couplets. In June 1370 he went abroad on the king's service, on an unknown errand, returning probably some time before Michaelmas. On Dec. 1, 1372, he started, with an advance of 100 marks in his pocket, for Italy, as one of three commissioners to treat with the Genoese as to an English port where they might have special facilities for trade. His accounts, delivered on May 23, 1373, show that he had also visited Florence on the king's business, and he possibly went also to Padua and there made the acquaintance of Petrarch.

In the second quarter of 1374, Chaucer lived in a whirl of prosperity. On April 23 the king granted him a pitcher of wine daily, subsequently commuted for an annuity of 20 marks. From John of Gaunt, who in Aug. 1372 had granted Philippa Chaucer £10 a year, he himself now received (June 13) a like annuity. On June 8 he was appointed (with a salary of £10 and an annual gratuity of £6 13s.4d.) comptroller of the Custom and Subsidy of Wools, Hides and Woodfells and also of the Petty Customs of Wine in the Port of London. Probably in anticipation of this appointment he had taken, on May 10, a lease for life from the city of London of the dwelling-house above the gate of Aldgate, and here he lived for the next 12 years. In 1375–76 two large windfalls came to him, the first being two wardships of Kentish heirs, one of whom paid him £104, the second a grant of £71 4s.6d. the value of some confiscated wool. In Dec. 1376 he was sent abroad on the king's service in the retinue of Sir John Burley; in Feb. 1377 he was sent to Paris and Montreuil in connection probably with the peace negotiations between England and France, and at the end of April (after a reward of £20 for his good services) he was again despatched to France. It is generally considered that this diplomatic period of his life was unprolific in poetry.

On the accession of Richard II., Chaucer was confirmed in his offices and pensions. In Jan. 1378 he seems to have been in France in connection with a proposed marriage between Richard and the daughter of the French king; and on May 28 of the same year he was sent (his last diplomatic journey) with Sir Edward de Berkeley to the lord of Milan and Sir John Hawkwood to treat for help in the king's wars, returning on Sept. 19. In April 1382 a new comptrollership, that of the petty customs in the Port of London, was given him, and shortly after he was allowed to exercise it by deputy, a similar licence being given him in Feb. 1385, at the instance of the earl of Oxford, as regards the comptrollership of wool. In Oct. 1385 he was made a justice of the peace for Kent. In Feb. 1386 we catch a glimpse of his wife, Philippa, being admitted to the fraternity of Lincoln cathedral in the company of Henry, earl of Derby (afterwards Henry IV.), Sir Thomas de Swynford and other distinguished persons. In Aug. 1386 he was elected one of the two knights of the shire for Kent, and with this dignity (one not much appreciated in those days) his good fortune reached its climax. In December he was superseded in both his comptrollerships, probably as a result of the absence of his patron, John of Gaunt, in Spain, and the supremacy of the duke of Gloucester. In the following year the cessation of Philippa's pension suggests that she died between midsummer and Michaelmas. In May 1388 Chaucer surrendered to the king his two pensions of 20 marks each, and they were regranted at his request to one John Scalby, an unusual transaction, pointing to a pressing need for ready money.

In July 1389, after John of Gaunt had returned to England, and the king had taken the government into his own hands, Chaucer was appointed clerk of works at various royal palaces at a salary of two shillings a day. To this post was subsequently added the charge of some repairs at St. George's chapel, Windsor. He was also made a commissioner to maintain the banks of the Thames between Woolwich and Greenwich, and was given by the earl of March (grandson of Lionel, duke of Clarence, his first patron) a sub-forestership at North Petherton, Devon; obviously a sinecure. While on the king's business, in Sept. 1390, Chaucer was twice robbed by highwaymen, losing £20 of the king's money. In June 1391 he was superseded as clerk of the works, and seems to have suffered another spell of misfortune, of which the first alleviation came in Jan. 1393, when the king made him a gift of £10. In Feb. 1394 he was granted a new pension of £20. In 1397 he received from King Richard a grant of a butt of wine yearly. For this he appears to have asked in terms that suggested poverty, and in May 1398 he obtained letters of protection against his creditors. On the accession of Henry IV. a new pension of 40 marks was granted him (Oct. 13, 1399) and Richard II.'s grants were formally confirmed. Though no instalment of the new pension was paid, on the strength of his expectations (Dec. 24, 1399), Chaucer leased a tenement in the garden of St. Mary's chapel, Westminster, and it was probably here that he died on the following Oct. 25. He was buried in Westminster Abbey, and his tomb became the nucleus of what is now known as Poets' Corner.

The portrait of Chaucer, which the affection of his disciple, Thomas Hoccleve, caused to be painted in a copy of the latter's *Regement of Princes* (now Harleian ms. 4,866 in the British Museum), shows him an old man with white hair; he has a fresh complexion, grey eyes, a straight nose, a grey moustache and a small double-pointed beard. His dress and hood are black, and he carries in his hands a string of beads.

Works.—Henry IV.'s promise of an additional pension was doubtless elicited by the *Compleynt to his Purs,* in the envoy to which Chaucer addresses him as the "conquerour of Brutes Albioun." Thus within the last year of his life the poet was still writing. Nevertheless, as early as 1393–94, in lines to his friend Scogan, he had written as if his day for poetry were past, and it seems probable that his longer poems were all composed before this date. In the preceding 15—or, if another view be taken, 20—years, his literary activity was very great, and with the aid of the lists of his works which he gives in the *Legende of Good Women* (lines 414–431), and the talk on the road which precedes the "Man of Lawe's Tale" (*Canterbury Tales,* B. 46–76), the order in which his main works were written can be traced with approximate certainty.

The development of Chaucer's genius has been attractively summed up as comprised in three stages, French, Italian and English, and there is a rough approximation to the truth in this formula, since his earliest poems are translated from the French or based on French models, and the two great works of his middle period are borrowed from the Italian, while his latest stories have no such obvious and direct originals, and in their humour and freedom anticipate the typically English temper of Henry Fielding. But Chaucer's indebtedness to French poetry was no passing phase. He knew the *Roman de la rose* as modern English poets know Shakespeare, and the full extent of his debt to his French contemporaries, not merely in 1369, but in 1385, and in 1393 (the dates are approximate), has only gradually been discovered. To this continuing French influence it was his good fortune to add lessons in plot and construction derived from Boccaccio's *Filostrato* and *Teseide,* as well as some glimpses of the higher art of the *Divina Commedia.* He shows acquaintance also with one of Petrarch's sonnets. His study of Italian models was thus an episode of unique importance in his literary life, but before it began he had already been making his own artistic experiments, and it is noteworthy that while he learnt much from Boccaccio he improved on his originals as he translated them. Doubtless his busy life in the service of the Crown had taught him self-confidence, and he uses his Italian models in his own way and with the most triumphant and assured success. When he had no more Italian poems to adapt he had learnt his lesson. In his "English" period we find him taking what might be little more than an anecdote and lending it body and life and colour with a skill never surpassed.

Early Period.—The most direct example of Chaucer's French studies is his translation of *Le Roman de la rose,* a poem written in some 4,000 lines by Guillaume de Lorris about 1237 and extended to over 22,000 by Jean Clopinel, better known as Jean de Meun, 40 years later. We know from Chaucer himself that he translated this poem, and the extant English fragment of 7,698 lines was generally assigned to him from 1532, when it was first printed, till its authorship was challenged in the early years of the Chaucer Society. The ground of this challenge was its wide divergence from Chaucer's practice in his undoubtedly genuine works as to certain niceties of rhyme, notable as to not rhyming words ending in *-y* with others ending *-ye.* It was subsequently contended, however, that the whole fragment is divisible linguistically into three portions, of which the first and second end respectively at lines 1,705 and 5,810, and that in the first of these three sections the variations from Chaucer's accepted practice are insignificant. Lines 1–1,705 have therefore been provisionally accepted as Chaucer's and the other two fragments as the work of unknown translators which somehow came to be pieced together. A rival theory proposed by Dr. Brusendorf assigns the whole fragment to a professional reciter writing down what he remembered of the parts of Chaucer's translation he was accustomed to recite, and varying when his memory failed.

While our knowledge of Chaucer's *Romaunt of the Rose* is in this unsatisfactory state, another translation of his from the French, the *Book of the Lyon* (alluded to in the "Retraction" found, in some manuscripts, at the end of the *Canterbury Tales*), which must certainly have been taken from Guillaume Michault's *Le Dit du lion,* has perished altogether. The strength of French influence on Chaucer's early work may, however, be amply illustrated from the first of his poems with which we are on sure ground, the *Book of the Duchesse,* or, as it is alternatively called, the *Deth of Blaunche.* Here not only are individual passages closely imitated from Machault and Froissart, but the dream, the May morning, and the whole machinery of the poem are taken over from contemporary French conventions. But even at this stage, Chaucer could prove his right to borrow by the skill with which he makes his materials serve his own purpose, and some of the lines in the *Deth of Blaunche* are among the most tender and charming he ever wrote.

Chaucer's *A.B.C.,* a poem in honour of the Blessed Virgin, of which the stanzas begin with the successive letters of the alphabet, is another example of French influence. It is taken from the *Pèlerinage de la vie humaine,* written by Guillaume de Deguilleville about 1330. The occurrence of some magnificent lines in Chaucer's version, combined with evidence that he did not yet possess the skill to translate at all literally as soon as rhymes had to be considered, accounts for this poem having been dated sometimes earlier than the *Book of the Duchesse,* and sometimes several years later. With it is usually moved up and down, though it should surely be placed in the '70s, the *Compleynt to Pity,* a fine poem which yet, from its slight obscurity and absence of Chaucer's usual ease, may very well some day prove to be a translation from the French.

Middle Period.—While Chaucer thus sought to reproduce both the matter and the style of French poetry in England, he found other materials in popular Latin books. Among his lost works are renderings of "Origenes upon the Maudeleyne," and of Pope Innocent III. on "The Wrecced Engendring of Mankinde" (*De miseria conditionis humanae*). He must have begun his attempts at straightforward narrative with the *Lyf of Seynt Cecyle* (the weakest of all his works, the second Nun's Tale in the Canterbury series) from the *Legenda Aurea* of Jacobus de Voragine, and the story of the patience of Grisilde, taken from Petrarch's Latin version of a tale by Boccaccio. In both of these he condenses a little, but ventures on very few changes, though he lets his readers see his impatience with his originals. In his story of Constance (afterwards ascribed to the Man of Lawe), taken from the Anglo-Norman chronicle of Nicholas Trivet, written about 1334, we find him strengthening another weak tale, but still without the courage to remedy its radical faults, though here, as with Grisilde, he does as much for his heroine as the conventional exaltation of one virtue at a time permitted. It is possible that other tales which now stand in the Canterbury series were written originally at this period. What is certain is that at some time in the '70s, independently of any glimpses he may have obtained of the *Divina Commedia* and of Petrarch's sonnets, two notable Italian poems by Boccaccio passed into Chaucer's possession and that the turning of the *Filostrato* into *Troilus and Criseyde* and the *Teseide* into "al the storye of Palamon and Arcyte" was his main poetic business during the next few years and vitally affected his development. He did not, however, work on these masterpieces uninterruptedly. Almost at the outset two court poems had to be written in connection with the betrothal and marriage of Richard II. to Anne of Bohemia, the *Hous of Fame* and *The Parlement of Foules.* The former begins with a dream on a certain tenth of December and Dr. Aage Brusendorf is almost certainly right in linking this with the formal appointment on Dec. 12, 1380, of an English embassy to treat for the marriage and the conception of the poem with Froissart's *Le Temple d'Honneur* in which a marriage is guardedly forecast. Unhappily, one or more leaves at the end of the archetype manuscript of Chaucer's poem were lost before other copies were made from it, so that the conjecture cannot be finally verified, but it offers a much needed clue to the meaning, which had previously been rashly connected with Dante's *Divina Commedia.* Written in octosyllabic couplets, like the *Romaunt of the Rose,* it shows Chaucer already possessed of the conversational ease which marks his later work, but the ease tempted him to extend the poem to a length out of keeping with his subject, and it is best known by the few lines in which he talks about himself. *The Parlement of Foules,* written in seven-line stanzas, commemorating the delay of over a year in the celebration of the marriage, and full of gaiety and humour, is in much better proportion.

Besides these two poems Chaucer about this time produced his most important prose work, the translation of the *De Consolatione Philosophiae* of Boethius. Reminiscences of this helped to enrich many of his subsequent poems and inspired five of his shorter pieces (*The Former Age, Fortune, Truth, Gentilesse* and *Lak of Stidfastnesse*), but the translation itself cannot be counted a success. To borrow Chaucer's own phrase, his "English was insufficient" to reproduce such difficult Latin. The translation is often barely intelligible without the original, and it is only here and there that it flows with any ease or rhythm.

Troilus and Criseyde.—A snatch of abuse of his scrivener shows that the translation of Boethius and *Troilus and Criseyde* were being copied for circulation at the same time and in the *Troilus,* after a good many half-successes, Chaucer achieved a great artistic triumph. He follows Boccaccio's *Filostrato* step by step, but he does not follow it as a mere translator. He had done his duty manfully for St. Cecyle, Grisilde and Constance, whom he was forbidden by the conventions of his originals to clothe with complete flesh and blood. In this great story of love and betrayal there were no such restrictions, and the characters, which Boccaccio's treatment left thin and conventional, became in Chaucer's hands convincingly human. No other English poem is so instinct with the glory and tragedy of youth, and in the details of the story Chaucer's gifts of vivid colouring, of humour and pity, are all at their highest. *Troilus and Criseyde* is written in seven-line stanzas; for re-telling from the *Teseide* the story of *Palamon and Arcyte* Chaucer used for the first time decasyllabic couplets, for which Guillaume Machault had provided him with a French model, with a great gain in swiftness and compression. The story has not the poignant interest of the *Troilus* (it is probably the "comedye" which in the epilogue to the earlier poems Chaucer promised to write), but Chaucer's skill is again at its highest. This time, while he takes Boccaccio's plot, he takes only as much of it as he wants, and what he takes he heightens and humanizes with the same skill as he had shown in transforming the *Filostrato.* Of the individual characters Theseus himself, the arbiter of the story, is developed as notably as Sir Pandarus in the *Troilus,* while the fair Emilye and her two lovers-at-first-sight receive just as much individuality as they can be given without burdening the story with a greater intensity than it will bear. With what revision we know not, the story was fitted into the *Canterbury Tales* and assigned to the chivalrous Knight; but that it was written soon after *Troilus* and the translation of Boethius, and before the *Legende of Good Women* (in which it is mentioned), should not be doubted, though other theories have been proposed.

When the *Teseide* had been used, Chaucer had no more Italian stories to translate and he turned to his Latin materials to compile a lectionary of Cupid's Saints for presentation to the queen. To atone for his portrayal of the disloyalty of Criseyde he accepted as a penance the painting of 19 women faithful to love, with Alcestis as their queen, enriching his scheme with a delightful prologue (extant in two rather widely differing forms) into which he introduces touches about his worship of the Deity and the controversy between the partisans of the Flower and the Leaf from his French friends, Froissart and Deschamps. Of the stories of constant women, those of Dido and Cleopatra are fully worthy of him. When, however, he had written eight and part of a ninth he wearied of the monotony of his theme, which he was beginning to treat with scant respect, and broke off.

Canterbury Tales.—Chaucer's failure to complete the scheme of the *Legende of Good Women* may have been partly due to the attractions of the *Canterbury Tales,* which were probably taken up in immediate succession to it. His guardianship of two Kentish wards, his justiceship of the peace, his representing the county in the parliament of 1386, his commissionership of the river-bank between Greenwich and Woolwich, all make it easy to understand his dramatic use of the merry crowds he saw on the Canterbury road, without supposing him to have had recourse to Boccaccio's *Decameron,* a book which there is no proof of his having seen. The pilgrims whom he imagines to have assembled at the Tabard inn in Southwark, where Harry Bailey was host, are said to have numbered "wel nyne and twenty in a company," and the Prologue gives full-length sketches (at least some of which Prof. Manly, in his *New Light on Chaucer,* has shown to have been drawn from life) of a Knight, a Squire (his son), and their Yeoman; of a Prioress, Monk, Friar, Oxford Clerk, and Parson, with two disreputable hangers-on of the church, a Summoner, and a Pardoner; of a Serjeant-at-Law and a Doctor of Physic, and of a Franklin, or country gentleman, Merchant, Shipman, Miller, Cook, Manciple, Reeve, Ploughman (the Parson's brother) and the ever-famous Wife of Bath. Five London burgesses are described in a group, and a Nun and Priest (altered possibly in a moment of hopefulness by Chaucer himself, to "priestes three") are mentioned as in attendance on the Prioress. Each of these, with Chaucer himself making the 29th, was pledged to tell two tales, but including one second attempt and a tale told by the Yeoman of a Canon, who overtakes the pilgrims on the road, we have only 20 finished stories, two unfinished and two interrupted ones.

As in the case of the *Legende of Good Women,* our loss is not so much that of the additional stories as of the completed framework. The wonderful character sketches of the Prologue are carried yet farther by the Talks on the Road which link the different tales, and two of these Talks, in which the Wife of Bath and the Pardoner respectively edify the company, have the importance of separate Tales, but between the Tales that have come down to us there are seven links missing, and it was left to a later and weaker hand to narrate, in the "Tale of Beryn," the adventures of the pilgrims at Canterbury.

The reference to the *Lyf of Seynt Cecyle* in the prologue to the *Legende of Good Women* gives external proof that Chaucer included earlier work in the scheme of the *Canterbury Tales,* and mention has been made of other stories which are indisputably early, while in the case of at least two, the Clerk's tale of Grisilde and the Monk's tragedies, there is evidence of early work being revised and supplemented. It is fortunately impossible to separate the prologue to the charmingly told story of "yonge Hugh of Lincoln" from the tale itself, and with the "quod sche" in the second line as proof that Chaucer was here writing specially for his Prioress we are forbidden to limit the new stories to any one metre or tone. There can be no doubt, however, that what may be called the Tales of the Churls (Miller, Reeve, Summoner, Friar, etc.), and the conversational outpourings of the Pardoner and Wife of Bath, form, with the immortal Prologue, the most important and distinctive additions to the older work. In these, and in the Pardoner's story of Death and the Three Revellers, and the Nun's Priest's masterly handling of the fable of the Cock and Fox, both of them free from the grossness which marks the others, Chaucer takes stories which could have been told in a short page of prose and elaborates them with all the skill in narration which he had sedulously cultivated. The conjugal reminiscences of the Wife of Bath and the Reeve's Tale with its abominable climax (lightened a little by Aleyn's farewell, lines 316–319) are among the great things in Chaucer, as surely as *Troilus* and *Palamon and Arcyte* and the *Prologue.* They help notably to give him the width of range which may certainly be claimed for him.

In or soon after 1391 Chaucer wrote in prose for an 11-year-old reader, whom he addresses as "Litel Lowis my son," a treatise on the use of the Astrolabe, its short prologue being the prettiest specimen of his prose. The wearisome tale of "Melibee and his wyf Prudence," which was perhaps as much admired in English as it had been in Latin and French, may have been translated at any time. The sermon on Penitence, used as the Parson's Tale, was probably the work of his old age. "Envoys" to his friends Scogan and Bukton, a translation of some balades by Sir Otes de Granson, and the *Compleynt to his Purs* complete the record of his minor poetry. We have his own statement that in his youth he had written many Balades, Roundels and Virelayes in honour of Love, and the two songs embedded respectively in the *Parlement of Foules* and the Prologue to the *Legende of Good Women* are charming and musical. His extant shorter poems, however, whether early or late, offer no excuse for claiming high rank for him as a lyrist. He had very little sheer singing power, and though there are fine lines in his short poems, witness the famous "Flee fro the prees and dwell with soothfastnesse," they lack the sustained concentration of great work. From the drama, again, Chaucer was cut off, and it is idle to argue from the innumerable dramatic touches in his poems and his gift of characterization as to what he might have done had he lived two centuries later. His own age delighted in stories, and he gave it the stories it demanded invested with a humanity, a grace and strength which place him among the world's greatest narrative poets, and which bring the England of his own day, with all the colour and warmth of life, wonderfully near to his readers.

The part played by Chaucer in the development of the English language has often been overrated. He neither corrupted it, as used to be said, by introducing French words which it would otherwise have avoided, nor bore any such part in fixing it as was afterwards played by the translators of the Bible. The practical identity of Chaucer's language with that of Gower shows that both merely used the best English of their day with the care and slightly conservative tendency which befitted poets. Chaucer's service to the English language lies in his decisive success having made it impossible for any later English poet to attain fame, as Gower had done, by writing alternatively in Latin and French.

Chaucer borrowed both his stanza forms and his "decasyllabic" couplets (mostly with an extra syllable at the end of the line) from Guillaume Machault, and his music, like that of his French master and his successors, depends very largely on assigning to every syllable its full value, and more especially on the due pronunciation of the final *-e.* The slower movement of change in Scotland allowed time for Chaucer to exercise a potent influence on Scottish poetry, but in England this final *-e,* to which most of the earlier grammatical forms by Chaucer's time had been reduced, itself fell rapidly into disuse during the 15th century, his disciples, Hoccleve and Lidgate, quickly lost touch with his rhythms and successive copyists reduced his text to a state in which it was only by accident that lines could be scanned correctly. For fully three centuries his reputation was sustained solely by his narrative power, his warmest panegyrists betraying no consciousness that they were praising one of the greatest technical masters of poetry. Even when thus maimed, however, his works found readers and lovers in every generation, and every improvement in his text has set his fame on a surer basis.

Bibliography.—The *Canterbury Tales* have always been Chaucer's most popular work, and, including fragments, upwards of 60 15th century manuscripts of it still survive. Two thin volumes of his minor poems were among the little quartos which Caxton printed by way of advertisement immediately on his return to England; the *Canterbury Tales* and *Boethius* followed in 1478, *Troilus* and a second edition of the *Tales* in 1483, the *Hous of Fame* in 1484. The *Canterbury Tales* were subsequently printed in 1492 (Pynson), 1498 (de Worde) and 1526 (Pynson); *Troilus* in 1517 (de Worde) and 1526 (Pynson); the *Hous of Fame* in 1526 (Pynson); the *Parlement of Foules* in 1526 (Pynson) and 1530 (de Worde), and the *Mars, Venus* and *Envoy to Bukton* by Julyan Notary about 1500. Pynson's three issues in 1526 almost amounted to a collected edition, but the first to which the title *The Workes of Geffray Chaucer* was given was that edited by William Thynne in 1532 for Thomas Godfray. Of this there was a new edition in 1542 for John Reynes and William Bonham, and an undated reprint a few years later for Bonham, Kele, Petit and Toye, each of whom put his name on part of the edition. In 1561 a reprint, with numerous additions, edited by John Stowe, was printed by J. Kyngston for J. Wight, and this was re-edited, with fresh additions by Thomas Speght, in 1598 for G. Bishop and again in 1602 for Adam Islip. In 1687 there was an anonymous reprint, and in 1721 John Urry produced the last and worst of the folios. By this time the paraphrasers were already at work, Dryden rewriting the tales of the Knight, the Nun's Priest and the Wife of Bath, and Pope the Merchant's. In 1737 (reprinted in 1740) the Prologue and Knight's Tale were edited (anonymously) by Thomas Morell "from the most authentic manuscripts," and here, though by dint of much violence and with many mistakes, Chaucer's lines were for the first time in print given in a form in which they could be scanned. This promise of better things was fulfilled by a fine edition of the *Canterbury Tales* (1775–78), in which Thomas Tyrwhitt's scholarly instincts produced a comparatively good text from second-rate manuscripts and accompanied it with valuable illustrative notes. The next edition of any importance was that edited by Thomas Wright for the Percy Society in 1848–51, based on the erratic but valuable British Museum manuscript Harley 7,334. In 1866 Richard Morris re-edited this text in a more scholarly manner for the Aldine edition of the British Poets.

In 1868 the foundation of the Chaucer Society, with Dr. Furnivall as its director and chief worker, and Henry Bradshaw as a leading spirit, led to the publication of a six-text edition of the *Canterbury Tales,* and the consequent discovery that a manuscript belonging to the earl of Ellesmere, though undoubtedly "edited," contained the best available text. The Chaucer Society also printed the best manuscripts of *Troilus and Criseyde* and of all the minor poems, and thus cleared the way for the "Oxford" Chaucer, edited by Prof. Skeat, with a wealth of annotation, for the Clarendon Press in 1894, the text of which was used for the splendid folio printed two years later by William Morris at the Kelmscott Press, with illustrations by Sir Edward Burne-Jones. A supplementary volume of the Oxford edition, entitled *Chaucerian and other Pieces,* issued by Prof. Skeat in 1897, contains the prose and verse which his early publishers and editors, from Pynson and Thynne onwards, included among his Works by way of illustration, but which had gradually come to be regarded as forming part of his text. Many of these pieces have now been traced to other authors, and their exclusion has helped to clear not only Chaucer's text but also his biography, which used (as in the "Life" published by William Godwin in two quarto volumes in 1803) to be encumbered with inferences from works now known not to be Chaucer's, notably the *Testament of Love* written by Thomas Usk. *See* Eleanor P. Hammond, *Chaucer; a Bibliographical Manual* (1909); J. S. P. Tatlock and A. G. Kennedy, *A Concordance to the Complete Works of Geoffrey Chaucer and to the Romaunt of the Rose* (Carnegie Institute, 1927). (A. W. P.)

CHAUDESAIGUES, a village of central France, in the department of Cantal, at the foot of the mountains of Aubrac, 19 mi. S.S.W. of St. Flour. Pop. (1936) 953. It has hot mineral springs, which at their maximum rank as the hottest in France. The water, which contains bicarbonate of soda, is employed medicinally, and also for washing fleeces, incubating eggs and various other economic purposes; and it furnishes a ready means of heating the houses of the town during winter. In the immediate neighbourhood is the cold chalybeate spring of Condamine. The warm springs were known to the Romans, and are mentioned by Sidonius Apollinaris.

CHAUFFEUR. In its anglicized sense, the common name for a professional driver of a motor vehicle. The word is French (from *chauffer,* to heat) and, primarily used for a man in charge of a forge or furnace, came to describe a stoker on a locomotive or steamship.

CHAULIAC, GUY DE (GUIDO DE CAULIACO) (*c.* 1300–1368), French surgeon, was born at Chauliac (Auvergne). He took holy orders and studied at Toulouse, Montpellier and Paris, and then went to Bologna to study anatomy under Nicolo Bertuccio. Chauliac was one of the most learned men of his time, and his book, *Chirurgia magna* (1363), passed through many translations and was for a long time the standard work on the subject, though it tended to retard progress in surgery by advocating meddlesome treatment of wounds. It was first printed in French at Lyons in 1478. In his *Capitulum singulare* he qualifies as an important medical historian. Guy died on July 25, 1368, at Avignon, where he was physician to the pope. He operated for hernia and cataract, which had hitherto been treated mainly by charlatans, and has left a description of the narcotic inhalation given to patients.

See Fielding H. Garrison, *History of Medicine,* p. 156–158 (1929); Arturo Castiglioni, ed. by E. B. Krumbhaar, *History of Medicine,* p. 345–347 (1941).

CHAULIEU, GUILLAUME AMFRYE DE (1639–1720), French poet and wit, was born at Fontenay, Normandy. His father, *maître des comptes* of Rouen, sent him to study at the Collège de Navarre. Louis Joseph, duke of Vendôme, and his brother Philippe, grand prior of the Knights of Malta in France, at that time had a joint establishment at the temple, where they gathered round them a very gay and reckless circle. Chaulieu received the abbey of Aumate and other benefices from the duke; and became the constant companion and adviser of the two princes. He made an expedition to Poland in the suite of the marquis de Béthune, but returned to Paris without securing any advancement. In his later years Chaulieu spent much time at the little court of the duchesse du Maine at Sceaux. There he became the trusted and devoted friend of Mdlle. Delaunay. Among his poems the best known are "Fontenay" and "La Retraite."

Chaulieu's works were edited, with those of his friend the marquis de la Fare, in 1714, 1750 and 1774. *See* also C. A. Sainte-Beuve, *Causeries du lundi,* vol. i; and *Lettres inédites* (1850), with a notice by Raymond, marquis de Berenger.

CHAUMETTE, PIERRE GASPARD (1763–1794), French revolutionary, was born at Nevers on May 24, 1763. Until the revolution he lived a somewhat wandering life, interesting himself particularly in botany. He was a student of medicine at Paris in 1790, became one of the orators of the club of the Cordeliers, and contributed anonymously to the *Révolutions de Paris.* As member of the insurrectionary Commune of Aug. 10, 1792, he was delegated to visit the prisons, with full power to arrest suspects. He was elected president of the Commune, defending the municipality in that capacity at the bar of the convention on Oct. 31, 1792. Chaumette was one of the ringleaders in the attacks of May 31 and of June 2, 1793, on the Girondists, towards whom he showed himself relentless. He was one of the promoters of the worship of reason, and on Nov. 10, 1793, he presented the goddess to the convention in the guise of an actress. On the 23rd he obtained a decree closing all the churches of Paris, and placing the priests under strict surveillance; but on the 25th he retraced his steps and obtained from the commune the free exercise of worship. Robespierre had him accused with the Hébertists; he was arrested, imprisoned in the Luxembourg, condemned by the revolutionary tribunal and executed on April 13, 1794. Chaumette was an ardent social reformer; he secured the abolition of corporal punishment in the schools, the suppression of lotteries, of houses of ill-fame and of obscene literature; he instituted reforms in the hospitals, and insisted on the honours of public burial for the poor.

CHAUMONT, a town of eastern France, capital of the department of Haute-Marne, a railway junction 163 mi. E.S.E. of Paris on the main line of the Eastern railway to Belfort. Pop. (1936) 17,389. Chaumont is situated on high ground at the confluence of the Marne and Suize. It received a charter from the counts of Champagne in 1190. The church of St. Jean-Baptiste dates from the 13th century, the choir and lateral chapels belonging to the 15th and 16th. The sculptured triforium (15th century), the spiral staircase in the transept and a Holy Sepulchre are of interest. The Tour Hautefeuille (a keep of the 11th century) is the principal relic of a château of the counts of Champagne; the rest of the site is occupied by the law courts. In 1814 Great Britain, Austria, Russia and Prussia concluded at Chaumont the treaty by which they bound themselves not to conclude a separate peace and to prosecute the Napoleonic war to a successful issue. Chaumont is the seat of a prefect and of a court of assizes, and has tribunals of first instance and of commerce. The main industries are glovemaking and leather dressing. The town has trade in grain, iron (mined in the vicinity) and leather.

CHAUNCEY, ISAAC (1772–1840), U.S. naval commander, was born at Black Rock, Conn., Feb. 20, 1772. He was brought up in the merchant service, and entered the U.S. navy as a lieutenant in 1798. The most active period of his life was that of his command on the Great Lakes during the War of 1812. He took the command at Sackett's harbour on Lake Ontario in Oct. 1812. Commodore Chauncey brought from 400 to 500 officers and men with him, and local resources for building being abundant, he had by November formed a squadron of ten vessels, with which he attacked the Canadian port, York, taking it in April 1813. The Americans had the advantage of commanding greater resources for shipbuilding. Sir James Yeo began by blockading Sackett's harbour early in 1814, but when the U.S. squadron was ready he was compelled to retire by the disparity of the forces. Commodore Chauncey was now able to blockade the British flotilla at Kingston. During his later years he served as commissioner of the navy, and was president of the board of naval commissioners from 1833 till his death at Washington, Feb. 27, 1840.

See Roosevelt's *War of 1812* (1882); and A. T. Mahan, *Sea Power in its Relations to the War of 1812* (1905); also *see* E. Channing, *History of the United States,* vol. iv (1926).

CHAUNCY, CHARLES (1592–1672), president of Harvard college, was born at Yardley-Bury, England, in Nov. 1592, and attended Trinity college, Cambridge. He was in turn vicar at Ware and at Marston St. Lawrence, but twice incurred censure from the authorities for nonconformity. His formal recantation in Feb. 1637 caused him lasting self-reproach. In this same year he emigrated to America, where he was an associate pastor at Plymouth, then pastor at Scituate (Mass.), and, from 1654 until his death, president of Harvard college. He died on Feb. 19, 1672. According to Mather, he was "a most incomparable scholar." His writings include: *The Plain Doctrine of the Justification of a Sinner in the Sight of God* (1659) and *Antisynodalia Scripta Americana* (1662).

His great-grandson, CHARLES CHAUNCY (1705–1787), a prominent U.S. theologian, was born in Boston (Mass.), on Jan. 1, 1705, and graduated at Harvard in 1721. In 1727 he was chosen as the colleague of Thomas Foxcroft in the First Church of Boston, continuing as pastor until his death. He condemned the "Great Awakening" as an outbreak of emotional extravagance in his sermon *Enthusiasm,* and in his *Seasonable Thoughts on the State of Religion in New England* (1743), written in answer to Jonathan Edwards' *Some Thoughts Concerning the Present Revival of Religion in New England* (1742). Before and during the War of Independence he ardently supported the patriot party. He died in Boston on Feb. 10, 1787. His publications include: *Salvation of All Men, Illustrated and Vindicated as a Scripture Doctrine* (1782) and *Five Dissertations on the Fall and its Consequences* (1785).

For Charles Chauncy *see* Cotton Mather's *Magnalia Christi Americana* (1702) and W. C. Fowler's *Memorials of the Chauncys* (1858). For the younger Chauncy *see* P. L. Ford's privately printed *Bibliotheca Chaunciana* (1884), and Williston Walker's *Ten New England Leaders* (1901).

CHAUNY, a town of northern France in the department of Aisne, 19 mi. S. by W. of St. Quentin by rail. Pop. (1946) 9,330. The town is situated on the Oise (which here becomes navigable) and at the junction of the canal of St. Quentin with the lateral canal of the Oise. It contains mirror-polishing works, chemical works and metal foundries. It was the scene of much fighting in the Hundred Years' War.

CHAUTAUQUA, Chautauqua county, N.Y., U.S., a summer centre of music, popular education and recreation, is located on the beautifully wooded west shore of Chautauqua lake. The resident population in 1950 was 4,082, but the summer program of symphony concerts, lectures, plays, operas, summer-school courses, religious works activities and recreation attracts an average of 50,000 summer visitors.

Originally established as a Sunday school assembly in 1874 by John Heyl Vincent and Lewis Miller, it operates about 30 public buildings and an outdoor amphitheatre seating 7,000 persons. Chautauqua maintains the Chautauqua Literary and Scientific circle, founded in 1878.

CHAUVIGNY, a town of western France in the department of Vienne, 20 mi. E. of Poitiers by rail. Pop. (1946) 3,914. The town is finely situated overlooking the Vienne, and has two interesting Romanesque churches, both restored in modern times. It was a strong fortress in the middle ages, and still possesses the ruins of no less than five castles, the chief of which is the Château Baronnial (11th and 15th centuries) the old seat of the bishops of Poitiers, who were lords of Chauvigny.

CHAUVINISM, a term for unreasonable and exaggerated patriotism, the French equivalent of "Jingoism." The word originally signified idolatry of Napoleon, being taken from a much-wounded veteran, Nicholas Chauvin, who, by his adoration of the emperor, became the type of blind enthusiasm for military glory.

CHAUX DE FONDS, LA, an industrial town in the Swiss canton of Neuchâtel, about 19m. by rail N.W. of Neuchâtel, at a height of about 3,250ft. in a valley of the same name in the Jura. Pop. (1930) 35,252; mainly Protestant (27,306) and French-speaking; of the Catholic faith, the majority are "Old Catholics." It is a centre of the watch-making industry. There are schools of watch-making and of industrial art.

See *Dict. hist. et biogr. de la Suisse,* ii.

CHAVANTEAN, a small independent linguistic stock of South American Indians, so called from the Chavantes or Caingangs, its most important tribe. The Chavantean tribes are found to-day on the upper Parana and Lower Paranapanema rivers, in the state of São Paulo, Brazil. They formerly occupied a somewhat larger territory. These Chavantes are to be carefully distinguished from the tribe of the same name in the States of Goyaz and Matto Grosso, who belong to the Ges stock. The Chavantes are quite dark-skinned, rather timid hunting folk, of very primitive culture. They are very little known. Both sexes wear small bast breech-clouts, but no other clothing. Their dwellings are tiny thatched huts, and their weapons the bow and spear. They have no pottery or textiles.

See H. von Ihering, *The Anthropology of the State of S. Paulo, Brazil* (2nd ed. S. Paulo, 1906).

CHAVASSE, FRANCIS JAMES (1846–1928), the son of Thomas Chavasse, of Sutton Coldfield, and brother of Sir Thomas Chavasse, the Birmingham surgeon, was born on Sept. 27, 1846. He was educated privately, and later at Corpus Christi college, Oxford. He was ordained in 1870, and in 1878 became vicar of St. Peter-le-Bailey, Oxford, and a year later principal of Wycliffe hall. In 1900, on the resignation of Dr. J. C. Ryle, the first bishop of Liverpool, Chavasse was appointed to the vacant see. He was remarkable for his ability in finding common interests for people of very different types and holding very different views, and in bringing tnem together to work for a common purpose. This gift proved invaluable in the execution of the great scheme for the building of Liverpool cathedral (on the plans designed by Sir Giles Gilbert Scott, R.A.) with which his name will always be associated. He resigned his bishopric in 1923, owing to his advanced years, and died on March 11, 1928.

CHAVES, a town of northern Portugal, in the district of Vila Real, 8 mi. S. of the Spanish frontier. Pop. (1940), 8,822. Chaves is the ancient *Aquae Flaviae,* famous for its hot saline springs, which are still in use. A fine Roman bridge of 18 arches spans the Tamega. Chaves was long one of the principal frontier fortresses, and may derive its present name from the position which makes it the "keys" (*chaves*) of the north. One of its churches contains the tomb of Alphonso I. of Portugal (1139–85).

CHEADLE, a small town in the urban district of Cheadle and Gatley (pop. 1938, 26,220), in Cheshire, England, 6m. S. of Manchester. The name occurs in the formerly separate villages of Cheadle Hulme, Cheadle Bulkeley and Cheadle Moseley. Cheadle is one of the numerous townships of modern growth which fringe the southern boundaries of Manchester, and practically form suburbs of that city. Stockport lies immediately to the east. There are cotton printing and bleaching works in the locality.

CHEADLE, market town of north Staffordshire, England, 10 mi. E. of Stoke, on the L.M.S.R. Pop. civil parish (1931) 6,754. The Roman Catholic church of St. Giles, with a lofty spire, was designed by Pugin and erected in 1846. There are three collieries in the neighbourhood, and a large textile manufactory in the town. Metal-working is also carried on.

CHEATING, "the fraudulently obtaining the property of another by any deceitful practice not amounting to felony, which practice is of such a nature that it directly affects, or may directly affect, the public at large" (Stephen, *Digest of Criminal Law*). Cheating is either a common law or statutory offence, and is punishable as a misdemeanour. An indictment for cheating at common law is of comparatively rare occurrence, and the statutory crime usually presents itself in the form of obtaining money by false pretences (*q.v.*).

CHEBICHEV, PAFNUTIY LVOVICH (1821–1894), after N. I. Lobachevskiy, the most distinguished of Russian mathematicians, was born at Borovsk on May 26, 1821. Educated at the University of Moscow in 1859, he became professor of mathematics in the University of St. Petersburg, a position from which he retired in 1880. He became a correspondent in 1860, and in 1874 *associé étranger* of the Institute of France. He was also a foreign member of the Royal Society of London. In 1841 he published a valuable paper, "Sur la convergence de la série de Taylor," in *Crelle's Journal.* He wrote much on prime numbers; in one paper ("Sur les nombres premiers," 1850) he established the existence of limits within which must be comprised the sum of the logarithms of the primes inferior to a given number. He devoted much attention to the problem of obtaining rectilinear motion by linkage. The "Chebichev's parallel motion" is a three-bar linkage, which gives a very close approximation to exact rectilinear motion, but he failed to devise one producing true rectilinear motion. Such a linkage was discovered by one of his pupils, Lipkin, who, however, had been anticipated by A. Peaucellier. His mathematical writings cover a wide range of subjects, such as the theory of probabilities, quadratic forms, theory of integrals, gearings, the construction of geographical maps, etc. He also published a *Traité de la théorie des nombres.* He died at St. Petersburg on Dec. 8, 1894.

CHEBOYGAN, a city of Michigan, U.S.A., on south channel of the Strait of Mackinac, at the mouth of the Cheboygan river; a port of entry and the county seat of Cheboygan county. It is on federal highways 23 and 27, and is served by the New York Central and the Detroit and Mackinac railways, by air and bus lines, and by lake steamers during the navigation season. The population in 1950 was 5,507. Cheboygan is in the heart of the summer resort region of northern Michigan, and is surrounded by a farming, stock-raising and fruitgrowing country. The city has sundry manufacturing industries, and is an important fishing port. There are large apple orchards and an apple juice factory. Cheboygan (at first called Duncan and later Inverness) was settled in 1846 and chartered as a city in 1889. Cheboygan is the home port of the United States coast guard icebreaker "Mackinaw."

CHECHENO-INGUSHETIA. This autonomous republic in the North Caucasian area of the Russian Soviet Federated Socialist Republic was created an autonomous republic in Dec. 1936. Area, 6,062 sq.mi. Pop. (1939) 697,408; 498,739 rural, 198,669 urban. It consists mainly of the densely wooded slopes of the Northern Caucasus, and extends from the Caucasus to the Terek river, and from North Ossetian A.S.S.R. and Kabardino-Balkaria to Daghestan. In the north the forest thins out and its place is taken by steppe with chestnut brown soil, less fertile than the black earth, but suitable for agriculture in years of good rainfall. The latter varies in quantity in the north, but is more abundant on the southern hill slopes. The density of population is about 115 per sq.mi.; the Chechens are the most numerous of the native hill tribes in the North Caucasian area, forming 58.4% of the total population. The Ingush represent only about 12.4% of the total population. The Chechen, Tchetchen (or Khists [Kisti], as they are called by the Georgians) call themselves "Nakhtche" (people). They fought fiercely against Russian aggression under Daûd Beg, Oman Khan and Shamyl, in the 18th century, and under Khazi-Mollah in the 19th century. Many of them migrated to Armenia in 1859, after the surrender of their chieftain Shamyl. They are Mohammedans, and they are governed by popular assembly in each commune, every man considering himself free and equal to his neighbour. Towards the north settled agriculture has been introduced by Russian immigrants and winter wheat, millet, oats and barley are grown. Working cattle are used in preference to horses. But, in the southern hill oak, beech, birch and pine forest and alpine pasture area, the Chechens are hunters or nomad herdsmen, taking their goats and sheep to the high meadows in the spring, and descending in autumn to the lower, more sheltered areas. They sow oats and barley under great difficulties, often having to remove the stones brought down by the spring floods from their tiny cultivated patches, and even in summer snow may fall.

Their goats supply them with milk, and their sheep with meat, leather and wool; koustar (peasant) industries include spinning, weaving, preparing leather and the making of knives and daggers. Bees are kept and a sawmilling industry is being developed.

Cultural life is at a low level: there is a high percentage of illiteracy, and this, combined with the absence of roads and the impossibility of using the mountain streams (the Sunzha and Argun and their tributaries) for passenger navigation, makes cultural and economic progress difficult. Many mountain Chechens and Ingush alike live in windowless hovels of mud and stone in the winter, and, in the summer, on the Alpine pastures, improvise shelters from boughs.

The two main roads are from Grozny to Shatoi on the Argun river, and a road farther east almost parallel to it, passing south into Daghestan. There is telegraphic communication along these roads.

From Gydermes junction a loop of the Caspian-Black sea railway passes through Grozny to Beslan, from which a branch goes to Orjonikidze (Vladikavkaz).

CHECKERS, the name by which the British game of draughts is known in the United States.

See DRAUGHTS OR CHECKERS.

CHEDDAR, town, Somersetshire, England, 22 mi. S.W. of Bristol by G.W.R. Pop. (1931) 2,154. To the west lies the low Axe valley, to the east rise immediately southwest the Mendip cliffs (600–800 ft.) of Cheddar gorge, with beautiful stalactitic caverns, of which Cox's and Gough's are best known. The remains discovered in the caves (particularly Gough's after 1928) and elsewhere in the neighbourhood give evidence of prehistoric and Roman settlements at Cheddar (*Cedre, Chedare*), which was a convenient trade centre. The manor of Cheddar was a royal demesne in Saxon times, and the witenagemot was held there in 966 and 968. It was granted by John in 1204 to Hugh, archdeacon of Wells. The bishop of Bath and Wells granted it to the king in 1553. It is now owned by the marquess of Bath. By a charter of 1231 extensive liberties in the manor of Cheddar were granted to Bishop Joceline, who in 1235 obtained the right to hold a weekly market and fair. By a charter of Edward III (1337) Cheddar was removed from the king's forest of Mendip. The market and stock fairs have long been discontinued, the former in about 1690. The name of Cheddar is given to a well-known species of cheese, the manufacture of which began in the 17th century in the town and neighbourhood.

CHEDUBA or **MAN-AUNG,** an island in the Bay of Bengal, situated 10 mi. from the coast of Arakan, between 18° 40′ and 18° 56′ N., and between 93° 31′ and 93° 50′ E. It forms part of the Kyaukpyu district of Arakan. It extends about 20 mi. in length from north to south, and 17 mi. from east to west, and its area of 220 sq.mi. supports a population of nearly 30,000. The channel between the island and the mainland is navigable for boats, but not for large vessels. The surface of the interior is richly diversified by hill and dale, and in the southern portion some of the heights exceed 1,000 ft. in elevation. There are various indications of former volcanic activity, and along the coast are earthy cones covered with green-sward, from which issue springs of muddy water emitting bubbles of gas. Copper, iron and silver ore have been discovered; but the island is chiefly noted for its petroleum wells. The inhabitants of the island are mainly Maghs. Cheduba fell to the Burmese in the latter part of the 18th century, and was taken by the British in 1824.

CHEERING, the uttering or making of sounds encouraging, stimulating or exciting to action, indicating approval or acclaiming or welcoming persons, announcements of events and the like. The word "cheer" meant originally face, countenance, expression (Low Lat. *cara*), and was at first qualified with epithets, both of joy and sorrow; compare "She thanked Dyomede for alle . . . his gode chere" (Chaucer, *Troylus*) with "If they sing . . . 'tis with so dull a cheere" (Shakespeare, *Sonnets*, xcvii.). An early transference in meaning was to hospitality or entertainment, and hence to food and drink, "good cheer." The sense of a shout of encouragement or applause is a late use.

Of the different words or sounds that are used in cheering, "hurrah," though now generally looked on as the typical British form of cheer, is found in various forms in German, Scandinavian, Russian (*urá*), French (*houra*); it is probably onomatopoeic in origin. The German *hoch*, the French *vive*, Italian and Spanish *viva, evviva*, are cries rather of acclamation than encouragement. The Japanese shout, *banzai*, became familiar during the Russo-Japanese War. In reports of parliamentary debates "cheers" indicates that approval was shown by emphatic utterances of "hear hear." Cheering may be tumultuous or it may be conducted rhythmically by prearrangement, as in the case of the "Hip-hip-hip" by way of introduction to a simultaneous "hurrah."

Rhythmical cheering has been developed to its greatest extent in America in the college yells, which may be regarded as a development of the primitive war-cry. The original yells of Harvard and Yale are identical in form, being composed of *rah* (abbreviation of *hurrah*) nine times repeated, shouted in unison with the name of the university at the end. The Yale cheer is given faster than that of Harvard. Many institutions have several different yells; the best known of these variants is the Yale cheer, partly taken from the *Frogs* of Aristophanes:

Brekekekéx, ko-áx, ko-áx,
Brekekekéx, ko-áx, ko-áx,
O-óp, O-óp, parabaloú,
Yale, Yale, Yale,
Rah, rah, rah, rah, rah, rah,
rah, rah, rah,
Yale! Yale! Yale!

The "triple cheer" of Princeton is:

H'ray, h'ray, h'ray,
Tiger, tiger, tiger,
Siss, siss, siss,
Boom, boom, boom,
Ah, ah, ah,
Princetón, Princetón, Princetón!

The "railroad cheer" is like the foregoing, but begun very slowly and broadly, and gradually accelerated to the end, which is enunciated as fast as possible. Many cheers are formed like that of Toronto university:

Varsitý, varsitý,
V-a-r-s-i-t-y (spelled)
VARSIT-Y (spelled *staccato*)
Vár-si-tý,
Rah, rah, rah!

The cheer of the United States Naval academy is an imitation of a nautical siren. The Amherst cheer is:

Amherst! Amherst! Amherst! Rah! Rah!
Amherst! Rah! Rah!
Rah! Rah! Rah! Rah! Rah! Rah! Amherst!

Besides the cheers of individual institutions there are some common to all, generally used to compliment some successful athlete or popular professor. One of the oldest examples of these personal cheers is:

Who was George Washington?
First in war,
First in peace,
First in the heárts of his countrymén,

followed by a stamping on the floor in the same rhythm.

College yells are used particularly at athletic contests. In any large college there are several leaders, chosen by the students, who stand in front and call for the different songs and cheers, directing with their arms in the fashion of an orchestral conductor. Cheering and singing form one of the distinctive features of intercollegiate and scholastic athletic contests in America.

CHEESE. The consolidated curd of milk is used as food in most parts of the world. The product is of many varieties, textures and flavours, depending on the animal source (mainly the cow, less frequently the sheep or goat and rarely the mare, llama, reindeer, buffalo, zebra or yak), acidity, fat and other characteristics of the milk and the nature of the processing and curing which it undergoes. The result is that 100 lb. of milk is reduced to 8–13 lb. of a highly nutritious, semistorable food. Cheese contains nearly all the fat, casein, calcium and vitamin A and part of the milk sugar and salts of the milk from which it was made. It is difficult to present comprehensive food value figures for such a variable food, but Cheddar and some other hard, whole-milk cheeses are about 25% protein and 31% fat and give approximately 387 cal. per 100 g. retail weight.

The beginning of cheese making and its use by early herdsmen thousands of years ago is unrecorded. History does record the use of cheese by many early peoples, and the Old Testament contains a number of references to it. The Greeks and Romans are supposed to have had cheese as a staple food at least a thousand years before the beginning of the Christian era. The Jews and the Romans are said to have recognized the strength-giving properties of cheese and to have fed it to their armies because of its convenient concentrated form, and the Greeks gave it to their wrestlers to increase their endurance.

Production and Processing.—Cheese making has largely moved from the individual art stage to one of scientific technology. High-quality, clean milk from healthy animals, without undesirable odours and not overripe, is preferable and even necessary. Pasteurization of milk for cheese making has come into general use in some areas for some types, permitting better control of quality, a more uniform product and better keeping characteristics. The first successful applications were to soft, unripened types, but later the process was adapted to the ripened cheese types such as Cheddar. Treatment of milk to get cheese and the processing of the green cheese, depending partly upon cheese type desired but also upon equipment and technology available, have many variations.

Among the simpler steps involved with the American type are the following: A lactic acid starter may be introduced to attain the degree of acidity desired, after which the temperature of the milk is raised to about 86° F., colour added and enough rennet or pepsin added to coagulate the milk into a firm, jellylike curd in about 30 undisturbed minutes. The curd is then cut and stirred, the curd and whey heated slowly to 100°–106° F. for one to two hours, at which time the curd reaches a desirable firmness, and the whey is removed. The curd is stirred, cooled to about 90° F. and salted, placed on a cap cloth, hooped and pressed under 40 to 60 lb. pressure for 30 to 60 minutes. Then the cap cloths are removed, surface fat is removed with warm water and the cheese is bandaged with light, unbleached cotton cloth; the cap cloths are replaced and the cheese is rehooped and pressed for 16 to 24 hours under 100–120 lb. of pressure, at which time it should have developed a sound rind. It is then cured, preferably at 50°–60° F. The bandage is removed if the humidity of the curing room is sufficiently high so that the rind does not become overdry and crack. In about six days the surface may be sufficiently dried to be paraffined, after which it is only necessary to turn the cheese periodically or otherwise care for it to keep it clean and free from mould. Depending partly on the temperature of the curing room, it may reach a desirable body and flavour for consumption in about six weeks, but it may be held five months or longer.

VARIETIES OF CHEESE

There are several possible ways of classifying cheeses, no one of which seems satisfactory for all purposes. For one purpose it may be more desirable to classify them according to methods of making; for another purpose the characteristics of the cheese may be more satisfactory. One common classification recognizes three groups—soft, semihard and hard. This grouping, however, is based almost entirely on the texture of the product when it is ready for consumption. In general the soft cheeses are those made by souring the milk with lactic acid; they are eaten within a few days after making. The hard cheeses are those made by coagulating the protein with rennet, cooking and pressing the curd and ripening with moulds or bacteria for several months or several years before they are ready to be eaten. Semihard cheeses fall between these two groups, and the process may have features in common with both.

All these types of cheese are known as the "natural" cheeses. Many of them are subjected to further treatment or processing, even smoking, which has the effect of producing an entirely new or different product, known as "processed cheese." In making processed cheese, one or more lots of a natural cheese or of several kinds of natural cheese or of cheeses of different ripeness or inferior texture and flavour may be ground up, melted and blended with various seasoning materials. The liquid is then forced into forms of the shape desired, cooled and packaged in containers for direct sale to consumers. The manufacture of processed cheese, though a comparatively modern phase of the cheese industry, developed rapidly.

Methods of making and handling cheese evolved more or less independently in widely separated regions. In many instances the practices were closely associated with local conditions of climate, agriculture and habits of the people, which not only resulted in characteristic differences in cheeses made in the different regions but also gave rise to a vast number of names. Apparently it was the custom of the earliest cheese-making peoples to name the product after the village or country in which it was made. In many instances local and regional names represent no real difference in type from that of cheese made under other names elsewhere, although the cheeses made in the various localities and countries may have certain distinguishing characteristics. Frequently these differences may be only in the shape or size of the cheese, or they may be in the flavour and texture resulting from different methods of cooking the curd or curing the cheese. Differences in ripening practices may give rise to considerable differences in quality even in cheese made from the same curd. Although cheese is marketed throughout the world under 400 to

500 different names, there are probably only about 18 distinct varieties.

Some of the distinctive differences in these varieties as briefed from K. J. Matheson (see *Bibliography,* below) are as follows:

Brick cheese is strictly an American product. Its name is supposed to have come from its shape or from the practice of using bricks to weight down the curd in the moulds. The curd is pressed in the small moulds—about 3 by 6 by 10 in.—for 24 hours, after which the prints are removed, salted and taken to the curing cellar where the cheese ripens in two or three months. Brick cheese has a strong, sweetish taste somewhat like Emmentaler or Swiss cheese and an aroma mildly resembling Limburger. The body of the cheese is rather elastic and contains numerous small, round holes or eyes.

Caciocavallo cheese is a peculiar kind of cheese made from either whole or partly skimmed milk of cows. It originated in Italy several centuries ago. One explanation of the name, which means literally "horse cheese," is that the cheese was first made in the region of Monte Cavallo; another is that the imprint of a horse's head appeared on each cheese as a trade mark of the original maker. The curd is moulded into any desired shape or size, usually about three pounds, and after the moulded shapes have been immersed in brine for several days they are suspended in pairs from the ceiling and smoked. The most common shape resembles a beet, the constriction at the top being caused by the string by which it hangs. This cheese is sometimes eaten while comparatively fresh, but is more frequently kept for months, then grated and used in soups or macaroni and similar foods. A small quantity is imported into the United States, and some is made in Wisconsin, Michigan and Pennsylvania.

Camembert cheese is a soft rennet cheese made from cows' milk. A typical cheese is about 4½ in. in diameter and 1 in. thick, and as marketed in the United States is usually found wrapped in paper and enclosed in a wooden box of the same shape. The cheese usually has a rind about ⅛-in. thick, which is composed of moulds and dried cheese. The interior is yellowish in color and waxy, creamy or almost fluid in consistency, depending largely upon the degree of ripeness. The flavour is similar to Limburger but not so strong. Four to six weeks of ripening is required before this cheese is in condition for the market. Camembert cheese is said to have originated in 1791 in the locality from which it derives its name in the northwestern part of France. Cheese of the same type, however, is made in other parts of France and also in other countries, including New York and Wisconsin in the United States.

Similar types are known as Brie, Coulommiers, Robbiola and Ripened Neufchâtel.

Cheddar cheese gets its name from the village of Cheddar in Somersetshire, England, where it was first made many years ago. It is very popular as a food product both in England and in the United States. It was exported from the United States as early as 1790 and is today the most important variety made in that country, its manufacture accounting for about 90% of the total cheese production. The cheese is made from whole milk of cows or from skim milk or partly skimmed milk. The term "Cheddar" as known and used today refers principally to a phase of the making process. The finished cheese may be white or yellow, and it may be used after only three or four months of ripening, when it has a very mild flavour, or after one or two years of curing to develop a sharp or snappy flavour. American Cheddar cheese is frequently known and retailed merely as American or "store" cheese, "cream," "Yankee," "Wisconsin" or "New York" cheese. In California this cheese is known as Jack or Monterey cheese. It is made in several sizes and shapes with more or less distinguishing names, such as Long Horns, Daisies, Twins, Flats and Cheddars or Exports. These sizes range from 5 to 16 in. in diameter, 4 to 16 in. in height and 10 to 100 lb. in weight. This variety has been packaged and cured in cans, to afford a convenient and attractive form in which to merchandise it. A one-way valve on the can permits ripening gases to escape and excludes air; thus curing in the can is possible.

Cottage cheese is an unripened, soft, sour-milk cheese made extensively in the United States, where it is often called Dutch cheese or smearcase. It is made both in the home and in the factory, from skim milk, with or without the addition of rennet. It is highly nutritious and palatable, contains all the food value of milk except the cream, and may be used as the main part of the meal or in salads, desserts or cooked dishes. Properly made, it has a clean, milk, acid flavour and smooth texture. Factory production increased markedly during and after World War I, as a result of educational campaigns directed toward the utilization of skim milk to conserve meats and other foods. The cheese is perishable and must be kept at low temperatures until consumed.

Cream cheese is a soft, mild, rich, uncured cheese made of cream or a mixture of cream and milk. In general, lactic acid culture, with or without rennet, is added to the pasteurized cream or cream mixture, which may be homogenized. It is held until it coagulates. The coagulated mass may be warmed and stirred; it is then drained. The curd may be pressed, chilled, worked, seasoned with salt; or it may be heated, with or without added cream or milk, until it becomes fluid and then homogenized or otherwise mixed. Flavouring materials, such as pimentos, pineapple or relish, may be added. It is packed usually in foil or in glasses with sealed metal tops. The finished cheese should contain not less than 33% of fat and not more than 55% of moisture.

Edam cheese is a hard rennet cheese produced in the Netherlands; it is also known as Katzenkopf, Tête de Maure and Manbollen. Formerly Edam cheese was made from whole milk on the farms in North Holland, but today it is usually made of skimmed milk. The genuine Edam cheese contains at least 40% fat, although many creameries make a cheese of the same shape with only 20% to 30% fat. All Edam cheese for export bears the government guarantee of the fat content. The cheese is round but flattened at the top and bottom, and the outside is coloured red; or the cheese is packed in tin foil and, for export to hot countries, in bladders or tins. When the cheeses are a few weeks old they are marketed and the ripening process continues in the warehouses of the cheese merchants. Some is made in Wisconsin, and the imported product is well known in all large markets.

Emmentaler cheese is a hard rennet cheese made from cows' milk and is somewhat sweetish in flavour. It is characterized by holes or eyes, about the size of a cent, about one to three inches apart throughout the cheese. This cheese originated in the Emmental valley of Switzerland and is a very old variety, reported as early as the middle of the 15th century in the canton of Emmental. Its manufacture in France in 1722 under the name of Gruyère is recorded. It is now made in every civilized country. That made in the United States is known as Domestic Swiss, and that in the region of Lake Constance is called Algau Emmentaler. Other local names are Bellunese, Formaggio Dolce, Fontine d'Aosta and Thraanen. Only the best grades are imported into the United States. The cheeses are like massive solid wheels, six inches thick and sometimes four feet in diameter, and weigh from 60 to 220 lb. each. Ripening requires three to six months. Scientific studies by the bureau of dairy industry of the U.S. department of agriculture established a controlled procedure in many factories, which facilitates the manufacture of a uniformly good-quality cheese. Whereas the original makers depended on nature to introduce the necessary bacteria into the milk, modern makers now introduce "pure cultures" to bring about the desired action as follows: (1) the *Lactobacillus bulgaricus* to check undesirable fermentation and to aid in controlling ripening, and (2) the use of an eye and flavour culture to aid in the development of eyes and flavour.

Gorgonzola cheese, known also as Stracchino di Gorgonzola, is a rennet Italian cheese made from whole milk of cows. Its name comes from Gorgonzola, near Milan, but very little of the cheese is now made there. The interior of the cheese is mottled or veined with a penicillium much like Roquefort. As seen on the markets of the United States, the surface of the cheese is covered with a thin coat resembling clay, said to be prepared by mixing barite or gypsum, lard or tallow and colouring matter. These cheeses are cylindrical, being about 12 in. in diameter and 6 in. in height. As marketed they are packed with straw in wicker baskets. Well-made cheeses may be kept a year or longer, but much is consumed fresh in the region where it is made. In England a similar type of cheese, known as Stilton, is made from cows' milk and is imported in quantities into the United States.

Gouda cheese is a sweet-curd Netherlands cheese made from cows' milk. The full-cream Gouda is mainly a farm product made chiefly in the provinces of South Holland and Utrecht, with an average fat content of 50%. Gouda made in creameries from partly skimmed milk has a fat content of 20% to 40%. The fat content is guaranteed by the government mark on the cheese. In shape Gouda cheese is cylindrical with the sharp edges rounded off. The cheeses weigh from 6½ to 44 lb. Ripening requires six to eight weeks. This cheese is commonly found on the larger markets in the United States.

Hand cheese is so named because originally it was moulded by hand into its final shape. It is a sour-milk cheese, very popular among German peoples, and is made in many countries. The process varies in different localities, but in general the curd is cooled in moulds, then ground fine in a curd mill (in some kinds caraway seed is added), then ripened on shelves in the curing room. The cheese has a sharp, pungent odour and taste, which is very disagreeable to most people unaccustomed to it. It is known by such local names as Thuringia Caraway cheese; Ihlefeld, in Mecklenburg; and Livlander in the U.S.S.R.

Limburger cheese is a soft rennet cheese made from cows' milk which may contain all the butter fat or may be partly or entirely skimmed. The best Limburger is undoubtedly made from the whole milk. This cheese has a very strong and characteristic odour and taste, weighs about two pounds and is about 6 by 3 in. in size. It requires about two months to ripen. The most common synonyms of Limburger are Backstein and Hervé. It has, however, many local names, such as Algau, Lanark, Marianhof, Morin, Saint Michels, Schutzen, Tanzenberg, Carinthian, Grottenhof, Emmersdorf, Briol and Lindenhof. Limburger cheese originated in the province of Lüttich, Belgium, in the neighbourhood of Hervé. Its manufacture spread to Germany and Austria, where it is very popular, and to the United States, where large quantities are made, mostly in New York and Wisconsin. Contrary to popular belief, Limburger is no longer imported into the United States, since the domestic product is of good quality and is made cheaply.

Neufchâtel cheese is a soft rennet cheese made extensively in France, from either whole or skim milk of cows. Bondon, Malakoff, Petit Carre and Petit Suisse are essentially the same as Neufchâtel but have slightly different shapes. Neufchâtel cheese is made in the same manner as cream cheese, except that a little less rennet is used. The standard package, wrapped in tin foil, is round and weighs 2½ to 3 oz., its dimensions being 1½ by 2½ in. Factories in the United States make a variation of the Neufchâtel cheese which is probably as good as the French variety. American makers attempt to vary this cheese by the use of condiments. Pimento, or Pepper Cream, is a Neufchâtel cheese in which one pound of red peppers is used for every ten pounds of cheese. The peppers are ground very fine and thoroughly mixed; the whole is then moulded and kept in a cold place.

Parmesan cheese is the name in common use outside Italy for the cheese made and known in that country for centuries as Grana, the term "grana" or "granona" referring to its granular appearance when broken, which is necessary because of the hardness of the cheese, cutting being practically impossible. There are two quite distinct kinds of cheese, one made in Lombardy and the other in Emilia. Parma, situated in Emilia, has long been an important commercial centre for both kinds, and from this fact the name of Parmesan results. The use of the term "Parmesan," however, is sometimes restricted to the cheese made in Lombardy, the term "Reggian" being used to designate that made in Emilia. The cheeses are ripened in a cool, well-ventilated room, where they may be stored for years, the surface being rubbed with oil from time to time. The exterior of the cheese is dark green or black, because of colouring matter rubbed on the surface. A greenish colour in the interior has been attributed to contamination with copper from the vessels in which the milk is allowed to stand before skimming. Parmesan cheese when well made may be broken and grated easily and may be kept for an indefinite number of years. It is grated and used largely for soups and with macaroni. A considerable quantity of this cheese is imported into the United States and sells for a very high price.

Pecorino cheese is a sheep's milk cheese made in Italy, and there are numerous more or less clearly defined kinds. The most common sort is the one designated Cacio Pecorino Romano, or merely Romano. This varies considerably in size and shape. A cheese of ordinary size is about 10 in. in diameter and 6 in. in thickness and weighs from 2 to 25 lb. The interior is slightly greenish in colour, somewhat granular and devoid of eyes or holes. Ripening requires eight months or longer. The Pecorino Dolce is artificially coloured with annatto and subjected to considerable pressure in the process of manufacture. Pecorino Tuscano is a smaller cheese than the Romano, measuring usually 6 in. in diameter and 2 or 4 in. in thickness and weighing from two to five pounds. Among the sheep's milk cheeses bearing local names are the following: Ancona, Cotrone, Iglesias, Leonessa, Puglia and Viterbo. In the manufacture of Viterbo cheese the milk is curdled by means of a wild artichoke, *Cynara scolymus*.

Roquefort cheese is a soft rennet cheese made principally from sheep's milk, although some cows' milk and goats' milk may be added. Numerous imitations, such as Gex and Septmoncel, are made from cows' milk. One of the most striking characteristics is the mottled or marbled appearance of the interior of the cheese, resulting from the development of a penicillium, which is the principal ripening agent. The manufacture of Roquefort has been carried on in the southeastern part of France at least since the beginning of the 18th century, and is particularly important in the village of Roquefort, from which the cheese derives its name. One interesting phase of the making process is the sifting of mouldy bread crumbs between layers of curd as it is placed in the forms or hoops, to bring about the desired ripening. Formerly the manufacture of the cheese up to curing time was carried on by the shepherds themselves, but today centralized factories collect the milk and make the cheese, which is still cured in the natural caves near Roquefort. The cheese may be sold after from 30 to 40 days or may remain in the caves as long as five months, depending on the degree of ripening desired. This type of cheese is made from cows' milk in Denmark. In the United States this type has been made since 1918, from cows' milk and with artificial curing conditions. Such American-made cheese has been ripened in natural caves along the Mississippi river in Minnesota and in an abandoned shaft of a coal mine in Pennsylvania.

Sapsago cheese is made principally in Glarus, Switz., from sour skim milk of cows. It is also known as Schabzieger, Glarnerkäse, Grünerkäse and Kräuterkäse. It is claimed that it was made in the 13th century; its authentic history at least dates back to the 15th century. Sapsago is a small, hard, green cheese flavoured with the leaves of an aromatic clover grown for the purpose. It is shaped like a truncated cone, 4 in. high, 3 in. in diameter at the base and 2 in. at the top. A comparatively small quantity is shipped into the United States under the name of Sap Sago, where it usually sells at a low price and is used as a grated cheese.

Trappist cheese originated with the Trappists in 1885 in the monastery of Mariastern, near Banjaluka, in Bosnia. Fresh milk is used and rennet is added. The ripening period of the smaller cheeses is from five to six weeks in summer, but the cheese is usually shipped at the end of four or five weeks. It is pale yellow in colour and has a remarkably mild taste. The smallest size of the cheese made in the monastery referred to has a diameter of 6 in. and a height of 2 in. and weighs two or three pounds. A larger size measures 9 in. in diameter and 2½ in. in height and weighs about ten pounds. There is also a still larger size. The cheese is exported to a large extent to Austria and Hungary, the most important centres of the trade in these regions being Gratz and Budapest. It is, however, found in all large cities of Austria, and the demand appears to be constantly increasing. This cheese is very probably the same as Port du Salut. A cheese which is probably identical with the Trappist, or Port du Salut, is made in the Trappist monastery at Oka, Que., and is known as Oka cheese.

TRADE AND CONSUMPTION

Cheese making was well established in European countries when the new settlers went to America, and it is evident the practices and methods they established were those with which they were familiar in their native countries. Thus Cheddar cheese became the first variety of importance in New England, where the English colonists settled, and Swiss cheese later became an important variety in Wisconsin, where immigrants from Switzerland established a settlement.

Originally, cheese was made only on the farm, both in Europe and in America. The earliest records indicating the growth and importance of cheese making in America are the export statistics of 1790, in which year the New England states, New York and Pennsylvania exported 145,000 lb. of farm-made cheese. It is generally believed that Jesse Williams of Oneida county, New York, was the first to operate under a factory system, in 1851. By 1870 the factory production of cheese made up more than half the total cheese made. Farm cheese production gradually declined and has almost completely disappeared.

Total cheese production in the U.S. in 1952 was 1,135,000,000 lb., representing utilization of 11,341,000,000 lb. or 10.3% of the total milk supply. Of the cheese total, more than 90% was the "American" (mostly Cheddar) type. Wisconsin was the leading state, with more than half the total production and a virtual monopoly of some types. Wholesale prices of Cheddar are based on the Plymouth Wisconsin Cheese exchange.

The average U.S. civilian in 1952 consumed 7.5 lb. of cheese, 36% more than before World War II but less than half as much as was used in some of the western European countries. Rationing of cheese was prevalent during the war and in the United Kingdom continued as late as 1952.

The world geography of cheese production depends not only upon the distribution of the dairy cow and milk production but also upon the comparative advantage of possible competitive uses of the milk. Use as fresh whole milk normally has highest priority. But in Europe, North America and Oceania (the main producing areas) about one-fifth of all whole milk used in manufacture in 1950 went into cheese making, as compared with about 16% before World War II, an increase made possible mainly by a decrease in the amount of milk used for butter. As compared with prewar output, the United States, largest producing country, was exceeding prewar levels in 1951 by approximately four-fifths and, on a per capita basis, by about 40%. Moreover, the U.S., which was a large net importer of cheese before the war, had become a major net exporter.

TABLE I.—*Estimated Cheese Output in Principal Producing Countries*
(In thousands of pounds)

Country	Average, 1934–38	1951
United States	643,234	1,157,560
France	584,000	617,000
Italy	523,518	613,000
Netherlands	200,000	265,257
New Zealand*	210,911	227,360
Argentina	67,873	186,210
Denmark	68,820	165,124
Sweden	76,059	120,007
Switzerland	111,729	116,848
United Kingdom	109,000	98,516
Australia*	48,400	93,242
Canada	119,924†	85,260
Norway	39,067	63,929
Union of South Africa	10,195	21,092

*Production year ending June 30. †Average, 1935–39.
Source: U.S. Department of Agriculture, *Foreign Crops and Markets*, vol. 65, no. 12, p. 249 (Sept. 22, 1952).

World trade in cheese in 1951 amounted to about 775,000,000 lb., nearly 30% more than before World War II. Some of the major exporting countries, particularly the United States, Italy, France and Canada, continued also to be large importers, emphasizing the fact that some of the numerous varieties serve special purposes. Bulk purchasing agreements, restrictive quotas and duties made the trade complex. At least 90% of New Zealand's exportable surplus was contracted to the United Kingdom at 176 shillings per hundredweight in 1952–53 for the first grade. In the United States several types of foreign cheese, amounting to about 27% of the imports, were freed from import controls in 1952, but quotas remained on several major types. The German Federal Republic substituted a 30% ad valorem duty for earlier weight duties.

TABLE II.—*International Trade in Cheese for the Major Trading Countries*
(In thousands of pounds)

Country	Average, 1934–38		1951*	
	Exports	Imports	Exports	Imports
Major exporting countries				
New Zealand	194,000	2	212,850	..
Netherlands	132,358	934	160,199	681
Denmark	18,067	33	101,132	42
United States	1,260	54,279	79,640	52,335
Australia	21,750	104	43,040	378
Switzerland	41,678	3,924	41,094	4,293
France	25,039	30,867	38,688	20,324
Italy	53,219	9,669	33,565	25,106
Canada	79,700	1,342	30,656	11,688
Major importing countries				
United Kingdom	2,987	319,028	..	435,105
Western Germany	..	22,000	3,871	93,208
Belgium and Luxembourg	344	50,563	1,018	69,939
Algeria	82	10,833	..	21,000

*Preliminary.
Source: U.S. Department of Agriculture, *Foreign Crops and Markets*, vol. 65, no. 5, p. 110 (Aug. 4, 1952).

BIBLIOGRAPHY.—K. J. Matheson, "Varieties of Cheese: Descriptions and Analyses," U.S. Department of Agriculture Bulletin 608 (1932); J. L. Sammis, *Cheese Making*, 12th ed. (1948); L. L. Van Slyke and W. V. Price, *Cheese* (1938); G. P. Sanders, L. A. Burkey and H. R. Lochry, "General Procedure for Manufacturing Swiss Cheese," U.S. Department of Agriculture Circular No. 851 (Sept. 1950); M. Dahnke, *The Cheese Cook Book* (1950). (O. E. R.; J. K. R.)

CHEETA, CHEETAH, CHITA or HUNTING LEOPARD (*Acinonyx jubata*), a member of the family Felidae, distinguished by its claws being only partially retractile (*see* CARNIVORA). The cheeta attains a length of three to four feet; it is of a pale fulvous colour, marked with numerous spots of black on the upper surface and sides and nearly white beneath. The fur is crisp, lacking the sleekness which characterizes the typical cats, and the tail is long and bushy at the tip. The cheeta is found on the plains of Africa and southern Asia, and has been employed for centuries in India and Persia in hunting antelopes and other game. It is taken to the field hooded and chained in a low car without sides. When the game is within about 200 yd., the cheeta is loosed. Over short distances, the cheeta can probably outrun any other animal. In India the name cheeta is applied also to the leopard.

BY COURTESY OF THE N.Y. ZOOL. SOC.
THE CHEETA, OR HUNTING LEOPARD

CHEF, in French, a chief or head person; in English-speaking usage, the head cook in a club or large private establishment, or the head of the kitchen department in a large hotel or commercial catering organization. In general a chef is responsible for the conduct and operation of the food preparation in a large kitchen. He directs the staff of cooks, bakers and others required to prepare food for serving. He plans meals, prepares menus and sees that sanitary practices are observed. If a chef-steward, he may be given complete control of kitchen, pantries and iceboxes, including all purchasing, and be expected to figure prices. If only a supervising chef, he is responsible only for the preparation of the food supplied to him from the stores department on requisition. He is usually expected to devise new recipes for preparing foods and more attractive ways for arranging them for service.

Every establishment preparing food on a large scale usually has a chef in charge of cooking operations. The constant growth of the hotel business and the commercial preparation of foods gives employment each year to a still larger number of chefs, though the requirements tend to become greater because of the demand for men having a more thorough knowledge of nutrition and food chemistry. For the most part, chefs are a product of an apprentice system. Young men start as assistant vegetable man, or even lower in the culinary scale, pass through a long line of specialized cooking positions such as vegetable cook, fry cook, roast cook (*rossetier*), roundsman, at times as baker or butcher, pastry man, cold meat chef (*garde manger*), until finally they become chefs, a process requiring from 4 to 8 years and frequent changes of employment. Schools for chefs and cooks are practically non-existent in the U.S.A., though not unknown in Great Britain. The leading chefs in English-speaking countries have usually served an apprenticeship in central Europe or in France, whence they depart after completing their service. In some commercial establishments trained chemists and graduates from university schools of home economics often serve as chefs, though usually under a different title.

CHEFOO, former treaty port on the rocky north coast of the Shantung peninsula in northeast China (37° 33′ N., 121° 22′ E). The port is naturally sheltered by outlying islands and in recent years these have been linked up by breakwaters to form a fully protected harbour. The port is more properly Yentai, Chefoo being a village across the harbour. Population (1931) 131,661. The tangled hill country of Shantung rises immediately behind Chefoo and its communications with the interior are only by pack-mule trails. A branch line of the Tsingtao-Tsinan railway was once projected. Chefoo was opened to foreign trade in 1863. It retained 10th place among Chinese ports until 1907, but decreased in importance after that year. It was the market for the tussore silk industry of the Shantung hills and raw silk constituted its staple export. A special trade had grown up between Chefoo in Shantung and the port of Antung across the Po Hai. After the Japanese occupation in 1938 the trade between Chefoo and Japan-controlled territory increased. The total value of imports in 1940 was $10,948,565 (U.S.) and that of the exports was $7,003,944 (U.S.). Of this $2,819,055 (U.S.) entered Chefoo from Japan and $4,254,042 (U.S.) from Kwantung-leased territory, while the largest part of the export, $2,795,756 (U.S.), went to the U.S.A. The treaty port status of Chefoo was ended as a result of the English and U.S. treaties with China, Jan. 11, 1943, in which the foreign rights and privileges in China were given up.

CHEHALIS, a city of Washington, U.S., 33 mi. S. by W. of Olympia, the county seat of Lewis county. It is on federal highway 99 and is served by four transcontinental railways and also by the Cowlitz, Chehalis and Cascade and the Chehalis and Western railways. Its manufacturing industries include lumber and shingle mills, brick and tile works, a cannery, drug manufacturing plant, fern packing and food-processing plants. The population in 1950 was 5,633.

CHEKE, SIR JOHN (1514–1557), English classical scholar, was one of the founders of Greek learning at Oxford. At St. John's college, Cambridge, where he became a fellow in 1529, he adopted the principles of the Reformation. In 1540, on Henry VIII.'s foundation of the regius professorships, he was elected to the chair of Greek. In a letter on the state of Greek learning at Cambridge to a fellow of St. John's college, Oxford, in 1542, his pupil, Roger Ascham, describes how Demosthenes had become as familiar as Cicero, and that Herodotus, Thucydides and Xenophon were more conned than Livy was in his student days. With Sir Thomas Smith, who shares with him the major part of the credit for the establishment of Greek studies at Cambridge, he introduced the "Erasmian" pronunciation of Greek in his lectures, rejecting the Italian and modern Greek method of giving various vowels and diphthongs the same sound, which the first western students had learned from Greek and Italian humanists. It was strenuously opposed in the university, where the "Reuchlinian" method favoured by Melancthon prevailed, and Bishop Gardiner, as chancellor, issued a decree against it (June 1542); but Cheke ultimately triumphed. On July 10, 1544, he was chosen tutor to Prince Edward, who retained him in that capacity after his accession to the throne. Cheke sat, as member for Bletchingly, for the parliaments in 1547 and 1552–1553; he was made provost of King's college, Cambridge (April 1, 1548), was one of the commissioners for visiting that university as well as Oxford and Eton, and was appointed with seven divines to draw up a body of laws for the governance of the church. On Oct. 11, 1551, he was knighted; in 1553 he was made one of the secretaries of State, and sworn of the privy council. He filled the office of secretary of State for Lady Jane Grey during her nine days' reign. In consequence Mary threw him into the Tower (July 27, 1553), and confiscated his wealth. He was released on Sept. 13, 1554, and granted permission to travel abroad. He went first to Basle, then visited Italy, giving lectures in Greek at Padua, and finally settled at Strasbourg, teaching Greek for his living. In the spring of 1556 he visited Brussels to see his wife; on his way back, between Brussels and Antwerp, he and Sir Peter Carew were treacherously seized (May 15) by order of Philip of Spain, hurried over to England, and imprisoned in the Tower. Cheke was terrified by a threat of the stake, and giving way, was received into the Church of Rome by Cardinal Pole, being cruelly forced to make two public recantations. He died in London on Sept. 13, 1557.

Thomas Wilson, in the epistle prefixed to his translation of the Olynthiacs of Demosthenes (1570), has a long and most interesting eulogy of Cheke; and Thomas Nash, in *To the Gentlemen Students,* prefixed to Robert Greene's *Menaphon* (1589), calls him "the Exchequer of eloquence, Sir Ihon Cheke, a man of men, supernaturally traded in all tongues." Many of Cheke's works are still in ms., some have been lost altogether. One of the most interesting from an historical point of view is the *Hurt of Sedition how greueous it is to a Communewelth* (1549), written on the occasion of Ket's rebellion, republished in 1569, 1576 and 1641, on the last occasion with a life of the author by Gerard Langbaine. Others are *D. Joannis Chrysostomi homiliae duae* (1543), *D. Joannis Chrysostomi de providentia Dei* (1545), *The Gospel according to St. Matthew . . . translated* (c. 1550; ed. James Goodwin, 1843), *De obitu Martini Buceri* (1551), (Leo VI.'s) *de Apparatu bellico* (Basel, 1554; but dedicated to Henry VIII., 1544), *Carmen Heroicum, aut epitaphium in Antonium Dencium* (1551), *De pronuntiatione Graecae . . . linguae* (Basel, 1555). He also translated several Greek works, and lectured admirably upon Demosthenes.

His *Life* was written by John Strype (London 1705, Oxford 1821); additions by J. Gough Nichols in *Archaeologia* (1860), xxxviii. 98, 127.

CHEKHOV, ANTON PAVLOVICH (1860–1904), Russian dramatist and story-writer, born on Jan. 17, 1860, in Taganrog on the Sea of Azov. This name is also spelled Tchekhov, Tchehov and Chehov. His father was a tradesman and the son of a serf. The writer was educated at the *gymnasium* of his native town, and in 1879 went to the University of Moscow, where he studied medicine. He took his degree in 1884 but practised very little (except during the cholera epidemic of 1892–93). He began his literary career while yet a student, and soon became one of the most welcome contributors to the comic papers. His early stories appeared over the signature Antosha Chekhonte. In 1886 some of his stories were published in book form (*Particoloured Stories*). The book had a great success and attracted the attention of the publisher and editor Suvorin, who became his friend.

In 1887 he produced his first play *Ivanov.* In 1890 he travelled to the convict island of Sakhalin and the result of his journey was *Saghalien Island* (1891), which had a considerable effect on the mitigation of the penal régime. From 1891 to 1897 he lived with his parents on a small estate he had acquired not far from Moscow. After 1897, as he was threatened with tuberculosis, he was forced to live the greater part of the year in the Crimea and abroad. In 1896 he produced his second play, *The Seagull,* which was a complete failure in St. Petersburg (Leningrad). But in 1898 it was revived by the Moscow Art theatre of Stanislavsky and proved a great success. Henceforward Chekhov's connection with that theatre became very close. *Uncle Vanya* (1899), *The Three Sisters* (1901) and *The Cherry Orchard* (1904) were produced there. In 1901 he married the actress Olga Knipper. In 1900 he was elected an honorary fellow of the Academy of Science, but resigned his fellowship when the election of Maxim Gorky was cancelled by the Government. He died on July 2, 1904, at Badenweiler in the Black Forest.

Early Work.—The early stories of Chekhov, up to about 1886, are chiefly humorous. They are, in Russia, the most widely popular part of his work, and more people know him by them than by *My Life* or *The Three Sisters.* Chekhov's humour is not strikingly above the level of the papers he wrote for. But very early he began to lay the foundations of that manner which is the essential Chekhov. Such a story as *The Chorus Girl* (1884) is almost a mature masterpiece. It was, however, only after 1886 that he found the necessary leisure and independence to give definite expression to his imaginative experience. The years 1886–88 are a period of transition during which he experimented in various directions. To these years belong a series of stories of atmosphere against a background of nature (*The Steppe, Happiness, Easter Eve*) where the lyrical element of his genius received its fullest expression, and short stories of morbid experience in which the knowledge of the doctor is balanced by the sense of form of the artist. By 1889, however, he had attained perfection in his style. To this and the following years belong a succession of masterpieces, the principal of which are *A Dreary Story* (1889), *The Duel, Ward No. 6* (1892), *The Teacher of Literature* (1894), *Three Years: An Artist's Story,* in Russian *The House with the Maisonette* (1895), *Peasants* (1897), *The Darling, Ionitch, The Lady with the Dog* (1898), *The New Villa* (1899), *The Bishop* (1902).

Chekhov's art has been described as psychological, but his psychology ignores the individual. His characters are not persons but just men and women, the genus *homo,* an indifferentiated mass of humanity, divided into watertight compartments by the phenomenon of individuality, which does not make one being different from another but only inaccessible to him. A typical story by Chekhov is the life-story of a "mood," of a state of mind, usually of the relation of one person to another and the gradual transformation of that state of mind under the action of the incessant infinitesimal and unforeseen pinpricks of life. Sensitiveness to these pinpricks is the main feature of Chekhov's people, of those at least who are made to kindle the reader's sympathy, and the standard by which Chekhov gauges the worth of a human being. Those who suffer and succumb are the higher race, those who do not are unfeeling brutes. Hence a deep-rooted aversion (present in pre-Chekhov Russian literature, especially in Turgenev, but enormously magnified by Chekhov) for the strong and efficient man. None but "Hamlets" may receive sympathy.

The construction of Chekhov's stories may be described as musical or infinitesimal. It is at once fluid and precise. They are built along exactly calculated curves, of which only certain points are marked in the story, but each two points are sufficient to calculate the whole curve. The curve is the mood which begins as almost a straight line, then under the influence of "pinpricks" begins to deviate and at last shoots out in an entirely opposite direction. By far the greater number of Chekhov's stories end on a minor note, "not with a bang but a whimper." A story where the direction is in the opposite way, as in *The Lady with the Dog* (where the hero begins by regarding his love for the lady as a mere insignificant intrigue and ends in self-forgetful passion), is an exception. The "pessimistic," destructive, descendant tendency of the Russian novelists of the mid and later 19th century reaches its extreme expression in Chekhov, all the more extreme as it is so consistently muffled and "understated." To him, better than to anyone, the words of Albert Thibaudet apply, that a Russian story is always the story of the undoing of a life.

Somewhat apart from the other stories of Chekhov stand, what are perhaps his two masterpieces, *My Life* (1895) and *In the Ravine* (1900). They have a clearer and harder outline; they are free from the atmospheric, autumnal haze that pervades the others, and animated by a more active sense of moral and human values. *My Life,* especially, is a creation of vast and pregnant significance, with a symbolical grasp that gives it an almost religious character.

Chekhov's dramatic work consists of the same element as his narrative work. It includes numerous one-act plays which were extremely popular in Russia. Belonging to a later period than the comic stories, they are also on a higher artistic level. The serious plays are five in number—*Ivanov, The Seagull, Uncle Vanya, The Three Sisters, The Cherry Orchard.* They have many points in common with his stories; one main difference is that while the stories invariably centre round a single person from whose standpoint the situation is developed, the dramas have no such central figure, and all the characters have more or less equal rights on the stage. The plays are, as it were, symphonies for an orchestra of parts, and the resultant is arrived at by the complex interaction of the various voices. They are plays of "atmosphere," the English word that comes nearest to the Russian *nastroenie* (Stimmung). The principal thing in them is not the action but the emotional accompaniment of the action. In the "de-theatricalisation" of the theatre, in the complete avoidance of all traditional stage effects (though he introduced a new kind of "atmospheric" effect, as the famous string bursting at the end of *The Cherry Orchard*), Chekhov is the logical limit of the preceding development of the Russian drama. He did not go much further in this respect than Turgenev or Ostrovsky, but he built a more consistent dramatic system with a completely adequate technique.

The Novelist's Influence.—The influence of Chekhov on Russian literature has not been extensive. The last realists (Andreyev, Gorky, Bunin, etc.) learned little from him, and soon after his death the rise of an entirely new movement put an end to all possibility of continuing in his tradition. His plays were imitated by Gorky, Andreyev and others, but they invariably missed the constructive principle without which the whole system is stultified. To the Russia of to-day Chekhov is perhaps more alien than any other Russian writer of his rank.

On the other hand, his vogue and his influence outside Russia have of recent years grown immensely and were in 1927 probably near their zenith. England has proved particularly sensitive to his charm. He is almost universally regarded as the greatest Russian writer and as the greatest story-teller and dramatist of modern times. (D. S. M.)

BIBLIOGRAPHY.—*The Tales of Tchehov* (13 vols., trans. C. Garnett, 1916–22); *Letters of A. Tchehov* (trans. C. Garnett, 1920); *The Notebooks of A. Tchehov, together with Reminiscences of Tchehov by Maxim Gorky* (trans. S. S. Koteliansky and L. Woolf, 1921); *The Plays of Tchehov* (2 vols. trans. C. Garnett, 1923, etc.); *Letters on Literary Topics* (trans. Louis Friedland, 1924); *The Life and Letters of A. Tchehov* (trans. S. S. Koteliansky and P. Tomlinson, 1925); *Letters of A. P. Tchehov to O. L. Knipper* (trans. C. Garnett, 1926); some hitherto unpublished letters have been edited by N. K. Piksanov at Moscow under the title of *Nesobrannye Pisma* (1928). *See* also L. Shestov, *Anton Tchehov* (1916); W. Gerhardi, *Anton Chehov* (1923); S. S. Koteliansky, *Anton Tchekhov, Literary and Theatrical Reminiscences* (1927).

CHEKIANG, the smallest but one of the most famous and densely peopled provinces of China. Area 40,169 sq.mi.; pop. 21,776,045 (1940). It is the most northerly of the coastal provinces of south China and is situated where the southwest to northeast ridges, so characteristic of southeast China, begin to sink beneath the alluvial plains of the delta of the Yangtze Kiang. The province falls naturally into two physiographic regions demarcated by the Tayu-ling, the northernmost ridge, which runs out to sea in the Chusan archipelago. The southern region consists of ridges and troughs parallel to the Tayu-ling and cut across by a number of transverse rivers. At the mouth of the largest of these, the Wu-kiang, lies Wenchow, the chief port of southern Chekiang. The northern region, drained for the most part by a single river, the Tsien-tang, with its outlet in Hangchow bay, consists essentially of the alluvial plains round the bay and of the foothills of the highlands. These northern plains are the most densely peopled part of the province participating in the life of the Yangtze delta and containing the well-known seaport of Ningpo and the beautiful capital city of Hangchow. This northern part of the province therefore resembles southern Kiangsu, while the rest is essentially similar to Fukien, which succeeds it on the south. Away from the plains around Hangchow bay flat land is rare and terraces stretch far up the mountain slopes.

The crops—wheat and beans, rice and cotton, tea and silk—are typical of mid-China, where the products characteristic of north and south overlap. On the slopes of the maritime ranges some of the best tea grown in the country is produced. The historical role of the province and many aspects of its culture reflect the pivotal position of Chekiang. Before the consolidation of China in the 3rd century B.C. north Chekiang was the core of the maritime state of Yüeh, which finally gained the mastery over the whole Yangtze delta. During the 12th and 13th centuries A.D. it had a larger significance, for Hangchow was then the capital of what remained of China to the Sung dynasty, retreating southwards before the Kin Tatars, and, after the Mongol conquest, it remained the acknowledged centre of Mangi. (*See* CATHAY.)

The province suffered severely through the Japanese invasion. After the fall of Hangchow, Christmas 1937, the Tsientang river temporarily formed the military line. Early in 1942 the Japanese attacked the airfields in western Chekiang and remained in possession of part of the territory. The occupation combined with deliberate destruction of Chinese sericulture brought great economic distress, little compensated by government sponsored development in the free part of the province.

Chekiang is linguistically divided. In the north, Wu dialects prevail, as in southern Kiang-su. The southwest speaks Mandarin as does neighbouring Kiangsi. In the south, Fukien dialects transgress the border.

CHELLEAN, the name given by the French anthropologist G. de Mortillet to the first epoch of the Quaternary period when the earliest human remains are discoverable. The word is derived from the French town Chelles in the department of Seine-et-Marne. The Chellean epoch was interglacial, warm and humid as evidenced by the wild growth of fig-trees and laurels. The animals characteristic of the epoch are the *Elephas antiquus,* the rhinoceros, the cave-bear, the hippopotamus and the striped hyaena. Man existed and belonged to the Neanderthal type. The implements characteristic of the period are flints chipped into leaf-shaped forms and held in the hand when used. There is clear evidence of phases of Chellean industry—both in a simple and an advanced stage.

See Gabriel de Mortillet, *Le Préhistorique* (1900); M. C. Burkitt, *Prehistory* (1925); H. Peake and H. J. Fleure, *Apes and Men* (1927).

CHELM (Russian *Kholm*), a town of Poland, in the province of Lublin, 45 mi. by rail E.S.E. of Lublin. Pop. (1931) 29,224. It was founded in 1223 by Prince Daniel of Volhynia. Germany occupied Chelm during World War II.

CHELMNO (German *Kulm*), a small town of Poland, in the province of Pomorze (Pomerania), 1 mi. E. of the Vistula. Pop. (1931) 12,533. It is surrounded by 13th century walls, and contains two Roman Catholic and two Protestant churches and a mediaeval town-hall. There are large oil mills and an important trade in agricultural produce, including fruit and vegetables. Granted in 1226 by Conrad of Mazovia to the Teutonic Order, it became the base for their conquest of Prussia and the seat of the first Prussian bishopric. It always retained a large Polish population, which revolted against the Order and was re-annexed to Poland by the peace of Thorn in 1466. It was part of Prussia from 1773 to 1918, and Germany occupied it again during World War II. It was a prominent member of the Hanseatic League.

CHELMSFORD, FREDERICK JOHN NAPIER THESIGER, 1ST VISCOUNT (1868–1933), British administrator, born on Aug. 12, 1868, was the eldest son of Frederick Augustus, 2nd Baron Chelmsford. He was educated at Winchester and Magdalen college, Oxford, and held a fellowship at All Souls from 1892 to 1899. Having been called to the bar he was a member of the London school board for four years, and in 1904–5 served on the London county council. In the latter year, when he succeeded his father as Baron Chelmsford, he was appointed governor of Queensland and he held that office till 1909. These years saw the inauguration of the new policy of replacing the repatriated Kanakas by white labour. It was also a period of bitter political conflict. Chelmsford's action in granting the request of the premier, Philp, for a dissolution of parliament led to widespread agitation for the appointment of local governors in Australia. In Aug. 1909 Chelmsford left Queensland for New South Wales, of which State he was governor till 1913. It was a period of great development for the colony, and also of great labour unrest.

Chelmsford, who was created G.C.M.G. in 1912, served in India with the Dorset regiment in the early part of the World War. From April 1916 to the spring of 1921 he was viceroy of India. During this period the system of dyarchy, founded upon the joint report of tne viceroy and the secretary of State, E. S. Montagu, was introduced. A considerable measure of autonomy was accorded to the provinces. The council of State and legislative assembly were to be elected, and the annual budget, with some reservations, submitted to the latter. Indians were given representation on the viceroy's council, and India was given the same power over tariffs as the Dominions.

But the new reforms were opposed by a combination of Hindus and Muslims under Gandhi, and a system of non-co-operation adopted, whilst the repressive legislation recommended by Mr. Justice Rowlatt's committee to deal with sedition provoked serious riots in Guzerat and the Punjab, culminating in the Amritsar disturbances (April 1919). However, an amnesty for political offences accompanied the promulgation of the reforms which were gradually accepted by moderate opinion. Meanwhile the viceroy had also to meet a Mohammedan agitation directed against British policy toward Turkey. This was actively supported by an Afghan army, after whose defeat the subsidy was withdrawn from the Amir, together with the privilege of importing arms from India. The new institutions were inaugurated by the duke of Connaught early in 1921. On his retirement Chelmsford was created a viscount and received Indian orders. He was first lord of the admiralty in Ramsay MacDonald's Labour Ministry of 1924. He died April 1, 1933. (G. LE G. N.)

CHELMSFORD, FREDERIC THESIGER, 1st BARON (1794–1878), lord chancellor of England, was the third son of Charles Thesiger, and was born in London on April 15, 1794. Young Frederic Thesiger was originally destined for a naval career, and he served as a midshipman on board the "Cambrian" frigate in 1807 at the second bombardment of Copenhagen. About this time he succeeded to a valuable estate in the West Indies, so he left the navy and studied law, with a view to practising in the West Indies, and eventually managing his property in person. But a volcano destroyed the family estate, and he was thrown back upon his prospect of a legal practice in the West Indies. He entered Gray's Inn in 1813, and was called on Nov. 18, 1818. Godfrey Sykes, whose pupil he was, advised him to try his fortunes in England. He accordingly joined the home circuit and practised at the Surrey sessions, also buying the right to appear at the old palace court (*see* LORD STEWARD).

In 1824 he distinguished himself by his defence of Joseph Hunt when on his trial at Hertford with John Thurtell for the murder of William Weare; and eight years later at Chelmsford assizes he won a hard-fought action in an ejectment case after three trials, to which he attributed so much of his subsequent success that when he was raised to the peerage he assumed the title Lord Chelmsford. In 1834 he was made king's counsel, and in 1835 was briefed in the Dublin election inquiry which unseated Daniel O'Connell. In 1840 he was elected M.P. for Woodstock. In 1844 he became solicitor-general, but having ceased to enjoy the favour of the duke of Marlborough, lost his seat for Woodstock and had to find another at Abingdon. In 1845 he became attorney-general, holding the post until the fall of the Peel administration on July 3, 1846. Thus by three days Thesiger missed being chief justice of the common pleas, for on July 6 Sir Nicholas Tindal died, and the seat on the bench, which would have been Thesiger's as of right, fell to the Liberal attorney-general, Sir Thomas Wilde. In 1852 he became M.P. for Stamford. On Lord Derby coming into office for the second time in 1858, Sir Frederic Thesiger was raised straight from the bar to the lord chancellorship (as were Lord Brougham, Lord Selborne, and Lord Halsbury). In the following year Lord Derby resigned. Again in 1866, on Lord Derby coming into office for the third time, Lord Chelmsforo became lord chancellor for a short period. In 1868 Lord Derby retired, and Disraeli, who took his place as prime minister, wished for Lord Cairns as lord chancellor. Lord Chelmsford died in London on Oct. 5, 1878. He had married in 1822 Anna Maria Tinling, and left four sons and three daughters, of whom the eldest, Frederick Augustus, 2nd Baron Chelmsford (1827–1905), earned distinction as a soldier, while the third, Alfred Henry Thesiger (1838–80), was made a lord justice of appeal and a privy councillor in 1877, at the age of 39, but died only three years later.

See *Lives of the Chancellors* (1908), by J. B. Atlay, who had the advantage of access to an unpublished autobiography of Lord Chelmsford.

CHELMSFORD, market town and municipal borough, and the county town of Essex, England, 30 mi. E.N.E. from London by the Eastern Region railway. Pop. (1938) 31,400. Area 7.4 sq.mi. It lies in the Chelmer valley at the confluence of the Cann, and has communication by river with Maldon and the Blackwater estuary 11 mi. east. Chelmsford (*Chilmersford, Chelmeresford, Chelmesford*) owed its mediaeval importance to its position on the road from London to Colchester. It consisted of two manors: that of Moulsham, which remained in the possession of Westminster abbey from Saxon times till the reign of Henry VIII and that of Bishop's hall which was held by the bishops of London from the reign of Edward the Confessor to 1545. The mediaeval history of Chelmsford centred round the manor of Bishop's hall. Early in the 12th century Bishop Maurice built the bridge over the Chelmer which brought the road from London directly through the town, thus making it an important stopping place. The town was not incorporated until 1888. In 1225 Chelmsford was made the centre for the collection of fifteenths from the county of Essex, and in 1227 it became the regular seat of assizes and quarter-sessions. The parish church of St. Mary is a Perpendicular building, largely rebuilt. The grammar school was founded in 1551 by Edward VI. In 1199 the bishop obtained the grant of a weekly market, and in 1201 that of an annual fair, now discontinued, for four days from the feast of St. Philip and St. James. The town has a large agricultural market and a corn exchange in the centre of the square. There are agricultural implement and iron foundries, electrical and engineering works and extensive corn mills. There is a racecourse 2 mi. S. of the town. The see of Chelmsford, founded in 1914, includes the whole of Essex and part of Suffolk and Kent. At the former radio station there the first wireless telephone broadcasting service in the world was transmitted Feb. 23, 1920. The borough is in the Chelmsford parliamentary division of Essex.

CHELMSFORD, a town of Middlesex county, Massachusetts, U.S., adjoining the city of Lowell. It lies on both sides of the Concord river and on the Merrimack, and is served by the New York, New Haven and Hartford railroad. Pop. (1950) 9,303. It has numerous factories. Chelmsford is first mentioned in the records of the state in 1655. Lowell was set off in 1826.

CHELSEA, a western metropolitan borough of London, England, bounded E. by the city of Westminster, N.W. by Kensington, S.W. by Fulham, and S. by the river Thames. Pop. (est. 1938) 56,050. Area, 1 sq.mi. Its chief thoroughfare is Sloane street, running south from Knightsbridge to Sloane square. From Chelsea King's road leads west, a commercial highway, named in honour of Charles II and recalling the private road from St. James's palace to Fulham. The main roads south join with the Victoria or Chelsea, Albert and Battersea bridges over the Thames. The Chelsea embankment, planted with trees and lined with fine houses and, in part, with public gardens, stretches between Victoria and Battersea bridges. The residential portion is eastern Chelsea near Sloane street and along the river. Chelsea, especially the riverside district, has many historical associations. At *Cealchythe* a synod was held in 787. A similar name occurs in a Saxon charter of the 11th century and in Domesday; in the 16th century it is *Chelcith.* The later termination *ey* or *ea* was associated with the insular character of the land, and the prefix with a gravel bank (*ceosol; cf.* Chesil bank, Dorsetshire); but the early suffix *hythe* commonly means a haven. The manor was originally in the possession of Westminster abbey, but its history is fragmentary until Tudor times. Henry VIII passed it to his wife Catharine Parr. It fell afterward to the Howards and the Cheynes, and later to the Cadogans. The memorials in St. Luke's (the old church) include those of Sir Thomas More (d. 1535); Lord Bray, lord of the manor (1539); Lady Jane Guyldeford (1555); Lord and Lady Dacre (1594–1595); Sir John Lawrence (1638); Lady Jane Cheyne (1698); Francis Thomas, "director of the china porcelain manufactory, Lawrence Street, Chelsea" (1770); Sir Hans Sloane (1753); Thomas Shadwell, poet laureate (1692); Woodfall, the printer of *Junius* (1844), and many others. The church, which had never been "restored," was ruined in World War II, though the chapel built by More still stands. Happily, most of the fine monuments were rescued, many almost undamaged. In the 18th and 19th centuries Chelsea was a literary and artistic quarter. Atterbury and Swift lived in Church lane, Steele and Smollett in Monmouth house. Later, Turner, Rossetti, Whistler, Leigh Hunt, Carlyle (whose house in Cheyne row is preserved as a public memorial), Lord Courtney, Count D'Orsay and Isambard Brunel are connected with Chelsea. At Lindsey house Count Zinzendorf established a Moravian society (*c.* 1750). Sir Robert Walpole's residence was extant till 1810; and till 1824 the bishops of Winchester had a palace in Cheyne walk. Queen's (Tudor) house was the home of D. G. Rossetti.

Ranelagh (*q.v.*) in the second half of the 18th century, and Cremorne gardens (*q.v.*) in the middle of the 19th, were famous places of entertainment. Don Saltero's museum contained curiosities from Sir Hans Sloane's famous collections. Sloane gave the Apothecaries' company ground for the Physick garden, which ceased in 1902 to be maintained by the company. The original Chelsea bun-house, claiming royal patronage, stood until 1839, and one of its successors until 1888. The porcelain works existed for some 25 years before 1769, when they were sold and removed to Derby. Chelsea Royal hospital for invalid soldiers, initiated by Charles II and opened in 1694 is well known. A system of outpensioning was found necessary from the outset, and it relieves large numbers throughout the empire. The picturesque building by Sir Christopher Wren, the great hall of which was damaged during World War II, stands in extensive grounds, which include the former Ranelagh gardens, site of the annual showing of the Royal Horticultural society. Crosby hall, with new buildings adjacent to it, was opened in 1927 as a residence hall for university women. The hall, built by Sir John Crosby in Bishopsgate in 1466, was removed thence to a site on Sir Thomas More's former garden in 1910 to save it from demolition. The Chelsea public library contains an excellent collection relative to local history. Chelsea returns one member to parliament.

CHELSEA, a city of Suffolk county, Massachusetts, U.S., on a peninsula between the Mystic and the Chelsea rivers and its inlets, opposite the Charlestown and East Boston districts of the city of Boston, bounded on the west by the city of Everett and on the north by the city of Revere. It has 3 mi. of water front with 35 ft. channel depth on upper Boston bay; and is served by the Boston and Maine and the Boston and Albany railways. It is within 1 mi. of Logan International airport. The 2 mi. Mystic River bridge, cantilever type, costing $27,000,000 was opened in 1950. The population in 1950 was 39,038, and in 1940 was 41,259 by the federal census.

The central part of the city was practically rebuilt after 1908, when, on April 12, it was swept by a fire which destroyed one-third of the city, including most public buildings. Chelsea is primarily an industrial city with about 200 factories. Its industries include lithography, shoes, shoe cut stock and findings, car wheels, rubber heels and soles, bakery products, foundry and machine-shop products, smoked and dried fish, furniture, fluorescent lighting, automatic machinery, chemicals, paints, varnishes and lacquers, wallpaper, elastic webbing, boxes, marine clocks and creosote products. It is a centre for junk salvage, with dealers in many kinds of waste material, metals, rags, paper, burlap, rubber, automotive, etc. Bulk oil wholesale plants occupy a large portion of the waterfront. A U.S. naval hospital and the Massachusetts Soldiers' home and hospital are situated there.

The Cary-Bellingham house, once the palatial home of Governor Bellingham, is an excellent example of colonial architecture, and is preserved as a historical relic, open to the public.

Chelsea (called Winnisimmet until 1739) was settled in 1624 by Samuel Maverick, a prominent loyalist and churchman, the first settler on Noddle's island (East Boston). It was set off from Boston as a separate town in 1739, and was chartered as a city in 1857. In May, 1775, a British schooner, the "Diana," in the Mystic river was captured by colonial militia under Gen. John Stark and Israel Putnam.

CHELSEA HOSPITAL. The Royal Hospital, Chelsea, to give the institution its full title, was founded by Charles II. Tradition has it that Nell Gwynne moved the king to build the hospital, but it is probable that the idea originated with Sir Stephen Fox, who had been a paymaster general to the forces. Sir Christopher Wren was the architect, and the building was completed in 1692. Many military trophies are preserved at the hospital, including the colours captured at Blenheim and Waterloo, and there is a fine collection of medals and pictures in the Great hall.

The candidates for a Chelsea in-pension must be out-pensioners, *i.e.* in receipt of either a service, disability or campaign pension. Candidates must be 55 years of age, unless through loss of limb or other disability, the result of army service, they are considered eligible for admission to in-pension at an earlier date. The establishment of in-pensioners is 558. The candidates must be capable of looking after themselves. In-pensioners may leave the hospital and revert to out-pension if they so wish, but unless there are some exceptional reasons such men are not again admitted to in-pension.

In addition to the in-pension establishment, the board of commissioners administer long service pensions, special campaign pensions, and deal with disability pensions other than those arising from World War I and earlier wars, which are administered by the ministry of pensions. They also approve, after investigation, the applications of pensioners who desire to receive a commuted sum in lieu of a portion of pension for the purpose of house purchase, etc. The number of men on the army pension list administered by the commissioners of the royal hospital was in 1927 approximately 103,000.

CHELTENHAM, a municipal and parliamentary borough of Gloucestershire, Eng., about 96 mi. W.N.W. of London. Pop. (1951) 62,823. Area 8 sq.mi. The town lies where the Chelt, a small tributary of the river Severn, breaks the western escarpment of the Cotswold hills. It is a residential, holiday and sporting centre and is also visited for its medicinal waters. There are three saline springs, the Pittville, Montpellier and Central spas. During the 20th century a number of light industries were established in and around the town. Four miles west is Staverton airport.

There was an early settlement at Cheltenham and a church existed there in 803. The manor belonged to the crown and was granted to Henry de Bohun, earl of Hereford, in the 12th century. In 1252 it was bought by the abbey of Fécamp in Normandy and afterward belonged to the priory of Cormeille. In 1415 it was confiscated, but at the dissolution it returned to the crown. It then became the property of the Dutton family. The town is first mentioned in 1223, when the benefit of the markets, fairs and hundred of Cheltenham was leased to it for three years. Henry III renewed the lease in 1226 and in 1230 granted a Thursday market and a three-day fair on July 24. It was governed by commissioners from 1852 to 1876, when it was incorporated. It became a parliamentary borough in 1832, returning one member. After the discovery of the mineral springs in 1716 and the erection of a pump room in 1738 Cheltenham rapidly became fashionable, the visit of George III and the royal princesses in 1788 ensuring its popularity. As an inheritance of those times the town is graced by much delightful Georgian building and wide tree-lined avenues and open spaces. Gustav Holst was born at Cheltenham in 1874.

Cheltenham is a well-known educational centre, the principal institutions being Cheltenham college (founded 1841); Cheltenham Ladies' college (1853); Dean Close school (1886); a grammar school (founded 1586; rebuilt 1883); and teachers' training colleges. The town hall, the opera house and the civic playhouse are used for entertainments. After World War II annual festivals of contemporary British music were launched. Race meetings are held under National Hunt rules, and county matches are played on the cricket ground with an important cricket festival in August.

CHELYABINSK, a region and town in the Uralsk area of the Russian S.F.S.R. The region has an area of 62,741 sq.mi. Pop. (1939) 2,802,949; urban 1,181,871; rural 1,621,078. It is dotted with forest, marsh and lake, but 59.2% is under cultivation (wheat, oats, rye, millet, peas, etc.). Cattle, sheep, horses and pigs are reared and coal is mined.

There are flour mills, brandy distilleries, breweries and other factories for food products. The town of Chelyabinsk, lat. 55° 8′ N., long. 61° 35′ E., pop. (1939) 273,127, is a trading centre for coal and Siberian grain. Manufactures of agricultural implements and leather goods are carried on, and the town has an elevator and a radio station. It is connected by rail with the north through Sverdlovsk (formerly Ekaterinburg), with the east, as the beginning of the trans-Siberian railway, and with the west through Zlatoust and Ufa. It was founded in 1658. During the Civil War following the 1917 revolution Chelyabinsk was for a time the headquarters of the Czechoslovak legion and the scene of much internecine warfare.

CHELYS, the common lyre of the ancient Greeks (Gr. χέλυς, tortoise), which had a convex back of tortoise shell or of wood shaped like the shell. According to tradition Hermes was attracted by sounds of music while walking on the banks of the Nile, and found that they proceeded from the shell of a tortoise across which were stretched tendons which the wind had set in vibration (*Homeric Hymn to Hermes*, 47–51). The word has been applied arbitrarily since classical times to various stringed instruments.

CHEMICAL ACTION is said to occur whenever the properties of a substance are so completely altered that we are entitled to regard the product as a new and distinct substance. In the burning of coal, for example, a combustible, black solid is chemically changed by union with the oxygen of the air, to produce ash, water vapour and gases, all of which differ from the original coal in all their important properties. The chemist pictures the properties of every substance as being determined by the chemical make-up of its molecules; *i.e.*, by the nature of the atoms which are contained in each molecule of the given substance, and the manner of their arrangement. Thus water is different from carbon disulphide because the molecules of water contain atoms which are different from those contained in molecules of carbon disulphide: on the other hand the molecules of grape sugar (glucose) and fruit sugar (fructose) contain identical atoms in identical proportions but the properties of these substances are nevertheless different because the atoms are differently arranged in the two kinds of molecules. (*See* REACTION KINETICS.)

The complete change of properties which is associated with chemical action is therefore to be considered as being accomplished by the recombination or rearrangement of atoms to produce new sorts of molecules. The science of chemistry (*q.v.*) is mainly concerned with the study of chemical change. The details thus far accumulated are commonly presented in chemical textbooks under headings that correspond with the various individual elements. The general results and such principles as are generally applicable to chemical change, form the subject matter of physical chemistry (*see* CHEMISTRY: *Physical*), and of these the present article deals with a few which are related most intimately to the factors that determine how quickly a given chemical change may be accomplished.

CHEMICAL REACTION VELOCITY

The variation in the speed of chemical change and its dependence on the nature of the reacting substances is illustrated on the one hand by the almost instantaneous change (explosive reaction) which transforms a stick of dynamite into gaseous products, and on the other, by the very slow change by which a steel girder is converted into a pile of iron rust, a process which may require thousands of years. It will only be possible to explain why some changes proceed so rapidly and others with such extreme slowness when we are able to state the cause of chemical change in general. At present, we can merely conclude that this is caused by the action of electrical forces, the nature of which we are beginning to understand as the result of recent observations which have provided us with information concerning the inner structure of the atoms themselves. (*See* ATOM.) It usually happens, as Julius Thomsen (1854) and Marcellin P. E. Berthelot (1867) first emphasized, that rapid and energetic chemical reactions take place with the liberation of greater quantities of heat than sluggish reactions although this rule is subject to many exceptions.

A second factor determining the speed of chemical change is the concentration of the reactants. By this we mean the amounts of the different reacting substances in unit volume. Thus C. F. Wenzel, in 1777, observed that metals dissolve in moderately concentrated acids more rapidly than they do in very dilute acids. Indeed it was soon recognized, as a result of the work of Claude Louis Berthollet in 1803, that whether a given chemical change or its reverse takes place sometimes depends only on the concentrations in which the several reacting substances are brought together. In such instances the effect of concentration outweighs the effect of the nature of the reacting substances, loosely termed "chemical affinity." The earliest accurate observations of the effect of concentration on the velocity of chemical changes were made by L. Wilhelmy (1850), who showed that the rate of conversion of cane sugar into glucose and fructose in the presence of an acid is at every moment very nearly proportional to the concentration of the cane sugar. These observations constituted the first definite proof that the influence of the concentration of a reacting substance can be quantitatively stated, but did not lead to any generalized statement.

It is only in the simplest type of chemical change, in which the change may be accomplished with a single molecule of a given reactant, that the velocity of the change is proportional to the first power of the concentration of that reactant If n molecules of a reactant are required to accomplish the chemical change the velocity of the change is proportional to the nth power of the concentration of that reactant. In many cases n will be indicated by the chemical equation for the change. Thus $2H_2 + O_2 = 2H_2O$, indicates that the formation of water from hydrogen and oxygen demands two molecules of hydrogen for every molecule of oxygen, and thus that the rate at which water is formed at any given temperature is proportional to the first power of the concentration of oxygen but to the square of the concentration of hydrogen. In more complicated reactions, however, the chemical equation gives no clue to the power to which the concentration must be raised in calculating reaction velocity, for the chemical equation often expresses only the total effect and final result of a series of simpler consecutive chemical changes, the slowest of which determines the speed at which the series of changes as a whole may be accomplished. Changes in pressure are without effect on the velocity of chemical change, save in so far as pressure may determine concentration, as happens especially with mixtures of gases.

A third factor which affects the velocity of chemical change is the temperature. With rare exceptions, which can be readily explained, an increase of temperature increases the rate at which a chemical change will take place. Milk quickly turns sour on a warm day, and a mixture of hydrogen and oxygen, prepared safely enough at room temperature, explodes when it is heated by an electric spark. Commonly an increase of 1° C. increases the velocity of a chemical change 10% or more, and most reactions at the temperature of boiling water proceed with several hundred times the velocity observed at room temperature. This striking effect of temperature is examined mathematically later.

A fourth factor is the presence or absence of particular substances which may increase or diminish the velocity of the chemical change, without being themselves permanently altered. Thus the velocity of a reaction between substances dissolved in water is different from the velocity of the same reaction, when the solvent is alcohol or benzene. Certain chemical reactions, including many of the most important in animals and plants, appear only to take place in the presence of these substances, which apparently need only be present in relatively small quantities. Changes of this sort are grouped under the head of catalytic action, or catalysis (*q.v.*); the substances essential to bring about the chemical changes between the reactants are called catalysts, or, in the case of the animal and plant ferments, enzymes (*q.v.*). The phenomena of catalysis and adsorption (*q.v.*) are closely connected with reaction velocity.

Finally, the velocity of a chemical change may be determined by the supply of energy to the reacting system from an external source. If this is light energy we have the phenomena of photochemistry (*q.v.*); if electrical energy, the velocity of the reaction will depend on the principles discussed under electrochemistry (*q.v.*), especially the laws of Faraday. The transformations of matter which occur in radioactive changes (*see* RADIOACTIVITY, NATURAL) differ from ordinary chemical changes in proceeding at rates which are determined entirely by the inner structure of the atoms of the radioactive elements, and are thus quite independent of the states of combination of those elements and even of the temperature.

CHEMICAL EQUILIBRIUM

Law of Mass Action.—We have referred to the observation of Berthollet that the concentration of the reactants is often sufficient to determine whether a given reaction or its reverse will take place. In this way we may explain why it so often happens that a chemical change fails to become complete, and comes to an apparent halt before the reacting material has been completely transformed. Evidently the forward reaction, transforming reactants A and B into resultants A′ and B′, is accompanied by a reaction which transforms A′ and B′ into A and B. Thus each reaction offsets the other, and the chemical change accordingly remains incomplete. The result is chemical equilibrium, commonly formulated with reversed arrows, thus:

$$A + B \rightleftarrows A' + B'$$

The proportions in which the different reactants are present in a mixture of substances which have attained a condition of chemical equilibrium are determined by a principle discovered by C. M. Guldberg and P. Waage in 1867. These investigators showed that the state of equilibrium attained in a reversible reaction can be interpreted on the assumption that the equilibrium state is the result of the equality of the speeds of the two opposed reactions, for each of which the velocity v or v' can be expressed in terms of a constant multiplied by the concentrations of the reacting substances, expressed by [A], [B], or [A′], [B′]. The velocities of the two opposed reactions are therefore given by $v=k$ [A].[B] and $v'=k'$ [A′].[B′]. At equilibrium these two velocities are equal, hence

$$k/k' = [A'][B']/[A][B] = K$$

in which K is the so-called equilibrium constant. If the reaction corresponds with

$$mA + nB \rightleftarrows m'A' + n'B',$$

the equilibrium constant may be written

$$K = \frac{[A']^{m'}[B']^{n'}}{[A]^m[B]^n}$$

The practical importance of a knowledge of equilibrium constants, calculated as just shown, will be realized when it is remarked that the equilibrium constant for any given reaction at a given temperature is independent of the concentrations in which the reactants are brought together. Thus when the numerical value of the constant has once been determined we may substitute this in the preceding equations, and determine the proportions in which the reactants and resultants will be intermingled when equilibrium is reached, starting from any given initial concentrations.

Though the mathematical expressions just given (commonly called mass-action expressions) may be regarded as empirical statements of actual laboratory experience with systems in chemical equilibrium, nevertheless they may readily be derived from the kinetic theory. It may be assumed in the simplest case that the interaction of two reactants A and B is the result of collision between the respective molecules. It follows that the rate of change should be proportional to the frequency with which such collisions occur The frequency with which a given molecule of A collides with molecules of B is proportional to the number of the latter in unit volume, *i.e.*, the molecular concentration of B; and in the same way the frequency of the collisions between a given molecule of B and the molecules of A is proportional to the molecular concentration of the latter. The total number of collisions between the molecules of A and B is therefore proportional to the product of the molar concentrations.

Kinetic considerations thus led to $v = k[A][B]$ which is the expression for the reaction velocity, embodied in mass-action expressions above. The coefficient k in this formula is called the specific reaction rate, and represents the velocity when the concentrations of the two reacting substances are each equal to unity. It depends on the nature of the reacting substances, the temperature, and the medium (solvent) in which the reaction occurs. In the case of gaseous reactions there is no solvent to be considered, but it may be noted that many apparently gaseous reactions are in reality surface reactions, *i.e.*, reactions which take place largely, if not entirely, on the surface of the walls of the containing vessel. (*See* ADSORPTION.)

Influence of Temperature on Reaction Velocity.—The principal weakness of the explanation which makes chemical change depend solely on collisions between molecules, is that the velocity should be approximately the same for all reactions of the same type under like conditions of temperature and concentration. Actually rate of chemical change is a highly specific quantity, which varies widely from one reaction to another. Moreover, if we conceive of reaction rate as depending altogether on the frequency of collisions between molecules, we find it impossible to account for the extraordinary influence of temperature on reaction rate. In the simplest cases, an increase of temperature of 10° C. would speed up the molecules sufficiently to make collisions between them several per cent more frequent, whereas reaction velocity in that temperature range is actually increased several hundred per cent. The simplest way of explaining this involves the assumption that molecular collision is not always followed by chemical change. Collision between molecules, when reactants A and B are transformed into resultants A′ and B′, is a necessary but not sufficient condition for reaction.

We have then to account for the fact that the proportion of the colliding molecules which react grows rapidly larger as the temperature is increased. We might assume that reaction takes place only when molecules collide that happen to have velocities exceeding some stated critical velocity Yet the proportion of such molecules, calculated from Maxwell's law of distribution of velocities, does not increase with increasing temperature in a way that fits the experimental facts.

Actually, as was first pointed out by Svante Arrhenius (1889), the specific reaction rate k for many common reactions varies with the temperature in a way that may be explained by assuming that only a very small proportion of the molecules are in a condition to react on collision. In other words the vast majority of collisions do not result in chemical change but this only takes place when the energy content of the colliding molecules is much greater than the average. The proportion (α) of the effective collisions increases rapidly with the temperature and if the extra energy (energy of activation) required at the absolute temperature T is represented by q, then the empirical relation of Arrhenius for the connection between reaction velocity and temperature may be put in the form

$$d\ln\alpha/dT = q/RT^2 \quad \text{or} \quad \alpha = e^{-q/RT}$$

At a given temperature, the value of α thus depends on the magnitude of q and diminishes as q increases. When the concept of active molecules is incorporated in the mass action equation, this becomes

$$v = k \, . \, e^{-q/RT} . [A] . [B]$$

in which q represents the extra energy of the impact which is required for the collisions between molecules of A and B to be effective.

This discussion neglects the possibility that even molecules possessed of the requisite supply of energy may not react when they collide unless they happen to be disposed in favourable positions with respect to each other at the moment of collision. A collision between molecules of ethyl alcohol and acetic acid, for example, would not be expected to produce a molecule of ethyl acetate unless the hydroxyl and carboxyl groups are favourably placed when collision takes place. Neglecting this difficulty, the coefficient k can be evaluated in terms of specific and general constants and the equation for the bimolecular reaction becomes

$$v = N\sigma^2\sqrt{[8\pi RT(1/m_A + 1/m_B)]} \, . \, e^{-(q_A+q_B)/RT} . [A] . [B]$$

in which N is the Avogadro number (6×10^{23}), σ is the mean diameter of the molecules and m_A and m_B are the molecular weights of A and B. This equation, due to W. C. McC. Lewis (1918) does actually enable us to calculate certain reaction rates with an accuracy which is satisfactory in view of the fact that the effective diameter of the colliding molecules is known only very roughly.

Unimolecular Reactions.—The assumption embodied in the preceding discussion, that chemical change occurs when molecules collide which happen to be possessed of a more-than-average supply of energy, at once meets the difficulty that many reversible reactions are known in which collisions between molecules appear to play no part. Thus when phosphorus pentachloride dissociates, forming phosphorus trichloride and chlorine, according to the equation $PCl_5 \rightleftarrows PCl_3 + Cl_2$, each molecule of PCl_5 would seem to decompose independently of other molecules in accordance with the ordinary law of chance. By some chemists it has been asserted that such chemical changes (called unimolecular reactions) are not really possible. The fact that they seem to be of frequent occurrence is presumed to be explained by the presence of traces of foreign substances, which, in acting as catalysts, provide the means for interpreting the mechanism on the basis of molecular collisions.

Recent work would, however, seem to have definitely established the occurrence of noncatalyzed gaseous reactions which proceed in accordance with the requirements of the unimolecular type of change over a wide range of concentration. An explanation of these has been sought in the radiation hypothesis, according to which the cause of the reaction is to be found in the selective absorption of radiant energy. The mechanism of the photochemical change would on this view by extended to all types of chemical reaction (*see* PHOTOCHEMISTRY). The wave length of the active radiation can be derived from the heat of activation of the molecules by Planck's relation, $q = h\nu$ (*see* QUANTUM MECHANICS), but in general the reacting substances afford no evidence of the requisite absorption bands. For this and other reasons the radiation hypothesis cannot be said to be acceptable. For a fuller discussion see *Trans. Faraday Soc.* (1922).

On the other hand, it seems probable that the apparently unimolecular reactions are primarily the result of molecular collisions, for it is only necessary to assume that the molecules activated by collision are for the most part deactivated by further collisions before they have time to reach that particular internal phase which is essential for chemical change to occur and the observed facts can be readily accounted for.

Since the molecules of the reaction products are the result of collisions between active molecules of the reactants and therefore, in general, distinguished by a high energy content, it follows that such "hot" molecules may hand on their excess of energy to other molecules of the reactants leading to a so-called chain reaction. Such chain reactions constitute a type which is illustrated by the combination of hydrogen and chlorine.

Chemical Activity.—Reference may now be made to the results which have followed from the application of thermodynamics to the problems of chemical action. Although the time factor is alien to the processes with which thermodynamics is concerned, the arguments peculiar to this branch of analysis can of course be applied to the states of equilibrium which are finally attained in reversible reactions. If the reacting substances are ideal gases (or solutes) thermodynamic reasoning leads to results which are identical with the expression for the law of mass action which follows from the kinetic theory. When the substances are not ideal, thermodynamics leads to the conclusion that the concentration terms in the mass-law expression should be replaced by the corresponding activities. The activity or effective concentration a of any substance is defined by the relation $\Delta F = RT \log a/a_0$, in which ΔF is the diminution of free energy associated with the reversible transformation of the substance from the condition defined by a to a standard condition defined by a_0. The activity in the standard condition may conveniently be taken as unity.

In practical applications the attempt is made to calculate activity or effective concentration by multiplying the actual concentration c, for the given substance, by an activity coefficient,

f, which is itself a function of the concentration. Then by substituting $a=fc$ for c, in the mass-action expressions given above, more nearly constant values for the equilibrium constant are found than would otherwise be obtained. To be fully satisfactory, this method would require that the activity coefficient, f, by means of which actual concentrations are converted into effective concentrations, should be independent of the nature of the reaction in which the given substance takes part. This has been found not to be the case. Accordingly J. N. Brönsted has introduced the assumption that the interaction of two substances A and B involves the intermediate formation of a "collision complex" X and this leads to $v=kc_A.c_B.f_A.f_B/f_X$ where f_X is the activity coefficient of the complex. In this connection it may be noted that the activity coefficients of ions depend largely on their charges and on the ionic strength of their environment. (Ionic strength is calculated by taking half the sum of products formed by multiplying the concentration of each cation or anion in the solution by the square of its valence.) In accordance with the theory of P. Debye and E. Hückel, the relation may be expressed in the form $-\log f=0.5x^2\sqrt{\mu}$ where x is the valence of the ion concerned and μ is the ionic strength of the solution in which it is present. This relation, when combined with Brönsted's reaction-velocity formula, affords results for ionic reactions of varied types which are in accord with experimental observations provided that the solutions are sufficiently dilute.

IONIC THEORY

Relative Strengths of Acids and Bases.—Although much recent work has been concerned with the precise significance of "active mass," the classical interpretation of this as synonymous with molecular concentration has yielded results of the greatest importance in the interpretation of the manifold phenomena associated with aqueous solutions of acids, bases and salts (*see* SOLUTION). Such substances are, in general, electrolytic conductors, and in accordance with the theory of Arrhenius are ionized to a greater or less extent. The traditional view, that salt formation corresponds with the neutralization of opposite qualities which characterize the acids and bases respectively, finds simple expression in the ionic theory, for, according to this, acids are substances which increase the hydrogen-ion concentration of water, while bases have the opposite effect. In aqueous solutions, the concentration of the hydrogen ion is directly connected with the hydroxyl-ion concentration, by the mass-action expression

$$K=\frac{[H^+].[OH^-]}{[H_2O]}$$

In all dilute aqueous solutions however the concentration of the un-ionized water $[H_2O]$ is nearly constant (55.5 moles per litre). Accordingly in all dilute aqueous solutions, whether acid, alkaline or neutral, the product of the two ion concentrations has a nearly constant value (10^{-14} at 25° C.). In neutral solutions hydrogen-ion (sometimes called hydrion) and hydroxyl-ion are present in equal concentrations 10^{-7} gram-ions per litre at 25° C.). In acid solutions the concentration of hydrogen-ion exceeds that of hydroxyl-ion; in alkaline solutions the reverse is true. Yet hydroxyl-ion is never completely absent from acid solutions, nor hydrogen-ion from alkaline solutions, for the concentrations of the two ions must always be so related that the ion product, $[H^+].[OH^-]$ has the constant value 10^{-14}, at 25° C. At higher temperatures the ion product increases very rapidly, attaining a value of about 60×10^{-14} at 100° C.

Equivalent solutions of different acids show very great differences in the hydrion concentration. These are exhibited very clearly when the electrical conductivities of such solutions are compared or when a comparison is made of the velocities with which certain reactions take place when these are subjected to the catalyzing influence of the various acids. The two series of numbers show a close parallelism which finds a simple interpretation in terms of the view that the differences between the acids are primarily caused by differences in their respective degrees of ionization. The conductivity is indeed proportional to the concentration of the ionized fraction of the acid and the catalytic effect is determined for the most part by the hydrion concentration. The application of the mass law to the equilibrium between the un-ionized acid and the corresponding ions, as represented by

$HA\rightleftarrows\overset{+}{H}+\overset{-}{A}$, gives

$$K=[\overset{+}{H}][\overset{-}{A}]/[HA]=(c\alpha)^2/c(1-\alpha)=c\alpha^2/(1-\alpha)$$

for the ionization constant, c being the molar concentration of the acid and α the fractional degree of ionization. In spite of the charges on the ions, this relation between the concentration of the acid and its degree of ionization is in very close agreement with the actual behaviour of weak or slightly ionized acids, as was clearly demonstrated by Wilhelm Ostwald. The results obtained in this connection constitute in fact the strongest and most comprehensive evidence as yet available in favour of the quantitative application of the law of mass action to states of equilibrium. The Ostwald dilution law does not hold for solutions of salts or more active (largely ionized) acids or bases. Many chemists have indeed arrived at the conclusion that most salts are completely ionized, at all concentrations. (*See* also HYDROGEN-IONS.)

Neutralization of Acids by Bases.—In the neutralization of an acid by the gradual addition of a base, the essential reaction consists in the combination of hydrogen ions with hydroxyl ions until the concentration of both reaches the value for pure water, viz., 10^{-7} gram-equivalents per litre (25°), which condition is shown by suitable indicators (*q.v.*). The constancy of the heat of neutralization of the strong acids by the strong bases is explained in this way. If one equivalent of a base BOH is added to a solution which contains one equivalent of each of two different acids HA_1 and HA_2, the relative proportions of the two acids which are neutralized afford a measure of the so-called relative affinities of the acids for the base. Because of such differences stronger acids tend to displace weaker acids from the corresponding salts. Such displacement effects, however, are not always the result of a difference in the affinities of the acids, for complications may occur in consequence of the removal of one of the resultant substances from the sphere of action in the form of an insoluble solid or a volatile gas; *e.g.*, the displacement of nitric acid by the relatively very weak acid hydrogen sulphide in accordance with $2AgNO_3 + H_2S \rightarrow Ag_2S + 2HNO_3$ is directly due to the insolubility of silver sulphide. The basic affinities of a pair of acids can in fact only be derived from a determination of the relative amounts which are neutralized by a base when the system is homogeneous. If x is the fraction of the acid HA, which is neutralized by the base, BOH, in the above solution, the resulting equilibrium can be represented by

$$(1-x)HA_1 + (1-x)BA_2 = xBA_1 + x\text{–}HA_2,$$

and the evaluation of x, which can be effected by a variety of physical methods, gives up the ratio $x/(1-x)$ which expresses the affinity of HA_1 relatively to HA_2. When such affinity values, referred to an acid chosen as standard, are compared, it is found that the acids form a series which is essentially the same as the series given by the relative conductivities and catalytic activities. It can be shown that this experimental result is generally consistent with the hydrion theory of acids for the application of the mass law to the equilibria which are involved in the above mentioned competition of two acids for a base shows that the affinity ratio $x/(1-x)$ is the ratio of the degrees of ionization of the two acids. The fact that $x/(1-x)$ is independent of the nature of the base is also explained at the same time. Similar considerations apply to the relative strengths of bases. At a given concentration their characteristic properties can be explained in terms of the hydroxyl-ion concentration. Since degrees of ionization vary with the concentration, it is convenient to eliminate the latter. This can be done by comparing the strengths of acids and bases in terms of the respective ionization constants.

BIBLIOGRAPHY.—J. H. van't Hoff, *Studies in Chemical Dynamics*, trans. T. Ewan (1896); J. W. Mellor, *Statics and Dynamics* (1914); G. N. Lewis and M. Randall, *Thermodynamics* (1923); H. S. Taylor, *A Treatise on Physical Chemistry* (1924); E. K. Rideal and H. S.

Taylor, *Catalysis in Theory and Practice* (1926); C. N. Hinshelwood, *The Kinetics of Chemical Change in Gaseous Systems.* (H. M. D.)

CHEMICAL APPARATUS. Chemical laboratory operations deal with gases, liquids and solids, and require for their manipulation a variety of specialized apparatus. Many of these find their counterpart in the home, since some of the unit operations such as heating, cooling, solution, etc., are a necessary part of our daily life. There is no fundamental difference between the laboratory Bunsen or Meker gas burner and the burner on the conventional kitchen gas-range. Frequently, the chemist may use the same glassware for a chemical manipulation that is used for baking or cooking in the home kitchen. In general, however, he must conduct his work with great care, as in analytical chemistry. The reagents are often corrosive and may be subjected to extremes of temperature or pressure, so that over a period of many years there has been devised a large number of items to facilitate chemical tasks.

Since chemical reactions can take place in the solid, liquid or gaseous phase a considerable proportion of laboratory apparatus is devoted to the processes of solution, extraction, filtration, precipitation, evaporation, distillation and desiccation. For these purposes flasks, beakers, suction pumps, suction flasks, water-baths, funnels, fractionating columns and stills are employed. Gases are conveniently manipulated in drying towers, aspirator pumps, gas generators, wash bottles and connections of glass tubing including stopcocks. Typical analytical chemical apparatus illustrated below includes crucibles, weighing bottles, burettes or burets, pipettes, graduates and graduated flasks.

Different pieces of apparatus may be connected with glass, rubber or plastic tubing. Stoppers of rubber or cork are used to make renewable seals at certain points such as thermometer inserts or connections between tubes. There is available a complete selection of glass apparatus such as flasks, condensers, columns and stopcocks comprising units of various sizes which fit together with either standard taper or hemispherical (semiball) joints to form gas-tight and liquid-tight seals. Since this glassware may be arranged at will to perform a large variety of unit operations it is gradually supplanting cork and rubber stopper closures in the more advanced laboratories. In order to ensure uniformity between the products of several manufacturers the United States bureau of standards has established tolerances for these joints and certifies master joints of steel for their checking. Both types of joints may be lubricated with rubber-petrolatum or synthetic ("Silicone") greases to render the joints completely gas-tight.

Physical measurements are an important part of laboratory practice and a chemical laboratory may employ a variety of measuring instruments. Mercury or liquid-in-glass thermometers, bimetallic thermometers, resistance thermometers and thermocouples are used for temperature measurement, whereas mercury or other fluid manometers and Bourdon gages are used to measure pressures. The chemical balance is used for weighing and it is constructed in many modifications depending upon the capacity and sensitivity demanded. The spectroscope (*see* SPECTROSCOPY) or spectrograph measures either the absorption or emission of light, and the colorimeter is used for exact colour comparison as in analytical determinations. Electrical measurements form the basis for the determination of hydrogen-ion concentrations (*q.v.*) using the *p*H meter, and reduction potentials are charted by the polarograph. Electrometric titrations as well as dyestuff indicators serve to determine the end-point in analytical titrimetry while burettes are available to measure amounts of liquids as small as $\frac{1}{1,000}$ ml. with analytical accuracy. The index of refraction of light determined with the refractometer furnishes a useful guide to the purity and identity of chemical compounds, while the microscope makes it possible to manipulate and to observe beyond the capacity of the unaided eye. (*See* CHEMISTRY: *Analytical Chemistry.*)

Laboratory technique is constantly being refined and improved. For the manipulation of a few milligrams of scarce or valuable material there has been developed a group of miniature beakers, flasks, funnels, etc., which is called microchemical equipment. Although some of these are merely small-scale models of the larger apparatus, others are truly novel in design and are cleverly adapted to ultra-precise work. A few of these are illustrated below.

The following list refers to the accompanying illustrations of apparatus commonly used in a chemical laboratory.

General Apparatus

1. Spatulas and spoons, for dealing with small quantities of material without touching by hand. They may be made of (*a*) porcelain, (*b*) steel, (*c*) silver or other corrosion-resistant materials.
2. (*a*) Pinchcock or spring clip (Mohr's pattern). (*b*) Screw clamp or clip (Hoffmann).
3. (*a*) Bunsen burner (Tirrill type) with adjustable gas and air flow. (*b*) Meker burner for producing an intense flame over a broad area. Used for heating crucibles to high temperatures. (*c*) Wing-top which slips onto top of Bunsen burner to form "fish-tail"-shaped flame.
4. Water-bath and rings on tripod. The bath is nearly filled with water which is heated by a burner underneath. Removal of one or more of the rings enables any circular vessel (*e.g.*, an evaporating basin) to rest in the hole of appropriate size, and its contents are slowly heated or evaporated. A constant-level device maintains the level of the water in the bath and obviates refilling.
5. (*a*) Support with iron rings, (*b*) clamps and (*c*) clamp fastener (boss).
6. Blast lamp or blast burner. Separate valves are provided for controlling the flow of oxygen and air which are mixed and fed to the gas through a central tube. The gas issuing from the outer sleeve forms a brush flame or a fine-pointed flame depending upon the adjustment of the mixture.
7. (*a*) Test-tube stand and test tubes. (*b*) Spring-clamp test-tube holder.
8. Water-jet suction pump, for use with filter flask and either Büchner funnel (fig. 9) or Gooch crucible (fig. 33). The stream of water is broken up at the jet A and entrains air in its passage down the tube B. This is capable of reducing the pressure as low as the vapour pressure of water.
9. Apparatus for filtering by suction. (*a*) Büchner funnel fitted with a cork or rubber stopper into a filter flask which is attached to a suction pump (see fig. 8) by means of rubber tubing. A circle of filter paper is placed on the perforated bottom and the material retained by it can be sucked dry, washed and pressed. (*b*) Hirsch funnel. (*c*) Sintered-glass funnel. (*d*) Ordinary funnel.
10. Evaporating dish or basin (porcelain or glass).
11. Casserole (porcelain).
12. Filter stand, funnel and beaker for gravity filtration. A filter paper is folded so as to fit into the funnel as shown; it retains solids while liquids filter into the beaker.
13. Mercury in glass thermometer. Numerous scales are available for both higher and lower temperature ranges.
14. Drying tower. Similar in function to fig. 15, but used where gases have to be passed through a granulated solid.
15. Wash-bottle for gases (Drechsel pattern). If the gas is bubbled through the liquid it can be freed from one or more impurities, *e.g.,* it can be dried by passage through concentrated sulphuric acid, or freed from carbon dioxide by a solution of sodium hydroxide.
16. Aspirator bottle. A cork carrying a tube is inserted into the top opening while a stopcock may be attached to the lower opening and the bottle is filled with water. On opening the stopcock, water will flow out and this will draw air through the tube which may be attached to any other apparatus.
17. Kipp gas generator. Hydrochloric acid (HCl) is allowed to run down the central tube and rise so as to act on the iron sulphide; if the tap is open hydrogen sulphide gas (H_2S) is expelled by the pressure of the "head" of acid; when the stopcock is closed the gas forces the acid into the top bulb and no more gas is produced. If marble (calcium carbonate) is used instead of iron sulphide, carbon dioxide (CO_2) is obtained. It may also be used to generate hydrogen gas by zinc metal and dilute sulphuric acid.
18. Desiccator. Concentrated sulphuric acid, granular calcium chloride or other desiccant is kept in the bottom; the material to be dried is spread on a watch-glass or evaporating dish resting on the gauze or on a perforated porcelain plate. An accelerated drying effect is produced by evacuating the desiccator through the stopcock tube by means of the suction pump shown in fig. 8.
19. Separatory funnels: (*a*) pear-shaped—also called a dropping funnel; and (*b*) cylindrical. If ether has been used to extract an organic substance from water, two layers are formed and the lower (aqueous) layer can be run off. Similarly, if chloroform had been used instead of ether, the lower layer would be the chloroform extract.
20. Pestle and mortar (of porcelain).

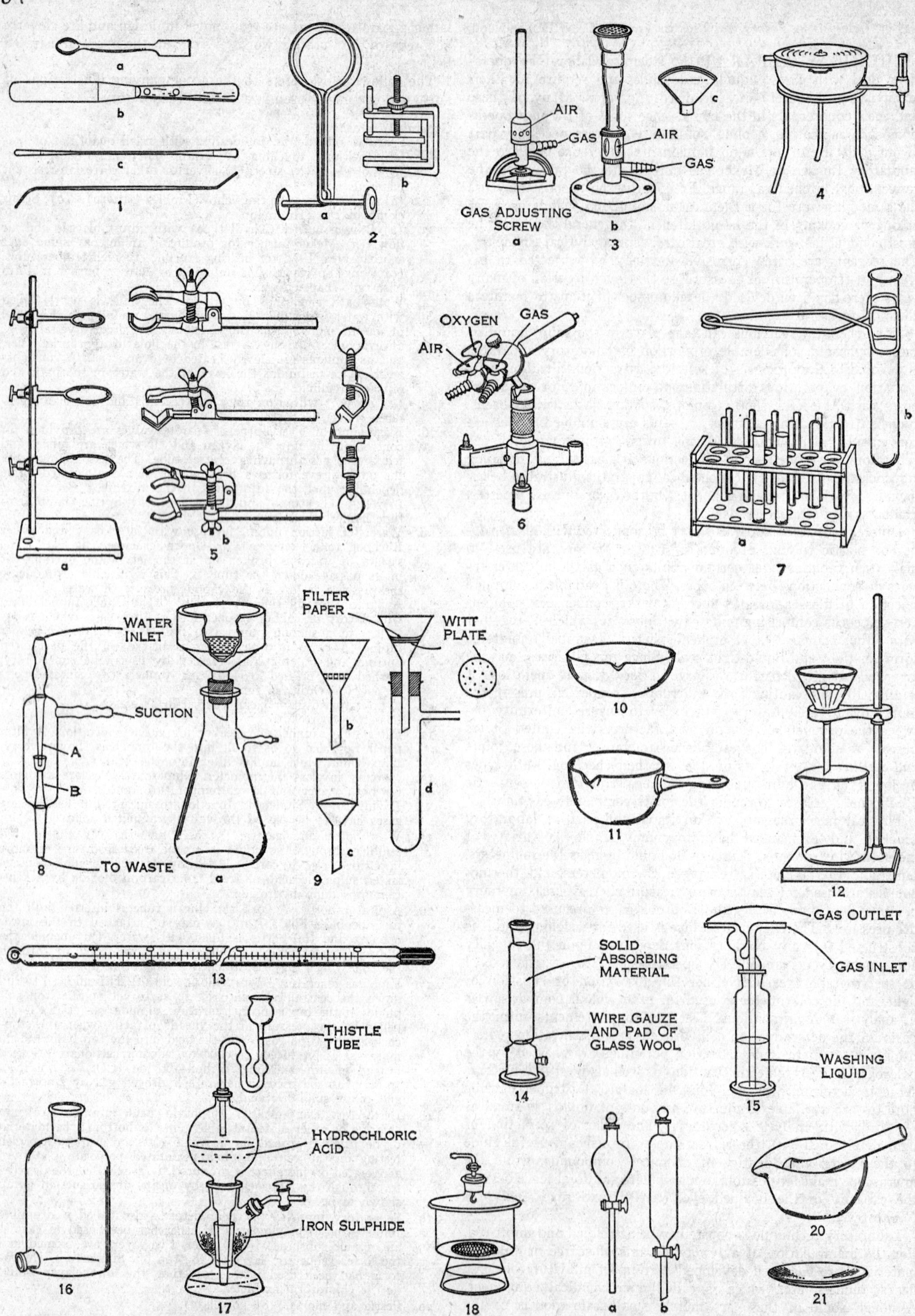

FIGS. 1 AND 9 FROM LOUIS FIESER, "EXPERIMENTS IN ORGANIC CHEMISTRY," COURTESY D. C. HEATH & COMPANY

FIGS. 1–21.—COMMON CHEMICAL APPARATUS (THE NUMBERS REFER TO DESCRIPTIONS IN THE TEXT)

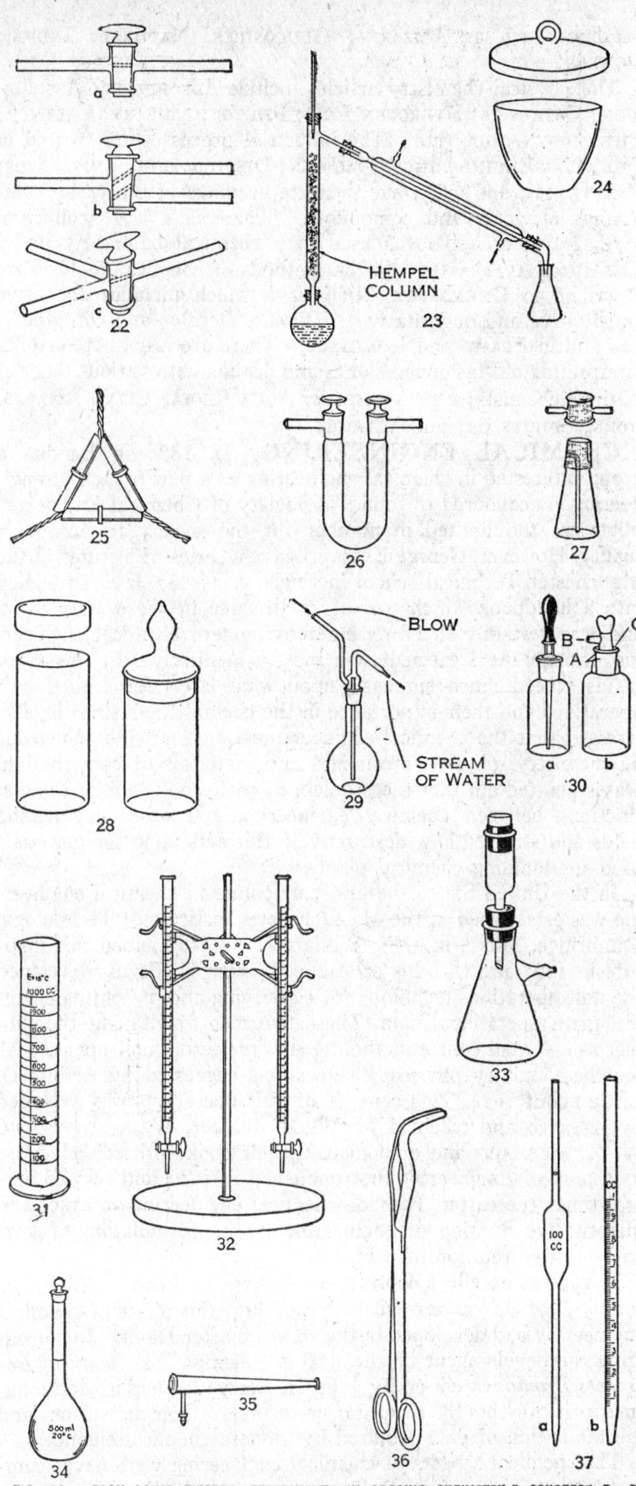

FIG. 23 FROM LOUIS FIESER, "EXPERIMENTS IN ORGANIC CHEMISTRY," COURTESY D. C. HEATH & COMPANY

FIGS. 22–37.—CHEMICAL APPARATUS USED FOR ANALYSIS

21. Watch-glass for covering beakers while evaporating liquid. It is usually supported on glass U-shaped rods hung on the edge of the beaker.
22. Stopcocks or taps. (*a*) A half turn shuts off the flow. (*b*) Three-way oblique bore plug. A half turn connects the lower limb with the left hand tube. (*c*) T-bore stopcock.
23. Distillation with a fractionating column. The liquid in the round-bottom flask is boiled and the vapours pass through the column where partial condensation occurs. The reflux liquid washes the ascending gases which then pass into water-cooled condenser where they are condensed to a liquid. A thermometer indicates temperature of the condensing liquid and an adapter leads to receiver which is an Erlenmeyer flask.

Apparatus Used in Analysis

24. Crucible and lid made of porcelain, quartz or platinum. Used for igniting precipitates.
25. Clay triangle for supporting crucible on tripod or ring.
26. U-tube. May be filled with granulated soda-lime to absorb carbon dioxide, or with pumice soaked in sulphuric acid to absorb water vapour. The ground-in stopcocks can be turned to shut off connection with the outer air.
27. Absorption bulb (Turner). Used for the absorption of carbon dioxide formed by the combustion of steel in oxygen. The stopper may be rotated so as to close both openings after the combustion has been completed.
28. Weighing bottles, for protecting material from the air while it is being weighed. A portion of the contained substance is shaken out and the whole reweighed, the amount of material thus taken being the difference in weight.
29. Wash bottle. A fine stream of water (or organic solvent) can be directed where required.
30. Dropping-bottles. (*a*) By slightly pressing the rubber nipple and releasing the pressure, a few drops are drawn up in the glass tube and can be squeezed out one at a time when the nozzle is withdrawn. (*b*) Liquid flows along the capillary tube at A when the bottle is tilted, and a drop falls from B, air entering through another channel at C. Used chiefly for indicators (*q.v.*).
31. Graduate or measuring cylinder.
32. Burettes in stand. Used for titrations. The volume of liquid delivered is accurately read on the graduated scale (*see* CHEMISTRY: *Analytical Chemistry*).
33. Gooch crucible with rubber cone, glass adapter and filter flask. The bottom of the crucible is perforated with small holes, and a mat of asbestos is formed on it by pouring in a pulp of asbestos and water, sucking it nearly dry and completely drying it in the oven. Used for filtering, washing, drying and weighing precipitates.
34. Volumetric flask. Contains the stipulated volume when filled to the mark with a liquid at 20° C., the temperature at which it was calibrated. Used for preparing "standard" solutions, *i.e.,* solutions containing a definite quantity of solid dissolved in an exact volume of solution.
35. Mouth blowpipe; used for directing a small flame jet onto the substance being analyzed (usually supported on a block of charcoal).
36. Crucible tongs; may be tipped with platinum for refined work.
37. Pipettes (not to scale). (*a*) If filled exactly to the mark by suction it will then deliver the stipulated volume on draining for 15 sec. after continuous flow has ceased. (*b*) Can be used for gradual addition of small quantities which are read off on the scale.
38. Graduated conical centrifuge tube for measuring small volumes of centrifuged solid or liquid at the bottom.
39. Electrically heated oven with thermostatic control for drying precipitates to constant weight.

Special Apparatus

40. Soxhlet extractor. The material to be extracted is placed in a "thimble" of filter paper. Ether or other volatile solvent is boiled in the flask and passes through the side tube A to the reflux condenser C. The condensed liquid drops into the thimble where it accumulates until it reaches the level of the top of the side arm B, and then siphons over into the flask. Several complete cycles are permitted to occur before the

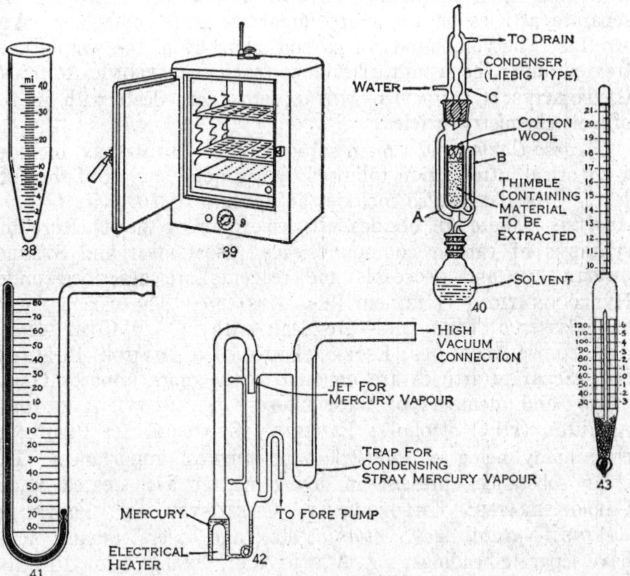

FIGS. 38–43.—CHEMICAL APPARATUS USED FOR ANALYSIS AND SPECIAL APPARATUS

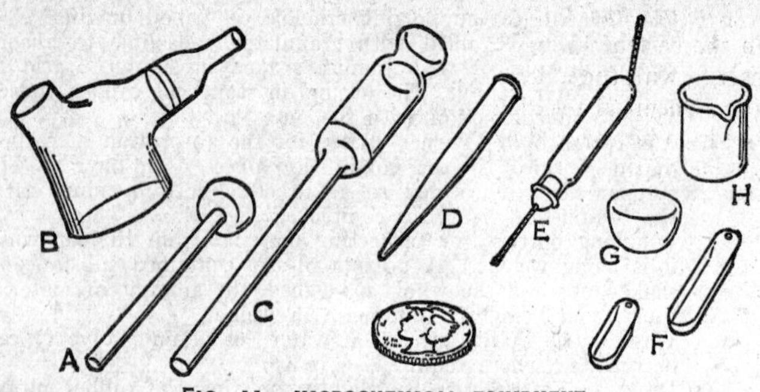

FIG. 44.—MICROCHEMICAL EQUIPMENT

Shown in size relationship to a ten-cent piece are: A. Porcelain filter stick for sucking liquids away from solids. B. Microfilter beaker. C. Sintered glass funnel. D. Microcentrifuge tube. E. Weighing tube (for protecting sample in boat from air during weighing. F. Microcombustion boats (small and medium size). G. 1-ml. porcelain crucible. H. 1-ml. glass beaker.

solvent flask is disconnected and the solvent evaporated to leave the extracted material.

41. Mercury manometer for vacuum distillations. The left-hand tube is completely filled with mercury as shown. When the side tube is connected to a system being evacuated the level in the left-hand tube drops while that in the right-hand tube rises, and the difference in height between the tops of the two mercury columns indicates the pressure in the system in millimetres of mercury.

42. Mercury vapour diffusion pump for producing high vacuum. The high velocity jet of mercury vapour permits diffusion of the other gases in the system into it. These are then removed by the fore pump after condensing the mercury in the condenser.

43. Hydrometer for determining the specific gravity of liquids. The instrument is floated in the liquid and the point on the scale in the stem coinciding with the surface level of the liquid indicates the specific gravity compared with water. A thermometer in the lower portion indicates the temperature of the liquid at the same time. Usually the liquid is brought to some specified temperature before the specific gravity is determined.

44. Microchemical equipment. (E. B. HG.)

CHEMICAL ARTICLES. The main article CHEMISTRY includes a general survey of the *History of Chemistry,* and also deals comprehensively with the various branches of this science; viz., *Inorganic, Organic, Physical* and *Analytical Chemistry.* These and their practical applications are treated in fuller detail in the chemistry articles appearing in this encyclopaedia. There are articles elucidating fundamental ideas and definitions and explaining chemical changes; *e.g.,* ACIDS AND BASES; ATOM; COMBUSTION; ELEMENTS, CHEMICAL; MOLECULE, CHEMICAL; OXIDATION AND REDUCTION; REACTION KINETICS. ATOM: *Atomic Weights* contains a list of the elements; these are described, with their chief compounds, in separate articles. There are also separate articles on the more important compounds, *e.g.,* AMMONIA. The compounds of carbon, apart from the simple ones treated under the separate headings (such as CARBONIC ACID AND CARBONATES; CARBONYLS, METAL; etc.), are dealt with in the organic chemistry articles.

Organic Chemistry, a main sub-section of CHEMISTRY, includes a historical introduction followed by a general survey of the subject. CHEMISTRY also includes an account of *Ultimate Organic Analysis.* There are, besides, articles explaining the structure and synthesis of carbon compounds, *e.g.,* ISOMERISM and STEREOCHEMISTRY; and processes and reagents are described under HYDROGENATION; GRIGNARD REAGENTS; etc. The various types and classes of compounds are dealt with in AZO COMPOUNDS; ALKALOIDS; ALCOHOLS; ESTERS; KETONES; CAMPHOR; PURINES; etc. Separate articles are devoted to the more important subgroups and members of these classes, *e.g.,* BUTYL ALCOHOLS; ALCOHOL (ethyl alcohol); BENZENE; CHLOROFORM; PYRIDINE; etc.; many being of industrial and medical importance. The chief substances present in living matter are treated under CARBOHYDRATES; CHLOROPHYLL, CHEMISTRY OF; PROTEINS; RESINS: *Natural and Synthetic;* etc.; and several organic acids have separate headings; *e.g.,* ACETIC ACID; OXALIC ACID; PHENOL OR CARBOLIC ACID; URIC ACID. Dyes and pigments are dealt with in DYES, NATURAL; and DYES, SYNTHETIC; and under various headings such as ALIZARIN; GLUCOSIDES, NATURAL; INDIGO; OCHRES; etc.

The physical chemistry articles include ADSORPTION; ASSOCIATION; CATALYSIS; HYDROGEN IONS; PHOTOCHEMISTRY; VALENCE; THERMODYNAMICS; etc. The industrial processes are treated in CHEMICAL ENGINEERING; COAL TAR; DISTILLATION; EXPLOSIVES; SUGAR; etc.; and under the separate headings of the various important elements and compounds. There is a large collection of diagrams of apparatus used in a chemical laboratory under CHEMICAL APPARATUS, and the methods of chemical analysis are described in CHEMISTRY: *Analytical,* which includes *Inorganic* (qualitative and quantitative), *Ultimate Organic* and *Gas Analysis;* and in FLAME and INDICATOR. There are also short articles interpreting old-fashioned names and dealing with various theories of the alchemists; *e.g.,* ALCHEMY; AQUA REGIA; ELIXIR; HARTSHORN, SPIRITS OF; and VITRIOL.

CHEMICAL ENGINEERING. In 1880 in London a group interested in chemical engineering as a new branch of engineering endeavoured to found "a Society of Chemical Engineers" but were too limited in number for the society to become a reality. However, George E. Davis gave a series of lectures in the Manchester Technical school in England in 1887, later embodied into a handbook which was of great value in those early years and was certainly the forerunner of modern chemical engineering, though the treatment was mostly qualitative. In this work Davis placed much emphasis upon what later were called unit operations and their importance in the chemical industry; he also stressed that the chemical engineer must have a wide knowledge of chemistry, physics, mechanics and materials of construction. Davis pointed out that the problem of corrosion is one of the distinctions between chemical engineering and other engineering fields and stressed how destructively this acts upon the materials used for building chemical plants.

In the United States the first curriculum in chemical engineering was established at the Massachusetts Institute of Technology, Cambridge, Mass., in 1888. William H. Walker joined this institute in 1903 and with his colleague, Warren K. Lewis, developed the unit operations technique for classifying and presenting chemical plant operational data. These two men first taught the subject as a formal course in about 1911; the term "unit operations" for these unitary physical changes was suggested by Arthur D. Little about 1914. This concept of unit operations was extended by research and teaching by W. H. Walker, W. K. Lewis and W. H. McAdams and embodied in their book entitled *Principles of Chemical Engineering* first published in 1923 and revised several times thereafter. It made chemical engineering an exact and quantitative division of engineering by its formulation of laws and its interpretation of data.

In 1950 an excellent book appeared by G. G. Brown *et al.,* called simply *Unit Operations* which showed how this phase of chemical engineering had developed in the 50 years after Davis. In considering the development of chemical engineering the *Chemical Engineers Handbook* edited by John H. Perry also had a wide influence as it presents the quantitative formulas, their derivations and the tabulation of data required by modern chemical engineers.

The chemical aspects of chemical engineering were never completely lost sight of in the development and education of the chemical engineer. Gradually the interests of the chemist gravitated more to the laboratory functions and teaching. Starting about 1930 in the United States much more emphasis was placed upon the chemical changes for chemical engineers. As the unit operations concept for the physical changes had been so successful, the term unit processes was suggested by P. H. Groggins in 1928 for the corresponding chemical changes.

Chemical engineering owes much to the presentation of the unitary aspect for both its physical and chemical changes; this led to the elucidation of general principles both from research in the laboratory and from observation in the plants. Thus, quantitative principles were evolved pertaining to the entire chemical industry.

Function or Work.—The chemical engineer has as his field the industries where the making of chemicals or chemical change is commercialized. These are called chemical process industries.

Here the chemical engineer is largely removed from the laboratory to the plant, leaving to the chemist the laboratory for control, research and teaching. The chemical engineer frequently carries on research for new chemical processes or for improving processes, though the initial laboratory investigation is usually reserved for the chemists. However, the chemical engineer takes a process from the laboratory through the pilot plant where he checks the equipment needed by actual trial; he then completes the design and installs the large-scale equipment in a manufacturing establishment. He runs the factory and the industrial chemical processes; the latter is probably the area that employs the greatest number of chemical engineers.

An increasing number of chemical engineers at mid-20th century were using their chemical engineering training as a foundation for sales, sales service and management. The over-all function of the chemical engineer is to run the chemical process industry in all its phases.

Physical Changes or Unit Operations.—Occasionally in the manufacture of a chemical the processes involve only unit physical operations with no chemical change taking place, as, for instance, in the rectification of impure alcohol, the distillation of petroleum into its various constituents or the crystallization of a pure salt from a mixture. As a rule, however, the unit operations such as mixing, heat transmission or flow of fluids are tied up intimately with the chemical change. The names of the principal unit operations following Perry's arrangement are:

1. Flow of fluids
2. Heat transmission
3. Evaporation
4. Distillation and sublimation
5. Gas absorption
6. Solvent extraction and dialysis
7. Humidification and cooling
8. Drying
9. Adsorption
10. Mechanical separations
11. Size reduction and size enlargement
12. Mixing of material
13. High-pressure technique
14. Movement and storage of materials

Brown's classification of the unit operations is newer and more scientific. In it the individual physical changes are arranged under solids, fluids, separation by mass transfer, and energy and mass transfer rates. Both Perry's *Handbook* and Brown's *Unit Operations* should be consulted for the quantitative data for chemical engineering unit operations.

Chemical Changes or Unit Processes.—Unit processes can be defined as the carrying on of a chemical change in an economical way in a manufacturing establishment. It is much more difficult to develop the unitary aspect of a chemical change because of the much greater complexity and the larger number of variables involved. However, the distinction between chemical reactions in the laboratory and the unit process in the factory is important because it involves large-scale equipment and economics as well as unit operations. The principal unit processes are listed as follows:

1. Combustion
2. Oxidation
3. Neutralization
4. Silicate formation
5. Causticization
6. Electrolysis
7. Double decomposition
8. Calcination
9. Dehydration
10. Nitration
11. Esterification
12. Reduction
13. Ammonolysis
14. Halogenation
15. Sulphonation
16. Hydrolysis
17. Hydrogenation
18. Alkylation
19. Friedel-Crafts
20. Condensation
21. Polymerization
22. Diazotization and coupling
23. Fermentation
24. Pyrolysis or cracking
25. Aromatization
26. Isomerization
27. Acylation
28. Oxo reaction

These unit chemical changes all have certain aspects in common, such as kinetics, equilibrium, reactants, equipment, material balances and energy balances. In presenting the chemical changes, the basic fundaments should be arranged under these divisions for all reactions or for all unit processes. In research, advanced study and in the details of industrial application there are enough differences to require a more detailed classification under the respective unit processes. There is no need to divide any unit process into the traditional inorganic and organic changes. For example, nearly the same conditions and equipment with a variation in reactants and catalysis have enabled an ammonia plant (inorganic) to be converted into a methanol (organic) establishment. The yields and conversions and other cost factors must always be considered. As research progressed a more quantitative foundation was placed under the respective unit processes.

Kinetics and Catalysis.—Because he is of necessity interested in the cost of his products, the chemical engineer is always concerned with the kinetics of the reaction; that is, the time required for a chemical reaction to proceed to a given extent. If this time needs to be reduced he turns to the use of catalysts to speed the course of the reaction. Indeed some of the most important work done by the chemical engineer in making chemicals at low cost for the consuming industries and the public has been in just such applications of basic physical chemistry to industrial chemical changes. In 1914 more suitable catalysts were discovered which increased the rate of the formation of ammonia. These reduced the cost of manufacturing ammonia and made it the basis of the present satisfactory condition of the world supply of nitrogen compounds. Ammonia could then be employed for the manufacture of many other nitrogen compounds, for fertilizers, explosives, resins, dyes and countless other applications. The kinetics of the reaction have a direct influence upon the expenditure for the equipment. If a given reaction can be made to proceed in one-half the time previously needed, it will require smaller equipment, and hence a decreased investment of capital for a plant to manufacture a required tonnage.

Equilibrium.—Likewise the chemical engineer is economically interested in how far a reaction will go, or its equilibrium. He will take advantage of the basic laws of physical chemistry, for instance that of mass action, to allow him to attain more favourable equilibrium conditions for a given reaction. This will influence the cost of the materials that enter into the making of a chemical such as ammonia or sulphur trioxide. If it is of sufficient interest, extensive equilibrium studies will be undertaken to determine the exact conditions of temperature, pressure and proportion of reactants that will furnish the most favourable result. Indeed these results will often be plotted as curves against the important variables. As was done in the case of ammonia, the chemical engineer will increase the pressure, following the principle of Le Chatelier, if there is a diminution in the relative number of molecules in the product. The higher pressure will cause a higher percentage of conversion of reactants to ammonia. On the other hand, this entails more expensive equipment to withstand these higher pressures. One of the functions of the chemical engineer is to balance the advantage of getting the more favourable equilibrium conditions against the expense entailed for both equipment and operation under this higher pressure.

Yields and Conversions.—The operational efficiency of chemical plants is interpreted in terms of the yield and conversion. These terms may be defined as follows:

$$\text{Percentage yield} = 100 \times \frac{\text{moles of main product}}{\text{moles of main product equivalent to net disappearance of chief reactant}}$$

$$\text{Percentage conversion} = 100 \times \frac{\text{moles of main product}}{\text{moles of main product equivalent to chief reactant charged}}$$

Considering the synthesis of ammonia at 300 atmospheres and 500° C. the yield is frequently about 98% while the conversion will be limited by the equilibrium figure of about 20%. This means that 80% of the charge does not react and must be recirculated. Somewhat similar figures prevail for the methanol synthesis.

The aim of the chemical engineer, concerned with the cost, is to have the conversion figures approach or equal the yield as closely as possible. This is, of course, not feasible with the ammonia reaction because of the low equilibrium results. As a corollary of the low ammonia and methanol conversions, larger equipment is required than would be necessary were the conversion figures nearer to those of the yield.

Flow Sheets.—The demand for a graphic and accurate presentation of a process led to flow sheets or flow diagrams. In these the raw materials are subjected to a co-ordinated sequence of unit chemical changes or unit physical changes to make the resulting product with or without by-products. These depict the flow and expenditure of material, energy, time and labour. The energy should include that for power, heat and chemical change. These flow sheets may be simply block type (fig. 1) or diagrammatic (fig. 2). In the latter the separate parts of the diagram

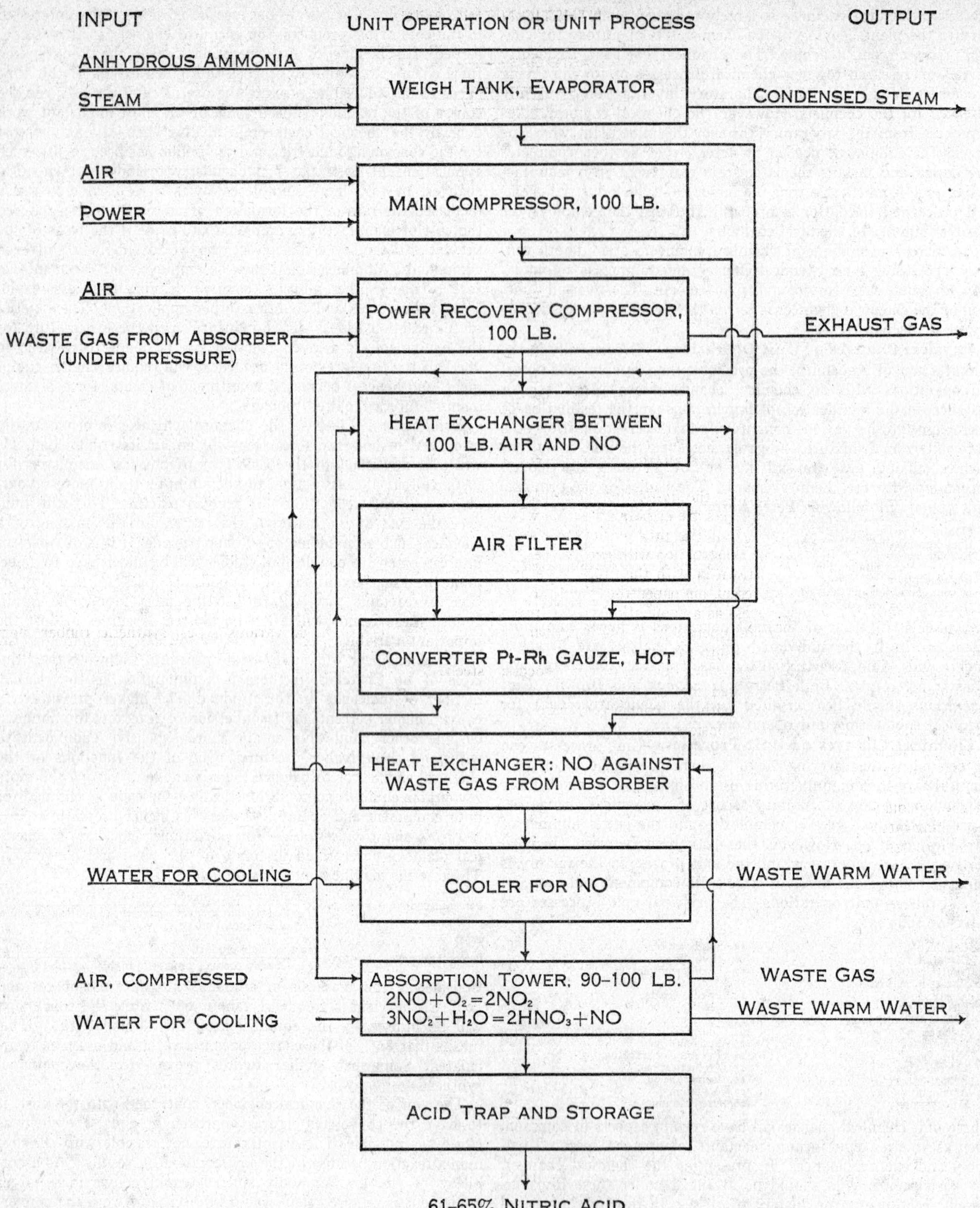

FIG. 1.—BLOCK STYLE OF FLOW SHEET FOR SYNTHETIC NITRIC ACID (100 LB. PRESSURE) FROM AMMONIA

SYNTHETIC NITRIC ACID

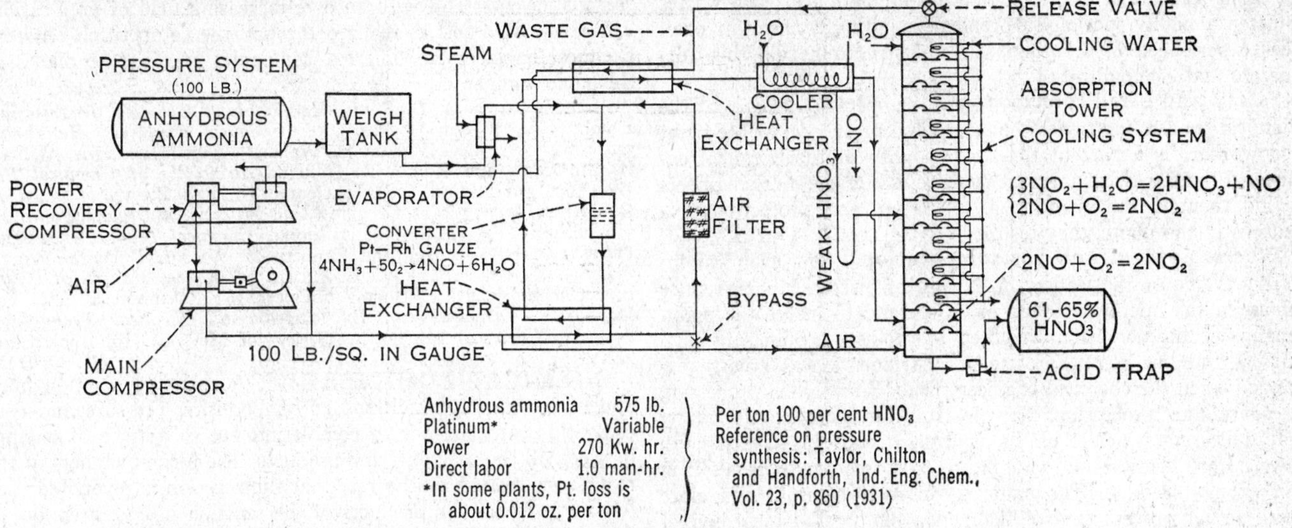

FROM R. NORRIS SHREVE, "CHEMICAL PROCESS INDUSTRIES," COURTESY MCGRAW-HILL BOOK COMPANY

FIG. 2.—DIAGRAMMATIC FLOW SHEET FOR SYNTHETIC (100 LB. PRESSURE) FROM AMMONIA

simulate the apparatus needed for the respective units. More complex or more complete flow sheets are elaborated as the work proceeds from the initial concept of the process until the final flow sheets become the basis for construction with each valve and pipe as well as all equipment drawn in with the proper size and position. Such flow sheets represent on paper the chemical engineer's concept of a given process as a summation of unit processes or chemical changes and unit operations or physical changes necessary to convert the materials into the finished products.

Material Balances.—In the economical design of any process, the amount of raw materials entered should be balanced against the materials leaving the process, with any chemical transformations calculated and taken into consideration. Such a balance shows at once any losses and may lead to reduced cost or point the way for proper investigation to reduce or remove such losses.

Energy Balances.—Similarly, such comparisons are made for energy by equating all energy entering a process against that leaving, taking into consideration any energy transformation in or out of the process. Much of the cost-reducing action of the chemical engineer is connected with his use of these two balances of material and energy. Indeed many flow sheets have as an essential part of their presentation the determination of these two balances (*see* fig. 2).

Pilot Plants.—After the chemist has worked out a process in the laboratory on the test-tube scale, it should be turned over to the chemical engineer for his quantitative design and for his operation on a pilot-plant scale. The pilot plant should be a small replica of what the designing engineer judges the large plant will be like. Here all phases of the unit chemical processes become intimately connected with unit physical operations. Although the chemical changes have been studied in the laboratory, and the best calculations and most suitable designs made, it is only in the pilot plant that they can be checked. The experienced chemical engineer, knowing with what materials he will deal in his process, designs the pilot plant to have minimum corrosion. He must test these conditions, however, in the pilot plant as well as investigate the application of the unit operations of heat transfer, mixing, distillation, filtration, etc. on this small-scale replica equipment. The chemical engineer determines in the pilot plant whether his design is efficient and if not, makes the correction on a small scale. One of the characteristics of the chemical process industry as run by the chemical engineer is the extensive use of pilot plants for precisely this determination. Indeed, in the development of a new process or improvement of an old process, the pilot plant is frequently the most important factor in ensuring success in the undertaking.

Materials of Construction.—Since corrosion of materials of construction is caused by chemicals, its avoidance is one of the most important principles in the design, operation or improvement of most any process in the chemical field. The proper choice of materials of construction offers the experienced chemical engineer an opportunity to design and supervise a chemical plant in a manner that will save costly breakdowns and repairs. Here great progress was made in discovering and applying many new materials of construction in the chemical plant. Among such can be named carbon of various types, synthetic rubber, new resins, new plastics and new alloys such as improved stainless steels. Likewise reductions in the price of long known but still costly metals, such as tantalum, were helpful. Because of this corrosion, the chemical engineer frequently designs equipment not according to a minimum for mechanical strength but with safety factor sufficiently large to allow for unavoidable corrosion.

Design and Equipment.—In the field of chemical engineering design, the type of equipment employed is of utmost importance as it is in all engineering. While almost all chemical engineers are concerned with design and equipment in certain phases of their work, a few work exclusively with the design and building of equipment. On the other hand, much of the progress in the chemical process industries is dependent upon improvements in the design of equipment. For large-scale operations the change from batch to continuous processes is an important step in the reduction of costs and in the maintenance of uniformity of quality. The use of pipes or towers in carrying on continuously the various steps required for manufacture in the petroleum industry has been one of the most important aspects of the large-scale and low-cost manufacturing as practised in this industry. The use of such equipment became more widespread in other phases of chemical processes as exemplified by the manufacture of a number of chemicals in continuous pipe autoclaves such as are used in one of the steps in making phenol from chlorobenzene.

Chemical Process Industries.—This classification, frequently used by the chemical engineer, was evolved out of the older applied or industrial chemistry. Under this designation an industry is classified by the chief product or classes of products from the industry such as rubber, alkali, plastics, petroleum, ceramics, cement, glass, electrolytic industry, nitrogen industry, paint, leather, vegetable oils, fats, pulp and paper, soaps, synthetic fibres, intermediates and dyes, organic chemicals and many others. It is the chief function of the chemical engineer to run these industries, design, improve and operate them. He naturally takes the basic principles involved in the physical changes or unit operations and chemical changes or unit processes and applies these to a specific industry in order to give better service to the consuming public by improving the quality and reducing the cost of his product.

Wastes.—The discharge of industrial wastes into the air, streams or on the land is objectionable, and often subject to stringent legislation. The reduction or elimination of such wastes is often a highly specialized problem requiring a chemical engineer experienced in the particular industry to handle this adequately and economically.

Safety and Fire Protection.—In the operation of any of the chemical process industries the safety and protection of the plant and workers is a part of the responsibility of the chemical engineer. In many cases insurance companies hire chemical engineers to aid them in the introduction of safety and protection procedures in the plants they insure.

Process Control and Instrumentation.—The chemical industry is one of the leaders in the use of instruments to reduce labour in the operation of its processes and to insure the maintenance of the conditions required to produce products of high quality and low cost. The use of instruments was greatly expanded when the chemical engineer turned from batch processing to continuous processing. New instruments were developed by manufacturers which even show initial trends in any changes, physical or chemical, and take means to correct these trends if in the wrong direction. The emphasis in instrumentation is more upon actual process control than upon simply the recording of temperature, pressure or other variables important though these latter still are.

Accounting and Cost Finding.—As an engineer is concerned with the making of useful products at a low cost in order to insure wide consumption, the economics of this process are constantly his responsibility. Any number of chemical companies take chemical engineers and train them specifically in accounting methods for the most efficient control of costs. As the chemical engineer, unlike the chemist, is always involved in the competitive production of his product, broad principles of economics as well as the details of his costs are an important part of his responsibility.

Plant Location.—Before the installation of any process, the proper location of the plant must be determined. This involves not only the sources of raw material, fuel and power but also labour supply, markets, transportation facilities and any local restrictive laws. Particularly in the chemical process industries, water resources are a decisive factor in the selection of a plant site. Frequently a chemical plant engaged in the manufacture of paper, plastics, dyes, intermediates or the like, will use many times the amount of water employed by the city or small town in which the plant is located. To save costs in the utilization of water, chemical plants find it necessary to have multiple supplies of varying purity according to the need. This may range from the use of surface water for sanitation to deep well water for cooling or distilled or deionized water for the making of pure chemicals.

State Registration.—In order to maintain standards and protect the public from untrained engineers, many states enacted laws with requirements for registration. Such registration is based on education, experience and examinations and is required when the public is involved in the work of the engineer. The requirement that engineers be registered is becoming more widespread.

Professional Societies.—In order to help continue the professional and technical growth of the chemical engineers and to facilitate exchange of information particularly in newer fields, professional societies are essential. They continue much of the educational work begun in the universities.

Among such professional societies is the American Institute of Chemical Engineers, founded in 1908. The institute has various classes of membership graded according to the experience and training of the chemical engineer. It publishes *Chemical Engineering Progress*. The Institution of Chemical Engineers of London, a comparable organization, publishes its *Transactions*.

The American Chemical society embraces both chemists and chemical engineers and includes not only the theoretical fundamentals but also the application of chemistry.

Responsibility.—The main responsibility of the chemical engineer is to run the chemical process industries. This responsibility is also directly connected with a larger contribution to society in supplying the products of the chemical industry at reasonable costs and with an ever-increasing field of application. The reasonable cost is realized through the competition between chemical engineers in different companies or different plants of the same company.

BIBLIOGRAPHY.—G. E. Davis, *Handbook of Chemical Engineering*, 2 vol. (1904); John H. Perry, ed. *Chemical Engineers' Handbook*, 3rd edition (1950); William H. Walker, Warren K. Lewis, William H. McAdams and Edwin R. Gilliland, *Principles of Chemical Engineering*, 3rd edition (1937); George Granger Brown *et al.*, *Unit Operations*, (1950) P. H. Groggins, *Unit Processes in Organic Synthesis*, 4th edition (1951); R. Norris Shreve, *Chemical Process Industries*, (1945); Olaf A. Hougen and Kenneth M. Watson, *Chemical Process Principles*, 3 vol. (1947); C. C. Furnas, ed. *Rogers Manual of Industrial Chemistry*, 6th edition, 2 vol., (1942); Raymond E. Kirk and Donald F. Othmer, eds., *Encyclopedia of Chemical Technology*, (1947); "Chemical Engineering Series" of McGraw-Hill Book Company. (R. N. S.)

CHEMICAL EQUILIBRIUM. A chemical reaction may, under appropriate conditions of temperature, pressure and concentration, proceed not to completion but to a state of balance between all the reactants and products. The incompleteness of the reaction is caused by the fact that the reaction is reversible; *i.e.*, by the fact that the products of the reaction in one direction, as soon as they begin to form, begin to react to produce the original reactants. A balance, called equilibrium, is attained when the two opposing reactions go on at equal rates; there is then no net change in the amounts of the substances involved. A change in temperature, pressure or concentration may temporarily upset the equality of the two rates so that one reaction gains over the other until equilibrium is again established.

It is not easy for a reader unfamiliar with chemistry to visualize simultaneous, opposing chemical reactions; so it is well to begin with a more "physical" equilibrium, that between a liquid and its vapour. The change from one to the other is quite reversible; liquids evaporate and vapours can be condensed to liquids. But if some liquid is introduced into a large, evacuated vessel, held at constant temperature, molecules rapidly pass from the liquid into vapour, until they reach a certain concentration, or pressure, at which the number evaporating per second per square centimetre of surface is just balanced by the number of vapour molecules being recaptured by the liquid per second per square centimetre. If some of the vapour is pumped out, the two rates are thrown temporarily out of balance; evaporation proceeds at the previous rate while condensation is reduced, but this difference of rates builds up the concentration of vapour till the balance is again restored. A rise in temperature brings about a new equilibrium, because the molecules are all made to move faster, making it easier for them to escape from their mutual attraction in the liquid and requiring a higher concentration of them in the vapour to restore equilibrium. The essential test for a state of equilibrium is the ability of the system to readjust so as to neutralize, so far as possible, the effect of the change. This general principle is known as the theorem of Le Chatelier. It applies not only to a physical equilibrium, such as that between liquid and vapour, but equally to a chemical equilibrium, such as that between calcium carbonate, $CaCO_3$, and its decomposition products, solid calcium oxide, CaO, and carbon dioxide gas, CO_2, the chemical equation for which is, $CaCO_3 = CaO + CO_2$. The reversibility of the reaction is proven on the one hand by the decomposition of limestone by heating in a lime kiln and, on the other, by the ability of CaO to absorb CO_2 at ordinary temperatures. The reversibility of a reaction is often indicated by writing double arrows with the equality sign, thus $\overset{\rightarrow}{\underset{\leftarrow}{=}}$, often abbreviated to $\rightleftharpoons$. These representations should not obscure the significance of the equality sign, which is the conservation of atoms and masses. The two reactions are complete under the respective conditions just stated, but this reversibility indicates that there are intermediate conditions under which equilibrium is possible. The relation between temperature, t, in degrees Centigrade, and equilibrium pressure, P, in atmospheres, for this particular equilibrium is as follows:

t	842	855	869	904	937;
P	0.45	0.53	0.67	1.16	1.77

An equilibrium involving two or more visually detectable and mechanically separable phases, solid, liquid or gas, is called a heterogeneous equilibrium; one existing within a single phase, either liquid or gas, is a homogeneous equilibrium. As an example of the latter we may consider the partial ionization of acetic acid into charged ions, according to the equation, $HC_2H_3O_2 \rightleftarrows H^+ + C_2H_3O_2^-$. If one gram-molecule, or mole, of the acid is dissolved in one litre of water, at 25° C., equilibrium is reached almost instantly with 0.0042 moles each of H^+ and $C_2H_3O_2^-$ and 0.9958 moles of un-ionized acid. If a little sodium acetate is added, which ionizes almost completely into Na^+ and $C_2H_3O_2^-$, the rate of reaction to the left is increased but the reaction to the right proceeds as before; consequently, the concentration of the H^+ is quickly reduced to such a value that the rates are again equal. Similarly, the addition of H^+ from another source, such as hydrochloric acid, would reduce the concentration of $C_2H_3O_2^-$ to a new equilibrium value. Dilution of the solution with water would diminish the rate of collision and recombination of the two ions until enough additional ions are formed to enable their rate of recombination again to equal their rate of formation. The fraction of the acid existing as ions is therefore increased by dilution.

These relations may be given an approximate quantitative formulation. The number of moles of acetic acid per litre decomposing per second into ions depends, at any one temperature, only on its concentration, which is customarily expressed by the formula in parentheses. The velocity of the reaction to the right, v_1, is $v_1 = k_1\ (HC_2H_3O_2)$ where k_1 is the constant of proportionality. The velocity of the reaction to the left, v_2, is similarly given by $v_2 = k_2\ (H^+)(C_2H_3O_2^-)$. At equilibrium, $v_1 = v_2$; therefore $(H^+)(C_2H_3O_2^-)/(HC_2H_3O_2) = k_1/k_2 = K$, the equilibrium constant. Its value for acetic acid can be obtained from the set of equilibrium concentrations previously given, as 1.8×10^{-5}. This constant expresses the strength of the acid and is valid for any set of concentrations at 25° C. In a solution of 0.1 mole of acetic acid per litre, for example, $(H^+) = (C_2H_3O_2^-)$ and $(HC_2H_3O_2)$ is still approximately 0.1; therefore, $(H^+)^2 = 1.8 \times 10^{-6}$ and $(H^+) = 1.3 \times 10^{-3}$. Again, in a mixture of an equal number of moles of $HC_2H_3O_2$ and $NaC_2H_3O_2$, $(HC_2H_3O_2) = (C_2H_3O_2^-)$ and hence $(H^+) = 1.8 \times 10^{-5}$. We thus have the means, by altering the relative amounts of acetic acid and acetate ion, of establishing any desired acidity through a wide range.

The following examples illustrate equations for equilibrium constants corresponding to equations for chemical reactions.

$$2SO_3 = 2SO_2 + O_2 \text{ (all gases)}: \frac{(SO_2)^2(O_2)}{(SO_3)^2} = K$$

Since the concentration of a gas is proportional to its partial pressure in a gas mixture, this equilibrium may also be expressed in terms of partial pressures, $P^2_{SO_2}P_{O_2}/P^2_{SO_3} = K_p$.

$$CO_2 + C \text{ (solid)} = 2CO;\ (CO)^2/(CO_2) = K \text{ or } P^2_{CO}/P_{CO_2} = K_p$$

Note that the concentration of solid carbon is not susceptible to change and therefore need not be expressed in the equilibrium equation.

$$3Fe \text{ (solid)} + 4H_2O \text{ (gas)} = Fe_3O_4 \text{ (solid)} + 4H_2 \text{ (gas)}$$

$$P_{H_2}{}^4/P_{(H_2O)^4} = K; \text{ or } P_{H_2}/P_{H_2O} = K'$$

$$Ca\ (OH)_2 \text{ (solid)} = Ca^{++} + 2OH^-;\ (Ca^{++})(OH^-)^2 = K$$

The effect of total pressure upon an equilibrium involving gases is to favour the state with a smaller number of gas molecules. Thus, in the following equilibria, $H_2 + I_2 = 2HI$, $2SO_2 + O_2 = 2SO_3$, $N_2 + 3H_2 = 2NH_3$, $CO_2 + C$ (solid) $= 2CO$, increasing the total pressure would have no effect upon the first; it would shift the second to the right, the third still more to the right and the fourth to the left. Each effect can be calculated quantitatively from the expression for the equilibrium constant and the condition that the total pressure is the sum of the partial pressures.

The effect of temperature upon an equilibrium depends upon the heat absorbed or evolved when the reaction occurs under equilibrium conditions. If a vessel containing an equilibrium mixture is transferred from a lower to a higher temperature, heat will, of course, flow into the mixture, and it will shift the equilibrium in that direction which absorbs heat. In the reactions,

$$H^+ + OH^- = H_2O + 13.7 \text{ kg.cal.},$$
$$N_2 + 3H_2 = 2NH_3 + 24.0 \text{ kg.cal.},$$
$$H_2 + I_2 \text{ (gas)} = 2HI - 2.8 \text{ kg.cal.},$$

the equilibria are shifted by rising temperature in favour of the substances on the left-hand side, in the first two cases, and in favour of more HI, in the third.

The effect of changing temperature is given quantitatively by the approximate equation,

$$\log_{10} \frac{K_1}{K_2} = \frac{\Delta H}{4.575} \frac{(T_2 - T_1)}{(T_1 T_2)}$$

where ΔH is the heat, in calories, absorbed by the reaction as written, and K_2 and K_1 are the equilibrium constants at the respective temperatures, T_2 and T_1, on the Kelvin scale.

The Haber process for the chemical utilization of the inert nitrogen of the air furnishes a striking instance of the practical fruits of the principles of equilibrium. The reaction, $N_2 + 3H_2 = 2NH_3$, does not take place at all when nitrogen and hydrogen are brought together under any ordinary conditions, whereas ammonia is easily decomposed on moderate heating. The principles of equilibrium teach that the equilibrium would be displaced in favour of ammonia by increasing pressure and lowering temperature. But lowering temperature normally decreases the velocity at which equilibrium is approached; so a compromise is necessary here, and a catalyst to increase speed is indicated. Proceeding in this way, Fritz Haber was able to obtain a small equilibrium concentration of ammonia, from which he calculated the equilibrium constant and the effect of temperature thereon. With this knowledge the desirable conditions could be predicted for obtaining an industrially profitable equilibrium concentration of ammonia.

Catalysts have been developed which cause the reaction to proceed at reasonable speed at 500° C. assisted by pressures of the order of 100 atmospheres, pressures unprecedented in technical processes at the time of Haber's investigation. These high pressures also shift the equilibrium strongly in favour of ammonia since four molecules become two in the reaction. Even so, the conversion to ammonia in one contact with the catalyst is only about 10%, but by liquefying and removing this ammonia, and repassing the nitrogen and hydrogen, augmented, over the catalyst, the equilibrium amount is again obtained, and so on. The ammonia thus obtained is used in part for refrigeration, in part oxidized to nitric acid for the multitude of uses of that important chemical and in large part converted into ammonium sulphate for fertilizer. It is safe to say that no amount of unscientific empiricism would ever have produced these results.

(*See* THERMODYNAMICS.) (J. H. HD.)

CHEMICAL SOCIETIES. Chemical organizations are among the most active agencies for promoting the increase and diffusion of chemical knowledge. At first, the chemists functioned purely within such general scientific bodies as the Royal Society of London. In the closing decades of the 18th century, however, a few chemical societies sprang up in England, Scotland and the United States. Some doubt exists as to the order of priority in which these societies were formed, but the most likely sequence seems to be: a London chemical society (1782); a chemical society at the University of Edinburgh (1785) composed of the students of Joseph Black; a chemical society at the University of Glasgow (1786), a chemical society in Manchester (prior to 1787); the Chemical Society of Philadelphia (founded by James Woodhouse in 1792); another chemical society in Glasgow (1798); and a chemical society of Edinburgh in 1800. The present Chemical Society of London dates from 1841.

There follows a list of some of the leading chemical societies in the principal countries of the world, together with some of their publications:

ARGENTINA. Buenos Aires, Asociación Química Argentina (founded 1912)—*Anales* (1913 *et seq.*). AUSTRALIA. Melbourne, Australian Chemical Institute (1917)—*The Australian Chemical*

Institute Journal and Proceedings (1934 *et seq.*); Melbourne, Society of Chemical Industry of Victoria (1900)—*Bulletin* (1887 *et seq.*). AUSTRIA. Vienna, Chemische-physikalische Gesellschaft (1869)—*Physik and Chimie* (1895–1938); Vienna, Verein Österreichischer Chemiker (1898)—*Österreichische Chemiker-zeitung.* BELGIUM. Brussels, Société Chimique de Belgique (1887)—*Bulletin;* Federation des Industries Chimiques de Belgique. CANADA. Toronto, Canadian Institute of Chemistry (1916)—*Canadian Chemistry and Process Industries* (1917 *et seq.*); Canadian Institute of Chemistry (1916)—*Canadian Chemistry and Metallurgy* (1916 *et seq.*). CZECHOSLOVAK REPUBLIC. Společnost pro Průmysl Chemiský v—*Kralovstrí Cheshem* (Prague). FRANCE. Association des Chimistes de Sucrerie et Distillerie de France et des Colonies (1882)—*Bulletin* (1883 *et seq.*); Paris, Cercle de Chimie (1917)—*Revue des Produits Chimiques;* Paris, Société Chimique de France (1857)—*Bulletin de la Société Chimique de France* (1858–1933), *Documentation* (1933 *et seq.*), *Memoires* (1934 *et seq.*); Société de Chimie Biologique—*Bulletin de la Société de Chimie Biologique* (1919 *et seq.*); Société de Chimie Industrielle (1917)—*Chimie et Industrie annales de Chimie Analytique* (1918); Union Internationale de Chimie (League of Nations, 1919)—*Comptes Rendus, Rapports.* GERMANY. Adolf-Baeyer-Gesellschaft zur Förderung der Chemischen Literatur; Halle, Deutsche Bunsen-gesellschaft für Angewandte Physikalische Chemie (1894); Berlin, Deutsche Chemische Gesellschaft (1867)—*Berichte, Chemisches Zentralblatt, Bibleographica Chemica* (1922 *et seq.*); Leipzig, Kolloid-Gesellschaft (1922?)—*Kolloid-Zeitschrift;* Berlin, Verein Deutscher Chemiker (1887)—*Angewante Chemie* (1887 *et seq.*), *Die Chemische Fabrik* (1928 *et seq.*); Berlin, Verein Deutscher Lebensmittelchemiker (1902)—*Vorratspflege and Lebensmittelforschung, Zeitschrift für Untersuchung der Lebensmittel;* Verein zur Wahrung der Interessen der Ehemireben Industrie Deutschlands—*Die Chemische Industrie* (1877 *et seq.*). GREAT BRITAIN. London, Biochemical Society (1911)—*Biochemical Journal;* Chemical Society (1841, incorporated 1848)—*Annual Reports* (1904 *et seq.*), *British Chemical and Physiological Abstracts* (1926 *et seq.*), *Journal of the Chemical Society* (1847 *et seq.*), *Memoirs and Proceedings* (1841–48), *Proceedings* (1885 *et seq.*); London, Faraday Society (1903)—*Proceedings* (1904–15), *Transactions* (1905); Oil and Colour Chemists' Association —*Journal;* London, Society of Chemical Industry (1881, inc. 1907)—*Journal* (1882 *et seq.*), *Report of the Progress of Applied Chemistry* (1916 *et seq.*); Society of Dyers and Colourists—*Journal;* Society of Leather Trades' Chemists—*Journal;* London, Society of Public Analysts (1874)—*The Analyst* (1887 *et seq.*). INDIA. Calcutta, Indian Chemical Society (1924)—*Monthly Journal, Quarterly Journal Industrial and News Edition, Report.* ITALY. Rome, Associazione Italiana di Chimica (1919)—*Annali di Chimica Applicata, Chimica e l'industria, Gazetta Chimica Italiana;* Associazone Italiana di Chemica Generale ed Applicata, *Gazzetta Chimica Italiana* (1871 *et seq.*); Milan, Associazione Italiana di Chimica Tessili e Coloristica (1925)—*Bollettina;* Societa di Chimica Industriale di Milana (1895)—*Annuario* (1896 *et seq.*), *Giornale di Chimica Industriale ed Applicato* (1919 *et seq.*). JAPAN. Tokyo, Nippon Kagaku Kai (1878)—*Journal* (*Nippon Kagaku Kai Shi*) (1880), *Bulletin* (1926); Kogyo Kagaku Kai (1898)—*Kogyo Kagaku.* LATVIA. Riga, Latvijas Kimijas Biedriba (1920). MAURITIUS. Port Louis, Société des Chimistes de Maurice (1910)—*Revue Agricole de l'Ile Maurice.* NETHERLANDS. Nederlandsche Chemische Vereeniging (1902)—*Chemisch Weekblad* (1903 *et seq.*), *Recueil des Travaux Chemiques des Pays-Bas;* Vereeniging van de Nederlandsche—*Chemische Industrie.* NORWAY. Oslo, Norsk Kjemisk Selskap (1893)—*Tidsskrift for Kjemi og Bergvesen.* POLAND. Warsaw, Polskie Towarzystwo Chemiczne (1919)—*Roczniki Chemji.* PORTUGAL. *Sociedade Chimica Portuguesa* (1912)—*Revista de Chimica Pura e Applicada* (1916 *et seq.*); Coimbra, Sociedade Portuguesa de Quimica e Fisica—*Revista de Chimica Pura e Applicada* (1905 *et seq.*). RUMANIA. Societatea de Chimie din România—*Buletinul Societații de Chimie din România.* RUSSIA. Russhoie Fiziho-chemitcheskoie Obschestro—*Zurnal* (1869 *et seq.*); Moscow, Lomonosovskoe Fiziko-Chemicheskoe Obschchestvo (1917)—*Vestnick.* SOUTH AFRICA. Capetown, Cape Chemical and Technological Society (1906); Johannesburg, Chemical, Metallurgical and Mining Society of South Africa (1894)—*Journal;* South African Chemical Institute—*Journal, Proceedings.* SPAIN. Madrid, Sociedad Espanola di Fisica y Química—*Anales.* SWEDEN. Kemist Samfundet i Stockholm—*Svensk Kemisk Tidskrift* (1889 *et seq.*); Kunglig Svenska Vetenskapsakademien (1739)—*Arkiv for Kemi, Minerdloge och Geologie* (1903 *et seq.*). SWITZERLAND. Basle, Basler Chemische Gesellschaft (1924); Société Suisse de Chimie (Schweizerische Chemische Gesellschaft)—*Helvetica Chemica Acta* (1918 *et seq.*). UNITED STATES. American Association of Textile Chemists and Colorists; American Ceramic Society (1899); American Chemical Society (1876)—*Journal* (1879 *et seq.*), *Chemical Abstracts* (1907 *et seq.*), *Journal of Industrial and Engineering Chemistry* (1909 *et seq.*), *Chemical Reviews* (1924 *et seq.*); American Electrochemical Society (1908); American Institute of Chemical Engineers (1908)—*Transactions* (1908); American Institute of Fertilizer Chemists (1919); American Leather Chemists Association (1903)—*Journal* (1906); American Oil Chemists Society (1903); American Pharmaceutical Association (1852)—*Journal, Yearbook;* American Society of Biological Chemists (1906)—*Journal of Biological Chemistry* (1919 *et seq.*); Association of Official Agricultural Chemists (1907)—*Journal* (1915).

BIBLIOGRAPHY.—American Chemical Society, *A Half Century of Chemistry in America, 1876–1926* (1926); R. S. Bates, *Scientific Societies in the United States* (1945); W. T. Bogert, "American Chemical Societies," *J. Am. Chem. Soc.* vol. xxx, pp. 163–182 (1908); H. C. Bolton, *Chemical Societies of the Nineteenth Century* (1902), *Early American Chemical Societies* (1897); *Chemical Abstracts,* vol. xxx, No. 22 (1936) lists chemical society publications, "Supplement" in *ibid.* vol., xxxvi, No. 24 (1942); Chemical Society, London, *Jubilee of the Chemical Society of London, Record of the proceedings together with an account of the history and development of the society, 1841–1891* (London, 1896); E. J. Crane and A. M. Patterson, *A Guide to the Literature of Chemistry* (1927); Callie Hull, Mildred Paddock, S. J. Cook and P. A. Howard, comps., *Handbook of Scientific and Technical Societies and Institutions of the United States and Canada, 4th ed., Bulletin of the National Research Council, No. 106* (1941); James Kendall, "Some Eighteenth-century Chemical Societies," *Endeavour,* vol. i, no. 3, pp. 106–109 (1942) "Old Chemical Societies in Scotland," *Chem. and Ind.,* vol. xv (1937); M. G. Mellon, *Chemical Publications, Their Nature and Use* (1940); *Minerva, Jahrbuch der Gelehrten Welt;* R. B. Pilcher, *The Institute of Chemistry of Great Britain and Ireland . . . History of the Institute: 1877–1914* (London, 1914); E. E. Reid, *Introduction to Organic Research* (1924); E. F. Smith, *Chemistry in America* (1914); B. A. Soule, *Library Guide for the Chemist* (1938); F. J. Wilson, "The Chemical Society of Glasgow, Minute Book of 1800–01" *Ann. Soc.,* vol. ii (1937); *Yearbook of Learned Societies* (British). (R. S. BA.)

CHEMICAL WARFARE. Chemical warfare relates to the employment of substances useful in war by reason of their direct chemical action. Chemistry has found application in military science throughout recorded history. It was not, however, until the 20th century that chemical warfare in the modern acceptance of that term became a distinct feature of military technique. Modern chemical warfare represents essentially the application of chemical energy in military action, in contrast to physical energy as represented by the impact of bullets or the shock of explosives. The substances employed in chemical warfare are known as "chemical agents." Those that react directly on the human organism are war gases. A second group of agents which are useful in obscuring distant objects are called smokes. A third group are incendiaries or fire-producers.

In each case the desired end is served by chemical reactions that take place after the appropriate agent has been released to atmospheric conditions of pressure and temperature. It is to be noted that these reactions are not necessarily instantaneous, as is the case where firearms or explosives are employed; chemical warfare agents on the contrary may act slowly and continue effective for extended periods of time.

Modern chemical warfare must be regarded as a product of industrial chemistry. Although the chemicals it employs have been known for many years, some of them for many centuries, yet only in relatively recent years has production capacity been available to permit the manufacture of the large quantities of these substances that are required for extended military operations.

Development.—The application of chemical warfare really commenced before recorded history by the use of fire and smoke to overcome an opponent. At the siege of Plataea in 429 B.C. burning pitch and sulphur were used. The so-called "Greek fire" was a mixture of highly combustible substances ignited on water. In 1855 Lord Dundonald proposed the use of burning sulphur on a large scale under favourable wind conditions during the siege of Sebastopol. During the U.S. Civil War it was proposed (1862) that shell containing chlorine be employed by the Union forces.

The science of chemistry advanced rapidly during the 18th and 19th centuries, and the use of toxic substances was foreseen and considered at the Hague Conference of 1899. With the exception of the United States, the great powers there pledged themselves not to use projectiles whose sole object was the diffusion of asphyxiating or harmful gases.

World War I.—The adoption of chemicals as weapons during World War I was logical in that the principal combatant nations were highly developed scientifically and industrially. A stalemate had been reached when both sides entrenched themselves so firmly that advance was impracticable without terrific losses. Means were sought to restore open warfare. At the outbreak of the war, none of the combatant nations was prepared to use or defend against chemicals.

The introduction of gas as an effective weapon in modern warfare actually dates from April 22, 1915, when the Germans launched a large-scale cylinder attack with chlorine against the Allied position in the Ypres salient where the British and French lines joined. Although intelligence reports had given warnings of an impending attack, little credence was given to them by the Allies. The attack came as a complete surprise to unprotected troops; its success was so far beyond German expectations that adequate reserves to exploit the breakthrough for a decisive stroke had not been provided. Within a few days Allied troops were equipped with pads of cotton dipped in a chemical solution and tied over the nose and mouth. These were soon followed by a crude form of respirator which was continually improved throughout the war both for comfort and efficiency. As protection was obtained against one chemical, the offense sought for and introduced new agents. These frequently required radical changes in the mask. Cloud gas attacks, although highly efficient, were entirely dependent on favourable wind conditions. Consequently the extensive use of gas shell was begun in 1916. This also permitted employment of a greater number of toxic substances.

Lacrimators, sneeze gases and vesicants were introduced as the war progressed, the Germans leading the way. Because of the manufacturing problem, many months were generally required for Allied retaliation in kind. In July 1917, the Germans introduced mustard gas, an extremely vesicant, highly persistent liquid, which causes severe, slow-healing burns. It was difficult to provide effective protection against this agent, which accounted for the majority of gas casualties during World War I.

Use After 1918.—Because of its controversial aspects, European powers have shrouded with silence their recent operations in the field of chemical warfare. However, all of the major world powers have maintained research facilities. Some have manufacturing facilities and chemical troops. The speedy conquest of Ethiopia by Italy has been ascribed to the extensive use of a vesicant material similar to mustard gas; against the unprotected native, its vesicant qualities proved irresistible. In China and in Spain, chemical warfare appeared chiefly as incendiaries, much damage thus being caused.

The use of toxic chemicals during the European war in 1939–40 had not been confirmed up to July 1940. Incendiary bombs were extensively used in air raids by both sides. Probably the chief use of chemical warfare was in the extensive adaptation of screening smoke tactics to both land and sea battles. Germany utilized smoke tactics with exceptional efficiency to blind observation, eliminate enemy-aimed fire and to immobilize enemy movements attempted within smoke. These tactics were especially effective during the closing weeks of the campaign in France to facilitate river crossings, establish bridgeheads, and to assist the rapid advance of infantry and tanks. On the sea, the German pocket battleship "Admiral Graf Spee" dispersed smoke in an attempt to blind its movements from enemy fire. This might have been more successful if a British observation plane had not been able to give accurate information as to course of the ship. During the spring of 1940 the German battleship "Scharnhorst," after being crippled in action, was hidden within a smoke screen laid by a friendly cruiser and was thus enabled to escape.

Chemical Agents.—The term gas is applied to those chemical agents used in war which, by ordinary and direct chemical action, produce a toxic or powerful irritant effect on the human body. Solids, liquids or true gases may be so employed; however, in their actual use on the battle area, the solid or liquid is converted by normal or artificial volatilization into a true gas or disseminated as minute solid or liquid particles called aerosols. Irritant smokes are types of aerosols included under the term gas because their principal use is for their physiological effect.

From the military viewpoint the most important classifications of chemical agents are in accordance with (1) physiological effect, (2) persistency and (3) tactical use.

Physiological effect classifies the chemical according to its primary action on the human body even though it may produce other secondary effects. The severity of effect is roughly proportional to the concentration (amount present in a unit volume of air) and the time of exposure.

Lung irritants act on the respiratory system and are often lethal. When breathed, they irritate and inflame the interior portion of the bronchial tubes and lungs, cause coughing, impede breathing, and, in severe cases, acute pulmonary oedema will result. Chlorine, phosgene and diphosgene are examples.

Vesicants or skin-blistering agents attack any part of the body with which the liquid or vapour comes in contact, especially moistened parts. They are absorbed or dissolved on exterior or interior parts of the body, followed by production of inflammation, burns and destruction of tissue. There is no immediate pain and effect is delayed for some period after exposure. Protection against this class is very difficult because of its insidious action by contact with the liquid or prolonged exposure to the vapour. Examples are mustard gas, lewisite and ethyldichlorarsine.

Sternutators or sneeze gases are also known as irritant smokes. They are disseminated into the air as minute solid or liquid particles which, if inhaled, cause sneezing, intense pain in the nose, throat and chest followed by violent nausea, headache, mental depression and physical weakness. No fatal cases have been recorded from this class; effect, although severe, is temporary, lasting about 12 hours. The charcoal and soda lime mixture of the gas mask canister will not remove these small particles from the air. A most efficient mechanical filter is necessary to give protection. Diphenylaminechlorarsine, an aromatic arsenical derivative, is an example.

Lacrimators or tear gases irritate the mucous membrane around the eyes, causing intense smarting and a profuse flow of tears with resultant hampering of vision. Effect from concentrations in the field is only temporary, recovery being complete within a few minutes after removal from the contaminated area. Chloracetophenone, brombenzylcyanide and xylyl bromide are examples.

The systemic poisons directly affect the heart action, nerve reflexes, or interfere with absorption and assimilation of oxygen by the body. Carbon monoxide and hydrocyanic acid, which pertain to this class, have never been effectively used in war because of their relative lightness compared with air with the consequent difficulty in placing satisfactory quantities on a given area.

The persistency of a chemical agent is determined by the length of time it will maintain an effective concentration without being renewed. Those chemicals which remain effective for longer than ten minutes after release in the open are defined as persistent. Usually dispersed in the liquid state, persistent agents contaminate the ground on which released and continue to give off dangerous vapour for long periods. Nonpersistent gases are those whose effectiveness in the open continues for less than ten minutes. They vaporize rapidly, forming concentrated clouds which drift with the wind, increasing in size but becoming diluted in gas content until they finally disappear.

Tactical classification, which is influenced by the persistency, is based on the primary military objective for which any particular chemical is used in the field. War gases are thus classified as casualty or harassing agents; smokes as screening agents; and the various fire producers as incendiaries.

No attempt will be made to enumerate all the chemical agents which might be used in war. Many thousands of compounds were thoroughly studied during World War I. Comparatively few were deemed worthy of test under battle conditions and of those only about a dozen were in actual use at the termination of that war. The majority of chemical warfare agents are organic compounds of which the theoretical number is almost limitless. From these, it is quite possible that more effective war chemicals will be found. On the other hand it is more probable that modification of types now known or more efficient methods of dispersion will first appear rather than entirely new discoveries.

To be useful as a chemical agent, certain requisites must be met. These include: adequate and utilizable physiological action, screening power, or incendiary effect; stability in storage and in contact with moisture; capability of manufacture on large scale at low cost from easily procurable, nonstrategic raw materials; suitability for safe handling, transporting and loading in munitions without corrosive effect on ordinary steel; capability of being disseminated in effective quantity under field conditions; gases, preferably much heavier than air, readily compressed to liquids and easily vaporized when released.

Brief descriptions of a few type chemical agents follow:

Phosgene under ordinary conditions is a colourless, nonpersistent gas with an odour varyingly described as of musty hay, green corn or green apples. Tactically, it is classified as a casualty agent. At low temperatures it is a clear, colourless, mobile liquid, which boils at 8.3°C. Under ordinary summer conditions, it will disappear from a given locality about as fast as the wind moves. Even in winter it evaporates very rapidly. In a light wind an effective concentration of phosgene can readily be produced. It is used commercially for dye manufacture. During World War I it was first employed by Germany in Dec. 1915, in a cloud gas attack from cylinders.

Chloropicrin derives its name from its principal method of commercial manufacture by the action of chlorine on picric acid. When free of impurities, it is a nearly colourless liquid of waterlike appearance except for a slight oiliness. It has a characteristic sweetish odour somewhat like flypaper and usually is first detected by lacrimatory effect on the eyes. It is a moderately persistent lung irritant but in addition causes lacrimation, nausea and vomiting. Tactically it may be classed as either a harassing or a casualty agent, depending on the concentration. Commercially, it is used as a seed fumigant and for insect control. Chloropicrin is said to have been first employed by Russia in 1916 and later was extensively employed by the Allies. It is neutralized by sodium sulphite solution in alcohol.

Mustard gas is a compound of carbon, hydrogen, sulphur and chlorine. It should not be confused with the true natural mustard oil or the artificial compounds having properties similar thereto. It was because of its sharp pungent odour and vesicant properties which resembled but greatly exceeded those of natural mustard oil that British soldiers first called it "mustard gas." The commercial product is a heavy oily liquid of dark colour and in low concentrations has the distinct odour of garlic or wild onions. This product freezes at about 10°C. It is one of the most persistent as well as one of the most toxic chemical agents. It is highly vesicant and is also a lung irritant. As the latter, in vapour form, after prolonged exposure, it attacks the whole respiratory system producing inflammation of the trachea and bronchi with necrosis of the mucous membrane and development of secondary bronchitis or bronchopneumonia. Upon slight contact with the liquid it is absorbed in the skin and produces serious burns. First employed by Germany at Ypres in July 1917, it was thereafter known to the French as Yperite. It hydrolizes slowly and may be neutralized by intimate mixture with bleaching powder, steam or gaseous chlorine.

Lewisite resembles mustard gas in many characteristics. It is a colourless or slightly yellow liquid freezing at —18.2°C. As usually prepared it is dark brown in colour with the faint odour of geraniums. Its vapour is distinctly irritating to the eyes and throat, sometimes followed by violent sneezing. It is absorbed by the skin or lung tissue and causes a serious blister. As it hydrolizes it liberates an oxide which poisons the body. It is a vesicant casualty agent, having a persistency of one to several days in summer and a week or more in winter. It is readily decomposed by water and may be neutralized by alcoholic sodium hydroxide spray. It was first made in the United States but has never been used in war. Lewisite has a distinct advantage over mustard gas in that blisters develop in about one hour, but has the disadvantage of rapid hydrolysis.

Hydrocyanic acid, though long known as one of the deadliest of compounds, was used with but little success during the period 1914–18. It is a paralysant acting vigorously on the central nervous system to produce quick death. Under ordinary conditions it is a colourless, mobile and volatile liquid with a slight odour of bitter almonds. It is a nonpersistent casualty agent. Because of its high volatility it is most difficult to maintain effective concentrations of hydrocyanic acid in the field; hence this compound has so far proven of little value in chemical warfare.

Diphenylaminechlorarsine, better known as adamsite, is representative of the large group of irritant smokes which may be used in war. Physically, in pure form it is a bright canary-yellow crystalline solid. Commercially, it is produced in a dark green or sometimes brownish colour. In solid state it is almost odourless, but when dispersed as an irritant smoke, a hazy yellow cloud is formed which gives a characteristic smoky odour. However, the first symptoms are usually a burning sensation in the nose and throat. It is classified as a nonpersistent harassing agent, but as such is extremely potent because very small concentrations with a brief period of exposure will prove effective. The headache, nausea and vomiting which it causes, followed by physical debility, render a person practically helpless. Effective use of the irritant smokes is largely dependent on penetration of the filtering device used with the gas mask. If protection is not assured, this group of agents has great potentialities in warfare.

White phosphorus, a pale yellowish, translucent crystalline solid of waxy consistency, is very active chemically and combines readily with oxygen. Hence unless protected from air it will burst spontaneously into flame. White phosphorus can be loaded into shell, bombs or grenades. When exploded by the bursting charge the solid phosphorus is broken into small fragments which are scattered in the air. The heat of explosion assists their immediate ignition, forming a cloud of phosphorus pentoxide. This smoke has the highest known obscuring power, yet is harmless when breathed. Fragments of considerable size are scattered about and continue to burn for some time, thus prolonging the emission of smoke. In addition, white phosphorus has limited incendiary value against readily combustible matter. Physiologically it may be classed as a casualty agent, since its ignited particles cause painful flesh burns that heal very slowly. Although primarily used for smoke production within the enemy lines, white phosphorus is also a formidable weapon against machine gun nests or troop concentrations.

FS, a mixture of sulphur trioxide about 55% and chlorosulphonic acid about 45% by weight, is an excellent cheap liquid smoke for release from containers or by dispersion from aeroplanes.

The thermits are mixtures of powdered aluminum and iron oxide which react chemically and generate intense heat. Hence they have powerful incendiary qualities and readily ignite any inflammable material. Allied to the thermits is the so-called electron bomb, used extensively in small scatter-type bombs during 1936–40 in Europe. This bomb has a case of magnesium alloy which is ignited by a chemical mixture and burns with intense heat.

Table I briefly summarizes characteristics of some important chemical agents used in war.

Protection.—Having in mind the three distinct types of agents employed in chemical warfare, protection is of interest principally as applied against gas, since smoke is harmless and protection against incendiary agents is limited to measures customarily followed in fire fighting. Against gas, protection has been highly developed. This type of defense is actually more effective than the protection that can be afforded against any other military weapon. In considering protection against war gases, it is necessary to distinguish between effect upon the respiratory organs and vesicant effect upon the body surface.

For protection against lung irritants, of which phosgene is typical, the gas mask is the primary protective device. The principle on which the military mask is based is that of filtering out or neutralizing noxious substances that may be present in inspired air. In order to accomplish this, air before it reaches the lungs must first pass through a filtering element containing materials that act mechanically or physically or react chemically with the toxic agents. For this reason a characteristic feature of the gas mask, from which its name is derived, is a tight-fitting facepiece so designed as to prevent air from reaching the respiratory organs from any direction except through the filter.

Since the mask must necessarily cover the entire face in order conveniently to permit normal respiration, it incidentally affords protection against lacrimators which, when the eyes are unprotected, cause intolerable eye irritation.

The principal materials used in gas mask filters (or canisters) are charcoal and soda lime. Charcoal absorbs and holds a relatively large volume of poisonous gases. Soda lime supplements the action of charcoal by neutralizing any toxic materials which might eventually be released by the charcoal and which otherwise would pass to the lungs with incoming air. Having a proper balance of charcoal and soda lime the gas mask may be worn with safety even after it has been used in concentrations of war gases.

Besides soda lime and charcoal, masks are sometimes provided with mechanical filtration intended to strain out finely divided solid particles (toxic smokes), which severely irritate the nasal passages. The life of a gas mask filter depends on two factors: the length of time it has been exposed in gas attacks and the concentrations of gas that have been encountered. Military masks generally remain serviceable even after use in several gas operations When the capacity of the filter is approaching exhaustion a slight odour of gas can be detected. This indicates that replacement with a fresh filter is necessary.

Although it is possible to design filtering devices that will neutralize any toxic substance, it is not feasible to combine in one mask protection against all toxics. Military masks are accordingly constructed with a view to counteracting those particular chemicals that are thought most likely to be used in war. The introduction of new types of military gases in future will undoubtedly be followed by appropriate modification of masks now considered standard.

For safeguarding of personnel while sleeping, messing or otherwise engaged where the mask cannot be worn, gasproof installations are provided. These are known as gas shelters or collective protectors. A typical installation is equipped with a filter similar in principle to that used in the gas mask, although much larger. Incoming air is drawn through this filter and thus purified, other outside air being excluded, so that all air within the enclosure may safely be inhaled.

Protection by filtration applies only to those chemical-warfare agents that are dispersed as true gases and which are therefore injurious when breathed. Agents dispersed in liquid form, which attack the body through the skin surface, necessitate a different type of protection.

Against liquid chemical agents, of which mustard gas is typical, special protective clothing is utilized. To insure complete protection for persons obliged to remain in contaminated areas, fabrics used in this clothing must be treated with moisture-resisting compounds (*e.g.*, oilskins), and garments must be designed positively to exclude air at all points. The gas mask is invariably worn with protective clothing, to prevent inhalation of noxious fumes which are always present where liquid agents are released.

No effort is made to destroy nonpersistent or highly volatile gases, since these are eliminated in due course by dilution and dispersion. However, ground or other surfaces saturated by persistent (liquid) chemicals may be treated to hasten decomposition of toxic materials. Chlorine is most effective for this purpose and is commonly applied in the form of chloride of lime.

The effective use of antigas equipment is dependent on thorough military training and organization. Training establishes skill in the use of protective devices; in locating and identifying gassed areas; and in the selection of positions that lack vulnerability to gas attack. Gas defense organization, based on the assignment of suitable gas specialists to various units, insures attention to all features of chemical security, including such matters as the alerting of troops to gas attack and the degassing of areas contaminated with persistent chemicals.

All measures for protection against gas contribute toward the development of gas discipline. When this is high, military organizations are able to face gas attacks with confidence born of the knowledge that gas casualties will be light and that gas will not unduly impede the attainment of objectives.

First Aid Treatment.—When protective devices are not available, the prompt application of certain simple first aid measures will frequently prevent the development of serious injury from exposure to war gases.

In all such cases the first requirement is immediate removal from the gassed area. For lung irritant casualties, treatment is then directed to conserving the supply of oxygen, all of which is needed for natural recuperation. Thus complete relaxation and rest are essential; warming of the body with loose coverings and drinking of hot coffee are helpful. Patients are evacuated by litter and special precautions are taken to prevent exertion for some time, since fatalities are liable to occur even after a lapse of a day or more when preventive measures are not enforced.

Contact with liquid vesicants necessitates different treatment which, however, must be promptly initiated in order to avoid serious burns. All clothing which may have become contaminated is quickly removed and portions of the body contacted by the liquid agent are repeatedly swabbed as soon as possible with a solvent such as gasoline or alcohol. In lieu of the latter, scrubbing with soap and water is helpful. Treatment administered as late as 30 minutes after exposure is seldom efficacious.

For the painful burns caused by contact of ignited fragments of white phosphorus with the skin, immediate relief is had by immersion in water. Application of an aqueous solution of copper sulphate enables the coated phosphorus particles to be removed, after which medical treatment is undertaken.

Lacrimation is soon counteracted by removal from the gassed area and exposure of the eyes to fresh air. From the effects of irritant smokes, relief is had by breathing low concentrations of chlorine and by flushing the nose with salt water or a weak solution of baking soda.

Protection of Civilian Population.—The potential threat of air-gas attack against congested population centres has forced wide adoption of protective measures for passive defense of noncombatants against chemical agents These measures are largely based on principles found effective for protection of military personnel. Gas masks designed for civilian use are ordinarily of lighter construction than those intended for use by soldiers in the field Gasproofed air raid shelters on the other hand are in most cases larger and more elaborate than are required for military operations. Civilian defense measures also include organization of medical aid for gas casualties, degassing squads and special fire-fighting units Civilian air-raid precautions in gas defense had become so highly developed and patently effective during the years immediately preceding 1939 as to assure a large degree of immunity from the effects of toxic gas in aerial bombardments of cities. To this fact may be ascribed, at least in a measure, failure to utilize chemical agents in the air attacks staged against European cities in 1939–40.

Dispersion of Agents.—With gas and smoke, military targets are areas rather than points against which fire of high explosives is usually aimed. Over these target areas the technique of chemical warfare is directed principally to establishing and maintaining an appropriate concentration.

The technical problems involved in dispersing chemical agents in war differ radically according to whether the medium employed is a volatile gas (or smoke) or a liquid. In the first instance it is necessary to generate an artificial cloud that will cover the selected area either (a) densely enough or (b) long enough to accomplish the desired result—since the effectiveness of chemical warfare agents is a product of two factors: concentration and length of exposure. The most efficient means for generating a gas or smoke cloud is by release from a stationary container (*e.g.*, cylinder). This was the method employed for the first use of gas in modern warfare (1915). It presents, however, certain practical disadvantages in military operations. A favouring wind is required to move the cloud to the target area, and where the distance the cloud must travel is very great the concentration will become unduly lowered before the target is reached. In order to overcome these difficulties, methods have been developed for projecting containers to the upwind side of distant targets and thus generating the cloud from a more advantageous position. This can be efficiently accomplished with smoke, but volatile gases do not lend themselves readily to dispersion at distances greater than 3,000 yards.

The principal methods by which volatile gases are dispersed, in the order of relative efficiency, are from (1) cylinders, (2) projectors, (3) shell. Efficiency of dispersion may be reckoned according to the ratio of the weight of the container to the weight of the agent it contains. This ratio is lowest for stationary cylinders, which can only be discharged within friendly lines. When the container is placed within a cannon and fired to the area of intended discharge it must necessarily be of heavier construction, its weight progressively increasing as weapons of greater range are employed.

The chemical projector discharges a container of relatively large volumetric capacity to ranges of approximately one mile. By employing a large number of these weapons in a single operation it is possible to establish effective concentrations of nonpersistent gas at some distance behind enemy lines.

The chemical mortar enables volatile gases to be released at distances of nearly 3,000 yd. But since the mortar projectile is much heavier, the proportion of gas it carries is accordingly lessened, thus reducing the size of gas cloud that can be established. On the other hand the chemical mortar can be fired repeatedly and the gas concentration can thus be maintained for a longer period than is possible with the projector.

The firing of nonpersistent gas containers from artillery weapons presents technical difficulties that have never been overcome nor have satisfactory aerial bombs been devised for this purpose. Liquid agents of the mustard gas type, however, may be employed in artillery of all calibres, the technique of firing being modified here to insure uniform distribution of impacts over the target area. The ideal shell for such use is of simple construction, designed to burst on or before impact so as to efficiently disperse the agent.

Aerial liquid-filled bombs may likewise be employed for dispersing persistent vesicants. Another effective method of aerial dispersion is that of sprinkling, where the agent is carried in tanks and discharged as a spray from low altitudes.

This represents possibly the most portentous form of chemical attack because the liquid chemical may thus be placed directly upon personnel.

TABLE I—*Characteristics of Some Important Chemical Agents Used in War*

Common name	Chemical name	Chemical formula	Physical state at 68° F. and 700 mm. pressure	Physiological effect	Elapsed time between exposure and effect	Lethal index (*) for mice and dogs (10 minute exposure)
Chlorine	Chlorine	Cl_2	Gas	Burns upper respiratory tract	Immediate; delayed in low concentrations	56,000
Phosgene	Carbonyl chloride	$COCl_2$	Gas	Causes lung oedema	Immediate	5,000
Hydrocyanic acid	Hydrocyanic acid	HCN	Gas	Paralysis of nerve centres	Immediate	2,000
Ethyldichlorarsine	Ethyldichlorarsine	$C_2H_5AsCl_2$	Liquid	⅙ as vesicant as mustard gas	30 min.	5,000
Chloropicrin	Trichlornitromethane	Cl_3CNO_2	Liquid	Burns respiratory tract. Lacrimates, causes nausea. Lung irritant	Immediate lacrimation; delayed lung action	20,000
Mustard gas	Bis Beta chlorethylsulphide	$(ClCH_2CH_2)_2S$	Liquid	Burns skin and lung tissue	4 to 24 hr.	1,500
Lewisite	Beta-chlorvinyldichlorarsine	$ClCH{:}\ CHAsCl_2$	Liquid	Burns skin and lung tissue. Arsenical poisoning in body	1 hr.	1,200
Adamsite	Diphenylaminechlorarsine	$C_6H_4NHAsClC_6H_4$	Solid	Headache, nausea, violent sneezing followed by temporary physical debility	5 to 10 min.	15,000
Chloracetophenone	Phenyl chlormethyl ketone	$C_6H_5COCH_2Cl$	Solid	Severe lacrimation and skin irritation	Immediate	8,500
Brombenzylcyanide	Brombenzylcyanide	$C_6H_5CHBrCN$	Solid	Severe lacrimation and nose irritation	Immediate	3,500
White phosphorus	White phosphorus	P_4	Solid	Incendiary effect	Immediate	
FM	Titanium tetrachloride	$TiCl_4$	Liquid	Eye irritation Prickly sensation on skin	Immediate	

*Product of the concentration (mg. per cu. m. of air) by number of minutes of exposure. These figures indicate the relative toxicity of war gases but do not necessarily represent their lethal effect on man. (After *A. M. Prentiss*)

Areas may also be contaminated by means of sprinklers operated from various types of vehicles. Another method applicable to delaying actions is by the use of land mines: tin containers which when statically detonated discharge their contents of liquid agent over the nearby ground.

The dispersion of smoke involves little deviation from the principles observed in the cloud-gas form of attack. The smoke cloud is in many tactical situations required for a longer period than may be the case with a gas cloud. Also with favourable wind conditions a much narrower screen of smoke will suffice to obscure vision. These factors make smoke well-adapted to discharge from artillery weapons. Liquid smoke agents (*e.g.*, titanium tetrachloride) may be discharged from aeroplane tanks, forming a smoke curtain that is of especial use in naval warfare.

Military Application.—The extent to which chemical warfare is employed in military operations may be said to depend principally upon its likely contribution to tactical success. Smokes and incendiaries have proven most valuable adjuncts to military force, so that these agents are commonly included in all modern armament. Gas on the other hand has been used but sporadically in battle after 1918, even though nonlethal types have found wide application in the control of domestic disturbances.

The casualties resulting from gas attacks made in Europe between 1915 and 1918 were impressive enough to justify regarding gas as a military weapon of considerable importance. However, the effectiveness with which gas may be counteracted by appropriate protective measures, which have been improved in recent years, introduces a factor that must be carefully evaluated in studying the possibilities of offensive gas warfare.

So long as antigas protection is highly maintained, the prospects for successful gas attack are materially lessened: when on the contrary gas defense is neglected, the gas weapon becomes one of exceptional potentiality.

The principal tactical value of the cloud-gas form of attack is in weakening defensive positions that successfully withstand assault. In warfare of continued movement this type of operation has limited value.

The most effective of all war gases is of the mustard gas type. This agent has important uses in both offensive and defensive action. The irritant smokes have definite possibilities when properly dispersed.

None of the gases so far employed in warfare satisfies the ideal of a substance, the use of which will permit an army to easily subjugate an opposing force.

The quest for such an agent may be unending, yet meanwhile the possibilities of chemical warfare will continue to receive close study.

Gas Warfare.—Gas (or chemical agents), which proved to be a weapon of considerable importance in military operations in World War I, was not employed during World War II. Only after the occupation of Germany and Japan by Allied forces in 1945 was the situation as to gas warfare in these countries fully disclosed. With data available, reasons why gas was not resorted to in World War II become clear.

Preparations made by Germany for gas warfare were found to have been extensive. The tonnage of chemicals produced by German chemical plants between 1939 and 1945 exceeded by nearly 50% the total amounts produced during World War I. Captured ammunition dumps contained large stores of gas-filled shells and bombs. Some were loaded with a new war gas while two more highly toxic agents had been discovered and were being processed for production.

Thus, Germany had at its disposal a powerful military weapon which was never brought into action, even in time of dire need. The official explanation given at German gas defense schools for this fact was that Hitler did not approve the use of gas. However, more cogent reasons deterred Germany, even though it was true that Hitler never put the weight of his authority behind the development of chemical warfare.

From the viewpoint of tactics, gas was inappropriate to the early stages of the war when German ground and air forces were most capable of employing it effectively. Later, when gas promised high tactical advantage, Germany had lost aerial supremacy over the reich and for this reason stood to lose on the strategic side any gains that might be made tactically.

To the German high command there was obviously no profit in releasing gas on the beach at Anzio if this meant retaliatory showering of chemical bombs on German cities.

Behind reasons of immediate military expediency other deterrents were also at work. Allied armies were well prepared, in both training and equipment, for defense against gas attack. At the same time Great Britain and the U.S. possessed ample stocks of gas-charged aerial bombs which were known to be located within striking distance of Berlin. Thus, the elements of surprise and preponderant initial advantage were denied Germany. The result was a situation of stalemate which the nazis seemed perfectly satisfied should continue while the attention of German scientists was being directed toward military novelties of apparently greater promise.

Japan, which had never been a serious contender in the field of toxic chemicals, was found to run a poor second to Germany in this connection. Japanese armament could have permitted only face-saving retaliation against a first-class power undertaking large-scale gas warfare. Emphasis was, therefore, placed on gas defense and on authoritative assurance "that Japan has never used, and never will use, gas against any enemy, unless the fact that the enemy has . . . is definitely established."

The Allies were in position to apply the pressure of gas to sensitive points almost at will throughout most of World War II. There were several occasions when such pressure could have been utilized to both tactical and strategical advantage. This can scarcely be said of either Germany or Japan. The Allied show of force in the field of gas warfare was, therefore, demonstrably in support of a firmly announced policy of the Allies to discourage the employment of this weapon.

The strong presentation of this policy to the Tokyo government by President Roosevelt in June 1942, which evoked the declaration above cited, resulted also in immediate cessation of incidents of Japanese use of gas on the Chinese mainland which up to that time had been reported with frequency. As the war progressed Japan adopted vigorous measures to avoid occasions which might even suggest intention to employ gas. Imperial directives were issued to field commanders forbidding use of toxic chemicals under all circumstances unless specifically ordered by highest authority.

In Germany, also, careful attention was given to avoidance of untoward events which might precipitate gas operations. Chemical troops carried only smoke-filled projectiles. Toxic munitions, which accumulated in considerable quantities toward the end of the war, were stored well inside the country; even stocks possessed by satellite nations were found to have been transferred to depots in central Germany. The nazi decision not to use gas was certainly not based on lack of ammunition.

The gas warfare policy of the Allies (with which the prewar unilateral policy of the U.S. coincided) left initiative entirely to the opponents. Attendant circumstances, however, were such as to make it inadvisable to accept this initiative. The future use of gas as a military weapon must be read in the light of this basic fact.

Chemical agents of toxicities greater than those known in 1918 were available for World War II. Development of air power, moreover, had greatly enhanced the capabilities of gas warfare. Thus, despite remarkable advances made with other weapons, gas was still to be rated as a relatively powerful instrumentality of war.

Whether or not this potentiality will actively be employed in the future is largely a question of whether the policy as to nonuse of the gas weapon can be continued in force. Measures that have so far sustained this policy are strong offensive preparations coupled with effective defensive procedures, both backed by extended research and production. During World War II the United States spent prodigious sums for these purposes; yet the results of such expenditures can be accepted as profitable.

At least it may be accepted, based on experience in the field of gas warfare, that peace-loving nations can possess a powerful military weapon and at the same time approach its use on grounds higher than those of military expediency. Thus, there is good reason to believe that the atomic bomb as well as gas will eventually prove to be a self-inhibiting agency of war.

BIBLIOGRAPHY.—A. A. Fries and C. J. West, *Chemical Warfare* (1921); V. Lefebure, *The Riddle of the Rhine* (1921); E. B. Vedder, *The Medical Aspects of Chemical Warfare* (1925); P. Bloch, *La Guerre Chemique* (1927); R. Hanslian, *Der Chemische Krieg* (1927); H. L. Gilchrist, *A Comparative Study of World War Casualties* (1931); H. Buscher, *Grun und Gelbkreuz* (1932); H. C. Foulkes, *Gas: The Story of the Special Brigade* (1934); A. M. Prentiss, *Chemicals in War* (1937); M. Sartori, *The War Gases* (1939); H. F. Thuillier, *Gas in the Next War* (1939); *Air Raids Precaution Handbooks*, British Home Office. (HA. SH.; G. J. B. F.)

CHEMILUMINESCENCE is cold light of chemical origin. This includes all forms of radiation—whether visible, infra-red or ultra-violet—emitted in excess of the black body radiation so far as the energy is supplied from simultaneously occurring chemical reactions.

Chemiluminescence is most commonly generated by oxidation. A large number of substances, such as formaldehyde, dioxymethylene, paraldehyde, acroleine, lophin, glucose, lecethin, cholesterin, luminesce if slowly oxidized in alkaline alcoholic solution (Br. Radziszewski, 1877–83). Another group of chemiluminescences described by M. Delépine (1910–12) is connected with the oxidation of sulphur compounds. The chemiluminescence of siloxene (H. Kautsky, 1921–25) is of special interest since its study has thrown much light on the mechanism of chemiluminescence. The widespread luminescence of living organisms like fireflies and luminous bacteria has been shown by R. Dubois (1885–87) to be based on the oxidation of a thermostable substance of unknown structure, luciferin, in the presence of a thermolabile enzyme, luciferase.

The light emitted in chemiluminescence can usually be ascribed to the transfer of the energy of oxidation to a molecule not itself undergoing oxidation in which light is thus generated. The chemiluminescence of siloxene, for example, was shown to be caused by the emission of light by unoxidized siloxene particles, and that of living organisms to light emission by unoxidized luciferase particles.

A chemiluminescent reaction which can be analyzed in detail is that between sodium vapour and the halogens or halogen-containing molecules such as $HgCl_2$ (M. Polonyi and collaborators, 1925–30). The halogen is introduced through a nozzle into a space containing sodium vapour, pressures being about 0.01 mm. Emission of the yellow D-line of sodium occurs with an efficiency (=number of light quanta per number of reacting molecules) which may rise to near unity for chlorine. The reaction with halogens (X_2) proceeds through $Na+X_2=NaX+X$ followed by a reaction of the halogen atom X with sodium vapour. The luminescence is caused by the transfer of the energy of the reaction $Na_2+X=NaX+Na$ to an Na atom which emits its characteristic radiation, the D-line. (*See* FLUORESCENCE AND PHOSPHORESCENCE.)

BIBLIOGRAPHY.—Geza Schay, *Hochverdunnte Flammen* (Berlin, 1930); E. Newton Harvey, *Living Light* (1940); E. J. Bowen, *The Chemical Aspects of Light* (1946). (M. POL.)

CHEMIN-DES-DAMES, BATTLE OF THE, 1918.

This is the name commonly given to the May offensive of the Germans in 1918, the third act of their plan to reach a military decision before the weight of U.S. numbers could turn the scales against them. It is alternatively called the Battle of the Aisne, 1918, or, less frequently, the Battle of Soissons-Reims. After the relative failure of the German offensives of March and April it was essential for the Germans, if they wished to preserve the initiative, to deliver another powerful blow without delay. The choice of the front of attack and the battleground fell on the oft-contested chain of heights between the Ailette and the Aisne, the Chemin-des-Dames.

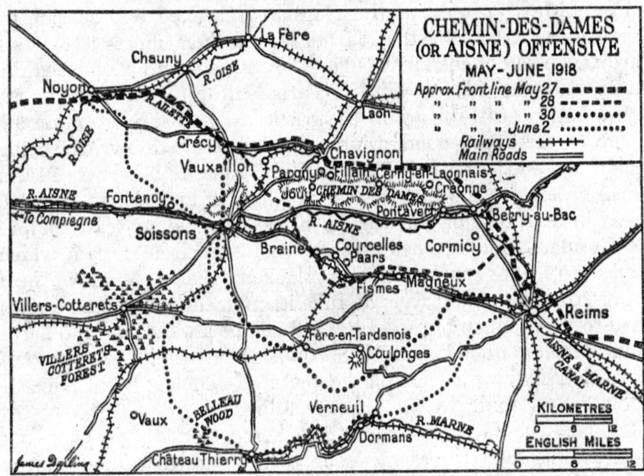

PLAN OF THE THIRD PHASE OF THE FINAL GERMAN OFFENSIVE IN 1918
The German attack, launched May 27 on a 30 mile front, took the Allies by surprise and drove them across the Aisne to the Marne. There, German efforts to push westward failed

Dispositions for the German Attack.—The German supreme command had decided to attack with the 7th and 1st armies against the sector between north of Soissons and Reims. If this attack proceeded favourably, it was to be prolonged on the right over the Ailette to the Oise and on the left as far as Reims. The German supreme command hoped that the push southward would succeed in reaching the neighbourhood of Soissons and Fismes, and by this means attract strong forces from Flanders so that it might be possible to continue the attack there according to plan. Preparations began about the middle of May. The 7th army under Böhm was charged with the main attack across the Chemin-des-Dames, the 1st army under Below with the neighbouring attack on the left in the direction of Compiègne. The right wing of the main attack, the 54th corps and the 8th Res. corps, had the task of pushing forward in a southwesterly direction on both sides of Soissons. The 25th Res. corps was to strike on both sides of Cerny-en-Laonnais direct toward Braisne, and on the east to take as much country as possible toward the south; the 4th Res. corps was to attack the high ground at the eastern end of the Chemin-des-Dames, immediately north of Craonne; in concert with this on the left the 65th corps was to occupy with its left wing the river bend north of Berry-au-Bac. Of the 1st army only one corps was to be launched at the outset to throw the opposing forces over the Aisne-Marne canal. The corps was to provide itself with bridgeheads in order to take the heights of Cormicy if the attack of the 7th army proceeded favourably.

For success there were two essentials; the first, surprise and the second, effective artillery preparation. Most elaborate and thorough precautions were taken to secure secrecy. As regards artillery preparation the ascent of the steep slopes on the heights of the Chemin-des-Dames was only possible if the Germans should succeed in silencing the bulk of the opposing guns. All registration was to be abandoned in order to surprise the enemy as much as possible. The first aim was to be a thorough gassing of the Allied position right down into the Aisne valley. Preparations were completed by the evening of May 26, 1918. At that moment four battle-worn British divisions were resting in this supposedly quiet sector. They had been sent to the French front, after strenuous exertions in the battles of the Lys, in return for French reinforcements which had gone north to the aid of the British in the later stages of that "backs to the wall" struggle. On the tranquil Aisne they could recuperate, while still serving a useful purpose as guardians of the trench-line. It was too quiet to be true. But the uneasiness of the local British commanders—shared by certain of their French neighbours—was slightly discounted by their Allied superiors. On May 25 they received from French headquarters the message that "in our opinion there are no indications that the enemy has made preparations which would enable him to attack to-morrow."

At 1 A.M. on May 27, 1918, a terrific storm of fire burst on the Franco-British front between Reims and north of Soissons, along the famous Chemin-des-Dames; at 4:30 A.M. an overwhelming torrent of Germans swept over the front trenches; by midday it was pouring over the many unblown bridges of the Aisne, and by May 30 it had reached the Marne—site and symbol of the great ebb of 1914. Happily, it proved to be "thus far, and no farther." Like the two great preceding offensives of March 21 and April 9, that of May 27 achieved astonishing captures of ground and prisoners, but it brought the Germans little nearer to their strategical object. And, even more than its predecessors, its very success paved the way for their downfall. To the reasons for this we shall come. But why, a month after the last onslaught, in the north, had come to an end, why, when there had been this long interval for preparation and for examination of the situation by a now unified command, should a surprise greater than any before have been possible?

It has long been known, of course, that the French command, that directly concerned with the safety of this Aisne sector, did not believe in the likelihood of an attack. Nor did the British higher command, which, however, was personally concerned with the front in the north. But the intelligence of another of the Allies, better placed to take a wide survey, did give the warning—only to be disregarded until too late. On May 13, a fortnight after the fighting in Flanders had died away, the British intelligence came to the conclusion that "an attack on a broad front between Arras and Albert is intended." Next day this was discussed at a conference of the intelligence section of the American Expeditionary Force, and the head of the battle order (of the enemy) section gave a contrary opinion holding that the next attack would be against the Chemin-des-Dames sector, and between May 25 and 30.

The warning in detail was conveyed to the French general headquarters, but fell on deaf ears. Why should credence be given to an opinion coming from such a new army, not yet tested in battle, over the verdict of war-tried and highly-developed intelligence services? The warning was reiterated, however, and the French intelligence was won over to its acceptance. But now, as at Verdun two years before, the operations branch opposed until too late the view of its own intelligence. This time, however, it was less blameworthy, for it was tugged the other way by the comforting assurances of the commander of the 6th French Army, in charge of the Chemin-des-Dames sector. This general, indeed, had a still heavier responsibility, for he insisted on the adoption of the long-exploded and wasteful system of massing the infantry of the defense in the forward positions. Besides giving the enemy guns a crowded and helpless target, this method ensured that, once the German guns had eaten up this luckless cannon-fodder, the German infantry would find practically no local reserves to oppose their progress through the rear zones. In similar manner all the headquarters, communication centres, ammunition depots and railheads were pushed close up, ready to be dislocated promptly by the enemy bombardment.

Pétain's instructions on a deep and elastic system of defense had evidently made no impression on this army command, so that it was still less a matter for wonder that the protests of junior British commanders met with a rebuff. It was unfortunate, also if perhaps less avoidable, that when the four British divisions forming the 9th corps (Hamilton Gordon) arrived from the north at the end of April, their depleted ranks filled up with raw drafts from home, they were hurried straight into the line, as the best place to complete their training. The backbone of the Aisne defenses was formed by the historic Chemin-des-Dames ridge north of the river. The eastern half of this "hog's back" was to be held by the British, with the 50th division (Jackson) on the left, next the 8th division (Heneker), and, beyond the end of the ridge, in the low ground from Berry-au-Bac along the Aisne and Marne canal, the 21st division (Campbell), joining up with the French troops covering Reims. The infantry of the 25th division (Bainbridge) was in reserve.

Altogether the French 6th army front was held by four French and three British divisions, with three and one respectively in reserve. Against these tired or raw troops, in the main attack from Berry-au-Bac westward, 15 German divisions, all but one brought up fresh, were to fall upon five, with two or more for the subsidiary attack between Berry-au-Bac and Reims, while 7 German divisions lay close up in support. Even so, the German superiority was not so pronounced as in the March and April offensives, whereas both the rapidity and the extent of their progress were greater. Yet this time the tactical surprise of the assault was unaided by the heavy ground mists which had previously helped so much by wrapping their initial advance in a cloak of invisibility. The conclusion is, therefore, that the advantage was in part the result of the strategic surprise the greater unexpectedness of the time and place—and in part to the folly of exposing the defenders so completely to the demoralizing and paralyzing effect of the German bombardment—by 3,719 guns on a front of under 40 mi. This last, indeed, was a form of surprise, for the object of all surprise is the dislocation of the enemy's morale and mind, and the effect is the same whether the enemy be caught napping by deception or allows himself to be trapped with his eyes open.

For three and a half hours, on May 27, the unfortunate troops had to endure a bombardment of exceptional intensity. And the ordeal of those hours of helpless endurance, amid the ever-swelling litter of shattered dead and untended wounded, was made more trying by crouching, semi-suffocated in gas masks. Then the gray waves advanced—relief, if only of action, at last. Three-quarters of an hour later they had reached the crest of the ridge in the centre near Ailles. This uncovered the flank of the left British division, the 50th, forcing its survivors to fall back down the other slope. Next to it, the 8th division was being forced to give way, although two of its brigades held on stubbornly for a time on the north bank of the Aisne. On the British right, the attack on the 21st division developed later; this division was awkwardly placed with the swampy Aisne and Marne canal running through the centre of its battle zone, but most of it was successfully extricated and withdrawn west of the canal. By midday the situation was that the Germans had reached and crossed the Aisne at most points from Berry-au-Bac to Vailly—helped by the fact that the order to blow up the bridges had been given belatedly. Hitherto the German progress had been evenly distributed, but in the afternoon a heavy sagging occurred in the centre, at the junction of the French and British wings, and the Germans pushed through as far as Fismes on the Vesle. This was natural, both because the joint is always the weakest point, and because the heaviest weight—more than 4 to 1—of the assault had fallen on the two French divisions in the centre and the left of the 50th division adjoining them.

This sagging, together with the renewed German pressure, compelled a drawing back of the flanks. On the east, or British flank, this operation was distinguished by a remarkable manoeuvre of the 21st division, wheeling back during the night through hilly, wooded country, while pivoting on and keeping touch with the Algerian division, which formed the right of the army. After a pause in the morning of May 28, the Germans forced the passage of the Vesle, and on the 29th they made a vast bound, reaching Fère-en-Tardenois in the centre, and capturing Soissons on the west, both important nodal points, which yielded them quantities of material. The German troops had even outstripped in their swift onrush the objectives assigned to them, and this, despite the counterattacks which Pétain was now shrewdly directing against their sensitive right flank. On the 30th the German flood swept on the Marne, but it was now flowing in a narrowing central channel, for this day little ground was yielded by the Allied right flank, where the 19th division as well as French divisions had come to reinforce the remnant of the original four British divisions, which next day were relieved.

From May 31 onward the Germans, checked on the side of Reims and in front by the Marne, turned their efforts to a westward expansion of the great bulge—down the corridor between the Ourcq and the Marne toward Paris. Hitherto the French reserves had been thrown into the battle as they arrived, in an attempt to stem the flood, which usually resulted in their being caught up and carried back by it. On June 1, however, Pétain issued orders for the further reserves coming up to form, instead, a ring in rear, digging themselves in and thus having ready before the German flood reached them a vast semicircular dam which would stop and confine its now slackening flow. When it beat against this in the first days of June its momentum was too diminished to make much impression, whereas the appearance and fierce counterattack of the 2nd U.S. division at the vital joint of Château-Thierry was not only a material cement, but an inestimable moral tonic to their weary allies. In those few days of "flooding" the Germans had taken some 65,000 prisoners, but whereas this human loss was soon to be more than made up by U.S. reinforcements, strategically the Germans' success had merely placed themselves in a huge sack which was to prove their undoing less than two months later (*see* Marne, Second Battle of the). As in each of the two previous offensives, the tactical success of the Germans on May 27 proved a strategical reverse, because the extent to which they surprised their enemy surprised and so dislocated the balance of their own command.

As the disclosures of General Kuhl have revealed, the offensive of May 27 was intended merely as a diversion, to attract the Allied reserves thither preparatory to a final and decisive blow at the British front covering Hazebrouck. But its astonishing opening success tempted the German command to carry it too far and too long, the attraction of success drawing thither their own reserves as well as the enemy's. Nevertheless it is a just speculation as to what might have resulted if the attack had begun on April 17, as ordered, instead of being delayed until May 27, before the preparations were complete. The Germans would have worn out fewer of their reserves in ineffectual prolongations of the Somme and Lys offensives, while the Allies would have still been waiting for the stiffening, moral and physical, of U.S. manpower. Time and surprise are the two supreme factors in war. The Germans lost the first and forfeited the second by allowing their surprise to surprise themselves. (B. H. L. H.)

CHEMIST, one who, for pleasure or profit, concerns himself with the acquisition of information relating to the composition and structure of substances and the changes of composition and structure which they undergo. The chemist traces his evolution from the Greek philosophers, who speculated without experiment as to the constitution of matter, through the mediaeval alchemists, who experimented with little logic, in the hope of transmuting one element into another. During the middle ages another sect, the iatrochemists, also existed, who carried out experiments which were to make chemistry more useful to medicine. Many types of chemists exist, classed usually according to the kind of matter or the kind of change with which they are most concerned. When the individual applies his information to the production, manufacture or commercial use of commodities, he is customarily considered an industrial chemist or chemical engineer.

CHEMISTRY. The science that is concerned with the composition of bodies and with the changes of composition they undergo. Analytical chemistry deals with the methods of separation of purer substances from mixtures, of elements from compounds, and with their estimation; synthetic chemistry treats of the methods by which complex bodies may be built up from simpler substances. In each case it is the changes of composition that concern the chemist. The combination of atoms, and the arrangement of atoms in a molecule, used to be regarded as the special province of the chemist; while the physicist dealt with changes of state and with the motions of the molecules: but today this distinction cannot be maintained.

With the rapid growth of modern chemistry it has become the practice to divide the theoretical study of the science into three main branches, and this conventional division is adopted in the present article, which, in addition, contains sections dealing with the history of chemistry and the practice of chemical analysis:—*History of Chemistry; Inorganic Chemistry; Organic Chemistry; Physical Chemistry; Analytical Chemistry* (*Inorganic Analysis, Ultimate Organic Analysis, Gas Analysis*).

HISTORY OF CHEMISTRY

Chemistry as a science had its origin in Egypt (*see* ALCHEMY)—the product on the one hand of much practical experience of workers in metals, glass and pottery, of users of dyeing and tanning materials; and on the other of Greek and Eastern speculation on the nature of the material world. The great school founded at Alexandria was the natural meeting place of the two streams, and from their union came in time the alchemy of the Arab conquerors, the iatrochemistry (*q.v.*) of the medical chemists and finally our modern science. In all the older cosmogonies we find the idea that there was some primordial element or principle from which the visible universe was derived. Perhaps the oldest speculations assigned to water this elementary character; its teeming life, its vivifying power, its solid deposits all marked it as the origin of things. The doctrine that water was the prime element—associated with the name of Thales—exerted an immense influence on scientific thought throughout the centuries. John van Helmont in the early 17th century thought he had proved it experimentally; it remained for Antoine Lavoisier in the late 18th to disprove it by mere decisive experiment. But water was not the only "element" that was regarded as primordial by Greek philosophers. That air could be condensed into clouds and clouds into rain was taught by Anaximenes; water could be evaporated into air, leaving solid earth behind. Everything therefore sprang from air. That fire was the first principle of things would appeal to those who came in contact with the fire worship of the Chaldeans, or with the religion of the Persians and Parsees, whom Zoroaster taught to look on fire as the symbol of goodness in creation. Heracleitus among the Greeks espoused the cause of fire, Pherecides that of earth; it was indeed easy to show that from combustible solids fire, air and water could be derived. That all four were primal elements, and that the varieties of matter were made from intermixture of these, was the conception of Empedocles, who regarded each element as distinct and unchangeable. But the doctrine of the four elements which gave so powerful an impulse and direction to chemistry was that taught by Aristotle. The importance of his doctrine lay not so much in the nature he assigned to matter, or to the modes in which qualities might be affixed to it, but in the broad principle that one kind of matter could be changed into another kind—in a word, that transmutation was possible. Underlying all tangible bodies was an indeterminate matter-stuff (ὕλη) on which properties might be impressed giving matter its particular form (εἶδος).

If such fundamental qualities as hotness and dryness (or their opposite qualities, coldness and wetness) are impressed on the matter-stuff, we may conceive two qualities combining to give a primal form of matter. For instance, the combination of dryness with heat gives fire, with cold gives earth: the combination of wetness with heat gives air, with cold gives water. Moreover these qualities are not unalterable. If the coldness of water is overcome by heat, the water changes to steam or air; if its wetness is overcome by dryness it leaves earth.

Aristotle's conception differed therefore not only from the unchangeable elements of Empedocles, but from the mechanical hypothesis of Democritus, who imagined the world built up by the fortuitous meeting of rapidly moving atoms—themselves of unalterable nature.

In Egypt the Aristotelian doctrine of the four elements readily took root. Working in metals had been practised for centuries not only along the valley of the Nile, but in the valleys of the Euphrates and the Indus, between which there had long existed intercourse.

How far the teaching of the Alexandrine school directly affected chemical practice among the Egyptians is doubtful. It is clear from the chemical writings that have been preserved—especially from the famous papyrus at Leyden—that the priests were well acquainted with methods for imitating gold and silver, and for covering metal vessels superficially with gold alloys so that the base metal could be removed and leave a pure gold surface which would "pass the test."

ALCHEMISTS AND IATROCHEMISTS

When the Arabs conquered Egypt in the 7th century and overran Syria and Persia, they brought a new spirit of enquiry to bear on the old civilizations they subdued. The great name that stands out in the alchemic period is that of Jabir—probably the same Geber of the Latin books *Summa Perfectionis* and *Liber Fornacum* of which the existing manuscripts date from the 13th century. Jabir ibn Hayyan accepted the Aristotelian doctrine of the four elements, but to these he added the special chemical elements mercury and sulphur, by which he meant not so much the two elements as met with in nature, but rather the principles giving metals their unalterable property, and the earthly impurity that it was possible to cleanse them from. Gold, unaltered by fire, contained a very pure mercury; lead and copper contained much sulphur. That gold could be extracted from copper pyrites, and that silver remained when galena was long roasted, were regarded as evidence that the lustrous crystals of pyrites and galena, looked on as metals, had been transmuted by purification from the sulphur or dross into the nobler metals.

The two alchemic elements were thus introduced; the third element "salt"—representing the residue that remained fixed after calcination—was added by the iatrochemists. These three elements constituted the *tria prima* of Paracelsus and his disciples of the 16th century. Jabir himself seems to have believed in the philosopher's stone, and the term Kimya may have signified the secret powder which had to be projected on the molten metal to cause transmutation.

A century after Jabir came Rhazes, physician and chemist; and he was followed by Ibn Sina, better known as Avicenna, who knew that metals could be changed in colour, but not really altered in substance.

In the 11th century Mansur distinguished between *natron* (sodium carbonate) and *qali* (potassium carbonate). He describes the preparation of a plaster of Paris, for use in surgery, by heating gypsum and mixing it with white of egg.

When the Arabs penetrated into Spain they brought with them their chemical knowledge and their love of learning. Through the Arab universities founded in Spain, the knowledge not only of alchemy, but also of much of Greek thought first illuminated the backward states of Europe. We cannot be sure of the origin of many of the Latin texts of the 12th and following centuries. It is said that the book translated from the Arabic by Robert of

Chester in 1144 contains passages which occur in the earlier alchemist manuscripts. It is even probable that the names which figure largely among the early chemists in Europe—Albertus Magnus, Roger Bacon, Raymond Lully, Vincent de Beauvais—are those of writers who made known not so much their own chemical experience as that of the Arabian alchemists. Albertus takes the same view as Avicenna concerning "chemical gold"—it is a superficial imitation, not real gold.

Paracelsus, the son of a physician, studied at Basle and at Würzburg, and after wandering through Europe returned to Basle in 1526 and was appointed professor of medicine. His first public act was to burn the works of Galen and of Avicenna, the great handbooks of medicine, and to proclaim that chemistry was not concerned with the transmutation of metals but was the handmaid of medicine. His reckless use of inorganic salts—many of them poisonous—led to his expulsion from Basle.

Contemporary with the restless and dogmatic Paracelsus, Agricola devoted many years to the study of ores and the preparation of pure metals and salts from them. His *De Re Metallica* records many first-hand experiments—on the amalgamation process of extracting gold, on the properties of bismuth, on flame-tests for various metals. A little later Libavius, a German physician, published his *Alchymia,* which may be regarded as the first European textbook of chemistry. Coming later still, Glauber made his reputation as a great practical chemist: he gave a clear description of the mineral acids and of *aqua regia* (*q.v.*), and he left his name attached to sodium sulphate.

Last of the iatrochemists came van Helmont, regarded by many as the link between the alchemists and the modern chemists. He rejected the *tria prima* of Paracelsus and the four elements of Aristotle, going back to the older doctrine of Thales that water was the origin of all things. His well-known experiment of growing a willow-shoot in dried earth, and watering it regularly until it had gained many pounds in weight without receiving any appreciable nutriment except from the water, is recalled now with a feeling that Nature had a sense of irony in deceiving the man who discovered carbonic acid gas.

He showed that an air was given off when an acid acted on limestone or potashes, and that this air extinguished a flame. The same air he found was produced in fermentation and occurred naturally in the Grotto del Cane. In his endeavours to prepare the air in closed vessels he discovered the enormous force developed by it; *Ideo, nominis egestate,* he writes, *halitum illum Gas vocavi, non longe a Chao veterum secretum* (*Opera Omnia,* Frankfurt, 1682, p. 69). The term *gas sylvestre,* applied to carbon dioxide, meant the wild chaotic air that could not be coerced into vessels. Van Helmont found he could make an inflammable air, *gas pingue,* by heating animal matter, but he did not further distinguish between his gases.

BIRTH OF MODERN CHEMISTRY

Boyle.—A new era began with Robert Boyle. In early life, a member of the "Invisible College" (the germ from which the Royal Society sprang), he was drawn in 1654 to Oxford where several of the members were in residence. Here he spent his most active years in experimental research. He established by careful experiments the law known by his name—that the volume of a given mass of air varies inversely as the pressure upon it. He determined the density of air and pointed out that bodies altered in weight according to the varying buoyancy of the atmosphere; and he compared the lower strata of the air to a number of sponges or small springs compressed by the weight of the layers above them. It is notable that not only the facts published by Boyle on the "Spring of the Air," but the very images he used were repeated by Edmè Mariotte 14 years later.

In 1661 Boyle published the *Sceptical Chymist,* in which he gravely questions the *tria prima:* "There are some bodies from which it has not yet been made to appear that any degree of fire can separate either salt, or sulphur or mercury, much less all three. Gold may be heated for months in a furnace without losing weight or altering, and yet one of its supposed constituents is volatile and another combustible. Neither can solvents separate any of the three principles from gold; the metal may be *added to,* and so brought into solution . . . but the gold particles are present all the time: and the metal may be reduced to the same weight, of yellow, ponderous malleable substance it was before."

Boyle gives many instances in which metals, such as lead or copper, may be dissolved in acids and their properties entirely disguised in the compound. The corpuscles of which the metal is composed, meeting with corpuscles of another kind, may be more disposed to unite with them than with the particles forming their original metallic cluster. From the coalition of two different corpuscles a new body may be formed "as really one as either of the corpuscles before they were confounded." We can trace here the modern idea of chemical affinity uniting atoms into compounds. Boyle devised a method for extracting the element phosphorus, which was long known as Boyle's phosphorus; he made many experiments on air and other gases. He prepared hydrogen by the action of acids on steel filings and on iron nails, and showed that it would burn with a strong flame though with little light. He collected the gas in an inverted glass flask over dilute acid, and showed that the imprisoned gas was permanent and "dilated itself" like air when the vessel was warmed.

In his "New Experiments touching the Relation betwixt Flame and Air" he showed that the flames of hydrogen, of sulphur, and of a candle were extinguished in the receiver of his air pump when the air was rarified. But, finding that gunpowder and fulminating gold would burn in his vacuum, he was forced to conclude that flame may exist without air: it was left to his assistant Robert Hooke to make the next advance.

By observing that wood charcoal was immediately dissipated into white ashes if the retort was opened in the air while still red-hot, Hooke grasped the fact that the air "preyed upon" or "dissolved" the charcoal; and he compared the active constituent of the air with that which is fixed in saltpetre. The oil rising as vapour from a lighted wick is not burnt inside the flame (which is dark) but only as it reaches the surrounding atmosphere where it meets the "nitre-air."

John Mayow made careful experiments on the burning of combustible bodies in air confined over water. He showed that part of the air disappeared both in combustion and respiration, and that the residue left would not support flame or life. This residue differed then from ordinary air. He did not isolate his nitre-air, nor show what became of it.

THEORY OF PHLOGISTON

The theory of phlogiston first proposed by Johann Joachim Becher and greatly advanced by Georg Ernst Stahl went back to the old idea of Jabir that combustible bodies lost something when they burnt. Becher's *terra pinguis* became Stahl's phlogiston, which was not fire itself but the material of fire. Metals were composed of a *calx,* different for each metal, combined with phlogiston, which was the same in all metals and common to all combustibles. When a metal, such as lead or tin, was calcined in the air, phlogiston was evolved and a calx was left behind. When a candle or charcoal was burnt in the air it gave off phlogiston (manifest as heat and light) and very little residue was left: wax and charcoal mainly consisted of the material of fire. When a calx was heated with charcoal out of contact with air the phlogiston of the charcoal recombined with the calx and the metal was regenerated. In this way a generalization was made which accounted for the two opposite processes of oxidation and reduction, and moreover was able to predict certain chemical consequences which were verified later by experiment. The heat given off by animal bodies and its restoration by food were also explained by phlogiston. The fact that combustion and life ceased in a confined volume of air was due to the swift whirling motion of the phlogiston that filled the air, which when saturated could take no more. In considering the wide acceptance of Stahl's theory it must be borne in mind that it gave expression to the very striking facts that in combustion something was emitted by the burning body, viz., *heat,* and in the reduction of a calx by charcoal something—potential energy, or the power of giving out heat again—was restored to it.

ANTIPHLOGISTIC EXPERIMENTS

Black and Cavendish.—The first blow to the phlogistic theory was dealt by Joseph Black, himself an adherent. It had long been known that limestone was turned into quicklime by heating, and that quicklime brought into contact with the mild alkalis rendered them caustic, returning itself to chalk. This was explained by supposing that the fire gave a "burning principle" to the limestone, which handed it on in turn to the mild alkali. Black, using the balance, found that both chalk and magnesia alba lost weight when they were heated, the loss being due to the escape of a gas previously fixed in them. The caustic lime and magnesia, freed from the gas, no longer effervesced with acids: moreover, the chalk and magnesia alba lost the same weight of gas whether they were strongly heated or were dissolved in an acid. The effervescence was obviously due to the escape of the air. Then an aqueous solution of the caustic lime or magnesia when exposed to the atmosphere gradually formed a white precipitate and lost its causticity as the "fixed air" from the atmosphere dissolved in the surface layer of the liquid. Caustic lime and magnesia act on the mild alkalis by combining with their fixed air, and not by an exchange of phlogiston. Black had proved by quantitative experiments the difference between the mild and caustic alkalis, and had shown that fixed air (CO_2) was a normal constituent of our atmosphere (1756).

Twenty years later Henry Cavendish published his researches on "Factitious Air," in which he described the preparation and properties of carbon dioxide and hydrogen. His work on hydrogen is of the first importance. "Inflammable air," he found, could be produced readily by the solution of zinc, iron and tin in dilute sulphuric or in hydrochloric acid. He collected and measured the gas over water, and found that a given weight of one of the metals gave the same measure of gas whichever acid was used as the solvent and however diluted the acid. He concluded therefore that the gas came from the metal and was either phlogiston or a compound of phlogiston with water.

Informed of Joseph Priestley's observations that in the explosion of inflammable air with common air a dew was deposited on the vessel and a loss of weight ensued, Cavendish carefully repeated the experiments and showed there was no loss of weight, while "almost all the inflammable air, and about one-fifth part of the common air, lose their elasticity and are condensed into a dew which lines the glass." He then burnt a quantity of hydrogen in air and, collecting the dew, found it had the properties of water; the two airs, he said, "are turned into pure water." Then Cavendish fired a mixture of hydrogen and oxygen, and was puzzled for some time by finding the condensed water to be acid. He proved this acid was caused by the presence of adventitious nitrogen (from the air) which was acted on in the explosion if the oxygen was in excess. Afterward he passed electric sparks through a mixture of air and oxygen in a bent tube over mercury in presence of potash. In this remarkable experiment he not only proved the composition of nitre, but proved that the nitrogen of the air could be completely removed with the exception of a small inert bubble of gas about one $\frac{1}{120}$ part of the whole. He had isolated argon (*q.v.*) from the air—by the same method used by Rayleigh and Ramsay more than 100 years later. Much has been written regarding the relative claims of Cavendish, Watt and Lavoisier regarding the discovering of the composition of water. It would seem clear that Cavendish alone established this by his exact quantitative work. Claims on behalf of James Watt have been advanced for having given the correct interpretation of the experimental results. Lavoisier is not entitled to any share in this discovery—his merit rests upon having expressed the results in language unhampered by the phraseology of the phlogistic theory of combustion.

Scheele and Priestley.—In contrast to the deliberative work of Black and Cavendish, the rapid series of experiments carried out by Karl Wilhelm Scheele in Sweden and by Priestley in England were remarkable for the brilliant observational powers brought into play and for the many discoveries that flowed from them.

Scheele found that various substances—especially bodies like sulphur and phosphorus—diminished the volume of air in which they were burnt; and the residual gas he found, against his expectation, to be lighter than ordinary air, and this lighter portion was no longer able to support combustion. The portion of the air concerned in the burning—his "fire-air" had disappeared. He burnt a jet of hydrogen in a measured volume of air over water, noticed how the flame died out, and then how the water rose in the vessel. Finding no evidence of any change in the water, he concluded that the missing air being neither condensed in the residual "foul air," nor dissolved in the water, must have escaped through the glass. The phlogiston (hydrogen) must have combined with the fire-air to form "caloric," and this had passed through the glass walls. He set himself to reverse the process. If caloric could be passed into a substance avid for phlogiston, the caloric might be broken up, the phlogiston retained and the fire-air liberated. Several bodies, he thought, would strongly attract phlogiston—such as nitric acid, pyrolusite (which he had himself investigated) and the red calx of mercury. When heat was applied to nitric acid, red fumes were evolved, and when these were absorbed by lime, a colourless gas remained, which supported combustion brilliantly. He had liberated the sought-for "fire-air." Similarly the calx of mercury, when heated in a vessel over a charcoal furnace, combined with the phlogiston of the caloric to form metallic quicksilver and the pure fire-air was set free. He added his fire-air to the residual "foul-air" in due proportion and found the mixture behaved as common air.

Scheele interpreted all his results in terms of the phlogistic theory. Thus when he first isolated chlorine by beating pyrolusite with hydrochloric acid, he imagined the pyrolusite had absorbed phlogiston from the acid, and he named the new gas "dephlogisticated marine acid." We owe to Scheele hydrofluoric, hydrocyanic, arsenic, tungstic and molybdic acids, and a long list of organic substances including glycerine and milk sugar, with oxalic, tartaric, citric, malic and other acids.

Scheele's discovery of fire-air, probably made in 1773, was not published until 1777. Meanwhile, on Aug. 1, 1774, Priestley had concentrated the sun's rays through his new burning-glass on the red calx of mercury contained in a glass vessel over mercury, and found an air was expelled from it very readily. This air he found was not soluble in water, "but," he writes, "what surprised me more than I can well express was that a candle burned in this air with a remarkably vigorous flame." Now Priestley had previously shown that the respiration of animals acted like burning bodies on common air, diminishing its volume and rendering it noxious. This new air, he found, differed from common air not only in supporting combustion more vividly but in prolonging the life of animals breathing it. His explanation was that while common air is always partially saturated with phlogiston and cannot make room for much more, the new air is uncontaminated and phlogiston can rapidly escape into it—as into a vacuum. He named the new gas therefore "dephlogisticated air," and the residual inert nitrogen he named "phlogisticated air."

Priestley was the first to prepare and describe the gases nitric oxide and nitrous oxide, which he collected over water, and the gaseous hydrogen chloride, ammonia, sulphur dioxide and silicon fluoride, which he collected over mercury.

Lavoisier.—The outstanding features of Lavoisier's work were the use of the balance and the clearness with which he interpreted quantitative results, a clearness founded on his conviction (partly gained from Black) that no ponderable matter disappears in any chemical change. He heated water in a sealed glass vessel for many days, and found the weight of the whole unaltered. On pouring out the water he found the glass had lost in weight, but on evaporating the water he recovered the lost weight in the alkaline silicates which had been dissolved from the glass.

In 1772 Lavoisier began his researches on combustion. When sulphur and phosphorus were burnt in air a portion of the air was fixed. The same thing was observed when lead and tin were calcined in air sealed in glass vessels: there was no change in weight until the vessels were opened and the air rushed in. In 1775, after hearing from Priestley of his "dephlogisticated air," and after repeating the experiment with the red calx of mercury, Lavoisier grasped the true explanation of combustion. The "pure" or "vital" air was combined with the metal in the calx, and this pure air formed that portion of common air which produced calcination by combining with the metal. Then followed the quantitative demonstration that mercury heated in common air slowly combined with the "vital" part and formed the red powder—*mercurius calcinatus:* from this powder, more strongly heated, the vital air was recovered, and this mixed with the inert "azote" (left in the first experiment) reformed exactly the original quantity of common air.

Finding that nonmetallic elements such as sulphur and phosphorus gave acids when combined with his vital air, and having shown that carbon yielded Black's fixed air (Bergman's aereal acid), Lavoisier adopted the name oxygen (acid-maker) for the substance which, combined with caloric, formed "oxygen gas." While the nonmetallic elements gave acids by their combination with oxygen, the metals gave calces—the oxides of the metals; and the union of the two kinds of oxides gave the various metallic salts. But, the phlogistonists could still object, this did not explain the formation of inflammable air when metals were dissolved in acids. Just the same salt was formed by the union of a calx with an acid as by the solution of the metal in the acid; but in the latter case the metal gave up its phlogiston as inflammable air. Moreover, unless the calx were originally present in the metal, there was no obvious source from which the metal could obtain the oxygen necessary to form the calx. It was a difficulty only to be solved by Cavendish's proof that water was formed when inflammable air was burnt. Informed of Cavendish's work, Lavoisier and Laplace repeated the experiment and by their correct interpretation supplied the missing data. In the solution of a metal by an acid, the oxygen of the water combines with the metal, liberating the inflammable air—now named hydrogen—while the two oxides (the calx and the acid) combine to form the salt. This was the deathblow to the phlogistic theory.

Founded on Lavoisier's oxygen theory, a new nomenclature was evolved, and this has largely survived to our day. It was perhaps natural that the new school should consider oxygen to be an essential constituent of all acids, and that the acid from sea salt, muriatic acid, should be regarded as formed by the union of an oxide of an unknown nonmetallic element murion with water, and that chlorine—Scheele's "dephlogisticated marine acid"—should be an oxygenated compound of this, or "oxy-muriatic acid."

THE ATOMIC THEORY

Before the publication of John Dalton's atomic theory, and indeed even before the formal enunciation of the law of the conservation of mass by Lavoisier, there was some recognition of the principle of equivalency in chemical combination. This can be traced back to Black's work on fixed air and magnesia alba about 1755. The subject of equivalency and the law of reciprocal proportions are usually identified with the name of J. B. Richter (1792), but experimental work on the neutralization of acids by bases, in which the principle of equivalency was recognized, were carried out at an earlier date by Cavendish. Clerk Maxwell, in his notes on Cavendish's electrical researches adverting to a particularly remarkable set of experiments carried out in 1777, pointed out that Cavendish must have carried out some equivalent weight determinations before this date but he did not publish them. The actual values were very similar to modern figures. On the subject of the determinations Maxwell remarked that "Cavendish was accustomed to compare the quantity of fixed air from different carbonates with that from 1,000 grains of marble. Now the modern equivalent weight of marble is 100, so that if Cavendish took 100 pennyweights as the equivalent weight of marble, the equivalents of other substances would be as he has given them."

In 1803 Claude Louis Berthollet published an important work entitled *Essai de statique chimique* which exercised considerable influence upon the progress of chemistry in more than one direction. Broadly speaking the *Essai* was an attempt to bring ideas regarding the course of chemical change and the composition of substances resulting therefrom under a few general principles. In this respect Berthollet made a marked advance upon the ideas regarding chemical affinity which were expressed during the 18th century by men such as T. O. Bergman and C. F. Wenzel. Berthollet was able to see the fallacies of Bergman's tables of affinity, and he pointed out that the course of chemical change was capable of modification by change in the relative quantities of the reacting substances. A most important feature of Berthollet's ideas was the recognition of a state of chemical equilibrium, and that the establishment of equilibrium was determined not only by the affinities of the reacting substances but upon their amounts. Berthollet regarded chemical affinity as akin to gravitational attraction, but at the same time he realized that it was a much more complex phenomenon. In spite of the limitations of his ideas, Berthollet must be regarded as a pioneer in the development of the law of mass action, a principle which was first clearly formulated by C. M. Guldberg and P. Waage in 1867.

Berthollet's brilliant ideas regarding the reversibility of chemical reactions unfortunately led him into serious errors regarding the constancy of composition of substances. The quantitative work of Black, Cavendish, and Lavoisier had all gone to show that compounds, however prepared, contain their constituents in definite proportions. Berthollet maintained a contrary opinion, and he asserted that the composition of compounds was determined by the conditions under which they are produced. This erroneous doctrine gave rise to a celebrated controversy with J. L. Proust, who was able to show as the result of his analytical work that the composition of compounds is constant and definite.

The controversy between Berthollet and Proust was followed in 1808 by the publication of Dalton's *New System of Chemical Philosophy,* vol. i, part i. In this work Dalton put forward his atomic theory. The origin of this theory has been the subject of some discussion. Among Dalton's contemporaries, including his biographer Henry, it was widely believed that Dalton derived his theory as the result of his experimental work on combination in definite and in multiple proportions. It seems certain, however, that Dalton had ideas regarding an atomic constitution of matter some years before the publication of the *New System,* and a careful examination of Dalton's notebooks by H. E. Roscoe and A. Harden led in 1896 to the conclusions expressed in their *New View of the Origin of Dalton's Atomic Theory* that the theory had been arrived at by deductive reasoning and not inductively as a result of a study of the laws of constant and multiple proportions. Dalton was known to be keenly interested in Isaac Newton's works, and it would seem that his study of the *Principia* and even more of the *Opticks* was the real source of his own atomic conceptions.

The study of quantitative relations between the volumes of gases taking part in chemical reactions dates back to the time of Cavendish, and in 1808 J. L. Gay-Lussac enunciated a general law, known by his name, which gave formal expression to such relations. Dalton, too, had done much experimental work in this direction, and he attempted, but without success, to discuss the results in terms of his atomic theory. In passing, it may be noted that while Dalton was a pioneer in scientific thought, as an experimentalist he was far from exact. Gay-Lussac's law which states that when gases combine together they do so in simple proportions by volume and the volume of the product, if gaseous, bears a simple relation to the volumes of the reacting gases, was a purely experimental generalization and was not accompanied with any theoretical discussion. Dalton ventured the suggestion that under identical conditions of temperature and pressure equal volumes of gases contain the same number of atoms, but he very soon found that this would lead to error. In 1811 A. Avogadro got over the difficulty by drawing a distinction between the ultimate particle of an element which can take part in a chemical change, the atom, and the ultimate particle of an element or compound which can exist by itself, this latter he termed a molecule. By replacing the word atom by the word molecule in Dalton's suggestion, the well-known hypothesis of Avogadro was formulated, viz., that under identical physical conditions equal volumes of gases contain the same number of molecules. This hypothesis, originally framed to explain Gay-Lussac's law, became the very corner-stone of modern chemistry. Every advance after that time in one way or another provided fresh evidence of its truth, so much so that it became customary to refer to Avogadro's *law.*

Although formulated three years after Gay-Lussac's law it took nearly half a century for Avogadro's ideas to secure general recognition among chemists. Dalton was antagonistic to the theorem after having seen the failure of his own attempt to discuss chemical combination in terms of gaseous volumes—indeed he challenged the accuracy of Gay-Lussac's law, relying upon the results of his own less accurate experiments. The state of chemistry for some 50 years after the publication of Avogadro's hypothesis was one of much confusion, no fewer than four "systems" of chemistry having been introduced between 1826 and 1858 associated with the names of J. J. Berzelius, L. Gmelin, C. F. Gerhardt, and S. Cannizzaro. Two important principles were introduced in 1819 which exerted much influence in fixing atomic weights and in the establishment of formulas, namely the law of Dulong and Petit and Mitscherlich's law of isomorphism. P. L. Dulong and A. T. Petit pointed out that the product of the specific heat of a solid element and its atomic weight was approximately constant, and E. E. Mitscherlich showed a connection between identity of crystalline form and of chemical composition. In 1826 J. B. A. Dumas devised a useful method for determining vapour densities by which molecular weights of substances could be determined in the vaporous condition. Berzelius carried out some good atomic weight determinations, and he made some use of the above-mentioned principles in establishing the formulas of inorganic compounds. Although some of his formulas were identical with those which are now in general use, others were not, and it is certain that in attempting to make use of volume relationships he failed to do so in a consistent and logical manner—in short his failure was due to neglect of Avogadro's principle. Gmelin's system was regarded by some as an improvement on that of Berzelius, but both were essentially founded upon gravimetric experiments; indeed Gmelin's atomic weights were what would now be termed equivalent weights. A much closer approach to the establishment of a satisfactory system of chemistry was realized by Gerhardt and strongly supported by A. Laurent. Both Gerhardt and Laurent stressed the molecule, not the atom, as the fundamental unit in chemistry. Gerhardt's system, in which due account was taken of Avogadro's rule, was largely successful with organic compounds, but with inorganic compounds it was somewhat of a failure. The final step, which resulted in the establishment of a completely logical system of chemistry with consistent formulas and atomic weights, was taken by Cannizzaro in 1858. He insisted upon the necessity of accepting Avogadro's hypothesis as universally applicable, and was able to explain the cause of certain apparent exceptions, resulting in the deduction of impossible formulas, as a consequence of thermal dissociation. Cannizzaro was able to deduce correct values for atomic weights by showing that, once the molecular weight of a compound had been established by a determination of its vapour density, the value of the atomic weight of some particular element in the compound must be fixed within a certain limit. By choosing a sufficient number of compounds of that element, he pointed out that there was reasonable probability of obtaining a compound containing only one atom of the element in the molecule of the compound, and thus of correlating the value of its equivalent weight with the atomic weight. Cannizzaro's system rapidly received general acceptance, but it is interesting to note that certain French chemists, particularly Sainte-Claire Deville, who had carried out much valuable experimental work on thermal dissociation, were unable to accept the explanation of the so-called abnormal vapour densities of substances like ammonium chloride and phosphorus pentachloride as being due to thermal dissociation. In short, they regarded such compounds as being exceptions to Avogadro's theorem. It was recognized by Cannizzaro, by H. Kopp, and by F. A. Kekulé that there was no question of any such exception, but that when values for the molecular weight of a compound in the vaporous state were obtained which were inconsistent with its formula, such results were due to an increase in the number of molecules in a given volume brought about by partial or complete thermal dissociation.

The experimental demonstration of this important principle was largely due to C. A. Wurtz.

The development of chemical theory between Dalton's time and that of Cannizzaro was much influenced by studies on electrolysis and on the reactions of organic compounds. In 1819 Berzelius put forward his dualistic theory of chemical combination, according to which salts were regarded as the products of the union of an electropositive (basic) oxide with an electronegative (acidic) oxide. With oxyacids and their salts this theory enjoyed some success. Its subsequent downfall was largely brought about by H. Davy's discovery of the elementary nature of chlorine, and also by Dumas' discovery that acetic acid could be converted into trichloracetic acid without causing a profound change in the nature of the product. Once it had been discovered that elements of opposite electrochemical character could replace each other in a compound, Dumas was able in 1839 to formulate his theory of types—an idea altogether at variance with the electrochemical ideas of Berzelius. Shortly before this time J. von Liebig and F. Wöhler had published their investigation on the radical of benzoic acid, and in 1841 R. W. Bunsen had begun his investigations on the cacodyl compounds. In these researches it had become recognized that a group of elements could take part in a number of reactions without the group thereby losing its individuality. In 1833 T. Graham showed that phosphoric and arsenic acids were capable of giving rise to more than one type of salt, and shortly afterward extended his work to organic acids and thus developed a theory of polybasic acids. Of other investigations which influenced the development of chemical theory, particular mention should be made of A. W. Williamson's experiments on etherification between 1850 and 1856. These and other departments of study all served, in one way or another, to elaborate the various theories of structure, known as the type and residue theories, associated particularly with the names of Gerhardt and Kekulé. (*See* historical introduction to CHEMISTRY: *Organic.*)

The various type theories gradually developed into a general theory of valency, largely as the result of the work of E. Frankland on organo-metallic compounds about 1852, and of H. Kolbe's experiments on the electrolysis of the salts of organic acids which were begun about 1845. Important theoretical developments were made by A. S. Couper in 1858 and especially by Kekulé from 1858 onward. Frankland and Kekulé were agreed in regarding valency as a property of an atom of an element expressing its capacity for saturation with hydrogen atoms, but they differed on the question of the variable or constant nature of valency. Kekulé saw that success in the development of organic chemistry would rest on the assumption of the constant quadrivalency of carbon, and accordingly he regarded other elements as having invariable valencies. Frankland preferred to regard an element such as phosphorus as being tervalent in the trichloride and quinquevalent in the pentachloride, and generally that valency was variable. Kekulé regarded phosphorus as definitely tervalent in all compounds. He regarded a substance such as phosphorus pentachloride as a "molecular" compound of the trichloride and chlorine and wrote the formula as PCl_3,Cl_2. Such formulas had much to recommend them; *e.g.,* the readiness with which the substances can undergo thermal dissociation, but it was soon found impossible to maintain a distinction between "atomic" and "molecular" compounds, so Frankland's view regarding the variable nature of valency received general acceptance.

Classification of the Elements.—In the early years of the 19th century several chemists; *e.g.,* J. W. Dobereiner and Dumas, attempted to establish relations between the values of the atomic weights of elements and their properties. Thus in several instances it was not difficult to show that there was a gradation of properties when three elements of similar nature and increasing atomic weight were considered together. Thus bromine which is intermediate in properties between chlorine and iodine has an atomic weight which is roughly the arithmetic mean of these two elements. Important advances in correlating the properties of elements with their atomic weights were made independently by A. E. B. de Chancourtois in 1862, by J. A. R. Newlands in 1866 who put forward his law of octaves, and by D. I. Mendeléyev in 1869 who elaborated a periodic system of classification. The ideas of de Chancourtois and of Newlands, which were fundamentally identical with those of Mendeléyev received almost no recognition, but Mendeléyev not only pointed out that when the elements were arranged in the order of ascending atomic weights similar elements occur at intervals of eight (Newlands' law of octaves) but was able to predict the existence of hitherto undiscovered elements and to correct the values of several erroneous atomic weights. Almost simultaneously with Mendeléyev, Lothar Meyer established the same principle, namely that the properties of the elements and of their compounds are a periodic function of their atomic weights, and he expressed his ideas graphically by plotting the atomic weights as abscissas against the atomic volumes of the elements as ordinates. Lothar Meyer, however, adopted a more restrained attitude to the whole subject, and he was opposed to altering the atomic weights of such elements which did not fit into the system.

Among the important theoretical aspects of the periodic classification, Mendeléyev drew attention to the valencies of the elements as measured by their combining capacities for hydrogen and for oxygen respectively. He pointed out that in a number of instances the sum of the "hydrogen" and of the "oxygen" valencies was equal to eight. Some 30 years later the same principle, expressed in electrochemical language, was formulated by R. Abegg, who regarded the elements as endowed with two different kinds of valency, namely a normal (electropositive) valency, and what he termed a contravalency of electronegative character. Thus phosphorus would have a normal valency of three in phosphine, PH_3, and a contravalency of five in the pentachloride, PCl_5. Abegg's theory amounted to a revival of Berzelius' dualistic theory welded on to the periodic system of classification. It attracted some attention at the time, but was less fruitful than an earlier conception of Werner's (*see* below).

Apart from a few elements which were discovered soon after Mendeléyev's formulation of the periodic law and were readily fitted into the table, a new situation arose after 1894 as the result of the discovery of the inert element argon by Lord Rayleigh and W. Ramsay, followed by that of helium in 1898, and of neon, krypton and xenon by Ramsay and M. W. Travers between 1898 and 1901, and the position of these elements in the periodic table required to be settled. Mendeléyev had previously drawn attention to the periodicity of electrochemical character shown by the elements, and accordingly Ramsay was able to show that the inert gases could be placed in a new group between the strongly electronegative halogens and the powerfully electropositive alkali metals, this position being in agreement with their atomic weights. The position to be assigned to the rare earths in the periodic table was a more difficult one, and remained unsettled until after H. G. J. Moseley's work on atomic numbers in 1913. This important generalization, according to which the atomic number as distinct from the atomic weight is regarded as the fundamental property of an element, gave a theoretical foundation for the periodic law and has been the means of removing some of the irregularities inherent in the original system; *e.g.*, inversion in the order of tellurium and iodine when considered with regard to atomic weights.

Until the closing years of the 19th century the atom had been regarded as the indivisible unit of elementary matter, although speculations regarding the possibility of the elements being composed of some fundamental substance had been advanced at various times. In 1815 W. Prout ventured the suggestion that the atomic weights were all integral numbers, being multiples of that of hydrogen. Accurate atomic weight research showed that such an idea was fundamentally erroneous, and accordingly Prout's hypothesis was abandoned, but it nevertheless continued to exercise a certain amount of interest for some chemists as it was well recognized that a large majority of the atomic weights tended to approach toward whole numbers. The correct explanation of the true significance of atomic weights, and generally of the elements as regards their places in the periodic table, was eventually given chiefly as a result of studies on radioactive phenomena and of analysis by rays of positive electricity during the early years of the 20th century. These investigations gave rise to a greatly extended conception of the nature of the elements (*see* ATOM; ATOMIC NUMBER; ISOTOPES, etc.).

Modern Views on the Elements and the Periodic Table.—Investigations of radioactive phenomena, particularly those of E. Rutherford and F. Soddy, had shown that certain elements of high atomic weight such as uranium, thorium, and radium, undergo spontaneous transformation into other products, and they explained these phenomena in terms of a theory of *atomic disintegration* in 1903. In the following year Ramsay and Soddy were able to demonstrate the formation of helium from radium by radioactive change, and in 1908 Rutherford and H. Geiger gave an experimental proof of the identity of the α-particle and the helium atom. As the atomic weight of helium is 4, it follows that whenever a radioactive atom suffers a loss of an α-particle its atomic weight must descend by 4 units. Gradually it was recognized that the final product of a succession of such changes would be lead, but if the origin of the lead was uranium its atomic weight would be 206, whereas if the source of the lead was thorium its atomic weight would be 208. The correctness of this reasoning was shown by the independent work of Soddy, T. W. Richards, K. Fajans and others since 1913 on the atomic weight of lead extracted from uranium and thorium minerals. The value of 207.1 for the atomic weight of ordinary lead is the mean value of the isotopes (a term attributable to Soddy) of which it consists. In 1911 J. J. Thomson introduced his method of analysis with positive rays and, a few years later, Aston introduced some improvements into the experimental method, particularly what he termed the mass spectrograph. With the aid of this apparatus F. W. Aston was able to show that a majority of the elements consist of isotopes, the atomic weights of which are whole numbers, and where an element has an atomic weight with a clearly defined figure after the decimal point, this is due to the value being an average one, just as in the case of the isotopes of lead. Thus in 1920 Aston showed that chlorine consists mainly of two isotopes having atomic masses of 35 and 37 mixed in such proportions as to agree with the atomic weight of 35.46 of this gas.

Much progress regarding the nature of the elements resulted from studies on X-rays, particularly from the work of the Braggs on the diffraction of these rays by crystals begun in 1912 and of the introduction of X-ray spectroscopy by Moseley in the following year. It was as a direct result of this latter work that atomic numbers were placed upon a sound experimental foundation. When the elements are arranged in the periodic table according to their atomic numbers, not only were the irregularities inherent in the older table removed, but, as the elements were now definitely "numbered," the difficult problem of the rare earths was solved, and some new elements were discovered by applying the methods of X-ray spectroscopy as an adjunct to the older methods of examining products from minerals. The numbering of the elements soon directed attention to some which, though undiscovered, were none the less believed to exist, namely those of atomic numbers 43, 61, 72, 75, 87 and 91. Particular interest is attached to the discovery of elements 72, 75, and 91. Element 91 was discovered in 1918 by O. Hahn and L. Meitner, and independently by Soddy and J. A. Cranston, by the methods of radioactivity, and is now known as protoactinium and is similar to tantalum. In 1923 G. Hevesy and D. Coster discovered element 72, which they termed hafnium and showed it to resemble zirconium. The discovery of element 75 was made in 1925 by W. and I. Noddack who recognized its relation to manganese.

Although modern atomic science dates from the beginning of the 20th century, and the views of chemists regarding the nature of the elements have thereby been greatly modified, it should be noted that many phenomena, formerly regarded from a purely empirical standpoint, have received much more enlightened explanations in consequence of our knowledge of atomic structure. The recognition of electrons as universal constituents of atoms was admitted toward the end of the 19th century. In 1904, J. J. Thomson regarded atoms as consisting of electrons embedded in a sphere of positive electricity, and he showed that considerations of this kind could furnish some explanation of the periodic system of the elements. Shortly afterward he showed that valency could be explained on an electrochemical basis. This idea was further elaborated by Kossel and independently by G. N. Lewis in 1916, the views of the former being chiefly concerned with ionizable substances, and those of the latter with nonelectrolytes. In developing his views, W. Kossel made some use of Abegg's conceptions of normal and contravalency and of the position of the inert gases in the periodic table, but without adopting any particular type of atomic model. Lewis, however, made use of a cubical atomic model, the electrons being situated at the corners—an arrangement which although theoretically unsound was nevertheless successful in giving expression in electronic language to the single, double and triple bonds of classical chemistry. In 1923 further fundamental contributions to an electronic theory of valency were made independently by T. M. Lowry and by N. V. Sidgwick. Sidgwick developed his views around the model atom of Rutherford and N. Bohr, and one of his outstanding achievements was the placing of A. Werner's theory of valency on a satisfactory electronic basis. Werner first put forward ideas in 1891, in which he drew a distinction between what he termed principal or primary valencies and secondary or auxiliary valencies, the former being concerned primarily with electrolytes, the latter more particularly with the attachment of substances such as water or ammonia to inorganic compounds. Although Werner developed his ideas in a purely empirical manner, and without entering into questions regarding the nature of valency, he made a definite advance upon the earlier ideas of Frankland and Kekulé, and in particular he provided the means of discussing isomerism among inorganic compounds. Kossel and Lewis had shown the possibility of explaining the two fundamental types of valency, namely electrovalency and covalency, on the basis of a transference and of a sharing of electrons respectively. Lowry and Sidgwick recognized a third type of valency, generally known as the co-ordinate link, in which donation of electrons is directive from some particular atom in a molecule to others, as distinct from the reciprocal sharing of electrons between atoms as in simple covalency. For further developments of electronic theories of valency *see* VALENCE.

About 1913 J. J. Thomson's conception of atoms, consisting of a uniform sphere of positive electricity with the electrons embedded within it, was abandoned in favour of an idea of Rutherford in which the mass of the atom, that is, the positive electricity, was concentrated into an extremely small central portion known as the nucleus, the electrons being disposed in orbits around it at considerable distances in comparison with the dimensions of the nucleus. Rutherford's conception was extended by Bohr, and was of immense importance in the development of atomic science. According to the conceptions inherent in the Rutherford-Bohr atom, it is the peripheral electrons which determine the ordinary chemical properties and reactions of an element, the nucleus being inert. In radioactive change, however, the nucleus is directly concerned. Until 1919 radioactivity had been regarded as fundamentally a property of elements of high atomic weight; *e.g.*, uranium, thorium and radium, but in that year Rutherford realized that it might be possible to attack the nuclei of elements of light atomic mass and thus effect artificial radioactive change. In this he was successful. He attacked nitrogen atoms with swiftly moving α-particles and obtained evidence of the liberation of hydrogen. This successful result was soon followed by experiments on the artificial disintegration of other elements, such as beryllium, boron, aluminium and phosphorus, and a considerable number of investigators have entered this field of research. After 1932 it became recognized, largely as the result of the work of J. Chadwick, of Irène Curie and F. Joliot, and of C. C. Lauritsen and H. R. Crane, that when the nuclei of elements of light atomic mass are bombarded with α-particles the attack may take place in two entirely different ways. It may result in the formation of a new and stable atomic nucleus with the emission of a proton, namely a particle of the mass of a hydrogen atom and carrying a positive charge. Alternatively, the product may consist in the formation of an unstable (radioactive) atomic nucleus accompanied with the emission of what Chadwick termed a neutron, namely an uncharged particle of mass similar to that of a proton. When the attack takes place in the latter way, the newly formed radioactive element undergoes atomic disintegration, with the production of a new and stable atomic nucleus and the emission of a strongly penetrating radiation derived from a positively charged electron, usually termed a positron.

It will thus be evident that the recognition of atoms as built up of protons and electrons—for many years a valuable basis for the study of fundamental questions in physics and chemistry—has become more complex. Theories concerning atomic structure must now take account of the discovery of the neutron and the positron. It is possible to regard the neutron and the proton on the one hand, and the positron and the electron on the other as modifications of two fundamental elementary particles—a modern development of the old problem regarding the nature of positive and negative electricity.

BIBLIOGRAPHY.—M. Berthelot, *Les Origines de l'Alchimie* (1885); A. Wurtz, *A History of Chemical Theory from the Age of Lavoisier to the Present Time*, tr. by H. Watts (1869); A. Ladenburg, *Lectures on the History of the Development of Chemistry since the Time of Lavoisier*, tr. by L. Dobbin (1900); E. von Meyer, *A History of Chemistry from the Earliest Times to the Present Day*, tr. by G. McGowan (third English ed., 1906); T. M. Lowry, *Historical Introduction to Chemistry* (1915, third ed., 1936); M. M. Pattison Muir, *A History of Chemical Theories and Laws* (1907); I. Freund, *The Study of Chemical Composition* (1904); T. E. Thorpe, *Essays in Historical Chemistry* (1902); H. Kopp, *Geschichte der Chemie*, four vol. (1843–47); J. M. Stillman, *The Story of Early Chemistry* (1924); J. Read, *Prelude to Chemistry* (1936); J. R. Partington, *A Short History of Chemistry* (1937); A. J. Berry, *Modern Chemistry; Some Sketches of its Historical Development* (1946). Chemical Society, *Annual Reports on the Progress of Chemistry* (1904 *et seq.*); *Memorial Lectures*, three vol. (1901, –14, –33); *Faraday Lectures* (1928). *Alembic Club Reprints*, several vol., at various dates. *Ostwald's Klassiker der exakten Wissenschaften*, numerous vol. at various dates.

(A. J. BY.; H. B. D.)

INORGANIC CHEMISTRY

Inorganic chemistry, which is concerned with the study of the elements and compounds other than those of carbon, was developed primarily through the investigations of minerals, whereas organic chemistry (*see* below) resulted from the study of substances of plant or animal origin. Although it was recognized that the two classes of substances were amenable to the same general chemical laws, it was supposed that a fundamental difference existed between the mineral (inorganic) substances and those which were the products of life processes (organic). However, during the middle of the 19th century it was found that organic substances could be prepared from their elements or from inorganic compounds, a fact which gave great impetus to the study of organic substances in the latter half of the century. Nevertheless, it is usual and convenient to divide chemical substances arbitrarily into the two classes, but to include the oxides of carbon, the carbonates, metallic carbonyls and certain other simple compounds of carbon as well as water and ammonia in the domain of inorganic substances.

Early Discoveries.—The earliest discoveries in inorganic chemistry were made in the metallurgical and medical arts and in the domestic economy of the ancients. Gold, silver, copper, tin, iron and lead, some of the simpler alloys, metallic salts and mineral products, and the rudiments of metallurgical, glass-making, enamelling, painting, dyeing, alchemical and medical arts were known to the ancient Chaldeans, Hindus, Chinese, Egyptians and Greeks, many centuries before the Christian era. By about the middle of the 17th century, the alchemists were acquainted with most of the common metals, their alloys and salts, a few acids, alkalis, medicinal minerals, and nonmetallic elements. In 1733 G. Brandt of Sweden isolated cobalt, and in 1750 A. F. Cronstedt prepared metallic nickel. These discoveries were followed by Henry Cavendish's recognition of elementary hydrogen in 1766, the isolation of nitrogen by Daniel Rutherford in 1772, manganese by J. G. Gahn in 1774, oxygen by Joseph Priestley and chlorine by K. Scheele in 1774, and molybdenum by P. J. Helm in 1782. Cavendish in 1784 made the far-reaching discovery that water is composed of two volumes of hydrogen to one of oxygen, and in the following year he succeeded in synthesizing nitric acid by passing electric sparks through moist air. His further discovery, that a minute residue of the air would not combine with oxygen, was ignored for more than a century, until Lord Rayleigh and Sir William Ramsay in 1895 proved that the inert residue consists of a mixture of the noble gases, argon, krypton, neon and xenon.

Other elements discovered during the 18th century include uranium, zirconium, titanium, wolfram (tungsten), platinum, beryllium, chromium, tellurium and a number of the rare earth metals, all of which are elsewhere fully discussed. The quantitative studies of chemical reactions by A. Lavoisier and others during the last part of the century led to a clarification of the nature of combustion and the abandonment of the doctrine of phlogiston. Laws governing chemical combinations were formulated and the atomic theory announced by J. Dalton in 1803 was generally accepted (see *History of Chemistry* above).

At the beginning of the 19th century the discovery of methods for the generation of the electric current gave to chemistry a most effective means for the separation of compounds into their elements. By the use of electrolysis, Sir Humphrey Davy in 1808 decomposed the supposed elements soda and potash and isolated the metals sodium and potassium. Shortly thereafter he obtained magnesium, calcium, strontium and barium from their respective oxides. With the new tools and techniques, chemistry and other sciences underwent a rapid growth. In addition to the striking developments in analytical and preparative chemistry there were numerous advances in the theoretical sciences; physical laws and principles were found to be applicable to chemical phenomena. Among all of the advances in theoretical, descriptive and industrial chemistry which took place in the 19th century, the two events which perhaps have contributed the most to inorganic chemistry are the formulation of the periodic law and the discovery of the electron.

The periodic law (*q.v.*) and the periodic classification of the elements, announced by D. Mendeléyev (1869), is the great fundamental generalization of chemistry, stimulating to research and serving as a framework for the organization of the vast amount of factual material which had been gathered and which had previously been organized only to a limited degree.

The profound and revolutionary effect of the discovery of the electron (1897), and the subsequent chain of related discoveries and theories, upon the character and scope of inorganic chemistry is treated after an introduction to chemical formulas and a few of the basic concepts.

Symbols and Formulas.—The chemical symbol for an atom of an element is either the capital letter of its English or Latin name, as C for carbon and K for potassium (Latin, *kalium*), or the capital letter followed by a small letter as Co for cobalt and Cr for chromium. A symbol is not merely an abbreviation but has a quantitative significance. It may represent one atom of the element whose weight relative to an arbitrarily selected unit is a number known as the atomic weight; or, alternatively it may represent a gram atomic weight or a gram atom which consists of 6.023×10^{23} atoms of the element and whose weight expressed in grams is numerically equal to the atomic weight. For example, the symbol C may stand for one atom of carbon whose relative weight is the pure number 12.010; or if more convenient it may stand for 12.010 grams of carbon which contains 6.023×10^{23} atoms (*see* ATOM).

A chemical formula represents a molecule of a substance which may be either an element or a compound. Since the formula is composed of symbols it shows qualitatively the constituent elements and quantitatively the number of atoms of each element in the molecule. Thus O_2, the formula for oxygen, indicates that the substance is an element and that a molecule of it consists of two atoms; He, the formula for helium, indicates that the molecule is monatomic and is identical with the atom; while Fe_2O_3 signifies that a molecule of ferric oxide consists of two atoms of iron and three atoms of oxygen and since it contains more than one element that the substance is a compound. Chemical formulas are established by experimental methods which involve a chemical analysis and the determination of the molecular weight of the substance. Empirical formulas are those which indicate the simplest ratio between the numbers of the component atoms while molecular formulas indicate further the actual number of atoms of each element in one compound molecule; *i.e.*, in the smallest portion of the compound that can exist as a separate entity. The empirical formula of hydrogen peroxide, for example, is HO but the molecular formula is H_2O_2. Empirical and molecular formulas of inorganic compounds are often identical. The establishment of an empirical formula requires only a chemical analysis of a compound and the atomic weight of the constituent elements, but that of a molecular formula requires, in addition, the molecular weight of the compound.

Once the molecular formula of a compound is determined it may in turn be used to calculate the molecular weight by addition of the atomic weights of all the atoms in the molecule. Hence the formula implies the molecular weight which may be a pure number expressing the relative weight of the molecule on the same arbitrary standard used for atomic weights or, alternatively it may represent a gram molecular weight or a mole which consists of 6.023×10^{23} molecules of the substance and whose weight in grams is numerically equal to the molecular weight (*see* MOLECULE, CHEMICAL).

Nomenclature.—By common agreement the formulas of inorganic compounds are usually written with the more electropositive element first and the electronegative element or radical last. The names of such compounds follow this order; for example, a compound of oxygen and fluorine is written OF_2 (oxygen fluoride) rather than F_2O. If the compound contains only two elements the name of the more electronegative element ends with the suffix *ide*. If the more electropositive element forms more than one compound with a given element, *i.e.*, has more than one valence (*q.v.*) the higher state of valence is given the suffix *ic* and for the lower *ous* is used, as in sodium chloride (NaCl), ferrous chloride ($FeCl_2$) and ferric chloride ($FeCl_3$) In some cases a prefix is used to inflect the electronegative element as in carbon monoxide (CO), carbon dioxide (CO_2) and chromium trioxide (CrO_3) as distinguished from chromic oxide (Cr_2O_3), sometimes called chromium sesquioxide, and a lower (divalent) valence state of chromium as chromous chloride ($CrCl_2$).

Inorganic compounds are generally classified in three groups: acids, bases, and salts. Conventional acids like sulphuric (H_2SO_4) and phosphoric (H_3PO_4) are prepared by a chemical combination of the acidic oxides (usually oxides of nonmetals) with water. Sulphur may be burned to sulphur dioxide (SO_2) which is further oxidized to sulphur trioxide (SO_3) which yields sulphuric acid (H_2SO_4). The phosphoric acid may be similarly prepared from phosphorus. These two acids which have high boiling points may in turn be used to prepare other acids from their salts as hydrochloric acid (HCl) by treatment of sodium chloride (NaCl) with sulphuric acid. The acids are named for the constituent element other than oxygen and hydrogen, usually a nonmetal. The names of the acids which contain no oxygen (binary acids) derived from the name of the nonmetal which is modified by the prefix *hydro* and the suffix *ic* as hydrochloric acid (HCl) and hydriodic acid (HI). The different oxygen acids of a nonmetal are distinguished from each other by the uses of the terminations *ic* and *ous* and the prefixes *per* and *hypo*. An acid in which the nonmetallic element is at a high state of oxidation (not necessarily highest) is designated by the termination *ic* with no prefix, and may be used as the starting point in the naming of the other acids of the nonmetal as for example the oxygen acids of chlorine: $HClO_4$, *per*chlor*ic* acid; $HClO_3$, chlor*ic* acid; $HClO_2$, chlor*ous* acid; HClO, *hypo*chlor*ous* acid.

The conventional bases of the water system are hydroxides of metals and are in some instances formed when the metal or basic oxide reacts with water; barium oxide, for example, (BaO) is converted to barium hydroxide [$Ba(OH)_2$]. Bases of this type are named for the metal with the uses of a suffix where necessary followed by the word hydroxide as cupr*ic* hydroxide [$Cu(OH)_2$] and cupr*ous* hydroxide (CuOH).

For purposes of nomenclature salts may be regarded as the products of reactions (neutralizations) of acids with bases. Although neutralization is one method of preparing salts, there are many more instances of naturally occurring salts being used to prepare acids or bases. Phosphoric acid is prepared from calcium phosphate; sodium hydroxide from sodium chloride. Whatever may be the source of the salt there is a generic relationship between a salt on the one hand and the base which contains the same metal and the acid which contains the same nonmetal or negative ion on the other. Sodium sulphate may be regarded as a salt of sodium hydroxide and of sulphuric acid. This relationship is indicated by the name. Salts bear the first name of the base and an additional word which is derived from the name of the acid as follows: the suffix *ate* is used for salts derived from acids whose names end in *ic* and the prefix (if any) used in the name of the acid is retained; the suffix *ite* is used for salts derived from acids whose names end in *ous* and the prefix (if any) used in the name of the acid is retained. For example: Na_2SO_4, sodium sulph*ate;* $FeSO_3$, ferrous sulph*ite;* $Cu(ClO_4)_2$, cupric *per*chlor*ate;* KClO, potassium *hypo*chlor*ite.*

There are additional systems of nomenclature for special classes of inorganic compounds, such as complex salts and hydrogen compounds of boron and silicon which are included in the appropriate articles.

The Scope of Inorganic Chemistry.—By the early part of the 20th century a very large amount of factual material concerning the preparation and properties of the important elements and compounds was known and had been consolidated and organized in accordance with the periodic classification. The empirical and in some cases the molecular formulas of the compounds had been determined by chemical means. Molecules were regarded as entities composed of atoms about which little was known, bound together by valence forces the nature of which was totally unknown. Considerable progress had been made in the development of structural formulas of organic compounds, these showing the arrangement of the atoms in molecules. The valence bonds were represented by lines drawn between symbols, a practice which is still in common use (see *Organic Chemistry,* below).

The discovery of the electron, of X-rays and of radioactivity, all within the three year period following 1895, marked the beginning of a new era in all of the sciences. The investigations which followed these discoveries provided the means, both experimental and theoretical, for studying the chemical bond, the structure of molecules, and the structure of the solid state. The emphasis in the field of inorganic chemistry was consequently shifted from the analytical and the preparative to the structural.

The Chemical Bond.—The early theories and concepts of atomic structure were used in attempts to explain the forces which bind atoms together in molecules. In 1916 G. N. Lewis and W. Kossel independently published papers which contain the basis of the present ideas of chemical bonds or the electron theory of valence. Later N. V. Sidgwick applied the electronic theory to a wide variety of compounds including complex salts. Both Kossel and Lewis maintained that atoms of the inert gases have complete outer or valence shells of electrons, two in helium atoms and eight in the others. Kossel held that other atoms could acquire the stable inert gas configuration by the loss or gain of electrons. Thus the sodium atom which has an electron configuration of 2,8,1 could attain the electron structure of neon (2,8) by the loss of the outer electron, while chlorine with a configuration of 2,8,7 could by the gain of one electron attain the electron structure of argon (2,8,8), forming respectively the ions Na^+ and Cl^- which together constitute the compound sodium chloride. Valence bonds of this type are formed by electrostatic attraction between the ions which result from the transfer of electrons from one atom to another and are called ionic bonds. Lewis suggested that some atoms might achieve the inert gas structure and at the same time be held together by sharing the electron pair between them, usually each atom contributing one of the paired electrons. To illustrate this type of bond the electron dot system, in which the outer electrons are represented by dots, is used. The hydrogen atom with one electron is written H·, the chlorine atom with seven valence electrons ·C̤̈l: and the hydrogen chloride molecule: H:C̤̈l:

Similarly the structural formula of the chlorine molecule Cl_2 is: :C̤̈l:C̤̈l: The chemical bond so constituted is called the covalent bond. Both the ionic and covalent bonds represent extreme types. The chlorine molecule is symmetrical as the electron pair is not preferentially drawn to either atom, whereas, in the hydrogen chloride molecule the electron pair is drawn to the atom of higher electronegativity (Cl) giving the molecule an electrical assymetry or polarity. That is, one end of the molecule is negative, the other positive and consequently the molecule has a dipole moment. The degree of polarity in covalent molecules may vary from those like chlorine in which there is no polarity to a high degree of polarity approaching the ionic type.

There are also double and triple covalent bonds which respectively involve the sharing of four and six electrons, ion-dipole bonds which result from the interaction of an ion with the oppositely charged end of a polar molecule, single electron bonds and triple electron bonds (*see* VALENCE).

Structural Chemistry.—The number of atoms of each element in a molecule and the molecular weight of the substance are determined by chemical or physical means. The determination of the structure, that is, the arrangement of the atoms in space, the interatomic distances and the bond angles involve an experimental study of how the substance interacts with energy. An aggregate of atoms which may be a molecule or an ion may absorb energy from a beam of light, X-ray or electrons and the modification of the beam observed; the group of atoms may acquire rotational or vibrational energy; or, it may react in a certain way in a magnetic or electrical field. The properties displayed by the group of atoms may be due to the nuclei or they may be due to the orbital electrons. The nuclei account for the mass and the scattering of other nuclei such as alpha-particles or deuterons and of fast moving electrons. The orbital electrons account for the scattering of X-rays, the absorption and emission of energy caused by movements of electrons from one quantum level to another and for magnetic properties caused by the movement of the electrons. Since the latter are charges in motion, they produce magnetic effects.

The data obtained from such studies are used to deduce the specific points of structure. Interatomic distances may be calculated from moments of inertia of atomic groups (the problem is difficult for more complex groups of atoms), from the scattering of X-rays which show the variation in electron density and permit the location of the nuclei, and from the scattering of electrons which is caused by the nuclei and from which their relative positions may be deduced. Neutron scattering is especially effective for compounds of hydrogen which do not readily respond to X-ray or electron scattering.

Unit cell constants in a crystal are determined by X-ray methods; the shape of a molecule may be approximately determined from the unit cell constants and confirmed by measurements of the dipole moment.

The internal energy of a molecule is of three kinds: electronic energy, energy of vibration of the nuclei and rotational energy. The loss or gain of any of these energies may be registered by appropriate spectroscopic methods which yield information concerning moments of inertia, molecular symmetry, force constants and dissociation energies.

Certain generalizations have been made concerning the relationship of the electronic structures of atoms and molecules to molecular configuration. For example, the compound boron trifluoride (BF_3) in which one s and two p orbitals are used for binding (the valence shell of boron contains one s and two p electrons which may pair with the electrons of fluorine) gives rise to a trigonal planar structure:

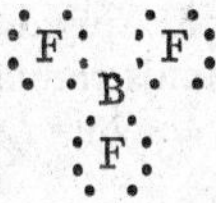

Nitrogen trifluoride utilizes for binding the three p orbitals of nitrogen (:Ṅ·) the pair consisting of s electrons, and such arrangement gives rise to a trigonal pyramidal (a triangular pyramid) structure with nitrogen at the apex:

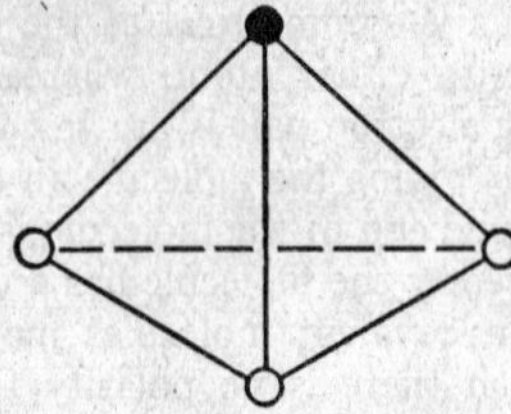

In addition to the utilization of the above physical techniques and theories, inorganic chemistry employs quantum mechanics, statistical mechanics, thermodynamics and natural and artificial radioactivity in its studies of structure and chemical reactions at various temperatures (high temperature chemistry is of special interest).

Preparative Inorganic Chemistry.—There is still considerable preparative chemistry in process which is of value per se and which is also concerned with problems structure. The fields in which considerable work has been done and is being done are: complex salts, hydrides of the light elements, and transuranic elements, the rare earths, rare elements such as beryllium, gallium and germanium, and metallic structure, all of which are treated extensively elsewhere. (*See* SPECTROSCOPY; CRYSTALLOGRAPHY: *Structure of Crystals;* ELECTRON DIFFRACTION; CO-ORDINATION COMPOUNDS; RADIOACTIVITY, ARTIFICIAL; RARE EARTHS.)

BIBLIOGRAPHY.—L. Pauling, *General Chemistry* (1947); M. Schlesinger, *General Chemistry* (1950); N. V. Sidgwick, *Chemical Elements and Their Compounds* (2 vol. 1950); J. W. Mellor, *A Comprehensive Treatise on Inorganic and Theoretical Chemistry* (1922); J. H. Emeléus and J. S. Anderson, *Modern Aspects of Inorganic Chemistry* (1948); O. K. Rice, *Electronic Structure and Chemical Binding* (1940); L. Pauling, *The Nature of the Chemical Bond* (1945); A. F. Wells, *Structural Inorganic Chemistry* (1945). (J. B. Ps.)

ORGANIC CHEMISTRY

The term organic chemistry came into use at the beginning of the 19th century. In its early usage it reflected, not a departmentalization of the science of chemistry, but rather the disposition of the chemists of the time (doubtless an inheritance from the alchemists) to classify substances on the basis of their origins. The assignment of matter of all kinds to the animal, vegetable or mineral kingdoms was at that time fairly general. Organic chemistry, therefore, was a convenient, inclusive term to designate the chemistry of substances of plant and animal origin, which were thought to be more closely related to each other than to substances of mineral origin.

Coexistent with this scheme of classification was a general conviction which further coloured the term and lent it additional implications—namely, that organic compounds (unlike mineral compounds) were necessarily the products of vital, or organic, processes exclusively, and could not be synthesized artificially in the laboratory, *cf.*, Leopold Gmelin, *Lehrbuch der Chemie* (1815).

In retrospect Friedrich Wöhler's classical conversion of ammonium cyanate, $NH_4^+CNO^-$, into urea, H_2NCONH_2 (1828), is often cited as the historic event that demonstrated the possibility of the preparation of organic compounds from inorganic materials. Many chemists of that time, however, argued that urea is, in fact, one of the end products of animal metabolism, and is, therefore, a result of the degradative rather than of the synthetic processes of living organisms, whereas others objected that the ammonia and the lead cyanate from which Wöhler's ammonium cyanate had been derived had been prepared in part from organic materials. The significance of Adolph Wilhelm Hermann Kolbe's synthesis of acetic acid, CH_3CO_2H (1845), was similarly discounted. It remained for Marcellin Berthelot to administer the *coup de grâce* to the notion of a vital force as an essential to the synthesis of organic compounds through the systematic series of researches described in his famous *La chimie organique fondée sur la synthèse* (1860).

Organic chemistry is often briefly, though not quite precisely, defined as the chemistry of carbon compounds. By common consent such carbon compounds as the metallic and ammonium carbonates, cyanides, carbides, cyanates and thiocyanates are relegated to the domain of inorganic chemistry, while such compounds as carbonic acid, the oxides of carbon and carbon disulphide are regarded as the joint property of organic and inorganic chemists.

At first thought it might appear absurd that a single element and its compounds should constitute the basis for one of the major branches of chemical science. The apparent absurdity diminishes, however, when relative volumes of subject matter are considered, for the known compounds of carbon far outnumber the noncarbonaceous compounds of all the other elements combined. Although no day-to-day census is possible, the number of known organic compounds must now approach, if indeed it has not already exceeded, 1,000,000.

EARLY DEVELOPMENT OF ORGANIC CHEMISTRY

The establishment of chemistry as a science may be said to have been achieved through the formulation and experimental justification of the concepts of: (1) conservation of matter; (2) chemical elements; (3) atomicity of matter and atomic weights; (4) stable aggregates of atoms; *i.e.*, molecules, and of molecular weights; (5) valence. The necessary experimental adjuncts to this primary evolution were the development of methods and techniques for: (1) the purification and identification of elements and compounds; (2) qualitative and quantitative analysis of compounds; (3) the determination of atomic and molecular weights. A further essential to rapid development of the science was the adoption of the modern system of chemical notation; *i.e.*, of molecular formulas and chemical equations, popularized, if not invented, by Jöns Jacob Berzelius (1819).

For the development of organic chemistry as an important branch of the science there were two additional necessities: (1) the demonstration of the generality of chemical laws and theories (specifically, of their applicability to organic compounds and reactions); (2) the formulation of a structural theory and of a convenient notation for its exploitation.

Re-exploration of the many blind alleys that chemists entered and the detours that they traversed in their progress toward these objectives would now be of interest only to the chemical historian. Indeed, anything beyond the barest outline of a few of the theories, discoveries and achievements that have proved to have survival value would be inordinately space-consuming, and, doubtless, tedious to the average reader. No more than a limited survey is attempted in the following discussion.

Chemists early discovered that organic substances yield water (H_2O) and "fixed air" (carbon dioxide, CO_2) when burned in oxygen. Antoine Laurent Lavoisier (1743–94), who perhaps, did more than any other one man to place chemistry on a quantitative basis, had shown that carbon, hydrogen and oxygen are the components of "spirits of wine" (ethyl alcohol, C_2H_5OH), and that carbon and hydrogen are among the chief components of other organic substances. Lavoisier's quantitative results were imperfect, partly because of impurities in the substances investigated (his alcohol undoubtedly contained water), partly because of defects in his methods and partly in consequence of his incorrect values for the compositions of water and carbon dioxide.

The first reasonably accurate investigations of the elementary compositions of organic substances were those of Louis Jaques Thénard and Joseph Louis Gay-Lussac, described to the scientific world in 1811. Regarding substances of vegetable origin they drew the conclusions that: (1) if oxygen is present in greater proportion (with relation to hydrogen) than in water, the substance is always acidic; (2) if hydrogen is present in excess, the substance is oily, resinous or alcoholic-like; (3) if hydrogen and oxygen are present in the same proportions as in water, the substance is analogous to the sugars, gums, starches or to wood fibre. Quite properly they limited their conclusions to the substances investigated by them, and pointed out that the validity of these statements as generalizations could be established only by the study of a greater number of vegetable substances. Regarding the substances of animal origin examined, they contented themselves with the observation that hydrogen was present in excess of the amount necessary to form water with the oxygen found, and that the excess was combined with nitrogen "in the form of ammonia"; *i.e.*, in the same proportions as in ammonia.

By that time Berzelius had perfected himself in the art of chemical analysis, devising many of his own methods. In the course of about ten years he established, almost singlehanded, the experimental basis of the laws of definite and multiple proportions which John Dalton (1766–1844) had deduced theoretically from his atomic theory. An idea of the Herculean labours he performed is to be derived from the fact that a summary of his analytical studies (1818) tabulated data for about 2,000 simple and compound substances.

In 1814 Berzelius extended his investigations to organic substances. He pointed out that, notwithstanding the apparent differences between inorganic and organic substances, existing knowledge of the elementary compositions of inorganic substances must be the only safe guide to a correct conception of the mode of combination of those substances produced under the influence of life processes. It was probably this point of view that motivated his approach to the investigation of organic substances by way of the alkaline salts of organic acids.

These studies led to the idea that many organic compounds are oxides, whose radicals are, however, compound, whereas those of inorganic oxides were generally thought to be simple; *i.e.*, elementary. The idea of a radical; *i.e.*, of a body, which although compound, plays the part of a simple body (atom) in its combinations with other bodies, was not original with Berzelius. Lavoisier may, perhaps, be credited with having crystallized the concept, and he published a list of acid radicals. In 1815 Gay-Lussac isolated cyanogen, which he believed to be the free radical (CN) of prussic acid (hydrogen cyanide, HCN), but which is now known to be the dimer $(CN)_2$, and Berzelius had called attention to the analogy between the ammonium radical (actually, ion, NH_4^+) and the alkali metals; *i.e.*, the alkali metal ions, but the concept did not immediately find general favour among chemists.

In the meantime Justus von Liebig developed for carbon and hydrogen (1831), and Jean Baptiste André Dumas for nitrogen (1833), the methods of quantitative estimation which form the basis of modern methods of organic analysis.

Eventually the radical theory came into its own with the appearance of the classical paper of Wöhler and Liebig on "the radical of benzoic acid" (1832), which, sharing the misconceptions of their time concerning atomic and molecular weights, they formulated as $14C + 10H + 2O$. (The modern version is C_7H_5O, or, more specifically, C_6H_5CO.) The benzoyl radical of Wöhler and Liebig was shown to be something more than a hypothetical concept like the organic radicals of Berzelius. These investigators had, so to speak, employed it as a building stone, taking it out of one compound and putting it into another almost at will. Impressive as this demonstration was in itself, it was generally regarded as more remarkable still that a ternary radical; *i.e.*, one composed of three elements, could be so manipulated.

Moreover, chemistry had been, from the time of Lavoisier, predominantly the chemistry of oxygen. Generally speaking, oxygen was regarded as the one element that confers distinctive properties upon its compounds; it was erroneously supposed to be an essential constituent of both acids and bases, giving rise to the former in combination with nonmetals, and to the latter in combination with metals. The chemical world was surprised and impressed to learn that oxygen might be a constituent of an organic radical in which it apparently played no more distinguished a role than did carbon and hydrogen.

According to Wöhler and Liebig, benzoic acid is benzoyl oxide (actually, hydroxide, $C_6H_5CO.OH$), oil of bitter almonds is benzoyl hydride (benzaldehyde, $C_6H_5CO.H$), the compound of benzoyl with chlorine is benzoyl chloride ($C_6H_5CO.Cl$), etc. Thus, the same oxygen-containing radical is a constituent of various substances which differ considerably from each other in their chemical properties.

As may be appreciated readily, this discovery received widespread and enthusiastic notice, and it constituted the stimulus for much laboratory research and even more blackboard chemistry. Shortly thereafter, Liebig published a memoir (1834), which, in historical perspective, is seen as the foundation of the general radical theory. A few years later (1837–43) Robert Wilhelm Eberhard von Bunsen carried out his famous series of researches on the cacodyl radical $[(CH_3)_2As]$.

The revival and elaboration of the radical theory also set in motion another train of chemical thought with which the names of Dumas, Auguste Laurent and Charles Frédéric Gerhardt are most closely associated. Wöhler and Liebig had pointed out that the place of hydrogen in oil of bitter almonds (benzaldehyde, $C_6H_5CO.H$), or of oxygen; *i.e.*, of hydroxyl, in benzoic acid ($C_6H_5CO.OH$), may be taken by chlorine, bromine, iodine or sulphur; *i.e.*, SH. All the resulting compounds have some chemical likeness to each other in that all react with water to form benzoic acid and an inorganic acid,

$$C_6H_5CO.X + H_2O \longrightarrow C_6H_5CO.OH + HX$$

Dumas found analogies to this persistence of chemical type throughout a series of compounds in the likenesses between chloral (CCl_3CHO) and acetaldehyde (CH_3CHO), and between trichloroacetic and acetic acids (CCl_3CO_2H and CH_3CO_2H, respectively); in a series of papers published in 1840, he developed his theory of chemical types.

According to Dumas, the reaction of a halogen, of oxygen or of various compound radicals with an organic compound containing hydrogen usually results in the elimination of one or more equivalents of hydrogen and the fixation of the same number of equivalents of halogen, or oxygen, or other reactant, as the case may be. This sort of reaction, he said, takes place, however, only in cases in which the chemical type is preserved; *i.e.*, in cases in which the original reactant and the product have the same fundamental chemical properties.

Dumas, at that time still an adherent to the electrodualistic theory of chemical combination, was careful to specify that when he used the word substitution he did so only in an empirical sense; he did not believe that an element like chlorine could actually take the place of, and play the part of, an element like hydrogen in an organic molecule.

Sir Humphry Davy had suggested in 1807 that the components of chemical compounds are held together by the force of electrical attraction. Berzelius, who had also performed electrochemical experiments with the aid of a voltaic pile, had adopted this idea, and had developed it into the doctrine that all atoms (and hence all radicals, which behave like atoms) are either positive or negative electrically. According to Berzelius only bodies of opposite electrical nature could combine. From his point of view, nothing could be more absurd than the idea that negative chlorine could replace positive hydrogen in a compound without essentially altering the nature of the compound.

Laurent, however, was no devotee of the dualistic theory, and he made it plain that when he used the word substitution in discussing reactions that change the composition of an organic compound without essentially altering its chemical type he intended the word to be taken in its most literal sense. Perhaps, as Dumas charged, after the weight of chemical evidence had forced him to alter his own opinions and join the camp of the antidualists, Laurent originally allowed his intuition to carry him beyond the point where he was completely supported by experimental fact. Be that as it may, Laurent had the courage of his convictions, and, in the main, he was justified by subsequent events.

To Gerhardt must be conceded the credit for effecting a synthesis of the radical and type theories, for making use of the principle of Amadeo Avogadro and André Marie Ampère to arrive at the simplest molecular formulas for organic compounds, and for being among the first to make systematic use of "rational" formulas. Gerhardt attempted to group all organic compounds under four types: hydrogen, hydrochloric acid, water and ammonia. Thus, ethyl alcohol (C_2H_5-O-H), ethyl ether ($C_2H_5-O-C_2H_5$), acetic acid (C_2H_3O-O-H) and acetic anhydride ($C_2H_3O-O-C_2H_3O$) were all regarded as belonging to the water ($H-O-H$) type. Similarly, ethyl hydride (ethane, C_2H_5-H), biethyl (normal butane, $C_2H_5-C_2H_5$), acetyl hydride (acetaldehyde, C_2H_3O-H) and acetyl-methyl (acetone, $C_2H_3O-CH_3$) all belonged to the hydrogen (H—H) type. Extensions of the system to the hydrochloric acid and ammonia types will be obvious to the reader without further examples.

On the whole, the period from 1838 to 1858 was, from a theoretical standpoint, one of groping in semidarkness, of no little confusion and of heated controversy, much of it fruitless. Nevertheless, during that period, Jeremias Benjamin Richter's rather restricted views on chemical equivalency were developed into a fairly comprehensive and useful concept of valency (*q.v.*), through the contributions of Sir Edward Frankland, Alexander Edward Williamson, William Odling and others.

In the year 1858 two notable clarifying and correlating articles appeared. In one of these Archibald Scott Couper, rejecting the type theory and basing his thesis on the idea of the valencies of the elements, proceeded to develop constitutional formulas for various compounds. Through no fault of Couper's the publication of his paper was delayed until after the other (Friedrich August Kekulé's) had appeared. With due allowance for Couper's misapprehensions concerning atomic and molecular weights, his formulas much more closely resemble those in present use than did Kekulé's formulas of that time. However, Couper's interest in chemistry lapsed, and he sank into scientific obscurity, whereas Kekulé continued to develop and apply his ideas and is now generally regarded as the founder of organic structural theory.

In his original paper on this subject, Kekulé accepted the type theory, generalized and extended it, at the same time avoiding the extremism that had misled some of his contemporaries, and used it in conjunction with the radical theory. He emphasized the fact that a compound may belong at the same time to more than one type, in that it may undergo one typical reaction under one set of conditions, and an entirely different reaction under another set of conditions. He regarded the assignment of compounds to types, not as an immutable classification to be determined by the constitution of the compound in question, but merely as a convenient means of emphasizing one or more of its chemical properties, and he held that the representation that tells the most about the chemical properties of a substance is the most rational.

Kekulé thus blurred the outlines of Gerhardt's too clear-cut type classification, and extended it by adding what might be called a methane type. This addition was more than a mere extension of area, however; it altered the complexion of the whole scheme. Instead of specific types like those of Gerhardt (hydrogen, hydrochloric acid, water, ammonia), Kekulé's idea embodies essentially the four general types: univalent, bivalent, trivalent and quadrivalent. Thus, compounds of hydrogen, chlorine or any other univalent atom or radical might be assigned to a univalent type which would include both the hydrogen and hydrochloric acid types of Gerhardt. Compounds of oxygen, the methylene radical ($H_2C=$) or any other bivalent atom or radical might be assigned to a bivalent type which would include the water type of Gerhardt, etc.

Finally, Kekulé pointed out that radicals are not necessarily indestructible; that they persist throughout a given series of reactions only to suffer disintegration in other reactions.

At that time Kekulé did not regard his "rational formulas" as "representative of groupings of atoms in existing compounds"; *i.e.*, as constitutional formulas, but rather as "expressions of certain relations in metamorphoses"; *i.e.*, in chemical reactions. Indeed, he specifically pointed out in a footnote that, although the constitution of matter must be regarded as the basis of a scientific problem, the answer to the question of the actual arrangement of atoms should be sought, not in the study of chemical transformations, but rather in the comparative study of physical properties.

Seven years later (1865–66) Kekulé proposed for benzene (C_6H_6) the constitutional formula that is still in use today, though with some modifications in its implications in the light of modern theories of valency and interatomic binding forces. Shortly thereafter (1867) he appended to a note on the constitution of mesitylene [*sym.*-$(CH_3)_3C_6H_3$] a discussion of his views on molecular diagrams and models in which he proposed the tetrahedral carbon atom that constitutes the cornerstone of modern structural theory. With proper scientific caution, Kekulé made it clear that he did not intend all the possible physical implications of his tetrahedral model for the carbon atom to be accepted literally. Nevertheless, it became apparent during his own lifetime (1829–96) that the tetrahedral model fulfilled strictly chemical necessities that he had not at first foreseen. As Adolph von Baeyer said (1890), paraphrasing Heinrich Rudolph Hertz's comment on James Clerk Maxwell's electromagnetic theory of light, it seemed that Kekulé's molecular models were "even cleverer than their inventor."

Although the fact has no bearing on their utility and sufficiency as unique designations for all possible isomers, it is of interest to note that modern methods of physical investigation; *e.g.*, X-ray and electron diffraction studies, and, in some cases, dipole moment studies, have shown Kekulé's models to be true indicators of molecular configuration; *i.e.*, of the arrangement of atoms in space.

ORGANOCHEMICAL MODELS AND NOTATION

At one time chemists supposed a compound to be uniquely identified by its elementary composition. This idea was perforce abandoned when Michael Faraday discovered (1825) a hydride of carbon (later called butylene) which had the same percentage composition (carbon, 85.7%; hydrogen, 14.3%) as the "olefiant gas" (ethylene) discovered a few years earlier by John Dalton (1820). On the strength of the fact that he found butylene to have twice the vapour density of ethylene, Faraday himself offered the correct explanation, namely, that the respective molecules, although containing like proportions of the same elements, must contain different numbers of atoms, and Dalton recognized the phenomenon as a special case supporting his theory of multiple proportions.

Up to about this time the necessities of compound designation were adequately fulfilled by molecular formulas, or would have been had chemists completely mastered the concepts of atomic and molecular weights and made adequate use of the potentially available methods for the determination of molecular weights. For instance, ethylene might, without ambiguity, have been designated by the formula C_2H_4, and butylene by the formula C_4H_8.

However, when Wöhler (1823) found that some of the cyanates he had prepared had not only the same percentage compositions, but apparently the same molecular weights as fulminates prepared by Liebig and by Gay-Lussac (as well as by himself), and that both corresponded to the molecular formula MCNO (in which M represents a univalent metal), a new explanation had to be sought. Chemists, generally, hesitated to attempt an explanation until a fact so unexpected in the light of the views then current had been incontrovertibly established, although Gay-Lussac did point out in a footnote that if Wöhler's analyses were indeed correct, a different mode of combination must be assumed to account for the differences in properties of two compounds of identical composition and molecular weight.

Berzelius (1827) commented on this remarkable discovery, but reserved judgment until the facts should have been more definitely established. Supplementary evidence was not long in appearing, however, for Berzelius himself (1830) found a similar example in his investigation of racemic and tartaric acids ($C_4H_6O_6$). Two years later (1832) he reviewed the field and proposed the adjective isomeric (from the Greek *ισομέρος*) to describe compounds of identical molecular formula, but unlike properties.

Instances of isomerism continued to multiply and were all accounted for by the general though rather vague assumption that the constituent atoms of isomeric substances must be linked together in different ways. The rapid development of a rational system of structural formulas out of Kekulé's model, and the subsequent contributions of Jacobus Henricus van't Hoff (1874), Jules Achille LeBel (1874) and Jacobus Wislicenus (1887), which eventually enabled chemists to deal adequately with problems of isomerism and to assign a unique formula to each known compound, are described in detail in the articles on ISOMERISM and STEREOCHEMISTRY.

For purposes of continuity in the present discussion, it is sufficient to point out here that the extended structural formulas of the organic chemist may be regarded as representing a conventionalization of one of several possible types of projection of tetrahedral models upon a plane surface. For example, the conventionalized projection I suggests to the eye the tetrahedral configuration of the methane molecule, but the projection II is of the type more commonly employed by the organic chemist.

```
    H                      H
    |                      |
    C—H                 H—C—H
  H/ \H                    |
                           H
    I                      II
```

If this point were not clearly understood the projections III A and III C might be interpreted as suggesting that there are two dichloromethanes (or methylene chlorides), but comparison with the projections III B and III D, which are perhaps more readily relatable by inspection to the corresponding tetrahedral models, reveals that all four diagrams represent a single configuration—the only one possible for CH_2Cl_2.

```
   Cl           Cl            Cl            Cl
   |            |             |             |
H—C—Cl          C          H—C—H            C
   |         H/ / \Cl         |          H/ / \H
   H           H              Cl            Cl
 III A        III B          III C         III D
```

As a matter of practice such detailed structural formulae for relatively simple compounds are used only for elementary pedagogical purposes. In current chemical literature molecular formulas, such as CH_4 for methane, $CHCl_3$ for chloroform and C_2H_4 for ethylene, are used whenever only a single configuration for the molecule indicated is possible. Even when several isomers are known it is usually possible to use a greatly simplified notation without ambiguity, as the following examples for C_4H_8 illustrate:

1-Butene	*cis*-2-Butene	*trans*-2-Butene
IV A	V A	VI A
	$H_3C(H)C{=}C(H)CH_3$ (V B)	$H(H_3C)C{=}C(CH_3)H$ (VI B)
$H_2C{=}CHCH_2CH_3$ IV B	V B	VI B
$H_2C{=}CHC_2H_5$ IV C	*cis*-$CH_3CH{=}CHCH_3$ V C	*trans*-$CH_3CH{=}CHCH_3$ VI C

Isobutylene (2-Methylpropene)	Methylcyclopropane	Cyclobutane (Tetramethylene)
VII A	VIII A	IX A
$H_2C{=}C(CH_3)_2$ (structure) VII B	CH_3–CH with ring H_2C—CH_2 VIII B	H_2C—CH_2 / H_2C—CH_2 IX B
$H_2C{=}C(CH_3)_2$ VII C	$(CH_2)_2CHCH_3$ VIII C	$(CH_2)_4$ IX C

In full detail one of the static forms of Kekulé's benzene formula would be represented as in X A; it is more often simplified as in X B and still more often as in X C. Indeed, X C is preferable, not only on the ground of simplicity, but because it correctly implies that all carbon-to-carbon bonds in benzene are equivalent.

X A X B X C

The convention of omitting the detailed designation of doubly bonded carbon atoms and of double bonds but retaining indications of hetero atoms; *i.e.*, atoms other than carbon, and of fully hydrogenated carbon atoms in the representation of unsaturated ring structures is common. (Unsaturated is here used in the structural sense. It does not necessarily imply that the compounds have the chemical properties associated with unsaturation in the olefin series, for example. See *Classification of Organic Compounds,* aromatic compounds, below.) Thus, furan (C_4H_4O) is often represented as in XI, thiophene (C_4H_4S) as in XII, pyrrole (C_4H_5N) as in XIII, thiazole (C_3H_3NS) as in XIV, pyran (C_5H_6O) as in XV and pyridine (C_5H_5N) as in XVI.

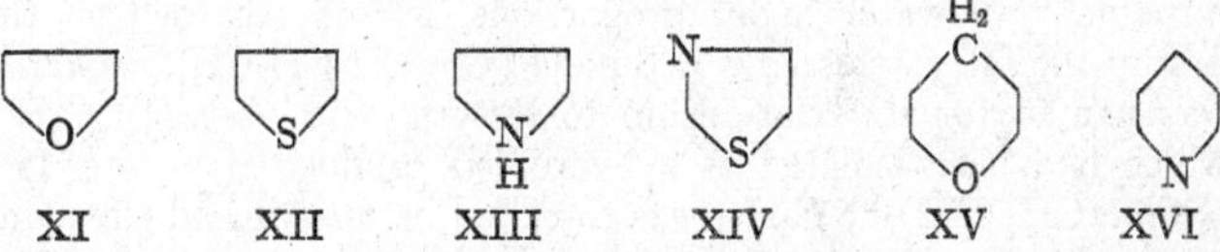

XI XII XIII XIV XV XVI

For some other types of compounds; *e.g.*, the steroids, it has been found simpler and more economical to adopt the different convention of omitting detailed representation of carbon atoms in the cyclic nucleus but of retaining indications of double bonds. Thus, for cholesterol ($C_{27}H_{46}O$) the simplified structural formula is XVII, in which the projecting lines indicate the locations of angular methyl (CH_3) groups.

$CH(CH_3)CH_2CH_2CH_2CH(CH_3)_2$

HO

XVII

Other conventions adopted for the convenient representation of stereoisomers are discussed in the article STEREOCHEMISTRY.

The writing of chemical equations is often similarly simplified by the organic chemist by the use of suitable symbols or abbreviations and by the omission of specific representations of reactants or by-products of secondary interest. For example, nitrobenzene ($C_6H_5NO_2$) may be reduced to aniline ($C_6H_5NH_2$) by the action of metallic iron in the presence of a mineral acid. In an elementary textbook on organic chemistry the process would be represented by a complete, balanced chemical equation of the form:

$$C_6H_5NO_2 + 2Fe + 7HCl \longrightarrow C_6H_5NH_2 . HCl + 2FeCl_3 + 2H_2O$$

Among the various other reactions that may be employed to effect this transformation is direct hydrogenation by means of hydrogen gas in the presence of a suitable catalyst:

$$C_6H_5NO_2 + 3H_2 \xrightarrow{(Cat.)} C_6H_5NH_2 + 2H_2O$$

Any of these processes might be indicated by the simplified equation indicating a hydrogenation reduction:

$$C_6H_5NO_2 \xrightarrow{[H]} C_6H_5NH_2$$

Similarly, the catalytic dehydrogenation of ethyl alcohol to yield acetaldehyde might be indicated by the equation

$$C_2H_5OH \xrightarrow[\text{(Cat.)}]{-H_2} CH_3CHO,$$

whereas the oxidation of ethyl alcohol by any of various oxidizing agents to yield acetic acid might be represented by

$$C_2H_5OH \xrightarrow{[O]} CH_3CO_2H$$

The application of heat is sometimes indicated by the symbol Δ in conjunction with the transitional arrow. Thus, the production of acetone by the heating of calcium acetate might be represented by:

$$(CH_3CO_2)_2Ca \xrightarrow{\Delta} (CH_3)_2CO + CaCO_3$$

(*See* also RESONANCE, THEORY OF.)

ORGANOCHEMICAL NOMENCLATURE

While the number of known organic compounds remained relatively small, it was the custom to name each new compound individually, usually with reference to its source, its properties or its relationship to a previously known compound. Thus, methane (CH_4) derived its name from the methylene radical (CH_2) which had been named because of its relationship to wood spirits (CH_3OH), for which a synthetic Greek name had been coined. Ethane (C_2H_6) was named because of its relationship to ether ($C_2H_5OC_2H_5$), notable for its volatility and inflammability. Propane (C_3H_8) was so-called because of its relationship to propionic acid ($C_2H_5CO_2H$), which was so named because, not being miscible with water in all proportions, it was regarded as the first of the fatty acids (*q.v.*). Butane ($CH_3CH_2CH_2CH_3$, $n\text{-}C_4H_{10}$) was named for its relationship to butyric acid ($n\text{-}C_3H_7CO_2H$), which had been isolated as a hydrolysis product of butter. Isobutane $CH(CH_3)_3$, $i\text{-}C_4H_{10}$ was so-called because it had the same composition and molecular weight as butane.

Such names are now known as trivial names, for they do not of themselves clearly indicate the structures of the compounds they represent.

As the number of known organic compounds grew, the necessity for a systematization of nomenclature became increasingly evident. Notwithstanding various sporadic attempts at reform and rationalization, the first significant and generally influential achievement in this respect was the formulation of a series of 52 rules by about 40 representatives of various countries at the Geneva congress of 1892. Some of the rules of the Geneva congress found general favour but others did not, and large parts of the field were left uncovered. In 1930 the "Definitive Report of the Commission on the Reform of the Nomenclature of Organic Chemistry" was unanimously adopted by the commission and council of the International Union of Chemistry, meeting at Liège, Belgium. Its 68 rules are based on those of the Geneva congress, but with many changes and additions. Further amplifications were adopted in 1936 and 1938. In general practice the rules of the International union require interpretation and extension. The most reliable guides to good usage in (English) organochemical nomenclature are the current annual and decennial subject indices of *Chemical Abstracts,* published by the American Chemical society. An excellent presentation of the International union rules, together with illustrations, interpretative discussions and supplementary appendixes is to be found in the introduction to the subject index for 1945, *Chemical Abstracts,* 39, pp. 5,867–5,975 (1945).

In the systematic nomenclature common or trivial names of long standing and universal adoption have been retained, and a certain flexibility is permitted in the systematic naming of other compounds. Therefore, many organic compounds may be said to have more than one correct name. Thus, the common name isobutane and the systematic name methylpropane are both correctly applied to the hydrocarbon $CH(CH_3)_3$. Normal pentane is both the common and the systematic name for the hydrocarbon $CH_3(CH_2)_3CH_3$. Isopentane and methylbutane are the common and systematic names respectively, for the hydrocarbon $CH_3CH_2CH(CH_3)_2$; neopentane and dimethylpropane are the common and systematic names, respectively, for the hydrocarbon $C(CH_3)_4$. Likewise, methyl alcohol (CH_3OH), the compound of a methyl radical with a hydroxyl group, is also correctly called carbinol, or methanol, the compound derived by substituting a hydroxyl group for a methane hydrogen atom; and ethyl alcohol (C_2H_5OH) may also be called methylcarbinol or ethanol. Acetic acid (CH_3CO_2H) is also ethanoic acid, the acid derived by converting one of the methyl groups of ethane to a carboxyl group (CO_2H), or methanecarboxylic acid, the acid derived by substituting a carboxyl group for a methane hydrogen atom. Acetone (CH_3COCH_3), the ketone derived from acetic acid (as by the pyrolysis of calcium acetate), is also dimethyl ketone, or propanone, the ketone structurally related to propane ($CH_3CH_2CH_3$).

For the simpler organic compounds, which are in most cases among those longest known, the common (or trivial) names are usually preferred by reason of long usage. For more complicated compounds common names are often preferable because the systematic names become inconveniently cumbersome. Camphor (XX), a ketone related to camphane (XIX), which is in turn a derivative of norcamphane (XVIII), one of the bicycloheptanes, furnishes an example:

```
 (6)      (1)       (2)
H2C ------CH------- CH2
 |         |         |
 |      (7)CH2       |
 |         |         |
H2C ------CH------- CH2
 (5)      (4)       (3)
```

Norcamphane (XVIII)
Bicyclo[2.2.1]heptane

```
             CH3
              |
H2C --------- C --------- CH2
 |            |            |
 |     H3C -- C -- CH3     |
 |            |            |
H2C --------- CH -------- CH2
```

Camphane (XIX)
1,7,7-Trimethylbicyclo[2.2.1]-heptane

```
             CH3
              |
H2C --------- C --------- C=O
 |            |            |
 |     H3C -- C -- CH3     |
 |            |            |
H2C --------- CH -------- CH2
```

Camphor (XX)
2-Camphanone
1,7,7-Trimethylbicyclo[2.2.1]-heptan-2-one

```
             CH3
              |
H2C --------- C --------- C=O
 |            |            |
 |     H3C -- C -- CH3     |
 |            |            |
H2C --------- CH -------- CH Br
```

α-Camphoryl bromide (XXI)
3-Bromo-2-camphanone
1,7,7-trimethyl-3-bromobicyclo[2.2.1]heptan-2-one

Obviously, a comprehensive treatment of the subject of nomenclature is neither possible nor necessary in an article of this kind. However, further nomenclatural information will be supplied wherever it is necessary to an understanding of the discussion in succeeding sections.

CLASSIFICATIONS OF ORGANIC COMPOUNDS

Aside from more or less artificial systems devised for indexing purposes, various methods of classifying organic compounds are in common use.

Classification Primarily on the Basis of Chemical Composition.—No serious attempt has been made to expand this method of classification into a general system, but it has been found useful in defining certain classes of compounds. To cite a few illustrative examples, hydrocarbons (*q.v.*), comprise the class of compounds composed solely of carbon and hydrogen.

The terpenes are a special class of hydrocarbons, defined by the general formula $(C_5H_8)_n$, and including: the hemiterpenes, C_5H_8, such as isoprene and pentadiene; the simple terpenes, $C_{10}H_{16}$, such as bornylene, camphene, limonene, pinene, terpinene, etc.; the sesquiterpenes, $C_{15}H_{24}$, such as cedrene, clovene, patchoulene, santalene, etc; the diterpenes, $C_{20}H_{32}$, the polyterpenes, $(C_{10}H_{16})_n$. For convenience other hydrocarbons derived by hydrogenation, or dehydrogenation of the parent terpenes, as well as various derived alcohols, aldehydes, ketones, acids, etc., are sometimes classed together with the terpenes as terpenoid substances.

The carbohydrates (*q.v.*), generally speaking, have the composition indicated by the general formula $C_x(H_2O)_y$. By common consent some compounds whose formulas correspond to the general formula; *e.g.*, acetic acid, CH_3CO_2H, $C(H_2O)_2$, are excluded from the classification because their chemical properties differ fundamentally from those of the majority of the carbohydrates; whereas other compounds; *e.g.*, rhamnose, $C_6H_{12}O_5$, whose formulas do not correspond exactly to the general formula, are arbitrarily classified with the carbohydrates because of their chemical characteristics.

Classification on the Basis of Structure.—Several classifications of general applicability, though rather limited utility, may be made on the basis of structure. For example, all organic compounds might be classified either as structurally saturated; *i.e.*, as containing only single bonds, or structurally unsaturated; *i.e.*, as containing one or more multiple bonds, or resonance hybrids thereof.

A different system of structural classification assigns all organic compounds to acyclic (open-chain), cyclic or hybrid cyclic-acyclic classes. The cyclic and cyclic-acyclic classes are subdivisible structurally into monocyclic, bicyclic, tricyclic or polycyclic classes. Bicyclic compounds may be of the spiro type (having one and only one atom common to each ring) as in the case of spiro[4.5]decane (XXII) or of the condensed-ring type (having two or more atoms common to each ring), as in the cases of norcamphane (XVIII) and naphthalene (XXIII).

$H_2C—CH_2$ $CH_2—CH_2$
H_2C C
$H_2C—CH_2$ $CH_2—CH_2$

XXII XXIII

Subclassification of cyclic compounds may also be made on the basis of composition into homocyclic and heterocyclic compounds. Rings of the former class are composed of carbon members only: benzene (X A, B, C), cyclobutane (IX A, B, C), norcamphane (XVIII), spiro[4.5]decane (XXII) and naphthalene (XXIII) are examples. Rings of the latter class include members other than carbon: furan (XI), thiophene (XII), pyrrole (XIII), thiazole (XIV), pyran (XV) and pyridine (XVI) are examples.

More limited classifications on the basis of structure are sometimes made for the purpose of defining types of compounds. For example, the steroids, of which cholesterol (XVII) may serve as an example, may be defined as derivatives or structural relatives of cyclopenta[*a*]phenanthrene (XXIV) or, as some organic chemists would prefer, of perhydrocyclopenta[*a*]phenanthrene (XXV).

H_2 C CH_2 CH_2

XXIV XXV

Classification on the Basis of Chemical Properties.—Organic compounds are often divided, primarily on the basis of chemical properties, into two classes—aliphatic and aromatic. The aliphatic compounds were originally so named because of their relationship to the fatty acids; the aromatic compounds were so-called because many of the earlier-known representatives of the class have distinctive odours, and were therefore described as aromatic. Although it is impossible to define the two classes concisely in a mutually exclusive manner, there is seldom any disagreement among organic chemists as to the assignment of a specific individual compound to its proper class. Briefly, and approximately, the acyclic and saturated, or more nearly saturated (structurally speaking), cyclic compounds belong to the aliphatic series; the more highly unsaturated cyclic compounds belong to the aromatic series. The acyclic hydrocarbons may, perhaps, be regarded as the prototypes of the aliphatic series, and benzene as the principal prototype of the aromatic series. Some compounds are in part aliphatic and in part aromatic; toluene ($C_6H_5CH_3$), ethylbenzene ($C_6H_5CH_2CH_3$), styrene ($C_6H_5CH{=}CH_2$) and stilbene ($C_6H_5CH{=}CHC_6H_5$) are examples. Such compounds are usually assigned to one class or the other with respect to the particular reaction under consideration. For example, in the reaction

$$C_6H_5CH_3 + Br_2 \longrightarrow BrC_6H_4CH_3 + HBr,$$

toluene reacts as an aromatic compound, whereas in the reaction

$$C_6H_5CH_3 + Br_2 \longrightarrow C_6H_5CH_2Br + HBr,$$

it reacts as an aliphatic compound. Because the two types of reaction—aromatic halogenation by hydrogen substitution and aliphatic halogenation by hydrogen substitution—differ in mechanism, it is possible to carry out either reaction to the almost total exclusion of the other by an appropriate selection of experimental conditions.

The ultimate criterion determining the assignment of a structurally unsaturated cyclic compound to the aromatic or aliphatic class is the similarity of its chemical properties to those of benzene on the one hand or to those of the olefins (*q.v.*), on the other. In general, aliphatic compounds (and especially unsaturated aliphatic compounds) are considerably more susceptible to oxidation than are aromatic compounds. It is usually possible, therefore, to effect selective oxidation of the aliphatic portion of a hybrid molecule without appreciable attack upon the aromatic portion. In the case of toluene, oxidation to benzoic acid may be carried out almost quantitatively by a suitable choice of oxidizing agent and experimental conditions:

$$C_6H_5CH_3 \xrightarrow{[O]} C_6H_5CO_2H + 1.5\ H_2O$$

The difference between aliphatic and aromatic halogenations by hydrogen substitution has already been mentioned. In general, the aliphatic halogenations are initiated or facilitated by the presence of organic peroxides or a small amount of oxygen in the reaction system, or by the application of light, and are favoured by relatively low initial halogen concentrations (constantly renewed as halogen is expended). In general, aromatic substitutive halogenations are favoured by relatively high initial halogen concentrations and are expedited by metallic halide catalysts such as ferric chloride ($FeCl_3$) or ferric bromide ($FeBr_3$).

Most unsaturated aliphatic compounds react additively with bromine, chlorine, hydrogen chloride, hydrogen bromide, hydrogen iodide and concentrated sulphuric acid at ordinary temperatures:

$$RCH{=}CH_2 + Br_2 \longrightarrow RCHBrCH_2Br;$$
$$RR'C{=}CHR'' + HCl \longrightarrow RR'CClCH_2R'';$$
$$RCH{=}CH_2 + H_2SO_4 \longrightarrow RCH(OSO_3H)CH_3$$

Aromatic hydrocarbons, although structurally unsaturated, do not undergo these reactions under the same conditions.

Many aliphatic compounds are oxidized by fuming nitric acid or by nitrating acid (a mixture of concentrated nitric and sulphuric acids) at room, or slightly elevated, temperatures. Under similar conditions aromatic compounds are nitrated:

$$C_6H_6 + HNO_3 \longrightarrow C_6H_5NO_2 + H_2O$$

Most saturated (aliphatic) hydrocarbons are unaffected by concentrated or fuming sulphuric acid at or near room temperature. Under similar conditions most aromatic compounds undergo sulphonation:

$$C_6H_6 + H_2SO_4 \longrightarrow C_6H_5SO_3H + H_2O$$

In addition to division into the two major classes, aliphatic and aromatic, organic compounds may be classified more minutely according to their so-called functional groups. The concept of function is essentially an editorial invention and has a significance established by usage rather than by precise definition. According to *Chemical Abstracts*, 39, p. 5,876 (1945), "It is customary to use the term 'function' to mean, in its broadest sense, any atom, group or arrangement which causes a compound to behave in some characteristic way." Nomenclaturally, some functions are denoted only by suffixes, some only by prefixes and many by either suffixes or prefixes according to circumstances.

In the broad sense of the foregoing quotation a carbon-to-carbon double bond is a function, denoted in the systematic nomenclature by the suffix -ene. Thus, the olefins (*q.v.*) comprise a class of acyclic unsaturated hydrocarbons characterized by the carbon-to-carbon double-bond function and designated in the systematic nomenclature by the generic term alkenes. Specific examples: 1-pentene (XXVI), *cis*-2-pentene (XXVII), *trans*-2-pentene (XXVIII).

$H_2C{=}CHCH_2CH_2CH_3$ XXVI

$(H_3C)(H)C{=}C(C_2H_5)(H)$ XXVII

$(H_3C)(H)C{=}C(H)(C_2H_5)$ XXVIII

Similarly, the acetylenes comprise a class of acyclic unsaturated hydrocarbons characterized by the carbon-to-carbon triple-bond function (denoted by the suffix -yne) and designated in the systematic nomenclature by the generic term alkynes. Specific examples: acetylene (ethyne), $HC{\equiv}CH$; methylacetylene (propyne), $HC{\equiv}CCH_3$; 1-butyne, $HC{\equiv}CC_2H_5$; 2-butyne, $H_3CC{\equiv}CCH_3$.

The organic acids fall into several classes corresponding to the several acidic functional groups. Among the more common organic acids are the carboxylic acids, characterized by the carboxyl group ($-CO_2H$), and the sulphonic acids (*q.v.*), characterized by the sulpho group ($-SO_3H$). Specific examples: acetic acid (ethanoic acid, methanecarboxylic acid, carboxymethane), CH_3CO_2H; benzoic acid (benzenecarboxylic acid, carboxybenzene), $C_6H_5CO_2H$; benzenesulphonic acid (sulphobenzene), $C_6H_5SO_3H$.

Among the compounds more or less closely related to the acids in a functional sense are the acyl halides, the esters (*q.v.*), the amides (*q.v.*) and the amidines (*q.v.*). All of these except the last may be regarded, formally, as organic acids in which an acidic hydroxyl group has been replaced by another group or atom. For example, a carboxylic acid may be represented by the general formula RCO.OH, and a sulphonic acid by the general formula $RSO_2.OH$. The corresponding acid halides may then be represented by the general formulas RCO.X and $RSO_2.X$, respectively, the corresponding esters by the formulas RCO.OR′ and $RSO_2.OR'$, respectively, and the corresponding amides by the formulas $RCO.NH_2$ and $RSO_2.NH_2$, respectively. The amidines are derivatives of the carboxylic acids and may be characterized by the general formula $RC({=}NH)NH_2$. Specific examples of acyl derivatives: acetyl bromide ($CH_3CO.Br$); methyl acetate ($CH_3CO.OCH_3$); acetamide ($CH_3CO.NH_2$); acetamidine $CH_3C({=}NH)NH_2$; benzenesulphonyl chloride ($C_6H_5SO_2.Cl$); benzenesulphonamide ($C_6H_5SO_2.NH_2$); ethyl benzenesulphonate ($C_6H_5SO_2.OC_2H_5$).

Another important class of acid derivatives comprises the acid anhydrides (*q.v.*). The anhydrides of the carboxylic acids are distinguished by the grouping

$$-C({=}O)-O-C({=}O)-$$

As the name suggests, these compounds may be regarded as dehydration products of the acids. As such they may arise, either from intermolecular dehydration of two molecules of monocarboxylic acid, or from intramolecular dehydration of one molecule of dicarboxylic acid.

$$2\,CH_3-C({=}O)-OH \longrightarrow CH_3-C({=}O)-O-C({=}O)-CH_3 + H_2O$$

(Acetic acid) (Acetic anhydride)

$$C_6H_4(COOH)_2 \longrightarrow C_6H_4(CO)_2O + H_2O$$

(Phthalic acid) (Phthalic anhydride)

Mixed anhydrides, derived from one molecule each of two different acids, are known; *e.g.*, acetic benzoic anhydride (XXIX).

$$CH_3-C({=}O)-O-C({=}O)-C_6H_5$$

XXIX

Another type of mixed anhydride is that exemplified by the anhydride of ortho-sulphobenzoic acid (XXX).

$$C_6H_4\langle C({=}O)-O-SO_2\rangle$$

XXX

Alcohols (*q.v.*), phenols and naphthols have in common the hydroxyl function (-OH) and are, therefore, hydroxylic compounds. This function is denoted by the prefix hydroxy- or by the suffix -ol. In terms of the general formula ROH, which may be applied to all monohydroxylic compounds, R signifies an aliphatic radical if the compound is an alcohol, a benzenoid radical if the compound is a phenol or a naphthalenic radical if the compound is a naphthol. Some authors loosely classify all aromatic hydroxylic compounds as phenolic substances. Specific examples: ethyl alcohol (ethanol, hydroxyethane), C_2H_5OH; benzyl alcohol (α-hydroxytoluene), $C_6H_5CH_2OH$; phenol (hydroxybenzene), C_6H_5OH; α-naphthol (1-naphthol, 1-hydroxynaphthalene, XXXI); β-naphthol (2-naphthol, 2-hydroxynaphthalene, XXXII).

XXXI (1-naphthol, OH) XXXII (2-naphthol, OH)

The carbonyl (>C=O) function is common to the aldehydes (*q.v.*), which may be characterized by the general formula RCHO, and the ketones (*q.v.*), which may be characterized by the general formula RCOR′. (Although this grouping also appears in the static formulas for the carboxylic acids and their functional derivatives, those compounds are usually regarded as belonging to separate classes of their own.) In the systematic nomenclature aldehydes are designated by the suffix -al, and ketones by the suffix -one. Specific examples: formaldehyde (methanal), HCHO; acetaldehyde (ethanal), CH_3CHO; acetone (propanone), CH_3COCH_3; diethyl ketone (3-pentanone), $(C_2H_5)_2CO$; cyclohexanone, $(CH_2)_5CO$.

The acetals and ketals are closely related to the aldehydes and ketones and have, respectively, the general formulas $RCH(OR')_2$ and $RR'C(OR'')_2$.

The amines (*q.v.*) may be regarded as organic derivatives of ammonia (NH_3). Primary amines correspond to the general formula RNH_2, secondary amines to the formula RR′NH and tertiary amines to the formula RR′R″N. The amines are characterized by the prefix amino- and the suffix -amine. Specific examples: methylamine (aminomethane), CH_3NH_2; aniline (phenylamine, aminobenzene), $C_6H_5NH_2$; diethylamine, $(C_2H_5)_2NH$; dimethylaniline (phenyldimethylamine, dimethylaminobenzene), $(CH_3)_2NC_6H_5$.

The organic cyanides are characterized by the nitrile (-CN)

function and have the general formula RCN. The appropriate prefix is cyano-, and the suffix -nitrile. Specific examples: acetonitrile (cyanomethane), CH_3CN; benzonitrile (cyanobenzene), C_6H_5CN.

Monohalogenated compounds may be designated by the general formula RX, in which X signifies a halogen—fluorine, chlorine, bromine or iodine. They may be named either as organic halides (specifically, fluorides, chlorides, bromides, iodides) or as halo-compounds (fluoro-, chloro,- bromo-, iodo-). Specific examples: ethyl bromide (bromoethane), C_2H_5Br; isopropyl iodide (2-iodopropane), $(CH_3)_2CHI$; chlorobenzene (phenyl chloride), C_6H_5Cl.

The foregoing summary is by no means an exhaustive compilation of types of organic compounds or of the functional groups that characterize them. A supplementary, though still incomplete, listing might include the following groups: azo- ($-N{=}N-$); hydrazino- (H_2NNH-); hydrazo- ($-HNNH$); hydroxamino- ($HONH-$); imino- (imido- in acid groups) ($NH{=}$); iodoso- ($OI-$); iodoxy- (O_2I-); isocyano- ($CN-$); isonitroso- ($HON{=}$); nitro- (O_2N-); nitroso- ($ON-$); phosphino- (H_2P-); phospho- (O_2P-); phosphono- [$(HO)_2OP-$]; selenyl- ($HSe-$); stibino- (H_3Sb-); sulphino- (HO_2S); sulphinyl- ($OS{=}$) sulphonyl- ($-SO_2-$); thiocarbonyl ($SC{=}$); thiocyano- ($NCS-$); triazo- (N_3-).

If a compound contains but one kind of functional group, it is said to be of simple function; if two or more of such groups are present the compound is said to be of multiple function. A compound of mixed or complex function is one which contains more than one kind of function.

Classifications on the Basis of Properties Other Than Chemical.—For various reasons groups of compounds widely divergent in structure and chemical nature, but having in common some other quality, characteristic or property, are sometimes classified together.

For example, the vitamins, comprising a considerable variety of structural and chemical types, have in common the quality that all are essential constituents of a normal diet, and that when they are absent from the diet or present in insufficient amount, one or more of a variety of deficiency diseases ensues.

The plastics are materials of high molecular weight formed by the condensation or polymerization of units of usually one or two, but always few, molecular species. In the broadest sense of the term the class includes: the thermosetting plastics; *e.g.*, Bakelite, which may be moulded by the application of heat and pressure, but which, once moulded, do not soften upon reheating; the thermoplastics; *e.g.*, Lucite, which may be reheated and remoulded indefinitely; the elastomers, which include the wide range of synthetic rubbers; the synthetic resins and many other substances.

The hormones, representing a variety of chemical types, are secretions of the endocrine glands and serve as the regulators of numerous and diverse bodily functions.

Dyes, or dyestuffs, may be divided into several chemical classes but have in common the ability to combine with and colour textiles or other materials.

ORGANIC REACTIONS

Organic reactions, like organic compounds, are subject to many schemes of classification and designation. Among the least systematic methods is that of designating a reaction or class of reactions by the name (or names) of its discoverer (or discoverers).

Sometimes this method of designation results in the co-classification of a wide variety of reactions which are only superficially related to each other, as for example, in the case of the Grignard reactions (named after Victor Grignard). The Grignard reactions may be defined as the reactions of the Grignard reagents (*q.v.*), or the organomagnesium halides (RMgX). Some idea of the considerable variety of reactions thus grouped in a single class may be formed from the following incomplete set of examples of typical Grignard reactions:

$CH_3MgCl + H_2O \longrightarrow CH_4 + MgClOH$;

$2i\text{-}C_4H_9MgBr + O_2 \longrightarrow 2i\text{-}C_4H_9OMgBr \xrightarrow{(H_2O)} 2i\text{-}C_4H_9OH + 2MgBrOH$;

$\alpha\text{-}C_{10}H_7MgBr + CO_2 \longrightarrow \alpha\text{-}C_{10}H_7CO_2MgBr \xrightarrow{(H_2O)} \alpha\text{-}C_{10}H_7CO_2H + MgBrOH$;

$C_6H_5CH_2C{\equiv}CMgBr + I_2 \longrightarrow C_6H_5CH_2C{\equiv}CI + MgBrI$;

$(C_6H_5)_3CMgBr + CH_2{=}CHCH_2Br \longrightarrow (C_6H_5)_3CCH_2CH{=}CH_2 + MgBr_2$;

$CH_3MgI + C_6H_5CHO \longrightarrow CH_3(C_6H_5)CHOMgI \xrightarrow{(H_2O)} CH_3(C_6H_5)CHOH + MgIOH$;

$CH_2{=}CHCH_2MgBr + CH_3COC_2H_5 \longrightarrow CH_3(C_2H_5)(CH_2{=}CHCH_2)COMgBr \xrightarrow{(H_2O)} CH_3(C_2H_5)(CH_2{=}CHCH_2)COH + MgBrOH$;

$C_6H_5MgBr + HC(OC_2H_5)_3 \longrightarrow C_6H_5CH(OC_2H_5)_2 + MgBrOC_2H_5$;

$2n\text{-}C_5H_{11}MgBr + CH_3CO_2C_2H_5 \longrightarrow CH_3(n\text{-}C_5H_{11})_2COMgBr + MgBrOC_2H_5 \xrightarrow{(H_2O)} CH_3(n\text{-}C_5H_{11})_2COH + C_2H_5OH + 2\,MgBrOH$;

$C_2H_5MgBr + C_6H_5COCl \longrightarrow C_2H_5COC_6H_5 + MgBrCl$;

$\alpha\text{-}C_{10}H_7MgBr + \alpha\text{-}C_{10}H_7CN \longrightarrow (\alpha\text{-}C_{10}H_7)_2C{=}NMgBr \xrightarrow{(H_2O)} (\alpha\text{-}C_{10}H_7)_2C{=}NH + MgBrOH$

Similarly, the Friedel-Crafts reactions (named after Charles Friedel and James Mason Crafts) embrace a variety of transformations, all having in common the characteristics that they result in substitutions in an aromatic ring and are catalyzed by anhydrous aluminum chloride ($AlCl_3$) or similar catalysts:

$C_6H_6 + CH_3Cl \xrightarrow{AlCl_3} C_6H_5{-}CH_3 + HCl$;

$C_6H_4(OH){-}OH + n\text{-}C_5H_{11}COCl \xrightarrow{AlCl_3} n\text{-}C_5H_{11}CO{-}C_6H_3(OH){-}OH + HCl$;

$CH_3{-}C_6H_5 + CH_3{-}C_6H_4{-}SO_2Cl \xrightarrow{AlCl_3} CH_3{-}C_6H_4{-}SO_2{-}C_6H_4{-}CH_3 + HCl$;

$C_6H_6 + COCl_2 \xrightarrow{AlCl_3} C_6H_5{-}COCl + HCl$;

$C_{10}H_8 + (H_2C{-}CO)_2O \xrightarrow{AlCl_3} C_{10}H_7{-}COCH_2CH_2CO_2H$

On the other hand, this method of classifying reactions sometimes leads to the designation of more or less closely related reactions by a number of different names depending upon the specific reactants involved or the catalysts employed, or both. For example, the aldol condensations, the Claisen, the Knoevenagel and the Perkin reactions are all catalyzed condensations involving a carbonyl group ($>C{=}O$) and a reactive methylidyne ($HC{\equiv}$), methylene ($H_2C{=}$) or methyl (H_3C-) group:

$2CH_3CHO \xrightarrow{OH^-} CH_3CH(OH)CH_2CHO$ (aldol);

$2CH_3CHO \xrightarrow[\Delta]{SiO_2} CH_3CH{=}CHCHO + H_2O$ (aldol + dehydration);

$C_6H_5CHO + CH_3COCH_3 \xrightarrow{OH^-} C_6H_5CH{=}CHCOCH_3 + H_2O$ (Claisen);

$CH_3COCH_3 + H_2C(CN)CO_2C_2H_5 \xrightarrow{(CH_2)_5NH} (CH_3)_2\ C{=}C(CN)CO_2C_2H_5 + H_2O$ (Knoevenagel);

$C_6H_5CHO + (CH_3CO)_2O \xrightarrow{CH_3CO_2Na} C_6H_5CH{=}CHCO_2Na + CH_3CO_2H$ (Perkin)

Among the numerous possible systematic classifications of organic reactions an arbitrary choice is made for the purposes of this discussion. According to the system adopted organic reactions fall into four principal classes: (1) those in which the original carbon skeleton of the chief reactant is unchanged but which result in the introduction, removal, replacement or alteration of substituent atoms or groups; (2) those in which the original carbon skeleton undergoes an alteration in structure, but without loss or gain of carbon; (3) those in which the carbon skeleton is augmented and (4) those in which a cleavage of one or more carbon-to-carbon bonds takes place, with fragmentation of the original carbon skeleton.

Class 1. Introduction, Removal, Replacement or Alteration of Substituent Atoms or Groups.—Although hydrogen is not ordinarily regarded as a substituent, for the term derives from the fact that the substituent group may be regarded, formally, at least, as having been substituted for hydrogen, the hydrogenation of unsaturated compounds properly falls in the class of reactions which do not alter the carbon skeleton. Such reactions are usually effected with the aid of a suitable catalyst, such as finely divided nickel, platinum or palladium, and hydrogen gas is usually introduced into the reaction system under pressure. Thus, acetylene (C_2H_2) may be partially hydrogenated to ethylene (C_2H_4) or fully hydrogenated to ethane (C_2H_6); or benzene (C_6H_6) may be hydrogenated to cyclohexane (C_6H_{12}):

$$HC{\equiv}CH \xrightarrow[\text{(Cat.)}]{+H_2} H_2C{=}CH_2 \xrightarrow[\text{(Cat.)}]{+H_2} H_3C{-}CH_3;$$

$$C_6H_6 + 3H_2 \xrightarrow{\text{(Cat.)}} (CH_2)_6$$

Large quantities of unsaturated vegetable oils, such as cottonseed and peanut oils, are partially hydrogenated in this way to produce solid or semisolid fats.

Reactions in which two or more reactant molecules combine to form a single molecule of product are sometimes called additive reactions or addition reactions. Reagents other than hydrogen, which react additively with many unsaturated compounds, either spontaneously or under the influence of catalysts, are the halogens (Br_2, Cl_2), the halogen acids (HI, HBr, HCl), sulphuric acid (H_2SO_4) and water (H_2O):

$$RC{\equiv}CH \xrightarrow{+Cl_2} RCCl{=}CHCl \xrightarrow{+Cl_2} RCCl_2CHCl_2;$$

$$RCH{=}CH_2 \xrightarrow{+HI} RCHICH_3;$$

$$RCH{=}CH_2 \xrightarrow{+H_2SO_4} RCH(OSO_3H)CH_3;$$

$$RC{\equiv}CH + H_2O \xrightarrow{(HgSO_4 + H_2SO_4)} [RC(OH){=}CH_2] \longrightarrow RCOCH_3$$

Sometimes the same product may be obtained either by an addition reaction of an unsaturated compound or by the replacement of hydrogen. For example, isopropyl bromide (2-bromopropane, $CH_3CHBrCH_3$) may be obtained either by the addition of hydrogen bromide to propylene (propene, $CH_3CH{=}CH_2$) or by the bromination of propane ($CH_3CH_2CH_3$):

$$CH_3CH{=}CH_2 + HBr \longrightarrow CH_3CHBrCH_3;$$

$$CH_3CH_2CH_3 + Br_2 \longrightarrow CH_3CHBrCH_3 + HBr$$

Among the hydrogen-substitution reactions that have attained considerable industrial importance are the aromatic sulphonations and nitrations by means of which many dyestuff and pharmaceutical intermediates and other commodities are produced. For example, the sulphonation of toluene ($C_6H_5CH_3$) yields a mixture of ortho- (XXXIII) and para-toluenesulphonic acids (XXXIV), the former of which finds one of its uses in the production of saccharin (XXXV).

$$C_6H_5CH_3 + H_2SO_4 \longrightarrow o\text{-}CH_3C_6H_4SO_3H + p\text{-}CH_3C_6H_4SO_3H + H_2O$$

XXXIII XXXIV

$$C_6H_4\langle^{C(=O)-NH}_{SO_2}\rangle$$

XXXV

Although the introduction of a sulpho or a nitro group into a benzene nucleus leads to a product less susceptible to further sulphonation or nitration than the original reactant, it is possible to introduce three nitro groups into toluene to produce 2,4,6-trinitrotoluene, commonly known as T.N.T.

$$C_6H_5CH_3 + 3HNO_3 \xrightarrow{(H_2SO_4)} CH_3C_6H_2(NO_2)_3 + 3H_2O$$

The removal of a functional group may sometimes be effected with the introduction of unsaturation or through the replacement of the functional group by hydrogen. Although the former process is in effect the reverse of an addition reaction, the halide obtained by addition of the appropriate hydrogen halide to the olefin obtained by dehydrohalogenation of a halide is not always identical with the original halide, as the following example illustrates:

$$(CH_3)_2CHCH_2Br + \text{alcoholic KOH} \longrightarrow (CH_3)_2C{=}CH_2 + KBr + H_2O;$$

$$(CH_3)_2C{=}CH_2 + HBr \longrightarrow (CH_3)_2CBrCH_3$$

Some other possible dehalogenations with resultant unsaturation are illustrated by the following examples:

$$RCHBrCH_2Br + 2KOH\ (alc.) \longrightarrow RC{\equiv}CH + 2KBr + 2H_2O;$$

$$RCHBrCH_2Br + Zn \longrightarrow RCH{=}CH_2 + ZnBr_2$$

The hydroxyl group is another functional group which may be removed with the introduction of unsaturation. In general tertiary alcohols are readily, secondary alcohols less readily and primary alcohols with relative difficulty, dehydrated to olefins. Some tertiary alcohols lose water quantitatively when distilled at atmospheric pressure; a wide variety of acidic catalysts, as well as alumina (Al_2O_3) and silica gel (SiO_2), have been used to facilitate more difficult dehydrations:

$$RR'C(OH)CH_2R'' \xrightarrow{\Delta} RR'C{=}CHR'' + H_2O;$$

$$RCH(OH)CH_2R'' \xrightarrow{(KHSO_4)} RCH{=}CHR' + H_2O;$$

$$RCH_2CHOH \xrightarrow{(Al_2O_3)} RCH{=}CH_2 + H_2O$$

The replacements of functional groups by hydrogen are in general oxidation-reduction reactions (*see* OXIDATION AND REDUCTION), usually called reductions because the principal organic reactant undergoes reduction. Many alkyl iodides are readily reduced by hydrogen iodide,

$$RI + HI \longrightarrow RH + I_2$$

The halogen of most alkyl halides may be directly replaced by hydrogen with the aid of catalysts of the type used to facilitate the hydrogenation of unsaturated compounds,

$$RX + H_2 \xrightarrow{\text{(Cat.)}} RH + HX$$

Occasionally, the replacement is effected indirectly, as by the formation and subsequent hydrolysis of a Grignard reagent,

$$RX \xrightarrow{Mg} RMgX \xrightarrow{H_2O} RH + MgXOH$$

Relatively few alcohols may be reduced directly;

$$ROH \xrightarrow{[H]} RH + H_2O$$

reduction is usually effected indirectly, either by conversion to a halide with subsequent reduction, or by dehydration and subsequent hydrogenation:

$$ROH \xrightarrow{HX} RX + H_2O \xrightarrow{[H]} RH + HX;$$

$$RR'C(OH)CH_3 \xrightarrow[\Delta]{(Cat.)} RR'C{=}CH_2 + H_2O \xrightarrow[(Cat.)]{+H_2} RR'CHCH_3$$

Unlike the alcohols, the aldehydes (RCHO) and ketones (RCOR′) are, in general, readily reducible to the corresponding hydrocarbons:

$$RCHO \xrightarrow{[H]} RCH_3 + H_2O;$$

$$RCOR'' \xrightarrow{[H]} RCH_2R' + H_2O$$

The replacement of one functional group by another may sometimes be effected by a true exchange reaction; more often it is accomplished by indirect means. Among the true exchange reactions may be cited: (1) the hydrolysis of many alkyl halides to the corresponding alcohols (usually alkali-catalyzed); (2) the conversion of secondary and tertiary alcohols to halides by treatment with the appropriate halogen acid; (3) the conversion of alkyl bromides or chlorides to iodides by treatment with potassium iodide (KI) and (4) the conversion of alkyl halides to amines (*q.v.*), by treatment with ammonia (NH_3). The latter process, however, invariably leads to a mixture of products, namely, the primary, secondary and tertiary amines:

(1) $RX + H_2O \xrightarrow{(OH^-)} ROH + HX;$
(2) $ROH + HX \longrightarrow RX + H_2O;$
(3) $RBr + KI \longrightarrow RI + KBr;$
(4) $RX + NH_3 \longrightarrow RNH_2 + NH_4^+X^- + R_2NH + R_3N$

In general nitro (NO_2) groups are converted to amino (NH_2) groups by any one of a variety of reduction processes,

$$RNO_2 \xrightarrow{[H]} RNH_2 + 2H_2O$$

Nitriles may be converted by partial hydrolysis to amides, or by complete hydrolysis to the corresponding carboxylic acids,

$$RCN \xrightarrow{+H_2O} RCONH_2 \xrightarrow[+HX]{+H_2O} RCO_2H + NH_4^+X^-$$

The carboxyl groups of carboxylic acids may be variously modified, and numerous interconversions of carboxylic acid derivatives are possible:

$$RCO_2H + R'OH \xrightarrow{(H^+)} RCO_2R' + H_2O;$$
$$RCO_2H + SOCl_2 \longrightarrow RCOCl + HCl + SO_2;$$
$$RCO_2R' + NH_3 \longrightarrow RCONH_2 + R'OH;$$
$$RCOCl + R'OH \longrightarrow RCO_2R' + HCl;$$
$$RCOCl + R'NH_2 \longrightarrow RCONHR' + HCl$$

In general, secondary alcohols (RR′CHOH) are readily converted to ketones (RCOR′) by mild oxidation,

$$RR'CHOH \xrightarrow{[O]} RCOR' + H_2O$$

Similarly, many primary alcohols (RCH_2OH) may be converted to aldehydes (RCHO) by dehydrogenation (which is essentially an oxidation process) by means of heating in the presence of a suitable catalyst,

$$RCH_2OH \xrightarrow[\Delta]{(Cat.)} RCHO + H_2$$

The converse reductions are likewise possible:

$$RCOR' \xrightarrow{[H]} RR'CHOH;$$
$$RCHO \xrightarrow{[H]} RCH_2OH$$

The foregoing examples are offered merely as illustrations; no attempt is made to present a complete résumé of organic reactions.

Class 2. Alteration in Structure of the Carbon Nucleus.—Among the many reactions that fall into this class are a variety of molecular rearrangements. Illustrative are: (1) the pinacol-pinacolone rearrangements

$$R_2C(OH)C(OH)R_2 \xrightarrow[(H_2SO_4)]{\Delta} R_3CCOR;$$

(2) the benzilic acid rearrangement

$$C_6H_5COCOC_6H_5 + KOH \longrightarrow (C_6H_5)_2C(OH)CO_2K$$

and (3) the Wagner rearrangements

$$R_3CCH(OH)R \xrightarrow{(H^+)} R_2C{=}CR_2 + H_2O$$

Also to be included in this category are various types of cyclization reactions of which the Wurtz-Fittig reaction of pentamethylene bromide to form cyclopentane and the acid-catalyzed cyclizations of derivatives of 2-benzyl-1-naphthoic acid to form derivatives of 1,2-benzanthrone may serve as illustrations:

$$Br(CH_2)_5Br + 2Na \longrightarrow (CH_2)_5 + 2NaBr;$$

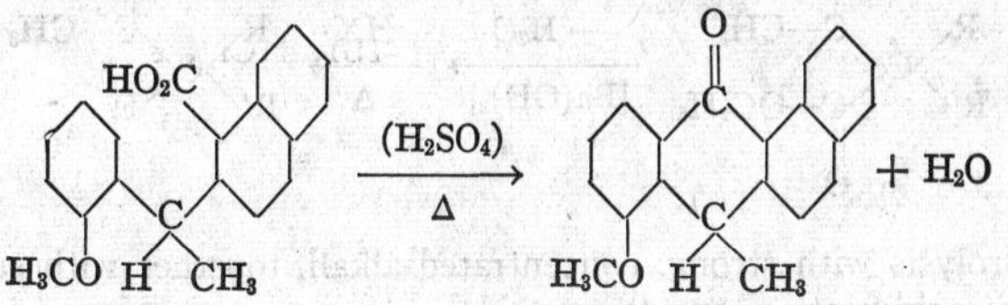

HO₂C … H₃CO H CH₃ $\xrightarrow[\Delta]{(H_2SO_4)}$ O … H₃CO H CH₃ + H_2O

Conversely, many decyclization reactions are known; among the simplest are the opening of the cyclopropane ring by reaction with a halogen or a halogen acid:

$$(CH_2)_3 + Br_2 \rightarrow Br(CH_2)_3Br;$$
$$(CH_2)_3 + HBr \rightarrow CH_3CH_2CH_2Br$$

Class 3. Augmentation of the Original Carbon Skeleton.—New carbon-to-carbon linkages may be established in a variety of ways. In some cases the Wurtz-Fittig reaction, the interaction of an organic halide (or halides) with a reactive metal like sodium (Na) or zinc (Zn), is applicable:

$$2RI + 2Na \rightarrow RR + 2NaI;$$
$$ArX + AlkX + Zn \rightarrow ArAlk + ZnX_2$$

The Grignard reagents (*q.v.*) (or organomagnesium halides) react with some alkyl and aralkyl halides, and with a variety of other types of organic compounds with the establishment of new carbon-to-carbon linkages. Several examples were cited at the beginning of this section.

The Friedel-Crafts reactions and some of the carbonyl condensations have also been illustrated previously in this discussion.

Among the numerous other methods of establishing carbon-to-carbon linkages are: the malonic ester syntheses, the acetoacetic ester syntheses and the Diels-Alder condensations.

The malonic ester syntheses are essentially methods for the production of substituted acetic acids of the types RCH_2CO_2H and $RR'CHCO_2H$.

$$\mathrm{H_2C(\overset{O}{\overset{\|}{C}}{-}OC_2H_5)_2 + NaOC_2H_5 \longrightarrow H{-}C(\overset{ONa}{\overset{|}{C}}{-}OC_2H_5)\!=\!\ldots(\overset{O}{\overset{\|}{C}}{-}OC_2H_5) \xrightarrow{+\ RX}}$$

$$\mathrm{\underset{H}{\overset{R}{>}}C(\overset{O}{\overset{\|}{C}}{-}OC_2H_5)_2 \xrightarrow[(H_2SO_4)]{+\ H_2O} \underset{H}{\overset{R}{>}}C{<}\overset{H}{}\ \overset{O}{\overset{\|}{C}}{-}OH}$$

$$\mathrm{\underset{H}{\overset{R}{>}}C(\overset{O}{\overset{\|}{C}}{-}OC_2H_5)_2 \xrightarrow{+\ NaOC_2H_5} R{-}C(\overset{O}{\overset{\|}{C}}{-}OC_2H_5){=}\underset{ONa}{\underset{|}{C}}{-}OC_2H_5 \xrightarrow{+\ R'X}}$$

$$\mathrm{\underset{R'}{\overset{R}{>}}C(\overset{O}{\overset{\|}{C}}{-}OC_2H_5)_2 \xrightarrow[(H_2SO_4)]{+\ H_2O} \underset{R'}{\overset{R}{>}}C{<}\overset{H}{}\ \overset{O}{\overset{\|}{C}}{-}OH}$$

The somewhat similar acetoacetic ester syntheses may also be used to produce substituted acetic acids of the types RCH_2CO_2H and $RR'CHCO_2H$, on the one hand, or methyl ketones of the types CH_3COCH_2R or $CH_3COCHRR'$, on the other, depending upon the method of hydrolysis adopted as the final step in the process. Mild alkaline hydrolysis, followed by acidification and heating, yields a ketone.

$$\mathrm{\underset{R'}{\overset{R}{>}}C{<}^{\overset{O}{\overset{\|}{C}}-CH_3}_{\underset{O}{\underset{\|}{C}}-OC_2H_5} \xrightarrow[{[Ba(OH)_2]}]{+\ H_2O} \xrightarrow[\Delta]{HX} \underset{R'}{\overset{R}{>}}C{<}^{\overset{O}{\overset{\|}{C}}-CH_3}_{H}}$$

Hydrolysis with strong, concentrated alkali, together with subsequent acidification, yields an acid.

$$\mathrm{\underset{R'}{\overset{R}{>}}C{<}^{\overset{O}{\overset{\|}{C}}-CH_3}_{\underset{O}{\underset{\|}{C}}-OC_2H_5} \xrightarrow[(KOH)]{+\ H_2O} \xrightarrow{HX} \underset{R'}{\overset{R}{>}}C{<}^{H}_{\underset{O}{\underset{\|}{C}}-OH}}$$

The Diels-Alder reaction is another synthetic device of remarkable breadth of applicability. It consists of an additive reaction between one molecule containing a suitably activated carbon-to-carbon double bond and another molecule containing two conjugated carbon-to-carbon double bonds ($C{=}C{-}C{=}C$). Many such reactions take place spontaneously at room temperature. The reaction between maleic anhydride and cyclopentadiene may serve as an illustrative example.

$$\mathrm{O{<}^{\overset{O}{\overset{\|}{C}}-\overset{H}{C}}_{\underset{O}{\underset{\|}{C}}-\underset{H}{C}}\ (\|) + \overset{H}{C}{=}CH{-}CH_2{-}CH{=}\underset{H}{C}\ (\text{ring}) \longrightarrow O{<}^{\overset{O}{\overset{\|}{C}}-CH}_{\underset{O}{\underset{\|}{C}}-CH}\ (\text{fused with } CH{-}CH{=}CH{-}CH,\ CH_2\ \text{bridge})}$$

So general is this reaction that maleic anhydride is often used as a specific test reagent for conjugated unsaturation in determinations of structure.

The numerous condensation, polymerization and copolymerization reactions resulting in plastics, synthetic resins and synthetic rubbers also fall into this class. Such products are of high molecular weight, and the reactions are by no means so simple and clear-cut as most of those previously discussed. However, the copolymerization of styrene ($C_6H_5CH{=}CH_2$) and butadiene ($CH_2{=}CHCH{=}CH_2$) to produce a synthetic rubber of the GR-S type may be represented in oversimplified fashion as follows:

$$n\ \mathrm{C_6H_5CH{=}CH_2} + n\ \mathrm{CH_2{=}CH{-}CH{=}CH_2} \xrightarrow{\text{(Cat.)}} [\mathrm{{-}CH_2CH{=}CHCH_2CH(C_6H_5)CH_2{-}}]_n$$

So many and so varied are the reactions of class three that the few examples cited can scarcely be said to constitute a representative sampling. They are, indeed, but a fraction of those with which every student of elementary organic chemistry is expected to acquaint himself.

Class 4. Degradations of the Carbon Skeleton.—All organic compounds, when heated to sufficiently high temperatures, undergo pyrolytic decomposition with cleavage of carbon-to-carbon bonds. In general, pyrolyses are of limited interest to theoretical organic chemists because many reactions occur simultaneously and give rise to mixtures of products. However, catalytically controlled pyrolysis is of great practical importance in the cracking of petroleum and has greatly increased the yields of gasoline obtainable from crude oils.

Some organic molecules are so constituted that moderate heating causes selective dissociation of a weak carbon-to-carbon bond (in some cases with the aid of catalysts, in others without). The more or less exceptional reactions of this kind are useful for preparational purposes. Among those most frequently employed are the decarboxylation reactions resulting in the loss of carbon dioxide from a carboxylic acid (RCO_2H).

Not all carboxylic acids are readily decarboxylated. Benzoic acid ($C_6H_5CO_2H$), for example, is so stable that thermal decomposition is accompanied by cleavage of the benzene ring. Examples of readily decarboxylated acids are to be found among the types having the following groupings: $>C(CO_2H)CO_2H$, $>COCO_2H$, $>C(NO_2)CO_2H$, $>C(OH)CO_2H$, $\mathrm{{-}\underset{\diagdown O \diagup}{CH{-}CHCO_2H}}$.

The substituted malonic acids belong to the first of these types, and the final stage of the malonic ester syntheses consists in a simultaneous hydrolysis and decarboxylation, usually effected by warming in the presence of aqueous sulphuric acid,

$$\mathrm{RR'C(CO_2C_2H_5)_2 \xrightarrow{H_2O} RR'C(CO_2H)_2 \xrightarrow[\Delta]{(H_2SO_4)}}$$
$$\mathrm{RR'CHCO_2H + CO_2}$$

Many acids, which are too stable for ready decarboxylation as such, lose carbon dioxide when first converted to their salts and then heated. For example, trichloroacetic acid (CCl_3CO_2H) may be converted to chloroform ($CHCl_3$) and a carbon dioxide by heating in the presence of aniline ($C_6H_5NH_2$) with which it forms a salt,

$$\mathrm{CCl_3CO_2H.H_2NC_6H_5 \xrightarrow{\Delta} CHCl_3 + CO_2 + C_6H_5NH_2}$$

The synthesis of cyclic ketones has been effected in an analogous manner by heating the calcium salts of dicarboxylic acids.

$$\mathrm{\begin{matrix} H_2C{-}CH_2{-}C{\overset{O}{\underset{O^-}{<}}} \\ | \\ H_2C{-}CH_2{-}C{\overset{O^-}{\underset{O}{<}}} \end{matrix}\ Ca^{++} \xrightarrow{\Delta} \begin{matrix} H_2C{-}CH_2 \\ | \\ H_2C{-}CH_2 \end{matrix}{>}C{=}O + CaCO_3}$$

Organic chemists make use of a wide variety of oxidative degradations, both for preparational purposes and as a means of establishing the structures of compounds of unknown constitution.

In general, it is possible to oxidize aliphatic side chains attached to aromatic nuclei to obtain the corresponding aromatic carboxylic acids. Thus, styrene may be oxidized to benzoic acid, and cymene to terephthalic acid.

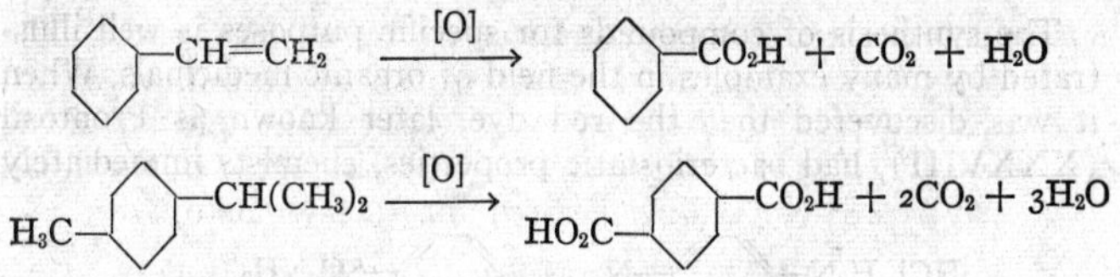

$$C_6H_5\text{—CH=CH}_2 \xrightarrow{[O]} C_6H_5\text{—CO}_2\text{H} + CO_2 + H_2O$$

$$H_3C\text{—}C_6H_4\text{—CH(CH}_3)_2 \xrightarrow{[O]} HO_2C\text{—}C_6H_4\text{—CO}_2\text{H} + 2CO_2 + 3H_2O$$

Selective oxidative cleavages may be effected at definite points in a carbon chain if certain structural features are present. For example, oxidative cleavage of a double bond may be accomplished in several ways. One method frequently employed in elucidations of structure is by ozonization and subsequent hydrolysis of the resultant ozonide in the presence of a reducing agent. (The ozonide formula used in the illustrative equation is probably not a true indication of structure.)

$$RR'C{=}CHR'' \xrightarrow{O_3} RR'C\text{—}CHR'' \ (O_3) \xrightarrow[\text{[H]}]{H_2O} RCOR' + R''CHO$$

Identification of the resultant aldehydes, or ketones, or both, serves to establish the location of the double bond and to reveal the structure of the original olefin. In special cases, an olefin of known structure may be so treated as a means of preparation of aldehydes or ketones.

Adjacent carbon atoms bearing hydroxyl groups [>CH(OH)—CH(OH)<], either present as such or resulting from oxidative treatment of double bonds, may be dehydrogenated by mild oxidation, with cleavage of the carbon chain and production of carbonyl compounds (aldehydes or ketones),

$$RR'C{=}CHR'' \xrightarrow{KMnO_4} RR'C(OH)\text{—}CH(OH)R' \xrightarrow{Pb(O_2CCH_3)_4} RCOR' + R''CHO$$

The haloform (CHX_3) reactions may be used to effect oxidative hydrolytic cleavage at a $-CH(OH)CH_3$ or $-COCH_3$ grouping. Because iodoform (CHI_3) is a yellow crystalline solid of highly distinctive odour, the iodoform reaction is used as a specific test for the presence of such groupings:

$$RCH(OH)CH_3 \xrightarrow{NaOX} RCOCH_3 \xrightarrow{NaOX} RCOCH_2X \xrightarrow{NaOX} RCOCHX_2 \xrightarrow{NaOX} RCOCX_3 \xrightarrow{H_2O} RCO_2H + CHX_3$$

Although oxidative cleavages are those of greatest variety and widest applicability, hydrolytic cleavages are possible in a few special cases. The final stage of the acetoacetic ester synthesis as employed for the production of substituted acetic acids is an example:

$$RR'C(COCH_3)CO_2C_2H_5 \xrightarrow{H_2O} RR'CHCO_2H + CH_3CO_2H + C_2H_5OH$$

SOME OBJECTIVES OF ORGANIC CHEMISTRY

Among the preoccupations of the organic chemist are the identification and determination of structure of natural and artificial compounds, the modification of natural compounds, the synthesis of natural compounds and the synthesis of artificial compounds for specific purposes.

The determination of the structure of a compound of unknown constitution is often a complicated task requiring the exercise of unusual ingenuity. However, one of the classical examples, Wilhelm Körner's "absolute method" for the identification of isomeric benzene derivatives (1874), is simple in principle. Prior to Körner's time, three dibromobenzenes were known. Granted the validity of Kekulé's benzene formula and the implied equivalency of the six carbon atoms and of the six carbon-to-carbon bonds of benzene, it was obvious that one isomer must be the ortho (1,2), one the meta (1,3) and one the para (1,4).

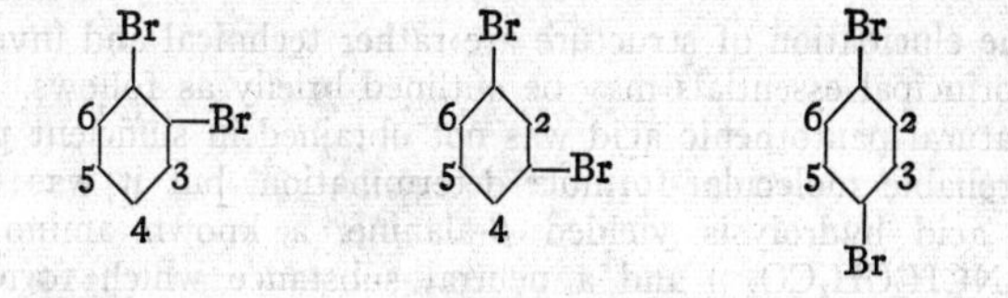

Ortho (1,2) Meta (1,3) Para (1,4)

Körner solved the problem of which was which by consideration of the geometry of the respective formulas. In ortho-dibromobenzene, the unsubstituted positions 3 and 6 are equivalent to each other, but different from positions 4 and 5, which are equivalent to each other. Hence, it should be possible to derive two isomeric tribromobenzenes (1,2,3 and 1,2,4) from 1,2-dibromobenzene. In meta-dibromobenzene, the unsubstituted positions 2 and 5 are unique, while positions 4 and 6 are equivalent to each other. Therefore, three isomeric tribromobenzenes (the 1,2,3, the 1,3,4 and the 1,3,5) are theoretically derivable from 1,3-dibromobenzene. In para-dibromobenzene, all the unsubstituted positions (2,3,5 and 6) are equivalent. Hence, but one tribromobenzene (1,2,4) is derivable from 1,4-dibromobenzene. The identical line of reasoning applies to the mononitrodibromobenzenes, with this difference, however, that, whereas there is a total of three isomeric tribromobenzenes, there are six nitrodibromobenzenes. Following this line of reasoning, though employing an indirect and somewhat more involved procedure than that implied, Körner prepared and identified the three isomeric dibromobenzenes, the three tribromobenzenes and five of the six nitrodibromobenzenes. Körner's method has been applied to the identification of many other benzene derivatives, although it sometimes presents considerable practical difficulties in the isolation of isomers produced in small amounts.

In general, however, the process is not so simple in principle, especially when relatively complicated substances of natural origin are involved. Although individual cases necessarily differ, a fairly representative structural determination might proceed substantially as follows. The molecular formula is derived by careful purification, accurate analysis and determination of molecular weight. Various functional groupings or structural features are identified by the application of specific tests or characteristic reactions. The substances may be subjected to various degradative processes in the hope that identifiable fragments may be isolated. When a satisfactory structural formula has been deduced, additional evidence of its validity may be supplied through synthesis of the compound by methods which leave little doubt of the structure of the product.

The elucidation of the structure of quinine (XXXVI) in 1908 when Paul Rabe proposed the correct formula for the closely

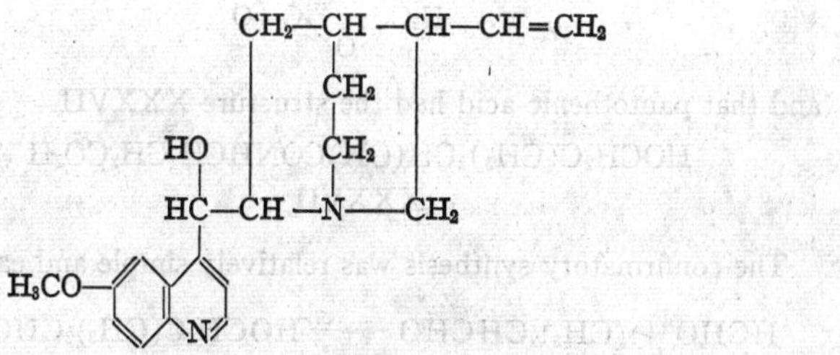

XXXVI

related cinchona alkaloid cinchonine, may be said to have followed substantially this pattern. It was not until 1944, however, that a total synthesis of quinine was achieved by R. B. Woodward and W. E. Doering through a long series of complicated reactions.

Another representative example, although one that presented unusual difficulties in the isolation and purification of minute quantities of compound from large quantities of starting material, was the determination of structure and the synthesis of pantothenic acid (XXXVII), one of the vitamins of the B complex, accomplished by two teams of research workers under the leadership of Roger J. Williams (1940). Although the complete details of the elucidation of structure are rather technical and involved, the principal essentials may be outlined briefly as follows.

Natural pantothenic acid was not obtained in sufficient purity for reliable molecular-formula determination, but it was found that acid hydrolysis yielded β-alanine, a known amino acid ($^{+}H_3NCH_2CH_2CO_2^{-}$) and a neutral substance which formed a salt on further hydrolysis with alkali. These observations suggested that the neutral substance was a lactone, or inner ester, of a hydroxy acid, probably a γ-hydroxy acid. It would therefore contain the grouping

>C—C<
>C C=O
O

Pantothenic acid, therefore, probably contained a peptide (—CONH—) linkage, and included the grouping

HO—C—C—C—C—NH—$CH_2CH_2CO_2H$
O

Sufficient quantities of the supposed lactone were obtained for determination of its molecular formula as $C_6H_{10}O_3$. By the Zerewitinoff method (reaction with a methylmagnesium halide, CH_3MgX, to form methane, CH_4) it was determined that the molecule contained one active hydrogen atom, which suggested a hydroxyl (—OH) group other than the one involved in lactone ring-formation.

The hydrolyzed lactone (though not the lactone itself) gave with ferric chloride ($FeCl_3$) a colour test characteristic of α-hydroxy acids. Further confirmation of the presence of an α-hydroxy group was obtained through the reactions

$$RCH(OH)CO_2H \xrightarrow[\Delta]{H_2SO_4} RCHO + HCO_2H;$$

$$HCO_2H \xrightarrow[\Delta]{H_2SO_4} CO + H_2O;$$

$$RCH(OH)CO_2H + (CH_3CO)_2O \longrightarrow RCH(O_2CCH_3)CO_2H + CH_3CO_2H$$

In view of the molecular formula determined, and of the results of certain other diagnostic tests that cannot be detailed here, it appeared possible that the lactone had the constitution

$(CH_3)_2C$—CHOH
H_2C C=O
O

and that pantothenic acid had the structure XXXVII.

$HOCH_2C(CH_3)_2CH(OH)CONHCH_2CH_2CO_2H$

XXXVII

The confirmatory synthesis was relatively simple and easy.

$$HCHO + (CH_3)_2CHCHO \longrightarrow HOCH_2C(CH_3)_2CHO \xrightarrow{HCN}$$

$$HOCH_2C(CH_3)_2CH(OH)CN \xrightarrow{H_2O}$$

$$[HOCH_2C(CH_3)_2CH(OH)CO_2H] \xrightarrow{-H_2O}$$

$(CH_3)_2C$—CHOH
H_2C C=O
O
$\xrightarrow{H_2NCH_2CH_2CO_2CH_2C_6H_5}$

$$HOCH_2C(CH_3)_2CH(OH)CONHCH_2CH_2CO_2CH_2C_6H_5 \xrightarrow{H_2O}$$

$$HOCH_2C(CH_3)_2CH(OH)CONHCH_2CH_2CO_2H$$

XXXVII

The synthesis of compounds for specific purposes is well illustrated by many examples in the field of organic medicinals. When it was discovered that the red dye, later known as Prontosil (XXXVIII), had bacteriostatic properties, chemists immediately

HCl. H_2N—⟨C₆H₃⟩—N=N—⟨C₆H₄⟩—SO_2NH_2
NH_2

XXXVIII

sought to discover the groupings responsible for its effectiveness, and soon found that the previously known sulfanilamide (XXXIX) had bacteriostatic properties similar to those of Prontosil itself.

H_2N—⟨C₆H₄⟩—SO_2NH_2

XXXIX

The race began immediately. The isomers of sulfanilamide were tested and found ineffective. Thousands of derivatives of sulfanilamide were prepared and investigated. Among the relatively few that were found to have properties superior in some respects to those of sulfanilamide were sulfapyridine (XL), sulfathiazole (XLI) and sulfadiazine (XLII).

H_2N—⟨C₆H₄⟩—SO_2NH—⟨pyridyl, N⟩

XL

H_2N—⟨C₆H₄⟩—SO_2NH—C(=N—CH=CH—S—)

S—CH
CH
N

XLI

CH
N CH
H_2N—⟨C₆H₄⟩—SO_2NH—C CH
N

XLII

The practice of taking a molecule of known properties as a model and attempting to synthesize compounds of similar or somewhat modified properties is illustrated by the synthetic antimalarials, of which Plasmochin (XLIII) and Atabrine (XLIV) may serve as examples. The structural relationship to quinine (XXXVI) is obvious.

H_3CO—⟨quinoline, N⟩
NH
H_3C—$CHCH_2CH_2CH_2N(C_2H_5)_2$.HCl

XLIII

H_3C—$CHCH_2CH_2CH_2N(C_2H_5)_2$.HCl
NH
⟨acridine, N⟩—Cl

XLIV

The so-called synthetic rubbers are examples of a similar practice. The hydrocarbon of natural rubber is a high-molecular-weight polymer of isoprene [$H_2C=C(CH_3)CH=CH_2$] which may be represented in simplified fashion as [—$CH_2C(CH_3)=CHCH_2$—]$_n$. However, the synthetic rubbers produced by the catalytic polymerization of isoprene are not duplicates of natural rubber and are inferior to it in several respects. A much closer approximation of some of the more desirable properties of natural rubber is achieved in the product of copolymerization of styrene and butadiene previously mentioned. A considerable variety of synthetic rubbers with special properties adapted to specialized uses have been produced. Some representative examples are indicated herewith:

$n\ H_2C{=}CClCH{=}CH_2 \longrightarrow [-CH_2CCl{=}CHCH_2-]_n,$

Neoprene GR-M;

$n\ H_2C{=}CClCH{=}CH_2 + n\ H_2C{=}C(CH_3)CH{=}CH_2 \longrightarrow$
$[-CH_2CCl{=}CHCH\ CH\ C(CH_3){=}CHCH_2-]_n,$

Neoprene FR;

$n\ H_2C{=}C(CH_3)CH{=}CH_2 + n\ (CH_3)_2C{=}CH_2 \longrightarrow$
$[-CH_2C(CH_3){=}CH_2C(CH_3)_2CH_2-]_n$, Butyl GR-I.

Another example of the synthesis of a compound to meet property specifications but without the attempt to duplicate any natural material is to be found in the synthetic fibre nylon. The process may be represented in simplified fashion as follows:

$$n\ HO_2C(CH_2)_4CO_2H + n\ H_2N(CH_2)_6NH_2 \longrightarrow [-OC(CH_2)_4CONH(CH_2)_6NH-]_n + H_2O.$$

In a sense this fibre may be said to be patterned after the natural fibres silk and wool, for it contains the peptide (−OCNH−) linkages common to them, but it has distinctive properties and is by no means either a synthetic silk or synthetic wool.

One of the early successes of the dyestuff chemists was the production of synthetic indigo (1897), which quickly drove the natural product from the market. The modern dyestuff industry, however, is concerned almost exclusively with purely artificial materials carefully tailored to property specifications and nowhere duplicated in nature.

The foregoing examples properly may be said to deal largely with practical applications of organic chemistry, which are by no means the sole preoccupation of organic chemists. Nevertheless, they do serve to illustrate, however imperfectly and incompletely, some of the activities and thought processes of the organic chemist. In the final analysis, the distinction between pure and applied chemistry is one of motivation rather than of the intrinsic nature of the work. Many studies of prime theoretical significance have been made in the hope of ultimate practical application, whereas many discoveries of great practical importance have been the by-products of pure research.

Bibliography.—Carl Schorlemmer, *The Rise and Development of Organic Chemistry* (London, 1894); Edv. Hjelt, *Geschichte der organischen Chemie* (Braunschweig, 1916); *Friedrich Richter, Beilsteins Handbuch der organischen Chemie,* Vierte Auflage, Bandes I–XXXIX, *Erstes Ergänzungswerk,* Bandes I–XXV, *Zweites Ergänzungswerk,* Bandes I–XIV (Berlin, 1918–51); J. Houben, *Methoden der organischen Chemie,* Dritte Auflage, Bandes I–IV (Leipzig, 1925–41); Henry Gilman, *Organic Chemistry,* vols. i, ii (New York and London, 1943); Roger Adams, *Organic Reactions,* vols. i, ii, iii, iv, v, vi (New York and London, 1951), *Organic Synthesis,* annual vols. 1–30 (1921–50), collective vol. i, 2nd ed. (1941), vol. ii (New York and London, 1943).

(P. H. O. R.)

PHYSICAL CHEMISTRY

The easiest definition of physical chemistry is that which describes it as the border-line subject between physics and chemistry, but this definition is not necessarily the most accurate. No greater clarity results by adopting the name "chemical physics." In fact, physical chemistry, since the first issue of the *Zeitschrift für physikalische Chemie* appeared in 1887, can claim to be a science in its own right. It certainly covers the ill-defined territory between physics and chemistry, as biochemistry does between chemistry and biology, and mathematical physics between mathematics and physics, but it can also stake a claim to quite a sizeable piece of land, as extensive and as cultivated as the regions conventionally allocated to the so-called pure sciences of physics and chemistry. We shall not here attempt a definition of physical chemistry, because, properly regarded, it is less a circumscription of subject matter than a method of approach, applicable equally to the problems of physics, chemistry, and biology. There can be no harm, however, in attempting to describe the physical chemist: he is a man who observes natural phenomena and records his observations, but maintains a judicious balance between the material changes themselves, the physical effects which accompany them and the mathematical machinery by means of which the whole can be most compactly condensed.

The three ordinary states of matter—solid, liquid and gaseous—fall within the province of physical chemistry, as do the metallic state, the interfacial state, the colloidal state, and, most important of all, the dissolved state of matter. The influence of heat, light and mechanical and electrical forces on the various states of matter forms the subjects of thermochemistry, photochemistry, piezochemistry and electrochemistry, which rank among the most important subdivisions of physical chemistry. A continuous treatment of these topics is to be found in textbooks, a selected list of which is appended. In this article various problems are discussed which, particularly during the 20th century, have been solved or are still being investigated in physical chemistry.

Adsorption.—When ethylene gas at atmospheric pressure is sealed in a vessel containing copper turnings, the pressure within the vessel gradually diminishes until it reaches a constant value. Similarly, when a solution of iodine is kept in contact with charcoal, the concentration of iodine diminishes until it reaches a constant value. Gas molecules in the first case and solute molecules in the second case have adhered to the surface of the solid. The phenomenon is known as adsorption, and occurs in varying degrees for all solutes and all gases kept over the surface of solids. Argon gas, for example, is adsorbed on the surface of potassium chloride crystals, and enzymes (*q.v.*) are adsorbed on kieselguhr. The extent of adsorption depends on specific properties of the adsorbed and the adsorbing molecules, on the temperature and on the concentration or pressure. The familiar facts have been utilized practically without being understood theoretically. The fairly general adsorbing power of charcoal, for example, explains its use in decolorizing solutions in the course of organic preparations, in protection against toxic vapours and in the treatment of digestive ailments. The reverse process, desorption, has been utilized in the isolation of pure enzymes. In an attempt to understand the mechanism of adsorption, many empirical relations appeared connecting the amount adsorbed with the principal variables, temperature and concentration. Curves showing the fractional adsorption as a function of the concentration at constant temperature are termed adsorption isotherms, and the empirical formulas advanced to account for these were numerous but unenlightening.

In 1916, Irving Langmuir (*q.v.*) proposed a theory of adsorption which was not only sufficient to explain the phenomena, but had extensive applications in other fields, which include statistical physics. His theory was simple. The surface of the solid, of area O cm.^{2}, is likened to a chess board, on which solute or gas molecules impinge. Some adhere to the unitary areas; others fly back to the bulk of the solution or the gas phase. When equilibrium is attained, a certain fraction, θ_s, of the area of the solid remains covered with adsorbed molecules. The fraction of free surface is then $(1-\theta_s)$. In deriving the theoretical expression for the adsorption isotherm, we shall use the terminology of solutions, though the formulas are applicable, *mutatis mutandis,* to gaseous systems. Let the total number of sites per unit area of surface, on which solute molecules can be adsorbed, be n_o, and the probability per second that an adsorbed molecule may become desorbed be ν_s. Then the total number of molecules escaping per second from a surface of area, O cm^2, is $On_o\,\nu_s\theta_s$. The total number of solute molecules reaching the surface from the solution in one second is proportional to the surface area, O, and to the concentration, n_s, of solute molecules. Denoting the proportionality factor by k_s, the number is thus k_sOn_s molecules per second. But only those which hit vacant sites are adsorbed. Hence the rate, of absorption is $k_sOn_s(1-\theta_s)$. At equilibrium, the rates of adsorption and desorption are equal. On solving for θ_s we find that $\theta_s = k_sn_s/(k_sn_s+\nu_sn_o)$, which is Langmuir's adsorption isotherm. From the form of this equation, we note that, at low concentrations, the fraction of the surface that is covered is proportional to the concentration of the supernatant solution, and is, in fact, $(k_s/\nu_sn_o)n_s$. At high concentrations, θ_s tends toward unity. The whole surface is then covered with adsorbed molecules, and the extent of adsorption becomes independent of the concentration. It is generally possible, by quite simple experiments, to measure the concentration, n_s^*, which corresponds to a surface which is only one-half covered. This concentration, from the isotherm equation, is seen to be $\nu_s n_o / k_s$.

Among the many recent applications of Langmuir's theory is the experimental determination of the number of catalytically active sites on the surface of a single enzyme. We have seen that $n_o = k_s n_s^* / \nu_s$. The proportionality factor, k_s, is given by classical theory in terms of the mass, m, of the solute molecule, the absolute temperature, T, and Ludwig Boltzmann's constant, k, which is numerically 1.372×10^{-16} erg/degree: $k_s = (kT/2\pi m)^{\frac{1}{2}}$. The probability per second, ν_s, that an adsorbed molecule will escape is given by quantal theory in terms of the energy, E, of adsorption, and Max Planck's constant, h, which is numerically 6.551×10^{-27} erg-second: $\nu_s = (kT/h)e^{-E/kT}$. We thus have $n_o = hn_s^*(2\pi mkT)^{-\frac{1}{2}}.e^{-E/kT}$. The application of this formula to experimental results on the inversion of cane sugar by saccharase shows that there are only a few active sites, probably eight, on the not inconsiderable surface of one enzyme.

Systems of greater complexity and interest are those in which the surface can simultaneously adsorb more than one kind of solute. Let us denote the second solute by the subscript, I. The fraction of the surface which, under equilibrium conditions, is covered by solute molecules of the first type is now $\theta_s = k_s n_s / [k_s n_s + \nu_s n_o + k_I n_I (\nu_s/\nu_I)]$. This formula, as Langmuir has shown, can explain a number of the idiosyncrasies of catalyzed reactions in solution. Inhibition of chemical reactions and the poisoning of catalysts by substances such as mercuric chloride are readily understood as a preferential adsorption of these compounds and a consequent exclusion of the reactants from the active centres. Similarly, many reactions proceed at rates which are inversely proportional to the concentration of products. These were discovered by Emil Schuetz in 1900, and include the digestion of proteins; they indicate that the greater the extent of reaction, the smaller the rate of the persisting reaction. Clearly, in such cases, the products are more firmly adsorbed than the reactants. There can be little doubt that the sensation of satiety finds its mechanistic basis here; so also does the protective effect so often exerted by the products of hydrolysis on the enzyme responsible for their appearance.

The energy which an adsorbed molecule must acquire before it can become dislodged must, in general, depend on how many of its neighbouring sites are occupied. The experimental dependence of the heat of adsorption on the extent of adsorption was established experimentally by J. K. Roberts a few years before his untimely death during World War II. It ranks as the greatest single extension of Langmuir's theory, and is proving to be one of the most fruitful fields for the investigation of surface catalysis. The discovery has had far-reaching applications in theoretical physics, which, in attempting to derive statistical laws for condensed systems, had previously been at a loss to know how to make allowance for the dependence of the molecular energy on the probability of occupation of neighbouring sites.

Diffusion.—The sugar at the bottom of a cup of tea does not take long to dissolve into a syrup, but, if it were not stirred, it would take a very long time to distribute itself throughout the whole volume of the beverage. The process whereby a quiescent solute at a high concentration moves isothermally to a region of low concentration is known as diffusion. It is analogous to thermal conduction and viscous flow, and differs from them only in that matter is transported in diffusion, whereas energy and momentum, respectively, are transported in the others. The exact mathematical theory of all three phenomena is difficult, but new laws of great beauty and simplicity have, nevertheless, been discovered by Albert Einstein during the first decade of the 20th century, and have had much to do with elucidating the nature of diffusion. They have been applied to determine the Avogadro number; *i.e.*, the number of molecules in one gram-molecule, to estimate the size of colloid particles, to evaluate the time taken by a given molecule in the gas phase or in solution to reach the walls of its container, and to develop the modern theory of liquids.

The number, dN, of molecules transported in a time interval, dt, across an area, O, is, according to Adolph Fick's law, proportional to both dt and O, and to the concentration gradient, dn/dx, at the plane crossed: $dN = -DO(dn/dx)dt$. The proportionality factor, D, is termed the coefficient of diffusion. Molecules are transported in the direction of increasing x only when the concentration gradient in that direction is negative. By subtracting from dN_1, the number of molecules crossing a given plane, the number dN_2, crossing a neighbouring and parallel plane at a distance, dx, from it, we obtain the net transport. Since dN/Odx is the increase in concentration between the planes, it may be denoted by dn, so that $dn/dt = D(d^2n/dx^2)$, which is a more general expression for the coefficient, D, of diffusion. When molecules at a concentration, n, move with an average velocity, v, the number which in one second cross unit area of a plane at right angles to the direction of motion is nv. The rate of transport of molecules across an area O cm.^{2} is thus $dN/dt = Onv$. Comparison with Fick's law indicates that the coefficient of diffusion is $D = -nv/(dn/dx)$. According to J. H. van't Hoff's laws, the osmotic pressure, π, of a solution containing n molecules per cubic centimetre is $\pi = kTn$. Any isothermal change in the osmotic pressure must therefore be the result of a change in the concentration, so that $d\pi = kTdn$. The additional force exerted in the direction of increasing x on an area, O, caused by a difference in concentration is thus $-Od\pi = -OkTdn$. The number of molecules exerting the force is the number contained in the volume element, Odx, which is $nOdx$. Hence the force exerted by each molecule is, on an average, $X = -(kT/n)(dn/dx)$. The uniform velocity, v, is the ratio of this force to the resistance factor, s. Thus $v = X/s$. Sir George G. Stokes's expression for the resistance factor in the case of a spherical molecule of radius, r, moving in a medium of viscosity, η, is $6\pi\eta r$. Hence $vn/(dn/dx) = -kT/6\pi\eta r$. According to our previous equation, the expression on the left side is simply the coefficient of diffusion with the sign reversed. It follows that $D = kT/6\pi\eta r$, which is Einstein's equation. The coefficients of diffusion and viscosity are not difficult to measure at a constant temperature, T, and the radii of particles diffusing in solution thus become directly measurable.

We have hitherto regarded diffusion as a property of molecules in systems of uneven concentration, and as the mechanism whereby uniformity of concentration is established. The process, however, must persist, though without a net transfer of matter, even in systems of uniform molecular concentration. We can, for example, apply the laws of diffusion to determine the fate of an arbitrarily selected group of molecules from one part of an equilibrated system to another. By solving the differential form of Fick's equation in the case of linear motion, it can readily be shown that the uniform velocity at the distance x is $v = D/x$. But $v = dx/dt$; hence $dx/dt = D/x$, which gives on integration: $x^2/2 = Dt +$ a constant. We choose the system of reference for the selected migrating molecules as that corresponding to $x = 0$ when $t = 0$, so that the square of the net displacement suffered by the selected molecules in time t, and measured along the x axis, is $x^2 = 2Dt$, which is the second of Einstein's diffusion laws. It has been verified by Jean Perrin in a series of well-known experiments, using colloidal particles, made visible in the ultramicroscope, and followed at time intervals of a few seconds. It is to be noted that, because the motion is a random one, the average distance traversed (or, more precisely, the square root of the average of the square of the distance) is proportional, not to the time, but to the square root of the time.

Einstein's treatment of diffusion has done much to stimulate work in the physical chemistry of solutions. In particular, attempts have been made to extend the treatment to the movement of molecules under the influences of forces other than the thermal and viscous forces to which the early work has been restricted. Only partial success has been achieved, in cases where the additional force is of a simple and well-known form. There is, however, no reason why the method should not ultimately prove helpful in the recognition of the type of force actually at work.

Perrin's experimental verification of Einstein's second law of diffusion has afforded one of the most accurate estimates of the Avogadro number. It is 6.063×10^{23} molecules per gram-mole. This fundamentally important constant has also been measured, with confirmatory results, in many other ways. It enables the physical chemists to compute, in all systems of interest, the actual number of molecules present. One drop of water, weighing five milligrams, is thus found to contain 168.3 million million million molecules.

Coagulation.—Colloid particles may be prepared, either in the gaseous phase or in solution, by a variety of methods. Aerosols, for example, may be made by mixing the vapour of the substance to be dispersed with a blast of air at a lower temperature, or by suddenly bursting a sample of liquid at great pressure into air at ordinary pressure. Collosols may be made by slow chemical reaction in dilute solution or, in the case of metals, by G. Bredig's method of sparking between electrodes immersed in the solvent. The chief characteristic of the dispersed phase in either system is its instability. The dispersed particles, when initially generated, are relatively small, but, with the passage of time, they become coarser, until they are large enough to come under the influence of gravity. The process of coarsening is termed coagulation, and it has been extensively studied. Experiment shows that the instantaneous rate at which the number of particles diminishes is proportional to the square of the concentration, n, of particles present at that instant. We may then write $-dn/dt = k_2 n^2$, where k_2 is the coefficient of coagulation. On integrating—and noting that the initial condition of $t=0$ corresponds to the initial concentration of $n=n_0$—we have $k_2 = (1/t) \times (1/n - 1/n_0)$. If we denote by $t_{\frac{1}{2}}$ the time required for the number of particles to be reduced to one-half of their original number, then clearly $k_2 = 1/t_{\frac{1}{2}} n_0$. These formulas are characteristic of bimolecular processes. The latter simply states that the product of the half life and the initial concentration for such processes is a constant, and that it is equal to the reciprocal of the bimolecular velocity coefficient. They have been abundantly verified for the process of coagulation in solution and in the gaseous phase. On rearranging the latter equation, in logarithmic form, we have $\log_{10} t_{\frac{1}{2}} = -\log_{10} k_2 - \log_{10} n_0$. A plot of the logarithm of the half life against the logarithm of the initial concentration should thus be a linear one, with a gradient of -1, and it should intercept the abscissa at a concentration numerically equal to the reciprocal of the bimolecular velocity coefficient. These generalities are illustrated in fig. 1, which has been drawn from P. Tuorila's data on the rate of coagulation of colloidal gold in water at 20° C. It will be noted that the initial concentration has been varied by a factor of more than 10,000, and that k_2 becomes 6.8×10^{-12} c.c./particle-second, which has a constant value over the whole range of concentrations. There can be no doubt that the coagulation of sols in aqueous solution takes place, as R. Zsigmondy first showed, as a result of binary encounters.

We next inquire, following M. von Smoluchowski, into the theoretical interpretation of the coefficient, k_2, and for this purpose must determine the frequency of binary collisions. The number of molecules of type A which, in one second, cross a spherical surface of radius, r, surrounding a molecule of type B is the product of the concentration of the A molecules by their velocity and by the spherical area. We have seen that the velocity is D/r, and, since the area is $4\pi r^2$, the number crossing per second is $4\pi D r n_A$. This equals the number of collisions, when r becomes the sum of the radii $(r_A + r_B)$ of the colliding partners. Hence ${}_1Z_A = 4\pi D(r_A + r_B) n_A$. The total number, ${}_AZ_B$, of collisions in unit volume is n_B times as great. Viewing the problem from the complementary angle of a stationary A molecule surrounded by approaching B molecules, and taking the mean, we obtain, for the number of binary collisions in unit volume and in unit time: ${}_AZ_B = 2\pi(D_A + D_B)(r_A + r_B) n_A n_B$. On making use of Einstein's first diffusion formula, we may rewrite this expression in terms of the viscosity, obtaining ${}_AZ_B = (kT/3\eta)(r_A + r_B)^2 n_A n_B / r_A r_B$, which, for particles of equal radii, reduces to $(4kT/3\eta) n^2$. Now if a collision between two particles is a sufficient condition for their coalescence, the coagulation coefficient, k_2, should equal $4kT/3\eta$. The viscosity of water at 20° C. being 0.01005 gram/cm.-second, the theoretical estimate of k_2 is seen to be 5.33×10^{-12} c.c. per particle-second, which is in good agreement with the experimental findings of Zsigmondy and of Tuorila. Moreover, the temperature dependence of the bimolecular velocity constant is correctly reflected by the ratio T/η. Smoluchowski's theory thus provides a fairly complete account of the kinetics of coagulation in solution, and establishes the fact that the rate of this process is simply the rate at which particles collide with one another. Points of refinement deal with the uneven distribution of particle size, and are relatively unimportant. There is also the possibility of preferential dissolution from the surface of the smaller particles.

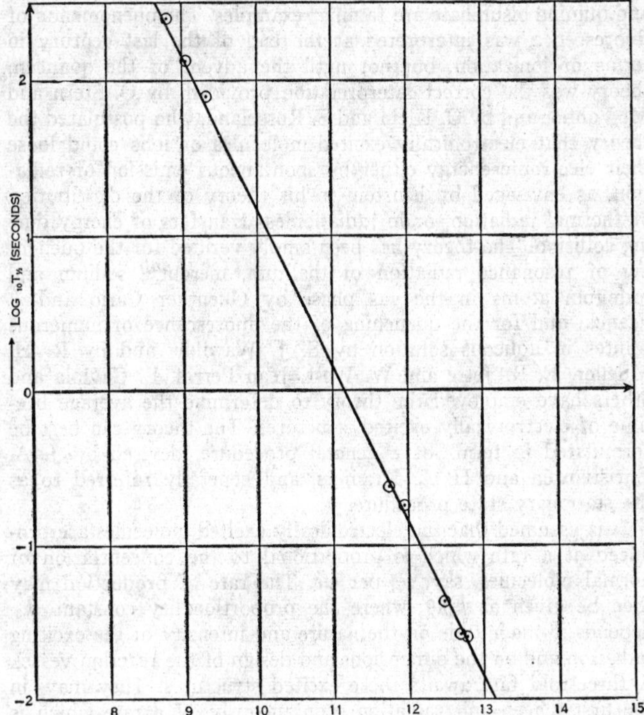

FIG. 1.—THE BIMOLECULARITY OF THE COAGULATION OF COLLOIDAL GOLD

Air at 20° C. is about 55 times less viscous than water at the same temperature. If, therefore, colloidal particles in air coagulate according to the same mechanism as colloidal particles in solution, the coagulation coefficient should be greater by about this factor, and should therefore be about 3×10^{-10} c.c. per particle-second. Smokes made from a variety of substances, such as magnesium oxide, cadmium oxide, long-chain fatty acids and resinous materials, have been examined by R. Whytlaw-Gray and H. S. Patterson, who find that k_2, though not exactly 3×10^{-10}, seldom varies beyond the limits of 5 and 8 in the same units. Vaporization from the particulate surface and the possible inadequacy of Stokes's expression for the frictional resistance factor are among the explanations offered for the slight discrepancy. Apart from points of detail, however, Smoluchowski's theory is as applicable to aerosols as to collosols. The point is an important one, as the work in the two phases has been carried out by different investigators, in different countries, and without liaison or much knowledge of one another's activities. It is, perhaps, one of the most attractive features of 20th century physical chemistry that theories, like that of Smoluchowski, sometimes emerge which, on being extensively applied, bring coherence to sets of phenomena which have been traditionally regarded as unrelated.

The Quenching of Resonance Radiation.—A substance that, while absorbing radiation of a given wave length, simultaneously emits radiation of a longer wave length, is said to fluoresce. Aqueous solutions of chlorophyll, fluorescein, disodiumuranine and quinine bisulphate are familiar examples. The phenomenon of fluorescence was interpreted at the end of the last century in terms of ionization, but not until the advent of the quantum theory was the correct interpretation provided, by O. Stern and M. Volmer and by O. Klein and S. Rosseland, who postulated the theory that electronically excited molecules or ions could loose their electronic energy either by spontaneous emission of radiation, as envisaged by Einstein in his theory of the distribution of thermal radiation, or in radiationless transfers of energy during collision. The theory has been amply verified for the quenching of resonance radiation of thallium, mercury, sodium and cadmium atoms in the gas phase by Guenther Cario and J. Franck, and for the quenching of the fluorescence of numerous solutes in aqueous solution by S. J. Wawilow and by R. H. Mueller, E. R. Jette and W. West. Jean Perrin, E. Gaviola and others have employed the theory to determine the average lifetime of electronically excited structures. The theory can best be formulated in terms of a general procedure, devised by J. A. Christiansen and H. A. Kramers, and generally referred to as the stationary state procedure.

It is assumed that the electronically excited molecules are produced at a rate which is proportional to the concentration of normal molecules, say, n_A per c.c. The rate of production may then be given as k_3n_A, where the proportionality constant, k_3, depends in magnitude on the nature and intensity of the exciting radiation and on the dimensions and design of the reaction vessel. A three-fold fate awaits these excited structures. They may, in the first place, emit radiation spontaneously, at a rate which is proportional to the concentration, a, of the excited structures. Let this rate of emission be denoted by k_1a, where k_1 is the decay constant, or the reciprocal of the mean life. They may, in the second place, be robbed of energy in collisions with normal molecules of their own kind: this rate is a bimolecular one, and may be denoted by k_4n_Aa. Finally, the excited molecules, atoms or ions may loose energy by transfer during collisions with molecules of another kind, which, let it be supposed, are present at a concentration n_B molecules per c.c.: this rate again is a bimolecular one, and may be expressed as k_2n_Aa. When a stationary concentration of excited molecules has been reached, the rate of production by absorption of light equals the sum of the three rates of destruction. We can thus solve for a, the concentration of excited molecules. But the rate of emission is known to be k_1a. Eliminating a from these two expressions, the rate, I, of emission is seen to be $k_1k_3n_A/(k_1+k_2n_B+k_4n_A)$. Maximum emission, I_o, coincides with absence of the quenching molecules, and is clearly $k_1k_3n_A/(k_1+k_4n_A)$. The ratio of the intensity of fluorescence in the absence of a quenching material to that in the presence of a quencher is $I_o/I=1+\frac{(k_2)}{(k_1+k_4n_A)}n_B$. If self-quenching is insignificant, the term k_4n_A can be ignored; the ratio I_o/I is then a linear function of the concentration of quenching molecules, and the gradient $d(I_o/I)/dn_B$ is the ratio of two velocity coefficients, k_2/k_1. The decay constant, k_1, is known from other sources, and the velocity coefficient governing the bimolecular process whereby excited molecules are deprived of their energy can thus be determined. When its magnitude is compared with the number of collisions, as given by the formula in the section on coagulation, we find varying results, according to the quenching molecule. Collisions between the quinine ion, electronically excited, and the normal iodide ion in water almost invariably lead to a radiationless transfer of energy. Collisions of the same organic ions with other inorganic quenchers are never quite so efficient. Inorganic ions, in fact, range themselves in an order of quenching efficiency that is the same as the order of electronic polarizability, coagulation power and lyophilic activity. The constant k_2 for gaseous processes, such as the damping of resonance radiation of sodium atoms by nitrogen molecules, is usually greater than the number of collisions occurring per c.c. per second. This result has generally been interpreted as indicating that the electronically excited atom has a larger radius than the normal atom. Certainly, if we apply to the experimental results the formulas of the kinetic theory of gases, we must employ a radius of capture which is considerably greater than the radius as measured by other means; but this explanation cannot be ultimately satisfactory, and the problem in the meantime is largely unsolved.

Perhaps the chief theoretical interest attaching to recent work on the quenching of resonance radiation in gases and of fluorescence in solution is that it brings to the fore the mechanism according to which, during collisions, energy of one kind is converted into energy of another kind. The present examples are confined to the conversion of electronic energy into some other form; *e.g.*, into kinetic energy, but the problem posed is a much more general one. When, for example, an atom of argon collides with a molecule of nitrogen, does the kinetic energy of the atom become exchanged for the kinetic energy of the molecule? Or does the atom during collision transmit its energy into vibrational energy of the molecule? In principle, these are questions which the quantum theory is able to answer but, in practice, little has yet been done in deriving the mathematical solution. A difficulty in the way is that one must possess complete information of the forces at work, and this is not always available. Assumptions as to the form of forces acting at short distances have been made, for example, by C. Zener, who has consequently arrived at a partial solution of the problem of conversion of energy from the kinetic to the vibrational kind. Arnold Eucken and his collaborators have pursued the same problem experimentally, using acoustical methods. The limit of accumulation of vibrational energy in a diatomic molecule corresponds to its dissociation into atoms, a process which is known to happen in certain cases of resonance quenching. Moreover, the most efficient quenchers are diatomic molecules whose energy of dissociation lies near to the quantum of energy emitted by the electronically excited atom. The theory of energy transfer during collisions is, as yet, in its infancy, and many more experimental guides such as those enumerated here will probably have to be discovered before any considerable growth can ensue.

Spectroscopy.—Studies made after 1930 of the radiation absorbed and emitted by chemical compounds in the gaseous and dissolved states of matter have given the physical chemist a more penetrating insight into the structure of molecules than would have been thought possible at the beginning of the 20th century. The key to the interpretation of the multitudinous spectra exhibited was provided by Ernest Rutherford and Niels Bohr in their treatment of the spectrum of the hydrogen atom. According to their well-known theory, the hydrogen atom can exist only in definite energy states; all conceivable energy states lying between these so-called "quantized" states are excluded from the realm of possibility. The energy levels are related to one another in the ratio of the inverse square of the integral ordinal numbers. To adopt an analogy effectively used by Bertrand Russell, it is as if the citizens of some fictitious town were allowed to possess curious sums of money, such as £100, £25, £11–2–2⅔, but not sums intermediate between these. All transactions would then be in terms of equally curious sums, such as £75, £13–17–9⅓, but not in intervening quantities. Analysis of the spectra of molecules shows that molecular electronic levels resemble atomic electronic levels. Vibrational energies in molecules are, however, almost directly proportional to integral ordinal numbers, and rotational energies are approximately proportional to the squares of integral numbers. Excluding the translational energy, the total energy of molecules may be considered as made up of three components, viz., the electronic energy, E_e, the vibrational energy, E_v, and the rotational energy, E_r. Then $E=E_e+E_v+E_r$. The difference between two neighbouring electronic energy levels in molecules is usually commensurable with the difference in the electronic levels in atoms. For every electronic energy level, there exists a number of vibrational levels, which lie relatively near to one another. Associated, in turn, with each vibrational energy level are many rotational levels, which, generally, lie still nearer together. The rotational energy, E_r, of a molecule in any given state depends not only on the rotational quantum number, J, but also on the vibrational quantum number, v, as well as on the electronic quantum number necessary to define completely a given molecular state. The vibrational level is also to some extent dependent on E_e, but the latter is independent of either J or v. The transition of a molecule from a state with energy E to one with a higher energy, E^1, is accompanied by the absorption of a quantum of radiation, hν, where h is Planck's constant, and ν is the frequency of the radiation absorbed. $\nu = (E^1 - E)h = \frac{E^1_e + E^1_v + E^1_r}{h} - \frac{E_e + E_v + E_r}{h} = \frac{E^1e - E}{h} + \frac{E^1_v - E_v}{h} + \frac{E^1_r - E_r}{h} = \nu_e + \nu_v + \nu_r.$ When both ν_e and ν_v are zero, all the absorption lines in the spectrum are the result of transitions between two states of the molecule with fixed electronic and vibrational quantum numbers; the lines of absorption are said to constitute a pure rotation band, and, since they occur between energy levels which lie very close together, the frequencies of the absorbed radiation are low, and therefore the wave lengths of the absorption lines are large. They are found in the infra-red region of the spectrum. When only $\nu_e = 0$, the lines may be caused by transitions between molecular states differing in both their vibrational and rotational quantum numbers; the lines constitute vibration-rotation bands, and often appear in the visible region of the spectrum. When ν_e, ν_v and ν_r have all positive values, the lines of absorption or emission correspond to transitions between molecules which have different electronic, vibrational and rotational energies. The whole band system may then extend right across from the far infra-red to the far ultra-violet regions. On account of the inequality $\nu_e > \nu_v > \nu_r$, it follows that the general position of a nonelectronic band is governed by the vibrational quantum number, while the structure of the various bands is determined by the rotational quantum numbers.

Special apparatuses and techniques pertain to the various spectra, and, although many physical chemists within recent years have devoted their time to the investigation of molecular spectra, the subject is so vast and the experimental intricacies attached to the various spectral regions so specific, that few investigators, if any, can claim to be directly acquainted with more than one technique. Experimentally, the investigators are grouped as infra-red, visible region and ultra-violet spectroscopists, and, as we shall see in the next section, as Raman spectroscopists. With the details of the investigations we are not here concerned. It is, however, necessary to outline the theoretical sections of the quantum theory which have been advanced by spectroscopic knowledge and to indicate briefly what information of value to the physical chemist has emerged in very simple cases.

According to the quantum theory, the rotational energy of a diatomic molecule, with a moment of inertia, I, is $E_r = J(J+1) \times \frac{h^2}{8\pi^2 I}$ where $J = 0, 1, 2, 3 \ldots$ The difference in energy between two neighbouring states is thus $J(J+1)(h^2/4\pi^2 I)$. The greater the rotational quantum number, the farther apart are the energies of any two neighbouring states. The emission frequencies form given states to those immediately below them are, by the Bohr frequency law, $(J+1)(h/4\pi^2 I)$. Transitions between systems performing simple harmonic motions, of which free rotation is an example, can take place only with unit change in the quantum number. The frequencies of the radiation absorbed or emitted by diatomic molecules in the infra-red region of the spectrum should therefore be $\frac{h}{4\pi^2 I}$, $2\frac{h}{4\pi^2 I}$, $3\frac{h}{4\pi^2 I}$, etc. Except for a small correction, this conclusion has been verified in the case of the hydrogen halides. Karl Czerny found that the pure rotational frequencies (in reciprocal seconds) of hydrogen chloride and hydrogen bromide are, respectively, $6.034 \times 10^{11} \times M$ and $5.002 \times 10^{11} \times M$, where M is 1,2,3,4, ... Now the moment of inertia is the product of the reduced mass of the rotator and the square of the distance apart of the nuclei. In this way it is possible to determine accurately the internuclear distances in simple molecules. The results for hydrogen fluoride, hydrogen chloride, hydrogen bromide and hydrogen iodide are, in Ångstrom units, 0.923, 1.281, 1.421, and 1.617 respectively. A more detailed analysis takes into account the fact that ordinary hydrogen chloride, for example, is a mixture of two kinds of molecules, one of which contains the chlorine atom of atomic weight 35, and the other the chlorine atom of atomic weight 37. The internuclear distance is found to be the same for the two molecules.

If the nuclei in a diatomic molecule were to vibrate harmonically with a frequency ν, the total vibrational energy of the molecule characterized by a quantum number, v, would be $E_v = (v+\frac{1}{2})h\nu$, and, by the Bohr frequency relationship, the frequency of the radiation absorbed or emitted would be $\nu_v = \nu$. But, since transitions between harmonically vibrating systems must coincide with unit changes in the quantum number, there should be only one absorption or emission line, and its frequency should be identical with the vibration frequency of the molecule. H. Deslandres has shown that the vibrational energy levels are more satisfactorily reproduced by the equation, $E_v = (v+\frac{1}{2})h\nu - x(v+\frac{1}{2})^2 h\nu$, in which the empirical factor, x, though numerically small, is never zero. It can be shown to be approximately equal to $h\nu/4D$, where D is the energy necessary to dissociate the molecule into atoms. The analysis of the vibrational spectra of simple molecules thus yields information on two important properties—the frequency of internuclear vibration, and the energy of dissociation. The vibration frequencies of the halogen molecules, in units of 10^{12} reciprocal seconds, are thus found to be 16.03 (Cl_2), 9.712 (Br_2) and 6.424 (I_2). The dissociation energies of the alkali metal diatoms, expressed in units of kilocalories per gram-molecule are, by the same method, found to be 26.275 (Li_2), 17.515 (Na_2) and 11.800 (K_2) (*see* fig. 3).

The absorption or emission lines in the electronic spectra of simple molecules can be represented semiempirically by equations of the Ritz-Rydberg form, which include terms inversely dependent on the square of an integral number. The constant term in the formula affords an analytical means of estimating the limit of absorption of electronic energy, and thus of the energy required to eject the least firmly bound electron. Ionization potentials of simple molecules and electron affinities of simple ions thus come within the reach of experiment. Both are of fundamental importance in the description of the electronic structure of molecules, a subject that, from the purely theoretical aspect, is fraught with complications.

From these elementary beginnings, modern physicochemical spectroscopy bifurcates. One branch seeks, with only qualified success, to extend to more complicated molecules the dynamic principles on which the spectra of diatomic molecules have been interpreted. The more complicated the molecule, the greater is the number of electrons and nuclei contained in it, and the more numerous, for that reason, are the ionization potentials and the internuclear frequencies. The other branch is directed to the applications of the spectra to the problems of chemical analysis, and has progressed further. Spectroscopic methods are now familiar not only for detecting impurities in suspect samples but also for estimating the composition of mixtures, the ordinary physicochemical analysis of which is too difficult. The preparation of vitamins from fish oils and the rectification of high-grade aviation spirit from natural petroleum are but two of the important industrial spheres in which spectroscopic analyses have proved to be supreme.

The Raman Effect.—In absorption spectra, atoms and molecules assimilate only those quanta of radiation to which they are constitutionally adapted. In Raman absorption, incident light of an arbitrary frequency is used. Moreover, the experimental technique is relatively simple. Raman instruments now accordingly take their place among the most useful tools of the physicochemical workshop. The research laboratories of all progressive universities and industries can boast of a Raman spectroscope.

It has been known since John Tyndall's time that a faint blue colour becomes visible from all directions when a beam of white light is passed through a pure transparent medium. Light of short wave length is more readily scattered than light of long wave length, as Lord Rayleigh emphasized in his explanation of the blueness of the sky. When, instead of white light, a beam of monochromatic radiation is allowed to pass through a homogeneous specimen of matter, light detected in a direction perpendicular to that of the incident beam is found to contain, in addition to the original radiation, light of other frequencies, in numbers and intensities which depend on the scattering medium. The displaced lines, on analysis after resolution in the detecting spectroscope, are found to be much fainter than the line resulting from the original light; exposures of several days are often necessary for the measurement of their position and intensity. The scattering of homogeneous radiation by chemical compounds is termed the Raman effect (*q.v.*). It was experimentally established by Sir C. V. Raman and K. S. Krishnan, in 1928, though its occurrence had been theoretically foreshadowed by A. Smekal, in 1923. Since its discovery, tens of thousands of compounds have been investigated by its means, with important consequences.

Let us consider a head-on collision between a quantum, $h\nu_1$, of incident light and an atom or molecule of mass, m, which is supposed to be moving with velocity v_1, and to possess an internal energy, E_1, in addition to its kinetic energy, $\frac{1}{2}mv_1^2$. The energy of the incident photon is $h\nu_1$, and, according to an important quantal law discovered by Louis de Broglie, its momentum is $h\nu_1/c$, where c is the velocity of light. The laws of the conservation of energy and momentum then give us the relations $h\nu_1+E_1+\frac{1}{2}mv_1^2=h\nu_2+E_2+\frac{1}{2}mv_2^2$ and $(h\nu_1/c)+mv_1=(h\nu_2/c)+mv^2$. The maximum energy exchange clearly occurs when $v_1=0$, and $\nu_2=0$; *i.e.*, when the whole kinetic energy of the incident photon is completely converted into kinetic energy of the atom or molecule which was initially at rest. We have only considered head-on collisions, but it can be shown by classical dynamics that the conclusion is a true one in general. It follows that the maximum gain in kinetic energy is $\frac{1}{2}mv_2^2=\frac{1}{2m}(mv_2)^2=\frac{1}{2m}\left(\frac{h\nu_1}{c}\right)^2$.

Under the most favourable conditions, therefore, the fraction of the incident energy, $h\nu_1$, which is convertible is $h\nu_1/2mc^2$. This is of a very small order of magnitude. When, for example, the 4358Å line of the mercury spectrum is used as incident radiation, and carbon tetrachloride as the scattering medium, the fraction proves to be less than 10^{-11}. Any change in the frequency of the light caused by its passage through the medium must accordingly be the result of a change in the internal energy of the molecule. The first of Smekal's equations now becomes, effectively, $\nu_1-\nu_2=(E_2-E_1)/h$. The difference between the frequencies of the incident and emergent radiation is termed the Raman frequency: it could with more logic be termed the Raman shift. We have, then, the relation $\nu_R=\nu_1-\nu_2$ where ν_R can be greater than, equal to or less than zero, according as the light is displaced toward the red end of the spectrum, is unaffected, or is displaced toward the ultra-violet end of the spectrum. The responsible collisions are said to be, respectively, inelastic, elastic or superelastic. The extent of the displacement in the two directions is the same, so that lines in the scattered radiation appear in pairs, equidistantly draping the undisplaced line. The intensities of the two displaced lines are, however, very different, and, by measuring the way in which the ratio of the two intensities varies with respect to the temperature, it has been possible to ascribe a numerical value to Planck's constant, h.

Although the occurrence of the Raman effect becomes intelligible in terms of Smekal's hypothesis, its true origin is to be traced to the fact that, on account of the vibratory motion executed by the atoms within a molecule, the molecular polarizability varies with the phase of intramolecular motion. The interplay between the variable internal field thus set up and the harmonic field caused by the electrical component of light results in the generation of three electromagnetic vibrations, of frequencies ν_L, $\nu_L+\nu_R$ and $\nu_L-\nu_R$, where ν_L is the frequency of the incident light, and ν_R is the Raman frequency.

The commonest source of light used is that given by the mercury vapour discharge tube, which emits strong radiation of wave lengths 5460.74, 4358.34 and 4046.56 Ångstrom units. These correspond to the reversal of the electronically excited mercury atom from the $2s$ state to the three $2p$ states. Two of these radiations may be cut out by suitable filters (such as quinine sulphate to eject the 4047 line), and as intense a beam of the monochromatic 4358 line as possible is used to irradiate the medium—generally in the pure liquid phase. The total light emitted is recorded on a photographic plate after resolution through a prism.

Experiment shows that the Raman shift, *i.e.*, the difference between the frequencies (or wave-numbers) of the incident and scattered radiation, is (1) independent of the frequency of the incident light; and (2) to a first approximation, independent of the state of the scattering substance. By virtue of Smekal's equations, the quantum $h\nu_R$ equals the difference between two stationary energy levels of the scattering molecule. The Raman wave numbers, in reciprocal centimetres, of the chloride, bromide and iodide of hydrogen in the gaseous phase are, respectively, 2880, 2558 and 2233. Very often the evidence afforded by Raman spectroscopy is complementary to that given by infra-red absorption spectroscopy, as lines missing in one may appear in other. In the case of the three heteronuclear diatomic molecules mentioned here, the missing null lines in the infra-red spectra of the gases have the wave numbers 2887, 2559 and 2240, respectively. Experiments show that the Raman wave numbers of these three compounds in the liquid state are about 80 less, and in the solid state about 130 less, than in the gaseous phase.

The Raman spectra of polyatomic molecules are naturally more complicated. An important guiding principle revealed by extensive experiments is that a given bond in a complicated molecule often gives rise to a Raman frequency which is but slightly affected by variations in the structure of the remaining portions of the molecule. All incompletely substituted aliphatic compounds, for example, exhibit a Raman shift in the neighbourhood of 2934 cm.$^{-1}$. A line near 1,700 cm.$^{-1}$ is invariably found in the Raman spectra of carboxylic acids, aldehydes, ketones, acid chlorides and esters, and is naturally attributed to the presence of the carbonyl group, $=C=O$. The exact value found for the methyl, ethyl, propyl, butyl and amyl esters of formic acid is 1718 ± 3, and for the corresponding values for the esters of chloroformic and acetic acids the values are, respectively, 1775 ± 5 and 1738 ± 2 reciprocal centimetres. These variations, though genuine, are not great enough to invalidate, as a guiding rule, the principle of a virtual independence of group frequencies. In this way, characteristic Raman shifts may be allotted to atom pairs in polyatomic molecules, such as the wave number 3050 for the –C–H pair in aromatic hydrocarbons and that of 2924 for the same pair in aliphatic hydrocarbons. The spectra of amines, alcohols and mercaptans similarly yield 3370 for the –N–H group, 3650 for the –O–H group and 2572 for the –S–H group.

Higher values of the Raman frequencies are obtained when the two atoms are joined by divalent bonds, and still higher values when the same two atoms are united by the tervalent bond. Thus, when the carbon-carbon, the carbon-nitrogen and the carbon-oxygen bonds are examined, each in the three valency states, the ratio of the Raman shifts are as 1:1.63:2.10. Now it can readily be shown that the average restoring force of a linear harmonic oscillator is proportional to the vibration frequency raised to the power of 3/2, and is in fact equal to $\pi\,(h\mu\nu^3)^{\frac{1}{2}}$, where μ is the reduced mass. We thus see, as A. Dadieu and K. W. F. Kohlrausch first pointed out, that, for univalent, divalent and tervalent bonds between the same pair of atoms, the average restoring forces stand in the ratio of 1 to 2.08 and to 3.05. The classical theory of valency is thus quantitatively vindicated by the study of the Raman affect. It is, thus, a natural result to find that the average restoring force exerted in the carbon-nitrogen bond contained in oximes, ketimines and isocyanates is intermediate in strength between the average forces exerted, on the one hand, in amines, amides and pyrroles, and, on the other hand, in nitriles, ferrocyanides and cyanamides.

Only a few instances can be cited of the further application of the Raman technique to physicochemical problems. In the familiar conversion of the keto to the enol modification suffered by ketonic compounds, the characteristic ethylenic lines at 1632 and 1725 cm.$^{-1}$, which are present in the spectrum of ethyl aceto-acetate, are found to be absent from the spectrum of ethyl-dimethyl-aceto-acetate, which shows, however, a doublet at 1707 and 1738, typical of the carbonyl group. In the polymerization of methyl methacrylate, the Raman line resulting from the—C=C—bond gradually vanishes, and is almost completely absent from the final polymer formed, which indicates the obliteration of the double bond during the linking up. The great similarity between the Raman spectra of the tertiary butane molecule and the tetra methyl-ammonium ion establishes a regular tetrahedral configuration for the latter. Finally, promising attempts have been made at computing, from a knowledge of the Raman frequencies, the specific heat of certain liquids and the latent heats of fusion of certain solids.

The Kinetic Theory of Gases.—With the exception of the atomic theory of matter, no theory has so powerfully influenced chemistry as the kinetic theory of gases. Its origin may be traced, through Pierre Gassendi in the 17th century, to the early speculations of the Greek philosophers, but its formulation as we now know it is due in equal measure to the German scientist, Ludwig Boltzmann, and the British scientist, J. C. Maxwell, whose classical theorems on the distribution, respectively, of energy and velocity, appeared in 1859. It is worthy of note that many of the ideas essential to the theory, though inaccurately formulated, were expressed in 1845 by J. J. Waterston, whose celebrated communication was not published until 1892. The original postulates are that the molecules constituting a gas are hard, perfectly elastic spheres, endowed with incessant translatory motion, and occupying a volume which is negligible compared with the total volume of the gas. The velocities, momenta, energies and directions of motion are not the same for all the molecules in any specimen of gas, but are distributed among them according to the formal laws of probability. Maxwell's first paper dealt chiefly with the distribution of velocities, and Boltzmann's with the distribution of energies.

Few of the postulates underlying the original theory are now regarded as valid, but enormous advances have been made by accepting them as working propositions, and by inventing additional postulates to explain divergences between theory and practice.

The kinetic theory of gases gives a logical meaning to the well-known laws of Robert Boyle, J. A. C. Charles and Amedeo Avogadro. Thomas Graham (1833) showed that the velocity of effusion of gases at a constant temperature should be independent of the pressure and inversely proportional to the square root of the molecular weight. He verified this theoretical deduction by measuring the rates of effusion of nitrogen and ethylene, which were found to be nearly equal, and the relative rates of effusion of hydrogen and oxygen, which were found to be 3.815:1.000, as compared with the anticipated value of 3.985. Atmolysis, the separation of gases by diffusion, was used by Sir William Ramsay and M. Travers to effect the isolation of helium from other gases, and by Lord Rayleigh and Ramsay in a partial separation of argon from nitrogen, using the celebrated churchwarden pipe technique. In this experiment, a mixture of gases of unequal molecular weight is made to flow through a tube which bifurcates into one tube of glass and one formed of two churchwarden pipes joined together. The lighter gas diffuses through the clay walls more readily than the heavier one, and partial separation can be effected. The formula (O_3) of ozone was first established as a result of diffusion experiments.

According to the kinetic theory, the specific heat of gases, and the ratio (γ) of the specific heat at constant pressure to that at constant volume, should be independent of the temperature and determined by the number of atoms in the molecule. The first of these conclusions has proved to be untrue, and the real effect, which is an increase in the specific heat with a rise in temperature, has only recently been understood, in terms of the quantum theory. The second conclusion, though limited in validity, has been of direct value to chemistry in allowing an experimental determination of the number of atoms in molecules. Rayleigh and Ramsay (1894) found γ, from the velocity of sound in the gas, to be nearly 1.67 in the case of argon, and concluded that this molecule was therefore monatomic.

Ramsay (1879) gave the first kinetic interpretation of the Brownian movement as the motion of small particles resulting from molecular impacts with molecules of the surrounding medium. This interpretation led later (1905) to the kinetic theories of the effect by Einstein and by Smoluchowski, and to the first reliable experimental value of the Avogadro number, by Perrin (1909). The Brownian movement of smoke particles studied by E. N. da C. Andrade and R. C. Parker (1937), offers direct visual evidence of the effects of collisions by gas molecules on the movements of small particles of suspensoid.

The coefficients of viscosity, diffusion and thermal conduction are given by the kinetic theory in terms of the molecular diameters (P. G. Tait, 1886). The three methods have afforded early values of molecular radii, which agree among themselves, and with those obtained by numerous other methods, of which only two—both due to Rayleigh—need be mentioned here. The first (1871) depends on the refraction of light by particles of molecular dimensions, and the second (1905) is based on the computed minimum thickness of an oil layer found necessary to stop the Brownian movement of camphor particles in the water-air interface. The value estimated by Rayleigh by the second method was 16×10^{-8} cm. His kinetic treatment of the effect forms the basis of the Langmuir-Adam-Rideal (I. Langmuir, N. K. Adam and E. K. Rideal) trough techniques for examining surface films.

The kinetic theory in its original form accounts only for the kinetic pressure exerted by a gas, and ignores intermolecular cohesion. The second factor is necessary to explain the condensation of gases into liquids, a process much investigated experimentally by T. Andrews (1876) in his work on critical phenomena and theoretically by James Thomson (1871) and J. D. van der Waals (1871) in their theories of the continuity of states. The existence of cohesive forces between molecules is manifested by the cooling which under ordinary conditions results during the expansion of a gas. By developing the porous plug experiment of J. P. Joule and James Thomson, both James Dewar (1900) and M. Travers (1900) succeeded in liquefying hydrogen, which is one of the two gases that Michael Faraday failed to liquefy by other means. It is the liquefaction of gases, and of helium in particular, that has enabled all the recent work to be done on physical and chemical properties of matter at low temperatures.

The classical work of Sir J. J. Thomson on the conduction of electricity through gases follows the observation of Sir William Crookes (1881) that the viscosity of gases at low pressures is less than that predicted by the kinetic theory.

The fundamental ideas of the kinetic theory of gases have been extensively applied to systems other than the gaseous system. In particular, they have greatly influenced the development of the theories of solution, which stimulated the precise experimental work of E. G. J. Hartley and the earl of Berkeley, and led to van't Hoff's hypothesis of osmosis.

The kinetic theory in its primitive form affords expressions for the number of collisions taking place in unit time between gas molecules and unit area of a surface and between gas molecules themselves in unit volume. The former of these expressions was compared by J. W. Strutt (afterward Lord Rayleigh) with the rate of reduction of solid silver oxide by gaseous ozone (1912), and the latter was compared by M. Trautz (1916) and W. C. McC Lewis with the rate of decomposition of gaseous hydrogen iodide (1918) The collision hypothesis, supplemented by the fundamental conception of a random distribution of energy, has since dominated the field of chemical kinetics and surface catalysis.

Extensions of the kinetic theory of gases to cover the repulsive and attractive forces exerted between the molecules have been made by A. W. Chapman (1915) and by Sir John Lennard-Jones (1924). The theory has also been extended to the kinetics of solutions (1933).

To the experimental chemist, the kinetic theory has given a picture of how molecules behave, and has made it possible for him to construct in his imagination the types of molecular interactions which constitute chemical change. It has given him a lively and interesting method of approach to many of his problems, a method which is neither as formal as that of thermodynamics nor as difficult as that of statistical mechanics.

The Maxwell-Boltzmann Law.—Reference has already been made to the theorems of Maxwell and of Boltzmann on the distribution, respectively, of momenta and energies among gaseous molecules. Boltzmann proved that the fractional number of molecules retained in a system at constant volume and temperature which possess an energy, *E*, per molecule, is proportional to the term $e^{-E/kT}$, where *e* is the base of the natural logarithms, *T* the absolute temperature on the Kelvin scale, and *k* a constant which is independent of the system, and is a universal constant now bearing Boltzmann's name. As *E* increases, the Boltzmann factor $e^{-E/kT}$ decreases. Hence, the number of molecules which are energetically well-endowed is relatively small, while the number of molecules with lower energies is large. Energy among molecules is thus like money among men; the poor are numerous, the rich few. This law has proved to be one of the securest possessions of natural science, and has survived the storms of quantal mechanics which within recent years have overthrown so many of the stately edifices constructed in the placid days of classical mechanics. Salvador de Madariaga has held that the derivation of the Maxwell-Boltzmann law offers the best example of pure logical deduction evinced since the middle of the 19th century. With its derivation we cannot here be concerned, but some indication must be given of its far-reaching effects on the development of many physicochemical themes.

When a liquid is kept in a closed vessel, like wine in a bottle, the molecules in the closed system distribute themselves between the condensed and vaporous phases in such a way that (except at the critical temperature) the molecular concentration in the vapour is considerably less than that in the liquid. The explanation, according to the Maxwell-Boltzmann law, is that only those molecules of the liquid which possess an energy *L* can vaporize. *L* is the latent heat of vaporization, and is usually large; hence the number of liquid molecules which have sufficient energy to detach themselves from their neighbours in the condensed state is relatively small. To revert again to our anthropomorphic analogy, it is as if transit from the liquid to the vapour states requires the expenditure of much energy, as the transit from a slum in England to a hotel on the Riviera requires the expenditure of much money.

A very similar state of affairs prevails in the case of electrons in metals. It is known that the atmosphere above the surface of a cold metal is electrically neutral. At high temperatures, however, all metals emit a stream of electrons which constitutes the so-called "thermionic current" now so extensively utilized in the construction of electronic tubes. O. W. Richardson discovered that the logarithm of the current is proportional to the reciprocal of the absolute temperature. In other words, the current itself has a strength which is proportional to $e^{-W/kT}$, where *W* is positive. In terms of the Maxwell-Boltzmann law, *W* can be identified as the work which must be expended to remove an electron from inside the metal. It is known as the thermionic work term, and has been shown by Einstein to be equal to the quantum, $h\nu$, of light necessary at the threshold frequency to emit electrons in the photoelectric effect.

It is well known that high altitude aviators must carry their own supply of oxygen with them, because the concentration of this vital gas at great heights is too attenuated to support life. The distribution of concentration with height is again governed by the Maxwell-Boltzmann law. The concentration, n_1, at a height H_1, is proportional to $e^{-mgH_1/kT}$, where *m* is the mass of one molecule, and *g* the gravitational constant. At the same temperature, but at another height, H_2, the concentration, n_2, is proportional to $e^{-mgH_2/kT}$. The ratio of the concentrations at two heights differing by *H* is thus $n_1/n_2 = e^{mgH/kT}$. The earth's atmosphere is not the most suitable medium for testing this equation, because the molecules are invisible, and because of the overwhelming complications due to meteorological factors. Working with colloid particles suspended in water at a constant temperature, however, the numbers may be counted by visible means, and the difference in height measured microscopically. This Perrin did in his classical researches which both verified the law and afforded an experimental determination of the Boltzmann constant, *k*.

The Maxwell-Boltzmann law forms the basis of the modern theories of electrolytic solutions, first proposed by S. R. Milner in 1917 and improved by P. Debye six years later. The electrolyte is regarded as dissociated completely or partially into ions, in a medium of uniform dielectric capacity. The random distribution of ions in solution differs from the random distribution of molecules in a gas, because of the strong Coulombic forces exerted between them. On applying the Boltzmann law to a determination of the ionic concentration in the neighbourhood of any selected ion, we see at a glance that the selected ion will be surrounded by a relatively high concentration of ions of the opposite sign, and by a relatively low concentration of ions of the same sign as its own. This uneven distribution of electrical charges leads to the formation, around each ion, of a cloud of ions, carrying a net charge of opposite sign to its own. The total electrostatic energy of ionic solutions is thus diminished, and is less than the electrostatic energy of the same number of ions in an infinitely dilute solution. In extremely dilute solutions of electrolytes of low valency type, the Milner-Debye theory has been corroborated in various ways, for example, by measuring cryoscopically the activity coefficients of electrolytes, by determining the ionic mobility in electrical fields and by estimating the effect of dilution on the heat of dissolution. The assumption that the Maxwell-Boltzmann law applies to electrolytic solutions is one of its least debatable ones, and is certainly a less dubious one than that of the invariance of the dielectric capacity of the medium.

The intensity of a line in the Raman spectrum is proportional to the stationary concentration of excited molecules in that state, transition from which causes the emission. If I_b and I_r stand, respectively, for the intensities of the lines displaced toward the blue and red ends of the spectrum from the central position of the undisplaced line, then the following expression holds, according to the Boltzmann law for the ratio of the intensities: $R = I_b/I_r = e^{-E_q/kT}/e^{-E_p/kT}$. But, from our discussion of the Raman effect, we know that $E_p - E_q = 2h\nu_R$; hence $R = e^{2h\nu_R/kT}$. As the temperature rises, the ratio approaches unity. By plotting $\log_{10}R$ against $1/T$, this relation has been verified independently by P. Daure and by L. S. Ornstein and J. Rekveld. The gradient determined from experiment yields the value of 4.79×10^{-11} degree-seconds for h/k. Taking *k* as 1.372×10^{-16} erg per degree, *h* thus becomes 6.56×10^{-27} erg-second, satisfactorily confirming the more accurate estimates based on the photoelectric effect and the spectrum of atomic hydrogen.

Finally, it has been shown by J. J. Hood (1878) and by S. A. Arrhenius (1889) that the logarithm of the velocity coefficient of a chemical reaction is linearly related to the reciprocal of the absolute temperature. The velocity itself is thus proportional to $e^{-E/kT}$, where E is termed the energy of activation. This relationship is the foundation of chemical dynamics.

In these instances of the application of the Maxwell-Boltzmann law, care has been taken to emphasize the proportionality between, rather than the identity of, the fractional number of energized molecules and the factor $e^{-E/kT}$. The ratio of the number of active molecules to the total number is equal to the exponential term only when the energy concerned can be expressed as the sum of two quadratic terms. A generalized form of the law has been derived by A. Berthoud (1911).

Chemical Kinetics.—Instructions for the preparation of chemical compounds frequently contain such phrases as "heat substance A with substance B for two hours." The time element is important in the process; its inclusion aims at the most abundant yield of the desired commodity. This process of preparing chemical compounds is, of course, one of the principal activities of the chemist. Organic chemists often know, almost by divination, how long to allow the reactants to react in order to obtain the best yield. Physical chemists have two guides to help them. One is thermodynamics, which can, in principle, tell them how far any reaction can go, given all the relevant thermal data; the other is chemical kinetics, which can, in most cases, tell them how fast the reactions can go. Chemical kinetics, since its inception by Ludwig Wilhelmy in 1850, has proved to be one of the most popular branches of physical chemistry, and one which has shown the most consistent and continuous growth. It introduces time as an essential variable in chemical systems. The laws of chemical kinetics, rigidly formulated, all contain time as a factor, and reduce, when the time is extended to infinity, to the equilibrium laws of chemical thermodynamics. The formal side of chemical kinetics deals with the velocity of chemical change in all systems. In its development, however, a machinery has been created for handling a variety of problems outside its formal sphere, and for the solution of problems which have proved too difficult for chemical thermodynamics or statistical physics. Adsorption, discussed in the first section of this article, provides a good example. Other problems which have been successfully approached by the method of chemical kinetics are the standard electrode process, overpotential, the conduction of electricity through gases, vaporization, enzyme structure, dissolution, the persistence of clouds and the disorderliness of simple binary systems in the condensed phases.

Clearly one condition that must be fulfilled before molecules can react is that they should meet. If an encounter between two molecules is a sufficient condition for reaction, the rate of chemical change should be equal to the rate of collisions. Two physical changes have already been discussed from this point of view, and it has been shown that the rate at which colloid particles in the gas phase and in solution coagulate and the rate at which electronically excited molecules in both systems are deprived of their energy are equal to the rate at which the molecules meet. Binary collisions are thus a necessary but not always a sufficient condition for the occurrence of these physical changes. When, however, we examine the rate of chemical processes in the light of the collision hypothesis, we find a wide disparity. Experiment shows that only a very small fraction of the total number of collisions is fruitful. M. Trautz, in 1916, and W. C. McC. Lewis independently in 1918, argued that, since only molecules possessing exceptional energies can undergo chemical change, the rate of reaction should be compared, not with the total rate of collisions, but with the rate of activating collisions, which, according to the Maxwell-Boltzmann law, is less by the factor $e^{-E/RT}$, where E is the energy of activation. Experiment shows that the energies of activation for the decomposition of ozone into oxygen, of hydrogen iodide into hydrogen and iodine and of nitrous oxide into nitrogen and oxygen are, respectively, 26,365, 47,275 and 61,550 calories per gram-mole. The Boltzmann factors are thus extremely small. Nevertheless, when multiplied by the total collision rate, they yield products which are experimentally indistinguishable from the rates of chemical reaction. This conclusion forms the basis of the collision theory of chemical change.

An application of the same reasoning by J. A. Christiansen, in 1924 to reactions in solution met with less success, in that a considerable discrepancy appeared between the observed rates and those computed on the basis of the collision theory. It was, therefore, maintained for some years that the theory, though apparently applicable to gases, was not, without drastic modifications, applicable to solutions. In 1932, however, it was revealed that hundreds of reactions in solution, some of which had been examined with great accuracy during the 19th century, fitted in perfectly with the predictions of the collision theory. Thousands more have since been discovered, and there now remains no doubt that the theory of activating collisions, sometimes in revised forms, is fundamentally sound. Among these numerous reactions are to be found the etherifications of alkyl halides by organic bases such as sodium methoxide, potassium phenoxide and alkali β-naphthoxides, the replacements of halogen and hydroxyl from aliphatic compounds by anions in various solvents, the union of ethyl bromide with diethylsulphide in hydrolytic media, and the formation of the bicarbonate ion from carbon dioxide and the hydroxyl ion in aqueous solution.

Occasionally when two chemical compounds interact, only one of them suffers chemical change, while the other which is termed a catalyst, emerges from the reaction unchanged. These catalytic reactions are essentially bimolecular, and their rates, with few exceptions, are also in agreement with the prediction of the collision theory. The catalytic mutarotation of the reducing sugars by hydrogen ions, the catalytic decomposition of ethylene di-iodide by iodine atoms, the catalytic mutarotation of beryllium benzoylcamphor by cresol, the catalytic conversion of the picryl ethers of benzophenone oximes by acetone and nitromethane are all processes the rates of which are given by the expression: Number of molecules reacting in unit volume in one second = number of collisions between catalyst and reactant in unit volume in one second $\times e^{-E/RT}$.

If only those molecules which possess considerable energies in excess of the average can react, on what, one may ask, is this energy expended? The answer was first given by W. Heitler and F. London, in 1927. Chemical change involves, first the loosening, and finally the breaking of a chemical bond and usually the simultaneous formation of a new bond. To break a bond requires energy; and this, duly compensated by energy liberated in the formation of another bond, constitutes the energy of activation. Heitler and London showed how the energy of activation could be calculated from first principles for very simple chemical changes, such as the following reaction between an atom, A, and a diatomic molecule, BC; $A+B\text{-}C \rightarrow A\text{-}B+C$. The initial system corresponds to a free atom, A, at an infinite distance from the stable molecule, BC, the atoms in which are at their normal, or equilibrium, distance apart. This state of affairs we may describe by saying that r_{AB} is infinite, and $r_{BC}=r^{\circ}_{BC}$. The final state, after the completion of reaction, corresponds to a free atom, C, at an infinite distance from the stable molecule, AB. This state of affairs may be summarized by saying that $r_{AB}=r^{\circ}_{AB}$, and that r_{BC} is infinite. Between these stages, the internuclear distances, r_{AB} and r_{BC}, must have had comparable magnitudes, and this very nearly corresponds to the activated state, as D. S. Villars (1930) independently concluded. The difference between the energy of the complex $A \ldots B \ldots C$ in the activated state and the energy of the initial system is the energy of activation. The solution of the dynamic problem is somewhat tortuous, and demands an exact knowledge of the forces exerted between the various atoms. The results of calculations on the energy of activation of the reaction between the bromine atom and the hydrogen molecule ($Br+H\text{-}H \rightarrow Br\text{-}H+H$) are shown graphically in fig. 2. From the energy contours, which are given in kilocalories per gram-mole, it is seen that the easiest of an infinite number of passages from the initial atomic configuration (top left-hand corner) to the final atomic configuration (bottom right-hand corner) requires an ascent of 22,000 calories, and that the two internuclear distances at this pass height are equal to 1.43×10^{-8}cm. The former value is in agreement, though not directly comparable, with the experimental values obtained by Max Bodenstein and H. Luetkemeyer, and later by F. Bach, K. F. Bonhoeffer and E. A. Moelwyn-Hughes, using both ordinary hydrogen and its heavy isotope.

The first calculations of the energy of activation of triatomic reactions according to the Heitler-London method were made by Henry Eyring and Michael Polanyi, on the ortho-para conversion of hydrogen, which as Adalbert Farkas and Bonhoeffer had shown, proceeds by the same mechanism as that previously established for the hydrogen-bromine reaction. Attempts at computing the energies of activation of more complicated reactions have also been made.

If all chemical reactions conformed to the collision theory, we would find chemical changes to proceed with wide ranges of velocities, from the fast reactions which require little energy, to the slow reactions which require much, but the changes would, as a rule, be orderly, and would never get out of hand. It is well known that many chemical reactions run riot; they proceed with accelerative rates and lead to explosions. The explanation of the occurrence of thermal explosions and of numerous phenomena with which they are akin has been given, principally by Max Bodenstein, R. Willstaeter, Fritz Haber, J. A. Christiansen, H. A. Kramers and N. Semenoff, in terms of the chain theory of chemical change. The primary notion is one of "hot" molecules; *i.e.*, of chemically reactive molecules produced during the activation process, and capable of retaining their energy until an opportunity

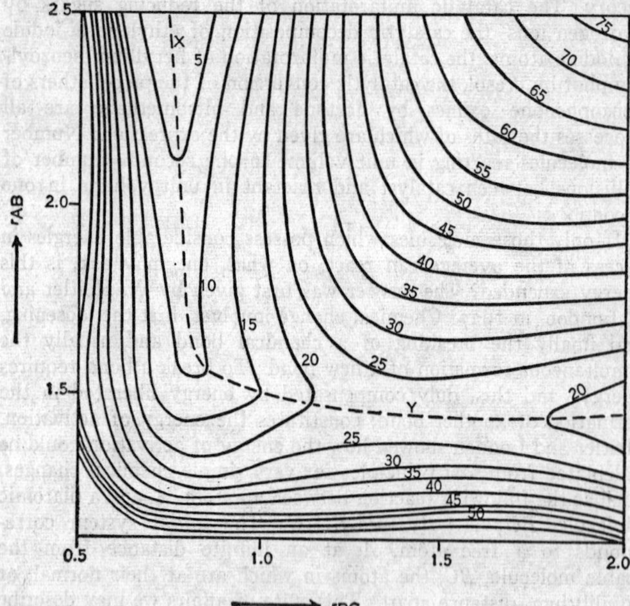

FIG. 2.—POTENTIAL ENERGY CURVES FOR THE SYSTEM Br..... H... H

affords of passing it on to fresh reactant molecules, which in turn become activated. One initial activation can thus lead to the conversion of many molecules. The average number so destroyed per unit activation is termed the chain length. This may amount to many thousands of molecules, not only in gases, but in solution, where deactivations by solvent molecules, though possibly not entirely absent, are by no means as probable as they were at one time thought to be. It can readily be shown that, if, in a system containing n molecules per c.c., the decomposition occurs by the mechanism under discussion, the rate of reaction becomes $-\frac{dn}{dt}=\frac{k_1 n^2}{(k_4/k_3)n+(1-\alpha)}$, where k_1 governs the rate of formation of active reactants by collisions between normal molecules, k_4 governs the rate of destruction of active reactants in deactivating collisions with normal molecules, and k_3 is the unimolecular constant for the spontaneous decomposition of active reactants. The important term, α, takes account of the fact that not all collisions between normal molecules and active products which lead to deactivation are effective in regenerating active molecules of reactants. In all thermal, or "quiet" reactions, α is zero. Chain reactions are characterized by real values of α. In simple cases, the chain length is simply the reciprocal of $(1-\alpha)$, which may be very large when α approaches unity. Branching chains are characterized by values of α exceeding unity, in which case the denominator in the general rate equation may become zero, and the rate itself may become infinite. This is what is generally meant by an explosion.

The chain theory has been employed to interpret numerous phenomena in the kinetics of chemical changes in gaseous and liquid systems. It can successfully account for the apparently unimolecular behaviour of molecules decomposing in systems of high concentration, though the rate of production of active molecules itself is a bimolecular process, and is therefore dependent on the square of the concentration, and for the distinction between the mechanism of hydrolytic and oxidative enzymic reactions.

The extensions of chemical kinetics resulting from the quantum theory are concerned with the more exact determination of the energy of activation, and with the possibility (precluded according to the classical theory) of the transit of a molecule over a potential barrier while not possessing sufficient energy to surmount it. The latter phenomenon is known as the tunnel effect, and is relevant only for light molecules penetrating barriers at low temperatures.

Intermolecular Energy.—When molecules come near enough to influence one another, at least two forces are brought into play: one of attraction, and one of repulsion. If molecules did not exert forces of attraction, they would not cohere, as they manifestly do in the liquid and crystalline state. Were there no forces of repulsion, the forces of attraction would be supreme, and nothing would prevent molecules from annihilating one another. Much as human conduct is determined by a conflict of loyalties, molecular behaviour is, to a large extent, determined by the balance struck between the forces which tend to pull molecules together and those which tend to push them apart. The detection of the kind of intermolecular force at work in particular systems has been an important new feature of the physical chemistry of the 20th century.

More is generally known about attractive than about repulsive forces. When, for example, two ions, of valencies z_A and z_B, are held at a distance, a, apart, there exists between them, *in vacuo*, an energy which C. A. Coulomb has shown experimentally to be inversely proportional to their separation. In fact, the energy is $u=z_A z_B\,\epsilon^2/a$, where ϵ is the electronic charge $(4.77\times10^{-10}$ electrostatic units). The force, X, is given by the general equation $X=\frac{du}{da}$, which, in the present example, becomes $z_A z_B\,\epsilon^2/a^2$. Thus, when both ions have charges of the same sign, their mutual energy and the force acting between them are positive, denoting repulsion. When the ions have charges of opposite signs, their mutual energy and the force acting between them are negative, indicating attraction. It is this Coulombic force which, as Ernest Rutherford and Niels Bohr first showed, accounts for the tenacity with which electrons in atoms are held to the positively charged nuclei. In crystalline salts, the units are positive and negative ions, such as the sodium and chlorine ions in common salt; and here also, the binding force is almost entirely due to the Coulombic attraction between the ions. It is thus easy to understand why the lattice energy (*i.e.*, the energy required to transform the crystalline salt into gaseous ions) is four times as great for a bi-bivalent salt as it is for a uni-univalent salt of the same molar volume. The Coulombic energy of a pair of ions separated by a medium of dielectric constant, D, is less than that *in vacuo* at the same separation by the ratio D:1. The dielectric constant of water at ordinary temperatures is about 80, hence the force attracting cations to anions in aqueous solution is relatively small, and can be effectively combated by the kinetic energy resulting from their motion.

The energy of interaction of an ion of charge $z_A\epsilon$ and a dipole of moment μ_B which is inclined at an angle of θ to the line joining their centres is given approximately by the equation $z_A\epsilon\mu_B\cos\theta/a^2$. The mutual energy may now be positive or negative even for a system containing the same ion, because $\cos\theta$ can be positive or negative. It is this term which explains the comparative stability of inorganic ions in solvents of high dielectric constant, such as water, alcohol and nitromethane. In solution, each ion attracts the solvent molecules, and forms a shell around itself, with each solvent molecule orientated in the position of minimum energy. The exact number of solvent molecules which forms the first sheath has not yet been established, although the co-ordination number of many ions in crystals of hydrated salts is known. When chemical reaction takes place between an ion and a polar molecule, the approach of the ion to the molecule is influenced by the position and magnitude of the dipolar groups which the latter contains. The interaction of the ion with all the dipoles constitutes an important component of the energy of activation, and thus modifies the velocity of reaction. In the light of these considerations, it is now, for the first time, becoming clear why the substitution of a given group in the benzene ring may hasten or retard chemical reaction, according to the position, relative to the point of attack, which it occupies.

When two dipoles interact, four angles, in addition to the distance apart of their centres, are required in order to express their mutual energy, which now varies inversely as the third power of the distance, as may easily be derived by applying Coulomb's law to the interaction due to each pole, or by carrying out experiments with bar magnets, which are the macroscopic and magnetic analogues of the microscopic and electric moments in molecules. The interaction of permanent dipoles probably explains most of the anomalous properties of binary liquid mixtures, such as that of acetone and chloroform.

The next force of physicochemical interest is that which comes into play when an ion approaches a nonpolar molecule. The field generated by the ion induces an electric moment in the molecule, and the net interaction energy that results is readily shown to be directly proportional to the square of the ionic charge and to the polarizability of the molecule, and inversely proportional to the fourth power of their distances apart. An example is afforded by the attraction of the highly polarizable iodine molecule for the iodide ion; iodine is very sparingly soluble in water, but readily soluble in aqueous iodides.

There are many forces which vary inversely as the seventh power of the intermolecular distance. The most important is the so-called "dispersion force," which London (1930) has shown to be related to the frequency of vibration of the electrons in the molecules. This is the force which accounts for the cohesion of nonpolar molecules in the condensed state. In the case of the inert elements, and of symmetrical molecules such as chlorine, carbon tetrachloride and benzene, the dispersion force is the only attractive one; it comes into play also even in polar cases, where it is often dominant. Deviations of the behaviour of real gases from that of ideal gases are in large measure caused by the presence of London forces.

As stated above, rather less is known of the repulsion forces. These may, it is thought, be exponentially related to the intermolecular distance, or they may vary inversely with respect to the distance raised to some power which must be higher than the power governing the attractive forces. If we provisionally adopt the latter supposition, the total interaction energy of a molecular pair, at a distance a apart, may be expressed as the sum of the repulsive and the attractive energies: $u = Aa^{-n} - Ba^{-m}$, where n is greater than m. This relationship was applied by Gustav Mie, in 1903, to a variety of chemical and physical problems. He showed how this equation, which represents the interaction energy of an isolated pair of molecules, can be extended to the evaluation of the interaction energy of a large number, mutually influencing one another, and derived, in terms of the constants, A,B, and the integers, m, n, illuminating expressions for the isotherms, the compressibilities and the expansivities of condensed systems. Mie's equation has, in later years, been applied by Max Born to the study of solids and by Lennard-Jones to the study of gases.

Other types of forces, which are only partially electrostatic in origin, are exerted between the atoms in a molecule, and give rise to the variety of chemical bonds. We have already seen that the average interatomic force between two atoms varies linearly with respect to their valencies. How the interatomic forces vary with the distance apart of the nuclei is a problem which is, as yet, only dimly understood. Progress is being made on empirical lines. There is, however, no obscurity about certain conditions which experiment imposes on the general nature of the force laws. It is certain, for example, that the force tending to restore the atoms to their equilibrium positions after they have been slightly displaced therefrom must increase in proportion to the displacement, and thus obey Robert Hooke's law. Only in terms of such an elastic force can the essential harmonicity of the interatomic vibrations, which is proved alike by infra-red and Raman spectroscopy, be understood. If, however, only elastic forces were at work, the more we drew the atoms apart, the stronger would be the forces of restitution, and the less would be the likelihood of bond cleavage. Experiment shows that, with increasing separation, the atoms come under the influence of a very weak force, which eventually vanishes as the interatomic distance reaches infinity. Finally, the interatomic forces must be consistent with the thermal and spectroscopic evidence on the energy of dissociation, as well as on the known values of the equilibrium separation and the fundamental vibration frequencies. These guides suffice to indicate the general way in which the force varies with the distance, and several empirical expressions embodying these essential features have been advanced. The most widely used is one given by Philip M. Morse, in 1929.

Rather special assumptions have to be made concerning the forces responsible for the properties of metals—their hardness, stability, lustre and high powers of conducting both heat and electricity. The essential features of the elementary model of metals is that the framework is provided by the nuclei, and that the whole of the volume of the metal is accessible to the valency electrons. High electrical conductivity is thus intelligible. The attractive energy is provided by the Coulomb forces between the cations and the mobile electrons, and the repulsive energy is provided by the kinetic energy of the electrons. The latter, according to the quantum theory, is much greater than one would expect on classical arguments, and has been evaluated by Enrico Fermi. The energy required to expel an electron from a metal, which can be measured photoelectrically or thermionically, thus equals in magnitude the difference between the Fermi and Coulomb energies. Such a simple model of metals, is, however, deficient in many ways. It cannot, for example, give an explanation of the elastic constants, such as the compressibility and the fundamental vibration frequency, which is consistent with the specific heat. Other forces must come into play in metallic cohesion, and research on their nature is being actively carried out by many investigators. A set of potential energy curves for the diatomic molecules of the alkali metals is shown in fig. 3, where the energy per pair of atoms is expressed as a function of the internuclear distance.

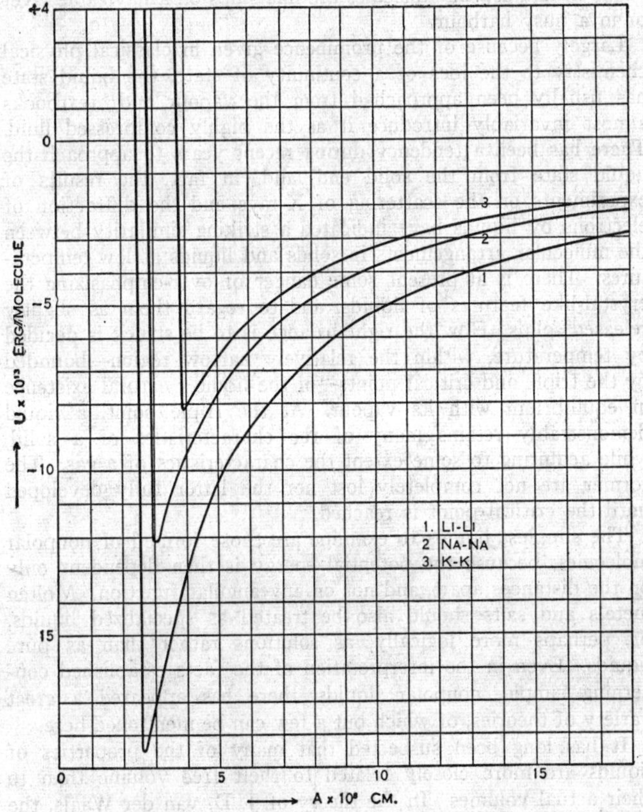

FIG. 3.—THE POTENTIAL ENERGIES OF PAIRS OF ALKALI METAL ATOMS

The Liquid State.—The liquid state has consistently been the most neglected of the various states of matter. Attention has been paid almost exclusively to the sister states called gaseous and crystalline. Classical kinetic theory has been progressively applied for 100 years to the study of the gaseous state, and the quantum theory has been vigorously used for nearly 50 years in the study of solids. It is only since the 1920s that either theory has been applied to liquids, except by a very small number of investigators, of whom Gustav Mie is the foremost. Two reasons may be advanced to explain the neglect. In the first place, the liquid state is the intermediate state of matter—that state which matter naturally assumes in passing from the solid to the vapour—and its properties are not so pronounced or sharp-edged as those of the extremes which flank it. In the second place, the classical theory appeared adequate to our knowledge of gases, and the quantum theory to our knowledge of solids. Neither suffices to explain what we know of liquids. The elucidation of their nature requires the full resources of both classical and quantal theories.

Solids are characterized by low potential energies, resulting from powerful cohesive forces, which tie the molecules together, usually in an orderly pattern, and prohibit motion, except an oscillation of small amplitude about the mean position of equilibrium. Gases are characterized by high potential energies, resulting from weak cohesive forces, which allow free motion and a completely random molecular distribution. A liquid, with its intermediate potential energies and moderate cohesive forces, has neither the orderliness of a crystal nor the randomness of a gas. Its molecules, though not constrained to vibrate about fixed positions in space, are, at the same time, not capable of unrestricted motion throughout the total volume.

The mean free path of a molecule in a crystal is less than, and of a molecule in a gas is greater than, the linear extension of the molecule. In a liquid, the mean free path is, under ordinary conditions, commensurate with the molecular dimensions. W. T. Kelvin once used a telling analogy of molecules with ships. In gases, the molecules are like ships on the high seas, which only seldom come within reach of one another; in solids, the molecules are like ships under construction in the dry docks of the building yard; in liquids, the molecules are like ships on a navigable river or in a busy harbour.

Largely because of the prominence given in classical physical chemistry to the idea of a continuity of state, the liquid state has usually been approached from the vapour end; textbooks almost invariably introduce it as the highly compressed fluid. There has been a tendency during recent years to approach the liquid state from the solid end, and, in fact, the results of experiments on the scattering of X-rays and the diffraction of electrons by liquids have indicated a striking similarity between the molecular arrangements in solids and liquids at low temperatures. There is at present some danger of over-emphasizing the crystal-like features of liquids, and to regard them as slightly released solids. How the right balance is to be struck is decided by temperature, within the relatively narrow region—bounded by the triple and critical points—of the liquid's natural existence in equilibrium with its vapour. At the triple point, a liquid demonstrably retains many of the characteristics of a solid, while acquiring to some extent the characteristics of a gas. The former are not completely lost nor the latter fully developed until the critical point is reached.

The simplest liquids to examine are those formed of nonpolar molecules, because the potential energy is then dependent only on the distances apart, and not on any angular function. Molten metals and salts should also be treated as specialized liquids, or, perhaps more logically, as solutions rather than as pure liquids. Even in the interpretation of the facts established concerning simple, nonpolar liquids, there has appeared a great variety of theories, of which but a few can be mentioned here.

It has long been suspected that many of the properties of liquids are more closely related to their free volume than to their actual volumes. In the theory of J. D. van der Waals, the free space in a gas consisting of noncompressible spheres is taken as the difference between the actual volume and a forbidden volume, the latter being identical with four times the sum of the volumes of the incompressible spheres. Coupled with a not unreasonable postulate concerning the attractive forces, this idea leads to the conclusion that the free space per molecule at the critical point is two-thirds of the critical molecular volume. An alternative assumption concerning the interaction energy led C. Dieterici to identify the forbidden volume with one-half the critical volume. Although neither conclusion can now be sustained, they both bring home the essential truth that the free volume in liquids increases as the temperature is raised. G. Jaeger's important extension of the free space theory is to allow for the possibility that the free space is a function, not only of the total volume and the total number of molecules, but of the temperature also. The extended theory is more consistent with the isotherms of the vapours and the internal pressures of the liquids. Although it is not always easy to evaluate the free volume in liquids, there is no difficulty in obtaining, at any temperature, the ratio of the free volume in the saturated vapour phase to the free volume in the liquid. Dieterici (1898) showed by the method of chemical kinetics and W. C. McC. Lewis (1912) by the method of thermodynamics that this ratio is simply the inverse of the Boltzmann factor, with the internal heat of vaporization as the energy term. At relatively low temperatures, the saturated vapour has a volume which is virtually identical with the free volume; under these conditions, the absolute free volume per molecule of liquid and the vapour pressure of the liquid in terms of its volume are readily obtained. The molecular free volume of water at 25° C., for example, is found to be 7.27×10^{-26}c.c.

In these early forms of the free space theory of liquids, the total free volume is assumed to be evenly distributed throughout the liquid, each molecule claiming, as it were, its own *Lebensraum*. The randomness of molecular distribution and energies envisaged in the kinetic theory suggests that the free space may be unevenly distributed. There can be, in other words, more free space in one region than in another. This argument leads naturally to the conception of holes in the liquid. Many versions of the theory of holes have been advanced during the 20th century (*e.g.*, by H. Eyring and by M. Fuerth). It is an attractive theory, capable of explaining phenomena not readily understood by other means, and one that is developing harmoniously with the theories of the solid state. The expansion of volume which most liquids enjoy on fusion can be attributed to the creation of holes; diffusion in liquids becomes readily intelligible; viscosity can be treated, not as the passage of molecules in the direction of viscous flow, but as the movement of holes in the opposite direction; liquids may be regarded as solutions of holes in matter, and vapours as solutions of matter in free space; the diminution of liquid density with an increase in temperature may be attributed to the increase in solubility of holes.

The cluster theory of fluids, developed by M. Reinganum in 1901, was revived in 1923 by Sir C. Venkata Raman, who applied it to the problem of the temperature dependence of the viscosity of liquids. The governing notion is one of localized molecular order, not extending to great distances. The representative molecule in a liquid is regarded as capable in maintaining order among the small number of members forming the family circle, while lacking control of those placed farther afield. Molecules in the orderly groups form clusters exothermally, and therefore in concentrations which diminish as the temperature is raised. The transport of momentum through the liquid is due not solely to the translation of molecules, but partly to the transmission of elastic waves through the groups of relatively stationary molecules. The cluster theory thus explains why the viscosity decreases somewhat rapidly with a rise in temperature. Direct experimental evidence for localized molecular order in certain liquids has been afforded by experiments on the scattering of X-rays, which afford a novel and fascinating method for tackling the long-neglected problem of the physical chemistry of liquids.

For other important physicochemical topics *see* related articles which will be found under their respective titles: LIQUID STATE, THE; SURFACE TENSION; SOLUTIONS; THERMOCHEMISTRY; ELECTROCHEMISTRY; RAMAN EFFECT; BAND SPECTRUM; REACTION KINETICS; ISOTOPES; RADIOACTIVITY, NATURAL; REFRACTION; VALENCE; HEAT; LIQUEFACTION OF GASES; VISCOSITY; PARACHOR; DISTILLATION; ADSORPTION; CATALYSIS; PHOTOCHEMISTRY; COLLOIDS.

BIBLIOGRAPHY.—W. C. McC. Lewis, *A System of Physical Chemistry*,

4th ed. (London, 1925); K. Jellinek, *Lehrbuch der physikalischen Chemie*, 2 Aufl. (Stuttgart, 1928–37); A. Eucken, *Grundriss der physikalischen Chemie*, 4 Aufl. (Leipzig, 1934); S. Glasstone, *Textbook of Physical Chemistry*, 2nd ed. (1947); E. A. Moelwyn-Hughes, *Physical Chemistry*, 2nd. ed. (Cambridge, 1947); J. Farringdon Daniels, *Outlines of Physical Chemistry* (1948). (E. A. M.-H.)

ANALYTICAL CHEMISTRY

Analytical chemistry has for its purpose the determination of the constituents of which a substance or mixture is composed by methods which are qualitative when the identity only is ascertained, or quantitative when the quantity or proportion is determined. If the constituent chemical elements only are determined the process is called an ultimate analysis; such analyses are often applied to organic compounds. In the analysis of inorganic substances additional information is usually obtained in regard to the state of association and oxidation of the elements. This is true because a large proportion of the methods for the analysis of inorganic substances involve treating an aqueous solution of the substance to be analyzed with known chemicals, termed reagents, which cause specific chemical changes or reactions. The chemical reactions of such substances in aqueous solutions are mainly those of electrically charged particles or ions, which they yield, and the nature of the ions may vary with the state of association and oxidation of the elements in their various compounds.

Analyses which are carried out in solutions are often called wet methods in order to distinguish them from dry methods whereby the material is examined in the dry state. The latter methods may involve observation of the effect of heat alone upon the substance, or treatment of the substance with a solid reagent at a temperature sufficient to cause fusion and the formation of characteristic compounds; or other physical phenomena, such as the spectrum obtained at high temperatures, may be observed.

The methods of quantitative analysis can be classified as follows: (1) Gravimetric, in which the constituent to be determined is weighed after being separated, usually by precipitation from an aqueous solution, in the elementary state or as some compound of definite composition. Such methods are called electrolytic when the precipitate is deposited on an electrode by passage of an electric current through the solution. (2) Volumetric, in which the volume of a reagent solution of known concentration required to cause a definite reaction is measured. In gas analysis the constituent is converted into a gas and the volume of the gas measured. (3) Instrumental, in which some physical property associated with the constituent to be determined is measured by means of an appropriate instrument. Some of these properties and the instruments used in measuring them are: colour, colorimeter; density, pycnometer; turbidity, nephelometer; spectrum, spectrograph; refractive index, refractometer.

Analytical methods are also classified as macro when the weight of the substance taken for the analysis is of the order of grams, as micro with milligram quantities and as ultramicro with microgram quantities.

INORGANIC ANALYSIS

Analytical chemistry, upon which all other branches of the science are ultimately dependent, has its source in the writings of the chemist-pharmacists of the iatrochemical period (1500–1700). Andreas Libavius and Otto Tachenius recognized many metals in solution together by their reactions in the wet way, but it was not until shortly before the phlogistic period (1700–1780) that any systematic progress was made, particularly by Robert Boyle, to whom we owe the term analysis. Many of the reactions still utilized in qualitative work were known to Boyle, who also introduced certain plant extracts, notably litmus, for the recognition of acids and bases. Active workers of the phlogistic period were Friedrich Hoffmann, Andreas Marggraf (who introduced the use of the microscope into chemistry), Karl Scheele and especially Torbern Bergman, who devised methods by which the metals might be separated into groups according to their behaviour with certain reagents. The blowpipe was introduced into dry qualitative analysis by the mineralogist, A. F. Cronstedt, who applied it to the examination of ores, although it was left to Jöns Berzelius and Johann Hausmann to bring about its general application. The colorations which sodium and potassium salts impart to the flame were known to Marggraf, but it is to Robert Bunsen, who, with Gustav Kirchhoff, devised spectrum analysis, that the full value of the flame test is due.

Although the work of the phlogistic period in this field was mainly of a qualitative character, some attempts of a quantitative nature were made by Marggraf and Joseph Black, while Bergman realized that elements need not be separated as such but might be isolated in the form of some suitable insoluble compounds. Martin Klaproth, who with Louis Vauquelin developed the quantitative analysis of minerals, proposed the ignition of precipitates before weighing them, if they were not decomposed thereby. Antoine Lavoisier, with his grasp of the importance of the composition by weight of chemical compounds, and because of his systematic use of the balance, must be considered as the first great exponent of quantitative analysis. The substantiation by Jeremias Richter, and independently by Joseph Proust, of the law of constant proportions and the formulation of the atomic theory by John Dalton combined to give a fresh impetus to the development of quantitative analysis, subsequently placed on a firm basis by Berzelius. The later researches of Heinrich Rose, Friedrich Wöhler and Karl Fresenius standardized various methods of analytical chemistry.

The quantitative precipitation of metals by the electric current, although known to Michael Faraday, was not applied to analytical chemistry until O. Wolcott Gibbs, in 1865, worked out the electrolytic separation of copper. Since then the subject has been extensively studied, particularly by Alexander Classen.

Volumetric analysis, possessing as it does many advantages over the gravimetric method, especially in technical work, was founded by J. L. Gay-Lussac, although rough application had been previously made; the advantages of his carefully worked out methods of chlorimetry (1824), of alkalimetry (1828) and of the chloride-silver titration (1832) were but slowly recognized. It was not until the application of potassium permanganate to the estimation of iron by F. Margueritte (1846) and of iodine and sulphurous acid to the estimation of copper and many other substances by Bunsen, that volumetric methods began to receive proper recognition. Significant contributions were made during the latter half of the 19th century, especially by K. F. Mohr and Jakob Volhard, and the subsequent development and application of these methods have been so extensive that for many purposes, particularly the control of industrial processes, gravimetric methods have been largely replaced.

Since the early part of the 20th century, there has been a rapid increase in the use of instrumental methods of analysis. Electrometric methods, especially potentiometric, have found general use as an aid to volumetric analysis. Polarographic methods involve the detection and estimation of substances by measurement of the potential and current required for partial electrolysis of the solution; usually one electrode consists of mercury dropping from a glass capillary. Coulometric methods involve a measurement of the quantity of electricity required to cause a specific reaction. Instruments based upon the use of the glass electrode in conjunction with vacuum tube amplification have largely replaced other methods for determining the effective acid concentration of solutions. Photo-electric colorimeters are used to measure the concentrations in solutions of those substances which are coloured, or which can be converted into compounds which are coloured; spectrophotometers are used to extend these measurements into the ultraviolet and infra red regions of the spectrum. The spectrograph and spectrographic methods, which depend upon the measurement of the light emitted by an element in a flame, arc or spark, have extensively replaced the use of conventional methods of qualitative analysis and are especially useful for the quantitative determination of the minor constitutents of substances.

The technique of quantitative microanalysis has been developed mainly by Fritz Pregl, although F. Emich had previously indicated the possibility of working with small amounts of inorganic materials. The same basic principles and methods hold as for macroanalysis, but apparatus and manipulation are necessarily modified when quantities of the order of a few milligrams only are being handled. During World War II these methods were extended to microgram quantities as the result of investigations on radioactive isotopes produced in extremely small quantities in connection with atomic fission research. (*See* ULTRAMICROCHEMISTRY.)

Qualitative Inorganic Analysis.—The complete qualitative analysis of a substance in the wet way is usually preceded by certain preliminary tests made by dry methods. The results of these tests may be useful in conducting and interpreting the subsequent analysis.

Dry Methods.—1. Effect of heat: The substance when heated in a hard glass tube may char or become tarry or smoke, indicating the presence of organic matter. Since many organic compounds interfere with the analysis in the wet way, organic matter should be eliminated by a preliminary treatment with nitric acid added to sulphuric or perchloric acid.

A test for organic matter can be made in a wet way by heating the substance with concentrated sulphuric acid and noting if charring occurs.

If the substance contains water an aqueous deposit will form on the cooler part of the tube. A white sublimate is given by ammonium halide salts, mercurous chloride and bromide, oxides of arsenic; a yellow sublimate may consist of sulphur (reddish brown when molten), arsenic sulphide and mercuric iodide (turning red on rubbing). A blackish deposit results from the condensation of violet iodine vapour or of mercuric sulphide, while most mercury compounds other than those mentioned give a gray deposit.

Metallic mercury and arsenic appear as minute globules and a gray mirror.

Oxygen results from the decomposition of peroxides, chlorates, nitrates, iodates and similar oxygenated compounds, and also from oxides of the noble metals; carbon dioxide from carbonates and organic substances, usually accompanied in the latter case by charring; sulphur dioxide from many sulphides and thiosulphates. Chlorine, bromine and iodine are evolved from certain halide salts, particularly in the presence of oxidizing agents, and oxides of nitrogen from nitrates. Some cyanides evolve cyanogen or hydrocyanic acid and possibly ammonia in the presence of water. All fluosilicates (silicofluorides) are decomposed on heating, evolving silicon tetrafluoride.

2. Flame tests: When volatilized in a nonluminous flame, the compounds of certain elements cause characteristic colours. Therefore this test is carried out by introducing into the flame by means of a platinum wire a portion of the substance, preferably moistened with hydrochloric acid since the chlorides are comparatively volatile salts. Sodium gives an intense yellow coloration; potassium, violet; rubidium and caesium, bluish-violet (the latter blue when really pure); calcium, red; strontium and lithium, crimson; barium, yellowish-green; and copper, bright green; while lead, arsenic and antimony (which should not be tested on platinum) give a grayish-blue. By observing the flame through a spectroscope much more definite information can be obtained. Of the rarer metals which give flame colours, indium (blue), thallium (green), caesium and rubidium (violet) were discovered by means of the spectroscope.

3. Spectrographic analysis: The development of spectrographic equipment and methods has greatly reduced the necessity for making complete qualitative analyses in the wet way, since it is possible in many cases for a trained analyst to obtain more quickly and easily by an emission spectra analysis much of the information given by a wet analysis.

4. Blowpipe and bead tests: The substance is placed in a depression on a charcoal block and heated in the reducing flame of a blowpipe. From the changes which occur and the residue which remains, information may be obtained as to the general nature of the material. Specific information as to certain elements may be obtained by treating the residue with certain reagents such as cobalt nitrate or sodium carbonate and again heating. The colourless beads obtained by fusing borax (sodium tetraborate) or microcosmic salt (sodium ammonium monohydrogen phosphate) on a small loop of platinum wire are capable of dissolving many metallic oxides or salts, often with the production of characteristic colours; the colour may differ according as the bead is heated in an oxidizing or reducing flame. These tests are of uncertain value when applied to complex mixtures and have been largely replaced for practical use by spectrographic methods or in some cases by wet tests employing organic reagents for the identification of specific elements by the formation of coloured precipitates or soluble compounds.

Wet Methods.—1. Specific tests: A large number of so-called spot tests for individual cations and anions have been developed, especially by Fritz Feigl. The material to be tested is dissolved, a drop of the solution placed in an indentation on a white tile (spot plate), a drop of reagent solution added and the mixture examined for a characteristic precipitate or coloration; as a modification the solution to be tested may be applied to a strip of paper impregnated with reagent, or drawn into a capillary tube containing reagent. The reagent frequently contains an organic compound capable of forming intensely coloured compounds with certain elements or radicals. When applied to complex mixtures the value of these tests is limited by the fact that several constituents may give similar reactions, and that other constituents may mask or cause failure of the test.

2. Systematic analyses: Systems for the complete qualitative analysis of a material in the wet way are based upon the principle of treating a solution of the material with a succession of reagents, each reagent causing the separation of a group of constituents. The groups are then treated successively with reagents which may divide a large group into subgroups or cause the separation of the constituents singly. After being separated, a constituent may be further treated to confirm its presence or to obtain information as to the amount present. Separate portions of the material are dissolved and different procedures are used for detecting the basic (metallic or cation) and acidic (anion) constituents.

Different procedures will also be used for dissolving the material and for the subsequent analysis according to whether the material is to be analyzed for only the common basic elements or for the rarer elements as well. The solution for the analysis of the common basic constituents is prepared by first treating the material successively with water, dilute nitric or hydrochloric acids, or a mixture of these concentrated acids. Any residue is usually treated separately with hydrofluoric acid in conjunction with fuming perchloric or sulphuric acid in order to eliminate silica. A refractory residue is then fused with sodium carbonate, with or without the addition of potassium nitrate.

The fusion mass is treated with water, whereby the acidic constituents are extracted; the carbonate-oxide residue is dissolved in an acid.

Separation of the Common Basic Constituents into Groups.—Most of the various systems which have been developed employ essentially the same reagents for the major group separations; minor modifications exist in some cases where the system is designed for a semimicro scale of operation or for elementary instruction.

The first group, called the silver group, is separated by the addition of a soluble chloride, preferably ammonium chloride. The precipitate consists of silver chloride, mercurous chloride and lead chloride. The precipitation of the lead is incomplete and in some systems is prevented by proper control of conditions. The next group, called the hydrogen sulphide group, is composed of those elements whose sulphides are precipitated by hydrogen sulphide from a solution in which the hydrogen and chloride ion concentrations are approximately 0.3 molal. This precipitate contains the sulphides of copper, lead, bismuth, cadmium, mercury, arsenic, antimony and tin. If not previously precipitated by chloride, silver and mercurous mercury would become constituents of this group. This large group is subdivided by treatment with an alkaline sulphide: if a reagent composed of ammonium sulphide and polysulphide and ammonium hydroxide is used, arsenic, antimony and tin are dissolved and constitute the tin group; if the reagent contains sodium sulphide and hydroxide, mercury is also dissolved. The elements in the residue constitute the copper group.

By neutralizing the acid filtrate from the hydrogen sulphide group with an excess of ammonium hydroxide and adding ammonium sulphide, the ammonium sulphide group is obtained, consisting of hydroxides of chromium and aluminum, and sulphides of iron, manganese, nickel, cobalt and zinc. If phosphate is present barium, strontium, calcium or magnesium may be partly precipitated; in this case the subsequent analysis of this group is modified to separate these elements. Various methods are used for the separation of this group into subgroups. If the system is to be used primarily for elementary instruction, the precipitate may be dissolved in a mixture of nitric and hydrochloric acids, and a slight excess of ammonia added, causing the precipitation of aluminum, chromium and iron (ferric) as hydroxides. In fact, in some cases this ammonia precipitation is made and these elements separated prior to the precipitation with ammonium sulphide. More commonly the ammonium sulphide group precipitate is dissolved in acid, the resulting solution treated with an excess of sodium hydroxide together with sodium peroxide. Ferric, nickelous, cobaltic hydroxides and manganese dioxide are precipitated and constitute the iron group; the solution contains aluminate, chromate and zincate and these elements constitute the aluminum group. Two alternative procedures are in general use for the separation of what is termed the alkaline earth group. In the first of these the filtrate from the ammonium sulphide group is evaporated until it is quite concentrated in ammonium salts, then ammonium carbonate is added thus precipitating barium, strontium and calcium carbonates. Or the filtrate is evaporated to a small volume, preferably to dryness, and the ammonium salts volatilized, then a reagent of concentrated ammonia and ammonium carbonate is added, followed by ethyl alcohol; under these conditions magnesium is also precipitated. The only elements remaining in the filtrate are sodium and potassium and they constitute the alkali group. Ammonium may be considered as a constituent of this latter group but a separate sample must be used for its detection since it has been introduced in the course of the analysis.

When the analysis is made on a macro scale, the precipitates obtained are usually separated by filtration; centrifugation is more extensively used if the analysis is made on a semimicro scale.

Analysis of the Groups.—Innumerable procedures have been suggested for the separation and identification of the individual elements. The methods given below are those which have been extensively used and are representative of the general principles involved.

The Silver Group.—The group precipitate is leached with hot water to remove the lead chloride; upon addition of acetic acid and a soluble chromate to the solution the formation of yellow lead chromate identifies lead. The residue is leached with ammonia.

Mercurous chloride is converted into a black residue of mercury and mercuric amidochloride; silver chloride dissolves and is reprecipitated by acidifying the ammonia solution.

The Copper Group.—The sulphide precipitate is dissolved in nitric acid (if mercuric sulphide is present it remains as a residue), sulphuric acid is added, the solution evaporated to fuming, then diluted; this precipitates lead sulphate. The precipitate is dissolved in ammonium acetate and yellow lead chromate precipitated by addition of a soluble chromate. Addition to the sulphuric acid filtrate of an excess of ammonia precipitates white bismuth hydroxide; treatment of the precipitate with an alkaline sodium stannite solution reduces the bismuth to the black metal. If copper is present the ammoniacal filtrate is blue because of the formation of the cupric tetrammine complex; in this case cyanide is added to form the colourless cuprous tricyano complex and the solution is treated with hydrogen sulphide to precipitate yellow cadmium sulphide.

The Tin Group.—The alkaline sulphide solution is acidified thus reprecipitating the sulphides. Upon treating this precipitate with potassium hydroxide and peroxide only mercuric sulphide is left as a residue. The residue is dissolved in hydrochloric acid to which sodium chlorate is added, then addition of excess of stannous chloride precipitates white mercurous chloride which becomes gray upon further reduction to mercury. Arsenic, antimony and tin are again precipitated as sulphides and the precipitate treated with hot concentrated hydrochloric acid which leaves only the arsenic sulphide. This is dissolved by means of sodium hydroxide and peroxide and the arsenic reprecipitated as magnesium ammonium arsenate. The concentrated hydrochloric acid solution is diluted sixfold, oxalic acid is added, and the reddish-orange antimony sulphide precipitated by means of hydrogen sulphide. The oxalic and hydrochloric acids are removed from the filtrate by adding sulphuric acid and evaporating to fuming; upon diluting the solution and treating it with hydrogen sulphide yellow tin sulphide is precipitated.

The Iron Group.—The sodium hydroxide-peroxide precipitate is dissolved in nitric acid and sodium chlorate added to the hot solution; brown to black manganese dioxide is precipitated. Addition of excess ammonia to the filtrate precipitates brown ferric hydroxide. The filtrate is made slightly acid with acetic acid and potassium nitrite added; cobalt is precipitated as the yellow potassium cobaltinitrite. Upon addition of dimethylglyoxime to the filtrate precipitation of the brilliantly red voluminous nickel dimethylglyoxime results.

The Aluminum Group.—The sodium hydroxide peroxide solution is acidified, then made just alkaline with ammonia thus precipitating aluminum hydroxide. Addition of sodium carbonate and boiling the solution until the ammonia is expelled precipitates the zinc as a basic zinc carbonate. The precipitate is dissolved in hydrochloric acid, the solution made alkaline with ammonia and ammonium sulphide added; white zinc sulphide is precipitated. The sodium carbonate solution is made acid with acetic acid and lead acetate added to precipitate yellow lead chromate.

The Alkaline Earth Group.—The precipitate produced by ammonium carbonate is dissolved in acetic acid, then potassium chromate added; yellow barium chromate precipitates. By neutralizing the solution and adding alcohol, yellow strontium chromate is precipitated. Addition of ammonium oxalate to the filtrate precipitates white calcium oxalate. Magnesium, when present in this group, is precipitated as magnesium ammonium phosphate.

The Alkali Group.—The filtrate from the ammonium sulphide precipitation is evaporated to dryness, then heated until ammonium salts are volatilized; otherwise, they would interfere with the test for potassium. The residue is dissolved in water and the solution divided into two portions. To one is added sodium cobaltinitrite which causes a yellow precipitate of potassium sodium cobaltinitrite; to the other is added a magnesium uranyl acetate reagent which causes a pale yellowish precipitate of sodium magnesium uranyl acetate. A separate portion of the original material to be analyzed is tested for ammonium by heating it with sodium hydroxide; ammonia is evolved and may be detected by its odour, or by its alkaline effect on litmus paper.

Systematic Qualitative Analysis for Common and Rare Elements.—The only system including the rare elements was developed by Arthur A. Noyes and William Crowell Bray (1927). This system is characterized by the separation of groups during the preparation of the solution of the material and by the use of separations depending upon the volability or extractability by immiscible solvents of the compounds of certain elements. The complete analysis is too extended to be given and only the principal groups separation are outlined below.

The Selenium Group.—The material is distilled with concentrated hydrobromic acid whereby selenium, arsenic and germanium are volatilized as the bromides.

Silicon, Osmium and Ruthenium.—Any solid residue is treated with hydrofluoric acid to eliminate silica as the volatile silicon tetrafluoride; the solution is then distilled with perchloric acid whereby osmium tetroxide is volatilized; by addition of concentrated nitric acid to the perchloric acid and repetition of the distillation ruthenium tetroxide is volatilized.

The Tungsten, Tantalum and Gold Groups.—The residual solution from the ruthenium distillation is diluted, formic acid added and the mixture heated. The resulting precipitate contains the oxides of tungsten, molybdenum, antimony and tin, the tungsten group; the oxides of tantalum, columbium and titanium (in part), the tantalum group; also metallic gold, mercury, platinum and palladium, the gold group. The tungsten and tantalum group elements are dissolved by treating the residue with hydrofluoric acid; the solution is fumed with sulphuric acid to eliminate the hydrofluoric acid, then an excess of ammonia and ammonium sulphide added. By this treatment the tantalum group elements are reprecipitated as oxides, the tungsten group elements are dissolved as sulpho-anions.

The Thallium Group.—Hydrobromic acid is added to the formic acid filtrate thus precipitating the bromides of silver, thallium (us) and lead (incompletely).

The Hydrogen Sulphide Group.—The hydrogen-ion concentration is adjusted to three-tenths molal and the solution is treated with hydrogen sulphide; this precipitates the sulphides of tellurium, molybdenum, iridium and rhodium (the tellurium group); and lead, bismuth, copper and cadmium (the copper group). The tellurium and molybdenum are removed separately, then the copper group elements precipitated as hydroxides.

The Ammonium Sulphide Group.—Small portions of the filtrate from the hydrogen sulphide group precipitation are tested for iron and phosphate. Additional iron is added to the main filtrate and a basic acetate precipitation made by adding ammonium acetate and boiling the solution. This process causes the precipitation of chromium, aluminum, indium, zirconium, titanium, gallium and vanadium together with the iron as hydrous oxides, basic acetates, phosphates or vanadates; the precipitation of gallium and vanadium is complete only when iron is present.

The precipitate is dissolved in hydrochloric acid and the iron and gallium extracted with ether. The hydrochloric acid solution is made alkaline and excess sodium peroxide added; indium, zirconium and thorium hydroxides are precipitated and these elements constitute the zirconium group.

The filtrate from the basic acetate precipitation is made alkaline with ammonia and then ammonium sulphide added. Beryllium and the rare earth elements are precipitated as hydroxides; manganese, zinc, cobalt, nickel and uranium as sulphides. The precipitate is dissolved in acid and excess sodium hydroxide and peroxide added; manganese, cobalt and nickel (the nickel group), and the rare earth elements (the rare earth group) are precipitated as oxides or hydroxides. The two sodium hydroxide filtrates are united.

The elements present are aluminum, chromium, vanadium, beryllium and zinc (the aluminum group).

The Alkaline Earth Group.—This group is precipitated and separated as in the system of analysis for the common elements (*see* above).

The Alkali Group.—The final filtrate is analyzed for lithium, rubidium and caesium in addition to sodium and potassium.

No provision is made in the system for the radioactive elements (other than uranium and thorium), rhenium, the inert gases, nor for any elements with atomic numbers greater than 92.

The Acidic Constituents.—The analysis for the acidic constituent (the acid radicals or anions) presents a more difficult problem and is of necessity less systematic than is that for the basic constituents. This is so because not only is it necessary to detect certain acidic elements, but also to establish their oxidation state and association with oxygen or other elements. For example, if sulphur is present the analysis should not only detect it, but should determine whether it is present in the material being analyzed as elementary sulphur, sulphide, sulphite, sulphate, the numerous other sulphur oxygen acids, or in combination with other elements as in thiocyanate. In addition, many of the anions are stable only in alkaline solutions or may react one with another upon acidification. Because of these facts appropriate tests are made in order to determine if certain groups of anions are present or absent.

The preliminary tests include those for anions which (1) act as (*a*) oxidizing agents, or (*b*) reducing agents; (2) form precipitates with silver ion in (*a*) neutral, or (*b*) acid solutions; (3) form precipitates with barium ion in (*a*) neutral, or (*b*) acid solutions, and (4) form precipitates with calcium ion in ammoniacal solutions.

The solution for the analysis for the anions is usually prepared by a treatment of the material with sodium carbonate solution. This reagent has the advantage that it removes most of the metals as carbonates or oxides; otherwise they would interfere with the subsequent analysis. In the systematic analysis a portion of the sodium carbonate solution is acidified with acetic acid; sulphide and cyanide are then volatilized as hydrogen sulphide and hydrogen cyanide and are collected in an alkaline solution. Addition of perchloric acid causes the volatilization of sulphite as sulphur dioxide. Addition of cadmium nitrate causes precipitation of cadmium ferrocyanide and ferricyanide. Addition of silver nitrate to the filtrate precipitates silver iodate, iodide, thiocyanate, bromide and chloride; the iodate is separated and the last four anions constitute the halide group. In case oxidizing agents were detected by the preliminary test, sodium nitrite is added to the filtrate; this causes the reduction of chlorate and bromate to chloride and bromide and their precipitation as the silver halides. Any iodate previously precipitated is reduced and precipitated as silver iodide. The filtrate is neutralized, then made just acid with acetic acid; silver phosphate, arsenate, arsenite and oxalate are precipitated (the phosphate group). From the filtrate, sulphate is precipitated as barium sulphate, then oxalate as calcium oxalate.

Tests are made on separate portions of the sodium carbonate solution for acetate, perchlorate, nitrate, nitrite, borate, peroxysulphate and periodate. The sodium carbonate treatment of the material may leave certain acidic constituents in the residue as insoluble compounds, therefore, this residue is decomposed with zinc and sulphuric acid and additional tests made for sulphide, cyanide, phosphate, arsenate, borate and the halides. A separate portion of the material is tested for carbonate.

BIBLIOGRAPHY.—Fritz Feigl, *Qualitative Analysis by Spot Tests*, Eng. trans. by Janet W. Matthews (1937); Arthur A. Noyes and W. C. Bray, *System of Qualitative Analysis for the Rare Elements* (1927). (E. H. St.)

QUANTITATIVE INORGANIC ANALYSIS

The branch of chemistry which deals with the determination of the amount or percentage of one or more constituents of a sample is known as quantitative analysis. This field is important because of its widespread use both in research and in industrial processes; whenever chemicals are used quantitative analyses are needed. Consequently every chemist is trained in analytical methods and in their applications and limitations.

A variety of methods is utilized for quantitative analyses; in fact, almost every property of matter can be made the basis for some analytical process. For convenience these methods may be broadly classified as chemical and physical, depending upon what properties are utilized. Chemical methods are those which depend upon reactions such as precipitation, neutralization, oxidation or, in general, the formation of a new compound. Physical methods are those which involve the measurement of some physical property such as density, refractive index, absorption or polarization of light, electromotive force, production of spectra, magnetic susceptibility and numerous others. Frequently an analysis will involve a combination of chemical and physical methods, the former for separating desired constituents from a sample and the latter for measuring the amounts present.

The Analytical Balance.—The basic tool in all quantitative analyses is the analytical balance, for the accurate weighing of samples and precipitates. The balance operates on the principle of levers, the weight of an object being determined by the sum of the weights of known mass which are required to balance the object. For usual analytical work the balance should be sensitive to or determine differences in mass of 0.1 mg. (about .000003 oz.).

In microanalyses the balance is about 1,000 times more sensitive and for special work balances of even higher sensitivity have been constructed. (*See* BALANCE.)

CHEMICAL ANALYSES

The major types of strictly chemical methods are known respectively as gravimetric and volumetric (or titrimetric) analyses. As the names imply, the former is based upon a measurement of the weight of a sample constituent and the latter upon the measurement of a volume of solution required to react with the sample. Application of these two methods may be illustrated by procedures which are used for the determination of chloride. In a gravimetric analysis the sample is treated with an excess of silver nitrate solution, which precipitates the chloride as silver chloride. The amount present is determined from the weight of silver chloride obtained. In a volumetric analysis the sample is treated with a solution of silver nitrate of known concentration and the volume of solution just required for reaction with all the chloride present is measured.

From this volume and the known concentration of the solution, the amount of chloride in the sample is computed.

The choice of method, gravimetric or volumetric, depends upon the conditions of the analysis. The accuracy of the two is about the same. Usually a volumetric analysis is far more rapid than a gravimetric after the necessary standard solutions are prepared. Consequently, whenever many samples are to be analyzed a volumetric method is chosen when one is available. But if only a few samples are analyzed it may be more convenient to use a gravimetric method than to prepare and standardize the solutions needed for the volumetric method.

Gravimetric Analyses.—In a gravimetric analysis the constituent sought is converted into a substance of definite composition, expressed by a chemical formula, in 100% yield. All operations in gravimetric analyses are directed toward the objectives of purity and yield. The following operations are common: (1) preparation of solution containing a known weight of the sample, (2) separation of the desired constituent in a pure condition of known composition, (3) weighing the isolated constituent, and (4) computing from the observed weight the amount of the sought constituent in the sample.

There are many methods for isolating the desired constituent from a solution of a sample. Most common is precipitation. A reagent is added which will form an insoluble compound with the desired constituent but will not precipitate other constituents of the sample. The precipitate obtained is separated by filtration, washed free of soluble impurities, dried or ignited to remove water, and weighed. Volatilization is used to separate a substance which can be readily converted into a gaseous compound. An example is the determination of carbonate in a mineral analysis. The sample is treated with an acid and carbon dioxide is evolved as a gas. The gas is absorbed in a weighed portion of an alkaline reagent and the amount of carbon dioxide is determined from the gain in weight of the absorbent. Electrodeposition is used for separation of certain metals which can be plated out by passage of an electric current through a solution. Copper in alloys is frequently determined by this method when interfering metals are not present in the sample.

(*See* ELECTROCHEMISTRY.)

The general methods of precipitation analyses are much like those of qualitative analyses (*see* section *Inorganic Analysis* above). If the sample is complex, *i.e.,* contains many constituents, it is necessary to separate the constituents into groups by successive addition of various reagents. Many of the reagents used for group separations are the same as those employed in qualitative analyses. After the groups are separated, each is redissolved and treated with specific reagents for precipitation of the constituents separately. The complete gravimetric analysis of a complex mineral may require several days, even with highly skilled operators.

The chief source of error in gravimetric analyses is in the purity of the separated constituent. In general the compounds precipitated are very insoluble and there is little error due to incompleteness of precipitation. It is a difficult matter, however, to obtain a precipitate which is 100% pure and exactly of the composition represented by a chemical formula and all gravimetric methods are subject to some degree of error because of this.

Volumetric Analyses.—In a volumetric analysis a solution of known concentration of the reagent is added to a solution of the substance to be determined until the quantity of the reagent is equivalent (*q.v.*) to the quantity of substance determined. All operations are directed toward the objective of measuring the amount of reagent equivalent to the constituent sought in the analysis. Not every chemical reaction can be utilized for volumetric procedures. The following conditions are necessary: (1) the reagent must react with only one constituent of the sample, (2) reaction must be rapid, so that each portion of reagent reacts as rapidly as added, (3) there must be some change in properties of the solution when the equivalence point is reached (usually a sudden change in concentration of ions present), and (4) an indicator (*see* INDICATORS) must be available to show the point at which equivalence is reached.

Operations of volumetric analysis are: (1) preparation of sample solution, (2) titration of sample solution with standard solution which contains a known concentration of the reagent chemical, and (3) computation of the amount of sought constituent in the sample, from the volume and concentration of reagent solution used. Titration, the determination of the amount of reagent equivalent to the sample, is done by adding the reagent slowly from a burette until the indicator shows a colour change. Ordinarily a 50 ml. burette is used and the analyst so chooses conditions that a volume of 30 to 40 ml. of reagent is required. In microchemistry the burette may have a capacity of 1 ml. or sometimes even less. Titrations are most commonly performed by use of chemical indicators, but various physical methods can also be used in special cases to show the equivalence point. A chemical indicator is a highly coloured substance which can react with one of the components of the system and show by a colour change when a component disappears or appears. A well-known example is starch, which gives with iodine an intense blue colour. If an iodine solution is being titrated the end point is marked by the disappearance of colour or conversely if iodine is the titration reagent the presence of an excess of iodine when the equivalence point is passed is marked by the appearance of blue colour.

All volumetric analyses must be preceded by standardization of the reagent solution. This is usually done by comparing the solution with a weighed sample of known purity. An acid solution, for example, is standardized by titration of a known weight of some pure basic substance such as sodium carbonate.

The determination of the amount of acid or base in a sample by titration with a standard solution of base or acid is known as neutralization. This type of volumetric analysis is widely used. Examples are the determination of the amount of free acid in vinegar or the amount of free base in lye. A variety of acid-base indicators is known. Most frequently used are phenolphthalein, methyl red and bromothymol blue. These differ among themselves in that they show colour changes at different hydrogen ion or *p*H values. In an acid-base titration it is important to select that indicator whose colour change corresponds to the hydrogen ion concentration of the equivalence point; use of the wrong indicator might lead to erroneous results.

Scores of volumetric methods are based upon oxidation-reduction reactions, in which there is a change in valence of some ion. A familiar example is the determination of iron by titration with permanganate or ceric sulphate solution. Prior to this determination it is necessary to reduce all the iron to the ferrous (Fe^{++}) condition and to remove from the solution all other reducing agents which might react with the standard solution of oxidizing agent. In the titration iron is oxidized to the ferric condition (Fe^{+++}). The amount present is computed from the volume of oxidizing agent required to react with the iron. If the standard solution used is potassium permanganate no indicator is required for the titration. Permanganate ion is so highly coloured that when the equivalence point is passed a drop or two of solution in excess will impart colour to the solution, thereby giving the end point. Oxidation indicators are known which can also be used. These are substances which are less readily oxidized than ferrous ion and consequently they are not affected until the equivalence point is reached and all the ferrous ion has been oxidized. At this point the indicator is oxidized and shows by a colour change that the end point is reached.

The most widely used standard oxidizing agents in mid-20th

century were potassium permanganate and ceric sulphate. Both of these are strong oxidizers and can be used to titrate numerous reducing agents, such as iron, titanium, vanadium, uranium, sulphides, nitrites, sulphites, oxalates, hydrogen peroxide, arsenic, antimony, molybdenum and many others, after a suitable solution of the sample is prepared with the sought constituent in its lower valence state. Another important class of oxidation-reduction (frequently called redox) determinations involves iodine. When potassium iodide is treated with any strong oxidizing agent iodine is liberated in equivalent amount. Titration of the liberated iodine gives an indirect measure of the amount of oxidizing agent which reacted with the potassium iodide. Thus this method can be used for analysis of any oxidizing agent which liberates iodine from potassium iodide.

The standard solution used to titrate the iodine may be either sodium thiosulphate or arsenious oxide.

Precipitation reactions can often be used for volumetric analyses when an indicator is available to show when the equivalence point is reached. A common example is the determination of chloride by titration with silver nitrate solution, as described above.

There are numerous substances for which there are no good volumetric methods. Examples are ions which are not readily oxidized or reduced and which do not give precipitates suitable for utilization in volumetric analyses, such as sodium, potassium, calcium, aluminum, etc. For some of these it is possible to devise an indirect method of volumetric analysis. Calcium for example can be determined volumetrically by first precipitating it as calcium oxalate, then dissolving the precipitate in sulphuric acid and determining oxalate by titration with potassium permanganate. Since the amounts of calcium and oxalate in the precipitate are equivalent the titration gives the equivalents of calcium in the sample.

Other Chemical Methods.—Some other chemical and physicochemical methods of less frequent use than gravimetric and volumetric analyses are listed below:

Colorimetric analyses are based upon the absorption of light by coloured substances in solution. They can be used when the sought constituent can be converted by chemical reaction into a coloured compound, in absence of other coloured compounds in the solution.

Nephelometric analyses are based upon the amount of turbidity in a solution and the effect of this turbidity upon the transmission of light.

This method is applicable only to the determination of small amounts of substances which yield a precipitate when treated with certain reagents.

Gas analysis depends upon selective absorption of constituents in a gaseous mixture and measurement of the changes in volume which occur when absorption has taken place. Prior to absorption carbon compounds are burned in excess oxygen, yielding carbon dioxide and water.

Fire assay is used to determine the amounts of precious metals in ores. The ore samples are heated with a flux and the metals are reduced to the free state. The free metals are then extracted from the flux by molten lead, which on cooling retains the precious metals as an alloy.

The amounts of precious metals are determined by dissolving (parting) the lead button in acids followed by chemical analysis of the solution or of the residue of metals which do not dissolve.

Computations of Chemical Analyses.—The basis for all quantitative computations is the weight relations expressed by a chemical equation. The equation

$$2NaOH + H_2SO_4 = Na_2SO_4 + 2H_2O$$

shows that two molecules of sodium hydroxide react with one molecule of sulphuric acid to give one molecule of sodium sulphate and two molecules of water. Since a molecule of sodium hydroxide weighs 40.00 atomic weight units (the sum of the atomic weights of Na, H and O) and a molecule of sulphuric acid 98.08 units then 2 × 40.00 units of NaOH react with 98.08 units of H_2SO_4 (*see* ATOM: *Atomic Weights*). The ratio of weights of NaOH and H_2SO_4 reacting are the same regardless of the units employed, whether these be grams, ounces, tons, etc.

In gravimetric analysis one computes from the weight of a precipitate the corresponding weight of the sought constituent by use of a factor based upon the atomic weights. Thus, from the weight of AgCl precipitate the weight of Cl is computed by the relation

$$\text{Weight Cl} = \text{Weight AgCl} \times \frac{\text{atomic weight Cl}}{\text{sum of atomic weights of Ag and Cl}}$$

In volumetric analyses the computations involve the volume and concentration of the reagent solution. The unit of concentration is conveniently chosen as the equivalent weight (*see* EQUIVALENT) and a solution which contains one equivalent weight of solute per liter is known as a 1 normal (1N) solution. Since titrations are made to the point that the equivalents of reagent equal the equivalents of sample, it follows from the definitions that the product, volume of reagent in liters times the normality of the reagent, is the total equivalents of reagent and therefore the total equivalents of the sought constituent in the sample. Multiplication of this value by the weight of one equivalent gives the weight of the sample constituent in grams. For example, if titration of a Cl sample requires 40.00 ml. 0.1N $AgNO_3$ solution, the weight of Cl in the sample is

$$\underset{\text{(vol. in liters)}}{40.00/1{,}000} \times \underset{\text{(normality)}}{0.1} \times \underset{\text{(eq.wt. Cl)}}{35.46} = \text{grams Cl}$$

Physical Methods.—As mentioned above, the variety of physical properties which can be used for analytical purposes is almost endless.

Only the more important physical methods of analysis can be mentioned here.

Spectrochemical.—The application of optical emission spectra to quantitative analyses was so well established by mid-20th century that in many control laboratories it had supplanted chemical analyses for numerous constituents. This was particularly true in the analysis of alloys for minor constituents. The basis for the method is the fact that the intensity of spectral lines (*see* SPECTROSCOPY) can be related to the concentration of the emitting element in the sample. Requirements are a spectroscope of sufficient dispersion in both the visible and the ultra-violet regions and a microphotometer for measurement of the blackness or density of the spectral line.

Before a spectrochemical method can be used it is necessary to work out curves relating line densities to concentrations, based upon samples of the general composition of those to be analyzed. This preliminary preparation of the working curve is based upon chemical analyses of the standard samples. It may require weeks of careful work to standardize conditions and develop the working curve for a given analysis. Consequently the spectrochemical method is not well suited to the analysis of occasional samples but it finds best application in routine analyses where large numbers of samples must be processed. Once methods are developed the spectrographic procedure is very rapid and accurate. It is possible to take molten metal samples from a furnace and to obtain an analysis for several constituents within 8 to 15 min. after the sample is withdrawn; this speed is far beyond that of any other method.

Light Absorption.—Colorimetry as described above has been in use many years for coloured substances. Recently this general method has been further developed and extended by spectrophotometry which is the measurement of the transmission of ultra-violet, visible and infra-red light of selected wave lengths. The spectrophotometer is an instrument arranged to give a light beam of a selected wave length range and to measure the fraction of this light absorbed by a sample solution. Many materials which are colourless in visible light, due to complete transmission of all components, will absorb strongly and selectively in the ultra-violet and infra-red regions. The analysis of solutions which contain such substances is based upon determination of the transmission curve and the quantitative measurement of the fraction of light absorbed at various wave lengths.

(*See* PHOTOMETRY.)

Polarimetry.—Polarimetry, or the measurement of rotation of polarized light has been used as an analytical method many years. An example is the analysis of sugar solutions whose concentrations can be read directly from the graduations on the scale of a special polarimeter.

Refractive Index.—Refractive index is often used to identify organic compounds and to measure the concentrations of solutions. A useful application is in the determination of the alcoholic content of beverages. Alcohol is distilled from the sample and collected in a measured volume of water. From the refractive index of the resulting solution the alcoholic content of the original sample is readily computed.

Polarograph.—This is an instrument arranged to trace a current-voltage curve during electrolysis of a solution at a dropping mercury electrode. S-shaped curves are obtained whose position on the voltage co-ordinate is characteristic of the material in solution and whose amplitude is proportional to the concentration.

The instrument has had extensive use in many analytical problems, particularly for the determination of small amounts.

***p*H Meters.**—The continuous and accurate determination of hydrogen-ion concentrations is important in many manufacturing processes. To facilitate this there have been developed many types of *p*H meters so arranged that the hydrogen-ion concentration is related to the voltage reading of the meter. By a slight modification these instruments can be used to detect potentiometrically the end point in oxidation-reduction and in certain precipitation titrations.

(*See* HYDROGEN-ION CONCENTRATION.)

X-ray Diffraction.—The characteristic X-ray diffraction pattern given by crystalline substances can be made the basis for qualitative and quantitative analyses where other methods are lacking. A beam of monochromatic X-rays is passed through a small tube of the powdered sample and the diffracted lines detected by their effect upon a photographic plate or film. The position of the lines serves to identify the crystalline species present and quantitative measurements of amounts present can be made by the intensity of the lines.

BIBLIOGRAPHY.—W. C. Pierce and E. L. Haenisch, *Quantitative Analysis*, 2nd ed. (1940); I. M. Kolthoff and E. B. Sandell, *Textbook of Quantitative Analysis* (1943); W. R. Brode, *Chemical Spectroscopy*, 2nd ed. (1943); I. M. Kolthoff and J. J. Lingane, *Polarography* (1941); John Howe Yoe, *Photometric Chemical Analysis* (1929); W. W. Scott, ed., *Standard Methods of Chemical Analysis* (1939).

(W. C. P.)

ULTIMATE ORGANIC ANALYSIS

The limited number of elements (carbon, hydrogen, oxygen, nitrogen, sulphur, halogens and occasionally phosphorus and some metals) employed by nature in building up her vast store of organic compounds would suggest that the analyses of such substances are simple operations, and this is true in so far as the determination of the elements present, their relative proportions, and the molecular complexity of the compound are concerned. Naturally such information tells us nothing of the *structure* of the compound and, indeed, leaves us much in the same position as we should be in if we were interested in some building and were supplied with the builder's estimate for material while denied access to the architect's drawings and plans. The problem of determining the manner in which the elements present in organic compounds are arranged, important as it is, lies outside the scope of the present article, which is limited to the description of the ultimate analysis. With the exception of oxygen, all the elements present in organic compounds can be estimated readily; oxygen is nearly always determined by difference, and in view of this fact it is of great importance that a careful qualitative examination be made of a substance, otherwise the results of the quantitative analysis may be interpreted erroneously.

Qualitative Tests for the Elements.—*Carbon and Hydrogen.*—The organic nature of a compound is generally indicated by its behaviour on being heated in air; solids usually melt, then burn with a more or less smoky flame, leaving a black residue of carbon. To test directly for carbon and hydrogen, a small quantity of the material intimately mixed with about 20 times its bulk of dry copper oxide powder is heated in a dry test tube closed by a cork carrying a delivery tube which dips into a solution of limewater. The copper oxide is reduced, the hydrogen is converted to water which bedews the cool part of the tube, and the carbon oxidized to carbon dioxide which forms a precipitate of chalk in the limewater.

Nitrogen, Halogens, Sulphur.—When organic compounds containing any or all of these elements are heated strongly with metallic sodium they are decomposed with the formation of sodium cyanide, halide and sulphide, respectively (Lassaigne's test). To test for these elements, therefore, 1 mg. of the substance and a small pellet of sodium (or potassium) are heated in a narrow test tube, gently at first and afterward more strongly, until the glass softens; the hot tube is shattered by plunging it into water, which converts any residual sodium into sodium hydroxide, yielding an alkaline solution of the sodium salts, which is boiled and filtered, and the filtrate is used in the following tests:

1. Nitrogen.—A portion of the filtrate is mixed with a solution of ferrous sulphate containing a small quantity of the ferric salt and boiled, thereby converting any sodium cyanide present to ferrocyanide, which gives a bluish-green solution and a precipitate of Prussian blue on adding hydrochloric acid.

2. Halogens.—A second portion of the alkaline filtrate is acidified with nitric acid and silver nitrate added, any precipitate of chloride, bromide or iodide, or a mixture of these, is examined in the usual manner. If the original substance also contains nitrogen or sulphur, the acid solution must be boiled to expel the hydrogen cyanide or hydrogen sulphide before adding the silver nitrate.

3. Sulphur.—A third portion of the alkaline filtrate is tested for sodium sulphide (1) by the formation of a deep violet colour when treated with a few drops of a freshly prepared solution of sodium nitroprusside; (2) by the evolution of sulphuretted hydrogen when acidified—this is readily detected by the odour and also by lead acetate test paper.

Phosphorus.—A small portion of the organic compound is intimately mixed with about ten times its bulk of a mixture of sodium carbonate and peroxide (2:3) and heated to fusion in a nickel crucible. The cold water extract of the melt is filtered, acidified with nitric acid, and tested for phosphoric acid with ammonium molybdate.

Metals.—(1) Volatile metals. (*a*) Arsenic.—The presence of arsenic in an organic compound is usually revealed by the formation of a dull gray mirror of the metal on the walls of the test-tube when the compound is fused with sodium as in Lassaigne's test. (*b*) Arsenic and Antimony.—A small quantity of the compound is fused with a mixture of sodium carbonate and peroxide as in the test for phosphorus. The fused melt is extracted with water, acidified and tested with sulphuretted hydrogen. (*c*) Mercury.—When an organic compound containing mercury is mixed with soda lime and heated in a long test tube, a mirror of metallic mercury is formed.

(2) Nonvolatile Metals.—Any of these metals that may occur in organic compounds are found as such or in the form of their carbonate or oxide in the ash left after the compound has been ignited on porcelain or silica. The ash is dissolved in dilute hydrochloric acid and the solution examined for metals in the usual manner.

Quantitative Analysis of Organic Compounds.—*Estimation of Carbon and Hydrogen.*—The carbon and hydrogen in an organic compound are estimated by completely oxidizing a weighed quantity of the substance and weighing the carbon dioxide and water thus formed. The simple method devised by Liebig in 1831 for carrying out this operation is in all essential principles the one still employed. A weighed quantity of the substance is heated in a tube filled with dry copper oxide, and the water and carbon dioxide are absorbed in weighed tubes filled with dried calcium chloride and potassium hydroxide solution or soda lime respectively. A current of dry air or oxygen is passed through the tube to sweep the products of combustion into the absorption apparatus. Fig. 4 shows the essential details of the apparatus required for these estimations; *a* and *b* are closely fitting, short

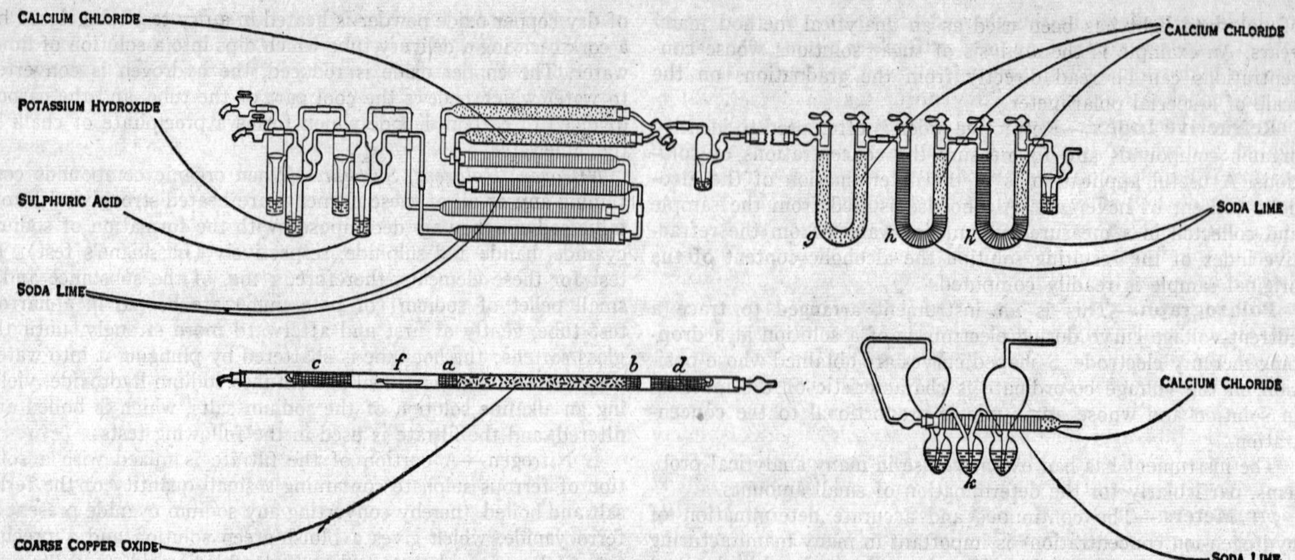

FIG. 4.—APPARATUS FOR QUANTITATIVE ESTIMATION OF CARBON AND HYDROGEN IN AN ORGANIC COMPOUND
THE PRINCIPLE DEPENDS ON OXIDIZING A WEIGHED QUANTITY OF THE COMPOUND AND THEN WEIGHING THE RESULTANT DIOXIDE AND WATER

spirals of copper gauze which serve to hold the copper oxide in position; the copper oxide is prepared by oxidizing copper wire; *c* and *d* are longer copper oxide spirals; *f* is the platinum or porcelain boat containing the weighed quantity of the compound.

In the absorption apparatus, the water is collected in the glass stoppered **U**-tube *g*, filled with calcium chloride (carefully freed from lime). The carbon dioxide is absorbed by the soda lime contained in the **U**-tubes *h* and h^1, the second limb of each tube containing a short filling of calcium chloride. The two soda lime tubes may be replaced by the apparatus *k*, of which the bulbs are charged with concentrated potassium hydroxide solution and the side tube filled with soda lime and calcium chloride. The apparatus for purifying the current of air or oxygen is connected with the anterior end of the tube and consists of a series of washing cylinders charged with potassium hydroxide or sulphuric acid, and **U**-tubes filled with soda lime or calcium chloride to remove moisture and carbon dioxide from the incoming gas. This apparatus is arranged in duplicate, one for the air and one for the oxygen supply. Any simple form of gas-heated furnace may be employed (fig. 5), or the tube may be heated electrically.

The combustion tube and its copper oxide charge are dried by heating the tube to a dull red heat for about an hour while a current of dry air is passed, the posterior end of the tube being protected by a calcium chloride tube. At the end of that time the fore part of the tube containing the oxidized spiral and the first six inches of copper oxide is cooled. While this process is in operation, the weighings are made. About 0.2 g. of the pure dry compound to be analyzed is weighed into the platinum or porcelain boat if the compound is a solid or a nonvolatile liquid. Volatile liquids are weighed in small thin glass bulbs drawn out to a capillary opening. The tubes for collecting the water and carbon dioxide are also weighed, and attached to the posterior end of the combustion tube. The boat and its contents are then introduced into the cooled anterior end of the combustion tube.

A slow current of air is passed through the tube, and the burners under the oxidized spiral in the rear of the boat are lighted. The heating is gradually extended toward the boat by moving forward the heated screen over the tube, or increasing the flame surface under the tube, the object being to distil the contents of the boat, or the volatile products of decomposition, on to the cold copper oxide where the combustion is completed. This most critical part of the operation must be carried out very slowly, and is finally completed in a current of oxygen which burns any residue of carbon left in the boat, and reoxidizes the reduced copper oxide. After displacing by air the oxygen in the apparatus, the absorption tubes are removed, closed, cleaned and allowed to cool in the balance room before being reweighed. From the weight of carbon dioxide and water yielded by the definite weight of the compound, the percentages of carbon and hydrogen in the compound are readily calculated.

The simple method described above applies to compounds containing carbon, hydrogen and oxygen only; if elements other than these are present the filling of the tube must be modified as follows: (*a*) *Nitrogen present.* The copper oxide spiral (*d*) is replaced by a similar spiral of freshly reduced copper to reduce any oxides of nitrogen that may be formed during the combustion. It is introduced into the end of the tube that has been previously cooled, before attaching the absorption apparatus. (*b*) *Halogens, sulphur or arsenic present.* The first six inches of copper oxide after the boat are replaced by a lead chromate cartridge, made by filling a hollow cylinder of copper gauze with freshly ignited fused lead chromate. The copper container becomes oxidized in the preliminary heating of the tube, nonvolatile lead compounds being formed with the sulphur or arsenic in the compound, and sparingly volatile compounds with the halogens. A short spiral of silver gauze should, therefore, be introduced at the posterior end of the tube when the compound contains halogens.

Estimation of Nitrogen.—The two methods in use for the estimation of nitrogen are (*a*) the absolute method (Dumas), in which the nitrogen in a known weight of the compound is eliminated in the gaseous form and estimated by direct measurement; (*b*) the Kjeldahl method, in which the nitrogen in a known weight of the material is reduced to ammonia and estimated volumetrically by titration. (*a*) The absolute method consists in the complete oxidation of a known weight of the compound by heating it with copper oxide in a tube in a current of carbon dioxide, passing the gaseous products of combustion over a heated copper spiral and collecting the nitrogen in a gas burette over strong potassium hydroxide solution. The gas is afterward transferred to a calibrated eudiometer tube and measured over water. The method of filling the tube is indicated in fig. 5. The three grades of coarseness in the copper oxide used are obtained by crushing the ordinary copper oxide made from wire, and passing it through two copper gauze sieves, 20 strands and seven strands to the centimetre respectively; the first retains the coarse and medium grades, and the second the coarse. The amount of the substance used in an analysis should be sufficient to give about 20 c.c. of nitrogen. The charged tube is placed in the furnace and connected with an apparatus for generating carbon dioxide and with a Schiff's nitrometer filled with a concentrated solution of potassium hydroxide. While the air in the apparatus is being displaced by carbon dioxide, the part of the tube containing the coarse copper oxide and reduced spiral is heated to dull redness. When no insoluble gas collects in the charged nitrometer, the current of carbon dioxide is stopped, and the nitrometer is filled with the potassium hydroxide solution which is allowed to overflow into the thistle funnel seal attached to the end of the capillary transferring tube. The burners under the copper oxide spiral are then lighted, and when this part of the tube is at a dull red heat, the heating is extended toward the mixture of the substance with copper oxide, and so regulated that not more than three bubbles of gas are ascending the nitrometer tube at the same time. Finally, when all the burners are lighted, the tube has attained a uniform dull red heat, and there is no further evolution of gas, a slow current of carbon dioxide is again passed through the tube to sweep out the remainder of the nitrogen. The nitrometer is then removed, the gas reduced to atmospheric pressure, by bringing the liquid in the open arm of the nitrometer to the same level as that in the closed arm, and after about 15 minutes transferred to a eudiometer tube over boiled-out water, which is then completely immersed in a tall glass cylinder of water containing also a thermometer. After about ten minutes the volume of the nitrogen (v) the temperature (t) and the barometer (p) are read. If p' is the tension of aqueous vapour under these conditions and w denotes the weight of substance taken, the percentage of nitrogen in the compound is given by the expression

$$N = \frac{v}{w} \times \frac{273 \times (p-p') \times 0.12507}{(273+t) \times 760}$$

(*b*) The Kjeldahl method is a modification of Will and Varrentrapp's method and is used for the estimation of nitrogen in such materials as foodstuffs, therapeutic substances, fertilizers, etc., in which the amount of nitrogen is small and many determinations have to be carried out simultaneously and rapidly. The method consists in decomposing the organic material by heating it with concentrated sulphuric acid; the carbon is oxidized and the nitrogen converted to ammonia which is retained as the sulphate, and afterward estimated in the usual manner by distillation (*see* AMMONIA). A weighed quantity of the material (0.5 to 5.0 g.) is placed in a long-necked, pear-shaped flask of 500 c.c. capacity, 20 c.c. of concentrated sulphuric acid are added, the flask is clamped in an inclined position and the contents heated gradually to avoid frothing. After the acid has been boiling for about 15 minutes, 10 g. of potassium sulphate are added, and the heating is continued until the contents of the flask are clear and a faint straw colour. In cases of not easily oxidizable materials, small quantities of certain metallic salts such as copper or mercuric sulphate or mercurous iodide may be added. Finally the cold acid liquid is transferred, with the washings of the flask, into the distilling flask of an ammonia distillation apparatus; after the contents of the flask have been made alkaline, the ammonia is distilled into a measured volume of standard sulphuric acid and estimated by titrating the excess of acid.

The Kjeldahl method can also be applied to the analysis of pure organic compounds, provided that those compounds which contain nitrogen combined directly with oxygen or with nitrogen as in nitro-, nitroso-, azo- or diazo-compounds or hydrazines, undergo a preliminary reducing operation.

Estimation of Halogens.—The estimation of halogens involves the complete decomposition of the compound, with the conversion of the halogen element into the hydracid or one of its salts, which is subsequently precipitated and estimated as the silver salt. (*a*) Liebig's is the oldest method and the one applicable to the largest number of organic compounds. It consists in decomposing a weighed quantity of the compound by heating it to redness with a large excess of pure lime in a glass tube sealed at one end, plunging the hot tube into cold water, dissolving the lime and calcium halide in cold dilute nitric acid, filtering, and estimating the halogen acid in the filtrate in the usual manner. Piria and Schiff modified the method in the direction of shortening the time of the operation, by replacing the lime by a mixture of lime and sodium carbonate, and the glass tube by two nickel crucibles, the smaller one containing the mixture of the substance being inverted in the larger, and the annular space between the two filled with the lime and sodium carbonate mixture. (*b*) Stepanoff's method, as modified by Bacon, is applicable to compounds in which the halogen is readily eliminated as hydracid by hydrolysis or by reduction. It consists in heating a weighed quantity of the compound with sodium and alcohol, and estimating the sodium halide in the resulting solution. (*c*) The method of Carius, as modified by Kuster, is the one most generally employed; it consists in the destructive oxidation of a weighed quantity of the compound (about 0.2 g.) by means of fuming nitric acid (2 c.c.) in the presence of silver nitrate in a sealed tube at a temperature of 250°–270° C.

The halogen is converted into the silver salt and is weighed as such.

Estimation of Sulphur.—The estimation of sulphur in organic compounds involves the destructive oxidation of the substance whereby the sulphur is converted to sulphuric acid and weighed as the barium salt. The two methods in general use are:—(*a*) The method of Carius, in which the operation is carried out as in the preceding case, no silver nitrate is required, but as the oxida-

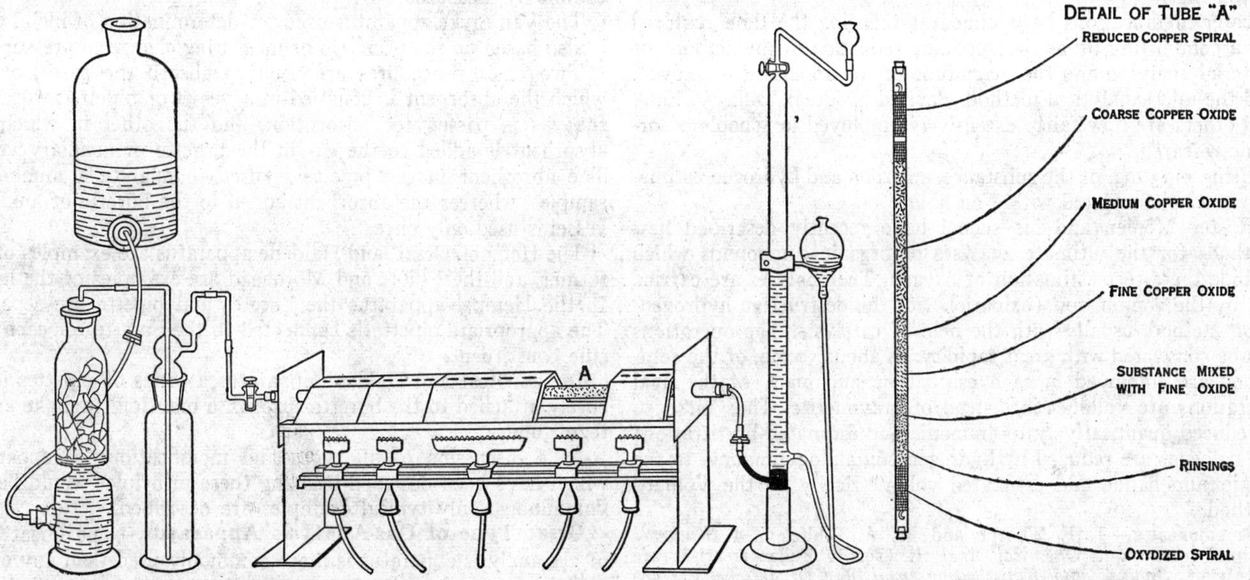

FIG. 5.—APPARATUS FOR ABSOLUTE METHOD (DUMAS) OF ESTIMATION OF NITROGEN IN AN ORGANIC COMPOUND

A KNOWN WEIGHT OF THE COMPOUND IS HEATED WITH COPPER OXIDE IN A CURRENT OF CARBON DIOXIDE; THE NITROGEN EVOLVED IS COLLECTED OVER A STRONG SOLUTION OF POTASSIUM HYDROXIDE AND THEN MEASURED IN A EUDIOMETER TUBE

tion is facilitated by the presence of a small quantity of bromine, a crystal of potassium bromide is placed in the tube containing the compound. The contents of the tube are diluted with water, the nitric acid removed by evaporation and the sulphuric acid precipitated and weighed as the barium salt. (*b*) The method of Asboth, in which the oxidizing agent employed is a mixture of sodium peroxide (three parts) and sodium carbonate (two parts). A weighed quantity of the substance (0.2 to 0.5 g.) is mixed with about 15 g. of the oxidizing mixture in a nickel crucible which is then carefully heated until the contents become liquid. When cold, the melt is extracted with water, and the soluble sulphate estimated in the usual manner.

Estimation of Phosphorus.—Organic compounds containing phosphorus are oxidized by fuming nitric acid, by concentrated nitric acid and potassium permanganate, or by chromic and sulphuric acids. The resulting phosphoric acid is precipitated as ammonium phosphomolybdate, and subsequently weighed as magnesium pyrophosphate.

Estimation of Metals in the Salts of Organic Acids and Bases. Gold, silver and platinum in organic salts are weighed as the metallic residue left after the organic material has been destroyed by igniting a weighed quantity of the dry salt in a platinum or silver crucible. Sodium, potassium, barium and calcium salts are decomposed by igniting a weighed quantity of the dry salt in the presence of pure sulphuric acid and weighing the sulphate of the metal.

Modern Modifications.—The methods described for the ultimate analysis of organic compounds leave nothing to be desired on the score of simplicity and accuracy, but many of them are very tedious in operation, and the modifications that have been introduced aim at reducing the time required for the analysis. The earlier attempts were directed toward the employment of more vigorous oxidizing agents than copper oxide, and of these the use of oxygen in the presence of a contact substance (Kopfer, 1876) has been employed with singular success by Dennstedt. He uses a platinum contact material, heated to bright redness, and passes the vapour of the substance over it in a rapid stream of oxygen. The carbon dioxide and water are collected and weighed in the usual manner. If the compound contains nitrogen, chlorine, bromine or sulphur, a boat containing lead peroxide heated to 320° C. is placed in the rear part of the combustion tube; this serves to break up any oxides of nitrogen that may be formed, and at the same time to absorb quantitatively the chlorine, bromine or sulphur, which can be estimated subsequently by the usual gravimetric methods. If iodine be present this can be retained by molecular silver contained in a second boat placed in the rear of the first.

Later modifications have aimed at reducing the time required for a combustion by a corresponding reduction in the amount of material analyzed and the magnitude of the apparatus employed, and the microanalytical methods devised by Pregl, Dubsky, Funk and others are now fairly extensively employed in schools of organic research.

Using 5–15 mg. of the substance, a carbon and hydrogen estimation can be completed within an hour.

H. ter Meulen and his school have recently described new methods for the ultimate analyses of organic compounds which include the direct estimation of oxygen. The analyses are carried out by the combustion (oxidation), or the destructive hydrogenation method, usually with the help of catalysts. The operations can be conducted with great rapidity, as about 50 mg. of the compound are employed in each estimation, and many of the final operations are volumetric instead of gravimetric. Thus nitrogen is reduced quantitatively to ammonia and estimated by titration; the halogens are reduced by hydrogen containing ammonia to the ammonium halide and estimated volumetrically by the Volhard method.

Bibliography.—J. F. Thorpe and M. A. Whiteley, *A Student's Manual of Organic Chemical Analysis* (1926). Fuller treatises are H. Meyer, *Analyse und Konstitutionsermittlung Organische Verbindungen*, 3rd ed. (1916); G. Lunge, *Technical Methods of Chemical Analysis*, 6 vol., 2nd ed. (1924); J. Houben, *Die Methoden der Organischen Chemie*, 3rd ed. (Leipzig, 1925). (M. A. W.)

GAS ANALYSIS

The field of gas analysis in a broad sense embraces the sampling and determination of all types of gaseous substances. The purpose of such analyses are many and varied. The following are a few typical examples: (1) evaluation of toxicity hazard of a particular gas, such as carbon monoxide in a vehicular tunnel; (2) determination of the composition of (a) fuel gases to ascertain heating value or for control of plant operations, (b) flue gases to evaluate efficiency of combustion, (c) exhaust gases from internal-combustion engines to establish proper carburettor adjustment for maximum efficiency, and (d) mine gases to evaluate explosion hazard and quality of air; and (3) determination of products of combustion of various types of materials to ascertain toxic constituents formed.

Numerous procedures and many types of specialized equipment have been developed for the determination of the various kinds of gases which occur under widely different conditions. The methods in general are based on chemical reactions or measurement of some specific property by physicochemical means.

The chemical reaction most commonly used is absorption of a specific gaseous constituent in a suitable liquid absorbent. The amount of gas present may then be estimated by (1) measuring the reduction in the volume of the sample due to absorption of the constituent, (2) titration of the absorbed gas with suitable reagent as acidimetric or iodometric determinations, (3) colorimetric comparison with standards, and (4) weighing of a precipitate such as barium carbonate.

Physicochemical measurements are made with such instruments as the interferometer, thermal conductivity apparatus, infra-red absorption spectrograph, mass spectrograph, combustible gas indicator, and many other indicators and recorders usually designed for the determination of a single gas.

This discussion is confined to typical conventional gas analysis methods and does not include discussion of such apparatus as the Van Slyke, Warburg-Barcroft and other specialized equipment which has been developed for a particular application or field of work as gas analysis in biological investigations.

Gas Volumetric Methods.—Virtually all conventional gas-analysis methods are based on the successive absorption of some constituents with suitable absorbents and combustion of other constituents. The volume of each gas removed is then determined by (1) measuring the change in volume at constant pressure and temperature or (2) measuring change in pressure at constant volume and temperature.

Apparatus used in the United States is designed to measure change in volume, whereas in England change in pressure is more commonly measured.

The Van Slyke apparatus used for determination of blood gases is also based on the principle of measuring change in pressure.

Two basic procedures are used to absorb the gases, one in which the absorbent is confined in a vessel or pipette into which the gas is passed for absorption, and the other in which the absorbent is added to the gas in the burette or auxiliary vessel. The absorbent in the pipette is used to analyze a number of samples, whereas the absorbent added to the burette or auxiliary vessel is used only once.

The Hempel, Orsat, and Haldane apparatus are examples of the former, and the Elliott and Morehead are examples of the latter. In the Hempel apparatus the burette and pipette are separate. The appropriate pipette is connected to the burette for each specific constituent.

In the Orsat and Haldane apparatus a series of pipettes is securely attached to the burette through a manifold to make an integral unit.

As a discussion of all types and modifications of apparatus which have been designed utilizing these principles would be too voluminous, only typical examples are described.

Orsat Type of Gas-Analysis Apparatus.—The Orsat type of gas-analysis apparatus is more commonly used than any other.

It is designed for various applications that range from small compact portable types with only one or two pipettes to large laboratory models having a half dozen or more pipettes.

The Orsat type of gas analysis apparatus (*see* fig. 6) consists essentially of: (1) burette, (2) pipettes, (3) copper oxide tube, (4) confining liquid, (5) compensator tube and (6) a water jacket for the burette and compensator tube. The burette is a cylindrical glass tube of 100 ml. capacity with carefully calibrated graduation marks to permit reading of gas volumes to a fraction of a milliliter. The burette is closed at the top with a stopcock, and the bottom is connected by a rubber hose to a reservoir for the confining liquid. The confining liquid may be water, a salt solution or mercury. As gases may dissolve in water or aqueous solutions, mercury is preferred and usually is employed in laboratory apparatus. Acid water or salt solutions are usually employed in portable units. The number and type of pipettes depend on the type of work to be done, but laboratory models usually have pipettes for the removal of carbon dioxide, illuminants, oxygen, carbon monoxide and for slow combustion of methane and ethane. The copper oxide tube is for the oxidation of carbon monoxide and hydrogen. The confining liquid not only confines the gas in the burette but also serves to draw the sample into the burette and forces it into the pipettes or copper oxide tube as required. Since the results of the analyses are based on change in volume due to absorption or combustion, it is essential that no changes in volume of sample occur due to changes in temperature, atmospheric pressure or water vapour. The water jacket surrounding the burette and compensator tube serves to control the temperature. Changes in pressure and water-vapour content due to slight changes in temperature are controlled by the compensator and by having a small amount of water on the mercury in the burette and in the compensator tube.

Analysis of Fuel Gas.—The use of the Orsat-type gas-analysis apparatus for the analysis of a fuel gas offers a typical example of the application and technique of gas analysis. The analysis of a fuel gas may require determination of the following constituents: carbon dioxide, illuminants, oxygen, carbon monoxide, hydrogen, methane, ethane and inert gases, mainly nitrogen. Illuminants include a number of unsaturated hydrocarbons, such as ethylene, propylene, butylene, benzene, toluene and acetylene.

Since the constituents are removed one at a time it is necessary that the absorbent used for the first constituent does not remove any of the other components. In other words, the order of removal of constituents is important and is fixed by the reagents used.

The following is the order in which the gases are usually determined and the reagents or reactions which are commonly used for the determination of the various gases:

(1) Carbon dioxide	Absorbed with potassium hydroxide
(2) Illuminants	Absorbed with fuming sulphuric acid
(3) Oxygen	Absorbed with alkaline pyrogallate
(4) Carbon monoxide	Absorbed with acid or ammoniacal cuprous chloride and cuprous sulphate-beta naphthol. Also determined by oxidation with heated copper oxide or by slow combustion with heated platinum spiral
(5) Hydrogen	Determined by oxidation with heated copper oxide or by slow combustion with oxygen
(6) Methane	Determined by slow combustion with oxygen
(7) Ethane	Determined by slow combustion with oxygen
(8) Nitrogen and other inert gases	Estimated by difference. Not determined directly

The potassium hydroxide solution is prepared by dissolving 30 g. of KOH in 100 ml. of distilled water. Sodium hydroxide also may be used; but it has the disadvantages of greater chemical action on the glass, and it forms a bicarbonate precipitate more readily than potassium hydroxide. The fuming sulphuric acid when fresh should contain 20% to 25% free sulphur trioxide. Bromine water (prepared by dissolving bromine in water until an excess of liquid bromine remains in the bottom of the pipette) also may be used to absorb illuminants, but should not be used when mercury is used as the confining liquid. Alkaline pyrogallate is prepared by dissolving 50 g. of pure pyrogallic acid in 150 ml. of distilled water, and mixing with a solution containing 1,200 g. of potassium hydroxide in 800 ml. of water. The mixture should be immediately protected from the air. Oxygen may be absorbed by other reagents such as white phosphorus, chromous chloride or acetate, and sodium hydrosulphite. There are objections to the use of these reagents and therefore alkaline pyrogallate is usually employed. For the absorption of carbon monoxide, acid cuprous chloride (450 g. of chemically pure cuprous chloride dissolved in 2,500 ml. of concentrated C.P. hydrochloric acid) is frequently used, but cuprous sulphate beta-naphthol is being used more than in the past. The latter is prepared from cuprous oxide, 20 parts; sulphuric acid, 200 parts; water, 25 parts; and beta-naphthol, 25 parts.

Analytical Procedure.—Before starting an analysis, the apparatus should be checked to be sure that it is in proper operating condition. It should be tested for leaks to assure that the sample is not lost or diluted with air. A small amount of water

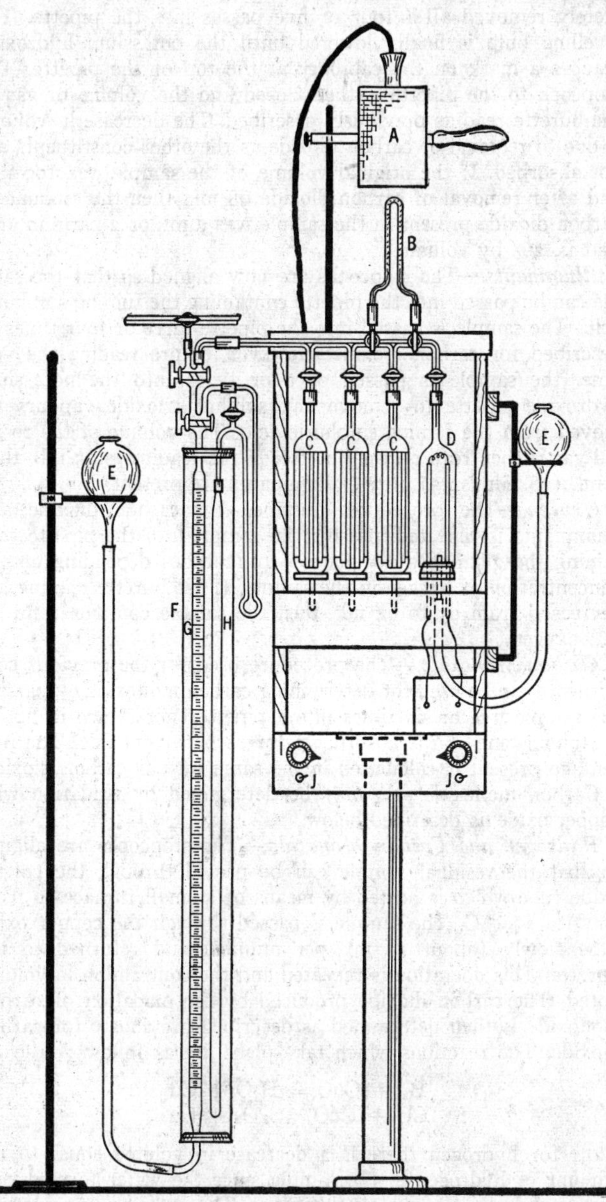

FIG. 6.—ORSAT-TYPE GAS-ANALYSIS APPARATUS. A. ELECTRIC FURNACE FOR COPPER OXIDE TUBE; B. COPPER OXIDE TUBE; C. ABSORPTION PIPETTES; D. COMBUSTION PIPETTE; E. LEVELLING BULBS; F. WATER JACKET; G. BURETTE; H. COMPENSATING TUBE; I. RHEOSTATS; J. SWITCHES

should be placed in the burette and in the compensator tube. The air in the compensator tube should be adjusted to atmospheric pressure. The capillary tubes of the manifold through which the sample is passed to the pipettes and copper oxide tube should be swept free of air by drawing a sample of air into the burette, absorbing the oxygen in the alkaline pyrogallate solution, and then passing the residual inert gas through the apparatus.

To obtain a sample for analysis, the mercury reservoir or levelling bulb is raised to free the burette of air. The burette is then connected to the gas sample container with capillary tubing and the levelling bulb lowered to draw the sample into the burette. The stopcock at the top of the burette is closed and the volume of gas in the burette is read at atmospheric pressure by adjusting the mercury in the levelling bulb and burette to the same level. The analyst is now ready to proceed with the analysis.

Carbon Dioxide.—The stopcocks are aligned so that the sample can be forced, by raising the levelling bulb, from the burette into the pipette containing the potassium hydroxide. The levelling bulb is alternately lowered and raised in order to pass the sample back and forth from the burette to the pipette. This procedure facilitates absorption of the carbon dioxide which should be completely removed after four or five passes into the pipette. The levelling bulb is finally lowered until the potassium hydroxide reaches a mark on the capillary at the top of the pipette. The stopcock to the pipette is then closed and the volume of gas in the burette read as previously described. The decrease in volume is due to removal of carbon dioxide as the other constituents are not absorbed. If the original volume of the sample was 100 ml., and after removal of carbon dioxide 98 ml., then the amount of carbon dioxide present in the sample was 2 ml. or 2 parts in 100, that is, 2% by volume.

Illuminants.—The stopcocks are now aligned so that the sample can be passed into the pipette containing the fuming sulphuric acid. The sample is passed into the pipette three or four times as described for carbon dioxide. However, before reading the volume, the sample is passed once or twice into the potassium hydroxide pipette to remove any sulphur trioxide vapours removed from the fuming sulphuric acid. The volume of the residual gas is then read on the burette. If the reading is 95 ml., then 3 ml. (98 minus 95) or 3% illuminants are present.

Oxygen.—The procedure described for carbon dioxide and illuminants is repeated, passing the sample into the pipette containing the alkaline pyrogallate 6 to 12 times depending on the concentration of oxygen in the sample. If the burette reading has decreased from 95 to 94 ml., then the sample contains 1 ml. or 1% oxygen.

Carbon Monoxide.—The procedure used for the previous constituents can be used for determining carbon monoxide by passing the sample five or six times into a pipette (not shown in fig. 6) containing one of the absorbents for carbon monoxide. The percentage present is calculated in the same way as carbon dioxide.

Carbon monoxide also may be determined by oxidation with copper oxide as described below.

Hydrogen and Carbon Monoxide.—The stopcocks are aligned so that the residual sample can be passed through the copper oxide tube which is heated by means of a small furnace to from 290° to 310° C. The sample is passed through the copper oxide tube slowly (about 10 ml. per minute) and returned to the burette. This operation is repeated and the contraction in volume noted. The carbon dioxide produced by the oxidation of carbon monoxide is then determined as described previously for carbon dioxide. The reactions which take place are as follows:

$$H_2 + CuO = H_2O + Cu$$
$$CO + CuO = CO_2 + Cu$$

Thus for hydrogen there is a decrease in volume equal to the amount of hydrogen in the sample since the water formed condenses and occupies a negligible space. The carbon monoxide produces an equal volume of carbon dioxide and therefore no change in volume. The volume of hydrogen in the sample equals the contraction of the sample after oxidation and the volume of carbon monoxide is equal to the volume of carbon dioxide produced.

Methane and Ethane.—At this stage in the analysis the residual gas may consist of methane, ethane and inert gases, mainly nitrogen. Since methane and ethane require oxygen for combustion, it is necessary to add oxygen. The residual gas is stored in the potassium hydroxide pipette and an excess of oxygen necessary for combustion of the methane and ethane is carefully measured in the burette. The oxygen is passed into the combustion pipette and the residual gas returned to the burette. The platinum spiral at the top of the combustion pipette is heated electrically to a bright yellow and the residual gas passed slowly (about 10 ml. per minute) into the combustion pipette. Methane and ethane are oxidized to carbon dioxide according to the following equations:

$$CH_4 + 2O_2 = CO_2 + 2H_2O$$
$$2C_2H_6 + 7O_2 = 4CO_2 + 6H_2O$$

On the basis of these reactions, the percentages of methane and ethane can be calculated as follows:

$$\text{Per cent of ethane} = \frac{(2 \times \text{carbon dioxide} - \text{contraction}) \times 100}{1.5 \times \text{ml. sample taken}}$$

$$\text{Per cent of methane} = \frac{(\text{carbon dioxide} - 2 \times \text{ethane}) \times 100}{\text{ml. sample taken}}$$

The sum of the percentages of all the constituents determined is then subtracted from 100 and the remainder is the percentage of nitrogen or inert gas in the sample.

In presenting the analytical procedure, only the basic steps have been described and no attempt has been made to incorporate numerous minor steps that are necessary to obtain accurate results.

To do so would require lengthy details which would add little and at the same time make it difficult to follow the general outline of the procedure.

Typical Values for Individual Constituents of Several Kinds of Fuel Gas

Kind of gas	Carbon dioxide	Illuminants	Oxygen	Carbon monoxide	Hydrogen	Methane	Ethane	Nitrogen
Natural	..	..	..	..	..	85.5	13.5	1.0
Blast furnace	10.8	..	..	28.2	0.8	..	..	60.2
Producer	5.6	..	0.4	25.4	15.2	1.4	..	53.0
Coal	2.1	3.3	0.4	8.2	50.5	28.6	..	6.9
Blue (water)	5.2	..	0.6	41.5	48.7	1.4	..	3.6
Carburetted water	2.7	9.2	0.7	33.6	35.2	12.4	..	6.2
Coke oven	1.9	3.5	0.3	6.4	52.5	30.6	..	4.8

Information on the composition of a fuel gas can be used in various ways, for example, calculation of heating value and specific gravity of the gas, data which are essential for the safe and efficient utilization of gaseous fuels.

Haldane Apparatus.—Another gas volumetric apparatus widely used for the analysis of mine atmospheres and samples that contain small quantities of carbon dioxide, combustible gases and oxygen, with an accuracy greater than that obtainable with the apparatus of the type previously described, is known as the Haldane apparatus. The basic principles of the apparatus and procedures are the same as for those of other gas volumetric methods of analysis. The conventional apparatus consists of a water-jacketed burette and compensator, two absorption and one combustion pipettes. The burette consists of an ungraduated bulb at the top having a volume of 15 ml. and a stem with a volume of 6 ml. graduated to 0.01 ml. Samples to be analyzed must not contain an explosive mixture of combustible gases, and there must be sufficient oxygen in the sample to burn completely all the combustible gases. Carbon dioxide is removed first, then the combustibles (methane, hydrogen and carbon monoxide), and finally oxygen. The oxygen determined is that remaining after combustion, and therefore it is necessary to add the amount consumed by the combustion.

Calculation of results is essentially the same as for the Orsat type of apparatus.

Bone-Wheeler Gas Analysis Apparatus.—The Bone-Wheeler gas-analysis apparatus is used to a considerable extent in England. Its use in the United States is very limited. This apparatus is based on the principle of measuring change in pressure at constant volume. Instead of removing the gases in a series of pipettes they are removed in a single absorption vessel. The reagent for a single constituent is added to the vessel and the gas removed, and the change in pressure at constant volume measured. The reagent for that gas is then removed from the absorption vessel and the reagent for the next gas added to the absorption vessel. In other words, instead of using a pipette in which a constituent can be removed from a number of samples, a small amount of new reagent is used for each constituent and is then discarded.

Although it has the advantage of requiring a small sample and is independent of the atmospheric pressure, disadvantages in operative procedures have prevented its wide application.

Sampling.—It is not within the scope of this article to discuss in any detail the various methods of collecting gas samples. However, regardless of refinements and care in analytical procedures no analysis can be more accurate than the sample. Therefore, it is of the utmost importance that the sample be properly taken and handled so that there is no possibility of contamination.

BIBLIOGRAPHY.—G. A. Burrell and F. M. Seibert, "Sampling and Examination of Mine Gases and Natural Gas," U.S. Bureau of Mines *Bulletin 197*, revised by G. W. Jones (1926); American Gas Association, *Gas Chemists' Handbook*, 3rd ed. (1929); V. J. Altieri, *Gas Analysis and Testing of Gaseous Materials* (1945). (H. H. SK.)

MICROANALYSIS

Chemical analysis becomes chemical microanalysis when the quantities of substance handled, examined, or measured are significantly (ten or more times) smaller than customary. Depending upon the reduction factor, one speaks of semimicro, micro or ultramicro procedures or methods. Since these terms convey no definite meaning, it appears preferable to follow Friedrich Emich's suggestion and to speak of a centigram, milligram, microgram, etc., scale so as to indicate the amount of material under investigation.

The emergence of microchemistry and microanalysis as a separate discipline was the result of the teachings of Emich who, about 1893, started a systematical development of micromethods of chemistry by embarking on a study of all kinds of chemical experimentation on an ever increasingly small scale. It may be said that the chemistry with which we are familiar is essentially independent of the scale of experimentation as long as approximately 1,000,000 molecules or approximately 10^{-16} g. = 0.0000001 mγ (milligammas), (1 gram = 1000 mg.; 1 mg. = 1000 γ; 1γ = 1000 mγ) of material are taking part in the reaction. Consequently, only the technique of handling, observation, and measurement must be changed with the scale of working. Emich developed micromethods of chemistry not only for the purpose of qualitative and quantitative analysis, but also for preparatory work, physicochemical studies and lecture demonstration.

Since most of our information regarding matter is derived from visual impressions, the microscope must be employed whenever the amounts of material become so small that the unaided eye can no longer be relied upon to report satisfactorily appearances and direct tools. The microchemical balance, originally designed by W. H. Kuhlmann in Hamburg, was drafted for service in microanalysis mainly because of its large carrying capacity of 20 g., which is required for the weighing of the absorption tubes of organic combustion analysis. A variety of microbalances with beams of vitreous silica and using different principles for weighing (elasticity and torsiòn forces, buoyant effect, electromagnetic attraction were designed by E. Salvioni, W. Nernst, B. D. Steele and K. Grant, R. W. Gray and Sir W. Ramsay, H. Pettersson, F. W. Aston, F. Emich and later by O. H. Lowry, H. V. Neher, P. L. Kirk with R. Craig, J. E. Gullberg and R. Q. Boyer, H. M. Barrett, A. W. Birnie and M. Cohen, C. H. Wilson and H. M. El-Badry, and F. C. Edwards and R. R. Baldwin for studies on very small quantities of material. Microscope and microbalances occupy a prominent position in microanalysis, but their role as necessary tools is incidental.

Determination of the rate of radioactive decay, spectroscopy, spectrophotometry, colorimetry, fluorimetry, nephelometry, polarography, chromatography and microbiological assay methods possess in certain instances high specificity and extraordinary sensitivity so as to give them a supreme position for the determination of trace constituents. Application of these methods on a small scale gives a further increase of their efficiency, and truly amazing limits may be obtained. Spectrophotometric measurements as performed by Paul L. Kirk with the use of a cell two millimetres in diameter and five centimetres long attain a sensitivity of 0.1 mγ. A. E. Mirsky and A. W. Pollister have performed colorimetric measurements in the microscopic image of tissue thin sections, and they were able to measure as little as 0.0001 m$\gamma$of tyrosine. Small-scale performance of microbiological assay allows accurate estimations of quantity with less than one milligamma of certain substances.

Also simple analytical test tube tests may be given sensitivities from 0.0001 to 0.00001 mγ or 10^{-13} to 10^{-14} g. by performing them with the use of micromanipulators under the high-power microscope. In general, one may state that the development of chemical microtechnique is now sufficiently advanced to permit, at least theoretically, performance of any analytical task on as small a scale as becomes necessary or seems desirable on the basis of practical considerations.

Microchemical methods are continuously gaining importance since all branches of research are by necessity turning to the study of increasingly smaller detail in their quest for final answers. The effects of trace constituents have become of ever-growing interest in the study of living matter as well as in the perfection of industrial processes and products and in the maintenance of all kinds of structures and equipment. In spite of the availability of especially suitable methods for the determination of traces, the co-operation of the microanalyst becomes increasingly desirable. In physiological and pathological studies on small animals as well as in the chemical laboratories of pediatric institutes, all chemical work must be performed on a small scale, since large samples of body liquids cannot be taken without upsetting the existing conditions. Finally, the chemical investigation of dangerous materials such as explosives or highly radioactive materials becomes less hazardous when done on a sufficiently small scale.

Qualitative Microanalysis.—Modern teaching of inorganic qualitative analysis is done on a semimicro or centigram scale with the use of spot tests for confirmatory tests. In at least one instance the milligram scale has been adopted, and the confirmatory tests are observed under the microscope. Schemes of analysis including rare elements have been tried on the centigram as well as on the milligram scale. A technique for efficient work on the microgram scale, with sensitivities from one to ten milligammas for the confirmatory tests, was developed during the late 1930s. Most operations are performed under the low-power microscope with the aid of simple manipulators having rack-and-pinion motions. The technique may be readily acquired, and the work may be conveniently observed by large audiences, if microprojection is used. The microgram technique is, of course, applicable to general chemical experimentation, and it seems to have been used in the study of the chemistry of small quantities of elements produced by the cyclotron or obtained as a consequence of atomic fission. Since most of the work is done by remote control, the technique is especially attractive for work with highly radioactive matter.

Since each element produces its own characteristic spectrum, an examination, by means of the spectroscope, of the flame or spark spectrum of a substance reveals the identities of the elements present. The delicacy of the method transcends that of the most sensitive chemical reactions. The presence of one-hundred-thousandth part of a milligram of lithium may be revealed by means of the spectroscope; or, again, five hundred-thousandths of a milligram of the rare gas, neon, present in the atmosphere, may be detected. In this manner the metallic elements gallium, rubidium, indium, caesium and thallium were discovered. The absorption spectra of many inorganic and organic substances are also characteristic, thus enabling the presence of these substances to be recognized. Examples are: copper sulphate; the blood pigments (haemoglobin and oxyhaemoglobin); and the porphyrins. (*See* SPECTROSCOPY.)

Far more widely employed, however, are the purely chemical

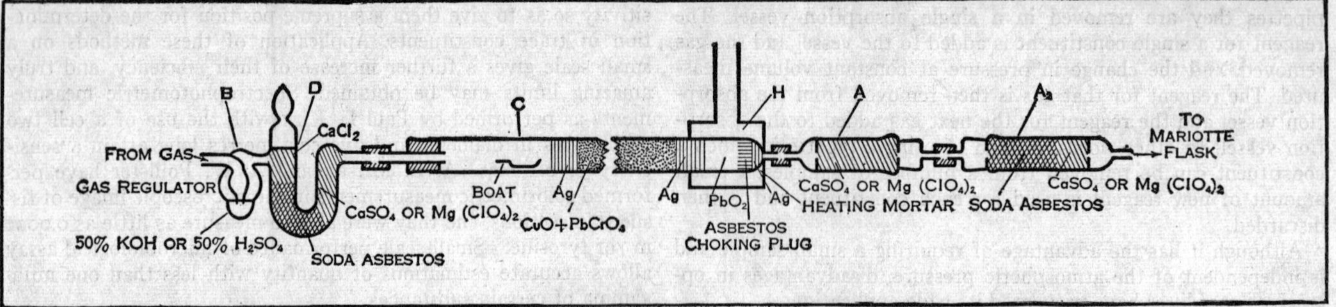

BY COURTESY OF THE SOCIETY OF CHEMICAL INDUSTRY

FIG. 7.—(B) BUBBLE COUNTER, (D) DRYING TUBE, (C) COMBUSTION TUBE, (H) HEATING MORTAR, (A_1) WATER-ABSORBING TUBE, (A_2) CARBON DIOXIDE-ABSORBING TUBE

methods which depend upon the production, on the addition of reagents to the sample or to its solution, of colorations or of colour changes; of precipitates having characteristic odour, colour or crystalline form; or of gases or liquids which can be distilled over and identified. These tests, many of which are very delicate, may be specific for particular compounds, radicals or elements; or for groups of these. Thus, the presence of 1 part of copper in 100,000,000 parts of water is shown by the blue colour produced on the successive addition of alcoholic hydrogen peroxide and guaiacum resin in pyridine. The presence of 1 part of gold in 20,000,000 parts of solution is revealed by the yellow coloration given with *o*-tolidine. Prussic acid (1 part in 2,000,000 of air) may be detected by means of the blue colour which it gives upon a test paper moistened with a solution containing *o*-tolidine, acetic acid and copper acetate. There are many hundreds of such tests, some of which are also quantitative.

Schemes of organic qualitative analysis may be carried out on a centigram or milligram scale by means of microtechniques developed mostly by Emich and his co-workers. The observation of *schlieren* for a criterion of purity was introduced by Emich and may find increasing application. Ludwig and Adelheid Kofler in Innsbruck, Austria, originated a system for the identification of organic compounds in simple mixtures, which is based on the determination of melting points under the microscope. Their technique also furnishes information on polymorphism and isomorphism, and it allows a quick survey of the melting point diagrams of mixtures.

Quantitative Microanalysis.—Complicated separations involving rare elements and followed by the determination of the isolated constituents have been carried out on the milligram scale. The most flexible technique of filtration is provided for such work by the use of Emich's filterstick, an immersion filter consisting essentially of a tube with a filter mat near its lower (immersed) opening. Any desirable material may be used for tube as well as for the filter mat. The foundation for gravimetric work on a microgram scale has been laid by Emich's systematic investigations on highly sensitive microbalances with beams of vitreous silica. Little progress has been made beyond the performance of simple residue determinations and electrolytic precipitations.

A systematic investigation of titrimetry, predominantly on the milligram scale, has been carried out by J. Mika. Titrimetric and colorimetric methods are, however, widely used on the microgram scale. A variety of burets have been developed for the purpose; some use the principle of the injection syringe, and others rely on the surface tension force originating in the fine tip to take the place of the stopcock of the customary buret. With the latter type it is possible to dispense and measure volumes of standard solutions down to 0.0002 cu.mm. by adopting the injection technique of the microbiologist and performing the titration in the field of a microscope.

Micromethods for the determination of density, some based on the use of pycnometers and some based on the principles of the floating and falling drop methods, have been applied to the determination of heavy water and to various biochemical studies. Of the gasvolumetric and manometric procedures, the very sensitive technique of D. D. van Slyke has demonstrated its great versatility. An ingenious adaptation of the principle of the Cartesian diver for gasvolumetric determinations on a microgram scale has been made by K. Linderstrom-Lang.

The milligram and centigram procedures of organic elementary analysis (determination of carbon, hydrogen, nitrogen, oxygen, sulphur, halide, phosphorus, arsenic, metallic constituents) have almost displaced the old macromethods, and the same may be said of the micromethods for the determination of the active groups in the molecule. Economy with regard to the material under investigation has become progressively more important as organic chemistry turned to the study of biochemical problems. The superiority of the micromethods in reliability and general efficiency is no longer questioned. The original methods of F. Pregl are still widely used with and without modifications. Micro adaptations of the tube filling of M. Dennstedt have been recommended by A. Friedrich and S. Ingram. In general, there is a tendency toward mechanizing the work with the use of automatic furnaces.

A brief outline of one of the most important processes is given below:

Determination of Carbon and Hydrogen.—A weighed quantity (three to five milligrams) of the substance, placed in a small platinum boat, is burned in a current of oxygen (dried by passage through the tubes B and D) in the apparatus shown in figure 7. The hard-glass tube, C, is 40 cm. in length, and contains a filling of chemicals (as indicated in the diagram) designed to arrest the escape of nitrogen, sulphur, halogens and other products which might vitiate the analysis. The remaining gaseous products of the combustion, water and carbon dioxide, are swept over with air, and are retained, respectively, in the tubes A_1 and A_2, which are weighed on the microbalance both before and after the experiment. From the gains in weight of these tubes, the amounts of hydrogen and carbon in the original material are calculated. The gas pressures at different points of the apparatus are carefully regulated, and the temperature of the lead peroxide is maintained at 180° C. by means of the external heating device shown at H. Practically all classes of organic substances may be analyzed with great accuracy in this apparatus.

Micromethods for the analysis of small samples of gases, originally introduced by C. Timiriazeff and A. Krogh, have been variously modified and refined for use in connection with chemical, industrial, biological, and medical work.

BIBLIOGRAPHY.—F. Emich, *Lehrbuch der Mikrochemie* (Munich, 1926); *Methoden der Mikrochemie* in Abderhalden's *Handbuch der biologischen Arbeitsmethoden*, Abt. i, Teil 3 (Vienna and Berlin, 1921); F. Emich–F. Schneider, *Microchemical Laboratory Manual* (1932); G. Klein and M. Strebinger, *Fortschritte der Mikrochemie* (Leipzig, 1928); reports in the *Annual Reviews of Biochemistry;* A. A. Benedetti-Pichler, *Microtechnique of Inorganic Analysis* (1942); N. D. Cheronis and J. B. Entrikin, *Semimicro Qualitative Organic Analysis* (1947); F. Schneider, *Qualitative Organic Microanalysis,* (1946); L. and A. Kofler, *Mikromethoden zur Kennzeichnung organischer Stoffe und Stoffgemische* (Innsbruck, 1948); F. Hecht and J. Donau, *Anorganische Mikrogewichtsanalyse* (Vienna, 1940); J. Mika, *Die exakten Methoden der Mikromassanalyse* (Stuttgart, 1939); P. L. Kirk, *Quantitative Ultramicroanalysis* (1950); F. Pregl, *Die quantitative organische Mikroanalyse* (Berlin, 1930); H. Roth and E. B. Daw, *Quantitative Organic Analysis of Fritz Pregl* (1937); J. B. and B. Niederl, *Micromethods of Quantitative Organic Elementary Analysis* (1942);

A. Friedrich, *Die Praxis der quantitativen organischen Mikroanalyse* (Leipzig and Vienna, 1933); R. F. Milton and W. A. Waters, *Methods of Quantitative Micro-Analysis* (1949); L. T. Hallett, a review in *Ind. Eng. Chem. Anal. Ed.*, 14:956–993 (1942); J. P. Peters and D. D. van Slyke, *Quantitative Clinical Chemistry, II. Methods* (1932); Fritz Feigl, *Qualitative Analysis by Spot Tests* (1948). (A. A. B.-P.)

CHEMISTRY, APPLIED: *see* CHEMICAL ENGINEERING.

CHEMNITZ, or KEMNITZ, **MARTIN** (1522–1586), German Lutheran theologian, born at Treuenbrietzen, Brandenburg, on Nov. 9, 1522. He went (1543) to the University of Frankfurt-on-Oder and then (1545) to the University of Wittenberg, where he heard Martin Luther preach but was more attracted by Philipp Melanchthon, who interested him in mathematics and astrology. He practised astrology, and this recommended him to Albert Frederick, duke of Prussia, who made him his librarian (1550). Returning in 1553 to Wittenberg, he lectured on Melanchthon's *Loci Communes,* his lectures forming the basis of his own *Loci Theologici* (published posthumously, 1591), an exposition of Lutheran theology. He moved to Brunswick on Dec. 15, 1554, to become coadjutor to the superintendent, Joachim Mörlin.

Against the Crypto-Calvinists he upheld the Lutheran view of the Eucharist in his *Repetitio sanae doctrinae de Vera Praesentia* (1560; in German, 1561). Other works include *Theologiae Jesuitarum praecipua capita* (1562), an attack on the society's principles; *Examen concilii Tridentini* (four parts, 1567–73); and *Corpus doctrinae Prutenicum* (1567), drawn up in conjunction with Mörlin. He resigned from his office as superintendent of Brunswick in 1584, and he died on April 8, 1586.

CHEMNITZ, a town of Germany, in the *Land* of Saxony, the capital of a governmental district, 50 mi. W.S.W. of Dresden and 51 mi. S.S.E. of Leipzig. Pop. (1939) 334,563.

Chemnitz (*Kaminizi*) was originally a settlement of the Sorbian Wends and became a market town in 1143. Its municipal constitution dates from the 14th century, and it soon became the most important industrial centre in the mark of Meissen. A monopoly of bleaching was granted to the town, and thus a considerable trade in woollen and linen yarns was attracted; paper was made here, and in the 16th century the manufacture of cloth was very flourishing. In 1546 the Benedictine monastery, founded about 1136 about 2 mi. north of the town, was dissolved. During the Thirty Years' War, Chemnitz was plundered by all parties and its trade was completely ruined, but at the beginning of the 18th century it had begun to recover. Further progress was made during the 19th century, especially after 1834 when Saxony joined the German *Zollverein.*

The town lies 950 ft. above sea, in a fertile plain at the foot of the Erzgebirge, watered by the river Chemnitz, an affluent of the Mulde. It is the chief manufacturing centre in the kingdom and ranks next to Dresden and Leipzig in point of population. It is well provided with railway communication, being directly connected with Berlin and with the towns of the Erzgebirge and Vogtland. The centre of the town is occupied by the market square, with the mediaeval *Rathaus,* now superseded by a modern building in the Post-strasse. The old inner town is within the old fortifications, and beyond lies industrial Chemnitz. There is an ancient Gothic church dedicated to St. James. To the northwest of the town is the Gothic church of a former Benedictine monastery, dating from 1514–1525, with a tower of 1897. The industry of Chemnitz has gained for the town the name of "Saxon Manchester." First in importance are its locomotive and engineering works. Next come its cotton-spinning, hosiery, textile and glove manufactures. It also has considerable dyeworks, bleachworks, chemical and woollen factories. The local communications are maintained by an electric tramway system.

Chemnitz is a favourite tourist centre for excursions into the Erzgebirge.

CHEMUNG CANAL, a canal and lock system completed in 1833, which connected the Susquehanna river with Seneca lake. It was 23 mi. long and had 49 locks, which were built of wood.

It was built during the era after 1826 when many states started ambitious inland water development projects.

CHEMURGY is not so new as its name. The latter was invented in 1935 and is said to be derived from two Greek words, the combination of which may be freely translated as "chemistry at work." Chemurgy, used in conjunction with the word "farm," gives us "farm chemurgic," which has been defined as "chemistry at work on the farm."

The farm chemurgic movement rose in the United States because of the distress caused by the enormous crop surpluses blocking the farmers' market in the late 1920s and middle 1930s. It was started in 1935 by a group of industrialists, agriculturists, and economists, who proposed to meet this problem in three ways: (1) By the discovery of new uses for established farm crops; (2) by the development of new crops to replace acreage already devoted to surplus crops; and (3) through the utilization of farm wastes, better described as "farm residues."

In a broad general sense, under the present marketing system, nearly all agricultural crops enter into industry, but these normal industrial applications are based on the old agricultural standards, food, raiment and shelter. These uses have not been changed essentially since the middle of the 19th century and have only been made more complex by the coming of the industrial age and the departure of most agricultural industry from the farm. The substitution of the power loom for farm weaving and the replacement by the tin can of the home container do not mean that more wool, cotton, or farm produce are consumed than previously, but merely that they are used elsewhere and travel farther than they did in the days when wool moved almost directly from the back of the sheep to the back of its owner. The controlling factors are financial rather than physical.

Many factors contributed to the building up of the burdensome crop surpluses of the 1920s and 1930s. The advent of automotive vehicles and the departure of the horse left available for farm products of other kinds the 30,000,000 ac. in the United States formerly devoted to forage crops, while the markets for these products remained stationary or nearly so. The introduction of the tractor greatly increased the productiveness of the farmer, while the development of high-yielding crop varieties and the extensive use of fertilizers led to a greater yield of crops per acre. Thus the farmers' productivity increased while the traditional uses for his products were either stationary or diminishing.

With the beginning of the 20th century, the so-called industrial utilization of all agricultural raw materials for purposes other than those of foods and feeds began to receive the attention of many organizations in the United States, notably that of the U.S. department of agriculture. Much work was done on the manufacture of alcohol from starchy crops; on the introduction of new crops for fibres, alcohol, and oil; and on the production of paper and furfural from corn stalks, wheat straw, corncobs, and other agricultural residues. Most of these investigations were completed on a laboratory and a pilot-plant scale and then abandoned because of unfavourable economic values. Matters stood at this point when the farm chemurgic movement was started. Those interested in improving the situation of the farmer—businessmen, agriculturists and scientists—got together to form a committee. This committee mailed out invitations for a conference of agriculture, industry, and science. The first meeting was held at Dearborn, Mich., in 1935. It resulted in the formation of the National Farm Chemurgic council, the central organization of the chemurgic movement in the United States. Its chief function by 1947 was to further and supervise the activities of local and regional groups interested in the advancement of chemurgic objectives. These groups sponsor local and regional conferences at which the chemurgic possibilities of the area are discussed by representatives of agriculture, science and business. The discussions cover a great variety of fields, all the way from working industrial developments and new research achievements to highly speculative suggestions for new crops. The result has been a distinct advance in state, industrial and government accomplishments in chemurgy. In fact, it may well be said that the chemurgic movement is responsible for the biggest government venture in this field—the establishment of the four regional research laboratories of the U.S. department of agriculture.

The background of the establishment of these laboratories is of interest.

The Bankhead-Jones bill, providing funds for additional research in the department of agriculture and the state agricultural experiment stations, became effective on July 1, 1935. The U.S. Regional Soybean Industrial Products laboratory was set up under the provisions of this bill on July 1, 1936. This was a real chemurgic laboratory, devoted primarily to finding new nonfood industrial uses for the soybean. Its success in the fields of paints and varnishes from soybeans, and plastics and fibres from soybean protein, led to the introduction in congress of a flood of other bills proposing the establishment of similar laboratories to do for other crops what soybean laboratory was doing for the soybean.

This agitation culminated in an amendment to the Agricultural Adjustment act of 1938. This amendment led to the establishment of the four regional research laboratories, whose chief functions were to be the study of new uses for agricultural raw materials. These laboratories, sometimes known as the "chemurgic laboratories," were established with a great deal of care. The sites were chosen with a view to such facilities as water, sewage disposal, transportation and easy access to possible industrial co-operators. The buildings were designed according to the latest construction developments, including ample provisions for work on a semi-industrial scale. They cost, fully equipped, around $2,000,000 each. Accommodations were planned for approximately 200 scientists and 100 auxiliary workers. The laboratories were located at Peoria, Ill.; New Orleans, La.; Philadelphia, Pa.; and Albany, Calif.; and were appropriately named for the four points of the compass.

The commodities to be studied were selected by a department of agriculture committee and were chosen primarily from among those agricultural products then in surplus. They were as follows: Northern laboratory: cereal crops, oilseeds of the area, agricultural residues; Southern laboratory: cotton, peanuts, sweet potatoes; Eastern laboratory: dairy products, tobacco, apples, white potatoes, vegetables, animal fats and oils, hides, skins and tanning materials; Western laboratory: fruits, vegetables, alfalfa, wheat, poultry products. In those cases where duplication of effort, resulting from the assignment of similar commodities to two laboratories, was thought possible, special care was taken in the arangement of the research program.

In due course, the laboratories were constructed and staffed, and work was begun on the commodities assigned to them. A number of important discoveries have been made and the use of agricultural commodities and their by-products has been greatly extended. For instance, the work of the Northern Regional Research laboratory on penicillin led to the additional use of 8,000,000 lb. of milk sugar and 12,000,000 lb. of corn steep liquor annually. The Eastern Regional Research laboratory has produced rutin from buckwheat, an accomplishment which was expected to lead to the planting of more than 50,000 ac. annually in buckwheat. (Rutin is a yellow substance, chemically a glucoside. In powder form it has proved beneficial in clinical tests for reducing the fragility of capillary blood vessels that accompanies some types of high blood pressure.)

The emphasis laid on government research in the preceding paragraphs should not be allowed to obscure other chemurgic investigations. Some of the agricultural experiment stations in the U.S. were engaged in such studies and there were many industrial organizations working on uses of agricultural commodities in fields quite apart from food, raiment and shelter. An outstanding illustration is found in the announcement of one large commercial organization that it had worked out processes by which 2,000,000 lb. of corncobs would be used annually as the basis for the manufacture of nylon. However, the basic elements of the process for the manufacture of furfural, an important step in this industrial sequence, were discovered in the department of agriculture in 1920. All of which demonstrates that chemurgy is an established influence in agricultural research.

As chemurgy develops further, it can and will have an outstanding influence on national economy in the U.S. No nation can live indefinitely on its capital and avoid bankruptcy. Agricultural commodities are reproducible and represent income rather than capital.

A nation which uses them largely in industry is simultaneously conserving its other resources. This is only one of the lessons of chemurgy. (H. T. H.)

See Wheeler McMillen, *New Riches from the Soil* (1946).

CHENAB, one of the "Five rivers" of the Punjab, Pakistan (the Greek Acesines). It rises in the snowy Himalayan ranges of Kashmir, enters Pakistani territory in the Sialkot district, and flows through the plains of the Punjab, forming the boundary between the Rechna and the Jech Doabs. Finally it joins the Jhelum at Trimmu.

The Chenab colony, resulting from the success of the Lower Chenab canal in irrigating the desert of the Bar, was formed out of the three adjacent districts of Gujranwala, Jhang and Montgomery in 1892. It lies in the Rechna Doab between the Chenab and Ravi rivers in the northeast of the Jhang district, and includes an irrigated area of more than 2,500,000 ac. The principal town is Lyallpur (pop. 1941, 69,930) called after Sir J. Broadwood Lyall, lieutenant governor of the Punjab. It is now an important trade centre, and gives its name to a district with an area of 3,224 sq.mi. and a population (1941) of 1,396,305. The Lower Chenab canal is now supplied with water from the Jhelum through the Upper Jhelum Canal, and the Chenab water is utilized for the upper Chenab canal.

This canal, opened in 1912, which has 173 mi. of main canals and distributaries, and irrigates more than 500,000 ac., forms part of the great Triple canals project.

CHÊNEDOLLÉ, CHARLES JULIEN LIOULT DE (1769–1833), French poet, was born at Vire (Calvados) on Nov. 4, 1769. He early showed a vocation for poetry, but the outbreak of the Revolution temporarily diverted his energy. Emigrating in 1791, he fought two campaigns in the army of Condé, and eventually found his way to Hamburg, where he met Antoine de Rivarol, of whose brilliant conversation he left an account. He also visited Mme. de Staël in her retreat at Coppet.

On his return to Paris in 1799, he met François Chateaubriand and his sister Lucille (Mme. de Caud), to whom he became deeply attached. After her death in 1804, Chênedollé returned to Normandy, where he married and became eventually inspector of the academy of Caen (1812–32). With the exception of occasional visits to Paris, he spent the rest of his life in his native province. He died at the château de Coisel on Dec. 2, 1833.

He published his *Génie de l'homme* in 1807, and in 1820 his *Études poétiques,* which had the misfortune to appear shortly after the *Méditations* of Alphonse Lamartine, so that the author did not receive the credit of their real originality.

Chênedollé had many sympathies with the romanticists, and was a contributor to their organ, the *Muse française*. His other works include the *Esprit de Rivarol* (1808) in conjunction with F. J. M. Fayolle.

The works of Chênedollé were edited in 1864 by Charles A. Sainte-Beuve, who drew portraits of him in his *Chateaubriand et son groupe* and in an article contributed to the *Revue des deux mondes* (June 1849).

BIBLIOGRAPHY.—E. Helland, *Étude biographique et litteraire sur Chênedollé* (1857); Cazin, *Notice sur Chênedollé* (1869); and L. de Samie, *Chênedollé* (1922).

CHENERY, THOMAS (1826–1884), English scholar and editor of the *Times,* was born at Barbados and educated at Eton and Caius college, Cambridge. Having been called to the bar, he went out to Constantinople as the *Times* correspondent just before the Crimean War, and it was under the influence there of Algernon Smythe (afterward Lord Strangford) that he first turned to those philological studies by which he became eminent. After the war he returned to London and wrote regularly for the *Times* for many years, eventually succeeding Delane as editor in 1877. He was then an experienced publicist, particularly well versed in oriental affairs, an indefatigable worker, with a rapid and comprehensive judgment, though he lacked Delane's intuition for public opinion. In 1868 he was appointed Lord Almoner's professor of Arabic at Oxford, and retained his position until he became editor of *The Times.* He was one of the company of revisers of the Old Testament. He was secretary for some time to the Royal Asiatic Society, and edited the Arabic classic *The Assemblies of Al-Harīrī* and the *Machberoth Ithiel.* He died in London on Feb. 11, 1884.

CHENG, Tscheng or Tschiang (Ger. *Scheng*), an ancient Chinese wind instrument in the nature of a primitive portable organ, containing the principle of the free reed which found application in Europe in the accordion, concertina, and harmonium. In shape the cheng resembles a closed teapot to the top of which are fitted bamboo pipes of graduated lengths and furnished in the side with an insufflation tube curved like a swan's neck or the spout of a teapot.

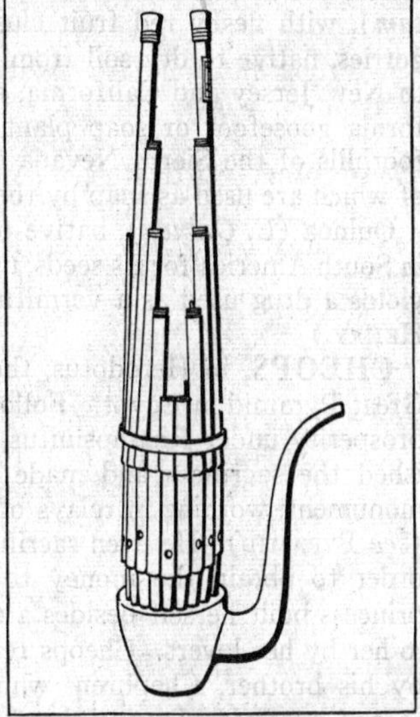
BY COURTESY OF THE METROPOLITAN MUSEUM OF ART

AN ANCIENT CHINESE WIND INSTRUMENT, ANTICIPATING THE PRINCIPLES OF THE HARMONIUM, PLAYED BY BLOWING THROUGH THE TEAPOT-LIKE SPOUT

CHÊNGTU, the administrative centre of the province of Szechwan and the regional capital of West China, situated 30° 40′ N., 104° 12′ E. In the north-west corner of the Red Basin of Szechwan there lies a smooth plain some 70 miles by 40, whose even surface contrasts strongly with the rest of the highly dissected Basin. Chêngtu is the centre of this plain which forms the deltaic fan of the Min-Ho below its debouchure at Kwan-hien from the high mountain country of north-west Szechwan. By means of a marvellous irrigation system, initially planned by Li Ping in the 3rd century B.C. and further elaborated at several subsequent periods, the river waters are now led off at Kwan-hien along innumerable irrigation channels to fertilize the whole plain instead of littering it with gravel as in its natural state. At the lower end of the plain the channels are drawn together and issue as two rivers, the Min-Ho, and the Chung-kiang, which join the Yangtze at Suifu and Luchow respectively. Although on the average 2,000 ft. above sea-level, the Chêngtu plain lies in a very sheltered position and yields exceptionally heavy crops of all the varied products typical of Middle China (*see* China).

Chêngtu also serves as the commercial outlet of the mountain country of north-west Szechwan, the pastoral products of which are utilized in the industries of the city. Because of its position at the contact of plain and mountain Chêngtu focuses the life of the sheltered agricultural Red Basin and the rugged pastoral mountain country of the west Szechwan border. The Red Basin of Szechwan lies in the far west of China and Chêngtu is placed on the western border of the Red Basin. After 1937, prominent Chinese universities moved to Chêngtu, including the University of Nanking, Yenching university, Ginling College for Women. Szechwan university and the West China Union university are also here. Manufacturing plants were established in Chêngtu for improved agricultural equipment. In the fall of 1940 the First National Forestry and Soil Conservation conference was held there. The population of Chêngtu was 440,988 (1934).

CHÉNIER, ANDRÉ DE (1762–1794), French poet, was born at Constantinople of a French father and a Greek mother. His parents returned to France in 1765, and though the father afterwards served as consul general in Morocco, the children (Marie-Joseph is noticed below) remained in France. André was educated at the college de Navarre in Paris, and after some months in the army at Strasbourg, returned to Paris, where he met the poets and artists of the day in his mother's salon. A visit to Italy in 1784 made a deep impression on his mind, and strengthened his passion for the antique. The next three years were spent in experimenting in eclogues and idylls in the classical manner. Of the works of this period the most famous is *La jeune Tarentine,* classical in form, but characterized by the grace and charm which informed all Chénier's work. He proposed to write and actually composed fragments of a poem modelled on Lucretius, *Hermès,* which was to cover the contents of the *Encyclopédie.* In 1787 he went to London as secretary to his relative, M. de la Luzerne, at that time French ambassador. London displeased him, and in 1790 he returned to France, and plunged into political writing. His prose *Avis au peuple français* (Aug. 24, 1790) was followed by the *Jeu de Paume,* a moral ode addressed to the painter Louis David. Chénier was a member of the Feuillant club, and contributed to the *Journal de Paris* the Iambes addressed to Collot d'Herbois *Sur les Suisses révoltés.* He escaped the massacres of September because his family got him away to Normandy, and after the execution of Louis XVI. he hid in an obscure refuge near Versailles. To this period belong his *Ode à Charlotte Corday* and his *Ode à Versailles.* His lines on the art of writing poetry are still quoted in French university circles.

But on Mar. 7, 1794, he was arrested in the house of Madame Piscatory at Passy. He was lodged first in the Luxembourg and then in Saint-Lazare. His imprisonment lasted 141 days. His brother, Marie-Joseph, a member of the Convention, could not save him, and he was guillotined on July 25, 1794, three days before Robespierre, whose death would have saved him. To this four months' imprisonment belong André Chénier's greatest poems, the *Jeune Captive,* the *Iambes* (in alternate lines of 12 and 8 syllables) attacking the Convention and conveyed sheet by sheet to his friends by a venal gaoler.

These circumstances explain how it was that the greatest French lyricist of the 18th century had to wait 20 years for the merest recognition of his genius. For only fragments of his work were known, and he only reached the full measure of his powers in the months before his tragic end. Only the *Jeu de Paume* and the *Hymne sur les Suisses* were known in his life time. The *Jeune Captive* and the *La Jeune Tarentine* were published in periodicals in 1795 and 1801. The first imperfect attempt to collect the body of his work was made in 1819. Since that date there has been unanimous acknowledgment of his genius, but the critics have been divided as to whether he should be classed, as Sainte-Beuve classed him, as the forerunner of Victor Hugo and the romanticists, or, as Anatole France would have it, as the last exponent of the art of the 18th century. Perhaps his influence was greatest on the classicists who led the reaction against the romanticists at the end of the 19th century, on Leconte de Lisle and Hérédia.

Bibliography.—The Chénier literature is enormous. His fate has been commemorated in numerous plays, pictures and poems, notably in the fine epilogue of Sully Prudhomme, the *Stello* of A. de Vigny, the delicate statue by Puech in the Luxembourg, and the well-known portrait in the centre of the "Last Days of the Terror." The best editions are still those of Becq de Fouquières (1862, 1872 and 1881), supplemented by those of L. Moland (2 vols. 1889) and R. Guillard (2 vols. 1899).

See also Sainte-Beuve, *Tableau de la Litt. fr.* (1828); Anatole France, *La Vie littéraire* vol. ii.; E. Faguet, *André Chénier* (1902).

CHÉNIER, MARIE-JOSEPH BLAISE DE (1764–1811), French poet, dramatist and politician, younger brother of André de Chénier, was born at Constantinople on Feb. 11, 1764. He was brought up at Carcassonne, and educated in Paris at the Collège de Navarre. After two years spent in the army he began to write plays on the Voltairian model. The notoriety attained by the later plays was due to political considerations rather than to any intrinsic literary merit. His *Charles IX.* was kept back for nearly two years by the censor; its production (Nov. 4, 1789) was an immense success, due in part to Talma's magnificent impersonation of Charles IX. Camille Desmoulins said that the piece had done more for the Revolution that the days of October, and a contemporary memoir-writer, the marquis de Ferrière, says that the audience came away "ivre de vengeance et tourmenté d'une soif de sang." The performance occasioned a split among the actors of the Comédie Française, and the new theatre in the Palais Royal, established by the dissidents, was inaugurated with *Henri VIII.* (1791), generally recognized as Chénier's masterpiece; *Jean Calas, ou l'école des juges* followed in the same year. In 1792 he produced his *Caius Gracchus,* which was proscribed in 1793 at the instance of the Montagnard deputy, Albitte, for an anti-anarchical hemistich (*Des lois et non du sang!*); *Fénelon* (1793) was suspended after a few representations; and in 1794 his *Timoléon,* set to Étienne Méhul's music, was also proscribed. This piece was played after the fall of the Terror, but the fratricide of Timoléon became the text for unfounded insinuations that, by his silence, Joseph de Chénier had connived at the judicial murder of André. In fact Joseph knew that André's only chance of safety lay in being forgotten by the authorities, and that intervention would only hasten the end. Joseph Chénier had been a member of the Convention and of the Council of Five Hundred, and had voted for the death of Louis XVI.; he had a seat in the tribunate; he belonged to the committees of public instruction, of general security and of public safety. Nevertheless, before the end of the Terror he had become a marked man. His purely political career ended in 1802, but from 1803 to 1806 he was inspector-general of public instruction. *Cyrus* (1804) was written in honour of Napoleon, but Chénier was temporarily disgraced in 1806 for his *Épître à Voltaire.* He died on Jan. 10, 1811. The list of his works includes hymns and national songs—among others, the famous *Chant du départ;* odes, *Sur la mort de Mirabeau, Sur l'oligarchie de Robespierre,* etc.; tragedies which never reached the stage, *Brutus et Cassius, Philippe deux, Tibère;* a *Tableau historique* (1808) of contemporary French literature; translations from Sophocles and Lessing, from Gray and Horace, from Tacitus and Aristotle; with elegies, dithyrambics and Ossianic rhapsodies.

See *Œuvres complètes de Joseph Chénier* (8 vols., 1823–26), containing notices of the poet by Arnault and Daunou; Charles Labitte, *Études littéraires* (1846); Henri Welschinger, *Le Théâtre révolutionnaire, 1789–1799* (1881); and A. Lieby, *Étude sur le théâtre de Marie-Joseph Chénier* (1902).

CHENILLE, a twisted velvet cord, woven so that the short outer threads stand out at right angles to the central cord, thus giving a resemblance to a caterpillar. Chenille is used as a trimming for dress and furniture. The word is French and means a hairy caterpillar.

CHENONCEAUX, a village of central France, in the department of Indre-et-Loire, on the right bank of the Cher, 20 mi. E. by S. of Tours on the Orléans railway. Pop. (1946) 222. Chenonceaux owes its interest to its château, a building in the Renaissance style on the river Cher. Founded in 1515 by Thomas Bohier (d. 1523), financial minister in Normandy, the château was confiscated by Francis I. in 1535. An isolated tower flanking a drawbridge is part of an earlier building of the 15th century. Henry II. presented it to Diane de Poitiers, who on his death was forced to exchange it for Chaumont-sur-Loire by Catherine de' Medici. The latter built the gallery which leads to the left bank of the Cher. Chenonceaux passed successively into the hands of Louise de Vaudémont, wife of Henry III., the house of Vendôme, and the family of Bourbon-Condé. It came into the possession of Claude Dupin (1684–1769) and in 1864 it was sold to the chemist Théophile Pélouze, whose wife executed extensive restorations.

CHENOPODIUM or Goosefoot, a genus of erect or sometimes prostrate herbs of the family Chenopodiaceae, comprising some 60 species, natives of temperate regions, some of which have cosmopolitan distribution as weeds. Inclusive of those introduced from the old world, some 25 species occur in North America. A well known representative is the common goosefoot (*C. album*), called also lamb's quarters and pigweed. It is native to Europe and Asia, is found in Great Britain, and is widely prevalent in North America as a naturalized weed. The green angular stem is often striped with white or red, and, like the leaves, often more or less covered with mealy particles. The leaves are entire, lobed or toothed and often more or less triangular in shape. The minute flowers are borne in dense axillary or terminal clusters. The fruit, usually enclosed by the persistent calyx, is a membranous utricle covering a small, black, often glossy seed.

Among other goosefoots found in Great Britain and also naturalized in North America are the maple-leaved goosefoot (*C. hybridum*), the nettle-leaved goosefoot or sowbane (*C. murale*), the oak-leaved goosefoot (*C. glaucum*), the many-seeded goosefoot (*C. polyspermum*), the city goosefoot (*C. urbicum*), and good-King-Henry (*C. Bonus-Henricus*). Other old-world species naturalized in North America are the Jerusalem oak (*C. Botrys*), the Mexican tea (*C. ambrosioides*) and the wormseed (*C. anthelminticum*).

Among native North American species are the red goosefoot (*C. rubrum*), growing on saline soils on sea coasts and in the interior, and found also in Europe; the strawberry blite (*C. capitatum*), with fleshy red fruit clusters somewhat resembling strawberries, native to dry soil from Nova Scotia to Alaska southward to New Jersey and California, and also in Europe; and the California goosefoot or soap plant (*C. californicum*), found in the foothills of the Sierra Nevada and coast ranges, the grated roots of which are used as soap by the Indians.

Quinoa (*C. Quinoa*), native to the Andean region, is cultivated in South America for its seeds, used as food. The wormseed (*q.v.*) yields a drug used as a vermifuge. (*See* the article Good-King-Henry.)

CHEOPS, in Herodotus, the name of the king who built the Great Pyramid in Egypt. Following on a period of good rule and prosperity under Rhampsinitus, Cheops closed the temples, abolished the sacrifices and made all the Egyptians labour for his monument, working in relays of 100,000 men every three months (*see* Pyramid). He even sacrificed the honour of his daughter in order to obtain the money to complete his pyramid; and the princess built herself besides a small pyramid of the stones given to her by her lovers. Cheops reigned 50 years and was succeeded by his brother, Chephren, who reigned 56 years and built the second pyramid. During these two reigns the Egyptians suffered every kind of misery and the temples remained closed. Herodotus continues that in his own day the Egyptians were unwilling to name these oppressors and preferred to call the pyramids after a shepherd named Philition, who pastured his flocks in their neighbourhood At length Mycerinus, son of Cheops and successor of Chephren, reopened the temples and, although he built the Third Pyramid, allowed the oppressed people to return to their proper occupations.

Cheops, Chephren and Mycerinus are historical personages of the fourth Egyptian dynasty, in correct order, and they built the three pyramids attributed to them here. But they are wholly misplaced by Herodotus. Rhampsinitus, the predecessor of Cheops, appears to represent Rameses III. of the twentieth dynasty, and Mycerinus in Herodotus is but a few generations before Psammetichus, the founder of the twenty-sixth dynasty. Manetho correctly places the great Pyramid kings in Dynasty IV. In Egyptian the name of Cheops (Chemmisor Chembis in Diodorus Siculus, Suphis in Manetho) is spelt Hwfw (Khufu), but the pronunciation, in late times perhaps Khöouf, is uncertain. How far we may accept Herodotus' view of the distress caused by the building of the pyramid is doubtful. Petrie thinks that he can trace a violent religious revolution with confiscation of endowments at this time in the temple remains at Abydos; but none the less the deities were then served by priests selected from the royal family and the highest in the land. Khufu's work in the temple of Bubastis is proved by a surviving fragment, and he is figured slaying his enemy at Sinai before the god Thoth. In late times the priests of Denderah claimed Khufu as a benefactor; he was reputed to have built temples to the gods near the Great Pyramids and Sphinx (where also a pyramid of his daughter Hentsen is spoken of), and there are incidental notices of him in the medical and religious literature. The funerary cult of Khufu and Khafrē was practised under the twenty-sixth dynasty, when so much that had fallen into disuse and been forgotten was revived. Khufu is a leading figure in an ancient Egyptian story (Papyrus Westcar), but it is unfortunately incomplete. He was the founder of the fourth dynasty, and was probably born in Middle Egypt near Beni Hasan, in a town afterwards known as "Khufu's Nurse," but was connected with the Memphite third dynasty. Two tablets at the mines of Wadi Maghara in the peninsula of Sinai, a granite block from Bubastis, and a beautiful ivory statuette found by Petrie in the temple at Abydos, are almost all that can be definitely assigned to Khufu outside the pyramid at Giza and its ruined accompaniments. His date, according to Petrie, is 3969–3908 B.C., but in the shorter chronology of Meyer, Breasted and others he reigned (23 years) about a thousand years later, *c.* 2900 B.C.

See Herodotus ii. 124; Diodorus Siculus i. 64; Sethevin Pauly-Wissowa's *Realencyklopädie, s.v.;* W. M. F. Petrie, *History of Egypt,* vol. i., and *Abydos,* part ii. p. 48; J. H. Breasted, *History.*

CHEPSTOW, market town, urban district and river port of Monmouthshire, England, on the Wye, 2 mi. above its junction with the Severn, and on the Western Region railway. Pop. (1951) 5,285. Area, 2.41 sq.mi. As the key to the passage of the Wye, Chepstow (*Estrighorel, Striguil*) was the site of British, Roman and Saxon fortifications. The Norman castle was built by William Fitz-Osbern to defend the Roman road into south Wales. The castle occupies a hill site on the western bank of the river. It was founded in the 11th and rebuilt in the 13th century. It was granted by Henry I to Walter FitzRichard of Clare, and after its reversion to the crown, Edward II granted it to Thomas de Brotherton. It passed, through Margaret, Lady Segrave, to the dukes of Norfolk, from whom, after again reverting to the crown, it passed to the earls of Worcester. It was confiscated by parliament but restored to the earls in 1660. The church of St. Mary, originally the conventual chapel of a Benedictine priory, has some old features. The borough must have grown up between 1310, when the castle and vill were granted to Thomas de Brotherton, and 1432, when John, duke of Norfolk, died seised of the castle, manor and borough of Striguil. In 1524 the earl of Worcester granted a new charter to the bailiffs and burgesses of the town, which had fallen into decay. This was sustained until the reign of Charles II, when, some dispute arising, the charter lapsed and the town was afterwards governed by a board of twelve. A port since early times, when the lord took dues of ships going up to the forest of Dean, Chepstow had no ancient market and no manufactures but that of glass, which was carried on for a short time within the ruins of the castle. A local trade during the 19th century was handicapped by the narrowness and depth of the channel and the consequent tidal bore. There is a racecourse 1½ mi. N.W. of the town.

CHEQUE or **CHECK.** A cheque, in the simple definition of the English law, "is a bill of exchange drawn on a banker payable on demand." It has proved in practice to be a credit instrument of astonishing usefulness. No one could have foreseen that the cheque would become the chief currency of domestic commerce in Great Britain and the United States. What is perhaps equally surprising is that the British and American example has not been more largely followed in other countries. Over 90 per cent of the internal financial and wholesale trading transactions of Great Britain and the United States are settled by cheque. On the continent of Europe the cheque system is comparatively undeveloped, but it is everywhere making headway, especially in France and Germany. That the cheque will eventually come into universal use cannot be doubted.

The word "cheque," of which "check" is a variant, originally signified the counterfoil or indent of an exchequer bill, or any draft form of payment, on which was registered the details of the principal part, as a "check" to alteration or forgery. The check or counterfoil parts remained in the hands of the banker, the portion given to the customer being termed a "drawn note" or "draft." From the beginning of the nineteenth century the word "cheque" gradually became synonymous with "draft" as meaning a written order on a banker by a person having money in the banker's hands, to pay some amount to bearer or to a person named. Ultimately, the word "cheque" entirely superseded the word "draft."

The law relating to cheques, which is generally one with that of bills of exchange, but has some different and supplemental points, is dealt with elsewhere (*see* BILL OF EXCHANGE). Here we note some of the chief precautions which should be used in drawing cheques.

Cheque Forms.—London banks use a form printed "or order"; the payees cannot obtain the money without "endorsing" the cheque. Therefore no other person could obtain the money without committing forgery. Further, the form may be printed "crossed"; two lines being printed across it. A cheque so crossed can only be cashed through a banker, so that, if we imagine the endorsement to be forged, the forger could not cash the cheque without the aid of a person with a banking account to put the cheque through for him. Further, the drawers of the cheque often take the precaution of adding the words "a/c Payees only" to the crossing. That means that no person other than the payees could obtain payment, even though a forger had signed the payee's name on the back.

In drawing cheque for eight pounds, for example, the words should be carefully written close to the printed words "the sum of," and also close to each other, to prevent the insertion of forged figures, while the space not needed for words is filled in with a thick wavy line. The "t" of "eight" and the "p" of pounds, are written closely together to prevent the insertion of a "y" to turn "eight" into "eighty." For the same reason, the figures are carefully written and the spaces between them filled with lines. As a further precaution, the words "under nine pounds" are written in the top left hand corner. A cheque thus drawn with care and intelligence can hardly be misused, but business firms often take the further precaution of using a machine which perforates the figures as it prints them. A cheque may legally be drawn upon a plain piece of paper, but this, fortunately for the bankers, is rarely done; it is only too likely to lead to mistake and loss. The adoption of an inimitable form of signature by those who draw many cheques should be carefully considered. It is a curious fact that wholly or partly illegible signatures are much safer than those carefully or very legibly written, for a well or beautifully written name is easily imitated by the forger.

Bankers issue to their customers on request cheque-forms either to "bearer" or to "order," and printed either crossed or left uncrossed. It is far the best way to use cheque forms printed "or order" and crossed. If it is desired to make the cheque payable to "bearer" this can be done by crossing out the word order and signing the alteration. Again, if it is desired to cancel the printed cross lines this can be done by writing across them "Pay cash" and signing the alteration.

The usual form of an American cheque carries at the top the date of issuance, the name of the bank on which it is drawn and a number for convenient identification. This is followed by the printed words "Pay to the order of" and a space in which is written the name of the payee. On the next line the amount in dollars is written out and the cents usually shown in figures. There is also provided a place for writing the whole amount of the cheque in figures. At the bottom appears the signature of the maker. To collect the cheque the payee must endorse it exactly as his name is written. When so endorsed the cheque is good in the hands of anyone, as is the case with a cheque made payable to cash. The signature of the person cashing it is usually required. The precautions stated above should be used in drawing the cheque.

The Cheque as Receipt.—The cheque form has come into common sense use as a means of giving a receipt conveniently and expeditiously. It is not surprising that it occurred to business men that as a cheque has to be endorsed on the back by the payee, it would make short work of detail by turning that endorsement into a definite receipt for the money paid. Accordingly, in an increasing number of cases, business firms print on the back of the cheques they use a form of a receipt for the payee to sign. As cheques are always sent back to the drawers when cleared by their bankers, the drawers have only to paste the returned cheques in their cheque book to have a complete and combined record of payments and receipts. A further development of the cheque form has naturally followed. The custom of endorsing a cheque on the back is a strange one. To find such an endorsement one has to turn the cheque over, and it is never well in matters of record to write or print on both sides of the paper. The endorsement on the back of a cheque, useful as it is, is thus seen as a combination of usefulness and inconvenience. Realising this, some business houses have boldly brought the endorsement on to the front of the cheque and at the same time made it a receipt form. This somewhat enlarges the size of the cheque form, but the complete record can be contrived within a space of 7 or 8 in. by 5 or 6 in. It is probable that so simple and convenient a method of combining payment, endorsement and receipt will come into wide use (*see* BILL OF EXCHANGE; BANKING; MONEY MARKET).

CHEQUERS. Chequers Court, near Wendover, Buckinghamshire, became an official residence of British prime ministers in 1921 through the generosity of its owners, Lord and Lady Lee of Fareham. The estate is about 1,500 ac. in extent.

Here Caractacus had a stronghold, of which the earthworks are still visible. "Radulphus," clerk to the Exchequer, was owner under Henry II., and the place appears to have taken its name from his office. In 1565, his descendant, William Hawtrey, remodelled the house and gave it much of its present character and appearance. In the 18th century, a unique collection (which still remains) of Cromwell portraits and other relics was brought by the Russells, who were descended from one of the Protector's daughters. The Russells maintained the Elizabethan house with little alteration, but Robert Greenhill, who inherited from them early in the 19th century, plastered the whole of the outside and redecorated the interior in Strawberry Hill Gothic fashion.

When the Lees entered on a long tenancy in 1909 they sought to reveal all the remaining ancient features, and to introduce others characteristic of the days of the Hawtreys and the Russells. In 1917 Lord and Lady Lee changed their tenancy into a freehold, and created a trust, which, on their deaths should make the house an adequate seat where the prime ministers could entertain guests. The original draft for the Chequers Trust declared that:—"The main features of the scheme are, therefore, designed not merely to make Chequers available as the official country residence of the prime minister of the day, but to tempt him to visit it regularly, and to make it possible for him to live there, even if his income should be limited to his salary. With this object a sufficient endowment is provided to cover the cost of a permanent nucleus staff of servants, of keeping up the gardens and grounds, of maintenance and repairs, and other necessary outgoings. There is also a residential allowance for the official occupant calculated in a fashion deliberately designed to encourage regular week-end visits." The draft, however, insisted upon the unaltered preservation of both house and contents.

In 1920 Lord and Lady Lee resolved that this scheme should not await their death but should take immediate effect. All the preparations for establishing and working the trust having been completed, the prime minister, Lloyd George, held his house-warming on Jan. 8, 1921. His successors have spent part of their time here during their terms of office and ministerial week ends at Chequers Court became a part of English political life.

CHER, a department of central France, embracing the eastern part of the ancient province of Berry, and parts of Bourbonnais, Nivernais and Orléanais, bounded north by the department of Loiret, west by Loir-et-Cher and Indre, south by Allier and Creuse, and east by Nièvre. Pop. (1946) 286,070. Area 2,820 sq.mi. Oolitic rocks occupy much of the department but are covered by Cretaceous and Tertiary deposits in the north. The higher well-drained land of the south and east is suitable both for cultivation and for pasturage. The valley of the Loire is especially fertile and the eastern, sunny slopes are noted for their vines, particularly in the neighbourhood of Sancerre. Wheat and oats are largely cultivated, while hemp, vegetables and fruits are also produced. The central districts are fertile but are low-lying and marshy, being often flooded by the Cher. The department contains much pasturage whence considerable trade in horses, cattle, sheep and wool for the northern markets. Many parts, also, are well-wooded. The chief rivers, besides the Cher and its tributaries, are the Grande Sauldre and the Petite Sauldre on the north, but the Loire, which forms the eastern boundary, and the Allier, though not falling within the department, drain the eastern districts, and are navigable. The Cher itself becomes navigable when it receives the Arnon and Yèvre, and communication is greatly facilitated by the Canal du Berry, the lateral canal of the Loire, which follows the left bank of that river, and the canal of the Sauldre. Mines of iron are worked and stone is quarried. There are brick, porcelain and glassworks, flour-mills, distilleries, oil-works, saw-mills and tanneries. Bourges and Vierzon are metallurgical and engineering centres. The department is served by the Orléans railway. It is divided into the two *arrondissements* (29 cantons, 290 communes) of Bourges and Saint-Amand-Mont-Rond, of which the former is the capital and the seat of an archbishop and of a court of appeal. The department belongs to the *académie* (educational division) of Paris. Bourges, Saint-Amand-Mont-Rond, Vierzon and Sancerre are the principal towns. Méhun-sur-Yèvre (pop. 4,616 in 1946), a town with porcelain manufactures, has a Romanesque church and a château of the 14th century. The church at St. Satur has a fine choir of the 14th and 15th centuries; those of Dun-sur-Auron, Plaimpieds, Aix d'Angillon and Jeanvrin are Romanesque in style, while that at Aubigny-Ville is of the 12th, 13th and 15th centuries. Drevant, on the site of a Roman town, preserves ruins of a theatre. The Pierre-de-la-Roche, at Villeneuve-sur-Cher, is the most notable megalithic monument.

CHERAT, a hill cantonment and sanatorium in the Peshawar district of the North-West Frontier province, Pakistan, 34 mi. S.E. of Peshawar. It is situated at an elevation of 4,500 ft. It was first used in 1861, and later was employed during the hot weather as a health station for the British troops quartered in the vale of Peshawar.

CHERBOURG, a naval station, fortified town and seaport of northwestern France, capital of an *arrondissement* in the department of Manche, on the English channel, 232 mi. W.N.W. of Paris on the Ouest-État railway. Pop. (1946) 40,042. Cherbourg is situated at the mouth of the Divette, on a small bay at the apex of the indentation formed by the northern shore of the Cotentin peninsula, backed by the steep Montagne du Roule.

Cherbourg is supposed to occupy the site of the Roman station of *Coriallum,* but nothing definite is known about its origin. The peninsula, stretching far towards the Isle of Wight, seems to have been used by prehistoric traders of the bronze age as a starting place for the British Isles. William the Conqueror, under whom the settlement appears as *Carusbur,* provided it with a hospital and a church; and Henry II of England on several occasions chose it as his residence. Under Philip Augustus it became of military importance; in 1295 it was pillaged by an English fleet from Yarmouth, and in the 14th century it frequently suffered during the wars against the English. Captured by the English in 1418 after a four months' siege, it was recovered by Charles VII of France in 1450. An attempt was made under Louis XIV to construct a military port. Fortifications constructed by Vauban in 1686 were dismantled in 1689. Harbourworks were begun under Louis XVI and continued by Napoleon I. It was left, however, to Louis Philippe, and Napoleon III, to complete them. By 1858, £8,000,000 had been expended on the works; in 1889, the harbour was farther extended.

The naval and commercial harbours are distant from each other about half a mile. The former consists of three main basins cut out of the rock, and has an area of 55 acres. The minimum depth of water is 30 ft. Connected with the harbour are dry docks, shipbuilding yards, magazines, rope walks, etc. There is a large naval hospital close to the harbour. The commercial harbour at the mouth of the Divette communicates with the sea by a channel 650 yd. long. It consists of two parts, an outer and tidal harbour $17\frac{1}{2}$ acres in extent, and an inner basin 15 acres in extent, with a depth on sill at ordinary spring tide of 25 ft. Outside these harbours is the triangular bay, which forms the roadstead of Cherbourg. The bay is naturally sheltered on every side but the north, where lies the huge breakwater, $2\frac{1}{4}$ mi. in length (begun by Louis XVI), with a width of 650 ft. at its base and 30 ft. at its summit, which is protected by forts, and leaves passages for vessels to the east and west. The transatlantic liners lie to within this *digue.*

Near the roadstead is the church of La Trinité, a good example of the Flamboyant style (1423–1504), and one of the few historic buildings of Cherbourg. A rich collection of paintings is housed in the *hôtel de ville.* A statue of the painter J. F. Millet, born near Cherbourg, stands in the public garden. Cherbourg is a fortified place of the first class, headquarters of one of the five naval arrondissements of France, and the seat of a sub-prefect. It has tribunals of first instance and of commerce, a chamber of commerce and a naval school. The chief industries of the town proper are fishing, sawmilling, tanning, shipbuilding, iron and copper founding and ropemaking. The bathing beach is frequented by local holidaymakers. Cherbourg is a port of call for transatlantic steamers. The chief exports are stone for road-making, butter, eggs and vegetables; the chief imports are coal, timber, superphosphates and wine from Algeria. Great Britain is the principal customer.

CHERBULIEZ, CHARLES VICTOR (1829–1899), French novelist and miscellaneous writer, was born at Geneva, where his father, André Cherbuliez (1795–1874), was a classical professor at the university. He resumed French citizenship and was elected a member of the Academy (1881). Cherbuliez wrote many novels, showing the influence of George Sand, of which the following are the best known: *Le Comte Kostia* (1863), *Le Prince Vitale* (1864), *Le Roman d'une honnête femme* (1866), *L'Aventure de Ladislas Bolski* (1869), *La Vocation du Comte Ghislain* (1888), *Le Secret du précepteur* (1893), *Jacquine Vanesse* (1898). He also contributed literary and historical studies to the *Revue des deux Mondes* and *Le Temps*, many of which were collected in book form in *L'Allemagne politique* (1870), *Études de littérature et d'art* (1873), *Profils étrangers* (1889), etc.

See E. Ritter, *Victor Cherbuliez* (1900).

CHERCHEL, a seaport of Algeria, in the *arrondissement* and department of Algiers, 55 mi. W. of the capital. Pop. (1948) 7,805. It is in an agricultural and vine-growing district. Commercially it is of no great importance. The artificial harbour gives excellent shelter to small vessels. The town is noted for the extensive ruins of former cities on the same site. Cherchel was a city of the Carthaginians, who named it Jol. Juba II. (25 B.C.) made it the capital of the Mauretanian kingdom under the name of Caesarea. Destroyed by the Vandals, Caesarea regained some importance under the Byzantines. Taken by the Arabs it was renamed Cherchel. Khair-ed-Din Barbarossa captured the city in 1520 and annexed it to his Algerian pashalik. In 1840 the town was occupied by the French. The ruins suffered from vandalism during the early period of French rule, many portable objects being removed to museums in Paris or Algiers, and most of the monuments destroyed for the sake of their stone. The museum contains some of the finest statues discovered in Africa.

See V. F. Godell, *Les monuments antiques de l'Algérie* (1901).

CHEREPOVETZ, a town and district in the Vologda region (*q.v.*) of the Russian Soviet Federated Socialist republic. The area of the district is 18,387 sq.mi., and the population 607,735, mainly rural. The soil is mainly of the podsolized bog type favourable to tree growth (*see* RUSSIA: *Soils and Their Influence*) and 76% of the district is forested. The climate is dry and cold, and the waterways are frozen six months in the year; of the average rainfall of 20 to 25 in., most falls in July and August. The summer temperature averages 65° F. Much timber is exported in a raw state to Leningrad and Moscow or abroad; there is little manufacture of furniture or other wooden goods. The timber is floated down the waterways on rafts when the spring thaws begin. During World War I and the Intervention (1914–21), sawmilling and timber works fell off, partly through the blockade of foreign markets and partly through the cessation of building operations. By 1924 it had reached only 50% of the 1913 level. Koustar (peasant) industries in charcoal burning and the production of pitch and tar are carried on in all the forest areas. Hunting is a profitable occupation, mainly for export. Squirrel, fox, marten and polecat fur have the widest sale; other animals hunted are otter and marsh otter, white hare, ermine, lynx, wolf and brown bear. During the war and civil war 1914–21, hunting practically ceased, and wolves and bears became so numerous that they attacked the villagers, and it was necessary to offer rewards for their heads. By 1925 the export of furs from the area reached two-thirds of the prewar level. In the sown area, the chief crops are rye, oats, barley, wheat and buckwheat, which together form 83.5% of the crops. Potatoes, flax and hay are also produced. In the famine year 1921–22, Cherepovetz had a good harvest, since it is largely under the influence of the western cyclonic system and was unaffected by the eastern drought conditions. Cattle, horses, sheep and pigs are reared and a co-operative system of dairy artels is developed for the supply of Moscow and Leningrad. Of industries other than timber working, only the production of matches and leather goods reached prewar level. Printing, the making of small metal goods and work on electric stations are slightly developed, the respective percentages being 1.6, 2.1 and .9. Roads are poor and in many areas do not exist at all, the only railway is the east to west line which links Leningrad with Vologda, and freightage is mainly by the waterways, especially that linking with the famous Marii network to Leningrad.

The town of Cherepovetz, lat. 59° 8′ N., long. 37° 55′ E., population 24,900, is the administrative centre. It is situated at the junction of the Yagorba and Sheksna rivers, which drain into the Volga, and during the spring thaws the banks of these streams are submerged. The Voskresensk monastery, of ancient foundation, certainly prior to the 15th century, led to a settlement of peasants near it, and this settlement was raised to town rank in 1780 and given the name of Cherepovetz. Its situation on the railway and waterways makes it a centre for the products of the province. Agricultural implements and boots and shoes are made in the town, and there are a brandy distillery and a timber mill.

CHERIBON (Tjerebon), Indonesia, formerly a residency of the island of Java, Dutch East Indies, bounded west by Batavia residency, south by Priangan residency, north by the Java sea, and east by the residency of Pekalongan: it is included in the government of West Java. Pop. (1930) 2,069,690, including 3,379 Europeans and Eurasians, and 36,905 foreign Asiatics, Chinese included. Although some Javanese live in the north, Cheribon is Sundanese country, its eastern boundary dividing the Sundanese from the Javanese territory of Central Java. Cheribon has been for centuries the centre of Mohammedanism in West Java, for it is here that the Mohammedan power was strongly established as early as 1526, under Gunung Jati and much of the opposition to Dutch rule at a later date came from this district. The native population is orderly and prosperous. The northern half of the residency is flat and marshy in places, while the southern half is mountainous. Southwest of the city of Cheribon stands the huge volcano Cherimaj, clad with virgin forest and plantations, and surrounded at its foot by rice fields. Sulphur and salt springs occur on the slopes of Cherimaj, and near Palimanan there is a cavernous hole called Guwagalang (or Payagalang), which exhales carbonic acid gas, and which is considered holy by the natives, and is guarded by priests. The principal products of cultivation are tea, rice, essential oils, sugar, cinchona, cassava and ground nuts and pulses, the tea and other plantations for the most part being owned by Europeans. The chief towns are Cheribon (pop. 54,079 with 1,653 Europeans and Eurasians and 8,191 Chinese), a seaport and the capital, and Indramayu (pop. 21,190). Cheribon has a good open roadstead, and quay and warehouse-accommodation for the lighters into which cargo is discharged. The town is very old and irregularly built; it is a regular port of call. Cheribon was the residence of the powerful sultans of Tjerebon, and their descendants live there still, on pension, the head of the house being styled the Sultan Sepoeh. Kuningan, famous for a breed of horses, is a hill resort (2,200 ft.) much resorted to by Europeans. Imports and exports respectively, in 1939 were, for Cheribon port, 22,636,000 and 9,371,000 guilders. The residency was occupied by Japan in March 1942.

CHERIMOYA or **CHERIMOYER** (*Annona Cherimola*), a sub-tropical fruit of the custard-apple family (Annonaceae), sometimes called Peruvian custard-apple. It is probably native to the mountains of Ecuador and Peru whence several centuries ago it spread by cultivation to Mexico, Central America and the West Indies; later to the Hawaiian islands, Mediterranean countries, Africa, India and Polynesia, and recently to the southern United States. It succeeds best in a comparatively cool and dry summer climate, and in the tropics must be grown at considerable elevation. It does well in protected foot-hill regions of California and also in southern Florida where there is little frost. The fruits are roundish to oblong conical, grayish-brown or nearly black, three to five pounds or more in weight, with the skin either smooth or with warty tubercles on the surface. The flesh is soft, sweet, rich and deliciously flavoured. Propagating is done by shield budding or cleft grafting on seedling stocks two years old, and stocks of other species of *Annona* are sometimes used. Mature trees are from 15 to 20 ft. high.

CHERKASSY (Cherkassi), a town in the Kiev region of the Ukrainian S.S.R., 49° 25′ N., 32° 3′ E. Pop. (1939) 51,693. It is situated near the right bank of the Dnieper, at the southeastern termination of a patch of forest. It has a radio station and is on the north to south railway which links Chernigov with Odessa. The inhabitants (Little Russians) are employed in agriculture and gardening. Sugar and tobacco are manufactured, and there are timber mills and veneering works and factories for nail and brick making. Cherkassy was an important town of the Ukraine in the 15th century, and under Polish rule, until the revolt of the Cossack hetman Chmielnicki (1648). It was annexed by Russia in 1795. German troops occupied it in 1941.

CHERNIGOV, a town and region in the Ukrainian S.S.R. The region has an area of 4,125 sq.mi., and is much smaller than the former Chernigov government. The Dnieper river forms its western boundary; its eastern boundary reaches long. 32° E. in the north, but toward the south is farther west and runs parallel with the left bank of the Desna river. Its northern boundary coincides with that of the Ukraine, and the region of Kiev lies to the south. The northwest between the Dnieper and the Desna is forested, with marshes near the rivers, but the area on the left bank of the Desna lies in the transitional forest-steppe zone. In the northwest lumbering and the production of woodenwares, tar, pitch and leather goods are the main peasant occupations, beekeeping forming a useful supplement. The sown area is small, the marshy and sandy soil being unfavourable to agriculture. The chief crops are rye and oats. Hemp is also cultivated. The Desna river and its tributaries are navigable in summer and form outlets for timber. The climate is severe, the rivers being frozen for about 130 days. The town of Chernigov, lat. 51° 31′ N., long. 31° 20′ E., has an average January temperature of 23° F.; July 68.5° F. Pop. (1939) 67,356. Chief occupations are the making of spirits, leather goods, especially footwear, and flour milling. The town is a river port, with an elevator and a radio station; it is the terminus of a branch railway. It has had a long and eventful history and was mentioned in the treaty of Oleg, 907, as next in importance to Kiev. In the 11th century it became the capital of the principality of Syeversk, and its cathedral dates from that time. The Mongol invasion, 1239, destroyed its prosperity. In the 14th century it was annexed by Lithuania, and as a part of the grand duchy of Lithuania entered in union with the kingdom of Poland and remained a part of the Polish-Lithuanian state until its occupation by the Russians in 1686. It was occupied by the Germans in 1941.

CHERNOV, VICTOR MIKHAILOVICH (Victor Olienin) (1876–1952), cofounder and leader of the Russian Social Revolutionary party, joined the revolutionary movement in 1893. He became a member of the party's central committee and editor of *Revolutionary Russia.* At the Zimmerwald conference of 1915 he supported the "defeatist" resolution of the party's left wing condemning the "imperialist war." After the revolution of March 1917 he returned to Russia and changed to a "defender" (*oboronets*) of his country against the German imperialist war. He edited the journal *Dielo Naroda* and opposed the left wing of the party and the Bolsheviks. He became minister of agriculture in the provisional coalition government of May 18, 1917, and was author of a project of radical legislation on agrarian reform. In September, however, he resigned after the anarchist peasant movement had seized lands from their owners. He was elected president of the Russian constituent assembly, which opened on Jan. 18, 1918, and, after one session, was dispersed by the Bolsheviks. During the civil war Chernov fought against the Reds and the Whites on the Volga. In 1918 he emigrated to Paris and devoted himself to literary work. At the outbreak of World War II he went to the United States, where he contributed to anti-Communist periodicals (notably *Sotsialisticheskii Vestnik*). He died in New York city on April 15, 1952.

CHERNYSHEVSKY, NIKOLAY GAVRILOVICH (1828–1889), Russian writer and political leader, was born at Saratov. His first works dealt with literary criticism (*The Aesthetic Relations of Art to Reality,* 1855, and *Studies of the Age of Gogol*). In the reform movement which set in after the Crimean War, he took an active part. His journal, the *Contemporary,* urged a program of education, more railways and a "rational distribution of economic forces"—in other words, emancipation of the serfs. On this last point he laid particular stress, and when the tsar Alexander put forward his first reform program (Jan. 1858), Chernyshevsky in the *Contemporary* ranked him higher than Peter the Great. The incompleteness of the agrarian reform, when promulgated, and the delays in its execution ended in turning Chernyshevsky against the government, and he and Dobrolyubov became the leaders of the Radical party which demanded immediate and wholesale reform. A visit to Hertzen in London convinced Chernyshevsky of the futility of the liberal movement and resulted in a rupture between the Liberals and Radicals. Chernyshevsky, now supported by the Nihilists, increased his agitation till his sudden arrest in 1862. He was tried in 1864 and sent for 24 years to Siberia. During his imprisonment in the fortress of St. Petersburg he had written his famous novel *Shto Delat* (*What Is to Be Done?,* 1863; Eng. trans. under the title *The Vital Question,* 1866)—a classic of the revolutionary movement which earned him his severe sentence. In 1883 he was transferred from north Siberia to Astrakhan, where he began to translate Weber's *Universal History.* In 1889 he was allowed to return to Saratov, where he died, broken in health, a few months after.

See G. Plekhanov, *N. G. Tschernyschewsky* (Stuttgart, 1894).

CHEROKEE. This tribe, of Iroquoian lineage, is one of the largest in the United States. They inhabited the southern Alleghenies, where the Carolinas, Georgia, Alabama and Tennessee adjoin. Their name seems to be of Muskogi origin and to mean "cave people." Encountered by De Soto in 1540, they first came into contact with the British in the latter half of the 17th century. They fought on the British side in the American Revolution, refusing to make peace until ten years after its termination. White settlement pressing in upon them, part of the tribe withdrew beyond the Mississippi, but the remainder, in 1820, formed a government modelled on that of the United States and soon after adopted the alphabet, or rather syllabary, invented by one of their half-bloods, Sequoyah. In 1838 the nation was reunited in Indian territory, now Oklahoma, where they were recognized as one of the "five civilized tribes" and set up their capital at Tahlequah, their government remaining effective until 1906, when all Cherokees became United States citizens. Their original numbers were about 15,000, making them one of the largest tribes in North America. Admixture of white and Negro blood, and adoption of aliens of all three races, as well as vigour of the Cherokee stock, have doubled this number. The Cherokee were divided into seven matrilineal clans. Their general culture was similar to that of the tribes of Muskogi stock to the south.

See Royce, *Bur. Am. Ethn. Rep.* v (1887); Mooney, *ibid.*, xix (1902).

CHEROKEE, a city of northwestern Iowa, U.S., on the west bank of the Little Sioux river, 60 mi. E.N.E. of Sioux City; the county seat of Cherokee county. It is a division point on the Illinois Central railroad. The population in 1950 was 7,705; in 1940 it was 7,469 by the federal census. Cherokee is the trade centre for a rich farming, dairying and stock-raising country. The state hospital for the insane is located there.

The first log house in the county was built in 1856, 4 mi. S. of the city, by Robert Perry, who soon thereafter met a colony of emigrants from Milford, Mass., and persuaded them to settle near by. Two black walnut logs from their first stockade are preserved as a historic relic, and the millstones from the first mill have been set up as a monument. When the railway reached the county (1871), the present town site was located about a mile from the old town. Just south of the city is Pilot Rock, a huge glacial boulder, 40 by 60 ft., which was a well-known landmark in the days of migration westward.

CHEROOT, a cigar made from tobacco grown in southern India and the Philippines. The quality of cheroots varies a great deal, but a good example is esteemed for its delicate flavour. A cheroot differs from other cigars in having both ends cut square, instead of one being pointed, and one end considerably larger than the other. Cheroot, which is also sometimes spelled "sheroot," is from the Tamil *shuruttu,* meaning a roll.

CHERRAPUNJI, a village in the Khasi hills district of Assam, India, notable as having one of the heaviest known rainfalls in the world. Its annual average is 429 in., but the fall varies greatly; 905 in. were registered in 1861 (366 in. falling in July) and only 283 in. in 1873. This excessive rainfall is caused by the fact that Cherrapunji stands on the edge of the plateau overlooking the plains, where it catches the full force of the monsoon from the Bay of Bengal.

CHERRY. Next to the peach and the plum the cherry is the most important stone fruit grown in the United States. The horticultural varieties which are of interest for their value as edible fruit belong to two groups, the sweet and the sour. Sweet cherry fruits are used principally for fresh fruit dessert, while the sours make up the great bulk of the frozen and canned cherries of commerce for use in bakeries, restaurants and homes for pies, preserves and sauce. This group is sometimes referred to as pie cherries.

Sweet cherries blossom early in the spring, and the flowers are very susceptible to cold and frost injury. The sour cherry tree is as hardy as some apple varieties, but its flower buds are also quite tender to cold after growth starts in late winter, and crops are frequently lost by freezes occurring near blossoming time. Chiefly because of the special climatic requirements of these two groups, the principal commercial production of sweet cherries in the United States is limited to the Pacific and intermountain states of the west, while the sour cherries are grown principally in districts near the Great Lakes in the states of Michigan, Wisconsin, Ohio, Pennsylvania and New York. However, the sour cherry is also grown as a dooryard or garden tree in many other parts of the country where winter temperatures are not too severe or the summers too hot and dry.

All varieties of cultivated cherry belong to two species. The sweet cherries, *Prunus avium,* are tall pyramidal trees with few or no suckers from the roots and with leaves downy on the underside. The sour cherries, *Prunus cerasus,* are small, broader trees with many suckers from the roots and with fruit sour to bitter in taste. Wild forms of the sweet cherry found growing in the United States and in Europe are also called mazzard, bird and wild sweet cherry.

The native habitat of the sweet cherry species is considered by many authorities to be western Asia, while that of *Prunus cerasus* seems to be close to that of *Prunus avium* in the region about the Caspian sea and extending into eastern Europe. These two species are widely distributed through the north temperate zone. The sweet cherry, *Prunus avium,* has been divided by botanists into different groups, but because of hybridization among the varieties it is rather difficult in many cases to classify them. Sweet cherries with soft, tender flesh form one group known by pomologists under the French group name *guigne* or the English *gean.* This group is also often referred to as the heart cherries. Some of the varieties, such as Wood, are light coloured with colourless juice, while that of others, such as Black Tartarian, are dark coloured with reddish juice. A second group includes those distinguished by the firm, crisp flesh of the fruits and often referred to as the Bigarreaus. Bing, a dark-red cherry, and Napoleon, a light-coloured one, are examples of this group. Like the sweet cherry, the sour cherry is also divided into groups based on the colour of the juice. Cherries with colourless juice are the Amarelles, these having pale red to red fruits more or less flattened at the ends. Montmorency is the most important variety of this group grown in the United States. The Morellos comprise a second group containing varieties such as English Morello, with very dark round to oval fruits and flesh with reddish juice. A group of cherries intermediate in type between the sweets and the sours is known as the dukes. These cherries, which are considered to be hybrids between *Prunus avium* and *Prunus cerasus,* have many characteristics of fruit, skin, flesh, juice colour and flavour, as well as of tree growth, that are intermediate between the sweets and sours. Three other species of cherry of low-growing bush or shrub form with edible fruit are the Nanking or bush cherry, *Prunus tomentosa,* an inhabitant of central Asia; the sand cherry, *P. pumila,* of the shores and beaches of the eastern United States; and the western sand cherry or Bessey cherry, *P. besseyi,* of the western United States.

The cherry is propagated by budding on the wild sweet or mazzard stock, or on the small, wild, inedible, sour cherry of southern Europe, *Prunus mahaleb.* The average annual commercial production of sweet cherries in the United States for the five-year period 1938–42 was slightly more than 79,000 tons, while the average production of sour cherries for the same period was 93,978 tons. In addition to dessert and culinary uses in the home, cherry fruit is also used in the making of liqueurs. Kirschwasser is made chiefly on the upper Rhine from a wild black sweet cherry, *Prunus avium.* Maraschino, a liqueur made from the marasca cherry, is used in Europe and the United States in the making of maraschino cherries. The marasca cherry is a native of the province of Dalmatia, Yugoslavia.

The black cherry, *Prunus serotina,* is native to most of the eastern half of the United States and adjacent areas of eastern Canada. Wood of this species has long been valued by cabinetmakers in making high quality furniture. (F. P. C.)

CHERRY VALLEY, a village of Otsego county, N.Y., U.S., in a township of the same name, 60 mi. N.W. of Albany. Pop. (1950) 760; (1940) 704. It is served by the Delaware & Hudson railway.

Cherry Valley is in the centre of a rich farming and dairying region, has a chair factory and is a tourist resort with sulphur and lithia springs. It was the scene of a terrible massacre during the War of Independence. The village was attacked on Nov. 11, 1778, by Walter Butler (d. 1781) and Joseph Brant with a force of 800 Indians and Tories, who killed about 50 men, women and children, sacked and burned most of the houses and carried off more than 70 prisoners, who were subjected to the greatest cruelties, many dying or being tomahawked before the Canadian settlements were reached.

Cherry Valley was incorporated in 1812.

CHERSIPHRON, a Cretan architect, the traditional builder (with his son Metagenes) of the great Ionic temple of Artemis at Ephesus in the 6th century B.C. Remains of this temple were found by J. T. Wood and brought to the British museum. A fragmentary inscription supports the statement of Herodotus that the pillars were presented by King Croesus.

CHERSO (CRES), one of the three major islands of the Quarnero group, lying off the east coast of the peninsula of Istria, Italy. With the adjacent island of Lussino (Losinj) it was transferred to Italy in the settlement after World War I and was included in Venezia Giulia, while Veglia (Krk), the third member of the group, was attached to Yugoslavia. In 1947 Cherso and Lussino also passed to Yugoslavia.

Cherso, 40 mi. long and 8 mi. wide, has a total area of 125 sq.mi. It is separated from Lussino by a navigable channel, crossed by a swing bridge, the channel being believed to be artificial and the result of Roman work. The Roman town of Ossero (Osor), now a village but formerly the capital of Cherso, stands where the two islands approach most closely. Lussino, though having an area of only 28 sq.mi., has a larger population than Cherso and contains in Lussin Piccolo (Mali Losinj) a harbour of some importance, while Cherso harbour has no great value. Both islands are structurally a part of the karst plateau of Istria, and show similar features, with numerous swallow holes and patches of fertile red earth. Wine, olive oil and fruits are produced in both, but Cherso, which is mountainous, rising to over 2,000 ft., is devoted largely to sheep raising.

Under the Austrians the population of Cherso, about 8,000, was registered as predominantly Serbo-Croat, the Italians forming a minority. But Cherso and Lussino formed together one district, and Italians so largely predominated in the latter island as to make the total figures for the two stocks practically equal. Since the Italians regarded the Austrian figures as favouring the Serbo-Croat element at their expense the frontier was drawn to include both islands within Italy. In 1947 Cherso was transferred to Yugoslavia.

See "The Austrian Littoral," Foreign Office *Peace Handbook,* 10.

CHERSONESE, CHERSONESUS or **CHERRONESUS,** a word equivalent to "peninsula" (Gr. χέρσος, dry, and νῆσος, island). In ancient geography the Chersonesus Thracica, Chersonesus Taurica or Scythica, and Chersonesus Cimbrica correspond to the peninsulas of the Dardanelles, the Crimea and Jutland; and the Golden Chersonese is usually identified with the peninsula of Malacca. The Tauric Chersonese was further distinguished as the Great, in contrast to the Heracleotic or Little Chersonese at its southwest corner, where Sevastopol now stands.

History.—The *Tauric Chersonese* (from the 2nd century A.D. called Cherson) was a Dorian colony of Heraclea in Bithynia, founded in the 5th century B.C. in the Crimea about two miles S. of the modern Sevastopol. After defending itself against the kingdom of Bosporus (*see* BOSPORUS CIMMERIUS), and the native Scythians and Tauri, and even extending its power over the west coast of the peninsula, it was compelled to call in the aid of Mithradates VI and Diophantus, *c.* 110 B.C., and submitted to the Pontic dynasty. On regaining a nominal independence, it came under the Roman suzerainty. In the latter part of the 1st century A.D., and again in the 2nd, it received a Roman garrison and suffered much interference in its internal affairs. In the time of Constantine, in return for assistance against the Bosporans and the native tribes, it regained its autonomy and received special privileges. It must, however, have been subject to the Byzantine authorities, as inscriptions testify to restorations of its walls by Byzantine officials. Under Theophilus the central government sent out a governor to take the place of the elected magistrate. Even so it seems to have preserved a measure of self-government and may be said to have been the last of the Greek city states. It had been the main emporium of Byzantine commerce upon the north coast of the Euxine. Through it went the communications of the empire with the Petchenegs and other native tribes, and more especially with the Russians. The commerce of Cherson is guaranteed in the early treaties between the Greeks and Russians, and it was in Cherson, according to Pseudo-Nestor's chronicle (*see* NESTOR), that Vladimir was baptized in 988 after he had captured the city. Its ruin was brought about by the commercial rivalry of the Genoese, who forbade the Greeks to trade there and diverted its commerce to Caffa and Sudak. The constitution of the city was at first democratic under *damiorgi,* a senate and a general assembly. Latterly it appears to have become aristocratic, and most of the power was concentrated in the hands of the first archon or *proteuon,* who in time was superseded by the *strategus* sent out from Byzantium. Its most interesting political document is the form of oath sworn by all citizens in the 3rd century B.C.

Remains.—The remains of the city occupy a space about two-thirds of a mile long by half a mile broad, enclosed by a Byzantine wall. Remains of a Greek wall going back to the 4th century B.C. have been found beneath this in the eastern or original part of the site. Many Byzantine churches, both cruciform and basilican, have been excavated. The latter survived here into the 13th century when they had long been extinct in other Greek-speaking lands. The churches were adorned with frescoes, wall and floor mosaics, and marble carvings similar to work found at Ravenna. The fact that the site has not been inhabited since the 14th century makes it important for our knowledge of Byzantine life. The city was used by the Romans as a place of banishment: St. Clement of Rome was exiled hither and first preached the Gospel; another exile was Justinian II, who is said to have destroyed the city in revenge. Its coins range from the 3rd century B.C. to about A.D. 200, and there are Byzantine issues.

BIBLIOGRAPHY.—B. Koehne, *Beiträge zur Geschichte von Cherronesus in Taurien* (St. Petersburg, 1848); art. "Chersonesos" (20) by C. G. Brandis in Pauly-Wissowa, *Realencyklopädie,* vol. iii, 221; A. A. Bobrinskoj, *Chersonesus Taurica* (St. Petersburg, 1905) (Russian); V. V. Latyshev, *Inscrr. Orae Septentr. Ponti Euxini,* vols. i and iv. Reports of excavations appear in the *Compte rendu* of the Imperial Archaeological Commission of St. Petersburg from 1888 and in its *Bulletin. See* also E. H. Minns, *Scythians and Greeks* (Cambridge, 1907). Rostovtseff. M., *Iranians and Greeks in South Russia* (Oxford, 1922).

CHERT, in geology, a rock consisting mainly of silica in a finely granular or chalcedonic form, closely allied to flint (*q.v.*). Cherts are probably formed in several different ways; for example, by solution and redeposition of the silica contained in the spicules of sponges and other siliceous organisms in sedimentary rocks, such as the Carboniferous limestone and Upper Greensand of England; by accumulation on the floor of the sea in ancient times of radiolaria and diatoms, like some of the modern deep-sea deposits; by precipitation of silica from magmatic solutions belonging to the later stages of submarine volcanic eruptions. In some instances it is uncertain which of these causes was concerned in their formation. Cherts rich in compounds of iron, of volcanic origin, were the primary source of the iron ore of the Lake Superior region of the U.S. The Rhynie cherts of Devonian age, in Scotland, are noteworthy for the preservation of the minute details of the structure of fossils embedded in them. (R. H. RA.)

CHERTSEY, urban district of Surrey, England, 22 mi. S.W. of London by the Southern Region railway. Pop. (1951) 31,029. Area 15.6 sq.mi. It is pleasantly situated on the right bank of the Thames, which is crossed by a bridge of seven arches, built of Purbeck stone in 1785. The first religious settlement in Surrey, a Benedictine abbey, was founded in 666 at Chertsey (*Cerotesei, Certesey*), the manor of which belonged to the abbot until 1539, when it became a possession of the crown. In the reign of Edward the Confessor Chertsey was a large village and was made the head of Godley hundred. Chertsey owed its importance primarily to the abbey, but partly to its geographical position. Ferries over the Redewynd were subjects of royal grant in 1340 and 1399; the abbot built a new bridge over the Bourne in 1333, and wholly maintained the bridge over the Thames when it replaced the 14th-century ferry. In 1410 the king gave permission to build a bridge over the Redewynd. As the centre of an agricultural district the markets of Chertsey were important and are still held.

Three days' fairs were granted to the abbots in 1129 for the feast of St. Peter ad Vincula by Henry III for Holy Rood day; in 1282 for Ascension day; and a market on Mondays was obtained in 1282.

Little remains of the abbey buildings, which fell into decay in the 17th century. The ground plan, however, can be traced and the fish ponds are complete. Among the abbots the most famous was John de Rutherwyk, who was appointed in 1307, and continued, till his death in 1346, to carry on a great system of alteration and extension. The house in which the poet Cowley spent the last years of his life remains. The town is the centre of a large residential district. Its principal trade is in produce for the London markets.

See Lucy Wheeler, *Chertsey Abbey* (London, 1905); *Victoria County History, Surrey.*

CHERUBIM are winged creatures associated in the Old Testament with the deity. The name, plural of the Hebrew *kĕrūb,* has no Hebrew etymology, and was taken over, with the conception, from older sources. Similar creatures are found in other oriental religions. The cherubim who guard Paradise (Gen. iii, 24) are introduced, without description, as well-known figures. The cherub appears also in Ezek. xxviii, 13–16, behind which passage lies another version of the Paradise story, but the text is too obscure to throw much light on his character. More illuminating is the vision of Ezekiel, ch. i., where the four "living creatures" attendant upon the divine chariot are undoubtedly cherubim, for they are expressly so named in Ezek. x. These have each four wings, and four faces—those of a man, a lion, an ox, an eagle. The two seraphim of Isa. vi belong to the same category, though these have six wings and, presumably, human faces. In Ezekiel and Isaiah these beings are connected with the divine throne. It is thus natural that we should find two gold cherubim covering the "mercy-seat" (Exod. xxxvii, 6–9, xxv, 18–22). Representations of cherubim are found also in the hangings of the shrine (Exod. xxvi, 1, 31), and figures of two cherubim, overlaid with gold, in Solomon's temple (1 Ki. vi, 23–28, viii, 6 *seq.*), others carved on the walls (vi. 29–32), and about the bases of the "molten sea" (vii. 29). So the temple of Ezekiel has carved decorations of cherubim, these with two faces, a man's and a lion's (xl. 18 *seq.*). The description of Yahweh riding "upon a cherub," Ps. xviii. 10, has for its parallel "upon the wings of the wind"; this, although in Babylonian myth the south wind has wings that can be broken, suggests that a mythological conception is used merely for poetical effect, a conclusion confirmed by the similar passage Ps. civ. 3, in which the cherub is replaced by clouds.

To sum up, the cherubim are hybrid creatures, with wings of birds, human or animal faces, regarded as attendants upon the divine throne, or guardians of specially sacred places. The four "living creatures" of Rev. iv. 6 are lineal descendants of those in Ezekiel's vision. In Jewish literature the cherubim appear as a class of angels. Representations of figures similar to the Old Testament cherubim have been discovered in many places, a pair from Dendera showing striking resemblance to those described in Exodus.

See the illustrations in Gressmann's *Altorientalische Texte und Bilder zum Alten Testamente,* nos. 378 *seq.;* Vincent, *Revue Biblique,* p. 487 *seq.* (1926). (W. L. W.)

CHERUBINI, MARIA LUIGI CARLO ZENOBIA SALVATORE (1760–1842), Italian musical composer, was born at Florence on Sept. 14, 1760, and died on March 15, 1842 in Paris. His father was *Maestro al Cembalo* at the Pergola theatre, and began to teach him music when he was six. By the time he was 16 he had composed a great deal of Church music, and in 1777 he went to Bologna, where for four years he studied under Sarti. This famous master well earned the gratitude which afterwards impelled Cherubini to place one of his double choruses by the side of his own *Et Vitam Venturi* as the crown of his *Treatise on Counterpoint and Fugue,* though the juxtaposition does Sarti's music no good. Cherubini also worked at operatic composition, and Sarti sometimes, like the great masters of painting, entrusted his pupil with minor parts of his own works. Cherubini's first complete opera, *Quinto Fabio* was produced in 1780 and was followed in 1782 by *Armida, Adriano in Siria,* and other works. In 1784 he was invited to London to produce two works for the Italian opera there, one of which, *La Finta Principessa,* was favourably received while the other, *Giulio Sabino,* was, according to a contemporary witness, "murdered" by the critics.

In 1786 he left London for Paris, which became his home after a visit to Turin in 1787–88 on the occasion of the production there of his *Ifigenia in Aulide.* His first French opera, *Dêmophon* (1788), which was not a popular success, already marks a departure from the Italian style, which Cherubini still cultivated in the pieces he introduced into the works of Anfossi, Paisiello and Cimarosa, produced by him as director of the Italian opera in Paris (established in 1789). In Paris Cherubini became a great composer. If his melodic invention had been as warm as Gluck's, his masterly technique would have made him one of the greatest composers that ever lived. But his personal character shows in its Johnsonian "anfractuosities" an un-Johnsonian "unclubability," which extends to the centre of his art and deprives even his finest music of the glow of inspiration that fears nothing.

With *Lodoiska* (1791) the series of Cherubini's master-pieces begins, and *Médée* (1797) shows his full powers. Cherubini's creative genius was never more brilliant than at this period, as the wonderful two-act ballet, *Anacreon,* shows; but his temper and spirits were not improved by a series of disappointments which culminated in the collapse of his prospects of congenial success at Vienna, where he went in 1805 in compliance with an invitation to compose an opera for the Imperial theatre. Here he produced, under the title of *Der Wasserträger,* the great work which, on its first production on January 7, 1801 (26 *Nivôse, An* 8) as *Les Deux Journées,* had thrilled Paris with the accents of a humanity restored to health and peace. It was by this time an established favourite in Austria. On February 25 Cherubini produced *Faniska,* but the war between Austria and France had broken out immediately after his arrival, and the run of *Faniska* was stopped by the bombardment and capitulation of Vienna.

His stay at Vienna is memorable for his intercourse with Beethoven, the most whole-hearted admirer he and his works have ever met in a century and a quarter. The mighty genius of Beethoven, which broke through all rules in vindication of the principles underlying them, was incomprehensible to Cherubini, in whose mind the creative faculties were finely developed, but whose critical faculty was supplanted by a mere disciplinary code inadequate even as a basis for the analysis of his own works. On the other hand, it would be impossible to exaggerate the influence *Les Deux Journées* had on the lighter parts of Beethoven's *Fidelio.* Cherubini's librettist was also the author of the libretto from which *Fidelio* was adapted, and Cherubini's score was a constant object of Beethoven's study, not only before the production of the first version of *Fidelio* (as *Leonore*) but also throughout Beethoven's life. Cherubini's record of Beethoven's character is contained in the single phrase, "Il était toujours brusque," a fine example of the pot's opinion of the kettle. The overture to *Leonore* merely puzzled Cherubini as to what key it might be in. Beethoven's brusqueness did not prevent him from assuring Cherubini that he considered him the greatest composer of the age and that he loved and honoured him. Cherubini's incapacity to understand Beethoven did not prevent him from working on the grand scale which Beethoven had by that time established as a permanent standard for musical art. The colossal breadth of the duet *Perfides ennemis* in *Médée* is almost inconceivable without the example of Beethoven's C minor trio, op. 1, No. 3, published two years before it. On the other hand the cavatina *Eterno iddio* in *Faniska* is of a terseness and depth not only worthy of Beethoven but surprisingly like him in style.

After Cherubini's disappointing visit to Vienna he did little until 1809 when his friends with much difficulty persuaded him to write a mass for the consecration of a church at the country seat of the prince de Chimay, where he was staying. With this mass (in F, for three-part chorus and orchestra), the period of his great Church music begins; although it was by no means the end of his career as an opera writer, which lasted as late as his 73rd year (1832). This third period is also marked by several instrumental compositions. An early event in the annals of the Philharmonic Society was the invitation of Cherubini to London in 1815 to produce a symphony, an overture and a vocal piece. The symphony (in D) was afterwards arranged, with a new slow movement, as the string quartet in C (1829), a curious illustration of Cherubini's notions of symphonic as well as of chamber-music style, for the quartet-writing is just like that of his other quartets; oil-painting restricted to black and white. Nevertheless the first three of the six string quartets written between 1814 and 1837 are interesting works performed with success at the present day, and the last three, discovered in 1889 are not without fine passages.

At the eleventh hour Cherubini received recognition from Napoleon, who, during the Hundred Days, made him chevalier of the Legion of Honour. Then, with the restoration of the Bourbons, Cherubini's position improved. He was appointed, jointly with Lesueur, as composer and conductor to the Chapel Royal, and in 1822 he obtained the permanent directorship of the conservatoire.

In 1833 Cherubini produced his last work for the stage, *Alì Baba,* adapted (with new and noisy features which excited Mendelssohn's astonished disgust) from a manuscript opera, *Koukourgi,* written 40 years earlier. It is therefore not one of the brighter rockets from what Mendelssohn called "the extinct volcano." But the requiem in D minor (for male voices), written in 1836, is one of Cherubini's greatest works, and, though not actually his last composition, is a worthy close to the long career of an artist of high ideals who, while neither by birth nor temperament a Frenchman, must yet be counted with a still greater foreigner, Gluck, as among the glories of French classical music. Cherubini's *Treatise on Counterpoint and Fugue* embodies his views as a theorist. Concerning one 16th century idiom, as natural in pure polyphony as "attraction of the relative" is in classical Greek. Cherubini remarks, "No tradition gives us any reason why the classics thus faultily deviated from the rule." On another point where there is a fine opportunity for stimulating a sense of harmonic values, he inculcates a mechanical pseudo-logic with the remark that "The opinion of the classics appears to me erroneous, notwithstanding that custom has sanctioned it, for on the principle that the discord is a mere suspension of the chord, it should not affect the nature of the chord. But since the classics have pronounced judgment we must of course submit." On the whole Cherubini's career as a teacher did more harm than good in his lifetime, and his *Treatise on Counterpoint and Fugue* continues at the present day to invest disastrous misinterpretations of classical art forms with the authority of a great composer.

And yet as a composer Cherubini was no psuedo-classic but a really great artist. His purity of style rarely joined itself to matter that could express the ideals he kept always in view. In his love of those ideals there was too much fear: but Beethoven's estimate of him is more just than the contemptuous neglect with which his art is treated now.

His principal works are summarized by Fétis as 32 operas, 29 Church compositions, four cantatas and several instrumental pieces, besides the treatise on counterpoint and fugue.

Good modern full scores of the two Requiems and of *Les Deux Journées* (the latter unfortunately without the dialogue, which, however, is accessible in a careful German translation in the *Reclam Bibliothek*), and also of ten opera overtures, are current in the Peters edition. Vocal scores of some of the other operas are not difficult to get. The great Credo is in the Peters edition, but is becoming scarce. The string quartets are in Payne's *Miniature Scores*. It is very desirable that the operas, from *Démophon* onwards, should be republished in full score.

(D. F. T.)

BIBLIOGRAPHY.—D. Denne-Baron, *Cherubini* (1862); E. Bellasis, *Cherubini* (1874 and 1912); Crowest, *Cherubini*, 1890; R. Hohenemser, *Luigi Cherubini, sein Leben und Seine Werke* (Leipzig, 1913); M. Quatrelles l'Epine, *Cherubini 1760–1842; Notes et Documents inédits* (Lille, 1913).

CHÉRUEL, PIERRE ADOLPHE (1809–1891), French historian, was born at Rouen. His most important work was done on the history of France in the 17th century. Among his books are *Histoire de l'administration monarchique en France depuis l'avènement de Philippe-Auguste jusqu'à la mort de Louis XIV*. (1855); *Dictionnaire historique des institutions, moeurs et coutumes de la France* (1855); *Journal d'Olivier Lefèvre d'Ormesson* (1860–62); editions of the *Lettres du cardinal Mazarin pendant son ministère* (6 vols., 1870–91), continued by the vicomte G. d'Avenel; of the *Mémoires du duc de Saint-Simon* (1856–58 and 1878–81); *Notice sur la vie et sur les mémoires du duc de Saint-Simon* (1876); *Histoire de la France pendant la minorité de Louis XIV*. (4 vols., 1880) and *Histoire de la France sous le ministère de Mazarin* (3 vols., 1882–83).

CHERUSCI, an ancient German tribe occupying the basin of the Weser to the north of the Chatti (*q.v.*). Together with the other tribes of western Germany they submitted to the Romans in 11–9 B.C., but in A.D. 9 Arminius, one of their princes, rose in revolt, and defeated and slew the Roman General Quintilius Varus, annihilating his army. Germanicus Caesar (*q.v.*) made several unsuccessful attempts to bring them into subjection again. By the end of the 1st century A.D. their prestige had declined, and their territory was eventually occupied by the Saxons.

BIBLIOGRAPHY.—*See* Tacitus, *Annals*, i. 2, 11, 12, 13; *Germania*, 36.

CHERVONETZ, the new Russian monetary unit, instituted in 1922 as part of the New Economic Policy. The old pre-World War I rouble had, owing to heavy war expenditure, the military-Communist era of 1917–22 and to post-war heavy budget deficits (balanced deliberately by fresh note emissions), depreciated to vanishing point. When the Soviet Government realized the need of a stable currency they instituted the chervonetz.

The chervonetz equals 10 pre-war roubles of 2s. 1½d. Chervonetz notes were issued by the new State bank, having a backing of 25% in gold, platinum or stable foreign exchange, the remaining 75% cover to consist of marketable goods, short-term securities or approved bills of exchange. These notes were from their inception restricted in their issue, so as to maintain the above provisions, and in particular steps were taken to discourage them from entering into internal circulation. They were used as the basis of the nation's currency system and foreign exchange rates were quoted in chervontsi.

Side by side with the chervonetz a new series of rouble notes was issued intended for internal use. These had no fixed conversion ratio against the chervonetz, and for the two years immediately succeeding their first appearance they were issued freely to balance successive budget deficits. Hence they in turn rapidly depreciated until the conversion ratio reached the astronomical figure of 200,000,000,000 roubles to one chervonetz.

In 1924 it proved possible to balance the budget and so to reorganize the internal currency. New currency rouble notes were issued, their volume being limited to half that of the chervontsi in circulation. Simultaneously the old Soviet or 1923 roubles were gradually withdrawn.

After 1924 the internal currency of the country consisted of stable rouble, currency notes and subsidiary coins. (*See* also ROUBLE.)

CHESAPEAKE AND DELAWARE CANAL, in the United States, connects Chesapeake City, Md., and Delaware City, Del., and provides a water route directly across Delaware and Maryland from Delaware bay to Chesapeake bay. It is 19 mi. long, 250 ft. wide and 27 ft. in depth. Its total cost was about $10,000,000.

CHESAPEAKE AND OHIO CANAL, in the United States, between Cumberland, Md., and Washington, D.C., was used formerly for the transportation of coal from the Cumberland region to the Potomac river.

The cost of construction with improvements was about $14,000,000. It is 184 mi. long, 68 ft. wide and 6 ft. in depth. The canal is no longer used for navigation.

CHESAPEAKE BAY, an arm of the Atlantic ocean on the east coast of the United States, is about 200 mi. long and varies in width from 4 to 40 mi.; the lower part of the bay cuts northward through the state of Virginia, and the upper part almost bisects Maryland.

The entrance to the bay is between Cape Charles on the north and Cape Henry on the south.

The Susquehanna river enters the head of the bay in the north; other tributaries include the Nanticoke, Choptank and Chester rivers on the east and the James, York, Rappahannock and Potomac rivers on the west. There are many inlets on the irregular shores of the bay.

The chief port is Baltimore, Md., at the head of the Patapsco river, one of the numerous deepwater estuaries. Oysters and crabs and Potomac herring, perch and other fish are found in great abundance in the waters of the bay. The bay area became a popular recreational centre.

The English settlers who founded Jamestown (*q.v.*) in May 1607 had anchored off Cape Henry in April of that year.

In the summer of the following year, Capt. John Smith began to explore Chesapeake bay and its tributaries. His party covered about 3,000 mi. in its search for data.

CHESELDEN, WILLIAM (1688–1752), English surgeon, was born at Somerby, Leicestershire, on Oct. 19, 1688. He studied anatomy in London under William Cowper (1666–1709), and in 1713 published his *Anatomy of the Human Body*. He became surgeon at St. Thomas's and St. George's hospitals, London. Cheselden is famous for his "lateral operation for the stone," which he first performed in 1727. He was one of the most famous and rapid operators in the preanaesthetic period. He also effected a great advance in ophthalmic surgery by his operation for the treatment of certain forms of blindness by the production of an "artificial pupil."

He attended Sir Isaac Newton in his last illness, and was a friend of Alexander Pope and of Sir Hans Sloane. He died at Bath on April 10, 1752.

See F. H. Garrison, *History of Medicine*, p. 343 (1929).

CHESHAM, an urban district and market town of Buckinghamshire, England, 26 mi. W.N.W. of London by the Eastern Region railway. Pop. (1951) 11,428. Area, 5 sq.mi. It is pleasantly situated in the narrow valley of the river Chess, flanked by low wooded chalk hills. St. Mary's church, which has some ancient frescoes, is mainly Perpendicular in style. Dairy utensils, chairs, malt-shovels, etc., are made of beech. Shoemaking is also carried on. Waterside, adjoining the town, has duck farms and extensive watercress beds, for which the Chess is noted.

CHESHIRE, a north-western county of England, bounded north by Lancashire, north-east by Yorkshire and Derbyshire, south-east by Staffordshire, south by Shropshire, west by Denbighshire and Flint, and north-west by the Irish Sea. Area 1,014.6 sq. m. The coast-line is formed by the estuaries of the Dee and the Mersey, which are separated by the low rectangular peninsula of Wirral. The Dee forms a great part of the county boundary with Denbighshire and Flint, and the Mersey the boundary along the whole of the northern side. The principal river within the county is the Weaver, which crosses it on a north-westerly course, and receiving the Dane at Northwich, discharges into the estuary of the Mersey south of Runcorn. The surface of Cheshire is mostly low and gently undulating or flat: the broken line of the Peckforton hills, seldom exceeding 600 ft. in height, is conspicuous. The northern part of the hills coincides approximately with the district called Delamere Forest, formerly a chase of the earls of Chester, and finally disforested in 1812. Southwards, commanding the narrow gap of the Gowy river on the west stands the Norman castle of Beeston. Distributed over the county, but principally in the eastern half, are many small lakes or meres, such as Combermere, Tatton, Rostherne, Tabley, Doddington, Marbury and Mere.

With the exception of some Carboniferous rocks on the eastern border, and a small patch of Lower Lias near Audlem, the whole county is occupied by Triassic strata. The great central plain is covered by Keuper Marls, rich grassland loams with many beds of rock-salt, mostly thin, though two are from 75 ft. to over 100 ft. thick. Thin beds and veins of gypsum are common in the marls. The striking features of the Peckforton Hills, which run north and south, bordering the valley of the Weaver on the west, are due to the repeated faulting of the Lower Keuper Sandstone, which lies upon beds of Bunter Sandstone. Besides forming this well-marked ridge, the Lower Keuper Sandstone, which is quarried in several places, forms several ridges north-west of Macclesfield and appears along the northern border and in the neighbourhood of New Brighton and Birkenhead. It is a good building stone and an important water-bearing stratum. At Alderley Edge ores of copper, lead and cobalt are found. West of the Peckforton ridge, Bunter Sandstones and pebble beds extend to the border. They also form low foothills between Cheadle and Macclesfield. They fringe the northern boundary and appear on the south-eastern boundary as a narrow strip of hilly ground near Woore. From Macclesfield northward through Stockport is a narrow tongue of coal-measures—an extension of the Lancashire coalfield. Coal is mined at Neston in the Wirral peninsula from beneath the Trias; it is a connecting link between the Lancashire and Flintshire coalfields. Glacial drift with northern erratics is thickly spread over all the lower ground; at Crewe the drift is over 400 ft. thick. Patches of drift sand, with marine shells, occur on the high ground east of Macclesfield at an elevation of 1,250 ft. The Cheshire lowland filled with prehistoric swamp and forest has not yielded large finds of ancient objects. A list of perforated stone axes is given in *Trans. Lancs. and Ches. Ant. Soc.*, vol. v., p. 327 (*see* also vol. xi., p. 171). Tranmere has yielded a stone-celt retaining part of its wooden handle. Copper was mined at some early period at Alderley Edge and stone hammers with a groove for attachment occur here. The type occurs in Shetland, Wales, South-West Ireland, Brittany, the Iberian Peninsula, Savoy, Austria and Egypt; it is well-known in the New World and the Cambridge Museum has specimens from Australia. A flat celt of copper or bronze is known from Grappenhall. Broxton has yielded one of the few trunnion celts of Britain (*see* Hemp, W. J. *Antiq. Journ.*, vol. v. 1925, p. 51) together with two palstaves and a spearhead. A dagger blade and a pommel have been found at Wilmslow and the surface of the upper Forest bed at Meols has yielded antiquities apparently of the Early Iron Age.

History.—The earliest recorded historical fact is the capture of Chester by the Northumbrian king Aethelfrith about 614. After a period of incessant strife between Britons and Saxons the district was subjugated in 830 and incorporated in the kingdom of Mercia. During the 9th century Aethelwulf held his parliament at Chester, and received the homage of his tributary kings from Berwick to Kent, and in the 10th century Aethelflaed rebuilt the city, and erected fortresses at Eddisbury and Runcorn. Edward the Elder garrisoned Thelwall and strengthened the passages of the Mersey and Irwell. On the splitting up of Mercia in the 10th century the dependent districts along the Dee were made a shire for the fortress of Chester. The shire is first mentioned in the Abingdon *Chronicle,* which relates that in 980 Cheshire was plundered by a fleet of Northmen. At the time of the Domesday survey the county was divided into twelve hundreds, exclusive of the six hundreds between the Ribble and the Mersey, now included in Lancashire, but then a part of Cheshire. Of the seven modern hundreds Bucklow alone retains its Domesday name. The hundreds of Atiscross and Exestan have been transferred to the counties of Flint and Denbigh, with the exception of a few townships now in the hundred of Broxton. Cheshire put up a determined resistance to the Conqueror and no Englishman retained estates of importance after the Conquest. It was constituted a county palatine, with an independent parliament consisting of the barons and clergy, and courts and all lands except those of the bishop were held of the earl. During the 12th and 13th centuries the county was impoverished by the constant inroads of the Welsh. In 1264 the castle and city of Chester were granted to Simon de Montfort. Richard II., in return for support made the county a principality, but the act was revoked in the next reign. In 1403 Cheshire was the headquarters of Hotspur. At the beginning of the Wars of the Roses Margaret collected a body of supporters from among the Cheshire gentry, and Lancastrian risings occurred as late as 1464. In 1643, Chester was made the headquarters of the royalist forces, while Nantwich was garrisoned for the parliament, and the county became the scene of constant skirmishes until the surrender of Chester in 1646.

In the reign of Henry VIII. the distinctive privileges of Cheshire as a county palatine were abridged. The right of sanctuary attached to the city of Chester was abolished and justices of peace were appointed as in other parts of the kingdom. An impression of the wealth of the rich agricultural county is to be seen in the numerous half-timbered houses and ancient manor-houses such as Bramhall Hall, near Macclesfield and Moreton Old Hall, near Congleton. The former dates from the 13th and 14th centuries, and contains a handsome panelled hall. Moreton Hall and several others, such as Brereton and Dorfold Halls, are Elizabethan. Vale Hall near Winsford incorporates fragments of a Cistercian monastery founded in 1277. Ecclesiastical architecture is not well represented outside Chester (*q.v.*), but Lower Peover, near Knutsford has a notable half-timbered church of 13th century date, restored in 1852. There is also a fine late Perpendicular church (with earlier portions) at Astbury near Congleton, and the churches of Banbury and Malpas are Perpendicular and Decorated. St. Michael's church and the Rivers chapel at Macclesfield are noteworthy. In the market-place at Sandbach are two remarkable sculptured Saxon crosses.

Agriculture and Industries.—From earliest times the staple products of Cheshire have been salt and cheese. The salt-pits of Nantwich, Middlewich and Northwich were in active operation at the time of Edward the Confessor, and at that date the mills and fisheries on the Dee also furnished a valuable source of revenue. Twelfth century writers refer to the excellence of Cheshire cheese. The trades of tanners, skinners and glove-makers existed at the time of the Conquest, and the export trade in wool in the 13th and 14th centuries was considerable. The soil of the county is varied and irregular; a large proportion is clay. About 75½% of the total area of 638,960 ac. was under cultivation in 1939. Oats were the most important cereal, occupying 35,224 ac., and over 52% of the cultivated land was in permanent pasture. The vicinity of such populous centres as Liverpool and Manchester stimulates dairying. The name of the county is given to a particular brand of cheese. Potatoes are by far the most important rootcrop and occupied 16,416 ac. in 1939. The damson is common among fruit trees, while the strawberry beds near Farndon and Holt are celebrated. Market-gardening is pursued in the neighbourhoods of Chester, Wallasey and Altrincham. In the first half of the 19th century the condition of agriculture in Cheshire was notoriously backward. In 1865–66 the county suffered from cattle plague, and at various times since diseases introduced from overseas through Liverpool have ravaged the county. The manufacture of textiles extends from its seat in Lancashire into Cheshire; and the whole northeastern tongue of the county is engaged in branches of the industry, particularly cotton-spinning. Metalworking is important, and embraces shipbuilding (Birkenhead) and galvanized iron products (Ellesmere Port). At Crewe are situated the great workshops of the London, Midland and Scottish railway company, to which the town owes its origin and rise. Chemical industries are of special importance, and are found along the Mersey; they are closely related to the salt industry. The Mersey shore also has machinery and ironworks, flour mills, tobacco and soap-works (Port Sunlight). Much sandstone is quarried, but the mineral wealth of the county lies in coal (around Congleton and Macclesfield) and especially salt.

Some rock salt is obtained at Northwich and Winsford, but most of the salt is extracted from brine both here and at Lawton, Wheelock and Middlewich. Subsidences frequently occur after the brine is pumped out; walls crack and collapse, and houses are seen leaning far out of the perpendicular.

Communications.—The county is well served with railways. The main line of the L.M.S.R. runs north from Crewe to Warrington with branches from Crewe diverging fanwise to Manchester, Chester, North Wales and Shrewsbury. The G.W.R. passes northward from Wrexham to Liverpool and Manchester. The heart of the county is traversed by the Cheshire lines of the L.M.S.R., serving the salt district, and reaching Chester from Manchester by way of Delamere Forest. In the west, between Chester, Connah's Quay and Liverpool, the L.N.E.R. operates. Many experiments in road building have been made in the Wirral. The river Weaver is locked as far up as Winsford, and the transport of salt is thus expedited. In the salt district of the Weaver, subsidence has resulted in the formation of lakes of considerable extent, which act as reservoirs to supply the navigation. Inland navigation is also provided by the Grand Trunk, Shropshire Union and other canals, and many small steamers are in use. The Manchester Ship canal passes through a section of north Cheshire, entering from the Mersey estuary by locks near Eastham, and following its southern shore up to Runcorn, after which it takes a course more direct than the river, and finally enters Lancashire at the junction of the Irwell with the Mersey, near Irlam.

Population and Administration.—The area of the administrative county is 973 sq.mi.; pop. (1951) 1,258,050. Cheshire has been described as a suburb of Liverpool, Manchester and the Potteries, and has been freely colonized from these populous industrial centres. On the short seacoast of the Wirral are found the popular resorts of New Brighton and Hoylake. The movement of population and the importance of the industries of the county have brought about a vast increase of population in modern times. Further movements during World War II raised the population of the whole county by 2% between Sept. 1939 and Feb. 1941. The county contains seven hundreds and four county boroughs, which are Birkenhead, Chester (a city), Stockport and Wallasey. The municipal boroughs are Altrincham, Bebington, Congleton, Crewe, Dukinfield, Hyde, Macclesfield, Sale and Stalybridge. Chester is the county town. There are 24 urban districts and 10 rural districts.

The county is in the North Wales and Chester circuit, and assizes are held at Chester. It has two courts of quarter sessions, and is divided into 17 petty sessional divisions. Cheshire is almost wholly in the diocese of Chester, but small parts are in those of Manchester, St. Asaph and Lichfield. There are nine parliamentary divisions returning one member each, namely Macclesfield, Crewe, Eddisbury, Wirral, Knutsford, Altrincham, Northwich, City of Chester and Stalybridge and Hyde; the county also includes the parliamentary boroughs of Birkenhead and Stockport, returning two members, and Wallasey, which returns one member. The National Trust owned 496 ac. in Cheshire in 1942.

Bibliography.—Sir John Doddridge, *History of the Ancient and Modern State of the Principality of Wales, Duchy of Cornwall, and Earldom of Chester* (London, 1630; 2nd ed. 1714); D. King, *The Vale-Royall of England, or the County Palatine of Cheshire Illustrated,* 4 parts (London, 1656); J. H. Hanshall, *History of the County Palatine of Chester* (Chester, 1817–1823); J. O. Halliwell, *Palatine Anthology* (London, 1850); G. Ormerod, *History of the County Palatine and City of Chester* (London, 1819; new ed. London, 1875–1882); J. P. Earwaker, *East Cheshire* (2 vols. London, 1877); J. Croston, *Historic Sites of Cheshire* (Manchester, 1883); and *County Families of Cheshire* (Manchester, 1887); W. E. A. Axon, *Cheshire Gleanings* (Manchester, 1884); Holland, *Glossary of Words used in the County of Cheshire* (London, 1884–1886); N. G. Philips, *Views of Old Halls of Cheshire* (London, 1893); *Land of Britain* (Report of Land Utilisation Survey) pt. 65 (London, 1941); *Survey of Merseyside* (Liverpool University Press, 1934). *See* also various volumes of the Chetham society and of the Record Society of Manchester, as well as the *Proceedings* of the Cheshire Antiquarian society, and *Cheshire Notes and Queries.*

CHESHUNT, an urban district of Hertfordshire, Eng., on the Lea, 16 mi. N. of London by the Eastern Region railway. Pop. (1951) 23,016. Area 13.3 sq.mi. Finds indicate the presence of a Romano-British settlement. There was a Benedictine nunnery there in the 13th century. A mansion in the vicinity, the Great house, belonged to Cardinal Wolsey. Theobalds Park was built in the 18th century. James I died there in the original mansion in 1625, and Charles I set out from there for Nottingham in 1642 at the outset of the Civil War. One of the entrances to Theobalds Park is old Temple Bar, moved from Fleet street, London, 1878. The church of St. Mary is Perpendicular, with modern additions. Cheshunt college (1792) was the successor of a college founded by the countess of Huntingdon in 1768 at Trevecca in Brecknockshire for the education of ministers of the Methodist connection. In 1905 it was converted into a theological college of the Church of England and later became known as Bishop's college. Cheshunt is an important centre of market gardening.

CHESIL BANK (A.S., *ceosol,* pebble bank), a remarkable beach of shingle on the coast of Dorsetshire, England. It is separated from the mainland for 8 mi. by an inlet called the Fleet, famous for its swannery, and continues in all for 18 mi. southeastward from near Abbotsbury, terminating at the so-called isle of Portland. At the Portland end it is 35 ft. above springtide level, and 200 yd. wide, while at the landward end the width is 170 yd. and the pebbles decrease in size. This accords with the general movement of shingle along this coast from west to east.

CHESNELONG, PIERRE CHARLES (1820–1899), French public official, was born at Orthez, Basses-Pyrénées. In 1848 he proclaimed himself a Republican. After the establishment of the Second Empire, however, he changed his views, and in 1865 was returned to the chamber as the official candidate for his native place. He at once became conspicuous, both for his eloquence and for his uncompromising clericalism, especially in urging the necessity for maintaining the temporal power of the papacy. In 1869 he was again returned and, devoting himself with exceptional ability to financial questions, was in 1870 appointed to report the budget.

During and after the war, for which he voted, he retired for a while into private life. But in 1872 he was again elected deputy, this time as a Legitimist, and took his seat among the extreme right.

He was the soul of the reactionary opposition that led to the fall of Thiers; and in 1873 it was he who, with Lucien Brun, carried to the comte de Chambord the proposals of the chambers. Through some misunderstanding, he reported on his return that the count had accepted all the terms offered, including the retention of the tricolour flag; and the count published a formal denial.

Chesnelong then devoted himself to the establishment of Catholic universities and to the formation of Catholic workingmen's clubs. He continued his vigorous polemic against the secularization of the educational system of France from his place in the senate, to which he was elected in Nov. 1876.

See M. de Marcey, *Charles Chesnelong*, etc., 3 vol. (1908); Mgr. Laveille, *Chesnelong, sa vie, son action catholique et parlementaire* (1913).

CHESNEY, CHARLES CORNWALLIS (1826–1876), British soldier and military writer, the third son of Charles Cornwallis Chesney, Bengal artillery, and nephew of Gen. F. R. Chesney, was born in County Down, Ire., on Sept. 29, 1826. Educated at Blundell's school, Tiverton, and afterward at the Royal Military academy, Woolwich, he obtained his first commission as second lieutenant of engineers in 1845, passing out of the academy at the head of his term.

His early service was spent in the ordinary course of regimental duty at home and abroad, and he was stationed in New Zealand during the Crimean War. Among the various reforms in the British military system which followed from that war was the impetus given to military education, and in 1858 Captain Chesney was appointed professor of military history at Sandhurst. In 1864 he succeeded Colonel (afterward Sir) Edward Hamley in the corresponding chair at the Staff college.

Chesney's first published work (1863) was an account of the Civil War in Virginia, which went through several editions. But the work which attained the greatest reputation was his *Waterloo Lectures* (1868), prepared from the notes of lectures orally delivered at the Staff college. Up to that time the English literature on the Waterloo campaign, although voluminous, was made up of personal reminiscences or of formal records, useful records for history rather than the history itself. The French accounts had mainly taken the form of fiction. Chesney's account illustrates both the strategy and tactics which culminated in the final catastrophe, and the mistakes committed by Napoleon are laid bare. For the first time, moreover, an English writer pointed out that the dispositions of Wellington were far from faultless. In the *Waterloo Lectures* the Prussians are for the first time credited by an English pen with their proper share in the victory. The work attracted much attention abroad as well as at home, and French and German translations were published.

Chesney was for many years a constant contributor to the newspapers and to periodical literature, devoting himself for the most part to the critical treatment of military operations and professional subjects generally. Some of his essays on military biography, contributed mainly to the *Edinburgh Review*, were afterward published separately (1874).

In 1868 he was appointed a member of the royal commission on military education, under the presidency first of Earl de Grey and afterward of Lord Dufferin, to whose recommendations were due the improved organization of the military colleges and the development of military education in the principal military stations of the British army.

In 1871, on the conclusion of the Franco-German War, he was sent on a special mission to France and Germany, and furnished to the government a series of valuable reports on the different siege operations which had been carried out during the war, especially the two sieges of Paris. These reports were published in a large volume, which was issued confidentially.

He was consulted by officers of all grades on professional matters, and few did more to raise the intellectual standard of the British officer. He constantly engaged in literary pursuits and managed also to devote a large part of his time to charitable and religious offices.

Chesney died after a short illness on March 19, 1876. He had become lieutenant colonel in 1873, and at the time of his death he was commanding royal engineer of the London district.

CHESNEY, FRANCIS RAWDON (1789–1872), British general and explorer, was the son of Capt. Alexander Chesney, an Irishman of Scottish descent who, having emigrated to South Carolina in 1772, served under Lord Rawdon (afterward marquess of Hastings) in the War of Independence and subsequently received an appointment as coast officer at Annalong, County Down, Ire. F. R. Chesney was born there on March 16, 1789.

Lord Rawdon gave the boy a cadetship at Woolwich, and he was gazetted to the royal artillery in 1805. But though he rose to be lieutenant general and colonel commandant of the 14th brigade royal artillery (1864), and general in 1868, Chesney is chiefly remembered for his connection with the Suez canal and with the exploration of the Euphrates valley, which started with his being sent to Constantinople in the course of his military duties in 1829 and his making a tour of inspection in Egypt and Syria. His report in 1830 on the feasibility of making the Suez canal was the original basis of Ferdinand de Lesseps' great undertaking. (In 1869 De Lesseps greeted him in Paris as the "father" of the canal.)

In 1831 Chesney introduced to the British government the idea of opening a new overland route to India, by a daring and adventurous journey (for the Arabs were hostile and he was ignorant of the language) along the Euphrates valley from Anah to the Persian gulf.

Returning home, Colonel Chesney (as he then was) busied himself to get support for the latter project, to which the East India company's board was favourable. In 1835 he was sent in command of a small expedition, for which parliament voted £20,000, in order to test the navigability of the Euphrates. After encountering immense difficulties from the opposition of the Egyptian pasha, and from the need of transporting two steamers (one of which was lost) in sections from the Mediterranean over the hilly country to the river, they successfully arrived by water at Bushire in the summer of 1836 and proved Chesney's view to be a practicable one.

In the middle of 1837 he returned to England and was given the Royal Geographical society's gold medal, having meanwhile been to India to consult the authorities there. But the preparation of his two volumes on the expedition (published in 1850) was interrupted by his being ordered in 1843 to command the artillery at Hong Kong.

In 1847 his period of service was completed, and he went home to Ireland to a life of retirement. But both in 1856 and again in 1862 he went to the east to take a part in further surveys and negotiations for the Euphrates valley railway scheme, which, however, the government would not take up in spite of a favourable report from the house of commons committee in 1871.

Chesney died on Jan. 30, 1872.

The chief works of Chesney are: *The Expedition for the Survey of the Rivers Euphrates and Tigris* (1850); *Observations on . . . Firearms* (1852); *The Russo-Turkish Campaigns of 1828 and 1829* (1854); *Narrative of the Euphrates Expedition* (1854).

See *The Life of Gen. F. R. Chesney* by his wife and daughter, ed. by S. Lane-Poole (1885).

CHESNEY, SIR GEORGE TOMKYNS (1830–1895), English general, brother of Col. C. C. Chesney, was born at Tiverton, Devon, on April 30, 1830. Educated at Blundell's school, Tiverton, and at Addiscombe, he entered the Bengal engineers as second lieutenant in 1848. He was employed for several years in the public works department. On the outbreak of the Indian Mutiny in 1857, he joined the Ambala column, was field engineer at the battle of Badli-ke-serai, brigade major of engineers throughout the siege of Delhi, and was severely wounded in the assault.

In 1860 he was appointed head of a new department in connection with the public works accounts. His work on *Indian Polity* (1868), dealing with the administration of the several departments of the Indian government, attracted wide attention and became a permanent textbook.

The originator of the Royal Indian Civil Engineering college at Cooper's Hill, Staines, he was also its first president from 1871 until 1880.

In 1871 he contributed to *Blackwood's Magazine*, "The Battle of Dorking," a vivid account of a supposed invasion of England by the Germans after their victory over France. The article was republished in many editions and translations and produced a profound impression.

Chesney was promoted to lieutenant colonel in 1869; colonel, 1877; major general, 1886; lieutenant general, 1887; colonel commandant of royal engineers, 1890; and general, 1892.

From 1881 to 1886 he was secretary to the military department of the government of India and was made a Companion (of the Order) of the Star of India and of the Indian Empire. From 1886 to 1892, as military member of the governor general's council, he carried out many much-needed military reforms.

He was made a Companion of the Bath at the jubilee of 1887, and a Knight Commander of the Bath on leaving India in 1892. In that year he was returned to parliament, in the Conservative interest, as member for Oxford, and was chairman of the committee of service members of the house of commons until his death on March 31, 1895.

Chesney wrote some novels, including *The Dilemma, The Private Secretary* and *The Lesters.*

CHESNUT, JAMES (1815–1885), U.S. senator and Confederate soldier, was born at Camden, S.C., on Jan. 18, 1815, the son of the owner of large plantations in Kershaw county, S.C. Chesnut was graduated from Princeton university in 1835 and admitted to the bar in 1837.

In 1840 he was elected to the lower house of the South Carolina legislature as a representative from Kershaw, and he served there, with the exception of the terms of 1846–47 and 1848–49, until 1852. Chesnut then became a state senator, serving as president of the senate from 1856 to 1858, when he was elected a U.S. senator. In the senate Chesnut, who had been graduated from Princeton with an honorary oration, soon became known as an eloquent defender of the institution of slavery.

After resigning from the U.S. senate on Nov. 10, 1860, he helped draw up the ordinance of secession at the South Carolina convention and the permanent constitution at the provisional congress of the Confederate states.

An aide to Gen. Pierre Beauregard during the Ford Sumter incident and at the first battle of Manassas, Chesnut later served as a colonel of cavalry under Jefferson Davis.

In April 1864 he became commander, with the rank of brigadier general, of the reserve troops in South Carolina.

After the war he participated in state politics and was a delegate to state and national conventions of the Democratic party.

He was married to Mary Boykin Miller, whose father, Stephen D. Miller, was governor of South Carolina from 1828 to 1830, on April 23, 1840.

Chesnut died near Camden on Feb. 1, 1885.

CHESS, a game for two players using a board and special pieces. From its pre-eminence among intellectual pastimes, it is called "the royal game." Probably originating in India during or before the 7th century (see *Origin of Chess,* below), chess spread to Persia, Arabia and thence to western Europe. Its name and the term "checkmate" derive from the Persian *shah,* "king," and *shah mat,* "the king is dead." The growth of an extensive occidental chess literature and the rise of international tournaments have standardized the game throughout European and American countries, but variants have survived in Japan and China.

The Board.—The chessboard comprises 64 squares, coloured alternately light and dark, in a large square. The players, designated White and Black, sit on opposite sides. In printed diagrams the Black side is by convention at the top. The board is placed so that each player finds a light square in the corner nearest his right hand. A row of eight squares parallel to the White and Black sides is called a *rank;* a row at right angles to the ranks is a *file.* The term *diagonal* is self-explanatory.

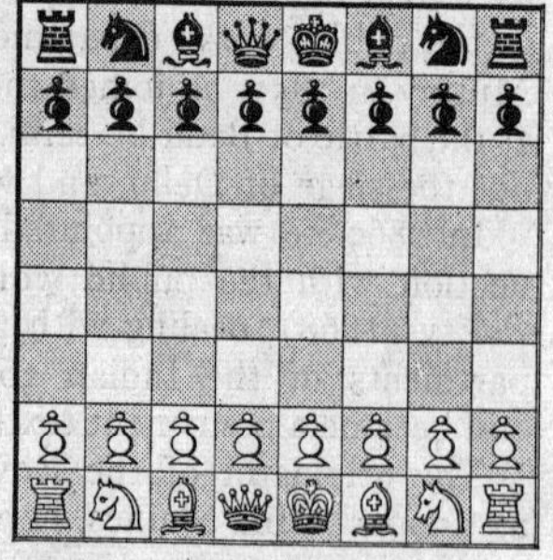

FIG. 1.—DIAGRAM SHOWING POSITION OF CHESSMEN AT BEGINNING OF GAME

Queen's rook (QR); queen's knight (QKt); queen's bishop (QB); queen (Q); king (K); king's bishop (KB); king's knight (KKt); king's rook (KR). The pieces in front of the principal pieces are the pawns (P)

The Pieces.—Each player has 16 pieces, which are placed on the board at the beginning of a game as shown in fig. 1. The pieces are distinguished by their shapes into six kinds: king, queen, rook, bishop, knight, pawn. The king moves in any direction, one square at a time. The queen, rook and bishop are "long-range" pieces, moving any distance along an unobstructed line. The rook moves only on the ranks and files, the bishop only on the diagonals. The queen combines the powers of rook and bishop, and thus moves on any open line. The knight move is from one corner to that diagonally opposite, in a rectangle three squares by two (*see* fig. 2). This is not a line move, but a move from point to point, and therefore cannot be obstructed by any neighbouring pieces. The term "piece" is often used in a restricted sense to exclude pawns. Any piece not a pawn captures in the same way it moves; that is, it may capture an adverse man standing on a square to which it can legally move. The capturing piece replaces the captured on the same square, and the captured man is removed from the board.

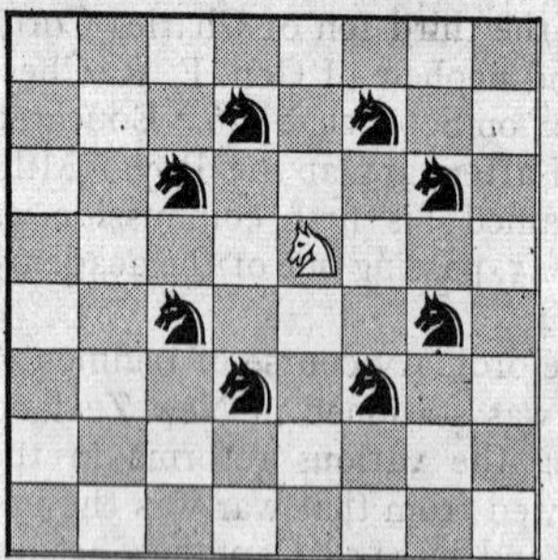

FIG. 2.—DIAGRAM SHOWING THE MOVE OF A KNIGHT

The White knight may move onto any of the squares occupied by the Black knights

The pawn has several peculiarities. It moves only forward, and when not capturing advances only on the file. For the first advance from its initial square on the second rank, the pawn has the option of moving one or two squares, but thereafter may move only one square at a time. If it reaches the eighth rank, farthest from the owner, the pawn is immediately replaced by a queen, rook, bishop or knight of the same colour, at the option of the owner. This *promotion* is also called *queening,* since the usual choice is a queen, the most powerful piece. A pawn may promote even though the piece chosen to replace it has not previously disappeared from the board by capture; *e.g.,* a player may have two or more queens. The pawn alone captures differently from its noncapturing move. It captures to either square that is adjacent and diagonally forward. If a pawn makes the double advance for its first move, an adverse pawn that could have captured it, had the first pawn moved only one square, may capture it *en passant,* in passing; but this "e.p." capture may be made only on the immediate turn, not later.

Castling is a compound move of the king and one rook that may be made, if at all, only once in a game. It is legal if neither the king nor the rook has yet moved; if all the squares between them on the rank are vacant and no adverse piece commands the two squares nearest the king; and if the king is not in check. The move is executed by moving the king two squares toward the rook, and then placing the rook on the square passed over by the king. Either the KR or the QR may be used in castling.

Notations.—In the descriptive notation (*see* fig. 3), each file is given the name of the piece originally posted on it, and the ranks are numbered from 1 to 8 away from the player. Each rank thus has a dual designation, according to the colour of the moving piece. A move is written in the form "P—QB4," the initial of the moving piece followed by the designation of the square moved to. The abbreviation "Kt" for knight is often replaced by "S" or "N." Indication of K—side or Q—side is omitted when no ambiguity would result; *e.g.,* "B—B4" when only one bishop can reach either of the B4 squares. The symbol "×" as in "P×P" indicates a capture and is read "takes." This notation was condensed in the middle 19th century from the earlier florid style; *e.g.,* "King's pawn to his fourth."

In the algebraic notation, each file and rank has a single designation, a letter and a number. A move is written in the form "Pc2—c4" or "c2—c4" or "c4." The initial for the pawn is usually omitted, as is also, in condensed style, the square of departure. Symbols used are as follows: (:) takes; (o–o) castles on K—side; (o–o–o) castles on Q—side; (†) or (+) check; (‡) or (#) checkmate; (!) best, or a good move; (?) questionable, or a poor move; (!?) is this best?

Game records are kept in columnar form, as below. The moves are numbered serially, both a White move and the Black reply having the same number.

	Descriptive			Algebraic	
	White	Black		White	Black
1	P—K4	P—K4	1	e2—e4	e7—e5
2	Kt—KB3	Kt—QB3	2	Sg1—f3	Sb8—c6
3	B—B4	B—B4	3	Bf1—c4	Bf8—c5
4	P—B3	Kt—B3!	4	c2—c3	Sg8—f6!
5	P—Q4	P×P	5	d2—d4	e5—d4:
6	P×P	B—Kt5ch	6	c3—d4:	Bc5—b4†

In annotation, moves are written linearly, thus: (Descriptive) 1 P—K4, P—K4; 2 Kt—KB3, Kt—QB3; 3. B—B4, B—B4; 4 P—QKt4, B×P; 5 P—B3. (Algebraic) 1 e4, e5; 2 Sf3, Sc6; 3 Bc4, Bc5; 4 b4, Bb4:; 5 c3. Occasionally, the descriptive notation is written in fractional form, the White moves being above the line and the Black moves below, thus:

$$\frac{1\ \text{P—K4}}{\text{P—K4}}\ \frac{2\text{Kt—KB3}}{\text{Kt—QB3}}.$$

In French and German, respectively, the names of the pieces are: king, *roi, König;* queen, *dame, Dame;* rook, *tour, Turm;* bishop, *fou, Läufer;* knight, *cavalier, Springer;* pawn, *pion, Bauer;* the game is chess, *les échecs, Schach.*

	a	b	c	d	e	f	g	h	
8	QR1 / QR8	QKt1 / QKt8	QB1 / QB8	Q1 / Q8	K1 / K8	KB1 / KB8	KKt1 / KKt8	KR1 / KR8	8
7	QR2 / QR7	QKt2 / QKt7	QB2 / QB7	Q2 / Q7	K2 / K7	KB2 / KB7	KKt2 / KKt7	KR2 / KR7	7
6	QR3 / QR6	QKt3 / QKt6	QB3 / QB6	Q3 / Q6	K3 / K6	KB3 / KB6	KKt3 / KKt6	KR3 / KR6	6
5	QR4 / QR5	QKt4 / QKt5	QB4 / QB5	Q4 / Q5	K4 / K5	KB4 / KB5	KKt4 / KKt5	KR4 / KR5	5
4	QR5 / QR4	QKt5 / QKt4	QB5 / QB4	Q5 / Q4	K5 / K4	KB5 / KB4	KKt5 / KKt4	KR5 / KR4	4
3	QR6 / QR3	QKt6 / QKt3	QB6 / QB3	Q6 / Q3	K6 / K3	KB6 / KB3	KKt6 / KKt3	KR6 / KR3	3
2	QR7 / QR2	QKt7 / QKt2	QB7 / QB2	Q7 / Q2	K7 / K2	KB7 / KB2	KKt7 / KKt2	KR7 / KR2	2
1	QR8 / QR1	QKt8 / QKt1	QB8 / QB1	Q8 / Q1	K8 / K1	KB8 / KB1	KKt8 / KKt1	KR8 / KR1	1
	a	b	c	d	e	f	g	h	

FIG. 3.—DESCRIPTIVE AND ALGEBRAIC SYSTEMS OF NOTATION
The descriptive system names the file after the piece on the first rank, as the "KR file" at the extreme right. The ranks are counted away from the player whose piece moves. In the algebraic system the files are lettered a to h, from White's left to right, and the ranks are numbered 1 to 8 from White to Black. In diagrams the bottom edge is always the White side

Object of Play.—The game is won by capturing the adverse king. The capture is never consummated; when the king is attacked and cannot escape, he is said to be *checkmated* and the game ends forthwith. Many games end by resignation of a player who sees that he cannot escape eventual defeat.

A threat to capture the adverse king is a *check,* and on making such a threat the player by custom says "Check!" The warning is not legally obligatory. A check must of course be averted or the game forfeited. The only ways of meeting a check are to move the king, capture the attacker or interpose on the line of check given by a distant queen, rook or bishop.

Check *by discovery* may be given by a long-range piece, by removal of a piece standing on a line between it and the adverse king. A piece that cannot move without discovering check upon its own king is said to be *pinned.* Even if completely immobilized by pin, a piece may exert check on the adverse king, for if the captures were actually consummated, the pinned piece would capture the adverse king one move ahead of the loss of its own king.

Value of the Pieces.—With only the kings otherwise left on the board, checkmate can be forced by a single "major piece," queen or rook, or by two bishops, or by a bishop and a knight, but not by two knights or any single "minor piece." (But a king accompanied by "officious friends," pawns that block rather than protect him, is sometimes mated by a single knight or bishop. *See* Problem No. 1, below.) A single pawn cannot give mate, but wins if it can be promoted. Two rooks normally draw against a queen, and may win. Two bishops can draw against a queen. But a queen wins against one rook or two minor pieces including a knight. One minor piece draws against a rook.

With additional pieces on the board, however, any "material superiority," even one pawn, spells potential victory. The superior fighting power can usually increase its own margin of advantage. In terms of the pawn as 1, the fighting power of the pieces is approximately: knight 3, bishop 3, rook 5, (king 5), queen 9. This scale gives a measure of whether material equality is disturbed by an exchange of captures of unlike pieces. The phrase "winning the exchange" is applied particularly to winning a rook for a minor piece, or two minor pieces for a rook. Any such gain in relative power is potentially decisive. The more disparate the pieces exchanged, however, the more the outcome is affected by the particular position. For example, the merits of one rook *v.* five pawns cannot be stated in general, as there is no "general position." Positional considerations often override the abstract evaluations. *Sacrifices* of material are often made for positional advantage. The knight and bishop are rated equal, but a bishop is more often favoured by the position than a knight, and two bishops are almost always markedly stronger than two knights.

Drawn Games.—A game may be abandoned as drawn for any of the following reasons. *Insufficient force:* The pieces remaining on the board do not suffice to force checkmate. *Stalemate:* The player in turn to move has no legal move but is not in check. *Perpetual check:* A player demonstrates that he can check the adverse king without cessation, and declares that he will do so. *Agreement:* The players agree to abandon the game (in tournaments, allowed only after Black has completed 30 moves). *Recurrence:* If the same position of all forces recurs three times, with the same player to move on each occasion, that player may claim a draw. *Fifty-move rule:* If during 50 moves on each side, no pawn has moved and no capture has been made, either may claim a draw, unless his opponent can demonstrate a forced checkmate or unless the position is one which is known theoretically to require more than 50 moves for a forced win.

Laws of Chess.—All countries outside the orient follow the laws of chess promulgated by the Fédération Internationale des Échecs. The principal provisions of the 1944 code are as follows:

White moves first. A completed legal move may not be retracted. A move is completed: in moving a man from one square to another, when the player has removed his hand from the man; in capturing, when the captured man has been removed from the board and the player has removed his hand from the capturing man; in castling, when the player has removed his hand from the rook; in promoting, when the player has replaced the pawn by the selected piece and removed his hand from the latter. A player may touch his own men for purpose of arranging them if he says "I adjust" or words to that effect; he must not touch an adverse piece to arrange, after commencement of play, but may call upon his opponent to do so. Except in arranging, if a player touches one of his own men, he must if possible move it; if he touches an adverse man, he must if possible capture it.

If a player makes an illegal move, and the opponent draws attention to the fact before touching any of his own men, the illegal move must be retracted and: if the move was noncapturing, the player must if able move the same piece; if the move was a capture, the player must if able move the same piece or capture the same piece, at the option of the opponent if he can comply in both ways. If during a game it is proved that an illegal move was made and not retracted, the position existing immediately before the illegal move must be reinstated and play continued from that point; if this position cannot be reinstated, the game is annulled. If a player entitled to direct a move in application of penalty names an illegal move, his right is abrogated. Castling may not be exacted as a penalty. A game is declared forfeited by a player who wilfully upsets the board or disarranges the men; refuses to comply with a requirement under the laws; refuses to conform to arrangements for the conduct of the game; or exceeds the time limit.

In tournament and match games, time is kept on each player, by separate clocks. Each player must complete 30 moves in his first two hours, 45 in his first three hours and so on by increments of 15 moves per hour. (This rate may be modified by regulations for a particular tournament.) A player's clock is set going as soon as it becomes his turn to move, and he may stop it only after making his move. The White player's clock is started at the time scheduled for commencement of a game, regardless of whether both players are present. A player who arrives more than an hour late (without excuse acceptable to the referee) forfeits the game.

If a game is not finished by the prefixed closing time for the session, it is adjourned. The player in turn to move takes whatever time he wishes for consideration, writes his move on a slip of paper, seals it in an envelope which he hands to the referee, and his clock is then stopped. At resumption of play, the referee sets up the position as it was left, opens the envelope, makes the indicated move and starts the opponent's clock. If the sealed move is illegal, and the mistake cannot be rectified to the satisfaction of the referee, he may declare the game forfeited by the player who sealed the illegal move.

Origin of Chess.—The origin of chess is lost in obscurity. Its invention has been variously ascribed to the Greeks, Romans, Babylonians, Scythians, Egyptians, Jews, Persians, Chinese, Hindus, Arabians, Araucanians, Castilians, Irish and Welsh. Some have endeavoured to fix upon particular individuals as the originators of the game; among others, upon Japheth, Shem, King Solomon, the wife of Ravan, king of Ceylon, the philosopher Xerxes, the Greek chieftain Palamedes, Hermes, Aristotle, the brothers Lydo and Tyrrhene, Semiramis, Zenobia, Attalus (d. *c.* 200 B.C.), the mandarin Hansing, the Brahman Sissa and Shatrenscha, stated to be a celebrated Persian astronomer. Many of these ascriptions are fabulous, others rest upon little authority, and some of them proceed from easily traceable errors, as where the Roman games of *ludus latrunculorum* and *ludus calculorum,* the Welsh recreation of *tawlbwrdd* (throw-board) and the ancient Irish pastime of *fithcheall* are assumed to be identical with chess; so far as the Romans and Welsh are concerned, the contrary can be proved, while from what little is known of the Irish game it appears not to have been a sedentary game at all. N. Bland, in his *Persian Chess* (London, 1850), endeavoured to prove that the Persians were the inventors of chess, and maintained that the game, born in Persia, found a home in India, whence after a series of ages it was brought back to its birthplace. The view which has obtained the most credence, however, is that which attributes the origin of chess to the Hindus. Thomas Hyde of Oxford, writing in 1694 (*De Ludis Orientalibus*), seems to have been the first to propound this theory, but he appears to have been ignorant of the game itself, and the Sanskrit records were not accessible in his time. About 1783–89 Sir William Jones, in an essay published in the second volume of *Asiatic Researches,* argued that Hindustan was the cradle of chess, the game having been known there from time immemorial by the name of *chaturanga;* that is, the four *angas,* or members of an army, which are said in the *Amarakosha* to be elephants, horses, chariots and foot soldiers. As applicable to real armies, the term *chaturanga* is frequently used by the epic poets of India. Sir William Jones's essay is substantially a translation of the *Bhawishya Purana,* in which is given a description of a four-handed game of chess played with dice. A pundit named Rhadhakant informed him that this was mentioned in the oldest law books, and also that it was invented by the wife of Ravan, king of Lanka (Ceylon), in the second age of the world in order to amuse that monarch while Rama was besieging his metropolis. This account claims for chess an existence of 4,000 or 5,000 years. Jones, however, grounded his opinions as to the Hindu origin of chess upon the testimony of the Persians and not upon the above manuscript, while he considered the game described therein to be more modern than the Persian game. Though sure that the latter came from India and was invented there, he admitted that he could not find any account of it in the classical writings of the Brahmans. He laid it down that chess, under the Sanskrit name *chaturanga,* was exported from India into Persia in the 6th century of our era; that by a natural corruption the old Persians changed the name into *chatrang,* but when their country was soon afterward taken possession of by the Arabs, who had neither the initial nor final letter of the word in their alphabet, they altered it further into *shatranj,* which name found its way later into modern Persian and ultimately into the dialects of India.

Anton van der Linde, in his exhaustive work *Geschichte und Litteratur des Schachspiels* (1874), had much to say of the origin theories, nearly all of which he treated as so many myths. He agreed with those who consider that the Persians received the game from the Hindus. The outcome of his studies appears to be that chess certainly existed in Hindustan in the 8th century, and that probably that country is the land of its birth. He inclined to the idea that the game originated among the Buddhists, whose religion was prevalent in India from the 3rd to the 9th century. According to their ideas, war and the slaying of one's fellow men, for any purposes whatever, is criminal, and the punishment of the warrior in the next world will be much worse than that of the simple murderer; hence chess was invented as a substitute for war. Van der Linde was in agreement with Sir William Jones in taking the view that the four-handed game of the original manuscript is a comparatively modern adaptation of the Hindu chess, and he altogether denied that there is any proof that any form of the game has the antiquity attributed to it.

H. J. R. Murray, in his monumental work *A History of Chess,* came to the conclusion that chess is a descendant of an Indian game played in the 7th century.

Altogether, therefore, we find the best authorities agreeing that chess existed in India before it is known to have been played anywhere else. In this supposition they are strengthened by the names of the game and of some of the pieces. *Shatranj,* as Duncan Forbes has pointed out, is a foreign word among the Persians and Arabians, whereas its natural derivation from the term *chaturanga* is obvious. Again *al-fil,* the Arabic name of the bishop, means the elephant, otherwise *alephhind,* the Indian ox. Our earliest authority on chess is Masudi, an Arabic author who wrote about A.D. 950. According to him, *shatranj* had existed long before his time; and though he may speak not only for his own generation but for a couple of centuries before, that will give to chess an existence of more than 1,000 years.

Early and Mediaeval Times.—The dimness which shrouds the origin of chess naturally obscures also its early history. We have seen that chess crossed over from India into Persia and became known in the latter country by the name of *shatranj.* Some have understood that word to mean "the play of the king"; but undoubtedly Sir William Jones's derivation carries with it the most plausibility. How and when the game was introduced into Persia we have no means of knowing.

The Persian poet Firdousi, in his historical poem the *Shahnama,* gives an account of the introduction of *shatranj* into Persia in the reign of Chosroes I. Anushirvan, to whom came ambassadors from the sovereign of Hind (India) with a chessboard and men, asking him to solve the secrets of the game, if he could, or pay tribute. The king asked for seven days' grace, during which time the wise men vainly tried to discover the secret. Finally, the king's minister took the pieces home and discovered the secret in a day and a night. He then journeyed to India with a game of his own invention, *nard,* which the Indians were unable to reconstruct.

Other Persian and Arabian writers state that *shatranj* came into Persia from India, and there appears to be a consensus that may be considered to settle the question. Thus we have the game passing from the Hindus to the Persians and thence to the Arabians, after the capture of Persia by the caliphs in the 7th century, and from them, directly or indirectly, to various parts of Europe, at a time which cannot be definitely fixed, but that was either in or before the 10th century. That the source of the European game is Arabic is clear enough, not merely from the words "check" and "mate," which are evidently from *shah mat* ("the king is dead"), but also from the names of some of the pieces. There are various chess legends having reference to the 7th and 8th centuries, but these may be neglected as historically useless; and equally useless appear the many oriental and occidental romances which revolve around those two great central figures, Harun al-Rashid and Charlemagne. There is no proof that either of them knew anything of chess or, so far as the latter is concerned, that it had been introduced into Europe in his time. True, there is an account given in Gustavus Selenus, taken from various old chronicles, as to the son of Prince Okar or Otkar of Bavaria having been killed by a blow on the temple, struck by a son of Pippin after a game of chess; and there is another well-known tradition as to the magnificent chessboard and set of men said to have been sent as a present by the empress Irene to Charlemagne. But both tales are not less mythical than the romance which relates how the great Frankish monarch lost his kingdom over a game of chess to Guérin de Montglave; for Van der Linde shows that there was no Bavarian prince of the name of Okar or Otkar at the period alluded to, and as ruthlessly shatters the tradition about Irene's chessmen.

With respect to Harun al-Rashid, among the various stories told which connect him with chess there is one that at first sight may seem entitled to some degree of credit. In the annals of the Moslems by Abulfeda (Abu'l Fida) there is given a copy of a letter stated to be "From Nicephorus, emperor of the Romans, to Harun, sovereign of the Arabs," which (using Forbes's translation), after the usual compliments, runs thus: "The empress (Irene) into whose place I have succeeded, looked upon you as a *Rukh* and herself as a mere Pawn; therefore she submitted to pay you a tribute more than the double of which she ought to have exacted from you. All this has been owing to female weakness and timidity. Now, however, I insist that you, immediately on reading this letter, repay to me all the sums of money you ever received from her. If you hesitate, the sword shall settle our accounts." Harun's reply, written on the back of the Byzantine emperor's letter, was terse and to the point. "In the name of God the merciful and gracious. From Harun, the commander of the faithful, to the Roman dog Nicephorus. I have read thine epistle, thou son of an infidel mother; my answer to it thou shalt see, not hear." Harun was as good as his word, for he marched immediately as far as Heraclea, devastating the Roman territories with fire and sword, and soon compelled Nicephorus to sue for peace.

Now the points which give authority to this narrative and the alleged correspondence are that the relations which they assume between Irene and Nicephorus on the one hand and the warlike caliph on the other are confirmed by the history of those times, while, also, the straightforward brevity of Harun's reply commends itself as what one might expect from his soldierlike character.

Still, the fact must be remembered that Abulfeda lived about five centuries after the time to which he refers. Perhaps we may assume that it is not improbable that the correspondence is genuine, but that the words *rukh* and *pawn* may have been substituted for other terms of comparison originally used.

As to how chess was introduced into western and central Europe nothing is really known. The Spaniards very likely received it from their Moslem conquerors, the Italians not improbably from the Byzantines, and in either case it would pass northward to France, going on thence to Scandinavia and England. Some say that chess was introduced into Europe at the time of the crusades, the theory being that the Christian warriors learned to play it at Constantinople. This is negatived by a curious epistle of St. Pietro Damiani, cardinal bishop of Ostia, to Pope Alexander II written about A.D. 1061, which, assuming its authenticity, shows that chess was known in Italy before the date of the first crusade. The cardinal, as it seems, had imposed a penance upon a bishop whom he had found diverting himself at chess; and in his letter to the pope he repeats the language he had held to the erring prelate; viz., "Was it right, I say, and consistent with thy duty, to sport away thy evenings amidst the vanity of chess, and defile the hand which offers up the body of the Lord, and the tongue that mediates between God and man, with the pollution of a sacrilegious game?"

Among those who took an unfavourable view of the game may be mentioned John Huss, who, when in prison, deplored his having played at chess, whereby he had lost time and run the risk of being subject to violent passions. Among authentic records of the game may be quoted the *Alexiad* of the princess Anna Comnena, in which she relates how her father, the emperor Alexius, used to divert his mind from the cares of state by playing at chess with his relatives. This emperor died in 1118.

Concerning chess in England there is the usual confusion between legend and truth. Snorre Sturleson relates that as Canute was playing at chess with Earl Ulf, a quarrel arose, which resulted in the upsetting of the board by the latter, with the further consequence of his being murdered in church a few days afterward by Canute's orders. Thomas Carlyle, in *The Early Kings of Norway,* repeats this tale, but Van der Linde treats it as a myth. The *Ramsey Chronicle* relates how Bishop Utheric, coming to Canute at night upon urgent business, found the monarch and his courtiers amusing themselves at dice and chess. There is nothing intrinsically improbable in this last narrative; but Canute died about 1035, and the date, therefore, is suspiciously early. Moreover, allowance must be made for the ease with which chroniclers described other games as chess.

As regards the individual pieces, the king seems to have had the same move as at present, but it is said he could formerly be captured. His "castling" privilege is a European invention; but he formerly leaped two and even three squares, and also to his Kt2. Castling dates no farther back than the first half of the 16th century. The queen has suffered curious changes in name, sex and power. In *shatranj* the piece was called *farz* or *firz* (also *farzan, farzin* and *farzi*), signifying a "counsellor," "minister" or "general." This was latinized into *farzia* or *fercia.* The French slightly altered the latter form into *fierce, fierge* and, as some say, *vierge,* which, if true, might explain its becoming a female. Another and much more probable account has it that whereas formerly a pawn on reaching an eighth square became a *farzin,* and not any other piece, which promotion was of the same kind as at draughts (in French, *dames*), so she became a *dame* or queen as in the latter game, and thence *dama, donna,* etc. There are old Latin manuscripts in which the terms *ferzia* and *regina* are used indifferently.

The queen formerly moved only one square diagonally and was consequently the weakest piece on the board. The immense power she now possesses seems to have been conferred upon her as late as about the middle of the 15th century. It will be noticed that under the old system the queens could never meet each other, for they operated on diagonals of different colours. The bishop's scope of action was also very limited formerly; he could move only two squares diagonally, and had no power over the intermediate square, which he could leap over whether it was occupied or not. This limitation of his powers prevailed in Europe until the 15th century.

This piece, according to Forbes, was called among the Persians *pil,* an elephant, but the Arabs, not having the letter *p* in their alphabet, wrote it *fil,* or with their definite article *al-fil,* whence *alphilus, alfinus, alifiere,* the latter being the word used by the Italians; while the French perhaps get their *fol* and *fou* from the same source. The pawns formerly could move only one square at starting; their powers in this respect were increased about the early part of the 16th century. It was customary for them on arriving at an eighth square to be exchanged only for a *farzin* (queen) and no other piece; the rooks (so called from the Indian *rukh* and Persian *rokh,* meaning "a soldier") and the knights appear to have always had the same powers as at present. As to the chessboards, they were formerly uncoloured, and it is not until the 13th century that we hear of checkered boards being used in Europe.

Development in Play.—The change of *shatranj* into modern chess took place most probably first in France, and thence made its way into Spain early in the 15th century, where the new game was called *Axedrez de la dama,* being also adopted by the Italians under the name of *scacci alla rabiosa.* The time of the first important writer on modern chess, the Spaniard Ruy Lopez de Segura

(1561), is also the period when the latest improvement, castling, was introduced, for his book (*Libro de la invencion liberal y arte del juego del Axedrez*), though treating of it as already in use, also gives the old mode of play, which allowed the king a leap of two or three squares. Shortly afterward the old *shatranj* disappears altogether. Lopez was the first who merits the name of chess analyst. At this time flourished the flower of the Spanish and Italian schools of chess—the former represented by Lopez, Ceron, Santa Maria, Busnardo and Avalos, the latter by Giovanni Leonardo da Cutri (Il Puttino) and Paolo Boi (Il Syracusano). In the years 1562–75 both Italian masters visited Spain and defeated their Spanish antagonists. During the whole 17th century we find but one worthy to be mentioned, Giacchino Greco (Il Calabrese).

The middle of the 18th century inaugurates a new era in chess. The leading man of this time was François André Danican Philidor. He was born in 1726 and was trained by M. de Kermar, sire de Légal, the star of the Café de la Régence in Paris, which was the centre of French chess until early in the 20th century. In 1747 Philidor visited England and defeated the Arabian player, Phillip Stamma, by 8 games to 1 and 1 draw. In 1749 he published his *Analyse des échecs*, a book which went through more editions and was more translated than any other work upon the game. During more than half a century Philidor travelled much but never went to Italy, the only country where he could have found opponents of first-rate skill. Italy was represented in Philidor's time by Ercole del Rio, Lolli and Ponziani. Their style was less sound than that of Philidor, but certainly a much finer and in principle a better one. As an analyst the Frenchman was in many points refuted by Ercole del Rio ("the anonymous Modenese").

Blindfold chess play, already exhibited in the 11th century by Arabian and Persian experts, was taken up afresh by Philidor, who played on many occasions three games simultaneously without sight of board or men. These exhibitions were given in London, at the Chess club in St. James's street, and Philidor died in that city in 1795. As eminent players of this period must be mentioned Count P. J. van Zuylen van Nyevelt (1743–1826) and the German player J. Allgaier (1763–1823), after whom a well-known brilliant variation of the king's gambit is named. Philidor was succeeded by Alexandre Louis Honoré Lebreton Deschapelles (1780–1847), who was also a famous whist player. The only player who is known to have fought Deschapelles not unsuccessfully on even terms is John Cochrane. He also lost a match (1821) to W. Lewis, to whom he conceded the odds of "pawn and move," the Englishman winning 1 and drawing the 2 others. Deschapelles's greatest pupil, and the strongest player France ever possessed, was Louis Charles Mahé de la Bourdonnais, who was born in 1797 and died in 1840. His most memorable achievement was his contest with the English champion Alexander Macdonnell, the French player winning in the proportion of 3 to 2.

The English school of chess began about the beginning of the 19th century, and Sarratt was its first leader. He flourished until 1820 and was followed by his great pupil W. Lewis, who will be remembered for his writings. His literary career belongs to the period from 1817 to 1848, and he died in 1870. Macdonnell (1798–1835) has been already mentioned. To the same period belong also Captain Evans, the inventor of the celebrated "Evans gambit" (1824), who died at an advanced age in 1872; George Perigal (d. 1854), who played in the correspondence matches against Edinburgh and Paris; George Walker (1803–79), chess editor of *Bell's Life* from 1835 to 1873; and John Cochrane (1798–1878), who met every strong player from Deschapelles down. In the same period Germany possessed but one good player, J. Mendheim of Berlin. The fifth decade of the 19th century is marked by the fact that the leadership passed from the French school to the English. After the death of La Bourdonnais, Fournié de Saint-Amant became the leading player in France; he visited England in the early part of 1843 and successfully met the best English players, including Howard Staunton (*q.v.*); but the latter soon took his revenge, for in Nov. and Dec. 1843 a great match between Staunton and Saint-Amant took place in Paris, the English champion winning by 11 games to 6 with 4 draws. During the succeeding eight years Staunton maintained his reputation by defeating Popert, B. Horwitz and Harrwitz. Staunton was defeated by Adolph Anderssen at the London tournament in 1851, and this concluded his match-playing career.

In the ten years 1830–40 a new school arose in Berlin, the seven leaders of which have been called "the Pleiades." These were Ludwig Bledow (1795–1846), Bilguer (1815–40), Hanstein (1810–50), Mayet (1810–68), Schorn (1802–50), B. Horwitz (1809–85) and von Heydebrand und der Lasa, once German ambassador at Copenhagen. As belonging to the same period must be mentioned the three Hungarian players Grimm, Szen and J. Löwenthal.

Among the great masters since the middle of the 19th century, Paul Morphy (1837–84), an American, has seldom been surpassed as a chess player. His career was short but brilliant. Born in New Orleans, La., in 1837, he was taught chess by his father when only ten years of age, and in two years' time became a strong player. When not quite 13 he played three games with Löwenthal and won two of them, the other being drawn. He was 20 years of age when he competed in the New York city congress of 1857, where he won the first prize. In 1858 he visited England and there defeated Boden, Medley, Mongredien, Owen, Bird and others. He also beat Löwenthal by 9 games to 3 and 2 draws. In the same year he played a match at Paris with Harrwitz, winning by 5 to 2 and 1 drawn; later he obtained a victory over Anderssen. On two or three occasions he played blindfolded against eight strong players simultaneously, each time with great success. He returned to the U.S. in 1859 and continued to play, but with decreasing interest in the game, until 1866. He died in 1884.

Wilhelm Steinitz (1836–1900) took the sixth prize at the London congress of 1862. He defeated Blackburne in a match by 7 to 1 and 2 draws. In 1866 he beat Anderssen in a match by 8 games to 6. In 1868 he carried off the first prize in the British Chess association handicap and in 1872 in the London grand tourney, also defeating J. H. Zukertort in a match by 7 games to 1 and 4 draws. In 1873 he carried off the first prize at the Vienna congress; and in 1876 he defeated Blackburne, winning seven games right off.

In Philidor's age it was considered almost incredible that he should be able to play three simultaneous games without seeing board or men, but Paulsen, Blackburne and Zukertort often played 10 or 12 such games, while as many as 28 and 29 were so played by Alexander Alekhine and M. V. Réti, respectively, in 1925. Again, in 1933, Alekhine played 32 and Koltanowski played 34 in 1937. Then, in 1943, Miguel Najdorf exceeded all performances with 40 at Buenos Aires.

In 1876 England was in the van of the world's chess army. English-born players then were Boden, Burn, Macdonnell, Bird, Blackburne and Potter; while among naturalized English players were Löwenthal, Steinitz, Zukertort (who died in 1888) and Horwitz. This illustrious contingent was reinforced in 1878 by Mason, an Irish-American, who went abroad for the Paris tournament; by Gunsberg, a Hungarian; and later by Teichmann, who also made England his home. English chess flourished under the leadership of these masters, the chief prizes in tournaments being consistently carried off by the English representatives.

Modern British Chess.—The British Chess federation was instituted in 1904, its first congress being held at Hastings in that year, when a British championship, a ladies' championship and a first-class amateur tournament were played. These competitions have been continued annually at the congresses of the federation, with the exception of the World Wars I and II periods and the years 1922 and 1927, when international tournaments were held in England. The holders of the British championship have been W. E. Napier, H. E. Atkins, R. C. Griffith, F. D. Yates, R. H. V. Scott, Sir G. A. Thomas, Sultan-Khan, W. Winter and W. A. Fairhurst.

In 1896 and following years matches between representative players of Great Britain and the United States, respectively, were played by cable, with the following results:

1896. U.S.	won by $4\frac{1}{2}$ games to $3\frac{1}{2}$
1897. Great Britain	" " $5\frac{1}{2}$ " " $4\frac{1}{2}$

1898. Great Britain won by 5½ games to 4½
1899. U.S. " " 6 " " 4
1900. U.S. " " 6 " " 4
1901. Drawn 5 games each
1902. U.S. won by 5½ games to 4½
1903. U.S. " " 5½ " " 4½
1907. Great Britain " " 5½ " " 4½
1908. U.S. " " 6½ " " 3½
1909. Great Britain " " 6 " " 4
1910. Great Britain " " 6½ " " 3½
1911. Great Britain " " 6 " " 4

By winning three consecutive matches Great Britain obtained permanent possession of the trophy.

The World Championship.—The strongest players of their time, and therefore regarded by later generations as "world champions" were: 1747–95, François Philidor, France; 1815–20, Alexandre Deschapelles, France; 1820–40, Louis de la Bourdonnais, France; 1843–51, Howard Staunton, England; 1851–58, Adolph Anderssen, Germany; 1858–59, Paul Morphy, United States; 1862–66, Adolph Anderssen, Germany. In 1866 Anderssen was defeated in a match by Wilhelm Steinitz of Austria, who then laid claim to the title "world champion"—rightly, for he was undoubtedly the strongest player of his day. Steinitz successfully defended his title in formal matches against Blackburne, Zukertort, Tchigorin (twice) and Gunsberg. His unparalleled reign of 28 years was brought to a close in 1894, when he was defeated by a young German player, Emanuel Lasker.

Lasker held the title almost as long as Steinitz, whom he defeated again in a return match two years later. Other challengers who failed were Frank Marshall, Siegbert Tarrasch, David Janowski and Carl Schlechter. Recognized as the logical challenger from about 1914 on was José R. Capablanca of Cuba, but a match was not arranged until 1921. With Capablanca leading 4–0, and 10 draws, Lasker resigned the championship, stating that the climate of Havana was dangerous to his health.

Capablanca held the title for six years. In 1927 he lost it to Alexander Alekhine in a struggle lasting nearly three months, at Buenos Aires. The score was 6–3, with 25 draws, the longest title match up to that time.

Alekhine, a Russian who acquired French citizenship, was defeated in 1935 by Max Euwe of the Netherlands, by the score of 9–8 with 13 draws. Two years later he regained the title in a return match, winning 11–6 with 13 draws. Alekhine twice defeated Efrem Bogoljubow in challenge matches, 1929 and 1934. The death of Alekhine in 1946 left the title vacant.

To establish a new champion, a tournament was held in 1948 among five players selected by world opinion as the strongest contenders. It was won by Mikhail Botvinnik of the U.S.S.R. The others were Samuel Reshevsky of the U.S., Max Euwe of the Netherlands, and Vassily Smyslov and Paul Keres, both of the U.S.S.R. In 1951 Botvinnik successfully defended his title in a drawn match with David Bronstein.

The victory of Reshevsky of the U.S. over Miguel Najdorf of Argentina, in a match in 1952, was hailed as establishing an unofficial championship of the western world, to offset the difficulties thrown in the way of a match between Botvinnik and any challenger from the non-Soviet sphere. In 1953 Russian players were permitted to leave the soviet domain to participate in foreign tournaments, and the way was opened for resumption of competition for the championship on a world-wide basis.

Tournaments.—The first modern international tournament was held in London in 1851. Several hundred tournaments were held after that time, and analysis of the game was greatly accelerated by the publication of all the games played in the major events. The principal tournaments from 1929 are as follows:

1929. Carlsbad. (1) Nimzowitsch, (2) Capablanca and Spielmann.
1929. Budapest. (1) Capablanca, (2) Rubinstein, (3) Tartakower.
1929. Barcelona. (1) Capablanca, (2) Tartakower, (3) Colle.
1929. Ramsgate. (1) Sultan-Khan, (2) Price and Michell.
1929. Bradley Beach. (1) Alekhine, (2) L. Steiner, (3) Kupchik and Turover.
1930. Hastings. (1) Capablanca, (2) Vidmar, (3) Yates.
1930. San Remo. (1) Alekhine, (2) Nimzowitsch, (3) Rubinstein.
1930. Frankfurt. (1) Nimzowitsch, (2) Kashdan, (3) Ahues and List.
1930. Liège. (1) Tartakower, (2) Sultan-Khan, (3) Ahues, Colle and Nimzowitsch.
1931. Hastings. (1) Euwe, (2) Capablanca, (3) Sultan-Khan.
1931. Bled. (1) Alekhine, (2) Bogoljubow, (3) Nimzowitsch.
1931. New York city. (1) Capablanca, (2) Kashdan, (3) Kevitz.
1932. Hastings. (1) Flohr, (2) Kashdan, (3) Euwe.
1932. London. (1) Alekhine, (2) Flohr, (3) Sultan-Khan and Kashdan.
1932. Pasadena. (1) Alekhine, (2) Kashdan, (3) Dake, Reshevsky and H. Steiner.
1932. Mexico City. (1) Alekhine and Kashdan, (3) Araiza.
1932. Berne. (1) Alekhine, (2) Euwe and Flohr.
1933. Hastings. (1) Flohr, (2) Pirc, (3) Sultan-Khan and L. Steiner.
1934. Hastings. (1) Flohr, (2) Alekhine and Lilienthal.
1934. Zürich. (1) Alekhine, (2) Euwe and Flohr.
1935. Hastings. (1) Euwe, Flohr and Thomas.
1935. Moscow. (1) Botvinnik and Flohr, (3) Lasker.
1935. Margate. (1) Reshevsky, (2) Capablanca and Thomas.
1935. Orebro. (1) Alekhine, (2) Lundin, (3) Stahlberg and Stoltz.
1936. Hastings. (1) Fine, (2) Flohr, (3) Tartakower.
1936. Bad Nauheim. (1) Alekhine and Keres, (3) Ahues.
1936. Moscow. (1) Capablanca, (2) Botvinnik, (3) Flohr.
1936. Zandvoort. (1) Fine, (2) Euwe, (3) Keres and Tartakower.
1936. Podebrad. (1) Flohr, (2) Alekhine, (3) Flotys.
1936. Nottingham. (1) Botvinnik and Capablanca, (3) Euwe, Fine and Reshevsky.
1936. Amsterdam. (1) Fine and Euwe, (3) Alekhine.
1936. Margate. (1) Flohr, (2) Capablanca, (3) Stahlberg.
1937. Hastings. (1) Alekhine, (2) Fine, (3) Eliskases.
1937. Margate. (1) Fine and Keres, (3) Alekhine.
1937. Ostend. (1) Fine, Grob and Keres.
1937. Kemeri. (1) Flohr, Petrow and Reshevsky.
1937. Semmering-Baden. (1) Keres, (2) Fine, (3) Capablanca and Reshevsky.
1938. Netherlands (A.V.R.O. tournament). (1) Keres, (2) Fine, (3) Botvinnik.
1939. Leningrad-Moscow. (1) Flohr, (2) Reshevsky, (3) Lilienthal, Loewenfisch, Makagonov and Ragozin.
1939. Hastings. (1) Szabo, (2) Euwe, (3) Landau and Pirc.
1939. Margate. (1) Keres, (2) Capablanca and Flohr.
1940. Salzburg. (1) Alekhine, (2) Keres, (3) Schmidt.
1941. Mar del Plata. (1) Stahlberg, (2) Najdorf, (3) Eliskases.
1942. Buenos Aires. (1) Najdorf and Stahlberg, (3) Frydman.
1942. Munich. (1) Stoltz, (2) Alekhine and Lundin.
1942. Mar del Plata. (1) Najdorf, (2) Stahlberg and Pilnik.
1943. Mar del Plata. (1) Najdorf, (2) Stahlberg, (3) Michel.
1943. Sverdlovsk. (1) Botvinnik, (2) Makagonov, (3) Smyslov and Kahn.
1944. Prague. (1) Alekhine, (2) Keres, (3) Katetov.
1944. Mar del Plata. (1) Najdorf and Pilnik, (3) Michel and Guimard.
1945. Mar del Plata. (1) Najdorf, (2) Pilnik, (3) Stahlberg.
1945. Hastings. (1) Tartakower, (2) Ekstrom, (3) Denker.
1946. London (two sections). (1) H. Steiner and Euwe.
1946. Groningen. (1) Botvinnik, (2) Euwe, (3) Smyslov.
1946. Prague. (1) Najdorf, (2) Stoltz and Trifunovich.
1946. Barcelona. (1) Najdorf, (2) Yanofsky.
1946. Hastings. (1) Alexander, (2) Tartakower, (3) Gudmundsson.
1947. Mar del Plata. (1) Najdorf, (2) Stahlberg, (3) Eliskases.
1947. Mar del Plata (sextangular). (1) Stahlberg.
1947. Venice. (1) Tartakower, (2) Canal and O'Kelly.
1947. Budapest. (1) Szabo, (2) Gligorich, (3) Foltys.
1947. Teplice. (1) O'Kelly and Piro.
1947. Hastings. (1) Szabo, (2) Grob, Muhring and Thomas.
1948. Karlovy Vary. (1) Foltys, (2) Barcza, (3) L. Steiner.
1948. Bad Gastein. (1) Lundin, (2) Benko and Rossolimo.
1948. Venice. (1) Najdorf, (2) Barcza and Canal.
1948. Mar del Plata. (1) Eliskases, (2) Stahlberg, (3) Medina.
1948. New York city. (1) Fine, (2) Najdorf, (3) Euwe and Pilnik.
1948. Hastings. (1) Rossolimo, (2) Koenig, (3) Muhring.
1949. Lucerne. (1) Unzicker, (2) Spanjaard, (3) Sämisch.
1949. Beverwijk. (1) Tartakower, (2) Schmidt, (3) Scheltinga.
1949. Mar del Plata. (1) Rossetto, (2) Eliskases and Guimard.
1949. Southsea. (1) Rossolimo, (2) Pachman, (3) Tartakower.
1949. Heidelberg. (1) Unzicker, (2) Rossolimo.
1949. Gijon. (1) Rossolimo, (2) O'Kelly, (3) Prins.
1949. Barcelona (first women's international). (1) Eileen Tranmer (England) and Mme. Chaude de Silans (France).
1949. Hastings. (1) Szabo, (2) Rossolimo, (3) Euwe and Evans.
1950. Southsea. (1) Tartakower and Bisguier.
1950. Mar del Plata. (1) Gligorich.
1950. Szcawnu Zdroj. (1) Keres, (2) Barcza and Taimonov.
1950. Venice. (1) Kotov, (2) Smyslov, (3) Rossolimo.
1950. Bled. (1) Najdorf, (2) Pilnik, (3) O'Kelly.
1950. Amsterdam. (1) Najdorf, (2) Reshevsky, (3) Stahlberg.
1950. Hastings. (1) Unzicker.
1951. London. (1) Gligorich, (2) Pirc, Stahlberg and Trifunovich.
1951. New York city. (1) Reshevsky, (2) Euwe and Najdorf.
1951. Southsea. (1) Rossolimo and Tartakower.
1951. Madrid. (1) Prins, (2) H. Steiner, Pilnik and Bernstein.

Chess by Radio.—The first international match to be conducted by radio was that between the United States of America and the Union of Soviet Socialist Republics, Sept. 1–4, 1945. The U.S. team comprised Arnold Denker, Samuel Reshevsky, Reuben Fine, Israel A. Horowitz, Isaac I. Kashdan, Herman Steiner, Albert S. Pinkus, Herbert Seidman, Abraham Kupchik and Anthony E. Santasiere. The Russian team was Mikhail Botvinnik, Vassily Smyslov, Isaac Boleslavsky, Salo Flohr, Alexander Kotov, Igor Bondarevsky, Andrea Lilienthal, Vyacheslav Ragozin, Vladimir Makagonov and David Bronstein. The Russian team won by 15½ to 4½. (See *Illustrative Game No. 11.*)

Fédération Internationale des Échecs.—This body is the central authority for chess matters. Most of the European countries and the U.S. are members. A tournament under the auspices of the federation was held at Budapest in 1926, and the following year a tournament was held at London between teams, each of four players, representing 16 nations attached to the federation. The tournament was won by Hungary with a score of 40 points out of a possible 60. Close behind came Denmark (second) and Great Britain (third). Hungary also won a similar tournament held at The Hague in 1928. The United States won at Prague, 1931; at Folkestone, 1933; at Warsaw, 1935; at Stockholm, 1937. The U.S. was not represented in 1939 at Buenos Aires, where Germany finished first.

Literature of the Game.—The most ambitious of early European writings on chess was the work of a Lombard, Jacobus de Cessolis (Jacopo Dacciesole), whose main object, however, though he gives the moves, etc., was to teach morals rather than chess. He was a Dominican friar and his treatise *Liber de Moribus Hominum et Officiis Nobilium* was written before the year 1300. It was afterward translated into several European languages, and in the year 1474 Caxton, under the title of *The Game and Playe of Chesse,* printed an English translation of the French version.

About 1500 appeared the *Göttinger Handschrift,* a work containing 12 different openings and 30 problems. The author of this manuscript is not known. Of Lucena, a Spanish author who wrote in or about 1497, we are better informed. His treatise, *Repeticion des amores e arte de axedres,* comprises various practical chess matters, including 150 positions, illustrated by 160 well-executed woodcuts. Various of these positions are identical with those in the *Göttinger Handschrift.*

In the 16th century works upon the game were written by Damiano, Ruy Lopez and Horatio Gianutio della Mantia; in the 17th century by Salvio, Polerio, Gustavus Selenus, Carrera, Greco, Fr. Antonio and the authors of the *Traité de Lausanne;* in the 18th century by Bertin, Stamma, Ercole del Rio, Lolli, Cozio, Philidor, Ponziani, Stein, Count P. J. van Nyevelt, Allgaier and Peter Pratt; in the 19th century by J. F. W. Koch and C. F. Koch, Sarratt, John Cochrane, William Lewis, Silberschmidt, Ghulam Kassim and James Cochrane, George Walker, A. Macdonnell, Jaenisch, Petroff, Bilguer, Von der Lasa, Staunton, Kling and Horwitz, Bledow, Dubois, Kieseritzki, Max Lange, Löwenthal, Dufresne, Neumann, Suhle, Zukertort, Preti, Steinitz and others.

English chess owes much to W. Lewis and George Walker. But to Howard Staunton must be ascribed the most important share in creating the later popularity which the game achieved in England. Staunton's first work, *The Chess Player's Handbook,* was published in 1847 and again (revised) in 1848. His other works are: *The Chess Player's Text-Book* and *The Chess Player's Companion* (1849) (the latter being a collection of his own games); the *Chess Praxis* (1860, republished in 1903); his posthumous work, *Chess Theory and Practice,* edited by R. B. Wormald (1876); and various smaller treatises.

The laws of the game as laid down in the *Praxis* formed the basis of the rules adopted by the British Chess association in 1862. Besides editing the *Chess Player's Chronicle* and the *Chess World,* he was the chess editor of the *Illustrated London News* from 1844 till his death in 1874.

BIBLIOGRAPHY.—*Elements of the Game:* E. E. Cunnington, *The Modern Chess Primer* (1920) gives a good grounding in the elements of the game and the student should master its contents. *General Treatises:* (*a*) Elementary: Lawrence H. Dawson, *A Short Guide to Chess* (1923); E. A. Greig, *Pitfalls of the Chess-Board,* rev. by W. A. Fairhurst (1927). (*b*) Fairly advanced: J. Mason, *The Art of Chess* (1913) and *The Principles of Chess* (1923); Emanuel Lasker, *Common Sense in Chess* (1896) and *Chess Strategy* (1922). (*c*) More advanced: J. R. Capablanca, *Chess Fundamentals* (1921); E. O. Znosko-Borowsky, *The Middle Game in Chess* (1922); M. V. Réti, *Modern Ideas in Chess* (1923); A. Nimzowitsch, *Die Blockade* and *Mein System* (1925); Kmoch, *Die Kunst der Verteidigung* (1927); Emanuel Lasker, *Lasker's Manual of Chess* (1927). *End Games:* The elements of the endings are dealt with in both *The Modern Chess Primer* and *The Art of Chess.* Other works which may be recommended to the more advanced student are: R. Fine, *Basic Chess Endings* (1943); Mieses, *Chess Endings from Modern Master-Play;* Tattersall, *A Thousand End-Games;* Rinck, *700 fins de partie* (1926) and Berger's monumental work, *Theorie und Praxis der Endspiele,* 2nd ed. (1921). *Openings:* The best work in English is undoubtedly R. C. Griffith and A. C. White's *Modern Chess Openings* (1925), revised by Reuben Fine (1939), upon the theory of the openings. The *Handbuch des Schachspiels* (8th ed. 1916, by Schlechter, with supplement, 1921, by Mieses) and *Lärobok i Schack* (1921) are decidedly more voluminous but less up-to-date. A mine of information is S. Tartakower's *Die Hypermoderne Schachpartie* (1924). Of works dealing with only one opening the following are useful: J. du Mont, *The Centre Counter* and *The Centre Game;* Maróczy, *Die Französische Partie* (1924); S. Tarrasch, *Die Verteidigung des Damengambits* (Gouda, 1924) and Tartakower, *Die Zukunftseröffnung* (1924); R. Fine, *Ideas Behind the Chess Openings* (1943); J. du Mont, *The Basis of Combination in Chess* (1942).

Collections of Games: A valuable—and, perhaps, the most enjoyable—form of chess study is the careful playing over of well-annotated master games. The following books are recommended: *Mr. Blackburne's Games at Chess* (1899); P. W. Sergeant, *Morphy's Games of Chess* (1916) and *Charousek's Games of Chess* (1919); P. W. Sergeant and W. H. Watts, *Pillsbury's Chess Career* (1923); Maróczy, *Hundert Schachpartien* (1921); J. R. Capablanca, *My Chess Career* (1920); S. Tarrasch, *Dreihundert Schachpartien* (1916) and *Die Moderne Schachpartie* (1916); A Alekhine, *My Best Games of Chess* (1927); A. Alekhine and H. Helms, *New York Tournament* (1924); F. Reinfeld, *Keres' Best Games of Chess* (1942); A. Alekhine, *The Nottingham Tournament Book* (1936); F. J. Wellmuth, *The Golden Treasury of Chess* (1943).

History: The best book on the history of the game is H. J. R. Murray, *A History of Chess* (1913). (G. E. S.; H. Hs.; G. Mh.)

Theories of Play.—One of the contributions of François Philidor was to draw attention to the importance of pawns as fighting units. He formulated the classic pattern of attack against the castled king—the advance of pawns to break up the pawns sheltering the enemy king and so open lines for the infiltration of pieces. The hundred years after the publication of his *Analyse des échecs* saw the discovery of a myriad permutations of the so-called "direct attack" and the rise of great masters of combination play, culminating in Adolph Anderssen. (See *Illustrative Game No. 1.*) By "combination" is understood the calculation of specific variations of play, in search of a way to force a more-or-less immediate decision.

The characteristic of the games of this era is the sacrifice, and the dominating motive is the desire to attack as quickly as possible. The analysis of openings was largely concerned with "gambits"—sacrifices of pawns, sometimes pieces, made to precipitate rapid contact with the enemy. It was even held by some that the Evans gambit was the only debut worthy of a gentleman, since this opening is particularly apt to lead to a "slugging contest."

In 1858–59 Paul Morphy created a sensation by trouncing all the masters who would meet him. His play introduced a new note, one that even today is basic in the teaching of beginners. Although second to none in combinative skill, Morphy delayed attacking until he had "completed his development." By simply bringing out his knights and bishops, posting the queen safe from harassment, and castling, Morphy repeatedly achieved a "won game" after a dozen moves. So effective was this procedure against the current fashion of attacking prematurely that it crystallized into a formula: move each centre pawn once, each bishop and knight once, get the queen off the back row, castle—before moving any piece a second time. The task of developing is not actually so easy: the opponent exerts threats that have to be parried. But it remains true that any relative loss of time in the opening can lead to a quick catastrophe. (See *Illustrative Game No. 2.*)

Rapid development, combinative attack—these principles seemed to be all-embracing and all-sufficient. Then came a pugnacious Austrian, Wilhelm Steinitz, whose play often violated classic principles. Yet with it he was able to win the world championship and to hold it longer that any other player. Steinitz lived to influence the theory of play more profoundly than any other player. His theories, at first seemingly antithetical to classic principles, were presently seen to be supplementary.

Steinitz started from the premise that there is no combination without positional advantage. That is, a specific winning sequence of moves cannot be found, if there is no superiority on which to base it. The player should therefore concern himself primarily with analyzing the position to detect its points of strength and weakness. On this score, Steinitz contributed a great deal of analysis on the nature of weaknesses, and the specific meaning of permanent as opposed to transient weaknesses. The objective of play, he said, is to gain a decisive positional superiority by "the accumulation of small advantages." An adverse weakness must be "nursed" and magnified until it becomes fatal: then the combination will spring of itself from the position. (See *Illustrative Game No. 4.*)

In pursuit of local advantages, Steinitz often moved the same piece several times in the opening, before completing his development. He demonstrated that the demands of the "close" game are somewhat different from those of the "open" game. It is indeed necessary to develop rapidly if centre pawns are exchanged early, opening lines of attack. But a slower development is feasible if the centre is kept closed; here it is often more important to get a single piece to its most effective post than to move all the pieces off the back row. Especially in his later years, Steinitz preferred to manoeuvre behind the lines before breaking the centre, so as to gain the maximum advantage from the break when it came. (See *Illustrative Game No. 5.*) This "hedgehog" policy forced upon him the necessity of defending accurately and economically against attack by a more-developed opponent, and his games are instructive for the resources of defense. It is said that Steinitz was never so happy as when sustaining a furious onslaught upon his king; proverbial are his remarks "When in doubt, take a pawn" and "A pawn is worth a little trouble."

The slow tempo of the Steinitz campaign was not for every taste, and it remained for Siegbert Tarrasch to show how to quicken it and open lines for direct attack without relinquishing vital positional advantages. Tarrasch made great contributions of his own to the theory. In play as well as in his writings he showed how positional weaknesses may be forced upon a player if he commands less terrain than his opponent. He formulated the theory of the centre. The opening, he said, is to be understood as a fight for control of the squares d4, d5, e4, e5. A piece standing in the centre has its maximum range, and the centre is the vital avenue of communication between the wings of the army. At first the centre must be controlled by pawns, to prevent its occupation by adverse pieces. He has an advantage who controls the greater number or the more advanced of central squares. (See *Illustrative Game No. 6.*)

A consequence of the Steinitz-Tarrasch analysis was that the opening 1 P—K4 came to be played much less in master tournaments, in favour of 1 P—Q4. The latter is the more likely to lead to a close game. The growing body of knowledge of opening variations tends to indicate that White retains the advantage of the first move longer in a close than in an open game. The queen's gambit came to be a dreaded weapon. (See *Illustrative Game No. 7.*) It was said, only half-jocularly, that "After 1 P—Q4, Black's game is in its last throes." However, Black's prospects brightened in the 20th century with the discovery of several new defensive systems.

In 1913 a young Russian master, Aaron Nimzowitsch, published articles assailing some of the cardinal points of the Tarrasch creed. After World War I he published *My System* and other books expounding certain ideas, as "centralization," "overprotection," "the homeopathic process." In definition these ideas do not seem to be out of the Steinitz-Tarrasch tradition, but their realization sometimes involves moves condemned by it. Nevertheless, Nimzowitsch achieved some notable tournament successes, and carried the Tarrasch principle of constraint to the extraordinary length of complete blockade. (See *Illustrative Game No. 8.*) A curious conclusion to be drawn is that, while the actual advance of a pawn wing may prove weakening, the mere inability to advance it at will is a positive weakness, often of decisive moment.

Nimzowitsch is credited with founding the self-styled "hypermodern school," of which the avowed exponents were Richard Réti, S. Tartakower and Efrem Bogoljubow. Réti (d. 1929) stated the principle of this school to be: "The golden rule is that there is no golden rule." Thus, any attempt to formulate its further principles is interdicted! In practice, the hypermoderns often go to great lengths to avoid releasing the tension in the centre, or even advancing the centre pawns at all, until pieces have been brought to bear upon it. This often involves the fianchetto of one bishop or both. (See *Illustrative Game No. 9.*)

The hypermoderns claim José R. Capablanca and Alekhine as exponents of hypermodern play, although both these world champions repudiated any conscious adherence. The Alekhine defense is cited as an example of relying on the evaluation of a particular position rather than upon general principles. After 1 P—K4, Kt—KB3; 2 P—K5, Kt—Q4; 3 P—QB4, Kt—Kt3; 4 P—Q4, White has three pawns in the centre, one being on the fifth rank, while Black has developed only a knight. By all classical precept, Black has wasted valuable time. Yet it has been abundantly demonstrated that Black can quickly catch up by attacking the advanced pawns. (See *Illustrative Game No. 10.*)

Illustrative Game No. 1.—Adolph Anderssen (1818–79) won first place in the first modern international tournament, London, 1851. His games are memorable for their slashing attacks and combinative brilliance. The famous game below was dubbed the "Immortal Partie."

London, 1851

	White Anderssen	Black Kieseritzki		White Anderssen	Black Kieseritzki
1	P—K4	P—K4	13	P—R5	Q—Kt4
2	P—KB4	P×P	14	Q—B3	Kt—Kt1 (*c*)
3	B—B4	P—QKt4	15	B×P	Q—B3
4	B×KtP	Q—R5ch	16	Kt—B3	B—B4 (*d*)
5	K—B1	Kt—KB3	17	Kt—Q5	Q×P (*e*)
6	Kt—KB3	Q—R3	18	B—Q6 (*f*)	B×R
7	P—Q3	Kt—R4 (*a*)	19	P—K5	Q×Rch
8	Kt—R4	P—QB3	20	K—K2	Kt—QR3 (*g*)
9	Kt—B5	Q—Kt4	21	Kt×Pch	K—Q1
10	P—KKt4	Kt—B3	22	Q—B6ch	Kt×Q
11	R—Kt1 (*b*)	P×B	23	B—K7 mate	
12	P—KR4	Q—Kt3			

(*a*) Threatening Kt—Kt6ch. But this lighthorse attack is backed by insufficient means. Black should have made a developing move, as B—Kt2 or even B—R3. (*b*) Commencing a combination based on the precarious position of the Black queen. (*c*) The only move to save the queen. (*d*) Perhaps better was B—Kt2 to keep out the terrible knight. But there is no move to parry all of White's threats. (*e*) Staying on the diagonal to defend KKt2. (*f*) The key move of the combination. Now if 18 . . . Q×Rch; 19 K—K2, Q×R then 20 Kt×Pch, K—Q1; 21 B—B7 mate. Or if 18 . . . B×B; 19 Kt×Bch, K—Q1 then 20 Q×P and mate cannot be averted. (*g*) To prevent the mate given in note (*f*).

Illustrative Game No. 2.—When Paul Morphy went to Europe in 1858 he met some unpleasant experiences with European masters jealous of their laurels. But Anderssen came out of retirement to play and lose a match to him in 1859, and he was generous in praise of the American genius. The present game was the seventh of the match.

	White Morphy	Black Anderssen		White Morphy	Black Anderssen
1	P—K4	P—Q4	14	Q×Kt	Q×B
2	P×P	Q×P	15	B—Q3 (*f*)	B—Kt5
3	Kt—QB3	Q—QR4	16	Kt—Kt5 (*g*)	KR—Q1
4	P—Q4	P—K4	17	Q—Kt4 (*h*)	B—B1
5	P×P	Q×Pch	18	KR—K1	P—QR4
6	B—K2	B—QKt5	19	Q—K7	Q×Q
7	Kt—B3 (*a*)	B×Ktch	20	R×Q (*i*)	Kt—Q4
8	P×B	Q×Pch	21	B×Pch	K—R1 (*j*)
9	B—Q2	Q—B4 (*b*)	22	R×KBP	Kt—B6
10	R—QKt1 (*c*)	Kt—QB3	23	R—K1	Kt×P
11	Castles	Kt—B3	24	R—B4	R—R3
12	B—KB4	Castles (*d*)	25	B—Q3	Resigns
13	B×P (*e*)	Kt—Q5			

(*a*) He could save the pawn and also develop by B—Q2, but he is perfectly willing to let Black waste further time to win it. (*b*) Black has won a pawn but lost the game. (*c*) Threatening B—Kt4 and also holding back the Black QB. (*d*) Giving back the pawn in order to get his king to safety. If 12 . . . Kt—Q4 then 13 R—Kt5 wins a piece. (*e*) More than regaining his pawn, for now he threatens B—Q6. (*f*) White's advantage is greater than it may seem. He has the "good" bishop for a king's-side attack, while Black's "bad" bishop cannot even be moved out to release the QR. Black indeed tries to develop it, but the effort is quickly refuted. (*g*) Threatening 17 Kt×RP, Kt×Kt; 18 Q×B. (*h*) Maintaining the threat and also forking the QKtP. To avoid immediate loss of a pawn Black is forced to retreat his bishop. (*i*) The exchange of queens has brought Black no relief. Useless to defend the KBP is 20 . . . R—B1, for then 22 Kt×BP, R×Kt; 23 B—B4 wins the exchange. (*j*) Forced, for if K—B1 then 22 R×Pch, K—K1; 23 R—K1ch leads to mate.

Illustrative Game No. 3.—J. H. Zukertort (1842–88) was a brilliant combination player. He reached the zenith of his powers in the London tournament of 1883, which he won without loss of a single game, although the entry list included all the greatest masters of the day, including Steinitz.

London, 1883

White Zukertort	Black Blackburne	White Zukertort	Black Blackburne
1 P—QB4	P—K3	17 QR—K1	R—B2
2 P—K3	Kt—KB3	18 P—K4	QR—QB1
3 Kt—KB3	P—QKt3	19 P—K5 (*b*)	Kt—K1
4 B—K2	B—Kt2	20 P—B4	P—Kt3
5 Castles	P—Q4	21 R—K3	P—B4 (*c*)
6 P—Q4	B—Q3	22 P×P e.p.	Kt×P (*d*)
7 Kt—B3	Castles	23 P—B5 (*e*)	Kt—K5
8 P—QKt3	QKt—Q2	24 B×Kt (*f*)	P×B
9 B—Kt2	Q—K2	25 P×KtP	R—B7 (*g*)
10 Kt—QKt5	Kt—K5	26 P×Pch	K—R1
11 Kt×B	P×Kt	27 P—Q5ch	P—K4
12 Kt—Q2	QKt—B3	28 Q—Kt4! (*h*)	R(B1)—B4
13 P—B3	Kt×Kt	29 R—B8ch	K×P (*i*)
14 Q×Kt	P×P	30 Q×Pch	K—Kt2
15 B×P	P—Q4	31 B×Pch	K×R
16 B—Q3	KR—B1 (*a*)	32 B—Kt7ch (*j*)	Resigns

(*a*) The subsequent course of the game shows that Black should have taken immediate measures to counteract the advance of the White KP. (*b*) This game and many others have shown the danger of allowing the KKt, the strongest defensive piece on the king's side, to be driven away from B3 by a supported pawn. (*c*) Necessary sooner or later so that KR2 can be protected along the rank. (*d*) If Q×P to get out of the pin, then 23 Q—K1 and the backward KP must fall. (*e*) Initiating a magnificent combination. (*f*) The combination has to be exactly calculated, for this exchange opens the way for a powerful counterattack on the QB file. (*g*) Best. Too slow is P×P; *e.g.*, 26 R—Kt3, Q—Kt2; 27 P—Q5, P—K4; 28 Q—Kt5. (*h*) The first point of the combination. If Q×Q then 29 B×Pch, K×P; 30 R—R3ch, K—Kt3; 31 R—Kt3ch, K—R3; 32 R—B6ch, K—R4; 33 R—B5ch, K—R3; 34 B—B4ch, K—R2; 35 R—R5 mate. (*i*) The second point. If Q×R then 30 B×Pch, K×P; 31 Q×Pch leads to mate. (*j*) The third point. If Q×B, then Q—K8 mate. After any other move, the queen is lost.

Illustrative Game No. 4.—Steinitz had his revenge for being outdistanced by Zukertort in the London tournament of 1883, by beating him in a match in 1885. According to Lasker, this match was a battle of "positional play" against "combination play," and it had far-reaching consequences upon chess theory.

White Steinitz	Black Zukertort	White Steinitz	Black Zukertort
1 P—K4	P—K4	18 Kt—Kt3	B—K3
2 Kt—KB3	Kt—QB3	19 R—K1	Kt—Kt2
3 B—Kt5	Kt—B3	20 P—KR4 (*e*)	Q—Q2
4 Castles	Kt×P	21 P—R5	B—B2
5 R—K1	Kt—Q3	22 P×P	B×P!
6 Kt×P	Kt×Kt	23 Q—K3	K—B2
7 R×Ktch	B—K2	24 Q—B4	R—K1
8 Kt—B3	Castles	25 R—K3	Kt—K3 (*f*)
9 B—Q3	B—B3	26 Q—KKt4	Kt—B1
10 R—K3	P—KKt3 (*a*)	27 Kt—B5	B—B4
11 P—QKt3	R—K1	28 Kt—R6ch	K—Kt2
12 Q—B3	B—Kt4 (*b*)	29 B×B (*g*)	Q×Q
13 R×Rch	Kt×R	30 Kt×Q	R×R
14 B—Kt2	P—QB3	31 BP×R	Kt×B
15 Kt—K4 (*c*)	B—K2	32 Kt×P (*h*)	
16 Q—K3	P—Q4	White won	
17 Q—Q4 (*d*)	P—B3		

(*a*) According to Steinitz, the king's-side pawns when under attack should not be moved unless there is no alternative. In his notes to this game he states that he considered this move a deliberate challenge to his theory. (*b*) Manifestly antipositional. The bishop is vitally needed at Kt2 to protect the "holes" in the pawn structure. (*c*) Nailing down the weakness of Black's KB3. (*d*) To force the following advance, which is a further weakening of the pawn wing. (*e*) An attacking move seen in many Steinitz games, made to "loosen up" the compromised pawns still further. (*f*) "From the 14th move until this moment Black, on the defense, has played good chess. Now White has no immediate threats and Black . . . is thrown on his own initiative . . . he has to originate a plan. But that is exactly what Zukertort did not understand . . . His right plan was to keep attention riveted on his weak points KB4, QB4 and KB3, and . . . work towards a draw by exchanging perilous pieces . . ."—Lasker.[1] (*g*) Actually Steinitz checked with the knight several times, to gain time, before making this move. (*h*) "All" that Steinitz has to show for his exertions is the win of a pawn. But this is enough to win the ending.

Illustrative Game No. 5.—Before completing his development, Steinitz moves his QKt three times, only to exchange it a few moves later. His games are full of such long-winded manoeuvres, in pursuit of modest but lasting positional advantages. Observe how carefully he refrains from P—Q4 until the move is decisive.

Havana, 1892

White Steinitz	Black Tchigorin	White Steinitz	Black Tchigorin
1 P—K4	P—K4	16 B—Kt3 (*i*)	Q—B3
2 Kt—KB3	Kt—QB3	17 Q—K2	B—Q2
3 B—Kt5	Kt—B3	18 B—K3	K—R1
4 P—Q3 (*a*)	P—Q3	19 Castles (Q)	QR—K1
5 P—B3 (*b*)	P—KKt3 (*c*)	20 Q—B1 (*j*)	P—QR4
6 QKt—Q2	B—Kt2	21 P—Q4 (*k*)	P×P
7 Kt—B1	Castles	22 Kt×P	B×Kt
8 B—QR4 (*d*)	Kt—Q2	23 R×B!	Kt×R
9 Kt—K3 (*e*)	Kt—B4	24 R×Pch! (*l*)	K×R
10 B—B2	Kt—K3 (*f*)	25 Q—R1ch	K—Kt2
11 P—KR4 (*g*)	Kt—K2	26 B—R6ch	K—B3
12 P—R5	P—Q4 (*h*)	27 Q—R4ch	K—K4
13 RP×P	BP×P	28 Q×Ktch	K—B4
14 P×P	Kt×P	29 Q—B4 mate	
15 Kt×Kt	Q×Kt		

(*a*) At variance from the then-fashionable practice of playing P—Q4 as soon as possible. (*b*) This pawn formation was frequently adopted by Steinitz after 1 P—K4. Its object is only remotely to enforce P—Q4; the primary purpose is to neutralize any effort by Black to break the centre. (*c*) The king's fianchetto was formerly much played against the Ruy Lopez, but it has dropped out of master practice as a result of Steinitz' victories against it. (*d*) Another of Steinitz' innovations was this manoeuvre B—Kt5—R4—B2 to preserve the KB, "the thorn of the Ruy Lopez." (*e*) The virtue of this post is that it discourages 9 . . . P—B4, for after 10 P×P Black could not retake with the rook, and so keep the file open. (*f*) Again P—B4 would be premature; *e.g.*, 11 P×P, B×P; 12 Kt×B, R×Kt?; 13 P—Q4. (*g*) This typical Steinitz attack is the more powerful since he has delayed castling and still has his rook on the file. (*h*) "The logical reaction against a wing advance is a break in the centre." Black expects to profit from opening lines against his "undeveloped" opponent. (*i*) But it is White who profits. To avoid the opening of the diagonal upon his king, Black might have tried 13 . . . RP×P but then would have had to reckon with an attack on the open KR file. (*j*) Meeting the immediate threat of Kt—B5. But the move also has a subtle attacking purpose. (*k*) This long-delayed advance is now devastating. Black can scarcely avoid the exchanges that follow, because of the awkward situation of his queen, knight and QB. (*l*) An unpleasant surprise. After 24 B×Ktch, R—B3 Black could still put up a defense.

Illustrative Game No. 6.—Siegbert Tarrasch was a prolific writer as well as a master player. He made large contributions to the Steinitz theory of positional play. Here he gives a classic demonstration of what ills may follow "surrender of the centre."

White Tarrasch	Black Schlechter	White Tarrasch	Black Schlechter
1 P—K4	P—K4	19 P—QB4! (*g*)	Kt—Q2
2 Kt—KB3	Kt—QB3	20 K—R1	P—B3
3 B—Kt5	P—Q3 (*a*)	21 Q—B2	Kt—K4
4 P—Q4 (*b*)	B—Q2	22 Kt—B3 (*h*)	Kt—B2
5 Kt—B3	Kt—B3	23 P—KKt4	Q—R4 (*i*)
6 Castles	B—K2	24 R—Q1	Q—Kt3
7 R—K1 (*c*)	Kt×QP	25 P—KR4	Kt—K4
8 Kt×Kt	P×Kt	26 R—Kt3	Kt—B2
9 B×Bch	Q×B	27 P—B3 (*j*)	Kt—R1
10 Q×P	Castles (K)	28 Kt—K2	Q—B2
11 P—QKt3 (*d*)	KR—K1	29 QR—KKt1	Q—B2
12 B—Kt2	B—B1 (*e*)	30 Kt—Q4	KR—K2
13 QR—Q1	Q—B3	31 P—Kt5	P×P
14 R—Q3	R—K3	32 R×P	P—KKt3
15 QR—K3	QR—K1	33 Kt—B5	R—K4
16 P—KR3 (*f*)	Q—Kt3	34 P—KB4	R×Kt (*k*)
17 Q—Q3	P—B3	35 P×R	B—Kt2
18 Kt—R4!	Q—B2	36 P×P	Resigns

[1]From Emanuel Lasker, *Lasker's Manual of Chess*, published by David McKay Co., Philadelphia.

(*a*) The defense favoured by Steinitz. (*b*) A precept of Tarrasch was to answer P—Q3 with P—Q4 (after 1 P—K4, P—K4). White thus attacks the Black KP; if Black plays P×P he "surrenders the centre" by leaving White a central pawn on the fourth rank, while Black's pawn is only on the third rank. (*c*) Prior to this move White could not win a pawn by B×Kt and P×P because his own KP would then be lost. But now he does threaten to win a pawn. This Tarrasch procedure against the Steinitz defense has caused it to be abandoned in master play. (*d*) Tarrasch emphasized that the player having the advantage of greater space should seek to avoid exchanges. If the bishop were developed at B4 or Kt5 it would soon have to be exchanged. (*e*) White threatened Kt—Q5. (*f*) Both to prevent Kt—Kt5 and to prepare the general advance of the king's-side pawns. (*g*) The paramount positional consideration is to prevent the liberating move P—Q4. (*h*) Still holding back the QP and preparing to swing the knight to the king's side. (*i*) It has been pointed out that Black could have played P—Q4 at this moment; *e.g.*, 24 KP×P, R×R; 25 R×R, R×R; 26 P×R, Q—Kt3. (*j*) Having parried Black's few threats, White is now ready to send the knight to KB5 and launch a decisive attack. Black's restriction in space prevents his getting the QR and KB into effective action. (*k*) If R×P then 35 Q—B3 is murderous.

Illustrative Game No. 7.—This game has been called the most important in history, for it exposed the inadequacy of the orthodox defense to the queen's gambit declined. Theorists have been occupied ever since with finding ways to circumvent the dread Pillsbury attack. Harry N. Pillsbury (1872–1906), U.S. champion, placed first at Hastings in a field that included Lasker, Steinitz, Tarrasch and Tchigorin.

Hastings, 1895

	White Pillsbury	Black Tarrasch		White Pillsbury	Black Tarrasch
1	P—Q4	P—Q4	27	R—B1 (*l*)	P—Kt5 (*m*)
2	P—QB4	P—K3	28	Kt—K2	Q—R5
3	Kt—QB3	Kt—KB3	29	Kt—Kt4	Kt—Q2 (*n*)
4	B—Kt5 (*a*)	B—K2	30	R(B4)—B2! (*o*)	K—Kt1
5	Kt—B3	QKt—Q2	31	Kt—B1	P—B6
6	R—B1	Castles	32	P—QKt3	Q—B3
7	P—K3	P—QKt3 (*b*)	33	P—KR3 (*p*)	P—QR4
8	P×P (*c*)	P×P (*d*)	34	Kt—R2	P—R5
9	B—Q3	B—Kt2	35	P—Kt4	P×P
10	Castles	P—B4	36	P×P	R—R1
11	R—K1 (*e*)	P—B5	37	P—Kt5	R—R6
12	B—Kt1	P—QR3	38	Kt—Kt4	B×P (*q*)
13	Kt—K5	P—Kt4	39	R—KKt2!	K—R1 (*r*)
14	P—B4 (*f*)	R—K1	40	P×P	P×P
15	Q—B3	Kt—B1	41	Kt×B!	R×Kt
16	Kt—K2 (*g*)	Kt—K5	42	Kt—R6	R—Kt2
17	B×B	R×B	43	R×R	K×R
18	B×Kt	P×B	44	Q—Kt3ch!	K×Kt (*s*)
19	Q—Kt3	P—B3 (*h*)	45	K—R1! (*t*)	Q—Q4
20	Kt—Kt4	K—R1 (*i*)	46	R—KKt1	Q×BP
21	P—B5	Q—Q2	47	Q—R4ch	Q—R4
22	R—B1	R—Q1 (*j*)	48	Q—B4ch	Q—Kt4
23	R—B4	Q—Q3	49	R×Q	P×R
24	Q—R4	QR—K1 (*k*)	50	Q—Q6ch	K—R4
25	Kt—B3	B—Q4	51	Q×Kt	P—B7 (*u*)
26	Kt—B2	Q—B3	52	Q×P mate	

(*a*) The key move of the Pillsbury attack. (*b*) Black's problem in the queen's-side openings is to find a way to get his QB into action. This immediate fianchetto was standard procedure for many years, and was stoutly championed by Tarrasch, but the Pillsbury system has caused it to be abandoned. (*c*) So as to keep the diagonal closed. By this exchange White cedes his opponent a pawn majority on the queen's side. As pointed out by Steinitz, this majority is a positional advantage, for if all the heavy pieces are exchanged the ending is often won for the player who has a pawn majority on the side remote from the kings. White therefore must strive to win in the midgame. While Black advances on the queen's wing, he must attack on the king's side. The particular importance of this game is that it finally convinced players that White's attack gets home first. (*d*) Capturing with the knight would let White play P—K4 soon, with greater control of the centre. (*e*) a wasted move. Pillsbury subsequently improved the system by leaving the rook on KB1. (*f*) Except that the KR should be on KB1, White has now achieved the "set position" for which the Pillsbury system strives. (*g*) This knight must eventually be swung to the king's side to reinforce the attack. (*h*) Though condemned by some annotators, this move seems necessary sooner or later to block the White KBP. (*i*) White threatened Kt×P. (*j*) Now Black wastes a move, since the rook goes to K1 two moves later. (*k*) White is preparing to attack the isolated KP with four pieces, so that Black must bring four to the defense. (*l*) Here and later White's manoeuvres seem maddeningly slow. But Pillsbury had a genius for calculating exactly the time available for an attack. (*m*) At last the counterattack gets under way, and the race is on in earnest. (*n*) He must pause to defend the KBP, else Kt×P will win. (*o*) Again preventing Q×P, for then 31 Kt—B4, B—B2; 32 Kt—Kt6ch, B×Kt; 33 P×B is too strong; *e.g.*, 33 . . . P—R3; 34 R×P, Kt×R; 35 R×Kt, P×R; 36 Q×RPch, K—Kt1; 37 Kt×P mate. (*p*) Commencing another seemingly slow manoeuvre, the advance of the KKtP. (*q*) Now if Black can parry the attack on his king, his two passed pawns must win. White must also reckon with a counterattack on his second rank; *e.g.*, if 39 Kt×B?, R×Kt; 40 R—KKt2, R—Kt7! (*r*) His KBP was attacked more times than it was defended, because of the potential pin of the KKtP. (*s*) Forced, for if K—B1, then 45 Q—Kt8ch and 46 Q×R. (*t*) The slowest-looking move of all! Yet to avoid mate Black has no resource but to give up his queen and knight. (*u*) Probably not an oversight, but desperation, hoping for 52 Q—K6ch and 53 Q×R, after which 53 . . . P queens ch might actually win.

Illustrative Game No. 8.—The importance of maintaining sufficient space to manoeuvre is discussed by A. Nimzowitsch in his book *Die Blockade*. He won several notable games by strangling the entire adverse army.

Copenhagen, 1923

	White Sämisch	Black Nimzowitsch		White Sämisch	Black Nimzowitsch
1	P—Q4	Kt—KB3	14	P—KR3	Q—Q2
2	P—QB4	P—K3	15	K—R2	Kt—R4 (*e*)
3	Kt—KB3	P—QKt3	16	B—Q2	P—B4! (*f*)
4	P—KKt3	B—Kt2	17	Q—Q1	P—Kt5 (*g*)
5	B—Kt2	B—K2	18	Kt—Kt1	B—QKt4
6	Kt—B3	Castles	19	R—Kt1 (*h*)	B—Q3
7	Castles	P—Q4	20	P—K4	BP×P!
8	Kt—K5	P—B3 (*a*)	21	Q×Kt	R×P (*i*)
9	P×P (*b*)	BP×P	22	Q—Kt5	QR—KB1
10	B—B4 (*c*)	P—QR3	23	K—R1	QR—B4
11	R—B1 (*d*)	P—QKt4	24	Q—K3	B—Q6 (*j*)
12	Q—Kt3	Kt—B3	25	QR—K1	P—R3 (*k*)
13	Kt×Kt	B×Kt		Resigns	

(*a*) The opening is all "book" so far. The natural move P—B4 has been shown to be somewhat hazardous. The object of P—B3 is to relieve the uncomfortable pin on the QB. Also played in this position is Q—B1. (*b*) In order to leave the Black QB locked behind its own centre pawns. (*c*) This post for the bishop is always dubious after its retreat to Kt3 has been blocked by the pawn advance. (*d*) The method of restraining the Black queen's-side pawns here attempted by White is shown to be futile. Necessary was the mechanical blockade, P—QR3 and P—QKt4. (*e*) White is laboriously preparing a pawn advance, but the misplaced bishop allows Black to strike first. (*f*) Threatening after due preparation to move P—B5 and smash the compromised king position. White's unmoved KP is an obstacle to bringing the queen's-side pieces over to the defense, hence White's ensuing plan to advance it. (*g*) Exacting heavy toll for White's failure to block the pawn, and his omission of moving the KP. The knight is forced back home, where it remains stalemated for the rest of the game. (*h*) At last White threatens to move P—K4, discovering attack on the knight by the queen. Black, having already won great superiority in space, ignores the threat. (*i*) "Two pawns, and a rook on the seventh rank, all for one knight!" remarks Nimzowitsch. (*j*) Shutting off access to the haven QKt3 and threatening R—K7. (*k*) "Announcing the *zugzwang*." White has no moves left; *e.g.*, 26 B—QB1, B×Kt, or 26 K—R2, QR—B6, or 22 QR moves, R—K7. After exhausting his pawn moves, White will be forced to move a piece and commence losing material.

Illustrative Game No. 9.—At move 8, Réti illustrates "the golden rule is that there is no golden rule" by switching from a "hypermodern" formation to a "classical."

New York city, 1924

	White Réti	Black Bogoljubow		White Réti	Black Bogoljubow
1	Kt—KB3	Kt—KB3	14	Kt×Kt	B×Kt
2	P—B4 (*a*)	P—K3	15	P—K4	P—K4 (*h*)
3	P—KKt3	P—Q4	16	P—B5	B—KB1
4	B—Kt2	B—Q3	17	Q—B2 (*i*)	P×QP
5	Castles	Castles	18	P×P	QR—Q1 (*j*)
6	P—Kt3	R—K1	19	B—R5 (*k*)	R—K4
7	B—Kt2	QKt—Q2	20	B×P	R×P
8	P—Q4 (*b*)	P—B3 (*c*)	21	R×R	B×R
9	QKt—Q2	Kt—K5 (*d*)	22	Q×B	R×B
10	Kt×Kt	P×Kt	23	R—KB1	Q—Q1 (*l*)
11	Kt—K5	P—KB4	24	B—B7ch	K—R1
12	P—B3 (*e*)	P×P	25	B—K8!	Resigns (*m*)
13	B×P (*f*)	Q—B2 (*g*)			

(*a*) The opening moves of the so-called Réti system. (*b*) One idea of the system is to avoid blocking the diagonal of the QB, making the break in the centre by P—Q3 and P—K4. But Réti perceives that reversion to the "normal position" of the queen's gambit declined is strongest against the formation adopted by Black. (*c*) Forced in order to retreat B—B2 in case White plays P—B5. This advance is powerful when Black cannot counter with P—K4. If the bishop were forced to retreat to B1, White would have time for P—QKt4 and

Kt—K5, with strangling effect. (d) Subsequent analysis indicates P—K4 to be Black's best move, but it is insufficient to overcome White's positional superiority. (e) White forces open the centre to capitalize the superior position of his pieces. (f) Of course not P×P, as the KP is to be used as a battering-ram. (g) One of Black's problems is to develop his QB. This move certainly seems to have better prospects than 13 . . . Kt×Kt; 14 P×Kt, B—B4ch; 15 K—Kt2, because White would then gain command of the open Q-file. (h) He must not allow P—K5, and P×P would leave his KP isolated. "Black appears to have surmounted the greater part of his early difficulty and it calls for exceptionally fine play on the part of White to make the hidden advantages of his position count so rapidly and convincingly."—Alekhine.[1] (i) Guarding his QB5 to threaten P×QP, and also threatening P×KBP. If Black now plays P×KP, then B×P and White wins either the KP or the KRP. (j) Indirectly guarding the QP; *e.g.*, 19 B×QP, B×KBP. (k) Initiating a beautiful combination that won this game the first brilliancy prize. (l) No better is 23 . . . Q—K2; 24 B—B7ch, K—R1; 25 B—Q5, Q—B3; 26 Q—B8. (m) To avert mate he must give up at least the bishop.

Illustrative Game No. 10.—This game was hailed as an example of the "hypermodern" style. Alekhine, however, vehemently repudiated the allegation.

Piestany, Czech., 1922

White Alekhine	Black H. Wolf	White Alekhine	Black H. Wolf
1 P—Q4	P—Q4	21 P—Q6	Kt×K3
2 Kt—KB3	P—QB4	22 R×Kt!	P×R
3 P—B4	BP×P	23 Kt—Kt5	Q—Kt1
4 P×P	Kt—KB3	24 Kt×KPch	K—B2
5 Kt×P	P—QR3 (a)	25 Kt—Kt5ch	K—B1
6 P—K4! (b)	Kt×KP	26 Q—Q5	R—Kt2
7 Q—R4ch (c)	B—Q2	27 Kt—K6ch	K—Kt1
8 Q—Kt3 (d)	Kt—B4	28 Kt×Rch	K×Kt
9 Q—K3 (e)	P—KKt3	29 P×P	Kt—B3
10 Kt—KB3 (f)	Q—B2	30 Q×P	R—R2
11 Q—B3	R—KKt1 (g)	31 R—K1	Q—Q3
12 B—K3	P—Kt3	32 P—K8(Kt)ch	Kt×Kt
13 QKt—Q2	B—Kt2	33 Q×Kt	Q×Kt
14 B—Q4	B×B	34 Q—K5ch	K—B2
15 Q×B (h)	B—Kt4	35 P—KR4	R×P (i)
16 B×Bch	P×B	36 Q—K8ch	K—Kt2
17 Castles	R—R5	37 R—K7ch	K—R3
18 P—QKt4	Q—Q1	38 Q—B8ch	K—R4
19 P—QR3	QKt—Q2	39 R—K5ch	K—Kt5
20 KR—K1	K—B1	40 R—Kt5ch	Resigns

(a) Black is reluctant to lose a tempo by 5 . . . Kt×P; 6 P—K4 or 5 . . . Q×P; 6 Kt—QB3. But the weak move chosen is at once shown by White to be a much more serious loss of time. (b) Giving up the KP to save the QP. The merit of this transaction is that the pawn at Q5 exerts a terrible cramp on the Black development. While the QP looks difficult to maintain in the long run, White actually succeeds in promoting it! (c) With the object of forcing Black to mask his own attack on the QP. Black cannot reply P—QKt4 because of 8 Kt×P, nor Q—Q2 because of 8 B—QKt5. If Kt—Q2, then 8 Kt—K6, P×Kt; 9 P×P would be unpleasant. (d) Black is kept busy meeting short threats. Now he has to defend the QKtP. (e) Holding back the KP; *e.g.*, 9 . . . P—K3?; 10 P—QKt4, Kt—R5; 11 P×P, etc. Black therefore decides to fianchetto his KB. (f) "This gain of time allows White to prevent 10—B—Kt2 followed by castling. Black's king being kept in the center, White's attack will be facilitated, thanks to his superior development . . . The advantage won results from repeated movements of the same pieces (here the first eleven moves contain four displacements of the queen and three of the king's knight). But the possibility of like maneuvers in the opening phase is *solely* attributable, I must reiterate, to the fact that the opponent has adopted faulty tactics, which must from the first be refuted by an energetic demonstration. It is clear, on the contrary, that in the face of correct development, similar anomalous treatment would be disastrous. It cannot therefore be any question of a 'Modern System', but just simply of exploiting in a rational manner the opponent's mistakes."—Alekhine.[2] (g) He cannot even play P—B3 in order to save the right to castle, for White also threatens P—QKt4 winning the knight. After the text move Black could answer P—QKt4 with B—Kt2. (h) Now observe the wretched state of Black's game! His king is held in the centre, his pawns are disorganized and the QP still hampers his development. (i) Against passive defense White plays R—K3 and R—KB3.

Illustrative Game No. 11.—The fear that chess is becoming exhausted is continually given the lie by the revival of old variations once thought to have been refuted. A galaxy of Russian chess stars has taken the lead in re-examining "the book."

[1]From Alekhine, "New York International Tournament, 1924," *American Chess Bulletin* (April 1, 1925).

[2]From Alekhine, *My Best Games of Chess* (1927), copyright by Harcourt, Brace and Co., Inc.

Radio Match, 1945

White Smyslov, U.S.S.R.	Black Reshevsky, U.S.	White Smyslov, U.S.S.R.	Black Reshevsky, U.S.
1 P—K4	P—K4	22 K—R1	Q×KP
2 Kt—KB3	Kt—QB3	23 B—Q2	Q×P
3 B—Kt5	P—QR3	24 B—B4	P—B4
4 B—R4	Kt—B3	25 B—K6ch	K—R1
5 Castles	Kt×P	26 B×QP	R—Q1
6 P—Q4	P—QKt4	27 QR—Q1	P—B5
7 B—Kt3	P—Q4	28 B×KtP	P—B6
8 P×P	B—K3	29 B—K5	P—Kt5
9 P—B3	B—QB4	30 B—QKt3	R—Q7
10 QKt—Q2	Castles	31 P—B4 (e)	P—KR4
11 B—B2	P—B4	32 R—QKt1	R—KB7
12 Kt—Kt3	B—Kt3	33 KR—K1	Q—Q7 (f)
13 KKt—Q4	Kt×Kt	34 QR—Q1	Q—Kt7
14 Kt×Kt	B×Kt	35 R—Q8ch (g)	K—R2
15 P×B	P—B5	36 B—Kt8ch	K—Kt3
16 P—B3	Kt—Kt6 (a)	37 R—Q6ch	K—B4
17 P×Kt	P×P	38 B—K6ch	K—Kt3
18 Q—Q3	B—B4	39 B—Q5ch	K—R2
19 Q×B (b)	R×Q	40 B—K4ch	K—Kt1
20 B×R	Q—R5 (c)	41 B—Kt6	Resigns
21 B—R3	Q×Pch (d)		

(a) The first 18 moves are identical with a game Duras-Maróczy, Ostend, 1906. After the sacrifice of the knight, Maróczy won, and the game was taken to indicate that 16 P—B3 by White is unsound. But in the Moscow championship tournament of 1942, Boleslavsky played it against Ragozin, captured the knight and won. The Russian analysts got busy and established to their satisfaction that the variation is playable for White. Smyslov was acquainted with this analysis, taking only eight minutes for his first 25 moves, while Reshevsky, who had not studied it, was consuming an hour and a half. (b) This is the improvement over Duras' play. White gets value for his queen in pieces, but it is not easy to see how he can withstand the advance of the Black queen's-side pawns. (c) By this threat of mate Black wins both White centre pawns, gaining himself a formidable supported passed pawn. (d) One point of the analysis is that Black cannot attack the bishop by P—KKt4, P—KR4 and P—KKt5. After playing BP×KtP White can move R—KB4 and the attack is smashed. (e) White now threatens 32 R×R, Q×R; 33 R—Q1, which previously could have been answered by Q—R3, check. (f) The effort to maintain the *status quo* by R—K7 would come to naught, as White would now be willing to play R×Q, for after the exchanges the Black rook would not attack the White KBP. (g) The White manoeuvres have cleared the Q-file for his rook, and now his superior forces institute an irresistible mating attack.

CHESS PROBLEMS

Chess problems are artificial positions, constructed to show dynamic possibilities of the pieces. Each is accompanied by a stipulation, as "(White to) mate in two moves." In the beginning, no doubt, problems were posed as mere puzzles, the sole interest being to discover the solution. But even from early times problem composers have been as much occupied with exploring strategic ideas as with baffling the solver. Today the chess problem is recognized as an aesthetic form, cast by accident of history in the form of a puzzle.

No. 1.—MATE IN FIVE No. 2.—MATE IN TWO No. 3.—MATE IN TWO

The first problems of which we have record were Arabian *mansubat* (betting problems). The earliest known manuscript was a collection by al-Adli, about A.D. 840; it was lost, but much of its contents was preserved in later collections. Chief of these is the compilation made by one who signed himself "Bonus Socius."

The National library at Florence contains a copy of the Bonus Socius manuscript, with 149 problems, believed to date from the late 13th century (1266?). Some of the problems no doubt were recorded from actual play, such as No. 1 (1 Sc3; 2 Se4; 3 Sd2; 4 Sf1; 5 Sg3). But there are many evidences of constructive editing, by deletion of superfluous pieces, and there are also outright inventions, such as No. 2 (1 Rh7—g7).

What is called the modern period began about 1840, in the compositions of an Englishman, Rev. Horatio Bolton (1793–1873); a Belgian, August d'Orville (1813–?); and the German master player Adolph Anderssen (1818–79). The beauty of "quiet" keys first began to be explored, as in No. 3 (1 Rd5). A great revival of interest culminated in the publication of a compilation of 2,000 problems, by A. Alexandre, at Paris, 1846. In 1845 was published the problem destined to become the most famous in history, the "Indian problem," No. 4 (1 Bc1; 2 Kb1 or other waiting move; 3 Rd2, Kf4; 4 Rd4 doublecheck mate). It was quoted in chess periodicals all over the world and stimulated intensive exploration of the strategy peculiar to problems. In the period 1845–61 were discovered many of the basic themes, as "Grimshaw induced interference," No. 5 (1 Bc8, B×B; 2 Qf6, Re6; 3 Qd4ch, K×Q; Sf5ch); "Novotny interference by obstruction," No. 6 (1 Sg3, Re8; 2 Rb2—c2, B×R; 3 Sf2—e4); and "Bristol clearance," No. 7 (1 Rh1, Bd7; 2 Qb1; 3 Qg1).

H. A. LOVEDAY 1845

No. 4.—MATE IN FOUR

W. GRIMSHAW 1850

No. 5.—MATE IN FIVE

A. NOVOTNY 1854

No. 6.—MATE IN FOUR

The later 19th century saw the emergence of several national schools with divergent ideals. The German school, including Philip Klett (1833–1910), Conrad Bayer of Austria (1828–97), Johann Berger (1845–1933; author of *Das Schachproblem*), J. Kohtz and C. Kockelkorn (authors of *Das Indische Problem,* 1903), emphasized strategy.

The Bohemian school, including J. Pospisil (1861–1916, author of *Ceske Ulohy Sachove,* 1888), Jan Dobrusky (1853–1907), G. Chocholous (1856–1930), M. Havel (1881–   ), emphasized "echoes"—reproduction of the same mating net in different orientations.

The English school, including B. G. Laws (1861–1932; author of *The Chess Problem Textbook,* 1886), C. Planck (1856–1935), A. F. Mackenzie (1861–1905; the blind composer of Jamaica), Godfrey Heathcote (1870–   ), emphasized economy and accuracy, especially as embodied in "model mates." (*See* No. 8 [1 Sd6, B×S; 2 Qe2, Bf4; 3 P×B]; No. 9 [1 Qe3, P×B; 2 Qb3ch, K×S; 3 Rc2. Or 1 . . . K×B; 2 Rc2, P×S; 3 Rd2]; No. 10 [1 Sa2, P×S; 2 Qc2. Or 1 . . . Kd2; 2 Kf3. Or 1 . . . Kd4; 2 Bf2ch. Or 1 . . . Ke2; 2 Sb4].)

F. HEALEY 1861

No. 7.—MATE IN THREE

J. KOHTZ AND C. KOCKELKORN 1905

No. 8.—MATE IN FOUR

M. HAVEL 1905

No. 9.—MATE IN THREE

The American school has been called cosmopolitan. Sam Loyd (1841–1911) was a master of the surprise move, but also pioneered in the discovery of many themes. (*See* No. 11 [1 Qf1, Bb2; 2 Qb1. Or 1 . . . Bc3 or d4; 2 Qd3. Or 1 . . . Be5 or f6; 2 Qf5. Or 1 . . . Pg3; 2 Sg6ch].)

The same wide range of interest and facility in many styles was displayed by W. A. Shinkman (1847–1933) and Otto Wurzburg (1875–   ).

National distinctions have tended to evaporate in the worldwide exchange of problem ideas. In the period 1913–24, the Good Companion club of Philadelphia, an international association of composers founded by J. F. Magee, Jr. (1867–   ), gave great impetus to the study of direct mates in two moves. Many new ideas were discovered by such men as G. Guidelli of Italy (1897–1924), A. Ellerman of Argentina (1893–   ), C. Mansfield of England (1896–   ), J. Schiffmann of Austria. More recently, new paths have been blazed by composers of the U.S.S.R., such as M. M. Barulin, A. P. Gulyaev and L. I. Kubbel. (*See* No. 12 [1 Be4]; No. 13 [1 Qf3]; No. 14 [1 S×P].)

G. HEATHCOTE 1904

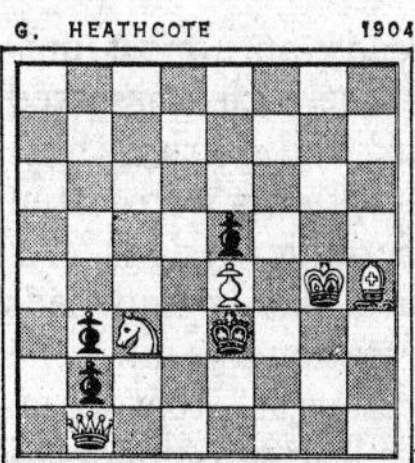

No. 10.—MATE IN THREE

SAM LOYD 1869

No. 11.—MATE IN THREE

C. MANSFIELD 1917

No. 12.—MATE IN TWO

A direct mate is a problem in which White is required to mate Black against his resistance. Many "unorthodox" forms have also been devised. In a selfmate, White must force Black to checkmate the White king, while Black seeks to avoid doing so. (*See* No. 15 [1 Rf2, K×R; 2 Qe2ch; 3 Qg2ch. Or 1 . . . Bg1; 2 Qg8ch; 3 Qg2ch].) In a helpmate, both sides conspire to mate one king, the difficulty being solely to weave a mating net. Other forms are the stalemate, maximate, reflex mate, and conditional mate. The properties of pieces with special powers have been investigated, such as the combination of a knight with queen, rook or bishop, under fanciful names, as chancellor, duke, templar, wazir, knight-rider, camel, giraffe, grasshopper. A pioneer in this field, called "fairy chess," was T. R. Dawson (1889–1952) of England.

J. SCHIFFMANN 1927

No. 13.—MATE IN TWO

M. BARULIN 1929

No. 14.—MATE IN TWO

O. WURZBURG

No. 15.—SELFMATE IN THREE

Modern interest in composition and solving is not confined to the difficulty, beauty and strategy of individual problems, but embraces the study of whole groups of problems and the classification of their themes. There exist large classified collections, such as that in the custody of C. S. Kipping of England (1891–   ), containing more than 150,000 examples. This collection was begun by Alain White of the United States, a composer and writer who has edited more than 40 compilations of problems in book form.

BIBLIOGRAPHY.—*Methods of Composition and Solution:* P. H. Williams, *The Modern Chess Problem* (1912); B. G. Laws, *Chess Problems and How to Solve Them* (1923); K. S. Howard, *The Enjoyment of Chess Problems* (1943). *History, Classification of Themes:* Alain White, *Simple Two-Move Themes* (1924); George Hume and Alain White, *The Good Companion Two-Mover* (1922); H. Weenink, *The Chess Problem* (1926). *Collections:* Alain White, the *Christmas Series* (more than 30 titles), *Sam Loyd and His Chess Problems* (1913), *A Sketchbook of American Chess Problematists* (1942) and *A Century of Two-Movers* (1941); Albrecht Buschke and others, *The Two-Move Chess Problem in the Soviet Union, 1923–1943* (1943); Frank Healey, *200 Chess Problems* (1908); F. Dedrle, *Echo* (1927). (G. MH.)

CHEST, a large box of wood or metal with a hinged lid. The term is used for many kinds of receptacles; and in anatomy indicates the portion of the body covered by the ribs and breastbone (*see* RESPIRATORY SYSTEM, ANATOMY OF). Chests as articles of furniture are of the greatest antiquity. The chest was the common receptacle for clothes and valuables, and was the direct ancestor of the "chest of drawers," which was formed by enlarging the chest and cutting up the front. It was also frequently used as a seat. Indeed, in its origin it took in great measure the place of the chair, which, although familiar enough to the ancients, was a luxury in the days when the chest was already an almost universal possession. In the early middle ages the rich possessed them in profusion, used them as portmanteaux, and carried them about from castle to castle. These portable receptacles were often covered with leather and emblazoned with heraldic designs. As houses gradually became more amply furnished, chests and beds and other movables were allowed to remain stationary; and the chest finally took the shape in which we best know it—that of an oblong box standing upon raised feet. As a rule it was made of oak, but sometimes of chestnut or other hard wood.

Types.—There are, properly speaking, three types of chest—the domestic, the ecclesiastical and the strong box or coffer. Old domestic chests still exist in great number and some variety, but the proportion of those earlier than the latter part of the Tudor period is very small; most of them are Jacobean in date. Very frequently they were made to contain the store of house-linen which a bride took to her husband upon her marriage. In the 17th century Boulle and his imitators glorified the marriage-coffer until it became a gorgeous casket, almost indeed a sarcophagus, inlaid with ivory and ebony and precious woods, and enriched with ormolu, supported upon a stand of equal magnificence. The Italian marriage-chests (*cassone, q.v.*) were also of a richness which was never attempted in England. The main characteristics of English domestic chests (which not infrequently are carved with names and dates) are panelled fronts and ends, the feet being formed from prolongations of the "stiles" or side posts. A certain number of 17th-century chests, however, have separate feet, either circular or shaped after the indications of a somewhat later style.

There is usually a strong architectural feeling about the chest, the front being divided into panels, which are plain in the more ordinary examples, and richly carved in the choicer ones. The plinth and frieze are often of well-defined *guilloche* work, or are carved with arabesques or conventionalized flowers. Architectural detail, especially the detail of wainscoting, has indeed been followed with considerable fidelity, many of the earlier chests being carved in the linenfold pattern, while the Jacobean examples are often mere reproductions of the pilastered and recessed oaken mantlepieces of the period.

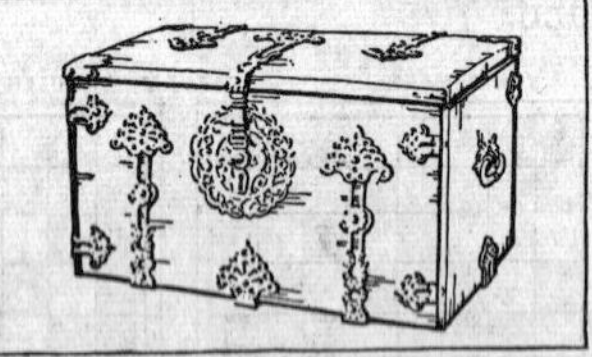

BY COURTESY OF THE VICTORIA AND ALBERT MUSEUM

A SPANISH TREASURE CHEST OF THE 17TH CENTURY

Occasionally a chest is seen which is inlaid with coloured woods, or with geometrical parquetry. Perhaps the most elaborate type of English parquetry chest is that named after the vanished Palace of Nonesuch. Such pieces are, however, rarely met with. The entire front of this type is covered with a representation of the palace in coloured woods. Another class of chest is incised, sometimes rather roughly, but often with considerable geometrical skill.

The more ordinary variety has been of great value to the forger of antique furniture, who has used its carved panels for conversion into cupboards and other pieces, the history of which is not easily unravelled by the amateur who collects old oak. Towards the end of the 17th century chests were often made of walnut, or even of exotic woods such as cedar and cypress, and were sometimes clamped with large and ornamental brass bands and hinges. The chests of the 18th century were much larger than those of the preceding period, and as often as not were furnished with two drawers at the bottom—an arrangement but rarely seen in those of the 17th century—while they were often fitted with a small internal box fixed across one end for ready access to small articles. The chest was not infrequently unpanelled and unornamented, and in the latter period of its history this became the ruling type.

Ecclesiastical Chests.—These appear to have been used almost entirely as receptacles for vestments and church plate, and those which survive are still often employed for the preservation of parish documents. A considerable variety of these interesting and often exceedingly elaborate chests are still left in English churches. They are usually of considerable size, and of a length disproportionate to their depth. This no doubt was to facilitate the storage of vestments. Most of them are of great antiquity. Many go back to the 14th century, and here and there they are even earlier, as in the case of the coffer in Stoke d'Abernon church, Surrey, which is unquestionably 13th-century work. One of the most remarkable of these early examples is in Newport church, Essex. It is one of the extremely rare painted coffers of the 13th century, the front carved with an upper row of shields, from which the heraldic painting has disappeared, and a lower row of roundels. Between is a belt of open tracery, probably of pewter, and the inside of the lid is decorated with oil paintings representing the Crucifixion, the Virgin Mary, St. Peter, St. John and St. Paul. The well-known "jewel chest" in St. Mary's, Oxford, is one of the earliest examples of 14th century work. Many of these ecclesiastical chests are carved with architectural motives—traceried windows most frequently, but occasionally with the linenfold pattern. There is a whole class of chests known as "tilting coffers," carved with representations of tournaments or feats of arms, and sometimes with a grotesque admixture of chivalric figures and mythical monsters. Only five or six examples of this type are known still to exist in England, and two of them are now in the Victoria and Albert museum, London. It is not certain that even these few are of English origin—indeed, very many of the chests and coffers of the 16th and 17th centuries are of foreign make. They were imported into England chiefly from Flanders, and were subsequently carved by native artisans, as was the case with other common pieces of furniture of those periods. The *huche* or "hutch" was a rough type of household chest.

TYPE OF CHEST USED IN THE DAYS OF THE STAGE COACH FOR TRANSPORTING VALUABLES ACROSS THE AMERICAN PRAIRIES

Coffer is the word properly applied to a chest which was intended for the safe keeping of valuables. As a rule the coffer is much more massive in construction than the domestic chest; it is clamped by iron bands, sometimes contains secret receptacles opening with a concealed spring, and is often furnished with an elaborate and complex lock, which occupies the whole of the underside of the lid. Pieces of this type are sometimes described as Spanish chests, from the belief that they were taken from ships belonging to the Armada. However, these strong boxes are frequently of English origin, although the mechanism of the locks may have been due to the subtle skill of foreign locksmiths. A typical example of the treasure chest is that which belonged to Sir Thomas Bodley, and is preserved in the Bodleian

VENETIAN CHEST OF THE 16TH CENTURY, IN THE MUSEO NAZIONALE OF FLORENCE, ITALY

library at Oxford. The locks of this description of chest are of steel and are sometimes richly damascened.

Another kind of chest in use in earlier days was that signified in the expression a "chest of viols." This took the form of a solidly constructed, baize-lined press or cupboard, designed to accommodate stringed musical instruments—in the case of a "chest of viols," six viols of varying sizes.

CHESTER, EARLS OF. The important palatine earldom of Chester was first held by a Fleming named Gherbod (fl. 1070), and then from 1071 by Hugh of Avranches (d. 1101), a son of Richard, viscount of Avranches. As the friend of St. Anselm, Hugh showed the customary liberality to religious houses. His life was spent in fighting in Wales and Normandy, and he died on July 27, 1101. Hugh's only son Richard, who was childless, was drowned in the "White Ship" in Nov. 1120. Among subsequent holders were Ralph, or Randulph, de Gernon (d. 1153), prominent in the civil wars under Stephen, fighting first on one side and then on the other; and his son Hugh de Kevelioc (1147–81), who shared in the rising against Henry II in 1173. The most celebrated of the earls was Ralph, Ranulf or Randulph, de Blundevill (*c.* 1172–1232), who succeeded his father Hugh de Kevelioc in 1181 and was created earl of Lincoln in 1217. He married Constance, widow of Henry II's son, Geoffrey of Brittany, and is sometimes called duke of Brittany and earl of Richmond. He fought in Wales, sided with John against the barons and fought for Henry III against the French invaders and their allies. In 1218 he went on crusade to the Holy Land and took part in the capture of Damietta. He died at Wallingford in Oct. 1232. Stubbs calls him "almost the last relic of the great feudal aristocracy of the Conquest."

In the *Vision of Piers Plowman* Ranulf's name is linked with that of Robin Hood. Ranulf being childless, in Nov. 1232 the earldom was granted to his nephew John the Scot, earl of Huntingdon (*c.* 1207–1237). In 1246 it was annexed to the English crown.

In 1254 Prince Edward, afterward Edward I, was created earl of Chester, and from that time the earldom always held by the heirs apparent to the English crown. From 1399 the earls of Chester were also princes of Wales, although the act of Richard II (1398), which created Chester into a principality to be held by the king's eldest son, was revoked by Henry IV.

CHESTER, county borough, city, seaport and the county town of Cheshire, Eng., 16 mi. S. of Liverpool. Pop. (1951) 48,237. Area, 6.5 sq.mi. It lies in a low plain on the Dee, principally on the north (right) bank, 6 mi. above the point at which the river opens out into its wide shallow estuary. It is an important railway centre.

History.—The Roman station of Deva was founded about A.D. 48 by Ostorius Scapula, and from its key position in relation both to the north Wales coastal route and to the northward avenue past the Mersey, it became an important military and commercial centre. In A.D. 78–79 it was the winter quarters of Agricola, and later became the permanent headquarters of the 20th legion, Valeria Victrix. Many inscriptions and remains of the Roman military occupation have been found, and the north and east walls stand in great part on Roman foundations. The Saxon form of the name was Leganceaster. About 614 the city was destroyed by Aethelfrith, and lay in ruins until 907, when Aethelflaed rebuilt the walls and restored the monastery of St. Werburgh. In the reign of Aethelstan there was a mint at Chester, and in 973 it was the scene of Edgar's triumph when, it is said, he was rowed on the Dee by six subject kings. It resisted the Conqueror, and did not finally surrender until 1070. On the erection of Cheshire into a county palatine after the Conquest, Chester became the seat of government of the palatine earls. The Domesday account of the city includes a description of the Saxon laws under which it had been governed in the time of Edward the Confessor. All the land, except the bishop's borough, was held of the earl, and assessed at 50 hides.

The earliest extant charter, granted by Henry II in 1160, empowered the burgesses to trade with Durham as freely as they had done in the reign of Henry I. From this date a large collection of charters enumerates privileges granted by successive earls and later sovereigns. Three from John protected the trade with Ireland. Edward I granted the citizens the fee farm of the city at a yearly rent of £100. In the 14th century Chester began to lose its standing as a port through the gradual silting up of the Dee estuary, and the city was further impoverished by the inroads of the Welsh. Continued misfortunes led to reductions of fee farm by Richard II and by Henry VI, who also made a grant for the completion of a new Dee bridge, the old one having been swept away by an unusually high tide. Henry VII reduced the fee farm to £20, and in 1506 granted "the Great Charter," which constituted the city a county by itself and incorporated the governing body under the style of a mayor, 24 aldermen and 40 common councilmen. This charter was confirmed by James I and Charles II. The charter of Hugh le Gros to the abbey of St. Werburgh includes a grant of the tolls of the fair at the feast of St. Werburgh for three days, and a subsequent charter from Ranulf de Blundevill (12th century) licensed the abbot and monks to hold their fairs and markets before the abbey gates. Friction between the abbot and civic authorities lasted until, in the reign of Henry VIII, it was decreed that the right of holding fairs was vested exclusively in the citizens. Charles II in 1685 granted a cattle fair to be held on the first Thursday in February. The city is divided into four principal blocks by the four principal streets—Northgate street, Eastgate street, Bridge street and Watergate street, which radiate at right angles from the cross and terminate in the four gates. These four streets exhibit in what are called "the rows" a characteristic feature of the city. In Eastgate street, Bridge street and Watergate street, the rows exist on each side of the street and form continuous galleries open to the street, from which they are approached by flights of steps. The rows are flagged or boarded under foot and ceiled above, thus forming a covered way, standing in the same relation to the shops, which are at their back, as the foot pavement does in other towns. On the west side of Northgate street, on the other hand, the row is formed out of the ground floor of the houses, having cellars beneath. The rows and the old half-timbered houses combine to give the city a picturesque and individual character. Among the ancient houses are Derby house, bearing the date 1591, Bishop Lloyd's house and God's Providence house in Watergate street and the Bear and Billet in Lower Bridge street; the last three date from the 17th century. A mortuary chapel of the early part of the 13th century exists in the basement of a house in Bridge street.

Chester is the only city in England that still possesses its walls perfect in their entire circuit of 2 mi. The gateways were all rebuilt at various dates: the north and east gates on the site of the Roman gates. The Grosvenor bridge (1832), a single span of stone 200 ft. in length, one of the largest in Europe, carries the road to Wrexham and Shrewsbury over the Dee on the southwest; while there is also an old bridge of seven arches. The castle, with the exception of Caesar's tower and a round tower with adjacent buildings, was taken down about 1790 and replaced by a barracks, county hall, jail and assize courts.

The cathedral church of Christ and the Virgin Mary stands toward the north of the city within the walls on an ancient site. In 1093 Hugh le Gros, earl of Chester, richly endowed the original foundation as a Benedictine monastery. The bishops of Mercia had apparently a seat at Chester, but the city had ceased to be episcopal until in 1075 Peter, bishop of Lichfield, removed his seat thence to Chester, having for his cathedral the collegiate church of St. John (*see* below). The see, however, was moved again to Coventry (1102), but Cheshire continued subject to Lichfield until in 1541 Chester was erected into a bishopric by Henry VIII, the church of the dissolved abbey of St. Werburgh becoming the cathedral. The diocese covers nearly all Cheshire, with small portions of Flintshire, Lancashire and Staffordshire. The cathedral, while not of first rank architecturally, gains in beauty from the tones of its red sandstone walls and from its picturesque close. It is cruciform with a central tower 127 ft. high. The nave is short (145 ft.), being of six bays; the southern arcade is Decorated, while the northern differs in detail. The basement of the northwestern tower is Norman and formed part of Hugh "Le Gros's" church. The north transept also retains Norman work, and its size shows the original plan, limited by the existence of the conventual buildings to the north. The south transept has aisles, with Decorated and Perpendicular windows. The fine organ stands on a screen across the north transept. The choir is a fine example of transitional Early English Decorated enhanced by the ancient carved wooden stalls unsurpassed in England. The Lady Chapel, east of the choir, is of rich Early English workmanship. Of the conventual buildings the cloisters are Perpendicular. The chapter-house, entered by a beautiful vestibule from the east cloister, is Early English (*c.* 1240). The refectory, adjoining the north cloister, is of the same period, with Perpendicular insertions; it retains its beautiful Early English lector's pulpit. An early Norman chamber, with massive pillars and vaulting, adjoins the west cloister, and may be the substructure of the abbot's house. The domestic buildings have been completely restored, the work being finished in 1928. The abbey gateway is of the 14th century. Within the walls there are several churches of ancient foundation: St. Peter's is said to occupy the site of a church erected by Aethelflaed, queen of Mercia, and St. Mary's dates from the 12th century. The church of St. John, outside the walls, which became the cathedral in 1075, is a massive early Norman structure, with later additions and restorations. It was a collegiate church until 1547. The Grosvenor Museum and School of Art, the foundation of which was suggested by Charles Kingsley the novelist, when canon of Chester cathedral, contains local antiquities and a fine collection of the fauna of Cheshire. The King's school, founded by Henry VIII (1541), was reorganized on the lines of a public school in 1873. Other educational institutions include the diocesan training college. Roodee, a level tract by the river at the base of the city wall, is appropriated as a race-course. An annual race-meeting is held in May. The town gains in prosperity from its large number of tourists. Manufactures are shot, white lead and paint, and tobacco and snuff. There is some shipping on the Dee but the river is principally used for pleasure vessels and rowing. The city of Chester parliamentary division, returning one member, includes the rural district of Chester and the urban district of Hoole. From 1553 Chester returned two members until 1885, when the representation was reduced to one member. The trades of tanners, skinners and glove-makers existed at the time of the Conquest, and the importation of marten skins is mentioned in Domesday. In the 14th century the woollen trade was considerable, and in 1674 weavers and wool-combers were introduced into Chester from Norwich. The restoration of the channel of the Dee opened up a flourishing trade in Irish linen, which in 1786 was at its height, but from that date gradually diminished.

See *Victoria County History, Cheshire;* R. H. Morris, *Chester in the Plantagenet and Tudor Reigns* (Chester, 1894); Joseph Hemingway, *History of the City of Chester* (2 vols., Chester, 1831).

CHESTER, a city of Delaware county, Pa., U.S., on the Delaware river, 13 mi. S.W. of Philadelphia. It is on U.S. highways 13 and 322, and is served by the Baltimore and Ohio, the Pennsylvania and the Reading railroads. The population in 1950 was 66,039 and was 59,285 in 1940 by the federal census. Chester has a good harbour, with considerable commerce. It is in an intensively industrialized area, with enormous shipbuilding plants, steel mills, automotive and locomotive works. Other manufactures of importance are cotton, silk and woollen goods, paper, iron, lace, hosiery and steel tubing. At the city of Chester is the Pennsylvania Military college, the second oldest military college in the United States. On the edge of the city is Crozer Theological seminary (Baptist), founded in 1867 by the family of John P. Crozer (1793–1866). Settled about 1645 by the Swedes and Finns, who called it Uplandt, Chester is the oldest town in Pennsylvania. It was the seat of the Swedish courts until 1682, when William Penn arrived. The spot where he landed is marked by a memorial stone, and Pusey house (built in 1683), which he occupied for a time, still stands. The old city hall (1724) is one of the oldest public buildings in the country. After the battle of Brandywine George Washington retreated to Chester, and here wrote his account of the battle. Soon after that it was occupied by the British. It was incorporated as a borough in 1701, and received a city charter in 1866. Its period of rapid growth began with the introduction of large manufacturing interests about 1850. In 1850 the population was 1,667; in 1880, 14,997; in 1900, 33,988. Between 1910 and 1920 it increased 50.6%. Annexations of territory brought the land area to 4.5 sq.mi.

CHESTER, a city of South Carolina, U.S., in the foothills of the Blue Ridge mountains, 65 mi. N.N.W. of Columbia; the county seat of Chester county. It is on federal highways 21 and 321, and is served by the Southern, the Seaboard, the Carolina and Northwestern and the Lancaster and Chester railways. The population was 6,893 in 1950 and was 6,392 in 1940 by the federal census.

The city is advantageously situated between the hydroelectric developments of the Broad and the Catawba rivers. Its manufactures include building products, cloth and yarn, flour and dairy products.

Chester was settled about 1732, was incorporated as a town in 1849 and as a city in 1893.

CHESTERFIELD, PHILIP DORMER STANHOPE, 4th Earl of (1694–1773), son of Philip Stanhope, 3rd earl (1673–1726), and Elizabeth Savile, daughter of George Savile, marquess of Halifax, was born in London on Sept. 22, 1694. The care of the boy devolved upon his grandmother, the marchioness of Halifax. His education, began under a private tutor, was continued (1712) at Trinity Hall, Cambridge; here he remained little more than a year, but seems to have acquired a considerable knowledge of ancient and modern languages. His university training was supplemented (1714) by a continental tour, untrammelled by a governor; at The Hague his ambition for the applause awarded to adventure made a gamester of him, and at Paris he began, from the same motive, that worship of the conventional Venus, the serious inculcation of which has earned for him the largest and most unenviable part of his reputation.

The accession of George I. brought him back to England. His relative, James Stanhope (afterwards 1st Earl Stanhope), the king's favourite minister, procured for him the place of gentleman of the bedchamber to the prince of Wales. In 1715 he entered the House of Commons as Lord Stanhope of Shelford and member for St. Germans. In 1726 his father died, and Lord Stanhope became earl of Chesterfield. He took his seat in the Upper House, and his oratory, never effective in the Commons by reason of its want of force and excess of finish, at once became a power. In 1728 Chesterfield was sent to The Hague as ambassador. In this place his tact and temper, his dexterity and discrimination, enabled him to do good service, and he was rewarded with Walpole's friendship, a Garter and the place of lord high steward. In 1732 there was born to him, by a certain Mlle. du Bouchet, the son, Philip Stanhope, for whose advice and instruction were afterwards written the famous *Letters.* He negotiated the second treaty of Vienna in 1731 and in the next year, being somewhat broken in health and fortune, he resigned his embassy and returned to England. A few months' rest enabled him to resume his seat in the Lords, of which he was one of the acknowledged leaders. He supported the ministry, but his allegiance was not the blind fealty Walpole exacted of his followers. The Excise bill, the great premier's favourite measure, was vehemently opposed by him in the Lords and by his three brothers in the Commons. Walpole bent before the storm and abandoned the measure; but Chesterfield was summarily dismissed from his stewardship. For the next two years he led the opposition in the Upper House, leaving no stone unturned to effect Walpole's downfall. In 1741 he signed the protest for Walpole's dismissal and went abroad on account of his health. He visited Voltaire at Brussels and spent some time in Paris, where he associated with the younger Crébillon, Fontenelle and Montesquieu. In 1742 Walpole fell, and Carteret was his real, though not his nominal, successor. Although Walpole's administration had been overthrown largely by Chesterfield's efforts the new ministry did not count Chesterfield either in its ranks or among its supporters. He remained in opposition, distinguishing himself by the courtly bitterness of his attacks on George II., who learned to hate him violently. In 1743 a new journal, *Old England; or, the Constitutional Journal,* appeared. For this paper Chesterfield wrote under the name of "Jeffrey Broadbottom." A number of pamphlets, in some of which Chesterfield had the help of Edmund Waller, followed. His energetic campaign against George II. and his government won the gratitude of the dowager duchess of Marlborough, who left him £20,000 as a mark of her appreciation. In 1744 the king was compelled to abandon Carteret, and the coalition or "Broad Bottom" party, led by Chesterfield and Pitt, came into office. In the troublous state of European politics the earl's conduct and experience were more useful abroad than at home, and he was sent to The Hague as ambassador a second time. The object of his mission was to persuade the Dutch to join in the War of the Austrian Succession and to arrange the details of their assistance. The success of his mission was complete; and on his return a few weeks afterwards he received the lord-lieutenancy of Ireland—a place he had long coveted.

Short as it was, Chesterfield's Irish administration was of great service to his country, and is unquestionably that part of his political life which does him most honour. To have conceived and carried out a policy, which, with certain reservations, Burke himself might have originated and owned, is no small title to regard. The earl showed himself finely capable in practice as in theory, vigorous and tolerant, a man to be feared and a leader to be followed; he took the government entirely into his own hands, repressed the jobbery traditional to the office, established schools and manufactures, and at once conciliated and kept in check the Orange and Roman Catholic factions. In 1746, however, he had to exchange the lord-lieutenancy for the place of Secretary of State. With a curious respect for those theories which his familiarity with the secret social history of France had caused him to entertain, he hoped and attempted to retain a hold over the king through the influence of Lady Yarmouth. The influence of Newcastle and Sandwich, however, was too strong for him; he was thwarted and over-reached; and in 1748 he resigned the seals. He declined any knowledge of the *Apology for a late Resignation, in a Letter from an English Gentleman to his Friend at The Hague,* which ran through four editions in 1748, but there is little doubt that he was, at least in part, the author.

The dukedom offered him by George II., whose ill-will his fine tact had overcome, was refused. He continued for some years to attend the Upper House and to take part in its proceedings. In 1751, seconded by Lord Macclesfield, president of the Royal Society, and Bradley, the eminent mathematician, he distinguished himself greatly in the debates on the calendar, and succeeded in making the new style a fact. Deafness, however, was gradually affecting him and he withdrew little by little from society and the practice of politics. In 1755 occurred the famous dispute with Johnson over the dedication to the *English Dictionary.* In 1747 Johnson sent Chesterfield, who was then Secretary of State, a prospectus of his *Dictionary,* which was acknowledged by a subscription of £10. Chesterfield apparently took no further interest in the enterprise, and the book was about to appear when he wrote two papers in the *World* in praise of it. It was said that Johnson was kept waiting in the anteroom when he called while Cibber was admitted. In any case the doctor had expected more help from a professed patron of literature, and wrote the earl the famous letter in defence of men of letters. Chesterfield's "respectable Hottentot," now identified with George, lord Lyttelton, was long supposed, though on slender grounds, to be a portrait of Johnson. During the 20 years of life that followed this episode, Chesterfield wrote and read a great deal, but went little into society.

In 1768 died Philip Stanhope, the child of so many hopes. His death was an overwhelming grief to Chesterfield, and the discovery that he had long been married to a lady of humble origin must have been galling in the extreme to his father after his careful instruction in worldly wisdom. Chesterfield, who had no children by his wife, Melusina von Schulemberg, illegitimate daughter of George I., whom he married in 1733, adopted his godson, a distant cousin, named Philip Stanhope (1755–1815), as heir to the title and estates. His famous jest (which even Johnson allowed to have merit) "Tyrawley and I have been dead these two years, but we don't choose to have it known"—is the best description possible of his humour and condition during the latter part of this period of decline. To the deafness was added blindness, but his memory and his fine manners only left him with life; his last words, "Give Dayrolles a chair," prove that he had neither forgotten his friend nor the way to receive him. He died on March 24, 1773.

As a politician and statesman, Chesterfield's fame rests on his short but brilliant administration of Ireland. As an author he was a clever essayist and epigrammatist. But he stands or falls by the *Letters to his Son,* first published by Stanhope's widow in 1774, and the *Letters to his Godson* (1890). The *Letters* are brilliantly written—full of elegant wisdom, of keen wit, of admirable portrait-painting, of exquisite observation and deduction. Against the charge of an undue insistence on the external graces of manner Chesterfield has been adequately defended by Lord Stanhope (*History,* iii. 34). Against the often iterated accusation of immorality, it should be remembered that the *Letters* reflected the morality of the age, and that their author only systematized and reduced to writing the principles of conduct by which, deliberately or unconsciously, the best and the worst of his contemporaries were governed.

See Chesterfield's *Miscellaneous Works* (2 vols. 1777); *Letters to his Son,* etc. ed. by Lord Mahon (5 vols. 1845–53, re-issued by the Navarre Society in 1926); and *Letters to his Godson* (1890) (ed. by the earl of Carnarvon). There are also eds. of the first series of letters by J. Bradshaw (3 vols. 1892) and Mr. C. Strachey (2 vols. 1901). In 1893 a biography, including numerous letters first pub. from the Newcastle Papers, was issued by Mr. W. Ernst; and in 1907 appeared an elaborate *Life* by W. H. Craig. *See* also *The Letters of Lord Chesterfield to Lord Huntingdon,* with intro. by A. F. Steuart (1923); R. Coxon, *Chesterfield and His Critics,* with selected essays and unpublished letters by Chesterfield (1925).

CHESTERFIELD, a market town and municipal borough in the Chesterfield parliamentary division of Derbyshire, England, 24 mi. N.E. of Derby by the L.M.S.R. and L.N.E.R. Pop. (1938) 64,730. Area 13.2 sq.mi. It is doubtful whether it was a Roman station. Chesterfield (Cestrefeld) owes its present name to the Saxons. It is mentioned in Domesday only as a bailiwick of Newbold. In 1204 John granted to the town all the privileges of a free borough enjoyed by Nottingham and Derby; but before this is seems to have had prescriptive borough rights. In 1598 it was incorporated by Elizabeth under the style of a mayor, six brethren and 12 capital burgesses, and was so governed till the Municipal act, 1835. In 1204 John granted two weekly markets and an annual fair of eight days at the feast of the Exaltation of the Holy Cross (Sept. 14). This fair, which is still held, is mentioned in the *quo warranto* roll of 1330. In 1266 the town was the scene of a battle between the royal forces and the barons. In 1586 it suffered from the plague, and the parliamentary forces were overthrown here during the Civil War.

Chesterfield lies at the junction of the Rother and Hipper, in an industrial district. The church of St. Mary and All Saints belongs principally to the Decorated period. It has a wooden spire, covered with lead, 230 ft. high, and possesses also an apsidal Decorated chapel. The Stephenson Memorial hall (1879) commemorates George Stephenson, the engineer. A new town hall was completed in 1938. The grammar school was founded in 1594. A technical college was opened in 1927. The industries of the town include mining, mechanical engineering, iron and brass founding and tanning. In the neighbourhood are ironstone and coal mines and sandstone quarries. There is also a manufactory of lint, cotton-wool, bandages, etc.

CHESTER-LE-STREET, urban district in the county of Durham, England, near the river Wear, where the latter changes its northward course and turns eastward to the sea. The town is 6 mi. north of Durham on the L. N. E. R. Pop. (1938) 17,080. Area 4.1 sq.mi. Chester-le-Street was a station on a branch of the Roman north road. Under the name of *Cunecastre* it was made the seat of a bishop in 883, and continued to be the head of the diocese until 995. During that time the church was the repository of the shrine of St. Cuthbert, which was then removed to Durham. The church of SS. Mary and Cuthbert has a remarkable series of monumental tombs. The proximity of the Durham coalfield and iron works gives employment to a large section of the population, but dependence upon these industries caused considerable unemployment during the depression of the 1930s.

CHESTERTON, GILBERT KEITH (1874–1936), English journalist and author, was born in London on May 29, 1874. He was educated at St. Paul's school, where, at an unusually early age, he gained the "Milton" prize for English verse. He left school in 1891 with the idea of studying art. But though he early developed, and indeed retained, a talent for draftsmanship of a very distinctive kind, his natural bent was literary, and he went through the usual apprenticeship of free-lance journalism, occasional reviewing and work in a publisher's office.

In 1901 he married Frances Blogg. In 1900 after having produced a volume of poems, *The Wild Knight* (1900), which led good critics to expect great things of him as a poet, he became a regular contributor of signed articles to *The Speaker* and the *Daily News*. From the first he stood out as the protagonist of revolt against the *fin-de-siècle* egotism and the weary omniscience of the previous generation, expressing for it the virile contempt of normal platitudinous man in a style unconventional, swashbuckling and dogmatic. As Addison turned the weapons of fashionable folly against itself by making vice ridiculous, so Chesterton laughed loud and long at the *blasé* self-sufficiency and the dingy little failings of the late Victorian wits. Never was conventionality defended in a manner so unconventional. Hence the legend of Chesterton as a "master of paradox," which originated among older Victorian contemporaries and persisted far longer than it was reasonable to expect, partly perhaps because the subject of the legend was more tickled by it than he need have been. Chesterton's early studies in this vein were reprinted in a series of volumes, *The Defendant* (1901), *Twelve Types* (1902), and *Heretics* (1905). Meanwhile he had laid the foundations of a more enduring reputation as a literary critic by his brilliant study of Browning in the "English Men of Letters" series (*Robert Browning*, 1903). This was followed (1906) by *Charles Dickens*, which has been described as "one of the best critical studies in the language." *Orthodoxy* (1908) and *What's Wrong with the World* (1910) succeeded *Heretics* as essays in religious thought and contemporary politics. To his hatred of the Victorian pessimists there had by now been added a hatred of Victorian economics. He had begun life as an orthodox Liberal but was seized with a growing distrust of the reality of modern party politics, coupled with a fierce dislike of the industrial capitalism which he found dominant in the two old parties. He reacted, however, ultimately as fiercely from Socialism, and, in company with Hilaire Belloc and others, propagated the Distributist theories with which his name is associated.

In fiction his fancy found free play, and the medium was well suited to the expression of his ideas. He produced *The Napoleon of Notting Hill* (1904), a fantastic dream-history of civil wars between the suburbs of London, in which the shattering sanity of romantic man is once more vindicated; *The Club of Queer Trades* (1905), wherein the germs of his later success in detective fiction may be noticed; *The Man Who was Thursday* (1908), and *The Ball and the Cross* (1909). In these works the tendency to commingle his philosophy with his fiction became even greater. An earlier generation than Chesterton's would have called the books allegories, probably with the enthusiastic assent of the author. During the same period Chesterton produced a quantity of verse, some good, some bad—none of it indifferent. At its best it is very good indeed. A well-known English critic once observed of his light verse that, whereas there had been many in all ages who could write comic verse, Chesterton was one of the very few who could write comic poetry. The compliment was deserved. His more serious verse has been held to give him rank as the last of the great rhetorical poets. Like all rhetorical poets he is sometimes tinselly, but his best poems show what rhetoric can be at its best. Of these are "Lepanto" (1911) and "A Song of the Wheels," written during the railway strike of 1911. *The Ballad of the White Horse* (1911) is uneven, but contains some of his finest work.

The year before the World War saw the issue of his *Victorian Age in Literature* (1913), in which he showed that he could write a hand-book without loss of those qualities of penetrating analysis and generous appreciation which he had already brought to the work of literary criticism. An excellent example is the way in which he put the case for Swinburne, a poet with whom fundamentally he had little in common. In the same year he produced *Magic*, a fanciful play in three acts, which was deservedly successful. It is a matter for surprise and regret that he never, until 1927, followed up this initial attempt at play-writing. Detective fiction claimed him for her own, and his "Father Brown" series (1911, 1914, 1926 and 1927) and *The Man Who Knew Too Much* (1922) showed that he could couple even the writing of sensational mystery stuff with an expression of the views which he had made peculiarly his own. *The Flying Inn* (1914) is yet another of his socio-political "allegories," interspersed with what are perhaps the most charming of his light verses, afterwards republished in *Wine, Water and Song* (1915). Another work of the same kind is *Manalive* (1915).

In 1922 an event happened which was of the utmost moment in Chesterton's life. He was received into the Roman Catholic Church. It was the natural result of a spiritual and intellectual development such as his had been; and it cannot be said profoundly to have modified this development, of which it was the outcome. For the student of his works in the future it will not be necessary sharply to divide, as has to be done in some cases, his "Catholic" from his "pre-Catholic" writings. The general doctrines which he was preaching in 1927 he was preaching in 1906. *Charles Dickens* might have been written by a Catholic, and *St. Francis of Assisi* (1923) by the "pre-Catholic" Chesterton.

During the War Chesterton published little of permanent value. His volume of suggestive and brilliant historical essays, called by some strange oversight *A Short History of England* (1917), is most worthy of note. Of his later works, *The Superstition of Divorce* (1920), *The New Jerusalem* (1920), *What I saw in America* (1922), *St. Francis of Assisi* (1923), *William Cobbett* (1925), *The Everlasting Man* (1925), *The Judgment of Dr. Johnson* (1927), *R. L. Stevenson* (1927), *Generally Speaking* (1929), and *The Poet and the Lunatics* (1929) are the chief.

It is difficult in the limits of such an article to appraise Chesterton's work adequately; but it is not difficult to see how his early reaction against the ideals (or lack of ideals) of the materialist civilization of the 19th century led him inevitably to champion the causes, lost or other, which he has championed (and here, be it said, that it is difficult to imagine that any cause is lost when Chesterton is defending it). He objected not so much to the civilization (for him, too, "Romance brought up the 9.15") as to the complacency of those who thought it the only, or the highest, form of civilization. And yet he could appreciate the great Victorians as could few of his contemporaries. The generation after the War returned to Trollope and Wilkie Collins. But it was Chesterton who was showing them the way 15 years earlier. Indeed, it is this quality of appreciating his opponent, which he himself so praises in Pope, which makes the literary Chesterton at once so lovable a personality and so deadly an antagonist.

If a prediction may be ventured, Chesterton will be remembered longest by his poems and his work in literary criticism. Many will regret that he tried his hand so little at play-writing, and spent so much time on polemical journalism. Nearly all will deplore the volume of his output. None will question the reality of his achievement at its highest, or the strength and purity of his influence. He died on June 14, 1936.

See *G. K. Chesterton: a Criticism* (published anonymously, 1908); "A Canterbury Pilgrim" in John Freeman, *English Portraits and Essays* (1924). (E. I. J.)

CHESTERTON, a suburb in the northeast of Cambridge borough, Cambridgeshire, England, on the river Cam. Pop. (1931) about 16,000. The church of St. Andrew is Decorated and Perpendicular, with remains of frescoes. The Cambridge university boat club and the various college boat clubs have boat-houses along the river. Market gardening is carried on in the neighbourhood. Pop. of rural district (est. 1938) 31,080.

CHESTNUT. In its true sense, this name applies only to the genus *Castanea,* which includes the following four species: (1) European chestnut, *C. sativa;* (2) American chestnut, *C. dentata;* (3) Japanese chestnut, *C. crenata,* and (4) Chinese chestnut, *C. mollissima.* Chinkapins also are members of the genus and therefore are closely related to chestnuts. There are a number of hybrids, of which none are well-known.

Chestnuts are deciduous, catkin-bearing trees of much value for many purposes. They produce food for man and many forms of animal life, tannin for the leather industry and firewood of certain value. The largest growers furnish excellent timber, much used for telephone poles, fence rails and posts, railroad ties, mine props, building material and to some extent material for interior finishing, although the grain is coarse and does not take a high polish. All species have remarkable capacity for self-replacement; that is, coppice growth springs up quickly when tops die because of disease or when trees are cut. The wood is outstanding in its resistance to decay either when exposed to weather or when in contact with soil.

There are two kinds of chestnut catkins, some of which are entirely staminate while a few others, in the upper parts of the clusters, have pistillate flowers at the base. Chestnut fruits develop from the latter as single or multiple spiny burs, with the usual number being three. Each normal bur contains three nuts, although here also there are freakish formations. All species thrive best in soils which are acid or neutral rather than strongly alkaline, loose and porous and somewhat dry. The trees are deep-rooted, and while many may die because of drought during the first one or two seasons after being transplanted, once they are well established they endure lack of soil moisture better than most species with which they are commonly associated. All occur in the less severe regions of the north temperate zone somewhat away from the seacoast. They seldom grow at altitudes of more than 4,000 ft. in Europe or the United States, 3,000 ft. in Japan or 8,000 ft. in China. No figures of nut production are available from any country.

The European chestnut is first in economic importance as its indigenous range includes much of southern Europe, northern Africa and southern Asia east to the Caucasus. It has long been grown successfully in England, Scotland, India and Australia. During the 19th century, it became widely established in the eastern parts of the United States and on the Pacific coast. It practically disappeared from the east during the first third of the 20th century, but in 1943 it was still being grown in California and the Pacific northwest. This species is probably the most massive grower of the genus, and few British writers on chestnut trees fail to mention certain individual specimens having tremendous crowns and trunks. The greatest of those so reported appears to have been the largest in a group of huge chestnut trees at the foot of Mount Etna in Sicily; this tree was estimated to have been possibly 2,000 yrs. old when it was finally destroyed by volcanic eruption. It was reported to have had a girth of 204 ft. in 1850.

The European chestnut is the principal source of chestnuts consumed in Europe and the United States. Of an average of 16,085,400 lbs. imported into the United States during the 5-year period ending June 30, 1941, 12,663,600 lbs. yearly came from Italy and 2,921,200 lbs. from Portugal. During the 5-year period ending June 30, 1936, an average of 819,000 lbs. were imported from Spain and 96,000 lbs. from France. The largest European chestnuts are called marrons. These are eaten raw, roasted or boiled. In many regions, chestnuts of secondary sizes are allowed to harden by becoming dry, after which they are ground into flour and substituted for cereals in making soups, breads and other foods. Chestnuts of the smallest sizes are used as food for livestock and wild life.

The American chestnut was once one of the nation's most valuable trees. Its original range extended from southern Maine, west to southeastern Michigan, south and west to southern Illinois, south and east to western Florida and northeast to New England, without reaching the Atlantic coast. It grew thickly over vast stretches of mountain land but thinned out rapidly at lower levels. In forests, trees often grew to 100 ft. in height and in open spaces, trunk diameters of 6–8 ft. were frequent. Maximum diameters of more than 12 ft. are authentic.

Nuts of the American chestnut are usually small in comparison with European chestnuts and less attractive in appearance because of being partially or completely covered by a gray tomentum. Among true chestnuts, however, the flavour of the American chestnut is equalled only by the Chinese chestnut, which rivals it closely. A number of varieties were named during the last decade of the 19th century, but only one—Hathaway of Michigan—was propagated to any extent.

Trees of both American and European species were largely killed throughout the entire east during the period 1900–35 by chestnut blight, a virulent fungus disease (*Endothia parasitica*) which was inadvertently introduced into the United States from the orient at the beginning of the century. Early efforts at control were made but with no practical success.

The Japanese chestnut is indigenous to Japan and Chosen. In the former country, chestnuts were important articles of food probably as early as 1700. The tree is usually a small grower, but heights of 60 ft. and trunk diameters of 3 ft. are on record. As most commonly known in the United States, where the species was introduced in 1876, the trees are precocious and prolific, and the nuts attractive in appearance, but rarely of fine texture or best flavour. Their eating qualities are much improved by boiling or roasting.

The Chinese chestnut grows to about the same size as the Japanese. Records show that it was introduced into the United States as early as 1853, but large importation and distribution of seed did not begin until the U. S. Department of Agriculture became active in this field in 1906. Between that time and the outbreak of World War II, many importations were made, and the species became well established in many quarters. The seedling trees vary greatly in form and general habit of growth, some being squat and awkward while others are tall and erect. Many are of intermediate form and therefore of the shape most desired by orchardists. As a rule the nuts are not so large as Europeans but they are of attractive, glossy appearance and very sweet. This chestnut appears to offer considerable inducement to conservative planters. The leading varieties are Bartlett, Carr, Hobson, Milford, Reliance, Stoke, Yankee and Zimmerman.

Chinkapin plants range from low shrubs to large trees, some species of which occasionally reach a height of 90 ft. The group differs from that of the chestnut mainly in that the nuts are small and single in the bur, and the burs form in racemes instead of clusters. Six species are known in the United States from middle Pennsylvania southward and two in China. (C. A. Rd.)

CHETTLE, HENRY (*c.* 1560–1607), English dramatist. In 1592 he published Robert Greene's *Groatsworth of Wit.* In the preface to his *Kind Herts Dreame* (end of 1592) he admits his editorship of that pamphlet, and incidentally he apologized to three persons (one of them commonly identified with Shakespeare) who had been abused in it. As early as 1598 Francis Meres includes him in his *Palladis Tamia* as one of the "best for comedy," and between that year and 1603 he wrote or collaborated in some 48 pieces. Of the plays usually attributed to Chettle's sole authorship only one was printed. This was *The Tragedy of Hoffmann: or a Revenge for a Father* (played 1602; printed 1631), a share in which Mr. Fleay assigns to Thomas Heywood. It has been suggested that this piece was put forward as a rival to Shakespeare's *Hamlet. The Pleasant Comedie of Patient Grissill* (1599), in which he collaborated with Thomas Dekker and William Haughton, was reprinted by the Shakespeare society in 1841. In Nov. 1599 Chettle received ten shillings for mending the first part of "Robin Hood," *i.e. The Downfall of Robert, Earl of Huntingdon,* by Anthony Munday; and in the second part, which followed soon after and was printed in the year 1601, *The Death of Robert, Earle of Huntingdon,* he collaborated with Munday. Both plays are printed in Dodsley's *Select Collection of Old English Plays* (edited by W. C. Hazlitt, volume viii). Chettle died before the appearance of Dekker's *Knight's*

Conjuring in 1607, for he is there mentioned as a recent arrival in limbo.

Hoffmann was edited by H. B(arrett) L(ennard) (1852), by Richard Ackermann (Bamberg, 1894), and J. S. Farmer in *Old English Plays, Students' Facsimile Edition* (1913).

CHETWODE, PHILIP WALHOUSE CHETWODE, 1ST BARON (1869–1950), British soldier, was born Sept. 21, 1869, and in 1889 was commissioned to the 19th Hussars from the militia. He saw active service in Burma and South Africa, and later became assistant military secretary to Sir John French at Aldershot. In 1905 he succeeded his father as 7th baronet. Promoted to the command of the 5th cavalry brigade in May 1914, his brigade accompanied the expeditionary force to France and helped to cover the retreat from Mons, bringing off at Cérizy one of the rare cavalry charges of World War I. He went to Egypt to command the desert column in 1916, and won distinction by the decisive surprise attack at Rafah, which finally freed Sinai from the Turks. After the second battle of Gaza in April 1917 he succeeded Gen. Dobell in command of the whole eastern force. When Gen. Allenby came out to take over the supreme command he based his plan on Chetwode's plans, and the latter, commanding the 20th army corps after the reorganization of the forces, played a distinguished part in the advance to Jerusalem and in the crowning victory in Sept. 1918. In Sept. 1920 Chetwode succeeded Gen. Harington as deputy chief of the imperial staff, and two years later became adjutant general to the forces. He was commander-in-chief of the army in India from 1930 to 1935. Sir Philip was gazetted field marshal in 1933. He was created baron in 1945. He died in London July 6, 1950.

CHEVALIER, ALBERT (1861–1923), English music-hall artist, began his connection with the variety stage while still a child. In 1869 he appeared at a "penny-reading" at Cornwall Hall, Notting Hill. After a brief experience as a clerk in a newspaper office, and as a pupil teacher, he appeared for a short time in 1877 with the Kendals and the Bancrofts. For some time he played "legitimate" parts with Hare (*q.v.*), Willie Edouin and others, and during his association with Edouin (1888–89) at the Strand theatre he introduced in burlesque his first cockney song, "Our 'armonic Club." The year 1891 was the turning point of his career, when he deserted the "legitimate" stage and appeared at the London Pavilion as a music-hall entertainer. Thereafter he speedily won the place to which his genius entitled him, among the first artistes of his generation. He toured throughout Great Britain and the United States, and in addition gave over 1,000 special recitals at the small Queen's Hall. As singer, composer or part composer, his name is associated with between 70 and 80 songs. In addition he wrote some 14 plays and sketches. In 1906 he appeared with Yvette Guilbert at the Duke of York's theatre, and in the name part of Sir James Barrie's *Pantaloon.* His last appearance was in Nov. 1922, in a play, *My Old Dutch,* written by himself and Arthur Shirley on the basis of his own famous song. He died on July 10, 1923. Chevalier's best known songs are: "Mrs. 'Enery 'Awkins," "Knocked 'em in the Old Kent Road," "My Old Dutch," "A Fallen Star," "Our Little Nipper," "Fair Flo." He wrote two records of his own experiences, *Before I Forget* (1901), and *Uninitiated* (1906).

In his own special line Chevalier is generally recognized as being an artist of the first rank. While not possessing the vast range of a Marie Lloyd, he yet developed his own specialty as it had never before been developed, and presented real character sketches of the life of the people, emphasizing the grave as well as the gay and bringing tears as readily as laughter. Subsequent cockney comedians have imitated his humour. None has even endeavoured to compete with him in the delineation of the pathetic. Another striking feature of his songs was the tuneful and haunting melodies to which they were set. This was a real feature of the music-hall stage in an era when the comedian tended to sing his patter to the baldest of extemporizations. (E. I. J.)

CHEVALIER, MICHEL (1806–1879), French economist, was born at Limoges. In his early manhood, while employed as an engineer, he became a convert to the theories of Saint-Simon; these he ardently advocated in the *Globe,* the organ of the Saint Simonians, which he edited until his arrest in 1832 on a charge of outraging public morality by its publication. He was sentenced to a year's imprisonment, but was released in six months through the intervention of Thiers, who sent him on a special mission to the United States to study the question of land and water transport. In 1836 he published the letters he wrote from America to the *Journal des Débats,* as *Lettres sur l'Amérique du Nord,* and in 1838 published *Des intérêts matériels de la France.* In 1850 he became a member of the Institute, and in 1851 published his *Examen du système commercial connu sous le nom de système protecteur.* He played an important part in bringing about the conclusion of the Cobden commercial treaty between France and Great Britain in 1860. He became a member of the Senate in 1860.

Among his other works are: *Cours d'économie politique* (1842–50); *Essais de politique industrielle* (1843); *De la baisse probable d'or* (1859, translated into English by Cobden, *On the Probable Fall of the Value of Gold,* Manchester, 1859); *L'Expédition du Mexique* (1862); *Introduction aux rapports du jury international* (1868).

CHEVALIER, ULYSSE (1841–1923), French bibliographer, was born at Rambouillet on Feb. 24, 1841. He published a great number of documents relating to the history of Dauphiné, *e.g.,* the cartularies of the church and the town of Die (1868), of the abbey of St. André-le-Bas at Vienne (1869), of the abbey of Notre Dame at Bonnevaux in the diocese of Vienne (1889), of the abbey of St. Chaffre at Le Monestier (1884), the inventories and several collections of archives of the dauphins of Viennais, and a *Bibliothèque liturgique* in six volumes (1893–97), the third and fourth volumes of which constitute the *Repertorium hymnologicum,* containing more than 20,000 articles. But his principal work is the *Répertoire des sources historiques du moyen âge.*

The first part of the *Répertoire, bio-bibliographie* (1877–78; 2nd ed., 1905), contains the names of all the historical personages alive between the years 1 and 1500 who are mentioned in printed books, together with the precise indication of all the places where they are mentioned. The second part, *Topo-bibliographie* (1894–1903), contains not only the names of places mentioned in books on the history of the middle ages, but, in a general way, everything not included in the *Bio-bibliographie.* The *Répertoire* is one of the most important bibliographical monuments ever devoted to the study of mediaeval history.

CHEVALIER, literally, a horseman. In feudal times the term was equivalent to knight (*see* KNIGHTHOOD AND CHIVALRY), and later it was also employed in France for the cadets of noble families, where it is still used for the lowest rank of certain orders, as Chevalier of the Legion of Hanover. The appellation of *Chevalier of St. George* was given to James Stuart, son of James II., the Old Pretender, and that of *The Young Chevalier* to Prince Charles Edward Stuart, the Young Pretender. The Seigneur de Bayard (*q.v.*) was known as the *Chevalier sans peur et sans reproche.*

CHEVAUX-DE-FRISE, a military obstacle, originating apparently in the Dutch War of Independence, and used to close the breach of a fortress, streets (French for "Friesland horses"; the Dutch *Vriesse ruyters,* "Frisian horsemen," and German *Spanische Reiter,* "Spanish horsemen"), etc. It was formerly often used in field operations as a defence against cavalry; hence the name, as the Dutch were weak in the mounted arm and had therefore to check the enemy's cavalry by an artificial obstacle. Chevaux-de-frise form an obstacle about 4 feet high, made of beams in which are fixed a number of spears, sword-blades, etc., with the points projecting outwards on all sides.

CHEVERUS, JEAN LEFEBVRE DE (1768–1836), French ecclesiastic, was born on Jan. 28, 1768, in Mayenne, France. He was made canon of the cathedral of Le Mans and began to act as vicar to his uncle in Mayenne, but owing to the Revolution he emigrated in 1792 to England, and thence in 1796 to Boston (Mass.). He spent several months in the Penobscot and Passamaquoddy missions and visited scattered Catholics. During the epidemic of yellow fever in 1798 he won great praise for his courage and charity; and his preaching attracted many

Protestants. In 1808 the pope made Boston a bishopric, suffragan to Baltimore, and Cheverus its bishop. Ill-health caused him to resign his bishopric and in 1823, Louis XVIII having insisted on his return to France, Cheverus became bishop of Montauban. He was made archbishop of Bordeaux in 1826; and in Feb. 1836, in accordance with the wish of Louis Philippe, he was made a cardinal, only five months before his death, which took place in Bordeaux on July 19, 1836.

See J. Huen-Dubourg, *Vie du cardinal de Cheverus* (Bordeaux, 1838); Eng. version by E. Stewart (Boston, 1839).

CHEVÉ SYSTEM. A method of teaching music to children in wide use in France. It is somewhat akin to the Tonic Sol-fa system, being based, like that, on the principle of a movable tonic as opposed to the older "fixed Do" method, but employs numerals for the written signs of the different notes instead of the sol-fa syllables, although the latter are retained for vocal purposes. The system was invented by a French mathematical professor, Pierre Galin (1786–1821); developed and advocated by one of his followers, Aimé Paris (1798–1866); and perfected and popularized, after much controversy and opposition, by the latter's brother-in-law, Émile Joseph Maurice Chevé (1804–64).

CHEVET, in architecture, the entire eastern termination of a church choir (*q.v.*), a term used especially for churches with apses (*q.v.*); also an ambulatory (*q.v.*) from which a series of radiating chapels open. It is a distinctly French development, appearing in a highly organized form in many 12th-century Romanesque churches; *e.g.*, Notre Dame du Port, Clermont-Ferrand and St. Paul, Issoire. It resulted from attempts to place as many subsidiary altars in chapels as possible, in close association with the high altar and the procession path around it. The development of the chevet produced many spaces of unusual shape whose vaulting was one of the great incentives toward the evolution of the ribbed and pointed vault; the chevet, therefore, plays an important part in the transition from Romanesque to Gothic. The radiating chapels are usually uneven in number, and the central one is frequently much larger than the others, dedicated to the Virgin Mary and known as the Lady chapel.

CHEVIOT, an incorporated city of Hamilton county, O., U.S., adjoining Cincinnati to the west, on the Chesapeake and Ohio railway. Pop. (1950) 9,944. It is a residential suburb. The village was incorporated in 1901. It was laid out in 1818 by John Craig, Sr., and was named after his native Cheviot hills of Scotland. It was first settled in 1805 by Enoch Carson.

CHEVIOT CLOTH. A woollen fabric made originally from the wool of the well-known breed of Cheviot sheep, and now made from other types of wool. Cheviot wool possesses good spinning qualities, since the staple is of a fine, soft and pliable character. The true Cheviot type of fabric has a crispness of texture similar to serge cloth (*q.v.*) except that it is of a slightly rougher and heavier type. Cheviot fabric may be produced either from woollen or worsted yarns according to the character and texture or feel desired in the finished fabric. Some qualities are produced from cross-bred worsted yarns which are adapted for furnishing the crispness of texture which is one of the distinguishing characteristics of the true Cheviot type of fabric. Cheviot suitings for sports wear are made from the harder spun worsted yarns, while some qualities are also made from Botany worsted. So-called cheviot suitings of inferior quality contain an admixture of cotton, while other low-grade cheviots are weighted with flocks. A stout, twilled, cotton fabric made from cotton warp and weft of coarse counts of yarn and woven with small dobby patterns or with fancy warp stripes, of brown or blue, with bleached weft, is also described as cheviot shirting. (H. N.)

CHEVIOT HILLS, a range forming about 35 mi. of the border between England and Scotland. The boundary generally follows the line of greatest elevation, but as the slope is more gradual southward than northward the larger part of the range is in Northumberland, Eng., and the lesser in Roxburghshire, Scot. The axis runs from northeast to southwest, with a northward tendency at the eastern end where the ridge culminates in the Cheviot, 2,676 ft. Its chief elevations from this point southwestward fall abruptly to 2,034 ft. in Windygate hill, and then more gradually to about 1,600 ft. above the pass, followed by a high road from Redesdale. Beyond this are Carter Fell (1,815 ft.) and Peel Fell (1,975 ft.), after which two lines of lesser elevation branch westward and southward to enclose Liddesdale. The rocks include Silurian, Old Red Sandstone (with lavas) and Carboniferous strata, and the hills are finely grouped, of conical and high-arched forms, and generally grass covered. Their flanks are scored with deep narrow glens in every direction, carrying the headwaters of the Till, Coquet and North Tyne on the south, and tributaries of the Tweed on the north. The range is famous for a valuable breed of sheep. It was the scene of many episodes of border warfare, and its name is associated with the ballad of *Chevy Chase.* The main route into Scotland from England lies along the low coastal belt east of the Till; the Till itself provided another and Redesdale a third. There are numerous ruins of castles and forts on the English side in this district.

CHEVRON, any ornament formed of two slanting lines meeting at an angle. In heraldry it is a bent bar. It is also one of the most common distinguishing marks for military and naval uniforms, where it is placed on the sleeves and serves either as a mark of honour or to indicate a special function. In architecture, the term is sometimes applied to the angle formed by the meeting rafters of a roof, but it is more commonly used for the purely decorative form. Chevrons joined together zigzag are one of the commonest of Romanesque geometric ornaments, especially in areas under Norman influence. It is a frequent decoration for arch mouldings and column shafts. The chevron appears early in primitive work and is found on pottery all over the world. It also occurs frequently in textiles, on Egyptian walls and ceilings and in Aegean art as a column decoration; *e.g.*, Tholos of Atreus at Mycenae, *c.* 1200 B.C. (For military use *see* INSIGNIA, MILITARY.)

CHEVROTAIN or MOUSE DEER, the representatives of the family Tragulidae. These tiny animals are not true deer, but constitute a special section of artiodactyles known as Tragulina (*see* ARTIODACTYLA). The typical genus, *Tragulus,* which is Asiatic, contains the smallest representatives of the family, the animals having more of the general aspects and habits of rodents than of ruminants. A number of species are known, inhabiting the Malay peninsula, the Malay archipelago, Ceylon and India. The second genus, *Hyemoschus,* is African, and distinguished by the feet being stouter and shorter, the outer toes better developed and the two middle metacarpals not welded together. The only existing species, *H. aquaticus,* is larger than any of the Asiatic chevrotains, which it otherwise resembles, but is said to frequent banks of streams and have much the habits of pigs. It is rich brown, spotted and striped with white. Remains of a form chiefly differing in size (*Dorcatherium*) have been found in the Miocene deposits of France.

BY COURTESY OF THE LONDON ZOOLOGICAL SOCIETY

CHEVROTAIN, OR MOUSE DEER, A TINY ANIMAL ABOUT THE SIZE OF A RABBIT

CHEWING GUM. Chewing gum is a confection product prepared from chicle and similar resilient substances, combined with sweetening and flavouring. For many centuries past, the Mayans and other Central Americans chewed chicle, the coagulated milky juice (latex) of the sapodilla tree, just as people in many lands chewed various resins, leaves and grasses for relaxation and enjoyment. From the Indians of New England, the American colonists learned to chew spruce tree resins, and spruce gum was marketed in the United States in the early 1800s as the first commercial chewing gum. Later, chewing gum made of paraffin wax was introduced. In the 1860s, the use of chicle as a chewing gum base was developed. Its resilient chewing quality and ability to carry flavours won preference for this type of gum and paved the way for the major rise in the popularity of chewing gum which began in the early 1900s with the advent of modern processing, packaging and promotional methods.

Modern chewing gum consists, by weight, of approximately 20% gum base, 19% corn syrup, 60% sugar and 1% flavouring. To insure uniform chewing texture, gum base may be blended of as many as 25 latex products and like materials. The latex products are obtained from trees growing wild in tropical forests. The trees are tapped with grooved cuts from which the latex flows into containers. The latex is then collected, boiled down and moulded into blocks. Chicle from Central America, leche caspi and sorva from the Amazon valley, and jelutong from British Borneo and Indonesia, are principal types of latex products used. Synthesized preparations having similar properties, such as vinyl resins and microcrystalline waxes, have been developed for use in combination with the tropical latex products. In the manufacturing process, the gum base ingredients are washed, ground, sterilized and blended. In mixing kettles, the melted base is combined with corn syrup, sugar and flavouring. The doughlike mixture is then rolled into sheets, and divided into sticks or pellets. Essential oils from mint plants—peppermint and spearmint—provide the two leading flavours. In food content, one stick of gum contains nine calories.

The use of chewing gum rises in periods of social tension, and it increased rapidly during and after World Wars I and II. In the United States annual per capita consumption went from 39 sticks in 1914 to 89 in 1924; from 98 in 1939 to 165 in 1953. In the latter year, there were 109 chewing gum factories in the world, located in 31 countries. Of these, 33 were in the United States and 10 in Great Britain. The English-speaking and Latin-American countries are the largest chewing gum consumers. Second to the United States in per capita consumption is Canada.

(P. H. E.)

CHEYENNE. This Algonkin tribe of the Great Plains, in Minnesota in the 17th century, drifted gradually westward and is now on reservations in Montana and Oklahoma. Their speech is closer than either Blackfoot or Arapaho to the central Algonkin dialects, so that their divergence from the main body of the family is evidently relatively late. After about 1850 the Sutaio, speaking a Cheyenne dialect, were part of the tribe, though in 1804 they were still separate. The Cheyenne took a leading part in the Custer massacre of 1876. They were a typical plains tribe—brave, warlike, nonagricultural, roving after buffalo or for adventure; they show the physical type at its best, being perhaps the tallest tribe in the area. The tribal fetish was a set of four sacred arrows. In 1945 the population was 4,815.

See Mooney, *Am. Anthr. Assoc. Mem.*, vol. i (1907); George Bird Grinnell, *The Cheyenne Indians*, 2 vol. (New Haven, 1923).

CHEYENNE, capital of Wyoming, U.S., and county seat of Laramie county; near the southeast corner of the state, on rolling plains east of the Laramie range, at an altitude of 6,062 ft. It is on federal highways 30, 85 and 87; is served by the Burlington, the Colorado and Southern and the Union Pacific railways; and is an important point on transcontinental air lines. Pop. (1950) 31,935; (1940) 22,474. The Union Pacific has extensive shops there, and there are meat-packing plants, brickyards and various other industries. The city is a supply point for an extensive grazing and dry-farming area, and ships quantities of cattle. The Frontier Days celebration, held for five days each summer, is a festival at which Indians, cowboys and plainsmen from Canada to Texas gather to give exhibitions of bronco busting, steer tying, Indian dances and other characteristic features of life in the old "wild west." Just northwest is Fort F. E. Warren and its manoeuvre reserve of 52,000 ac. Cheyenne was founded in 1867, when the Union Pacific reached the spot. It was made the capital of the state and was incorporated in 1869.

CHÉZY, ANTOINE LÉONARD DE (1773–1832), French orientalist, born at Neuilly on Jan. 15, 1773. He was the first occupant of the chair of Sanskrit in the Collège Royal de France (1815), at that time the only chair of Sanskrit in Europe. Among his works were *Medjnoun et Leila* (1807), from the Persian; *Yadjnadatta-badha* (1814) and *La Reconnaissance de Sacountala* (1830), from the Sanskrit; *L'Anthologie érotique d' Amarou* (1831), published under the pseudonym A. L. Apudy.

See the *Memoires* of the Académie des Inscriptions (new series, vol. xii), where there is a notice of Chézy by Silvestre.

CHHATARPUR, a town and district of Vindhya Pradesh, India. The town (pop. 1941, 13,210) is 70 mi. by road southwest of Banda on the Gwalior-Allahabad railway line; it was named after Chhatar Sal, the founder of Bundelkhand independence, and contains his cenotaph. Paper and coarse cutlery are manufactured. The town is the seat of a college of Agra university.

CHHATARPUR DISTRICT absorbed on Jan. 1, 1950, the former princely state of Chhatarpur (area 1,170 sq.mi.; pop. 1941, 184,720), which during British rule had been in the Bundelkhand subagency of the Central India agency. The population of the district was 481,140 according to the 1951 census. The state was founded in the 18th century by Kunwar Sone Sah, a Rajput of the Ponwar clan. On the establishment of British supremacy in Bundelkhand he received a *sanad* in 1806 confirming him in the possession of his state. In 1854 it would have lapsed to the British government for want of direct heirs but, in 1862, because of the loyalty of the Chhatarpur chiefs during the mutiny, it was conferred on Jagat Ray. (C. C. D.)

CHHATTISGARH, a natural region of south-central India, an administrative division of Madhya Pradesh and a former states agency. Chhattisgarh is a huge, undulating laterite plain, treeless except for the mango groves planted by generations of villagers round the village sites. The formation of the country and the soil are distinct from all other parts of Madhya Pradesh. On the crests of the undulations the red laterite, locally known as *bhata*, comes to the surface. In the depressions between these crests is black soil, gradually turning to brown and then to yellow as the ground rises. The Mahanadi river flows north and east across the division on its way to the Bay of Bengal.

In the past Chhattisgarh was remote and isolated, being shut off by the Maikal range from the Nagpur division on the west and by miles of hills and forests in the wilder states bordering it on the north, east and south. This isolation allowed a very ancient dynasty, the Hai Hai Bansis of Raipur and Ratanpur, to remain undisturbed for about seven centuries, but in 1743 Maratha forces took the country without a blow. (For its history thereafter *see* CENTRAL PROVINCES AND BERAR.) The division now comprises six districts: Bastar, Bilaspur, Drug (Durg), Raigarh, Raipur and Sirguja (Surguja).

Aboriginals occupied the hilly and jungly surroundings of the great plain. The open country is populated by Hindu castes and outcasts, of whom the Chamars, originally leatherworkers but now cultivators, in the 19th century under reforming leaders revolted against the oppression of the Brahmins and high-caste Hindus. The "Satnami" Chamars, as they are called, worshippers of the "true Name" (Satnam) are monotheists and total abstainers from alcohol, some sections also prohibiting tobacco. They freely slaughter cattle and have other customs repugnant to Hindus; between Chamars and Hindus there is hereditary hostility. There are also in Chhattisgarh many disciples of the saint Kabir (Kabirpanthis; *q.v.*), but this sect is not peculiar to the division.

The division covers an area of 40,434 sq.mi. and had a population in 1951 of 6,408,524. Satnami Chamars number nearly 500,000; Hindus proper and animists preponderate. The Chhattisgarh peasant (ryot) speaks a corrupt dialect of Hindi, akin to the dialect of Baghelkhand.

The laterite ridges of Chhattisgarh are either barren or produce nothing but catch crops of coarse rice when the rains are favourable. The depressions between are more fertile and often rich. The rich soils also are mainly under rice, but produce a second crop of pulses and oilseeds if the late rains are propitious. The western part of the plain produces a fair amount of wheat and cold-weather field crops.

The great rice crop of Chhattisgarh was once almost at the mercy of a droughty season, being broadcasted and unirrigated. It is a country with thousands of shallow village tanks unsuited for irrigation, wells are comparatively few and tank water is used indiscriminately for men and cattle, both for drinking and washing purposes. Wells are sparingly used, even when constructed at the expense of public funds, as the water is pronounced "tasteless." As a consequence, cholera is likely to be rife in the hot season and at its worst in times of drought and famine. The railway and government irrigation works have worked wonders in improving the country, and education has made considerable though slow progress. Chhattisgarh has often been described as one of the granaries of India, but lack of irrigation, rough cultivation and excessive fragmentation of holdings, whereby one man holds numbers of tiny, scattered rice plots instead of compact holdings, has resulted in precarious and most uneconomical agriculture. Many storage tanks have been constructed by the government in Raipur and Drug districts and a few in Bilaspur, and after 1914 two major works, the Mahanadi and Tendula canals enabled very large areas to receive protection. Large works were also constructed at Bilaspur, but the people are very slow in learning how to utilize irrigation to the best purpose.

Under British paramountcy the Chhattisgarh States Agency, a subagency of the Eastern States Agency, comprised Bastar, Chhuikhadan, Jashpur, Kalahandi, Kanker (Kankar), Kawardha, Khairagarh, Korea, Patna, Raigarh, Sakti, Sirguja, Changbhakar, Nandgaon, Sarangarh and Udaipur states. Following the independence of India, Kalahandi and Patna were merged with Orissa state and the remainder with Madhya Pradesh on Jan. 1, 1948. The total area of the subagency was 37,688 sq.mi.; total pop. (1941) 4,050,000. The headquarters of the states agency, like those of the division, were at Raipur.

CHHINDWARA, a town and district in the Nagpur division of Madhya Pradesh, India. The town (pop., 1951, 27,652), 64 mi. N.N.W. of Nagpur, is the district headquarters and a market town with small local industries; situated on the Satpura plateau about 2,000 ft. above sea level, it is a pleasant place with a fairly temperate climate. It is connected by the Central railway with Betul, Nagpur and Jubbulpore.

Chhindwara District (area 7,794 sq.mi.) had a population in 1951 of 1,080,491; about 75% were Hindus and most of the rest Gonds and other aboriginal tribes. In the north of the district, bordering the Mahadeo range and Hoshangabad district, are hills rising to about 3,000 ft. and containing some sal forest. The rugged country immediately south of the hills constitutes the *Jagirs* or feudal estates of the Gond chiefs, who once preyed upon travellers and raided the open country on their borders. South of the *Jagirs* is the more level Satpura plateau, extending from Betul in the west to Seoni in the east and drained by the Pench and Kanhan rivers. The southern and eastern parts of the plateau include the fertile wheat plain of Chaurai. On the south again the country drops into the Nagpur plain, to which it geographically belongs. This is a rich cotton and *jowar* (big millet) area and is the richest and most populous part of the district; the language of the area is Marathi. On the southeast the plateau, here called the Lahmarpani, projects into the plain, and this part is noted for its breed of cattle. The lowlands of the district are hot and the uplands have a temperate climate. There are fairly extensive coal fields to the north of Chhindwara, connected by narrow-gauge railway with that town and by broad-gauge line with Betul. In the south, near the Nagpur district border, are valuable deposits of manganese.

CHIABRERA, GABRIELLO (1552–1638), Italian poet, was born at Savona, It. He studied philosophy at the Jesuits' college in Rome and entered the household of a cardinal. He mixed in the literary society of his day, but presently was drawn into a quarrel which compelled him to leave Rome. He retired to Savona, where he read Pindar and Anacreon and, no doubt, Pierre de Ronsard. He determined to enrich Italian poetry with new forms, and his imitations from the classics include some successful innovations in Italian verse, which were adopted by the lyrists of the next century. The mass of Chiabrera's work is great: epics, pastorals, odes, lyrics, satires, dramas and religious and didactic poems. His best poetry, however, is to be found not in his more ambitious works but in his gracefully musical *canzonette,* described as *anacreontiche.* His autobiographical sketch is also extremely interesting. The simple old poet, with his adoration of Greek (when a thing pleased him greatly he was wont to talk of it as "Greek poetry"), his delight in journeys and sightseeing, his dislike for literary talk save with intimates and equals, his vanities and vengeances, his pride in the memory of favours bestowed on him by popes and princes and his quiet Christianity, is a figure deserving perhaps of more study than is likely to be bestowed on his work in grafting a new Hellenic style onto Italian poetry or on that "new world" of art which he fancied his own.

Bibliography.—Editions of Chiabrera's works are those of Rome, 3 vol. (1718), of Venice, 4 vol. (1730), of Leghorn, 5 vol. (1781), and of Milan, 3 vol. (1807). *See* also G. Taccetta, *Gabriello Chiabrera e la sua produzione epica* (Catania, 1921); F. Neri, *Il Chiabrera e la Pléiade française* (Turin, 1920); F. L. Mannucci, *La Lirica di G. C.* (Naples, 1925); E. N. Girardi, *Esperienza e poesia di Gabriello Chiabrera* (Milan, 1950).

CHIANA (anc. Clanis), a river which rises in the Apennines south of Arezzo, It., runs through the valley of Chiusi and, after receiving the Paglia just below Orvieto, falls into the Tiber after a course of 60 mi. In Roman times it often caused floods in the valley of Clusium. In the middle ages the whole of its valley from Arezzo to Chiusi was an uninhabitable swamp; but at the end of the 18th century the engineer Count Fossombroni moved the watershed about 25 mi. farther south, so its waters now flow partly into the Arno and partly into the Tiber.

CHIANG KAI-SHEK (or Chiang Chieh-shih; Chiang Chung-sheng) (1887–), Chinese soldier and statesman, was born in a village near Ningpo, not far from Shanghai, in the province of Chekiang. He was thus a native of southeast China, where the inhabitants differ somewhat from the other Chinese as regards both culture and language. Chiang's forebears were middle-class farmers and merchants, but he early decided upon a military career. In spite of his southern background he was accepted as a cadet in the newly established Paoting Military academy. In 1907 he was sent by the Chinese imperial government to Japan to complete his military education. While in Japan Chiang came under the influence of some Chinese expatriates, Cantonese for the most part, who were followers of the radical revolutionary leader Sun Yat-sen.

When the Chinese revolution broke out in 1911, Chiang secretly made his way back to China to aid the revolutionary cause. Though the revolution was successful, Chiang gained nothing personally, as he remained loyal to the group led by Sun Yat-sen, which was soon ousted from all governmental posts in the new republic headed by Yuan Shih-k'ai. In the years which followed, Sun continued to agitate against the new regime in the hope of establishing a more radical type of government. For some time Chiang remained a minor and rather obscure military official in the employ of Sun's revolutionary group, now known as the Kuomintang or Nationalist party. By 1920, however, most of Chiang's immediate superiors were either dead or in disgrace, and Chiang became one of Sun's most trusted and influential assistants. By this time Sun, though not a Communist, had decided to work in close co-operation with the Soviet government. On his order Chiang made a brief visit to Russia to study the Soviet military organization and on his return to China was made head of the Whampoa Military academy for the training of officers for the revolutionary or Kuomintang army. Whampoa was near Canton, which by this time had passed under Kuomintang control. Chiang soon became suspicious of the Russians, but they continued to exert strong influence over both the Whampoa academy and the higher echelons of the Kuomintang army. For a time it looked as if the Russian agents Michael Borodin and B. K. Galen would become the real leaders of the revolutionary movement, but Chiang managed to keep some check upon their powers.

In 1925 Sun Yat-sen died, and Chiang soon became recognized as one of Sun's principal political heirs. He secured the appointment as commander in chief of the Kuomintang army. By the end of the year he had brought the whole of Kwangtung and Kwangsi provinces under the control of the Kuomintang executive committee. In 1926 Chiang made his amazing advance northward through Hunan to the Yangtze river. In the following months the Kuomintang secured control over all the important cities in the Yangtze valley. This great military success was marred by internal dissensions. The Kuomintang had long included a number of different groups and cliques; the two most important were a left-wing group willing to follow Russian Communist leadership, and a right-wing group which demanded social and economic change but which was definitely anticommunist and looked to Chiang for leadership. In 1927, after lengthy political and military manoeuvres, the right-wing or Chiang group won control over the party organization. The Soviet agents were sent back to the U.S.S.R. and a national capital was set up at Nanking, where Chiang had established military control. Some party leaders continued to express dissatisfaction, however, and in Aug. 1927 he announced his resignation, though he continued to play an active role behind the scenes.

While still in his teens Chiang had married a girl from his native village. He had long since divorced her, though retaining custody of the two sons born of this marriage. In 1927, while still in nominal retirement, Chiang was married for a second time, to Soong Mei-ling, sister-in-law of Sun Yat-sen, thus further identifying himself with the constitutional element in the Kuomintang. Eventually, through his wife's influence, Chiang was persuaded to become a Christian, joining the Methodist Church.

As he had anticipated, all sections of the Kuomintang soon felt the need of Chiang's military leadership, and in 1928 internal differences were glossed over and Chiang was recalled to serve as commander in chief (or generalissimo) of the revolutionary army, and thereafter he remained in effective control of the Kuomintang government, though at some periods he was content with real power and permitted other persons to assume nominal leadership. In 1928 the Kuomintang army again drove north and this time succeeded in capturing Peking, the ancient capital. By this action China was, in name, reunited under a single government. In point of fact, however, even when Chiang was at the height of his power the Kuomintang never had effective control over the whole of China. In some of the outlying provinces semi-independent war lords remained in power, though such men were persuaded to join the party and in theory ruled as deputies of the Kuomintang government. More serious trouble came from the Communists.

After the collapse of the left-wing branch of the Kuomintang, a few fanatical Chinese Communists, led by Mao Tse-tung determined to establish a state and a government of their own, and as time went on they were joined by an appreciable number of disgruntled intellectuals and dissatisfied peasants. At first Communist activity centred in a small area of southeastern China, but in 1935 the Communists migrated in a body to northwestern China, where the terrain was more defensible and where it was easier to maintain contact with the Russians.

For a time the most serious threat to Chiang's government came from the Japanese. In 1931 Japan seized control of Manchuria and in the following years seriously threatened other portions of northeastern China. In consequence there was considerable pressure on Chiang to cease all operations against the Communists and even to join with them in opposing the Japanese. Affairs reached a head in Dec. 1936 with the "kidnapping" of Chiang by Chang Hsüeh-liang, with the idea of forcing Chiang to join the Communists in a united front. Chiang was subsequently released without making any commitments, but for several years thereafter the Nationalists and the Communists had a tacit understanding that the major effort of both groups would be concentrated on the common enemy. These efforts were not successful. In 1937 Japan began a major war on China and won a number of important victories, occupying most of eastern China. Chiang was forced after several moves to locate his capital in Chungking in the far west. Chiang was now in a desperate condition, but he refused to come to terms with the invaders. His position was greatly helped by the entrance of the United States into the Pacific war in Dec. 1941. Japan's surrender in 1945 removed one major threat to Chiang's regime, and the Kuomintang was soon able to reoccupy a large portion of China.

Attempts were then made at political reform, and a new democratic constitution was adopted in 1946 which permitted groups outside the Kuomintang to participate in the functions of government. In 1948 under the operations of this constitution Chiang was elected president. Meanwhile the Communist menace continued to grow in magnitude, in spite of the efforts made by the U.S. to induce the Nationalists and the Communists to form a coalition government. With Soviet aid the Communists were able to secure Manchuria and seize great quantities of war material which the Japanese had left behind, while the Nationalists were not able to secure adequate supplies. In 1948 the Communists marched south and by the end of the year had control over most of China north of the Yangtze. In view of the desperate military situation Chiang retired from the presidency in Jan. 1949. The vice-president, Li Tsung-jen, became acting president with the hope that he would be able to negotiate a peace with the Communists on honourable terms. These hopes were soon blasted as the Communists demanded unconditional surrender, and when this was refused they crossed the Yangtze and began the conquest of south China. They were uniformly successful, and in a few months Nationalist resistance in China proper collapsed. Many Nationalist leaders, in despair, accepted Communist domination, but in Dec. 1949 Chiang reemerged from retirement and established headquarters in Formosa (Taiwan), which thus became the bastion of noncommunist China. He was followed by the more intrepid of the Kuomintang leaders and by about 500,000 Nationalist troops. In the following years the government was thoroughly reorganized and numerous political and economic reforms were carried out, including the distribution of land among the peasants. Chiang was re-elected president in 1954; the U.S. and several other countries continued to recognize Chiang as the head of the legal Chinese government. After 1950 the U.S. also gave the Chiang regime substantial economic and military aid. (W. M. McG.)

CHIAPAS, a Pacific coast state of southern Mexico on the Guatemalan frontier, bounded by the states of Tabasco on the north and Veracruz and Oaxaca on the west. Pop. (1950) 907,026, largely Indians; area 28,732 sq.mi., largely forested. The Sierra Madre crosses the southern part of the state parallel with the coast, separating the low, humid, forested districts on the frontier of Tobasco from the hot, drier, coastal plain on the Pacific. The mountain region includes a fertile temperate plateau which is one of the best parts of Mexico and contains the larger part of the population of the state, but isolation and lack of transportation facilities have retarded its development.

The extension across the state to the Guatemalan frontier of the Pan-American railway (from Ixtepec, on the Tehuantepec national line) and the Inter-American highway improved the industrial and social conditions of the people. The principal industries are agriculture, which is very backward, stock raising, timber cutting, fruit farming and saltmaking. Coffee is cultivated on the Pacific slope of the Sierra Madre at elevations of 2,000 to 4,000 ft., and production has met with considerable success. Rubber plantations have also been laid out, principally by U.S. companies. The exports include mahogany, dyewoods, cattle, hides, coffee, rubber, fruit and salt. The mineral resources include gold, silver, copper and petroleum. The capital, Tuxtla Gutierrez (pop. 15,883), is on the plateau, 3½ mi. from the Río Sabinas, and 138 mi. N.E. of the Pacific port of Tonala. The former capital, San Cristobal (pop. 11,768), about 40 mi. E. of Tuxtla, is an interesting old town and the seat of the bishopric of Chiapas, founded in 1525 and made famous through its associations with Las Casas. Tapachula (pop. 15,187), the capital of the department of Soconusco, 18 mi. from the Guatemalan frontier, is a commercial town of the coffee district. It is 24 mi. inland from the small port of San Benito, is 559 ft. above sea level and has a healthful climate.

CHIAROSCURO, the disposition of light and shade in a painting (Ital. *chiaro,* light; *oscuro,* shade); the term is applied to an early method of printing woodcuts in various tones from several blocks, and also to a picture in black and white or brown and white only. It has also come to mean the atmospheric effect produced by the handling of high lights and shadows.

CHIAVARI, a town near the mouth of the Entella, Liguria, It., province of Genoa, 24 mi. S.E. by rail from Genoa. Pop. (1951) 20,324 (commune). It is in a fertile plain surrounded by mountains except on the southwest, where it comes down to the sea. It trades in farm products, and makes lace, light wicker-seated bentwood chairs and silk.

CHIAVENNA (anc. *Clavenna*), a town of Lombardy, Italy, in the province of Sondrio, 17 mi. by rail north of Colico, which lies at the north end of the Lake of Como. Pop. (1936) 3,803 (town); 5,379 (commune). It is on the right bank of the Mera, at the mouth of the Val Bregaglia, through which the road to the Maloja pass and the Engadine runs to the east. This line was followed by a Roman road, which took the Julier route to Coire (anc. *Curia*). The Splügen route, also used by the Romans, runs north from Chiavenna to Coire: the modern road was constructed by the Austrians in 1819–21. Chiavenna's ruined castle was the seat of the counts who ruled the valley from the time of the Goths till 1194, when the district was handed over to the bishops of Coire. In the 14th century the Visconti, as masters of the Valtellina, bought the "county" of Chiavenna from the bishop of Coire; but it was taken by the canton of the Grisons in 1525, and the castle dismantled. In 1797 Chiavenna became part of the Cisalpine republic, and thenceforward followed the fortunes of Lombardy. Chiavenna has cotton factories and breweries, and is a depot for the wine of the district because of the coolness of the caves which are used as cellars.

CHIBCHAN, an important linguistic stock of South American and Central American Indians. The tribes to be included within this stock and its precise geographic limits are still open to discussion. Beginning with the Ulvan tribes along the Honduras-Nicaragua border southward and eastward through Nicaragua, Costa Rica and Panama, the larger proportion of all the tribes belonged to Chibchan stock. In Colombia they probably held most of the drainage basins of the Magdalena and Cauca rivers. The region of the Cordillera Central, between these streams, was, however, held by tribes classed as Paniquitan (*q.v.*), who are regarded by some as constituting a distinct stock. Rivet would include as Chibchan also the Barbacoan (*q.v.*) and Coconucan (*q.v.*) tribes farther south, extending as far as the equator in western Ecuador. There has been considerable difference of opinion as to whether the direction of movement of the stock has been southward into South America or from the southern continent into North America. The more recent opinion seems to favour the former view, but the question cannot by any means be regarded as settled. The stock has received its name from the Chibchas (*q.v.*), the most important tribe of the stock at the time of the Spanish conquest.

See H. Beuchat and P. Rivet, *Affinités des langues du sud de la Colombie et du nord de l'Equateur,* vol. xi (Museon, 1910); W. Lehmann, *Zentral Amerika* (Berlin, 1920).

CHIBCHAS, a small group of tribes of South American Indians, occupying at the time of the Spanish conquest the high valleys in the vicinity of Bogotá and Tunja in Colombia. In their culture the Chibchas and other related tribes in the vicinity ranked next to that developed by the Inca and their predecessors in Peru and Bolivia. They were, however, on a distinctly lower level, for although a sedentary, agricultural folk, skilful weavers and artificers in gold, they had little copper and no bronze. They were also much inferior in pottery making, had no knowledge of stone or sun-dried brick construction and had no means of record, such as the Peruvian quipu. Just prior to the advent of the Spanish, the Zipa, or chief, of the Chibchas at Bogotá had been successful in extending his political control over several of the tribes farther north, and seems to have initiated a movement which, but for the Spanish conquest, might have paralleled the military expansion of the Aztecs in Mexico. Like the latter, the Chibchas employed human sacrifice in their religious ceremonials. In one of these, the chief, or "king," was smeared with a sticky substance and then powdered with gold dust, which was subsequently washed off by bathing in a sacred lake. It was this practice which, at least in part, gave rise to the legend of "El Dorado." The dead were buried in well-graves, which sometimes attained a depth of 30 or 40 ft.

BIBLIOGRAPHY.—L. F. de Piedrahita, *Historia general de las conquistas del Nuevo Reyno de Granada* (Verdussun, 1688); P. Simon, *Noticias historiales,* etc. (Bogotá, 1882); P. de Aguado, *Historia de Santa Marta y Nuevo Reino de Granada,* new ed. (Madrid, 1916).

CHIBOUQUE or CHIBOUK, a long Turkish pipe (Fr. form of the Turk. *chibūk,* "a stick"), often ornamented with precious stones.

CHICA, an orange-red pigment or dyestuff obtained from the leaves of *Bignonia chica* by the Orinoco Indians.

CHICACOLE, a town of British India in the Ganjam district of Madras, situated on the right bank of the river Languliya, crossed there by a bridge, 4 mi. from the sea. Pop. (1941) 22,249. Under Mohammedan rule it was the capital of one of the Northern Circars, and afterward of a British district. Several old mosques remain.

The town was formerly famous for its muslins.

CHICAGO, a city, a port of entry and the county seat of Cook county, Ill., the second city of the United States in population, commerce and manufacture; pop. (1910) 2,185,283; (1920) 2,701,705; (1930) 3,376,438; (1940) 3,396,808; (1950) 3,606,436, an increase of 6.2% over 1940. The increase in the decade 1920–30, partly as a result of annexations, was 674,733, the largest gross gain in the history of the city.

The population of the metropolitan district of Chicago, embracing suburbs of the city both in Illinois and Indiana, but excluding adjacent communities in Wisconsin, was 5,475,535 in 1950, an increase of 14% over 1940. As is the case with most U.S. cities, the growth of the population of Chicago has decreased relatively to the growth of the outlying communities of its metropolitan area. The rate of regional growth about the city increased as the rate of strictly urban growth declined, largely because of the extension of motor traffic and hard-surfaced highways. The almost negligible increase of the population of the city of Chicago proper from 1930 to 1940 represented a net balance of gains in half the city's wards and losses in the other half.

Chicago is situated at the southwest corner of Lake Michigan (lat. 41° 50′ N., long. 87° 38′ W), about 913 mi. distant by railway from New York city, 912 mi. from New Orleans, La., 2,265 mi. from Los Angeles, Calif., and 2,330 mi. from Seattle, Wash. The climate is very changeable and is much affected by the lake; changes of more than 30° in temperature within 24 hrs. are not rare, and changes of 20° are common. The city lies 598 ft. above sea level.

The greatest railway centre of the United States, Chicago for several decades was practically the only commercial outlet of the great agricultural region of the northern Mississippi valley. Trunk lines reach east to Montreal, Que., Boston, Mass., New York, Philadelphia, Pa., Baltimore, Md. (the nearest point on the Atlantic coast, 854 mi.); south to Charleston, S.C., Savannah, Ga., Florida, Mobile, Ala., New Orleans, Port Arthur, Tex., and Galveston, Tex.; west to the Pacific at Los Angeles, San Francisco, Calif., Seattle and Vancouver, Wash., and to most of these by a variety of routes. Thirty-two trunk lines operated by 22 railway companies enter the Chicago terminal district. In this terminal system about 4½% of the total freight tonnage of the United States is loaded and 6¼% unloaded annually. Chicago is also the greatest Canadian railway centre from a traffic standpoint.

The Canadian National lines and the Canadian Pacific enter it through subsidiaries.

The passenger-terminal situation, like the intramural rail-transit problem, was altered to fit the great city, which grew up around the original railheads and then passed miles beyond them. In 1911 the passenger station of the Chicago and North Western railway, a dignified structure costing $20,000,000, was opened for service. The railways using the Union station directly south of this terminal—the Pennsylvania, the Burlington, the Gulf Mobile and Ohio and the Milwaukee road—completed in 1925 their terminal at a cost of $75,000,000. With the construction of a great postal-terminal building near by, this completed the rearrangement of the terminals of the railroads on the west side of the Chicago river. But the far more numerous railways entering four passenger terminals on the south side spent years working out a plan for consolidation and rearrangement, still incomplete at mid-20th century. Decline of railway passenger traffic because of automotive and aerial competition and weakened railway finances during the depression of the 1930s diminished interest in these projects. But the straightening of the Chicago river followed by the building of through streets through the area foreshadowed its better use. Building of industrial structures over railway tracks and lease of railway "air rights" began. The first railway electrification was completed July 21, 1926, when the Illinois Central railway opened its electrified suburban passenger service over the 30 mi. from Matteson, Ill., to Randolph street at a total cost of $40,000,000.

With its suburbs within the area of the Chicago railway-terminal district, Chicago occupies a crescent-shaped area, the concave side of which is the shore of Lake Michigan. This Chicago district is 1,119.29 sq.mi. in extent, about the size of Rhode Island, and lies along the lake shore for about 55 mi. (the incorporated city proper for 26.5 mi.). The city proper has a land area of 206.7 sq.mi. It spreads loosely and irregularly backward from the lake over a shallow alluvial basin, which is rimmed to the west by a low moraine water parting that separates the drainage of the lake from that of the Mississippi valley. The city site has been built up out of the Lake Chicago of glacial times, which exceeded in size Lake Michigan. Three lakes—Calumet, almost five square miles, Hyde and part of Wolf—with a water surface of about six and one-half square miles lie within the municipal limits. The original elevation of what is now the business heart of the city was only about seven feet above the lake, but the level was greatly raised—in some places more than ten feet—over a large area between 1855 and 1860. The west side, especially the northwest near Humboldt park, is much higher (highest point, 75 ft.). A narrow inlet from the lake, the Chicago river, runs west from its shore about a mile, dividing then into a north and south branch, which run respectively to the northwest and the southwest, thus cutting the city into three divisions known as the north, the west and the south sides. The river no longer empties into Lake Michigan since the completion of the drainage canal. Its commercial importance is still great; but with the change in the character of lake traffic it diminished, and this stream and harbour upon which Chicago's history and greatness were based are looked upon primarily as an obstruction to urban street traffic. Agitation for the abolition of the river as a shipway and for the substitution of fixed bridges for the draw, lift and bascule types became active. Ship traffic on the lake became principally a matter of the transport of bulk cargoes of iron ore, coal, coke and limestone direct from mine rail terminals to the great iron, steel and cement plants with their own docks on the south shore of Lake Michigan. Traffic shifted to the ports on the southern extremities of the city, Calumet Harbor, Indiana Harbor, etc.; and steamers formerly docking in the river call at the Navy pier or dock in the outer harbour. Some lake cargo destined for Chicago is landed at Milwaukee, Wis., and comes in by rail.

Upon the completion of the Illinois waterway, connecting Chicago, through the Illinois and Mississippi rivers, with New Orleans by a barge route of nine-foot draft, the Chicago river became an important link for through water traffic; but it was proposed to obviate this by widening a direct canal to connect the south lake harbour with the drainage canal to constitute a link of the waterway.

The improvement of the city's outer harbour by the federal government was begun in 1833. Great breakwaters protect the river mouth from the silting shore currents of the lake and afford secure shelter in an outer roadstead from its storms, and there is a smaller inner basin (about 450 ac., 16-ft. depth) as well. The river itself has about 15 mi. of navigable channel, in part lined with docks. Its channel was repeatedly deepened and, especially from 1896, after its control as a navigable stream passed (1890) to the federal government, widened and straightened by the removal of jutting building constructions along its shores. Grain elevators of enormous size, coalyards and warehouses once crowded close upon it. In 1927 the south bank of the river from the Michigan avenue bridge to Lake street, the northern boundary of the loop business district, was completely denuded of abutting buildings by the opening of the two-level Wacker drive, a broad boulevard upon a gigantic concrete structure occupying the space of former blocks of buildings and streets. This construction, which cost about $28,000,000, and which connects with the Michigan avenue bridge and the two-level boulevards approaching it, was the first item of a program designed to convert the entire south and east banks of the river into broad traffic arteries. Its extension southward from Lake street was begun in 1949. Farther south, under an agreement of the railways, property owners and the city, the south branch of the river, which curves to the east for about a mile of its length, was moved westward for a maximum distance of a quarter of a mile, to allow the construction of wide streets leading from the south into the loop district.

The plan of the city was originally regular (*i.e.*, rigidly rectangular) and the original streets were wide according to the standards of the days of horse-drawn traffic. The original plan was altered by the construction of a great number of boulevards in the outer areas which, in connection with the growth of the park system and the construction of driveways in the parks, provided numbers of diagonal traffic arteries. The recovery of land from the lake and the construction of a great parkway system along the lake front also led to the belting of the downtown areas on the east with a number of north and south boulevards not in keeping with the original plan of the city. The initiation and completion of these projects were so rapid and the number of new plans in various stages of execution so great that the older parts of Chicago were profoundly altered, especially during the great building boom of 1922–28.

Rapid transit by rail did not keep pace with these improvements in streets. One result was that a number of outlying business, hotel and apartment centres grew up, which began in the aggregate to rival the loop, the former business, financial, theatrical and hotel centre. Chicago developed into a series of urban centres rather than a centralized city on the usual U.S. model. Notwithstanding the growth of these outlying centres, however, the construction of great buildings within the loop from 1922 to 1928 proceeded at a pace never approached before, while the opening of Wacker drive and the Michigan avenue bridge enabled the business district to break out of the narrow confines of the former loop district—the one and one-half square miles lying between the lake, the main Chicago river and the south branch of the river. This northward advance of the business district was accompanied by the construction of numbers of the tower type of office building. This forest of bold and graceful towers relieved the former drab monotony of downtown Chicago. The construction of so many great office buildings and hotels in the downtown district made the problem of street congestion increasingly acute despite the enormous expenditures upon new boulevards. Hope for any material relief from the construction of the freight tunnels vanished with the advent of the popular-priced automobile, and the capacity of these underground freight arteries is such that they can handle only a trifling percentage of the movement of goods in the district. A belt of "badlands"—deteriorated residence, shop and factory property—surrounds the business district except on the northeast. There a great section crowded with expensive family and apartment hotels grew up on the lands reclaimed from the lake in the section called "Streeterville"—named from a belligerent old squatter who long claimed title to these accretions because his schooner had stranded on that shore. Chicago's architectural achievements are yet blighted by the use of soft coal, which after a time smears a drab colour on the finest structures. Vigorous efforts to combat this nuisance have had small results. Yet the sky line, the immensity of the traffic movement and the massiveness of its central district give the city a distinct tone, found nowhere else.

The unstable soil of sand, clay and boulders that underlies the city is unfavourable to tall constructions, and necessitates extraordinary attention to foundations. The bedrock lies, on an average, 50 ft. below the level of the lake (in places more than 100). The foundations are often sunk to the rock in caissons, the buildings resting on monster columns of concrete and steel. In other cases great "pads" of the same materials, resting or "floating" upon the clay, sustain and distribute the weight of the building.

Buildings notable for their architectural boldness and the

beauty which resulted from the conversion of the economics of the tall structure to aesthetic purposes are the Chicago temple, a spire above an office pile, the Tribune tower, distinguished for its flying buttresses, the Wrigley building with its campanile tower and the Civic Opera building, which faces across the river the Daily News building and plaza. A large part of the business of the former dry goods wholesale district is housed in the huge Merchandise Mart on the north bank of the river.

The Board of Trade building topped by a statue of Ceres poised 612 ft. in the air is at the south end of the financial district of LaSalle street.

Older buildings associated with the city's history or notable architectural triumphs of their day are the Auditorium—now occupied by Roosevelt college—the Continental Illinois bank, the Monadnock, the People's Gas building, the LaSalle, Blackstone and Sherman hotels and the Marquette building. There are a number of enormous retail stores. The largest, and one of the finest in the world, is that of Marshall Field and Co.

The city hall and county building (cost $8,617,626) is an enormous double structure in a free French Renaissance style, with columned façades.

The federal building (finished in 1905; cost $4,750,000) is a massive edifice (a low rectangle surmounted by a higher inner cross and crowned with a dome). The public library (1893–97, $2,125,000) is constructed of dark granite and limestone, with rich interior decorations of varied frescoes, mosaics, ornamental bronze and iron work and mottoes. The Art Institute of Chicago, Orchestra hall and the Museum of Science and Industry are also noteworthy. The Chicago Natural History museum, completed in 1920 at a cost of $6,000,000, is a white marble structure in Ionic style, 350 ft. wide and 700 ft. long.

Navy pier, completed in 1915, projects 3,000 ft. into Lake Michigan, north of the mouth of the Chicago river and combines the functions of an enormous dock, a school (University of Illinois's Chicago undergraduate division) and a playground. It has two exhibition halls, each one-half mile in length, one of which has the largest unobstructed floor space of any exhibit hall in the United States. The movement of wealthier residents to surrounding communities left the city proper without any notable street of private homes, although many of the older boulevards are fringed by dignified houses. The physical growth of Chicago after 1909 was guided by a definite plan laid down by the Chicago Plan commission, created by the city council during the administration of Mayor Fred A. Busse. The plan had its genesis in a report of Daniel H. Burnham and was submitted by the Commercial club to the city and adopted as an enduring policy. It took cognizance of the natural features of Chicago's site and environs and proposed the gradual adaptation of the city then existing, and the city as it grew, to the best uses of its natural setting—from a commercial, industrial, social and cultural standpoint. The plan was constantly modified and expanded to keep pace with new conditions and problems. Railroads, public utility companies and industrialists co-operated to carry out its designs. The Chicago plan demonstrated that the most intensive modern industrialism and commercial activity can be profitably harmonized with beauty, social welfare and ample recreational and cultural centres for the people of a metropolitan city.

Public Works and Communications.—Local transit is provided for by suburban railway service, motorbuses, elevated electric roads and a system of electric surface cars. Two great public works demand notice: the water system and the drainage canal. Water is pumped from Lake Michigan through several tunnels connecting with cribs located from two to five miles from shore. The cribs are heavy structures of timber and iron loaded with stone and enclosing the intake cylinders, which join with the tunnels well below the bottom of the lake. The first tunnel was completed in 1867. The tunnels form a 100-mi. labyrinth under the lake and city. The average amount of water pumped per day at mid-20th century was 971,000,000 gal. Because of pollution of lake water from the wastes of Indiana cities, not participating in the drainage system of the Chicago sanitary district, this water has been chlorinated at the intakes. The wastes of the city—street washings, building sewage, the offal of slaughterhouses and wastes of distilleries and rendering houses—were originally turned into the lake, but before 1870 it was discovered that the range of impurity extended a mile into the lake, halfway to the water crib; and it became evident that the lake could not be indefinitely contaminated. The Illinois and Michigan canal was once thought to have solved the difficulty. It connected with the main (southern) branch of the Chicago river, five miles from its mouth, and with the Illinois river at La Salle, and was the natural successor in the evolution of transportation of the old Chicago portage, one-half mile in length, between the Chicago river and the headwaters of the Kankakee. It was so deepened as to draw water out from the lake, whose waters thus flowed toward the Gulf of Mexico; but it proved inadequate for the disposal of sewage. A solution of the problem was imperative by 1876, but almost all the wastes of the city continued nevertheless to be poured into the lake. In 1890 a sanitary district, including part of the city and certain suburban areas to be affected, was organized, and preparations made for building a greater canal that should do effectively the work it was once thought the old canal could do. The new drainage canal, one of the greatest sanitary works of the world, constructed between 1892 and 1900 under the control of the trustees of the sanitary district of Chicago, joins the south branch of the Chicago with the Des Plaines river, and so with the Illinois and Mississippi. The canal, or sewer, is flushed with water from Lake Michigan, and its waters are pure within a flow of 150 mi. Its capacity, which was not at first fully utilized, is 600,000 cu.ft. per minute, sufficient to renew entirely the water of the Chicago river daily. A system of intercepting sewers to withdraw drainage from the lake was begun in 1898; and the construction of a canal to drain the Calumet region was begun in 1910. This system was later changed and extended to deliver all sewage to plants for oxidation and chemical treatment. The drainage canal is the backbone of a great system of feed-water lateral canals and underground sewers. The drainage canal became the nucleus of the Lakes to the Gulf waterway, under construction by the state of Illinois to connect the drainage canal with the Illinois river, the federal government undertaking the improvement of the rivers to the gulf. The canal also made possible the development at Lockport of hydroelectric power, which is used by the sanitary district and for street lighting in Chicago.

The lowering of lake levels which resulted brought protests and litigation from other lake cities. Shipping interests blamed the drainage canal for the lower levels and the shoaling of port and dock channels. The sanitary district denied responsibility for more than six inches of the fall in the levels of Lakes Michigan, Huron and Erie, and offered to construct compensating weirs to retain levels in the St. Clair river, connecting Lakes Huron and Erie, and in the Niagara river. Litigation against the sanitary district by the other lake states was defended in the United States supreme court by the state of Illinois, assisted by other states of the Mississippi valley interested in maintaining the diversion of lake water into the Mississippi drainage system in aid of navigation.

The first adverse decision by the supreme court was handed down Jan. 5, 1925. Finally, that tribunal decreed that the diversion of water should be reduced to 1,500 cu.ft. per second by 1938. The sanitary district was given time to construct sewage purification works, but its extravagance and depleted resources would have made that impossible had it not been for the aid of the federal treasury extended as grants to relieve unemployment. The works prior to 1950 cost $262,000,000.

Chicago was early a centre of aerial transport. The first municipal airport was established in 1927 and by mid-century the three city-owned airports were handling more than 3,250,000 air passengers annually. Plane arrivals and departures at the Midway (Municipal) airport averaged more than 600 daily. Twelve major air lines provided 450 regularly scheduled trips per day. In addition, many other lines provided air-freight and air-express services.

Atrophy of the city's internal traction and elevated systems after 1907 was partially compensated for by the establishment of numerous motorbus lines on the boulevards and parkways, and by the extension and modernization of electric railways in the outlying regions. Numerous bus lines connecting Chicago with other towns and cities came into competition with the railways. Another great improvement was begun in 1901 by a private telephone company. This is an elaborate system of freight subways, more than 62 mi. of which, underlying the entire business district, had been constructed before 1909. It is the only subway system in the world that seeks to clear the streets by the lessening of trucking, in place of devoting itself to the transportation of passengers. Direct connection is made with the freight stations of all railways and the basements of important business buildings, and coal, building materials, ashes and garbage, railway luggage, heavy mail and other kinds of heavy freight are removed and delivered. Telegraph and telephone wires are carried through the tunnel, and can be readily repaired. The subway was opened for partial operation in 1905. However, street traffic growth was so great and the capacity of the tunnels so small, that the 125 locomotives and 2,500 cars operated in the tunnels at mid-century were handling less than 10% of railway freight loaded or unloaded in the business district.

Parks.—The park system may be said to have been begun in 1869, and in 1870 aggregated 1,887 ac. Chicago then acquired the name of the "Garden City," still emblazoned on the municipal coat of arms. But other cities later passed it, and in 1904 Chicago ranked only 32nd among U.S. cities of more than 100,000 population in per capita holdings of park acreage. The area of the city's parks is 7,327 ac., but this was extended all along the lake front by the reclamation of land from the lake for parks, bathing beaches and an island airport (Meigs field) near the business district.

In addition to the city park system, the Cook county forest preserves, a broad belt of wooded lands, 38,000 ac. in extent, acquired over many years, form a belt north, south and west of the city. The value of this great playground is attested by a census of visitors for one year which totalled 5,500,000. In the same year 4,582,000 persons bathed at the city's supervised bathing beaches and 3,700,000 children were counted at the city's playgrounds. The large and small parks number 300. There are 71 bathing beaches and public pools, 25 free public golf courses and 98 public playgrounds. The park in each district, usually located near a school, is almost all-inclusive in its provision for all comers, from babyhood to maturity, and is open all day.

The older parks include several of great size and beauty. Lincoln park, near the lake shore of the north side, was much enlarged by an addition reclaimed from the lake. It has fine monuments, conservatories, a zoological garden and the collections of the Academy of Sciences. Jackson park, on the lake shore of the south side, was the main site of the World's Columbian exposition of 1893. It is joined with Washington park by the Midway Plaisance, a wide boulevard. Along the Midway are the buildings of The University of Chicago. On the west side of the city are three large parks—Douglas, Garfield (with a fine conservatory) and Humboldt, which has a remarkable rose garden—and in the extreme south side several others, including Calumet, by the lake side, and Marquette. The shore of the north side is quite free, and beginning a short distance above the river is skirted for almost 30 mi. by Lake Shore drive and Sheridan road. In Grant park is the building of the Art institute, the Shedd aquarium, the Adler planetarium, the Chicago Natural History museum and Soldier Field, a great stadium devoted to sports and pageants, with a capacity of about 200,000. About two-thirds of the city's frontage on the lake is composed of parks or boulevards. The inner boulevards and the drives through the lake-front parks are parked ways ranging from 150 to 300 ft. in width. (L. H. L.; X.)

Art and Music.—The history of Chicago as an art and music centre has been impressive. The city has produced important composers, headed by John Alden Carpenter; painters like G. P. A. Healy and Oliver Dennett Grover; and sculptors like Lorado Taft. Its Art Institute of Chicago is outstanding among the great world museums in its collections of 19th- and 20th-century paintings. The Symphony orchestra is one of the four or five great U.S. orchestras. Its Civic Opera house, built in 1929 by Samuel Insull, is the best equipped scenically in the Americas or Europe. Chicago opera, under the regime of Mary Garden and with the financial backing of Mrs. Rockefeller McCormick challenged the supremacy of New York's Metropolitan during the second decade of the 20th century. With the crumbling of the Insull financial empire and the financial depression of the 1930s, however, opera sank to a low ebb.

Art started in Chicago in 1855 when an Irish carpenter, Martin O'Brien, set aside a small corner of his shop for the framing of Currier & Ives prints, and later for the sale of prints and paintings. On April 13, 1861, O'Brien opened an adjoining shop devoted exclusively to his growing picture business. It became the favourite meeting place of G. P. A. Healy, back from Europe, where he had painted European aristocracy and royalty. In 1866 O'Brien's customers and others formed an association for the purpose of studying art history and methods, "copying in oil" the paintings in the establishment and even posing models. They rented rooms in a neighbouring building, called themselves the Chicago Academy of Design, and were beginning to flourish when the Chicago fire of 1871 put an end to their activities.

The club was kept loosely intact, and in 1878 started again, this time incorporating as the Chicago Academy of Fine Arts, and electing as president George Armour. In 1882 the academy changed its name to the Art Institute of Chicago, reorganized and elected a new president, Charles L. Hutchinson. Under Hutchinson's administration, which continued to 1924, the institute built its museum and school on the lake front, and assembled under its roof the collections of the Potter Palmers, the Logans, Nickersons, Ayers, Buckinghams, Butlers, Leiters, Ryersons and Hutchinsons. On loan in the museum in 1924, too, was the Birch-Bartlett collection, to be accepted later as a gift, the first great collection of the European moderns in a U.S. public museum.

The Art Institute of Chicago remained the centre of the city's art activities, more intimately than in any of the great capitals of the world. New York city, London, Paris, Rome and other large cities all have two or three or more public galleries, rivalling each other in importance. The Arts Club of Chicago, which opened the day the Armistice was signed in 1918, was for a time a rival, bringing to Chicago the art of the 20th-century European moderns. But the Art institute, accepting slowly and steadily the innovators, finally absorbed the function of the Arts club. Numerous commercial galleries, starting with O'Brien's pioneer shop, and numerous art organizations were established and flourished in Chicago and its suburbs.

The musical history of Chicago starts even earlier than its art history. There were enough people on the mud flats along Lake Michigan as early as 1850 to encourage a music teacher, John Dyrenfurth, to found a philharmonic society with himself as conductor. In 1854 Dyrenfurth encouraged a concert troupe to visit Chicago. Theodore Thomas was first violinist. Three years later the Mendelssohn Singing society was organized by George P. Upton. This society later became the Apollo Musical club, still in existence at mid-20th century. In 1869 Thomas visited the town again, this time as conductor of a travelling orchestra of 40 pieces. He booked another concert for Oct. 9, 1871, but the Chicago fire intervened. After the fire he returned repeatedly with his orchestra, and eventually, in 1891, he came to stay. He organized a local orchestra, which he called the Chicago Symphony orchestra. In 1904 he and his orchestra moved into the new Orchestra hall, across the street from the Art Institute of Chicago, and there it remained. Thomas himself promoted the building of the hall, with a long list of subscribers donating. Thomas conducted the orchestra until his death in 1905 and was succeeded by Frederick Stock (1872–1942).

Meanwhile, the Auditorium was built to house opera, which had made its Chicago debut July 30, 1850, in Rice's theatre. Before the second act was over, fire broke out, and it was several years before Chicagoans were to see the finish of the opera *La Somnambula.* A more substantial *première* was staged on April 20, 1865, when the Grau Grand Opera company sang *Il Trovatore.* This *première* was a delayed performance, having been scheduled for April 17, but postponed because of the assassination of Abraham Lincoln in Washington, D.C.

The Auditorium was dedicated Dec. 9, 1889, with Pres. Benjamin Harrison as guest of honour and Adelina Patti singing with the Apollo club. The next night, Patti and the Grau Grand Opera company sang *Romeo and Juliet,* and opera was an established institution in Chicago. The city depended on the Grau company and other touring organizations, including the Metropolitan and the Manhattan companies until 1910, when it organized its own opera, with leading citizens contributing. This Chicago Opera company brought in Mary Garden eventually, not only as a prima donna but as an artistic manager, and started a real rivalry with the Metropolitan of New York city.

Numerous minor orchestras and opera companies also were established in Chicago, along with scores of singing societies, notably the Paulist choir. During the depression of the 1930s, the city of Chicago and the Works Progress administration presented open-air symphony concerts in Grant park to crowds which on some nights numbered 500,000 people. Both the opera and the symphony organizations also went into the open air in Ravinia park, 25 mi. N. of Chicago, for performances rivalling those presented downtown in the regular seasons. (C. J. Bt.)

Libraries.—At the head of the libraries of the city stands the public library, established in 1872, the nucleus of which was a collection of books from England, Ireland, Germany, France and other countries, after the great Chicago fire of 1871, a collection to which many contemporary literary and other celebrities made contributions. The library was opened in 1874. The main library in 1950 had 2,196,742 vol., in addition to independent collections ranging from 5,000 to 50,000 in 34 general branches, 15 branch library buildings and 27 subbranches.

The circulation of books in 1949, in addition to those used on the main shelves of the central library, was 8,719,880. The John Crerar library, endowed in 1889 by John Crerar, wealthy manufacturer of railway supplies, had in 1950, about 700,000 vol. on social, physical, natural and medical sciences and their applications. It occupies a large building across the street from the main building of the public library at Randolph street and Michigan avenue. The Newberry library, endowed by a bequest of Walter L. Newberry, in 1950 contained 650,000 vol., chiefly in the field of the humanities, history and literature. These three libraries cooperate to avoid useless duplication and each has certain special fields. Other important collections are the library of The University of Chicago; the Burnham Library of Architecture and the Ryerson library in the Art institute, devoted to fine arts and travel; the libraries of Northwestern university (including the Elbert H. Gary law library), the Chicago Natural History museum, the Museum of Science and Industry, the Illinois Institute of Technology, Loyola university, Garrett Biblical institute; the Virginia collection of the McCormick Historical Association library; and the Municipal Reference library, containing a great collection of documents and data on municipal government in Chicago and elsewhere. Many trade, engineering and professional organizations maintain special libraries at their national or sectional headquarters in Chicago.

Universities and Colleges.—The leading university is The University of Chicago (*see* CHICAGO, THE UNIVERSITY OF). The professional departments of Northwestern university are mostly located in Chicago while the academic and theological departments are in the suburb of Evanston. Northwestern university was organized in 1851 by the Methodist Episcopal Church and retained nominal relations with the denomination. In 1950–51 it had a student enrolment of 20,196 with 1,848 instructors. Loyola university, with a beautiful 25-ac. campus, De Paul university and Mundelein college for women are the principal Catholic schools of the city. Other schools of importance are: Illinois Institute of Technology, George Williams college, North Park college, Roosevelt college, occupying the former Auditorium building on Michigan avenue, three public junior colleges and the Chicago Teachers' college of the city's board of education. The University of Illinois, at Champaign-Urbana, maintains an undergraduate division at Chicago, as well as its professional colleges of medicine, dentistry and pharmacy. Theological schools independent of the universities include the Presbyterian Theological seminary, the Chicago Theological seminary (Congregational, opened 1858, and including German, Danish-Norwegian and Swedish institutes), the Seabury-Western Theological seminary at Evanston, a German Lutheran theological seminary and an Evangelical Lutheran theological seminary. There are a number of independent medical schools and schools of dentistry and veterinary surgery.

Newspapers.—The morning newspapers published in English are the *Tribune* and the *Sun-Times* (tabloid), established as the *Sun* in 1941 and merged with the *Times* in 1947.

The afternoon papers are the *Daily News,* the *Herald-American* and the *Sun-Times.* The last two publish an edition Sunday mornings, as does the *Tribune.* Formerly supporting more than a dozen dailies, many of pronounced partisan affiliations, the city of Chicago has no daily newspapers that have other than nominal political-party connections. In the number of publications, though not in circulation, the foreign-language press outstrips the English publications—foreign-language dailies including publications in Polish, Yiddish, German, Swedish, Czech, Greek and Italian. The city is the largest U.S. printing centre in point of volume of output, and many trade, labour, scientific and religious publications are included in its total of approximately 800 periodicals. In 1920 the city's first financial daily, the *Chicago Journal of Commerce,* was established. The Joseph Medill school of journalism, named after the founder of the *Chicago Tribune,* was opened as a part of Northwestern university in 1921, the *Tribune* underwriting any deficits for a period of years.

Industry and Commerce.—Chicago's situation at the head of the most southwestern of the Great Lakes has given it great importance in trade and industry. The growth of its trade has been enormous. After the beginning of the 20th century, however, Chicago underwent an industrial and commercial transformation roughly parallel to that of the U.S. as a whole. The city's paramount position as a great market in the 19th century was associated with the extractive industry of the U.S. economy of that day, and Chicago's trade consisted principally in the assembly and distribution of the raw crops and resources of fields and forests; its industries were mainly processing raw products, such as meat packing, woodworking, flour milling, tanning, etc. While these great industries remained important, Chicago's leading position in regard to them, except in meat packing, disappeared, but this was made up many times by the growth of an intensive industrialism. The city made great strides as a centre of the iron and steel industry, including many other products such as cement. The Calumet steel and iron region south of the city made tremendous progress after the founding of the steel city of Gary in 1906 just across the Indiana state boundary, and in manufacturing plants for heavy iron and steel products the Chicago region came to stand to the Pittsburgh, Pa., district—U.S. leading steel region—in the ratio of 10 to 13, while the operations became more continuous in the Chicago district.

The last years of the 19th century showed, however, an inevitable loss to Chicago in the growth of Duluth, Minn., Kansas City, Mo., and other rivals in strategic situations. In particular, the struggle of the north and south railway lines in the Mississippi valley to divert grain and other freight to ports on the Gulf of Mexico caused great losses to Chicago. An enormous increase in the cereal trade of Philadelphia, Baltimore, Newport News, Va., and Norfolk, Va., was partly because of the traffic eastward over lines south of Chicago. The traffic of the routes through Duluth and Canada did not, indeed, represent actual losses, for the traffic was largely a new growth; but there was nevertheless a considerable drain to these routes from U.S. territory which was once tributary to Chicago. Altogether the competition of the Gulf roads and the lines running southwest from Duluth had largely excluded Chicago by 1899 (according to its board of trade) from the grain trade west of the Missouri river; its facilities for receiving and distributing remained nevertheless unequalled, and it continued practically to monopolize the traffic between the northern Atlantic seaboard and the central west. The city's position as a gateway for passing trade is indicated by the fact that one-eighth of the traffic of its railway terminals is through traffic.

New York alone among U.S. cities has a greater trade. Chicago is the greatest railway centre, the greatest grain market, the greatest livestock market and meat-packing centre in the world and holds world primacy in a large number of smaller manufacturing industries.

Chicago has never participated to a great extent in international finance. The collapse of the speculative boom of 1929 and the bankruptcy of the Insull utility investment corporations checked a promising growth of domestic finance and investment banking.

Annual bank clearings for 1949 totalled $35,806,000,000, more than double the clearings of 1940. In April 1949 Chicago banks had loans and discounts of $1,944,756,000, deposits of $8,617,358,000, cash resources of $2,263,468,000 and savings deposits of $1,755,152,000.

The city's wholesale trade was estimated in 1875 at $293,900,000. In dollar value it reached a peak of $5,870,166,410 net sales disclosed by the census of distribution for 1929. In the ensuing depression money value declined greatly, physical volume to a lesser extent. The retail trade of the city reported by the census of 1949 amounted to $4,270,000,000 in net sales, the wholesale trade to $13,500,000,000. The Chicago board of trade remains the greatest speculative grain market in the world.

The grain elevators are still among the sights of Chicago. They are enormous storehouses into which the grain is elevated from ships and cars, sorted into grades and reloaded for shipment, all the work being done by machinery. Chicago's direct foreign trade is mostly by rail through other ports, although vessels of less than 14-ft. draught come in from the Atlantic on special trade voyages.

The Chicago industrial district, comprising the counties of Cook, Du Page, Kane, Will and Lake in Illinois and Lake in Indiana is the second largest in the United States. In 1950 the district had 10,500 manufacturing establishments, 1,000,000 factory wage earners and produced goods valued at $11,000,000,000. In 1937, during economic depression, the number of establishments was only 9,019. The number of wage earners was 538,775 and the value of goods produced was $4,711,428,323. As many as 192,000 families were on public relief rolls in Cook county at one time during the depression, at a monthly expense of $6,063,207.

The value added by manufacture in the Chicago metropolitan area of the following products in 1947 included: food and kindred products $714,614,000; textile-mill products $38,037,000; apparel and related products $222,905,000; lumber and products, except furniture, $35,144,000; furniture and fixtures $116,893,000; paper and allied products $122,656,000; printing and publishing industries $498,878,000; chemicals and allied products $385,123,000; petroleum and coal products $181,044,000; primary metal industries $678,036,000; fabricated metal products $495,435,000; machinery, except electrical, $700,787,000; electrical machinery $624,389,000; transportation equipment $236,237,000; instruments and related products $123,221,000; and miscellaneous manufactures $172,746,000. The International Harvester company, successor to the McCormick Harvester company, is the largest manufacturer of agricultural machinery in the world and the Western Electric company holds the same position in the manufacture of telephone equipment. The Pullman company manufactures railway freight and passenger cars. Meat packing, for which Chicago is best known, is the greatest local industry. In the enormous stockyards (about 500 ac. in area) from two-thirds to four-fifths of the cattle and hogs received are killed and sent out in various forms of prepared meats and by-products (lard, fertilizers, glue, butterine, soap, etc.). About 2,525,000 people (32% women) were gainfully employed in the Chicago metropolitan area at mid-20th century. This compared with 1,880,000 employed in 1939. Manufacturing accounted for 43% of the total; wholesale and retail trade 21%; service establishments 12%; transportation, communication and public utilities 9%; finance 5%; and miscellaneous 10%.

Public Utilities.—The development of manufacturing in Chicago went hand in hand with an equally remarkable development of public utility services, without which Chicago's industrialism would be impossible, for much of its factory industry is due to an abundance of cheap electric power, supplied by a highly efficient system of interconnected generating stations. The electrical output was 5,574,961,000 kw.hr. in 1929; in 1949, 11,987,651,000 kw.hr. There were 1,595,000 consumers of electric light and power in Chicago in the latter year. The company serving the incorporated city consumed about 9,035,918 tons of coal annually and for condensing purposes alone pumped an average of 1,978,000,000 gal. of water per day, more than the daily pumpage of the city water works. The local gas industry served more than 900,000 consumers within the incorporated city and is interconnected by pipe lines with the natural gas fields of Texas and with producing plants and consumers within a wide radius of the city. It makes use of surplus by-product gases generated in the steel and iron industry. Telephonic communication is in almost universal use by householders and by mid-century the work of converting the telephone system to the automatic switching type was virtually complete.

Administration.—Chicago is governed under a general city charter law of Illinois of 1872, accepted by the city in 1876, but the charter has been amended in some minor particular at every biennial session of the Illinois state legislature since that date. The essential framework of government, however, remains as it was originally adopted, and the efforts of municipal reformers to institute a complete new system of local government have been defeated, even when submitted to a referendum of the voters. Although the government remains apparently archaic and highly complicated, it really works about as well as that of the average U.S. municipality, and the faults of municipal government and politics in Chicago relate rather to the polyglot character of the population than to the form of government. Chicago remains a good example of the councilmanic form of municipal government, once almost universal in the U.S., but the legal and *de facto* powers and influence of the mayor have grown, even as the power of the presidential office has grown at the expense of congressional prestige and effectiveness in the federal government. A common council consisting of one alderman from each of the 50 wards is elected quadrennially. It controls the budget, police, excise, city contracts and franchises. The latter are subject to popular referendum, however. The council confirms appointments by the mayor and may pass legislation by a two-thirds vote, in spite of his veto. The mayor, selected every four years, is the executive head of the city. He appoints a cabinet, consisting of the heads of city departments, but most city employees are under a civil service law and are removable only under processes and tribunals provided by that law. There are several commissions in charge of city functions—such as the school board, the public-library board, the commission in charge of elections and that in charge of the Municipal Tuberculosis sanitarium. Administration of several pension funds for city employees is also committed to a number of commissions.

Like most U.S. cities Chicago has a dual city and county government. Cook county, which contains Chicago, retains practically all of the extensive government functions of rural counties of the type which arose in Virginia and the southern colonies, and in which the county was the real unit of local government. This complication of dual government in Cook county extends to the suburbs of Chicago, which have separate municipal organizations, while the county itself was laid out after 1848 in townships, somewhat on the New England town model. It was not until 1900 that the town organizations within the territory gradually annexed to the original village of Chicago were deprived of their political structure and divested of governmental functions within the city, and as late as 1903 ten townships exercised taxing power within the municipal area. A plan for the consolidation of local government was rejected by the people in 1920. In addition to the original duplications of government, new quasi-governmental bodies were set up for special purposes and in some cases were granted police and tax powers.

There are more than 400 distinct political units in Cook county, empowered to levy 600 different sorts of taxes. The average citizen of Chicago is under the jurisdiction of or in contact with 25 different kinds of governments. But in 1934 the voters approved the consolidation of 22 formerly independent park districts, and these great properties with annual budgets of many millions passed under a board of five appointed by the mayor. Formerly they were a species of independent principalities within the city. Officials of some were appointed by the governor of Illinois, some were elected by the judges of the courts, some by the voters of the districts. They had powers of police, taxation and debt incurment.

In 1906 the archaic system of administering petty justice through the justices of the peace was abolished and a co-ordinated municipal court with numerous judges and a chief justice was established. The juridical system is complicated by the fact that the circuit court is a constitutionally established court of the state of Illinois. The superior, municipal and other special courts are created by statute. The sanitary district, practically an independent government in itself, with powers of tax levy and debt making, is superimposed over the territory of Chicago and Cook county. Both the state of Illinois and the federal government also extended the legislative and administrative regulation of industry and commerce, and maintain large staffs of officials in Chicago. The school board has been nominally separate from and almost independent of the city government in its powers since 1857. The forest preserves adjacent to the city's boundaries are also quasi-governmental bodies exercising some sovereign powers.

The initiative and referendum in local matters have been made possible by the state, and this power has been frequently exercised. Increases of the public debt are subject to popular vote, but financial arrangements under such a complex system of government are naturally loose and inefficient, co-ordinated budgeting being virtually impossible. The grant of independent taxing power to so many governmental bodies, in the Chicago area, as elsewhere in the U.S., is one result of state constitutional limitations upon the public debt. Chicago, as a municipal corporation, is prohibited from incurring debt in excess of 5% of the value of the property within the city. The inevitable result of such a restriction, whenever a great public necessity arose, was the creation of another taxing body not limited by pre-existing debt limits covering a given territory, within the jurisdiction of an existing governmental body.

Finances.—The budget for the city of Chicago proper for 1950 called for the expenditure of $188,236,912, including $26,398,855 by the water department, $6,110,000 by the Municipal Tuberculosis sanitarium, $5,215,000 by the public library board, $3,529,000 by the board in charge of firemen's pensions, $4,400,000 by the board administering police pensions and $7,360,000 by the board in charge of pensions for other municipal employees. Other funds in the budget out of which a variety of expenses are met, such as police, fire department and street and bridge maintenance, are the corporate fund of $81,329,663 and the debt service funds, amounting to $17,150,935. The separate school-board budget totalled $129,217,692; the park budget, $19,188,718; county budget, $37,346,365. In 1935 Chicago's revenues were disorganized and sadly deficient as the result of the worst financial crisis in the city's history. The full effect of the economic depression of 1929 struck the city in the midst of a general reassessment of real property to adjust gross inequalities of tax burdens. Taxpayers refused or were unable to pay their taxes. Forty-one per cent of taxes due were delinquent in 1933. Teachers and other public employees went for months without pay. Subventions from the federal government in the form of relief allotments and make-work grants helped the city tide over its crisis while rigid retrenchments were instituted. During the crisis the city sold tax-anticipation warrants and practically lived on future revenues, the collection of much of which was dubious.

Transit Problems.—Chicago's conspicuous failure as a city has been in the lack of providing adequate rapid-transit facilities.

At the mayor's election in 1905 the successful political party stood for municipal acquisition of all roads. Meanwhile, under the State Referendum act, the city in 1902 voted overwhelmingly for municipal ownership and operation (142,826 to 27,990); the legislature in 1903 by the Meuller law gave the city the requisite powers; the people accepted the law, again declared for municipal ownership, for temporary compulsion of adequate service and against granting any franchise to any company, by four additional votes similarly conclusive. At last, after tedious negotiations, a definite agreement was reached in 1906 assuring an early acquisition of all roads by the city. The issue of bonds for municipal railways was, however, declared unconstitutional that year. At the municipal elections of 1907 there was a complete reversal of policy; a large majority voted this time against municipal ownership in favour of leaving the working of the street railways in private hands and strengthening the powers of municipal control. For 20 years after 1907 the surface-car lines of Chicago were operated under unified management and rendered excellent service. The system was completely rebuilt, and that work led to the repaving of the city, so that the coming of the automobile age found Chicago comparatively well-equipped for motor transport. But with the growth of the city and the congestion of the streets by motor traffic, transportation by surface electric railways became too slow to meet the demands of the population. In the meantime, the construction of elevated railway lines practically ceased, except for extensions outside the incorporated city limits where the political factor did not enter into calculations. But construction of a subway did not begin until Dec. 17, 1938, when boring of 8.75 mi. of tube 40 to 50 ft. under State, Dearborn, Lake and other streets was begun. In two years the tubes were virtually completed to their connections with the elevated system outside the congested districts, but construction of stations and equipment remained to be done. Money from the city's accumulated traction fund was supplemented by a grant from the Federal Public Works administration to defray the cost of the project. The first unit —about four and three-fourths miles, mostly under State street— began operation in Oct. 1944. The second unit—the Milwaukee-Dearborn, about four miles—was opened in 1951.

Under the franchise arrangement of 1907 the city received 55% of the divisible net receipts of the surface lines—after payment of 5% on agreed capital, which with interest earned on the fund amounted to $47,518,060.66 Jan. 31, 1947. The city also has power to subject adjacent property to special assessments in aid of subway construction. When the 1907 franchise expired in 1927, no agreement was reached.

The lines were operated under temporary agreements pending an adjustment of the conflicting claims and proposals.

The Chicago Transit authority (C.T.A.) was created by act of the Illinois legislature, known as the Metropolitan Transit Authority act, approved April 12, 1945. By reason of this act, and proper municipal legislation, the C.T.A. on Sept. 30, 1947, acquired the properties of the Chicago surface and elevated railway lines. The authority functions as a semipublic body, publicly owned but privately financed to the extent of $105,000,000 through the sale of bonds to private investors. It acquired an exclusive 50-year franchise from the city.

The administrative agency of the C.T.A. is the Chicago Transit board, politically independent, and consisting of seven members who establish C.T.A. policy. The top operating officer of the system is the general manager.

The C.T.A. lines at mid-20th century comprised one of the largest local transit systems in the world, operating gasoline, diesel and trolley buses, streetcars, elevated and subway trains. C.T.A.'s operating territory included Chicago and 85 other municipalities in Cook county. Surface operations included 805.52 mi. of streetcar routes, 540.64 mi. of diesel and gasoline-bus lines and 59.34 mi. of trolley-bus lines. In 1949, 724,851,315 passengers were carried on these lines.

The rapid-transit operations embraced 77.22 route mi. of elevated railroad and 4.9 route mi. of subway lines; 161,570,270 passengers were carried in 1949. Motorbuses carried 100,196,910.

Education and Charity.—The school board is appointed by the mayor. Since 1904 a merit system has been applied in the advancement of teachers; civil service rules cover the rest of the employees. There are free evening schools. Vacation schools were begun in 1896. As far as possible the school buildings are kept open for school lectures and entertainments, serving as social centres; thus, a more adequate use is made of the large investment which they represent.

In all the public schools, manual training, household arts and economy, and commercial studies are a part of the curriculum.

A department of scientific pedagogy and child study (1900) seeks to secure a development of the school system in harmony with the results of scientific study of children (the combination of hand and brain training, the use of auditovisual methods, an elastic curriculum during the adolescent period, etc.). Enrolment in the schools in Sept. 1950 totalled 380,610. The teaching staff numbered 13,565. In 1950 the sum of $5,786,177 was devoted to new school buildings. There were 47 high schools and 343 grade schools in that year.

Hospitals, infirmaries, dispensaries, asylums, shelters and homes for the defective, destitute, orphaned, aged, erring, friendless and incurably diseased; various relief societies; and associations that sift the good from the bad among the mendicant, the economically inefficient and the viciously pauper represent the charity work of the city. The most important charitable societies of the city are the United Charities of Chicago (1909), the United Hebrew charities (1857) and the Associated Jewish charities (1900). A famous institution is Hull house, a social settlement of women, which aims at being a social, charitable and educational district centre. It was established in 1889 by Jane Addams, who became the head worker, and Ellen Gates Starr. It includes an art building, a free kindergarten, a fine gymnasium, a crèche and a diet kitchen and supports classes, lectures and concerts. It has had a very great influence throughout the United States.

The major portion of social work in Chicago is performed by 38 general-welfare agencies, 24 general-health agencies, 110 hospitals and 73 dispensaries, 55 infant-welfare centres, 34 agencies for family relief and rehabilitation, 148 child-caring institutions, 70 boarding clubs and hotels for men and women, 29 employment and vocational-guidance organizations, 60 homes and emergency shelters for adults, 49 summer camps, 60 institutions for civic, legal and protective work. There are also institutions for the shelter of abandoned and stray dogs, cats and other animals. The total financial outlay, public and private, for such work was estimated by the Welfare council of metropolitan Chicago at $114,347,700 for 1948. One of the most important municipal undertakings is the Municipal Tuberculosis sanitarium, erected after 1909, in which year a site of 164 ac. was acquired in the northwestern part of the city.

Population.—Of the total population of Chicago as counted in 1940, 672,705 out of a total of 3,396,808 were foreign-born immigrants, 2,441,859 of native white and of mixed parentage, 277,731 Negro and 4,513 were of other races including Chinese, Japanese and American Indian. The effect of the restrictive immigration laws enacted after World War I was notable in the population of Chicago. A heavy influx of native-born white population from the farms and smaller cities, the growth of the Negro population and an increased influx of Mexicans, not subject to the quota restrictions imposed upon Europe and the eastern hemisphere, had discernible effects, but the business and political life of the city remained influenced by national and racial blocs. There are about 42 nationalistic and racial organizations of one kind or another which maintain secretariats in the business district, and many others with headquarters in outlying parts of the city. The largest, most completely organized and politically influential nationalistic groups are the Germans and Irish—very much "Americanized" and losing cohesion—Poles, Swedes, Czechs, Italians, Yiddish-speaking Jews. There are still approximately 40 or more languages spoken in Chicago, and many sections of the city are to all intents and purposes foreign quarters, but the process of assimilation made the city much more homogeneous than it was at the beginning of the 20th century. In 1920 the Negro population was 109,594, an increase of 148.5% over the preceding census. The influx of Negroes was due to the demand for unskilled labour, especially in the packing industry, during World War I, when European immigration was slight. A shortage of housing facilities for these Negro labourers was one of the underlying causes of the race riots of 1919. The Negro influx slackened during the industrial depression of 1920–21, to be resumed in 1923, but in the depression years it again declined. Negroes continued to come to Chicago throughout the decade 1940–50. Increases in the population also occurred through an excess of births over deaths. The estimate for 1950 was about 500,000.

The Chicago Housing authority is a municipal corporation, empowered by the state of Illinois, with five commissioners, serving without pay as appointees of the mayor of the city subject to state housing board approval, to build and operate public-housing projects in Chicago with federal, state and local funds and to aid in clearing and redeveloping the city's blighted areas.

Partly because of the high percentage of youthful adults in the population of Chicago, drawn to the city from other lands and from the rural districts and smaller cities of the United States, the death rate of the city is among the lowest urban rates in the U.S. Births maintain a lead over deaths, so that the city has a substantial, natural rate of increase of population, irrespective of immigration. The growth of Chicago has been remarkable even for U.S. cities. Any resident of four-score years living in 1900 had seen it grow from a frontier military post among the Indians to a great metropolis, fifth in size among the cities of the world. In 1828 what is now the business centre was fenced in as a pasture; in 1831 the Chicago mail was deposited in a dry-goods box; the tax levy of 1834 was $48.90, and a well which constituted the city water works was sunk at a cost of $95.50; in 1843 pigs were barred from the town streets. Such facts impress upon one, as nothing else can, the rapid growth of the city.

History.—The river Chicago (an Indian name of uncertain meaning, but possibly from Ojibwa *she-kag-ong*, "wild onion place") was visited by Louis Jolliet and Jacques Marquette in 1673, and later by René Robert Cavellier, sieur de la Salle and others. It became a portage route of some importance, used by the French in their passage to the lower Illinois country. In 1804 the United States established Ft. Dearborn there. In 1812, during the Indian War of Tecumseh, the garrison and settlers, who had abandoned the fort and were retreating toward safety, were attacked and overpowered by the savages about 2 mi. S. of the fort. The fort was re-established and fitfully occupied until its final abandonment in 1837.

When Cook county was organized in 1831, Chicago, then a tiny village, became the seat of justice. It became a town in 1833 and a city in 1837. By that time Chicago was confident of its future. The federal government had begun the improvement of the harbour, and the state had started the Illinois and Michigan canal. There was a federal land office also, and the land speculator and town promoter had opened a chapter of history more picturesque, albeit sordid, than in any of the old French days. The giant growth of the lake trade had drawn attention before railway connection was secured with the east in 1852, making progress even more rapid thereafter. During the Civil War a large prison camp for Confederate prisoners, Camp Douglas, was maintained at Chicago. In 1870 the city had 306,605 inhabitants and was already a commercial centre of immense importance. In 1871 it suffered a terrible calamity. On Oct. 8 a fire broke out near the lumber district on the west side. Two-thirds of the city's buildings were wood, and the summer had been excessively dry, while to make conditions worse a high and veering wind fanned the flames. The conflagration leaped the river to the south and finally to the north side, burned over an area of three and one-third miles, destroyed 17,450 buildings and property valued at $196,000,000 and rendered almost 100,000 people homeless; 250 lost their lives. The flames actually travelled two and one-fourth miles in an air line within six and one-half hours. Thousand of persons, fleeing before the flames and firebrands, sought refuge on the shore and even in the waters of the lake. Robbery, pillage, extortion, orgies and crime added to the general horror. In the south side the fire was checked on the 9th by the use of gunpowder; in the north (where the water works were early destroyed) it had extended almost to the prairie when rainfall finally ended its ravages, after about 27 hr. of destruction. A vast system of relief was organized and received generous aid from all parts of the world.

The money contributions from the United States and abroad were $4,996,782; of this, foreign countries contributed nearly $1,000,000 (England half of this). These funds, which were over and above gifts of food, clothing and supplies, were made to last

CHICAGO AERIAL SURVEY CO.

THE CHICAGO LAKE FRONT, LOOKING NORTH

Showing the buildings lining Michigan avenue, the railroad yards, Grant park and Lake Shore drive (extreme right)

CHICAGO

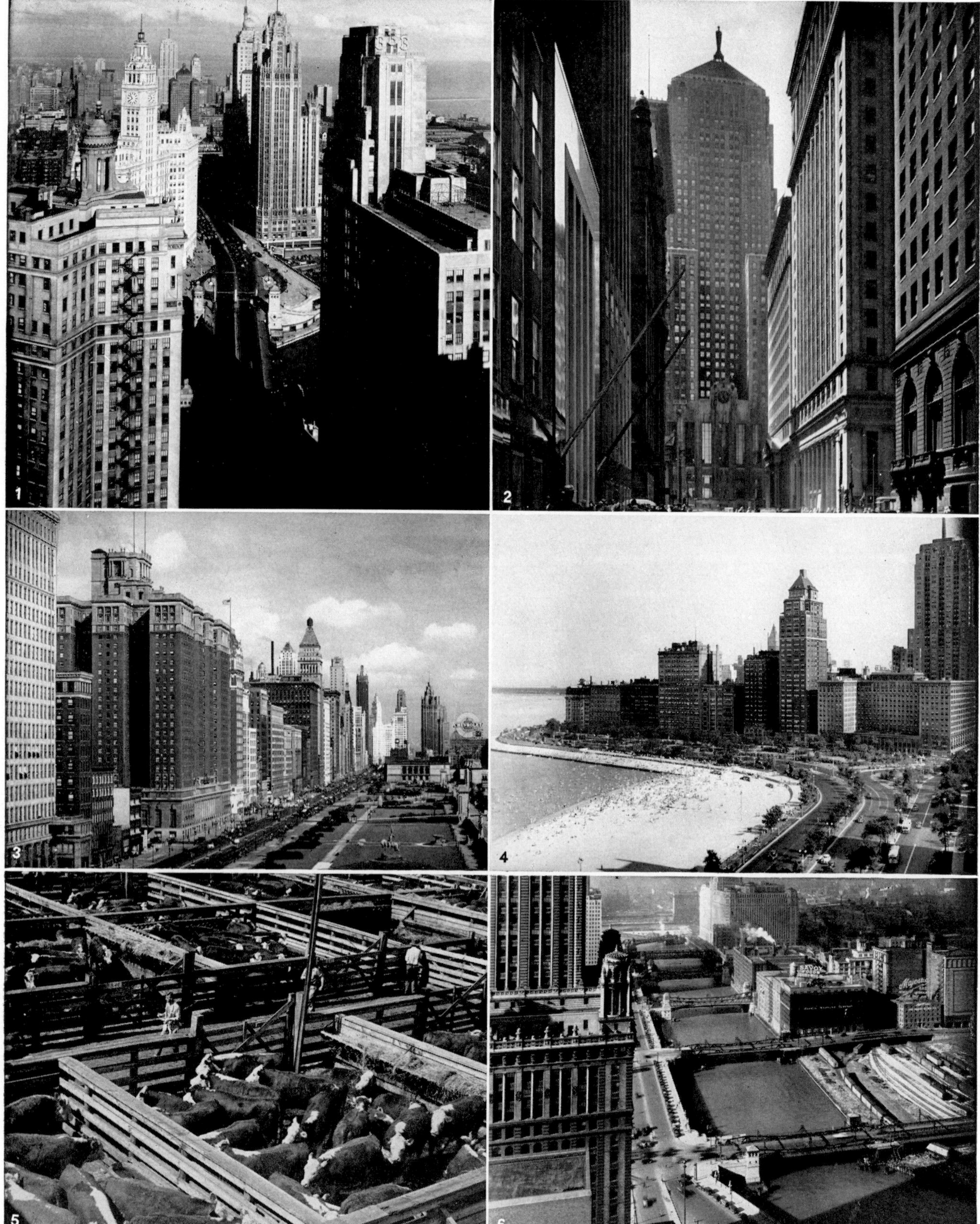

BY COURTESY OF (5) UNION STOCK YARDS; PHOTOGRAPHS (1-4, 6) KAUFMANN & FABRY PHOTO, (5) J. F. ABERNATHY

DOWNTOWN CHICAGO AND A VIEW OF THE UNION STOCK YARDS

1. Michigan avenue, looking north toward the clock tower of the Wrigley building (second building left), across the avenue from the Tribune tower
2. La Salle street, in the financial district. In the background is the Board of Trade building
3. A view along Michigan avenue. The low building at the right is the Art institute
4. The "gold coast" residential section of downtown Chicago, and Oak street beach
5. Cattle pens at the Union Stock Yards in Chicago during the yarding period before sale on the open market. There are approximately 13,000 pens in the yards for the housing of livestock.
6. Six of the bridges spanning the Chicago river near its entrance into Lake Michigan. In centre background is the Merchandise Mart

till the close of 1876 Out of them temporary homes were provided for nearly 40,000 people; barracks and better houses were erected, workmen were supplied with tools and women with sewing-machines; the sick were cared for and the dead buried; and the poorer classes of Chicago were probably never so comfortable as during the first two or three years after the fire. The rebuilding of the city was accomplished with wonderful rapidity. The business district was largely rebuilt within a year, and within three there were few scars of the calamity. Wood was barred from a large area, and a new Chicago of brick and stone, larger, finer and wealthier, had taken the place of the old. Business and population showed no setback in their progress. The solidity and permanence of this prosperity were confirmed during the financial panic of 1873, when Chicago banks alone, among those of the large cities of the country, continued steadily to pay out current funds.

In its later history Chicago became a storm centre of labour troubles, some of them of especially spectacular character. There were great strikes in the packing industry in 1886, 1894 and 1904. But more noteworthy are the railway strike of 1894 and the unsuccessful teamsters' strike of 1905. The former began in the works of the Pullman Car company, and its leader was Eugene Victor Debs. When the contentions of the Pullman employees were taken up by the American Railway union, the strike immediately extended to tremendous proportions. Chicago, as the greatest railway centre of the country and the home of the strike, was naturally the seat of the most serious complications. There was much rioting and destruction of property, and the railway service was completely disorganized. Pres. Grover Cleveland, on the ground of preventing obstruction of the mail service, and of protecting other federal interests, ordered a small number of federal troops to Chicago. Gov. J. P. Altgeld denied the inability of the state to deal with the difficulty, and entered a strong protest against federal interference; but he did nothing to put down the disorder. Federal troops entered the state, and almost immediately the strike collapsed. The high officials of the Railway union, for ignoring a court injunction restraining them from interfering with the movement of the mails, were imprisoned for long terms for contempt of court.

Out of the strike in the McCormick works in 1886 there sprang another famous incident in Chicago's history. The international anarchists of Chicago had been organized in groups about two years earlier, and were very active. They were advocating a "general strike" for an eight-hour day, and the tense excitement among the labourers of the city, because of the McCormick strike, induced unusually extreme utterances. There was a riot at the McCormick works on May 3, in which several men were killed by the police. An anarchist meeting was called for the next day at the Haymarket, a square in Randolph street, and when the authorities judged that the speeches were too revolutionary to be allowed to continue, the police undertook to disperse the meeting. A bomb was thrown, and many policemen were injured, seven fatally. No person could be proved to have thrown the bomb, or to have been directly implicated in its throwing; but on the ground that they were morally conspirators and accomplices in the killing, because they had repeatedly and publicly advocated such acts against the servants of government, 7 anarchists were condemned to death. An application to the United States supreme Court for a writ of error was unanimously refused.

Four were hanged, one committed suicide, two had their death sentence commuted to life imprisonment; an eighth was sentenced to imprisonment for 15 years. Governor Altgeld in 1893 pardoned the three in prison on the ground that the jury was "packed" and consequently incompetent, that no evidence connected the prisoners with the crime and that the presiding judge was prejudiced (*see* an article by Judge J. E. Gary, who presided at the trial, in the *Century Magazine* [April 1893]).

Chicago remained essentially a union town. Organization of unskilled workers gained after 1936, causing one bitter riot with ten deaths in 1937. After World War I the effect of the greater mechanization of industry, the increased productivity of labour, the immigration restrictions and the maintenance of high wage rates without strikes was evidenced in greater industrial tranquillity. In the building trades, however, labour unionism remained a powerful factor, despite a great deal of faction and many charges of corruption and of collusion between labour leaders and gangsters pursuing unlawful avocations. A later phase of trade-union organization was the extension of unionism among small merchants and shopowners, for purposes of price maintenance and limitation of competition. The extension of this form of organization was linked with bombing, terrorism and extortion, but the greater part of the trade-union movement in Chicago was not affected by such methods.

The 400th anniversary of the discovery of America was commemorated by the World's Columbian exposition held at Chicago. The site was in Jackson park and the adjoining Midway, and included 686 ac., of which 188 were covered by buildings. On Oct. 21, 1892—corresponding to Oct. 12, 1492, O.S.—the grounds were formally dedicated, and on the following May 1, opened to the public, continuing open for six months. The number of paid admissions was 21,500,000; of total admissions, 27,539,521. The buildings, planned by a commission of architects, of whom John W. Root and Daniel H. Burnham of Chicago were responsible for the general scheme, formed a collection of remarkable beauty.

Forty years later Chicago threw open the gates of its second international exposition, A Century of Progress, celebrating the centennial of the incorporation of the municipality. In the 1933 period the paid attendance was 22,320,456 and in 1934, 16,314,480. Bold experimental architecture and startling effects in colour and lighting were the dominant features of the exposition, which laid emphasis upon scientific and technological development. The success of the exposition in the midst of a world-wide depression had a stimulating effect upon the city's morale as well as its business.

In the late '90s the city began a great civic awakening. A civil service system was inaugurated in 1895. The salaries of the councilmen were raised with good results. Numerous reform associations were started to rouse public opinion, such as the Citizens' Association of Chicago, organized in 1874, the Civic federation (1894), the Municipal Voters' league (1896), the Legislative Voters' league (1901), the Municipal Lectures association (1902), the Referendum League of Illinois (1901), the Civil Service Reform Association of Chicago, the Civil Service Reform Association of Illinois (1902), the Merchants' club, the City club (1903), Law and Order league (1904) and Society of Social Hygiene (1906); and many of the women's clubs took an active part. They stood for effective enforcement of the laws, sanitation, pure food, public health, the improvement of the schools and the widening of their social influence and (here especially the women's clubs) aesthetic, social and moral progress. The Merchants' club reformed the city's bookkeeping, and secured the establishment (1899) of the first state pawnbrokers' society. The Civic federation demonstrated (1896) that it could clean the central streets for little more than half what the city was paying (the city later saved the difference); it originated the movement for vacation schools and other educational advances, and started the Committee of One Hundred (1897), from which sprang various other reform clubs. The Municipal Voters' league investigated and published the records of candidates for the city council, and recommended their election or defeat. Moreover, a municipal museum was organized in 1905, mainly supported by private aid, but in part by the board of education, in order to collect and make educational use of materials illustrating municipal administration and conditions, physical and social.

The reform movement in its various phases came to its full tide under the administration of Carter H. Harrison, Jr., who was elected to his fifth term in 1911, thereby equalling his father's record of elections to the highest office within the gift of the people of the city. In 1912 State's Attorney John E. W. Wayman closed the city's tolerated vice district, and it was not allowed to operate thereafter.

With the adoption of the prohibition amendment to the federal constitution in Jan. 1919, and the flocking to the city of many adventurous characters attracted by the building boom and the prosperity following the war, there was a growth of violent crime in Chicago. The huge profits of the illicit liquor trade led to the organization of powerful criminal gangs to exploit the traffic, and competiton between these organizations led to murder and banditry, which attracted world-wide attention. The most notorious gang leader of this period was Al ("Scarface") Capone.

Growth of the gang system coincided with an era of spoils politics under Mayor William Hale Thompson, Republican (1915–23 and 1927–31). The reformist interlude of Mayor William E. Dever, Democrat (1923–27) did not abate growing disorders. In 1931 Chicago returned to its normal Democratic moorings under Mayor Anton J. Cermak, a machine politician but a man of forceful character who began a cleanup of the city. He was shot by a criminal anarchist who was attempting to kill President-elect Franklin D. Roosevelt and hit Cermak by mistake at Miami, Fla.

Cermak died March 6, 1933, but his organization remained firmly entrenched under Mayor Edward J. Kelly, Democrat. Repeal of national prohibition in 1933 followed by vigorous police and court offensives for a brief time quelled the organized criminal elements.

Under the centralized regime introduced by Cermak, Chicago politics, long a quasi-tribal and feudal system under ward and district leaders, developed along the lines of Tammany in New York —domination by a powerful organization brooking no rebellion within its ranks. In this change Chicago witnessed the passing of the last of its frontier-town characteristics, which persisted for a century.

Kelly, together with "Pat" Nash, built the Cermak political machine into one of the most powerful vote-getting organizations in the country. Kelly became strong enough, with the help of the bosses of other cities, to defeat the nomination of Henry A. Wallace as vice-president in 1944 and nominate Harry S. Truman, paving his way to the presidency.

Lawlessness, which flourished gangland style during the prohibition era, continued on the same violent scale. In 1947 Chicago had another mild reform when Kelly stepped out as mayor and another Democrat, Martin H. Kennelly, a prominent businessman, took over as mayor.

Nash had died and Kelly went into nominal retirement from politics before his death in 1950. His successor as head of the powerful Democratic machine was Jacob M. Arvey, an attorney who had risen in party ranks under the Kelly regime.

Because of its central location, Chicago has been the United States' most famous convention city and the scene of much national political history. Lincoln (1860), U. S. Grant (1868), James A. Garfield (1880), Cleveland (1884 and 1892), Harrison (1888), Theodore Roosevelt (1904), William Howard Taft (1908), Warren G. Harding (1920) and F. D. Roosevelt (1932, 1940) were all nominated for president in Chicago in addition to a number of unsuccessful candidates nominated in stirring conventions.

BIBLIOGRAPHY.—Annual *Reports* of city departments, school board, park commissioners, etc; *Reports* of the Bureau of the Census; files of the Chicago press; *Report* of the Committee on Co-ordination of Chicago Railway Terminals, engineers' reports on Chicago traction situation; corporation statements of public utility companies; *Reports* of the Chicago Board of Trade; documents in the Municipal Reference Library of Chicago; A. T. Andreas, *History of Chicago* (1884–86); R. Blanchard, *Discovery and Conquest of the Northwest with the History of Chicago* (1898–1903); J. Kirkland, *Story of Chicago* (1892); issues of the *Fergus Historical Series* (1876 *ff.*); S. E. Sparling, *Municipal History and Present Organization of the City of Chicago* (1898); T. J. Riley, *A Study of the Higher Life of Chicago* (1905). Periodical literature contains a vast amount of information on Chicago's progress and conditions that is elsewhere unobtainable; exact references may be obtained in Poole's *Index to Periodical Literature* and *Reader's Guide to Periodical Literature.* (L. H. L.; F. F. Rx.)

CHICAGO, BURLINGTON & QUINCY RAILROAD COMPANY, popularly known as the "Burlington route," incorporated in Illinois Feb. 12, 1849, as the Aurora Branch Railroad company, and adopted its present name Feb. 14, 1855. The railroad commenced operation in 1850 over 12 mi. of track between Aurora, Ill., and West Chicago. Thereafter, by construction and by acquisition of other lines, it grew to about 9,000 mi., extending from Chicago and St. Louis, Mo., to Minneapolis, Minn., Omaha, Neb., Kansas City, Mo., Denver, Colo., and Billings, Mont. More than 97% of the capital stock of the Burlington is owned in equal parts by the Northern Pacific and Great Northern railways, with which it connects at St. Paul, Minn., and Billings to form through routes to the Pacific northwest. The Burlington, in turn, controls the Colorado and Southern railway, which provides a rail route from Wyoming to the Gulf of Mexico. The Burlington system, including the Colorado and Southern and subsidiaries, totals about 11,000 mi. in 14 states.

In 1951 the company, excluding its interest in subsidiary companies, had an investment in railway operating property of about $626,000,000 and $171,000,000 of funded debt and $171,000,000 par value capital stock outstanding.

The railroad was handling more than 50,000,000 tons of commercial freight each year, of which approximately 40% was mine products, 20% agricultural products, 5% livestock and animal products, 5% lumber and forest products and 30% manufactures and miscellaneous freight.

It carried 4,038,511 passengers during 1950 besides a heavy commutation traffic in Chicago suburban territory. On April 9, 1934, the Burlington inaugurated America's first diesel-powered streamline train, the "Zephyr."

CHICAGO, MILWAUKEE, ST. PAUL AND PACIFIC RAILROAD COMPANY. The Chicago, Milwaukee, St. Paul and Pacific Railroad company, incorporated March 31, 1927, was organized under the laws of the state of Wisconsin in order to take over the properties of the Chicago, Milwaukee and St. Paul Railway company, a Wisconsin corporation (organized May 5, 1863, as the Milwaukee and Saint Paul Railway company, "Chicago" having been added to its name Feb. 11, 1874), after receivership and mortgage foreclosure proceedings, culminating in sale of the property on Nov. 22, 1926; and reorganized after bankruptcy by amendment of charter but without change of name, effective Dec. 1, 1945.

The company's history from its early days on records the acquisition of smaller lines until a system developed, extending from Chicago and Milwaukee, Wis., to Saint Paul, Minn., Kansas City, Mo., Omaha, Neb., and many points in the states of Wisconsin, Iowa, Minnesota, North Dakota and South Dakota. On Jan. 1, 1913, it acquired the property of its subsidiary, the Chicago, Milwaukee and Puget Sound Railway company, which operated 2,081 mi. of road, including branch lines, extending from Mobridge, S.D., to Seattle and Tacoma, Wash. Subsequently, other lines were acquired, including the Idaho and Washington Northern railroad, Big Blackfoot Railway company, Tacoma Eastern Railroad company, Puget Sound and Willapa Harbor Railway company, Seattle, Port Angeles and Western Railway company, Bellingham and Northern Railway company, Milwaukee Terminal Railway company, Gallatin Valley Railroad company and Chicago, Milwaukee and Gary Railway company. The properties of the Chicago, Terre Haute and Southeastern Railway company (known as the Terre Haute), which had been operated by the Milwaukee or its predecessors since July 1, 1921, under a 999-year lease, were conveyed to the Milwaukee company by deed dated Dec. 31, 1948. On Dec. 31, 1950, the company operated 10,671 mi. of railroad, of which 9,843 were solely owned, 165 jointly owned and 663 operated under trackage rights. It operated in the states of Idaho, Illinois, Indiana, Iowa, Kansas, Michigan, Minnesota, Missouri, Montana, Nebraska, North Dakota, South Dakota, Washington and Wisconsin. The company on that date owned 838 steam, 60 electric and 232 diesel-electric locomotives; 58,787 freight-train cars; 1,119 passenger-train cars, 13 rail-motor cars; 1 tugboat; 5 car barges; and 3,375 units of company service equipment. (J. W. Ss.)

CHICAGO, ROCK ISLAND AND PACIFIC RAILROAD COMPANY, a U.S. railroad extending from Chicago, Ill., westward, northwestward and southward. It dates from a special act of the Illinois state legislature, approved Feb. 27, 1847, and amended Jan. 27, 1851. Construction began in Chicago Oct. 1, 1851, and the first train ran from Chicago to Joliet, Ill., a distance of 40 mi., on Oct. 10, 1852. The road reached the Mississippi river on Feb. 22, 1854, and there was constructed there the first bridge over that river between Rock Island, Ill., and Davenport, Ia., which was opened on Sept. 1, 1854.

At the close of 1950 the Rock Island comprised about 8,000 mi. running through 14 middle western states, and extending from Chicago to Denver and Colorado Springs, Colo., and Santa Rosa, N.M., and from St. Paul, Minn., to Fort Worth, Dallas and Houston, Tex., with lines into St. Louis, Mo., Memphis, Tenn., Kansas City, Mo., Omaha, Neb., Des Moines, Ia., Oklahoma City, Okla., Topeka, Kan., Eunice, La., and the principal Mississippi valley centres. The total capitalization of all the Rock Island lines as of Dec. 31, 1950, was approximately $295,436,542, including $211,409,442 of capital stock. The railroad on that date was largely dieselized.

CHICAGO, THE UNIVERSITY OF, an institution of higher learning in Chicago, Ill., was founded in 1891 and opened on Oct. 1, 1892. It is privately supported and coeducational. Though originally established as a Baptist university, requirements for Baptist membership on the board of trustees were progressively relaxed by the Northern Baptist convention, and the university is now nondenominational.

The university is approximately 8 mi. S. of the downtown section of Chicago, with frontage for three-fourths of a mile on both sides of the Midway plaisance, which links Jackson and Washington parks. The campus of 110 ac. has more than 100 buildings, most of which are collegiate Gothic in architectural style and grouped in quadrangles. Newer buildings, however, departed from the Gothic style, though general uniformity was maintained with limestone exteriors.

Growth of the university in facilities, program and influence was rapid, largely because of the combination of John D. Rockefeller, its founder, who provided liberal and consistent financial support, and William Rainey Harper, who served as the first president until Jan. 10, 1906. Harper had original educational ideas and enthusiasm, and he gathered a distinguished faculty, including nine presidents of colleges and universities. From the start, therefore, the university was eminent in research and advanced study.

Although the university gained an international reputation as a centre of research, it also was continuously concerned with the development of undergraduate education. Harper established junior and senior college divisions, of two years each, which prevailed until 1930, when the Chicago plan was instituted. This program was extended in 1941 to provide a four-year liberal education curriculum, beginning at the end of the sophomore year of high school. Under that plan, year-long integrated courses covering the broad fields of knowledge were developed. Students met the requirements for the bachelor's degree by passing, either through comprehensive examinations or placement tests taken at the beginning of their residence, 14 required courses. At the beginning of the academic year 1954 the plan was modified to relocate undergraduate education primarily at the end of high school, and to provide approximately half of the requirements in specialized fields. Early admission was continued, as was the four-year program entirely in liberal arts for students so electing, but the large majority of entering students were high-school graduates. Many of the innovations of the Chicago plan, including the integrated courses, early admission of qualified students and renewed attention to liberal education, had a wide influence on collegiate programs of the country.

An administrative reorganization also was made in 1930, establishing largely the present university organization: the College; four divisions—the physical, biological and social sciences and the humanities; six professional schools—business, divinity, law, library science, medicine and social service administration; the library; the press; and University college (for study off-campus, at a downtown centre and through correspondence). This grouping includes the Oriental institute, engaged in research on earlier civilizations; Yerkes observatory, Williams Bay, Wis. (whose astronomers also staff, under a co-operative agreement, the University of Texas' McDonald observatory, Mt. Locke, Tex.); the laboratory schools (nursery, elementary and high school); an orthogenic school; the University clinics; and two basic research organizations, established in 1945, the Institute for Study of Metals and the Enrico Fermi Institute for Nuclear Studies (named in honour of Fermi in 1955). Much of the research and advanced study is conducted through interdivisional and interdepartmental committees. The University of Chicago Press, the oldest in continuous publication in the country, publishes a number of learned journals and an average of 50 books a year.

In addition to the building during Harper's administration, there was extensive construction during the period 1924–32, which trebled floor space. Principal units built after World War II were new hospitals, the administration building, the accelerator building (housing a 450,000,000-ev synchrocyclotron and a 100,000,000-ev betatron) and laboratories for the new institutes in nuclear energy and metals.

Harper, a professor of biblical literature at Yale university before he became the university's first president, was succeeded in 1907 by Harry Pratt Judson. Judson had served as dean of the faculty under Harper and was the first head of the political science department. He consolidated and co-ordinated the university, following its rapid development and expansion under Harper. Judson retired in 1923 and was succeeded by Ernest DeWitt Burton, a New Testament scholar who was also a member of the original faculty. In his two-year administration, terminated by his death, Burton displayed remarkable qualities of enthusiasm and leadership, initiating a program of expansion and implementing it with the university's first public campaign for funds, an effort that produced $9,500,000 in gifts.

Max Mason, a mathematical physicist, succeeded Burton in 1925, and on July 1, 1929, Robert M. Hutchins, dean of the law school of Yale university, became the fifth president at the age of 30. Under Hutchins the Chicago plan for undergraduate education, mentioned previously, was introduced and the faculties were reorganized. Hutchins' title was changed by trustee action to that of chancellor in 1945, and Ernest C. Colwell became president, serving in that office until June 30, 1951.

Hutchins resigned on Dec. 19, 1950 (effective June 30, 1951), as chancellor of the university and as a member of its board of trustees to join the Ford foundation as an associate director.

Lawrence A. Kimpton, vice-president of the university in charge of development, was elected chancellor on April 12, 1951. Kimpton readjusted the undergraduate curriculum to fit the prevailing 8–4–4 divisions by years of U.S. education and took action to balance the university budget and reverse the trend toward deterioration of the area close to the university.

In 1954 Kimpton began a further phase of his administrative program, including a campaign to raise $32,700,000 for use over a ten-year period and a series of important appointments to the faculty.

In the latter 1950s there were enrolled in any one quarter approximately 5,100 full-time students. (W. V. M.)

CHICAGO ACADEMY OF SCIENCES, THE, an institution organized at Chicago, Ill., on Jan. 13, 1857, "to promote and diffuse scientific knowledge," and one of the oldest scholarly bodies existing in Illinois. The collections of the academy, considered at the time among the most valuable in the United States, were in the Chicago fire of 1871.

With the erection of the new building in Lincoln park in 1893 by Mathew Laflin, a new impetus was given to the establishment of a fine scientific museum. Exhibits featuring the wildlife, flora and physical characteristics of the Chicago region were opened daily to the public. (H. K. G.; X.)

CHICAGO AND NORTH WESTERN RAILWAY COMPANY, comprising 7,923 mi. operated as of Dec. 31, 1950, in Illinois, Iowa, Nebraska, Wyoming, Wisconsin, Michigan, Minnesota, South and North Dakota. It owned (1950) 736 steam locomotives and 336 diesel-electric power units, not including 6 diesel-electric power units jointly owned with the Union Pacific railway; 1,179 passenger-train cars; and 45,171 freight-train cars.

The balance sheet, as of Dec. 31, 1950, showed investment in property, less depreciation and amortization, of $366,848,157, investments including capital and other reserve funds and sinking funds of $78,447,814 and total assets of $512,844,979. Capital stock consisted of $81,554,400 common and $91,390,300 preferred.

Its funded debt held by the public was $177,472,669. The Interstate Commerce commission's bureau of valuation reported, as of Dec. 31, 1949, that cost of reproduction less depreciation, value of lands and rights, working capital and material and supplies aggregated $728,512,485. Gross operating revenue for 1950 was $188,901,154 and net railway operating income was $9,132,-717. It was the first railroad to operate into the city of Chicago, commencing in Oct. 1848, and expanding from that date to its present proportions.

CHICAGO HEIGHTS, a city of Cook county, Ill., U.S., on federal highway 30, 28 mi. S. of Chicago. It is served by the Chicago and Eastern Illinois, the Chicago, Milwaukee, St. Paul and Pacific, the Elgin, Joliet and Eastern, the New York Central, Baltimore and Ohio Chicago terminal and the Chicago Heights Terminal Transfer railways. In 1900 the population was 5,100; in 1920, 19,653; in 1940, 22,461; and in 1950, 24,369 by the federal census.

Chicago Heights is an important industrial centre, manufacturing chemicals, alloy and steel products, glass specialties, roofing, textiles, school supplies, fertilizers, paints and various other commodities. The city was incorporated in 1901.

CHICAGO SANITARY AND SHIP CANAL, in the United States, is an engineering development of special importance to the city of Chicago and surrounding districts. It was first opened in 1900 and the cost of construction with improvements has been about $70,000,000. Before the construction of the canal Chicago discharged sewerage into Lake Michigan, which was also the source of the water-supply. Such serious contamination resulted that ultimately the extension of water intake pipes for a distance of 4mi. out into Lake Michigan failed to avoid dangerous pollution.

A few miles west of the city, a low limestone ridge marks the division of the watersheds leading to the Des Plaines and Chicago rivers. The Des Plaines, to the west of the ridge, flows southwest to the Illinois river and thence to the Mississippi river. The Chicago river, to the east of the ridge, normally drains into Lake Michigan. A canal channel was dug through the ridge by which the Chicago was connected with the Des Plaines river and at the same time the flow in the Chicago river was reversed from east to west. The sewage of the city is collected in great central city mains, passed through sewage treatment plants and the purified effluent turned into the canal and carried down to the Gulf of Mexico. The canal is 34mi. long, 160ft. wide and 24ft. in depth. In 1939 an average of 1,500 cu.ft. per second was being drawn from Lake Michigan to carry away the drainage of Chicago. Another phase of the project, completed in 1933, was the creation of an all-water route with a minimum depth of 9ft. between the Great Lakes and the Gulf of Mexico.

CHICANE, the pettifogging subterfuge and delay of sharp law-practitioners, also any attempt to gain unfair advantage by petty tricks. A more common English form of the word is "chicanery." Chicane was also used until recent years as a term in the game of bridge for the points a player might score if his hand contained no trumps. Chicane is no longer scored, but the term is still used. The word is French, derived either from *chaugān,* Persian for the stick used in the game of polo, still played on foot and called *chicane* in Languedoc (*cf.* the military use of *chicaner,* to take advantage of slight variations in ground), or from *chic,* meaning little or petty, from the Spanish *chico,* small.

CHICHA, a fermented liquor resembling beer made by the natives of South America from Indian corn.

CHICHELEY, HENRY (1364–1443), English archbishop, founder of All Souls college, Oxford, was born, the son of a yeoman, at Higham Ferrers, Northamptonshire. He seems to have passed from Winchester college to New college, Oxford, where he took his B.A. in 1392. He was then ordained sub-deacon, but he already held the living of Llanvarchell, in the diocese of St. Asaph. About 1394 he went up to London to practise as an advocate in the principal ecclesiastical court, the court of arches, and from that time an extraordinary number of posts fell to him. In 1396 he was presented to the rectory of St. Stephen's, Walbrook, and, being ordained deacon and priest later on in the year, he was made archdeacon of Dorset in 1397, and in 1399, canon of the collegiate church of Abergwili, North Wales. In Feb. 1402, he was allowed to use a bull of the pope "providing" him to the chancellorship of Salisbury cathedral and canonries in the nuns' churches of Shaftesbury and Wilton, and in Jan. 1402–3 he became archdeacon of Salisbury. In May 1404, Boniface IX. provided him to a prebend at Lincoln, notwithstanding that he already held prebends at Salisbury, Lichfield, St. Martin's-le-Grand and Abergwili, and the living of Brington.

In July 1405, Chicheley began his diplomatic career by a mission to the new Roman pope, Innocent VII., who was professing his desire to end the papal schism by resignation, if his French rival at Avignon would do likewise. In 1406 he was appointed to treat for peace with the French king, and in the following year he was sent to the new pope, Gregory XII., to end the schism. The pope provided him to the bishopric of St. David's and gave him a bull granting him the right to hold all his benefices with the bishopric.

In Jan. 1409, Chicheley was chosen by the convocation of Canterbury to attend the Council of Pisa, which withdrew obedience from both existing popes and in June elected a new pope. Chicheley now became the subject of a leading case, the court of king's bench deciding, after three successive terms, that he could not hold his previous benefices with the bishopric, and that a papal bull could not supersede the law of the land (*Year-book* ii. H. iv. 37, 59, 79). Accordingly he had to resign livings and canonries wholesale (April 28, 1410), and was enthroned at St. David's in May, 1411. He was with the English force under the earl of Arundel which accompanied the duke of Burgundy to Paris in Oct. 1411, and there defeated the Armagnacs; and in July 1413 was sent by Henry V., with the earl of Warwick, to France to conclude peace. On the death of Archbishop Arundel he was nominated to the archbishopric.

These dates are important as they save Chicheley from the charge, versified by Shakespeare (*Henry V.* act i. sc. 2) from Hall's *Chronicle,* of having tempted Henry V. into the conquest of France for the sake of diverting parliament from the disendowment of the Church. As a matter of fact, the parliament at Leicester, in which the speeches were supposed to have been made, began on April 30, 1414 before Chicheley was archbishop, and the rolls of parliament show that he was not present in parliament. Moreover, parliament was so far from pressing disendowment that on the petition of the Commons it passed a savage act against the heresies "commonly called Lollardry" which "aimed at the destruction of the king and all temporal estates," making Lollards felons and ordering every justice of the peace to hunt them down.

Chicheley was present at the siege of Rouen, and the king committed to him the negotiations for the surrender of the city in Jan. 1419 and for the marriage of Katherine. He crowned Katherine at Westminster (Feb. 20, 1421), and in Dec. baptized her child, Henry VI.

Chicheley is renowned chiefly for his educational foundations. He endowed a chest or loan fund for poor scholars at New college, and another for the university at large. He founded at least three colleges, one at Higham Ferrers and two at Oxford. The licence for the first was given by Henry V. in May 1422. It was closely modelled on Winchester college, and to it was attached an almshouse for 12 poor men. His first Oxford college, St. Bernard's, was founded under licence in mortmain in 1437 for Cistercians. It was suppressed with the Cistercian abbeys in 1539 and granted in 1546 to Christ Church, Oxford, who sold it to Sir Thomas Pope in 1553 for the present St. John's college. The patent for All Souls college, dated May 20, 1438, is for a warden and 20 scholars, to be called "the Warden and College of the souls of all the faithful departed," to study and pray for the souls of Henry V. and Henry VI. and all Englishmen who had died in the wars with France. A papal bull for the college was obtained on June 21, 1439; and further patents for endowments from May 11, 1441, to Jan. 28, 1443, when a general confirmation charter was obtained, for which £1,000 (£30,000 at least of our money) was paid. Only about a quarter of the whole endowment was derived from alien priories bought by Chicheley from the crown. The rest, particularly the manor of Edgware, which made the fortune of the college, was bought from private owners. Early in 1443 the college was opened by Chicheley with four bishops in state. The statutes, not drawn up until April 2, 1443, raised the number of the college to 40, 16 of whom were to be "jurists" and 24 students of arts and philosophy or theology.

Chicheley died on April 12, 1443, and was buried in Canterbury cathedral.

CHICHEN-ITZÁ or **CHICHEN,** the ruins of an ancient Mayan city of that name, in the south-central part of the State of Yucatán, Mexico, near the boundary of Quintana Roo, about 20° 30′ N. lat. and 88° 30′ W. longitude. The dry, waterless region round about Chichen-Itzá is of limestone formation, with only an underground water supply, available in but a few places called *cenotes* by the Mayans, where the limestone cap has fallen into the caves through which the water flows. Two large *cenotes* determined the location of the city and gave it its distinctive name, *Chi,* which in Mayan means mouths, *chen,* wells, and *Itzá* the name of the particular Mayan tribe or group which first settled there, the whole meaning the "Mouths of the Wells of the Itzá."

Founded not later than A.D. 530, the settlement for about the first century constituted but a frontier post of a Mayan civilization, "The Old Empire," which at that time was flourishing in the much greater centres to the southward—Copan, Tikal, Quiriqua, Palenque and a dozen other equally important cities. When about a century later these great flourishing southern cities were finally abandoned, Chichen-Itzá was also temporarily abandoned, A.D. 668, and the Itzá trekked westward across Yucatán to a new capital, Chakanputun, south of the modern Campeche. Chakanputun was burned in A.D. 944 and the "Holy Men of the Itzá" led their people back to the "Mouths of the Wells of the Itzá" where, in A.D. 964 they re-established their *lares* and *penates* and rebuilt their shrines and altars.

It was the period of the founding of "The New Empire" with Uxmal, Mayapan, and a group of satellite cities, sharing with Chichen-Itzá a superb renaissance of Mayan culture and power. In A.D. 1004 the three greater cities formed an alliance, the League of Mayapan, and the calm and order and prosperity that followed gave rise to a golden age of Mayan religion, science and art, with majestic temples and superb sculptures scattered about the land. At Chichen most of the middle section of the city lying south and west of the Thousand Columns, was built at this time, graced by the Akab'tzib (House of the Dark Writing), the Chichanchob (Red House), the House of the Deer, and parts of the Monjas (Monastery).

In 1201 the League of Mayapan was disrupted by an attack of the Mayapan people upon the Chichen-Itzá because of conspiracies against the League by Chac Xib Chac (The Very Red Man), the Itzan ruler. With the aid of Toltec and Aztec allies from Central Mexico the Mayapan people conquered the Itzans. Henceforth the city was held in thrall by the Toltec-Aztec allies of the Mayapan group. These Toltec-Aztec conquerors brought with them the worship of the fair, golden-haired god, Quetzalcoatl, the "Feathered Serpent," who became "Kukulcan," the Itzan equivalent. During this period Chichen-Itzá rose to heights of prosperity, prominence and architectural development surpassing anything in its earlier history, and highly adorned temples, sanctuaries and shrines rose as if by magic; the principal temple, the so-called Castillo, covering an acre of ground and rising 100 ft. above the plain; the Thousand Columns enclosing a central plaza of more than 5 ac. with pyramid temples, colonnaded halls, sunken courts, terraces and theatres; the Tlachtli-ground or Ball Court; the Temple of the Jaguars; the Temple of the Tables; the Astronomical Observatory; the High Priest's grave; and a host of others.

The two *cenotes,* or wells, upon which the city depended for its very life, constituted the religious, as well as the economic, centre of the city and its culture. Young Itzan maidens were sacrificed to the gods of the wells, as were all kinds of valuables, in gruesome spectacles that drew thousands to share in the ceremonies and the rites, and gave to the city its "holy" character. The natural setting of the wells, the grandeur of the temples built beside them, the austerity and dignity of the rites, all contributed to the lure, and made Chichen-Itzá the Mecca of the Mayan world for almost two and one-half centuries until about the middle of the 15th century when it was rather suddenly and finally abandoned, only a few stragglers making their homes there and doing homage to the old gods.

See S. G. Morley, "Chichen-Itzá, An Ancient American Mecca," *Natl. Geog. Mag.*, vol. xlvii., No. 1, pp. 63–95 (Jan. 1925). (W. E. E.)

CHICHERIN, GEORGHY VASILIEVICH (1872–1936), Russian statesman, the son of an official in the ministry for foreign affairs, was born in Karaul, province of Tambov. He was educated at a Russian Higher school, and at St. Petersburg (Leningrad) university, and entered the diplomatic service in the archives department of the foreign office. From 1897 onward he was gradually drawn into the revolutionary movement. He resigned from the diplomatic service in 1904, renouncing his estates, and went to Berlin, where he followed closely the German Social-Democratic movement. He was at first attached to the Russian socialist-revolutionary party, but later joined the social-democratic party. He was prevented by illness from taking part in the revolution in 1905. He spent 12 years in revolutionary activities in London, Paris and Berlin, being elected secretary of the foreign central bureau of the Russian Social-Democratic party in 1907. In the same year he was arrested in Berlin for the possession of a false passport, and banished from Prussia. During the World War he assisted the anti-war Labour elements in Great Britain, and organized the relief of Russian political refugees, a philanthropic work which had a revolutionary aspect in maintaining contact with Russian revolutionaries. After the Bolshevik revolution in November, when Russia was no longer considered an ally, but an enemy, Chicherin was imprisoned in Brixton gaol on the ground of "enemy associations." On Jan. 3, 1918 he was exchanged for Sir George Buchanan by the Soviet Government, and banished from England. He returned to Russia, and was appointed People's Commissary for foreign affairs in March 1918. In 1922 he headed the Soviet delegation to the conference at Genoa (April 10–May 19) (*q.v.*), of which the unexpected result was a separate treaty between Soviet Russia and Germany. Chicherin conducted Russian policy continuously, from 1918 to 1930, having a longer tenure of office than any contemporary European foreign minister. (For the policy for which he was responsible during this period, *see* RUSSIA.)

CHICHESTER, a city and municipal borough in the Chichester parliamentary division of Sussex, England, 69 mi. S.W. of London by the Southern railway. Pop. (est. 1938) 16,460. Area, 4.48 sq.mi. It lies in the coastal plain at the foot of a spur of the South Downs, a mile from the head of Chichester harbour, an inlet of the English channel. The Romano-British town on this site was perhaps Regnum or Regni. Situated on one Roman road in direct connection with London and another leading from east to west, Chichester (*Cesseceastre, Cicestre*) remained of considerable importance under the South Saxon kings and it had a mint in 928. Domesday book speaks of 97½ haws, or building plots, in Chichester and a charter of Henry I mentions the borough, but the earliest extant charter is that of Stephen, about 1135, granting the burgesses the rights of a borough and gild merchant, as they held them in the time of William I. This grant shows the Chichester gild merchant to be possibly the oldest in the country. This was confirmed by Henry II *c.* 1155. By a charter of Edward II, the customs of wool, hides and skins were reserved to the king. Edward III directed that the Sussex county court should be held at Chichester. Confirmations of the previous charters were granted by many later sovereigns. James II in 1685 granted the charter now in force. Chichester returned two members to parliament from 1295 to 1867, and one member from then until 1885. Throughout the middle ages Chichester was a place of great commercial importance, Edward III establishing a wool staple there in 1348. Chichester had five fairs in 1889; all but Sloe fair (*c.* 1107–08) were abolished. Fuller mentions the Wednesday market as being famous for corn, while Camden speaks of that on Saturday as the greatest for fish in the county.

The cathedral church of the Holy Trinity was founded towards the close of the 11th century, after the see had been removed to Chichester from Selsey in 1075. It was consecrated in 1108; Bishop Ralph Luffa (1091–1123) was the first great builder, followed by Seffrid II (1180–1204), but disastrous fires led to further building throughout the 13th century. Norman work appears in the nave (arcade and triforium), choir (arcade) and elsewhere; but there is much very beautiful Early English work, as in the choir above the arcade. The nave is remarkable in having double aisles on each side, the outer pair being of the 13th century. The church is also unique among English cathedrals for its detached campanile, a massive and beautiful Perpendicular structure with the top story octagonal. Modern restorations, which include the fine central tower and spire (originally 14th century), the Decorated Lady Chapel and the Perpendicular cloisters, have been effected with great care. The library is a fine late Norman vaulted room; and the bishop's palace retains an Early English chapel. The cathedral is 393 ft. long within, 131 ft. across the transepts, and 90 ft. across the nave with its double aisles. The height of the spire is 277 feet. At the junction of the four main streets of the town, which preserves its Roman plan, stands an octagonal market cross, in ornate Perpendicular style, built by Bishop Story, *c.* 1500, perhaps the finest of its kind in the United Kingdom. The hospital of St. Mary was founded in the 12th century, but the existing buildings are transitional from Early English to Decorated. Its use as an almshouse is maintained. Other ancient buildings are St. Olave's church, in the construction of which Roman materials were used; the Guildhall, formerly a Grey Friars' chapel, of the 13th century; the Canon gate leading into the cathedral close; and the Vicars college. The city retains a great part of its ancient walls, which have a circuit of about a mile and a half, and at least in part, follow the line of Roman fortifications. There is a theological college, a women teachers' training college and a blue-coat school. A new county office building was opened in 1938. The town has a large cattle market and a considerable agricultural trade, but no outstanding industry. A canal connects with Chichester harbour. The diocese includes the whole county of Sussex except a few parishes, with very small portions of Kent and Surrey.

See *Victoria County History,* "Sussex"; Alexander Hay, *History of Chichester* (Chichester, 1804).

CHICHESTER OF BELFAST, ARTHUR CHICHESTER, Baron (1563–1625), lord-deputy of Ireland, second son of Sir John Chichester of Raleigh, Devonshire, was educated at Exeter college, Oxford. He commanded a ship against the Spanish Armada in 1588, and is said to have served under Drake in his expedition of 1595. Having seen further service abroad, he was sent to Ireland at the end of 1598 and was appointed by the earl of Essex to the governorship of Carrickfergus. When Essex returned to England Chichester served under Mountjoy in the war against the rebellious earl of Tyrone, and in 1601 Mountjoy recommended him to Cecil as the fittest person to be entrusted with the government of Ulster. On Oct. 15, 1604, Chichester was appointed lord-deputy of Ireland. He announced his policy in a proclamation wherein he abolished the semi-feudal rights of the native Irish chieftains, substituting for them fixed dues, while their tenants were to become dependent "wholly and immediately upon his majesty." Tyrone and other Irish clan chieftains resented this summary interference with their ancient social organization, and their resistance was strengthened by the ill-advised measures against the Roman Catholics which Chichester was compelled to take by the orders of the English ministers. He himself was moderate and enlightened in his views on this matter, and it was through his influence that the harshness of the anti-Catholic policy was relaxed in 1607. Meantime his difficulties with the Irish tribal leaders remained unsolved. But in 1607, by "the flight of the Earls," he was relieved of the presence of the two formidable Ulster chieftains, the earls of Tyrone and Tyrconnell. Chichester's policy for dealing with the situation thus created was to divide the lands of the fugitive earls among Irishmen of standing and character; but the plantation of Ulster as actually carried out was much less favourable and just to the native population than the lord-deputy desired. In 1613 Chichester was raised to the peerage as Baron Chichester of Belfast, and in the following year he went to England to give an account of the state of Ireland. On his return to Ireland he again attempted to moderate the persecuting policy against the Irish Catholics which he was instructed to enforce; and although he was to some extent successful, it was probably owing to his opposition to this policy that he was recalled in Nov. 1614. The king, however, told him, "You may rest assured that you do leave that place with our very good grace and acceptation of your services"; and he was given the post of lord-treasurer of Ireland. After living in retirement for some years, Chichester was employed abroad in 1622; in the following year he became a member of the Privy Council. He died on Feb. 19, 1625, and was buried at Carrickfergus.

CHICHIBU, PRINCE: *see* Yoshihito.

CHICKADEE, common American name (derived from the call-note) for the black-throated, black-capped titmouse (*Parus atricapillus*), of the northern states and Canada. The brown-capped chickadee (*P. hudsonicus*) is resident in Canada and northern New England. The smaller Carolina chickadee (*P. carolinensis*) breeds in the southeastern states. The mountain chickadee (*P. gambeli*) is resident in the Rocky Mountains and westward, and has a white stripe over the eye. The Alaska chickadee (*P. cinctus alascensis*) is also found in eastern Siberia. The chestnut-backed chickadee (*P. rufescens*) lives on mountains from Alaska to Montana and California. Others are found in Mexico. All are closely allied with the old world titmice, but have no crest. (*See* Titmouse.) (G. F. Ss.)

CHICKAMAUGA. The battle of Chickamauga was fought (Sept. 19–20, 1863) in northern Georgia between the Federal army of the Cumberland under Rosecrans and *Bragg's* Confederate army. It was the one great Confederate victory in the West, rendered indecisive by subsequent events. *Bragg,* afraid of being surrounded in Chattanooga, evacuated the town, which Rosecrans occupied (Sept. 9), and withdrew to Lafayette, where he awaited reinforcements from Virginia under *Longstreet* before fighting a pitched battle. Rosecrans, when *Bragg* was found not to be retreating on Rome, hastily concentrated his three corps (Sept. 17), his left (Crittenden) on West Chickamauga creek at Lee and Gordon's mills, 12 m. S. of Chattanooga, and his right (McCook) at Stevens' gap in Lookout mountain. *Hood* with three brigades joined *Bragg* (Sept. 18), who that day had begun to move down the east bank of the creek to outflank Crittenden at the mills. His right column crossed 4 m. below, and the movement was to be taken up by the other columns in succession from right to left. *Bragg* expected to envelop Crittenden and drive Rosecrans back upon Lookout mountain, cutting him off from Chattanooga. Only two Confederate columns crossed that day; three more divisions followed early next morning. But during the night Rosecrans, who had been shifting his army all day to the left, moved Thomas's corps from the centre to the extreme left, to secure his line of retreat to Chattanooga. Thomas's night march defeated *Bragg's* plan. He was now forced to deliver battle north of the mills, to prevent his own right from being turned. Thick woods concealed the movements of both armies, and the fighting consisted of a series of independent engagements, in which each side alternately outflanked and was outflanked by the other. The battle began (Sept. 19) with Thomas sending a division on a reconnaissance towards the creek. It encountered dismounted cavalry. Both sides hurried up reinforcements and the fighting spread southward, until the whole of Rosecrans' and the greater part of *Bragg's* forces had been drawn in. The general result was favourable to Rosecrans. He had strengthened his hold on the roads in his rear, but he had put in all his forces, except three brigades of Granger's reserve corps, which were holding Rossville gap, whereas *Bragg* had still three divisions in hand and during the night was joined by three fresh brigades.

For the morrow's battle *Bragg* reorganized his army in two wings, the right under *Polk,* the left under *Longstreet,* who arrived at 11 p.m., and decided to persevere with his progressive order of attack. *Polk* was ordered to advance at sunrise (Sept. 20), but the battle only began some hours later. Thomas had strengthened his line during the night with breastworks. *Polk's* right overlapped Thomas's left, and two brigades worked round the breastworks into his rear, but were driven out by his reserves. *Polk's* frontal attacks were repulsed, but Thomas urgently called for reinforcements to secure his left. Rosecrans, believing that *Bragg* was massing all his troops against Thomas, ordered the best part of three divisions to the left. The withdrawal of a fourth (Wood's), due to a misunderstanding, opened a gap in the Federal line, into which *Longstreet* stepped. He had organized a heavy column of attack with eight brigades in three lines and another division forming a flankguard on his left. The Federal right wing, now numbering less than 7,000 men, was swept off the field, but not being pursued, rallied in McFarland's gap. Rosecrans, McCook and Crittenden were all caught in the rout and went to Chattanooga. The break in the Federal line occurred about noon. Thomas was left with five divisions (including one from each of the other two corps) and two or three brigades to withstand *Bragg's* whole army. *Longstreet,* swinging to the right, endeavoured to reach Thomas's rear. Four of Thomas's divisions continued to hold the breastworks in *Polk's* front, but Brannan's division and part of Wood's formed a fresh line nearly at right angles with Thomas's main position along Horseshoe ridge, a spur projecting from Missionary ridge. *Longstreet* had almost enveloped Brannan's right, when two of Granger's brigades under Steedman came to the rescue, and after a desperate struggle dislodged the attacking force, and the Federals held the ridge against renewed assaults, until *Longstreet,* having vainly called for reinforcements from *Polk's* wing, put in his reserve division. The Federals were then driven back from the ridge, with the loss of three regiments captured, to the Snodgrass hill, an elevation 50 ft. lower and over 200 yd. to the rear. Thomas, on receiving an order about 4.30 P.M., had already ordered his left wing to withdraw. *Polk,* who had remained inactive since his repulse in the morning, about 4 P.M. had recommenced his attacks, but the four Federal divisions succeeded in extricating themselves. The right, on Snodgrass hill, was then withdrawn, before *Longstreet* could renew the attack. The Confederate pursuit was halted at 6 P.M., at which hour the whole field was in their possession. Thomas took up a position for the night covering Rossville, and *Bragg's* army being too exhausted to attack next day, after dark (Sept. 21) the Federals withdrew unmolested to Chattanooga. The two armies were probably of about equal strength, from 60,000 to 65,000 each. The percentage of losses was heavier than in any other battle of the Civil War, the casualties on either side exceeding 16,000.

See Gracie, *Truth about Chickamauga* (1911); Geer, *Campaigns of the Civil War* (1926). For a very different version, claiming a Federal victory, *see* Massachusetts Military Historical Society, vol. vii.

(W. B. Wo.)

CHICKASAW, an American Indian people of Muskogi stock for long resident in northern Mississippi, and later forming one of the "five civilized tribes" of Oklahoma. They were foes of the French, friends of the British, and fierce fighters. They never numbered more than about 5,000, which is also their present population, although this comprises many individuals of mixed blood. (*See* MUSKOGIAN INDIANS.)

CHICKASHA, a city of Oklahoma, U.S., on the Washita river, 45 mi. S.S.W. of Oklahoma City; the county seat of Grady county. It is on federal highways 81 and 277, and is served by the Rock Island and the Frisco railways. By the federal census of 1950 the population was 15,753, as compared with 14,111 in 1940. Chickasha is the trade centre of a diversified farming, livestock and dairy region. The city has cotton gins, compresses, flour and oil mills. The Chickasha natural gas field is one of the largest in the world. The Oklahoma College for Women, one of the highest ranking colleges of its kind, is located there. Chickasha was founded in 1892. In Indian language Chickasha means rebel.

CHICKEN POX or varicella, a contagious disease characterized by an eruption of vesicles in the skin. The disease usually occurs in epidemics, and the patients are generally between two and six years old. The incubation period is at least two weeks; there are practically no prodromal symptoms, though slight fever for about 24 hr. may precede the eruption. A number of raised red papules appear on the back or chest; in from 12 to 24 hr. these develop into tense vesicles filled with a clear fluid, which in another 36 hr. or so becomes opalescent. During the fourth day these vesicles shrivel up, and the scabs fall off, leaving as a rule no scar. Fresh spots appear during the first three days, so that at the end of that time they can be seen in all stages of growth and decay. The eruption is most marked on areas covered by clothing, but it also occurs on the face and limbs and on the mucous membrane of the mouth and palate. The temperature rarely rises above 102° F. The disease runs a favourable course in most cases, and after-effects are rare. The patient should be isolated. The diet should be light, and the patient should be prevented from scratching the spots, which would lead to ulceration and scarring. After the first few days there is no necessity to confine the patient to bed. In the large majority of cases, it is easy to distinguish the disease from smallpox, but sometimes it is difficult. The chief points in the differential diagnosis are as follows: (1) In chicken pox the rash is chiefly on the trunk, and less on the limbs and face; (2) some of the vesicles are oval, whereas in smallpox they are always hemispherical. They have not at the outset the hard shotty feeling of the more virulent disease; (3) the vesicles attain their full growth within 12 to 24 hr.; (4) the rash appears "in crops"; (5) there is no prodromal period.

The disease is believed to be caused by a filterable virus. A curious and imperfectly understood relationship exists between chicken pox and herpes zoster (shingles). Contact with chicken pox gives rise in some individuals to herpes zoster, while the reverse may also occur though to a lesser extent. There also appears to be a certain degree of cross immunity between the two diseases.

CHICKWEED (*Stellaria media* or *Alsine media*), an annual herb of the pink family (Caryophyllaceae), called also satinflower, tongue-grass and winter weed. It is native to Europe and Asia and widely naturalized throughout North America and other regions. The plant has weak, reclining, much-branched stems, oval or ovate leaves about 2 in. long and small white flowers. In mild climates it is found blooming throughout the year; in colder regions, as in the northeastern U.S., it withstands severe frosts and may be discovered blossoming under light snow in midwinter. Various other species of *Stellaria* and also of *Arenaria* are known as chickweeds. Closely allied are the mouse-ear chickweeds (*Cerastium* sp.), various species of which are found in Great Britain, North America and other temperate regions. Most plants called chickweed, though abundant as weeds, are readily eradicated by cultivation. Perennial species are sometimes persistent in lawns.

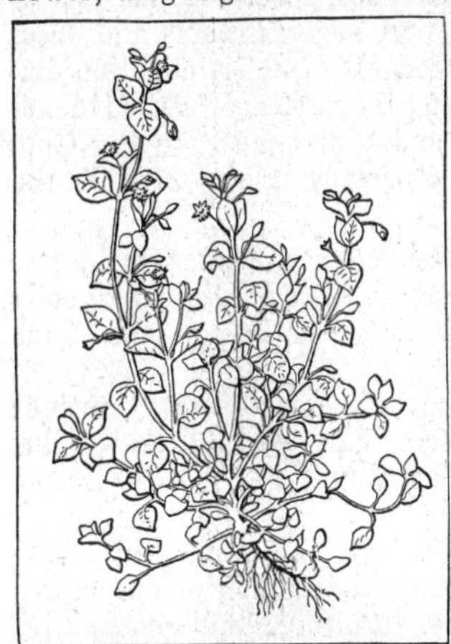

BY COURTESY OF IOWA GEOLOGICAL SOCIETY

CHICKWEED, A COMMON GARDEN WEED USED AS FOOD FOR CAGED BIRDS

CHICLANA DE LA FRONTERA, a town of southern Spain, in Cádiz province, 12 mi. S.E. of Cádiz. Pop. (1940) 14,337 (mun., 17,047). Owing to its position in the fertile valley of the Irio, facing the Gulf of Cádiz, 3 mi. W., Chiclana is the centre of a great fruit and vine growing district, and is the favourite summer residence of wealthy Cádiz merchants. Its hot mineral springs also attract many visitors. About 5 mi. S. is Barrosa, where the British under Sir Thomas Graham (Lord Lynedoch) defeated the French under Marshal Victor, March 5, 1811.

CHICLE or **CHICLE-GUM,** the coagulated milky juice (latex) of the sapodilla or naseberry (*Sapota achras*), a tropical American tree of the family Sapotaceae, the fruit of which is widely used in all tropical regions. The latex was first taken to the United States as a substitute for rubber or balata, but beginning about 1890 was imported in increasing quantities, being the basic ingredient of modern commercial chewing gum. The latex is collected by tapping the trunk after the manner followed for gathering balata and gutta percha (*q.v.*); zigzag deep cuts are made to a height of 30 ft. or more up the trunk. The very viscous "milk" oozes out and runs slowly down to a receptacle placed at the base of the tree, the flow lasting for hours and amounting at times to many quarts. The *chicelero* collects the chicle from his "walk" of trees once a day, gathering about a ton per season from 200 to 300 or more trees, which are rested from four to seven years between tappings, about 15% being lost by this treatment.

Practically all the gum comes from Yucatan and adjacent El Petén in Guatemala from wild trees, but attempts to grow it in plantations have been started in British Honduras. The coagulated raw gum is boiled in large kettles until a water content of about 33% is attained; the semisolid mass is then poured into wood forms and moulded into *marquetas* or blocks of about 25 lb. weight, which are packed for transportation in bales of four blocks each.

For manufacture into chewing gum the grayish-brown blocks are remelted, foreign matter is removed, sugar and flavouring substances are added and the finished product moulded and wrapped in packages.

After 1924 the scarcity of chicle resulted in the importation into the U.S. of jelutong from the East Indies, a gum derived from *Dyera costulata* (family Apocynaceae), often called wild rubber. It is mixed with chicle to make chewing gum.

CHICO, a city of Butte county, Calif., U.S., 96 mi. N. of Sacramento on federal highway 99E and the Southern Pacific and Western Pacific railways. The population in 1950 was 12,210; in 1940, 9,287. Almonds, prunes and other fruits, alfalfa, rice and other grains are produced in the region. The city has a match factory, rice mills, fruit-packing houses and creameries, and manufactures steel, aluminum, metal tubes, portable homes, packing cases, millwork, concrete pipe, beet sugar, brooms and sheet metal. Chico State college and a federal plant-introduction station are situated there. In Bidwell park (2,400 ac.) is the Hooker oak which has a diameter of 9 ft. and a spread of 150 ft. Gold and silver are mined in the county, especially around Oroville, the county seat.

CHICOPEE, a city of Hampden county, Mass., U.S., just north of Springfield, on the east bank of the Connecticut river at the mouth of the Chicopee, and served by the Boston and Maine railroad.

It has an area of 22.9 sq.mi., and includes five villages: Chicopee Center, Chicopee Falls, Willimansett, Fairview and Aldenville. The population in 1950 was 48,939; it was 41,664 in 1940 by the federal census.

The Chicopee falls 70 ft. there in less than 3 mi., furnishing power for numerous factories. Among the leading manufactures are radios and electrical appliances, furniture, knit goods, tires and sporting goods.

Chicopee was settled about 1638; was set off from Springfield as an independent town in 1848; and was chartered as a city in 1890. The name is an Indian word meaning "cedar tree." Chicopee Falls was the home of Edward Bellamy.

The bronze-casting industry (later abandoned) was founded there by Nathan Peabody Ames (1803–47), a swordmaker, who in 1836 began the manufacture of cannonballs and church bells. Some of the finest bronze work in the country was done there, including the doors of the national capitol.

CHICORY, *Cichorium intybus* (family Compositae), in its wild state is a native of Great Britain, occurring most frequently in dry chalky soils and by roadsides. It has a long fleshy taproot, a rigid branching hairy stem rising to a height of 3 to 5 ft., the leaves around the base being lobed and toothed, not unlike those of the dandelion. The flower heads are of a bright blue colour, few in number, and measure nearly an inch and a half across. Common chicory is cultivated extensively on the continent of Europe—the Netherlands, Belgium, France, Germany. Its roots roasted and ground are used as a substitute for, adulterant of, or addition to coffee; both roots and leaves are employed as salads; and the plant is grown as a fodder or herbage crop for cattle. In Great Britain it is chiefly in connection with coffee that chicory is employed. A large proportion of the chicory root used for this purpose is obtained from neighbouring continental countries; but a considerable quantity is cultivated in England, chiefly in Yorkshire. It gives the coffee additional colour, bitterness and body.

The blanched leaves are much esteemed by the French as a winter salad, *Barbe de capucin.* In Belgium a variety of chicory called *Witloef* (or witloof) is preferred. There, also, the fresh roots are boiled and eaten with butter, and throughout the continent the roots of witloof are stored for use as salads during winter.

In North America chicory is an introduced weed which has become widely distributed. It is abundant in pastures and along roadsides in the eastern United States and Canada, and is usually considered a pest. As a cultivated crop common chicory is grown to some extent for its root. Witloof chicory (French endive) is grown to some extent as a forcing crop. The roots are grown in the open during the summer and are taken up in the fall to be forced during the winter. If the seed is sown early in the spring in temperate regions having a growing season of five and one-half to six months, the plants may go to seed instead of forming large storage roots suitable for forcing. In such regions seed should be sown in June. The roots may be forced under greenhouse benches, in cellars or out of doors. (*See* also ENDIVE.)

CHICOUTIMI, industrial town and capital of Chicoutimi county, Quebec, on the Saguenay river, 227 mi. N. by E. from Quebec, on the Canadian National railway; it is also connected with Quebec by regular steamship lines. Pop. (1951) 23,216. It is the centre for one of the greatest hydro developments in North America for aluminum production at near-by Arvida. The district has pulp, paper, furniture and textile plants. (C. CY.)

CHIDAMBARAM, a town of India, in the South Arcot district of Madras, 7 mi. from the coast and 151 mi. S. of Madras by rail. Pop. (1941) 26,212. The fine pagodas at Chidambaram are the oldest in the south of India. The northern frontier of the ancient Chola kingdom is supposed to have been there. The principal temple is sacred to Siva, and is visited by huge numbers of pilgrims.

CHIEF (Fr. *chef,* head; Lat. *caput*), the head or upper part of anything and so, in heraldry, the upper part of the escutcheon, occupying one-third of the whole. The phrase "in chief" (Med. Lat. *in capite*) is used in feudal law of the tenant who holds his fief immediately from the lord paramount (*see* FEUDALISM).

CHIEF JUSTICE. By mid-20th century, every U.S. state constitution with the exception of one carried a section providing for a highest appellate court. Each had a presiding officer—entitled the chief justice in 44 states, the chief judge in Maryland and New York, the president in West Virginia and the presiding judge in South Dakota. Until 1951 the supreme court in Delaware was presided over both by a chancellor and a chief justice, but under a reorganization that year a separate supreme court was created headed by a chief justice.

The manner of selection and terms of office of the chief justices varied widely among the states. The most common single method of selecting the chief justice is appointment by members of the court. This occurred in 28 states under various forms of a rotation system in the 1950s. In 16 of these states rotation took place within a specified period ranging from six months to four years; in 7 the justice with the shortest term left to serve became chief justice for the remainder of his term on the bench; and in 5 the senior justice became chief justice for the remainder of his term.

In the rest of the states the chief justice was specifically designated for his office. Nine states provided for his popular election; eight states for appointment by the governor; and three states for selection by the legislature.

Terms served by the chief justices differed as widely in the states as the methods for their selection. In the 1950s they ranged from six months in Indiana and Iowa to life tenure in Massachusetts and New Hampshire.

In at least 19 states terms of office of chief justices were identical with those of the associate justices. These states generally included those in which the chief justice is elected to his office or where he is appointed by the governor or legislature. Tenure in this group ranged from 6 to 15 years. Those states selecting their chief justices by rotation, seniority or in accordance with the principle of the shortest term to serve commonly provided for much briefer tenure. In ten such states at mid-century he served two years; in five, one year; and in two, six months.

There were a number of states in which the chief justices had an indeterminate period of office. Thus, in Tennessee the chief justice served at the pleasure of the court; in Maryland it was reported that the term was undefined, although presumably as long as he sat on the court. Besides judicial responsibilities, the chief justice of the court of last resort has innumerable administrative duties. Although most details can be delegated to the clerk's office, many of these functions can be executed by him alone; and his immediate responsibility for administrative matters never can be delegated.

The powers of the chief justices vary sharply among the states. For example, in New Jersey, under the new constitution of 1948, the chief justice was made permanent administrative head of all of the courts in the state with powers of assigning judges to equalize case loads, of requiring judicial statistics on number of cases handled and hours in which the court held session, among others. He was provided with a well-staffed administrative office whose director was appointed by the chief justice. The director was made responsible for all fiscal and business activities of the court. In most states, however, the chief justice does not have supervisory powers over other courts in the state and is not adequately provided either with legal or administrative assistance.

One of the most important developments in judicial administration took place in 1949 when the Conference of Chief Justices was organized. The conference met annually thereafter and provided a forum to discuss improvements in judicial administration by the highest judicial officers in each of the states. The conference requested the Council of State Governments to act as its secretariat, and the council issued a series of reports and memoranda on judicial administration for consideration by the executive and legislative branches in the various states as well as by the judicial departments. (S. Sr.)

CHIEF RENT: *see* Quit Rent.

CHIEFS. Chieftainship occurs among many but not all primitive peoples at all levels of culture. Its essential feature is the fact that there is always some individual person who is regarded as the official head of the community, and who acts as its leader, ruler and representative. Almost everywhere he bears some distinctive title; and by virtue of his office he frequently enjoys special rights and privileges, and is held in a high degree of honour and appreciation by the other members of the community.

Forms of Chieftainship.—The institution varies according to the size and structure of the community. Among the lower hunting peoples, where the political unit is a small local group, there is generally only a single chief; and this is also the case even among such relatively advanced peoples as the Bantu tribes of South Africa. Elsewhere there may be found a dual chieftainship, as, *e.g.*, under the dual organization (*q.v.*), where each moiety often has a chief of its own. Or, as among many North American and Melanesian tribes, there may be a division of functions resulting in the occurrence of two chiefs, one of whom is generally associated with the economic and religious side of tribal life, while the other is associated with the military and profane aspects. Thus, among the Mekeo peoples of New Guinea, each clan possesses two chiefs, the high chief and the war chief, while among the neighbouring Roro peoples, the high chief is associated with another, whose business it is to see that the orders of the high chief are carried out. In both cases the functions of the high chief are mainly of a sacred kind. Again, as in Polynesia and parts of Africa, where the community is divided into a number of distinct social classes, there may be several chiefs or grades of chiefs. In general, with the advance in political organization, political powers and functions are multiplied and diversified, and this increasing complexity of duties and functions requires the existence of different grades of officers. Thus, the highly organized Iroquois and Creek of North America have civil chiefs and sub-chiefs, chosen for personal merit, and permanent and temporary war chiefs. These several grades of chiefs bear distinctive titles, indicative of their diverse jurisdiction.

In most communities the office of chief is hereditary within a certain family or group of families, so that only members of this family or group of families can become chiefs. Where inheritance is thus recognized it is almost always reckoned in the male line. The chieftainship goes only exceptionally to a woman, and then usually only in default of a suitable male successor. Female chiefs occur sporadically, especially in parts of Africa, but there is hardly a single people among whom the chiefs are regularly women. The rule of descent generally follows that of the community. Where it is patrilineal, the chief is usually succeeded by one of his sons, most frequently the eldest, but primogeniture is by no means universal. In matrilineal societies, the successor is normally a brother of the chief, or one of his sister's sons. Even where the office is thus inherited, however, the succession is often dependent upon the fulfilment of certain conditions. If the rightful heir is regarded as incompetent, or is physically unsound, or suffers from some other disability, he may be passed over. Sometimes he is required to pass through certain tests before he is allowed to take up office.

In other communities the chief is elected. Where this is the case, the choice is often determined by personal qualities or attributes, such as bravery in war, skill in hunting, fishing or some other occupation, ability in council or debate, knowledge of tribal lore and tradition, wealth, generosity, character and so on. Sometimes the chief is elected for a certain period only, as among certain North American tribes, where special war chiefs are chosen to hold office only as long as the war lasts.

Powers and Functions.—These vary considerably; in many parts of the world the office is unaccompanied by the exercise of authority or political functions; at any rate, as far as the administration of justice is concerned. This is the case especially in Oceania and America; in Africa, on the other hand, the chief is often not only the chief judge of his people, but also the law-giver. But his other activities extend over a very wide range. He is often a prominent figure in the economic life of the tribe, and directs hunting, fishing, planting, harvesting, pastoral migrations and trading, according to the mode of life of the people. In many tribes he is regarded as the owner of the tribal land, and regulates its distribution and tenure. He is generally the wealthiest man in the tribe, and often has a very definite function as a sort of tribal banker, providing his people with feasts and, if need be, with the necessities of life, in return for the tribute which they pay him. In war, he is often the actual leader, fighting at the head of the tribe, and where he is too old or too sacred to do that, he plans campaigns and creates *morale* by incantations and medicines. In a number of cases he assigns wives, manages marriages, confirms inheritances, and otherwise makes his influence felt at many junctures of family life.

The chief plays an extremely important part in the religious life of the community. He acts as priest in public rites, prayers and sacrifices; he is frequently the chief magician of his people, and is often held responsible for the weather and the crops, for the health of his subjects and the fertility of their herds. So that, especially among the more highly organized peoples, he is often regarded as sacred or even divine, both during his lifetime and after his death. There are almost always special prohibitions and obligations regulating the relations between him and his subjects, and some form of etiquette and ceremonial to be observed in approaching him. His own health and soundness are in some cases of vital importance to the community. For their sake he must observe many irksome rules of conduct and diet, neglect of which is regarded as harmful not only to himself but also to his people; and bodily weakness may render him liable to deposition and even death.

Origin.—Of the various theories put forward to explain the existence of chiefs, one of the most famous is that in which Sir

James Frazer argues that the chief developed out of the medicine man, and was primarily a magician, his juridical and other functions being a subsequent development. By Davy's theory the chieftainship arose through the concentration of wealth in the hands of one man, whose superior economic position gave him authority over the rest. Rivers, again, stresses the fact that chiefs usually have customs peculiar to themselves, frequently with a similarity between the functions of chiefs in different societies widely separated; and he therefore thinks that the strong basis of "group sentiment" in the government of early societies changes to that of individual authority by the advent of a race of rulers, "enterprising strangers," imposing their ideas upon a community, and becoming chiefs.

There is something to be said for each of these theories, but while each of them lays stress upon a factor of great importance, none of them is exclusive. There is no single factor which can be regarded as having produced chieftainship, which is probably the resultant of a whole series of different factors acting in different combinations in different parts of the world. The essential fact about chieftainship, wherever it occurs, is that it serves as a means of concentrating the activities of the community under the direction of one person. The chief is not merely the representative and leader of the community; he is also frequently the symbol of its corporate unity.

See J. G. Frazer, "The Magic Art and the Evolution of the Kingship" (*The Golden Bough*, vols. i and ii, 1911); R. H. Lowie, *Primitive Society* (1920); G. Davy, *La Foi Jurée* (1922); W. H. R. Rivers, *Social Organisation* (1924). (I. S.)

CHIEMSEE, also called *Bayrisches Meer,* the largest lake in Bavaria, lies 1,600 ft. above the sea, between the rivers Inn (to which it drains through the Alz) and Salzach. With a length of 6 and a breadth of 9 mi., it has an area of about 33 sq.mi., and contains three islands, Herrenwörth, Frauenwörth and Krautinsel. The first is beautifully wooded; it was the seat of a bishop from 1215 to 1805, until 1803 it contained a Benedictine monastery, and today it is remarkable for its castle. The shores of the lake are flat on the north and south sides, but its other banks are flanked by undulating hills. The waters are clear and well stocked with trout and carp; but the fishing is strictly preserved, and steamers ply on the lake.

CHIENGMAI, chief city of northern Thailand (Siam) and terminus of the 467-mi. railway from Bangkok. Pop. (est. 1937) 60,000. The massive but decaying walls of the old city enclose an area of about .4 sq.mi. on the bank of a tributary of the Menam Chao Phya river. The rather fertile valley is 20 mi. wide by 80 mi. long, and is surrounded by high, wooded mountains, inhabited by tribesmen, chiefly Karens. The city has outgrown the walls, and the business district is outside the walled area The last *chao,* or hereditary chief, died in 1939. His son received a pension but did not succeed him. The population consists of Laos (closely related to the Thai), Thai, Chinese and Shans. The American Presbyterian mission commenced work in 1867, its chief local institutions having been Prince Royal college, McCormick hospital, Dara academy and the Chiengmai Leper asylum. Leprosy abounds there, and the asylum had 1,200 outpatients. The Roman Catholic mission had two schools.

From the 13th century until its absorption in the 18th century, the Lao or northern Thai kingdom of Chiengmai fought chronic wars with its ambitious southern Thai neighbour. Twice it was conquered and ruled by Burma, but regained its independence when Burmese rule subsided. The distinction between the Lao of Thailand and the Thai has been almost obliterated. Chiengmai was broken up into a number of tribal states, each with a hereditary chief, co-operating with Thai officials. The small surrounding states of Nan, Prè, Lampun, Lampang and Tern also had hereditary chiefs, but only Lampun has a surviving ruler of the old type. Chiengmai was a provincial or circle headquarters for northwestern Thailand until about 1932, when the circles were abolished.

Roads and trails radiate in several directions and Chiengmai has long been the trading centre of this area—meeting place of Chinese, Burmese, Shan and Thai merchants. The hills are rich in teak, and two large British companies extracted large quantities of this valuable wood. Rice is the chief crop, minor crops being legumes, tobacco and cotton.

CH'IEN LUNG or **K'IEN LUNG** (1711–1799), Chinese emperor, the fourth of the Ch'ing dynasty, was born Sept. 25, 1711. He succeeded his father, Yung Ch'eng, as emperor in 1736. At that time he dropped the name Hung-li, which he had previously borne, and was thereafter known as Ch'ien Lung. When he first came to the throne, Ch'ien Lung was much influenced by his ministers but by 1750 he was in almost complete personal control of the imperial power. About this time he began a succession of wars and campaigns which had substantially increased the territory under Chinese domination by the time of his retirement. Rebellions were put down in several parts of the empire during his reign; the territories of Ili, Turkistan, Kuldja and Kashgaria were conquered; and Tibet, Burma, Nepal and Annam were scenes of successful military ventures, some of these territories paying tribute to China for many years afterward. Ch'ien Lung is perhaps best known as a patron of the arts. He himself was a poet, the author of some thousands of verses, but he encouraged not only writers but painters, pottery makers, musicians and scholars. In 1772 he authorized the collection of all important writings extant in the kingdom This collection he ordered housed and catalogued in the Imperial library, together with a history and criticism of each work. During Ch'ien Lung's reign attempts were made by the British to increase trade with China. A mission for this purpose, sent in 1793 under the leadership of Lord George Macartney, came to nought, however, and trade with a number of countries continued, as before, exclusively at the port of Canton. In 1796, having reigned 60 years, Ch'ien Lung voluntarily abdicated, not wishing to rule a greater length of time than his illustrious grandfather, K'ang Hsi. It is probable, however, that he continued to have much influence over his son and successor, Chia Ch'ing, until his death on Feb. 7, 1799.

CHIERI, a town and episcopal see of Piedmont, Italy, province of Turin, 13 mi. S.E. by rail and 8 mi. by road from the town of Turin. Pop. (1936) 9,601 (town); 13,736 (commune). Its Gothic cathedral (1037, rebuilt 1405), is the largest in Piedmont, and has a 13th-century octagonal baptistery. Subject to the bishop of Turin in the 9th and 10th centuries, it became independent in the 11th century. In 1347 it submitted voluntarily to Count Amedeus VI of Savoy and finally came under Savoy in the 16th century. In 1785 it was made into a principality of the duke of Aosta. It was an early centre of trade and manufacture; and in the middle of the 15th century produced about 100,000 pieces of cotton goods per annum.

CHIETI, a city of the Abruzzi, Italy, the capital of the province of Chieti, and the seat of an archbishop, 140 mi. E.N.E. of Rome by rail, and 9 mi. W. of Castellammare Adriatico. Pop. (1936) 17,575 (town), 30,266 (commune). It is situated at a height of 1,083 ft. above sea level, 3 mi. from the railway station, from which it is reached by an electric railway. It commands a splendid view of the Apennines on every side except the east, where the Adriatic is seen. It is an active modern town, upon the site of the ancient Teate Marrucinorum, the chief town of the Marrucini Some scanty remains of the theatre, of a temple (?) and some large reservoirs exist. The Gothic campanile of the cathedral is fine. Close by is the town hall, which contains a small picture gallery. The de Laurentiis family possesses a private collection of some importance. To the north of Chieti is the octagonal church of S. Maria del Tricaglio, erected in 1317. The order of the Theatines, founded in 1524, takes its name from the city. Under the Lombards Chieti formed part of the duchy of Benevento; it was destroyed by Pippin in 801, but was soon rebuilt and became the seat of a count. The Normans made it the capital of the Abruzzi.

CHIFFON. In dress fabrics, one of the most delicate, gauze-like and transparent of all silk tissues. Chiffon consists of a plain woven texture produced from very fine and hard-twisted warp and weft of corresponding denier (counts), with a corresponding number of warp threads and picks per inch, and a soft dull finish. So very delicate and flimsy is the chiffon texture, that it is easily distorted and pulled out of shape.

The term chiffon has different meanings in different countries. Thus, in France, it signifies a rag; in Rumania, a bleached cotton shirting; in Germany it means a stout, fine, plain woven linen fabric with a smooth finish, and used for shirtings and other garments for underwear; in England, chiffon net (also nun's veiling) signifies a very fine and delicate quality of silk net used as lace and for veils. Chiffon twist signifies a hard-twisted silk thread spun with about 50 or more twists per inch, and used in the production of chiffon tissues.

CHIFFONIER, a piece of furniture differentiated from the sideboard by its smaller size and by the enclosure of the whole of the front by doors. Its name (which comes from the French for a rag-gatherer) suggests that it was originally intended as a receptacle for odds and ends which had no place elsewhere, but it now usually serves the purpose of a sideboard. It is a remote and illegitimate descendant of the cabinet; it has rarely been elegant and never beautiful. It was one of the many curious developments of the mixed taste, at once cumbrous and bizarre, which prevailed in furniture during the Empire period in England. The earliest chiffoniers date from that time; they are usually of rosewood; their "furniture" (the technical name for knobs, handles and escutcheons) was most commonly of brass, and there was very often a raised shelf with a pierced brass gallery at the back. The doors were well panelled and often edged with brass-beading, while the feet were pads or claws, or sphinxes in gilded bronze.

CHIGGER. A name used for a mite (*see* HARVEST-BUG) and for a flea (*see* JIGGER, CHIGGER or CHIGOE).

CHIGI-ALBANI, a Roman princely family of Sienese extraction descended from the counts of Ardenghesca. The earliest authentic mention of them is in the 13th century, and they first became famous in the person of Agostino Chigi (d. 1520), a banker who built the palace and gardens afterwards known as the Farnesina, decorated by Raphael. Pope Julius II made him practically his finance minister. Fabio Chigi, on being made pope (Alexander VII) in 1655, conferred the Roman patriciate on his family, and created his nephew Agostino prince of Farnese and duke of Ariccia, and the emperor Leopold I created the latter *Reichsfürst* (prince of the Holy Roman empire) in 1659. In 1712 the family received the dignity of hereditary marshals of the Church and guardians of the conclaves, which gave them a very great importance on the death of every pope.

See A. von Reumont, *Geschichte der Stadt Rom,* vol. iii. (1868); *Almanach de Gotha;* V. Frittelli, *Albero genealogia della nobile famiglia Chigi* (1922).

CHIGWELL, an urban district of Essex, England, with stations (Chigwell Lane and Chigwell) on the L.N.E.R., 13 mi. N.E. of London. Pop. (1951) 51,775. Area 14 sq.mi. The village, which is mentioned in Domesday, lies in a branch of the Roding valley, fragments of Hainault forest lying to the south and east, bordering the village of Chigwell Row. The scenery of the neighbourhood is described in Dickens's *Barnaby Rudge,* and the King's Head inn, Dickens's "Maypole," still stands. The old grammar school was founded by Samuel Harsnett, archbishop of York (d. 1631), whose fine memorial brass is in St. Mary's church, a Perpendicular structure with a Norman south door.

CHIHLI: *see* HOPEI.

CHIHUAHUA, a northern frontier state of Mexico, bounded N. and N.E. by the United States (New Mexico and Texas), E. by Coahuila, S. by Durango, and W. by Sinaloa and Sonora. The population in 1950 was 841,077, and the area, 94,806 sq.mi. The surface of the state is in great part an elevated plain, sloping gently toward the Rio Grande. The western side, however, is much broken by the Sierra Madre and its spurs, which form elevated valleys of great fertility. An arid sandy plain extending from the Rio Grande inland for 300 to 350 mi. is quite destitute of vegetation where irrigation is not used. The more elevated plateaus and valleys have the heavier rainfall, but over most of the state it is less than 20 in.; an impermeable clay substratum prevents its absorption by the soil, and the bare surface carries it off in torrents. The great Bolsón de Mapimí, an enclosed depression, in the southeastern part of the state, was once considered to be an unreclaimable desert, but experiments with irrigation have shown its soil to be highly fertile. The only river of consequence is the Conchos, which flows north and northeast into the Rio Grande across the whole length of the state. In the north there are several small streams flowing northward into lakes. Agriculture has made little progress in Chihuahua, and the scarcity of water has been a serious obstacle to its development outside the districts where irrigation is practicable. Stock-raising is an important industry in the mountainous districts of the west, where there is excellent pasturage for the greater part of the year. The principal industry of the state, however, is mining—its mineral resources including gold, silver, copper, mercury, lead, zinc and coal.

The silver mines of Chihuahua are among the richest in Mexico and include the famous mining districts of Batopilas, Chihuahuilla, Cosihuiriachic, Jesús María, Parral and Santa Eulalia or Chihuahua el Viejo. There are more than 100 of these mines. The state is well served by trunk-line railways and by several short branches to the mining districts.

Chihuahua originally formed part of the province of Nueva Viscaya, with Durango as the capital. In 1777 the northern provinces, known as the Provincias Internas, were separated from the viceroyalty, and in 1786 the provinces were reorganized as intendencias, but Chihuahua was not separated from Durango until 1823.

An effort was made to overthrow Spanish authority in 1810, but its leader Hidalgo and two of his lieutenants were captured and executed, after which the province remained passive until the end of the struggle.

The people of the state have been active partisans in most of the revolutionary outbreaks in Mexico, and in the war of 1862–66 Chihuahua was loyal to Juárez. The principal towns are the capital Chihuahua, pop. (1950) 110,779; Parral, 120 mi. S.S.E. of the state capital, in a rich mining district, with a population (1940) of 24,231; Ciudad Juárez across the Rio Grande from El Paso, pop. (1950) 128,782; Camargo, pop. (1940) 7,705; Santa Barbara (1940) 13,902; and Jiménez, 120 mi. S.E. of Chihuahua, pop. (1940) 5,175.

CHIHUAHUA, a city of Mexico, capital of Chihuahua state, about 1,000 mi. N.W. of Mexico City and 225 mi. S. by E. of El Paso. Pop. (1940) 56,805; (1950) 110,779. The city stands in a beautiful valley opening northward and hemmed in on all other sides by spurs of the Sierra Madre. It is 4,635 ft. above sea level, and its climate is mild and healthful. The city is laid out regularly, with broad streets, and a handsome plaza with a monument to Hidalgo and his companions of the revolution of 1810, who were executed there. The most noteworthy of its public buildings is the fine old parish church of San Francisco, begun in 1717 and completed in 1789, one of the best specimens of 18th-century architecture in Mexico. It was built, it is said, with the proceeds of a small tax on the output of the Santa Eulalia mine. Other prominent buildings are the Government palace, the Porfirio Díaz hospital, the old Jesuit college (now occupied by a modern institution of the same character), the mint, and an aqueduct built in the 18th century. Chihuahua is served by the Mexican National, the Kansas City, Mexico and Orient (Santa Fe) and the Mexico North-Western railways. Mining is the principal occupation of the surrounding district, the famous Santa Eulalia or Chihuahua el Viejo mines being about 12 mi. from the city. Manufacturing is making good progress, especially the weaving of cotton fabrics by modern methods. The manufacture of gunpowder for mining operations is another old industry.

Chihuahua was founded between 1703 and 1705 as a mining town, and was made a villa in 1715 with the title San Felipe el Real de Chihuahua. Because of the rich mines in its vicinity it soon became one of the most prosperous towns in northern Mexico, although the state was constantly raided by hostile Indians. In 1763 it had a population of nearly 5,000. The war of independence was followed by a period of decline, owing to political disorder and revolution, which lasted until the presidency of Gen. Porfirio Díaz. In the war between Mexico and the United States, Chihuahua was captured on March 1, 1847, by Col. A. W.

Doniphan, and again on March 7, by Gen. S. Price. In 1864 President Juárez made the city his provisional capital for a short time.

CHIKMAGALUR, a town and district of Mysore state, republic of India. The town, about 90 mi. N.W. of Mysore city, had a population of 21,744 in 1951.

CHIKMAGALUR (formerly KADUR) DISTRICT has an area of 2,771 sq.mi. Pop. (1951) 417,538. The larger part consists of the Malnad or hill country, which contains some of the wildest mountain scenery in southern India. The western border is formed by the Ghats, of which the highest peaks are the Kudremukh (6,207 ft.) and the Meruti Gudda (5,444 ft.). The centre is occupied by the horseshoe range of the Baba Budans, containing the highest mountain in Mysore, Mulainagiri (6,310 ft.), and enclosing the Maidan or plain country, a fertile, well-watered region, with the famous "black cotton" soil. The principal rivers are the Tunga and Bhadra, which rise near each other in the Ghats and unite to form the Tungabhadra, a tributary of the Kistna. The eastern region is watered by the Vedavati (Hagari). From all the rivers water is drawn off into irrigation channels by means of anicuts or weirs. The chief natural wealth of Chikmagalur is in its forests, which contain large supplies of the finest timber, especially teak, and provide shelter for the coffee plantations. Iron is found and smelted, and there is corundum in some places. The staple crop is rice, chiefly grown on the hill slopes, where the natural rainfall is sufficient, or in the river valley, where the fields can be irrigated. The district is served by the Southern railway, on which, 23 mi. N.E. of Chikmagalur, is Kadur, from which the district formerly took its name.

CHILACHAP, or TJILATJAP, a port in Java, Indonesia, on the southern coast, in the residency of Banjumas, west of Schildpadden bay. Its harbour, the most favoured by nature in the whole of Java, is formed by the island of Nusa Kambangan, which is long and narrow and lies close to the shore opposite Chilachap, beyond which it projects for a considerable distance and thus protects it from the heavy monsoon seas and swell of the Indian ocean. With the exception of Segoro Wedi bay, Chilachap is the only harbour on the south coast of Java which affords protection during the southeast monsoon, and it is the most important.

The town of Chilachap, which has a population of 28,309, including 670 Europeans and Eurasians, and 1,626 foreign Asiatics, stands on a tongue of land flanked on the east by Schildpadden bay, and on the west by the estuary of the river Donan. The entrance to the harbour is between a projecting headland of Nusa Kambangan and South point, on the tongue of land opposite, and is 1½ mi. wide, but because of a sandbank the navigable channel, which varies in depth from 29 ft. to 48 ft., is narrow. The port has two concrete wharves, 1,350 ft. and 400 ft. in length, respectively, affording mooring places for vessels drawing up to 30 ft. of water at low tide. Chilachap is connected by rail with Batavia, Surabaya, Surakarta and Samarang by a junction with the main Batavia-Surabaya line at Maos. Japanese troops occupied Chilachap shortly after their invasion of Java in World War II.

CHILAS, an important settlement far up the Indus; headquarters of the Chilas subdivision (2,800 sq.mi.) of the Gilgit agency, lying within the Shinaki tribal territory. The settlement is about 100 mi. N.N.E. of Abbottabad, North-West Frontier province, Pakistan. The Chilas settlement, situated 4,010 ft. above sea level, holds an important position with reference to the Kashmir-Gilgit route via Astor. It is connected with Gilgit via Bunji by a metalled road. Chilas also offers a route to Gilgit from the Kaghan valley in Hazara through Babusar pass, shorter than from Kashmir through Burzil pass and gaining importance with the development of the Kaghan valley.

The Chilas valley is rich and green. Although it was included in the British territory in 1893, it kept its autonomy.

CHILBLAIN (*pernio*) is a chronic condition of inflammation and swelling usually of the toes, feet or fingers, accompanied by intense itching. The condition is frequently precipitated by impaired and weak circulation in the extremities and may follow prolonged exposure to cold and dampness or sudden changes in temperature. Ulceration may occur. To minimize the possibilities of chilblain formation, warm loose hose and warm shoes should be worn, and the feet and hands should be dried carefully and rubbed briskly after each washing.

CHILD, SIR FRANCIS (1642–1713), English banker, was a Wiltshire man, who, having apprenticed to a goldsmith, became himself a London goldsmith in 1664. In 1671 he married Elizabeth (d. 1720), daughter of another goldsmith named William Wheeler (d. 1663), and with his wife's stepfather, Robert Blanchard (d. 1681), took over about the same time the business of goldsmiths hitherto carried on by the Wheelers. This was the beginning of Child's bank. Child soon gave up the business of a goldsmith and confined himself to that of a banker. He inherited some wealth and was very successful in business; he was jeweller to the king and lent considerable sums of money to the government. Being a freeman of the City of London, Child was elected a member of the court of common council in 1681; in 1689 he became an alderman, and in the same year a knight. He served as sheriff of London in 1691 and as lord mayor in 1699. His parliamentary career began about this time. In 1698 he was chosen member of parliament for Devizes and in 1702 for the City of London, and was again returned for Devizes in 1705 and 1710. He died on Oct. 4, 1713, and was buried in Fulham churchyard. Sir Francis, who was a benefactor to Christ's hospital, bought Osterley park, near Isleworth, later the residence of his descendant, the earl of Jersey.

Child had 12 sons. One, Sir Robert, an alderman, died in 1721. Another, Sir Francis (*c.* 1684–1740), was lord mayor of London in 1732, and a director of the East India company. He was chosen member of parliament for the City of London in 1722 and was member for Middlesex from 1727 until his death. After the death of the younger Sir Francis at Fulham on April 20, 1740, the banking business passed to his brother Samuel, and the bank passed to his descendants, retaining its identity until May 1924, when it was absorbed by Glyn Mills and Co. Child's bank was at first conducted at the Marygold, next Temple bar in Fleet street, London, and later occupied the site formerly covered by the Marygold and the adjacent Devil tavern.

CHILD, FRANCIS JAMES (1825–1896), U.S. scholar and educator, was born in Boston, Mass., Feb. 1, 1825. He graduated at Harvard in 1846, taking the highest rank in his class; remained as a tutor in various subjects; and after two years of study in Europe succeeded Edward T. Channing in 1851 as Boylston professor of rhetoric, oratory and elocution; and in 1876 became professor of English at the same institution. Child studied the English drama and Germanic philology, the latter at Berlin and Göttingen during a leave of absence, 1849–53; and he took general editorial supervision of a large collection of the British poets. He edited Edmund Spenser (5 vol., 1855), and published an important treatise in the *Memoirs of the American Academy of Arts and Sciences* for 1863, entitled "Observations on the Language of Chaucer." His largest undertaking, however, grew out of an original collection of *English and Scottish Ballads* (8 vol., 1857–58). He accumulated, in the university library, one of the largest folklore collections in existence, studied manuscript rather than printed sources and carried his investigations into the ballads of all other tongues, meanwhile giving a sedulous but conservative hearing to popular versions still surviving. His final collection was published as *The English and Scottish Popular Ballads,* first in ten parts (1882–98) and then in five quarto volumes, which remain the authoritative treasury of their subject. Child worked—and overworked—to the last, dying in Boston Sept. 11, 1896, having completed his task save for a general introduction and bibliography. A sympathetic biographical sketch was prefixed to the work by his pupil and successor George L. Kittredge.

See also Gameliel Bradford, *As God Made Them* (Boston, 1929).

CHILD, SIR JOHN (d. 1690), English deputy governor of Bombay from 1679 to 1681 and president of Surat from 1682 to 1690, was the first person to be placed in control of all the East India company's factories in India. In 1672 he married Susannah, daughter of Capt. John Shaxton, who commanded the Bombay garrison. He was implicated in the mutiny of Shaxton's troops two years later but was restored to favour through the influence of his namesake, Sir Josia Child, the powerful governor of the company in London. Like his patron he was utterly unscrupulous and had a passion for intrigue. His tyrannical behaviour as president led to Capt. Richard Keigwin's rebellion at Bombay in 1683. Acting under instructions from London, Child became involved in war with the Mogul emperor Aurangzeb, but the seizure of Surat by Mogul troops forced him to sue for peace. He was not the strong governor that historians had depicted, and his career was a series of ignominious failures.

See R. and O. Strachey, *Keigwin's Rebellion* (Oxford, 1916), which gives evidence that the two Childs were in no way related. (C. C. D.)

CHILD, SIR JOSIA (1630–1699), English merchant, economist and governor of the East India company, was born in London in 1630, the second son of Richard Child, a London merchant of old family. After serving his apprenticeship in the business to which he succeeded, he started on his own account at Portsmouth, as victualler to the navy under the Commonwealth, when about 25. He amassed a comfortable fortune and became a considerable stockholder in the East India company. He was returned to parliament in 1659 for Petersfield; and in later years sat for Dartmouth (1673–78) and for Ludlow (1685–87). He was made a baronet in 1678. His advocacy, both by speech and by pen, under the pseudonym of Philopatris, of the East India company's claims to political power, as well as to the right of restricting competition with its trade, brought him to the notice of the shareholders, and he became a director in 1677, and, subsequently, deputy governor and governor. In order to control the company's affairs in India he got rid of John Pettit, the senior and best-qualified candidate for the presidency of Surat, in favour of a subservient protégé named John Child. He was for a considerable time virtually the sole ruler of the company and directed its policy as if it were his own private business. He has been credited with the change from unarmed to armed traffic; but the actual renunciation of the Roe doctrine of unarmed traffic by the company was resolved upon in Jan. 1686, under Gov. Sir Joseph Ash, when Child was temporarily out of office. He died on June 22, 1699.

Child made some important contributions to the literature of economics; especially *Brief Observations Concerning Trade and the Interest of Money* (1668) and *A New Discourse of Trade* (1668 and 1690). He made various proposals for improving British trade by following Dutch example and advocated a low rate of interest as the "*causa causans* of all the other causes of the riches of the Dutch people." This low rate of interest he thought should be created and maintained by public authority. Child, while adhering to the doctrine of the balance of trade, observed that a people cannot always sell to other countries without ever buying from them and denied that the export of the precious metals was necessarily detrimental. He had the mercantilist partiality for a numerous population and propounded a new scheme for the relief and employment of the poor; he advocated the reservation by the mother country of the sole right of trade with its colonies.

See R. and O. Strachey, *Keigwin's Rebellion* (Oxford, 1916).

CHILD, LYDIA MARIA (1802–1880), U.S. author and reformer, was born at Medford, Mass., Feb. 11, 1802, and died at Wayland, Mass., Oct. 20, 1880. One of the most prominent women of her day, Mrs. Child's present claims to remembrance are the contemporaneous popularity of her stories *Hobomok* (1824), *The Rebels* (1825) and *Philothea* (1836); her editorship of the *Juvenile Miscellany*, the first children's monthly periodical in the United States; and her efforts in behalf of the slaves, freedmen and Indians, including her stirring *Appeal for That Class of Americans Called Africans* (1833) and her editing of the *Anti-Slavery Standard* (1840–44) in association with her husband.

In spite of the 35 editions of her *Frugal Housewife* (1829) and the German, the eight American and the 12 English editions of her *Mother's Book* (1831), these and her many other stories and books on feminism, religion, biography and history have been superseded by later works.

Bibliography.—*Letters of Lydia Maria Child* (1882), with a biographical introduction by J. G. Whittier, appendix by Wendell Phillips; also, a chapter in T. W. Higginson's *Contemporaries* (1899).

CHILDEBERT, the name of three Frankish kings.

Childebert I (d. 558) was one of the four sons of Clovis. In the partition of his father's realm in 511 he received as his share the town of Paris, and the country to the north as far as the river Somme, and to the west as far as the English channel, with the Armorican peninsula. In 524, after the murder of Chlodomer's children, Childebert annexed the cities of Chartres and Orleans. He took part in the various expeditions against the kingdom of Burgundy, and in 534 received as his share of the spoils of that kingdom the towns of Mâcon, Geneva and Lyons. When Vitiges, the king of the Ostrogoths, ceded Provence to the Franks in 535, the possession of Arles and Marseilles was guaranteed to Childebert by his brothers. Childebert also made a series of expeditions against the Visigoths of Spain. In 542 he took possession of Pampeluna with the help of his brother Clotaire I, and besieged Saragossa, but was forced to retreat. From this expedition he brought back to Paris a precious relic, the tunic of St. Vincent, in honour of which he built at the gates of Paris the famous monastery of St. Vincent, known later as St. Germain-des-Prés. He died without issue in 558, and was buried in the abbey he had founded, where his tomb has been discovered.

See "Nouveaux documents sur le tombeau de Childebert à Saint-Germain-de-Prés," in the *Bulletin de la Société des Antiquaires* (1887).

Childebert II (570–595), king of Austrasia, was a son of Sigebert. When his father was assassinated in 575, Childebert was taken from Paris by Gundobald, one of his faithful *leudes,* to Metz, where he was recognized as sovereign. He was then only five years old, and during his long minority the power was disputed between his mother, Brunhilda, and the nobles. Chilperic, king at Paris, and King Gontran of Burgundy, sought alliance with Childebert, who was adopted by both in turn. But after the assassination of Chilperic in 584, and the dangers occasioned to the Frankish monarchy by the expedition of Gundobald in 585, Childebert threw himself unreservedly into the arms of Gontran. By the pact of Andelot in 587 Childebert was recognized as Gontran's heir, and with his uncle's help he quelled the revolts of the nobles and succeeded in seizing the castle of Woëwre. Many attempts were made on his life by Fredegond, who was anxious to secure Gontran's inheritance for her son Clotaire II. On the death of Gontran in 592, Childebert annexed the kingdom of Burgundy, and contemplated becoming sole king of the Franks. He died, however, in 595. Childebert II had had relations with the Byzantine empire, and fought in 585 in the name of the emperor Maurice against the Lombards in Italy.

Childebert III was one of the last and feeblest of the Merovingians. A son of King Theuderich III, he succeeded his brother Clovis III in 695, and reigned until 711.

See B. Krusch, "Zur Chronologie der merowingischen Könige," in *Forschungen zur deutschen Geschichte,* vol. xxii, pp. 451–490. (C. Pf.)

CHILDERIC, the name of three Frankish kings.

Childeric I (*c.* 437–481), king of the Salian Franks, succeeded his father, Merwich (Merovech), as king about 457. With his tribe he was established around the town of Tournai, on lands which he had received as a *foederatus* of the Romans, and for some time he kept the peace with his allies. About 463, in conjunction with the Roman general Egidius, he fought against the Visigoths, who hoped to extend their dominion to the banks of the Loire; after the death of Egidius he assisted Count Paul in attempting to check an invasion of the Saxons. Paul having perished in the struggle, Childeric defended Angers against the Saxons, recovered from them the islands they had seized at the mouth of the Loire and destroyed their forces. The Saxon chief Odoacer now agreed to serve the Romans and the two chieftains, now reconciled, intercepted a band of the Alamanni. These are all the facts known about him. The stories of his early life by the Franks, of his stay of eight years in Thuringia with King Basin and his wife (or sister) Basine, of his return when a faithful servant advised him that he could safely do so by sending to him half of a piece of gold which he had broken with him and of the arrival at Tournai of Queen Basine, whom he married, are preserved by Gregory of Tours, and have found a place in French epic poetry. After the fall of the western empire in 476 there is no doubt that

Childeric regarded himself as freed from his engagements toward Rome. He died in 481 and was buried at Tournai, leaving a son Clovis (*q.v.*), afterward king of the Franks. His tomb was discovered in 1653, when numerous precious objects, arms, jewels, coins and a ring with his name and the image of a long-haired warrior, were found.

Childeric II (*c.* 653–675), king of Austrasia, was a son of the Frankish king Clovis II, and in 660, although a child, was proclaimed king of Austrasia, while his brother Clotaire III ruled over the rest of the dominions of Clovis. After the death of Clotaire in 670 he became ruler of the three Frankish kingdoms, Austrasia, Neustria and Burgundy. He was murdered in 675 while hunting. He was buried at St. Germain near Paris.

Childeric III (d.*c.* 751), king of the Franks, was the last of the *fainéant* Merovingian kings. The throne had been vacant for seven years when the mayors of the palace, Carloman and Pippin the Short, decided in 743 to recognize Childeric as king. We cannot say whose son he was, or what bonds bound him to the Merovingian family. He took no part in public business, which was directed, as before, by the mayors of the palace. When in 747 Carloman retired into a monastery, Pippin resolved to take the royal crown for himself. Childeric was dethroned in 751 and placed in the monastery of St. Omer. (C. Pf.)

Bibliography.—J. J. Chiflet, *Anastasis Childeric I. Francorum regis* (1655); W. Junghans, *Kritische Untersuchungen zur Geschichte der fränkischen Könige Childerich und Clodovech* (1857); J. B. D. Cochet, *Le Tombeau de Childeric I., roi des Francs* (1859); G. Kurth, *Histoire poétique des Merovingiens* (1893); E. Lavisse, *Histoire de France,* vol. 6 (Paris, 1903); and authorities quoted under Gregory of Tours.

CHILDERMAS: *see* Innocents' Day.

CHILDERS, HUGH CULLING EARDLEY (1827–1896), British statesman, was born on June 25, 1827. On leaving Cambridge he went out to Australia in 1850. In 1852 he was appointed auditor-general in Melbourne, and in 1853 collector of the customs; he carried through a bill for the establishment of the University of Melbourne, and was its first vice-chancellor. In 1856 he represented Portland in the new parliament of Victoria, and was commissioner of trades and customs in its first cabinet. In 1857 Childers returned to England as agent-general of the colony, and in 1860 entered parliament as liberal member for Pontefract. In 1865 he became financial secretary to the treasury. He occupied various posts in the Gladstone ministries. As secretary for war from 1880 to 1882 he was responsible for the administration of the Transvaal War in 1881 and the Egyptian War in 1882. During his term of office the territorial system was introduced, with other administrative reforms of the army. From 1882 to 1885 he was chancellor of the exchequer, and the beer and spirit duty in his budget of 1885 was the occasion of the government's fall. In 1886 he was returned as a Home Ruler (one of the few Liberals who adopted this policy before William Gladstone's conversion) for south Edinburgh, and was home secretary in Gladstone's ministry of 1886. The withdrawal of the financial clauses of the first Home Rule bill was largely the result of his threat of resignation. He retired from parliament in 1892, and died on Jan. 29, 1896.

See the *Life of Childers,* by his son (1901).

CHILDERS, ROBERT CAESAR (1838–1876), English oriental scholar, son of the Rev. Charles Childers, English chaplain at Nice, studied Pāli during his residence (1860–64) as a civil servant in Ceylon. In 1869 he published the first Pāli text ever printed in England, and began to prepare a Pāli dictionary (2 vol., 1872–75), which was awarded the Volney prize by the Institute of France. In the *Journal of the Royal Asiatic Society* he published the *Mahā-parinibbāna Sutta,* the Pāli text giving the account of the last days of Buddha's life. In 1872 he was appointed sublibrarian at the India office, and in 1873 first professor of Pāli and Buddhist literature at University college, London. He died in London on July 25, 1876.

CHILDERS, ROBERT ERSKINE (1870–1922), Irish politician, the son of Robert C. Childers of London, was educated at Haileybury and Trinity college, Cambridge. From 1895 to 1910 he was a clerk in the British house of commons. He served as a trooper in the South African War in 1900 and from 1910 to 1914 was engaged in political work and writing for Irish home rule. During World War I he served in the royal naval air service and in the royal air force, in which he attained the rank of major and won the D.S.C. From 1917 to 1918 he served on the secretariat of the Irish convention. On his demobilization he returned to Ireland and was elected to *dail eireann* as deputy for Wicklow in May 1921. He was principal secretary to the Irish delegation of plenipotentiaries to Westminster, Oct.–Dec. 1921. He afterward opposed the Anglo-Irish treaty of 1922, supported Eamon de Valera in the *dail* and joined the Republicans when they again took up arms. He was captured in Wicklow Nov. 10, 1922, and tried by military court martial on Nov. 17, on the technical charge of having possession of an automatic pistol without proper authority. He was found guilty of treason, and executed on Nov. 24, 1922.

Among his publications are: vol. v of the *Times* history of the South African war, dealing with the guerilla campaigns; a brilliant story, *The Riddle of the Sands* (1903); *The Framework of Home Rule* (1911); *Military Rule in Ireland* (1920).

CHILD PSYCHOLOGY AND DEVELOPMENT. General psychology seeks to give both a description and explanation of the mental processes of adults—processes such as those of learning, perceiving, thinking and motivation. Child psychology is that branch of psychology which devotes itself to the investigation of the processes of psychological growth and adjustment in human beings from conception to adulthood.

Child psychologists strive not only to plot the course of behaviour, ability and attitude change which characterizes the progress of individuals as they mature but also to describe and explain the differences observed between children in the many aspects of their development. With this objective, the discipline, it should be expected, would have nebulous bounds since it is recognized that the individual and his functional environment are interdependent as are also all of the functions of the person to some degree. In order to achieve its purposes, child psychology has cross-fertilized with other sciences such as cultural anthropology, sociology, psychiatry, pediatrics, nutrition and physiology. Vitamin deficiencies and hormone irregularities are not without influence on behaviour and attitude. Comparisons of the behaviour of children in different cultures have thrown into relief the moulding effect of the social milieu.

Child psychology has a rather short history, most of its development as a science having been achieved in the 20th century.

Methods and Techniques of the Science.—The techniques whereby the specific mental functions and behaviour patterns of children are described and analyzed are essentially those used in general psychology since the same processes are studied, though procedural adjustments must often be made to the level of skill and the motivation of young subjects.

The data of child psychology are obtained from a variety of sources. Most frequently children are observed directly either in a casual or in a systematic and controlled way. Casual observation often makes it possible to catch behaviour on the wing; controlled observation is usually necessary to provide detailed descriptions of behaviour and analyses of the influences which alter it. By controlled observation is meant a procedure whereby conditions within and/or about the subjects being studied, as well as the methods of the observer, are regulated or arranged. The controls imposed vary with the purposes of the investigator.

In addition to learning about pre-adult humans through their own direct observations, investigators may gain insights through reports others give of children in questionnaires, interviews or in less formal ways; through records kept by some agency such as a school or clinic, as well as through a study of the things children create; *e.g.,* their drawings and compositions. Introspections by a child himself or by an adult on his own childhood may also shed light on how human beings develop psychologically. That not all evidence of the kinds enumerated can be trusted, however, suggests that the task of data gathering must be surrounded by such safeguards as will ensure accuracy. Since, moreover, much mental behaviour is covert and has to be inferred from behaviour that can be directly observed, the pitfalls which interfere with accurate inference have also to be avoided.

Quantified descriptions of various qualities children have—their abilities, skills, interests, values, social-emotional characteristics

—are achieved usually through tests (objective and projective), ratings and rankings, simple counts and what are known as time-sampling methods.

Since the investigator as he observes children directly in their activities may not be able to see and hear quickly enough to give an accurate report of what happens, he may find it profitable to obtain a permanent record which can then be analyzed at leisure. Hence, cinematic and sound recording are among the routine techniques of the child psychologist. The movie and the wire or plastic sound records obtained can be presented at any desired tempo and can be reviewed an indefinite number of times.

To discover the usual course of developmental change in children, two chief methods have been employed. The same group of subjects is followed through a period of years, or different groups of children at successive ages are studied. The latter cross-sectional method is less time-consuming since the investigator is not obliged to wait for his subjects to grow up; but the resulting composite image is likely to give us the impression that development in the case of the individual is smoother and more regular than it actually is. In fact, no child, as he matures, may follow exactly the pattern of the mean.

Whereas from some points of view the first method, the longitudinal, is preferable—since it yields a picture of the development of each individual as well as of the trend in the total group—it is not often used, not only because of the slow rate at which data can be accumulated but also because subjects are lost with great rapidity because of the difficulty of sustaining co-operation and of population mobility. An investigator might well lose two-thirds of his subjects over a period of 18 years. Those subjects who were still available at the termination of such a long study would, doubtless, be a highly selected group and hence would not depict well what is typical.

MENTAL DEVELOPMENT

Both the fact that people differ and the fact that they are alike in many of the aspects of their development need consideration. This first section will sketch roughly what tends to be the rather usual pattern of unfolding in children in a culture such as that of the United States; *i.e.*, give a sort of developmental time schedule for the average child. A brief discussion of the problem of individual differences is reserved for a later section.

Although the most striking characteristics of development are that it is continuous, irreversible and its parts all interrelated, any description of its course must be cross-sectional and selective—deal with discrete bits of behaviour at arbitrarily chosen landmarks. The reader must fill in with his imagination the gaps between the segments selected for mention.

Prenatal Development.—If the beginning of psychological life is to be understood, the child must be studied before birth. Because of the fact that the prematurely delivered foetus which is more than six months of age can live, if given proper care, and hence can be available for visual inspection, the behaviour and ability of the foetal infant during the last three months of the prenatal period are better understood than are those of younger foetuses. Direct observation of aborted foetuses who are younger than six months must be distorted by the fact the infant is dying when under visual scrutiny. Some of the indirect means devised to throw light on the activities of young foetuses involve the use of palpation, X-rays, the stethescope, the electrocardiograph and introspections by the pregnant mother on the felt movements of the child she is carrying.

Many behaviour patterns once thought to appear only after birth we now know can be elicited much earlier. By the 2nd month after conception, for example, a primitive sort of sucking response can be aroused; by the 11th week, grasping; by the 4th month, rudimentary respiratory movements; and by the 7th month, the corneal reflex. Quickening may be felt by the mother as early as the 16th week. The foetus' heart begins to beat at about the 3rd week.

There is evidence that learning can occur before birth, but how much and what is usually learned is not clear. While the one-time belief that a mother could "mark" her child physically by the specific thoughts and feelings she experienced while pregnant has long been exploded, it is not out of the realm of the possible that her mental state, since it affects her physiological condition, may have some influence on the foetus' psychological life. We know it can influence the foetus physically.

The Newborn.—The neonate is no automaton, no mere bundle of reflexes, but rather an organism with an extensive repertoire of responses so co-ordinated as to make possible, if it is given some protection, its survival in this everchanging and infinitely complex world. Its responses are, to be sure, largely vegetative, but the psychological registration of these in feeling should not be overlooked. A few hours after birth, for example, crying on the part of the infant will accompany the "hunger" contractions of its stomach. The newborn can be roused via all sense modes if the stimuli are such as to have organic significance. Sometimes the infant's response is seen chiefly in increased or decreased movement of a massive sort or in changes in circulation or breathing. Often, however, the response appears more specific and localized—such as fixating, converging on or following a light or closing the hand when the palm is stimulated. The neonate reacts less vigorously to pain than do older children and, strangely enough, it does not shed tears when it cries. Whether its discriminations embrace those between the various colours or beween different odours is still something of a moot question, but it seems not unlikely that it can sense certain gross differences within these modalities.

The baby who has just arrived seems capable of being upset not only by interference with its biological needs (*e.g.*, by food, water and air lacks, too great heat or cold and by pain) but also by sudden intense light, sound or equilibratory stimuli. There is disagreement, however, as to whether it can be said that the new infant shows differentiated emotions. It seems clear enough, even though an occasional faint smile may be seen flickering across the newborn's face, that pleasant excitement is generally lacking. How safe it is to assume that differentiation has occurred in the area of unpleasant emotion (*e.g.*, that anger and fear have emerged) is a point that is debatable.

Even though the newborn sleeps about 20 hrs. a day and spends much of his waking time in nursing, he is still a learner. Conditioning with respect to certain details of the feeding routine are some of the learnings that have been reported to have occurred within four to five days of birth.

The Yearling.—By one year the infant has made great strides and has quite a distinct personality. The yearling seems to be making his most dramatic advances in locomotion. Not only has he greatly expanded his horizon by learning to sit alone, but he can voluntarily change the horizons upon which he looks; for he can creep, pull himself to standing and walk, if led by the hand. The experience of stepping out on his own usually comes a couple of months later.

Manual explorations, too, are among his enthusiasms. He seems to have a compulsion to touch and finger articles and grabs avidly for most everything in sight. Even so tiny an object as a crumb may attract his attention and, when it does, he can appropriate it with a neat pincer grasp. But his manipulation does not stop with mere grasping and holding, as it did earlier. The objects he picks up are likely to be combined in some activity. The yearling enjoys putting objects into containers, such as a ball into a box. The object, to be sure, does not stay put long, for he retrieves it promptly with the same flourish displayed in depositing his cache. If we would point to his lacks rather than achievements in the case of manual skills, we might mention his awkward voluntary release of objects whose position he is trying to control. He tends to have difficulty, for instance, according to Arnold Gesell, in dropping a pellet into the mouth of a small bottle, and he does well if he can build a block tower of even two blocks.

In self-help he is beginning to make progress. He drinks from a cup easily and can hold it alone, although, of course, he needs both hands to steady it. Bits of solid food such as meats he finger-feeds himself. If he uses a spoon, he tends to turn it over as he lifts it to his mouth, rather than to keep it upright, with the result that any self-feeding he does with a spoon may consign more food to his chin and bib than mouth.

That his infancy is about behind him is attested by the fact that he is now on a three-meal-a-day schedule. If he has a bottle, it usually is just one a day. His social advance is revealed also by his sensitivity to approval and disapproval. He can even inhibit his impulses a bit if the person who is requesting him to refrain from some act remains close at hand and frowns or displays some other sign of disapproval. The baby of a year is likely to shy away from strangers, an attitude which, while it does not seem like a social advance, does reflect his budding understanding of human groups and alliances.

In the matter of verbal communication the year-old infant has not made much progress. He has spoken his first word but at best this is little more than a vocal stunt which he performs on request. In spite of his lack of verbal skill, it must not be overlooked that he is making progress in important aspects of language. His eager interest in the world about him and the resulting perceptual differentiations he makes as well as the understandings he gains will provide him with meanings without which the words he is soon to acquire would be hollow shells.

The Toddler.—By two years the child is a toddler and explorer. He can even run. He is likely to fall frequently not only because of his light mass, small base and relatively high centre of gravity but also because of his lacks in foresight and learned motor skills. The climbing of stairs and the walking of simple inclines fascinate him. When he climbs stairs, he marks time (*i.e.,* brings one foot up to the level of the other before advancing) and holds on to the balustrade. He thinks it a feat to jump down one step without falling. Not only can he carry himself almost anywhere he wants to by walking and running, but before he is three he is frequently a master of one form of vehicular locomotion; *i.e.,* he can ride a tricycle, if given opportunity to learn.

In manual skills, as in locomotor, he has made progress. His hand preference is fairly well established. He helps, when being dressed, chiefly by holding his various members in readiness; but pulling off his cap, shoes, stockings and mittens are not beyond him. If his food is soft or finely cut, he can feed himself with a spoon, though the activity takes considerable concentration. The spoon he holds fist-fashion. He can drink from a cup and not infrequently holds it with one hand. His improvement in co-ordination is revealed by the fact that he is seen frequently pushing a baby carriage, covering a doll, putting pegs into a simple peg board. Opening and closing containers and screwing and unscrewing are sources of great delight. Although he is usually unable to make a representative drawing (his are scribbles), the two-year-old likes pictures and tends to puff with pride as he names the common objects and animals portrayed in his picture book. He can often recite a short nursery rhyme or supply the final words to the lines of the rhyme as the adult reads a familiar jingle. In fact, his verbal skill is considerable; a vocabulary in use of approximately 300 words has been estimated as about average. One-word sentences, however, predominate in his speech, though he is beginning to put words together. When the two-year-old refers to himself, he usually does so by name. Pronouns are rather conspicuously absent from his speech, but before he is three the first person singular and the pronominal adjective, "mine," may be overworked, especially when he is playing with his peers. The two-year-old, in addition to knowing his name, knows his sex and that he is a little person; i.e., he has begun that classification and diagnosis of himself which will occupy him endlessly in his life.

As might be expected, since correct pronunciation involves fine auditory perception and delicate motor control, the toddler's pronunciation is far from perfect, letters in his words being frequently omitted and misplaced or wrong ones substituted.

It is possible to guide the behaviour of the two-year-old somewhat by simple directions; for instance, he can hold a limited task in mind, such as returning with the toy he has been sent into the next room to fetch. Control of him, however, has still to be chiefly nonverbal. Nor has he internalized to any extent the mechanisms which would help him inhibit his impulses. If told not to do something, he cannot yet be trusted to desist when the adult's back is turned. This is not necessarily because he is perverse but merely that he has not yet formed the mental cues which will help him to remember and control. His conscience, like his good intentions, is short-lived and poorly formed.

That he has come a great way in his socialization is indicated by the fact that he has fairly dependable bowel control. In the matter of bladder control his success is not so great. While daytime accidents are not usually frequent, he is likely to wet himself at night. He is down to one nap a day and this usually in the afternoon. Awake now about ten hours a day, he has much time for getting acquainted with his universe. No wonder he learns rapidly.

In his social relations the young two-year-old is more adult-centred than peer-centred. At nursery school, for instance, he is more inclined to ignore or play alongside other children than to play co-operatively with them. Objects and materials seem to interest him more than do children, though he may spend considerable time watching the latter and may snatch things from them if they have something that appeals to him. In the main, he has few techniques of defense.

If the adults caring for the toddler are and have been relatively fearless and have dealt with him wisely, he is likely to have few fears. Among the fears common at this age, says Arthur T. Jersild, are those of animals, falling, sudden loud noises, strangers and strange settings. When distressed, the two-year-old cries readily and, when thwarted, often merely explodes—lies down on the floor and kicks or bangs his head but fails to direct his attack toward those who have interfered with his desires. He is easily made cranky by hunger, fatigue and colds and has little self-control. In general, he lacks sympathy with and insight into the sufferings of others. If another child cries he may, however, watch in a rather troubled way.

The School Entrant.—The fact that formal education usually begins around six years indicates the belief of society that the child by this age can take reasonably good care of himself and can work with a group. The six-year-old's control of his body is shown by his ability to climb almost anything in sight, skip, hop and gallop, as well as run fleetly.

He grasps a knife, fork, spoon and pencil with a fingerhold—a form which makes for much finer control than the fisthold which characterized him at two years. In the matter of dressing and undressing, he is quite independent, only an occasional snugly fitting rubber or awkwardly placed button producing calls for help. With assistance on ears and back, he may give himself an acceptable bath. He can tie a bow knot, use a pair of scissors with fair control, paste and hammer, as well as saw in a fashion. His wood products, such as boats and wagons, begin to resemble what he is trying to represent. His drawings, too—people, houses, trains, autos, planes and flowers are among his favorite themes—are now recognizable. For the spatial relationships of the major parts of the objects he tries to represent he has some feeling, but his sense of proportion is none too good; those parts in which he has a special interest or for which he has enthusiasm are usually portrayed disproportionately large. The doors and windows in the houses he draws provide more than adequately for exit and light.

That in representing he pays attention to more than the spatial relationships of the parts is apparent in that, when painting or colouring, he tends to portray objects in realistic colours. When he strings beads he often follows a pattern instead of merely interesting himself in getting the beads on the string, as he did earlier. This following of a bead pattern may involve other discriminations such as those of simple number. In fact, the school entrant has made significant progress in the development of a conception of number. According to Lewis M. Terman, he can count 13 pennies and can select out of a pile, on request, groups of objects numbering as many as 10.

The most significant achievement of the sixth year, in the case of the schoolchild in the U.S., is that of learning to read. Reading, however, might better be designated word-calling at first, for only gradually does the child learn to read along continuously and get ideas from his reading.

With baby talk largely a thing of the past, and in spite of the fact that he is beginning to shed his milk teeth, the school entrant's enunciation is not unlike an adult's. In his six years he has acquired an active vocabulary of about 2,500 words. Compound and complex sentences are common among his verbal products, his sentences averaging around five words. This fact indicates his thinking has reached a respectable degree of abstractness since qualifiers are not unusual. The six-year-old's use of the present, past and future tenses reflects some understanding of time, though he does show his youth by the extent to which he lives in the present—by his relatively infrequent references to the past and future and also by his inability to work toward a remote goal.

Important in revealing his social progress is the fact that the six-year-old cries relatively infrequently, in contrast with the two-year-old, expressing his displeasure and wants more often in words. If he is angry he tends to work his way through the difficulty by the use of language rather than as he did earlier by loud lament or physical force. Emotional explosions as undirected as tantrums occur rather seldom. Instead, his attacks, when he is annoyed, tend to be well directed, whether they are verbal or physical.

Having to defend himself and his status in a society which is highly competitive, a child of six in the U.S., for instance, is already rivalrous and status-conscious. Despite rivalrous attitudes, however, it is not beyond him to share spontaneously some of his possessions, to take turns and to listen quietly when another person has the floor. It is sometimes, of course, difficult to persuade him that these procedures are in his interest. With guidance in a project, he may be able to take a role which complements the roles of others and to sustain this role for a number of days. Among his play activities are likely to be such co-operative enterprises as playing school, house, store and war. In such techniques for manipulating others as flattery, bribery, bargaining, threats and forming counteralliances he tends to be fairly well practised.

The child of six can enter into the more intimate types of social relationships, too. He usually has a special friend or two whom he seeks out and, if need be, defends, albeit his alliances are not distinguished for their permanence. Among racially mixed groups he is likely to prefer those of his own race. Association with those of other races tends, notwithstanding, to be free and easy. Also he associates with the members of both sexes rather willingly, though he is seen more with the members of his own sex.

A further sign of his increasing socialization is the fact that when not too sorely tempted, the six-year-old can control himself, even in the absence of the enforcing authority. He does have a conscience and finds it difficult to bear or conceal guilt. Since the school entrant is governed little by broad principles, his morals tend to be specific to the situation; he may be honest or generous in one situation and dishonest or selfish in another.

Among the fears common in children of this age, according to A. T. Jersild, are likely to be those of the dark, robbers, animals, being alone, dangers associated with imaginary creatures, and bodily injury through drowning, fire or traffic accidents. Those fears of sudden loud noises and high places so characteristic of young children have in most cases disappeared. It is conspicuous that the fears of the child of six are roused less than they were at a younger age by present events and more by symbols of objects, persons or situations which he believes threaten his welfare. These threats may, of course, be more imaginary than real. Indeed the boundary between the real and imaginary is still somewhat blurred at times for the six-year-old. When he listens to the radio, which he likes to do, he often believes the action and characters are real.

Because he has just entered school and is having to work out adjustments to a new and usually taxing social environment, he may be more emotional, explosive and less well-adjusted than he was somewhat earlier. Insecure in the school environment and in his relations with his new companions, he may take out his irritations on the members of his family. It is well to realize also that his parents may have been dwarfed some in significance by the emergence of the teacher as a new authority.

The Preadolescent.—Since girls are more accelerated in their development, the picture given in this section is chiefly of girls of about 10 years and boys of about 11. The picture, it should be added, blurs sex differences even more than has been the case thus far.

The preadolescent period is often called the gang age, since children of this age seem to go in packs. Informal clubs, pass words and code language are their special joy and are signs of the increasing dependence of preadolescents on their peers and their decreasing dependence on adults. In their social interplay children just entering the second decade tend to be somewhat rough. The flaunting of untidiness is not unusual among them, and the lack of social amenities in her preadolescent son has been many a mother's despair. Practical jokes, such as poking and tripping, and slapstick comedy are forms humour takes. The comic strips (usually not comics but pictorial detective and adventure stories) are read avidly and programs of similar type on the radio are listened to. Favourite play activities for boys of this age in the United States, for instance, are roller skating, bicycling, romping, carpentering, chasing, swimming, coasting, skating, marbles, baseball and football. The girls tend to favour more quiet play, although rope jumping, jacks and hopscotch are at the peak of their popularity. Popular among girls, too, are sewing clothes for dolls, playing the piano for fun and listening to the radio.

A deep gulf separates the boys and girls, partly because the members of each sex are not equally vigorous and hence have developed dissimilar play interests, and partly because they are so anxious to conform to the pattern society holds for their sex that they feel they cannot run the risk even of association with the opposite sex.

The interracial distance, like the intersex distance, tends to be great in the preadolescent period.

At 10 to 11 years, then, it is clear the child tends to be leaguing himself strongly with his peers and those of his own social group. It should be no surprise to find that he is less respectful of adult authority than he was earlier. A number of these young children even engage in some of the minor forms of delinquency such as petty larceny. These delinquencies are usually committed in gangs.

If we look back and consider from where these preadolescent children have come, their school accomplishments seem considerable. Reading for them is usually no longer a difficult task. Although the comics rank high in the materials read by boys and girls of preadolescent years in the United States these children tend to enjoy books also. The boys are inclined to like particularly books of adventure, mystery and magic, tales of children of other lands and realistic accounts of animals. Girls tend to like stories of home and school life.

There is some evidence that the average preadolescent's comprehension vocabulary may be as extensive as 12,500 words. The 10-to-11-year-olds express themselves easily in speaking, the average length of their sentences being between six and seven words, and among their verbal products will be found virtually all important language forms.

In contrast with their verbal skill, children of this age still do not have much fluency in communication through writing. Their themes and letters lack flexibility as well as variety of expression. They have the motor ability to write easily, their expression being blocked among other things by their preoccupation with the details of spelling and of written forms. They typically have only a limited command of the intricacies of capitalization, punctuation and paragraphing but do apply the simpler rules successfully.

Their progress in mathematics has usually carried them to a level at which they can deal with the elements of addition, subtraction, multiplication, division and with simple decimals.

The Adolescent.—Adolescence is the period, usually from 11 or 12 to 22 or 23 years (boys later than girls), when the individual is completing his growth and the development of the structures and functions which make procreation possible. The onset of menstruation is generally taken as the beginning of adolescence in girls, a custom which should not blind us to the fact that significant hormonal and growth changes precede this event. In the male no such convenient landmark is available. The menarche occurs most frequently in girls between 12 and 14 years, although the range of ages at which it appears is great, while puberty in boys is delayed on the average from a year and a half to three years longer.

When the individual begins to take on the physique of the adult and experiences the effects of his altered physiology, life tends to change rapidly for him. While societies differ greatly in the clarity with which they define the adolescent's role for him, in U.S. society the route from childhood to adulthood is not well outlined. The young adolescent finds the people about him treating him in varying degrees as an adult. Since children in the United States are usually not active participators in the work of adults, an adolescent may find that his mother, who still thinks of him as a child, gives him little responsibility and humours him, whereas the proprietor of the drug store where he serves as errand boy expects of him mature judgment and dependability. Forced into the role of an adult one minute and that of a child the next, the youth tends to be confused.

As he comes to think of himself as grown, we find the adolescent asserting his independence and wanting to be responsible for his own destiny. With respect to peer dictates, however, he is inclined to be a severe conformist. Whether or not he is to wear a certain type of clothing when his friends do is a momentous matter. When the code of his peers conflicts with that of his home, the latter sometimes is sacrificed, though as a rule not without struggle. Delinquency and radicalism approach their maximum at this period.

The young adolescent tends to spend much time with his peers; this is the age of the drugstore and pool-hall gangs. Clubs and teams are matters of much importance. The adolescent is increasingly able, as he matures, to submerge his interests as he elevates those of his group. His friendships tend to be intense, both with older persons and with his peers, keeping his life from assuming too pale a cast. He loves idealistically, even though rather egotistically, and is anxious to be approved. Members of the opposite sex who were heartily scorned a few years earlier are now often worshipped. Strong heterosexual interests, along with physical maturation, tend to appear earlier in girls than in boys. With these interests comes concern over grooming. The adolescent's looks are likely to be the source of much anguish to him—a few unwanted pounds or inches may make life miserable, and sad is the youth if acne mars his skin. Much conflict stems from the fact that adolescents differ greatly in the time at which they experience their growth spurt and sexual ripening. A youngster who is still in his prepubertal period at 15 when all his friends have taken on adult appearance is likely to doubt his normality. He may even find himself rejected by his peers.

Since the role of the male in the United States is that of wage earner and provider, boys in that land approaching adulthood become increasingly concerned with the problem of selecting an occupation and earning money. Girls, too, give some heed to the problem of their future work, for no longer is it lacking in respectability for women to engage in gainful occupation, even after marriage.

Though young in experience, adolescents tend to be strong in physical capacity. Girls, it has been reported, reach the peak of such motor abilities as running and throwing at about 14 years—while boys approach their peak in these skills about 3 years later. The sexes become sharply differentiated in strength and endurance, on the average, after 13 years.

It is difficult to say when the peak in intellectual capacity is reached. In simple functions like memory span the maximum occurs earlier than is true in the case of the more complex cognitive activities. The adolescent who remains in such stimulating environments as a university seems to increase his score in tasks of the type included in the so-called intelligence up to at least 20 years. The adolescent's command of language improves steadily with the years, and the average high-school senior has a comprehension vocabulary, according to one estimate, of 15,000–18,000 words. Whether or not a youth's vocabulary increases after he leaves high school will depend largely on the demands of his social and occupational environments.

INDIVIDUAL DIFFERENCES

As was stated earlier, the developmental picture just sketched is that of the average child and in one culture. But each child is unique, and few are average in even most respects. Among children are the feeble-minded and the geniuses, the right-handed and left-handed, the stutterers and those with fluent speech, the delinquent and the moral conformist, those who attack every one who crosses their path and those who seldom think a hostile thought. Suffice it to say that the genes inherited and the environments, intra-uterine and postnatal, which have surrounded the children cause the heterogeneity we find in the child population. Both nature and nurture influence every trait and behaviour a child displays, but in the case of some qualities the dissimilarities children exhibit are more frequently reflections of the varied environmental pressures to which the children have been subjected, whereas in the case of other qualities the population variance seems to derive more from genetic influences.

Not a great deal is known of the role heredity plays in producing psychological variance, though such evidence as is available suggests that in some areas the weight of heredity is great. More is known about the likely effects of at least some environmental forces. Environmental effects can best be gauged either by studying the same individuals under different circumstances, for then surely heredity is held constant, or by comparing individuals such as identical twins, who have developed from the same fertilized egg and, hence, have the same genes. It is impossible, on the other hand, to hold environmental forces completely constant, while heredity is varied. Even children growing up in the same household may have different nurturing. The fact of family resemblance alone proves nothing conclusive about the effects of either nature or nurture.

Environmental Influences.—The forces in the environment which cause people to differ are, of course, almost infinite in number. Among important classes or complexes of these influences are those of race, nation, social and income class, individual family attitudes and practices, schooling, disease and nutrition. That code of behaviour, values and practices to which groups such as a race, nation or social class hold their members we customarily call culture. The details of such a code, for conformity with which the child is rewarded and for deviation from which he is punished, are astoundingly numerous. Children are made to follow the endless minutiae of the group's feeding rituals, to learn the group's language with all that implies in the way of the determination of thought, to respond in certain ways to each class of person (*e.g.,* their elders, their peers, the younger, the sick or those in various social and occupational positions) and to conduct themselves in accordance with the behaviour forms considered appropriate for each type of situation and setting. Most of what is to be valued and what is to be abhorred is dictated.

Within each such group as a race or nation there are subgroups, each with its code. The family is an important subgroup since it is the chief conveyor to the child of the social traditions of the race, nation and social class to which it belongs as well as of its own unique traditions. It is an agency which tends to make its influence felt during most of the individual's life and is especially strategic because of its functions of ministration and protection. If a child's parents are cautious, they will warn him innumerable times of dangers and hazards; if they are hostile, he will have felt the chill of their irritation, hate and resentment with untold frequency. It is no wonder, then, we find that children whose parents are rejecting tend to be hostile, tense, distractible and avid for attention; or that children who are overprotected tend to be tender, adult-centred and conforming. A child from an upperclass family lives by a code of manners and morals so different from that of a lowerclass child that the two may find it difficult to converse. One class may value formal education and the fruits thereof, disapprove physical attack as a means of settling difficulties and put rigid taboos on certain sex practices such as masturbation, while another class sanctions the exact opposite of these values and behaviour patterns.

Disease and malnutrition also contribute to individual differences among children. An infection resulting in encephalitis has the power to change the whole course of the individual's life—make a dissenter out of a docile soul, a mental defective out of a genius or a cripple out of an athlete. Malnutrition, like disease, may warp the body, ready it for invasion by bacteria and viruses and colour the individual's whole outlook by limiting his energy

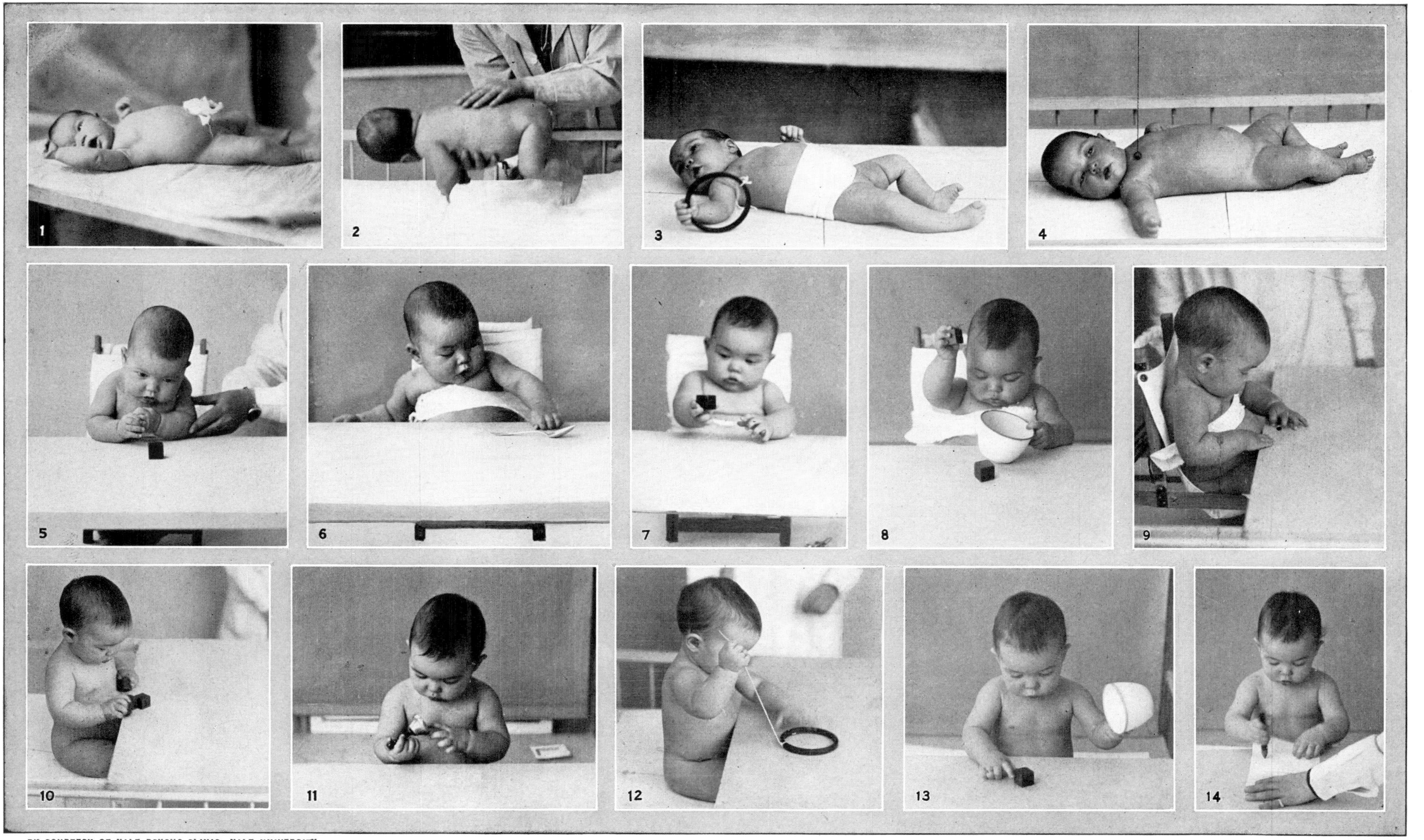

BY COURTESY OF YALE PSYCHO-CLINIC, YALE UNIVERSITY

GROWTH OF CHILD BEHAVIOUR FROM BIRTH TO FIRST BIRTHDAY

These pictures of a normal infant under systematic observation, were made in the photographic laboratory of The Yale Psycho-Clinic. They show characteristic behaviour patterns at advancing age levels as follows:

1. At *one week* of age the infant stares at large objects. Lies with head on side, extending arm on same side (tonic neck reflex; cf. 3 and 4)
2. At *6 weeks* of age, lifts head when held in ventral suspension
3. At *8 weeks* clasps a ring, without visual regard
4. At *12 weeks* follows with eyes a small moving ball
5. At *16 weeks* intently regards cube on table
6. At *20 weeks* makes crude approach on spoon
7. At *24 weeks* picks up cube on the table
8. At *28 weeks* bangs a cube on the table
9. At *32 weeks* plucks a tiny pellet
10. At *36 weeks* holds two cubes and attends to a third
11. At *40 weeks* explores the clapper of a bell
12. At *44 weeks* secures a ring by pulling a string
13. At *48 weeks* lifts a cup to secure a cube
14. At *52 weeks* makes a crude imitative scribble with crayon

or disturbing his body's functioning. Rickets, pellagra and beriberi are forms of malnutrition with massive cumulative psychological effects.

BIBLIOGRAPHY.—"Adolescence," *43rd Yrbk. Nat. Soc. Stud. Educ.*, part i (1944); L. Carmichael (ed.), *Manual of Child Psychology* (1946); A. Gesell *et al.*, *The First Five Years of Life* (1940), *The Child from Five to Ten* (1946); A. T. Jersild, *Child Psychology* (1947); L. M. Terman and M. A. Merrill, *Measuring Intelligence* (1937). (H. L. K.)

CHILDREN, CARE OF: *see* INFANCY.

CHILDREN, DISEASES OF. The major developments in this special branch of medical science, known also as pediatrics, took place after the turn of the 20th century. Prior to that time there existed but little knowledge of, or interest in, the special problems of child health. Infants and young children were regarded merely as "miniature adults," whose physical, mental and emotional disorders required no special consideration beyond that afforded mature persons. As a result of this attitude and the undeveloped state of medical science and practice, the incidence of disease and the mortality rates among children were appalling; 20% to 40% of all infants born alive died during the first year of life. Of the total deaths in the population, three out of four occurred in children under 12 years of age. However, as a result of revolutionary advances in the field of pediatrics and intensive application of sound public health principles, death rates among children at mid-20th century were reduced to one-tenth of those figures in some parts of the world.

One of the most important steps in the development of modern pediatrics was the recognition by physicians of certain fundamental differences between the child and the adult. Conditioned by his state of immaturity, the infant or young child differs from the mature person physiologically, psychologically, immunologically and anatomically. The constant changes in functional patterns incident to growth and development impose different standards for health appraisal and for nutritional, medicinal and other health requirements in the very young. Throughout the wide range of diseases affecting infants and children, the concept of prevention predominates over that of treatment in the mind of the properly trained physician. Fortunately, advances in the basic sciences of nutrition, microbiology, immunology, epidemiology, hygiene and sanitation made it possible for medical practitioners and public health officers to exercise a large measure of control over many of the most devastating physical diseases. Improvements in diagnostic laboratory techniques together with revolutionary developments in chemotherapy and in pediatric surgery reduced the dire effects of certain nonpreventable diseases to a minimum.

The diseases which affect infants and children may be classified according to the nature of their causes, the particular organ systems primarily involved or a combination of these methods. Since pediatrics is based upon the science of growth and development of the individual, the pediatric physician must take into account, so far as is feasible, all conditions that influence the orderly course of these normal processes from the moment of conception throughout the periods of infancy, childhood and adolescence. For example, such determining factors as heredity, prenatal influences (including maternal illness) and injuries incident to the process of birth, explain most cases referred to as diseases of the newborn.

Examples of the hereditary diseases are haemophilia, erythroblastosis foetalis, familial periodic paralysis, certain nervous and mental diseases and a tendency to allergic disorders, such as eczema and bronchial asthma. Of the congenital diseases known to be acquired in utero by the infant as a result of maternal disease, syphilis, certain anomalies (*e.g.*, congenital cataracts and possibly malformations of the heart) and toxoplasmosis are best understood. Prematurity of birth, which constitutes the major cause of an excessively high rate of mortality among infants, is due in the main to foetal anomalies or to impaired health in the mother during her period of gestation. Accidents incident to the birth process, such as asphyxia, brain haemorrhage, fractures and muscular paralyses, may result in immediate death or may be followed by such sequelae as retarded mental development, epilepsy and cerebral palsy.

Serious accidents (including poisoning) which involve children are largely preventable. Yet, as a result of personal carelessness and lack of education in accident prevention, such mishaps were still responsible at mid-century for more deaths and more permanent disabilities than many of the more serious infectious diseases.

Disorders of nutrition, together with the alimentary or enteral diseases, presented the most serious of all problems involved in the care of infants and young children prior to the time when their specific causes were discovered. Later, however, it became possible to prevent the major number of these or to effect a cure in most instances after the disease has been allowed to develop. The nutritional requirements of children for normal growth and development and for normal functioning of the various organ systems of the body differ quantitatively from those of mature men and women. On the basis of age and size, the growing individual needs much more of the essential food substances than do adults. These nutrients are water, protein (essential amino acids), "energy foods" (fats and carbohydrates), vitamins and minerals (calcium, iron, iodine, magnesium, potassium, sodium, phosphorus, chloride, sulphur and the so-called essential trace elements).

Prolonged deficiency of intake in the case of any one or any combination of these essential nutritional factors causes more or less specific symptom complexes. For example, unless water is furnished for young children and infants in required amounts, a state of underhydration ensues. This is manifested by dryness of the skin and mucous membranes, interference with normal circulatory and secretory functions and obvious discomfort from intense thirst. Severe protein privation in the young interferes with building new, and maintaining pre-existing, protoplasm in the living cells of the body and interferes with blood protein formation. Insufficient intake of fats and carbohydrates to satisfy the energy needs of the body likewise limits growth. Of the minerals, calcium and phosphorus are required in optimal amounts for bone formation and for certain other vital cellular functions. Magnesium plays a role in cellular function somewhat similar to that of calcium. Sulphur derived from certain essential amino acids of the diet (methionine and cystine) plays its specific role in the formation of certain all-important substances, such as enzymes, insulin and glutathione. Iodine is essential for synthesis of the hormone thyroxin in the thyroid gland, which is essential for normal growth and development. Iron is an essential constituent of the red blood cell pigment, haemoglobin, which carries oxygen from the lungs to all parts of the body. A deficient intake of this element results in the development of a common form of anaemia. The monovalent elements (namely, sodium, potassium and chloride), which constitute the chief electrolytes in the body fluids, together with the phosphate and bicarbonate ions, serve essential roles in maintaining the normal chemical environment of all living cells, as well as the normal acid-base balance. Alterations in their concentrations in the body fluids, whether caused by certain endocrine disorders, kidney disease, diarrhoea, vomiting or profuse sweating, produce serious illness.

Specific diseases develop from vitamin deficiencies in the diet. Deprivation of vitamin A manifests itself as xerophthalmia and also as "night blindness" arising from disturbed function of the retinal pigments. A variety of disease states occur in infants and growing children deprived of different members of the vitamin B complex. The best known of these are beri beri (caused by lack of thiamine); pellagra (deficiency of niacin); ariboflavinosis (lack of riboflavin) and megaloblastic anaemia of infants (lack of folic, or folinic, acid). Scurvy is caused by inadequate amounts of ascorbic acid (vitamin C) in the diet. Rickets is caused by a deficiency of vitamin D in the diet, unless the skin is exposed directly to ultra-violet light waves. Haemorrhagic disease of the newly born infant is caused by a relative deficiency of vitamin K in the mother's diet during her period of pregnancy. These deficiency diseases rarely occur, however, if the diet contains sufficient amounts of natural foods, including milk, meats, egg yolk, fish liver oils, fresh citrus fruits, green vegetables, salt and water. Cure of existing vitamin deficiency diseases is accomplished most promptly by administration of the missing vitamin in concentrated or synthetic forms.

Many serious diseases of childhood are caused by pathogenic or parasitic living organisms. Such diseases are classified into general categories according to the type of organism responsible for the particular disease state. For example, there are (1) the bacterial diseases, caused by microscopically visible germs; (2) the viral diseases, caused by specific viruses too small to be seen with ordinary optical microscopes; (3) the rickettsial diseases, caused by an intermediate type of micro-organism; (4) the mycotic diseases, caused by invasion of the tissues by certain plant moulds or mould-like organisms; (5) the animal parasitic diseases, caused by unicellular animal parasites; and (6) the diseases caused by infestation with comparatively larger and more complex animal parasites, such as worms.

The specific infectious diseases in the foregoing categories are too numerous to be discussed in detail here. However, those contagious diseases customarily referred to as "childhood diseases" (measles, mumps, whooping cough, diphtheria, scarlet fever, German measles [or rubella], infantile paralysis, smallpox and chicken pox [*qq.v.*]) deserve special mention. All are known to be caused by specific viruses, excepting diphtheria (*C. diphtheriae*), whooping cough, or pertussis (*H. pertussis*), and scarlet fever (hemolytic streptococcus). Smallpox and whooping cough, like typhoid fever, can be prevented by vaccination. Diphtheria can be prevented by injections of minute amounts of modified diphtheria toxin (toxoid). Treatment of this disease with serum containing antitoxin is usually successful too. Tetanus, or "lockjaw," can likewise be prevented by its specific toxoid and can be treated by tetanus antitoxin. Treatment by means of the antibiotic drugs is successful in whooping cough and scarlet fever. Measles can be prevented temporarily by means of human gamma globulin or convalescent serum.

The common respiratory diseases of infancy and childhood, such as common colds, infantile virus pneumonitis, influenza, atypical pneumonia (all caused by specific viruses) and the bacterial pneumonias (caused by various types of pneumococci, streptococci, staphylococci and *H. influenzae*) are more serious infections in infants than in older children. While attempts to prevent them by vaccination had met with no success by mid-century (except for short periods in the case of influenza), sulfonamide and antibiotic drug therapy had proved to be amazingly effectual in the treatment of those infections caused by bacteria. Unfortunately, such therapeutic agents are far less, if at all, effective in the treatment of respiratory diseases caused by viruses.

Tuberculosis is improved only temporarily by antibiotic drugs. Immunization by attenuated tubercle bacilli (BCG [Bacillus-Calmette Guérin]) remained of uncertain value. Among populations where the disease incidence is comparatively low and where it is feasible to discover and isolate active cases through community-wide programs of tuberculin testing and chest X-ray surveys, attempts to immunize by vaccination would appear to be unnecessary.

Congenital syphilis can be prevented by active antibiotic or arsenical drug treatment of the infected mother before the infant is born or it may be cured in the affected baby or older child by use of these drugs.

Meningitis, lymphadenitis and bacteriemia, caused by meningococci, streptococci, pneumococci, staphylococci, *H. influenzae* and certain other bacteria, can usually be treated successfully with sulfonamide and antibiotic drugs. Infections caused by the gonococcus yield readily to modern chemotherapy also, as do typhoid, typhus and malarial fever.

Many of the congenital malformations of the heart and blood vessels, the gastrointestinal tract, the nervous system and the extremities are amenable to surgical treatment.

The underlying cause of *rheumatic fever* remained unknown, but streptococcic infections accentuate the symptoms. Control of such infections by drugs is beneficial. ACTH and cortisone were still in the experimental stage of development as possible treatments for acute rheumatic fever at mid-20th century. They might prove of great importance in diminishing the incidence of this most common cause of death in children between the ages of 5 and 19.

Advances in endocrinology made possible the successful hormone treatment of such disorders as diabetes mellitus, spontaneous hypoglycaemia, diabetes insipidus, parathyroid tetany, adrenal insufficiency, adrenal hyperactivity, pituitary insufficiency, hypothyroidism and certain diseases of the sex glands.

Mental, emotional and social maladjustments in children tardily gained recognition as having health significance quite comparable with that of the common physical or organic diseases. The functional and organic components of a child's illness may at times be so thoroughly fused as to require use of the special techniques of the psychiatrist for its successful diagnosis and treatment. Appreciation of this fact gave origin to the branch of child psychiatry designated as psychosomatic pediatrics. Prevention of such disorders by consistent application of proper mental hygiene is important.

BIBLIOGRAPHY.—Irvine McQuarrie (ed.), *Brennemann's Practice of Pediatrics*, vol. 1–4 (1951); Waldo E. Nelson (ed.), *Mitchell-Nelson's Textbook of Pediatrics*, 5th ed. (1950); Wilbur C. Davison, *The Compleat Pediatrician*, 6th ed. (1949); Leonard Parsons, *Pediatrics* (1948). (I. McQ.)

CHILDREN: PROTECTIVE LAWS. The wide powers of life and death allotted to the head of a family under the *patria potestas* of Roman law were not applied under European feudal systems of law although on the continent of Europe, where the laws were modelled on Roman civil law, stress was placed on the importance of the family and strict controls by curatorship and by the family council were imposed over children, particularly as regards their rights of inheritance to property. The system as developed in England recognized rights of wardship over children enabling a feudal lord, on the death of a tenant leaving an infant heir, to administer the tenant's estate as guardian during the minority of the heir. The guardian was made responsible for waste entailing forfeiture of the land wasted and threefold damages.

Guardianship, whether of the natural parent or other guardian, was recognized as including the right of custody of the child, control of his religious training and education, consent to his marriage, the right of chastisement and the right of enjoyment of his services; and, in addition, control of his estate subject to the use of a sufficient portion for his maintenance, education or training. In England, the court of chancery, in the delegated exercise of the authority of the sovereign as *parens patriae*, assumed wardship if rights of guardianship were abused and applied the property so far as necessary for the maintenance of the child. This jurisdiction was later vested in the chancery division of the high court.

The courts gradually acquired control over abuse of the power of chastisement and heard actions or prosecutions for assault against the person concerned, whether the parent, guardian or teacher or an employer in the case of an apprentice or servant. If attended by fatal results, the charge was for murder or manslaughter.

After 1601, under the English poor law, provision was made for destitute children either in association with their parents or otherwise by the grant of relief by overseers or guardians of the poor. In 1889, power was conferred on poor-law guardians to assume parental rights of control over deserted children and, in 1899, the control was extended to orphans and children of parents who were disabled, in prison or unfit to have them in care. Similar powers were developed in continental countries, particularly in France and later in Belgium and Denmark.

Development proceeded in Great Britain and in Europe, the aims being the prevention of ill-treatment and cruelty, child-life protection, the regulation of dangerous performances, employment restrictions and the compilation of a general children's charter. In England ill-treatment attracting legal punishment consisted originally of blows or threats and was extended to neglect to supply necessaries. The Offences Against the Person act, 1861, imposed punishment for the exposure of infants and for the neglect or ill-treatment of apprentices or servants. The Poor Law Amendment act, 1868, made it an offense for parents to neglect to supply necessaries (*e.g.*, food, lodging, clothing and medical aid) for their children. At the instigation of the National Society for the Prevention of Cruelty to Children, a series of statutes aimed at preventing cruelty to children in their homes was passed in 1889 and progressively extended between 1894 and 1933.

Child-life protection was applied in baby-farming cases in 1897 and 1908 in regard to infants maintained by foster parents for reward, the age limits rising from seven to school-leaving age by the acts of 1932 and 1948. These powers were transferred to the Public Health Acts code in 1936. Penalties for the employment of children up to the age of 16 in dangerous performances were imposed by the statutes of 1879, 1897 and 1932. Restrictions on the employment of children in casual occupations and amusements were imposed in 1903 and extended by the Education acts of 1918 and 1921 and the Children act of 1932. The employment of children between 9 A.M. and 6 P.M. or in injurious work or in street trading was prohibited and local authorities were enabled to make regulative bylaws.

A series of children's charters commencing in 1908 controlled the sale of tobacco and the exclusion of children from licensed bars, and introduced supervision by probation officers and other fit persons, detention in industrial or reformatory schools and the hearing of charges in juvenile courts. The Children and Young Persons act of 1932 extended the control to children in need of care and protection and introduced inspection of voluntary homes by the secretary of state. The statutes were consolidated in 1933. After investigation by the Curtis committee of 1946, the act of 1948 placed on local authorities responsibility for the care of children deprived of normal home life, enlarged their powers of assumption of parental rights over children in their care, and increased their responsibility to act as fit persons at the request of the courts.

MODERN BRITISH LAW

This can be examined under six main heads; viz., legal status, care of children in special categories, protection, welfare, employment and court proceedings.

Legal Status.—Guardianship is regulated by the acts of 1886 and 1925, dealing with control of the person of the child, including custody, training and education. Control of the child's estate is usually vested in trustees during the minority of the child. Affiliation orders may be made against the putative father of an illegitimate child and the child may be legitimated under an act of 1926 by the subsequent marriage of its parents with entitlement to property rights as if born legitimate. The adoption of children is governed by the act of 1950, preventing exploitation of the child and securing its supervision by the local authority during a probationary period. On adoption, the child loses succession rights in the old family and acquires corresponding rights in the new one.

Care of Children in Special Categories.—This is prescribed for five categories of children; viz., according to whether they are deprived of normal home life, in need of care and protection, beyond parental control, handicapped in mind or body, or suffering from mental illness (whether mental deficiency or insanity). The care of these children is shared by local authorities, voluntary organizations and state institutions. The children are either boarded out with foster parents or housed in special homes or institutions. Voluntary institutions are controlled by the secretary of state. Children suffering from mental illness are treated mainly in hospitals provided by the minister of health and the compulsory detention of such children is supervised by the board of control, specially appointed to protect the liberty of the subject.

Children deprived of normal home life, whether orphaned, abandoned or neglected, are committed to the care of local authorities who may in suitable cases assume parental rights. Care may last until the child reaches the age of 18 and may be extended to 21 if necessary. Maintenance contributions are recoverable from parents.

Children in need of care and protection, if under 17, may be brought before the juvenile courts (Children and Young Persons act, 1933). They include children falling into bad associations through lack of parental care and the victims of violence or immorality. Any such child may be sent to an approved school or committed to the care of a probation officer or other fit person. Special medical or other treatment may be recommended.

Children beyond control of their parents or guardians, if under 17, may be brought before the juvenile courts and dealt with like children in need of protection. If they are already in the care of a local authority, they can be sent to approved schools on the order of the juvenile court.

Handicapped children suffering from disability of mind or body can, under the Education act, 1944, be provided by the local authorities with treatment in special schools. This applies to pupils who are blind or deaf or partially so, delicate, diabetic, educationally subnormal, maladjusted, physically handicapped or defective in speech. Medical examination may be enforced and so may attendance at the special school selected until the age of 16. Further assistance between the ages of 16 and 21 is given by the local authority under the National Assistance act, 1948, in the form of provision of work at home or elsewhere and rehabilitation facilities.

Children who are mentally ill receive treatment under the Mental Deficiency acts, 1913 to 1938, the Lunacy and Mental Treatment acts, 1890 to 1930, and the acts relating to criminal lunatics. Treatment of a defective includes supervision in his home or care in an institution, including detention under the order of the judicial authority or the secretary of state. Insane children are treated at out-patient child guidance clinics provided by regional hospital boards and centres provided by local education authorities. In-patient treatment is provided in general or mental hospitals. At a mental hospital, the child may be treated as a voluntary or temporary patient under the Mental Treatment act, 1930. If a reception order is made by a justice of the peace, after certification under the Lunacy acts, the child is detained in a mental or registered hospital or a licensed home.

Protection.—Children maintained for reward apart from their parents are regulated by part VII of the Public Health act, 1936, and part XIII of the Public Health (London) act, 1936, as amended by the Children act, 1948. The protection extends until the age of 15 but may be extended to the age of 18. Local authority visitors inspect the homes of the children and give directions as to their health and care. The local authorities may regulate the number of children kept in the homes and apply to the court for orders of removal of children from unsatisfactory premises to places of safety. Under the Nurseries and Child-Minders Regulation act, 1948, nurseries and child-minders are regulated by local health authorities who keep registers of children looked after for the day or for any longer period not exceeding six days, issue certificates of registration and inspect the premises and the children therein and the arrangements for their welfare. Registration may be refused if the child-minder is unfit to look after children or if the premises are unfit for their reception.

Offenses against children, including cruelty or exposure to moral or physical danger, are regulated by part I of the Children and Young Persons act, 1933. Causing suffering or injury to health is punishable by fine or imprisonment. Other offenses include the causing of seduction, prostitution or begging, the sale of intoxicants, presence or employment in licensed premises, taking articles in pawn from children and exposing infants under seven to the risk of burns. Attendants must be provided where large numbers of children attend entertainments. Assault, rape and abduction are dealt with under the Offences against the Person act, 1861, and protection from prostitution and sexual offenses is ensured under the Criminal Law Amendment act, 1885. Incest is punishable under the Punishment of Incest act, 1908.

Maintenance allowances are payable in respect of children under the state schemes set up under the Family Allowances act, 1945, the National Insurance act, 1946, and the National Assistance act, 1948.

Employment is regulated by part II of the Children and Young Persons act, 1933, ss.58 to 60 of the Education act, 1944, and the acts relating to factories, shops and mines. The restrictions relate to hours of employment, employment while of school age, intervals for meals and rest and holidays. Bylaws may be made by the local education authorities and control is exercised over street trading and entertainments.

Criminal Proceedings.—Various rules protect children as regards these proceedings, including their separation from adults, the granting of bail, the notification of proceedings to parents, guardians and local authorities and the presence of children during court trials. Most charges against children are heard in juvenile courts and detention is usually prescribed in places other than prisons.

CONTINENTAL DEVELOPMENTS

Towards the end of the 19th century, the importance of child welfare increased in several European countries owing to a fall in the birth rate. In France, premiums were granted for large families (of four or more children). Medical attendance before and after childbirth was made available for the poorer classes and women were allotted rest allowances after childbirth. Employers co-operated in arranging free medical attention for mothers and infants. Breast-feeding and milk distributing centres were provided. Institutions were provided for destitute children by the public assistance scheme. Regulation of employment and special courts for juveniles were established. Similar provision was made in Belgium by the *Oeuvre Nationale de l'Enfance* (an independent public agency assisted by state grants) and the Office for the Protection of Children (under the ministry of justice). In Denmark, child welfare was fostered on public-assistance lines in 1933, and in 1939 maternity aid institutions were established. The Netherlands relied for similar services on private societies (the Green Cross and the White and Yellow Cross) assisted by state grants. Progress in Norway was slower owing to the lack of constitutional powers covering social welfare. In Sweden, social family measures limited in scope were enacted to combat the decline in population.

Progress in child protection received a setback in World War I, which was followed by an effort to restore the previous standards. Co-operation between the nations was secured through the League of Nations and the International Labour office, resulting in international conventions to protect mothers and children, particularly as regards their employment, and to control prostitution. World War II had catastrophic consequences caused by the disruption of families, the problem of refugees and the plight of homeless and undernourished children. Under the auspices of the United Nations an International Children's Emergency fund was created.

In France after World War II the act of 1945 established maternal and child welfare services as part of the public health service of each departmental area. Children deprived of family support were placed under supervision or transferred to state guardianship. Milk distribution to children was secured. Services for defective and delinquent children were improved. Homes and approved schools were provided by the *Direction de l'Education surveillée* under the minister of justice. Agencies for social security and family allowances were operated.

In Belgium the older services were reinstated and measures taken for the health and care of young workers. Similar action was taken in Denmark and the Netherlands after World War II. Norway modernized its statutes concerning child protection and welfare and set up a central organization. Family allowances were introduced. Sweden improved its maternity services, adopted family allowances, set up compulsory sickness insurance and formed child welfare boards in most towns to supervise private and municipal welfare institutions.

BIBLIOGRAPHY.—Elsie Edith Bowerman, *Law of Child Protection* (1933); A. E. Williams *Barnardo of Stepney, the Father of Nobody's Children* (1943); *Curtis Report on Care of Children* (H.M.S.O., London, 1946); Sir William Clarke Hall, *Law Relating to Children and Young Persons,* ed. by A. C. L. Morrison, 3rd ed. (London, 1947); A. C. L. Morrison, *Children Act, 1948* (London, 1948); A. C. L. Morrison, *Outlines of Law for Social Workers* (London, 1948); John Moss, *Hadden's Health and Welfare Services Handbook* (London, 1949); Harry Samuels, *Factory Law,* 4th ed. (London, 1948); J. A. F. Watson, *British Juvenile Courts* (London, 1948); J. Gazdar, *National Insurance,* (London, 1947); Charles Winter, *Children and Young Persons Under the Law* (London, 1949); United Nations Department of Public Information, *Year Book of the United Nations* (1947 *et seq.*); United Nations Department of Social Affairs, *Annual Report on Child and Youth Welfare* (1948). (C. WTR.)

UNITED STATES

The tendency of U.S. law has been to enlarge the rights of the child and the measure of protection afforded to him against ill-usage, exploitation and conditions affecting his health, morals and general well-being. While the laws of the various states and the judicial decisions interpreting them differ in details, certain general principles were quite widely accepted by mid-20th century.

The first duty of the parents of children is to provide them with support. This obligation rests principally upon the father but the mother is required to do so upon the death of the father. The Social Security Act of 1935, with its federal subsidy of aid to dependent children (A.D.C.), recognized the difficulties a widow might have in supporting her child and also giving it the necessary care and supervision. Any relative of first or second degree providing care for a child and satisfying the legal test for dependency was made eligible for A.D.C., which was more inclusive than the mothers' pension laws operative in most of the states before 1935.

The father of stepchildren is not obligated to provide for them unless he voluntarily undertakes to do so. In the case of an illegitimate child, the mother is liable for its support, and in some states she and her child are eligible for A.D.C. The father may be required to provide support if his paternity has been legally adjudged or if he voluntarily acknowledges it and assumes the duty of support. The precise extent of the duty of support is determined by the law of the particular jurisdiction. Generally it includes food, shelter, clothing, medical care and education. Compulsory education laws require the attendance of children at school and impose a penalty upon the parents for noncompliance. At the same time, child labour laws prohibit the employment of the child during the time when he is required to be in school or in dangerous occupations.

Generally speaking, the father has the control and custody of the child and he may determine where it shall live although the modern tendency is to recognize a larger right in the mother as to these matters. Either or both parents may be deprived of custody by conduct harmful to the child. In case of the father's death, the mother assumes full custody and control. An illegitimate child becomes legitimate upon the subsequent marriage of its parents. In a few states, legitimation can be effected through a judicial proceeding instituted for the purpose or through the process of legal adoption. A legitimated child assumes the same relation to the parent or parents as if born in lawful wedlock. Where a child becomes an orphan or where his parents prove to be wholly unfit to care for him properly, he may be committed in a legal proceeding, usually through the juvenile court, to the guardianship of a suitable person, a public welfare agency or a private social agency. Guardians may be appointed either to conserve the property of the child or to provide care and maintenance, or both.

A guardian does not assume the full status of a parent. This relationship is established only through the process of legal adoption by which the child becomes the lawful child of his adoptive parents. The tendency of legislation in the 20th century has been to safeguard adoption proceedings by requiring that the child shall remain in the prospective foster home for a trial period, usually six months, before the proceeding is completed. At mid-20th century such laws existed in 40 states, and agencies commonly required a trial period of one year. In 41 states the law (mandatory in 36 states) provided for a social investigation of the foster home by an official or someone designated by the court and a report presented to the court having jurisdiction of the proceeding as to whether the foster parents are proper persons to adopt the child and their home a suitable one for the purpose.

Because of the abuses arising out of the casual transfer of children from parents to irresponsible people, many states passed laws prohibiting any transfer of parental control except upon a court order; *i.e.,* through guardianship or adoption proceedings or upon order of a juvenile court. Few adoption agencies relied only upon a parent's surrender, even where it had become the only legal requirement. The law in many jurisdictions prohibited the bringing of children into one state from another for purposes of permanent care until after investigation and approval by the authorities of the state to which the child is brought.

In addition to the duty of support the parent must shield the child from evil surroundings and may not impose injury or cruelty upon him. The parent may use physical force to protect the child from danger and, under proper circumstances, to impose reasonable parental correction. The conduct of any adult which tends to deprave the morals of a child or endanger his health or well-being is punishable as a criminal offense.

The White House Conference on the Care of Dependent Children called by Pres. Theodore Roosevelt in 1909 incorporated among its conclusions the following: "To engage in the work of caring for needy children is to assume a most serious responsibility, and should, therefore, be permitted only to those who are definitely organized for the purpose, who are of suitable character, and who possess, or have reasonable assurance of securing, the funds needed for their support. . . ." This conference and succeeding White House conferences on child welfare in 1919, 1930, 1940 and 1950 emphasized the need for organization and development of a strong department of public welfare in each state with functions to include the licensing of voluntary child-care agencies and institutions and the supervising of similar services wherever operated by cities, counties or the states.

At mid-20th century there was great variation in the state laws for proper care of dependent children and in the administrations of the public welfare departments responsible for enforcing such laws. These variations had been reduced, however, by the provisions of the Social Security act, and the federal grants-in-aid under this act, which first became available in 1936. This act and succeeding annual appropriations by the congress authorized and subsidized the child welfare services as well as aid to dependent children and other forms of public assistance. Child welfare services gave priority to various social services for children in rural areas, and as a result many counties organized such programs in conformity with plans drawn up by state welfare departments, which in turn required approval by the U.S. children's bureau. An important element in the plans was the provision, with federal funds, for professional training for the social workers essential to effective service. Child welfare services include work with delinquent, emotionally disturbed and mentally handicapped children as well as those who are dependent, covering services to children in their own homes as well as in foster homes.

The responsibility for licensing a children's institution, a child-placing agency or a day-care centre usually is carried by the children's division of the state department of public welfare, with the responsibility to license foster homes usually carried by a county department of public welfare. Other public officials who sometimes share in the inspection prerequisite to issuance of a license are public health officers and fire marshals. In some jurisdictions the only license required for a foster home or a day-care centre is issued by the health department.

Laws governing guardianship and custody, administered by local courts, differed greatly at mid-century, though in many states their original characteristics, derived from the English Poor law, had little adaptation to modern social and economic conditions. Indenture of children, though still practised, was widely condemned in the early years of the 20th century. The obsolete laws authorizing indenture in the statutes of most of the older states were repealed, though it was as late as 1946 in Mississippi. The rights of children born out of wedlock were recognized in the revision of legal requirements for birth registration to the extent that in some states a birth card, supplying data needed for enrolment in school and satisfaction of the child labour laws, became the common document issued in lieu of a complete birth certificate. The original record and information about parentage remained available only for restricted use and in the child's interest. Safeguards assuring rights of inheritance to adopted children were developed, especially in preventing hasty and illegal adoptions. Hazards to children of unmarried mothers, comprising the majority of those placed for adoption, still persisted as evidenced by the operation of baby farms and the prevalence of black-market adoptions in which the rights of the child received secondary consideration.

Beginning in 1911, protective legislation for children was markedly accelerated by the work of state commissions for the study and revision of child welfare laws. This movement was no doubt stimulated in part by the British Children Act of 1908, sometimes referred to as the "Children's Magna Charta." While this act was mainly a codification of existing law on the subject, in the process of compilation and revision distinct advance in protective measures was made. The White House Conference on the Care of Dependent Children recommended periodic review and revision of child welfare legislation. In 1911 the first state commission was appointed for this purpose. By mid-century almost all states and the District of Columbia had followed the precedent set by Ohio. Stimulated by the National Commission on Children and Youth appointed during World War II by the U.S. children's bureau, committees and councils in most of the states urged further revision of children's codes. The year 1947, when most of the state legislatures held their biennial sessions, was one of unprecedented activity, one-half of the states then making changes in their adoption laws.

States were influenced after World War II by the Veterans' administration, especially in making more adequate provisions for guardianship of children of veterans.

Large numbers of children became beneficiaries of life insurance carried by their fathers and others became entitled to benefits under old aid and survivors insurance administered by the Federal Security agency.

The National Conference on Prevention and Control of Juvenile Delinquency, held in Washington in 1946 was attended by about 800 officials and professional workers experienced in serving children. Their findings dwelt on the interrelationship of housing, recreation, education, religious training and family relationships and the need for recognition of these forces by the entire community and especially by those who enact and enforce laws and administer training schools for delinquents.

Recommendations pertaining to the protection of children, passed at the Midcentury White House Conference on Children and Youth, held in 1950, included the following:

"That children of migrant and seasonal workers be given all the protections and services available to other children, with special regard to transportation, housing, sanitation, health and educational services, social benefits, and protection under labor laws.

"That standards be developed for juvenile services by police departments.

"That, in accordance with state-wide standards, courts of superior jurisdiction, with judges qualified in the law with an understanding of social and psychological factors, and with qualified probation staff and auxiliary personnel be available for all cases involving children with problems that require court action in rural and urban areas.

"That the preventive and treatment functions of social agencies, police, courts, institutions, and after-care agencies be coordinated so as to insure continuity of service.

"That states and other appropriate public bodies establish and enforce standards covering the employment of youth in all occupations, such standards to include minimum age and wages, as well as hours of work, night work, protection from hazardous occupations and provisions for workmen's compensation; and that, under these conditions, employers in cooperation with labor be urged to provide appropriate work experience for youth on a part-time basis.

"That communities foster cooperative community councils representative of all community interests to study and advance better conditions and opportunities for young workers.

"That citizens be encouraged to support adequate appropriations and qualified staff to administer and enforce basic legislative standards of states, and other appropriate public bodies, covering the employment of youth."

Bibliography.—John S. Bradway, *Law and Social Work* (1929); White House Conference on Child Health and Protection, *The Delinquent Child* (1932), *Organization for the Care of Handicapped Children, National, State, Local* (1932), *Dependent and Neglected Children* (1933); Grace Abbott, *The Child and the State*, 2 vol (1938); David M. Schneider, *The History of Public Welfare in New York State, 1609–1866* (1938); David M. Schneider and Albert Deutsch, *The History of Public Welfare in New York State, 1867–1940* (1941); Henry W. Thurston, *Concerning Juvenile Delinquency* (1942); Children's Bureau, Federal Security Agency, *Final Report: White House Conference on Children in a Democracy* (1943); S. P. Breckinridge and Mary Stanton, "The Law of Guardian and Ward with Special Reference to the Children of Veterans," *Social Service Review* (Sept.

1943); Child Welfare League of America, *Child Welfare Bibliography* (1944) with annual supplements; Emma O. Lundberg, *Our Concern—Every Child* (1945); U.S. Department of Justice, *Reports of National Conference on Prevention and Control of Juvenile Delinquency* (1946); Children's Bureau, Federal Security Agency, *Public Social Services to Children—a Decade of Progress, 1935–1945* (1946); P. S. de Q. Cabot, *Juvenile Delinquency, A Critical Annotated Bibliography* (1946); Emma O. Lundberg, *Unto the Least of These: Social Services for Children* (1947); Russell Sage Foundation, *Social Work Yearbook, 1949* (1949). (W. Ho.; H. W. Hk.)

CHILDREN'S BOOKS. Children's "books" in Europe, like other books, were in use before the invention of printing. Such works as *Gesta Romanorum,* the riddles and scholastic exercises of Aelfric and Alcuin, versions of Aesop's *Fables,* etc., were all used by children. They are, however, a piece of social history rather than of specialized literature. The early printed (and ms.) "books of courtesy"—which contained rules of conduct in polite society—are also social documents, and may be set apart with abecedaria, hornbooks, battledores and pure schoolbooks. They lived a changed life later in works like Francis Osborne's *Advice to a Son* (1656), and Chesterfield's *Letters.* With the Reformation, secular books gave way to fierce moral tales which dealt out hell-fire punishment to sinners, as typified by James Janeway's *Token for Children* (1720). But the greatest of all Puritans was one of the first to see that something less stark was needed. John Bunyan's *Book for Boys and Girls; or, Country Rhimes for Children* (1686: later renamed *Divine Emblems*), popular for more than a century, contained rough but kindly "natural history" verses and vigorous "morals."

The Fairy Tale.—Meanwhile, oral tradition was preserving vernacular folklore, destined to be the bedrock of children's literature in the form of fairy stories and versions of the Arthurian and Robin Hood romances. There was no printed version, however, before the crudely printed chapbooks which spread over England in the late 17th and early 18th centuries—the library of Steele's little godson (*Tatler,* No. 95). Here the child found action and romance—the same ingredients which in part accounted for the popularity of *Pilgrim's Progress* (1678), *Robinson Crusoe* (1719) and *Gulliver's Travels* (1726). The fairy tale also invaded England from court—Louis XIV's—when Perrault's *Histoires ou Contes du Temps Passé* (1696 in French, probably 1729 in English; better known as *Mother Goose's Fairy Tales*), and the Comtesse D'Aulnoy's tales (1707) were translated.

This was not enough to make a literature. Other developments were needed. Isaac Watts created one with his moral but technically excellent verses (1715). But the real beginning lay in four volumes and in the personality of one man. A few well-known rhymes had appeared incongruously in severer treatises; but the nursery-rhyme was first thoroughly collected in *Tommy Thumb's Pretty Song Book* (1744), *The Top Book of All, Mother Goose's Melody,* and *Gammer Gurton's Garland* (all ascribed to 1760).

The man was John Newbery, who in 1744 published his first children's book, *The Little Pretty Pocket Book.* Before his death in 1767 this friend of Goldsmith had built up a business which itself lasted into the 20th century, and had founded a new branch of the book trade. There is no space here to enumerate his "pretty gilt toys for girls and boys" (so-called from their gay Dutch-paper bindings). In form (strongly bound, not ill-printed, before long quite tolerably illustrated) as well as in substance, they decided the nature of children's books for three or four generations, even though fashion in expression changed.

The Moral Tale.—Their contents were soon influenced by wider issues than the bookseller probably foresaw. Philosophy and even politics intervened. Maria Edgeworth (1767–1849), the best of all storytellers of this period for children, and her friend Thomas Day (*Sandford and Merton,* 1783–89) deliberately put into nursery tales the doctrines of Rousseau. Arnaud Berquin ("l'ami des enfants") translated Day into French, and was himself translated copiously, with other French writers. Maria Edgeworth's work prepared the way for the freer, more realistic stories of Mrs. D. M. Craik, Mrs. J. H. Ewing, Mrs. Alfred Gatty, Mrs. M. L. Molesworth and Charlotte M. Yonge. The active Quakers (like Priscilla Wakefield) wrote many moral tales. Mrs. Trimmer, remembered for her *Robins* (1786; originally called *Fabulous Histories*), at once combated Jacobinism, on behalf of the church, and desired fairy tales to be suppressed as immoral. Mrs. Sherwood also wished to depose Titania; but her *Fairchild Family* (1818, etc.) remained popular for at least four generations. Ann and Jane Taylor (1804, etc.) of a notable Nonconformist family, put the "cautionary tale" into nimble verses, of which "Twinkle, twinkle, little star" will never die; with them should be associated Elizabeth Turner (1807, etc.). The Lambs were, in a sense, of the same school; Blake is splendidly apart from all tendencies.

The Return of Fantasy.—Fantasy returned in 1806, when 40,000 copies of Roscoe's *Butterfly's Ball* and Mrs. Dorset's *Peacock at Home* were sold. The tide of reaction against "amusement with instruction" came to a head in 1824, when the *German Popular Stories* of the brothers Grimm began to appear in English, with Cruikshank's illustrations. Hans Andersen was translated in 1841, levity (even naughtiness) condoned by Catherine Sinclair in *Holiday House* (1839), and absurdity made sublime by Edward Lear's *Book of Nonsense* (1846).

This new freedom infected even "Felix Summerly" (Sir Henry Cole, an adviser of the prince consort) who introduced the Seven Champions and other fabulous monsters into his chaste and well-produced *Home Treasury.* There followed what may be called the Parley epoch, in which a number of Peter Parleys—the chief an American, S. G. Goodrich—vied in amassing instruction in easy-going form.

In 1865 or 1866 and in 1872 appeared the greatest of all children's books, the two *Alice* volumes of Lewis Carroll (C. L. Dodgson), with whom is indissolubly associated John Tenniel. These inspired, finely imaginative tales finally routed didacticism and moralizing and passed at once not only into the affections of the whole English-speaking world, but also into its arsenal of quotations. They made possible the success of the good modern fairy tale (the poor one is a perpetual trap for inexperienced writers), like those of Kingsley, George Macdonald and Mrs. Molesworth; of such books as Mrs. Ewing's *Lob-lie-by-the-Fire;* of the magical *Peter Pan* (1911); of such delicate modern art as A. A. Milne's *Winnie-the-Pooh* (1926) and Kenneth Grahame's *Wind in the Willows* (1908); John Masefield's *Midnight Folk* (1927) and the writings of Walter De La Mare.

The animal story, a prominent feature of the 20th century, had its beginnings in the late 18th century; but the animals remained characterless until *Black Beauty* appeared (1877) and Kipling was inspired to write his *Jungle Books* (1894–95). Animal stories of the more fanciful type are closely allied to the fairy tale; Beatrix Potter's excellent little books (1902–30), illustrated with charm and delicacy by the author herself, are outstanding examples.

Other developments were the adventure story (a parallel growth to the adult novel), firmly established by *Coral Island* (1857); the boys' school story, notably *Tom Brown's Schooldays* (1856) and *Stalky and Co.* (1899) and its sentimental counterpart for girls; Edith Nesbit's own particular blend of fantasy and reality; and the appearance in the latter half of the 19th century of literature of appeal to the older child, as opposed to the "babies'" nursery stories of earlier days.

Illustrations were counted a necessity in children's books from the beginning but did not reach satisfactory artistic standards until the work of Bewick and Blake appeared in the 18th century. Walter Crane (1845–1915), Kate Greenaway (1846–1901) and Randolph Caldecott (1846–86) contributed outstanding work in line and colour. Modern colour lithography made possible the reproduction of fine work by Kathleen Hale (in the *Orlando* series), Clarke Hutton and Edward Ardizzone (all 20th century).

During the 20th century a new type of children's book has developed; nonfiction which seeks not to educate, but to interest, and in so doing, often imparts more knowledge than a text book. The articles in Arthur Mee's *Children's Encyclopedia* (1906) were a landmark in this type of literature. The major development, however, has been in children's fiction. With the publication of Arthur Ransome's *Swallows and Amazons* (1930) emerged the realistic children's novel, with good characterization and plot within the bounds of possibility. Written in easy, colloquial style and peopled with lively children, creators of their own fun, Ransome's works have many able imitators.

The school story has given way to the family story, such as Eve Garnett's *Family from One End Street* (1937) and many series of holiday adventures. Novels have been written especially for the young adolescent; for example, career stories such as Richard Armstrong's *Sea Change* (1948).

BIBLIOGRAPHY.—*Cambridge History of English Literature*, vol. xi, bibl. (Cambridge, 1914); C. Welsh, *A Bookseller of the Last Century* (John Newbery) (London, 1885); L. F. Field, *The Child and His Book* (London, 1891); A. W. Tuer, *History of the Horn-Book*, 2 vol. (London, 1896), *Pages and Pictures from Forgotten Children's Books* (London, 1898), *Stories from Old Fashioned Children's Books* (London, 1900); E. Godfrey, *English Children in the Olden Time* (London, 1907); F. V. Barry, *A Century of Children's Books* (London, New York, 1923); F. J. H. Darton, *Children's Books in England; Five Centuries of Social Life* (Cambridge, New York, 1932); Dorothy M. (Neal) White, *About Books for Children* (Wellington and Toronto, 1946); J. A. Smith, *Children's Illustrated Books* (London, 1949); G. Trease, *Tales Out of School* (London, 1949); K. M. Lines, *Four to Fourteen*, a select list of contemporary children's literature (London, Toronto, 1950); F. Eyre, *20th Century Children's Books* (London, 1952; Boston, 1953). (F. J. H. D.; D. D. C.)

UNITED STATES

Colonial Period to 1800.—The Puritan exodus from the old world which began with the landing of the *Mayflower* in 1620, brought to American shores "the people of a book, and that book was the Bible." This meant a people so deeply concerned with religion that their first responsibility to their children was to indoctrinate them with their beliefs. As early as 1632 there are references to hornbooks, those little paddles with an alphabet and the Lord's prayer pasted on, but the first real book for children published in the new world was John Cotton's *Spiritual Milk Drawn Out of the Breasts of Both Testaments, Chiefly for the Spiritual Nourishment of Boston Babes in Either England* (1646). It was an example of theological didacticism, for the instruction of "babes," with the intent of stiffening their resistance to sin by lurid pictures of hell and only faint hopes of heaven. *Spiritual Milk* was followed by the famous *New England Primer*, printed in Boston, sometime before 1690. It began with the alphabet "In Adam's fall/We sinned all" and as the years went by and new editions succeeded each other, its theology grew steadily grimmer. But by the time the American Revolution began, theology had diminished in favour of appropriate patriotic sentiments. *Spiritual Milk* and the *Primer* were followed by some terrifying booklets dealing with the "joyful deaths" of pious children. These must have induced more night terrors than love of reading, but dreadful as they were, they bear witness to the Puritans' recognition of books as the tools of learning.

In Worcester and Boston, Isaiah Thomas (1749–1831) imported and later pirated his own editions of John Newbery's popular books for children. The most famous of these was the immortal *Mother Goose* (1785), the edition of nursery rhymes Oliver Goldsmith is supposed to have compiled. In New York city, another printer, Hugh Gaine (1726 or 1727–1807), brought out *The Wonderful Life and Surprising Confessions of the Renowned Hero Robinson Crusoe* (1775). Also in circulation were *Aesop's Fables in Verse, Watts' Divine Songs for Children,* and little chapbook versions of such fairy tales as "Cinderella" and "Tom Thumb." So perhaps small Puritans, struggling with the harrowing *Spiritual Milk,* may have been heartened now and then by stray glimpses of happier reading matter.

Nineteenth Century.—In 1831, a little book called *Mary Lothrop Who Died in Boston* made its appearance and seems to have terminated the morbid emphasis on the brevity of a child's life. In 1819 Washington Irving's *Sketch Book* appeared with that still popular fairy tale of the new world, "Rip Van Winkle." Then came those remarkable books by James Fenimore Cooper of which *The Last of the Mohicans* (1826) and *The Deerslayer* (1841) became the most popular both in the U.S. and Europe. His heroic Indians and Irving's fantasy gave children their first taste of native romanticism and good writing.

Then earnestness set in, this time in the form of educational didacticism which pursued children through one long series of books after another. Samuel Goodrich, who wrote under the name of Peter Parley, turned out about five or six books a year; *Tales of Peter Parley about America* (1827) was typical. The books contained laudatory biographies, bits of science, history and geography, amazingly dull in style but popular both in England and the United States. Even more popular were the innumerable books of Jacob Abbott. By 1834 his *Rollo* books were underway. *Rollo Learning to Talk* was followed by 28 volumes which accompanied Rollo around the world with a steady barrage of information.

Book series were momentarily interrupted by Susan Warner's Sunday school best seller, *The Wide, Wide World* (1850), and a few years later, *Queechy*. Girls liked these books and the tears shed by the orphaned heroines were matched by the tears of young readers. Then, back to the series again, with the first appearance of the priggish *Elsie Dinsmore* (1868) by Martha Finley (pseudonym for Farquharson) who carried her heroine through 26 volumes. Elsie's sentimentality was paralleled by stereotyped success stories for boys written by Horatio Alger. His *Ragged Dick* (1867), in the rags-to-riches pattern was a typical example. Two entertaining series of stories about normal children and family life were *The Five Little Peppers and How They Grew* (1881) by Margaret Sidney, pseudonym of Harriet Mulford Lothrop, and the well written books by Laura Richards—*Queen Hildegarde* (1889) and *The Three Margarets* (1897).

In the field of verse, Clement Moore's ballad, "A Visit from St. Nicholas" (1822) delighted children. Some of the better poems of Eugene Field (1850–95) and James Whitcomb Riley (1849–1916) are still to be found in modern anthologies and Laura Richards' *In My Nursery* (1890) began the gay nonsense verses which she continued to write in the next century. *The Brownies, Their Book* (1887), by Palmer Cox, launched a series of picture stories in verse about the antics of a band of brownies. These elves were individualized and favourite characters were the Dude or the Cowboy or the Policeman, perhaps.

Suddenly among those minor works, great books appeared. Nathaniel Hawthorne's *A Wonder-Book For Boys and Girls* (1852) and *Tanglewood Tales* (1853) reduced myth to child's size but were full of the enchantment of wonderful storytelling. Mary Mapes Dodge's *Hans Brinker or the Silver Skates* (1865) charmed children with its story of Holland. Louisa M. Alcott's *Little Women* (1868) has been so beloved by girls that it has appeared in one new edition after another. It gave girls an intimate picture of a loving, struggling family, with memorable characterizations of four sisters, and a happy element of romance. For boys there were two major books—*The Adventures of Tom Sawyer* (1876) and *The Adventures of Huckleberry Finn* (1884), by Mark Twain (pseudonym for Samuel L. Clemens). The heroes, like Clemens himself, knew everyone in the village from the town drunkards to the deacons of the church. Adventure, humour and authentic portrayals of boy nature made these books unrivalled Americana and good literature.

In different vein another great originator, Howard Pyle, retold the epics. Of these, his *Merry Adventures of Robin Hood* (1883), with Pyle's own illustrations, remained over the years the best version of that hero tale. His stories in folklore style came next —*Pepper and Salt* (1887) and *Wonder Clock* (1887). His two books on mediaeval times, *Otto of the Silver Hand* (1888) and *Men of Iron* (1891) set high standards for historical fiction. In 1883 Joel Chandler Harris' *Nights with Uncle Remus* introduced children to the rich humour of American Negro folk tales and in 1880 Lucretia Hale's droll *The Peterkin Papers* set children and adults to chuckling.

So the 19th century progressed from religious and educational didacticism, stereotypes and sentimentality to sound folklore, myth, and epics, drolls, realistic stories of family life, unsurpassed historical fiction and Americana. Nor were these books the product of ordinary writers condescending to the juvenile field. They were created by men and women of established literary reputations. Their work and that of writers abroad lifted children's books from the trivial to an area of literature worthy of respect and study.

Twentieth Century.—The notable books with which the 19th century closed were forerunners of a phenomenal flood of books for children in the 20th century. Causes are matters of speculation. The rise of kindergartens, and later nursery schools, brought with them a new concern for the needs of young children. The development of laboratory psychology, psychiatry and adult education fostered a broader knowledge of childhood and adolescence. Innumerable research studies in reading skills led to a new evaluation of books. By 1900 children's rooms were established in public libraries and by 1940 libraries began to appear in elementary schools. Before 1915 library and teacher training schools had added courses in children's literature to their curriculums. Between 1920 and 1930, scholarly reviews of children's books were underway. Children's Book Week was a nation-wide observance by 1919 and *The Horn Book Magazine,* devoted to children's literature, was launched in 1924. In 1922 Frederick Melcher, editor of *Publishers' Weekly,* established the Newbery Medal, an annual award for the most distinguished literature for children written in this country. The Caldecott award for the best picture book was added in 1938. Both called attention to the fact that in books for children there can and should be elements of distinction.

Picture stories attained distinction with Wanda Gag's *Millions of Cats* (1928), told and illustrated in folk tale style. She was an innovator few have equalled. Marjorie Flack's *Angus and the Ducks* (1930) began a series of dog stories for the nursery age. *Make Way for the Ducklings* (1941) by Robert McCloskey and *Little House* (1942) by Virginia Burton, both won Caldecott medals. Maude and Miska Petersham, Berta and Elmer Hader, Ingri and Edgar d'Aulaire, Leo Politi, Will Lipkind and Nicolas Mordvinoff, Roger Duvoisin and others made picture stories beloved by children everywhere.

Folk and Fanciful Tales.—In 1909 Kate Douglas Wiggin and Nora Archibald Smith compiled a fine edition of *The Arabian Nights.* But it was Gudrun Thorne-Thomsen's collection of Norse tales, *East o' the Sun and West o' the Moon* (1912) together with her storytelling that started a wave of interest in European folk tales. Major compilations were made by Padraic Colum, Ruth Sawyer, James Cloyd Bowman, Parker Fillmore and others. In 1924 Esther Shephard made the first collection of the American tall tale stories, *Paul Bunyan,* the lumberjack hero. To these James Cloyd Bowman added *Pecos Bill, the Greatest Cowboy of All Time* (1937). Glen Rounds, Richard Chase, Anne Malcolmson and Irwin Shapiro also contributed to the store of folk tales of the United States.

Modern fanciful tales were few at the beginning of the century but soon included such original inventions as Carl Sandburg's *Rootabaga Stories* (1922), Dr. Seuss' (pseudonym for Theodor Seuss Geisel) *500 Hats for Bartholomew Cubbins* (1938) and the same year, *Mr. Popper's Penguins* by Richard and Florence Atwater. The *Cat Who Went to Heaven* (1930) by Elizabeth Coatsworth, *Rabbit Hill* (1944) by Robert Lawson, *Miss Hickory* (1946) by Carolyn Bailey and *Twenty-One Balloons* (1947) by William Pène du Bois, all won Newbery medals, and E. B. White's *Charlotte's Web* (1952) had equal originality and distinction. These were examples of fantasy without benefit of fairies!

Realism.—Realistic animal stories were increasingly popular after the publication of Ernest Thompson Seton's *Wild Animals I Have Known* (1898) and Jack London's *The Call of the Wild* (1903). These set new standards of fidelity to animal lore, well maintained with two Newbery winners—*Smoky* (1925) by Will James and *King of the Wind* (1948) by Marguerite Henry. *Kildee House* (1948) by Robert Montgomery and books by Jim Kjelgaard, Joseph Lippincott, John and Jean George afford outstanding examples of authentic animal stories.

The world of here and now came alive for 20th-century children with Kate Douglas Wiggin's *Rebecca of Sunnybrook Farm* (1903) and Frances Hodgson Burnett's *The Secret Garden* (1909). Both books developed strongly individualized child characters and unusual story interest. After those books, realism developed along many lines. Stories of everyday children, earnestly doing their best but finding themselves in ludicrous situations were Eleanor Estes' *The Moffats* (1941–43) and Robert McCloskey's *Homer Price* (1943). The regional books of Lois Lenski, such as her *Strawberry Girl* (1945; Newbery Medal) and Doris Gates' *Blue Willow* (1940), gave children serious but appealing pictures of underprivileged families. Grace Moon and Ann Nolan Clark wrote authentic stories of American Indians. Other racial and religious minorities were sympathetically presented by Marguerite De Angeli, Mabel Leigh Hunt and Florence Crannell Means. Popular stories about peoples of other countries were written by Kate Seredy, Armstrong Sperry, Monica Shannon and Elizabeth Lewis, all winners of Newbery Medals.

Historical Fiction and Biography merged in children's literature and included some of the strongest books the United States had produced. Laura Richards' *Florence Nightingale, the Angel of the Crimea* (1909) and Albert Bigelow Paine's *Girl in White Armor* (1927) were vigorous beginnings. The latter was an unforgettable picture of Joan of Arc. Hendrick Van Loon's *Story of Mankind* (1925), Newbery winner, gave further impetus to vivid biography which Elizabeth Janet Gray, James Daugherty, Clara Ingram Judson, Genevive Foster and the *The Landmark Books* further illumined. Cornelia Meigs' *Master Simon's Garden* (1916) launched historical fiction that was authentic, well-written, and with a lasting message for the modern world. Rachel Field's historical novel, *Calico Bush* (1931), was her best book and Esther Forbes' Newbery winner, *Johnny Tremain* (1943), was rated as one of America's greatest juvenile books. Laura Ingalls Wilder's splendid eight volume saga of a pioneer family began with *Little House in the Big Woods* (1932). Walter Edmonds, Elizabeth Coatsworth, Stephen Meader and Rebecca Caudill also made notable contributions to this field.

Poetry for children in the United States developed a fresh, native melody and an awareness of the child's interests. The poets of childhood used successfully those qualities of poetry that most delight a child and so prepare him for an appreciation of adult poetry later on. *Under the Tree* (1922) by Elizabeth Madox Roberts was the voice of a creative artist speaking as a child. *Taxis and Toadstools* (1926) by Rachel Field, presented a child's-eye view of city and country. Vachel Lindsay's *Johnny Appleseed and Other Poems* (1928) and Carl Sandburg's *Early Moon* (1930) introduced free verse and a vigorous masculine note to children's poetry. The southwest, with its Indians and deserts came alive in Mary Austin's *Children Sing in the Far West* (1928) and Rosemary and Stephen Benét enlivened American history with their penetrating vignettes of famous heroes in *The Book of Americans* (1933). Harry Behn's *Little Hill* (1949) had child appeal and lyric charm. Moreover, such poets as Edna St. Vincent Millay, Sara Teasdale and others wrote occasional poems for children which added to the child's store of authentic poetry.

Bibliography.—Clifford K. Shipton, *Isaiah Thomas, Printer, Patriot, and Philanthropist* (Rochester, N.Y., 1948); P. L. Ford, *The New England Primer* (New York, 1897), and edited *The Journals of Hugh Gaine* (New York, 1902); R. V. Halsey, *Forgotten Books of the American Nursery, a History of the Developments of the American Story-Book* (Boston, 1911); Elva S. Smith, *The History of Children's Literature* (Chicago, 1937), syllabus with bibliographies; Cornelia Meigs, Anne Eaton, Elizabeth Nesbitt and Ruth Hill Viguers, *A Critical History of Children's Literature* (New York, 1953), traces children's books from earliest times to 1950 with chapters on books in the United States; Joseph Auslander and F. E. Hill, *The Winged Horse* (Garden City, N.Y., 1927) history of the development of poetry over the years; Iona and Peter Opie, *The Oxford Dictionary of Nursery Rhymes* (London, Toronto, 1951), origins and history of over 500 nursery rhymes with American variants and editions; Sister Monica Mary Kiefer, *American Children Through Their Books, 1700–1835* (London, Philadelphia, 1948), an outstanding study of the changing status of American children as revealed in their books, fine bibliography of early books; Paul Hazard, *Books, Children and Men* (Boston, 1944) a French professor of comparative literature surveys the books of many countries; Lillian H. Smith, *The Unreluctant Years* (Chicago, 1953) emphasizes qualities of good writing in children's books; May Hill Arbuthnot, *Children and Books* (Chicago, 1947) analyzes books as literature and children's responses to them; Annis Duff, *Bequest of Wings* (New York, 1944) pleasant account of a family's use of books with children; Anne Thaxter Eaton, *Reading with Children* (New York, Toronto, 1940) brief accounts of children's enjoyment of different types of books; Anne Carroll Moore, *My Roads to Childhood* (New York, 1939) a children's librarian looks at memorable books; May Hill Arbuthnot, *The Arbuthnot Anthology of Children's Literature* (Chicago, 1953) examples old and new, of poetry, fairy tales, realistic fiction of many types and biographies, with evaluations and bibliographies; Stanley J. Kunitz and Howard Haycraft, eds., *The Junior Book of Authors,* revised ed. (New York, 1951), brief sketches of the lives and writing of authors of children's books; Elizabeth Rider Montgomery, *The Story Behind Modern Books* (New York, Toronto, 1949), how or why artists and authors happened to create their books; Helen Ferris, ed., *Writing Books for Boys and Girls* (New York, 1952), writers and artists tell how they work; Jean Poindexter Colby, *The Children's Book Field* (New York, 1952), a juvenile editor considers what makes a good book for children and how it is produced; Bertha E. Mahony, Louise Payson Latimer and Beulah Folmsbee, *Illustrators of Children's Books* (Boston, 1947), the history of illustration, together with a critical evaluation of outstanding artists. (M. H. A.)

CHILDREN'S COURTS or Juvenile Courts, a special system of tribunals for dealing with juvenile offenders, which has found its widest development in the United States. The earliest trace of such institutions is however contained in a Swiss ordinance of the year 1862. In 1869 Massachusetts adopted the same principle when a plan was introduced of hearing charges against children separately and apart from the ordinary business of the lesser tribunals. The system of probation, by which children were handed over to the kindly care and guardianship of an appointed officer and thus escaped legal repression, was created about the same time in Boston, Mass., and produced excellent results. The probation officer is present at the judge's side when he decides a case, and is given charge of the offender, whom he takes by the hand either at his parent's residence or at school, and continually supervises, having power if necessary to bring him again before the judge. The example of Massachusetts in due course influenced other countries, and especially the British colony of South Australia, where a state children's department was created at Adelaide in 1895, and three years later a juvenile court was opened there for the trial of persons under 18 and was conducted with great success, though the system of probation officers was not introduced.

The movement when once fully appreciated went ahead very rapidly and most civilized countries throughout the world have now adopted it. France, Germany, Spain, Holland, Belgium, Austria, Hungary, Sweden and Switzerland have all established these courts. In Paris the splendid work of M. Henri Rollet secured the foundation of such a court in 1912, while the Berlin children's court, established in 1923, is a particularly well worked and efficient one. Italy, Czechoslovakia, Yugoslavia, Poland, Bulgaria and Esthonia are making arrangements not yet completed. Norway, Denmark and Finland deal with children's cases under a special code, while the Soviet Government of Russia entrusts the whole matter to the education authorities. In India, Madras secured a Children Act under which the powers conferred were to be exercised "only by a juvenile court." Bengal followed in 1922, and the Indian Government are now striving zealously to establish the principle throughout India. Australia, Canada, South Africa and New Zealand all have children's courts in good working order, and in Melbourne, Sydney, Cape Town and Johannesburg they are particularly flourishing. Japan introduced a very interesting system for dealing with offenders under the age of 18 in juvenile courts in the year 1922, Brazil in 1923 and the Argentine in 1924. Amsterdam has tried the new experiment of instituting a police service especially for children, many of its members being women. The republic of Colombia insists that all juvenile offenders shall be examined by a medical man who is present in court as an assessor.

In England the Home Office recommended London police magistrates to keep children's cases separate from those of adults; the same practice or something analogous obtained in many county boroughs, such as Bath, Birmingham, Bristol, Bolton, Bradford, Hull, Manchester, Walsall, Halifax and others, and the Children Act, 1908, definitely established children's courts. This act enacted that courts of summary jurisdiction when hearing charges, etc., against children or young persons should, unless the child or young person is charged jointly with an adult, sit in a different building or room from that in which the ordinary sittings of the court are held, or on different days or at different times. Furthermore, provision must be made for preventing persons apparently under the age of 16 years whilst being conveyed to or from court, or whilst waiting before or after their attendance in court, from associating with adults, unless such adults are charged jointly with them. The act prohibits any persons other than members and officers of the court, the parties to the case, their solicitors, counsel and other persons directly concerned in the case, from being present in a juvenile court, except by leave of the court. Bona-fide press representatives are also excepted. The main object of the whole system is to keep the child, the embryonic offender who has probably erred from ignorance or the pressure of circumstances or misfortune, altogether free from the taint or contagion that attaches to criminal proceedings. The moral atmosphere of a legal tribunal is injurious to the youthful mind, and children who appear before a bench, whether as accused or as witness, gain a contemptuous familiarity with legal processes.

The most beneficial action of the children's court comes from its association with the system of personal guardianship and close supervision exercised by the probation officers, official and voluntary. Where the intervention of the newly constituted tribunal can not only save the child from evil association when first arrested, but can rescue him without condemnation and committal to prison, its functions may be relied upon to diminish crime by cutting it off at the source. Much depends upon the quality and temperament of the presiding authority. Where a judge with special aptitude can be appointed, firm, sympathetic, tactful and able to gain the confidence of those brought before him, he may do great good by dealing with each individual and not merely with his offence, realizing that the court does not exist to condemn but to strengthen and give a fresh chance. Where the children's court is only a branch of the existing jurisdiction worked by the regular magistrate or judge fulfilling his ordinary functions and not specially chosen, the beneficial results are not so noticeable. The Juvenile Courts (Metropolis) Act, 1920, has given legislative authority to this principle by enacting that the home secretary in selecting as presidents of such courts certain metropolitan magistrates "shall have regard to their previous experience and their special qualifications for dealing with cases of juvenile offenders."

In view of the fact that about 50% of regular criminals begin a life of crime when under 21 years of age, the importance of the juvenile courts can hardly be exaggerated. Rightly, sympathetically and firmly dealt with whilst still young, the vast majority of these potential criminals would become good citizens of the State. Bad surroundings, evil companions, undesirable parents, mental and physical deficiencies and various psychological causes are responsible for most juvenile delinquency. The responsibility for discovering, removing or eliminating these causes rests with the children's courts, and too much care, time and effort cannot be expended in the carrying out of this work. The younger the offender, the greater is the need for efficient diagnosis of the underlying causes of his wrongdoing. That the Home Office is fully alive to this necessity is shown by the very careful report of the juvenile offenders committee published in 1927. Valuable as probation has proved itself to be in the adult courts, it is of even greater value in the children's courts. The legislature, recognizing this importance in all courts, has greatly strengthened the system by the passing of the Criminal Justice Act, 1925, the first ten sections of which deal exclusively with the question of probation. It enacts that "one or more probation officers shall be appointed for every probation area," but in country districts combined areas may be created. The secretary of State is empowered to make rules (which have now been promulgated and are in force) governing the appointment, qualifications and salaries of probation officers and the constitution, procedure, powers and duties of the probation committees. *See* also CHILDREN: PROTECTIVE LAWS; INFANT; JUVENILE DELINQUENCY.

(W. C. HA.)

UNITED STATES

Legal and Historical Background.—The juvenile court as a distinct organization originated in America but takes its root in legal and philosophical assumptions current in the 19th century. Its immediate aim was to preserve children from the abuses of criminal procedure. Its principles involve a revolutionary change of attitude. The 17th and 18th centuries record great severities. A child of ten who confessed to killing his bed-fellow was punished with the death penalty, because "sparing of this boy simply on account of his tender years might be of dangerous consequences to the public by propagating a notion that children might commit such atrocious crimes with impunity." "In 1828 in New Jersey, a boy of 13 was hanged for murder committed when he was 12. A survey in Illinois revealed that in 1898 575 children between 10 and 16, were confined in the Chicago jail, and 1,983 boys were committed to city prison." Similar conditions existed in every part of the United States.

At first there was no thought of modifying court procedure. The idea was stressed that after conviction the confinement should be apart from adult criminals. Rise of children's reformatories made this possible in New York (1825), Pennsylvania (1828), and Massachusetts (1847). There was also some provision for separate hearings for children, and for probation in Massachusetts between 1870 and 1880, and in New York in 1892. In 1899 the first juvenile court was organized (Cook county, Chicago, Ill.). It brought under one jurisdiction children who violated laws and dependent children, provided identical procedure for both, established probation, decreed that adjudication be deemed not a conviction of crime, but the placing of the child in the relation of ward to the State. The care for the delinquent child was to "approximate as nearly as may be that which should have been given by the parents." Instead of warrant of arrest, examination by a police judge, bail, indictment, jury trial and sentence, there was substituted complaint, investigation by probation officer, petition, informal hearing and commitment. Fines, imprisonment and penal treatment were abolished. The movement spread with rapidity. By

1904 ten States had juvenile courts; after the first ten years, 20 States and the District of Columbia; by 1914, 30 States; and in 1928 only two States (Wyoming and Maine) were without juvenile courts.

This rapid expansion, without trained personnel, led to a period of critical inquiry. The State supreme courts, however, have upheld the constitutionality of the original statutes. Juvenile court ideals have not been applied throughout the rural districts and small towns. In 1918 the Children's Bureau, Washington, D.C., estimated that of 175,000 cases of children in the U.S. courts, approximately only 50,000 went before courts adapted to handle them.

The juvenile court principle is, first, that the child is not an ungrown adult, but a distinct being, physically, mentally, emotionally and socially; the child's response to life is different; secondly, that the State should not proceed against the child as prosecutor, but exercise the chancery power of *parens patriae* to protect the child.

Age-limits.—The legal meaning of the term "child" is defined by statute, which limits the age of criminal responsibility. Under the English common law, no child under seven was held responsible for crime. Belgium in recent years has raised this to 16, the period *sans discernment.* In the United States the tendency is to increase it to 18 and even 21 (excepting offences punishable by death or life-imprisonment). In approximately one-third of the States jurisdiction of the juvenile court extends to children under 16, in one-third to children under 17, and in the remaining third to children under 18 and above.

It is argued that the older child is entitled to trial by jury, and will not be injured by penal treatment. There is however scientific evidence that the child is not capable of complete integration, or maturation, until 21 or beyond, a belief crystallized in the practice of civilized countries to keep him under legal disabilities as regards contract, voting and marriage until age of majority is reached. In the opinion of many experts it is only a question of time until the juvenile court age-limit will be the same as the recognized age of majority.

Treatment.—The psychological importance of the first offence cannot be overstated. Police methods of apprehension and investigation should be eliminated. The child's court hearing in the better sort of American courts is informal. A well trained juvenile court judge does not proceed to disposal unaided. He seeks the wisdom of the clinic and the social worker. If the child has constructive possibilities he may safely be placed on probation.

Foster homes are used in some parts of America for the placement of delinquent children from unfit homes. Maintenance is supplied by public or private agencies. Correctional institutions are used for cases where an extended period of training is indicated, or where the child is under physical or mental handicaps. Some correctional institutions have supplied individual education, notably for girls, in Sauk Center, Minn., Sleighton Farms, Penn., Samarcand, N.C., Gainsville, Texas, and for boys, in New Jersey, California and elsewhere. In these training schools self-government and expert scientific guidance have met with success. Other social resources are clubs for boys and girls in industry, habit clinics, child guidance clinics, religious agencies, Big Brothers or Big Sisters, and Juvenile Protective agencies. These work most effectively under a co-ordinated philosophy of child care. To achieve this a conference is often held for social diagnosis.

Thus the old sentiments of revenge and deterrence give way to a concerted effort to understand, and to remove underlying causes. In this way sponsors of children's courts have become leaders in the scientific and humanitarian movement to prevent delinquency and to increase human happiness.

BIBLIOGRAPHY.—U.S. Children's Bureau publications, especially *Juvenile Court Standards;* Jane Addams, *Spirit of Youth and the City Streets* (1909); J. W. Mack, *The Juvenile Court* (1909); W. Healy, *The Individual Delinquent* (1917); Judge Baker Foundation, *Case Studies* (Boston, 1922–23); the Commonwealth Fund Program, *Pamphlets* (1923–24–25); B. B. Lindsey, *Twenty-five Years of the Juvenile and Family Court of Denver* (1925); C. Burt, *The Young Delinquent* (1925); E. J. Cooley, *Probation and Delinquency* (1927); H. H. Lou, *Juvenile Courts in the U.S.* (1927); H. C. Parsons, *Report* of Mass. State Probation Commission; *Report* of the Departmental Committee on the Treatment of Young Offenders, (1927); T. W. Trought, *Probation in Europe,* (1927). (M. V. W.)

CHILDREN'S GAMES. The traditional games still played by children are nearly all very old. Many have been played in one form or another since the beginning of recorded history and perhaps longer. Some now confined to children, like Hide-and-Seek or Blindman's Buff, were commonly played by adults until at least as late as the 15th century. Others, like the simpler ball and skipping games, were originally not pastimes at all, but primitive rituals seriously performed to avert evil or to make the crops grow. They survive in juvenile play because the children imitated these rites, as they also imitated the domestic, hunting, farming and fighting lives of their elders. The resulting games were handed on to their successors who, with the innate conservatism of childhood, continued to play them long after the customs from which they sprang had vanished from the adult world. Thus modern games often contain fossilized relics of ancient belief.

Some games have flourished for centuries in particular countries and closely resemble others found elsewhere. Time has naturally modified some details, but the general plan usually remains the same so that the modern form, even with its variations, would probably be quite easily recognized by a child of classical or earlier times. Buck Buck, for instance, has scarcely changed since Petronius described it in his *Satyricon.* He tells us that boys in his day leaped upon the bent backs of others and beat them on the shoulders, crying *Bucca, bucca, quot sunt hic?* In like fashion, English lads today climb on a companion's back and cry "Buck, buck, how many horns do I hold up?" Greek and Roman boys trundled hoops in spring, and their sisters skipped with ropes of plaited vine strands. Virgil in his *Aeneid* speaks of whirling tops lashed round empty courts, and in Homer's *Odyssey* there is a description of Nausicaa playing ball with her maidens. All these pastimes are as popular now as they were in pre-Christian periods; and probably pursuit and combat games in the far past ran along much the same lines as Touch, Prisoner's Base, King of the Castle, Cowboys and Indians (lately translated into Gangsters and G-men or Spacemen and Martians) and We Are the Romans now.

Certain games tend to become fashionable at particular seasons. Tops normally come in during March, and are superseded about mid-April by skipping ropes. Hopscotch is also principally a March game, and so is kite flying, probably because March is a windy month. Marbles are popular in September and then give way to Conkers when the horse chestnuts are ripe. This does not mean, of course, that such games are never seen at any other time. But there are, nevertheless, definite seasons when they become a craze.

Traditional games may be roughly divided into two main categories: games of skill and chance and dramatic games in which a story or ritual is acted, with or without song accompaniment. Pursuit and combat games are essentially dramatic because they imitate hunting and war. The songs once attached to the more boisterous forms have mostly been lost, but frequently a counting-out or choosing rhyme is used. There are countless such rhymes.

Many skipping games, Thread-the-Needle, and Oats and Beans and Barley Grows derive from agricultural ritual dances. In the last named the players act the sowing of the seed; in the French game called *L'Avoine* they sow, reap, bind and thresh the crop. Courtship, wedding and funeral games are especially popular with girls, though boys often condescend to take part. One of the best-known funeral games is Jenny Jones, which should rightly be Jenny Jo, meaning sweetheart. This has a long and complicated song carrying the heroine through numerous domestic tasks to her death and then discarding one colour after another till black is finally chosen for her funeral. Sally Waters, Poor Mary Lies a-Weeping and In and Out the Window are singing marriage games. So also are Drop Handkerchief and Nuts in May, which represent marriage by capture, the bride being pursued in the first and dragged away in the other. The singular title of Nuts in May is really a corruption of knots (or posies) of May.

An extremely interesting type of dramatic game is that in which two players form an arch with uplifted arms and the rest hurry through until one is caught by the sudden lowering of the arch.

In some variants a choice is offered to the prisoner, who passes to left or right behind the leaders and takes part in a tug of war at the end. London Bridge is Falling Down is probably the best known of these games, and certainly the most interesting, for the words show clearly that it is based upon foundation sacrifice. In Scotland a similar game is called Broken Bridges; in America, Charleston Bridge; in France *Pont-Levis*. The Scandinavian version is *Brö Brö Brille*. Other English arch games are The Robbers are Coming to Town, How Many Miles to Babylon, and Oranges and Lemons, in which most of London's old City churches are mentioned by name.

Among the older games of skill are Fivestones (often called Dabs or Daubbins), which is played with pebbles, Knucklebones, Marbles, Guggles, played with coloured shells, Peg in the Ring, played with tops, Hopscotch and Merelles. The aim in each is to win something from another player. All were commonly played by men in country districts until well into the 19th century.

BIBLIOGRAPHY.—G. F. Northall, *English Folk-Rhymes* (London, 1892); A. B. Gomme, *Children's Singing Games* (London, 1894), *The Traditional Games of England, Scotland and Ireland,* 2 vol. (London, 1894–98), *Old English Singing Games* (London, 1900); P. B. Green, *History of Nursery Rhymes* (London, 1899); R. C. Maclagan, *The Games and Diversions of Argyllshire* (London, 1901); J. Strutt, *The Sports and Pastimes of the People of England,* rev. by J. C. Cox (London, 1903); R. Ford, *Children's Rhymes, Children's Games, Children's Songs, Children's Stories,* 2nd ed. (Paisley, 1904); L. Eckenstein, *Comparative Studies in Nursery Rhymes* (London, 1906); C. J. Sharp, *English Folk Songs* (London, New York, 1921); H. Bett, *The Games of Children* (London, 1929); Norman Douglas, *London Street Games,* 2nd ed. (London, 1931); I. Williams, *English Folk-Song and Dance* (London, New York, 1935); R. W. Henderson, *Bat, Ball and Bishop: the Origin of Ball Games* (New York, 1947); L. Daiken, *Children's Games Throughout the Year* (London, New York, 1949), *Children's Toys Throughout the Ages* (London, Toronto, 1953); I. and P. Opie (eds.), *The Oxford Dictionary of Nursery Rhymes* (Oxford, New York, 1951); L. Gordon, *Peepshow Into Paradise: a History of Children's Toys* (London, 1953; New York, 1954). (C. S. HE.)

AMERICAN GAMES

Games played by children in the United States fall into two categories: traditional and improvised. The traditional games are those handed down from generation to generation, usually with fixed rules. Improvised games are invented on the spur of the moment by the players, with the rules made up as the game develops. Dramatic play falls between these two, because certain kinds of make-believe occur in generation after generation, with the broad outlines of the play remaining the same, but with the details varying from child to child.

In general, very young children play improvised games. At about four or five, traditional circle games with songs and pantomime are introduced. After that, a continuous acquisition of skills and game forms takes place, with the younger children learning from those slightly older.

Circle and Singing Games.—Among the first traditional games played are Ring Around the Rosy, Farmer in the Dell, Looby-Loo, Oats, Peas, Beans and London Bridge. At about six or seven years, the children begin to play games which involve chasing or tagging, like Drop the Handkerchief, Cat and Rat and Button, Button. Double circle games are often played at parties or on playgrounds under the direction of a leader. These include tag games such as Three Deep, partner-finding games similar to Odd Man Out and simple group dances like Grand Right and Left. Some ball games and stunt games are also played in the form of a circle. Among these are Jump the Rope, Passball, Touchball and Dodgeball.

Running, Chasing and Hiding Games.—Perennial favourites in this group are plain Tag, Hide-and-Seek and various types of foot races. Interest in these usually starts when the children enter elementary school and continues until they are about 12 or 13 years old.

The simplest forms of these games involve pitting one individual against a number of others. More complex forms, in which teams of players operate as a unit, also exist. In Crows and Cranes, for example, the players are divided into two groups, each of which chases the other at a prearranged signal until all the players on one side are caught. In other games one group hides while the other searches, and relay races offer victory to the speediest team. Team games appeal most to children past the age of eight.

Running games without chasing are also popular. In these the players compete to secure objects, places or partners or to avoid punishment.

Ball and Goal Games.—Baseball is undoubtedly the favourite ball game among boys in the U.S. Between the ages of 8 and 11 both boys and girls play some form of this game. After 11, girls tend to drop out of the play. Younger children and girls usually play a modified version of the game called Softball, in which the ball used is larger and softer than the official baseball. Other games derived from Baseball include Hand Baseball, Playground Kickball and Fungo Baseball, which eliminates pitching.

Football takes over during the fall season. A goal game played by two teams, it involves also some elements of combat. Although seven-year-olds try to play it, its demands are such that it can rarely be played correctly by boys younger than 14 or 15.

Other popular goal games are Basketball and Shinny, a derivative of Field Hockey. Shinny can be seen most often on city streets, played on roller skates, with pieces of broomstick and a tin can for a puck.

Games involving getting a ball over a net or hitting it against a wall are numerous. Among these, Handball, Tetherball, Wall Tennis and Table Tennis (Ping-pong) are played most frequently informally. In recreation and physical-education programs Dodgeball and Newcomb, which serves as an introduction to Volleyball, are favourites.

Special Games of Childhood.—Many of the games mentioned above are played by adults as well as by children; they may in fact be derived from adult games. A number of others, however, are uniquely characteristic of the culture of child groups. Among these are combat games like the Cowboys and Indians of small boys; these change later to Storming the Fort and Tug of War. Informal wrestling is a boy's "game" at seven and eight. Marbles and Darts are target games that start early, and Mumblety-Peg is a contest of skill which the possession of a pocket knife seems to inspire. Leapfrog attracts both boys and girls until the end of elementary school.

Young girls have their own play rituals. One, Two, Three O'Leary, played with a rubber bounce ball, Jacks (using a small rubber ball and metal or plastic jackstraws), rope jumping to the tune of "Hot Peppers" or "Double Dutch" and Hopscotch must be in the repertoire of any six- to ten-year-old who wants to keep up with her age mates. Simon Says and May I? are popular games which require alertness, while Statues falls into the category of stunt games. Follow the Leader attracts boys as well as girls.

Games commonly played during quiet times may be divided into those needing special equipment and those needing little or none. The former group includes games of skill like Checkers and games of chance like Old Maid. Paper-and-pencil games, guessing games, spelling games, stunts and string games make up the second group. Twenty Questions, I Spy, Ghost, Charades, Ticktacktoe, Consequences, Cat's Cradle and Paper, Stone and Scissors are examples of these. Special party games include Pin the Tail on the Donkey, Post Office, Spin the Bottle and stunt races like the potato or three-legged race.

BIBLIOGRAPHY.—W. W. Newell, *Games and Songs of American Children* (New York, 1884); D. A. Hindman, *Handbook of Active Games* (New York, 1951); E. Gardner, *Handbook for Recreation Leaders* (1937); R. E. Hartley, "Children Grow Through Play," in S. M. Gruenberg (ed.), *The Encyclopedia of Child Care and Guidance* (New York, 1954). (R. E. H.)

CHILDRESS, a city in the "panhandle" of Texas, U.S., near the Red river and the Oklahoma border; the county seat of Childress county. It is on federal highways 287 and 83; is served by the Fort Worth and Denver City railway and has an airport about 5 mi. W. Pop. (1950) 7,619. Cattle, hogs, wheat, cotton and grain sorghum are raised in the vicinity. Gypsum and gypsites are found. The city has cotton compresses, gins, cottonseed oil mill, railway repair shops and packing plants; other products include bedding, soft drinks and dairy products. Settled in 1888, it was incorporated in 1892.

CHILDS, GEORGE WILLIAM (1829–1894), U.S. publisher, was born in Baltimore, Md., on May 12, 1829. In 1847 he established a bookshop in Philadelphia, and two years later organized the publishing house of Childs and Peterson. In 1864, with Anthony J. Drexel, he purchased the *Public Ledger.* He died at Philadelphia, Feb. 3, 1894. Childs was known for his public spirit and philanthropy. He erected memorial windows to William Cowper and George Herbert in Westminster abbey (1877) and to Milton in St. Margaret's, Westminster (1888), a monument to Leigh Hunt at Kensal Green, to Shakespeare a memorial fountain at Stratford-on-Avon (1887) and monuments to Edgar Allan Poe and to Richard A. Proctor. He gave Woodland cemetery to the Typographical Society of Philadelphia for a printers' burial ground, and with Anthony J. Drexel founded in 1892 a home for union printers at Colorado Springs, Colo.

His *Recollections* were published in Philadelphia in 1890.

CHILD WELFARE AND CHILD LABOUR. The heavy toll inflicted on children by the wars of the 20th century impelled such recognition and measurement of their needs as modern skills would permit. Expansion and improvement of services to children was marked during the second quarter of the century, calling for financial support in large measure from governments and individuals and the recruitment and training of professional workers in all parts of the world.

Origins of Child Welfare.—Child welfare had some recognition in ancient legal codes and much religious sanction in the teachings of Buddhism, Christianity and Judaism. Hospices for the care of travellers, the sick and the poor authorized by the early Christian church at the council of Nicaea in A.D. 325 were among the first known facilities for the protection of children as well as adults. Concepts of communal responsibility for child welfare acquired gradually extended horizons, both in oriental and western countries.

The development of social security and social services under governmental auspices focused attention on the age-old needs of children. In several countries there was an organization of services to children following wars, epidemics or famines severe enough to create large numbers of orphans. Wars, even civil wars as in Switzerland at the end of the 18th century and in the United States after the middle of the 19th century, left orphans and half-orphans to an extent that warranted the establishment of institutions for dependent and neglected children. World Wars I and II were followed by the organization of relief, health services and facilities for child welfare on a scale without precedent in history but still small in proportion to the destruction of homes and the impoverishment of family life which these conflicts produced.

Far more significant than the emergency wartime and postwar efforts to relieve misery was the development of international planning in behalf of the children of the world. A better world for children was envisaged in the Universal Declaration of Human Rights, approved Dec. 10, 1948, by the general assembly of the United Nations. Their interests were especially stressed in: "The family is the natural and fundamental group unit of society and is entitled to protection by society and the State" (article 16, section 3), and "Motherhood and childhood are entitled to special care and assistance. All children, whether born in or out of wedlock, shall enjoy the same social protection" (article 25, section 2). Steps toward enactment of a Declaration of the Rights of the Child were taken within the United Nations in 1950. A draft declaration was prepared for consideration in turn by the Economic and Social council, the Commission on Human Rights and the general assembly.

There had been little international exchange of information about child welfare before the early years of the 20th century, when the development of education, health and social services led to the organization of professional societies in many countries.

International Conferences.—International conferences of professional workers serving children had been held under various auspices, however, some devoted entirely to child welfare and some covering several fields of work but dealing largely with child welfare. Ten congresses with delegates from Europe and America, including the United States, were held in London, Eng., and six European cities, the first and last being in Paris, Fr., in 1883 and 1933, respectively. Two congresses, limited to the Balkan countries, were held in 1936 and 1938, respectively. The International Conference of Social Work held the following seven sessions: Paris, 1928; Frankfurt-on-Main, Ger., 1932; London, 1936; Atlantic City, N.J., with concluding meetings at New York city in 1948; Paris, 1950; Madras, India, 1952; and Toronto, Ont., 1954. The last six of these conferences brought together the same professions and organizations which previously had organized the international child welfare congresses.

The Pan American Child congress held the following sessions: Buenos Aires, Arg., 1916; Montevideo, Urug., 1919; Rio de Janeiro, Braz., 1922; Santiago, Chile, 1924; Havana, Cuba, 1927; Lima, Peru, 1930; Mexico City, Mex., 1935; Washington, D.C., 1942; Caracas, Venez., 1948; and Panamá, 1955. Resolutions passed by the congress led to organization of the International American Institute for the Protection of Childhood in Montevideo in 1927. The World Federation for Mental Health founded in 1948 was an outgrowth of the first International Congress on Mental Health. The Latin American Conference on Nutrition was under the auspices of the Food and Agriculture organization.

The League of Nations.—Article 23 of the covenant of the League of Nations requested member states to endeavour to secure and maintain fair and humane conditions of labour for adult and child workers, to take measures for the prevention and control of disease and to entrust the League with general supervision over the execution of agreements on the traffic in women and children.

The agencies given responsibility for services authorized by the League were the International Labour organization, which continued after dissolution of the League as one of the international bodies safeguarding the rights of children; the Health organization, which was succeeded by the World Health organization; and the Advisory Committee on Social Questions and the Social Questions section of the League secretariat.

In 1921 the League appointed an Advisory Committee on Traffic in Women and Children, replaced in 1925 by the Advisory Commission for the Protection and Welfare of Children and Young People, with two subcommittees, the Traffic in Women and Children committee and the Child Welfare committee.

Among the subjects studied by the Child Welfare committee between its appointment in 1925 and its reorganization in 1936 were: the age of marriage and consent; legal status of illegitimate children; juvenile courts and their related services; motion pictures and child welfare; and measures taken in various countries for the protection of children and young persons from the consequences of economic depression.

United Nations Agencies.—The United Nations created or encouraged the organization of services entirely or partly concerned with the welfare of children, and co-ordinated the work of these and other international agencies serving children, some of which were in existence before the UN was organized in 1945. Co-ordination of the work of the various specialized agencies and the UN became a principal responsibility of the Economic and Social council and the Administrative Committee on Co-ordination consisting of the secretary-general of the UN and the executive officers of the specialized agencies. The unprecedented organization and expansion of relief and child welfare services during the decade prior to mid-century made their co-ordination a tremendous and urgent task.

The United Nations International Children's Emergency fund, after 1953 called the United Nations Children's fund (UNICEF), was established in Dec. 1946 by the general assembly of the UN for the relief and rehabilitation of children in war-torn countries and for child health throughout the world. Though not a direct descendent, UNICEF inherited much of the responsibility for feeding children and providing other child welfare services which had been a part of the load carried by the United Nations Relief and Rehabilitation administration. Though UNICEF received much less financial support than UNRRA, it was less restricted in the number of countries it could enter and less subject to military and political controls. UNICEF was supported by voluntary contributions from governments and individuals; by 1955 nearly $200,000,000 had been provided from 48 countries, about 70% of which was from the United States. The work of the UNICEF was not restricted by national boundaries as were many international services. It maintained programs on both sides in war-torn China and operated freely in the four zones in Germany and Austria and in the countries of central and eastern Europe. Prior to 1950 the fund provided a daily supplementary meal for 4,000,000 to 6,000,000 children and nursing and pregnant women. The program in the east, including the East Indies, consisted mostly of supplying medicines and equipment and training local personnel in techniques for the control of specific child welfare problems. In Europe and North Africa much progress was made in the world-wide campaign to test 100,000,000 children for tuberculosis. A resolution adopted by the general assembly of the UN, Dec. 1, 1950, revised the policy of the UNICEF. Relief programs were replaced by emergency and long-range projects whereby supplies, training and advice were provided in underdeveloped countries with a view, wherever appropriate, to strengthening the permanent child health and child welfare programs of the countries assisted. By 1954 most of these countries had realized the advantages of UNICEF services and instead of matching UNICEF funds, as in previous years, they provided several times as much as the UN appropriations for advancing the welfare of their own children. Thus facilities for manufacturing powdered milk had been developed in the near east, Asia and Latin America where formerly milk and other relief supplies had been imported.

The World Health organization (WHO), created July 22, 1946, from its beginning gave priority to children in much of its work. In addition to the joint programs in which it promoted the mass feeding of children, improved nutrition and instituted more effective methods of food production, the representatives of WHO surveyed the tuberculosis problem in many countries and set up laboratories for the manufacture of Bacillus-Calmette Guérin (BCG) vaccine. Outstanding among its achievements was its campaign against malaria. WHO also issued daily radio warnings of epidemics of smallpox, cholera and other pestilential diseases. Venereal diseases, in some areas affecting nearly half the population, were combated; prenatal and infantile syphilis were treated with penicillin in mass campaigns in several countries. The sanitation program of the WHO led to improvement of water supply and sewage disposal systems and destruction of disease-carrying insects. With such improvements the death rate among infants in some areas was cut from 30 to 3 per 100 births in a comparatively short time. The WHO and the Food and Agriculture organization (FAO) jointly promoted a "food for health" program, stressing health education of the public.

The United Nations Department of Social Affairs made a comparative survey of juvenile delinquency in five regions: (1) Asia and the far east; (2) Europe; (3) Latin America; (4) the middle east; and (5) North America. Reports of findings, published in 1952 and 1953, were widely circulated and studied in preparation for a world conference on the prevention of crime and the treatment of offenders planned for 1955.

The International Refugee organization (IRO) was established as a nonpermanent specialized agency under a constitution approved by the general assembly of the UN on Aug. 20, 1948, and discontinued in 1952. Children, often without trace of their parents, constituted a large portion of the 1,600,000 refugees and displaced persons remaining in need of protection and sustenance in Europe and the middle and far east at that time. Prior to 1948, approximately 7,000,000 persons had been repatriated with the help of the military and UNRRA.

The United Nations Korean Reconstruction agency (UNKRA) was the channel through which much relief and child care were provided war orphans and other children in South Korea. By 1954 the total spent by all relief agencies, including UNKRA, exceeded $500,000,000. Nearly one-third of the 150,000 severely deprived war orphans or other homeless children were given care in about 350 orphanages. The foreign military forces, mostly from the United States, made large contributions to these efforts, as did religious bodies and nonsectarian relief agencies such as the American-Korean foundation. UNKRA and UNICEF, by 1954, were operating about 100 feeding stations from which powdered milk was made available to more than 1,000,000 persons, mostly children. UNKRA also assisted the government of South Korea in reorganizing and expanding its public schools.

Private Agencies.—Children were also well served during and after the World War II years by sectarian relief agencies under Jewish, Protestant or Roman Catholic auspices, such aid coming from the more favoured parts of Europe and overseas. Many were privately aided through the Cooperative for American Remittances to Everywhere (CARE). Steps to co-ordinate the financial and service activities of private relief agencies had been taken with the organization in 1943 of the American Council of Voluntary Agencies for Foreign Service, with membership including 52 agencies.

The United States Committee for the Care of European Children, in existence from 1940 to 1953, brought thousands of children to temporary or permanent homes in the United States. During World War II most of these were British children, many of whom returned to their homes in the United Kingdom. After the war nearly all children brought to the United States were from camps for displaced persons in western Europe. The preparation of these children for immigration under quota regulations, their transportation under escort and their reception was one of the greatest child welfare achievements during and after the war. The Committee safeguarded these children before and after placement, including the many who were legally adopted, by utilizing the country's network of competent governmental, sectarian and nonsectarian child care agencies. Except for temporary reception service in institutions most of the care thus provided was in foster homes or the homes of relatives or friends.

DEVELOPMENTS IN VARIOUS COUNTRIES

The nations of the British commonwealth during the period 1930–50 developed health and social services for children and social insurance which did much to offset the demoralizing influences of World Wars I and II. Family allowances, first provided in Australia and New Zealand, were introduced in the United Kingdom under the Beveridge plan and in Canada under the Marsh plan for social security. These allowances, recognizing the size of each family, permitted better balanced diets. The Children bill enacted by the British parliament in June 1948 transferred from local authorities to the home office responsibility for services to children up to the age of 18 who were deprived of normal home life. This national authority, with jurisdiction over juvenile courts and legislation for the protection of children, was authorized to decide whether a child was to receive foster care in an institution or a foster home, without restrictions previously imposed by the Poor law and its means test for determining public responsibility.

Sweden and Switzerland sustained their previously superior services in the fields of education, health and welfare and carried to adjoining war-torn countries material aid and cultural leadership. Among those countries seriously damaged by World War II which took steps to improve their services to children was Finland, which extended its well-baby clinics and anticipated in its public health law the development of such clinics in every community. France also extended its school health services and maintained its social security benefits for maternity leave and related services. Poland sharply reduced its infant mortality rate, stressing the needs of farm communities and mothers and children, and increasing the facilities for training physicians. The U.S.S.R. extended various services for children after the war.

India held a child welfare exhibition in New Delhi in 1949, one of several activities following the second annual session of the All India Conference of Social Work held in Dec. 1948.

Brazil's progress in the development of maternal and child health services was reflected in the findings of the second Brazilian Conference on Child Care and Pediatrics held in 1948. Uruguay developed a unified health and welfare service, the Council of the Child, an outgrowth of a children's code enacted in 1934. Aid to mothers unable to provide adequate support for their children was authorized. Care of dependent children in foster homes was also extended under the Uruguayan program.

United States.—The child population of the United States had an unprecedented increase in the decade prior to mid-century. The 1947 record total of approximately 3,720,000 births was in sharp contrast with the 2,360,000 (approximate) born in 1940. During the three years following 1947 the number of births occurring annually remained at about 3,500,000, but rose steadily thereafter until in 1954 it exceeded 4,000,000. The country was embarrassed by the limited facilities and services for children available in the fields of education, health and social service and the lack of suitable housing for the large number of new families during and after World War II.

A three-year nation-wide study of child health services, completed in 1949 by the American Academy of Pediatrics with the assistance of other agencies, notably the children's bureau and the public health service of what was then the Federal Security agency, gave a comprehensive appraisal of health services. Two over-all needs emphasized were the inadequacy of the general practitioner's training in pediatrics and the scarcity of health services and hospital facilities for children in rural areas.

About 4,000,000 children, 5 to 17 years old, were not enrolled in any school at mid-century. The shortage of teachers and school buildings had become acute and efforts to secure enactment of legislation for federal aid to public schools had been unsuccessful.

Social services to children, first developed under sectarian and other private auspices, were greatly extended after passage of the Social Security act in 1935. Aid to dependent children, which soon became effective in all states, was available at mid-century to about 1,500,000 children and 585,000 families. In June 1954 aid was provided for 1,565,000 children and 581,000 families. Children in rural communities and in areas of special need were provided with various social services under the child welfare services provision of this act. The children's bureau of the department of health, education and welfare continued to provide federal supervision of child welfare services, just as the bureau of public assistance supervised aid to dependent children and aid to the blind, all administered by state and county authorities.

Maternal and child services for crippled children had become major items in the budget and program of the children's bureau. One of the most widely circulated of all federal publications was *Infant Care,* a pamphlet which had reached millions of American mothers.

The National Commission on Children and Youth, created during World War II by the children's bureau, played an important role in planning for the mid-century White House Conference on Children and Youth. It also helped co-ordinate the child welfare work of federal and national agencies in education, health, recreation and social service, giving attention to problems such as the day care of children of working mothers.

The mid-century White House Conference on Children and Youth was held in Washington in Dec. 1950. More than 5,000 workers and other interested citizens and youth themselves were invited by Pres. Harry S. Truman to constitute this, the largest of the five successive White House conferences on child welfare, held at ten-year intervals beginning in 1909. The fields of service represented included education, health, recreation, religion and welfare. The conference focused attention on existing services to children, developments during the previous decade and unmet needs as determined by preconference studies.

The development of child guidance clinics, well advanced by 1940, was slowed down by the scarcity of psychiatrists and psychologists in wartime. The appropriation of public funds, including federal provisions for research and training of psychiatrists, a repercussion from the military reliance upon such services, included child guidance and the treatment of mentally disturbed children in the programs thus supported.

After World War II facilities for the study and treatment of emotionally disturbed children were developed under various auspices. The Child Welfare League of America, under a grant from the Marshall Field foundation, in 1952 published the report of a two-year study of resident treatment centres for emotionally disturbed children operated under private auspices. The states which established similar institutions included Connecticut, Kansas, Massachusetts, New Hampshire, New Jersey, New York and Ohio. The U.S. public health service facilities at Bethesda, Md., include seven research institutes, one of which, established in 1953, is a clinical centre where a small group of emotionally disturbed children receive study and treatment.

Child development, which had become the object of research by pediatricians, psychologists, nutritionists, educators and social workers, had absorbed the attention of many leaders and organizations. In addition to research, these programs included training of workers in several professions and extensive efforts in parent education. Outstanding among the centres engaged in this work at mid-century were the Rochester Child Health project (Rochester, Minn.), The University of Chicago, Columbia and Yale universities and the state universities of California, Iowa, Minnesota and Ohio.

CHILD LABOUR

The movement for the legal regulation of child labour began at the close of the 18th century when, with the rapid development of large-scale manufacturing in Great Britain, the exploitation of very young children in industrial work attracted public notice. The first child labour law, adopted in England in 1802 in an attempt to control the evils of apprenticing pauper children to cotton-mill owners, was ineffective for lack of provisions for enforcement. The Factory act of 1833 was the first law with a system of factory inspection.

The first International Labour conference, in Berlin, Ger., in 1890, did not reach agreement on standards and was followed by similar conferences and other international efforts. The International Association for Labour Legislation, established at Basle, Switz., in 1900, a private organization with branches in at least 16 countries, promoted child labour provisions as part of other international labour legislation. Such organizations successfully urged inclusion in the treaty of Versailles of 1919 provision for the International Labour organization (ILO), affiliated with the League of Nations and including all members of the League.

The International Labour office, a part of the ILO, drafted conventions which were submitted to member countries through the International Labour conference for ratification, with ratification including an obligation to enact a law carrying out provisions of the convention.

The 1944 International Labour conference adopted a declaration redefining the aims and purposes of the ILO. Further action in 1945 and 1946 provided that any member of the UN might become a member of the ILO by declaring its formal acceptance of the obligations of membership. Other countries could be enrolled as members upon vote of the conference.

Reverses in the enactment and enforcement of child labour legislation came during and after World War II. In the struggle for survival of individuals, families and nations, children throughout the world were required to do the work of adults, some even as soldiers. In the most devastated countries, young children sank to levels unprecedented in the 20th century, engaging in hazardous work and some even in such occupations as smuggling and prostitution. Consequently, postwar international and national efforts to reduce and control child labour included a comprehensive and searching review of the basic rights of children and families and pointed to correlations between low family incomes and the exploitation of children. Among the several international conventions adopted after the war was a revision in 1948 of the 1919 convention concerning the night work of youth employed in industry. Regional international conferences of the ILO gave special attention to conditions of work of children engaged in agriculture, other than on the home farm; child labour in the coal and inland transport industries; and elemental protective measures in the middle east, Asia and Latin America.

The ILO submitted a report on child labour in relation to compulsory education for consideration at the 14th International Conference on Public Education held in Geneva, Switz., in 1951. This provided a basis for international study of the minimum age of admission to work and the age of compulsory school attendance. Measures for the protection of young workers in Asian countries, on the agenda of the Asian regional conference of the ILO held in Tokyo in 1953, recognized the growing desire for education among the peoples of Asia and outlined legislation and steps for realization of objectives in the control of child labour and the provision of both elementary and vocational education. A member of the staff of the ILO made a study of juvenile employment in Latin America, published in the *International Labour Review* in March 1954.

Child Labour in the U.S.—Approximately 2,000,000 U.S. children between the ages of 14 and 17 were employed part time or full time at mid-century, according to estimates of the U.S. census bureau. Nearly half of these worked 35 hours or more weekly.

Early efforts to control child labour, prior to 1850, sought to prohibit employment of children under the age of ten in factories—a problem then also being combated in England. This was in contrast with federal regulations which in 1950 specified for certain employment a minimum age of 16. But in agriculture, especially as migrant labourers, children nine years of age and even younger still were employed in the United States at mid-20th century. Wartime employment of children reached a peak in 1945 of almost 3,500,000 workers 14 to 17, with summer employment bringing the total to about 5,000,000.

Most child labour legislation continued to be a state responsibility. Only 19 states in 1949 prohibited employment of children under 16 during school hours, and some of these states exempted children in agriculture and other industries. All states required school attendance up to 16 years of age or higher, though many were exempted and in some states the laws were poorly enforced.

Federal legislation, though limited, had effected certain nation-wide controls. Two federal child labour laws, declared unconstitutional in 1918 and 1922, were followed by the Fair Labor Standards act of 1938. This act, applying only to the production of goods for interstate or foreign commerce, established a minimum age of 16 and, in occupations particularly hazardous, 18. An amendment effective Jan. 25, 1950, prohibited employment of children under 16 years of age in agriculture during school hours, but did not apply to children working for their parents or those in intrastate agriculture. (*See* also CHILDREN: PROTECTIVE LAWS.)

BIBLIOGRAPHY.—Emma O. Lundberg, *Unto the Least of These* (New York, 1947); American Academy of Pediatrics, Committee for the Study of Child Health Services, *Child Health Services and Pediatric Education*, 2 vol. (Cambridge, Mass., London, 1949); Child Welfare League of America, Child Welfare (issued monthly), *Child Welfare Bibliography* (New York, 1944, with annual supplements), *Residential Treatment of Emotionally Disturbed Children* (New York, 1952); Children's Bureau, Department of Health, Education and Welfare, *Infant Care* and other pamphlets, *The Child* (issued monthly); Clara D. Rackham, *Factory Law* (London, 1938); International Labour Organization, *Bulletin of the I.L.O., Legislative Series* (1919–), *Report of the Director General* (1949), *Reports of the I.L.O. to the United Nations* (1st, 1947; 3rd, 1949), *Measures for the Protection of Young Workers in Asian Countries, Including Vocational Guidance and Training* (1953); U.S. Federal Interagency Committee on Migrant Labor, *Migrant Labor, a Human Problem* (Washington, D.C., 1947); Wage and Hour Public and Contracts Division, U.S. Department of Labor, *A Guide to Child-Labor Provisions of the Fair Labor Standards Act* (Washington, D.C., 1948); American Association of Social Workers, *Social Work Year Book* (1954); Department of Social Affairs of the UN, *A Comparative Survey on Juvenile Delinquency,* part 1, "North America" (English), part 2, "Europe" (French), part 3, "Latin America" (Spanish) (1952).

(H. W. HK.)

CHILE, a republic on the Pacific coast of South America, occupies the western slope of the continent south of Peru. It is a narrow ribbonlike country, averaging only 110 mi. in width, but extending about 2,650 mi. in length, from 17° 30′ S. to 55° 59′ S. In the northern hemisphere this distance would be equivalent to the stretch from southern Mexico to southern Alaska. Although Chile has a greater inhabited latitudinal range than any other country in the world, about 90% of the people live in middle Chile, from 30° S. to 42° S. The total area of the country is 286,323 sq.mi., slightly less than the combined areas of England, Scotland and France, but middle Chile is hardly bigger than England and Scotland alone, and one-third of it is exceedingly rugged. In addition to its main area Chile owns the Juan Fernández Islands, Easter Island, and a number of other islands in the South Pacific ocean, and lays claim to a sector of Antarctica from 53° W. to 90° W. In northern and middle Chile the country is composed of three parallel strips: the Andes on the east, the coast range on the west and a series of lowlands between. South of 42° S. there is no central lowland, a discontinuous island chain standing guard before a fjorded mountainous coast. Northern Chile is a desert, notable for the production of copper and nitrates; southern Chile is a cold, wet region of little attractiveness and limited economic potential; but middle Chile is climatically most agreeable, and is the centre of agriculture, livestock ranching and industry.

Physical Features.—The northern coast of Chile conveys the impression of a great land barrier with a remarkably even sky line. This barrier consists of a coastal range with gently rounded upper surfaces that descend only slightly to the floors of the interior basins, or pampas, whereas the seaward face is generally a steep escarpment that drops from an elevation of 2,000 or 3,000 ft. directly into the sea. This coastal bluff is a serious obstacle to transportation and settlement. Only in isolated spots is there a sufficiently wide bench or alluvial fan for a town site. South of Valparaíso the coastal escarpment is more broken and the elevations assume the characteristics of a mountain chain. From Chiloé south, subsidence has taken place, and only the higher parts of the coastal range reach above sea level as a series of islands.

The great barrier ranges of the Andes, which make up fully a third of the country, may be divided about 27° S. into a shorter northern and a longer southern section. The southern part is composed of a single rather narrow range, whereas the northern is made up of two or more roughly parallel ranges enclosing a series of plateau surfaces whose major development, because of the narrow shape of Chile, is to be found in Bolivia and Argentina. The Andes increase progressively in height from an elevation of 6,000 or 7,000 ft. at the southern end until they culminate at 32° 39′ S. in Aconcagua, which, with an elevation of 22,835 ft., is the highest peak in the western hemisphere. The peak, however, is located just across the border in Argentina. Uspallata pass, el. 12,650 ft., lies immediately south of Aconcagua, and is the most important international pass in South America. Below it at 10,469 ft. is the tunnel of the transcontinental railway that connects Valparaíso with Buenos Aires. Farther south the lower average elevation of the mountain ranges results also in lower passes. In the lake district south of 39° S. most of the passes are under 5,000 ft., a circumstance that greatly facilitates trans-Andean communication in that area. The Strait of Magellan in the extreme south is a sea level pass through the Andes. The southern Andes are intensively glaciated—U-shaped valleys and glacially-sculptured peaks being the rule. Large glaciers are still to be found in many places, and extensive moraines are in evidence, many of them acting as dams for lakes. A series of young volcanic cones are superimposed on the Andes between 34° and 43° S., some of them of striking beauty and symmetry.

North of 30° the Andes are divided into several chains of which the western forms the major eastern boundary of northern Chile. Two railroads lead across it into Bolivia, the one from Arica at 13,956 ft. and the other from Antofagasta at 12,972 ft. In 1948 the Transandine railroad of the north was opened through Socompa pass (el. 12,657 ft.), connecting Antofagasta with Salta, Argentina. The extreme ruggedness, the aridity and the cold of this section limit crop raising and grazing, but it is highly mineralized, although handicapped by lack of water. One of the largest copper deposits known is located at Chuquicamata (22° 19′ S. lat.) at an elevation of 9,300 ft. It has been worked since 1915 by U.S. interests. This enterprise is by far the most important economic activity in northern Chile.

Between the coast range and the Andes lies the so-called longitudinal valley. This is not a true valley but an irregular depression, in places 25 to 50 mi. wide and at times reaching an altitude of 3,000 to 4,000 ft. In some sections it is broken by isolated groups of mountains or by spurs from the main range, which divide the portion above 30° S. into a series of basins, locally known as pampas. The most northern of these is the Tamarugal extending north from the river Loa. This differs from the others in that the ground water in places lies within four or five feet of the surface. Although on the whole this pampa is very barren of vegetation there are remnants of what once must have been extensive thornwood areas. The desert of Tarapacá lies in the western part of the Tamarugal pampa and furnishes a portion of Chile's nitrate. About 60% of total production in 1952 came from the neighbouring province of Antofagasta, and a very small amount came from Atacama still farther south. In this province the desert pampas end with an irregular mass of low mountains which occupy the whole belt between the ranges, until approximately the latitude of Valparaíso. There begins the central valley, one of the finest agricultural valleys in the world, which is continued south until approximately 40°. The longitudinal valley then gives way to a series of lakes, and then to a complex series of beautiful islands which are but sparsely inhabited.

Geology.—Along the coast of Chile lies a belt of rocks formed mainly of old granite and schist and overlying Cretaceous and Tertiary deposits; farther inland is the western cordillera of the Andes, which is composed chiefly of intrusive masses, volcanic rocks and folded Mesozoic beds. The deposit in the great longitudinal valley of Chile, which lies between these two zones, is formed of débris that is in places more than 300 ft. thick. In northern Chile the rocks of the coastal zone, which disappear northward beneath the Pacific, consist mainly of isolated masses that stand close to the shore or that project into the sea. South of Antofagasta these old rocks, which there begin to rise to higher levels, form a nearly continuous belt along the coast, extending southward to Cape Horn and occupying the greater part of the islands of southern Chile. They are greatly folded and are doubtless Palaeozoic. In northern Chile the Cretaceous and Tertiary beds of the coastal zone are of small extent, but in southern Chile the Mesozoic beds, which are at least in part Cretaceous, form a rather wide band. The Tertiary coastal beds include both marine and terrestrial deposits, and most of them appear to be of Miocene or Pliocene age. The whole of the northern part of Tierra del Fuego consists of plateaus formed of horizontal Tertiary beds. The northern part of the Chilean Andes, which is the western cordillera of Bolivia, consists almost entirely of Jurassic and Cretaceous sediments and Tertiary eruptive rocks. The Mesozoic beds are thrown into a series of parallel folds, which run in the direction of the mountain chain. Into these folded beds are intruded granitic and other igneous rocks of Tertiary age, and upon this foundation rise the cones of Tertiary and later volcanoes. Triassic rocks are found only at La Ternana, near Copiapó, where coal seams containing upper Triassic (Rhaetic) plants have been found, but the entire Mesozoic series appear to be represented at different places. The Mesozoic rocks are chiefly marine sandstone and limestone, but they include also tuff and conglomerate of porphyry and porphyrite. These porphyritic rocks, which form a characteristic element of the Southern Andes, are volcanic, and as they contain marine fossils they must have been laid down beneath the sea. They are not confined to any one geologic horizon but occur at different levels in the Jurassic beds and at some places in the Cretaceous. Here and there they may be traced laterally into the more normal marine deposits of the same age. A large part of the Andes is covered by the products of the great volcanoes that still form the highest summits. The volcanic rocks are liparite, dacite, hornblende andesite and pyroxene andesite. The recent lavas of the volcanoes in southern Chile are olivine-bearing hypersthene andesite and basalt.

(W. H. Hs.; G. McL. Wo.; H. J. Bn.)

Ports.—As outlets for its products Chile is unusually rich in ports, but singularly unfortunate in harbours. Nearly all of these are mere open roadsteads, requiring the transfer of goods by lighters. Moreover the heavy swells along the major part of the coast frequently cause the transfer of goods to be abandoned temporarily for hours, or even days. Of the 57 ports listed relatively few are very important in international trade, and because of the abrupt slope of the ocean bottom artificial protection is both costly and difficult. Many breakwaters have been constructed of recent years, however, particularly at Antofagasta and Valparaíso, but without securing thoroughly safe anchorage at these ports. Valparaíso, with its modern wharves and other harbour facilities, also illustrates the case of an older port which is favoured by the government in its fight for continued supremacy. In colonial times it was selected as the outlet for central Chile because the traffic of that day could pass from the capital to the coast without encountering any considerable ford. Better natural harbours are to be found in the vicinity, both to the north and south of it, and Valparaíso today is meeting serious competition from San Antonio, 50 mi. below, which ships the large copper output from the Rancagua district and is gaining in general commerce. Valparaíso is also handicapped by the unwise selection of the route for the railroad leading to the interior, although a modern highway joining it to Santiago has overcome the difficulties to some extent. Antofagasta is the leading nitrate port and shares with Tocopilla the exports and imports passing to and from the copper centre at Chuquicamata. Arica, the northernmost port, gains its economic importance as an outlet of the Bolivian plateau but formerly played a more conspicuous part as a diplomatic pawn. This port and its fellows in the north, like Valparaíso, are hampered by railway conditions. Talcahuano in the south is the chief naval station of the country as well as the commercial outlet of an extensive section. Near by, Coronel is one of the three ports serving the coal producing district as Cruz Grande, north of Valparaíso with its direct docking facilities, serves the iron mines of El Tofo. Valdivia, through its port, Corral, and Constitución are able to make some commercial use of the rivers on which they are located. Punta Arenas on the Strait of Magellan gives Chile the distinction of having the most southerly port in the world.

(W. H. Hs.; I. J. C.; H. J. Bn.)

Rivers.—Because of the general outline and topography of the country, the rivers are short and unimportant except for the life giving waters they may bring, and have little or no significance in directing the settlement or trade of the country. In the north they are few, and for a distance of approximately 600 mi., the waters of only one, the Loa, reach the sea throughout the year. This stream, the longest in Chile (273 mi.), has made possible certain settlements. The Copiapó, 186 mi. long, marking approximately the southern limit of the northern desert, once discharged its waters into the sea, but rarely does so now, as the needs for irrigation are greater than the supply. The rivers to the south are better fed at their heads and flow through much less arid regions. Some of them become raging torrents at certain times of the year, and a number have been harnessed for the production of electricity. The electrification of the road in the Chilean section of the transcontinental is complete, together with the main line to the capital and other minor developments. With the increased demand for electric current has come also the storage of waters for irrigation.

Lakes.—The lakes of Chile have little significance in the life of the people. In the north occur occasional salt playas, which are dry the greater part of the year. In central Chile, south of the Bío-Bió river, there is a series of very picturesque lakes in the provinces of Cautin and Llanquihue. The largest of these lakes are Ranco and Llanquihue, the former with an estimated area of 200 sq.mi., the latter 300 sq.mi. Because of its natural beauty, the lake region has become a resort place for Chileans and tourists at all seasons of the year.

Climate.—Not many countries have the climatic extremes of Chile. The north is an absolute desert, but there is a gradual increase in precipitation through central Chile until it reaches a total in south Chile not surpassed by any extra-tropical region. The strong permanent high pressure area formed over the Pacific at about 30° dominates the climatic conditions of northern Chile, accounting for its northward flowing winds and consequently for the great aridity of the region. South of this high pressure area is a region of variable winds that accompany the passage of cyclones moving from west to east across the South Pacific ocean. The cyclonic belt moves north in the winter and south in summer, at times causing violent winds to sweep the Andean passes between Chile and Argentina. In central Chile it makes its influence felt as far north as the region of Coquimbo, where it produces winter rains. At Santiago, this migration is shown in a winter rainfall (3.4 in. in July, 0 in. in January, annual 14.4 in.). In certain years or series of years this migration does not take place or goes on beyond the normal and the result is either great droughts or heavy rains.

South of the southern tip of Chile is a belt made up of numerous low pressure areas, with unusually high barometric gradients, which produce very strong winds averaging over 30 mi. per hour, and reaching velocities three or even four times as high. These moving low pressure areas give a constant succession of storms

PHOTOGRAPHS, (TOP LEFT) FENNO JACOBS FROM THREE LIONS, (TOP RIGHT) PIX FROM PUBLIX, (CENTRE LEFT) PHILIP GENDREAU, (CENTRE RIGHT, BOTTOM) RAYS FROM MONKMEYER

VIEWS OF CHILEAN CITIES AND MOUNTAINS

Top left: Market place of Santiago
Top right: Ski lift and view of Grand Hotel Portillo in the Andes
Centre left: Ships in the harbour at Valparaíso
Centre right: Portico of the national congress building, Santiago
Bottom: Osorno volcano as seen from across Lake Todos los Santos

CHILE

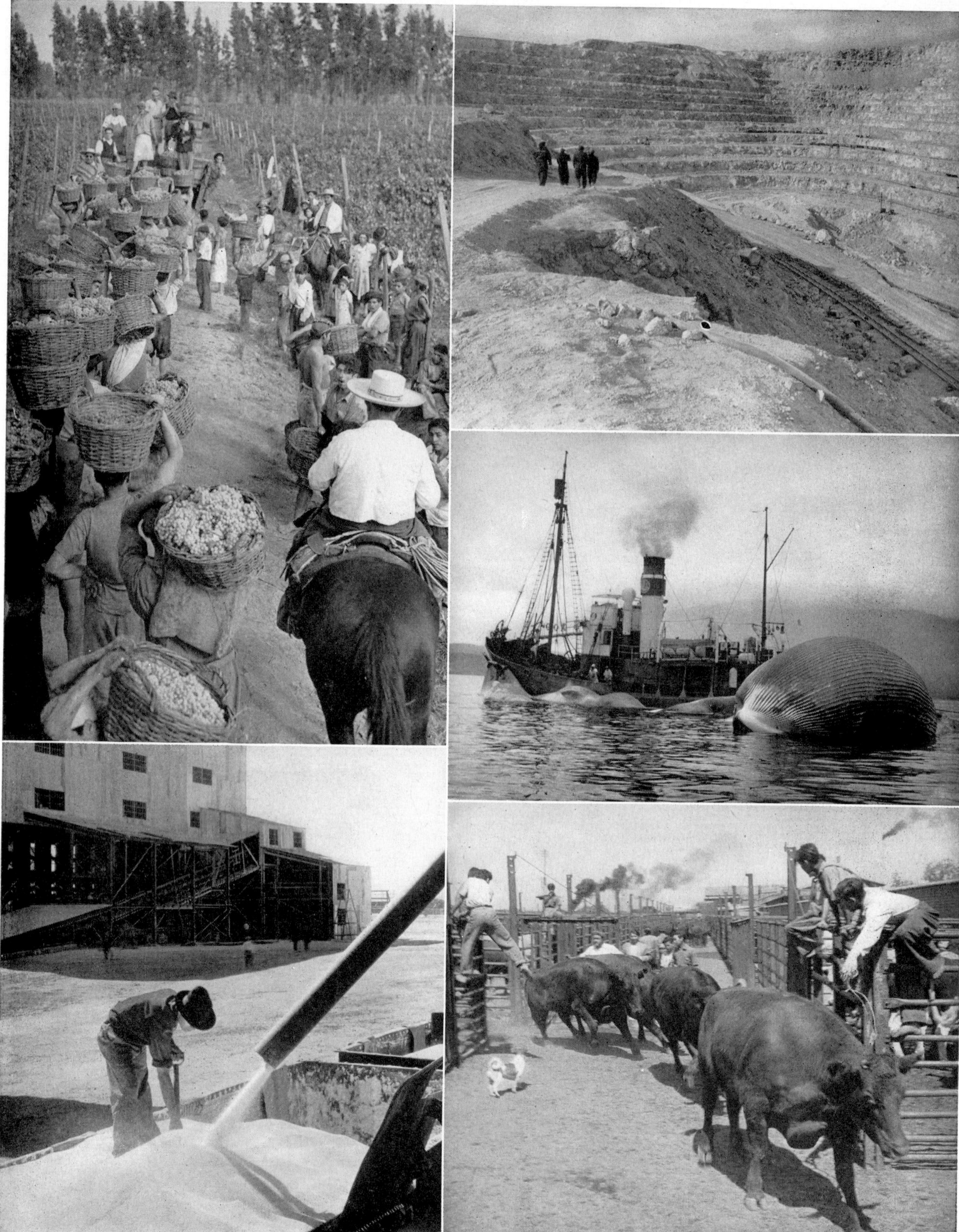

BY COURTESY OF (BOTTOM LEFT) PAN AMERICAN UNION, (BOTTOM RIGHT) UNITED NATIONS; PHOTOGRAPHS (TOP LEFT, CENTRE RIGHT) PIX FROM PUBLIX, (TOP RIGHT) STOPPELMAN—PIX FROM PUBLIX

CHILEAN AGRICULTURE AND INDUSTRY

Top left: Vineyard workers carrying baskets of grapes to carts. Chile exports several millions of gallons of wine annually
Top right: View of the open-pit copper mines near Chuquicamata
Centre right: Whaler preparing to unload its catch of blue whales at processing plant
Bottom left: Natural nitrate being loaded on railway cars
Bottom right: Steers arriving in the livestock pens at Santiago

for which the passage around the Horn has been renowned ever since its discovery, and farther northward give the lower part of Chile its westerly winds and immense rainfall.

North Chile is quite the driest region of which there is any record. During a 21-year period Iquique had an average rainfall of 1.5 mm. (0.06 in.) and Arica for a 19-year period had less than one-half as much. These averages do not represent normal conditions but show that north Chile is not entirely rainless. On the Andean slopes of this region, periodic summer rains fall as low as 8,000 ft. with occasional heavy snows. These may produce stream floods, which spread mud and gravel over the valley and give rise to temporary salt lakes. Needless to say such rains are calamitous; nitrates are destroyed, the work of the *salitreras* paralyzed, and the homes of the people, because of the poor mud roofs, practically ruined. This absolute desert condition does not change until in the latitude (27°) of Caldera or Copiapó, where a mean rainfall of about 15 mm. (0.6 in.) prevails.

The rainfall increases rapidly to the south, being 141 mm. (5.6 in.) at La Serena (30°); 500 mm. (19.7 in.) at Valparaíso (33°). The increase southward is still fairly regular reaching 2,707 mm. (107 in.) at Valdivia (39° 50′). From there south, the rainfall is more or less uniform except for local modifications with the striking maximum of 5,379 mm. (216 in.) for south Chile at Balúa Felix (53°).

The Chilean rains definitely come from the west. The western Andean slopes are wetter than the valley areas in all latitudes, and this is very noticeable even on the Andean slope of the northern desert region, where a rainfall map, however, shows all of Chile north of 31° with less than 10 inches. This dry area thrusts a finger down the central valley nearly as far south as Santiago. The 10 to 20 in. rainfall area, whose southern coastal limit is at Valparaíso, sends a strong arm down the valley nearly as far as Concepción, with a rain belt on either side of 20–40 in. and with a belt along the western slope of the Andes, overlooking the beautiful agricultural valley, of 40 to 80 inches. This belted arrangement is still more marked in the southern rainy section. The various islands and embayments show a rainfall of 80–200 in., the mountainous area directly to the east has a precipitation of over 200 in., while over in Argentina the rainfall gradually decreases again to less than 20 in.

Irrigation is needed throughout the central valley, not only because of the low rainfall but more especially because the greater part occurs in the winter. This discrepancy becomes less marked from north to south. At La Serena over 98% of the rain comes in the six winter months and 82% in the three colder months. The percentages at Santiago for the same periods are respectively 90 and 73; for Concepción 83 and 61.

Even at Punta Arenas 61% of the precipitation is during the six winter months. This seasonal distribution has given Chile an irrigated agriculture with an intensive rather than an extensive use of the land and with the climatic life of the Mediterranean.

In general, for its latitude, the temperature is low. The cold Humboldt current, which strikes Chile in the vicinity of 40° S., flows northward along the entire coast, and keeps the temperatures down and very uniform. The average summer temperature, even at Arica, does not rise above 75° F. Similarly the mean at Iquique is only 66° F., and at Antofagasta 65° F., although southward the temperature is somewhat lower as at Valparaíso, where it is only 58° F. At the latter place, the mean monthly temperature varies from 63.5° F. in summer to 52° F. in winter, and the thermometer seldom rises to 85° or falls below 38°. Santiago at an altitude of 1,740 ft. has recorded extremes of 96° F. and 25° F., and on rare occasions snow falls in the city. At Valdivia in the southern end of the central valley, January is the warmest month with 61.5° F. and July the coldest with 45° F. Because of the winter rainfall and the attendant cloudiness, the sensible winter temperatures are somewhat lower than the records indicate. But there is no doubt that the main inhabited parts of Chile enjoy some of the most healthful climates of South America.

(H. J. Bn.; W. H. Hs.)

Vegetation.—With more than 70% of Chile mountainous, with altitudes from sea level to more than 20,000 ft., with rainfall from practically nothing to more than 200 in. annually, and temperatures from very hot to cold, it is readily understandable that the flora is remarkably diverse. Three main plant zones, correlated chiefly with changes of altitude and climate, are evident.

(1) An almost rainless desertlike area, between 19° and 30° 50′. The Chilean coast from the Peruvian border to 20° S. lat. is nearly barren, more nearly approaching an absolute desert than any other part of the world. South of 20° the heavy winter fogs of the coastal hills account for a seasonal flora, prominent in Antofagasta and Atacama provinces. Between 24° and 26° 50′ there are four main types of vegetation in the coast range, varying from drought-resisting desert shrubs, such as *Chuquiragua ulicinia* and cacti, above and below the fog belt, to a more varied plant formation within the fog belt, containing among other species various cacti, *Oxalis gigantea, Proustia tipia,* and *Alstroemeria violacea.*

(2) "Mediterranean" zone, between 30° 50′ and 37°, having dry summers and rather rainy winters. This zone is diversified, and the flora varies with the altitude. Near sea level *Solanum maritimum* is common. Up to 2,500 ft., characteristic plants are *Crinodendron patagua* and *Bellota miersii.* Over large areas in these lower altitudes species of *Adesmia* and *Acacia* are common. On certain favoured slopes Quillai (*Quillaja saponaria*), *Cryptocarya,* and *Lithraea,* among others, are found. Other plants at this altitude favour running or seasonally dry streams. Up to 4,500 ft. *Valenzuelia* and other shrubs grow. Below the snow line (about 14,000 ft. in central Chile) are developed the conspicuous cushion or mound plants, chiefly *Azorella* and *Laretia acaulis.* Many spring-flowering (October and November) plants, belonging to such genera as *Valeriana, Anemone, Cardamine, Libertia,* and *Oxalis,* are found in this zone.

(3) A humid area from 37° to 56°, between Concepción and Tierra del Fuego, with rain the year round in some places exceeding 200 in. There is developed a dense, rich, temperate, rain forest slightly south of Valdivia to Magellan strait. Several species of false beech (Nothofagus), nine kinds of conifers, including *Saxegothea, Libocedrus, Dacrydium, Fitzroya, Podocarpus, Araucaria,* and *Pilgerodendron,* many of the myrtle family (Myrtaceae), *Lomatia, Embothrium,* and *Weinmannia* constitute some of the principal trees in these forests. A motley variety of vines, shrubs, ferns and mosses abound, while in more open parts of the rain forest are found solid thickets of the wild bamboo, *Chusquea.*

Many distinct genera and species of plants are known only from Chile. Many of the Chilean plants are Andean in origin and relationship, others are subantarctic. Examples of relict and isolated assemblages of plants occur in the flora, suggesting correlation with past climatic and geological changes and events.

(J. A. Sk.)

Fauna.—Except at the extreme south, where low passes lead to Patagonia, and at the north, where the deserts of both coast and highland merge with those of Peru and Bolivia, Chile is cut off from the rich life of South America by the barrier of the Andes, which extends north and south for hundreds of miles with scarcely a pass below the snow line.

The larger Chilean mammals are the puma and guanaco, the Andean wolf and the *huemul* (a large deer), the foxlike *chilla,* and two kinds of wild cats. The mountain rodents include the almost extinct chinchilla. The South Chilean forest has distinct types of marsupials (especially *Rhyncholestes*), Darwin's fox, and the little spike-horned pudu, smallest of deer. Though rich in small birds, Chile does not have many of the more conspicuous South American bird types.

The Chilean bullfrog, *Calyptocephalella,* with a bony casque, is regularly eaten. The tiny Darwin's frog, *Rhinoderma,* is remarkable in that the male takes the developing eggs into his enlarged vocal pouch, where they transform into tiny froglets. The native fresh-water fishes are extremely few. The successful introduction of North American trout into the lakes of southern Chile has made them attractive resorts for fishermen. (K. P. S.)

Population.—Quite commonly Chile is spoken of as a "white man's country." This is true when compared with the plateau countries to the north, but the qualification is more a matter of class than of blood. There was abundant opportunity for miscegenation during the colonial period as the fierce Araucanian Indian remained unconquered for three centuries and the conflict with him called for an endless succession of Spanish soldiers, who in turn left in their wake a large number of half-breed children.

From such unions came the foundation of the Chilean race. The mixture occurred so long ago that its results are now expressed in racial unity and common characteristics and are quite unnoticed in the country itself.

In the forested region south of the Bío-Bío river are the Araucanian Indians who proved such valiant and unconquerable foes during both the Inca and Spanish regimes. Their definite overthrow as an independent people came only in 1882 when seasoned troops from the battlefields of the north pushed through the *frontera* and put an end to their resistance. The Araucanian strain in Chilean blood is considerable although not so noticeable as the blood of other tribes for it has not resulted in deterioration. Pride in the Araucanian heritage is reflected even in the national anthem. About 90% of the Indians (127,151 in 1952) live in the provinces of Malleco and Cautín.

Beyond lie Valdivia and Llanquihue. It is in this region that German colonists of the mid-19th century encountered extraordinary hardships. But they introduced much-needed handicrafts, iron- and woodworking, tanning, shoemaking and the like, and soon drew large numbers of Chileans to their settlements. The Germanization of south Chile has not been a matter of sheer numbers, but results from a far-reaching cultural influence that if more widespread might prove a great blessing.

In the extreme south one still encounters some remnants of the Fuegians, an indigenous people of extremely low culture, and in the north the Changos may represent survivors of an earlier native stock. In other parts of the country a plentiful sprinkling of English, Irish and Scotch names denotes an infusion of northern European blood, while Spaniards, Italians and Slavs bespeak a continued connection with southern Europe.

Chile, however, has never attracted a large immigration, and the influence of immigrants in the composition of the Chilean people has not been large.

The 1952 census showed a population of 5,930,809 (2,911,129 men and 3,019,680 women) as compared with 5,023,539 in 1940, 4,287,445 in 1930 and 3,731,573 in 1920. The density of population per square mile in the whole country was 20.7 in 1952, but there was a wide variation in density among regions. The northern desert region, with more than one-third of the total area, had 6½% of the population and a density of less than 4 per square mile. On the other hand the central Mediterranean region, with only 18% of the national area, had 65% of the total population and a density of 76 per square mile.

The mainland forest region, with 13% of the area, had 26% of the population and a density of 38 per square mile, but the archipelagic zone of the forest area, with 27% of the total area, had 2% of the population and a density of little more than 1 per square mile. Atlantic Chile, with 7% of the area, had 1% of total population, most of its inhabitants being concentrated in the city of Punta Arenas.

Chile has one of the highest birth rates in the world. Before 1930 the rate averaged 40 per 1,000 with only minor fluctuations. After 1930 a slow decline set in which was maintained with small variations, the 1946, 1950 and 1951 rates of 32.4 per 1,000 being the lowest recorded in the 20th century. There was an increase to 33.5 in 1952 and 36.1 in 1953.

The high birth rate is characterized by a large number of illegitimate births. A record peak of 39.1% was recorded in 1917; thereafter there was a progressive decline to a record low of 17.8% in 1953.

The death rate showed a progressive decline after 1900. The average rate per 1,000 in 1905–09 was 32.5, while in 1930 it was 24.7; in 1940, 21.6; in 1950, 15.7; and in 1953, 13.2.

The increase in Chile's population was accompanied by a strong trend toward urbanization. The 1952 census classified 60% of the population as urban and 40% as rural; the corresponding percentages in 1940 were 52 and 48.

Major cities (1952 census) were Santiago, 1,348,283; Valparaíso, 218,829; Concepción, 119,887; Viña del Mar, 85,281; and Antofagasta, 62,272.

TABLE I.—*Provinces* and Population*
(Census Figures of 1930, 1940 and 1952)

Province	Area in sq.mi. 1930	Population	Area in sq.mi. 1940	Population	
		Census of 1930		Census of 1940	Census of 1952
Aconcagua	5,798	463,544	3,940	118,049	128,378
Antofagasta	47,502	178,765	47,515	145,147	184,779
Arauco	..	..	2,222	66,107	72,289
Atacama	30,835	61,008	30,843	84,312	80,154
Aysén	38,511	9,711	34,357	17,014	26,262
Bío Bío	6,155	180,688	4,343	127,312	138,411
Cautín	10,517	383,791	6,707	374,659	365,072
Chiloé	12,733	183,499	9,052	101,706	100,401
Colchagua	6,167	295,971	3,423	138,036	139,531
Concepción	4,422	329,495	2,201	308,241	411,559
Coquimbo	15,397	198,336	15,401	245,609	262,067
Curicó	..	..	2,215	81,185	89,391
Linares	..	..	3,791	134,968	146,257
Llanquihue	..	..	7,107	117,225	139,922
Magallanes	52,271	37,913	52,285	48,813	55,091
Malleco	..	..	5,512	154,174	159,486
Maúle	5,962	197,468	2,172	70,497	72,181
Ñuble	5,485	231,890	5,487	243,185	251,607
O'Higgins	..	..	2,746	200,297	224,637
Osorno	..	..	3,867	107,341	123,059
Santiago	6,557	967,603	6,559	1,261,717	1,752,773
Talca	5,935	218,227	3,722	157,141	173,793
Tarapacá	21,341	113,331	21,346	104,097	102,789
Valdivia	10,731	236,115	7,723	191,642	232,647
Valparaíso	..	..	1,860	425,065	498,186
Antárida	..	..	..	..	87
Total	286,322	4,287,445	286,396	5,023,539	5,930,809

*This table represents the distribution of territory established in 1928 and 1940. In 1928 the former province of Valparaíso was annexed as a department to Aconcagua and the former province of Llanquihue was made a department of Chiloé, while the territory included in the old provinces of O'Higgins, Curicó, Linares, Arauco, and Malleco was divided among the neighbouring provinces. At the same time the new territory of Aysén was created from the lower part of Llanquihue and upper Magallanes. The populations here given for 1930 are for the provincial boundaries then in force.

Government.—Technically Chile is a unitary republic with responsibility centred in the president, who is elected for six years and cannot succeed himself. After experimenting for more than 30 years with a pseudo-parliamentary government, Chile in 1925 reverted to the presidential type.

The constitution which was adopted in that year provides for direct elections, for suffrage and citizenship without class distinction, for the separation of Church and State and for an independent president.

The validity of a president's election is finally determined by a special tribunal made up of former presiding officers of the senate and chamber of deputies and members of the supreme and appellate courts.

The president selects the members of the supreme court from a list of five proposed by the court itself, designates members of the courts of appeals, of which there are eight, from lists submitted by the supreme court, and appoints judges of first instance from lists submitted by the court of appeals in the jurisdiction concerned.

The president cannot remove judges but he is empowered to transfer them, when necessary, within the jurisdictions to which they belong. Judges are removable by a two-thirds vote of the supreme court.

The president names the *intendentes* of the provinces, the governors of departments, and *alcaldes* in municipalities or communes of more than 10,000 inhabitants. He also has the power to remove these officials and indirectly controls their subordinates. The constitution provides for provincial elective assemblies, but so far no measures have been taken to carry out this provision or to give greater power in local affairs to the *intendentes* and governors. The taxpayers are empowered to name communal committees (*juntas de vecinos*), non-political in character, who advise in local administrative and economic matters. Since 1935, women and foreigners residing for 5 years in the country may vote in municipal elections.

Congress consists of a senate and chamber of deputies. The former is composed of 45 members, five from each of the nine groups of provinces into which the republic is divided. Each senator holds office for eight years, and half the seats are renewable at the end of four years. The chamber of deputies numbers 132 members, one for each 30,000 inhabitants or major fraction. Electors are registered citizens over 21 years who are able to read and write. The ordinary session of congress lasts from May 21 to Sept. 18. It passes on the budget but the president may increase or decrease items within the limits therein prescribed, but congress may by a two-thirds vote pass a bill over his veto. Members of the cabinet are ineligible for seats in congress, but may speak in its sessions. They are subject to impeachment by congress and to removal from office for cause.

Credit and Finance.—The monetary unit is the peso, divided into 100 centavos. The peso was established at a gold valuation of 6*d*, or 12.17 cents, U.S. currency, in July 1931. By agreements with the International Monetary fund it was officially revalued on Dec. 18, 1946, at 3.22 cents, or 31.1 pesos to the dollar, and on Oct. 5, 1953, at 0.91 cents, or 110 pesos to the dollar. Effective Nov. 11, 1954, the official rate for most transactions was changed to 0.5 cents. The free market (curb) rate was 0.33 cents on Dec. 31, 1954. Foreign exchange control was initiated in July 1931 and various economic factors after that date fostered the growth of an intricate system designed to meet the peculiar needs of the Chilean economy. Beginning in 1947 most operations in foreign exchange were carried on within the framework of an annual foreign exchange budget prepared by the National Foreign Trade council in collaboration with the Central bank.

Chile's physical expanse has always made the collection of public revenue difficult and costly. Moreover, the dominant landowning class resisted any attempt to tax the land and its production and the remainder of the population had little to be taxed. As a result, import and export taxes were relied upon from an early date as the two principal sources of public revenue. From 1880 to 1930 nitrate taxes accounted for more than 40% of all public revenue and up to 1917 they produced 50% or more of the national revenue. With the growth of competition from synthetic nitrates in the 1920s, export taxes were lowered but still accounted for 25% of the revenue. As a result, the collapse of foreign trade in the early 1930s seriously affected public finance.

Over the next 20 years the national revenue was slowly placed on a broader base, and by 1953 the distribution was approximately as follows: internal direct taxation 25%; internal indirect taxation 45%; customs duties 5%; national services 3%; miscellaneous 22%. Table II shows ordinary public revenue and expenditure for five years. Ordinary state expenditure by ministries was constituted as follows in 1953: commerce and economic development 34%; education 14%; public works and transport 13%; defense 13%; health 10%; interior 9%; others 7% (including presidency, congress, foreign relations, justice and agriculture).

TABLE II.—*Ordinary Public Revenue and Expenditure, 1945–54*
(in 000,000 pesos)

Item	1945	1950	1952	1953	1954*
Revenue	5,531	18,887	36,184	43,722	62,952
Expenditure . . .	5,741	20,637	41,987	54,125	62,952

*Budget estimate.
Source: Servicio Nacional de Estadística.

The total budgetary deficit for the years 1950 through 1953 was 19,588,557,487 pesos.

The external debt of Chile grew very slowly during the 19th century. During the first Ibáñez regime (1927–31) large amounts, mostly U.S. dollars, were borrowed for public works programs. With the onset of the depression and the loss of foreign trade, Chile was unable to meet these obligations and its first default on its foreign debt occurred in 1931. Under Gustavo Ross, as minister of the treasury after 1932, service on part of the foreign debt was resumed. Favourable economic conditions during World War II permitted partial liquidation of the debt and thereafter the income from the Nitrate and Iodine corporation and the tax on copper companies made further reduction possible. Between 1934 and Dec. 31, 1953, the debt was reduced from £29,600,000, $264,600,000 and 120,600,000 Fr. Swiss to £17,440,974, $106,595,500 and 85,832,400 Fr. Swiss. Large development expenditures, however, sharply increased the internal debt; it stood at 10,363,370,454 pesos on Dec. 31, 1953.

The Central bank was established in 1925 upon the advice of the Kemmerer commission. It is modelled on the U.S. federal reserve system and is the only bank of issue. Of its capital, 10% is owned by the treasury and the balance, in varying proportions, by other banks, domestic and foreign, and the public. It was given control over the lending powers of other banks in June 1953.

Supervision of insurance companies is exercised by the superintendency of insurance, corporations and stock exchanges, which is part of the ministry of the treasury. All insurance companies must obtain authorization to do business; authorization is not granted to foreign companies not already doing business in Chile.

Foreign Investment.—Although a relatively small country, Chile has attracted sizable amounts of private foreign investment. In the last part of the 19th and the early years of the 20th century there was a growing amount of foreign investment in the exploitation of mineral resources, particularly nitrate, and in railway construction. The immediate post-World War I period was marked by large investments in copper mining. With the growth of national sentiment in the early 1930s, foreign-owned firms became the target of increasing government controls, but foreign investments nevertheless continued to expand both before and after World War II. In 1929 U.S. direct investments were valued at $422,600,000; in 1936, $483,700,000; in 1943, $328,300,000; in 1950, $540,100,000; and in 1953, $666,000,000. Of U.S. investments in 1950, mining and smelting accounted for $350,600,000; transportation, communications and public utilities $137,000,000; and manufacturing $29,000,000. At the end of 1953 Chile was fourth in Latin America with respect to the amount of U.S. investment. Other direct foreign investments approximated $144,000,000, in large part British, at the end of 1950. A considerable reduction in British investments took place during World War II. The most important post-World War II U.S. investments were the Chile Exploration company's construction at Chuquicamata of a new plant to utilize copper sulphide ores and the Bethlehem Steel company's development of the iron ore reserves of Romeral.

Development Corporation.—The Chilean Development corporation (Corporación de Fomento de la Producción de Chile), established in 1939, presents an outstanding example of successful national planning aided by international co-operation. Under its basic law it is charged with directing the economic development of the country. Freed of customary controls by government departments, it is directed by a presidentially appointed council which is presided over by the minister of economy and commerce. In practice, its projects were financed by foreign loans matched by the corporation's funds, grants from the government and private Chilean capital. From its inception in 1939 until the end of 1952 it received more than $125,000,000 in credits from the U.S. Export-Import bank and $17,300,000 from the International Bank for Reconstruction and Development, Chile being the first country to receive (in 1948) facilities from the latter bank for development, as opposed to reconstruction. Almost one-half the credits were used for construction of the Huachipato steel plant; the remainder was used in a wide range of projects, including agricultural mechanization, hydroelectric plants, the Romeral iron mine, road-making equipment, irrigation projects and a rayon plant.

Education.—Chilean education in the colonial period was limited and was conducted by the church. The first public education system was organized around the middle of the 19th century. A program of school building was inaugurated during the prosperous years of the 1880s and was continued into the 20th century, but it was not until 1920 that primary education between the years of 7 and 15 was made compulsory. From 1900 to 1920 the number of elementary schools rose from 1,547 to 3,148 and by 1947 the number had increased to 5,635.

At mid-20th century the administration of the school system

was highly centralized under the ministry of education. State-authorized private schools continued, however, to play an important role. The system was organized along three separate levels—primary, secondary and university. Between 1937 and 1951 enrolment of primary pupils increased from 587,108 to 721,879; of the latter, 100,934 were enrolled in private schools. Attendance as a percentage of those of school age was only 51.1 in 1948 and a high percentage abandoned school after learning the rudiments of reading and writing, which had the effect of producing a high proportion of semiliterates. This tendency was greater in the public than in the private schools and also among boys than girls. Out of each 100 who started the first grade in 1943, only 19 were in the sixth grade in 1948. Illiteracy was estimated at 49.7% in 1920, 25.2% in 1931 and at about 20% at mid-20th century.

In 1952 there were 101 public secondary schools with 54,666 students enrolled and 231 private schools with 31,512 students. In 1949 another 67,000 pursued agricultural, vocational, industrial, technical, commercial, artistic and nursing courses. Normal-school enrolment was 3,583 in 1948.

The University of Chile, Santiago (founded 1842), is the official university; it had 6,903 students in 1950, about 10% of whom were foreigners. The Catholic University of Chile, Santiago (founded 1888), had 1,914 students and the Catholic University of Valparaíso, 642 students. The University of Concepción, which has many features analogous to modern English universities, had 1,433 students. The privately endowed Santa María Technical university, Valparaíso, offered excellent technical and engineering courses comparable to those of the pre-World War II German universities.

In 1949 Chile had 39 daily newspapers with an aggregate daily circulation of 456,000. There were in all 318 newspapers and 676 magazines. Motion-picture theatres numbered 410 in 1951 with seating capacity of 300,000.

Social Conditions.—Labour organizations before the 20th century were of the beneficiary type, the pioneer being the Typographical union organized in 1853. The extractive industries gave impetus to the formation of a formal labour movement in the last years of the 19th century, and by 1903 workmen's associations or trade unions (*sindicatos*) had about 63,000 members centred in the province of Valparaíso. This number grew to 92,000 by 1910 and in 1909 the Labour Federation of Chile was organized. It adhered to the third international in 1921 and much of its program, which as adopted in 1919 was frankly Communist, was embodied in the social legislation of 1924–26. After 1920 unions abandoned the policy of abstention from politics.

Conditions in the early 1930s stimulated the conversion of the labour movement into a popular mass organization. In 1936 rival labour organizations formed the Chilean Trades Union congress (Confederación Nacional de Trabajadores de Chile) which included 50% of Chilean industrial workers and a larger proportion of miners and became a strong supporter of the popular front. After World War II a rift, brought into the open by the general strike of 1946, occurred between Communist and other elements in the confederation, with the coal-mining unions supporting the Communist element, the nitrate and railway workers' unions being more or less divided and the copper-mining unions and most of the important manufacturing unions of Santiago and Concepción supporting the Socialists. The confederation withdrew from the Latin American Federation of Labour (C.T.A.L.) in June 1947 on the ground that that organization had succumbed to Communist influence, and Bernardo Ibáñez, a founder of the confederation, was elected president of the anti-Communist Inter-American Federation of Labour in 1948. At mid-20th century the majority of Chilean industrial labour was represented by well-organized and highly aggressive unions.

Table III.—*Trade Unions and Members, 1935–52*

Year	Totals		Professional		Industrial		Agricultural	
	Unions	Members	Unions	Members	Unions	Members	Unions	Members
1935	669	83,262	414	35,820	255	47,442	—	—
1940	1,888	162,297	1,259	70,357	629	91,940	—	—
1945	1,581	232,714	1,023	92,953	558	139,761	—	—
1950	1,907	260,143	1,270	111,994	626	147,306	11	843
1952	1,997	284,418	1,343	128,329	639	155,054	15	1,035

Source: Servicio Nacional de Estadística.

The progress of the Chilean labour movement was not accomplished without violence. There was a bitter general strike at Santiago and Valparaíso early in the 20th century and the Iquique strike in 1907 resulted in the death of 1,000 persons. Strikes were prevalent in the 1920s and 1930s, and severe post-World War II inflation prompted many crises. In the latter period the operations of a number of foreign interests, including the copper and nitrate companies, were seriously hampered by protracted labour disputes, work stoppages and strikes. In 1953 there were 208 strikes, legal and illegal, involving 123,103 persons. The Labour code provided that no work stoppage could occur in any establishment employing ten or more workmen or employees until the code's provisions for conciliation were exhausted.

Chilean labour and social legislation is among the most extensive in Latin America. Although there were some earlier enactments, labour legislation had its formal beginnings in the decree law of Sept. 8, 1924, which with supplemental legislation was codified as the Labour code of 1931, the first labour code to be promulgated in Latin America. The code regulates in detail employer-employee contracts, hours and wages, vacations and holidays and workmen's compensation. It provides that at least 85% of all employees of any one employer must be Chilean and that at least 85% of any one employer's payroll must be paid to Chileans. The code also provides for the compulsory sharing of profits by labour. It places on the employer the responsibility for work accidents and diseases except those caused intentionally, those caused by exterior *force majeure* and those not arising in the ordinary course of employment. Employers may relieve themselves of responsibility by insuring either with the State Workmen's Compensation fund (Caja de Accidentes de Trabajo) or with a private insurance company authorized to do business in Chile.

The Chilean national system of social insurance, initiated in 1926, covered at mid-20th century virtually the whole working population under the aegis of a number of organizations of social prevision which are under the general supervision of the ministry of health, social insurance and social assistance. The basis of the system is a compulsory *caja,* or guild structure, related to the type of employment. The system is financed by employer, employee and state contributions. The law applicable to manual workers provides sickness, invalidism and old-age insurance; that applicable to salaried employees also provides for other benefits, including family allowances, unemployment benefits, dismissal wages, medical benefits and borrowing privileges.

The largest *caja* is that covering manual workers (Caja de Seguro Obligatorio), which had 1,050,000 active participants in 1952. The next largest are those covering salaried employees of private commercial, industrial, agricultural and mining companies (120,000) and state, semistate and journalistic employees (84,000). Others cover the armed forces, police, municipal employees, merchant marine and railway workers.

At the end of 1952 all the *cajas* had total assets of 27,537,835,359 pesos, of which 7,553,446,133 pesos represented mortgage investments and 5,906,193,178 pesos, investments in real estate. Total receipts in 1952 were 13,428,079,638 pesos; expenditures, 8,987,332,046 pesos.

Considerable progress was made after 1925 in the fields of public health and sanitation and as a result there was a sharp reduction in the death rate. In 1951 Chile had a total of 3,251 physicians, or 1 per 1,800 inhabitants, as compared with a rate of 1 per 750 inhabitants in the U.S. The Chilean rate was surpassed in South America only by those of Argentina and Uruguay. In 1951 there were 33,738 hospital beds.

Mining.—At mid-20th century Chile was the leading mineral-producing country in South America, and the mineral extractive industry largely determined the financial and economic policy of the nation. The industry dates back to colonial days, but the modern history of the development of mining is predominantly the history of nitrate and copper operations. Nitrate was predominant from the 1880s until the early 1930s when competition from synthetic nitrate and the depression brought about a decline in importance. Thereafter, copper was the predominant force in the industry.

Nitrate.—Chile has a complete monopoly of the production of natural sodium nitrate acquired as a result of the acquisition of the northern desert area through the War of the Pacific (1879–83). The deposits, which vary considerably from area to area both in thickness and depth, occur from Arica to Copiapó in the central zone between the coastal plateau and the Andes. The beds vary in width from 5 to 40 mi. and occur at altitudes from 4,000 to 9,000 ft. The ordinary workings are by the open-pit method, and most of the *caliche,* or ore, is mined by hand methods, although electrical equipment is also used. The Guggenheim process of treating ore, introduced in 1926, permitted a considerable reduction in costs and a more complete recovery of nitrate than the old Shanks process that had prevailed from 1884.

TABLE IV.—*Mineral Production, 1944–53*
(in metric tons)

Mineral	1944	1948	1950	1952*	1953*
Coal	2,279,438	2,270,862	2,216,819	2,450,074	2,335,970
Copper	498,520	445,067	362,939	408,633	363,135
Iodine†	1,328,572	1,951,071	473,475	818,336	175,840
Iron ore	18,413	2,710,941	2,953,233	2,365,512	2,903,435
Nitrate of soda	990,709	1,834,981	1,607,529	1,427,817	1,420,243
Petroleum‡	..	..	100,227	144,643	200,065
Sulphur	25,575	13,335	15,472	48,588	..
Gold†	6,342	5,105	5,984	5,507	4,065
Silver†	30,996	26,810	29,430	38,766	46,588

*Provisional figures. †Kilograms. ‡Cubic metres.
Source: Servicio Nacional de Estadística.

The origin of these immense deposits is more or less conjectural. The theories roughly fall into two groups, the organic and the inorganic. The theories of origin through organic means are: (1) from seaweed; (2) from guano; and (3) from fixation of atmospheric nitrogen by bacteria. However, none of these theories is taken very seriously at the present time. The inorganic origin has been attributed to: (1) the electric fixation of atmospheric nitrogen; and (2) to the concentration of the nitrates coming directly from tuffs and lava flows. The latter postulates, probably the more scientific, present fewer difficulties. Of this group, two theories stand out most prominently. The one (J. T. Singewald, Jr., and B. L. Miller, "The Genesis of the Chilean Nitrate Deposits," *Econ. Geol.,* xii, 1917) "is that the nitrate deposits have resulted from the accumulation, by means of evaporation of the minute nitrate content of the underground waters of the region. In other words, they represent a sort of efflorescence of soluble salts out of the ground water." The other (W. L. Whitehead, "The Chilean Nitrate Deposits," *Econ. Geol.,* ix, 1920) and later suggestion is that the source of the salts is from the Mesozoic rocks of the region which in extent correspond remarkably with the nitrate fields. Ammonium salts were probably sufficiently common in the volcanic rocks of the region to account for the present deposits. The process of reconcentration, through oxidation with alkaline earth, has been going on since early Pliocene time. Under desert conditions the salts derived from sources on steep slopes and hilltops were carried down by dews, fogs or infrequent rains to be deposited during evaporation in the gravels below. There in periods of high humidity, sodium nitrate, a deliquescent substance, was separated from the accompanying sodium chloride and sodium sulphate, to be precipitated during dry weather lower in the gravel.

The importance of these deposits to Chile can be gauged with little certainty. It has been estimated that between 1880 and 1910 Chile derived from the export tax on nitrate alone an average annual income of $10,000,000 gold and up to 1920 one of twice that amount. For many years this nitrate trade constituted more than half the total value of its exports, and the tax thereon of $10.60 U.S. gold per ton collected by the government constituted not only the largest item of its revenue, but also for some years exceeded all other revenues combined. The prosperity of the whole country and the financial condition of the national treasury were to a very large measure determined by the condition of the nitrate industry.

Nitrate production increased steadily to a peak of 3,000,000 tons in 1914 and in 1910 Chile produced 64% of the world's nitrogen requirements. Thereafter, the industry began increasingly to feel the effect of competition from synthetic nitrates, although this was offset somewhat by the development of low-cost production processes. However, the world depression of 1930 and subsequent collapse of world trade had a catastrophic effect on the industry. As a result, the government in 1934 instituted a monopoly over the production and sale of nitrate through the vehicle of the Chilean Nitrate and Iodine Sales corporation. This organization determines the amount of nitrate to be produced each year, allocates the production among the producing companies, fixes sales prices and concludes all sales of nitrate and iodine. By joining a world cartel it succeeded in increasing sales abroad and with the general improvement of market conditions in the 1940s the industry recovered somewhat. In the mid-1950s, however, it had a doubtful future. Chile is the world's largest supplier of iodine, which is a by-product of the nitrate industry. The supply varies with the quantity of nitrate treated.

Copper.—Chile also has rich and abundant low-grade copper deposits. Some of the richer ores were worked by the Spaniards as early as 1601 and by the Indians long before. In the latter half of the 19th century Chile was a leading copper centre of the world, in 1876 producing 38% of the total supply.

With the development of the copper deposits in the United States, Chilean production fell off to only 4% of the world total in 1906. It surpassed nitrate in importance after 1932, but the depression of 1930 and the discovery of new ore bodies in Africa caused a period of stagnation, which was ended by market recoveries in the late 1930s and the advent of World War II. Copper exports reached a record peak of almost 500,000 tons during the war. In the postwar period the industry was faced once again with the problem of expanded production and contracting markets. It was also hampered by high taxes and government regulation. More than 95% of Chilean copper is produced by U.S. companies operating at three centres: one in the north at Chuquicamata; another near Rancagua at El Teniente; and the third at Potrerillos near Chañaral. The Chuquicamata deposit has the greatest reserves known to exist; they were estimated at mid-20th century at 1,000,000,000 tons of 2% ore.

Iron ore.—Chile has numerous large high-grade iron-ore deposits, the three best known being El Tofo, Romeral and Algarrobo, all in the coastal zone. El Tofo, the first deposit to be developed, was worked by a subsidiary of the Bethlehem Steel corporation. Shipments to the U.S. of the ore, which runs about 60% iron, began in 1922. The mining and loading on steamers of the ore is considered a model of efficiency. Shipments were suspended during World War II. In 1952 Bethlehem also began working the El Romeral deposit; shipments were made via Guayacán, near Coquimbo, for the benefit of both the domestic and U.S. market.

Other Minerals.—Petroleum was discovered late in 1945 at Cerro Manantiales and San Sebastián on Tierra del Fuego; commercial production began in 1950. Development of the field entailed the construction of a 46-mi. pipeline from the producing area to a port and of submarine lines at Bahía Gente Grande (Caleta Clarence) for loading oil at deepwater stations. Production and refining is under the control of the Development corporation.

Chile is rich in sulphur deposits which occur in the Andean cordillera from the extreme north to the southern limits of Mediterranean Chile.

The coals of Chile are noted for their quantity rather than their quality. They occur on the coast south of Concepción and are of Tertiary age. They vary considerably in quantity, improving with depth. The product has been described as second-class steamer coal, on the average 25% inferior to the Welsh product. There are four principal coal fields in the vicinity of the Bío-Bío, of which the most important, Coronel and Lota, are worked under the sea by means of inclined drifts (*chiflones*) on the longwall system. In addition there is a small lignite deposit near Magallanes mined only for local use.

Alluvial workings for gold were long a feature of the mining industry, but at mid-20th century the emphasis was on the exploitation of lode gold and the extraction of gold from copper ore. More than 50% of the country's silver production also came from copper ore. Silver mining was concentrated in Antofagasta province, near Taltal. Valuable molybdenum concentrates are recovered from copper refining by differential flotation at the El Teniente copper mine. Other mineral resources included mercury, calcium borate (source of borax), phosphates, kaolin, limestone, quartz, barium sulphate, gypsum and large reserves of manganese ore.

Agriculture.—The agriculture of Chile is confined almost wholly to the central valley. The available productive land is extremely limited, the amount devoted to cereals and other food crops being estimated at not more than 4% of the total area of the country; orchards, vines, planted woodlands, grasses and alfalfa (lucerne) occupy a somewhat smaller area; and the natural pasturage occupies a smaller area still. This 10% or 12% of the area, together with the 20% to 22% in natural forests and woodland, mostly in southern Chile, make up the productive land—about one-third of the total area of the country.

TABLE V.—*Crop Sowings and Production, 1943–53*
(in 000)

Crop	Sowings (hectares)			Production (quintals*)		
	1943–48†	1950–51	1952–53	1943–48†	1950–51	1952–53
Wheat	777.5	816.1	779.1	9,576.0	9,751.1	9,891.9
Barley	51.1	50.7	56.9	848.1	527.1	837.5
Oats	87.8	98.9	98.8	841.9	820.5	914.1
Rice	37.9	23.4	31.6	1,212.1	402.8	926.1
Beans	82.3	72.6	80.2	718.8	618.9	813.6
Maize	47.7	55.5	48.0	646.1	709.9	798.6
Potatoes	52.4	53.2	54.2	5,130.0	4,242.4	5,374.1
Tobacco	2.9	3.5	2.2	58.9	71.1	49.6

*One quintal=101.43 lb. †Average, crop years 1943–44 through 1947–48.
Source: Servicio Nacional de Estadística.

In 1953 Chile had 2,409,109 cattle (compared with 2,634,499 in 1938) and in 1951, 6,500,000 sheep (5,749,069 in 1936), 650,000 pigs, 830,000 goats and 600,000 horses. More than half the sheep are concentrated in the far south in the Magallanes pampa region, northern Tierra del Fuego and parts of Aysén province. Exports of wool averaged 7,932 metric tons a year in the years 1951–53, more than half of which went to the United Kingdom; the domestic textile industry also consumed considerable quantities.

By far the major part of the cropland is made possible only by irrigation, which was practised in limited areas of northern Chile even during prehistoric times. The chief areas now under irrigation lie along the river terraces within the cordillera, upon the piedmont to the west or within the central valley. The available streams from the Loa to the Bío-Bío are the chief sources of water. Some of the irrigation projects are of long standing and on a large scale, and carry water in canals more than 100 mi. besides furnishing extensive electric power. Many of the undertakings are privately owned, others belong to associations and others, some very large, were financed by the government.

Although agriculture in the central valley lays the foundation for the social and political structure of the country and affords a large share of the products for local consumption, it has little influence on trade balances. Socially the bulk of the people are organized around the large feudal estates and suffer little change in condition whether crops are good or bad. The owner may be more or less affluent from year to year, but this adds little to his comforts or discomforts, and he always remains on the social and political register of the country. In the northern valleys maize (corn) is the chief food crop and besides there is a great variety of subtropical fruits. The best developed type of feudal estate may include about 250 ac. of irrigated fields and 2,000 ac. or more of hillside land, which offers excellent range for livestock during the rainy season. These *propriedades agricolas* are mixed farms producing a large variety of grains and fruits and alfalfa, some horses and a larger number of cattle and sheep, but never many hogs. The growing of livestock on irrigated land, however, is not profitable. As a result Chile, with less than half the cattle of Cuba, became dependent upon Argentina for part of its meat supply.

The central valley, which is similar to that of California, favours the growing of fruits, and apples, pears, peaches, apricots, plums, prunes, cherries, table grapes, raisins, oranges, lemons and figs are produced in commercial quantities. Markets have been developed in the U.S. and Europe.

Chile is an important wine producer. In 1952 there were 32,154 vineyards covering 97,603 ha.; production by 27,129 vineyards harvesting grapes from 84,752 ha. was 58,100,000 gal. (1942–50 average: 81,900,000 gal.). Production is concentrated in the central valley, with the provinces of Santiago, Talca and Linares accounting for more than one-half the national total.

In the second quarter of the 20th century agricultural and pastoral production increased 30% over the 1923–27 level. Most of the increase took place in the 1930s and thereafter there was little change. There was, however, a change of emphasis, with the production of beans, peas, lentils, fruit and wine increasing and that of fodder barley, meat and wool tending to decline.

The waters off the coast of Chile are rich in fish. Production in 1953 included 87,075 metric tons of wet fish and 19,663 tons of shellfish. Between 1944 and 1953 there was an almost uninterrupted increase in production which in 1953 was three times that in 1944. Talcahuano and ports in Arauco and Tarapacá are the principal bases for the industry.

Southern Chile has vast forest resources, but at mid-20th century they were relatively unexploited. Nevertheless, development had permitted the creation of a considerable export trade, notably in pine, laurel, beech and other woods, and the satisfaction of most domestic needs, once-substantial imports, largely from the U.S., having been almost entirely eliminated. A U.S. forest service mission estimated in 1943 that the forested area covered 40,000,000 ac., a large part of which had to be discounted because of inaccessibility or the nature of the woods. It has been estimated that forest fires destroy three times as much timber as the country uses annually. Two-thirds of forestry production comes from the provinces of Cautín and Valdivia, which have the most accessible and valuable stands.

Manufacturing.—Chilean manufacturing industries produce principally for the domestic market, which is limited by low per capita purchasing power and also by inadequate transportation and communications facilities. Industry made important advances after 1930 and by the mid-1950s it supplied all of Chile's essential needs for some articles, including woollen textiles, footwear, paper other than newsprint, cement, explosives and glassware, and an increasing proportion of other items, including cotton textiles, clothing, paint, iron and steel and some building materials.

TABLE VI.—*Production of Principal Factories, 1930–53*

Commodity and unit	1930	1937	1947	1950	1953
Coke, 000 metric tons	49	71	109	122	110
Cement, 000 metric tons	161	313	602	519	762
Beer, 000 hl.	552	699	852	915	1,240
Cotton cloth, 000 m.	..	12,860	35,942	36,531	38,594
Pig iron, 000 metric tons	—	7*	11	109	286
Steel, 000 metric tons	..	..	31	56	313
Manufactured gas, 000,000 cu.m.	..	77	132	150	153
Electricity, 000,000 kw.hr.	301	477	1,083	1,520	1,991

*1940.
Sources: Servicio Nacional de Estadística; UN Statistical Office.

The basic pattern of Chilean industry was set prior to World War I, when sugar refineries, food and beverage industries, woollen and cotton mills and a cement plant were already in existence. The early and middle 1930s saw a considerable expansion of industrialization, and in the ten years between 1928 and 1938 the index of factory production increased 66%. The expansion was promoted by a desire to alleviate the severity of the economic dislocation caused by the depression and had the twofold objective of helping to free the economy from its dependence on mineral exports and raising the standard of living.

By far the most important landmark in the history of Chilean industrialization was the creation in 1939 of the Development corporation. In the following years it engaged in a program of widespread industrialization which was aided by high protective tariffs and exchange controls. Despite difficulties caused by World War II, industrial production increased 60% between 1937 and

1946. Expansion continued in the immediate postwar period, aided by increased mineral exports leading to increased purchasing power and by the large accumulations of foreign exchange. Thereafter, however, foreign exchange shortages and increasing competition from some lines of foreign goods forced a slackening of the pace from time to time. An important milestone in Chilean industrialization was the coming into operation in 1950 of the Huachipato steel plant near Concepción, which was built under the direction of the Development corporation at a cost of close to $100,000,000.

TABLE VII.—*General Index of Industrial Production, 1947–53*
(1936–38=100)

Industry	1947	1948	1949	1950	1951	1952	1953
Food (11.6)*	183.4	193.1	195.7	201.8	211.0	221.7	262.8
Sugar (14.5)	122.3	126.0	138.5	137.4	138.8	155.8	165.5
Beer (1.8)†	130.6	135.9	142.1	141.2	141.1	165.6	191.5
Clothing (10.0)	117.5	113.1	100.7	102.4	99.6	103.8	113.1
Chemical (7.5)	111.8	115.8	117.3	118.7	131.9	136.2	128.3
Pig iron (2.0)‡	437.7	558.9	724.1	471.1	1,579.2	1,976.7	2,096.7
Gas, coke (3.0)	151.6	165.2	171.6	171.6	163.3	159.0	171.5
Electric energy (7.6)	231.6	249.3	274.0	325.1	359.5	400.4	425.8
Construction (11.7)	177.3	161.5	158.4	159.5	146.8	144.9	193.8
Other (30.3)	148.1	150.4	149.7	150.2	148.5	160.7	168.4
General index	158.0	162.7	168.7	168.5	193.4	212.8	232.6

*Weight accorded in general index. †Includes carbonated beverages. ‡Base adjusted, Jan. 1951.
Source: Servicio Nacional de Estadística.

At mid-20th century almost three-fourths of all manufacturing production was concentrated in the provinces of Santiago (more than 50%) and Valparaíso, reflecting the great concentration of population there. The province of Concepción was third in rank and, with the coming into operation of the Huachipato steel plant, growing rapidly in importance. The remainder of industry was widely scattered. In 1940 there were 4,169 industrial establishments with 116,493 employees; by 1948 these had increased to 5,585 establishments with 296,000 employees. Despite its great advances, manufacturing was still secondary to mining and agriculture in the economic framework of the country.

In order of importance, the food, beverage and tobacco industry ranked first, followed by metals and metal products (including machinery), textiles, chemicals and leather and rubber goods.

Chile is exceeded only by Brazil in South America in the amount of hydroelectric power potentially available. The great bulk of available power is located in the central portion from La Serena to Puerto Montt. The Development corporation made hydroelectric development a central part of its program, and great advances were made. Nevertheless, at mid-20th century power shortages continued to hamper industrial development.

Foreign Trade.—Minerals have played a dominant role in Chilean foreign trade since the mid-19th century, when trade first became an important factor in the economy. Throughout that period there was no fundamental variation in the pattern of foreign trade. In 1913 minerals accounted for 88% of exports and agricultural and pastoral products for 12%; in 1953 minerals accounted for 79%, agricultural and pastoral products for 8% and manufactured and other products for 13%. Within this pattern, however, there were important changes. In 1913 nitrate accounted for 80% of exports and copper for 7%. The decline of nitrate in importance was accompanied by an increase in the importance of copper, which surpassed nitrate in 1932 and thereafter held first place. In 1953 copper produced 57% of exports, nitrate 15% and other minerals 7%. The proportion of agricultural and pastoral products remained fairly uniform, while the proportion of manufactured products grew because of increased processing of foodstuffs and industrial expansion, and in 1953 metallurgical products accounted for 7% of exports. On the other hand, the proportion of manufactured imports decreased in relation to pastoral, agricultural and mineral imports, a change brought about by increased dependence on imported foodstuffs, increased consumption of imported raw materials by industry and the increasing importance of petroleum imports. Leading imports in 1953 were machinery (20%), chemicals and drugs (15%), transport materials (12%), agricultural products (12%) and metallurgical products (9%).

TABLE VIII.—*Foreign Trade, 1938–53*
(in 000,000 U.S. dollars)

Item	1938	1946	1947	1948	1949	1950	1951	1952	1953
Exports	131	213	276	328	295	282	371	454	409
Imports	103	197	266	269	305	248	329	371	335

Source: International Monetary Fund.

Two world wars and also the change in the character of mineral exports wrought fundamental changes in the geographical pattern of foreign trade. Before World War I most of the exports went to the United Kingdom and other European countries, and the United Kingdom supplied about 35% of the imports, followed by Germany, 25%, the U.S., 17%, and France and Belgium, each 9%. This pattern was dislocated during World War I but was partially restored in the interwar period, although the U.S., largely at the expense of the United Kingdom, became the largest single trading partner, accounting for between one-quarter and one-third of the foreign trade. World War II effected a greater dislocation in the pattern, and trade became predominantly hemispheric in direction. This trend continued during the postwar period, and European nations recovered only a part of their prewar shares. Chief customers in 1953 were the U.S. (64%), Argentina (11%), Germany (5%), the United Kingdom (4%) and Uruguay and Brazil (each 2%); chief suppliers, the U.S. (53%), Argentina (9%), Germany (6%), the United Kingdom (6%) and Peru (5%). As is shown by Table VIII, Chile almost invariably has a favourable balance of trade. Actually, however, on account of large foreign investments in copper and nitrate, the sales of those exports do not return to Chile in foreign exchange the full amount of the selling price, with the result that the apparently favourable balance is often illusory.

Transport and Communications.—Chile is linked with Argentina, Bolivia and Peru by five international rail lines—Arica to Tacna, Peru; Arica to La Paz, Bolivia; Antofagasta to La Paz; Los Andes to Mendoza, Arg. (the famed Trans-Andean line); and Antofagasta to Salta, Arg. (completed in 1948). Internally, the northern two-thirds of Chile is spanned by a 1,450-mi. longitudinal state-owned line running from Pueblo Hundido in the north to Puerto Montt in the south. Numerous short lines connect this line with the coast and the interior. There are also numerous short industrial lines operated principally by the mining companies. The railway system (excluding branch lines and sidings) totalled 5,434 mi. in 1949, of which 3,859 mi. were owned by the state railways. In 1953 the international railways carried 362,000 passengers and 1,053,000 metric tons of freight, the domestic state lines, 22,178,000 passengers and 8,184,000 tons of freight and the private lines, 4,438,000 passengers and 3,626,000 tons of freight.

The mountainous terrain of most of Chile made highway construction quite difficult. Nevertheless, at mid-20th century Chile had a fairly extensive road system aggregating about 32,000 mi., of which 65% was unimproved and only 900 mi. were classified as arterial. The Santiago area and the Mediterranean central valley were best served by roads. Road construction was being pushed in the southern third of the country below Puerto Montt, the southern railway terminus. At the end of 1953 Chile had 47,739 automobiles (an increase of 67% over 1946), 4,501 buses and 38,647 trucks. About 55% of the automobiles were located in the province of Santiago; Chiloé had only 29 automobiles and Aysén, 48.

Maritime communication is of vital importance to Chile, both internationally and internally. Coastal shipping between Chilean ports is the monopoly of Chilean vessels, which operate between all ports from Magallanes in the south to Arica in the north. The extreme north and the extreme south are almost entirely dependent on coastwise shipping for the movement of goods. Of the 10,054 vessels of 19,077,233 net tons entering and clearing Chilean ports in 1953, 7,309 vessels of 7,778,000 tons were Chilean vessels engaged in coastal trade. Valparaíso is the nucleus of the coastal trade and also by far the leading port for imports, followed in that regard by Antofagasta and Talcahuano. Antofagasta and San Antonio are the leading export ports, accounting for more than

50% of the exports by value in 1953; they owe their position to the copper mines at Chuquicamata and El Teniente. Next in importance are Tocopilla, a nitrate port, and Chañaral, port for the Potrerillos copper mine. On June 30, 1953, the Chilean merchant marine had 96 vessels (100 tons and more) aggregating 200,719 gross tons.

The development of air transport was of outstanding importance to Chile because of its geographical situation. Between the late 1930s and the mid-1950s there were enormous increases in traffic on both domestic and international routes. Santiago was the terminus of several international routes, and the number of passengers entering and leaving Chile by air exceeded that of all other means of transport combined. Routes of the National Air Line (L.A.N.) covered the whole length of the country and extended to Buenos Aires. In 1953 L.A.N. carried 133,933 passengers, compared with 18,103 in 1944. Airfields were numerous, but the number suitable for larger four-engined aircraft was limited.

The internal telegraphic service is largely government-controlled; international telecommunication service is provided largely by All America Cables and an affiliate of Cable and Wireless Ltd. The internal telephone service, under control of private companies, is not highly developed; there were 140,769 telephones in 1953, about 90% of which were served by the Chile Telephone company. Commercial radio broadcasting is quite highly developed.

Defense.—Compulsory military service prevails in Chile. Every able-bodied man over 20 years of age is due to receive 18 months' training. Following the months of active service they belong to the first reserve for 12 years and to the second reserve until the completion of their 45th year. At mid-20th century the active army was composed of about 1,900 officers and 18,500 men. It was organized into three army corps, one army division, one cavalry division and one railway regiment.

The influence of the German military system was strong prior to World War II. The air force was organized in 1918 under British instruction. It was strengthened during World War II and is equipped largely with U.S. matériel.

Military, naval and aviation schools are maintained by the government.

The Chilean navy took its rise in 1817 with the capture of a Spanish frigate and brigantine at anchor in Arica bay. This initial success, brought about by a Scotsman, Capt. William McKay, was brilliantly continued during the four years that Thomas Cochrane served Chile and cleared the west coast of Spanish vessels. These operations, loyally supported by the supreme director, Bernardo O'Higgins, made possible the success of José de San Martín in Peru, and left a definite British impress upon the navy of Chile. It was the "Cochrane" which won the naval battle of Angamos in 1879. The officers of the Chilean navy maintain a more aristocratic tradition than the other branches of service. This led the major part of them under their leading officer, Capt. (later President) Jorge Montt, to support congress in 1891 against Pres. José Balmaceda.

In 1954 the Chilean navy had one old battleship, the "Almirante Latorre," a 28,950-ton vessel completed in 1915 and refitted in England in 1929–31, and two modern cruisers, the "Capitán Prat" (10,000 tons) and the "O'Higgins" (9,700 tons), both completed in 1938 and acquired from the United States in 1951. It also had 6 destroyers, 6 frigates and escort vessels, 7 submarines, a submarine depot ship, 6 transports and other ancillary craft. Active strength, including marines and coastal artillery, was about 13,000 officers and men. (I. J. C.; J. W. Mw.)

HISTORY

In the 15th century the Peruvian Indians invaded the country—even then known as Chile—and dominated it as far south as the Rapel river (34° 10′ S.). Their control may have furthered the later conquest by the Spaniards. The latter made their first attempt to occupy the region under Diego de Almagro, associate and subsequent rival of Pizarro. After Almagro's death the conqueror of Peru granted Chile to his favourite aide, Pedro de Valdivia. That invader founded Santiago (Feb. 12, 1541), and after establishing other fortified towns north and south of that centre and east of the Andes, lost his life in a general uprising of the Araucanian Indians, under their celebrated *toqui,* or war-chief, Caupolicán. The greater part of his settlements were destroyed, although La Serena and Concepción remained as the outposts of the future colony to the north and the south, while Cuyo held the same position east of the Andes.

The Colonial Period.—With this inauspicious beginning Chile entered upon its three centuries of colonial history. In such phases of its development as were affected by the administrative and commercial control of the homeland it differed in no wise from its neighbours. Its population took no part in political affairs, aside from membership in the town councils. It accepted ecclesiastical control in its scant educational facilities as well as in spiritual matters. It endured all the vagaries of Spain's trade restrictions, varied by the piratical and contraband practices of its enemies. Chile differed from other Spanish colonies in that its remote position forced upon the people a more thorough isolation, while continued conflicts with the Araucanians tended to harden the settlers, and the scarcity of precious metals turned them toward farming.

By the end of the 17th century this population numbered 100,000. A century later it approached a half million. This included 300,000 *mestizos* (mixed bloods), half as many *Criollos* ("Creoles," *i.e.,* natives of European descent), some 20,000 *Peninsulares* (recently arrived Spaniards, among whom Basque immigrants from northern Spain formed an energetic commercial element), and a smattering of negroes and recently emancipated Indians. This hardy population had progressed far towards racial unity but the *mayorazgos,* a system of transmitting estates by entail, gave enhanced importance to a few leading families. The people, set down in the midst of resources that were barely touched, were stimulated to activity by a bracing climate, but were pitifully handicapped by ignorance, isolation, and the lack of political experience.

Independence and Self-government.—None of the above conditions that hampered Chile in common with its fellow colonies provoked the movement for independence. Nor was this act due to the rise of the United States nor to the French Revolution. It was the intervention of Napoleon in Spain—an act that in 1808 threw each part of the Spanish monarchy on its own resources—that led Chile to take the first halting step toward self-government. This occurred on Sept. 18, 1810, when an open *cabildo* or general town meeting in Santiago accepted the resignation of the president-governor and in his stead elected a *junta* (board) of seven members.

JARS USED IN MAKING WINE

This act divided the people (not including, of course, the ignorant masses) into two general groups. The first, which was composed exclusively of Creoles was headed by the *cabildo,* or town council of Santiago. The *audiencia* headed the second, which largely represented peninsular interests. The former group wished to organize for local protection during the intervention and possibly for more complete self-government thereafter. The peninsulars followed reluctantly, for they preferred to keep intact the existing system which insured them special privileges.

The creole leaders gained their immediate point—a recognized position in the new *junta,* took measures for the defence of the province, opened its ports to general trade, abolished the *audiencia,* when that body encouraged a reactionary uprising, and summoned a national congress. By this time Concepción, under the leadership of Juan Martínez de Rozas, broke away from the conservative leaders of the Santiago *cabildo.* This split enabled an ambitious popular leader, José Miguel Carrera, to dissolve congress, some two months after it finally organized, banish Rozas, and assume dictatorial powers, but this did not occur before congress had assumed administrative control of the colony, broken relations with Peru, abolished slavery, established a press, encouraged education and suggested further important steps towards self-government—all in the name of the captive king. Affairs in Chile now assumed the aspect of civil war between those of its people who favoured the former autocracy, as represented by the viceroy of Peru, and those who espoused self-government under a more liberal monarchy. Owing to divisions among the autonomists, who called themselves partisans of Carrera or of Bernardo O'Higgins, who had superseded him, the royalists gained the upper hand at Rancagua, Oct. 7, 1814, and brought to an end that first phase of the Chilean War for independence known as *la patria vieja* (the Old Country).

Two and a half years of repression under the restored government effectually cured the Chilean people of further loyalty to Spain. During this period José de San Martín patiently gathered an army at Mendoza and led it early in 1817 across the Andes. With this force, in which O'Higgins commanded a contingent, he defeated the royalists at Chacabuco, on Feb. 12, and made his associate supreme director of Chile. Their first task was to meet the inevitable counter attack under Osorio, the victor of 1814, who surprised and routed the patriot forces at Cancha Rayada. But with a reorganized force San Martín met and crushed the royalists at Maipú, April 5, 1818. This victory made good the declaration of independence which had been formally proclaimed on the first anniversary of Chacabuco.

During the next 15 years Chile passed through a period of political uncertainty that fortunately was less prolonged and less anarchic than her neighbours experienced. For five years O'Higgins maintained a fairly efficient personal rule, slightly modified by constitutional offerings of his own devising. After his abdication in 1823 there followed a more unsteady dictatorship under Ramón Freire, which was modified in 1826 by an ill advised attempt at federalism and two years later by the liberal but unworkable constitution of 1828. During this period the Spaniards were finally expelled from Chiloé and that island and the contiguous area incorporated with the country. Aided by a naval contingent under Lord Cochrane (earl of Dundonald) the Chileans united with other patriotic forces in freeing Peru and thus assuring their own security. Then followed recognition by Brazil, Mexico, the United States, and Great Britain. Through the last named country Chile was enabled to float its first external loan.

In domestic affairs the country was less fortunate. A few social reforms, initiated by O'Higgins and Freire, did little to remove the discontent engendered by years of warfare, to counteract the hostility of the Church, or to straighten out financial tangles. Politics

PRIMITIVE METHOD OF MAKING ROPE FROM HEMP FIBRE IN CHILE

was almost wholly personal and merely served to reveal political incapacity. Matters reached a crisis in 1829 with the outbreak of civil strife between Freire, who seemed the only hope of liberalism, and Joaquín Prieto, a successful military chief whom the reactionaries accepted. The conflict was decided at Lircay, April 17, 1830, with the utter defeat of the Liberal forces.

This victory made Prieto president of Chile, but his chief minister, Diego Portales, became its controlling spirit. This conservative leader, the Alexander Hamilton of Chile, aimed at something more substantial than mere military control. He wished to establish the credit of the country and assure its orderly progress. He proposed to continue in power those aristocratic elements that had softened the rigours of colonial control and had kept the struggle for independence clear of unproductive radicalism. With the aid of the *Pelucones* ("Bigwigs"), he centred administration in a President of almost dictatorial powers, whose acts were subject to limited revision by Congress. It was this combination of aristocratic supervision with autocratic administration that constituted the main feature of the Constitution of 1833.

The Autocratic Republic (1831–61).—The government under the new constitution soon faced a series of intrigues that in 1835 called Portales from retirement, and forced the re-election of Prieto. In furthering his efforts to preserve the constitution and to develop the resources of the country Portales now systemized the revenues, reorganized the treasury and refunded the public debt. But the benefits of this policy were measurably neutralized by his severity. Further dissatisfaction was aroused by a conflict with the Peru-Bolivian confederation, in the midst of which a regiment stationed near Valparaiso revolted and seized and assassinated the dictatorial minister, June 6, 1837. His death, regarded as a national calamity, served to fix his policy upon the country more firmly than ever. The war that he had brought about ended with the overthrow of the confederation at Yungay (Jan. 20, 1839). This victory assured the predominance of Chile on the west coast and made its successful general, Manuel Bulnes, the next president.

The first half of Bulnes's double term (1841–51) was an era of conciliation, of material progress, and of cultural awakening. The public debt was liquidated and the customs better regulated. Steamship lines were established, coal mines were opened, and the output of copper and silver was greatly increased. Colonies of Germans were located in the south and in 1849 the Strait of Magellan occupied. This last move provoked a series of boundary disputes with Argentina which were further complicated by similar controversies with Bolivia. Per contra Spain now recognized the independence of Chile, and Peru settled the debt—a legacy of the period of independence—that had helped provoke war between them.

Intellectual expression kept pace with material progress. The National Institute improved its course of instruction. In 1843 the University of Chile opened its doors under the direction of Andrés Bello, a naturalized Venezuelan who later codified the civil law of Chile and attempted to nationalize its language. The Argentine refugee, Domingo F. Sarmiento, headed the first Normal School (1842) and for several years served on the editorial staff of *El Mercurio*. Literary expression manifested itself especially in the press, where José Victorino Lastarria represented reviving liberalism, and Francisco Bilbao, more definitely the revolutionary philosophy of 1848. Growing demands for religious toleration led the State to legalize the marriage of dissenters and to exercise some control over clerical appointments.

After two decades of effective rule the Conservative Party found its supremacy threatened when in 1850 it brought Manuel Montt forward as the successor of Bulnes. But the administration ruthlessly suppressed opposition, which culminated in an unsuccessful revolt, and ushered in the decennium (1851–61) which closed the "autocratic republic." Montt was a fit executive for the period. A pedantic devotion to law and order motivated his policy but once assured of these essentials he devoted himself to developing his country's resources. He introduced the telegraph, began the construction of railways, started the hall of congress and various public buildings, and encouraged the founding of savings banks, the Mortgage Loan Bank, and other financial institutions. Agriculture was aided by the suppression of tithes and of the *mayorazgos*, by the subdivision of rural properties, and by modifying the *alcabalas*. He provided for better primary instruction, for more normal schools, and for public libraries. The discovery of gold in California created for a few years a better market for Chilean flour, but later led to a disastrous financial reaction.

Montt's insistence upon the authority of the State provoked a controversy over the appointment of the archbishop of Santiago and split his party. In a quarrel over the budget the malcontents were joined by a new party—the Radical—and the combined opposition forced the president to reconstruct his cabinet. This incident was later interpreted as a step toward fixing its responsibility to Congress. When opposition in 1859 became open revolt, Montt with the aid of his efficient co-labourer, Antonio Varas, rigorously suppressed it. It was felt inadvisable, however, to force the election of the latter as his successor.

The Liberal Republic (1861–91).—Joaquín Pérez was a compromise president. He began his administration in a spirit of conciliation and supported by a fusion of Liberals and Conservatives carried it on for ten years without recourse to the "extraordinary faculties," which preceding presidents occasionally used. The opposition maintained by the "Montt-Varistas" (Nationalists) and by the Radicals, mollified by religious and civil concessions, finally secured a constitutional amendment against the re-election of the president. The Radicals also sponsored closer relations with their west coast neighbours, when in 1866 Chile was drawn into the war between Peru and Spain, of which the outstanding event was the wanton bombardment of Valparaiso by the Spanish fleet. The growth in public revenues, which were doubling each decade, permitted this administration to complete the railway between Valparaiso and the capital and to increase expenditures for such public services as the police, the postoffice, and highways. A new commercial code went into effect in 1867 and two years later was held the first National Exposition of Agriculture—both marks of a healthy expansion in production. Colonization was extended into the south at the expense of the Araucanians.

Federico Errázuriz Zañartu (1871–76) continued the record of Pérez for efficient public service. He pushed forward the construction of railways, improved the water front at Valparaiso and finished the edifices for congress, for the University, and for the Agricultural Exposition. At the same time his colleague, Benjamin Vicuña Mackenna transformed and beautified Santiago. The opening of new silver mines and the exploitation of guano deposits and of nitrate greatly stimulated business activity. But still more significant were the political changes of the period. Such issues as the secularization of cemeteries, civil marriage, the separation of Church and State brought the Conservatives forward as champions of ecclesiastical privilege, with the Radicals, aided by a press that was practically free, as their chief opponents. Fundamental changes in the penal code and in the organic Law of Tribunals subjected clerics to civil procedure, restricted the "extraordinary faculties" of the president, and rendered those holding judicial appointments ineligible for other political offices. Amendments to the constitution enlarged the powers of the chamber of deputies, provided for the election of its members by cumulative voting, and made the ministry more thoroughly subject to congress.

His successor, Aníbal Pinto (1876–81) suspended specie payments to meet the economic crisis caused by the exportation of gold and silver, and in 1881 finally settled the long-standing dispute with Argentina over the Strait of Magellan. The quarrel with Bolivia over the guano deposits at Atacama proved insoluble. An attempt had been made in 1866 to settle it by dividing the revenues of the disputed territory. The discovery of silver mines at Caracoles and of nitrate deposits near Antofagasta increased the tension and ultimately led to the War of the Pacific.

Hostilities began in 1879 with the occupation of Antofagasta by Chilean troops. Bolivia immediately declared war and appealed to Peru for aid under the terms of an alliance made in 1873. Chile rejected Peru's offer of mediation and declared war against both republics. The first stages of the conflict were marked by naval engagements at Iquique and at Angamos, Oct. 8, 1879. The latter victory gave Chile command of the sea. After brilliant campaigns the Chileans speedily occupied the province of Tarapacá and followed this with the capture of Arica. Here in Oct. 1880, the contestants met in conference under the auspices of the United States but failed to come to terms. Chile, determined to force a territorial indemnity, then transferred her arms to the vicinity of Lima and in Jan. 1881, after desperate fighting occupied the city. Then followed two years of desultory guerrilla warfare, after which the Peruvians brought together a government that in 1883 accepted the Treaty of Ancón. Under this pact Peru unconditionally ceded Tarapacá to Chile and gave that country control for ten years over Tacna and Arica. At the end of that period, according to the third article of the treaty, a plebiscite should determine whether the provinces were to continue under Chile or return to Peru, the country winning the plebiscite being then obligated to pay the other 10,000,000 pesos. In 1884 Chile and Bolivia agreed to a truce by which the latter yielded to Chile for an indefinite period the province of Antofagasta—its only outlet to the sea.

In the midst of hostilities Domingo Santa María succeeded to the presidency. While bringing the war to a close he also subdued the Araucanian Indians. These successes in the north and south increased the territory of the republic by a third. Within the five years of Santa María's administration (1881–86) the public revenues more than doubled and continued to increase. The government, therefore, was able to meet all existing obligations, to encourage immigration and aid agriculture and mining—in short, to do everything except redeem its paper money. The peso depreciated to about half its value; prices rose accordingly. Thus in a period of apparent national prosperity the masses of the people suffered greatly.

More significant than fiscal issues was the election of an archbishop in Santiago—an act which revived the fervid discussion of "theological reforms." The authorities secularized the cemeteries and recognized civil marriage by law, but failed to bring about the separation of Church and State. At the same time congress extended individual guarantees, assumed the power to override the president's veto by a two-thirds vote, curtailed the powers of local officials, and established manhood suffrage. Yet the president, as before, intervened in the following election and despite prolonged opposition, secured the choice of his designated successor, José Manuel Balmaceda (1886–91).

The new president was a reformer who showed a tendency to use autocratic methods. Yet at the outset he attempted to reconcile his enemies and even permitted them to name the archbishop. Substantial increases in the revenue, especially from the export tax on nitrates, enabled him to initiate a veritable "dissipation of progress," including commendable attention to educational affairs. The system of secondary and higher education had been revised under the law of 1879. Medical instruction was now improved and a pedagogical institute founded for the training of secondary teachers. In fiscal affairs a more just system of taxation was introduced, a tribunal of accounts created, and part of the public debt paid. But the Government made no attempt to abandon the system of paper money. It supplied the army and navy with better equipment and made efforts to encourage immigration.

These improvements were accompanied by complaints of wastefulness and of unnecessary increases in the civil service. At this period also occurred extensive strikes among the labourers, due in part to the depreciation of the currency and to the introduction of workmen from abroad. These conditions gave rise to a new party—the Democrats. The old parties were thoroughly disorganized and at outs with the executive, despite his conciliatory attitude. Cabinets were formed and dissolved mechanically. The president used his influence to elect new members to congress, only to have them join the opposition. The real issue at stake was the election of 1891, which Balmaceda, as usual, planned to dominate in favour of a friend. Congress attempted to checkmate the scheme by adjourning in 1890, without voting supplies. Balmaceda thereupon selected a group of advisers headed by his favoured candidate and announced that he would collect taxes for 1891 under the budget of the preceding year. This step was clearly illegal, but the president's worst offence was his open challenge to the aristocratic and clerical influences that had hitherto dominated the country.

His opponents, who comprised a majority of both houses of congress, did not hesitate to declare themselves in revolt. Led by the vice president of the senate and the president of the chamber of deputies and supported by the navy under Capt. Jorge Montt, they fled northward and established themselves at Iquique. Utilizing the revenues of the nitrate fields, they recruited an army from the labourers and prepared to fight the dictatorial president. He in turn declared Montt and his levies traitors and raised a force of 40,000 men to combat them. He filled up Congress with his supporters and directed an election in June, when his friend Claudio Vicuña was chosen to succeed him. He aroused further vindictive feeling by the execution in August of several youths belonging to leading families of the country.

Meanwhile his enemies in the north sought to purchase a supply of arms in the United States. Their vessel, the "Itata," evaded the American authorities, but after reaching Chile was forced to return without landing its cargo. The revolutionists finally obtained arms from Europe with which they met and defeated the Balmacedists at Concón and then utterly overwhelmed them at Placilla. Their victory was largely due to the scattering of the president's forces, to treachery in his ranks, and especially to the resentment inspired by his recent arbitrary course. Balmaceda abdicated on the evening of his defeat, took refuge in the Argentine legation and there, on the evening of Sept. 18, the last day of his administration, committed suicide. The contest had cost 10,000 lives and had added materially to the public debt, but it apparently decided that Congress and not the president should control the country.

The Democratic Republic (1891–1924).—The triumphant Congressionalists speedily restored order and in November elected their leader, Admiral Jorge Montt as president. The new president proved a straight-forward, conciliatory official. He and his associates extended amnesty to the greater part of their opponents and assumed the debts contracted by both factions in the late contest. Then they proceeded to consolidate the pretentious parliamentary régime for which they had contended. The Municipal Law of 1892 by which the victors hoped to provide more definitely for local participation in affairs and to forestall further executive interference in elections, was accompanied by a new law of parliamentary incompatibility, which prevented any one drawing a salary from the State from holding a legislative office and definitely shifted the control of elections from the executive to Congress. Political campaigns were henceforth carried on by party groups, seven or more in number, whose leaders resided in the capital and directed the activities of their representatives in each of the communes into which the country was divided.

These party groups now became mere personal followings, which could determine action only through precarious combinations. In presidential elections, however, the parties generally formed themselves into two general groups—the Alliance and the Coalition—of which the former embraced the more liberal elements. Yet there was nothing fixed in these combinations. In 1896 the Coalition carried the election of Federico Errázuriz, son of the former president, by a very narrow majority; in 1901 the vote went the other way in favour of Germán Riesco and swung back again five years later.

At this election in 1906 certain groups that were disgusted with sterile political combinations united to form a "National Union." They proposed to bring about "administrative regeneration" in the government and fittingly chose as their candidate, Pedro Montt, son of the man whose earlier administration still suggested law and stability. Although Montt had been defeated in 1901 the "National Union" now put him into office by an overwhelming majority. But the new executive was unable to bring about the redemption of the currency and only after the greatest efforts was he authorized to start construction on the Longitudinal railway. On the completion of the Transandine railway in 1910 President Montt, accompanied by a brilliant entourage, journeyed to Buenos Aires, where the presidents of Argentina and Chile celebrated together the common struggle for independence. In the midst of preparations for the return celebration in Santiago, the president fell ill and in August died while on his way to Europe. Montt's successor also died in September, and Emiliano Figueroa, head of the cabinet, presided over the centennial festivities, and directed the election for president, which took place a few days later. After a prolonged contest within their party the Liberals placed in nomination Ramón Barros Luco, a veteran publicist, whom the Conservatives accepted and who was elected without opposition; but this result did not insure administrative stability nor repress the growing influence of money. Cabinet changes occurred as frequently as before.

Bribery, despite severe laws against it, replaced executive intervention as the controlling factor in all elections, and made procedure therein a matter of purchase and of fraud.

In respect to international affairs the quarter century that followed the Civil War presents a more flattering record. The resentment aroused against the United States over the "Itata affair" led to the still more irritating "Baltimore incident," which was finally settled by Chile's offer of compensation. The Alsop claim, growing out of the war with Bolivia, was finally arbitrated in 1911 by King George V. With the turn of the century there was a recurrence of border quarrels with Argentina, in two regions—the Puna de Atacama in the north and the Patagonian area in the south.

The former was settled in 1899 by arbitration of the U.S. minister in Buenos Aires, but without appeasing popular agitation in either country. In May 1902 the two countries signed treaties which provided for the arbitration of disputes between them, for naval equality during five years and for limitation of armaments. The last two points made this treaty a pioneer. Moreover each country was to remain neutral with respect to affairs upon the other's coast. Some months later the British king, who had been asked to arbitrate the dispute in Patagonia, announced his award, which proved to be a virtual division of the contested area. Thus was ended a controversy that had lasted more than a half century (1847–1902).

In commemoration of this settlement the two nations later joined in erecting on their common boundary above the tunnel of the Transandine railway the famus statue known as the "Christ of the Andes."

In 1904 Chile signed with Bolivia the pact of Santiago by which the former gained full sovereignty in the Atacama region. A secret article of the treaty assured Bolivia an outlet through Tacna-Arica. As a temporary substitute for this corridor Chile agreed to construct a railway from Arica to La Paz (which was completed in 1915) and in 1928 to turn over to Bolivia the portion in the latter's territory. Meanwhile Bolivian goods were given free entry and shipment in bond at Arica. These arrangements created a better sentiment between the two peoples. Chile and Peru, however, could not agree upon terms for holding the plebiscite under the treaty of Ancón. All attempts to arbitrate the question failed. Chile began, after 1908, to interpret the disputed clause as a disguised cession and in 1913 the two countries agreed to postpone for 20 years any further attempts to carry out its provisions.

Through Chile's understanding with Brazil and Argentina and through the participation of the three in the controversies between the United States and Mexico, the country gained marked prestige in Pan American affairs.

The irredeemable paper money affected adversely the volume of trade, and caused a moratorium during the war scare of 1898. Industry which was checked by the Civil War showed a favourable turn before the end of the century. This process was hastened by the protective policy of the government and by its measures to encourage the colonization of the Magellan area and to develop its wool interests and gold washings. The financial crisis of 1907 gave a set-back to industry, already suffering from the great earthquake of 1906.

These successive disasters, however, affected the country less than had at first been feared.

The rise in the cost of living led to demands for increased salaries and wages—demands that in the case of workmen were not granted without frequent resort to strikes. A series of these in 1905 terrorized Santiago and led to bloodshed. Serious disturbances also marked outbreaks at Iquique in 1907 and later in the coal fields of Lota. A few publicists now began to call attention to the misery and squalor that afflicted the Chilean masses and to the general lack of public sanitation. Agricultural labourers in times of scarcity showed a tendency to migrate, especially to Argentina. Because of this continued public neglect the population of Chile failed to keep pace with its growth in wealth and productivity.

A better situation obtained in cultural activities. A freer press supplied both books and periodicals to wider circles of readers. Primary instruction, both public and private, received fresh impetus from new normal schools, while the Pedagogic Institute (founded in 1889) exerted a marked effect on secondary education. Progress was shown in the establishment of trade schools and in the betterment of professional instruction. A General Congress of Instruction, held in 1902, and a General Congress of Secondary Instruction held ten years later, greatly stimulated the production of didactic treatises and the development of a professional spirit. A reputable group of scientific writers and of historians, of litterateurs and of artists registered the intellectual and social advance of the country and with these cultured and zealous Church officials kept pace.

In the presidential election of 1915 Chile was hampered both by disturbances caused by the World War and by local political strife. In spite of the unanimity that marked the choice of Barros Luco in 1910 and of his general conciliatory policy, partisan spirit showed itself in the intervening elections and forced numerous cabinet changes. Accordingly the Alliance and the Coalition now put forward separate candidates and thus precipitated an exciting campaign in which neither received an actual majority. Congress, with whom final decision rested, chose Juan Luis Sanfuentes, the candidate of the Coalition, who succeeded in reorganizing public administration, in improving the army and navy, in extending railroads, encouraging the commercial marine, constructing port works and public buildings, and beginning the National Library. These improvements were effected despite the grave financial and industrial depression that rested upon the country during the early months of the war, and despite cabinet changes and the later renewal of difficulties with Peru.

Chile had already experienced some trouble in maintaining neutrality when Sanfuentes became president. The country was terribly affected by the loss of European markets. Prussian methods in the army and German scholars among her educators, not to mention a thrifty German population in southern Chile and extensive German business connections, inclined large sections of the people to favour the Central Powers. In 1915 the German cruiser "Dresden" was sunk by a British squadron while supposedly interned in Chilean waters. England apologized for the affront and owing to the clever management of Agustín Edwards, the Chilean minister in London, suffered no further trouble from the incident. Gradually as the war continued public opinion in Chile veered toward the Allies, but the Government maintained its neutrality and continued therein after the United States entered the struggle. Nor did the country fail to reap material rewards from the increase in its trade which in 1916 surpassed that of any previous year and two years later had still further doubled in amount.

The difficulties of the war period were surpassed by those that followed the Armistice. Anti-Peruvian riots at Iquique and Antofagasta in 1918 caused the withdrawal of consular agents from both countries. In the following year Bolivia and Peru, encouraged by the attitude of President Wilson, talked of carrying their grievances to Versailles or to Geneva. By 1920 Peru and Chile were on the verge of hostilities. A *coup d'état* in Bolivia, where Chile was supposed to be exercising too much influence, relieved the situation, and left affairs in train for a more definite *rapprochement* the following year. In the first assembly of the League of Nations Chile gained an important chairmanship and in 1922, its delegate, Agustín Edwards, presided over the assembly.

Post-war recovery was retarded by the slump in nitrate and the ensuing labour disturbances. In the midst of these difficulties occurred the memorable election of 1920. Arturo Alessandri, the candidate of the Liberal Alliance, had served with distinction in Congress and cabinet. He launched his candidacy in 1918 and based his platform on an extensive social program. This precipitate act, typical of the man, increased his prestige as a candidate. As representative of the middle classes and the labour groups, he covered the country in a veritable whirlwind campaign. At the election on June 25, 1920, it was announced that he had received 179 electoral votes to 175 for his opponent. Numerous charges of fraud, however, cast doubt upon the result. The canvass of the voters rested with congress, where each chamber favoured a different candidate. There was a demand for a special court of honour to determine the dispute. In the face of popular clamour, which culminated in a general strike, congress appointed the court and on the basis of its decision gave Alessandri 177 valid votes against 176. The settling of the election by this method, probably saved the country from a revolutionary outbreak.

In his message of June 1, 1921, President Alessandri outlined a program of political and social reform. He wished to improve the conditions of labour and the status of women; to decentralize administration, separate Church and State, change the parliamentary system, establish executive responsibility, and elect the president and vice president by popular vote. A split in the ranks of the Alliance (following a general election to the chamber of deputies) added to the strength of the Conservative groups. In despair at his failure to overcome political opposition and faced with adverse economic conditions Alessandri tendered his resignation Nov. 17, 1921, but was persuaded to continue in office. Some slight betterment in the nitrate industry eased labour conditions, while the adoption of a protocol for the arbitration of the Tacna-Arica dispute diverted attention from domestic difficulties. The Fifth Pan American Congress, which was held at Santiago in April and May, 1923, served momentarily to distract attention from pressing local problems; but fiscal and business affairs showed an alarming uncertainty that was further increased by continued manifestations of unrest among students and labourers. Parliamentary government in Chile seemed hopeless.

Reform and Readjustment.—At the beginning of 1924 affairs in Chile were in an alarming state of uncertainty. Unsuccessful attempts were made to modify by general party agreement the ineffective parliamentary system, to hold a fair election for members of congress, and to carry out the presidential program of reform. With the failure of these efforts, Alessandri determined at all cost to secure control of the reactionary senate. He personally took part in the campaign that preceded the March election and as a result of his intervention, coupled with an extensive but as it proved unnecessary use of military pressure, he carried both houses of congress and for the first time seemed in a position to control public policy.

Congress, however, failed to follow his urgings. The opponents of the administration plotted its overthrow. Unmindful of its increasing unpopularity congress, late in August, intensified the general unrest by proposing to pay its members. Thus it brought upon itself charges of gross selfishness as well as of general incapacity. Army officers attended the sessions of the senate in token of disapproval and in reply to a demand for their punishment forced, on Sept. 5, the installation of a military junta to direct affairs. The president at first agreed to accept its supervision in return for support of his program but soon resigned and left the country. The junta, presided over by General Luis Altamirano, dissolved congress with evident public approval, proposed some fiscal measures, and issued a few "decree-laws" in the way of reform. Then its members seemed to fall under reactionary influences. In Feb. 1925, a second *coup d'état,* directed by the younger army officers, dismissed Gen. Altamirano and his colleagues and recalled Alessandri. A young cavalry officer, Major Carlos Ibáñez, took a conspicuous part in this overturn.

The recalled president received a delirious ovation. He had come back on condition that he be permitted to carry out his program for political and social reform. His way was smoothed by an agreement between the Conservative and Radical parties for the separation of Church and State. The decision in the Tacna-Arica controversy, shortly handed down by President Coolidge, also promised to strengthen his cause. His first care was to prepare a new constitution. This task, after some consideration of a convention, was turned over to a general committee—hand picked, indeed, but fairly representing all shades of public opinion. A smaller committee, of which Alessandri was chairman, actually prepared the document, which was then submitted to popular vote along with an alternative proposal for a modified "parliamentary" system. The new pact, based on what may be termed "presidential" principles was overwhelmingly successful, although some political groups abstained from voting.

The selection of the new executive caused further difficulty. An attempt to present a single candidate failed. Then Colonel Ibáñez, who had been promoted and was then serving as minister of war, announced his candidacy, thereby disrupting the cabinet and forcing the president's resignation. In alarm at the prospect of military domination most of the political factions came to a belated agreement upon Señor Emiliano Figueroa as a joint candidate. He triumphed at the polls although the leader put forward at the last moment by the more radical elements received a large vote in the capital and industrial centres. In Santiago a general strike followed the election but the acting president, Señor Barros Borgoño, handled the situation firmly, and in Dec. 1925, turned the administration over to president-elect Figueroa.

Each shifting authority of this tumultuous year furthered measures to rehabilitate finances. Unable to secure domestic agreement as to methods, the government finally invited Professor E. W. Kemmerer, of Princeton university, and a group of associates, to study the situation. A decree-law of Sept. 1925, finally embodied the results of their investigation. This act thoroughly revised the fiscal system and created a national bank for the triple purpose of administering the finances of the government, of reducing general rates of interest, and of regulating the other banks of the country. Other decree-laws provided for extensive social legislation, including the regulation of labour conditions and of public health. With the promise of greater stability under the new constitution, Chile seemed destined to experience an important social and industrial advance.

The new administration failed to meet expectations. For some months, indeed, President Figueroa held together a meritorious cabinet, but the legislative factions could not keep from tinkering with executive affairs The Tacna-Arica plebiscite did not materialize and this failure rested heavily on the administration. Many features of the social program were premature and still others proved unpopular. No serious friction occurred over the separation of Church and State, because under agreement, the Government was to continue its ecclesiastical subsidies for five years longer. The national revenues failed to respond to the strain resting upon them.

Changes in 1926 in the ministry of foreign affairs and in that of finance failed to restore public confidence. The one point of stability in the midst of general uncertainty was the ministry of war, still directed by Colonel Ibáñez. A general disruption in the cabinet, late in the year, made the colonel its head, without depriving him, however, of his military control. This new position enabled him to establish a veritable dictatorship, under which Conservatives, Communists, Radicals, Liberals and Democrats were alike proscribed. By such measures he dominated congress and essayed to reform the judiciary, even proceeding to arrest, and finally to banish, the presiding judge of the supreme court, who was President Figueroa's brother.

Before this extreme measure was carried out the president himself quitted office. The executive duties thereby devolved upon Colonel Ibáñez, who continued more openly but not less effectively his policy of administrative reform. In July 1927 an election was held which confirmed Ibáñez as President with virtually dictatorial powers. His administration rested upon a combination of military force and public largess. For a time, through borrowings abroad, he was able to bestow unexampled prosperity on the country. When in 1929 this source of income failed, the true test of his power occurred. In May 1930, came the first proposal to reduce the budget, but it was not accepted. A succession of ministers essayed the hopeless task of reducing expenditures, but when the foreign credit ceased and the efforts to float the nitrate industry likewise failed, the Ibáñez administration of military repression came to an end in July 1931.

Juan Estéban Montero, a liberal law professor, took over temporary rule and, despite his protest, was formally elected president. He inherited a huge deficit from the preceding administration, and faced such additional problems as unemployment, partial crop failure, and an abrupt drop in the revenues. When he proved unequal to the task for which he had been elected, a military revolution, fomented in the aviation school early in June 1932, placed Carlos Dávila in power. After a few days of kaleidoscopic political changes, he essayed a socialistic régime which in September came to an end through a second military revolution. Quarrels between military leaders led the president of the Supreme Court to assume temporary civilian rule. He in turn was followed by Arturo Alessandri, former president of radical tendencies, who now seemed the only hope of the Liberal-Conservative elements. Chosen as chief executive in October, he assumed office in December, with a promise to restore the badly shattered political and economic reputation of the country.

This promise he carried out with reasonable success during the next six years. He rigidly suppressed sporadic attempts at insurrection. Fiscal affairs were entrusted to Gustavo Ross as minister of finance. Within two years the latter had balanced the budget, reorganized Cosach by making it a general sales corporation, and was using the nitrate industry for international trade on a quota basis. By manipulating a portion of the proceeds from this industry, he arranged for token payments on the interest of the foreign debt and sought to redeem the bonds at a fraction of their face value. This arrangement was accepted by Great Britain, but rejected by American, French, and Belgian creditors. In his five years of incumbency, however, Ross did much to restore Chile to a pay-as-you-go basis.

The general economic situation gradually forced the country into a strongly nationalistic policy. Unable to accept adequate imports, the country turned to domestic production. The renewal of gold washings, further issues of paper money, better crops and better prices in time relieved unemployment. Foreign trade increased; public works, especially in the capital and larger cities, helped to meet economic needs. In the midst of continued depression elsewhere, Chile developed a more adequate system of social and economic procedure. The Government encouraged a system of sanitation and public health that easily gave it leadership in Latin America.

The year 1936 marked the 400th anniversary of Diego de Almagro's discovery of Chile. It likewise reopened an era of political strife. Alessandri had attempted to administer affairs with a cabinet representing all the more conservative elements. The Radical Party which had supported him in 1932 found itself divided into rightist and leftist factions. The leftist bloc in Congress attempted to force the ministers of interior and of defence to resign in Feb. 1936, but only succeeded in obstructing the president's legislative program and in precipitating a general strike of railroad employees. This enabled the president to crush the opposition by suspending Congress, declaring martial law and arresting some 600 members of the opposition. When normal procedure was resumed, the president found himself confronted by a Popular Front, from which he tried to detach the Radicals by an offer of three cabinet posts, but they refused unless other leftist parties were also given recognition. This refusal, coupled with frays between Socialist and Nazi groups, with demands for the resignation of the minister of finance, led Alessandri later in the year to ask for dictatorial powers on the pretext of suppressing Communism. This enabled him to gain the congressional election of 1937 by a small majority. The Republican militia, a volunteer force of 50,000 that had supported the Alessandri government for four years, was formally dissolved in July 1936, but reappeared in October as Acción Nacional, definitely pledged to oppose both Communism and Naziism. To meet the demands of radical elements, the Government suggested laws calling for a living wage to workmen, low cost dwelling projects, public works, and adult education. A surplus from 1935 and 1936 enabled the Government to make payments on the foreign debt. Resources mounted, but not so fast as public expenditures or the living cost.

The congressional election of 1937 was but the preliminary

skirmish to the presidential election of 1938. The Radicals, holding the key to the situation, attempted to hold seats in the rightist cabinet and at the same time adhere to the leftist program. Minister Ross resigned his cabinet post in order to force them out of the ministry and to prepare for his own campaign as the Conservative candidate.

Alessandri perforce had to carry on with a cabinet wholly rightist, made up of Conservatives, Liberals and Democrats. As a precautionary measure, the government, on April 10, 1937, banned Nazi mass meetings or parades. Ex-President Ibáñez returned from exile and after some uncertain manoeuvres, became the candidate of the Nacista group. The leftists at first were inclined to support Col. Marmaduke Grove, a socialistic leader in the tempestuous days of 1932, but after bringing the middle-class Radicals into the Popular Front, accepted Pedro Aguirre Cerda, a capitalist and educational leader of moderate social views, as their candidate.

The election of 1938 was marked by bitter discussion, accompanied by resort to violence. Ross was charged with using his position as president of the Nitrate Sales corporation to close the plants and scatter the labourers so as to keep them from voting. A scene of disorder, marked by the wild pistol shot of a Nazi member, greeted President Alessandri when in May he delivered his last annual message before both houses of congress. The arrest and punishment of this member further alienated the leftist groups. Weeks later some young Nazis attempted to seize buildings near the presidential palace, but were quickly subdued with considerable loss of life. Their leader, Deputy J. González von Marées, received a 20-yr. prison sentence. (W. H. Hs.; I. J. C.)

Ibáñez was also arrested, but he was released just before the election and left Chile. Aguirre Cerda was elected by a margin of 4,111 out of 443,525 votes cast and was inaugurated on Dec. 24. The president's first official act was to pardon González von Marées, presumably for the support that the Nacista had thrown to the Popular Front ticket late in the campaign. Ibáñez returned to Santiago Dec. 31 and was welcomed by uniformed Nacista. In Aug. 1939 an unsuccessful coup was led by Gen. Ariosto Herrera and Ibáñez, who had been considered a government adherent.

The government's constructive program was soon seriously interrupted by the disastrous earthquake of Jan. 24, 1939, and by domestic political opposition. The greatest specific achievements were in improved housing.

Chile promptly declared its neutrality in World War II, and participated in the first inter-American foreign ministers' conference at Panamá in September and October 1939.

When President Aguirre Cerda became seriously ill in Nov. 1941, Jerónimo Méndez, little-known president of the Radical party, was named interior minister, and when Aguirre Cerda temporarily withdrew he became acting president. President Aguirre Cerda died Nov. 25, 1941.

In the Feb. 1942 presidential elections, Juan Antonio Ríos, Radical party candidate, won an easy victory; Ibáñez was second.

Ríos' Administration.—Ríos was inaugurated on April 1 for a six-year term. He did not immediately change the policy of neutrality, but congressional debates on it became intense. Socialists were especially active anti-noninterventionists. A great uproar followed the charge made by U.S. Undersecretary of State Sumner Welles on Oct. 8, 1942, that two Latin-American countries (unnamed but interpreted as Chile and Argentina) were used as bases of axis activities. The government began a campaign against axis spies, and broke with the axis powers on Jan. 20, 1943, leaving Argentina as the only American republic maintaining relations. Chile continued, however, to maintain friendly relations with Argentina, and on March 3, 1944, became the first government to recognize the revolutionary Argentine government headed by Gen. Edelmiro Farrell.

Debates in the congress in Feb. 1945 over Chile's war status led President Ríos to assert on Feb. 14 that Chile recognized a state of belligerency with Japan but not with Germany because "that nation is defeated." Ambassador Marcial Mora signed the United Nations pact for Chile at Washington, D.C., on Feb. 14. The senate and the chamber of deputies, on April 5 and 11, respectively, approved a declaration of war, and the president and his cabinet signed it April 11. Ill health forced Ríos to withdraw from active participation in the government on Jan. 17, 1946. In the election of Sept. 4, 1946, Gabriel González Videla won and congress accordingly confirmed his election.

González' government on Oct. 21, 1947, severed diplomatic relations with the Soviet Union, charging inspiration of communist unrest among the coal miners, and on June 22, 1948, a long-fought measure outlawing the Communist party became law.

Return of Ibáñez.—In Oct. 1952 Gen. Carlos Ibáñez del Campo, the former president whose administration had been based on virtually dictatorial powers, was named president by congress, since no candidate in the September election of that year had an absolute majority. Congress in Feb. 1953 voted the president extraordinary economic and administrative powers to facilitate his struggle against inflation and his program for reorganization of the government. Despite these measures, the first half of Ibáñez' six-year term was characterized by excessive ministerial instability and persistently rising inflation, the latter complicated by labour difficulties. Partially because of the narrow majority and the unpredictability of the administration's parliamentary support—the Agrarian Labor party was alone among the major groups backing the president—Ibáñez found it necessary to reorganize his cabinet no fewer than ten times before the end of 1955. On the labour front, martial law was declared in July 1955, when the country was virtually paralyzed by a transport and communication workers' strike. Inflation-inspired demands for wage increases ranging between 60% and 100% touched off a wave of strikes at its peak in August, with about 55,000 workers enforcing stoppages. Branding many of these as illegal, the government imprisoned about 1,000 strikers.

Bibliography.—The most complete general work is that of Diego Barros Arana, *Historia general de Chile* (16 vols., Santiago, 1884–1902), which covers the period up to 1830 and is virtually continued in his *Un decenio de la historia de Chile, 1841–51.* A convenient summary is to be found in Luis Galdames' *Estudio de la Historia de Chile* (8th ed., Santiago, 1937), (Eng. trans. in 1940 by I. J. Cox, Chapel Hill, N.C.). A. U. Hancock's *History of Chile* is an available English text; but H. C. Evans, Jr., in *Chile and its Relations with the United States* (Durham, N.C., 1927), summarizes clearly the major phases of the country's development during the colonial period, as does I. J. Cox in *Argentina, Brazil and Chile Since Independence,* (Washington, 1935) pp. 279–414.

M. L. Amunátegui contributes for the colonial period the *Descubrimiento y conquista de Chile* (Santiago, 1885) and *Los Precursores de la independencia de Chile* (1870) and numerous other studies. Agustín Edwards' *Peoples of Old,* (London, 1929) deals in popular fashion with the Indians. The standard work on the Indians is Ricardo E. Latcham, *La prehistoria Chilena,* (Santiago, 1928). Abbe Eyzaguirre's *Histoire du Chile* (Lille, 1855) deals with the Church during this period while Horacio Lara's *Cronica de la Araucania* is devoted to the Indians. Crescente Errázuriz, *Historia de Chile* (Santiago, 1911–12) treats of the conquest by Valdivia and the period immediately following. R. B. Cunningham Graham's *Pedro de Valdivia, Conqueror of Chile,* (London, 1926) is a scholarly narrative of the conquest. The monumental editorial works of José Toribio Medina, *Colección de documentos ineditos para la historia de Chile* (Santiago, 1888–1902), his *Cosas de la colonia* (Santiago, 1889), and his *Colección de historiadores i de documentos relativos a la independencia de Chile* (Santiago, 1900–14) form a veritable mine for research on the colonial and revolutionary periods. His *Historia de la Literatura Colonial de Chile,* i-iii (Santiago, 1878), reviews the cultural history of the period. His *Biblioteca hispano-americana, 1493–1810* (Santiago, 1898–1907) is a detailed bibliography in seven volumes. Alejandro Fuenzalida Grandón's *La Evolucion Social de Chile* is an important contribution to colonial social life, as is his *Lastarria i su Tiempo, (1817–1888),* (Santiago, 1911), to that of the 19th century. Ramón Briseño, *Memoria historico-critica del derecho publico chileno* (Santiago, 1849) is still the standard work on the early constitutions of Chile.

A. Chisholm, *The Independence of Chile,* reviews the struggle against Spain. John J. Mehegan, *O'Higgins of Chile,* (London, 1913), popularizes the life of that hero. A. Edwards' *Bosquejo historico de los partidos politicos chilenos* (Santiago, 1936) and his *La fronda aristocratica* (Santiago, 1928) review the struggle and subsequent national events. His *El Gobierno de Don Manuel Montt, 1851–1861,* (Santiago, 1932), gives the best treatment of that administration. L. Galdames presents a detailed study of certain phases of the period in *La evolución constitucional de Chile,* vol. i. (Santiago, 1926), and José Guillermo Guerra's *Constitucion de 1925* (Santiago, 1929) affords the best commentary on the present Constitution. The *Historia general de la republica de Chile* (Santiago, 1866–82) by B. Vicuña Mackenna and collaborators still has an important place for the revolutionary period. The same author's *Vida de O'Higgins* (Santiago, 1882) and his *Don Diego Portales* (Valparaiso, 1863) are useful supplemental works. Thomas Cochrane, Earl of Dundonald, *Narrative of Services, etc.* (London, 1859) treats of events during the War of Independence from the viewpoint of the outsider.

R. Sotomayor Valdés, *Historia de Chile, 1831–71* (Santiago, 1875) covers less than a decade of the period indicated. P. P. Figueroa, *Historia de la revolucion constituyente, 1857–59* (Santiago, 1895); F. Fonck, *Chile in der Gegenwart* (Berlin, 1870); Sir T. Holdich, *Countries of the King's Award* (London, 1904); I. Errázuriz, *Historia de la administración Errázuriz* (Santiago, 188?); Joaquím Nabuco, *Balmaceda* (Santiago, 1914); Barros Arana, *La Guerra del Pacifico* (Santiago, 188?), F. Velasco, *Memorias sobre la revolucion de 1891* (Santiago, 1926), C. Walker Martínez, *La Administracion de Santa María* (Santiago, 1888–89), are works devoted to individuals and men of importance in the national period. W. J. Dennis in *Tacna and Arica* (New Haven, 1931), summarizes the nitrate war of 1879. Ricardo Salas Edwards, *Balmaceda y el parlamentarismo en Chile* (Santiago, 1925) is the latest review of that epoch. A. Roldán, *El desarrollo constitucional de Chile* (Santiago, 1925) is the best text for the legal background. Alberto Cabero, *Chile y los Chilenos* (Santiago, 1926), combines social, political, industrial features of Chilean life. A. Coester in *Literary History of Spanish America* (2nd ed., New York, 1928) has an interesting chapter on Chile. G. F. Scott Elliot, *Chile* (London, 1907) and L. E. Elliot, (New York, 1922) and Fred H. Carlson, *Geography of Latin-America,* ch. v. (New York, 1936) are suggestive descriptive works. Occasional articles in *Revista Chilena de historia y geografia* (Santiago, 1911 *et seq.*) and in *Chile* (New York, 1926–31) have historical notes. Carlos Keller R., *Sinopsis Geográfico-Estadistica de la Republica de Chile* (Santiago, 1933) presents a summary of all public activities. *See* also G. J. Butland, *Chile: an Outline of Its Geography, Economics and Politics,* rev. ed. (London, New York, 1953); P. T. Ellsworth, *Chile, an Economy in Transition* (New York, 1945); L. J. Hughlett (ed.), *Industrialization in Latin America* (New York, 1946; London, 1947); J. R. Stevenson, *The Chilean Popular Front* (Philadelphia, London, 1942); G. Wythe, *Industry in Latin America* (New York, 1945; London, 1946).

(W. H. Hs.; I. J. C.; G. I. B.)

CHILEAN CIVIL WAR (1891). The Chilean civil war grew out of political dissensions between the president of Chile, J. M. Balmaceda, and his congress (*see* CHILE: *History*), and began in Jan. 1891. On the 6th, at Valparaiso, the political leaders of the Congressional Party went on board the ironclad "Blanco Encalada," and Capt. Jorge Montt of that vessel hoisted a broad pennant as commodore of the Congressional fleet. Preparations had long been made for the naval *pronunciamiento,* and in the end but few vessels of the Chilean navy adhered to the cause of the "dictator" Balmaceda. But amongst these were two new and fast torpedo gunboats, "Almirante Condell" and "Almirante Lynch," and in European dockyards (incomplete) lay the most powerful vessel of the navy, the "Arturo Prat" and two fast cruisers. If these were secured by the Balmacedists the naval supremacy of the congress would be seriously challenged. The rank and file of the army remained faithful to the executive, and thus in the early part of the war the "Gobernistas," speaking broadly, possessed an army without a fleet, the congress a fleet without an army. Balmaceda hoped to create a navy; the congress took steps to recruit an army by taking its sympathizers on board the fleet. The first shot was fired, on Jan. 16, by the "Blanco" at the Valparaiso batteries, and landing parties from the warships engaged small parties of Government troops at various places during January and February. The dictator's principal forces were stationed in and about Iquique, Coquimbo, Valparaiso, Santiago and Concepción. The troops at Iquique and Coquimbo were necessarily isolated from the rest and from each other, and military operations began, as in the campaign of 1879 in this quarter, with a naval descent upon Pisagua followed by an advance inland to Dolores. The Congressional forces failed at first to make good their footing (Jan. 16–23), but, though defeated in two or three actions, they brought off many recruits and a quantity of munitions of war. On the 26th they retook Pisagua, and on Feb. 15, the Balmacedist commander, Eulogio Robles, who offered battle in the expectation of receiving reinforcements from Tacna, was completely defeated on the old battle-field of San Francisco. Robles fell back along the railway, called up troops from Iquique, and beat the invaders at Haura on the 17th, but Iquique in the meanwhile fell to the Congressional fleet on the 16th. The Pisagua line of operations was at once abandoned, and the military forces of the congress were moved by sea to Iquique, whence, under the command of Col. Estanislao Del Canto, they started inland. The battle of Pozo Almonte, fought on March 7, was desperately contested, but Del Canto was superior in number, and Robles was himself killed and his army dispersed. After this the other Balmacedist troops in the north gave up the struggle. Some were driven into Peru, others into Bolivia, and one column made a laborious retreat from Calama to Santiago, in the course of which it twice crossed the main chain of the Andes.

The Congressional *Junta de Gobierno* now established in Iquique prosecuted the war vigorously, and by the end of April the whole country, from the Peruvian border to the outposts of the Balmacedists at Coquimbo and La Serena, was in the hands of the "rebels." The *Junta* now began the formation of a properly organized army for the next campaign, which, it was believed universally on both sides, would be directed against Coquimbo. But in a few months the arrival of the new ships from Europe would reopen the struggle for command of the sea. The Congressional Party could no longer aim at a methodical conquest of successive provinces, but was compelled to attempt to crush the dictator at a blow. Where this blow was to fall was not decided up to the last moment, but the instrument which was to deliver it was prepared with all the care possible under the circumstances. Del Canto was made commander-in-chief, and an ex-Prussian officer, Emil Körner, chief of staff. Balmaceda could only wait upon events, but he prepared his forces as best he was able, and his *torpederas* constantly harried the Congressional navy. By the end of July Del Canto and Körner had done their work as well as time permitted, and early in August the troops prepared to embark, not for Coquimbo, but for Valparaiso itself.

The expedition by sea was admirably managed, and Quinteros, north of Valparaiso and not many miles out of range of its batteries was occupied on Aug. 20, 1891. Balmaceda was surprised, but acted promptly. The first battle was fought on the Aconcagua at Concón on the 21st. The eager infantry of the Congressional army forced the passage of the river and stormed the heights held by the Gobernistas. The killed and wounded of the Balmacedists numbered 1,600, and nearly all the prisoners, about 1,500 men, enrolled themselves in the rebel army, which thus more than made good its loss of 1,000 killed and wounded. The victors pressed on towards Valparaiso, but were soon brought up by the strong fortified position of the Balmacedist Gen. Barbosa at Viña del Mar, whither Balmaceda hurried up all available troops from Valparaiso and Santiago, and even from Concepción. Del Canto and Körner now resolved on a daring step. Supplies of all kinds were brought up from Quinteros to the front, and on Aug. 24, the army abandoned its line of communications and marched inland. The flank march was conducted with great skill, little opposition was encountered, and the rebels finally appeared to the south-east of Valparaiso. Here, on the 28th, took place the decisive battle of La Placilla. The splendid fighting qualities of the Congressional troops and the superior generalship of their leaders prevailed in the end over every obstacle. The Government army was practically annihilated. Valparaiso was occupied the same evening and Santiago soon afterwards. There was no further fighting, for so great was the effect of the battles of Concón and La Placilla that even the Coquimbo troops surrendered without firing a shot.

BIBLIOGRAPHY.—Lieut. Sears and Ensign Wells, U.S.N., *The Chilean Revolution of 1891* (Office of Naval Intelligence, Washington, 1893); *The Capture of Valparaiso, 1891* (Intelligence Department, War Office, London, 1892); H. Kunz, *Taktische Beispiele aus den Kriegen der neuesten Zeit; der Bürgerkrieg in Chile* (1901); *Revista Militar de Chile* (Feb.–March 1892); Sir W. Laird Clowes, *Four Modern Naval Campaigns* (1902); M. H. Hervey, *Dark Days in Chile; an Account of the Revolution of 1891* (1892); F. Velasco, *La Revolución de 1891* (1914); and C. Mondiola Gana, *Páginas de la Guerra Civil de 1891* (1915).

CHILE-PERUVIAN WAR (1879–82). The proximate cause of this war was the seizure, by the authorities of Bolivia, of the effects of the Chilean Nitrate Company at Antofagasta, then part of the Bolivian Province of Atacama. The first act of hostility was the despatch of 500 soldiers to protect Chilean interests at Antofagasta. This force, under Col. Sotomayor, landed and marched inland; the only resistance encountered was at Calama on the river Loa, where a handful of newly raised militia was routed (March 23, 1879). About the same time Chilean warships occupied Cobija and Tocopilla, and Sotomayor, after his victory at Calama, marched to the latter port. Bolivia had declared war on March 1, but Peru not till April 5: this delay gave the Chileans time to occupy every port on the Bolivian coast. Thus the Chilean admiral was able to proceed at once to the blockade of the southern ports of Peru, and in particular Iquique, where there took place the first naval action of the war. On May 21, the Chilean sloop "Esmeralda" and the gunboat "Covadonga"—both small and weak ships—engaged the Peruvian heavy ironclads "Huascar" and "Independencia." After a hot fight the "Huascar" sank the "Esmeralda," but Carlos Condell in the "Covadonga" manoeuvred the "Independencia" aground and shelled her into a complete wreck. The Chileans now gave up the blockade and concentrated all their efforts on the destruction of the "Huascar," while the allies organized a field army in the neighbourhood of Tacna and a large Chilean force assembled at Antofagasta.

On Oct. 8, 1879, the "Huascar" was brought to action off Angamos by the "Blanco Encalada," and the "Almirante Cochrane." Although hopelessly outmatched the "Huascar" made a brave fight. When she finally surrendered she had but one gun left in action, her fourth commander and three-quarters of her crew were killed and wounded, and the steering-gear had been shot away. The Peruvian navy had now ceased to exist. The Chileans resumed the blockade, and more active operations were soon undertaken. The whole force of the allies was about 20,000 men, scattered along the seaboard of Peru. The Chileans on the other hand had a striking force of 16,000 men in the neighbourhood of Antofagasta, and of this nearly half was embarked for Pisagua on Oct. 26. The expeditionary force landed, in the face of considerable opposition, on Nov. 2, and captured Pisagua. From Pisagua the Peruvians and Bolivians fell back along the railway to their reinforcements, and when some 10,000 men had been collected they moved forward to attack the Chilean position of San Francisco near Dolores station (Nov. 19). In the end the Chileans were victorious, but their only material gain was the possession of Iquique and the retreat of the allies, who fell back inland towards Tarapacá. The tardy pursuit of the Chileans ended in the battle of Tarapacá on the 27th, in which more men were killed than were wounded, the Chileans suffering a complete defeat. For some inexplicable reason the allies made no use of their victory, continued to retreat and left the Chileans in complete possession of the Tarapacá region. With this the campaign of 1879 ended. Chile had taken possession of the Bolivian seaboard and of the Peruvian province of Tarapacá, and had destroyed the hostile navy.

The objective of the Chileans in the second campaign was the Province of Tacna and the field force of the allies at Tacna and Arica. The invasion was again carried out by sea, and 12,000 Chileans were landed at Pacocha (Ylo), far to the north of Arica. Careful preparations were made for a desert march, and on March 12, 1880, the advanced corps started inland for Moquegua, which was occupied on the 20th. Near Moquegua the Peruvians, some 2,000 strong, took up an unusually strong position in the defile of Cuesta de los Angeles. But the great numerical superiority of the assailants enabled them to turn the flanks and press the front of the Peruvian position, and after a severe struggle the defence collapsed (March 22). In April the army began its advance southward from Moquegua to Tacna. Arica was also watched, and the blockade was extended north of Lima. The land campaign had in the meanwhile culminated in the battle of Tacna (May 26), in which the Chileans attacked at first in several disconnected bodies, and suffered severely until all their forces came on the field. Then a combined advance carried all before it. The allies engaged under Gen. Narciso Campero, the new president of Bolivia, lost nearly 3,000 men, and the Chileans, commanded by Manuel Baquedano, lost 2,000 out of 8,500 on the field. The defeated army was completely dissolved, and it only remained for the Chileans to march on Arica from the land side. The navy co-operated with its long-range guns, on June 7 a general assault was made, and before nightfall the whole of the defences were in the hands of the Chileans. Their second campaign had given them entire possession of another strip of Peru (from Pisagua to Ylo), and they had shown themselves greatly superior, both in courage and leadership, to their opponents.

The Chilean army was reorganized during the summer, and prepared for its next operation, this time against Lima itself. Gen. Baquedano was in command. The leading troops disembarked at Pisco on Nov. 18, 1880, and the whole army was ready to move against the defences of Lima six weeks later. These defences consisted of two distinct positions, Chorrillos and Miraflores, the latter being about 4,000 yd. outside Lima. The first line of defence was attacked by Baquedano on Jan. 13, 1881. The defenders had 22,000 men in the lines, the Chileans engaged about 24,000. The battle of Chorrillos ended in the complete defeat of the Peruvians, less than a quarter of whose army rallied behind the Miraflores defences. Two days later took place the battle of Miraflores. Here the defences were very strong and the action began with a daring counter-attack by some Peruvians. Neither party had intended to fight a battle, for negotiations were in progress, but the action quickly became general. Its result was, as before, the complete dissolution of the defending army. Lima, incapable of defence, was occupied by the invaders on the 17th, and on the 18th Callao surrendered. The resistance of the Peruvians was so far broken that Chile left only a small army of occupation to deal with the remnants of their army. The last engagement took place at Caxacamara in Sept. 1882, when the Peruvians won an unimportant success.

BIBLIOGRAPHY.—T. B. M. Mason, *The War on the Pacific Coast, 1879–1881* (U.S. Office of Naval Intelligence, 1883); Capt. Châteauminois (trans.), *Mémoire du Ministre de la Guerre du Chili sur la guerre Chilo-Peruviénne* (1882); Barros Arana, *Hist. de la guerre du Pacifique* (1884); Sir W. Laird Clowes, *Four Modern Naval Campaigns* (1902); R. Markham, *The War between Peru and Chile* (1883); Pascual Ahumada y Moreno, *Guerra del Pacífico, Recopilación Completa de Todos los Documentos Oficiales, Correspondencia, etc.* (1884–89); I. Santa María, *Guerra del Pacífico* (1919); C. V. C. Varigny, *La Guerra del Pacífico* (1922); Gonzalo Bulnes, *Chile and Peru; the Causes of the War of 1879* (1920).

CHILI or CHILE, the pods of several kinds of peppers, notably the capsicum, used as a condiment. A dish of meat and beans, called chili con carne, highly flavoured with chili, is popular in the United States; it is generally, though erroneously, believed to have originated in Mexico. In tropical countries chilies are used in many ways to flavour foods.

CHILIA (KILIYA), a town formerly in Bessarabia, Rum., in the department of Ismail, on the Chilia branch of the Danube. Pop. (1930) 17,049. Anciently known as Chilia, Chele or Lycostomium, it was a place of banishment for Byzantine political dignitaries in the 12th–13th centuries, a Genoese trading settlement 1381–1403, then Walachian, Moldavian and Hungarian. It was taken by Turkey in 1484, by Russia in 1812 and by Rumania in 1918. Ceded with Bessarabia to the U.S.S.R. in June 1940, it was regained by Rumania during the axis attack on the U.S.S.R. in 1941. In 1947 it was returned to the Izmail oblast, Ukrainian S.S.R. The official name is Kiliya.

CHILIASM, the belief that Christ will return to reign for a thousand years (from Gr. χιλιασμός, χίλιοι, a thousand), the doctrine of the Millennium (*q.v.*).

CHILLÁN, a city and the capital of the province of Ñuble, in the southern part of central Chile, 246 mi. by rail south-southwest of Santiago and about 56 mi. direct (108 by rail) northeast of Concepción. Pop. (1952) 52,576. Chillán is one of the most active commercial cities of central Chile, and is surrounded by a rich agricultural and grazing country. Chillán was founded by Ruíz de Gamboa in 1580. Its present site was chosen in 1836. The original site, known as Chillán Viejo, was the birthplace of the liberator, Bernardo O'Higgins. Chillán was severely damaged by an earthquake in 1939. The hot sulphur springs of Chillán, known since 1660, are about 45 mi. east-southeast. They issue from the flanks of the Volcán Viejo, about 7,000 ft. above sea level. The highest temperature of the water issuing from these springs is a little over 135°. The principal volcanoes of the Chillán group are the Nevado (9,528 ft.) and the Viejo. After a two-century repose, Nevado de Chillán erupted violently in 1861 and 1864 and slightly in later years.

CHILL HARDENING, the process of hardening the surface of a metal by rapidly cooling it while it is molten or at a very high temperature. Usually the chilling is done by plunging the object in a bath of water or oil. In the case of railway and other wagon and car wheels, a "chill mould" is used, consisting of a sand mould with the outer part (which forms the rim) made of cast iron. When the wheel is cast, the rim cools very rapidly because the iron part of the mould absorbs and conducts away the heat from it, and the consequent chilling hardens the rim. Chill hardening is sometimes combined with case hardening. (*See* FOUNDING; CASE HARDENING; IRON AND STEEL.)

CHILLIANWALLA, a village of British India in the Punjab, situated on the left bank of the river Jhelum, about 85 mi. N.W. of Lahore. It is memorable as the scene of a battle on Jan. 13, 1849, between a British force commanded by Lord Gough and the Sikh army under Sher Singh. The loss of the Sikhs was estimated at 4,000, while that of the British in killed and wounded amounted to 2,800, of whom nearly 1,000 were Europeans and 89 were British and 43 native officers. An obelisk erected at Chillianwalla by the British government preserves the names of those who fell. (*See* SIKH WARS.)

CHILLICOTHE, a city of northern Missouri, U.S., on the Grand river, 80 mi. N.E. of Kansas City; the county seat of Livingston county. It is on federal highways 36 and 65 and is served by the Burlington, the Chicago, Milwaukee, St. Paul and Pacific, and the Wabash railways and by bus lines; it has a municipal airport. Pop. (1950) 8,649. Coal and limestone abound in the vicinity, and much livestock is raised. The city has various manufacturing industries, and is one of the principal assembling points for dairy products in the state. The state industrial school for girls and a business college are there.

Chillicothe was settled about 1830. The town was laid out in 1837 on land granted by the federal government, and the city was incorporated in 1855. A famous tavern of the '50s, kept by "Uncle Johnny" Graves, is now a beautiful private residence. A tablet on the county courthouse commemorates the death, in 1868, of Nelson Kneass, composer of the music for "Ben Bolt," who drifted there with a travelling theatrical troupe.

CHILLICOTHE, a city of Ohio, U.S., on the Scioto river, 50 mi. S. of Columbus; the county seat of Ross county. It is on federal highways 23, 35 and 50, and is served by the Baltimore and Ohio and the Norfolk and Western railways. Pop. (1950) 20,121. It is the trade centre of a rich agricultural region. The city has railway repair shops, paper mills, a shoe manufacturing industry and an aluminum fabricating industry. There are ancient mounds (Mound City Group National monument) 4 mi. north. Chillicothe was founded in 1796. On the Camp Sherman site of 1914–18 are a veterans' hospital and a federal reformatory. Chillicothe was the capital of the Northwest territory in 1800–03, and the capital of Ohio in 1803–10 and 1812–16.

CHILLINGWORTH, WILLIAM (1602–1644), English divine, was born at Oxford in Oct. 1602. He was persuaded by a Jesuit to embrace Catholicism and went to study at the Jesuit college at Douai. After a short stay, however, he left Douai in 1631 and returned to Oxford. On grounds of Scripture and reason he at length declared for Protestantism but declined a preferment offered to him in 1635. His principal work was *The Religion of Protestants a Safe Way to Salvation* (1637).

CHILLIWACK, an incorporated city of British Columbia, Can., on the Fraser river, 70 mi. E. of Vancouver. Pop. (1951) 5,663. It is on the trans-Canada highway, is served by the Canadian National railways and is connected by ferry with Harrison Mills on the Canadian Pacific line. Sawmilling and timber manufactures, canning, mineral water and dairy produce works are of importance. The fertile district east and west of the city, incorporated as the municipality of Chilliwack (pop., 1951, 13,677), is devoted chiefly to hop culture, dairy farming and small fruit growing, and has been extended by the drainage of Sumas lake (30,000 ac.).

CHILOÉ, a province of southern Chile, and also the name of a large island off the Chilean coast forming part of the province. The province (area 9,052 sq.mi., pop., 1951, 95,893) is composed of numerous islands and a section of the mainland which border on the gulfs of Ancud and Corcovado. The mainland portion of the province is extremely rugged and is virtually uninhabited, such colonies, towns and Indian settlements as there are being principally on the island of Chiloé. The island, which is some 90 mi. long by 35 mi. wide, lies within the temperate rainforest belt of South Chile. where frosts are rare, summers are cool, and rainfall is abundant throughout the year. Both the coast range of western Chiloé and the rolling plains of the east are heavily forested with large evergreens (mostly broad-leaved) such as *alerce, roble, ciprés,* cinnamon trees and filberts. For four centuries these dense forests, which are too wet to be burned, have provided an effective barrier to the majority of white settlers who have tried to clear the land for cultivation and pasturage. Logging operations have never been developed on an extensive commercial scale, and most of the timber that is cut is consumed locally. Ancud, the capital of the province (pop. 4,327 in 1940), is situated at the N. end of the island on the sheltered bay of San Carlos. Castro, the oldest and only other sizable town in the province (pop. 4,786 in 1940), is on the eastern shore of the island, 55 mi. S.E. of Ancud by rail.

CHILON, of Sparta, son of Damagetus, one of the Seven Sages of Greece, flourished about the beginning of the 6th century B.C. In 560 (or 556) he acted as ephor, an office which he is even said to have founded. According to Chilon, the great virtue of man was prudence, or well-grounded judgment as to future events.

A collection of the sayings attributed to him will be found in F. W. Mullach, *Fragmenta Philosophorum Graecorum,* i; *see* Herodotus, i, 69; Diogenes Laertius i, 68; Pausanias iii, 16, x, 24.

CHILPERIC, the name of two Merovingian Frankish kings.

CHILPERIC I (d. 584) was one of the sons of Clotaire I. On his father's death in 561, fearing that, as he was illegitimate, his brothers would deprive him of his share of the patrimony, he seized the royal treasure at Berny and entered Paris, prepared to bargain. The resulting division of the patrimony gave Chilperic the old Salian territories of the modern Picardy, Flanders and Hainaut; this included Soissons. When Charibert died in 567, Chilperic's share of his property included lands and cities in the west and in Aquitaine. Distrust of his brothers, fear for his insecure eastern frontier and the perpetual need of land and treasure for his followers caused Chilperic to attack Sigebert's town of Reims. There followed a series of campaigns in which Reims and Soissons were the key points. Sigebert's marriage to the Visigothic princess Brunhilda (Brunechildis), daughter of King Athanagild, seemed to endanger Chilperic's possessions in Aquitaine; so Chilperic put away his wife and married Galswintha, Athanagild's elder daughter. This prudent step angered his followers, who hated the Arian Visigoths. Galswintha was shortly murdered, to be replaced by Chilperic's former mistress, Fredegond (*q.v.*). This lady was Gregory of Tours's pet aversion, but Chilperic's subjects seemed to prefer her to her predecessor. The consequent vendetta with Sigebert and Brunhilda, in which Guntram of Burgundy acted occasionally as arbitrator, lasted, almost without pause, for 40 years and was castigated by Gregory of Tours as *bella civilia.* After Sigebert's murder in 575, Chilperic became effectively master of the *regnum Francorum.* The Visigothic king Leovigild sought the hand of his daughter Rigunthis for his heir Reccared. Chilperic was assassinated near Chelles in 584.

Chilperic was naturally ferocious and appeared to Gregory of Tours as the Nero and the Herod of his time. But he was the ablest and most interesting of the grandsons of Clovis. As a bastard he had to fight for his existence; yet, a builder of circuses, he seems to have had ideas about a king's duties that were Roman or Byzantine rather than Germanic. His fiscal measures were vigorous and provoked the hatred of the church (which suffered from them). His court circle had something more than pretensions to culture; it appreciated poetry and even theological discussion. Chilperic held his own views on the doctrine of the Trinity and revised the Latin alphabet to suit his tastes. It is a pity that our sources allow us to get no nearer to the motives of his wild, unhappy career.

CHILPERIC II (d. 720), son of Childeric II, was already middle-aged when, in 715, he was taken from a monastery to become king of Neustria, his name being changed from Daniel. He appears to have been the tool of Ragenfrid, his mayor of the palace; and after Ragenfrid's defeat by Charles Martel and the Austrasians, Chilperic fell into the hands of Odo of Aquitaine, who, himself defeated, surrendered him to Charles. On the death of Clotaire IV of Austrasia in 719, Chilperic became king over the whole *regnum Francorum.* Charters were issued in his name, and from these the abbey of St. Denis was a notable beneficiary.

(J. M. W–H.)

CHILTERN HILLS, a range of chalk hills in England extending from southwest to northeast through parts of Oxfordshire, Buckinghamshire, Hertfordshire and Bedfordshire. Considerable areas are cared for by the National trust. The Chilterns form a well-marked escarpment facing northwestward, with a long south-eastern slope, and run from the Thames in the neighbourhood of Goring to the headwaters of its tributary the Lea between Dunstable and Hitchin, the crest line between these two points being about 55 mi. These hills are part of a larger chalk system, continuing the line of the White Horse hills from Berkshire, and themselves continued eastward by the East Anglian ridge, a series which represents the edge of the chalk rising from beneath the Eocene deposits of the London basin. The greatest elevation in the Chilterns is between Watlington and Tring, where they reach 800–900 ft. Toward the Thames gap to the west the elevation falls away only a little, but eastward the East Anglian ridge seldom exceeds 500 ft. Several passes through the Chilterns are used by roads and railways converging on London. The hills were formerly covered with beech, which is still the characteristic growth and the main raw material of the chair and furniture manufactures of High Wycombe.

CHILTERN HUNDREDS. An old principle of English parliamentary law declared that a member of the house of commons, once duly chosen, could not *resign* his seat. This rule was a relic of the days when the local gentry had to be compelled to serve in parliament. The only method, therefore, of avoiding the rule came to be by accepting an office of profit from the crown, a statute of 1707 enacting that every member accepting an office of profit from the crown should thereby vacate his seat, but should be capable of re-election, unless the office in question had been created since 1705, or had been otherwise declared to disqualify for a seat in parliament. Before this time the only course open to a member desiring to resign was to petition the house for its leave, but except in cases of incurable ill-health, the house always refused it. Among the posts of profit held by members of the house of commons in the first half of the 18th century are to be found the names of several crown stewardships, which apparently were not regarded as places of profit under the crown within the meaning of the act of 1707, for no seats were vacated by appointment to them. The first instance of the acceptance of such a stewardship vacating a seat was in 1740, when the house decided that Sir W. W. Wynn, on inheriting from his father, in virtue of a royal grant, the stewardship of the lordship and manor of Bromfield and Yale, and *ipso facto* vacated his seat. On the passing of the Place act of 1742, the idea of utilizing the appointment to certain crown stewardships (possibly suggested by Sir W. W. Wynn's case) as a pretext for enabling a member to resign his seat was carried into practice. These nominal stewardships were eight in number, but only two survived to be used in this way in contemporary practice—those of the Chilterns and Northstead; and when a member wishes to vacate his seat, he is accordingly spoken of as taking the Chiltern Hundreds. The Chiltern Hundreds formed a bailiwick of the ordinary type. They are situated on the Chiltern hills, Buckinghamshire. The appointment of steward was first used for parliamentary purposes in 1750, the appointment being made by the chancellor of the exchequer (and at his discretion to grant or not), and the warrant bestowing on the holder "all wages, fees, allowances and other privileges and pre-eminences." Up to the 19th century there was a nominal salary of 20s. attached to the post. It was laid down in 1846 by the chancellor of the exchequer that the Chilterns could not be granted to more than one person in the same day, but this rule has not been strictly adhered to, for on four occasions subsequent to 1850 the Chilterns were granted twice on the same day. The Chilterns might be granted to members whether they had taken the oath or not, or during a recess, though in this case a new writ could not be issued until the house met again. Each new warrant expressly revoked the grant to the last holder, the new steward retaining it in his turn until another should be appointed.

See parliamentary paper—*Report from the Select Committee on House of Commons (Vacating of Seats)* (1894).

CHILWA (incorrectly SHIRWA), 15° 15′ S., 35° 40′ E.; a shallow lake of brackish water in the Nyasaland Protectorate abutting on Mozambique. Its area varies with the rainfall, but never exceeds 100 sq.mi. Formerly, at a period of higher level, it appears to have drained northward to the Lujenda branch of the Rovuma. There are four islands, one rising 500 ft. above the water level. The lake was discovered by Livingstone in 1859.

CHIMAERA. A term applied botanically to certain types of plants formerly regarded as "graft hybrids." The term graft hybrid suggests a plant produced by the fusion of vegetative cells derived respectively from two plants grafted together. That hybrid plants do in fact originate in such a way is, however, regarded by most botanists as problematical. It is true that plants composite in nature and having some of the characteristics of the two plants employed may result from an operation of grafting, but these are usually interpreted as arising in an entirely different way without the fusion of cells that would justify the appellation of hybrid. The term graft hybrid has been replaced in general by "plant chimaera" or simply "chimaera," since, like the mythological monster so-called, plant chimaeras are composite in nature and origin.

Many of these plants have been long known in gardens, being grown as curiosities rather than for their decorative value. The earliest to be described in scientific literature was the Bizzaria orange which appeared in a garden in Florence in 1644, arising as an adventitious bud from the region where a scion of sour orange (*Citrus aurantium*) had been grafted on a stock of citron (*Citrus medica*). Others are the so-called *Crataego-mespilus* forms, arising in a similar way following the grafting of medlar (*Mespilus germanica*) on hawthorn (*Crataegus monogyna*); the *Pyro-cydonias* from the grafting of pear (*Pyrus communis*) on quince (*Cydonia vulgaris*); and, best known of all, *Cytisus adami* (or *Laburnum adami*) from the grafting of the small purple-flowered broom (*Cytisus purpureus*) on the common laburnum (*Laburnum vulgare*). In all these instances the history of origin is the same; the plants at present in existence have been derived by vegetative propagation from an adventitious shoot that arose at the junction of scion and stock.

While all the examples mentioned above originated as the result of a horticultural operation, their production was unintentional. Knowledge of the subject passed into a new phase with Hans Winkler's experiments in 1907 deliberately designed to produce graft hybrids. In these experiments black nightshade (*Solanum nigrum*) was grafted on tomato (*Solanum lycopersicum*). After the graft had taken, a transverse cut was made through it at the junction of the stems. From the exposed surface numerous buds developed which grew into new shoots, all of which were shoots either of nightshade or of tomato except one; this, arising at the junction of the two tissues, had the characters of nightshade on one side and tomato on the other. Winkler called this shoot a *chimaera,* since it was partly of one species and partly of another. In the following two years large-scale experiments were carried out resulting in the production of many thousands of shoots from decapitated grafts. Most of these were either pure nightshade or pure tomato, some were chimaeras of the kind already described, but in addition there were a few shoots showing characters intermediate between scion and stock. These differed among themselves as to the extent to which they resembled scion or stock and Winkler gave them special names, believing them to be true graft hybrids.

Fig. 1.—Stages in the production of a chimaeral branch; Winkler's method. Dotted line indicates position of cut. n, nightshade; t, tomato; sc, sectorial chimaera

In 1909 Erwin Baur published observations on variegated plants, in particular the garden geranium (*Pelargonium zonale*).

In such plants branches sometimes occur in which one side is green and the other colourless, corresponding structurally to the tomato-nightshade branch to which Winkler first applied the term chimaera. In the present instance the distribution of the two kinds of tissue constituting the branch is dramatically obvious owing to the difference in colour. Such a branch, called by Baur a *sectorial chimaera,* when cut through transversely usually presents an appearance as shown at A in fig. 2. The nature of any lateral shoot arising from it depends on the place of origin; shoots arising at b and d will be pure green and pure white respectively, while one arising at c will possess a sectorial structure like the parent branch. If a shoot arises as at d where, as often occurs, a superficial strip of one component overlaps the other, a *periclinal chimaera* will result—an arrangement in which a "core" of green tissue is invested by a "skin" of colourless tissue, one, two, or more cell layers thick, depending on the thickness of the overlap; or vice versa. If the bud arises at the extreme edge of the overlap, the superficial "skin" may occupy only part of the surface of the shoot, a condition described as mericlinal. Thus, a branch having a sectorial structure gives rise during growth, not only to occasional sectorial branches like itself, but to branches that are pure for either component, periclinal, or mericlinal. In contrast to this instability, a branch that has once acquired a periclinal pattern shows very great stability of structure during growth, producing lateral branches that are all periclinal chimaeras like the parent branch.

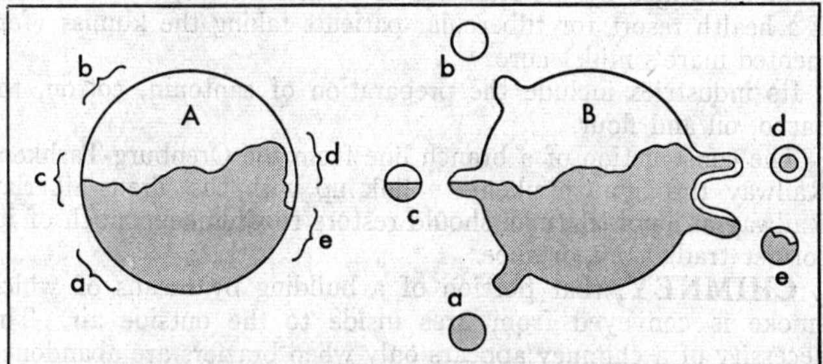

Fig. 2.—A. Diagram of a cross section of the stem of a sectorial chimaera consisting of green and colourless tissue; the line of junction between the two tissues is often very irregular
B. Illustrating how there may arise from such a stem pure green (a), pure white (b), sectorial (c), periclinal (d), or mericlinal (e), branches, depending on the position of lateral bud formation

Baur's experience with these chimaeras of *Pelargonium* composed of green and colourless tissue led him to suggest that Winkler's so-called graft hybrids between nightshade and tomato were in reality periclinal chimaeras, and he provided cogent evidence that two of the plants to which Winkler had given special names were built up of a core of tomato with a skin of nightshade one and two cell layers thick respectively, and two of the others of a core of nightshade with skins of tomato one and two cell layers thick. After some hesitation Winkler fully concurred with Baur's interpretation. (A fifth form obtained by Winkler unfortunately died before it could be fully investigated.)

Attention was then turned to *Cytisus adami* and the other long-known "graft hybrids." The general consensus of opinion in 1944 was that these also are periclinal chimaeras: *Cytisus adami,* for example, consisting of a core of laburnum invested with a one-layered skin of *Cytisus purpureus,* the *Crataego-mespili* having a core of hawthorn covered with skins of medlar differing in thickness in the different forms, and so on.

Owing to the fact that in flowering plants the reproductive cells arise from the layer second from the surface at the growing point, seedlings from periclinal chimaeras are all pure core if the skin is but one cell layer thick, and all pure skin tissue if the skin consists of more than one layer; they are never periclinal chimaeras like the parent plant. Also, while stem branches or stem cuttings reproduce the periclinal condition, root cuttings yield invariably plants of core tissue only owing to the endogenous manner in which lateral roots are formed.

Apart from being an occasional product of grafting, chimaeras also arise in nature, most frequently, no doubt, as the result of a sudden mutation in some cell or cells of a growing region. The new kind of tissue may be conspicuously different from the old as when it is colourless instead of being green, but far more commonly the difference is evident only on special investigation as when the number of chromosomes is altered. Thus, chimaeras are of far greater frequency than the readily recognizable examples met with might suggest. In contrast to the graft-hybrid interpretation which predicates a blending of the two components, the chimaera hypothesis regards the components as maintaining their identity, but arranged in a definite pattern at the growing point; the manner in which vegetative growth occurs in flowering plants is responsible for the way this pattern is transferred from the growing point to the mature tissues. The whole behaviour of these plants in reproduction and vegetative growth, as well as the nature and arrangement of their mature tissues accords well with the supposition that they are chimaeras. The alternative graft-hybrid hypothesis cannot be said to be theoretically impossible, but it may be regarded as improbable in view of what is known of plant behaviour and as lacking positive support from indubitable evidence. Nevertheless it still has its supporters, few though they may be, as exemplified by Trofim Lysenko and his followers, representing one Russian school of thought.

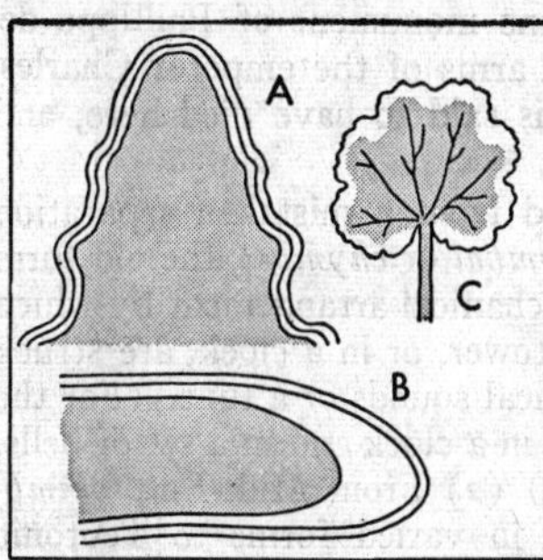

Fig. 3.—A. Longitudinal section through the growing point of a periclinal chimaera in which the cells of the central core possess potentially green plastids while in the two outer cell layers the plastids lack the capacity to become green
B. Transverse section near the edge of a leaf derived from such a growing point. Owing to the whole of the marginal tissue, apart from the epidermis, being derived from the second layer of the growing point, the leaf has a white margin
C. Superficial appearance of a leaf from such a periclinal chimaera. The central part of the leaf, as well as the stem, appears green since the green core tissue shows through the two enveloping layers of colourless cells

While in no sense conclusive, it is at least significant that variegated foliage as described above for *Pelargonium zonale* is commonly met with in flowering plants of all kinds, but never occurs in groups such as the ferns with a single-celled growing point. This is what would be expected if such variegation is correctly interpreted as a consequence of the possession of a growing point having a chimaeral structure, for which a multicellular growing point is a necessity.

Bibliography.—R. J. Chittenden's article "Vegetative Segregation," *Bibliographia Genetica* (1927); and F. E. Weiss's review in *Biological Reviews* (1930) give detailed accounts in English of many aspects of chimaeras; Krenke's volume, translated from Russian into German under the title *Wundkompensation, Transplantation und Chimaeren bei Pflanzen* (1933) gives a later and more general discussion of the subject. All three are provided with full bibliographies. *Plant Chimaeras and Graft Hybrids,* by W. Neilson-Jones (1934) will be found to provide a general treatment of all aspects of the subject up to that date within a relatively small compass. Later experimental work, which is not extensive, must be sought in scientific journals.

(W. N. J.)

CHIMAERA. In Greek mythology a chimaera was a fire-breathing female monster resembling a lion in the fore part, a goat in the middle, and a dragon behind (*Iliad,* vi, 179). She devastated Caria and Lycia until finally she was slain by Bellerophon (*q.v.*). In art the Chimaera is usually represented as a lion, with a goat's head in the middle of the back, as in the bronze Chimaera of Arezzo (5th century). The word is now used generally to denote a fantastic idea or fiction of the imagination.

Chimaera, or *chimère,* in architecture, is a term loosely used for any grotesque, fantastic or imaginary beast used in decoration.

CHIMAY, a town in the extreme southeast of the province of Hainaut, Belgium, dating from the 7th century. Pop. (1939) 3,250. Owing to its proximity to the French frontier it has undergone many sieges, the last of which was in 1640, when Turenne reduced it to ruins. The town is chiefly famous for the castle and park that bear its name. Originally a stronghold of the Cröy family, it has passed through the D'Arenbergs to its present owners, the princes of Caraman-Chimay. The castle, which in

1640 possessed seven towers, has now only one, which is in ruins; a château was built in the Tudor style in the 18th century. This domain carried with it the right to one of the twelve peerages of Hainaut. The church contains a fine monument of Phillippe de Cröy, chamberlain and comrade in arms of the emperor Charles V. Jean Froissart, the chronicler, is said to have died here, and has a statue in the square.

CHIME. (1) Probably derived from a mistaken separation into two words, *chimbe bell,* of *chymbal* or *chymbel,* the old form of "cymbal," Lat. *cymbalum.* A mechanical arrangement by which a set of bells in a church or other tower, or in a clock, are struck so as to produce a sequence of musical sounds or a tune. (For the mechanism of such an arrangement in a clock and in a set of bells, *see* the articles CLOCKS and BELL.) (2) From Mid. Eng. *chimb,* a word meaning "edge," common in varied forms to Teutonic languages, *cf.* Ger. *Kimme,* the bevelled rim formed by the projecting staves at the ends of a cask.

CHIME-BELLS, a mediaeval instrument consisting of a set of small bells of varying pitch which were arranged in a frame and struck with a hammer after the manner of a glockenspiel. They ranged in number from four or five up to as many as 14 or 15. The chime-bells were known also under the Latin name of *cymbalum.*

CHIMERE, in modern English use the name of a garment worn as part of the ceremonial dress of Anglican bishops. It is a long sleeveless gown of silk or satin, open down the front, gathered in at the back between the shoulders, and with slits for the arms. It is worn over the rochet, and its colour is either black or scarlet (convocation robes). The origin of the chimere has been the subject of much debate; but it is practically proved to be derived from the mediaeval tabard, an upper garment worn in civil life by all classes of people both in England and abroad. It has therefore a common origin with certain academic robes (*see* ROBES: *Academic Costume*). The word "chimere," which first appears in England in the 14th century, is of uncertain origin. It occurs in different forms in various languages (Lat. *chimera,* Fr. *simarre,* Ital. *zimarra*) and may possibly be derived from the Greek χειμέριος, "wintry." This derivation is made plausible by the original character of the chimere; for the word properly applies to the sleeveless tabard which tended to supersede, from the 15th century onwards, the inconvenient *cappa clausa* (a long closed cloak with a slit in front for the arms) as the out-of-doors upper garment of bishops. The chimere was, moreover, a cold weather garment. In summer its place was taken by the tippet. In the Anglican form for the consecration of bishops the newly consecrated prelate, hitherto vested in rochet, is directed to put on "the rest of the episcopal habit," *i.e.* the chimere. The robe has thus become in the Church of England symbolical of the episcopal office, and is in effect a liturgical vestment. The civil quality of the garment still survives; the full dress of an Anglican prelate at civil functions of importance (*e.g.* in parliament, or at court) is still rochet and chimere. The continental equivalent of the chimere is the *zimarra* or *simarre,* which is defined by foreign ecclesiologists as a kind of *soutane* (cassock), from which it is distinguished by having a small cape and short, open arms (*manches-fausses*) reaching to the middle of the upper arm and decorated with buttons. In France and Germany it is fitted more or less to the figure; in Italy it is wider and falls down straight in front. Like the *soutane,* the *zimarra* is not proper to any particular rank of clergy, but for bishops and prelates it is ornamented with red buttons and bindings. It is worn by university professors. A black *zimarra* lined with white, and sometimes ornamented with a white binding and gold tassels, is worn by the pope.

BIBLIOGRAPHY.—*See* the *Report* of the sub-committee of Convocation on the ornaments of the church and its ministers, p. 31 (London, 1908); the Rev. N. F. Robinson, "The black chimere of Anglican Prelates: a plea for its retention and proper use," in *Transactions of the St. Paul's Ecclesiological Soc.* vol. iv. pp. 181–220 (London, 1898); Herbert Druitt, *Costume on Brasses* (London, 1906); G. Moroni, *Dizionario dell' erudizione storico-ecclesiastica* (Venice, 1861), vol. 103, *s.v.* "Zimarra"; X. Barbier de Montault, *Traité pratique de la construction, etc., des églises,* ii. 538 (Paris, 1878).

CHIMKENT, a town in the Syr Daria province of the Kazak (Kirghiz) A.S.S.R. of the R.S.F.S.R., Lat. 42° 20′ N., Long. 69° 40′ E. Pop. (1939) 74,185, mostly Sarts. It lies in a fertile valley between the Alexander range and the Ala-tau, and is the centre of a grain, fruit growing and cattle rearing district, watered by streams from the Ala-tau. Above the town are the ruins of its citadel, stormed by the Russians in 1864. Its clear, dry air makes it a health resort for tubercular patients taking the kumiss (fermented mare's milk) cure.

Its industries include the preparation of santonin, cotton, tobacco, oil and flour.

The construction of a branch line from the Orenburg-Tashkent Railway through Chimkent to link up with the Trans-Siberian Railway at Semipalatinak should restore to Chimkent much of its former trading importance.

CHIMNEY, that portion of a building by means of which smoke is conveyed from fires inside to the outside air. The necessity of a chimney appears only when braziers are abandoned in favour of large fireplaces. Thus in northern Europe in the 12th century the primitive hole in the roof yielded to a hollow flue leading from a fireplace by the wall to the outside; but a specific architectural form of flue was not developed until the 15th century. The 13th and 14th century type was a simple, round, vertical conduit of stone, with a conical cap and openings at the sides under the cone. A remarkable example occurs in the monastic kitchen of the Abbey of Fontevrault, France, dating from the end of the 12th century. In the early 15th century the re-duplication of fireplaces led to the grouping of several flues inside a vertical, and generally rectangular, mass of masonry, which was carried well above the roof, and occasionally decorated. In France, in the latter half of the century, this decoration was of great richness, consisting of late Gothic pinnacles and niches, and in the châteaux of the Francis I. period, chimneys vied with dormers in their lavish detail. Heraldic ornaments, pilasters and entablatures abound. In England, decorative effect was obtained by grouping the flue tops as independent features, usually in brick, above a stone base; each flue was then treated as a separate shaft with base and cap, polygonal or twisted; *e.g.,* Compton Wynyates and Hampton Court palace. In the early Renaissance, the flues were sometimes treated like little classic columns, as at Burleigh House. With the development of classicism, the chimney became simple

A. FRENCH RENAISSANCE CHIMNEY (FRANCIS I. PERIOD), CHÂTEAU OF BLOIS; B. ENGLISH TUDOR, FROM COVENTRY; C. AMERICAN COLONIAL, WARRIER HOUSE, PORTSMOUTH, N.H. (EARLY 18TH CENTURY)

again, a mere rectangular mass of masonry. In colonial work in America, the chimney is either a large square mass in the centre of the roof or else developed as an important feature of the end gable walls. In the Italian Renaissance the chimney is merely utilitarian and, whenever possible, is hidden. (T. F. H.)

CHIMNEY AND FIREPLACE CONSTRUCTION

Correct chimney construction is absolutely essential to economical home heating. The ideal and most efficient chimney is vertical, with round flue and smooth interior surfaces (fig. 1). All chimneys should be built with "fire-clay" flue linings (not "flue-tile," "terra-cotta" or "clay" flue lining). Faulty chimney construction practically always shows its shortcomings by its effect upon some other feature of the plant. A lighted paper thrust in the bottom and sucked up and consumed with a roar is often erroneously taken to indicate a good draught. Chimney draught can be known definitely only by measurement with the proper instrument, a draught gage. Chimney height and temperature inside and outside the chimney determine intensity of draught in a correctly built chimney.

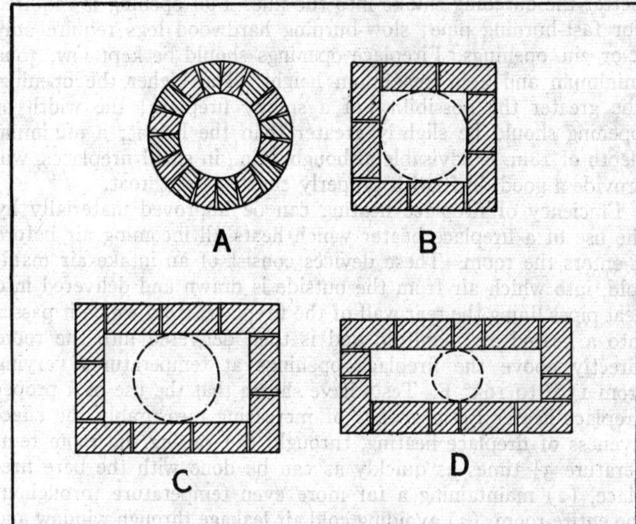

FIG. 1.—EXAMPLES OF CHIMNEY CONSTRUCTION. A. ROUND FLUE; B. SQUARE FLUE; C. OBLONG FLUE; ELONGATED OBLONG FLUE. TYPE A IS THE BEST, TYPE B, SECOND BEST, TYPE C, NEXT PREFERABLE, TYPE D, POOR CONSTRUCTION

Factors that contribute to faulty chimneys are: (1) Insufficient height to assure proper draught and avoid interfering air currents (fig. 2); the top of a chimney should extend at least 3ft. above flat roofs and at least 2ft. above the ridge of peaked roofs; extensions, if used, should be fitted with air-tight joints; (2) omission of flue-lining to ensure continued tightness, so that heat and weathering cause mortar gradually to disintegrate and result in a leaky chimney (fig. 2); (3) offsets and bends are likely to reduce the chimney free area and present difficulties in construction that militate against tightness and inside smoothness; loose bricks and mortar may fall and lodge in such a way as to cause objectionable restricted areas and provide lodgement for dangerous soot accumulations (fig. 2); (4) careless and improper installation of the smoke pipe into the chimney (fig. 3); (5) openings into a chimney for other than the smoke pipe of the boiler; such should never be permitted, they are apt to check and interfere with the draught; (6) lack of a tightly-fitting cover for the clean-out door; (7) failure to support the chimney properly; it should never be based on timber construction and when resting upon the ground sufficient masonry foundation should be provided to prevent settling; (8) improper laying of brick; it should never be laid on edge, should be properly bonded and sufficient mortar used between the bricks to fill all voids. Size and height of chimneys depend upon the total heat demands of the structure to be served, the type and number of boilers and the fuel to be used. Reputable manufacturers specify draught requirements for their respective equipment and state the required flue areas, sizes and heights of chimneys; these should be observed. Irrespective of fuel used, the minimum effective area[1] inside the flue lining for any installation should be not less than 70 sq.in. and the short cross-sectional dimension should be never less than six-tenths of the greater dimension. The minimum chimney height above the grate should be 35ft. if erratic draughts are to be avoided.

A chimney that is not tight will fail to draw properly. Force or direction of wind, the amount of moisture in the air or the quality of the fuel may aggravate the trouble. A smoke test will prove leaks and every flue should be tested before a boiler is connected thereto, by building a paper, straw, wood or tar-paper fire at the base of the flue. When the smoke is passing in dense volume if the stack be tightly blocked by laying a wet blanket over it, the leakage will be immediately evident by the appearance of smoke at the opening, or from an adjoining flue indicating leakage between the flue joints.

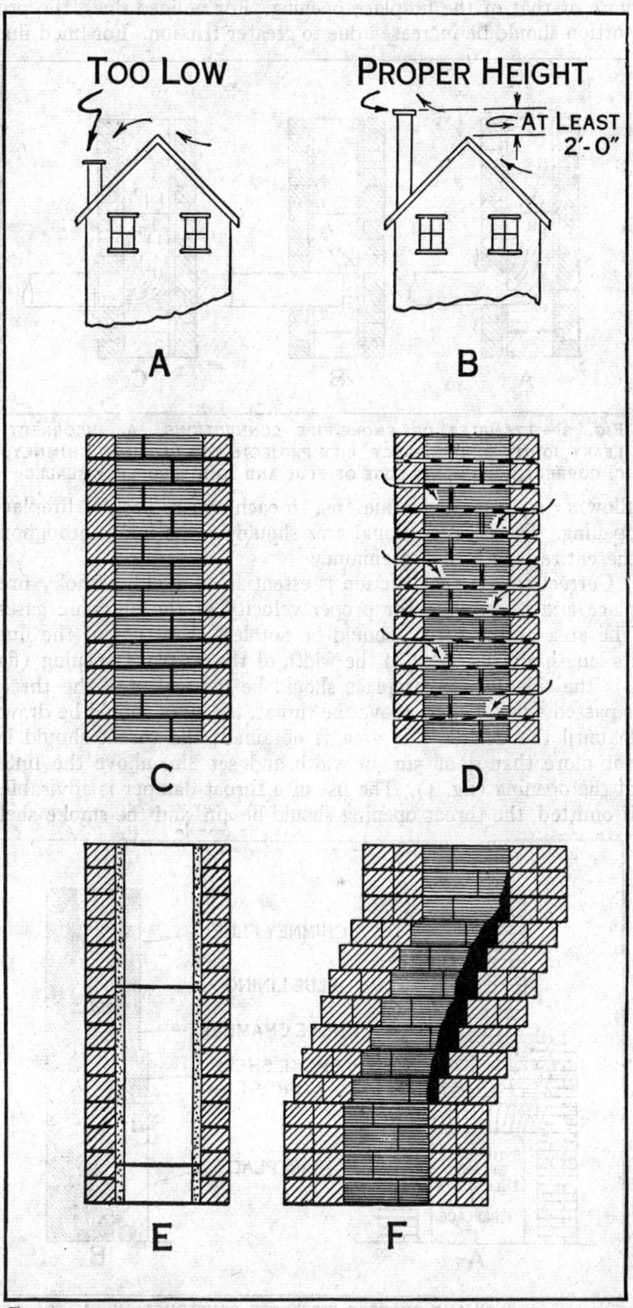

FIG. 2.—EXAMPLES OF CHIMNEY CONSTRUCTION. A. TOP TOO LOW, EDDY CURRENTS CAUSE DOWN DRAFT; B. TOP CARRIED PROPER HEIGHT; C. UNLINED FLUE BEFORE USE; D. UNLINED FLUE, LEAKS CAUSED BY HOT GASES AND WEATHERING; E. LINED FLUE, A PREVENTION AGAINST LEAKS; F. OFFSETS TO BE AVOIDED

If a leakage is not obviously evident, further inspection by means of a mirror held at the proper angle at the base of a straight flue should be made for minor obstructions such as broken tile, mortar accumulations, birds' nests, partly burned paper, soot or tarry deposits; or removal may be accomplished by passing up and down the flue a weighted bag of hay or straw attached to the end of two ropes.

[1]Effective area of a flue, broadly speaking, is the theoretical cross-sectional area occupied by the column of smoke and gases rising with spiral motion up the flue.

Fireplaces.—A satisfactory open fireplace requires: (1) a flue of proper area, (2) fireplace throat correctly proportioned and located, (3) a correctly built smoke shelf and chamber, (4) sufficient chimney height, (5) a shape for radiating maximum heat into the room. The area of a lined flue should equal one-tenth or more of that of the fireplace opening. For unlined flues, the proportion should be increased due to greater friction. For lined flue, allow 13 sq.in. of clear flue area to each square foot of fireplace opening. The cross-sectional area should be the same throughout the entire length of the chimney.

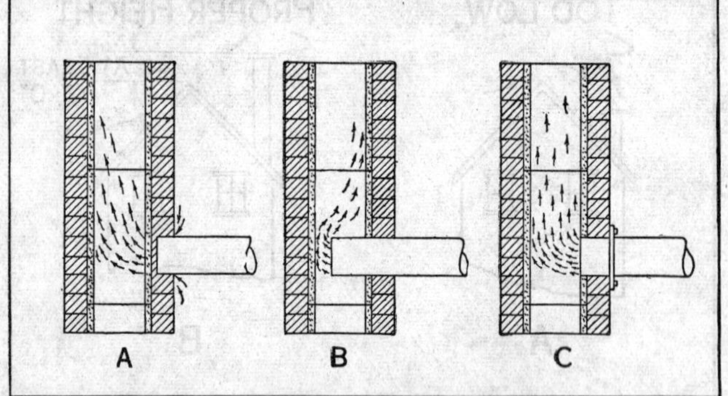

FIG. 3.—EXAMPLES OF SMOKE-PIPE CONNECTIONS. A. INCORRECT, LEAKY JOINT; B. INCORRECT, PIPE PROJECTS TOO FAR INTO CHIMNEY; C. CORRECT, PIPE MEETS EDGE OF FLUE AND JOINT PROPERLY SEALED

Correct throat construction is essential, to avoid a smoky fireplace and to provide for proper velocity of the outgoing gases. The area of the throat should be not less than that of the flue, its length always equal to the width of the fireplace opening (fig. 4); the sides of the fireplace should be vertical until the throat is passed (fig. 4); and above the throat, the sides should be drawn in until the desired flue area is obtained; the throat should be not more than 4 or 5in. in width and set 8in. above the lintel of the opening (fig. 4). The use of a throat damper is advisable; if omitted, the throat opening should be 4in. and the smoke shelf always included. A smoke shelf and chamber are absolutely essential. The shelf is formed by setting back the brick work at the top of the throat to the line of the flue wall, making the shelf equal in length to that of the throat. No shelf should be less than 4in. and may vary from this to 12in. or more, depending on depth of fireplace; the level of the shelf should be 8in. above the fireplace opening (fig. 4). The smoke chamber acts as a reservoir to hold accumulated smoke temporarily when a gust of wind across the chimney top momentarily dampers the chimney, as well as to lessen the down draft and prevent smoke being forced into the room. All smoke chamber walls should be smooth inside. The back of a fireplace should pitch forward from a point a little less than half-way from the hearth to the top of the opening and the sides should be beveled, as straight back and sides do not radiate heat as well.

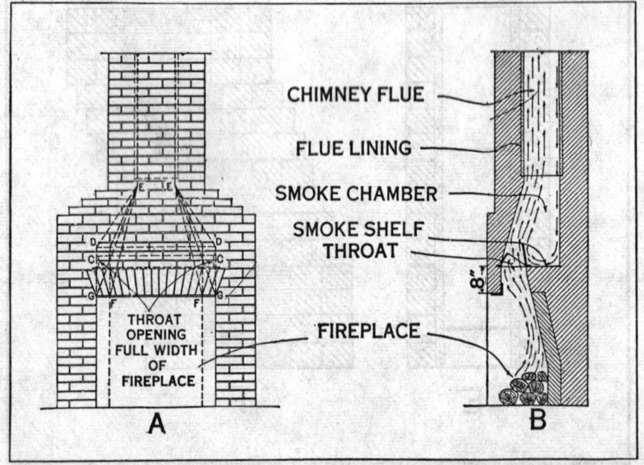

FIG. 4.—FAULTY AND CORRECT FIREPLACE CONSTRUCTION. A. TOP OF THROAT DAMPER IS AT DD, SMOKE SHELF AT CC. SIDE WALL SHOULD NOT BE DRAWN IN UNTIL THE HEIGHT DD IS PASSED. IF DRAWN IN AS INDICATED BY EF AND EG, THE WIDTH OF THROAT BECOMES LESS THAN THE WIDTH OF THE OPENING AND CAUSES THE AIR CURRENTS TO PILE UP RESULTING IN A SMOKY FIREPLACE. B, CORRECT FIREPLACE CONSTRUCTION

The use of a throat damper affords means for regulating a fire. The type with lid hinged at rear, rather than in the centre, directs better the outgoing smoke into the flue. Full opening is required for fast-burning pine; slow-burning hardwood logs require only 1 or 2in. openings. Fireplace openings should be kept low, 30in. minimum and 42in. maximum height. The higher the opening, the greater the possibility of a smoky fireplace; the width of opening should be slightly greater than the height; a minimum depth of 18in. is advisable although 12in., in small fireplaces, will provide a good draft with properly constructed throat.

Efficiency of fireplace heating can be improved materially by the use of a fireplace heater which heats all incoming air before it enters the room. These devices consist of an intake air manifold, into which air from the outside is drawn and delivered into heat pipes lining the rear wall of the fireplace, from which it passes into a heated air manifold and is then delivered into the room directly above the fireplace openings at temperatures varying from 135° to 195° F. Tests have shown that the use of a proper fireplace heater is the means of increasing measurably the effectiveness of fireplace heating, through, (1) raising the room temperature 3¼ times as quickly as can be done with the bare fireplace, (2) maintaining a far more even temperature throughout the entire room, (3) avoiding cold air leakage through window and door cracks and (4) by producing a greater heating effect with less fuel than when no heater is used. (A. M. D.)

See J. J. Norman, *Design of a Brick Chimney* (1913); J. G Mingle, *Draft and Capacity of Chimneys* (1925); A. Custodis, *Radical Brick Chimneys* (1924).

CHIMNEY-PIECE, in architecture, originally a hood, projecting from the wall over a grate, built to catch the smoke and lead it up to the chimney flue; later, any decorative development of the same type or for the same purpose; a mantel or mantelpiece. Like the chimney (*q.v.*), the chimney-piece is essentially a northern mediaeval development. Its earliest form, a simple hood, sometimes with shafts below, at the wall, is shown in the king's house at Southampton and at Rochester castle, England (12th century). Later, the spaces under the ends of the hood were made solid, so that the fireplace became a rectangular opening, and in some cases the fireplace was recessed into the wall. Late mediaeval fireplaces are of great size and richness, *e.g.* the triple fireplace in the great hall of the Palais des Comtes at Poitiers, and the earlier fireplaces in the château of Blois.

During the Renaissance fireplace openings were decorated with columns, pilasters and entablatures, and occasionally the front of the wall or hood above the overmantel was enriched. North Italian palaces are full of examples of great delicacy. In France the fireplaces at Blois and Chambord are famous. In England, the same formula appears in naïve and complex types, with the usual Elizabethan and Jacobean *mélange* of misunderstood classic and Flemish motives—strap work, gaines, etc. In France, after a brief classicism under Henry II. and Henry IV., the chimney-piece became a centre of fantastic design. Although the opening was usually small, the decoration was rich, and commonly characterized by the use of a great mirror as an overmantel. The detail assumed the classic extravagance of the Louis XIV. style, the swelling curves and bulbous shells of the Louis XV. and the distinguished restraint of the Louis XVI. styles, but almost always retained the same general proportions and the mirror. German design largely followed that of France; chimney-pieces are less numerous there, however, owing to the use of porcelain stoves.

In England the Renaissance chimney-piece was at first treated, with simple architraves, frieze and cornice, in such a way as to serve as mantel shelf, occasionally with rich panelling above, and much breaking or keying of the mouldings. Later, consoles, caryatides and columns were used, although occasionally a simple moulding of sweeping profile replaced the architrave, and the shelf was omitted. In the last half of the 18th century the char-

FRENCH GOTHIC 15TH CENTURY
(IN CLUNY MUSEUM, PARIS)

AMERICAN COLONIAL 1762
POWELL HOUSE, PHILADELPHIA

ENGLISH JACOBEAN, 17TH CENTURY
STOKESAY CASTLE, ENGLAND

MODERN ENGLISH
(STUDIO OF F. R. WALKER)

MODERN ENGLISH CHIMNEY PIECE BY COURTESY OF "THE AMERICAN ARCHITECT"

CHIMNEY-PIECES FROM THE 15TH TO THE 20TH CENTURIES

The early fireplaces of the Gothic period were enormous in order to permit the burning of large logs, but the manner in which they smoked led to a continued decrease in size, which reached a climax in modern English chimney-pieces designed for burning coal. The projection of the chimney breast has always been realized as a decorative opportunity and was developed in nearly all the Renaissance styles

acteristic English chimney pieces, in the style of Robert Adam, owed much to Louis XVI influence. In American colonial work there is an almost exact following of English precedent, and occasional examples can be traced to definite plates in English architectural books.

CHIMPANZEE, the popular name of one of the African anthropoid apes (*Pan troglodytes*), characterized by being smaller than the gorilla (*q.v.*). It has very large, outstanding ears and its abundant hair is black in colour. Frequently the area around the mouth is white. Males are only slightly larger than females; they weigh about 120 lb. and standing erect may be about 4½ ft. in height. The chimpanzee is found from French Guinea to western Uganda and Belgian Congo. A pygmy species (*Pan paniscus*) occurs on the south side of the Congo river, but the various forms farther north, although they show great variation, are probably only races of the common species. The nomenclature of the chimpanzee is greatly complicated, partly because of confusion with the orangutan by early writers. *Anthropopithecus, Troglodytes* and *Simia* are frequently used as generic names, although the last has been ruled invalid for any animal.

Chimpanzees are forest animals living in small family groups—an adult male, one or several females, infants and several partly grown young. It takes 9 to 12 years for them to reach maturity. The territory of such a band is about ten miles square. These apes spend most of their time in the trees, where they construct crude sleeping platforms high above the ground. On the ground chimpanzees walk on all fours, using the knuckles of the hands. The skin shows friction ridges and is horny, like that of the palm. They occasionally stand upright, but rarely walk in this position unless trained. Chimpanzees have a sense of rhythm, shown by a kind of dance, and they drum on trees or the ground, producing a primitive music. Their food includes many fruits, shoots of certain plants, occasionally varied by insects and birds' eggs. They raid cultivated fields of cane, pineapple, cacao or bananas.

The popular interest in this ape lies in its resemblance to man. Physiologically and anatomically it is more like man than like the tailed monkeys. Its intelligence is also manlike, as has been amply shown by experiments and studies by psychologists Wolfgang Köhler, Robert M. Yerkes and others. The lack of capacity for speech seems absolutely to preclude the attainment of a culture or social inheritance. (*See* PRIMATES.)

See R. M. Yerkes, *Almost Human* (New York, 1925); R. M. Yerkes and A. Yerkes, *The Great Apes* (New Haven, Oxford, 1929); W. Köhler, *The Mentality of Apes* (New York, 1926). (J. E. HL.)

CHIN, a Burmese term for a hillman applied in particular to branches of the Kuki (*q.v.*) race, inhabiting the hills along the west bank of the Chindwin river south of Manipur.

CHINA, a vast country of eastern Asia, bordering the U.S.S.R. and the Mongolian People's Republic for more than 6,000 mi. on the north and west; it is flanked by Korea on the northeast; the Yellow sea, East China sea and South China sea on the east; Indochina and Burma on the south; and the Karakoram and Himalaya ranges on the southwest. Including Manchuria, Sinkiang and Tibet on the mainland and Formosa (Taiwan) and numerous smaller islands, China has a total area of approximately 3,876,956 sq.mi. with a population of about 475,000,000 (1950 official est.). After the victory of the Chinese Communists and the flight of the Nationalist government to Formosa (Dec. 8, 1949), China was virtually divided into two entities: Communist China on the mainland and the Nationalist government on Formosa.

The Central People's (Communist) government in Peking, which was formally inaugurated in Oct. 1949, was founded on the principles of Marx, Lenin and Stalin and of Mao Tse-tung's New Democracy. (The Chinese Communist party was founded in Peking in 1921.) The Nationalist government in Taipei, Formosa, was based on Sun Yat-sen's Three Principles of the People and the five-power constitutional system. Its official name is Chung-Hua Min-Kuo; *i.e.*, Republic of China.

Following are the main sections of the article:

INTRODUCTION

Agricultural China.—Less than half of China's total area is essentially Chinese. The country's civilization has always rested upon agriculture, and Chinese culture has extended as a dominant institution only into those areas where cultivation is possible. The majority of political China is either too dry, too hilly or too cold for farming; these vast spaces, while relatively empty and hence relatively easily incorporated into the Chinese polity, are inhabited for the most part by non-Chinese people whose cultures and economies are markedly distinct from the human patterns of agricultural China.

"China proper," as this agricultural area is often called, consists of 18 provinces, bounded by the sea to the east, the mountains to the south and west and the desert to the north. The Great Wall, completed, from earlier walls, as a continuous unit by the emperor Ch'in Shih Huang Ti in the 3rd century B.C., still serves to mark a line between farming and grazing along the desert border of agricultural China in the north and northwest. Not all of the area of the 18 provinces is arable, however, and in fact mountains, hills and climate, especially in the west and south, combine to keep almost three quarters of it out of cultivation. In many of the areas—for example, the southwest—the population is still largely non-Chinese. Agriculture also increasingly spread out beyond the limits of China proper after the middle of the 19th century as population pressure mounted. Southern Manchuria and the moister parts of Inner Mongolia have in particular been largely occupied by Chinese farmers. But the 18 provinces of China proper do contain the bulk of the agricultural land, the great majority of the Chinese people and the roots and body of Chinese civilization.

Manchuria was sparsely settled before 1900. Chinese political claims to it were weak but were made effective by the mass immigration of farmers. Southern Manchuria has rich resources of broad, level land, coal, iron, timber and water power, which were largely developed by the Japanese during their period of control from 1931 to 1946. Under Chinese Communist control after 1947, the original three provinces of Heilungkiang, Kirin and Liaoning were redivided into nine administrative units. Manchuria's current distinction from China lies to a considerable degree in the commercialized and industrialized nature of its economy, a reflection of accessible resources and of heavy Japanese and Russian investment in railways and manufacturing between 1890 and 1946.

Mongolia is a vast steppe bordering on the desert of central Asia. The moister southern sections, designated as Inner Mongolia (or the Chinese provinces of Ningsia, Suiyuan, Chahar and Jehol—not part of the 18 provinces), have especially since the end of the 19th century been infiltrated by Chinese farmers and drawn more firmly under Chinese political control. The remaining drier sections, known as Outer Mongolia and sparsely though almost exclusively occupied by Mongols, are oriented to the Soviet Union. Outer Mongolia's independent status as the Mongolian People's Republic was recognized by both the Nationalist and Communist governments of China in agreements with the Soviet Union.

Sinkiang is the westernmost extension of political China, a desert corridor between the two arms of the mountain mass of central Asia, the Tien Shan and Kuen-Lun (Kunlun) ranges. Its earlier name of Eastern or Chinese Turkistan reveals its non-Chinese culture, as well as the reason for the repeated assertion of Chinese control: it is the traditional overland connection with the west. Most of Sinkiang's people belong culturally to the Turkish group, and life centres in the scattered string of oases from east to west along the base of the mountain escarpment. These oases, following both the northern and southern margins of the desert basin, nourished the old silk route from China to Europe and the middle east. At Kashgar and Yarkand passes lead out of the desert basin and across the Pamirs into Russian Turkistan and Afghanistan. Another route westward runs north of the basin through the oases of Hami and Urumchi into the steppe of Dzungaria, which is also included in the province of Sinkiang. Chinese authority in Sinkiang tended to be increasingly nominal after 1900, and Russian influence grew. The Chinese Communist government established its control in Sinkiang in late 1949.

Tibet, like Mongolia, has two parts, though it is less usable from a human point of view. The terms "hither" and "farther" Tibet record this division, the first referring to the borderland areas in the east fronting on agricultural China and low enough or with a series of narrow river valleys to permit farming. About 80% of Tibet's cultivated area and the majority of its population are there. Most of hither Tibet is included in the Chinese provinces of Sikang and Chinghai (or Koko-nor) (not part of the 18 provinces), reflecting not only the penetration of agriculture but the need for a buffer against nomadic raids from farther Tibet. Most of farther Tibet is too high, rugged and cold for agriculture. It is extremely thinly occupied by a non-Chinese population whose support comes largely from nomadism based on the yak, from the raising of barley in a few favoured places, and from the trade routes connecting India, China and central Asia which pass through the country, with their most notable focus at Lhasa, the capital. Chinese sovereignty over all of Tibet has usually accompanied the rise of a strong dynasty in China. As central authority in China weakened during the 19th century the theocratic government at Lhasa became increasingly independent. Though Great Britain and Russia recognized China's suzerainty by treaty in 1907, Tibet remained very loosely attached until the Chinese Communist government carried out a military occupation as far as Lhasa in 1951 and obtained an agreement conferring on Peking all control of foreign affairs, currency and defense.

The interaction between agricultural China and the outer areas of political China is in part a measure of their differences, but equally of the attractive power, wealth and prestige of Chinese civilization. Despite the distinctions outlined above, "greater China" is a living entity, with a degree of unity which belies its regional distinctiveness.

China Proper.—It is neither practicable nor useful to generalize in physical detail about an area as diverse as China. The outer areas, for all their community with China proper, must be treated separately. Even within the 18 provinces, an area which reaches across 20° of latitude and 28° of longitude, there is great physical variation. "China" as used hereinafter refers exclusively to China proper.

THE LAND

Rivers and Their Basins.—Physiographically, China proper is centred on three great river systems, each rising in the high escarpment of the west and running fortunately across the greatest extent of the country from west to east, so that they complement the north-south sea route. Roughly the northern quarter is drained by the Hwang-ho (Yellow river), the middle half by the Yangtze river and the southern quarter by the Si Kiang (West river). Of these the Yangtze is by far the most important, since the varied waterways of its basin (exclusive of the almost myriad canals in the delta area) are navigable by steamships or junks or both for about 20,000 mi. Approximately half of China's people live in the Yangtze basin, and it includes the richer and more productive half of the country. The usefulness of the Yangtze itself is greatly implemented by the fact that it receives a series of navigable tributaries from both north and south, each draining its own productive area. (Alternate north and south tributaries also join with the relatively even moist climate of central China to maintain navigability and to lessen the danger of floods.) These include, in ascending order, the Kan, from the south, with its mouth at Kiukiang; the Han, from the north, with its mouth at Hankow; the Siang, from the south, with its mouth in Tungting lake, draining into the Yangtze; and the Kialing, from the north, with its mouth at Chungking. As a result, much of the trade of both north and south China (as well as nearly all the trade of central China) drains via the Yangtze, which is itself navigable for ocean-going ships as far upstream as Hankow, 630 mi. from the sea.

The Hwang is a typical arid-climate river, running as it does through dry northwest China, north in a great loop into the Ordos desert of Inner Mongolia, and finally down across the semiarid north China plain. It is characterized by a high silt content, by violent seasonal fluctuations in volume and by recurrent and disastrous changes of course. It is thus almost useless for navigation, although small native craft use it along scattered stretches in Honan and between Paotou and Lanchow-fu (Lanchou) farther west. The river's most dramatic effect on the land is its frequent floods, hence the epithet "China's sorrow." Silting of the bed increased as cultivation of the hillsides in the Hwang watershed spread during the historical period; natural and artificial levees along much of the river's lower course have prevented the regular release of silt, and thus the bed lies in many places above the level of the surrounding plain.

The inevitable break-through of pent-up floodwaters may be permanent, in the form of a new course, but even on a smaller scale the destruction and loss of life are great. However, silt deposition from the Hwang and its tributaries over the north China plain has helped to make this the most fertile major agricultural area in China. The Hwang's course has seldom been constant for more than 100 years during the historical period, and changes have taken it both north and south of the Shantung peninsula. The Si Kiang or West river is a lesser stream than the Yangtze or the Hwang, and its watershed is restricted by the high relief characteristic of south China. It is navigable by steam launches for about 250 mi. from its mouth near Canton, but it lacks major navigable tributaries on the scale of the Yangtze, and its basin is far less productive. Nevertheless, as the largest river in south China, which also contains south China's largest lowland area, it is the most obvious core of this extensive region.

Rivers are important in China not only as physiographic classifiers but for two more pragmatic and particular reasons. First, in this largely preindustrial economy and except for the arid north, rivers are the cheapest and almost the only practicable means of transport for many bulk goods moving beyond local markets. Railway development was still in its infancy in the 1950s, largely restricted to a few major trunk routes, and in any case still too expensive to compete effectively with water transport. Second, China, aside from the north, is not on the whole an area of naturally fertile soils, and high relief further limits agriculture. But in the river valleys fertile alluvial soil and level land are available, plus water for irrigation, which is even more important in the north than in the south. As a result of these two sets of factors, China's population is markedly concentrated along its rivers and reaches its highest and most extensive density at their mouths, where the advantages for transport and agriculture are at the maximum. Hence the primacy of Shanghai among China's cities, the prominence of Canton, Hong Kong, Nanking and Hankow, and the deltaic emphasis of settlement in both north and south.

Relief.—China has often been schematically divided between the mountainous south and the more level north, but topographic distinctions are also clear as between east and west. The north China plain extends for the most part less than 400 mi. from the coast, and beyond are the rugged uplands of Shansi, Shensi and Kansu. Most of this northwest area, sometimes called "Loessland," is overlain by a thick mantle of fine-grained wind-deposited alluvium, or loess, between 50 and 250 ft. deep. The landscape has a characteristic carved appearance, since the loess is easily etched and dissected by erosion. This loess soil is highly fertile and, where water is available, very productive, but both rainfall and water for irrigation are scarce; there is also relatively little land level enough for cultivation, and the greater part of it lies in the northwestern section where rainfall is least. Cultivation has made increasing use of the hillsides, usually by means of terracing, though even in this form it does not prevent erosion of the soft loess. Irrigation water is most often available only in the deeply entrenched stream valleys, and hence cannot generally be used for cultivation on the interfluvial uplands despite the fertility of their soils. Wind-deposited loess occurs also outside Loessland proper, notably in a relatively thinner cover over most of eastern Honan seaward from the Fu Niu Shan; as a secondary fluvial deposit it is spread more uniformly over the north China plain, mixed with other Hwang silt, and thus augments the fertility of this lowland area.

In the east, the north China plain encompasses one of China's major concentrations of settlement and agriculture. Fertile soil and low relief combine to outweigh the manifold disadvantages of aridity. Proximity to the sea helps to make up for the lack of inland water transport, and over this generally dry and level land roads are easily built. A considerable volume of trade moves overland between the northwest and Tientsin, the commercial and industrial centre of north China and, after neighbouring Peking, the leading railway centre of China proper. A narrow coastal corridor between the sea and the mountains of Jehol links the north China plain with the plain of southern Manchuria. It has been a persistent route of invasion and became the focus of rail lines linking Manchuria with China.

In central and south China east-west topographic distinctions are less strong but still apparent. In the western half there are only rare and limited breaks in the jumbled sea of mountains which covers the area, while in the eastern half the Yangtze has created an extensive lowland as far west as Tungting lake, 700 mi. from the sea. In the south the Si Kiang has duplicated this pattern on a much smaller scale. It is nevertheless true that south China as a whole is a land of mountains and that it contrasts markedly with the more uniform and level terrain of much of the north.

There are very few well-defined mountain ranges within China proper. Where they occur, their effects are the more pronounced. The Tsinlingshan, running roughly east and west from southeastern Kansu to central Honan, where it largely disappears, marks one of the sharpest physical and cultural lines in China, between the dry brown plain of the north and the green hills of the south. Farther eastward, however, there is no such striking demarcation, though the Hwai Yang Shan along the provincial boundary between Honan and Hupeh helps somewhat to carry on the north-south boundary. Beyond Nanking begins the open coastal plain, where the old deltas of the Hwang merge with those of the present Hwai and Yangtze and north and south meet unhindered over a wide zone of transition. Central China, or the Yangtze basin, is in many respects not only transitional between north and south but a distinct geographic region. It lacks both the aridity of the north and the excessive relief of the south; its lowlands include not only the delta and lacustrine plains farther upstream but also the Red basin of Szechwan, considerably less level but one of China's primary areas of settlement and agriculture. There the Yangtze emerges from the plateau escarpment of the mountain mass of central Asia and is joined by three major tributaries; the rivers have between them carved out an extensive and fertile basin, and their continuing role in the province, China's largest in terms of both area and population, is revealed in the name "Szechwan," which means four rivers (the Min, Lu, Kialing and Yangtze).

South of the Yangtze basin the only significant gaps in the confused mass of mountains are the delta of the Si and the succession of smaller flood plains and deltas northward from Canton along the coast. Running roughly northeast-southwest approximately 200 mi. inland from this coast are the only major discernible ranges in south China, the Wu Kung, Ta Yü and Yün Ling. Difficult, broken country, however, extends almost to the coast between Hangchow and Swatow, and this succession of barriers has tended to cut off southeast coastal China from the main body of the country, to the extent that many of the people are either non-Chinese in origin or still retain a different language or dialect. The drowned coast line includes many fine harbours, and this is China's maritime region, with long-standing commercial relations overseas, a large investment in trade, shipping and fishing and a virtual monopoly of overseas emigrants. This is also the only significantly forested area of China proper, and while the stands are difficult of access on the steep slopes which cover the region, and their total is not very large, their timber helps to support the fishing and trading specialties and is also a leading export.

A second discernible topographic region in the south is the misnamed "plateau" of Yünnan and Kweichow in the southwest. It is so heavily dissected that the term "plateau" hardly fits the case; level land is almost as scarce there as in the southeast and is for the most part confined to a series of old intermontane lake beds now largely dry. The area owes its distinction to remoteness, to a dry climate, to a high average elevation (over 5,000 ft. for most of Yünnan) and to the consequence of its high relief in the fact that Chinese settlement has not yet spread significantly into the hills, which are still occupied by non-Chinese tribes. This country, in effect the foothills of the great Tibetan escarpment, actually continues northward through the western part of Szechwan and into Kansu. The southwest has periodically enjoyed closer relations with the Indochinese peninsula (to whose present inhabitants the non-Chinese tribes of the southwest are closely related) than with China, though access even in this direction is difficult. The gorges of the Salween, Mekong and lesser streams, plus the tropical rain forest and climate, interpose a formidable barrier.

Chinese occupation of the land south of the Yangtze basin did not begin until about the Christian era and is still not complete in the southwest. Its slow and often-interrupted progress during 2,000 years is a reflection of the basically inhospitable nature of the land for agriculture. The non-Chinese linguistic or ethnic islands in the southeast and southwest are samples of what mountains and isolation have made of the pattern of human occupancy. The only easy overland connection, and by far the most important, between the south and the Yangtze basin is the twin route leading from Canton via the Pei (North) river or one of its tributaries and across one of two low saddles into the headwaters of the Siang or Kan rivers, each leading to the Yangtze. These mountain passes, Cheling (1,400 ft.) and Meiling (1,000 ft.), have helped to keep Canton in much closer relationship with the rest of China than has been possible for most of the south, and have implemented Canton's traditional function before 1842 as the overseas trade centre for the whole of China, despite its off-side location. Modern China's only direct north-south rail line from Peking via Hankow to Canton runs through the Cheling pass.

The Coast Line.—China's north-south dichotomy is re-emphasized by the break in the nature of its coast line which occurs in the area of Hangchow bay. South of this area is a submerged coast with numerous good natural harbours, while to the north an emergent coast line provides almost no naturally usable harbours with the exception of the rocky promontory of Shantung. Shantung, originally an island in the Yellow sea, has been tied to the land by silt deposition from the Hwang, but the general lack of easy transport connections with the hinterland, especially by river, has greatly reduced the usefulness of the major harbours at Tsingtao and Chefoo. Elsewhere along the north China coast the originally poor harbours are continually menaced by silt from the arid-climate rivers and from the Yangtze in the case of Shanghai. Tientsin, 40 mi. from the sea on the Pei river, was forced to remove its port to Taku-Tangku at the river's mouth, but even there sand bars made it necessary for deep-draught shipping to load and unload by lighter at sea. The Communist government built an artificial harbour near Tangku, but it was too shallow for large transpacific shipping. Shanghai's problem is less crucial but still serious. Other north China ports such as Sinhai (Tunghai or Haichow) and Chinwangtao have had to rely on artificial harbours as well as on constant dredging.

What south China gains in number of good harbours it largely loses in ports which are inaccessible to a productive hinterland because of mountain barriers and lack of navigable inland waterways. The Si makes Canton an exception, though its deltaic harbour is poor, and also accounts substantially for the commercial prominence of Hong Kong, a rocky island off the mouth of the Si with a large and deep protected roadstead. However, not Hong Kong but Shanghai, despite its poor harbour, is normally by far the largest port in China, by virtue of the Yangtze river and its access to a huge, productive hinterland.

Climate.—It is difficult to generalize about so large an area and one which contains such climatic extremes. North China as a whole has a continental climate of hot summers and cold winters, with the extremes becoming more pronounced farther inland. Continentality is accentuated by the monsoon wind system of east Asia, which, while less marked than in south Asia or India, produces in north China predominantly inblowing, warm maritime airs in summer and predominantly cold, dry, outblowing airs from Siberia and inner Asia in winter. The mountains of the northwest tend to exclude the maritime airs (which bring moisture as well as warmth), and their penetration is further offset by the counterinfluence of the warm Kuro Shiwo or Japan current off the coast. Close to the sea, in the eastern sections of the north China plain, winters are relatively mild, with only one month having an average temperature below freezing. This area also receives the inblowing summer winds from the sea in fair amount, and, while the rainfall which they bring to north China is highly unreliable, their southeasterly origin makes for a summer which at its height is nearly as warm as that in south China, although less prolonged. In the northwest winters are rigorous, in the full grip of the outblowing airs from inner Asia, and summers are considerably cooler than on the plain.

North China's great climatic problem is rainfall. This is everywhere a marginal area, more because of the great yearly fluctuation in precipitation than because of the average annual amount. Average annual variability in north China as a whole is approximately 30%; in the loess area of the northwest it reaches 40%. With an annual rainfall average for all north China of between 20 and 25 inches, this is a precarious situation. Annual variability is frequently matched by seasonal variability, which can be fully as serious. Considerably more than half the annual precipitation usually comes in June, July and August, when it is most needed for the planting season and the early growth of crops. But it is often delayed beyond the end of the planting season and may either largely fail or come so late that it is of no use for the current agricultural year and instead produces disastrous floods. Unfortunately the population of north China has increased up to the maximum for optimum climatic conditions, and in at least one-third of the years conditions are far from optimum. Hence the cruel and long-established cycle in north China of one major famine approximately every three years, periodically worsened by floods. Winter precipitation is far too slight to support crops even if the temperatures allowed it, although the thin and sparse winter snows occasionally help to moisten the soil for spring. The winter winds from inner Asia, however, are mainly dry, and their violence picks up clouds of dust from the loess highlands and the bare parched plain to make dust storms a prominent feature of all north China from October to April. The north depends on drought-resistant crops rather than on rice—wheat, kaoliang and millet most importantly. No part of the north has adequate rainfall, but the western parts, farther from the sea, are especially arid; for the north China plain alone the annual average is about 22 in., while for the loess highlands it is about 15 in.

The isohyet (line) of 40 in. annual rainfall runs in the eastern half of China roughly along the valley of the Hwai river, and in the west through northern Szechwan. South of this line rainfall generally is adequate and reasonably reliable. Average annual variability is less than 15%. Seasonal distribution is also favourable, with a peak in June-July-August but with adequate and reliable amounts occurring throughout the year, including the winter months. This and the mild temperature regime make winter crops possible and largely save south China from recurrent famines. Annual rainfall reaches and exceeds 70 in. in parts of Kwangtung and Fukien, but the general average for China south of the Yangtze (exclusive of the southwest) is about 55 in. During the summer months this is likely to come as heavy showers, and, given the relatively high annual total, the soils of south China are badly leached. Winters are mild, though in the lower Yangtze basin the Siberian high penetrates enough to put average temperatures for three months into the 40's and to make many dry, clear, cold days or nights with temperatures below freezing. Nevertheless the growing season in the Yangtze basin averages more than 300 days, and winter crops, especially of beans or wheat, are universal.

In Kwangtung, Kwangsi and Fukien, while there may be occasional frosts, there are barely two months with average temperatures under 60°, and the growing season is virtually unbroken, allowing two crops of rice per year plus a winter crop. Summer in the south is hot, humid and long; Kwangtung and Kwangsi have four months with average temperatures over 80°, which is not surprising considering the southeasterly origin of the prevailing summer winds and the fact that Canton itself lies 21 mi. S. of the Tropic of Cancer. At the other extremity, Szechwan and the lower Yangtze basin each have three humid months over 80°, although the maxima are less than for Kwangtung and Kwangsi.

This temperature and rainfall regime is the result of a modified monsoonal wind system, plus a cyclonic pattern which moves over China especially in winter from west to east. The major cyclonic storm track follows the Yangtze valley, bringing the gentle *pai yü* (plum rains) in early and middle spring to coincide with the rice-planting season. Winter rains of both cyclonic and maritime origin are general over most of south China, and there is no marked dry period. Mountain protection and the influence of the sea help to exclude the Siberian high and to keep southern winters mild. Even Szechwan, far from the sea but ringed by high mountains, has a generally milder winter than the relatively open plain of the lower Yangtze. The great and destructive climatic anomaly of the south is typhoons, although they are largely limited to the coastal strip south of Shanghai. They quickly lose their violence inland from the coast, and north of Shanghai they are infrequent and not severe. Typhoons may occur throughout the year along the southeast coast, but they are commonest in late summer (mid-July to mid-September); they account for much of the summer rainfall as well as damage to coastal shipping and settlement.

The southwest is climatically a distinct region; its mountain barriers and distance from the sea keep it on the fringes of monsoonal influence, and it is also off the track of most of the cyclonic storms. Average annual rainfall (derived from both the Indian and Pacific oceans) is about 40 in. but is markedly concentrated in summer; for the balance of the year it is minimal, and the winter and spring landscape is bare and brown enough in the western sections to be reminiscent of north China. However, its southerly latitude and degree of mountain protection against the Siberian high keeps winters mild, and only two months have average temperatures under 50°. In summer the hot, humid maritime airs seldom penetrate, and the generally high average elevation helps to produce a cool and bracing atmosphere. Yünnan and eastern Kweichow should be distinguished climatically, the latter having slightly greater precipitation but many more rainy days, which are less strongly concentrated in summer, and lacking the higher elevations of Yünnan. Yünnan is famous for its magnificent cumulus clouds and bright blue sky (the name may be translated as "south of the clouds" or "southern cloud land"), which contrast sharply with the gray, dripping winters of neighbouring Kweichow and Szechwan and which are suggestive of a semineutral position between monsoonal and cyclonic influences.

Regional Summary.—On the basis of the foregoing sections, China may grossly but usefully be divided into six major regions, characterized in brief as follows:

1. The north China plain (Hopei and parts of Shantung, Kiangsu and Honan): semiarid, level, rich alluvial soil, dense agricultural settlement, several prominent trade and manufacturing centres; the consistent military and political focus of China and with most of its railways.

2. The northwest, including the loess area (Shansi, Shensi, Kansu and parts of Honan): arid, deeply eroded mountains, severe continental climate, rich loess soil, relatively sparsely populated, few large cities or railways; the vestibule of China's gateway to the west and probably the site of the earliest Chinese civilization.

3. The Red basin of Szechwan: moderate climate with adequate rainfall, moderate relief (dissected by four rivers), including several densely settled agricultural areas; demarcated and isolated by mountains on all sides, but tied to the east by the Yangtze; a few large trading cities but little manufacturing.

4. The lower Yangtze basin (most of Hupeh, Hunan, Anhwei, Chekiang, Kiangsi and Kiangsu): moderate climate, much level alluvial land, very dense agricultural settlement and heavy rice production; China's major trade artery, with many large commercial and manufacturing cities, including Shanghai.

5. The southeast (Kwangtung, Kwangsi, Fukien and parts of Chekiang and Kiangsi): subtropical climate, heavy relief, isolated by mountains and oriented to the sea, very dense agricultural settlement on the deltas, sparsely occupied uplands, series of maritime trading centres along the coast; retains many non-Chinese features.

6. The southwest (Yünnan and parts of Kweichow and Szechwan): moderate, bracing climate, fairly heavy relief, isolated by mountains and distance, Chinese occupancy largely confined to the occasional intermontane basins, few large cities, little trade or manufacturing, very sparse non-Chinese settlement on the uplands; connections with the Indochinese peninsula. (R. M.)

Bibliography.—G. B. Cressey, *China's Geographic Foundations* (New York, 1934); L. D. Stamp, *Asia: An Economic and Regional Geography* (New York, London, 1929); W. G. Kendrew, *The Climates of the Continents* (Oxford, 1922); C. C. Chu, *Climatic Provinces of China* (Nanking, 1929); for climatic statistics see *La Pluie en Chine* and *La Température en Chine* by the Zicawei Press (Shanghai).

GEOLOGY

The geological pattern of China and its dependencies is determined by two series of structural axes, one extending east-west in central Asia and the other northeast-southwest in the coastal regions. The more important and more recent axes are marked by mountain ranges. They intersect and interfere with one another in much of China proper, produce many complexities and enclose several important structural and depositional basins, such as the Red basin of Szechwan and the Shensi basin to the north, and the modern alluvial areas in the lower Hwang and Yangtze river valleys, as well as many smaller ones.

The earth movements, involving both folding and faulting, responsible for the present geological structure began in very ancient times and have continued at intervals to the present. The most important were: (1) pre-Cambrian (widespread, in several stages); (2) post-Silurian (minor except in south); (3) post-Devonian (in southeast); (4) Upper Carboniferous (in southwest and in Nan Shan, where granite intrusions are numerous); (5) mid-Permian (Kuen-lun mountain axis and its extension into central China, lava flows in southwest); (6) post-Triassic (general uplift of eastern Asia, folding in southwest and east central China); (7) post-Jurassic (widespread, most important in Tsinling axis of central China); (8) post-Cretaceous (widespread, lava flows in Manchuria and southeast China, igneous intrusions in south with which metalliferous deposits are associated); (9) late Tertiary (particularly in north China and Mongolia); and (10) Recent (central Asian highlands).

Because of structural complexity, rocks of all geologic ages are widely but irregularly distributed, and the only considerable areas of comparatively undisturbed strata occur in the basins. The total thickness of sedimentary rocks is very great, but in a country of such size the thickness and also the lithologic nature of beds of equivalent age vary greatly in different areas.

The pre-Cambrian rocks constitute three great systems: Tai Shan (oldest), Wutai and Sinian (youngest). The first consists of highly metamorphosed sedimentary and igneous rocks, mostly gneiss and schist, and the second is made up of less metamorphosed sediments. The last is mainly sedimentary and consists of arkosic clastics below grading up into thick cherty limestone; it also includes sedimentary iron ore, tillite and local lava flows. These are unmetamorphosed except where involved in much later mountain-forming disturbances and generally resemble overlying Palaeozoic formations.

The Palaeozoic succession begins with Lower Cambrian sandstone and grades upward into thick later Cambrian and Ordovician limestone. Toward the end of the Ordovician period all China north of the Tsinling axis was gently uplifted, and subsequent deposits are absent from that region.

Silurian, Devonian and Lower Carboniferous strata are confined to south China and include graptolite-bearing shale (Silurian), plant-bearing nonmarine beds (Devonian) and much limestone. The lower parts particularly were deposited in very shallow water.

Upper Carboniferous strata overlap extensively onto Ordovician and older rocks in north China, and Permian strata are almost equally extensive. In south and central China these beds are mainly limestone, but in the north they include the most important coal deposits of the country, and red beds become conspicuous in the upper part.

Sinian and Palaeozoic sediments accumulated in a broad depression extending northeast-southwest and connecting with similar east-west depressions on either side of the Tibetan region. Successive mountain uplifts encroached upon these depressions and reduced in size and multiplied in number the depositional basins of later times, which shifted to some extent with respect to each other.

Nonmarine strata become progressively more important in the Mesozoic, and thick red beds are present in many areas. Rock salt occurs in the Triassic of Szechwan, coal in the Jurassic and gypsum in the Cretaceous.

Tertiary strata, mostly nonmarine red beds, occur especially in the north, where they are many thousands of feet thick. They include some lignite, gypsum, fresh-water limestone and lava flows. The youngest of these beds are nearly horizontal except adjacent to very recently uplifted mountains. Oil is produced from the Tertiary in the northwest.

Deposits of Pleistocene and Recent age include thick piedmont gravels in central Asia, the loess of north China and extensive alluvium in the Hwang, Yangtze and other river valleys.

(J. M. Wr.)

Bibliography.—B. Willis *et al., Research in China,* 3 vol. (Washington, 1907); L. de Launay, *La Géologie et les richesses minérales de l'Asie* (1911); S. Li, "An Outline of Chinese Geology," *Geological Magazine* (1921); A. W. Grabau, *Stratigraphy of China,* Chinese Geological Survey (1924–); *Bulletins* and *Memoirs* of the Chinese Geological Survey; S. Li, *The Geology of China* (New York, London, 1939).

ANIMAL LIFE

Profusion of vegetation and variety of relief have fostered the development of a fauna of great diversity and have permitted the survival of animals elsewhere extinct. Notable among such survivals are the great paddlefish (*Psephurus*) of the Yangtze, the small species of alligator in east central China and the giant salamander (related to the Japanese giant salamander and the American hellbender) in western China. The diversity of animal life is perhaps greatest in the ranges and valleys of the Tibetan border, to which region the remarkable giant panda is confined. The takin or goat antelope, numerous species of pheasants and a variety of laughing thrushes are to be found in all the Chinese mountains. China seems to have been one of the chief centres of dispersal of the carp family and also of old world catfishes.

The regional affinities of the Chinese fauna are complex. In the northeast there are relations with the animal life of the Siberian forests. The Mongolian deserts bring animals from central Asia into suitable steppe areas in northern China. The life of the great mountain ranges is Palaearctic, but with distinctively Chinese species or genera. To the southeast, the lowlands and mountains alike lead directly into the oriental region. This part of China presents a complete transition from the temperate zone Palaearctic life to the wealth of tropical forms distinctive of southeastern Asia. Tropical types of reptiles and amphibians and of birds and mammals predominate in the southernmost Chinese provinces. (K. P. S.)

VEGETATION

The natural vegetation of China ranges from boreal taiga to rain forest and from barren tundra and desert to the littoral vegetation of the coral islands in the tropical seas. In general, the entire territory of China is dominated by two great plant formations: the grassland-desert of the northwestern half of China and the woodland of the southeastern half.

Six major forest types are recognized:

1. The mixed northern hardwood forest is best developed in the northeastern provinces. A similar type appears also in the higher elevations of the northern provinces above the deciduous oak belt. The primary components are maple (eight species), linden (five) and birch (nine), intermixed with white pine (*Pinus koraiensis*), oak, walnut, *Maackia, Phellodendron*, elm, *Kalopanax* and other minor accessories.

2. The deciduous oak forest is the major type of the northern provinces. Relics of natural forest indicate that the primary components are *Quercus aliena, Q. liaotungensis, Q. dentata* and *Q. variabilis*. The common associates are ash, hornbeam, elm, *Pistacia, Prunus*, walnut and hackberry. Pine (*Pinus tabulaeformis*), arborvitae and juniper grow on exposed ridges. The denuded slopes are covered with *Vitex, Zizyphus, Lespedeza*, grasses and thickets of *Cotinus, Deutzia, Spiraea*, wild roses and lilacs.

3. The mixed mesophytic forest of the Yangtze valley is richest in composition of all the deciduous forests. Preserved in this temperate clime are a number of relics of Tertiary flora (notably *Ginkgo, Metasequoia*) of more than 60,000,000 years ago, and polytopic genera which are represented also in North America (*e.g., Liriodendron, Sassafras, Cladrastis, Gymnocladus*). The forest components include: *Aesculus, Aphananthe, Carya, Castanea, Cephalotaxus, Cercidiphyllum, Cryptomeria, Cunninghamia, Cupressus, Daphniphyllum, Diospyros, Ehretia, Emmenopterys, Eucommia, Fagus, Fraxinus, Halesia, Idesia, Magnolia, Nyssa, Paulownia, Pseudolarix, Pseudotsuga, Quercus, Torreya, Trema and Zelkova.*

4. The evergreen oak forest extends over the hilly areas of the southern and southwestern provinces, Taiwan and Hainan Island. It is composed of more than 150 species of evergreen cupuliferous trees (*Quercus, Pasania, Castanopsis, Castanea*) and numerous evergreen trees of the Lauraceae, Theaceae, Magnoliaceae and Hamamelidaceae. Bamboo and secondary growth of *Pinus massoniana* and *Liquidambar* cover large areas south of the Yangtze.

5. Rain forest occurs only along the southern fringe of China from the Yünnan-Assam border to the lowlands of Kwangtung, Hainan and Taiwan.

6. The montane coniferous forest of the Greater Hsingan range is essentially of larch (*Larix gmelini*), but spruce (*Picea obovata, P. jezoensis*) and fir (*Abies holophylla, A. nephrolepis*) form dense forest on the eastern rampart bordering Korea. The montane coniferous forest of the southwestern plateau is composed of a multitude of conifers, including spruce (eight species), fir (ten), hemlock, larch and *Pseudotsuga*. Montane coniferous forests appear also on the high peaks of the northern provinces (*Picea asperata, P. neoveitchi, Abies nephrolepis*), Sinkiang (*Picea schrenkiana*) and Taiwan (*Picea morrisonicola, Abies kawakami*), right under the Tropic of Cancer.

A vast expanse of grassland extends from the plain of the

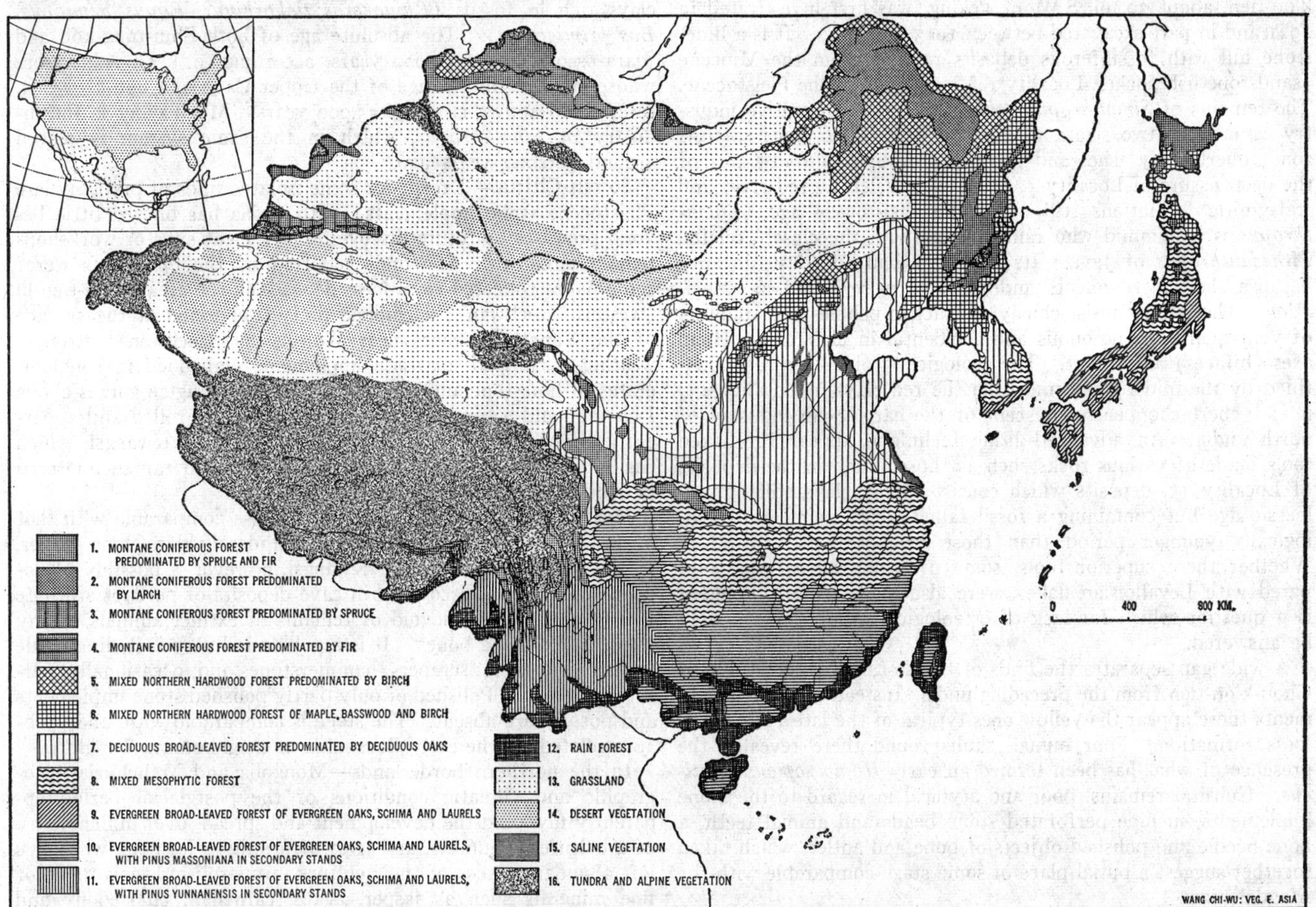

DISTRIBUTION OF THE MAIN TYPES OF NATURAL VEGETATION OF CHINA, MONGOLIA, KOREA AND JAPAN

northeastern provinces westward to the Tien Shan, interspersed with salt lakes (*nor*), gravel desert and sand dunes. Thick clumps of *Stipa splendens* are the most conspicuous feature. The arid areas support only xerophytes and halophytes. Orchards, vineyards and luxuriant groves of poplar and elm, however, thrive in the oases. Marshes of cattail and *Phragmites* teem with nesting geese, ducks and swans in summer. The vegetation of the Sidzang plateau (Tibet) is scanty, consisting only of scattered cushion plants with thick rootstocks. But the Tsangpo (upper Brahma-putra) valley is well wooded. Rice and corn are planted successfully in Zayul district. (W.)

Bibliography.—N. Shaw, *Chinese Forest Trees and Timber Supply* (1914); E. Wilson, *A Naturalist in Western China;* K. Ward, "From the Yangtze to the Irrawaddy," *Geographical Journal* (July 1923); A. de C. Sowerby, *The Natural History of China,* Smithsonian Institution, annual report, 1923 (Washington, 1925); Y. Chen, *Manual of Chinese Trees;* C. W. Wang, *Vegetation of Eastern Asia.*

ARCHAEOLOGY

To the Chinese scholar up to the 20th century, archaeology was a discipline closely linked with historical and literary studies. Archaeological materials were valued according to whether they verified or illustrated the past as encompassed in the classics and annals. Epigraphy, therefore, naturally became all-important, while objects without inscriptions were neglected. Thus the documents of the scriptless prehistoric past remained practically outside the sphere of scholarly research in China until duly authorized westerners began to organize explorations in the field from about the early 1920s onward. Their activities, soon shared by the Chinese themselves, resulted in geological, palaeontological and archaeological discoveries of the utmost importance. Progressing at a fast pace, these activities came to a standstill when the Chino-Japanese War started in 1937. Much of the material which had accumulated up to that time became accessible in publications and discussions carried on later.

Palaeolithic in North China.—The famous site of Chou-k'ou-tien, about 30 mi. S.W. of Peking, was first investigated in 1921 and in part excavated between 1923 and 1937. It is a limestone hill with fossiliferous deposits ranging from the Miocene (sandstone fish pocket, Locality 14) to the end of the Pleistocene. The remains of *Sinanthropus pekinensis* and his primitive industry came from two strata (sands and breccias, *Hyaena sinensis* zone; overlaid by ashes and travertine, *Hyaena ultima* zone) of the deep fissure of Locality 1, which was sealed by red clays and stalagmitic formations still of middle Pleistocene age. *Sinanthropus* is a hominid who ranks in age with the closely related *Pithecanthropus* of Java. Its discovery had added significance because skeletal fragments and artifacts were found in association. The latter consist chiefly of cracked pebbles and splinters of vein quartz, monotonous and accidental in character. Hand axes (bifaces) are absent. The geologically oldest artifact identified by the mid-1950s came from the red clays in Locality 13; it is a chert chopper reminiscent of the early Soan industry of north India. An advanced lithic technique appears in flaked tools made of various rocks such as those found in the deposits of Locality 15, deposits which consist of red clays still of preloessic age but containing a fossil fauna which points to a geologically younger period than those of Localities 13 and 1. Whether these superior tools, some of which have been compared with Levalloisian flakes, were also made by *Sinanthropus* is a question which for lack of osteological proof cannot safely be answered.

A wide gap separates the finds of the so-called Upper Cave of Chou-k'ou-tien from the preceding finds. Instead of the red sediments there appear the yellow ones typical of the late Pleistocene loess formation. Four human skulls found there revealed the presence of what has been termed an early *Homo sapiens asiaticus.* Cultural remains, poor and atypical in regard to the stone implements, include perforated stone beads and animal teeth, a bone needle and polished objects of bone and antler, which taken together suggest a burial place of some stage comparable with the Magdalenian.

Ordos Industries.—Several important Upper Palaeolithic sites have been discovered along the southern fringe of the Ordos steppe, the area skirted by the great bend of the Hwang-ho. They belong in their entirety in the late Pleistocene, the time of the formation of the yellow earths (loess), but vary in age. None of them yielded skeletal remains of man. A series of very hard quartzite implements, mostly made of round pebbles chipped along one edge, as well as some flakes, came from the basal gravels underneath the loess, the maximum thickness of which does not exceed, according to Pierre Teilhard de Chardin, 50 m. and often is far less. Finds of this category were reported from Ch'ing-yang-fu, Yu-fang-t'ou, Chungar, Pao-te and Wu-pao. In the loess stratum itself, two dwelling places and workshop sites were explored: Shui-tung-kou, close to the Hwang-ho opposite Ningsia, and Sjara-osso-gol, southeastern Ordos.

Shui-tung-kou.—This is a loess-filled depression, stretching east-west for 10 mi., where five hearths with ashes and a great number of artifacts were located at various depths in a stratum of loess measuring 15 m. A rich and diversified lithic industry comprising such types as scrapers, points and gravers reminiscent of Mousterian and Aurignacian types suggests a stage more developed than that of the aforementioned group; yet tools of the primitive "Soan chopper" variety occurred in the same assemblage. The materials used, chert and silicified limestone, were taken from the gravel of streams embedded in the yellow loam which were later buried under renewed deposits of aeolian loess dust.

Sjara-osso.—The site of Sjara-osso is remarkable on two accounts; viz., the extraordinary depth of the fossiliferous beds of dune sands and lacustrine clayey sediments overlying the Palaeolithic floor, and the smallness of the lithic implements, chiefly scrapers and points, made of small siliceous pebbles such as are available in this area. Typologically, this "micro-industry" is considered by Henri Breuil as advanced beyond the Shui-tung-kou stage. However, it is separated from the Neolithic horizon of the same site by no less than 55 m. of deposits, sands and sandy clays rich in fossils (*Rhinoceros tichorhinus, Equus hemionus, Bos primigenius*). The absolute age of both Shui-tung-kou and Sjara-osso is about 50,000 years, according to J. G. Andersson, whose estimate of the age of the Upper Cave of Chou-k'ou-tien, referred to above, is about 25,000 years. Much older is the industry of *Sinanthropus,* which in the same system is placed around 500,000 years ago.

South China.—Except for some isolated finds of probably late Pleistocene stone implements, south China has offered little beyond promises of future discoveries. Ancient sites or workshops remain unknown. The finds reported by the mid-1950s were: some flakes collected from loess deposits in the area of Ta-tien-lu (western Szechwan); a chipped flinty tool found at the surface of the Yangtze terraces near Wan-hsien (Szechwan); strongly weathered chipped quartzite implements embedded in conglomerates of limestone and river gravels in the Yangtze gorges above I-ch'ang; and a quartzite chopper (?), heavily rolled and apparently reworked by Mesolithic cave dwellers of Kwangsi, which has some claim to be the oldest implement so far encountered in south China.

Mesolithic Phase.—A Mesolithic phase comparable with that of post-Pleistocene Europe has not been identified in China proper. In the southerly province of Kwangsi, however, a possibly Mesolithic culture was discovered in cave deposits of perhaps still late Pleistocene age but devoid of remains of extinct animals or any strongly fossilized bones. It is a pebble industry including crude types of choppers, scrapers, hammerstones and, occasionally, perforated stones. Polished or only partly polished stone implements and pottery are absent. The stage is comparable with, and probably related to, the early Bacsonian of neighbouring Tongking.

In the northern borderlands—Mongolia and Manchuria—geographic and climatic conditions of the postglacial period apparently favoured the development and spread, over millenniums, of a culture of hunters, and later of primitive farmers, who have left abundant traces of their culture in microlithic tools made of fine minerals such as jasper, agate, carnelian, chalcedony and flint. The commonest shapes among those tools are small and slender flakes and the conical cores, or micronuclei, from which these flakes were obtained. The foremost site in Mongolia is that of Shabarakh-Usu in the Gobi desert. Widely diffused to the east, into Manchuria, and southward (Ordos), and no doubt related to Siberian microlithic cultures, this Shabarakh or Gobi culture corresponds to the Tardenoisian and Azilian of Europe, but differs from the latter in that the "geometric" silices are wanting. In regard to China it should be observed that microlithic chipped implements are not encountered to the south of the line of the (much later erected) Great Wall; it appears as though this gigantic limes followed a cultural borderline of hoary age and remarkable stability.

Neolithic Stage.—This northern orbit seems to have undergone a gradual transition toward a primitive Neolithic culture of sedentary farmers and husbandmen. This can be observed at two sites in Jehol, Lin-hsi and Ulan Hata (Ch'ih-feng), which were discovered by Émile Licent and Teilhard de Chardin in 1924. The artifacts at Lin-hsi were found either embedded in a post-Pleistocene layer of black earth on top of Quaternary white sands above ancient schist, or exposed on the sand where the black earth had been blown away. Crude rhyolithic pebble tools and blades as well as nuclei of fine siliceous rocks occurred side by side with grinding stones and pestles usually made of granite. A few hoelike implements and perforated round pebbles were recovered. Polished implements were rare, and true axes or celts were absent. The pottery encountered in the stratum of black earth was a hand-made, poorly fired ware. Bones of the domesticated horse, ox and sheep, but none of wild game, were found.

Geologically and archaeologically similar conditions prevail at the site to the south of the "red rock," which gave Ulan Hata its name. In addition to the Lin-hsi inventory mentioned above, however, this site yielded rather advanced types in stone as well as pottery, the later age of which seems unquestionable but could not be ascertained stratigraphically. To these later types belong more or less wholly polished hatchets; a polished, rectangular ax with perforation; broad knives with perforations; and stone beads. In pottery there appeared round, obtusely pointed solid legs of tripods, as well as vases of fine red clay, occasionally with a white slip and, most characteristic, with spiral decoration painted in black.

The "Mongolian Neolithic," typified by the presence of microliths, agricultural tools and some pottery such as are known from Lin-hsi, expands north into north Manchuria (Hailar; Ang-ang-ch'i near Tsitsihar), where it assumes or retains a character that has been described as Maglemosian, since the finds speak of a stronger dependence on fishing and hunting there; farther west it was traced in the Gobi (later Shabarakh) and southwest in the Ordos (Sjara-osso, surface finds). This culture, which must have comprised the wide territories to the north of the yellow clay or loess of China proper and to the south of the Siberian forest zone, seems to have vanished without further local developments, presumably because of an increasing desiccation and the desertlike conditions resulting therefrom. Some traces of it were found in sites spreading between western Kansu (Chu-chia-chai; Lake Koko-nor) and the Gulf of Liaotung (Sha-kuo-t'un in Liaoning), where—similar to what was noted in Ulan Hata—a new late Neolithic culture with painted pottery and polished stone tools supervened. These "mixed sites," on the whole, have to be understood as evidence of an expansion of the new culture into the southern fringes of the territory previously and perhaps still held by the makers of the microliths.

The rare case of what appears to be an intrusion of north Eurasian *Kammkeramik* in a south Kansu site (Ch'i-chia-p'ing) visited and described by Andersson, a ware with comb stamped ornaments entirely foreign in China, probably belongs in the period preceding the appearance of the painted pottery.

Yangshao Painted Pottery Culture.—The period between the late Palaeolithic of the Upper Cave at Chou-k'ou-tien and the appearance of the Painted Pottery or Yangshao culture in north China, a period of many millenniums, is (in contrast with Mongolia) archaeologically obscure. Except for a series of limestone and quartzite artifacts of Palaeolithic character collected by C. C. Young and W. C. P'ei at Yang-shao-ts'un in 1934, there are no finds to shed light on that long period. But this is an isolated and puzzling case which does not go far in altering the apparent fact of an archaeological blank, Andersson's "Neolithic hiatus." Climatic conditions may account largely for this hiatus. The final Pleistocene, when the loess formation was still in progress, was a cold and semiarid phase; afterward, in postglacial times, the river valleys and plains may have been swamplands.

Then suddenly, at the very end of the Neolithic, at a time only four thousand years distant from our own, the hitherto seemingly empty land becomes teeming with busy life. Hundreds, not to say thousands of villages occupy the terraces overlooking the valley bottoms. Many of these villages were surprisingly large and must have harboured a considerable population. Their inhabitants were hunters and stock-raisers but at the same time agriculturalists, as is evidenced by their implements and by the finding of husks of rice in a potsherd at Yang-shao-ts'un. The men were skilled carpenters and their womenfolk were clever at weaving and needlework. Their excellent ceramics, with few or no equals at that time, indicate that the then inhabitants of Honan and Kansu had developed a generally high standard of civilization. There must have been, by some means or other—new inventions or the introduction of new ideas from abroad—a rather sudden impetus that allowed the rapid spread of a fast growing population. (From J. G. Andersson, *Researches into the Prehistory of the Chinese,* Bulletin of the Museum of Far Eastern Antiquities, no. 15, p. 297 [Stockholm, 1943].)

It was in 1921 at Yang-shao-ts'un (Mien-ch'ih-hsien, western Honan) that Andersson discovered the culture so succinctly described in his above-quoted words. Further explorations revealed that this culture had covered the wide area between western Kansu and northern Honan, with extensions into Szechwan, Jehol and Liaoning, and that the ancient settlements were close to the rivers Hsi-ning, T'ao, Wei, upper Kialing and Han and to the Hwang-ho where it flows eastward after the great Ordos bend. The surprising and basic fact arising from this discovery is that China falls in line with west Asian and Indian sequences. For not only does there appear in China a painted ware, but, exactly as in the west, this ware is gradually replaced by a burnished black ware. This is, or was, however, a complicated process, far from being clarified by adequate field work. The observations made up to the mid-1950s are summed up in brief below.

Stratigraphy.—In most of the dwelling sites explored, the cultural stratum was rather shallow, but in two very large ancient villages, Hsi-yin-ts'un (southwestern Shansi) and Yang-shao-ts'un (western Honan), partial excavations revealed cultural strata varying between 2.50 to 4.00 m. and 2.50 to 3.00 m., respectively. However, judged by the occurring types of pottery shards, no clear subdivision or stratigraphic sequence was seen in either place. Andersson stated that Yangshao represents one single cultural stage comprising both painted and burnished black wares. The only stratigraphic change noted by P. L. Yüan, Li Chi and Liang Ssu-yung at Hsi-yin-ts'un in 1926 was a slight increase in the percentage of the black shards as compared with the painted shards in the upper layers, while the percentage of the cruder pottery, gray and reddish, with or without cord impression, remained constant throughout. In a few northern Honan sites, on the other hand, excavated by staff members of the Academia Sinica in 1931 and 1932, a stratigraphic sequence of painted pottery overlaid by black pottery and, topmost, gray Shang pottery was observed (Hou-kang, 1931; Kao-ching T'ai-tzu near Hou-chia-chuang, 1932; Ta-lai-tien near Hsün-hsien, 1932). In other sites in northern as well as western Honan, however, black pottery associated with, or overlaid by, gray pottery but with no trace of painted pottery was found to be a recurring and typical assemblage (Ssu-p'an-mo and Huo-chia Hsiao-chuang, near An-yang, north Honan; Pu-chao-chai, Yang-ho-ts'un, Hsi-chun-ts'un, in west Honan). Field observations made in the upper Wei valley by W. C. P'ei in 1947 tended to show that the ceramic wares in the many prehistoric sites of that area—the main route from Kansu to Honan—suggest three stages, early, middle and late, characterized by painted pottery first of good style, then of degenerate style and finally by the utter decay and disappearance of the painted pottery. From Kansu came the finest of the painted ceramics but little of stratigraphic interest. No more than two significant observations can be reported. Andersson noted at Hsin-tien (T'ao river valley) that Yangshao ware was overlaid by a stratum of Hsin-tien ware. Hsia Nai, who in 1945 excavated a tomb containing Ch'i-chia pottery as burial gifts (Pan-shan hills, Ning-ting-hsien), picked two Yangshao painted shards from the refill close to the bottom of the pit. Evidently the two shards were manufactured, used and discarded some time before the grave with its entirely different pottery was dug.

From the foregoing notes some inferences can be drawn. In Honan and Shensi, the painted ware preceded, but apparently overlapped with, the black pottery, and the latter in turn preceded a Bronze Age gray ware. In Kansu, where the black pottery seems to be almost absent, only a very few shards being reported, the Yangshao ware is older than the Hsin-tien ware of the beginning metal age and older than the (unpainted) Ch'i-chia ware, which is unknown in Honan.

Painted Pottery Styles.—The phenomenon of clearly differentiated styles of ornament was observed only in Kansu. Named after type sites in Kansu, most of these styles suggest an evolutionary sequence and, consequently, relative dates: (1) Pan-shan, (2) Ma-ch'ang, (3) Hsin-tien and (4) Sha-ching. The Pan-shan style is distinguished by an amphora type, of noble shape and with exquisitely painted ornaments, among which a design of rotatory S curves running horizontally round the vessel predominates. Other frequent patterns are rhombic chequers, diamonds, zigzags and a gourd motif. One tomb of this phase which Andersson was able to excavate at Pien-chia-kou (Pan-shan hills, T'ao valley) contained the skeleton of a man of about 40, in a flexed position and sprinkled with ochre, as well as eight fine painted vases, four crude, unpainted pots and four stone tools. The Ma-ch'ang wares are of reddish clay and are painted, sometimes carelessly, with black ornaments such as large concentric circles, rhombic T hooks and large meander bands consisting of parallel lines; the beautiful dynamic spiral patterns have disappeared. It was with the pottery of the following Hsin-tien stage that some minor bronze objects came to light, none of them, by the way, typically Chinese (Shang). These Hsin-tien wares retain the meander as the predominating motif of their sparse decoration, while their shapes mark a departure from the Pan-shan-Ma-ch'ang tradition. Sha-ching, the fourth phase, appears to have derived from Hsin-tien.

More closely comparable with the repertory of ornamental designs found in Shansi, among which stand out large, flowerlike, sweeping patterns (Ching-ts'un, Wan-ch'üan-hsien, southwestern Shansi), are decorations known from minor find spots in south Kansu. The exact relationship of these latter styles to those of the above-described sequence is not fully clarified, but it appears likely that they postdate the Pan-shan style; they presuppose the spiral motif, which here is transformed into free and asymmetrical curvilinear patterns foreign to the geometric development of the Ma-ch'ang phase.

Ma-chia-yao and Lo-han-t'ang in central Kansu, two large dwelling sites, exhibit designs that may well stand midway between Pan-shan and these south Kansu styles.

The range of ornamental patterns known from Shansi and Honan is comparatively narrow; to put it in the briefest interpretive statement, it may be said that after a splendid manifestation in Shansi (Ching-ts'un and Hsi-yin-ts'un) decline set in in west Honan (Yang-shao-ts'un), followed by a rapid decay in north Honan, so that a loss of diversity and freshness becomes the more noticeable the farther east we move.

Stone Implements.—The following four tools are, according to Andersson, characteristic of the Pan-shan phase: heavy axes of rectangular cross section with rounded-off corners, flat adzes, small adzes and rectangular or trapezoidal knives with one or two perforations. There are pendants and beads of jade, amazonite, turquoise and marble and perforated disks of jade, which in more regular shapes reappear in Shang and Chou times. The techniques of sawing and drilling hard stones thus were familiar to those vase painters. The occurrence of composite tools such as bone knives set with small flint blades (Lo-han-t'ang and Chu-chia-chai, west Kansu) point to connections with the Gobi microlithic cultures.

Lungshan Black Pottery Complex.—It was noted above that a black ware is associated with the painted ceramics in Shansi and Honan. In the eastern provinces of Shantung, Kiangsu, Anhwei and Chekiang, however, only the black wares are found, without any traces of painted pottery. The existence of a culture or cultural phase traceable through this black ware became known through the excavation in 1930 and 1931 of Ch'eng-tzu-yai, a mound near the railway station of Lungshan, east of Tsinan (west Shantung).

The typical black pottery is a very thin ware with a blackish or brownish body and a burnished, shiny, black surface. The shapes are distinguished by angular silhouettes that bespeak the potter's wheel. Save for some occasional incised geometric design of great simplicity, there is no decoration. Among the vessels are found types not known in painted pottery, such as tripods, spouted vases with bulbous hollow legs and, most characteristic, bowls on high ringed stems. Specimens of these stemmed bowls were unearthed not only in Shantung but also as far south as the Hangchow bay (Liang-chu, Chekiang) and in westerly Szechwan (Han-chou, north of Chengtu). Sparse occurrences of black pottery have been reported from outlying regions such as northwest Kansu (Chu-chia-chai), south Szechwan (upper Yangtze) and Liaotung (Port Arthur). The centres of the black pottery culture appear to have been located in Shantung and the Huai (Hwai) river valley, areas held by tribes which as late as the Chou dynasty had not yet been assimilated (Tung I and Huai I).

It is certain that the Lungshan culture preceded the Bronze Age level of Anyang (north Honan), site of the last Shang capital between 1300 and 1028 B.C., and that several Lungshan features live on in the Shang culture: bone oracles, shapes of vases (in gray Shang pottery and in bronze) and tamped earth structures. Even so there is no evidence of a genetical relationship between the basically premetallic Lungshan culture and the Shang civilization of Anyang, unless it should emerge with new discoveries relating to the archaeologically still wholly obscure span of approximately two centuries of Shang rule before 1300 B.C.

Chronology and Western Connections.—An earlier Lungshan (I) without metal was found to be separated by a thin, sterile, sandy layer from a later Lungshan (II) with scarce bronze objects at Ch'eng-tzu-yai. It is likely that Lungshan II, as assumed by R. von Heine-Geldern, belongs in the early Shang period (1523?–1301 B.C.), and that Lungshan I accordingly dates from the first half of the 2nd millennium, beginning perhaps around 1800 B.C. Consequently the painted pottery must be placed, in its beginnings in Kansu, around or shortly before 2000 B.C., because its secondary styles in Shansi and Honan overlap with the black pottery.

Both the painted Yangshao and the black Lungshan ceramics appear to have come to China from the west, where possible prototypes of similar shapes, ornamentation and techniques are widespread. In the case of the painted pottery, moreover, an apparent want of archaic forerunners, hence the phenomenon of a sudden unfolding, make it almost necessary to think of outside stimuli. These may have come from Iran, where similar shapes of tripods (Giyan, Djamshidi and Kamterlan), urns (Musyan and Persepolis) and steamers (Giyan) occur, dating from around 2000 B.C., or from south Russia (Tripolye B), where both the shapes of the urns and their *décor* of running spirals offer striking parallels, pointed out by L. Bachhofer, to the Chinese types. For the black pottery, close similarities to north Iranian and east Caspian types of stemmed bowls dating from about 2000 B.C. (Tepe Hissar and Shah Tepe) seem to warrant actual connections through cultural transmissions or, possibly, according to Heine-Geldern, migrations. Even a type of tripod with hollow legs, which is widely regarded as uniquely and specifically Chinese, occurs as far west as Anatolia (Manisa, 3rd millennium).

The approximate dates of the western—Asiatic and European—relevant material agree fairly well with the rough estimates of which the Chinese evidence admits.

Late Neolithic of South China.—The beginning of exploration dates only from about 1932, along the coast between Hong

Kong and Swatow, an area which under the ancient Yüeh had remained independent until as late as 111 B.C., when it was finally subdued by Han Wu Ti. Field observations made by J. Shellshear, D. J. Finn and R. Maglioni (which led to the recognition of several late Neolithic and chalcolithic cultures) were summed up by Maglioni in an attempt to arrive at a coherent if preliminary and admittedly still obscure picture. This includes three Neolithic stages, termed—after a district in Kwangtung—Hoifung (Mandarin: Haifeng) I (Sov), Hoifung II (Sak) and Hoifung III (Pat), and a chalcolithic and bronze period which is but a continuation of the Pat culture modified by the acquaintance with metal. The various stages are differentiated on the basis of the ceramic wares and stone or bronze tools as well as the sites discovered. In most cases these sites revealed objects of only one of the three cultures; among more than 20 sites in the Hoifung district, only two or three showed a mixture of remains of two different cultures.

Hoifung I combines a short ax of lenticular cross section with flattened sides, a derivative of the *Walzenbeil*, as its most typical tool with three kinds of pottery: (1) cord-impressed ware, (2) smoothly finished wares with incised or stamped geometric *décor* around the neck and (3) footed dishes with cutouts in the foot and with red and white paint. This culture is believed to be closely related to Indochina. Hoifung II possesses a wider variety of axes, which again resemble Indochinese types and like these latter are very often ground only near the cutting edge, and leaf-shaped arrowheads as well as stone bracelets. Besides corded ware and another coarse pottery tempered with sand, there appears a fine and thin ware with the *décor* always stamped. A tree pattern deserves to be noted, for it occurs also in the first stage.

The Hoifung III settlements were found almost everywhere near those of the preceding (Sak) phase, pointing to a shift in population, perhaps an invasion. The stone industry differs considerably from the earlier ones. Tools are polished all over, and the finest of them are made of beautiful hard stones or jade. Most typical is the stepped adz with a tang of elliptic cross section distinctly set off from the angular body, a boatbuilders' tool that forms one important link with Neolithic Formosa, the Philippines and Polynesia, while it seems to have remained unknown in northern China. Other polished stone objects such as arrowheads, spearheads and halberds reminiscent of the Chinese *ko* clearly suggest northern connections, and in contrast with the preceding stages there are no Indochinese types present. There is a wide variety of beads, bracelets, pendants and amulets. The pottery of this (Pat) stage likewise exhibits new features. One of them is a stamped "net pattern" of raised lines running obliquely over the surface, a pattern which is paralleled in Ch'eng-tzu-yai, the black pottery site in west Shantung. Others, according to Maglioni, are wares of vitrified clay and even glazed wares, the inclusion of which in this late or post-Neolithic assemblage may need further substantiation. The rise of the Yüeh people is believed to have occurred in the early metal age, partly as a result of ethnic movements and fusions at the time of incipient metallurgy, a factor which transformed the culture termed Pat or Hoifung III without breaking its continuity.

By the mid-1950s no dependable clue had been provided for the chronology of those prehistoric cultures, whose correlations with those of the surrounding areas remained to be clarified.

Early Bronze Age in North China.—This age is likely to antedate the highly advanced stage from after 1300 B.C. known through excavations of the large and rich Shang site near Anyang (north Honan). However, no site of a Bronze Age phase earlier than Anyang has been discovered. Scanty occurrences of primitive metal objects from several painted pottery sites in remote Kansu and Jehol, which probably date from before 1300, shed little light on what happened in the Shang domain before Anyang, say between 1400 and 1300. Those primitive objects consist of single round and conical buttons, compounded buttons, round buttons with striated rims, small buttons in aggregates of six, funnel- and bell-shaped pendants, a bronze armlet with overlapping ends, simple, "shapeless" bronze knives, a thin blade considered to be a razor, small bronze tubes, some arrowheads and the like, such as were found in west Kansu (Hsia-hsi-ho and Ch'ia-yao), central Kansu (Hsin-tien, Hui-tsui and Ssu-wa-shan) and Jehol (Ulan Hata)—a far cry from the elaborate bronze art of Anyang.

Anyang, therefore, appears as an unheralded, surprising and sudden manifestation of Chinese metallurgy as well as of Chinese art forms, which in contrast with the "international" character of the Neolithic potter's art, with its many parallels in western Asia and southeastern Europe, are profoundly dissimilar from those of any other ancient civilization. Even so, some of the outstanding cultural possessions of the Shang people again are paralleled in the west and ultimately may have come thence: the horse-drawn war chariot, a developed system of script and the technique of bronze casting as such.

The excavations carried out by the Academia Sinica in 15 campaigns between Oct. 1928 and June 1937, in an area stretching more than three miles along the Huan river to the west of the city of Anyang, revealed a considerable number of individual sites of varying age and importance. These sites, which are not equally well explored, form, according to Shih Chang-ju, six groups:

1. Hsiao-t'un: large dwelling site of Lungshan and Shang periods. Dwelling, storage and refuse pits; remains of water ditches or canals; pounded earth foundations of houses; foundation burials; individual and collective burials, horse burials, chariot burials and sacrificial burials of oxen, sheep and dogs, all of Shang age; later burials from Sui to Manchu dynasties.
2. Ssu-p'an-mo, Wang-yü-k'ou, Huo-chia Hsiao-chuang: Shang dwelling sites and cemeteries.
3. Hou-kang, Kao-ching-t'ai-tzu, T'ung-lo-chai: three successive stages, painted, black and gray potteries.
4. Hou-chia-chuang (Northwest Hill): Shang cemetery; "royal tombs."
5. Fan-chia-chuang: cemetery, little explored.
6. Ta-ssu-k'ung-ts'un, Nan-pa-t'ai, Hou-chia-chuang "South Field": Shang sites of slightly varying character.

Although the finds were published only in part, enough became known to enable us to form an idea of the range of Shang art and of what either links it to, or separates it from, the past.

Clear links with older cultures exist in the case of the gray pottery, which in a coarsened fashion continues the black pottery traditions. They exist also in the case of many types of bronze vessels, the shapes of which were dependent on then-current pottery prototypes. To ceramic traditions points also a limited but common repertory of geometric ornaments such as diapers, angular meanders and T hooks, found on gray pottery and bronzes as well as on a peculiar new kind of ceramic ware, the Shang white pottery. This is a heavy, hard-fired, whitish ware distinguished by its carved *décor*.

The same white pottery, on the other hand, marks a new departure, being carved in a technique foreign to the Neolithic potters and decorated also with animal images of the abstract, heraldic style that is one of the Shang novelties in archaic bronzes as well as on carved bones and ivories. A bone carver's tradition looms as the uniting agency behind the abstract animal imagery in all those mediums including wood, but the origins of this tradition are unknown. Another new feature is small animal sculptures in jade; they have no precursors whatever in Neolithic sites, while in a general way they are reminiscent of much earlier animal amulets in stone such as were unearthed at Ur, Erech, Tepe Gawra and Khafaje in Mesopotamia.

Among the magnificent bronze weapons of the Shang there are types of tanged axes which appear to be autochthonously Chinese. Others are suggestive of foreign connections. Some rarer types of shaft-hole axes recall designs current in Mesopotamia, Luristan and Persia. The spearheads, socketed celts and certain kinds of daggers and knives, on the other hand, have close analogies in east Russia, Siberia, Mongolia and the Ordos steppe inside the great bend of the Hwang-ho. Conditions thus would seem to repeat a pattern observed when dealing with the Neolithic painted ceramics, which likewise point toward south Russia and the ancient near east as centres of diffusion.

Ordos.—On the evidence of numerous stray finds of bronze objects made there, the Ordos region and adjacent Inner Mongolia form part of the geographical and cultural continuum of the Eurasian steppe belt, an area that was to remain alien to that of the Chinese culture. The Ordos bronzes have close affinities in the Bronze Age inventory of central and south Siberia (Minusinsk, Tomsk, Altai and Kazakhstan), east Russia (Ananino and Perm) and south Russia (Kuban), and after they became known in the 1920s were rightly recognized as related to Scythian art. However, older, pre-Scythian strains are also present in Ordos art. In fact, it seems that the Bronze Age sequence established for Siberia is fully answered by the Ordos bronze material so far known, whereas correspondences with Shang art appear to be limited to the types mentioned above. These types belong, in Siberia, in the periods called Andronovo (*c.* 1700–1300 B.C.) and Karasuk (*c.* 1300–1000 B.C.). It is the influence of these cultures, including early Ordos, which in the author's opinion accounts also for the lesser bronze finds in several Kansu and Jehol painted pottery sites.

The Karasuk phase is archaeologically important in that it offers early examples of what is known as the Eurasian animal style. This culture has been explained as the result of an amalgamation with Mongoloid elements which, absent in the older Andronovo population, were traced in the skeletal remains of the Minusinsk area. Even so, most of the Karasuk inventory, whether metal tools or pottery, is linked with Andronovo, and the animal sculptural adornments of daggers and knives (which might be taken as testimony of influences from Anyang or the Shang cultural sphere at large) agree so well with older Siberian animal sculpture in stone, antler and bone that there is little need to look to China for their origin; particularly since the comparable specimens from Anyang appear to be novelties with no background of native traditions. A grave disadvantage in an attempt at disentangling these Bronze Age Chino-Siberian relations is the lack of scholarly excavations in the Ordos region; no ancient settlements, burials, skeletal materials, pottery or other tomb furniture were known in the mid-1950s. Evidence, therefore, rests with the stray finds of metal tools and chronology. Taking this latter fully into account, it can only be assumed that metallurgy came to China from the northwest, ultimate filiations with Mesopotamia notwithstanding.

Perhaps no other single factor so aptly illustrates the degree of obscurity prevailing in regard to the pre-Anyang period (before 1300 B.C.) as does the Chinese script. Appearing in the archaic but essentially developed system of the oracle inscriptions on tortoise shells and animal bones found in Hsiao-t'un, one of the Anyang sites, this script, an eminent achievement of Chinese civilization, undoubtedly presupposes some span of time prior to Anyang for its evolution. Yet not the faintest trace of any pictographic writing before Anyang has been discovered. It is justifiable, therefore, to conceive of the creation of the Chinese script some time during the obscure two centuries or so before Anyang, a creation which save perhaps for the basic idea of writing was entirely indigenous.

BIBLIOGRAPHY.—*Books and Articles:* J. G. Andersson, *The Cave-Deposit at Sha-kuo-t'un in Feng-t'ien* (Peking, 1923) and *Researches Into the Prehistory of the Chinese* (Stockholm, 1943); T. J. Arne, *Painted Stone Age Pottery From the Province of Honan, China* (Peking, 1925); C. W. Bishop, "The Rise of Civilization in China With Reference to Its Geographical Aspects," *Geographical Review,* vol. xxii (1932); H. G. Creel, *The Birth of China* (London, 1936; New York, 1937); N. Egami, K. Komai and S. Gotō, *Tōa Kōkogaku* (*East Asian Archaeology*) (Tokyo, 1939); Liang Ssu-yung, *New Stone Age Pottery From the Prehistoric Site at Hsi-Yin Tsun, Shansi, China,* Memoir No. 37, American Anthropological Association (Berkeley, 1930); É. Licent, *Les Collections néolithiques du musée Hoang-ho Pai-ho de Tientsin* (Tientsin, 1932); Max Loehr, *Zur Ur- und Vorgeschichte Chinas,* Saeculum III (1952); R. Maglioni, "Archaeology in South China," *Journal of East Asiatic Studies,* University of Manila, vol. ii (1952); Hallam L. Movius, Jr., "The Lower Palaeolithic Cultures of Southern and Eastern Asia," *Transactions* of the American Philosophical Society, new series 38 (1948); N. Palmgren, *Kansu Mortuary Urns of the Pan Shan and Ma Chang Groups* (Peking, 1934); P. Teilhard de Chardin, *Early Man in China* (Peking, 1941); P. Teilhard de Chardin and Pei Wen-chung, *Le Néolithique de la Chine* (Peking, 1944); Wu Chin-ting, *Prehistoric Pottery in China* (London, 1938).

Serials and Periodicals: Artibus Asiae; Archaeologia Orientalis (Tokyo and Kyoto); *Archaeologia Sinica,* Academia Sinica (Nanking); *Bulletin* of the Geological Society of China; *Bulletin* of the Museum of Far Eastern Antiquities (Stockholm); *Chung-kuo K'ao-ku Hsüeh-pao* (*Chinese Journal of Archaeology*) (Shanghai); *Kōkogaku Zasshi* (*Archaeological Journal*) (Tokyo); *Memoirs* of the Geological Society of China; *Palaeontologia Sinica,* Geological Survey of China; *T'ien-yeh K'ao-ku Pao-kao* (*Reports on Field Archaeology*) (Shanghai, 1936).

(M. L.)

HISTORY

EARLY PERIOD

Introduction; The Influence of Physical Environment.—Throughout its course the history of China has been profoundly affected by physical environment. In the first place, what is known as China proper is singularly fitted for a large and civilized population. Fertile valleys, the loess soil, great alluvial plains, a fairly large supply of minerals, a favourable climate and a rainfall which is usually adequate combine to make the region a natural seat for powerful and highly cultured peoples. In the second place, the mountains and rivers within China proper offer no insuperable obstacles to the union of the region under one rule. This is especially true of the part of China embracing the Yangtze valley east of the gorges and the valleys of the Hwang, the Hwai and the Pei (North) rivers. China is fairly easily welded into an empire.

On the other hand, these internal barriers, especially those in the west and southwest, are sufficiently marked to stimulate a strong provincial feeling and dialectal differences. Not infrequently—often for centuries—they have permitted political division. In the third place, the great plateaus, deserts and mountains by which China proper is surrounded have been sources of periodic invasions. The sturdy dwellers in these relatively inhospitable wastes naturally looked with covetous eyes upon the fertile and wealthy plains to the south and east. The necessity of defense against them was constant with every government of China; hence the Great Wall; hence, too, the attempt to control them by the conquest of their homes—Tibet, Sinkiang, Mongolia and Manchuria; hence, too, the periodic infusion of new blood and the highly mixed character of the present Chinese population. In the fourth place, these land barriers, together with the ocean, until the 19th century prevented close, continuous contacts with other seats of culture—India, Persia, Mesopotamia, the Mediterranean and Europe. Many contributions have come from without, notably Buddhism. Yet, while absorbing foreign elements, the civilization that developed in China retained a distinctive character partly because of the considerable isolation. The breaking of these barriers by the west was responsible for the stupendous revolution of the 20th century. In the fifth place, the seas played a relatively minor part in shaping Chinese civilization, which at its beginning was continental. Only as coastal regions were absorbed politically, as naval technology developed and as centres of civilization grew in Korea, Japan and southeastern Asia did maritime commerce become increasingly important. Extensive migration by sea was limited to the past several centuries. Geographical environment, in short, encouraged the Chinese to become a numerous, highly civilized, fairly well-unified though mixed people, isolated and nearly self-contained.

Origins.—The origins of the Chinese people and their civilization are still undetermined. It need not be assumed, indeed it is unlikely, that the people were of one original stock or that the civilization spread from one centre either within or outside the modern boundaries. It appears more likely that many different ethnic groups and many separate centres of primitive culture gradually merged and mingled to produce the civilization that has been continuously unfolding and spreading over this continental region. Archaeology revealed the existence of Neolithic culture in numerous sites in China. This culture bore fundamental resemblances to the Neolithic in many parts of the Eurasian continent but also had some distinctive features. In different parts of China, moreover, there were from early times regional variations. There was apparently a continuity of population from Neolithic times into the historic period, and there are some evidences of cultural continuity as well.

The sources of information available allow no simple conclusion about the complex question of the connection between the civilization of China and other ancient centres to the west.

The oldest Chinese historical literature, that in the *Shu Ching* (*Canon of History*)—parts of it the so-called "ancient text," a late forgery—and the earliest extant collection of ancient songs and poems, the *Shih Ching* (*Canon of Odes*), cannot be depended upon for information earlier than the 1st millennium B.C., and much of that is by no means uncontested. The earliest documents in even these books show a civilization which is already far removed from primitive conditions and contain no certain proof of either a native or a foreign origin for the Chinese. Archaeology has only begun to help. Researches in central Asia disclosed extremely ancient seats of culture east of the Caspian and suggested the possibility of migrations from what is now Sinkiang and Mongolia and possibly from farther west, and also the possibility of very early transmission of some art forms from western Asia and southeastern Europe. Remains of a Neolithic culture in Honan and elsewhere, with vessels and implements resembling those in use by the Chinese in historic times, were brought to light. The excavations at Anyang in Honan told much of the second traditional dynasty, the Shang, but gave evidence of nothing but a native origin for the rich bronze culture and its highly sophisticated writing. All that can be said with certainty is that clear glimpses of what can be called with assurance Chinese culture are caught first in the present area of Honan, Shantung and Shensi, that at the time from which we have remains it was already old, and that it and the people who possessed it were probably the result of several strains from different parts of Asia. Much and perhaps all of Chinese culture may have developed in China itself.

Mythical and Legendary Period.—The Chinese, like other peoples, have accounts which attempt to trace their history to its beginnings. Chinese myths speak of gods and demigods in what became Kansu and Shensi, of a first man, P'an Ku, who was endowed with supernatural powers and was the first ruler of the world, and of several series of emperors who were followed by Sui Jên, the "Fire Producer," who learned how to kindle fire by watching a bird produce sparks by pecking at a tree. The legendary Fu Hsi is thought of as having introduced matrimony, substituting the patriarchate for the matriarchate, as the inventor of the *pa kua*, or trigrams, much used in divination, as having taught his people hunting, fishing and the care of flocks, as the originator of musical instruments, as having substituted a kind of hieroglyphs for a system of knot writing previously used, and as having arranged a calendar. Fu Hsi is supposed to have been followed by Shên Nung, to whom is ascribed the introduction of agricultural implements and the tilling of the fields and the discovery of the medicinal properties of plants.

Shên Nung in turn was succeeded by Huang Ti, or the Yellow Emperor, who is held to have extended the boundaries of the empire, to have regulated the calendar, to have been the first builder of houses and cities, to have organized a board of historiographers and to have improved commerce. His consort is said to have invented the manufacture of silk.

Various dates are assigned to these last three rulers, but most chronologies agree in placing them somewhere in the 3rd millennium B.C. Whether these emperors ever existed is uncertain. At best they are but legendary figures.

Huang Ti is supposed to have been followed by four other rulers, and these in turn by the famous rulers Yao, Shun and Yü. These three are the first monarchs mentioned in the *Shu Ching* and were regarded by Confucius as models. Dates and details are still extremely uncertain, for most of those usually given are of late origin. Even the historicity of the three is to be viewed with decided doubt. Yü is held to have dealt successfully with the problem of draining away the waters of a great flood and to have founded the first dynasty, the Hsia (to which are ascribed the doubtful dates of 2205–1765 B.C. and whose very existence is questioned). It is said to have come to a close with the reign of an intolerable tyrant, Chieh Kuei, and to have been overthrown by T'ang, who in turn founded another dynasty, the Shang or Yin. The Shang dynasty is said by some to have lasted from 1765 to 1122 B.C., by others from 1523 to 1027 B.C.

Beginnings of History; The Shang Dynasty.—The existence of the Shang, however, has been amply demonstrated by modern archaeology. What have been some of the most brilliant and startling of relatively recent archaeological discoveries revealed the Shang to have had bronze utensils of unusual beauty and skill of construction and writing out of which came the present Chinese system. There was an elaborate system of divination by heating bones and tortoise shells and interpreting the cracks which came with cooling. There were chariots and horses and domesticated cattle, pigs, sheep, dogs and chickens. There were buildings of some size. The cowrie, a shell, was used for money. Stone was sculptured. The family was important and was reinforced by ancestor worship (at least in the royal house). Various spirits and deities were revered. The Shang dynasty, like its predecessor, is said to have been brought to its end by the misdeeds of its last ruler, Chou Hsin.

The Chou Dynasty.—Condign punishment was inflicted on Chou Hsin by the rulers of the principality of Chou. Chou was on the western frontier, a buffer against the constant pressure of invaders who would seize the fertile plains. It may itself have been founded by a fresh wave of immigrants from the northwest closely related to those controlled by the Shang.

One of the rulers of Chou, Wên Wang, who, so the records claim, had devoted himself to governing well his little state, protested against the cruelties of Chou Hsin and was incarcerated for his pains. While in prison he is said to have produced the *I Ching*, or *Canon of Changes*, a volume based upon the trigrams and later viewed with great veneration and incorporated into the Confucian canon. The book is, however, undoubtedly of much later origin. Wên Wang's son, Wu Wang, eventually obtained his father's release and then, after his father's death, with the aid of a coalition of princes, overthrew Chou Hsin and established himself as the first monarch of the Chou dynasty. Wu Wang was greatly aided by his distinguished brother, Chou Kung, or the duke of Chou, whose regency during the minority of the second emperor of the dynasty is held by orthodox historians to have been ideal. The Chou dynasty lasted until 249 B.C. and so had a longer life than any other which has held the throne of China.

The nearly nine centuries of the Chou dynasty witnessed many important developments. First of all, the area of the realm was greatly extended. Expansion carried the Chinese and their culture to the sea on the east, to the Yangtze river on the south and to the eastern borders of Szechwan. The "barbarians" in these regions appear to have adopted Chinese culture and to have been assimilated by the conquerors. This expansion was for the most part not the result of any leadership provided by the imperial house. After the death of its founders, the dynasty produced few monarchs of outstanding ability. One, Mu Wang, is reported to have been a great traveller and to have extended his journeys to the mysterious "Royal Lady of the West" (Hsi Wang Mu). Most of the emperors, however, were distinctly mediocre, and some are remembered chiefly for their folly. The spread of Chinese power was the result chiefly of the energies of adventurers and the activities of heads of subordinate principalities.

The realm, as it expanded and as the quality of the Chou declined, tended to break up into semi-independent states. These made war on one another, concluded peace and developed the rudiments of international law, with scant attention to the authority of the imperial house. The power of the central administration more and more fell into abeyance, until, finally, the result was a condition which in many respects resembled European feudalism.

The Chou dynasty is memorable for a marked development in culture. Agriculture was highly developed through irrigation and the regular division of lands, some of the metals were in use, literature had come into existence, including poetry, history and state archives, schools were to be found, and industry and commerce had sprung up. As in the Shang, there were bronze implements and utensils, although not so skilfully cast as under the earlier dynasty. Religion was highly developed, with divination, the worship of ancestors and of spirits of hills, rivers, stars and other natural objects, and adoration of a supreme being variously called Shang Ti and T'ien. Much emphasis was placed on ceremonies and ritual, both in religion and in official intercourse, and a keen sense of ethical values had developed, reinforced by the belief that the supreme being was on the side of righteousness and hated iniquity. Then, as in modern times, the family was the dominant social unit. Knowledge of the period is not sufficiently complete to enable us to trace all the growth in culture which occurred, nor is it known how much this was attributable to influences from peoples outside the expanding frontier.

Some developments, however, are known, chief among them being the expansion of thought and the rise of schools of philosophy. Most of the thinkers seem to have been associated with the government. Certainly the problem which chiefly engaged their attention was the welfare of society. Cosmogony did not greatly concern them. To their minds, however, the disorder which attended the breakdown of the central government and the division of the country into warring states dominated by autocratic rulers was of great moment, and they sought to build a new order which would bring happiness to all. More is said elsewhere of the teachings of the Chou philosophers. It is sufficient to state here that Confucius (551–479 B.C.) sought to save society by a return to the way of the ancients. This he believed to involve an emphasis upon ethics—especially upon moral education—and upon ceremonies. By the leadership and example of the educated, and by the careful regulation of society by the ceremonies which had come down from the past, he would bring in a golden age.

In his train and approving his solution came others, chief among them Mencius (372 or 385–289 B.C.), who stressed the essential goodness of human nature and the right of subjects to revolt against a persistently unjust ruler. Another school, Taoism, had as its foundation classic the *Tao Tê Ching* and attributed this to one Lao Tzŭ (Lao-tse), who is said to have been an older contemporary of Confucius. The authorship and the dates of Lao Tzŭ are highly doubtful. The solution for the woes of mankind offered by the *Tao Tê Ching* was conformity to the way of the universe. The way of the universe was believed to be the absence of all man-made restraints and freedom from elaborate regulations and from what passed for civilization. This solution was, obviously, quite different from that advocated by Confucius, and members of the two schools engaged in frequent controversy. Belonging to the school of the *Tao Tê Ching*—Taoism—were many other thinkers, notably Chuang Tzŭ (*c.* 369–286 B.C.). A book bearing his name is a witty exposition of the Taoist view that happiness may be achieved only by the free development of man's nature and that the best way of governing is through non-government.

Mo Ti, who lived between the times of Confucius and Mencius and who was the precursor of two schools which for several centuries were to have great vogue but were eventually to disappear, taught that institutions should be submitted to the pragmatic test—were they of benefit to society? He was deeply religious, believed that T'ien (Heaven) loved men and that all men should love one another. It was his doctrine of universal love as the basis of ethics which brought against him the vigour of Mencius' dialectic. Yang Chu, a contemporary of Mencius, declined to trouble himself about society, maintained that death ended all and held that each man should live for himself and for his own pleasure. Hsün Tzŭ, born in 340 B.C., denied immortality and the existence of spirits and held that man, although bad by nature, could be improved by regulations and ceremonies. The legalists, as their name indicates, wished autocratic rule through the enforcement of law rather than the Confucian influence of moral example.

These and others show how diverse and vigorous was the thought of the age. Never again was Chinese philosophy to be so creative and so untrammelled by the past. Systems then begun were to persist until modern times.

The Ch'in Dynasty.—The philosophers, for all their theories, were unable to prevent the progressive disintegration of the realm. Under the last Chou emperors internal strife so increased that the final 250 years of the dynasty are dubbed Chan Kuo, "the Contending States." Individualism was the order of the day. In the general anarchy the Chou dynasty as last disappeared. The end of the Chou and the union into one empire of the large territory over which the Chinese people and culture had now spread were achieved by the rulers of the state of Ch'in. Ch'in, on the northwestern frontier, like the state of Chou before Wu Wang, had been a buffer against the barbarians. Its princes at last conquered their rivals and took the emblems of imperial power from the weaklings of the Chou line. The last of the Chou was deposed in 249 B.C. The welding of the new domains of the Ch'in into a unified state was the work of the Ch'in ruler who ascended the throne in 246 B.C. and who styled himself Shih Huang Ti, the "First Emperor." Assisted and perhaps inspired and directed by his minister, Li Ssŭ, and utilizing the principles of the legalists, Ch'in Shih Huang Ti abolished the political system of the Chou, with its many petty states and hereditary princes, and divided the country into 36 provinces, over each of which he set officials appointed by and directly responsible to himself. As an emblem and centre of his power he built a capital near the present Sian (Hsi-an, Shensi province). He introduced a uniform system of laws, weights and measures, thus aiding both unity and commerce. He extended the boundaries of the empire, carrying his arms into what became Fukien, Kwangtung and Kwangsi and against the barbarians—the Hsiung Nu—on the northern and western frontiers. To defend his borders on the side from which they were most frequently attacked, he constructed the Great Wall. This had probably already existed in part, but he completed and strengthened it. Later orthodox scholars held his name in reproach for one of the signal acts of his reign, the "burning of the books." What motives lay behind this deed we do not know; he probably believed that the scholars who were advocating political philosophies contrary to the legalist school on which he was building his regime were enemies of the new order he was trying to establish. Whatever his motives, he had the existing literature collected and burned, exempting only copies he preserved in the imperial library and books dealing with divination, pharmacy, medicine, agriculture and arboriculture. He commanded scholars to desist from discussing the past. The old order did not expire without a struggle. Ch'in Shih Huang Ti died in 210 B.C., and almost as soon as his strong hand was removed the structure he had erected collapsed. Insurrection broke out, the feeble "Second Emperor" was murdered (207 B.C.), and military chieftains set to fighting for the throne.

The Han Dynasty.—Out of the renewed civil strife one of the contestants, Liu Pang, shortly emerged victorious and founded the Han dynasty (202 B.C.—Liu Pang counted his reign as having begun in 206 B.C.). The effort of Ch'in Shih Huang Ti had not been in vain. The "feudalism" of the last years of the Chou had been so badly shattered that Liu Pang found it possible to unite the country quickly. At the beginning the Han attempted to rule the empire by a system which was a combination of that instituted by the Ch'in and of "feudalism." Members of the emperor's family were placed over the main divisions of the realm. This compromise carried with it the seeds of the old pernicious particularism, however, and after about a century the principle of hereditary local power was curtailed and the practice was adopted of governing through a civil service recruited on the basis of worth. Worth was to be discovered in part by means of examinations. Confucianism in a modified form rather than legalism became orthodox. Greatly enlarged by later dynasties, the practice of recruiting officials by means of examinations was to be a means of holding the country together. It was one of the most successful political devices ever invented.

With the consolidation of China went foreign conquests. The major ones date from the long and brilliant reign of Wu Ti (140–87 B.C.). The Han arms were directed chiefly against the barbarians on the northwest, especially the Hsiung Nu. Alliances against this common foe were made with central Asiatic peoples. To effect the alliances Chang Ch'ien was sent to the west and went as far as Bactria. The power of the Hsiung Nu was broken and the Han rule was extended into what is now Sinkiang. In the dry air of the far northwest remains of fortresses and walls built by the Han to guard the frontier have survived to our own day. The Han also carried their arms south of the Yangtze as far as Tongking and to the northeast into Korea.

With unity, increased prosperity and conquests came foreign trade. The caravan routes to the west had been made safe by the defeat of the Hsiung Nu, and products from central Asia and even from the outposts of the Hellenistic world reached China, and Chinese goods were sent in exchange.

Literature and art revived. The first emperor of the Han declined to remove the prohibition of Ch'in Shih Huang Ti against the ancient books. The ban was lifted by his successor, however; documents which had escaped the holocaust were brought out from their hiding places, and scholars devoted themselves to restoring the texts and writing commentaries on them. The Han could not boast of as much original philosophical thought as could the Chou: it may be that the emphasis placed by the state upon the study of the classics of the Confucian school discouraged originality. Taoism was espoused by many in high position, but it degenerated more and more into magic and the search for the elixir of life and for means of transmuting the baser metals into gold. Historiography was greatly developed, however, the outstanding work being the monumental *Historian's Records* (*Shih Chi*) of Ssu-ma Ch'ien. Poetry, too, revived. In art the Han period showed some new forms, several of them possibly influenced by contacts with central Asia and the west.

The Han rule suffered a temporary interruption when, in the 1st century of the Christian era, Wang Mang, one of the most interesting social and economic innovators in Chinese history, set aside an infant emperor (A.D. 8) and for a few years ruled as the emperor of the Hsin dynasty. Princes of the Han, however, defeated and killed him, and in A.D. 23 restored the dynasty. The capital was now moved from Ch'ang-an (Sian) in the later Shensi province to Loyang in the later Honan province. The dynasty after this interruption is known as the Later or—because of the change of capital—Eastern Han, as distinguished from the Earlier or Western Han.

The Later Han renewed the conquests in the west, and under Gen. Pan Ch'ao the Chinese became masters of parts of central Asia. A Chinese embassy reached the Persian gulf. Partly because of the control by the Han of the caravan routes to central Asia and partly because of the possession of Tongking and the south, commerce was maintained with the Roman orient—known to the Chinese as Ta Ts'in—both by land and by sea. Chinese silks were carried to the Mediterranean world, and products from central Asia and the Hellenistic world were brought to China.

Through these contacts with the west came Buddhism. The story which attributes its introduction to a dream of the Emperor Ming is a pious fabrication of a later age, but that it entered China under the Han is certain. The Later Han continued the patronage of letters, and especially of the Confucian school, which had been accorded by the Earlier Han. Literature flourished and was furthered by the invention of paper (*c.* A.D. 105).

The annals of the Han dynasty, like those of both its predecessors and successors, are punctuated by rebellions and intrigues. As the imperial line became weak, these succeeded in bringing it to an end, and a period of disunion followed which was to last for nearly four centuries. So thoroughly had the Han emperors welded China together, however, that cultural unity and the vision of a single empire were never lost, and to this day the Chinese call themselves the "Sons of Han." Under the Ch'in and the Han China had for the first time become a great state.

Three and One-Half Centuries of Disunion (the "Three Kingdoms").—The Later Han technically came to an end in 220. It was succeeded by three states—the "Three Kingdoms"—Wei in the north, ruled by the successors of Ts'ao Ts'ao, minister and betrayer of the last of the Han; Wu in the central and lower part of the Yangtze valley, with its capital at Nanking; and Shu, in Szechwan, whose monarchs, of the house of Han, claimed title to the entire empire and which, for its Han connection, is known as the Minor or Shu Han. The period was one of almost constant war and is famed for the exploits of its chief figures, popularized for later ages by the stage and the historical novel *San Kuo Chih Yen I*. Liu Pei, first prince of the Minor Han, was aided by Chang Fei and Kuan Yü, the latter of whom was later deified as the god of war, Kuan Ti. He was also assisted by Chu-ko Liang, who was noted as a strategist and as the inventor of war machines. The fortunes of war varied, but not one of the three kingdoms was able long to conquer the other two.

To domestic dissension was being added foreign invasion. Peoples from the north and west—Mongols, Hsiung Nu and Turks—took advantage of the internal weakness of the fertile lands to the east and south and seized much of the territory north of the Yangtze. Many ephemeral states and dynasties followed, the invaders striving to establish themselves in the north and the Chinese, from the south, endeavouring to beat them back. The period is accordingly known as the epoch of the northern and southern dynasties. The most prominent among many dynasties of the period were the Eastern Chin (A.D. 317–420), with its capital at Nanking; the Sung (420–479, called Liu Sung to distinguish it from the later and more famous Sung dynasty), also with its capital at Nanking; the Northern or Yüan Wei (386–535) of the Toba Tatars, with its capital at the modern Tatung in Chahar, and at its end dividing into the Western and the Eastern Wei, followed by the Northern Ch'i and the Northern Chou. In the south ruled the Ch'en.

The period was one of transition in civilization. Many of the invaders adopted Chinese culture, but they could not but modify it. Buddhism now achieved popularity, perhaps in part because with the breakdown of central authority the Confucian school could not offer the resistance that it could under the Han. Many of the monarchs espoused the foreign cult, missionaries came in numbers, and Chinese, the best known of whom was Fa-hsien, went on pilgrimages to the sacred sites in India and returned with Buddhist scriptures.

By the time the empire was once more united, Buddhism had become an integral part of its life and was having profound effects upon other religions, popular thought, literature and art. The Buddhist sculptures of the period are noteworthy. During the last years of disunion and during the first century or two of the union which followed, Buddhism was more prosperous than it was ever again to be in China. The many new sects which arose within it testified to its vigour. Taoism, too, under the stimulus of Buddhism, developed as an organized church and became a great popular religion.

Though it was a period of disunion and turmoil, the 3rd to 6th centuries showed great increases in knowledge of medicine, mathematics, astronomy, botany and chemistry. Through foreign missionaries and returning pilgrims, merchants and embassies, the Chinese became much better informed about the outside world. Sea connections and commerce between China and southern Asia increased. The lower Yangtze region became more highly developed economically and culturally.

The Sui and the T'ang.—After the long period of division, union was once more achieved, first under the Sui dynasty (A.D. 589–618) and then under the T'ang (618–906). Under the second emperor of the T'ang, T'ai Tsung (627–649), China became more powerful than it had been since the Han and was for a time the strongest and largest empire on earth. Under the T'ang Chinese arms were carried again into Korea, into Turkistan, across the Pamirs to northwest India and into Tibet. To China, and especially to the T'ang court at Ch'ang-an, the later Sian, journeyed peoples of many lands and faiths. Moslems, Nestorians and followers of Manichaeism came, and Persians sought aid against the Moslem Arab wave of invasion. The Nestorians had missionaries and churches in China and, apparently, a fairly extensive literature. Japanese carried home ideas which were to continue the revolution in the life of their nation that contact with China immediately before the T'ang had begun. Chinese Buddhist pilgrims also continued to visit India.

Under the T'ang the bureaucracy and its accompanying civil service examinations were further developed, and the latter were capped by the foundation of the Han Lin academy, in later years charged with the compilation of histories, the drafting of decrees and other literary labours.

In the prosperous and peaceful T'ang period, painting reached new heights and China's most famous poets wrote. Among the latter the most distinguished were the realistic Tu Fu and the Bohemian and attractive Li Po. From the T'ang dynasty dates the earliest-known printing, and paper money made its tentative appearance.

Of the many rulers of the T'ang little need be said here. Besides T'ai Tsung the best remembered was probably Hsüan Tsung (Ming Huang) (reigned 712–756). Under him lived the greatest poets and painters. In him the dynasty reached its apex, and toward the close of his reign a disastrous rebellion broke out which marked the beginning of the dynasty's decline. After him invasions and rebellions decimated the population, and in 907 the dynasty was brought to an end.

The Five Dynasties (907–960).—Following the T'ang various aspirants for imperial honours fought for the throne, and in quick succession there followed five ephemeral dynasties, known as the Later Liang, the Later T'ang, the Later Chin, the Later Han and the Later Chou. Their assumption of famous names did not prevent the early demise of each, and in 960 the last gave way to the Sung dynasty.

The Sung Dynasty (960–1279).—The Sung dynasty, founded by Chao K'uang-yin, began auspiciously. Most of the country was reduced to submission, the capital was placed at Kai-feng, near the site of the glories of some earlier dynasties, and under the first few rulers the civil service was so developed and improved that it became a model for later times.

This did not prevent the former, however, from arrogating ever more authority to the throne. Before long evil days came. An attempt to conquer the K'itan, a people of Mongol tongue who ruled the Liaotung peninsula, proved unsuccessful, and the K'itan occupied portions of the empire adjoining their domains and were prevented from further depredations only by the payment of tribute. On the northwest another kingdom, that of Hsi Hsia, threatened the frontiers and fought both the Sung and the K'itan. The Sung called to their assistance the Chin ("Golden") Tatars, but after expelling the K'itan the Chin made themselves masters of the territory north of the Yangtze and the Sung were constrained to move their capital to Hangchow. In the wake of the Chin came the Mongols. The great Mongol general Temuchin, or Jenghiz Khan (*q.v.*), invaded China early in the 13th century. By 1223 he had possession of most of the country north of the Hwang-ho, having defeated the Chin. Before his death (1227) Jenghiz had made further inroads on the Chin and had defeated the Hsi Hsia. Jenghiz' successor, Ogdai, formed an alliance with the Sung, and the two made an end of the Chin. The allies then fell out, and the Mongols under Ogdai, Mangu and Kublai pressed south, until, after the last of the Sung monarchs had in despair cast himself into the sea, Kublai in 1279 became emperor of all China.

The military misfortunes of the Sung did not prevent the dynasty from synchronizing with one of the great creative periods of Chinese culture. Painting, under the influence of Buddhism and Taoism, reached a very high point. Philosophical schools contended with each other, and one, culminating in Chu Hsi (1130–1200), gave Confucianism the form which until the 20th century was to be regarded as orthodox. Notable histories were written, among them that of Ssŭ-ma Kuang. An interesting experiment in economic and political reorganization was made under the leadership of Wang An-shih (1021–86). Wang An-shih was a brilliant and thoroughgoing radical. He sought to change the existing educational system and make it of more practical use. He issued original commentaries on the classics, reading new meanings into these ancient documents. For 18 years, as prime minister, he inaugurated and superintended what resembled the later European socialism. His object was to make the state better fitted to cope with its foreign enemies. To this end he would have the government take over the entire management of commerce, redivide the land, regulate prices, make loans to farmers at moderate rates of interest and place more of the burden of taxation on the rich. He also put upon every family the burden of military defense and appointed a commission to fix a national budget. Wang inevitably had many enemies and critics, one of the chief being Ssŭ-ma Kuang. These eventually forced his retirement and restored the *status quo*.

The Mongol Dynasty (1260–1368).—The Mongol or, as it was officially known, the Yüan dynasty was not of long duration. The reign of Kublai was brilliant. From his capital at Khanbaliq, or Cambaluc, on approximately the site of the modern Peking, he ruled not only over China but over most of the vast Mongol empire, with its western frontiers in Mesopotamia and Europe. Expeditions were sent into Champa, Annam, Burma and Java and against Japan. Under him, however, Mongol power reached its climax. The invasions to the south ended in a somewhat inglorious retirement, the attempt on Java was unsuccessful, and the armadas against Japan met with overwhelming disaster. The Mongols ruled China largely as conquerors and brought in many foreign troops and hordes of foreign officials.

After Kublai the ability of the monarchs rapidly declined, rebellions arose, the Mongols were expelled, and in 1368 the most successful of their opponents, a former Buddhist monk, Chu Yüan-chang, became the first emperor of a new dynasty, the Ming.

The Yüan dynasty, brief though it was, was not without notable developments. The Grand canal was completed, and drama and the novel first became important. The safety of the trans-Asiatic trade routes under Mongol rule and the Mongol method of government brought many foreigners into China. Nestorian Christianity had survived on the edges of the empire since the T'ang and now reappeared in China. Moslems entered in fairly large numbers, and even Armenians were to be found. Now for the first time western Europeans made their way to China.

The eastward expansion of Europe in the crusades and Italian commerce, and the burst of missionary enthusiasm through the Franciscan and Dominican orders, brought Europeans to the western fringes of the Mongol empire. It was natural that European merchants and missionaries should make their way to China—or Cathay, as they called it. Most notable among the merchants were the Venetians Nicolo and Maffeo Polo, and the son of Nicolo, Marco. Marco Polo was for years in the service of Kublai and, returning to Venice, wrote the account of his travels which has made him famous. Friars were sent as envoys to the Mongol rulers in central Asia, but so far as is known the first to reach China was the Franciscan Giovanni di Monte Corvino, who arrived at Cambaluc in 1294 and there, in the ensuing three decades or more, built up a Christian community of several thousands. When news of his success reached Europe he was created archbishop of Cambaluc, and reinforcements were sent him.

In the course of the next few years numbers of other missionaries arrived, notably a papal legate, Giovanni de' Marignolli. With the collapse of Mongol rule, however, the trade routes became unsafe and an antiforeign reaction set in; Europeans, both merchants and missionaries, disappeared from China, and the Catholic Nestorian communities passed out of existence.

The Ming Dynasty (1368–1644).—This new and purely Chinese dynasty was not noteworthy for its brilliance. Under it, however, the empire was fairly prosperous. The first emperor, Chu Yüan-chang, better known by his reign title, Hung Wu, unified the country and established his capital at Nanking. His fourth son, the third emperor, commonly known by his reign title, Yung Lo, came to the throne through a sea of blood but proved an able ruler. He was a great builder: he established his seat at Peking, and the palaces and temples which through succeeding centuries made the city architecturally one of the outstanding capitals of the world were largely his work. He was a patron of literature. He sent expeditions to the south and southeast as far as Java and Ceylon. One of the princes of Ceylon was brought captive to China, and for years tribute came from the island. Under a succeeding monarch an expedition was sent by sea as far as the Persian gulf. Under the Ming emperors, moreover, Korea was invaded, Annam for a time became subject to China, and frequent wars with the Mongols usually kept those ancient enemies at bay. As time passed, the decline which was the inevitable fate of dynasties brought weakness to the empire. The Japanese invaded Korea, and for decades Japanese pirates ravaged the coasts.

The Ming period brought a restoration of Chinese culture after a long period of foreign domination. All forms of intellectual and artistic life flourished; there was a growth of academies, libraries and book printing. In philosophy the neo-Confucian school of Chu Hsi was dominant, but Wang Yang-ming (1472–1529) founded an influential school of thought which maintained that reality and truth lie in the mind and that knowledge is achieved intuitively. Scholars were active, studying and reinterpreting the Confucian canon, writing treatises on philology and geography or monographs on arts and sciences, preparing dictionaries and an illustrated encyclopaedia. In literature the novel developed into an important new genre. Architecture, landscape painting and ceramics showed vitality.

An important development was the introduction of new crops and the spread of their use. Cotton, introduced in the 13th century, was now widely cultivated; cotton cloth began to be worn throughout the empire. New world plants such as maize, or Indian corn, sweet potatoes and peanuts enriched the diet and allowed the profitable cultivation of unused land. Tobacco entered toward the end of the dynasty. These crops and others adopted during the 17th century helped make possible the large growth in population during the next dynasty.

The Ming period was made memorable by the renewed coming of Europeans. The European voyages and conquests of the 16th century brought the Portuguese to India, Malacca, China and Japan and the Spaniards to the Philippines. The first Portuguese reached China about 1514 and within a few years had established themselves at several ports. The first comers were so truculent, however, that before long they were driven out or massacred. For a brief time the Portuguese traded from the island of Shang-ch'uan, south of Canton, but shortly afterward were permitted to form a settlement at Macao—the exact date is uncertain, but was probably between 1552 and 1560—and retained that as their base. Missionaries came. St. Francis Xavier died on Shang-ch'uan (St. John Island) in 1552 while engaged in a vain attempt to enter the empire. His fellow Jesuits renewed the effort and before the close of the century had established themselves in several cities in the interior. The ablest of their number was Matteo Ricci (1552–1610), an Italian who arrived in China in 1582 and in 1601 succeeded in effecting a residence in Peking. Ricci and his associates commended themselves to the scholar-official class by their knowledge of science, especially of mathematics and astronomy, and were placed in charge of the government's bureau of astronomy in Peking.

MODERN PERIOD

The Manchus.—The weakening Ming dynasty was overthrown by invaders from the northeast, the Manchus. The Manchus had been welded into a formidable force by Nurhachu (1559–1626) and before his death had aspired to the empire. Their opportunity came when, in 1644, a rebel, Li Tzŭ-ch'eng, made himself master of Peking and the Ming emperor committed suicide. A Ming general, Wu San-kuei, joined forces with the Manchus to oust Li, and a Manchu prince was placed on the throne. Ming claimants did not tamely submit, and it was not until 1662 that the last of them, driven, after stubborn resistance, to the Burmese borders of Yünnan, came to his end. Somewhat later, the successors of Koxinga, who had been implacable toward the Manchus and had harried the south coast and had ruled Formosa, were eliminated.

For a century and a half the Manchu (or the Ch'ing dynasty, 1644–1911) provided the throne with able rulers. The monarchs whose reigns were named K'ang Hsi (1662–1722) and, after the brief interlude of Yung Chêng (1723–35), Ch'ien Lung (1736–96) had, from the standpoint of foreign conquests and domestic prosperity, as brilliant careers as the empire had known.

The Manchus ruled as conquerors and maintained permanent garrisons in strategic centres throughout the country, but they adopted Chinese culture, perpetuated the time-honoured administrative machinery and laws, associated Chinese with themselves in the highest boards at Peking and opened to them all the provincial offices. They guarded against revolt by forbidding a Chinese to hold office in his native province, by frequently shifting officials and by dividing the administrative responsibility for each province among several officers who could serve as checks on one another. They vigorously put down revolts, notably that of Wu San-kuei, to whose aid they largely owed the throne. They ruled Manchuria and conquered Mongolia; under K'ang Hsi they added Tibet and Formosa to their possessions and, under Ch'ien Lung, Ili and Turkistan. Ch'ien Lung's armies penetrated Burma, Nepal and Annam, and Korea paid tribute.

Never had the empire covered so much territory, and never had it been so populous. With the reign of Ch'ien Lung the dynasty passed its zenith, and after it the quality of the ruling house declined. In the later years of Ch'ien Lung and under Chia Ch'ing (1796–1820), Tao Kuang (1821–50), Hsien Fêng (1851–61) and T'ung Chih (1862–75) numerous rebellions kept part or all of the country in turmoil.

In culture, the China of the Manchus was largely a continuation of that of the Ming. Ceramics were elaborated, but painting did not equal that of the Sung. Scholarship flourished under imperial patronage with the compilation of vast encyclopaedias, dictionaries, geographies and other compendiums of knowledge. Historical and textual criticism reached its maturity in the School of Han Learning, a movement which undertook to restudy the authenticity of all ancient works and to strip away the accretions of later centuries. This movement challenged the very basis of Sung neo-Confucianism. But a return to orthodoxy, fostered by the emperor Ch'ien Lung, marked the latter part of the dynasty.

Pressure by Europeans to gain a foothold in China became an increasingly serious problem. Catholic missionaries continued to come. To the Jesuits were added in the 17th century Franciscans, Dominicans and Augustinians from the Philippines, Franciscans from Italy and members of the Société des Missions Étrangères of Paris. In 1692 K'ang Hsi issued what amounted to an edict of toleration, and for a number of years the church prospered greatly. Missionaries and Christian communities were in all provinces, and by 1700 the Catholics in the empire probably numbered more than 300,000. Then came a series of reverses. A prolonged controversy over the question of what Chinese term should be used for God and of what attitude should be taken by Christians toward certain Chinese rites, among them the honours paid to ancestors and to Confucius, divided the foreign staff. When Rome finally spoke, the decision antagonized K'ang Hsi and the Chinese scholar class. Repeated persecutions arose—only in part because of the decision on the rites; in 1773 papal orders dissolved the Society of Jesus, and the Lazarists, in spite of valiant attempts, could not fully take its place. Religious indifference in Europe, the French Revolution and the wars of Napoleon cut off support from home. By 1800 the Catholics in the empire numbered only about 200,000 and were badly demoralized. Between 1600 and 1800, however, Catholic missionaries had helped to acquaint China with European science and religion and, by their writings, had spread in Europe a knowledge of China.

European merchants did not penetrate the empire as did the missionaries, but they continued to come. Although their commerce declined, the Portuguese retained Macao. The French, Dutch and British opened trade with China, and in 1784 came the first ship from the United States, the precursor of many more. By the middle of the 18th century British trade was more important than that of any other occidental people and was the official monopoly of the English East India company. Chinese teas, silks and cottons were in great demand in Europe, and for a time were paid for largely by specie. Eventually, however, the importation of opium, chiefly from India and on British ships, brought a reversal of the balance of trade.

Commerce was carried on under great restrictions. By the close of the 18th century only one port, Canton, was open to merchants from abroad. The Europeans were there confined to a small area—the "factories"—and were ordered to spend the quiet months in Macao. Business could be conducted only through an officially designated group of Chinese merchants, the Co-hong. The absence of fixed tariff charges, the exactions of venal officials, the unwillingness of the Chinese to permit official intercourse on the basis of equality, the prohibition against a Chinese teaching a foreigner the language, the subjection of the foreigner to Chinese laws and courts were all galling to the westerner.

Russia had little if any better treatment. K'ang Hsi had momentarily checked the Russian advance by the capture of Albazin (1685) and there followed the first treaty to be signed with a European power, that of Nerchinsk (1689), which, with its successor, the treaty of Kyakhta (1727), provided for trade, diplomatic intercourse—in part through a resident Russian mission in Peking—and the extradition of criminals.

Repeated attempts were made to obtain better terms. Portuguese, Dutch and British embassies travelled to Peking, notably those of the British in 1793 and 1816, led respectively by Earl Macartney and Earl Amherst, but to no avail. The Chinese had never been accustomed to dealing with other governments on the basis of equality and regarded all foreign envoys as bearers of tribute.

The First War With Great Britain and the First Group of Foreign Treaties (1839–44).—Such a condition of affairs could not endure. The industrial revolution inaugurated a period of renewed expansion of the occident, and the west desired admission to China to market the products of its factories and to obtain raw materials. This was also the period of the important clipper ship trade between the United States and China.

Pressure first came from Great Britain, the European nation in which the industrial revolution began. On demand from British merchants, the monopoly of the China trade by the English East India company was abolished (1834), and friction between the English and Chinese increased. Lord Napier was appointed the first "superintendent" of British trade in Canton (1834), but Chinese officials looked upon him as merely a head merchant and refused to deal with him as an equal. Lord Napier died while still in this anomalous position, and his successors were unable to effect any improvement in the situation. Armed conflict was all but inevitable. British merchants were insisting upon more privileges than the Chinese were willing to concede, and British and Chinese ideas of international intercourse were fundamentally at variance—the one government being accustomed to a family of equal nations, the other knowing only an empire and subject peoples. Conceptions of law differed, the Chinese, with their emphasis on group responsibility, holding the entire British community liable for the misdemeanour of any of its members and insisting upon a life for a life, even when death had been accidental, and the British contending that upon the individual and not the community should be placed the responsibility for misdeeds.

The conflict came to a head over the question of the importation of opium. This had long been prohibited by the Manchu government, but foreign merchants brought it in ever-increasing quantities and corrupt Chinese and Manchu officials connived at its introduction. After many futile attempts at enforcement, Peking at last took vigorous action and dispatched a special commissioner, Lin Tsêhsü, to stamp out the trade. Lin arrived at Canton in 1839 and promptly set about his task. Foreign merchants were compelled to surrender their stocks of opium for destruction, and pressure was put upon them to give bond not to engage further in the importation of the drug. The British objected to what seemed to them high-handed measures, and in Nov. 1839 hostilities broke out. The Chinese were repeatedly defeated. The war dragged out until 1842, however, for the British contented themselves largely with attacks on centres south of the Yangtze, and their victories alternated with unsuccessful attempts at negotiation. Finally, when Chinkiang—at the intersection of the Yangtze and the Grand canal—was taken and Peking's communications with the south were threatened, the imperial authorities were frightened into concessions, and on Aug. 29, 1842, the treaty of Nanking was signed.

This document provided for the cession of the island of Hong Kong to Great Britain, for the opening to foreign residence and commerce of five ports, Canton, Amoy, Foochow, Ningpo and Shanghai, for liberty to appoint consuls at each port, for communication between British and Chinese officials of the same rank on the basis of equality, for an indemnity to the British, for the abolition of the Co-hong and for a "fair and regular tariff." In 1843 regulations for trade were agreed upon and published, and a supplementary treaty was signed which fixed the tariff rates, assured to the British most-favoured-nation treatment and contained the beginnings of extraterritoriality. Other western nations took advantage of China's defeat. The U.S. sent a commissioner, Caleb Cushing, who negotiated a treaty which conceded, in general, the same commercial privileges to Americans which had been granted to the British and which, among other things, removed U.S. citizens engaged in the opium traffic from the protection of their government, elaborated extraterritoriality and provided for the revision of the treaty at the end of 12 years. In 1844 the French obtained a treaty which had much the same provisions for trade and official intercourse as were guaranteed by the British and U.S. documents. At the instance of the French, imperial edicts were issued providing for the toleration of Catholic Christianity and for the restoration of the church property which had been sequestered in the persecutions of the previous century. In the next few years the Belgians and the Swedes were also given treaties.

The Second Foreign War and the Second Group of Treaties, 1856–60.—The years between 1842 and 1856 were in effect a period of troubled truce. The treaties of 1842 and 1844 were satisfactory neither to foreigners nor to Chinese. From the standpoint of the foreigner they did not grant enough. No provision was made for travel in the interior, for residence in places other than the five open ports or for direct diplomatic intercourse through representatives resident in Peking. The Chinese, on the other hand, believed that the treaties conceded too much, and, since they had been extracted by force, the authorities were not disposed to abide by them any more than they were compelled to do. The Chinese were no further inclined than formerly to treat western "barbarians" as equals. Clashes were frequent. Moreover, the British treaties said nothing about opium, and the traffic in the drug continued, a constant source of friction.

While the Americans, the British and the French were demanding that revision of the treaties which had been promised in the documents of 1844, war between the British and the Chinese broke out over a comparatively minor incident—as is often the case in times of international tension—the violation by the Chinese of a British flag and the arrest of the crew, all Chinese, on a Chinese-owned but British-registered craft, the lorcha "Arrow" (Oct. 8, 1856). The French, then closely associated with the British through the Crimean War, found in the judicial murder of a Roman Catholic missionary, Chapdelaine, in Kwangsi (Feb. 29, 1856), an occasion for joining in the conflict.

The two powers did not at first press the war, for they were just emerging from the struggle in the Crimea and difficulties with Persia in 1856–57, and the Indian mutiny, which blazed out in 1857, engrossed the attention of the British. Late in 1857, however, the British and French took Canton, and in the following year their squadrons went north to Tientsin, thence to threaten Peking into submission. The Taku forts, commanding the entrance to Tientsin, were captured, and to save the capital the Chinese granted the desired treaties. The Russian and U.S. representatives, although not in the war, were on hand to profit by the French and British successes and also obtained treaties. The Russians obtained all the Chinese territory north of the Amur.

The treaties of Tientsin (1858) in general contained the following provisions: (1) the tariff was modified, and by the fixing of a rate for opium the importation of that drug was legalized; (2) the residence in Peking of diplomatic representatives of the powers was promised; (3) foreigners were to be permitted to travel in the interior; (4) the activities of Christian missionaries were sanctioned, and Christians, both foreign and Chinese, were guaranteed freedom in the practice of their faith; (5) foreign merchant vessels were allowed on the Yangtze; (6) several additional ports were opened to foreign residence and trade, includ-

PHOTOGRAPHS, (TOP LEFT) TAGER—PIX, (TOP RIGHT) WIDE WORLD, (CENTRE LEFT) HARRISON FORMAN, (CENTRE RIGHT) FRITZ HENLE, (BOTTOM) EASTFOTO

SCENES IN CHINA

Top left: Street scene in Canton
Top right: Chinese fishing junk, off the coast of Hong Kong, British crown colony
Centre left: Farmers of a labour pool sharing a meal
Centre right: Marble pagoda, Peking
Bottom: Bactrian camels crossing a wasteland of Inner Mongolia

CHINA

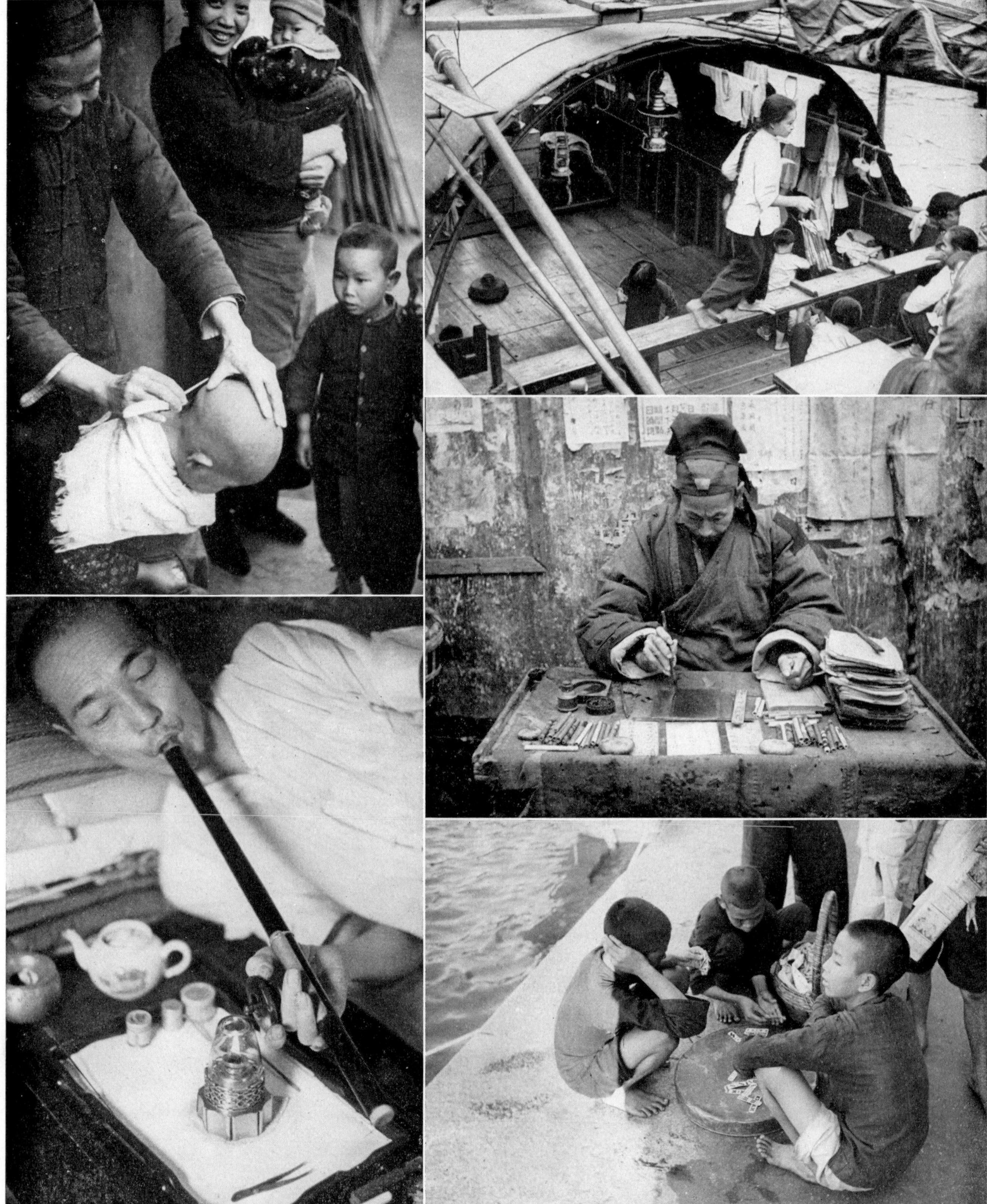

PHOTOGRAPHS, HARRISON FORMAN

CHINESE PEOPLE

Top left: A village barber shaves the head of a young customer in his "shop" on the street
Top right: Interior of a Chinese fishing vessel used as a home. The coastal and river cities of southeast China have a large floating population
Centre right: Public letter writer of Szechwan. Literacy in China is low
Bottom left: Opium smoker. China is an important producer of the drug
Bottom right: Boys playing dominoes on the waterfront, Shanghai

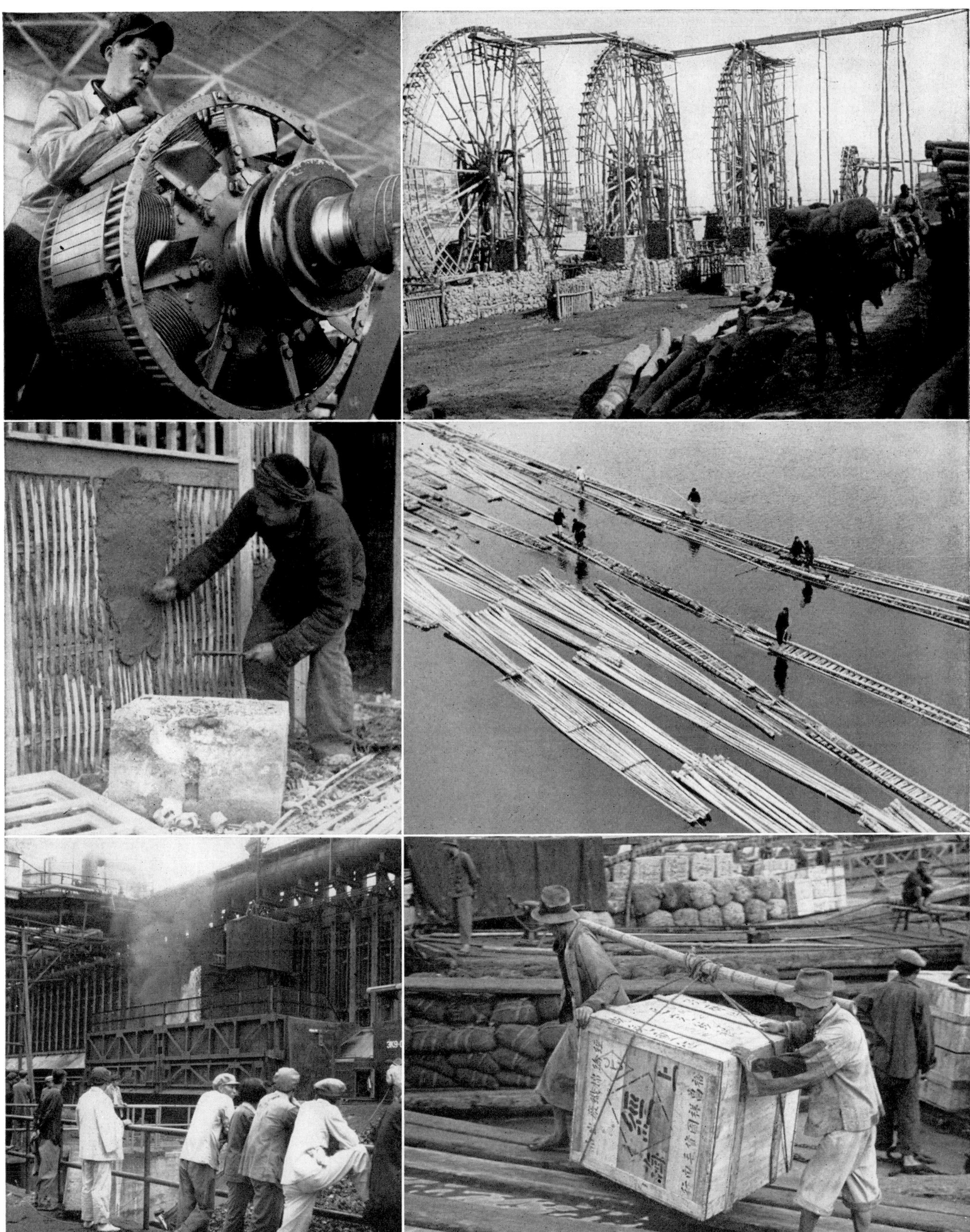

PHOTOGRAPHS, (TOP LEFT, BOTTOM LEFT) EASTFOTO, (OTHERS) HARRISON FORMAN

CHINESE INDUSTRY

Top left: Worker adjusting a generator rotor at an electric machinery plant, Harbin

Top right: Wooden wheels used to lift water from the Hwang-ho (Yellow river) over the wall of the city of Lanchow, capital of Kansu province

Centre left: Construction worker applying plaster to bamboo latticework on a house wall

Centre right: Bamboo tied into rafts to be floated downriver to market cities

Bottom left: Coke-oven batteries at Anshan, a metallurgical centre, northeast China

Bottom right: Coolies moving cargo on a water front. Manual labour continues to be most important in the transportation of goods in China

CHINA

PHOTOGRAPHS, (TOP LEFT) QUENTELL VIOLETT FROM BLACK STAR, (TOP RIGHT, BOTTOM LEFT) BOB KLEIN FROM BLACK STAR, (CENTRE LEFT) HORACE BRISTOL FROM PHOTO-REPRESENTATIVES, (CENTRE RIGHT, BOTTOM RIGHT) PAUL BERG—"POST DISPATCH" PICTURES FROM BLACK STAR

FORMOSA (TAIWAN), NATIONALIST CHINESE STRONGHOLD

Top left: Keelung harbour, north Formosa
Top right: Construction workers preparing foundation of building
Centre left: Army recruit
Centre right: South Chungking road, a street in the business section of Taipei, capital of Formosa
Bottom left: Mother and child before a shop in a village market place
Bottom right: A labourer eating his dinner at a sidewalk restaurant as cooks prepare dish in boiling cauldron; Taipei

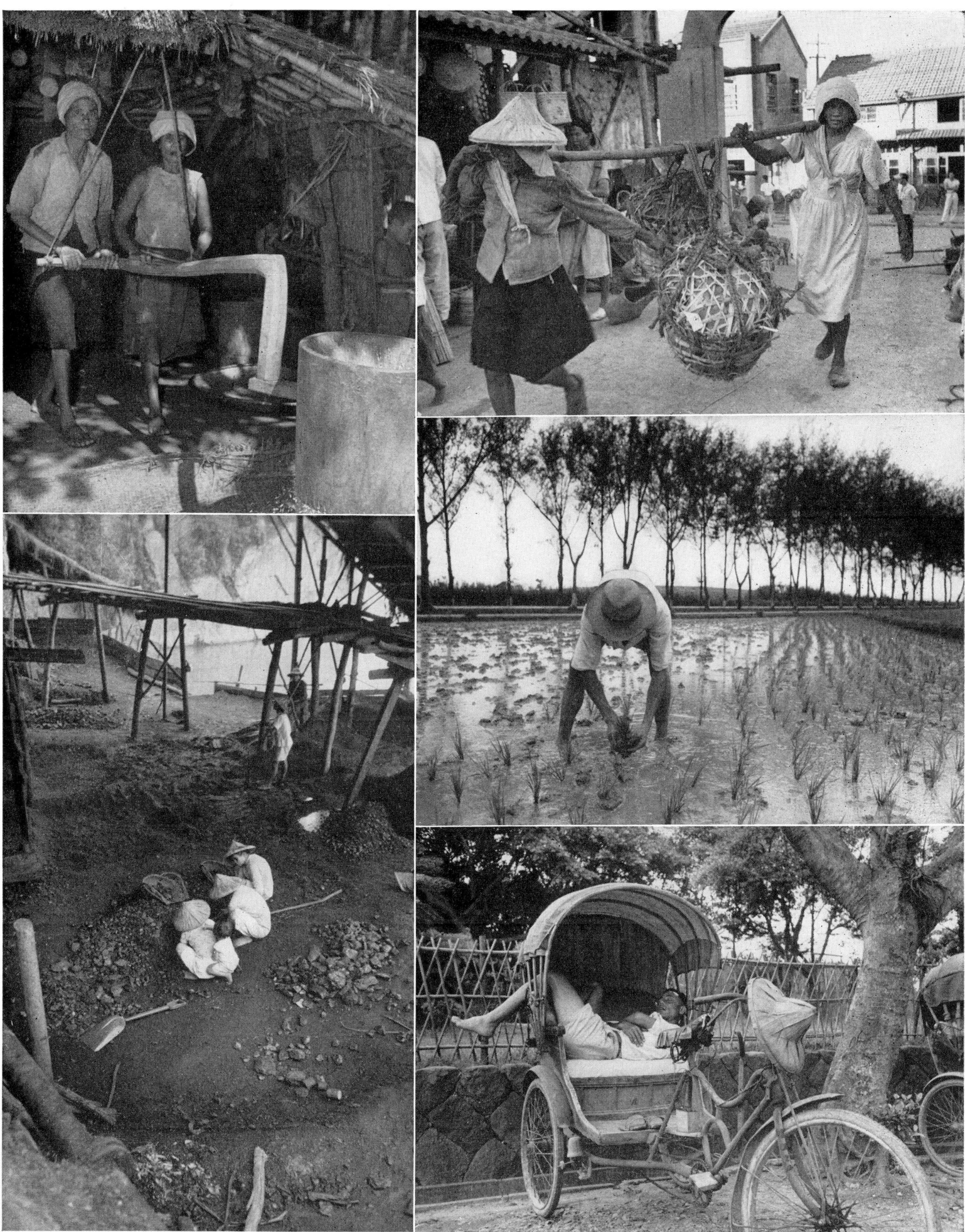

PHOTOGRAPHS, (TOP LEFT) PAN-ASIA FROM BLACK STAR, (OTHERS) PAUL BERG—"POST DISPATCH" PICTURES FROM BLACK STAR

PEOPLE OF FORMOSA AND THE PESCADORES

Top left: Women of the Ami tribe grinding rice with primitive machine. The Amis are one of the aboriginal tribes of Formosa

Top right: Farm women carrying produce to market on a bamboo pole; Makung, Penghu Island, Pescadores

Centre right: Rice worker transplanting seedlings. Rice is a principal crop of Formosa

Bottom left: Women grading coal by hand at a mine in northern Formosa

Bottom right: Taipei "pedicab" driver relaxing. The pedicab replaced the ricksha as the principal form of urban transportation

ing Chefoo and Newchwang in the north, one on Hainan, two on Formosa and four on the Yangtze; (7) extraterritoriality was further elaborated; (8) regulations for trade, including the collection of customs, were developed; and (9) indemnities were promised.

When, in 1859, the envoys came to complete the ratification of the treaties and to take up their residence in Peking, they found the road by Tientsin blocked. The Chinese, moreover, proposed the reconsideration of the treaties. The British and French attempted to force their way past the Taku forts and were repulsed. The two powers accordingly renewed the war and in 1860 fought their way through Tientsin to Peking. Peking was captured, the emperor fled to Jehol, and the British, in retaliation for the violation of a flag of truce and the death of some of its bearers, set fire to such of the summer palace as had escaped marauding Chinese troops. The Chinese were now constrained to sign conventions by which they agreed to observe the treaties of 1858, to pay an additional indemnity, to open Tientsin to trade and to permit—more definitely than agreed upon in 1858—the permanent residence of foreign ministers in Peking. The British were ceded the Kowloon promontory opposite Hong Kong, and through the French was obtained treaty sanction for what had been promised earlier, the restoration of confiscated Catholic Church property. In the Chinese, although not in the official (French), text of the French convention was also permission for French missionaries to lease or buy land and build houses in the interior. The Russians, still fishing in troubled waters, obtained a modification of their frontier by which the territory east of the Ussuri was awarded to them. This territory had a long stretch of coast which included the site of Vladivostok.

The treaties of 1842–44 and 1858–60 defined the legal basis on which intercourse between the occident and China was to be conducted. They were later modified in details, but until 1943 in their main outlines they were the basis of the legal status of foreigners in China.

While at the time they seemed to solve a troublesome situation, they weakened Chinese sovereignty and threatened the existence of the state—partly by removing foreigners from Chinese jurisdiction, partly by their regulation of the tariff and partly by making Christian communities *imperia in imperio*.

The T'ai P'ing Rebellion and Other Revolts.—In addition to the problem of the occidentals, China was confronted by serious internal problems. By 1800 the population probably was three times as large as it had been at the beginning of the dynasty. Agriculture, industry and commerce had not been able to expand so rapidly. In some regions landlordism was widespread. Furthermore, the government had been growing corrupt; taxes grew heavier and the officials squeezed the people. After more than a century of internal peace rebellions began to break out. The great rebellion of the White Lotus society (1796–1803) in the western provinces was followed by many lesser uprisings which, though suppressed, were signs of serious socio-economic maladjustment. The dynasty was approaching a crisis.

In south China, particularly in Kwangtung, a number of additional factors stimulated disorder. The Hakka were an ethnic group which had migrated centuries before from north China and settled in Kwangtung and Kwangsi. They were in frequent conflict with the longer-established local population, and when economic troubles grew these conflicts increased. Secret societies with an anti-Manchu purpose were strong in south China. The illegal opium trade, carried on by smugglers, encouraged gangsterism and piracy, which became linked with the underground secret societies. After about 1820 opium was beginning to drain silver from China, which disturbed the economy, particularly that of Kwangtung. The first Anglo-Chinese war was a blow to the prestige of the Manchu dynasty. It also broke the government's naval power and weakened its ability to maintain order in Kwangtung against the league of pirates, gangsters and secret societies. During the 1840s in Kwangtung and Kwangsi the people suffered severe famines. Banditry increased; disorder was spreading. Conditions—both general and specific—made an uprising almost inevitable.

The T'ai P'ing rebellion, one of several that concurrently shook the imperial structure to its foundations, also had another ingredient—Christianity. The leaders of this rebellion were mostly Hakka. One of them, Hung Hsiu-ch'üan, an unsuccessful competitor in the civil service examinations, suffered a serious illness accompanied by bizarre visions. He later interpreted these in the light of some books prepared by Protestant missionaries which had been given to him years before in Canton. Believing he had been called by God to wean the Chinese from the worship of idols, he and his first convert, Fêng Yün-shan, began preaching their new religion in Kwangtung and Kwangsi. Their followers, mostly impoverished Hakka, were formed into religious communities that by 1848 were being welded into fighting units.

About this time Hung had an opportunity to study Christianity for about two months with a U.S. missionary in Canton. Conflicts between the Society of God Worshippers, mostly Hakka, and the non-Hakka authorities in Kwangsi burst into rebellion in 1850. By this time there were some secret society and pirate adherents in the movement.

Under skilful leadership and against very weak resistance from the government, the T'ai P'ing rebellion swept north from Kwangsi into Hunan and from there down the Yangtze, gathering thousands of supporters, until in 1853 the rebels took Nanking. Their serious expedition to the north failed, but at Nanking they ruled for more than a decade, a fanatical sect whose faith was an ill-assorted blend of misunderstood Christianity and native Chinese beliefs. They showed an utter lack of ability to organize their conquests and owed their temporary success more to the weakness of the imperial government than to their own prowess. They were eventually (1864) put down, chiefly by Tsêng Kuo-fan but with the aid of a picturesque foreign-officered force which was headed first by an American, Frederick Townsend Ward, and later by an English major, Charles George Gordon. The rebellion had cost millions of lives and had wasted some of China's fairest provinces.

During the T'ai P'ing rebellion the imperial government, in desperate straits for revenue, resorted to likin (internal transit taxes on commerce) and, the crisis once past, continued it. During the rebellion, too, as a convenience for the imperial authorities, the system began of collecting the maritime customs through the agency of foreigners. This expedient was first adopted in Shanghai but proved so acceptable to both Chinese and foreigners that it was extended to other ports. The imperial maritime customs service so developed was in 1863 placed under the direction of Robert Hart, and through his genius was officered by an able foreign staff and became not only a dependable source of revenue but an agency for the charting and lighting of the coasts and the inauguration of a postal system.

Other rebellions threatened the power of the Manchus, especially in Shensi, Kansu and Sinkiang, but these were all suppressed. The Manchu dynasty, indeed, for the moment took on a new lease of life. Able Chinese came to its support. The empress dowager, Tz'ŭ Hsi, who had had the good fortune to bear the heir of Hsien Fêng, ruled as coregent during the minority of her son, the emperor T'ung Chih, and then on his death (1875) obtained the succession for another minor—known by his reign name of Kuang Hsü—and was dominant not only during his boyhood but after her nominal retirement (1889). Unscrupulous but vigorous, she probably prolonged the life of the dynasty.

Increasing Foreign Pressure on China, 1860–94.—The years between 1860 and 1894 were marked by no major crises in China's foreign relations, and Chinese life and culture went on nearly unaltered by the presence of the westerner. Pressure was steadily accumulating, however, occasional minor clashes occurred, and the stage was being set for revolutionary changes.

From time to time new ports were opened, and through these and the ones previously available foreign commerce was growing. As before 1860, the British continued to lead. In the treaty ports foreign colonies arose, and in some of them special districts were set aside, usually either as "concessions" or "settlements" (some of them dated from before 1860), which, as a development of extraterritoriality, were under the administration of the foreigners, through the consuls, and some of them with a council elected by the foreign taxpayers.

Christian missionaries, both Roman Catholic and Protestant, rapidly increased in number. The first Protestant missionary, Robert Morrison, of the London Missionary society, arrived in 1807, and under the impulse of the vigorous new life of Protestantism in Europe and the U.S. during the ensuing century representatives of many societies followed—British, American and European. Protestant missionaries emphasized the translation and distribution of the Scriptures and of religious and secular literature, preaching, schools, medical relief and the formation of churches. They were largely responsible for China's first contacts with western education and medical science.

Roman Catholics reinforced their missionary staffs, emphasizing the winning of converts and the care of children in orphanages. By 1890 Protestant Chinese numbered about 50,000 and Roman Catholic Chinese about 500,000.

The growing pressure of the west began slowly to take effect. Before 1895 no startling changes in the structure of Chinese life occurred, but here and there were indications that China would not remain as it had been. In the first place, it somewhat grudgingly began to enter into the diplomatic life of the world. In 1866 a Manchu was sent to Europe with Robert Hart to observe and report. In 1867 Anson Burlingame, who was retiring as United States minister in Peking, was asked to head a mission to present China's case to the governments of the west. Burlingame went first to the United States and there negotiated a treaty (1868) which among other things promised respect for the territorial integrity of China and freedom of immigration of Chinese labourers to the United States and reciprocal rights of residence and travel. From Great Britain and France the mission obtained assurances that pressure would not be applied inconsistent with the independence and safety of China. In 1870, after visiting several courts, and while in St. Petersburg, Burlingame died and his colleagues returned to China. The mission was much criticized, especially for Burlingame's optimistic speeches, but—with the exception of a much earlier one to Russia (1733)—it was China's first formal embassy to that west with which it must henceforth deal.

Before 1880 resident envoys had been appointed to most of the leading capitals of the world. In 1873 and again in the early 1890s the foreign envoys in Peking were given audience by the emperor, but always with a subtle suggestion that they were considered as coming from tributary states. Not until 1894 were they received on the basis of full equality.

In the 1870s, at the instance of Yung Wing, who had graduated from Yale university in 1854, the Chinese government sent several scores of youths to the United States to be educated, but in 1881 a conservative brought about their recall. Two government schools were founded to train men for diplomatic service. By 1894 telegraph lines and a few miles of railway were built, and some attempts were made to reorganize China's naval and military forces and to construct coast defenses according to western models.

The Chino-Japanese War and the Beginning of Rapid Changes.—China could not hope long to remain semi-isolated. The occident was continuing to expand, Japan, at China's very doors, was rapidly adopting and adapting western culture, and the Middle Kingdom must sooner or later adjust itself to the new world.

The beginning of rapid change was brought by war with Japan. Korea had long been in an ill-defined position of vassalage to China. Japanese, on the other hand, had invaded the peninsula at least twice, the latest occasion having been in the last decade of the 16th century. With its reorganization in the 1860s and 1870s, Japan again began to exert influence in Korea, and in doing so came into conflict with China, for the latter, under the advice of Li Hung-chang, was inclined—with some vacillation—to assert more actively than in the past its authority as suzerain. Japan refused to recognize China's suzerainty and the two nations came to blows over the dispatch of troops by both to put down an insurrection in Korea. War was declared Aug. 1, 1894, and China was quickly and overwhelmingly defeated. By March 1895 the Japanese had successfully invaded Shantung and Manchuria, had captured Wei-hai-wei and Port Arthur, fortified posts which commanded the sea approaches to Peking, and the Chinese sued for peace. By the resulting treaty (of Shimonoseki) China recognized the independence of Korea, ceded to Japan Formosa, the adjoining Pescadores Islands and the Liaotung peninsula (in Manchuria), agreed to pay an indemnity of 200,000,000 taels, opened four more ports to trade and promised a satisfactory treaty of commerce. Russia was not disposed to see Japan make gains which would threaten Russian ambitions in the far east, and, backed by its ally, France, and by Germany—which professed fear of the "yellow peril"—protested against the cession of the Liaotung territory. Japan had no other recourse but submission, and the retrocession to China was made in return for a face-saving increase in the indemnity. The war had demonstrated the utter failure of Chinese attempts at "self-strengthening" during the past three decades. Its "modern armies" had proved incapable of defending the country and its western-style navy had been destroyed.

The victory of Japan was the signal for a scramble among the powers for leases, concessions and special privileges. The weakness of the Middle Kingdom had been unmistakably disclosed and for a few years it looked as though the powers, driven by earth hunger and fear of one another, would partition it. Russian, French, British and German bankers angrily contested for shares in the loans through which China was to pay the Japanese indemnity. In 1895 Russia obtained permission to carry the Trans-Siberian railway directly across Manchuria instead of by the longer all-Russian route of the Amur and Ussuri. France secured a "rectification" of the frontier in the Mekong valley and railway and mining privileges in China. Great Britain, alarmed, demanded and received concessions on the Burmese frontier. Rumours were soon afloat (1896) of further grants to Russia in Manchuria and of a promise to that same power of a lease on Kiaochow bay in Shantung. Russia, too, extended its influence in Korea. In Nov. 1897 German forces seized Tsingtao, giving as an excuse the murder of German missionaries in Shantung, and the following March that port and land controlling Kiaochow bay were leased to Germany for 99 years, and railway and mining concessions in Shantung were assured. Russia made the German seizure of Tsingtao the signal for the occupation of Port Arthur and Talien (Dairen or Dalny), and in March 1898 a portion of the Liaotung peninsula which included these two ports was leased to Russia for 25 years. Within a few weeks France was given a 99-year lease to Kwangchowwan in Kwangtung, and Great Britain acquired Wei-hai-wei "for so long a period as Port Arthur shall remain in the occupation of Russia." Great Britain also acquired a 99-year lease on an additional portion of the Kowloon promontory, opposite Hong Kong.

Concurrently with the seizure of these leaseholds, the powers delimited "spheres of interest," by which they meant, by implication, prior rights to provide capital for the development of mines and railways, and the promise of nonalienation of territory to another power. In case China should be partitioned, spheres of interest might become formal annexations. In 1897 France secured from China a "declaration of nonalienation" of Hainan to any third power. In 1898 Great Britain obtained a similar declaration for the provinces adjoining the Yangtze, France for the provinces bordering on Tongking and Japan a promise that none of Fukien would be alienated to any power whatsoever. Germany claimed Shantung as its sphere and Russia the territory north of the Great Wall. In 1899 Russia and Great Britain agreed not to interfere in each other's preserves. Great Britain, too, exacted from China a promise that the inspector-general of the maritime customs should be of British nationality, at least so long as the trade of Great Britain exceeded that of any other country.

Still another form of the struggle for a slice of the Chinese melon was the competition for the privilege of providing capital for railways. The details of the story are extremely complicated, but in general the results were that Russia acquired a monopoly on railway building in Manchuria; Belgian financiers—behind whom France and Russia were suspected to stand—provided the money for the road from Peking to Hankow; Germans furnished the capital for lines in Shantung and for the northern section of the road from Tientsin to Pukow (on the Yangtze, opposite Nanking), Britons for the southern half of the road and the line from Shanghai to Nanking, and France was granted concessions for railways in its sphere of interest—Kwangtung, Kwangsi and Yünnan. A U.S. syndicate was given the concession for a road from Hankow to Canton, but the Belgians later acquired a controlling interest in the company and the Chinese, irritated, bought back the grant. The French got from the Russo-Chinese bank the contract for a road connecting Tai-yüan with the Peking-Hankow line, and a Franco-Belgian syndicate the contract for a line from Kai-fêng to Loyang. Mining concessions, which need not be enumerated here, were also obtained by various foreign groups.

To prevent the threatened disruption of China three major and widely different efforts were made. One was by the United States. In the autumn of 1899, John Hay, the U.S. secretary of state, asked from England, France, Russia, Germany, Japan and Italy assurances that within their respective spheres of interest they would not interfere with any treaty port or vested interest, that no preferential harbour dues or railway charges would be given their subjects and that the Chinese government should collect the customs duties and only according to the Chinese tariffs. This "open-door policy" was not, strictly speaking, new, but was founded upon the most-favoured-nation clauses. Nor was it entirely disinterested. The United States held aloof, to be sure, from the scramble for leases and concessions, but this was partly because the U.S. was too engrossed in developing the virgin resources of its own land to engage in ventures abroad. On its acquisition of Hawaii and the Philippines, however, the United States had awakened to a livelier interest in the far east, and did not wish doors to be slammed in the faces of its merchants and bankers. All the powers assented to the U.S. note, although Russia did so with slight reservations.

The other major efforts to save China were by the Chinese themselves. After the war with Japan clubs sprang up advocating "reform"—organization on the occidental pattern. That, so the members urged, had been the secret of Japan's victory. The great viceroy Chang Chih-tung came out with a widely read pamphlet, *Learn*, urging reform, although without the abandonment of the best of China's heritage. Some of the extremists, notably the brilliant but erratic K'ang Yu-wei and his disciple Liang Ch'i-ch'ao, a master of Chinese style, obtained the ear of the emperor, and for a little more than three months in the summer of 1898 edict after edict poured forth from Peking ordering some of the changes which the radicals desired. Compared with what was to happen in the next 25 years, these were moderate enough, but at the time they seemed revolutionary.

The civil service examinations were to be reformed, new schools with western as well as Chinese subjects were to be founded, western military methods and equipment were to be introduced and steps taken looking toward a national army based on conscription, reforms in the courts of law were projected, a government bureau to translate foreign works and a ministry of arts, commerce and agriculture were to be established, patent and copyright laws were to be introduced and rewards offered to authors and inventors, annual budgets of receipts and expenditure were sanctioned and many sinecure offices were abolished.

Skilled statesmen might have succeeded in carrying through these reforms without provoking a major crisis, but the young emperor knew little of the world of men outside his palace walls, and his radical advisers had little or no experience in government. The inevitable storm, therefore, was intensified, and in Sept. 1898 the empress dowager suddenly intervened and inaugurated a third effort to save China—by a return to the conservative *status quo*. The coup d'état was precipitated by the emperor's plan to thwart the reactionaries by placing restrictions on the empress dowager and executing her most loyal henchman, Jung Lu. Information seems to have come to Jung Lu through Yuan Shih-k'ai, and Tz'ŭ Hsi acted promptly. On Sept. 22, 1898, she reassumed the reins of government. She kept the emperor a virtual prisoner and but for the powers might have had him assassinated. As many reformers as could be apprehended were executed, and most of the reform decrees were annulled. Tz'ŭ Hsi attempted to restore the government as it had been and to strengthen it to resist foreign encroachments.

The Boxer Uprising, 1900.—On the heels of the conservative reaction, and in part as a consequence of it, came a blind attempt, largely popular but sanctioned by the extremists, to oust the foreigner once and for all. In 1898 and 1899 unrest was widespread, induced partly by the talk of reform, partly by the aggressions of the powers and partly by the vigorous reaction led by the empress dowager. The government, in an attempt to provide for the national defense against foreign aggression, ordered the revival of the village trainbands or militia and put the plan into effect first in the northeastern provinces. Into these trainbands came many of the local rowdies, and here and there disorderly secret societies affiliated with them. The members practised rites which they believed would make them invulnerable to bullets and came to be known to foreigners as "Boxers"—a loose translation of the Chinese name for the bands, I Ho T'uan or I Ho Ch'üan, "Righteous Harmony Bands" or "Righteous Harmony Fists."

One of the favourite mottoes of the Boxers was "Protect the country, destroy the foreigner." By the autumn of 1899 the Boxers were beginning to persecute Christians—as "secondary foreign devils"—especially in Shantung, where the antiforeign Yü Hsien was governor. The powers, alarmed, brought pressure, and, while they obtained the recall of Yü Hsien, he was soon appointed to the governorship of Shansi and unrest increased. An English missionary was murdered the last day of 1899, and by the following June the attacks on Chinese Christians became more frequent and foreigners were in grave danger.

In early June 1900 an unsuccessful attempt of the powers to throw additional troops into Peking aggravated the situation, and when, on June 17, foreigners seized the Taku forts to open the way to Tientsin and Peking, the storm broke. Against the counsel of saner heads, the empress dowager ordered all foreigners to be killed. The German minister was murdered, and the other foreign ministers and their staffs, missionaries and hundreds of Chinese Christians were besieged in the legation quarter and in the Catholic cathedral in Peking. Scores of Roman Catholic and Protestant missionaries and thousands of Chinese Christians were done to death, principally in Hopei, Shansi and Manchuria. The powers declared that they were not waging war on China but were simply seeking to rescue their nationals and to suppress the Boxers. The viceroys in the Yangtze valley and the south opposed Boxerism and accordingly remained neutral and endeavoured to repress antiforeign outbreaks within their jurisdiction. That attitude was also taken by high officials in most of the west and north. The disorders, therefore, were chiefly confined to the northeast. An international force captured Peking on Aug. 14, 1900, the court fled to Sian, and the foreign troops proceeded to loot the capital and then to relieve scattered groups of missionaries and Christians who had been standing siege and to disperse the Boxer remnants.

Although the powers had not declared war on China, they deemed a formal settlement necessary to exact reparation and to guard against a recurrence of the outbreak. After negotiations, which were prolonged by disagreements among the victors, in Sept. 1901 a protocol was finally signed.

This document provided for the punishment, by China, of some of the officials held chiefly responsible; for memorial monuments for some of the murdered foreigners; for formal missions of apology to Berlin for the death of the German minister; for the suspension for five years of civil service examinations in towns where foreigners had been killed or mishandled; for the prohibition for at least two years of the importation of arms and ammunition; for an indemnity of 450,000,000 taels, to be paid in 39 years and to be secured by the revenues of the imperial maritime customs; for the fortification and policing by foreigners of the legation quarter, the razing of the Taku forts and the maintenance by foreign troops of communication between Peking and the sea; for edicts against antiforeign agitation; for the amendment of the existing commercial treaties; and for transforming the foreign office (Tsungli Yamen) into the chief of the ministries of state, under the name of the Wai Wu Pu.

The Era of Change to the Overthrow of the Manchus, 1900–11.—The Boxer year inaugurated momentous changes. The empire was clearly at the mercy of the powers, and foreigners acted as though they were living in a conquered country. With the exception of Manchuria, encroachments on Chinese sovereignty were less marked than in 1898 and 1899. The Russians continued their aggressions. The disorders of 1900 had spread to Manchuria, and thither Russia quickly dispatched large bodies of troops, ostensibly to protect its subjects and investments. The Russian forces ruthlessly suppressed all opposition and occupied much of the three provinces. Late in 1900 an agreement between China and Russia promised the latter extensive control in southern Manchuria and was modified only on protest from the other powers. Both Great Britain and Japan were alarmed, the former because of its general fear of Russia in the east and the latter because of the threat to Korea, where Russian machinations were increasing. In defense against the common foe, the Anglo-Japanese alliance was formed (Jan. 30, 1902). Russia, subjected to pressure from these two powers and the United States, promised to respect the commercial rights of all nations, and agreed with China (1902) gradually to withdraw Russian troops from Manchuria. However, Russia found pretexts for delays and sought from China, in return for evacuation, compensations which would have strengthened its hold on the debated territory.

Great Britain, the United States and Japan sought to check Russia. Japan was especially concerned and strove by direct negotiations with St. Petersburg to obtain recognition of its interests in Korea and the promised evacuation of Russian troops from Manchuria. Russia was obdurate and Japan had recourse to arms (Feb. 1904). In the ensuing months the Japanese captured Port Arthur, drove the Russians out of southern Manchuria and destroyed the Russian fleets. In 1905 Pres. Theodore Roosevelt proffered his good offices, hostilities were suspended, and by the resulting treaty of Portsmouth (Sept. 5, 1905) Russia recognized Japan's interest in Korea, transferred to Japan Russian rights in the Liaotung peninsula, ceded to Japan the southern section of the Manchurian railway and the southern half of Sakhalin, and both powers agreed to withdraw their troops from Manchuria, to use the railways in Manchuria, except those in the Liaotung peninsula, only for economic and industrial and not for strategic purposes, and not to obstruct "measures common to all countries which China may take for the development of the commerce and industry of Manchuria."

The war merely substituted Japan for Russia in southern Manchuria, and the former was no more scrupulous in respecting China's rights than was the latter. Many Japanese contended, indeed, that having spent blood and treasure for Manchuria they had better rights there than the Chinese. By the annexation of Korea (1910) Japan moved its boundary to the southeastern edge of Manchuria and strengthened its interests in Kirin and Liaoning, the southern two of the three provinces.

The suppression of the Boxer outbreak by the powers and the subsequent war between Japan and Russia seriously weakened China. The governmental machinery, which had worked fairly well as long as China had not been in intimate touch with nations as powerful as itself, proved inadequate to meet the strain imposed by the coming of the occident. The Manchus would have to show unusual ability if they were to save their throne, and the Chinese if they were to avoid anarchy.

After 1900 and especially after 1905 both Chinese and Manchus set about the reorganization of the country. Even the most conservative could not fail to read the signs of the times, and the empress dowager, doubtless reluctantly and with many misgivings, attempted to direct the reform which she could no longer avert. In 1902 the court returned to Peking and the empress dowager set herself to win the friendship of the foreigners, addressing herself especially to the ladies of the legations.

Much more important was the sanction which she gave to decrees which sought to aid and to regulate the introduction of western civilization.

In 1902 orders were issued to remodel public instruction by the creation of new schools and by the introduction of western subjects in the curriculum. In Sept. 1905 a decree was promulgated abolishing that most characteristic feature of the old educational system, the civil service examination. Partly as a result of these orders and partly in consequence of the general movement for reform, schools teaching Chinese and western subjects sprang up by the thousand. The old examination stalls were razed and on some of the sites rose buildings dedicated to the new learning. Many temples were converted for educational purposes. By the end of 1910 there were 35,198 government schools with 875,760 pupils. Protestant mission institutions, once the unpopular representatives of a new learning, were now thronged and new ones were opened. Students by the thousand flocked to Japan, there to study in modern schools, and hundreds went to Europe and the U.S. When in 1908 the United States announced its purpose to return a portion of its share of the Boxer indemnity, the sums remitted were set aside for scholarships to enable Chinese to study in the U.S. With the new schools came a flood of literature treating of western ideas, and publishing houses, notably the Commercial Press, arose to give it circulation.

With educational reform went efforts to put the country in a better state of defense. The foreign drilling of the northern army continued; throughout the country troops were trained in the new ways, greater honours were paid to military officers, and in 1906 steps were taken toward the creation of a national force as contrasted with the older provincial forces.

In 1910 slavery was abolished, but since that institution was never so prominent in China as in parts of the occident the step did not entail marked revolution. Vigorous efforts were made to stamp out the opium trade, an imperial edict of Sept. 1906 inaugurating the campaign. The British government, under whose protection much of the foreign trade in the drug was carried on, in 1907 agreed to reduce the importation concurrently with the progressive abolishment of the domestic growth of the poppy, at a rate which would extinguish the trade in ten years. The restriction on poppy growing proved so much more rapid than was anticipated that in 1911 Great Britain agreed to the complete exclusion of the foreign drug from the provinces where the culture had ceased.

Governmental reorganization also was undertaken. In 1902 a commission on juridical reform was established and in 1905 reported, recommending the modification of the laws. As a beginning, torture, except in criminal cases, and certain cruel forms of punishment were ordered to be abolished. The reorganization of laws and judiciary was not sufficiently thoroughgoing, however, to cause the powers to dispense with extraterritoriality. The reform of the currency was discussed, but nothing effective was accomplished, and with the appearance of new coins the previous confusion became worse confounded.

Most important of all the governmental reforms was the attempt to introduce a constitution with representative assemblies. In 1905 a commission was sent abroad to study constitutional methods, and on its return in 1906 a promise was made to introduce a parliamentary form of government. That same year, as a preliminary, changes were made in the organization of the central administrative boards in Peking.

In Aug. 1908 an edict promised the convocation of parliament in nine years, but the death of the emperor and of the empress dowager in November of that year brought postponement. The new emperor, a nephew of the childless Kuang Hsü, was an infant of 2½ years, and his father, Prince Ch'un, was appointed regent. The new reign was given the title of Hsüan T'ung. Shortly after its beginning the regency was deprived of the support of one of the strongest Chinese by the forcible retirement of Yuan Shih-k'ai, as a punishment, so rumour had it, for his alleged betrayal of the regent's brother, the late emperor, in 1898.

Constitutional reform was only delayed by the change in rulers, and that briefly. In 1909 provincial assemblies met, chosen by a limited electorate, and in Oct. 1910 the national assembly convened, half of it elected and half appointed by the throne. The national assembly demanded the right to legislate, but for the time could gain merely the promise of the convocation of a parliament with legislative powers in 1913 rather than in 1917.

Along with changes in education and government went other sweeping alterations in the nation's life. Several of the railways authorized before 1900 were constructed, bringing great modifications in transportation. Foreign shipping increased on the coastal waters and the Yangtze, telegraph lines were extended, and the business of the post office multiplied. Foreign commerce more than doubled in the decade after 1901, and foreign merchandise penetrated to the remotest hamlets. The numbers of missionaries rapidly increased, and both the Catholic and Protestant communities showed a phenomenal growth.

After 1900 a more radical movement looking toward overthrow of the Manchu dynasty began to gain strength among Chinese abroad and to penetrate secretly into the empire. Revolutionary leaders found recruits among the thousands of Chinese students studying in Japan. On their return to China many of these students secured positions of influence in education, journalism and the army. Magazines preaching revolution as well as those urging reform were printed in Japan and smuggled into China.

Merchants overseas contributed funds. Anti-Manchu secret societies in south and west China were rejuvenated. Several short-lived uprisings occurred. Sun Yat-sen and Huang Hsing were but two of many revolutionary leaders.

The Passing of the Manchus.—In 1912 the rising tide of change swept aside the Manchus. Ever since the conquest in the 17th century most of the Manchus had lived in comparative idleness, supposedly a standing army of occupation, but in reality inefficient pensionaries. All through the 19th century the dynasty had been declining, and in the death of the empress dowager it lost its last able leader. In 1911 the emperor was an infant and the regency utterly incompetent to guide the nation through the stormy waters ahead. The unsuccessful contests with foreign powers had shaken not only the dynasty but the entire machinery of government. The ferment of new ideas was already weakening the ancient wineskins, and only strong and wise leadership could prevent loss to both. Under the circumstances almost any incident might have toppled the Manchus off the throne.

The chain of events immediately leading to the revolution began with the signing (April 5, 1911), with a four-power group of foreign bankers, of the Hukwang railway loan agreement for the construction of roads in central China. The Peking government decided to take over from a local company a line in Szechwan, on which construction had been barely begun, and to apply part of the loan to its completion. The sum offered did not meet the demands of the stockholders, and in Sept. 1911 the dissatisfaction boiled over into open revolt. On Oct. 10, in consequence of the uncovering of a plot in Hankow which had little or no connection with the Szechwan episode, a mutiny broke out among the troops in Wuchang, and this is regarded as the formal beginning of the revolution. The mutineers soon captured the Wuchang mint and the arsenal at Wuchang, and city after city declared against the Manchus. The regent, panic-stricken, granted the assembly's demand for the immediate adoption of a constitution, and urged Yuan Shih-k'ai to come out of retirement and save the dynasty. Yuan, after much hestitation, accepted on his own terms, and at the end of October took the field at the head of the northern armies. In November he was made premier.

Had Yuan acted vigorously he might have suppressed the uprising and so have delayed the inevitable. He dallied, however, and by the end of the year 14 provinces had declared against the Manchus, in several cities Manchu garrisons had been massacred, the regent had been forced out of office, a provisional republican government had been set up at Nanking, and the archrevolutionist Sun Yat-sen had returned from abroad and had been elected president.

In December Yuan agreed to an armistice and entered upon negotiations with the republicans. On Feb. 12, 1912, the boy emperor was made to abdicate the throne in a proclamation which transferred the government to the people's representatives, declared that the constitution should thenceforth be republican and gave Yuan Shih-k'ai full powers to organize a provisional government. The Nanking authorities agreed that the emperor was to retain his title for life and to receive a large pension. To unify the country, Sun Yat-sen resigned the presidency and Yuan was chosen in his place. Li Yuan-hung, who had come into prominence in Wuchang in the initial stages of the rebellion, was elected vice-president. A provisional constitution was promulgated in March 1912 by the Nanking parliament, and in April the government was transferred to Peking.

The republic, established with such startling rapidity and comparative ease, was destined to witness the progressive collapse of national unity and orderly government. The causes for this chaos were, in the main, three. In the first place, traditional processes were being repeated. The demise of every dynasty had been followed by civil strife, in which rival military chieftains struggled for the throne. The disorder usually lasted for decades, and once, after the downfall of the Han dynasty, was prolonged for nearly four centuries.

The peaceful transfer of power to Yuan Shih-k'ai under the guise of a republic for a time mitigated the struggle and even seemed to have averted it. Yuan, however, did not prove strong enough to hold the country together. Until after 1928 no one else came as near to success as did he, and the country was broken up into ever-smaller fragments, most of them ruled by military chieftains. Figures came and went from the political stage with bewildering rapidity, and after Yuan's death (1916) the political map was seldom the same two years in succession.

In the second place, the chaos was accentuated by new ideas from the west. The governmental machinery which on the whole had worked better over a longer period than any other ever devised for so numerous a people was being abandoned. It was ill adapted to the new conditions, and theoretical radicals, imbued with occidental ideas, and militarists tended to ignore it or to modify it more greatly than at any time since the Han. Such thoroughgoing political experimentation meant chaos, and new institutions were not quickly evolved for so enormous a section of mankind.

In the third place, the disorder was increased by the interference of foreigners. Japan was vitally concerned in the fate of its huge neighbour. Its population was steadily increasing, no adequate relief could be had through emigration, and its only recourse was to add to its income by engaging in industry and commerce. If it were to do this, it must have access to raw materials, including coal and iron, and to markets. For these it most naturally looked to the adjoining continent and especially to China. Japan's life depended, therefore, upon keeping open the door into China, and it is not surprising that it sought to control portions of the republic and at times meddled in Chinese politics. To Japan were added the western powers, especially Russia. Beginning about 1922, but especially after 1925, Russian Communists sought to extend their influence into China and to foment the kind of revolution which they had achieved at home.

It must be noted, however, that foreign activities helped to bring union as well as disunion. Resentment against the foreigner was the one issue on which the vocal elements of the nation could unite; railways and telegraph lines—both of foreign origin—helped to bind the country together, and the foreign-controlled customs service and the foreign-organized postal system were the only governmental agencies which continued to function over all the country.

The Republic Under Yuan Shih-k'ai.—For four years Yuan Shih-k'ai was able to delay the further disintegration of China. He faced no easy task. The radicals, who in Aug. 1912 took the party name of Kuomintang, regarded him with suspicion, and, obtaining a majority in the parliament which assembled in 1913 under the provisional constitution of 1912, demanded a type of government in which the legislature should be supreme and the president a figurehead. Rival military leaders were beginning to appear, and grave financial difficulties faced a government whose fiscal machinery, already decrepit, had been disturbed by the revolution. The confidence of the powers, moreover, was not yet given the new regime.

In the face of all these difficulties Yuan for a time achieved marked success and gradually restored in the provinces the authority of the central government. In April 1913, after prolonged negotiations, he concluded a "reorganization" loan with a financial group representing Great Britain, France, Russia, Germany and Japan. The loan, a large one, was secured by a lien on Chinese revenues, chiefly on the income from the salt monopoly —now put under foreign supervision. His financial position and the moral support of the powers thus assured, Yuan proceeded to defy the members of the Kuomintang. The latter had sought to block the loan and saw in its conclusion grave danger to themselves. They continued obstructionist policies, and, as Yuan still prevailed, in the summer of 1913 some of them, including Sun Yat-sen and Huang Hsing, declared a "punitive" expedition against him and for a while held Nanking. Yuan promptly put down the rebellion, and, after obtaining the ratification of the articles of the "permanent" constitution which had to do with choosing the president, and being elected under them (Oct. 1913), he outlawed the Kuomintang (Nov. 1913) and unseated its members of parliament. A few weeks later he disbanded what remained of parliament, replacing it with an administrative council selected by himself. In March 1914 the provincial assemblies were dissolved. A new constitution, framed by a body controlled by Yuan, was promulgated in May 1914. The president's power was greatly strengthened, his term was lengthened to ten years, and he might be rechosen by the council of state or control the election of his successor. In 1914 Yuan performed the imperial ceremonies in the Temple of Heaven at the winter solstice. He seemed to be winning against the opposition and in 1915 prepared to take the further step of having himself formally chosen and proclaimed emperor.

However, opposition developed both within China and among various foreign powers, particularly Japan, which was supported by its wartime allies Great Britain, France and Russia. A rebellion broke out in Yünnan and spread to other provinces of the south. The Kuomintang established a rival government at Canton. Opposition was so formidable that Yuan rescinded the monarchy in March 1916; on June 6 he died.

With Yuan removed, the country appeared quickly to unite. Li Yuan-hung, unopposed, succeeded to the presidency; Tuan Ch'i-jui, appointed by Yuan in the last few weeks of his life, continued as premier and brought to the support of the new government some of the northern military chiefs. The parliament of 1913, reassembling, brought back to Peking many of the Kuomintang. The government seemed to be further strengthened by the election to the vice-presidency of Fêng Kuo-chang, dominant in the lower part of the Yangtze valley.

The very strength of the new government was, however, its weakness, for it was made up of elements which were fundamentally discordant and which any crisis might set at loggerheads. This crisis was to grow out of international reactions in which China was inextricably involved.

Foreign Relations, 1911–17.—The revolution did not immediately bring marked change in China's foreign relations. Tibet and Outer Mongolia, at best never very firmly attached to the empire, took the opportunity afforded by the shift in governments to effect their virtual independence, and Great Britain in the former case and Russia in the latter were not slow to attempt to extend their influence over territories which abutted so directly upon their own. China recognized the autonomy of Outer Mongolia in return for the acknowledgment of Chinese suzerainty, but it was less pliant in yielding to British ambitions in Tibet. On the whole, the powers made little objection to the establishment of the republic.

The outbreak of World War I, however, brought serious difficulties. With Europe absorbed in internecine strife, Japan saw a golden opportunity to extend its power in China. The Anglo-Japanese alliance afforded it a welcome excuse for seeking to eliminate Germany from the far east. Accordingly, in Aug. 1914 Japan dispatched an expedition to Shantung and, with the cooperation of a small British force, captured Tsingtao and the other German possessions in the province.

The occupation of the German properties in Shantung was only a beginning. In Jan. 1915 Japan presented to Peking a formidable array of 21 demands in five groups.

1. In Shantung, China was to agree to any transfer of German possessions to Japan that the latter might obtain. China was not to alienate to a third power any territory in the province; it was to declare additional cities to be open ports and was to grant certain railway privileges.

2. In south Manchuria and eastern Inner Mongolia, the leases of Port Arthur, Dairen (Dalny) and the railways were to be extended to 99 years. Anywhere in these regions, Japanese might lease land and travel or reside. There were also demands for mining and railway privileges and for Japanese control of loans and the employment of Japanese official advisers.

3. The Han-yeh-p'ing company, the largest Chinese iron-mining and smelting concern, was to be made a Chino-Japanese enterprise, and China was not to sell its interest in it without Japan's consent.

4. China was to promise not to cede or lease to any third power any harbour, bay or island along its coast.

5. China was to employ Japanese as advisers to the central government; the police departments in certain districts were to be jointly administered by Japanese and Chinese; China was either to buy 50% or more of its munitions from Japan or to establish a Chino-Japanese arsenal which was to use Japanese materials under the direction of Japanese; Japanese were to be granted the privilege of buying land in the interior for schools, hospitals and churches; certain railway concessions in the Yangtze valley were to be promised; and Japan was to be allowed to scrutinize all proposed loans of foreign capital for mines and works in Fukien.

Japan attempted to keep the demands secret, but they became known and a wave of indignation swept over China; criticism also was expressed publicly and vigorously in Great Britain and the United States. The Japanese were constrained to make important concessions, but they had the upper hand and knew it; they presented an ultimatum to which China, helpless, had no recourse but submission. By a series of treaties and exchange of notes China agreed to the first three groups, with important modifications in its favour; group 4 was met by a presidential mandate which directed that no part of China's coast should be ceded to any power; and group 5 was reserved for further negotiations except for a promise from China that no nation should be permitted to construct a dockyard, a coaling station or a naval base on the coast of Fukien.

In February and March 1917 Japan made secret arrangements with Great Britain, France and Italy whereby those powers assured their support to Japanese demands at the peace conference for the former German holdings in Shantung.

China's Entrance Into World War I and Further Internal Difficulties.—As World War I progressed, pressure was brought upon China to enter the struggle on the side of the Allies. In Feb. 1917 the United States invited the Chinese government to follow its example in protesting against Germany's submarine campaign and severing diplomatic relations, and the Franco-Japanese secret notes of March 1, 1917, promised Tokyo's support to the effort to induce Peking to take the step. On Feb. 9 the Chinese foreign office sent warning to Germany and on March 14 broke off diplomatic intercourse.

The question whether China should actually declare war became an issue which precipitated a contest among the principal military successors of Yuan Shih-k'ai for control of the government. The step was taken on Aug. 14, 1917, when China formally declared war on Germany. The country had already begun, however, to disintegrate politically.

The Kuomintang members of the dismissed parliament denounced the Peking government as illegal, and, under the leadership of Sun Yat-sen, in Sept. 1917 organized a provisional government which they declared to be the only constitutional one in China. The powers did not grant it recognition, however, and it maintained a precarious and chequered existence, usually with headquarters at Canton. In the north Tuan Ch'i-jui and his supporters, the so-called Anfu group, were for several years in the ascendant.

China's Part in World War I.—In the meantime World War I was drawing to a close. China's internal discord and financial straits were such that it could take no active part in the struggle, although it permitted the recruiting of about 175,000 of its citizens for labour battalions for service behind the lines in France, Mesopotamia and Africa.

China gained slightly by its entry into the war. It took over the German and Austrian concessions in the ports, cancelled the unpaid portions of the Boxer indemnities due its enemies and was permitted to suspend for the time payments on the sums due to the Allies. China was assured a seat at the peace conference.

In contrast with these gains, however, was an increased control by Japan. In Nov. 1917 the United States, in an effort to adjust its difficulties with Japan, entered upon the Lansing-Ishii agreement (terminated March 30, 1923), by which it recognized that because of "territorial propinquity . . . Japan had special interests in China," and so seemed to have delivered the latter over to the island empire. The Anfu clique around Tuan Ch'i-jui concluded agreements with Japan for the construction of railways in Shantung, Manchuria and Mongolia (Sept. 1918) and borrowed extensively from the Japanese on the security—some of it extremely dubious—of railways, mines, forests, telegraphs, taxes and bonds.

The Peace Conference.—To the peace conference which terminated the war the Chinese sent an able delegation representing, by a strange but characteristic anomaly, both the Peking and the Canton governments. The delegation asked not only for the restoration to China of the former German properties in Shantung, but for the cancellation of spheres of influence, the withdrawal of foreign troops, post offices and wireless and telegraphic communications, the abolition of consular jurisdiction, tariff autonomy, the relinquishment of leased territories and the restoration of foreign concessions and settlements. China was, however, doomed to disappointment. The U.S. delegation favoured the restoration of the Shantung properties, but against it were the agreements of 1917 between Japan and the European Allies. By the treaty of Versailles, therefore, Japan was confirmed in the possession of its holdings in Shantung. The remaining questions were held not to come within the purview of the conference.

When news of the Versailles settlement reached China there was immediate widespread protest. Students in Peking began a demonstration on May 4, 1919, against the pro-Japanese government. This patriotic movement spread rapidly to other cities and won the support of other groups in the population. The Peking government had to instruct the Paris delegation to refuse to sign the treaty with Germany. A very effective nation-wide boycott against Japanese goods was also instituted by patriotic groups. This patriotic outburst, known as the May 4 movement, had wide ramifications. It developed under the leadership of western-trained professors and their university students into a broad movement for reform and rejuvenation of Chinese life in all aspects.

China was not, however, to emerge from the war without some gains. It obtained membership in the League of Nations by signing the treaty with Austria, for that document did not contain the objectionable Shantung clauses, and in its separate treaty with Berlin the German share of the Boxer indemnity and German extraterritorial privileges were cancelled. A significant breach had been made in the wall of foreign "rights" in China.

The Washington Conference.—After the war the U.S. continued its active participation in Chinese affairs by bringing about (1920) a financial consortium whose purpose it was to assume international control of all further foreign loans to China and so to prevent the granting of special privileges to individual nations.

In 1921 and 1922, moreover, the United States called the Washington conference (*q.v.*), and China again had the opportunity to lay its case before the world and to ask for the elimination of the special privileges that foreigners enjoyed within its borders. Not all the agreements and treaties which arose out of the conference affected China, but the Chinese question loomed larger than any other except possibly that of disarmament. The most important actions, in so far as they concerned China, were as follows:

1. The treaty limiting naval armaments and fortifications had the effect of confirming Japan in the domination of the north-eastern coast of Asia. No sea power could now hope easily to penetrate by force through its curtain of islands to the coast of China, as the United States and Great Britain found to their sorrow after 1941.

2. Nine powers agreed by treaty to respect the sovereignty, independence and territorial and administrative integrity of China, to give China opportunity to develop a stable government, to maintain the principle of equal opportunity in China for the commerce and industry of all nations and to refrain from taking advantage of conditions in China to seek special privileges that would abridge the rights of subjects or citizens of friendly states.

3. The customs schedule of duties was within four months to be raised to an effective 5%, and provision was made for the convening of a special tariff conference and for the periodical re-adjustment of the customs tariff.

4. A board of reference was to be established in China to which questions connected with the enforcement of the "open door" and equal railway rates could be referred.

5. A resolution expressed the sympathy of the powers with China's desire to see removed "immediately or as soon as circumstances will permit existing limitations upon China's political, jurisdictional and administrative freedom," and provided for the early establishment of a commission to inquire into the practice of extraterritoriality in China and the progress in judicial reforms.

6. On Jan. 1, 1923, foreign postal agencies in China were to be abolished.

Several other resolutions expressed the good intentions of the powers toward China.

The Washington conference also afforded Japan and China an opportunity to come to an understanding over the thorny Shantung question. Following the signing of the treaty of Versailles, Japan had made attempts to adjust the dispute, but always on conditions which had been repulsed by the Chinese. Now, however, Japan adopted a much more conciliatory attitude, and an agreement was reached whereby the former German holdings in Shantung were to be returned to China. However, the Japanese retained a share in some mines in the province and large commercial interests and landholdings in Tsingtao.

Several of the promises made to China at Washington were carried out. The foreign post offices were discontinued at the designated time. A special conference on the tariff convened in Peking in Oct. 1925 and, going beyond the assurances previously given, permitted the consideration of the entire question of tariff autonomy. Because of the disintegration of the Chinese government, the gathering broke up before a treaty was framed, but the foreign delegates agreed to the removal of tariff restrictions and consented to the putting into effect of the Chinese national tariff law on Jan. 1, 1929. The Chinese for their part promised to enforce the national tariff law and to abolish likin, long obnoxious to foreigners, on the same date.

Japan, moreover, continued conciliatory. While it declined to accede to the Chinese demand, made in 1923, for the abrogation of the agreements of 1915, until 1931 it entered upon no new marked aggression.

The powers also seemed about to remit the unpaid portions of the Boxer indemnity. The United States acted finally in May 1924, and Great Britain, France, Japan and Russia took preliminary steps looking toward the same end. All plans for remission, however, called for the allocation of the funds to educational or other cultural projects.

Domestic Politics After World War I.—While China was making progress toward regaining the special privileges which had been wrested from it by the powers, internally its government was rapidly disintegrating.

At the close of World War I, it will be recalled, Hsü Shih-ch'ang was in the presidential chair and Tuan Ch'i-jui was in control. A separate government was maintained at Canton, largely by members of the Kuomintang, under the leadership of Sun Yat-sen. For a time Sun was ousted from Canton by a Kwangsi faction, but he was restored by Ch'en Ch'iung-ming, and in April 1921 he was elected "president of the Chinese republic" by such members of the parliament of 1913 as could be got together. However, he secured only a precarious foothold in Canton and a part of Kwangtung. Most of southern China was a medley of petty factions and quarrelling war lords.

Conditions were little better in the north. In 1920 the outstanding leaders were Wu P'ei-fu, his titular superior, Ts'ao Kun, and Chang Tso-lin, the master of wealthy Manchuria. In the summer of 1920 these three united to drive Tuan and the Anfu leaders out of power. Wu P'ei-fu and Chang Tso-lin could not long co-operate, and in 1922 Wu defeated the latter and drove him back into Manchuria.

Wu now took steps which he hoped would unify the country. Hsü Shih-ch'ang resigned the presidency, Li Yuan-hung was reinstated in that office, and the parliament of 1913 was recalled to Peking. Thus the last officers around whom the entire country had seemed to unite were put back into power.

Hopes for a unified China, however, proved illusory. Funds were insufficient, cabinets unstable, parliament venal and militarists intransigent. The disintegration that set in after the death of Yuan Shih-k'ai became complete. China was torn by rival military factions which year after year launched campaigns against each other, conscripted troops, levied burdensome taxes and disrupted the economy.

Nationalism and Communism.—During the early years after World War I two interrelated developments of great significance occurred: the rise of nationalism and the emergence of the Chinese Communist movement. The Communist party was founded by a group of intellectuals, some of them leaders in the May 4 movement, who had turned to Marxism for a possible solution to China's weakness and political instability. With the help of an adviser from the Comintern, the party was organized in July 1921, though there were then only a few score members. The party devoted itself at first to organizing labourers and publishing propaganda journals. In Moscow the Communist international at its second congress in July-August 1920 had adopted a strategy with respect to colonial peoples that called in the first place for co-operation between Communists and other parties in movements for national liberation. Applied to China, this strategy was interpreted to require an entente between the Communist party and the Kuomintang. It took several years for Comintern agents to convince both parties of the desirability of this program. By the summer of 1923, however, the details had been worked out and the U.S.S.R. had promised help to Sun Yat-sen, who was attempting to establish a government in Canton.

In Sept. 1923 Mikhail M. Grusenberg, better known as Michael Borodin, arrived in Canton and soon became Sun Yat-sen's adviser in a program of reorganizing the Kuomintang into a strong, disciplined and centralized party. Communists were to be admitted to the Kuomintang as individuals and to assist in an attempt to reunite the country and free it of foreign encroachments. Russian advisers, money and arms flowed into Canton to aid in the creation of a Nationalist army. After Sun's death on March 12, 1925, his party glorified him as a national hero and elevated his Three Principles of the People—nationalism, democracy and livelihood—into a bible.

In the latter part of 1925 the Nationalist movement was directed sharply against Great Britain, the occasion being a sequence of clashes between British authorities and Chinese in Shanghai and Canton during which many Chinese were killed. Hong Kong was tied up for months by boycott and widespread strikes. Patriotic students flocked to the Kuomintang and many into the Communist party as well. Communist members of the Kuomintang were particularly active in the anti-imperialist movement and in organizing labourers and poor peasants to demand better economic conditions. The movement at Canton under the leadership of Borodin and some of Sun's more radical lieutenants veered increasingly to the left. In the meantime the new Nationalist army was consolidating the power of the Kuomintang in Kwangtung.

Not all leaders of the Nationalist party approved of the Communists, but some hoped to use them to achieve Nationalist aims. The Communists likewise hoped to use the Kuomintang. Great tension existed within the coalition.

In the summer of 1926 the Nationalist armies, led by Chiang Kai-shek, began a triumphant march northward, and by winter they had driven Wu P'ei-fu into Honan and practically eliminated him, were in possession of the Wuhan cities—Hankow, Wuchang and Hanyang—and the Kuomintang had moved its capital to Hankow.

The victories had been achieved as much by skilful propaganda as by force of arms. Wherever the Nationalist forces came, trained agitators directed popular sentiment against the treaties and foreign merchants and against Christian schools, churches and hospitals as imperialistic.

Kuomintang agitators also organized labourers and peasants to make exorbitant demands of employers and landlords, and in some places, notably Hunan and Hupeh, a reign of terror followed in which many of the propertied class were dispossessed and even executed.

Educated Chinese, weary of the long civil strife and smarting over China's feeble position among the nations, hailed the advance of the Kuomintang as the harbinger of better days. That advance continued with amazing rapidity, and by March 1927 the Chinese had taken over the British concessions in Hankow and Kiukiang; British and U.S. merchants and missionaries were being evacuated from much of the Nationalist territory; Sun Chuang-fang, recently strongly entrenched in Chekiang and Kiangsu, was in full flight, his armies a disorganized rabble; and only strong forces of foreign marines kept the Nationalist armies out of the foreign settlements in Shanghai. The northern military chiefs, alarmed, had put themselves under the direction of Chang Tso-lin to stem, if possible, the oncoming flood.

The radicalism of the Communists during the northern expedition inevitably produced a reaction. Merchants, landlords, army officers and many other groups who found themselves menaced offered support to conservative leaders in the Kuomintang if they would rid the party of its radical wing. With victory in sight, tension between right and left grew sharper. Chiang Kai-shek became the centre of the anti-Communist movement. In March 1927 Nationalist troops, entering Nanking, looted foreign dwellings, robbed foreigners and killed several of them, until further loss of foreign lives was prevented by the fire of British and U.S. gunboats in the Yangtze river. One effect of this incident was to widen the breach within the Kuomintang.

In the Chinese section of Shanghai, labour unions under leadership of the left wing had risen in a general strike, disarmed police and driven out some of the northern troops. On April 12, shortly after the Nationalist army arrived in Shanghai, Chiang Kai-shek instituted a bloody purge to stamp out the Communists and left Kuomintang elements in the city. The purge quickly spread to other regions under control of conservative military commanders. Chiang then set up a government in Nanking as a rival to the one in Hankow. The irreconcilable cleft between Communists and Nationalists dates from this period.

The Nationalist advance was halted by these internal dissensions, and the party continued to divide. By autumn 1927 the anti-Communist reaction was in full swing, Borodin and other Russian advisers were ousted from Hankow, and in many places Chinese Communists were being hunted down and executed.

In 1928 the Nationalists reorganized under moderate and conservative leaders and with headquarters at Nanking, began a new northward advance. Chiang Kai-shek led, in co-operation with Fêng Yü-hsiang and Yen Hsi-shan. A serious clash with Japanese troops occurred in May in Chinan, and a partial reoccupation of Shantung by Japan followed. In spite of this, however, the Nationalists pushed on and in June entered Peking. Chang Tso-lin was killed by a bomb as he was retiring into Manchuria, and his son, Chang Hsüeh-liang, succeeded to the command of his forces. Because of Japanese opposition, Manchuria did not formally join the Nationalists, but Chang Hsüeh-liang was given a place on the chief council of the Nanking government. The major armed opposition to their rule having been eliminated, the Nationalists moved the capital from Peking (now renamed Peiping, "Northern Peace") to Nanking and in October set up an administration reorganized to conform to Sun Yat-sen's program, with Chiang Kai-shek as the ranking official.

Events From 1928 to 1937.—In domestic politics the years from 1928 to 1937 were stormy but on the whole witnessed marked progress toward a more stable regime. Throughout them all, the most prominent figure in the central government was Chiang Kai-shek. In 1927 he married Soong Mei-ling, a sister of Mme. Sun Yat-sen, and so, in a sense, strengthened his claim to the inheritance of the leadership of the Kuomintang. Much of the time, moreover, two of his brothers-in-law occupied prominent posts in the central government—T. V. Soong, who proved an extraordinarily able minister of finance, and H. H. K'ung, who had married one of the Soong sisters.

So strong and vigorous a man as Chiang Kai-shek inevitably had his enemies. However, he retained control of the army and, accordingly, continued the dominant leader.

The chief internal movements against the authority of Chiang Kai-shek after 1928 can be quickly summarized. Yen Hsi-shan and Fêng Yü-hsiang could scarcely be expected to submit tamely to the leadership of this young arrival from the south. In the summer of 1930 they joined forces against Chiang. By autumn of that year, however, Chiang had vindicated his power against them. The "Young Marshal," Chang Hsüeh-liang, until the autumn of 1931 in possession of the major military machine in the north, continued loyal to Nanking and to Chiang.

More serious was the recalcitrancy of the south and west. Only slowly, and then largely because of the necessity of presenting a common front against the Japanese, did Kwangtung, Kwangsi, Yünnan, Kweichow and Szechwan fall into line with Nanking.

The greatest domestic menace to Chiang Kai-shek and the Kuomintang, however, was the Communist movement. After the purges of mid-1927 the Communist party turned to armed force to overthrow its rival. Only gradually was it able to create armed bands of peasants and deserting soldiers, seize control of inaccessible bits of territory and begin to create soviet districts. It appealed to tenant farmers, landless labourers and others upon whom the existing rural order bore most heavily. Terror was widely used, and persons of property were cruelly dealt with. In essence the movement fed on peasant revolt. By 1930 the Red army had become a sizable force and soviet regions covered large areas in Kiangsi, Fukien, Hunan and Hupeh.

The Nanking government launched five campaigns between Dec. 1930 and Oct. 1933 in an attempt to destroy the Red army and capture the soviet bases. Finally by Oct. 1934 the main Red forces were driven out of their chief base in southern Kiangsi. They executed a long retreat, marching and fighting through most of the southern and western provinces of China, arriving in north Shensi one year later. In the meantime Japan had seized Manchuria and was seeking to detach north China (*see* below). The Communists skilfully employed the rising patriotic sentiment to blunt the Nationalist attacks against themselves, urging an end of civil war and a united front of all parties and armies against Japan. This program appealed especially to the Manchurian troops of Chang Hsüeh-liang who were being used to fight the Communists in north Shensi. When Chiang Kai-shek went late in 1936 to Sian to push the campaign, he was seized by Chang Hsüeh-liang, who demanded the end of the civil war against the Communists, a reorganization of the government with more toleration for the opposition and, above all, a united front against Japan.

Although Chiang Kai-shek was released without publicly acceding and Chang Hsüeh-liang was technically punished, in effect the dramatic incident was the precursor to the easing of the war against the Communists and to the eventual co-operation of the latter in the defense against Japan.

In many ways advance was being registered by the Nationalist government. A better class of official was gradually introduced, partly through the initiative of Chiang Kai-shek. In many districts and in some of the provinces, men with modern training, less venal and with more of the community spirit than the typical war lord, were coming into power. Many felt the importance of improving the conditions of those rural masses who constituted the vast majority of the population. The government had no fundamental program to reform the socio-economic maladjustment in rural areas, however. Government energies were concentrated elsewhere. Education throughout the country was improved, with schools of better equipment and quality and with increasing enrolments. The government, too, became increasingly interested in public health. Previously physicians with modern training had come almost entirely from schools founded by Christian missionaries. Now the state was assuming more of the burden of public health, both by the organization of schools of modern medicine and by community-wide campaigns for the control of disease.

The improvement in internal order must not be exaggerated. Much of it depended precariously upon the life of one man, Chiang Kai-shek. Dissensions among leaders had not been eliminated. Over several provinces even of China proper Nanking exercised no effective control. In the outlying dependencies, only in Sinkiang, in portions of Inner Mongolia and here and there on the borders of Tibet did Nanking exert even a shadow of power. The world-wide financial depression brought embarrassment, especially beginning in 1934 with a marked rise in the price of silver and, accordingly, with a fall in other price levels. In the autumn of 1935 the government felt itself forced to nationalize all the silver and to go officially on a managed currency. Yet nearly every year witnessed some gains. Even those provinces which did not tolerate the interference of Nanking in their internal affairs usually permitted the Nationalist government to speak for them in relations with other nations.

One post office administration and one customs service extended throughout the country. In educational matters practically all the provinces co-operated with Nanking. Painfully and with occasional relapses China was advancing toward unification and a better and more stable government.

For more than two years after 1928 China seemed to be making progress toward emancipation from the "unequal treaties." In 1929 the British returned to Chinese administration their concession in Chinkiang and the next year their concession in Amoy. In 1929 Belgium consented to the cancellation of its concession in Tientsin. In 1928 and 1929 nearly all the western powers formally assented to the resumption by China of its tariff autonomy, followed in 1930 by Japan. On Feb. 1, 1929, accordingly, the Chinese government put into effect a schedule of duties determined by itself. Moreover, effective Chinese control over the customs administration increased. China, too, seemed to be making headway toward the abolition of extraterritoriality. Several of the smaller powers assented to the jurisdiction of Chinese laws and courts over their citizens. In July 1928 the Nanking government announced that all "unequal treaties . . . which have already expired shall *ipso facto* be abrogated" and that it would take immediate steps to end those "unequal treaties which have not yet expired and conclude new treaties." A number of the powers against which China adopted specific measures protested. Eventually several assented, but only on certain conditions. However, Great Britain, Japan, France and the United States, together with some of the smaller countries, held out. In Dec. 1929 Nanking announced that extraterritoriality would come to an end on Jan. 1, 1930, but postponed putting the order into effect pending suitable provision for the trial of cases involving foreigners. The needed regulations were framed and were announced to be operative on Jan. 1, 1932. Before that day arrived, however, events in Manchuria precluded carrying out the plan.

For several years after 1927 the relations of Nanking with Moscow were much of the time either strained or decidedly unfriendly. The Nanking government had been established in an anti-Communist reaction and could scarcely be expected to look upon the U.S.S.R. with cordiality. The joint operation by Russians and Chinese of the Chinese Eastern railway, in Manchuria, made for irritation. In 1929, indeed, the Chinese dismissed and arrested the Soviet officials associated with the railway. In Jan. 1930 a Russian invasion forced the Chinese to assent to the restoration to the Soviet Union of its former share in the control of the line. The U.S.S.R., moreover, had the sovietized Outer Mongolia in its orbit and appeared to threaten the remnants of Chinese authority in Sinkiang. By the end of 1932, however, Russo-Chinese relations became much more friendly, especially since both nations found common cause in their apprehension of Japan.

Japanese Aggression.—It was from Japan, as it has been suggested, that the greatest external menace arose to the territorial integrity and independence of China. Since the Washington conference the attitude of the Japanese government toward China had usually been one of moderation and restraint.

In Manchuria, however, a serious conflict was brewing. There the Chinese were especially restive under the privileges held by the Japanese. Chinese formed the vast majority of the population, and the legal title of the region was held by China, yet Japan controlled much of south Manchuria through its railways and its leasehold on the Liaotung peninsula, and in other ways compromised Chinese sovereignty. The Chinese began building a series of railroads which would in part encircle the Japanese lines, debouch at Hulutao, a port which the Chinese were developing, and make them partially independent of the Japanese. Chang Hsüeh-liang, the ruler of Manchuria, was disposed more and more to ally himself with Nanking and to sympathize with the Kuomintang and its desire to rid China of foreign control.

The Japanese, on the other hand, had large investments in Manchuria. Because of the rapidly increasing population of their islands and the necessity which they were under of finding markets and raw materials for the industries which were their only relief, they looked upon Manchuria as their life line against national ruin, as a bulwark against the U.S.S.R. and as a source of food, coal and oil in case they should go to war with a naval power. In the summer of 1931 the friction expressed itself in minor incidents. The element in control of the main body of the Japanese forces in Manchuria believed that the time had passed for temporizing and compromise, and on the night of Sept. 18–19, 1931, alleging that Chinese had blown up part of the track of the South Manchuria railway near the city, seized Mukden.

In the next few weeks the Japanese occupied other cities in Manchuria and demolished Chang Hsüeh-liang's power north of the Great Wall. Having destroyed the only effective Chinese rule in Manchuria, the Japanese, compelled to preserve order to protect their own interests and not disposed to annex the region outright, stimulated native leaders, largely Chinese, to set up local governments. Early in 1932 these were organized, with Japanese direction, into a new state called Manchoukuo which on Feb. 18, 1932, declared its independence and called to its head P'u Yi, the last Manchu emperor of China.

Later in the year Japan accorded Manchoukuo official recognition and entered into a defensive alliance with it.

Nanking, unable to offer effective armed resistance to Japan, presented its case to the League of Nations. The League found in it the most difficult crisis which that young organization had yet faced, attempted to induce Japan to withdraw its troops to the zone of the South Manchuria railway, and in time appointed a commission, headed by Lord Lytton, to investigate.

The commission's report, made in the autumn of 1932, in the main found Japan to be at fault and proposed a procedure for settling the dispute which would preserve China's sovereignty. On Feb. 24, 1933, the assembly of the League took action against Japan, recommending a method of effecting an adjustment which Japan would not accept. Soon thereafter Tokyo announced its resignation from the League.

The United States, at times acting in close co-operation with the League, attempted to induce Japan to keep the peace and declined to recognize Manchoukuo. The U.S.S.R., while deeply interested, was not disposed to go to war to keep Japan out of the Russian sphere of influence in northern Manchuria.

The Chinese, powerless to oppose effective military resistance, had at hand a weapon in the boycott. They invoked this at great cost to Japanese trade. The Japanese objected, friction became acute and fighting broke out in Jan. 1932 at Shanghai; in the ensuing warfare Japanese forces laid waste a large portion of the city. The Chinese offered a much sturdier defense than had been expected, but eventually were driven back. Due in part to the good offices of the League, fighting ceased in March 1932.

Chinese anti-Japanese activities continued in Manchuria, largely through irregulars. Chang Hsüeh-liang, for a time with his headquarters at near-by Peiping (Peking), was a source of irritation. The Japanese, too, wished to add the province of Jehol to Manchoukuo. In Jan.-Feb. 1933, Manchoukuoan-Japanese forces occupied Jehol, and Chang Hsüeh-liang, his prestige badly damaged, soon resigned and left for Europe. When he returned, it was to a post in Hupeh and then in Shensi. In April 1933 the Japanese, annoyed by raids from south of Jehol, advanced within the Great Wall. The Chinese were forced to withdraw and on May 31 Nanking found it advisable to enter into a truce, setting up a demilitarized zone south of the Great Wall, in the northeastern part of the province of Hopei. Strangely enough, however, in all this time war was not officially declared and regular diplomatic relations were maintained between the two governments. The truce of May 1933 established a *modus vivendi* which was practically a treaty of peace and which tacitly (although not explicitly) acquiesced in the Japanese occupation of Manchuria. The articulate among the Chinese, however, remained unreconciled to the existence of Manchoukuo. Moreover, for a number of years only two foreign powers besides Japan, Italy and the small Central American El Salvador, formally accorded the new state official recognition.

Japan, however, persevered in consolidating its position in Manchoukuo. It acted against banditry and entered upon a vast program of railway building which opened up more of the land and connected it with Korea. In 1934 P'u Yi was officially crowned monarch of the new state.

After long negotiations, moreover, Japan obtained the sale of the Russian interest in the Chinese Eastern railway and thus eliminated the last legal trace of the former Russian sphere of influence.

Japan was not content with confining its control of China to regions north of the Great Wall. In the spring of 1934 a pronouncement from Tokyo in effect declared all China to be a Japanese preserve in which no power could take important action without the consent of the island empire. In 1935, moreover, Japanese forced the withdrawal from Hopei and Chahar of any officials and armed forces and the disbandment of any organization which might prove unfriendly to Japan. The provinces of Hopei and Chahar passed partly into Japanese control, and Suiyuan, Shansi and Shantung were threatened. Chiang Kai-shek dared not offer open opposition for fear of bringing a Japanese avalanche upon his head.

In July 1937 what proved to be a life and death struggle broke out between China and Japan. The opening incident was a minor clash between Chinese and Japanese troops not far from Peiping on the night of July 7. The conflict soon ceased to be localized. The Japanese came to feel that since Chiang Kai-shek and the Nationalist government would not yield to their wishes they must be eliminated. To the Japanese, the rising tide of nationalism in China, directed, as much of it was, against them, had become intolerable. Governments, so they held, must be set up in China which would co-operate with Japan.

The Chino-Japanese War, 1937–45.—The war, which remained undeclared until Dec. 9, 1941, may be divided into three phases—a period of rapid Japanese advance until the end of 1938, a period of virtual stalemate until 1944, and the final period when United Nations counterattack, principally in the Pacific and on Japan's home islands, brought about Japan's surrender.

In July 1937 the Chinese people were determined to resist further Japanese aggression. Practically all regional military and political groups rallied to support the National government and Chiang Kai-shek in their decision to oppose Japan by every means. The Communists, who had urged a united front against Japan since 1935, pledged their support and put their armies nominally under command of the government. From a strictly military point of view, however, Japan was so much better prepared than China that its armies achieved rapid initial success.

Within the course of two years Japan obtained possession of most of the ports, of the majority of the chief cities as far west as Hankow and of the larger part of the railways. Peiping and Tientsin were occupied in July 1937. After fierce fighting, the Chinese armies were driven out of the Shanghai area by the middle of Nov. 1937. Nanking fell in mid-Dec. 1937. The capital was moved west to Hankow. The Japanese followed and took that city in Oct. 1938. In the same month, the Chinese lost Canton. The Japanese pressed northward and westward from Peiping along the railway lines into Shansi and Inner Mongolia. They dominated Shantung. They took possession of the Peiping-Hankow, the Tientsin-Pukow and the Lunghai railways and of the lines in the lower part of the Yangtze valley. They had complete command of the sea. Always superior in the air, before many months they had all but destroyed the Chinese air force and bombed Chinese cities at will. The loss of life, particularly to Chinese, both soldiers and civilians, was enormous.

Yet the Chinese did not yield and the war was prolonged far beyond Japan's expectations. Chiang Kai-shek moved his capital to Chungking, in Szechwan, at the western end of the difficult Yangtze gorges. Much of China's leadership migrated to the far west, to Szechwan and Yünnan. In Free China, they prepared for prolonged resistance. In occupied China Japan was unsuccessful in inducing many Chinese of standing to take office in the governments which it endeavoured to set up. Even there Japan's control was confined to the cities and the railway lines; outside these it was challenged, often successfully, by guerrilla bands which professed allegiance to the Nationalist government. The Communist regime was particularly successful in using guerrilla methods to resist Japan. The rapid Japanese advances broke down the established patterns of politico-military control. Communists troops and organizers moved into the vast rural areas behind Japanese lines. They organized village self-defense units, created local governments and expanded their own armies, the 8th route army operating in the mountains and plains of north China and the new 4th army in the lower Yangtze valley.

During the stalemate phase of the war, beginning in 1939, Japan tried to subdue Chinese resistance by the slow strangulation of blockade. China's main seaports were occupied, from the south to the north. In at least one, Foochow, the occupation was only intermittent, but in most of them it was continuous. When, in 1940, France fell to the Germans, Japan took the occasion to advance in French Indochina and to seal access to Free China by the railroad which led from the coast to Kunming (Yünnanfu) and by crude highways from the Indochinese coast to the interior. For a time Japan induced the English, fighting as they were with their backs to the wall, to close the difficult road which led from Burma to Yünnan. After a time the English reopened the road. Then, following years of increasing tension, came the sudden outbreak of war, precipitated by the Japanese attack on Pearl Harbor (Dec. 7, 1941), between the United States and Great Britain on the one hand and Japan on the other.

The Japanese, taking advantage of their preparedness on land, sea and air and of their favourable geographic position, quickly made themselves dominant on the coasts of east Asia. Their capture of Hong Kong and of Burma in 1942 shut doors by which some goods had moved in and out of Free China.

The only routes which now remained to connect the fighting Chinese with their friends abroad were the long and difficult roads across Sinkiang and the air passage from Assam to Free China. Over the latter, freight and passengers were conveyed by heroic airmen, and that in spite of the perils of high altitudes and of Japanese planes. Through the venality of Japanese officials and the skill of blockade runners, some goods trickled through the Japanese lines along the coast.

During the war of endurance China was divided into three regions—Free China under control of the Nationalist government, Communist China and the regions occupied by Japan. The regimes in each area were pitted against the other two.

Nationalist China had serious economic and social problems. The relatively backward western provinces, with almost no modern industry or transport facilities, were strained to support the huge armies and the government. Free China was crowded with refugees and some of its cities were mercilessly bombed. The shortage of manufactured goods and the costs of war brought on inflation which was intensified by the government's fiscal policy and which caused great hardship to troops, government workers, teachers, wage earners and students. It encouraged hoarding, speculation and graft. The army, unable to take the offensive against the superior Japanese forces, steadily deteriorated. Graft became widespread among the officers, while the undernourished conscripts no longer had much will to fight.

In schools and colleges shortage of books and equipment, malnutrition and attempted regimentation by government thought-police all had a deteriorating effect.

The government, too, was deeply affected by the war. It had lost its industrial and financial base in east China and the flower of its armies. The strong public support it enjoyed during the early years of resistance waned and turned to apathy or hostility. This was the result of many factors. The government was blamed for the ills of inflation, corruption and heavy taxation. The strains of war tore at the united front.

When the Communists began to reappear as rivals rather than subordinates, the government retaliated with repressive measures which it applied also to other groups. Essentially an authoritarian regime, it tended to become more repressive and less efficient as the war dragged on. Yet with all these difficulties, Free China under Chiang Kai-shek's leadership refused to surrender or negotiate with Japan.

The scattered areas controlled by the Communist party and its armies grew during the war until near the end they covered large parts of north and east China. In these "border regions" and "liberated areas" the regime was, by nearly unanimous report, popular with the people.

This was partly the result of economic and social reforms which bettered the conditions of the peasantry and partly the result of the system of local government which encouraged wide participation of the public through mass organizations even though control was held firmly by the party. The army was also popular because of its good discipline and close relations with the common people upon whom it depended for existence.

During the stalemate period relations between the Nationalists and the Communists were embittered by many military clashes for which each side blamed the other. The Communists did everything possible to strengthen themselves, while the government tried to keep them confined by blockade and other means. In effect the civil war was merely submerged, after 1938, in the larger war with Japan.

In the occupied regions Japan tried to win support and lessen its military burden by setting up a puppet regime at Nanking (1940). To head this, it obtained Wang Ching-wei, an erstwhile intimate companion of Sun Yat-sen, who professed to be carrying on the latter's tradition. Japan also went through the motions of restoring to Chinese administration the French concession and the international settlement in Shanghai, for it had taken these over after the attack on Pearl Harbor.

Yet Japan was no more successful than earlier in inducing many Chinese of ability and integrity to serve in these administrations. Obviously, too, no important step could be taken by these regimes without the approval of the Japanese authorities.

In the last phase of the war, from early 1944 to Aug. 1945, some help was beginning to come to China from the outside, chiefly from the United States. Aeroplanes and various kinds of war *matériel* were being flown from India over "the hump," as the mountain barrier was called. Chinese pilots and mechanics were being trained. No longer could the Japanese bomb Chinese cities at will. Some of their own strongholds were bombed by U.S. and

Chinese planes. Americans were also training and equipping in India Chinese forces which had taken refuge there after the fall of Burma. Yet the main theatre of war was far from China, whose armies by then were too debilitated to play an important part in the final campaigns

The Nationalist government had been seriously undermined by seven years of war and inflation, while Communist strength had grown. As Japan withdrew divisions to fight on Pacific islands, the Communist armies were able to move in and organize more "liberated areas." The danger of fratricidal war after Japan's defeat became obvious. Patriotic Chinese of all parties hoped to find some way to restore national unity and avoid a ruinous civil war. The U.S. government was drawn into China's domestic crisis since the United States provided the main external supports—financial, military and diplomatic—for the Nationalist government and since the U.S. was eager that China should take a place after the war as a stabilizing influence in the far east. In various ways United States representatives in China tried to bring about a reconciliation between the Kuomintang and the Communists. A fundamental difficulty—besides the bitter distrust and intransigence of both Chinese parties—lay in the United States' position of trying to mediate between them while supporting one side, the Nationalists, as the government of China.

CHINA AFTER WORLD WAR II

Civil War.—Within five years of the victory over Japan the Nationalist government had been driven from the mainland by the Communists, who then became masters of the country. Japan's defeat set off a struggle for control of occupied China extending from Manchuria in the north to Canton in the south. Nationalist troops, transported by the U.S. army air force and navy, were able to take over key cities and most railway lines in east and north China. But Communist troops, moving out from their guerrilla bases, occupied much of the hinterland in the north and in Manchuria. The stage was set for full-scale renewal of civil war.

For more than a year the U.S. government attempted, through its ambassador, Patrick J. Hurley, and then through Gen. George C. Marshall, to mediate and prevent this conflict. During Jan. and Feb. 1946, it appeared that agreements laying the basis for peace had been reached. On Jan. 10 the Nationalists and Communists concluded a cease-fire agreement to be administered by a tripartite committee (Kuomintang, Communist and U.S.) which would send out truce teams to stop conflicts that flared up. A Political Consultation conference representing all parties, meeting Jan. 10–31, worked out plans for an interim coalition government to function until a new constitution should be adopted by a representative national assembly. On Feb. 25, 1946, a military reorganization plan worked out with the help of General Marshall, to merge and consolidate the hostile armies, was agreed upon by representatives of the government and of the Communist party. Within a few months, however, these agreements were undone. During all of 1946 the U.S. government, acting through General Marshall and his aides, strove for peace. The hostility, ambition and distrust of both Chinese parties made peace impossible.

The civil war was fought out from 1946 to 1950. In that period the great strategic advantage of the Nationalists was reversed. During 1946 and early 1947 they succeeded in taking most of the railways and in recapturing important cities in the north. As Soviet troops withdrew from Manchuria the Nationalists sent in their best armies to try to hold the vital railways and industrial centres. But they were overextended. Communist forces, retrained and re-equipped with Japanese arms, gradually shifted from guerrilla warfare to large-scale offensive campaigns. In 1948 they turned the tide, destroying the Nationalist armies in Manchuria and winning impressive victories in north China. By the end of the year the Nationalist government was in desperate straits. Its armies were disintegrating. Inflation was destroying the economy. The Kuomintang was torn by factional strife. The public was withdrawing its support of the regime.

In 1948 the Communists began a southward march. They captured Nanking, the Nationalist capital, on April 24, 1949; the substitute capital of Canton, on Oct. 15; then Chungking, the wartime capital to which the government returned for final refuge, on Nov. 30. On Dec. 8, 1949, the government declared Taipei in Formosa to be the National capital.

Communist Regime.—During 1949 the Communists laid the foundation for a national government. In September the Chinese People's Political Consultative conference, a body having the appearance of a constitutional convention, met in Peiping to establish a new government. The conference included representatives of many parties, professions, organizations, and ethnic minorities, but selection was determined by the Communist party, which dominated the gathering behind the scenes. The climax of its meetings was the announcement of the establishment of the Chinese People's Republic on Oct. 1, 1949.

The Central People's government of the People's Republic of China was established at Peking (renamed by the conference). While having the appearance of a coalition government, it was essentially a Communist dictatorship.

Government was only one of the agencies employed by the Communist leaders to control the country and carry out their policies. Other agencies included the party itself, numerous mass organizations and the armed forces. The Communist party, a highly centralized and strongly disciplined organization, had from 6,000,000 to 7,000,000 members in the early 1950s. Its central committee, or a smaller group within it, determined party policy, carried out by a network of regional, provincial, municipal and lesser committees. The party structure paralleled and party officials controlled each level of the government, of the army and of the mass organizations. The rank-and-file members provided the motive force for carrying out the party's will in factories, villages, street associations and army units throughout the country. After coming to power the party established many types of mass organizations or extended those it had previously created. Associations of peasants, youth, women and labourers enrolled millions or scores of millions of members. Every profession and occupation was organized. Each of these centrally controlled bodies served as an agency to mobilize support for the regime and its programs. At the same time they provided the Chinese people with greater opportunity for participation in government, particularly local government, than ever before.

The party, through the government, established a monopoly of all organs of information—radio, press, motion pictures, etc.—and the entire educational system. All coercive bodies such as the army, the police and the courts came under its control. The government did not hesitate to use terror, including widespread executions and forced labour, to eliminate or control potential opponents. It was through these means that the new regime, with a large measure of popular support, was able to unify the country more completely than any other had done since the height of Manchu power.

In foreign policy the regime was firmly in the world Communist camp. The government was quickly recognized by the Soviet Union and its satellite countries. A treaty of friendship, alliance and mutual assistance between the People's Republic of China and the Soviet Union was signed in Moscow on Feb. 14, 1950. It linked the two countries in a defensive alliance. By the terms of a supplementary agreement, the U.S.S.R. promised to transfer to the People's Republic of China before the end of 1952 all its rights in the Chinese Changchun railway (the former Chinese Eastern and South Manchuria railways) and to withdraw its troops from Port Arthur and turn over the naval base to China's control; Dairen (Dalny) was also to be returned. The U.S.S.R. also extended a five-year credit of U.S. $300,000,000. Subsequent treaties and agreements bound the two countries closely together. Communist China's entry into the Korean conflict toward the end of 1950 tightened this alliance and tended to isolate China from the non-Communist world. The balance of China's foreign trade shifted from Japan and the west to the Soviet Union and its satellites.

The non-Communist governments of the world were divided over the issue whether to recognize the new Chinese government or continue to deal with the Nationalist government on Formosa. Burma, India, Pakistan, Indonesia, Sweden, Denmark, Finland and Switzerland quickly established relations with the new government. Great Britain and certain other countries offered recognition, but the Communist regime made no effort until 1954 to establish relations. The question which government should represent China in the United Nations was also controversial.

Tibet was brought back under Chinese control through a military campaign beginning in Oct. 1950 and through negotiations during April and May of 1951. The Central People's government promised Tibet "national regional autonomy under the unified leadership of the Central People's Government" but took over the country's defense, communications and external relations. The agreement was signed on May 23, 1951, in Peking and was ratified by the dalai lama in October. In a treaty between India and China signed April 29, 1954, India recognized China's full sovereignty over Tibet and gave up certain privileges previously acquired there by Great Britain.

After winning control of the country, the Communist regime launched a series of nation-wide reforms which attempted to refashion nearly every aspect of Chinese life. Here only a few may be described. Of fundamental significance was the land redistribution program. In this the regime undertook to expropriate the land of all landlords and of "opponents of the state" and distribute it to farm labourers, tenants and poorer peasants. Within a few years, throughout a territory larger than Europe, ownership of land was redistributed and landlords were eliminated as an economic class. This was only the first step toward collectivization. Other intermediate stages were mutual aid teams and agricultural co-operatives, which were gradually developed on an ever-expanding scale throughout the land. Marketing and distribution of most of the products of Chinese agriculture was brought under co-operatives and state trading companies. These and other measures were designed to increase greatly the nation's agricultural output and place it at the service of the state for its program of economic development.

China's economic development was planned and controlled by the state. The first several years after 1949 were devoted to rehabilitation and to establishing the mechanism of economic controls. Communication facilities were restored, inflation was halted, and state banking and state trading companies were established. The war in Korea prevented much new capital construction except of railways and flood-control systems, but in 1953 the government launched the first five-year plan and announced a "high tide of construction" to transform China from an agricultural to an industrial country. Visitors to China in 1954 and 1955 reported impressive results.

The Communist regime actively extended education, which was brought completely under state control. Schools and colleges operated by western missionaries were confiscated. In the revised system emphasis was laid upon expanded educational facilities, ideological uniformity and technical training. A central purpose of the new system was to bring education within the reach of all workers and peasants. Mass education to eliminate illiteracy was pushed vigorously. Elementary education was to be available to all children. Teachers were retrained through "ideological remoulding campaigns," and new textbooks, much influenced by Soviet counterparts, were produced. Secondary and higher education became increasingly technical in order to train engineers, agronomists, medical personnel and technicians needed for the country's reconstruction.

The emancipation of women from their inferior position in the old society was announced as another aim of the Communist regime, carrying forward a movement which had been developing during previous decades of the 20th century. Legislation strengthened women's rights in property ownership, employment and health insurance. The marriage law, promulgated in May 1950, made child marriage and concubinage illegal, and stressed the right of young women to choose their own marriage partners. Women were given franchise equal to that of men.

During 1953–54, elections were held throughout China for "people's congresses" at village, county, municipal, provincial and national levels. To prepare for elections a population count was made as of June 30, 1953. According to official announcement, China's total population was found to be 601,938,035 (this included 7,591,298 for Taiwan and 11,743,320 estimated for Chinese abroad). On Sept. 20, 1954, the new National People's congress adopted a constitution of the People's Republic of China, the first constitution since China came under Communist control.

Nationalist Government on Formosa.—The Nationalist government meanwhile maintained itself on Formosa, which had reverted to Chinese control upon Japan's surrender in Aug. 1945. When the island became the government's last refuge late in 1949 it was necessary thoroughly to reform the inefficient, "carpet-bag" administration which had operated there during most of the civil war period. The Kuomintang party was reorganized with a view to its revitalization. The government bureaucracy, superimposed upon the provincial administration, was reduced and rationalized. The armed forces which had fled from the mainland were reorganized and, with help from a United States military mission and large U.S. financial grants, were revived into a more effective fighting force to defend the island and, according to Nationalist hopes, to lead in a reconquest of the mainland. In these efforts to establish a secure base Chiang Kai-shek took the lead as head of the Kuomintang, president of the republic and commander in chief of the armed forces. His power within the regime became even more absolute than before.

An attempt was made to provide Formosa with an efficient administration having due regard for the welfare of the people. This was necessary in order to restore confidence in the Nationalist government both at home and abroad. Elections in 1950–51 for magistrates, mayors and councils introduced a measure of local self-government. (The councils were given only advisory, not legislative, power.)

In the civil service the proportion of Formosans, especially in higher positions, was markedly increased. The former Japanese educational system was completely reorganized and extended so that more than 80% of children of elementary school age were in schools by 1952. Facilities for secondary and higher education were also greatly expanded.

The island's economy was brought back to the productive levels of the prewar Japanese administration or improved. During four years, 1949–53, the Nationalist government peacefully carried out a land reform program including reduction of land rents to 37.5% of the yield, sale of government land to cultivators, and government purchase of landlord's land and sale to tenant cultivators. As a result 5,800,000 ac. of land were transferred to tenants, and the percentage of Formosa's farmland cultivated by owners increased from 50.5% to 75.4%. With help of the Joint Commission on Rural Reconstruction, composed of Chinese and Americans, significant improvements were made in irrigation, cropping methods, animal husbandry, organizing of farmers' associations and agricultural extension. But the island's economy had to support the Nationalist government, armed forces numbering 500,000 and about 1,000,000 refugees from the mainland. Only with extensive economic aid from the U.S. was that possible. Inflationary pressures were held in check with greatest difficulty.

On April 28, 1952, the Nationalist government on Formosa and the government of Japan signed a separate peace officially ending the war which had begun in fact on July 7, 1937. Yet the two Chinese political regimes—Nationalist and Communist—which had been at war most of the time since 1927, confronted each other across the Formosan strait in a continuation of the contest for support of the Chinese people and the nations of the world.

BIBLIOGRAPHY.—For Chinese works *see* CHINESE LITERATURE.

General Histories: Henri Cordier, *Histoire générale de la Chine* (1920–21); Otto Franke, *Geschichte des Chinesischen Reiches* (1930–52); K. S. Latourette, *The Chinese: Their History and Culture*, 3rd ed. (New York, 1946); L. Carrington Goodrich, *A Short History of the Chinese People*, rev. ed. (New York, 1951); C. P. Fitzgerald, *China: A Short Cultural History,* ed. by C. G. Seligman (London, 1935; New York, 1938); Wolfram Eberhard, *A History of China,* tr. by E. W. Dickes (Berkeley, London, 1950); Owen Lattimore, *Inner Asian Frontiers of China* (New York, Oxford, 1940). For an account of Chinese history writing *see* C. S. Gardner, *Chinese Traditional Historiography* (1948). For a bibliography of works in western languages *see* H. Cordier, *Bibliotheca Sinica,* 2nd ed. (1904–08, supp. 1924). A guide is L. C. Goodrich and H. C. Fenn, *A Syllabus of the History of Chinese Civilization and Culture,* 5th ed. (New York, 1951).

Ancient and Middle Periods: E. Chavannes, *Mémoires historiques de Se-ma Ts'ien* (1895–1905); H. Maspero, *La Chine antique* (1927); H. G. Creel, *The Birth of China* (London, 1936; New York, 1937); D. Bodde, *China's First Unifier* (New York, London, 1938); Pan Ku, *The History of the Former Han Dynasty,* trans. by H. H. Dubs (Washington, 1938–44; London, 1939–45); Woodbridge Bingham, *The Founding of the T'ang Dynasty* (Washington, 1941); Karl A. Wittfogel and Fêng Chia-shêng (eds.), *History of Chinese Society: The Liao (907–1125)* (Philadelphia, 1949); H. D. Martin, *The Rise of Chingis Khan and His Conquest of North China* (Baltimore, 1950; Oxford, 1951); René Grousset, *Histoire de l'Extrême-Orient,* vol. ii (1929).

Modern Period: A. W. Hummel (ed.), *Eminent Chinese of the Ch'ing Period, 1644–1912,* 2 vol. (Washington, London, 1944–45); L. C. Goodrich, *The Literary Inquisition of Ch'ien-lung* (Washington, London, 1935); S. Y. Teng, *New Light on the History of the Taiping Rebellion* (Cambridge, Mass., 1950); J. K. Fairbank, *The United States and China* (Cambridge, Mass., Oxford, 1948); Meribeth E. Cameron, *The Reform Movement in China, 1898–1912* (Stanford, 1931; Oxford, 1932); H. F. MacNair, *China in Revolution* (Chicago, Cambridge, 1931); Kiang Wen-han, *The Chinese Student Movement* (New York, Oxford, 1948); Hu Shih, *The Chinese Renaissance* (Chicago, Cambridge, 1934); Ch'ien Tuan-shêng, *The Government and Politics of China* (Cambridge, Mass., Oxford, 1950); Lyon Sharman, *Sun Yat-sen* (New York, 1934); P. M. A. Linebarger, *The China of Chiang K'ai-shek* (Boston, 1941); Edgar Snow, *Red Star Over China,* rev. ed. (New York, 1938); Conrad Brandt, B. Schwartz and J. K. Fairbank (eds.), *A Documentary History of Chinese Communism* (Cambridge, Mass., London, 1952); Benjamin Schwartz, *Chinese Communism and the Rise of Mao* (Cambridge, Mass., 1951; Oxford, 1952); Harold Isaacs, *The Tragedy of the Chinese Revolution,* rev. ed. (Stanford, 1951; Oxford, 1952); Richard L. Walker, *China under Communism: the First Five Years* (New Haven, 1955).

China's Relations With the Occident: F. Hirth, *China and the Roman Orient* (1885); G. F. Hudson, *Europe and China* (New York, London, 1931); H. Yule, *Cathay and the Way Thither,* new. ed. by H. Cordier (1916); A. C. Moule, *Christians in China Before the Year 1550* (New York, London, 1930); A. H. Rowbotham, *Missionary and Mandarin: The Jesuits at the Court of China* (Berkeley, 1942); K. S. Latourette, *A History of Christian Missions in China* (New York, London, 1929); H. B. Morse, *The International Relations of the Chinese Empire,* 3 vol. (New York, 1910–18); H. F. MacNair and D. F. Lach, *Modern Far Eastern International Relations* (New York, London, 1950); Ssu-yü Teng and J. K. Fairbank, *China's Response to the West: a Documentary Survey, 1839–1923* (Cambridge, Mass., 1954); U.S. Department of State, *United States Relations With China* (1949).

(K. S. L.; C. M. W.)

ETHNOLOGY

Two forms of early man are found in China: chronologically, the giant ape (*Gigantopithecus blacki*) and Peking man (*Sinanthropus pekinensis*). The existence of the first was evidenced by three teeth found in south China and corroborated by some larger specimens of the Java man (*Pithecanthropus erectus*). Remains of the Peking man were much more abundantly found in a cave southwest of Peking. Most original remains of the Peking man disappeared in the China sea somewhere en route either to Japan or to the Philippines during World War II. The authenticity of the giant ape was in dispute in the mid-1950s, and the conditions of its existence remained unknown. The Peking man had tools of the Old Stone Age type, including crude flints, bone and ornaments such as beads and perforated teeth and shells. It is doubtful that Peking man was ancestral to modern Chinese, for most or all of his points of resemblance with the Chinese are also shared by other living races, notably those of Europe.

Early Origins.—While there is evidence in Chinese myths and tradition, early history and archaeology that the original Chinese came to China via Sinkiang (Chinese Turkistan), there is also a likelihood that they might have reached the continent from the north, via Mongolia. H. L. Movius, Jr., based the latter contention on the following grounds: (1) The Old Stone Age implements found with the Peking man are of the chopper type, different from all Old Stone Age tools found in Europe and elsewhere. (2) The Old Stone Age tools found in the Ordos region of Mongolia seem to have much in common with those of the Yenisei-Baikal region of Siberia, on the one hand, and with the pebble tools of the type used by the Peking man.

There is much more abundant evidence of New Stone age developments among the Chinese in north central China, in the basin of the lower Hwang-ho, the major home of the prehistoric Chinese. The first part of this development was characterized by polychrome pottery of two general varieties: a hand-made red and design-painted kind and a coarser, gray, unpainted ware. The second part, probably overlapping somewhat with the former, was characterized by a kind of all-black ware, fine, thin, wheel-turned and burnished. With this ware was also found a white variety made of kaolin. Both parts of these cultural developments were associated with other items. Coexisting with polychrome pottery were agriculture, stock raising, houses with roof entrances and possibly some metal. The most outstanding things associated with the black wares were the walled cities which remained an important Chinese culture trait throughout their later history.

The bronze culture which followed that of the black wares marked the beginning of Chinese written history. The inscriptions on the many hundreds of oracle bones uncovered in Anyang in the same general area of the Stone Age cultures depict a civilization with dynasties, commanding armies of 1,000 to 5,000 men, great subterranean tombs, horse teams yoked to spoked chariots, silk, clothes with sleeves, animal and human sacrifices, writing and bronze vessels and implements made both with moulds and by the melted-wax method. This culture developed at least 1,000 years after the rise of its Sumerian and Egyptian counterparts, but within a short period it seems to have achieved equal splendour, with a characteristic Chinese colouring and style. (See *Archaeology,* above.)

Influences on Other Peoples.—From north central China the Chinese extended their influence over the rest of China, including not only the original 18 provinces but also Manchuria and Formosa, while keeping and amplifying their own peculiar cultural integrity and form remarkably well. It is highly probable that racially the Koreans and at least some Japanese and Indochinese were of Chinese origin.

The racial influence of the Chinese on their other neighbours is less pronounced, although they have continuously absorbed some of the aboriginal peoples in China as they replaced them as well as invaders from outside, notably the Manchus, who ruled China for nearly 300 years. Yet in spite of this history of mixture, the modern Chinese as a whole show a higher degree of homogeneity than the peoples of Europe. The skin colour is generally light yellow, fair in some regions and brownish in others. The hair is usually black and straight, while occasionally a strain of waviness is present. The Mongolian eye fold is conspicuous as with all Asian peoples. The stature is generally medium, but in a few provinces such as Fukien and Hupeh it is not unusual to find adult men more than six feet tall. The head form ranges from long to broad, while the width of the nose is medium.

The cultural influences of the Chinese over their neighbours as well as the country's intruders have been more spectacular than their physical absorption of them. The Japanese received from the Chinese the entire Confucian ethics, although keeping their own variety of ancestor worship and political organization, and the Chinese version of Buddhism. The Korean family relationship and court manners and organization were practically copies of those of China. In much of Indochina the same imitation occurred. The styles of clothing and hairdress of modern Japan and Korea were those prevailing in China about T'ang times, while the premodern official garments and paraphernalia of the several states in Indochina were those prevailing in China up to the 17th century. The most extraordinary Chinese influence on Japan and Korea was linguistic. Both the Japanese and the Koreans borrowed the Chinese written language after, probably, the 5th century A.D. Although the Japanese and the Koreans each later acquired an alphabetic system of their own, even today they continue to cling to the Chinese characters to parallel their phonetic scripts.

Regional Differences.—There are certain obvious regional differences in China, not only in topography and climate but also in culture of the inhabitants. China south of the Yangtze is subtropical; in the Hwang-ho region and north of it, it is frigid, while in that region which lies between it is temperate. In the south the rainfall is from 40 to 75 in. annually, whereas in the north it ranges from 25 to 10 in. Topographically the variation is equally extreme. In south China, parts of north China and especially west China are many hills and mountains. Most of the plateau of Tibet comes to three miles in elevation, with many peaks reaching five miles. On the other hand, east China is close to sea level, being an alluvial plain. In Sinkiang the oasis of Turfan is as low as 928 ft. below sea level.

China can be differentiated into at least three agricultural regions. In the south and the southwest rice is the principal crop, and the average farm or area of cultivation is three acres or less. In the north, inside the great wall, the principal crop is wheat, and the usual size of a farm is about five acres. In Manchuria in the northeast, the average farm is much larger—about 15 ac. or more—and the principal crops are corn and sorghum.

Historically there have been many differences between the northern and southern peoples. More southerners than northerners have participated in China's political, intellectual and artistic life. The relatively few Chinese who migrated after about 1750 to the south seas and the west were practically all southerners. Modern revolutions in China from the T'ai P'ing to the Communist were all led by southerners. For these reasons, the southerners in China have been described as more progressive and the northerners more conservative, the former as more urban, the latter more rural.

The differences among the different regions of China, however, are overshadowed by the many basic similarities. Throughout China persist the same pattern of family and filial piety, the practice of ancestor worship and the observance of the same major festivals, as well as similar marriage and funeral practices. Even the diversity of dialects has been much exaggerated. In all there are probably not more than eight mutually unintelligible dialects, seven of which are spoken in the narrow coastal belt stretching from Shanghai to Canton. The rest of China speaks one variety or another of Mandarin, with regional differences not greater than those, for example, between Chicago, Ill., and Houston, Tex. Furthermore even the mutually unintelligible dialects are practically identical in grammar. Only one written language prevails among all literate Chinese regardless of geographical origin.

Religion.—For untold years writers have spoken of the Chinese as having three major religions: Confucianism, Taoism and Buddhism. This is a misconception. Individual westerners usually not only adhere to one faith but also to one denomination or even to one branch of that denomination. Members of different churches of the same sect have a sense of rivalry. Such phenomena are unknown to the Chinese. The average Chinese tends to have something to do with any or all religions but adheres exclusively to none.

The most universal system of belief in China is ancestor worship. First, it is a part of the filial duty of sons to provide for their parents before and after death, for the dead are believed to have the same needs as the living. Second, like the father-son relationship within the family, the relationship between the departed ancestors and their living descendants is also reciprocal. The conduct of the living affects the welfare of the dead, and the actions of the latter in the spirit world continue to help the living. Many Chinese folk tales and novels depict this belief. Third, the interest of the departed ancestors is largely confined to their own lineal descendants, just as the duty of worship on the part of the living is confined to the lineal ancestors. It is because of ancestor worship that the Chinese construct elaborate tombs and graveyards for the dead. Here again the elaborate tombs and graveyards are not merely for the comfort of the dead. By means of *feng shui* ("wind and water" or geomancy) the Chinese arrange the burial grounds of their dead so that the graveyards will promote the prosperity of and ensure good luck for the descendants.

Ancestor worship is, however, part of a wider belief system of the Chinese. The departed ancestors are spiritual beings closest to the living descendants, but each descendant is also affected by a tremendous hierarchy of nonancestral gods. In its bare outline this spiritual hierarchy is not dissimilar to that of the traditional Chinese government. At the very top is the Supreme Ruler of Heaven and his ministers and their assistants. In the middle are the judges who scrutinize individual merit and demerit to mete out reward or punishment. Then there are the local gods, temples for whom are found in nearly every Chinese village and town. In addition there is the western paradise which seems to have come to China by way of Indian Buddhism. It is in this hierarchy of gods that Confucianism, Taoism and Buddhism find their places. The scholars of China studied the Confucian classics assiduously and raised controversies over them, just as a few learned monks and philosophers also elaborated and discussed the Buddhist scriptures and the essential meaning of the original teachings of the Indian holy man. But to the ordinary believing Chinese, Confucius and his many disciples, Buddha and his many early followers, true or fancied, as well as the many spirits of Taoist origin, were merely intermediary between the Supreme Ruler of Heaven and man. In fact, it is not unusual to find, in many public prayer meetings called to deal with emergencies such as a drought, earthquake or epidemic, the tablets of Mohammed and Jesus Christ placed side by side with those of Confucius, Buddha and Lao Tzŭ (Lao-tse; alleged founder of Taoism), all in a position subordinate to that of the Supreme Ruler of Heaven. In such a prayer meeting, the officiating priests can literally invent any variety of god as they see fit, with no danger of being questioned by the people who provide their support.

The essential character of the Chinese approach to religion is polytheistic, as contrasted with the monotheistic western approach. The latter approach maintains that one and only one God is true and all others are false and therefore must be eradicated and their believers either won over peacefully or forced to change their creed. To the Chinese, however, gods may be higher or lower to one another, more or less powerful than one another, but they coexist, and there is no question of the followers of one group of gods being committed to the transformation or the annihilation of believers in other kinds of deities. Hence theological elaboration for purposes of strengthening a given religion and missionary activities for its spread are as characteristic of the western ways of religion, including Mohammedanism, as they are atypical of the Chinese. Since western forms of belief centre in one God, the magical arts such as horoscope and divination tend to have no place in the regular churches and remain as personal predilections of the relative minority. On the other hand, gods being many and often strange, the Chinese find it necessary to resort, as a matter of regular and formal religious practice, to horoscope, divination and many other similar practices to ascertain the wishes of the gods or to ensure their good graces for private purposes. For the same reason, Chinese Moslems, although they number several million, concentrated in the northwest but also scattered in different parts of China from Yünnan to Manchuria, are described by western observers as not fanatical at all. Mohammedans who served as officials in the Chinese imperial court used to worship at the Temple of Heaven with the emperor, and Mohammedan inhabitants in many parts of the country take active part in rain pleading and other pagan ritual parades. This is why Christianity failed to gain a substantial foothold in China. It is obviously difficult for the average Chinese with his particular religious and cultural background to commit himself irretrievably to one God and forget about all others. Most Chinese Christians, to please their parents, will have no compunction in undergoing two marriage ceremonies, one Christian and one pagan, or in having duplicate funerals for their parents in the same manner. This is probably also why, of the less than 1% of the Chinese population which was converted to Christianity, 90% were Catholics and 10% Protestants. Catholicism, with its many saints, elaborate ritual and a purgatory from which the suffering souls can be raised by the merits of the living, is more in consonance with the Chinese religious orientation than Protestantism.

Non-Chinese Groups.—The greatest concentration of aboriginal tribes in China is in the southwest. Tribal peoples are also found in smaller numbers in the extreme southern provinces such as Kwangsi, Kwangtung and Hainan Island and central provinces such as Hunan. The ethnological classification of these peoples has never been clear. Tribally they are known by such names as the Chung Chia, Miao (Miaotsze), Kachin, Keh-Lao, Loi, Lolo, Yao, Mo-so, Min Chia, etc. One linguistic analysis divides them into three groups, Lolo, Shan and Miao; another into Mon-Khmer, Shan and Tibeto-Burmans. But linguistic affiliation is no assurance of extensive cultural connection. In fact, some of these groups, notably the Min Chia who inhabit western Yünnan, were so assimilated into the Chinese way of life that they became more Chinese than the Chinese. Others, such as some of the Lolo, in the Yünnan-Szechwan-Tibetan border region, maintained their tribal entity so exclusively that Chinese who entered their area unprotected were captured as slaves. The largest of these groups is probably the Miao, which is divided into several branches. The smallest is probably the Mo-so. Some of these are also more closely related to the peoples of Thailand, Burma and Indochina than to the Chinese. In all probability, the aboriginal groups in southwest and south China were the original inhabitants of the continent and were driven out or replaced by and amalgamated with the Chinese, much like the American Indians with reference to the Americans and the Ainus with reference to the Japanese.

In the north and northwest, other non-Chinese groups either predominate or are present in large numbers. The Mongols in Inner Mongolia have become largely assimilated to the Chinese, but those in Outer Mongolia maintain their tribal entity as well as religious hierarchy. In the Manchurian-Siberian border, a certain number of Tungus tribes live. They are more closely related to the aboriginal tribes in Siberia than to the Mongols. In the northwest, in the province of Sinkiang (Chinese Turkistan), many Arabs, Turks, Uighurs and Kazaks live side by side with their Chinese neighbours, both Mohammedan and non-Mohammedan. Lastly, the Tibetans located south of Sinkiang and west of Yünnan maintained their cultural entity and political semi-independence for many centuries. They and the Mongols to the north share the same branch of Buddhism, namely Lamaism, and the highest religious authorities in Mongolia acknowledge the nominal supremacy of the religious ruler of Tibet. When possible, from time to time, many pilgrims found their way from Mongolia to Tibet. Culturally the Tibetan family is one of the three examples in the world where polyandry prevails. The Tibetans have for many years been the object of attempts at domination or infiltration by the British, the Russians and the Chinese, with the latter claiming nominal suzerainty over the territory. By the mid-1950s the Chinese Communists had undoubtedly obtained more complete control over Tibet as a whole than any of the preceding powers.

In general a majority of the non-Chinese groups are agriculturalists, with the exception of the Mongols in the north and a few groups in the northwest. A majority of them speak some Chinese dialects. Among the illiterate there is the tendency to use Chinese written characters for amulets, a practice they share with the illiterate Chinese. The Lolos are said to have invented a sort of phonetically based system of writing extracted from the Chinese written characters. Physically, all of the non-Chinese peoples, except a few Caucasoid groups in Sinkiang and a small group of Jews in Honan, north China, are varieties of the Mongoloid division of mankind.

See K. S. Latourette, *The Chinese: Their History and Culture,* 3rd ed. (New York, 1946); F. L. K. Hsu, *Under the Ancestors' Shadow* (New York, 1948). (F. L. K. H.)

THE PEOPLE AND THEIR CIVILIZATION

Introduction.—China during the 20th century experienced the most momentous transformation in its history, one affecting every aspect of life: economic, social and political, intellectual, ethical and cultural. Changes were at first sporadic and unco-ordinated, the automatic result of infiltration of alien ideas or modifications by way of goods and techniques imported from the occident. Then under the modern-minded Nationalist government and particularly under the Communist regime there occurred a purposeful, co-ordinated remoulding of the society and economy and a systematic attempt to refashion the habits and even the ethics of the entire people.

China's traditional civilization—over the centuries and millenniums—was essentially indigenous, and it was continuously developing and elaborating. It has never been static and it has intermittently absorbed cultural contributions from abroad. Yet because of its remoteness from other centres of high civilization and because of difficult geographical barriers, the Chinese developed their civilization in relative isolation. Furthermore, in comparison with their non-Chinese neighbours, they possessed a highly sophisticated culture. As dispensers of civilization to surrounding peoples, the Chinese developed a strong sense of superiority. As a result of these factors—the long, continuous and somewhat isolated development of a highly elaborated civilization and the strong cultural pride—there was a powerful resistance to change when this ancient culture was brought into active contact with the entirely different civilizations of Europe. Throughout the 19th century the European conception of the Chinese was of a people immobile, uniform, unchanging and virtually unchangeable. During the 19th century European culture affected little more than the fringes of China and its external political framework. Its influence later, however, began to penetrate to the very foundations of Chinese civilization, bringing about changes in the social and economic fabric, and in the traditional philosophy and ethical outlook of the people, of greater significance than the more dramatic changes in the political sphere. The ultimate effects on the structure of Chinese society of the alterations in its material environment and on the Chinese mind and character of the flood of new ideas, at once disintegrating and liberating, are beyond prophecy, but no generalizations can be valid which do not allow for the great vitality and adaptability of the people. In the consideration of the various aspects of Chinese life it seems better to stress those elements inherited from the past which count for most in the present and the future and to indicate the character of the new forces than to attempt an adequate description of the traditional civilization.

POPULATION

It has been said with some force that estimates of the total population of China have "assumed the importance of an indoor sport unencumbered by any definitely established rules." One reasonable estimate of China's population, the post office census of 1926, returned a total of more than 485,000,000 for China proper (including Manchuria). Allowing 11,000,000 for Mongolia, Tibet and Sinkiang, a round total of 496,000,000 is reached. At the other end of the scale, the census of the board of the interior in 1910, shortly before the fall of the Manchus, put the figure for China proper with Manchuria as low as between 323,000,000 and 343,000,000. The total population of China may reasonably be put at about 400,000,000, but authorities differ vigorously as to whether it is less than or more than this figure. According to official estimates, the population in 1950 was 475,000,000. Particularly important is the extraordinarily uneven distribution and almost unparalleled density in certain areas. The bulk of the population of China is contained in the following regions:

1. The central portion of the north China plain around the convergence of the provinces of Hopei, Shantung and Honan and a section of the valley of the tributary Wei river.
2. The triangular tract of the Yangtze delta with its apex at Nanking.
3. A relatively narrow coastal belt extending southward from the Yangtze mouth through Chekiang, Fukien and Kwangtung to the Si Kiang or Canton delta, where it widens considerably.
4. The central (Hupeh) basin with the Wuhan cities (Hankow, Hanyang, Wuchang) as its node and extending up the radial valleys converging on it (Han, Siang, Kan, etc.).
5. The Red basin of Szechwan, isolated far in the west beyond the Yangtze gorges.

The northern belt of maximum population is essentially one of peasant farmers, depending upon the land; large cities are rare and industries relatively few. In the Yangtze delta, the coastal zone and the Canton delta agriculture greatly predominates, but in addition there are old and new industries and active river and maritime commerce. The merchant classes form a bigger element, and great cities are numerous. That these great regions as a whole, but particularly the northern plains, are supersaturated with human beings relative to the present means of subsistence there can be no question. It is attested by the appalling frequency of famines in the north (about one in every three years) and to a lesser extent in the lower Yangtze, and by a very low standard of comfort which allows of no margin.

Outside these regions, population is dense only in isolated valleys or small basins. In the provinces of the loess plateau (Shensi and Shansi) the density is moderate and the population fairly evenly distributed. The same may be said of the south China plateau as a whole. In both, well-peopled valleys contrast with sparsely occupied highlands. The southwestern provinces (Kweichow, Yünnan and Kwangsi), Kansu, the provinces of Inner Mongolia in the northwest and the Manchurian provinces in the northeast all have distinctly low densities. The possibility of lessening the pressure of population, if that could be accomplished, would depend upon developing industries and new agricultural techniques, internal migration and gradual changes in reproduction patterns.

Migration.—The Chinese have been throughout their history a colonizing people, but the mobility of movement from congested and overpeopled regions to sparsely occupied areas was constantly held in check by the great reluctance, for reasons connected with their social philosophy (*see* below), to leave their ancestral homes. This is least true of southeast China. There has long been an increasing stream of Chinese emigrants from Fukien and Kwangtung, with their densely peopled coasts, to the rich peninsulas and islands to the south, where they helped to develop the far eastern tropics. In Malaya Chinese form more than one-third of the total population. In the Philippines, in Java and many other parts of Indonesia, in Thailand (Siam), in Indochina and in Burma their vigour, frugality and tenacity make them a prosperous and progressive element. These same qualities often constitute a menace to the economic prospects of the less energetic native peoples. These important and thriving Chinese communities retain close contact with their ancestral provinces, the latter receiving large remittances from them and being influenced by them in many ways.

The peoples of the congested districts of the north in Shantung, Hopei and Honan were until relatively recently somewhat less adventurous. The rich grasslands of Manchuria beyond the Great Wall only became available for agricultural settlement under the Manchu dynasty, and economic development was very slow until after the Russo-Japanese War of 1904–05. With the rapid development of railways and new industries, Manchuria became a very attractive field. North China, on the other hand, was devastated by famines and the ravages of civil war. The almost intolerable conditions of life in many districts so weakened old prejudices that a tremendous mass movement toward Manchuria set in. It was no longer a mainly seasonal migration of males, but a wholesale exodus of entire families. The increase of population in Manchuria in the four years 1923–27 was estimated at 2,000,000 and the exodus from north China during the summer of 1928 at 40,000 a week. During the period of Japanese control of Manchuria, 1931–45, migration was slow but steady. After the area came under control of the Communist regime, it was developed as an agricultural-industrial base, and migration, particularly of skilled workers and technicians, was encouraged. To this field of colonization in the north must be added the adjacent districts of Inner Mongolia on the Chinese side of the Gobi desert, with very considerable pastoral possibilities which the Peking-Kalgan-Suiyuan railway made accessible. However, this is a marginal region in which the small and fluctuating rainfall makes settlement and livelihood precarious. In spite of climatic limitations, northern China has thus had a "land of promise" along its whole northern border, but except for some sections of Manchuria this nearly reached the saturation point. The tendency to overpopulation, which is the root cause of the grinding mass poverty of so many districts and which underlies so many of China's problems, results essentially from social causes. The Communist regime attempted by a drastic reorganization of the society and economy to solve this fundamental problem, but with what success it is difficult to predict.

CHINESE SOCIETY

The Family System.—In preceding paragraphs the diversity of China has been emphasized. But more significant than the diversity is the cultural unity which held Chinese civilization intact for more than four millenniums. The basis of this fundamental unity was the family system which dominated Chinese society and permeated almost every aspect of economic and political life. The sanctity of the family found expression in what the western world would regard as an excessive reverence for ancestors. It is the cornerstone of the Confucian teaching, which gives first place to the virtue of filial piety and discourages children from going far away from their aging parents. It is the *raison d'être* of much of the ceremonial prescribed by the etiquette to which Confucius and all his interpreters attached immense importance.

Associated with the family have been the elaborate and expensive rites connected with marriage and death, the maintenance of ancestral halls, the family reunions at fixed seasons, the erection of memorial arches to virtuous widows who refused to remarry, and countless other symbolic acts.

In comparison with the family, the individual has counted for little. To it he has owed implicit loyalty. Marriage, for example, has been a contract between two families arranged without reference to the individuals concerned, usually when they were both young children and often without their having seen each other. The family in its extended form as a clan has served the function of insurance and benevolent societies in Europe, and the provision of clan funds for education enabled many a promising boy to qualify for public office.

The association of families in a community provided a system of local government enabling village and district life to maintain an effective organization even during periods of political anarchy. The village attempted to avoid relations with officials of the central government or to reduce them to a minimum. The group of elders, selected from the wisest and most experienced heads of families, combined many of the duties of an English parish council, board of guardians and bench of justices of the peace, and dealt with the higher state officials. Their meeting place, the village temple, became the centre of social life. So, too, the offices connected with the affairs of the village were held in succession by the principal family heads.

Thus the basis of the system of government became patriarchal. The old China was in a sense a social democracy of myriad families whose relations were determined by an elaborate social code requiring obedience to an emperor who was himself regarded as at once the supreme patriarch and the "son of heaven," with power equalled only by his responsibility. If by his actions he incurred the wrath of the Spiritual Father on the immense family which he represented, he had plainly "exhausted the mandate of heaven" and revolt against him was justified.

The bureaucracy through which he worked was immensely complex and intended to counterweigh local and provincial interests, but the same patriarchal conception was seen in the functions of the head of the *hsien,* the one state official with whom the masses in the countryside and smaller towns came into contact. The *hsien* magistrate was entrusted with a great variety of duties and under the old regime essentially represented government to the people. In the city of Peking the Temple of Confucius, with a large hall preserving the ancestral tablet of the sage enshrined in an alcove, adjoined the Hall of Classics, where the emperor came on state occasions and whose courtyard contained 300 stone steles on which the complete texts of the "nine classics" were inscribed. The juxtaposition of two of the most famous buildings in the country symbolized the intimate relationship between the massive social fabric based upon the family and the traditional scholarship of China. This scholarship, of high antiquity and unique continuity, furnished alike the sanction of the social system, its support and its cultural background. Ethical teaching about social obligations, summarized in the five relationships (sovereign and subject, parent and child, husband and wife, elder brother and younger brother, friend and friend), lay at the heart of a moral code already hallowed by antiquity when Confucius gave it coherence.

It was largely through schools provided by the family or clan for its own members that the rudiments of its teaching were given to the rising generation. By a graded system of public examinations, proficiency in this learning in its more advanced aspects was tested as the qualification for public office, on the principle that only those who understood the foundations on which society rested were fit to be entrusted with affairs of state. Thus the scholars were the governing class and the social aristocracy during long periods of the past 2,000 years. They enjoyed immense prestige and ranked first in the four recognized groups (scholars, farmers, artisans, traders). They could not transmit their offices to their children, but in practice retired officials had exceptional means for giving their children the necessary education, so that many families had at once wealth, usually invested in country estates, and literary traditions, and constituted the literati or gentry, the notables of the countryside and small towns. Yet they were never a caste apart, and their ranks were open to any peasant's or craftsman's son who could qualify. The recognition of an aristocracy of learning, the recruitment of the civil service by competitive public examinations (from the time of the Han dynasty) and the absence of caste distinctions were three outstanding features of the old Chinese civilization complementary to the patriarchal system and adapting it to a complex state organization.

To the family system China largely owes the remarkable social stability which has enabled it to survive the many shocks which the political fabric has received and to outlive many far more highly organized communities. Many of the most attractive aspects and some of the most fundamental virtues of the Chinese character are bound up with it.

Yet the cult of the family is an important cause of the intense pressure of population in the land. Among the peasantry there was need for sons to work the fields, although economic pressure also acted to limit family size. Among the gentry which had its economic basis in farm lands rented to tenants, families tended to be large and to consist of several generations of adults and children living together. Concubinage was not uncommon in this class. The social premium on male progeny (to ensure the perpetuation of the family line) led to early marriage, concubinage and a high birth rate, and the first result of this chronic tendency to overpopulation, in a country so largely composed of peasant proprietors, where no law of primogeniture existed, was naturally the excessive subdivision of land. The abnormally low standard of living and the absence of any economic reserve explain the existence of a "submerged tenth" of desperate men, ready to adopt brigandage. Hence the contrast between the singularly peaceful and law-abiding character of the Chinese as a whole and the frequent disorder and terrorism in country districts when authority is relaxed. Hence, too, the ease with which armies can be raised in a country essentially unwarlike and the extreme difficulty of disbanding them once they have come into existence. Excessive emphasis on the family also proved a potent cause of China's political weakness, since family interests were constantly preferred to those of the state. Nepotism, in fact, has been described as a religious duty in China, an obligation to use public office for the benefit of the family group as the supreme object of loyalty. Many individuals attained to a larger vision, but usually there was a marked contrast between the admirable honesty and trustworthiness of the Chinese in their individual and trade relations and the corruption which tended to characterize their public life and to ruin large-scale undertakings lying outside the traditional group organizations. The state, as such, traditionally meant very little to the vast majority of the Chinese people. China has been a civilization rather than a national entity in the European sense.

Industry's Influence.—Even before the Communist regime began its effort to reduce the control of the family in favour of that of the state, many influences were at work in modern China to reduce the importance of the family and to disintegrate the traditional structure of Chinese society. One of these was modern industry. The most important effects of industrialization are at present localized in the cities of the Yangtze and Canton deltas, the central basin, at nodal points along the main railways, at several of the seaports and in Manchuria. The Communist regime exerted great effort in the attempt to industrialize China. In these centres there is a large and increasing class of industrial workers of a type quite new to China. They are losing touch with the corporate life of the countryside and are increasingly detached from the traditional social heritage. A large proportion of them are women, and the entrance of women into large-scale factory industry implies at once their growing economic independence and the breakdown of the clan system.

Nor is that all. Industry and commerce in China were formerly almost entirely controlled by the guild system. The guilds are group organizations of various types, but like the family organization all make the well-being of the individual dependent on his obedience to the code governing the interests of his craft or trade or, in the case of provincial and city guilds, of his locality. Large-scale industries of western type employing the new class of artisans are for the most part outside the guild system, and the workers, often living under conditions similar to those of the factory towns of England in the early days of the Industrial Revolution, proved to be open to the appeal of new influences such as the western trade-union movement and communism.

That the old capacity for combination was capable of taking new forms was shown by the many examples in modern times of relatively successful strikes and boycotts. Under the Communist regime, however, all labour was organized into unions under control of the party. The ever-widening use of machine-made goods, manufactured abroad or in China's new factories, seriously disrupted the peasant economy, which depended upon subsidiary handicraft industries to supplement farm income. The destruction of cottage industry and the increased commercialization of agriculture to the disadvantage of the small farmer acted, in combination with many other factors, to pauperize the peasantry. This general tendency likewise disrupted the traditional social order.

Modern Educational System and Linguistic Reforms.—Of the new cultural forces which tended to disrupt the traditional family and other phases of the hereditary culture the most outstanding, before the advent of the Communist regime, were the modern educational system, the student movement and the penetration of new ideas from Europe, the U.S. and modernized Japan. The sudden abolition of the old classical system of examinations in the last years of the Manchu dynasty marked a dramatic break more fundamental in effect than the abolition of the imperial office seven years later. In spite of many difficulties, a system of schools gradually emerged in which, while western subjects and methods predominated, traditional language and literature still found a place. The most revolutionary of the social influences of the new education were: (1) The granting of educational facilities to women and the introduction of coeducation in primary schools. In conjunction with the economic forces already noticed, this produced a remarkable change in the status of women and the relations between the sexes. Many young persons now arrange their own marriages without consultation with their elders. (2) Western science, very imperfectly organized in China, but implying a mental discipline of a kind quite foreign to the old literary training. (3) The ideal of mass education. In respect for learning no country excelled China, but in the past it was always associated with a relatively small group of scholars. Both the Nationalist and the Communist regimes worked hard to extend the public educational system. Because of the huge population, the country's poverty and the decades of war and political disorder, the creation of a modern national educational system has been a slow process. The mass education movement was aimed to overcome China's widespread illiteracy. There were few more promising features in modern China than the almost passionate enthusiasm with which the students and teachers of secondary schools and colleges organized the popular educational movement, devoting evenings and parts of vacations to the conduct of free schools for poor children and adults. The mass education movement, inaugurated by a returned student from the United States, greatly aided the progress toward literacy. Mass education was pushed with energy by the Communist regime. In the linguistic field the popular vernacular (*Pai-hua*)of the Mandarin dialect became the accepted medium for new literature, in place of the old classical and "dead" language. The change was comparable in character and importance to the adoption of the vernacular as the medium of literary expression in place of Latin in Chaucer's England and Dante's Italy. Further, out of the vast number of Chinese characters, 1,000 (or even 600) of the most essential were selected for use in the people's schools—hence often called "foundation character schools" —and were used exclusively in the writing of appropriate popular books. A standard form of the Mandarin vernacular (*Kuo-yü*) was taught in the schools throughout the country, a procedure which tended toward uniformity in the spoken tongue and toward national linguistic unity.

The "New Tide."—These important linguistic reforms, especially the development of the new national language (*Pai-hua*), were to a large extent the outcome of the remarkable movement known as the "new tide" or Chinese renaissance that flourished during several decades after 1915. This movement, associated with the new intelligentsia in the chief centres of thought, such as the National university at Peking, owed its origin to returned Chinese graduates of foreign universities (especially Paris and certain U.S. universities) and in particular, on its literary side, to Hu Shih, often called the "father of the Chinese renaissance." This renaissance was an intellectual ferment similar in many ways to that which characterized the revival of learning in Europe. On its literary and linguistic side it was essentially constructive while critical in many other respects. Especially notable was its vigorous and unsparing attack on the inferior status of women, child betrothals and costly expenditure on funeral rites. On its more speculative side it was concerned with what its exponents described as a "revaluation" of Chinese thought and philosophy in the light of western science and knowledge. In the sphere of religion it was for the most part sceptical and rationalistic and helped to give birth to a widespread but transient anti-Christian movement in the ranks of "Young China." At the same time the movement in many of its aspects included some of the most distinguished of the leaders of Chinese Christianity.

Religion.—The disintegrating effects of the new influences inevitably invaded the religious sphere, but in many respects the break with the past in this field was less complete and revolutionary than in some other aspects of life; however, there was, even before the Communist regime, some change, and traditional religion and religious observances were greatly weakened. Of the three historic religions of China (*see* under *History*), Taoism in its later phases has been little more than a congeries of superstitions which must gradually lose their vitality. The same may be said of the cruder side of popular Buddhism, especially in its northern form (Lamaism), but in its more philosophical aspects Buddhism has a definite adaptability and is by no means a negligible factor. Confucianism, although it has a religious aspect, denotes a social code and an attitude toward life rather than a religion. Although obviously weakened by the changed conditions, it retains great vitality; it forms the mental background and in part orients the lives of many educated Chinese who hold no definite religious beliefs. The average attitude of the majority of educated Chinese may probably be described as an agnosticism coloured and softened by Confucian and Buddhist tendencies.

The influence of Christianity proved considerably greater than the relatively very small number of its adherents would indicate, and the Christian community played a part in the public life of China out of all proportion to its numbers. Under the Communist regime foreign Christian missionary enterprises were nationalized and almost all missionaries compelled to leave. Yet an indigenous Christian church, subservient to the regime, was not discouraged. While the Communist revolution was corrosive of all the older religions in China, "Marxism and the thought of Mao Tse-tung" was elevated to a national cult.

Thus in modern China the mature old civilization has been changing under pressure from within and without. Yet many-sided as is the revolution through which the country is passing, prolonged as must be the social turmoil and difficult the integration, there are many elements in the heritage of the past still vital and making for stability. (L. H. D. B.; K. S. L.; C. M. W.)

ECONOMIC AND POLITICAL CONDITIONS

DEFENSE

Historical.—Up to the date of the reforms of 1905–06 the Chinese constitution provided for two sorts of military organization, the Manchu army and the Chinese armies in the provinces. When the dynasty was originally established in 1644, the victorious troops, composed mostly of Manchus but including also Chinese and Mongols, remained in Peking as a hereditary national army. Every adult male was entitled by birth to be enrolled as a soldier under one of the eight banners and, after enrolment, to draw an allowance of tribute rice, whether or not employed on active service. Some were sent to garrison such places as Canton, Foochow, Hangchow, etc., but the bulk of them, both in Peking and in these garrisons, lost all military value. The other military organization, the provincial forces, was styled the army of the green standard and resembled a local constabulary rather than an army. Its soldiers were poorly paid, virtually untrained and badly armed. Their ineffectiveness as a military force was fully exposed by the outbreak of large-scale rebellions in the 1850s and 1860s. Such rebellions as the T'ai P'ing, the Nien and the northwest Moslem spread over many provinces. Their eventual suppression was accomplished not by the decayed regular provincial forces or the Manchu army but by the newly organized Hunan and Anhwei "braves" or irregulars. It was also the leaders of the new forces who made a few beginnings at building modern arsenals and in training troops in modern ways. After the war with Japan in 1894–95, some of the corps of braves were quartered near Peking and Tientsin and became spoken of generally as the army of the north. By 1900 this was the only real fighting force of China. After the Boxer rising of 1900 an imperial decree ordered the reorganization of the military forces of the empire and something was accomplished on provincial lines, especially in Hopei, but little was done toward establishing an army on European lines until after the Russo-Japanese War of 1904–05, when various military schools and training organizations were established (or provided for on paper).

By 1910 some progress had been made toward evolving an efficient body of officers. An army board was organized and progress made with a general staff. Service, mostly voluntary, was for three years with the colours, three in the reserve and four in the territorial army. Reservists were called up annually for training and territorials once in two years. The Japanese system of training was followed.

China, although a belligerent on the side of the Allied powers, took no effective part in the victory which they achieved over the Central Powers in World War I. The country was in the throes of internecine strife. In the spring of 1919 the governments of Great Britain, Spain, Portugal, the United States, Russia, Brazil, France and Japan agreed "effectively to restrain their subjects and citizens from exporting to or importing into China arms and munitions of war and material destined exclusively for their manufacture, until the establishment of a government whose authority is recognized through the whole country." The governments of the Netherlands, Denmark, Belgium and Italy adhered to the agreement and the diplomatic body appealed to the Chinese government to prohibit imports. No effective action was taken, and the Soviet government added its activities to those of the nationals of some of the signatory powers in carrying on this traffic, with deplorable results. The import of war material, of which a large surplus remained for disposal in belligerent countries at the time of the Armistice, was largely supplemented from the resources of numerous arsenals and factories in Chinese territory, such as those at Mukden, Paoting, Tehchow, Chinan, Tai-yuan, Kai-fêng, Kunghsien, Sian, Hanyang, Nanking, Shanghai, Changsha, Chêngfu, Foochow, Canton, Swatow, Kiungchow (Ch'iung-shan), Kunming (Yünnanfu) and Kalgan.

Army.—Any attempt to describe the army in modern China in terms of accurate statistics is futile. For years after the revolution of 1911 various war lords had larger or smaller units in various stages of equipment and poor training and discipline. Most of these armies were in theory part of the national forces, but in practice they were not co-ordinated under any general staff or supreme command. Their total enrolment ran into the millions, but few if any were effective fighters. They were largely a refuge for the riffraff and the unemployed, a way of taking care of some of the many millions who were thrown out of their normal occupations by civil strife and natural disasters in a land in which the margin of subsistence was always slender. The transition from bandit to soldier and from soldier to bandit was usually easy and was very frequent. Equipment was inferior and discipline, training and leadership worse. Battles between the war lords were aptly characterized as "much noise, little fighting, less damage." Loss of life, except through disease and to noncombatants through starvation occasioned by the destruction of the means of subsistence, was slight. The coming of the Nationalist government in 1927 brought some improvement. The prolonged struggle against the Communists and preparation against the Japanese menace forced progress. Such leaders as Chiang Kai-shek, Li Tsung-jen and Pai Chung-hsi, especially the first, brought various advances. Schools for officers turned out a better leadership. Here and there arsenals began to supply native-made equipment, mostly small arms and trench mortars. German officers supervised the training of the army.

At the outbreak of the war with Japan in 1937 the Chinese army was well past the 1,000,000 and possibly the 2,000,000 mark. But in officers' training and mechanized equipment it was still far behind its opponent. Many of the best troops were sacrificed in the early stages of the war. New armies were recruited in "Free China," to the west of the Japanese lines. Some troops were drilled and equipped in India, mainly by Americans. The Communists who fought with the Nationalists against the Japanese under the united front policy used guerrilla tactics and expanded their forces rapidly behind enemy lines. Before the Japanese invasion of China in 1937 and after the successive campaigns waged by the Nationalist army against the Communists, the Communist army that retreated to Shensi amounted to fewer than 30,000 men. By 1940 it had grown to 500,000. After the conclusion of World War II, the Nationalist army was estimated to be more than 3,000,000 and the Communist army was estimated to be almost 1,000,000 with a militia of more than 2,000,000. In 1949 the mainland of China was overrun by the Communist army. Only one-tenth of the Nationalist army retreated to Formosa (Taiwan); most of the rest surrendered. The Chinese army on the mainland in 1953 was composed of the following: four field armies of 22 army corps divided into 70 armies, including special service corps, estimated at more than 2,000,000; the military district armies estimated at 2,000,000; and a militia of more than 12,000,000. There were also the people's security forces of 250,000, whose duties were the suppression of local disturbances.

Air Forces.—Up to the early 1950s all aeroplanes had been of foreign make. When the Communists took over the Chinese mainland, they captured 183 aeroplanes from the Nationalists. Before the Korean war, there was only one pilot-training academy in the northeast. Together with aircraft purchased from the Soviet Union, there were fewer than 600 planes, including about 30 jets. The objective was to match the air power of Formosa. After the Korean war, pilot-training academies were established in the various military districts and the number of planes was increased to more than 1,200 in 1952, including a large number of jets. Two paratroop headquarters were also established in Peking and the Wuhan area. The total personnel of the air forces on the mainland reached an unprecedented 200,000.

Foreign Troops.—Though not strictly germane to the subject of Chinese armies, it is important in this connection to consider the presence of foreign troops in various parts of China. In the north, Peking and Tientsin, they had the right, by the protocol of 1901, to put the legation quarter in a state of defense and to occupy selected points between Peking and the sea. Japan had troops in the South Manchuria railway zone under a treaty of Dec. 1905 with the Chinese government. Foreign garrisons in the north, distributed between Peking, Tientsin, Tangku, Tongshan, Chinwangtao and Shanhaikwan, were strongly reinforced in 1927, during the conflict between north and south. The total number at the end of 1927 was 11,880, compared with 4,740 in 1926. The nationalities, in order of numbers, were U.S., French, British, Japanese and Italian. The Shanghai defense force, amounting to a mixed division with armoured cars and attached troops, was in 1927–28 gradually reduced in strength to about a brigade. The Japanese invasion which began in 1931 in Manchuria and by stages, chiefly following July 1937, extended to the rest of China, strikingly altered this picture. After 1931 the Japanese army dominated Manchuria. Forces of possibly as many as 1,000,000 or more men were poised on the northern borders, ready to resist a Soviet advance or to take advantage of Soviet weakness to acquire eastern Siberia or Outer Mongolia. After 1937 Japanese forces were also distributed widely through occupied China south of the Great Wall. They may have totalled another 1,000,000 or more. Foreign troops of other nationalities were withdrawn before Dec. 1941. The Japanese domination ended with the conclusion of World War II. On the Chinese mainland in 1952 Soviet troops totalling about 60,000 men were disposed in the Port Arthur and Dairen area as agreed by the People's Republic of China and the Soviet Union on Feb. 14, 1950. Some Russian troops were also reported to be disposed along the Chinese Changchun railway in the northeast, in Peking, Tientsin and Tsingtao, in north China and in Ili, Urumchi and other places in Sinkiang. (G. G. A.; K. S. L.; C.-L. C.)

Navy.—The beginning of a navy in China dates from about 1867, approximately the same period as that which saw the introduction of the telegraph into the country. A shipyard at Foochow turned out a few small composite gunboats, and a training ship was bought and placed under the command of a British officer. Several armoured cruisers were ordered from England, while naval bases were fortified at Port Arthur and Wei-hai-wei.

Forts were also built and guns mounted at Foochow, Shanghai, Canton and other points which appeared vulnerable from the sea. Money for those purposes was forthcoming from the customs duties on foreign trade.

The Chinese fleet had not, however, developed into a formidable force when, in 1884, France had occasion to take reprisals against China for attacks by irregular troops in Tongking. A wretched collection of craft, the chief of which was the "Yang-Woo," a composite cruiser, was practically wiped out by a French squadron in seven minutes in the river Min, where it had taken cover, near Foochow.

In 1894, when China found itself at war with Japan, the former country had an appreciable fleet, in fact one which on paper was stronger than its adversary's, but because of the disorganized state of administration only one out of the four squadrons into which it was organized took part in the hostilities. This squadron consisted of two small battleships, the "Chen Yuen" and "Ting Yuen," built in Germany, five other small armoured vessels and six sloops. It had attained a good standard of discipline and efficiency under Capt. W. M. Lang of the British navy, but after his departure, and by the time war broke out, the ships had deteriorated and the personnel had relapsed into their normal state of inefficiency. The squadron was defeated by the Japanese fleet at the battle of Yalu.

In 1909 an effort was made to re-establish a fleet, and a naval commission under Tsai Hsün, a brother of the emperor Kuang Hsü, was sent to Europe to obtain the necessary information and advice. Various societies had already started in several provinces to collect funds for naval purposes.

At this time the fleet consisted of four armoured cruisers, some modern gunboats built in Japan, a few miscellaneous vessels and some old torpedo boats, but the efforts of China to create and maintain a navy were never crowned with success, chiefly because of the corruption of the government and the irresponsibility of the officers. No marked improvement was made by the Nationalist government. In their invasion of China the Japanese had unchallenged control of the sea.

In 1952 the Peking government had three fleets with bases at Dairen, Tsingtao and Canton. There were altogether about 350 ships totalling more than 90,000 tons; personnel totalled about 30,000. Naval academies were established in Antung and Tsingtao. There was in addition a marine corps of 50,000 men.

(E. A.; K. S. L.; C.–L C.)

AGRICULTURE

Characteristics of Chinese Agriculture.—Chinese agriculture is distinguished primarily by its intensity. This is made possible only by the unremitting labour which the struggle for existence demands and the traditional skill born of 40 centuries of transmitted experience. The maintenance of soil fertility under constant intensive cultivation for such an immense period is in part secured by replenishment with canal mud, as in the Yangtze delta, or by the silt deposited by river floods (otherwise disastrous), but in the main by the use of night soil and every other possible kind of manure, applied to the land in primitive but effective fashion. Soil is composted with organic matter and ashes and then dried and pulverized to form a plant food. Deforestation took place not simply to make room for more arable land but as the result of a constant quest for green manure. In hilly districts, such as the loess plateau and the Red basin, the fields on the valley slopes are terraced and rimmed so that the runoff may be retained until the suspended matter has settled. Again, in crop rotations, legumes have long been grown to fertilize the soil. A system was evolved whereby two, three or even four crops are grown in the same ground space each year, while as many as three crops, each in a different stage of development, grow simultaneously in one field. In few countries has the practice of multiple cropping been so perfected. The great traditional skill of the Chinese has raised their agriculture to the level of an art; they show, moreover, remarkable ingenuity in adapting means to ends, as in the many uses to which they put bamboo or millet. Their implements, moreover, are effective, if primitive. On the other hand, the typical Chinese farmer traditionally knows nothing of science as applied to proper seed selection, experiments in better crop rotation or animal breeding and the fighting of plant and animal pests. His methods are essentially conservative and traditional, and little use is made of chemical fertilizers. Notwithstanding great industry at certain seasons, there is much idle time in winter, especially in the north, which the development of small rural industries on a co-operative basis would employ to great advantage in the farming community. There is little combination for the purchase of seeds or implements or for the marketing of produce. Important experiments to remedy these defects have been begun. Some have been undertaken by local governments and some by the ministry of agriculture. Others have been associated with agricultural colleges or departments. By the early 1950s these colleges had graduated more than 6,000 students, serving in agricultural and related fields. More effective utilization of agricultural resources in terms of greater output per hectare and greater output per man-hour, and improvement in marketing and rural finance, would improve the general welfare of the Chinese farmers.

Agricultural Regions.—The salient characteristics of the major agricultural regions can be summarized most easily in relation to the scheme of the natural divisions of China, except that the essential features of crop production and farming methods in the Red basin closely resemble those of the lower Yangtze valley.

1. The Tsinlingshan mountain complex delimits the agricultural "province" of north China. There severe winters and the short and rather uncertain rainy season preclude winter crops. It lies beyond the limit of the cultivation of wet rice, which as a staple crop is replaced by millets and wheat. Rice, it is true, is a subordinate crop in favoured districts of north China; it is known, however, as small rice and is really a glutinous millet. Most people live on wheat, kaoliang and millet, while meat and potatoes play a part in the diet. Soybeans, too, are important. Barley and maize are extensively grown.

The soils of the loess lands are of unusual fertility because of their fine texture, their porous and friable nature and the presence in them of soluble mineral matter for plant nourishment. On the other hand, the region is the driest in China, and, except in the basins, is incapable of manual irrigation. Arable cultivation is therefore often precarious, and there is greater reliance on sheep and cattle.

In the extreme northwest pastoral products and some associated manufactures of coarse woollens and cloths are important products. There occurs the greatest concentration of sheep, raised primarily for wool. Cattle, elsewhere in China almost exclusively draught animals, are raised in the northwest for dairy and leather products; there are distinct prospects for leather and woollen manufactures in parts of the loess belt. In the loess basins such as Tai-yuan and Tatung, where well irrigation and terrace cultivation reduce the risk of crop failure, the hardier cereals are often accompanied by fruit culture (apples, pears, plums, walnuts, apricots, strawberries and the jujube) and also by cotton. (For agriculture in the northwest *see* KAN-SU and SHENSI.)

The plain of north China east of the Taihang Shan, which forms the edge of the loess plateau, has a slightly higher rainfall, but risk of flood is much higher and the great problem is the control of the Hwang-ho, Hwai and northern rivers. Main reliance is on wheat, barley, millet, buckwheat and maize, together with vegetable crops, especially rape, beans and peas. Rice is grown in southern Shantung and northern Kiangsu (*i.e.*, on the borders of the Yangtze "province") and cotton and hemp in Shantung and Hopei, but there is little room for any but subsistence crops. In Shantung there are three crops in two years, the usual rotation being wheat in spring, beans in autumn and finally millet, which is gathered in the following September. As an alternative, wheat or barley in winter and spring may be followed by large or small millet, sweet potatoes, soybeans or peanuts in summer. Animals are less important than in the northwest, but in the parts of Hopei adjacent to Mongolia there is the largest concentration of horses, mules and draught animals to be found in China proper.

2. The Yangtze "province," with rich alluvial basins, relatively high, well-distributed rainfall, seasonal rhythm of moist, subtropical summers and mild winters and magnificent natural waterways, is one of the most favoured agricultural regions in the world and the premier granary of China, supporting nearly half its total population. The combination of summer "wet" crops and winter "dry" (temperate) crops gives it a marvellous range of production, and most of the staple products of China, whether subsistence or commercial crops, find there their optimum conditions. It is easily first in the production of rice, the chief food of all central and south China. If Chekiang is included, it produces more than 68% of the total output of silk, the oldest and most famous of Chinese commercial products, and about 50% of that of cotton, one of the chief factors in the new industrial development. It is also the largest centre of tea production. In some districts, as in parts of the Yangtze delta and the central basin, the rotation is determined by the needs of a special crop. In the normal agricultural year barley, wheat, beans and peas are sown early in winter and harvested in May (wheat in June), followed by sesame, sown after the wheat harvest and ripe early in September, while rice may be either an early crop, planted early in April and ready for harvesting 90 days later, or a late crop planted in early June and harvested after 110 days. If rice is grown for commercial purposes it receives special attention and the fields are ploughed and prepared in early winter. Cotton lands also require special preparation. While this is the regime of the lowland basins, the uplands of central China, especially between the Tungting and Poyang lakes, are associated with the cultivation of the tea plant and the tallow tree.

3. The southeast China highlands are not unlike those of central China, and the ranges of Fukien form the second great tea

district, but the valleys and basins, with more abundant rainfall and warm winters, can grow subtropical crops all the year round. In the most favoured regions such as the Canton delta there are two or even three rice crops a year, and the sugar cane finds its optimum conditions. Largely confined to this section of China are the pineapple, spice-yielding plants such as cinnamon and cassia, ginger and aniseed. The southern coast of Kwangtung and the island of Hainan, with an exceptionally high rainfall and uniformly hot conditions, are particularly associated with these tropical cultures. On the other hand, the climate of southeast China is too moist for cotton and for the "dry" cereals which form the winter crops of the Yangtze valley.

4. The southwest is the least developed of all the major regions of China. The high plateaus are scenes of pastoralism and sporadic cereal and poppy cultivation, but the deeply cut and generally narrow valleys, with a damp, unhealthful climate and often still choked with luxuriant jungle vegetation, were not so intensively developed as the more open and accessible basins of the southeast.

Special Products and Associated Manufactures.—Of necessity subsistence crops are of far greater importance in China than commercial products, and this is strikingly shown by the fact that the three greatest food crops—rice, wheat and millets—occupied in 1953 approximately 54% of the cultivated area.

Rice, the staple food in central and south China, took up no less than 28% and had first choice of the land. More than half the land under cultivation in Kiangsu, the richest province, was devoted to it. Yet only four provinces, Hunan, Anhwei, Kwangsi and Kiangsi, normally have a surplus over local needs, and before World War II large imports were made each year from other lands in the far east.

Wheat comes second to rice in importance and replaces it as a food crop in north China. In some northern districts it occupies 40% of the cultivated land, but there must be considerable imports of wheat and flour. The number of wheat eaters steadily increased in northern China, especially in the towns. The annual output, however, could be increased through both extension of the wheat area by "dry" farming in the marginal lands of Manchuria and by an increase of the rate of yield. Flour milling made notable advances, especially in Manchuria.

Millets and kaoliang (sorghum), whose distribution is rather wider than that of wheat, occupied, in 1953, 15% of the cultivated land area of China. They are dominant in Hopei, Shantung and Honan, where they take up approximately one-third of the agricultural surface. Apart from the grain, their by-products are of great value, and in north China the stalks and fibre of the kaoliang replace, for many purposes, bamboo, which reaches its northerly limit in the Hwai river valley.

Tea has long been the chief beverage in China, and since about the 8th century A.D. the cultivation of the tea plant has been a great agricultural industry, localized mainly on the uplands of central China and on the ranges of the maritime provinces but important also in Szechwan. Black, green and brick teas result from different processes of manufacture. The tea plant in China is mainly grown in patches round the homestead, and the methods of both cultivation and preliminary preparation after the picking of the leaves (usually in April, mid-May and August) are traditional and not based on scientific knowledge. Mainly for this reason the chief European markets for black tea were largely lost by China in the later 19th century, when the plantation system, with its associated scientific processes of manufacture, was developed in India and Ceylon. Export of tea from India and Ceylon was 5 times the export from China in 1937 and 20 times in 1947. Brick tea, made by pressing damp leaves into a bricklike mould, found its chief market in Tibet, the U.S.S.R. and interior Asia. Chief ports for tea export have been Hankow (black and brick tea), Kiukiang and Foochow (black tea), Hangchow, Ningpo and Kiukiang (green tea). Experimental stations and investigation bureaus for more scientific cultivation and preparation of tea were opened in the Yangtze valley and at Foochow, and a small beginning was made with the plantation system.

For sericulture, the most far-famed and ancient of its industries, China has many natural advantages, including two or more leafings of the mulberry as compared with one in the Mediterranean countries, and abundant, cheap and traditionally skilled labour in the manipulation of the cocoons and in weaving. In the production of raw silk there are many regional specializations in accordance with the variation of soil and climatic conditions. The silk of the north (Shantung and Manchuria) is chiefly "wild," the product of silkworms fed on oak leaves and manufactured into coarse-textured tussahs and pongees; the Canton delta, where there are as many as six or seven leafings of the mulberry, produces soft Canton silk and Szechwan a special yellow variety. But the most renowned silk region is the lower Yangtze valley, the finest white silk in the world (tsatlee) coming from around the Tai-hu. Exports to European and particularly U.S. markets, although considerable, were surpassed by those of Japan, which added scientific technique to the natural advantages for silk production which it shares with China, where the industry is carried on by peasants on traditional lines. Serious efforts were made by special departments of several colleges and by the International Committee for the Improvement of Sericulture in China to improve the mulberry plantations and to eradicate silkworm diseases, which greatly impair the prosperity of the industry. A more revolutionary change was indicated by the development of large steam filatures and weaving mills at Canton, Shanghai, Soochow, Hangchow, Hankow, Chefoo, Chinkiang and other towns. Even under prevailing conditions, raw silk and cocoons formed more than 9% of the total value of Chinese exports in 1933 and came first in all exports. In contrast, tea, which in 1820 constituted 75% and in 1867, 60% of all Chinese exports, accounted for little more than 5% in 1933.

The most remarkable agricultural development in China during modern times was the rapid growth of the bean industry. Beans long had been grown as an article of food, but the development of the culture on a commercial basis was quite modern and was the result of the realization of the many valuable qualities of the soya variety, which is admirably adapted to north China, and particularly Manchuria.

On the one hand, it has a higher food value than any other seed, which, in conjunction with its cheapness, makes it an effective substitute for milk, meat or the staple grain foods of north China; on the other, its by-products—bean oil as a cooking sauce, as a base in soap manufacture and as a lubricant for various purposes, and bean cake as a fertilizer and cattle food—are of great commercial value.

Beans became one of the major crops in China, next in importance only to rice, wheat and millet. Bean production was one of the principal factors in the rapid economic development of Manchuria. (*See* MANCHURIA.)

Of the purely industrial crops of China, cotton is important. The soil and climatic conditions of many districts of the Yangtze valley and the adjacent parts of the plain of north China approximate those of the cotton belt of the United States. But the industry suffered from many disadvantages: the short staple of the native varieties, primitive methods of seed selection and cultivation, lack of transport and of banking and credit facilities to deal with the movement of crops, and the existence of taxes, which greatly raised its price. Much important work was done by provincial associations and agricultural colleges and departments to improve native varieties and to acclimatize and then distribute seeds of American cottons. It would seem to be established by experiments that late-maturing American cottons will not succeed in the Yangtze delta, with its humid early autumn climate, but can be acclimatized in the central basin and parts of north China where September and October are normally dry, sunny months. An endeavour was made to produce longer-stapled Chinese cottons for the deltaic area.

The great development of cotton mills in China in the first half of the 20th century was the most important aspect of the new industrialism. They were, however, very strictly localized. Of 144 cotton mills in China in 1937, more than 40% were in Shanghai, the great textile centre, and half the remainder were in the Yangtze delta and the central basin. Of the grand total,

96 were Chinese-owned with 2,764,000 spindles and 25,503 looms, and 48 were foreign-owned (mainly Japanese) with 2,503,000 spindles and 37,528 looms.

At the end of World War II, the Japanese-owned textile mills were taken over and operated by the Chinese government. In 1951 production of cotton yarn and cloth on the mainland had exceeded prewar levels. On Formosa there was also a great increase in cotton textiles in 1951. There were 950,000 spindles and 5,392 looms.

The opium poppy has been one of the chief and most widely distributed products of China's fields, and the area devoted to it, reduced to a minimum by the prohibition orders of 1906 and subsequent years, greatly increased during the period of civil war, with its military exactions of illicit revenues. In west China the Nationalist government by forcible measures greatly reduced its growth. During World War II, in some Japanese-controlled areas, a marked increase in opium production as well as in the consumption of opium and its derivatives occurred.

Other important Chinese products, which cannot be separately described, include fibre crops, especially ramie in the Yangtze valley, tobacco (very widely distributed), peanuts, many kinds of vegetable oils, cane sugar and a great variety of medicinal plants and spices.

So great is the need for subsistence crops in China that grazing grounds for sheep and cattle are virtually confined to the dry northwest and to mountain pastures. In the rest of China there is no dairy industry, and cattle are used primarily as draught animals. Moreover, there is a lack of pasture grasses, partly because of the type of rainfall. On the other hand, animals such as swine, goats and poultry, which can subsist on by-products of the farm, are kept in large numbers. Scientific animal breeding has been developed little. Modern China's timber resources are very meagre.

China has an important source of wealth in its sea and river fisheries, which are rich and varied and supplemented by artificial breeding in tanks. The coastal fisheries of Shantung, Chekiang and Kwangtung are especially valuable, and they include some of the world's greatest fishing centres. Fish, both fresh and salted, is a staple article of diet in many districts.

MINERAL WEALTH AND MINING

Coal.—Coal is by far the most important mineral of China, but there is as yet no certainty regarding even the approximate amount of the coal reserves. The revised estimate (1945) of the Chinese geological survey was 265,331,000,000 tons. Through the efforts of survey parties sent out by government agencies, new coal reserves were found in various parts of the country, especially in north China. It indicates a bulk which is probably the greatest in the far east, sufficient to form the fuel basis of a fairly extensive industrial development in China. Of the total amount of the coal reserve estimate, Shansi province alone is responsible for almost one-half.

The annual production of coal in 1938 was 38,900,000 tons. Production in 1951, although only 69% of the peak level of 56,300,000 in 1942, was higher than the prewar average. Coal mines are all intimately related to the existing railway systems, mainly concentrated in north China, and are therefore chiefly located on the small fields scattered around the edges of the north China and south Manchurian plains.

The only really important mine in south China is that of Pingsiang among the hills of the Hunan-Kiangsi border, and this too is linked with the railway system. Much the largest concerns are the Fushun in the northeast and the Kailan in Hopei, whose fields, though small, have each an important strategic position, being in close contact with the railway focuses of south Manchuria and of north China, respectively.

The production of Fushun has been the larger of the two. From these and from other mines in Shantung and along the eastern fringes of the Shansi coal field, coal is exported along the railways and by coasting steamer to the commercial and industrial centres, of which the Yangtze delta is the chief. Chinwangtao, a port close to the Kailan mines, developed a larger coal-shipping trade than any other port east of Suez.

Iron, Oil and Other Minerals.—China's resources of iron are more meagre than those of coal. The 1947 estimate of the Chinese geological survey was 2,554,896,000 tons, while that of the bureau of mineral exploration of the National Resources commission was 5,065,838,000 tons. In 1953 new deposits of iron were located at Penki (Pen-ch'i) in the northeast and at Lungyen in north China. These were not sufficient to form the permanent basis of an iron industry of the magnitude of that of the U.S. On the other hand, the Chinese industry, with a capacity of 1,000,000 tons of pig iron, produced only two-thirds that amount; thus there was room for very considerable expansion.

Mining is most active along the lower Yangtze valley (Tayeh in particular) and in south Manchuria (An-shan in particular), and these two regions are also the chief centres of iron smelting. Before World War II, China was the principal supplier of iron ore to Japan's iron and steel industry, the major utilizable iron resources being virtually controlled by Japan. The 1936 ore production was 3,360,000 tons. Wartime disruption brought operation to extremely low levels, only 150,000 tons being produced in 1947. Rapid recovery began to take place after 1950, but in 1952 the production was still below the prewar level.

Oil reserves in China have always been greatly underestimated. Extensive surveys were undertaken but they had not been completed by 1953. The known oil reserves in China have been estimated at 778,855,000 tons, including 520,000,000 tons of oil shale. Small deposits of lead, zinc, silver, copper and tin have long been worked in many parts of the country. The most important copper and tin mines all lie in Yünnan and adjacent southwest Szechwan. Of some rare metals, particularly antimony and tungsten, China became the leading producer of the world.

In conclusion it may be said that China, though not richly endowed with all kinds of minerals, has many varieties of them which are necessary for its future economic development. These minerals had not been fully exploited by the early 1950s. With improved transport facilities and more favourable economic conditions, China might develop great mining activities.

MANUFACTURING

From what has been said in the preceding sections it must be clear that industrial development in the modern occidental sense of that term was still in its infancy in the early 1950s. In the older, premachine age, manufacturing was in the handicraft stage and was carried on in countless small units organized by guilds. Handicrafts persisted as the prevailing method of manufacture. Some were weakened by competition with foreign machine-made goods or, in cottons, by modern factories in China. Factory development was mainly, although not exclusively, in the manufacture of cotton textiles. There also were established silk filatures, flour mills, match factories and some steel works. Industrial development was retarded by civil strife and foreign wars, since both domestic and foreign capital were reluctant to invest extensively in equipment which might be destroyed by contending armies.

Before the war with Japan began in 1937, industry had been developed mainly in the lower reaches of the Yangtze valley. After 1937 industrial development made rapid progress in the interior provinces. After the government laid special emphasis on the heavy and the basic chemical industries, the growth of the heavy industries overtook that of the light industries.

COMMERCE

Currency and Banking.—At the dawn of the 20th century China's only domestic coinage was copper, in coins known by the foreigners as "cash." This could be employed only for relatively small transactions. Larger transactions were in silver bullion. The unit was the tael (Chinese liang), which varied in weight from locality to locality and agency to agency. Silver dollars of foreign minting, largely Spanish and Mexican, had been imported and were in increasing circulation. Domestic banks were chiefly for the purpose of facilitating internal commerce and exchange, although some received deposits and made loans. In the larger ports there were foreign banks, chiefly British.

In the course of the 20th century the "cash" largely disappeared. Silver coins corresponding to the dollar and called yuan were minted, and a subsidiary coinage, theoretically decimal, appeared. The yuan or dollar was legally substituted for the tael. There was much use of paper money, but silver remained the basis of the currency. In the 1930s the country was drained of much of its silver by purchase from abroad. Remaining stocks of silver were nationalized in Nov. 1935. From that time only the paper money issued by the government banks was allowed to circulate. In 1953 the official currency was the jenminpi or People's bank note on the mainland; on Taiwan it was the hsintaipi or new Taiwan dollar. There was an extensive development of banks, both government and private, of occidental types. The capital of these modern banks, however, was not made available to industries, except in the form of short-term loans. Investment banking, necessary to the industrialization of the country, was one line of activity which had not yet developed.

Foreign Trade.—The origin and characteristics of the system by which the foreign trade of China was organized from the middle of the 19th century down to relatively recent times are explained in the section on *History*. Some changes of great importance are indicated below. Tables I–IV, showing the total foreign trade for 1933 and 1947 according to the returns of the Chinese maritime customs, may be taken as fairly typical of the prewar years and the first few postwar years in spite of the disturbed political conditions.

Of the total shipping engaged in 1947, 41,733 were steamers with an aggregate tonnage of 18,331,569 and 23,006 were Chinese junks with an aggregate tonnage of 1,701,722. These figures were considerably below prewar figures.

An important feature shown by Tables I and II is the considerable excess of imports over exports; with the exception of certain years in the 1880s, this was a constant characteristic of Chinese foreign trade from 1869. The interpretation of this excess is by no means easy. It cannot be explained, as in the case, for example, of Great Britain, by so-called "invisible" exports in the form of shipping services paid for by imports or by interest on capital invested abroad, which again swells the import list. China has, however, an important asset, which is in some respects comparable with the latter, in the extensive remittances made to their ancestral homes by emigrants (numbering more than 10,000,000) to Thailand, Malaya, Indonesia, Indochina, Burma, the Philippines, the Americas and Europe. But, important as this factor is, it does not seem sufficient to cover what the official returns describe as an "unfavourable balance."

Before 1918 China was bound by a number of unfavourable treaty agreements. After 1918 the organization of Chinese foreign trade entered on a new and momentous phase. By the treaty of Versailles Germany surrendered its concessions at Hankow and Tientsin, and the U.S.S.R., too, as a result of World War I, lost and later renounced its treaty privileges. At the Washington conference (1921–22) the nine-power treaty on the Chinese customs tariff decreed *inter alia* "a general revision of the tariff, to make it a more effective instrument of revenue." In 1925 and 1926 an international conference was held in Peking to deal with the problem of the tariff. In 1928, 1929 and 1930 all the powers, including Japan, consented to the resumption by China of tariff autonomy. In 1929 China made these agreements effective by inaugurating a system of duties fixed by itself.

After the Japanese occupation of Manchuria in 1931 and especially after the Japanese attack on China in 1937, China's foreign trade was greatly modified by the progressive Japanese aggression. More and more Japan endeavoured to bring within its economic empire the portions of China which it occupied. Japan did this in part through various companies organized specifically for this purpose. Obviously Japan's plan was to integrate all of east Asia into an economic whole in which it would be dominant and in which Chinese economy would be made to subserve Japanese ends. As the war progressed, Japan strove by the slow strangulation of an increasing blockade to cut off from the outside world Free China. By successive steps various Chinese ports were seized, access from west China to the sea by way of Indochina was cut off, and the capture of Hong Kong and the conquest of Burma in 1942 shut these doors to the outside world. By 1943 such foreign trade as Free China had was either by air transport from India or through the Japanese blockade. During these years no reliable figures on trade could be had.

China had a big import surplus in 1946 and 1947 which was financed largely by foreign aid. The composition of imports to China in those years changed considerably as the result of deliberate policy. In the 1930s, rice and wheat headed the import list. In 1947 raw materials (mainly raw cotton), capital goods and chemicals headed the import list. In exports, wood oil had become increasingly important.

Foreign trade in 1948 was considerably reduced because of civil strife but began to increase in 1949 under the Peking government. Various measures of import and export control were adopted, such as the state monopoly in the export of bristles, soybeans and mineral oils, and the allocation of foreign exchange for the import of machinery and essential raw materials.

After 1949 the direction of foreign trade of the mainland of China shifted considerably, reflecting developments in the political and economic structure of the area and in the international situation. Imports from the United States decreased considerably in 1949 and 1950. Imports from the United Kingdom also decreased, but imports from Hong Kong increased substantially, since Hong Kong, more than during earlier years, served as an entrepôt for the mainland of China through which commodities were imported from other countries with which the Peking government had strained diplomatic relations. In Dec. 1950 the United States announced the ban on transportation or discharge

Table I.—*Foreign Trade of China, 1933 and 1947*

Principal commodities imported directly from abroad				
Commodity	1933		1947	
	In thousands of standard $	Per cent	In millions of Chinese national $	Per cent
Rice	150,272	11.2	187,343	1.7
Kerosene oil, liquid fuel and lubricating oil	115,435	8.6	993,253	9.3
Raw cotton	98,152	7.3	1,982,264	18.6
Metals and ores	97,067	7.2	790,802	7.4
Wheat	87,725	6.6	61	
Cotton goods	71,255	5.1	27,995	0.3
Chemicals	51,383	3.8	649,313	6.1
Paper	43,826	3.3	653,150	6.1
Sugar	42,026	3.1	28,109	0.3
Dyes and pigments	40,127	3.0	491,691	4.6
Machinery	39,181	2.9	882,857	8.2
Timber	37,314	2.8	351,193	3.3
Wool and cotton unions and woollen goods	31,724	2.4	380,320	3.6
Flour	29,699	2.2	154,270	1.4
Tobacco	29,644	2.2	297,692	2.8
Others	380,737	28.3	2,811,013	26.3
Total net imports	1,345,567		10,681,326	

Principal commodities exported directly to foreign countries				
Commodity	1933		1947	
	In thousands of standard $	Per cent	In millions of Chinese national $	Per cent
Raw silk, cocoons, etc.	57,736	9.4	297,274	4.7
Cotton yarn	40,007	6.5	419,815	6.6
Eggs and poultry products	36,480	6.0	146,098	2.4
Tea	34,210	5.6	230,172	3.6
Ores, metals, minerals and manufactures thereof	32,366	5.3	342,791	5.3
Skins, hides and leather	31,920	5.2	121,832	1.9
Wood oil	30,261	5.0	969,239	15.2
Raw cotton	30,229	5.0	2	
Peanuts and peanut products	23,866	3.9	41,619	0.7
Silk piece goods	20,789	3.4	139,462	2.1
Seeds and seedcake	18,838	3.1	105,679	1.7
Coal	5,078	0.8	21,316	0.3
Beans and bean products	5,044	0.8	243,539	3.8
Cereals	806	0.1	6,136	0.1
Others	244,198	39.9	3,291,530	51.6
Total net exports	611,828		6,376,504	

The equivalent of the standard dollar in terms of the U.S. dollar in 1933 was 0.26347 and of pence sterling 14 13/16. The equivalents of Chinese national $1,000 in terms of U.S. currency in the months of 1947 varied from a high of U.S. $0.29674 in January to a low of U.S. $0.0128 in December, and the average for the year was approximately U.S. $0.09.

TABLE II.—*Foreign Trade of China with Principal Countries, 1933 and 1947*

Country	Direct imports	Percentage of total imports	Direct exports	Percentage of total exports	Excess of Imports	Excess of Exports
	1933, in thousands of standard $					
United States	296,101	22.01	113,065	18.48	183,036	
Great Britain	153,557	11.41	48,723	7.96	104,834	
Japan	130,798	9.72	95,800	15.66	34,998	
Germany	107,653	8.00	20,783	3.40	86,870	
Hong Kong	44,174	3.28	120,729	19.73		76,555
Other countries	613,284	45.58	212,728	34.77	400,556	
Total	1,345,567		611,828		733,739	
	1947, in millions of Chinese national $					
United States	5,356,537	50.15	1,486,177	23.30	3,870,360	
India	965,128	9.03	202,087	3.17	763,041	
Great Britain	732,501	6.86	418,341	6.56	314,160	
Canada	405,855	3.80	22,724	0.36	383,131	
Hong Kong	196,271	1.84	2,179,373	34.18		1,983,102
Other countries	3,025,034	28.32	2,067,802	32.43	957,232	
Total	10,681,326		6,376,504		4,304,822	

TABLE III.—*Tonnage of Vessels Engaged in Carrying Trade Entered and Cleared at the Ports of China, 1933 and 1947*

1933 Flag	1933 Tons	1933 Per cent	1947 Flag	1947 Tons	1947 Per cent
British	58,215,213	42.3	U.S.	5,334,730	26.6
Chinese	37,254,843	27.1	Chinese	5,033,608	25.2
Japanese	20,168,140	14.7	British	4,872,091	24.4
Norwegian	5,750,291	4.1	Norwegian	1,088,981	5.4
U.S.	5,350,526	3.9	Netherlands	1,062,946	5.3
Other flags	10,640,161	7.9	Other flags	2,641,135	13.1
Total	137,379,174		Total	20,033,491	

TABLE IV.—*Percentage of the Value of Direct Foreign Trade in Principal Ports of China, 1933 and 1947*

Port	1933, per cent	1947, per cent
Shanghai	53.37	69.39
Tientsin	10.62	5.61
Canton	6.11	5.10
Tsingtao	5.70	1.08
Kowloon	5.10	10.20
Other ports	19.10	8.62

by U.S. ships or aircraft of strategic materials shipped from or transhipped through the United States to the Chinese mainland, Hong Kong and Macao. Subsequently trade with the Soviet Union and the eastern European countries increased considerably.

Trade with the Soviet Union was only 0.4% of total trade in 1936 and 8% in 1949. Trade and credit agreements were signed with the Soviet Union in February and April 1950. In 1950 the Soviet Union accounted for 19.84% of total imports and 26.58% of total exports; in 1951, 44.70% of total imports and 51.51% of total exports. Trade agreements were also signed with eastern European countries such as Poland, Czechoslovakia, Hungary and eastern Germany. These countries accounted for 1.37% of total imports and 3.87% of total exports in 1950; in 1951, for 25.30% of total imports and 26.43% of total exports. Imports from the Soviet Union and eastern European countries consisted mainly of industrial raw materials, industrial machinery, equipment and parts, and communication and transportation equipment and parts. Exports to those countries consisted of soybeans, silk, tea, wool and agricultural by-products.

In Formosa, most of the import and export business before and during World War II was with Japan. After the war, the Chinese mainland was Formosa's supplier-buyer. However, in 1949 Formosa lost this market.

In Dec. 1949 private trading was resumed between Formosa and Japan. Of the U.S. $93,000,000 exports in 1951, purchases by Japan amounted to U.S. $38,790,000, including sugar, rice and tea, and out of the imports of U.S. $84,000,000, Japan supplied U.S. $39,920,000 worth of commodities.

COMMUNICATIONS

Transportation.—In modern times for the most part freight was still moved in China as it always had been, by human labour, with animals as supplementary carriers. The wheelbarrow and carrying pole are the commonest means of transport for small merchandise. In north China wheeled vehicles, mostly the springless Pekingese cart, are used to a considerable extent on the sandy tracks, while in the centre and south the sedan chair is still in evidence, and rickshas are in general use in and around the larger cities. The Tsinlingshan roughly defines the northern limit of the general use of water transport, which in north China becomes subordinate to the cumbrous cart, drawn by horse, mule, bullock or mixed team. In the utilization of inland waterways no people have excelled the Chinese. The natural routes provided by the Yangtze and its great tributaries and to a lesser extent by the Si Kiang and other rivers of southeast China bear an enormous amount of junk traffic, while steamboats, large and small, increased especially in the lower Yangtze.

From an early stage of Chinese history the rivers have been supplemented by canals. The most famous of these was the Grand canal, at its fullest development reaching from Tung-chow, just outside Peking, to south of the Yangtze. In later years much of it suffered from accumulations of silt and lack of repair. In central and south China the great bulk of inland trade is carried on by waterways, and many millions of Chinese spend their lives in boats. At various periods of Chinese history extensive systems of "imperial" highways were constructed, radiating from the capital, but these were seldom kept in repair for long and most became mere tracks. However, after the "good roads movement" was launched in 1921, broad macadamized thoroughfares, capable of carrying heavy traffic, were constructed around many of the more progressive cities. Motor services came into existence, and highways were increased from 1,185 km. in 1921 to 115,702 km. in 1936. By 1950 the 200,000-km. mark was reported to have been passed. Most of these roads had only dirt surfaces, but some had been given rock dressings. Notable was a road which, under the pressure of military necessity, the Chinese built from Yünnan to Burma.

Passenger and freight transport by air were also developed after 1929. It was both retarded and stimulated by the war with Japan.

Railways.—The program of railway construction, which in the early years of the 20th century was making fair progress, was almost entirely held up during the 1920s because of civil war. It was resumed in the 1930s.

After 1937 some old railways were destroyed during the war while new ones were being built. Under the Communist regime railway construction continued to progress. All in all, the total length was approaching the 30,000-km. mark, which was, however, a low figure for a country like China. The outstanding feature of the railway system, so far as it has been completed, is the concentration in north and northeast China and the lower Yangtze valley. Thence diverge:

1. The Peking-Kalgan-Suiyuan-Paotou line, which ascends the scarps leading to the high Mongolian plateau and is intended to develop the pastoral and potential agricultural resources of Inner Mongolia and northwest China. This line is notable as having been constructed and maintained by the Chinese without external assistance.

2. The two great trunk railways traversing the plain of north China from north to south: (*a*) the Peking-Hankow railway (1,215 km.), whose route lies along the western border of the plain, and, with the equally long line from Hankow (terminus at Wuchang, across the Yangtze from Hankow) to Canton (1,096 km.), forming the north-south artery par excellence; (*b*) the Tientsin-Pukow railway (1,010 km.), running through the eastern part of the plain, links Peking with the Shanghai-Nanking line and the lower Yangtze valley.

3. The Peking-Tientsin-Mukden railway, traversing the coastal sill between the edge of the Mongolian plateau and the sea, joins the two great northern centres with the metropolis of south Manchuria and makes contact with the complex and rapidly expanding railway system of Manchuria. (Manchurian railways total about 12,000 km., including the Chinese Eastern and the South Manchuria railways which were merged after World War II

as the Chinese Changchun railway jointly managed by China and the U.S.S.R. until Dec. 31, 1952, after which it came under full Chinese administration.)

The most important transverse line is the east-west Lunghai railway (1,227 km.), which from the port of Lienyün in northern Kiangsu crosses both the north-south trunk lines and runs through Süchow and Kai-fêng to Loyang, Sian and Paoki. Continuations were projected to Lanchow-fu, in Kansu, and to Chêngtu, in Szechwan. (Construction was under way in 1953.)

Apart from small branch lines, mainly tapping coal fields, there are two important railways connecting with the main systems: the Shantung railway joining Chinan on the Tientsin-Pukow line with the seaport Tsingtao (Kiaochow), and the Shansi railway linking the Peking-Hankow line with Tai-yuan.

Shanghai is the focus of a distinct system: (1) Shanghai-Nanking, (2) Shanghai-Hangchow-Ningpo and (3) Shanghai-Woosung (the first railway built in China, 1876).

From Hangchow a railroad stretches westward through Nanchang and Changsha and was projected to reach Kwei-yang and Kunming. Kiukiang on the Yangtze was connected with Nanchang. Hengyang on the Hankow-Canton line in Hunan was connected with Kwei-lin in Kwangsi.

In the south, Canton has a similar role. Apart from the Canton-Hankow line, already mentioned, short railways connect the southern metropolis with Kowloon, opposite Hong Kong, and with Samshui. Another important railway in China is the trunk line, completed by the French in 1909, which runs from Haiphong in Indochina to Kunming in southwest China, part of its course being in Chinese territory. There are short local lines running inland from Amoy, Swatow and Macao, respectively. The railway between Chêngtu and Chungking (823 km.) in Szechwan was completed in 1952. Work was begun on a number of other lines in west China designed to connect some of the main cities in Szechwan and Yünnan, and Kweichow with Hunan.

Postal Services.—The postal service of China began in 1879 and was greatly improved after 1889. As a result of the Washington conference and in acknowledgment of the efficiency of the Chinese postal service, all the foreign powers concerned agreed to withdraw their postal agencies from China on Jan. 1, 1923.

Postal service was maintained with surprising efficiency in spite of civil and foreign wars. Wireless and telephone services are fairly widely distributed.

ADMINISTRATION

Sun Yat-sen's Three Principles.—After the revolution of 1911, which abolished the imperial office and the time-honoured machinery of administration, China passed through a bewildering series of political changes and civil wars (*see* under *History*). On the eve of the outbreak of the Chino-Japanese hostilities of 1937 a quieter phase had supervened and constructive forces were obviously at work, but the factors in the political situation were still extremely complex and the legacy of militarism which the civil wars had bequeathed increased the difficulty of administrative reconstruction. In 1928 a constitution was promulgated embodying certain principles to which, in theory at any rate, all Chinese Nationalists adhered. The constitution and the administrative arrangements which it contemplated were the work of the Kuomintang or the Nationalist party, which was not only supreme in China at that time but was the only party whose existence was recognized. Sun Yat-sen, the founder of the Kuomintang, was after his death regarded in some sense as its patron saint, his will or statement of three essential principles being regarded as a kind of instrument of government. The Three Principles of the People have been translated as:

1. Nationalism (national emancipation and racial equality).
2. Democracy (political rights for the people).
3. Livelihood (economic welfare of the people).

Under the first principle Sun states what is necessary for the development of a strong national consciousness so that China can escape from the position of being "a colony of every Great Power." One of the steps on which he insists is that "we must organize our people into one strong organic group. This can be accomplished only by utilizing such strong units as clans and local organizations." Many old characteristics must be revived, including "our old learning as found in the *Great Learning*" and "we must revive our creative power, the power which we once had in inventing new things." He adds, "We must do all these things, but, aside from that, we must also go out to learn what is best in the West."

Under the second principle Sun first states the case for democracy and maintains that China in this respect has little to learn from the west, since "the West has, in the last century, progressed much more rapidly in material things than in those that concern man and his welfare. In politics, very little advance has been made." He makes the interesting point that whereas the western peoples had formerly too little personal freedom and had to fight hard for liberty, in China "our people have had too much personal freedom" and, as a result, "have become a plate of sand . . . helpless in the face of foreign imperialism and its economic conquest." "So what we need now is not to fight for more personal freedom, but to sacrifice some of our personal freedom, in order to gain our national freedom." China has to face two problems, in the solution of which, he maintains, it is helped neither by its own nor by western experience: how to have a strong central government and at the same time to remove the fear of the people of such a government. To build up a powerful government machinery and to enable the people fully to exercise their power and control of the machinery two things are essential: (*a*) the organizing of government "on the five principles—legislative, judicial, executive, entrance to public office by examination, and censorship"; (*b*) safeguarding the people with "the power of election, power of recall, power of initiation of new laws, and power of revision or abolition of old laws."

Under the third main principle Sun insists that "we must centre all our problems around the welfare of the people" and avoid the western mistake of taking "material problems as the central point in human history." "None of the forms of Socialism developed in the west are fitted for our own country." China has to avoid the dangers of industrialism. "Our great and immediate problem is not economic inequality but economic poverty, not a fight against capitalists, but the prevention of the rise of capitalists in the future. Our method of solving this problem is to develop State industry."

He enumerates a series of measures for increasing production and concludes: "On the one hand there is an urgent need of improving our old methods of raising raw materials. On the other hand, we have to develop our own textile industry as rapidly as possible. This is at present hindered by the treaties which forbid us to have tariff autonomy. So our first step in solving the problem (of clothing) is to remove all unequal treaties so that we may carry out a policy of protection."

The official program of the Kuomintang, passed at a plenary session of the central executive committee, with delegates from all provincial committees, in Oct. 1926 at Canton, was essentially an elaboration of the main points and an application of the abstract principles contained in the famous will.

Nationalist Constitution.—Sun Yat-sen contemplated three stages in the political development of the country. The first was to be military rule. This was to be followed by political tutelage under the Kuomintang, and this in turn was to be succeeded by government under a constitution which presumably would be democratic. In theory, the first stage ended in 1928. In practice, military and party rule went along together. The Kuomintang brought together in Nanking a national assembly which adopted the constitution of the Republic of China on Dec. 25, 1946, based on Sun's teachings. In general the structure of government provided for in that constitution was maintained by the Nationalist government on Formosa in the early 1950s after that government was driven from the Chinese mainland in 1949. The following are the chief features of the organization of the National government as stipulated by the constitution:

1. The president is the head of the state, elected once in six years, vested with supreme power. He controls the army, navy and air force and is alone competent to declare war, conclude peace and negotiate treaties with foreign states. He represents the nation in international affairs and at the same time is commander in chief of all the forces.

2. Five yuan (or councils) for the following functions: executive, legislative, judicial, examination and control (*i.e.*, censorship or supervision). Of these the executive yuan is the highest administrative organ of the national government, composed of ministries and commissions to which are entrusted various executive duties. The president of the executive yuan is nominated and appointed by the president with the consent of the legislative yuan. Members of the legislative yuan are elected once in three years and members of the control yuan once in six years. It will be observed that the five yuan or councils are in accordance with Sun's proposals under his second essential principle. The control yuan exercises the functions of the censorate under the imperial regime. The examination yuan supervises the system of public examinations as the test of admission to public office, which was originated in the 7th century.

Communist Government.—The Peking government was inaugurated on Oct. 1, 1949, under the name of the Central People's government. The leaders of the new government drew upon Marxism-Leninism-Stalinism for inspiration and patterned some of their techniques of government after those worked out by the U.S.S.R. The following are the chief features of the organic law of the Central People's government of the People's Republic of China, passed by the first plenary session of the Chinese People's Political Consultative conference (P.P.C.C.) on Sept. 27, 1949:

1. A government council consisting of a chairman and six vice-chairmen and 56 members, elected by the P.P.C.C., "represents the People's Republic of China in international relations, and assumes leadership of the state authority at home."

2. The council controls four organs, namely (*a*) state administration council, (*b*) people's revolutionary military council, (*c*) supreme people's court and (*d*) people's procurator-general's office. The state administration council consists of a premier, a number of deputy premiers, a committee on political and legal affairs, a committee on finance and economics, a committee on culture and education, a committee on people's supervision and 30 ministries, bureaus, offices and commissions.

Under the Peking government there were established six large regional divisions, two autonomous governments (Inner Mongolia and Tibet), 28 provinces, eight administrative districts and 13 municipalities placed directly under the control of either Peking or the administrative regions.

EDUCATION

A national system of education was first established during the last years of the Manchu dynasty, but it was reorganized under the republic. The school system was organized as follows:

1. A two-year kindergarten.
2. A six-year primary school course (covering approximately the ages 6 to 12) divided into two grades, lower and higher, the former of four years' and the latter of two years' duration. In theory this was obligatory. In Formosa there were 1,289 primary schools with an enrolment of 976,462 in 1952. The ratio of the number of children attending school to the number of children of school age reached 81.49%. On the mainland there were approximately 450,000 primary schools with an enrolment of 38,700,000 in 1952, estimated to be about 50% of the number of children of school age.
3. A six-year middle or secondary school course (age 12–18), similarly divided into senior and junior grades, the higher tending to be vocational in character. In Formosa there were 129 middle schools with an enrolment of 85,682 in the spring of 1952. On the mainland there were 4,015 middle schools with an enrolment of 1,290,000 in 1951.
4. A four-year university course. There are also normal schools, both lower and higher, for the training of primary and middle school teachers, respectively, and also higher professional or technical colleges of various types.

In Formosa there were one national university, three provincial colleges and three polytechnic institutes with a total enrolment of 7,965 in 1952, as compared with 2,983 in 1947 and 5,906 in 1950. On the mainland there were 218 institutions of higher education with an enrolment of 219,700 in 1953, as compared with 129,000 in 1946.

A complete reorganization of higher educational institutions was undertaken on the mainland after 1951. In big cities such as Shanghai and Peking the old universities were in some cases divided up and in others combined so that each administrative region had only one university for the arts and sciences. In 1953 there were 13 universities in different parts of China; 20 polytechnic institutes, formed by rearranging the technical colleges of the old universities; 26 newly established special technological institutes, such as the steel institute and the mining institute; 29 agricultural forestry colleges; seven institutes for finance and economics; two special colleges newly established in the northeast and in Sinkiang to train students from the national minorities; and other special institutes. As the result of government policy, students majoring in technology rose to 35.4% in 1952 as compared with 18.9% in 1946.

BIBLIOGRAPHY.—*Racial Characteristics of the Chinese People:* S. M. Shirokogoroff, *Anthropology of Northern China* (1923); E. Huntington, *The Character of Races* (New York, London, 1924); L. H. D. Buxton, *China, the Land and the People* (Oxford, 1929).

Population: W. W. Rockhill, *Enquiry Into the Population of China* (1904); H. F. MacNair, *The Chinese Abroad* (New York, 1924); P. M. Roxby, "The Distribution of Population in China," *Geographical Review* (1925); Chi Li, *The Formation of the Chinese People* (Cambridge, Mass., Oxford, 1928); W. F. Willcox, "A Westerner's Effort to Estimate the Population of China," *Journal of the American Statistical Association* (Sept. 1930); Ch'ên Ta, *Population in Modern China* (Chicago, 1946).

Chinese Society: D. H. Kulp, *Country Life in South China* (New York, 1925); K. A. Wittfogel, "Die Theorie der orientalischen Gesellschaft," *Zeitschrift für Sozialforschung* (1938); Fei Hsiao-tung, "Peasantry and Gentry," *American Journal of Sociology,* vol. lii, no. 1 (1946); Olga Lang, *Chinese Family and Society* (New Haven, Oxford, 1946).

Philosophy and Religion: J. J. M. de Groot, *The Religious System of China* (1892–1911); Sir C. Eliot, *Hinduism and Buddhism,* 3 vol. (New York, 1921); K. S. Latourette, *A History of Christian Missions in China* (New York, London, 1929); E. R. Hughes (ed. and tr.), *Chinese Philosophy in Classical Times* (New York, London, 1942); Fêng Yulan, *A History of Chinese Philosophy,* vol. i, *The Period of the Philosophers From the Beginnings to Circa 100 B.C.,* trans. by Derk Bodde (Princeton, 1952; London, 1953); Charles Moore (ed.), *Essays in East-West Philosophy* (Honolulu, 1951).

Agriculture: W. Wagner, *Die chinesische Landwirtschaft* (1926); W. H. Mallory, *China: Land of Famine* (New York, 1926); F. H. King, *Farmers of Forty Centuries,* ed. by J. P. Bruce (New York, 1927); K. A. Wittfogel, *Wirtschaft und Gesellschaft Chinas* (1931); J. L. Buck, *Land Utilization in China,* 3 vol. (Chicago, 1937; Oxford, 1938); T. H. Shên, *Agricultural Resources of China* (Ithaca, Oxford, 1951).

Industry: D. K. Lieu, *China's Industries and Finance* (New York, 1927); H. F. Bain, *Ores and Industry in the Far East* (New York, 1927); R. H. Tawney, *Land and Labour in China* (London, New York, 1932); Fong Hsien-ding, *The Post-War Industrialization of China* (Washington, 1942); Juan Vei-chow, "Mineral Resources of China," *Economic Geology* (1946); D. K. Lieu, *China's Economic Stabilization and Reconstruction* (New Brunswick, N.J., 1948).

Commerce: H. B. Morse, *The Trade and Administration of China,* 3rd rev. ed. (New York, 1921); C. S. See, *The Foreign Trade of China* (New York, 1919); C. F. Remer, *The Foreign Trade of China* (New York, 1926); J. Arnold, *China, A Commercial and Industrial Handbook* (1926); *Annual Reports of the Maritime Customs of China; The China Year Book;* the *Chinese Economic Journal* (monthly); *Chinese Economic Bulletin* (weekly); *China Handbook; Economic Survey of Asia and the Far East.*

Government: Sun Yat-sen, *The San Min Chu I,* trans. by F. W. Price, ed. by L. T. Chen (New York, London, 1927); *The Civil Code of the Republic of China,* trans. by C. L. Hsia and J. L. E. Chow (Shanghai, 1931); M. S. Bates and F. W. Price, "Kuomintang," in *Encyclopaedia of the Social Sciences,* vol. viii, pp. 610–614; Ch'ien Tuan-shêng, *The Government and Politics of China* (Cambridge, Mass., Oxford, 1950). (P. M. R.; K. S. L.; C.-L. C.)

CHINA (ware): *see* CHINAWARE.

CHINABERRY (*Melia azedarach*), a member of the Meliaceae or mahogany family and also known as China tree, pride of India and Indian lilac, is a spreading, mostly deciduous tree that may reach a height of 50 ft. The leaves are twice pinnate, the fragrant, purplish flowers are in open panicles 4–6 in. long, and the fruit is a globular, yellow, smooth drupe to $\frac{3}{4}$ in. in diameter, hanging after the leaves fall. Although native to Asia it has become naturalized in tropical America and is much grown in the southern United States from southeastern Virginia to Texas. It grows with great rapidity and forms a desirable, dense shade. The variety *umbraculiformis,* known as the Texas umbrella tree, has drooping foliage and radiating branches which give the tree the appearance of a giant umbrella. (J. M. BL.)

CHINA CLAY (KAOLIN), an essential ingredient in the manufacture of china or porcelain. The word "kaolin" is derived from the Chinese Kau-ling ("high ridge"), a hill east of Kingte-chen, whence the earliest samples of the clay sent to Europe were obtained by François Xavier Dentrecolles (1662–1741), a French Jesuit missionary. His specimens, examined in Paris by R. A. Ferchault de Réaumur, showed that true porcelain was manufactured from a paste containing two essential ingredients: china clay, a pure white clay; and china stone, a variety of granite consisting mainly of orthoclase feldspar. The china clay confers plasticity on the paste and secures retention of form for the ware when exposed to the heat of the kiln; the china stone gives the characteristic translucency. Some of the earliest discoveries of china clay in Europe were at Aue, near Schneeberg in Saxony, and at St. Yrieux, near Limoges in France. In England it was discovered in Cornwall about 1750 by William Cookworthy of Plymouth, who in 1768 took out his patent for making porcelain from china clay and china stone. These raw materials were found first at Tregonning hill, near Breage, and afterward at St. Stephen's-in-Brannel, near St. Austell; and their discovery led to the manufacture of true porcelain at Plymouth and subsequently at Bristol.

The china clay rock of Cornwall and Devon is a granite with its orthoclase feldspar decomposed to a soft, white, powdery substance which, when wet, acquires the characteristic plasticity of clay. The other components of the granite, the quartz and mica, are unaffected, and although they are subordinate to the decomposed feldspar or kaolin their presence retains for the rock the appearance of a weathered granite. Although kaolinization can undoubtedly result from weathering, the evidence in this case indicates that the alteration consists in the removal of the alkalies and the formation of a hydrated silicate of aluminum having the formula $Al_2O_3.2SiO_2.2H_2O$. This substance, known as kaolinite (*q.v.*), constitutes the bulk of refined china clay, the impurities of the commercial article being finely divided quartz and mica (muscovite). It is not possible to remove the whole of these impurities by washing, and this accounts for the difference in composition between pure kaolinite and a refined Cornish clay as shown by the analyses below.

	Kaolinite	China clay
SiO_2	46.3%	48.3%
Al_2O_3	39.8%	37.6%
Fe_2O_3		0.5%
CaO		0.1%
K_2O, Na_2O		1.5%
H_2O	13.9%	12.5%

Note: 1% of alkalies in china clay is equivalent to 8.5% of muscovite.

Physically china clay is a white, soft powder consisting of crystals and groups of crystals which may be observed in the electron microscope and which range in size from 0.2 μ to 50 μ across, the larger size in the form of composite columns of crystals called vermicules from their appearance in the optical microscope. According to the degree of refining, a china clay may contain all its particles below 3 μ or below 50 μ. It will form with water a smooth mixture whose viscosity may be greatly influenced by the presence of certain deflocculating salts, particularly silicates and phosphates, which permit concentrations up to 70% of solids to be achieved in some cases. This property has commercial significance in the ceramic industry in the casting process and in the paper industry in high-speed paper-coating processes. The whiteness of china clay, a property important in most of its uses, is largely dependent on the absence of iron as an impurity. The qualities for which china clay is esteemed in the arts vary according to the application of the material. In the paper industry it is used as a filler for paper where whiteness combined with a medium grain size providing high retention in the fibres together with absence of abrasive impurities are required. In the coating of paper very white, fine-grain china clays are used generally in combination with other minerals in the classical brush-coating processes and alone in the high-speed machine-coating processes. China clay is much used in ceramics and forms the refractory basis of the article during the sintering or firing process. In all ceramic composition it contributes to the plasticity in the unfired state and, in compositions containing no other clay, is the main source of plasticity. It is widely used as a refractory. In the associated mineral china stone, the feldspar is only partially decomposed, and the higher percentage of alkalies leads to its employment as a flux in combination with china clay to produce a ceramic body. By such combinations vitreous ceramic materials such as porcelain and bone china are produced at temperatures substantially lower than the melting point of china clay itself. China clay has a lesser though widely distributed use in a variety of industries, the next important to the above being the rubber industry, in which it is used as a filler and reinforcing agent.

In order to prepare china clay for the market the china clay rock is subjected to the action of a water jet; the bulk of the quartz and any undecomposed feldspar are arrested in sand pits, which, in their modern form, are mechanically operated. The slurry is pumped to the surface of the pit, which may be 250 ft. deep and several acres in area. After further separation of coarser impurities, various particle-size classification processes are applied, resulting in a series of products in the finest of which 80% of the particles may be less than one micron in diameter. The refined clay, as a suspension in water, is then led to settling pits or tanks, in which the clay concentrates and water is removed. The concentrate is filter-pressed to reduce the water content and then dried in mechanical driers. A number of chemical and physical refining processes will have been applied to special types of clay to suit the properties to particular purposes. China stone is quarried and ground without levigation.

(F. H. Ha.; N. O. C.)

UNITED STATES

In the United States the term "china clay" and "kaolin" are synonymous. They designate relatively pure clays of highest quality which fire white or nearly white. Either residual (primary) or sedimentary (secondary) kaolins were reported in 24 states in the mid-1950s. Major production was concentrated in Georgia and South Carolina, Georgia alone accounting for more than 70% of the domestic production of nearly 2,000,000 tons yearly. Other producing states included Alabama, California, Florida, Illinois, North Carolina, Pennsylvania, Texas, Utah and Virginia. Also of interest are the extensive ball clay deposits of western Kentucky and Tennessee. These fine-grained, extremely plastic clays, closely related to kaolins, are consumed almost entirely by the ceramic industry.

The extensive kaolin deposits of Georgia and South Carolina occur on the coastal plain in an irregular belt along the fall line. These beds of sedimentary kaolin are 5 to 40 ft. thick, with up to 60 ft. overburden. Dry Branch and McIntyre, Ga., and Aiken county, S.C., are major production centres. Georgia kaolins tend to be more fine-grained and plastic than South Carolina kaolins. Open-pit mining is employed, and the yields from processing the Georgia and South Carolina kaolins range from 80%–99%.

The commercial Florida kaolins occur in Putnam county in a sedimentary rock stratum about 10 feet below ground level at about the water table. Hydraulic mining is thus logically employed. The deposits yield roughly 15% clay and 85% sand and gravel. The commercial kaolin separated in processing is fine-grained and very plastic, often being termed ball-kaolin.

The residual North Carolina kaolins are mined principally in mountainous Avery and Mitchell counties. These kaolins occur in dikes and lenses resulting from decomposition of pegmatite granite. The average depth of the kaolin mines, excluding overburden, is about 40 ft. A yield of about 15% commercial kaolin plus some by-product mica results from processing.

In the United States most of the kaolins are produced in several grades, ranging from crude lump clay to air-floated material. The wide differences in the raw kaolin itself, plus variations in refinement and sizing, accommodate all reasonable market demands. Refining and beneficiating processes range from air separation of dry-ground raw kaolin to elaborate water washing, separation, settling, classification and chemical treating.

The paper industry uses half of all kaolin produced, for filling and coating purposes. The other half is consumed primarily for rubber filling and ceramic products (refractories, whitewares, cement, vitreous enamel, etc.), with some being used in oil refining, fertilizers, insecticides, chemicals, paint and linoleum.

Bibliography.—Heinrich Reis, "Report of Committee on Geologic Surveys," *Bulletin of the American Ceramic Society*, vol. xxiv (1945); Jasper L. Stuckey, "Kaolins of North Carolina," *Transactions of the American Institute of Mining and Metallurgical Engineers*, vol. clxxiii (1947); J. M. Huber, Inc., *Kaolin Clays, and Their Industrial Uses* (New York, 1949); Brooke L. Gunsallus and Bernice V. Russ, "Clays," *Minerals Yearbook 1952*, Bureau of Mines, U.S. Department of the Interior (Washington, 1955); Ralph E. Grim, *Clay Mineralogy* (New York, 1953). (R. Rl.)

CHINAN or Tsinan, a large and historic city and the capital of the province of Shantung in north China, 36° 43′ N., 116° 37′ E. Chinan is situated at the northern base of the ancient highlands of Shantung (near Tai-shan, the sacred mountain) where they sink beneath the alluvium of the Hwang-ho and along an important spring line which fostered very early settlement. Its early history is bound up with that of the ancient states of Chi and Lu in the classical (Chou) period; when the present province of Shantung—closely corresponding to the territory of the two feudal states—was created under the Ming dynasty (1368–1644), Chinan, a natural focus of mountain and plain, was selected as administrative centre. The change in the course of the Hwang-ho in 1854 brought it within 5 mi. of Chinan. But the destruction of the dikes as a war measure in 1938 turned most of the water into the regions south of Shantung, while in 1943 the Japanese military began work to divert the Hwang-ho north into the Wei river. Formerly, Chinan controlled the Hwang-ho bridge of the Tientsin-Pukow railway (completed 1912). This railway runs parallel to, and fulfils the function once served by, the now dilapidated Grand canal. Chinan is the junction of this arterial railway with the Shantung railway running eastward by way of the Poshan coal field to the port of Tsingtao on Kiaochow bay, which from 1898 until 1915 was leased territory in control of Germany, afterward falling into the hands of Japan. Although by the Shantung treaty, arranged at the time of the Washington conference (1922), Japan on certain conditions surrendered Tsingtao to China, its influence and interests in the Shantung railway were still very strong, as was shown by the dispatch of Japanese troops to Chinan in 1928, when the Nationalist armies were advancing northward. In contact with foreign influences along the two railways, in communication with the sea by a canal fed from the local springs and the market for one of the richest parts of the great plain, Chinan was much affected by western industrial methods, seen especially in flour milling and cotton manufacture. The city was voluntarily opened to foreign commerce in 1904, and a large "settlement" grew up in the Shang-pu or trading quarter, outside the west gate of the city. Pop. (est. 1936) 472,300.

Occupied by Japan from 1937 to 1945, Chinan was captured by Communist forces in 1948.

CHINANDEGA, an important city of Nicaragua, Central

America, capital of the department of the same name. It is 13 mi. N.N.E. of the Pacific port of Corinto, on the Pacific railway; population (1950) 13,146. It is 22 mi. from León and 74 mi. from Managua, the national capital. Chinandega is the centre of the sugar-producing area of Nicaragua and a high grade of sugar is manufactured and exported to the western United States and to other Central American countries. Corn, rice, potatoes, vanilla and cotton are also grown.

Chinandega was partly destroyed by fire during one of the battles of the revolution of 1927 in which American marines and aeroplanes took an active part.

CHINAWARE, a name given to a hard, translucent type of pottery.

Earthenware is sometimes quite thin, and it is a common error not to discriminate between this and the ware which is properly called china.

A simple test for china is its translucency, which allows the outline of a finger to be seen if held between a piece of ware and the light.

Another and more accurate test is that of applying red ink to the ware under the glaze. If the ink is absorbed, then it is considered that the ware is not china. A portion of the glaze must be thoroughly removed before the ink can be applied.

The actual meaning of "vitrified" causes some trouble and the following is the definition: vitrified pottery is nonporous; unvitrified pottery is porous. Vitrified china has been defined as follows: vitrified china is glazed chinaware having a white body and burned to such a temperature that a dense, practically nonabsorbent body is produced.

"Practically" is a much abused adverb, and one is left wondering whether or not a slightly absorbent ware with a white body would pass as vitrified.

Porcelain, which may be regarded as synonymous with china, is not easily defined in scientific terms, for several specimens of ware, which may be correctly regarded as true porcelain, will vary in actual composition.

J. W. Mellor, F.R.S., said that the most practical definition he could give is the following: "Porcelain is a body which in moderately thin layers is translucent."

CHIEF CENTRES OF PRODUCTION

Commercially, the chief centres of production, with international importance, are the potteries of Limoges, Fr., Staffordshire, Eng., Czechoslovakia, Germany (Thuringia and Bavaria) and Japan. Copenhagen, Den., produces a very fine china, but this, although sold commercially, is not strictly a competitive production.

England.—Bone china, the porcelain in which bone ash is an important constituent, is made almost entirely in England, and it is claimed that it is more durable than the feldspar china of the continent of Europe.

This type of porcelain was introduced by the famous potter Josiah Spode of Stoke-on-Trent in 1799. Alexandre Brogniart, director of the national factory at Sèvres, referring to this, said:

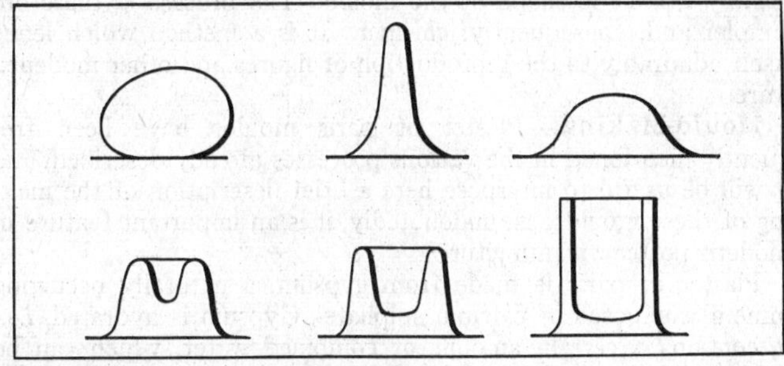

FROM BINN, "POTTERS' CRAFT" (VAN NOSTRAND)

PROGRESS OF A BALL OF CLAY ON THE POTTER'S WHEEL

"Spode produced a better porcelain than any that had yet been made in England. He endeavoured to equal the soft porcelain of Sèvres, which his paste closely resembled. He introduced, or at any rate perfected, the use of calcined bones in the body of the ware."

Spode's formula was later adopted by all the leading manufacturers throughout the five towns in north Staffordshire, and also by the Coalport, Derby and Worcester factories. Of the manufacturers of china in England, the greater part have their factories at Longton, one of the five towns mentioned above.

Japan.—Some of the ware of Japan has a world-wide reputation and is distinctly oriental in its decoration; but the Japanese rapidly copied western methods, and the decorations of their commercial products are often distinguished from the wares of European countries only with difficulty. They realized that in order to sell in another country, they must decorate their ware to appeal to the taste of the potential buyers. The U.S. proved to be the best customer of Japan for porcelain.

The cheaper types of china are made in the area of Nagoya, but the Imari porcelain (a very high-class product) is produced at Arita. Toy tea sets and dolls are important items in the Japanese porcelain trade, and the annual production of these wares is great. Porcelain insulators are also exported in large quantities, and many users of wireless materials will probably have handled this particular ware.

RAW MATERIALS

The raw materials needed for the manufacture of china are china clay or kaolin, china stone, bone and feldspar. (*See* CHINA CLAY.)

China Stone.—This is an important ingredient in the china body, and it is mined by inserting explosive charges in holes drilled by compressed air boring machines.

The stone has four recognized qualities or grades: hard purple (a white, hard rock with a purple tinge); mild purple (similar but softer); dry white or soft (a soft white rock); buff (similar to dry white, but with a slight yellow tinge).

Silica is the principal constituent, amounting to more than 80% in the two purple and the buff varieties, and about 74% in the dry white. Alumina is the next important ingredient, amounting to about 18% in the dry white and from 7% to 10% in the other varieties. The most effective constituents are the alkalies and lime which make up the balance of the composition. China stone gives the china body its translucency resulting from its feldspar content. Its function, hence, is that of a flux.

Bone Ash.—This, as already stated, is used in the English china industry where the bone china is almost exclusively produced. Animal bones are used and, as a result of its vast business of cattle rearing and slaughtering, South America is the chief source of supply. The bones are calcined and ground to a fine powder.

Feldspars.—The feldspars are silica compounds of alumina and alkalis (chiefly potash and soda), with small proportions of iron oxide, lime and magnesia. Norway is a principal source of supply, but large quantities are also found in Czechoslovakia. Canada is an important feldspar-producing country.

The Norwegian feldspar is largely used in Europe. The mineral is exported both in lump and as a powder.

MAKING THE WARE

The Slip.—The slip, it should be explained, is the china clay and other ingredients mixed with water to a thin consistency. Metallic impurities, which would spoil the finished ware, are removed by a series of magnets, which, in one method, are arranged in what is known as a cascade; *i.e.*, the watery mass flows over small falls, the metallic parts being retained by the magnets and the remainder passing on. As the slip has to pass over a series of small falls in cascade fashion, any pieces of metal are certain to be extracted. (Prior to this process the various ingredients have been weighed and mixed in an agitator known as a blunger.)

The slip is, of course, too thin in consistency for moulding into ware, and must be made into a firm and plastic condition. This is done in a filter press, an appliance used in many trades. Briefly, this consists of a number of cloth bags in square frames, which are screwed together horizontally, the whole resembling a "square" loaf, cut into slices, but retaining the shape of the loaf. By pressure, the surplus water is removed and the clay, now in flat slabs, is rolled up and passed on to the "pug mill." This piece of machinery may be likened to the domestic mincer or meat grinder. Blades, revolving in a manner popularly known as the "spiral," knead the clay and force it through a circular opening, from which it emerges as a huge "sausage."

In the pottery industry, as in all other artistic crafts, mechanical means cannot effectively replace the dexterity of man or woman. The "pug mill," *e.g.*, is an admirable method for kneading the clay, but it cannot do it so effectively as an experienced pottery worker. Such a man would cut a lump of clay into two pieces and bang one on to the other, a process which he repeats many times. Obviously this is a slower and more expensive method, and cannot be used for the cheaper types of ware.

Throwing.—The clay is now ready for making into the ware. Everyone has heard of the potter's wheel, but many have probably not seen one or have an incorrect impression of this simple appliance, which plays such an important part in the making of some delightful pieces of pottery. It is not a wheel, as generally understood, but a circular, horizontal disc, which revolves at the will of the thrower. A ball of clay is thrown on to the "wheel," and then the "thrower," after getting it into the condition of plasticity he considers most correct, deftly transforms the ball of clay into whatever shape he is proposing to make, by pressing it with his fingers as the "wheel" revolves. In this way a symmetrical form is obtained. The art of the potter is infinite, and it is little wonder that his skill in transforming an ugly ball of clay into a bowl or vase of beautiful contour has moved poets to acclaim his craft.

For domestic articles, such as cups, the thrower may be aided by a mould, which is made of plaster of paris. The inside of the mould will correspond to the shape of the outside of the cup. It is a simple matter—to the experienced thrower—to press the clay into the mould until the desired thickness is obtained. The plaster of paris absorbs some of the moisture in the clay, which, besides contracting, becomes correspondingly harder, and therefore much more easily handled by the potter. The cup is then passed on to a man who turns (or trims) it on a lathe. The cup, of course, is not complete without a handle, which could not be thrown on the wheel. It is therefore "cast," the clay taking the shape of a plaster of paris mould. After trimming, the handle is affixed to the cup by dipping the ends in some "slip." When joining together two pieces of clay, it is important to ensure, as far as possible, that the percentage of moisture is approximately the same in each, for if one is drier than the other, unequal contraction will take place, with the result that the two will part company. This is one of the many contingencies that the potter has to guard against, and it will readily be seen that a large amount of skill and experience is necessary for the production of good pottery.

Turning.—This important operation in the manufacture of pottery has been mentioned above. It will be obvious that the products from the thrower's hands will need trimming if a smooth finish is required. Some potters, particularly those known as "artist potters," who, however, usually work with coarser "bodies" (heavier types of clay), like to leave the marks of the thrower's hands, just as some take a pride in the hammer marks on hand-wrought silver ware. In commercial production, particularly if moulds are used, as mentioned in the previous paragraph, a little trimming is necessary. When the ware is moulded, a process that will be described later, turning will be an essential operation.

It must be remembered that the clay, when it reaches the lathe, is becoming harder; at this stage it is known as "green hard," a condition which has been likened to hard cheese, while another description is "leather hard." In such a condition the cup or other article can be shaved or trimmed on a lathe just as a piece of wood can. Any unevenness can be removed, while, if a "foot" for the ware is required, this can be formed by the turner. An additional advantage of the lathe is the speed with which the ware may be "embossed" with decorations, such as beads, etc. While the ware revolves, the turner presses against it a little wheel, which has the decoration engraved upon it, in reverse.

The lathe used for this work resembles in many respects the machine used for wood or metal turning. The principal difference is the method of holding the article to be turned. In the pottery industry, the ware is placed in a "chum," a hollow drum that grips the piece at about half its length. When the exposed half has been finished, the ware is reversed and the process continued.

In the case of cups, and other ware requiring handles, it will be obvious that the turning must be done before the handle is applied.

Jolleying.—Although the methods of the early potter have remained almost unaltered in many respects, the large output of the modern factories makes it necessary to provide a means whereby a more rapid production of ware can be maintained. The "jolley" takes the place, to some extent, of the thrower; but man's skill is still needed to ensure the output of good pottery. Again, we have a small revolving disk, and on this a mould of the exterior of the article to be made is placed. Into this a slab or "bat" of clay is thrown. The mould forms one side of the piece of ware (the exterior), and the interior is shaped by a "profile" which is brought down by a lever and cuts away the clay to the desired thickness, the mould on the platform being revolved during the process.

For flat ware, such as plates and saucers, the procedure is slightly different. Such pieces are made upside down, the bottom of the plate, or saucer, being uppermost. The mould in this case will furnish the shape of the interior or top of the ware, while the profile, which is lowered on to the revolving slab of clay by the lever, will form the underside.

When the piece of ware has been fashioned on this machine, it is taken, still on the mould, to a drying chamber. Here the clay contracts and the saucer, or whatever it may be, is lifted away and passed on for finishing. This means the trimming of the edges, and smoothing with a flannel and fine sandpaper. It it should be a cup, a handle has, of course, to be applied.

Pressing.—This process consists of placing soft clay, which has been beaten out to the required thickness, into plaster of paris moulds, which may form one half of the ware. When the halves have been made they are brought together to form the whole, the joints being finished off. After sufficient water has evaporated, the ware can be removed, and handles, knobs, feet, or any other parts which have been fashioned in a like manner, are then attached.

Casting.—Many will have a passing acquaintance with this process, for the method of casting metals is well known; in the pottery industry the "slip" takes the place of the molten metal. The "slip" is poured into plaster of paris moulds, which absorb some of the moisture, leaving a layer of clay. When the clay is of sufficient thickness, the surplus "slip" is poured away, and the mould, with its clay lining, is taken to the drying room, where the ware contracts and hardens, making it suitable for removing and finishing off as in the case of pressed ware. The moulds may form only part of the finished article, the remainder being made in other moulds. When ready, the pieces from each mould are joined together. It will be seen that casting is similar to pressing, except that the potter is able to commence with an easily handled material (the "slip") which, owing to its limpidness or low viscosity, rapidly takes the shape of the mould. The process is therefore simpler and, consequently, cheaper. It is a method which lends itself admirably to the reproduction of figures and other modelled ware.

Mould-Making.—Plaster of paris moulds have been frequently mentioned in the various processes already described, and it will be useful to interpose here a brief description of the making of these moulds, as, undoubtedly, it is an important feature in modern pottery manufacture.

Plaster of paris is made from gypsum, a naturally occurring mineral composed of calcium sulphate. Gypsum is hydrated, *i.e.,* it contains a certain amount of combined water, which can be driven off by heat. When it has been calcined an amorphous powder is left, known as partially hydrated calcium sulphate, or plaster of paris.

This material has a peculiar property in that it swells when water is added, forming an absorbent solid, which lends itself readily to the formation of various shapes by carving, turning on the lathe, etc. Every cup, jug, or other piece of ware produced, must, of course, have had an original from which it is duplicated. The original is modelled in clay and is solid, *i.e.*, it gives the shape of the *exterior* only. From this model the plaster of Paris mould is prepared. This is a process that needs special care, for upon the mould the accuracy of all the reproductions depends. The mould may be in three parts, two halves, forming the sides, and a bottom. From this mould a duplicate of the original can be produced, and, in turn, moulds for reproductions. The number of pieces of a mould will depend upon the shape of the article to be made.

Modelling.—As stated above, every piece of ware produced must have had an original, which may vary from an ordinary teapot to a dainty shepherdess, or a group of several figures. The modeller's skill in this matter may be likened to that of the artist who paints a picture for reproduction. The modeller creates and the craftsman copies.

But the task is not ended when the modeller has finished his work; considerable skill is required to reproduce his work faithfully. When the modeller's work takes the shape of a figure in fanciful pose, many moulds have to be made, and the number may be as high as 28. Arms, legs, hands, head and many other parts have to be moulded separately and then joined to make the figure created by the modeller. As the pieces are often hollow, it will readily be seen that great care must be exercised by the man whose occupation it is to assemble the various parts, as undue pressure on the pieces would cause distortion and the spirit of the modeller's art would be lost.

A further difficulty, which affects the modeller, is that allowance must be made for contraction. The mould from his model will, of course, give a piece of ware corresponding, in its raw state, to the original; but when the reproduction has lost its moisture and has been further contracted by the firing, the figure (or whatever it may be) will be much smaller. This shrinkage may be as much as one-tenth. Obviously the modeller must keep this in mind when at work on an original.

Firing.—The processes described have led up to the first firing of the ware, when what is known as "biscuit" is produced.

The shape of a pottery oven, or kiln, will be familiar, by photographs and drawings, to many. The huge, bottle-shaped ovens are peculiar to the pottery industry. They are heated by fires placed at intervals at the base. Coal is the fuel principally employed, but electrically heated ovens have made an appearance, while oil and gas have their advocates. On the Continent and in the Far East wood often plays an important part in the firing.

As thousands of pieces of ware may be fired at one time, the arrangement in the oven needs special care. It would not, of course, be possible just to stack clay cups on top of one another; even if they kept in position, the weight on those below would, at least, cause distortion. The ware is therefore placed in "saggars," which are largely fireclay receptacles resembling big cheeses in shape. In these the "green" ware is placed, separated by ground flint, which, owing to its very high melting, or fusing point, will not affect the ware in the oven. The "saggars," when filled, are "placed" in the ovens, special care being taken to see that they are perfectly level. As a rule, hollow ware (such as cups) is placed at the top of the oven and flat ware (such as plates) at the bottom. When filled, the ovens are sealed up and the heating is commenced, continuing for about 50 to 60 hours. For the first 24 hours the firing is slow, *i.e.*, the temperature is not raised unduly, to drive out the moisture. The temperature will then be increased until it reaches about 1,300° C. A necessary precaution is to ensure that the temperature never falls back. This is part of the fireman's responsibility; he must also know when the firing is complete. He has means of testing the rate of progress of the firing, but the control of the temperature and the length of time given needs skilful judgment. Very useful pyroscopes for determining the proper heat treatment attained in an oven are employed frequently. Some are small tetrahedra, called cones, compounded from a series of ceramic mixtures. These cones are placed in the oven where they may be observed by the fireman. As a certain temperature is reached, depending somewhat on the rate of temperature increase, they bend so that the apex gradually touches the base. The finishing point of the firing may thus be indicated. These pyroscopes are called Seger cones after their inventor. Other temperature indicators are Holdcroft's thermoscopes. These are small bars supported at their ends in a horizontal position. When the critical temperature of a bar is reached it sags in the middle. The Seger cones and Holdcroft's thermoscopes are given a variety of numbers, the refractoriness of the cone or bar increasing as the numbers go up. Pyrometers, scientific instruments for measuring heat, may be employed instead of the pyroscopes. When the firing is complete the oven is allowed to cool; this takes about the same time as the firing—50 to 60 hours.

The biscuit ware, when it leaves the oven, must be translucent, and it is the aim of all the makers to obtain a ware with a perfect translucent body, free from blemishes.

Glazing.—When the "biscuit" ware produced by the first firing has been sorted (for the rejection of any pieces containing flaws), and cleaned, it is ready for the "dipper," the man who dips the piece into a tub of glaze. The glaze is made from a variety of ingredients which, when fused, form what might be termed "glass," for the glaze on a piece of china is really a glass. Lead is an important ingredient in many glazes and the question of lead poisoning has long been a problem in the pottery industry; but this is being overcome by the introduction of low-solubility glazes.

It may appear a simple matter to dip a cup into a tub of glaze, but here, as in most of the processes through which the ware has to pass, the skill of the worker is all important.

The ware, with its coating of glaze, has now to be fired again, when the opaque covering will be rendered translucent. The china is arranged in saggars, the round, cheese-shaped, fireclay receptacles already mentioned, but this time the saggar will be glazed inside, otherwise trouble would arise owing to absorption. The saggars are "placed" or stacked in the oven. This oven is known as the "glost" oven, and the man who stacks the saggars containing the glazed ware is called a "glost placer." Before the ware reaches the "glost placer" it passes through a drying room and is cleaned. Where there are small holes in the ware, in pepper pots, for instance, any glaze filling the openings must be entirely removed.

The saggars are arranged in the oven, as in the case of biscuit ware, but this time rolls of fireclay are placed between the saggars. This clay, by the pressure of the saggar above, effectively prevents any products of combustion from reaching the glaze, which, obviously, would be spoiled.

Decorating.—In the early days of pottery making, decoration was not as we understand it to-day—it was confined more to shapes than applied colours. Those who are familiar with the Greek urns will readily appreciate the beauty of the outlines; but in the 20th century pottery is judged more by the decorative scheme. Our modern potters do, of course, pay considerable attention to shapes; but the general public, with an appetite for colour, looks for applied decoration.

The limitations, and the great skill required by the pottery artist, are little known to the average purchaser in a retail establishment. Unlike most other decorative processes, the colours, especially if under the glaze, have to be subjected to a very high temperature for the glaze itself demands this, and therefore many pigments are unsuitable, as they would be destroyed by the heat. Metallic oxides are used, such as cobalt oxide for blue, uranium oxide for yellow, chromium oxide for green, iron oxides for reds and reddish browns.

Underglaze decoration is particularly suitable for household ware, as it is indestructible, and cannot be worn off in use. On the commoner types of domestic china the design would probably be "printed," a process which is carried out as follows. A copper plate is engraved with the design, which is filled with colour mixed with oil. The printer cleans off any surplus colour and then applies a sheet of tissue paper (which has been water sized) to the plate. The copper plate, with the paper above, is then passed through a roller press, which causes the decoration to adhere to the paper. The tissue is now pressed on to the ware, and on its removal, by soaking in water, the decoration remains behind. The design will probably be in outline and this may be filled in by hand, an operation cleverly carried out by girls. When the decoration is complete the next step is to remove the oil, for this would interfere with the application of the glaze. To do this the ware is placed in a kiln, where it is fired at a low temperature, though a sufficiently high one to destroy the oil and leave the colour "fixed." The china is now ready for the glaze, and is finished as already described. Hand-painted work can also be done under the glaze—with a limited palette.

For overglaze decoration a much wider range of colours is possible. A flux is added so that the resulting colours are really glasses, although enamels, as they are called in the industry, is a better term, which will be readily understood if one thinks of the enamelled ware in jewellers' shops—not the air-dried enamel used by house decorators.

Many pieces of domestic ware have a gold band or a gold treatment somewhere in the decoration. This is applied in two forms: "best" gold and "liquid" gold, which is an alloy. The "best" gold comes out of the kiln in a dull condition, but can be burnished to a bright tone. The "liquid" is bright when it leaves the kiln, but it has not the beauty or the wearing qualities of the other. There is a type of decoration known as "acid gold." A design is etched on to the glaze with hydrofluoric acid, which eats away the glaze unprotected by a "resist." The etched part may be coated with "best" gold, which, after being fired, is burnished, with the result that the gold in the depressions formed by the etching remains dull, while the burnished part is bright.

The decoration particularly suitable for rapid production is that of lithography. Lithographed designs are quite common for the cheaper classes of ware, and, while they may not always appeal to the critical eye, nevertheless satisfy a large percentage of the population.

The design is made up on several stones, one for each colour. These colours are transferred to sheets of paper, so that the complete decoration is obtained on one sheet. We have now what is commonly termed a "transfer." This is applied to the ware, the design remaining after the removal of the paper. The colours are fired in the enamel kiln.

A type of decoration that has not been employed to any great extent since the 19th century is that obtained by building up flowers, in clay, petal by petal, on the ware. This calls for exceptional skill on the part of the artist.

Very fine effects are obtained with a process of decoration known as "pâte-sur-pâte." Commercially various designs are modelled in white clay and affixed to the ware.

THE USES OF CHINA

Owing to its acid and heat resisting properties china finds a special use in chemical industries. It will often be found in large industrial concerns where cleanliness is of great importance. It is even employed in grinding—porcelain balls pound materials in a cylindrical machine known as a "ball mill." Porcelain is also used for the linings of these mills.

It is a splendid material for insulating, and consequently is much used by the electrical industry. In Central Europe the bowls of tobacco pipes are composed of porcelain.

Its use in domestic ware is well known, while almost everyone possesses a dainty figure or some other piece of ornamental porcelain. (*See* also POTTERY AND PORCELAIN; EARTHENWARE.)

See Emile Bourry, *A Treatise on Ceramic Industries* (trans. from the French with some additional notes by Alfred B. Searle), giving a complete description of pottery processes; *The Manual of Practical Potting* (ed. Charles F. Binns); Rudolf Hainbach, *Pottery Decorating* (English trans. published); William Burton, *Porcelain*, describing the nature, art and manufacture of porcelain; A. Malinovzsky, *Ceramics*, a book for chemists and engineers in the pottery industry; C. F. Binns, *The Potter's Craft*, for the studio potters, schools, etc.; Chas. J. Noke and H. J. Plant, *Pottery*, a small popular book by two men well known in the pottery industry; *A Text Book for Salespeople engaged in the Retail Section of the Pottery and Glass Trades*, written by an expert committee in conjunction with the Education Committee of the Pottery and Glass Trades' Benevolent Institution for the guidance of students. (G. C.)

UNITED STATES CHINAWARE

Earthenware.—The tableware made in the United States represents to a very large extent a high grade of white earthenware, also called semi-vitreous or white ware. This product is made in 60 potteries and its composition is approximately as follows: Ball clay 24%, feldspar 12, china clay or Kaolin 29, flint 35. The use of American clays has steadily replaced the imported materials. The biscuit firing is done at about 2,282° F, pyrometric cone 9, the glost firing at 2,150°, cone 5, and the decorating firing at 1,330°, cone .017. The glaze is invariably a boro-silicate of the alkalies, lime, lead and zinc. The operations are practically the same which prevail in Staffordshire (England) except that both the bisque and the glost firing are carried to a higher temperature.

The use of tunnel kilns for all three firings has become very extensive. Ivory coloured ware is produced in large quantities and this colour is obtained through the use of larger amounts of American ball clay and the introduction of yellowish firing kaolins. The tendency towards the application of vivid coloured glazes is very marked at the present time. Considerable under-glaze decoration is applied. The principal centre of the white earthenware industry is near East Liverpool, O., including potteries located just across the Ohio river, at Newell and Chester, W. Va. Within a short distance of East Liverpool factories are operating at Sebring, East Palestine, Minerva, and Carrollton, O. Formerly, a considerable quantity of white ware was produced at Trenton, N.J. But this activity has diminished to comparatively small operations.

Vitreous Ware.—The demand for non-absorbent, vitreous table ware for hotels and restaurants has stimulated the American potters to develop such a product quite obviously from the semi-vitreous type of body through the increase in fluxing material and the raising of the bisque firing temperature. Thus, the composition of a vitreous body would be as follows: Feldspar 15%, flint 38, ball clay 6, china clay or kaolin 40, whiting 1. The biscuit firing is carried to cone 11, or about 2,300° F. The resulting product shows the "stony" type of vitrification as distinguished from the "glassy" structure, possesses great toughness and mechanical strength and is translucent but markedly less so than the hard fire porcelains of continental Europe and bone china. The processes are essentially the same as practised in the earthenware manufacture except that, previous to the biscuit firing, the green flat ware is sanded, in which operation sand is shaken between the individual plates of a bung. The glaze is practically the same as that of earthenware though it is fired to a somewhat higher temperature. Under-glaze decoration is used to a large extent though largely confined to lines and plain printing. However, increased application is being made of polychrome lithographic transfer, decalcomania, as the development of the industry extends to the production of household china. Over-glaze decoration is also applied. The vitreous tableware industry is scattered and factories are located at Trenton, N.J., Syracuse, N.Y., Beaver Falls, Pa., New Castle, Pa., Wheeling and Clarksburg, W.Va., and Wellsville, O.

Belleek China.—There is produced in the United States a highly decorated grade of china, known as the Belleek type, which is named after a similar porcelain produced in Ireland. This product has attained an international reputation under the name of Lenox china. The porcelain is highly translucent, of an ivory colour and has a texture well suited for ornate decoration. The main flux of the body is a pre-fused, glassy mass, composed of feldspar, flint and alkalies. The body thus consists of this flux, feldspar, china and ball clay. The biscuit firing temperature is considerably below the maturing point of the other types of porcelain. The glaze is a very brilliant boro-silicate of the alkalies, lime, lead and zinc.

The principal production of this type of china is at Trenton, N.J.

Hard Fire China.—Hard fire china, similar to the porcelains of Austria, Czechoslovakia, France and Germany, with a low temperature biscuit and high glost fire, is produced only by two factories and on a comparatively small scale. The body employed is somewhat more silicious than the typical European product.

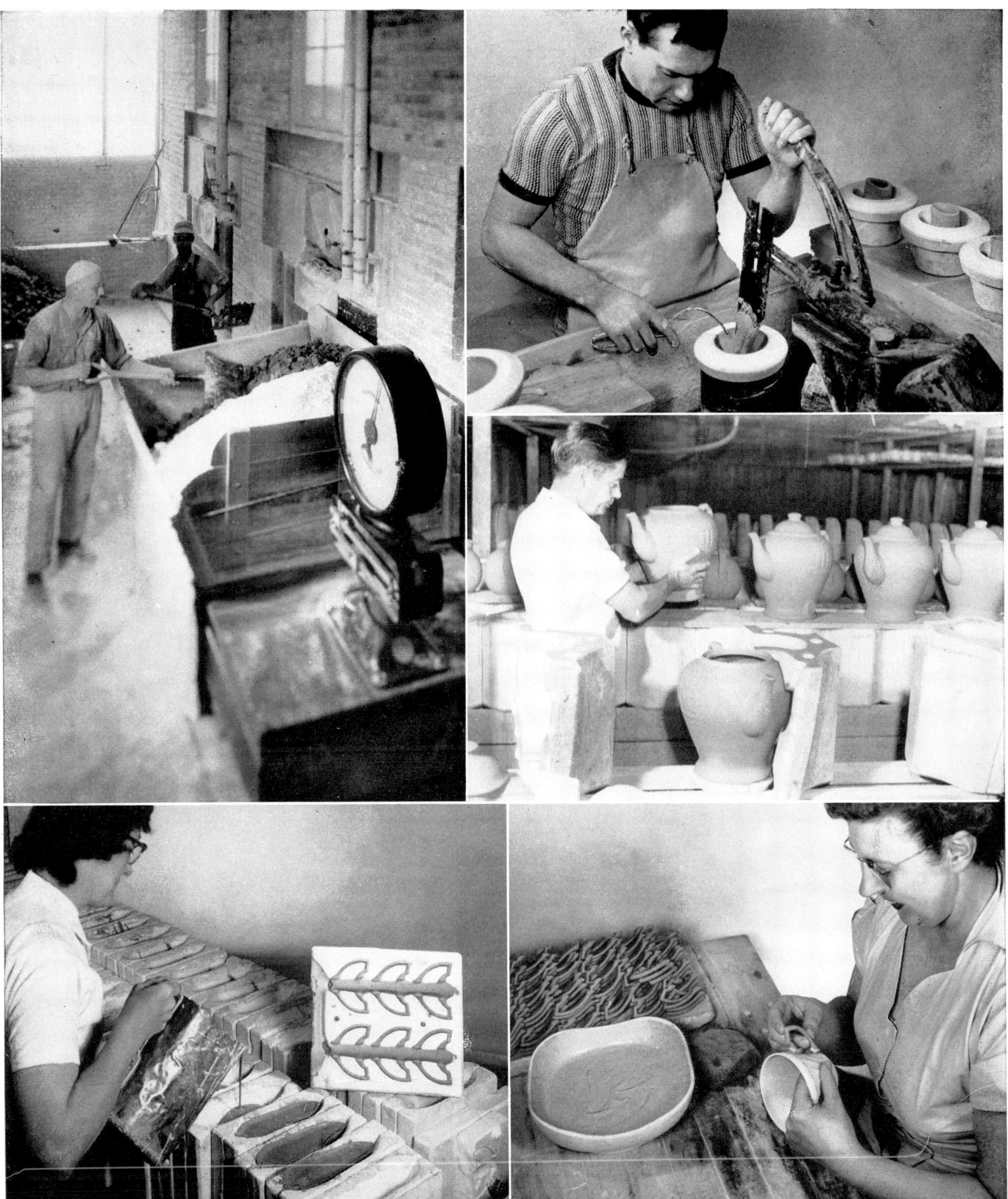

ALL PHOTOS BY COURTESY OF UNITED STATES POTTERS ASSOCIATION

STAGES IN THE MANUFACTURE OF POTTERY AND CHINAWARE

Top left: Careful weighing and blending of materials, an important step in the manufacture of fine chinaware

Top right: Forming a cup in the jigger. Liners have been thrown in the moulds on the right to ensure uniformity in the finished cups

Centre right: Casting of hollow pieces. Liquid slip—a controlled solution of water and various minerals in suspension—is poured into a plaster mould. Capillary attraction draws moisture to mould, forming a solid wall of clay on the inside of the mould

Bottom left: Cup handles are cast on "trees" for easy removal from the mould. They are trimmed and finished before being attached to cups

Bottom right: Handles being joined to cups after being dipped in an adhesive solution of clays

CHINAWARE

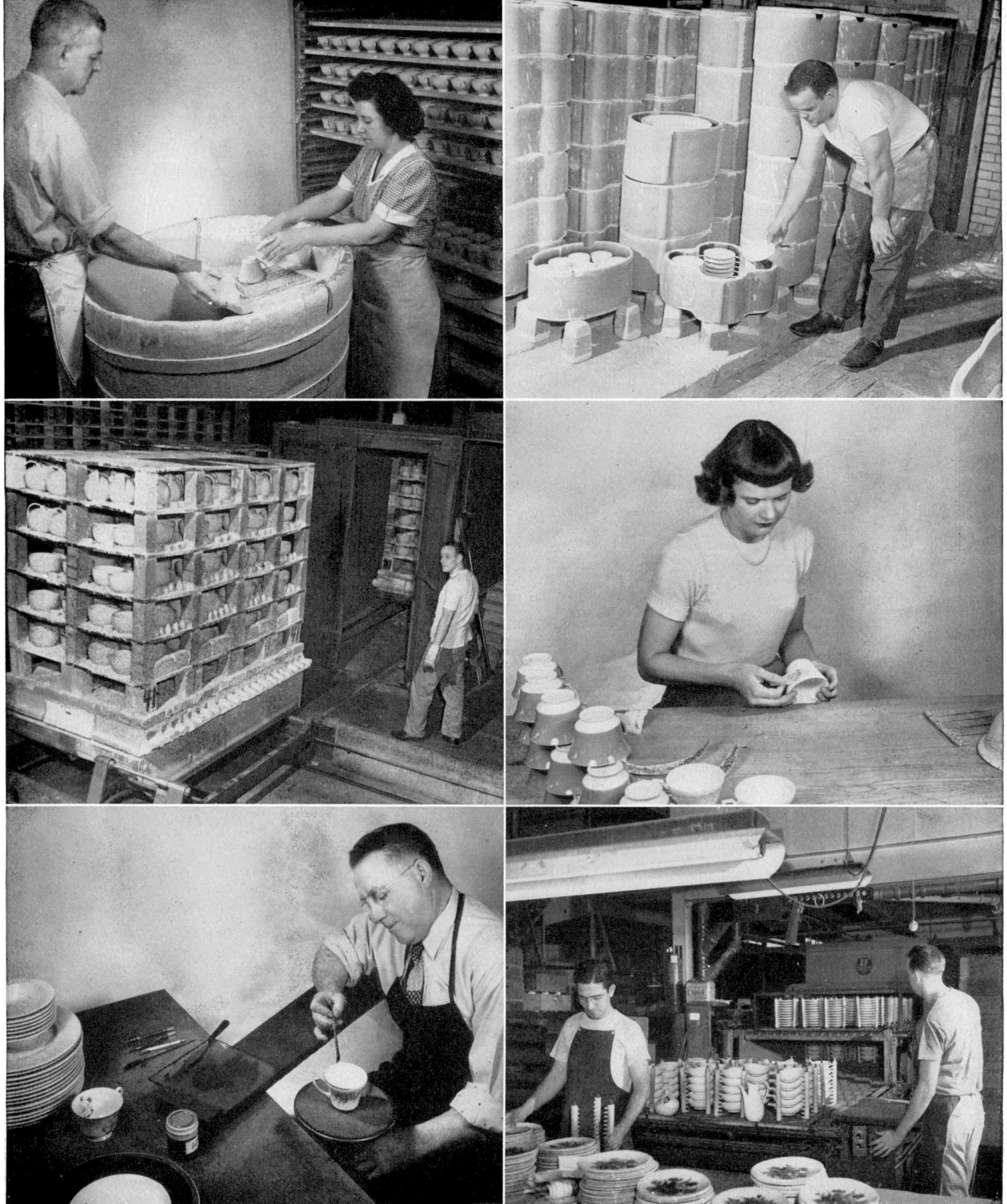

ALL PHOTOS BY COURTESY OF UNITED STATES POTTERS ASSOCIATION AND (CENTRE RIGHT) O. H. BIZZELL, (BOTTOM RIGHT) DON ECKERT STUDIO

FIRING AND DECORATING

Top left: Dipping cups into tubs of glaze, a process to which all china for domestic purposes is subjected. This glaze after firing in a kiln makes an extremely hard and durable finish

Top right: A "sagger" in which glazed ware is being arranged for firing. The pieces are packed separately, extreme care being taken that no mark is left on the glaze

Centre left: Kiln fireman removing car of ware from firing kiln

Centre right: Applying decalcomania decoration to ware. Decal is placed over previously applied varnish and rubbed to make it adhere smoothly

Bottom left: Liner applying gold or other colours to ware in final decoration

Bottom right: Final firing in electric kiln to burn decoration into finished ware which has approximately the composition: Kaolin, 50%, feldspar, 25% and flint, 25%. The glost firing temperature is somewhat lower than that of European practice, being close to 2,410° F., or cone 12. There are indications that a considerable expansion in the production of hard fire porcelain is to be looked for in the near future. Laboratory and technical porcelain is being produced by two factories.

The subject of high fire porcelain cannot be dismissed without referring to an American development which works with exceedingly high temperatures. Through the introduction of synthetic mixtures or of natural minerals of the sillimanite group which have the general composition, $Al_2O_3SiO_2$, aluminous porcelains are produced which show remarkable mechanical strength and resistance to thermal shock. These properties are associated with the development within the fired body, of a crystalline compound, mullite, which has the composition, $3Al_2O_32SiO_2$. This compound is formed in all porcelains but in these special bodies, through the deliberate exclusion of nearly all crystalline silica and its replacement by the aluminum silicate just referred to, a large proportion of the mass consists of mullite. The porcelains are fired at temperatures between 2,650–3,000° F., cones 17 to 30. The dense crystalline structure and low thermal expansion are responsible for the high mechanical strength and resistance to thermal shock. This type of porcelain is marketed in the form of insulators for spark plugs and other electrical purposes, laboratory and technical ware, special refractories, etc. Products of this kind are known on the market as sillimanite porcelain.

Bone china, as made in England, is produced in the U.S. only in small quantities, because of the lack of the specially skilled and trained workers required in its manufacture. (A. V. B.)

CHINCHA ISLANDS, 14 or more small islands in the Pacific ocean, about 12 mi. from the coast of Peru, to which country they belong, opposite the town of Pisco, and 106 mi. from Callao, 13° 38′ S., 76° 28′ W. The largest of the group, known as the North Island or Isla del Norte, is only four-fifths of a mile in length, and about a third in breadth. They are of granitic formation and rise from the sea in precipitous cliffs, worn into countless caves and hollows. Their highest points attain an elevation of 113 ft. The islands have yielded a few remains of the Chincha Indians. They were formerly noted for vast deposits of guano, and its export was begun by the Peruvian government in 1840. The supply, however, was exhausted in 1874. In 1853–54 the Chincha islands were the chief object in a contest known as the Guano war between President Echenique and General Castilla; and in April 1864 they were seized by the Spanish rear admiral, Pinzón, in order to bring the Peruvian government to apologize for its treatment of Spanish immigrants. The government enforces strong regulations for the protection of the sea birds, and repairs the cliffs with cement as needed to ensure the continuance of guano deposits.

CHINCH BUG, a North American heteropterous insect (*Blissus leucopterus*) occurring in most parts of the United States, but particularly destructive to grain crops in the valleys of the Mississippi, Missouri and Ohio rivers. It is a most destructive native insect, and has frequently damaged crops to the extent of many million dollars in a single year. It was first noticed in North Carolina, at the close of the Revolutionary War, was first described and named by Thomas Say in 1831, and with the growth of agriculture in the middle west, soon became a pest of the first importance. By 1871 it had damaged the wheat, oat and barley crops of several midwestern states to the estimated amount of $30,000,000. The loss in 1887 to maize, wheat and oats was estimated at $79,000,000. Federally supported and organized programs, conducted to protect crops from the insects, have been successful. In one year, for instance, it was estimated that through a combined federal and state expenditure of $1,212,776 in a co-operative effort to control the chinch bug, at least $25,500,000 worth of corn was saved from destruction.

Originally the chinch bug fed upon wild grasses, but when the cultivation of wheat reached its native haunts it multiplied enormously. It is a small black and white insect, about ⅙ in. long, and when full grown has a long-winged and a short-winged form. The adult bugs hibernate in sheltered places, usually clustering about the roots and bases of grassy plants. In the spring they lay their eggs behind the lower blades of the grain or in the ground around the plants.

The young, when hatched, are bright red in colour, and begin at once to suck the sap of the plants. They grow rather rapidly and shed their skins five times, the adult being the sixth stage. (*See* fig. 6 under HEMIPTERA.) By the time the majority are full grown, or even before, the wheat has become too hard to suck, or harvest begins, and they are then compelled to migrate in search of food. The cropping systems prevalent in the middle west at once offer new sources of food.

In seasons of abundance the bugs march in throngs from the wheat to the maize. The full-grown individuals do not generally take wing, but walk along the ground. Occasionally, however, at this time they take wing and scatter. There is generally a second generation on maize, the adults appearing in the autumn and flying back to their winter quarters at the roots of wild grasses or other sheltered places. The chinch bug is most susceptible to weather conditions, and with wet weather in the late spring and toward the end of July the young are either destroyed by the water or develop an epidemic fungous disease.

In dry weather, however, they flourish. Seasons in which they occur in great numbers are rarely consecutive. Outbreaks have lasted for two or three years, but, in the same locality, years of abundance are apt to be separated. Serious damage may be obviated by proper cropping of farms, reducing the acreage of small grains and using the land for immune crops. Resistant varieties of grains have also been found.

At the time of migration, millions may be destroyed by barriers of various kinds, including ditches, and lines of coal tar, creosote or gas tar, or creosoted paper fences.

See *Farmers' Bulletin* No. 1780, U.S. dept. of agriculture; and *Iowa Extension Circular* No. 213. (L. O. H.; X.)

CHINCHILLA, a small gray hopping rodent (*Chinchilla lanigera*), the size of a squirrel, inhabiting the eastern slopes of the Andes in Chile and Bolivia, at altitudes between 8,000 and 12,000 ft. It typifies not only the genus *Chinchilla,* but the family Chinchillidae (*see* RODENTIA). The chinchilla is about 10 in. in length, exclusive of the long tail, and in the form of its head somewhat resembles a rabbit. It is covered with a dense soft fur of a delicate French gray, darkly mottled on the upper surface and dusky white beneath, the ears being long, broad and thinly covered with hair. Chinchillas live in burrows. They associate in communities, forming their burrows among loose rocks, and coming out to feed in the early morning and toward sunset. They feed on roots and grasses, and when eating they sit on their haunches, holding their food in their forepaws. The fur (*q.v.*) of this rodent was prized by the ancient Peruvians, and the skins are exported in numbers to the markets, where they are made into muffs, tippets and trimmings. That chinchillas have not under such circumstances become extinct is owing to their fecundity, the female producing five or six young twice a year. The Peruvian chinchilla (*C. brevicaudata*) is larger, with relatively shorter ears and tail; while still larger species constitute the genus *Lagidium,* ranging from the Andes to Patagonia, and distinguished by having four in place of five front toes, more pointed ears, and a somewhat different skull. (*See* also VISCACHA.)

THE CHINCHILLA, A NATIVE OF THE SOUTH AMERICAN ANDES. ITS FUR IS EXTREMELY VALUABLE AND THE SPECIES IS NEARLY EXTINCT

CHINDE, a town of Portuguese East Africa and the seat of a district in the province of Zambezia, is situated at the mouth of the Chinde branch of the Zambezi river in 18° 40′ S., 36° 30′ E. Pop. (1936) was 3,894, of which some 150 were Europeans. Chinde, having superseded Quelimane, is the chief port for the Zambezi valley and the starting point for river traffic to the interior (to Tete and Sena). The harbour, which at high water has a depth of 18 to 19 ft., has remained undeveloped, serving primarily the lower Zambezi valley where sugar, cotton, ground-nuts and sisal are grown. A slip serves the stern-wheel river steamers which connect with the steamers visiting the port and ply up and down the river to Chindio and Tete. After the completion of the railroad from Beira to Tete and British Nyasaland in 1939, it lost much of its former importance which depended largely on the shipping to the British protectorate.

Unlike most Portuguese towns in East Africa, Chinde is a new settlement owing its origin to the discovery by D. J. Rankin in 1888 that the Chinde branch of the Zambezi was navigable from the ocean. In 1891 the British government leased a British concession of 20 ac. in order to permit storage and the entry of duty-free goods destined for Nyasaland. When, in 1923, following the opening of the Beira-Chindio in 1922, the concession ceased to exist, Chinde's commercial decline began. Previous to this the town was almost completely destroyed by a cyclone on Feb. 24, 1922, at which time more than 100 persons were killed.

The climate of Chinde is tropical and during the southern winter rather healthful; during the rainy season, which lasts from Dec. to March, it is unpleasant, particularly on account of the prevalence of malaria. Rainfall is rather heavy (about 58 in. annually), contributing to erosion, which makes the continual reconstruction of Chinde's buildings necessary. (H. A. WF.)

CHINDWIN, river of Burma, the largest tributary of the Irrawaddy, called Ningthi by the Manipuris. It is formed by the junction of the Tanai, the Tawan and the Tarôn or Turông, but there is doubt as to which is the main stream. The Tanai rises on the Shwedaung-gyi peak of the Kumôn range, 12 m. N. of Mogaung, and flows due north until it reaches the Hukawng valley, when it turns to the west and meets the Tarôn or Turông river. The last-named flows into the Hukawng valley from the north. Its sources are in the hills to the south of Sadiya, rising from 10,000 to 11,000 ft. above sea-level. It flows in a general east to west direction as far as its junction with the Loglai. It then turns south and breaks into the Hukawng valley a few miles north of Saraw and meets the Tanai about 10 m. above Kintaw village. Below the Hukawng valley the Chindwin is interrupted at several places by falls or transverse reefs. At Haksa goods have to be transhipped from large boats to canoes. Not far below this the Uyu river comes in on the left bank at Homalin, and from this point downwards steamers ply for the greater part of the year. The Uyu flows through a well-cultivated valley, and during the rainy season it is navigable for a distance of 150 m. from its mouth by steamers of light draught. Below Kindat, the only considerable affluent of the Chindwin is the Myit-tha, which drains the Chin hills. The Chindwin rises considerably during the rains, but in March and April is so shallow in places that navigation is difficult even for small steam launches. Whirlpools, narrows and sandbanks also cause great trouble. The extreme outlets of the river are 22 m. apart, the interval forming a succession of long, low, partially populated islands. The most southerly mouth of the Chindwin is, according to tradition, an artificial channel, cut by one of the kings of Pagān. It was choked up for many centuries, until in 1824 it was opened out by an exceptional flood.

CHINDWIN, UPPER and LOWER, two districts in the north-west border division of Burma. Upper Chindwin has an area of 16,037 square miles. Pop. (1941), 209,575. Lower Chindwin has an area of 3,480 square miles. Pop. 427,340. For further details *see* BURMA.

CHINESE ARCHITECTURE. The art of building in China has always been closely dependent on the intimate feeling of the Chinese people for the significance and beauty of nature. They arranged their buildings with special regard to the "spirits of earth, water and air," their ambition being not to dominate nature by their creations, as Westerners mostly do, but to co-operate with it, so as to reach a perfect harmony or order of the same kind as that which is reflected in the creations of nature. It was less the outward forms that interested them than the inner meaning, the underlying creative forces. This is most evident in the arrangement of some of the great tombs and shrines or in open-air altars dedicated to the divinities of heaven and earth. But it is also reflected in profane buildings such as the imperial palaces, which were planned and built according to sidereal or cosmological considerations. This appears even from the name used for the present and some earlier imperial palaces: Tzu Chin Ch'eng, the so-called Purple (or Violet) Forbidden City, of astronomical origin: the Heavenly Lord or Ruler Above was supposed to occupy a circumpolar constellation composed of 15 stars called the Purple Protected Enclosure, and as this was situated in the centre of the celestial world, so was the palace of the emperor, the human representative of the highest divine principle, supposed to be in the middle of the human world.

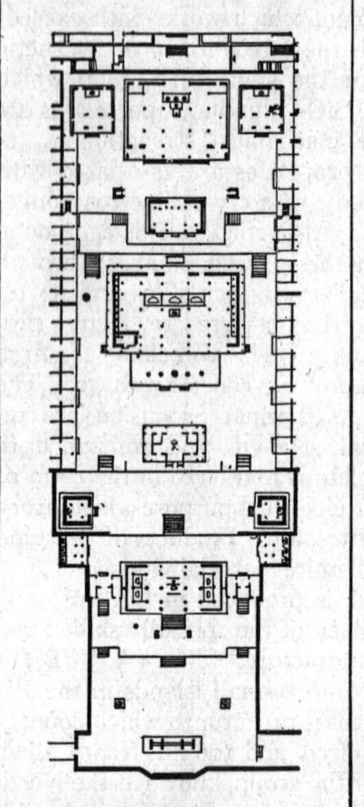

CHINESE TEMPLE PLAN
Showing the usual arrangement of placing the main buildings in a row, the one behind the other

The general arrangement and planning of the Chinese buildings have indeed very little in common with such artistic points of view as have been applied in Western architecture; they result rather from religious and philosophical ideas which have their roots in most ancient traditions. This accounts also for the uniformity, not to say monotony, of early Chinese architecture. The principles of construction have remained the same during many centuries, as have also the plans of the temples and palaces. The modifications of style which have been introduced are of comparatively small importance. It thus becomes possible to draw some conclusions from relatively late examples about the earlier buildings, which unfortunately are practically all destroyed; the wooden material has poorly withstood the ravages of fire and warfare, and the people have never made any serious efforts to protect their old buildings. It was mainly for the dead that the Chinese created more permanent abodes, and thus the tombs are the most ancient architectural monuments still existing in China. Besides these there are some cave temples hollowed out in the mountain sides and a few stone and brick pagodas of early date which will be mentioned later.

The Walls of China.—The earliest architectural monument above the soil in China is the "Great Wall," a massive fortification running along the northern and north-western frontier of the country. It was erected by the great Emperor Ch'in Shih Huang Ti shortly after he had reunited the different parts of the country into an empire (228 B.C.). No doubt minor parts of such a wall had existed before his time, but he planned his defence against the nomadic tribes on a very much larger scale than had any previous ruler. It is stated that nearly 750km. of the wall were built during his reign. Whatever truth this statement may contain, the fact remains that he laid the foundation of one of the world's grandest constructions, which, after many enlargements and restorations in the course of time, is still of great importance. The structural character of the wall is quite simple. It is built mainly of earth and stone, varies in height between 6 and 10 metres and is mostly covered by a coating of bricks. On the ridge of the wall runs a passage three or four metres wide between crenellated parapets, and at regular intervals square watchtowers rise above the ridge on which fires were lighted as soon as any danger was sighted. In spite of this uniformity, the wall is intimately connected with the landscape, rising in many parts almost like one of nature's own creations, accentuating the sharp ridges of the mountain chains and winding according to the undulations of the ground. It is the greatest and most monumental expression of the absolute faith of the Chinese in walls.

Walls, walls and yet again walls, form the framework of every Chinese city. They surround it, they divide it into lots and compounds, they mark more than any other structures the basic features of the Chinese communities. There is no real city in China without a surrounding wall, a condition which indeed is expressed by the fact that the Chinese used the same word *ch'eng* for a city and a city wall; there is no such thing as a city without a wall. It is just as inconceivable as a house without a roof. These walls belong not only to the provincial capitals or other large cities but to every community, even to small towns and villages. There is hardly a village of any age or size in northern China which has not at least a mud wall or remains of a wall around its huts and stables. No matter how poor and inconspicuous the place, however miserable the mud house, however useless the ruined temples, however dirty and ditch-like the sunken roads, the walls are still there and as a rule kept in better condition than any other building. Many a city in north-western China which has been partly demolished by wars and famine and fire and where no house is left standing and no human being lives, still retains its crenellated walls with their gates and watchtowers. These bare brick walls with bastions and towers, sometimes rising over a moat or again simply from the open level ground where the view of the far distance is unblocked by buildings, often tell more of the ancient greatness of the city than the houses or temples. Even when such city walls are not of a very early date (hardly any walls now standing are older than the Ming dynasty) they are nevertheless ancient-looking with their battered brickwork and broken battlements. Repairs and rebuildings have done little to refashion them or to change their proportions. Before the brick walls there were ramparts round a good many of the cities and towns as still may be seen at some out-of-the-way places; before the towns were built there were villages or camps of mud and straw huts surrounded by fences or ramparts of a temporary character.

Types and Construction of Buildings.—Whether the buildings were imperial tombs, Buddhist temples or memorial shrines dedicated to great philosophers or, on the other hand, of a profane nature, such as imperial palaces, dwelling-houses or administration offices, all were arranged within walls and in closed compounds according to similar principles. Characteristic of all these extensive compounds is the clear development of a main central axis running from north to south. The principal buildings, their courts and gateways are all placed in a row, one behind the other, while the secondary buildings are arranged at the sides of the courtyards, the façades, the doors and the gates of the principal buildings all facing south, an orientation which evidently was based on religious traditions. It was not by adding to the height of the buildings but by joining more courts to the compounds that these architectural compositions could be enlarged. There are princes' palaces in Peking which have as many as 20 courtyards and some of the large temples or monasteries have a still larger number of such units. As each compound is enclosed by a high wall it is quite impossible to obtain any idea of the arrangements from the outside, and at the larger palaces the different courtyards are also divided the one from the other by secondary walls with decorative gateways. The courts vary in size and the streets follow along the walls. Through such an arrangement the inner portions of the Purple Forbidden City of Peking became almost labyrinthine.

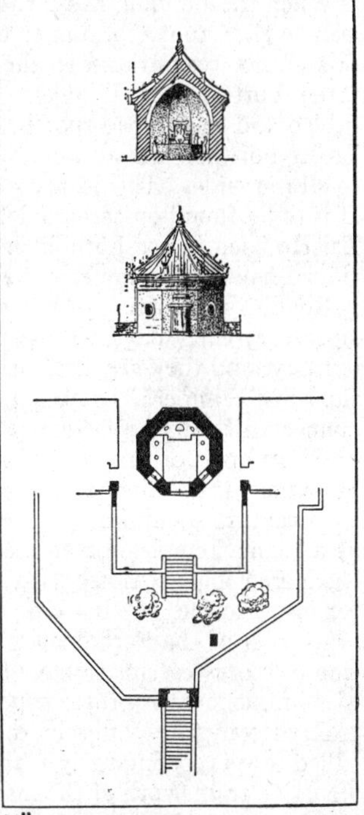
YÜ HUANG MIAO ON PIAO SHAN NEAR TSINANFU

The types of the principal buildings also remain the same, independently of their use as temples, palaces or dwelling-houses. The most common among these types is the hall, *tien, i.e.,* an oblong, rectangular room, usually divided by rows of round pillars or columns into three or more naves of which the foremost is usually arranged as an open portico; in other cases the open colonnade is continued all around the building. The interior is, as a rule, lighted by small windows placed quite low, but exceptionally there may be a second row of windows, giving a brighter effect; these are at a higher level. Very important for the decorative effect of the buildings is the broad substructure, the terrace and the far projecting roof. When the substructure is made higher, a so-called *t'ai* is created, *i.e.,* a shorter hall or a centralized building in two storeys on a high terrace with battered walls. Such *t'ai* are often mentioned in the old descriptions of palaces and cities. They seem to have been quite common since earliest times. In the Forbidden City of Peking this type of building is beautifully developed at the outer gates as, for instance Wu Men, where the great pavilion rises on a monumental terrace. Other characteristic examples of *t'ai* are the drum and bell towers which rise in the centre of many of the old cities in northern China, but similar buildings have also been used as storehouses, watchtowers and observatories. The general name for larger, many storeyed buildings is *lou,* a name which, however, is not used for the pagodas, whereas small buildings of two or more storeys often are called *ko,* and the open small pavilions *t'ing.* Furthermore, one finds in some of the palatial compounds as well as at many private dwelling-houses, particularly where they are connected with gardens, so-called *lang, i.e.,* long open galleries which serve to connect larger buildings.

WU-LIANG TIEN, SUCHOW, A 2-STOREYED HALL WITH BARREL VAULTS

Considering the most common Chinese buildings such as the *tien,* the *t'ai* and the *t'ing* in their entirety, we may be struck by the fact that the main body of the structures appears much less than in Western buildings. It is, figuratively speaking, pushed into the background by the broad terrace and the far projecting roof which throws a broad shadow over the façade. These two elements are of the greatest importance for the general effect of the structure. The terrace may be developed in various steps and provided with marble balustrades and decorative staircases, as, for instance, at the imperial palace and many large temples, or it may be simply a stone-lined substructure with one or two steps; but it always contributes to lift the building and to form a kind of counterbalance to the projecting roof. It is, however, at the *t'ai* that the substructures become of greatest importance. They may reach a height of 10 or 12 metres and be covered by a hall or pavilion of tower-like effect.

The buildings which rise on the terraces are made of wood; their structural frame is pure carpenters' work. The walls may look massive and appear to support the roof but, practically speaking, they have no structural importance. They are simply filled with brick or clay between the supporting columns. In the larger buildings the outer wall on the façades is usually not placed in the foremost row of columns but this is reserved as an open gallery. In some instances the portico is double, in other cases it is reduced to a few intercolumns in the middle. The building thus consists of a nave and aisles some of which might be completely or partly divided by filled-in walls, by which various rooms are created which indeed may be quite freely increased or decreased, the middle one being, as a rule, the broadest. The intervals between the columns are on the whole quite wide, and sometimes it happens that some columns are excluded in the midst of the building in order to create more free space. But the Chinese hall is not a longitudinal structure like the Greek temples (which also originally were built of wood); it expands transversally to the central axis which is indicated by the entrance door on the middle of the façade. The two short sides with the gables serve no other purpose than to end the hall; they have no decorative importance and no such emphasis as in the classic temples; sometimes they are hardly meant to be seen. The side walls may project as a kind of ante-room to the portico or the corners may be accentuated by columns. The Chinese builders were never so particular or consistent in the placing of the columns as the classical architects. They employed a material which allowed greater freedom than the marble beams and they yielded less to purely artistic considerations than to practical wants. The beauty and strength of their architecture depend mainly on the logical clearness of the constructive framework.

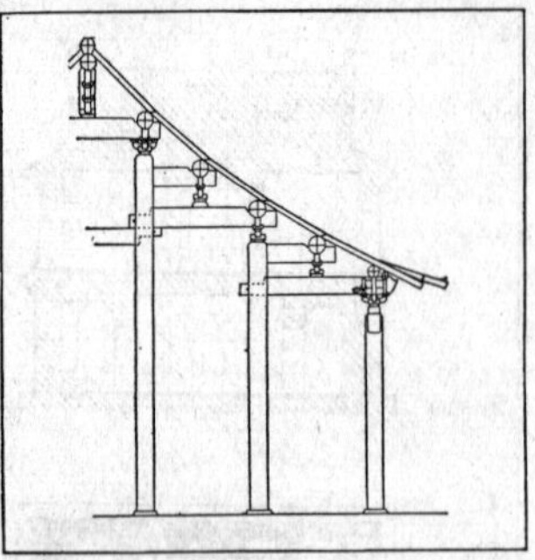

ROOF CONSTRUCTION ACCORDING TO YING TSAO FA SHIH (1103)

This comparative freedom in the placing of the columns is rendered possible also by the fact that they are not supporting posts as in the classical buildings. They are not provided with capitals and they do not support the entablature, but they are tied both longitudinally and transversally by beams which may cut into, or run through, the posts. The ends of the transverse beams often project in front of the columns, and the longitudinal beams form a kind of architrave which keeps the outer colonnade together. In larger buildings of comparatively late periods brackets or cantilevers are sometimes introduced on the columns below the tie beams but the real bracketing system which serves to support the eaves of the roof is situated above these. The roof brackets are, in their simplest form, two-armed and project in the earlier buildings only from the heads of the columns; but in the later buildings they become manifolded and are placed on the beams as well as on the posts, sometimes so close together that they create the impression of a cornice. It is mainly in the modifications of the bracketing system that one may trace an evolution of Chinese architecture.

The constructive system demanded that the buildings should be developed horizontally rather than vertically. Nevertheless, many of the large halls are erected in two storeys, though the second is often nothing more than a decorative superstructure without floor or windows. The lower storey forms a kind of outer compartment to the building and is covered by a lean-to shed roof while the main span or saddle roof covers the central portion of the building which rises to a greater height. Sometimes there is a coffered or painted ceiling over this portion but more often, particularly in the temples, the trusses and beams of the roof construction are left entirely uncovered.

Roofs.—It is evident that the development of the roof on the Chinese buildings is closely connected with the placing of the entrance door. This is not to be found on the short (gable) ends of the building but in the middle of the southern façade, which usually has also a free-standing row of columns. Most of the important buildings are indeed placed so that they can be appreciated only in full-front view, and their peculiar decorative effect thus becomes dominated by the broad high-towering roof. Whatever the original reason for this particular kind of roof may have been, it was gradually more and more developed from a decorative point of view. The builders may have felt the need of modifying the impression of weight and breadth, inevitably adhering to the enormous roof masses, and this was most successfully done by curving the sides and accentuating the tension and rhythm of the rising lines. This tendency becomes perhaps more evident in minor decorative buildings such as pavilions and pagodas, not to speak of small ornamental works in clay and metal on which the roof appears almost as a crown. The common dwelling-houses in northern China have, on the contrary, much smaller and less curving roofs and, if we may judge from reproductions of earlier buildings, such as the reliefs from the Han tombs in Shantung and some small clay models dating from the Han and Wei dynasties, it seems that the curved roof was then not very far developed. In the T'ang time (7th to 9th century) the characteristic shape of the roof was, however, fully developed.

It is possible that the origin of the far projecting and strongly curved roof may be looked for in primitive thatch-covered huts of a kind similar to those which still are to be seen on the Indo-Chinese islands. If so, it would first have been introduced in southern China (where indeed the curving and projecting roof always was more strongly developed than in the north), and later on, when the whole country became more of a cultural unit, in the northern provinces. When the Chinese once had realized the fine decorative effect of these roofs, they developed them freely at the expense of the main body of the building. The larger the roofs, the stronger becomes the effect of shade under the eaves and the more they seem to be disengaged from the supporting framework and to soar in the air. In many instances the roofs crown the building rather than cover it, and their decorative ornamentation with figures and animals on the ridges and on the corner ribs serve also to strengthen the impression of a decorative superstructure.

When the building has a roof in two storeys the lower one is a lean-to shed roof; the upper one, a span-roof—but the gables of this do not reach down to the eaves: they are cut at one-half or three-fourths of their height. This peculiar combination of the gabled and the hipped-roof is very common both in China and in Japan, but there are also buildings with complete hip-roofs sloping to all four sides. This is, according to the Chinese, the finest form. It is to be found on ceremonial edifices such as the big central hall Tai Ho Tien in the Forbidden City, Peking, and some of the sacrificial halls at the imperial tombs.

Buildings consisting of two superimposed halls have been in use since very early days, as may be seen on some reliefs of the Han dynasty, and they are also mentioned in many of the old descriptions of the imperial palaces, where such buildings sometimes were connected by flying bridges. Very characteristic and well-developed examples of this type of structure are still to be seen at Yung Ho Kung (the Yellow Temple) in Peking, which was erected in the 17th century as an imperial residence but afterwards consecrated as a Llama temple. Later Llamaistic buildings (from the Ch'ien Lung era) show at times an even further development in height, as for instance the Yu Hua Ko, a temple standing at the north-western corner of the Forbidden City. In southern China the distribution of storeys seems to have been still freer; there are large temples in Suchow with three superimposed halls and other more centralized structures built in the same way, which indeed may be called towers, particularly if they are placed on terraces. The constructive framework of the main roof consists generally of various beams arranged step-wise one above the other and supporting on their ends the purlins (*q.v.*). In smaller buildings all the transversal beams may be supported by columns which increase in length towards the middle of the room, the central one reaching up to the main ridge. It is, however, more common that only the lowest or the two lower beams rest directly on pillars, while the upper ones are carried by brackets and small posts rising from the lower beams. The purlins laid on these supports are arranged rather closely, so that the rafters may be stretched in curves, the projecting ones being spliced and bent upwards. The well-developed system of brackets and cantilevers which support this projecting part of the roof will be specially discussed later because it is in this that one may follow the development and decay of Chinese architecture.

The outer aspect of the roof is determined by the alternatively convex and concave tiles and the strongly accentuated corner ridges which curve at the ends in a kind of snout and often are provided with series of fantastic human and animal figures, called *k'uei lung tzŭ*. The main ridge-post is very high and decorated at both ends with a kind of fish-tailed owl, called *ch'ih wen,* which had a symbolic significance and served to protect the building against fire and other calamities. On ordinary buildings the roof tiles are of unglazed, lightly baked grey clay, but on the present imperial buildings all the roofs are laid with yellow glazed tiles, while some of the temples and smaller buildings erected for various members of the imperial family have deep-blue roof tiles. Green tiles are sometimes used on pavilions, gates and walls.

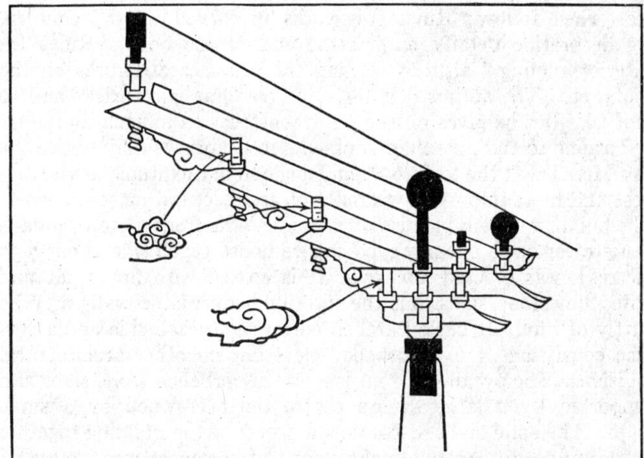

BRACKETING SYSTEM FROM A PAVILION AT THE CONFUCIUS TEMPLE IN CHÜFU. YÜAN PERIOD

The columns as well as the filled-in walls between them have usually a warm vermilion tone which becomes most beautiful when softened by dampness and dust. The beams and the brackets below the eaves are painted with conventionalized flower ornaments in blue and green, sometimes with white contours. The door panels of more important buildings are provided with ornaments in gold, but their upper part serves as windows and is fitted only with open lattice-work. On the whole it seems as if later times had tried to gain by decorative elaboration whatever of constructive significance and beauty had been lost.

Minor Pavilions and Gateways.—Besides the longitudinal halls in right angle to the central axis, indicated by the entrance door, there are more centralized structures on a quadrangular, polygonal or round plan, *i.e.,* pavilions or towers, which may be more than two storeys high. The most primitive type of pavilion is a square hut with corner posts which carry a flat or tent-shaped roof. Such pavilions are often seen in pictures representing famous philosophers meditating on nature. Unless they are quite open the walls may be made of bamboo or basket-work. The more elaborate pavilions on a polygonal or round plan developed in connection with the Chinese garden and have been abundantly used in the imperial parks since early times. Such kiosks, tea-houses and pavilions were placed on spots with historical associations or on hills or promontories where the view was particularly beautiful. Their shape and style were developed with a view to the rockeries and the growing trees; how well they fitted into such surroundings may still be seen in the wonderful gardens around the sea palaces in Peking. These small pavilions, half hidden between the trees, clinging on the rocks or rising on stones out of the mirroring water, often give us a more vivid and immediate impression of the charm and naturalness of Chinese architecture than the larger buildings. It was also pre-eminently through such small decorative structures that Chinese architecture became known and appreciated in the 18th century in Europe.

On the larger pavilions the roofs are usually divided into two or three storeys, thus adding greatly to the picturesque effect of the building, particularly when it is erected on a polygonal plan which gives it a number of projecting corner snouts. Beautiful examples of this kind of pavilion may be seen at the "Coal Hill" in Peking as well as in Pei Hai and other imperial parks. They have no walls, simply open colonnades supporting the roof which may give the impression of hovering in the air. When the portions between the successive roofs are enlarged and provided with balconies or colonnades the pavilion becomes a real tower, such as for instance the Fo Hsiang Ko (Buddha's Perfume Tower), which rises above the lake at the Summer palace.

Related to the pavilions by their open decorative effect, yet forming an architectural group of their own, are the *p'ai lou, i.e.,* free-standing gateways with three or more openings, which span the streets in many Chinese cities or mark the entrance to some sacred precincts, such as tomb or temple areas. The object of their erection was often to commemorate some outstanding local character or some important event in the history of the place or simply to mark a spot notable for its beauty or its sacredness. The earliest *p'ai lou* were, no doubt, simply large gateways made of wood and provided with inscribed tablets. These could easily be developed into more important structures by adding at the sides more posts and gateways, and they were soon executed in stone as well as in wood. From an architectural point of view they may be divided into two principal groups: the one consisting of *p'ai lou* with very tall side posts reaching above the transversal beams (which may be covered by small roofs); the other, of *p'ai lou* with shorter side posts covered by the roofs, so that the whole gateway has more likeness to a façade or an open flat pavilion. The supporting masts, which may be 4 or 8 or 12 according to the size and importance of the structure, are placed on stone plinths, sometimes decorated with lions, and tied together not only by cross-beams in two or three horizontal rows, but also by carved or painted panels or, in the case of stone *p'ai lou,* by flat slabs decorated with reliefs. Over each one of the openings is a separate small span-roof resting on brackets and usually covered with glazed pantiles. The *p'ai lou* thus contain some of the most characteristic features of traditional Chinese architecture, viz., the supporting posts, the curving saddle-roofs on double or triple rows of brackets, and the carved or painted friezes. They are essentially wooden structures. The whole character of these buildings as well as their decoration has been developed with a view to the special requirements of the material, but that has not prevented the Chinese from executing the same type of structure also in brick and in stone. The largest among them stand at the Ming tombs near Nankow and at the tombs of the Ch'ing emperors at Hsi Ling and Tung Ling, but the most elaborately decorated marble *p'ai lou* may be seen in some of the old cities in Shantung, such as Chüfu and Weihsien.

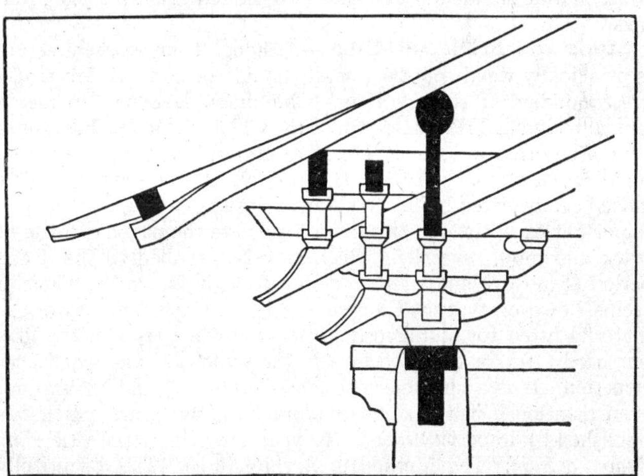

BRACKETING SYSTEM ON BELL-TOWER AT SHAO LIN SSU. YÜAN PERIOD

Closely connected with the *p'ai lou* are those highly decorative sham façades which used to be erected in front of important shops. They also consist of tall masts tied by cross-beams with manifold rows of brackets which support small roofs in one or two storeys.

Under these are panels decorated with human figures in relief or with brightly coloured floral designs in open-work into which the signboards of the shops are inserted. High masts or pillars are indeed much in favour in China; they are mostly used pair-wise, either free-standing in front of palaces (as the *hua piao*) or at the gateways of the dwelling compounds. Another type of gateway which is quite common consists of broad pillars made of masonry

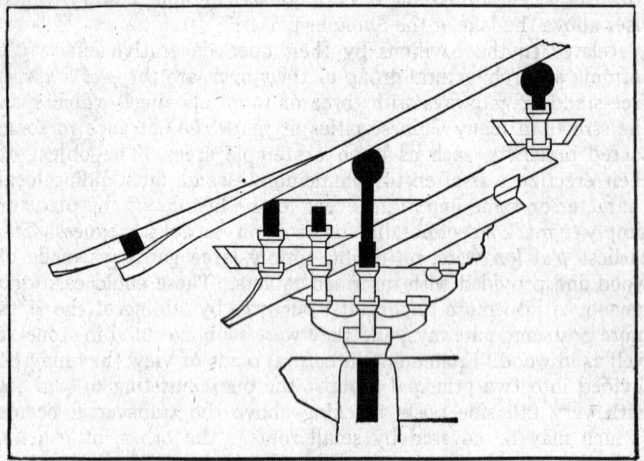

BRACKETING SYSTEM FROM THE CH'U TZU AN, SHAO LIN SSU, SUNG STYLE

and coated with glazed tiles, often with ornaments in various colours. When a span-roof connects the deep pillars a kind of small gatehouse may be created.

Of considerable importance also for the outward effect of the Chinese buildings are the balustrades which line the terraces and staircases in front of the buildings. They are in northern China mostly made of white marble and composed of square posts ending in sculptured finials between which ornamented panels and moulded railings are inserted. Such marble balustrades may be seen at most of the important temples and, in their richest development, on the terraces of the Three Great Halls (San Ta T'ien) in the Forbidden City in Peking. Here they are repeated in three different tiers and broken in many angles, according to the shape of the terraces, producing a splendid decorative effect, particularly as the white marble stands out in contrast to the red colour of the buildings.

Stone and Brick Buildings.—Although Chinese architecture is principally wood construction, it should not be forgotten that a great number of stone and brick buildings have been made in China, including bridges, for which the Chinese since earliest times have used brick and stone. The great majority of the still existing buildings in masonry are of comparatively late periods; very few indeed can be dated before the Wan Li era (1573–1619). The only important exceptions to this general rule are the pagodas made of brick and mud, several of which may be ascribed to the T'ang period (618–907) and a few to even earlier times. On the whole, it seems, however, that the Chinese regarded brick and stone work as material fitted for storehouses, walls, substructures and the like, but hardly for real architecture in the same sense as wood construction. It is a characteristic fact that brick buildings are not even mentioned in the standard work on architecture which was published by imperial order in the year 1103 under the title *Ying Tsao Fa Shih* (The Method of Architecture). This beautifully illustrated work in eight volumes (which has been issued in a modern reprint) is founded on the practical experience of architects and decorators, which the author, Li Chieh, collected from various sources. It gives everything that an educated Chinese towards the end of the Sung period considered the fundamentals of architecture. No stone or brick houses are mentioned, not even columns, door-frames or floors of stone. The only stoneworks particularly described are the plinths and corner pilasters, stairs, balustrades, dragon heads on staircases, thresholds and stones for the door-posts, besides canals, sluices, platforms, terraces, etc. The measures and instructions for the execution of all these various kinds of stonework are very accurate, but they are of no great importance for the architectural style. The constructive methods are treated only in the third part of the book, which contains "Rules for large work in wood," *i.e.,* framework of buildings, posts, trusses, rafters, etc. Then follows a chapter called "Rules for smaller works in wood," *i.e.,* doors, windows, partition walls, coffered ceilings, screens, cornices, gutters, staircases, door-panels, balustrades, besides Buddhist and Taoist house shrines, or *Fa yüeh,* decorative gate-façades erected in front of important houses, etc. Then follow "Rules for works in carved wood," concerning decorative details, and at the end of the book, "Rules for exterior roofing," also concerning the ornamental figures on the roofs, etc. The author devotes some paragraphs to bricks and to roof tiles but he gives no rules for construction in such materials.

Turning to the existing monuments in China, we may notice the Ssu Men Ta, at the temple Shen Tung Ssu in Shantung, as the earliest and most important example of architectural masonry work. The building, which in spite of its name—the Four-Gate pagoda—is no tower but a one-storeyed square house (each side about 7·35 metres), was erected A.D. 534. It is coated with finely cut and fluted limestone slabs, but the interior body of the walls may be partly of mud. It has an arched entrance on each side and a cornice consisting of five corbelled tiers but no other architectural divisions. The pyramidal roof is made of corbelled stone slabs and supported by a large square centre pillar crowned by a small stūpa. The solid and self-contained aspect of the building together with its fine proportions make it one of the most remarkable of Chinese architectural monuments. It is possible that similar buildings existed in earlier times when stone and brick may have been more freely used; the type may be observed, for instance, in the more or less house-shaped tomb pillars of the Han dynasty in Szechuan and Honan.

The next in date among the masonry buildings are some real towers or pagodas of the Sui and T'ang periods which will be mentioned later; most of them are made of packed clay or dirt in combination with stone or brick. Still more common is the combination of brick and wood construction. It can be carried out in different ways, either by lining a real wooden structure with brick walls or by placing a bracketed span-roof on strong brick walls, eventually adding pillars for interior support if the walls are too wide apart. This method of construction has been used in most of the outer city gate-towers, of which the oldest now preserved are from the beginning of the Ming period, and also in numerous watchtowers and storehouses on the walls that enclose the cities of northern China. A particularly fine example is the famous bell tower at Peking, often considered as a monument of the Yuan dynasty, though it was completely renewed during the reign of Chi'en Lung. All these buildings exhibit on the outside massive brick walls more or less regularly divided by windows or by rows of square loopholes which give to the battered façades of the big gate-towers a fortress-like appearance. The shape of the high roofs is, however, the same as on ordinary wooden structures, and if one examines these masonry buildings more closely, one usually finds wooden columns inserted in the walls as well as detached in the interiors.

The substructures of the gate and bell towers are in most cases pierced by tunnels or barrel vaults serving as passages. These may be either round or somewhat pointed, as for instance on the drum tower in Peking which actually dates from the Yuan period. The vaults are constructed with great care and precision, sometimes reaching a span of nearly 15 metres. Vaulting (but not the system of voussoirs) was undoubtedly known in China in early times; it was used in the tomb chambers which were covered with bricks, in the tunnels leading to these; when heavy brick walls were erected around the cities, barrel vaults followed suit for the entrances. The step from such constructions in brick to the building of cupolas is not a very long one. We do not know exactly when cupolas first came into use, but we have reason to assume that they were well developed in the T'ang period. As an evidence of this the mosque in Hangchow may be mentioned because the farthest rooms of this building are covered by three cupolas on pendentives (*q.v.*). The mosque may have been renewed in later times but in close adherence to the original model which, of course, was of Persian origin. Another kind of cupola is to be found over the hall of the big bronze elephant on the Omi mountain in Szechuan erected during the reign of Wan Li (1573–1619). The transition of the square room into a round cupola is here also accomplished by means of pendentives but outwardly the building is covered by a tent-shaped roof. One of the small sanctuaries on Piao shan near Tsinanfu is an example of a more pointed cupola.

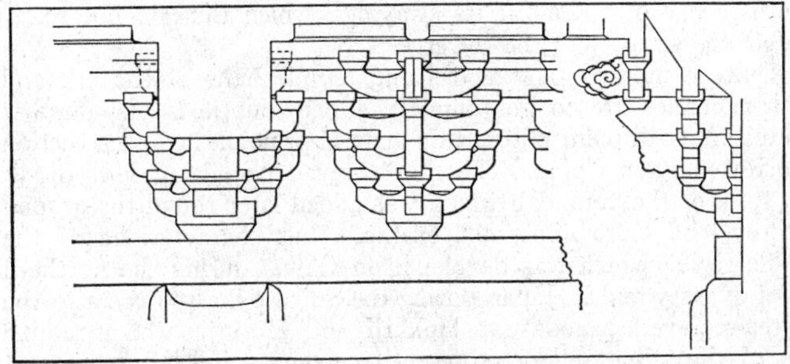

BRACKETING SYSTEM OF CHIEN CH'ING KUNG, FORBIDDEN CITY, PEKING

At the end of the Ming period buildings with classical orders in one or two storeys began to appear. Internally these were covered by longitudinal or transversal barrel vaults, but outwardly they were provided with the usual span and shed-roofs. Among the best examples of this kind of building may be mentioned the Wu Liang Tien in Suchow and Shuan Ta Ssu in Taiyuanfu, besides the two halls on Wu Tai Shan. The façades are divided by arches and columns, but these are partly inserted in the wall and the capitals are stunted or turned into cantilevers, the entablature reduced to an architrave, the cornice replaced by rows of brackets above which the upturned eaves project in the usual manner. This combination of classical orders and Chinese brackets is indeed characteristic evidence of how foreign the principles of Greek architecture always remained to the Chinese. Such buildings may have been inspired by Indian models, but the Chinese modified them quite freely by grafting on the pseudo-classical models elements inherited from their indigenous wooden architecture.

An entirely different type of masonry work is illustrated by the buildings made after Tibetan models mostly as late as in Ch'ien Lung's reign. The towers and sham fortresses on the slopes of the Western hills in Peking, which were erected in order to give the Chinese soldiers an opportunity to practise assaults, are well known by all tourists. Still larger and more important Tibetan buildings may be seen at Jehol, the famous summer resort of the Manchu emperors in northern Chihli, where an entire Llama cloister was erected after the model of the famous Potala in Lassa, the residence of the Tibetan pope-kings. This enormous brick façade in some nine or ten storeys must in its absolute bareness have appeared quite dreary to the Chinese. They have tried to give it some life or colour by surrounding the windows with pilasters and canopies made of glazed tiles, but the sombre and solid character still dominates, giving evidence of a foreign culture transplanted into Chinese surroundings.

Historical Development.—Buddhist temples and pagodas have existed in China since the end of the Han dynasty, and though the earliest ones are no longer preserved, we may obtain some idea about them from old reproductions and contemporary Japanese buildings made after Chinese models. The first messages of the new religion were brought to the Chinese at the beginning of our era, but it was not until the 2nd century A.D. that it became more widely spread, largely due to the pilgrims who journeyed between China and India. They brought news not only of the writings and images of the new religion but also of its buildings. It has been reported that small bronze models of the famous stūpa of Kanishka at Peshawar (erected in the 1st century A.D.) were brought to China by Hui Sheng, a monk who took part in a mission to India in the year 518. No doubt, other pilgrims did the same, and there may have been many small models of this much admired religious monument in China. As far as one may judge by later Indian reproductions, reverting more or less directly to the famous pagoda of Kanishka, it was built on a square platform, but the main section of it seems to have been round or bottle-shaped and divided by projecting cornices into three or more storeys. Very characteristic of this pagoda was the high mast with its nine superposed metal disks and crowning lotus bud. At present there are no such pagodas preserved in China, but ancient engravings on stone give us reason to believe that they have existed.

The oldest pagoda in China still standing is at Sung Yüeh Ssu, a temple on the sacred mountain Sung Shan in Honan. According to historical records, it was built about 523, when the palace previously existing here was consecrated as a temple. The tower is made of mud and brick on an octagonal base and reaches a height of nearly 30 metres. The lowest section consists of a plain plinth above which follows a main storey divided by pilasters and windows in a kind of aedicula (*q.v.*). The upper section of the tower has the shape of a convex cone, divided by narrow cornices into 15 low, blind storeys. It is crowned by a large bud or cone with nine rings, an equivalent to the mast with the metal disks which is usually found in the wooden pagodas. The early date of the building is verified by the style of the lion reliefs and the mouldings of the main storey.

The character of the whole structure is solid and severe, at the same time the incurvation of the outline prevents any impression of rigidity.

There is no other pagoda of as early date but the type returns with some modifications in some later pagodas, as for instance, the Pei T'a (the North tower) and the Nan T'a (the South tower) at Fang Shan in Chihli. The former, which was built at the beginning of the 8th century, shows a more typically Indian style with its bottle-shaped top, part being on a terraced substructure while the latter, which was built at the beginning of the 12th century, has a stiffer appearance without any incurvation of the outline or narrowing towards the top. It is divided by bracketed cornices into 11 storeys and reveals by its form and details a closer connection with traditional Chinese constructions. To the same group of buildings belong also the pagodas at Chêngtingfu, Mu T'a (T'ien Ning Ssu) built about 1078 in nine storeys with wooden cornices, and the Ching T'a built at a somewhat later period, and furthermore the two big pagodas near Peking, known as Pa Li Chuan and T'ien Ning Ssu, which were erected during the Chin and Yüan dynasties (in the 12th and 13th centuries). They show some likeness to the Nan T'a at Fang Shan, but their dimensions are much larger and their high plinths are richly decorated with figure reliefs in baked clay. Both have 13 low blind storeys and make quite an imposing effect by their great height, but they lack the elastic incurvation which gives to the pagoda at Sung Yüeh Ssu such an harmonious character.

ROOF TILES ON A HALL IN THE FORBIDDEN CITY, PEKING

Many of the early pagodas in China were, no doubt, constructed of wood and have perished, because of the unresisting material. There are records of a very large wooden pagoda erected in A.D. 516 at Lo-yang at the order of the Empress Dowager Hu. According to Chinese chronicles this was 1,000ft. high (a statement which must not be taken literally but merely as a general indication of unusual height) and consisted of nine storeys. Above the tower rose a mast 100ft. high carrying 30 gilt metal discs which, as well as the chains by which the mast was tied to the four corners, were hung with no less than 500 gilt bells. This noble edifice became, however, the prey of fire in 534. The description must have been based on hearsay, but it nevertheless has some interest as testimony of the existence of wooden pagodas in China at an early date. It is also confirmed by several reproductions of pagodas found among the cave sculptures from the beginning of the 6th century at Yun Kang and Lung Men. Here one may see executed in relief pagodas with three as well as with five storeys illustrating exactly the same architectural type as found in the earliest Japanese pagodas from the beginning of the following century. They are built on a square plan with corner posts and projecting roofs over the successive storeys and crowned by high masts carrying discs and ending in the form of large buds or small stūpas. In the successive storeys on some of these pagodas are placed Buddhist statues.

Excellent examples of the same type of pagoda may be seen at some of the old temples near Nara in Japan, as, for instance,

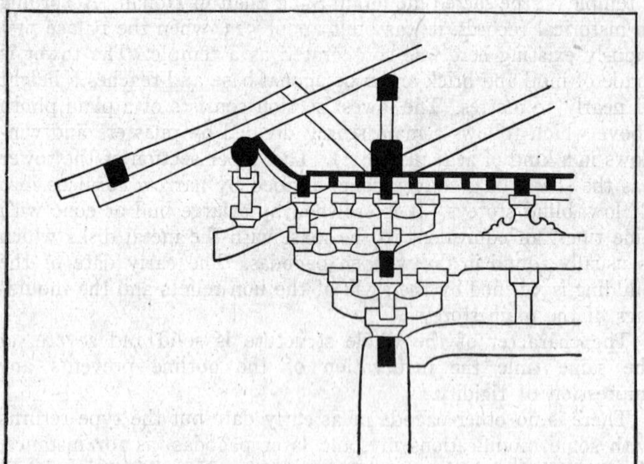

BRACKETING SYSTEM ON THE KONDO OF TOSHODAIJI. T'ANG STYLE

Horyuji and Hokkiji which were erected at the beginning of the 7th century in the Suiko period by builders from Korea or China. The pagoda at Hokkiji has five storeys; the bracketed roofs project quite far but narrow gradually towards the top so that the appearance of heaviness is avoided. Each side has four carrying posts with projecting cantilevers, which at the corners are placed diagonally and cut into the shape of clouds, a motif which is particularly characteristic of this period. The rafters are square and rather substantial; the far projection of the eaves is produced by a very clever construction which no doubt was developed in China before it was introduced in Japan, although the earliest Chinese examples no longer exist. The principle of this system consists in the redoubling of the rafters below the eaves: instead of placing the outermost purlins directly on the cantilevers, which project from the posts, supporting shorter rafters are introduced which are fastened in the beams and trusses of the roof and which carry by means of vertical struts or cushions the further projecting upper rafters. These may be made longer and the roof is lifted higher, the effect becoming lighter than in buildings where the purlins rest directly on cantilevers or beams. This constructive system with redoubled rafters remained in use until the Yüan period, perhaps even later, though the form of the lower rafters as well as other details becomes modified. Furthermore one may notice in these early buildings the very solid and broad shape of the various members, as, for instance, the comparatively short columns with entasis (*q.v.*) and the very broad and heavy cantilevers cut into the shape of clouds at their lower side. The trusses and beams of the roof, to which the rafters are tied, are solid and strong, the various parts being tied together with consummate skill.

The essential parts of the buildings and the method of construction are the same in the pagodas and in the temple halls of this period, as may be learned from a closer study of the Golden Hall or Kondo of Horyuji, an oblong, quadrangular room with a colonnade and a roof in two storeys. A very important member added to the pagodas is, however, the mast which runs through the whole height of the tower. The purpose of this mast is not really constructive, it is not meant to support the tower, but simply to form a spire rising high above the roof and carrying the nine metal rings or discs. The builders usually did not tie the mast very tightly to the framework of the tower, because if the whole structure were suspended on the mast, the security of the tower would be jeopardized by the unavoidable swaying of the mast. In some comparatively recent examples one may find the mast suspended in the beams of the tower, but here the intention evidently was to lift it a little above the ground in order to avoid the still greater danger that might arise through the gradual sinking of the tower which would then, so to speak, be carried by the mast or hang on it. In the oldest pagodas which for the longest time have withstood storms and earthquakes the mast is a relatively free-standing post within the structure, always with plenty of room for its swayings, which thus do not really affect the security of the tower.

Quite a number of pagodas and temple halls of the 7th and 8th centuries are to be found in Japan, but it is our purpose here simply to point out certain general principles of construction borrowed from China. The five-storeyed pagoda at Horyuji is, in spite of the verandah which was added later round the ground storey, the most important example, but characteristic of the same style (which was developed in China, during the northern Wei dynasty and in Japan during the Suiko dynasty) are also the three-storeyed pagodas at Hokkiji and Horinji, which remind us of the stone reliefs representing pagodas in the grottoes at Lung Men and Yun Kang.

Inportant modifications of the old style may be observed on the beautiful pagoda of Yakushiji which was erected at the beginning of the 8th century in close adherence to Chinese constructions from the beginning of the T'ang period. It is a three-storeyed tower, but each one of the storeys is provided with a closed balcony carried on cantilevers, so that the pagoda at first sight gives the impression of a six-storeyed building. The intermediate shed-roofs are of the same shape, though smaller than those which cover the main storeys; a kind of rhythmic division is thus created, and the decorative effect becomes more interesting than in the earlier pagodas. Of great importance for the horizontal articulation are also the far-projecting carrying beams of the balconies, as well as the repetition of the three-armed brackets in double tiers under the eaves of the six successive roofs. The bracketing system has here attained its highest development, the lower brackets being used as supports for the upper ones which reach farther out and are provided with cushions. Their transversal arms replace the formerly used cantilevers, and on the top of them may be one more tier of similarly shaped brackets, as on other buildings of the same period. It should be observed that all the brackets are complete, the lower ones being so arranged that they carry a continuous beam and also the transversal arms of the upper brackets, while these serve as supports for the upper beams under the eaves and for the rafters. In order to strengthen the vertical construction, struts with cushions are often placed on the hammer-beams in the intervals between the brackets.

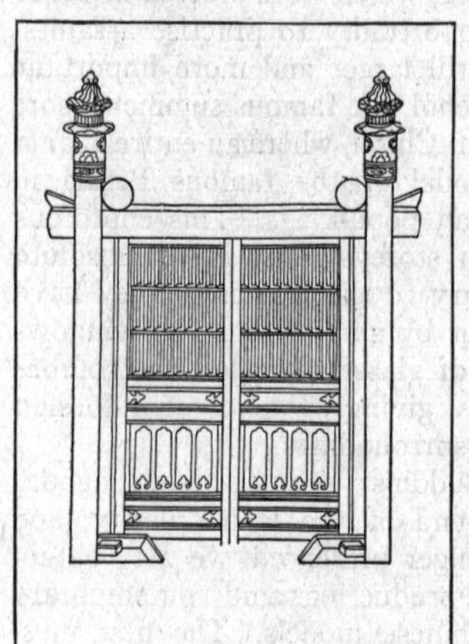

OUTER GATEWAY ACCORDING TO YING TSAO FA SHIH (1103)

The same characteristic forms and constructive features return in some contemporary temples and pagodas which thus also testify that the parts to which we have paid special attention are typical features of the architecture of this period. Interesting in this connection are the two large temple halls at Toshodaiji, another temple not far from Nara, *i.e.*, the Kodo (Hall of Teaching) and the Kondo (the Golden Hall). The former once formed a part of the imperial palace at Nara but was moved to its present place when the temple was erected in 759. The building is quite simple, an oblong, one-storeyed hall with double rows of columns all around, the inner row standing free in the room, the outer being filled out to form a wall. The columns are not quite as heavy as on the buildings of the preceding period and the inter-columns are very long. The brackets are introduced only in one tier but between them are struts which contribute to support the roof.

PHOTOGRAPH, COPR. OSVALD SIRÉN

THE GREAT WALL OF CHINA

The Great Wall of China at the Nank'ou pass, Chih-li; 228 B.C. It is 1,400 miles long, with square watch-towers at intervals

TWO CITY WALLS

1. Portion of the city wall of Peking; west side, outer view. It is provided with 44 bastions and coated with bricks. The battlements are beginning to crumble. It had been constantly rebuilt or repaired from the end of the 15th to the middle of the 19th century. Its two gates are the Hsi Chih men (north) and Ping Tzu men (south), connecting city and suburbs

2. Portion of the city wall and the double bastion at south gate in Si-an, Shen-si, built at the end of the 14th century, and repaired in places. It encloses an almost square city, and has double gate-towers, square bastions and round corner-towers

EXAMPLES OF THE CHINESE PAGODA, OR TEMPLE-TOWER

1. The Nan t'a (south tower), at Fang Shan, Chih-li; 11th century
2. The Pa Li Chuan pagoda near Peking; 13th century
3. Pagoda of Sung Yueh Ssu, at Sung Shan, Hon-an; A.D. 523
4. Pei t'a (north tower), at Fang Shan, Chih-li; 8th century

BUDDHIST BUILDINGS

1. Ssu Mên T'a, the Four Gate pagoda at Shen Tung Ssu, Shantung; middle of 6th century
2. Wu Liang Tien, a temple in Su-chow, Chakiang; 17th century
3. The Drum Tower in Peking; erected in 1273

CHINESE MEMORIAL GATEWAYS

1. P'ai-lou or memorial gateway built of wood, at the lake of the Summer Palace, Peking. These characteristic structures, usually of wood, mark the entrance to a sacred or beautiful spot or commemorate some event or person
2. Marble P'ai-lou at the Altar of Heaven, Peking. This illustrates the type of p'ai-lous with tall side-posts reaching above the transverse beams
3. Marble P'ai-lou over the main street in Wei-hsien, Shantung. In this type of p'ai-lous, the shorter side-posts are covered by roofs, making the gateway resemble an open pavilion. This is one of the more elaborate examples, with three openings and storeyed roofs

The same principles of construction are still further developed on the Kondo of Toshodaiji which, with the exception of its entirely rebuilt roof, is an unusually imposing example of T'ang architecture. The building stands on a comparatively broad and high platform, but it is provided with a colonnade only on the front. The columns have a slight entasis and rest on moulded plinths. They are tied together, as usual, by a long architrave-beam and provided with quadrangular cushions from which the three-armed brackets project. These carry the upper longitudinal beam and a second tier of brackets. Above this follows a third row of brackets which is almost hidden below the far projecting eaves. The rafters project between the arms of the uppermost brackets and abut against the tranversal arms of the second row of brackets. The rafters are doubled, the upper ones being supported by struts which also carry the outermost purlins, and the two layers are furthermore tied by braces. The whole system is carried out with perfect logic in a method which may be termed the highest perfection of wooden construction.

How closely this building depends on Chinese models is proved by the reproduction of a similar temple hall on a large stone gable above one of the gateways to the Ta Yen T'a pagoda at Sianfu. This remarkable engraving which we reproduce from a copy executed by a Japanese artist for Prof. Sekino, is of great historical importance, because it evidently reproduces a Chinese temple on which we may observe the same constructive details as pointed out on the Kondo of Toshodaiji. It matters little that the columns have been made spiky and the roof too small, as long as we recognize the principle of the whole constructive system, *i.e.,* the brackets and the struts, of which the lower ones have the same kind of curving legs as may be seen on some Japanese buildings of the 9th and 10th centuries.

Before following the further development of the traditional wooden construction during the Sung and the Yüan dynasties it is necessary to mention a group of buildings which illustrates another side of T'ang architecture. These are pagodas in what is popularly called the "Indian style," that is to say, buildings made of packed mud and brickwork which rise in terraces on a square plan. The most important among these pagodas stand in the neighbourhood of Sianfu within or just outside the district which once was occupied by Ch'angan, the capital of the T'ang emperors. In the first place should be mentioned the Ta Yen T'a (the Large Pagoda of the Wild Geese) which was founded in the year 652 by the great Buddhist pilgrim and teacher, Hsüan Chuang. It was then made of clay and brick in five storeys; later on, though still in the T'ang period, some storeys were added, and after some vicissitudes, the tower was rebuilt between 931 and 933. Later repairs have been carried out in the Ming and Ch'ing periods. The present pagoda, which has five storeys, seems however to correspond quite well to the T'ang building. It stands on a fairly high terrace and is at the base about 25·5 metres square, its full height being almost 60 metres. Its general shape reminds us of an elongated pyramid with truncated top. The successive storeys, which are accentuated by corbelled cornices, grow lower and narrower towards the top. The uppermost has a pyramidal roof crowned by a glazed cone which is now well covered by small trees and bushes. The coating of the walls is made of yellowish, lightly burnt bricks. They are quite plain except for some very thin pilasters and the arched gateways and a window on each side. The interior division is made by beams and wooden floors and the staircase which still exists makes it possible to ascend to the top. The imposing effect of this tower depends on its fine proportions and well balanced, massive form, which is strengthened by its position on a natural elevation.

Not far from this stands a smaller pagoda called Hsiao Yen T'a (the Small Tower of the Wild Geese), erected 707–709. This tower had originally 15 storeys but of these hardly 13 are now preserved. The storeys are very low but, as in the previous instance, accentuated by corbelled cornices. Only the ground floor is a little higher and on the northern and southern side provided with vaulted entrances. The upper storeys have small vaulted windows on the façade but otherwise no openings or divisions, and it is impossible to know whether they ever had any floors because there is no longer any staircase. Externally the tower differs from the Ta Yen T'a by the fact that it is not a stepped pyramid but a square tower with a slight curve on its middle part.

In still worse repair is the Hsiang Chi Ssu, situated a little farther southward from Sianfu. It was erected in 681 according to the same general design as Hsiao Yen T'a, probably in 11 or more storeys, of which, however, only ten remain. The outline is not curved but rises straight towards the top which is largely ruined. The storeys are quite low but provided with an horizontal and vertical moulding possibly suggested by wooden buildings. The dependence on wooden architecture is still more evident in another pagoda situated in the same neighbourhood called Hsing Chiao Ssu, which was erected in 839 at the place where the remains of the great pilgrim, Hsüan Chuang, were removed in 669. It is a comparatively small tower measuring only about 20 metres in height and 5·35 on each side, but it presents an unusual historical interest by the fact that some of the most characteristic elements of wooden architecture have here been faithfully reproduced in brickwork. The storeys are not only marked by corbelled cornices but also with rows of three-armed brackets which rise from a kind of horizontal beam and provided furthermore, in the two upper storeys, with carrying posts in the shape of half columns. This close adherence to wood constructions may also be taken as an evidence of the greater age of the wooden pagodas in China as compared with the brick pagodas, which probably were developed through influence from India.

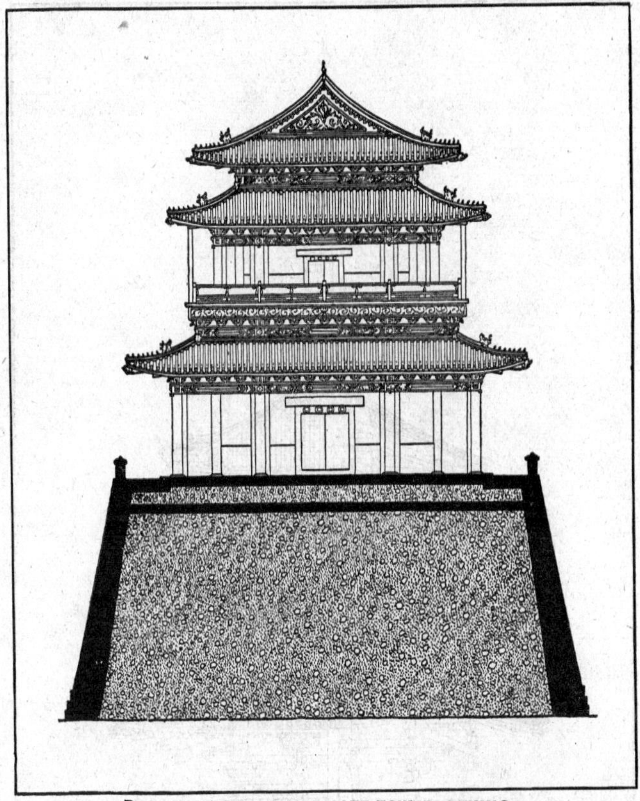

P'ING TZU MEN, INNER GATE-TOWER, PEKING

On each side of the Hsing Chia Ssu are smaller three-storeyed pagodas erected to the memory of other monks, both having three divisions without any cornices. Such minor quadrangular towers of three to five storeys dating from the T'ang, Sung and Yüan dynasties are often to be found on tombs or other memorable places. One of the largest and most beautiful among them is the Pai T'a Ssu in the same neighbourhood south of Sianfu; others are to be found at Shen Tung Ssu in Shantung and at Fang Shan in Chihli. The same architectural shape may also be observed in the celebrated pagoda Pai Ma Ssu near Honanfu which was not built until the Sung period, though it often has been mentioned as one of the oldest pagodas in China, probably owing to the legend connected with the Pai Ma Ssu temple. It is supposed to have been founded by Indian missionaries, who carried the first *sutras* to China, but as a matter of fact, the present pagoda was preceded by an earlier one in wood, which perished by fire in 1126. Other characteristic buildings are the Chiu T'a Ssu, or Nine-towered Pagoda, near Lin Cheng in Shantung, and the Lung Kung T'a at Shen Tung Ssu, an impressive square tower in three high divisions, which are encumbered by sculptural decoration.

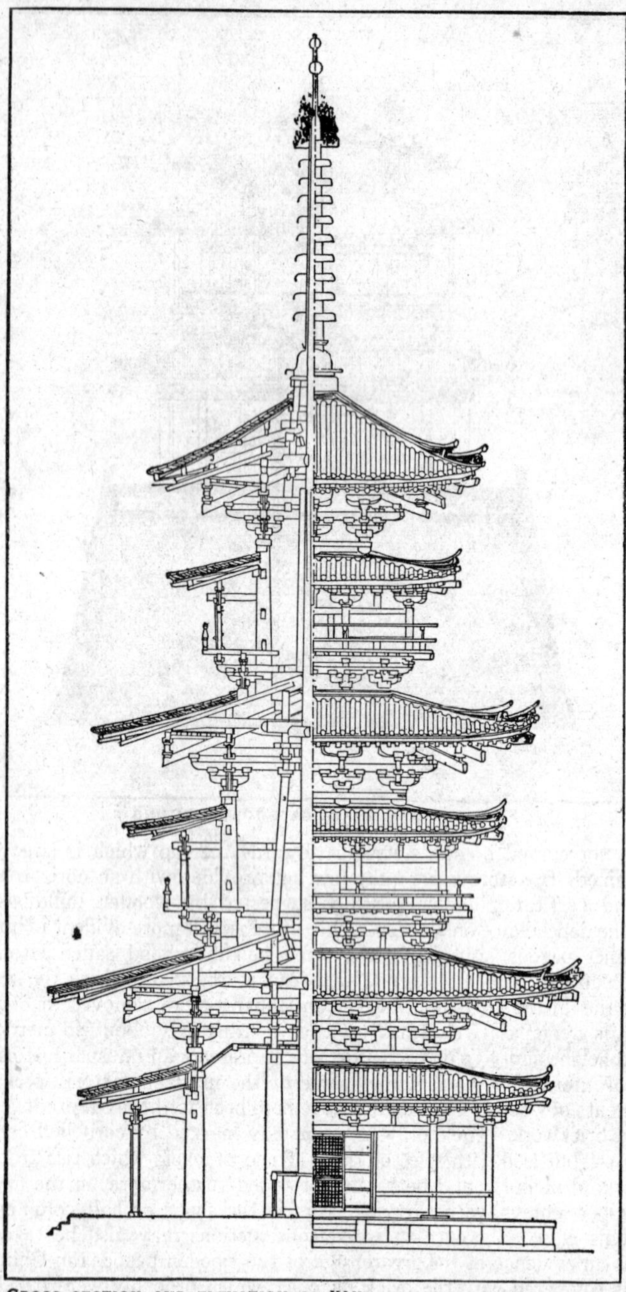

CROSS SECTION AND ELEVATION OF YAKUSHIJI PAGODA. 8TH CENTURY

Although the greater part of the buildings which still remain in China from the T'ang and Sung dynasties are pagodas made of mud and brick there are also some examples of temples constructed at least in part of wood, dating from the end of the Sung period. The most authentic and important of these is the Ch'u Tzu An hall at Shao Lin Ssu, the famous temple on the slope of Sung Shan in Honan, where the miraculous Bhodidharma, the founder of the Dhyana or Zen Buddhism, is said to have remained several years. According to an inscription, the Ch'u Tzu An was erected about the year 1125 or shortly before. It is a small, square building (measuring about 11 metres on each side) standing, as usual, on a stone terrace. Each side has four hexagonal stone pillars but only those of the façade are even partly visible, the others being completely embedded in the brick walls. In the room are two pairs of smaller and two pairs of larger hexagonal pillars, all decorated with Buddhist reliefs, and the gateway is framed by carved stone beams. Thanks to these solid stone supports the building still stands, but the roof, which is made of wood, threatens to fall in (if it has not already done so). At the writer's visit to the place in 1921 large pieces of the eaves were missing, and perhaps now the building has no other roof than the sky. The most interesting parts of this structure, however, are not the carved stone pillars but the brackets under the eaves which illustrate how these were used in the Sung period. The modifications in comparison with the bracketing system of the T'ang dynasty are quite noteworthy. Thus we find that the brackets emerge not only from the pillars but also, between these, from the horizontal beam. They are placed more closely together than previously, forming a kind of cornice. In the lower tier the brackets have three arms but in the upper tier the transversal arms have been cut by the under rafters, which are pointed and project like beaks or long paws. They are tied by means of braces to the brackets and carry at both ends struts (vertical posts) on which the purlins or corresponding beams rest. This change may be said to imply that the lower rafters have lost their original character and become a sloping cantilever transversing the lower brackets which they lengthen, thus making them better fitted to support the far projecting roof. The modification has evidently a practical purpose, though it hardly improves the original bracketing system, as exemplified on the T'ang buildings.

The evolution continued in this same direction; the three-armed constructive brackets gave place to two-armed ones transversed by thin sloping beams or rafters, cut like beaks at the end. These project successively, the one tier reaching beyond the other, each one carrying its row of brackets which serve to support the longitudinal beams or a kind of struts for the purlins. The former system may be observed on the Bell Tower at Hsiao Lin Ssŭ, which according to an inscription was erected about the year 1300, where the third storey has no less than four tiers of gradually projecting brackets with beaks. The latter method is quite common; as an example may be mentioned one of the pavilions at the Confucius temple at Chüfu, also of the Yüan dynasty, where the horizontal pieces form a support for several sloping cantilevers (or rudimentary lower rafters) which have been joined into a kind of bed for the struts and purlins of the roof.

Chinese buildings dating from the Sung and Yüan dynasties are scarce indeed, but our knowledge of the architecture of these

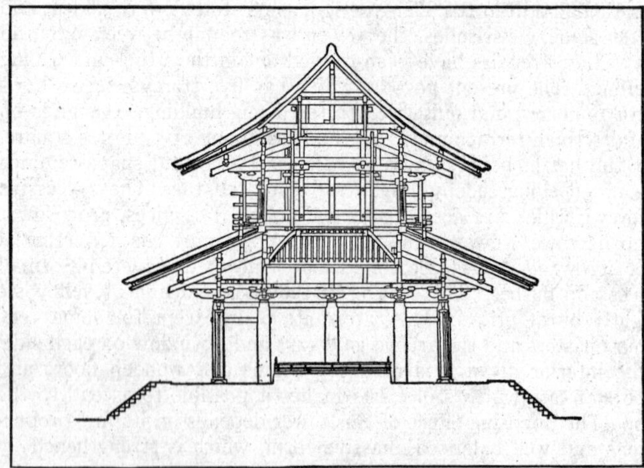

CROSS SECTION OF THE KONDO OF HORYUJI, BUILT IN 7TH CENTURY

times may be supplemented by observations on Japanese buildings from the 12th and 13th centuries, *i.e.*, the Kamakura period. In Japan this was a time of great building activity and, according to the best informed Japanese authorities, remarkable for its close imitation of the contemporary Chinese models. Quite important in this respect is the Shariden (Chu Tsu An) of the Zen temple Engakuji in Kamakura, built according to the same principles as the above-mentioned Chinese hall, though with an extraordinarily large and high roof covered with straw. This is carried by brackets of the same type as those which were observed at Chu Tsu An of Hsiao Lin Ssu. The brackets are placed so closely together that they form a continuous cornice. The purely Chinese origin of the constructive system of the Shariden of Engakuji may be confirmed through a comparison with some of the illustrations in the above-mentioned architectural treatise *Ying Tsao Fa Shih* published in 1103. On the buildings or schematic designs reproduced here we find brackets of exactly the same type as those described above, though their significance is partly obscured by the addition of some large transverse beams which probably have their origin in the imagination of the draughtsman.

The Japanese called this constructive system which they have borrowed from northern China, "karayo," while another somewhat different contemporary method was called "tenjiku," because it was considered to have been derived from India via southern China. It was used principally at large gates and temple buildings, to which one desired to give a particularly imposing appearance by the development of their upper portions. This was achieved by multiplying the brackets and transforming them into straight arms or cantilevers projecting stepwise from the posts. A good example of the *tenjiku* style is the Nandaimon gate at Todaiji, which was erected in 1199. It has five spans of columns on the long sides and a roof in two storeys, of which the lower one is supported by seven tiers and the upper by six tiers of cantilevers projecting from each column. At the corners are added diagonal cantilevers to form a support for the corner beaks. This kind of construction seems, however, never to have won much popularity in northern China; it is so simple and natural that it hardly can be credited with particular artistic importance. Projecting roof beams have indeed been used in many countries to support the eaves, but the characteristic feature of the *tenjiku* buildings is that the cantilevers are multiplied or massed together by the insertion of intermediate pieces into large composite brackets.

The further development of the wood construction in China after the end of the Yüan dynasty is a question which hardly needs to be discussed, because no real progress can be observed, but rather a gradual decline, which becomes evident in the more and more arbitrary treatment of the bracketing system. At the beginning of the Ming dynasty one may still find buildings constructed in the same style as those of the Yüan period, *i.e.*, with beak-formed pieces laid transversally across the brackets, but the projecting pieces become often clumsy and out of proportion to the brackets. A fine example of early Ming architecture is the Bell Tower in Sianfu, the lower roof of which rests on a double row of brackets of the same type as those of the Yüan buildings. On the other hand, the tower of the eastern gate of T'a Tung Fu, erected in 1371, shows beak-shaped pieces projecting from very feeble brackets.

A STONE ENGRAVING ON THE DOOR GABLE AT TA YAN T'A, SIANFU

The question how long a really constructive bracketing system remained in use in China is difficult to answer without more detailed investigations than have hitherto been made. It is evident however, that already during the latter half of the Ming period simpler methods were applied, as may be seen for instance on the earliest buildings in the Forbidden City in Peking. It is true that the outer appearance was kept up by fixing multiple rows of brackets and pointed beaks below the eaves, but these have no real constructive function. The purlins rest on projecting beams or on struts standing on the columns. The closely arranged and freely multiplied brackets and beaks which we find on the big palace halls and imposing gate towers in Peking are nothing but ornamental cornices, the decorative effect of which nobody will deny. The roof would indeed rest just as well on the building even if these sham brackets were taken away. The forms are still the same as before but they have lost much of their significance because they lack inner necessity. The particular quality and importance of the old architecture of China depended on its firm and clearly developed wood construction. It was purely carpenters' art, and based on the special requirements of the material. Each part had a definite function which was not concealed by any superimposed decoration. This architecture was logical and purposeful and it remained a living art as long as the original principles of construction were kept up, but once these were encroached upon by purely decorative tendencies, both vitality and further growth were at an end. (*See* also JAPANESE ARCHITECTURE.) (O. S.)

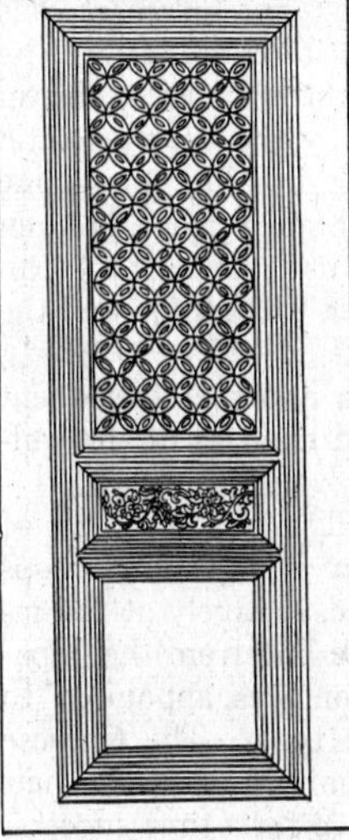

DOOR PANEL ACCORDING TO YING TSAO FA SHIH (1103)

BIBLIOGRAPHY.—The only original Chinese work on architecture is the *Ying Tsao Fa Shi* (1103; 2nd ed., 1145; reissued by the Shanghai Commercial Press). Good accounts of the work were given by P. Demieville in *Bulletin de l'École Française d'Extrême-Orient*, tome xxv. (1925), and Percival W. Yetts in the *Burlington Magazine* (March, 1927), the latter containing a discussion of earlier European books dealing with Chinese architecture. Of greater importance are, however, the works published by various Japanese authorities on their own early buildings since these are closely connected with those of China. See *Japanese Temples and their Treasures* (last ed. 1915); also articles in the *Kokka* and other Japanese reviews, especially C. Ito and J. Tsuchija's report about the imperial palaces in Peking, in the *Bulletin of the School of Engineering of the Tōkyō Imper. University* (1905), a kind of text for the portfolio publications; *Photographs of Palace Buildings of Peking* and *Decoration of the Palace Buildings of Peking* (1906). *See* also Boerschmann, *Baukunst und religiöse Kultur der Chinesen* (1911–14) and *Chinesche Architektur* (1925); Osvald Sirén, *The Walls and Gates of Peking* (1924), and *The Imperial Palaces of Peking* (Paris, 1926); Tokiwa and Sekino, *Buddhist Monuments in China* (Tōkyō, 1926–27), of which only one part has been issued in English.

The drawings of this article are executed partly on the basis of sketches by Prof. Sekino and partly after photographs by the author.

CHINESE EASTERN RAILWAY. In 1895 there was formed, under Russian charter, but with a predominance of French capital and with some capital owned by the Chinese Government, the Russo-Chinese Bank. When, in 1896, Russia obtained from China permission to shorten the Trans-Siberian railway by building a line across Northern Manchuria, the bank formed the Chinese Eastern Railway Company. Only Russians and Chinese were to be shareholders, and a Chinese appointed by Peking was to be president. After 80 years the line was to revert to China free of charge, or the Chinese Government might purchase it at the end of 36 years. The original board of directors was entirely Russian, and the capital stock was all owned by the Russo-Chinese Bank. In 1898 a convention between China and Russia provided for the construction by the company of the South Manchurian line of the Chinese Eastern railway from Harbin to Port Arthur and Dairen (Dalny). The roads so provided for were completed in 1905 and for that purpose the Russian Government advanced about 800,000,000 roubles. In 1905, as a result of the Russo-Japanese War, the South Manchurian railway south of Changchun passed into the hands of Japan.

In 1910 the Russo-Chinese Bank was amalgamated with the Northern Bank to form the Russo-Asiatic Bank, and the new institution became heir of the Russo-Chinese Bank's interest in the Chinese Eastern railway. The new bank had a Russian charter, but the majority of its stock was in French hands. The Chinese government remained a part owner. In 1915 an agreement was formed for the operation by the Chinese Eastern railway of the short private line connecting Tsitsihar and the main line, and in March 1916 an agreement was entered into by the Russo-Asiatic Bank and the Chinese government for the building of a line from Harbin to Blagovyeshchensk with a branch from Mergen to Tsitsihar. In a treaty of July 3, 1916, Russia ceded to Japan 60 mi. of the Chinese Eastern railway between Changchun and the Sungari river.

World War I and the Russian Revolution and the consequent disintegration in Siberia threw the traffic and finances of the railway into confusion.

In pursuance of the Chino-Japanese military agreement of 1918, made after China entered World War I, Japanese troops appeared in the Chinese Eastern railway zone. Largely at the insistence of the United States, and to save the line from the Japanese, an international, interallied commission was appointed to operate the road. This control lasted until 1922. The Chinese saw in the disturbed conditions an opportunity to extend their control over the railway, and beginning in 1920 for a time successfully asserted themselves.

At the Washington conference in 1921–22, a resolution was adopted stating that better protection should be given the railway, that the personnel should be more carefully selected, and the funds more economically used. The powers other than China also made reservations under which the consular body in Harbin interfered when in Aug. 1923 the Chinese attempted to seize the land department of the railway.

The Russo-Chinese agreement of May 31, 1924, contained a long article which, among other things, had an assurance that China might buy back the railway and a provision for a conference to settle more definitely the future of the road. Simultaneously, another agreement was adopted for the joint administration of the railway pending the final adjustment.

In July 1929, sharp dissension culminated in the seizure of the road by the Chinese. A Russian invasion, however, compelled the restoration of the *status quo*.

After the establishment of the Japanese-dominated state of Manchoukuo relations between the joint owners became strained. To remove the friction, negotiations were begun in 1933 for the sale of Russia's share. These resulted in an agreement, Sept. 19, 1934, whereby Manchoukuo was to pay the equivalent of 140,000,000 yen (1 yen=$.4985 at par), one-third in cash and the remainder in kind. The transfer was completed March 23, 1935. The road was renamed the North Manchurian railway and became part of the system operated by the (Japanese) South Manchuria Railway company. Renamed the Chinese Changchun railway, the Manchurian rail system was jointly controlled by China and the U.S.S.R. after World War II.

As part of a series of agreements signed between the Chinese People's Republic and the U.S.S.R. in Moscow on Feb. 14, 1950, the U.S.S.R. promised to transfer the full ownership and control of the Chinese Changchun railway to China. The transfer became effective on Dec. 31, 1952. (K. S. L.; X.)

CHINESE EMIGRATION. From the fact that in 1718 the Chinese government banned emigration, it may be inferred that some Chinese had left for neighbouring countries, but there were no reliable statistics for about another century, when Chinese emigration, especially to other Asiatic lands, increased greatly. Overpopulation, wars, famines, political unrest, lawlessness, low wages, high land prices and recruitment of labourers by foreigners exerted pressures that account for Chinese migration until it was restricted or prohibited by the receiving countries.

From 1820, when one Chinese entered the United States, until the middle of the 19th century, fewer than 100 Chinese went to the United States; but with the gold rush that started in California in 1849 there began a period of increased Chinese immigration, especially to California, which made Chinese immigration a dominant issue in California politics from 1860 to 1890. For a time the immigrants were welcomed as cheap labour that was needed for the menial tasks of a pioneering, aggressive community preoccupied with railroad building and gold prospecting; but when unemployment developed, the welcome turned into racial animosity and agitation for state and national restrictive or exclusionary measures.

It was charged that the immigrants were unassimilable and subject to grave personal vices. For their part, the immigrants complained that they were excluded from the rest of society by discriminatory laws and customs.

The Burlingame treaty of 1868 gave Chinese subjects in the United States the right to privileges enjoyed by citizens of the most-favoured nation, but soon this treaty was effectively abrogated by congressional acts, the constitutionality of which was upheld by the supreme court. In 1879 congress passed a bill to exclude Chinese labourers; it was vetoed by the president. In 1882 congress passed an act to suspend Chinese immigration for ten years. An act of 1892 extended the suspension for another ten years. In 1902 the statutory policy became one of permanent exclusion. In a message to congress, Pres. Franklin D. Roosevelt asked for an end of this policy, and in 1943 congress complied (at that time China was an ally of the United States in World War II and was to be one of the Big Five of the projected United Nations). The Immigration and Nationality act of 1952 repealed all racial exclusionary provisions except that (1) persons who are related by as much as one-half of their ancestry to peoples indigenous to an Asia-Pacific triangle, defined by the act, are charged, for immigration quota purposes, to the countries of Asia, wherever they may have been born or however long their ancestors may have made their homes outside the land of their origin; and (2) a quota limit of 100 was placed on entries from any colony. The former provision assured that immigrants of Chinese descent, regardless of nationality, are not to exceed the annual Chinese quota of 105.

Despite restrictions, from 1820 to 1949, 397,602 Chinese immigrants were admitted into the United States; and of this total, 50,264 were admitted in the years 1921–1949, the so-called restrictive period of U.S. immigration policy, and 118,393 in the selective period 1881–1920.

Available statistics for the number of Chinese residing abroad show that the largest migrations from China were to other Asiatic countries, and the smallest were to Europe. Thus (the figures are for 1922) Burma had 134,600; the East Indies, 1,023,500; Formosa, 2,258,650; Java, 1,825,700; Korea, 11,310; Siam, 1,500,000; Straits Settlements, 432,764; and the Philippines, 55,212. Australia had 35,000. Brazil had 20,000; Canada, 12,000; Cuba, 90,000; Mexico, 3,000; Peru, 45,000. South Africa had 5,000; and all of Europe, only 1,760. A total of more than 8,000,000 Chinese resided abroad. In the 1920s and 1930s there was a considerable Chinese migration to Manchuria—nearly 1,000,000 went there in 1928, and from 1925 to 1929 at least 2,000,000 settled there. Chinese immigration has been prohibited by the statutes or administrative action of many countries, among them Canada and Australia.

Chinese immigration to occidental countries failed to bring about distinctive, lasting effects upon the culture of the receiving countries. This may be explained by the inimical acts of the occidental peoples which permitted but few contacts. Immigration restrictions have, however, reduced tensions; Chinatowns are disappearing, and the Chinese are becoming absorbed in the general life of the community, leaving no specific significant trace of their own culture.

Bibliography.—*See* the critical bibliographies in David F. Bowers (ed.), *Foreign Influences in American Life* (Princeton, London, 1944); Senate Committee on the Judiciary, "The Immigration and Naturalization Systems of the United States," *Report 1515* (Washington, 1950); M. R. Konvitz, *The Alien and the Asiatic in American Law* (Ithaca, N.Y., and London, 1946), *Civil Rights in Immigration* (Ithaca, N.Y., and London, 1953); United Nations Department of Social Affairs, *Demographic Yearbook* (New York, London, 1948 *et seq.*).

(M. R. K.)

CHINESE LANGUAGE. In treating of Chinese, it will be convenient to distinguish, broadly, the spoken from the written language because for reasons connected with the peculiar nature of the script, the two soon began to move along independent and largely divergent lines.

Although Chinese, like other living languages, must have undergone gradual changes in the past, so little can be stated with certainty about these changes that an accurate survey of its evolution is quite out of the question. Obviously a different method is required when we come to the written characters. We have hardly any clue as to how Chinese was spoken or pronounced in any given district 2,000 years ago, although there are written remains dating from long before that time; and in order to gain an insight into the structure of the characters now existing, it is necessary to trace their origin and development.

We find a number of dialects, all clearly of a common stock, yet differing widely from one another. Most of these dialects fringe the coast-line of China, and penetrate but a comparatively short way into the interior. Starting from the province of Kwangtung in the south, where the Cantonese and, farther inland, the Hakka dialects are spoken, and, proceeding northwards, we pass in succession the following dialects: Swatow, Amoy (these two may almost be regarded as one), Foochow, Wenchow, Ningpo and Wu. Farther north the great dialect popularly known as Mandarin (*Kuanhua* or "official language"), sweeps round behind the narrow strip of coast occupied by the various dialects above-mentioned, and dominates a hinterland constituting nearly four-fifths of China proper. Mandarin, of which the dialect of Peking, the capital 1421 to 1928, is now the standard form, comprises a considerable number of sub-dialects, some of them so closely allied that the speakers of one are wholly intelligible to the speakers of another, while others (*e.g.*, the vernaculars of Yangchow, Hankow or Mid-China and Ssŭ-ch'uan) may almost be considered as separate dialects. Cantonese is supposed to approximate most nearly to the primitive language of antiquity, whereas Pekingese perhaps has receded farthest from it. For all practical purposes Mandarin, in the widest sense of the term, is by far the most important as the native speech of the majority of Chinese and the recognized vehicle of oral communication between all Chinese officials, even when they come from the same part of the country and speak the same *patois*. All examples of phraseology in this article will therefore be given in Pekingese.

The dialects proceed from the same parent stem, are spoken by members of the same race, are united by the bond of writing, the common possession of all, and share alike in the two most salient features of Chinese as a whole: (1) they are all monosyllabic, that is, each individual word consists of only one syllable; and (2) they are strikingly poor in vocables, or separate sounds for the conveyance of speech. The number of these vocables varies from between 800 and 900 in Cantonese to no more than 420 in the vernacular of Peking. This scanty number is eked out by interposing an aspirate between certain initial consonants and the vowel, so that for instance *p'u* is distinguished from *pu*. The latter is pronounced with little or no emission of breath, the "p" approximating the farther north one goes (*e.g.*, at Niuchwang) more closely to a "b." The aspirated *p'u* is pronounced more like our interjection "Pooh!" The number of vocables in Pekingese has slowly but surely diminished. Thus the initials *ts* and *k*, when followed by the vowel *i* (with its continental value) have gradually become softer and more assimilated to each other, and are now both pronounced *ch*. Again, all consonantal endings in *t* and *k*, such as survive in Cantonese and other dialects, have entirely disappeared from Pekingese, and *n* and *ng* are the only final consonants remaining. Vowel sounds, on the other hand, have been proportionately developed, such compounds as *ao, ia, iao, iu, ie, ua* occurring with especial frequency. One and the same sound has therefore to do duty for different words. Some sounds may have fewer meanings than ten attached to them, but others will have many more. Thus the following represent only a fraction of the total number of words pronounced *shih* (something like the "shi" in shirt): 史 "history," 使 "to employ," 屍 "a corpse," 市 "a market," 師 "an army," 獅 "a lion," 恃 "to rely on," 侍 "to wait on," 詩 "poetry," 時 "time," 識 "to know," 施 "to bestow," 是 "to be," 實 "solid," 失 "to lose," 示 "to proclaim," 視 "to look at," 十 "ten," 拾 "to pick up," 石 "stone," 世 "generation," 食 "to eat," 室 "a house," 氏 "a clan," 始 "beginning," 釋 "to let go," 試 "to test," 事 "affair," 勢 "power," 士 "officer," 誓 "to swear," 逝 "to pass away," 適 "to happen."

Use of Couplets.—To supplement this deficiency of sounds several devices are employed through the combination of which confusion is avoided. One of these devices is the coupling of words in pairs in order to express a single idea. There is a word 哥 *ko* which means "elder brother." But in speaking, the sound *ko* alone would not always be easily understood in this sense. One must either reduplicate it and say *ko-ko*, or prefix 大 (*ta*, "great") and say *ta-ko*. Simple reduplication is mostly confined to family appellations and such adverbial phrases as 慢慢 *man-man*, "slowly." But in a much larger class of pairs, each of the two components has the same meaning. Examples are: 恐怕 *k'ung-p'a*, "to be afraid," 告訴 *kao-su*, "to tell," 樹木 *shu-mu*, "tree," 皮膚 *p'i-fu*, "skin," 滿盈 *man-ying*, "full," 孤獨 *ku-tu*, "solitary." Sometimes the two parts are not exactly synonymous, but together make up the sense required. Thus in 衣裳 *i-shang*, "clothes," *i* denotes more particularly clothes worn on the upper part of the body, and *shang* those on the lower part. In another very large class of expressions, the first word serves to limit and determine the special meaning of the second: 奶皮 "milk-skin," "cream"; 火腿 "fire-leg," "ham"; 燈籠 "lamp-cage," "lantern"; 海腰 "sea-waist," "strait." There are, besides, a number of phrases which are harder to classify. Thus, 虎 *hu* means "tiger." But in any case where ambiguity might arise, *lao-hu*, "old tiger," is used instead of the monosyllable. 狐 (another *hu*) is "fox," and 狸 *li*, an animal belonging to the smaller cat tribe. Together, *hu-li*, they form the usual term for fox. 知道 *chih tao* is literally "to know the way," but has come to be used simply for the verb "to know." These pairs or two-word phrases are of such frequent occurrence, that the Chinese spoken language might almost be described as bi-syllabic. Suffixes or enclitics are attached to many of the commonest nouns. 女 *nü* is the word for "girl," but in speech 女子 *nü-tzŭ* or 女兒 *nü-'rh* is the form used. 子 and 兒 both mean child, and must originally have been diminutives. The suffix 兒 belongs especially to the Peking vernacular. The use of numeratives is quite a distinctive feature of the language. The commonest of them, 個 *ko*, can be used indifferently in connection with almost any class of things, animal, vegetable or mineral. But there are other numeratives (at least 20 or 30 in everyday use) which are strictly reserved for limited classes of things with specific attributes. 枚 *mei*, for instance, is the numerative of circular objects such as coins and rings; 顆 *k'o* of small globular objects—pearls, grains of rice, etc.; 口 *k'ou* classifies things which have a mouth—bags, boxes and so forth; 件 *chien* is used of all kinds of affairs; 張 *chang* of chairs and sheets of paper; 隻 *chih* (literally half a pair) is the numerative for various animals, parts of the body, articles of clothing and ships; 把 *pa* for things which are grasped by a handle, such as fans and knives.

The Tones.—The tones may be defined as regular modulations of the voice by means of which different inflections can be imparted to the same sound. To the foreign ear, a Chinese sentence spoken slowly with the tones clearly brought out has a certain sing-song effect. It is absurd to suppose the tones were deliberately invented in order to fit each written character with a separate sound. It is considered that tones were the automatic result of the elision of prefixes, some of which as elsewhere may have served as classifiers. A tone is as much an integral part of the word to which it belongs as the sound itself; like the sound, too, it is not fixed once and for all, but is in a constant, though very gradual state of evolution. This is proved by the great differences of intonation in the dialects. Theoretically, four tones have been distinguished (the even, the rising, the sinking and the entering) each of which falls again into an upper and a lower series. But only the Cantonese dialect possesses all these eight varieties of tone (to which a ninth has been added), while Pekingese has only four: the even upper, the even lower, the rising and the sinking. It appears that down to the 3rd century B.C. the only tones distinguished were the 平 "even," 上 "rising" and 入 "entering" Between that date and the 4th century A.D. the 去 sinking tone was developed. In the 11th century the even tone was divided into upper and lower, and a little later the entering tone finally disappeared from Pekingese. For centuries their existence was unsuspected, the first systematic classification of them being associated with the name of Shên Yo, a scholar who lived A.D. 441–513. The Emperor Wu Ti one day said to him: "Come, tell me, what are these famous four tones?" "They are 天子聖哲 whatever your Majesty pleases to make them," replied Shên Yo, skilfully selecting for his answer four words which illustrated, and in the usual order, the four tones in question. Not every single word in a sentence must necessarily be given its full tonic force. Quite a number of words, such as the enclitics, are not intonated at all. In others the degree of emphasis depends partly on the tone itself, partly on its position in the sentence. In Pekingese the 3rd tone (really the 2nd in the ordinary series, the 1st being subdivided into upper and lower) is particularly important, and next to it in this respect comes the 2nd (that is, the lower even, or 2nd division of the 1st). It may be said, roughly, that any speaker whose 2nd and 3rd tones are correct will at any rate be understood, even if the 1st and 4th are slurred over.

The Characters.—A page of printed Chinese or carefully written manuscript consists of a number of wholly independent units, each of which would fit into a small square, and is called a character. These characters are arranged in columns, beginning on the right-hand side of the page and running from top to bottom. They are *words*, standing for articulate sounds expressing root-ideas, but, unlike our words, are not composed of alphabetical elements or letters. Clearly, if each character were a distinct and arbitrarily constructed symbol, only those gifted with exceptional powers of memory could ever hope to read or write with fluency. This, however, is far from being the case. Most Chinese characters are susceptible of some kind of analysis. Means of communication other than oral began with the use of knotted cords, similar to the *quipus* (*q.v.*) of ancient Mexico and Peru, and were displaced later on by the practice of notching or scoring rude marks on wood, bamboo and stone. The first four numerals, as written with simple horizontal strokes date from this early period. In Chinese writing, a few characters, even in their present form are pictures of objects, pure and simple. Thus, for "sun" the ancient Chinese drew a circle with a dot in it: ⊙, now modified into 日; for "moon" ☽, now 月; for "God" they drew the anthropomorphic figure [illegible], which in its modern form appears as 天; for "mountains" [illegible], now 山; for "child" [illegible], now 子; for "fish" [illegible], now 魚; for "mouth" a round hole, now 口; ψ for "hand" now 手; for "well" 丼, now written without the dot. These picture-characters, then, accumulated little by little, until they comprised all the common objects which could be easily and rapidly delineated—sun, moon, stars, various animals, certain parts of the body, tree, grass and so forth to the number of two or three hundred. The next step was to a few compound pictograms: 旦 the sun just above the horizon = "dawn"; 林 trees side by side = "a forest"; 舌 a mouth with something solid coming out of it = "the tongue"; 言 a mouth with vapour or breath coming out of it = "words."

While writing was still in its infancy, it must have occurred to the Chinese to join together two or more pictorial characters in order that their association might suggest to the mind some third thing or idea. "Sun" and "moon" combined in this way make the character 明, which means "bright"; woman and child make 好 "good"; "fields" and "strength" (that is, labour in the fields) produce the character 男 "male"; the "sun" seen through "trees" 東 designates the east; 家 has been explained as (1) a "pig" under a "roof," the Chinese idea, common to the Irish peasant, of home, and also (2) as "several persons" under "a roof," in the same sense; a "woman" under a "roof" makes the character 安 "peace"; "words" and "tongue" 話 naturally suggest "speech"; two hands (友, in the old form 㕛) indicate friendship; "woman" and "birth" 姓 = "born of a woman," means "clan-name," showing that the ancient Chinese traced through the mother and not through the father. This class of characters, correctly called ideograms, as representing ideas and not objects, is comparatively small. As there was nothing in the character *per se* which gave the slightest clue to the sound of the word it represented, each character had to be learned and recognized by a separate effort of memory. The first step in a new, and, ultimately the right direction, was the borrowing of a character already in use to represent another word identical in sound, though different in meaning. Owing to the scarcity of vocables there might be as many as ten different words in common use, each pronounced *fang*. Out of those ten only one, we will suppose, had a character assigned to it—viz., 方 "square" (originally said to be a picture of two boats joined together). But among the other nine was *fang*, meaning "street" or "locality," in such common use that it became necessary to have some means of writing it. Instead of inventing an altogether new character, as they might have done, the Chinese took 方 "square" and used it also in the sense of "locality." This was a simple expedient, no doubt, but one that applied on a large scale would lead to confusion. The difficulty which presented itself was overcome as in speech by adding to *fang* "square," another part meaning "earth," in order to show that the *fang* in question had to do with location on the earth's surface. The whole character thus appeared as 坊. Nothing was easier now than to provide signs for the other words pronounced *fang*. "A room" was 房 door-*fang;* "to spin" was 紡 silk-*fang;* "fragrant" was 芳 herbs-*fang;* "to enquire" was 訪 words-*fang;* "an embankment," and hence "to guard against," was 防 mound-*fang;* "to hinder" was 妨 woman-*fang*. This class of characters, which constitutes at least nine-tenths of the language, has received the convenient name of *phonograms*. The formation of the phonogram, or phonetic compound, did not always proceed along such simple lines as in the examples given above. In the first place, most of the phonetics now existing are not simple pictograms, but themselves more or less complex characters made up in a variety of ways. Again, the sound is in most cases given by no means exactly by the so-called phonetic, a fact chiefly due to the pronunciation having undergone changes which the written character was incapable of recording. There are extreme cases in which a phonetic provides hardly any clue at all as to the sound of its derivatives. In general, the "final" or rhyme is pretty accurately indicated, while in not a few cases the phonetic does give the exact sound for all its derivatives. A considerable number of phonetics are nearly or entirely obsolete as separate characters, although their family of derivatives may be a very large one. 臤, for instance, is never seen by itself, yet 堅 緊, and 賢 are among the most important characters in the language.

The whole body of Chinese characters, then, may conveniently be divided up, for philological purposes, into pictograms, ideograms and phonograms. The first are pictures of objects, the second are composite symbols standing for abstract ideas, the third are compound characters of which the more important element simply represents a spoken sound. In a strict sense, even the first two classes do not directly represent either objects or ideas, but rather stand for sounds by which these objects and ideas have previously been expressed. It may, in fact, be said that Chinese characters are "nothing but a number of more or less ingenious devices for suggesting spoken words to a reader."

The "Six Scripts."—The Chinese themselves at a very early date (probably many centuries B.C.) evolved a six-fold classification of characters, the so-called 六書 *liu shu*, very inaccurately translated by the Six Scripts, which may be briefly noticed:—

1. 指事 *chih shih*, indicative or self-explanatory characters. This is a very small class, including only the simplest numerals and a few others such as 上 "above" and 下 "below."
2. 象形 *hsiang hsing*, pictographic characters.
3. 形聲 *hsing shêng* or 諧聲 *hsieh shêng*, phonetic compounds.
4. 會意 *hui i*, suggestive compounds based on a natural association of ideas. To this class alone can the term "ideographs" be properly applied.
5. 轉注 *chuan chu*. The meaning of this name has been much disputed, some saying that it means "turned round"; *e.g.*, ⦾ *mu* "eye" is now written 目. Others understand it as comprising a few groups of characters nearly related in sense, each character consisting of an element common to the group, together with a specific and detachable part; *e.g.*, 老, 考 and 耇, all of which have the meaning "old." This class is concerned only with peculiarities in the use of characters.
6. 假借 *chia chieh*, borrowed characters, that is, characters adopted for different words simply because of the identity of sound. The period of "borrowed characters" did not last very long, though traces of it are thought to be seen in the habit of writing several characters, especially those for certain plants and animals, indifferently with or without their radicals.

Styles of Writing.—In the earliest inscriptions (Shang dynasty, 18th century B.C.), the so-called 古文 *ku-wen* or "ancient figures," all the above-mentioned forms occur. None are wholly pictorial, with one or two unimportant exceptions. In the following specimen only the last character is unmistakably pictorial: This is read: 申作寶鼎 "Shên made [this] precious *ting*."

In 1903 a large number of inscribed bone fragments were excavated in the north of China, which have furnished a list of nearly 2,500 separate characters, of which not more than about 600 have been so far identified. They appear to be responses given by professional soothsayers to private individuals who came to them seeking the aid of divination in the affairs of their daily life. The bones were ancient but some at least of the inscriptions have been forged. It is difficult to fix their date with much exactitude. The script, though less archaic than that of the earlier bronzes, is of an exceedingly free and irregular type. Some attribute them to the Shang, or Yin dynasty (1765–1122 B.C.) in accord with Chinese tradition. Others think that they represent a mode of writing already obsolete at the time of their production, and retained of set purpose by the diviners from obscurantist motives, dating them about 500 years later, or only half a century before the birth of Confucius, long after the appearance of a new and more conventionalized form of writing, called in Chinese 篆 *chuan*, which is commonly rendered by the word Seal, for the reason that many ages afterwards it was generally adopted for use on seals. Under the Chou dynasty, as well as the two succeeding it, the meaning of the word was not "seal," but "sinuous curves," as made in writing. This epoch possibly marks the first introduction into China of the brush in place of the bamboo or wooden pencil with frayed end which was used with some kind of colouring matter or varnish, and the introduction of a supple implement like the brush at the very time when the forms of characters were fast becoming crystallized and fixed, would account for a great revolution in the style of writing. Authentic specimens of the 大篆 *ta chuan*, older or Greater Seal writing, are exceedingly rare. But it is generally believed that the inscriptions on the famous stone drums, now at Peking, date from the reign of King Hsüan, and they may therefore with practical certainty be cited as examples of the Greater Seal in its original form. These "drums," really ten roughly chiselled mountain boulders, were discovered in the early part of the 7th century, lying half buried in the ground near Fêng-hsiang Fu in the province of Shensi. On them are engraved ten odes, a complete ode being cut on each drum, celebrating an imperial hunting and fishing expedition in that part of the country. Great strides had been made in this writing towards symmetry, compactness and conventionalism. The vogue of the Greater Seal appears to have lasted until the reign of the First Emperor, 246–210 B.C. (*see* CHINA: *History*), when further modification took place. For centuries China had been split into a number of practically independent States, and this circumstance seems to have led to considerable variations in the styles of writing. Having unified the empire, the First Emperor proceeded, on the advice of his minister Li Ssŭ, to standardize its script by ordaining that only the style in use in his own State of Ch'in should henceforward be employed throughout China. This new style of writing was the Greater Seal characters in the form they had assumed after several centuries of evolution, with numerous abbreviations and modifications. It was afterwards known as the 小篆 *hsiao chuan*, or Lesser Seal, and is familiar from the *Shuo Wên* dictionary. Though an improvement on what had gone before, something less cumbrous was felt to be necessary by the clerks who had to supply the immense quantity of written reports demanded by the First Emperor. Thus a simpler and more artistic form of writing was in use, though not universally, not long after the decree abolishing the Greater Seal. This 隸書 *li shu*, or "official script," as it is called, shows a great advance on the Seal character. It is perhaps likely to have been directly evolved from the Greater Seal. It differs from the modern character only in minor details. The Lesser Seal was evidently obsolete at the time of the compilation of the *Shuo Wên*, about 100 years after the Christian era. The Greater Seal and still earlier forms of writing had fallen into utter oblivion before the Han dynasty was 50 years old.

Out of the "official script" two other forms were soon developed, viz., the 草書 *ts'ao shu*, or "grass character" which so curtails the usual strokes as to be comparable to a species of shorthand, requiring special study, and the 行書 *hsing shu* or running hand, used in ordinary correspondence. Some form of grass character is mentioned as in use as early as 200 B.C. or thereabouts, though how nearly it approximated to the modern grass hand it is hard to say; the running hand seems to have come several centuries later. The final standardization of Chinese writing was due to the great calligraphist Wang Hsi-chih of the 4th century, who gave currency to the graceful style of character known as 楷書 *k'ai shu*, sometimes referred to as the "clerkly hand." When block-printing was invented some centuries later, the characters were cut on this model, which still survives at the present day. The script of China has remained practically unchanged ever since. The manuscript rolls of the T'ang and preceding dynasties, discovered by Sir Aurel Stein in Turkestan, show a style of writing not only clear and legible but remarkably modern in appearance.

Grammar.—No set of rules governing the mutual relations of words has ever been formulated by the Chinese, apparently because the need of such rules has never been felt. The most that native writers have done is to draw a distinction between 實字 and 虛字 "full" and "empty words," respectively, the former being subdivided into 活字 "living words" or verbs, and 死字 "dead words" or noun-substantives. By "empty words" particles are meant, though sometimes the expression is loosely applied to abstract terms, including verbs. The above meagre classification is their nearest approach to a conception of grammar in our sense. Every Chinese character is an indivisible unit, representing a sound and standing for a root-idea. Being free from inflection or agglutination of any kind it is incapable of indicating in itself either gender, number or case, voice, mood, tense or person. No Chinese character can be definitely regarded as being any particular part of speech or possessing any particular function absolutely, apart from the general tenor of its context. Thus, taken singly, the character 上 conveys only the general idea "above" as opposed to "below." According to its place in the sentence and the requirements of common sense, it may be a noun meaning "upper person" (that is, a ruler); an adjective meaning "upper," "topmost" or "best"; an adverb meaning "above"; a preposition meaning "upon"; and finally a verb meaning "to mount upon," or "to go to." It would puzzle grammarians to determine the precise grammatical function of any of the words in the following sentence, with the exception of 何 (an interrogative, by the way, which here happens to mean "why" but in other contexts is equivalent to "how," "which" or "what"): 事何必古 "Affair why must ancient," or in more idiomatic English, "Why necessarily stick to the ways of the ancients in such matters?" Or take a proverbial saying like 少所見多所怪 which may be correctly rendered "The less a man has seen the more he has to wonder at." It is one thing, however, to translate it correctly, and another to explain how this translation can be inferred from the individual words, of which the bald equivalents might be given as: "Few what see, many what strange." To say that "strange" is the literal equivalent of 怪 does not mean that 怪 can be definitely classed as an adjective. On the other hand, it would be dangerous even to assert that the word here plays the part of an active verb, because it would be equally permissible to translate the above, "Many things are strange to one who has seen but little."

There are certain positions and collocations of words which tend to recur, but the number of qualifications and exceptions which will have to be added is so great as to render the rule itself valueless. 馬上 means "on a horse," 上馬 "to get on a horse." But it will not do to say that a preposition becomes a verb when placed before the substantive, as many other prepositions come before and not after the words they govern. If we meet such a phrase as 警寇, literally "warn rebels," we must not mentally label 警 as a verb and 寇 as a substantive, and say to ourselves that in Chinese the verb is followed immediately by its object. Otherwise, we might be tempted to translate, "to warn the rebels," whereas a little reflection would show us that the conjunction of "warning" and "rebels" naturally leads to the meaning "to warn (the populace or whoever it may be) *against* the rebels." Each particular passage is best interpreted on its own merits, by the logic of the context and the application of common sense. The beginner must accustom himself to look upon each character as a root-idea, not a definite part of speech.

The Book Language.—In the beginning, all characters doubtless represented spoken words, but there was no need to reproduce in writing the bisyllabic compounds of common speech because *chien* "to see," in its written form 見, could not possibly be confused with any other *chien*, and it was therefore unnecessary to go to the trouble of writing 看見 *k'an-chien* "look-see," as in colloquial. All superfluous particles or other words that could be dispensed with were ruthlessly cut away, and all the old classical works were composed in the tersest of language, far removed from the speech of the people. The passion for brevity and conciseness resulted often in such obscurity that detailed commentaries on the classics have always constituted an important branch of Chinese literature. After the introduction of the improved style of script, and when the mechanical means of writing had been simplified, literary diction became freer and more expansive, to some extent, but the classics were held in such veneration as to exercise the profoundest influence over all succeeding schools of writers, and the divorce between literature and popular speech became permanent. No book of any first-rate literary pretensions would be easily intelligible to any class of Chinese, educated or otherwise, if read aloud exactly as printed. The public reader of stories is obliged to translate, so to speak, into the colloquial of his audience as he goes along. There is no inherent reason why the conversation of every-day life should not be rendered into characters, as is done in foreign handbooks for teaching elementary Chinese; one can only say that the Chinese do not think it worth while. There are a few words, indeed, which, though common enough in the mouths of genteel and vulgar alike, have positively no characters to represent them. On the other hand, there is a vast store of purely book words which would never be used or understood in conversation.

The book language is nice in its choice of words, and obeys special rules of construction. Of these, perhaps the most apparent is the carefully marked antithesis between characters in different clauses of a sentence, which results in a kind of parallelism of rhythmic balance. This parallelism is a noticeable feature in ordinary poetical composition, and may be well illustrated by the following four-line stanza: "白日依山盡 The bright sun completes its course behind the mountains; 黃河入海流 The yellow river flows away into the sea. 欲窮千里目 Would you command a prospect of a thousand *li*? 更上一層樓 Climb yet one storey higher." In the first line of this piece, every single character is balanced by a corresponding one in the second: 白 white by 黃 yellow, 日 sun by 河 river, and so on. In the 3rd and 4th lines, where more laxity is generally allowed, every word again has its counterpart, with the sole exception of 欲 "wish" and 更 "further." Some of the early Jesuit missionaries, men of great natural ability who steeped themselves in Oriental learning, have left very different opinions on record. Chinese appeared to be as admirable for the superabundant richness of its vocabulary as for the conciseness of its literary style. And among modern scholars there is a decided tendency to accept this view as embodying a great deal more truth than the other.

The Chinese language has to assimilate the vast stock of new terminology which closer contact with the West would necessarily carry with it, by the conjunction of two or more characters already existing; of this 昇降機 (rise-descend-machine) for "lift," and 議政國會 (discuss-govern-country-assembly) for "parliament" are examples. Even a metaphysical abstraction like the Absolute has been tentatively expressed by 絕對 (exclude-opposite); but in this case an equivalent was already existing in the Chinese language.

A drastic measure, strongly advocated in some quarters, is the entire abolition of all characters, to be replaced by their equivalent sounds in letters of the alphabet. Under this scheme 人 would figure as *jên* or *ren*, 馬 as *ma*, and so on. But the proposal has fallen extremely flat. The vocables are so few that only the colloquial, if even that, could possibly be transcribed in this manner. Any attempt to transliterate classical Chinese would result in a mere jumble of sounds, utterly unintelligible, even with the addition of tone-marks. There is another aspect of the case. The characters are a potent bond of union between the different parts of the country with their various dialects, and the script, in spite of certain disadvantages, has hitherto triumphantly adapted itself to the needs of civilized intercourse.

BIBLIOGRAPHY.—P. Premare, *Notitiae Linguae Sinicae* (1831); Ma Kien-chung, *Ma shih wên t'ung* (1899); L. C. Hopkins, *The Six Scripts* (1881) and *The Development of Chinese Writing* (1910); H. A. Giles, *A Chinese-English Dictionary* (2nd ed., 1910); B. Karlgren, *Sound and Symbol in Chinese* (1923).

CHINESE LITERATURE is not the oldest in the world, but it has the longest history of any written in a single language, continuously producing works of historical, intellectual and artistic interest for more than 2,500 years. The people's speech varied in different areas and changed with time, but because of the nature of their writing (*see* CHINESE LANGUAGE) and the early standardization of orthography, educated persons could read the national literature no matter where or when it was written.

Writing in the living language was a late development, and although masterpieces appeared in it, for a thousand years they remained outside the four standard Chinese categories of literature. These were:

The Classics.—These refer not to great writings throughout Chinese history, but to the heterogeneous scriptures (*ching*) making up the canon of the Confucian school of thought. They derive their status from association (in part actual, in part contrived much later) with Confucius himself (550 or 551–479 B.C.). It is certain that he used some form of the *Shu Ching* (*Classic of Documents*) and *Shih Ching* (*Classic of Songs*) in his teachings, less certain that he set great store by the *I Ching* (*Classic of Divination*). He probably compiled the *Ch'un Ch'iu* (*Springs and Autumns*), a bare chronicle of his native state of Lu which, accompanied by three early commentaries, accounts for three among the classics. The *Tso Chuan* probably was not a commentary in origin, being largely narrative; its literary interest is considerable.

The remarks of Confucius and some of his students are preserved in elliptical style in the *Lun Yü* (*Analects*). His later admirer Mencius was similarly immortalized in the more fluent book *Meng Tzu*, which likewise eventually became a classic. Since the 12th century these two texts have been associated with the *Ta Hsüeh* (*Great Learning*) and *Chung Yung* (*Happy Mean*) in a group constituting the four books emphasized by the neo-Confucians (*see* below, *Philosophical Works*). The latter two are really chapters extracted from the *Li Chi*, one of three classic collections of public and private ritual compiled toward the time of Christ, as was the *Erh Ya*.

This is a kind of lexicon, perhaps deriving its canonical status from a Chinese concept of the nature and power of the word—spoken or written—almost as mystical as the Christian concept of the Logos. Last but not least influential of the 13 classics is the spurious *Hsiao Ching* (*Classic of Filial Piety*). All are accompanied by numerous, sometimes divergent commentaries and subcommentaries.

Forming the core of education for government service (the primary aim of all education in prerepublican China), the classics permeated Chinese life. Their historical and philological importance is great, but except for the *Songs* (*see* below, *Poetry*) their intrinsic literary interest is far outweighed by their influence on later writings, which are often incomprehensible without recognition of their allusions to the classics. Chinese literary theory related all subsequently acknowledged literary forms to one or another of the classics.

Historical Writings, Including Biographies, Travelogues, Geographies, etc.—Historiography derives from the *Classic of Documents* through the *Springs and Autumns* chronicle. The so-called commentary *Tso Chuan* and other works of its period undoubtedly contain some genuine historical data. The first general history of China was the *Shih Chi* (*Historian's Records*) of Ssu-ma Ch'ien (145–?87 B.C.), who to some extent rationalized legend and proceeded with increasing historicity down to his own Han times. The monumental work was substantially a selection of extant texts, to which the compiler appended his own judgments. His method set the pattern for most subsequent histories, which were divided into (1) annals of imperial reigns; (2) tables of government organization, etc.; (3) treatises on such subjects as the calendar, economy and geography; and (4) biographies. Pan Ku (A.D. 32–92) intended his *History of the Han Dynasty* as a continuation of the *Historian's Records*. Each later dynasty officially sponsored such a continuation for its predecessor, usually compiled by a committee from the records of the fallen dynasty (*e.g.*, the "Veritable Records" of each emperor's reign). These and Ssu-ma Ch'ien's pioneer work make up the 25 standard histories.

The *Draft History of the Ch'ing Dynasty*, completed in 1928, never received official status, but it remains an indispensable source for the period it covers. The others are of similar value, though none deals in detail with events not connected with the court or government. The same applies generally to the independently written histories; *e.g.*, the celebrated *Tzu Chih T'ung Chien* (*Comprehensive Mirror for Aid in Governing*), a general history by Ssu-ma Kuang (1019–86), of which a later abridgment and various continuations formed the basis of the first European history of China. Aside from formal histories, innumerable other texts—biographical, geographical, technological, miscellaneous—can be used with critical care to fill in the background. Modern Chinese historians have produced many books and studies on currently accepted principles, including those of Marxism.

Philosophical Works other than those considered classics are catalogued together with all sorts of polemical and theoretical treatises and include some works of a religious nature but little on Buddhism, which had its own extensive canon outside the four classifications.

Early attempts to persuade men to courses of action (or inaction), by composition in a written language long based on symbols for concrete ideas and relatively simple extensions of them, were important in developing that language into a flexible medium for expository prose.

Persuasion rather than mere conviction was the aim; philosophy in China has been concerned mostly with principles for the guidance of human behaviour rather than with metaphysics or systems of logic. Hence it was usually political or antipolitical. Confucius' time was one of disunion and social breakdown; he preached return to a traditional age of sage kings who were in harmony with the Way of Heaven and governed by example. There were now many rival kingdoms, but Confucius maintained that a true king would receive the voluntary submission of all. A subject could at least become a gentleman (the Chinese term meant a prince's son, but the sage gave it a moral sense) with such virtues as humanity, justice and reciprocal fidelity between parents and children, superiors and inferiors.

Confucius emphasized, as manifestations of these qualities and as disciplines in preserving them, strict observance of time-honoured public and private rituals and manners. These ideas can be pieced together from the laconic *Analects;* they were developed, with certain divergencies, by similarly oriented teachers such as Mencius and Hsün Tzu.

To some other thinkers, the existence of political structures, rules of conduct and reverence for the past meant only that men had deviated from the Way (*Tao*), which could only be followed intuitively and could never be embodied in records or words. Yet these mystical Taoists wrote numerous books themselves. The *Tao Te Ching* (*Scripture of the Way and Its Power*) is one of the most frequently and divergently translated Chinese texts. Its alleged author, Lao Tzu (Lao-tse), was supposed to have lived in the time of Confucius, but at least parts of it are later than some of the *Teachings of Chuang Tzu*.

The latter contains passages of brilliant style and wit. Unlike many later Taoist writings, with their esoteric recipes for direct immortality, it more than once counsels accepting death with equanimity.

Few of these early writings were by a single hand, hence they are not always consistent. Taoism and Confucianism, often in conflict, were not mutually exclusive. Many writers classified under one school show elements of the other. Mo Ti stood apart from either in preaching universal love, a beneficent deity, and interceding spirits, while opposing useless ceremony. The legalists put no faith in good intention or example and called for explicit, rigorous law under absolute totalitarianism. Their program achieved the first unification of China, but the Ch'in dynasty (249–207 B.C.) was short-lived, and Confucianism became orthodox under the succeeding Han.

Scholar-administrators fostered acceptance of a textual canon which would be of higher authority than that of changing rulers, and of which they themselves would be the recognized interpreters. Thereafter Confucianism developed mostly through commentary on fixed texts.

Occasional independent philosophers appeared (*e.g.*, the skeptic Wang Ch'ung and the youthful metaphysician Wang Pi). Taoism in one direction degenerated into magic and became a popular religion, which soon had the powerful competition of imported Buddhism. Confucianism, with its noncommittal position on the supernatural and its emphasis on obligations, remained the official standard, but even emperors often favoured one or the other of its competitors.

Eventually the traditionalist philosophy vitiated its rivals by borrowing from them. Neo-Confucianism, as articulated by Chu Hsi (1130–1200) in a feat of syncretism comparable to that of

St. Thomas Aquinas, remained grounded on the classics but invested them with an eclectic metaphysic and cosmology. Its conservative ethic dominated Chinese mores, as Chu Hsi dominated scholarship, until modern times.

An influential modifier, Wang Yang-ming (1472–1528), gave the pursuit of knowledge a subjective interpretation suggestive of Zen Buddhism. The school of "Han Learning" from the 17th century sought an objective view of history, but its followers confined their investigations largely to textual problems.

At the turn of the 20th century, conditions brought political theory again to the fore. K'ang Yu-wei and, at first, Liang Ch'i-chao tried to rehabilitate Confucianism as a modernized state religion; Sun Yat-sen attempted to combine the western liberal tradition and some elements of Marxism with Chinese concepts. After 1949 the Communist state imposed an orthodoxy more absolute than Confucianism ever enjoyed.

Of professional philosophers, outside the field of action, the best-known Chinese name at mid-century was that of Fung Yu-lan, whose works show in different phases the influence of neo-Confucianism, western neorealism and Taoist transcendental thought.

Collected Works, as a standard classification, include all the poems, essays, letters and occasional pieces by a given man, but not a single drama or novel.

Until the 19th century the professional author, receiving money for publications, was virtually unknown in China. However, nearly all educated men were professional writers, their ability to compose documents being their primary qualification for civil employment.

Anything else they wrote was incidental, but could hardly be called avocational since proficiency in verse and certain other accepted forms was required for the government examinations as well as by social exigency. Actually a talent for literature often had a great deal to do with a man's reputation and consequently with his advancement. Production of less dignified genres, on the contrary, was harmful to an official career and hence usually unacknowledged.

Poetry in China from the beginning made rhyme as important as rhythm. The ancient *Classic of Songs* is a collection of folk songs (polished by court scribes), ceremonial odes and dynastic hymns, all from North China. Later commentators interpreted even the love songs as moral and political allegories. Similar treatment was inflicted on the next-oldest preserved poetry, which originated farther south in the incantations (often erotic) of male and female shamans. These inspired the melancholy rhapsodies associated with the vague figure of Ch'ü Yüan, central among which stands the luxuriant, obscure "Li Sao" ("Falling into Trouble"). Partly from these, in turn, came the rhymeprose (*fu*), with a short prose introduction and strongly rhythmical sections making free use of rhyme. It was characterized by virtuoso piling up of words for cumulative effect, as already in the goddess-haunted "Rhymeprose on Mount Kao-t'ang" attributed to one Sung Yü (third century B.C.?).

Eventually some writers used the *fu* for more formal or more realistic subjects, as Lu Chi (A.D. 261–303) in his brilliant "Rhymeprose on Literature"—the first systematic Chinese essay on literary form and theory—and Yü Hsin (513–581) in his great "Lament for the South" on the fall of the Liang dynasty. But during Han times, when the *fu* was the chief rhythmic vehicle for the literati, it remained predominantly descriptive.

Meanwhile the Han imperial music bureau had started writing down the songs of the people for adaptation to court use. These lyrics and ballads (called *yüeh-fu* poems), more varied in theme and expression than the ancient *Classic of Songs,* gradually inspired literary men to simpler poetry mixing personal sentiments with folk themes.

The Wei dynasty prince Ts'ao Chih (192–232) raised this combination to poetic heights. Even more individual was the recluse T'ao Ch'ien (365–427), one of China's greatest poets. He spent nearly all his life on a small farm close to nature, which permeates his poems both realistically and philosophically. He also took considerable comfort in wine. Coterie poets of this period of disunion were more self-consciously unconventional, often proclaiming their scorn of official life, celebrating wine and fantasy. Others devoted themselves to erotic themes, praising beautiful women in the ornamental palace style, a pastiche of cliché. After the reaction against this preciosity, poets seldom wrote about sexual or romantic passion, at least for circulation.

The T'ang dynasty (618–907) is often called the golden age of Chinese poetry, because it produced galaxies of major and minor poets and because early in this period was crystallized the verse form par excellence. The regulated poem (*lü-shih*) is so considered because it fully yet compactly exploits the tonal resources of the Chinese language. It consists of a stanza of eight five-word or seven-word lines with a complex pattern of tonal or pitch contrasts. In such brief space there is no place for connectives; the style is inevitably elliptical and allusive. Even more concentrated is the stop-short (*chüeh-chü*) containing only four such lines.

Able poets sometimes violated the rules and often wrote freer "old-style" types of verse; no Chinese literary form, once established, was ever abandoned completely.

T'ang poetry reflects the dynastic glory and sophisticated cosmopolitan life of the period but also the hazards of political careers and the hardships of internal war and disaster. One of history's most lavish patrons of the arts was the emperor Ming Huang (Hsüan Tsung), yet his reign was broken by a rebellion which sent his pensioners scurrying about the empire in search of food and shelter. The insouciant Li Po, once a favoured guest at court, in his wanderings continued to write virtuoso fantasies and heightened evocations of landscape with the same ease as before. A legend grew up that he drowned while drunkenly trying to embrace the moon's reflection. Tu Fu, a man of soberer character, a conscientious minor official and a painstaking writer, put into his poems the hardships and sorrows of his own life and those of the common people.

For his broad humanity coupled with meticulous craftsmanship many Chinese consider him their greatest poet. Some of his and Li Po's poems were messages to each other. Meetings and partings of friends is a ubiquitous subject in Chinese poetry, often treated with deep feeling as between these two, perhaps oftener as a social-literary convention.

In later and calmer T'ang times the ballads and lyrics of a gentler poet, Po Chü-i (772–846), made his name a household word. One of the most appealing of Chinese poets, he is also one of the most translatable. More difficult are the poems of his contemporary Han Yü, chiefly known as a model prose writer. He championed a return to the simplicity characteristic of Chinese prose before it accumulated a set of elaborate rules involving verbal parallelism and verselike regularity. As a poet he wrote largely in regulated verse, but brought to it an unhackneyed vocabulary and employed harsh combinations when he wanted a harsh effect.

Equally original, at about the same time, was the short-lived Li Ho, whose strange satanic poems have been compared with those of the French symbolists.

Toward the end of the T'ang a previously subliterary form, the *tz'u,* began to enjoy a measure of artistic status. Young men set their own words to songs they heard in the brothels and teahouses, following the rhythm and melody of a given song so that the resulting love poem was often in uneven lines. Some of the loveliest and saddest are by Li Yü (937–978), second and last ruler of the ephemeral Southern T'ang, who died a prisoner of the Sung.

In the Sung dynasty (960–1279) the *tz'u* was adapted to more varied subjects, and much of the best poetry of the period was in this form, though its origin prevented inclusion in a man's collected works. Sung writers also revitalized the rhymeprose, while making of it less rhyme and more prose; the "prose *fu*" of Ou-yang Hsiu are especially noteworthy. The most popular Sung poet, Su Tung-p'o, reworked as a *tz'u* one of his two famous *fu* about his visits to the Red cliff on the Yangtze. The most prolific of all Chinese poets, Lu Yu, especially wrote patriotic pieces urging defense of Sung China against its encroaching enemies. For several centuries after its fall, the finest verse appeared in opera librettos.

Drama or opera evolved slowly from court ballets, street entertainments and variety shows. The theatre as an integral artistic and popular institution emerged in the Yüan dynasty (1279–1368). For its character and history, *see* DRAMA. Despite or rather because of its great popularity, the drama was not a respected medium for literary talent, partly because the narrative and dialogue parts were written in the language of everyday life. There was little precedent for writing down such language, and doing so could not advance a man's career in an officialdom for which even the entrance examinations were in the terse literary language.

In the Yüan period China was ruled by the Mongols, and the classical examinations counted for little. Apparently some educated Chinese to whom office under the conquerors was either closed or repugnant, having time on their hands, took an interest in the theatre and began to write for it, doubtless not without pay. Verses for the arias more or less remained in the literary language, being made intelligible to the ear through colloquial asides by the performers.

Fiction existed in written form from early times, in the sense of elaborations on history and anecdotes in philosophical writings. Nobody knows how much of the *Intrigues of the Warring States* or the *Tso Commentary* is factual, how much hearsay or invention. Even in later times, hero tales and ghost stories were intended to be taken as true reports. The poet T'ao Ch'ien wrote a famous prose allegory, "The Peach Blossom Source," but not until the T'ang period did the literary tale come into its own. From frequent use of the supernatural such tales were called *ch'uan-ch'i*, "narrations of strange things." Many were love stories. They were still written in the scholar's language, and could scarcely be read by any other class; the masses depended on itinerant storytellers in the streets.

These entertainers seem to have kept simple outlines or prompt books in the vernacular, which printers began to bring out in illustrated popular editions, which fell into the hands of scholars who read them in private and polished them for diversion. They expanded the outlines, adding new incidents and subplots, retaining as chapter endings the storyteller's allurement: "And if you don't know what happened then, listen to the next episode."

Thus the novel was born. For centuries it remained outside the pale of recognized literature, unsigned or attributed to a rival, since discovery might ruin the author's official career. Authorship was often composite, different readers making any alterations or additions they liked; numerous variant editions appeared. The *Romance of the Three Kingdoms,* prototype of many novels based on historical characters and themes, existed in fairly extended form as early as the Yüan period, but the present 120-chapter version probably dates from the 16th century. The *Water Margin* (retitled *All Men Are Brothers* in one translation) deals sympathetically with the exploits of a band of robbers in the 12th century. The *Journey to the West* (partially translated as *Monkey*) by a known author, Wu Ch'eng-en (?1500–80) is a satirical allegory written in the manner of an interminable but amusing fairy tale.

The first novel of everyday life, divorced from legend, history and the street entertainer's conventions, was *Chin P'ing Mei* (completely translated as *The Golden Lotus*), written anonymously in Ming times. Its theme is the ruin caused by selfish pursuit of pleasure; because of its frequent pornography, probably introduced to ensure readers, it has been especially denounced. Yet it is a truly great realistic novel, complex in plot and convincing in characterization.

The 18th-century *Dream of the Red Chamber* (*Hung Lou Meng*) is a sentimental but psychologically penetrating love story developed against the background of a large family and its declining fortunes. Ts'ao Chan left this novel unfinished at his death, and Kao E carried it to a conclusion. The death of one of its two heroines has called forth at least as many tears as Samuel Richardson's *Pamela,* written not much earlier.

Several Ch'ing dynasty novels sharply satirized official corruption and inefficiency. In the last years of the Chinese empire an unsuccessful businessman and reformer, Liu E (1857–1909), wrote the semiautobiographical *Travels of Lao Ts'an,* which has little plot but is unified by an original personality. It reflects his multiform interests, including the Sherlock Holmes stories, but primarily his anxiety over the future of China, represented in a dream by a floundering ship with an irresponsible and vicious crew.

The colloquial short story developed concurrently with the novel, retaining the oral storyteller's clichés to an even greater extent. Stories of exemplary conduct were rather conventional; love stories showed far more realism and invention. Three definitive anthologies published in late Ming times are known collectively as the *San Yen.*

In the Ch'ing dynasty the literary-language tale of ghosts and marvels was revived, with especial artistry in P'u Sung-ling's *Strange Stories from the Liao-chai Studio.*

Women Writers, exceptional in premodern China because of educational and social limitations, were by no means unknown. Pan Ku's sister, Pan Chao, contributed substantially to his *History of the Han Dynasty.* It became a convention for men to write love poetry from a woman's standpoint, reserving the masculine first person for poems of friendship; but countless anonymous love poems are traditionally attributed to various women. Known poetesses include Ts'ai Yen, who wrote 18 memorable stanzas about her long captivity by a border tribe in late Han times; Yü Hsüan-chi, a Taoist nun and mistress of more than one T'ang poet; and Li Ch'ing-chao (Sung dynasty), famous for her *tz'u.* Female professional authors appeared in the 20th century (*e.g.,* leftist short story writer and poetess Ting Ling).

The Literary Revolution which followed the political one of 1911 virtually abolished the terse traditional style; the mainstream of literature shifted to an approximation of the vernacular. This change, championed in 1917 by Hu Shih and Ch'en Tu-hsiu amid a storm of controversy, came about largely for practical rather than purely literary reasons.

A modern China must aim at nation-wide literacy, impossible if education should remain divorced from speech patterns, and at assimilation of the theoretical and practical knowledge of the rest of the world. Even in the new *pai-hua* (plain speech) style, officially taught in the schools after 1920, new terms had to be coined, eventually becoming idiomatic.

Authors freely borrowed both ideas and techniques from Europe and America, where some of them studied. Western literary trends reflected in China generally were those of several decades past: Ts'ao Yü's play *Thunder and Rain* shows the influence of Ibsen, Mao Tun's novel *Midnight* that of Zola and Tolstoy. Although the high place occupied in European literature by fiction and drama had much to do with the reappraisal of China's own popular literature, the traditions of that literature (other than its use of the vernacular) were more honoured than imitated. The new writings were nearly always bound up with some aesthetic or political program, their authors associating themselves with magazines or manifestoes. Groups dissolved and shifted overnight as iconoclasts became conservatives and aesthetes turned reformers.

Caught between opposing political forces some turned from programs to scholarship, while the most active writers tended more and more to the left. Lu Hsün (1881–1936), whose brief but bitter *Ah Q* is the classic of modern Chinese fiction, was forced into the extreme camp by circumstance rather than by firm conviction, though the Communists later made his works "revolutionary" classics. At mid-20th century the outstanding literary name in Communist China was that of Kuo Mo-jo, an archaeologist, playwright, poet and critic who attained high office as a sort of cultural commissar.

Cut off from the mainland, Nationalist Chinese writers abroad and on the island stronghold of Formosa found it hard to produce creative works rooted in their native soil, but not being bound by an all-pervasive authority they could maintain a higher level of objective literary criticism and scholarship.

Modern Chinese poetry threw off restrictions of form and content, but merely exchanged Chinese models for foreign ones, principally the imagists and Whitman in reverse chronological order. Traditional forms were not completely abandoned—even Communist leader Mao Tse-tung wrote *tz'u* verses—but no general revitalization of them appeared imminent.

Chinese literature obviously would remain in transition until the nation became sufficiently unified and stabilized to achieve again a homogeneous culture of its own. Whether the novels, plays and poems of the future would be anything like those of the past would depend on whether native traditions were to be reassimilated and transformed.

The Communists undertook to reinterpret the whole of China's past literature, for instance revising the still popular traditional plays to emphasize social and economic contrasts in them. But no very individual creative artistry could operate in either traditional or new mediums as long as both were to be rigorously controlled. Meantime contemporary Chinese literature continued to share one important characteristic with that of the past, namely its predominantly didactic nature.

Bibliography.—Marcel Granet, *La Pensée chinoise,* chapters 1–2 (1934); Lien-sheng Yang, *Topics in Chinese History* (Cambridge, Mass., and London, 1950); Fêng Yu-lan, *A History of Chinese Philosophy,* Eng. trans. by Derk Bodde, rev. ed., 2 vol. (Princeton and London, 1952–53); James R. Hightower, *Topics in Chinese Literature,* rev. ed. (Cambridge, Mass., and London, 1953), with extensive bibliography of translations (note addenda); Bernard S. Solomon, *The Veritable Record of the T'ang Emperor Shun-tsung* (Cambridge, Mass.; London, 1955); John L. Bishop, *The Colloquial Short Story in China* (Cambridge, Mass.; London, 1955); John L. Bishop, "Chinese Poetics: Prosodic Elements in T'ang Poetry," *North Carolina Studies in Comparative Literature,* vol. 12 (Chapel Hill, N.C., 1955); Yi-tsi Mei, "Tradition and Experiment in Modern Chinese Literature," *ibid.*; Achilles Fang, "From Imagism to Whitmanism in Recent Chinese Poetry—A Search for Poetics That Failed," *ibid.* (G. W. Br.)

CHINESE MUSIC. Music played a great part in the origins of ancient Chinese civilization. The pitch pipe of the normal pitch (called *huang-chung*) was the basis of the Chinese system of measures, of the calendar and of their astronomical calculations.

A Musical System.—According to tradition, the emperor Huang Ti (*c.* 2697 B.C.) sent his minister Ling-lun to the Kuenlun mountains in northwest China to cut a pitch pipe from a species of bamboo which gave the note *huang-chung.* Eleven other notes were derived from this note by the following process: a third part of the nine-inch pipe *huang-chung* was cut off, thus producing a second pipe, *lin-chung,* which was six inches long ($9\times\frac{2}{3}$) and gave the fifth. The second pipe was divided into three parts, and one of the third parts was added to it (8 in. or $6\times\frac{1}{3}$); this gave the descending fourth (*tai-tsu*) from the second pipe, and so on.

This was the origin of the 12 Chinese pitch pipes: *huang-chung* (Ć), *ta-lu* (Ć#), *tai-tsu* (D́), *chia-chung* (D́#), *ku-hsi* (É), *chung-lu* (F́), *jui-pin* (F́#), *lin-chung* (Ǵ), *i-tse* (Ǵ#), *nan-lu* (Á), *wu-i* (Á#), and *ying-chung* (B́). The Chinese system of fifths is first mentioned in the work *Lu-Tsu-Chun-Chiu,* which dates from the 3rd century B.C.—about the time when the Pythagorean musical system was made known in Greece by the pupils of Pythagoras.

As the circle of fifths could not be closed because of the (Pythagorean) comma, the Chinese made a number of attempts in the course of the ages to divide the octave into 60 notes (King-fang, *c.* 40 B.C.), 360 notes (Chien-lo-chih, *c.* A.D. 430), 18 notes (Tsai-yuan-ting, *c.* A.D. 1180) and 12 notes (Ho-cheng-tien, *c.* A.D. 420 and Wang-po, *c.* A.D. 958), equal and unequal temperament respectively. The old system of fifths still continued however to be the prevailing system.

Finally, Prince Chu-tsai-yu, in 1595, a century earlier than Andreas Werkmeister (1691) in Europe, fixed the 12 pitch pipes in equal temperament; in order to obtain the nearest semitone he divided the length of a pitch pipe by 1.0594631 or $\sqrt[12]{2}$ and its diameter by 1.0292857 or $\sqrt[24]{2}$. The mathematical and physical basis was confirmed by experiment by the Belgian authority on acoustics, V. C. Mahillon.

The ancient Chinese scale has five tones: *kung* (C), *shang* (D), *chiao* (E), *chih* (G) and *yu* (A). Later, under the Chou dynasty (1122–255 B.C.), two further notes, *pien-chih* (F#) and *pien-kung* (B), were added.

Each note of this scale of five or seven notes can be used as the primary note of a scale, and this gives five or seven modes, just as in Greek music there are the Doric mode, the Phrygian, etc. As each of these five or seven modes can be transposed in 12 ways, there are 60 or 84 keys in Chinese music. (X.)

Musical Practice.—The ancient theory and the classical music of past centuries were connected almost exclusively with the rites and ceremonies of the temples of worship and of the court. One of the old literary classics, the *Li Chi* or *Book of Rites,* contains many allusions to music; and one whole section (said to be a later interpolation) is devoted wholly to music in its ethical, ritual and symbolic aspects. The imperial ministry of rites once included a bureau of music, but the function of that office seems to have been entirely a matter of ceremonial tradition and to have had no connection with the practice of music in its popular forms. The performance of ritual music was continued in certain places up to recent times with a scrupulous adherence to tradition. The solemn celebration of the highest office of the Confucian worship is accompanied by a traditional orchestra of 44 pieces. Taoist temples are content with about six instruments. In the Confucian solemn rite the emperor himself was supposed to be the chief celebrant.

The pentatonic, nonharmonic music for this celebration has often been reproduced in European notation in the books on Chinese music, particularly the solemn march to which the imperial worshipper proceeded to the door of the temple and the concluding monodic hymn to Confucius (*Ta tsai K'ung tsen*) in which all the instruments and voices took part.

Music outside the temples is more popular in character and has probably been subjected to more frequent changes in style; although even here the tenacious conservative instincts of the Chinese handed down a more archaic type of music to the present day than is known in the occidental countries. The practice of this music by individuals, particularly by amateurs of high social status, for their own aesthetic satisfaction is not so widespread in China as in the west.

Home or household music seems to have been more highly developed in Japan than in China. There is, in China, no well-organized class of professional music teachers. Most musicians acquire their art in a purely empirical way, although there is a considerable body of books containing the notations of tunes for various instruments. This notation is not a staff notation, but a tablature system; that is, a series of signs or symbols for the individual tones, frets or finger positions.

BY COURTESY OF THE METROPOLITAN MUSEUM OF ART

CHINESE GONG AND STICK. A MUSICAL PERCUSSION INSTRUMENT NOW USED CHIEFLY IN THE THEATRE

Vocal music has an important place in the temples and still more in the theatre. Apart from this it is not cultivated as an art co-ordinate with instrumental music to the same extent as in western nations, although the singing of songs and ballads is not uncommon.

Musical Instruments.—The number of instruments used by

the Chinese is comparatively large. Moule lists and describes not fewer than 130. Many of them are, to be sure, mere toys or signal instruments of no great musical importance. They are used by mountebanks at fairs or markets, and by hawkers or beggars. European writers about Chinese instruments devote much space to the description of the ancient classic instruments used in temple worship, many of which have long since gone out of common use. They are largely percussion instruments, including many forms of highly ornamented drums (*Ying ku,* 應鼓; *po fu,* 搏附; *pang ku,* 梆鼓), sonorous stones single (*t'e k'ing* 特磬) or arranged in chimes (*pien k'in* 編磬) or bronze bells used in the same manner (*po chung* 鎛鍾; *pien chung* 編鍾). The *k'in* 琴 is a narrow hollow box 3 to 4 ft. in length, with slightly convex upper surface. It has five, or in more modern instruments, seven silk strings plucked with the fingers, and was still used until fairly recent times for refined artistic music. Its Japanese counterpart is the *koto.* A larger instrument constructed on the same principle, but having in earlier times as many as 50 strings, later only about 25, is the *se,* rarely used except in ceremonies. The ancient instruments were classified by the older theory according as they produced the sound of stone, metal, silk, bamboo, wood, skin, gourd and earth. The most important instruments still in use are the two-stringed fiddle, *hu k'in,* 胡琴; the four-stringed moon guitar, *y"ueh k'in,* 月琴; the four-stringed, pear-shaped, balloon guitar, *p'i p'a,* 琵琶; the three-stringed guitar with a very long neck, *san hsien,* 三絃; a first cousin of the Japanese *samisen.* Of the flute type are the straight (direct) flute *hsiao* 簫; and the transverse flute *ti,* 笛. Reed instruments are represented by the gentle *kuan tzu* 管子, a straight bamboo tube, 8 to 10 in. long, with a rice straw serving as a double reed or oboe mouthpiece; and the shrill, *so na* 鎖吶, a double reed instrument with a conical wooden body ending in a metal "bell," often called the Chinese clarinet. The *sheng* 笙 consists of a lacquered wooden body (formerly a gourd or calabash), about the shape and size of a tea cup, and a mouthpiece through which the player inhales the air. On the body are grouped 13 to 17 speaking pipes, slender bamboo tubes each provided with a thin, free reed of metal. Each tube has a hole below the reed and the pipe speaks only when the hole is stopped by the player's finger. The *yang k'in,* 洋琴, or foreign psaltery, consists of a trapezoidal sound box about 2 ft. in width over which are usually stretched 14 to 20 double, triple or quadruple sets of metal strings which are played by striking them with two light bamboo rods.

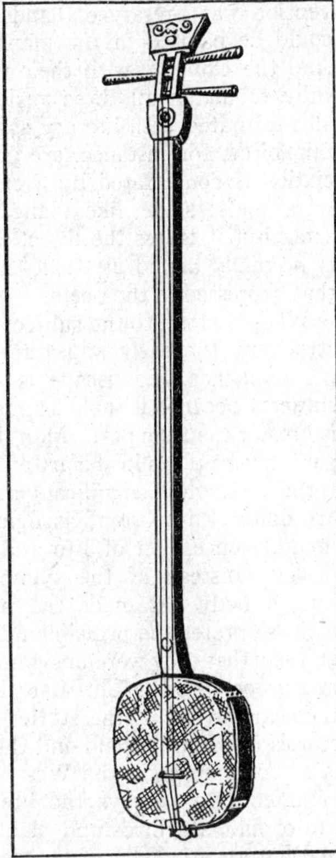

BY COURTESY OF THE METROPOLITAN MUSEUM OF ART
THE THREE-STRINGED CHINESE BANJO, SHOWING LONG NECK

Modern percussion instruments, used chiefly in the theatre, include the large gong (*lo* 鑼), cymbals (*po* 鈸), a flat circular drum, struck with a pair of light sticks (*pang ku* 梆鼓) and sharply resonant wooden blocks or castanets (*pe pan* 拍板). Before the revolution of 1911–12, professional musicians had no high social standing. Those who played in the theatre commanded more respect than the players in funeral or wedding processions. Courtesans and beggars who played and sang, and ballad singers were of the lowest rank. The Chinese theatre makes copious use of music, the drama being practically a music drama. A relatively very small part of the play is given over to unaccompanied spoken dialogue. The recitative portions are either punctuated by the percussion instruments or are invested with a continuous rhythmic accompaniment of these instruments which often drown out the actor-singer's voice. The lyric portions of the performance are accompanied by the fiddles, guitars, flutes or pipes. The protagonist selects the tunes from among a large number of well-known conventional strains or motives, said to be very old. The instrumentalists accompany in unison, although, since they play without

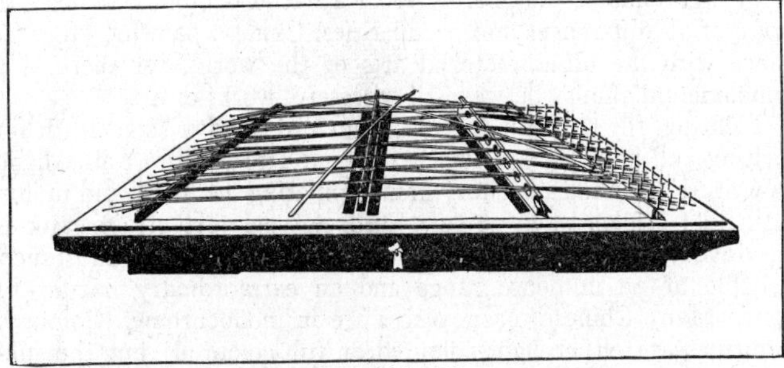

BY COURTESY OF THE METROPOLITAN MUSEUM OF ART
CHINESE DULCIMER (YANG CH'IN), HAVING 16 SETS OF STRINGS, 4 IN EACH SET, AND PLAYED WITH TWO BAMBOO BEATERS

written music, embellishments and variations are produced *ad libitum,* and there are at times instances of the use of double notes and traces of an embryo type of contrapuntal invention. The Chinese ideal of good vocal performance, particularly for the male actors, requires a high, forced falsetto tone production.

All of this music, as well as the popular music of funeral and wedding processions and of street songs is, like the sacred music, distinctly pentatonic. But where, as in the popular orchestra or solo performance, the art of improvisation and embellishment has free play, the larger intervals of the five-tone scale are frequently filled out in runs and figures, as a careful analysis of phonograph records (Erich Fischer) has shown. But even here the importance of the pentatonic skeleton or foundation is beyond doubt and is easily sensed by the European hearer. Since the revolution the influence of Western music has become more marked.

BIBLIOGRAPHY.—J. A. Van Aalst, *Chinese Music* (1884); A. C. Moule, "A List of the Musical and Other Sound-Producing Instruments of the Chinese," *Journal of the North-China Branch of the Royal Asiatic Society* (vol. xxxix., 1908); Louis Laloy, *La Musique Chinoise* (1910); Erich Fischer, "Beiträge zur Erforschung der chinesischen Musik," *Sammelbände der Internationalen Musik-Gesellschaft* (vol. xii., 1911); Maurice Courant, "Sur La Musique Classique des Chinois," *Encyclopédie de La Musique* (1914); G. Soulié de Morant, *Théatre et Musique en Chine* (1926). (O. K.)

CHINESE PAINTING. The first thing to be said about Chinese painting is that very little is known of its actual achievements. We have indeed ample records of the lives and works of innumerable painters, from the first centuries of our era onwards, and a mass of criticism. Chinese paintings also exist in vast quantities. But it must be realized that of genuine, or probably genuine, works of the great masters of the best periods, very few indeed remain. It is impossible to doubt, from the evidence of what has survived, and from literary records, that Chinese painting, with its majestic and continuous tradition of more than 1,500 years, is one of the greatest schools of painting that the world has seen. But we are quite without the means of comparing Chinese painting as a whole with the paintings of Italy, or any other European school, the successive masterpieces of which are known and accessible to every student.

It is true that during the 20th century the almost complete ignorance which prevailed on the subject till the end of the 19th century has been greatly lessened. Important discoveries have been made, and it is impossible to predict what may yet be discovered. The fundamental difficulties, however, of the study of Chinese painting are likely to remain; the extreme rarity, namely, of certain and documented works, on which an accurate conception of the greater masters' style can be based. The practice of repeating famous designs with variations, of copying ancient works, which has prevailed in all ages, makes it possible to have a general idea of the styles of certain periods and certain masters.

But immense and repeated destruction accounts for the rarity of ancient pictures in China itself. In Japan collections have been made, centuries ago, and religiously preserved; and these paintings form the best foundation for study, though in many cases the traditional attributions have been abandoned by modern criticism.

General Characteristics.—Painting is the pre-eminent art of China. It is right that the art of any nation should be judged by a world standard, not merely from a national point of view. In spite of all differences and peculiarities, Chinese painting takes its place with the other pictorial arts of the world, for there is a fundamental affinity between all successful works of art.

Painting, for the Chinese, is a branch of handwriting. Both for writing and painting a brush is used; and to acquire a fine hand in writing demands a mastery in manipulating the brush and modulating its strokes such as few European painters attain. Ink is the favourite medium; but Chinese ink is a wonderful substance, capable of an immense range and an extraordinary beauty of tone. Many Chinese masterpieces are in monochrome. Coloured paintings are either light-coloured or full-coloured; but the ink-drawing remains almost always the foundation of the design. Fresco-painting, technically a different method from the fresco-painting of Europe (*see* Church's *Chemistry of Paints and Painting*, p. 307, 1915), was largely practised—and probably the grandest art of China was in this form—but the frescoes of the finest period seem all to have been destroyed. The great mass of Chinese pictures, however, are paintings on silk or, less commonly, absorbent paper, the pigments being water-colours or body-colours (*see* R. Petrucci, *Encyclopédie de la Peinture Chinoise*, 1918, a translation of a well-known treatise illustrated with woodcuts called the *Mustard Seed Garden*. *See* also Ferguson's *Chinese Painting*). Paintings are usually in the form of hanging pictures or of horizontal scrolls, in both cases normally kept rolled up. The latter form involves a mode of composition peculiar to Chinese art, though imitated by the Japanese. These paintings, often of great length, are unrolled bit by bit and enjoyed as a reader enjoys reading a manuscript. A succession of pictures is presented, though the composition is continuous. Thus, in the case of landscape, for which this form has been used with most felicity, one seems to be actually passing through the country depicted. Other forms are the framed picture and the small album picture; screens also were employed for painting.

Chinese technique admits of no correction. The artist closely observes and stores his observations in his memory. He conceives his design, and having completed the mental image of what he intends to paint, he transfers it swiftly and with sure strokes to the silk. The communication through the sensitive and powerful strokes of the brush of something personal and unique must, in such an art, count for much in the spectator's appreciation. The qualities prized by the Chinese in a small ink-painting of bamboos, a favourite subject alike with beginners and masters, are those prized in a piece of fine handwriting, only there is added a keen appreciation of the simultaneous seizure of life and natural character in the subject. In the *Mustard Seed Garden* treatise cited above, it is said that in a master's work "the idea is present even where the brush has not passed." And this emphasis on the value of suggestion, of reserves and silences, is important to notice, because no other art has understood, like the Chinese, how to make empty space a potent factor in the design. It may be that Chinese painting relies too much on suggestion, presuming in the spectator a sensibility and a fineness of organization which are found but in choice societies; on the other hand it avoids that laborious accumulation of unessential phenomena which in European art has proved the death of so many pictures by accomplished hands. A certain slightness, comparatively speaking, is inevitable in Chinese paintings, partly because of the water-colour medium, partly because suggestion is preferred to statement, partly because so many of the artists were amateurs and not professionals. It is remarkable, however, how solid and structural a Chinese landscape can be. The greater painters gave much thought and pains to elaborating a convention by which the sense of shape and mass can be given to rock forms, for instance, without losing directness and vitality of brush stroke, the sense of handwriting. Each successful convention was preserved, handed down and imitated. Mountains could be painted in the manner of this old master or of that. And the Chinese, with their passion for codification, have carefully tabulated all these various methods. The painter's art is also saturated with literary associations. Certain flowers and certain birds, for instance, are painted together because their association is consecrated by a classic poem. Many of the painters were poets; some, like Wang Wei, equally distinguished in both arts. But it is less the direct illustration of a poem or story that is normally aimed at, than the evocation of a mood similar to that expressed in the poem.

When we turn to the subject-matter of Chinese painting, we are struck by the early appearance of landscape art and its actual predominance. Landscape is accounted the most important of subjects because it includes man and all living things; the whole is greater than the part. Man does not play the central and heroic part that he plays in the art of Europe, for which the nude human form is the most significant and expressive of motives. Flowers are quite as important as figures. This difference in the fundamental conception of life and the universe makes itself felt in design. Instead of the symmetry which contemplation of the human body has made the basis of Western composition, the Chinese prefer the principle of balance. They contemplated trees and saw that they were unsymmetrical but perfectly poised. Where in Europe we have Christian themes, in China we have Buddhist themes; instead of the stories of classic mythology we have the stories of Taoist legend and the fairy tale. Genre-painting (*q.v.*) is as common as in the West, though portraiture is perhaps less common. But always the life of the world outside man,—the life of animals, birds and plants—plays a much larger part than in Western art. The life of action counts for less, and the contemplative life for more.

HISTORY

Early Periods.—From literary references we can infer that painting was practised in China several centuries at least before Christ, chiefly in the form of portraiture. It is not till we come to the Han dynasty, that we have any more tangible evidence, though there exist some rude designs in red on jade which may be a thousand years earlier. Designs on lacquer of the 1st century A.D., found in Korea by Mr. Umehara, and in Chinese Turkistan by Sir Aurel Stein; some rough paintings on tiles (Eumorfopoulos collection), and other decorations; outline drawings on vases of rather later date, give some hint of what painting in the Han period was like. We see that a Chinese type of decorative design, animated by movement in the forms, was already matured. The incised stone friezes of the period are clearly translations of paintings, and these give an idea of the character of pictorial design and the range of subject—scenes from history and legend, ceremonies, dances, mythical creatures, and all the fairy world of Taoism.

In the 4th century, however, flourished an artist who ranks among China's most famous masters: Ku K'ai-chih. There exist two rolls attributed to him: one, *The Admonitions of the Instructress in the Palace*, is in the British Museum; the other, illustrating a poem on a river nymph, is in the Freer collection at Washington. These paintings are by different hands. The one in the Freer collection is altogether drier in handling, and may be a Sung copy. The British Museum roll is of a marvellous subtlety and distinction; the line is intimately expressive. Its actual date is disputed, but it is generally thought to be, if not an original, a T'ang copy. In any case there is no doubt that both of these paintings represent the design of the Chin dynasty (A.D. 265–420). They are, therefore, extremely precious documents, and their value is increased by the fact that while the British Museum roll depicts scenes of court life, with all the details of dress and accessories of singular refinement, the Freer roll, with its dragon chariot and floating fairies, gives the imaginative or fanciful side of the art of the period. In both cases the landscape element is quite primitive. The landscape introduced into the London painting is indeed in strong contrast with the consummate grace and expressiveness of the tall and slender figures, and the air of a mature and fine civilization which they seem to breathe. Far from being primitive, the figure-drawing seems to belong to the close of a tradition rather than its beginning; and we may conjecture behind it the ruder, masculine style of Han gradually subtilized and transformed in the direction of elegance and charm. Ku K'ai-chih famed especially for his portraits, painted all kinds of subjects, including Buddhist themes. But if we may take these two pictures attributed to him as typical of the period, we find no trace of Indian influence in them.

Of about the 6th century are some of the earliest wall paintings in the rock temples at Tun-huang, on China's western frontier (*see* Pelliot, *Grottes de Touen-houang,* vol. iv.), full of animated movement, containing figures of the same slender and elegant type as those in the Ku K'ai-chih roll. But these are provincial in manner.

It was in the 6th century that the famous six canons of Hsieh Ho, himself a painter, were formulated. The exact meaning of the first and most important of these has been disputed, but it is clear that the emphasis is laid on creative inspiration, conceived not as a personal gift, but as the spirit of the cosmos entering into the artist and enabling him to produce in his forms the movement of life.

The legends of the great masters tell, not of the deceptive appearance of reality in their paintings, but of their being so informed with passionate life that they assumed material existence and motion. The emphasis on movement is significant. Even in decorative designs the forms seem to move and flow.

The T'ang Dynasty (A.D. 618–907).—In the 7th century the empire, after a period of division, was consolidated under the great T'ang dynasty, which lasted for 300 years. This was undoubtedly the period of China's grandest art. It is true that almost all the painting of the time has perished; but all the available evidence confirms the testimony of the Chinese historians and critics to the greatness of the T'ang masters. Some fragments of a painting of a spring festival, found by Sir Aurel Stein in 1914 at Turfan, and some other paintings found in the same locality by the Otani expedition, are precious relics of early T'ang art, for they show us something of the pictorial style of the early 8th century. Here we find the new T'ang ideal of feminine beauty: a more massive form, compared with the slender elegance of preceding periods; a full, rounded face, with hair heaped around and above the head, and an air of smiling health. Precisely the same types and the same pictorial motives are found in the few pictures surviving from this period in Japan. And it is from the early painting of Japan, closely modelled on Chinese prototypes, that we can most safely infer the great style of T'ang. This kind of painting is mostly Buddhistic, and the grandest T'ang works were of Buddhist inspiration. Supreme among them, according to all testimony, were the works of Wu Tao-tzū, acknowledged to be the greatest of all Chinese painters.

China, during this epoch, was open to foreign influences as she has never been since. Her empire expanded westward; her suzerainty extended as far as the Caspian. Envoys and tribute-bearers were constantly coming or going; there was a great interest in foreign ways, dresses and customs; Indians, Persians, Turks and Syrians met in the capital, which was truly a world centre. But the influence of greatest moment was Buddhism, now accepted with fervour. Great numbers of Indian monks, some of them doubtless artists, were settled in China. Chinese pilgrims journeyed to India and brought back sacred manuscripts and images. But Chinese art, strong in its own traditions, was able to assimilate the Indian formulae and create a Buddhist art of extraordinary splendour. Among the earliest of the T'ang masters may be mentioned Wei-ch'ih I-sēng, who came from Khotan to China about 630. A copy of a picture of Vaisravana by this artist is in the Freer collection at Washington; and his style is perhaps to be discerned in a remarkable roll in Mr. Berenson's collection. Yen Li-pēn (born *c.* 600), was famous for his portraits of national worthies, foreign envoys and Buddhist pictures. We know his work only through copies. With Wu Tao-tzū, T'ang painting underwent a transformation. His early style was fine and delicate; later, it became broad and of amazing power. He painted over 300 Buddhist frescoes, as well as paintings of all kinds of subjects on silk. All have perished. One or two of his designs have been preserved by being engraved on stone, and some paintings and drawings are extant which may be copies from his work. The majestic fresco *Three Bodhisattvas,* given to the British Museum by Mr. Eumorfopoulos, dating probably from the 12th century, presumably preserves the T'ang tradition, and from it we may infer the yet grander and more magnificent creations of Wu Tao-tzŭ and his followers. All records agree in emphasizing the overwhelming power of his creations and also the almost sculptural character of his figures. Of actual and authenticated work by a known T'ang artist we have only five portraits of priests (much damaged) painted about 800 by Li Chēn and preserved in Japan. These are in a contained and rather austere style. But our chief documents for T'ang Buddhist painting are the pictures recovered from Tun-huang, on the western frontier of China, by Sir Aurel Stein and Prof. Pelliot. These are now in the British Museum, at Delhi and in Paris. A certain number are dated, with dates of the 9th and 10th centuries. Those which are in Chinese style may be taken to reflect the central tradition of Buddhist painting, though in a more or less provincial form. Of much the same character is a large Buddhist picture of the 9th century in the Boston Museum.

The Tun-huang pictures are largely devoted to the cult of Amitabha Buddha, who presides over the Western Paradise, and of his spiritual son Avalokitesvara, or Kuan-yin, the genius of Compassion, who in later times assumes a feminine form. There are many pictures of the Paradise, in which we see a host of blessed beings presided over by a Buddha (usually, but not always, Amitabha) gathered round a sacred concert, where a dancer performs to music on a terrace raised above the lotus-lake. Some of these complex compositions, containing a great number of figures, are remarkable for the harmonious serenity of the design —there is no confusion or awkwardness in the arrangement—and the varied beauty of the colouring. Other votive pictures portray the great Bodhisattvas, especially Kuan-yin, or scenes from the Buddha legend. In the former case, the forms, draperies and ornaments are closely modelled on Indian prototypes; in the latter, types, dress and architecture are purely Chinese. From the small scenes sometimes painted at the sides of the large pictures we get a hint of the secular style of the period both in figure and landscape. The figures of donors, which are also fairly frequent, give us contemporary costume. Though mostly the work of artisans rather than artists, the value of these paintings as documents is very great, and a few are of real beauty as works of art.

In this era landscape became important as an independent art. The character of Chinese landscape is seen in the word for landscape, *shan-sui* (山水), mountain and water. Li Ssŭ-hsün (b. 651) was the first eminent painter who devoted himself mainly to landscape. He painted in greens and blues, with gold outline. None of his works exist, but copies preserve the characteristics of his style. His son, Li Chao-tao, developed this technique. A small picture in the Boston Museum, ascribed to him but probably of later date, gives a good idea of this "miniature" kind of landscape-painting. A very different tradition in landscape was founded by Wang Wei (b. 699), who was equally famous as a poet. He matured a style of ink-painting, in which the landscape became the counterpart of an emotion, more subjective and more "impressionist" in method than the work of Li Ssŭ-hsün and his school. Copies exist (one is in the British Museum, and an earlier one in the Freer collection) of a famous roll by Wang Wei, *Scenery of the Wang Ch'uan.* The painting was engraved on stone when it began to decay. Rubbings have been published by Dr. B. Laufer in *Ostasiatische Zeitschrift* (April 1912).

Ts'ao Pa and his greater pupil, Han Kan, were especially famous for their paintings of horses. Han Kan found endless subjects in the fine horses sent as tribute from Central Asia. He worked in the 8th century for the emperor Ming Huang. A contemporary, Han Huang, painted buffaloes and rustic scenes. The splendidly modelled pottery figures of horses and camels found in T'ang tombs give us a clue to the vigour and breadth of the animal painting of these masters, whose original work has perished.

Admirable *genre* pictures and scenes from court life were also painted in this era. Chou Fang is known by versions (one in China and one in a New York private collection) of his *Listeners to Music,* a design in which the Chinese genius for eloquent spacing is conspicuous. The beautiful picture in the Boston museum of *Ladies Beating and Preparing Silk* probably preserves a T'ang design.

The Five Dynasties (A.D. 907–960).—In this short period a great many artists are recorded, of whom Hsü Hsi was famous as a flower-painter and Chou Wên-chü for his pictures of women. Still more celebrated was Huang Ch'uan, who painted landscape, birds, flowers, etc., and who is said to have started what is called the "boneless method"; *i.e.,* painting without a drawn outline.

The Sung Period (A.D. 960–1279).—Under the emperors of the Sung dynasty China was re-united. The emperor Hui Tsung was himself a painter and a great collector. In his reign the Academy of Painting became very prominent and attracted artists from all parts. A certain realism was inculcated, but in style a fastidious simplicity was to be aimed at. The small album-painting of a bird in a bough in the Eumorfopoulos collection, and similar paintings in famous albums in Japan, some of which are attributed to Hui Tsung, illustrate the ideals of the time. Flower-painting, hardly existent in the T'ang period, was now a favourite theme, and some painters, like Wên T'ung, specialized in ink-painting of the bamboo. Of the flower-painters Chao Ch'ang was the most celebrated. The most eminent master in landscape of Northern Sung was Kuo Hsi, who wrote an essay on landscape, partly translated by Waley (*Chinese Painting,* pp. 189–194). Mi Fei invented a new style in landscape, without outline and with boldly brushed-in wooded peaks rising above rain and mist. His style is preserved in many pictures, though again few or none are likely to be actually by his hand. Chao Ta-nien painted autumn and winter scenes; Fan K'uan was famous for his snow-scenes.

But the most famous name in the art of Northern Sung is Li Lung-mien (*c.* 1040–1106). Much of his work consisted of copies from earlier masters. He had a reverential passion for tradition. At first he painted horses, but soon abandoned such subjects for Buddhist themes. Rarely using colour, he drew with a delicate, nervous line. Copies of his works are numerous, and a few originals have been reproduced in the *Kokka.* He is revered by the Chinese as a perfect type of Chinese culture; judged purely as an artist, he would not have so great a fame.

In 1127 the Tatars occupied northern China. The emperor Hui Tsung was taken prisoner and died in exile. Hang-chow became the new capital of what is known as Southern Sung. The changed temper of the times is reflected in the art of a people no longer greatly interested in external events which they were helpless to transform. The passion for romantic solitudes, for soaring peaks and plunging torrents, which had always haunted certain minds, eager to escape from the pressure of official life and ceremonious routine, became a mastering inspiration. The Zen sect of Buddhism, now dominant, with its reliance on intuition, its contempt for all outward forms, replaced the votive picture of single or assembled Bodhisattvas, glowing with colour and gold, by pictures of Arhats in intense contemplation, or by swift ink-sketches of Zen saints; even a poising bird or blossoming spray could become in this mode of thought as "religious" a theme as the glorified Buddha. The emphasis was all on the interior mind. This temper, to which Taoist love of freedom and fluidity contributed much, gives a peculiar poetic character to the art of Southern Sung. Some there were, like Li Sung-nien, who kept to the older traditions and painted scenes from history and legend, and sets of pictures on weaving and agriculture. But the genius of the age is seen rather in Li T'ang (to whom are attributed a roll in a Japanese collection and a beautiful small picture in the Boston Museum), and still more in his famous pupils, Hsia Kuei and Ma Yüan. Owing to the enthusiasm with which the landscapes of this school were collected in Japan, we are able to judge of its productions from concrete examples. Though this school soon fell out of favour in China, it represents to Europe Chinese landscape at its finest; synthetic in conception, impassioned in execution, it unites simplicity with grandeur. Hills and high places had always been regarded with reverence as the abode of spirits. We find no counterpart to the feeling of aversion or disgust which the Alps inspired in Europeans down to so late a period. And though the Chinese have always been an agricultural people, it is not the relation of toiling man to the fruitful earth which inspires their typical landscape art. It is a more cosmic inspiration; a feeling of affinity between the human spirit and the energies of the elements,—the winds, the mists, the soaring peaks, the plunging torrents. Technically, Chinese landscape design differs from European. The high horizon precludes the need for uniting sky and ground, divided by the natural horizon of sight, by means of vertical lines and masses. The eye passes from the foreground, so often a source of trial and difficulty to the European painter, to the central motive of the picture, usually a mountain form.

The Yüan or Mongol Period (A.D. 1279–1368).—In this comparatively short period there was a tendency to go back to the style of ancient masters. Chao Mêng-fu is perhaps the most famous painter of the time. Countless pictures of horses now in Western collections are attributed to him, few of them with any probability. He also painted landscapes and flowers. Another fine painter was Jên Jên-fa, of whom there is a good example in the Eumorfopoulos collection, and others in Japan. The four chief landscape masters were: Huang Kung-wang, Wang Mêng, Ni Tsan, and Wu Chên. The two latter led roaming lives and had nothing of the professional about them. Ni Tsan painted suggestions of landscape in ink, in a reticent, delicate manner. Wu Chên, known as the "Priest of the Plum-blossom," excelled in paintings of bamboos. Ch'ien Hsüan is a master whose name is very frequently forged on paintings; he painted birds, flowers, also figures. Wang Yo-shui was famous for flowers. Yen Hui is greatly admired in Japan for his pictures of Taoist sages, but is less known in China.

The Ming Dynasty (A.D. 1368–1644).—The art of the Ming period is characterized as a whole by a gradual fading out of the interior glow which under Buddhist and Taoist inspiration had suffused the creations of earlier periods. Concentrated in herself, China had no longer any stimulating contact with the world without; and her art became concerned rather with the beauty of material things than with the expression of the interior spirit. At the same time a reverential conservatism prescribed for the painter both subject and manner of treatment. The painters of this period are so numerous that only a few outstanding masters can be mentioned. The first Ming emperor re-established the Academy of Painting, with the aim of emulating the glories of Sung art. Gifted painters flocked to his court. Lin Liang painted ink-pictures of eagles, wild geese, flowers, etc., in a style of extraordinary breadth and power. A good example is in the British Museum, which also has a fine *Fairy and Phoenix* ascribed to Wu Wei, a master who strove to recapture something of the strong brush-work of Wu Tao-tzŭ. Very typical of early Ming art are the bird and flower pictures of Pien Ching-chao (Pien Wên-chin) and of Lü Chi, in which a certain solidity and a decorative richness of colour combine with powerful drawing in a large design. In landscape, Tai Chin, accounted one of the foremost Ming painters, led a new movement and had many followers. His style was broad and free, with little or no colour. Another school preferred minuteness of detail, with an ornamental use of colour, especially a rich blue. Of this school were Chou Ch'ên and T'ang Yin, who also excelled in figures.

Tung Ch'i-ch'ang (1554–1636), eminent as a critic as well as a painter and calligrapher, despised these "professionals" and their laborious technique. He is associated with the "Learned Man's Painting," in which refined taste and literary associations counted for much more than mere accomplishment. Tung Ch'i-ch'ang claimed that this style originated with Wang Wei in the 8th century, the founder of the Southern school. (In distinguishing the Northern and Southern schools, he tried to give these rather shadowy terms a geographical foundation which does not really

LANDSCAPES OF THE SUNG PERIOD (960–1279)

1. A landscape scroll, attributed to Tung Yüan, 10th century, but probably 12th–13th century
2. Dragons and a waterfall among cavernous rocks, by Ch'ên Jung, 12th century, southern Sung school. Ch'ên Jung was especially skilled in painting dragons, symbolic of the powers of nature

BY COURTESY OF (1, 2, 3, 4) THE MUSEUM OF FINE ARTS, BOSTON, (5, 6) THE TRUSTEES, THE BRITISH MUSEUM

SIX CHARACTERISTIC PAINTINGS, 4TH TO 14TH CENTURY

1. Chinese herdsman, a painting of the mid-12th century, Sung period. **2.** A man on a water-buffalo attributed to Li T'ang (*c.* 1100), of the Northern Sung school. **3.** Landscape with bridge and willows, by Ma Yuan, a landscape painter of the late 12th and early 13th century. His work shows the vigor of the Northern Sung school combined with delicacy and sensitiveness. **4.** Detail, from "Ladies Beating and Preparing Silk," a genre painting attributed to the artist-emperor, Hui Tsung (1082–1135), Sung dynasty. It probably preserves a T'ang design. **5.** Portrait of a Buddhist priest, a Chinese fresco of the 14th century. **6.** "Harmonious Family Life," part of "The Admonitions of the Instructress in the Palace," attributed to Ku K'ai-chih (4th century), one of China's earliest painters

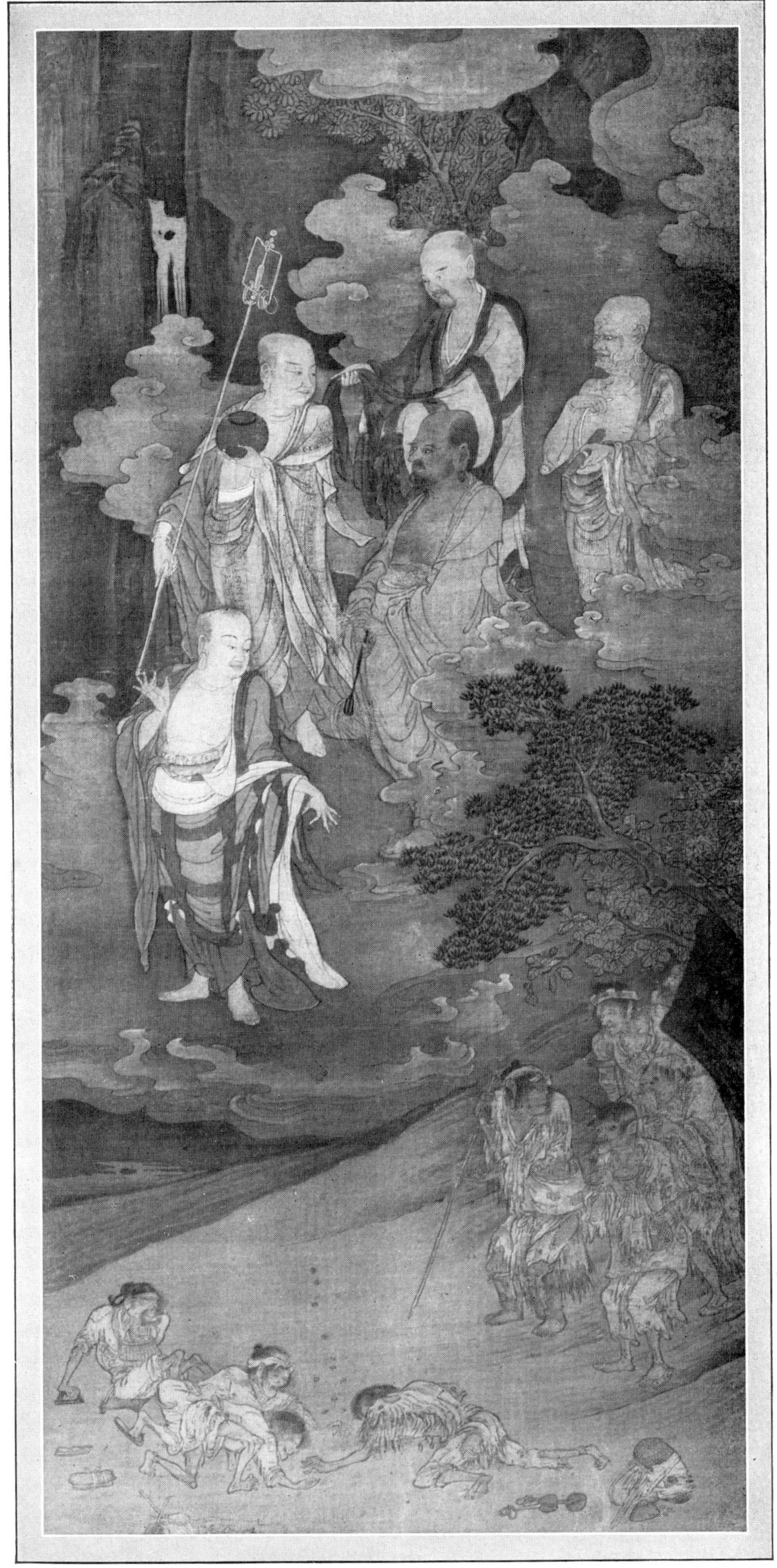

BY COURTESY OF THE MUSEUM OF FINE ARTS, BOSTON

FIVE ARHATS BESTOWING ALMS

One of a set of 100, representing the Five Hundred Arhats; by Lin T'ing Kuei and Chou Chi-ch'ang. The set was painted in Ningpo and is dated A.D. 1178. Colours on silk

A SNOW SCENE

Painting, Sung period or later

exist.) The Southern school, adorned in the earlier part of this period by Shên Chou and Wên Chêng-ming, two much-admired masters, had by the close of the dynasty become triumphant and supreme. Among bird and flower painters of the 16th century, Chou Chih-mien may be mentioned as one of the most distinguished, though his work is rare.

The Ch'ing (Manchu) Dynasty (A.D. 1644–1911).—Painting in the 17th and 18th centuries is very largely devoted to landscape in the style of the Southern school, which in the later developments of the literary man's style becomes loose, slight, capricious and eccentric. Among gifted amateurs of the beginning of the dynasty, Chu Ta is much admired for his ink-sketches of flowers, rocks, etc. More important artists of the K'ang Hsi period are "the four Wangs, Wang Shih-min, Wang Chien, Wang Hui and Wang Yuan-ch'i.

Another great figure in the 17th century is Yün Shou-p'ing, also called Nan-t'ien, the most famous flower painter of the Ch'ing period. Wu Li, who was converted to Christianity and became known as Father Acunha, painted landscapes. The influence of the Jesuits was considerable for a time in China, but had no lasting effect on the arts. The Jesuit Giuseppe Castiglione was made to learn the Chinese style of painting under the name Lang Shih-ning. Chiao Ping-chêng, however, learnt something of European perspective and taught it to Lêng Mei and other artists. Chiao Ping-chêng's sets of pictures of agriculture and weaving were engraved in 1696. Shên Nan-pin went to Japan and stayed at Nagasaki (1731–33); his work had a very stimulating effect on the naturalistic movement in Japan. Apart from this naturalistic movement, the modern painting of China seems to show little new life, and though good painters flourished in the 19th century, they were mostly content with exercises in the various manners consecrated by the past.

BIBLIOGRAPHY.—S. Omura, *Chinese Painters,* vol. viii.–xii.; H. A. Giles, *Introduction to the History of Chinese Pictorial Art;* A. Waley, *Introduction to the Study of Chinese Painting* and *Index of Chinese Artists;* L. Binyon, *Painting in the Far East;* R. Petrucci, *Encyclopédie de la Peinture Chinoise;* F. Hirth, *Scraps from a Collector's Notebook;* J. C. Ferguson, *Chinese Painting.* (L. Bi.)

CHINESE PAVILION, TURKISH CRESCENT, TURKISH JINGLE, or JINGLING JOHNNY, an instrument consisting of a pole about 6ft. high terminating in a conical metal cap or pavilion, hung with small jingling bells and surmounted by a crescent and a star. The Turkish crescent, or "jingling Johnny," as it was familiarly called in the British army bands, was introduced by the Janissaries into western Europe, but it has fallen into disuse now, having been replaced by the *glockenspiel* or steel harmonica.

CHINESE SCULPTURE. The historical records about sculptural works in China do not begin until the Ch'in dynasty (249–206 B.C.); the earliest refer to the 12 colossal statues of "the giant barbarians" and the bell-frames in the shape of monsters "with stags' heads and dragons' bodies," which the great emperor Ch'in Shih Huang Ti ordered to be cast from the weapons of war collected throughout the kingdom. These enormous bronze statues which were placed before one of the imperial palaces near Hsien Yang, on the Wei river in Shensi, are mentioned by Lu Chia, an author who lived from the Ch'in to the Han dynasty, and by several later chroniclers such as Chang Heng (d. A.D. 139) who speaks of "the metal barbarians sitting in a row." At the end of the later Han dynasty Tung Chow melted "ten bronze men into small cash, also the bell-frames"; the two remaining ones he set up inside the Ch'ing Ming gate at Ch'angan but these were also lost during the 4th century, when a local ruler tried to remove them but found them too heavy for the muddy roads, the result being that one was melted down into cash, the other thrown into the river. Nothing, however, is known about the artistic character of these statues, but their well recorded history proves that they were considered extraordinary both for their motives and their size.

Ch'in Dynasty.—The only sculptures now remaining which possibly might be attributed to the Ch'in dynasty are some decorative animals in bronze. Most of these are of small size and placed on the lids of sacrificial vessels, but nevertheless with a well developed sculptural character. A larger example,—sometimes ascribed to the Ch'in period—is a statuette, that represents a reclining bull (now in the possession of L. Wannieck, Paris). It is said to have been found together with some bronze vessels, decorated in Ch'in style, at Li Yü in northern Shansi, but to judge by its style, it can hardly have been executed before the 6th century A.D. (Northern Wei dynasty). We illustrate it, however, as a particularly fine example of early Chinese animal sculpture.

Among other bronze animals which have been ascribed to the Ch'in period should be mentioned a large dragon or hydra with crested neck and flame-like wings at the shoulders and the loins, in the collection of A. Stoclet, Brussels. It is in marked contrast to the bull, fierce, fantastic, grotesque to the utmost without any connections with nature, and must, indeed, be earlier in date, though hardly of the Ch'in period. Other fantastic animals such as interwinding dragons or felines appear at the handles of some large bells in Ch'in style.

New efforts were evidently made in different directions during this short period which, in the field of art, was simply an introduction to the classic age of the Hans. The rigid ceremonial art of earlier times is gradually modified by a more direct and vivid interest in nature. The Chou art (1122–249 B.C.) was pre-eminently symbolic and geometrical. The art of the Ch'in and the Han periods aimed at the presentation of the actual rhythm of things, the inherent life and significance of the artistic forms.

The Han Dynasty.—Most of the Han monuments have evidently been destroyed; yet, to judge from those which remain as well as from minor plastic creations in bronze and clay, Chinese sculpture was at this early period much better fitted to treat animal motives than human shapes. It is only in the reliefs that the human figures reach an importance comparable to that of the animals, and these are, on the whole, more like paintings translated into stone than real sculptures. With the exception of the small tomb statuettes made as substitutes for real people, human representations are quite rare and artistically much inferior to the representations of animals. The Chinese have never considered the human figure an artistic motive in itself, but simply used it for expressing an action or a state of consciousness. They have taken greater interest in types, postures and motives of drapery than in the bodily form or the muscular organism. The case is quite different with the animal sculptures. They may adhere to certain types or formulae characteristic of the period to which they belong but their artistic importance depends mainly on the rendering of their organic form and vitality. The best among them are monumental creations, hardly inferior to animal sculptures of any other period or nation. The conventionalization, which is more or less preponderant during the early epochs, does not convey an element of immaterial abstraction but serves to accentuate the muscular organism, the energy of movement, the monumentality of the form, all that makes the animals great and convincing as works of art.

Bronze, Clay and Stone Work of the Han.—Among the great number of wild and domestic animals represented in bronze, clay and stone during the Han period we may choose as examples some bears executed in bronze. The majority of these bears are quite small, intended to serve as feet for sacrificial vessels, but there are also some of a larger size which have the character of free standing sculptures. The two best are in the Gardner museum in Boston. These are represented in a squatting posture, stretching their heads forward with a friendly roar. The modelling of the limbs is not carried very far, yet it is sufficient to awake an impression of suppleness and force. The artist has not been afraid of exaggerations in the characterization of the lumpy forms or the telling postures. The heavy weight of the body supported by the broadly placed forepaws, the elastic power of the enormous legs, the softness of the bulky paws and the long nose which seems to form a direct continuation of the ears, are rendered with a power of conviction and a sense of monumental unity that are rarely found in later animal sculptures.

It should also be noticed that in their representations of animals the Chinese have quite often combined two or more into a group. They have composed them in the most intricate positions and built up groups which satisfy the highest requirements of plastic art. Most of these groups are on a relatively small scale, but they are nevertheless truly monumental. The finest results are achieved in groups of fighting animals, because the bodies are here represented in their highest tension, in the full development of their muscular effort, and so closely interlaced that they complete each other perfectly in the expression of the plastic idea. The same is also true of some of the animals which are composed into an architectural unity with monuments such as the tomb pillars in Szechuan (which will be mentioned below).

Tomb Statuettes of the Han.—The greatest variety of animal types may however be found among the clay statuettes made for the tombs. The material was most easily handled and thus invited all sorts of individual variations, and as these clay sculptures were executed as substitutes for living animals, which in earlier times followed their dead masters into their tombs, it was natural that they should be made as lifelike as possible. The majority are domestic animals such as horses, sheep, dogs, pigs, hens and ducks in various sizes, the smallest hardly more than two or three inches high, the largest measuring a foot or more. They were usually executed in clay moulds but sometimes modelled by hand, and the best among them have retained a spontaneous freshness and vivacity which make them very entertaining. Proportions and shapes are treated with a great deal of freedom. The dogs have enormous heads, the horses have necks which curve like high arches, and the pigs have snouts like bowsprits, yet the exaggerations serve simply to accentuate the typical features of the various animals.

Besides the animals there are human *ming ch'i,* or tomb statuettes, made as substitutes for living people, such as servants, and wives who formerly were buried alive with the husbands. Most common amongst these statuettes from the Han period are the slender ladies in long robes with wide sleeves reminding one of the Japanese kimonos. They stand usually in very quiet postures simply with a slight inclination of the large round head, but occasionally we find them represented in a dancing movement, though with closed feet, swinging their bodies and their arms in a rhythmic fashion.

Stone Sculptures of the Han.—Stone sculptures on a large scale were, no doubt, also executed in steadily increasing numbers during the Han period, though comparatively few of them have been preserved. Among the earliest which can be approximately dated are the animals at the tomb of General Ho Ch'ü Ping, situated at the Wei river some 20 m. N.W. of Sianfu. They were discoverd by Ségalen and Lartigue during their explorations in 1914 and more completely dug out by the latter in 1923. Lartigue has also published them in an article in the German magazine *Artibus Asiae* (1927) in which he presents some evidence for the supposition that these statues were executed about 117 B.C., the year of the death of the famous general. He thinks that the statues, which represent a horse standing over a fallen warrior, a reclining horse and a buffalo, were placed in front of the mound, and that their present quite irregular positions have been caused by the shifting of the mud. Besides these, complete sculptures may, however, be seen in the neighbourhood of the mound, a large block with a mythological figure, executed in relief, and fragments of some animal sculptures which seem to indicate that this large composition never was completely finished. It is difficult to appreciate the artistic importance of these large statues without seeing the originals, but if we may draw some conclusions from the reproductions, the sculptures are comparatively undeveloped from an artistic point of view. This is particularly true of the main statue, the horse standing over a fallen warrior. The composition is indeed significant but the formal treatment does not seem to do justice to the motive. The short-legged horse with an enormous head is more bulky than monumental, and the figure under its belly is simply a large block. Here is little of that intrinsic energy which is so prominent in some of the minor sculptures already mentioned. This impression is, however, to some extent counteracted by the reclining horse and the buffalo which, even if they are heavy and bulky with stumpy legs, reveal a very sensitive artistic treatment, particularly in their expressive heads. Here one may discover a touch of that excellent animal psychology which is one of the greatest assets of Han art, a characterization which, to some extent, makes up for the shortcomings in other directions.

Sculpture Developed For the Dead.—Other stone sculptures from the beginning of the Han dynasty which might serve for comparison have not come to light, though it is more than probable that they have existed, because this tomb was hardly an isolated case, and broadly speaking sculpture in stone as well as in clay had its origin in the decoration and the arrangement of the tombs. It was for the dead rather than for the living that the Chinese developed their creative activity in the field of the plastic arts. As proof of this may be quoted not only the various classes of clay and stone sculptures mentioned above, but also numerous reliefs executed for the decoration of the "spirit chambers" of the tombs and the sculptural pillars placed in front of the mounds. These monuments marked as a rule the beginning of the "shen tao" (spirit path) which led up to the tomb and which in later times was farther and farther extended in a straight line from the mound towards the south. The interior of the tomb consisted often of two or more chambers (as also may be observed in contemporary Korean tombs), the first being a kind of ante-room called the "spirit chamber," where the soul of the deceased was supposed to dwell, while the coffin was placed, together with various vessels and other paraphernalia of bronze or clay, in the back room. The main decoration, be it in sculpture or painting, was concentrated in the ante-room where the walls often were covered with representations from ancient history and mythology or with illustrations with a moral import.

BY COURTESY OF THE METROPOLITAN MUSEUM OF ART
SCULPTURE OF THE SUI PERIOD

Tomb Pillars.—Quite a number of the decorative pillars which formed the gateway to the "spirit road" are known from central and western China, particularly the provinces of Honan, Shantung and Szechuan. They are usually constructed on a rectangular plan of large and well-fitted stone blocks reaching a total height of 15 to 18 feet. When completely preserved they consist of a moulded pedestal, a very broad shaft and a cornice over which the roof projects quite far. But the form varies somewhat in the different provinces; thus the pillars in Honan, of which the best known stand at Têng Fung Hsien on Sung Shan, are very broad and provided with projecting buttresses. Otherwise they are quite simple without any particular development of the cornices and decorated with ornaments and figures in very low relief. The earliest of these Honan pillars is dated A.D. 118, the latest A.D. 175.

The pillars in Szechuan have usually no buttresses, but they are higher and characterized by a richer architectural composition; their upper parts, the cornices and friezes under the projecting roof are particularly well developed. We find here, reproduced in stone, the beam ends and brackets so characteristic of Chinese wooden architecture, and between these are sculptural decorations executed in high relief, sometimes almost in the round. These pillars are all from the later Han dynasty, but only one of them, the pillar of Fung Huan at Ch'iu Hsien, is dated by an inscription which contains the year A.D. 121.

Symbolic Decorations of the Han.—More important for their sculptural decorations are, however, two pillars in the same neighbourhood erected at the tomb of a man called Shen. On their shafts are representations of the symbols of the four directions; *i.e.*, the red bird of the South, the white tiger of the East, the blue dragon of the West and the black tortoise of the North, animal representations which, with regard to energetic rhythm of line and grand decorative stylization, may be compared to the best works in bronze or clay known from this classic epoch. At the corners of the entablature are seated human figures which seem to carry the projecting beams on their shoulders, and, on the middle of the south side, a kind of *t'ao t'ie* (glutton) appears between the beams. All these figures are executed practically in the round and most skilfully composed into the architectural scheme of the monument. The very high frieze is divided into two sections, of which the lower one is decorated with hunting scenes in quite low relief and the upper one with some larger figures in high relief. One may observe here men riding on stags, horse-like animals running along with the swiftness of the wind, and hunters who aim with their bows above their heads or grasp the passing leopard by its tail. Here is the same free-play with animal and human forms as may be observed on some of the inlaid bronze vessels or on the glazed Han urns with relief friezes. The motives seem to have some reference to the life beyond the tomb, though they represent this with a naturalness and an intensity of movement which make them appear like scenes from real life. The style reveals something of the same energy and nervous tension that characterizes the small bronze ornaments of this period, and it can hardly be explained without accepting an influence from west Asiatic sources, though the Chinese transformation of the west Asiatic tradition is more complete in the large stone sculptures than in most of the minor bronze ornaments.

Dramatic Expression of the Pillars.—The majority of the tomb pillars in Szechuan, of which at least a score were discovered by Ségalen and Lartigue during their exploration in 1914, show the above mentioned combination of friezes with flat reliefs and tri-dimensional representations of animals and human figures on the entablature. The motives vary, some being historical or legendary, others religious or mythological, but they are all more or less imbued with a dramatic expression, and executed in a form of high decorative beauty.

Much simpler than these are the pillars which stood at the entrance to the tomb of the Wu family at Ch'ia Hsiang in Shantung. They were erected about the year A.D. 147 and they are still in their original place, although the tomb-area has become a large pit, usually filled with water. The pillars are provided with buttresses and a small superior storey on the projecting roof, but their sculptural decoration consists simply of quite low reliefs representing dragons, tigers and birds, in decorative translation, besides legendary illustrations with a moral import, framed by geometrical ornaments of the same kind as may be found for instance on the mirrors of the Han period.

Reliefs of the Han.—The same kind of motive, executed in a strictly conventionalized linear style, appears also on the large stone slabs which used to be arranged along the walls of the ante-chamber in the tomb, but which are now transferred to a primitive little store-room where they stand without any kind of order. These reliefs from the Wu Liang Tzu tomb have become known all over the world through numerous series of rubbings taken of them since the 18th century, and reproduced in many Chinese and European publications. Two or three of the reliefs have found their way into Western collections, though it should be noticed that the majority of the stone reliefs, said to come from Wu Liang Tzu, are simply modern imitations, made on the basis of rubbings.

Legendary Motives.—Nothing is more entertaining than to follow, with the aid of Chavannes interpretations, the legendary motives represented in these reliefs and thus to learn something about classical Chinese examples of filial piety, matrimonial fidelity, the faithfulness of loyal citizens, the valour of great heroes, not to mention the quasi-historical traditions about the great Yü and Ch'in Shih Huang Ti or the mythological stories about the king of the East, Tung Wang Kung, and the queen of of the West, Hsi Wang Mu. Very common motives in these reliefs are the long processions of riders and carriages and the rows of men on horseback escorting a carriage, which may be representations of the journey of the deceased to Hades.

The compositions are arranged in horizontal storeys, with single rows of figures, animals, trees, houses and the like, appearing as silhouettes against a neutral background. The artistic expression lies mainly in the contours, and in the engraved lines; the modelling of the forms is very slight. These reliefs may thus hardly be called sculpture in the real sense of the word, but rather paintings or drawings translated into stone. We have reason to suppose that they were made after such patterns and reproduce popular wall paintings which existed in some contemporary palaces, a supposition which is supported by the poet Wang Yen Shou, who describes the wall paintings in the Ling Kuang palace executed about the middle of the 2nd century A.D. He mentions in his description mythological illustrations of the same kind as may be seen in the Wu Liang Tzu reliefs besides "many riotous damsels and turbulent lords, loyal knights, dutiful sons, mighty scholars, faithful wives, victors and vanquished, wise men and fools," motives which correspond more or less to those appearing on the stone reliefs from Wu Liang Tzu and other places in Shantung.

Bactrian Types.—It has been claimed that the proud horses of these reliefs were of Bactrian origin. This is possible but the Chinese sculptors were certainly less guided by observation of nature than by artistic models, be it in bronze, clay or textile. They have accepted and further developed a definite type of horse which probably existed in the art of the Hellenized west-Asiatic countries.

Less Hellenistic and more definitely Scytho-Iranian in character are the winding dragons and heraldically placed tigers which appear in one or two of these reliefs. They belong to the same great family of ornamental animals which we also met on the stone pillars in Szechuan, and may thus be said to form some additional proofs of the general acceptance of this kind of animal sculpture during the Han period.

Still more remarkable examples of the same stylistic current are the two lions which stood at the entrance to the tomb of the Wu family (at the sides of the above-mentioned pillars) but which are now more or less buried in the mud. The anatomical character of the only visible one is rather free. It is, indeed, no common lion but a descendant of those proud animals which stood at the royal palaces in Susa and Persepolis and whose artistic pedigree may be traced to Chaldean and Assyrian art. The form is supple, the body is thin, the whole animal is dominated by the broad curving neck which comes so far to the front that the head almost disappears and the neck continues in the enormous jaws. At the shoulders one may observe traces of small wings, though they have been practically worn off by time. Such a creation has hardly been shaped from nature. Even if single lions now and then were sent as tributes from western Asiatic nations to the Chinese emperor, these were hardly known by the people in the provinces, and as there were no other lions in China, we may well suppose that the inspiration for such animal representation was drawn from examples of Iranian art rather than from living models.

Animal Statues.—To the same group of animal statues from the end of the Han-epoch may also be assigned two winged tigers at the tomb of K'ao Yi at Ya Chou Fu in Szechuan, which have been published by Ségalen and Lartigue, and the enormous seated lion—which has served as a plinth for a pillar in the Okura museum in Tokyo. There are furthermore some minor animal statuettes of the same type but they hardly need detain us as they only verify what has already been said about the artistic style and derivation of these sculptures. Nor do we need to stop at the human figures executed in stone on a large scale, because their artistic importance is much inferior to that of the animals.

Animal Sculptures of the Six Dynasties Period.—During the centuries which followed the fall of the Eastern Han dynasty (A.D. 214) artistic activity in China lost some of its intensity. The times were restless, filled with war and political upheaval. The empire was again divided into several minor States, to begin with, the Three Kingdoms, Wu, Shu and Wei, and later on, after 223, into a northern and a southern half, the former being under the domination of the Tartars, among whom the Toba tribe came out the strongest and took the name of the Northern Wei dynasty, while the latter was ruled over by a number of short-lived native dynasties—Sung, Ch'i, Liang and Ch'en—which had their headquarters at Nanking. We know very little about the artistic activity during these times but it seems that the stylistic traditions of the Han period remained in force also during the 3rd and 4th centuries of our era. Some tomb reliefs, mainly from Shantung, executed in a kind of coarser Han style, may well be of this transition period, and the same may be said of a number of minor plastic works in bronze and clay.

The general evolution can be followed most closely through the small tomb statuettes; they reflect the variations in taste and fashion better than the large stone sculptures. Among them are real *genre* figures represented in various occupations such as music-making, feeding the hens, or with children in their arms, and we may observe how the fashion is changed from the simple "kimono" to an elegantly draped mantle over a tightly-fitting undergarment and how the head-dress becomes higher and more decorative. These tomb statuettes and minor animals in terracotta originate mainly from Honan, whereas the larger stone sculptures of this same period are executed for the reigning dynasties in Nanking. These monuments which form one of the most important groups within the domain of Chinese sculpture, have been more or less identified and reproduced by various explorers.

The largest among these lions and chimaeras measure up to 10 or 12 ft. in length and may still be seen at their original places, but some smaller ones, 4 to 6 ft. long, have found their way to Western collections. They all represent winged, lion-like animals but it is possible to distinguish two main types, *i.e.*, the chimaeras, which are a kind of cross between dragons and lions, and the real lions which have wings on their shoulders but no feathers or scales on their bodies and no ornamental beard. The former seem to have been considered the nobler, because they were employed as guardians at the tombs of emperors, whereas the lions stood at the tombs of princes and dukes.

Early Chimaeras.—The earliest chimaera which can be dated stands at the tomb of Emperor Sung Wen Ti (d. 453). It is a colossal and, in spite of its dilapidation, still imposing animal, largely covered up by a heap of refuse, so that the statue had to be dug out whenever it was photographed. The upper part of the head is lost and the surface of the grey limestone is very much worn but it is still possible to see that the body as well as the legs have been covered by ornamental scales or feathers and that the animal had wings not only at the shoulders but also at the ears.

The second earliest in date of the chimaeras which still remain at their original sites is the one at the tomb of Emperor Ch'i Wu Ti (d. 493). The dimensions are somewhat smaller but the animal is more completely preserved. The long body has a more dragon-like character, the legs are comparatively short and the tail well developed. The most imposing part is, however, the enormous head with the open jaws from which the ornamental beard hangs like a long tongue. One may here observe three pairs of wings as well as feathers drawn in spirals over the whole body.

Sixth-century Chimaeras.—The same proud bearing characterizes the chimaera at the tomb of Emperor Liang Wu Ti (d. 549). The movement of the long and supple body is still better developed and it receives a most effective continuation in the enormous curve of the neck. The animal is moving forward in an ambling fashion; we feel its vigour and suppleness. The wings and the feathers are indicated in quite low relief or simply engraved.

This nobility and energy are carried still further in the two large chimaeras which now stand in the University Museum at Philadelphia. We have no information whence they come, but they illustrate a further evolution of the style of the chimaeras at the tomb of Emperor Liang Wu Ti, which would date them shortly after the middle of the 6th century. It is possible that they stood at the tomb of some of the emperors of the short Ch'en dynasty which followed after the Liang, such as Ch'en Wu Ti (d. 559) or Ch'en Wen Ti (d. 566). In comparison with these beasts, the earlier chimaeras appear almost like domestic animals. The fantastic wildness and the seething energy are here given free outlet. The legs are stretched, the bodies drawn, the head is wildly thrown backwards, the chest pushed forward into a large curve, and all these movements are accentuated by engraved lines which give the impression of taut steel springs. Besides these large ones several minor chimaeras are known but none of them reaches the extraordinary expressiveness of the last-mentioned.

Winged Lions.—The largest of the winged lions still remain *in situ,* not far from Nanking; their weight and colossal dimensions have made their removal impossible, but some of them are so far decayed that, if nothing is done to protect them, they will soon disappear. The earliest and most important stand at tombs of various members of the Liang family, *i.e.,* the brothers of the Emperor Wu Ti, Prince Hsiao Hsiu (d. 518), Prince Hsiao Tan (d. 522) and the cousin of the emperor, Duke Hsiao Ching (d. 523). Besides these, two or three pairs of large lions are in the same neighbourhood, at Yao Hua Men, to the east of Nanking, but they are later and artistically inferior. The anatomical difference between the lions and the chimaeras is, as already said, not very important. The former as well as the latter are feline animals with an enormous curving neck and wings, but they are not provided with scales or feathers, nor do they have any ornamental beard like the chimaeras, only a large tongue which hangs down from the open jaws over the projecting chest. They are all represented in an ambling posture, majestically walking or coming to a sudden standstill, when the fore-legs are strained and the hind-legs bent. The head is lifted high on the proudly curving neck, the forms are full, the limbs heavier than in the chimaeras. Their massiveness is at least as imposing as the concentration of power in their enormous limbs. Most eaten by frost and water are the lions at the tomb of Duke Hsiao Ching which is now covered by a watery rice field in which the lions sink up to their shoulders.

SCULPTURE OF THE NORTHERN WEI PERIOD

Lions of Hsiao Hsiu Tombs.—Better preserved and more completely visible are the two colossal lions at the tomb area of Hsiao Hsiu, now covered by the village Kan Yu Hsiang, and here remains one row of the other monuments which flanked the "spirit road," *i.e.,* two large tablets with inscriptions carried by tortoises and a fluted column on a plinth composed of winding dragons. This seems to be the earliest preserved "tomb alley" in China, an arrangement known from a great number of later tombs. The lions are of the same family as those already described, the fact that they have wings is in itself a proof of their dependence on Persian art. It should, however, be remembered that the Achaemenian and Sassanian animals were descendants of the Assyrian which must be regarded as the fore-fathers of all the greatest Asiatic and a good many European lion sculptures. To what extent the Chinese really knew such models is a question which cannot be discussed here; it is in any case evident that they transformed the foreign models quite freely, not to say fantastically, in harmony with their native traditions. These animal sculptures form stylistically a direct continuation of the plastic art of the Han period. Yet, they indicate that a new wave of Western influence reached China at this time on a more southern route than through the north-western nomads. These lion sculptures do not appear in the northern provinces which were dominated by the Tartars. They belong to the more southern provinces where the old Chinese civilization and the creative spirit of the "Han people" never were completely subdued by foreign elements.

Religious Sculpture of the Six Dynasties.—When Buddhist sculpture was introduced into China it had passed through a long evolution in India and Central Asia; the principal iconographic motives, symbols and attributes were all developed into definite forms; the Chinese took them over just as they took over Buddhist scriptures; and whatever modifications they may have introduced concerned more the artistic interpretation than the motives themselves. It should never be forgotten that they were greater artists than any other people of the Far East, and when Buddhist art took root in China, the country was by no means devoid of sculptural monuments. There were (as we have previously seen) artistic traditions which could not be forgotten, only modified when applied to Buddhist motives. The Buddhas and Bodhisattvas were, of course, represented in human shapes but the artists could not enhance their significance by accentuating their physical organisms or their likeness to ordinary human beings, nor could they change their general shapes or postures if they wanted to be understood. The iconographic rules are indeed much more exacting in Buddhist than in Christian art, and the motives are more limited in their artistic scope.

Religious Symbolism.—The great majority of the Buddhist sculptures represent isolated figures, seated or standing in very quiet postures without any attempt at movement, except certain symbolic gestures. The heads are made according to quite definite types, somewhat changing with the periods and localities, but it is rare to meet heads with individual expression or portraitlike features. The bodies are as a rule entirely covered by long mantles or rich garments according to the rôle or meaning of the figure; they have hardly any importance of their own but serve simply as a substratum for the rich flow of the mantle folds which, particularly in the early sculptures, conceal the forms much more than they accentuate them. Even in figures which are represented almost nude, such as the guardians at the gate (*Dvarapalas*), the representation is not really naturalistic; their Herculean forms and muscular movements are altogether exaggerated and their significance is symbolic.

The earliest dated Buddhist sculptures in China, known to us, are small bronze statuettes of a greater historical than artistic importance. Some of them are provided with inscriptions which make it possible to fix their date, the earliest being of the years 437 and 444, whereas the earliest dated Buddha in stone is of the year 457. These small statuettes represent standing or seated Buddhas or Bodhisattvas against a leaf-shaped nimbus decorated with engraved flame-ornaments. The figures are mostly of a very moderate artistic importance recalling by their types and draperies the Graeco-Buddhist art of north India. The large nimbuses behind these small figures constitute, however, a feature which is not known in Gandahara sculpture.

Yün Kang Cave Temples.—The greatest *ensemble* of early Buddhist sculptures in China is to be found at the Yün Kang cave temples near Ta Tung Fu in Shansi where the Northern Wei dynasty had its capital until 494, when it was removed to Loyang in Honan. The work at these cave sculptures started about the middle of the 5th century and was continued towards the latter part of the 6th century. Amongst the rich material displayed at this place one may observe different stylistic currents, some originating from Central Asia and India, others more closely connected with earlier forms of Chinese art. Here are ornaments of a distinctly Iranian character, and architectural forms of the same type as on reliefs from Taxila and Peshawar, but also some decorative motives recalling the art of the Han period. Among the figures there are some curious examples which form a link with Central Asiatic art, *e.g.*, the five-headed and six-armed god who sits on a large bird with a pearl in its beak. This is no doubt the Garuda-raja, the bird of Vishnu, which also may be seen in some paintings from Tun Huang. This and other Hindu divinities of a similar kind, which appear in the Buddhist pantheon at Yün Kang, testify that artistic influence from central and western Asia reached China in connection with the introduction of Buddhism.

Artistic Expression.—Most famous among the figures here are the colossal Buddhas and Bodhisattvas which, however, seem to us artistically least interesting. A certain conventional type and fold design have in these figures been enormously enlarged without any intensification of the rhythmic motives or the artistic expression. More artistic expression and beauty may be found in some other figures at Yün Kang which are less closely allied to Indian models and more imbued with the traditional Chinese feeling for rhythmic lines and elegant form. The figures themselves are quite thin and flat, sometimes hardly modelled into full cubic volume, and they are entirely covered up by very long and heavy garments. The folds of these are pressed and pleated on the very thin shapes and uniformly arranged on both sides of the figures in long concave curves, forming a kind of zigzag pattern at the border; the contours are very tense, with the elasticity of drawn bow-strings. When this type of draping is fully developed the drawn out, curving mantle-folds may suggest wings.

Temple Grottoes at Lung Men.—The same energetic style as in the best Yün Kang sculptures may also be observed in some of the statues in the famous temple grottoes at Lung Men in Honan which were begun shortly after the Northern Wei dynasty had transferred its capital to Loyang (494). During the last decade these caves have been so badly destroyed that hardly 10% of the original sculpture still remains; all the rest is either smashed or beheaded, some of the heads being replaced by clay substitutes of a very provincial type. The most beautiful and earliest sculptures at Lung Men are to be found in the so-called Lao Chun Tung cave which is decorated from ceiling to floor with a great number of niches of varying sizes in which Buddhas and Bodhisattvas are grouped, either alone or together with adoring bikshus or other attendants. The majority of these sculptures were executed in the 3rd or 4th decade of the 6th century, but only some of the minor reliefs remain still in a fair condition. Yet some characteristic positions may be observed, for instance the cross-ankled Bodhisattvas which represent Maitreya, the coming Buddha, while the Buddha Sakyamuni is seated with legs straight down. The stylization of the folds is carried out according to the same patterns as in the Yün Kang caves, but the stone is harder and the technique is superior to that of the earlier Yün Kang sculptures. Some of these Lung Men sculptures have certainly been among the finest works of their kind in China.

Another variation of the Northern Wei period style may be observed in the sculptures which decorate the temple caves at Shih Ku Ssu, near Kung Hsien in Honan. The work was here started about the same time as at Lung Men but the material is of a softer kind and the technique is not quite so fine. The large central Buddha at this place, which now stands up to its knees in mud, is a broad and block-like figure modelled in very large planes, with a remarkable cubistic tendency, which also may be observed in several minor heads from the same place, now dispersed in various European and American museums.

Buddhist Stelae.—Besides these cave sculptures of the Northern Wei period should be mentioned a large number of Buddhist stelae, *i.e.*, slabs with figures in high relief, varying in size, some up to 12 ft. high, others quite small. Their decoration consists generally of a combination of niches with Buddhist figures and ornamental borders. On the back of these slabs are often found long rows of figures in flat relief representing the donors of the monuments. This form of stelae was probably developed from the earlier type of inscribed memorial stones, as used in China since the Han dynasty. It is worth noticing that we find at the top of the Buddhist stelae the same kind of winding and interlacing dragons as on the slabs which were raised at the tombs; their fierceness and energy of movement seem to reveal their derivation from the Sibero-Asiatic art, based on Scythian traditions which, indeed, had a great influence on the development of the ornamental style of this period.

Transition Period.—The stylistic ideals of the Northern Wei period retained their importance until the middle of the 6th century. About this time a new wave of artistic influence reached China from northern India. It may be quite clearly observed in some of the monuments which were executed during the Northern Ch'i and Northern Chou dynasties (550–581). The best cave sculptures from this time existed, at least a few years ago, at T'ien Lung Shan not far from Taiyuan-fu in Shansi. They were started in the Northern Ch'i period and continued, with some intermissions during the Sui and T'ang dynasties.

Sculptures at T'ien Lung Shan.—The earliest sculptures at T'ien Lung Shan are to be found in the caves no. 2, 3, 10 and

16, probably executed between 560 and 580. The system of decoration in the first two caves consists of three large groups, one on each wall representing a seated Buddha accompanied by two Bodhisattvas and, in some instances, also by adoring monks and donors, characterized with striking realism. The main figures are executed in very high relief, giving almost the impression of free-standing forms, yet there is a certain flatness about them, noticeable particularly in the Bodhisattvas which stand turned half-way towards the central Buddha and whose garments —arranged in pleated folds—spread out in wing-like fashion at the sides. They are not very far removed stylistically from corresponding figures on later Wei monuments, though their heads are less archaic both in shape and expression.

The maturest examples of this transition period—possibly executed as late as 580—are to be found in the 16th cave at T'ien Lung Shan, where all the three walls are decorated with large groups of Buddhas with Bodhisattvas and other attendants placed on raised platforms, the fronts of which were decorated with representations of dwarf musicians. The central Buddhas are lifted into commanding positions on high pedestals in the form of lotus-flowers or altars; their shapes are full and well rounded, their heads comparatively small for the strong bodies. They are all seated in the same cross-legged posture, with bare feet and hands in the *abhaya* and *vara mudra* (gestures signifying "without fear" and "charity"). Their mantles, which are made of a very thin material, are draped only over the left shoulder, leaving the right bare, and the folds have practically no relief. Buddhas clothed in this fashion are very rare in Chinese art; they may occasionally be found in later T'ang sculpture but at this early period they are certainly surprises.

Foreign Influence.—The most probable explanation of this apparent anachronism in the style of the Buddhas seems to be that they were made from foreign models or by foreign artists while the less important side figures were carved in accordance with the indigenous principles of style. The figures are altogether Indian in spirit and form. It is hard to believe that Chinese artists would have been able to reproduce Mathura models so faithfully as we find them here, and it may at least be claimed that they have never done it better, either before or after. Possibly some Indian artist, well acquainted with the Mathura school, worked for some time at T'ien Lung Shan.

The same general types and principles of style which characterize the sculpture at T'ien Lung Shan may also be found in some isolated statues coming from this or a similar centre of sculptural activity. The most characteristic feature of all these figures is the cylindrical shape indicated in the legs and arms, as well as in the shape of the whole body, which often stands like a column on the lotus pedestal. Nothing can be more unlike the comparatively flat and angular shapes of the Northern Wei figures, which even when they have a more developed plastic form are linear rather than rounded.

Sculptures from Chihli Province.—Another provincial variation of the transition style may be seen in the sculptures from Chihli, the present metropolitan province, and particularly from Ting Chou where the supply of a beautiful white marble was abundant. The artistic quality of these sculptures is however quite uneven; the best of them stand on the highest level of Buddhist art in China, while the poorest are hardly more than ordinary artisans' work. Several figures of this group might be quoted as proofs of what already has been said about the plastic formula during this transition period. Their shapes are more or less cylindrical, their heads mostly large and heavy. One may notice a general tendency to make the figures narrower towards the feet and to broaden them towards the shoulders. The thin garments fit tightly over the bodies and their softly curving folds are indicated in quite low relief or simply with incised lines. Good examples of such statues are in the Metropolitan Museum in New York. If we place such a figure beside some characteristic example of the Northern Wei art, we may observe two opposite tendencies of style. In the earlier works the mantle folds and the contours are stretched and bent outward at the feet, the shoulders are narrow, the heads small; the rhythm is rising. In the later ones the rhythm is falling instead of rising, the tempo is slow, not without heaviness; there is no bending of the contours, they are falling almost straight down; the mantle hangs over the body and it is only towards the feet, where the circumference becomes smaller, that a certain acceleration of the tempo is noticeable.

The Sui Dynasty.—The sculptures of the Sui period (589–618) form, stylistically, a direct continuation of those of the transi-

BY COURTESY OF THE METROPOLITAN MUSEUM OF ART
SCULPTURE OF THE TRANSITION PERIOD OF THE NORTHERN CH'I DYNASTY

tion period during the Northern Ch'i and Chou dynasties. Most of them are still examples of the transition style, but a few may well be classified among the most perfect works of religious statuary in China. Conditions were particularly favourable for the flourishing of religious art, and the formal development had not yet passed the point where it becomes an end in itself. Sui sculpture is, on the whole, quite restrained in its formal modes of expression and its interest in nature is slight, but it marks nevertheless a distinct progress in the representation of actual forms.

T'ien Lung Statues.—Some good examples of the particular style of this period are to be found in the 8th grotto at T'ien Lung Shan which is in part preserved, although the soft material has been worn by time and water and some of the statues have been smashed and decapitated. Coming to these statues from a study of the sculptures in cave 16 at the same place (mentioned above), the first thing that strikes one is that they are not at all Indian in their general appearance. The Buddhas are seated in the same postures as the earlier ones but vested in the Chinese fashion with an upper garment covering both shoulders and with a less hieratic bearing of the stiff bodies. The shoulders are not so broad, the waist less curving, the forms are quite undifferentiated, but the heads have increased in size and have a more human air. They are certainly more Chinese, though in a provincial sense, and they are executed by inferior artists with little feeling for rhythmic lines and decorative beauty.

Most interesting are the two pairs of Dvarapalas (guardians) outside this cave. One pair is placed at the sides of the entrance, the other at each side of a tablet near by which still contains traces of an inscription of the Sui dynasty (said to be dated from about 589). The attitudes of these guardian figures are dramatic, not to say strained. The movement of the arms is jerky, the turning of the heads, which are looking over the shoulder, is violent. The impetuosity is, indeed, much greater in these figures than in the Dvarapala statues at the earlier caves, but whether they have gained in sculptural quality as much as in dramatic force is less certain.

Typical expressions of the plastic formula of the Sui period are also to be found among the sculptures from Chihli, easily recognizable by their material which is a micaceous white marble. Common to them all is the general shape which is no longer simply pillar-like or cylindrical, but ovoid. The contours are swelling out over the hips and elbows and gradually draw closer toward the feet and over the head. Thus a general formula is created, and it is often repeated on a smaller scale in the heads. The same rhythm is taken up by the folds which in some of the figures form a succession of curves over the front endowing them with a more complete harmony and repose than may be expressed by any other shape or formula known to us.

Shantung Sculptures.—The richest and most varied provincial group of sculptures from the Sui period is to be found in Shantung. The religious fervour and interest in establishing Buddhist temples and sanctuaries seem to have been particularly great in this part of the country and, to judge from the sculptures still preserved in several of these caves, there must have existed an important tradition of religious art which was now revived by various masters of no common ability. The earliest caves are at T'o Shan and Yü Han Shan; at the latter place many of the figures are dated in the 4th, 5th and 6th year of the K'ai Huang era (584–586), but unfortunately they are largely restored with plaster and crude colouring.

The great sculptures in the second and third cave at T'o Shan belong practically to the same stylistic group as those at Yü Han Shan. None of them bears a definite date, but, to judge from their style, they must have been executed about the same time as those mentioned above, *i.e.,* about the middle of the '80s. The typical Sui formula for single figures has been enlarged on an enormous scale, not without some loss of plastic beauty and intimacy. The great Buddhas which are seated in cross-legged position on a low pedestal impress us more as a kind of architectural monolith than as plastically conceived sculptures. It is only the folds of the hem, falling over the pedestal, that have a livelier rhythm; here one may observe the very characteristic meandering wave-line which returns in most sculptures of the Sui period, and some overlapping larger curves divided by the no less significant ear-like curves.

Passing from the cave sculptures at T'o Shan to those at Yün Men Shan, which is situated across the valley, means moving into a quite different artistic centre. There are only a few large statues at Yün Men Shan and some of these are in a deplorable state of preservation, but whatever remains here is of remarkably fine artistic quality. No doubt, these sculptures are a little later than those in the caves at T'o Shan, though hardly more than ten years; the dates that are found in some of the small niches at the side of the main figures range from 596 to 599. The figures are not placed in real caves but in flat niches, and may thus be seen to more advantage than most cave sculptures in their original position; the actual play of light and shade adds something to the plastic effect.

The Yün Men Shan Buddha.—The principal group consists of a seated Buddha accompanied by a standing Bodhisattva and another figure which may have been a Dvarapala (now practically destroyed). Close to this is another still flatter niche which never contained any central statue, only a large tablet, which is now removed, and on each side of it two monumental Bodhisattvas.

The great Buddha is seated on a dais in the traditional posture with the legs crossed in front, and entirely covered by the wide mantle. The bearing of the body is, however, quite different; instead of the old stiffness there is a certain ease in the posture, a repose without any strain. He seems to lean against the wall of the niche, moving the head slightly forward as if intent on looking at something in front. The upper garment which is fastened with a string knot on the left shoulder is draped in quite broad curves between the knees. The folds are not simply ornamental or expressive of a linear rhythm, but modelled with fine gradations of light and shade, sometimes even undercut. They have become means of primary importance for creating a sculptural effect. The head is treated in a new individual manner with broad effects of light and shade. The eyes are not closed or half closed, as in most of the earlier Buddhas, but wide open, and the eyelids are undercut, which adds greatly to the impression of life. The lips are also separated by a deep shadow, as if they were opening. The whole treatment is quite exceptional and bears witness to an impressionistic style; strictly speaking, it remains an isolated phenomenon in Chinese sculpture.

The T'ang Dynasty.—It would indeed be wrong to imagine that there is an absolute break or a deep-rooted difference between the sculpture of the Sui and that of the T'ang period; quite the opposite. T'ang sculpture is stylistically an immediate successor to the art of the Sui period. When we, for convenience sake, use the dynastic names and dates also in the domain of art, it should be clearly understood that they do not signify here the same kind of opposites or renewals as in the political history of the country. Artistic evolution in China is a slow and gradual process, which only to a minor degree is conditioned by the political events.

It may also be recalled that the T'ang dynasty reigned during a longer time than most of the preceding dynasties (618–907), and the plastic arts remained by no means the same during this whole period. The production of sculpture was very intense during the first 100 years of the period, but became soon afterwards comparatively weak and insignificant. In speaking about T'ang sculpture we mean the art up to about 725, which may be considered the most mature and perfect kind of Buddhist sculpture in China. It reflects something of the same creative and expansive power that we may observe in other manifestations of T'ang culture. Its best products are characterized by a plenitude, not to say magnificence, that can hardly be found in the art of earlier epochs. The forms grow full and strong, the decoration becomes rich and exuberant, gradually approaching what we should call baroque.

An important element in this evolution was due to the growing inter-communication between China and the western Asiatic centres of artistic activity, particularly the Sassanian empire. Many new impulses were derived thence and grafted upon the old stock of Chinese art, modifying it more and more in the direction of Western ideals of style. Generally speaking, it may be said that the current that came from India was of the greatest importance for the Buddhist sculpture, while the influences from Persian art are most plainly discernible in the ornamentation of minor objects in bronze and silver.

In order to illustrate these two main currents, as well as other important elements of style in the plastic art of the T'ang period, it would be well to take into consideration other artistic products besides stone sculptures, such as objects in bronze, silver, clay and lacquer, which reflect the aesthetic ideals of the time, but this would carry us beyond the limits of this short study. Buddhist statues still form the most important province within the plastic arts of the T'ang period, though it should also be remembered that some large tomb sculptures were executed at this time, including magnificent representations of lions and horses at the tombs of the great emperors, T'ai Tsung (d. 649) and Kao Tsung (d. 683).

The Shensi Sculptures.—The early T'ang sculptures from Shensi, which then was the metropolitan province, are made in a very hard, grey limestone or in a dense yellowish marble. The fine quality of the material demands a highly developed technique in order to yield good plastic effects and ornamental details, and it may well be admitted that as far as workmanship goes many of these statues stand on the highest level of Chinese sculpture, but the artistic quality is often less remarkable. The earliest dated statue of this period known to us is of the year 639; it represents a Buddha seated in cross-legged position on a high, draped pedestal placed in front of a background slab which is bordered like a nimbus with flame ornaments. The figure is draped in a mantle which covers both shoulders, arms and feet, leaving only a small part of the chest bare. The folds are highly conventionalized in the form of thin, rounded creases and arranged in long curves over the body, the legs and the upper part of the pedestal. The decorative effect is altogether more powerful and concentrated than in earlier statues of a similar kind, and the execution is masterly. Although made in stone, the statue gives the impression of a work cast in bronze, an impression which is supported by the dark metallic hue of the hard stone.

Influence of Indian Art.—Some Bodhisattva statues, of which two may be seen in the University museum in Philadelphia, illustrate still better an increasing influence from Indian art not only by their costumes and decorative ornaments but also by their bearing and formal character. They stand no longer in stiff upright positions with the weight of the body evenly divided on both feet; the one leg is slightly curved and moved backward, the other serves as a support for the body which consequently is curving, a movement which is continued in the neck and in the more or less marked inclination of the head. The upper part of the body is bare, except for the jewelled necklaces and the narrow scarf draped over the shoulder; the chest is well developed and the waist rather narrow. The *dhoti,* which is tied with a sash round the hips, falls in a series of curving folds over each leg, and these are indicated in the same fashion as the folds of the Buddha mentioned above. It should also be noticed that these figures do not wear a crown or a diadem on their heads like the early Bodhisattvas, but a high head-dress made up of thick winding plaits, a feature which also adds to their feminine aspect.

A kind of masculine pendant to these Bodhisattvas may be found among the statues of *bikshus* or monks, executed either as individual *post mortem* portraits or as parts of altar groups (examples of such statues may be seen in the museums in Philadelphia and Boston). They are less conventionalized, less dependent on foreign models and made in closer adherence to actual life. Their heads are portrait-like, their mantles arranged in a more or less natural fashion, thus, in many instances, approaching the small clay statuettes made for the tombs during the T'ang period as well as in earlier times. Some of these portrait statues may indeed be placed on a level with the best Roman sculptures. They are character studies, not so far individualized as Renaissance portraits, but very striking types, observed in actual life. It is also worth noticing how much freer and more plastic the draping of the mantle becomes in these statues. A figure such as the headless monk in the Boston museum might have been made by a Roman artist.

Honan Sculptures.—When we pass from the metropolitan province of Shensi into the adjoining province of Honan we may at once observe that the general character of the sculptures becomes modified. The provincial schools and stylistic differentiations seem on the whole to have become more developed at this time than at earlier epochs; it is now easier to distinguish the provincial currents.

The statues made in Honan, and particularly at the great artistic centre of Lung Men, where the decoration of the caves was continued during the 7th century, are generally more elegant than those originating from Shensi, though not always executed in such perfect technique. Unfortunately, the great majority of the early T'ang sculptures at Lung Men are partly or wholly destroyed—the heads being dispersed all over the world—so that it is now next to impossible to find there complete and good specimens of moderate size; we find them more easily in museums and private collections.

One of the finest examples is a large Bodhisattva statue, originally at Lung Men, but now in private hands in Peking. It may be taken as a representative of a large group of standing Bodhisattvas which all show the Indian influence grafted in Chinese types and shapes, a combination which in this particular instance has led to a perfectly harmonious result. The whole figure from the head-dress down to the feet is dominated by the softly gliding movement of the double S-curve (as in some Gothic madonnas) which would appear almost too accentuated, if it were not so perfectly balanced by the position of the arms. The contemporary Bodhisattvas from Shensi, represented in a similar position, appear quite stiff and hard beside this elegant and yet so dignified figure.

The Vairochana Buddha.—The colossal statues on the open terrace, which rises above the river at Lung Men, reflect in the most monumental form the religious pathos of the fully developed T'ang art. This is true particularly of the central figure, the great Vairochana Buddha; the side figures, two Bodhisattvas and two *bikshus* are decidedly inferior. The hands are destroyed, the lower part of the figure has suffered a great deal, but I doubt whether it ever made a stronger impression than to-day when it rises high and free in the open air over the many surrounding niches in which time and human defilers have played havoc with most of the minor figures. The upper part of this giant is well preserved and more dominating now than ever. Long ages have softened the mantle folds and roughened the surface of the grey limestone which is cracking all over, but they have not spoilt the impression of the plastic form. It may still be felt under the thin garment: a very sensitively modelled form, not a dead mass, though unified in a monumental sense. According to the inscription on the plinth the statue was made about 672–675.

The great power which is here reflected in such a harmonious and well-balanced form finds further dramatic expression in the

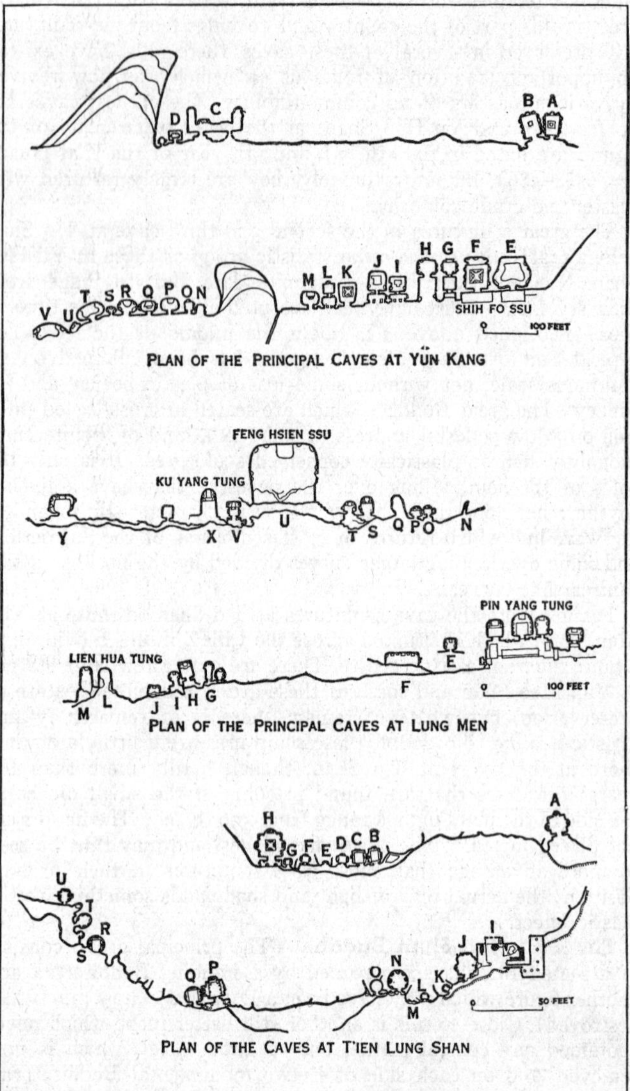

PLANS OF THE PRINCIPAL CAVES AT YÜN KANG, LUNG MEN AND T'IEN LUNG SHAN

Dvarapalas which stand at the entrance to the so-called "lion cave." The bestial heads of the figures are amazing and terrible, and even the naked form is by no means represented from a naturalistic point of view, but as a symbol of strength and vigilance. Other Dvarapalas of the same date are sometimes represented in livelier postures, bending sideways or lifting one hand to deal a killing blow to any approaching enemy. The plastic effect is decidedly of a baroque nature, a tendency which is characteristic of the mature T'ang art whenever it leaves the well-trodden path of the traditional religious imagery and ventures on more naturalistic and dramatic representations.

Later T'ien Lung Shan Sculptures.—Another fairly homogeneous local group of T'ang sculpture may be observed in some of the later caves at T'ien Lung Shan where the artistic activity must have been kept up ever since the middle of the 6th century. During all these generations T'ien Lung Shan seems to have remained a special centre of Indian influence. Unfortunately, none of these sculptures is dated, and in some respects they fall outside

FROM (1) THE OPPENHEIM COLLECTION, (2) THE WANNIECK COLLECTION, (4) THE GARDNER COLLECTION, (5) "MISSION ARCHÉOLOGIQUE EN CHINE" BY SEGALEN-VOISINS AND LARTIGUE (PAUL GEUTHNER); PHOTOGRAPHS, (3) COPR. OSVALD SIRÉN

ANIMALS IN EARLY CHINESE SCULPTURE

1. Bear in gilt bronze; Han dynasty (206 B.C.–A.D. 220)
2. Reclining bull, bronze; North Wei dynasty (A.D. 386–636)
3. Dog, in clay; Han dynasty (206 B.C.–A.D. 220)
4. Two bears, gilt bronze; Han dynasty (206 B.C.–A.D. 220)
5. Reclining horse, from the tomb of General Ho Ch'iu P'ing, Shen-si, (*c.* 117 B.C.)

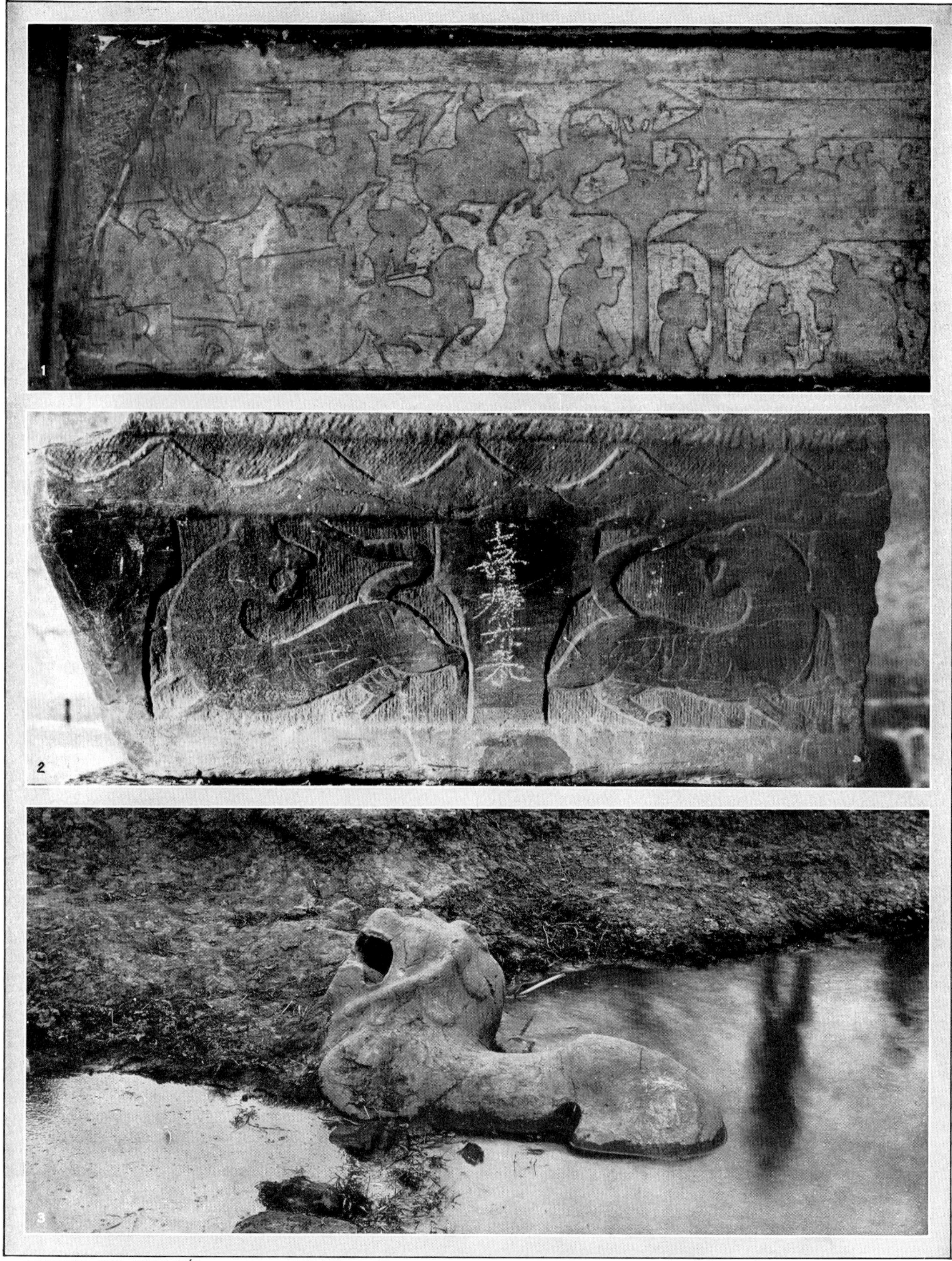

SCULPTURES AT THE TOMB OF WU LIANG TZU, SHANTUNG

1. Men coming in carts and on horseback to a festival in a house; stone relief from the tomb shrine of Wu Liang Tzu; A.D. 147

2. Two tigers; stone relief from the same tomb

3. Statue of a guardian lion at entrance of the same tomb

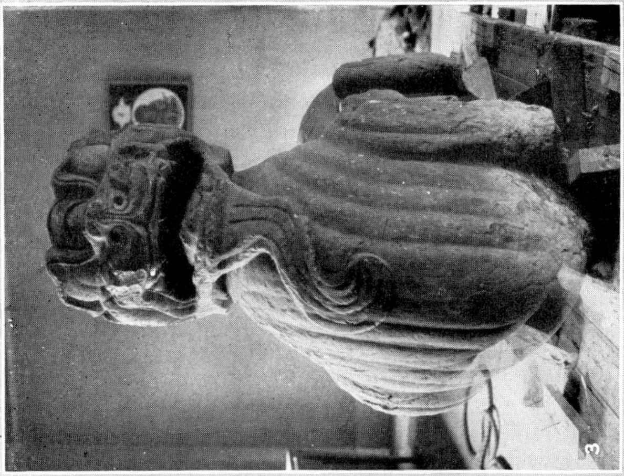

MONSTERS IN CHINESE SCULPTURE

1. Winged lion; statue at the tomb of Prince Hsiao Hsiu (d. A.D. 518), near Nanking. 2. Chimaera; statue at the tomb of the Emperor Ch'i Wu Ti (d. A.D. 493), near Nanking. Chimaeras usually guarded the tombs of emperors; lions those of princes and dukes; the largest are 10–12 ft. long. 3. Chimaera; statue from an imperial tomb of the 6th century A.D. 4. Chimaera; statue from an imperial tomb. 5. Statue of winged lion at the tomb of Duke Hsiao Ching (d. A.D. 523), near Nanking

CHINESE SCULPTURE

LARGE AND SMALL WORKS OF CHINESE SCULPTURE

1. Pillars forming the entrance to the tomb-area of Wu Liang Tzu, Shantung, A.D. 147
2. Pillar at the tomb of Fung Huan, Sze-Ch'uen, A.D. 121
3. Pillars at tomb of Shen, Sze-Ch'uen
4. Seated Bodhisattva, marble statue, late T'ang dynasty
5. Tomb-statuettes in clay, Han dynasty, in a private collection in Berlin
6. Praying monk, a marble statue, 12th–13th century A.D.

DIVINITIES IN CHINESE SCULPTURE

1. Seated Buddha, colossal statue at Yun Kang, Shan-si, 6th century. 2. Seated Bodhisattva, early 6th century, from Yun Kang, Shan-si. 3. Hindu divinities and a guardian at entrance to a cave, Yun Kang, 6th century. The sculptures of the cave temples (5th–6th centuries) show strong influences from the art of Central and Western Asia. 4. Portion of a wall in the Lao Chun cave, Lung-Men, Ho-nan, early 6th century

RELIGIOUS SCULPTURES OF THE 6TH CENTURY A.D.

1. Buddha accompanied by two Bodhisattvas, Cave 2 at T'ien Lung Shan, Shan-si, middle 6th century. 2. Standing Bodhisattva, marble statue of Sui period, about 600. 3. Standing Buddha; statuette in gilt bronze, dated 537. 4. Guardian at entrance of Cave 8, T'ien Lung Shan, Shan-si, North Ch'i period, middle of the 6th century

CHINESE SCULPTURES OF THE SUI PERIOD

1. Seated Buddha accompanied by two Bodhisattvas and two monks, Cave 16 at T'ien Lung Shan; Sui period, end of 6th century
2. Colossal Buddha in a cave at T'o Shan, Shantung; end of 6th century
3. Seated Buddha accompanied by a Bodhisattva, in a niche at Yun Men Shan, Shantung
4. Upper part of a Bodhisattva, Yun Men Shan, Shantung

CHINESE SCULPTURE: 7TH, 13TH, AND 14TH CENTURIES

1. Standing Bodhisattva, marble statue, end of T'ang period, now in a private collection in the United States
2. Kuanyin Bodhisattva, wooden statue, 13th century
3. Kuanyin Bodhisattva, wooden statue, 13th century
4. Virudhaka, one of the four Lokapâlas (guardians of the universe), relief on the Chü Yung Kuan Gate, Nank'ou, Chih-li, dated 1345
5. Girl playing the lute, marble statue, end of T'ang period

the general stylistic current of T'ang art. Some of them show plastic motives which really did not come into vogue until some time after 700, but this may be due to the fact that they were made under foreign influence. The earliest among these sculptures are remarkably fresh and subtle while the later ones are comparatively heavy and commonplace works. The best specimens of the earlier types are to be seen in caves 6 and 14, while the later ones are found in caves 17, 19, 20 and 21.

The main group on the back wall of cave 6 consists of a Buddha seated cross-legged on a high pedestal accompanied by two side figures, which, however, are almost eaten away by time and running water, but there is a Bodhisattva on the side wall which can still be enjoyed. The figure is seated on a round lotus pedestal with the legs folded but not crossed. He leans toward the right side and turns slightly in the waist, a movement which is accentuated by the turning of the head in the same direction. The left hand is placed on the leg in front as if to give added support to the body and make the free attitude still more restful. The body is entirely bare, except for a jewelled necklace and the narrow scarf which is draped in a diagonal curve from the right shoulder. The ease of the posture in conjunction with the sensitive modelling of the youthful body endow this figure with a sensual charm which is very seldom found in Chinese statues. It would hold its place beside the most exquisite French sculptures of the 18th century and yet it impresses us just as much by its dignity and composure.

A similar artistic conception is expressed in a still ampler form in a Bodhisattva statue in cave 16. The posture of the figure is a kind of *lalitasana* (position of ease). It is seated with the one leg pendant, the other bent crosswise over the seat, but the foot is not placed on the opposite leg. The left elbow is practically touching the knee, as if to support the body which leans over toward the side, turning at the same time slightly in the waist. The movement of the head follows in the opposite direction, producing thus a contraposto effect which, although not very pronounced, serves to bring out the beauty of the ripe body and the supple limbs. It may not have quite the charm of the one noticed above, but it shows an astonishingly free treatment of the mantle, the material being a kind of *draperie mouillée.*

None of the other caves at T'ien Lung Shan contains statues of a corresponding importance, although there are some which reveal the strong Indian influence both in their general shapes and in the treatment of their garments. The heads, which in late years have been knocked off and spread all over the Western world, are sometimes beautiful, though less expressive than the best heads from Lung Men or earlier centres of Buddhist sculpture in China.

Changes in Style.—Similar tendencies toward a freer plastic style may also be observed in contemporary sculptures from Shensi and Chihli. Among them may be seen beautiful Bodhisattvas which not only bend in the waist but also turn on the hips, making thus quite complicated movements, which tend to bring out the beauty and significance of their corporeal form. By these freer postures their likeness to ordinary human beings becomes more striking. They sometimes remind one of the complaint of the philosopher from the end of the T'ang period who said that the artists were losing their reverent attitude toward the religious motives and were representing the Bodhisattvas in the shape of court ladies.

The difference between the religious and the secular motives seems, as a matter of fact, to become less and less important, and one meets with quite realistic *genre* figures not only in clay but also executed on a large scale in stone, very much according to the same formula as the Bodhisattvas. As a good example of this class of work may be mentioned a statue of a young lady (in the Academy of Art in Tokyo) who sits on a bank with crossed legs playing a lute, while a dog and a cat are frolicking at her feet, a statue without any religious pretext, with the same amount of free and elegant realism as we know from the tomb statuettes in clay and from some T'ang paintings. Works of this kind indicate that the sculptors no longer remained satisfied with the purely religious inspiration but turned their attention towards nature and human life. If the evolution had continued along these lines, the plastic arts in China might have become just as expressive and varied in their interpretations of purely artistic problems as Renaissance sculpture in Europe, but the creative power turned more and more from sculpture to painting.

Quite interesting as examples of the new tendencies of style are certain statues made at Ting Chou in Chihli, a centre of sculptural activity which, as we have seen, was important ever since the Northern Wei period. The best of these are surprisingly free and illustrate a new interest in movement and in the full development of the human figure. Among them may be mentioned a large statue of a headless Bodhisattva in the collection of Mrs. J. D. Rockefeller Jr. in New York, which is represented in a forward stride. The figure is composed in a similar way to some early Renaissance statues represented in a walking posture, *e.g.,* St. John the Baptist —and shows the same shortcomings in the stiff limbs and the stilted rhythm, but also the same endeavour to treat the plastic form in the full round.

There are many other statues illustrating this tendency. The most original is perhaps a bare-headed monk who stands turned sideways with hands folded before the chest and head thrown back, looking almost straight upwards (in the collection of General Munthe, Peking). The movement expresses an intense religious devotion, not in the usual restrained and well-balanced form but with the flow of human feeling which leads our thoughts away from the Orient toward the most emotional religious art of Europe, such as we know it from the late Gothic and Baroque periods. The impressionistic treatment of the soft and heavy mantle points in the same direction.

The Post-T'ang Periods.—The production of religious sculpture decreases more and more towards the end of the T'ang period. Very few dated specimens are known from the 9th century, while those from the 8th are quite numerous. During the following periods of the Five Dynasties and the Northern Sung the creative energy of the nation, which in former times, particularly when religious devotion ran high, had been largely directed to the production of sculpture, turned to painting, which now definitely took the lead among the fine arts in China. The change in the relative importance of sculpture and painting is also illustrated by the fact that sculpture responded more and more to the influence of painting, an influence which became evident not only in the new impressionistic tendencies of style but also by the fact that other materials than stone and bronze came into vogue, particularly wood, clay, iron and lacquer-work, and these were usually treated with colour. Many of the new compositions introduced about this time were derived from contemporary paintings. It is true for instance of the very popular Kuanyin Bodhisattvas in the *maharajalila* (posture of royal ease) executed in stone, clay and wood, and it may also be observed in the combination of the figures with backgrounds treated like rocky landscapes or some kind of scenery with trees, buildings, animals and small human beings.

This more or less pictorial kind of sculpture spread all over northern China during the 12th and 13th centuries, when Buddhist art enjoyed a short period of reflorescence, and wooden sculpture particularly reached a high degree of perfection. A great number of wooden statues have in later years been brought from China to various Western collections, *e.g.,* the museums in Philadelphia, Chicago and Toronto which alone contain more such statues than can be mentioned here. The majority of these represent either standing Bodhisattvas in long garments which often take on a fluttering movement toward the feet, or Kuanyins on rocky seats in the *maharajalila* posture. One of the standing figures in Toronto is said to have been dated by a tablet inserted in the figure in the year 1106, while one of the seated Kuanyins, lately belonging to the Ton Ying company in New York, carries an inscription with the date 1168. Similar ones are to be found in the British Museum, in the museums in Boston and Chicago, in the Musée Guimet and Collection Jean Sauphar in Paris, etc.

It is during this period that Kuanyin, the Bodhisattva of Mercy, definitely changes into a feminine being usually represented in a free and elegant form, whether she be seated on a rock by the water in the *maharajalila* posture, as in so many of these wooden figures, or is standing, bending forward as if lending a listening ear to the invocations of her adorers. The womanly beauty is much more accentuated in these figures than any bodhisattvic qualities. The form has lost all its abstract serenity and become fluttering and emotional, but it is sometimes highly decorative in a new and more limited sense. Many of these figures seem to have been conceived not for a moral purpose, like the old Buddhas and Bodhisattvas, but simply to please the eye and the sentimental longings of the worshippers. Besides these wooden sculptures there are a good many made in stone, particularly series of Arhats, who are usually represented in series of 16 or 18, according to definite types and with more realistic than artistic expression. Interesting series of such Arhats executed in stone may be seen at the Yen Sha Tung and Ling Yen Ssu caves near Hangchow, as well as in the museum at Toronto. They are very uneven in quality and, on the whole, more interesting from an historical than from an artistic point of view.

Yuan Dynasty.—After the establishment of the Yüan dynasty (1280–1368) the position of the fine arts in China, including sculpture, changed considerably. The Mongols brought no new positive inspiration, on the contrary they destroyed more than they built up, except perhaps in the art of war. Art was useful to them only in so far as it could support and glorify the temporal power of the emperor and his generals. The religious attitude of the Yüan emperors was on the whole tolerant, but officialdom was then thoroughly Confucian and the Buddhists were pushed into the background. Taoism seems now to have held its place by the side of Buddhism. The cave sculptures at Hao Tien Kuan, south of T'aiyüan-fu in Shansi, executed at the end of the 13th century, are in this respect very interesting. Some of the compositions illustrating scenes from the life of the Taoist philosopher Pi Yün Ssu, besides a great number of other Immortals, reveal an evident interest in nature as, for instance, the old man on his deathbed; he is represented lying soundly asleep on the Chinese "kang" clad in a long garment. The most successful portions in these grottos are, however, the purely decorative compositions, the low reliefs on the walls representing clouds and phoenixes, and the two guardians at the sides of one of the entrances whose fluttering draperies are arranged in ornamental curves. All these decorative designs are characterized by a buoyancy and a vigour which are hardly to be found in Chinese sculpture of the immediately preceding period. The motives are used for decoration rather than for the expression of purely plastic ideas. The pictorial tendency which characterizes the sculptures of the preceding period is still existent, although it has become coarser and of a more superficial kind. The same stylistic tendencies are also quite noticeable in a number of other sculptures of the same period, such as the four *Lokapalas* (guardians of the world) on the Chü Yung Kuan gate at Nank'ou, executed in 1345, and the Buddhist figures in a niche at Lung Tung Ssu near Tsinan-fu in Shantung, executed in 1318, not to speak of minor detached statues, dated at the beginning of the 14th century.

Ming Period.—When we enter into the Ming period (1368–1644) the dramatic power of expression seems to dry up more and more and the general artistic level is certainly not raised, although the production of Buddhist sculptures goes on with increasing abundance. Among the most popular and common creations of this time may be mentioned, for instance, series of Arhats in iron (good examples of such series are in the museums at Toronto and Gothenburg) which, however, seldom rise above the level of ordinary mass products made according to standard models. Similar motives are also treated in wood and lacquer, sometimes with good decorative effect, though with no more individual characterization. The sculpture of the Ming period is generally at its best when it takes up purely realistic motives instead of the traditional hieratic figures. It may thus become quite enjoyable in minor representations of mourners, musicians or similar *genre*-like motives, presented without any tendency to archaic restraint which otherwise is so apparent in the plastic arts of the Ming.

Summary.—Trying to sum up the general course of development of Chinese sculpture from the 10th to the 15th century in a few words, we have to remember first the comparatively low level of religious sculpture towards the end of the Sung dynasty, particularly after the capital was moved from Kaifêng to Hangchow; secondly, the re-awakening of religious imagery in the northern provinces after the Tartar dynasties had got a firm hold on this part of the country (a flourishing sculptural activity, particularly in wood, developed there in the provinces of Chihli and Shansi); and thirdly, that with the Yüan dynasty a new foreign element appears which perhaps may be called Mongolian and which expresses itself on the one hand in a somewhat dry realism and on the other hand in a whirling linear ornamentation. The religious figures have still some life and expression of their own, though no real spirituality. This development was no longer continued during the Ming period. Whatever creative power may have been left did not turn towards the production of religious sculpture. It is true that a lot of statues, or rather statuettes, in bronze, wood, porcelain and ivory were produced but no great religious works, whether in stone or other materials. The Ming sculptors have given their best in the field of decorative art such as columns, balustrades, and other architectural details, but they created no new types of plastic works, whether religious or secular. They sought their inspiration much more in the imitation of earlier models than in any fresh efforts in the field of sculpture. (*See* also SCULPTURE; CHINA; BUDDHA AND BUDDHISM; INDIAN AND SINHALESE ART AND ARCHAEOLOGY; CHINESE ARCHITECTURE.)

BIBLIOGRAPHY.—E. Chavannes, *Mission archéologique dans la Chine septentrionale* (1909–15); S. Omura, *History of Chinese Art; Sculpture*, text in Japanese (1915); T. Sekino, *Sepulchral Remains of the Han Dynasty in Shantung*, text separate in Japanese (1920); S. Taketaro and Nakagawa, *Rock Carvings from Yün Kang Caves*, no text (1921); S. Tanaka, *T'ien Lung Shan, no text* (1923); L. Ashton, *Introduction to the Study of Chinese Sculpture* (1924); V. Ségalen, "Premier exposé des résultats archéologiques dans la Chine occidentale par la mission G. de Voisins, J. Lartigue, V. Ségalen," *Journal Asiatique*, tome v3, vi2, vii3; O. Sirén, *Chinese Sculpture from the 5th to the 14th Century*, 3 vol. plates, 1 vol. text (1925), and *Studien zur Chinesischen Plastik der Post-T'ang Zeit* (1927); V. Ségalen, G. de Voisins and J. Lartigue, *Mission Archéologique en Chine*, no text (1926); O. Sirén, *A History of Early Chinese Art* (1929). (O. S.)

CHINGFORD, a municipal borough in the Epping parliamentary Division of Essex, England, 12 mi. N.E. of London by the L.N.E.R. Pop. (1938) 37,510. Area 4.5 sq.mi. It lies between the river Lea and the western outskirts of Epping forest. The church of All Saints has Early English and Perpendicular remains. The half-timbered Queen Elizabeth's, or Fair Mead, hunting lodge is preserved there. Chingford was incorporated in 1938 and adopted a town planning scheme.

CHINGLEPUT, town and district, British India, in the Madras presidency. The town, situated 36 mi. by rail from Madras, and a junction for a branch line to Arkonam, had a population in 1941 of 17,829. With Chandragiri in North Arcot, Chingleput was once the capital of the Vijayanagar kings, after their overthrow by the Mohammedans at Talikota in 1565. In 1639 a chief, subject to these kings, granted to the East India Company the land on which Fort St. George now stands. The fort built by the Vijayanagar kings in the 16th century, which was of strategic importance, was taken by the French in 1751, and retaken in 1752 by Clive, after which it proved invaluable to the British. It withstood Hyder Ali and afforded a refuge to the natives; and in 1780, after the defeat of Colonel W. Baillie, the army of Sir Hector Munro took refuge here. It is now partially ruined. The town is noted for its manufacture of pottery, and carries on a trade in rice. It is the centre of a Scotch Free Church mission, and has a reformatory school.

THE DISTRICT OF CHINGLEPUT surrounds the city of Madras, stretching along the coast for about 115 miles. The administrative headquarters are at Saidapet. Area 3,074 sq.mi. Pop. (1941) 1,823,955. Salt is extensively manufactured along the coast, and fishing carried on. There are cotton and silk mills, tanneries, stone quarries and soapworks.

CHIN HILLS, a constituent hill-group of the mountain arc stretching from the Arakan Yoma northwards to the Patkai hills, between Burma and India. This mountain arc, compressed at either end, has advanced farthest towards the west in the centre where the long parallel folds are most numerous and the arc broadest. The Chin hills form the highest part of this central stretch. They consist simply of a succession of long narrow troughs and ridges, from 5,000 to 9,000 ft. high, with little flat land either in the valley bottoms or on the ridge tops. There is a marked climatic contrast between the humid tropical conditions of the deeply cut valleys and the cooler temperatures of the ridges. This contrast is reflected in the vegetation. Above 3,000 ft. the tropical forest gives way to oak and pine woods which in turn give way above 7,000 ft. to the rhododendron. A migratory form of agriculture, the *taungya* system, is practised in these hillside woods where the greater part of the population is centred. Clearings are made and the wood burnt for fertilizer. Such clearings are cultivated for two or three years and then abandoned. Bamboo, bracken and elephant grass then spring up with such vigour that natural re-afforestation is impossible. The main crop cultivated by this method is *jowar* millet contrasting with rice in the plains of Lower Burma. Some rice is, however, grown in the Chin hills on the lower slopes on terraces constructed with the help of felled timber.

The north-south trend lines of Indo-China as a whole have permitted the flooding of the region with "Mongoloid" peoples coming down from the north and have hindered east-west movement of both peoples and culture. The Arakan Yoma-Patkai mountain arc, of which the Chin hills form a part, exemplifies these features. It constitutes a frontier zone between Indian and Burmese cultures and its hill-tribes remained independent of British administration until the close of the 19th century. The Chin hills, lying on the Irrawaddy side of the watershed, were eventually occupied to prevent the raids by hill-folk on the plains of Burma. They are now administered primarily with the object of preserving the peace and of building up a sound government on the basis of the tribal system. The substitution of peaceful agriculture for raiding is producing changes in the distribution of population; the defensive hill-sites are being deserted and population is becoming concentrated on the more easily cultivable land. The whole of the southern part of the Arakan Yoma-Patkai mountain arc from the Chin hills southward into the Arakan Yoma is occupied by the Chin peoples who belong to the Southern Mongoloid race group and are linguistically a branch of the Tibeto-Burmans. The Chin hills proper are occupied by only the northern tribes of the Chin peoples. **Area of the district** 10,377 **sq.mi. Population (1941)** 186,405. (P. M. R.)

CHINKIANG, former treaty port of China on the south bank of the Yangtze Kiang, 32° 11′ N., 119° 24′ E., 160 mi. above Shanghai and 43 mi. below Nanking. It lies where the north-south route of the Grand canal from Hangchow to Peiping crosses the east-west route of the Yangtze river. So long as the Grand canal, linking the Yangtze delta with the imperial capital, remained an arterial line of communication, Chinkiang retained its significance. But traffic on the Grand canal became after 1850 increasingly local and its function as a north-south link was later usurped by the Tientsin-Pukow (Tsin-Pu) railway, which comes down to the Yangtze opposite Nanking, itself the terminus of a railway from Shanghai.

Chinkiang, although a station on the Shanghai-Nanking railway, had therefore given place to Nanking in the command of the Yangtze crossing. Moreover the port of Chinkiang was experiencing local difficulties through silting. In consequence, while, since the first decade of the 20th century, the trade of neighbouring ports had continued to increase, that of Chinkiang had been arrested.

The port was functioning for a time almost solely as a distributing place of imported goods. In 1926 the excess of imports over exports was in the proportion of 15 to 1. With the fall of Chinkiang into Japanese hands, Dec. 1937, the Japanese controlled the river trade. The population was given as 216,803 in 1937.

CHINO-JAPANESE WAR (1894–95). The causes of this conflict arose out of the immemorial rivalry of China and Japan for influence in Korea. In the 16th century a prolonged war in the peninsula had ended with the failure of Japan to make good her footing on the mainland—a failure brought about largely by lack of naval resources. In more modern times (1875, 1882, 1884) Japan had repeatedly sent expeditions to Korea, and had fostered the growth of a progressive party in Seoul. The difficulties of 1884 were settled between China and Japan by the convention of Tientsin, wherein it was agreed that in the event of future intervention each should inform the other if it were decided to despatch troops to the peninsula. Nine years later the occasion arose. A serious rebellion induced the Korean Government to apply for military assistance from China. Early in June 1894 a small force of Chinese troops was sent to Asan, and Japan, duly informed of this action, replied by furnishing her minister at Seoul with an escort, rapidly following up this step by the despatch of about 5,000 troops under Maj.-Gen. Oshima. A complicated situation thus arose. Chinese troops were present in Korea by the request of the Government to put down rebellion. The Japanese controlled the capital, and declined to recognize Korea as a tributary of China. But they proposed that the two Powers should unite to suppress the disturbance and to inaugurate certain specified reforms. China considered that the measures of reform must be left to Korea herself. The reply was that Japan considered the Government of Korea "lacking in some of the elements which are essential to responsible independence." By the middle of July war had become inevitable unless the Peking Government were willing to abandon all claims over Korea, and as Chinese troops were already in the country by invitation, it was not to be expected that the shadowy suzerainty would be abandoned.

At Seoul the issue was forced by the Japanese minister, who delivered an ultimatum to the Korean Government on July 20. On the 23rd the palace was forcibly occupied. Meanwhile China had despatched about 8,000 troops to the Yalu river. The outbreak of war thus found the Japanese in possession of Seoul and ready to send large forces to Korea, while the Chinese occupied Asan (about 40m. south of the capital) and had a considerable body of troops in Manchuria in addition to those despatched to the Yalu river. To Japan the command of the sea was essential for the secure transport and supply of her troops. Without it the experience of the war of the 16th century would be repeated. China, too, could only utilize overland routes to Korea by submitting to the difficulties and delays entailed.

By the time war was finally declared (August 1), hostilities had already begun. On July 25 Oshima set out from Seoul to attack the Chinese at Asan. On the 29th he won a victory at Sönghwan, but the Chinese commander escaped with a considerable part of his forces by a détour to Ping-Yang (Phyöng-Yang). Meanwhile a portion of the Japanese fleet had encountered some Chinese warships and transports off Phung-Tao, and scored an important success, sinking, amongst other vessels, the transport "Kowshing" (July 25). The loss of more than 1,000 Chinese soldiers in this vessel materially lightened Oshima's task. The intention of the Chinese to crush their enemies between their forces at Asan and Ping-Yang was completely frustrated, and the Japanese obtained control of all southern Korea.

Reinforcements from Japan were now pouring into Korea, and Gen. Nozu, the senior Japanese officer present, soon found himself in a position to move on Ping-Yang. Three columns converged upon the place on Sept. 15 and carried it after severe fighting.

Nearly all the troops on either side had been conveyed to the scene of war by sea, though the decisive contest for sea supremacy was still to be fought. The Chinese admiral Ting with the Northern squadron (which alone took part in the war) had hitherto remained inactive in Wei-hai-wei, and on the other side Vice-Admiral Ito's fleet had not directly interfered with the hostile transports which were reinforcing the troops on the Yalu. But two days after the battle of Ping-Yang, Ting, who had conveyed a large body of troops to the mouth of the Yalu, encountered the Japanese fleet on his return journey off Hai-Yang-Tao on Sept 17. The heavy battleships "Chên-Yuen" and "Ting-Yuen" constituted the strongest element of the Chinese squadron, for the Japanese, superior as they were in every other factor of success, had no vessels which could compare with these in the matter of protection. Ting advanced in a long irregular line abreast; the battleships in the centre, the lighter vessels on the wings. Ito's fast cruisers steamed in line ahead against the Chinese right wing, crushing their weaker opponents with their fire. In the end the Chinese fleet was defeated and scattered, but the two heavy battleships drew off without serious injury. This battle of the Yalu gave Japan command of the sea, but Ito continued to act with great caution. The remnants of the vanquished fleet took refuge in Port Arthur, whence after repairs Ting proceeded to Wei-hai-wei.

The victory of Ping-Yang had cleared Korea of the Chinese troops, but on the lower Yalu—their own frontier—large forces threatened a second advance. Marshal Yamagata therefore took the offensive with his I. Army, and on Oct. 24 and 25, under great difficulties—though without serious opposition from the enemy—forced the passage of the river and occupied Chiu-lien-chêng. Part of the Chinese force retired to the north-east, part to Fêng-hwang-chêng and Hsiu-yuen. The Japanese I. Army advanced several columns towards the mountains of Manchuria to secure its conquests and prepare for a future advance. Gen. Tachimi's brigade, skirmishing with the enemy on the Moukden and Liao-Yang roads, found the Chinese in force. A simultaneous forward move by both sides led to the action of Tsao-ho-ku (Nov. 30), after which both sides withdrew—the Chinese to the line of the mountains covering Hai-chêng, Liao-Yang and Moukden, with the Tatar general Ikotenga's force 14,000 strong, on the Japanese right north-east of Fêng-hwang-chêng; and the Japanese to Chiu-lien-chêng, Takushan and Hsiu-yuen. The difficulties of supply in the hills were almost insurmountable, and no serious advance was intended by the Japanese until Jan. 1895, when it was to be made in co-operation with the II. Army. This army, under Marshal Oyama, had been formed in September and at first sent to Chemulpho as a support to the forces under Yamagata; but its chief task was the siege and capture of the Chinese fortress, dockyard and arsenal of Port Arthur.

The Liao-Tong peninsula was guarded by the walled city of Kin-chow and the forts of Ta-lien-wan (Dalny under the Russian régime, and Dairen under the Japanese) as well as the fortifications around Port Arthur itself. On Oct. 24 the disembarkation of the II. Army began near Pi-tse-wo, and the successive columns of the Japanese gradually moved towards Kin-chow, which was carried without difficulty. Even less resistance was offered by the modern forts of Ta-lien-wan. The Japanese now held a good harbour within a few miles of the main fortress. Here they landed siege artillery, and on Nov. 17 the advance was resumed. The attack was made on the 19th at dawn. Yamaji's division (Nogi's and Nishi's brigades), after a trying night march, assaulted and carried the western defences and moved upon the town. Hasegawa in the centre, as soon as Yamaji began to appear in rear of his opponents in the northern forts, pushed home his attack with equal success, and by 3 P.M. practically all resistance was at an end. The Japanese paid for this important success with but 423 casualties. Meanwhile the Chinese general Sung, who had marched from Hai-chêng to engage the II. Army, appeared before Kin-chow, where he received on the 22nd a severe repulse at the hands of the Japanese garrison. Soon after this overtures of peace were made by China; but her envoy, a foreigner unfurnished with credentials, was not received by the Tokyo Government.

The Japanese I. Army (now under Gen. Nozu) prepared, in spite of the season, to move across the mountains, and on Dec. 3 Gen. Katsura left Antung for Hai-chêng, which was safely occupied on Dec. 13. In the meantime Tachimi had moved northward from Fêng-hwang-chêng in order to distract the attention of the Chinese from Hai-chêng, and there were some small engagements between this force and that of Ikotenga, who ultimately retired beyond the mountains to Liao-Yang. Sung had already left Kai-ping to secure Hai-chêng when he heard of the fall of that place; his communications with Ikotenga being now severed, he swerved to the north-west and established a new base at Niu-chwang. Once on his new line Sung moved upon Hai-chêng. As it was essential that he should be prevented from joining forces with Ikotenga, Gen. Katsura marched out of Hai-chêng to fight him. At Kang-wang-tsai (Dec. 19) the Chinese displayed unusual steadiness, and it cost the Japanese some 343 casualties to dislodge the enemy. The victors returned to Hai-chêng exhausted with their efforts, but secure from attack for some time to come. The advanced troops of the II. Army (Nogi's brigade) were now ready to advance, and only the Kai-ping garrison barred their junction with Katsura. At Kai-ping (Jan. 10) the resistance of the Chinese was almost as steady as at Kang-wang-tsai, and the Japanese lost 300 killed and wounded in their successful attack. In neither of these actions was the defeated force routed, nor did it retire very far. On Jan. 17 and again on the 22nd Ikotenga attacked Hai-chêng from the north, but was repulsed.

Meanwhile the II. Army, still under Oyama, had undertaken operations against Wei-hai-wei, the second great fortress and dockyard of northern China; and it was hoped that both armies would accomplish their present tasks in time to advance in the summer against Peking itself. On Jan. 18 a naval demonstration was made at Têng-chow-fu, 70m. west of Wei-hai-wei, and on the 19th the Japanese began their disembarkation at Yung-chêng Bay, about 12m. from Wei-hai-wei. The landing was scarcely opposed, and on the 26th the Japanese advance was begun. The south-eastern defences of Wei-hai-wei harbour were carried by the 6th Division, whilst the 2nd Division reached the inner waters of the bay, driving the Chinese before them. The fleet under Ito co-operated effectively. On the night of Feb. 4–5 the Chinese squadron in harbour was attacked by ten torpedo boats. Two boats were lost, but the armour-clad "Ting-Yuen" was sunk. On the following night a second attack was made, and three more vessels were sunk. On the 9th the "Chên-Yuen" was sunk by the guns in one of the captured forts. On the 12th Admiral Ting wrote to Admiral Ito offering to surrender, and then took poison, other officers following his example. Wei-hai-wei was then dismantled by the Japanese, and the II. Army concentrated at Port Arthur for the advance on Peking.

While this campaign was in progress the Chinese despatched a second peace mission, also with defective credentials. The Japanese declined to treat, and the mission returned to China. In February the Chinese made further unsuccessful attacks on Hai-chêng. Yamaji near Kai-ping fought a severe action on Feb. 21, 22 and 23, at Taping-shan against a part of Sung's army under Gen. Ma-yu-kun. This action was fought with 2ft. of snow on the ground, the thermometer registering zero F, and no less than 1,500 cases of frost-bite were reported. It was the intention of Gen. Nozu, after freeing the Hai-chêng garrison from Ikotenga, to seize Niu-chwang port. Two divisions converged on An-shan-chan, and the Chinese, threatened in front and flank, retired to Liao-Yang. The Japanese then moved on Niu-chwang, and Yamaji's 1st Division at Kai-ping joined in the advance. The column from An-shan-chan stormed Niu-chwang, which was obstinately defended, and cost the stormers nearly 400 men. All three divisions converged on Niu-chwang port (Ying-kow), and the final engagement took place at Tien-chwang-tai, which was captured on March 9. The Chinese forces in Manchuria being thoroughly broken and dispersed, there was nothing to prevent the Japanese from proceeding to the occupation of Peking, since they could, after the break-up of the ice, land and supply large forces at Shan-hai-kwan, within 170m. of the capital. Seven divisions were at Port Arthur ready to embark when negotiations were reopened. Li Hung-Chang proceeded to Shimonoseki, where the treaty was signed on April 17, 1895. An expedition was sent towards the end of March to the Pescadores, and later the Imperial Guard Division was sent to Formosa.

It is impossible to estimate the Chinese losses in the war. The Japanese lost 4,177 men by death in action or by sickness, and 56,862 were wounded or disabled by sickness, exclusive of the losses in the Formosa and Pescadores expeditions. Nearly two-thirds of these losses were incurred by the I. Army in the trying winter campaign in Manchuria.

Bibliography.—The most important works dealing with the war are: von Kunowski and Fretzdorff, *Der japanisch-chinesische Krieg* (Leipzig, 1895); von Müller, *Der Krieg zwischen China und Japan* (Berlin, 1895); Vladimir, *China-Japan War* (London, 1896); Jukichi Inouye, *The Japan-China War* (Yokohama, etc., 1896); du Boulay, *Epitome of the Chino-Japanese War* (London, 1896), the official publication of the British War Office; Atteridge, *Wars of the Nineties*, pp. 535–636 (London, 1899); Bujac, *Précis de quelques campagnes contemporaines: II. La Guerre sino-japonaise* (Paris and Limoges)

CHINON, a town of western France, capital of an arrondissement in the department of Indre-et-Loire, on the bank of the Vienne, 32 m. S.W. of Tours. Pop. (1936) 4,511. It lies under a rocky height crowned by ruins of the famous castle, its narrow, winding streets containing many turreted houses of the 15th and 16th centuries. Chinon (Caïno) existed before the Roman occupation of Gaul, and was from early times an important fortress. It was occupied by the Visigoths, and subsequently, after forming part of the royal domain, came to the counts of Touraine and from them to the counts of Anjou, in 1044. In the next century it passed to Henry II. of England, who died there, but it was won back to France by Philip Augustus in 1204, after a year's siege. Of its oldest church, the Romanesque St. Mexme, only the façade and nave are left. The church of St. Etienne dates from the 15th century, that of St. Maurice from the 12th, 15th and 16th centuries. The castle, which has undergone considerable modern restoration, consists of three separate strongholds. That to the east, the Château de St. Georges, built by Henry II. of England, has almost vanished, only the foundation of the outer wall remaining. The Château du Milieu (11th to 15th centuries) comprises the keep, the Pavillon de l'Horloge and the Grand Logis, where the first meeting between Joan of Arc and Charles VII. took place. Of the Château du Coudray, which is separated by a moat from the Château du Milieu, the chief remains are the Tour du Moulin (10th century) and two later towers. A statue of Rabelais, who was born in the vicinity of the town, stands on the river-quay. Basket and rope manufacture, tanning and cooperage are among the industries.

CHINOOK. This important American Indian people held Columbia river from the mouth to the Dalles, and adjacent territory. Their culture was a localized form of the North Pacific Coast (*q.v.*) type, with plank houses, good canoes, trade, slavery, potlatch distributions of property, but without secret societies or totemic art. The language is distinctive, and a selection of words from it, much simplified phonetically and the grammar wholly done away with, forms the basis of the Chinook jargon. This trade language contains also French, English, Nutka and other Indian ingredients, and prevails from Oregon to Alaska. The Chinook were organized by settlements rather than tribes; some of their divisions are known as Clatsop, Wasco and Wishram. Estimated at 16,000 in 1805, they decreased (from disease) to a twentieth in the next 50 years, and now number perhaps 200–300, known under different names on several reservations containing ethnic mixtures.

See Lewis and Clark, *Original Journals* (1904); F. Boas, *Bur. Am. Ethn.* Bull. 20 (1895); E. Sapir, *Publ. Am. Ethn. Soc.*, vol. ii. (1909). (A. L. K.)

CHINOOK, the name given to a wind which blows from west or north over the Rocky Mountains, where it descends as a dry wind, warm in winter and cool in summer. It is due to a cyclone passing northward, and continues for a few hours to several days. It moderates the climate of the eastern Rockies, the snow melting quickly on account of its warmth and vanishing on account of its dryness, so that it is said to "lick up" the snow from the slopes.

CHINQUAPIN, the name given to several North American shrubs or small trees belonging to the genus *Castanea* of the Fagaceae (beech family). The most important of these is *C. pumila,* a shrub or small tree found chiefly in dry soils from New Jersey to northern Florida and westward to southwestern Missouri and eastern Texas. In Arkansas and Texas, where it attains its best development, it occasionally reaches a height of 45 ft. and a diameter of 30 in. It is closely related to the chestnut, *C. dentata,* from which it differs in its much smaller leaves, which are white-woolly beneath, and its usually solitary nut, which like that of the chestnut is very sweet and edible.

On the Pacific slope the name chinquapin is given to two species of *Castanopsis,* a genus closely allied to *Castanea.* Golden chinquapin (*Castanopsis chrysophylla*) found from southern Washington to southern California, is a magnificent tree which occasionally attains a height of 150 ft. and a trunk diameter of 8 ft. The lance-shaped evergreen leaves, 3 to 5 in. long, are clothed beneath with minute golden-yellow persistent scales. The fruit is similar to that of the chestnut and contains one or two hard-shelled nuts with a sweet kernel. The wood is reddish-brown, straight grained, easily worked and takes an excellent finish, yet it is not extensively utilized. The bark, although devoid

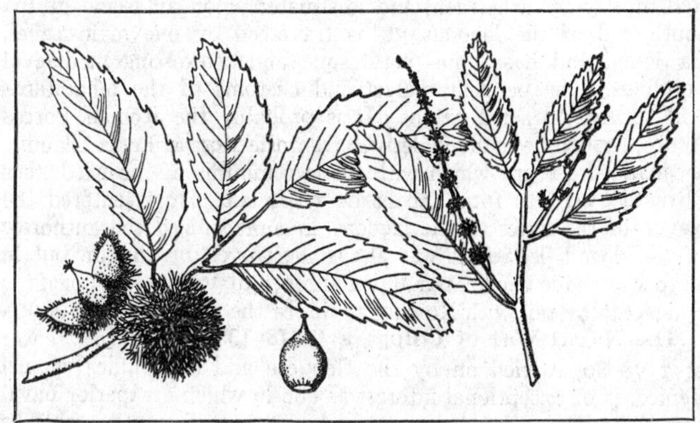

CHINQUAPIN. BRANCH (LEFT) SHOWING SPINY BURR AND SOLITARY NUT; BRANCH (RIGHT) WITH MALE FLOWERS

of tannin, is sometimes used to adulterate that of the tanoak (*Lithocarpus densiflorus*), with which it is often associated in the forest. Bush chinquapin (*C. sempervirens*) is a small spreading shrub of dry mountain slopes in California. Some authorities regard it as a variety of the golden chinquapin. (E. S. Hr.)

CHINSURA, a town of British India, on the Hooghly river, 24m. above Calcutta, formerly the principal Dutch settlement in Bengal. The Dutch erected a fortified factory here in 1656. In 1759 a British force under Col. Forde was attacked by the garrison of Chinsura on its march to Chandernagore, but in less than half an hour the Dutch were entirely routed. Chinsura was taken by the British in 1781 on the outbreak of war with Holland and restored to the Dutch in 1783. Again, in 1795, during the Napoleonic wars, the settlement was occupied by a British garrison. At the peace of 1814 it was a second time restored to the Dutch. It was among the cessions in India made by the king of the Netherlands in 1825 in exchange for the British possessions in Sumatra. The Dutch church, commissioner's house, and cemetery (extended since 1825) are memorials of Dutch rule. Chinsura is included in the Hooghly-Chinsura municipality (pop. [1941] 49,081), and contains the Hooghly college.

CHINTZ, a word derived from the Hindu *chīnt,* spotted or variegated. This name was given to a kind of stained or painted calico produced in India. It is now applied to a highly glazed printed calico, commonly made in several colours on a light ground and used for bed hangings, covering furniture, etc.

CHINWANGTAO, 39° 56′ N., 119° 38′ E., former treaty port on the shores of the Gulf of Liaotung in northeast China; the port was created by, and the harbour is the property of, the Kailan Mining administration, which works the Kaiping coalfield some 100 miles away. Export trade originated almost entirely from the coalfield and comprised not only coal but also coke, firebricks and cement manufactured at Tangshan, the new industrial town on the coalfield. Chinwangtao had also the largest glass factory in China. As it was the only ice-free port on the shallow gulf of Liaotung Chinwangtao had developed as a winter out-port to Tientsin, and to a lesser extent to Newchwang as well. This out-port function did not remain quite so important as at the beginning of the 20th century. The navigation of the Hai-ho could be kept open whenever the winds were off-shore and much of the trade that formerly went through Newchwang had since the advent of the Japanese been diverted through the ice-free Dairen. The port was first opened to foreign trade in 1901. After the Manchurian incident the Japanese pressure led to intensive smuggling of Japanese goods into North China largely through Chinwangtao. With establishment of the East Hopei autonomous puppet regime, Dec. 1935, smuggling continued disguised as a special tariff. After the Japanese invasion trade increased from $1,-024,120 (U.S.) to $21,399,938 for import and from $2,099,392 to $4,324,975 for export, 1936–39, with Manchuria and Japan holding the largest percentages. Pop. 20,020.

CHIOGGIA, a town and episcopal see of Venetia, Italy, in the province of Venice, from which it is 18½ mi. S. by sea. Pop. (1936) 23,577 (town), 42,569 (commune). Chioggia is inhabited mostly by fishermen, and is situated upon an island at the south end of the lagoons. It is traversed by one main canal, La Vena, and has some picturesque and interesting mediaeval buildings. The peculiar dialect and customs of the inhabitants still survive to some extent. It is probably the Roman Portus Aedro, though its name is derived from the Roman Fossa Claudia, a canalized estuary which with the two mouths of the Meduacus (Brenta) went to form the harbour. In A.D. 672 it entered the league of the cities of the lagoons, and recognized the authority of the doge. In 809 it was almost destroyed by Pippin, but in 1110 was made a city, remaining subject to Venice. Chioggia is connected by rail with Rovigo, 35 mi. to the southwest. (X.)

The Naval War of Chioggia (1378–1380).—The naval war of 1378–80, carried on by the Genoese and their allies against Venice, is of exceptional interest as one in which a superior naval power, having suffered disaster in home waters, was yet able to win by holding out till its squadrons in distant seas could be recalled for its defence.

Venice was mainly concerned for the safety of her trading stations in the Levant and the Black sea. The more powerful of her two fleets was sent to the eastern Mediterranean under Carlo Zeno, and the smaller to operate against the Genoese in the western Mediterranean, under Vettor Pisani. The possessions of Venice on the mainland were assailed by the lord of Carrara and the Hungarians, but this danger seemed trifling so long as Venice could keep the sea open to her trade.

At first she was entirely successful. While Carlo Zeno harassed the Genoese stations in the Levant, Pisani brought one of their squadrons to action in May, 1378, to the south of the Tiber, and defeated it. If Pisani had sailed direct to Genoa itself, which was thrown into a panic, he might have dictated peace, but he thought his squadron too weak, and followed the Genoese galleys which had fled to Famagusta in Cyprus. During the summer of 1378 he was employed partly off Cyprus, but mainly in taking and capturing the Istrian and Dalmatian towns which supported the Hungarians. He was ordered to winter on the coast of Istria, where his crews suffered from exposure and disease. Genoa now decided to attack Venice at home while the best of her ships were absent with Carlo Zeno, and sent a strong fleet under Luciano Doria. Pisani had been reinforced early in the spring of 1379, but when he was sighted by the Genoese fleet off Pola on May 7, he was slightly out-numbered, and his crews were still weak. He would have preferred to avoid action and to threaten the Genoese fleet from his base on the Istrian coast, but he was forced into battle by the Senate, and was defeated with great loss. On the other hand Luciano Doria himself was killed, and the Genoese, who had suffered severely, did not at once follow up their success. On the arrival of Pietro Doria, with reinforcements, they appeared off the Lido, the outer barrier of the lagoon of Venice, and in July began combined operations against Chioggia, co-operating with the Carrarese and the Hungarians. The Venetians had closed the passages through the outer banks except at the southern end, at the island of Brondolo, and the town of Chioggia. The barrier here approaches close to the mainland, and the position facilitated the co-operation of the allies; but Chioggia is some distance from Venice, which could only be reached across the lagoon, where the Venetians had taken up the buoys and had a light squadron. The allies, after occupying the island of Brondolo, attacked, and took the town of Chioggia on Aug. 13.

There was nothing now to prevent them from advancing on Venice itself except the difficult navigation of the lagoon. The Senate applied for peace, but the Genoese offered impossible terms. Pisani, who had been imprisoned after the defeat at Pola, was released and named commander-in-chief. The heavy Genoese vessels were much hampered by the intricate passages through the lagoon, and by using his own local knowledge, Pisani completely turned the tables on the invaders by a succession of night attacks, during which he sank vessels in the canals leading through the lagoon to Venice, and in the fairways leading from Chioggia to the open sea. The Genoese were thus blockaded, Pisani having stationed his galleys in the open sea outside Brondolo. The Venetians themselves were in great distress; Carlo Zeno had long since been ordered home, but he was delayed by the difficulty of communication under 14th century conditions, and the besiegers of Chioggia were at the end of their strength when his fleet reached Brondolo on Jan. 1, 1380. The Genoese held out in the hope of relief from home, but it was not until May, 1380, that Matteo Maruffo arrived with reinforcements. By this time the Venetians had recovered the island, and their fleet occupied a fortified anchorage so that Maruffo could do nothing, and on June 24, 1380, the Genoese defenders of Chioggia surrendered. Venice, being now safe at home, recovered the command of the sea, and before the close of the year was able to make peace as a conqueror.

BIBLIOGRAPHY.—Horatio F. Brown, *Venice* (1839); S. Romanin, *Storia documentata di Venezia* (1855); W. C. Hazlitt, *History of the Venetian Republic* (1860). (G. A. R. C.; W. C. B. T.)

CHIOS, an island on the west coast of Asia Minor (ancient Greek Χίος) about 30 mi. long from north to south, and from 8 to 15 mi. broad. Population, 75,680. The north end is mountainous with steep coasts; southwards there is open country, and great fertility. The capital, Chios, on the east coast, has a small safe harbour, and mediaeval fortifications. Population, 22,122. The climate is healthy; oranges, olives and even palms grow freely; the figs were famous in antiquity, but wine and gum mastic have always been the principal products. The latter, collected from a wild shrub, gives flavour and name to a popular Greek liqueur (*masticha*). Antimony, calamine and marble are worked; there is a tanning industry, and considerable coasting trade.

There are few remains of ancient Chios (on the same site as the modern); traces of a theatre and a temple of Athena Poliuchus; and about 6 m. N. of the city the curious "School of Homer," a sanctuary of Cybele, with altar and figure of the goddess with two lions, in the native rock of a hill-top. On the west coast is a rich monastery with a church founded by Constantine IX. Monomachus (1042–54). In antiquity Chios was famous for its school of epic poets, the Homeridae, who claimed descent from Homer, and probably did much to popularize the *Iliad* and *Odyssey* in early Greece.

To Glaucus of Chios was ascribed the invention of iron-welding, early in the seventh century B.C., and his masterpiece, the support of a large bowl, was shown at Delphi: for his place in ancient art and craftsmanship *see* J. G. Frazer *Pausanias*: note on x. 16. 1. (vol. v. pp. 313–4); and for the beautiful and instructive coinage, P. Gardner, *History of Greek Coinage* (index) and the *British Museum Catalogue* (*s.v.*).

The early history of Chios is obscure. There were Greek legends of Leleges, Pelasgi from Thessaly, a Cretan foundation "in the days of Rhadamanthus" (13th century), and of eventual colonization by Ionians from Attica four generations later. Early kings and tyrants are little more than names, but the long friendship with Miletus is significant and determined the hostility of Chios to its neighbours, Phocaea, Erythrae and Samos. The Chian colony at Maroneia on the coast of Thrace reinforced the wine-trade of the mother city. Like Miletus, Chios in 546 submitted to Cyrus as eagerly as Phocaea resisted him. When Miletus revolted, 100 Chian ships joined in offering desperate opposition at Lade (494). Persian reprisals were severe, and temporarily successful, for Chian ships, under the tyrant Strattis, served in the Persian fleet at Salamis. But in 479 Chios joined the Delian League and long remained a firm ally of the Athenians, retaining political independence and a navy of its own. But in 413 the island revolted, and was not recaptured. After the Peloponnesian War it renewed the Athenian alliance, but in 357 again seceded. It was reputed one of the best-governed states in Greece, for although it was governed alternately by oligarchs and democrats neither party persecuted the other severely. Late in the 4th century, however, civil dissension left it a prey to Idrieus, the dynast of Caria (346), and to the Persian admiral Memnon (333). During the Hellenistic age Chios retained its independence, supported the

Romans in their Eastern wars, and was made a "free and allied state." Under Roman and Byzantine rule industry and commerce were undisturbed, its chief export at this time being the "Arvisian wine," of the north-west coast (*Ariusia*). After temporary occupations by the Seljuk Turks (1089–1092) and by the Venetians (1124–1125, 1172, 1204–1225), it was given in fief to the Genoese family of Zaccaria, and in 1346 passed definitely into the hands of a Genoese *maona*, or trading company, which was organized in 1362 under the name of "the Giustiniani," and alone exploited the mastic trade; but the Greeks were allowed to retain their rights of self-government and continued to exercise their industries. In 1415 the Genoese became a tributary to the Ottomans and, in spite of occasional secessions which brought severe punishment (1453, 1479), the rule of the Giustiniani was not abolished till 1566. But capture and reconquest from the Florentines (1595) and the Venetians (1694–1695), greatly reduced the number of the Latins and wrecked its prosperity. Worst of all were the massacres of 1822, which followed upon an attack by Greek insurgents against the will of the natives. Many survivors fled to Syra (*q.v.*) and founded its prosperous carrying trade. But the island's natural resources made its recovery sure, and its efficient and peaceable inhabitants passed quietly from Turkish to Greek rule during the Balkan War of 1912.

BIBLIOGRAPHY.—Strabo xiv. pp. 632 f.; Athenaeus vi. 265–266; Herodotus i. 160–165, vi. 15–31; Thucydides viii. 14–61; *Corpus Inscr. Atticarum*, iv. (2), pp. 9, 10; H. Houssaye in *Revue des deux mondes*, xlvi. (1876), pp. i. ff.; T. Bent in *Historical Review* (1889), pp. 467–480; Fustel de Coulanges, *L'Ile de Chio* (ed. Jullian, Paris, 1893); for coinage, B. V. Head, *Historia numorum* (Oxford, 1887). pp. 513–515, and NUMISMATICS: *Greek Coins*.

BY COURTESY OF THE AMERICAN MUSEUM OF NATURAL HISTORY

CHIPMUNK (TAMIAS STRIATUS), FOUND IN EASTERN UNITED STATES AND CANADA

CHIPMUNK, the name for small striped ground squirrels (*Tamias striatus* and numerous species of the genus *Eutamias*) found in North America and eastern Asia. They are 5 or 6 in. long, with a tail about 4 in., reddish or grayish brown in colour.

(J. E. HL.)

CHIPPENDALE, THOMAS (*c.* 1718–1779), the most famous of English cabinet-makers, was the son of John Chippendale, a joiner of Otley, Yorkshire. He was baptised at Otley on June 5, 1718. The materials for the biography of Chippendale are scanty, but it is known that he came to London when he was about 20, and at the end of 1749 established himself in Conduit court, Long Acre, whence in 1753 he removed to No. 60, St. Martin's lane, which with the addition of the adjoining three houses remained his factory for the rest of his life.

It has always been exceedingly difficult to distinguish the work executed in Chippendale's factory and under his own eye from that of the many copyists and adapters who throughout the second half of the 18th century plundered remorselessly. Apart from his published designs, many of which were probably never made up, we have to depend upon the very few instances in which his original accounts earmark work as unquestionably his. For Claydon house, in Buckinghamshire, he executed much decorative work, and the best judges are satisfied that the Chinese bedroom there was designed by him. At Harewood house, in Yorkshire, we are on firmer ground. The house was furnished between 1765 and 1771, and both Robert Adam and Chippendale were employed upon it. Indeed, there is unmistakable evidence to show that certain work, so closely characteristic of the Adams that it might have been assigned to them without hesitation, was actually produced by Chippendale, whose bills for this Adam work are still preserved. For Nostell Priory, Yorkshire he made a quantity of fine furniture in 1766, the bills for which are also in existence there. Stourhead, the famous house of the Hoares in Wiltshire, contains much undoubted Chippendale furniture, which may, however, be the work of his son Thomas Chippendale II.; at Rowton castle Shropshire, Chippendale's bills as well as his works still exist.

Our other main source of information is *The Gentleman and Cabinet Maker's Director,* which was published by Thomas Chippendale in 1754. This folio, the most important collection of furniture designs issued up to that time in England, contains 160 engraved plates, and the list of subscribers indicates that the author had acquired a large and distinguished body of customers. There was a second edition in 1759, and a third in 1762.

The *Director* contains examples of each of the manners which Chippendale practised. Occasionally we find in one piece of furniture a combination of the three styles which he most affected at different periods (Louis XV., Chinese and Gothic) and it cannot be said that the result is as incongruous as might have been expected. Some of his most elegant and attractive work is derived directly from the French.

The primary characteristic of his furniture is solidity, but it is a solidity which rarely becomes heaviness. Even in apparently slight work, such as the ribbon-backed chair, construction is always the first consideration. It is indeed in the chair that Chippendale is seen at his best and most characteristic. From his hand, or his pencil, we have a great variety of chairs, which, although differing extensively in detail, may be roughly arranged in three or four groups, which it would sometimes be rash to attempt to date. He introduced the cabriole leg, which, despite its antiquity, came immediately from Holland; the claw and ball foot of ancient Oriental use; the straight, square, uncompromising early Georgian leg; the carved latticework Chinese leg; the pseudo-Chinese leg; the fretwork leg, which was supposed to be in the best Gothic taste; the inelegant rococo leg with the curled or hoofed foot; and even occasionally the spade foot. His chair-backs were very various. His efforts in Gothic often took the form of the tracery of a church window, or even of an ovalled rose window. His Chinese backs were distinctly geometrical, and from them he would seem to have derived some of the inspiration for the frets of the glazed bookcases and cabinets which were among his most agreeable work. The most attractive feature of Chippendale's most artistic chairs (derived from Louis Quinze models) is the back, which, speaking generally, is the most elegant and pleasing thing that has ever been done in furniture. He took the old solid or slightly pierced back, and cut it up into a light openwork design exquisitely carved (for Chippendale was a carver before everything) in a vast variety of designs ranging from the elaborate and extremely elegant ribbon back, to a comparatively plain but highly effective splat. His armchairs, however, often had solid or stuffed backs. Next to his chairs, Chippendale was most successful with settees, which almost invariably took the shape of two or three conjoined chairs, the arms, backs and legs identical with those which he used for single seats. He was likewise a prolific designer and maker of bookcases, cabinets and escritoires with doors glazed with fretwork divisions, cases for long clocks, and a great number of tables, some of them with a remarkable degree of Gallic grace. He was especially successful in designing small tables with fretwork galleries for the display of china. His mirrors, which were often in the Chinese taste or extravagantly rococo, are remarkable and characteristic. Some of Chippendale's most graceful work was lavished upon the woodwork of the lighter, more refined and less monumental four-poster. His claims to distinction are summed up in the fact that his name has by general consent been attached to the most splendid period of English furniture.

Chippendale was buried on Nov. 13, 1779, at the church of St. Martin-in-the-Fields. Of his 11 children, THOMAS CHIPPENDALE II. succeeded to the business of his father and grandfather, and for some years the firm traded under the style of Chippendale and Haig. The factory remained in St. Martin's lane, but in 1814 an additional shop was opened at No. 57, Haymarket, whence it was in 1821 removed to 42, Jermyn street. Like his father, Thomas Chippendale II. was a member of the Society of Arts; and he is known to have exhibited five pictures at the Royal Academy between 1784 and 1801. He died at the end of 1822 or the beginning of 1823.

See Oliver Brackett *Thomas Chippendale, a Study of his Life, Work and Influence* (1924).

CHIPPENHAM, market town and municipal borough in the Chippenham parliamentary division of Wiltshire, England, 94 mi. W. of London by the G.W.R. on the south side of the Upper Avon. Pop. (1938) 10,120. Area 1.9 sq.mi. St. Andrew's church, originally 12th century Norman, has been enlarged in different styles. Chippenham (*Chepeham, Chippeham*) was the site of a royal residence where, in 853, Aethelwulf celebrated the marriage of his daughter Aethelswitha with Burgred, king of Mercia. The town figured prominently in the Danish invasion of the 9th century, and in 933 was the meeting-place of the witan. In the Domesday survey Chippenham appears as a Crown manor. The town was governed by a bailiff in the reign of Edward I; it was incorporated in 1553, but in 1685 received a new charter which was soon abandoned in favour of the original grant. The derivation of Chippenham from *cyppan,* to buy, implies that the town possessed a market in Saxon times. The neighbouring Cotswold hills preserve many relics of early man, and their grasslands produced the sheep which gave Chippenham its fame as a woollen centre from the 16th century. On the decline of this trade the grain and cheese markets developed. Condensed-milk making, bacon curing and engineering are carried on.

The town sent two members to parliament until 1867, and one until 1885.

CHIPPEWA. The Canadian branch of the Chippewa, one of the largest tribes north of Mexico, lives in the woodlands north and west of Lake Superior. Their culture was typical in many respects of the central Algonquians. Moose, deer, beaver and rabbits were snared or killed with arrows; wild-fowl were shot or clubbed, and fish were speared or taken with hook and line. Wild rice was collected as a staple food in the vicinity of Lake Superior; maple sugar was manufactured, and nuts, berries and edible roots are still gathered in large quantities. In their search for game the Chippewa travel long distances, by canoe in summer, or in winter on snow-shoes, dragging their goods on toboggans. These wanderings, however, usually lead back to semi-permanent settlements, where formerly bark houses were used in warm weather, and oval, rush-covered lodges in winter. In pre-Columbian days, utensils were almost entirely of wood or bark, basketry being weakly developed. Clothing was of skins, while bags, belts and garters were woven on heddle looms out of bark or wild hemp fibre. Expert artificers in wood, Chippewa stone work was limited to arrow points and a few tools, while native copper, mined near Lake Superior, was pounded into serviceable shapes.

BY COURTESY OF THE SMITHSONIAN INSTITUTION

CHIPPEWA INDIAN, IN HIS TRIBAL DRESS

Politically, there is no Chippewa "tribe," since the numerous sub-divisions have no single, central authority. Each inhabits a certain locality, and the members enter into definite relations with one another. There is an ill-defined kind of council, consisting of practically all the males of the community, which elects a chief, whose powers are even more shadowy than those of the body that selects him. Social divisions are more definite, since, in addition to the family, there are exogamic patrilineal clans of a totemic nature. Individual ownership of material objects prevails, but land was probably held, in former times, by groups of kindred.

The Chippewa have firm belief in a cosmic force animating all nature which frequently manifests itself in animals, mythical or real. Like their eastern kinsmen, the concept of a guardian spirit was important, and shamanism with conjuring flourished. Entry to the next world depended largely upon membership in the *Midéwiwin,* "Great Medicine Society," a secret organization entered after elaborate initiation. Symbolic pictographs drawn upon bark were perhaps originally connected with this society. (See *Handbook of the American Indian,* 1906.)

CHIPPEWA FALLS, a city of northwestern Wisconsin, U.S.A., on the Chippewa river, 100 mi. E. of St. Paul, the county seat of Chippewa county. It is on federal highway 53, and is served by the Chicago and North Western, the Chicago, Milwaukee, St. Paul and Pacific and the Soo Line railways. The population in 1950 was 11,072. The city has machine shops and a packing plant, and its manufactures include woollen goods, shoes, gloves, pumps, sashes and doors, milk products and cement silos. The first settlement was made in 1837. The city was chartered in 1870.

CHIPPING CAMPDEN, market town, Gloucestershire, England, 29 mi. N.E. from Gloucester by the G.W.R. Pop. (1931) 1,645. It is situated toward the north of the Cotswold hills. A ruined 16th century manor house, some almshouses and the church complete a picturesque group of buildings. The house of William Grevel (d. 1401), a great wool merchant, is noteworthy.

Apart from a mediaeval tradition that a conference of Saxon kings was held there, the earliest record of Campden (*Campedene*) is in Domesday, when earl Hugh held it. The manor passed in 1173 to Hugh de Gondeville, and about 1204 to Ralph, earl of Chester. These lords granted charters which are known from a confirmation dated 1247. In 1605 Campedene was incorporated, but was never represented in parliament. The corporation was abolished in 1885. Camden speaks of the town as a market famous for stockings, a relic of its mediaeval importance as a mart for wool which gave it the name of Chipping.

CHIPPING NORTON, municipal borough, Oxfordshire, England, 16 mi. N.W. of Oxford by a branch of the G.W.R. Pop. (1938) 3,369. It lies on the steep flank of a hill, and consists mainly of one very wide street. Chipping Norton (*Chepyngnorton*) was of some importance in Saxon times. At the Domesday survey it was held by Ernulf de Hesding and assessed at 15 hides with three mills. It returned two members to parliament as a borough in 1302 and 1304–1305, but was not represented after this date. Fairs were granted in 1205 to William Fitz-Alan and in 1276 to Roger, earl of March. In the reign of Henry VI the market was held on Wednesday, and a fair was held at the Translation of St. Thomas Becket. James I annulled the former two fairs, and granted others. He also granted the first and only charter of incorporation. The church of St. Mary the Virgin on the lower slope is a fine building in the Decorated and Perpendicular styles. The trade is still mainly agricultural, though woollen goods are manufactured. The borough is in the Banbury division of Oxfordshire. Area, 3.8 sq.mi.

CHIQUITAN, an independent linguistic stock of South American Indians, so called from the Chiquitos who are the best known of its tribes. The stock occupies a considerable area in eastern Bolivia, in the forested hilly country on the northern border of the Chaco. In recent times they have held the area between the headwaters of the Guapore on the north and the hills on the northern bank of the Otuquis river on the south, and between the San Miguel river in the west and the Paraguay in the east. It is probable that they formerly extended farther west to the foothills of the Andes and may have been forced eastward as a result of the displacements of peoples consequent on the invasion and settlement of the Chiriguanos in the early 16th century. The Chiquitos were a rather warlike and originally mainly nomadic hunting and fishing folk of simple culture. Their name, meaning "little ones" in Spanish, was given them on account of the very small doorways of their tiny thatched huts, through which one had to crawl on hands and knees. They seem to have had some palisaded strongholds and to have used poisoned arrows. Some of the tribes made good pottery and simple textiles. They had no canoes. Monogamy was the rule except for the chiefs, who were not hereditary but chosen for valour and ability. The youth before marriage lived apart in a special house. The shamans appear to have used snakes a good deal in connection with their religious ceremonies. The best known tribe of this stock to-day is the Lenguas.

See J. P. Fernandez, *Relacion historial de las missiones de los Indios que llaman Chiquitos, etc.* (Madrid, 1726).

CHIRICAHUA NATIONAL MONUMENT, a tract of 10,529.8 ac. (about 16 sq.mi.) in the Coronado national forest in Arizona, U.S.A., remarkable for its "pinnacle" formations. The original tract of 4,480 ac. was set apart as a Government reservation in 1924 but was enlarged to the present area in 1938.

CHIROL, SIR VALENTINE (1852–1929), British journalist, was born on May 23, 1852, and educated in France and Germany. He graduated Bachelier-ès-lettres of the University of Paris. From 1872 to 1876 he was a clerk in the Foreign Office and afterwards travelled throughout the Near and Far East. He succeeded Sir Donald Mackenzie Wallace in 1899 as foreign editor of *The Times*. He retired from the service of *The Times* in 1912, and then became a member of the Royal Commission on Indian Public Services (1912–16). He wrote authoritative works on India, Egypt and the Far and Near East, and in 1927, he published a volume of reminiscences entitled *Fifty Years in a Changing World* to which a second volume, *With Pen and Brush in Eastern Lands*, was added in 1929. He was knighted in 1912 and died in London on Oct. 22, 1929.

CHIROMANCY, the art of telling character or fortune by studying the lines of the hands (*see* PALMISTRY).

CHIRON or **CHEIRON,** in Greek mythology, one of the Centaurs, the son of Cronus and Philyra, a sea nymph. He dwelt at the foot of Mount Pelion, and was famous for his wisdom and knowledge of the healing art. He offers a remarkable contrast to the other Centaurs in manners and character. Many of the most celebrated heroes of Greece were brought up and instructed by him (Apollodorus iii, 10. 13). Accidentally pierced by a poisoned arrow shot by Heracles, he renounced his immortality in favour of Prometheus, and was placed by Zeus among the stars as the constellation *Sagittarius*.

CHIROPODIST (Podiatrist). One who diagnoses and treats conditions affecting the feet. The first podiatrist was Dr. Lyon who, in 1785 in England, applied for a licence to limit practice to the foot alone. Chiropody practice in the United States was governed by law in all but two states in 1941. Competent podiatrists have the degree of doctor of surgical chiropody (D.S.C.) from recognized schools.

CHIROPRACTIC, "a system of therapeutics based upon the theory that disease is caused by interference with nerve function. Its theory is based upon the premise that all other systems and physiologic processes of the human body are controlled and coordinated by the nerve system. Its therapeutics attempts to restore normal function of the nerve system by manipulation and treatment of the structures of the human body, especially those of the spinal column." Daniel David Palmer began to formulate its theory in 1895, and established the Palmer School of Chiropractic at Davenport, Ia., in 1903. Later others were founded in different parts of the United States and, by 1941, the National Chiropractic association had extended accredited ratings to 12 colleges teaching a scientific course of four collegiate years. The practice of chiropractic has been accorded legislative recognition in 42 states, the District of Columbia, Alaska, Hawaii and several provinces of Canada. It is estimated that there are about 18,000 chiropractors practicing in the United States and Canada.

CHIROPTERA, the order of mammals containing the bats. They are the only members of this class which can truly fly and their forelimbs are modified to form wings, whence the name Chiroptera (from the Greek, meaning "hand-wings").

Bats not very different from those that still exist have been found in the early part of the Eocene period, indicating that the order is an ancient one. No animals are known that connect the bats closely with other groups of mammals, but the great resemblances between them and some of the Insectivora (*q.v.*) indicate these are probably the most closely related order. The existence of the so-called "flying lemur," *Cynocephalus,* suggests how the transformation from tree-living to flying took place. This animal possesses extensive folds of skin connecting its neck, wrists, ankles and tail, and even between the fingers and toes. These membranes enable it to glide long distances between trees and even to control its course somewhat during the glide. The ancestral bats progressed further in this direction. They developed extremely long forearm and fingers and extended the skin web between these. Their breast muscles increased in power until they were able to beat the forelimbs and wing membranes against the air and thus propel themselves through it. The side and tail membranes support bats in the air between wing beats, and the latter acts as a powerful brake when the end is brought forward under the body. The impervious nature of the wing membranes, their elasticity, and the manner in which they fold up on the fingers, somewhat as an umbrella does on its stays, tend to make the flight of bats both efficient and erratic.

Once this ability to fly was achieved, the bats underwent evolutionary diversification chiefly in minor details. Often the various stages in these modifications still persist in the various living species, and it is possible partly to reconstruct the changes. The upper armbone, or humerus, in the weaker flying bats has its usual simple ball-and-socket articulation with the shoulder blade, while the groups which fly best, the families Vespertilionidae and Molossidae, have developed a second joint between the greater tubercle of the humerus and the scapula. These swift-flying bats have a short upper arm as compared with the forearm, and the third finger is much longer than the others. The humerus has a small but well developed crest for the attachment of the deltoid and pectoral muscles; its shaft is rounded and it varies in shape from somewhat curved in the lower bats to almost straight in the higher groups. Of the two bones generally found in the forearm, the radius alone is well developed, the ulna being little more than a thread and often almost completely fused with the radius. A bone is developed in the tendon of the triceps muscle near the elbow, somewhat resembling the kneecap and with a similar function. The wristbones, six in number, are small. The metacarpal bones, except for that of the thumb, are greatly lengthened, forming the chief supports of the wing. The short thumb is separate from the rest of the wing; its claw is sharp and hooked in most bats, and it is used to grapple the surface in crawling; and some species occasionally swing from branches by the thumb. In certain bats the thumb is provided with a round adhesive disk by means of which they can rest upside down on a smooth surface, such as a banana leaf (fig. 18).

The second, or index finger, except in the fruit bats and the mouse-tailed bat, has lost its terminal joints, consisting only of the metacarpal and a poorly developed cartilage. This finger is generally closely associated with the middle, or third finger, and strengthens it. The third, fourth and fifth fingers have three joints or phalanges as a rule, but the last of these is usually cartilaginous. When bats rest, the phalanges are often bent, sometimes in zigzag fashion to fold the wing more completely.

The shoulder girdle is well developed, with a stout curved clavicle, or collarbone, and broad scapula, or shoulder blade. The coracoid process of the latter is large, usually curved outward but occasionally inward and dorsally. Its base articulates with the secondary articular process developed from the greater tubercle

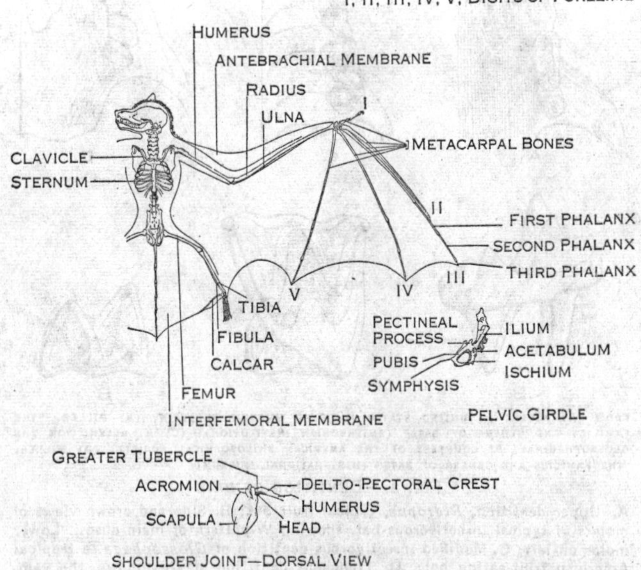

FIG. 1.—SKELETON AND WING MEMBRANES OF A BAT (MYOTIS)

of the humerus. The sternum, or breastbone, consists of three parts, the more or less T-shaped presternum or manubrium, the body of the sternum and the xiphisternum. The presternum is large, strongly keeled for the attachment of the flying muscles of the breast, while the lateral processes articulate with the clavicle and first rib. The keel continues down the body of the sternum, gradually becoming lower. The xiphisternum is short, often expanded posteriorly and partly cartilaginous.

The thorax is capacious, to accommodate the large heart and lungs, and the ribs are often flattened and close together. The first rib consists of two parts; it is usually thickened and much shorter than the others. The ventral segment frequently articulates with the clavicle. In the horseshoe and leaf-nosed bats (Rhinolophidae) the first or first two ribs are fused with both the sternum and their vertebrae to form a solid ring supporting the shoulder girdle. The pelvic girdle is weaker than the pectoral; its dorsal border is usually almost straight and almost on the same plane as the sacrum. The ilia are generally narrow but occasionally shelflike, while the pubis and ischium are generally narrow. A well developed pectineal process extends forward from the pubis and in the Hipposiderinae it unites with a process from the ilium to form a large foramen. The acetabulum or hip socket is often incomplete, dorsally or ventrally or both.

The hind limbs support the side membrane and that of the tail. The head of the femur is almost in the same axis as the shaft, so that the thigh projects almost at right angles to the body. The knee bends outward and backward rather than forward like that of terrestrial mammals. The foot is weak—the toes all about the same size and armed with sharp hooked claws by which the bat hangs, as a rule, when resting. The heel bone bears a long cartilaginous process, the calcar, rarely rudimentary or absent, which supports part of the posterior margin of the interfemoral membrane extending from the tail or hinder part of the body to the hind limbs.

The tail varies greatly in the different groups of bats; in primitive forms it is long and generally free from the membrane. Only one of the fruit bats has a long tail, as long as the hind limbs, the genus *Notopteris,* found in the southwestern Pacific. In other fruit bats the tail is either very short or absent. Most of the insectivorous bats have a well developed tail, but the mouse-tailed bat, *Rhinopoma,* has a long tail almost completely free from the interfemoral membrane. In the sheath-tailed bats (Emballonuridae) the tail is partly enclosed in the membrane but its distal end projects through the dorsal surface. In most other families the tail extends to the end of the large interfemoral membrane, as its median support.

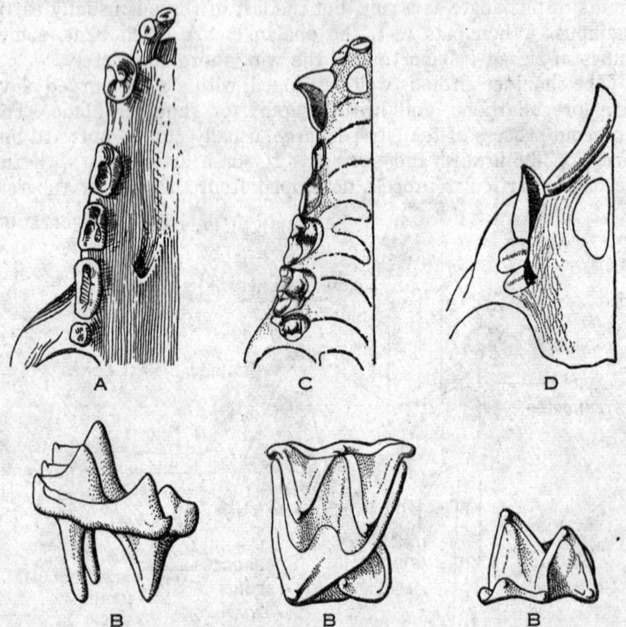

FROM (A) MILLER IN UNITED STATES NATIONAL MUSEUM BULLETIN; (B) MILLER, "THE FAMILIES AND GENERA OF BATS" (SMITHSONIAN INSTITUTION); (C) H. ALLEN, "ON THE GLOSSOPHAGINAE" BY COURTESY OF THE AMERICAN PHILOSOPHICAL SOCIETY; (D) MILLER, "THE FAMILIES AND GENERA OF BATS" (U.S. NATIONAL MUSEUM)

FIG. 2.—DENTITION OF BATS

A. Upper dentition, *Pteropus,* typical fruit bat; B. Side and crown views of molars of typical insectivorous bat, showing W-pattern of main cusps. Lower molar on left; C. Modified insectivorous dentition of *Glossophaga,* a tropical American fruit-eating bat; D. Trenchant dentition of *Desmodus,* the vampire bat

The skull varies a great deal in the different groups and it is used to characterize these. There is a tendency for the facial portion to become shortened in the more progressive forms, but all extremes are found from elongate snout to a short massive one.

The teeth comprise incisors $\left(\frac{2-1}{3-0}\right)$ canines $\left(\frac{1}{1}\right)$, premolars $\left(\frac{3-1}{3-2}\right)$ and molars $\left(\frac{3-1}{3-1}\right)$, totalling from 38 to 20. The cheek teeth of fruit bats have poorly marked cusps, their squarish crowns bearing a large outer and a smaller inner cusp, which become gradually reduced toward the posterior end of the series. The pattern of these teeth of fruit bats has probably been simplified from the insectivorous pattern. In the molars of insectivorous bats the cusps on their surfaces show a W-pattern in both upper and lower teeth, the upper ones broader, with an additional shelf and "talon" cusp. They thus resemble closely the teeth of certain insectivorous mammals of similar food habits, the hedgehogs, the jumping shrews, moles and shrews. The cusps on the cheek teeth of the vampires are greatly simplified, the teeth being specialized into blades for cutting. The milk teeth are quite unlike those of the permanent series, being slender and hooklike, sometimes with forked or trifid tips, and are soon shed.

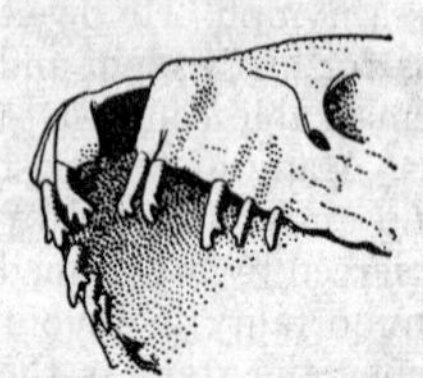

FROM MILLER, "THE FAMILIES AND GENERA OF BATS" (SMITHSONIAN INSTITUTION)

FIG. 3.—DECIDUOUS DENTITION OF PROMOPS, AN INSECTIVOROUS BAT

The brain is not highly developed; the cerebral hemispheres are smooth or only slightly furrowed and do not extend back over the cerebellum. However, bats have a delicate sense of touch; tactile hairs exist on the region around the mouth, on the flying membranes and ears. Each hair is provided with a nerve ending that surrounds its base. The expanded ears and noseleaves may also serve as organs of touch, although special nerves are not known. The sense of scent appears to be only moderately well developed, but hearing is keen, especially for notes higher than those heard by the human ear. This is of great importance in flight, for the bat emits high-pitched cries continuously and solid objects reflect these sounds, warning the bat of obstacles. The eyes of bats, although small, are far from blind; bats see fairly well but depend more on their hearing to find food and to avoid collisions. In no animal are the ears so developed or so variable in form; in many insectivorous species they are longer than the head, while in the Eurasian long-eared bat their length nearly equals that of the body. The "earlet," or tragus, is generally large in the insectivorous bats but is never present in the Megachiroptera nor in the insectivorous Rhinolophidae.

The stomach is of two types, corresponding to the two suborders, Megachiroptera and Microchiroptera. In the latter group the stomach is simple and almost spherical. In the fruit bats the narrow oesophagus gradually enlarges just before reaching the stomach. The stomach is enlarged transversely, with a large cardiac sac and a tapering pyloric portion which gradually passes into the intestine. The vampire bat, one of the Microchiroptera, feeds on blood; its stomach has a long tubular cardiac portion, folded on itself, but the pyloris is hardly distinguishable from the small intestine. The intestine is short in insectivorous bats, in some of which it is shorter than in any other mammal, but may be four times the body length in the fruit-eating types.

As a rule bats produce only a single young at a birth, but among the insectivorous types two or even four young may occur. These are born with closed eyes and nearly naked; they are able to climb up the mother's skin to the nipples, where they attach by the delicate hooklike deciduous teeth. The young bats remain attached to the mother for some time and she may fly about with them while hunting her prey. In many species of the northern hemisphere the mating period is in the fall; the sperm remain inactive during the winter. Early in spring, when the bats become active again, ovulation occurs in the females and the egg cells are fertilized. The penis is pendulous; often there is a bone in its distal part. The uterus of females is primitively double; in some species the uterus consists of a rounded body with long horns, while in others the horns are greatly reduced. A simple uterus is formed in some of the Phyllostomidae. The placenta is discoidal and deciduate, as in the Primates. Bats are divisible into two suborders: the Megachiroptera and the Microchiroptera.

MEGACHIROPTERA

The first of these suborders comprises the fruit bats, generally of large size. The crowns of their cheek teeth show only poorly marked cusps which never form a W-pattern. The bony palate extends behind the last molar, narrowing slowly backward. The greater tubercle of the humerus is poorly developed and does not articulate with the scapula. The second finger is partly independent from the third and retains three phalanges, the terminal one generally with a claw. The margins of the ear unite to form a ring at the base. The tail, often absent, is free from the interfemoral membrane. This group is limited to the tropical and subtropical parts of the eastern hemisphere. All the members of this suborder are included in the single family Pteropodidae, which may be divided into four subfamilies.

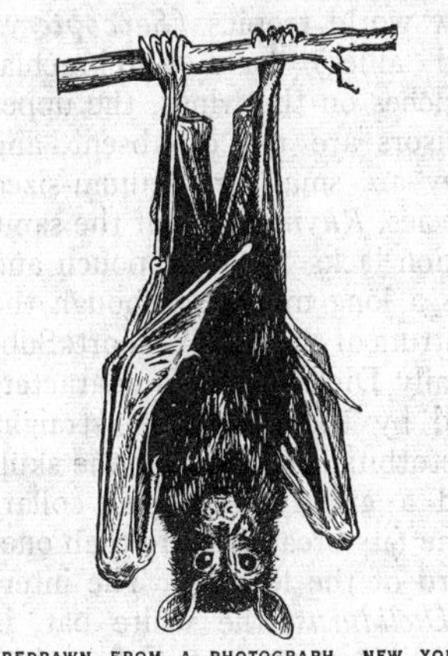

REDRAWN FROM A PHOTOGRAPH, NEW YORK ZOOLOGICAL SOCIETY

FIG. 4.—FLYING FOX (PTEROPUS)

The subfamily Pteropodinae contains a large majority of the frugivorous genera. It is characterized by having a normal tongue, blunt-crowned cheek teeth, canines which are vertically directed and the lower pair separated from each other by the incisors, and premaxillary bones which are separated or only barely united.

The Pteropodinae may be divided into three tribes. The pteropodine tribe is characterized by having the occipital part of the skull deflected (the alveolar line projected backward passes above the occipital condyle); the muzzle is long, about equal to the postorbital part of the head. The first representatives of this group, the flying foxes (*Pteropus*) are found from the Comoro Islands and Madagascar to southern Japan, Samoa and Tasmania; they have foxlike faces, two lower incisors on each side and no tail; the occiput of the skull is elongated and tubular. Most species have a brilliantly coloured mantle, although this varies from light yellowish buff or even whitish to dark brown or blackish. *Styloctenium wallacei* of Celebes resembles *Pteropus*, but the lower incisors are 1–1; its general colour is pale grayish to warm cinnamon above, with a white shoulder patch, light cinnamon under parts and a whitish or creamy mantle. The dog-faced bats (*Rousettus*), found throughout Africa and east to the Solomon Islands, have a short tail, the occiput of the skull is not tubular and the muzzle is shorter and coarser than that of *Pteropus*; in colour they are generally dark dull brown. The yellow fruit bat (*Eidolon*) occurs in Africa, from Southern Arabia and the Sudan to Namaqualand; it differs from other fruit bats in having a bony external ear tube. *Boneia bidens* of Celebes combines characters of *Pteropus* and *Rousettus*, having a tail, tubular occiput of the skull, but its incisors are $\frac{1-1}{2-2}$. The spinal-winged bat (*Dobsonia*) is found from Celebes and Bali to the Solomon Islands and Queensland; its wings are attached to the mid-line of the back rather than to the sides of the body and the index finger of the wing has no claw; in colour the various species are dark brown, usually with an olive cast, lighter on the underparts; the muzzle is heavy, shorter than in *Pteropus*, and the cheek teeth are heavy and crowded.

The epomorphorine tribe contains only African species. It is characterized by the brain case being flattened posteriorly (the alveolar line produced posteriorly passes below the occipital condyle or through its lower part); the muzzle is generally long but may be quite short; the upper cheek teeth are three or four on each side; there are whitish hair tufts before, and usually behind, the ear. *Plerotes*, known only from Angola, has narrow, weak cheek teeth, four in number above; the occiput of the skull is deflected more than typical of this group, and in coloration it is a dull fawn. The epaulet bats (*Epomophorus*) vary from small short-faced species to larger, long-faced types. They are fawn-coloured; the males have erectile whitish or yellowish shoulder pouches, from which the species received its common name. The hammer-headed bat (*Hypsignathus*) of the Congo and West Africa has an enormous muzzle, especially the adult males, swollen, pendulous lips and extensive cheek pouches; it is grayish-brown in colour. The males emit loud cries during the night, frequenting mangroves and palms along the river. *Casinycteris* of the Cameroons is a short-faced, broad-headed species, differing from all its relatives by the reduced palate, which ends shortly behind the last molar; it is fawn-coloured, with a white blaze on the face.

The short-faced fruit bats of India and the Malay region, east to the Molucca Islands, Timor and the Philippines, form the third, or cynopterine, tribe. They have the occipital region on the same plane as the upper alveolar line. *Cynopterus* occurs throughout the range of the group, including about a dozen species; a small tail is present; the lower incisors are 2–2, while the cheek teeth are $\frac{4-4}{5-5}$. *Sphaerias* of Burma is like *Cynopterus* but the calcar or spur, which usually supports the interfemoral membrane, is absent, as is also the tail. *Balionycteris* has spotted wings, the tail is absent and the cheek teeth are $\frac{5-5}{5-5}$; it occurs in Borneo. *Ptenochirus* has lower incisors 1–1, cheek teeth $\frac{4-4}{5-5}$, a short tail or none. The typical species occurs in the Philippines; related forms are found on the Malay peninsula, Borneo and Sumatra. The flying foxes and their relatives feed on many fruits, such as figs, guavas, bananas, dates and others. Flowers and their buds are frequently taken and some species have been known to gnaw bark of young trees. In the tropics some fruit or flowers are almost always available.

FROM DOBSON, "PROCEEDINGS OF THE ZOOLOGICAL SOCIETY"

FIG. 5.—TUBE-NOSED FRUIT BAT, NYCTIMENE

The subfamily Nyctimeninae includes two genera of tube-nosed fruit bats. They are short-faced, with their nostrils drawn out into tubes; their lower canines are in contact, the lower incisors being absent; and in the skull the premaxillary bones are strongly united. The tail is about as long as the lower leg. The wings and ears are usually yellowish spotted. *Paranyctimene* has sharp-cusped cheek teeth, while those teeth in *Nyctimene* are almost as blunt as in most fruit bats. Both of these may feed on insects rather extensively, in addition to fruit.

The subfamily Harpyionycterinae contains only a single genus, *Harpyionycteris*. Like *Nyctimene*, it has the premaxillary bones broadly fused; the canines slant forward, crossing when the jaws are closed, the lower incisors are usually absent. The cheek teeth each show five or six sharp cusps. The skull is like that of the pteropodine fruit bats, with a long face. The harpy fruit bat is chocolate brown in colour, small in size and the tail is absent. It is known only from the Philippine Islands and Celebes.

The subfamily Macroglossinae includes a number of small, long-faced fruit bats, generally less than 5 in. in head and body length. The long, narrow tongue is free for its anterior two-thirds, protrusile and armed with recurved filiform papillae. Their cheek teeth are narrow, incisors greatly reduced in size, the mandibular symphysis is long and the brain case strongly deflected. They feed on soft fruits, the nectar and pollen of flowers, probably also on insects found in them. Bats of this group are found from India to the Fiji Islands and Australia, while one form occurs in West Africa. Two sections of Macroglossinae have been distinguished. The macroglossine tribe, with a narrow ascending process of the premaxillary bone, contains three genera. *Eonycteris,* characterized by relatively large cheek teeth $\left(\frac{5}{6} \text{ or } \frac{5}{5}\right.$ on either side), a short tail and the index finger without a claw, is found from Burma to the Philippines and Celebes. *Megaloglossus,* characterized by bilobed lower incisors, no tail, and males with pale neck-ruffs, has an African distribution from Liberia to the Belgian Congo. *Macroglossus* occurs from India to the Solomon Islands and northern Australia; cranially the brain case is strongly deflected, the infraorbital canal generally long; the index finger is clawed and there is no tail. The notopterine tribe, the skull with the ascending process of the premaxilla broad, contains three genera. *Melonycteris* of New Guinea and the Bismarck archipelago is golden brown in colour above, with dark under parts and small white epaulettes in males; the index finger bears a claw; the tail is absent; the skull is almost semicircular in dorsal outline and the infraorbital canal is long. *Nesonycteris* of the Solomon Islands has under parts paler and duller than the russet-brown back; the index finger is clawless; there is one minute lower incisor on either side instead of two. The long-tailed flower bat (*Notopteris*), of New Caledonia, the Carolines, the New Hebrides and Fiji Islands, is the only fruit bat with a tail reaching to the heel; the wings take origin from the middle of the back; cranially it resembles *Melonycteris* and *Nesonycteris* but has only one upper and one lower incisor on each side.

MICROCHIROPTERA

The second and larger suborder contains the insectivorous bats, most of which are of relatively small size. Their teeth are usually adapted for cutting up hard-bodied insects, the sharp cusps being arranged in W-pattern (fig. 2 B). The rim of the ear does not form a ring, as in the fruit bats. The angular process of the mandible is long and slender. The greater and lesser tubercles of the humerus are well developed and the former usually articulates with the scapula. The index finger never bears a claw and, except in a few species, lacks bony phalanges. As the suborder contains 600 or more different forms, it will be possible only to outline the various families and subfamilies, with special mention of some of the more important types.

The Microchiroptera may be divided into four superfamily groups, including 15 recent families.

(1) Superfamily Emballonuroidea is characterized by the premaxillaries being generally free, the ascending process the most important part. The greater tubercle of the humerus is small; only in the Noctilionidae does it articulate to a small degree with the scapula. The third digit bears two well developed phalanges. The teeth are normal.

Family Rhinopomidae includes only the genus *Rhinopoma,* the mouse-tailed bat, found from Egypt to Burma and Sumatra. The interfemoral membrane is small, while the tail is slender and extremely long. The muzzle is broad, with a poorly developed nose-leaf; the ears are long and the index finger has two bony joints. The skull has a short rostrum, the dorsal surface of which exhibits a depression; there are no postorbital processes.

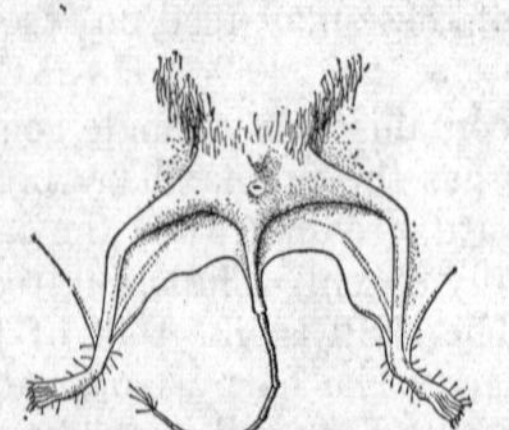

FROM ALLEN, LANG AND CHAPIN IN "BULLETIN OF THE AMERICAN MUSEUM OF NATURAL HISTORY"

FIG. 6.—TAIL OF THE MOUSE-TAILED BAT (RHINOPOMA)

Family Emballonuridae, the sheath-tailed bats. The tail projects through the interfemoral membrane on the upper side. The basal phalanx of the third finger folds back on the upper side of the metacarpal bone when the wing is folded. The face is pointed, the nostrils project in front of the lips and there is no nose-leaf. The skull shows postorbital processes and the premaxillary bones are independent, without palatal processes. In subfamily Emballonurinae the postorbital processes are long and curved, the clavicle or collarbone is normal (its greatest breadth less than a quarter of its length). Bats of this group in the old world: *Emballonura,* with incisors $\frac{2-2}{3-3}$ and of small size, is found in Madagascar, the Malay region and eastward to Samoa; *Taphozous,* the tomb bats, has incisors $\frac{1-1}{2-2}$, a deep depression in the forehead of the skull, often a glandular throat-sac—bats of this genus are medium-sized or large and occur from Africa and southern Asia to the Philippines and Australia; *Coleura,* of eastern Africa and the Seychelle Islands, resembles *Emballonura* but has one upper incisor on each side. The sheath-tailed bats of the new world tropics (*Saccopteryx* and allies) have antebrachial pouches on the wings, the upper incisors are 1–1 or absent, and they are small or medium-sized species. *Rhynchiscus* of the same region lacks the wing pouch and has a long muzzle, although the rostrum of the skull is short. Subfamily Diclidurinae is characterized by the short and straight postorbital processes of the skull and a greatly expanded collar-bone (its breadth more than one-third of the length). The interfemoral membrane is glandular. *Diclidurus,* the white bat, is widely distributed in tropical America. *Drepanonycteris* has whitish head, shoulders and underparts, but the back becomes brownish.

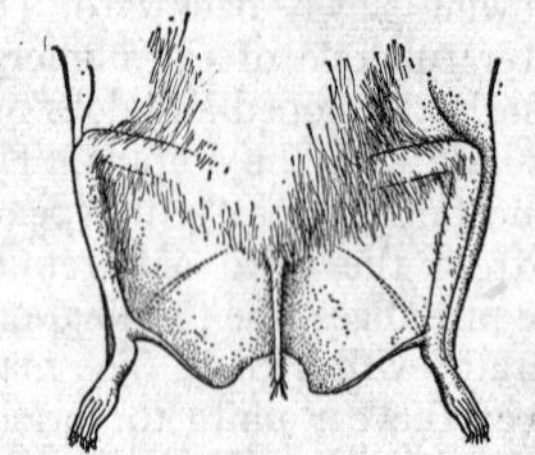

FROM ALLEN, LANG AND CHAPIN IN "BULLETIN OF THE AMERICAN MUSEUM OF NATURAL HISTORY"

FIG 7.—A. HEAD OF SHEATH-TAILED BAT (TAPHOZOUS); B. TAIL AND INTERFEMORAL MEMBRANE

Family Noctilionidae, the hare-lipped bats of tropical America and the West Indies, have a curiously folded upper lip, the middle forming an inverted V. The second finger has a rudimentary phalanx and the terminal phalanges of the third and fourth fingers fold under when at rest. The hind feet and claws are large and the ears long and pointed. There are cheek pouches but no nose-leaf. The incisors are $\frac{2-2}{1-1}$; both nasal and palatal processes of the premaxillaries are developed and these bones unite with the maxillaries in adults. The shoulder joint is strengthened by a small articulation of the greater tubercle of the humerus with the scapula. The hip-bones are solidly attached to the spinal column, the ischia fused together and with the under side of the sacrum, and the symphysis pubis is absent in females. These large or medium-sized bats feed chiefly on fish, which they catch with their long feet. Two genera, *Noctilio* and *Dirias,* are distinguished, the latter by minor dental characters and shorter legs and feet.

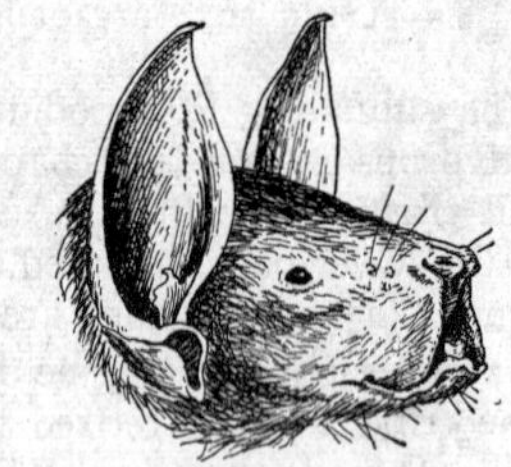

FIG. 8.—HARE-LIPPED BAT (NOCTILIO)

FIG. 9.—SLIT-FACED BAT (NYCTERIS)

(2) Superfamily Rhinolophoidea contains bats characterized by degenerate premaxillary bones, without nasal processes, and often partly or wholly cartilaginous. The nostrils open in a complicated nose-leaf or margined by cutaneous outgrowths forming a deep longitudinal groove. The ears are large and the third finger bears only two phalanges.

Family Nycteridae, the slit-faced bats, are so called from a deep slit down the front of the face, into which the nostrils open. The edges of this are swollen but do not form a nose-leaf. The tail is long, included in the interfemoral membrane to the tip. The ear is large, with a simple tragus. The skull has poorly developed postorbital processes on the sides of an extensive frontal basin; the premaxillaries are represented only by their palatal portions. The humerus exhibits a poorly developed greater tubercle which does not articulate with the scapula. Only the single genus *Nycteris* is extant, found throughout Africa except for the northwest, and from Borneo and Java to Celebes and Timor.

FROM ALLEN, LANG AND CHAPIN, "BULLETIN OF THE AMERICAN MUSEUM OF NATURAL HISTORY"
FIG. 10.—FALSE VAMPIRE (LAVIA FRONS)

Family Megadermidae, the false vampires, are distributed from India and southern China to the Philippine Islands and Java, and in Australia and tropical Africa. The muzzle bears a nose-leaf; the tragus of the ear is large and bifid and the tail is short. The premaxillaries are almost completely cartilaginous and there are no upper incisors. *Megaderma* (including *Lyroderma* of many authors) ranges from southern Asia to Java and the Philippines; it is distinguished by having $\frac{5-5}{5-5}$ cheek teeth and only slightly concave frontal region. *Macroderma,* the Australian false vampire, is one of the largest of the insectivorous bats, the head and body length 4.92–5.11 in. It is pale grayish green, almost whitish in colour and has 4–4 upper cheek teeth and conspicuously concave frontal part of the skull. *Lavia* (including *Cardioderma* of some authors) of the savanna country of Africa, agrees with *Macroderma* in dental formula and cranially. In colour these bats are bright greenish gray.

FIG. 11.—HORSESHOE BAT (RHINOLOPHUS)

Family Rhinolophidae, the horseshoe and leaf-nosed bats, inhabits the tropical and temperate parts of the old world. The ears are large and lack a tragus and a complicated nose-leaf is developed. The tail is generally shorter than the hind legs. The rostrum of the skull is short, the nasal cavities inflated, and the premaxillaries are partly cartilaginous, the only ossified parts being a palatal strap bearing the small incisors. The greater tubercle of the humerus is large, articulating with the shoulder blade, and the first ribs, last cervical and first thoracic vertebrae tend to fuse with each other and the presternum to form a broad bony ring. The pelvic girdle is weak, the dorsal and ventral margins of the hipbone are almost parallel, the obturator foramen small. Two subfamilies may be recognized: the Rhinolophinae, with three joints in the second to fifth toes, the nose-leaf pointed above and broad below; the Hipposiderinae, with squarish nose-leaf, the toes with only two phalanges, the basal joint and the one bearing a claw. Subfamily Rhinolophinae, the horseshoe bats, contains only two genera. *Rhinolophus* is found throughout the tropical and temperate regions of the old world, from England and Japan to South Africa and Australia. Almost 100 species are recognized, ranging from small to medium in size (up to about 3.34 in. head and body length). *Chilophyla,* found only in the Philippines, has a broad, poorly differentiated horseshoe, the ears large and rounded. The thumb has a long metacarpal included in the antebrachial membrane, which forms a pouch. This rare bat is dull fawn colour, with long soft hair. Subfamily Hipposiderinae, the leaf-nosed bats, restricted to the tropics or warmer regions, are found throughout Africa and southern Asia, east to Australia and the Solomons. In addition to the characters given above, the thoracic ring is more extensive than in the Rhinolophinae, the hipbone contains a secondary pre-acetabular foramen and the lumbar vertebrae tend to fuse. The typical genus, *Hipposideros,* has a range coextensive with that of the subfamily. Some species are large, *H. gigas* being as much as 4.92 in., while others vary from 1.57 in. to 3.46 in. head and body length. Many species are represented by bright red varieties. One grizzled brown species of Africa, *H. cyclops,* has a curious eversible pouch on the forehead, containing stiff whitish hairs. Other genera differ in precise dental formula and minor cranial characters. *Anthops* of the Solomon Islands has an extremely short tail and a rosette-like nose-leaf covering the face; at the top of this there are three hemispherical bodies, the rounded surfaces directed forward.

FROM ALLEN, LANG AND CHAPIN, "BULLETIN OF THE AMERICAN MUSEUM OF NATURAL HISTORY"
FIG. 12.—LEAF-NOSED BAT (HIPPOSIDEROS CYCLOPS)

FROM DOBSON, "CATALOGUE OF THE CHIROPTERA" (BRITISH MUSEUM)
FIG. 13.—CHIN-LEAF BAT, MORMOOPS BLAINVILLII

(3) Superfamily Phyllostomatoidea is characterized by complete premaxillary bones in the skull, fused with each other and the maxillaries, and there is no postorbital process. The ears are moderately large, with a tragus. The third finger has three bony joints beyond the metacarpal, while the index finger has one phalanx. Many species have a nose-leaf. The shoulder joint includes both the head of the humerus and the greater tubercle (except in the Chilonycterinae).

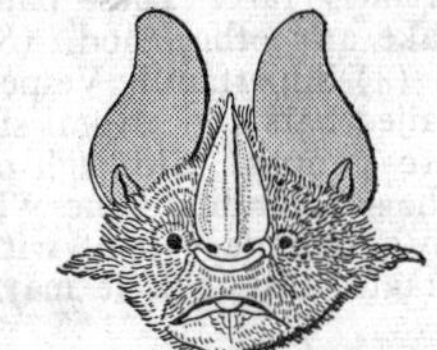
FIG. 14.—JAVELIN BAT (PHYLLOSTOMUS)

Family Phyllostomatidae have well developed molar teeth, adapted for crushing insects or fruit. It is restricted to tropical and subtropical America. Subfamily Chilonycterinae contains three genera, differing from their relatives in having a primitive shoulder joint in which the humerus takes no part. The muzzle does not bear a nose-leaf but the lower lip is decorated with platelike outgrowths of skin. The tail membrane is large, supported in part by a long calcar or "spur." Two genera are noteworthy: *Pteronotus,* with wings attached along the mid-dorsal line, and *Mormoops,* with extremely shortened head, highly elevated brain case and extraordinary development of the cutaneous outgrowths on the chin (fig. 13). Subfamily Phyllostomatinae contains bats with a nose-leaf, usually shaped like a spearhead, on the muzzle. The greater tubercle of the humerus forms a secondary shoulder joint as it does in the following groups of this family. The molars have cusps arranged in the normal W-pattern. The best known genera are: *Phyllostomus,* the spear-nosed bat, represented by several species, 2.95 in. to 4.33 in. in head-body length and heavily built, with a well developed nose-leaf (fig. 14), short tail and incisors $\frac{2-2}{2-2}$; *Vampyrus,* the largest American bat, has a wing spread of about 27.55 in. and a head-body length of about 5.51 in., and *Macrotus* with large oval ears, head and body about 3.93 in. in length, is found as far north as California. The first two feed on other bats, small mammals and birds, in addition to fruit and insects, and are confined to tropical America and the West Indies. Subfamily Glossophaginae includes the long-nosed flower bats, adapted for feeding on nectar and pollen by their long brush-tipped tongue. In the skull, the zygomatic arch is slender or incomplete. The cheek teeth are long and narrow but show the W-pattern indistinctly, and the lower incisors are rudimentary. The nose-leaf is well developed though simple, and the ears small and separate. Subfamily Carolliinae is characterized cranially by incomplete zygomatic arch and cheek teeth simplified from the normal W-pattern to form cutting blades, the third molar patternless or with two low cusps. These bats feed on fruit, especially bananas, and are often very common. Subfamily Sturnirinae contains a single tailless, fruit-eating species, *Sturnira lilium,* with broad cheek teeth, the crowns of which have a longitudinal groove or valley laterally margined by two cusps. The muzzle is broad, with a normal nose-leaf. The males of this species have tufts of deep red stiff hair on the shoulders. Subfamily Stenoderminae includes a number of genera, short-faced and with a high brain case for the most part, the nose-leaf usually present, although sometimes rudimentary or absent; the tail is generally missing. The molar teeth are broad and short, the lateral cusps well developed, forming a cutting edge, a smaller medial cusp separated from these by a wide concavity, the enamel of which is often wrinkled. One of the best known genera is *Artibeus,* one form of which rarely reaches southern Florida. These bats are often large (up to 4.13 in. head and body length), marked by white lines on the head. *Uroderma* has similar head markings but in addition has a

FROM DOBSON, "CATALOGUE OF THE CHIROPTERA" (BRITISH MUSEUM)
FIG. 15.—LONG-TONGUED FLOWER BAT (CHOERONYCTERIS)

white stripe extending from the shoulders to the hind quarters. *Centurio,* the centurion bat, lacks a nose-leaf but the skin of the entire face is folded in grotesque fashion. Subfamily Phyllonycterinae resembles the Glossophaginae externally, with long rostrum, extensile tongue, armed with bristle-like papillae at the tip. The zygomatic arch is likewise incomplete. The upper molars, however, are triangular in crown view, without distinct cusps, most of the crown surface occupied by a groove. Such teeth could be best derived from the stenodermine or sturnirine pattern. The habits of this group are undoubtedly like those of the Glossophaginae. They are confined to the Bahama Islands and Greater Antilles.

BY COURTESY OF ANTHONY, "NATURAL HISTORY"

FIG. 16.—VAMPIRE BAT (DESMODUS)

Family Desmodontidae, the vampire bats, is restricted to the warmer regions of America north to southern Mexico. They agree with the Phyllostomatidae in most characters of the wing and limb girdles. The skin around the nostrils is folded, forming a poorly developed nose-leaf. The fibula is large, reaching the head of the tibia, and the teeth are specialized for cutting, being narrow blades without any crushing surface. The cheek teeth are reduced and of little function. The stomach is reduced to a long slender tube, folded upon itself. Three genera are recognized, of which *Desmodus* is the best known, *Diaemus* and *Diphylla* being extremely rare. These bats feed on blood, apparently being unable to take any other food. (*See* VAMPIRE.)

(4) Superfamily Vespertilionoidea includes the typical bats, the free-tailed bats and several small families. In this group the premaxillaries are complete, although often separated by a gap, and are fused with the surrounding bones. The greater tubercle of the humerus articulates in a secondary joint with the scapula. The ears are provided with a tragus, although it may be small. Except for the Australian long-eared bat, *Nyctophilus,* the muzzle does not bear a nose-leaf. The molars show a well-marked W-pattern.

FROM DOBSON, "CATALOGUE OF THE CHIROPTERA," COURTESY OF THE BRITISH MUSEUM

FIG. 17.—LONG-LEGGED BAT (CHILONATALUS)

Family Natalidae, the long-legged bats, includes several delicately built genera from the American tropics and subtropics. In all but one genus (*Nyctiellus*) the ears are funnel-shaped. The muzzle is long and relatively broad. The lumbar vertebrae are fused together, except for the last two, the presternum large and strong, with a well developed backward slanting keel. The third finger has two phalanges. The brain case is domelike, rising high above the rostrum.

AFTER DOBSON IN "THE PROCEEDINGS OF ZOOL. SOC." BY COURTESY OF THE COUNCIL

FIG. 18.—SUCTIONAL DISKS IN THYROPTERA
(A) Side, (B) concave surface of thumb disk, (C) foot, with disk and calcar

Family Furipteridae is restricted to the tropical parts of South America. The bats of this group resemble the preceding but the thumb is vestigial, included in the wing membrane to the base of the functionless claw. The premaxillary bones have a poorly developed palatal branch and are widely separated from each other. The two genera recognized, *Furipterus* and *Amorphochilus,* both have high-crowned skulls.

Family Thyropteridae, containing only a single genus, is restricted to tropical America, north as far as Honduras. The thumb and the sole of the foot (fig. 18) bear sucking-disks and the former has also a well developed claw. The lumbar vertebrae are independent. The dental formula on either side agrees with the Natalidae (incisors $\frac{2}{3}$, canines $\frac{1}{1}$, premolars $\frac{3}{3}$, molars $\frac{3}{3}=38$) and contains one more upper premolar than in the Furipteridae.

Family Myzapodidae contains only the sucker-footed bat of Madagascar related to the Natalidae and Thyropteridae. The index finger has a cartilaginous rod in addition to the metacarpal, probably representing the phalanges, while the third finger exhibits three bony phalanges. The thumb and sole of the foot bear adhesive disks; the toes have only two phalanges. The tragus is fused with the ear conch on the anterior side, and the ear opening is partly closed by a mushroomlike process. Cranially the premaxillary bones are complete, surrounding the incisive foramen. The teeth number 38, including incisors $\frac{2}{3}$, canines $\frac{1}{1}$, premolars $\frac{3}{3}$ and molars $\frac{3}{3}$ on each side.

FROM ALLEN, "BATS" (HARVARD UNIVERSITY PRESS)

FIG. 19.—MOUSE-EARED BAT (MYOTIS LUCIFUGUS) IN FLIGHT

Family Vespertilionidae contains the typical insectivorous bats and is almost world-wide in distribution. The muzzle and lips are simple; except for one subfamily (Nyctophilinae) there is no nose-leaf and the ears are separate. The long tail extends to the edge of the broad interfemoral membrane and rarely projects more than one vertebral joint beyond it. The two incisors on each side of the upper jaw are separated by a considerable gap. The secondary shoulder joint is well developed, the greater tubercle projecting well above the head and articulating with a large facet on the shoulder blade. The ulna is usually fused with the proximal end of the radius, the shaft of the ulna reduced to a poorly ossified thread. The family is divided into six subfamily groups.

Subfamily Vespertilioninae contains about 20 genera and is as widely distributed as the family, being found on the continents to the limits of tree growth and on all but a few mid-oceanic islands. The best known genera are: the mouse-eared bats (*Myotis*), with about 75 species, found on all the continents, characterized by $\frac{6\text{–}6}{6\text{–}6}$ cheek teeth; the pipistrelles (*Pipistrellus*), with nearly as wide a range and almost as many species, have cheek teeth $\frac{5\text{–}5}{5\text{–}5}$, incisors $\frac{2\text{–}2}{3\text{–}3}$, and are usually smaller, only rarely more than 2.75 in. head and body length; the serotines and brown bats (*Eptesicus*), also widely distributed and represented by numerous species, have $\frac{4\text{–}4}{5\text{–}5}$ cheek teeth; the long-eared bats (*Plecotus*) are widely distributed in the northern hemisphere and have ears almost as long as their bodies. Numerous other bats belong here.

FROM ALLEN, LANG AND CHAPIN IN "BULLETIN OF THE AMERICAN MUSEUM OF NATURAL HISTORY"

FIG. 20.—WING OF BENT-WINGED BAT (MINIOPTERUS)

Subfamily Miniopterinae. The bent-winged or long-fingered bats, represented by a single genus (*Miniopterus*), occur in southern Europe, Africa, Asia and the Pacific islands east to the Loyalties. The first phalanx of the third finger is short, only about a third as long as the second phalanx; this second phalanx and the equivalent joint of the fourth finger are folded back on the under side of the metacarpals when the bat rests. The crown of the skull is domelike and high and the cheek teeth are $\frac{5\text{–}5}{6\text{–}6}$. Long-fingered bats are usually small, with large wings.

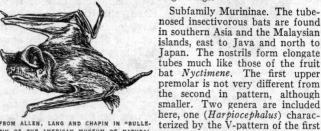

FROM ALLEN, LANG AND CHAPIN IN "BULLETIN OF THE AMERICAN MUSEUM OF NATURAL HISTORY"

FIG. 21.—FREE-TAILED BAT (TADARIDA)

Subfamily Murininae. The tube-nosed insectivorous bats are found in southern Asia and the Malaysian islands, east to Java and north to Japan. The nostrils form elongate tubes much like those of the fruit bat *Nyctimene.* The first upper premolar is not very different from the second in pattern, although smaller. Two genera are included here, one (*Harpiocephalus*) characterized by the V-pattern of the first two upper molars, unlike the more normal W-pattern of *Murina.*

Subfamily Kerivoulinae. The trumpet-eared bats are confined to the tropical and subtropical regions of the old world, east as far as the Solomon Islands. The well developed ears are funnel-shaped, with long slender tragi. The sternum differs from that of other bats by its shortness, less than twice as long as the breadth of the presternum, and only four or five ribs articulate with it. The skull is high-crowned and the teeth number 38 (incisors $\frac{2}{3}$, canines $\frac{1}{1}$, premolars $\frac{3}{3}$, molars $\frac{3}{3}$). Three genera are known: one (*Anamygdon*) is confined to the Solomons; *Phoniscus,* with four-lobed lower incisors, occurs from the Malay peninsula and Sumatra to New Guinea; *Kerivoula,* with three-cusped lower incisors, is widely distributed in the warmer parts of the old world.

Subfamily Nyctophilinae contains two genera confined to Australia and New Guinea, and one found in North America. The muzzle is truncate, the nostrils opening beneath a horseshoelike ridge or small nose-leaf. *Antrozous,* of western North America from Texas to the Pacific and from Oregon to central Mexico, has long ears and incisors $\frac{1-1}{2-2}$. *Nyctophilus,* the long-eared bat of Australia and New Guinea, has incisors $\frac{1-1}{3-3}$, and there is a small nose-leaf.

Subfamily Tomopeatinae includes only a single genus, *Tomopeas,* found in Peru. The ear resembles that of the Molossidae, without anterior basal lobe and the tragus short and blunt. The upper lip is widely spreading but not heavily wrinkled. The seventh cervical vertebra is fused with the first dorsal, as in the free-tailed bats. Externally *Tomopeas* resembles a small pipistrelle.

Family Mystacinidae includes only the New Zealand bat, one of two species found in New Zealand. The feet are short and broad, the claws bearing accessory talons at the base. The fibula is complete and relatively large, forming with the tibia a stout lower leg. The tail projects from near the middle of the upper surface of the interfemoral membrane. The third finger bears three bony phalanges, the first of which is bent back on the upper surface of the metacarpal when at rest. In the vespertilionine skull, the premaxillary bones are complete, isolating two small incisive foramina.

Family Molossidae contains the mastiff, or free-tailed bats. The group is found in the warmer parts of both hemispheres, north to southern Europe and Asia, east to New Guinea, Australia and Norfolk Island; in America, north to the central United States and throughout the West Indies. In these bats the double articulation of the shoulder joint is perfected. The wing is long and narrow, the fifth finger much shortened, and the membranes thick and leathery. The tail projects beyond the interfemoral membrane, which can be contracted or expanded along the tail, somewhat like an awning. The ears are frequently joined across the forehead, the tragus much reduced. The muzzle is obliquely truncate, the upper lip broad and wrinkled, usually sprinkled with short spoon-tipped hairs. The lower leg is stout and contains a complete fibula, relatively strong and bowed out. Cranially, the premaxillaries are either united medially, enclosing the small incisive foramina, or are separated by a narrow space. About 12 genera are recognized. *Cheiromeles,* containing a single species, *C. torquatus,* from the Malay peninsula and the islands, east to Java and north to Palawan, is one of the strangest appearing bats, with long pig-like snout, widely separated ears, almost naked, wrinkled skin and large opposable first toe. A large pouch under each wing may serve to carry the young. This bat is one of the largest of the insectivorous group (head and body 5.31 in., tail 1.77 in. and forearm about 3.34 in. *Tadarida* has a range coextensive with that of the family, being found in the tropics and warm parts of the old and new world. The ears are large and rounded, arising from the middle of the head or joined by a narrow ridge. The fur covering the body is extremely fine and oily and males of many species have erectile crests on the forehead. Most species have the premaxillaries incomplete, the upper incisors separated by a space, but all gradations exist between this condition and complete premaxillae, with the upper incisors almost in contact. The upper cheek-teeth are 5-5 in number, the last molar often narrow, with a simplified V-pattern. Several species found in Malaysia, central Africa and the West Indies have elongate skulls and very large ears. *Myopterus,* an African genus, has transparent flesh-coloured wings and creamy white under parts. The ears in this bat are pointed and more erect than is usually the case in the Molossidae. The upper lip is not wrinkled; in front it is covered with relatively large "spoon-hairs." The upper incisor teeth are strongly in contact with each other and with the canine; the cheek-teeth are $\frac{4}{5}$ on each side. The skull is long and low, with sagittal crest poorly marked. *Molossops,* represented by several South American species, has procumbent upper incisors and broad low skull with large antorbital ridge but weak sagittal crest. The premaxillaries are complete, enclosing the small incisive foramina. The ears are rounded and short. *Eumops,* with numerous species, is found from southwestern United States to Argentina. They vary in size from large (4.43 in. head and body length) to medium (3.54 in.). The upper incisors are large, closely pressed together and procumbent, the skull is long and low with poorly developed sagittal crest. The cheek-teeth are generally $\frac{5}{5}$ on each side but the first upper premolar is sometimes absent. The ears are large, joined across the forehead, rounded or somewhat squarish and extending beyond the muzzle. *Molossus* is generally small, with short, rounded skull in which the sagittal crest is well developed. The first upper premolar is absent or a mere vestige, and the last upper molar is narrow, with a V-shaped crest. The other cheek-teeth are massive.

EXTINCT BATS

The frail skeletons of bats are rarely preserved as fossils but several deposits have yielded extremely fine specimens. The oldest forms come from the Eocene and even then showed most of their present-day structure; some were sufficiently different to be referred to separate families. Others were members of the Rhinolophidae. In a little later deposit representatives of the Megadermidae, Emballonuridae, Vespertilionidae and Molossidae were found. The first known pteropodid comes from the Oligocene of Italy. By the Pliocene most bat fossils can be referred to existing genera but even late Pleistocene deposits contain a few extinct genera and numerous extinct species.

Bibliography.—G. E. Dobson, *Catalogue of the Chiroptera* (British Museum, Natural History, 1878); K. Andersen, *Catalogue of the Chiroptera,* vol. i; *Megachiroptera* (British Museum, Natural History, 1912); G. S. Miller, Jr., "Families and Genera of Bats," *U.S. National Museum, Bull. 57* (1907); G. M. Allen, *Bats* (1940); G. G. Simpson, *Bull. Amer. Mus. Nat. Hist.,* vol. 85, pp. 54–61 (1945).

(J. E. Hl.)

CHIRU, a graceful Tibetan antelope (*Pantholops hodgsoni*), of which the bucks are armed with long, slender and heavily ridged horns of a peculiar type. Chiru are very wary and difficult to approach; they are generally found in small parties. They inhabit the desolate plateau of Tibet, at elevations of between 13,000 and 18,000 ft., and have a thick coat, formed of close woolly hair of a gray-fawn colour. The most peculiar feature about the chiru is its swollen, puffy nose, probably connected with breathing a rarefied atmosphere. The chiru is allied to the saiga (*q.v.*).

CHIRURGEON, one whose profession it is to cure disease by operating with the hand. The word in its original form is now obsolete. It derives from the Mid. Eng. *cirurgien* or *sirurgien,* through the Fr. from the Gr. words meaning *hand* and *work;* from the early form is derived the modern word "surgeon." "Chirurgeon" is a 16th century reversion to the Greek origin. (*See* Surgery.)

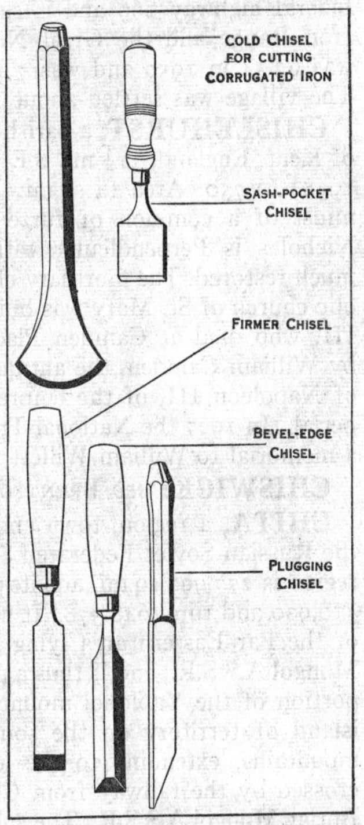

CHISELS IN COMMON USE FOR CUTTING METAL, STONE OR WOOD USED IN CARPENTRY AND OTHER TRADES

CHISEL, a sharp-edged tool for cutting metal, wood or stone. There are numerous varieties of chisels used in different trades; the carpenter's chisel is wooden-handled with a straight edge, transverse to the axis and bevelled on one side; stone masons' chisels are bevelled on both sides, and others have oblique concave or convex edges. A chisel with a semicircular blade is called a "gouge." The tool is worked either by hand-pressure or by blows from a hammer or mallet. The "cold chisel" has a steel edge, highly tempered to cut unheated metal. The derivation is from O.Fr. *cisel,* modern *ciseau,* late Lat. *cisellum,* a cutting tool, from *caedere,* to cut. (*See* Tool.)

CHISHOLM, HUGH (1866–1924), editor of the *Encyclopædia Britannica,* was born in London on Feb. 22, 1866. He was of Scottish descent, the son of Henry Chisholm, who became warden of the standards in the Board of Trade. Educated at Felsted school and Corpus Christi college, Oxford, of which he was a scholar, he graduated in 1888 with a first class in *literae humaniores.* He then read for the bar, being called at the Middle Temple in 1892, but occupied himself also with occasional journalism and finally adopted that profession. From 1892 to 1897 he was assistant editor, and from 1897 to the end of 1899 editor, of the *St. James's Gazette,* and during these years he also contributed numerous articles on political, financial and literary subjects to the weekly journals and monthly reviews, becoming known as a literary critic and Conservative publicist.

On resigning the editorship of the *St. James's,* he became a leader writer for *The Standard,* and later, in 1900, was invited to join *The Times,* under whose management he acted as the responsible co-editor, with Sir Donald Mackenzie Wallace and President A. T. Hadley of Yale university, of the new volumes, constituting the tenth edition (1902), of the *Encyclopædia Britannica,* becoming in 1903 editor-in-chief of the 11th edition.

Rejoining *The Times* in 1913 as day editor, he became financial editor at the end of that year, and occupied this responsible position all through the momentous period of World War I, resigning his connection with *The Times* in March 1920, in order to reassume the editorship of the *Encyclopædia Britannica* and to organize the publication of the new volumes constituting the 12th edition. In 1893 Chisholm married E. Beatrix Harrison, of Ardkeen, County Down, Ireland, and had three sons. He died in London on Sept. 29, 1924.

CHISHOLM, a mining village of St. Louis county, Minn., U.S., on the Mesabi iron range, 75 mi. N.W. of Duluth. It is on federal highway 169 and is served by the Duluth, Missabe and Iron Range and the Great Northern railways. The population was 6,854 in 1950 and was 7,487 in 1940 by the federal census. The village was settled about 1901.

CHISLEHURST, a parish and, with Sidcup, an urban district of Kent, England, 11¼ mi. S.E. of London, by the S.R. Pop. (est. 1938) 61,750. Area 14 sq.mi. It is 300 ft. above sea level in the midst of a common of furze and heather. The church of St. Nicholas is Perpendicular with Early English portions, though much restored. The mortuary chapel attached to the Roman Catholic church of St. Mary was built to receive the body of Napoleon III, who died at Camden Place in 1873. This house was built by William Camden, the antiquary, in 1609. It was the residence of Napoleon III, of the empress Eugénie and of the prince imperial. In 1927 the National Trust secured 88 ac. of Pettswood as a memorial to William Willett, founder of "summer time."

CHISWICK: *see* BRENTFORD AND CHISWICK.

CHITA, a region, town and river in the Far Eastern area of the Russian Soviet Federated Socialist Republic. The area of the region is 277,992 sq.mi. and its population (1939) 1,159,478, urban 510,900 and rural 648,578. It consists of the southwestern tongue of the Far Eastern area lying between Mongolia and the Buriat Mongol A.S.S.R., and is thus a plateau area, with the southwestern portion of the Yablonoi mountains rising above the plateau. An island of territory on the southeastern slopes of the Yablonoi mountains, extending to the left bank of the Onon river, and crossed by the railway from Chita to Manchuria, belongs to the Buriat Mongol A.S.S.R. The subalpine conditions and the extreme continental character of the climate are unfavourable to agriculture except along the valleys of the Shilka and its tributaries, the Ingoda and Onon. Rye is the main crop, though oats, wheat, buckwheat, barley, grass and potatoes are also grown. Herding of horses, cattle, sheep and goats is, however, more important than cultivation, and only .9% of the region is ploughed land. But the essential wealth of the region is in its forests and minerals. Timber and fur (especially fox and squirrel) are exported, the latter being sent to the Irbit and Gorky fairs. The mineral wealth of the region is very great, gold is produced in quantity. Brown coal is mined, and used mainly for the railway and for the town of Chita, and iron ore is mined in quantity. It is almost the only area in U.S.S.R. where wolfram, bismuth and molybdenum are found. There are tin mines near the Onon river and precious stones, *e.g.,* crystal, topaz, aquamarine, amethyst, tourmaline and beryls occur. Mining in the area ceased during the civil war following the 1917 revolution, but most of the mines were working again after 1925. Much of the rolling stock of the railway was destroyed in this period and great damage done to the permanent way, and this hampered the reorganization of the mining industry. Manufactures are little developed, the chief being metal goods and leather. A few electric stations exist. The district is noted for contraband trade with Manchuria and Mongolia.

The town of Chita, lat. 52° N., long. 113° 25′ E. pop. (1939) 102,555, is on the Chita river above its confluence with the Ingoda. With the coming of the Trans-Siberian railway and the increasing exploitation of the mineral, timber and fur wealth of the region, the population and importance of the town developed. Its industries include iron founding, fur and leather dressing, soap boiling, chemical works and boxmaking. The Russian Geographical society has a museum in the town. The Dekabrists, exiled after the Dec. 1825 plot, by their improvements in draining and levelling, converted Chita from a village to a prosperous settlement.

CHITALDROOG, a district and town in the native state of Mysore, India. The district has an area of 4,022 sq.mi. and a population (1931) of 656,569. The rainfall is low, and the Vedavati or Hagari river, in whose valley the town lies, is mostly dry in the hot season. Several parallel chains of hills, reaching an extreme height of 3,800 ft., cross the district; otherwise it is a plain. The chief crops are cotton and rice, and manganese is worked. The west of the district is served by the Madras and Southern Mahratta railway. The largest town in the district is Davangere with cotton factories and a trade in cotton and grain. The town of Chitaldroog, which is the district headquarters (pop. 1941, 14,528) has a considerable trade in cotton. It possesses massive fortifications erected under Hyder Ali and Tippoo Sahib toward the close of the 18th century; and near it on the west are remains of a city of the 2nd century A.D. It is the terminus of a railway from Chikjajur.

CHITARRONE: *see* LUTE; THEORBO.

CHITIMACHA, a tribe of American Indians living on the shores of Grand lake and the banks of Grand river in Louisiana at the time the French settled that region. The Chitimachan linguistic group included three tribes: the Chitimacha, Washa and Chawasha. The name comes from the Choctaw: *chuti,* cooking pot, *masha,* they possess (they have cooking vessels). They called themselves *Pantchpinunukansh,* "men altogether red," a designation apparently made after the coming of the whites. War with the French over the murder of the missionary St. Cosme in 1706 was concluded by presentation of the head of the murderer. They were strict monogamists, and women evidently had authority in their government. What remains of the tribe is scattered.

CHITON, a genus of Amphineura (*q.v.*). (*See* also MOLLUSCA.)

CHITRAL, a native state in the North-West Frontier Province of India. The State of Chitral (*see* also HINDU KUSH) is somewhat larger than Wales, and supports a population of about 35,000 rough, hardy hillmen. Both the state and its capital are called Chitral, the latter being situated about 47 mi. from the main watershed of the range of the Hindu Kush, which divides the waters flowing down to India from those which take their way into the Oxus. The state is important because of its situation at the extremity of the country over which the government of India exerts its influence, and for some years before 1895 it had been the object of the policy of the government of India to secure an effective guardianship over its northern passes. This policy resulted in a British agency being established at Gilgit (Kashmir territory). Chitral can be reached either by the long circuitous route from Gilgit, involving 200 mi. of hill roads and the passage of the Shandur pass (12,250 ft.), or (more directly) from the Peshawar frontier at Malakand by 100 mi. of route through the independent territories of Swat and Bajour, involving the passage of the Lowarai (10,450 ft.). It is held by a small force as a British outpost.

The district of Chitral is called Kashgar by the people of the country. It was under Chinese domination in the middle of the 18th century, and was a Buddhist centre of some importance in the early centuries of our era. The aboriginal population is probably to be recognized in the people called Kho (speaking a language called Khowar), who form the majority of its inhabitants. Upon the Kho a people called Ronas, who form the chief caste and fighting race of the Chitral districts, have been superimposed; they came originally from the north, but have adopted the language and fashions of the conquered Chitrali. (X.)

The Siege of Chitral.—The town of Chitral is chiefly famous for a siege which it sustained in the spring of 1895. Owing to complications arising from the demarcation of the boundary of Afghanistan which was being carried out at that time, and the ambitious projects of Umra Khan, chief of Jandol, who was a tool in the hands of Sher Afzul, a political refugee from Chitral supported by the amir at Kabul, the mehtar (or ruler) of Chitral was murdered, and a small British and Sikh garrison subsequently besieged in the fort. A large force of Afghan troops was at that time in the Chitral river valley to the south of Chitral, nominally holding the Kafirs in check during the progress of boundary demarcation. It is considered probable that some of them assisted the Chitralis in the siege. The position of the political agent Dr. Robertson (afterward Sir George Robertson) and his military force of 543 men (of whom 137 were noncombatants) was at one time critical. Two forces were organized for the relief. One was under Sir R. Low, with 15,000 men, who advanced by way of the Malakand pass, the Swat river and Dir. The other, which was the first to reach Chitral, was under Colonel Kelly, commanding the 32nd Pioneers, who was placed in command of all the troops in the Gilgit district, numbering about 600 all told, with two guns, and instructed to advance by the Shandur pass and Mastuj. This force encountered great difficulties owing to the deep snow on the pass (12,230 ft. high), but it defeated the Chitrali force opposed to it and relieved Chitral on April 20, the siege having begun on March 4. Sher Afzul, who had joined Umra Khan, surrendered, and eventually Chitral was restored to British political control as a dependency of Kashmir. (T. H. H.)

CHITTAGONG, town and port of British India, giving its name to a district and division of Bengal. It is situated on the right bank of the Karnaphuli river, about 12 mi. from its mouth. It is the terminus of the Assam-Bengal railway and a port of call for the Clan line of steamers. The municipal area covers about 9 sq.mi.; pop. (1941) 92,301. Tea is brought from Assam for export to Europe; mineral oil comes in bulk from Burma, is put into tins here and distributed by rail; other exports are jute, raw cotton, rice and hides.

The district of Chittagong occupies a strip of coast and hills between the Bay of Bengal and the mountains. Its area is 2,569 sq.mi.; in 1941 the population was 2,153,296. A few unimportant ranges rise within the northeastern portion, the highest hill being the sacred Sitakund, 1,155 ft. high. The principal rivers are the Karnaphuli, on which Chittagong town is situated, navigable by sea-going ships as far as Chittagong port, the Halda and the Sangu. The wild animals include tigers, elephants, leopards and deer. The northern portion of the district is traversed by the Assam-Bengal railway. Tea cultivation is moderately successful; there were 21 gardens with an output of 1,250,000 lb. in 1921. Chittagong was a famous seaport known to the Portuguese as Porto Grande, and described by de Barros in 1552 as "the most famous and wealthy city of the kingdom of Bengal"; it has been generally identified with the City of Bengala mentioned by Portuguese and other writers. Conquered by the Mohammedans in the 14th century, it passed under the rule of the Arakanese in the next century. The piratical raids of the Arakanese and their Portuguese mercenaries led to the despatch of a strong force by Shaista Khan, the Mughal Nawab of Bengal, which in 1666 captured the town and occupied the district. The Portuguese also had a settlement at Dianga, where 600 of them were massacred by the Arakanese in 1607. Chittagong was ceded to the East India company by Nawab Mir Kasim Ali in 1760.

The Chittagong Hill Tracts is an independent district occupying the hill country between Chittagong proper and the Lushai hills. The highest point is 4,034 ft. above sea level. Its area covers 5,007 sq.mi.; pop. (1941) 247,053. The inhabitants are either descendants of Arakanese or aboriginal tribes, such as Maghs, Tipperas and Chakmas: seven-tenths are Buddhists. The Hill Tracts are grouped in three circles, each under a chief, who is responsible for the collection of revenue and the internal management of the villages. The headquarters are at Rangamati, which was wrecked by a cyclone in Oct. 1897.

The division of Chittagong lies at the northeast corner of the Bay of Bengal, extending northward along the left bank of the Meghna. It consists of the districts of Chittagong, the Hill Tracts, Noakhali and Tippera. Its area covers 11,765 sq.mi.; the population in 1941 was 8,477,890.

CHITTOOR, a town and district of the Madras Presidency, British India. The district, which has an area of 5,951 sq.mi. and a population (1941) of 1,632,395, was formed in recent years from the northern part of North Arcot. It is in great part hilly, being traversed by spurs of the Eastern Ghats radiating east and south. The surface in the hill-country is rocky, save for patches of stunted jungle, but the narrow valleys between the hills are fertile, and the hills themselves are highly mineralized, showing copper and iron especially. The chief crops are rice, millet and oil-seeds. Chittoor (pop. 1941, 27,835) is the chief town, with a station on the Madras and South Mahratta railway, 100 mi. by road from Madras. It contains a native college, mission training school, a hospital and a sanatorium. There is a trade in granite, a distillery and a tannery, but Chittoor is not an important centre. Hyder Ali died here in 1782.

CHITTY, SIR JOSEPH WILLIAM (1828–1899), English judge, was born in London. He was the second son of Thomas Chitty, a celebrated special pleader and writer of legal text-books. Joseph Chitty was educated at Eton and Balliol college, Oxford, and elected to a fellowship at Exeter college. He became a member of Lincoln's Inn in 1851, was called to the bar in 1856, and made a queen's counsel in 1874, electing to practise in the court of the Master of the Rolls, Sir George Jessel, before whom he was very successful. In 1880 he entered the house of commons as Liberal member for Oxford (city); in 1881, however, he was selected to fill the vacancy in the chancery division caused by the elevation of the master of the rolls to the court of appeal by the Judicature Act. In 1897 he was promoted to the court of appeal.

See E. Manson, *Builders of our Law* (1904).

CHIUSI, a town of Tuscany, Italy, province of Siena, 55 mi. S.E. by rail from the town of Siena, and 26 mi. N.N.W. of Orvieto by the main line from Rome to Florence. Pop. (1936) 2,534 (town), 8,043 (commune). The ancient name was Clusium (*q.v.*). It is on a hill 1,305 ft. above sea level, and is surrounded by mediaeval walls, in which, in places, fragments of the Etruscan wall are incorporated. The cathedral of S. Secondiano is a basilica with eighteen ancient marble columns. It has fine choir books from Monte Oliveto Maggiore (*see* Asciano). Chiusi was devastated by malaria in the middle ages (*see* Chiana). Nine miles by road to the northwest are the baths of Chianciano.

CHIVALRY, the knightly class of feudal times. (*See* Knighthood and Chivalry.) The primary sense in the middle ages is "knights" or "fully armed and mounted fighting men." Thence the term came to mean that gallantry and honour expected of knights. Lastly, the word came to be used in its general sense of "courtesy." In English law chivalry meant the tenure of land by knights' service. The *Court of Chivalry* was a court instituted by Edward III, of which the lord high constable and earl marshal of England were joint judges, having summary criminal jurisdiction as regards all offences of knights, and generally as to military matters. When the earl marshal alone presided it was a court of honour deciding as to precedence, coats of arms, etc. This court sat for the last time in 1737. The heraldic side of its duties is now vested in the earl marshal as head of the Heralds' college.

CHIVASSO, a town and episcopal see of Piedmont, Italy, province of Turin, 18 mi. N.E. by rail from that town, 600 ft. above sea level. Pop. (1936) 6,002 (town); 11,590 (commune). It is on the left bank of the Po, near the influx of the Orco. The cathedral (15th century) has a fine façade, with statues in terracotta. A tower remains of the old castle of the marquesses of Monferrato, who possessed the town from 1164 to 1435. It was an important fortress in the middle ages and until the French dismantled it (1804). Chivasso is the junction of branches for Aosta, Asti, and Casale Monferrato.

CHIVES (*Allium Schoenoprasum*), hardy perennial plant, with small narrow bulbs tufted on short root-stocks and long cylindrical hollow leaves. It is found in the north of England and in Cornwall, growing in rocky pastures throughout temperate and northern and in the mountain districts of southern Europe and in Asiatic Russia. It is cultivated for its leaves, which are used in salads and soups as a substitute for young onions; it will grow in any good soil.

CHLOPICKI, GREGORZ JOZEF (1772–1854), Polish general, was born in Podolia. In 1787 he enlisted in the Polish army and fought in the campaigns of 1792–94. He served with the new Italian legion at the storming of Peschiera, at Modena, Busano, Casabianca and Ponto, and in 1807 commanded the first Vistula regiment. In Spain he obtained the Legion of Honour for his heroism at Epila and the storming of Saragossa. Chlopicki accompanied the Grande Armée into Russia (1812). On the reconstruction of the Polish army in 1813 he was made a general of a division, afterward joining the Russian army with the rank of general officer.

He held aloof at first from the Polish national rising of 1830, but at the request of his countrymen he accepted the dictatorship on Dec. 5, 1830. Lacking faith in the success of the movement, he clung to the hope of negotiation with Russia and acted purely on the defensive. On Jan. 17, 1831, he resigned and became a private, until he was forced to retire into private life owing to serious wounds received at Olszyna.

See Josef Maczynski, *Life and Death of Joseph Chlopicki* (Pol.) (Cracow, 1858); Ignacy Pradzynski, *The Four Last Polish Commanders* (Pol.) (Posen, 1865).

CHLORAL or TRICHLOROACETALDEHYDE, first prepared by J. von Liebig in 1832, is a heavy, oily and colourless liquid, of specific gravity 1.541 at 0° C., boiling point 97.7° C., and the formula $CCl_3.CHO$. It has a greasy, somewhat bitter taste and gives off a vapour at ordinary temperature which has a pungent odour and an irritating effect on the eyes. The word "chloral" is derived from the first syllables of "chlorine" and "alcohol," the names of the substances employed for its preparation. Chloral is soluble in alcohol and ether, in less than its own weight of water and in four times its weight of chloroform. It deliquesces in the air and is converted by water into a hydrate, with evolution of heat; it combines with alcohols and mercaptans. With an alkali, chloral gives chloroform (*q.v.*) and a formate; oxidizing agents give trichloroacetic acid, $CCl_3.CO_2H$. When kept for several days, as also when placed in contact with sulphuric acid or a very small quantity of water, chloral undergoes spontaneous change into the polymeride metachloral $(C_2HCl_3O)_x$ of uncertain molecular weight and structure, a white substance slowly volatile in the air and reconverted into chloral without melting at 180° C. Two different, and presumably stereoisomeric parachlorals, $(C_2HCl_3O)_3$, having also been reported to be formed by the action of sulphuric acid upon chloral.

Chloral is prepared by passing dry chlorine into cooled absolute alcohol; toward the end of the operation the liquid is heated nearly to boiling. The alcohol is converted finally into a syrupy fluid, from which chloral is procured by treatment with sulphuric acid (P. Fritsch, 1894). The crude chloral is distilled over lime and is purified by further treatment with sulphuric acid and by redistillation. A mixture of starch or sugar with manganese peroxide and hydrochloric acid may be employed instead of alcohol and chlorine (A. Staedeler, 1847).

Chloral hydrate, $CCl_3.CH(OH)_2$, forms oblique rhombic prisms, perfectly transparent and only slightly odorous. The melting point of pure chloral hydrate is 57°, the boiling point 96°—98° C. When heated with sulphuric acid it is converted into anhydrous chloral and chloralide, $C_5H_2Cl_6O_3$. When mixed with water, chloral hydrate causes a considerable degree of cold; and, as with camphor, small fragments of it placed on the surface of water exhibit gyratory movements. Chloral hydrate does not restore the colour to a solution of fuchsine decolorized by sulphurous acid; this absence of aldehydic property indicates that the water present is combined in the molecular condition. Chloral may be estimated by distilling the hydrate with aqueous calcium hydroxide and measuring the volume of chloroform produced, or by hydrolysis with a known volume of standard alkali and back titration with standard acid. Chloral hydrate has the property of checking the decomposition of many albuminous substances, such as milk and meat; and a mixture with glycerin, according to J. Personne, is suitable for the preservation of anatomical preparations.

Pharmacology and Therapeutics.—The alkaline hydrolysis of chloral hydrate, with production of chloroform and formates, led O. Liebreich to the conjecture that a similar decomposition might be produced in the blood, and he introduced the drug in 1869 as an anaesthetic and hypnotic. It later became known, however, that the drug circulates in the blood unchanged and is excreted as urochloralic acid. In large doses chloral hydrate is a depressant to the circulation and the respiration, and also lowers the temperature. In therapeutic dosage the drug is a powerful and safe hypnotic, acting directly on the brain and producing no preliminary stage of excitement. About 20 minutes after taking such a dose, the patient falls into a refreshing sleep which, lasting several hours, is not distinguishable from natural sleep and is without disagreeable after-symptoms. Chloral hydrate rapidly induces a depression of the anterior horns of gray matter in the spinal cord, and, as strychnine poisoning is accompanied by violent stimulation of these areas, chloral hydrate is a valuable antidote in such cases. It should not be hypodermically injected since it is irritating to the tissues. It can be applied locally as a rubefacient. Its action on the spinal cord has been employed with success in cases of tetanus, whooping cough, urinary incontinence and strychnine poisoning. It is used by doctors to allay spasms in infancy and childhood and also in certain complications of pregnancy and labour.

Toxicology.—In cases of acute poisoning by chloral hydrate, the symptoms may be summarized as those of profound coma. The treatment is to give gastric lavage, to keep up the temperature by hot bottles, etc., and to use artificial respiration in extreme cases. Strychnine injections are much less likely to save life after poisoning by chloral hydrate than chloral hydrate is to save life in poisoning by strychnine. Metrazol and ephedrine may be useful.

Habitual use of chloral as a drug results in chronic poisoning. The victim is usually excited, loquacious, easily fatigued and suffers from attacks of readily induced syncope. The patient may succumb to a dose only slightly larger than usual. There is no specific remedy; the patient must be persuaded to put himself under restraint, and the drug must be stopped at once and entirely.

CHLORATES: *see* CHLORINE.

CHLORINE, a chemical element of the halogen (*q.v.*) family. This strong-smelling, greenish-yellow gas was first prepared in 1774 by K. W. Scheele from muriatic (hydrochloric) acid (HCl) and pyrolusite (MnO_2); it was then known as dephlogisticated muriatic acid. C. L. Berthellot, believing that the muriatic acid had combined with the oxygen from the pyrolusite, called it oxymuriatic acid. Because he was unable to decompose it, H. Davy (1810) contended that the so-called oxymuriatic acid was an element and showed further that muriatic acid itself contains only hydrogen and the new element, chlorine. Hence in its reaction with pyrolusite, muriatic acid loses hydrogen rather than gains oxygen. Davy's views eventually prevailed, chlorine was accepted as an element, and Antoine Lavoisier's theory that all acids contain oxygen was discarded. The name "chlorine" is taken from the greenish-yellow (Greek χλωρός) colour of the gas.

Chlorine is never found uncombined in nature. Estimated to account for 0.15% of the earth's crust, it occurs most abundantly in soluble chlorides, such as sodium chloride in salt water and rock salt, and in smaller quantities in such insoluble materials as horn silver (AgCl). Chlorine as chloride is an essential constituent of animal life.

Preparation.—The element may be prepared on a laboratory scale by treatment of hydrochloric acid, or any soluble chloride in acid solution, with strong oxidizing agents such as manganese dioxide, potassium permanganate or potassium dichromate. Concentrated sulphuric acid, however, will not liberate chlorine. The essential change in the preparation of the element from chloride is the removal of an electron from the chloride ion, $2\bar{C}l \rightarrow Cl_2 + 2e$. Chlorine may also be prepared by the reaction of a hypochlorite with an acid. Since chlorine is readily available in cylinders of various sizes, preparation in the laboratory is of little practical importance. (For the preparation of chlorine on a large scale, *see* section *In Industry*, below.)

Physical Properties.—Chlorine, having an atomic weight of 35.457, is a mixture of two isotopes of weights 35 and 37, 24.6% of its atoms being the heavier isotope. The radioactive isotopes Cl_{33}, half life 2.4 sec.; Cl^{34}, half life 33 min.; Cl^{36}, half life $>10^3$ years; and Cl^{38}, half life 37 min., have been made artificially. All atoms have the electron configuration: $1s^2$, $2s^2$, $2p^6$, $3s^2$, $3p^5$. The atom has a high affinity, 3.75 ev, for an additional electron, the acquisition of which gives it a complete external octet and a charge of -1 as chloride ion. The chloride ion in crystals has a radius of 1.81 Å. Elementary chlorine in the vapour state consists of diatomic molecules, of molecular weight 70.91. The density of the gas at 0° C. and 1 atm. is 3.214 g. per litre, 1.6% greater than the density corresponding to a molecular weight of 70.91. At 1,000° C. less than 0.01% of the molecules dissociate. Chlorine boils at -34.7° C. at 1 atm., freezes at -102° C., its critical temperature is 184° C., critical pressure 76.1 atm. and critical density 0.573 g./ml. The vapour pressure of liquid chlorine in atmosphere at T° Kelvin is $\log P = -1{,}499.5/T - 4.022 \log T + 15.844$. The heat of fusion of chlorine is 22.9 cal./g., the heat of vaporization 62.2 cal./g. The heat capacity of chlorine gas at constant pressure is 0.226 cal./g. at room temperature, $8.28+0.56\times10^{-3}T$ cal./mol. at T° K. and of liquid chlorine 16 cal./mol. The entropy at 298.1° K. is 53.31 cal./mol./degree. The gas is moderately soluble in water, at 20° C. to the extent of 0.09 mol./litre at 1 atm.

FIG. 1.—CYLINDRICAL DIAPHRAGM CELL

Hydrogen is set free at the perforated cathode as the brine percolates through it, leaving caustic soda in solution. The chlorine is set free at the carbon anodes

Chemical Properties.—Chlorine is a member of Group VII of the periodic system. While it is essentially an electronegative element, tending to go to the chloride ion of oxidation state -1, chlorine is also known in the $+1$, $+3$, $+4$, $+5$ and $+7$ states of oxidation. Chlorine combines directly with all but a few elements; oxygen, fluorine, nitrogen, carbon and the inert gases being exceptions. The binary compounds thus formed are called chlorides (*see* HYDROCHLORIC ACID AND HYDROGEN CHLORIDE). Many of these reactions occur at room temperature; *e.g.*, with powdered antimony $2Sb+3Cl_2=2SbCl_3$. If free from moisture, chlorine is much less reactive, and higher temperatures are required for reaction, thus permitting the storage of dry liquid chlorine in steel cylinders. Chlorine reacts at high temperatures with certain oxides in the presence of carbon to form chlorides; *e.g.*,

$$Al_2O_3+3Cl_2+3C=2AlCl_3+3CO.$$

With water at 0° C., chlorine forms a crystalline hydrate, $Cl_2.8H_2O$, which decomposes on warming. This compound is of historical interest for, while experimenting with the hydrate, Michael Faraday in 1823 discovered that chlorine became liquid under pressure at low temperatures and later succeeded in liquefying a number of other substances which were previously known only in the gaseous state. A solution of chlorine in water contains a small amount of hydrochloric and hypochlorous acid because of the reversible reaction,

$$Cl_2+H_2O=H^++\bar{C}l+HOCl,$$

$K=4.8\times10^{-4}$ at 25° C. Since the hypochlorous acid slowly loses its oxygen, the solution of chlorine in water is unstable, the chlorine eventually being all transformed to hydrochloric acid. Chlorine is readily absorbed in basic solutions, for the neutralization of the hydrochloric and hypochlorous acids prevents equilibrium being established. The reaction at room temperatures may be represented by

$$Cl_2+2O\bar{H}=\bar{C}l+O\bar{C}l+H_2O,$$

thus producing a mixture of chloride and hypochlorite (*see* BLEACHING POWDER). In hot concentrated alkali, chlorine forms chloride and chlorate,

$$3Cl_2+6O\bar{H}=5\bar{C}l+\bar{C}lO_3+3H_2O.$$

Chlorine is a strong oxidizing agent. In aqueous solution the electrode potential

$$\tfrac{1}{2}Cl_2(g)+e=\bar{C}l$$

is 1.358 v. at 25° C. Hence chlorine displaces bromine and iodine, which have lower potentials, from bromides and iodides. In aqueous solution chlorine oxidizes and is itself reduced to chloride by such ions as sulphide, thiosulphate, sulphite, ferrous and stannous. Chlorine combines with carbon monoxide to form carbonyl chloride (phosgene), $COCl_2$; with sulphur dioxide to form sulphuryl chloride, SO_2Cl_2; and with nitric oxide to form nitrosyl chloride, NOCl. Many organic compounds are chlorinated by chlorine. Hydrocarbons react with chlorine, by addition of chlorine to double bonds, or substitution of hydrogen by chlorine. In some cases, as with turpentine, the reaction is violent, all the hydrogen is removed as hydrogen chloride, and a residue of carbon is left.

Chlorine is an active poison and was the first gas used in chemical warfare in World War I. It causes suffocation, constriction in the chest, tightness in the throat and oedema of the lungs after severe exposure. As little as 2.5 mg. per litre in the atmosphere causes death in a few minutes, but less than 0.0001% by volume may be tolerated for several hours. Its strong odour, however, gives warning of its presence at much lower concentrations than are dangerous.

Oxides of Chlorine.—Four oxides, chlorine monoxide (Cl_2O), chlorine dioxide (ClO_2), chlorine hexoxide (Cl_2O_6) and chlorine heptoxide (Cl_2O_7), are known. ClO_4 or Cl_2O_8 has been made in solution by the reaction of iodine with silver perchlorate dissolved in benzene. All the oxides are unstable and reactive and cannot be produced by direct synthesis. Chlorine monoxide is made by the reaction of chlorine with mercuric oxide,

$$HgO+2Cl_2=HgCl_2+Cl_2O.$$

In an industrial process chlorine monoxide is formed by the reaction of chlorine on solid sodium bicarbonate,

$$2Cl_2+2NaHCO_3=Cl_2O+2NaCl+2CO_2+H_2O.$$

It is slightly darker yellow than chlorine, condensing to a liquid at 2° C. and solidifying at -116° C. Chlorine monoxide is the anhydride of hypochlorous acid, readily dissolving in water to form the acid,

$$Cl_2O+H_2O=2HClO.$$

Chlorine dioxide is formed by the action of strong acids on chlorates, best with oxalic acid,

$$2KClO_3+3H_2C_2O_4=2ClO_2+2H_2O+2CO_2+2KHC_2O_4.$$

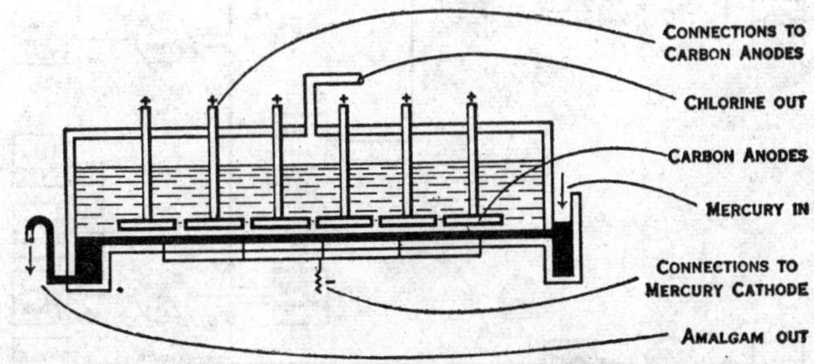

FIG. 2.—PRINCIPLES OF A MERCURY CELL

Mercury enters the cell at one end, propelled by a mechanical device. Brine flows through the cell in the same direction as the mercury (entrance and exit not shown). The mercury-sodium amalgam formed by the electrolysis leaves the cell and travels to a separate chamber in which it is brought into contact with water. After extraction of the sodium, the mercury returns to the cell and repeats the cycle

In the industrial preparation of sodium chlorite, chlorine dioxide is first formed by the reaction of hydrochloric acid on calcium chlorate,

$$Ca(ClO_3)_2+4HCl=CaCl_2+2ClO_2+Cl_2+2H_2O,$$

the accompanying chlorine being removed by absorption on lime.

Chlorine dioxide decomposes explosively to Cl_2+O_2. It is a gas with a much stronger yellow colour than chlorine, liquefying at 10° C. and solidifying at −76° C. It is not an acid anhydride, hardly reacting with water and but slowly with alkalies to give a mixture of chlorite and chlorate. Chlorine hexoxide, formed by the action of light or ozone on chlorine dioxide, is a red oil, freezing at −1° C., decomposing slowly at higher temperatures. Chlorine heptoxide, the anhydride of perchloric acid, is formed by removal of water from that acid by phosphorus pentoxide. It is a colourless liquid boiling at 80° C. and freezing at −91.5° C. It explodes with shock.

Hypochlorous Acid and Hypochlorites.—In these compounds chlorine exists in the +1 state of oxidation. Hypochlorous acid, HOCl, is quite weak, $K=4\times10^{-8}$ at 25° C., and unstable, decomposing to hydrochloric acid and oxygen. The hypochlorite ion is stable in alkaline solution. Hypochlorites are formed in solution by the neutralization of hypochlorous acid or by the absorption of chlorine monoxide or chlorine by alkaline solutions. If chlorine is employed an equivalent amount of chloride is formed along with the hypochlorite. Because of the weakness of hypochlorous acid, hypochlorites are considerably hydrolyzed and preparation of the pure salts is difficult. Only a hydrated calcium hypochlorite, $Ca(OCl)_2.2H_2O$, is available in solid form, although solid sodium hypochlorite has been prepared. Sodium and calcium hypochlorite are widely used in bleaching and disinfecting, their effectiveness being attributed to their oxidizing powers. They are also effective oxidizing agents in preparative chemistry, lead dioxide for example being formed from lead acetate by the action of sodium or calcium hypochlorite in basic solution.

Chlorous Acid and Chlorites.—Salts of chlorous acid, $HClO_2$, are called chlorites and contain the ion $\bar{Cl}O_2$, in which chlorine is in the +3 oxidation state. Sodium chlorite is made by passing chlorine dioxide into alkaline solution containing carboniferous material,

$$4ClO_2+4NaOH+Ca(OH)_2+C=4NaClO_2+CaCO_3+3H_2O.$$

Chlorites are generally soluble and stable in alkaline solution. Chlorous acid, although somewhat stronger than hypochlorous acid, is much less stable, and on acidifying a solution containing a chlorite, decomposition to ClO_2 occurs rapidly. Sodium chlorite is employed in bleaching.

Chlorates and Chloric Acid.—Chlorine in the +5 oxidation state occurs in chloric acid and its salts the chlorates. Chlorates

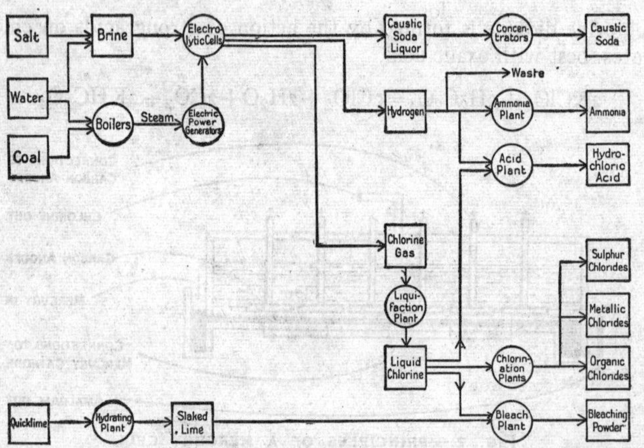

FIG. 3.—THE MANUFACTURE OF CHLORINE AND ITS DERIVATIVES

The diagram shows, from left to right the manufacture of chlorine from salt, water and coal, the principal industrial compounds formed and the commercial utilization of the by-products

are formed in solution by the reaction of chlorine with hot alkalies, or on mixing, at the proper temperature, the anode and cathode solutions resulting from electrolysis of sodium chloride solution. The chlorate is generally separated from the accompanying chloride by crystallization of the potassium salt which is only moderately soluble, but other chlorates may be made by either of these methods. A solution of chloric acid ($HClO_3$) may be prepared by adding sulphuric acid to a solution of barium chlorate and filtering to remove the precipitated barium sulphate. By evacuating at room temperature the solution may be concentrated to about 50% $HClO_3$, but in more concentrated solution decomposition is rapid. Chloric acid is a strong acid, hence chlorates are not hydrolyzed in solution. Chlorate ion is stable in neutral or basic solution, but in acid solution chlorates are readily reduced to chloride by such reagents as sulphur dioxide. Potassium chlorate, a white crystalline material melting at 350° C., is unstable with respect to the decomposition $2KClO_3=2KCl+3O_2$, and other chlorates decompose similarly. This reaction is highly exothermic and irreversible, but the decomposition is relatively slow below 400° C. It is markedly susceptible to catalysts; a mixture of potassium chlorate and manganese dioxide decomposes smoothly at moderate temperatures and serves as a source of small amounts of oxygen in the laboratory. A mixture of potassium chlorate and a reducing material such as charcoal or sulphur is dangerously explosive. Because they serve as a concentrated source of oxygen, chlorates are employed in fireworks, matches, etc. Potassium chlorate is claimed to be an effective antiseptic in the treatment of ulcers of the mouth, but in larger quantities is definitely poisonous. Sodium chlorate is sold commercially for use as a weed killer.

Perchlorates and Perchloric Acid.—In these compounds chlorine is in its highest oxidation state, +7. Potassium perchlorate may be made by carefully heating the chlorate,

$$4KClO_3=3KClO_4+KCl,$$

and separating the perchlorate, which is less soluble than either the chloride or chlorate, by crystallization. Commercially, however, it is made by electrolysis of chlorate solutions at high current density. The perchlorates in general are soluble, their solutions are stable, and even in strongly acid solution are reduced with difficulty. A perchlorate may be distinguished from a chlorate by treating in acid solution with sulphur dioxide, which reduces the latter readily but does not affect the perchlorate. Barium and magnesium perchlorates form stable hydrates and are employed as drying agents to remove moisture from gases. Perchloric acid is made by treatment of potassium perchlorate with sulphuric acid and separation of the perchloric acid by vacuum distillation. While perchloric acid is much more stable than chloric acid, the pure acid decomposes slowly at 92° C. At ordinary temperatures perchloric acid is a liquid with a strong affinity for water. It forms a stable hydrate, $HClO_4.H_2O$, which is a solid below 50° C. although the anhydrous acid only freezes at −112° C. It is commonly sold in 60% solution and finds application in analytical chemistry. It is one of the strongest acids. The concentrated acid is a powerful oxidizing agent and in contact with reducing materials violently explosive, as are the solid perchlorates at higher temperatures. Solid perchlorates lose oxygen on heating as do the chlorates but are somewhat more stable. They may be used in place of chlorates in explosives and fireworks, as they are considered safer to handle.

IN INDUSTRY

Almost since its discovery chlorine has been produced on a large scale for use in industry. The long-obsolete Weldon process was first employed, making use of the reaction of hydrochloric acid with manganese dioxide,

$$MnO_2+4HCl=Cl_2+MnCl_2+2H_2O,$$

by which K. W. Scheele first discovered chlorine. At best, only about one-third of the hydrochloric acid is transformed to chlorine in the process, and the lack of materials in which these corrosive substances could be handled made the Weldon process difficult and expensive. About 1868 Henry Deacon developed a process by which chlorine was made by the reaction of hydrogen chloride gas and atmospheric oxygen. The reaction employed,

$$4HCl+O_2=2Cl_2+2H_2O,$$

is reversible and incomplete. The rate of reaction was found to be satisfactory when the gases were passed over pumice in contact with cupric chloride, a catalyst, at about 430° C. Under these

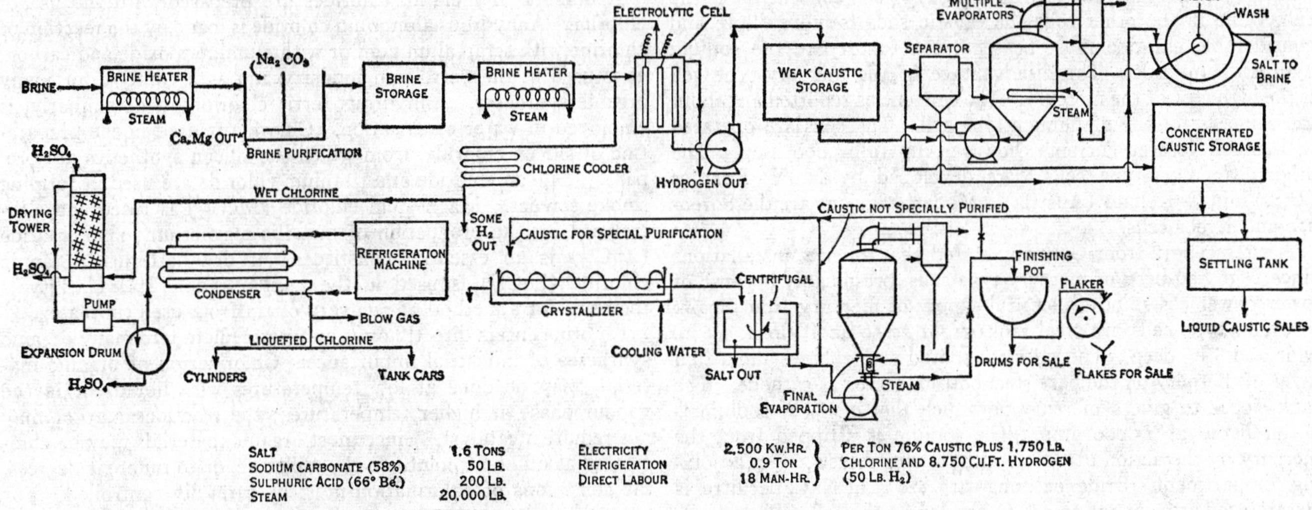

FROM C. L. MANTELL IN "CHEMICAL AND METALLURGICAL ENGINEERING"

FIG. 4.—ELECTROLYTIC CAUSTIC SODA AND CHLORINE

Flow sheet showing the several stages from brine, the raw material, to caustic soda and chlorine, the products

conditions about 70% of the hydrogen chloride could be converted to chlorine. The hydrogen chloride required in the Deacon process was largely a by-product of the LeBlanc soda process (*see* ALKALI MANUFACTURE). With the decline of the latter, the Deacon process was abandoned, and electrolytic methods became the sole source of industrial chlorine.

Electrolytic chlorine was first produced successfully on a commercial scale about 1890. The following half century saw an enormous increase in the amount of chlorine produced. Technical improvements greatly increased the efficiency of production, but the process remained basically unchanged. The raw materials are salt (NaCl) and water; the products chlorine, sodium hydroxide (alkali or caustic soda) and hydrogen. The change which is brought about by electrical energy may be represented by

$$\underset{\text{salt}}{2NaCl} + \underset{\text{water}}{2H_2O} = \underset{\text{chlorine}}{Cl_2} + \underset{\text{sodium hydroxide}}{2NaOH} + \underset{\text{hydrogen}}{H_2}$$

Although the electrolysis of salt produces equivalent amounts of both chlorine and caustic soda, the chlorine is regarded as the primary product and the caustic soda a by-product because, without a market for chlorine, the caustic soda so produced cannot compete economically with caustic from the ammonia-soda process.

Two distinct types of cell are employed, the diaphragm cell (fig. 1) and the mercury cell (fig. 2). In both, the electrolyte is a strong solution of salt (brine). Calcium and magnesium ions are precipitated from the brine before it enters the cell by addition of sodium carbonate, since these ions would otherwise precipitate in the cell and interfere with its operation. Both types employ graphite anodes but differ in the cathode material. Iron cathodes are generally used with the diaphragm-type cell, while a mercury cathode is the distinct feature of the mercury-type cell. In electrolysis of sodium chloride solution, the reaction at a graphite anode is the liberation of chlorine gas,

$$2\overline{Cl} = Cl_2 \stackrel{+}{+} 2e.$$

Small amounts of oxygen usually accompany the chlorine, thus reducing the efficiency of operation (*see* ELECTROCHEMISTRY). At an iron cathode, hydrogen is discharged. Discharge of sodium does not occur in the presence of water, for the potential required to discharge sodium is much greater than that at which hydrogen is set free. The hydrogen comes from the water, leaving hydroxyl ion in solution,

$$H_2O + 2e = H_2 + 2\overline{O}H.$$

The cathode and anode solutions must be kept separate for, with chlorine formed at the anode and sodium hydroxide at the cathode, mixing of the solutions would result in the formation of hypochlorite instead of evolution of chlorine. The diaphragm, commonly made of asbestos paper, serves this purpose. The diaphragm is adjacent to, and supported by, the cathode. Later practice favoured the nonsubmerged diaphragm, where the brine seeps through the diaphragm and is electrolyzed, and the alkaline solution trickles to the bottom of the cell. The cathode liquors average 110 to 120 g. NaOH per litre and 140 to 170 g. NaCl per litre. An outlet above the cathode allows the hydrogen to escape or to be collected. The anode section generally has a concrete cover with an opening for collection of the chlorine. Some of the diaphragm-type cells in common use at mid-20th century were the rectangular Allen-Moore and Hooker type S (U.S.), the Hargreaves-Bird (British), Krebs (French), Billiter (German) and the cylindrical Vorce (U.S.). The bell jar cell, without diaphragm and with a slowly streaming electrolyte, has been employed in Europe.

Factors influencing the design of cells are the initial cost, life period, purity of product and efficiency with which electrical energy is utilized. Theoretically, the decomposition of aqueous sodium chloride solution requires about 2.2 v., but in operation the voltage drop per cell is found to be from 3.3 to 4.5 v. Hence, although the current efficiency in the modern cell is more than 90%, the energy efficiency is only 50%–60%. The excess voltage required results from energy lost as heat because of the resistance of the electrolyte, which may be minimized by having large electrodes close together, and to overvoltage effects at the electrodes. The overvoltage is largely a property of the electrode material, in the choice of which resistance to chemical action and cost must be considered. The commoner types of cell operate at 1,000–5,000 amp., but the current density in amperes per square inch of electrode surface is only 0.12–0.50. An average yield per kilowatt hour is about two-thirds pound of chlorine and the same weight of sodium hydroxide. The different types of cell vary considerably in size, from the cylindrical Vorce cell, only 26 in. in diameter, to the Billiter cell, 18 ft. long, 10 in. wide and 2 ft. deep.

The operation of the diaphragm-type cell is accompanied by decreased efficiency because of the clogging of the diaphragm, which must be renewed at intervals of from one month to a year, varying with the different types of cell. In the Hargreaves-Bird cell, steam and carbon dioxide enter the cathode compartment, changing the sodium hydroxide to sodium carbonate. The diaphragm in this cell has a long life which is attributed to the action of the steam.

In the mercury-type cell sodium is discharged into the mercury cathode at the bottom of the cell, and no hydrogen is evolved. Mechanical agitation moves the amalgamated mercury to a separate compartment of the cell where it is made the anode, causing the sodium to go back into solution as sodium hydroxide, while hydrogen is discharged from an ion cathode above. The over-all reaction is the same as with the ion cathode-type cell. The advantage of the mercury-type cell is that the caustic soda solution is free from chloride and may be produced at as high as 50% concentrate in the cell, while in the other cells the caustic soda is more dilute and considerable chloride must be separated to prepare the sodium hydroxide for sale. The disadvantage of the mercury-type cell is the high cost of the mercury. The efficiencies reported are about the same as for the diaphragm-type cell. The cells are operated with much greater currents, however, up to 15,000 amp. The original mercury-type cells were developed by H. Y. Kastner (U.S.) and C. Kellner (Austria). Modern versions are the Sorenson and Krebs cells.

A 1945 report from Germany stated that all new installations since 1936 had been of mercury-type cells, presumably because of lower power costs and a plentiful supply of mercury from Spain. The new-type cells are steel tanks from 20 to 40 ft. long, 25 in. wide and 8 in. deep. The sides are coated with rubber, and a thin layer of mercury on the bare steel bottom serves as cathode. The tank slopes to give a mercury flow such that 0.2% of sodium is accumulated at 15,000 amp. The sodium is stripped from the mercury by the action of water, without electrolysis, in an adjoining compartment. Brine, entering with 310 g. of NaCl per litre, is electrolyzed at from 70° to 90° C. and leaves the cell with 220–270 g. of salt per litre. The loss of mercury is reported to be from 1% to 7% per year.

Chlorine from the cells is freed from moisture by the action of concentrated sulphuric acid, cooled and liquefied by compression. The liquefied chlorine is sold in steel cylinders and tank cars. The large chlorine-caustic soda plants are generally located at points where both salt and electrical power are cheapest. However, some paper mills and rayon manufacturers, which are large users of both chlorine and caustic soda, run their own electrolytic plants. In this case the chlorine need not be liquefied and may be piped directly to the point of use. Chlorine produced as a by-product of the preparation of metallic sodium by the electrolysis of fused sodium chloride is a minor source of chlorine for industry.

Uses.—Originally the only large consumers of chlorine were the paper and textile industries, and most of the chlorine produced was consumed in the manufacture of bleaching powder for their uses. (*See* BLEACHING; BLEACHING POWDER.) Early in the 20th century began the shipment and use of liquid chlorine, which could be used directly in bleaching, and the proportion used in the manufacture of bleaching powder declined. Chlorine is an effective germicide, and chlorination of municipal water supplies has become general. In some instances chlorine is used to disinfect sewage. The rise of the rayon industry, which employs chlorine for the bleaching of pulp, provided a major outlet for industrial chlorine. Although the amount of chlorine employed for bleaching and disinfecting was undoubtedly increasing, the fraction of the total chlorine production going into this field was declining because of the tremendous increase in the amount of chlorine consumed by the chemical industry.

Chlorine has become widely used in the production of both organic and inorganic chemicals (fig. 3). Chlorine reacts with carbon disulphide to form carbon tetrachloride and sulphur chloride,

$$CS_2+3Cl_2=CCl_4+S_2Cl_2.$$

Carbon tetrachloride is largely used as a solvent, in fire extinguishers and in dry cleaning. Sulphur chloride, also made by combining sulphur and chlorine, is used in the vulcanization of rubber and as a chlorinating agent in organic syntheses. Sulphur chloride was used in the preparation of mustard gas, an important chemical warfare agent in World War I. Another important chlorinating agent, thionyl chloride ($SOCl_2$), is made by the reaction of chlorine, sulphuric acid and sulphur chloride. Thionyl chloride is used to form the acid chlorides of organic acids, which are valuable intermediates in organic syntheses. Chlorine combines with phosphorus to form phosphorus trichloride (PCl_3), which may be oxidized by potassium chlorate to phosphorus oxychloride ($POCl_3$), which is another useful chlorinating agent in forming acid chlorides from organic acids. Chlorine and carbon monoxide form carbonyl chloride, or phosgene ($COCl_2$), which has been employed in chemical warfare and is also used in metallurgy to transform certain oxides to chlorides.

A number of metallic chlorides are prepared with the use of chlorine. Anhydrous aluminum chloride is made by the reaction of chlorine with scrap aluminum or with aluminum oxide and carbon. It is used in the petroleum industry and as a catalyst for many organic syntheses. Anhydrous ferric chloride, made similarly, is employed in water clarification. Chlorine is used in the preparation of silicon chloride, from which the silicon synthetics are prepared. Silicon chloride and titanium chloride are used in forming smoke screens. Magnesium chloride ($MgCl_2$) is fused and electrolyzed for the production of metallic magnesium; zinc chloride ($ZnCl_2$) is an essential constituent of dry batteries. Stannic chloride ($SnCl_4$) is used in the textile trade. Its volatility is the basis for a method of recovery of tin from used tin plate.

Chlorine enters directly or as an intermediate into many organic syntheses of industrial importance. Chlorination of organic materials may be done at low temperatures with liquids or in the vapour phase at higher temperatures; the reactions may or may not require a catalyst. Since most organic materials may be chlorinated at different points on the molecule, or to different degrees, the conditions of chlorination must be carefully controlled. For example, the chlorination of a compound containing a benzene nucleus with an aliphatic side chain occurs in the benzene nucleus when the temperature is low in the presence of certain catalysts, but in the side chain at elevated temperatures or in the presence of sunlight.

Of the chlorinated derivatives of methane (CH_4), carbon tetrachloride (CCl_4) has been mentioned. Chloroform ($CHCl_3$) is used as a solvent and in medicine. Methyl chloride (CH_3Cl) is used as a refrigerant. Dichlor-difluoro-methane (CCl_2F_2), known as freon, is used as a household refrigerant. Ethyl chloride (C_2H_5Cl), a derivative of ethane (C_2H_6), is used in the production of lead tetraethyl. Unsaturated hydrocarbons, such as acetylene, combine directly with chlorine to form liquids such as acetylene tetrachloride ($CHCl_2$-$CHCl_2$) which are largely used as solvents and in dry cleaning.

Chlorinated aromatics serve as intermediates in the dye industry. Chlorobenzene (C_6H_5Cl) is hydrolyzed to produce phenol (C_6H_5OH). The insecticide DDT is dichloro-diphenyl-trichloroethane, $(Cl.C_6H_4)_2CH$-CCl_3. Paradichlorobenzene ($C_6H_4Cl_2$) is used as a moth repellent. Chlorine is an essential raw material in manufacture of many plastics, nylon and synthetic rubber.

BIBLIOGRAPHY.—F. Ephraim, *Inorganic Chemistry,* 3rd ed. by P. C. L. Thorne and A. M. Ward (New York, London, 1939); L. Gmelin, *Handbuch der anorganischen Chemie,* 8th ed. (Berlin, 1927); J. W. Mellor, *Comprehensive Treatise on Inorganic and Theoretical Chemistry,* vol. ii (New York, 1927); F. Ullmann, *Enzyklopädie der technischen Chemie,* 2nd ed. (Berlin, 1930); C. L. Mantell, *Industrial Electrochemistry,* 2nd ed. (New York, 1940). (R. P. S.)

CHLORITE, a group of green micaceous minerals which are hydrous silicates of aluminum, magnesium and ferrous iron. The name was given by A. G. Werner in 1798, from χλωρῖτις, "a green stone." Several species and many rather ill-defined varieties have been described, but they are difficult to recognize. Like the micas, the chlorites (or hydromicas) are monoclinic in crystallization and have a perfect cleavage parallel to the flat face of the scales and plates. The cleavage, however, is not quite so prominent as in the micas, and the cleavage flakes though pliable are not elastic.

The chlorites usually occur as soft (H. = 2–3), scaly aggregates of a dark-green colour. They vary in specific gravity between 2.6 and 3.0, according to the amount of iron present. Well-developed crystals are met with only in the species clinochlore and penninite; those of the former are six-sided plates and are optically biaxial, while those of the latter have the form of acute rhombohedra and are usually optically uniaxial. The species prochlorite and corundophilite also occur as more or less distinct six-sided plates. These four better-crystallized species were grouped together by G. Tschermak as orthochlorites, the finely scaly and indistinctly fibrous forms being grouped by the same author as leptochlorites.

Chemically, the chlorites are distinguished from the micas by the presence of a considerable amount of water (about 13%) and by not containing alkalies; from the soft, scaly, mineral talc they differ in containing aluminum (about 20%) as an essential constituent. The magnesia (up to 36%) is often in part replaced by ferrous oxide (up to 30%), and the alumina to a lesser extent by ferric oxide; alumina may also be partly replaced by chromic oxide, as in the rose-red varieties kämmererite and kotschubeite.

The chlorites usually occur as alteration products of other minerals, such as pyroxene, amphibole, biotite, garnet, etc., often occurring as pseudomorphs after these, or as earthy material filling cavities in igneous rocks composed of these minerals. Many altered igneous rocks owe their green colour to the presence of secondary chlorite. Chlorite is also an important constituent of many schistose rocks and phyllites, and of chlorite-schist it is the only essential constituent. (L. J. S.)

CHLOROFORM (Trichloromethane, $CHCl_3$) is the most potent and most rapidly acting of the volatile anaesthetics. It is a clear, colourless, noninflammable, sweet-smelling fluid with a pleasant but burning taste; molecular weight 119.5; boiling point 61° C. (142° F.), specific gravity of the fluid 1.476 and specific gravity of the vapour 4.1. It is manufactured by chlorination of alcohol or acetone in an alkaline solution. When heated in air or exposed to light it can eventually form phosgene ($COCl_2$), a poisonous gas, and it is decomposed by alkali to formate, a relatively harmless salt. Chloroform dissolves in 210 volumes of water, and it is miscible with alcohol, ether, benzene and with fixed and volatile oils.

It was prepared in 1831 simultaneously by Samuel Guthrie in the United States, J. von Liebig in Germany and E. Soubeiran in France. Sir James Young Simpson of Edinburgh first used it as an anaesthetic in 1847. Chloroform anaesthesia was used extensively, particularly in obstetrics, but fell into disrepute because of its dangers. Because of its extreme potency overdosage may easily occur, resulting in damage to the heart (depression of the myocardium, arrythmia, tachycardia, ventricular fibrillation) and to the liver (immediate or delayed degeneration). The blood pressure may fall because of decreased tone in the peripheral blood vessels. It is more often administered by dropping it upon an open mask or by blowing the vapour into the airway.

R. Waters *et al.* re-evaluated chloroform anaesthesia and showed that the toxicity of chloroform relative to the anaesthetic dose is not greater than that of most other anaesthetics, though overdose and sudden changes in concentration are more difficult to avoid because of its potency. Inadequate oxygenation and accumulation of carbon dioxide caused either by depression of the respiration or rebreathing of the same atmosphere under the mask are responsible for the majority of complications.

Correctly used there still remained indications for chloroform anaesthesia; *e.g.*, in obstetrics, in warm climates and in circumstances where there would be a danger of explosion from other anaesthetics. Where high temperature would evaporate ether too rapidly, chloroform is more useful because of its higher boiling point. A patient anaesthetized with chloroform recovers in ½ hour to 2 hours.

About 90% of the agent in the body is exhaled through the lungs while the rest is excreted in the urine and faeces.

In anaesthetic concentrations the vapour is not irritating to the respiratory tract. Liquid chloroform is used as a counterirritant or rubefacient in a number of liniments and ointments. Chloroform water U.S.P. is frequently used as a constituent of cough medicines and sedatives and as a carminative. In instances where a higher concentration of chloroform is desired, chloroform spirit N.F. is useful (85% to 91% alcohol by volume). (D. W. B.)

CHLOROMYCETIN (chemical name Chloramphenicol) is an antibiotic substance originally obtained from cultures of the actinomycete *Streptomyces venezuelae* and used in the treatment of many infectious diseases. It was the first of the broad-spectrum antibiotics to be reported, being characterized and identified by Paul R. Burkholder in 1947.

Chemical synthesis of the substance was reported in 1950, at which time the official name "chloramphenicol" was applied to the compound.

Chloromycetin has been found to be effective against a wide variety of infectious agents, including both gram-negative and gram-positive bacteria, certain rickettsiae, spirochaetes and viruses. It acts to inhibit the growth and multiplication of the microorganisms sensitive to it. Chloromycetin usually is given orally and is rapidly absorbed from the gastrointestinal tract, diffusing readily into the body tissues and fluids.

Gastrointestinal disturbances and diarrhoea are not commonly seen following the administration of chloromycetin, and, because of the rapid inactivation of the antibiotic in the digestive tract, little inhibition of the normal bacterial flora of the large bowel is observed.

In rare instances, the administration of chloromycetin has been complicated by the development of an aplastic anaemia due to depression of the bone marrow by the drug.

See H. Welch and C. N. Lewis, *Antibiotic Therapy* (Washington, 1951; London, 1952). (T. W. L.)

CHLOROPHYLL, CHEMISTRY OF. The green pigment which is present in leaves and algae is known as chlorophyll. Attempts to prepare the colouring matter of leaves in a pure form have shown that it is not homogeneous. R. Willstätter was able to separate it into four components: two green ones, chlorophylls *a* and *b* ($C_{55}H_{72}O_5N_4Mg$ and $C_{55}H_{70}O_6N_4Mg$); and two yellow ones, carotene ($C_{40}H_{56}$) and xanthophyll ($C_{40}H_{56}O_2$). At the same time, he found that the ratio of the blue-green chlorophyll *a* to the yellow-green chlorophyll *b* is 3:1, while that of xanthophyll to carotene is 2:1. The proportion of chlorophyll *a*+*b* to xanthophyll+carotene is about 3:1.

Later work (V. Lubimenko, 1921; A. Stoll and E. Wiedemann, 1938) showed that these pigments are not present in the leaf in the free state but are combined with a protein in the form of chloroplastin. Consequently, they pass into ether from an aqueous solution of the leaf pigment only after splitting the organic complex (called "symplex" by Willstätter, 1934). Chloroplastin is decomposed not only by high concentrations of salt but also by the presence of alcohol or acetone, so that the normal extraction process using these solvents liberates the individual pigments.

The separation of the carotenoids and the chlorophylls is achieved by distribution between suitable solvents, according to the method of Willstätter and Stoll (1913). Later, the technique of chromatographic analysis was employed to prepare the components in a pure state and to test their homogeneity. This led to preparations which careful spectrographic analyses proved to be of uniform composition (A. Winterstein and G. Stein, 1934; G. Mackinney, 1940–42; F. P. Zscheile, 1934–43). The pure chlorophylls are dark-green amorphous waxes; crystalline derivatives can be obtained only by degradation and elimination of the phytol. The methods employed for the identification of the chlorophylls and for their quantitative determination are based upon characteristic absorption and fluorescence spectra (C. Dhéré and O. Biermacher, 1914–36; A. Hagenbach, F. Auerbacher and E. Wiedemann, 1936; A. Stern and co-workers, 1936–38; F. P. Zscheile and D. G. Harris, 1943). In ether solution the absorption maxima correspond to the following wave lengths (A. Winterstein and G. Stein, 1933):

chlorophyll *a*: 663 623 607 577 534 507 494 432 mμ
chlorophyll *b*: 644 614 594 567 542 503 456

The connection between fluorescence and the part played by chlorophyll in photosynthesis has been thoroughly investigated (J. Franck, 1935–42; A. Kautsky, 1932–39; E. W. McAlister, 1937–41; E. C. Wassink, 1937–46).

The essential chemical properties of the chlorophylls and their most important derivatives will be discussed in relation to the formula depicted for chlorophyll *a*. The characteristic features of the structure of chlorophyll are the porphin system, the magnesium atom with its complex linkage, and the phytyl radical (R. Willstätter and A. Stoll, 1913).

The components of the porphin system were ascertained by Willstätter (1904–12) when he carried out his first work on the degradation of the chlorophylls. The nature of the 16-membered ring system, composed of four pyrrole rings linked by methine bridges (α-δ), was then elucidated by H. Fischer (1915–30), who confirmed the formula suggested by W. Kuester in 1912 for haemin. The stage of hydrogenation of the chlorophyll nucleus

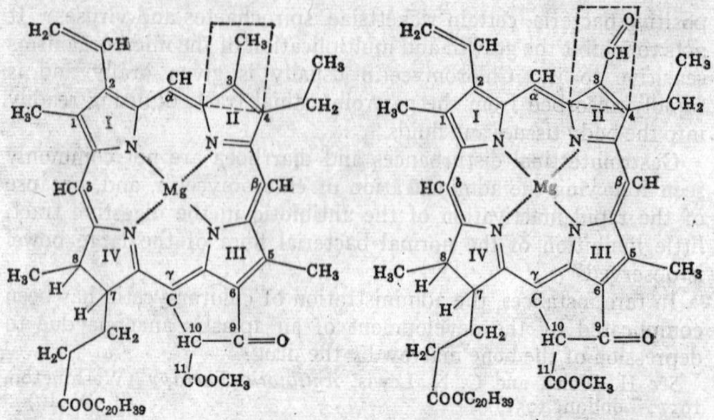

CHLOROPHYLL *a* AND CHLOROPHYLL *b*. THE DIFFERENCE IN THE TWO STRUCTURES IS INDICATED BY THE AREAS WITHIN THE DOTTED LINES

is that of the phorbins; *i.e.*, dihydroporphyrins. The chlorophylls therefore contain two hydrogen atoms more than the porphyrins, which possess the maximum possible number of double bonds in the ring system.

The structure of the porphin system and of the individual substituents was established by H. Fischer by degradation reactions and by the syntheses of numerous porphyrins, including most of those obtained by degradation of chlorophylls.

The discovery that magnesium, bound in the form of a metallic complex, forms an essential component of the molecules of the natural chlorophylls caused great surprise at the time (R. Willstätter, 1904), and this type of magnesium linkage remained unique. It may be that the magnesium has a share in the part played by chlorophyll in the assimilation process. The magnesium atom also constitutes a characteristic difference between the chlorophylls and the blood pigment haemin, which is an iron complex but otherwise possesses a similar structure, including a porphyrin system whose substituents agree closely with those of the chlorophyll porphyrins. On treating the chlorophylls with acids, the magnesium atom is easily split off, the colour then changing from pure green to brownish green. The magnesium can be replaced by copper, zinc or other metals. The corresponding copper complexes are stable and are used as industrial pigments; *e.g.*, in the soap and cosmetic industries.

The structure of the simple unsaturated alcohol phytol, $C_{20}H_{40}O$, was elucidated by F. G. Fischer (1928) by total synthesis, which showed it to be an isoprene derivative. It was subsequently demonstrated that phytol, as a structural component of vitamins E and K_1, is connected with special physiological functions:

$$H_3C{-}\underset{\displaystyle CH_3}{CH}{-}(CH_2)_3{-}\underset{\displaystyle CH_3}{CH}{-}(CH_2)_3{-}\underset{\displaystyle CH_3}{CH}{-}(CH_2)_3{-}\underset{\displaystyle CH_3}{C}{=}CH{-}CH_2OH.$$

Before discussing the individual reactions by which derivatives of chlorophyll may be formed, it should be mentioned that chlorophyll *b* differs from chlorophyll *a* only in having an aldehyde group in position 3 in ring II in place of a methyl group; *i.e.*, it has an oxygen atom in place of two hydrogen atoms. Most reactions, therefore, follow the same course with both components, so that they can be discussed as one.

Among the simple reactions which leave the phorbin system intact and do not alter the relative positions of the substituents, the action of the specific enzyme, chlorophyllase, and the reactions with dilute acids and alkalies (*see* table) are worthy of mention.

In green leaves, chlorophyll is accompanied by the enzyme chlorophyllase, the quantity of which naturally varies according to the variety of plant. Its specific action is the removal of the phytyl group, which is replaced by water, methyl or ethyl alcohol according to the nature of the medium present (R. Willstätter and A. Stoll, 1910; C. Weast and G. Mackinney, 1940). In this way, chlorophyllides are produced, which still contain magnesium. The reaction is reversible, since chlorophyllase can also be used to introduce phytol (R. Willstätter and A. Stoll, 1910), as well as other higher alcohols (H. Fischer, 1938), into the chlorophyll molecule.

Dilute acids split off the magnesium from chlorophyll and chlorophyllides with the formation of phaeophytin and the corresponding phaeophorbides, respectively. This reaction is also reversible, since it is possible by means of the Grignard reagent (R. Willstätter and L. Forsén, 1911) or magnesium alcoholate (A. Stoll and E. Wiedemann, 1933; H. Fischer, 1934) to reintroduce the magnesium.

By the action of hot alkalies, both the chlorophylls and the phaeophytins and phaeophorbides are converted into tricarboxylic acids by saponification of the phytyl- and methylester groups and the cleavage of the carbocyclic side ring (C_6–C_γ). Thus, the chlorophylls yield the isochlorophyllins, which are converted by acidification into chlorin e_6 in the case of chlorophyll *a*, and into rhodin g_7 in the case of chlorophyll *b*, these end products being also obtained by the above reaction from the phaeophorbides and their esters.

The determination of the structure of the chlorophylls and their primary derivatives was carried out by way of the related porphyrins. These are obtained by degradation of the phorbins with alkali, or by treatment with hydrogen iodide. This reagent reduces only the double bonds. During the subsequent working up, aerial oxidation takes place until the ring system is completely dehydrogenated. As will be described later, at the same time a vinyl group is converted to an ethyl group during the reduction. It therefore follows that the most important phaeoporphyrins, phaeoporphyrin a_5 in the *a* series and phaeoporphyrin b_6 in the *b* series, formed in this way are isomers of the phaeophorbides *a* and *b*. The numerals added as subscripts indicate the number of oxygen atoms present. Phaeoporphyrin a_5 still contains the carbocyclic side ring from C_6 to C_γ which, as an acetoacetic ester group, is responsible for the ready transformation into the tricarboxylic acids chlorin e_6 and chloroporphyrin e_6, respectively.

In order to confirm this acetoacetic ester grouping, it was essential to demonstrate the presence of an enolizable keto group, which was achieved by the preparation of oxime and benzoyl derivatives of phaeophorbide *a*. By oximation of phaeophorbide *b* it was possible to prove the presence of a further carbonyl group in addition to the keto group, so that a dioxime and two monoximes were obtained in this case (A. Stoll and E. Wiedemann, 1934).

Enolization in the carbocyclic side ring is also proved by the so-called phase test, which is characteristic of the intact chlorophyll molecule. On shaking an ethereal chlorophyll solution with concentrated alcoholic alkali, the green colour changes suddenly to brown, followed, after several minutes, by a return of the green colour owing to hydrolysis of the carbocyclic ring. Oxidized chlorophyll derivatives, which form even on standing in alcoholic solution, especially on the alkaline side, no longer give the phase test and are known as allomerized chlorophyll derivatives and purpurins (J. B. Conant, 1931–34; A. Stoll and E. Wiedemann, 1932–35; H. Fischer and co-workers, 1933).

The presence of the vinyl group in position 2 of the chlorophyll molecule was proved by hydrogenation and by a specific oxidation reaction (oxoreaction). Its position was confirmed by elimination of the acetyl group thus produced and identification of the resulting porphyrin (H. Fischer and co-workers, 1935).

The green compounds, the phorbins, to which the chlorophylls and their primary derivatives belong, arise from the red porphyrins by the reduction of one of the double bonds in the nucleus. The natural phorbins are further characterized by the above-mentioned vinyl group in place of the ethyl group in position 2. The fact that the phorbins are dihydroporphyrins was proved by oxidation of their copper complexes (H. Fischer and K. Herrle, 1937; H. Wenderoth, 1939; H. Gibian, 1942). The placing of the two hydrogen atoms in positions 7 and 8 in the pyrrole ring IV followed from the optical activity of chlorophyll derivatives in which other asymmetric centres had been eliminated (H. Fischer and H. Wenderoth, 1940). The optical rotation in acetone is $[\alpha]^{25}_{720} = -262°$ for chlorophyll *a*, and $[\alpha]^{25}_{720} = -267°$ for chlorophyll

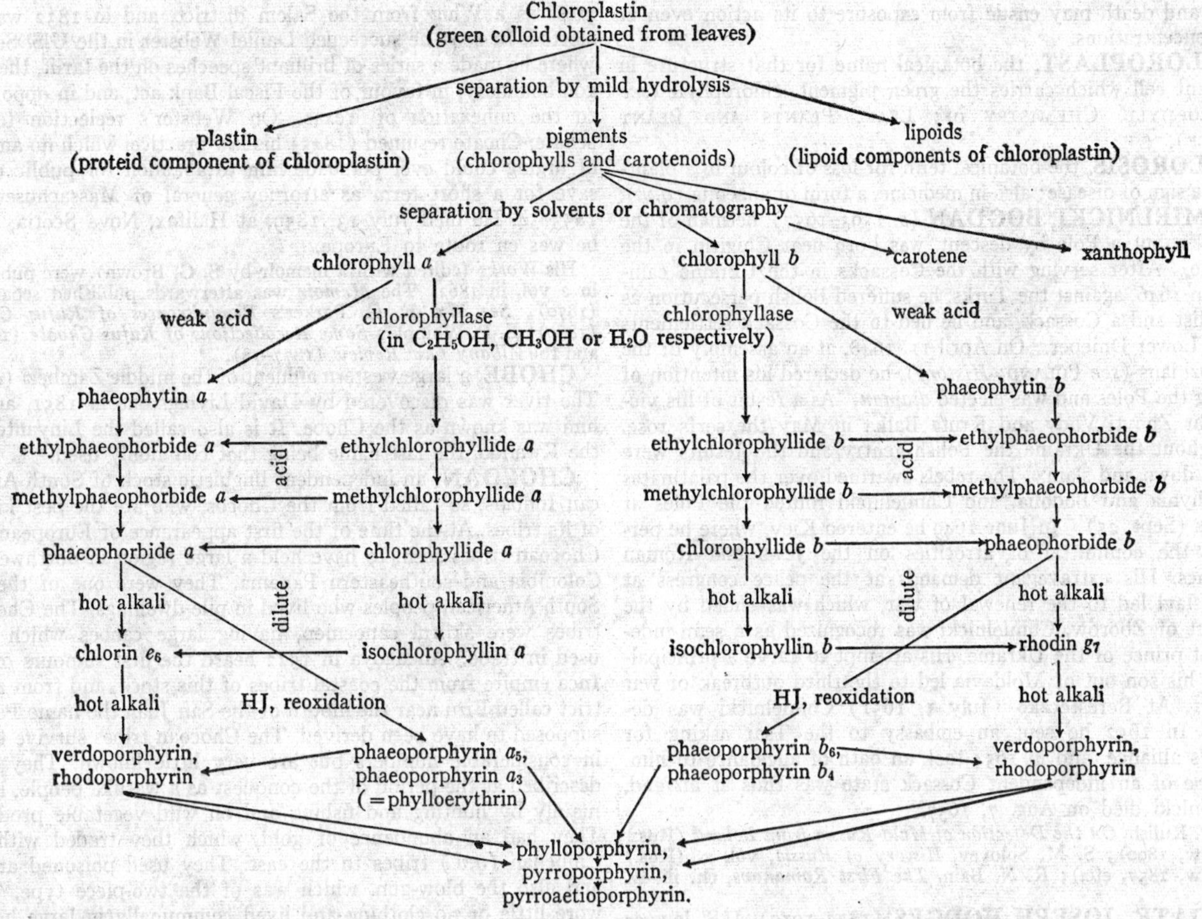

b (A. Stoll and E. Wiedemann, 1933).

In principle, the conversion of porphyrins into green compounds can be achieved by hydrogenation. The main obstacles which have so far prevented a total synthesis of the chlorophylls are the severity of the conditions which have to be employed and the simultaneous reduction of the 2-vinyl group if previously introduced. In the case of simple porphyrins, it has been possible to effect the introduction of hydrogen in the required 7:8 position (A. Treibs and E. Wiedemann, 1928; H. Fischer and H. Helberger, 1929; H. Fischer and H. Wenderoth, 1940). The introduction of magnesium, of the phytyl and vinyl radicals and of the carbocyclic side ring has been carried out successfully.

As precursors of the chlorophylls in plants, protochlorophylls were found which are converted into chlorophylls on exposure to light (N. A. Monteverde and V. Lubimenko, 1894–1912). It is probable that these protochlorophylls belong to the porphyrins but otherwise possess the same structure as the chlorophylls (K. Noack, 1928–31; A. Seybold, 1937).

A chlorophyll derivative has been found in photosynthetic bacteria and has been named bacteriochlorophyll (C. B. van Niel, 1932–36). Its structure can be derived from that of chlorophyll *a* by the addition of two H atoms to the double bond in ring II and by replacing the vinyl group in position 2 by an acetyl group (H. Fischer and co-workers, 1937–38).

Compared with the spectra of the chlorophylls, the absorption bands of bacteriochlorophyll are shifted into the infra-red (C. B. van Niel, 1938).

Only brief reference can be made to the part played by the leaf pigments in the assimilation of carbon dioxide without discussing the many theories relating to this phenomenon. An important result is the confirmation that the assimilatory quotient of the expired oxygen to the assimilated carbon dioxide is always equal to 1 (R. Willstätter and A. Stoll, 1917). The separation of the chain of reactions into individual stages, as was possible with other natural chemical processes, had not been achieved by the 1950s. A step in this direction was indicated by the reduction of carbon dioxide by organic material in the absence of light which is observed in special cases with algae and bacteria (G. B. van Niel, 1931–46; H. Gaffron, 1940).

The function of chlorophyll in photosynthesis has been defined as that of an energy transformer or of an assimilatory ferment (R. Emerson, 1936; A. Stoll, 1936).

The part played by carbon dioxide in photosynthesis was elucidated by use of radioactive carbon (Calvin and Benson, 1947).

The combination of chlorophyll with protein in chloroplastin is of special significance for this function, since only as a result of this combination is chlorophyll able to remain resistant to light (Lubimenko, 1921). Chloroplastins from different plants are not identical. A characteristic of chloroplastin is its great tendency toward agglomeration, and even the smallest molecular weights measured by the ultracentrifuge on electrophoretically homogeneous chloroplastin preparations run into several millions (A. Stoll and E. Wiedemann, 1938–47). (A. STL.)

In the 1950s chlorophyll was exploited commercially as a deodorant. It was incorporated into a variety of products, including tooth paste and dog food.

CHLOROPICRIN, product of the distillation of bleaching powder with many nitro compounds (*e.g.*, picric acid, nitromethane), may be prepared also by the action of concentrated nitric acid on chloral or chloroform, or by the action of aqua regia (*q.v.*) upon almost any organic substance. The commonest method of preparation (A. W. von Hofmann, 1866) consists of adding a solution (saturated at 30° C.) of one part of picric acid to a paste of ten parts of bleaching powder and water. A violent reaction occurs and chloropicrin (nitrochloroform, trichloronitromethane), $NO_2.CCl_3$, distils over, generally without external heating. It is a colourless liquid of boiling point 112° C. and of specific gravity 1.692. It is almost insoluble in water but is readily soluble in alcohol; it has a sharp smell, and its vapour powerfully affects the eyes. Chloropicrin has been employed in chemical warfare (*q.v.*) as a lachrymatory, irritant and lethal agent. High concentrations of this chemical cause fatal lung injuries and death may ensue from exposure to its action even at low concentrations.

CHLOROPLAST, the botanical name for that structure in the plant cell which carries the green pigment, chlorophyll (*see* CHLOROPHYLL, CHEMISTRY OF; LEAF; PLANTS AND PLANT SCIENCE).

CHLOROSIS, the botanical term for loss of colour in a plant-organ, a sign of disease; also in medicine, a form of anaemia (*q.v.*).

CHMIELNICKI, BOGDAN (*c.* 1593–1657), hetman of the Cossacks, but a Pole by descent, was born near Chigirin in the Ukraine. After serving with the Cossacks in the Ukraine campaign in 1646, against the Turks, he suffered Polish persecution as a royalist and a Cossack, and he fled to the Cossack settlements on the Lower Dnieper. On April 11, 1648, at an assembly of the Zaporozhians (*see* POLAND: *History*), he declared his intention of fighting the Poles and was elected *ataman.* As a result of his victories at Zhovti Vody and Kruta Balka in May the serfs rose. Throughout the Ukraine the Polish gentry and the Jesuits were hunted down and slain. The rebels swarmed over the palatinates of Volhynia and Podolia, and Chmielnicki routed the Poles at Pilawce (Sept. 23). In June 1649 he entered Kiev, where he permitted the committal of atrocities on the Jews and Roman Catholics. His extravagant demands at the peace congress at Pereyaslavl led to the renewal of war, which was ended by the compact of Zborow. Chmielnicki was recognized as a semi-independent prince of the Ukraine. His attempt to carve a principality for his son out of Moldavia led to the third outbreak of war in 1651. At Beresteczko (July 1, 1651) Chmielnicki was defeated. In 1652 he sent an embassy to the Tsar asking for Russia's alliance, and in 1654 took an oath of allegiance to him. All hope of an independent Cossack state was thus at an end. Chmielnicki died on Aug. 7, 1657.

See P. Kulish, *On the Defection of Malo-Russia from Poland* (Rus.) (Moscow, 1890); S. M. Solovev, *History of Russia,* vol. x. (Rus.) (Moscow, 1857, etc.); R. N. Bain, *The First Romanovs,* ch. iii.–iv. (1905).

CHOATE, JOSEPH HODGES (1832–1917), U.S. lawyer and diplomat, was born at Salem, Mass., on Jan. 24, 1832. He was the son of Dr. George Choate, a physician of considerable note. He was admitted to the bar in 1855 and in 1856 began practice in New York city. Choate was associated with many of the most famous litigations in American legal history, including the Tilden, A. T. Stewart and Stanford will cases, the Kansas prohibition cases, the Chinese exclusion cases, the Maynard election returns case and the income tax suit. In 1871 he became a member of the "Committee of Seventy" in New York city, which was instrumental in breaking up the "Tweed Ring." His greatest reputation was won, perhaps, in cross-examination. In politics he allied himself with the Republican party on its organization, being a frequent speaker in presidential campaigns, beginning with that of 1856. He never held political office but he was ambassador to Great Britain from 1899 to 1905. In England he won great personal popularity, and accomplished much in fostering the good relations of the two great English-speaking powers. He was one of the representatives of the U.S. at the second peace congress at The Hague in 1907. Upon the outbreak of World War I he ardently supported the British and Allied cause and severely criticized President Wilson's hesitation to recommend America's immediate co-operation, but shortly before his death retracted his criticism. He died in New York on May 14, 1917. Among his last works were *Abraham Lincoln and Other Addresses in England* (1910) and *American Addresses* (1911).

See *The Choate Story Book* (1903); T. G. Strong, *Joseph Choate, New Englander, New Yorker, Lawyer, Ambassador* (1917); *Joseph Choate, a Great Ambassador* (1918); Edward Sandford Martin, *The Life of Joseph H. Choate* (1920); *Arguments and Addresses of Joseph Hodges Choate,* edit. Frederick C. Hicks (1926).

CHOATE, RUFUS (1799–1859), U.S. lawyer and orator, was born at Ipswich (Mass.) on Oct. 1, 1799. He graduated at Dartmouth college in 1819 and spent a year in the law school of Harvard university. He was admitted to the Massachusetts bar in 1823 and practised for five years, during which time he served in the Massachusetts house of representatives (1825–26) and in the state senate (1827). In 1830 he was elected to congress as a Whig from the Salem district, and in 1832 was re-elected. In 1841 he succeeded Daniel Webster in the U.S. Senate, where he made a series of brilliant speeches on the tariff, the Oregon boundary, in favour of the Fiscal Bank act, and in opposition to the annexation of Texas. On Webster's reelection to the senate, Choate resumed (1845) his law practice, which no amount of urging could ever persuade him to abandon for public office, save for a short term as attorney general of Massachusetts in 1853–54. He died July 13, 1859, at Halifax, Nova Scotia, while he was en route to Europe.

His *Works* (edited with a memoir by S. G. Brown) were published in 2 vol. in 1862. The *Memoir* was afterwards published separately (1870). *See* also E. G. Parker's *Reminiscences of Rufus Choate* (1860); E. P. Whipple's *Some Recollections of Rufus Choate* (1879); and the *Albany Law Review* (1877–78).

CHOBE, a large western affluent of the middle Zambezi (*q.v.*). The river was discovered by David Livingstone in 1851, and to him was known as the Chobe. It is also called the Linyante and the Kwando, the last name being that commonly used.

CHOCOAN, an independent linguistic stock of South American Indians, so called from the Chocos, who are the best known of its tribes. At the time of the first appearance of Europeans the Chocoan tribes seem to have held a large region in northwestern Colombia and southeastern Panamá. They were one of the few South American peoples who lived in pile dwellings. The Chocoan tribes were skilful canoemen, having large canoes which they used in trade. Andagoya in 1522 heard the first rumours of the Inca empire from the coastal tribes of this stock, and from a district called Biru near the mouth of the San Juan the name Peru is supposed to have been derived. The Chocoan tribes survive today in considerable numbers but are very little known. They were described at the period of the conquest as a warlike people, living mainly by hunting and fishing and on wild vegetable products. They had an abundance of gold, which they traded with the Chibchan (*q.v.*) tribes to the east. They used poisoned arrows and also the blow-gun, which was of the two-piece type. They wore little or no clothing and lived communally in large houses of thatch, set on very high piles or sometimes in trees.

See P. Simon, *Noticias historiales de las Conquistas de Tierra Firme en las Indias Occidentales* (Bogota, 1882); W. Lehmann, *Zentral Amerika* (Berlin, 1920).

CHOCOLATE, a preparation of the cacao bean and sugar, usually flavoured, and either used as a food or mixed with hot water and milk as a drink. It is also widely used to flavour other types of food such as ice cream, bakery products and candy. Cocoa and chocolate for eating are comparatively modern preparations, whereas drinking chocolate, of a sort, has been known to Europeans since the discovery of America. The original of the modern chocolate was *chocolatl,* a frothy beverage taken cold and held in high esteem in Mexico by the Aztecs. As *chocolatl* apparently consisted simply of the roasted and ground cacao bean flavoured with peppers and other spices, it was both bitter and pungent. The Spaniards greatly improved it by adding sugar and guarded the secret of its preparation for nearly a century, when it became known in Italy, Germany and France. In 1657 a Frenchman opened a shop in London, at which solid chocolate for making the beverage could be purchased at 10*s.* to 15*s.* a pound. At this price, only the wealthy could afford to drink it; hence the appearance in London, Amsterdam and other European capitals of the fashionable chocolate houses, some of which developed later into famous clubs. About 1700 the English improved chocolate by the addition of milk. The reduction of the cost of the beverage was hampered in Great Britain by the imposition of high import duties on the raw cacao bean, and it was not until 1853, when Gladstone lowered the duty to a uniform rate of 1*d.* a lb., that chocolate became popular.

Cakes of chocolate are still the accepted material in France from which to prepare a cacao beverage, but elsewhere cocoa powder has for many years been more generally used. While the use of chocolate for drinking has declined, the amount of chocolate eaten has greatly increased.

Method of Manufacture.—In the manufacture of chocolate, cocoa beans are first cleaned to remove stones, dirt and other foreign matter and then roasted. The roasting process develops

PHOTOGRAPHS, PIX-MELVIN

MANUFACTURE OF CHOCOLATE CANDY

1. Placing solid blocks of chocolate into a melter, where they are heated to liquid form
2. After melting, the chocolate is poured onto a marble slab for cooling and working
3. Making chocolate-covered creams. The cream fillings are first poured into moulds
4. The entire tray of moulds filled with the cream centres is covered with liquid chocolate, then allowed to harden

CHOCOLATE

PHOTOGRAPHS, PIX-MELVIN

MAKING VARIOUS KINDS OF CANDIES

1. Revolving pens in which nut fillings of candies are covered with an equal distribution of chocolate
2. Workman inspecting finished chocolate-covered almonds in a revolving pen
3. Hand-dipping centres in liquid chocolate
4. Wrapping pieces of candy in tin foil
5. Packing candy in boxes

flavour, colour and serves to loosen the kernel or nib from the shell. Beans are then cracked and the shell is removed by a winnowing process. The nibs are generally ground through stone mills. During the grinding the heat of friction melts the cocoa butter present, and the resulting product comes from the mills in liquid form. It is known in the trade as "chocolate liquor." This liquor can then be cooled and moulded into cakes for use in other branches of the food industry or can be given further processing to prepare sweet chocolate, milk chocolate or cocoa powder. The U.S. standard for chocolate liquor calls for a minimum of 50% fat and a maximum of 8% ash, and 7% crude fibre on a fat and moisture-free basis. The ash and fibre limits are intended to prevent adulteration with shells.

In the manufacture of sweet chocolate, granulated or pulverized sugar is mixed with the chocolate liquor and the resulting paste is ground by passing it over steel roll refiners. As the addition of sugar reduces the over-all fat content, additional cocoa butter must be supplied to the mix to maintain sufficient fat to permit further processing and moulding. A typical sweet chocolate contains 42% chocolate liquor, 42% sugar and 16% added cocoa butter. The finer qualities of sweet chocolate are further processed to improve and develop their flavour in machines known as "Conges." This processing may take up to 96 hours. After the processing, the sweet chocolate is cooled and moulded into cakes for use by the candy industry as a coating for centres or it may be cast directly into small bars suitable for eating.

Milk chocolate is sweet chocolate in which the flavour has been modified by the addition of whole milk solids. The U.S. standard calls for a minimum of 12% whole milk solids, but most good quality chocolates may contain as much as 20 to 22% whole milk solids.

The cocoa butter required for the manufacture of sweet chocolate is obtained by pressing chocolate liquor.

Sweet chocolate in block form is recognized as a compact and valuable foodstuff. Blocks or bars are sold plain and in combination with nuts and fruits. During World War II, the high food value of chocolate was recognized through its use by the armies as an emergency ration, and at sea as a lifeboat ration. It is unique among foods because of its high calorific value combined with small bulk.

Because of shipping shortages in World War II, it was rationed in Great Britain and the United States. The method employed in the U.S. was to limit the quantity which manufacturers could grind to a fraction of the amount which the same manufacturer had ground in 1941. This fraction was changed from time to time as was found necessary to maintain a reserve stock of cocoa beans in the U.S.

Chocolates or Chocolate-covered Confectionery.—Chocolate is used for covering all manner of confections. It is prepared by the methods outlined above, but more cocoa butter is added to make it flow readily. The best work is done by hand: the vanilla crême, caramel or other confection is laid on a fork and dipped beneath the molten chocolate and then turned on to a sheet of paper. A mechanical coverer or "enrober" invented in 1903 is much used; in this machine the crêmes move on a woven wire band through a cascade of liquid chocolate.

Production of Chocolate and Cocoa Trades.—According to the United States biennial census of manufactures of 1940 the total values of products of manufactures of chocolate and cocoa was $99,-018,203. Of this amount, $39,516,767 represented the value of 216,-821,762 lb. of chocolate (not including chocolate coatings); $32,194,541 the value of 339,530,664 lb. of chocolate coatings; $13,199,965 the value of 153,440,919 lb. of powdered cocoa; $6,880,433 the value of 57,205,043 lb. of cocoa butter; and $1,159,041 the value of other products, chiefly chocolate and cocoa specialties. In the 39 reporting establishments there were 6,464 wage earners, who received $7,711,129 in wages. During the calendar year ending Dec. 31, 1939, the United States imported 545,010,374 lb. of raw cocoa, valued at $28,547,394; of prepared cocoa (not including confectionery), 3,587,000 lb., valued at $432,000. The United Kingdom imported 147,298 tons of raw cocoa valued at $16,076,714 in 1938, of which 78,130 tons were retained for home consumption. For the general facts of the industry, see COCOA; CONFECTIONERY MANUFACTURE.

BIBLIOGRAPHY.—*See* for cacao cultivation: J. H. Hart, *Cacao* (1911) and C. J. J. van Hall, *Cocoa* (1914). For chemistry and manufacture *see:* R. Whymper, *Cocoa and Chocolate* (1921). A popular work on cultivation and manufacture is A. W. Knapp, *Cocoa and Chocolate* (1920). On pp. 191–203 is a full bibliography.

(A. W. KN.; X.)

CHOCTAW, a prominent tribe in southern Mississippi, of Muskogi stock (*see* MUSKOGIAN INDIANS). Their name is apparently a corruption of the Spanish *chato,* flattened, which referred to their practice of flattening the heads of male infants. They farmed intensively. The Choctaws were allies of the French, enemies of the British and of most of the Muskogians. In the later 18th century they began drifting west of the Mississippi, and about 1832 the majority moved to what is now eastern Oklahoma, where they remained self-governing and semi-civilized until their absorption into American citizenship in 1906. They number about 17,500 exclusive of Negro freedmen included in the "nation," but include many of mixed blood; the original population seems to have been only slightly larger.

CHODKIEWICZ, JAN KAROL (1560–1621), Polish general. In 1599 he was appointed *starosta* of Samogitia, and in 1600 acting commander-in-chief of Lithuania. In the war against Sweden for the possession of Livonia he repulsed the duke of Sudermania, afterwards Charles IX, from Riga, and in 1604 captured Dorpat. At Kirkholm (Aug. 27, 1605) he annihilated a large Swedish army; but he was hampered always by the Polish diet which denied him adequate supplies, and after helping to defeat the rebels in Poland and to relieve Riga when the Swedes again invaded Livonia, he was sent against Moscow with an army which mutinied for lack of pay and was compelled to retreat to Smolensk. On being reinforced by Prince Wladislaus, however, he took the fortress of Drohobu in 1617, and on the conclusion of the Muscovite war by the treaty of Deulina he was sent to defend the southern frontier against the Turks. He died on Sept. 24, 1621, after forcing the Ottoman army to raise the siege of Khotin.

See Adam Stanislaw Naruszewicz, *Life of J. K. Chodkiewicz* (Pol.) 4th ed. (Cracow, 1857–58); Lukasz Golebiowski, *The Moral Side of J. K. Chodkiewicz as indicated by his Letters* (Pol.) (Warsaw, 1854).

CHODOWIECKI, DANIEL NICOLAS (1726–1801), German genre painter and engraver of Polish descent, was born at Danzig on Oct. 13, 1726, and died at Berlin on Feb. 7, 1801. He began engraving in 1758. After designing and engraving several subjects from the story of the Seven Years' War, Chodowiecki produced the famous "History of the Life of Jesus Christ," a set of admirably painted miniatures, which made him popular at once. Few books were published in Prussia for some years without plate or vignette by Chodowiecki. The catalogue of his works (Berlin, 1814) includes over 3,000 items, the most famous being the picture of "Jean Calas and his Family." He became director of the Berlin Academy in 1797. The title of the German Hogarth was disclaimed by Chodowiecki himself. He actually had only one point in common with Hogarth—the practice of representing actual life and manners.

See Von Oettingen, *Daniel Chodowiecki* (1895).

CHOERILUS. (1) An Athenian tragic poet, who exhibited plays as early as 524 B.C. He was said to have competed with Aeschylus, Pratinas, and even Sophocles. According to F. G. Welcker, however, the rival of Sophocles was a son of Choerilus, who bore the same name. Suidas states that Choerilus wrote 150 tragedies and gained the prize 13 times. His works are all lost; only Pausanias (i, 14) mentions a play by him entitled *Alope.* Choerilus was also said to have introduced considerable improvements in theatrical masks and costumes.

See A. Nauck, *Tragicorum Graecorum Fragmenta* (1889); F. G. Welcker, *Die griechischen Tragödien,* pp. 18, 892.

(2) An epic poet of Samos who flourished at the end of the 5th century B.C. After the fall of Athens he settled at the court of Archelaus, king of Macedonia, where he was the associate of Agathon, Melanippides and Plato, the comic poet. The only work that can with certainty be attributed to him is the Περσηΐς or Περσικά, a history of the struggle of the Greeks against Persia. The treatment of contemporary events was a new departure in epic; he apologizes in the introductory verses (preserved in the scholiast on Aristotle, *Rhetoric,* iii, 14). The *Perseis* was at first successful, but later critics reversed this favourable judgment. Aristotle (*Topica,* viii, I) calls Choerilus's comparisons far-fetched and obscure, and the Alexandrians displaced him by Anti-

A, PERSHORE ABBEY, ENGLISH DECORATED GOTHIC (14TH CENTURY); B, THE CERTOSA, PAVIA, ITALIAN RENAISSANCE; C, HALBERSTADT CATHEDRAL, GERMAN GOTHIC (14TH–15TH CENTURIES). D, F, CHOIR, LIVERPOOL CATHEDRAL, MODERN ENGLISH GOTHIC; E, J, CHOIR, YORK CATHEDRAL, ENGLISH DECORATED GOTHIC (14TH CENTURY); G, RESTORATION OF 13TH CENTURY STATE OF THE CHOIR OF NOTRE DAME, PARIS, FRENCH GOTHIC; H, L, CHOIR OF DURHAM CATHEDRAL, ENGLISH ROMANESQUE AND GOTHIC (STALLS, 17TH CENTURY; SCREEN, 19TH CENTURY). K, CHOIR, LINCOLN CATHEDRAL, EARLY ENGLISH GOTHIC (12TH–13TH CENTURIES); M, CHOIR STALLS, ELY CATHEDRAL, ENGLISH DECORATED GOTHIC (14TH CENTURY); N, RETRO CHOIR ("ANGELS CHOIR") LINCOLN CATHEDRAL (13TH CENT.)

machus in the canon of epic poets.

G. Kinkel, *Epicorum Graecorum Frag.* i. (1877); for another view of his relations with Herodotus *see* Müder in *Klio* (1907), 29–44.

(3) An epic poet of Iasus in Caria, who lived in the 4th century B.C. He accompanied Alexander the Great on his campaigns as court-poet. He is well known from the passages in Horace (*Epistles,* ii. 1, 232; *Ars Poëtica,* 357), according to which he received a piece of gold for every good verse he wrote in honour of the deeds of his master.

See G. Kinkel, *Epicorum Graecorum Fragmenta,* i. (1877); A. F. Näke, *De Choerili Samii Aetate Vita et Poësi aliisque Choerilis* (1817), where the above poets are carefully distinguished; and the articles in Pauly-Wissowa's *Realencyklopädie,* iii. 2 (1899).

CHOEROBOSCUS, GEORGIUS, also called CHARTOPHYLAX (*c.* A.D. 60), deacon and professor at the oecumenical school at Constantinople. A course of his lectures on grammar has come down to us in the shape of notes taken by his pupils. He drew from the best authorities—Apollonius Dyscolus, Herodian, Orion, Theodosius of Alexandria. These lectures were much used by Constantine Lascaris in his Greek grammar and by Urban of Belluno (end of 15th century). Other works: commentary on the canons of Theodosius on declension and conjugation, which is extant; a treatise on orthography, of which a fragment (on quantity) has been preserved; a tract on prosody; commentaries on Hephaestion and Dionysius Thrax; and grammatical notes on the Psalms.

BIBLIOGRAPHY.—*See* A. Hilgard, *Grammatici Graeci,* iv. (1889–94), containing the text of the commentary on Theodosius and a full account of the life and writings of Choeroboscus; L. Kohn in Pauly-Wissowa's *Realencyklopädie,* iii. 2 (1889); C. Krumbacher, *Geschichte der byzantinischen Literatur* (1897); Reitzenstein, *Etymologika,* 190, n. 4.

CHOIR, the body of singers who perform the musical portion of the service in a church, or the place set apart for them (O.F. *cuer* from Lat. *chorus,* Fr. *choeur*). Any organized body of singers performing full part choral works or oratorios is also called a choir. The word was originally applied to all the clergy taking part in services of the church.

In English cathedrals the choir is composed of men (vicars-choral or lay clerks) and boys (choristers). They are divided into two sets, sitting on the north and south side of the chancel respectively, called *cantoris* and *decani* from being on the same side as the *cantor* (precentor) or the *decanus* (dean). Surpliced choirs of women have occasionally been introduced, notably in the United States and the British colonies, but the practice has no warrant of traditional usage. (*See* VESTMENTS.) In England at the Reformation the choir services (Mattins, Evensong) replaced the Mass as the principal popular services, and, in general, only the choir vestments were retained in use. In the English cathedrals the members of the choir often retain privileges reminiscent of an earlier definite ecclesiastical status.

In architecture, (1) any part of a church intended for choir use, and (2), more commonly, the eastern end of a church, almost synonymous with chancel (*q.v.*). In developed churches of the middle ages, the choir is just to the west of the altar rail, usually between that and the crossing, although in some churches of England and Spain the space extends well into the nave (*q.v.*). In some modern churches members of the choir are placed in a western gallery; in Non-conformist churches they are frequently placed over and behind the pulpit. The choir stalls of Gothic churches such as Amiens, Exeter, Lincoln are works of great richness. In the illustration, Figure A. is from Gardner, *A Guide to English Gothic Architecture,* permission of the Cambridge University Press; C. and N. are by permission from Sir Banister Fletcher, *History of Architecture on the Comparative Method,* 8th ed. 1928 (Batsford); F. from Atkinson and Bagenal, *Theory and Elements of Architecture,* permission of Benn & Co.; L from Greenwell, *Durham Cathedral,* permission of Andrews & Co. (*See* also CHORAL SINGING; FESTIVALS, MUSICAL.)

CHOISEUL, CÉSAR, DUC DE (1598–1675), French marshal and diplomatist, known for the best part of his life as the marshal du Plessis-Praslin, came of the old French family of Choiseul, which arose in the valley of the Upper Marne in the 10th century. Entering the army he took part in the siege of La Rochelle, assisted to defend the island of Ré against the duke of Buckingham, and accompanied the French forces to Italy in 1629. In 1630 he was appointed ambassador at the court of the duke of Savoy, and was engaged in diplomatic and administrative work in Italy till 1635, when war was declared between France and Spain. Plessis-Praslin distinguished himself in the Italian campaign which followed, and after further service in Italy he was made a marshal of France (1645). During the first War of the Fronde he assisted Condé in the brief siege of Paris; and in the second war, remaining loyal to the queen-regent and the court party, he defeated Turenne and the allied Spaniards and rebels at Rethel (or Blanc-Champ) in 1650. He became minister of state in 1652, and in November 1665 was created duc de Choiseul. He was concerned in some of the negotiations between Louis and Charles II. of England which led to the Treaty of Dover, and died in Paris on Dec. 23, 1675.

CHOISEUL, ÉTIENNE FRANÇOIS, DUC DE (1719–1785), French statesman, was the eldest son of François Joseph de Choiseul, marquis de Stainville (1700–1770), and bore in early life the title of comte de Stainville. Born on June 28, 1719, he entered the army, and during the War of the Austrian Succession served in Bohemia in 1741 and in Italy, where he distinguished himself at the battle of Coni, in 1744. From 1745 until 1748 he was with the army in the Low Countries, being present at the sieges of Mons, Charleroi, and Maestricht. He acquired a large fortune by his marriage in 1750 with a daughter of the marquis de Châtel.

Choiseul gained the favour of Madame de Pompadour, and was given the appointment of ambassador to Rome in 1753, where he was entrusted with the negotiations concerning the disturbances called forth by the bull *Unigenitus.* In 1757 his patroness obtained his transfer to Vienna, where he was instructed to cement the new alliance between France and Austria. He then replaced Antoine Louis Rouillé (1689–1761) as minister for foreign affairs, and therefore had the direction of French foreign policy during the Seven Years' War. At this time he was made a peer of France and created duc de Choiseul. Although from 1761 until 1766 his cousin César, duc de Choiseul-Praslin, was minister for foreign affairs, yet Choiseul continued to control the policy of France until 1770, and during this period held most of the other important offices of state. As the author of the "Family Compact" he sought to retrieve by an alliance with the Bourbon house of Spain the disastrous results of the alliance with Austria, but his action came too late. He reformed both the army and navy, and although too late to prevent the loss of Canada and India, he developed French colonies in the Antilles and San Domingo, and added Corsica and Lorraine to the crown of France. His management of home affairs in general satisfied the *philosophes.* He allowed the publication of the *Encyclopédie* and procured the banishment of the Jesuits and the temporary abolition of the order by Pope Clement XIV.

Choiseul's fall was caused by his action towards the Jesuits, and by his support of their opponent La Chalotais, and of the provincial parlements. After the death of Madame de Pompadour in 1764, his enemies, led by Madame du Barry and the chancellor Maupeou, were too strong for him, and in 1770 he was ordered to retire to his estate at Chanteloupe. Greatly to his disappointment Louis XVI. did not restore him to his former position, although the king recalled him to Paris in 1774, where he died on May 8, 1785.

BIBLIOGRAPHY.—P. Calmettes, *Choiseul et Voltaire* (1902); G. Mangras, *Le duc et la duchesse de Choiseul* (1902) and *La disgrace du duc et de la duchesse de Choiseul* (1903); *Memoires du duc de Choiseul,* ed. F. Calmettes (1904); A. Bourguet, *Le duc de Choiseul et l'alliance espagnal* (1906) and *Études sur la politique étrangère du duc de Choiseul* (1907). *See* also *Cambridge Modern History,* Bk. vi.

CHOISY, FRANÇOIS TIMOLEON, ABBÉ DE (1644–1724), French author, was born in Paris on Aug. 16, 1644, and died in Paris on Oct. 2, 1724. His father was attached to the household of the duke of Orleans, and the lad became famous in court circles for his extravagance, his adoption of female dress and his numberless intrigues. He had been made an abbé in his childhood, and poverty drove him to live on his benefice at Sainte-Seine in Burgundy, where he found a kindred spirit in Bussy-Rabutin. He visited Rome in the suite of the cardinal de Bouillon in 1676, and shortly afterwards a serious illness brought about a sudden conversion. In 1685 he accompanied the chevalier de Chaumont on a mission to Siam. He was ordained priest, and received various ecclesiastical preferments. He wrote voluminous historical works, but is remembered by his gossiping *Mémoires* (1737), which contain remarkably exact portraits of his contemporaries, although he has otherwise small pretensions to historical accuracy.

The *Mémoires* passed through many editions, and were edited in 1888 by M. de Lescure. Some admirable letters of Choisy are included in the correspondence of Bussy-Rabutin. Choisy is said to have burnt some of his indiscreet revelations, but left a considerable quantity of unpublished ms. Part of this material, giving an account of his adventures as a woman, was surreptitiously used in an anonymous *Histoire de madame la comtesse de Barres* (Antwerp, 1735), and again with much editing in the *Vie de M. l'abbé de Choisy* (Lausanne and Geneva, 1742), ascribed by Paul Lacroix to Lenglet Dufresnoy; the text was finally edited (1870) by Lacroix as *Aventures de l'abbé de Choisy*. *See* also Sainte-Beuve, *Causeries du lundi*, vol. iii.

CHOKE BORE, the bore of a gun narrowed at the muzzle to concentrate the shot.

CHOKE-DAMP, also known as "black-damp" and "stythe," is a mixture of carbon dioxide and nitrogen, pure choke-damp according to Dr. J. Haldane, containing about 13% of the former and 87% of the latter; but probably the relative proportions are variable. Choke-damp, which in this connection is more frequently known as "stythe," is found in old, abandoned, or worked portions of the mines—especially wet mines—where the ventilation is stagnant, and on the occasion of a fall in the atmospheric pressure emerges from the "wastes" ("goaves") and makes its appearance in the workings, and, being heavier than air, lies along the floor of the mine gradually ascending as it increases in volume.

Choke-damp is the result of the absorption of the oxygen in the air by the coal substance in the mine and the formation of carbon dioxide in the process; it is also produced by the decay of timber, the breathing of men and animals, the burning of lamps and candles, and the firing of explosives. Spontaneous combustion, or self-heating of coal, which is a characteristic of some coal mines, is merely the rapid absorption of oxygen by the coal, which produces carbon dioxide and carbon monoxide in the process.

Carbon monoxide is known to miners as "white-damp" but is present only in minute quantities in the mine. It is the result of incomplete combustion, may be caused by the exploding of gunpowder and other explosives, and is always present in the "after-damp" resulting from an explosion of fire-damp or of coal dust.

Whereas carbon dioxide, if present in sufficient quantity, extinguishes light and life mainly by suffocation, carbon monoxide, if present in the air to an extent greater than 1%, can be detected by a cap on the ordinary flame of a safety lamp. It is a virulent poison, its destructive effect being due to its action on the haemoglobin of the blood with which it chemically combines, robbing the body of its oxygen. But haemoglobin when saturated with carbon-monoxide cannot take up oxygen. An atmosphere containing as low as 0·2% of the dangerous gas will cause in time complete helplessness and loss of consciousness. An analysis of after-damp made by Dr. Bedson after the Usworth explosion (County Durham) in 1885 showed it to contain—

	%
Carbon dioxide (CO_2)	4·54
Carbon monoxide (CO)	2·48
Methane (CH_4 the chief constituent of fire-damp)	8·68
Oxygen	7·23
Nitrogen	76·80

Analyses of after-damp by Mr. W. I. Orsman in 1892 showed it to be composed of—

	%
Oxygen	3·9
Nitrogen	75·9
Carbon dioxide	12·1
Carbon monoxide	8·1

The bodies of persons killed by after-damp in which carbon monoxide was the fatal agent, present a pink and healthy look due entirely to its coloration effect, and *rigor mortis* is not present. (R. R.)

CHOKING, the obstruction of a passage. In animals choking is the interference with breathing caused by obstruction or compression of the larynx, windpipe or other respiratory passages and may lead to suffocation (*see* TRACHEOTOMY). In electricity, a *choking coil* is designed so that it will pass alternating currents of low but not of high frequencies (*see* RADIO RECEIVER).

In internal combustion engines (*q.v.*) a *choke tube* is a constriction in a pipe, which increases the velocity of the fluid in its neighbourhood and thus reduces the pressure (*see* HYDROMECHANICS: *Hydrodynamics*); this results in the liquid from the carburettor being sucked into the tube.

CHOLAS, a Hindu dynasty which became the paramount power in southern India toward the end of the 10th century A.D. From the 3rd century to the 9th Chola history is obscure. The *Purananuru*, one of the eight major anthologies of the early Tamil classics, contains the names of a number of Chola kings, of whom Karikala was the most famous; but in the absence of inscriptions their chronology is merely conjectural. There is apparently no truth in the legend that Karikala invaded Ceylon and transported thousands of its inhabitants to work as slaves on the banks of the Cauvery. The first ruler for whom there is definite historical evidence is Vijayalaya (*c.* 836–870). Under his son Aditya I (*c.* 870–907) the Pallavas were defeated and the Chola dominions extended until they bordered on those of the Rashtrakutas of the Deccan. The reign of his son Parantaka I (907–953) saw a further extension of their power from the Velur river to Cape Comorin, but toward the end of his days the Chola kingdom was overrun by the Rashtrakutas under Krishna III. With the accession of Rajaraja the Great, in 985, the Cholas regained their lost possessions and became the paramount power in southern India. Rajaraja's conquests included the Chera and Pandya country, Vengi and Kalinga. With the aid of a powerful fleet he annexed the Maldive Islands and conquered Ceylon, destroying its ancient capital of Anuradhapura. He was a great builder of stone temples to which the magnificent Siva temple at Tanjore still bears witness. The Chola empire reached its greatest extent in the reign of his son Rajendra I (1012–44). It is usually supposed that he reached the Ganges during one of his expeditions, but the evidence of the Tiruvalangadu plates proves that the expedition was undertaken by one of his generals and that Rajendra himself never advanced beyond the Godavari. To celebrate this achievement he assumed the title of Gangaikonda and built a new capital city, Gangaikondacholapuram, to the northeast of Tanjore. Modern scholarship inclines to the belief that he undertook a naval expedition against the Sailendra empire of Srivijaya and its dependencies in the Malay peninsula and archipelago, but there is no evidence that any territory was annexed to the Chola empire. (For the identification of Kadaram with the kingdom of Palembang in Sumatra *see* G. Coedès, "Le Royaume de Crivijaya," *Bulletin de l'École Française d'Extrême-Orient*, vol. xviii [Paris, 1918]). His son Rajadhiraja had to wage continual wars against neighbouring princes who were anxious to wipe out the humiliation they had suffered at the hands of the Cholas; he was killed in 1052 at the battle of Koppam on the banks of the Tungabhadra. In 1070 the direct Chola line appears to have become extinct and under Kulottunga I (1070–1120) the eastern Chalukya and Chola kingdoms were united. The empire now began to disintegrate; Ceylon recovered its independence and Gangavadi was lost to the rising power of the Hoysalas of Mysore. By the year 1267 the Chola empire had ceased to exist, and it was not until the end of the 14th century that its place was taken by the mighty Hindu empire of Vijayanagar.

Chola administration was well organized, especially in the sphere of local government.

There were two types of village assemblies, a general assembly of the whole village known as the *ur*, and the *sabha* which was composed entirely of Brahmans.

See K. A. N. Sastri, *The Colas*, 3 vol. (Madras, 1935–37); L. de la Vallée Poussin, *Dynasties et histoire de l'Inde depuis Kanishka jusqu'aux invasions musulmanes* (Paris, 1935). (C. C. D.)

CHOLERA is a term that has been applied to a wide variety of acute diarrhoeal diseases of short duration. Cholera nostra, simple cholera, European cholera, British cholera and cholera infantum or summer diarrhoea of infants are relatively mild enteric diseases characterized by sudden onset, acute diarrhoea sometimes accompanied by vomiting, low fatality and recovery in one to five days. These diseases are of diverse, and in many instances uncertain, aetiology. Known aetiologic agents include the paratyphoid bacilli (*Salmonella*), certain of the dysentery bacilli, especially the Sonne and Newcastle types, and some members of the genus *Proteus*. It is probable that certain of the lesser known enteric bacilli, such as the paracolon bacilli, are causally associated with this kind of disease in man. In many instances these infectious agents are transmitted by food, and differentiation of food-borne infections and food poisoning is not sharp; it is not unlikely that in the past food poisoning such as that produced by ingestion of staphylococcal enterotoxin was classed as simple cholera. These diseases are, however, to be distinguished from the acute, specific and highly fatal infection with *Vibrio cholerae* known as true cholera, Indian cholera or, most commonly, Asiatic cholera. In modern medical literature the generic use of the term cholera fell into disrepute, and came to refer almost invariably to Asiatic cholera. These enteric diseases of man are unrelated to fowl cholera, an epidemic haemorrhagic septicaemia of chickens caused by the bacillus *Pasteurella aviseptica*, or to hog cholera which is of virus aetiology; man is not susceptible to infection with either of these agents.

Historical.—References to acute, epidemic diarrhoeal disease are not uncommon in historical literature. As early as the 5th century B.C. Thucydides described the occurrence of such a disease in Athens, and the earliest report in the Indian literature of what may have been cholera is that of Susrata in the 7th century. A.D. The *χολερα* of Hippocratic writings does not refer to diarrhoeal disease. The earlier descriptions are equally applicable to bacillary dysentery, and it was not until the 15th century that acute, epidemic diarrhoeal disease which was probably cholera was described; such, for example, was the epidemic disease that brought about the destruction of Ahmed Shad's army in 1438, and that described by Jacobus Bontius in the Netherlands Indies in 1629. According to the Chinese writers, cholera reached China from India in 1669.

Cholera, however, was probably endemic in India, in the delta of the Ganges river and in lower Bengal, in remotest antiquity. With increasing facilities for travel, the disease spread from India overland through Persia into Russia, and by sea routes to China and the far east on the one hand, and on the other through Arabia into Asia Minor and Egypt and thence into Europe proper. Later it became apparent that there was also an endemic focus of infection in central China, in the valley of the Yuan river which flows into the Yangtze river through Tung Ting lake, and from which the disease spread down the valley of the Yangtze and into the coastal areas. Whether this endemic centre was a recent development or only recently discovered is problematical, but it was not associated with the great pandemics of the 19th century and early part of the 20th century.

The first of the great pandemics began in India in 1817, and spread by land to China in 1818, to Ceylon in 1819 and by sea to Mauritius and East Africa in 1820, to the Philippines, China and Japan in 1822 and by land to Persia and Arabia in the same year and thence to Russia through Astrakhan in 1823, but this pandemic did not reach Europe proper. Another pandemic wave began in India in 1826 and followed a similar course, but spread farther, reaching European Russia, via China, Manchuria and Mongolia, and through Astrakhan. It reached Moscow in 1830 and spread from Moscow to St. Petersburg, into Germany and across the North sea to Great Britain, reaching Edinburgh in 1832. The infection was carried from Europe to North America, entering Canada in 1832 and spreading south to Fort Dearborn (Chicago) and down the Mississippi valley. It appeared concurrently in New York city and Boston and spread south and west, so that by 1836 cholera was present in most of the U.S. and did not disappear until 1838. The pandemic wave occurring between 1840 and 1849 and that of 1863–66 reached Europe by overland routes via Mecca and Egypt and spread to North America, giving rise to the outbreaks of 1867 and 1873. Another pandemic began in India in 1879 and the disease reached Europe through Egypt by 1883, affecting especially the Mediterranean ports of France, Spain and Italy. It was during this epidemic that Robert Koch carried out his studies on the aetiology of the disease (*see* below). Another serious outbreak spread from India in 1891 and was carried to Europe by pilgrims returning from Mecca, reaching that continent the following year and primarily affecting European Russia. It was in this outbreak that the Russian composer Peter Ilich Tschaikovsky died of cholera. Still another great pandemic began in 1902, spreading from India to China and the Philippines, and to Europe by 1908 and 1910. With the development of knowledge of the aetiology of the disease and efficacious methods of control, no pandemic spread occurred after 1910. Cholera recurs annually in India in epidemic form and with great loss of life, usually not less than 200,000 deaths per year. The disease has spread into eastern Europe on occasion, as during the Balkan War in 1913; there were a few cases in central Europe during World War I, and several small outbreaks in Russia and Poland in the 1920s; an epidemic also occurred in Egypt during the late summer and early autumn of 1947. Epidemic cholera occurs with some frequency in the far east, especially in Burma, Indochina, the China coast and Manchuria, and sporadic cases occur in the Philippines and Indonesia. While the epidemic disease is readily controlled by sanitary measures, these are not available under primitive conditions, and should such preventive measures break down on any large scale, the rapidity of travel customary in the 20th century would make possible the spread of cholera in pandemic proportions in a matter of a few weeks or months.

The Cholera Vibrio.—Although Félix Pouchet reported finding vibrios in the stools of cholera patients as early as 1849, it was not until 1883 that the causal agent of the disease was isolated and studied by the German bacteriologist Robert Koch. He cultured a small, slightly curved bacillus from the dejecta of cholera patients, first in Cairo and the following year in India, now known as *Vibrio cholerae*. Its aetiologic relation to the disease was suggested by its occurrence in enormous numbers in the stools of infected persons, substantiated by fatal infection of the guinea pig on intragastric inoculation and proved beyond reasonable doubt by accidental laboratory infections of man with pure cultures of the microorganism. The cholera vibrio is a member of a large group of gram-negative, comma-shaped bacteria that are morphologically indistinguishable from one another. This group is ordinarily divided into two parts, the one made up of the non-cholera vibrios, and the other of the cholera and choleralike or paracholera vibrios. The former includes a variety of saprophytic forms found in water and soil, together with some species that are pathogenic for lower animals, such as those producing a fatal septicaemia in birds, contagious abortion of sheep and the like. The members of the latter group are parasites of man, and the paracholera vibrios have been found with some frequency in association with mild diarrhoeal disease. The best known of the choleralike vibrios are the El Tor vibrios which were first isolated at the quarantine station at Tor (*see* map) in 1906 from pilgrims suffering from diarrhoea, and afterward were found repeatedly under similar circumstances. The question of the pathogenicity of these vibrios was raised again in the Celebes epidemic of 1938. The disease was identical with true cholera on clinical grounds, but was apparently caused by an El Tor vibrio; the development of the far eastern phase of World War II prevented

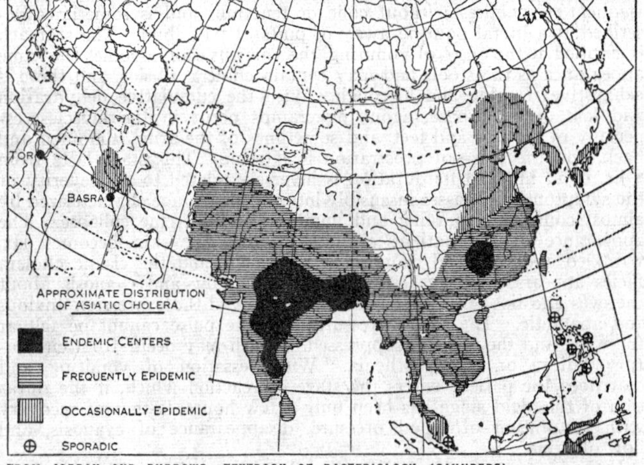

FROM JORDAN AND BURROWS, TEXTBOOK OF BACTERIOLOGY (SAUNDERS)

APPROXIMATE DISTRIBUTION OF ASIATIC CHOLERA IN THE DECADE 1930 TO 1940

detailed study. It was urged by some workers that the paracholera vibrios associated with diarrhoeal disease in man are variants of the true cholera vibrio, and that the transformation is reversible; this theory was not generally accepted and the question of the relation of these forms to human disease was still an open one at mid-20th century.

The cholera vibrio is characterized physiologically by its rapid growth, requirement for free access to oxygen, tolerance of alkali and marked susceptibility to deleterious factors in the environment. It may be isolated from contaminated specimens by culture on a medium of high alkalinity. An enriched medium containing defibrinated blood or haemoglobin and adjusted to *p*H 9.5 is used; the best known of these media are Adolf Dieudonné's medium and that of Col. Edward Bright, G. A. Vedder and W. van Dam. Because of its relatively slight resistance the vibrio dies out in a matter of a few days at best on contaminated leafy vegetables and similar foods and does not persist in water so long as does the typhoid bacillus. The differentiation of the cholera vibrio from closely related vibrios is of considerable importance. While these vibrios commonly give the cholera-red or nitrosoindole reaction in nitrate-peptone water culture, and usually ferment sucrose and mannose but not arabinose, strains are biochemically heterogeneous and cannot be identified on the basis of cultural reactions alone. They are, however, closely related immunologically in that they contain a common heat stable somatic *O* antigen and fall into a serologic group designated *O* subgroup I; provisional identification may be made by agglutination with monospecific antiserum. Certain of the El Tor vibrios are members of this group also, but the El Tor vibrios form a soluble haemolysin acting on goat red blood cells while the cholera vibrios do not. The two may be differentiated by the Greig test in which equal volumes of peptone water culture of the vibrio and a 5% suspension of goat erythrocytes are mixed, incubated and read for haemolysis. The cholera vibrio is, therefore, defined as a nonhaemolytic vibrio of *O* subgroup I. Serologic types of the cholera vibrio, arising from minor differences in the *O* antigen and demonstrable by the use of absorbed antiserums, were described by Japanese workers in 1913 and 1921. These were designated the Inaba or original type, the Ogawa or variant type, and the Hikojima or middle type. The first two are distinct from one another and the last is related to both end types. These serologic types do not differ in pathogenicity.

Cholera in Man.—Under natural conditions cholera is exclusively a disease of man. Susceptibility of individuals varies widely and is markedly influenced by predisposing factors such as low gastric acidity and gastrointestinal disturbance arising from purging, alcoholism, infection with other enteric bacteria and the like. The vibrio enters the body via the mouth, usually in contaminated water or food, and sets up an infection in the small intestine, seldom penetrating the tissues beyond the superficial layers of the mucosa. The incubation period is short, probably never longer than five days and sometimes less than one. The vibrio does not form an extracellular toxin, but the cell substance is toxic, and with proliferation and disintegration of the vibrios within the lumen of the bowel, the endotoxin is liberated and symptoms appear. The disease usually develops in three relatively well-defined stages; the stage of evacuation, the stage of collapse or algid stage and the stage of reaction. The onset is usually abrupt and characterized by a purging diarrhoea followed by copious vomiting. The lower bowel is emptied of faecal matter early in the disease, and the stool takes on the typical rice-water appearance, a nonoffensive, whitish, opaque, albuminous fluid containing flakes of mucus and having a slight albuminous odour. The diarrhoea is both profuse and frequent, is painless without colic or tenesmus and is sometimes described as a literal pouring away of pints of pale fluid. The stomach is emptied at the onset of vomiting, the vomitus soon assumes the same appearance as the stools and may contain cholera vibrios, and there is exhaustive retching and hiccough. With the cumulative dehydration and loss of fixed base, agonizing cramps occur in the muscles, especially of the legs and feet, and sometimes of the arms, abdomen and back, and the sense of prostration is extreme. This stage lasts from 2 hr. to 12 hr., and its duration is inversely related to the severity of the symptoms. It passes insensibly into the algid stage characterized by almost continuous purging and vomiting and extreme collapse. The appearance of the patient changes rapidly, the skin becomes lax, wrinkled and cold and clammy to the touch, and the classic cholera facies appears, with eyes sunken, cheeks hollow and cyanosis about the eyes and lips; the voice becomes husky and the expression anxious and apathetic. The blood pressure falls, the pulse cannot be felt at the wrist and the urine is suppressed. Death may occur from circulatory failure or from asthenia. With cessation of vomiting and diarrhoea the patient enters the stage of reaction which, if the duration of the algid stage has been only a few hours, is that of recovery with restoration of blood pressure, disappearance of cyanosis, and flow of urine.

If the impairment of renal function has been serious with damage to the kidney parenchyma, flow of urine is not resumed, and death may result in four to five days.

The pathology of the disease is sometimes attributed to the action of absorbed toxin, but is equally well accounted for on the basis of the extreme dehydration, hypochloraemia, acidosis and impairment of renal function. The severe dehydration results in a similarity between the patient with cholera and the one in shock, but it is not complete because plasma elements other than fluid and electrolytes are not lost in cholera. The specific gravity of the blood rises to as high as 1.064 with polycythaemia and disproportionate leucocytosis. The outstanding post-mortem changes are the marked rigidity, with almost immediate stiffening of the limbs after death, and the pronounced dehydration of the tissues, though the body is usually well nourished because of the relatively short duration of the disease. Convalescence is commonly uneventful, with disappearance of vibrios from the stools in ten days to two weeks, but cardiac failure may result from slight exertion. The case fatality rate is usually 40% to 60% in untreated cases, but may be reduced to 10% to 20% by adequate treatment.

Treatment is both symptomatic and specific. The former is directed toward the replacement of fluid, the maintenance of blood and tissue chloride and the counteraction of acidosis. This may be achieved through the intravenous administration of hypertonic alkaline salt solution. Sterile stock solutions of hypertonic saline, alkaline saline, alkaline hypotonic saline and bicarbonate are mixed in proportions indicated by the state of the patient, and the amount administered is determined by the degree of dehydration as shown by the specific gravity and pressure of the blood. Collapse is favourably affected by atropine and pitressin, and the pain of muscular cramps may be relieved by whiffs of chloroform. Use of morphine and alcohol in any form is avoided. Specific treatment, such as the therapeutic use of anticholera serum and the administration of potassium permanganate or kaolin for neutralization of the toxin, has been disappointing, although cholera bacteriophage by mouth seems to have some small favourable effect. Certain drugs of the sulfonamide group, especially sulfaguanidine, were given extensive trial in Indian clinics with, on the whole, encouraging results, and the chemotherapy of cholera appears promising.

A majority of cases of cholera, especially during an epidemic, can be diagnosed on clinical grounds alone, and during an epidemic all suspected cases should be treated as cholera, and all contacts as potential cases. Diagnosis of the isolated case is more difficult, but the more important from the public health point of view. The disease may be confused with fulminating bacillary dysentery, with the algid and choleraic forms of malaria, trichinosis, food poisoning of staphylococcal or streptococcal aetiology, mushroom poisoning or poisoning with antimony or arsenic. The bacteriological diagnosis of cholera is dependent upon the isolation and identification of the vibrio. The demonstration of typical vibrios in a gram-stained smear from a flake of mucus is suggestive, and the vibrio may be isolated by culture on a selective medium and identified by agglutination with specific *O* antiserum and a negative reaction to the Greig test.

Immunity.—Infection with the cholera vibrio provokes an immune response as indicated by the appearance of bacteriolysins, agglutinins and other antibodies in the blood serum. Immunity to subsequent infection is not of a high order, however, nor does it persist for more than one to two years at the most. Prophylactic immunization was practised almost from the time of the discovery of the cholera vibrio, beginning with the work of Jaime Ferran in Spain and that of Waldemar Haffkine in India. A variety of immunizing preparations was used, including living vibrios, bacteriophage lysate and bilivaccine by mouth as well as the usual type of vaccine. Modern vaccines consist of suspensions of cholera vibrios killed by heat or phenol in isotonic saline in a concentration of 8,000,000,000 per millilitre and are administered in two parenteral inoculations of 0.5 and 1.0 ml. one week apart. The vaccines used in India contained the Inaba type only, but bivalent vaccines containing equal proportions of the Inaba and Ogawa types are widely used. Immunity appears as early as the third to fifth day after inoculation but is effective for less than a year, and reinoculation should be practised at intervals of six months. The results of phophylactic inoculation have been to some degree conflicting. For example, an extensive immunization program carried out in Indochina in the 1930s apparently produced no immunity to the disease, but field studies in India consistently gave encouraging results. In such a study carried out in Madras during the severe epidemic of 1941-42 the incidence of the disease was reduced more than 90% by prophylactic immunization.

Immunization does not, however, reduce the severity of the disease in the individual.

Epidemiology and Control.—The dissemination of cholera is dependent upon connecting links between infected faecal material and the mouths of susceptible persons. The vehicle is most often water, but the disease is also transmitted by foods consumed in the raw state and by direct or indirect personal contact. The explosive character of the epidemic is attributable to the simultaneous infection of large numbers of persons, as by a common water supply, coupled with the short incubation period, and its dramatic aspect is accentuated by the high case fatality rate. When the epidemic has run its course in a nonendemic area, the disease dies out completely because of the fragility of the vibrio and the absence of the chronic carrier state in cholera, and subsequent epidemics are dependent upon reimportation of the infection. In endemic areas, however, the infection persists in a smouldering form and, while the mechanism of its maintenance is not altogether clear, it is highly probable that it depends on the occurrence of mild cases of the disease transmitted from person to person under the relatively primitive conditions prevailing. For example, in India water is stored in tanks which serve for the disposal of faecal material and as a source of water for washing and drinking purposes; such water supplies are seldom protected by the usual sanitary measures such as chlorination, filtration or other means of purification. Habitual defecation in open fields about inhabited areas and the use of fresh night soil as fertilizer in truck gardens makes possible dissemination of the infection by flies, on the surfaces of leafy vegetables and the like. Under ordinary circumstances spread of the disease into Europe is prevented by inspection at the quarantine stations at Tor and Basra (*see* map), and it is readily controlled by the usual sanitary practices, especially water purification and sewage disposal. This was strikingly illustrated in the Balkan War in 1913 in which infection was widespread in the Bulgarian army about Sofia, but cases in the capital were largely imported and the disease showed little tendency to spread; Sofia was efficiently sewered and had an excellent water supply.

Ultimate control of the disease depends upon the development of a higher standard of living in the primitive parts of the far east, and under ideal conditions cholera could probably be stamped out entirely.

BIBLIOGRAPHY.—E. R. Stitt, *Diagnosis, Prevention and Treatment of Tropical Diseases,* 7th ed., rev. by R. P. Strong (1944); L. E. Napier, *The Principles and Practice of Tropical Medicine* (1946); T. T. Mackie and others, *A Manual of Tropical Medicine* (1945); J. E. Ash and S. Spitz, *Pathology of Tropical Diseases* (1945); W. Burrows, *Jordan-Burrows Textbook of Bacteriology,* 15th ed. (1949).

(W. BU.)

CHOLET, a town of western France, capital of an *arrondissement* in the department of Maine-et-Loire, 33 mi. E.S.E. of Nantes. Pop. (1946) 26,086. Cholet stands on high ground on the right bank of the Le Moine, which is crossed by a 15th-century bridge. Megalithic monuments are numerous in the neighbourhood. The town owes the rise of its prosperity to the settlement of weavers there by Edouard Colbert, count of Maulévrier, a brother of the great Colbert. It suffered severely in the War of La Vendée of 1793. A public garden occupies the site of the old castle. The town possesses a sub-prefecture, a tribunal of first instance, a chamber of commerce and a board of trade-arbitrators.

There are granite quarries in the vicinity. The chief industries are the manufacture of linen and of preserved foods. Cholet is an important centre for the sale of fat cattle, sheep and pigs, for which Paris is the chief market.

CHOLON ("great market"), a town of French Indo-China, the largest commercial centre of Cochin-China, 3½ mi. S.W. of Saigon, with which it is united by railway, tramways, roads and canal. Cholon was founded by Chinese immigrants about 1780 and is situated on the *Arroyo Chinois* at the junction of the Lo-Gom and a canal. Its waterways are frequented by innumerable boats and lined in some places with native dwellings built on piles, in others by quays and houses built by the French, who have also carried out drainage schemes, installed electric lighting in the main streets and erected factories, schools, hospitals and administrative buildings. Its population is almost entirely Asiatic. In 1880 the population was 45,000; in 1936 it was about 145,000. Of these about half were Chinese, divided into congregations according to their place of origin. During the rice season the town is visited by a large floating population. Pre-1941 Cholon had a municipal council, composed of French, Annamese and Chinese traders. An administrator of native affairs, nominated by the governor, fills the office of mayor.

The rice trade, almost monopolized by the Chinese, is the leading industry.

Tanning, dyeing, copper-founding, glass, brick and pottery manufacture, stone working, timber sawing and junk building are other industries.

CHOLONAN, a linguistic stock of South American Indians, so called from the Cholones, its most important tribe. The Cholonan Indians live in eastern Peru, between the eastern crest of the Andes and the upper Huallaga river, from the Monzon in the south to the Mayo in the north. Missions were established among them in the 17th century, so that they have now largely lost their original culture. They are sedentary agriculturists, and still retain the use of the blow-gun, widely distributed among the neighbouring tribes to the north and east.

They live in cane-walled, thatched-roof houses, but, unlike their neighbours to the north and east, do not use the hammock for sleeping.

They appear to have had elaborate puberty ceremonies for the young men.

See E. Poeppig, *Reise in Chile, Peru und auf dem Amazonenstrome,* etc. (Leipzig, 1835).

CHOLULA, an ancient town of Mexico, in the state and on the plateau of Puebla, eight miles by rail W. by N. of the city of that name, and situated about 6,912 ft. higher than sea level. Pop. (1940) 8,424. The city's commercial and industrial standing is overshadowed by that of its larger, more modern neighbour, with which it is connected by tramway. At the time of the Spanish conquest, Cholula—then known as Cholo-lan—was a large and important town, consecrated to the worship of the god Quetzalcoatl, who had here one of the most imposing temples in Anahuac, built on the summit of a truncated pyramid, the largest of its kind in the world. This pyramid, constructed of sun-dried bricks and earth, 177 ft. high, and covering an area of nearly 45 ac., is the most conspicuous object in the town and was built probably as an imposing site for a temple. Nothing definite is known of its age and history, as the fanatical zeal of Cortés and his companions destroyed whatever historical data the temple may have contained. Cholula was visited by Cortés in 1519 during his eventful march inland to Montezuma's capital, Tenochtitlán, when he treacherously massacred its inhabitants and pillaged the city, pretending to distrust the hospitable inhabitants. Cortés estimated that the town then had 20,000 habitations, and its suburbs as many more, but this was undoubtedly a deliberate exaggeration. The Cholulans were of Nahuatl origin and were semi-independent, yielding only a nominal allegiance to Montezuma. They were a trading people, holding fairs, and exchanging their manufactures of textiles and pottery for other produce. The pyramid is believed to have been built by a people occupying this region before the Cholulans.

CHOPIN, FRÉDÉRIC FRANÇOIS (1810–1849), Polish musical composer and pianist, was born at Zelazowa-Wola, near Warsaw, on Feb. 22, 1810 (*not* Mar. 1, 1809). His father, of French origin, born at Nancy in 1770, had married a Polish lady, Justine Krzyzanowska. Frédéric was their third child. His first musical education he received from Adalbert Ziwny, a Czech musician, who is said to have been a passionate admirer of J. S. Bach. He also received a fair general education at the recently-founded Lyceum of Warsaw, where his father was professor of French. His musical genius opened to Chopin the best circles of Polish society, at that time unrivalled in Europe for its ease of intercourse, the beauty and grace of its women, and its liberal appreciation of artistic gifts. These early impressions were of lasting influence on Chopin's development. While at school he received thorough instruction in the theory of his art from Joseph Elsner, a learned musician and director of the conservatoire at Warsaw. When in 1829 he left his native town for Vienna, where his *début* as a pianist took place, he was in all respects a perfectly formed and developed artist. There is in his compositions little of that gradual progress which, for instance, in Beethoven, necessitates a classification of his works according to different periods. Chopin's individuality and his style were distinctly pronounced in that set of variations on "La ci darem" which excited the wondering enthusiasm of Robert Schumann. In 1831 he left Vienna with the intention of visiting London; but on his way to England he reached Paris and settled there for the rest of his life. Here again he soon became the favourite and musical hero of society. His connection with Mme. Dudevant, better known by her literary pseudonym of George Sand (*q.v.*), is an important feature of Chopin's life. When in 1839 his health began to fail, George Sand went with him to Majorca, and it was mainly owing to her tender care that the composer recovered his health for a time. Chopin declared that the destruction of his relations with Mme. Dudevant in 1847 broke up his life. The association of these two artists has provoked a whole literature of the nature of their relations, of which the novelist's *Un Hiver à Majorque* was the beginning. The last ten years of Chopin's life were a continual struggle with the pulmonary disease to which he succumbed in Paris Oct. 17, 1849. The year before his death he visited England, where he was received with enthusiasm by his numerous admirers.

Chopin died in the arms of his sister, who hastened from Poland to his death-bed. He was buried in the cemetery of Père Lachaise.

In looking through the list of Chopin's compositions, teeming with mazurkas, valses, polonaises, and other forms of national dance music, one might hardly suppose that here one of the most melancholy natures revealed itself. This seeming paradox is explained by the type of Chopin's nationality, of which it has justly been said that its very dances are sadness intensified. Yet notwithstanding its strongly pronounced national characteristics, Chopin's music is always expressive of his individual feelings and sufferings in the highest possible degree. He is indeed the lyrical composer *par excellence,* and the intensity of his expression finds its equal in literature only in the songs of Heinrich Heine, to whom he has been so often likened. Such high-strung passion cannot be prolonged, and hence it was in works of small compass, such as the nocturne and the étude, that Chopin found the happiest expression of his genius. In compositions of larger scope he was out of his element, and even the beauty of his melodies and harmonies cannot wholly banish the impression of incongruity. Fortunately, he himself had an unerring sense of his own limitations, though there could be no greater mistake than to suppose that because he wrote in the smaller forms he was not, even so, one of the greatest of masters. Chopin's piano-playing was as exquisite as his music, and many accounts left by his contemporaries have testified to the irresistible fascination which he exercised by performances described as the last word in delicacy, subtlety and refinement.

It is well to sift the posthumous works from those published under Chopin's direction, for the last three mazurkas are the only things he did not keep back as misrepresenting him. On these principles his mature works are summed up in the 42 mazurkas (Opp. 6, 7, 17, 24, 30, 33, 41, 50, 56, 59, 63, and the beautiful contribution to the collection *Notre temps*); seven polonaises (Opp. 26, 40, 53, 61); 24 preludes (in all the major and minor keys), Op. 28, and the single larger prelude, Op. 45; 27 études (12 in Op. 10, 12 in Op. 25, and 3 written for the *Méthode des méthodes*); 18 nocturnes (Opp. 9, 15, 27, 32, 37, 48, 55, 62); 4 ballades, in forms of Chopin's own invention (Opp. 23, 38, 47, 52); 4 scherzos (Opp. 20, 31, 39, 54); 8 waltzes (Opp. 18, 34, 42, 64); and several pieces of various description, notably the great fantasia, Op. 49, and the impromptus, Opp. 29, 36, 51. The posthumous works number 35 pieces, besides a small volume of songs a few of which are of great interest.

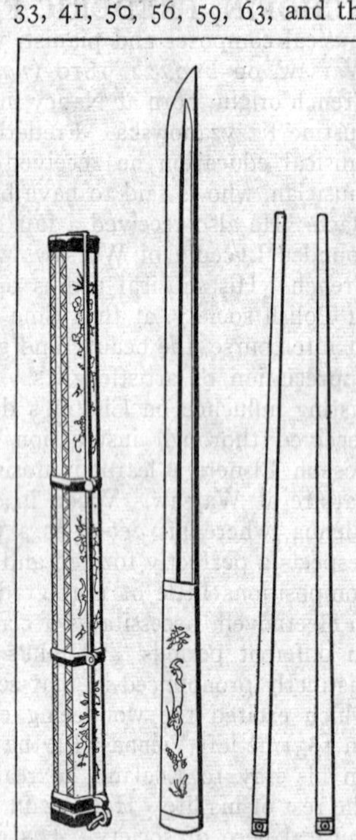

BY COURTESY OF THE TRUSTEES OF THE BRITISH MUSEUM

CHINESE CHOPSTICKS. TO THE LEFT IS A LONG, SLENDER KNIFE WITH ITS ENGRAVED CASE

The editions of Chopin's works by his pupil Mikuli and by Klindworth are full of valuable elucidation as to methods of performance, but unfortunately they do not distinguish the commentary from the text. The critical edition published by Breitkopf and Härtel, with all its mistakes, is absolutely necessary for students who wish to know what Chopin wished to put into the hands of players of independent judgment.

The Chopin literature is very extensive. The standard biography is the English work of Prof. F. Niecks (1888), while other leading works are those by Liszt, Karasowski and Huneker. *See* also W. H. Hadow, *Studies in Modern Music,* Henry Bidou, *Chopin* (1927) and G. Ashton Jonson's useful *Handbook to Chopin's Works.*

CHOPSTICKS, the "pidgin-English" name for the pair of small tapering sticks used by the Chinese in eating. (Chinese *kwai-tse* "the quick ones," "chop"-quick.) They are made of wood, bone, or ivory, somewhat longer and thinner than a lead-pencil. Held between the thumb and fingers, they are used to take up portions of food, cut up into small pieces. Many rules of etiquette govern the proper conduct of the chopsticks; laying them across the bowl is a sign that the guest wishes to leave the table; they are not used during a time of mourning, when food is eaten with the fingers; and various methods of handling them form a secret code of signalling.

CHORALE, a term in music used by English writers to indicate the hymn-tunes composed or adopted for use in church by the German reformers (Lat. *Choralis*). German writers, however, apply the terms "Choral" and "Chorale-geesang," as Luther himself would have applied them, to any solemn melody used in the church. It is thus the equivalent of canto fermo; and the German rhymed versions of the biblical and other ancient canticles, such as the Magnificat and the Te Deum, are set to curious corruptions of the corresponding Gregorian tunes, which adaptations the composers of classical German music called chorales with no more scruple than they applied the name to tunes of secular origin, German or foreign. The peculiarity of German chorale-music, however, is that its use, and consequently much of its invention, not only arose in connection with the Reformation, by which the liturgy of the church became "understanded of the people," but also that it belongs to a musical epoch in which symmetry of melody and rhythm was beginning to assume artistic importance. The growing sense of form shown by some of Luther's own tunes (*e.g., Vom Himmel hoch, da komm' ich her*) soon advanced, especially in the tunes of Crüger, beyond any that was shown by folk-music; and it provided a massive bulwark against the chaos that was threatening to swamp music on all sides at the beginning of the 17th century.

By Bach's time all the polyphonic instrumental and vocal art-forms of the 18th century were mature; and though he loved to derive the design as well as the details of a large movement from the shape of the chorale tune on which it was based, he became quite independent of any aid from symmetry in the tune as raw material. The chorus of his cantata "Jesus nun sei gepreiset" is one of the most perfectly designed and quite the longest of movements ever based upon a chorale-tune treated phrase by phrase. Yet the tune is one of the most intractable in the world, though its most unpromising portion is the basis of the most impressive feature in Bach's design (the slow middle section in triple time.)

In recent times the great development of interest in folk-music, and the discovery of the unique importance of Bach's work, have combined to tempt writers on music to over-estimate the distinctness of the art-forms based upon the German chorale. There is really nothing in these art-forms which is not continuous with the universal practice of writing counterpoint on a canto fermo. Thus Handel in his Italian and English works wrote no entire chorale movements, yet what is the passage in the "Hallelujah" chorus from "the kingdom of this world" to the end, but a treatment of the second part of the chorale "Wachet auf"? Again, to return to the 16th century, what are the hymns of Palestrina but figured chorales? In what way, except in the lack of symmetry in the Gregorian phrasing, do they differ from the contemporary setting by Orlando di Lasso, also a Roman Catholic, of the German chorale "Vater unser im Himmelreich"? In later times the use of German chorales, as in Mendelssohn's oratorios and organ-sonatas, has had rather the aspect of a revival than of a development; though the technique and spirit of Brahms's posthumous organ chorale-preludes is thoroughly modern and vital.

One of the most important, and practically the earliest collection of "Chorales" is that made by Luther and Johann Walther (1496–1570), the "Enchiridion," published in 1524. Next in importance we may place the Genevan Psalter (1st ed., Strasbourg, 1542, final edition 1562), which is now conclusively proved to be the work of Bourgeois. From this Sternhold and Hopkins borrowed extensively (1562). The psalter of C. Goudimel (Paris, 1565) is another among many prominent collections showing the steps towards congregational singing, *i.e.,* the restriction to "note-against-note" counterpoint (*sc.* plain harmony), and, in 12 cases, the assigning of the melody to the treble instead of to the tenor. The first hymn-book in which this latter step was acted on throughout is Osiander's "Geistliche Lieder . . . also gesetzt, das ein christliche Gemein durchaus mitsingen kann" (1586). But many of the finest and most famous tunes are of much later origin than any such collections. Several (*e.g.*, "Ich freue mich in dir") cannot be traced before Bach, and were very probably composed by him. (D. F. T.)

CHORAL SINGING. In Great Britain choral singing, from 1913 to 1928, falls into three periods—the splendid activity which was checked by the World War, the struggles during that dark period, and the efforts since 1919 to find means of meeting the new situation. In the first period there was extraordinary vitality and much new impetus.

Some Notable Figures.—The old tradition of solid, square-toed choralism had been shaken to the roots by the personality of Dr. (now Sir) Henry Coward, the Sheffield chorus master. He had turned the big, heavy, unwieldy body of the provincial choral society into a living, sensitive, functioning organism, and his exploits had created a sensational interest in this form of art. Some of his disciples, no doubt, carried his ideas too far and lost sight of the end in exploiting the means. There were other notable workers in the field, with different aims, each contributing to the general good. Harry Evans, by his work in Wales and Liverpool, his keen personality and penetrating insight, made a great impression on the choral world. He was particularly successful in modern works for large choirs, exploiting vivid colouring. His comparatively early death in 1914 was a severe loss.

Two other choirs, also under men of outstanding personality, were beginning to attract attention. Both were breaking away from the lines traditionally followed by the average British choral society. In 1904 Charles Kennedy Scott, an able and versatile musician, founded in London the Oriana Madrigal Society, a small body originally intended to arouse interest in the English madrigal school. It eventually widened its scope and devoted much attention to modern British unaccompanied choral works, and in the period in question it was becoming firmly established in public notice. The choice of programmes struck out new lines and gave fresh ideas to choral conductors all over the world.

In Glasgow an amateur musician, Hugh S. Roberton, was attracting attention by the skilled singing of his Orpheus Choir, a body of about 120 singers, concentrating mostly on Scottish song arrangements and unaccompanied works on a small scale. Dr. E. C. Bairstow, organist of York Minster since 1913, was proving himself one of the most able choral conductors in the land, and a church musician who made the services at the Minster among the finest of the world.

The period being described was also remarkable for experiments in choral composition. The new technique acquired by large choral societies and the enormous strides made by choirs in touch with the competition festival movement opened up new possibilities to composers. The most daring experimentalist was Sir Granville Bantock, who wrote (1912–14) *Atalanta in Calydon* and *The Vanity of Vanities*. Entitled choral symphonies, they are divided into four movements on the lines of the traditional orchestral form, and are written for unaccompanied voices. The voices are disposed in 20 and 12 parts respectively, not with a view to polyphonic writing, but to obtain contrasts of colour on the lines of strings, wind and brass of the orchestra. Many highly original effects are obtained, and severe problems set for choir and trainer.

Recent Developments.—On the conclusion of the World War the task of reconstruction proved even greater than had been anticipated. Traditions had been broken and the formerly constant supply of tenors and basses was not and has not been recaptured. Subscribers who had supported institutions for many years as a duty did not resume their help. The war, too, had accelerated a change of taste which had gradually been coming about. Standard societies had always been able to rely upon the popular oratorios of Handel and Mendelssohn to crowd houses and fill coffers. *The Messiah* had paid many and many a deficit. But, generally speaking, this was no longer the case. Moreover, costs of halls, orchestra, printing and advertising, were all higher, and in addition there was the devastating entertainment tax. Consequently few societies could meet their expenses.

On the other side of the account, however, there was a new awakening of competition festivals, which, firmly established before the war, have attained an extraordinary vitality since. One great value of this movement is that it affords a *raison d'être* for the existence of every kind of society, except the larger bodies. Rural festivals bring into existence choirs in the smallest of villages, and the larger festivals stimulate the virtuosity of the leading bodies. Choirs connected with churches and chapels, women's institutes, guilds, boy scouts, all sorts of male, female and mixed organizations, are encouraged, improved and given a new outlook. In this way the problem of finding an audience for a concert and making ends meet may be avoided.

There has been a remarkable development of male voice choirs, mostly of working men, often connected with factories or works of various kinds, and these have, to a certain extent, thinned the male ranks of mixed choirs. A keen sense of sportsmanship and comradeship results in much more intensive work than is customary with mixed choirs. "Trade" bodies were willing to submit to 60 or 70 rehearsals of a single part song. A much higher standard of music is now obtained through the influence of these festivals. The singing of madrigals has received an immense impetus. Choral arrangements of folk songs and compositions by the best of our modern composers are being brought within the ken of many thousands of people. For some festivals choirs prepare choruses from an important work which is finally given by combined forces. In this way tiny rural villages know their Bach cantatas, and are even intimate with the B minor Mass and other large-scale compositions.

Another striking development of importance has been the growth of "works" choirs, some of which are very fine bodies. The Glasgow police and tramways choirs and the L.N.E.R. Musical Society are examples. One interesting fact is being disclosed by this activity. It was thought that the best choral singing was to be found only in Yorkshire, and that other parts of the country could not hope to rival that county. But the opinion of most adjudicators is that first-rate work can be produced anywhere. Without doubt the most robust voices come from this northern county, and in other parts of the country the current quality is less adapted to powerful and brilliant results, but a good conductor can produce superlatively good results from material existing in any district in the British Isles. Adjudicators of the widest experience have found astonishing results in places which were supposed to be unmusical. The general consensus of opinion among critics at the Leeds festival of 1925 was that although vocally the choir there was perhaps the finest in the world, technically it was inferior to many bodies in other parts of the country. This change of centre foreshadows a new era in choral singing.

Some Notable Choirs.—In London the Oriana Choir continues to do good work, forming a model for madrigal singing, and producing the latest works of modern British composers. In 1919 the Philharmonic Choir was formed in order that a large choral body might be affiliated with the Philharmonic Society. Kennedy Scott was appointed conductor, and he had proved as brilliant with a large choir as with a small one. Among the important works produced, in addition to classics, have been Bax's motets and the choral works of Delius. In particular, the performance of the *Mass of Life* in April 1925, reached a remarkable standard. London possesses, for the first time in its history, both a large and a small choir which can give performances unexcelled anywhere else in the kingdom. A junior philharmonic choir, composed of young women, is now in existence. Besides giving concerts of its own, it forms a source from which experienced singers can be drafted into the main body.

In Scotland.—The Glasgow Orpheus Choir has reached a state of popularity unprecedented in the history of choral singing, and maintains the level of its superlatively polished performances. It attracts crowded audiences in Glasgow, gives concerts all over Scotland, and makes annual raids into England. It has done much to stimulate choral singing; its policy has been to afford opportunities for the training of conductors, and to give advice and assistance on the question of formation of new choirs. It is probably the first time that any choir has undertaken missionary work on such a large scale. A most successful tour was made in Canada and the United States of America, in the summer of 1926, and the reputation of British choral singing was brilliantly enhanced. In Manchester the Hallé Choir (chorus master, Mr. Dawber) has within late years won fresh honours at the concerts conducted by Sir Hamilton Harty.

Changes of Taste.—A significant feature in recent years has been the greatly increased interest in Bach. At the beginning of the century Bach was considered suitable for only the finest choirs, and especially cultured audiences. His cantatas were almost unknown in Britain. Now large and small societies produce his larger works frequently, and his church cantatas are being regularly performed. Reference may be made in this connection to an experiment, the founding of the Newcastle-upon-Tyne Bach Choir in 1915 to perform the works of the master, not with the wrong proportions of an orchestra of 50 and a choir of 300, but with forces approximating to those used in his day. The choir, after a period of experiment, was fixed at 40, ten to a line. The orchestra varies according to the work concerned; in some cases it is practically equal to the choir in numbers. Besides all the large works of Bach and the motets, about 80 of his cantatas have been given. A three days' Bach festival was given in London in Feb. 1921. British composers are also included in the scheme of work, over 60 having been represented. It gave in Newcastle cathedral in 1924 the first known complete performance of Byrd's recently discovered *Great Service,* and the Carnegie United Kingdom Trust sent the choir to give three performances of it in St. Margaret's, Westminster, London, in November of the same year. Several choirs have been formed on its lines, in Doncaster, Stockton, Leicester, Liverpool, and are helping to spread a knowledge of Bach unrivalled in any other country outside Germany if, indeed, that country is not now outdistanced in this direction by Great Britain. A Bach Cantata Club began operations in London in Feb. 1926, under the direction of C. K. Scott.

The Newcastle-upon-Tyne Bach Choir was invited to sing at the festival of the International Society for Contemporary Music, in Frankfurt-on-Main in July 1927, and afterwards made a short tour of German university towns, singing unaccompanied British music ranging from Byrd to Holst.

Advance in Technique.—It is impossible in a short article even to mention all the manifestations of choral singing throughout Great Britain. As a result of the competition festival movement, new conductors of merit are appearing everywhere. Works which, a few years ago, were looked upon as extremely difficult, for instance, Elgar's *Gerontius,* are now sung in many small towns. The work in question will receive 50 to 60 performances every winter. To take a single example, an isolated town like Kendal, with a population of 14,000, can produce such works as Holst's *Cloud Messenger* and Vaughan Williams' *Sea Symphony.*

At the same time the improved standard of choral singing has inspired a series of fine works by British composers. Vaughan Williams' unaccompanied *Mass,* and his oratorio, *Sancta Civitas,* Holst's *Hymn of Jesus* and first choral symphony, and a remarkable group of unaccompanied motets by Arnold Bax, are a tribute alike to the technical efficiency of choral bodies and to the vitality and high level of the great tradition of native compositions for choirs.

Community singing has been another development of the movement and was inaugurated in 1915 on the lines of successful gatherings in Australia. Meetings were organized at which folk, national, and simple classical songs were sung in unison, and easy rounds were rehearsed, the music being taught by pattern, so that no technical knowledge was demanded from the singers. This "caught on" in a remarkable way, and the movement promises to become a permanent feature of national life, closely allied with the folk dance revival. Notable leaders are Gibson Young (who was one of the prime movers in Australia), Geoffrey Shaw, Sir Richard Terry, and Sir Hugh Allen.

In the Dominions.—British choirs overseas bid fair to follow the good example of the Mother Country. Dr. Fricker, late of Leeds, is doing splendid work in Toronto. The Winnipeg Male Voice Choir, under Hugh Ross (since conductor of the Schola Cantorum in New York) impressed visiting adjudicators greatly. British adjudicators returning from recent competitive festival tours, report that choral activity may outdistance the Mother Country in a short time, and speak enthusiastically of a remarkable standard of performance. Possibly by virtue of its climate, Australia produces splendid women's voices, which rather overweigh the men's. South Africa is producing some astonishing results with native races, especially in schools, where early maturity enables fully fledged four-part singing to be cultivated. There is much choral activity in the main centres of that continent. (W. G. W.)

THE UNITED STATES

The early growth of choral music in the United States, as elsewhere, was associated with the Church. It was the Puritans of New England rather than the Dutch colonists of New York who were mainly responsible for the earliest developments, and this although the Pilgrim fathers brought to America a hatred of musical culture that is without parallel in history. Over a century of controversy was required, indeed, before the Church reluctantly accepted organized singing in "the new and ruleable way," which simply meant singing from the printed page rather than constantly repeating the traditional tunes from memory. Even late in the 18th century some localities still sang in "the usual way," which often consisted of the congregation's singing parts of two or three different tunes to one stanza of a hymn, or even singing different tunes at the same time. These melodies were sung so slowly that it was often necessary to take breath twice on one and the same tone or word-syllable.

In the face of such a handicap, it is surprising that early choral singing developed as rapidly as it did. But the acceptance of organized singing in the Church brought with it the advent of the singing school, with its psalm-tune teacher, and thereafter the choral society was a natural development. An early, but it must be admitted not too well authenticated, report describes a performance of the *Messiah* with organ accompaniment in the New York Trinity church as long ago as Jan. 9, 1770, less than 28 years after the original production of the work.

Early Organizations.—Probably the first stable organization of amateur singers in America was the Stoughton Musical Society, founded in Stoughton, Mass., by the first American composer, William Billings, in 1786. This antedates by five years the famous Berlin *Singakademie.* A rapid growth of similar choral societies followed, so that by 1812 the regularly established amateur choruses in America already outnumbered those of Germany, although the latter were doubtless vastly superior in quality. Of more lasting influence than the Stoughton Society was the Handel and Haydn Society, founded in Boston in 1815. This, while it lasted, became to America what the *Singakademie* of Berlin was to Continental Europe—the model for all similar organizations throughout its native country. It may be added that this society, whose present conductor is Thompson Stone, actually negotiated with Beethoven for a new choral work.

Henceforward, choral societies appeared in rapid succession. The short-lived Handel and Haydn Society of New York gave way to the New York Choral Society and the New York Sacred Music Society, both established in 1823, though the former only lasted a year. In 1844 the Musical Institute of New York was founded, but by 1850 it was saved only by an amalgamation of the three New York choral groups, the Vocal Society, the Sacred Music Society and the American Musical Institute, all combining to form the New York Harmonic Society. As a result of a controversy the short-lived Mendelssohn Society was formed in 1863, but nothing of a permanent nature was established until 1873, when Dr. Leopold Damrosch organized the New York Oratorio Society, which remains to-day as probably the foremost choral organization in the United States.

In recent years the Harvard and Radcliffe Glee clubs have taken part in notable choral performances with the Boston Symphony orchestra under Koussevitzky.

New York Oratorio Society.—Starting with a group numbering from 15 to 20, and giving its first concert with only 60 voices, Dr. Damrosch lived to direct such a festival as that of 1881 when he conducted a chorus of 1,200 and an orchestra of 250. At his death the work was continued by his son Walter and later, for a short period, by Frank Damrosch. Louis Koemmenich, a German conductor, did much for the development of the Oratorio Society. After 1921 the society was under the leadership of Albert Stoessel, who, in its annual Christmas production of the *Messiah,* and performances of other compositions of the great classical masters, as well as of modern works, had continued the traditions of the organization. In 1927 the society gave the first complete performance in New York of Bach's *B Minor Mass.* The Oratorio Society shares with the more recent Schola Cantorum of New York, founded by Kurt Schindler in 1909 (Hugh Ross, conductor), the responsibility of providing New York with choral music.

It was due largely to the singing schools of New England that choral culture found its way to other sections of the country. In the west, Cincinnati became a choral centre, developing around the German population who were responsible for the first American *Sängerfest* in 1849, just four years after such reunions had been introduced in Würzburg, Germany. Theodore Thomas was responsible for the first of the famous Cincinnati festivals, in 1873. With one exception they have taken place biennially since that time. The director in 1931, 1933, 1935, 1937 and 1939 was Eugene Goossens.

Of eastern choral festivals, two are of outstanding importance. The annual Worcester (Mass.) music festival was established in 1858 under the name of Musical Convention. In 1873 it became the Worcester County Musical Festival. The annual Bach festival at Bethlehem, Pa., is devoted to the works of the great master, and was responsible for the first complete American performance of the *B Minor Mass.* To-day the choral societies in the United States are almost innumerable; Philadelphia alone boasts over 60, and the number of such bodies throughout the whole country is being added to every year.

BIBLIOGRAPHY.—Elson, *The History of American Music;* Key, *International Music Year Book;* Krehbiel, *Choral Music in New York;* Mees, *Choirs and Choral Music;* Bauer, *Music Through the Ages.*

(A. STO.)

CHORAL SYMPHONY, a symphony including choral movements or numbers. Beethoven's ninth symphony, with vocal finale for four solo singers and chorus, is the most famous of all such works. Another is Mendelssohn's *Hymn of Praise.* Among more recent composers Mahler wrote several choral symphonies.

CHORAZIN and **BETHSAIDA.** Towns in the neighbourhood of Capernaum (Mth. xi., 21; Lk. x., 13). Since the 18th century the former has been identified with a ruined site *Khirbet Kerāzeh* about 2 m. N. of *Tell Hûm* (Capernaum). Amongst the ruins are the remains of a synagogue built of black basalt. Scholars are divided as to whether *one* Bethsaida is to be sought or *two.* Those who favour one generally locate it east of the Jordan at *Et-Tell* or *El-'Ardj* (either site answering the description of Bethsaida-Julias of Josephus, *Antiq.* xviii. 2. 1) or at *Mas 'adiyeh.* Those who would look for a separate "Bethsaida of Galilee" (John xii., 21) have advocated variously *Tell Hūm, 'Ain et-Tābighah, Khirbet* (*Khān*) *Minyeh* or *'Ain et-Tīneh.* Now that *Tell Hūm* has been identified with Capernaum, the identification of *Khirbet Minyeh* with Bethsaida is being urged.

CHOREA: *see* ST. VITUS'S DANCE.

CHORIAMBIC VERSE or **CHORIAMBICS,** lyric verse based on the choriambus, a group of four syllables, – ⏑ ⏑ – (*i.e.,* choree or trochee+iamb). It is especially characteristic of Aeolic verse, as that of Alcaeus, Sappho, and their Latin imitator Horace, but is not confined to it. Regularly, one or more choriambi are preceded, or followed, or both, by other groups of syllables, as

hoc dea ue|re Sybarim | cur properas | amando (Greater Sapphic).

integer ui | tae sceleris | que purus (Sapphic hendecasyllable).

sic fra|tres Helenae | lucida si|dera (Lesser Asclepiad).

tu ne | quaesieris | scire nefas | quem mihi quem | tibi
(Greater Asclepiad).

These and other varieties are arranged into various stanzas. These are essentially metres meant for song, not recitation, and are used to express emotion, serious or trivial. *See* GLYCONIC; SAPPHIC METRE.

Modern music often contains choriambi, but the few attempts at these in modern verse are mere *tours de force* as Gilbert Murray's:—

"an old | eagle, a blind | eagle who waits | hungry and cold | and still."

CHORICIUS, of Gaza, Greek sophist and rhetorician, flourished in the time of Anastasius I. (A.D. 491–518). He was the pupil of Procopius of Gaza, who must be distinguished from Procopius of Caesarea, the historian. His declamations, often accompanied by commentaries, include, besides panegyrics, funeral orations, and stock themes, *Epithalamioi,* or wedding speeches. Choricius was also the author of so-called *Ekphraseis,* descriptions of works of art after the manner of Philostratus. His moral maxims were largely drawn upon by Macarius Chrysocephalas, metropolitan of Philadelphia (middle of the 14th century), in his *Rodonia* (rose-garden). A special feature of Choricius' style is the avoidance of hiatus, peculiar to what is called the school of Gaza.

Editions by J. F. Boissonade (1846, supplemented by C. Graux in *Revue de philologie,* 1877), and R. Förster (1882–94); *see* also C. Kirsten, "Quaestiones Choricianae" in *Breslauer philologische Abhandlungen,* vii. (1894); G. Pietsch, "De Choricio Patrocli declamationis auctore" in same publication (1910), and article by W. Schmid in Pauly-Wissowa's *Realencyklopädie,* iii. 2 (1899). On the Gaza school *see* K. Seitz, *Die Schule von Gaza* (Heidelberg, 1892).

CHORIN, AARON (1766–1844), Hungarian rabbi and pioneer of religious reform, born at Weisskirchen, Moravia, on Aug. 3, 1766, educated at Prague, and became rabbi at Arad in 1789. His *Emek ha Shaweh* (Vale of the Plain) of 1803 was declared heretical by the orthodox party, but he continued to favour such reforms as modification of the traditional laws, vernacular prayers, and the use of the organ. Chorin was also interested in the promotion of schools, seminaries, and professions among the Jews. He died on July 26, 1844.

See L. Low: *Gesammelte Schriften* vol. ii. (Szegedin, 1889).

CHORIZONTES ("separators"), the name given to the Alexandrian critics who denied the single authorship of the *Iliad* and *Odyssey,* and held that the latter poem was the work of a later poet. The most important of them were the grammarians Xeno and Hellanicus; Aristarchus was their chief opponent (*see* HOMER).

CHORLEY, a municipal borough, Chorley parliamentary division, North Lancashire, England, 22 mi. N.W. from Manchester, on the L.M.S.R. and the Leeds and Liverpool canal. Pop. (est. 1938) 30,140. Area, 6.7 sq.mi. The town is situated on the "fall-line" between a westward projection of the Pennines and the North Lancashire plain. The church of St. Lawrence is mainly Perpendicular and contains fine woodwork. Textiles, railway-wagon making and metal-working are the chief industries, but there are several coal mines and stone quarries. There is a large reservoir of the Liverpool corporation water works with a capacity for 48,300,000 gal. The beautiful Elizabethan mansion of Astley hall, with park, was presented to Chorley as a World War I memorial. The corporation bought Duxbury park (541 ac.) in 1932.

CHORLU or CORLU, a town of European Turkey, in the vilayet of Adrianople; on the left bank of the Chorlu, a small left-hand tributary of the Ergene, 25 mi. N.E. of Silivri on the Sea of Marmora, and about 75 mi. by rail from Istanbul. Population (1940) 16,979. Chorlu has a station on the Istanbul-Edirne railway.

It manufactures woollen cloth (*shayak*) and native carpets, and exports cereals, oilcloth, carpets, cattle, poultry, fresh meat, game, fruits, wine, alcohol, hides and bones.

CHOROGRAPHY. (1) A description or delineation on a map of a district or tract of country (from the Gr. χώρα, a tract of country, and γράφειν, to write). The word is common in old geographical treatises, but is now superseded by the wider use of "topography."

(2) A system of notation to indicate the steps and movements in dancing.

CHOROTEGA, a group of linguistically related Indian tribes located on the west coasts of Honduras (Choluteca), Nicaragua (Mangue), and Costa Rica (Orotiña). Other groups are found in southern Mexico. All have lost their tribal identity, although the Mangue dialect is still in existence. Archaeological evidence assigns to the Chorotega an important place in the aboriginal culture history of Central America, for early phases of the Chorotega underlie the most ancient remains of the Maya.

See S. K. Lothrop, "Pottery of Costa Rica and Nicaragua," *Contributions from the Museum of the American Indian, Heye Foundation,* vol. viii., 1926, p. 20–100.

CHOROTES, a tribe of South American Indians belonging to the Matacan (*see* MATACO) linguistic stock. The Chorotes live in southern Bolivia on the eastern side of the upper Pilcomayo river. They are a tall, long-headed folk, with a simple semi-nomadic type of culture. The dress of both sexes is a short kilt of skins or coarse woollen cloth. Today, at least, the Chorotes practise some agriculture. They live in small, rudely thatched huts. They have no canoes. The bow is the main weapon. Simple pottery and netted bags are made. Village chiefs are hereditary and have considerable power. The women select their husbands.

See E. Nordenskiold, *Indianerleben; El Gran Chaco* (Leipzig, 1913).

CHÓRUM or ÇORUM, the chief town, pop. (1950) 22,835, of the vilayet of the same name in Turkey, altitude 2,300 ft., on the edge of a plain, almost equidistant from Amasia and Yozgat. Pop. of vilayet (1950) 342,290. The ancient *Euchaïta,* 15 mi. E., was attacked by the Huns A.D. 508, and became a bishopric at an early period. It contained the tomb of the revered St. Theodore, who slew a dragon in the vicinity and became one of the great warrior saints of the Greek Church. (*See* J. G. C. Anderson, *Studia Pontica.*)

CHORUS (Gr. χορός), properly a dance, and especially the sacred dance, accompanied by song, of ancient Greece at the festivals of the gods. The word χορός seems originally to have referred to a dance in an enclosure, and is therefore usually connected with the root appearing in Gr. χόρτος, hedge, enclosure, Lat. *hortus,* garden, and in the Eng. "yard," "garden" and "garth." In the chorus sung in honour of Dionysus the ancient Greek drama had its birth. From that of the winter festival, consisting of the κῶμος or band of revellers, chanting the "phallic songs," with ribald dialogue between the leader and his band, sprang "comedy," while from the dithyrambic chorus of the spring festival came "tragedy." (For the history of the chorus in Greek drama *see* DRAMA: *Greek Drama.*)

The chorus as a factor in drama survived only in the various imitations or revivals of the ancient Greek theatre in other languages. A chorus is found in Milton's *Samson Agonistes.* The Elizabethan dramatists applied the name to a single character employed for the recitation of prologues or epilogues. Apart from the uses of the term in drama, the word "chorus" has been employed chiefly in music. It is used of any organized body of singers, in opera, oratorio, cantata, etc., and, in the form "choir," of the trained body of singers of the musical portions of a religious service in a cathedral or church. As applied to musical compositions, a "chorus" is a composition written in parts, each to be sung by groups of voices in a large body of singers. The word is also used of that part of a song repeated at the close of each verse, in which the audience or a body of singers may join with the soloist.

In the early middle ages the name *chorus* was given to a primitive bagpipe without a drone. Giraldus Cambrensis in his *Topographia Hiberniae* mentions it as one of the three instruments of Wales and Scotland, though there is some reason to believe that he may have been confusing it with the crot or crwth, an entirely different instrument. It is further recorded that King James I. of Scotland was renowned for his skill as a performer on various musical instruments, one of which was the chorus.

CHOSE, a term used in law in different senses. *Chose local* is a thing annexed to a place, as a mill. A *chose transitory* is that which is movable, and can be carried from place to place. But the use of the word "chose" in these senses is practically obsolete, and it is now used only in the phrases *chose in action* and *chose in possession.* A "chose in action," in its more limited meaning, denotes the right to sue for a debt or damages, whether arising out of a contract or a tort. Less accurately, the money itself which could be recovered is frequently termed a chose in action, as is also sometimes the document evidencing a title to a chose in action, such as a bond or a policy of insurance, though strictly it is only the right to recover the money which can be so termed. Choses in action were either *legal* or *equitable.* Where the chose could be recovered by an action at law, as a debt (whether arising from contract or tort), it was termed a legal chose in action; where the chose was recoverable only by a suit in equity, as a legacy or money held upon a trust it was termed an equitable chose in action.

The courts of Common law did not originally (except in the case of negotiable instruments) recognize the assignment of choses in action. Any attempt to assign a chose in action was invalid, and if the debtor paid the assignee, he could be compelled to pay the debt over again to the assignor. The only way in which a debt could be transferred was by a new contract of a trilateral nature in which the debtor was released by the assignor, and consented, in consideration of such release, to become liable to the assignee. This was a novation, not an assignment. But courts of equity at an early date gave effect to an assignment of a chose in action for valuable consideration, treating the assignee as an agent of the assignor with an irrevocable authority to collect and keep the proceeds. By the end of the eighteenth century the law courts adopted a similar doctrine permitting the assignee to sue in the assignor's name. *Winch* v. *Keeley,* 1 T.R. 619. In America statutes known as real party in interest statutes are common permitting the assignee to sue in his own name. In England under the Judicature Act of 1783 as amended by the Law of Property Act, 1925, permits the assignee to sue in his own name without joining the assignor, provided (a) the assignment was absolute and not by way of charge only; (b) the assignment was in writing; and (c) notice in writing was given to the debtor or party to be charged.

See Williston, Contracts, c. 14.

A chose in possession is opposed to a chose in action, and is a thing in actual physical possession. A chose in possession is freely transferable by delivery.

CHOSEN: *see* KOREA.

CHOSROES (koz'rō-ēz), in middle and modern Persian *Khosrau* ("with a good name"), a common name, borne by a king of the Iranian legend (Kai Khosrau); by a Parthian king, commonly called by the Greeks Osroes; and by the following two Sassanid kings.

1. CHOSROES I., "the Blessed" (*Anushirvan*), A.D. 531–579, successor of Kavadh I., and the most famous of the Sassanid kings. At the beginning of his reign he concluded an "eternal" peace with the emperor Justinian, who wanted to be free for the conquest of Africa and Sicily. But successes against the Vandals and Goths caused Chosroes to renew the war in 540. He invaded Syria and took Antioch, and during the next years fought successfully in Lazica or Lazistan (the ancient Colchis, *q.v.*), on the Black sea, and in Mesopotamia. In 545 an armistice was concluded and in 562 a peace for 50 years, in which the Persians left Lazistan to the Romans, and the Romans paid subsidies to Persia. Meanwhile in the east the Hephthalites had been attacked by the Turks, who now appear for the first time in history. Chosroes united with them and conquered Bactria, while he left the country north of the Oxus to the Turks. He also assisted the dynasts of Yemen to expel the Ethiopians and Yemen became dependent on Persia. In 571 a new war with Rome broke out about Armenia, in which Chosroes conquered the fortress Dara on the Euphrates, invaded Syria and Cappadocia, and returned with large booty. During the negotiations with the emperor

Tiberius, Chosroes died in 579, and was succeeded by his son Hormizd IV.

Although Chosroes had extirpated the heretical Persian sect of the Mazdakites (*see* KAVADH) he was a tolerant adherent of Zoroastrian orthodoxy. He introduced a system of taxation, based upon a survey of landed possessions begun by his father.

2. CHOSROES II., "the Victorious" (*Parvez*), 590–628, son of Hormizd IV and grandson of Chosroes I, was raised to the throne by the magnates who had rebelled against his father in 590. At the same time the general Bahram Chobin proclaimed himself king. The war with the Romans, begun in 571, had not yet ended. Chosroes fled to Syria, and persuaded the emperor Maurice (*q.v.*) to send help. Many acknowledged Chosroes, and in 591 he was brought back to Ctesiphon and Bahram Chobin beaten. Peace with Rome was then made, Maurice merely restoring the former frontier and abolishing the subsidies which had formerly been paid to the Persians. When in 602 Maurice was murdered by Phocas, Chosroes began war with Rome to avenge his death. His armies plundered Syria and Asia Minor, and in 608 advanced to Chalcedon. In 613 and 614 Damascus and Jerusalem were taken by the general Shahrbaraz, and the Holy Cross seized. Soon after, Egypt fell. The Romans could offer little resistance, as they were torn by internal dissensions, and pressed by the Avars and Slavs. At last, in 622, the emperor Heraclius (successor of Phocas in 610) was able to take the field. In 624 he advanced into northern Media, where he destroyed the great fire temple of Gandzak (Gazaca); in 626 he fought in Lazistan, while Shahrbaraz advanced to Chalcedon and tried in vain to conquer Constantinople. In 627 Heraclius defeated the Persian army at Nineveh and advanced toward Ctesiphon. Chosroes fled, and as his despotism and indolence had roused opposition, his eldest son, Kavadh II, whom he had imprisoned, was set free and proclaimed king. Four days afterward, Chosroes was murdered (Feb. 628). Meanwhile, Heraclius returned in triumph to Constantinople; in 629 the Cross was given back to him and Egypt evacuated, while the Persian empire, from the apparent greatness which it had reached ten years earlier, sank into hopeless anarchy.

See PERSIA: *Ancient History*, and the references there given. For the Roman wars *see* authorities quoted under MAURICE and HERACLIUS.

CHOTA NAGPUR, a division of British India in Bihar, consisting of five British districts, viz., Hazaribagh, Ranchi, Palamau, Manbhum and Singhbhum. Chota Nagpur consists of a hilly, forest-clad plateau, inhabited mostly by aboriginal races, between the basins of the Son, the Ganges and the Mahanadi. The total area is 27,112 sq.mi. The population in 1941 was 7,516,349. The principal agricultural products are rice, Indian corn, pulses, oilseeds and potatoes. A small quantity of tea is grown in Ranchi district. The principal jungle products are timber, lac, tussur silk and *mahuá* flowers, which are used as food and also distilled into a strong country liquor. Chota Nagpur contains the Jharia, Giridih, Bokaro, Karanpura, Ramgarh and Daltonganj coal fields. It has other valuable mineral resources. Mica is mined in Hazaribagh and iron ore in Singhbhum, where the output is already nearly 500,000 tons; there is a belt of copper ore in the latter district, where also manganese ore, gold, chromite and apatite occur; and important deposits of bauxite have been found in Ranchi and Palamau.

The indigenous inhabitants consist of non-Aryan tribes, the principal of whom are the Hos, Oraons, Santals, Mundas and Bhumij. Except in Palamau these tribes were never subdued by the Mohammedans, who contented themselves with occasional expeditions and an irregular tribute of diamonds. Until the country passed under British rule, moreover, there was very little communication between Chota Nagpur and the plains of India, with the result that the tribes have preserved to a large extent their languages, customs and primitive religions.

CHOUANS, the name given to the bands of peasants, mainly smugglers and dealers in contraband salt, who rose in revolt in the west of France, in 1793, and joined the royalists of la Vendée (*see* FRANCE: *History*). The Breton word *chouan* means "screech-owl," and is supposed to have been originally applied as a nickname to Jean Cottereau (1767–94), the leader of the revolt, and afterward extended to his followers. In any case, it was appropriate; for they were night birds and used the hoot of an owl as a signal. The motive for revolt was less devotion to the monarchy than resentment at interference of the new republican government with their old habits; the ruin of their contraband trade by the abolition of the *Gabelle* (*q.v.*); the attacks by the convention on the priesthood, and, above all, the enforcement of conscription. Their methods of warfare were barbarous and were met by barbarous reprisals. A vivid picture of these wild people is given by Honoré de Balzac in his novel *Les Chouans.*

CHOUETTE, a method whereby three or more persons may participate in a two-hand game. The three or more players establish an order of precedence, by lot or in any other way. Highest in precedence is "in the box" and plays against next highest, who is "captain." All other players bet that the captain (with whom they may consult) will win. If the man in the box wins, he collects the agreed stake from each other player individually; the captain becomes lowest in precedence. If the captain wins, he is in the box for the next game. The player previously in the box pays the agreed stake to each other player individually and becomes lowest in the order of precedence. In either case, the player who was next under the captain in precedence becomes the captain for the next game. (A. H. MD.)

CHOUGH (*Pyrrhocorax pyrrhocorax*), a bird of the crow family. It inhabits mountains and rocky coasts in Europe and North Africa. The combined effects of persecution by man and competition with the jackdaw (*q.v.*) have reduced its numbers greatly and it is now rare. Recognized by its black plumage and bright red legs and red, curved beak, the Cornish chough is more slenderly built than the crows. It is less common in Great Britain and Ireland, though a breeding resident. The Alpine chough (*P. graculus*), smaller and with a yellow bill, is gregarious. It is a European species.

CHOUTEAU, AUGUSTE (1739–1829), American pioneer, was born in New Orleans, La., in 1739. With his younger brother Pierre (1749–1849), he was the founder of the city of St. Louis, Mo. In Aug. 1763, they joined the expedition of Pierre Ligueste Laclède who had received a commission from the director-general of Louisiana to establish the fur trade in the country west of the Mississippi. In this party Auguste was given command of the boat, and in Oct. 1763, they reached the settlement of Sainte Genevieve. In the winter they ascended to a point about 60 miles upstream and chose a site on the western bank for their chief trading station, which they named St. Louis. On Feb. 15, 1764, a party under the direction of Auguste Chouteau began active trading operations. The two brothers remained in the new settlement and built up a profitable fur trade with the Indians of the north and west. Auguste died in St. Louis on Feb. 24, 1829. His son Pierre Chouteau (1789–1869), developed an immense business in furs, becoming an associate of John Jacob Astor (*q.v.*).

CHRESTIEN, FLORENT (1541–1596), French satirist and Latin poet, the son of Guillaume Chrestien, a French writer on physiology, was born at Orleans on Jan. 26, 1541. A pupil of Henri Estienne, the Hellenist, at an early age he was appointed tutor to Henry of Navarre, afterward Henry IV, who made him his librarian. Brought up as a Calvinist, he became a convert to Catholicism. He was one of the authors of the *Satyre Ménippée*, the famous pasquinade in the interest of his old pupil, Henry IV, and his works include a Latin version of *Hero and Leander* and French versions of Buchanan's *Jephthé* and Oppian's *De Venatione.* He died at Vendôme on Oct. 26, 1596.

CHRÉTIEN DE TROYES, a native of Champagne, and one of the famous French mediaeval poets. We possess very few details as to his life, and opinion differs as to the exact date to be assigned to his poems. We know that he wrote *Le Chevalier de la Charrette* at the command of Marie, countess of Champagne (the daughter of Louis VII and Eleanor of Aquitaine, married to the count of Champagne in 1164), and *Le Conte du Graal,* or *Perceval* for Philip, count of Flanders, guardian of the young king, Philip Augustus from 1180 to 1182. As Chrétien refers to the story as the best tale told *au cort roial* it was probably composed during the regency. It was left unfinished, and later continued by three writers, Wauchier de Denain, Gerbert de Montreuil and Manessier. The second of these says definitely that Chrétien died before he could complete his poem. The extant works in their chronological order are, *Érec, Cligēs, Le Chevalier de la Charrette* (*Lancelot*), *Le Chevalier au Lion* (*Yvain*) and *Le Conte du Graal* (*Perceval*) all dealing with Arthurian legend. Besides these he himself mentions a *Tristan,* and certain translations from Ovid's *Ars amatoria,* and *Metamorphoses.* A portion of this last was found by Gaston Paris, included in the translation of Ovid by Chrétien Legouais; of the *Tristan* no trace has yet been discovered. There is also a poem, *Guillaume d'Angleterre,* the authorship of which is a matter of debate. Prof. Foerster claimed it as by Chrétien, and included it in his edition of the poems, but Gaston Paris never accepted it.

Chrétien's poems enjoyed widespread favour, and of the three most popular (*Érec, Yvain* and *Perceval*) there exist old Norse translations, while the first two were admirably rendered into German by Hartmann von Aue. There is an English translation of the *Yvain, Ywain and Gawain,* and there are Welsh versions of all three stories, though their exact relation to the French is still a matter of debate. Chrétien's style is easy and graceful, he is analytic but not dramatic, in depth of thought and power of characterization he is decidedly inferior to Wolfram von Eschenbach, and as a poet he is probably to be ranked below Thomas, the author of *Tristan,* and the translator of Thomas, Gottfried von Strassburg. Much that has been claimed as characteristic of his work has been shown by M. Willmotte to be merely reproductions of literary conceits employed by his predecessors. In the words of so competent a judge as M. J. Bédier he appears to have been "not so much a creative artist as a clever compiler" and this probably represents what will be the final verdict on his work.

Bibliography.—Chrétien's poems, except the *Perceval,* have been critically edited by Prof. Foerster. There is so far no edition of the *Perceval* save that printed from the Mons ms. by M. Potvin (6 vols., 1866–71, out of print and difficult to procure). Prof. Baist published a private and limited edition of ms. 794 of the *Bibl. Nationale.* Dr. Mary Williams is publishing an edition of the Gerbert continuation in the *Classiques Français du Moyen Age.* For general criticism of Chrétien's work, *see* Willmotte, *L'Évolution du roman français aux environs de 1150* (1903); also J. L. Weston, *Legend of Sir Lancelot* and *Legend of Sir Perceval* and for an appreciation, M. Borodine, *La Femme et l'amour au XIIe siècle, d'après les poèmes de Chrétien de Troyes* (1909).

CHRISM, a mixture of olive oil and balm, used for anointing in the Roman Catholic church in baptism, confirmation and ordination, and in the consecrating and blessing of churches, altars, chalices, baptismal water, etc. (through Med. Lat. *chrisma,* from Gr. χρῖσμα, an unguent). The consecration of the chrism is performed by a bishop during the High Mass on Maundy Thursday. In the Orthodox Church the chrism contains, besides olive oil, many precious spices and perfumes, and is known as "muron" or "myron." The "Chrisom," originally a head-cloth to prevent the chrism from being rubbed off a newly-baptized child's forehead, came to mean the white baptismal robe, which was used as the child's shroud if it died within the month, but was otherwise given to the church by the mother at her churching. Children dying within the month were called "chrisom-children" or "chrisoms," as in Mrs. Quickly's description of Falstaff's death (Shakespeare, *Henry V.,* ii. 3).

CHRIST, the Anointed One (Gr. Χριστός), equivalent to the Hebrew Messiah: the title given in the New Testament to Jesus of Nazareth. (*See* Jesus Christ; Messiah; Christianity.)

CHRIST, WILHELM VON (1831–1906), German classical scholar, was born at Geisenheim, on Feb. 8, 1831, and died on Feb. 8, 1906, at Munich, where he had been professor from 1860 to 1902. His most important works are his *Geschichte der griechischen Literatur* (5th ed., 1908 f.), a history of Greek literature down to the time of Justinian, one of the best works on the subject; *Metrik der Griechen und Römer* (1879); editions of Pindar (1887); of the *Poëtica* (1878) and *Metaphysica* (1895) of Aristotle; *Iliad* (1884).

See O. Crusius, *Gedächtnisrede* (Munich, 1907).

CHRISTADELPHIANS, sometimes also called Thomasites, a community founded in 1848 by John Thomas (1805–1871), who, after studying medicine in London, migrated to Brooklyn, N.Y., U.S.A. (Χριστοῦ ἀδελφοι, "brothers of Christ"). There he at first joined the "Campbellites," but afterwards struck out independently, preaching largely upon the application of Hebrew prophecy and of the Book of Revelation to current and future events. Both in America and in Great Britain he gathered a number of adherents, and formed a community which has extended to several English-speaking countries. They believe that they alone hold the true interpretation of Scripture. Their theology is strongly millenarian, centring in the hope of a world-wide theocracy with its seat at Jerusalem. No statistics of the community are published.

See R. Roberts, *Dr. Thomas, his Life and Work* (1884); and F. J. Powicke, art. "Christadelphians" in Hastings' *Encyclopaedia of Religion and Ethics.* The community publishes a monthly magazine, *The Christadelphian,* in Birmingham.

CHRISTCHURCH, municipal borough, Southampton, England, at the confluence of the rivers Avon and Stour, 1½ mi. from the sea, and 25½ mi S.W. of Southampton on the S.R. Pop. (est. 1938) 14,050. Area 8 sq.mi. The neighbourhood was of great importance in late pre-historic times. Much of the late Bronze and early Iron age intercourse of Britain with the continent seems to have focused on Hengistbury Head and Christchurch. The town is mentioned in Saxon documents under the name of Tweotneam or Tweonaeteam, which long survived in the form Christchurch Twineham. In 901 it was seized by Aethelwald, but was recaptured by Edward the Elder. In Domesday, under the name of Thuinam, it appears as a borough belonging to the king, who held 31 messuages there. Henry I granted Christchurch (about 1100) to Richard de Redvers, who erected the castle. Only fragments remain, but the ruined Norman House apparently dates from the later part of the 12th century. The famous Augustinian priory church of the Holy Trinity is cruciform in plan, lacking a central tower but having a Perpendicular tower at the west end. The nave and transepts are principally Norman, and very fine; the choir is Perpendicular. Early English additions appear in the nave, clerestory and elsewhere, and the rood-screen is of ornate Decorated workmanship. The priory attained to such fame that its name of Christchurch finally replaced the older name of Twineham. It was dissolved in 1539.

The first charter was granted by Baldwin earl of Devon about 1150; Baldwin, the seventh earl, granted to the burgesses the tolls of the fair at St. Faith and common of pasture in certain meads shortly after 1257. The Holy Trinity fair is mentioned in 1226.

Christchurch was not incorporated till 1886. The town has never enjoyed any great prosperity, though the salmon fisheries have always been famous. It is mainly residential and is a holiday resort. There is a small harbour.

From 1571 the borough was represented in the house of commons by two members until the Reform act of 1832 reduced the number to one.

Christchurch is included in the New Forest and Christchurch division of Southampton.

CHRISTCHURCH, a city of New Zealand, near the east coast of South Island, to the north of Banks peninsula, in Selwyn county; the capital of the provincial district of Canterbury and the seat of a bishop. Pop. (1936) 92,189 (132,559 including suburbs).

Christchurch stands on the great Canterbury plain; a background is supplied by the distant mountains to the west and by the nearer hills to the south. The small river Avon winds through the city. Christchurch is chiefly dependent on the rich agricultural district which surrounds it, the plain being mainly devoted to cereals and grazing. It is also the site of a number of important industries, including particularly meat freezing and woollen manufacturing. Railways connect with Blenheim to the north and with Dunedin and Invercargill to the south, with many branches through the agricultural districts; also with Lyttelton, the port of Christchurch, 8 mi. southeast. The principal public buildings include the government offices, the museum, with its fine collection of remains of the extinct bird, moa, and the McDougall Art gallery. There is a fine Gothic cathedral built from designs of Sir G. Gilbert Scott in Early English style, with a tower and spire 240 ft. high. Among the city's many noted educational institutions is Canterbury University college, a constituent college of the University of New Zealand. There is a Roman Catholic pro-cathedral attached to a convent of the Sacred Heart. A large extent of open ground comprises Hagley park, recreation grounds, and the Botanical gardens, which are among the largest and finest in the dominion. Wide streets cross one another for the most part at right angles, and there are well-planted parks, avenues and private gardens. The foundation of Christchurch is connected with the so-called "Canterbury Pilgrims," who settled in this district in 1850. Lyttelton was the original settlement, but Christchurch came into existence in 1851, and is thus the latest of the settlements of the original colony.

The city became a municipality in 1862. In 1903 several populous suburban boroughs were amalgamated with Christchurch.

See *City of Christchurch, New Zealand, Yearbook* (annual).

CHRISTENSEN, JENS CHRISTIAN (1856–1933), Danish politician, was born in North Jutland. The son of a peasant farmer, he was an elementary school teacher from 1877 to 1901. In 1890 he entered Parliament and eventually became leader of the Liberal party. In 1901 he was Minister of Education in the first Liberal government, and from 1905 to 1908 was Prime Minister. In 1909 he was Minister of Defence and in this capacity carried through the Army bill. From 1912 to 1913 he was Speaker of the *Folketing* (Lower House), from 1916 to 1918 minister without portfolio, and Minister of Worship from 1920 to 1922. He retired from politics in 1924. He has published a book, *Fra min Barndom og Ungdom* (1925).

CHRISTIAN II. (1481–1559), king of Denmark, Norway and Sweden, son of John (Hans) and Christina of Saxony, was born at Nyborg Castle on July 1, 1481, and succeeded his father as king of Denmark and Norway in 1513. As viceroy of Norway (1502–12) he had already displayed singular capacity. Patriotism, courage, statesmanship—these qualities were indisputably his; but unfortunately they were vitiated by obstinacy, suspicion and a sulky craftiness, beneath which simmered a very volcano of revengeful cruelty. Christian's succession to the throne was confirmed at the *Herredag* or assembly of notables from the three northern kingdoms, which met at Copenhagen in 1513. A decision as to the Swedish succession was postponed, as the Swedish delegates refused to accept Christian as king. On June 11, 1514, he was crowned king of Denmark and Norway at Copenhagen, and on the same day he married, by proxy, Isabella, sister of the future emperor Charles V. The wedding was celebrated on Aug. 12, 1515. But he would not give up his liaison with Dyveke, a Dutch girl of bourgeois origin, and on the death of the unfortunate girl in 1517, under suspicious circumstances, Christian revenged himself by executing the magnate Torben Oxe, who was supposed to have been Dyveke's murderer, despite the strenuous opposition of Oxe's fellow peers; henceforth the king lost no opportunity of depressing the nobility and raising plebeians to power. His chief counsellor was Dyveke's mother Sigbrit, a born administrator and a commercial genius of the first order. Christian first appointed her controller of the Sound tolls, and ultimately committed to her the whole charge of the finances. A *bourgeoise* herself, Sigbrit soon became the soul of a middle-class inner council, which competed with the *Rigsraad* itself. The patricians naturally resented their supersession and nearly every unpopular measure was attributed to the influence of 'the foul-mouthed Dutch sorceress who hath bewitched the king."

Meanwhile Christian was preparing for the inevitable war with Sweden, where the Patriotic Party, headed by the freely elected governor Sten Sture the younger, stood face to face with the philo-Danish Party under Archbishop Gustavus Trolle. Christian, who had already taken measures to isolate Sweden politically, hastened to the relief of the archbishop, who was beleaguered in his fortress of Stäke, but was defeated by Sture and his peasant levies at Vedla and forced to return to Denmark, while the castle was destroyed and the archbishop deposed and imprisoned. A second attempt to subdue Sweden in 1518 was also frustrated by Sture's victory at Bränkyrka. A third attempt made in 1520 with a large army of French, German and Scottish mercenaries proved successful. Christian had persuaded Pope Leo X. to excommunicate Sture and to lay Sweden under an interdict. Sture was defeated at Bogesund and mortally wounded at the battle of Tiveden, on Jan. 19, and the Danish army, unopposed, was approaching Uppsala, where the members of the Swedish *Riksråd* had already assembled. The senators consented to render homage to Christian on condition that he gave a full indemnity for the past and a guarantee that Sweden should be ruled according to Swedish laws and custom; and a convention to this effect was confirmed by the king and the Danish *Rigsraad* on March 31. But Sture's widow, Dame Christina Gyllenstjerna, still held out stoutly at Stockholm, and the peasantry of central Sweden, stimulated by her patriotism, flew to arms, defeated the Danish invaders at Balundsäs (March 19) and were only with the utmost difficulty finally defeated at the bloody battle of Uppsala (Good Friday, April 6). In May the Danish fleet arrived, and Stockholm was invested by land and sea on Sept. 7. Christina surrendered on the promise of a general amnesty. On Nov. 1, the representatives of the nation swore fealty to Christian as hereditary king of Sweden, and on Nov. 4 he was crowned by Gustavus Trolle in Stockholm cathedral. The next three days were given up to banqueting, but on Nov. 7 "an entertainment of another sort began." On the evening of that day a band of Danish soldiers broke into the great hall and carried off several carefully selected persons. By 10 o'clock the same evening the remainder of the king's guests were safely under lock and key. All these persons were charged with heresy and violence against the church by archbishop Trolle, who presided over their trial on the following day. At 12 o'clock on the night of Nov. 8 the patriotic bishops of Skara and Strängnäs were led out into the great square and beheaded. The executions, known as the "Stockholm bath of blood," continued throughout the following day; in all, about 82 people, most of them noblemen, were thus murdered. Sten Sture's body was dug up and burnt, as well as the body of his little child. Dame Christina and many other noble Swedish ladies were sent as prisoners to Denmark. Christian suppressed his political opponents under the pretence of defending an ecclesiastical system which in his heart he despised.

With his brain teeming with great designs Christian II. returned to his native kingdom. Deeply distrusting the Danish nobles with whom he shared his powers, he sought helpers from among the wealthy middle classes of Flanders. In June 1521 he paid a sudden visit to the Low Countries, and remained there for some months. He visited most of the large cities, took into his service many Flemish artisans, and made the personal acquaintance of Quentin Matsys and Albrecht Dürer, the latter of whom painted his portrait. Christian also entertained Erasmus, with whom he discussed the Reformation, and let fall the characteristic expression: "Mild measures are of no use; the remedies that give the whole body a good shaking are the best and surest." On his return to Denmark on Sept. 5, 1521, Christian proceeded at once to inaugurate the most sweeping reforms. Soon after his return, in 1521 and 1522, he issued his great *Landelove,* or Code of Laws. For the most part this is founded on Dutch models, and testifies in a high degree to the king's progressive aims. Provision was made for the better education of the lower, and the restriction of the political influence of the higher clergy; there were stern prohibitions against wreckers and "the evil and unchristian practice of selling peasants as if they were brute beasts"; the old trade guilds were retained, but the rules of admittance thereto made easier, and trade combinations of the richer burghers, to the detriment of the smaller tradesmen, were sternly forbidden. Unfortunately these reforms, excellent in themselves, suggested the standpoint not of an elected ruler, but of a monarch by right divine. Some of them were even in direct contravention of the charter; and the old Scandinavian spirit of independence was deeply wounded by the preference given to the Dutch.

Sweden too was now in open revolt; and both Norway and

Denmark were taxed to the uttermost to raise an army for the subjection of the sister kingdom. In Jan. 1521 a young Swedish noble, Gustave Eriksson Vasa, at the head of a small force of dalesmen, led a revolt against Christian. (For the ensuing struggle which terminated the union between Denmark and Norway, *see* GUSTAVUS I. ERIKSSON and SWEDEN: *History.*) On June 6, 1523, Gustavus Eriksson was elected king of Sweden. Foreign complications were added to these domestic troubles. With the laudable object of releasing Danish trade from the grinding yoke of the Hansa, and making Copenhagen the great emporium of the north, Christian had arbitrarily raised the Sound tolls and seized a number of Dutch ships which presumed to evade the tax. Thus his relations with the Netherlands were strained, while with Lübeck and her allies he was openly at war. Finally Jutland rose against him late in 1522, renounced its allegiance and offered the Danish crown to Duke Frederick of Holstein (Jan. 20, 1523). So overwhelming did Christian's difficulties appear that he took ship to seek help abroad, and on May 1 landed at Veere in Zealand. Eight years later (Nov. 1531) he attempted to recover his kingdoms, and obtained some support from Olaf, archbishop of Trondhjem, who feared for the safety of the church under Frederick's rule. Christian landed with a small army of Dutch mercenaries on the Norwegian coast and proclaimed himself king at Oslo (Nov. 29). But he wasted time and opportunities; his fleet was destroyed by a Danish force, and it was arranged that he should negotiate with Frederick in person, on the understanding that if the negotiations broke down he should be allowed to return to Norway. When he reached Denmark, however, he was thrown into prison, first in Sonderborg Castle, afterwards in Kalundborg Castle. He died in Jan. 1559.

See K. P. Arnoldson, *Nordens enhet och Kristian II.* (Stockholm, 1899); Paul Frederik Barfod, *Danmarks Historie fra 1319 til 1536* (1885); *Danmarks Riges Historie,* vol. 3 (1897–1905); R. N. Bain, *Scandinavia,* chap. 2 (Cambridge, 1905). (R. N. B.; X.)

CHRISTIAN III. (1503–1559), king of Denmark and Norway, was the eldest son of Frederick I. of Denmark and his first consort, Anne of Brandenburg. Educated by German Lutheran teachers, Christian travelled in Germany in 1521 and was present at the Diet of Worms. On his return he found that his father had been elected king of Denmark in place of Christian II. Christian's unconcealed Lutheran views brought him into collision with the Catholic *Rigsraad,* and the religious intolerance which he showed in his capacity of stadtholder of the Duchies in 1526, and as viceroy of Norway in 1529, greatly provoked the Catholic party. On the death of Frederick I. in 1533 confusion arose over the election of his successor. Christian was supported by the nobility of Denmark; a strong Catholic party wished to put his younger brother, Hans, who was a child and still a Catholic, on the throne; while the peasants and burghers hoped for the restoration of the captive Christian II. (*q.v.*), and allied themselves with the citizens of Lübeck, who were led by Count Christopher of Oldenburg. Duke Christian crushed the rising of the peasants, made peace with Lübeck and in March 1535 was proclaimed king of Denmark at Viborg.

Christian III.'s triumph brought about the fall of Catholicism. On Aug. 12, 1536, the archbishop and bishops were arrested; on Oct. 30 a national assembly abolished episcopacy, made over the episcopal property to the Crown and established the Lutheran Church in Denmark, with the king as its head. The royal charter issued the same day proclaimed the Crown of Denmark, hitherto elective, hereditary in Christian's line.

The first six years of Christian's reign in Denmark were marked by a contest between the Danish *Rigsraad* and the German counsellors, both of whom sought to rule "the pious king" exclusively. Though the Danish party won a signal victory at the outset, by obtaining the insertion in the charter of provisions stipulating that only native-born Danes should fill the highest dignities of the State, the king's German counsellors continued paramount during the earlier years of his reign. The ultimate triumph of the Danish party dates from 1539, the dangers threatening Christian III. from the emperor Charles V., and other kinsmen of the imprisoned Christian II., compelling him to lean exclusively on Danish magnates and soldiers. The complete identification of the Danish king with the Danish people was accomplished at the *Herredag* of Copenhagen, 1542, when the nobility of Denmark voted Christian a twentieth part of all their property to pay off his heavy debt to the Holsteiners and Germans.

The pivot of the foreign policy of Christian III. was his alliance with the German Evangelical princes, as a counterpoise to the persistent hostility of Charles V., who was determined to support the hereditary claims of his nieces, the daughters of Christian II., to the Scandinavian kingdoms. War was actually declared against Charles V. in 1542, and though the German Protestant princes proved faithless allies, the closing of the Sound against Dutch shipping proved such an effective weapon in King Christian's hand that the Netherlands compelled Charles V. to make peace with Denmark at the Diet of Spires on May 23, 1544. The foreign policy of Christian's later days was regulated by the Peace of Spires. He carefully avoided all foreign complications; refused to participate in the Schmalkaldic War of 1546; mediated between the emperor and Saxony after the fall of Maurice of Saxony at the battle of Sievershausen in 1553, and contributed essentially to the conclusion of peace. King Christian III. died on New Year's day, 1559. Though not, perhaps, a great, he was, in the fullest sense of the word, a good ruler. A strong sense of duty, genuine piety and a cautious, but by no means pusillanimous common-sense, coloured every action of his patient, laborious and eventful life. He found Denmark in ruins; he left her stronger and wealthier than she had ever been before.

See *Danmarks Riges Historie,* vol. iii. (Copenhagen, 1897–1901); Huitfeld, *King Christian III.'s Historie* (Copenhagen, 1595); R. N. Bain, *Scandinavia,* ch. iv., v. (Cambridge, 1905).

CHRISTIAN IV. (1577–1648), king of Denmark and Norway, the son of Frederick II., king of Denmark, and Sophia of Mecklenburg, was born at Fredriksborg castle on April 12, 1577, and succeeded to the throne on the death of his father (April 4, 1588); during his minority which lasted till Aug. 17, 1596, the government was carried on by a regency of four. The young king's court was one of the most joyous and magnificent in Europe; yet he found time for work of the most various description, including a series of domestic reforms (*see* DENMARK: *History*). New fortresses were constructed under the direction of Dutch engineers. The Danish navy was developed and improved. In the war with Sweden, generally known as the "Kalmar War" (*see* SWEDEN: *History*), Christian compelled Gustavus Adolphus to give way on all essential points (treaty of Knäred, Jan. 20, 1613). After this war Christian made efforts to improve the army, which was composed mainly of mercenaries, though it was not until after the Thirty Years' War that any effective reforms were carried through. He then turned his attention to Germany. His object was twofold: first, to obtain the control of the great German rivers, the Elbe and the Weser; secondly, to acquire the secularized German bishoprics of Bremen and Werden as appanages for his younger sons. He skilfully took advantage of the alarm of the German Protestants after the battle of White Hill in 1620, to secure the coadjutorship to the see of Bremen for his son Frederick (Sept. 1621), a step followed in November by a similar arrangement as to Werden; while Hamburg by the compact of Steinburg (July 1621) was induced to acknowledge the Danish overlordship of Holstein. The growing ascendancy of the Catholics in North Germany in and after 1623 almost induced Christian, for purely political reasons, to intervene directly in the Thirty Years' War. The solicitations of the Western Powers led him in 1625 to plunge into war against the combined forces of the emperor and the League. For this defeat at Lutteram-Barenberge and the invasion of Jutland by Tilly and Wallenstein *see* THIRTY YEARS' WAR. In his extremity Christian now formed an alliance with Sweden (Jan. 1, 1628), whereby Gustavus Adolphus pledged himself to assist Denmark with a fleet in case of need, and shortly afterwards a Swedo-Danish army and fleet compelled Wallenstein to raise the siege of Stralsund. Declining to form a further alliance with Sweden for the defence of the North, and of Protestantism, Christian concluded a separate peace on May 12, 1629 with the emperor at Lübeck, without any diminution of territory, at the price of abandonment of the Protestant cause. Unfortunately Christian would neither conciliate Sweden, henceforth his most dangerous enemy, nor guard himself against her by a definite system of counter-alliances. By mediating in favour of the emperor, after the death of Gustavus Adolphus in 1632, he tried to minimize the influence of Sweden in Germany, and his whole Scandinavian policy was so irritating and vexatious that Swedish statesmen made up their minds to wage war with Denmark. In May 1643 the Swedish *Riksråd* decided upon war; on Dec. 12 the Swedish marshal Lennart Torstensson, advancing from Bohemia, crossed the northern frontier of Denmark; by the end of Jan. 1644 the whole peninsula of Jutland was in his possession. This totally unexpected attack, conducted from first to last with consummate ability and lightning-like rapidity, had a paralysing effect upon Denmark. Yet in his sixty-seventh year Christian IV. once more displayed something of the magnificent energy of his triumphant youth. Night and day he laboured to levy armies and equip fleets. Fortunately too for him, the Swedish government delayed hostilities in Scania till Feb. 1644, so that the Danes were able to make adequate defensive preparations and save the important fortress of Malmö. Torstensson was unable to cross from Jutland to Fünen for want of a fleet, and the Dutch auxiliary fleet which came to his assistance was defeated between the islands of Sylt and Rönnö on the west coast of Schleswig by the Danish admirals. Another attempt to transport Torstensson and his army to the Danish islands by a large Swedish fleet under Klas Fleming was frustrated by Christian IV. in person on July 1, 1644. On that day the two fleets encountered off Kolberg Heath, S.E. of Kiel Bay, and Christian displayed a heroism which endeared him ever after to the Danish nation. Darkness at last separated the fleets; and though the battle was a drawn one, the Danish fleet showed its superiority by blockading the Swedish ships in Kiel Bay. But the Swedish fleet escaped, and the annihilation of the Danish fleet by the combined navies of Sweden and Holland at the end of September exhausted the military resources of Denmark and compelled Christian to accept the mediation of France and the United Provinces. Peace was finally signed at Brömsebro in 1645. (*See* DENMARK: *History*.)

The last years of the king were still further embittered by struggles with the nobility to whom he was forced to concede more and more power. He died at Copenhagen in Feb. 1648. During his reign Norway made great strides in economic and administrative prosperity under his son-in-law, Hannibal Sehested (*q.v.*), as Stadtholder. (*See* NORWAY: *History*.)

See *Life* (Dan.), by H. C. Bering Liisberg and A. L. Larsen (Copenhagen, 1890–91); *Letters* (Dan.), ed. Carl Frederik Bricka and Julius Albert Fridericia (Copenhagen, 1878); *Danmarks Riges Historie*, vol. 4 (Copenhagen, 1897–1905); R. N. Bain, *Scandinavia*, cap. vii. (1905).

CHRISTIAN V. (1646–1699), king of Denmark and Norway, the son of Frederick III. of Denmark and Sophia Amalia of Brunswick-Luneburg, was born on April 15, 1646, at Flensburg, and succeeded to the throne on Feb. 9, 1670. Christian was very popular among the lower orders, but hated the old noble families, and tried to establish a new nobility by creating two new orders, consisting largely of officials and upper middle class families, which were to take precedence of the older ones. Under the guidance of his great chancellor Griffenfeldt (*q.v.*), Christian carried his ideas of absolute government into practice, introducing extreme centralization into the organization of civil and military affairs. Griffenfeldt pursued an ambitious policy of foreign alliances, but aimed at keeping peace, and for a brief period Denmark seemed to have a chance of regaining her position as a great power; but Christian sacrificed Griffenfeldt to the jealousy of his adversaries, and sentenced him to life-long imprisonment. After this the financial position of the state grew steadily worse, owing partly to the extravagance of the court, partly to the unremunerative war with Sweden (1675–79). Christian was a weak despot, though his personal courage and affability made him popular among the lower orders. During his reign a new code of laws was drawn up for Norway, begun in 1661 and completed in 1683. He died in a hunting accident on Aug. 25, 1699.

See P. E. Holm, *Danmarks indre Historie under Enevaelden* (Copenhagen, 1881–86); A. D. Jörgensen, *Peter Griffenfeldt* (Copenhagen, 1893); R. N. Bain, *Scandinavia* cap. x., xi. (Cambridge, 1905).

CHRISTIAN VII. (1749–1808), king of Denmark and Norway, was the son of Frederick V., king of Denmark, and his first consort Louise, daughter of George II. of Great Britain. He became king on his father's death on Jan. 14, 1766. Badly educated, systematically terrorized by a brutal governor and hopelessly debauched by corrupt pages he grew up a semi-idiot. After his marriage in 1766 with Caroline Matilda (1751–1775), daughter of Frederick, prince of Wales, he abandoned himself to the worst excesses. He ultimately sank into a condition of mental stupor and became the obedient slave of the upstart Struensee (*q.v.*) who, after the dismissal of Bernstorff in 1770, controlled all affairs of State. After the fall of Struensee (the warrant for whose arrest he signed with indifference) in 1772, for the last 26 years of his reign, he was only nominally king, his half-brother, Prince Frederick, acting as regent. He died on March 13, 1808. In 1772 the king's marriage with Caroline Matilda, who had been seized and had confessed to criminal familiarity with Struensee, was dissolved, and the queen, retaining her title, passed her remaining days at Celle in Hanover, where she died on May 10, 1775.

See E. S. F. Reverdil, *Struensee et la cour de Copenhague, 1760–1772* (1858); *Danmarks Riges Historie*, vol. v. (Copenhagen, 1897–1905); and for Caroline Matilda, Sir F. C. L. Wraxall, *Life and Times of Queen Caroline Matilda* (1864), and W. H. Wilkins, *A Queen of Tears* (1904).

CHRISTIAN VIII. (1786–1848), king of Denmark and Norway, the only son of Frederick (d. 1805, half brother to Christian VII and son of Frederick V), was born on Sept. 18, 1786, at Christiansborg castle. His first marriage with his cousin Charlotte Frederica of Mecklenburg-Schwerin was dissolved in 1810. In May 1813 he was sent as stadtholder to Norway to promote the loyalty of the Northmen to the dynasty, which had been very rudely shaken by the disastrous results of Frederick VI.'s adhesion to the falling fortunes of Napoleon. Though his endeavours were opposed by the so-called Swedish party in Norway, which desired a dynastic union with Sweden, he was elected regent of Norway by an assembly of notables on Feb. 16, 1814. This election was confirmed by a *Storthing* held at Eidsvold on April 10 and on May 17 Christian was elected king of Norway. On being summoned by the commissioners of the allied powers at Copenhagen to bring about a union between Norway and Sweden in accordance with the terms of the treaty of Kiel, he replied that, as a constitutional king, he could do nothing without the consent of the *Storthing*, to the convocation of which a suspension of hostilities on the part of Sweden was the condition precedent. A short campaign ensued, in which Christian was easily worsted by the superior skill and forces of the Swedish crown prince (Bernadotte). The brief war was finally concluded by the convention of Moss on Aug. 14, 1814 (*see* NORWAY: *History*). Henceforth Christian's alleged democratic principles made him suspect, and he and his second wife, Caroline Amelia of Augustenburg, whom he married in 1815, lived in comparative retirement. It was not till 1831 that old King Frederick gave him a seat in the council of state. On Dec. 13, 1839 he ascended the Danish throne as Christian VIII. The Liberal party had high hopes of "the giver of constitutions," but he disappointed his admirers by steadily rejecting every Liberal project. He came into conflict with the German element in the duchies of Schleswig and Holstein by issuing (March, 1844) a patent permitting, under certain circumstances, the use of the Danish language in the estates. By his Open Letter of July 8, 1846, in which he declared that the *Kongelov*, Danish royal law in the matter of the succession applied to Schleswig and Lauenburg, though its application to parts of Holstein was doubtful, and by the Constitution of Jan. 28, 1848, he raised the Schleswig-Holstein question in a form which involved his successor in the War of 1848. (*See* SCHLESWIG-HOLSTEIN QUESTION.) He died at Plön on Jan. 20, 1848.

See Just Matthias Thiele, *Christian den Ottende* (Copenhagen, 1848); Yngvar Nielsen, *Bidrag til Norges Historie* (Christiania, 1882–86). A. J. Lange, *Christian Frederik som Norges Statholder regent og Konge* (1914).

CHRISTIAN IX (1818–1906), king of Denmark, was a younger son of William, duke of Schleswig-Holstein-Sonderburg-Glücksburg (d. 1831), a direct descendant of the Danish king Christian III by his wife Louise, a daughter of Charles, prince of Hesse-Cassel (d. 1836), and grand-daughter of King Frederick V. Born at Gottorp on April 8, 1818, Christian entered the army, and served with the Danish troops in Schleswig during the insurrection of 1848. In 1842 he married Louise (1817–1898), daughter of William, prince of Hesse-Cassel (d. 1867), and cousin of King Frederick VII. The reigning king, Frederick VII, being childless, the representatives of the great powers met in London and settled the crown on Prince Christian (May 1852), an arrangement confirmed in Denmark in 1853. The "protocol king," as Christian was sometimes called, ascended the throne on Frederick's death in Nov. 1863. By putting into force (Nov. 18) the recently drafted constitution under which Schleswig was to be incorporated with Denmark, he came into conflict with the German confederation. (*See* SCHLESWIG-HOLSTEIN QUESTION.) The German-Danish War followed, which ended by the separation (Oct. 13, 1864) of the duchies from Denmark. Within the narrowed limits of his kingdom Christian's difficulties were more protracted and hardly less serious. During almost the whole of his reign the Danes were engaged in a political struggle between the "Right" and the "Left," the former being supported in general by the *Landsting*, and the latter by the *Folketing*. The king was for many years successful in preventing the radicals from coming into office, but in 1901 he was forced to assent to the formation of a "cabinet of the Left" (*see* DENMARK: *History*). In his later years he occupied a patriarchal position among the sovereigns of Europe to many of whom he was related. His eldest son Frederick had married a daughter of Charles XV of Sweden; his second son George had been king of the Hellenes since 1863; his youngest Waldemar (1858–1939) was married to Marie d'Orléans, daughter of Robert, duc de Chartres. Of his three daughters, Alexandra married Edward VII of Great Britain; Dagmar (Marie Feodorovna), the tsar Alexander III; and Thyra, Ernest Augustus, duke of Cumberland. One of his grandsons, Charles, who married Princess Maud of England, became king of Norway as Haakon VII in 1905, and another, Constantine, crown prince (afterwards king) of Greece, married a sister of the German emperor William II. Christian was also the ruler of Iceland. He died at Copenhagen on Jan. 29, 1906, and was buried at Roskilde.

See Barfod, *Kong Kristian IX's Regerings-Dagbog* (Copenhagen, 1876); and *Hans Majestet Kong Kristian IX* (Copenhagen, 1888).

CHRISTIAN X, king of Denmark and Iceland (1870–1947), was born on Sept. 26, 1870, at Charlottenlund castle, near Copenhagen, the eldest son of Crown Prince Frederick, later King Frederick VIII (1906–12), and Louise, princess of Sweden and Norway. After matriculating in 1889, the prince embarked upon a military career, becoming chief of the royal guard, and attained the rank of major general. He married, in 1898, Alexandrine, duchess of Mecklenburg-Schwerin and they had two sons, Crown Prince Frederick (b. 1899) and Prince Knud (b. 1900). In 1906 he became crown prince and in 1912 ascended the throne.

During World War I the necessity of friendly intercourse between the Scandinavian kingdoms resulted in several meetings among the three kings, of which the first was held at Malmö in Dec. 1914. On June 5, 1915, King Christian signed the new constitution of Denmark which extended the franchise to women. He signed, on Dec. 1, 1919, the Federal act, whereby Denmark acknowledged Iceland as an independent kingdom and king of Iceland was incorporated in the king's title. In 1944, however, Iceland completely severed its ties with Denmark. In July 1920 he rode over the old frontier into Slesvig Nord, which had been ceded to Denmark by the Treaty of Versailles, and received an enthusiastic reception from the people. When the Germans occupied Denmark in 1940, King Christian retained control of the internal organization of the country, and endeared himself to his people by his "passive resistance." During October of 1942 he became ill with pneumonia after a fall from his horse, and the crown prince was named regent temporarily. After his recovery he continued to withstand nazi pressure, although he was compelled to make a speech in May 1943 warning his people against the growing sabotage of munitions and railways. Open rebellion against the occupation forces broke out in Aug. 1943, and King Christian was made a virtual prisoner at Sorgenfri castle and later at the palace of Amalienborg in Copenhagen. He opened the free Danish parliament on May 9, 1945, after the surrender of the German forces. He died at Amalienborg castle on April 20, 1947.

CHRISTIAN, WILLIAM (1608–1663), Manx politician, a son of Ewan Christian, one of the Manx deemsters, was born on April 14, 1608, and was known as *Illiam Dhone,* or Brown William. In 1648 the lord of the Isle of Man, James Stanley, 7th earl of Derby, appointed Christian his receiver-general; and when in 1651 the earl crossed to England to fight for Charles II he left him in command of the island militia. Derby was taken prisoner at the battle of Worcester, and his famous countess Charlotte de la Tremouille, who was residing in Man, sought to obtain her husband's release by negotiating with the victorious parliamentarians for the surrender of the island. At once a revolt headed by Christian broke out, partly as a consequence of this step, partly owing to the discontent caused by some agrarian arrangements recently introduced by the earl. The rebels seized many of the forts; then Christian in his turn entered into negotiations with the parliamentarians; and probably owing to his connivance the island was soon in the power of Col. Robert Duckenfield, who had brought the parliamentary fleet to Man in Oct. 1651. The countess of Derby was compelled to surrender her two fortresses, Castle Rushen and Peel castle, while Christian remained receiver-general, becoming governor of the island in 1656. Two years later, however, he was accused of misappropriating some money; he fled to England, and in 1660 was arrested in London. Having undergone a year's imprisonment he returned to Man, hoping that his offense against the earl of Derby would be condoned under the Act of Indemnity of 1661; but, anxious to punish his conduct, Charles, the new earl of Derby, ordered his seizure; he refused to plead, and a packed house of keys declared that in this case his life and property were at the mercy of the lord of the island. The deemsters then passed sentence, and in accordance therewith Christian was shot on Jan. 2, 1663. This arbitrary act angered Charles II and his advisers; the deemsters and others were punished, and some reparation was made to Christian's family. Christian is chiefly celebrated through the Manx ballad *Baase Illiam Dhone,* which was translated into English by George Borrow, and through the reference to him in Sir Walter Scott's *Peveril of the Peak.*

See A. W. Moore, *History of the Isle of Man* (1900).

CHRISTIAN CATHOLIC CHURCH, the name assumed by a religious organization founded at Zion (*q.v.*) city near Chicago, Ill., in 1896, by John Alexander Dowie (*q.v.*). Its members added to the usual tenets of Christianity a special belief in faith healing, and laid much stress on united consecration services and the threefold immersion of believers. To assist Dowie, assistant overseers were appointed, and the operations of the community included religious, educational and commercial departments. After 1903 considerable dissension arose among Dowie's followers: he was deposed in 1906; and after his death in 1907 his assistant Wilbur Glenn Voliva became general overseer of the organization.

See art. "Enthusiasts (religious)," by G. H. Gray and W. T. Whitley in Hastings, *Encyclopaedia of Religion and Ethics,* vol. v, p. 320; and K. Harlan, *John Alexander Dowie and the Christian Catholic Church,* Evansville, Wisconsin, 1906.

CHRISTIAN ENDEAVOUR SOCIETIES, organizations formed for the purpose of promoting spiritual life among young people. They date from 1881, in which year Dr. Francis E. Clark (*q.v.*) formed a Young People's Society of Christian Endeavour in his (Congregational) church at Portland, Maine, U.S.A. The idea was taken up elsewhere in America and spread to other countries, till, under the presidency of Dr. Clark, a huge number of affiliated societies came into operation throughout the world. They take as their motto "For Christ and the Church," and have done much, especially in the nonepiscopal churches, to prepare young men and women for active services in the Church. The organization is international and interdenominational, a World's Christian Endeavour Union being formed in 1895.

See Francis E. Clark, art. "Christian Endeavour," in Hastings' *Encyclopaedia of Religion and Ethics,* vol. iii. 571 ff. (with reff.) and *Memories of Many Men in Many Lands* (1922); J. R. Fleming, *The Christian Endeavour of the Future* (1903).

CHRISTIANIA, the capital of Norway; *see* OSLO.

CHRISTIANITY, regarded historically as one of the great religions of the world, owes its rise to Jesus of Nazareth, in ancient Galilee (*see* JESUS CHRIST). By reverent disciples His ancestry was traced to the royal family of David and His birth is ascribed by the church to the miraculous act of God. At 30 years of age Jesus Christ appeared in public, and after a short period (we cannot determine how long, but possibly 18 months) he was crucified, upon the accusation of His countrymen, by the Roman authorities.

Relation to Judaism.—His career is understood only in the light of His relation to Judaism (*see* JUDAISM). This faith, in a peculiarly vivid fashion, illustrates the growth and development of religion, for its great teachers in the highest degree possessed what the Germans call God-consciousness. When the national independence of Israel was destroyed, the prophetic teaching held the people together in the hope of a re-establishment of the Kingdom when all nations should be subject to it and blessed in its everlasting reign of righteousness and peace (Isa. xlix., lx.).

Some of the prophets associated the restoration of the Kingdom with the coming of the Messiah, the anointed one, who should re-establish the line of David (Isa. ix. 6 f., xi. 1 f.; Micah v. 2; Ezek. xxxiv. 23, xxxvii. 24; Zech. ix. 9; Ps. ii. 72). Others said nothing of such a one, but seemed to expect the regeneration of Israel through the labours, sufferings and triumphs of the righteous remnant (Isa. liii., Ezek. xxxvi.–xxxvii.). By the strong emphasis upon righteousness, the tribal Lord of Israel was revealed as the universal God, of one relationship to all men. This monotheism was not primarily cosmological nor metaphysical, but ethical. The Jews showed little capacity for abstract reasoning and never pursued their inquiries to the discovery of ultimate principles. Thus they did not develop a systematic cosmology, nor formulate a system of metaphysics. Their religion was pre-eminently "theocratic"; God was thought of as King, enthroned in heaven and supreme.

But the prophetic teaching was obscured in part by the nationalism of the prophets themselves, who exalted Israel as at once God's instrument and the peculiar object of His love. Inevitably the freedom, spirituality and universality of the prophetic teaching were obscured. In the 1st century A.D. the national and priestly elements were supreme. The triumph of Israel was to be accomplished by the miraculous power of a Messiah who should descend out of heaven. His coming was delayed, in part by the opposition of demons, in part by the failure of the people to obey the law, which embraced both moral and ceremonial elements derived from varied sources, but by the people was all alike regarded as of divine origin. It was to be obeyed without question and without inquiry as to its meaning, because established by God; it was contained in the Sacred Scriptures (*see* BIBLE: *Old Testament*), which had been revealed by God supernaturally, and its meaning was set forth by schools of learned men whose interpretations were authoritative. The priesthood held still the ancient ideas. Salvation was for the nation, and the individual was not necessarily participant in it; life after death was disbelieved or held as the existence of shades; there could be no resurrection of the body and no immortality (in the Greek sense); and with these beliefs were associated a certain worldliness and want of fervour. The more actively and aggressively religious party, on the other hand, adopted the belief in the resurrection of the body, and in the individual's participation in the Messiah's kingdom; all the pious would have their share in it, while the wicked would be outcast. But these doctrines were variously conceived. By some the Messianic kingdom was thought of as permanent, by others as intermediary, the external kingdom being transcendent. So too some thought of a literal resurrection of the body of flesh and blood, while others thought that it would be transformed. The rudiments of some of these ideas can be found in the prophets, but their development took place after the exile, and indeed for the most part after the conclusion of the writings accounted canonical. Thus too the belief in a kingdom of demons held a large place in the mind of the people, though the references to such evil beings are almost absent from the sacred writings of the Old Testament. Again it is to the East that we must look for the origin of these ideas.

The Teaching of Jesus.—Jesus completed the prophetic teachings. He employed the old phraseology and imagery, but He was conscious that He used them in a new sense, and that He preached a new gospel of great joy. Jesus was not a historian, a critic or a theologian. He used the words of common men in the sense in which common men understood them; He did not employ the Old Testament as now reconstructed by scholarship or judged by criticism, but in its simple and obvious and traditional sense, and His background is the intellectual and religious thinking of His time. The ideas of demons and of the future, of the Bible and many other traditional conceptions, are taken over without criticism. So the idea of God which He sets forth is not that of a theologian or a metaphysician, but that of the unlearned man which even the child could understand. Yet though thus speaking in untechnical language, He revolutionized His terms and filled them with new meaning. His emphasis is His own, and the traditional material affords merely the setting for His thought. He was not concerned with speculative questions about God, nor with abstract theories of His relationship to the soul and to the world. God's continual presence, His fatherly love, His transcendent righteousness, His mercy, His goodness, were the facts of immediate experience; not in proofs by formal logic but in the reality of consciousness was the certainty of God. Thus religion was freed from all particular and national elements in the simplest way: for Jesus did not denounce these elements, nor argue against them, nor did He seek converts outside Israel, but He set forth communion with God as the most certain fact of man's experience and as simple reality made it accessible to everyone. Thus His teaching contains the note of universality—not in terms and proclamations but as plain matter of fact. His way for others to this reality is likewise plain and level to the comprehension of the unlearned and of children.

For Him repentance (change of mind, μετάνοια) is placed first. The intricacies of ritual and theology are ignored, and ancient laws which contradict the fundamental beliefs are unhesitatingly abrogated or denied. He seizes upon the most spiritual passages of the prophets, and revives and deepens them; He sums up His teaching in supreme love to God and a love for fellow-man like that we hold for ourselves (Mark xii. 29–31). This supreme love to God is a complete oneness with Him in will, a will which is expressed in service to our fellow-men in the simplest and most natural relationship (Luke x. 25–37). Thus religion is ethical through and through, as God's inner nature, expressed in forgiveness, mercy, righteousness and truth, is not something transcendental, but belongs to the realm of daily life. We become children of God and He our Father in virtue of a moral likeness (Matt. v. 43–48), while of any metaphysical or (so to speak) physical relationship to God, Jesus says nothing. With this clearly understood, man is to live in implicit trust in the divine love, power, knowledge and forgiveness. Hence he attains salvation, being delivered from sin and fear and death, for the divine attributes are not ontological entities to be discussed and defined in the schools, but they are realities, entering into the practical daily life. Indeed they are to be repeated in us also, so that we are to forgive our brethren as we ask to be forgiven (Matt. vi. 12; Luke xi. 4).

As religion thus becomes thoroughly ethical, so is the notion of the Messianic kingdom transformed. Its essential characteristic is the doing of the Father's will on earth as in heaven. Jesus uses parable after parable to establish its meaning. It is a seed cast into the ground which grows and prospers (Matt. xiii. 31–32); it is a seed sown in good ground and bringing forth fruit, or in bad ground and fruitless (Luke viii. 5–8; Mark iv. 1–32); it is a pearl of great price for which a man should sell all that he possesses (Matt. xiii. 44–46); it is not come "with observation," so that men shall say "lo here and lo there" (Luke xvii. 20–21); it is not of this world, and does not possess the characteristics or the glory of the kingdom of the earth (Luke xxii. 24–26; Mark x. 13–16); it is already present among men (Luke xvii. 21). Together with these statements in our sources are still mingled fragments of the more ordinary cataclysmic, apocalyptic conceptions, which in spite of much ingenious exegesis, cannot be brought into harmony with Christ's predominant teaching, but remain as foreign elements in the words of the Master, possibly brought back through His disciples, or, more probably, used by Jesus uncritically—a part of the current religious imagery in which He shared.

Originality.—It is often declared that in these teachings there is nothing new, and indeed analogies can be found for many sayings; yet nowhere else do we gain so strong an impression of originality. The net result is not only new but revolutionary; so was it understood by the Pharisees. They and Jesus spoke indeed the same words and appealed to the same authorities, but they rightly saw in Him a revolutionist who threatened the existence of their most cherished hopes. The Messianic kingdom which they sought was opposed point by point to the kingdom of which He spoke, and their God and His Father—though called by the same sacred name—were different. Hence almost from the beginning of His public ministry they constantly opposed Him, the conflict deepening into complete antagonism.

Jesus Christ has been termed unique, one of the common people yet separated from them, and this description applies to the breadth, depth and reality of His sympathy. In the meagre records of His life there is evidence that He deemed no form of suffering humanity foreign to Himself. This was not a mere sentiment, nor was His sympathy superficial, for it constituted the essential characteristic of His personality—"He went about doing good." In Him the will of the Father for the redemption of the race was incarnate. This led Him into the society of those outcasts who were condemned and rejected by the respectable and righteous classes. In contemptuous condemnation He was called the friend of the outcasts (Matt. xi. 19; Mark ii. 16–17), and on His part He proclaimed that these sinners would enter into the Kingdom of Heaven before the self-righteous saints (Matt. xxi. 31); even the most repulsive forms of disease and sin drew from Him only loving aid, while he recognized in all other men who laboured for the welfare of their fellows the most intimate relationship to Himself; these constituted His family, and these were they whom His Father will bless.

Jesus recognized His unique position; He could not be ignorant of His powers. Even the prophets had spoken in the name of God; they accepted neither book nor priesthood as authoritative, but uttered their truth as they were inspired to speak, and commanded men to listen and obey. As in Jesus the whole prophetic line culminates, so does its consciousness; reverent toward the Holy Scriptures, He spoke not as their expositor but with a power which invests His words with immediate and full authority. The prophets used the formula, "Thus saith the Lord," but He goes beyond them and speaks in His own name. He believed Himself to be the Messiah of whom the prophets spoke, and only through this self-consciousness can we explain His mission and the career of His disciples. The prophets up to John foretold the coming of the kingdom (Matt. xi. 11–13; Luke xvi. 16), but Jesus opened its doors and made possible entrance into it. Where He is there it is, and hence those who follow Him are God's children, and those who refuse His message are left outside in darkness. He is to sit as enthroned, judge and king, and by Him is men's future to be determined (Matt. xxv. 31 f.; Mark xiii. 26); indeed it was His presence more than His teaching which created His Church. Great as were His words, greater was His personality. His disciples misunderstood what He said, but they trusted and followed Him. By Him they felt themselves freed from sin and fear—and under the influence of a divine power.

Messianic Claims.—Though His claims to authoritative pre-eminence thus took Him out of the class of prophets and put Him even above Elijah and Moses (Mark ix. 2–7; Luke vii. 28; Luke x. 23–24), and though naturally this self-assertion seemed blasphemous to those who did not accept Him, yet as He had transformed the traditional notion of the kingdom, so did He the current thought of the Messiah. The pre-eminence was not to be of rank and glory but of service and self-sacrifice. In His kingdom there can be no strife for precedence, since its King comes not to be ministered unto but to minister and to give His life in the service of others (Mark ix. 33 f., x. 42–45). The formal acknowledgment of the Messiah's worth and position matters little, for to call Him Lord does not ensure entrance into His Kingdom (Matt. vii. 21–23). It is those who fail to recognize the spirit of sympathy and self-sacrificing service as divine and blaspheme redeeming love who are in danger of eternal sin (Mark iii. 28–29). All who do the will of the Father, *i.e.,* who serve their fellows, are the brethren of Christ, even though they do not call Him Lord (Mark iii. 31–35; Matt. vii. 21): and those are blessed who minister to the needy even though ignorant of any relation to Himself (Matt. xxv. 37–40). Finally, membership in His own selected company, or a place in the chosen people, is not of prime importance (Mark ix. 38–40; Luke xiii. 24–30).

Jesus also refuses to conform to the current ideas as to the establishment of the kingdom. The tradition of the people implied a sudden appearance of the Messiah, but Jesus made no claims to a supernatural origin and was content to be known as the son of Joseph and Mary (Mark vi. 3–4). His kingdom is not to be set up by wonders and miraculous powers, nor is it to be established by force (Matt. xxvi. 52); such means would contradict its fundamental character, for as the kingdom of loving service it can be established only by loving service. Even the disciples of Jesus could not grasp the simplicity and profundity of His message; still less could His opponents. He was accused of blasphemy to the ecclesiastical authorities and of insurrection to the civil rulers. He was condemned and crucified. His followers were scattered. Of His work nothing remained, not a written word, nor more than the rudiments of an organization. The decisive event, which turned defeat into victory and re-established courage and faith, was the belief in the reappearance to His disciples. Our sources will not permit the precise determination of the order or the nature of these appearances, but in any case from them arose the faith which was the basis of the Christian Church and the starting-point of its theology.

The death of Jesus as a criminal, and His resurrection, profoundly aroused the belief and hopes of the little group of Jews who were His followers. It is not His word but His person which assumes first place, and faith is acceptance of Him—crucified and risen—as Messiah. Hence His followers early acquire the name Christian from the Greek form of the word. With this emphasis upon the Messiah the Jewish element would seem to be predominant, but as a matter of fact it was not so. The earlier group of disciples, it is true, did not appreciate the universality of the teaching of Jesus, and they continued zealous for the older forms; but Paul through his prophetic consciousness grasped the fundamental fact and in this respect became Jesus' true interpreter. As a result Christianity was rejected by the Jews and became the conquering religion of the Roman empire. In this it underwent another modification of far-reaching consequence.

In our earliest sources—the epistles of St. Paul—Christ is the pre-existent divine man from heaven, He is before and above all things, and had come to earth by a voluntary act of self-humiliation. In the Johannine writings He is the Son of God—the Logos who in the beginning was with God—of Whom are all things—Who lightens every man—and Who was incarnate in Jesus. Here the cosmological element is again made prominent though not yet supreme, and the metaphysical problems are so close at hand that their discussion is imperative. Even in Paul the term Messiah thus had lost its definite meaning and became almost a proper name. Among the Greek Christians this process was complete. Jesus is the "Son of God"; and the great problem of theology becomes explicit. Religion is in our emotions of reverence and dependence, and theology is the intellectual attempt to describe the object of worship. Doubtless the two do not exactly coincide, not only because accuracy is difficult or even impossible, but also because elements are admitted into the definition of God which are derived from various sources quite distinct from religious experience. Like all concepts the meaning of religious terms is changed with a changing experience and a changing world-view. Transplanted into the world where Greek ideas were prevalent, inevitably the Christian teaching was modified—indeed transformed. Questions which had never been asked came into the foreground, and the Jewish presuppositions tended to disappear, and the Messianic hopes were forgotten or transferred to a transcendent sphere beyond death. When the empire became Christian in the 4th century, the notion of a kingdom of Christ on earth to be introduced by a great struggle all but disappeared, remaining only as the faith of obscure groups. As thus the background is changed from Jewish to Greek, so are the fundamental religious conceptions.

The Semitic peoples were essentially theocratic; they used the forms of the sensuous imagination in setting forth the realities of the unseen world. They were not given to metaphysical speculation, nor long insistent in their inquiries as to the meaning and origin of things. With the Greeks it was far otherwise: for them ideas and not images set forth fundamental reality, and their restless intellectual activity would be content with nothing but the ultimate truth. Their speculation as to the nature of God had led them gradually to separate Him by an infinite distance from all creation, and to feel keenly the opposition of the finite and the infinite, the perfect and the imperfect, the eternal and the temporal. To them, therefore, Christianity presented itself not primarily as the religion of a redemption through the indwelling power of a risen Saviour, as with Paul, nor even as the solution of the problem how the sins of men could be forgiven, but as the reconciliation of the antinomy of the intellect, indicated above. The incarnation became the great truth: God is no longer separated by a measureless distance from the human race, but by His entering into humanity He redeems it and makes possible its ultimate unity with Himself. Such lines of thought provoke discussion as to the relationship of Jesus to God the Father, and, at a later period, of the nature of the Holy Spirit who enters into and transforms believers.

Greek philosophy in the 2nd century A.D. had sunk for the most part into scepticism and impotence; its original impulse had been lost, and no new intellectual power took its place; only in Alexandria was there a genuine effort made to solve the fundamental problems of God and the world; and mingled with the speculations of the Greek philosophers were the ancient legends of gods and heroes, accepted as inspired scripture by the people, and by the philosophers in part explained away by an allegorical exegesis and in part felt increasingly as a burden to the intelligence. In this period of degeneracy there were none the less an awakening to religious needs and a profound longing for a new revelation of truth, which should satisfy at once the intellect and the religious emotions.

Christianity came as supplying a new power; it freed philosophy from scepticism by giving a definite object to its efforts and a renewed confidence in its mission. Monotheism henceforth was to be the belief not of philosophers only but even of the ignorant, and in Jesus Christ the union of the divine and the human was effected. The Old Testament, allegorically explained, became the substitute for the outgrown mythology; intellectual activity revived; the new facts gained predominant influence in philosophy, and in turn were shaped according to its canons. In theology the fundamental problems of ontological philosophy were faced; the relationship of unity to multiplicity, of noumenon to phenomena, of God to man. The new element is the historical Jesus, at once the representative of humanity and of God. As in philosophy, so now in theology, the easiest solution of the problem was the denial of one of its factors: and successively these efforts were made, until a solution was believed to be found which satisfied both terms of the equation and became the fundamental creed of the Church. Its moulds of thought are those of Greek philosophy, and into these were run the Jewish teachings. We have thus a peculiar combination—the religious doctrines of the Bible, as culminating in the person of Jesus, run through the forms of an alien philosophy.

The Doctrine of the Trinity.—The Jewish sources furnished the terms Father, Son and Spirit. Jesus seldom employed the last term and Paul's use of it is not altogether clear. Already in Jewish literature it had been all but personified (*cf.* the *Wisdom of Solomon*). Thus the material is Jewish, though already doubtless modified by Greek influence: but the problem is Greek; it is not primarily ethical nor even religious, but it is metaphysical. What is the ontological relationship between these three factors? The answer of the Church is given in the Nicene formula, which is characteristically Greek, and which affirms that God, the infinite, the absolute, the eternal, is yet not separated from the finite, the temporal, the relative, but, through the incarnation, enters into humanity (*see* ARIUS and ATHANASIUS "THE GREAT"). This entering into humanity is not an isolated act but continues in all the children of God by the indwelling Spirit. Thus, according to the canons of ancient philosophy, justice is done to all the factors of our problem—God remains as Father, the infinitely remote and absolute source of all; as Son, the Word Who is revealed to man and incarnate in Him; as Spirit, Who dwells even in our own souls and by His substance unites us to God.

Jesus was the central fact of faith, because he had led the disciples to God. After the resurrection He was the object of praise, and soon prayers were offered in His name and to Him. Already to the apostle Paul He dominates the world and is above all created things, visible and invisible, so that He has the religious value of God. Metaphysics and speculative theories were valueless for Paul; he was conscious of a mighty power transforming his own life and filling him with joy, and that this power was identical with Jesus of Nazareth he knew. In all this Paul is the representative of that which is highest and best in early Christianity. Speculation and hyperspiritualization were ever tending to obscure this fundamental religious fact: in the interest of a higher doctrine of God His true presence in Jesus was denied, and by exaggeration of Paul's doctrine of "Christ in us" the significance of the historic Jesus was given up. The Johannine writings, which presupposed the Pauline movement, are a protest against the hyperspiritualizing tendency. They insist that the Son of God has been incarnate in Jesus of Nazareth, and that our hands have handled and our eyes have seen the word of life. This same purpose, namely, to hold fast to the historic Jesus, triumphed in the Nicene formula; Jesus was not to be resolved into an aeon or into some mysterious *tertium quid*, neither God nor man, but to be recognized as very God who redeemed the soul. Through Him men were to understand the Father and to understand themselves as God's children.

It is apparent that such a doctrine as the Trinity is itself susceptible of many explanations, particularly as to the distinction and relation between God the Eternal Son and God the Holy Spirit; and minds differently constituted lay emphasis upon its different elements. Especially is this true as its Greek terminology was translated into Latin, and from Latin came into modern languages—the original meaning being obscured or disguised, and the original issues forgotten. For some the first thought of God, the infinite and ultimate reality lying beyond and behind all phenomena, predominates. With these the historic manifestation of Jesus becomes only a guide to lead us to that immediate apprehension of God which is the end of theology, and to that immediate union with God which is the end of religion. Such an end is accomplished either by means of pure thought or by a oneness of pure feeling, giving as results the theological or philosophical construction of the idea of God, or a mystical ecstasy which is itself at once immediate, inexplicable and indescribable. On the other hand, minds of a different and more concrete character so emphasize the distinctions God, Son and Holy Spirit, that a tritheistic construction appears—three individuals in the one Godhead: these individuals appearing, as for example, in the Father and the Son, even in opposition to each other. In general we may say then that the Trinity takes on three differing aspects in the Christian Church: in its more common and easily apprehended form as three Gods; in its ecclesiastical form as a mystery which is above reason to be accepted by faith; in its philosophic form as a metaphysical interpretation of the finite, the infinite and the relation between them.

To some Christians the doctrine of the Trinity appeared inconsistent with the unity of God which is emphasized in the Scriptures. They therefore denied it, and accepted Jesus Christ, not as incarnate God, but as God's highest creature by Whom all else was created, or as the perfect man who taught the true doctrine of God. The first view in the early Church long contended with the orthodox doctrine, but finally disappeared, and the second doctrine in the modern Church was set forth as easily intelligible, but has remained as a form of "heresy."

The Cross and the Atonement.—Allied with the doctrine of God which seeks the solution of the ultimate problem of all philosophy, the doctrine of salvation has taken the most prominent place in the Christian faith: so prominent, indeed, that to a large portion of believers it has been the supreme doctrine, and the doctrine of the deity of Jesus has been valued only because of its necessity on the effect of the atonement. Jesus alone of the great founders of religion suffered an early and violent death, even the death of a criminal. It became therefore the immediate task of His followers to explain this fact. This explanation was the more urgent because under the influence of Jewish monotheism the rule of God was accepted as an undoubted presupposition, so that the death of Jesus must be in accordance with His will. The early Church naturally used the term and phrases of the prophets. He died the death of a criminal, not for His sins, but for ours. Isaiah liii. was suggested at once and became the central explanation: Christ is the suffering servant Who is numbered with the transgressors and Who bears the sins of many.

It is remarkable that in the earliest centuries of Christian thought there is only the most slender support for theories of the Atonement which became widely current at a later time. The early Fathers did not regard the sufferings of Christ as a vicarious satisfaction of God's wrath, where He underwent punishment due to us and His obedience is imputed to us. Whenever they use language which seems to convey such ideas, they as it were instinctively safeguard it by the idea of our union with Christ, where we share in His obedience and His passion, and only so far as we make them our own do we actually appropriate the redemption He won for us. Their main thought is that man is reconciled to God by the Atonement, and not God to man; the change which it effects is a change in man rather than a change in God. Many centuries later the familiar outlines of the theory of vicarious atonement were drawn, and carved into a rigid scheme by the Reformers. They were deeply convinced that human sin is the violation of an eternal law which has its basis in the very being of God and is the expression of God's justice, which must be satisfied. This is the conviction embodied in the Protestant creeds, and worked out by means of metaphors so legal and even mechanical in character that modern theology has been marked by a widespread revolt against every form of it.

A large part of the history of Christian doctrine deals with controversies arising from theories of the Atonement (*q.v.*); but excepting in relatively narrow circles these theories have been seriously studied only by professed theologians. That Christ died for us, and that we are saved by Him, is indeed the living truth of the Church in all ages, and a false impression of the fact is given by dwelling upon theories as if they were central. At best they bear only the relationship of philosophy to life.

These hopes and theories of salvation do not indeed wholly explain the power of Christianity. Jesus wearied Himself with the healing of man's physical ailments, and He was remembered as the great physician. Early Christian literature is filled with medical terms, applied (it is true) for the greater part to the cure of souls. The records of the Church are also filled with the efforts of Jesus's followers to heal the diseases and satisfy the wants of men. A vast activity animated the early Church: to heal the sick, to feed the hungry, to succour the diseased, to rescue the fallen, to visit the prisoners, to forgive the erring, to teach the ignorant, were ministries of salvation. A mighty power impelled men to deny themselves in the service of others, and to find in this service their own true life. None the less the first place is given to the salvation of the soul, since, created for an unending existence, it is of transcendent importance. While man is fallen and by nature vile, nevertheless his possibilities are so vast that in comparison the affairs of earth are insignificant. The word, "What shall it profit a man if he gain the whole world and lose his own soul?" comes to mean that the individual soul outvalues the whole world. With emphasis upon God as creator and ruler, and upon man as made in God's image, endowed with an unending existence, and subject to eternal torture if not redeemed, the concept of personality has been exalted at the expense of that of nature, and the future has been magnified at the expense of the present. Thus a future heaven is man's true home, and theology instead of philosophy or natural science is his proper study.

Indeed, intellectual interest centred in religion. Natural science was forsaken, except in so far as it ministered to theology. Because the Old Testament contained references to the origin and the objects of the universe, a certain amount of natural science was necessary, but it was only in this connection that it had any value. By Augustine's time this process is complete. His writings contain most of the knowledge of his age, but it is strictly subordinate to his theological purpose. Hence, when the barbarians submerged southern Europe, theology alone survived. The Church entered upon a new task. In the beginning Christianity had been the teacher of religion to highly civilized peoples —now it became the civilizing agent to the barbarians, the teacher of better customs, the upholder of law and the source of knowledge. The learned men were monks and priests, and the universities were Church institutions.

The Sacraments and Salvation.—Belief in mysterious powers attached to food, feasts, ceremonial rites and sacred things is all but universal. Primitive man seldom connects sacrifice with notions of propitiation, indeed only in highly ethicized religions is the consciousness of sin or of guilt pre-eminent. Sacrifice was believed to exert an influence on the deity which is quasi-physical, and in sacrificial feasts God and worshipper are in mysterious union.

So universal are such ideas that the problem in particular religions is not their origin but their form. In the Old Testament repeatedly they are found in conflict with the prophetic ideals. Sometimes the prophets denounce them, sometimes ignore them, sometimes attempt to reform and control them. Jesus ignores them, His emphasis being so strong upon the ethical and spiritual that the rest is passed by. In the early Church, still Jewish, the belief was in the coming of a mysterious power from God which produced ecstasy and worked wonders. Paul also believes in this, but insists that it is subordinate to the peaceable fruits of righteousness. With the naturalization of the Church in the Gentile world ethical ideas became less prominent, and the sacramental system prevailed. By baptism and the Lord's Supper grace is given (*ex opere operato*), so that man is renewed and made capable of salvation. Already in the 2nd century baptism was described as a bath in which the health of the soul is restored, and the Lord's Supper as the potion of immortality. Similar notions present in the ethnic faiths take the Christian facts into their service, the belief of the multitude without essential change remaining vague and undefined. While the theologians discussed doctrine the people longed for mystery, as it satisfied their religious natures; by sacraments they felt themselves brought into the presence of God, and to sacraments they looked for aid. Many sacraments were adopted by portions of the Church, until at last the sacred number seven was agreed upon.

In the earliest period the services were characterized by extreme freedom, and by manifestations of ecstasy which were believed to indicate the presence of the spirit of God; but as time went on the original enthusiasm faded away, the cult became more and more controlled, until ultimately it was completely subject to the priesthood, and through the priesthood to the Church. The power of the priesthood had its centre in the sacrament of the Eucharist (*q.v.*), and in the Roman communion the structure of the sacred edifice, the positions and attitudes of the priest and the congregation, the order of service, emphasize the mystery and the divine efficacy of the sacrament. The worshipper feels himself in the immediate presence of God, and enters into physical relations with him; participation in the mass also releases from guilt, as the Lamb of God offered up atones for sin and intercedes with the Father in our behalf. Thus in this single act of devotion both objects of all cults are attained.

Organization.—As the teaching and person of Jesus were fitted into the framework of Greek philosophy, and the sacraments into the deeper and broader forms of popular belief, so was the organization shaped by the polity of the Roman empire. Jesus gathered His group of followers and committed to it His mission, and after His resurrection the necessities of the situation brought about the choice of quasi-officials. Later the familiar polity of the synagogue was loosely followed. A completer organization was retarded by two factors, the presence of the apostles and the inspiration of the prophets. But when the apostles died and the early enthusiasm disappeared, a stricter order arose. Practical difficulties called for the enforcement of discipline, and differences of opinion for authority in doctrine; and, finally, the sacramentarian system required a priesthood. In the 2nd century the conception of a Catholic Church was widely held and a loose embodiment was given it; after the conversion of the empire the organization took on the official forms of the empire. Later it was modified by the rise of the feudal system and the re-establishment of the modern European nationalities.

The polity of the Church was more than a formal organization; it touched the life of each believer. Very early, Christianity was conceived to be a new system of law, and faith was interpreted as obedience. Legalism was joined with sacramentarianism, doubling the power of the priest. Through him Church discipline was administered, a complete system of ecclesiastical penalties, *i.e.,* penance, growing up. It culminated in the doctrine of purgatory, a place of discipline, of purifying suffering after death. The Roman genius for law strengthened and systematized this tendency.

The Roman Church.—The hierarchy which centres in the pope constitutes the Church of which the sacramental system is the inner life and penance is the sanction. It is thus a divine-human organization. It teaches that the divine-human Son of God established it, and returning to heaven committed to the apostles, especially to St. Peter, his authority, which has descended in an unbroken line through the popes. This is the charter of the Church, and its acceptance is the first requisite for salvation; for the Church determines doctrine, exercises discipline and administers sacraments. Its authority is accompanied by the spirit of God, who guides it into truth and gives it miraculous power. Outside the Church are only the "broken lights" of man's philosophy and the vain efforts of weak human nature after virtue.

Christianity in its complete Roman development is thus the coming of the supernatural into the natural. The universe falls into these orders, the second for the sake of the first, as nature is of and for God. Without Him nature at its highest is like a beautiful statue, devoid of life; it is of secondary moment compared even to men, for while it passes away he continues for ever. Man is dependent, therefore, not upon nature, but upon God's grace for salvation, and this comes through the Church. Thus the Church ever receives God and has a twofold nature; its sacraments through material and earthly elements impart a divine power; its teachings agree with the highest truths of philosophy and science, yet add to these the knowledge of mysteries which the unaided reason of man could never apprehend. Theology is the queen of the sciences, and nothing should be taught in school or university which contradicts its conclusions. Moreover, nothing should be done by the State which interferes with the transcendent interest committed to the Church. Thus the Church touches and controls all realms of life, and the cycle is complete.

The Reformation.—The idea of the Roman Church was imperfectly embodied at the best; the divine gift was in earthen vessels. The world was never completely cast out; indeed the Church became the scene for ambition and the home of luxury and pleasure. It was entangled also in the political strife of the feudal ages and of the beginning of modern empires. Its control of the sciences embroiled it with its own philosophers and scholars, while saints and pure-minded ecclesiastics attempted, without success, its reform from within. Finally, through Luther, the explosion came, and western Christendom broke into two parts—Catholic and Protestant.

Protestantism in its primary principle is the return to primitive Christianity. The whole development which we have traced, culminating in the ecclesiastical-doctrinal system of the Roman Church, is regarded as a corruption, since foreign and even heathen elements have been brought in, so that the religion established by Christ is obscured or lost. For Protestants the Bible only now becomes the infallible inspired authority in faith and morals. Interpretations by the Fathers or by the councils are to be taken only as aids to its understanding. But in Protestantism reason and the light of nature are in themselves as impotent as in the Roman Church. The Bible interpreted by man's unaided intelligence is as valueless as other writings, but it has a sacramental value when the Holy Spirit accompanies its teaching, and the power of God uses it and makes the soul capable of holiness. In all this the supernatural is as vividly realized as in the Roman Church; it is only its mediation which is different.

These principles are variously worked out in the different churches and variously expressed. In part because of historical circumstances, the divergence from the older systems is more marked in some Protestant churches than in others, yet on the whole these two principles determine cult and in part organization. As in the Roman Church cult centres in the mass, so in the original Reformed Church it centred in the sermon. The ancient Jewish prophetic office was revived, yet with a difference: the ancient prophets acknowledged no external authority, but the Protestant preacher is strictly subordinate to the Scriptures of which he is the interpreter. Besides the sermon, the sacraments are observed as established by Christ—two in number, baptism and the Lord's Supper. But these do not exert a quasi-physical or magical influence, *ex opere operato.* Unless there be faith in the recipient, an understanding of the meaning of the sacrament and an acceptance of it, it is valueless or harmful. Prayer and praise also are effective only as the congregation intelligently joins in them.

The emphasis upon the believer and his freedom from all external authority do not result in a thoroughgoing individualism. Luther clearly held to the unity of all Christians, and Protestants are agreed in this. For them, as for the Roman Church, there is a belief in a catholic or all-embracing Church, but the unity is not that of an organization; Christians are one through an indwelling spirit; they undergo the same experience and follow the same purpose.

Historically these principles were only in part embodied, for the Reformation was involved in political strife. The Reformers turned to the Government for aid and protection, and throughout Europe turmoil and war ensued. In consequence, in the Protestant nations the State assumed the ultimate authority over the Church. Moreover, in the early days of the Reformation the Catholic Church charged it with a lawless individualism, a charge which was seemingly made good by an extreme divergence in theological opinion and by riots in various part of the Protestant world. The age was indeed one of ferment, so that the foundations of society and of religion seemed threatened. The Reformers turned to the State for protection against the Roman Church, and ultimately as a refuge from anarchy, and they also returned to the theology of the Fathers as their safeguard against heresy. Instead of the simplicity of Luther's earlier writings, a dogmatic theology was formed, and a Protestant ecclesiasticism established, indistinguishable from the Roman Church in principle. The main difference was in the attitude to the Roman allegiance and to the sacramentarian system. There was thus by no means a complete return to the Bible as the sole authority, but the Bible was taken as interpreted by the earlier creeds and as worked into a doctrinal system by the scholastic philosophy. Thus Protestantism also came to identify theology with the whole range of human knowledge, and in its official forms was as hostile to the progress of science as was the Roman Church itself.

Many Protestants rebelled against this radical departure from the principles of the Reformation and of biblical Christianity. To them it seems the substitution of the authority of the Church for the authority of a living experience, and of intellectual adherence to theological propositions for faith. The freedom of the individual was denied. Protestantism divided into many sects and denominations, founded upon special types of religious experience or upon particular points in doctrine or in cult. Thus Protestantism presents a wide diversity in comparison with the regularity of the Roman Church (*see* REUNION, CHURCH).

Christianity and the Modern World.—The coming of the northern peoples into the Roman world profoundly modified Christianity. It shared indeed in the dreariness and corruption of the times commonly called the "dark ages," but when at last a productive period began the Church was the first to profit by it. Since all educated men were priests, it assimilated the new learning—the revived Aristotelianism—and continued its control of the universities. In the 13th century it was supreme, and Christianity was identified with world systems of knowledge and politics. Both were deemed alike divine in origin, and to question their validity was an offence against God. Christianity thus had passed through three stages in politics as in science. At first it was persecuted by the State, then established by it, and finally dominated over it; so its teaching was at first alien to philosophy and despised by it, next was accepted by it and given form and rights through it, and finally became queen of the sciences as theology and ruled over the whole world of human knowledge. But the triumph by its completeness ensured new conflicts; from the disorder of the middle ages arose states which ultimately asserted complete autonomy, and in like fashion new intellectual powers came forth which ultimately established the independence of the sciences.

In the broadest sense the underlying principle of the struggle is the reassertion of interest in the world. It is no longer merely the scene for the drama of the soul and God, nor is man independent of it, but man and nature constitute an organism, humanity being a part of the vaster whole. Man's place is not even central, as he appears a temporary inhabitant of a minor planet in one of the lesser stellar systems. As in the political world the States gained first the undisputed control of matters secular, rejecting even the proffered counsel of the Church, and then proceeded to establish their sovereignty over the Church itself, so was it in the empire of the mind. The rights gained for independent research were extended over the realm of religion also; the two indeed cannot remain separate, and man must subordinate knowledge to the authority of religion—or make science supreme, submitting religion to its scrutiny and judging it like other phenomena. Under this investigation Christianity does not appear altogether exceptional. Its early logic, ontology, and cosmology, with many of its distinctive doctrines, are shown to be the natural offspring of the races and ages which gave them birth. Put into their historical environment they are found to be steps in the intellectual development of man's mind. But when put forward as absolute truths to-day, they are put aside as anachronisms not worthy of dispute. The Bible is studied like other works, its origins discovered and its place in comparative religion assigned. It does not appear as altogether unique, but it is put among the other sacred books. For the great religions of the world show similar cycles of development, similar appropriations of prevalent science and philosophy, similar conservative insistence upon ancient truth, and similar claims to an exclusive authority.

With this interest is involved an attitude of mind toward the supernatural. As already pointed out, nature and super-nature were taken as physically and spatially distinct. The latter could descend upon the former and be imparted to it, neither subject to nature nor intelligible by reason. In science the process has been reversed; nature ascends, so to speak, into the region of the supernatural and subdues it to itself; the marvellous or miraculous is brought under the domain of natural law, the canons of physics extend over metaphysics, and religion takes its place as one element in the natural relationship of man to his environment. Hence the new world-view threatens the foundations of the ecclesiastical edifice. This revolution in the world-view is no longer the possession of philosophers and scholars, but the multitude accepts it in part. Education in general has rendered many familiar with the teachings of science, and, moreover, its practical benefits have given authority to its maxims and theories.

The *Roman Catholic Church* uncompromisingly reasserts its ancient propositions, political and theological. The cause is lost indeed in the political realm, where the Church is obliged to submit, but it protests and does not waive or modify its claims (*see* the *Syllabus* of 1864, par. 19 *seq.,* 27, 54 and 55). In the Greek and Protestant churches this situation cannot arise, as they make no claims to governmental sovereignty. In the intellectual domain the situation is more complex. Again the Roman Church unhesitatingly reaffirms the ancient principles in their extreme form (*Syllabus,* par. 8–9–13; *Decrees of the Vatican Council,* ch. 4, especially canon 4–2); the works of St. Thomas Aquinas are recommended as the standard authority in theology (Encyc. of Leo XIII., *Aeterni Patris,* Aug. 4, 1879). In details also the conclusions of modern science are rejected, as for example the origin of man from lower species, and, in a different sphere, the conclusions of experts as to the origins of the Bible. Faith is defined as "assent upon authority," and the authority is the Church, which maintains its right to supremacy over the whole domain of science and philosophy.

The *Greek Church* remains untouched by the modern spirit. With characteristic oriental conservatism it claims the title of "Orthodox" and retains the creed and organization of the early Church. The *Protestant Churches* also are bound officially to the scholastic philosophy of the 17th century; their confessions of faith still assert the formation of the world in six days, and require assent to propositions which can be true only if the old cosmology be correct.

Compromises.—On the other hand there are individuals and even large bodies of Christians who are intent upon a reinterpretation. Even in the official circles of the Church, not excepting the Roman Church, there are many scholars who find no difficulty in maintaining communion while accepting the modern scientific view of the world. This is possible to some because the situation in its sharp antithesis is not present to their minds: by making certain compromises on the one side and on the other, and by framing private interpretations of important dogmas, they can retain their faith in both and yet preserve their mental integrity.

Thus the crisis is in fact not so acute as it might seem. No great institution lives or dies by logic. Christianity rests on great religious needs which it meets and gratifies, so that its life (like all other lives) is in unrationalized emotions. Reason seeks ever to rationalize these, an attempt which seems to destroy yet really fulfils. As thus the restless reason tests the emotions of the soul, criticizes the traditions to which they cling, rejects the ancient dogmas in which they have been defined, the Church slowly participates in the process; silently this position and that are forsaken, legends and beliefs once of prime importance are forgotten, or when forced into controversy many ways are found by which the old and the new are reconciled; the sharpness of distinctions can be rubbed off, expressions may be softened, definitions can be modified and half-way resting-places afforded, until the momentous transition has been made and the continuity of tradition is maintained. Finally, as the last step, even the official documents may be revised.

Philosophy and Ethical Redemption.—The intellectual crisis cannot be ignored in the interest of the practical life. Men must rationalize the universe. On the one hand there are churchmen who attempt to repeat the historical process which has naturalized the Church in alien soils by appropriating the forces of the new environment, and who hold that the entire process is inspired and guided by the spirit of God. Hence Christianity is the absolute religion, because it does not preclude development but necessitates it, so that the Christianity that is to come shall not only retain all that is important in the Christianity of the past and present but shall assimilate new truth. On the other hand some seek the essential Christianity in a life beneath and separable from the historic forms. In part under the influence of the Hegelian philosophy, and in part because of the prevalent evolutionary scientific world-view, God is represented under the form of pure thought, and the world process as the unfolding of Himself. Such truth can be apprehended by the multitude only in symbols which guide the will through the imagination, and through historic facts which are embodiment of ideas. The Trinity is the essential Christian doctrine, the historic facts of the Christian religion being the embodiment of religious ideas. The chief critical difficulty felt by this school is in identifying any concrete historic fact with the unchanging idea, that is, in making Jesus of Nazareth the incarnation of God. God is reinterpreted, and in place of an extra-mundane creator is an omnipresent life and power. The Christian attainment is nothing else than the thorough intellectual grasp of the absolute idea and the identification of our essential selves with God. With a less thoroughgoing intellectualism other scholars reinterpret Christianity in terms of current scientific phraseology. Christianity is dependent upon the understanding of the universe; hence it is the duty of believers to put it into the new setting, so that it adopts and adapts astronomy, geology, biology and psychology.

From all these efforts to reconstruct systematic theology with its appropriations of philosophy and science, groups of Christians turn to the inner life and seek in its realities to find the confirmation of their faith. They also claim oneness with a long line of Christians, for in every age there have been men who have ignored the dogma and the ritual of the Church, and in contemplation and retirement have sought to know God immediately in their own experience. To them at best theology with its cosmology and its logic is only a shadow of shadows, for God reveals himself to the pure in heart, and it matters not what science may say of the material and fleeting world. This spirit manifests itself in wide circles in our day. The Gordian knot is cut, for philosophy and religion no longer touch each other but abide in separate realms.

In quite a different way a still more influential school seeks essential Christianity in the sphere of the ethical life. It also would disentangle religion from cosmology and formal philosophy. It studies the historic development of the Church, noting how element after element has been introduced into the simplicity of the gospel, and from all these it would turn back to the Bible itself. In a thoroughgoing fashion it would accomplish what Luther and the Reformation attempted. It regards even the earliest creeds as only more or less satisfactory attempts to translate the Christian facts into the current language of the heathen world. But the process does not stop with this rejection of the ancient and the scholastic theology. It recognizes the scientific results attained in the study of the Bible itself, and therefore it does not seek the entire Bible as its rule of truth. To it Jesus Christ, and He alone, is supreme, but this supremacy does not carry with it infallibility in the realm of cosmology or of history. In these too Jesus participated in the views of His own time; even His teaching of God and of the future life is not lacking in Jewish elements, yet none the less He is the essential element in Christianity, and to His life-purpose must all that claims to be Christianity be brought to be judged. To this school Christianity is the culmination of the ethical monotheism of the Old Testament, which finds its highest ideal in self-sacrificing love. Jesus Christ is the complete embodiment of this ideal, in life and in death. This ideal He sets before men under the traditional forms of the Kingdom of God as the object to be attained, a Kingdom which takes upon itself the forms of the family, and realizes itself in a new relationship of universal brotherhood. Such a religion appeals for its self-verification not to its agreement with cosmological conceptions, either ancient or modern, or with theories of philosophy, however true these may be, but to the moral sense of man. On the one hand, in its ethical development, it is nothing less than the outworking of that principle of Jesus Christ which led Him not only to self-sacrificing labour but to the death upon the cross. On the other hand, it finds its religious solution in the trust in a power not ourselves which makes for the same righteousness which was incarnate in Jesus Christ.

Thus Christianity, as religion, is on the one hand the adoration of God, that is, of the highest and noblest, and this highest and noblest as conceived not under forms of power or knowledge but in the form of ethical self-devotion as embodied in Jesus Christ, and on the other hand it meets the requirements of all religion in its dependence, not indeed upon some absolute idea or omnipotent power, but in the belief that that which appeals to the soul as worthy of supreme worship is also that in which the soul may trust, and which shall deliver it from sin and fear and death. Such a conception of Christianity can recognize many embodiments in ritual, organization and dogma, but its test in all ages and in all lands is conformity to the purpose of the life of Christ. The Lord's Prayer in its oldest and simplest form is the expression of its faith, and Christ's separation of mankind on the right hand and on the left in accordance with their service or refusal of service to their fellow-men is its own judgment of the right of any age or Church to the name Christian.

Christianity has passed through too many changes, and it has found too many interpretations possible, to fear the time to come. Thoroughgoing reconstruction in every item of theology and in every detail of polity there may be, yet shall the Christian life go on—the life which finds its deepest utterance in the words of Christ, "Thou shalt love the Lord thy God with all thy heart and thy neighbour as thyself"; the life which expresses its profoundest faith in the words Christ taught it to pray, "Our Father"; the life which finds its highest rule of conduct in the words of its first and greatest interpreter, "Let this mind be in you which was also in Christ Jesus our Lord."

The view that Jesus deliberately founded a Church (an ecclesiastical institution), appointed the Apostles its rulers, settled its rites, gave it its doctrine and guaranteed its fidelity, can only be maintained by discarding history altogether. In the 19th century this was transformed into the view that Jesus planted "in germ" what has grown to be the present Catholic doctrine and order. Among those who differ only in detail about what happened, there are, however, diametrically opposite judgments of the value of the change. (i.) Liberal Protestant scholars, on the whole, regard it as the kind of corruption to which religions are always subject as they absorb alien elements with their imperfectly instructed converts. They find the essential Christian element to be a power, shown by no other religion, first of elevating and spiritualizing these alien elements and then of eliminating them. This they ascribe to the higher idea of redemption inseparable from the faith in Christ (which, however much overlaid, has always wrought like leaven), and to what goes with it—the Revelation of the Father. Thus, for them, an essential quality of Christianity is its power to regenerate itself by a return to the Jesus of the Gospels. They would maintain that all other religions have their place, but it is as a preparation, or if their elements remain in Christianity, it is only as a temporary substitute for the true Christian redemption. (ii.) Liberal Catholic scholars on the other hand regard it as the highest perfection of Christianity that it can thus "syncretize" (absorb and transform) what has appealed to human need in any religion. By this comprehensiveness, they maintain, Christianity, from being an enthusiastic but incoherent movement, grew into a permanent and effective institution, with its original puritanism enriched in all kinds of religiously valuable ways.

The foregoing statement is a definition not of two positions but of two *directions,* and allows for various intermediate doctrines and interpretations. All these are naturally exemplified in the principal branches of organized Christianity, and reference must be made to the various articles on these subjects: ROMAN CATHOLIC CHURCH; ENGLAND, CHURCH OF; PRESBYTERIANISM; LUTHERANS; CONGREGATIONALISM; METHODISM; etc.

BIBLIOGRAPHY.—On such a vast subject we can here refer to only a few of those books which give guidance for further study and are typical of each of its main lines. For Roman Catholicism: P. Batiffol, *L'Église naissante et le catholicisme* (4th ed., 1909); Wilhelm and Scannell, *Manual of Catholic Theology* (1899); C. S. Devas, *The Key to the World's Progress* (1906); and many articles in the *Catholic Encyclopaedia.* For Anglicanism: *Lux Mundi* (1890); Gore, *Orders and Unity* (1909); *The Reconstruction of Belief* (1927); Darwell Stone, *The Church, its Ministry and Authority* (1902); A. C. Headlam (Bishop of Gloucester), *The Church of England* (1927). For the Free Churches: *Towards Reunion,* by Church of England and Free Church writers (1919); G. K. A. Bell, *Documents on Christian Unity*

(1924); G. K. A. Bell and W. Robertson (eds.), *The Church of England and the Free Churches* (1925); A. E. Garvie, "Christianity" in James Hastings' *Encyclopaedia of Religion and Ethics*, 12 vol. (1908–22), for liberal Evangelicalism; J. E. Carpenter (ed.), *Freedom and Truth* (1925), for Unitarian Christianity. *See* also James Drummond, *Via, Veritas, Vita* (Hibbert Lectures, 1894); and Charles Beard, *The Reformation of the Sixteenth Century in Its Relation to Modern Thought and Knowledge* (Hibbert Lectures, 1883; new ed., 1927).

For the principles of Protestantism as a religion: A. Ritschl, *Christian Doctrine of Justification and Reconciliation* (Eng. trans., 1900), most important for its present influence (for a critical estimate, Garvie, *The Ritschlian Theology*, 1897); E. Troeltsch, *Die Absolutheit des Christenthums* (1902); W. Hermann, *Communion of the Christian with God* (Eng. trans., 1895), a discussion in the spirit of Luther; A. Sabatier, *Religions of Authority and the Religion of the Spirit* (Eng. trans., 1904). On primitive Christianity, *see* Harnack, *Mission and Expansion of Christianity in the First Three Centuries* (Eng. trans., 1904); Wernle, *Beginnings of Christianity* (Eng. trans., 1904); Weizsacker, *The Apostolic Age* (Eng. trans., 1897); Edwin Hatch, *Influence of Greek Ideas and Usages upon the Christian Church* (Hibbert Lectures, 1888).

(G. W. Kn.; S. H. M.)

CHRISTIAN OF BRUNSWICK (1599–1626), bishop of Halberstadt, a younger son of Henry Julius, duke of Brunswick-Wolfenbüttel, was born in Groningen, Neth., on Sept. 20, 1599. Having succeeded his father as "bishop" of Halberstadt in 1616, he obtained some experience of warfare under Maurice, prince of Orange, in the Netherlands. Raising an army he entered the service of Frederick V, elector palatine of the Rhine, and attacked the lands of the elector of Mainz and the bishoprics of Westphalia. After some successes he was defeated by Johann (later Count van) Tilly at Höchst, Prus., in June 1622; then, dismissed from Frederick's service, he entered that of the United Provinces, losing an arm at the battle of Fleurus. In 1623 he was beaten by Tilly at Stadtlohn, Prus., and driven back to the Netherlands. When in 1625 Christian IV, king of Denmark, entered the arena of the war, he took the field again in the Protestant interest, but after some successes he died at Wolfenbüttel, Ger., on June 16, 1626. (*See* also THIRTY YEARS' WAR.)

BIBLIOGRAPHY.—Count van Tilly, *Relacion de la vitoria que de dar al Conde de Tylli contra el Duque Cristiano de Bronzuyque* (Madrid, 1623).

CHRISTIANSAND, a fortified seaport of Norway, the chief town of the diocese (*stift*) of Agder on a fjord of the Skagerrack, 175 mi. S.W. of Oslo. Pop. (est. 1936) 18,781. It stands on a square peninsula flanked by the western and eastern harbours and by the Otter river, among wooded hills and islands. It is a fishing centre (salmon, mackerel, lobsters), with sawmills, woodpulp factories, shipbuilding yards and mechanical workshops. The port is the largest on the south coast; coast and foreign steamers on the way north to Oslo ordinarily touch there. The Saetersdal railway follows that valley north to Byglandsfjord (48 mi.), whence a good road continues to Viken i Valle at the head of the valley. Flekkerö, a neighbouring island, is a favourite pleasure resort. The town was founded in 1641 by Christian IV.

CHRISTIAN SCIENCE, the religion founded by Mary Baker Eddy; the religion represented by the Church of Christ, Scientist. Applicable to health, as the Christian religion originally was, Christian Science is a religious teaching and practice based on the words and works of Christ Jesus. As defined by Mrs. Eddy, it is "divine metaphysics"; it is "the scientific system of divine healing"; it is "the law of God, the law of good, interpreting and demonstrating the divine Principle and rule of universal harmony" (*Science and Health, with Key to the Scriptures*, p. 111, 123; *Rudimental Divine Science*, p. 1). For many years prior to 1866 Mrs. Eddy had observed and studied mental causes and effects. Profoundly religious, she was disposed to attribute causation to God and to regard Him as divine Mind. At Lynn, Mass., in that year, she recovered almost instantly from a severe injury after reading an account of healing in the Gospel according to St. Matthew ix, 1–8. The discovery of what she named Christian Science ensued from this incident. As she has said, "I knew the Principle of all harmonious Mind-action to be God, and that cures were produced in primitive Christian healing by holy, uplifting faith; but I must know the Science of this healing, and I won my way to absolute conclusions through divine revelation, reason and demonstration" (*Science and Health*, p. 109).

At Boston, Mass., in 1875, Mrs. Eddy published her principal work, first called *Science and Health* but afterward entitled *Science and Health, with Key to the Scriptures*. It is known also as the Christian Science textbook. Occasionally revised by the author, "only to be a clearer and fuller expression of its original meaning" (p. 361), this book received from her its final revision in 1907. It is read in Christian Science services in connection with the Bible, and is to be found in all Christian Science reading rooms as well as in public libraries. (For other works on Christian Science by Mrs. Eddy, *see* the bibliography under EDDY, MARY BAKER.) Mrs. Eddy also attached great importance to periodical literature. Publications of the church, issued by the Christian Science Publishing society, include *The Christian Science Journal* (1883); the *Christian Science Quarterly* (1890); the *Christian Science Sentinel* (1898); *The Herald of Christian Science*, published in seven foreign languages and in Braille in English; and the *Christian Science Monitor* (1908). All except one of these periodicals circulate chiefly among people who have some degree of interest in Christian Science, but the *Christian Science Monitor* has become established as an excellent newspaper in the estimation of many people who are entirely indifferent toward the religion which it promotes but does not obtrude or even stress.

At first, Mrs. Eddy did not expect to found a distinct church or denomination; she hoped that her discovery would be accepted soon by existing churches. In a short time, however, a distinct church became needed to facilitate co-operation and unity between Christian Scientists, to present Christian Science to other people and to maintain the purity of its teaching and practice. Accordingly, at Boston, in 1879, Mrs. Eddy with her followers founded the Church of Christ, Scientist. Soon the original organization became inadequate for the growing denomination. To the first congregation in Boston there were added numbers of Christian Scientists at other places. Local churches as well as a central organization or Mother Church became necessary. Therefore, in 1892, Mrs. Eddy with her followers founded the Christian Science Mother Church, The First Church of Christ, Scientist, in Boston, of which the local churches throughout the world are regarded as branches.

Mrs. Eddy passed away in 1910. Until then she had initiated every step in the progress of Christian Science. Nothing of moment was done without her approval. Furthermore, although the organic law of the Christian Science movement, its *Church Manual*, confers extensive and sufficient powers upon an administrative board, the Christian Science board of directors, yet this board always had functioned under her immediate supervision. Mrs. Eddy's demise, therefore, immediately tested the adequacy of the *Church Manual* as an organic law and the loyalty of Christian Scientists to this law, in the absence of its author. Nevertheless, the period since 1910 has been the most fruitful and prosperous in the history of Christian Science.

The theology of Christian Science begins with the propositions that God is the only might or Mind; that He is "the divine Principle of all that really is" (*Science and Health*, p. 275). To define God further, it employs frequently the word Good, besides such terms as Life, Truth, Love, Soul, Spirit and Infinite Person. Next to God, the name Jesus and references to him occur most frequently in the authorized literature of Christian Science. Concerning Jesus the Christ and his relation to God and men, Christian Science distinguishes between what is in the New Testament and what is in the creeds, doctrines and dogmas of later times. Accordingly, Christian Scientists speak of him oftenest as the Way or Way-shower and they regard his atonement, his chief work, as "the exemplification of man's unity with God, whereby man reflects divine Truth, Life and Love" (*Science and Health*, p. 18).

The most distinctive feature of Christian Science teaching is its absolute distinction between what is real and what is apparent or seeming but unreal. This distinction Mrs. Eddy explains, for instance, as follows: "All reality is in God and His creation, harmonious and eternal. That which He creates is good, and He makes all that is made. Therefore the only reality of sin, sickness or death is the awful fact that unrealities seem real to human, erring belief, until God strips off their disguise. They are not true, because they are not of God" (*Science and Health,* p. 472). Contrary to common misapprehension, Christian Science does not ignore what it regards as unreal. This religion teaches its adherents to forsake and overcome every form of error or evil on the basis of its unreality; that is, by demonstrating the true idea of reality. This it teaches them to do by means of spiritual understanding, spiritual law and spiritual power.

In this connection, Christian Science maintains that the truth of being, the truth concerning God and man, includes a rule for its practice and a law by which its practice produces effects. To a certain extent Jesus declared this rule and law when he said, "Ye shall know the truth, and the truth shall make you free" (John viii, 32). Accordingly, for an individual to gain his freedom from any form of error or evil, he should know the truth, the absolute truth of being, applicable to his case; and Christian Science further teaches that this practice is effective when employed by one individual for another, because such is the unity of real being and such is the law of God. For these reasons, evidently Jesus could and did declare the possibility of Christian healing in unlimited terms. *See* Matthew x, 5–10, and xxviii, 16–20; Mark xvi, 14–18; John xiv, 12.

The practice of Christian Science is not merely mental; it must be also spiritual. Indeed, it is truly mental only as it is absolutely spiritual. The nonspiritual elements in the so-called human mind do not contribute to harmony or health. The practitioner must know or realize spiritually, and his ability to do this is derived from the divine Mind. Therefore, he must agree with the Teacher and Way-shower who said, "I can of mine own self do nothing" (John v, 30), and must prepare for the healing ministry and keep himself in condition for it by living the life of a genuine Christian. The practice of Christian Science is not limited, as is commonly supposed, to the healing of the sick. On the contrary, Christian Scientists regard their religion as applicable practically to every human need.

While the adherents of Christian Science are chiefly found among people who read English, it has followers among Christian people everywhere and also among Jews.

In Jan. 1950 there were 3,006 branches of the Mother Church, in addition to which there were 108 college and university organizations besides many groups not yet formally organized. Of these churches, there were in the United States 2,251; in Great Britain, 344; in Germany, 119; and in other countries, 292.

(C. P. S.; X.)

BIBLIOGRAPHY.—Mary Baker Eddy, *Science and Health, with Key to the Scriptures,* rev. ed. (1910); Edward A. Kimball, *Lectures and Articles on Christian Science* (1921); Charles Herman Lea, *A Plea for the Thorough and Unbiased Investigation of Christian Science* (London, 1923).

CHRISTIAN SOCIALISM is a term that has been used to denote a wide variety of social doctrines and movements which have attempted to give a basic, structural application to the social principles of Christianity. In the 19th century the term socialism in this context was employed in a loose sense, denoting, in opposition to *laissez-faire* individualism, a Christian demand for some form of political or economic action in the interest of all the people. Christian Socialists usually did not demand the common ownership and control of the means of production and exchange. Roman Catholic Christian socialism, for example, promoted certain reforms to improve social relations, but its ultimate aim, in accord with papal encyclicals, was the establishment of a neofeudal corporative system, an order quite different from what is usually called socialism. In the 20th century, Christian social and industrial reform movements have been more and more referred to as the Christian social, the Protestant social or the Catholic social movement. The term Christian socialism tends to be reserved for those movements which attempt to combine the fundamental aims of socialism with the religious and ethical convictions of Christianity. It is this sort of Christian socialism that is mainly dealt with here.

Christian Socialism in England.—Although anticipations of Christian socialism are to be found in early Christian "communism of love" and in the radical sects of the middle ages, of the "left wing" of the Reformation and of the 17th century (*e.g.,* the Levellers in England), the term Christian socialism was first appropriated by the Broad Churchmen, J. F. D. Maurice, Charles Kingsley (the novelist), J. M. Ludlow and others, who entered on public propaganda immediately after the collapse of the chartist uprising of 1848. Their general purpose was to vindicate for "the Kingdom of Christ" its "true authority over the realms of industry and trade" and "for socialism its true character as the great Christian revolution of the 19th century." Four years after Karl Marx characterized religion as "opiate for the people," Kingsley (probably unaware of Marx's phrase) asserted that the Bible had been wrongly used as "an opium-dose for keeping beasts of burden patient while they were being overloaded" and as a "mere book to keep the poor in order" (in *Politics for the People,* 1848). Greatly stirred by the sufferings of the poor, the group vigorously criticized socially conservative Christianity and *laissez-faire* industrialism, extolling "the Bible principles" of self-sacrifice and co-operation as against self-interest and competition.

Reviving the co-operative movement, they favoured copartnership and profit-sharing in industry; they organized the Council for Promoting Working Men's Associations, which gave rise to or encouraged producers' and consumers' co-operatives; they aided in securing the enactment in 1852 of the Industrial and Provident Partnerships bill, the Magna Carta of the modern co-operative movement; and they instituted workers' education by founding the Working Men's college in London (1854). The movement as such continued for only a decade.

In 1877 Stewart Headlam founded the (Anglo-Catholic) Guild of St. Matthew, which espoused a composite of doctrines drawn from Maurice, from Tractarianism and from Fabian socialism. Somewhat similar if less definitely socialistic ideas gained influence after the turn of the century through the support of certain high churchmen who founded the Christian Social union (1889).

Subsequent to Headlam's effort numerous Christian Socialist organizations were formed, both in the established church and among the free churches. Prominent among these were the interdenominational Christian Socialist league, originating in the early 1880s, the labour churches (organized in 1891), and the (Anglican) Church Socialist league (founded in 1906), which emanated from the industrial north of England and brought the churches closer to labour and Socialist movements. Following internal dissension the Church Socialist league was succeeded in 1923 by the League of the Kingdom of God, which called for a generically Catholic Christian sociology looking toward the establishment of a neomediaeval social system. The (official Anglican) Industrial Christian fellowship, founded in 1919, was of a mediating character. The later (predominantly Free Church) Socialist Christian league and the (Anglo-Catholic) Order of the Church Militant made explicit demand for the communal control of the means of life and regarded socialism as the economic expression of Christianity. The Malvern declaration of 1941, drawn up by Anglicans under the leadership of Archbishop William Temple, was considered to be left-wing in character, but it was criticized for its "vagueness" by the Council of Clergy and Ministers for Common Ownership (founded in 1942). More sympathetic to Marxist philosophy was the (Free Church) Christian Left, which, under the leadership of John Macmurray, flourished in the 1930s and which viewed it to be "the religious mission of the working class to achieve Socialism."

Christian Socialism on the Continent.—The precursors of this movement on the continent are dealt with in another place. Roman Catholic Christian socialism (now called the Catholic social movement) was the first of its kind on the continent, but it was not socialistic except in the sense of a clerical socialism.

In France the Protestant Association for the Practical Study of Social Questions (founded in 1888) was mainly concerned with the need for social reform. T. Fallot, one of its principal founders, opposed bourgeois, individualistic Protestantism and strove for a Protestant socialism that would achieve liberty through co-operation and through resisting an "artificial and deadly" equalitarian socialism. Until World War I, Protestant left-wing views were for the most part mildly social-reformist in character. In the 20th century Protestant Socialists found their most effective mediums of expression in the periodical *Le Christianisme Social* (founded in 1877), edited by Élie Gounelle, and in the Fédération du Christianisme Social. In this group one of the most influential Christian Socialists of the second quarter of the century was André Philip, an economist, a prolific writer on Christianity and socialism and a leader in labour and government circles.

Outstanding among German Protestant Christian Socialists in the 19th century were Rudolf Todt, Adolf Stöcker (who deviated into anti-Semitism), Friedrich Naumann and J. C. Blumhardt. The state Socialists Todt and Stöcker (anti-Marxist and in the throne and altar tradition) were, like the Catholic groups, opposed by the Social Democrats. Naumann took a more democratic attitude toward the worker and also believed it desirable for churchmen to co-operate with a revisionist social democracy. A still more favourable attitude toward social democracy was adopted by Blumhardt, who held that the Kingdom of God can be hindered by the churches and can be advanced by seemingly anti-Christian secular movements; indeed, he joined the Social Democratic party.

In the early part of the 20th century Hermann Kutter, "the Zürich Savonarola," held that the Social Democrats were revolutionary because God is; God's Kingdom must go forward in a revolutionary way despite, and even because of, the sluggishness of the churches. Leonhard Ragaz of Zürich, who looked forward to a Socialist society organized in freedom and love, was the connecting link with postwar movements in Switzerland and Germany. Christian socialism now assumed a great variety of forms. Some Christian Socialists (1) held that socialism is the logical consequence of Christianity, (2) others made socialism into a religion, (3) others tried to bring about understanding and interpenetration between the churches and the organized Socialist proletariat and (4) still others tried to uncover the roots of both Christianity and Marxist socialism toward the end of understanding more critically the affinities and the needed correctives. Representative of the fourth type was the League of Religious Socialists of south Germany, which included both Protestants and Catholics in its membership. Philosophically and theologically the most important and fruitful was the (Berlin) Kairos circle, which belonged to the fourth type mentioned and which for the decade preceding the nazi revolution was under the leadership of the theologian Paul Tillich. After 1933 Tillich went to the U.S., where his religious socialism exercised an influence.

Movements similar to the above-mentioned types have appeared also in other European countries; they were especially successful in the Scandinavian countries. Of intellectual significance in the 1930s and 1940s was the religious-Socialist "personalist" philosophy of the one-time Marxist, theosophical Russian Orthodox writer Nicolas Berdyaev, whose antecedents appear in the writings of 19th-century Russian lay theologians such as Theodore Dostoievski and Leo Tolstoy.

Developments in America.—As the result of the absence of an archaic period in the history of the U.S., neofeudal and patriarchal forms of Christian socialism have played a small role; Puritan activism, the enlightenment and radical democratic tendencies have been more in evidence. Although ethical rationalism and deism exercised considerable influence in 18th-century religion and politics, although semi-Utopian Fourierist communities were established in the 1840s and 1850s and although progressive social concerns during this period found strong advocates in the Unitarians W. E. Channing, Joseph Tuckerman and Theodore Parker, a social Christianity was not widely expounded until after the Civil War. Its outstanding leaders down to the 1930s were R. H. Newton (an Episcopalian), Washington Gladden, Josiah Strong, G. D. Herron (Congregationalists), Shailer Mathews (a Baptist), Bishop Francis J. McConnell (a Methodist) and F. G. Peabody and J. H. Holmes (Unitarians). Of these men only Herron and Holmes were Socialists.

As early as 1849 Henry James, Sr., had argued the identity of the aims of Christianity and socialism. Largely under the leadership of W. D. P. Bliss, an Episcopalian who had been a member of the Knights of Labor, the Society of Christian Socialists was organized in 1889. Vigorously criticizing economic individualism and its ruinous progeny of plutocracy, industrial crises and wage slavery, the society attempted to show that "the aim of socialism is embraced in the aim of Christianity."

In the first quarter of the 20th century numerous Christian Socialist or quasi-Socialist groups were formed, as for example the nondenominational Christian Socialist fellowship (1906), the (pacifist) Fellowship of Reconciliation (started in England in 1914 and extended to the U.S. in 1915), the (Episcopalian) Christian Socialist league (1911–19), followed by the Church League for Industrial Democracy.

This period was the heyday of the Social Gospel movement, which, in the spirit of evolutionism and evangelical humanitarianism, interpreted the Kingdom of God as requiring social as well as individual salvation. Its most influential exponent was Walter Rauschenbusch (a Baptist), who demanded "a new order that would rest on the Christian principles of equal rights and democratic distribution of economic power." He distinguished sharply between the ultimate presuppositions of Christian socialism and those of secular socialism. Influences from this movement extended to Japan (*e.g.*, through T. Kagawa), China, South America and India.

Following World War I, Marxist doctrine and also radically democratic doctrine began to play a larger role. Harry F. Ward (a Methodist) and his disciples were moving toward a Christian Marxism which showed a marked sympathy with Russian communism. In the 1930s and 1940s a neo-Marxist and theologically neo-orthodox Christian socialism gained wide attention under the leadership of Reinhold Niebuhr (an Evangelical); attacking the "Utopian naturalism" of Marxism and the overoptimism of the "liberal" Social Gospel, the nondenominational Fellowship of Socialist Christians, founded in 1932, undertook a "Christian espousal of socialism" as the logical next step in a technical society; and the group published a magazine, *Christianity and Society.* The National Religion and Labor foundation (1932 *et seq.*), the Fellowship of Southern Churchmen (1934 *et seq.*) and the (Canadian) Fellowship for a Christian Social Order (1934 *et seq.*) advocated similar economic policies, as did the United Christian Council for Democracy (1936 *et seq.*) which provided a means of common action for the left-wing organizations of six liberal Protestant denominations. Beginning in 1939 *The Protestant Digest*, later named *The Protestant,* a journal edited by Kenneth Leslie (a Baptist), served as a medium of expression for Christian, Jewish and secular left-wing and neo-Marxist viewpoints. The Highlander Folk school (Monteagle, Tenn., 1932 *et seq.*) espoused a Christian Socialist gospel, co-operatives, unionism and adult education among rural and industrial workers. In most of these groups social planning tended to replace gradualist socialism as the remedy proposed for the ills of capitalism.

Although it has not been markedly successful in attracting the alienated working classes to the churches, Christian socialism has done much to stimulate churchmen to give a radical social application to Christian ethics in an industrial society.

Bibliography.—W. D. P. Bliss and R. M. Binder (eds.), *New Encyclopedia of Social Reform*, new ed. (1908); Gerda Soecknick, *Religiöser Sozialismus der neueren Zeit* (1926); J. Lewis, Karl Polanyi and D. K. Kitchin (eds.), *Christianity and the Social Revolution* (1936); Donald O. Wagner (ed.), *Social Reformers* (1934), an anthology with bibliographies; C. H. Hopkins, *The Rise of the Social Gospel in American Protestantism, 1865–1915,* no. 14 in "Yale Studies in Religious Education" (1940); Paul Tillich, *The Protestant Era* (1948). For extensive bibliography *see* H. W. Laidler, *Social-Economic Movements,* chap. 43, in "Crowell's Social Science Series" (1944). (J. L. A.)

CHRISTIANSUND, a seaport on the west coast of Norway, in Romsdal *amt* (county), 259 mi. N.E. by N. of Bergen, in the latitude of the Faeroe Islands. Pop. (1936) 14,646. It is built on four small islands, by which its harbour is enclosed. The chief exports before World War II were wood, cod, herrings and fish products, and butter to Great Britain. The town is the chief port of the Nordmöre district. Till 1742, when it received town privileges from Christian VI, Christiansund was called Lille-Fosen.

CHRISTIAN UNITY: *see* Reunion, Church.

CHRISTIE, RICHARD COPLEY (1830–1901), English scholar and bibliophile, was born on July 22, 1830, at Lenton, Notts., the son of a millowner. He was educated at Lincoln college, Oxford, was called to the bar at Lincoln's Inn in 1857 and in 1872 became chancellor of the diocese of Manchester. He resigned this position in 1893. He held numerous appointments, notably the professorships of history (from 1854 to 1856) and of political economy (from 1855 to 1866) at Owens college, Manchester. He always took an active interest in this college of which he was a governor; in 1893 he gave the Christie library building designed by Alfred Waterhouse, and in 1897 he devoted £50,000 of the funds at his disposal as trustee of Sir Joseph Whitworth's estate for the building of Whitworth hall, which completed the front quadrangle of the college. He was an enthusiastic book collector and bequeathed to Owens college his library of about 75,000 vol., rich in a complete set of books printed by Etienne Dolet, a wonderful series of Aldines, and of volumes printed by Sebastian Gryphius. His *Etienne Dolet, the Martyr of the Renaissance* (1880) is the most exhaustive work on the subject. He died at Ribsden on Jan. 9, 1901.

CHRISTIE, SIR WILLIAM HENRY MAHONEY (1845–1922), British astronomer, son of Samuel Hunter Christie, professor of mathematics at the royal military academy, Woolwich, was born at Woolwich on Oct. 1, 1845. He was educated at King's college school, London, and at Cambridge. In 1870 Christie was appointed chief assistant to Sir George Airy at the royal observatory, Greenwich, and in 1881 astronomer royal.

While Christie was at the observatory, the work was considerably extended, and it was largely because of him that regular spectroscopic and photographic observations were started. Some of these photographs form a valuable part of the work of the observatory, and the observations are still continued. Between 1890 and 1898 Christie supervised the construction of a new building and the erection of a 30-in. reflector and a 26-in. photographic refractor, enabling the observatory to take part in the international photographic map of the heavens; the measurements and publication of results occupied a number of years. Christie erected a wooden building for magnetic observations, designed a new altazimuth to replace a faulty one which had been used by Airy and also designed a "duplex" micrometer for identifying stars on overlapping plates. Christie wrote a number of papers embodying his work on the solar eclipses observed in Japan (1896), India (1898) and Portugal (1900), on the measurement of double stars, on the observations of Eros for determining the solar parallax and on the duration of exposure in photographing stars.

Christie received the C.B. on the occasion of Queen Victoria's Jubilee and the K.C.B. in 1904. He died on Jan. 22, 1922, while on a voyage to Mogador, Morocco, and was buried at sea.

CHRISTINA (Maria Christina) (1858–1929), queen regent of Spain (1885–1902), widow of Alphonso XII and mother of Alphonso XIII, was born at Gross Seelowitz, Aus., on July 21, 1858, being the daughter of the archduke Charles Ferdinand and the archduchess Elizabeth of Austria. In 1879 she married Alphonso XII of Spain, whom she had met at the court of Vienna when he was only a pretender in exile, before the restoration of the Bourbons, and whose first wife, Mercedes, daughter of the duc de Montpensier, had died childless. Queen Christina bore her husband two daughters—Doña Mercedes, born on Sept. 11, 1880, and Doña Maria Theresa, born on Nov. 12, 1882. On her husband's death on Nov. 25, 1885, she became regent, and during the long minority of the posthumous son of Alphonso XII, later Alphonso XIII, she exhibited her wisdom, tolerance and unselfishness.

In spite of the excessive rotation of political parties under Práxedes Sagasta and Antonio Canovas del Castillo, the restlessness of the army, the economic depression and the disastrous war of 1898 with the United States, in which Spain renounced its rights over Cuba, Puerto Rico and the Philippines, the country, under Christina, won the respect of the great powers, and opposition from the former royal family gradually diminished. Her regency ended in 1902, when Alphonso XIII came of age.

Christina died Feb. 7, 1929.

CHRISTINA (1626–1689), queen of Sweden, daughter of Gustavus II and Marie-Eleonore of Brandenburg, was born at Stockholm, Swed., on Dec. 8, 1626. Her father was killed at Lützen (1632) when she was only six years old.

She was educated principally by the learned Johannes Matthiae, in as masculine a way as possible, while the chancellor, Count Axel Oxenstjerna, instructed her in politics. Christina became queen on her 18th birthday (Dec. 8, 1644). From the moment when she took her seat at the head of the council board she impressed her veteran counsellors with the conviction of her genius. Unfortunately her brilliant and commanding qualities were vitiated by an inordinate pride and egoism, which exhibited themselves in an utter contempt for public opinion, and a prodigality utterly regardless of the necessities of the state. She maintained a luxurious court, frequented by French artists, scholars and philosophers, and seemed to consider Swedish affairs as far too petty to occupy her full attention. Her unworthy treatment of the great chancellor was mainly caused by her jealousy of his extraordinary reputation. Recognizing that he would be indispensable as long as the Thirty Years' War lasted, she used every effort to bring it to an end; and her impulsive interference seriously hampered the diplomacy of the chancellor, and materially reduced the ultimate gain of Sweden. Yet she gave fresh privileges to the towns; she encouraged trade and manufactures, especially the mining industries of the Dales; in 1649 she issued the first school ordinance for the whole kingdom; she encouraged foreign scholars to settle in Sweden; and native science and literature, under her liberal encouragement, flourished as they had never flourished before. In one respect, too, she showed herself wiser than her wisest counsellors. The senate and the estates, naturally anxious about the succession to the throne, had repeatedly urged her majesty to marry, and had indicated her cousin, Charles Gustavus, as her most fitting consort. Wearied of their importunities, Christina settled the difficulty by appointing Charles her successor, and at the *riksdag* of 1650 the Swedish crown was declared hereditary in Charles and his male heirs.

In the summer of 1651 Christina was, with difficulty, persuaded to reconsider her resolution to abdicate, but three years later the nation had become convinced that her abdication was highly desirable.

There were many causes which predisposed her to what was, after all, anything but an act of self-renunciation. First of all she could not fail to remark the increasing discontent with her arbitrary and wasteful ways. Within ten years she had created 17 counts, 46 barons and 428 lesser nobles; and, to provide these new peers with adequate appanages, she had sold or mortgaged crown property representing an annual income of 1,200,000 rix-dollars. Signs were also not wanting that Christina was growing weary of the cares of government, while the importunity of the senate and *riksdag* on the question of her marriage was a constant source of irritation. From 1651 there was a notable change in her behaviour. She cast away every regard for the feelings and prejudices of her people. She ostentatiously exhibited her contempt for the Protestant religion. Her foreign policy was flighty to the verge of foolishness. She contemplated an alliance with Spain, a state quite outside the orbit of Sweden's influence, the first fruits of which were to have been an invasion of Portugal.

She utterly neglected affairs in order to plunge into a whirl of dissipation with foreign favourites. The situation became impossible, and it was with an intense feeling of relief that the Swedes saw her depart, in masculine attire, under the name of Count Dohna. At Innsbruck she openly joined the Catholic Church, was rechristened Alexandra and kept up a royal household in Rome, surrounded by cardinals. In 1656, and again in 1657, she visited France, on the second occasion ordering the assassination of her major-domo, Giovanni Monaldischi, for continuous betrayal of her confidence.

Twice she returned to Sweden (1660 and 1667) in the vain

hope of recovering the succession, finally settling in Rome, where she died on April 19, 1689, poor, neglected and forgotten.

(R. N. B.; X.)

Bibliography.—F. W. Bain, *Queen Christina of Sweden* (1890); R. N. Bain, *Scandinavia* (Cambridge, 1905); H. E. Friis, *Dronning Christina* (Copenhagen, 1896); C. N. D. Bildt, *Christina de Suède et le conclave de Clement X* (1906); *Drottning Kristinas sista dagar* (Stockholm, 1897). Of the many books telling the fantastic story of Christina's later years *see* A. Barine, *Princesses and Court Ladies*, (Eng. trans., 1906); F. H. Gribble, *The Court of Christina of Sweden* (1913), *The History of the Intrigues and Gallantries of Christina, Queen of Sweden, and of Her Court Whilst She Was at Rome*, Eng. trans. by P. Hollingworth (1697; repr. 1927).

CHRISTISON, SIR ROBERT, Bart. (1797–1882), Scottish toxicologist and physician, was born in Edinburgh on July 18, 1797. He studied in London under John Abernethy and Sir William Lawrence, and in Paris under Pierre J. Robiquet and M. J. B. Orfila. In 1822 he became professor of medical jurisprudence at Edinburgh. In 1829 his *Treatise on Poisons* was published, and he became medical officer to the crown in Scotland, and from that time till 1866 he was called as a witness in many celebrated criminal cases, notably in the case of William Burke and William Hare (1829). Instructions drawn up by him for the examination of dead bodies for legal purposes became the accepted guide for the purpose. He may be said to have placed legal jurisprudence on a scientific basis. In 1832 he gave up the chair of medical jurisprudence for that of medicine and therapeutics, which he held till 1877. His work on the pathology of the kidneys and on fevers brought him many honours, including a baronetcy in 1871. Christison died at Edinburgh on Jan. 23, 1882.

See *The Life of Sir Robert Christison* (1885–86), edited by his sons, which contains his autobiography, with chapters on his work by Gairdner and T. R. Fraser.

CHRISTMAS (*i.e.*, the mass of Christ), in the Christian Church, the festival of the nativity of Jesus Christ. The history of this feast coheres so closely with that of Epiphany (*q.v.*), that what follows must be read in connection with the article under that heading.

Origin.—Christmas was not among the earliest festivals of the church, and before the 5th century there was no general consensus of opinion as to when it should come in the calendar, whether on Jan. 6, March 25 or Dec. 25. The earliest identification of Dec. 25 with the birthday of Christ is in a passage, otherwise unknown and probably spurious, of Theophilus of Antioch (*c.* 180), preserved in Latin by the Magdeburg centuriators (i, 3, 118), to the effect that the Gauls contended that since they celebrated the birth of the Lord on Dec. 25, they ought to celebrate the resurrection on March 25. A passage, almost certainly interpolated, in Hippolytus' (*c.* 202) commentary on Daniel iv, 23, says that Jesus was born at Bethlehem on Wednesday, Dec. 25, in the 42nd year of Augustus, but no feast is mentioned, and such a feast, indeed, would conflict with the then orthodox ideas. As late as 245 Origen (hom. viii on Leviticus) repudiated the idea of keeping the birthday of Christ, "as if he were a king Pharaoh."

The first certain mention of Dec. 25 is in the calendar of Philocalus (354), which was first published entire by Theodor Mommsen in *Abhandlungen d. sächs. Akad. d. Wissensch.* (1850), and is dealt with in Joseph Strzygowski's *Kalenderbilder des Chron. vom Jahre 354* (1888). This states that in "Year 1 after Christ the Lord Jesus Christ was born on Dec. 25, a Friday, and 15th day of the new moon"—though, in fact, Dec. 25, a.d. 1, was a Sunday. Here again no festal celebration of the day is attested.

Clement of Alexandria (*c.* 200) mentions several speculations on the date of Christ's birth, and condemns them as superstitious. Some chronologists, he says, alleged the birth to have occurred in the 28th year of Augustus, on 25 Pachon (an Egyptian month); *i.e.*, May 20. Others assign it to 24 or 25 Pharmuthi (April 19 or 20). Clement himself sets it on Nov. 17, 3 b.c.; and the anonymous author of a Latin tract, *De Pascha computus* (written in Africa, 243), sets it, "by private revelation," on Wednesday, March 28, the supposed anniversary of the creation of the sun, which typifies the Sun of Righteousness.

Similar symbolical reasoning led Polycarp (in a fragment preserved by an Armenian writer, Ananias of Shirak, dated before 160) to set His birth on Sunday, when the world's creation began, but His baptism on Wednesday, as the analogue of the sun's creation. On such grounds certain Latins as early as 354 may have transferred the birthday from Jan. 6 to Dec. 25, which was then a Mithraic feast, the *natalis invicti solis* or birthday of the unconquered Sun of Philocalus. The Syrians and Armenians, who clung to Jan. 6, accused the Romans of sun worship and idolatry, contending that the feast of Dec. 25 had been invented by disciples of Cerinthus and its lections by Artemon to commemorate the *natural* birth of Jesus. Ambrose (*On Virgins*, iii, ch. 1) seems to imply that as late as the papacy of Liberius (352–356) the birth was feasted together with the marriage at Cana and the "feeding of the four thousand," which were never feasted on any other day but Jan. 6.

Chrysostom, in a sermon preached at Antioch on Dec. 20, 386 or 388, says that the feast of Dec. 25 was known in the west, from Thrace as far as Cadiz, from the beginning. It certainly originated in the west, but spread quickly eastward. In 353–361 it was observed at the court of Constantius; Basil of Caesarea (d. 379) adopted it; Honorius, emperor (395–423) in the west, told his mother and brother Arcadius (395–408) in Byzantium how the new feast was kept in Rome, separate from Jan. 6 with its own *troparia* and *sticharia;* and they adopted it. The patriarchs Theophilus of Alexandria, John of Jerusalem and Flavian of Antioch were won over to it under Pope Anastasius, 398–401. John or Wahan of Nice (Combefis, *Historia monothelitarum*) affords the above details. The new feast was communicated by Proclus, patriarch of Constantinople, to Sahak, Catholicos of Armenia, about 440; and the Armenians within the Byzantine pale adopted it for about 30 years, but finally abandoned it, together with the decrees of Chalcedon, early in the 8th century. Many writers of the period 375–450 (*e.g.*, Epiphanius, Cassian, Asterius, Basil, Chrysostom and Jerome) contrast the new feast with that of the baptism as that of the birth *after the flesh*, implying that the latter was generally regarded as a birth according to the spirit. Hermann Usener notes that in 387 the new feast was reckoned according to the Julian calendar by writers of the province of Asia, who in referring to other feasts use the reckoning of their local calendars. As early as 400 in Rome an imperial rescript includes Christmas (with Easter and Epiphany) among the three feasts on which theatres must be closed. Epiphany and Christmas were not made judicial *non dies* until 534.

For some years in the west (as late as 353 in Rome) the birth feast was appended to the baptismal feast on Jan. 6 and was altogether supplanted by it in Jerusalem from about 360 to 440, when Bishop Juvenal introduced the feast of Dec. 25, which about the same time was finally established in Alexandria. The *quadragesima* of Epiphany (*i.e.*, the presentation in the Temple) continued to be celebrated in Jerusalem on Feb. 14 until the reign of Justinian. In most other places it had long before been put back to Feb. 2 to suit the new Christmas. But in Jerusalem, as Armenian historians record, the transference occasioned riots.

In Britain, Dec. 25 was a festival long before the conversion to Christianity, for Bede (*De temp. rat.*, ch. 13) relates that "the ancient peoples of the Angli began the year on Dec. 25 when we now celebrate the birthday of the Lord; and the very night which is now so holy to us, they called in their tongue *modranecht* (*môdra niht*), that is, the mothers' night, by reason we suspect of the ceremonies which in that night-long vigil they performed." In England the observance of Christmas was forbidden by act of parliament in 1644; Charles II revived the feast, but the Scots adhered to the Puritan view. Outside Teutonic countries Christmas presents are unknown. Their place is taken in Latin countries by the *strenae*, French *étrennes*, given on New Year's day. The setting up in Latin churches of a Christmas crèche is said to have been originated by St. Francis.

(X.)

Christmas Customs.—Christmas customs are an evolution from times that long antedated the Christian period—a descent from seasonal, pagan, religious and national practices, hedged about with legend and tradition. Their seasonal connections with the pagan feasts of the winter solstice relate them to the beginning of time and their legacy in the birthday of Christ makes them shareholders in the most significant event in the history of the world—an event that gave it a new date, anno Domini.

In the beginning many of the earth's inhabitants were sun worshippers because the course of their lives depended on its yearly round in the heavens, and feasts were held to aid its return from distant wanderings. In the south of Europe, in Egypt and Persia, the sun gods were worshipped with elaborate ceremonies at the season of the winter solstice, as a fitting time to pay tribute to the benign god of plenty, while in Rome the Saturnalia reigned for a week. In northern lands mid-December was a critical time, for the days became shorter and shorter and the sun was weak and far away. Thus these ancient peoples held feasts at the same period that Christmas is now observed; they built great bonfires in order to give the winter sun god strength and to bring him back to life again. When it became apparent that the days were growing longer, there was great rejoicing because of the promise of lengthening days to follow. Thus, the central idea of the winter solstice—the return of light—became the hope of the world in the birth of Christ, the light of the world.

The exact day and year of Christ's birth have never been satisfactorily settled, but when the fathers of the church in A.D. 440 decided upon a date to celebrate the event, they wisely chose the day of the winter solstice which was firmly fixed in the minds of the people and which was their most important festival. Because of changes in man-made calendars, the time of the solstice and the date of Christmas vary by a few days.

The transition from paganism to Christianity was gradual but became apparent after the fall of Rome (A.D. 476) when the church was the one organization which had the strength and wisdom to withstand the disorganized centuries of the dark ages. During this time great progress was made by the Christian leaders in extending the new faith.

When missionaries were sent from Rome to the outlying provinces in 601, their instructions given by Pope Gregory I made clear the policy of the church: "Let the shrines of idols by no means be destroyed but let the idols which are in them be destroyed. Let water be consecrated and sprinkled in these temples; let altars be erected . . . so that the people, not seeing their temples destroyed, may displace error, and recognize and adore the true God. . . . And because they were wont to sacrifice oxen to devils, some celebration should be given in exchange for this . . . they should celebrate a religious feast and worship God by their feasting, so that still keeping outward pleasures, they may more readily receive spiritual joys." (Bede, *Ecclesiastical History of the English Nation.*)

For several centuries Christmas was solely a church anniversary observed by religious services. But as Christianity spread among the people of pagan lands, many of the practices of the winter solstice were blended with those of Christianity because of the liberal ruling of Gregory I, the Great, and the co-operation of the missionaries.

Thus, Christmas became both religious and secular in its celebration, at times reverent, at others gay. From the pagan accent on light it is not difficult to trace the rise of lights and open fires —from the bonfires of sun worship and their variant, the yule log, to the many customs centring around the candle and its legends to light the Christ child.

Many customs besides those of light and fire date back in some way to these pre-Christian origins, among them Christmas decorations. The Romans ornamented their temples and homes with green boughs and flowers for the Saturnalia, their season of merrymaking and the giving of presents; the Druids gathered mistletoe with great ceremony and hung it in their homes; the Saxons used holly, ivy and bay.

It is generally believed that the first Christmas tree was of German origin dating from Boniface, English missionary to Germany in the 8th century, who replaced the sacrifices to Odin's sacred oak by a fir tree adorned in tribute to the Christ child. Accounts persist that Martin Luther introduced the tree lighted with candles. It is known that the German prince Albert, soon after his marriage to Queen Victoria, introduced it into England, and that German immigrants brought the custom to the United States.

Music early became a marked feature of the season. But the first chants, litanies and hymns were in Latin and too theological for popular use. The 13th century found the rise of the carol written in the vernacular under the influence of Francis of Assisi: carol meaning a song in which a religious topic is treated in a style that is familiar or festive. From Italy, it passed to France and Germany, and later to England, everywhere retaining its simplicity, fervour and mirthfulness. Music in itself has become one of the greatest tributes to Christmas, and includes some of the noblest compositions of the great musicians, especially George Frederick Handel's *Messiah* with its "Hallelujah Chorus."

Anthems sung by choirs with organ accompaniment and hymns and carols sung by the congregation constitute modern Christmas church music. As a setting for the music and services of the Protestant churches, evergreen trees and branches and other seasonal decorations transform the church, pulpit and choir loft, combining thus the details of customs that have evolved with the centuries.

In Roman Catholic churches the heart of the celebration is the crèche, or crib, the realistic tableau in miniature of the nativity, another custom introduced in an Italian church by Francis of Assisi in 1224, in his efforts to bring Christmas to the people. The secular singing of folksongs and carols on the Christmas theme by minstrels and waits was customary, especially in England. House-to-house singing survives in many communities.

In keeping with the religious significance of Christmas, the church, as early as the 6th century, set apart the four Sundays preceding Christmas as a time of devotional preparation, known as the Advent season, which ends with Christmas eve. From this date on, the Catholic Church held a midnight mass as one of the solemnities of Christ's birthday. Equally solemn is the Christmas morning service in Lutheran churches, especially the Swedish; the service was put at an early hour by the Lutherans because the shepherds, the first to worship Him, came early and then returned to their work.

Merrymaking came to have a share in Christmas observance through popular enthusiasm even while emphasis was on the religious phase. The mediaeval secular celebrations were no matter of a day or two but lasted for a season extending from Christmas eve to Epiphany, and in some localities even longer, from St. Thomas' day to Candlemas. In England Christmas became increasingly the great festival of the year from the 11th to the 17th centuries, with observance from Christmas eve to Twelfth day. In the holly-decked great halls of the feudal lords, whose hospitality extended to all their friends, tenants and household, wassailing, feasting, singing and games, dancing, masquerading, mummers presenting pantomimes, and masques were all part of the festivities. A lord of misrule and his jester directed the revels and kept them uproarious, from the dragging in of the yule log to the end of the holiday. The Christmas feast, brought in state into the hall, heralded by the lord of misrule and the minstrels headed by the chief cook carrying the boar's head followed by the servants bearing an incredible number of dishes, was the outstanding event. But the wild licence of these celebrations, with no semblance of the inner vision and meaning of Christmas, came under the disfavour of the Puritans and were forbidden by parliament in 1644, after the Puritans came into power.

England gradually found Christmas again and made it both a church ceremonial and a home festival. There are family reunions, gifts, decorations, carols and parties, and a pantomime for the children, whose day it is and for whom Father Christmas, the English counterpart of Santa Claus, was introduced. It is a season of good will with much hospitality, roast goose and plum pudding being associated with the day. The true spirit of the day prevails, as set forth in the immortal *A Christmas Carol* by Charles Dickens, written in the year 1843.

Although many of the picturesque customs were suppressed, they have contributed vicariously to modern observance through Christmas pageants, in the designs of Christmas cards and favours and in adapted formalities of social functions. Descriptive accounts and crude drawings found in old household or day books and other chronicles, together with the narratives in ballads and carols, have aided in this artistic restoration, keeping the old English Christmas always present.

The Scandinavian countries have always had a natural tendency for the keeping of Christmas, because of the northern location and their winter solstice traditions; they have transplanted their customs wherever they have settled. Elaborate preparations are begun weeks in advance, and there is a great amount of cooking of special meats and baking of breads, fancy cakes, cookies and other special foods.

Germany has also kept Christmas with much heartiness in the old manner with emphasis on home celebrations and attendance at church services. The observance centres around the Christmas tree, and carols include "O Tannenbaum" and "Stille Nacht."

In the Netherlands and Belgium the feast of St. Nicholas, Dec. 6, is the children's holiday, when the customs associated with Christmas and feasting are observed. Dec. 25 is a religious holiday, with services in the churches and quiet family gatherings at home, where Christmas cakes and other favours are served. One of the traditions of Christmas is Santa Claus, a contraction for St. Nicholas who was born in the 3rd century; he became a bishop and gained distinction in the councils of the church, being especially famed for unexpected gifts, and later associated with the giving of presents during the season at the end of the year. He seems to have been first adopted by the Netherlands as the patron saint of children, and there, on St. Nicholas eve, they leave their wooden shoes, filled with hay for the saint's white horse. He is real to children the world over, under such various names as Kris Kringle, La Befana, Yule Tomten and Christkindli.

New Year's day came to be the great festival in France and Scotland, many of the Christmas customs being observed on that day. The religious features are prominent in France, especially the crèche in churches and homes and the midnight mass followed by elaborate Christmas suppers. The Feast of the Kings, or Epiphany, finishes the holiday season with traditional parties.

The Italian Christmas is a sacred holiday, observed with solemn ceremonies including a midnight mass in the churches. Though there are home customs and special foods, gifts are reserved for Epiphany.

The *Presepio,* or miniature representation of the nativity, rather than the Christmas tree, came to be the holiday symbol in Italian homes.

Christmas in the United States, composed of threads from many countries and reflecting their customs in church and home, has evolved into a celebration that is more or less uniform, with some variations according to sections and origins, such as those of the Pennsylvania Germans in Bethlehem and the Scandinavians in Wisconsin and Minnesota. The festive aspects were not accepted in New England until about 1875, because of Puritan influence.

For generations Christmas customs have focused around the fact that it belongs to the season of frost and snow. Transplanted to a tropical climate, its celebration would, of course, be different in many ways.

In tropical Mexico, where Roman Catholicism is the state religion, every home is decorated with flowers and has an altar erected with a representation of the nativity, in preparation for the *Posadas*. This means "resting place" and commemorates the journey Mary and Joseph took from Nazareth to Bethlehem. The *Posadas* begin on Dec. 16, and groups of nine families hold one every night before Christmas eve, meeting in the different homes. Carrying candles and following an image of the Virgin and Joseph; they re-enact the search for shelter, stopping at the door of each room and pleading for entry. In the last room they are admitted and there sing their thanks.

Christmas in Brazil, for example, falls in midsummer, giving it the characteristics of a summer festival with flowers for decorations, fireworks, picnics, fiestas and boating excursions. The religious phase is the same as in other Catholic countries, with a *Presepio* in homes and churches; the midnight mass, with an out-of-door procession of the priests to the church, is a colourful part of the festival. Family suppers are served on Christmas eve; the people hold carnivals in the streets, and everywhere there is much gaiety. Various customs brought by people from the United States have crept in, including Papa Noel, dressed like Santa Claus. Both Christmas and King's day, as Epiphany is called, serve as gift-giving occasions.

BIBLIOGRAPHY.—W. F. Dawson, *Christmas, Its Origin and Association* (1902); E. L. Urlin, *Festivals, Holy Days, and Saints' Days* (1915); Sir James George Frazer, *The Golden Bough,* abr. ed. (1922); T. G. Crippen, *Christmas and Christmas Lore* (1936); W. M. Auld, *Christmas Traditions* (1931); R. E. Haugan (ed.), *Christmas; an American Annual of Christmas Literature and Art,* 17 vol. (1931–47); A. C. Hottes, *1001 Christmas Facts and Fancies* (1937); Dorothy Gladys Spicer, *Book of Festivals* (1937); A. R. Wright, *British Calendar Customs: England,* vol. 3 (1941); John Hadfield (ed.), *Christmas Companion* (1939); Mary Emogene Hazeltine, *Anniversaries and Holidays,* 2nd ed. (1944). (M. E. HE.)

CHRISTMASBERRY (*Photinia arbutifolia*), a handsome American shrub or small tree of the rose family (Rosaceae), called also California holly and toyon, native chiefly to the chaparral (*q.v.*) belt of the Sierra Nevada and coast ranges.

It grows from 5 to 15 ft. high and bears oblong, pointed, evergreen leaves and numerous small, white flowers in large, terminal clusters, followed in late autumn by bright red, hollylike fruits. It is very popular for Christmas decoration, being sold in Pacific coast cities in the same manner as holly in the eastern United States.

CHRISTMAS ROSE: *see* HELLEBORE.

CHRISTODORUS, of Coptos in Egypt, epic poet, flourished during the reign of Anastasius I (A.D. 491–518). According to Suidas, he was the author of Πάτρια, accounts of the foundation of various cities; υδιακά, the mythical history of Lydia; Ἰσαυρικά, the conquest of Isauria by Anastasius; three books of epigrams; and many other works.

In addition to two epigrams (*Anthol. Pal.*, vii, 697, 698) we possess a description in hexameters of 80 statues in the gymnasium of Zeuxippus at Constantinople; this forms the second book of the Palatine anthology. Some critics regard it as important for the history of art and a model of description; others consider it valueless.

See F. Baumgarten, *De Christodoro poëta Thebano* (1881), and his article in Pauly-Wissowa's *Realencyklopädie,* iii, 2 (1899); W. Christ, *Geschichte der griechischen Literatur* (1898).

CHRISTOPHE, HENRY (1767–1820), Negro king of Haiti. After purchasing his freedom from slavery he played a prominent part in the insurrection against the French and in the rising of 1803. He was general in chief of the army during the short-lived government of Jean Jacques Dessalines. Appointed president of Haiti in 1807, after the ensuing civil war, he was crowned king on June 2, 1812.

Under him the country prospered, but his cruelty led to an insurrection, and being deserted by his troops, he shot himself on Oct. 8, 1820. (*See* HAITI: *History.*)

See J. Vandercook, *Black Majesty* (1928).

CHRISTOPHER, SAINT (CHRISTOPHORUS, CHRISTOFERUS), patron saint of ferrymen, is honoured in the Latin Church on July 25 and in the Greek Church on May 9. He appears to have been born a pagan in Syria, to have been baptized by Babylas, bishop to Antioch; he preached in Lycia and was martyred *c.* A.D. 250 during the persecution under the emperor Decius. The more conspicuous of the legends which collected about this nucleus of possibility are included in the Mozarabic *Breviary* and *Missal,* the best known being given in the *Golden Legend* of Jacopus de Voragine. According to this, Christopher was a giant in search of a master stronger than himself. He left the service of the king of Canaan because the king feared the devil, and that of the devil because the devil feared the Cross. He was converted by a hermit; but since he had neither the gift of fasting nor that of prayer, he decided to devote himself to a work of charity, and set himself to carry wayfarers over a bridgeless river.

One day a little child asked to be taken across, and Christopher took him on his shoulders. When halfway over the stream, he staggered under what seemed to him a crushing weight; but he reached the other side and then upbraided the child for placing him in peril. "Had I borne the whole world on my back," he said, "it could not have weighed heavier than thou!" "Marvel not!" the child replied, "for thou hast borne upon thy back the world and Him who created it!"

See Bolland, *Acta Sanct.*, vi, 146; Guenebault, *Dict. iconographique des attributs, des figures et des légendes des saints* (Paris, 1850); Smith and Wace, *Dictionary of Christian Biography.*

CHRISTOPHORUS, pope or anti-pope, elected in 903 against Leo V, whom he imprisoned. In Jan. 904 he was treated in the same fashion by his competitor, Sergius III, who had him strangled.

CHRISTOPOULOS, ATHANASIOS (1772–1847), Greek poet, was born at Castoria in Macedonia. He studied at Buda and Padua, and became teacher of the children of the Vlach prince Mourousi. After the fall of Mourousi in 1811 he was employed by Prince Caradja, hospodar of Moldavia and Walachia, in drawing up a code of laws for that country. On the removal of Caradja, he retired into private life and devoted himself to literature. He wrote drinking songs and love ditties which are very popular among the Greeks. He also wrote *Politika Parallela* (a comparison of various systems of government), translations of Homer and Herodotus, a tragedy and some philological works on the connection between ancient and modern Greek.

His *Hellenika Archaiologemaia* (Athens, 1853) contains an account of his life.

CHRIST'S HOSPITAL (the BLUE COAT SCHOOL) was originally one of three royal hospitals in the city of London, founded by Edward VI. Christ's hospital was specially devoted to fatherless and motherless children. The buildings of the monastery of Grey Friars, Newgate street, were appropriated to it; liberal public subscription added to the king's grant endowed it richly, and the mayor, commonalty and citizens of London were nominated its governors in its charter of 1552. Not long after its opening Christ's was providing home and education (or, in the case of the very young, nursing) for 400 children. The popular name of the Blue Coat school is derived from the dress of the boys—originally (almost from the time of the foundation) a blue gown, with knee breeches, yellow petticoat and stockings, neckbands and a blue cap. The petticoat and cap were given up in the middle of the 19th century. In 1902 the buildings on the Newgate street site were vacated by the school, which was moved to new buildings at Horsham. It includes a preparatory school for boys, established in 1683 at Hertford, where the buildings have been enlarged for the use of the girls' school on the same foundation.

CHRISTUS, PETRUS (d. 1472/73), Flemish painter, born at Baerle in Brabant, in 1444 acquired citizenship rights at Bruges, where he worked until his death. Following the example of Jan van Eyck, he added a date and signature, usually in the form "PETRUS XPI," to some of his pictures. These include "Edward Grymeston," 1446 (earl of Verulam's collection), "A Carthusian," 1446 (New York), "St. Eligius," 1449 (New York, Lehman coll.), "Virgin and Child," 1449 (Lugano, Thyssen coll.), altar wings with "Annunciation," "Nativity" and "Last Judgment," 1452 (Berlin) and the "Virgin With SS. Jerome and Francis," probably 1457 (Frankfurt). Among others ascribed to him are two versions of the "Nativity" (Washington, D.C.; New York, Wildenstein), three versions of the "Lamentation Over the Dead Christ" (Brussels; New York; Paris), the "Virgin With a Carthusian" (Berlin) and two portraits (Berlin; London).

Christus appears as the closest of Jan van Eyck's followers, yet some of his motifs and compositions show that he was no stranger to the different tradition exemplified by the Master of Flémalle and Rogier van der Weyden. These borrowings from more powerful spirits tend to overshadow and confuse his personal development. Compared with Van Eyck's all-seeing eye or with Rogier's emotional force his pictures seem empty, conventional and phlegmatic. Nevertheless, they remain admirable for their careful construction and jewellike execution. The Frankfurt "Virgin With Saints" is the earliest Netherlandish picture with a single vanishing point.

See W. H. J. Weale, *Peintres Brugeois: les Christus* (Bruges, 1909); M. J. Friedländer, *Die Altniederländische Malerei,* vol. i (Berlin, 1924), xiv (Berlin, 1937). (D. KG.)

CHRISTY, HENRY (1810–1865), English ethnologist, was born at Kingston-on-Thames, Eng., on July 26, 1810. From 1850–58 he travelled in Europe and America, studying ethnology. In 1858 the discoveries by Boucher de Perthes of flint implements in France and England were first held to have proved the great antiquity of man. Christy joined the Geological society, and with his friend Edouard Lartet explored the caves in the valley of the Vézère. An account of the explorations appeared in *Comptes rendus* (Feb. 29, 1864) and *Transactions of the Ethnological Society of London* (June 21, 1864). He died, on May 14, 1865, leaving a half-finished book, entitled *Reliquiae Aquitanicae,* which was issued in parts and completed first by Lartet and, after the latter's death in 1870, by Rupert Jones. Christy's archaeological collection was placed in the British Museum in 1884.

CHROMATES AND DICHROMATES: *see* CHROMIUM.

CHROMATIC, a term meaning "coloured," used in science, particularly in the expression "chromatic aberration" or "dispersion" (*see* ABERRATION OF LIGHT). In Greek music *χρωματική μουσική* was one of three divisions—diatonic, chromatic and enharmonic—of the tetrachord. Like the Latin *color,* *χρῶμα* was often used of ornaments and embellishments, and particularly of the modification of the three *genera* of the tetrachord. The chromatic, being subject to three such modifications, was regarded as particularly "coloured." To the Greeks chromatic music was sweet and plaintive. From a supposed resemblance to the notes of the chromatic tetrachord, the term is applied to a succession of notes outside the diatonic scale, and marked by accidentals. A "chromatic scale" is thus a series of semitones.

CHROMATOMETER or TINTOMETER, an instrument for standardizing the *intensity* and *hue* of a given colour (*q.v.*). The specimen is compared with a standard by viewing the two simultaneously and interposing in front of the standard various standard coloured plates until a match is obtained. Instead of the plates, strata liquids of the three primary colours may be used. (*See* also COLORIMETER.)

CHROME STEEL: *see* IRON AND STEEL; STAINLESS STEEL.

CHROMITE, a member of the spinel group of minerals; an oxide of chromium and ferrous iron, $FeCr_2O_4$. It is the chief commercial source of chromium and its compounds. It crystallizes in regular octahedra, but is usually found as grains or as granular to compact masses. In its iron-black colour with submetallic lustre and absence of cleavage it resembles magnetite (magnetic iron ore) in appearance, but differs from this in being only slightly, if at all, magnetic and in the brown colour of its powder. The hardness is $5\frac{1}{2}$; specific gravity, 4.5. The theoretical formula $FeCr_2O_4$ corresponds with chromic oxide (Cr_2O_3) 68%, and ferrous oxide 32%; the ferrous oxide is, however, usually partly replaced by magnesia, and the chromic oxide by alumina and ferric oxide, so that there may be a gradual passage to picotite or chrome spinel. Much of the material mined as ore does not contain more than 40% to 50% of chromic oxide. The earliest-worked deposits of chromite were those in the serpentine of the Bare hills near Baltimore, Md. The principal producing areas of chromite are, in the order of their importance, Southern Rhodesia, U.S.S.R., Turkey, Union of South Africa, Philippines, Cuba, Yugoslavia, India, Greece and New Caledonia. Chrome ore is used in manufacturing special steels and alloys, as a metallurgical refractory and in manufacturing chemicals. Chemical uses include dyeing, tanning and for pigments. (W. F. FG.)

CHROMIUM is a metallic chemical element, called so from the Greek *χρῶμα*, colour, because of the varied colours of its compounds. In 1798 L. N. Vauquelin and M. H. Klaproth simultaneously and independently discovered a new element in addition to lead in the mineral crocoisite or crocoite (lead chromate, $PbCrO_4$) first described by J. G. Lehmann in 1762. The metal was not isolated, however, until 1859, when F. Wöhler obtained small quantities of it by reduction of the trichloride with potassium. Because of the difficulty of reduction and of electrodeposition, the metal remained a chemical curiosity for many decades, although it was in 1950 produced on a large scale for use in stainless and alloy steels. Its symbol is Cr, and it has an atomic number of 24 and an atomic weight of 52.01.

Stable isotopes of the following mass numbers are known: 50 (4.49%), 52 (83.77%), 53 (9.43%), 54 (2.30%) and the artificially radioactive isotopes 51 (half life 26.5 days) and 55 (2.3 hr.). The distribution of the 24 electrons in the various quantum groups, $1s^2$, $2s^2$, $2p^6$, $3s^2$, $3p^6$, $3d^5$, $4s^1$, is indicated by the superscripts. The valence electrons are in the $3d$ and $4s$ states and thus are 6 in number.

Occurrence and Production.—Igneous rocks contain on the average 0.037% chromium, usually as compounds of Cr_2O_3. The metal is not found free in nature. The principal commercial ore is chromite, $FeCr_2O_4$ or $FeO.Cr_2O_3$. The world production of crude chromite (approximately 50% Cr_2O_3) was 1,744,000 metric tons in 1943 and the five largest producing countries were: Cuba (354,152 tons), U.S.S.R. (325,000 tons), Southern Rhodesia (266,272 tons), Turkey (196,836 tons) and Union of South Africa (163,232 tons). In addition to chromite and crocoisite, chromium is also found as sesquioxide in chrome ochre, Cr_2O_3, as potassium chromate, K_2CrO_4, as redingtonite (a hydrated sulphate), as phosphochromates, as basic chromates, as ferrous thiochromite, $Fe(CrS_2)_2$, and in various other combinations. The green colour of emerald, serpentine, chrome mica and chrome garnet is due to chromium, as is also the red colour of ruby, and some sapphires and spinels.

Metallurgy and Uses.—In the metallurgy of the element, chromite is usually reduced to ferrochrome, $FeCr_2O_4+4C=Fe+2Cr+4CO$. Low chrome steel contains 0.5% to 1% of Cr which increases the hardness and tensile strength. Stainless steel (6%–30% Cr) is very resistant to chemical oxidation and is widely used in the manufacture of cutlery, turbine blades and apparatus for the chemical industries. These steels are generally made by the addition of ferrochrome to steel scrap in an electric furnace, but some are made directly in the open-hearth furnace. Other alloys are nichrome (60% Ni, 15% Cr and 25% Fe), used as resistance wire, and stellite (60% Co, 15% Cr, 20% W and 5% Mo), employed for high-speed cutting tools. Chrome plating on steel or copper has become highly important in the automobile industry. The metal cannot be deposited from pure chromic-acid solutions, but the electrolytic deposition proceeds if a high concentration of sulphate as chromic sulphate or sulphuric acid is present. The metal may also be prepared by the Goldschmidt process in which the sesquioxide is reduced by aluminum. The distillation of chromium amalgam at 350° C. in hydrogen yields a pyrophoric (spontaneously inflammable) powder form of the metal. A large fraction of the chromite production is used in the manufacture of refractory chrome bricks for lining metallurgical furnaces. Among the more important chromium pigments are: chrome oxide green, Cr_2O_3, a highly stable pigment; zinc yellow, a basic potassium zinc chromate, used as a corrosion inhibitor; chrome orange, basic lead chromate, similar use; and chrome yellow, lead chromate, used in paints and printing ink. The most important commercial salt is sodium dichromate, $Na_2Cr_2O_7$. It may be prepared by fusing the ore with sodium carbonate in air and extracting with dilute acid. Chrome tanning is in general use in the leather industry. In one method, the hides are first treated with a weak acidified bath of sodium dichromate. The hides are then transferred to a second bath containing an acid solution of sodium thiosulphate which reacts to form basic chromic sulphates and rapidly converts the hide into leather.

Properties.—Chromium is a steel-white metal, harder than iron, cobalt or nickel, and capable of taking a brilliant polish. It is nonmagnetic at ordinary temperatures, but becomes magnetic at −15° C. The melting point is 1,900° C. and the boiling point 2,482° C., the melting point being higher than that of manganese, iron, cobalt or nickel, though the boiling point is less than that of any of these. The density of the metal varies from 6.7 to 7.1. The electrolytically deposited metal occludes about 250 times its volume of hydrogen. It has a normal body centred crystal structure at room temperature, but a hexagonal and a complex cubic structure exist at high temperatures. Its coefficient of thermal expansion is 8.2×10^{-6} at 20° C., and its resistivity, 2.6×10^{-6} ohm cm. at 0° C.

Though pyrophoric in the finely divided condition, chromium in the massive form is not affected by moist air and only very slowly by dilute acids. Neither fuming nitric acid nor aqua regia attacks it, but with hot concentrated sulphuric acid it gives sulphur dioxide and a dark solution. Warm dilute hydrochloric or sulphuric acid slowly dissolves the metal, hydrogen being evolved with the formation of chromous salts. Heated in hydrogen chloride, the metal yields crystalline colourless chromous chloride, while chlorine yields violet chromic chloride. Chromium is not attacked even by fused alkalies, but fused potassium nitrate or chlorate oxidizes it rapidly to potassium chromate. Heated with sulphur or in hydrogen sulphide, chromium yields chromous sulphide, CrS, whereas with carbon, silicon or boron, various carbides, silicides or borides are formed. Though a chromium carbonyl, $Cr(CO)_6$, is known, it is not formed by heating chromium in carbon monoxide, but by treating chromic chloride with carbon monoxide in the presence of magnesium phenyl bromide. Pyrophoric chromium combines directly with nitrogen to form a magnetic nitride.

Chromium amalgam also combines with nitrogen to form chromic nitride (CrN), chromous nitride (Cr_3N_2) being formed by heating chromium to 850° C. in ammonia.

In addition to the metal, the element exists in the +2 (chromous), +3 (chromic) and +6 (chromate) valence states. The potentials of the oxidation-reduction couples relating the oxidation states are: $Cr=Cr^{++}+2e^-$, +0.86 v.; $Cr^{++}=Cr^{+++}+e^-$, +0.41 v.; and $2Cr^{+++}+7H_2O=Cr_2O_7^{--}+14H^++6e^-$, −1.36 v.

Chromous Compounds.—As indicated by the potential values, chromous ion may be formed by the reaction $Cr + 2Cr^{+++} = 3Cr^{++}$. The reduction of chromic to chromous also goes readily with zinc. The chromous ion is such a powerful reducing agent that it is readily oxidized to the chromic state even by weak oxidizing agents such as hydrogen ion, $2Cr^{++} + 2H^+ = 2Cr^{+++} + H_2$. The properties of chromous ion are similar to those of ferrous. The colour in aqueous solutions is blue. Chromous fluoride, CrF_2, is green; potassium chromous carbonate, $K_2Cr(CO_3)_2.3H_2O$, is yellow; and chromous acetate, $Cr(CH_3CO_2)_2$, is red. The hydroxide is but slightly soluble and is readily oxidized in air, $4Cr(OH)_2 + O_2 + 2H_2O = 4Cr(OH)_3$. The sulphide and carbonate, like the ferrous salts, are not readily soluble.

Chromic Compounds.—In the properties of its hydroxide and the solubilities of its compounds, chromic ion resembles aluminum ion. However, in its capacity to form double and complex salts, it shows similarity to the cobaltous ion. The hydrous oxide, $Cr_2O_3.nH_2O$, dissolves readily in both acids and strong bases but is readily precipitated by ammonium hydroxide from solutions of its salts. The acidic nature of the oxide gives rise to an extended series of chromites, among these are a number of natural and artificial gemlike minerals called chrome spinels; for example, nickel spinel, $NiO.Cr_2O_3$. The carbonate and sulphide are hydrolyzed to the hydrous oxide. Chromic sulphate forms chrome alums of the type $RCr(SO_4)_2.12H_2O$. The anhydrous chloride, $CrCl_3$, is a beautiful violet colour and dissolves but slowly in water. The aqueous solution of the chloride generally contains the violet ion $[Cr(H_2O)_6]^{+++}$ when the solution is dilute but the ion $[Cr(H_2O)_4Cl_2]^+$ when the chloride concentration is high. Equilibrium is established but slowly between the two ionic species.

Chromic ion forms many complexes, especially with the halides, cyanide, thiocyanates and ammonia. In nearly all these salts it is possible to discern six nonionizing groups attached or co-ordinated to the chromium atom, which is accordingly said to possess the co-ordination number six like cobalt. In the case of the ammonia-addition compounds (*see* AMMINES) whole series are known which are indistinguishable in appearance and general properties from the corresponding cobaltammines. These comprise such types as luteochromic ammines, $Cr(NH_3)_6Cl_3$, purpureo-ammines, $CrCl(NH_3)_5SO_4$, and among many others, praseo-ammines, $CrCl_2(NH_3)_4NO_3$. Complex salts are also formed by replacing ammonia with pyridine, ethylenediamine and similar organic bases. Some of these complex salts have been shown to be capable of existing in optically active forms, thus proving that the groups co-ordinated to the chromium atom are not planar but have a spatial distribution which is octahedral. The use of chrome alum and chromic fluoride as mordants in fixing soluble dyestuffs on fabrics has been shown to be due to the capacity of the chromium atom to enter into complex formation with the dyestuffs, yielding highly insoluble compounds, often of different colour from the combined dyestuff, firmly fixed on or in the fibre. It is probable that the use of chromium compounds in tanning is due to complex reaction with the organic substances present in hides.

Chromates and Dichromates.—The +6 state of chromium is represented by compounds of the two ions, yellow-coloured chromate, CrO_4^{--}, and orange-red-coloured dichromate, $Cr_2O_7^{--}$. In water solution there exists the equilibrium, $2CrO_4^{--} + 2H^+ = Cr_2O_7^{--} + H_2O$. The value for the equilibrium constant $(C_2O_7^{--})/(CrO_4^{--})^2(H^+)^2$ is 4.2×10^{14}. Thus, in high acid, the ionic species is largely $Cr_2O_7^{--}$ and in alkali CrO_4^{--}. In acid solution, powerful oxidizing agents such as sodium bismuthate are required to oxidize chromic to dichromate, $2Cr^{+++} + 3NaBiO_3 + 4H^+ = Cr_2O_7^{--} + 3Bi^{+++} + 3Na^+ + 2H_2O$. Alkali chromates may be prepared by roasting chromites in air (O_2 oxidizing agent) or by treating chromite with sodium peroxide, $2CrO_2^- + 3HO_2^- = 2CrO_4^{--} + H_2O + OH^-$. Chromic anhydride, CrO_3, or chromium trioxide, may be crystallized from a concentrated solution of an alkali chromate in concentrated sulphuric. It is readily soluble in water, forming chromic and dichromic acids. There are many slightly soluble chromates, but they dissolve in strong acid because of the formation of dichromate ion, $2PbCrO_4 + 2H^+ = 2Pb^{++} + Cr_2O_7^{--} + H_2O$. In very concentrated acid higher polychromate ions exist, and salts of trichromate and tetrachromate may be prepared such as $K_2Cr_3O_{10}$ and $K_2Cr_4O_{13}$. Chromates and dichromates are all therapeutically dangerous, very strongly caustic and destructive of red corpuscles of the blood.

Normal chromates are known of nearly all the stronger bases, both organic and inorganic, and are generally yellow. Ammonium, lithium, sodium, potassium, cuprous, cupric, rubidium, caesium, magnesium, calcium, zinc, cobalt and nickel chromates are soluble in water; strontium and the rare-earth chromates are sparingly soluble in water; mercuric chromate is decomposed by water, while silver, thallous, mercurous, cadmium, barium and lead chromates are insoluble in water. With the exception of cuprous, mercurous and magnesium dichromates which are unknown, all the metals forming soluble chromates also yield soluble red dichromates.

Chromates and polychromates are readily reduced by hydrochloric acid, sulphurous acid, hydrogen sulphide, ferrous salts, alcohol, etc., with formation of chromic salts or hydroxide. The chromates of the strongly basic elements are not readily decomposed by heating, but those of the feebler bases yield chromium sesquioxide and oxygen. Ammonium chromate, on heating or exposure to air, loses ammonia and yields the dichromate, which decomposes with explosive violence on further heating, leaving a residue of chromium sesquioxide, while nitrogen, ammonia, oxides of nitrogen, water and oxygen are also formed.

On treatment of chromates or dichromates with concentrated cold solutions of the halogen acids, or phosphorus halides, salts are obtained, derived from hypothetical half-acid halides; for example, hydrochloric acid and potassium dichromate yield potassium chlorochromate, a salt of the unknown chlorochromic acid $HCrO_3Cl$ or $CrO_2Cl.OH$, the half-acid chloride of chromic acid $CrO_2(OH)_2$. Fluorochromates, chlorochromates, bromochromates and iodochromates of some of the strong bases are known. If chromates or dichromates are treated with a large excess of hydrofluoric or hydrochloric acid, chromyl fluoride, CrO_2F_2, and chromyl chloride, CrO_2Cl_2, are formed. These compounds, which are red volatile liquids yielding red vapours, are the acid fluoride and acid chloride of chromic acid. The bromine and iodine analogues are unknown.

Though chromates and dichromates are readily decomposed by warm solutions of hydrogen peroxide to form oxygen and chromic salts or chromic hydroxide, cold solutions yield little or no oxygen and form peroxidized compounds, nearly all of which yield hydrogen peroxide by suitable treatment and all readily evolve oxygen. It is accordingly inferred that all contain sexivalent chromium as in chromates and dichromates, the extra equivalents of oxygen being in the same form as in hydrogen peroxide. The highest stage of peroxidation is found in the red perchromates of the general formula R_3CrO_8. These salts are obtained by the action of 30% hydrogen-peroxide solutions on alkaline solutions of the chromates at low temperatures. They are unstable at ordinary temperatures and occasionally evolve oxygen explosively. The acid corresponding to these salts has not been isolated. When 97% hydrogen peroxide is added at −30° C. to chromium trioxide, a dark-blue crystalline acid is formed, having the empirical formula H_7CrO_{10} or $H_3CrO_8.2H_2O$. An intense blue coloration is formed on adding hydrogen peroxide to an acidified solution of a chromate, the reaction being sufficiently delicate to detect traces of either reagent. The blue colour is extracted by ether, and the ethereal solution on neutralization by alkalies yields dark-blue salts. These salts have the general formula RH_2CrO_7 and are as unstable as the more oxygenated red salts. If the red or blue salts are treated with excess of an organic base such as pyridine, blue or violet salts are obtained having the general formula $RCrO_5$. If the red perchromates are heated with ammonia to about 40° C., or with potassium-cyanide solution, derivatives of a chromium peroxide of the formula CrO_4 or Cr_2O_8 are obtained. This peroxide may be regarded as an acid anhydride, formed by the loss of a molecule of hydrogen peroxide from two molecules of the acid $HCrO_5$, or one molecule of the dimeric acid $H_2Cr_2O_{10}$. The derivatives of this peroxide yield oxygen and chromates with alkalies, and oxygen, hydrogen peroxide and chromic salts with acids.

Analytical.—Chromium can be detected in compounds by the formation of a green borax bead, by the yellow colour of chromates formed on fusion with potassium nitrate, by the formation of red chromyl chloride and by the blue colour of peroxychromic acid. In the general systematic separation, chromium is precipitated with aluminum since they are not precipitated by H_2S in 03n H^+, but do precipitate with NH_4OH as the hydrous oxides. When this precipitate is treated with sodium peroxide, the chromium is oxidized to chromate and may be identified by the precipitation of lead chromate from a dilute acid solution after first destroying the excess peroxide by heating. Chromates may be quantitatively determined by reduction with ferrous, $Cr_2O_7^{--} + 6Fe^{++} + 14H^+ = 2Cr^{+++} + 6Fe^{+++} + 7H_2O$, or by reduction with excess of iodide and the titration of liberated iodine with thiosulphate.

BIBLIOGRAPHY.—J. A. Newton Friend (ed.), *Text-book of Inorganic Chemistry*, vol. vii, part 3 (1926); U.S. Bureau of Mines, *Minerals Yearbook* (1940, 1941 and 1944); Leopold Gmelin, *Gmelin und Krauts Handbuch der anorganischen Chemie*, vols. i–iii, 7th ed. (1905); J. W. Mellor, *A Comprehensive Treatise on Inorganic and Theoretical Chemistry*, vol. xi (1931); W. M. Latimer, *Oxidation States of the Elements and Their Potentials in Aqueous Solutions*, Chap. XVI (1938); Mutual Chemical Company of America, *Chromium Chemicals* (1941); *Trans. Electrochemical Soc.*, vol. 80 (1941). (J. D. M. S.; W. M. LA.)

CHROMOLITHOGRAPH: *see* LITHOGRAPHY; COLOUR PRINTING.

CHROMOSOME. So called because of their affinity for certain dyes, the chromosomes are minute bodies seen in the dividing cells of which the bodies of animals and plants are composed. Their characteristic configurations and remarkable behaviour in cell division, in the process of development and in the union and formation of the reproductive elements have been the subject of a large body of research, since their discovery in 1873 by Anton Schneider, Flemming, Otto Bütschli and others. The progress achieved during the three decades that followed their discovery made it possible, when J. G. Mendel's law of segregation was rediscovered in the opening years of the 20th century, to identify the structural mechanism predicted by him. From that time on intensive study of the behaviour of the chromosomes in relation to breeding experiments resulted in the building up of one of the most spectacular generalizations of modern biology. An exposition of this chromosome hypothesis is given in the article CYTOLOGY. The word was first used by Wilhelm von Waldeyer-Hartz (1888). (*See* also HEREDITY; GENE.) (L. T. H.)

CHROMOSPHERE is the name which was given by Sir J. Norman Lockyer in 1868 (at the suggestion of William Sharpey, then secretary of the Royal society) to the layer of the sun's atmosphere, just outside the photosphere, which is observed visually when the sun is totally eclipsed and is spectroscopically observable at other times. Observations of the chromosphere had in fact been made before 1868. Thus, C. A. Young (*The Sun,* 1882) mentions that Captain Stannyan, in a report on the eclipse of 1706 observed by him at Berne, Switz., noticed "a blood-red streak of light visible for six or seven seconds upon the western limb," just before the emergence of the sun. It was observed also by Edmund Halley in 1715, and by François Arago, Sir George Airy, Angelo Secchi and others at eclipses in the 19th century. Attention was, however, directed mostly at that time to solar prominences, and the chromosphere escaped serious study. In 1868 Pierre Janssen and Lockyer independently discovered that solar prominences, hitherto only observed at total eclipses, could be seen in full daylight by means of the spectroscope—the principle being that the white light from the sky surrounding the sun's disk was weakened by dispersion on passing through the spectroscope, while any monochromatic constituent of the light from the prominences passed through undispersed and gave rise to a bright line. Lockyer shortly afterward (Nov. 5, 1868) noticed that the prominences jutted out from a continuous spherical envelope surrounding the sun. This envelope was at all times visible in the red (C or Hα) and blue (F or Hβ) lines of hydrogen and in the yellow (D_3) line of the then unidentified element helium. It was to this continuous envelope that Lockyer gave the name chromosphere, in reference to the colour effects seen in the spectroscope.

At a time of total solar eclipse, at the moment of second contact, the chromosphere becomes visible as a thin red crescent, about 10 sec. in thickness, on the east side of the disk. The advancing moon rapidly covers up the layer, which reappears at the western limb just before third contact. The red colour is due to the visual dominance of the Hα line of hydrogen.

Astronomers soon recognized that in the chromosphere they must be viewing tangentially the upper layers of the same gases which, when projected against the bright disk, produce the ordinary Fraunhofer absorption spectrum of sunlight, and it was natural to look for confirmation of this. The complete spectrum of the light from the chromosphere might be expected to correspond with the Fraunhofer spectrum, a bright line in the chromospheric spectrum corresponding to each dark line in the Fraunhofer spectrum. This was first verified by Young at the total eclipse of Dec. 22, 1870. Placing the slit of his spectroscope tangential to the advancing limb of the moon, he saw the Fraunhofer spectrum suddenly replaced by a spectrum of bright lines which lasted only two or three seconds. This spectrum was hence called by Young the "flash spectrum." In Young's own words, "as the moon advances, making narrower and narrower the remaining sickle of the sun's disk, the dark lines of the spectrum remain sensibly unchanged though becoming somewhat less intense. A few, however, begin to fade out, and some even turn partially bright a minute or two before totality begins. But the moment the sun is hidden, through the whole length of the spectrum, in the red, the green, the violet, the bright lines flash out by hundreds and thousands, almost startlingly; as suddenly as stars from a bursting rocket, and as evanescent, for the whole thing is over in two or three seconds."

Photography was first successfully applied to the photography of the flash spectrum by A. Fowler and W. Shackleton at the eclipse of April 16, 1893. The flash spectrum may be observed by the use of a tangential slit, as in Young's original observation. But the crescent of atmosphere left exposed by the moon's disk during the period of the flash is so thin that it behaves as a crescent-shaped slit. A direct photograph of the flash spectrum with a prismatic camera without slit reveals a series of crescents, one corresponding to each bright line in the flash spectrum. Each gives an image of the chromosphere and prominences in the corresponding radiation. The thicker the atmosphere as viewed in the light of a particular radiation, the longer will be the arc in the photograph, and it is a matter of simple geometry to deduce the height of the chromosphere in any given radiation from a measurement of the distance from cusp to cusp, using the known diameters of the sun and moon. The following table shows chromospheric heights derived in this way by Lockyer (eclipse of 1898), S. A. Mitchell (1905), C. R. Davidson and F. J. M. Stratton (1926) and D. H. Menzel (1931).

Heights of Elements in Chromosphere from Lengths of Arcs

Element	Radiation	Lockyer 1898	Mitchell 1905	Davidson and Stratton 1926	Menzel 1931
		Km.	Km.	Km.	
H	λ6563Hα	7,500	..	8,400	..
	λ4861Hβ	..	8,000	8,400	9,000
	λ4341Hγ	..	8,000	8,000	..
He	λ4713	..	3,900	6,000	..
	λ5876(D_3)	..	7,500	7,500	..
	λ4471	6,500	7,500	7,400	..
	λ4026	4,500	6,000	4,400	..
He+	λ4686	..	1,580	2,200	..
Na	λ5896, λ5890(D_1,D_2)	..	1,200	1,000	..
Ca	λ4227	3,500	5,000	2,500	..
Ca+	λ3968, λ3933(H,K)	9,500	14,000	9,200	10,000
Sr+	λ4215, λ4077	4,500	6,000	5,200	..

Number of Atoms at a Height H in Kilometres

Menzel, all atoms:

From multiplet intensities.................. $\exp\left(-\frac{H}{4050}\right)+59\exp\left(-\frac{H}{1560}\right)$

From microphotometer intensities........... $\exp\left(-\frac{H}{3580}\right)+56\exp\left(-\frac{H}{1650}\right)$

Mitchell and Williams:

Singly ionized titanium...................... $\exp\left(-\frac{H}{5000}\right)+60\exp\left(-\frac{H}{2000}\right)$

Iron (of excitation potential 1 v.)............ $\exp\left(-\frac{H}{3333}\right)+50\exp\left(-\frac{H}{1667}\right)$

Pannekoek and Minnaert:

Hydrogen.................................. $\exp\left(-\frac{H}{617}\right)$

Apart from the heights to which the various elements are detected in the chromosphere, the question of greatest interest concerns the distribution of density in the chromosphere. The table also shows the results of various investigations by Menzel, Mitchell and Emma T. R. Williams, and Antonie Pannekoek and Marcel G. J. Minnaert.

As regards wave length, the flash spectrum is an almost exact copy of the Fraunhofer spectrum. The Balmer series of hydrogen extends, however, much further (Stratton and Davidson at Sumatra, in 1926, observed 36 members of the series); also helium is prominent in the flash, while it appears only fitfully and faintly in the Fraunhofer spectrum. But the intensities of the lines in the flash are markedly different from the intensities in the Fraunhofer spectrum. Lines faint in the Fraunhofer spectrum give rise to short intense arcs in the flash; this is easily explained since the faint lines in the Fraunhofer spectrum are probably produced by low-lying vapours at a high temperature, which accordingly shine brightly when viewed tangentially. But in addition many lines are enormously increased in intensity in the flash. It was pointed out by Lockyer that such lines are almost invariably "enhanced" lines; *i.e.*, lines which are relatively strengthened from arc spectra to spark spectra. For example the D-lines of sodium (arc lines) are relatively inconspicuous in the flash; the blue line λ4227 of calcium is much less intense and extends to a smaller height than the H and K lines; the enhanced lines of iron, scandium, titanium and chromium are all strengthened in the flash, and usually extend to greater heights than the unenhanced lines. The flash spectrum, in fact, resembles in many ways the spectrum of stars much hotter than the sun. This was for many years a difficulty, for it was hard to believe that the high-level chromosphere could be hotter than the low-level reversing layer.

The explanation was given by Megnad Saha in 1920. Enhanced lines are now known to be due to the ionized atom (*i.e.*, the atom which has lost one or more electrons) and Saha showed that ionization was promoted not only, as in Lockyer's experiments, by high temperature but also by low pressure. At high temperatures the process of the dissociation of an atom into an electron and a positive ion goes on of its own accord, according to the reversible equation

$$A \rightleftharpoons A^{+} + e^{-}$$

until a balance is obtained between the rate of dissociation and the rate of recombination. Reduction of pressure reduces the rate of recombination, while leaving the rate of ionization unchanged, and so favours an increased degree of ionization. Saha showed that at a given temperature and pressure the degree of ionization was calculable, given the ionization potential of the atom. The following table gives the percentage ionization of calcium at 5,000° C. at the pressures mentioned.

Pressure (atmospheres)	10^{-1}	10^{-2}	10^{-3}	10^{-4}	10^{-5}	10^{-6}
Percentage ionization	6.5	20.2	54.5	90	99	(100)

The pressure at the base of the chromosphere is probably less than 10^{-6} atm., and so in the high-level chromosphere calcium must be almost completely ionized. The spectrum must, therefore, be that of the ionized atom, not the neutral atom; hence, the predominance of enhanced lines in the chromospheric spectrum. Similar calculations apply to other elements. The D-lines of sodium, for example, which are due to the neutral atom, are not found in the upper chromosphere, because any sodium there would be completely ionized; the lines of the ionized atom are too far in the ultra-violet to be observable.

The question remains why the chromosphere should extend to such great heights in certain elements. Gravity at the solar surface is about 27 times as powerful as at the earth's surface, and it is readily calculated that under gravity only the solar atmosphere would have a thickness which would be measured in tens of kilometres instead of thousands. (E. A. Mi.)

An explanation with specific reference to the ionized calcium chromosphere was given by E. A. Milne in a series of papers published during the years 1924–27. This theory of Milne is based on the following considerations: when an atom absorbs a quantum of light, and thereby undergoes a transition from one stationary state to another, it experiences a blow in the direction in which the light was moving. In the case of the sun this blow will be in the outward direction. After a short interval the atom must re-emit the quantum, suffering thereby a blow from the recoil, but the recoil blows will be random in direction and will neutralize one another on the average. The net result is that in a succession of absorptions and emissions the atom experiences a series of outward blows. An atom of ionized calcium in the high-level chromosphere experiences about 20,000 such blows per second and this is just sufficient to keep it suspended against gravity. In other words, the pressure of radiation is able to support the ionized calcium atom against gravity and this would account for the enormous extension of the calcium chromosphere. This theory of Milne, attractive in many ways, encounters certain difficulties. For one thing, the density distribution which it predicts does not seem to be in accord with the observations. For another, it appears too special in the sense that it is unable to account for the extent of the other atoms in the chromosphere. This latter failure of Milne's theory, particularly in the case of hydrogen, throws serious doubts on the adequacy of the whole picture; for hydrogen is the most abundant constituent of the chromosphere. These remarks apply not only to Milne's theory but also to other variants of it, as given, for example, by S. Chandrasekhar.

In view of the difficulties encountered by theories based on support from radiation pressure, W. H. McCrea has advanced an alternative theory based on the notion of turbulence. McCrea supposes that the chromospheric gases can be divided into volume elements of finite extent V such that the atomic motion in each group is temperature motion (the temperature corresponding to the ionization and excitation exhibited by the chromosphere) but the elements V themselves have a Maxwellian distribution in velocity corresponding to a temperature $\mathbf{T}$ characterized by a mean velocity C. In the case of an atmosphere consisting of nothing but neutral hydrogen we can expect a relation of the form

$$k\mathbf{T} = kT + \tfrac{1}{3}MC^2,$$

where M is the mass of the hydrogen atom and k is the so-called Boltzmann constant. The pressure p will be given by

$$p = nk\mathbf{T}$$

where n is the number of hydrogen atoms per cubic centimetre. Under these circumstances it is not difficult to visualize that the density distribution in the chromosphere will imitate an isothermal atmosphere at the fictitious temperature $\mathbf{T}$. The density distributions in the chromosphere as indicated by the observations would lead to a temperature $\mathbf{T}$ of the order of 18,000° corresponding to a velocity C of about 18 km./sec. It would not seem impossible that turbulent motions of this magnitude exist in the chromosphere. Indeed, there are observations which would lead one to suspect velocities of exactly this order.

Finally, we may refer to an outstanding problem of the chromosphere. The high-level chromosphere rotates around the sun's axis faster than the reversing layer, and moreover does not have the retardation experienced by the latter. No satisfactory explanation had been suggested up to mid-20th century. (Su. C.)

Bibliography.—General accounts of the chromosphere are contained in the following standard works: E. Pringsheim, *Physik der Sonne* (1910); C. G. Abbot, *The Sun* (1911); H. Dingle, *Modern Astrophysics* (1924); S. A. Mitchell, *Eclipses of the Sun* (1923); F. J. M. Stratton, *Astronomical Physics* (1926). *See* also A. S. Eddington, *Stars and Atoms* (1927) and F. J. M. Stratton, *Modern Eclipse Problems* (Halley Lecture, 1927). J. N. Lockyer's early researches on the chromosphere are contained in *Contributions to Solar Physics* (1874) and *Chemistry of the Sun* (1887). Original records of eclipse observations on the chromosphere are given in the following fundamental memoirs: *Phil. Trans. Roy. Soc.*, vol. 187A (1896, J. N. Lockyer, A. Fowler and W. Shackleton); *Mem. Roy. Astron. Soc.*, vol. 54 (appendices) (1901 and 1902, J. N. Lockyer; 1901 and 1903); J. Evershed, vol. 57 (appendix) (1906, F. W. Dyson); *Astrophys. Journ.*, vol. 38 (1913, S. A. Mitchell); *Mem. Roy. Astron. Soc.*, vol. 64 (1927, C. R. Davidson and F. J. M. Stratton). For the rotation of the chromosphere *see* W. S. Adams, *Astrophys. Journ.*, vol. 29 (1909). Saha's fundamental paper on ionization in the chromosphere occurs in *Phil. Mag.*, vol. 40 (1920). The mathematical theory of the equilibrium of the chromosphere is given in E. A. Milne's papers in *Monthly Notices R.A.S.*, vol. 84–87 (1924–27). See also *Monthly Notices*, vol. 87 (1927, S. R. Pike and P. A. Taylor). For recent views on the height of the chromosphere *see* correspondence in *Observatory*, vol. 48, 49 (1925, 1926, J. Evershed, S. A. Mitchell, E. A. Milne, A. A. Buss and G. Abetti); Sir Frank Dyson and R. van der R. Woolley, *Eclipses of the Sun and Moon* (1937); D. H. Menzel, *Lick Obs. Publ. 17*, part I (1931); S. Chandrasekhar, *Monthly Notices R.A.S.*, 94:13 (1933); W. H. McCrea, *Monthly Notices R.A.S.*, 89:718 (1929). (E. A. Mi.; Su. C.)

CHRONAXIE or Chronaxia, a term introduced by Louis Lapicque in 1909 to define the character of the stimulus which is required to excite various types of living tissue, particularly muscle and nerve. The most convenient form of stimulus is an electric current, since this can be made to excite (*i.e.*, to cause the tissue to display its characteristic activity) without doing any damage. It is found that a current must fulfil three conditions if it is to excite: (1) it must flow for more than a certain minimal duration; (2) the final strength must exceed a certain value; and (3) the rate of increase of the current from zero must exceed a definite velocity. The need for a minimal duration is shown by the fact that a current alternating at 1,000,000 cycles a second is powerless to excite any tissue in the body; and the modern surgical technique of diathermy is based on this.

The curve relating minimal duration and minimal strength has the form shown in the figure, and as a first approximation it obeys the formula of Weiss, $i = a + \frac{b}{t}$, where i is the current, t its duration and a and b are constants. Lapicque has shown that curves of the same form are obtained from the most diverse tissues, ranging from the human nerve, where the minimal duration is less than .0001 sec., to the cells of a plant where it may be longer than 1 sec. Thus, the character of the stimulus for a given tissue can be defined at once if we know the constants a and b for that tissue. The constant a (the rheobase) is given by the minimal current strength at long durations. The other constant b is the more important, for it determines the slope of the curve, it can be fixed by measuring the chronaxie, which is equal to

$\frac{b}{a}$ and is the least duration required when the current strength is $2a$. The true form of the curve differs somewhat from that given by Weiss's equation, and it has been used as a basis from which to deduce the mechanism of excitation. In Lapicque's hands the measurement of the chronaxie has also been used to investigate the passage of the state of excitation from one tissue to another (*e.g.*, from nerve to muscle). (E. D. A.)

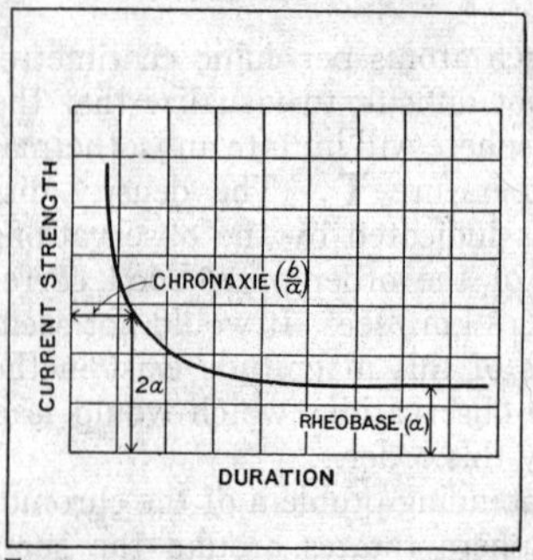

FORM OF A STIMULATING CURRENT IN LIVING TISSUE

The curve shows the relation between the strength and the duration of the smallest current which will excite a living cell. The chronaxie and the rheobase are the two constants which define the curve

CHRONICLE. The historical works written in the middle ages are variously designated "histories," "annals" or "chronicles" (from Gr. χρόνος, "time"); it is difficult, however, to give an exact definition of each of these terms, since they do not correspond to determinate classes of writings. Perhaps the most reasonable definition is that given by H. F. Delaborde at the École des Chartes that chronicles are accounts of a universal character, while annals relate either to a locality, or to a religious community or even to a whole people, but without attempting to treat of all periods or all peoples. The primitive type, he says, was furnished by Eusebius of Caesarea, who wrote (*c.* 303) a chronicle in Greek, which was soon translated into Latin and frequently recopied throughout the middle ages; it embraced the history of the world since the creation. It is certain, however, that mediaeval authors or scribes were not conscious of any clear distinction between annals and chronicles; indeed, they often apparently employed the terms indiscriminately.

In any case, chronicles and annals (*q.v.*) have points of great similarity. Chronicles are accounts generally of an impersonal character, and often anonymous, composed of passages copied from sources which the chronicler is seldom at pains to indicate, and of personal recollections the veracity of which remains to be determined. Some of them are written with so little intelligence that the work of composition seems a mere piece of drudgery imposed on the clergy and monks by their superiors. To distinguish what is original from what is borrowed, to separate fact from falsehood and to establish the value of each piece of evidence is thus a difficult undertaking, and one which has exercised the sagacity of scholars, especially since the 17th century.

The Christian chronicles were first written in the two learned languages, Greek and Latin. At an early stage we have proof of the use of national languages, the most famous instances being the Anglo-Saxon Chronicle (*q.v.*), the most ancient form of which goes back to the 10th century, and the so-called Chronicle of Nestor, in Palaeo-Slavonic, written in the 11th and 12th centuries. In the 13th and 14th centuries the number of chronicles written in the vulgar tongue continued to increase more rapidly on the continent than in England. From the 15th century, with the revived study of Greek and Roman literature, the traditional form of chronicles, as well as of annals, tended to be replaced by another based on the models of antiquity—that of the historical composition combining skilful arrangement with elegance of style. It was not, however, until the 17th century that the traditional form became practically extinct.

See E. Bernheim, *Lehrbuch der historischen Methode,* 4th ed. (1903); H. Bloch, "Geschichte der deutschen Geschichtsschreibung im Mittelalter" in the *Handbuch* of G. von Below and F. Meinecke (Munich, 1903 *et seq.*); Max Jansen, "Historiographie und Quellen der deutschen Geschichte bis 1500," in Aloïs Meister's *Grundriss* (Leipzig, 1906); and the introduction to A. Molinier's *Les Sources de l'histoire de France* (1904). (C. Bem.)

CHRONICLES, BOOKS OF, two Old Testament books of the Bible. The name is derived from *Chronicon,* first suggested by Jerome as a rendering of the title which they bear in the Hebrew Canon; viz., *Events of the Times.* (1 Chron. xxviii, 24; Esth. x, 2, etc.) The Greek translators divided the long book into two, and adopted the title Παραλειπόμενα, "Things Omitted" (*scil.* in the other historical books).

Authorship and Date.—The book of Chronicles begins with Adam and ends abruptly in the middle of Cyrus' decree of restoration, which reappears complete at the beginning of Ezra. A closer examination of those parts of Ezra and Nehemiah which are not extracted from earlier documents or original memoirs leads to the conclusion that Chronicles-Ezra-Nehemiah was originally one work, displaying throughout the peculiarities of language and thought of a single editor, who, however, cannot be Ezra himself as tradition states. The style of the language, and also the position of the book in the Jewish Canon, stamp the book as one of the latest in the Old Testament. In 1 Chron. xxix, 7, which refers to the time of David, a sum of money is reckoned by darics, which certainly implies that the author wrote after this Persian coin had been long current in Judaea. In 1 Chron. iii, 19 *et seq.*, the descendants of Zerubbabel seem to be reckoned to six generations (the Septuagint reads it so as to give as many as 11 generations), and this agrees with the suggestion that Hattush (v, 22), who belongs to the fourth generation from Zerubbabel, was a contemporary of Ezra (Ezra viii, 2). With this it accords that in Nehemiah five generations of high priests are enumerated from Joshua (xii, 10 *et seq.*), and that the last name is that of Jaddua, who, according to Josephus, was a contemporary of Alexander the Great (333 B.C.). A date some time after 332 B.C. is now accepted by most modern critics. (*See* EZRA AND NEHEMIAH, BOOKS OF.)

Scope and Object.—The writer lived a considerable time after Ezra and stood entirely under the influence of the religious institutions of the new theocracy. This standpoint determined the nature of his interest in the early history of his people. The true importance of the history of Israel centred in the fact that this petty nation was the people of Yahweh, the spiritual God. The tragic interest which distinguishes its annals from the forgotten history of Moab or Damascus lies wholly in that contest which vindicated the reality of spiritual things and the supremacy of Yahweh's purpose, in the political ruin of the nation which was the faithless depository of these sacred truths. After the return from the Exile it was impossible to write the history of Israel's fortunes otherwise than in a spirit of religious pragmatism. But within the limits of the religious conception of the plan and purpose of the Hebrew history more than one point of view might be taken up. The book of Kings looks upon the history in the spirit of the prophets—in that spirit which is still echoed by Zech. i, 5 *et seq.*, but which had become extinct before the chronicler wrote. The New Jerusalem of Ezra was organized as a municipality and a church, not as a nation. The centre of religious life was no longer the living prophetic word but the ordinances of the Pentateuch and the liturgical service of the sanctuary. The religious vocation of Israel was no longer national but ecclesiastical or municipal, and the historical continuity of the nation was vividly realized only within the walls of Jerusalem and the courts of the Temple, in the solemn assembly and stately ceremonial of a feast day. These influences naturally operated most strongly on those who were officially attached to the sanctuary. To a Levite, even more than to other Jews, the history of Israel meant above all things the history of Jerusalem, of the Temple and of the Temple ordinances. Now the writer of Chronicles betrays on every page his essentially Levitical habit of mind. It even seems possible from a close attention to his descriptions of sacred ordinances to conclude that his special interests are those of a common Levite rather than a priest, and that of all Levitical functions he is most partial to those of the singers, a member of whose guild he may have been. From the standpoint of the post-Exilic age, the older delineation of the history of Israel, especially in the books of Samuel and Kings, could not but appear to be deficient in some directions, while in other respects its narrative seemed superfluous or open to misunderstanding, as for example by recording, and that without condemnation, things inconsistent with the later post-Exilic law. The history of the ordinances of worship holds a very small place in the older record. Jerusalem and the Temple have not that central place in the book of Kings which they occupied in the minds of the Jewish community after the Exile. Large sections of the old history are devoted to the religion and politics of the ten tribes, which are altogether unintelligible and uninteresting when measured by a strictly Levitical standard; and, in general, the whole problems and struggles of the prophetic period turn on points which had ceased to be cardinal in the life of the New Jerusalem, which was no longer called to decide between the claims of the word of Yahweh and the exigencies of political affairs and social customs, and which could not comprehend that men absorbed in deeper spiritual contests had no leisure for the niceties of Levitical legislation. Thus, there seemed to be room for a new history, which should confine itself to matters still interesting to the theocracy of Zion, keeping Jerusalem and the Temple in the foreground, and developing the divine pragmatism of the history, not so much with reference to the prophetic word as to the fixed legislation of the Pentateuch, so that the whole narrative might be made to teach that the glory of Israel lies in the observance of the divine law and ritual.

Contents.—For the sake of systematic completeness the book begins with Adam, as is the custom with later oriental writers. The early history is contracted into a series of tribal and priestly genealogies, which were doubtless by no means the least interesting part of the work at a time when every Israelite was concerned to prove the purity of his Hebrew descent (*cf.* Ezra ii, 59, 62). Commencing abruptly (after some Benjamite genealogies) with the death of Saul, the history becomes fuller and runs parallel with the books of Samuel and Kings. The limitations of the compiler's interest in past times appears in the omission, among other particulars, of David's reign in Hebron, of the disorders in his family and the revolt of Absalom, of the circumstances of Solomon's accession and of many details as to the wisdom and splendour of that sovereign, as well as of his fall into idolatry. In the later history the ten tribes are quite neglected ("Yahweh is not with Israel," II Chron. xxv, 7), and political affairs in Judah receive attention, not in proportion to their intrinsic importance, but according as they serve to exemplify God's help to the obedient and His chastisement of the rebellious. That the compiler is always unwilling to speak of the misfortunes of good rulers is not necessarily to be ascribed to a deliberate suppression of truth, but shows that the book was throughout composed not in purely historical interests, but with a view to inculcating practical lessons. The more important additions to the older narrative consist partly of statistical lists (I Chron. xii), partly of full details on points connected with the history of the sanctuary and the great feasts or the archaeology of the Levitical ministry (I Chron. xiii, xv, xvi, xxii–xxix; II Chron. xxix–xxxi, etc.), and partly of narratives of victories and defeats, of sins and punishments, of obedience and its reward, which could be made to point a plain religious lesson in favour of faithful observance of the law (II Chron. xiii, xiv, 9 *et seq.;* xx, xxi, 11 *et seq.*, etc.). The minor variations of Chronicles from the books of Samuel and Kings are analogous in principle to the larger additions and omissions, so that the whole work has a consistent and well-marked character, presenting the history in quite a different perspective from that of the old narrative.

Value.—For a critical study of the book it is necessary to compare carefully Chronicles with the parallel narrative in Samuel–Kings. "A careful comparison of Chronicles with Samuel and Kings is a striking object lesson in ancient historical composition; it is an almost indispensable introduction to the criticism of the Pentateuch and the older historical works" (W. H. Bennett, *Chronicles,* p. 20 *et seq.*). Where Chronicles directly contradicts the earlier books there are few cases in which an impartial historical judgment will decide in favour of the later account, and in any point that touches difference of usage between its time and that of the old monarchy it is of no authority. A certain freedom of literary form was always allowed to ancient historians; and the typical speeches in Chronicles are of little value for the periods to which they relate, especially where they are inconsistent with the evidence from earlier writings. According to the ordinary laws of research, the book, being written at a time long posterior to the events it records, can have only secondary importance, although here and there valuable material has been preserved. It must be remembered that the earlier books contain only a portion of the material to which the compilers had access. Hence, it may well happen that the additional details, which unfortunately cannot be checked, were ultimately derived from sources as reputable as those in the books of Samuel, Kings, etc. As examples may be cited Rehoboam's buildings, etc. (II Chron. xi, 5–12, 18 *et seq.*); Jeroboam's attack upon Abijah (II Chron. xiii, *cf.* I Kings xv, 7); the invasion of Zerah in Asa's reign (II Chron. xiv; *see* ASA); Jehoshaphat's wars and judicial measures (II Chron. xvii, xx; *see* I Kings xxii, 45); Jehoram's family (II Chron. xxi, 2–4); relations between Jehoiada and Joash (II Chron. xxiv, 3, 15 *et seq.*); conflicts between Ephraim and Judah (II Chron. xxv, 6–13); wars of Uzziah and Jotham (II Chron. xxvi, *et seq.*); events in the reign of Ahaz (II Chron. xxviii, 8–15, 18 *et seq.*); reforms of Hezekiah (II Chron. xxix *et seq.*, *cf.* Jer. xxvi, 19); Manasseh's captivity, repentance and buildings (II Chron. xxxiii, 10–20; *see* II Kings xxi and MANASSEH); the death of Josiah (II Chron. xxxv, 20–25). In addition to this, reference may be made to such tantalizing statements as those in I Chron. ii, 23 (R.V.); iv, 39–41; v, 10, 18–22; vii, 21 *et seq.;* viii, 13; xii, 15—examples of the kind of tradition, national and private, upon which writers could draw. Although in their present form the additional narratives are in the chronicler's style, it is not necessary to deny an older traditional element which may have been preserved in sources now lost to us.

BIBLIOGRAPHY.—Robertson Smith's famous article in the 9th edition of the *Encyclopædia Britannica* was modified by his later views in *Old Testament in the Jewish Church,* pp. 140–148. Later literature is summarized by Driver in his revision of Smith's article in *Ency. Bib.* and in his *Literature of the Old Testament,* by F. Brown in Hasting's *Dict. Bib.* and by Elmslie (in the Cambridge Bible).

(W. R. S.; S. A. C.)

CHRONOGRAPHS. A chronograph is an instrument for making a graphical record by means of which a sequence of events may be accurately co-ordinated with the passage of time. The name is also frequently applied to instruments which give visual indication of the time between two events without making a permanent graphical record. Such instruments are more properly called chronoscopes. A third use of the term is to designate the complete instrumentation used in measuring the velocity of a projectile or other moving object.

VELOCITY CHRONOGRAPHS

The velocity, V, of an object can be determined as the quotient of the increment of its path ds by the time increment dt required to traverse ds. The velocity chronograph consists of two screens, or signalling devices, placed at either end of the path increment, ds, and of the chronograph proper, which records the elapsed time, dt, between the two signals. In the design of the velocity chronograph the first consideration is the accuracy required. For example, in the analysis of the dispersion of projectiles fired from modern cannon with a velocity of about 3,000 ft. per second it is often desired to measure the velocity with an error in the order of 1 ft. per second, or .03%. If the distance between screens is 100 ft. it must be known within $\frac{1}{3}$ in. and the time of flight between screens, which is about $\frac{1}{30}$ sec., must be known within $\frac{1}{100,000}$ sec. As regards knowing the distance between screens the problem is not so much one of measuring the distance accurately, since ordinary surveying methods are sufficient, as it is in designing a screen which gives a signal when the projectile is at a definite position with respect to the screen. Specially designed devices are also required in the measurement of the time.

At least eight different types of screens have been used in the measurement of projectile velocities, the selection depending upon the conditions of the tests and the accuracy required. Perhaps the oldest and most widely used screen, the *Le Boulengé screen* named after Capt. Paul Émil le Boulengé, of the Belgian artillery, who invented it as a component of the Le Boulengé chronograph, consists of a frame on which a fine wire is strung in many loops to form a fine network. A signal is produced when an electric current passing through the wire is interrupted as the projectile pierces the network. Since electrical contact may be made through the projectile itself, this type of screen is subject to excessive errors. The mass of the wire itself may also appreciably change the velocity of the projectile. An improved screen of the same type has recently been designed in which the electrical current is conducted through a grid printed with conducting ink on a thin sheet of paper.

The *Aberdeen screen* first used extensively at the Aberdeen Proving Ground of the U.S. army ordnance department consists of two conducting foils separated by an insulating sheet. A signal is generated when contact is made between the two foils by the nose of the projectile. This screen has the advantage that it can be used many times. However, it may appreciably alter the velocity of the projectile, and there is intrinsic uncertainty in the time at which contact is first established.

The *solenoid screen,* widely used in many proving grounds, avoids the two main objections to the Le Boulengé and Aberdeen screens. It derives its signal from the voltage generated by magnetic induction when the magnetized projectile passes through a large circular coil of wire. The current induced in the circuit containing the solenoid coil flows first positively as the magnetic flux through it increases; when the magnetic centre of the projectile reaches the centre plane of the coil the current reverses quickly and flows in the negative direction; finally, as the projectile recedes from the coil, the current falls gradually to zero. The sharp crossover from positive to negative current is generally used as the signal for marking the time of passage of the projectile. Although the exact point in the projectile whose passage through the coil produces this signal is never known, it may be assumed that the same point produces the signal in two successive coils. However, there may be some error caused by differences in yaw of the projectile as it passes through the two coils, or by differences in the centring alignment of the coils with respect to the trajectory. *Electrostatic induction* has also been used to produce signals. In this case the screen consists of an insulated loop of wire which forms an antenna through which the projectile passes after it has acquired a static charge of electricity. The potential of the antenna gradually rises as the projectile approaches; it reaches a maximum when the projectile is centred in the loop and then it falls again gradually to zero as the projectile recedes. By means of a suitable amplifier the point of maximum potential can be converted into a pulse of short duration which serves as the desired signal.

Photoelectric screens have been used in two forms. In the telephoto screen an image of the silhouette of the projectile against the light background of the sky is projected by means of a lens onto an opaque disk containing a transparent slit at its centre. As the image passes over the slit, a photocell located behind the disk receives less illumination and there is a change in current through the cell. The sudden increase in illumination when the square base of the projectile image leaves the slit is converted in the amplifier into a sharp pulse which serves as the signal. This type of screen can be used with 90 mm., or larger, shell at distances of 200 ft. from the trajectory, and it thus forms a useful component of a field chronograph. It has the advantage of convenience in setting up, especially for firing tests at high angles of elevation. In another form of photoelectric screen the projectile is fired between a linear light source and a parallel slit behind which is mounted a photocell. The light cut off from the photocell by the shadow of the projectile causes a change in current which is used to generate a signal in much the same way as in the telephoto screen. This type of screen is used extensively in closed ranges for measuring velocities and drag coefficients of small arms projectiles.

Acoustic screens operating from the impact of the bow shock-wave of the projectile upon a microphone have also been used, but variations in the distance between microphone and trajectory introduce errors. The change in the angle of the bow wave with velocity of the projectile is another source of error if the projectile experiences an appreciable change in velocity between the two screens.

For the most accurate measurements of velocity the method of *spark photography* has distinct advantages. In one form the projectile is fired between a photographic plate and a spark gap. An acoustic pickup or one of the other forms of screens already described may be used to trigger the spark while the projectile is in front of the plate. The electric pulse generated by the spark constitutes a signal of less than one microsecond duration and the exact position of the projectile at the instant the spark is fired can be inferred from measurements made on the shadow of the projectile recorded on the plate. In another form used by the German army during World War II a photograph of the projectile is made with two stereoscopic cameras of conventional design using the light of an electric spark for illuminating the projectile against a dark background. After developing the plates, the exact position of the projectile at the instant the spark was fired was reconstructed by reprojecting the images, using the cameras themselves as projectors. Again the spark served as a signal for the time measurements.

Time Measurements.—Up to the end of World War I most ordnance testing establishments measured the time of flight of projectiles between two screens by means of the *Le Boulengé chronograph.* In this instrument the distance of free fall under the acceleration of gravity is used as the basis of the time measurements. The signal from the first screen breaks the current in an electromagnet allowing a weight, in the form of a long rod, to fall freely. The time corresponding to a distance of fall of s cm. is given in seconds by the well-known equation

$$t=\left(\frac{2s}{g}\right)^{\frac{1}{2}}$$

where g is the acceleration of gravity in c.g.s. units and has a value ranging from 978.039 to 983.217 at sea level depending upon the location. The signal from the second screen releases a second weight which falls against a trigger allowing a knife to fly out and mark the falling rod. If both weights are released simultaneously, the knife makes a mark at a distance s_o corresponding to the dead time,

$$t_o=\left(\frac{2s_o}{g}\right)^{\frac{1}{2}}.$$

The actual time of flight is given by the difference $t-t_o$. Under the conditions of measurement an error of .001 in. in the measurement of the distances s and s_o corresponds to an error of $\frac{1}{20,000}$ sec. in time of flight. The actual errors are somewhat more than this and partly for this reason the instrument has been largely superseded by other more accurate methods.

The *Aberdeen chronograph* was developed during World War I for the U.S. army as a convenient and more accurate instrument than the Le Boulengé chronograph. It consists of a hollow cylindrical drum rotated by a synchronous motor operating from alternating current with an accurately controlled, or accurately measured, frequency of 60 cycles per second. A strip of waxed paper is held by centrifugal force against the inside surface of the drum and it is marked by sparks, triggered by the signals from the screens, which jump through the paper between sharp metallic needle points, mounted close to the inner surface of the paper, and the drum. The paper speed is exactly 1,500 cm. per second and an error of $\frac{1}{4}$ mm. in the measurement of the distance between two spark marks corresponds to an error of $\frac{1}{60,000}$ sec. An instrument of similar design with a more slowly rotating drum is used for measuring the time between the firing of a gun and the bursting of the explosive shell.

The *drum camera chronograph* is used extensively for measuring velocities of machine-gun bullets fired in a burst of many rounds, and as a general utility chronograph. In this instrument a strip of photosensitive paper is attached to the outer surface of a drum which rotates inside of a light-tight box, and at the same time moves slowly along its axis to prevent overlapping of traces made on successive turns. A light beam reflected from the mirror of an oscillographic galvanometer enters the box through a slit and makes a trace on the paper; deflections produced by signals from the screens are thus recorded. On the same record another galvanometer, driven by a standard 1,000-cycle frequency generator, produces time marks at one millisecond intervals. The timing galvanometer is usually arranged to vibrate in the direction of motion of the photosensitive paper and with an amplitude such that the forward velocity of the beam of light at the centre of its swing, where it crosses the slit, is the same as that of the paper. Thus, during that phase of the motion, a sharp, intensely exposed line is produced on the paper, while in the opposite phase of the motion the light is not in contact with the paper long enough for production of a photographic image. In a more refined version of the drum camera chronograph the image of the luminous spot of a cathode-ray tube is focused onto the paper. The signals from the screens are applied to the transverse deflecting plates of the cathode-ray tube and time marks are made by deflecting the beam at one

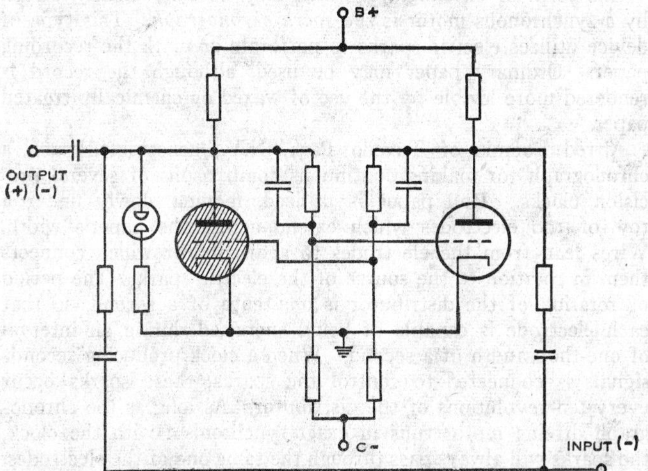

DIAGRAM OF ONE ELEMENT OF THE ELECTRONIC COUNTER CHRONOGRAPH

This circuit is stable with either of the tubes in the conducting state (indicated by the shading) while the other is nonconducting. Each negative pulse applied to the input terminal causes a reversal in the state of the circuit; positive pulses similarly applied have no effect. Negative output pulses are generated when the circuit goes into the state indicated, and these actuate the next stage. Thus, each stage of a circuit, containing several such elements connected in series, sends out half as many negative pulses as are applied to it. The final state of the circuit from which the number, *N*, of pulses applied to it can be determined, is indicated by neon lamps

millisecond intervals to form short pips on the trace. From such a record the time between two signals can be determined with an error of about two microseconds. The *raster chronograph* is a modification of the latter type of drum camera designed to give higher time resolution. In this instrument the cathode-ray beam is swept transversely with sawtooth motion at an accurately controlled frequency of 1,000 cycles per second. The signals are applied to the longitudinal plates, deflecting the beam in the direction of motion of the paper. Thus, the linear distance on the record corresponding to one millisecond is equal to the amplitude of the sweep. The drum speed need be sufficient only to separate one sweep from the next. Another form of raster chronograph capable of a tenfold higher resolution of time than the rotating drum type is one in which the cathode-ray beam scans the screen with several linear horizontal sweeps, each being separated from the preceding one by a small vertical distance to prevent overlap. The signals are applied to the vertical plates, and a photograph of the entire pattern is taken with an ordinary camera. If the lines of the raster are swept with a frequency of 10,000 sawtooth cycles per second and the position of the signals can be determined within 1% of the sweep amplitude, the times can be determined within one microsecond.

During the years just preceding World War II, and during that war, the *electronic counter chronograph* came into use on an ever-increasing scale. This device is based upon an electronic counting circuit first used by Wynn-Williams in England for counting radioactive rays registered by a Geiger counter. It has the great advantage that the time, in units of ten, or even of one, microseconds, can be read directly from the face of the instrument. The complete instrument consists of three parts, a crystal-controlled oscillator, which supplies consecutive pulses at the rate of 100,000 per second (or in the faster instrument at some higher rate), a gate circuit which is opened by the signal from the first screen and is closed by the signal from the second screen, and a counting circuit which registers the number of pulses getting through the gate during the interval while it is open.

In its simplest form the counting circuit consists of a cascaded series of similar circuit elements, each of which may be called a binary pair. One such binary pair consists of two electronic triodes connected together with resistors and capacitors in a so-called trigger circuit which allows one of the triodes to be in a conducting state while the other is held in the nonconducting state. A negative pulse applied to the input point of the circuit reverses the state of the circuit putting the triode which was formerly conducting into the nonconducting state. A small neon tube connecting across one of the triodes glows when that side of the circuit is nonconducting. Finally, a negative pulse is generated by such a binary pair at every second alternation, and this may be used as the input pulse for the next binary pair in cascade. If a series of such circuits is restored to an initial state in which all neon glow tubes are extinguished and then a sequence of pulses is fed into the input point of the first stage the first lamp will glow after one pulse has been received, the second will glow after two pulses, the first and second will glow after three pulses, the third will glow after four pulses and so on. The total count is equal to the sum of a series of terms of the form 2^n where n has the values 0, 1, 2—etc., corresponding to the first, second, third, etc., stages, respectively, and only those terms are to be included in the sum for which the corresponding neon lamps are glowing. By a slight modification of a circuit containing 4 such stages it may be made to recycle to the initial state after 9 pulses have been received, instead of after the 15th as would be the case without the modification. Thus, four binary pairs can be made to form a decade counter and the resulting numbers come out in the decimal system. The conventional electronic counter chronograph for use in measuring the speed of projectiles contains four such decades and it is pulsed at the rate of 100,000 pulses per second. Its range of measurement thus extends from 0.00001 sec. to 0.1 sec. and it gives the time between two signals to the nearest 0.00001 sec. Other counting circuits have operated at more than 1,000,000 pulses per second, and 10,000,000 pulses per second may not be impossible to count in this way.

The development of microwave techniques for radar during World War II afforded the means for designing the *microwave Doppler chronograph* which gave promise of having many practical advantages for measuring the velocities of projectiles under field conditions. In this instrument electromagnetic radiation in the three-centimetre band of wave lengths is projected from behind the gun along a beam which intersects the trajectory and is as nearly parallel to it as the configuration of the gun will allow. Radiant energy reflected backward from the base of the projectile is modified in frequency by the Doppler effect and is received in the same instrument and allowed to beat against the outgoing frequency. Each of the resulting beats corresponds to an increment in the path of the radiation of one wave length of the initial frequency. Half of this distance multiplied by the secant of the angle between the trajectory and the line joining the projectile with the microwave projector is the corresponding distance through which the projectile has moved. In the microwave chronograph an electronic counter records the total number of such units of distance, while another electronic counter records the number of oscillations of a quartz crystal for measurement of the time. The quotient of the former by the latter number is proportional to the velocity of the projectile. (T. H. J.)

ASTRONOMICAL CHRONOGRAPHS

For many years the most common form of time-recording device in astronomical work was the *writing chronograph,* and instruments of this type are still widely used. A writing chronograph utilizes one or more pens, or scribers, writing on paper which moves at a uniform speed beneath them. Sometimes paper tape in roll form is used, while in other cases paper sheets are wrapped around cylindrical drums on which the pens draw spiral lines. The motion of the paper is actuated by weight-driven or electric motors, the speed being usually controlled by centrifugal governors. In the most common form of the single-pen drum chronograph the drum makes either one or two revolutions per minute. The pen is actuated by an electromagnet which is opposed by a spring. When the electric current flowing in the magnet is interrupted, the spring pulls the pen a short distance to the side, producing a jog in the line. A clock or chronometer is connected to produce timing signals, either on every second or on certain seconds of the minute. When such a sheet is removed from the drum, the record for each minute (or half minute) appears as one line across the sheet, and the jogs in the line produced by the timing signals serve as marks for setting a scale. The timing signals should be of short duration so that they will interfere as little as possible with the signals to be measured. In the usual forms of the single-pen chronograph it is possible to make measurements accurately to the hundredth of a second. When two pens are used, one of them serves to record the timing signals and the other the signals which are to be measured, thus eliminating interference between the two sets of signals. Several pens are used when signals from more than one source are to be recorded simultaneously.

Efforts to reduce the labour of the measurements which are necessary with the writing chronograph have led to the development of *printing chronographs.* These devices generally print from rotating type wheels which are driven by governor-controlled motors. In a typical instrument of this kind, manufactured by William Gaertner of Chicago, there are three wheels alongside each other carrying type to print the minute, second and hundredth of a second. The governor is adjusted to run slightly faster than the controlling clock or chronometer. If the type wheels reach the position corresponding to the beginning of a second before a synchronizing signal from the clock is received, the clock wheels are automatically disengaged from the driving motor and held motionless until such a signal is received. In this manner the type wheels are retarded every few seconds by a hundredth of a second, and are thereby kept in fairly close agreement with the clock. The signals, the times of which are to be measured, are connected so that they cause a set of hammers to press the paper against the type wheels. It is necessary that the hammers rebound quickly from the paper, so that the record made by the fastest of the type wheels will not be blurred.

There are of course numerous variations of these instruments. The U.S. naval observatory employs a type of printing chronograph which prints a series of small marks instead of figures, and the time to the nearest five-thousandths of a second is read from the position of these marks. The instrument prints eight columns at once. Its printing wheels are not synchronized with a clock, but the clock signals are printed in one of the columns, thus providing a standard for calibrating the readings in the other columns.

All of the instruments thus far described are limited in their accuracy by the fact that they employ moving mechanical parts. A certain time is required for the motion of these parts, and this time varies according to the strength of the electric current which actuates them, as well as from various other causes. The writing chronograph of one pen is basically the best in this respect, since its travel time is eliminated if it is the same on the clock signals and the signals to be measured. Although such instruments are usually read only to the hundredth of a second, by using a sufficiently fast and uniform drive for the paper they could doubtless be made accurate within two or three thousandths of a second. When more than one pen is used, however, an error of several hundredths of a second can easily arise from the variable lags and uncertain relative positions of the different pens. The chronographs which print figures are also subject to similar errors, mostly because of the variable reaction times of the hammers. The fact that the type wheels are usually slightly out of synchronism with the master clock also contributes to this error.

The elimination of the errors which are caused by the moving mechanical parts has been made possible by the use of electron tubes and their associated equipment. These tubes make it possible for very feeble currents to control powerful ones without the use of mechanical relays, and with negligible time delay. Moreover, they have made possible a new type of time keeper, the quartz crystal-controlled oscillator. In this device the vibrating crystal takes the place of the pendulum. Since the frequency of the crystal oscillations is high, a means is provided of dividing the second into small parts. Alternating current of various frequencies may be generated, making it possible to operate synchronous motors in unison with the crystals.

One form of chronograph which may be conveniently driven by a synchronous motor is the *spark chronograph.* This type of device utilizes electric sparks to perforate or mark the recording paper. Ordinary paper may be used, although the record is rendered more legible by the use of waxed or chemically treated paper.

Alfred Loomis of Tuxedo Park, N.Y., constructed such a chronograph for making continuous comparisons of several precision clocks. Roll paper is utilized, moving slowly under a row of 100 electrodes which extend across the paper's width. Wires lead from the electrodes to a distributor which connects them in rotation to the source of the electric spark. The period of rotation of the distributor is one-tenth of a second, so that each electrode is capable of being energized during an interval of one-thousandth of a second. When a clock producing seconds signals is connected to control the sparks, these sparks occur every ten revolutions of the distributor. As long as the chronograph driving motor runs in exact synchronism with the clock, the sparks will always pass through the same one of the electrodes. As a result a straight line of perforations will be produced on the paper. If the signal clock gains or loses with respect to the chronograph mechanism, however, the line of perforations will move diagonally across the paper. Several clocks may be connected to the recorder at the same time. Each clock then produces a line of perforations on the sheet, and the relative inclinations of these lines indicate the relative rates of the clocks. The differences of the times indicated by the various clocks may be read off at any time, so far as the hundredth and thousandth parts of the second are concerned, but the whole seconds and tenths must be otherwise determined.

Later designs of the spark chronograph have eliminated the wiring between the distributor and the spark electrodes. The national bureau of standards has an instrument in which this is accomplished by causing the paper to pass between a metal cylinder, rotating several times per second, and a metal strip or comb. The length of the cylinder is about equal to the width of the paper. The sparks jump from a ridge on the cylinder to the metal strip. The ridge is spiral in shape and extends just one turn around the cylinder. As the cylinder makes each revolution the point on the spiral which is closest to the paper and the metal strip therefore moves across the width of the paper. The records secured are similar to those described.

The U.S. naval observatory developed a *photographic chronograph* which makes use of a flashing gas-filled lamp, and records figures showing the times of signals in minutes, seconds and thousandths. A 1,000-cycle alternating current, controlled by a crystal oscillator, is used to drive a synchronous motor at 10 r.p.s. A dial attached to the motor shaft is engraved from 00 to 99 to indicate the hundredth and thousandth parts of the second. Other slower moving dials are located alongside to show the tenths of seconds, whole seconds and minutes. All of these dials are in a dark box. When signals are received, they cause the flashing lamp to illuminate the figures. A suitable lens

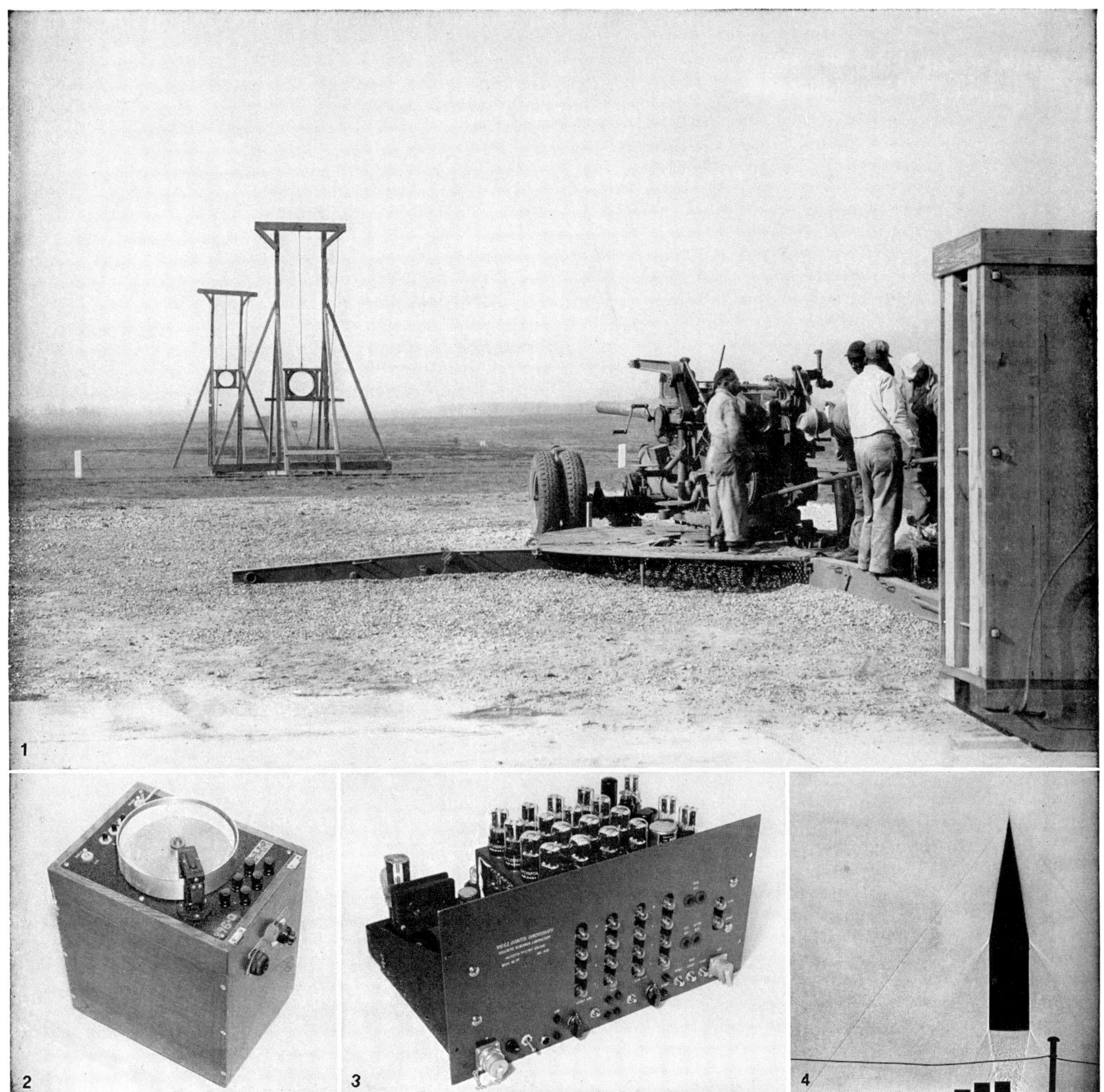

BY COURTESY OF BALLISTIC RESEARCH LABORATORIES, ABERDEEN PROVING GROUND, MD.

1. Solenoid screens on a 100-ft. base line for measuring velocities of projectiles fired at low angles. The wooden frames support wire coils in which signals are generated when the magnetized projectile passes through
2. The Aberdeen chronograph, showing the hollow drum which contains the record paper. Spark points which mark the paper when excited by signals from the screens are mounted under the bracket projecting into the drum
3. An electronic counter chronograph with a capacity of 10,000 counts
4. One of a pair of spark photographs used for determining the successive positions of a projectile in the precise measurement of its velocity. The illuminating spark, which is triggered after a brief time delay by a voltage pulse induced by the projectile on the antenna wire at the left, has a duration of about one-tenth microsecond. The position of the projectile is determined with reference to the notches in the mask along the lower edge of the plate. The time between the two sparks used in making a pair of such plates is measured by a megacycle counter chronograph

forms a reduced image on microfilm. The accuracy of the device is such that the ten-thousandth of a second may be estimated from the position of the figures showing the thousandth of a second, with an error of one or two ten-thousandths. (P. Sr.)

CHRONOLOGY, a time scale, a system of reckoning time massively. In testimony of the social memory and of the classification and exploitation of social experiences embedded therein mankind has learnt to recognize the orderly recurrence of natural phenomena and to base thereon his calendar (*q.v.*).

Astronomy.—Every science has now its chronology. The astronomer reminds us that "looked at in the astronomical time-scale, humanity is at the very beginning of its existence—a new born babe, with all the unexplored potentialities of babyhood" (J. H. Jeans in *Nature,* Supplement [March 1928]); so that the chronology of the astronomer "uses a clock which does not tick seconds but years: its minutes are the lives of men." It tells us "that light travelling 186,000 mi. a second, takes about 140,000,000 years to come to us from the most remote objects visible in the biggest telescope on earth" (*ibid.*).

Geology.—We turn now from chronology of this vastness—to the chronology of this habitable globe, to the time scale of geology (*q.v.*) which is based for its larger divisions on the record of physical events, displaying ice ages, periods of mountain building, of tectonic activity. By the aid of palaeontology, smaller divisions are established: yet here again we deal with vast figures.

Anthropology.—The earth (*q.v.*) must be 2,000,000,000 years old and man from the best evidence now available has existed thereon for something like 300,000 years.[1] Where then—with a 12-in. measure as our scale—shall we place the beginnings of our race? Each division of an inch stands for 160,000,000 years, so we divide the last of our inches of our scale by 50 and there place the first appearance of man. Where shall we place the Piltdown man (*see* Man, Evolution of), or Heidelberg man? Divide one fiftieth of an inch into tenths and mark the fifth of these divisions as the age of Piltdown man.

Archaeology.—Where shall we put the beginnings of the Neolithic age, when agriculture, domestication, settled life, metallurgy all have their beginning? It is so near us that we cannot mark it successfully. We can no longer use our big scale. We must change our scale and take a scale of 12 in. to represent the 300,000 years of man's existence. Each inch stands for 25,000 years and we must place the dawn of what is essential to modern life about halfway in the last or 12th of our inches. Ur and its treasures go to 3500 B.C. or 5,000 years ago and are one fifth of an inch from to-day. Egypt is but a century or two later. The Indus civilization comes next and then that of China. The archaic culture of Central America is 3,000 years old, but by then great empires in the east had waxed and waned and disappeared. Egypt was then old Egypt; and the Greeks like Herodotus were as children in cultural growth.

History.—Again we must change our scale. If we take the Neolithic age as 12,000 years ago, as a basal point (ignoring thereby all the Palaeolithic and Eolithic periods), each inch stands for 1,000 years. The discovery of the new world called America comes half way in the last inch upon this scale and there is so much to cram into the last tenth of the last inch that we are almost tempted to augment our scale once more.

Dynastic Reckoning.—When we come to the great civilizations of antiquity in the valleys of the Euphrates, the Tigris and the Nile or in China, we find established the method of chronological computation by reckoning dynasties of rulers. Social continuity finds its expression and its measure in this development of social organization. But dynasties are human, and disappear. Within the framework of historical chronology we may at will establish periods based on the varying phases and variable elements of human culture. The founders of great religions are remembered in the chronologies of their followers. There are great periods in art, in literature, in science, not inaptly recorded and recollected and concentrated by the names of great individuals. It is still true that the world forgets. The record of their existence and often their deeds are being revealed to us by archaeology (*q.v.*) so that we seem to know more of them and their forerunners than they even knew themselves. Yet in their flourishing days, which by scale of time are so near to us and by scale of culture seem so different, there was behind them a long past, unheeded, ignored, yet potent in their lives as their achievements are still potent in and even essential to our lives. (*See* Calendar.)

[1] Sir A. Keith places the Piltdown skull as of 1,000,000 years ago.

CHINESE

From the time of the emperor Yao, upward of 2,000 years B.C., the Chinese had two different years—a civil year, regulated by the moon, and an astronomical year, which was solar. The civil year consisted in general of 12 months or lunations, but occasionally a 13th was added to preserve its correspondence with the solar year. Even at that early period the solar or astronomical year consisted of $365\frac{1}{4}$ days, like our Julian year, arranged in the same manner, a day being intercalated every fourth year. The civil day begins at midnight and ends at the midnight following.

Since the accession of the emperors of the Han dynasty, 206 B.C., the civil year of the Chinese has begun with the first day of that moon in the course of which the sun enters into the sign of the zodiac which corresponds with our sign Pisces. From the same period also they have employed, in the adjustment of their solar and lunar years, a period of 19 years, 12 of which are common, containing 12 lunations each, and the remaining 7 intercalary, containing 13 lunations. It is not, however, precisely known how they distributed their months of 30 and 29 days, or, as they termed them, great and small moons.

The Chinese divide the time of a complete revolution of the sun with regard to the solstitial points into 12 equal portions, each corresponding to 30 days, 10 hours, 30 minutes. Each of these periods, which is denominated a *tsieh,* is subdivided into two equal portions called *chung-ki* and *tsie-ki,* the *chung-ki* denoting the first half of the *tsieh,* and the *tsie-ki* the latter half. The *tsieh* are thus strictly portions of solar time, and give their name to the lunar months, each month or lunation having the name of the *chung-ki* or sign at which the sun arrives during that month. As the *tsieh* is longer than a synodic revolution of the moon, the sun cannot arrive twice at a *chung-ki* during the same lunation; and as there are only 12 *tsieh,* the year can contain only 12 months having different names. It must happen sometimes that in the course of a lunation the sun enters into no new sign; in this case the month is intercalary, and is called by the same name as the preceding month, with the addition of the word *jun* (intercalary). (X.)

EGYPTIAN

The chronology of Ancient Egypt has been ascertained by means of the statements of classical authors, by regnal years and other indications on the monuments, by the results of close archaeological study, and the ascertaining of certain fixed astronomical data, checked by comparison with the known chronology of the ancient nations which afford synchronisms with events in Egyptian history. The Egyptians never possessed a regular era, as the Assyrians did with their list of *limmu* officials (*see* Babylonia and Assyria). Only once is an era mentioned, in the description of Rameses II, mentioning the 400th year of the Hyksos king (?) Nubti which fell in his reign. We only hear of such and such a regnal year of a king or, in early days, of the years of certain fiscal numberings. Regular regnal annals are very rarely preserved, though we have fragments of them in the Old Kingdom in the Palermo stone, and there is of course the famous *Turin Papyrus of Kings,* which is invaluable even in its mutilated condition. Under the 12th and 22nd dynasties the custom of the association of fathers and sons on the throne enables us to check the chronology of the overlapping years of those periods (as when the 10th year of one king is stated to be the first of another), and so reconstitute the length of the dynasty with some accuracy. The use of synchronisms with Mesopotamian history is evident when we see that the reign of Rameses II is contemporary with that (of certain date) of Shalmaneser I of Assyria (*c.* 1250 B.C.), a datum with which other synchronisms agree. And dates fixed astronomically are of great importance. The Egyptian did not note eclipses as the Mesopotamian did, so that we have not this evidence. But we have the observations of the heliacal risings of the star Sothis (Sirius), which have supplied us with certain fixed dates which are of great importance, the more so as they agree with the results obtained from synchronisms. The Egyptian calendar was regulated by the observations of the heliacal risings of Sirius, which were supposed to take place on the first day of the first month of the year. But as an additional leap year day was not intercalated every four years in addition to the year of 360–5 "epagomenal" days, the months gradually lost all relation to the seasons, and it was not till 1,460 years after the last accurate coincidence that the heliacal rising of Sirius again took place accurately on the first day of the first month. When it did the event was celebrated as the beginning of a new "Sothic cycle." We know that a new cycle began either in 139 or in 143 A.D. An Alexandrian mathematician calls the initial year of the preceding cycle (1321 or 1317 B.C.) the "epoch of Menophres." The "throne-name" of Rameses I., who began to reign, it is known from the synchronism of Rameses II. with Shalmaneser III., about 1320 B.C., is Menpehtira or more shortly Menpehra' (a form that constantly occurs), which is obviously "Menophres." Now it would appear from contemporary evidence that Sothis rose heliacally on the first day of the month Pharmouthi in the seventh year of Senusret III., of the 12th Dynasty; so that it would seem easy to calculate that the seventh year of that king should be 1876 or 1872 B.C. (although another computer [Nicklin] has arrived at the date 1924 B.C. for the same year), on the assumption that this king reigned during the immediately preceding cycle which began in 2781 or 2778 B.C. Here, since synchronisms fail us, our knowledge of the historical development of Egyptian civilization and art comes to our aid to assure us that this must have been so, in spite of the fact that it is very difficult to square the lengthy list of kings given us by the Egyptians themselves with so short an interval as the two hundred years only which, if this conclusion is right, can have elapsed between the end of the 12th Dynasty and the beginning of the 18th. If it is right, the 12th Dynasty must have ended about 1788 B.C., and we know that the 18th cannot have begun later than 1580, from our full knowledge of the length of the reigns of that dynasty, confirmed by records of certain new-moon festivals at the time, as well as by synchronisms. So short is this period that Prof. Sir Flinders Petrie has preferred the view that Senusret and the 12th Dynasty really belong to the preceding cycle, and so go back to the fourth millennium B.C. This view however goes clearly against our archaeological knowledge. The resemblances between the culture of the early 18th Dynasty and the 12th are enough to forbid us to suppose that 1600 years elapsed between them, an epoch as long as that which separates Augustus from Queen Elizabeth. And our knowledge of the development of Minoan civilization (*see* AEGEAN CIVILIZATION) confirms this prohibition. The 12th Dynasty was contemporary with the Second Middle Minoan period; the early 18th with the First Late Minoan period. No student of Minoan archaeology could admit that these two Cretan epochs were separated by more than two or three centuries; 16 is impossible. Yet the fact remains that only two centuries or at the most three between the 12th and the 18th Dynasties are rather hard to accept. Four would seem more probable; and so it remains a moot question whether or not something has happened, some mistake in the observation of the star, or some unrecorded modification of the calendar, which would invalidate the modern calculation of the distance of time between Senusret and Rameses I. If, however, it is maintained that no such mistake is possible, then we must accept 1788 as the latest date of the end of the 12th Dynasty, 1861 B.C., as the earliest. The length of the dynasty we know from its recorded reigns to have been 212 years, so that it began about 2000 B.C. or about a century earlier, unless we choose to allow a little more time for a possible error, and suppose a date for it of *c.* 2212–2000 B.C. Further back we reach a state of great uncertainty. There are no synchronisms and no Sothic records to help us. The length of time between the beginning of the 12th Dynasty and the end of the 6th is unknown, but it cannot have been longer than two or three centuries. The Turin papyrus comes to our help with the statement that 955 years elapsed between the beginning of the 1st Dynasty and the end of the 8th, a statement that agrees with historical and archaeological probability, and if we reckon the latter at about 2400 B.C. we reach 3350 as that of "Menes," the conflate founder of the kingdom (=the historical kings "Scorpion," Narmerza, and "Ahai") (*see* EGYPT: *History; Art*). But Prof. Meyer now takes *c.* 3200 B.C. as the date of "Menes," assuming, as we have not, that the Sothic date of Senusret III. is incontrovertible. We have assumed 2212 as the beginning of the 12th Dynasty, and 2370 as that of the beginning of the 11th. The 8th may well have been contemporary with the 9th and 10th (Herakleopolites) and have lasted until *c.* 2400. If the "Kahun" date is correct, as Meyer assumes, and the end of the 8th dynasty is brought down to 2300, the Sothic cycle that began in 2781 or 2778 B.C. will then have fallen about the time of the 3rd Dynasty. If 2400 is taken as the date it will have fallen as late as the 5th. In either case, the yet earlier cycle-era in 4241 or 4238 B.C. will belong well before the beginning of the kingdom. And it has been supposed that the calendar must have been invented at that time, because the calendar was known before the 4th Dynasty. But the invention of a calendar presupposes a settled state and civilization, not the undeveloped culture of the predynastic period, though we do not know that there did not exist in Lower Egypt before the unification a political state where culture was sufficiently developed for such an invention to be made, and there have been considered to exist indications of the existence of such a state. Still, eight centuries between the invention and the unification under Menes is a very long time for such a hypothetical civilization to have endured apart from the fact that such an invention as a calendar must have occurred at the end of its development rather than its beginning; and recently a suggestion has been made by Dr. Scharff that revolutionizes our ideas on this point. This is that since the older date is so improbable the invention of the calendar in reality took place in 2781–2778 B.C., and since it was known before the time of the 4th Dynasty, this dynasty must in reality be later than that date, so that this Sothic cycle probably began about the time of the 3rd Dynasty. And it is significant that it is precisely in the time of the 3rd Dynasty, in the reign of king Zoser, that the great development of Egyptian culture took place that is ascribed to the inspiration of that king's minister, Imhotep, who was later deified as the patron of art and learning, including medicine, architecture, astronomy and science generally. It is then surmised that the calendar was invented by Imhotep or in his time, and that therefore the date 2781–2778 falls in the reign of Zoser. Now if this new surmise is correct, the 1st Dynasty will have begun rather later than 3200 B.C., and then the end of the 8th Dynasty will certainly fall about 2300. But in this case we shall have to assume the astronomically calculated "Kahun" date of Senusret III. to be unquestionably correct, as Meyer does, and must accept two centuries only between the 12th Dynasty and the 18th, in spite of the long Turin list of kings of this period, who then must have been mostly very ephemeral rulers. In any case the ancient list-compilers were evidently as much at sea in the two "intermediate" periods (6th–12th and 12th–18th Dynasties), as we are, for they suffered from absence of reliable material just as we do.

In later days, after the time of Rameses II., we have various data to help us. The date of Sheshonk (Shishak), the contemporary of Rehoboam and founder of the 22nd Dynasty, is fixed to *c.* 930 B.C. by Assyrian and biblical evidence, and for the Ethiopian kings, Shabak, Taharka and the rest, we have the fixed synchronisms with Assyrian kings whose dates are fixed by the *limmu*-lists. From the time of Psammetichus I., the founder of the 26th Dynasty, Babylonian and Greek authorities assist us, and his date is definitely known to be 663 (651 independent of Assyria)–609 B.C. After him we are dealing with the known facts of general ancient history as reported by the classical historians.

BIBLIOGRAPHY.—E. Meyer, *Die ältere Chronologie Babyloniens, Assyriens u. Aegyptens* (1925), *Aegyptische Chronologie, Bbh. Berlin Acad.* (1904), *Nachfrage zur äg. Chr., do.* (1907); T. Nicklin, "The Origin of the Egyptian Year," *Class. Rev.* 1900, pp. 146–148; H. R. Hall, *Anc. Hist. Near East* (1924), p. 15 ff. Cambr. Anc. Hist. i. p. 166 ff; Scharff, *Grundzüge d. Aegyptische Vorgeschichte* (1927), p. 46 ff; "Beitrag zur Chronologie der 4ten Aegyptischen Dynastie," *Orientalische Litterarische Zeitung* (1928) p. 73 ff. (H. R. H.)

BABYLONIAN AND ASSYRIAN

Evidence of Babylonian documents, from 330 B.C. onward, dated by kings' regnal years has settled many points in relation to the chronology of late as well as of early periods, though this evidence has been much discussed and often wrongly represented. It is now fairly clear that the era of the Arsacid dynasty was reckoned from 1st Nisan, 246, and that apparent divergences from this reckoning depend on ancient scribal errors or modern errors of interpretation. The Seleucid era was reckoned from 1st Nisan 311. There was no difference between "civil" and "religious" reckoning, as has sometimes been maintained. The reckoning of the Seleucid era from 311 B.C. must have been introduced in or before 305 B.C.; the years before that were actually spent by the Babylonians in a state of confusion as to dating which was introduced with the advent of Alexander the Great. The confusion was due in part to the use of two systems; in one reckoning, the year dates according to the Macedonians was used, in another a dating strictly true of Babylon only, but this will not explain every case. The effect of this may be seen from the following list:—

Year	King	Numbering (a)	Numbering (b)
330-329	Alexander the Great	7th	1st
323-322	Philip Arrhidaeus	2nd	1st
317-316	Alexander IV	.	1st
316-315	Antigonus	1st	2nd

The exact method of dating between 311 and 305 is not certain; a broken document renders it possible that 311 was called "the seventh year of Alexander and Seleucus," *i.e.,* that Seleucus associated his name with the king's for the first time, and that would account for the Babylonian reckoning of the Seleucid era. It should be noted that from the advent of Alexander the year reckoning commenced immediately from the accession of the king.

From 626 B.C.–331 B.C.—The ordinary Babylonian reckoning of regnal years, always observed before the Macedonian invasion, was from the 1st Nisan after a king's accession; months or days prior to Nisan were reckoned "beginning of kingship." There are two sources for the chronology of the New Babylonian and Persian empires, the canon of the Greek historian Ptolemy, and the reckoning which can be traced almost month by month and day by day; the tablets give names of rebels against the Persian kings otherwise unknown, and allow of more accuracy in dating, *e.g.,* the coregency of Cambyses to the first year only of his father's reign.

New Babylonian Empire	Accession	1st full year
Nabopolassar	626	625
Nebuchadrezzar II	605	604
Evil-Merodach	562	561
Neriglissar	560	559
Labashi-Marduk	556	
Nabu-na'id	...	555
Persian Empire.		
Cyrus	539	538
Cambyses	...	529
"Smerdis," Nebuchadrezzar III	...	522
Darius I	522	521
Xerxes I	486	485
Artaxerxes I	465	464
Darius II	...	423
Artaxerxes II	...	404
Artaxerxes III (Ochus)	...	358
Arses	...	337
Darius III	...	335

Between 648 and 626 B.C.—The dating of the New Babylonian empire secures the long uncertain dating of the fall of Nineveh; a chronicle, dating by the regnal years of Nabopolassar, places that event in 612 B.C. The period from 648 to 626, the accession year of Nabopolassar, is still very obscure; the statements of Ptolemy's canon cannot exactly accord with the facts. Dating by Sin-sharishkun, the last king of Assyria up to the 7th year has been found at Sippar; since this year must at latest be 616, his first full year must at latest be 622. A certain Sin-shum-lishir, intervened between Assur-etil-ilani, who reigned at least four years, and Sin-sharishkun, so that reckoning by Ashur-etil-ilani commenced in 627 at latest. Between 648 and 626 documents were dated by Kandalanu, the Kineladan of Ptolemy's canon; that this was a name assumed by Assur-bani-pal as king of Babylon is doubtful, as there are good grounds for assuming that cuneiform scribes distinguished between the two. But since a building inscription dating from Assur-bani-pal's 30th year has been found in Babylon, *i.e.,* 639 B.C., the Assyrian must have claimed the kingship also.

From 911–648 B.C.—Assyrian chronology depends on lists of eponymous officials called *limmu,* by whom years were dated. These lists were drawn up in two ways; the first class consists of simple lists of names, the second gives in a column opposite the name an entry concerning the events of the year. An entry opposite the name Pur-Sagale reads, "Governor of Gozan. Revolt in the city of Ashur. In Siwan there was an eclipse of the sun," and this eclipse has been astronomically fixed as having taken place on June 15, 763 B.C. This fixes the years of all *limmus* in the continuous list which reaches from 890–648. There are discrepant versions of these *limmu* lists which affect the reigns of Adad-nirari III and Shalmaneser III; these kings are allowed 29 or 28 and 35 or 34 eponyms to their reign. The weight of authority seems to lie with the lower numbers, but the question is not definitely settled; otherwise the Assyrian chronology of the period is fixed.

The Babylonian chronology of the time is less certain. Ptolemy's canon and cuneiform documents give the regnal years from Nabonassar's first year, 747 B.C. The belief that some kind of era commenced then is baseless; it was chosen by Ptolemy for some accidental reason, perhaps because that was the first fixed point that was known to him, but not for any scientific reason. Before Nabonassar, the continuous king-list is now known to have included between Shamash-mudammiq, who was reigning about 910 B.C., and Nabonassar 16 names, an average of about 10 years apiece, but the exact lengths of reigns cannot yet be ascertained.

Babylonia		*Assyria*	
Shamash-mudammiq, abt.	910	Adad-nirari II	911–889
Nabu-shum-ukin		Tukulti-Enurta II	889–884
Nabu-apal-iddin	?–851	Assur-nasir-pal II	884–859
Marduk-bel-usate	851–850	Shalmaneser III	859–824
Marduk-zakir-shum	850–839		
Marduk-balatsu-iqbi	?–811		
Bau-akh-iddin	810	Shamshi-Adad V	824–812
(Five names missing including Adad-shum-ibni)		Adad-nirari III	811–782
Marduk-bel-zeri			
Marduk-apal-usur		Shalmaneser IV	782–772
Eriba-Marduk		Assur-dan III	772–754
Nabu-shum-ukin		Ashur-nirari V	754–745
Nabonassar	747–732	Tiglathpileser III	745–727
Nabu-nadin-zer	733–732		
Nabu-shum-ukin	732		
Ukin-zer	731		
Pulu (-T.-P.III)	731–727	Shalmaneser V	726–722
Ululai	726–722	Sargon II	722–705
Merodachbaladan II	721–710		
Sargon	709–705	Sennacherib	705–681
Sennacherib	705–703		
Merodachbaladan III	703–702		
Bel-ibni	702–700		
Assur-nadin-sum	699–694		
Nergal-ushezib	693–692		
Mushezib-Marduk	692–689		
Sennacherib	688–681		
Esar-haddon	680–669	Esar-haddon	680–669
Shamash-shum-ukin	668–648		
Kandalanu	647–626	Assur-bani-pal	668–638 (?)

From About 1380–911 B.C.—There are broken *limmu* lists which once gave the eponymous officials from about 1200 B.C.; in their present state they give a framework for the Assyrian kings from about 1068–911, the margin of error within which is not more than ten years. Complete king-lists for Assyria being now obtained from broken documents, approximate dates for the kings of the 13th century can be based on intervals sometimes mentioned between them and later kings. The approximate date of Ashur-uballit can be determined from his correspondence with Akhnaton, the Pharaoh of Egypt, with a marginal error of ten years, as about 1380.

Babylonian chronology depends upon the cases where the number of years are known, and on synchronisms with the Assyrian kings. The result can only be an approximation with a margin of error perhaps exceeding a decade. The arrangement is then roughly:—

Babylonia	*Assyria*	
Burnaburiash	Ashur-uballit . .	1380–1335
Karaindash		
Kadashman-kharbe		
Shuzigash		
Kurigalzu III. (23 years)	Enlil-nirari . . .	1335–
	Arik-den-ili . . .	–1311
Nazimaruttash (26 years)	Adad-nirari I. . .	1310–1280
Kadashman-turgu (17 years)	Shalmaneser I. . .	1280–1250
Kadashman-Enlil (6 years)		
Kudur-Enlil (9 years)		
Shagarakti-shuriash (13 years)	Tukulti-Enurta I. .	1250–1216
Kashtiliash (8 years)		
Enlil-nadin-shum ($1\frac{1}{2}$ years)		
Kadashman-Kharbe ($1\frac{1}{2}$ years)		
Adad-shum-iddin (6 years)		
Adad-shum-nasir (30 years)	Ashur-nadin-apal .	1215–1212
	Ashur-nirari III. . .	1211–1206
	Enlil-kudur-usur .	1205–1201
Meli-shipak (15 years)	Enurta-apal-ekur .	1200–1188
Merodachbaladan I. (13 years)	Ashur-dan I. . .	1187–1150
Ilbaba-shum-iddin (6 years)		
Enlil-nadin-akhkhe (3 years)		
Marduk-shapik-zeri (17 years)		
Enurta-nadin-shum (6 years)		
Nebuchadrezzar I.	Enurta-tukulti-Ashur	
	Mutakkil-Nusku	
Enlil-nadin-apal	Ashur-resh-ishi I. .	?–1099
Marduk-nadin-akhkhe	Tiglathpileser I. . .	1098–1068
Itti-Marduk-balatu	Enurta-apal-ekur II .	1067–
Marduk-shapik-zer-mati	Ashur-bel-kala	
Adad-apal-iddin (22 years)	Eriba-Adad II.	
	Shamshi-Adad IV. .	–1048
Marduk-akhkhe-eriba ($1\frac{1}{2}$ years)	Ashurnasirpal I. . .	1047–1027
Marduk-zer (12 years)	Shalmaneser II. . .	1026–1015
Nabu-shum-libur (8 years)	Ashur-nirari V. . .	1014–1009
Simmash-Shipak (18 years)	Ashur-rabi II. . .	1008–?
Ea-mukin-zer (5 months)		
Kashshu-nadin-akhkhe (3 years)		
Eulmash-shakin-shum (17 years)		
Enurta-kudur-usur (3 years)		
Shiriqtum-Shuqamuna (3 mos.)		
Marbiti-apal-usur (6 years)		
Nabu-mukin-apal (36 years)	Ashur-resh-ishi II. . .	?–964
Enurta-kudur-usur	Tiglathpileser II. . .	963–933
Marbiti-akh-iddin	Ashur-dan II. . . .	932–912

Before 1380 B.C.—All earlier chronology must be subject to considerable margin of error. It depends on (1) Babylonian king-lists which give the number of regnal years; in many instances, where these figures can be checked by other sources, they are proved unreliable; (2) statements of Assyrian kings about their predecessors; the figures given are sometimes round numbers, and are never absolutely reliable; (3) dead reckoning on the basis of generations, coupled with the use of the rare synchronisms known between the two countries.

The Babylonian king-list allows 36 kings, and 576 years 9 months for the period during which the country was ruled by Kassite kings. Enlil-nadin-akhkhe, the last of the dynasty, succeeded to the throne in the time of Ashur-dan I., roughly about 1170, within a decade, and ruled three years: this would place Gandash, the first king, about 1743–42, but an increased margin of error must be allowed owing to the inaccuracy of the list. The 13th Kassite king, Ulam-Buriash, may have ruled about 1530–20; he occupied the Sea-land, the marshes at the head of the Persian gulf, when the last independent king of the Sea-land fled to Elam. This Sea-land dynasty numbered, according to variant accounts, 11 or 12 kings, who ruled for the long period of 368 years, which would place Iluma-ilum, the first king, about 1900 B.C., if the last king fled just before 1530. But Iluma-ilum can be proved by various documents to be a contemporary of Samsu-iluna and Abi-eshu', kings of the 1st dynasty of Babylon. Iluma-ilum is said to have reigned 60 years, and Samsu-iluna and Abi-eshu' reigned respectively 38 and 28; it is not probable that Samsu-iluna began to reign before Iluma-ilum, and if he be assigned a date about 1900–1863, the end of the 1st dynasty is brought to about 1746, almost immediately before the accession of the first Kassite king. This cross-reckoning is satisfactory in itself and supported by the Assyrian king-list. There were 42 kings between Ilushuma, an early governor of Ashur, and Ashur-uballit, about 1380. According to kings' statements Ilushuma lived about 2000 B.C., and this accords roughly with other statements about his son. It is certain from an entry in a chronicle that Ilushuma carried out some military enterprise in Babylonia in the time of Sumu-abu, the first king of the 1st dynasty. If the 1st dynasty ended about 1746–45, the first king dated about 2045–44 to 2032–31. This would accord with the Assyrian statements.

Some modern authorities hold that a fixed dating, not based on the king-lists, can be secured from tablets dealing with observations of Venus. From an entry for the sixth year of Ammizaduga they calculate certain astronomical possibilities, and check the date obtained—one out of four or five possible—by calculations as to the probable period of the date-harvest. Arguing on these lines they hold the sixth year of Ammizaduga to be 1916–15, which would place the commencement of the 1st dynasty in 2170, its close in 1871; another, arguing on the same lines, would date these events 2049–1750. The former, if correct, will necessitate the abandonment of a great deal of Babylonian historical writing as worthless; the question is at present open, and scholars differ by some 120 to 130 years for this period.

Accepting the dating 2045–1745, admittedly open to a margin of error, for the 1st dynasty as fairly accurate, the date lists for the kings' reigns provide an accurate scheme which correct the king-lists in many places. These date-lists arose from the custom of naming a year by some event; in some cases the event was one of religious importance, and may actually have taken place in the year so named, but where military campaigns are mentioned the event probably belongs to the previous year. These date lists establish a synchronism between Hammurabi and Rim-Sin which leads to a date about 2175 for the commencement of the rival dynasties of Isin and Larsa, subject to an error not greater than the date given for the 1st dynasty. Similarly, the 3rd dynasty of Ur of which date-lists are extant may be dated 2282-2175 with the same error. Probably less than seven years actually passed between the accession of Utu-khegal, who ended the oppression by the foreign dynasty of Gutium, and Ur-Nammu's assumption of sovereignty in 2282; this places the Gutium dynasty about 2375–2287, with an increased margin of error. Dating earlier than this is a matter of speculation, for the king-lists, which are complete, give figures that cannot be checked, and for earlier dynasties quite impossible reigns are assigned. There is a general probability that Sargon of Agade commenced his reign between 2550 and 2525, and that the 4th dynasty of Kish began to rule not earlier than 2580. An estimate for the 1st dynasty of Ur, the third after the Flood, based upon comparison with objects from Lagash and the generations, would assign a date between 3000 and 2900 for the commencement of that dynasty, the earliest historical kings known belonging to it. (S. Sm.)

Bibliography.—F. X. Kugler, *Sternkunde und Sterndienst in Babel* (1914–24); *Cambridge Ancient History*, vols. i. and ii. (1923–24; bibl.); Sidney Smith, *Early History of Assyria* (1928; bibl.).

HINDU

The early Hindu astronomers selected a period in the course of which a given order of things is completed by the sun, moon and planets returning to the state of conjunction from which they started. This is known as the Great age of 4,320,000 sidereal solar years, the aggregate of the *Krita* or Golden age, the *Trēta* or Silver age, the *Dvāpara* or Brazen age, and the *Kali* or Iron age (in which we now are). There is, however, the system of the *Kalpa* or aeon, consisting of 1,000 (or 1,008) Great ages.

The Hindus now recognize three standard sidereal solar years determined in that manner. (1) A year of 365 days 6 hours 12 min. 30 sec. according to the *Āryabhaṭīya,* otherwise called the *First Ārya-Siddhānta,* which was written by the astronomer Āryabhaṭa (b. A.D. 476); this year is used in the Tamil and Malayāḷam districts, and in Ceylon. (2) A year of 365 days 6 hours 12 min. 30·915 sec. according to the *Rājamṛigā ka,* a treatise based on the *Brāhma-Siddhānta* of Brahmagupta (b. A.D. 598) and attributed to king Bhōja, of which the epoch, the point of time used in it for calculations, falls in A.D. 1042: this year is used in parts of Gujarāt (Bombay) and in Rājputānā and other western parts of Northern India. (3) A year of 365 days 6 hours 12 min. 36·56 sec. according to the present *Sūrya-Siddhānta,* a work of unknown authorship which dates from probably about A.D. 1000: this year is used in almost all the other parts of India. According to modern science, the true mean sidereal solar year measures 365 days 6 hours 9 min. 9·6 sec., and the mean tropical year measures 365 days 5 hours 48 min. 46·054440 seconds.

The result of the use of this sidereal solar year is that the beginning of the Hindu astronomical solar year, and with it the civil solar year and the lunar year and the nominal incidence of the seasons, has always been, and still is, travelling slowly forward in our calendar year by an amount which varies according to the particular authority. For instance, Āryabhaṭa's year exceeds the Julian year by 12 min. 30 seconds. This amounts to exactly one day in 115⅕ years, and five days in 576 years. Thus, if we take the longer period and confine ourselves to a time when the Julian calendar (old style) was in use, according to Āryabhaṭa the Mēsha-saṁkrānti began to occur in A.D. 603 on March 20 and in A.D. 1179 on March 25. The intermediate advances arrange themselves into four steps of one day each in 116 years, followed by one step of one day in 112 years: thus, the Mēsha-saṁkrānti began to occur on March 21 in A.D. 719, on March 22 in A.D. 835, on March 23 in A.D. 951, and on March 24 in A.D. 1067 (whence 112 years take us to March 25 in A.D. 1179). It is now occurring sometimes on April 11, sometimes on the 12th; having first come to the 12th in A.D. 1871. (*See* CALENDAR: *Hindu.*)

Eras.—The Kalachuri or Chēdi era, commencing in A.D. 248 or 249, is known best from inscriptional records, which range from the 10th to the 13th century A.D., of the Kalachuri kings of the Chēdi country in Central India; and from them it derived its name. In earlier times, this era was well established, without any appellation, in Western India, in Gujarāt and the Ṭhāṇa district of Bombay, where it was used by kings and princes of the Chalukya, Gurjara, Sēndraka, Kaṭachchuri and Traikūṭaka families. It is traced back there to A.D. 457, to the reign of a Traikūṭaka king named Dahrasēna. Beyond that point, we have at present no certain knowledge about it. But it seems probable that its founder was an Ābhīra king Īśvarasēna, or his father Śivadatta, who was reigning at Nāsik about A.D. 248–249.

The Gupta era, commencing in A.D. 320, was founded by Chandragupta I., the first paramount king in the great Gupta dynasty of Northern India. When the Guptas passed away, their reckoning was taken over by the Maitraka kings of Valabhī, who succeeded them in Kāṭhiāwār and some of the neighbouring territories; and so it became also known as the Valabhī era.

From Halsī in the Belgaum district, Bombay, we have a record of the Kadamba king Kākusthavarman, which was framed during the time when he was the Yuvarāja or anointed successor to the sovereignty, and may be referred to about A.D. 500. It is dated in "the eightieth victorious year," and thus indicates the preservation of a reckoning running from the foundation of the Kadamba dynasty by Mayūravarman, the great-grandfather of Kākusthavarman. But no other evidence of the existence of this era has been obtained.

The records of the Gāṅga kings of Kaliṅganagara, which is the modern Mukhaliṅgam-Nagarikaṭakam in the Gañjām district, Madras, show the existence of a Gāṅga era, which ran for at any rate 254 years. And various details in the inscriptions enable us to trace the origin of the Gāṅga kings to Western India, and to place the initial point of their reckoning in A.D. 590, when a certain Satyāśraya-Dhruvarāja-Indravarman, an ancestor and probably the grandfather of the first Gāṅga king Rājasiṁha-Indravarman I., commenced to govern a large province in the Koṅkaṇ under the Chalukya king Kīrtivarman I.

An era beginning in A.D. 605 or 606 was founded in Northern India by the great king Harshavardhana, who reigned first at Ṭhāṇēsar and then at Kanauj, and who was the third sovereign in a dynasty which traced its origin to a prince named Naravardhana. This era continued in use for apparently four centuries after Harshavardhana, though his line ended with him.

The inscriptions assert that the Western Chālukya king Vikrama or Vikramāditya VI. of Kalyāṇi in the Nizam's dominions, who reigned from A.D. 1076 to 1126, abolished the use of the Śaka era in his dominions in favour of an era named after himself. He or his ministers adopted, for the first time in that dynasty, the system of regnal years, according to which, while the Śaka era also remained in use, most of the records of his time are dated, not in that era, but in the year so-and-so of the Chālukya-Vikrama-kāla or Chālukya-Vikrama-varsha, "the time or years of the Chālukya Vikrama." There is some evidence that this reckoning survived Vikramāditya VI. for a short time. But his successors introduced their own regnal reckonings; and that prevented it from acquiring permanence.

In Tirhut, there is still used a reckoning which is known as the Lakshmaṇasēna era from the name of the king of Bengal by whom it was founded. The exact initial point of this reckoning appears to be in A.D. 1119. This era prevailed at one time throughout Bengal, from a passage in the *Akbarnāma,* written in A.D. 1584, which specifies the Śaka era as the reckoning of Gujarāt and the Dekkan, the Vikrama era as the reckoning of Mālwā, Delhi and those parts, and the Lakshmaṇasēna era as the reckoning of Bengal.

The Rājyābhishēka-Śaka, "the era of the anointment to the sovereignty," was in use for a time in Western India. It dated from the day Jyaishṭha śukla 13 of the Śaka year of 1597 current, =June 6, A.D. 1674, when Śivajī, the founder of the Marāṭhā kingdom, had himself enthroned.

There are four reckonings which it is difficult at present to class exactly. Two inscriptions of the 15th and 17th centuries, recently brought to notice from Jēsalmēr in Rājputānā, present a reckoning which postulates an initial point in A.D. 624 or in the preceding or the following year, and bears an appellation, Bhāṭika, which seems to be based on the name of the Bhaṭṭi tribe, to which the rulers of Jēsalmēr belong. No historical event is known, referable to that time, which can have given rise to an era. It is possible that the apparent initial date represents an epoch, at the end of the Śaka year 546 or thereabouts, laid down in some astronomical work composed then or soon afterwards and used in the Jēsalmēr territory. But it seems more probable that it is a purely fictitious date, set up by an attempt to evolve an early history of the ruling family.

In the Tinnevelly district of Madras, and in the territories of the same presidency in which the Malayāḷam language prevails, namely, South Kanara below Mangalore, the Malabar district, and the Cochin and Travancore States, there is used a reckoning which is known sometimes as the Kollam or Kōlamba reckoning, sometimes as the era of Paraśurāma. The years of it are solar: in the southern parts of the territory in which it is current, they begin with the month Siṁha; in the northern parts, they begin with the next month, Kanyā. The initial point of the reckoning is in A.D. 825; and the year 1076 commenced in A.D. 1900. The popular view about this reckoning is that it consists of cycles of 1,000 years; that we are now in the fourth cycle; and that the reckoning originated in 1176 B.C. with the mythical Paraśurāma, who exterminated the Kshatriya or warrior caste, and reclaimed the Koṅkaṇ countries, Western India below the Ghauts, from the ocean. But the earliest known date in it, of the year 149, falls in A.D. 973; and the reckoning has run on in continuation of the thousand, instead of beginning afresh in A.D. 1825. It seems probable, therefore, that the reckoning had no existence before A.D. 825. The years are cited sometimes as "the Kollam year (of such-and-such a number)," sometimes as "the year (so-and-so) after Kollam appeared"; and this suggests that the reckoning may possibly owe its origin to some event occurring in A.D. 825, connected with one or other of the towns and ports named Kollam, on the Malabar coast; perhaps Northern Kollam in the Malabar district, perhaps Southern Kollam, better known as Quilon, in Travancore. But the introduction of Paraśurāma into the matter, which would carry back (let us say) the foundation of Kollam to legendary times, may indicate, rather, a purely imaginative origin. Or, again, since each century of the Kollam reckoning begins in the same year A.D. with a century of the Saptarshi reckoning, this reckoning may be a southern offshoot of the Saptarshi reckoning, or at least may have had the same astrological origin.

In Nēpāl there is a reckoning, known as the Nēwār era and commencing in A.D. 879, which superseded the Gupta and Harsha eras there. One tradition attributes the foundation of it to a king Rāghavadēva; another says that, in the time and with the permission of a king Jayadēvamalla, a merchant named Sākhwāl paid off, by means of wealth acquired from sand which turned into gold, all the debts then existing in the country, and introduced the new era in commemoration of the occurrence. The era may have been founded by some ruler of Nēpāl: but nothing authentic is known about the particular names mentioned in connection with it. This era appears to have been discarded for State and official purposes, in favour of the Śaka era, in A.D. 1768, when the Gūrkhas became masters of Nēpāl; but manuscripts show that in literary circles it has remained in use up to at any rate A.D. 1875.

Inscriptions disclose the use in Kāṭhiāwār and Gujarāt, in the 12th and 13th centuries, of a reckoning, commencing in A.D. 1114, which is known as the *Simha-samvat*. No historical occurrence is known, on which it can have been based, and the origin of it is obscure.

The eras mentioned above have for the most part served their purposes and died out. But there are three great reckonings, dating from a very respectable antiquity, which have held their own and survived to the present day. These are the Kaliyuga, Vikrama and Śaka eras. The Kaliyuga era is the principal astronomical reckoning of the Hindus. It is frequently, if not generally, shown in the almanacs: but it is not now in practical use for civil purposes; and in previous times we have instances of its use in inscriptions from Southern India, one of A.D. 634, one of A.D. 770, three of the 10th century, and then, from the 12th century onwards, but more particularly from the 14th, a certain number of instances extremely small in comparison with the use of the Vikrama and Śaka eras and other reckonings: from Northern India the earliest known instance is A.D. 1169 or 1170, and the later ones number only four. Its years are by nature sidereal solar years, commencing with the Mēsha-samkrānti, the entrance of the sun into the Hindu constellation and sign Mēsha, *i.e.*, Aries (for this and other technical details, *see* above, under the Calendar); but they were probably cited as lunar years in the inscriptional records which present the reckoning; and the almanacs appear to treat them either as Mēshādi civil solar years with solar months, or as Chaitrādi lunar years with lunar months *amānta* (ending with the new-moon) or *pūrṇimānta* (ending with the full-moon) as the case may be, according to the locality. Its initial point lay in 3102 B.C.; and the year 5002 began in A.D. 1900.

The Vikrama Era, the earliest of all the Hindu eras, is the dominant era and the great historical reckoning of Northern India—that territory on the north of the rivers Narbadā and Mahānadī to which part of the country its use has always been practically confined. Like, indeed, the Kaliyuga and Śaka eras, it is freely cited in almanacs in any part of India; and it is sometimes used in the south by immigrants from the north: but it is, by nature, so essentially foreign to the south that the earliest known inscriptional instance of the use of it in Southern India only dates from A.D. 1218, and the very few later instances, prior to the 15th century A.D., come, along with that of A.D. 1218, from the close neighbourhood of the dividing-line between the north and the south. The Vikrama era has never been used for astronomical purposes. Its years are lunar, with lunar months, though sometimes regarded as solar, with solar months, when cited in almanacs of Southern India which present the solar calendar. Originally they were Kārttikādi, with *pūrṇimānta* months (ending with the full-moon). They now exist in the following three varieties: in Kāṭhiāwār and Gujarāt, they are chiefly Kārttikādi, with *amānta* months (ending with the new-moon); and they are shown in this form in almanacs for the other parts of the Bombay Presidency: but there is also found in Kāṭhiāwār and that neighbourhood an Āshāḍhādi variety, commencing with *Āshāḍha śukla* 1, similarly with *amānta* months; in the rest of Northern India, they are Chaitrādi, with *pūrṇimānta* months. The era has its initial point in 58 B.C., and its first civil day, *Kārttika śukla 1,* is Sept. 19, in that year if we determine it with reference to the Hindu Tulā-samkrānti, or October 18, if we determine it with reference to the tropical equinox. The years of the three varieties, Chaitrādi, Āshāḍhādi and Kārttikādi, all commence in the same year A.D.; and the year 1958 began in A.D. 1900.

The Śaka Era, which had its origin in the south-west corner of Northern India, is the dominant era and the great historical reckoning of Southern India. It is also the subsidiary astronomical reckoning, largely used, from the 6th century A.D. onwards, in the *Karaṇas,* the works dealing with practical details of the calendar, for laying down epochs or points of time furnishing convenient bases for computation. As a result of that, it came to be used in past times for general purposes also, to a limited extent, in parts of Northern India. And it is now used more or less freely, and is cited in almanacs everywhere. Its years are usually lunar, Chaitrādi, and its months are *pūrṇimānta* (ending with the full-moon) in Northern India, and *amānta* (ending with the new-moon) in Southern India; but in times gone by it was sometimes treated for purposes of calculation as having astronomical solar years, and it is now treated as having Mēshādi civil solar years and solar months in those parts of India where that form of the solar calendar prevails. It has its initial point in A.D. 78; and its first civil day, *Chaitra śukla* 1, is March 3 in that year, as determined with reference either to the Hindu *Masanikrānti* or to the entrance of the sun into the tropical Pisces. The year 1823 began in A.D. 1900. (X.)

GREEK

The difficulty besetting Greek chronology, for ancient and modern investigators alike, is the absence, for the earlier periods especially, of a universally understood era, corresponding to our reckoning, B.C. or A.D., or the Muslim, dating from the Hejira. Generally speaking, each state had its own fashion of dating, the usual method of specifying time being to name the annual magistrate who was then in office, as "in the archonship of Apsephion," or a king, priest etc., as "in the reign of King Agis," "in the third year of such a one's tenure of office as priestess of Hera at Argos." This had the grave disadvantage that unless a list of the functionaries in question was available, the date was unintelligible. Hence the best-known of them, the Athenian archons, were most commonly referred to, and often several parallel dates were given, as "when Chrysis had been priestess at Argos for 47 years, Aenesuis being then ephor at Sparta, Pythodorus having yet four months left of his archonship at Athens" (Thucydides, ii.,2,1; =April, 431 B.C.).

Dating by Olympiads.—Gradually, however, the system of dating by Olympiads came into use; this was much more convenient, for the successive celebrations of the festival at Olympia were numbered, not merely named, and the date of the first was conventionally fixed at 776 B.C. of our reckoning. This is due largely to the Alexandrian chronologists, Eratosthenes and the rest, who also drew up the received list of Olympiads. There remained, however, a further difficulty, viz., that various Greek civic years started at different times (*see* CALENDAR: *Greek*); hence there was often used a conventional Olympiad, beginning at the Attic new year, the summer solstice.

The diligence of the Alexandrians resulted in a fairly satisfactory chronology being drawn up for the fully historical periods, *i.e.*, back to about 600 B.C.; from about 500 onwards the number of dates which are seriously doubtful, where the ancient evidence survives, is comparatively small, although minor divergencies are common. But for earlier times, and especially before the beginning of the series of Olympiads (itself not very dependable until Olymp. 50), even the ancient investigators had but few documents to go upon, and were obliged to trust largely to genealogies. By comparing these, they made out a pre-historic and proto-historic chronology, arrived at by allowing three generations to a century. Supposing the genealogies to be authentic and complete, this was a tolerably accurate method; but, although they contained a large element of real tradition, we know enough of them to be sure that they were often interpolated, telescoped by the omission of obscure persons, and otherwise corrupted; so that the earlier dates, such as that of the fall of Troy, must be taken as being, at best, very rough approximations.

The ancient chronologists are represented, for us, by a few historians, such as Diodorus of Sicily, who adopt the annalistic method, and by the Christian chronologists, such as Eusebius and his Latin translator and continuator, S. Jerome, also by later writers, such as Iulius Africanus and Georgius Syncellus. The desire of apologists to prove the Biblical revelation earlier than any other led to the prominence of this branch of learning among them, and to the creation of a new, Hebraizing chronology, made by combining the existing systems with data from the Old Testament. Although uncritical and biased, these writers are of immense value to modern historians of antiquity.

Contribution of Archaeology.—Further help is given by the results of modern archaeology. By careful and minute study of the details of artistic technique, the stratification of material remains of all sorts, the styles of pottery, coins, and other common objects, and comparison with the comparatively few pieces which are in some way dated (*e.g.*, by bearing the name of an owner or dedicator whose epoch is accurately known) it is possible, not only to determine often within a few years and not infrequently with much greater exactness the date of objects found, but also by working backwards to come to reasonable conclusions as to the epoch of many events long previous to documentary history, whereof only vague accounts, largely mythological, had come down to us. Thus, the stratification of the seven cities at Hissarlik, the ancient Troy, has given us a relative chronology, or order of events, for the history of that place; while careful comparison of the finds there with those from Cretan and Mycenaean sites, and of these again with certain Egyptian and other documents which can be at least approximately dated, is gradually enabling us to fix, at any rate within a century or so, the absolute date of Agamemnon's expedition. But at present such dates must be largely provisional, and subject to revision, sometimes of a sweeping kind, in the light of further discoveries. For instance, there are differences of some four centuries in the dating of the Dorian invasion, and even doubts as to its historicity.

It is usual, in giving an ancient date, to extend the Julian period backwards and speak, for instance, of March 2, 290 B.C., meaning the day which would have been so styled if the Greeks of that time had had our calendar and could have foreseen when our era would begin. As these imaginary Julian years frequently cut across the real Greek ones, it is best, when the year only is given, to use a double date and say, for instance, 501/500 B.C.

In dealing with events in late Greek history (Roman and Byzantine epochs) we frequently find non-Greek systems used, such as the Julian calendar. For these, *see* under *Roman Chronology*.

The most important ancient works are cited in the text. For modern authorities, *see* CALENDAR: *Greek*; GREECE: *History; Ancient to 146 B.C.: General*. Of modern writers, Clinton (*Fasti Hellenici*, 3 vols., 1834) is still useful, although needing much correction in detail.

ROMAN

Roman chronology was in antiquity wholly dependent upon Greek methods, and hence suffered from all the drawbacks of the latter (*see* above, *Greek*), together with a further one, viz., the scarcity and untrustworthiness of native documents. Working along the lines of the Alexandrians, several Roman scholars, notably Varro and Atticus (the friend of Cicero) arrived at chronological schemes for the early history of Rome, whereof considerable fragments have come down to us in the various historians and antiquarians whose works survive, in lists of magistrates such as the fragmentary Fasti Capitolini, and in S. Jerome's chronicle. They are without exception highly untrustworthy for the regal period and the earlier centuries of the Republic (*see* ROME: *Ancient History*), but at least provide us with an epoch by which to reckon: that from the conventional date (753 B.C. of our reckoning) of the foundation of Rome.

Founding of Rome.—Even this date was by no means a matter on which unanimity was reached; that given is the one which ultimately found most favour, and to which the majority of ancient authors refer when they use the expression *a.u.c.* (*ab urbe condita*, or *anno urbis conditae*). The official method of dating was by consuls, as *M. Messalla et M. Pupio Pisone consulibus* (abbreviated *cos.* or *coss.*), "in the consulship of Marcus Messalla and Marcus Pupius Piso" (Caesar, *de bell. Gall.*, 1, 2, 1 (61 B.C.). This never quite went out of use; but under the empire, official documents emanating from the emperors or referring to them reckoned by their years of tribunician power, to which were frequently added other, less regularly recurring, distinctions, such as the consulate or the salutation as *imperator*, *e.g., Imperator Caesar Vespasianus Augustus pontifex maximus, tribuniciae potestatis viiii, imp(erator) xiix, consul viii, i.e.*, "Vespasian (name and titles in full), in the ninth year of his tribunician power, having been saluted *imperator* 18 times, consul for the eighth time" (A.D. 77; from an official letter *C.I.L., II*, 1423). As, however, documents relating to the emperors are very numerous, this method of dating seldom raises much difficulty; our list of consuls also, for the fully historical periods, is tolerably complete. Naturally, in dealing with pre-Caesarian years (*see* CALENDAR: *Roman*) calculations more or less elaborate are needed to convert the year *urbis conditae* into the conventional Julian year (*see* above, *Greek*). These are based on a few facts, such as the mention of an eclipse or other event which we can date accurately. One such eclipse was that of the sun on Oct. 19, 202 B.C.; we gather from various authors that its civic date was about the beginning of December, and this enables us to calculate the condition of the calendar at that time.

Julian Calendar.—The reformed calendar of Julius Caesar was not imposed by Rome on her empire, but naturally it was widely adopted in various modifications. It became the calendar of Christian Rome and also of Constantinople; but gradually a change was made in the era; the supposed date of the birth of Christ replacing that of the foundation of the city (Christian or Dionysian era). This, however, was very slow to win official recognition, despite its convenience; Charlemagne appears to have been the first secular authority to use it. Before that, Christian chronologists used frequently to reckon in years of Abraham, *i.e.*, from his birth, which was placed by Eusebius at a date corresponding to Oct. 2016 B.C.

More important for the determining of Roman imperial dates, than the former, and for some of the later Republican dates also, are the provincial eras and the indictions. It was a wide-spread custom in Hellenistic times to count years from some notable event. The accession of the reigning king was, and continued to be, commonly used, and this, as we have seen, was followed by the emperors; but the Seleucidae and their subjects counted from 312/11 B.C., the date of Seleucus Nicator's decisive victory at the battle of Gaza and his capture of Babylon. In like manner a few Roman chronologists counted from 45 B.C., the date of the Julian reform; and Spain had an era of its own, beginning with 38 B.C., a date chosen for no very obvious reason. Again, several independent cities, such as Antioch, had local eras. When, therefore, we find a year mentioned in an inscription or other piece of evidence, it is necessary to know where this was written, and thus whether the Seleucid era, or that of Spain, or Antioch, or some other place, is meant; or, if the author be a historian, whether he may be using some peculiar era of his own, counting, for example, from the date which he accepts for the fall of Troy, or from the death of Alexander the Great.

The indictions are late, but important for late events, for they appear in all manner of official documents, ecclesiastical and secular. Properly, *indictio* means an assessment of taxes; *nec novis indictionibus pressi ad vetera tributa deficiunt,* says the younger Pliny (*Paneg.* 29), "the provincials are not so ground down with fresh exactions as to be unable even to pay the old taxes." Under Diocletian, a five-yearly assessment was ordered, and three of these periods grouped together made what was now called an indiction. One authority traces this arrangement back to comparatively early times, making the first indiction begin in 49 B.C.; but the real date seems to be A.D. 297, although even at the beginning of the empire the germ of such a system existed in Egypt. Its chronological importance is, that it provided a means of dating, without mentioning the several emperors who, by Diocletian's arrangement, ruled simultaneously. A disadvantage was that the cycle began on different days at different times and places. Despite these differences, and the fact that *indictio* meant now the whole cycle, now a year of it, it remained in use until the middle ages, and here and there even later.

See CHRONOLOGY: *Greek;* CALENDAR: *Greek;* CALENDAR: *Roman;* also Clinton, *Fasti Romani,* vol. i., 1845, vol. ii., 1850; Seeck, art. "Indictio," in Pauly-Wissowa, *Realencyclopädie,* and literature there cited. (H. J. R.)

JEWISH

The era which is in present vogue among Jews (*Anno Mundi, li-yitzirah* or *libriath olam,* from the creation of the world) appears not to have come into popular use before the 9th century, though possibly it may have been known to learned writers earlier. The era is supposed to begin, according to the mnemonic *Beharad,* at the beginning of the lunar cycle (*see* CALENDAR: *Jewish*) on the night between Sunday and Monday, Oct. 7, 3761 B.C., at 11 hours 11⅓ minutes P.M. This is indicated by *be* (*beth,* two, *i.e.,* 2nd day of week), *ha* (*he,* five, *i.e.,* fifth hour after sunset) and *Rad* (*Resh, dalet,* 204 minims after the hour). Rühl's theory that this era existed already in A.D. 222 is disputed by Poznanski on strong grounds. In the Bible various eras occur, *e.g.,* the Flood, the Exodus, the Earthquake in the days of King Uzziah, the regnal years of monarchs and the Babylonian exile. During the exile and after, Jews reckoned by the years of the Persian kings. Such reckonings occur not only in the Bible (*e.g.,* Daniel viii., 1) but also in the Assouan papyri. After Alexander, the Jews employed the Seleucid era (called *Minyan Shetaroth,* or era of deeds, since legal deeds were dated by this era). So great was the influence exerted by Alexander, that this era persisted in the East till the 16th century, and is still not extinct in south Arabia. This is the only era of antiquity that has survived. Others, which fell into disuse, were the Maccabaean eras, dating from the accession of each prince, and the national era (143–142 B.C.), when Judaea became free under Simon. That the era described in Jubilees (*see* CALENDAR: *Jewish*) was other than hypothetical, is probable. Dates have also been reckoned from the fall of the second Temple (*Le-Ḥorban hab-bayyith*). The equation of the eras is as follows: 1 after destruction = A.M. 3831 = 383 Seleucid = A.D. 71. Jewish chronology falls into two periods, biblical and post biblical. With the latter alone is this article concerned; for the former *see* BIBLE: *Old Testament: Chronology* and *New Testament: Chronology.* The earliest Jewish chronologies have not survived. Demetrius, a Jew of Alexandria, wrote a treatise in which he endeavoured to deduce the dates of Hebrew history from the Scriptures. Of this work only a very few remnants are extant; they have been published by C. Müller (*Fragmenta Hist. Graecorum,* iii. 214–217). The *Book of Jubilees,* written in the second pre-Christian century, subordinates chronology to its peculiar views on the calendar and theology. For present purposes Josephus must be left out of account, for chronology and history are separate studies. The most important and the earliest of all surviving chronologies is the *Seder 'Olam Rabbah.* This Hebrew book is mentioned in the Talmud; the author and date are unknown, but the authorities cited in the book belong almost exclusively to the 2nd century A.D. According to R. Johanan, the work was transmitted by R. Jose ben Halafta, a pupil of Aqiba, and it is possible that this tradition is correct. The author was possibly the first to make use of the era of Creation. Owing to defective sources he makes many errors in the Persian period. The chronology extends from the creation of Adam to Bar Kochba's fight for liberty in Hadrian's days, but the period from Alexander to Hadrian is compressed into the end of one chapter. The best edition is that of B. Ratner (Wilna, 1897). Various Latin translations exist (*vide* bibliography in *Jewish Encyclopedia, s.v.*).

The *Seder 'Olām Zūta,* a smaller work, was written probably in the 8th century; it completes the *Rabbah* and is based on it. The object of the book, which enumerates the 39 generations of Babylonian exitarchs, is to show that the latter were lineal descendants of David. The best text is that of Neubauer, *Mediaeval Jewish Chronicles,* ii., 67.

Megillat Ta'anith, or scroll of Fasting, is a chronicle rather than a chronology, since the events are grouped according to the months of the year and not in chronological sequence. The book enumerates 35 eventful days in five groups: I., pre-Maccabaean; II., Maccabaean; III., pre-Sadducean; IV., pre-Roman; V., the Diaspora. The author was probably, as stated in the Talmud (Sabbath 13 *b*), Hananya ben Hezekiah of the family of Garon, and the date would be about A.D. 7. A Latin translation exists (*vide* bibliography, *s.v.* in *Jewish Encyclopedia,* to which add the edition of Solomon Zeitlin, New York, 1922).

Tanna debe Eliyahu, a composite Midrash finally redacted in the 10th century, can scarcely be termed a chronology, since the underlying theme is the growth of the world-system; human history is arranged in *Shiṭṭōth* (series) in order to bring the moral into prominence. The absence of dates excludes this book from the category of chronology proper, although it contains much historical information.

For modern purposes the best chronology is that at the end of H. Graetz's *History of the Jews* in the American edition. Others are included in the bibliography in the *Jewish Encyclopedia, s.v.* Chronology. *See* also M. L. Margolis and A. Marx, *History of Jewish People* (1927). (H. M. J. L.)

MAYA AND MEXICAN

For technical terms relating to the calendar, which must be used to explain the chronology, the reader is referred to article CALENDAR: *Maya and Mexican.*

Maya: The Long Count.—The Maya calendar is based upon a year of 365 days, but it seems clear that the Mayas themselves recognized no such period. In their view 365 days was one tun (360-day period) and five days, and they so expressed the distance from a month-day in one year to the same month-day in the following year; *e.g.,* from 9 Imix 19 Zip to 10 Cimi 19 Zip. They never used a year of 365 days in counting the distance in time from one date to another. No glyph for the 365-day year is found, and there is no word with that meaning in the Books of Chilan Balam. It has been stated that haab meant 365-day year, but in fact it means tun (360-day period). All authorities agree, however, as to the method of counting time. The units used are the kin or day, the uinal of 20 days, the tun of 18 uinals, the katun of 20 tuns, and the cycle of 20 katuns. The Maya name for the cycle is unknown, and until proof is available it is undesirable to give it a hypothetical Maya name. In transcribing Maya numerals the numbers are written with a dash between each. Thus 9–10– 6– 5– 9 means 9 cycles, 10 katuns, 6 tuns, 5 uinals, and 9 kins. By this method the Maya counted the time elapsed from a certain day, 4 Ahau 8 Cumhu, which was the starting-point of their era, and thereby fixed dates in the Long Count, as the Maya era is called. What is called an Initial Series shows the position of a date in the Long Count. Thus 8 Muluc 2 Zip will recur every 52 years, but if it is expressed as an Initial Series date, 9–10– 6– 5– 9, 8 Muluc 2 Zip, its position in time is fixed, as its distance from the starting-point of the Long Count is given. In the Inscriptions an Initial Series always begins the inscription (hence the name) and commences with an "introducing glyph" which appears merely to mean "This is an Initial Series." Then follow the Maya numerals written in descending order, that is commencing with the largest period (cycle) and ending with the kin, and then the terminal date (in the above example, 8 Muluc

2 Zip). More often than not, the day number and day name (as 8 Muluc) are separated from the month day (as 2 Zip) by a Supplementary Series. In such cases the month day regularly follows the last glyph of the Supplementary Series. A date which is not fixed in the Long Count is called a "Calendar Round date," as it can recur every 52 years.

Another method of giving dates is by "period-endings." This somewhat resembles the European method of giving the last two figures of the year without the century. Thus '98 may mean 1798 or 1898, etc., recurring every 100 years. But the Maya method differs in that it always denotes a certain day instead of a larger period such as a year, and further it is a day terminating a certain round number. It is as if the European method only denoted Dec. 31, and then only when it ended a decade or century. The most usual period-ending is the katun-ending. This is expressed by (1) a glyph meaning "ending," (2) the number of the katun, (3) the Calendar Round date on which a katun of such a number ended. Example: "Ending Katun 13, 8 Ahau 8 Uo." Such a date cannot occur again in the Long Count for 374,400 years, so it is fixed as effectually as if the Initial Series had been given. The "ending sign" may be omitted. Less common are cycle-ending dates, as "2 Ahau 3 Uayeb ending Cycle 2." These cannot recur for 748,800 years. Very common are the lahuntun-endings, expressed by a special glyph meaning "end of Tun 10" together with the Calendar Round date. This means Tun 10 from the last katun-ending. These cannot recur for 18,720 years. Also common are the hotun-endings, expressed by a special glyph meaning "end of Tun 5" and the Calendar Round date. This Tun 5 may mean either Tun 5 from the last katun or Tun 5 from the last lahuntun (therefore Tun 15 from the last katun). These cannot recur for 9,360 years and are, therefore, practically as much fixed as the others. Example: "4 Ahau 13 Mol, Hotun." This must be 9–11–15– 0– 0 4 Ahau 13 Mol, because that date does not end Tun 5 or 15 elsewhere in cycles 8, 9 or 10 or indeed for 9,360 years before or after. No other satisfactory case of tun-ending occurs in the old empire except the 13– tun ending, expressed by glyphs meaning "ending Tun 13" and the Calendar Round date. These cannot recur for 18,720 years. As all period-endings denote the ends of even periods in the Long Count which itself starts from 4 Ahau 8 Cumhu, they must themselves all end on a day Ahau.

Many dates in the inscriptions are connected with other dates by "Secondary Series" numbers. If a date is connected by a Secondary Series with another date which is fixed in the Long Count, then the former date is called a Secondary Series date and is, of course, itself fixed in the Long Count, as it can be calculated by the Secondary Series from the known date. Example: "6 Imix 19 Zotz, connected by Secondary Series of 2–1–13–19 with 4 Ahau 13 Mol." But the latter is fixed by a period-ending in same inscription as 9–11–15– 0– 0 4 Ahau 13 Mol. so the former is 9–9–13– 4– 1 6 Imix 19 Zotz. But dates may be connected by a Secondary Series, and neither of them may be fixed in the Long Count, in which case both are merely Calendar Round dates.

All Initial Series in the Dresden Codex, and all except two in the inscriptions, start from 4 Ahau 8 Cumhu. But there are two Initial Series in the inscriptions which start from a date 4 Ahau 8 Zotz which occurred 13 cycles before the date 4 Ahau 8 Cumhu, the starting-point of all the rest. In the Dresden Codex a "great cycle" is used containing 20 cycles. Dr. Sylvanus G. Morley shows that this was used in the inscriptions, and also a great-great cycle of 400 cycles, and a great-great-great cycle of 8,000 cycles. This has been confirmed by Long's discovery of a new interpretation of an inscription at Palenque.

It will be noted that all the Maya time periods (except the tun) are each 20 times the next lower one. In the inscriptions these numbers are written with the glyphs for the periods as well as the numbers. Thus 9–10– 0– 0– 0, if an Initial Series, is expressed by glyphs reading 9 cycles, 10 katuns, 0 tuns, 0 uinals, 0 kins. This is similar to the usual mode of writing measures; *e.g.*, 10ft. 11in. Secondary Series are written in the same manner except that in them the lowest denomination (kin) comes first and the highest last. There are only three or four Secondary Series which do not follow this order, all at Palenque. But in the Dresden Codex the glyphs for the periods are omitted, and the value of the numbers depends upon position alone, as in the Arabic numerals.

Cyrus Thomas remarks that there is nothing to show that the 4 Ahau 8 Cumhu to which the Initial Series count back is the same in actual time in all. This is so, because 4 Ahau 8 Cumhu will recur every 52 years. But Thomas agrees that the assumption that it is the same actual day in all gives the most credible result, as this makes the terminal dates of the inscriptions fall within a reasonable distance of each other, and no doubt the assumption is correct. The earliest dated monument is Stela 9 at Uaxactun, 8–14–10–13–15 and the latest in the old empire is Stela 12 at the same site and is 10– 3– 0– 0– 0. This gives an extreme range of 1– 8– 9– 4– 5 (about 561 years), quite a probable time for any phase of civilization to last. But since the Maya erected the first dated monument about 3,443 years after the beginning of their era, it is clear that 4 Ahau 8 Cumhu represents no historical event and must have fallen long before there was any Maya civilization. Like the Julian period used by astronomers, it was a date calculated by skilled chronologists long after the invention of the calendar, doubtless with the object of harmonizing lesser periods.

But in general the range of Maya dates is even shorter. Many of the monuments record only one date, and where there are several the last date, or at least the last period-ending, seems generally to be the contemporaneous one. Now the dated monuments are very rare in cycle 8, more numerous, but still confined to a few sites, from 9– 0– 0– 0– 0 to 9– 10– 0– 0 0, become very numerous from 9–10– 0– 0– 0– to 9–15– 0– 0– 0, increase much more after 9–15– 0– 0– 0, reach a maximum in 9–18– 0– 0– 0, and then suddenly diminish, becoming much fewer after 9–19– 0– 0– 0, and ceasing after 10– 3– 0– 0– 0. The style of the monuments likewise shews a steady advance in art up to about 9–18– 0– 0– 0. Change is also observable in the method of dating. In cycle 8 the monuments were erected on casual dates which did not end any tun or other time period, and the dates were usually shewn by Initial Series, but early in cycle 9 the practice was adopted of setting up the monuments to mark each hotun. Unfortunately hotun is used by Maya scholars in this case to mean the end of either a katun, lahuntun, or hotun, that is, it means any number of tuns of the Long Count which is divisible by five. Initial Series were still used, and at about 9– 8–15– 0– 0 the practice began of giving several dates on a monument besides the Initial Series, the last one marking the hotun. After 9–10– 0– 0– 0 monuments dated by period-endings became fairly frequent, and after 9–15– 0– 0– 0 the Initial Series became rarer, and monuments were dated mostly by period-endings or Calendar Round dates. Geographically we also see change. The old empire area was roughly triangular with Uaxactun and Tikal in the north-east, Copan and Quirigua in the south-east, and Piedras Negras in the west. Uaxactun and its neighbour, Uoluntun, alone show dates in cycle 8. In the first half of cycle 9 the monuments are almost confined to Uaxactun, Tikal, Copan and Piedras Negras, outliers in the area, while after 9–10– 0– 0– 0 they are numerous everywhere till 9–18– 0– 0– 0, when they cease at Piedras Negras and the west, ceasing at Quirigua and Copan and the south-west after 9–19– 0– 0– 0. Some new cities appear towards the close of cycle 9 in the north-east, and the closing date is at Uaxactun and Xultun near it. It is noteworthy that Uaxactun and Tikal, though at the north-east of the old empire, are almost in the centre of the whole Maya area if we consider the old and new empire territories together, and these sites were probably the original seats of the Maya.

The New Empire.—The Long Count was wanting in the new empire. Instead they used the U Kahlay Katunob, which was a simplification of the older period-ending method. The cycle had entirely dropped out of use, and the only periods were the katun and the tun, the katun being the more important. The katuns were cited by the day Ahau with its day number on which they ended. Thus "Katun 13 Ahau" or simply "13 Ahau." Such a date can recur every 13 katuns (about 256 years) because in that time the 13 day numbers will be exhausted. The order of succession is 13. 11. 9. 7. 5. 3. 1, 12. 10. 8. 6. 4. 2. Often nothing was mentioned save the katun in which the event occurred, so that not only could the katun recur about every 256 years, but the event might have occurred anywhere within the katun, leaving about 20 years uncertainty. At times an event is described as occurring in tun so-and-so of such a katun, thus fixing it within a period of 360 days within the katun. But if the Calendar Round date is given as well, as *e.g.*, "Katun 13 Ahau, Tun 13, 9 Imix 18 Zip," then (depending upon what date it is) the date can either only occur once in 18,720 years or can occur twice in that time, at intervals of 7,436 years and 11,284 years respectively.

Correlations.—The state of knowledge about the Maya of the old empire has no parallel in archaeology. While on the one hand we do not even know the names of the peoples who erected the monuments, much less their history, nor even if they spoke Maya, seeing that all knowledge of the calendar is based upon Landa's account of the new empire, yet so accurate were their dates that it is possible to date the monuments with regard to each other to the exact day. But widely different views are held by scholars as to the correlation with Christian chronology. The principal elements of the problem are: (1) correlation of the old and new empire chronologies, (2) correlation of the new empire and Christian chronologies, (3) correlation with astronomical discoveries of Teeple. (1) If the month-days on which the katuns of the new empire ended had been stated, there would have been an absolute correlation with the old empire. A tun ends on the same day number every 13 tuns, but will end on the same month-day only every 73 tuns, and on the same day number and month-day only every 949 tuns. Similarly a katun will only end on the same day number and month-day every 949 katuns (18,720 years). But as the new empire method did not state the month, the Katun 13 Ahau which occurred in the 16th century is identified with various katuns of the Long Count by different writers. The Books of Chilan Balam carry back the new empire chronology to about A.D. 163. Mr. J. Eric Thompson alone shortens this. (2) Opinions differ as to what year in the 16th century a katun 13 Ahau ended in, so the new empire chronology is only loosely correlated with Christian chronology within the limits of about a katun. The Maya year was a shifting one and Landa says that in his time Pop began on July 16 O.S. This was in or near 1553. No correlation can stand which does not agree with Landa's statement, consequently all are ruled out but the three given below. (3) Teeple shows certain lunar and Venus dates agreeing with Thompson, but probably the last word has not yet been said on this subject.

The Bowditch correlation depends on a statement as to the month-day and has considerable historical evidence in its favour. Thompson's correlation depends on another statement as to the month-day and raises some difficulties owing to the shortness of its chronology. Dr. Herbert J. Spinden's correlation is at variance with both of these month-dates and also with Teeple's results. Moreover, the astronomical observations on which he relies have been shown by further measurement to be incorrect. The dates of 4 Ahau 8 Cumhu in these correlations are in the Gregorian Calendar (astronomical reckoning):—

Bowditch, Joyce and Long	Feb. 10	3641 B.C.
Spinden	Oct. 14	3373 B.C.
Thompson	Aug. 13	3113 B.C.

As the Maya chronology was the only efficient one in pre-Columbian America it would, if fixed, throw much light on that of America as a whole. Excavation of Maya sites has yielded objects obtained in trade from both northwards and southwards, so that if the correlation was established, the period when these neighbouring cultures flourished could be approximated.

Solving Dates.—A word in conclusion on solving dates. Given such a series as 9–10–6–5–9 and that its starting-point is a known date such as say 4 Ahau 8 Cumhu, the day name can at once be determined by counting the kin number (in this case 9) from the starting-point; thus 9 days from Ahau will reach Muluc. But the finding of the day number and the month-day is a more difficult matter. It is possible to reduce the whole series to single days and then find the day number by dividing by 13 and counting the remainder forward from the day number of the starting point, similarly to find the month-day by dividing the total number of days by 365 and counting forward the remainder from the month-day of the starting-point. But the student is advised not to use this time-wasting method. Many problems can be solved by tables, of which the best are J. T. Goodman's and those of Mr. Thomas A. Joyce, but not all cases can be directly done by tables, and though they are valuable for checking results, it is well to be able to calculate independently of them. By far the best rule is that of Mr. Raymond K. Morley (*see* Bibliography), by which all series can be quickly calculated without any tables.

Cakchiquel Calendar.—This is the only era found in ancient America except the Maya. It was a pure vigesimal count, the units being the *kih* or day; the *vinak* (meaning "twenty") or 20 *kih*, the *a* or 20 *vinak*, and the *may* or 20 *a*. No higher units are known or were required, as the era only started from the day 11 Ah, the date of the revolt of the Tukuche tribe, equivalent to May 20 1493 O.S. This era is altogether unique, not only from its purely vigesimal character, but also that it only commenced in the lifetime of persons who were living at the Spanish conquest. No hint of any other era appears in the Annals, before the revolt, but the use of the special words such as *a* and *may* shows that such a mode of counting from some other epoch or epochs had been previously known. The Cakchiquel, living southwards of the old empire, like the Yucatan Maya to the north of it, used a later simplification of the older time counts. Dates were expressed thus: On 1 Ah was completed 1 *may* and 5 *a;* after the revolt, on 12 Camey (a certain event occurred). Sometimes the number of *vinak* and *kih* was also given.

Mexican Calendar.—There was no chronological system beyond the calendar round. The codices show no means of giving the numbers of years elapsed from one date to another except the clumsy one of stating the year-bearers of all the intervening years. The calendar round began with the year 2 Acatl, in which year the great festival of the "year-binding," *xiuhmolpilli,* was held. The codices denote such a year by a special sign along with the year-bearer, but this is merely the same thing as noting the occurrence of such an event in that year. The sign for the year-binding was never used as an arithmetical sign to show that 52 years or a multiple thereof had elapsed. To do this they had to set out all the individual years. Naturally, there is much confusion in Mexican history and the same event is placed by different authorities at varying numbers of calendar rounds before the Spanish conquest. Mexico surrendered to Cortez on the day 1 Coatl, year 3 Calli, which was Aug. 13 1521 O.S. This was 3 Xocouetzi, as the year-bearers were taken from 1 Toxcatl instead of from the first month of the year. The explanation is probably that the monthly festivals were displaced in the shifting calendar to agree with the seasons, but this question is very obscure.

Bibliography.—C. P. Bowditch, *The Numeration, Calendar Systems, and Astronomical Knowledge of the Mayas* (Cambridge, U.S.A. 1910); T. A. Joyce, *Mexican Archaeology* (London, 1914), and *Guide to the Maudslay Collections of Maya Sculptures* (British Museum, 1923); S. G. Morley, *An Introduction to the Study of Maya Hieroglyphs* (Washington, Bureau of American Ethnology, 1915), and *The Inscriptions at Copan* (Washington, Carnegie Institution, 1920); R. K. Morley, "Computations for the Maya Calendar" in *American Anthropologist* (1918); R. C. E. Long, "Maya and Christian Chronology," *Journal Royal Anthropological Institute* (1923), "The Age of the Maya Calendar," *Journal Royal Anthropological Institute* (1924), "Maya High Numbers," Man. No. 39 (1923), "The Bowditch and Morley Correlations of Maya Chronology," Man. No. 2 (1925); J. E. Teeple, "Maya Inscriptions, Glyphs," C. D. & E. of the Supplementary Series, and "Further Notes on the Supplementary Series," in *American Anthropologist* (1925); also "Maya Inscriptions, The Venus Calendar and another Correlation," in *American Anthropologist* (1926); H. J. Spinden, *The Reduction of Mayan Dates* (Cambridge, U.S.A., Peabody Museum); J. E. Thompson, *A Correlation of the Mayan and European Calendars* (Chicago, Field Museum of Natural History, 1927).

The student is recommended to read first Joyce's *Guide*, then his *Mexican Archaeology*, then Morley's *Introduction* (with good bibliography), and then Bowditch. The last two are absolutely essential. Morley's *Copan*, a truly great book, presupposes a knowledge of the subject and contains an extensive bibliography. (R. C. E. L.)

MUSLIM

The Muslim Calendar (*see* CALENDAR: *Muslim*) may evidently be carried on indefinitely by successive addition, provided care be taken to allow for the additional day occurring in bissextile and intercalary years. The purely lunar years of this calendar are partitioned into cycles of 30 years, 19 of which are common years of 354 days each, the remaining 11 being intercalary years having an additional day appended to the last month. The mean length of the year is, therefore, $354\frac{11}{30}$ days (354 days, 8 hours, 48 minutes). This gives $29\frac{191}{360}$ days (29 days, 12 hours, 44 minutes) as a period of mean lunation, and this differs from the astronomical mean lunation by only 2·8 seconds. This small error amounts to a day in about 2,400 years.

To find if a year is intercalary or common, divide it by 30; the quotient will be the number of completed cycles and the remainder will be the year of the current cycle; if this last be one of the numbers 2, 5, 7, 10, 13, 16, 18, 21, 24, 26, 29, the year is intercalary and consists of 355 days; if it be any other number, the year is ordinary.

Year of the current cycle (y)				Number of the period of seven cycles = $\left(\frac{C}{7}\right)_r$						
				0	1	2	3	4	5	6
0	8	..	..	Mon.	Sat.	Thur.	Tues.	Sun.	Frid.	Wed.
1	9	17	25	Frid.	Wed.	Mon.	Sat.	Thur.	Tues.	Sun.
*2	*10	*18	*26	Tues.	Sun.	Frid.	Wed.	Mon.	Sat.	Thur.
3	11	19	27	Sun.	Frid.	Wed.	Mon.	Sat.	Thur.	Tues.
4	12	20	28	Thur.	Tues.	Sun.	Frid.	Wed.	Mon.	Sat.
*5	*13	*21	*29	Mon.	Sat.	Thur.	Tues.	Sun.	Frid.	Wed.
6	14	22	30	Sat.	Thur.	Tues.	Sun.	Frid.	Wed.	Mon.
*7	15	23	..	Wed.	Mon.	Sat.	Thur.	Tues.	Sun.	Frid.
..	*16	*24	..	Sun.	Frid.	Wed.	Mon.	Sat.	Thur.	Tues.

To find from this table the day of the week on which any year of the Hejira begins, the rule to be observed will be as follows:—

Rule.—Divide the year of the Hejira by 30; the quotient is the number of cycles, and the remainder is the year of the current cycle. Next divide the number of cycles by 7, and the second remainder will be the Number of the Period, which being found at the top of the table, and the year of the cycle on the left hand, the required day of the week is immediately shown.

The intercalary years of the cycle are distinguished by an asterisk.

For the computation of the Christian date, the ratio of a mean year of the Hejira to a solar year is:

$$\frac{\text{Year of Hejira}}{\text{Mean solar year}} = \frac{354\frac{11}{30}}{365\cdot2422} = 0\cdot970224.$$

The year 1 began July 16, 622, Old Style, or July 19, 622, according to the New or Gregorian Style. Now the day of the year answering to July 19, is 200, which, in parts of the solar year, is 0·5476, and the number of years elapsed $= Y-1$. Therefore, as the intercalary days are distributed with considerable regularity in both calendars, the date of commencement of the year Y expressed in Gregorian years is:

$$0\cdot970224\ (Y-1)+622\cdot5476,$$
$$\text{or } 0\cdot970224\ Y+621\cdot5774.$$

This formula gives the following rule for calculating the date of the commencement of any year of the Hejira, according to the Gregorian or New Style.

Rule.—Multiply 970,224 by the year of the Hejira, cut off six decimals from the product, and add 621·5774. The sum will be the year of the Christian era, and the day of the year will be found by multiplying the decimal figures by 365.

The result may sometimes differ a day from the truth, as the intercalary days do not occur simultaneously; but as the day of the week can always be accurately obtained from the foregoing table, the result can be readily adjusted.

CHRONOMETER. A marine timekeeper, used for determining longitude at sea. The word was originally used to denote any time-measuring instrument. The first instance of its employment in its accepted modern meaning is to be found in Jeremy Thacker's "The Longitudes Examined . . ." (London, 1714). On the Continent the analogous term "chronométre" is still used to describe any high-class timekeeper, whether for marine purposes or otherwise.

History.—The possibility of determining longitude at sea by the use of a timekeeper was first pointed out by the Flemish astronomer Gemma Frisius, in a work on navigation published at Antwerp in 1530. At that date, however, and for long afterwards, the mechanical difficulties in the way of constructing an accurate marine timekeeper appeared to be insurmountable. The first attempt to put Frisius' suggestion into practice was made in 1662–70 by the celebrated Dutch scientist, Christiaan Huygens, of Zulichem, who constructed several marine timekeepers controlled by pendulums and subjected them to actual tests at sea. It was found that the timekeeping of the machines was quite unreliable, owing to the effects of temperature and of the ship's motion. Many later inventors fared no better, but during 1729–60 John Harrison, a self-taught Yorkshire carpenter, invented and constructed four practical marine timekeepers, with the fourth of which (now preserved, in going order, at Greenwich Observatory) he won the reward of £20,000 offered in 1714 by the British Government for any means of determining a ship's longitude within 30 nautical miles at the end of a six weeks' voyage. It may be noted that a timekeeper fulfilling this condition would have to keep time within three seconds per day—a standard which, at the date when the reward was offered, had not been attained by the best pendulum clocks on shore.

Harrison's mechanism, although unquestionably efficient, was complicated, delicate and costly—the Board of Longitude paid Larcum Kendall, a London watchmaker, £450 for a duplicate of the No. 4 timekeeper. Accordingly, it had little direct effect upon the evolution of the modern chronometer. But in 1765 Pierre Le Roy, of Paris, invented and constructed a marine timekeeper whose mechanism embodied, in an embryonic but perfectly recognizable form, practically all the essential features of the modern chronometer. This machine, or a contemporary duplicate, is preserved in the Conservatoire des Arts et Métiers in Paris. Le Roy's work was followed up by Ferdinand Berthoud in France and by John Arnold and Thomas Earnshaw in England. The last-named produced, as early as 1785, several chronometers which, both in appearance and mechanism, are scarcely distinguishable from the machine of to-day.

Description.—The modern chronometer is, broadly speaking, a large, well-made watch, suspended in gimbals (a set of two bearings at right-angles, connected by a ring) and so poised as to remain horizontal whatever the inclination of the ship. It is thus safeguarded from those alterations of position which slightly affect the timekeeping of even the best watches. In addition, it differs somewhat in its mechanism from an ordinary watch, the spiral balance-spring and lever escapement of the latter being replaced by a helical balance-spring and a spring-detent or "chronometer" escapement. This form of escapement is mechanically superior to any other, and requires no oiling, but it is unsuitable for use in pocket watches, as if stopped it has no tendency to re-start itself. For the purpose of equalizing the force of the mainspring, almost all chronometers are fitted with a device known as a "fusee," which has for some time past been discarded in watches, and their compensation-balances, by which the effects of heat and cold upon their timekeeping are practically nullified, also differ in some respects from the ordinary watch type, as well as being considerably larger and heavier.

Accuracy.—The modern chronometer is capable, with fair usage, of going with what must be regarded, in view of the unfavourable conditions to which it is necessarily exposed on board, as astonishing accuracy. Both during the official tests at Greenwich Observatory (which has been held annually, on practically unaltered lines, from 1844 to 1914) and in their subsequent service afloat, many hundreds of chronometers have shown themselves capable of keeping time in all ordinary variations of temperature for six months at a time with an error not exceeding a second a day—an amount which, in a month's voyage along the equator, would involve an error in the ship's final position of less than eight nautical miles. (*See* also NAVIGATION.)

U.S. Marine Chronometer.—During the years 1942 to 1944 a marine chronometer of very high precision was developed in the United States by the Hamilton Watch company. In general appearance, this chronometer is like any other, but certain changes have been made in the escapement. The hairspring used is made of nickel steel, similar to elinvar; the balance wheel is uncut and has a stainless steel rim with an invar arm. There are a number of timing screws, as in a watch, which permit very close adjustment of the rate. This chronometer shows a practically uniform variation with temperature, with daily rates at 5° C. and 35° C. differing by only a few tenths of a second. The rate during run-down remains uniform for 48 hours after winding.

See R. T. Gould, *The Marine Chronometer, its History and Development* (1923), a general history of the subject. (R. T. Go.; X.)

CHRYSANTHEMUM, a genus of nearly 300 species of annual or perennial herbs of the family Compositae; popularly the name given to forms of certain old world species of this genus which have been remarkably developed by cultivation. Most varieties of the so-called Chinese and Japanese chrysanthemums extensively grown by gardeners and florists are blended hybrids or other forms derived from *C. morifolium* and *C. indicum*, natives of eastern Asia. Other species of interest to flower growers are *C. coccineum* (pyrethrum), *C. parthenium* (feverfew), and *C. frutescens* (marguerite). Other representatives of the genus are *C. balsamita* (costmary) and *C. leucanthemum* (ox-eye daisy), the latter often a pestiferous weed. The common chrysanthemum has probably been known for at least 2,000 years. In Japan, where it can be traced back many centuries, it is the national flower. Breynius in 1689 was the first European to mention the chrysanthemum, giving it the name of *Matricaria japonica maxima*. Pierre Louis Blancard introduced the first large-flowering chrysanthemum into England in 1789. This first flowered in 1790. Just when the plant was first introduced into the United States is uncertain, although horticultural chrysanthemums were exhibited in Philadelphia in 1827 and in Boston the next year. The work of hybridization was first taken up by Dr. H. P. Walcott and later in the '80s by John Thorpe, who organized the Chrysanthemum Society of America in 1890. The only species of economic importance are certain forms of *C. coccineum*, much grown for the aromatic flower heads, the source of pyrethrum powder, widely used in insecticides. Chrysanthemums are popular with the gardeners, both professional and amateur, as an exhibition flower because of their great size and variety of shape and colour, and also because some varieties are extremely hardy, which permits their use in the perennial garden. Chrysanthemums owe their popularity with commercial florists not so much to their value as a crop as to the fact that they may be planted in the late spring and early summer when the greenhouse otherwise would be empty. Moreover, the chrysanthemum is a quick-maturing crop, many varieties being grown without artificial heat, since they bloom from late August to December.

The cultural requirements for chrysanthemums may be adjusted to many rotation schemes, so that the same greenhouse may be used for growing other floral crops, such as calendulas, sweet peas, stocks, snapdragons, annuals and lilies.

Classification of Types.—(1) *Incurved Chinese types* are nearly globular in form and regular in outline; the florets are smooth, rounded or somewhat toothed at the top, and sufficiently long to form a graceful curve (commercial varieties are Maj. Bonaffon, Mrs. Nellie T. Ross, Citronelle). (2) *Japanese types* are varieties with long loosely arranged florets; the florets may be flat, fluted, quilled or tubulated and may be incurved or reflex. Many exhibition varieties (Mrs. H. S. Firestone, F. E. Nash, Miss Ruth C. Twombly, Majestic), come in this type. (3) *Anemones* have high, neatly formed centres with elongated quilled florets, surrounded by flat, more or less horizontally arranged ray flowers. Examples are Gorza, Chestnut, Mapleleaf. (4) *Pompons* may be somewhat flat or nearly globular, generally very neat and compact, formed of short, flat, fluted or quilled florets. The florets of each bloom are all of one form, such as the varieties Varsity, Co-ed, Baby, Pink Dot and Nuggets. (5) *Singles* are arranged sufficiently close together to form a regular fringe. There may be one or two rows of ray flowers and sometimes as many as three or five. The centres of the florets are always tubular, either short or somewhat elongated. Golden Mensa, Mrs. E. D. Godfrey and Margaret Waite are good examples. (6) *Cascades*, derived from a wild Japanese species, comprise a group of showy pot plants which by pinching make handsome, usually drooping, very floriferous sprays of bloom.

During 1936–38 a group of chrysanthemums was launched under the name of *azaleamum*. Most of them were related to old varieties such as Amelia, etc., with no relationship to azalea.

Propagation.—The chrysanthemum is generally propagated by cuttage, seedage or division. Cuttage is by far the most satisfactory, since insects and diseases may be controlled by the careful selection of clean stock. Plants grown from cuttings make better growth, give better flowers and are easier to stake and tie in the garden. Nearly all chrysanthemums grown in commercial greenhouses are produced from cuttings. Division is practised by many outdoor gardeners. Seedage is practised only by breeders who seek new varieties.

Plants for propagation are packed in flats, benches or cold frames, after the flowering season, and wintered over in either a cold greenhouse or frame. In March or April the strong shoots are ideal for making cuttings 2 to 4 in. long. If aphides are present, the cuttings should be placed in a 1-to-500 or 1-to-800 solution of nicotine sulphate in water before planting. Clean sand is best for rooting cuttings, which should be firmly packed and watered. The bed should be lightly shaded for a few days to prevent wilting.

Wilted cuttings generally die, but if they root the resulting plants are stunted. Syringing on warm days will help to keep the cuttings fresh. A temperature of 50° F. is sufficient, but quicker rooting is obtained if 60° F. is maintained.

When the roots are about ½ in. long the plants should be potted in a fibrous loam soil. If allowed to remain too long in the cutting bed, they become hard and are not responsive to good culture. The plants are usually ready for their permanent quarters by early June or July. A good fibrous, well-drained loam is the ideal soil medium for chrysanthemums. If this soil is packed before planting or directly afterward, the new growth becomes firmer and the internodes shorter. Newly set plants should be watered only lightly, since wet soil is unfavourable for their growth. The tops of the plants may, however, be syringed often to keep them fresh.

The planting distances vary with the different types. Commercial growers vary the planting of the large flowering chrysanthemums as follows: 6 in. by 6 in., 7 in. by 8 in., 7½ in. by 8 in., 10 in. by 10 in. Pompons are planted 12 in. by 12 in. and 12 in. by 15 in. inside, while outdoors 15 in. by 15 in. and 18 in. by 18 in. is the general practice.

As soon as the plants are placed they should be staked and tied. The tying should be done as the plant grows so that the stem will remain straight. When the stem becomes 6 in. long the plant should be "topped" (top pinched out), if more than one stem is desired. Topping should continue for small-flowered plants until August. Watering, syringing and tying are of chief importance during the summer months.

The plants should be kept as cool as possible by spraying and syringing and by wetting the walks.

In the late summer and early fall "disbudding" becomes a factor. The first bud to appear is generally the crown bud. This bud will flower early and give a large flower, but the shape, colour and habit are not as desirable for commercial use as are flowers from lateral buds. The crown bud is surrounded by vegetative shoots, one of which may be saved to produce the desired flower bud. The terminal bud of the final shoot is surrounded by other buds, which should be removed if only one large flower is desired.

If the soil is a good composted fibrous loam, no fertilizer should be given until the bud is selected. Thereafter, liquid manure should be given once a week until the buds show colour. Continued use of any fertilizer, especially those that are too strong, will cause the flowers to "blast" and "burn." The foregoing cultural directions apply equally as well to the chrysanthemums in the garden. Systematic fumigation and the propagation of clean stock are the greatest factors in the prevention and control of pests. Upwards of 500 named varieties of the chrysanthemum are listed in catalogues and horticultural works, and new forms are constantly being produced.

For more extensive details, *see* L. H. Bailey, *The Standard Cyclopedia of Horticulture* (1933); for list of recognized American varieties, *see Standardized Plant Names* (Salem, Mass., 2nd edition, 1939). *See* also E. A. White, *The Chrysanthemum and Its Culture* (1930).
(H. O. Y.; N. Tr.)

CHRYSANTHIUS, Greek philosopher of the 4th century A.D. He was a pupil of Aedesius and an exponent of the mystical side of Neoplatonism (*q.v.*). Invited by the emperor Julian to assist in the scheme for the revival of Hellenism, he declined, probably foreseeing its failure. As high-priest of Lydia he kept the respect of Christians and pagans alike.

CHRYSELEPHANTINE, the architectural term given to statues which were built up on a wooden core, with ivory representing the flesh and gold the drapery (Gr. χρυσός, gold, ἐλέφας, ivory). The most celebrated examples are by Pheidias, the statue of Athena in the Parthenon and of Zeus in the temple at Olympia.

CHRYSENE, a hydrocarbon discovered by Laurent in the high boiling point fractions of coal tar distillate, is produced in small quantity in the distillation of amber, or on passing the vapour of benzyl-α-naphthylmethane through a red-hot tube. When impure, it is of a yellow colour; hence its name (χρύσεος, golden yellow). Chrysene, $C_{18}H_{12}$, 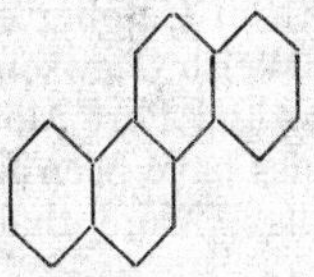 crystallizes in colourless plates or octahedra (from benzene), which exhibit a violet fluorescence, and melt at 250° C. It boils at 448° C. Chromic acid in glacial acetic acid solution oxidizes it to chrysoquinone $C_{18}H_{10}O_2$, which, distilled with lead oxide, gives chrysoketone $C_{17}H_{10}O$. *See* A. E. Everest, *The Higher Coal-tar Hydrocarbons* (1927).

CHRYSIPPUS (*c.* 280–206 B.C.), Greek philosopher, third leader of the Stoics, born at Soli, Cilicia (Diog. Laert. vii. 179). He came to Athens and studied possibly under Zeno, certainly under Cleanthes. It is said also that he became a pupil of Arcesilaus and Lacydes, heads of the middle academy. His chief fame rested on his controversies in the academy, for which he was called "the column of the portico." Diogenes Laertius says "without Chrysippus there had been no Porch." Of the 750 treatises with which he is credited only fragments survive. The style is said to have been crabbed, the argument lucid.

See G. H. Hagedorn, *Ethica Chrysippi* (1715); J. F. Richter, *De Chrysippo Stoico fastuoso* (1738); F. Baguet, *De Chrysippi vita doctrina et relinquiis* (1822); C. Petersen, *Philosophiae Chrysippeae fundamenta* (1827); A. B. Krische, *Forschungen auf dem Gebiete der alten Philosophie* (1840); R. Nicolai, *De logicis Chrysippi libris* (1859); R. Hirzel, *Untersuchungen zu Ciceros philosophischen Schriften,* ii (1882); A. Gercke, "Chrysippea" in *Jahrbücher für Philologie*, suppl. vol. xiv (1885); L. Stein, *Die Psychologie der Stoa* (1886); J. E. Sandys, *Hist. Class. Schol.* i, 149; E. Brehier, *Chrysippe* (Les Grands philosophes, Paris, 1910). *See* also Stoics.

CHRYSOBERYL, a yellow or green gem stone, remarkable for its hardness, being exceeded in this respect only by the diamond and corundum. The name suggests that it was formerly regarded as a golden variety of beryl. Its composition is $BeAl_2O_4$ or $BeO.Al_2O_3$. It is yellow or pale green, occasionally passing into shades of dark green and brown. Chrysoberyl is often mistaken by its colour for chrysolite (*q.v.*), and has indeed been termed oriental chrysolite, but it is a much harder and denser mineral. A contrast of their chief characters is as follows:

	Chrysoberyl	Chrysolite
Hardness	8.5	6.5 to 7
Specific gravity	3.65 to 3.75	3.34 to 3.37
Chemical composition	$BeAl_2O_4$	Mg_2SiO_4

Chrysoberyl is not infrequently cloudy, opalescent and chatoyant, and is then known as "cymophane" (Gr. κυμα, cloud). The cloudiness is referable to the presence of multitudes of microscopic cavities. Some of the cymophane, when cut with a convex surface, forms the most valuable kind of cat's-eye (*see* Cat's-eye). A remarkable dichroic variety of chrysoberyl is alexandrite (*q.v.*).

Most chrysoberyl comes from Brazil, chiefly from the district of Minas Novas in the state of Minas Gerais, where it occurs as small water-worn pebbles. The cymophane is mostly from the gem gravels of Ceylon. Chrysoberyl is a constituent of certain kinds of granite, pegmatite and gneiss. In the U.S. it occurs at Haddam, Conn.; Greenfield Center near Saratoga Springs, N.Y.; Greenwood, Me.; and Manhattan Island. It is known also in the province of Quebec and near Gwelo, Rhodesia.

CHRYSOCOLLA, a hydrous copper silicate occurring as a decomposition product of copper ores. It is never found as crystals, but always as encrusting and botryoidal masses. It is green or bluish-green in colour, and often has the appearance of opal or enamel, being translucent and having a conchoidal fracture with vitreous lustre; sometimes it is earthy in texture. Not being a definite crystallized substance, it varies widely in chemical composition, the copper oxide (CuO), for example, varying in different analyses from 17% to 67%. The hardness (2–4) and specific gravity (2.0–2.8) are also variable. The mineral occurs in the upper parts of veins of copper ores, and has resulted from their alteration by the action of waters containing silica in solution. Pseudomorphs of chrysocolla after various copper minerals (*e.g.,* cuprite) are not uncommon. Chrysocolla is found in most copper mines. The name chrysocolla (from χρυσός, gold, and κόλλα, glue) was applied by Theophrastus and other ancient writers to materials used in soldering gold, one of which, from Cyprus, may have been identical with the mineral now known by this name. Borax, which is used for this purpose, has also been called chrysocolla.

CHRYSOLITE, a transparent green gem stone. The name chrysolite, meaning "golden stone" (χρυσός and λίθος), has been applied to various yellowish gems, notably to topaz, to some kinds of beryl and to chrysoberyl. The true chrysolite of the modern mineralogist is a pale green olivine (*q.v.*).

CHRYSOLORAS, MANUEL (or Emmanuel) (*c.* 1355–1415), a pioneer in spreading Greek literature in the west, was born at Constantinople. He was a pupil of Gemistus Pletho (*q.v.*). In 1393 the emperor Manuel Palaeologus sent him to Italy to seek the aid of the Christian princes against the Turks. About 1395 he became professor of Greek at Florence, where he taught for three years and became famous as a translator of Homer and Plato. In 1413 he went to Germany on an embassy to the emperor Sigismund, to fix the site of a general council. It was decided to hold the meeting at Constance, and Chrysoloras was on his way thither, having been chosen to represent the Greek Church, when he died suddenly on April 15, 1415. Only two of his works have been printed, his *Erotemata* (published at Venice in 1484), which was the first Greek grammar in use in the west, and *Epistolae III de comparatione veteris et novae Romae.*

John Chrysoloras, a relative of the above, who, like him, had studied and taught at Constantinople and had then gone to Italy, shared Manuel's reputation as one of those who spread the influence of Greek letters in the west. His daughter married Filelfo (*q.v.*).

CHRYSOPRASE is a transparent variety of cryptocrystalline silica of an apple-green colour (Gr. χρυσός, gold, and πράσον, leek), the latter being caused by the presence of nickel, probably in the form of hydrous silicate. A very similar artificial gem may be prepared by immersing chalcedony in solutions of nickel salts. On exposing a natural chrysoprase to light or heat its colour becomes paler, though this may be restored by placing the stone in a damp medium. It is surprising that the colour of the natural gem should be susceptible to the action of light and heat, while the artificial product is quite unaffected. (Max Bauer, *Precious Stones,* trans. by L. J. Spencer, 1904.)

CHRYSOSTOM (St. John Chrysostom) (Χρυσόστομος, golden-mouthed) (A.D. 345–407), the most famous Greek father, was born at Antioch about A.D. 345. At the school of Libanius, the sophist, he gave early indications of his mental powers and love of classical culture. On being baptized (*c.* 370) by Meletius, bishop of Antioch, he retired to the desert, where for ten years he led a life of asceticism and study. Illness compelled him to return to the world, and in 381 he was ordained deacon and in 386 priest. He won great reputation by his preaching at Antioch, especially by his homilies on *The Statues,* delivered when the people feared the consequences of the destruction of the statues of the emperor Theodosius during a riot.

On the death of Nectarius, Chrysostom was appointed bishop of Constantinople (398). In this capacity he won the love of the people by his eloquent and devout homilies and by the application of his ample revenues to the establishment of hospitals. But his reforming zeal also made him many enemies. The clergy were forbidden to keep lay sisters as servants, aimless monks were confined to their monasteries and the extravagances of the court were strongly denounced. His enemies found a pretext for revenge in the shelter which he had given to four Nitrian monks who had been excommunicated by their bishop, Theophilus of Alexandria. Theophilus was invited to Constantinople (403) and, charging Chrysostom with Origenism, thrice summoned him to appear before a synod. He refused to appear and finally was declared deposed, arrested and exiled. The threats of the people, however, led the empress Eudoxia to recall him. Shortly afterward his denunciation of the honours addressed to a statue of the empress almost within the precincts of St. Sophia led to the calling of a second council, which again deposed him (404) for having resumed his functions without its permission. The people fired the cathedral and the senate house, but Chrysostom was hurried away to Cucusus (Cocysus) among the ridges of Mt. Taurus. His correspondence with the different churches and the recognition of his orthodoxy by Pope Innocent I and the emperor Honorius caused the emperor Arcadius to order his removal to the extreme desert of Pithyus. He died on the way at Comana in Pontus in 407. His exile gave rise to a schism and the Johannists (as they were called) only returned to communion with the bishop of Constantinople after the relics of the saint were brought back (437) and the emperor had publicly implored divine forgiveness. The feast of St. John Chrysostom falls on Nov. 13 in the Greek Church and on Jan. 27 in the Latin Church.

He elevates the ascetic element in religion and stresses the importance of knowing the Scriptures. In exegesis he is pure Antiochene, basing his expositions upon thorough grammatical study and not on the allegorical interpretation of Origen and the Alexandrian school. His writings contain the germ of later Eucharistic teaching and the invocation of the saints, but give no direct expression of the primacy of the pope or the necessity of private confession. As early as 425 Chrysostom was cited by the Greeks and Latins as a great authority.

His voluminous works include the early monastical treatises, including *On Priesthood,* the many homilies and commentaries written during his priesthood and episcopate, the best known being those *On the Statues* and on *Genesis, Psalms, Matthew and Romans,* and the letters which belong to the time of his exile and are valuable sources of history. The best edition is that of Migne (*Patrol. Graec.*, xlvii–lxiv) but many of the treatises have been edited more recently. English translations of some of the homilies and commentaries are in the Oxford Library of the Fathers. The most valuable authorities for his life are the ecclesiastical histories of Palladius, Socrates, Sozomen and Theodoret.

See W. R. Stephens, *St. John Chrysostom* (1871); F. H. Chase, *Chrysostom, a Study in Biblical Interpretation* (1887); Naegle, *Die Eucharisticlehre Des hl. Joh. Chrysostom* (Freiburg, 1900); C. Baur, *S. Jean Chrysostome et ses oeuvres* (Louvain, 1907); J. M. Vance, *Beiträge Byzantinischen Kulturgeschichte aus den Schriften des Chrysostom* (Jena, 1907); A. Harnack, *Hist. of Dogma,* iii and iv.

CHRYSOTILE, a variety of serpentine, a hydrous silicate of magnesia, characterized by a fine, more or less silklike fibrous structure; this is the principal fibrous mineral used in commerce under the name asbestos (*q.v.*). (The name is derived from the Greek χρυσός, gold, and τίλος, down or hair, literally hair of gold.)

CHUB (*Leuciscus cephalus*), a cyprinid fish distinguished from others of the family in English rivers by the broad head and strong jaws and by feeding to a considerable extent on little fish. In England a length of 2 ft. and a weight of 8 lb. is reached, but on the continent 12 lb. In America the name is applied to other large-headed cyprinids; *e.g.,* the river chub (*Hybopsis kentuckiensis*) and the silver chub (*Semotilus corporalis*).

CHUBB, THOMAS (1679–1746), English deist, was born at East Harnham, near Salisbury, on Sept. 29, 1679. The son of a maltster, he was apprenticed to a glovemaker and subsequently worked for a tallow chandler. Later he lived for several years in the house of the master of the rolls, Sir Joseph Jekyll, apparently as a servent. He died in Salisbury on Feb. 8, 1746. He appeared as an author during the Arian controversy with an essay, *The Supremacy of the Father Asserted,* published on Whiston's authority in 1715. Mainly interesting as showing the spread of rationalism in the popular mind of the period, he was regarded by Voltaire as one of the most logical of his school. (*See* DEISM.) His chief works are *Discourse Concerning Reason* (1731); *True Gospel of Jesus Christ* (1739); and *Posthumous Works* (1748).

CHUBUT, a territory of the southern Argentine republic, part of what was formerly called Patagonia, bounded north by Río Negro, south by the military zone of Comodoro Rivadavia, east by the Atlantic and west by Chile. Pop. (1947) 58,856; area 65,669 sq.mi. Except for the valleys in the Andean foothills, which are fertile and well forested, and the land along the banks of the Chubut river, which flows entirely across the territory from the Andes to the Atlantic, the country is a steppeland covered with scanty dwarfed vegetation, with occasional shallow saline lakes. The larger rivers are the Chubut and the Senguer, the latter flowing into Lake Colhué Huapí. There are a number of large lakes among the Andean foothills, the best known of which are Fontana, Menéndez and General Paz, and, in the interior, Colhué Huapí and Musters, the latter named after the English naval officer who traversed Patagonia in 1870. Petroleum was found in the southern part of the territory toward the close of 1907, at a depth of 1,768 ft., and is being exploited. Chubut is known chiefly by the Welsh colony near the mouth of the Chubut river and its branch, the 16th of October colony, farther up the river. The chief town of the Welsh, Rawson, is the capital of the territory (pop. 1947, 9,605) and Port Madryn on Golfo Nuevo is its best port. Other colonies have been founded in the fertile valleys of the Andean foothills. More than 5,000,000 head of sheep grazed in Chubut in 1948. (C. E. Mc.)

CHUCK-A-LUCK or CHUCKERLUCK is a simplified version of the French game hazard. A layout numbered from one to six inclusive, a table, three dice and a dice cup are the essentials. Many times the dice are kept in a wire cage shaped like an hourglass. When the cage is reversed the dice fall through the centre opening to the bottom half. In this form the game is often referred to as the bird cage.

Players can wager any amount within the minimum and maximum limits on one or more of the six numbers. When all bets are down the dice are thrown, or the wire cage is upended. The uppermost faces of the three dice determine the outcome. If the player's selected number shows on one dice, he wins the amount he wagered; if on two dice, he wins double; if on three dice, he wins triple. The house breaks even when three different numbers are thrown; averages a profit of one unit when a pair and a single are thrown; averages a profit of two units when three of a kind are thrown. This amounts to 7.87% of the total.

Crown and anchor, known throughout the Commonwealth of Nations and often played in states contiguous to Canada, uses the same equipment as chuck-a-luck except for the markings on the dice. Instead of dots, the six sides bear various symbols: anchor, crown, club, diamond, heart and spade. The layout used displays these same symbols. Method of play, amount of pay-off and house percentage are identical with chuck-a-luck.

Hazard is the game from which chuck-a-luck evolved. In the United States almost all houses with hazard layouts refer to the game as chuck-a-luck.

The only material difference is in the layout. Besides the six chuck-a-luck numbers the hazard layout provides spaces for wagering on odd or even; on high or low; on triples (called raffles); and on any number the dice may total, from 4 to 17. Three, the lowest number possible, and 18, the highest number possible, can only be made with triples so they are not included in the regular line.

The pay-off on single numbers is the same as in chuck-a-luck. A player betting on high, low, odd, or even, collects even money if he wins. The banker's advantage lies in the fact that he does not pay off if triples show. There are 216 possible combinations of 3 dice, 6 of which are triples. On this type of wager the house advantage is 2.78%.

If a player bets that any three of a kind will come up, he collects 30 to 1. (Correct odds—35 to 1; house advantage—13.9%.) If he bets that a particular triple will show, and he wins, he collects 180 to 1. (Correct odds—215 to 1; house advantage—16.2%.)

The percentage in favour of the house when a player bets on any particular number varies considerably, as shown by this table:

Combination	*Actual Odds*	*House Pays*	*House Advantage*
4 or 17	71 to 1	60 to 1	15.3%
5 or 16	35 to 1	30 to 1	13.9%
6 or 15	23 to 1	18 to 1	20.8%
7 or 14	67 to 5	12 to 1	9.7%
8 or 13	65 to 7	8 to 1	12.5%
9 or 12	8 to 1	6 to 1	22.2%
10 or 11	7 to 1	6 to 1	12.5%

To explain how the percentages are figured: suppose the chosen number is 6. There are 10 ways to make 6 with three dice—1–1–4, 1–4–1, 1–2–3, 1–3–2, 2–2–2, 2–1–3, 2–3–1, 3–1–2, 3–2–1, 4–1–1. The house does not pay off when 6 is made with three deuces, leaving 9 winning combinations for the player. There are 216 possible combinations. Deduct the 9 winning combinations. The odds are 207 to 9, or 23 to 1. The house pays 18 to 1. The difference between these two figures—24 for the house, 19 for the player—constitutes the house "edge" (advantage)—5/24 of 100 is 20.8%.

Should the house use a layout which reads 18 for 1, instead of 18 to 1, its percentage is increased, in this case 4.2%.

Poker dice requires five dice, a dice cup and a mat. The object is to score as high a poker hand as possible (*see* POKER). The ace has the highest value, the deuce the lowest. The hands run the same as in poker: five of a kind; four of a kind; full house; three of a kind; two pair; one pair. Usually the straight is not played, but when it is it ranks between three of a kind and a full house. Most players make the ace "wild," counting for any number the player wishes.

The first player throws all five dice. He may then put aside any combination he wishes, place the remaining dice in the cup, and throw again. Should he wish to play the first five thrown, he may do so. On the other hand, he may if he wishes pick up all five dice. It is sometimes played that each player in his turn is entitled to three casts of the dice. Subsequent players do likewise. The one getting the highest poker hand wins. Often the game is played with dice bearing regular playing card denominations: ace, king, queen, knave (jack), ten and nine. Occasionally pentagonal dice with values from ace to ten are used.

Many variations of poker dice are played as "counter games," so called because they are played on the counters of small retail stores with the merchant as banker. Each player has an equal chance. The advantage to the banker lies in the fact that the player must take his winnings, if any, in merchandise, upon which the owner of the store makes a profit. Such games therefore come under the heading of "trade stimulators."

Twenty-six is a counter game played for direct profit by the banker. Ten dice, a dice cup and a score card are required. The house always banks the game. The player first chooses any number from 1 to 6. The ten dice are thrown from the cup, the operator counts the number of times the selected number has shown, marks the total on the score card, and replaces the dice in the cup. The player is allowed 13 throws in all. If the number named by the player appears less than 11 times, or more than 25 times, the house pays the winner four units for every unit wagered. Sometimes the pay-off is increased if the player throws the chosen number more than 26 times.

Manufacturers of the paraphernalia guarantee their customers a profit of 15%. The dice girls who usually handle the game claim that the actual percentage is higher, often running as much as 20%. (S. M. M.)

CHUGUYEV, a town in the Kharkov county of the Ukrainian S.S.R., on the right bank of the Donetz river where the railway linking Kharkov to Kupyansk crosses the river; 49° 49′ N. lat., 36° 41′ E. long. Pop. (1926) 13,311.

CHUKCHI, a Mongoloid people inhabiting northeastern Siberia between Bering strait, Chaun bay and the Anadyr river. Culturally they belong to the circumpolar area, along with the Eskimo of North America and the Lapps, Samoyedes and other peoples of arctic Eurasia. Their language, however, is related only to those of the neighbouring Koryak and Kamchadal.

The Chukchi number about 12,000. Approximately 3,000 Maritime Chukchi live in permanent villages along the Arctic and Pacific coasts, subsisting primarily by fishing and the pursuit of seals, walrus and whales. About 9,000 Reindeer Chukchi wander in the interior, hunting, gathering and grazing their herds of domesticated reindeer on the tundra. Both groups live today in skin tents, but the Maritime Chukchi once occupied semisubterranean dwellings. Each community is politically independent under a nominal headman.

A man obtains a wife by serving her father for two or three years, after which he returns with his family to his own relatives. Polygamy is general and wife lending common. Clans are lacking, marriage with a first cousin is permitted and kinship conforms to the Eskimo pattern. Old people are respected, but when decrepit they sometimes commit suicide or compel their relatives to kill them.

The Chukchi people the unseen world with nature spirits who control natural phenomena, benevolent celestial spirits who receive sacrifices, evil spirits who cause sickness and death and various mythical monsters. Men who receive a "call" become shamans. They can commune with spirits, cause injuries through incantations and cure disease in spiritualistic seances. Summoning their familiar spirits by singing and drum beating, they become possessed by them, dance with frenzy and ventriloquistic utterances and ultimately fall into a trance, during which they purportedly visit the spirit world and rescue the wandering soul of the patient.

BIBLIOGRAPHY.—W. Bogoras, *The Chukchee* (1904–09); H. U. Sverdrup, *Hos Tundrafolket* (1938); T. Odulok, *Snow People*, tr. by J. Cleugh (London, 1934); A. E. Nordenskiöld, *The Voyage of the Vega* (1882); W. H. Hooper, *Ten Months Among the Tents of the Tuski* (1853). (G. P. MK.)

CHULALONGKORN, PHRA PARAMINDR MAHA (1853–1910), king of Thailand (Siam), eldest son of King Maha Mongkut, was born on Sept. 20, 1853, and succeeded his father on the throne on Oct. 1, 1868. The young king, who had according to custom been brought up in a Buddhist monastery, again retired into seclusion until he came of age in 1873, the government being entrusted to a regency. He then took the step, unprecedented for an eastern Asiatic potentate, of travelling outside his dominions, in India and the Dutch East Indies. The fruits of his appreciation of foreign institutions appeared in the reforms which he instituted in Thailand: the abolition of slavery, the simplification of court etiquette, the grant of liberty of conscience, the erection of schools and hospitals and the further development of the army and navy. He established a standard coinage, postal and telegraph services, and arranged for the policing, sanitation and lighting of Bangkok. Several of his sons, including the crown prince, were educated in England, and he himself visited Europe in 1897. He died at Bangkok on Oct. 23, 1910.

CHUMBI VALLEY, a valley connecting Tibet (*q.v.*) with the frontier of India. On the southern slopes of the Himalayas about 9,500 ft. above the sea, the valley is wedged in between Bhutan and Sikkim, and does not belong geographically but only politically to Tibet. The valley is sparsely cultivated on small flats by the river.

CHUNAR, a town and ancient fortress in Mirzapur district, Uttar Pradesh, India, on the south bank of the Ganges, 16 mi. S.S.W. of Benares. Pop. (1951) 8,176. The fort is on the summit of an abrupt rock commanding the river. It was once a place of great strength and contains the remains of a Hindu palace with interesting carvings. The town was once a European settlement for the invalid or veteran battalion of the East India company's army. In the church, the school, some ruined houses and the graveyards are traces of that colony of war-worn exiles. The chief industry is quarrying the excellent Chunar sandstone, which was used notably for the buildings and sculptures of the Maurya and Gupta dynasties. In 1530 Chunar became the residence of Sher Shah the Afghan, and 45 years later was recovered by the emperor Akbar after a siege of six months. It fell to the English under Col. John Carnac in 1763 after long resistance. A treaty with the nawab of Oudh was signed there by Warren Hastings on behalf of the East India company in Sept. 1781, and for a time it enjoyed military importance as the frontier post of the company's jurisdiction.

CHUNCHO (Anti), a term used to distinguish several South American Indian tribes on the eastern slope of the Andes, *e.g.*, the Arawakan (*q.v.*), Campa and others, from the Quéchua (*q.v.*) (Quichua) and the Aymara of the highlands. (J. H. Sd.)

CHUNGKING, former treaty port and commercial emporium of the isolated but important and densely peopled inland basin of Szechwan in western China. Pop. (1942) *c.* 1,000,000.

It is built on a rocky peninsula at the confluence of the Kialing, the most easterly of the great rivers draining the Red basin, with the Yangtze, the arterial line of communication in middle China. Chungking is therefore the natural gateway through which Szechwan communicates with the rest of China and the ocean. Moreover it gathers up the trade of eastern Tibet and of much of the north of Kweichow and Yünnan.

Chungking claims a history of more than 4,200 years. It was the birthplace of the imperial consort of the legendary Emperor Yu of the Hsia dynasty of the 22nd century B.C. When Emperor Wu of the Chou dynasty became ruler of China he made the viscount of Pahtzeku ruler over the territory now called Chungking and its neighbouring towns. It was made a kingdom about 340 B.C. Pahtzekuo was absorbed, as a county, under the Ch'in dynasty. The region of Chungking served occasionally as basis for independent rebellious leaders as Gen. Min Yu-chen at the end of the Yüan dynasty in 1367–68 and Chang Hsien-chung in 1645–51 at the end of the Ming dynasty. The Sino-British treaty of Chefoo in 1876 and the treaty of Peking in 1890 opened Chungking as a treaty port. The Japanese gained the right to establish a concession in Chungking after the treaty of Shimonoseki in 1895. The Japanese concession established in 1901 was taken over by the Chinese when war broke out in 1937.

Chungking became a municipality in Feb. 1923; on Nov. 20, 1937, Chungking became the wartime capital of China. In May 1939 it was placed under the control of the executive yuan and became a special municipality. After being officially named an auxiliary capital in Oct. 1940, its municipal limits were extended to include the four districts of Hsiaolungkan, Shapingpa, Tzechikow and Koloshan. Total area after expansion equalled 116 sq.mi. Extensive damage was caused by the repeated bombings by the Japanese from 1938 to 1941. Large sections of the downtown area were destroyed.

CHUPATTY. An Anglo-Indian term for an unleavened cake of bread. The word represents the Hindustani *chapati,* and is applied to the usual form of native bread, the staple food of upper India. The chupatty is generally made of coarse wheaten flour, patted flat with the hand and baked upon a griddle. In 1857 chupatties were circulated as a sign of discontent.

CHUPRIYA or Cuprija, a city in the Morava department of Serbia, Yugo. The old name was Korea Margi. (Pop., 1948, 9,819.) It is on the railway from Belgrade to Nish, and on the Morava, which is navigable up to this point by small sailing vessels. A light railway runs to Senje, which has lignite and other collieries that were seriously damaged in World War I. Fine Serbian cattle are bred in the neighbouring lowlands, and the town has a large sugar-beet factory and considerable trade in plums and farm produce. A government nursery for mulberry trees has been started; sericulture, which flourished in the middle ages, died down under Turkish rule. There is a government stud farm in the district. In World War I Chupriya was the central ammunition depot of the Serbian army; in World War II it was occupied by Germany. Cloth is woven, and there are glassworks at Paracin, 5 mi. S. Jagodina, 8 mi. N.W., is an important market town. Both are connected with Chupriya by rail and road.

The 14th-century Ravanitsa monastery, with a ruined fort and an old church (their walls and frescoes pitted by Turkish bullets), is about 7 mi. distant. Legend says that there the Serbian tsar Lazar (1374–89) was visited by an angel who bade him choose between an earthly and a heavenly crown. In accordance with his choice Lazar fell fighting at the battle of Kossovo. He was buried at Ravanitsa, but his body was afterward removed. His crucifix is treasured among the monastic archives, which also contain a charter signed by Peter the Great of Russia (1672–1725). Manasia (Manasiya), the still more celebrated foundation of Stephen, the son and successor of Lazar, lies 12 mi. N. of Ravanitsa. Built in a cleft among the hills, this monastery is enclosed in a fortress whose square towers and curtain without loopholes or battlements remain largely intact. Within the curtain stand the monastic buildings, a large garden and a cruciform chapel, with many curious old stone carvings, half hidden beneath whitewash. Numerous gifts from the Russian court, such as gospels lettered in gold and silver relief and jewelled crucifixes, are preserved on the spot, but the valuable library was removed in the 15th century to the monastery of Hilendar on Mt. Athos.

CHUQUISACA, a department of southeast Bolivia. It lies partly upon the eastern plateau of Bolivia and partly upon the great plains of the upper La Plata basin; area, 19,893 sq.mi. The Pilcomayo, a large tributary of the Paraguay, crosses northwest to southeast the western part of the department. The climate of the lowlands is hot, humid and unhealthful, but that of the plateau is salubrious, though subject to greater extremes in temperature. The seasons are sharply divided into wet and dry, the eastern plains becoming great lagoons during the wet season and parched deserts during the dry. The mineral resources are important, but are less developed than those of Potosí and Oruro. Grazing is the principal industry of the plains, and cattle, sheep, goats and llamas are raised and cereals grown in the fertile valleys of the plateau. Rough highways connect Chuquisaca with its neighbours on the north and west, and pack animals are the common means of transporting merchandise. The only railway and the best highway in the department connect Sucre with Potosí. Pop. (1950) 282,980, largely Indians and mestizos. The plateau Indians are generally Aymaras, but on the eastern plains there are considerable settlements of partly civilized Chiriguanos, of Guaraní origin. The department is divided (1950) into ten provinces, the greater part of the lowlands being unsettled and without effective political organization. Its principal towns are Sucre (*q.v.*), the capital, San Lucas, Tarabuco and Yotala.

CHUR, the capital of the Swiss canton of the Grisons (Fr. Coire, Ital. Coira). It lies 1,950 ft. above sea level on the valley floor of the Vorder Rhein in the angle between the Plessur and the Rhine, and is overshadowed by the Mittenberg and Pizokel, hills that guard the entrance to the deep-cut Schanfigg (Plessur) valley. Pop. (1950) 19,382. In 1920, 12,644 were German-speaking, 1,871 were Romansch and 943 Italian. Protestants numbered 9,783 and Roman Catholics 5,733. The old city is on the west, and includes the cathedral church of St. Lucius (traditionally a 2nd-century British king), which was built between 1178 and 1282 on the site of an older church. Opposite is the Bishop's palace and not far off is the Episcopal seminary (built on the ruins of a 6th-century monastic foundation). The Raetian museum contains a great collection of objects relating to Raetia. Chur is 74 mi. by rail from Zürich: it is the meeting point of routes from Italy over many Alpine passes (the Lukmanier, the Splügen, the San Bernardino) and is the centre of an active trade, particularly in wine from the Valtelline. Electric trains run to Davos, St. Moritz, Arosa and Andermatt.

The episcopal see is first mentioned in 452, but probably existed a century earlier. The bishop soon acquired great temporal powers, and became a prince of the empire in 1170. In 1392 he became head of the League of God's House (originally formed against him in 1367), one of the three Raetian leagues, but in 1526, after the Reformation, lost his temporal powers, having fulfilled his historical mission. The bishopric still exists, with jurisdiction over the cantons of the Grisons, Glarus, Zürich and the three forest cantons, as well as over Liechtenstein. The guild constitution of the city of Chur lasted from 1465 to 1839.

Bibliography.—W. von Juvalt, *Forschungen über die Feudalzeit im Curischen Raetien,* 2 parts (1871); C. Kind, *Die Reformation in den*

Bisthümern Chur und Como (1858); Conradin von Moor, *Geschichte von Curraetien*, 2 vol. (1870–74); P. C. von Planta, *Verfassungsgeschichte der Stadt Cur im Mittelalter* (1879); *Das Bürgerhaus d. Schweiz*, vol. xiv (1924).

CHURCH, FREDERICK EDWIN (1826–1900), American landscape painter, was born at Hartford (Conn.) on May 4, 1826. He was a pupil of Thomas Cole at Catskill (N.Y.), where his first pictures were painted. Developing unusual technical dexterity, Church from the beginning sought for his themes such marvels of nature as Niagara Falls, the Andes, and tropical forests—he visited South America in 1853 and 1857—volcanoes in eruption, and icebergs, the beauties of which he portrayed with great skill in the management of light, colour, and the phenomena of rainbow, mist and sunset, rendering these plausible and effective. In their time these paintings awoke the wildest admiration and sold for extravagant prices, collectors in the United States and in Europe eagerly seeking them, though their vogue has now passed away. In 1849 Church was made a member of the National Academy of Design. His "Great Fall at Niagara" (1857) is in the Corcoran Art Gallery, Washington (D.C.), and a large "Twilight" is in the Walters Gallery, Baltimore (Md.). Among his other canvases are "Andes of Ecuador" (1855), "Heart of the Andes" (1859), "Cotopaxi" (1862), "Jerusalem" (1870), and "Morning in the Tropics" (1877). He died on April 7, 1900, at his house on the Hudson river above New York city, where he had lived and worked for many years. He was the most prominent member of the "Hudson river school" of American artists.

CHURCH, GEORGE EARL (1835–1910), American geographer, was born in New Bedford (Mass.), on Dec. 7, 1835. He was educated as a civil engineer, and was early engaged on the Hoosac tunnel. In 1858 he joined an exploring expedition to South America. During the American Civil War he served (1862–65) in the Army of the Potomac, rising to the command of a brigade and the rank of colonel; and in 1866–67 he was war correspondent of the *New York Herald* in Mexico. He explored the Amazon (1868–79), and gradually became the leading authority on that region of South America. In 1880 he was appointed U.S. commissioner to report on Ecuador, and in 1895 visited Costa Rica to report on its debt and railways. He wrote extensively on South and Central American geography, and became a vice-president of the Royal Geographical Society (London), and in 1898 president of the geographical section of the British Association.

CHURCH, SIR RICHARD (1784–1873), British military officer and general in the Greek army, was the son of a Quaker, Matthew Church of Cork. He was born in 1784, and at the age of 16 ran away from home and enlisted in the army. For this violation of its principles he was disowned by the Society of Friends, but his father bought him a commission in the 13th (Somersetshire) Light Infantry. He served in the demonstration against Ferrol, and in the expedition to Egypt under Sir Ralph Abercromby in 1801. He accompanied the expedition which landed in Calabria, and fought a successful battle against the French at Maida on July 6, 1806. In the summer of 1809 Church sailed with the expedition sent to occupy the Ionian islands. Here he formed a Greek regiment in English pay. It included many of the men who were afterwards among the leaders of the Greeks in the War of Independence. Church drew up a report on the Ionian islands for the Congress of Vienna, in which he advocated the retention of the islands under the British flag and the permanent occupation by Great Britain of Parga and of other formerly Venetian coast towns on the mainland, then in the possession of Ali Pasha of Iannina. In 1817 he entered the service of King Ferdinand of Naples as lieutenant-general, with a commission to suppress the brigandage then rampant in Apulia. In 1820 he was appointed governor of Palermo and commander-in-chief of the troops in Sicily. The revolution which broke out in that year led to the termination of his services in Naples.

In 1827 Church became commander-in-chief of the Greek army. The rout of his army in an attempt to relieve the acropolis of Athens, then besieged by the Turks, proved that it was incapable of conducting regular operations. The acropolis capitulated, and Sir Richard (he had been knighted by George IV.) turned to partisan warfare in western Greece. Here his activity had beneficial results, for it led to a rectification in 1832, in a sense favourable to Greece, of the frontier drawn by the Powers in 1830 (*see* his *Observations on an Eligible Line of Frontier for Greece*, 1830). Church had, however, surrendered his commission, as a protest against the unfriendly Government of Capo d'Istria, on Aug. 25, 1829. He lived for the rest of his life in Greece, was created general of the army in 1854, and died at Athens on March 30, 1873.

See *Sir Richard Church*, by Stanley Lane Poole (1890); Z. D. Feniman, *Some English Philhellenes* (1917); *Sir Richard Church in Italy and Greece*, by E. M. Church (Edinburgh, 1895), based on family papers (an Italian version, *Brigantaggio e società segrete nelle Puglie, 1817–1828*, executed under the direction of Carlo Lacaita, appeared at Florence in 1899). The ms. correspondence and papers of Sir Richard Church, in 29 vols., now in the British Museum (add. mss. 36,543–36,571), contain invaluable material for the history of the War of Greek Independence, including a narrative of the war during Church's tenure of the command, which corrects many errors in the published accounts and successfully vindicates Church's reputation against the strictures of Finlay, Mendelssohn-Bartholdy and other historians of the war (see *Cam. Mod. Hist.* x. p. 804).

CHURCH, RICHARD WILLIAM (1815–1890), English divine, son of John Dearman Church, brother of Sir Richard Church (*q.v.*), a merchant, was born at Lisbon on April 25, 1815, his early years being mostly spent at Florence. He went up to Wadham college, Oxford, in 1833, took first-class honours in 1836, and in 1838 was elected fellow of Oriel. He was appointed tutor of Oriel in 1839, and was ordained the same year. He was an intimate friend of J. H. Newman at this period, and closely allied to the Tractarian party. In 1841 No. 90 of *Tracts for the Times* appeared, and Church resigned his tutorship. In 1844–45 he was junior proctor, and in that capacity, in concert with his senior colleague, vetoed a proposal to censure Tract 90 publicly. In 1846 Church, with others, started *The Guardian* newspaper, and he was an early contributor to *The Saturday Review.* He accepted in 1852 the small living of Whatley in Somersetshire, near Frome. In 1869 he refused a canonry at Worcester, but in 1871 he accepted, most reluctantly (calling it "a sacrifice *en pure perte*"), the deanery of St. Paul's, to which he was nominated by W. E. Gladstone. Dean Church died on Dec. 9, 1890.

His chief pub. works are a *Life of St. Anselm* (1870); the lives of *Spenser* (1879) and *Bacon* (1884) in Macmillan's "Men of Letters" series; an *Essay on Dante* (1878); *The Oxford Movement* (1891), together with many other vols. of essays and sermons. A coll. of his journalistic arts. was pub. in 1897 as *Occasional Papers.*

See *Life and Letters of Dean Church*, by his daughter, M. C. Church (1895); memoir by H. C. Beeching in *Dict. Nat. Biog.;* and D. C. Lathbury *Dean Church* (1907).

CHURCH. The word church refers both to the Christian religious community and to the building used for Christian worship. This article, after discussing the etymology of the word itself, will deal separately with these two subjects.

Etymology of the Word Church.—According to most authorities, the word is derived from the Gr. κυριακὸν (δῶμα), "the Lord's (house)," and is common to many Teutonic, Slavonic and other languages, under various forms—*e.g.,* Scottish *kirk*, Ger. *kirche*, Swed. *kirka*, Dan. *kirke*, Russ. *tserkov*, Bulg. *cerkova*, Czech. *cirkev*, Finn. *kirkko*, etc. The word was originally applied to the building used for Christian worship, and subsequently extended to the Christian community (*ecclesia*) itself. Conversely, the Greek word *ecclesia* (ἐκκλησία) was transferred from the community to the building, and is used in both senses, especially in the modern Romance and Celtic languages (*e.g.,* Fr. *église*, Welsh *eglwys*, etc.). The Gothic New Testament of Ulfilas has *aikklesjo*.

A. THE CHURCH: THE RELIGIOUS COMMUNITY

The English word "church" represents the Greek ἐκκλησία (naturalized in Latin as *Ecclesia*) in its specifically Christian use. Other uses of the Greek word shed no light on this, and may prove misleading if brought into comparison. As so used, its earliest appearance that we can date is in the Epistles of St. Paul, where it is evidently a familiar term. In the earliest of them the apostle writes, "ye have heard of my manner of life in time past in the Jews' religion, how that beyond measure I persecuted the Church of God, and make havock of it." This phrase, *the Church of God* (τὴν ἐκκλησίαν τοῦ Θεοῦ), has a history behind it, which will show exactly in what sense it was here used.

In the Old Testament are two Hebrew words *'edah,* and *ḳahal,* which in the LXX. are indiscriminately rendered συναγωγή or ἐκκλησία. In the Pentateuch both alike signify the general assembly of the people of Israel during the Wanderings. The word ἐκκλησία, which is so far confined to Deuteronomy is in this connection a natural Hellenism. Elsewhere they mean the people itself, especially in its relation to God, with little or no reference to assembling. Striking examples are Nehemiah xiii. 1 where the phrase is ἐκκλησία θεοῦ, and Ps. lxxiv. 2, τῆς συναγωγῆς σου. The word συναγωγή is the more frequent, and this alone survived in current use among Hellenistic Jews in the sense of a local congregation, the familiar *synagogue.* What has to be considered is the reason why the other word was revived in Christian use. The origin and the essential character of the Church are involved in this enquiry.

As historical sources there is nothing else, except in some sections of the Acts, so entirely contemporary as St. Paul's Epistles; but in the Gospels and in the rest of the Acts, though the language may be coloured by later thought or experience, valuable material can be found. It is clear that the gospel began as a proclamation of the Kingdom of God (or of Heaven) having close affinity both with older Messianic prophecy referring to the lineage of David, and with more recent apocalyptic dreams. The proclamation was renewed in both aspects by the Apostles on the basis of belief in the resurrection and ascension of Jesus as the Christ. They gathered at Jerusalem a considerable number of disciples, forming a close community which was entered by the rite of baptism. There is reason to think that it was organized as a synagogue, one of the many in Jerusalem. In Aramaic "synagogue" is *knishta.* The Church is still so called by the Aramaic Christians of Palestine. Hence, perhaps, the word *synagogue* in James ii. 2. In the 4th century Epiphanius writes clumsily of the Ebionites, συναγωγὴν καλοῦσι τὴν ἑαυτῶν ἐκκλησίαν καὶ οὐχὶ ἐκκλησίαν (*Adv. Haeres,* i. ii. 18). We hear of it later (Acts xv.) as governed by James with a bench of Presbyters, the usual equipment of a synagogue. Some Pharisees and some priests joined, and the disciples regularly took part in the worship of the Temple; but the high priest and the Sanhedrim were hostile, making intermittent attempts to suppress the movement.

The episode of Stephen was a turning point. It is evident that this Hellenistic Jew was out of sympathy with the dominant religious sentiments of Jerusalem, probably shared by the Apostles and most of their disciples. He seems to have anticipated revolutionary changes, involving the suppression of the Mosaic ordinances and even of the Temple. His defence before the Sanhedrim was a rapid survey of Old Testament history. That history is a record of repeated relapses and ruin of God's chosen people, followed by the recovery of a small remnant, the common subject of prophecy. Stephen is just approaching a prophetic warning when he is silenced. It is probable that this worked in the mind of St. Paul, as preparation for his conversion. It became a prominent element in his teaching that the prophetic doctrine of the Remnant was being fulfilled. The Jewish people as a whole had fallen away by their rejection of Jesus as Messiah; those who accepted him were the faithful remnant which was to be the beginning of a reconstitution of God's people. He develops the argument in Romans ix., xi., but the conclusion is condensed into one remarkable sentence, Philip iii. 3, "We are the circumcision, who worship by the spirit of God, and glory in Christ Jesus, and have no confidence in the flesh." In current speech "the circumcision" meant the Jewish people regarded as bound in covenant to God. The actual rite of circumcision was being abandoned by Christians, and the sentence may be paraphrased: "Not those who practise the circumcision of the flesh, but the believers in Jesus as the Christ, are all that circumcision signifies, the covenanted People of God." It is the proper conclusion of Stephen's interrupted argument. St. Paul himself, having heard the argument and taken an active part in the persecution that followed, was soon afterwards convinced of its truth. So he said that he had persecuted "the *ecclesia* of God."

Why that Greek word? It occurs in Stephen's defence, but we do not know that he spoke in Greek. It would be familiar to any diligent reader of the LXX. and peculiarly appropriate, as it appears in Nehemiah xiii. 1, where ἐκκλησία Θεοῦ means the returning exiles, the Remnant on which the people of God was to be reconstructed. Its use appears to be a deliberate archaism; the exact equivalent συναγωγή being current, but unsuitable because of its immediate associations. In the Aramaic of the Christians of northern Syria *'edta,* a variant of the Hebrew *'edah,* is a precisely similar archaism. A common place of origin is, perhaps, to be found at Antioch. Hort's hesitating suggestion that it may have been derived from the saying of our Lord recorded in Matt. xvi. 18 is unacceptable in view of the improbability that Greek was the language used on that occasion. If not, the use of ἐκκλησία there will be due to later coloration.

The use of the word thus indicates the definite application of the prophetic teaching about the Remnant to the new Christian community. This application was not peculiar to St. Paul; it is found also in the words quoted by James in Acts xv. 16, "I will build again the tabernacle of David which is fallen, and I will build again the ruins thereof." The rest of his quotation marks a second crisis: "That the residue of men may seek the Lord, and all the Gentiles, upon whom my name is called." It was not long after the episode of Stephen that St. Peter startled the community at Jerusalem by baptizing Cornelius the centurion at Caesarea, an example which appears to have been soon followed at Antioch. The Jewish Commonwealth had always been open to proselytes who received circumcision and undertook to observe the Mosaic law, but these new entrants did not conform to either condition. When the community at Jerusalem consented, perhaps reluctantly, to the innovation, a complete break with Judaism was bound to come. St. Paul was inclined to press it, arguing (rather inconsistently with the doctrine of the Remnant) that Jews and Gentiles had to enter equally into the new covenant (*Gal.* iii.), but he afterwards spoke of the Gentiles as engrafted into the stock of Israel (*Rom.* xi. 17).

The Church now became a Diaspora, like that of Judaism, extended in all directions by the work of the Apostles and their helpers, but retaining its headquarters at Jerusalem. Consequently, the word *ecclesia* speedily went the same way that the word *synagogue* had gone; from being the designation of the whole People of God, it became the designation also of local groups. This development was already complete when St. Paul addressed his first extant epistle to "the Churches of Galatia." Of the organization of these Churches we know very little, for our only informants had no occasion to describe what was familiar to those for whom they were writing. Two opinions on the subject stand in sharp contrast. The one is linked with Luther's conception of an "invisible" Church, the members of which are known only to God. Rudolph Sohm is the ablest recent exponent of this idea. According to him, believers in Jesus as Christ were at first united only by a spiritual nexus; but before long there was an inevitable attempt to bind together all putative believers in an external organization, which eventually claimed to be the true Church of God, thus corrupting the pure spirituality of the Gospel. The other opinion postulates a completely organized society, existing from the beginning and continuing, not indeed without changes, but in consistent development through subsequent ages. In reply to Sohm, Harnack stated this with much exaggeration, asserting that the Church began with an "abundant and elaborate equipment," and even with a "legal code" of complicated structure.

The truth seems to lie in a synthesis of the ideal and the actual contained in these extremes. Lightfoot constructed such a synthesis in his essay on *The Christian Ministry.* What discipleship meant was a spiritual union with the risen Christ, but this union was held to be mediated by the rite of baptism. According to St. Paul, to be baptized was to "put on Christ," (*Gal.* iii. 27). Those who thus "live by the Spirit" must also "walk by the Spirit"

(*Gal.* v. 25). But this spiritual walking was strictly controlled by the Apostles, who ruled the several Churches in a most peremptory manner, "So ordain I in all the Churches" (I. *Cor.* vii. 17) says St. Paul about the conduct of marriage. Their control secured some measure of uniformity; "We have no such custom, neither the Churches of God" (I. *Cor.* xi. 16) was sufficient reason for repressing an innovation. To keep things in order they visited the Churches, personally or by delegates, and in case of need wrote directive letters. In a striking metaphor they are to the Church as the foundation to a house (*Eph.* ii. 20), and this cannot refer only to the original preaching of the Twelve, for St. Paul certainly included Barnabas and himself. Thus the Apostolate extended as the Church extended, and was in the way of becoming a permanent institution. Of the interior order of the local Churches we know at least the existence of Presbyters, some of whom were called ἐπίσκοποι or overseers. Details must be treated elsewhere. The Church of the first age, therefore, certainly had an official equipment and some rules of conduct, but probably nothing so elaborate as Harnack supposed. Nor was this equipment alien to the spiritual character of the Church, for every function depended on a special gift of the Spirit, however mediated (I. *Cor.* xii.; *Eph.* iv.). (*See* MINISTRY, THE CHRISTIAN; EUCHARIST.)

For 30 years after St. Paul's latest epistle we are left without information. The *First Epistle of Clement* supplies nothing new, but 20 years later the *Epistles of Ignatius* show a development. The five Churches in Asia which he addresses are equipped with a hierarchy of deacons and presbyters under a chief who bears the old title of ἐπίσκοπος (*bishop*) but no longer as a subordinate; he appears to execute in that one Church all the functions of an apostle. It is a disputed question whether his office has grown out of the presbyterate or is a continuation of the apostolate. If he were invariably attached to a single city, the former theory would be strengthened; but it is not so, for Ignatius calls himself "bishop of Syria," and some years later a single bishop is found serving the whole of Gaul north of the Narbonensian province, a truly apostolic charge. The system of city-bishops became general within the Roman empire, but in northern Europe and elsewhere the system of regionary bishops has always prevailed from the earliest times.

In Ignatius we find the important word "Catholic" describing the whole Church as distinct from local Churches. It is evidently a current term. He relates the bishop to a local Church as Jesus Christ to the Catholic Church (*Smyrn.* viii. 2). But in the *Martyrium Polycarpi,* some years later, the Church of Smyrna is called Catholic, perhaps as locally representing the whole. The word afterwards takes on a much larger content, indicating adhesion to the Christian religion as a whole, in contrast with the particularities of heresy, and so can be applied even to individual persons.

The First Reasoned Theory.—The 3rd century presents to us for the first time in its history a reasoned theory of the Church in the writings of St. Cyprian. He bases it on the episcopate, which he entirely identifies with the apostolate. Bishops are appointed by Christ himself, as the Apostles were, though the divine appointment is mediated by consecration, and even by some elements of popular election. The episcopate is one, and he illustrates its unity by terms borrowed from the Roman law of corporations. Nevertheless in each single place there is a single bishop who represents the whole, and of that place those inhabitants who communicate with the bishop, and none else, are in the communion of the Catholic Church. He has been generally followed, except in two particulars. He maintained: (1) that all bishops are precisely equal in authority, and (2) that a bishop is responsible only to God, and can be removed from his place, as he was appointed, only by God. The latter contention was confronted, in his own practice, by the obvious difficulty of ascertaining when the Divine judgment has fallen. A solution was soon found in the obvious inferiority of a single bishop to a council of bishops, which could therefore depose him. The case of Paul of Samosata settled this. Irenaeus had already noted the special weight of authority (*potentior principalitas*) exerted by the bishop of Rome, and this was equally true of the other great capital cities, Alexandria and Antioch; Constantinople was afterwards added next to Rome, and the honorary addition of the restored Jerusalem completed the system of the patriarchates which dominated the Church in the eastern half of the Roman empire from Italy to the Euphrates. In the same part of the empire there was a similar aggrandisement of the bishop seated in the metropolis of each province, who presided over a manageable council of comprovincial bishops, and acquired a commanding influence in their appointment; a system which with some differences, was gradually extended westward, and into the countries beyond the empire.

Such is the working system of the Catholic Church, evolved from elements which we can discern in the first age. From the 5th century onward it has been complicated by claims made for the Church of Rome based on the promise of the Keys to St. Peter in Matt. xvi. 19. This requires separate treatment. It has been complicated also by obstinate schisms. Donatism in Africa was a passing trouble. Such also was the Arianism of the Goths, which for three centuries delayed the settlement of the Church in the new nations carved out of the Western empire. More permanent has been the separation, much more racial than theological, of Nestorians and Monophysites in the East from the orthodoxy of Constantinople. A succession of temporary quarrels between Constantinople and Rome led to the great breach of 1054 still continuing. (*See* PAPACY.)

In the 16th century the Reformation shattered the unity of the Western Church, contrary to the intention of the promoters, who aimed at reforming the whole Church "in head and members." The predestinarianism alike of Luther and of Calvin brought in the theory of the Invisible Church mentioned above, reducing the hierarchy to the level of a not indispensable expedient. Luther, regarding the Visible Church in this light, gave the chief control of it to the civil magistracy, in which he was followed or preceded by the Swiss Reformers and by those of the middle Rhine. Calvin established at Geneva a system of Presbytery, modelled on indications drawn from the Pauline Epistles and the Acts, acting in close connection with the magistracy and this was carried by his disciple, Theodore Beza, to the Reformed of France, in complete independence of a hostile State. The Genevan model was extended to the Netherlands, and the independent Presbytery of Beza was planted in Scotland by John Knox, to be afterwards perfected by Andrew Melville. This Presbyterianism followed with some exaggeration the lines of the Cyprianic episcopacy, while dropping the title of *bishop,* with all the associations which had gathered round it. In the Scandinavian countries the historic episcopate was retained by the reformers, and in England the organized administration connected with it also remained almost intact. The doctrinal aspects of the Reformation do not concern us here. (*See* REFORMATION.)

English Puritanism began as a demand for further reformation on the Swiss model, and with Thomas Cartwright took the form of an assertion of the Divine right of Presbyterianism, but a native development became much more important. Robert Browne, and after him Henry Barrow, deduced from the doctrine of the Invisible Church their conception of the "gathered Church," a group of believers voluntarily associated in complete independence, which they declared to be the only true Visible Church of the New Testament. This *Independency,* dominant during the crisis of the Civil War, survived its political failures, and remains, with various modifications, one of the chief factors in the Protestantism of English-speaking countries, where a "Church" is usually taken to be such an association, whether in its original form of a single congregation or in a close-knit and extensive system like those of the various Methodist connections. These developments will be found severally treated elsewhere. In their mutual antagonisms the idea of the Christian Church as a whole has been almost lost sight of, but it has recently revived in more friendly discussion, and is found to be firmly rooted in history.

BIBLIOGRAPHY.—Hort, *The Christian Ecclesia;* Lightfoot, *The Christian Ministry;* Sohm, *Wesen und Ursprung des Katholizismus;* Harnack, *Enstehung und Entwickelung der Kirchenfassung,* etc. (Eng. trans. by Pogson, *The Constitution and Law of the Church in the*

First Two Centuries); Lindsay, *The Church and the Ministry in the Early Centuries;* Gore, *The Church and the Ministry* (ed. 1919); Swete, *Essays on the Early History of the Church and the Ministry, by Various Writers;* Lacey, *The One Body and the One Spirit.*

(T. A. L.)

B. THE CHURCH BUILDING

It is generally held that the Church, when established as part of the organization of the Roman Empire, adopted for its buildings the plan of the secular basilica, and the name basilican has been given to the plan consisting of a long hall or nave with aisles, and with a projecting semicircular apse at the end opposite the main entrance. It should be remembered that the secular basilica followed no stereotyped form of plan, and that other influences may have combined to determine the plan assumed by the Christian church fabric. Further, although the term basilica was very commonly applied to early Christian churches, it was by no means confined to aisled buildings, but was also used of simpler structures. The internal arrangement of the apse, however, closely resembled that of the apse of the basilican law-court. The altar, on the chord of the apse, took the place of the altar on which oaths were taken by deponents: the seats of the bishop and clergy, ranged behind it, corresponded to those of the secular magistrates. The *cancelli* or screen, which divided the tribunal from the body of the court, became the barrier between the congregation and the sacred rites, and gave its name to the chancel of the church.

Circular Plan.—An alternative plan to that of the long aisled nave was the circular or polygonal plan, radiating from a central point, of which the most famous example is the church of San Vitale at Ravenna. This had its origin in the plan of the Christian baptistery, which was symbolically derived from the centralized plans of funeral monuments. The centralized church-plan, however, was provided with an encircling aisle or ambulatory, above which was a tribune or gallery, and with a chancel for the altar. Thus the fundamental characteristic of the Christian church-plan is its division into the nave for the worshippers and the chancel for the altar and clergy. Covering the main entrance to the nave there was frequently a narthex or vestibule, originally used by catechumens or by penitents excluded from participation in the holy mysteries. In the earliest churches the chancel was at the west end of the building, and the celebrant at the altar faced the congregation, but eventually the custom of placing the chancel at the east end of the church, which first appears in the basilicas of Ravenna prevailed, the celebrant still facing eastward. Beneath the altar there was often a crypt, the *martyrium* or *confessio,* so called from its traditional identity with the place of death or burial of the saint to whom the church was dedicated. The choir of singers was accommodated on the altar platform on either side of which were the *ambones* or pulpits from which the epistle and gospel were read.

In the larger Romanesque churches of western Europe, the aisled nave was practically universal, and the problem of covering these long structures with vaults of stone produced the characteristic art of the middle ages. Towers rose at the west ends of the aisles, and the erection of a tower on piers and arches between nave and chancel led to the development of the transept or cross-arm for purposes of abutment. It was, however, at the east end of the church that the principal development of plan took place. An aisled presbytery was interposed between the apse and the nave, and the aisles were in many instances continued round the apse, forming an ambulatory with a ring of chapels opening eastward from it. This arrangement, dictated by the requirements of processions and by the need of additional altars, became the regular plan of the French Gothic church, producing those magnificent *chevets* of apse and chapels which are the greatest masterpieces of mediaeval art. The process of enlargement and rebuilding, which attained its height in the thirteenth century, was due to the necessity of a larger ritual space and to the multiplication of endowments for masses. The east arms of churches were reconstructed on a large scale. Behind the altar in many churches rose the shrine of the local saint, the object of pilgrimages which enriched the church and its fabric. A Lady chapel, where the mass of the Blessed Virgin was celebrated daily, was often the most prominent of the chapels at the east end of the church, though its position on the plan varied. The transepts had their eastern aisles of chapels, and the spaces between the buttresses of the nave were utilised for the same purpose.

The Small Parish Church, usually an aisleless structure with nave and chancel, and with western or central tower, also underwent enlargement as local needs demanded. The nave was aisled; the chancel was lengthened; chapels were added at various points in the plan, which sometimes became extremely complex. Such enlargements and additions did not imply growth of population and the consequent need of a larger area for worshippers. Their cause was local anxiety to contribute to the pious work of church-building, and, where the means of benefactors allowed, to provide altars at which masses, maintained by their endowments, could be celebrated for the health of their souls. In certain districts church-building was encouraged by agricultural or commercial prosperity, by the existence of gilds which vied with one another in founding chantries, and by abundance of good local material and ease or cheapness of carriage. The architectural history of parish churches was much affected by the division of responsibility for cost between the rector, who met the repairs of the chancel, and the parishioners, who maintained the rest of the building by their contributions to the fabric fund or "works," under the administration of the church wardens, the *custodes fabricae* or *operis.*

It is often stated that the church architecture of the middle ages was dictated by an elaborate scheme of religious symbolism. While symbolical ideas entered into the adoption of certain types of plan, as in the transference, already mentioned, of the mausoleum plan to the baptistery, experience shows that the lay masons who usually carried out the work of building were guided by practical considerations, structural and ritual, whose free and natural expression would have been fettered by adherence to artificial rules of symbolism. Anomalies or deviations from regularity of plan, for which deep significances have been sought, can generally be assigned to errors of setting-out or to imperfect workmanship. The beauty and nobility of mediaeval church architecture is the result of the perfectly natural and unaffected response of the builders to the necessities of construction and to the immediate demands of the religious cult for which they laboured.

Artistic Development.—In some later mediaeval churches, especially those of friars, wide naves were provided for preaching purposes. Usually the interior of the church was broken up by the screens which enclosed the chapels in the aisles and beneath the arches. Between the nave and chancel was the screen, the western counterpart, with open tracery in its panels, of the closed iconostasis of the Eastern Church: above it was the loft or gallery and the beam on which stood the crucifix. In cathedral and collegiate churches the screen was habitually a solid erection of stone, shutting off the choir services from the nave; while in monastic churches, including several of the English cathedrals, there were two transverse screens, the choir-screen with its *pulpitum* or loft to the east, and the rood-screen a bay or two west of it. As the middle ages advanced, with the growth of specialization in various departments of church fittings, the church became more and more the frame and setting for works of art in stone, marble, alabaster, wood and stained glass. From the beginning colour played a large part in internal effect, as in the mosaic incrustation of early Christian churches. Rough walls were plastered and pictures or patterns painted on the dry surface or in fresco. The window-openings were filled with stained glass; pigments were lavishly employed on ceilings, on the surface of piers and vaults, and on furniture. In such prodigality of colour the mediaeval mind found the fullest satisfaction of its religious ideals. By the contemplation of the works of art that filled his church, Suger, the great abbot of Saint-Denis, tells us that he felt himself lifted in spirit from the world to a purer clime; and in Italy and Flanders the art of painting grew to perfection in the decoration of church walls and altars.

The Renaissance.—In countries which embraced the Reformation, the work of church-building was checked. The prime motive which up to that time had prompted the rebuilding or extension of so many churches was gone and existing buildings fully met the requirements of reformed worship. But in any case the Gothic art of the middle ages was already disappearing before the revival of classic art which had its birth in Italy. The ruthlessness which mediaeval artists had shown to the work of their predecessors was pursued by the architects of the Renaissance, who thought nothing of sweeping away great historic monuments like St. Peter's at Rome to make way for buildings in their new style. At the same time, while this implied a change in methods of construction and decoration, those methods were adapted to the traditional Christian church plan, and the combination of classical architecture with mediaeval traditions of planning and design is nowhere more clearly seen than in St. Paul's Cathedral and in other churches designed by Wren and the English architects who followed in his footsteps. While the church plan, during the period of Renaissance influence, underwent some simplification, and the idea of the large auditorium or hall of worship superseded the practice of the middle ages and survived in the churches of the Gothic revival, it still retained the fundamental character of the plan which had approved itself as suitable for the needs of the early Church and had reached its highest development in conformity with the requirements of mediaeval ritual. (A. H. T.)

See RELIGIOUS AND MEMORIAL ARCHITECTURE.

CHURCH AND STATE. The relation of Church and State in England, conveniently summed up in the word "establishment," is curiously complicated, including elements of great antiquity and arrangements made as recently as the year 1919. The antiquary, the historian, the lawyer, and the ecclesiastic find ample materials for their several studies in the Church of England as by law established. With the partial exception of Sweden, England was the only country in which the Reformation did not involve an almost complete breach with the system of the mediaeval Church. The main lines of the existing ecclesiastical system are mediaeval—the hierarchy, the parochial system, the convocations, the presence of the archbishops and bishops in the House of Lords, the canon law in so far as it was perpetuated by the legislation of Henry VIII., and the ecclesiastical courts. The Reformation effected a threefold change—social, doctrinal and constitutional. By the abolition of the monasteries, and the confiscation of the monastic property, the spiritual estate was weakened and impoverished: by the changes in doctrine and discipline the Church of England abandoned the distinctive beliefs and devotions of mediaeval Christianity; and by the acceptance of the royal supremacy, it not only repudiated the authority of the Roman pope, but received the status and constitution of an independent national Church. Since the 16th century the acceptance of the policy of religious toleration by the State, and the evolution of democracy, have affected importantly the system of the Established Church. The growth of nonconformity, the expansion of the insular kingdom into the British empire, the secularisation of parliament, and the development of denominational self-assertion within the Church itself have all affected the existing relations of Church and State in England. Establishment in its present form may be conveniently considered under five heads, viz., the royal supremacy, the authority of parliament, the ecclesiastical courts, patronage, the tenure of the ancient endowments.

The Royal Supremacy.—Henry VIII. forced the convocations to recognize his "headship" of the Church of England, but mitigated the unquestionable innovation by the pretence that he was but vindicating and restoring to the Crown the authority in ecclesiastical matters which was inherent in the monarchy by divine right, and had been recognized in practice until the usurpation of the Roman popes had obscured and superseded it. The revolutionary statutes which abolished the papal authority, and severed the national Church from the larger ecclesiastical system of which it had hitherto formed part, adopted a demurely constitutional tone, emphasizing the ancient independence and imperial self-sufficiency of the realm under its monarch. Thus the Restraint of Appeals, A.D. 1533, begins:

> Where by divers sundry old authentic histories and chronicles it is manifestly declared and expressed, that this realm of England is an empire, and so hath been accepted in the world, governed by one supreme head and king, having the dignity and royal estate of the imperial crown of the same, unto whom a body politic, compact of all sorts and degrees of people, divided in terms, and by names of spiritualty and temporalty, be bounden and ought to bear, next to God, a natural and humble obedience, etc.

That the royal authority over the Church in England had been very great in the past, and that the power of the popes had grown to exorbitant proportions in the period immediately preceding the Reformation, were unquestionable facts, and they gave plausibility to a contention which was, none the less, essentially untrue. The supremacy which the royal headship implied was a new thing in Christendom, and had no real precedents in history. It owed its origin to the novel conditions of the age, and its form to the masterful despot who arrogated it to himself. The functions withdrawn from the pope were accumulated on the monarch. Henry VIII., uniting in his own hands the plenitude of power both civil and spiritual, became in Bishop Stubbs's notable phrase, "the pope, the whole pope, and something more than the pope." (*Lectures on Mediaeval and Modern History*, p. 301.) So monstrous a claim could not be maintained. Under Elizabeth the royal supremacy was defined and delimited, and the much debated title, "head of the Church," was laid aside. Article XXXVII., which still binds the English clergy, claims for the sovereign "that only prerogative, which we see to have been given always to all godly Princes in holy Scriptures by God himself; that is, that they should rule all estates and degrees committed to their charge by God, whether they be Ecclesiastical or Temporal, and restrain with the civil sword the stubborn and evildoers." The Article adds that "the Bishop of Rome hath no jurisdiction in this Realm of England." So long as the royal supremacy was exercised by a sovereign who was himself a Christian man this definition served well enough: but the development of the English constitution from the practical autocracy of the Tudor sovereigns to the limited monarchy of their latest successors, has had its effect on the ecclesiastical system, and raised some formidable questions, of which the answer is not yet apparent.

Parliament.—The legislative authority of the mediaeval Church had been "spiritual." In the last resort the Church in England was governed by the canons of general councils and by the decretals of the popes. These controlled the action of the provincial convocations, which held the status of subordinate legislatures. The abolition of extra-national authorities, papal and conciliar, left nothing but the convocations of Canterbury and York in existence. In these circumstances the king and parliament may be said to have taken over the legislative functions of the pope and the general council. The Church of England before the Restoration was governed by ordinances and statutes. Church and nation were identified, at first practically, and then theoretically. The identification was defended with impressive eloquence by Hooker (d. 1600) and became the assumption of the English establishment. The convocations continued to legislate under the severe limitations imposed by 25 Henry VIII. cap. 19. (The Submission of the Clergy and Restraint of Appeals, 1534), and the mediaeval canon law retained under the same act a carefully restricted authority, but the right of parliament to legislate for the national Church even in "spiritual" matters was asserted and acted upon. The right was grounded on the Christian character of parliament, and on its essential function. Only by recognizing the legislative supremacy of parliament could the unity of the church-nation be secured. The 17th century witnessed the triumph of constitutional government, and the beginning of religious toleration. Legislative authority once shared between king and parliament became vested in parliament alone. The national Church was no longer governed partly by royal ordinance. James II.'s claim to the dispensing power was disallowed. While, however, the Act of Settlement (1701), provided that "whosoever shall hereafter come to the possession of this Crown shall join in communion with the Church of England, as by law established," it did not provide against the danger implicit in a change in the religious character of parliament. The danger of Roman Catholic members was indeed guarded against by the Test act (1673); but 45 Presbyterians were admitted by the Act of Union with Scotland, A.D. 1707, and in the course of the 19th century parliament was opened to Nonconformists, Roman Catholics, Jews, and nonbelievers of every description. Parliament, thus frankly divorced from an ecclesiastical character, retained its ecclesiastical functions unaltered. The anomaly was apparent and increasingly resented as the Church of England, waking from the deep slumbers of the 18th century, felt and acted as a spiritual society. The influence of the Oxford movement tended powerfully in the same direction. In 1852 the convocations, which had been suspended for 135 years, again were permitted to function. Parliament ceased to be the sole organ of ecclesiastical legislation and henceforth found its action conditioned by the constitutional rights of a clerical legislature, subordinate indeed, but as ancient as itself, and within its own sphere as independent. Nor was this all. While parliament became patently unqualified for ecclesiastical legislation, its secular task, ever waxing with the expansion of the empire, and the complexity of social life, required its undivided concern. Urgent ecclesiastical reforms were postponed for no better reason than the congestion of parliamentary business. Accordingly the demand for better legislative machinery became general, and, in the general reconstruction of the national system which followed World War I, was met by the Enabling act (1919). A new body, the national assembly, was created consisting of three "houses"—the diocesan bishops, the members of both convocations and elected laity. To this body legislative authority, subject to the veto of either house of parliament, was given. Measures affecting the Church of England passed by the national assembly, certified as constitutional by an ecclesiastical committee created for the purpose, and approved by both houses of parliament, were to have the force of statutes on receiving the royal assent. The constitution of the national assembly both reserved unaltered "the powers belonging to the convocations of the provinces of Canterbury and York or of any House thereof," and prohibited the assembly from "exercising any power or performing any function distinctively belonging to the bishops in right of their episcopal office."

This devolution of legislative power by parliament to the assembly did not destroy the right of parliament to make laws for the Church of England, but rendered the exercise of that right abnormal and improbable. The right of a spiritual society to be truly autonomous in spiritual matters is obviously patient of large secular control in other directions: but the line between spiritual and secular is not always easy to trace, and the intermingling of secular and ecclesiastical interests in an anciently Christian community is extremely close. The Enabling act, however, carries the possibility of future trouble. In twice rejecting the Prayer Book measure (1927 and 1928) the house of commons has precipitated a conflict on a plainly spiritual issue, which must affect gravely the Establishment itself and may even bring about its destruction.

The Ecclesiastical Courts.—The unique character of the English Reformation as at once conservative and revolutionary is nowhere better exhibited than in the ecclesiastical courts. They are the provincial and diocesan courts of the mediaeval church, but they are held in the king's name, the law they administer is the king's ecclesiastical law, and they are subject to the appellant authority of the king's privy council. The modern system has departed in some important respects from that which the Reformation created. It is much more nakedly secular, for the study of canon law having practically ceased, and the race of canonists having died out, there was left no effective check on the secularizing tendency of the lawyers, who of old time cherished a professional dislike of the ecclesiastical jurisdiction, and sought after a simplification of the legal system which paid little heed to tradition and the claims of the "spiritualty." In the course of time, notably during the 19th century the limits of ecclesiastical jurisdiction have been greatly contracted by the withdrawal of suits relating to wills, marriage and tithes. Acts of parliament are administered in the ecclesiastical courts, not any more the mediaeval canon law, save where this has acquired statutory force from the provisional legislation of Henry VIII. The ecclesiastical judges are laymen and they acknowledge the supreme appellant authority of the judicial committee of the privy council. This progressive secularization of the church's legal system did not provoke resentment until, largely as a consequence of the Oxford movement, the ecclesiastical courts had to deal with suits affecting the interpretation of rubrics and doctrinal standards. That such subjects, affecting the worship and belief of churchmen, should be handled by secular lawyers, who might not even themselves be Christians, offended the new sense of ecclesiastical independence and did violence to the religious conscience of many devout persons. The courts were denounced as "Erastian," and a disposition manifested itself to repudiate their authority. This disposition has certainly been strengthened by the course of national politics. A breach has opened between the general sentiment of English churchmen and the settled policy of the state in the matters of religious education and the marriage law, which is not likely to be closed, and which tends to create an attitude of apprehension and suspicion not favourable to the easy working of the establishment. A commission charged to make recommendations for the reform of the ecclesiastical courts was appointed by the national assembly and issued its report. The general discontent with the existing courts, and the widely extended disposition to ignore their verdicts, add an element of special embarrassment to the problem of maintaining discipline in the church.

Patronage.—No part of the establishment is more distinctive, and none more perplexing than "patronage," that is the process by which clergymen are appointed to office. It presents a curious blending of ancient and modern elements. The higher ecclesiastics—bishops, deans, some canons and many incumbents—are appointed by the crown on the nomination of the prime minister. In the case of the ancient sees, the mediaeval process is still followed, viz., *congé d'élire* to the dean and chapter accompanied by letters missive containing the name of the person whom they are desired to elect, confirmation by the archbishop, consecration, homage, and enthronement in the cathedral. In the case of modern sees which have no cathedral chapters, the bishop is appointed by letters patent. Two archbishops and 24 bishops sit in parliament—the archbishops and the bishops of London, Durham and Winchester by right of their sees, the other bishops by seniority of their consecration. The incumbents are nominated to the bishop of the diocese by patrons, who are either public (the lord chancellor, the bishops, colleges, the deans and chapters and other ecclesiastics holding patronage by title of their benefices) or private. The bishop has a limited power of refusing institution, but, in the absence of disqualification duly proved, he must institute and induct the patron's nominee to the benefice. This system is criticized as providing no adequate protection of parishioners against unsuitable appointments, and various projects for amending it have been advanced; but it is generally allowed that patronage, although anomalous in theory does not work badly, and there is no agreement as to a satisfactory substitute. The system is closely bound up with the method by which the parochial clergy are remunerated. The parish is also a benefice, and the incumbent possesses a life tenure of the endowment attached to it. This also is much objected to by reformers, but it does not lack apologists. Opinion, however, seems to be tending toward an age limit, which would remedy the principal fault of the existing system, viz., the incompetence of aged and ailing clergymen. A recent measure securing a modest pension at the age of 70 has laid the foundation for further reforms.

Tenure of the Ancient Endowments.—The Church of England is an endowed church, and, if it were disestablished, its claim to retain possession of the ancient endowments would certainly be disallowed. These endowments—fabrics, tithes, glebes, investments—are held by a multitude of corporations, sole and aggregate, on a service tenure, which is stated in the statutes which prescribe the functions of the bishops and clergy. Disestablishment would involve the dissolution of all these corporations. Such property as might be left to the disestablished church would be held under conditions which the Act of Disestablishment and Disendowment would create. It is the tenure of the endowments which forms now the most important aspect of the English establishment, and the prospect of their partial or total loss constitutes the weightiest of all arguments against disestablishment. Statesmen shrink from the grievous social and economic disturbance which disendowment would involve. Churchmen dread the loss of the material resources which maintain throughout the country the ministrations of religion. Neither the reluctance of the first nor the apprehensions of the last could avert the catastrophe if a breach between Church and State on a point of religious principle were to take place and prove incapable of remedy.

SCOTLAND

If the establishment in England is the most complicated, that in Scotland is the simplest which Christendom includes. In Scotland a "clean sweep" of the mediaeval system was effected. The Church was equipped with a new polity and in the course of history acquired an unprecedented independence. Its constitution as set out in the Church of Scotland Act, 1921, exhibits the model of "a free Church in a free State," such as Cavour projected in the middle of the 19th century. The 3rd Article "declaratory of the Constitution of the Church of Scotland in Matters Spiritual" runs thus:

This Church, as part of the Universal Church wherein the Lord Jesus Christ has appointed a government in the hands of Church office-bearers, receives from Him, its Divine King and Head, and from Him alone, the right and power subject to no civil authority to legislate and to adjudicate finally, in all matters of doctrine, worship, government, and discipline in the Church, including the right to determine all questions concerning membership and office in the Church, the constitution and membership of its Courts, and the mode of election of its office-bearers and to define the boundaries of the spheres of labour of its ministers and other office-bearers. Recognition by civil authority of the separate and independent government and jurisdiction of this Church in matters spiritual, in whatever manner such recognition be expressed, does not in any way affect the character of this government and jurisdiction as derived from the Divine Head of the Church alone, or give to the civil authority any right of interference with the proceedings or judgments of the Church within the sphere of its spiritual government and jurisdiction.

Partly, this unique independence may be ascribed to the presbyterian polity which, while magnifying the ministry, gave comparatively little importance to any section of it. There was nothing in Scotland parallel in political function to the episcopate in England. Partly, the emphasizing of ecclesiastical independence has grown from the union of the kingdoms, at first personal and then, since 1707, parliamentary also. When the centre of national government had been removed to London, and Scottish business became a comparatively subordinate element in British politics, the Church of Scotland ceased to move the anxious concern of statesmen, while it acquired in the popular regard an ever greater importance as the principal, almost the only surviving, witness of an independent Scottish nationality. In more recent times, in Scotland as elsewhere, the secularization of society has deprived all ecclesiastical concerns of much of their former importance. The attendance of the king's commissioner at the annual meeting of the general assembly, and the appointment of a number of presbyterian ministers as royal chaplains, form the chief tokens of that connection with the State which is the core of establishment. The State exercises no control over legislation, or ecclesiastical courts or patronage. Establishment in Scotland has no practical importance, though unquestionably its sentimental value as a solemn recognition of national Christianity is still great, and its abolition would be regretted by many, probably by most, Scottish citizens.

THE UNITED STATES AND THE BRITISH DOMINIONS

Save in Great Britain, there is no established Church throughout the English-speaking communities, though the relations of the Churches to the State are everywhere friendly. Bryce's description of the situation in the United States holds good throughout the British Dominions:

The legal position of a Christian church is in the United States simply that of a voluntary association, or group of associations, corporate or unincorporate, under the ordinary law. There is no such thing as a special ecclesiastical law; all questions, not only of property but of church discipline and jurisdiction, are, if brought before the courts of the land, dealt with as questions of contract; and the court, where it is obliged to examine a question of theology, as for instance whether a clergyman has advanced opinions inconsistent with any creed or formula to which he has bound himself—for it will prefer, if possible, to leave such matters to the proper ecclesiastical authority—will treat the point as one of pure legal interpretation, neither assuming to itself theological knowledge, nor suffering considerations of policy to intervene.

Religious bodies are in so far the objects of special favour that their property is in most States exempt from taxation; and this is reconciled to theory by the argument that they are serviceable as moral agencies, and diminish the expense incurred in respect of police administration.

It would perhaps be true to say that there is an informal establishment of Christianity though not of the Churches. It is assumed that society is Christian. Religious acts inaugurate the sessions of the representative assemblies, and no public function would be considered complete without them. Undoubtedly this informal establishment by public opinion and social habit is menaced by the increasing secularization of society, but it is still strongly entrenched in the public sentiment of all English-speaking communities. Establishment in the true sense is limited to England and Scotland, and only in England does it possess any importance or present any legal and constitutional problems.

(H. H. H.)

For special relationships between Church and State in Europe (anticlericalism, *Kulturkampf*), *see* ANTICLERICALISM; FRANCE: *History;* GERMANY: *Mediaeval History, History from 1519 to 1648,* etc.

CHURCH ARMY, an English religious organization, founded in 1882 by the Rev. Wilson Carlile (afterwards prebendary of St. Paul's), who banded together in an orderly army of "soldiers" and "officers" a few working men and women, whom he and others trained to act as "Church of England evangelists" among the outcasts and criminals of the Westminster slums. Previous experience had convinced him that the moral condition of the lowest classes of the people called for new and aggressive action on the part of the Church, and that this work was most effectively done by laymen and women of the same class as those whom it was desired to touch. It is essentially a working men's and women's mission to working people. As the work grew, a training institution for evangelists was started in Oxford but soon moved (1886) to London where, in Bryanston Street near the Marble Arch, the headquarters of the army are now established. Working men are trained as evangelists and working women as mission sisters. Officers and sisters are paid a limited sum for their services either by the vicar or by voluntary local contributions. Church Army mission and colportage vans circulate throughout the country parishes, if desired, with itinerant evangelists who hold simple missions without charge and distribute literature. Each van missioner has a clerical "adviser." Missions are also held in prisons and workhouses, at the invitation of the authorities. In 1888 (before the similar work of the Salvation Army was inaugurated) the Church Army established labour homes in London and elsewhere, with the object of giving a "fresh start in life" to the outcast and destitute. The Army has lodging homes, employment bureaus, cheap food depots, old clothes department, dispensary and a number of other social works. There is also an extensive emigration system under which carefully tested men and families of good character, chiefly of the unemployed class, are placed in permanent employment in Canada through the agency of the local clergy.

See Carlile, art. "Church Army" in Hasting's *Encyclopaedia of Religion and Ethics;* Rowan, *Wilson Carlile and the Church Army; The Church Army Review,* and other publications of Headquarters.

CHURCH ASSEMBLY: *see* CANON LAW: *Canon Law in England and in the Anglican Communion;* CONVOCATION; and ENGLAND, THE CHURCH OF.

CHURCH COUNCIL: *see* COUNCIL and CHURCH HISTORY.

CHURCHES OF CHRIST. The Churches of Christ are the conservative wing of the U.S. religious movement which began with the work of Thomas Campbell, a Presbyterian minister. In the *Declaration and Address* (1809), Campbell stated the principle that "where the Scriptures speak, we speak; where they are silent, we are silent." He and his son, Alexander, hoped to lead all Christian denominations into a single body united by adherence to the New Testament, considered as the final authority in all matters of church government and patterns of worship. The New Testament was to be treated as a religious constitution whose directions were to be minutely and literally followed. The Campbells seceded from the Presbyterian Church, and from 1813 till 1830 the movement was nominally Baptist. From the Baptists came the practice of total immersion as the only acceptable type of baptism. But beginning as early as 1826 many of the followers of the Campbells withdrew from the Baptist connection and organized Disciple congregations. (*See* DISCIPLES OF CHRIST.) These Disciples rejected all the historic creeds and the traditional dogmas, and many of them spoke of churches still using such creeds and dogmas as "man-made" in contrast with their own practice of following closely the text of the New Testament in polity, worship and organization.

As early as 1906 the conservative group, which constituted about one-fourth the Disciples, came to be recognized as a separate body. This group thought that the larger group had permitted unscriptural practices to creep into the church.

The Disciples and the Churches of Christ are congregational in their church government. They accept only two sacraments—baptism by immersion and the Lord's Supper, the communion service which is celebrated each Sunday, or Lord's Day, as they prefer to call it. Worship consists in reading the Bible and preaching, the observation of the Lord's Supper as a memorial and not a sacrifice, the contribution of money to the Lord's work, praying and singing without instrumental accompaniment. These conservatives objected to modernism, higher criticism of the Bible, missionary societies, mechanical instruments in worship services and acceptance of members from other church bodies which do not practice immersion on confession of faith. They do not fraternize with interdenominational agencies. The local churches, which are self-governing, have two classes of officials—elders and deacons. Persons are admitted to the church when three requirements are met: faith in Jesus Christ as the Son of God, repentance from sin and baptism by immersion.

About 80% of the Churches of Christ are in rural areas, and the greatest concentration is in Texas, Tennessee, Arkansas, Oklahoma, Alabama and Kentucky. Local churches maintain missionaries in Germany, the Netherlands, Belgium, France and other countries. There were about 12,000 churches in the United States, and outside the United States there were about 170 churches at mid-20th century. In the United States there were 16 colleges controlled by members of the churches, 15 homes for the aged and orphans and 45 periodicals published by individual members. There were approximately 800,000 members.

The title Church of Christ is used by other groups, including several old Congregational churches in New England. The title is frequently used by churches which belong to the Disciples and which have introduced practices regarded as unauthorized in

Scripture by the conservatives. (J. H. Cb.)

Bibliography.—Earl Irwin West, *The Search for the Ancient Order: Restoration Movement, 1844–1906*, 2 vol. (1949–50); John F. Rowe, *A History of Reformatory Movements*, 10th ed. (1938); George A. Klingman, *Church History for Busy People*, 4th ed. (1943); L. G. Tomlinson, *Churches of Today*, 3rd ed. (1943).

CHURCH HISTORY. In the following account of the historical evolution of the Church, the subject will be treated in three sections:—(A) The ancient Church to the beginning of the pontificate of Gregory the Great (A.D. 590); (B) The Church in the middle ages; (C) The modern Church.

A. THE ANCIENT CHURCH

The crucifixion of Jesus Christ resulted in the scattering of His followers, but within a short time they became convinced that He had risen from the dead, and would soon return to set up the expected Messianic kingdom, and so to accomplish the true work of the Messiah (*cf.* Acts i. 6 ff.). They were thus enabled to retain the belief in His Messiahship which His death had threatened to destroy permanently. This belief laid upon them the responsibility of bringing as many of their countrymen as possible to recognize Him as Messiah, and to prepare themselves by repentance and righteousness for the coming kingdom (*cf.* Acts ii. 21, 38, iii. 19 *et seq.*). In Jerusalem the new movement had its centre, and the church established there is rightly known as the mother church of Christendom. The life of the early Jewish disciples, so far as can be judged from our very meagre sources, was very much the same as that of their fellows. They continued faithful to the established synagogue and temple worship (*cf.* Acts iii. 1), and did not think of founding a new sect, or of separating from the household of Israel (*cf.* Acts x. 14, xv. 5, xxi. 21.) There is little evidence that their religious or ethical ideals differed in any marked degree from those of the more serious-minded among their countrymen, for the emphasis which they laid upon the need of righteousness was not at all uncommon. In their belief, however, in the Messiahship of Jesus, and their consequent assurance of the speedy establishment by Him of the Messianic kingdom, they stood alone. The first need of the hour, therefore, was to show that Jesus was the promised Messiah in spite of His crucifixion, a need that was met chiefly by testimony to the resurrection, which became the burden of the message of the early disciples to their fellow-countrymen (*cf.* Acts ii. 24 ff., iii. 15 ff., v. 31). It was this need which led also to the development of Messianic prophecy and the ultimate interpretation of the Jewish Bible as a Christian book (*see* Bible). The second need of the hour was to bring the nation to repentance and righteousness in order that the Kingdom might come (*cf.* Acts iii. 19).

Its Early Difficulties.—Meanwhile the new movement spread quite naturally beyond the confines of Palestine and found adherents among the Jews of the dispersion. Among the Christians who did most to spread the gospel in the Gentile world was the apostle Paul, whose conversion was the greatest event in the history of the early Church. In his hands Christianity became a new religion, fitted to meet the needs of all the world, and freed entirely of the local and national meaning which had hitherto attached to it. Paul saw in Jesus much more than the Jewish Messiah. He saw in Christ the divine Spirit, who had come down from heaven to transform the lives of men, all of whom are sinners. The Kingdom of which the early disciples were talking was interpreted by Paul as righteousness and peace and joy in the Holy Ghost (Rom. xiv. 17), a new principle of living, not a Jewish State. But Paul taught also, on the basis of a religious experience and of a distinct theory of redemption, that the Christian is freed from the obligation to observe the Jewish law. He thus did away with the fundamental distinction between Jews and Gentiles. The transformed spiritual life of the believer expresses itself not in the observance of Jewish law, but in love, purity and peace. This precipitated a very serious conflict, of which we learn something from the Epistle to the Galatians and the Book of Acts (xv. and xxii.).

It was Christianity in its universal form which won its great victories, and finally became permanently established in the Roman world. The appeal which it made to that world was many-sided. It was a time when men were awaking to the need of better and purer living. To all who felt this need Christianity offered high moral ideals, and a tremendous moral enthusiasm, in its devotion to a beloved leader, in its emphasis upon the ethical possibilities of the meanest, and in its faith in a future life of blessedness for the righteous. It was a time of great religious interest, when old cults were being revived and new were finding acceptance on all sides. Christianity, with its one God, and its promise of redemption and a blessed immortality based upon divine revelation, met as no other contemporary faith did the awakening religious needs. It was a time also of great social unrest. With its principle of Christian brotherhood, its emphasis upon the equality of all believers in the sight of God, and its preaching of a new social order to be set up at the return of Christ, it appealed strongly to multitudes, particularly of the poorer classes. That it won a permanent success, and finally took possession of the Roman world, was due to its combination of appeals.

Christianity was essentially a proselytizing religion, not content to appeal simply to one class or race of people, and to be one among many faiths, but believing in the falsity or insufficiency of all others and eager to convert the whole world, but it did not win its victory without a struggle. Superstition, misunderstanding and hatred caused the Christians trouble for many generations, and governmental repression they had to suffer occasionally, as a result of popular disturbances. No systematic effort was made by the imperial authorities to put an end to the movement until the reign of Decius (250–251), whose policy of suppression was followed by Diocletian (303 ff.) and continued for some years after his abdication. In spite of all opposition the Church steadily grew, until in 311 the emperor Galerius upon his death-bed granted it toleration; and in 313 the emperors Constantine and Licinius published the edict of Milan, proclaiming the principle of complete religious liberty, and making Christianity a legal religion in the full sense.

Constantine, recognizing the growing strength of the Church and wishing to enlist the loyal support of the Christians, treated them with increasing favour, and finally was baptized upon his death-bed (337). Under his successors, except during the brief reign of Julian (361–363), when the effort was made to reinstate paganism in its former place of supremacy, the Church received growing support, until, under Theodosius the Great (379–395), orthodox Christianity, which stood upon the platform adopted at Nicaea in 325, was finally established as the sole official religion of the state, and heathen worship was put under the ban. The union between Church and State thus constituted continued unbroken in the East throughout the middle ages. The division of the Empire resulted finally in the division of the Church, which was practically complete by the end of the 6th century, but was made official and final only in 1054, and the Eastern and Western halves, the Greek Catholic and the Roman Catholic Churches, went each its separate way.

For long after the establishment of Christianity as the State religion, paganism continued strong, especially in the country districts, and in some parts of the world had more adherents than Christianity, but at length the latter became, at any rate nominally, the faith of the whole Roman world. Meanwhile already before the 3rd century it went beyond the confines of the Empire in Asia, and by the end of the period was strong in Armenia, Persia, Arabia and even farther east. It reached the barbarians on the northern and western borders at an early day, and the Goths were already Christians of the Arian type before the great migrations of the 4th century began. Other barbarians became Christian, some in their own homes beyond the confines of the Empire, some within the Empire itself, so that when the hegemony of the West passed from the Romans to the barbarians the Church lived on. Thenceforth for centuries it was not only the chief religious, but also the chief civilizing, force at work in the Occident.

The Christian Life.—The most notable thing about the life of the early Christians was their vivid sense of being a people of God, called and set apart. They regarded themselves as separate from the rest of the world and bound together by peculiar ties: their citizenship was in heaven, not on earth (*cf.* Phil. iii.

20, and the epistle to Diognetus, c. 5), and the principles and laws by which they strove to govern themselves were from above: the present world was but temporary, their true life was in the future; Christ was soon to return, and the employments and labours and pleasures of this age were of small concern. The belief that the Church was a supernatural institution found further expression in the conviction of the presence and power of the Holy Spirit, supposed to be manifest in various striking ways, in prophecy, speaking with tongues and miracle-working. In this idea Paul also shared, but he carried the matter farther than most of his contemporaries and saw in the Spirit the abiding power and ground of the Christian life. Not simply in extraordinary phenomena, but also in the everyday life of Christians, the Holy Spirit was present, and all the Christian graces were the fruits (*cf.* Gal. v. 22). A result of this belief was to give their lives a peculiarly enthusiastic or inspirational character. Theirs were not the everyday experiences of ordinary men, but of men lifted out of themselves and transported into a higher sphere. With the passing of time the early enthusiasm waned, the expectation of the immediate return of Christ was widely given up, the conviction of the Spirit's presence became less vivid, and the conflict with heresy in the 2nd century led to the substitution of official control for the original freedom (*see* below). The late 2nd century movement known as Montanism was in essence a revolt against this growing secularization of the Church, but the movement failed, and the development against which it protested was only hastened. The Church as an institution now looked forward to a long life upon earth and adjusted itself to the new situation, taking on largely the forms and customs of the world in which it lived. This did not mean that the Church ceased to regard itself as a supernatural institution, but only that its supernatural character was shown in a different way; the early conviction of the essential difference between the life of this world and that of the next lived on, and, as the Church became increasingly a world-institution, found vent in monasticism, which was simply the effort to put into more consistent practice the other-worldly life, and to make more thoroughgoing work of the saving of one's soul.

There were Christian monks as early as the 3rd century, and before the end of the 4th monasticism (*q.v.*) was an established institution both in East and West. The monks and nuns were looked upon as the most consistent Christians, and were honoured accordingly. Those who did not adopt the monastic life endeavoured on a lower plane and in a less perfect way to realize the common ideal, and by means of penance to atone for the deficiencies in their performance. The existence of monasticism made it possible at once to hold up a high moral standard before the world and to permit the ordinary Christian to be content with something lower. With the growth of clerical sacerdotalism the higher standard was demanded also of the clergy, and the principle came to be generally recognized that they should live the monastic life so far as was consistent with their active duties in the world. The chief manifestation of this was clerical celibacy, which had become widespread already in the 4th century. Among the laity, on the other hand, the ideal of holiness found realization in the observance of the ordinary principles of morality recognized by the world at large, in attendance upon the means of grace provided by the Church, in fasting at stated intervals, in eschewing various popular employments and amusements, and in almsgiving and prayer. Christ's principle of love was widely interpreted to mean chiefly love for the Christian brotherhood, and within that circle the virtues of hospitality, charity and helpfulness were widely exercised.

Worship.—The primitive belief in the immediate presence of the Spirit affected the religious services of the Church. They were regarded in early days as occasions for the free exercise of spiritual gifts. As a consequence the completest liberty was accorded to Christians to take such part as they chose, it being assumed that they did so only under the Spirit's prompting. But the result of this freedom was confusion and discord, as is indicated by Paul's 1st Epistle to the Corinthians (*see* ch. xi., xiv.). This led to the erection of safeguards. Particular Christians were designated to take charge of the services, and orders of worship were framed out of which grew ultimately elaborate liturgies (*see* LITURGY). The Lord's Supper first took on a more stereotyped character, and prayers to be used in connection with it are found in the *Didachē* (ch. ix., x.). There developed in the 3rd or 4th century what is known as the *arcani disciplina,* or secret discipline of the Church, involving concealment from the uninitiated and unholy of the more sacred parts of the Christian cult, such as baptism and the eucharist, with their various accompaniments, including the Creed and the Lord's Prayer. The same interest led to the division of the services into two general parts, which became known ultimately as the *missa catechumenorum* and the *missa fidelium,*—that is, the more public service of prayer, praise and preaching open to all, including the catechumens or candidates for Church membership, and the private service for the administration of the eucharist, open only to full members of the Church in good and regular standing. Meanwhile, as the general service tended to grow more elaborate, the *missa fidelium* tended to take on the character of the current Greek mysteries (*see* EUCHARIST). Many of the terms in common use in them were employed in connection with the Christian rites, and many of the conceptions, particularly that of sharing in immortality by communion with deity, became an essential part of Christian doctrine. Thus the early idea of the services, as occasions for mutual edification through the interchange of spiritual gifts, gave way in course of time to the theory that they consisted of sacred and mysterious rites by means of which communion with God is promoted. The emphasis accordingly came to be laid increasingly upon the formal side of worship, and a value was given to the ceremonies as such, and their proper and correct performance by duly qualified persons, *i.e.,* ordained priests, was all-important.

Doctrine.—Two tendencies appeared in the thought of the primitive Church, the one to regard Christianity as a law given by God for the government of men's lives, with the promise of a blessed immortality as a reward for its observance; the other to view it as a means by which the corrupt and mortal nature of man is transformed, so that he becomes a spiritual and holy being. The latter tendency appeared first in the New Testament in Paul, and afterwards in the Gospel and 1st Epistle of John. The former found expression in most of our New Testament writings, in all of the apostolic fathers except Ignatius, and in the Apologists of the 2nd century. The two tendencies were not always mutually exclusive, but the one or the other was predominant in every case. Towards the end of the 2nd century they were combined by Irenaeus, bishop of Lyons. To him salvation bears a double aspect, involving both release from the control of the devil and the transformation of man's nature by the indwelling of the Divine. Only he is saved who on the one hand is forgiven at baptism and so released from the power of Satan, and then goes on to live in obedience to the divine law, and on the other hand receives in baptism the germ of a new spiritual nature and is progressively transformed by receiving the body and blood of the divine Christ in the eucharist. This double conception of salvation and of the means thereto was handed down to the Church of subsequent generations and became fundamental in its thought.

The twofold conception referred to had its influence also upon thought about Christ. The effect of the legal view of Christianity was to make Christ an agent of God in the revelation of the divine will and truth, and so a subordinate being between God and the world, the Logos of current Greek thought. The effect of the mystical conception was to identify Christ with God in order that by His incarnation the divine nature might be brought into union with humanity and the latter be transformed. In this case too a combination was effected, the idea of Christ as the incarnation of the Logos or Son of God being retained and yet His deity being preserved by the assertion of the deity of the Logos. The recognition of Christ as the incarnation of the Logos was practically universal before the close of the 3rd century, but His deity was still widely denied, and the Arian controversy which distracted the Church of the 4th century concerned the latter question. At the council of Nicaea in 325 the deity of Christ received official sanction and was given formulation in the original Nicene Creed. Controversy continued for some time, but finally the Nicene decision was recognized both in East and West as the only orthodox faith. The deity of the Son was believed to carry with it that of the Spirit, who was associated with Father and Son in the baptismal formula and in the current symbols, and so the victory of the Nicene Christology meant the recognition of the doctrine of the Trinity as a part of the orthodox faith.

The assertion of the deity of the Son incarnate in Christ raised another problem which constituted the subject of dispute in the Christological controversies of the 4th and following centuries. What is the relation of the divine and human natures in Christ? At the council of Chalcedon in 451 it was declared that in the person of Christ are united two complete natures, divine and human, which retain after the union all their properties unchanged. This was supplemented at the 3rd council of Constantinople in 680 by the statement that each of the natures contains a will, so that Christ possesses two wills. The Western Church accepted the decisions of Nicaea, Chalcedon and Constantinople, and so the doctrines of the Trinity and of the two natures in Christ were handed down as orthodox dogma in West as well as East.

Meanwhile in the Western Church the subject of sin and grace, and the relation of divine and human activity in salvation, received special attention; and finally, at the 2nd council of Orange in 529, after both Pelagianism and semi-Pelagianism had been repudiated, a moderate form of Augustinianism was adopted, involving the theory that every man as a result of the Fall is in such a condition that he can take no steps in the direction of salvation until he has been renewed by the divine grace given in baptism, and that he cannot continue in the good thus begun except by the constant assistance of that grace, which is mediated only by the Catholic Church. This decision was confirmed by Boniface II., and became the accepted doctrine in the Western Church of the middle ages.

Organization.—The origin and early development of ecclesiastical organization are involved in obscurity.

In the earliest days the Church was regarded as a divine institution, ruled not by men but by the Holy Spirit. At the same time it was believed that the Spirit imparted different gifts to different believers, and each gift fitted its recipient for the performance of some service, being intended not for his own good but for the good of his brethren (*cf.* 1 Cor. xii.; Eph. iv. 11). The chief of these was the gift of teaching, that is, of understanding and interpreting to others the will and truth of God. Those who were endowed more largely than their fellows with this gift were commonly known as apostles, prophets and teachers (*cf.* Acts xiii. 1; 1 Cor. xii. 28; Eph. ii. 20, iii. 5, iv. 11). The apostles were travelling missionaries or evangelists; there were many of them in the primitive Church, and only gradually did the term come to be applied exclusively to the twelve and Paul. There is no sign that the apostles, whether the twelve or others, held any official position in the Church: that they had a large measure of authority goes without saying, but it depended always upon their brethren's recognition of their possession of the divine gift of apostleship, and the right of Churches or individuals to test their claims and to refuse to listen to them if they did not vindicate their divine call was everywhere recognized. Witness, for instance, Paul's reference to false apostles in 2 Cor. xi. 13, and his efforts to establish his own apostolic character to the satisfaction of the Corinthians and Galatians (1 Cor. ix. 1 ff.; 2 Cor. x. 13; Gal. i. 8 ff.), and the reference in Rev. ii. 2 to the fact that the Church at Ephesus had tried certain men who claimed to be apostles and had found them false.

Between the apostles, prophets and teachers no hard-and-fast lines can be drawn. The apostles were commonly missionary prophets, called permanently or temporarily to the special work of evangelization (*cf.* Acts xiii. 1), while the teachers seem to have been distinguished both from apostles and prophets by the fact that their spiritual endowment was less strikingly supernatural. The indefiniteness of the boundaries between the three classes, and the free interchange of names, show how far they were from being definite offices or orders within the Church.

But at an early day we find regular officers in this and that local Church, and early in the 2nd century the three permanent offices of bishop, presbyter and deacon existed at any rate in Asia Minor. Their rise was due principally to the necessity of administering the charities of the Church, putting an end to disorder and confusion in the religious services, and disciplining offenders. Regular officers within the local Churches gradually made their appearance, sometimes simply recognized as charged with responsibilities which they had already voluntarily assumed (*cf.* 1 Cor. xvi. 15), sometimes appointed by an apostle or prophet or other specially inspired man (*cf.* Acts xiv. 23; Titus i. 5; 1 Clement 44), sometimes formally chosen by the congregation itself (*cf.* Acts vi.). These men naturally acquired more and more, as time passed, the control and leadership of the Church in all its activities, and out of what was in the beginning more or less informal and temporary grew fixed and permanent offices, the incumbents of which were recognized as having a right to rule over the Church, a right which once given could not lawfully be taken away unless they were unfaithful to their trust. Not continued endowment by the Spirit, but the possession of an ecclesiastical office now became the basis of authority. The earliest expression of this genuinely official principle is found in Clement's Epistle to the Corinthians (ch. xliv.).

The earliest distinct evidence of the organization of Churches under a single head is found in the Epistles of Ignatius of Antioch, which date from the latter part of the reign of Trajan (*c.* 116). Ignatius bears witness to the presence in various Churches of Asia Minor of a single bishop in control, with whom are associated as his subordinates a number of elders and deacons. This form of organization ultimately became universal. Where there were one bishop and a number of presbyters and deacons in a church, the presbyters constituted the bishop's council, and the deacons his assistants in the management of the finances and charities and in the conduct of the services.

Meanwhile the rise and rapid spread of Gnosticism (*q.v.*) produced a crisis in the Church of the 2nd century, and profoundly affected the ecclesiastical organization. The views of the Gnostics, and of Marcion as well, seemed to the majority of Christians destructive of the gospel, and it was widely felt that they were too dangerous to be tolerated. The original dependence upon the Spirit for light and guidance was inadequate. The men in question claimed to be Christians and to enjoy divine illumination as truly as anybody, and so other safeguards appeared necessary. It was in the effort to find such safeguards that steps were taken which finally resulted in the institution known as the Catholic Church. The first of these steps was the recognition of the teaching of the apostles as the exclusive standard of Christian truth. This found expression in the formulation of our New Testament, and of an apostolic rule of faith, of which the old Roman symbol, the original of our present Apostles' Creed, is one of the earliest examples. Over against the claims of the Gnostics that they had apostolic authority, either oral or written, for their preaching, were set these two standards, by which alone the apostolic character of any doctrine was to be tested (*cf.* Irenaeus, *Adversus Haereses,* i. 10, iii. 3, 4; Tertullian, *De Prescriptione Haereticorum*). But these standards proved inadequate to the emergency, for it was possible, especially by the use of the allegorical method, to interpret them in more than one way, and their apostolic origin and authority were not everywhere admitted. In view of this difficulty, it was claimed that the apostles had appointed the bishops as their successors, and that the latter were in possession of special divine grace enabling them to transmit and to interpret without error the teaching of the apostles committed to them. This is the famous theory known as "apostolic succession." The idea of the apostolic appointment of church officers is as old as Clement of Rome, but the use of the theory to guarantee the apostolic character of episcopal teaching was due to the exigencies of the Gnostic conflict. Irenaeus (*op. cit.* iii. 3, iv. 26, 33, v. 20), Tertullian (*op. cit.,* 32) and Hippolytus (*Philosophumena,* bk. i., preface) are about our earliest witnesses to it, and Cyprian sets it forth quite clearly in his epistles. The Church was thus in possession not only of authoritative apostolic doctrine, but also of a permanent apostolic office, to which alone belonged the right to determine what that doctrine is. The combination of this idea with that of clerical sacerdotalism completed the Catholic theory of the Church and the clergy. Saving grace is recognized as apostolic grace, and the bishops as successors of the apostles become its sole transmitters. Bishops are therefore necessary to the very being of the Church, which without them is without the saving grace for the giving of which the Church exists (*cf.* Cyprian, *Ep.* 33, "ecclesia super episcopos constituitur"; 66, "ecclesia in episcopo"; also *Ep.* 59, and *De unitate ecclesiae* 17).

These bishops were originally not diocesan but congregational, that is, each church, however small, had its own bishop. This is the organization testified to by Ignatius, and Cyprian's insistence upon the bishop as necessary to the very existence of the Church seems to imply the same thing. Congregational episcopacy was the rule for a number of generations. But after the middle of the 3rd century diocesan episcopacy began to make its appearance here and there, and became common in the 4th century under the influence of the general tendency toward centralization, the increasing power of city bishops, and the growing dignity of the episcopate (*cf.* canon 6 of the council of Sardica, and canon 57 of the council of Laodicea; and see Harnack, *Mission und Ausbreitung*, pp. 319 *seq.*). This enlargement of the bishop's parish and multiplication of the churches under his care led to a change in the functions of the presbyterate. So long as each church had its own bishop the presbyters constituted simply his council, but with the growth of diocesan episcopacy it became the custom to put each congregation under the care of a particular presbyter, who performed within it most of the pastoral duties formerly discharged by the bishop himself. The presbyters, however, were not independent officers. They were only representatives of the bishop, and the churches over which they were set were all a part of his parish, so that the Cyprianic principle, that the bishop is necessary to the very being of the Church, held good of diocesan as well as of congregational episcopacy.

The belief in the unity of the entire Church had existed from the beginning. Though made up of widely scattered congregations, it was thought of as one body of Christ, one people of God. This ideal unity found expression in many ways. Intercommunication between the various Christian communities was very active. Christians upon a journey were always sure of a warm welcome and hospitable entertainment from their fellow-disciples. Messengers and letters were sent freely from one church to another. Documents of various kinds, including gospels and apostolic epistles, circulated widely. Thus in various ways the feeling of unity found expression, and the development of widely separated parts of Christendom conformed more or less closely to a common type. It was due to agencies such as these that the scattered churches did not go each its own way and become ultimately separate and diverse institutions. But this general unity became official, and expressed itself in organization, only with the rise of the conciliar and metropolitan systems. Already before the end of the 2nd century local synods were held in Asia Minor to deal with Montanism, and in the 3rd century provincial synods became common, and by the council of Nicaea (canon 5) it was decreed that they should be held twice every year in every province. Larger synods representing the churches of a number of contiguous provinces also met frequently; for instance, in the early 4th century at Elvira, Ancyra, Neo-Caesarea and Arles, the last representing the entire Western world. Such gatherings were specially common during the great doctrinal controversies of the 4th century. In 325 the first general or oecumenical council, representing theoretically the entire Christian Church, was held at Nicaea. Other councils of the first period now recognized as oecumenical by the Church both East and West are Constantinople I. (381), Ephesus (431), Chalcedon (451), Constantinople II. (553). All these were called by the emperor, and to their decisions he gave the force of law. Thus the character of the Church as a State institution voiced itself in them (*see* COUNCIL).

The theory that the bishops are successors of the apostles, and as such the authoritative conservators and interpreters of apostolic truth, involves of course the solidarity of the episcopate, and the assumption that all bishops are in complete harmony and bear witness to the same body of doctrine. This assumption, however, has not always been sustained by the facts. Serious disagreements even on important matters developed frequently. As a result the oecumenical council came into existence especially for the purpose of settling disputed questions of doctrine, and giving to the collective episcopate the opportunity to express its voice in a final and official way. At the council of Nicaea, and at the oecumenical councils which followed, the idea of an infallible episcopate giving authoritative and permanent utterance to apostolic and therefore divine truth, found clear expression, and has been handed down as a part of the faith of the Catholic Church both East and West.

Meanwhile the Roman episcopate developed into the papacy, which claimed supremacy over the entire Christian Church, and actually exercised it increasingly in the West from the 5th century on. This development was forwarded by Augustine, who in his famous work *De civitate Dei* identified the Church with the Kingdom of God, and claimed that it was supreme over all the nations of the earth, which make up the *civitas terrena* or earthly state. Augustine's theory was ultimately accepted everywhere in the West, and thus the Church of the middle ages was regarded not only as the sole ark of salvation, but also as the ultimate authority, moral, intellectual and political. Upon this doctrine was built, not by Augustine himself but by others who came after him, the structure of the papacy, the bishop of Rome being finally recognized as the head under Christ of the *civitas Dei*, and so the supreme organ of divine authority on earth (*see* PAPACY and POPE).

B. THE CHRISTIAN CHURCH IN THE MIDDLE AGES

The middle ages came into being at the time when the political structure of the world, based upon the conquests of Alexander the Great and the achievements of Julius Caesar, began to disintegrate. They were present when the believers in Mohammed held sway in provinces which Alexander had brought under the influence of Hellenism; while the Lombards, the West Goths, the Franks and the Anglo-Saxons had established kingdoms in Italy, Spain, Gaul and Britain.

The East.—Ancient and mediaeval times were not separated by so deep a gulf in the East as in the West; for in the East the Empire continued to exist, although within narrow limits, until towards the end of the middle ages. Constantinople only fell in 1453. Ecclesiastical Byzantinism is therefore not a product of the middle ages; it is the outcome of the development of the eastern half of the empire from the time of Constantine the Great. Imperial power extended equally over State and Church. Since the emperor ruled the Church there was no longer any question of independence for the bishops.

The *orthodoxy* of the Eastern Church was also a result of the Church's development after the time of Constantine. In the long strife over dogma the old belief of the Greeks in the value of knowledge had made itself felt, and this faith was not extinct in the Eastern Church. But the strife over dogma ended with the 7th century. After the termination of the Monothelite controversy (638–680), creed and doctrines were complete; it was only necessary to preserve them intact. Theology, therefore, now resolved itself into the collection and reproduction of the teaching of ancient authorities. The great dogmatist of the Eastern Church, John of Damascus (*c.* 699–753), who stood on the threshold of the middle ages, formulated clearly and precisely his working principle: to put forward nothing of his own, but to present the truth according to the authority of the Bible and of the Fathers of the Church.

In the Eastern Church the religious interest concerned itself more keenly with the mystic rites of divine worship than with dogma. Here was more than knowledge; here were representations of a mystic sensuousness, solemn rites, which brought the faithful into immediate contact with the Divine, and guaranteed to them the reception of heavenly powers. We may gauge the energy with which the Greek intellect turned in this direction if we call to mind that the controversy about dogma was replaced by the controversy about images. This raged in the Eastern Church for more than a century (726–843), and only sank to rest when the worship of images was unconditionally conceded. In this connection the image was not looked upon merely as a symbol, but as the vehicle of the presence and power of that which it represented.

Consistent with this circle of ideas is the cultivation of religious experience. A beginning had been made, in the 5th century, by the Neo-platonic Christian who addressed his contemporaries under the mask of Dionysius the Areopagite. He is the first of a series of theological mystics which continued through every century of the middle ages. It is this striving after religious experience that gives to the Oriental *monasticism* (*q.v.*) of the middle ages its peculiar character; in it the old Hellenic ideal of the wise man who has no wants, *αὐτάρκεια*, was from the first fused with the Christian conception of unreserved self-surrender to God as the highest aim and the highest good.

The Eastern Church, then, throughout the middle ages, remained true in every particular to its ancient character. It did not develop as did the Western Church during this period, but room for *expansion* was found in the new nations which had sprung into existence since the beginning of the middle ages: the Bulgarians, the Serbians, and the multifarious peoples grouped under the name of Russians. One outcome of this expansion was the impossibility of continuing to share the life of the Western Church. Neither in the East nor in the West was a *separation* desired; but it was inevitable, since the lives of East and West were moving in different directions.

Since the time when the church of eastern Syria had decided, in opposition to the church of the Empire, to cling to the ancient views of Syrian theologians—therefore also to the teaching and person of Nestorius—her relations were broken off with the church in western Syria and in Greek and Latin countries; but the power of *Nestorian* Christianity was not thereby diminished. Separated from the West, it directed its energies towards the East, and here its nearest neighbour was the Persian church. The latter followed, almost without opposition, the impulse received from Syria; from the rule of the patriarch Babaeus (498–503) it may be considered definitely Nestorian. Thus there survived in mid-Asia a widely-scattered remnant, which, although out of touch with the ancient usages of Christian civilization, yet in no way lacked higher culture. Nestorian philosophers and medical practitioners became the teachers of the great Arabian natural philosophers of the middle ages, and the latter obtained their knowledge of Greek learning from Syriac translations of the works of Greek thinkers.

Political conditions at the beginning of the middle ages favoured the Nestorian church, and the fact that the Arabs had conquered Syria, Palestine and Egypt, made it possible to exert an influence on the Christians in these countries. Of still more importance was the brisk commercial intercourse between central Asia and the countries of the Far East; for this led the Nestorians into China. But with the consolidation of Mohammedan power the greater part of Nestorian Christendom was swallowed up by Islam, and only remnants of this once extensive church have survived until modern times. The middle ages were even more disastrous for *Monophysite* Christianity; in their case there was no alternation of rise and decline, and there is only a long period of gradual exhaustion to chronicle, alike in Syria and in Egypt.

The West.—(i.) During the *early middle ages* the central fact in the history of the Church is the influence of the foundation of the Teutonic States. While the Eastern Church was stereotyping those peculiar characteristics which made her a thing apart, the Church of the West was brought face to face with the greatest revolution that Europe has ever experienced. At the end of the 6th century all the provinces of the Empire had become independent kingdoms, in which conquerors of Germanic race formed the dominant nationality. This is the great fact which stands out at the beginning of the history of the Church in the middle ages. The continuity of the political history of Europe was violently interrupted by the Germanic invasion, but not that of the history of the Church. Creed and dogma, above all, remained unchanged. The doctrinal decisions of the ancient Church remained the indestructible canon of belief, and what the theologians of the ancient Church had taught was reverenced as beyond improvement. The entire form of divine worship remained therefore unaltered. Even where the Latin tongue was not understood by the people, the Church preserved it in the mass and in the administration of the sacraments, in her exorcisms and in her benedictions. The organization of ecclesiastical offices; and the property and social status of the Church and of the hierarchy, remained unchanged.

Nevertheless, the new conditions did exercise the strongest influence upon the character of the Church. The churches of the Lombards, West Goths, Franks and Anglo-Saxons, all counted themselves parts of the Catholic Church; but the Catholic Church had altered its condition; it lacked the power of organization, and split up into territorial churches. Under the Empire the oecumenical council had been looked upon as the highest representative organ of the Catholic Church; but the earlier centuries of the middle ages witnessed the convocation of no oecumenical councils. Under the Empire the bishop of Rome had possessed in the Church an authority recognized and protected by the State; among the new territorial churches, respect for Rome and for the successor of Peter was not forgotten but had altered in character; legal authority had become merely moral authority; its wielder could exhort, warn, advise, but could not command. The bishops continued to meet in synods as before, but the councils became territorial synods; they were called together at irregular intervals by the king, and their decisions obtained legal effect only by royal sanction.

In the middle ages *the civilizing task of the Church* was first approached in England. Aldhelm (d. 709) and the Venerable Bede (d. 735) were the first scholars of the period. England was also the home of Winfrid Bonifatius (St. Boniface, d. *c.* 757), who, in co-operation with the bishops of Rome, began the reorganization of the Frankish church, which had fallen into confusion and decay during the political disorders of the last years of the Merovingians. It was Boniface, too, who, with the aid of numerous English priests, monks and nuns, introduced the literary culture of England into Germany.

Charlemagne (d. 814) built on the foundations laid by St. Boniface. The importance of Charlemagne's work, from the point of view of the Church, consists in his having led back the Frankish Church to the fulfilment of her functions as a religious and civilizing agent. This was the purpose of his ecclesiastical legislation. The principal means to this end taken by him was the raising of the status of the clergy. For the purpose of carrying out his ideas Charlemagne gathered round him the best intellects of Europe. None was more intimately associated with him than the Anglo-Saxon Alcuin (d. 804); but he was only one among many. Under this guidance theology flourished in the Frankish empire. It was as little original as that of Bede; for on the continent, too, scholars were content to think what those of old had thought before them. But in so doing they did not only repeat the old formulae; the ideas of the men of old sprang into new life. This is shown by the searching discussions to which the Adoptionist controversy gave rise. At the same time, the controversy with the Eastern Church over the adoration of images shows that the younger Western theology felt itself equal, if not superior to the Greek.

The second generation of Frankish theologians did not lag behind the first. Hrabanus of Fulda (who died archbishop of Mainz in 856) was in the range of his knowledge undoubtedly Alcuin's superior. He was the first learned theologian produced by Germany. His disciple, Abbot Walafrid Strabo of Reichenau (d. 849), was the author of the *Glossa Ordinaria,* a work which formed the foundation of biblical exposition throughout the middle ages. France was still more richly provided with theologians in the 9th century: her most prominent names are Hincmar, archbishop of Reims (d. 882), Bishop Prudentius of Troyes (d. 861), the monks Servatus Lupus (d. 862), Radbert Paschasius (d. *c.* 860), and Ratramnus (d. after 868); and the last theologian who came into France from abroad, Johannes Scotus Erigena (d. *c.* 880). The real strength of Erigena was in the field of speculative metaphysics; the controversy about predestination, which, in the 9th century, Hincmar and Hrabanus fought out with the monk Gottschalk of Fulda, as well as the discussions that arose from the definition of the doctrine of transubstantiation by Radbert, enable us to gauge the intellectual energy with which theological problems were being handled.

Charlemagne followed his father's policy in carrying out his ecclesiastical measures in close association with the bishops of Rome. The relation was one of co-operation, without supremacy on either side. There were, indeed, forces tending in the contrary direction; and these were present in the Frankish empire. Evidence of this is given by the canon law forgeries of the 9th century: especially the great collection of the Pseudo-Isidorian Decretals (*see* DECRETALS), the fundamental idea being that all lay control in ecclesiastical affairs is wrong. For the moment, however, this party met with no success. Of more importance was the fact that at Rome the old conditions, the old claims, and the old law were unforgotten. For example, Nicholas I. (858–867) drew a picture of the divine right and unlimited power of the bishop of Rome, which anticipated all that the greatest of his successors were, centuries later, actually to effect. The time had not, however, yet come for the establishment of the papal world-dominion. For, while the power of Charlemagne's successors was decaying, the papacy itself became involved in the confusion of the party strife of Italy and of the city of Rome, and was plunged in consequence into such an abyss of degradation (the so-called Pornocracy), that it was in danger of forfeiting every shred of its moral authority over Christendom.

(ii.) During the central period of the Middle Ages the antagonism between the German conception of ecclesiastical affairs and Roman views of ecclesiastical law found inevitable expression. This was most obvious in the matter of appointment to bishoprics. At Rome canonical election was alone regarded as lawful; in Germany, on the other hand, developments since the time of Charlemagne had led to the actual appointment of bishops being in the hands of the king, although the form of ecclesiastical election was preserved.

The practice customary in Germany was finally transferred to Rome itself. The desperate position of the papacy in the 11th century obliged Henry III. to intervene. When, in Dec. 1046, after three rival popes had been set aside, he nominated Suidgar, bishop of Bamberg, as bishop of Rome before all the people in St. Peter's, the papacy was bestowed in the same way as a German bishopric; and what had occurred in this case was to become the rule. By procuring the transference of the patriciate from the Roman people to himself Henry assured his influence over the appointment of the popes, and accordingly also nominated the successors of Clement II.

His intervention saved the papacy. For the popes nominated by him, Leo IX. in particular, were men of high character, who exercised their office in a loftier spirit than their corrupt predecessors. They placed themselves at the head of the movement for ecclesiastical reform. But it was not possible for the relation between Empire and Papacy to remain what Henry III. had made it.

The original sources of this reform movement lay far back, in the time of the Carolingians. It has been pointed out how Charlemagne pressed the monks into the service of his civilizing aims; but he thereby alienated monasticism from its original ideals. These, however, had far too strong a hold upon the Roman world for a reaction against the new tendency to be long avoided. This reaction began with the reform of Benedict of Aniane (d. 821), the aim of which was to bring the Benedictine order back to the principles of its original rules. In the next century the reform movement acquired a fresh centre in the Burgundian monastery of Cluny. A large number of the reformed monasteries attached themselves to the congregation of Cluny, thus assuring the influence of reformed monasticism upon the Church, and securing likewise its independence of the diocesan bishops, since the abbot of Cluny was subordinate of the pope alone (*see* CLUNY, BENEDICTINES, and MONASTICISM). Everywhere the object was the same: the supreme obligation of the Rule, the renewal of discipline, and also the economic improvement of the monasteries. The reform movement had originally no connection with ecclesiastical politics; but that came later when the leaders turned their attention to the abuses prevalent among the clergy, to the conditions obtaining in the Church in defiance of the ecclesiastical law. "Return to the canon law!" was now the battle-cry. The programme of reform thus included the freeing of the Church from the influence of the State, the recovery of her absolute control over all her possessions, the liberty of the Church and of the hierarchy.

As a result, the party of reform placed itself in opposition to those ecclesiastical conditions which had arisen since the conversion of the Teutonic peoples. It was, then, a fact pregnant with the most momentous consequences that Leo IX. attached himself to the party of reform. For, thanks to him and to the men he gathered round him (Hildebrand, Humbert and others), their principles were established in Rome, and the pope himself became the leader of ecclesiastical reform. But the carrying out of reforms led at once to dissensions with the civil power, the starting-point being the attack upon simony, this term covering all transferences by laymen of ecclesiastical offices or benefices, even though no money changed hands in the process. Thus the lord who handed over a living was a simonist, and so too was the king who invested a bishop. The Church at first concentrated her attack upon investiture. In 1059 the new system of papal election introduced by Nicholas II. (*see* CONCLAVE) ensured the occupation of the Holy See by a pope favourable to the party of reform; and in 1078 Gregory VII. issued his prohibition of lay investiture. In the years of conflict that followed Gregory looked far beyond this point; he set his aim ever higher, until, in the end, his idea was to concentrate all ecclesiastical power in the hands of the pope, and to raise the papacy to the dominion of the world. Thus was to be realized the old dream of Augustine: that of a Kingdom of God on earth under the rule of the Church. But it was not given to Gregory to reach this goal, and his successors had to return again to the strife over investiture; and the long struggle ended in a compromise by the Concordat of Worms (1122), the essential part of which was that the Empire accepted the canonical election of bishops, while the Church acknowledged that the bishop held his temporal rights from the Empire, and was therefore to be invested with them by a touch from the royal sceptre. A similar solution was arrived at in England. In France the demands of the Church were successful to the same degree as in England and Germany, but without any conflict. Thus the Germanic element in the law regarding appointment to bishoprics was eliminated. Somewhat later it disappeared also in the case of the churches of less importance, patronal rights over these being substituted for the former absolute ownership. The pontificate of Alexander III. (1159–81) decided this.

The Teutonic peoples had been taking the lead in the expansion of Christianity; but the spirit of the Latin races now began to assert itself. Scholasticism, the new theology, had its home in the Latin countries. Reason as well as authority had been appealed to as the foundation of theology; but for the theologians of the 9th and 10th centuries, whose method had been merely that of restatement, *ratio* and *auctoritas* were in perfect accord. Then Berengar of Tours (d. 1088) ventured to set up reason against authority: by reason the truth must be decided. This involved the question of the relation in theology of authority and reason, and of whether the theological method is authoritative or rational. These questions Berengar could not settle; he was ruined by his opposition to Radbert's doctrine of transubstantiation. The Lombard Anselm (d. 1109), archbishop of Canterbury, was the first to deal with the subject. He took as his starting-point the traditional faith; but he was convinced that whoever has experience of the truths of the faith would be able to understand them, by the exercise of his natural reason.

It was a bold conception—too bold for the mediaeval world, for which faith was primarily the obligation to believe. It was easy, therefore, to understand why Anselm's method did not become the dominant one in theology. Not he, but the Frenchman Abelard (d. 1142), was the creator of the scholastic method. Abelard, too, started from tradition; but he discovered that the statements of the various authorities are very often in the relation of *sic et non*, yes and no. Upon this fact he based his pronouncement as to the function of theology: it must employ the dialectic method to reconcile the contradictions of tradition, and thus to shape the doctrines of the faith in accordance with reason. By teaching this method Abelard created the implements for the erection of the great theological systems of the schoolmen of the 12th and 13th centuries: Peter Lombard (d. 1160), Alexander of Hales (d. 1245), Albertus Magnus (d. 1280) and Thomas Aquinas (d. 1275). They adventured a complete exposition of Christian doctrine that should be altogether ecclesiastical and at the same time altogether rational. In so doing they set to work to complete the development of ecclesiastical dogma; the formulation of the Catholic doctrine of the Sacraments was the work of scholasticism.

Canon law is the twin-sister of scholasticism. At the very time when Peter Lombard was shaping his Sentences, the monk Gratian of Bologna was making a new collection of laws. It was not only significant that in the *Concordia discordantium canonum* ecclesiastical laws, whether from authentic or forged sources, were gathered together without regard to the existing civil law; of even greater eventual importance was the fact that Gratian taught that the contradictions of the canon law were to be reconciled by the same method as that used by theology to reconcile the discrepancies of doctrinal tradition. Thus Gratian became the founder of the science of canon law, a science which, like the scholastic theology, was entirely ecclesiastical and entirely rational (*see* CANON LAW).

Like the new theology and the new science of law, the new monasticism was also rooted in Latin soil. The duty of the priest-monk is not only to work out his own salvation, but, by preaching and cure of souls, to labour for others. This was the dominant idea of the order of friars preachers founded in 1216 by St. Dominic (*see* DOMINIC, SAINT; DOMINICANS). It was also the basis of the order of friars minor, founded in 1210 (*see* FRANCIS OF ASSISI, ST.; FRANCISCANS). This alone would serve to indicate the remarkable deepening of the religious life that had taken place in the Latin countries. In the 12th century the most influential exponent of this new piety was Bernard (*q.v.*) of Clairvaux, who taught men to find God by leading them to Christ. Contemporary with him were Hugh of St. Victor (*q.v.*) and his pupil Richard of St. Victor (*q.v.*), both monks of the abbey of St. Victor at Paris, the aim of whose teaching was a mystical absorption of thought in the Godhead and the surrender of self to the Eternal Love. Under the influence of these ideas, in part purely Christian and in part Neoplatonic, piety gained in warmth and depth and became more personal; and though at first it flourished in the monasteries, and in those of the mendicant orders especially, it penetrated far beyond them and influenced the laity everywhere. The new piety did not set itself in opposition either to the hierarchy or to the institutions of the Church, such as the sacraments and the discipline of penance, nor did it reject those foreign elements (asceticism, worship of saints and the like) which had passed of old time into Christianity from the ancient world. Its temper was not critical, but aggressively practical.

All this meant a mighty exaltation of the Church, which ruled the minds of men as it had hardly ever done before. Nor was it possible that the position of the bishop of Rome, the supreme head of the Western Church, should remain unaffected by it. Two of the most powerful of the German emperors, Frederick I. and his son Henry VI., struggled to renew and to maintain the imperial supremacy over the papacy. But when at the peace of Venice (1177) Frederick recognized Alexander III. as pope, he relinquished the hope of carrying out his Italian policy; while Henry died at the early age of thirty-two (1197), before his far-reaching schemes had been realized.

The field was thus cleared for the full development of papal power. This had greatly increased since the Concordat of Worms, and reached its height under Innocent III. (1198–1216). Innocent believed himself to be the representative of God, and as such the supreme possessor of both spiritual and temporal power. He therefore claimed in both spheres the supreme administrative, legislative and judicial authority. The bishops described themselves as holding office "by grace of the Apostolic See," for they administered their dioceses as plenipotentiaries of the pope; and even the criminal jurisdiction of the church (*see* INQUISITION) became more and more concentrated in his hands. And just as he considered himself entitled to appoint to all ecclesiastical offices, so also he invested the emperor with his empire and kings with their kingdoms. Not only did he despatch his decretals to the universities to form the basis of the teaching of the canon law and of the decisions founded upon it, but he considered himself empowered to annul civil laws. Thus he annulled the Great Charter in 1215. Just as the Curia was the supreme court of appeal in ecclesiastical causes, so also the pope threatened disobedient princes with deposition, *e.g.*, the emperor Otto IV. in 1210, and John of England in 1212. But the papal claim to supreme temporal authority proved impossible to maintain, although Innocent III. had apparently enforced it. The long struggle against Frederick II., carried on by Gregory IX. (1227–41) and Innocent IV. (1243–54), did not result in victory; no papal sentence, but only death itself, deprived the emperor of his dominions; and when Boniface VIII. (1294–1303), who gave the papal claims to universal dominion their classical form, quarrelled with Philip IV. of France about the extension of the royal power, he could not but perceive that the national monarchy had become a force which it was impossible for the papacy to overcome.

(iii.) At the close of the middle ages we come to a period of disintegration. While the Church was yet at the height of her power began the great revolution which was to end in the disruption of that union between the Temporal and the Spiritual which, under her dominion, had characterized the life of the West. The Temporal now claimed its proper rights. The political power of the Empire, indeed, had been shattered; but this left all the more room for the vigorous development of national states, notably of France and England. At the same time intellectual life was enriched by a wealth of fresh views and new ideas, partly the result of the busy intercourse with the East to which the Crusades had given the first impetus, and which had been strengthened and extended by lively trade relations, partly of the revived study, eagerly pursued, of ancient philosophy and literature (*see* RENAISSANCE). The life of the Church, moreover, was affected by the economic changes due to the rise of the power of money as opposed to the old economic system based upon land.

The effects of these changes made themselves felt on all sides, in no case more strongly than in that of the papal claims to the supreme government of the world. Theoretically they were still unwaveringly asserted; but after Boniface VIII. no pope seriously attempted to realize them; to do so had in fact become impossible, for from the time of their residence at Avignon (1305–77) the popes were in a state of complete dependence upon the French crown. In France Philip IV.'s jurists maintained that the temporal power was independent of the spiritual. In Italy, a little later, Dante championed the divine right of the emperor (*De Monarchia*, 1311). In Germany, Marsiglio of Padua and Jean of Jandun, the literary allies of the emperor Louis IV., ventured to define anew the nature of the civil power from the standpoint of natural law, and to assert its absolute sovereignty (*Defensor pacis*, *c.* 1352); while the Franciscan William of Occam (d. 1349) examined, also in Louis' interests, into the nature of the relation between the two powers. He too concluded that the temporal power is independent of the spiritual, and is even justified in invading the sphere of the latter in cases of necessity.

While these thoughts were filling men's minds, opposition to the papal rule over the Church was also gaining continually in strength. The reasons for this were numerous, first among them being the abuses of the papal system of finance, which had to provide funds for the vast administrative machinery of the Curia. There was also the boundless abuse and arbitrary exercise of the right of ecclesiastical patronage; and further the ever-increasing traffic in dispensations, the abuse of spiritual punishments for worldly ends, and so forth. No means, however, existed of enforcing any remedy until the papal schism occurred in 1378. Such a schism as this, so intolerable to the ecclesiastical sense of the middle ages, necessitated the discovery of some authority superior to the rival popes, and therefore able to put an end to their quarrelling. General councils were now once more called to mind; but these were no longer conceived as mere advisory councils to the pope, but as the highest representative organ of the universal Church, and as such ranking above the pope, and competent to demand obedience even from him. The council of Constance (1414–18) did actually put an end to the schism; but the reforms begun at Constance and continued at Basel (1431–49) proved insufficient. Above all, the attempt to set up the general council as an ordinary institution of the Catholic Church failed; and the Roman papacy, restored at Constance, preserved its irresponsible and unlimited power over the government of the Church (*see* PAPACY; CONSTANCE, COUNCIL OF; and BASEL, COUNCIL OF). Neither France nor Germany, however, was prepared to forgo the reforms passed by the council. France secured their validity, as far as she herself was concerned, by the Pragmatic Sanction of Bourges (July 7, 1438); Germany followed with the Acceptation of Mainz (March 26, 1439). The theory of the papal supremacy held by the Curia was thus at least called in question.

The antagonism of the opposition parties was even more pronounced. The tendencies which they represented had been present when the middle ages were yet at their height; but the papacy, while at the zenith of its power, had succeeded in crushing the attacks made upon the creed of the Church by its most dangerous foes, the dualistic Cathars (*q.v.*), Waldenses (*q.v.*) and kindred enthusiasts, who everywhere kept alive mistrust of the temporal power of the Church, of her priesthood and her hierarchy. In England the hierarchy was attacked by Wycliffe (d. 1384), its greatest opponent before Luther. Starting from Augustine's conception of the Church as the community of the elect, he protested against a church of wealth and power, a church that had become a political institution instead of a school of salvation; and against its head, the bishop of Rome. Wycliffe's ideas, conveyed to the continent, precipitated the outbreak of the Hussite storm in Bohemia (*see* HUSS; WYCLIFFE; LOLLARDS). This was open opposition; but there was besides another opposing force which, though it raised no noise of controversy, was far more widely severed from the views of the Church than either Wycliffe or Huss, namely the Renaissance, which began its reign in Italy during the 14th century. The Renaissance meant the emancipation of the secular world from the domination of the Church, and it contributed in no small measure to the rupture of the educated class with ecclesiastical tradition. Beauty of form alone was at first sought, and found in the antique; but, with the form, the spirit of the classical attitude towards life was revived. The men of the Renaissance wished to enjoy the earth by means of secular education and culture, and an impassable gulf yawned between their views of religion and morality and those of the Church. Theology could no longer provide a reconciliation. Since the time of Duns Scotus (d. 1308) theologians had been conscious of the discrepancy between Aristotelianism and ecclesiastical dogma. Faith in the infallibility of the scholastic system was thus shaken, and the system itself was destroyed by the revival of philosophic nominalism, which had been discredited in the 11th century by the realism of the great schoolmen. It now found a courageous supporter in William of Occam, and through him became widely accepted. But nominalism was powerless to inspire theology with new life; on the contrary, its intervention only increased the inextricable tangle of the hairsplitting questions with which theology busied itself.

In the meantime the Roman claim to the supreme government of the Church was steadily maintained. In 1512 Julius II. called together the 5th Lateran general council, which expressly recognized the subjection of the councils to the pope and also declared the constitution of Boniface VIII. (*see* above) valid in law. But the papacy that sought to win back its old position was no longer the same as of old. Eugenius IV.'s successor, Nicholas V. (1447–55), was the first of the Renaissance popes. Under his successors the views which prevailed at the secular courts of the Italian princes came likewise into play at the Curia: the papacy became an Italian princedom. Innocent VIII., Alexander VI., Julius II. were in many respects remarkable men, but they were scarcely affected by the convictions of the Christian faith. The terrible tragedy which was consummated on May 23, 1498, before the Palazzo Vecchio, in Florence, casts a lurid light upon the irreconcilable opposition in which the wearers of the papal dignity stood to mediaeval piety; for Savonarola was in every fibre a loyal son of the mediaeval Church.

Twenty years after Savonarola's death Luther made public his theses against indulgences. The Reformation which thus began brought the disintegrating process of the middle ages to an end, and at the same time divided Western Catholicism in two. Yet we may say that this was its salvation; for the struggle against Luther drove the papacy back to its ecclesiastical duties, and the council of Trent established mediaeval dogma as the doctrine of modern Catholicism in contradistinction to Protestantism.

C. THE MODERN CHURCH

The issue in 1564 of the canons of the council of Trent marks a very definite epoch in the history of the Christian Church. Up till that time, in spite of the schism of East and West and of innumerable heresies, the idea of the Church as Catholic, not only in its faith but in its organization, had been generally accepted. From this conception the Reformers had, at the outset, no intention of departing. Their object had been to purify the Church of mediaeval accretions, and to restore the primitive model in the light of the new learning; the idea of rival "churches," differing in their fundamental doctrines and in their principles of organization, existing side by side, was as abhorrent to them as to the most rigid partisan of Roman centralization. The actual divisions of Western Christendom are the outcome, less of the purely religious influences of the Reformation period than of the political forces with which they were associated and confused. Thus over a great part of Europe the Catholic Church was split up into territorial or national churches, which, whatever the theoretical ties which bound them together, were in fact separate organizations, tending ever more and more to become isolated and self-contained units with no formal intercommunion, and, as the rivalry of nationalities grew, with increasingly little even of intercommunication.

It was not, indeed, till the settlement of Westphalia in 1648, after the Thirty Years' War, that this territorial division of Christendom became stereotyped, but the process had been going on for 100 years previously; in some States, as in England and Scotland, it had long been completed; in others, as in S. Germany, Bohemia and Poland, it was defeated by the political and missionary efforts of the Jesuits and other agents of the counter-Reformation. In any case, it received a vast impetus from the action of the council of Trent. With the issue of the Tridentine canons, all hope even of compromise between the "new" and the "old" religions was definitely closed. Considered from the standpoint of the world outside, the Roman Church is, no less than the Protestant communities, merely one of the sects into which Western Christendom has been divided—the most important and widespread, it is true, but playing in the general life and thought of the world a part immeasurably less important than that filled by the Church before the Reformation, and one in no sense justifying her claim to be considered as the sole inheritor of the tradition of the pre-Reformation Church.

If this be true of the Roman Catholic Church, it is still more so of the other great communities and confessions which emerged from the controversies of the Reformation. Of these the Anglican Church held most closely to the tradition of Catholic organization; but she has never made any higher claim than to be one of "the three branches of the Catholic Church," a claim repudiated by Rome and never formally admitted by the Church of the East. The Protestant churches established on the continent, even where —as in the case of the Lutherans—they approximate more closely than the official Anglican Church to Roman doctrine and practice, make no such claim. The Bible is for them the real source of authority in doctrine; their organization is part and parcel of that of the State. They are, in fact, the State in its religious aspect, and as such are territorial or national, not Catholic. This tendency has been common in the East also, where with the growth of racial rivalries the Orthodox Church has split into a series of national churches, holding the same faith but independent as to organization.

A yet further development, of comparatively recent growth, has been the formation of what are now commonly called in England the "free churches." These represent a theory of the Church practically unknown to the Reformers, and only reached through the necessity for discovering a logical basis for the communities of conscientious dissidents from the established churches. According to this the Catholic Church is not a visibly organized body, but the sum of all "faithful people" throughout the world, who group themselves in churches modelled according to their convictions or needs. For the organization of these churches no divine sanction is claimed, though all are theoretically modelled on the lines laid down in the Scriptures. It follows that, while in the traditional Church, with its claim to an unbroken descent from a divine original, the individual is subordinate to the Church, in the "free churches" the Church is in a certain sense secondary to the individual. The believer may pass from one community to another without imperilling his spiritual life, or establish a new church without necessarily incurring the reproach of schism. From this theory, powerful in Great Britain and her colonies, supreme in the United States of America, has resulted an enormous multiplication of sects.

Hence, from the period of the Reformation onward, no historical account of the Christian Church as a whole, and considered as a definite institution, is possible. The stream of continuity has been broken, and divides into innumerable channels. The only possible synthesis is that of the Christianity common to all; as institutions, they are divided, though they possess many features in common. The history of the various branches of the Christian Church since the Reformation will therefore be found under their titles: ROMAN CATHOLIC CHURCH; ENGLAND, THE CHURCH OF; PRESBYTERIAN; CONGREGATIONALISM; METHODISM; and others. The references given under the titles CHRISTIANITY, HERESY, and REUNION, CHURCH, may be mentioned here also.

The first real Church History was written by Eusebius of Caesarea in the early part of the 4th century. His work was continued in the 5th century by Philostorgius, Socrates, Sozomen and Theodoret, and later by Evagrius, Theophanes and others. In the West the history of Eusebius was translated into Latin by Rufinus and continued to the end of the 4th century. In the 6th century Cassiodorus had a translation made of the histories of Socrates, Sozomen and Theodoret, and brought down to 518. It was called *Historia Ecclesiastica Tripartita,* and during the middle ages was the principal textbook of Church History in the West. During the 5th, 6th and following centuries numerous works were produced containing more or less ecclesiastical material: biographies, chronicles, cloister annals and especially many local and territorial histories such as Gregory of Tours, *History of the Franks,* and Bede's *Ecclesiastical History of England.* The Protestant Reformation led to a new development of historical writing. In 1559 and following years a number of Protestant scholars published the *Magdeburg Centuries* to prove the primitive character of Protestantism, and were followed by Baronius (*Annales Ecclesiastici,* 1588 ff.) on the Roman Catholic side. Both works became the model for many others.

Church history began to be written in a genuinely scientific spirit in the 18th century under the leadership of Mosheim, whose most important work is his *Institutiones Historiae Ecclesiasticae* (1755), and was carried further through the new historical spirit of the 19th century in a series of works of which the most important are those of Gieseler, *Lehrbuch der Kirchengeschichte* (1826 ff. Eng. tr. by H. B. Smith), with copious citations from the sources, and still valuable; Neander, *Allgemeine Geschichte der Christlichen Religion und Kirche* (1825 ff., Eng. tr. by Torrey), with special stress on the religious side of the subject (*cf.* also Schaff, *History of the Christian Church,* 5th ed. 1889 ff.); Ferdinand Christian Baur of Tübingen (*Das Christenthum und die christliche Kirche,* 1853 ff.) whose many historical works were dominated by the principles of the Hegelian philosophy and exhibit both the merits and defects of that school; and Albrecht Ritschl (*Entstehung der alt katholischen Kirche,* 2nd ed. 1857), who broke away from the Tübingen school and built up new points of view. Among many more recent books may be mentioned that of W. Moeller, *Lehrbuch der Kirchengeschichte* (1889 ff., 2nd ed. by von Schuberth, 1898 ff., enlarged and improved), the translation of the latter being still the most useful textbook in English. Many references to historical works on specific branches of the subject will be found in the relative articles.

There are many editions of the works of the Fathers in the original, the most convenient, in spite of its defects, being that of J. P. Migne (*Patrologia Graeca,* 166 vols., Paris, 1857 ff.; *Patrologia Latina,* 221 vols., 1844 ff.). Of modern critical editions, besides those containing the works of one or another individual, the best are the Berlin edition of the early Greek Fathers (*Die griechischen christlichen Schriftsteller der ersten drei Jahrhunderte,* 1897 ff.), and the Vienna edition of the Latin Fathers (*Corpus scriptorum ecclesiasticorum Latinorum,* 1867 ff.), both of first-rate importance. There is a convenient English translation of most of the writings of the ante-Nicene Fathers by Roberts and Donaldson (*Ante-Nicene Christian Library,* 25 vols., Edinburgh, 1868 ff., American reprint, 9 vols., 1886 ff.). A continuation of it, containing selected works of the Nicene and post-Nicene period, was edited by Schaff and others under the title *A Select Library of Nicene and post-Nicene Fathers* (series 1 and 2; 28 vols., Buffalo and N.Y., 1886 ff.).

On early Christian literature, in addition to the works on Church history, see especially the monumental *Geschichte der altchristlichen Litteratur bis Eusebius,* by Harnack (1893 ff.). The brief *Geschichte der altchristlichen Litteratur in den ersten drei Jahrhunderten,* by G. Krüger (1895, English translation, 1897) is a very convenient summary. Bardenhewer's *Patrologie* (1894) and his *Geschichte der altkirchlichen Litteratur* (1902 ff.) should also be mentioned. Upon the spread of the Church during the early centuries see especially Harnack, *Mission und Ausbreitung des Christenthums in den ersten drei Jahrhunderten,* Eng. tr. *The Mission and Expansion of Christianity* (1907). An interesting parallel to the spread of Christianity in the Roman empire is afforded by the contemporary Mithraism; *see* Cumont's *Les Mystères de Mithra* (1900, Eng. tr., 1903). *See* also Hatch, *Influence of Greek Ideas and Usages upon the Christian Church,* 1890; Anrich, *Das antike Mysterienwesen in seinem Einfluss auf das Christentum,* 1894, Wobbermin, *Religionsgeschichtliche Studien zur Frage der Beeinflussung des Urchristentums durch das antike Mysterienwesen,* 1896; and for the organization of the early church, Harnack, *Mission und Ausbreitung des Christenthums,* pp. 337 *seq.,* and to the same writer's *Texte und Untersuchungen,* ii. 5 (Eng. tr. *Sources of the Apostolic Canons,* 1895); Fulbert Cayré, A.A.; *Precis de Patralogie,* French 1930, 1931; English 1936, 1940. **(A. C. McG.; A. Hk.; W. A. P.; X.)**

CHURCHILL, CHARLES (1731–1764), English poet and satirist, was born in Westminster, in Feb. 1731. His father, a clergyman, destined his son for the Church, and Charles was ordained in 1756. He was married at the age of 18, but his married life was unhappy and in 1761 he separated from his wife. He had lived a poverty-stricken life until that year, when he published, anonymously and without advertisement, the *Rosciad* at the price of a shilling. This brilliant but merciless satire described one by one the faults and eccentricities of the leading actors and actresses of the London stage, David Garrick almost alone escaping censure. It lay but a few days unnoticed in the bookshops; it was soon taken up with enthusiasm and the secret of its authorship publicly debated. It was attributed to Robert Lloyd, an amiable Welsh poet who, on Churchill's acknowledging the authorship, became his great friend. Churchill followed up the *Rosciad* with the *Apology,* in which his strictures were repeated and even Garrick was threatened. The actor sent through Lloyd an anxious and alarmed letter which flattered the poet by showing the fear which he already inspired. More, perhaps, even than his new-found power, Churchill enjoyed the wealth which his poems brought him. He paid his debts, made an allowance to his wife and started on a career of loose living and dandiacal dressing, which led, in 1763, after protests from his parishioners and his bishop, to his being forced to resign his living. He defended in 1761 his method of life in a poem called *Night,* of which Smollett's *Critical Review* said in Dec. 1761, not unfairly, "This Night, like many others at this time of the year, is very cold, long, dark and dirty." With Sir Francis Dashwood and John Wilkes (*q.v.*) he drank wine in the globe at the top of West Wycombe church, and indulged in even less seemly pranks; he may even have been one of the famous Medmenham monks.

He became, in 1762, along with Lloyd, a close ally of Wilkes and assistant editor of the *North Briton* throughout its career, assisting its furious political campaign by rhymed satires which were almost equally feared: *The Prophecy of Famine* (1763), an attack on Lord Bute and the Scots, an *Epistle to William Hogarth* (1763), a reply to Hogarth's attack on Temple and Pitt; *The Duellist* (1763), an attack on Samuel Martin, M.P., who had attempted to kill Wilkes, and *The Candidate* (1764), an exposure of "Jemmy Twitcher," Lord Sandwich, Wilkes' chief enemy. His other completed works are *The Ghost, The Conference, The Author* (1763), *The Farewell, Independence, The Times* and *Gotham* (1764), of which the last is perhaps the best. He died of a fever on a visit to Wilkes in exile at Boulogne on Nov. 4, 1764.

Churchill was elephantine in figure: he has drawn his own picture in *Independence:—*

Vast were his bones, his muscles twisted strong;
His face was short, but broader than 'twas long;
His features, though by nature they were large,
Contentment had contrived to overcharge,
And bury meaning, save that we might spy
Sense lowering in the penthouse of his eye;
His arms were two twin oaks; his legs so stout
That they might bear a Mansion House about;
Nor were they, look but at his body there,
Designed by fate a much less weight to bear.

Churchill excelled in invective and malicious portraiture, as of Warburton, the pedantic and ambitious bishop of Gloucester:—

Who was so proud, that should he meet
The Twelve Apostles in the street,
He'd turn his nose up at them all
And shove his Saviour from the wall.
(*The Duellist.*)

In his lifetime he was grossly overpraised and his death was lamented as a privation equal to the loss of Hogarth. Since then he has suffered an almost total eclipse. But he possesses great merits: his English is clear and vigorous, his wit and talent for invective are undoubted, and his poetic genius, of a Juvenalian character, much above the average. But it requires a great knowledge of 18th century politics and an equally great interest to appreciate his merits, and for that reason he is never again likely to be widely read.

See his *Collected Poems,* edited by W. Tooke with a biography and letters (1804), and re-edited by J. L. Hannay (1892), and the books cited under Wilkes, John. (R. W. P.)

CHURCHILL, LORD RANDOLPH HENRY SPENCER (1849–1895), English statesman, third son of John, 7th duke of Marlborough, by Frances, daughter of the third marquess of Londonderry, was born at Blenheim palace, on Feb. 13, 1849. He was educated at Eton and at Merton college, Oxford. In 1874 he was elected to parliament in the Conservative interest for Woodstock.

In 1878 he forced himself into public notice as the exponent of a species of independent Conservatism. He directed a series of furious attacks against some of the occupants of the front Ministerial bench. Sclater-Booth (afterwards 1st Lord Basing), president of the Local Government Board, was a special object of attack, and denounced as the "crowning dishonour to Tory principles." In the new parliament of 1880, Churchill began to play a more notable rôle. With the assistance of Sir Henry Drummond Wolff, Sir John Gorst and occasionally of Arthur Balfour, and one or two others, he constituted himself at once the audacious opponent of the Liberal Administration and the unsparing critic of the Conservative front bench. The "fourth party," as it was nicknamed, was effective in awakening the Opposition from the apathy which had fallen upon it after its defeat at the polls. Churchill roused the Conservatives and gave them a fighting issue, by putting himself at the head of the resistance to Charles Bradlaugh, the member for Northampton, who, though an avowed atheist or agnostic, was prepared to take the parliamentary oath. He continued to play a conspicuous part throughout the parliament of 1880–85, dealing his blows with almost equal vigour at Gladstone and at the Conservative front bench, some of whose members, and particularly Sir Richard Cross and W. H. Smith, he assailed with extreme virulence.

From the beginning of the Egyptian imbroglio Lord Randolph emphatically opposed almost every step taken by the Government. He declared that the suppression of Arabi Pasha's rebellion was an error, and the restoration of the khedive's authority a crime. He was equally severe on the domestic policy of the Administration, and was particularly bitter in his criticism of the Kilmainham Treaty and the *rapprochement* between the Gladstonians and the Parnellites. It is true that for some time before the fall of the Liberals in 1885 he had considerably modified his attitude towards the Irish question, and was himself cultivating friendly relations with the Home Rule members, and even obtained from them the assistance of the Irish vote in the English constituencies in the general election. By this time he had definitely formulated the policy of progressive Conservatism which was known as "Tory democracy." He declared that the Conservatives ought to adopt, rather than oppose, reforms of a popular character, and to challenge the claims of the Liberals to pose as the champions of the masses. His views were to a large extent accepted by the official Conservative leaders in the treatment of the Gladstonian Franchise bill of 1884. Lord Randolph insisted that the principle of the bill should be accepted by the Opposition, and that resistance should be focussed upon the refusal of the Government to combine with it a scheme of redistribution. The prominent, and on the whole judicious and successful, part he played in the debates on these questions, still further increased his influence with the rank and file of the Conservatives in the constituencies. At the same time he was actively spreading the gospel of democratic Toryism in a series of platform campaigns. In 1883 and 1884 he invaded the Radical stronghold of Birmingham itself, and in the latter year took part in a Conservative garden party at Aston Manor, at which his opponents paid him the compliment of raising a serious riot. He gave constant attention to the party organization, and was an active promoter and first member of the Primrose League, which owed its origin to the happy inspiration of one of his own "fourth party" colleagues.

In 1884 the struggle between stationary and progressive Toryism ended in favour of the latter. At the conference of the Central Union of Conservative Associations, Lord Randolph was nominated chairman, notwithstanding the strenuous opposition of the parliamentary leaders of the party. The split was averted by Lord Randolph's voluntary resignation; but the episode had confirmed his title to a leading place in the Tory ranks. It was further strengthened by the prominent part he played in the events immediately preceding the fall of the Liberal Government in 1885; and when Childers's budget resolutions were defeated by the Conservatives, aided by about half the Parnellites, Lord Randolph Churchill's admirers were justified in proclaiming him to have been the "organizer of victory." Owing to Lord Randolph's refusal to serve under Sir S. Northcote's leadership, Lord Salisbury had great difficulty in forming a cabinet in June 1885. Finally a way out of the *impasse* was found by elevating Northcote to the peerage (as earl of Iddesleigh) and giving the leadership in the House of Commons to Sir M. Hicks Beach. Lord Randolph was given the India Office, where "the India Council would be a check on him." (*Letters of Queen Victoria,* second series, vol. iii., p. 663.) During the few months of his tenure of this great post the young free-lance of Tory democracy attended to his departmental duties and mastered the complicated questions of Indian administration. In the autumn election of 1885 he contested Central Birmingham against Bright, and though defeated here, was at the same time returned by a very large majority for South Paddington. In the Home Rule controversy, both in and out of parliament, Lord Randolph again bore a conspicuous part. He was now the recognized Conservative champion in the lower chamber, and when the second Salisbury Administration was formed after the general election of 1886 he became chancellor of the exchequer and leader of the House of Commons. His management of the House was on the whole successful, and was marked by tact, discretion and temper. But he had never really reconciled himself with some of his colleagues, and there was a good deal of friction in his relations with them, which ended with his sudden resignation on Dec. 20, 1886. Various motives influenced him in taking this step; but the only ostensible cause was that put forward in his letter to Lord Salisbury, read in the House of Commons on Jan. 27, in which he stated that his resignation was due to his inability, as chancellor of the exchequer, to concur in the demands made on the Treasury by the ministers at the head of the naval and military establishments and that a better foreign policy might obviate the necessity for such demands. Although he himself refrained from offering any public explanation of his conduct, nor in any way sought to bring about a reconciliation with Salisbury, Lord Randolph Churchill's prestige was so great that a reconstruction of the cabinet proved a task of great difficulty. At length Goschen was induced to accept the chancellorship, and Churchill disappeared from any effective part in the leadership of the Conservative Party.

He continued, for some years longer, to give a general, though decidedly independent, support to the Unionist Administration. On the Irish question he was a very candid critic of Balfour's measures, and one of his later speeches, which recalled the acrimonious violence of his earlier period, was that which he delivered in 1890 on the report of the Parnell commission. He also fulfilled the promise made on his resignation by occasionally advocating the principles of economy and retrenchment in the debates on the naval and military estimates. In April 1889, on the death of Bright, he was asked to stand for the vacant seat in Birmingham, and the result was a rather angry controversy with Chamberlain, terminating in the so-called "Birmingham compact" for the division of representation of the Midland capital between Liberal Unionists and Conservatives. But his health was already precarious, and he bestowed much attention on society, travel and sport. He was an ardent supporter of the turf, and in 1889 he won the Oaks with a mare named the Abbesse de Jouarre. In 1891 he went to South Africa, in search both of health and relaxation. He travelled for some months through Cape Colony, the Transvaal and Rhodesia, and recorded his impressions in a book entitled *Men, Mines and Animals in South Africa.*

In the general election of 1892 he once more flung himself, with his old vigour, into the strife of parties. His seat at South Paddington was uncontested, and when parliament met he returned to the Opposition front bench to take a leading part in debate, attacking Gladstone's second Home Rule bill with especial energy. He died in London on Jan. 24, 1895.

Lord Randolph Churchill married, in Jan. 1874, Jennie, daughter of Leonard Jerome of New York, U.S.A., by whom he had two sons. In 1900 Lady Randolph Churchill married G. Cornwallis-West.

An authoritative biography of Lord Randolph, by his son Winston appeared in 1906; and a brief and intimate appreciation by Lord Rosebery, inspired by this biography, was published a few months later. Lord Randolph's earlier speeches were edited, with an introduction and notes, by Louis Jennings (2 vols., 1889). *See* also H. W. Lucy, *Diary of Two Parliaments* (1892); and Mrs. Cornwallis-West, *The Reminiscences of Lady Randolph Churchill,* (*i.e.,* of the author) (1908); *The Letters of Queen Victoria,* second series, 3 vols. (1926–28).

CHURCHILL, WINSTON (1871–1947), U.S. writer, was born in St. Louis, Mo., Nov. 10, 1871. He was graduated from the United States naval academy in 1894, soon devoting himself to writing. His first novel, *The Celebrity,* appeared in 1898. His next, *Richard Carvel* (1899), a novel of Maryland in the time of the Revolution, had a sale of nearly 1,000,000 copies. Then followed *The Crisis* (1901), the heroine of which is a descendant of his former hero, Richard Carvel; and *The Crossing* (1904). His other works include: *Coniston* (1906); *Mr. Crewe's Career* (1908); *A Modern Chronicle* (1910); *The Inside of the Cup* (1913); *The Dwelling Place of Light* (1917); *The Uncharted Way* (1941). Although his later work consisted chiefly of problem novels, his romantic tales of America's past were most popular. From 1903 to 1905 he was a member of the New Hampshire legislature, and in 1913 he was a candidate for the governorship as a Progressive.

He died Mar. 12, 1947, in Winter Park, Fla.

CHURCHILL, SIR WINSTON LEONARD SPENCER (1874–   ), British statesman, son of Lord Randolph Churchill and Jennie, daughter of Leonard Jerome, of New York city, was born on Nov. 30, 1874, at Blenheim palace, Oxfordshire. He was educated at Harrow and Sandhurst. Entering the army in 1895, he saw active war service with the Malakand field force (1897) and the Tirah expeditionary force (1898); attached to the 21st Lancers, he also served with the Nile expeditionary force and was present at the battle of Omdurman (1898). These campaigns gave him material for two brilliant books, *The Story of the Malakand Field Force* (1898) and *The River War* (1899). During the South African War (1899–1902) he was correspondent for the *Morning Post* and wrote an account of his experiences as *London to Ladysmith via Pretoria* (1900). He was taken prisoner by the Boers, but escaped.

Churchill was elected Conservative M.P. for Oldham in 1900 (having unsuccessfully contested the seat in 1899), and immediately made his mark in a house which expected great things from his father's son. He excelled in the set speech elaborately prepared on the classic models, but was not at first a ready speaker. Lord Balfour once said of him that he carried "heavy but not very mobile guns," and it was only later that he became a master in the cut and thrust of debate. He had a filial reverence for the political memory of his father and his *Life of Lord Randolph Churchill* (1906) is one of the most interesting political biographies in the language.

In 1904, when Joseph Chamberlain's tariff reform campaign seemed likely to turn the Conservatives into a party of protection, Churchill crossed the floor of the house and joined the Liberals. In the general election of 1906 he was returned for North-West Manchester and became undersecretary for the colonies in the Campbell-Bannerman government, 1905–08.

He soon won renown by his skill and authority in defending the policy of conciliation and self-government for South Africa. With his admission to the cabinet in 1908 as president of the board of trade his standing increased. His platform oratory had a vivacity, a boldness and an epigrammatic quality that stirred popular gatherings. Into the conflict that followed the rejection of the Lloyd George budget by the house of lords he threw himself with characteristic impetuosity. As home secretary (1909–11) he was responsible for carrying the Trade Boards act, directed against sweated industries, but was rather less successful in coping with the industrial disturbances of 1911.

Transferred to the admiralty later in the year, Churchill was explicitly enjoined by Herbert Asquith to put the navy into a state of "instant and constant readiness" in case of a German attack. He was not at first successful in creating the naval war staff which was generally thought desirable, but he did introduce many valuable reforms, both administrative and technical. When war came in 1914, it found the navy both efficient and prepared.

Churchill, who had been one of the most convinced supporters of the declaration of war on Germany, was the most strenuous advocate of aggressive land and sea campaigns. He carried out the Dardanelles enterprise of 1915 in face of the disapproval of the first sea lord, Sir John Fisher. Churchill left the admiralty for the duchy of Lancaster when the expedition proved a failure and Fisher resigned. When the Liberal government collapsed in the ensuing political crisis, Churchill abandoned politics for soldiering; he went on active service in France, where he commanded the 6th Royal Scots Fusiliers.

David Lloyd George, returning to power in 1917, recalled Churchill to office, first as minister of munitions and then as combined war and air minister (1918–21). But apart from his conspicuous part in the Irish settlement, Churchill began to be less in agreement with the premier. Lloyd George disapproved of the costly British intervention in the U.S.S.R. that Churchill promoted. To be given the colonial office instead of the exchequer in 1921 was a severe disappointment. In the collapse of the coalition in 1922 Churchill lost even his seat in parliament, after representing Dundee since 1908.

Two years of retirement followed, filled, with characteristic versatility, by painting and writing. In 1924 he was returned to parliament from Epping as a Constitutionalist. Stanley Baldwin appointed him chancellor of the exchequer and in 1925 he rejoined the Conservative party. He presided over the return to the gold standard (1925), with the accompanying "revenue duties" and the derating scheme of 1928, measures not unproductive of controversy either then or since. In the same period he completed his work *The World Crisis* (1923–29).

With the fall of the Conservative government in 1929 a breach developed between Churchill and Baldwin. It began over India, where Churchill was opposed to any abdication of British imperial power—an opposition which led to his exclusion from the National government of 1931. In the nine years that followed Churchill led the life of a private member of parliament, writing the life of his great ancestor the 1st duke of Marlborough and only intervening in public debate on issues that profoundly moved him. As the Ramsay MacDonald, Baldwin and Neville Chamberlain governments pursued their policies of conciliation and surrender to the threats of Adolf Hitler, Churchill's protests became ever louder and more insistent. From 1936 to 1938 he particularly warned against German rearmament and British unpreparedness. In the commons' debate on the Munich agreement he asserted that it was "a defeat without a war" and "only the beginning of the reckoning." In March 1939 he pressed for an all-party government and in May urged an immediate agreement with the U.S.S.R.; to both proposals Chamberlain was cool.

However, on the British declaration of war on Sept. 3, 1939, Chamberlain in response to a wide popular demand appointed Churchill to his old post at the admiralty. His energy was soon felt not only within the department but also in the work of the cabinet. But the Norwegian defeats of April and May 1940 shook public confidence in Chamberlain's leadership, and on May 10, when the German armies entered the Low Countries, Chamberlain resigned to make way for the one leader, Churchill, who could form a national coalition government. Three days later Churchill made his celebrated speech to the commons in which he said, "I have nothing to offer but blood, toil, tears and sweat." Parliament gave him a unanimous vote of confidence.

This confidence was sustained throughout the four and one-half years that followed, stimulated by Churchill's rocklike trust in Allied victory and his frank, memorable and dynamic oratory. The story of his war premiership is the history of the British war effort because more nearly than any other war leader in British history he both directed and personified it, combining with the premiership the ministry of defense and taking a tirelessly energetic personal interest in every detail of administration. At moments of crisis he crystallized the national will, as in his memorable declaration on the occasion of Dunkirk, "We shall go on to the end, whatever the cost may be," or in the decision to reinforce the middle east in the dangerous autumn of 1940, or in the pledge to the U.S.S.R. on June 22, 1941, "Any man or state who marches with Hitler is our foe."

To nothing did Churchill more earnestly devote himself than to the construction and maintenance of what he called the "Grand Alliance." From the outset he looked forward to the day when, "The New World, with all its power and might," would step "forth to the rescue and the liberation of the Old." Churchill's conduct of relations with the United States and its wartime president, Franklin D. Roosevelt, was a remarkable blend of tact and candour, of a determination, as he said, not to "liquidate" the British empire and yet of a willingness to pool sovereignty and resources in a common cause.

With the U.S.S.R. he strove unceasingly to break down the barriers of misunderstanding—witness his dispatch to Moscow of Lord Beaverbrook in Sept. 1941, and of Anthony Eden in November and his own visit to Joseph Stalin in Aug. 1942. In Dec. 1941 he went to Washington, D.C., for the first of a series of conferences with Roosevelt. The year 1942 saw British reverses in Burma, Malaya and Hong Kong; but as U.S. strength gathered and the Russians fell back on Stalingrad, there was pressure on Churchill to agree to the early opening of a second front in Europe. Churchill thought this premature and successfully opposed it.

Even for 1944 he personally advocated an invasion of central Europe from the Mediterranean to coincide with the Normandy landings. However, Churchill's loyalty to an agreed strategy was as complete as his advocacy of his own views was powerful. Never in history had allied forces co-operated so harmoniously as in the strategy hammered out at the six planning conferences with Roosevelt and other leaders which Churchill attended in 1943.

The successes of 1944 brought new problems. At home and abroad Churchill was attacked for supporting allegedly reactionary regimes in Belgium, Italy and Greece. Meanwhile, his conversations in Moscow in October revealed the entering wedge of disagreements with the U.S.S.R. about eastern Europe.

The next year brought victory and great popular acclaim for Churchill. But the general election of June showed that this acclaim did not extend to Churchill, the Conservative party leader. Churchill bore the brunt of the election campaign himself, broadcasting and touring the country. But, although he retained his own seat, his party was severely defeated, and he began a long vigil as leader of the opposition.

During the first Labour government after World War II (1945–50) Churchill, still boundlessly energetic in his seventies, did not confine himself to parliamentary activities, master of debate though he still showed himself to be. He also embarked on a full-scale history of World War II (6 vol., 1948–53). His concern for British security and world peace did not flag. On March 5, 1946, in a speech at Fulton, Mo., he sharply criticized growing Soviet imperialism and advocated a "fraternal association" of the English-speaking peoples. On Sept. 19, 1946, at Zürich, Switz., he urged a closer unity in Europe, following it up with personal support for the Council of Europe, the first assembly of which he attended at Strasbourg, Fr., in 1949.

In the 1950 general election Churchill again led the Conservative party, and the Labour majority was reduced to seven. After his party won the election of Oct. 1951, Churchill again became prime minister. Here his single-minded devotion was to the cause of world peace, and his efforts were continuously bent on the realization of "talks at the summit" with Soviet leaders. However, age obliged his resignation on April 5, 1955, with these hopes unrealized although, by one of history's ironies, his chosen successor, Sir Anthony Eden, was able a few weeks later to announce to a British electorate Soviet and U.S. agreement to a four-power conference at Geneva, Switz.

Winston Churchill was named a knight of the Order of the Garter by Queen Elizabeth II on April 24, 1953. (H. G. N.)

CHURCHILL (Missinnippi or English), the name of a river of the province of Saskatchewan and province of Manitoba, Canada. It rises in La Loche (or Methy) lake, a small lake in 56° 30′ N. and 109° 30′ W., at an altitude of 1,577 ft. above the sea, and flows east-northeast to Hudson's bay, passing through a number of lake expansions. Its principal tributaries are the Beaver (305 mi. long), Sandy and Reindeer rivers. Between Frog and Methy portages (480 mi.) it formed part of the old *voyageur* route to the Peace, Athabasca and Mackenzie. It is still navigated by canoes, but has many rapids.

The Churchill is 1,000 mi. long. Churchill, at its mouth, is the best harbour in the southern portion of Hudson's bay. The river has enormous undeveloped water powers.

CHURCHING OF WOMEN, the Christian ceremony of thanksgiving on the part of mothers shortly after the birth of their children. Unlike the Mosaic ceremony (Lev. xii), it is not a rite of purification from uncleanness. In ancient times the ceremony was usual but not obligatory in England. In the Greek and Roman Catholic Churches today it is encouraged. No ancient form of service exists, and that which figures in the English Prayer Book of today dates only from the middle ages. In the Prayer Book of 1549 the rite was called the Purification of Women; but this was altered in 1552 to the modern form, Thanksgiving of Women after Childbirth. (*See* Hooker, *Eccl. Pol.,* V, lxxiv.) Custom differs, but the usual date of churching was the 40th day after confinement, in accordance with the biblical date of the presentment of the Virgin Mary and the Child Jesus at the Temple. It was formerly regarded as unlucky for a woman to leave her house to go out at all after confinement till she went to be churched. It was not unusual for the churching service to be said in private houses. In some parishes there was a special pew known as the "churching seat." The words in the rubric requiring the woman to come "decently [*i.e.,* suitably] apparelled" refer probably to the custom of wearing a veil upon the head.

In the *Roman Ritual* (tit. vii, c. 3) the rite is called "The Blessing of a Woman after Childbirth." The mother is to kneel at the church door (more commonly at the altar rail), holding a lighted candle. The priest, vested in surplice and white stole (symbolizing gladness), sprinkles her with holy water and recites Psalm 23 (R.V. 24). Then, offering her the end of the stole that hangs to his left, he leads her into the church, saying in Latin: "Enter into the temple of God, adore the Son of Blessed Mary the Virgin, who has granted thee [the grace of] the birth of a child." The mother "kneels before the altar and prays, thanking God for the gifts given her"; and the priest utters a prayer for her temporal and eternal happiness and that of her child. Finally, he invokes upon her the abiding "peace and blessing" of the Trinity.

CHURCH OF THE BRETHREN: *see* GERMAN BAPTIST BRETHREN.

CHURCH OF THE NAZARENE: *see* NAZARENE, CHURCH OF THE.

CHURCH RATE, the name of a tax formerly levied in each parish in England and Ireland for the benefit of the parish church. Out of this rate were defrayed the expenses of carrying on divine service, repairing the fabric of the church and paying the salaries of the officials connected with it. The church rate was made by the churchwardens, together with the parishioners duly assembled after proper notice in the vestry or the church, and was a personal charge imposed on the occupier of land or of a house in the parish. Though it was compulsory, much difficulty was found in effectually applying the compulsion. This was especially so in the case of Nonconformists, who had conscientious objections to supporting the Established Church; and in Ireland, where the population was preponderatingly Roman Catholic, the grievance was specially felt and resented. The agitation against church rates led in 1868 to the passing of the Compulsory Church Rate Abolition act. By this act church rates were made no longer compulsory on the person rated but were made merely voluntary, and those not willing to pay them were excluded from inquiring into, objecting to or voting in respect of their expenditure.

CHURCH STRETTON, urban district, Shropshire, Eng., situated on a low watershed in a narrow longitudinal valley between the Longmynd and the Caradoc ranges. Pop. (1951) 2,580. Area 9.5 sq.mi. It takes its name ("Street Town") from the Roman road joining Viroconium and Caerleon, on which it lies. The Western Region railway from Shrewsbury to Ludlow and the main road parallel to it make use of this gap, where the railway reaches a height of 600 ft. As a market town Church Stretton serves the hilly country between Wenlock Edge and Longmynd, but the area is limited by hill barriers and much trade drifts to Shrewsbury on the north and Craven Arms and Ludlow on the south. The neighbourhood has numerous prehistoric camps and barrows, while a remarkable ridgeway or "portway" runs along the summit of the Longmynd.

CHURCHWARDEN, in England, the guardian or keeper of a church and representative of the body of the parish. The office dates from the 14th century, when the responsibility of providing for the repairs of the nave and of furnishing the utensils for divine service was imposed on the parishioners. Resident lay householders of a parish are those primarily eligible as churchwardens, but nonresident householders who are habitually occupiers are also eligible, while there are a few classes of persons who are either ineligible or exempted. The appointment of churchwardens is regulated by the 89th canon, which requires that the churchwardens shall be chosen by the joint consent of the ministers and parishioners, if it may be; but if they cannot agree upon such a choice, then the minister is to choose one and the parishioners another. If, however, there is any special custom of the place, the custom prevails, and the most common custom is for the minister to appoint one and the parishioners another. This was established by English statute, in the case of new parishes, by the Church Building and New Parishes acts, 1818–84. There are other special customs recognized in various localities; *e.g.,* in some of the larger parishes in the north of England a churchwarden is chosen for each township of the parish; in the old ecclesiastical parishes of London both churchwardens are chosen by the parishioners; in some cases they are appointed by the select vestry or by the lord of the manor, and in a few exceptional cases are chosen by the outgoing churchwardens. Each churchwarden after election subscribes before the ordinary a declaration that he will execute his office faithfully.

The duties of churchwardens comprise the provision of necessaries for divine service; the keeping of order during the divine service and the giving of offenders into custody; the assignment of seats to parishioners; and the presentment of offenses against ecclesiastical law. By the Parochial Church Councils (Powers) measure, 1921, no. 1, made under the Church of England Assembly (Powers) act, 1919, c. 76, all powers, duties and liabilities of the churchwardens relating to (1) the financial affairs of the church, (2) the maintenance and insurance of the fabric, goods and ornaments and (3) the maintenance of the churchyard (even when closed) were transferred to the parochial church councils. The property in the movable goods and ornaments remained in the churchwardens.

In the Protestant Episcopal Church in the United States, churchwardens discharge much the same duties as those performed by the English officials; their duties, however, are regulated by canons of the diocese, not by canons general. In the United States, too, the usual practice is for the parishes to elect both the churchwardens.

BIBLIOGRAPHY.—J. H. Blunt, *Book of Church Law,* 7th ed. (1894); C. G. Prideaux, *Churchwarden's Guide,* 16th ed. (1895); J. Steer, *Parish Law,* 6th ed. (1899).

CHURCHYARD, THOMAS (*c.* 1520–1604), English author, was born at Shrewsbury. He served in the household of Henry Howard, earl of Surrey, and in 1541 became a soldier of fortune. During the next 30 years he fought in almost every campaign in Ireland, Scotland and the Low Countries, now in the service of the emperor Charles V, now in the English service, at last under the prince of Orange. His last campaign was the defense of Zutphen in 1572.

Churchyard was employed to devise a pageant for the queen's reception at Bristol in 1574 and again at Norwich in 1578. He had published in 1575 *The firste parte of Churchyarde's Chippes,* the modest title which he gives to his works. No second part appeared, but there was a much enlarged edition in 1578. A passage in *Churchyarde's Choise* (1579) gave offense to Elizabeth I, and the author fled to Scotland, where he remained for three years. He was not restored to favour until about 1584, and in 1593 he received a small pension from the queen. The affectionate esteem with which he was regarded by the younger Elizabethan writers is expressed by Thomas Nashe, who says (*Foure Letters Confuted*) that Churchyard's aged muse might well be "grandmother to our grandiloquentest poets at this present."

His writings, with the exception of his contributions to the *Mirror for Magistrates,* are chiefly autobiographical in character or deal with the wars in which he had a share. They are very rare, and have never been completely reprinted. Churchyard lived right through Elizabeth's reign and was buried in St. Margaret's church, Westminster, on April 4, 1604.

BIBLIOGRAPHY.—The extant works of Churchyard, exclusive of commendatory and occasional verses, include: *A lamentable and pitifull Description of the wofull warres in Flanders* (1578); *A gen-*

eral rehearsall of warres, called Churchyarde's Choise (1579), really a completion of the *Chippes*, and containing, like it, a number of detached pieces; *A light Bondel of livelie Discourses, called Churchyarde's Charge* (1580); *The Worthines of Wales* (1587), a valuable antiquarian work in prose and verse, anticipating Michael Drayton; *Churchyard's Challenge* (1593); *A Musicall Consort of Heavenly harmonie . . . called Churchyard's Charitie* (1595); *A True Discourse Historicall, of the succeeding Governors in the Netherlands* (1602).

The chief authority for Churchyard's biography is his own "Tragicall Discourse of the unhappy man's life" (*Churchyarde's Chippes*). George Chalmers published (1817) a selection from his works relating to Scotland, for which he wrote a useful life. *See* also an edition of the *Chippes* (ed. J. P. Collier, 1870), of the *Worthines of Wales* (Spenser Soc., 1876) and a notice of Churchyard by H. W. Adnitt (*Transactions* of the Shropshire Archaeological and Nat. Hist. Soc., reprinted separately 1884).

CHURCHYARD, a piece of consecrated ground attached to a parochial church, and used as a burial place. It is distinguished from a cemetery (*q.v.*), which is also a place of burial, but is separate and apart from any parochial church. (*See* BURIAL.)

CHURL. In Old English law the word *ceorl* denoted the ordinary free man, who formed the basis of Anglo-Saxon society. In the course of time he lost much of his original independence, and after the Norman Conquest became included within the great class of villeins (*see* VILLEINAGE) who were regarded in law as personally unfree. It is largely owing to this depression that the word "churl" came to bear a derogatory sense. Nevertheless, even in Anglo-Norman law the *ceorl* had not wholly sunk into a servile position; he retained the wergild of a free man until the whole system of wergilds became obsolete, and he was long subject to the duty of attending public courts such as that of the Hundred (*q.v.*). His depression was due essentially to economic causes; men of his class suffered heavily in the wars of the 10th and 11th centuries and the lawyers of a later time who regarded their descendants as legally dependent upon their lords were only recognizing accomplished facts.

CHURN: *see* DAIRY MACHINERY AND EQUIPMENT.

CHURRIGUERESQUE, in architecture, the late, luxuriant, Spanish baroque style, so called from its most famous architect, Don José Churriguera (d. 1725). *See* RENAISSANCE ARCHITECTURE.

CHURUBUSCO, a village of Mexico on the river of the same name, about six miles south of the capital. It contains a massive stone convent. It was here that Major General Winfield Scott in his brilliant southern campaign of the war between Mexico and the United States (1846–48) fought the battle of that name as an aftermath of the action at Contreras the same day (August 20, 1847). Brigadier General Worth, who had been acting as rear guard at San Agustín, moved forward toward San Antonio to find, after trying a turning movement, that, on account of the victory at Contreras, the strong fortifications before him had been evacuated by General Santa Anna's Mexicans. Worth pressed on to meet stout and unexpected resistance at the bastioned bridgehead of Churubusco. Scott, taking charge of Pillow's and Twiggs' troops, a part of whom he sent to reinforce Worth, decided upon a turning movement. Sending Pierce and Shields over a road around Santa Anna's right flank, he ordered them to strike the Mexican general in rear. Though the untrained militia making the detour did not at first acquit themselves well, Worth stubbornly pressed in front and, after severe charging in which his troops succeeded in turning Santa Anna's left flank, was able to take the bridgehead and the well fortified convent beyond. The pursuit continued for over two miles. In addition to the guns and ammunition taken, the Mexican losses probably mounted to 10,000. The Americans lost about 950.

BIBLIOGRAPHY.—Justin H. Smith, The *War with Mexico*, Vol. I. (1919); George B. McClellan, *The Mexican War Diary* (1917); C. M. Wilcox, *History of the Mexican War* (1892); W. A. Ganoe, *The History of the United States Army* (1924); Original Correspondence and Reports in Old Files Section, Adjutant General's Office, Washington, D.C. (W. A. G.)

CHUSAN, an island archipelago off the Chinese coast. It represents the submerged terminus of the Tayu-ling, the dominating range of Chekiang, which is linked on south-westwards with the high ranges along the Fukien-Kiangsi border. The outermost islands of the archipelago lie across the entrance to Hangchow bay. Their shores are becoming choked with silt from the Yangtze estuary, which opens out just to the north of them, in perhaps the same way as at an earlier period the hills along the E. side of the Tai-hu became linked together by stretches of alluvium. If this interpretation is correct, the shallow Hangchow bay may in time become a second Tai-hu. By reason of its character as a rocky island and of its proximity to the Yangtze estuary, Chusan island, the largest of the archipelago, was during the Ming Dynasty (1368–1644) an entrepôt for trade with Japan. Until the modern development of Japan, Japanese relations with China were naturally most intimate in the neighbourhood of the Yangtze estuary. The Japanese use of Chusan at that time is somewhat comparable to the British use of Hongkong at a later period.

CHUTE, a channel or trough, artificial or natural, down which objects, such as timber, coal or grain may slide, identical in meaning and pronunciation with "shoot." A channel cut in a dam on a river for the passage of floating timber, and in Louisiana and on the Mississippi a channel at the side of a river or narrow way between an island and the shore. The "water-chute," a steep wooden slope terminating in a shallow lake down which run flat-bottomed boats, is a Canadian pastime, which has been popular in London and elsewhere.

CHUTNEY, a sweet pickle or relish prepared from sweet fruits such as mangoes, raisins, etc., with acid flavouring from tamarinds, lemons, limes and sour herbs, and with a hot seasoning of chillies, cayenne pepper and spices. The word is an anglicized form of the Hindustani *chatni*.

CHUVASH, an A.S.S.R. in the Russian Soviet Federated Socialist Republic, created as an autonomous area by decree in June 1920 and declared an autonomous soviet socialist republic in April 1925. Area 6,911 sq.mi. Its boundaries are: west, Gorki (formerly Nizhegorod); south, Ulianovsk; east, Tatar A.S.S.R.; north, Marii A.S.S.R. East of the Gorki province, from the junction of the Sura river with the Volga river, begins the forest area in which many Finno-Turkish tribes maintained their linguistic and racial individuality against the advancing waves of Slav colonization. Of these tribes the Chuvash occupy the area between the right bank of the Sura and Volga and are thus nearest to Moscow. The population (1939) 1,077,614 (urban, 131,533; rural, 946,081) includes Chuvash 80%, Great Russians 18%, Tatars and Marii (Cheremiss). The urban population is 85% Great Russians. In the south and west the republic is forested, but toward the north and east the forest remains only in patches. Deforestation became a serious problem, for much of the timber cut was not replaced. From ancient times lumbering, sawmilling and the making of wooden articles (*e.g.*, furniture, oak rivets, barrels, wagons, shovels) were the chief industries of the Chuvash. In modern times light manufacturing and machine production made industry equal in importance to agriculture. The chief industrial items exported are wood (mainly oak) articles and construction materials.

Agriculture was not well developed because of poor soil and climatic conditions and the primitive methods adopted. The soils are podsolized or degraded soils and liched black soils (*see* RUSSIA: *Soils and Their Influence*). The climate is severe; snow covers the ground from October to April, and the rivers are frozen. There are fierce storms in winter and spring, and in June and July thunderstorms are frequent. The prevailing winds are southwesterly, and in the hot summer they bring sand from the steppe, so that the crops are covered with dust. Oats and rye, once the main crops, were varied by the introduction of buckwheat, potatoes, fodder crops, hemp, flax and tobacco. Peas and lentils are also grown. The chief agricultural exports are oats, by waterway to Leningrad and by rail to Moscow, and eggs and poultry. Small quantities of honey, apples and hops are also exported. Though Chuvash horses, cattle, sheep and pigs are underfed and undersized, cattle, meat, wool and hides are exported. The standard of living is low and the imports are mainly salt, kerosene and iron goods, but in spite of the few cultural needs of the people there are many bazaar centres and several annual fairs.

Cheboksary, on the Volga river, the administrative centre, is a river port with an electric plant, a radio station and a Chuvash regional museum, and its fair is the most important. It also has sawmills, printing works, dried fruit, starch and syrup industries, and it produces flour, alcohol and leather goods. The Yadrinsk oil-pressing factory was established at Cheboksary. Hemp, fulling and metal industries of a *koustar* (peasant) and semi-*koustar* type were set up, as were several steam flour mills. The Volga and Sura rivers provide navigable waterways in the summer. The Kazan to Kanash railway, linking through Arzamas in the Gorki province, is the shortest route to Moscow. Kanash (formerly Shikhran) is an important timber and grain centre. It is also the centre of the railroad system of Chuvash, one of the best developed in the U.S.S.R., with four lines radiating from it. One of the branches leads to Cheboksary and was built just before World War II. Another goes southwest through Alatyr, also a grain and timber centre, with an elevator. The Alatyr district is noted for its *koustar* furniture industry, and Alatyr is the largest city in the republic. It has locomotive and car factories, metalworking and sawmilling industries, and clothes and knitted goods are manufactured there. Located at smaller cities in Chuvash are a shipbuilding yard and a chemical plant which produces phosphate meal and other chemicals from the phosphorite and oil shale deposits which are fairly extensive in the area.

In order to combat illiteracy, which was still prevalent after World War I, the soviet government inaugurated a policy of instruction in the vernacular, which belongs to the Tatar or Turkish group but has many Finno-Ugrian idioms. A Chuvash daily paper was issued and in Cheboksary a theatre was established. The Chuvash are of Finno-Tatar origin, rounded-headed, flat-featured and light-eyed; they are thought by some to be the descendants of the ancient Bolgars. Their preferences tend toward agriculture rather than toward industrial occupations.

CHVALA, EMANUEL (1851–1924), Czechoslovak composer and critic, was born in Prague on Jan. 1, 1851. He studied both piano and theory of composition. In 1878 Josef Sladka suggested he attempt musical criticism, and it was in this field that he made his greatest contribution to Czechoslovak art. He wrote articles for Sladka's publication *Lumir,* and he also contributed to *Dalibor, Politik* and other journals. His essays in German, *A Quarter Century of Bohemian Music: 1862–87,* helped to introduce the music of his land to a wider audience. His compositions include songs and chamber and piano music. A concert overture; a *sinfonietta, Impressions of Spring;* and *Wake-Night,* a tone picture, were considered the most successful of his works. Simultaneously with his musical career, Chvala was director in chief of Czechoslovakia's state railways. He died in Prague on Oct. 28, 1924.

CHWANBEN: *see* SIKANG.

CIALDINI, ENRICO (1811–1892), Italian soldier, politician and diplomatist, was born in Castelvetro, Modena. In 1831 he took part in the insurrection at Modena, fleeing afterward to Paris, whence he proceeded to Spain to fight against the Carlists. Returning to Italy in 1848, he commanded a regiment at the battle of Novara. In 1859 he organized the alpine brigade, fought at Palestro at the head of the 4th division, and in the following year invaded the marches, won the battle of Castelfidardo, took Ancona and subsequently directed the siege of Gaeta. In 1861 his intervention envenomed the Cavour-Garibaldi dispute. Placed in command of the troops sent to oppose the Garibaldian expedition of 1862, he defeated Garibaldi at Aspromonte. Between 1862 and 1866 he held the position of lieutenant royal at Naples, and in 1864 was created senator. On the outbreak of the war of 1866 he resumed command of an army corps, but dissensions between him and La Marmora contributed to the defeat of Custozza. In 1867 he attempted unsuccessfully to form a cabinet sufficiently strong to prevent the threatened Garibaldian incursion into the papal states, and two years later failed in a similar attempt, through disagreement with Lanza concerning the army estimates. On Aug. 3, 1870, he pleaded in favour of Italian intervention in aid of France, a circumstance which enhanced his influence when in July 1876 he replaced Nigra as ambassador to the French republic. This position he held until 1882, when he resigned because of the publication by Mancini of a dispatch in which he had complained of arrogant treatment by Waddington. He died at Leghorn on Sept. 8, 1892.

BIBLIOGRAPHY.—G. Marcotti, *Il Generale Enrico Cialdini* (Florence, 1892); N. Nisco, *Il Generale Cialdini e i suoi tempi* (Naples, 1893); Prince Adam Wiszniewski, *Le Général Cialdini,* etc. (1913).

CIAMICIAN, GIACOMO LUIGI (1857–1922), Italian chemist, was born at Trieste on Aug. 22, 1857; his father was of Armenian origin. He was educated at Trieste and Vienna but took his doctorate in 1880 at the University of Giessen because he lacked the classic requirements demanded by all the other universities. He became assistant to Stanislao Cannizzaro (*q.v.*) and later reader in the Institute of General Chemistry of the University of Rome. In 1887 he was appointed professor of general chemistry in the University of Padua. In 1889 he accepted the chair of chemistry at the University of Bologna and retained this post until his death on Jan. 2, 1922. From 1910 to 1922 he was a member of the Italian senate, concerning himself mainly with education and the chemical industry.

Ciamician's most important researches were in organic chemistry. He stressed its application to biological chemistry rather than the discovery of new compounds. An investigation on the compounds in animal tar led him early in his career to the important researches on pyrrole. A monograph, *Il Pirralo e i suoi derivati* (1888), gained the royal prize of the Accademia dei Lincei. Ciamician was also a pioneer in the chemistry of vegetable products. At first he worked on organic compounds of vegetable origin and later became interested in the chemistry of the substances in the living plant and their biological significance. The essential oil of celery was the subject of an important early investigation; later he inoculated plants and seeds with alkaloids and with their constituents. His researches on the chemical action of light, many of them carried out in conjunction with Paul Silber of Rome, are noteworthy. The rear of the chemistry building was filled with shelves where hundreds of bottles and sealed tubes were exposed to the sun's rays. In addition there are a number of investigations by Ciamician in physical chemistry. Some of his earliest work was on the spectra of homologous elements; later researches were on theory of electrolytic dissociation, on solvates, on the nature of chemical affinity and on the valency of atoms. He published about 170 papers and delivered invited lectures before the German and French chemical societies and the International Congress of Applied Chemistry at New York city in 1912. A street in Trieste was named for him.

For biographical details *see* W. McPherson, *Journal of the American Chemical Society,* vol. 44, Proceedings 101 (1922); R. Nasini, *Journal of the Chemical Society,* Transactions 996 (London, 1926); R. Fabré, *Bull. soc. chim. France* [4] vol. 41, p. 1562 (1927); C. Harries, *Berichte d. deutschen chemischen Gesellschaft,* vol. 55 A, p. 19 (1922).

CIANO, GALEAZZO (1903–1944), Italian statesman, was the son of Count Costanzo Ciano (1876–1939), naval hero of World War I and a long-time legislative aide of Mussolini. The son entered diplomatic service in a South American embassy and was later consul general at Shanghai. In 1930 he married Mussolini's daughter Edda. In 1934 he became minister of propaganda, and during the conquest of Abyssinia he led a squadron of bombing planes. He was a member of the grand fascist council and in 1936 became minister of foreign affairs, a post he held until Jan. 1943, when Mussolini took over the ministry of foreign affairs himself, at the same time appointing Ciano ambassador to the Vatican. Ciano retained this position only six months, resigning in July 1943. On Jan. 11, 1944, Ciano and four other former members of the grand fascist council, all of whom had previously been convicted by a special fascist tribunal of high treason for plotting the overthrow of Mussolini, were executed in Verona.

CIBBER (or CIBERT), **CAIUS GABRIEL** (1630–1700), Danish sculptor, was born at Flensburg. He was the son of the king's cabinetmaker and was sent to Rome at the royal charge while yet a youth. He went to England during the Protectorate, or during the first years of the Restoration. Besides the famous statues of "Melancholy" and "Raving Madness" ("great Cibber's brazen brainless brothers"), now in the Guildhall, London, Cibber produced the bas-reliefs round the Monument on Fish street hill. The several kings of England and the Sir Thomas Gresham, executed by him for the Royal Exchange, were destroyed with the building itself in 1838. Cibber was long employed by the fourth earl of Devonshire, and many fine specimens of his work are to be seen at Chatsworth. Under that nobleman he took up arms in 1688 for William of Orange, and was appointed, in return, carver to the king's closet. He died rich, and, according to Horace Walpole, built the Danish church in London, where he lies buried beside his second wife, to whom he erected a monument. She was a Miss Colley, of Glaiston, granddaughter of Sir Anthony Colley, and the mother of Colley Cibber.

CIBBER, COLLEY (1671–1757), English actor and dramatist, was born in London on Nov. 6, 1671, the eldest son of Caius Gabriel Cibber, the sculptor. Sent in 1682 to the free school at Grantham, Lincolnshire, the boy distinguished himself by an aptitude for writing verse. He was removed from school in 1687 on the chance of election to Winchester college. His father, however, had not then presented that institution with his statue of William of Wykeham, and the son was rejected, although through his mother he claimed to be of "founder's kin." The boy went to London, and indulged his passion for the theatre. He was on his way to Chatsworth, the seat of William Cavendish, earl (afterwards duke) of Devonshire, for whom his father was then executing commissions, when the news of the landing of William of Orange was received; father and son met at Nottingham, and Colley Cibber was taken into Devonshire's company of volunteers. Afterwards he enrolled himself (1690) as an actor in Betterton's company at Drury Lane. On his more than meagre earnings, which rose to £1 per week, supplemented by an allowance of £20 a year from his father, he contrived to live with his wife and family—he had married in 1693—and to produce a play, *Love's Last Shift, or the Fool in Fashion* (1696). Of this comedy Congreve said that it had "a great many things that were like wit in it"; and Vanbrugh honoured it by writing his *Relapse* as a sequel. Cibber played the part of Sir Novelty Fashion, and his performance as Lord Foppington, the same character renamed, in Vanbrugh's piece established his reputation as an actor. In 1698 he was assailed with other dramatists, by Jeremy Collier in the *Short View.* In Nov., 1702, he produced, at Drury Lane, *She Wou'd and She Wou'd Not; or the Kind Impostor,* one of his best comedies; and in 1704, for himself and Mrs. Oldfield, *The Careless Husband,* which Horace Walpole classed, with Cibber's *Apology,* as "worthy of immortality." In 1706 Cibber left Drury Lane for the Haymarket, but when the two companies united two years later he rejoined his old theatre through the influence of his friend Colonel Brett, a shareholder. Brett made over his share to Wilks, Estcourt and Cibber. Complaints against the management of Christopher Rich led, in 1709, to the closing of the theatre by order of the crown, and William Collier obtained the patent. After a series of intrigues Collier was bought out by Wilks, Doggett and Cibber, under whose management Drury Lane became more prosperous than it ever had been. In 1715 a new patent was granted to Sir Richard Steele, and Barton Booth was also added to the management. In 1717 Cibber produced the *Nonjuror,* an adaptation from Molière's *Tartuffe;* the play, for which Nicholas Rowe wrote an abusive prologue, ran eighteen nights, and the author received from George I., to whom it was dedicated, a present of two hundred guineas. Tartuffe became an English Catholic priest who incited rebellion, and there is little doubt that the Whig principles expressed in the *Nonjuror* led to Cibber's appointment as poet laureate (1730). It also provoked the animosity of the Jacobite and Catholic factions, and was possibly one of the causes of Pope's hostility to Cibber. Numerous "keys" to the *Nonjuror* appeared in 1718. In 1726 Cibber pleaded the cause of the patentees against the estate of Sir Richard Steele before Sir Joseph Jekyll, master of the rolls, and won his case. In 1730 Mrs. Oldfield died, and her loss was followed in 1732 by that of Wilks; Cibber now sold his share in the theatre, appearing rarely on the stage thereafter. In 1740 he published *An Apology for the Life of Colley Cibber, Comedian . . . with an Historical View of the Stage during his Own Time,* which gives the best account there is of Cibber's contemporaries on the London stage.

In 1742 Cibber was substituted for Theobald as the hero of Pope's *Dunciad.* Cibber had introduced some gag into the *Rehearsal,* in which he played the part of Bayes, referring to the ill-starred farce of *Three Hours after Marriage* (1717). This play was nominally by Gay, but Pope and Arbuthnot were known to have had a hand in it. Cibber refused to discontinue the offensive passage, and Pope revenged himself in sarcastic allusions in his printed correspondence, in the *Epistle to Dr. Arbuthnot* and in the *Dunciad.* To these Cibber replied with *A Letter from Mr. Cibber to Mr. Pope, inquiring into the motives that might induce him in his satirical works to be so frequently fond of Mr. Cibber's name* (1742). Cibber scored with an "idle story of Pope's behaviour in a tavern" inserted in this letter, and gives an account of the original dispute over the *Rehearsal.* By the substitution of Cibber for Theobald as hero of the *Dunciad* much of the satire lost its point. Cibber's faults certainly did not include dullness. A new edition contained a prefatory discourse, probably the work of Warburton, entitled "Ricardus Aristarchus, or the Hero of the Poem," in which Cibber is made to look ridiculous from his own *Apology.* Cibber replied in 1744 with *Another Occasional Letter . . .* , and altogether he had the best of the argument. When he was 74 years old he made his last appearance on the stage as Pandulph in his own *Papal Tyranny in the Reign of King John* (Covent Garden, Feb. 15, 1745), a miserable paraphrase of Shakespeare's play. He died on Dec. 11, 1757.

Cibber's reputation has suffered unduly from the depreciation of Pope and Johnson. "I could not bear such nonsense" said Johnson of one of Cibber's odes, "and I would not let him read it to the end." Fielding attacked Cibber's style and language more than once in *Joseph Andrews,* and elsewhere. Nevertheless, Cibber possessed wit, unusual good sense and tact; and in the *Apology* he showed himself the most delicate and subtle critic of acting of his time. He was frequently accused of plagiarism, and did not scruple to make use of old plays, but he is said to have been ashamed of his Shakespearian adaptations, one of which, however, *Richard III.* (Drury Lane, 1700), kept its place as the acting version until 1821. Cibber is rebuked for his mutilation of Shakespeare by Fielding in the *Historical Register for 1736,* where he figures as Ground Ivy.

Charlotte, Colley Cibber's youngest daughter, married Richard Charke, a violinist, from whom she was soon separated. She began as an understudy to actresses in leading parts, but quarrelled with her manager, Charles Fleetwood, on whom she wrote a one-act skit, *The Art of Management* (1735). She also wrote two comedies and two novels of small merit, and an untrustworthy, but amusing, *Narrative of Life of . . . Charlotte Charke, . . . by herself* (1755), reprinted in Hunt and Clarke's *Autobiographies* (1822).

The *Apology* was edited in 1822 by E. Bellchambers and in 1889 by R. W. Lowe, who printed with it other valuable theatrical books and pamphlets. It is also included in Hunt and Clarke's *Autobiographies* (1826, etc.). Cibber's *Dramatic Works* were published in 1760, with an account of the life and writings of the author, and again in 1777. Besides the plays already mentioned, he wrote *Woman's Wit, or the Lady in Fashion* (1697), which was altered later (1707) into *The Schoolboy, or the Comical Rivals; Xerxes* (1699), a tragedy acted only once; *The Provoked Husband* (acted 1728), completed from Vanbrugh's unfinished *Journey to London; The Rival Queens, with the Humours of Alexander the Great* (acted 1710), a comical tragedy; *Damon and Phyllida* (acted 1729), a ballad opera; and adaptations from Beaumont and Fletcher, Dryden, Molière and Corneille. A bibliography of the numerous skits on Cibber is to be found in Lowe's *Bibliographical Account of English Theatrical Literature.*

CIBBER, SUSANNAH MARIA (1714–1766), wife of T. Cibber, was an actress of distinction. She was the daughter of a Covent Garden upholsterer, and sister of Dr. Arne (1710–78) the composer. Mrs. Cibber had a beautiful voice and began her career in opera. She was the original Galatea in Handel's *Acis and Galatea,* and the contralto arias in the *Messiah* are said to have been written for her. She played Zarah in Aaron Hill's version of Voltaire's *Zaïre* in 1736, and it was as a tragic actress, not as a singer, that her greatest triumphs were won. From Colley Cibber she learned a sing-song method of declamation. Her mannerisms, however, did not obscure her real genius, and she freed herself from them entirely when she began to act with Garrick, with whom she was associated at Drury Lane from 1753. She died on Jan. 30, 1766. She married Theophilus Cibber in 1734, but soon separated from him. Appreciations of Mrs. Cibber's fine acting are to be found in many contemporary writers, one of the most discriminating being in the *Rosciad* of Charles Churchill.

CIBBER, THEOPHILUS (1703–1758), Colley Cibber's son; also an actor and playwright, was born on Nov. 26, 1703. In 1734 he was acting-manager at the Haymarket, and later played at Drury Lane, Lincoln's Inn Fields and Covent Garden. His best impersonation was as Pistol, but he also distinguished himself in some of the fine-gentleman parts affected by his father. He was one of the ringleaders in the intrigues against John Highmore, who had bought a share in the patent of Drury Lane from Colley Cibber. Theophilus Cibber, with a number of other actors, seceded from Drury Lane, and in thus depreciating the value of the patent, for which his father had received a considerable sum, acted with doubtful honesty.

In 1753 appeared *An Account of the Lives of the Poets of Great Britain and Ireland,* with the name of "Mr. Cibber" on the title page. The five volumes of *Lives* are chiefly based on the earlier works of Gerard Langbaine and Giles Jacob and the ms. collections of Thomas Coxeter (1689–1747). The book is said to have been largely written by Robert Shiels, Dr. Johnson's amanuensis. Theophilus Cibber perished by shipwreck on his way to Dublin to play at the Theatre Royal.

CIBORIUM, in classical Latin a drinking-vessel (Gr. *κιβώριον,* the cup-shaped seed-vessel of the Egyptian water-lily, and hence a cup). In the early Christian church the ciborium was a canopy over the altar (*q.v.*), supported on columns, and from it hung the dove-shaped receptacle in which was reserved the consecrated Host. The name was early transferred to the receptacle, and in the Western church the canopy was known as a baldachin (Ital. *baldacchino,* from *Baldacco,* Bagdad, whence came the rich brocade used for canopies, etc.). At the present day in the Roman church the term "pyx" (*πύξις*, a boxwood vessel) is used for the receptacle in which the viaticum is carried to the sick or dying. Mediaeval pyxes and ciboria are often beautiful examples of the goldsmith's, enameller's and metal-worker's craft. They usually take the shape of a covered chalice or of a cylindrical box with cover surmounted by a cross. An exquisite ciborium, probably of English 13th century make, fetched £6,000 at Christie's in 1908: copper-gilt, ornamented with champlevé enamels, with Biblical subjects in medallions on the outside (coloured illustration in catalogue of Burlington Fine Arts Club Exhibition, 1897).

CIBRARIO, LUIGI, Count (1802–1870), Italian statesman and historian, was born in Usseglia. His verses to King Charles Albert, then prince of Carignano, on the birth of his son Victor Emmanuel, led to a long friendship. He entered the Sardinian civil service, and in 1824 was appointed lecturer on canon and civil law. He was sent to search the archives of Switzerland, France and Germany for charters relating to the history of Savoy. During the war of 1848, after the expulsion of the Austrians from Venice, Cibrario was sent to that city with Colli on an abortive mission to secure its union with Piedmont. After the battle of Novara (1849) and the abdication of Charles Albert he visited the ex-king at Oporto on behalf of the Senate. In May 1852 he became minister of finance in the reconstructed d'Azeglio cabinet, and later minister of education in that of Cavour. He strongly supported Cavour's Crimean policy (1855), and, as minister for foreign affairs during the war, he seconded Cavour in procuring the admission of Piedmont to the congress of Paris on an equal footing with the great powers. On retiring from the foreign office Cibrario was created count. After the war of 1866 by which Austria lost Venetia, Cibrario negotiated the restitution of state papers and art treasures removed by the Austrians from Lombardy and Venetia to Vienna. He died in Oct. 1870, near Salò, on the lake of Garda. His most important work was his *Economia politica del medio evo* (Turin, 1839), popular then, but now of little value. His *Schiavitù e servaggio* (Milan, 1868–69) gave an account of the development and abolition of slavery and serfdom.

His biography has been written by F. Odorici, *Il Conte L. Cibrario* (Florence, 1872).

CICADA (Cicadidae), insects of the homopterous division of the Hemiptera (*q.v.*), generally of large size with the femora of the forelegs spined below, two pairs of large membranous wings and prominent eyes. Cicadas are remarkable for the shrill noise emitted by the males, which has been variously compared to a knife-grinder, scissors-grinder or even a railway whistle, and may be heard in concert at a distance of a quarter of a mile or more. The sound-producing organs are a kind of drum on each side of the base of the abdomen. These drums vibrate by the action of powerful muscles and the sound can be modified by the so-called mirrors or sounding boards. Although no auditory organs are known in the females, the song of the males is regarded as a sexual call.

One of the best-known species is the periodical cicada (*Magicicada septendecim*) of eastern N. America, often known as the 17-year "locust" which appears in great numbers and often causes much concern. It has two races, a 13-year race in the southeastern United States which requires 13 years from egg to adult and a 17-year race in the northeastern United States which requires 17 years from egg to adult. There are 17 different broods of the 17-year race in different parts of the United States and 13 different broods of the 13-year race. Since there is some overlapping of the different broods, some confusion has arisen in the minds of some people in regard to the regularity of this insect. By means of a saw-like instrument the eggs are laid in the twigs of trees, and the nymphs, upon hatching, drop to the ground, where they bury themselves. They feed by sucking juices from the roots of forest and fruit trees and finally change into the so-called "pupae." In the latter stage the insect crawls from the ground, grasps a suitable support and emerges as a full-fledged cicada. In some cases these "pupae" construct curious earthen chimneys wherein they live before turning into adults. The life-histories of cicadas are all very similar. Other common North American species seem to require from one to five years to complete their life histories with a few adults emerging every year. Over 2,000 kinds are known and they are most abundant in the tropics. One species occurs in the southern counties of England, but is rare; 170 species are known in the United States. *See* J. G. Myers, *Insect Singers: a Natural History of the Cicadas* (1929). (Z. P. M.)

CICELY, *Myrrhis odorata* (family Umbelliferae), a perennial herb with a leafy hollow stem, 2 to 3 ft. high, much divided leaves, whitish beneath, a large sheathing base, and terminal umbels of small white flowers, the outer ones only of which are fertile. The fruit is dark brown, long (¾ to 1 in.), narrow and beaked. The plant is a native of central and southern Europe, and is found in parts of England and Scotland in pastures, usually near houses. It has aromatic and stimulant properties and was formerly used as a pot-herb.

CICERO, the name of two families of ancient Rome. It may perhaps be derived from *cicer* (pulse), in which case it would be analogous to such names as *Lentulus, Tubero, Piso.* Of one family, of the plebeian Claudian *gens,* only a single member, Gaius Claudius Cicero, tribune in 454 B.C., is known. The other family was a branch of the Tullii, settled from an ancient period at Arpinum. This family, four of whose members are noticed specially below, did not achieve more than municipal eminence until the time of M. Tullius Cicero, the great orator.

(1) Marcus Tullius Cicero (106–43 B.C.), Roman orator and politician, was born at Arpinum on Jan. 3, 106 B.C. His mother, Helvia, is said to have been of good family. His father was by some said to have been descended from Attius Tullius, the Volscian host of Coriolanus, while spiteful persons declared him to have been a fuller; in any case he was a Roman knight with property at Arpinum and a house in Rome. His health was weak, and he generally lived at Arpinum, where he devoted himself to literary pursuits. Cicero spent his boyhood partly in his native town and partly at Rome. The poet Archias, he says, first inspired him with the love of literature. He was much impressed by the teaching of Phaedrus, the Epicurean, at a period before he assumed the *toga virilis;* he studied dialectic under Diodotus the Stoic, and in 88 B.C. attended the lectures of Philo, the head of the Academic school, whose devoted pupil he became.

He studied rhetoric under Molo (Molon) of Rhodes, and law under the guidance of Q. Mucius Scaevola, the augur and jurisconsult. After the death of the augur, he transferred himself to the care of Q. Mucius Scaevola, the *pontifex maximus,* a still more famous jurisconsult, nephew of the augur. His literary education at this period consisted largely of verse-writing and making translations from Greek authors. We hear of an early poem named *Pontius Glaucus* the subject of which is uncertain, and of translations of Xenophon's *Oeconomica* and the *Phenomena* of Aratus. Considerable fragments of the latter work are still extant. To this period also belongs his *de Inventione rhetorica,* of which he afterwards spoke lightly (*de Orat.* i. 5), but which enjoyed a great vogue in the middle ages. Cicero also, according to Roman practice, received military training. At the age of 17 he served in the social war successively under Pompeius Strabo and Sulla (89 B.C.). In the war between Marius and Sulla his sympathies were with Sulla, but he did not take up arms (*Sext. Rosc.* 136, 142).

His forensic life begins in 81 B.C., at the age of 25. A speech delivered in this year, *pro Quinctio,* is still extant; it is concerned with a technical point of law and has little literary merit. In the following year he made his celebrated defence of Sextus Roscius on a charge of parricide. He subsequently defended a woman of Arretium, whose freedom was impugned on the ground that Sulla had confiscated the territory of that town. He then left Rome on account of his health, and travelled for two years in the East. He studied philosophy at Athens under various teachers, notably Antiochus of Ascalon, founder of the Old Academy, a combination of Stoicism, Platonism and Peripateticism. In Asia he attended the courses of Xenocles, Dionysius and Menippus, and in Rhodes those of Posidonius, the famous Stoic. In Rhodes also he studied rhetoric once more under Molo, to whom he ascribes a decisive influence upon the development of his literary style. He had previously affected the florid, or Asiatic, style of oratory then current in Rome. The chief faults of this were excess of ornament, antithesis, alliteration and assonance, monotony of rhythm, and the insertion of words purely for rhythmical effect. Molo, he says, rebuked his youthful extravagance and he came back "a changed man."

He returned to Rome in 77 B.C., and appears to have married at this time Terentia, a rich woman with a domineering temper, to whom many of his subsequent embarrassments were due.[1] He engaged at once in forensic and political life. He was quaestor in 75, and was sent to Lilybaeum to supervise the corn supply. His connection with Sicily let him to come forward in 70 B.C., when curule-aedile elect, to prosecute Gaius Verres, who had oppressed the island for three years. Cicero seldom prosecuted, but it was the custom at Rome for a rising politician to win his spurs by attacking a notable offender (*pro Caelio,* 73). In the following year he defended Marcus Fonteius on a charge of extortion in Gaul, using various arguments which might equally well have been advanced on behalf of Verres himself.

In 68 B.C. his letters begin, from which (and especially those to T. Pomponius Atticus, his "second self") we obtain wholly unique knowledge of Roman life and history. In 66 B.C. he was praetor, and was called upon to hear cases of extortion. In the same year he spoke on behalf of the proposal of Gaius Manilius to transfer the command against Mithridates from Lucullus to Pompey (*de Lege Manilia*), and delivered his clever but disingenuous defence of Aulus Cluentius (*pro Cluentio*). At this time he was a prospective candidate for the consulship, and was obliged by the hostility of the nobles towards "new men" to look for help wherever it was to be found. In 65 B.C. he even thought of defending Catiline on a charge of extortion, and delivered two speeches on behalf of Gaius Cornelius, tribune in 67 B.C., a leader of the democratic party. In 64 B.C. he lost his father and his son Marcus was born. The optimates finally decided to support him for the consulship in order to keep out Catiline, and he eagerly embraced the "good cause," his affection for which from this time onward never varied, though his actions were not always consistent.

The public career of Cicero henceforth is largely covered by the article on ROME: *Ancient History.* The year of his consulship (63) was one of amazing activity, both administrative and oratorical. Besides the three speeches against Publius Rullus and the four against Catiline, he delivered a number of others, among which that on behalf of Gaius Rabirius is especially notable. The charge was that Rabirius (*q.v.*) had killed Saturninus in 100 B.C., and by bringing it the democrats challenged the right of the senate to declare a man a public enemy. Cicero, therefore, was fully aware of the danger which would threaten himself from his execution of the Catilinarian conspirators. He trusted, however, to receive the support of the nobles. In this he was disappointed. They never forgot that he was a "new man," and were jealous of the great house upon the Palatine which he acquired at this time. Caesar had made every possible effort to conciliate Cicero,[1] but, when all overtures failed, allowed Publius Clodius to attack him. Cicero found himself deserted, and on the advice of Cato went into exile to avoid bloodshed. He left Rome at the end of March 58, and arrived on May 23 at Thessalonica where he remained in the deepest dejection until the end of November, when he went to Dyrrhachium (Durazzo) awaiting his recall. He left for Italy on Aug. 4, 57, and on arriving at Brundisium (Brindisi) found that he had been recalled by a law passed by the *comitia* on the very day of his departure. On his arrival at Rome he was received with enthusiasm by all classes, but did not find the nobles at all eager to give him compensation for the loss of his house and villas, which had been destroyed by Clodius. He was soon encouraged by the growing coolness between Pompey and Caesar to attack the acts of Caesar during his consulship, and after his successful defence of Publius Sestius on March 10 he proposed on April 5 that the senate should on May 15 discuss Caesar's distribution of the Campanian land. This brought about the conference of Luca (Lucca). Cicero was again deserted by his supporters and threatened with fresh exile. He was forced to publish a "recantation," probably the speech *de Provinciis Consularibus,* and in a private letter says frankly, "I know that I have been a regular ass." His conduct for the next three years teems with inconsistencies which we may deplore but cannot pass over. He was obliged to defend in 54 Publius Vatinius whom he had fiercely attacked during the trial of Sestius; also Aulus Gabinius, one of the consuls to whom his exile was due; and Rabirius Postumus, an agent of Gabinius. On the other hand, he made a violent speech in the senate in 55 against Lucius Piso, the colleague of Gabinius in 58. We know from his letters that he accepted financial aid from Caesar, but that he repaid the loan before the outbreak of the civil war. There is no doubt that he was easily deceived. He was always an optimist, and thought that he was bringing good influence to bear upon Caesar as afterwards upon Octavian. His actions, however, when Caesar's projects became manifest, sufficiently vindicated his honesty. During these unhappy years he took refuge in literature. The *de Oratore* was written in 55 B.C., the *de Republica* in 54, and the *de Legibus* at any rate begun in 52. The latter year is famous for the murder of Clodius by T. Annius Milo on the Appian Way (on Jan. 18), which brought about the appointment of Pompey as sole consul and the passing of special laws dealing with rioting and bribery. Cicero took an active part in the trials which followed both as a defender of Milo and his adherents and as a prosecutor of the opposite faction. At the close of the year, to his annoyance, he was sent to govern Cilicia under the provisions of Pompey's law (*see* POMPEY and ROME: *Ancient History*). His reluctance to leave Rome, already shown by his refusal to take a province, after his praetorship and consulship, was increased by the inclination of his daughter Tullia, then a widow, to marry again.

[1]According to Plutarch she urged her husband to take vigorous action against Catiline, who had compromised her half-sister Fabia, a vestal virgin; also to give evidence against Clodius, being jealous of his sister Clodia.

[1]Caesar, at one time, offered him a place on the coalition, which on his refusal became a triumvirate (*Att.* ii. 3. 3; *Prov. Cons.* 41), and afterwards a post on his commission for the division of the Campanian land, or a *legatio libera.*

During his absence she married the profligate spendthrift, P. Cornelius Dolabella.

The province of Cilicia was a large one. It included, in addition to Cilicia proper, Isauria, Lycaonia, Pisidia, Pamphylia and Cyprus, as well as a protectorate over the client kingdoms of Cappadocia and Galatia. There was also danger of a Parthian inroad. Cicero's legate was his brother Quintus Cicero (below), an experienced soldier who had gained great distinction under Caesar in Gaul. The fears of Parthian invasion were not realized, but Cicero, after suppressing a revolt in Cappadocia, undertook military operations against the hill-tribes of the Amanus and captured the town of Pindenissus after a siege of 46 days. A *supplicatio* in his honour was voted by the senate. The early months of 50 were occupied by the administration of justice, chiefly at Laodicea, and by various attempts to alleviate the distress in the province caused by the exactions of his predecessor, Appius Claudius. He had to withstand pressure from influential persons (*e.g.*, M. Brutus, who had business interests in his province), and refused to provide his friends with wild beasts for their games in Rome. Leaving his province on the earliest opportunity, he reached Brundisium on Nov. 24, and found civil war inevitable. He went to Rome on Jan. 4, but did not enter the city, since he aspired to a triumph for his successes. After the outbreak of war he was placed by Pompey in charge of the Campanian coast. After much irresolution he refused Caesar's invitations and resolved to join Pompey's forces in Greece. He was shocked by the ferocious language of his party, and himself gave offence by his bitter jests (Plut. *Cic.* 38). Through illness he was not present at the battle of Pharsalus, but afterwards was offered the command by Cato the Younger at Corcyra, and was threatened with death by the young Cn. Pompeius when he refused to accept it. Thinking it useless to continue the struggle, he sailed to Brundisium, where he remained until Aug. 12, 47, when, after receiving a kind letter from Caesar, he went to Rome. Under Caesar's dictatorship Cicero abstained from politics. His voice was raised on three occasions only: once in the senate in 46 to praise Caesar's clemency to M. Claudius Marcellus (*pro Marcello*), to plead in the same year before Caesar for Quintus Ligarius, and in 45 on behalf of Deiotarus, tetrarch of Galatia, also before Caesar. He suffered greatly from family troubles at this period. In 46, he divorced Terentia, and married his young and wealthy ward, Publilia. Then came the greatest grief of his life, the death of Tullia, his beloved daughter. He shortly afterwards divorced Publilia, who had been jealous of Tullia's influence and proved unsympathetic. To solace his troubles he devoted himself wholly to literature. To this period belong several famous rhetorical and philosophical works, the *Brutus, Orator, Partitiones Oratoriae, Paradoxa, Academica, de Finibus, Tusculan Disputations,* together with other works now lost, such as his *Laus Catonis, Consolatio* and *Hortensius.*

His repose was broken by Caesar's murder on March 15, 44, to which he was not a party. On March 17 he delivered a speech in the senate urging a general amnesty like that declared in Athens after the expulsion of the Thirty Tyrants. When it became apparent that the conspirators had removed only the despot and left the despotism, he again devoted himself to philosophy, and in an incredibly short space of time produced the *de Natura Deorum, de Divinatione, de Fato, Cato maior* (or *de Senectute*), *Laelius* (or *de Amicitia*), and began his treatise *de Officiis.* To this period also belongs his lost work *de Gloria.* He then projected a journey to Greece in order to see his son Marcus, then studying at Athens, of whose behaviour he had heard unfavourable reports. He reached Syracuse on Aug. 1, having during the voyage written from memory a translation of Aristotle's *Topica.* He was driven back by unfavourable winds to Leucopetra, and then, hearing better news, returned to Rome on Aug. 21. He was bitterly attacked by Marcus Antonius (Mark Antony) in the senate on Sept. 1 for not being present there, and on the next day replied in his First *Philippic.* He then left Rome and devoted himself to the completion of the *de Officiis,* and to the composition of his famous Second *Philippic,* which was never delivered, but was circulated, at first privately, after Antony had made his departure from Rome on the way to Cisalpine Gaul on Nov. 28.

Cicero returned to Rome on Dec. 9, and from that time forward led the republican party in the senate. His policy, stated briefly, was to make use of Octavian, whose name was all-powerful with the veterans, until new legions had been raised which would follow the republican commanders. Cicero pledged his credit for the loyalty of Octavian, who styled him "father" and affected to take his advice on all occasions. Cicero, an incurable optimist in politics, may have convinced himself of Octavian's sincerity. The breach, however, was bound to come, and the saying, maliciously attributed to Cicero, that Octavian was an "excellent youth who must be praised and—sent to another place," neatly expresses the popular view of the situation. Cicero was sharply criticized by M. Junius Brutus for truckling to Octavian while showing irreconcilable enmity to Antony and Lepidus (*ad Brut.* i. 16. 4, i. 15. 9); but Brutus was safe in his province, and it is difficult to see what other course was open to a politician in Rome. Whether Cicero was right or wrong, none can question his amazing energy. He delivered his long series of Philippics at Rome, and kept up a correspondence with the various provincial governors and commanders, all short-sighted and selfish, and several of them half-hearted, endeavouring to keep each man in his place and to elaborate a common plan of operations. He was naturally included in the list of the proscribed, though it is said that Octavian fought long on his behalf, and was slain near Formiae on Dec. 7, 43. He had a ship near in which he had previously attempted to flee, but being cast back by unfavourable winds he returned to his villa, saying, "Let me die in the country which I have often saved." His head and hands were sent to Rome and nailed to the rostra, after Fulvia, wife of Antony and widow of Clodius, had thrust a hairpin through the tongue.

Works.—The literary works of Cicero may be classed as (i.) rhetorical; (ii.) oratorical; (iii.) philosophical and political; (iv.) epistolary.

(i.) *Rhetorical.*—His chief works of this kind are: (*a*) *de Oratore,* a treatise in three books dedicated to his brother Quintus. The discussion is conducted in the form of a dialogue which is supposed to have occurred in 91 B.C. chiefly between the two orators L. Crassus and M. Antonius. The first book deals with the studies necessary for an orator; the second with the treatment of the subject matter; the third with the form and delivery of a speech. Cicero says of this work in a letter (*Fam.* i. 9. 23) that it "does not deal in hackneyed rules and embraces the whole theory of oratory as laid down by Isocrates and Aristotle." (*b*) *Brutus,* or *de claris oratoribus,* a history of Roman eloquence containing much valuable information about his predecessors, drawn largely from the *Chronicle* (*liber annalis*) of Atticus. (*c*) *Orator,* dedicated to M. Brutus, sketching a portrait of the perfect and ideal orator, Cicero's last word on oratory. The sum of his conclusion is that the perfect orator must also be a perfect man. Cicero says of this work that he has "concentrated in it all his taste" (*Fam.* vi. 18. 4). The three treatises are intended to form a continuous series containing a complete system of rhetorical training.

It will be convenient to mention here a feature of Ciceronian prose on which singular light has been thrown by recent inquiry. In the *de Oratore,* iii. 173 *sqq.,* he considers the element of rhythm or metre in prose, and in the *Orator* (174–226) he returns to the subject and discusses it at length. His main point is that prose should be metrical in character, though it should not be entirely metrical, since this would be poetry (*Orator,* 220). Greek writers relied for metrical effect in prose on those feet which were not much used in poetry. Aristotle recommended the paean ⏑⏑⏑–. Cicero preferred the cretic –⏑–, which he says is the metrical equivalent of the paean. Demosthenes was especially fond of the cretic. Rhythm pervades the whole sentence but is most important at the end or *clausula,* where the swell of the period sinks to rest. The ears of the Romans were almost incredibly sensitive to such points. We are told that an assembly was stirred to wild applause by a double trochee –⏑–⏑.[1] If the order were changed, Cicero says, the effect would be lost. The same rhythm should be found in the *membra* which compose the sentence. He quotes a passage from one of his own speeches in which any change in the order would destroy the rhythm. Cicero gives various *clausulae* which his ears told him to be good or bad, but his remarks are desultory as also are those of Quintilian, whose examples were largely drawn from Cicero's writings. It was left for modern research to discover rules of harmony which the Romans obeyed unconsciously. Other investigators had shown that Cicero's *clausulae* are generally variations of some three or four forms in which the rhythm is trochaic. Dr. Thaddaeus Zielinski of Warsaw, after examining all the *clausulae* in Cicero's speeches, finds that they are governed by a law. In every *clausula* there is a basis followed by a cadence. The basis consists of a cretic or its metrical equivalent.[2] This is followed by a cadence trochaic in character, but varying in length. The three favourite forms are (i.) –⏑–⏓, (ii.) –⏑––⏑⏓, (iii.) –⏑––⏑–⏓. These he styles *verae* (V). Other frequent *clausulae*, which he terms *licitae* (L), are those in which a long syllable is resolved, as in verse, into two shorts, e.g., *ēssĕ vĭdĕātŭr*. These two classes, V and L, include 86% of the *clausulae* in the orations. Some rarer *clausulae* which he terms M (=*malae*) introduce no new principle. There remain two interesting forms, viz., S (=*selectae*), in which a spondee is substituted for a trochee in the cadence, *e.g.*, –⏑––––⏓, this being done for special emphasis, and P (= *pessimae*), where a dactyl is so used, *e.g.*, ⏑––⏑⏑⏓, this being the *heroica clausula* condemned by Quintilian. Similar rules apply to the *membra* of the sentence, though in these the S and P forms are more frequent, harmony being restored in the *clausula*.

These results apply not only to the speeches but also to the philosophical writings and the more elaborate letters, and with modifications to other rhythmical prose, *e.g.*, that of Pliny and Seneca. Rhythm was avoided by Caesar who was an Atticist, and by Sallust, who was an archaist. Livy's practice is exactly opposite to that of Cicero, since he has a marked preference for the S forms, thereby exemplifying Cicero's saying that long syllables are more appropriate to history than to oratory (*Orator*, § 212).

(ii.) *Speeches.*—These were generally delivered before the senate or people, if political in character, and before jurors sitting in a *quaestio*, if judicial. The speech against Vatinius was an attack upon a witness under examination; that *de Domo* was made before the Pontifices; that *pro C. Rabirio perduellionis reo* in the course of a *provocatio* to the people; and those *pro Ligario* and *pro rege Deiotaro* before Caesar. The five orations composing the *Actio Secunda in Verrem* were never spoken, but written after Verres had gone into exile. The Second *Philippic* also was not delivered but issued as a pamphlet. Cicero's speech for Milo at his trial was not a success, though, as Quintilian (ix. 2. 54) quotes from it, as taken down by shorthand reporters, an example of a rhetorical figure well used, it cannot have been such a failure as is alleged by later writers. The extant speech was written by Cicero at his leisure. None of the other speeches is in the exact form in which it was delivered. Cicero's method was to construct a *commentarius* or skeleton of his speech, which he used when speaking. If he was pleased with a speech he then wrote it out for publication. Sometimes he omitted in the written speech a subject on which he had spoken. A record of this is sometimes preserved: *e.g.*, "de Postumi criminibus" (*Mur.* 51), "de teste Fufio" (*Cael.* 19). These *commentarii* were published by his freedman Tiro and are quoted by Asconius (*ad Orat. in Toga Candida*, p. 87).

Cicero in his speeches must be given all the privileges of an advocate. Sometimes he had a bad client; he naïvely confesses the straits to which he was put when defending Scamander (*Clu.* 51; *cf. Phil.* xiii. 26). He thought of defending Catiline, though he says that his guilt is clear as noon-day (*Att.* i. 1–2 and ii. 1). Sometimes the brief which he held at the moment compelled him to take a view of facts contrary to that which he had previously advocated. Thus in the *pro Caecina* he alleges judicial corruption against a witness, Falcula, while in the *pro Cluentio* he contends that the offence was not proved (*Caec.* 28, *Clu.* 103). He says quite openly that "it is a great mistake to suppose that statements in his speeches express his real opinions" (*Clu.* 139). It is therefore idle to reproach him with inconsistencies, though these are sometimes very singular. Thus in the *pro Cornelio* he speaks with praise of Gabinius, who, when a colleague vetoed his proposal, proceeded to depose him after the precedent set by Tiberius Gracchus (Asconius *in Cornel.* p. 71). In the *pro Cluentio*, 111, he contends that nothing is easier than for a new man to rise at Rome. In the *pro Caelio* he says that Catiline had in him undeveloped germs of the greatest virtues, and that it was the good in him that made him so dangerous (*Cael.* 12–14). He sometimes deliberately puts the case upon a wrong issue. In the *pro Milone* he says that either Milo must have lain in wait for Clodius or Clodius for Milo, leaving out of sight the truth, that the encounter was due to chance. He used to boast that he had cast dust into the eyes of the jury in the case of Cluentius (Quintil. ii. 17–21).

Cicero had a perfect mastery of all weapons wielded by a pleader in Rome. He was specially famous for his pathos, and for this reason, when several counsel were employed, always spoke last (*Orat.* 130). A splendid specimen of pathos is to be found in his account of the condemnation and execution of the Sicilian captains (*Verr.* [*Act.* ii.] v. 106–122). Much exaggeration was permitted to a Roman orator. Thus Cicero frequently speaks as if his client were to be put to death, though a criminal could always evade capital consequences by going into exile. His enemies scoffed at his "tear-drops." He indulged in the most violent invective, which, though shocking to a modern reader, *e.g.*, in his speeches against Vatinius and Piso, was not offensive to Roman taste (*de Orat.* ii. 216–290). He was much criticized for his jokes, and even Quintilian (ii. 17–21) regrets that he made so many in his speeches. He could never resist the temptation to make a pun. It must be remembered, however, that he was the great wit of the period. Caesar used to have a collection of Cicero's *bons mots* brought to him. Cicero complains that all the jokes of the day were attributed to himself, including those made by very sorry jesters (*Fam.* vii. 32. 1). A fine specimen of sustained humour is to be found in his speech *pro Murena*, where he rallies the jurisconsults and the Stoics. He was also criticized for his vanity and perpetual references to his own achievements. His vanity, however, as has been admirably remarked, is essentially that of "the peacock, not of the gander," and is redeemed by his willingness to raise a laugh at his own expense (Strachan-Davidson, p. 192). Some critics have impugned his legal knowledge, but probably without justice. It is true that he does not claim to be a great expert, though a pupil of the Scaevolas, and when in doubt would consult a jurisconsult; also, that he frequently passes lightly over important points of law, but this was probably because he was conscious of a flaw in his case.

(iii.) *Political and Philosophical Treatises.*—These are generally written in the form of dialogues, in which the speakers sometimes belong to bygone times and sometimes to the present. The first method was known as that of Heracleides, the second as that of Aristotle (*Att.* xiii. 19. 4). There is no reason to suppose that the speakers held the views with which Cicero credits them, or had such literary powers as would make them able to express such views (*ib.*, xiii. 12. 3). The political works are *de Republica* and *de Legibus*. The first was a dialogue in six books concerning the best form of constitution, in which the speakers are Scipio Africanus Minor and members of his circle. He tells us that he drew largely from Plato, Aristotle, Theophrastus and writings of the Peripatetics. The famous "Dream of Scipio" recalls the "Vision of Er" in Plato's *Republic* (Book x. *ad fin.*). The *de*

[1] *Orator*, § 214: "'patris dictum sapiens temeritas fili cōmprŏbāvĭt'—hoc dichoreo tantus clamor contionis excitatus est ut admirabile esset. Quaero, nonne id numerus efficerit? Verborum ordinem immuta, fac sic: 'Comprobavit fili temeritas' jam nihil erit."

[2] This theory is partly anticipated by Terentianus Maurus (*c.* A.D. 290), who says of the cretic (v. 1440 *sqq.*):—

"Plurimum orantes decebit quando paene in ultimo
Obtinet sedem beatam, terminet si clausulam
Dactylus spondeus imam, nec trochaeum respuo;
Plenius tractatur istud arte prosa rhetorum."

Legibus, a sequel to this work in imitation of Plato's *Laws,* is drawn largely from Chrysippus.

Cicero as a philosopher belonged to the New Academy. The followers of this school were free to hear all arguments for and against, and to accept the conclusion which for the moment appeared most probable (*Acad.* ii. 131). Thus in the *Tusculan Disputations* v. he expresses views which conflict with *de Finibus* iv., and defends himself on the ground that as an Academic he is free to change his mind. He was much fascinated by the Stoic morality, and it has been noticed that the *Tusculan Disputations* and *de Officiis* are largely Stoic in tone. He has nothing but contempt for the Epicureans, and cannot forgive their neglect of literary style. As Cicero's philosophical writings have been severely attacked for want of originality, it is only fair to recollect that he resorted to philosophy as an anodyne when suffering from mental anguish, and that he wrote incredibly fast. He issued two editions of his *Academica.* The first consisted of two books, in which Catulus and Lucullus were the chief speakers. He then rewrote his treatise in four books, making himself, Varro and Atticus the speakers. His works are confessedly in the main translations and compilations (*Att.* xii. 52. 3); all that he does is to turn the discussion into the form of a dialogue, to adapt it to Roman readers by illustrations from Roman history, and to invent equivalents for Greek technical terms. This is equally true of the political treatises. Thus, when Atticus criticized a strange statement in *de Republ.* ii. 8, that all the cities of the Peloponnese had access to the sea, he excuses himself by saying that he found it in Dicaearchus and copied it word for word (*Att.* vi. 2. 3). In the same passage he used an incorrect adjective, *Phliuntii* for *Phliasii;* he says that he had already corrected his own copy, but the mistake survives in the single palimpsest in which this work has been preserved. The only merits, therefore, which can be claimed for Cicero are that he invented a philosophical terminology for the Romans, and that he produced a series of manuals which from their beauty of style have had enduring influence upon mankind.

The most famous of these treatises are the following:

De Finibus, on the Supreme Good. In Book i. L. Manlius Torquatus explains the Epicurean doctrine, which is refuted in ii. by Cicero. In iii. and iv. M. Porcius Cato sets forth the doctrine of the Stoics which is shown by Cicero to agree with that of Antiochus of Ascalon; in v. M. Pupius Piso explains the views of the Academics and Peripatetics.

Tusculanae Disputationes, so called from Cicero's villa at Tusculum in which the discussion is supposed to have taken place. The subjects treated are:—in Book i., the nature of death and the reasons for despising it; Book ii., the endurance of pain; pain is not an evil; Book iii., wisdom makes a man insensible to sorrow; Book iv., wisdom banishes all mental disquietude; Book v., virtue is sufficient to secure happiness. The materials are drawn largely from works of Dicaearchus.

De Deorum Natura.—The dialogue is placed in 77 B.C. In Book i. Velleius attacks other philosophies and explains the system of Epicurus. He is then refuted by Cotta. In Book ii. Balbus, speaking as a Stoic, discusses the existence of the gods, nature, the government of the world and providence. In Book iii. Cotta criticizes the views of Balbus. The statement of the Epicurean doctrine is drawn from the work of Phaedrus, περὶ θεῶν the criticism of this from Posidonius. The Stoic teaching is derived from Cleanthes, Chrysippus and Zeno, and is criticized from the writings of Carneades and Clitomachus.

De Officiis, addressed to his son Marcus. In this the form of dialogue was not employed. The material is chiefly drawn from Stoic sources, *e.g.,* works of Panaetius in Books i. and ii., of Posidonius and Hecato in Book iii.

The *Academica,* as they have come down to us, are a conflation from the two editions of this work. They consist of the second book from the first edition, and a portion of the first book from the second edition.

Cato maior, or *de Senectute,* a dialogue placed in 150 B.C., in which Cato, addressing Scipio and Laelius, set forth the praises of old age. The idea is drawn from Aristo of Chios, and the materials largely derived from Xenophon and Plato.

Laelius, or *de Amicitia,* a dialogue between Laelius and his sons-in-law, in which he sets forth the theory of friendship, speaking with special reference to the recent death of Scipio. Cicero here draws from a work of Theophrastus on the same subject and from Aristotle.

(iv.) *Letters.*—Those preserved are (1) *ad Familiares,* i.–xvi.; (2) *ad Atticum,* i.–xvi.; (3) *ad Quintum,* i.–iii., *ad Brutum,* i.–ii. Some 35 other books of letters were known to antiquity, *e.g.,* to Caesar, to Pompey, to Octavian and to his son Marcus.

The collection includes nearly 100 letters written by other persons. Thus, the eighth Book *ad Fam.* consists entirely of letters from Caelius to Cicero when in Cilicia. When writing to Atticus Cicero frequently sent copies of letters which he had received. There is a great variety in the style not only of Cicero's correspondents, but also of Cicero himself. Caelius writes in a breezy, school-boy style; the Latinity of Plancus is Ciceronian in character; the letter of Sulpicius to Cicero on the death of Tullia is a masterpiece of style; Matius writes a most dignified letter justifying his affectionate regard for Caesar's memory. Several of his correspondents are indifferent stylists. Cato labours to express himself in an awkward and laconic epistle, apologizing for its length. Metellus Celer is very rude, but gives himself away in every word. Antony writes bad Latin, while Cicero himself writes in various styles. We have such a *cri de coeur* as his few words to one of the conspirators after Caesar's murder, "I congratulate you. I rejoice for myself. I love you. I watch your interest; I wish for your love and to be informed what you are doing and what is being done" (*Fam.* vi. 15). When writing to Atticus he eschews all ornamentation, uses short sentences, colloquial idioms, rare diminutives and continually quotes Greek. This use of Greek tags and quotations is also found in letters to other intimate friends, *e.g.,* Paetus and Caelius; also in letters written by other persons, *e.g.,* Cassius to Cicero; Quintus to Tiro, and subsequently in those of Augustus to Tiberius. It is a feature of the colloquial style and often corresponds to the modern use of "slang." Other letters of Cicero, especially those written to persons with whom he was not quite at his ease or those meant for circulation, are composed in his elaborate style with long periods, parentheses and other devices for obscuring thought. These are throughout rhythmical in character, like his speeches and philosophical works.

We know from Cicero's own statement (*Att.* xvi. 5. 5) that he thought of publishing some of his letters during his lifetime. On another occasion he jestingly charges Tiro with wishing to have his own letters included in the "volumes" (*Fam.* xvi. 17. 1). It is obvious that Cicero could not have meant to publish his private letters to Atticus in which he makes confessions about himself, or those to Quintus in which he sometimes outsteps the limits of brotherly criticism, but was thinking of polished productions such as the letters to Lentulus Spinther or that to Lucceius which he describes as "very pretty" (*Att.* iv. 6. 4).

It is universally agreed that the letters *ad Familiares* were published by Tiro, whose hand is revealed by the fact that he suppresses all letters written by himself, and modestly puts at the end those written to him. That Cicero kept copies of his letters, or of many of them, we know from a passage in which, when addressing a friend who had inadvertently torn up a letter from him, he says that there is nothing to grieve about; he has himself a copy at home and can replace the loss (*Fam.* vii. 25. 1). Tiro may have obtained from Terentia copies of letters written to her. It has been suggested that he may also have edited the letters to Quintus, as he could obtain them from members of the family. The letters *ad Familiares* were generally quoted in antiquity by books, the title being taken from the first letter, *e.g., Cicero ad Varronem epistula Paeti.*

While the letters *ad Familiares* were circulated at once, those to Atticus appear to have been suppressed for a considerable time. Cornelius Nepos (*Att.* 16) knew of their existence but distinguishes them from the published letters. Asconius (p. 87), writing under Claudius, never quotes them, though, when discussing Cicero's projected defence of Catiline, he could hardly have failed to do so, if he had known them. The first author who quotes them is Seneca. It is, therefore, probable that they were not published by Atticus himself, who died 32 B.C., though his hand may be seen in the suppression of all letters written by himself, but that they remained in the possession of his family and were not published until about A.D. 60. At that date they could be published without expurgation of any kind, whereas in the letters *ad Familiares* the editor's hand is on one occasion (iii. 10. 11) manifest. Cicero is telling Appius, his predecessor in Cilicia, of the measures which he is taking on his behalf. There then follows a lacuna. It is obvious that Tiro thought the passage compromising and struck it out. In the letters to Atticus, on the other hand, we have Cicero's private journal, his confessions to the director of his conscience, the record of his moods from day to day, without alterations of any kind.

Cicero's letters are the chief and most reliable source of information for the period. It is due to them that the Romans of the day are living figures to us, and that Cicero, in spite of, or rather in virtue of his frailties, is intensely human and sympathetic. The letters to Atticus abound in the frankest self-revelation, though even in the presence of his confessor his instinct as a pleader makes him try to justify himself. The historical value of the letters, therefore, completely transcends that of Cicero's other works. It is true that these are full of information. Thus we learn much from the *de Legibus* regarding the constitutional history of Rome, and much from the *Brutus* concerning the earlier orators. The speeches abound in details which may be accepted as authentic, either because there is no reason for misrepresentation or on account of their circumstantiality. Thus the *Verrines* are our chief source of information for the government of the provinces, the system of taxation, the powers of the governor. They tell us of the monstrous system by which the governor could fix upon a remote place for the delivery of corn, and so compel the farmer to compound by a payment in money which the orator does not blame, on the ground that it is only proper to allow magistrates to receive corn wherever they wish (iii. 190). From the speech *pro Cluentio* (145–154) we gain unique information concerning the condition of society in a country town, the extraordinary exemption of *equites* from prosecution for judicial corruption, the administration of domestic justice in the case of slaves examined by their owner (*ib.*, 176–187). But we have always to be on our guard against misrepresentation, exaggeration and falsehood. The value of the letters lies in the fact that in them we get behind Cicero and are face to face with the other *dramatis personae;* also that we are admitted behind the scenes and read the secret history of the times. One of the most interesting documents in the correspondence is a despatch of Caesar to his agent Oppius, written in great haste and in disjointed sentences. It runs as follows: "On the 9th I came to Brundisium. Pompey is at Brundisium. He sent Magius to me to treat of peace. I gave him a suitable answer" (*Att.* ix. 13, A). In the *de Bello civili,* on the other hand, Caesar who wishes to show that he did his best to make peace, after stating that he sent his captive Magius to negotiate, expresses mild surprise at the fact that Pompey did not send him back (*Bell. Civ.* i. 26). We hear of the extraordinary agreement made by two candidates for the consulship in Caesar's interest with the sitting consuls of 54 B.C., which Cicero says he hardly ventures to put on paper. Under the terms of this the consuls, who were *optimates,* bound themselves to betray their party by securing, apparently fraudulently, the election of the candidates while they in turn bound themselves to procure two ex-consuls who would swear that they were present in the senate when supplies were voted for the consular provinces, though no meeting of the senate had been held, and three augurs who would swear that a *lex curiata* had been passed, though the *comitia curiata* had not been convened (*Att.* iv. 18. 2). But perhaps the most singular scene is the council of three great ladies presided over by Servilia at Antium, which decides the movements of Brutus and Cassius in June 44 B.C., when Cassius "looking very fierce—you would say that he was breathing fire and sword"—blustered concerning what he considered an insult, viz., a commission which had been laid upon him to supply corn. Servilia calmly remarks she will have the commission removed from the decree of the senate (*Att.* xv. 11. 2).

(v.) *Miscellaneous.*—It is not necessary to dwell upon the other forms of literary composition attempted by Cicero. He was a fluent versifier, and would write 500 verses in one night. Considerable fragments from a juvenile translation of Aratus have been preserved. His later poems upon his own consulship and his exile were soon forgotten except for certain lines which provoked criticism, such as the unfortunate verse:

"O fortunatam natam me consule Romam."

He wrote a memoir of his consulship in Greek and at one time thought of writing a history of Rome. Nepos thought that he would have been an ideal historian, but as Cicero ranks history with declamation and on one occasion with great *naïveté* asks Lucius Lucceius (*q.v.*), who was embarking on this task, to embroider the facts to his own credit, we cannot accept this criticism (*Fam.* vi. 2. 3).

(vi.) *Authenticity.*—The genuineness of certain works of Cicero has been attacked. It was for a long time usual to doubt the authenticity of the speeches *post reditum* and *pro Marcello.* Recent scholars consider them genuine. As their rhythmical structure corresponds more or less exactly with the canon of authenticity formed by Zielinski from the other speeches, the question may now be considered closed. Absurd suspicion has been cast upon the later speeches *in Catilinam* and that *pro Archia.* An oration *pridie quam in exsilium iret* is certainly a forgery, as also a letter to Octavian. There is a "controversy" between Cicero and Sallust which is palpably a forgery, though a quotation from it occurs in Quintilian (iv. 1. 68). Suspicion has been attached to the letters to Brutus, which in the case of two letters (i. 16 and 17) is not unreasonable since they somewhat resemble the style of *suasoriae,* or rhetorical exercises, but the latest editors, Tyrrell and Purser, regard these also as genuine.

After Cicero's death his character was attacked by various detractors, such as the author of the spurious *Controversia* put into the mouth of Sallust, and the calumniator from whom Dio Cassius (xlvi. 1–28) draws the libellous statements which he inserts into the speech of Q. Fufius Calenus in the senate. Of such critics, Asconius (in *Tog. Cand.* p. 95) well says that it is best to ignore them. His prose style was attacked by Pollio as Asiatic, also by his son, Asinius Gallus, who was answered by the emperor Claudius (Suet. 41). The writers of the silver age found fault with his prolixity, want of sparkle and epigram and monotony of his *clausulae.* A certain Largius Licinius gained notoriety by attacking his Latinity in a work styled *Ciceromastix.* His most devoted admirers were the younger Pliny, who reproduced his oratorical style with considerable success, and Quintilian (x. 1. 112), who regarded him as the perfect orator, and draws most of his illustrations from his works. At a later period his style fascinated Christian writers, notably Lactantius, the "Christian Cicero," Jerome and St. Augustine, who drew freely from his rhetorical writings.

(2) QUINTUS TULLIUS CICERO, brother of the orator and brother-in-law of T. Pomponius Atticus, was born about 102 B.C. He was aedile in 67, praetor in 62, and for the three following years propraetor in Asia, where, though he seems to have abstained from personal aggrandizement, his ill-temper gained him an evil notoriety. After his return to Rome, he heartily supported the attempt to secure his brother's recall from exile, and was nearly murdered by gladiators in the pay of Clodius. He distinguished himself as one of Julius Caesar's legates in the Gallic campaigns, served in Britain, and afterwards under his brother in Cilicia. On the outbreak of the Civil War between Pompey and Caesar, Quintus, like Marcus, supported Pompey, but after Pharsalus he deserted and made peace with Caesar, largely owing to the intercession of Marcus. Both the brothers fell victims to the proscription which followed Caesar's death, Quintus being put to death in 43, some time before Marcus. His marriage with Pomponia was very unhappy, and he was much under the influence of his freedman Statius. Though trained on the same lines as Marcus he never spoke in public, and even said,

"One orator in a family is enough, nay even in a city." Though essentially a soldier, he took considerable interest in literature, wrote epic poems, tragedies and annals, and translated plays of Sophocles. There are extant four letters written by him (one to his brother Marcus, and three to his freedman Tiro) and a short paper, *de Petitione Consulatus* (on canvassing for the consulship), addressed to his brother in 64. A few hexameters by him on the 12 signs of the zodiac are quoted by Ausonius.

(3) Marcus Tullius Cicero, only son of the orator and his wife Terentia, was born in 65 B.C. At the age of 17 he served with Pompey in Greece and commanded a squadron of cavalry at the battle of Pharsalus. In 45 he was sent to Athens to study rhetoric and philosophy, but abandoned himself to a life of dissipation. It was during his stay at Athens that his father dedicated the *de Officiis* to him. After the murder of Caesar (44) he attracted the notice of Brutus, by whom he was offered the post of military tribune, in which capacity he rendered good service to the Republican cause. After the battle of Philippi (42), he took refuge with Sextus Pompeius in Sicily, where the remnants of the Republican forces were collected. He took advantage of the amnesty granted by the Treaty of Misenum (39) to return to Rome, where he took no part in public affairs, but resumed his former dissipated habits. In spite of this, he received signal marks of distinction from Octavian, who not only nominated him augur, but accepted him as his colleague in the consulship (30). He had the satisfaction of carrying out the decree which ordered that all the statues of Antony should be demolished, and thus "the divine justice reserved the completion of Antony's punishment for the house of Cicero" (Plutarch). He was subsequently appointed proconsul of Asia or Syria, but nothing further is known of his life. In spite of his debauchery, there is no doubt that he was a man of considerable education and no mean soldier, while Brutus, in a letter to his father (*Epp. ad Brutum*, ii. 3), even goes so far as to say that the son would be capable of attaining the highest honours without borrowing from the father's reputation.

(4) Quintus Tullius Cicero (*c.* 67–43 B.C.), son of Quintus Tullius Cicero (brother of the orator). He accompanied his uncle Marcus to Cilicia, and, in the hope of obtaining a reward, repaid his kindness by informing Caesar of his intention of leaving Italy. After the battle of Pharsalus he joined his father in abusing his uncle as responsible for the condition of affairs, hoping thereby to obtain pardon from Caesar. After the death of Caesar he attached himself to Mark Antony, but, owing to some fancied slight, he deserted to Brutus and Cassius. He was included in the proscription lists, and was put to death with his father in 43. In his last moments he refused under torture to disclose his father's hiding-place. His father, who in his concealment was a witness of what was taking place, thereupon gave himself up, stipulating that he and his son should be executed at the same time.

Bibliography.—It is impossible to mention more than a few works as the literature is so vast. (1) *Historical.*—J. L. Strachan-Davidson, *Cicero and the Roman Republic* (Heroes of the Nations series, 1894); G. Boissier, *Cicéron et ses amis* (1865); W. Warde Fowler, *Social Life at Rome* (1908); introduction to R. Y. Tyrrell and L. C. Purser's edition of the letters (1904–18); Th. Zielinski, *Cicero im Wandel der Jahrhunderte* (3rd ed., Leipzig, 1912). (2) *Literary.*—M. Schanz, *Geschichte der römischen Literatur*, i., 194–274 (München, 1890). (3) *Linguistic.*—H. Merguet, *Lexikon zu den Schriften Ciceros* (Jena, 1887–94); J. Le Breton, *Études sur la langue et la grammaire de Ciceron* (1901); E. Norden, *Die antike Kunstprosa* (Leipzig, 1898); Th. Zielinski, "Das Clauselgesetz in Ciceros Reden" in *Philologus* (Leipzig, 1904); L. Laurand, *Études sur le style des discours de Cicéron* (1907). Much information on points of Ciceronian idiom and language will be found in J. S. Reid's *Academica* (London, 1885), *de Finikus*, i.–ii. (Cambridge, 1925) and G. Landgraf's *Pro Sext. Roscio* (Erlangen, 1884). (4) *Legal.*—A. H. J. Greenidge, *The Legal Procedure of Cicero's Time* (Oxford, 1901). (5) *Philosophical.*—An excellent account of Cicero as a philosopher is given in the preface to Reid's editions of the *Academica.* (6) *Editions* (critical) of the complete texts.—Baiter-Halm (1845–61); C. F. W. Müller (1880–96); Oxford Classical Texts. (A. C. C.)

CICERO, a town of Cook county, Ill., U.S., about 7 mi. S.W. of the loop, and bounded by Chicago on the north, east and south. Pop. (1950) 67,195; (1940) 64,712 by the federal census. Cicero is an important industrial centre, manufacturing electrical equipment, iron and steel, enamelware, castings, asbestos, copper, brass and printing machinery. Cicero was settled about 1849, and was incorporated in 1867. The town achieved notoriety during the 1920s and later as the headquarters of Alphonse ("Scarface Al") Capone (1899–1947) and other Chicago gangsters who built vast criminal syndicates to run speak-easies during the period of prohibition and later expanded their activities along many other lines, principally gambling and prostitution.

CICERONE, a guide, one who conducts visitors to museums, galleries, etc., and explains matters of historic or artistic interest. The word is presumably taken from Marcus Tullius Cicero as a type of learning and eloquence. According to a quotation (1762) cited by the *New English Dictionary* the word seems first to have been applied to "learned antiquarians who show and explain to foreigners the antiquities and curiosities of the country."

CICHLID. The fishes of the family Cichlidae are perches with a single nostril on each side and with the lower pharyngeals coalesced or united by suture. They are found in lakes, rivers and brackish lagoons of Central and South America, Africa and Syria, Madagascar and India. This distribution was formerly considered to favour the idea of the persistence of the connection between South America and Africa into the Eocene, but the value of the Cichlids in this relation is discounted by the fact that many species enter brackish water and some the sea. Their presence in Madagascar, where none of the true freshwater African families is represented, indicates that their dispersal has been accomplished in a manner different from these.

The American species number about 250, the African 400; none of the genera is common to the two continents. The Indian *Etroplus* is an isolated genus, related only to *Paretroplus* of Madagascar, in which island the genera are peculiar, the two others being related to African genera. In the African Cichlid fauna an extraordinary diversity and specialization is attained in the great lakes, Tanganyika having 100 species, nearly all belonging to genera found only in the lake, and Nyassa having nearly as many endemic species, some of which have evolved on parallel lines to those of Tanganyika. The lacustrine genera differ from each other, especially in modifications of the mouth and teeth, enabling these fishes to make use of every kind of animal and vegetable food available in the lakes. Many Cichlids are beautifully coloured, and are favourite aquarium fishes. *Herichthys cyanoguttatus* of Mexico, covered with bright blue spots, is one of the really handsome species. *Pterophyllum scalare* of the Amazon has the body very deep and strongly compressed and the dorsal and anal fins high. *Tilapia nilotica,* the bolti of the Nile, reaches a length of 18 inches.

In many Cichlids the female fish keeps the eggs in her mouth until they hatch, and for a time swims with her brood, opening her mouth for the little fishes to swim in when danger threatens. In other species the eggs are laid in a hollow scooped out by the male; both parents guard the nest until the eggs hatch, when the mother takes the young into her mouth. (C. T. R.)

CICISBEO (chĭ-chĭs-bā'ō), the term in Italy (17th century onwards) for a dangler about women. The cicisbeo was the professed gallant of a married woman, who attended her at all public entertainments, it being considered unfashionable for the husband to be her escort.

CICOGNARA, LEOPOLDO, Count (1767–1834), Italian archaeologist and writer on art, was born at Ferrara. A residence of some years at Rome, devoted to the study of the antiquities and galleries, was followed by visits to Naples and Sicily. He then visited Florence, Milan, Bologna and Venice, acquiring a complete archaeological knowledge of these and other cities. In 1795 he took up his abode at Modena, and was for 12 years engaged in politics, becoming minister plenipotentiary of the Cisalpine Republic at Turin. Napoleon decorated him with the Iron Crown; and in 1808 he was made president of the Academy of the Fine Arts at Venice. In 1808 appeared his treatise *Del bello ragionamenti.* This was followed (1813–18) by his *magnum opus*, the *Storia della scultura dal suo risorgimento in Italia al* *secolo di Napoleone.* The book was designed to complete the works of Winckelmann and D'Agincourt, and is illustrated with 180 plates in outline. His *Fabbriche più cospicue di Venezia,* two superb folios containing about 150 plates, was published (1815–20) under the auspices of Francis I of Austria. Charged by the Venetians with the presentation of their gifts of the empress Caroline at Vienna, Cicognara added to the offering an illustrated catalogue of the objects it comprised; this book, *Omaggio delle Provincie Venete alla maestà di Carolina Augusta,* has since become of great value to the bibliophile. In 1821 he published at Pisa a *catalogue raisonné,* rich in bibliographical lore, of his fine library, the result of 30 years of loving labour, which in 1824 was purchased *en bloc* by Pope Leo XII and added to the Vatican library. Cicognara's work in the academy at Venice, of which he became president in 1808, led to the foundation of a gallery for the reception of Venetian pictures.

See Zanetti, *Cenni biografici di Leopoldo Cicognara* (Venice, 1834); Malmani, *Memorie del conte Leopoldo Cicognara* (Venice, 1888).

CICONIIDAE: *see* Jabiru; Stork.

CID, THE (Arabic *sid,* "lord"), is the popular sobriquet by which Rodrigo Díaz de Vivar (?1043–1099), most famous of mediaeval Spanish captains, has been known in Spain since his own day. It is frequently linked with another sobriquet, of Romance origin, *Campeador,* "winner of battles." There is a substantial heroic history of Rodrigo Díaz, in both poetry and prose, originating in the 12th century, but this is of more concern to the student of literature than to the historian (*see* Spanish Literature). There are, however, some acceptable historical sources from which his biography may be established. These include some contemporary documents, the *Historia Roderici* (a very nearly contemporary private Latin chronicle of his life) and a detailed narrative of his conquest of Valencia written by Ibn Alkama, an Arab historian living in the city at the time.

Rodrigo Díaz was born at Vivar, near Burgos, about 1043, his father, Diego Laínez, being a member of the Castilian squirearchy. He was brought up at the court of Ferdinand I by the latter's eldest son, Sancho. Details of his early career are uncertain, but he seems to have distinguished himself in Ferdinand's later campaigns and, when Sancho succeeded to the Castilian throne (1065), the young Cid was appointed to the high military office of standard-bearer. His successful generalship during Sancho's reign established his military reputation.

The Cid had taken a prominent part in the campaign which enabled Sancho to seize the throne of León from his younger brother, Alphonso. His position was, therefore, of some difficulty when Sancho was killed at the siege of Zamora (1072) and Alphonso returned from exile to become king of both León and Castile. Nevertheless, he remained at Alphonso's court for nearly a decade and, in 1074 even married the king's own niece, Jimena, daughter of the count of Oviedo. In 1079 the Cid was with the army of Alphonso's tributary, Mutamid (al-Motamid) of Seville, when Mutamid defeated an invasion by Abdullah of Granada. Alphonso's favourite, Count García Ordoñez, happened to be on the Granadine side and was captured by the Cid. This affair renewed Alphonso's dormant suspicions of him, and when it was followed, in 1081, by an unauthorized incursion on a large scale into the Moorish kingdom of Toledo, over which Alphonso had established a protectorate, the Cid was ordered into exile.

He now removed himself to the Moorish kingdom of Saragossa, whose kings he served for a number of years, leading successful campaigns on their behalf against the count of Barcelona (1082) and Sancho Ramírez of Aragon (1084). He also became chief political adviser to his Moorish employers (who regarded him highly) and acquired that familiarity with Islamic politics, law and customs which was to prove invaluable for his later career.

A temporary reconciliation with Alphonso in 1083 had soon broken down, but the king's difficulties in meeting the invasion of Spain by the Almorávides led him to readmit the Cid to his favour in 1087. The Cid's interests were by this time wholly concentrated on eastern Spanish affairs, and he turned his attention to the task of securing Alphonso's suzerainty over the extensive Moorish kingdom of Valenicia. In 1089 he extracted a written assurance from Alphonso that any lands won by him from the Moors would belong to himself and his heirs in perpetuity. When, later in the same year, he was again banished, he proceeded with the subjugation of Valencia more or less as a private venture.

The conquest of Valencia by the Cid was an extremely complicated affair: it began in 1089, when he made its king, al-Kadir, his tributary; entered its second stage in 1092, when al-Kadir was murdered by the cadi Ibn Yehhaf; and ended in June 1094, when the city capitulated to the Cid's troops after a prolonged siege. During these proceedings, the Cid relied on his talent for political intrigue almost as much as on military force, playing off against each other both the rival groups within the city and his own rivals for its control outside it—Alphonso himself, the Almorávides and the king of Saragossa. Several months after the surrender the Cid broke the terms of the capitulation that he had made with Ibn Yehhaf and executed him in a brutal manner; motives of cupidity and vengeance were responsible, at least in part, for this act. Determined Almorávide attempts to recover the city were defeated by the Cid at the battles of Cuarte (1094) and of Bairén (1097). The semiroyal status that the former squire from Vivar had by now achieved was shown when, soon afterward, his daughters Cristina and María married the Navarrese prince Ramiro and Raymund Berenguer, count of Barcelona, respectively.

The Cid died in Valencia on July 10, 1099. Three years later his wife, Jimena, had to give up the city, as it was impossible to hold it indefinitely against the Almorávides. The Cid's body was removed to the monastery of San Pedro de Cardeña, near Burgos, where the monks gradually made it the centre of an elaborate cult which sought to portray the Cid as a near saint.

The task of evaluating the Cid's career historically is a delicate one because of his status as a national hero. It is clear from all sources that he was a remarkably successful field commander, consistently achieving brilliant victories over superior enemy forces by boldness in action balanced, however, by cunning and careful preparation. There is little evidence of any religious motive behind his career, particularly before the coming of the Almorávides. The force which drove him seems to have been the pursuit of power and wealth. In these respects his attitude was entirely typical of that of other Christian Spaniards in pre-Almorávide Spain. The truth behind his quarrels with Alphonso VI is uncertain, but it would be rash to absolve the Cid of all blame by attributing responsibility to that exceptionally able monarch. The deeds of the Cid cannot be said to have made any great material contribution to Spanish history: he did not take part in Alphonso's most critical campaigns; his greatest achievement, the conquest of Valencia, proved ephemeral.

Nevertheless the Cid's life fired the popular imagination as that of no other mediaeval Spaniard was able to do. This was the result not only of his invincibility in the field but also of the fact that, after his career as a courtier had been ruined, he had continued to win fame, riches and rank solely by the exercise of his sword and his intelligence despite the king's disapproval and the active opposition of the great magnates.

Bibliography.—Ramón Menéndez Pidal, *La España del Cid,* 4th ed. (Madrid, 1947). There is an abridged English translation of the 1st edition of this work by H. Sunderland, *The Cid and His Spain* (London, 1934). The text of the *Historia Roderici Campidocti* is published by Menéndez Pidal, *op. cit.,* ii, pp. 919–969, and by R. Foulché-Delbosc in the *Revue hispanique,* xxi (Paris, 1909). For Ibn Alkama's account of the conquest of Valencia, *see* E. Lévi-Provençal, "La Toma de Valencia por el Cid," *Al-Andalus,* xiii (Madrid, 1948). (P. E. R.)

CIDER or Cyder is an alcoholic beverage made from apples; it is produced by the vinous fermentation of the expressed juice of the fruit. (In the United States the name is applied also to the unfermented juice.) Although any kind of apples can be used for the purpose, special vintage varieties distinguished by chemical and other characters rendering them unsuited for the most part for table use are required for a beverage of fine quality. The making of cider has been attempted wherever the apple is grown extensively, but a flourishing commercial industry has been established only where true vintage fruit can be obtained.

The Cider Districts.—The cider apple orchards of the world are mainly confined to certain districts of France and England.

The former country possesses the largest acreage and ranks as the chief producing centre, its average annual output of fruit being sufficient to permit of a considerable export trade to adjacent countries after home requirements have been satisfied. The cider orchards of France are chiefly concentrated in Normandy and Brittany, where the soil and other local conditions are particularly well suited to the production of fruit of a high order of vintage quality. The average annual output of cider in France is roughly 40,000,000 gal. In England, where the acreage under cider fruit is also extensive, the orchards are almost entirely confined to the western and southwestern counties, in particular Hereford, Worcester, Gloucester, Monmouth, Somerset and Devon. In that area, according to the returns of the ministry of agriculture and fisheries, the extent of grass orcharding is approximately 50,000 ac., of which the major part is planted with cider apple trees. Cider fruit growing has also spread into the counties bordering that area. In other parts of Great Britain the cider industry is limited to a few scattered localities, of which parts of Norfolk, Suffolk and Kent are the most important. Efforts have been made to develop the industry in Ireland with some success, but in this case the quantity of fruit grown specially for the purpose is small. The cider-making industry in Germany has attained considerable dimensions, but it has been in the past to some extent dependent on supplies of imported French fruit. Of the other European countries, Spain and Switzerland notably have obtained repute.

Farm Cider and Factory Cider.—While in France and Germany the cider industry has long been of considerable commercial importance and the manufacture of the beverage has been carried on in factories of some magnitude, in England before the beginning of the 20th century cider making was chiefly confined to the farms upon which the fruit was grown. The product was mainly consumed on the farm and the surplus disposed of in the immediate locality. Except for the output of a few old-established factories the distribution and consumption of cider were confined almost exclusively to the west of England. Thereafter there was a remarkable change. The introduction of improved methods of making as the result of research and education aided by the ministry of agriculture led to a marked improvement in the quality of the article placed upon the market, which was followed by the widespread adoption of cider as a popular beverage throughout the country generally. Many new factories in the cider-making area were established and the major part of the fruit which was formerly made into cider on the farms was now sold by the farmers to the factories. There was a gradual elimination of making on farms where the product was formerly indifferently prepared.

Legal Standards.—As a commercial article English cider has been handicapped by its extreme variability in character. No legal definitions or standards have been imposed other than regulations relating to metallic contamination and the National Mark Scheme for Cider introduced in World War II. A wide variety of types has therefore been placed upon the market. In France, where hitherto the industry has been of much greater commercial importance, cider has to conform to a series of regulations defining the respective standards of the beverage to which the name may be applied. These regulations, originally introduced in 1905 and modified in 1933, lay down that no beverage may be offered for sale under the name of cider unless produced exclusively by the fermentation of the juice from fresh apples, or a mixture of fresh apples and pears extracted with or without the addition of potable water. The term *cidre pur jus* is reserved for cider made without addition of water. The term *cidre* may be applied only to a beverage containing at least 3.2% (weight by volume) alcohol actual or potential, 1.3% (wt./vol.) dry extract at 100° C. (sugar not included) and 0.13% (wt./vol.) ash (apart from any salt added as a specific treatment). All ciders containing smaller quantities must be designated as *boisson de pommes*.

In England, though no corresponding regulations exist, the application of the name of cider to beverages other than those of which apple juice is the basis is an offense under the Merchandise Marks acts, as illustrated by cases where legal proceedings have been taken successfully against the use of the name for synthetic carbonated drinks flavoured with artificial apple essence.

Constituents of Cider.—Even in the most strictly restricted class, that of *cidre pur jus*, the French regulations permit a great elasticity in the nature of the beverage offered for sale. The primary reason for variability lies in the nature of the raw material. The more important constituents of apple juice are sugars, malic acid and "tannin." (The term "tannin" is used comprehensively by cider makers to include a group of constituents giving an astringent and bitter flavour to the juice; chemically they may not all be true tannins.) If allowance is made for seasonal effects on composition and the kinds of apples used and no account is taken of extreme cases, the total sugar content of a freshly expressed juice may range from 6% to 20%, the acid from 0.1% to 1.25% and the tannin from 0.05% to 0.75%. Further, since the extent of the ensuing fermentation is related to the nitrogenous content of the juice, which also varies widely, it proceeds in some cases till the whole of the sugar is fermented (unless prevented by special treatment), and in others ceases prematurely and leaves more or less of the sugars unfermented. According to the nature of the juice used, therefore, the finished article may be sweet or dry, strongly or very lightly alcoholic, highly acid or of a very low grade of acidity and strongly astringent and bitter or almost entirely lacking in that character.

The variations here indicated are attributable primarily to the varieties of apples from which the juice is derived. By a suitable blending of different sorts, juices of any desired standard of composition can be secured. In practice individual makers aim at definite standards suited to the taste of their customers and some degree of uniformity is thus attained, but as the predominating kinds of apples grown in different areas vary widely and other local influences, such as those of soil and climate, come into play, ciders tend to show marked distinctive local characters. French ciders generally are characterized by low acidity and a bittersweet flavour. Those of the English cider area north of Bristol are usually light and brisk as compared with the typical heavy subacid and bittersweet Somerset ciders and the less heavy but luscious Devon type of rather low acidity and astringency.

Classification and Composition of Cider Apples.—The varieties of cider apples are grouped into three classes, commonly termed sharp, sweet and bittersweet respectively. The classification is based upon chemical composition. The sharp class includes all varieties yielding the juices which normally contain not less than 0.45% of total acid, expressed as malic acid. The latter is the predominating acid, but various other organic acids are also present in very small amounts. Varieties of the sweet class are characterized by juices containing normally less than 0.45% of total acid, expressed as malic acid, and also less than 0.2% of tannin. Bittersweet apples contain normally in their juices acids in corresponding amount to those of the sweet class and are specially characterized by a relatively large quantity of tannin, which normally exceeds 0.2%.

According to this classification all table varieties of apples, dessert and culinary, fall within the sharp class and form a distinct section of it characterized by an extremely low tannin content, which rarely exceeds 0.1% in the juice. The typical sharp vintage apple contains generally a substantially larger amount. This high-acid, low-tannin character of the eating apple and other features usually associated with that type of composition render such fruit inferior for cider making, primarily because of the unbalanced flavour of the product. The number of varieties of cider apple occurring in the orchards of England and France is very large, certainly running into thousands. Many are of very low vintage quality and are being eliminated gradually in favour of those proved by research and experience to be worthy of more extended cultivation. A complete list of the latter is too lengthy for inclusion here, but the following selection is representative of high-grade English and French varieties.

English Varieties. *Sharp*—Backwell Red, Coleman's Seedling, Crimson King, Frederick, Kingston Black, Improved Foxwhelp, Langworthy, Stoke Red. *Sweet*—Court Royal, Sweet Alford, Sweet Coppin. *Bittersweet*—Ashton Brown Jersey, Belle Norman, Brown Snout, Bulmer's Norman, Dabinett, Dove, Ellis Bitter, Hangdown, Kingston Bitter, Red Jersey, Tremlett's Bitter, White Norman, Yarlington Mill.

FRENCH VARIETIES. Bédan, Binet Rouge, Doux Amer, Ecarlatine, Frequin Audièvre, Frequin Rouge, Michelin, Muscadet, Reine des Pommes, Reinette Obry, Tardive Forestier.

Cider Making.—Methods of cider making have undergone great changes since the early years of the 19th century. Then the fruit was crushed to a pulpy mass by heavy revolving stone rollers in a circular stone trough, similar to a mortar mill, and the pulp transferred by shovels to a cumbrous wooden press worked by hand, the time occupied in milling and pressing a single lot of fruit often extending to more than 24 hours. The modern grater form of mill now in general use is a steel cylindrical revolving drum in which are fixed toothed knives in such fashion that their edges project about $\frac{1}{16}$ in. above the surface of the drum. The latter is power driven at 2,000 r.p.m. The fruit falling upon it is grated almost instantaneously to a very fine pulp from which, because of its extreme state of disintegration, the juice can be expressed with great ease and speed. This pulp, technically termed pomace, is delivered from the mill direct onto the bed of the press, where it is built up into a "cheese," consisting of a series of layers, each wrapped in an open-meshed cloth or net of cotton or other strong fibre and separated from its neighbours by slatted wooden racks to facilitate the drainage of the juice. Power-driven hydraulic presses have now largely superseded the old screw type. Later types of mill, such as the hammer, are, moreover, considered in some respects to represent an advance on the grater. With machinery of this type the whole series of operations can be completed within 20 minutes after the delivery of the fruit to the mill. With fruit in good condition, a yield of juice varying from 75% to 80% of the weight of the fruit can be obtained.

Juice extracted by this method is comparatively clear and free from fragments of pulp and can therefore be placed directly into fermenting vats or casks without any intervening treatment being required to remove the suspended solid matter. The operation of keeving, formerly an important stage in the clearing of the juice, is thus no longer necessary and the risk of taint from acetic fermentation greatly reduced.

In some factories a diffusion process, analogous to that used in the extraction of sugar from sugar beet, is substituted for that of direct expression of the juice by pressure.

Subsequent treatment is determined by the type of cider to be produced. If a sweet cider is required, the fermenting juice must be filtered at a comparatively early stage to make it possible to retain the desired percentage of unfermented sugar. If a dry cider is wanted, fermentation is allowed to proceed till the whole or the greater part of the sugar is converted into alcohol. Filtration is then required for the purpose of clarifying the liquor rather than for checking fermentation. Various types of filters are in use. They differ in constructional details rather than in principle, which consists of the forcing under pressure of the turbid liquor through a thick layer of paper pulp or other suitable fibrous material. In many cases a single filtration suffices to clear the cider to a brilliant condition; occasionally for sweet ciders a second filtration is necessary to prevent further fermentation. Many makers use a centrifuge beforehand to facilitate filtration. After filtration the cider is fit for consumption at any time, though age, within limits, brings improvement in flavour. Made by the process here outlined, cider generally requires filtration within three months of the time of milling and is in its best condition for consumption during the summer following making. Specialized forms of treatment are sometimes practised for the production of a more fully matured article, which may require two or three years to reach prime condition.

While there is still a wide demand for draught cider, bottled cider has grown greatly in popularity. The latter is usually conditioned by carbonation, although natural conditioning by the champagne process is utilized for ciders of the highest quality.

Cider Disorders and Preservatives.—Attempts have been made to eliminate the risks of various bacterial disorders by pasteurization of the freshly expressed juice and subsequent fermentation by added pure cultures of selected kinds of yeasts; and some measure of success has been achieved. Most makers, however, still adhere to the older method of natural fermentation resulting from the wild yeasts naturally present on the surface of the apples and rely on strict attention to cleanliness at all stages of production to minimize the risks of disorders. The practice of washing the fruit in running water prior to milling is being increasingly adopted to ensure the maximum of cleanliness.

The chief disorders to which cider is subject are acetification, ropiness, lactic fermentation and "sickness," each caused by specific microorganisms, and discoloration, attributable generally to contamination with iron. To check fermentation and prevent the development of bacterial disorders preservatives such as salicylic acid were formerly largely used. Under the regulations relating to the use of preservatives in foods and drinks which came into force in Great Britain in 1927 no preservative other than sulphur dioxide is permissible for cider. The maximum allowed is 14 gr. of free and combined sulphur dioxide per gallon.

General.—The wholesome properties of pure cider are widely recognized. In affections of a gouty or rheumatic nature positive benefit frequently results and regular cider drinkers are rarely troubled by stone, gravel and similar disorders. The malic acid of cider is regarded as a powerful diuretic which stimulates the kidneys and prevents accumulation of uric acid within the system.

The improved position of the cider industry and the marked developments in technique have been greatly assisted by the researches and educational work on the subject conducted in France at the Station Pomologique at Caen, in Germany and in Switzerland at the research stations of Geisenheim-am-Rhein and of Wädenswil respectively, and in England at the National Fruit and Cider institute established at Long Ashton, near Bristol, and now associated with the University of Bristol.

BIBLIOGRAPHY.—National Fruit and Cider Institute, Long Ashton, *Reports, 1903–12* (Bath, 1905–13), continued as *The Annual Report of the Agricultural and Horticultural Research Station of the University of Bristol* (Bath, 1914–); G. Warcollier, "Pomologie et cidrerie" in G. Wery, *Encyclopédie Agricole* (Paris, 1920), *The Principles and Practice of Cider-Making,* trans. by V. L. S. Charley (London, 1949); Ministry of Agriculture and Fisheries, *Bulletin No. 104: Cider Apple Production* (H.M.S.O., London, 1953). (B. T. P. B.)

UNITED STATES

There is confusion in the United States about the proper terminology for unfermented and fermented juices of the apple. In contrast with European practice cider in the U.S. refers to unfermented juice of the apple. Unfermented apple juice is commonly called cider or fresh cider in contrast with the fermented product, hard cider. The processing industry, however, usually refers to unfermented juice containing less than 0.5% alcohol, by volume, as apple juice, regardless of its method of preservation.

Ordinarily, apple juice is made from second-grade or cull fruit. The apples must be free from decay and worms and must be properly ripened. To obtain an apple juice of high flavour it is important to blend several varieties of apples together to get the proper balance between aroma, acids, sugars and astringent components of the fruit. For example, a typically good blend for apple juice would be 50% Baldwin, 25% Northern Spy, 12½% Cortland and 12½% Russet apples.

Apples to be made into juice must be inspected so that decayed and seriously damaged fruits can be graded out. The fruit is thoroughly washed in water. When spray residues are a problem the apples must be washed in a hot acid or alkaline wash and rinsed with water to reduce the residues below the legal tolerances.

The apples are ground up in grater mills or hammer mills so that pressing can be facilitated. If a juice with the natural colour and flavour is desired a solution of ascorbic acid (vitamin C) is sprayed on the milled pomace before pressing. More commonly, normal oxidation is allowed to take place so that the juice has an amber colour.

The ground pomace is then pressed out in rack-and-cloth types of presses. The ground pulp is placed in layers about two to three inches deep within cloths. These enclosures of pulp, called "cheeses," are built up one on top of the other and separated by wooden racks. A hydraulic press then expresses the juice out of the pomace or pulp. Usually only a single pressing is made but occasionally the pomace is broken up and pressed again under a higher pressure press. The average yield of juice from apples is about 150 gal. of juice per ton of fruit from the first pressing and 20 gal. per ton from the second pressing. The pomace is ordinarily dried for later processing for pectin extraction.

A considerable amount of apple juice is consumed in the cloudy state in which it comes from the presses. The juice in any case is usually allowed to stand in settling tanks for a short time or is screened to remove the large cell masses. There has been a strong trend toward more clarification than is possible with a simple sedimentation process or screening in order to get a clear product.

Clarification accomplishes a breaking up of the colloidal system of the juice. One of the most widely used systems is the addition of pectin-decomposing enzymes. The enzyme preparation is mixed with the juice and is allowed to stand for several hours or more before the clarified juice is siphoned off. Apple juice is also clarified by using precipitating agents such as gelatin in combination with tannin. The colloidal material may also be removed by mixing the juice with fuller's earth or bentonite clay. Flash heating the juice to 180° F. for about 20 seconds followed by rapid cooling has been used as a means of clarification.

To get complete removal of suspended material from clarified apple juice it is necessary to filter or centrifuge after clarification. Filtration is not always done, however. When clarification is fairly complete, passing the juice through a porous filter composed of diatomaceous earth will give a brilliantly clear juice. If unclarified juice is to be filtered it must be passed through successively retentive filters. High-speed centrifuging may be used prior to filtration on unclarified juice to prevent clogging of the filters. Filtration is carried out in a plate-and-frame type of filter under pressure. After filtration the apple juice may or may not be fortified with ascorbic acid (vitamin C) to make it comparable to citrus juices in nutritional value.

Practically all of the apple juice is preserved by flash pasteurization. Microorganisms are killed by pasteurizing the juice at 170° to 200° F. for one to three minutes. The juice is packaged in sterile cans or bottles. For highest quality juice, freezing is the best method of preservation. The juice is frozen at 0° to −40° F. and stored at 0° F. in tin containers allowing 10% room for expansion in the container during freezing. Some juice is preserved by using chemicals such as sodium benzoate (0.1% dissolved in a small amount of water). Such juice can be kept for a month at room temperature but some flavour is usually imparted by such chemicals. Apple juice is sometimes sterilized by special filters which actually remove yeasts and other microorganisms that cause spoilage. Only highly clarified juices can be sterilized by filtration and sterile conditions must prevail in the packaging rooms.

Apple juice concentrate has the advantage over many other forms of apple juice in that there is a more natural flavour and there are considerable savings in container, shipping and storage costs. Low-temperature evaporation of the water out of the juice is accomplished by using vacuum and boiling off the water at less than 150° F. In another process an apple essence is prepared by concentrating the volatile fractions of the apple juice up to 150 times that of the original juice. Apple juice can also be concentrated by freezing followed by centrifuging.

BIBLIOGRAPHY.—R. M. Smock and A. M. Neubert, *Apples and Apple Products* (New York, 1950); D. K. Tressler and M. A. Joslyn, *The Chemistry and Technology of Fruit and Vegetable Juice Production* (New York, 1954).

(R. M. Sk.)

CIENFUEGOS (originally FERNANDINA DE JAGUA), third largest commercial city of Cuba, on the southern coast, 192 mi. by rail S.E. of Havana in the province of Las Villas (formerly named Santa Clara province). Population of the *municipio* (1943 census), 94,810, 52,910 of whom live in Cienfuegos. Area of *municipio*, 598 sq.mi.

The city, located on a broad, level peninsula opposite the narrow entrance of the magnificent Bay of Jagua or Cienfuegos, is noted for its wide, straight streets, beautiful parks, attractive buildings and scenic surroundings. It is served by the United Railways of Havana and is connected by a branch road with the Central highway of Cuba. Domestic and foreign air lines use its airfield.

The fertile country which surrounds Cienfuegos produces henequen, coffee, rice, tobacco, honey, fruit (especially mangoes and avocados), cattle and large quantities of sugar. Large sugar *centrales* (estates) are located within short distances of the city, such as the *central* Soledad, where Harvard university long maintained botanical gardens for research in tropical agriculture; but the major centres of sugar cultivation are located elsewhere.

The site of Cienfuegos was visited by Columbus in 1494, but the Bay of Jagua and its environs attracted no permanent settlement until 1738, in which year a small fortress (converted into the fort of Nuestra Señora de los Angeles de Xagua in 1745) was erected at the entrance of the port. In 1817 a French colonel from Louisiana (Luis d'Clouet) presented to the captain general of Cuba (Don José Cienfuegos) a project for colonizing the Bay of Jagua. In the same year the foundation of the colony of Fernandina de Jagua was authorized by royal order. D'Clouet, accompanied by 46 colonists, arrived from Bordeaux, Fr., on April 8, 1819; in 1820, 282 more colonists arrived. A poll in 1824 revealed that there were 1,238 inhabitants in the settlement. After a storm had destroyed the village in 1825 it was rebuilt and named Cienfuegos in honour of the man who had participated so actively in its founding.

(R. W. Rd.; X.)

CIEZA, a town of southeastern Spain, in the province of Murcia, on the Madrid-Cartagena railway, and junction for a line to Valencia. Pop. (1950) 23,328 (mun.). Cieza stands on the right bank of the Segura river, in a narrow bend of the valley which is enclosed on the north by mountains, providing good building stone and low timber, and on the south broadens into a fertile plain, producing grain, wine, olives, raisins, esparto, oranges and other fruits. The district greatly developed with improved communications, and Cieza became a flourishing town with flour, paper, sawmilling industries and brandy distilleries.

CIEZA DE LÉON, PEDRO DE (*c.* 1519–1560), Spanish soldier and historian, was born at Seville. He sailed for the new world, possibly in Heredia's expedition of 1532, more probably with Duran in 1534, reaching Cartagena in November. In 1535 he went with Heredia's brother Alonzo to Darien, and in 1538 with Vadillo on an appalling journey up the valley of the Cauca; Vadillo was eventually deserted by his men, and Cieza de León later joined Jorge de Robledo, who consolidated the discoveries in the Cauca valley, and on his death served under Belalcazar, governor of Popayan, who had beheaded Robledo. It was in 1541, in the Cauca valley, that he started his diary. In 1547 the troops from Popayan marched to join President Gasca against Pizarro, a long journey, the details of which he carefully noted. In 1549 he went to look at the mines of Porco and Potosí, and then to Cuzco to confer with a surviving descendant of the Incas; in 1550 he left for Spain. The first part of his *Crónica de Perú* was published at Seville in 1553.

The scheme of his *Crónica de Perú* was as follows: part i, geography; part ii, early history; part iii (lost), conquest; and part iv (of which books 1, 2 and 3 have been found), civil wars. The first part is a minute topographical review, founded on his diary, with an account of the customs and religion of the people as he found them, given with unusual accuracy of observation and without concealing his respect for the Inca civilization. Part ii, referred to inaccurately by Prescott as *Sarmiento,* gives the history of Peru under the Incas. The manuscript was preserved in the Escorial library and published in 1880.

C.I.F., in commerce, a short form of "cost, insurance, freight." Thus, if an article is quoted C.I.F. London it means that the quotation is inclusive of (1) the price of the article, (2) the cost of insurance to London and (3) the cost of freight to London. In the official trade returns of the United Kingdom the import values are usually recorded by the customs statistical department at C.I.F. values.

CIGAR. The word cigar is derived from the Spanish *cigarro,* which in turn probably was derived from Mayan *sik'ar,* found commonly by early explorers in Cuba and Yucatan. Indians rolled single leaves or wrapped tobacco in its own leaf or in leaves of other plants and understood curing and fermentation of the leaf to improve taste. The industry was carried by the Spaniards to Haiti about 1530 and later to Europe and North America. Early production in the colonies consisted mostly of "Spanish" cigars, the leaf being obtained in the West Indies trade. Stogies were made as early as 1785 by the Pennsylvania Dutch in York county and were carried west by drivers of Conestoga wagons, from which the name was derived. Connecticut in 1810 established factories making Long Nines and Windsor Particulars, which were peddled by farmers' wives. Imports of cigars from New Orleans in 1800, as well as from Cuba, were part of the same trade pattern. Sizes and shapes of cigars were irregular, often tied in bunches which were sold for a few pennies, or bundled in lots of 100 and packed in barrels and chests.

Composition.—Three components—filler, binder and wrapper—are found in cigars. Filler tobacco is grown in Cuba, Puerto Rico, Pennsylvania and Ohio. Binders are produced in Connecticut, Massachusetts and Wisconsin; wrappers in Connecticut, Florida, Cuba and Indonesia. Havana cigars are made entirely from Cuban tobacco.

Processing.—The cured leaf as received from the farms needs to be sweated, or fermented, before use in the cigar, to reduce the content of harsh and bitter compounds and develop the mild and aromatic properties. Wrapper leaves, tied in hands of 40–50 leaves, are placed in orderly piles, or bulks, of several thousand pounds in a regulated atmosphere. Heat is generated by the tobacco, whereupon the bulk is taken apart and rebuilt, often five or six times. Two subsequent fermentations, the first in wooden cases, the second in bales, precede its use in cigars. Binders are usually packed in wooden cases, placed in a sweat room near 100° F. for several weeks, stored under cooler conditions for nearly a year and sometimes after being remoistened briefly exposed to high temperature and humidity. Fillers, likewise packed in wooden cases, undergo a slow fermentation for one to several years, then are moistened, repacked and submitted to a moist hot atmosphere (about 110° F. with 60% relative humidity). This resweat is interrupted periodically by unpacking and airing the leaves, an operation which may be repeated only once or twice or as many as 10 or 12 times. The severity of fermentation is greatest for fillers, least for wrappers.

How Cigars Are Made.—Whereas early cigar making was entirely by hand, machines now perform most of the steps. In hand work, the midribs, or stems, are removed from the moistened leaves, the half leaves being laid in pads or strips. Strips of filler are bunched to the necessary size and shape and cut evenly on a block with a half-round knife. The binder is cut in a half-moon shape, within which the filler is evenly and smoothly rolled. The wrapper is usually cut narrower than the binder, care being taken to wrap the cigar spirally so that the diagonal veins in the leaf lie lengthwise along the cigar. Opposite diagonal wrapping of binder and wrapper is practised for the right-hand and left-hand halves of the leaves. Finally, for sealing the mouth end or head of the wrapper tragacanth, a product of Iran, is customarily used as an adhesive.

Long hardwood moulds, originally made in Osnabrück, Ger., in 1870, are used in the manufacture of moulded or shaped cigars. This semihand-making or German method is used in the smaller factories for lower-priced cigars. Each matrix holds 20 bunches of hand prepared filler and binder. In team work, trios of cigarmakers are employed, two to wrap and one to break and bind the bunches and load the moulds, each team making approximately 1,000 cigars a day.

Cigar machines were first used in 1919 at Newark, N.J. Later improvements enabled machines to make up to 13 cigars a minute, an approximate rate of 600 to 700 an hour being common. One person feeds the strip filler, the second feeds the binder mechanism, the third feeds the wrapper and the fourth inspects the finished product, which is automatically cut, rolled and pasted. Nearly any size or shape can be produced. Long filler cigars (filler strips the length of the cigar), which command slightly higher prices, scrap filler and ribbon filler are all machine made.

Banding and Packing.—Bands are placed on the cigar or printed on the protective covering (usually cellophane) which preserves the natural humistatic condition of the cigar; this is accomplished by a machine at the rate of 30,000 cigars daily, with band, cellophane, tin foil or any combination of similar wrapping. One person operates the machine.

Boxes of wood, metal, paper and glass are used to package the cigars. Selectors and packers, working under proper lighting, arrange the cigars according to colour and perfection of wrappers. The top row of each box of flat four-row packs is shaded almost imperceptibly to please the eye. Colours commonly recognized are claro (light yellow), colorado claro (light red or brown), colorado (brown), colorado maduro (dark brown), maduro (deep brown), oscuro (almost black). During the McKinley era dark cigars were generally preferred, and experts still believe them to be mildest and tastiest, because the so-called lighter, and particularly the greenish, colours may be bitter. Modern opinion favours the claro shades. Actually, the thin elastic sheen of the wrapper, especially of shade-grown Connecticut, has little influence on smoking quality. As a rule, wrappers have a neutral taste and are selected more for beauty and service than for smoking value. The smoker looks for a pleasant aroma, delicate blend, even burn and white ash.

Terms descriptive of shape of cigars still follow the Spanish nomenclature, as do many brand names. These include straight shapes, such as Londres or London, blunt on the tuck or lighting end; perfecto, pointed at both ends; concha, small perfecto; puritano, adaptation of the perfecto; panatela, long and thin; breva, short and stubby; corona, thick and straight; imperiale, long perfecto; and numerous modifications.

Factory Equipment.—Technological advances in cigar factories cover a wide range. Hand stemming had largely disappeared by mid-20th century. Threshed, cut and shredded filler was prepared to size by rapid machine cutters. Equipment for drying and moistening the leaf, exact control of fermentation processes, and mechanical conveyors and hoists improved the ease of handling and increased the uniformity of the product. Fluorescent lighting with tubes of differing colour permit accurate and constant evaluation of leaf colours. Both from the viewpoint of the product and the workers, it is desirable to keep the air at a proper temperature and moisture content. Air-conditioning equipment and electrostatic precipitrons combine to provide the desired conditions. Precautions for the health and safety of the employees are numerous and effective. Delicate control equipment of laboratory precision is commonly used. Machines are also used for pasting revenue stamps and labels on every box, for attaching special wrappers (commonly used for the Christmas trade), as well as for packaging for shipment.

Research.—Chemical research made great strides, beginning in 1930 in the biochemistry laboratory of the Connecticut Agricultural Experiment station under H. B. Vickery. Specialized analytical methods showed that during curing, rapid starvation of leaf cells was succeeded by extensive breakdown of pigments, leaf proteins and carbohydrates. Basic knowledge thus gained was applied to widely separated plant phenomena. R. F. Dawson made use of tomatoes grown on tobacco roots and the opposite combination (technically known as reciprocal grafts). The leaves and fruit of tomatoes grown on tobacco roots contained nicotine; tobacco plants grown on tomato roots contained no nicotine. By this classic method, he showed that tobacco roots made nicotine and the leaves stored it. Later the laboratory of the General Cigar company under W. G. Frankenburg studied the changes occurring in tobacco during fermentation. Further breakdown of some components affected by curing occurred, but new chemical groups related to colour and aroma were also involved. The relation of low nicotine content to high smoking quality was shown, followed by proof of the breakdown of nicotine into a wide variety of products.

Production.—In the United States, cigar production first passed the 1,000,000,000 mark in 1870; successive increases of 1,000,000,000 occurred in 1879, 1882, 1890, 1900 and 1902. The 7,000,000,000 mark was reached in 1906, but it was not until 1920 that the all-time high of 8,266,770,593 occurred. The decline which became evident in 1921 reached its full impetus in the 1930s, falling below 5,000,000,000. After 1940 a moderate but quite steady increase occurred with consumption in the 1950s approximately 6,000,000,000. (O. E. S.)

Great Britain and Europe.—Though the connoisseur favours Havana- or Jamaican-made cigars as the ideal smoke, there are, nevertheless, many discriminating cigar smokers who are satisfied with the best-quality British-made cigars, which, so far as flavour and aroma are concerned, are little below the imported article and have the advantage of lower price. They are, in fact, manufactured of all-Havana leaf of good quality and are hand-made, their lower price being the result of the difference in customs duty on imported manufactured cigars and the unmanufactured leaf imported by the British manufacturers. Cheaper domestic cigars are made of Sumatra, Borneo, Java, Brazilian and Jamaican leaf, with or without Havana fillers or wrappers according to price. No detailed statistics were made available of sales or production of domestic cigars, but they were considerably lower after than they were before World War II. That the reason for this was high prices was borne out by the enormous increase in the sales of miniature cigars, or whiffs, which suggested that the taste for the cigar-type of smoke was still prevailing and that only the high price held the public back. Whiffs are machine-made; some are all-Havana, others part-Havana. Most of the big manufacturers were breaking sales records each year in the early 1950s.

On the continent of Europe the domestic cigar is a good deal cheaper than in Great Britain because of the lower import duties on leaf tobacco. The Dutch are big cigar manufacturers and use mostly East Indian and Brazilian leaf, which were so cheap that they could export to Great Britain, pay the manufacturers' import rate of duty and still sell at less than many British brands. They were gaining in popularity in Britain in the mid-1950s, not only because of price but also because of their mildness. Germany also is a cigar-smoking nation and has a big domestic production, using mostly East Indian and some domestic-grown leaf. In the mid-1950s German manufacture barely met home consumption. The basis of most continental cigar brands is East Indian, Brazilian and some Havana leaf. (D. Sg.)

Bibliography.—R. F. Dawson, "Basic Research in Tobacco Chemistry," *J. Chem. Ed.*, 30:404–406 (1953), "Chemistry and Biochemistry of Green Tobacco," *Ind. Eng. Chem.*, 44:266–270 (1952); W. G. Frankenburg, "Chemical Changes in the Harvested Tobacco Leaf," *Adv. Enzym.*, 6:309–387 (1946); H. B. Vickery and A. N. Meiss, "Chemical Investigations of the Tobacco Plant," *Conn. Agr. Exp. Sta. Bull. 569* (1953). (O. E. S.)

CIGARETTE. A cigarette is literally a little cigar—finely cut tobacco rolled in paper. The word is undoubtedly from the Spanish *cigarito*, which was introduced to Europe after 1518, when Spaniards found Aztecs wrapping tobacco in cornhusks. The use of cigarettes spread to all parts of Europe, including Turkey and Russia. A great popularity in England followed the Crimean War, but in the United States cigarettes were virtually unknown before 1860.

The U.S. Cigarette Industry.—Early manufacture in the United States was entirely by hand, either in factories or by the smoker (the "roll-your-own" method). The paper was often any type available, but later it was imported from France, where linen was reworked for this purpose. Equipment in early factories was extremely simple. Essentially the process consisted of hand-rolling on a table followed by pasting and hand-packaging. In 1883 girls working in these factories earned a maximum of $9 for rolling 15,000 to 18,000 cigarettes per week. The tobacco was reduced to granules or flakes by hand-crushing or beating before use.

The first shredding or cutting machine was patented in 1860 by W. H. Pease, but was not widely used for many years. A crude cigarette-manufacturing machine was exhibited at the Philadelphia Centennial exposition in 1876. In 1880 James A. Bonsack patented a cigarette machine with several basic features. The prepared tobacco was fed onto a continuous strip of paper which entered a forming tube. In the tube the paper formed a cylinder, passing a pasting brush before being closed. A rotary cutting knife was activated by differential gears to permit intermittent action, and cut the cigarette into the proper length. In 1884 a printing attachment was added. Each of these crude machines did the work of about 50 hand-rollers, approaching 100,000 cigarettes per day, and reduced the cost of manufacture from 80 to 30 cents per 1,000. Production increased from 500,000,000 cigarettes in 1880 to 1,000,000,000 in 1885 and 4,000,000,000 in 1895.

Consumer preference for tobacco products thereafter shifted enormously. Plug or chewing tobacco and snuff were dominant in 1850, while pipe smoking reached its peak in the next half century. Cigars continued in unchallenged favour until 1920, when their consumption was equalled by cigarettes, and thereafter cigarettes reached half of total tobacco consumption by 1938 and three-fourths by 1950.

The composition of the American cigarette changed several times. Turkish cigarettes, composed wholly of tobacco imported from the orient, were favoured first, but their popularity was soon shared by Virginia types, using tobacco from the Carolinas and Virginia. (The preference for Virginia cigarettes still applied in Great Britain and the commonwealth countries in the 1950s.) With the outbreak of World War I the supply of oriental tobacco to the United States was virtually cut off, and the supply of flue-cured became inadequate. The American blend, which then appeared, contained Burley and Maryland tobaccos in addition to flue-cured and Turkish, and continued thereafter with no marked changes.

Mechanization entered the cigarette industry to a marked degree in the first half of the 20th century. Tobacco from the farm may have the midribs removed by a stemming machine, so-called green stemming. After drying, packing in hogsheads and aging up to three years, the tobacco is moistened and stemmed if this was not previously done. With certain classes of tobacco a thresher can be used for the same purpose. Blowers are used to remove dust and foreign matter.

A series of treatments alternately using moist and dry heat is used for the domestic types. Blending of all types in the proper proportions is done in revolving drums. This is followed by a storage known as bulking to ensure equal distribution of moisture. Cutting is done by machines equipped with self-sharpening rotary blades which shred the tobacco into strips only a few hundredths of an inch wide. After several days' storage, the blended mixture is made into cigarettes.

In general, four classes of tobacco are used in American blend cigarettes. Flue-cured or bright, the largest component, is grown in Virginia, North Carolina, South Carolina, Georgia and Florida. A high sugar and low nicotine content is desirable in bright tobacco.

Burley, an air-cured class, second in importance, is grown in Kentucky, Tennessee, Ohio, Indiana, Missouri, Virginia, West Virginia, North Carolina and limited areas in other states. In the cigarette, Burley counteracts the acid smoke of bright to produce a neutral reaction.

Maryland, also an air-cured type, has limited use to improve burning properties and aid aroma.

Turkish tobacco, imported into the U.S. mainly from Turkey and Greece, but also from Syria, Yugoslavia and Italy, is classed as aromatic tobacco but is also desirable for low nicotine content and mild taste. A modest quantity of aromatic tobacco is grown in the mountainous parts of North Carolina.

Standard machines produce 1,200 cigarettes a minute. Packaging machines, working twice as fast, wrap 20 cigarettes at a time in paper-backed foil, paper label and cellophane and affix the revenue stamps. Refinements in cigarette-making machinery resulted in notable increases in speed of operation. Uniformity was improved, for example, by microfeed controls, in which twin beams of nucleonic particles compare the density of the cigarette rod with a standard. The current thus generated and amplified finally regulates automatically the feed mechanism. Filter-tip attachments insert a double-length filter plug between two cigarettes, detach the tipping material and cut the assembly in two.

While packages of 20 cigarettes wrapped in paper and foil are the most common unit, sliding boxes of 20s, "flat 50s" and tins of 50 are available. Cartons of 10 packages are packed in cases of 50 cartons for shipment. All of the packing is done by automatic machines.

Dependence of the U.S. industry on France for cigarette paper was no longer necessary after development of a domestic paper industry in the early 1930s. Linen paper of the highest purity, made from flax straw, supplies the demand for writing, printing and cigarette papers. (O. E. S.)

Production of cigarettes in the U.S. increased rapidly during and after World War I, from about 18,000,000,000 in 1915 to 124,000,000,000 in 1930. A similar rise occurred during and after World War II, from about 190,000,000,000 in 1940 to more than 400,000,000,000 in the early 1950s. Thereafter consumption tended to drop, probably as the result of medical reports linking cigarette smoking with cancer of the lungs, and also of the switch of many smokers to king-size (longer) cigarettes.

Great Britain.—In Great Britain the tobacco used in cigarettes is mostly bright flue-cured, better known as Virginia. The leaf first must be moistened to make it pliable for stemming (*i.e.*, removing the stalk or midrib). The next process is to cut the leaf into fine shreds. The cut tobacco is then conditioned, usually in large rotary drums where it is first subjected to heat to remove excess moisture and then cooled. Handmade cigarettes are relatively rare, but several "roll-your-own" machines which any person can use to make a cigarette have been developed.

In factory production cigarette-making machines produce from 1,000 to 1,600 cigarettes per minute. The cigarette paper is put up in bobbins of definite width and is fed into a narrow trough at the side of the machine. The name of the brand is imprinted on the paper at regular intervals so that it will appear on each finished cigarette. The shredded cuts of tobacco fall upon the paper, which moves into a funnel-shaped tube, passing a device which gums the edges, the paper then being automatically folded over the tobacco. The end of the cigarette moves under a knife which cuts it into sections of the desired length.

In Great Britain the type of package used is known as a slide and shell package, usually containing 10 or 20 cigarettes. The cigarettes are automatically packed by modern machinery, by which they are counted, wrapped in foil and placed in a cardboard slide. The slide is then inserted into a shell of cardboard. The machines are also capable of placing an insert in the package if necessary. The packages of many of the more popular cigarettes in Great Britain are wrapped in moistureproof cellophane in order to protect them from the varied conditions of humidity prevalent in the British Isles.

The cigarette business in Great Britain grew from year to year. In the 1950s approximately 195,000,000 lb. of tobacco were used annually in cigarettes for home consumption. Tobacco brought into Britain is taxed with heavy import duty, which is a great source of income to the British government. Virginia tobacco, grown in the United States, is predominantly used in cigarettes made in England; however, a great deal of tobacco (grown from seed imported from the United States) is shipped into England from various parts of the commonwealth and is blended in varying degrees with that imported from America. Turkish and Egyptian cigarettes were at one time popular in the British Isles, but in the 1950s accounted for only a very small business. Turkish tobacco, used widely in the United States, is imported mainly from Greece and Turkey. (X.)

Continental Europe.—Development of the cigarette industry in France, Belgium and other western European countries is quite comparable to that in the United States and Great Britain. The mechanization of the industry is aided by the use of different machines developed in several countries, notably Sweden and Switzerland. One of the cigarette factories in Switzerland uses a thermal pump, whereby water from very deep wells serves to cool the building in summer and to heat it in the winter. Average cigarette consumption in European countries usually ranges from one-third to two-thirds the U.S. usage. (O. E. S.)

CIGNANI, CARLO (1628–1719), Italian painter, was born at Bologna (May 15, 1628) and trained there chiefly under Francesco Albani. He faithfully continued the Bolognese Baroque tradition in his use of ample, generalized forms, fluently turning poses, deep colours and blended contrasts of light and shadow. In sentiment, also, his work is characteristic of this tradition. It was a tradition which derived its elements in the first place from Correggio, but Cignani was in addition influenced by Correggio directly and his masterpiece, the "Assumption of the Virgin" in the cupola of Forlì cathedral, is closely based on the former's cupola in Parma cathedral. He executed numerous altarpieces, mythological scenes and several fresco decorations (*e.g.*, in the ducal palace, Parma). There is a "Magdalene" by him in the Dulwich College picture gallery in London, Eng. Cignani died at Forlì on Sept. 6, 1719.

His son Felice Cignani (1660–1724) and nephew Paolo Cignani (1709–64) were also painters.

See T. Gerevich in Thieme-Becker, ***Künstlerlexikon***, vi, (Leipzig, 1912), p. 576 ff. (M. W. L. K.)

CIGOLI, Lodovico Cardi da (1559–1613), Italian painter, architect and poet, was born at Cigoli, Tuscany, on Sept. 12, 1559; he worked both in Florence and in Rome, where he died, June 8, 1613. Trained under Alessandro Allori and Santi di Tito, he reflected the many crosscurrents in Italian art between the decline of Michelangelesque Mannerism and the beginnings of the Baroque. Thus there are few consistent characteristics in his earlier work beyond some north Italian strength of colour and lighting. He was an innovator in sentiment rather than in style and, like Federico Baroccio, foreshadowed Baroque emotions. From 1595 onward he began to reflect the new realistic tendencies. These qualities are well illustrated in his "Ecce Homo" (*c.* 1607; Pitti palace, Florence). His architecture (*e.g.*, the court of the Palazzo Nonfinito, Florence, 1604) shows the elements of Palladian classicism, which he first learned from Bernardo Buontalenti.

See G. Battelli, *Lodovico Cardi detto il Cigoli* (Florence, 1922). (M. W. L. K.)

CILIA, in biology, the threadlike processes by the vibration of which many lowly organisms move through water. They are also found on certain cells of both lower and higher organisms to create a current (*e.g.*, on the gill of oysters and the lining of the bronchioles of the lungs in man). The singular is cilium.

CILIATA, one of the divisions of Infusoria characterized by the permanent possession of cilia or organs derived from these (membranelles, etc.), and all parasitic. They are the most highly differentiated Protozoa (*q.v.*).

CILICIA, a district of Asia Minor, extending along the south coast between Pamphylia and Syria. Its northern limit was the crest of Mt. Taurus. It was divided into Cilicia Trachea and Cilicia Pedias.

Cilicia Trachea is a rugged mountain district formed by the spurs of Taurus, which often terminate in rocky headlands with small sheltered harbours—a feature which, in classical times, made the coast a resort of pirates and, in the middle ages, led to its occupation by Genoese and Venetian traders. The district is watered by the Geuk Su (Calycadnus) and is covered to a large extent by forests, which supply timber to Egypt and Syria. There were several towns but no large trade centres.

Cilicia Pedias included the rugged spurs of Taurus and a large plain of rich stoneless loam. Its eastern half is studded with isolated rocky crags, which are crowned with the ruins of ancient strongholds and broken by the low hills that border the plain of Issus. The plain is watered by the Cydnus (Tarsus Chai), the Sarus (Sihun) and the Pyramus (Jihun) and is extremely productive. Through it ran the great highway, between the east and the west, on which stood Tarsus on the Cydnus, Adana on the Sarus, and Mopsuestia (Missis) on the Pyramus. The great highway from the west, on its long rough descent from the Anatolian plateau to Tarsus, ran through a narrow pass between walls of rock called the Cilician Gate (Ghulek Boghaz). After crossing the low hills east of the Pyramus it passed through a masonry (Cilician) gate, Demir Kapu, and entered the plain of Issus. From that plain one road ran southward to Alexandretta and thence crossed Mt. Amanus by the Syrian Gate, to Antioch and Syria; and another ran northward and crossed Mt. Amanus by the Amanian Gate, to North Syria and the Euphrates. By the last pass, which was apparently unknown to Alexander, Darius crossed the mountains prior to the battle of Issus. Both passes are short and easy, and connect Cilicia Pedias with Syria rather than with Asia Minor. In Roman times Cilicia exported the goat's-hair cloth, *cilicium*, of which tents were made.

Under the Persian empire Cilicia was apparently governed by

tributary native kings, who bore a name or title graecized as Syennesis; but it was officially included in the fourth satrapy by Darius. Xenophon found a queen in power, and no opposition was offered to the march of Cyrus. Alexander found the gates open when he came down from the plateau in 333 B.C., and it may be inferred that the great pass was not under direct Persian control. After Alexander's death it fell to the Seleucids, who, however, never held effectually more than the eastern half. Cilicia Trachea became the haunt of pirates, who were subdued by Pompey. Cilicia Pedias became Roman territory in 103 B.C., and the whole was organized by Pompey (64 B.C.) into a province, of which at one time Cicero was governor. It was reorganized by Caesar (47 B.C.), and about 27 B.C. became part of the province Syria-Cilicia-Phoenice. Under Diocletian (*c.* A.D. 297), Cilicia, with the Syrian and Egyptian provinces, formed the Diocesis Orientis. In the 7th century it was invaded by the Arabs, who held the country until it was reoccupied by Nicephorus II in 965.

The Seljuk invasion of Armenia was followed by an exodus of Armenians southwards, and in 1080 there was founded in the Cilician Taurus a small principality, which gradually expanded into the kingdom of Lesser Armenia. This Christian kingdom—situated in the midst of Muslim states, hostile to the Byzantines, giving valuable support to the crusaders, and trading with the great commercial cities of Italy—had a stormy existence of about 300 years. When Levond V died (1342), John of Lusignan was crowned king as Gosdantin IV; but he alienated the Armenians by attempting to make them conform to the Roman Church, and at last the kingdom, a prey to internal dissensions, succumbed (1375) to the attacks of the Egyptians. Cilicia Trachea was occupied by the Osmanlis in the 15th century, but Cilicia Pedias was only added to the empire in 1515.

From 1833 to 1840 Cilicia formed part of the territories administered by Mohammed Ali of Cairo, who was compelled to evacuate it by the allied powers. By the treaty of Sèvres (*see* TURKEY) part of Cilicia was granted to France, but on Oct. 20, 1921, after unsuccessful conflicts with the Nationalist troops, the French withdrew all claim to this area.

BIBLIOGRAPHY.—Besides the general authorities for Asia Minor, see *Cambridge Ancient History,* vol. iii. (with useful bibliography); J. R. S. Sterrett, *Wolfe Expedition* (1888); G. L. Schlumberger, *Un Empereur byzantin* (1890); D. G. Hogarth and J. A. R. Munro, *Mod. and Anc. Roads in E. Asia Minor* (R.G.S. Supp. Papers, iii.) (1893); R. Heberdey and A. Wilhelm, *Reisen in Kilikien* (1896); D. G. Hogarth, *A Wandering Scholar* (1896). *See* also authorities under ARMENIA and MOHAMMED ALI.

CILLI, ULRICH, COUNT OF (1406–1456), son of Frederick II, count of Cilli, and Elizabeth Frangepan. About 1432 he married Catherine, daughter of George Brankovich, despot of Serbia.

His influence in the troubled affairs of Hungary and the empire, of which he was made a prince by the emperor Sigismund (1436) led to feuds with the Habsburgs, the overlords of Cilli. Finally he made an alliance with the Habsburg king Albert II, and after his death (1439) Alrich took up the cause of his widow, Elizabeth, and presided at the coronation of her infant son Ladislaus V. Posthumus (1440). A feud with the Hunyadis followed, embittered by John Hunyadi's attack on George Brankovich of Serbia (1444) on his refusal to recognize Ulrich's claim to Bosnia on the death of Stephen Tvrtko (1443). In 1446 Hunyadi, then governor of Hungary, harried the Cilli territories in Croatia-Slavonia; but his power was broken at Kosovo (1448), and Count Ulrich was able to lead a successful crusade, nominally in the Habsburg interest, into Hungary (1450). In 1452 he forced the emperor Frederick III to hand over the boy king Ladislaus V to his keeping, and became thus virtual ruler of Hungary, of which he was named lieutenant by Ladislaus in 1456. The Hunyadis now conspired to destroy him. On Nov. 8, in spite of warnings, he entered Belgrade with the king; the next day he was attacked by Laszlo Hunyadi and his friends, and put to death. With him died the male line of the counts of Cilli.

CILLI (Slovene *Celje*), a town of Slovenia, Yugoslavia, on a branch of the Zagreb-Fiume railway, lies picturesquely with remains of walls and towers on the river Sann, on an important road north to Marburg (Maribor) and south to Ljubljana. Pop. (1931) 7,602. The city was annexed by Germany in 1941. Probably a Celtic settlement, the Romans took it (15 B.C.) and Claudius made it a Roman municipium (A.D. 50), naming it Claudia Celeja. It prospered greatly, and its temple of Mars was widely famed. Its museum contains many Roman remains, and the Roman sewerage system was rediscovered in the second half of the 19th century and is now in use. It was incorporated with Aquileia under Constantine, and was destroyed by Slavs at the end of the 6th century. The counts of Cilli, at one time in authority in Croatia, at another in Bosnia, had their castle, Ober Cilli, on the Schlossberg (1,320 ft.), southeast of the town. Its ruins, the Cilli throne and the family tomb remain. Under the Cilli (1350–1455) the town prospered; on their extinction it became subject to Austria. The fine church (14th century) has a beautiful chapel and is justly renowned. The so-called German church (Romanesque) belonged to the Minorite monastery (founded 1241, closed 1808). Antimony and zinc are mined near by, and enamelled iron utensils are made. Ten miles northwest are the baths and ruined castle of Neuhaus, after 1643 called Schlangenburg.

See E. Glautschnigg, *Cilli und Umgebung; Handbuch für Fremde* (Cilli, 1887).

CIMA, GIAMBATTISTA (CIMA DA CONEGLIANO, *c.* 1459–1517), Italian painter of the Venetian school, probably a pupil of Bartolomeo Montagna, and later influenced by Giovanni Bellini. He was born at Conegliano on the southern slopes of the Alps. His earliest dated picture is the altarpiece of 1489 in the Museo Civico of Vicenza. He was then 30 years old and his style was fully developed and altered very little during the course of his long life. In 1492 he settled in Venice. In 1493 he was commissioned to paint an altarpiece for the cathedral of Conegliano which is still in its original place. Most of his important works are in Venice in the churches of S. Giovanni in Bragora, S. Maria dell'Orto, the Carmine, and in the Academy; there are also pictures by him at Bologna, Modena and Parma and in many of the great galleries in Europe.

See V. Botteon, *Ricerche intorno alla vita e alle opere di G. Cima* (1893); R. Burckhardt, *Cima da Conegliano* (1905).

CIMABUE, name of a Florentine painter Cenni di Pepo active in the 13th and the beginning of the 14th century. Some Italian painters preceded Cimabue—particularly Guido of Siena and Giunta of Pisa; but though he worked on much the same principle as they, and to a like result, he was held up to admiration as the "Father of Italian Painting" by Florentine writers, inspired by local patriotism. There is no documentary evidence that a single picture attributed to Cimabue was painted by him.

His fame rested chiefly on a colossal "Madonna and Child with Angels," the largest altarpiece produced up to that date, which was painted in tempera for the chapel of the Rucellai in St. Maria Novella, Florence; but research proved this work to be by the Siennese Duccio.

Among paintings still extant attributed to Cimabue are the following:—In the Uffizi in Florence, a "Madonna and Child," with eight angels, and some prophets in niches—better than the Rucellai picture in composition and study of nature, but more archaic in type, and the colour now spoiled (this work was painted for the Badia of St. Trinita, Florence); in the National Gallery, London, a "Madonna and Child with Angels," which came from the Ugo Baldi collection, and had probably once been in the church of St. Croce, Florence; in the Louvre, a "Madonna and Child," with twenty-six medallions in the frame, originally in the church of St. Francesco, Pisa. In the lower church of the Basilica of St. Francesco at Assisi, Cimabue, succeeding Giunta da Pisa, is said to have adorned the south transept—painting a colossal "Virgin and Child between Four Angels," above the altar of the Conception, and a large figure of St. Francis. In the upper church, north transept, he has the "Saviour Enthroned and some Angels," and, on the central ceiling of the transept, the "Four Evangelists with Angels." It is, however, impossible to say whether Cimabue was at Assisi or not.

In the closing years of his life he was appointed capomaestro of the mosaics of the cathedral of Pisa, and was afterwards, hardly a year before his death, joined with Arnolfo di Cambio as architect for the Cathedral of Florence. In Pisa he executed a Majesty in the apse—"Christ in glory between the Virgin and John the Evangelist," a mosaic, now much damaged. This was probably the last work that he produced.

He was the master of Giotto, whom (is the tradition) he found a shepherd boy of ten, in the pastures of Vespignano, drawing with a coal on a slate the figure of a lamb. Cimabue took him to Florence, and instructed him in the art; and after Cimabue's death Giotto occupied a house which had belonged to his master in the Via del Cocomero. Another painter with whom Cimabue is said to have been intimate was Gaddo Gaddi.

Giovanni Cimabue was buried in the cathedral of Florence, St. Maria del Fiore, with an epitaph written by one of the Nini:

> Credidit ut Cimabos picturae castra tenere,
> Sic tenuit vivens; nunc tenet astra poli.

Here we recognize distinctly a parallel to the first clause in the famous triplet of Dante:

> Credette Cimabue nella pintura
> Tener lo campo; ed ora ha Giotto il grido,
> Si che la fama di colui' oscura.

Bibliography.—Vasari, ed. Frey (1911); Crowe and Cavalcaselle, ed. Langton Douglas (1903); J. Strzygowski, *Cimabue und Rom* (1888); J. P. Richter, *Lectures on the National Gallery* (1898); H. Thode, *Franz v. Assisi* (1904).

CIMAROSA, DOMENICO (1749–1801), Italian musical composer, was born at Aversa, in the kingdom of Naples, Dec. 17, 1749. His parents were poor, but anxious to give their son a good education, and after removing to Naples they sent him to a free school connected with one of the monasteries of that city. He obtained a free scholarship at the musical institute of Santa Maria di Loreto, where he remained for eleven years, studying chiefly the great masters of the old Italian school. Piccini, Sacchini and other musicians of repute are mentioned amongst his teachers. At the age of twenty-three Cimarosa began his career as a composer with a comic opera called *Le Stravaganze del Conte,* first performed at the Teatro dei Fiorentini at Naples in 1772. The work met with approval as did its successors *Le Pazzie di Stellidanza e di Zoroastro,* a farce full of humour and eccentricity, and another comic opera called *L'Italiana in Londra.* From 1784–87 Cimarosa lived at Florence, and wrote the following works for the theatre of that city:—*Caio Mario;* the three biblical operas, *Assalone, La Giuditta* and *Il Sacrificio d'Abramo;* also *Il Convito di Pietra;* and *La Ballerina amante,* a pretty comic opera first performed at Venice with enormous success.

About the year 1788 Cimarosa went to St. Petersburg (Leningrad) by invitation of the empress Catherine II. In 1792 he went to Vienna at the invitation of the emperor Leopold II. Here he produced his masterpiece, *Il Matrimonio segreto* which ranks amongst the highest achievements of light operatic music. In 1793 he returned to Naples, where *Il Matrimonio segreto* and other works were received with great applause. Amongst the works belonging to his last stay in Naples may be mentioned the charming opera *Le Astuzie feminili,* which during recent years has been adapted with great success as one of the productions of the Diaghilev Ballet.

This period of his life is said to have been embittered by the intrigues of envious and hostile persons, amongst whom figured his old rival Paisiello. During the occupation of Naples by the troops of the French Republic, Cimarosa joined the Liberal party, and on the return of the Bourbons, was, like many of his political friends, condemned to death. By the interces ion of influential admirers his sentence was commuted into banishment. But his health was broken, and after much suffering he died at Venice Jan. 11, 1801, of inflammation of the intestines. The nature of his disease led to the rumour of his having been poisoned by his enemies, which, however, a formal inquest proved to be unfounded.

CIMBALO: *see* Cembalo.

CIMBRI, a Teutonic tribe which in 113 B.C. defeated the consul Gnaeus Papirius Carbo near Noreia. They had been wandering along the Danube for some years, warring with the Celtic tribes on either bank. After the victory of 113 B.C. they passed westwards over the Rhine, threatening the territory of the Allobroges. Their request for land was not granted, and in 109 B.C. they defeated the consul Marcus Junius Silanus in southern Gaul, but did not at once follow up the victory. In 105 B.C. they returned to the attack under their king, Boiorix, and annihilated the Roman armies at Arausio (Orange). Again the victorious Cimbri turned away from Italy, and, after attempting to reduce the Arverni (*q.v.*), moved into Spain, where they failed to overcome the desperate resistance of the Celtiberian tribes. In 103 B.C. they marched back through Gaul, which they overran as far as the Seine, where the Belgae made a stout resistance. Near Rouen the Cimbri were reinforced by the Teutoni and two cantons of the Helvetii. They marched southwards by two routes, the Cimbri moving on the left towards the passes of the eastern Alps, while the newly arrived Teutoni and their allies made for the western gates of Italy. In 102 B.C. the Teutoni and Ambrones were totally defeated at Aquae Sextiae by Marius, while the Cimbri succeeded in passing the Alps and driving Q. Lutatius Catulus across the Adige and Po. In 101 B.C. Marius overthrew them on the Raudine Plain near Vercellae. Their king, Boiorix, was killed, and the whole army destroyed. The Cimbri were the first in the long line of the Teutonic invaders of Italy.

The original home of the Cimbri has been much disputed. From information gained from the *Monumentum Ancyranum* and the map of Ptolemy, it may reasonably be conjectured that they came from the peninsula of Jutland, where their name may be preserved in Himmerland (Aalborg). Strabo and other early writers related a number of curious facts concerning the customs of the Cimbri, which are of great interest as the earliest records of the manner of life of the Teutonic nations.

Bibliography.—Livy or Florus, *Epitome of Roman History,* lxiii., lxvii., lxviii.; Pomponius Mela, *De situ orbis,* Bk. III. iii.; C. Plinius Secundus, *Nat. Hist.,* Bk. IV. xiii. and xiv., all in Bibliotheca Script. Graec. et Roman. Teubneriana, Leipzig; Plutarch, "Marius," in vol. ix. of Plutarch's *Lives,* with Eng. trans., B. Perrin (1920); Strabo, *Geography,* Bk. VII. i. and ii., with Eng. trans., H. L. Jones (1917–27), both in the Loeb Classical Library; Ptolemy, *Geography,* Bk. II. xi., ed. O. Cuntz (1923). For *Monumentum Ancyranum see* Ancyra.

CIMICIFUGA, a genus of herbs of the family Ranunculaceae, comprising 12 species widely distributed in the north temperate zone; the bugbanes. The root of *C. foetida* was used as a preventive against vermin and that of the North American black snake-root (*C. racemosa*) as an emetic.

CIMINIA, VIA, an ancient road of Italy, which diverged from the Via Cassia at Sutrium, and led along the east side of the Lacus Ciminius (Macaulay's "Ciminian mere," mod. Lago di Vico, an extinct crater basin) out of which it climbed on the north to 2,785 feet. Thence it descended and rejoined the Via Cassia at Aquae Passeris, a few miles north of Viterbo. The Ciminian hills are still wooded, and of great beauty. Caprarola on the east slopes of the crater, contains a very fine palace built for Alessandro Farnese in 1547–59 by Vignola, with the interior decorated by the Zuccari brothers; other villages in the district (notably Soriano with the Palazzo Chigi, which also has a fine castle of 1278), also contain good specimens of his architecture; while S. Martino al Cimino has a fine French Gothic 13th century church.

See S. Bargellini *I Monti del Cimino* (Bergamo, *Arti Grafiche,* 1914, well illustrated).

CIMMERII, an ancient people of the far north or west of Europe, first spoken of by Homer (*Odyssey,* xi. 12–19), who describes them as living in perpetual darkness. Herodotus (iv. 11–13), in his account of Scythia, regards them as the early inhabitants of South Russia (after whom the Bosporus Cimmerius [*q.v.*] and other places were named), driven by the Scyths along by the Caucasus into Asia Minor, where they maintained themselves for a century. But it is quite possible that some Cimmerii made their raids across the Hellespont, having been cut off by the Scyths as the Alani (*q.v.*) were by the Huns. Certain it is that in the middle of the 7th century B.C., Asia Minor was ravaged by northern nomads (Herod. iv. 12), one body of whom is called in Assyrian sources *Gimirrai* and is represented as coming through the Caucasus. They were probably Iranian speakers, to judge by the few proper names preserved. The name has also been identified with the biblical Gomer, son of Japheth (Gen. x. 2, 3). Later writers identified them with the Cimbri of Jutland, who were probably Teutonized Celts, but this is a mere guess due to the similarity of name.

For the Cimmerian invasions described by Herodotus, *see* Scythia; Lydia; Gyges.

CIMON (*c.* 507–449 B.C.), Athenian statesman and general, was the son of Miltiades (*q.v.*) and Hegesipyle, daughter of the Thracian prince Olorus. Cimon's first task in life was to pay the fine (about £12,000) which had been imposed on Miltiades after the Parian expedition. After winning a high reputation in the second Persian invasion, he served under Aristeides with the Athenian fleet and later (477, see *Camb. Anc. Hist.*, vol. v. App. B) became sole commander. His first success was the expulsion of Pausanias from Byzantium. Having captured Eion (at the mouth of the Strymon), he expelled the Persian garrisons from the entire seaboard of Thrace with the exception of Doriscus, and, having captured Scyros (470), confirmed his popularity by transferring thence to Athens the supposed bones of Theseus. In 466 Cimon proceeded to liberate the Greek cities of Lycia and Pamphylia, and at the mouth of the Eurymedon he defeated the Persians decisively by land and sea.

The Persian danger was now over, and the immediate purpose of the Delian League was achieved. Already, however, Athens had introduced the policy of coercion which was to transform the league into an empire, a policy which, after the ostracism of Themistocles and the death of Aristides, must be attributed to Cimon, whose fundamental idea was the union of the Greeks against all outsiders (*see* Delian League). Carystus was compelled to join the league; Naxos (*c.* 469) and Thasos (465–463), which had revolted, were compelled to accept the position of tributary allies. In 464 Sparta was in difficulties, owing to the revolt of her Helots. Cimon persuaded the Athenians to send aid, on the ground that Athens could not "stand without her yokefellow" and leave "Hellas lame." The expedition was a failure, and Cimon was attacked by the democrats led by Ephialtes. The history of this struggle is not clear. The ordinary account is that Ephialtes during Cimon's absence in Messenia overthrew the Areopagus (*q.v.*) and then obtained the ostracism of Cimon, who tried to reverse his policy. It may be pointed out that when the Messenian expedition started, Cimon had twice within the preceding year triumphed over the opposition of Ephialtes, and that presumably the Cimonian party was predominant until after the expedition proved a failure. It is therefore unlikely that, immediately after Cimon's triumph in obtaining permission to go to Messenia, Ephialtes was able to attack the Areopagus with success. The chronology would thus be: ostracism of Cimon, spring, 461; fall of the Areopagus, summer, 461.

A more difficult question is involved in the date of Cimon's return from ostracism. The ordinary account says that he was recalled after Tanagra (457) to negotiate the Five Years' Truce (451 or 450). Some writers, maintaining that Cimon did return soon after 457, say that the truce which he arranged was really the four months' truce recorded by Diodorus (only). To this there are two main objections: (1) if Cimon returned in 457, why does the evidence of antiquity connect his return specifically with the truce of 451? and (2) why does he after 457 disappear for six years and return again to negotiate the Five Years' Truce and to command the expedition to Cyprus? It seems much more likely that he returned in 451, at the very time when Athens returned to his old policy of friendship with Sparta and war against Persia (*i.e.*, the Cyprus expedition).

Cimon died in Cyprus (449), and was buried in Athens. Later Attic orators speak of a "Peace" between Athens and Persia, which is sometimes connected with the name of Cimon and sometimes with that of Callias. If any such peace was concluded, it cannot have been soon after the battle of the Eurymedon as Plutarch assumes. It can have been only after the evacuation of Cyprus (*i.e.*, *c.* 448). There are weighty reasons which render it improbable that any formal peace can have been concluded at that period between Athens and Persia (see further Ed. Meyer's *Forschungen*, ii.).

Cimon's services in consolidating the empire rank with those of Themistocles and Aristeides. He is described as genial, brave and generous. The one great principle for which he is memorable is that of the balance of power between Athens and Sparta, as respectively the naval and military leaders of a united Hellas. It has been the custom to regard Cimon as a man of little culture. The truth is that, as in politics, so in education and attitude of mind, he represented the ideals of an age which, in the new atmosphere of democratic Athens, seemed to savour of rusticity and lack of education.

Bibliography.—The lives of Cimon by Plutarch and Cornelius Nepos are uncritical; the conclusions above expressed are derived from a comparison of Plutarch, *Cimon*, 17, *Pericles*, 10; Theopompus, frag. 92; Andocides, *de Pace*, §§ 3, 4; Diodorus xi. 86 (the four months' truce). *See* histories of Greece (*e.g.*, Grote, ed. 1907), *Cambridge Ancient History*, vol. v., c. ii. and iii.; also Pericles; Delian League, with works quoted.

CIMON OF CLEONAE, an early Greek painter, who is said to have introduced great improvements in drawing. He represented "figures out of the straight, and ways of representing faces looking back, up or down; he also made the joints of the body clear, emphasized veins, worked out folds in garments" (Pliny).

CINCH, a Mexican saddle girth; figuratively, a secure hold.

CINCHONA, an important genus of shrubs and trees, family Rubiaceae, closely related to coffee and ipecac. The 38 species are found on the warm, moist Amazonian slopes of the Andes from Colombia to Bolivia at elevations of 5,000–8,500 feet, a few above and some below this. They have opposite leaves and pink or whitish, sometimes fragrant, usually cymose, flowers in lilac-like clusters. A few of the species are of world importance because their bark is the only source of quinine (*q.v.*) the specific for malaria, and widely used in the treatment of influenza, the common cold and some other diseases.

Some species also yield totaquina. The medicinal value of cinchona bark was unknown to the Incas, and it is not mentioned in Gracilasso de la Vega's *Royal Commentaries on the Incas* or in Pedro de Cieza de Leon's *Chronicles of Peru*, published in 1553.

The oft repeated tale of the first use and introduction of cinchona bark to Europe by the Countess of Chinchon in 1638 was completely disproved by A. W. Haggis in 1941, as the wife of the Viceroy of Peru never had malaria, died at Cartagena on her way to Spain and hence could not have carried cinchona bark to Europe. Who took it there, and when, will probably never be settled. It was known to the Jesuits at Lima about 1630, hence its common appellation of Jesuits' bark and Peruvian bark. The first mention in European medical literature was by Herman van der Heyden, in his *Discours et advis sur les flus de ventre douloureux*, Antwerp, 1643.

For the next two hundred years cinchona bark was ruthlessly exploited especially after the isolation of its chief constituent by Pelletier and Caventou in 1820 had demonstrated that the quinine content dictated its price. Bark depletion seemed so inevitable that Hasskarl for the Dutch and Sir Clements Markham for the English were sent to South America between 1859–63 in an attempt to introduce cinchona culture to Java and India. Both expeditions failed because they did not secure varieties of high quinine content. In December 1865 there arrived in Java a pound of seed from Charles Ledger of Puño, Peru, collected on the banks of the upper Marmoré River in Bolivia.

The progeny of these, and subsequent skilful cultivation by the Dutch, resulted in Java becoming the world source of cinchona bark and hence of quinine. Part of the Ledger seed was planted by the British at their government cinchona station in Madras, where it failed. That failure was disastrous, for India has the highest incidence of malaria in the world and the inferior Indian varieties have never yielded enough quinine. Private planters have abandoned its culture for more profitable crops; and government plantations are supplemented by importation from Java. Dutch bark production yielded 1017 tons of quinine in 1941, all derived from *Cinchona ledgeriana*. The only other species grown commercially in Java is *C. succirubra,* which yields quinidine, cinchonine and cinchonidine. (N. Tr.)

CINCHONA BARK, ALKALOIDS OF. About 30 distinct alkaloids have been isolated from cinchona bark, of which quinine is by far the most important, followed by quinidine, cinchonidine and cinchonine. Because of the therapeutical importance of cinchona bark and its four principal alkaloids most of the national pharmacopoeias prescribe methods of estimating these constituents in the bark and lay down standards both for the bark and for quinine. Thus, the British Pharmacopoeia requires that red cinchona bark should yield from 5% to 6% of alkaloids, of which not less than half must consist of quinine and cinchonidine, and for quinine sulphate a test is prescribed which excludes all but a minimum quantity of cinchona alkaloids, other than quinine. (For further information *see* Alkaloids.)

Quinine, $C_{20}H_{24}O_2N_2$.—This alkaloid is rarely seen or used, except in the form of its salts with acids. Though it contains two atoms of nitrogen it behaves as a monoacidic base yielding a sulphate of the formula $(C_{20}H_{24}O_2N_2)_2$, H_2SO_4, $7H_2O$, popularly known as quinine. It crystallizes in bulky masses of colourless, glistening needles, which become dull on exposure to air because of the loss of five of their molecules of water of crystallization, so that the thoroughly stable, air-dry salt has the composition $(C_{20}H_{24}O_2N_2)_2$, H_2SO_4, $2H_2O$. It is sparingly soluble in water, more so in alcohol and still more in a mixture of alcohol and chloroform. The solutions are laevorotatory and those in water, especially when acidified, are strongly fluorescent. Two other sulphates, $C_{20}H_{24}O_2N_2$, H_2SO_4, $7H_2O$ (so-called bisulphate) and $C_{20}H_{24}O_2N_2$, $2H_2SO_4$, $7H_2O$ (so-called tetra-sulphate), are known and are used when more soluble salts are required. Quinine hydrochloride, $C_{20}H_{24}O_2N_2$, HCl, $2H_2O$, which closely resembles the ordinary sulphate in appearance but has the advantage of being a little more soluble in water, is also in use. In addition, a great variety of special salts have been made in attempts to combine the therapeutic advantages of quinine with those of medicinally valuable acids; *e.g.,* quinine salicylate, acetylsalicylate, valerianate, cacodylate, etc.

On reduction quinine furnishes hydroquinine, which also occurs in cinchona bark and is the raw material for the production of a series of drugs in which the side chains of quinine are modified to enhance its therapeutic properties in certain directions. The best known of these modified cinchona alkaloids is eucupin.

Quinidine, $C_{20}H_{24}O_2N_2$ (also called conquinine).—This alkaloid, which is a dextrorotatory isomeride of quinine, crystallizes from alcohol in colourless prisms and melts when dry at 171.5° C. It forms two series of salts analogous with those of quinine.

Cinchonine $C_{19}H_{22}ON_2$.—This alkaloid crystallizes from alcohol in rhombic prisms and melts at 264° C. It is dextrorotatory in solution and like the other cinchona alkaloids yields two series of salts with acids.

Cinchonidine, $C_{19}H_{22}ON_2$.—This laevorotatory isomeride of cinchonine (*see* above), is one of the chief constituents of the mixture of alkaloids present in red cinchona bark, the variety now generally produced for making galenical preparations of cinchona. It crystallizes from alcohol in large colourless prisms, melting at 207° C., and corresponds with quinine in being laevorotatory in solution, but is unlike it in showing no fluorescence in dilute sulphuric acid. It forms two series of salts, analogous with those of quinine described above.

These four cinchona alkaloids have been the subject of investigations designed to determine their constitution and permit of their synthesis, almost continuously since they were discovered in 1820.

The reactions of the four alkaloids can all be accounted for on the basis of the structural formula below, which was developed by P. Rabe (1909), and which represents them as containing a quinoline (left) and a quinuclidine (right) nucleus, joined by a secondary alcohol group.

The difference between the two pairs (1) quinine and quinidine and (2) cinchonine and cinchonidine, is that in the first pair, R on the quinoline nucleus is a methoxyl (CH_3O) group, while in the second pair, R is hydrogen. Within each pair, the two alkaloids differ in the spatial arrangement of the H and OH of the secondary

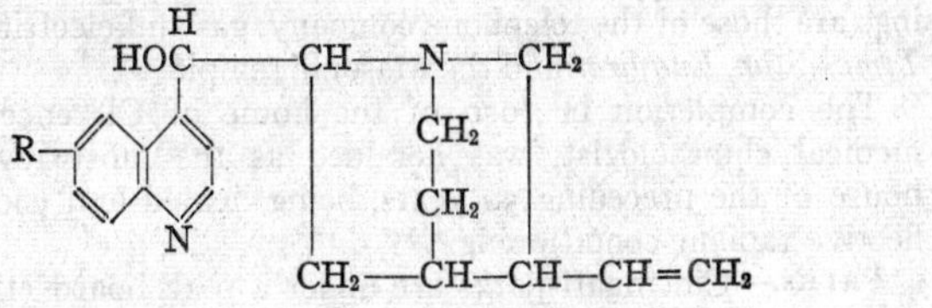

Cinchona Alkaloids, Type Formula

alcohol group (*see* Stereochemistry). Confirmation of the structures assigned to the cinchona alkaloids involved great difficulty. It was attained in 1931 with the synthesis of hydroquinine and hydroquinidine by Rabe, and with that of quinine itself by R. B. Woodward and W. E. Doering in 1944.

Further it should be noted that there is now some reason to believe that the protozooicidal action of these alkaloids, to which is due their value in malaria, is associated mainly with the quinoline nucleus, while their action on the heart, which has led to the use of quinidine in cardiac therapeutics, is due to the quinuclidine nucleus, since sparteine, which also contains this nucleus, is stated to exert a similar action. (*See* also Quinine.) (T. A. H.; L. F. Sl.)

CINCINNATI, a city and the county seat of Hamilton county, Ohio, U.S., 39° 8′ N., 84° 30′ W., on the north bank of the Ohio river opposite the mouth of the Licking, about 116 mi. S.W. of Columbus, about 281 mi. by rail S.E. of Chicago and about 755 mi. (by rail) W.S.W. of New York city. Through the city flows Mill creek; to the east the Little Miami and to the west the Great Miami empty into the Ohio. Population (1950) 503,998. Previous census reports were (1810) 2,540; (1830) 24,831; (1850) 115,435; (1870) 216,239; (1890) 296,908; (1910) 363,591; (1930) 451,160; (1940) 455,610. The resident birth rate in 1949 was 24.6 per thousand and the death rate 12.7 per thousand.

Cincinnati is on two plateaus—one about 60 ft., the other 100–150 ft., above low water—and on hills (400–460 ft.) which enclose these terraces on three sides. The city datum is 546.9 ft. above sea level, zero river gauge 430.06 ft., low-water mark 431.96 ft. The low-water record is 1.9 ft. (Sept. 1881) and high-water 79.9 ft. (Jan. 26, 1937). About half the river plain (average above sea level 550 ft.) lies south of the Ohio in Kentucky, where Covington, Newport and other suburbs are located. Cincinnati has a river frontage of about 27 mi., extends back about 6 mi. in the valley of Mill creek and occupies a total area of 75 sq.mi. It was connected in 1867 with Covington by a suspension bridge (1,057 ft. between towers; total 2,252 ft.). Two bridges lead to Newport; one to Ludlow; and one to West Covington.

On the terraces the streets generally intersect at right angles, but on the hills irregularly. The wholesale district is for the most part, in the "bottoms." Manufacturing is scattered widely, with the largest concentration also in the "bottoms" area of the city. Other important areas are lower Mill creek valley, St. Bernard-Ivorydale, North Norwood and Oakley.

Many of the finer residences are on the picturesque enclosing hills; but there is a tendency toward more remote and larger estates. Among Ohio suburbs are Norwood (pop. 35,001); Cheviot (pop. 9,944); Reading (pop. 7,836); St. Bernard (pop. 7,066); Wyoming (pop. 5,582); Lincoln Heights (pop. 5,531).

Average summer temperature is 75° F.; autumn 57°; winter 34°; spring 54°; yearly average 55°. Mean annual precipitation is 40.63 in. Average wind velocity is 7.1 mi. per hour.

Buildings.—The U.S. government building, Union terminal, Hamilton county courthouse and the city hall are monumental structures. Notable among the hundreds of churches are St. Peter in Chains (1844), used as the cathedral until superseded by St. Monica in 1938; St. Francis de Sales; the First (1835) and Second Presbyterian (1872); Christ Church (1835); and the Jewish temples. A distinctive feature of downtown Cincinnati is the number of church spires and steeples. It is the seat of a Roman Catholic archbishopric and a Protestant Episcopal bishopric.

Tallest buildings are the Carew Tower (574 ft.) and Union Central building (495 ft.). The Terrace Plaza, completed in 1948, is a combination department store and hotel. Other notable buildings are those of the telephone company, gas and electric company, *Times-Star*, *Enquirer* and the Masonic temple.

The completion in 1950 of the home of Clarence A. Mills, medical climatologist, was heralded as the most revolutionary house of the preceding 50 years, being heated and cooled by reflective radiant conditioning.

Parks.—Cincinnati parks are under a park board (three members) appointed by the mayor, created in 1908 when the city owned 485 ac. of parks. In 1950 the total area was 3,655 ac. In general the parks are located on hilltops, affording a view of the downtown area, the Ohio river and the neighbouring hills, but many small parks such as Lytle (1 ac.) and Washington (5 ac.) are located downtown.

Eden park, closest of the large parks, has 184 ac. It was originally a vineyard belonging to Nicholas Longworth, great-grandfather of the speaker of the house of the same name, and called the Garden of Eden. Located there are the Cincinnati Art museum and Art academy and the Irwin M. Krohn conservatory, with displays of tropical and greenhouse plants and special flower exhibits, particularly at Thanksgiving and Easter. Mount Airy forest (1,364 ac.) was the first municipal forest in the United States. More than 1,125,000 trees had been planted by mid-20th century and 12 mi. of pedestrian and 14 mi. of equestrian trails laid out.

Burnet Woods (109 ac.) adjoining the campus of the University of Cincinnati, has many fine plant and tree specimens and the Trailside museum, headquarters for park nature activities. Alms park (85 ac.) overlooks the Ohio river with an especially fine view. Ault park (237 ac.), another hilltop park, features ornamental trees, shrubs and flowers. The Cincinnati Zoological Garden was founded in 1875 and acquired by the city in 1933. Its 57 ac. house birds, beasts and reptiles in natural settings. During the summer season wild animals are kept in barless grottoes surrounded by water-filled moats. An amphitheatre with about 1,000 seats was completed in 1951.

Education.—In 1950 there were 63 elementary, 9 junior high, 5 senior high, 4 vocational and 10 special schools in the public school system, with total enrolment of 59,091. The system of publicly supported education is completed by the University of Cincinnati, the first municipal university chartered in Ohio under the earliest municipal university statute in the United States (1870). The university was formed by uniting the Cincinnati Astronomical society (1842) and McMicken university (1859), later joined by Cincinnati college (1819) and the Medical College of Ohio (1819). The campus adjoins Burnet Woods. Included are a graduate school, teachers' college, colleges of engineering, business administration, medicine, law, applied arts, nursing and health, home economics, and an evening college. The "co-op" system of combining college instruction with practical paid training in industry under actual commercial conditions was originated at the university by Dean Herman Schneider. The college of law developed from the law school of Cincinnati college, and the college of medicine from the Medical College of Ohio (1820), each the first in the new west. University enrolment in 1950 was 15,170, 7,274 in day classes and 7,896 in the evening college. The faculty exceeded 1,200. The University observatory dates from 1843. In 1868 its director, Cleveland Abbe, inaugurated a system of daily weather reports from which the U.S. weather bureau developed. Newer buildings are McMicken hall, the Student Union building and the University library. Support is derived from endowments, fees and municipal taxes.

There were 61 elementary Catholic parochial schools in 1950, with enrolment of 17,497, and 15 diocesan high schools with enrolment of 5,993; also Concordia Lutheran parochial school. The Athenaeum of Ohio was incorporated in 1928 to control the Roman Catholic institutions of higher learning: Mount St. Mary of the West seminary, St. Gregory seminary and teachers' college. The Institutum Divi Thomae was established in 1935 as the department of scientific research of the Athenaeum.

Xavier university, Roman Catholic, founded by Bishop Fenwick in 1831, is located on Victory parkway. Enrolment in 1950 was 2,851—1,415 day, 163 graduate, 1,147 evening and 126 Milford preparatory seminary. The faculty numbered 150.

Hebrew Union college (1875) is the oldest rabbinical school in the United States. In Jan. 1950 it merged with the Jewish Institute of Religion of New York city (1922). Its library contains the largest collection in the U.S. of the minute books of U.S. congregations and an important collection of Judaica. The Ohio Mechanics' institute (1828) prepares skilled workmen and industrial executives. It offers instruction in a wide variety of trades—mechanical, chemical and electrical—in day, evening and summer classes. Salmon P. Chase college (Cincinnati Y.M.C.A.) includes a college of law (1893) and an evening college of commerce (1920) and opened also (1946) a day school. There are also the College of Pharmacy and Our Lady of Cincinnati college (Roman Catholic).

The Public library, established in 1867, includes the main library, 40 branches, 3 bookmobiles and 296 smaller agencies serving city and county. It had 156,797 registered cardholders and 1,584,667 vol. in 1950. Among special libraries are the County Law library and the Lloyd library, outstanding in pharmacy, botany, chemistry and natural sciences. The library of the Historical and Philosophical Society of Ohio, on the University of Cincinnati campus, contains an important collection of books, newspapers, maps and manuscripts.

Hospitals and Charity.—The General hospital (850 beds), completed in 1915, occupies a plot of 27 ac. Built on the pavilion plan, it consists of 24 interconnected buildings, including the Hospital for Contagious Diseases. Near by are the University of Cincinnati college of medicine, the Children's (1883) and the Christian R. Holmes (1929) hospitals. Private general hospitals include Bethesda, Christ, Deaconess, Jewish, Good Samaritan, Our Lady of Mercy and St. Mary hospitals, St. Francis and St. George. Special hospitals are Chronic Disease (county), Longview (state) and Cincinnati sanitarium for the mentally ill, and Dunham (county) for tuberculosis patients. A Veterans' administration hospital was under construction (1950).

There are numerous charitable institutions. The Community Chest, organized in 1915, has been a major factor in their support. In 1950 more than $2,657,000 was raised for allocation among 82 health and welfare agencies.

Water Supply.—The municipally owned water works were placed in service in 1907. Water is taken from the Ohio river on the Kentucky side several miles above the discharge from the city sewers. It comes through a seven-foot gravity tunnel under the river to the Ohio side, the water being thence elevated by four steam-driven pumping engines (daily capacity 30,000,000 gal.) and four electrically driven pumps (daily capacity 15,000,000 gal.) into settling basins (capacity 400,000,000 gal.). From this point the water flows by gravity through chemical house and filter house (rapid sand filters capacity 200,000,000 gal.), thence through two tunnels, one seven feet in diameter and four miles long leading to a pumping station with 103,000,000 gal. per day capacity, and the other eight feet in diameter and two and one-half miles long to a station with 100,000,000 gal. capacity.

Because of the diversified topography there are three pumping districts. In the business district, Eden park reservoir stores 96,000,000 gal. (three average days' supply); in the eastern hills, the Mt. Auburn and Eastern Hills tanks and reservoirs contain 42,000,000 gal. (two days' supply), and in the western hills two groups of tanks contain 12,300,000 gal. (two days' supply). The daily average consumption at mid-20th century was 82,000,000 gal. The system is entirely self-supporting.

Transportation.—Cincinnati at mid-century had about 845 mi. of paved streets and sewers. The city is served to a great extent by two transit systems—the Cincinnati Street Railway company, operating over a major portion of the area north of the Ohio river on a service at cost system; and the Cincinnati, Newport and Covington Railway company, connecting Cincinnati with near-by Kentucky cities. These systems are supplemented by several suburban bus lines.

Eight railroads operating 12 trunk lines radiate from the city. The single Union terminal, unusually fine and commodious, accommodates 17,000 people and more than 100 trains daily. The Cincinnati Southern railway (336 mi.) from Cincinnati to Chattanooga, Tenn., is municipally owned. It was leased to the Cincinnati, New Orleans and Texas Pacific Railway company until 2026 at a rental of $1,350,000 per year plus a percentage of net profit. In 1950 there were seven certificated water freight carriers and two passenger excursion steamboats. Six scheduled airlines operated from the Lunken Municipal airport and the Greater Cincinnati airport, Boone county, Ky.

Administration.—A home-rule charter was adopted in 1917 and amended in 1924 to establish a city-manager form of government. A revised charter was adopted in 1926, effective from Jan. 1927. There is a council of nine, nominated by petition and elected at large for two years; the council elects one of its members as presiding officer, who becomes the mayor. The mayor presides at meetings of the council. He appoints the city auditor and members of independent commissions and boards.

The city manager is chosen by the council for an indefinite term. He makes most of the executive and administrative appointments, prepares the budget, supervises the various public services and keeps the council informed of the city's condition.

The bonded debt in 1950 was $77,117,330.81; the net amount not self-supporting was $41,766,064.10. The tax rate for 1950 was $26.10, of which $11.72 was for the city and the remainder for state, county and educational purposes. Between 1940 and 1950 the citizens of Cincinnati voted $81,325,000 in bonds for public improvements in city and county.

Industries.—Cincinnati has a diversity of industry. As listed by the U.S. census of manufactures of 1947, the Cincinnati metropolitan area had 1,700 establishments, employing 135,774 people, whose total salaries and wages amounted to $382,935,000; the value added by manufacture was $777,201,000. In the production of soap, machine tools, playing cards and electrotypes, Cincinnati led the world. There were 43 men's and boys' suits and coats establishments with a value added by manufacture of $23,906,000; 22 machine-tool firms with a value added of $46,542,000, paper and allied products, 44 firms with a value added by manufacture of $38,236,000; wholesale meat packing, 26 firms and an added value of $11,236,000; printing and publishing, 271 firms with an added value of manufacture of $62,637,000. Cincinnati is also a leader in the production of office furniture, laundry machinery, printing inks, books, shoes, sheet metal products, engineering appliances, coffins, plastics, radio and television sets, sporting goods, malt liquors, chemicals and still-mill products.

A great bituminous coal centre, Cincinnati at mid-century was handling more than 520,000 cars annually with a tonnage of 29,120,000 and more than 4,000,000 additional tons on the river. An indication of the city's business stability was the fact that 77 business establishments had enjoyed a continuous existence of more than 100 years. Bank clearings for 1949 amounted to $8,516,752,660, and bank debits $10,187,117,000.

Art, Music and Literature.—Musical development began in 1810–20; by 1825 musical academies, choral societies performing the works of George Frederick Handel and Franz Joseph Haydn, and musical publications were quite numerous. Joseph Tosso, famed for performances of the "Arkansas Traveler," went to Cincinnati in 1820 and remained for 60 years. The drama was popular. It was, however, the large influx of Germans in the 1840s and later that promoted music most. Stephen Foster spent several years there. A sängerfest was held in 1849 and again in 1870, when a hall was built for it. Under Theodore Thomas (1835–1905) the Cincinnati Musical Festival association was incorporated, and its biennial May festivals began in 1873. In 1875–78 was built the Springer Music hall, and the Cincinnati College of Music was endowed in 1878. Theodore Thomas was its director in 1878–81; a statue of him by Clement J. Barnhorn stands in Music hall. Until his death Thomas was director of the May festivals. The sängerfest met in Cincinnati for the third time in 1879 and its jubilee was held there in 1899. Choral societies have been important in musical life, as has the Cincinnati Conservatory of Music (1867), the Cincinnati Symphony orchestra (1893) and the Cincinnati Summer opera (1920) with first-rate performances given at the Cincinnati Zoo.

A number of early U.S. artists, such as Frederick Eckstein and Hiram Powers, lived in Cincinnati, where German influence greatly promoted art. In 1877 the Women's Art Museum association brought about the building of the Art museum. A school of design (1869) was a part of the university until 1884, when it was transferred to the museum. An art academy was erected in 1887 near the Art museum. Frank Duveneck was for some time director of the academy, and the Duveneck room in the museum contains a great many of his works. Henry Farny was another artist of repute. The Taft House museum (1932) is the gift of their home and art collection by Mr. and Mrs. Charles P. Taft. Built in 1819–20, it is one of the finest examples of the Early Federal style of architecture. The Rookwood pottery was the first (1880) in the United States to devote exclusive attention to artware. The earlier wares were yellow, brown and red, then came deep greens and blues, followed by mat-glazes and by "vellum" ware (1904), a lustrous pottery resembling old parchment, with decoration painted or modelled or both. Lithographing became important in Cincinnati in the first half of the 19th century.

Principal daily newspapers in 1950 were the *Post,* founded 1881 as the *Penny Paper;* the *Times-Star,* which traced its descent from the *Cincinnati Times* (1840); and the *Enquirer* (1841). There was also the *Union,* a Negro weekly (1907), the Catholic *Telegraph-Register* (1821) and the *American Israelite* (1854). The *Freie Presse,* a weekly, was the only German language paper. The city's Literary club celebrated its centennial in 1949.

In the centre of the city is the Tyler Davidson bronze fountain (1871) on Fountain square. It was designed by August von Kreling and comprises 15 bronze figures cast at the royal bronze foundry in Munich, Ger.; the base is of porphyry. Other notable monuments are those to James A. Garfield by Charles H. Niehaus, the William Henry Harrison by L. T. Rebisso, George Grey Barnard's Lincoln, the Galbraith memorial, the Ft. Washington monument, McCook and Hecker busts and a monument to Ohio volunteers killed in the Civil War.

History.—The site of Cincinnati was a centre of the mound-builder civilization. Forts, burial mounds and other remains of their activities have been found there. René Robert Cavalier, sieur de la Salle is said to have been the first white man to pass this point on his way down the river in 1669. The Indians in the Ohio valley belonged to the Algonquin family. From the Wabash to the two Miamis were tribes of the Miamis.

On a journey to the Miami country in 1787, John Cleves Symmes (1742–1814), New Jersey congressman, was so attracted by its fertile valleys and clear streams that he purchased the land between the Miami rivers. Columbia, the first settlement, was founded near the mouth of the Little Miami in 1788. It was followed, six weeks later, by a town opposite the mouth of the Licking river, and in Feb. 1789 by a third settlement at North Bend. The second of these was destined to grow and become a large city. Named Losantiville by John Filson, schoolmaster and surveyor, he intended it to mean "the town opposite the mouth of the [L]icking." Gen. Arthur St. Clair or Israel Ludlow, a surveyor, changed the name of Losantiville to Cincinnati in 1790, in honour of the Society of the Cincinnati (*q.v.*). St. Clair created Hamilton county with Cincinnati as county seat. With the coming of soldiers to Fort Washington, it became the centre of activities against the Indians. Gen. Anthony Wayne's victory at Fallen Timbers (1794) ended Indian warfare and opened the country to settlement. In 1802, with 700 inhabitants, the military post was incorporated as a town and in 1819 became a city (pop. 10,283).

In 1811 the "New Orleans," first steamboat on western waters, passed Cincinnati and opened a new era. By 1826 steamboat building had become an important industry and the town was a busy port. During the 1830s and 1840s Ohio's canals further stimulated Cincinnati boatbuilding and by serving as feeders greatly swelled trade on the Ohio river. River commerce was at its height in 1852, with 8,000 steamboat arrivals.

In 1842 Cincinnati was one of the few U.S. cities liked by Charles Dickens, but by the late 1840s another British visitor, a Mrs. Houston, called it "a city of pigs, a monster piggery." Small wonder that it received the nickname of "Porkopolis"; between 1842 and 1852, 27% of the hogs packed in the United States were packed there. Although there were still 33 large-scale pork-packing houses in Cincinnati in 1859, the grain fields were moving west and the meat-packing industry went with them to Chicago and St. Louis, Mo. Cincinnati's northern neighbours surpassed it in population and industry and it lost its position as third largest city in the United States.

In the 1850s the Germans began coming in great numbers, and by the 1870s they had made the city almost bilingual. Until World War I, German was taught in all public and parochial schools. By the 1890s the section north of the canal was known as the "Over-the-Rhine" region.

Although Cincinnati had close commercial and cultural ties with the south, it became an important station on the "Underground railroad" prior to the Civil War, and sided with the North when war came. In 1862 there was a threatened invasion by a Confederate force under Gen. Kirby Smith and for a time the city was under martial law, but the invasion did not take place.

Residential development began to climb up to the hilltops. In the 1870s five inclined-plane railways were built, all later abandoned. The rugged terrain encouraged the growth of independent neighbourhoods, many of them retaining their identities. In 1925 Cincinnati adopted a city master plan. Realizing that this plan needed revamping, city officials in 1944 authorized the City Planning commission to bring it up to date. The Metropolitan Master plan was completed in 1948 at a cost of more than $250,000. It called for the redevelopment of the downtown river front, a system of motor expressways and off-street parking facilities, the reclamation of blighted areas and the protection of residential neighbourhoods.

Bibliography.—Charles Cist, *Cincinnati in 1841* (1841); H. A. Ford and Mrs. K. B. Ford, *History of Cincinnati* (1881); Federal Writers' project of Ohio, *Cincinnati Guide* (1943); C. T. Greve, *Centennial History of Cincinnati* 2 vol. (1904); Alvin Harlow, *Serene Cincinnatians* (1950); Charles P. Taft, *City Management* (1933); Iola O. Hessler, *Cincinnati Then and Now* (1949); D. J. Kenney, *Illustrated Guide to Cincinnati* (1893); Cincinnati, City Planning Commission, *Cincinnati Metropolitan Master Plan and the Official City Plan of the City of Cincinnati Adopted November 22, 1948* (1949); Charles Frederick Goss, *Cincinnati the Queen City*, 4 vol. (1912).

(E. L. Hs.)

CINCINNATUS, LUCIUS QUINTIUS (b. *c.* 519 B.C.), one of the heroes of early Rome. He worked his own small farm. A persistent opponent of the plebeians, he resisted the proposal of Terentilius Arsa to draw up a code of written laws applicable equally to patricians and plebeians. Twice he was called to the dictatorship of Rome (458 and 439). In 458 he defeated the Aequians in a single day, and after entering Rome in triumph with large spoils returned to his farm. The story of his success, related five times under five different years, possibly rests on an historical basis, but the account given in Livy is incredible.

See Livy iii. 26–29; Dion. Halic. x. 23–25; Florus i. 11. For a critical examination of the story *see* Schwegler, *Römische Geschichte*, bk. xxviii. 12; E. Pais, *Storia di Roma*, i. ch. 4 (1898).

CINCLIDAE: *see* Dipper.

CINDERELLA, the heroine of an almost universal fairy-tale (*i.e.*, little cinder girl). Its essential features are (1) the persecuted maiden whose youth and beauty bring upon her the jealousy of her step-mother and sisters; (2) the intervention of a fairy or other supernatural instrument on her behalf; (3) the prince who falls in love with and marries her. In the English version, a translation of Perrault's *Cendrillon*, the *glass* slipper which she drops on the palace stairs is due to a mistranslation of *pantoufle en vair* (a *fur* slipper), mistaken for *en verre*. It has been suggested that the story originated in a nature-myth, Cinderella being the dawn, oppressed by the night-clouds (cruel relatives) and finally rescued by the sun (prince).

See A. Lang, *Perrault's Popular Tales* (1888); Marian Rolfe Cox, *Cinderella; Three Hundred and Forty-five Variants* (1893).

CINEAS, a Thessalian, the chief adviser of Pyrrhus, king of Epirus. He was regarded as the most eloquent man of his age. He tried to dissuade Pyrrhus from invading Italy, and after the defeat of the Romans at Heraclea (280 B.C.) was sent to Rome to discuss terms of peace. These terms, which are said by Appian (*De Rebus Samniticis*, 10, 11) to have included the freedom of the Greeks in Italy and the restoration to the Bruttians, Apulians and Samnites of all that had been taken from them, were rejected. Two years later Cineas was sent to renew negotiations on easier terms. The result was a cessation of hostilities, and Cineas crossed over to Sicily to prepare the ground for Pyrrhus's campaign. Nothing more is heard of him. He is said to have made an epitome of the *Tactica* of Aeneas, probably referred to by Cicero, who speaks of a Cineas as the author of a treatise *De Re Militari*.

See Plutarch, *Pyrrhus*, 11–21; Justin xviii. 2; Eutropius ii. 12; Cicero, *Ad Fam.* ix. 25.

CINEMATOGRAPHY: *see* Motion Pictures: *Technology*.

CINERARIA, cultivated ornamental plants originated from species of *Senecio*. There are two distinct types, the garden species, of which one of the most common is a Dusty Miller, *S. cineraria* and the greenhouse varieties of *S. cruentus*, commonly referred to as Cinerarias.

Greenhouse cinerarias are of two types: one a dwarf, compact growing plant with large flowers in dense clusters; the other a taller growing variety with larger, more spreading clusters of small star-shaped flowers. These are known horticulturally as stellate varieties of *Cineraria cruentus*. Both are easily grown from seed and are sold commercially as potted plants. The very free-flowering stellate varieties are more popular than are the large-flowered types and through a careful selection and crossing of varieties many beautiful colours are available.

For a succession of blooming plants during the late winter and spring months seeds are first sown in August in the cool greenhouse. As soon as the seedlings can be handled conveniently they are put in $2\frac{1}{4}''$ pots. Later they are shifted to 3″ pots as the root system develops. The final shift into 6″ flowering pots is made early in January. Soil for cinerarias should be of a light, porous character and a mixture of one-half fibrous loam, one-half leaf mould with a liberal sprinkling of sharp sand suits them admirably. They grow best in a night temperature of from 45° to 50° F. with an increase of about 10° during the day. The soft succulent character of foliage and stems makes cinerarias especially liable to be attacked by green fly. The plants should be frequently fumigated with nicotine preparations or sprayed with nicotine solutions.

CINGOLI (anc. Cingulum), a town of the Marches, Italy, province of Macerata, about 14 mi. N.W. direct, and 17 mi. by road from the town of Macerata. Pop. (1936) 1,751 (town); 15,496 (commune). Cingulum, a town of Picenum, founded by Caesar's lieutenant, T. Labienus, at his own expense in 63 B.C., played an important part in the civil wars owing to its lofty site (2,300 ft.).

Remains of the ancient city walls survive and there are interesting works of art in the Gothic church of S. Esuperanzio.

CINNA, a Roman patrician family of the gens Cornelia. The most prominent member was Lucius Cornelius Cinna, who, after serving in the war with the Marsi as praetorian legate, became consul in 87 B.C. After Sulla's departure for the East, riots broke out in Rome, and Cinna was expelled. He at once collected an army, Marius joined him, and the two captured Rome. Proscriptions followed, and the death of Marius (Jan. 86) left Cinna leader of the party. L. Valerius Flaccus became his colleague, and afterwards Cn. Papirius Carbo. In 84, however, Cinna, who was still consul, was forced to advance against Sulla; but while embarking his troops for Thessaly, he was killed in a mutiny. His daughter Cornelia was the wife of Julius Caesar, but his son, L. Cornelius Cinna, praetor in 44 B.C., sided with Caesar's murderers.

The hero of Corneille's tragedy *Cinna* (1640) was the Cn. Cornelius Cinna pardoned by Augustus for conspiracy.

CINNA, GAIUS HELVIUS, Roman poet of the later Ciceronian age, the friend of Catullus, whom he accompanied to Bithynia in the suite of the praetor Memmius. Suetonius, Valerius Maximus, Appian and Dio Cassius all state that, at Caesar's funeral, a certain Helvius Cinna was killed by mistake for Cornelius Cinna, the conspirator. The last three writers mentioned above add that he was a tribune of the people, while Plutarch states that the Cinna who was killed by the mob was a poet. This points to the identity of Helvius Cinna the tribune with Helvius Cinna the poet. The chief objection to this view is based upon two lines in ninth eclogue of Virgil, supposed to have been written 41 or 40 B.C., which seem to imply that Helvius Cinna was then alive. But such an interpretation of the passage is not absolutely necessary. Cinna's chief work was a mythological epic poem called *Smyrna*. A *Propempticon Pollionis,* a send-off to (Asinius) Pollio, is also attributed to him. In both these poems, the language of which was so obscure that they required special commentaries, his model appears to have been Parthenius of Nicaea.

See A. Weichert, *Poëtarum Latinorum Vitae* (1830); L. Müller's edition of Catullus (1870), where the remains of Cinna's poems are printed; A. Kiessling, "De C. Helvio Cinna Poëta" in *Commentationes Philologicae in honorem T. Mommsen* (1878); O. Ribbeck, *Geschichte der römischen Dichtung,* i (1887); Teuffel-Schwabe, *Hist. of Roman Lit.* (Eng. trans. 213, 2–5); Plessis, *Poésie latine* (1909).

CINNABAR, sometimes written cinnabarite, is red mercuric sulphide (HgS), or native vermilion, the common ore of mercury (Ger. *Zinnober*). The name comes from the Greek κιννάβαρι, used by Theophrastus and probably applied to several distinct substances. Cinnabar is generally found in a massive, granular or earthy form, of bright red colour, but it occasionally occurs in crystals with a metallic adamantine lustre. The crystals belong to the hexagonal system and are generally of rhombohedral habit, sometimes twinned. Cinnabar presents remarkable resemblance to quartz in its symmetry and optical characters. Like quartz it exhibits circular polarization, and A. des Cloizeaux showed that it possessed 15 times the rotatory power of quartz (*see* LIGHT).

Cinnabar has a high refractive power, its mean index for sodium light being 3.08 (*see* REFRACTION). The hardness of cinnabar is 3, and its specific gravity 8. Cinnabar is the principal ore of mercury. The chief producing areas are Almaden, Sp., where it has been mined for 2,000 years, and Idria, It. The finest specimens come from Kweichow and Hunan, China. Hepatic cinnabar is an impure variety in which cinnabar is mixed with bituminous and earthy matter. Metacinnabar is a black cubic dimorphous form of mercury sulphide. (W. F. FG.)

CINNAMIC ACID or Phenylacrylic Acid, is present in Peru and Tolu balsams, in storax and in some gum benzoins, combined with benzyl alcohol as an ester. Its formula is $C_6H_5.CH:CH.COOH$. It can be prepared by the reduction of phenyl propiolic acid with zinc and acetic acid, by heating benzal malonic acid, by the condensation of ethyl acetate with benzaldehyde in the presence of sodium ethoxide or by the so-called "Perkin reaction," which is the method commonly employed.

In this process benzaldehyde, acetic anhydride and anhydrous sodium acetate are heated to about 180° C.; the mixture is made alkaline with sodium carbonate, and excess of benzaldehyde removed by a current of steam. The residual liquor is acidified with hydrochloric acid. The cinnamic acid, which is precipitated, is then recrystallized from hot water. Cinnamic acid crystallizes in needles or prisms, melting at 133° C. It exists in two stereoisomeric varieties, one of which is trimorphous. On nitration it gives a mixture of ortho- and paranitrocinnamic acids, the former of which is of historical importance as by converting it into orthonitrophenylpropiolic acid A. Baeyer was enabled to carry out a complete synthesis of indigo (*q.v.*).

Cinnamic acid and its esters are employed in perfumes production. Various cinnamic acid preparations were used in the treatment of tuberculosis with disappointing results.

CINNAMON, the inner bark of *Cinnamomum zeylanicum,* a small evergreen tree belonging to the family Lauraceae, native to Ceylon. The leaves are large, ovate-oblong in shape, and the flowers, which are arranged in panicles, have a greenish colour and a rather disagreeable odour. The tree is grown at Tellicherry, in Java, the West Indies, Brazil and Egypt, but the produce of none of these places approaches in quality that grown in Ceylon. In 1940 imports of cinnamon oil into the United States were 184,673 lb., valued at $112,000. Ceylon cinnamon of fine quality is a very thin, smooth bark, with a light-yellowish brown colour, a highly fragrant odour and a peculiarly sweet, warm and pleasing aromatic taste. Its flavour results from an aromatic oil. This is prepared by pounding the bark, macerating it in sea water and then quickly distilling the whole. It is golden-yellow, with the peculiar odour of cinnamon and a hot aromatic taste. Cinnamon is principally employed in cookery as a condiment and flavouring material, being largely used in the preparation of some kinds of chocolate and liqueurs. It is also used in soap perfumes. Being a more costly spice than cassia, that comparatively harsh-flavoured substance is frequently substituted for or added to it.

CINNAMON STONE: *see* GARNET.

CINNAMUS (KINNAMOS), **JOHN,** Byzantine historian. He was imperial secretary to Manuel I Comnenus (1143–1180), whom he accompanied on his campaigns in Europe and Asia Minor. He appears to have outlived Andronicus I, who died in 1185. Cinnamus was the author of a history of the period 1118–76, which thus continues the *Alexiad* of Anna Comnena, and embraces the reigns of John II and Manuel I, down to the unsuccessful campaign of the latter against the Turks, which ended with the rout of the Byzantine army at Myriocephalum. Cinnamus was probably an eyewitness of the events of the last ten years which he describes. The work breaks off abruptly, and there are indications that it is an abridgement. The text is in a very corrupt state. The author's hero is Manuel; he is strongly impressed with the superiority of the east to the west, and is a determined opponent of the pretensions of the papacy; but he cannot be reproached with undue bias.

C. Tollius *Editio princeps* (1652); in Bonn, A. Meincke, *Corpus Scriptorum Hist. Byz.* (1836), with Du Cange's valuable notes; Migne, *Patrologia Graeca,* cxxxiii; *see* also H. von Kap-Herr, *Die abendländische Politik Kaiser Manuels* (1881); C. Neumann, *Griechische Geschichtsschreiber im 12 Jahrhundert* (1888); C. Krumbacher, *Geschichte der byzantinischen Litteratur* (1897).

CINO DA PISTOIA (1270–1336), Italian poet and jurist, whose full name was GUITTONCINO DE' SINIBALDI, was born in Pistoia, of a noble family. He studied law at Bologna under Dinus Muggelanus (Dino de Rossonis, d. 1303) and Franciscus Accursius, and in 1307 is understood to have been assessor of civil causes in his native city. In that year, however, Pistoia was disturbed by the Guelph and Ghibelline feud. Cino was a Ghibelline, and had to leave Pistoia. Pitecchio, a stronghold on the frontiers of Lombardy, was yet in the hands of Filippo Vergiolesi, chief of the Pistoian Ghibellines; Selvaggia, his daughter, was beloved by Cino (who was probably already the husband of Margherita degli Unghi); and Cino betook himself to Pitecchio. He was not with the Vergiolesi at the time of Selvaggia's death (1310) at the Monte della Sambuca, in the Apennines, whither the Ghibellines had been compelled to shift their camp. In 1313 the emperor died, and the Ghibellines lost their last hope. Cino appears to have thrown up his party and to have returned to Pistoia. Thereafter he devoted himself to law and letters. After filling several high judicial offices, a doctor of civil law of Bologna in his 44th year, he lectured and taught from the professor's chair at the universities of Treviso, Siena, Florence and Perugia in succession.

Cino, the master of Bartolus and of Joannes Andreae, the celebrated canonist, was long famed as a jurist. His commentary on the statutes of Pistoia, written in two years, is said to have great merit; while that on the code (*Lectura Cino Pistoia super codice,* Pavia, 1483; Lyons, 1526) is considered by Savigny to exhibit more practical intelligence and more originality of thought than are found in any commentary on Roman law since the time of Accursius. He was the friend and correspondent of Dante's later years, and possibly of his earlier also, and was certainly, with Guido Cavalcanti and Durante da Maiano, one of those who replied to the famous sonnet *A ciascun' alma presa e gentil core* of the *Vita Nuova.* In the treatise *De Vulgari Eloquio* Dante refers to him as one of "those who have most sweetly and subtly written poems in modern Italian." Petrarch coupled Cino and Selvaggia with Dante and Beatrice in the fourth chapter of his *Trionfi d'Amore.* As a poet Cino has moments of true passion and fine natural eloquence. Of these qualities the sonnet in memory of Selvaggia, *Io fui in sull' alto e in sul beato monte,* and the canzone to Dante, *Avegnachè di omaggio più per tempo,* are interesting examples.

The textbook for English readers is D. G. Rossetti's *Early Italian Poets,* which contains a memoir of Cino da Pistoia and some admirably translated specimens of his verse. *See* also Ciampi, *Vita e poesie di messer Cino da Pistoia* (Pisa, 1813).

CINQ-MARS, HENRI COIFFIER RUZÉ D'EFFIAT, MARQUIS DE (1620–1642), French courtier, was the second son of Antoine Coiffier Ruzé, marquis d'Effiat, marshal of France (1581–1632), and was introduced to the court of Louis XIII by Richelieu, who had been a friend of his father and who hoped he would counteract the influence of the queen's favourite, Mlle. de Hautefort. He became the king's accredited favourite, master of the wardrobe and master of the horse. After distinguishing himself at the siege of Arras in 1640, Cinq-Mars became restive. He had fallen in love with Louise Marie de Gonzaga, afterward queen of Poland, who was not disposed to favour a suitor who could not satisfy her ambition. Cinq-Mars demanded a high military command, but Richelieu opposed his pretensions and the favourite talked rashly about overthrowing the minister. He was probably connected with the abortive rising of the count of Soissons in 1641; however that may be, in the following year he formed a conspiracy with the duke of Bouillon and others to overthrow Richelieu. This plot was under the nominal leadership of the king's brother, Gaston of Orléans. The plans of the conspirators were aided by the illness of Richelieu and his absence from the king, and at the siege of Narbonne Cinq-Mars almost induced Louis to agree to banish his minister. Richelieu, however, recovered; Gaston betrayed the conspirators, and Richelieu laid before the king the proofs of the treasonable negotiations of the conspirators for assistance from Spain. Cinq-Mars was tried, admitted his guilt and was executed at Lyons on Sept. 12, 1642. His conspiracy was the subject of A. de Vigny's novel *Cinq-Mars.*

See D'Hancour, *La Conspiration de Cinq-Mars* (1902); Vicomtesse de Gallard, *Lettres de Bullion et de Richelieu* (Paris, 1903).

CINQUECENTO, a term used to describe that period of the Italian Renaissance between 1500 and 1600. The word is often applied to the artistic styles prevalent at that time, and particularly to the classicism of the high Renaissance.

CINQUEFOIL, a decorative form of five lobes or cusps.

CINQUE PORTS, the name of an association of maritime towns in the southeast of England, exercising a jurisdiction dating from about the time of the Norman conquest, organized, it seems on French lines, in the 13th century, and still surviving. The ports originally constituting the body were only five in number—Hastings, Romney, Hythe, Dover and Sandwich; but to these were afterward added the "ancient towns" of Winchelsea and Rye with the same privileges, and other places, both corporate and noncorporate, which, with the title of limb or member, held a subordinate position. To Hastings were attached the corporate members of Pevensey and Seaford and the noncorporate members of Bulvarhythe, Petit Iham (Yham or Higham), Hydney, Bekesbourn, Northeye and Grenche or Grange; to Romney, Lydd, and Old Romney, Dengemarsh, Orwaldstone and Bromehill or Promehill; to Dover, Folkestone and Faversham, and Margate, St. John's, Goresend (now Birchington), Birchington Wood (now Woodchurch), St. Peter's, Kingsdown and Ringwould; to Sandwich, Fordwich and Deal, and Walmer, Ramsgate, Reculver, Stonor (Estanor), Sarre (or Serre) and Brightlingsea (in Essex). To Rye was attached the corporate member of Tenterden, and to Hythe the noncorporate member of West Hythe. The jurisdiction thus extends from Seaford in Sussex to Birchington near Margate in Kent, and includes part of the Essex coast.

The duty of the Cinque Ports until the reign of Henry VII was to furnish nearly all the ships and men that were needful for the king's service; and for a long time after they were required to give large assistance to the permanent fleet. In return for their services the ports enjoyed extensive privileges (*cf.* S. Jeake's *Charters of the Cinque Ports,* still the chief authority).

The highest office in connection with the Cinque Ports is that of the lord warden, who is also constable of Dover castle; the two offices have for centuries been held by the same persons, but are still distinct. He has a maritime jurisdiction as admiral of the ports. His power was formerly of great extent, but he has now practically no important duty to exercise. Walmer castle was for long the official residence of the lord warden, and its use as such, though intermittent, is not obsolete. In 1941 King George VI appointed Winston Churchill lord warden.

The court of admiralty for the Cinque Ports exercises a coordinate but not exclusive admiralty jurisdiction over persons and things found within the territory of the Cinque Ports. At an inquisition taken at the court of admiralty, held by the seaside at Dover in 1682, the limits of its jurisdiction were declared to extend from Shore Beacon in Essex to Redcliff, near Seaford, in Sussex; and with regard to salvage, they were to comprise all the sea between Seaford in Sussex to a point five miles off Cape Grisnez on the coast of France, and the coast of Essex. An older inquisition of 1526 is given by R. G. Marsden in his *Select Pleas of the Court of Admiralty,* II, xxx (London, 1894). The judge sits as the official and commissary of the lord warden, just as the judge of the high court of admiralty sat as the official and commissary of the lord high admiral. And, as the office of lord warden is more ancient than the office of lord high admiral (*The Lord Warden* v. *King in his office of Admiralty,* 1831, 2 Hagg, Admy. Rep. 438), it is probable that the Cinque Ports' court is the more ancient of the two.

The jurisdiction of the court is in theory concurrent with that of the king's court of admiralty, subject to some statutory modifications. Cases of collision have been tried in it (the "Vivid," 1 *Asp. Maritime Law Cases,* 601), but of late mainly salvage cases (the "Clarisse," *Swabey,* 129; the "Marie," *Law. Rep.* 7 P.D. 203).

Robert Joseph Phillimore succeeded his father as judge of the court from 1855 to 1875. As he was also the last judge of the high court of admiralty, from 1867 (the date of his appointment to the high court) to 1875, the two offices were, probably for the only time in history, held by the same person. His patent had a grant of the "place or office of judge official and commissary of the court of admiralty of the Cinque Ports, and their members and appurtenances, and to be assistant to my lieutenant of Dover castle in all such affairs and business concerning the said court of admiralty wherein yourself and assistance shall be requisite and necessary." Of old the court sat sometimes at Sandwich, sometimes at other ports, but the regular place for the sitting of the court was for a long time St. James's church, Dover. For convenience the judge later sat at the royal courts of justice, but the last full sitting was in 1914. The office of marshal in the high court is represented in this court by a sergeant, who also bears a silver oar.

The registrar who, according to general civilian practice, can act as the judge's deputy, deals at Dover with the small matters which keep the jurisdiction alive. An appeal is to the king in council, advised by the judicial committee. For details of the jurisdiction *cf.* the Cinque Ports act, 1821. The judge's only active duty is to take part in the installation of a new lord warden.

The Cinque Ports from the earliest times claimed to be exempt from the jurisdiction of the admiral of England. Their early charters do not, like those of Bristol and other seaports, express this exemption in terms. It seems to have been derived from the general words of the charters which preserve their liberties and privileges.

The lord warden's claim to prize was raised in, but not finally decided by, the high court of admiralty in the "Ooster Ems," 1 C. Rob, 284, 1783. No trace was found of any later attempt to assert it.

BIBLIOGRAPHY.—S. Jeake, *Charters of the Cinque Ports* (London, 1728); Sir T. Mantell, *Cinque Ports, Brotherhoods and Guestlings* (Dover, 1828); E. Knocker, *An Account of the Grand Court of Shepway* (London, 1862); M. Burrows, *Cinque Ports* (London, 1888); J. H. Round, *Feudal England* (London, 1895); F. M. Hueffer, *The Cinque Ports* (Edinburgh, 1900); *Indexes of the White Book and of Black Book of the Cinque Ports* (London, 1905); Benoist-Lucy, *Les Cinq-Ports* (1911); A. G. Bradley, *An Old Gate of England* (London, 1918); K. M. E. Murray, *The Constitutional History of the Cinque Ports* (Manchester, 1935); J. B. Jones, *The Cinque Ports,* 2nd ed. (Dover, 1937); H. S. Giffard, *The Laws of England,* ed. by Viscount Hailsham, 2nd ed. (London, 1931); *Encyclopaedia of the Laws of England,* 3rd ed. (London, 1938); Sir F. Pollock, "Cinque

Ports Jurisdiction," *Law Quart. Rev.*, 41:453 (London). The archives of the Cinque Ports are not gathered together in one place; the chief repositories are at New Romney, Dover and Rye.

CINTRA, town of central Portugal (modern spelling, Sintra), 17 mi. W.N.W. of Lisbon by the Lisbon-Caçem-Cintra railway and 6 mi. N. by E. of Cape da Roca, the westernmost promontory of the European mainland. Pop. (1950) 7,150. Cintra is magnificently situated on the northern slope of the Serra da Cintra, a rugged mountain mass, largely overgrown with pines, eucalyptus, cork and other forest trees, above which the principal summits rise in a succession of bare and jagged gray peaks, the highest being Cruz Alta (1,736 ft.). Every educated Portuguese is familiar with the verses in which the beauty of Cintra is celebrated by Byron in *Childe Harold* (1812), and by Camoens in the national epic *Os Lusiadas* (1572). One of the highest points of the Serra is surmounted by the Palacio da Pena, a fantastic imitation of a mediaeval fortress, built on the site of a Hieronymite convent by the prince consort Ferdinand of Saxe-Coburg (d. 1885); while an adjacent part of the range is occupied by the Castello des Mouros, an extensive Moorish fortification containing a small ruined mosque and a very curious set of ancient cisterns.

In the town itself the most conspicuous building is a 14th-15th-century royal palace, partly Moorish, partly debased Gothic in style, and remarkable for the two immense conical chimneys. The 18th-century Palacio de Seteaes is said to derive its name ("Seven Ahs") from a sevenfold echo; here, on Aug. 22, 1808, was signed the convention of Cintra, by which the British and Portuguese allowed the French army to evacuate the kingdom. Beside the road which leads for 3½m. W. to the village of Collares, celebrated for its wine, is the Penha Verde, an interesting country house and chapel, founded by Dom João de Castro (1500–1548), fourth viceroy of India. Castro also founded the Capuchin convent of Santa Cruz, better known as the Cork convent. Beyond the Penha Verde, on the Collares road, are the palace and park of Montserrate. The palace was originally built by William Beckford, the novelist and traveller (1761–1844), and was purchased in 1856 by Sir Francis Cook, an Englishman, who afterwards obtained the Portuguese title viscount of Montserrate. The park, with its tropical luxuriance of vegetation and its variety of lake, forest and mountain scenery, is by far the finest example of landscape gardening in the Iberian Peninsula, and probably among the finest in the world.

CIPHER or **CYPHER,** the symbol o, nought, or zero (Arab. *ṣifr*, void), and so a name for symbolic or secret writing (*see* CODES AND CIPHERS), or for shorthand (*q.v.*), and also in elementary education for doing simple sums ("ciphering").

CIPPUS (Lat. for a "post" or "stake"), in architecture, a low pedestal, either round or rectangular, set up by the Romans for various purposes such as military or mile stones, boundary posts, etc. The inscriptions on some in the British Museum show that they were occasionally funeral memorials.

CIPRIANI, GIOVANNI BATTISTA (1727–1785), Italian painter and engraver, Pistoiese by descent, was born in Florence in 1727. He studied first under Ignatius Heckford or Hugford, and afterwards under Antonio Domenico Gabbiani. He was in Rome from 1750 to 1753, where he became acquainted with Sir William Chambers, the architect, and Joseph Wilton, the sculptor, whom he accompanied to England in Aug., 1755. When Chambers designed the Albany in London for Lord Holland, Cipriani painted a ceiling for him. He also painted part of a ceiling in Buckingham Palace, and a room with poetical subjects at Standlynch in Wiltshire. Some of his best and most permanent work was, however, done at Somerset House, London, built by his friend Chambers. He not only prepared the decorations for the interior of the north block, but, says Joseph Baretti in his *Guide through the Royal Academy* (1780), "the whole of the carvings in the various fronts of Somerset place—excepting Bacon's bronze figures—were carved from finished drawings made by Cipriani." These designs include the five masks forming the keystones to the arches on the courtyard side of the vestibule, and the two above the doors leading into the wings of the north block, all of which are believed to have been carved by Nollekens. The grotesque groups flanking the main doorways on three sides of the quadrangle and the central doorway on the terrace appear also to have been designed by Cipriani. The central panel of the library ceiling was painted by Sir Joshua Reynolds, but the four compartments in the coves, representing Allegory, Fable, Nature and History, were Cipriani's. These paintings still remain at Somerset House, together with the emblematic painted ceiling, also his work, of what was once the library of the Royal Society. He was an original member of the Royal Academy (1768), for which he designed the diploma so well engraved by Bartolozzi. He was much employed by the publishers, for whom he made drawings in pen and ink, sometimes coloured. His friend Bartolozzi engraved most of them. Drawings by him are in both the British Museum and Victoria and Albert Museum, London. His best autograph engravings are "The Death of Cleopatra," after Benvenuto Cellini; "The Descent of the Holy Ghost," after Gabbiani; and portraits for Hollis's memoirs, 1780. He painted allegorical designs for George III.'s state coach—which is still in use—in 1761, and repaired Verrio's paintings at Windsor and Rubens's ceiling in the Banqueting House at Whitehall. He designed nymphs and *amorini* and medallion subjects to form the centre of Pergolesi's bands of ornament, and they were continually reproduced upon the elegant satin-wood furniture which was growing popular in his later days. Almost certainly some of the beautiful furniture designed by the Adams was actually painted by Cipriani himself. He also occasionally designed handles for drawers and doors. Cipriani died at Hammersmith in 1785 and was buried at Chelsea, where Bartolozzi erected a monument to his memory. He had married an English lady, by whom he had two sons.

CIRCAR, an Indian term applied to the component parts of a *subah*, or province, each of which is administered by a deputy-governor. In English it is principally employed in the name of the Northern Circars, used to designate a now obsolete division of the Madras presidency, which consisted of a narrow slip of territory lying along the western side of the bay of Bengal from 15° 40′ to 20° 17′ N. lat. These Northern Circars were five in number, Chicacole, Rajahmundry, Ellore, Kondapalli and Guntur, and their total area was about 30,000 sq. miles.

The district corresponds in the main to the modern districts of Kistna, Godavari, Vizagapatam, Ganjam and a part of Nellore. It was first invaded by the Mohammedans in 1471 and conquered by them in the following century, but they appear to have acquired only an imperfect possession of the country, as it was again wrested from the Hindu princes of Orissa about the year 1571. In 1687 the Circars were added, along with the empire of Hyderabad, to the empire of Aurangzeb. In 1759, by the conquest of Masulipatam, the dominion of the maritime provinces on both sides, from the river Gundlakamma to the Chilka lake, was transferred from the French to the British. But the latter left them under the administration of the nizam, with the exception of the town and fortress of Masulipatam, which were retained by the English East India company. In 1765 Lord Clive obtained from the Mogul emperor Shah Alam a grant of the five Circars. Hereupon the fort of Kondapalli was seized by the British, and in 1766 a treaty of alliance was signed with Nizam Ali, by which the company, in return for the grant of the Circars, undertook to maintain troops for the nizam's assistance. By a second treaty, signed in 1768, the nizam acknowledged the validity of Shah Alam's grant and resigned the Circars to the company, receiving as a mark of friendship an annuity of £50,000. Guntur, as the personal estate of the nizam's brother, was excepted during his lifetime under both treaties. He died in 1782, but it was not till 1788 that Guntur came under British administration. In 1823, the claims of the nizam over the Northern Circars were bought out by the company, and they became a British possession.

CIRCASSIA: *see* CAUCASIAN AREA, NORTH; KARACHAEV; KABARDA-BALKARIA; INGUSHETIA; ADIGEI.

CIRCASSIANS. The Cherkesses or Circassians differ from the other tribes of the Caucasus in origin and language. They designated themselves by the name of Adigheb, that of Cherkesses being a term of Russian origin. The government under which they lived was a peculiar form of the feudal system. The free Circassians were divided into three distinct ranks, the princes or *pshi,* the nobles or *uork* (Tatar *usden*), and the peasants or *hokotl.* They were also divided into numerous families, tribes or clans, some of which were very powerful and carried on war against each other with great animosity. The slaves, of whom a large proportion were prisoners of war, were generally employed in the cultivation of the soil, or in the domestic service of some of the principal chiefs.

The will of the people was the supreme source of authority; and every free Circassian had a right to express his opinion in those assemblies of his tribe in which the questions of peace and war, almost the only subjects which engaged their attention, were brought under deliberation. The princes and nobles, the leaders of the people in war and their rulers in peace, were only the administrators of a power which was delegated to them. The administration of justice was regulated solely by custom and tradition, and in those tribes professing Mohammedanism by the precepts of the Koran. The most aged and respected inhabitants of the various auls or villages frequently sat in judgment, and their decisions were received without a murmur by the contending parties. The Circassian princes and nobles were professedly Mohammedans; but in their religious services many of the ceremonies of their former heathen and Christian worship were still preserved. A great part of the people had remained faithful to the worship of their ancient gods—Shible, the god of thunder, of war and of justice; Tleps, the god of fire; and Seosseres, the god of water and of winds. One of their marriage ceremonies was that the young man who had been approved by the parents, and had paid the stipulated price in money, horses, oxen, or sheep for his bride, was expected to come with his friends fully armed and to carry her off by force from her father's house. Every free Circassian had unlimited right over the lives of his wife and children. Although polygamy was allowed by the laws of the Koran, the custom of the country forbade it. The respect for superior age was carried to such an extent that the young brother used to rise from his seat when the elder entered an apartment, and was silent when he spoke. Circassians were distinguished for the most generous hospitality and implacable vindictiveness. The individual who had slain any member of a family was pursued with implacable vengeance by the relatives, until his crime was expiated by death. The murderer might, indeed, secure his safety by the payment of a certain sum of money, or by carrying off from the house of his enemy a newly-born child, bringing it up as his own and restoring it when its education was finished. In either case, the family of the slain individual might discontinue the pursuit of vengeance without any stain upon its honour. The man closely followed by his enemy, who, on reaching the dwelling of a woman, had merely touched her hand, was safe from all other pursuit so long as he remained under the protection of her roof. The commission of theft was not considered so disgraceful as its discovery. The Circassian father was always willing to part with his daughters to Turkish merchants for the harems of Eastern monarchs. But no degradation was implied in this transaction, and the young women themselves were generally willing partners in it. Herds of cattle and sheep constituted the chief riches of the inhabitants. The princes and nobles, from whom the members of the various tribes held the land which they cultivated, were the proprietors of the soil. The Circassians carried on little or no commerce.

CIRCE, in Greek legend, a famous sorceress, the daughter of Helios and the ocean nymph Perse. She was able by means of drugs and incantations to change human beings into the forms of wolves or lions, and with these beings her palace was surrounded. Odysseus visited her island, Aiaie, with his companions, whom she changed into swine, but the hero, protected by the herb *molu,* which he had received from Hermes, compelled her to restore them to their original shape. He lived with her for a year, and when he determined to leave, she instructed him how to sail to the House of Hades in order to learn his fate from the prophet Teiresias. Upon his return she also gave him directions for avoiding the dangers of the journey home (Homer, *Odyssey,* x.–xii.; Hyginus, *Fab.* 125). Graeco-Italian tradition placed her island near Italy, or located her on the promontory Circei. *Cf.* PICUS, SCYLLA AND CHARYBDIS.

See C. Seeliger in W. H. Roscher's *Lexikon der Mythologie.*

CIRCEIUS MONS (mod. MONTE CIRCEO), an isolated promontory on the south-west coast of Italy, about 80m. S.E. of Rome. It is a ridge of limestone about 3½m. long by 1m. wide at the base, running from east to west and surrounded by the sea on all sides except the north. The land to the north of it is 53ft. above sea-level, while the summit of the promontory is 1,775ft. The origin of the name is uncertain: it has naturally been connected with the legend of Circe. It is true that the promontory ceased to be an island at a very early date; but it looks exactly like one from a distance. Upon the east end of the ridge are the remains of an *enceinte,* forming a rectangle of about 200 by 100yds. of very fine polygonal work. It seems to have been an acropolis, and contains no traces of buildings, except for a subterranean cistern, circular, with a beehive roof of converging blocks. The modern village of S. Felice Circeo occupies the site of the ancient town, the citadel of which stood on the mountain top, for its mediaeval walls rest upon ancient walls of Cyclopean work of less careful construction than those of the citadel, and enclosing an area of 200 by 150yds.

Circeii was founded as a Roman colony at an early date. At the end of the republic, the city of Circeii was no longer at the east end of the promontory, but at the south end of the Lago di Paola (a lagoon—now a considerable fishery—separated from the sea by a line of sandhills and connected with it by a channel of Roman date; Strabo speaks of it as a small harbour). The transference of the city did not, however, mean the abandonment of the east end of the promontory, on which stand the remains of several very large villas. An inscription, indeed, cut in the rock near S. Felice, speaks of this part of the *promonturium Veneris* (the only case of the use of this name) as belonging to the city of Circeii. For its villas Cicero compares it with Antium, and both Tiberius and Domitian possessed residences there. The villa of the latter indeed, on the east shores of the Lago di Paola, has been mistaken for the Roman town of Circeii. It extends over an area of some 600 by 500yds., consisting of fine buildings along the lagoon, including a large open *piscina* or basin, surrounded by a double portico, while farther inland are several very large and well-preserved water-reservoirs, supplied by an aqueduct of which traces may still be seen. The beetroot and oysters of Circeii had a certain reputation.

The view from the highest summit of the promontory (which is occupied by ruins of a platform attributed with great probability to a temple of Venus or Circe) is of remarkable beauty; the whole mountain is covered with fragrant shrubs. From any point in the Pomptine Marshes or on the coast-line of Latium the Circeian promontory dominates the landscape in the most remarkable way.

See G. Lugli, *Forma Italiae* 1. i. 2. (1928), the Italian archaeological survey.

CIRCLE, a curve consisting of all those points of a plane which lie at a fixed distance from a particular point in the plane, called the *centre.*

The circle is the simplest and most useful *plane curve* and alone possesses the property of being exactly alike at all points. If the curve be turned in its plane about its centre, the new position taken up is the same as the original position. This property constitutes the "roundness" of the circle, and distinguishes it from other plane curves. A circle may be traced upon a plane by the continuous movement of a point rigidly connected with the centre, as in the use of compasses, and it is in part the simplicity of this construction which explains the fundamental importance of this curve. The tracing of a circle is a much simpler problem than the tracing of a straight line, since the common method of drawing the latter, with the aid of a ruler, only reproduces the straight line already constructed along the ruler's edge. A difference in the use of the word "circle" is observable between the older writers and those of the present century. With the former the word is understood to mean the part of the plane enclosed by the curve, while the curve itself is called the *circumference.* The latter consider the circle and its circumference identical, except that the latter is often spoken of as the measure of the former; and the enclosed portion of the plane is spoken of as the *interior,* not as the circle itself.

The straight line joining the centre to a point on the circle, *e.g., OP* or *OQ* (fig. 1) is called a *radius;* from the definition of a circle, the radii drawn to various points on the circle are equal. A straight line drawn through the centre and having its ends on the circle, *e.g., EOH* (fig. 1) is called a *diameter;* evidently all diameters of the same circle are equal in length, and twice as long as a radius. A straight line, such as *ABC* (fig. 1), joining *any* two points on a circle is called a chord; and the greatest possible chord is a diameter. The portion of the circle intercepted between two points is called an *arc.* Any two points on the circle divide it into two arcs; thus, in fig. 1, *ADC* is the *minor arc,* and *APEC* the *major arc,* between *A* and *C.* The figure composed of an arc and the chord joining its extremities is a *segment* of the circle. In fig. 1, *ADCB* and *APECB* are respectively the minor and major segments made by the chord *AC.* A *sector* of a circle is the figure formed by two radii and one of the arcs joining their extremities. The angle between these radii and within the sector is called the angle of the sector. Thus *ODKC* (fig. 1) is a sector, and *DOC* its angle.

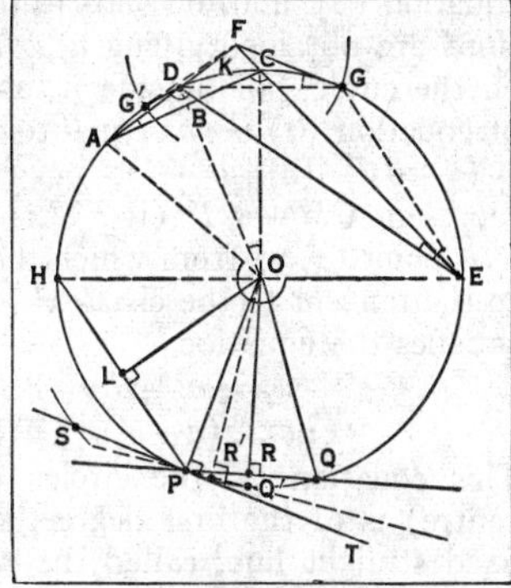

FIG. 1.—THE CIRCLE AND ITS PARTS Showing the radius OP or OQ, diameter EOH, chord ABC, minor arc ADC, major arc APEC, minor and major segments ADCB and APECB, sector ODKC and the angle of sector DOC

Geometrical Properties.—A number of properties of the circle are direct results of the symmetry and regularity of the curve. For instance, if two chords in the same circle are equal, the arcs corresponding to them are equal; if two sectors of the same circle have equal angles, they have equal arcs, and contain equal areas, etc. A useful property of this kind is that *every chord is bisected by the perpendicular drawn to it from the centre.* This allows the centre to be found when the circle is given, and to draw the circle when three points on it are given. Thus, to construct the circle through *H, P* and *Q,* draw the perpendicular bisectors *LO* and *RO* to *HP* and *PQ* as in fig. 1, and take as centre the point *O* where these meet.

A less evident property is that, *when any arc is taken, the angle between the lines joining its end-points to the centre is double the angle between the lines joining these end-points to any point on the remaining part of the circle, each angle being measured in the position facing the arc.* In fig. 1, by using the minor arc *CD,* the angle *COD* is double the angle *CED,* and also double the angle *CAD.* By using the major arc *APE,* the outer (reflex) angle *AOE* is double either *ACE* or *ADE.* An immediate consequence is that the angle *ACE* is equal to the angle *ADE.* Here *A, C, D* and *E* are any four points on a circle so placed that *C* and *D* lie on the same arc having *A* and *E* for end-points. The theorem is commonly stated in the form: *angles in the same segment are equal.* (To exhibit the segment it is necessary to join *AE.*) It is a property of wide application, and numerous instances of it may be seen in fig. 1 by joining various pairs of points. Thus the angles *CAD, CED, CGD, CQD* (when the lines *CQ, QD* and *CG* are drawn), are equal. In particular, *the angle in a semi-circle is a right angle.* Closely related to this is the theorem that *a four-sided figure whose four corners all lie on the same circle has the sum of either pair of opposite angles equal to two right angles.* The converse is true that if the sum of one of the pairs of opposite angles of a four-sided plane figure is two right angles, a circle may be drawn to pass through the four corners.

It is readily seen that a straight line whose shortest distance from the centre is less than the radius cuts a circle in two points, and that a line whose shortest distance is greater than the radius does not meet the circle at any point. The intermediate case occurs when the line is at a distance from the centre equal to the radius, as is the case with *SPT* (fig. 1). Such a line has only one point in common with the circle; it is said to *touch* the circle and is called a *tangent* to the circle. The tangent at any point of a circle is the line through that point drawn at right angles to the radius; thus *OPT* is a right angle. The tangent at *P* is the limiting position approached by a chord *PQ,* drawn through *P,* as the other extremity *Q* approaches *P.* The chord must be prolonged as shown in the figure, in order that it may not be lost as its length vanishes. It is known that the perpendicular *OR* from the centre falls on the middle point of the chord. As *Q* moves to *Q′, R* moves to *R′,* and, as *Q* approaches *P, R* approaches *P* also. Finally the right angle *ORQ* approaches the limiting position *OPT,* and the chord *PQ,* prolonged sufficiently, is finally represented by the tangent *PT* at right angles to the radius *OP.* This second view of a tangent, as the limiting form of a short chord, is more generally applicable than the former, being valid for curves other than circles. It also enables many tangent theorems to be recognized as the limiting forms of related theorems on chords, and leads to a better understanding of tangent relations.

From a point *F* outside a circle two tangents may be drawn. The *points of contact G* and *G′* of these may be found by first drawing the tangent at a point *P* on the circle, finding with the compasses a point *S* on this such that $OS=OF$, and then finding *G* and *G′* on the circle and at distance from *F* equal to *PS. The angle made by a tangent with a chord through its point of contact is equal to the angle in the segment on the other side of the chord.* Thus the angle *FGD* is equal to the angle *GED.* An important theorem on intersecting chords follows readily from the law of equal angles in a segment. *If two chords intersect, the product of the distances of the extremities from the point of intersection is the same for either chord.* Thus, in fig. 1, *AC* and *DE* intersect at *B.* The figure represents the case where *AB* contains 4·5 units, *BC* 3·2 units, *DB* 1 unit, and *BE* 14·4. It will be seen that $4{\cdot}5\times3{\cdot}2=1\times14{\cdot}4$. The relation remains true when the chords have to be prolonged to meet outside the circle, as *AD* and *CE,* meeting at *F.* In the figure $AF=7{\cdot}2$, $DF=3{\cdot}2$, $CF=1{\cdot}6$ and $EF=14{\cdot}4$, so that $AF\times DF=CF\times EF$, each being 23·04. In the case of external intersection each of the equal products is also equal to the *square of the tangent from the point of intersection.* In the figure, $FG=4{\cdot}8$, the square of which is 23·04. This is one of the cases where the tangent represents a chord whose ends are coincident.

Circle Constructions.—The circle plays an important part in the problems of constructive geometry. This will be easily understood when it is remembered that, in the traditional view, a geometrical solution means a solution by ruler and compasses; that is, the only steps available are to rule a straight line through two given points and to draw a circle having a given centre and radius. It is therefore a matter of importance to the student of geometry to be able to construct circles to satisfy various standard sets of conditions; and several of these processes will be indicated briefly:

1. *Circle through three given points.* The method of finding the centre by the right bisectors of the joining lines has already been given. When the three points are thought of as the corners of a triangle, the circle is said to be *circumscribed* to the triangle.

2. *Circle touching three given straight lines.* Bisect the angles between two of the lines *l* and *m,* obtaining a pair of bisector lines *a* and *b.* Bisect in the same way the angles between *l* and the third line *n* by a pair of bisectors *c* and *d.* The centre of a circle touching *l* and *m* must be equidistant from *l* and *m,* and so must lie either on *a* or on *b.* The centre of a circle touching *l* and *n* must be either on *c* or on *d.* Four solutions are obtained, the positions of the centre being the intersections of *a* and *c,* of *a* and *d,* of *b* and *c,* and of *b* and *d.* The circle that lies between the given lines and touches them is said to be *inscribed* to the triangle.

3. *Circle through two given points and touching a given line* (which does not pass between the points). Let *A* and *B* be the

given points, and l the given line (fig. 2). Let AB cut l in O. Draw any circle c through A and B, by taking as centre any point on the right bisector of AB. Draw the tangent OT touching c at T. Find points H and K on l so that $KO=OH=OT$. The circle c_1 through A, B and H and the circle c_2 through A, B and K will each be a solution of the problem. The proof is briefly that $OH^2=OK^2=OT^2=OA.OB$, so that OH and OK are each of the right length for a tangent from O.

4. *Circle through a given point and touching two given lines.* Let l and m (fig. 2) be the given lines, and A the given point. Draw n, the bisector of that angle between l and m in which A lies. Draw AL perpendicular to n and prolong to B so that $LB=AL$. The circles c_1 and c_2 constructed as in 3 to pass through A and B and to touch l will then constitute the two solutions of the problem.

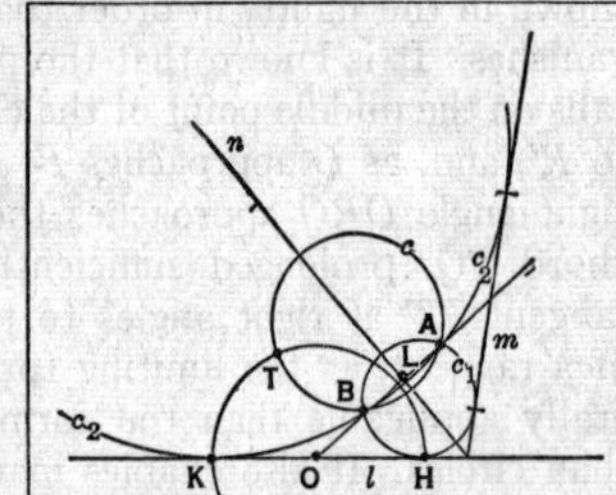

FIG. 2.—SHOWING THE CONSTRUCTION OF A CIRCLE THROUGH TWO GIVEN POINTS AND TOUCHING A GIVEN LINE, AND THROUGH A GIVEN POINT TOUCHING TWO GIVEN LINES

Circle constructions in which some of the conditions are that the circle should touch certain given circles require refined geometrical methods. A celebrated case of this type is Apollonious's problem: —*to construct a circle to touch three given circles.* If the three circles are entirely external to one another, this problem admits of eight solutions. A number of problems of this kind, due to Jakob Steiner and others, are discussed by Coolidge (*see* bibl.). It is often useful to remember that a circle through two given points may have its centre anywhere on the right bisector of their joining line, and that a circle touching two given intersecting straight lines has its centre anywhere on either of the lines bisecting the angles between them. A circle through a given point and touching a given line has its centre on a curve known as a parabola; but this fact is not of much direct assistance in finding constructions.

In many cases a point moving under specified conditions traces a circular path. The definition of the circle shows that this curve is the *locus* (or path) of a variable point whose distance from a fixed point remains constant. But there are numerous other ways in which the circular path may be recognized. If the base of a triangle is fixed, and the angle at the vertex is of constant magnitude, the moving vertex traces an arc of a circle as long as it remains on the same side of the fixed base; the property involved here is that of equal angles in a segment. If the base of a triangle is fixed, and the other two sides are in constant ratio, the moving vertex traces a circle which encloses one of the fixed vertices. If the sum of the squares of the distances of a variable point from two fixed points is constant, the point traces to a circle whose centre is half-way between the two fixed points.

Analytic Treatment.—We may take for axes of reference two lines OX and OY at right angles; and, drawing PN perpendicular to OX from any point P, denote by x and y the measurements ON and NP. The two quantities x and y are called the co-ordinates of P, and the position of P depends on their values. the point P is denoted by (x, y).

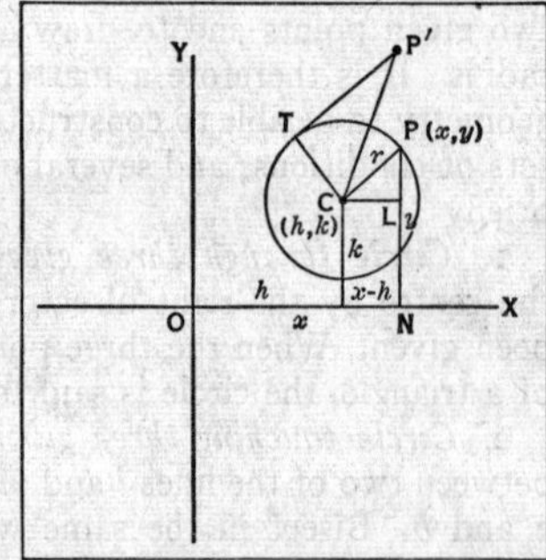

FIG. 3.—ANALYSIS OF THE CIRCLE TO DETERMINE ITS EQUATION

If C is a fixed point (h, k), P will be restricted to a circle of centre C and radius r provided $CP=r$; *i.e.*, $CP^2=r^2$, or $CL^2+LP^2=r^2$, if CL is perpendicular to NP; therefore

$$(x-h)^2+(y-k)^2=r^2 \qquad (1)$$

This is the *equation of the circle.* The variable point P will lie on the circle if, and only if, (1) is satisfied.

The equation $x^2+y^2+2ax+2by+c=0$ . . . . (2) may be written in the form $(x+a)^2+(y+b)^2=a^2+b^2-c$, which is equivalent to (1) if $h=-a$, $k=-b$ and $r^2=a^2+b^2-c$. The last of these conditions is not possible for any real value of r if a^2+b^2-c is negative; but, if a^2+b^2-c is positive, the equation (2) is seen to represent a circle whose centre is $(-a,-b)$ and *radius* $\sqrt{(a^2+b^2-c)}$. The constants a, b and c in (2) may be determined to satisfy specified conditions, and the circle becomes then definitely fixed. For instance, if the circle is to pass through three given points, the co-ordinates of these must satisfy the equation (2), and, on substituting them for x and y, three equations are obtained giving a, b and c. If the point (x, y) is not on the circle, but outside it, as at P' (fig. 3), the left-hand side of equation (2) is *not* equal to zero, but, when written as $(x+a)^2+(y+b)^2-(a^2+b^2-c)$, or $(x-h)^2+(y-k)^2-r^2$, is seen to represent CP'^2-CT^2 (if $P'T$ is a tangent), which is $P'T^2$.

A point (x, y) from which the tangent to the circle (2) is equal to the tangent to the circle $x^2+y^2+2a'x+2b'y+c'=0$ . . . . . . (3) satisfies the equation

$$x^2+y^2+2ax+2by+c=x^2+y^2+2a'x+2b'y+c';$$
$$\textit{i.e.,}\ 2(a-a')x+2(b-b')y+(c-c')=0.$$

This equation (if the circles (2) and (3) have not the same centre) is of the first degree, so that the point (x, y) lies on a fixed straight line, called the *radical axis* of the circles. If the circles (2) and (3) have two points in common, the radical axis is the line joining these points. The equation $x^2+y^2+2kx+c=0$ represents, for different values of c, different circles of which any two have OY for radical axis. These circles are said to form a *coaxial system.* If c is negative, all the circles pass through the same two points on OY. If c is positive, none of the circles intersect. In either case one circle of the system may be found to pass through any given point not on OY.

The equation of the tangent at a point (x_1, y_1) on the circle (2) may be shown to be

$$x_1x+y_1y+a(x+x_1)+b(y+y_1)+c=0. \qquad (4)$$

If, however, (x_1, y) is not on, but outside the circle, equation (4) represents the *polar* of (x_1, y_1) that is the straight line joining the points of contact of tangents from (x_1, y_1).

Mensuration of the Circle.—The ratio of the length of the circumference to the diameter is the same for all circles. This number can only be calculated approximately, and is 3·14159265358979323846 as far as 20 places of decimals. The true value of this number is always denoted by π, and has been recognized from antiquity as a most important constant. $\frac{22}{7}$ may be used as a rough approximation to π. Mathematicians have devoted an incredible amount of time to the calculation of this number, even reaching hundreds of decimal places. It is difficult to believe, however, that more than about ten figures could ever be put to any practical use; in fact 3·1415926 is likely to serve well enough. If r is the radius, the length of the whole circumference is $2\pi r$.

Let s measure the arc AB, c the chord AB, and h the distance from the middle of the arc to the chord. By dividing up the area of the sector AOB as suggested (fig. 4), and reasoning from the sum of a number of small triangles, it is inferred that the *area of the sector* is $\frac{1}{2}rs$; and the area of the whole circle is $\frac{1}{2}r\times 2\pi r=\pi r^2$.

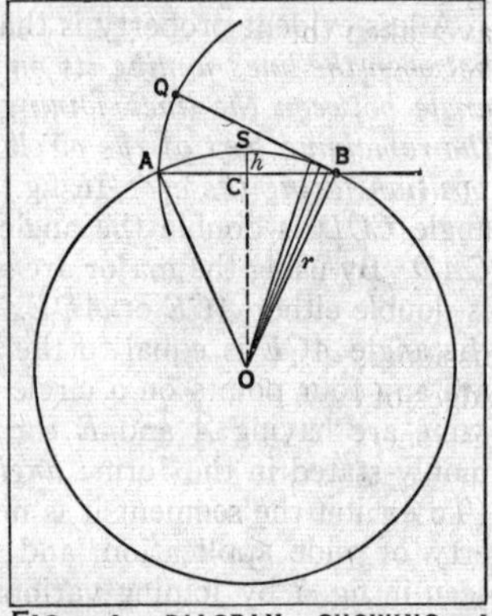

FIG. 4.—DIAGRAM SHOWING A METHOD OF DETERMINING THE AREA OF A CIRCLE

It has long been known that no construction by ruler and compasses can furnish a straight line of length equal to that of the circumference of a given circle, or a square equal in area to a given circle; though in ancient times "squaring the circle" was considered an important unsolved problem. Also a straight line cannot be constructed equal to any given arc of a circle, though approximate methods exist which work well for an arc which is not too large compared with the radius. For instance, produce *AB* to *P*, making $BP=\frac{1}{2} AB$. With centre *P* and radius *PA* draw an arc cutting at *Q* the tangent at *B*. Then $BQ =$ the arc *AB* approximately. For an arc forming a quarter circle the error is about one part in 300. For $\frac{1}{36}$ of the circumference the error is less than one in a million. An approximate relation between *c*, *h* and *s* is $s=c+8h^2/(3c)$. For a value of *h* less than $\frac{1}{12}$ of *c*, this gives *s* to within $\frac{1}{10,000}$ of its value. The radius of the circle does not appear in this relation. As an example of its use, if $c=144$, and $s=144\cdot2$, then $h=3\cdot3$.

BIBLIOGRAPHY.—Euclid, *Elements*, Bk. III; J. L. Coolidge, *A Treatise on the Circle and the Sphere* (1916); H. S. Hall and F. H. Stevens, *A School Geometry* (1924); D. M. Y. Sommerville, *Analytical Conics* (1924).

CIRCLEVILLE, a city of Ohio, U.S., on the Scioto river, 25 mi. S. of Columbus; the county seat of Pickaway county. It is on federal highways 22 and 23 and is served by the Norfolk and Western and the Pennsylvania railways. The population in 1950 was 8,723. Canned vegetables, straw paper for boxes, advertising novelties, products from corn cobs, stock feeds and soybean meal and oil are among its manufactures. An annual pumpkin show is held. The city was laid out (1806) within a circular embankment of prehistoric origin, with an octagonal courthouse in the centre and circular streets around it. The courthouse was burned in 1841, and no trace remains of the original plan or of the ancient earthworks. The city was chartered in 1853.

CIRCUIT is a path for transmitting electrical energy.

CIRCUIT RIDER, a preacher or minister who supplies several localities, preaching at each in succession and thereby forming a "circuit." Francis Asbury, a follower of John Wesley inaugurated the custom in the United States in Nov. 1771, and for 45 years travelled on horseback, at the rate of 5,000 m. a year, preaching twice a day on weekdays and three times on Sunday. Each circuit was under the supervision of a Wesleyan conference preacher and he might have any number of lay-assistants. Any young man who showed aptness for public speaking and willingness to endure the hardships of travelling in the saddle for weeks at a time over a wild and rough country, might become an assistant and finally a circuit rider. The salary was $64 a year until 1800, when it was raised to $80 a year, with the horse furnished by the circuit. There were almost no meeting houses and services were held in log cabins, bar-rooms or in the open. Circuit riders were a considerable religious and moral force, especially along the frontier.

CIRCUITS, in a legal sense, are the periodical progresses of the judges of the superior courts of common law through the several counties of a given region for the purpose of administering civil and criminal justice. These modern circuits in progresses have taken the place of the *eyres* or *itinera* of the ancient system. The word circuit is also applied to the rotative sittings of judges of county courts in the various towns of the districts over which they preside.

It is provided by s. 70 of the Supreme Court of Judicature (Consolidation) Act, 1925, that judges of the king's bench division of the high court and every judge of the probate division (if the state of business of that division permit) together with such commissioners of assize as may be appointed by letters patent shall be judges of assize. By virtue of their commission all judges and commissioners of assize are entitled within the districts fixed by their commission (including the counties palatine of Lancaster and Durham) to exercise all the powers of civil or criminal jurisdiction capable of being exercised by the high court, including (s. 71) the trial of revenue causes or proceedings. It is further provided by the act (s. 77) that: If at any time it appears to the lord chief justice that there is no business, or no substantial amount of business, to be transacted at the assizes about to be held at any particular place on a circuit, he may, with the concurrence of the lord chancellor, direct that assizes shall not on that occasion be held at such place.

The general regulation of circuits throughout England and Wales, in modern times, was originally provided for by s. 23 of the Judicature Act, 1875 (now replaced by s. 70 of the Supreme Court of Judicature [Consolidation] Act, 1925). By this section power was conferred on the Crown by order in council to make regulations respecting circuits, including the discontinuance of any circuit, and the appointment of the places at which assizes are to be held on any circuit. Under this power, an order in council, dated Feb. 5, 1876, was made reconstructing and remodelling the circuit system throughout England and Wales. By virtue of this order the then existing circuits were discontinued and were replaced by fresh circuits. These, after various mutations, are now settled as follows: the northern, the north-eastern (taken from the northern), the midland, the south-eastern, the Oxford, the western, and the north Wales (with Chester) and south Wales (divisional) circuits. The delimitation of these circuits together with the names of the towns throughout England and Wales at which assizes are held are set out in some 14 orders in council, all of which are printed in *Statutory Rules and Orders*. Birmingham was first constituted a circuit town in the year 1884 and, by arrangement, the work there became the joint property of the midland and Oxford circuits. There are alternative assize towns in the following circuits, viz., on the western circuit, Salisbury and Devizes for Wiltshire and Wells and Taunton for Somerset; on the south-eastern, Ipswich and Bury St. Edmunds for Suffolk; on the north Wales circuit, Welshpool and Newtown for Montgomery; and in the south Wales (division), Cardiff and Swansea for Glamorgan.

The approximate dates for the holding of circuit assizes are: winter (about the middle of January), summer (about the middle of May), and autumn (about the middle of October). Spring assizes for both civil and criminal business are held in April and May in two circuits only, viz., at Manchester and Liverpool on the northern, and at Leeds on the north-eastern. In the past considerable difficulty was experienced in coping with assize work in the provinces and at the same time maintaining the efficiency of the common law sittings in London. With the object of obviating this as far as possible it has been arranged that certain of the common law judges shall remain in London during the whole of the circuits, and the others until their respective commission days which are generally arranged to fall on varying dates.

Counsel are not expected to practise on a circuit other than that to which they have attached themselves, unless they receive a special retainer. They are then said to "go special," and the fee in such a case is 100 guineas for a king's counsel and 50 guineas for a junior. In such cases it is customary to employ in the action one member of the circuit on which the counsel has come special. Certain rules have been drawn up by the bar council for regulating the practice as to retainers on circuit: (1) A special retainer must be given for a particular assize (a circuit retainer will not, however, make it compulsory upon counsel retained to go the circuit, but will give the right to counsel's services should he attend the assize and the case be entered for trial); (2) if the venue is changed to another place on the same circuit, a fresh retainer is not required; (3) if the action is not tried at the assize for which the retainer is given, the retainer must be renewed for every subsequent assize until the action is disposed of, unless a brief has been delivered; (4) a retainer may be given for a future assize, without a retainer for an intervening assize, unless notice of trial is given for such intervening assize. There are also various regulations enforced by the discipline of the circuit bar mess.

In Scotland the judges of the supreme criminal court, or high court of justiciary, form also three separate circuit courts, consisting of two judges each; and the country, with the exception of the Lothians, is divided into corresponding districts, called respectively the northern, western and southern circuits. On the northern circuit, courts are held at Inverness, Perth, Dundee and Aberdeen; on the western, at Glasgow, Stirling and Inveraray; and on the southern, at Dumfries, Jedburgh and Ayr. (W. W.-P.)

UNITED STATES

The United States is organized in 11 judicial circuits (including the District of Columbia as a circuit), a U.S. court of appeals being in each circuit. In the mid-1950s the number of judges on the bench of each court of appeals varied from three to nine. Cases were usually heard, however, in divisions of three judges, though the judges might sit *en banc* with all present. The chief judge was appointed on the basis of seniority in commission, and one of the U.S. supreme court justices was assigned to each circuit as circuit justice. These courts have appellate jurisdiction over most of the matters determined by the U.S. district courts, but certain matters are taken directly to the supreme court. They are also authorized to review and enforce the orders of various federal administrative agencies.

U.S. Judicial Circuits.—The states and territories of the United States were organized in judicial circuits in the mid-1950s as follows: first, districts of Maine, New Hampshire, Massachusetts, Rhode Island and Puerto Rico; second, districts of Vermont, Connecticut, northern, southern, eastern and western New York; third, districts of New Jersey, eastern, middle, and western Pennsylvania, Delaware and the Virgin Islands; fourth, districts of Maryland, northern and southern West Virginia, eastern and western Virginia, eastern, middle and western North Carolina and eastern and western South Carolina; fifth, northern, southern and middle Georgia, northern and southern Florida, northern, middle and southern Alabama, northern and southern Mississippi, eastern and western Louisiana, northern, southern, eastern and western Texas and Canal Zone; sixth, districts of northern and southern Ohio, eastern and western Michigan, eastern and western Kentucky and eastern, middle and western Tennessee; seventh, districts of northern and southern Indiana, northern, eastern and southern Illinois and eastern and western Wisconsin; eighth, districts of Minnesota, northern and southern Iowa, eastern and western Missouri, eastern and western Arkansas, Nebraska, North Dakota and South Dakota; ninth, districts of northern and southern California, Oregon, Nevada, Montana, eastern and western Washington, Idaho, Arizona and territories of Alaska, Hawaii and Guam; tenth, districts of Colorado, Wyoming, Utah, Kansas, eastern, western and northern Oklahoma and New Mexico; and the judicial circuit of the District of Columbia, with the chief justice of the supreme court as circuit justice.

CIRCUITS, ENGINEERING. There are many ways of classifying the systems designed, analyzed and synthesized by engineers, one of which is to imagine all engineering systems composed of one or more of four basic elements: circuits, processes, energy converters and structures.

A structure may be defined as an engineering system constructed, or existing in nature, to support or retain objects against the effect of the force fields that may be acting upon it or them. Examples are bridges, buildings, highways, dams, transformer cores, etc.

An energy converter is a device which transforms energy from one form to another such as a battery, internal-combustion engine, photoelectric cell, microphone and nuclear reactor.

A process is a progressive action or series of controlled events in the regular course of performing an intended engineering operation such as manufacturing a machine, reduction of an ore, refining of crude oil and production on assembly lines.

A device through which energy, information or matter flows is termed a circuit—the subject of the present article. Examples are an electrical circuit, pipe lines for oil or water, thermal circuits, etc.

Actual engineering systems are usually composed of more than one of the elements, and particular parts of a system may partake of the nature of more than one element. For example, a vacuum tube consists of a structure for supporting the various parts and may also be considered as an energy converter as well as a part of an electrical circuit. It is difficult to classify engineering systems according to these elements; however, the idea of "elements" is most useful in the analysis and synthesis of engineering problems.

The circuit concept has been found very useful for the study of electrical and nonelectrical engineering problems, whether static or dynamic. The employment of the general idea that cause is proportional to effect leads to the following mathematical expression:

$$\text{Cause} = Z\ (\text{effect}). \qquad (1)$$

In this expression Z is a proportionality factor, which can oftentimes be interpreted as an opposition. For instance, Ohm's law for a constant continuous direct current may be written as:

$$v = iR. \qquad (2)$$

Here the voltage, v, may be considered as the cause for the effect, which is the flow of current, i, against an opposition or resistance, R.

On the other hand, if the current is considered the cause, then:

$$i = v\left(\frac{1}{R}\right). \qquad (3)$$

In this instance v is the effect and $\frac{1}{R}$ the opposition.

In some electrical circuits the opposition is made up of a resistance and a reactance. The resistance part opposes the continuous flow of current, and the reactance opposes the change. The total resistance is often termed the impedance.

In electrical engineering the cause was originally designated as being the electromotive force and the current as effect, hence the opposition or impedance was the proportionality factor connecting the cause and effect. Later, in considering electronic circuits, the current was adopted as the cause and the voltage the effect.

The flow of heat through the wall of a building may be analyzed on the basis of a thermal circuit. Here the cause is the difference in temperature between the inner and outer surfaces, while the effect is the heat transfer, the opposition being the thermal resistance and/or thermal capacity of the material. A pipe line through which water flows at a steady rate may be considered a fluid circuit. As an approximation the pressure drop constitutes the cause, the effect is the quantity of water flowing (or a function of this quantity), and the opposition is the frictional effect which opposes the flow of material through the pipe. One might even consider an oversimplified learning circuit as consisting of a teacher (the transmitter) and the student (receiver), connected by an imaginary circuit having an opposition. In this case, the cause would be a stimulus sent by the teacher, the effect the response of the student and the opposition the vocal, auditory and other neural or intellectual blocks and resistances that constitute the impedance of the learning circuit. In this case the response is equal to the ratio of the stimulus to the opposition. For a given stimulus, the greater the opposition of the learning circuit, the smaller would be the response. If one wished to portray the actual learning circuit, it would be necessary to establish a very complicated network consisting of many other factors such as feedback.

Feedback, or the process of transferring energy or information from the output of a circuit to its input, is a very important concept in complex circuit analysis and synthesis. Control by feedback plays a dominant part in industry and everyday life. Feedback control is an operation which reduces the difference between the actual state or condition of a system and an arbitrarily desired state or condition in response to the detected difference between them. In order to illustrate a simple feedback control system, consider a bimetallic thermostat and related circuits for the control of a home gas furnace. The desired temperature is set by adjusting the dial on the thermostat. This control unit then detects or senses any differences between the actual and desired temperatures. The difference is also termed an error. If an error or difference exists, a pair of contacts in the thermostat closes or opens the circuit, thereby initiating the desired action. If the house is too warm, the feedback control shuts off the furnace, and if the temperature falls below the desired value the furnace is turned on. Changes in temperature, which are classed as disturbances as far as the control system is concerned, result from changes in the atmospheric conditions. The control of body temperature in human beings is an excellent example of feedback control. This amazing body temperature regulation is accomplished in a feedback control system which is based in part on a balance of the heat losses through conduction, convection, radiation and evaporation of water and energy gains by metabolism and the muscle action.

In the analysis and synthesis of engineering circuits, it becomes apparent that to produce an effect there must be a cause. The cause, effect and opposition are related in such a manner that the cause is proportional to the effect. In order to illustrate this relationship for a mechanical system, imagine a block of wood sliding down a steep, inclined plane in such a manner that the velocity of the block increases with the distance travelled. The cause which accounts for the movement of the block is the resultant of the downward gravitational force component and the backward frictional force between the block and the plane. The effect is manifest as an acceleration of the block, and the opposition is represented by the mass of the block. Hence the net driving force or cause equals the product of the acceleration and the mass of the block. This is immediately recognized as one of Newton's laws of motion.

In engineering circuits, the cause variable is often referred to as a driving potential. Hence the cause variables for several circuits are: for a thermal circuit, the temperature difference; for a fluid circuit, the pressure difference; and for an electrical circuit, the voltage or current. All engineering circuits show some form of opposition; otherwise a finite cause could produce enormous effects, which is contrary to experience.

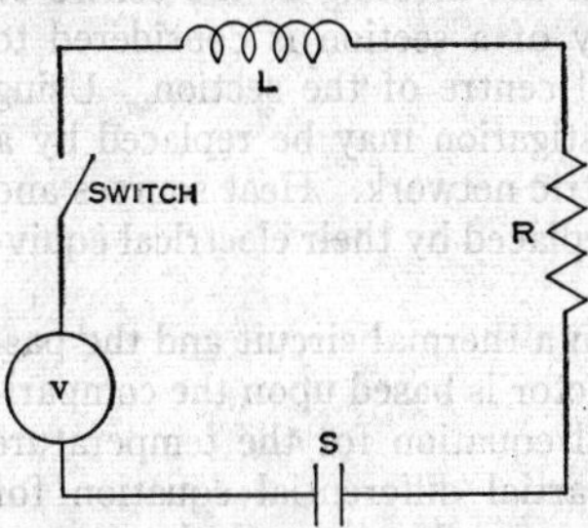

FIG. 1.—PLANER ONE LOOP *LRS* NETWORK (*see* TEXT FOR FURTHER EXPLANATION)

For convenience, the opposition variable may be divided theoretically into two classes: one in which energy is converted into another form, the other in which energy is stored. Mechanical friction would serve as an example of opposition wherein energy is converted. An electric capacitor is a unit in a circuit where potential electrical energy is stored.

A circuit is usually composed of a number of units joined together by connectors. The effect variable is the same at any given time throughout the unit, while the cause variable varies across the unit. For convenience the symbols C, E and Z will be employed to designate the cause, effect and opposition quantities.

According to the general relation it may be stated that the opposition is equal to the ratio of the cause to the effect variable, or

$$Z = C/E.$$

The product of the cause and effect variable often represents apparent power. For example, in an electric circuit the power term may be expressed as the product of voltage and current.

According to the laws of conservation of mass and energy, neither can be created nor destroyed. From these laws, two very important propositions result. The first is that the summation of the effect variables about a point in a circuit must be equal to zero. Also, it may be concluded that for a closed circuit the summation of the cause variables across the individual units must be equal to zero.

When applied to an electrical circuit, these two are recognized as the potential and current laws established by Gustav Robert Kirchhoff in 1857. The Kirchhoff potential law states that the vector sum of the potential differences across the individual unit in any closed path in an electrical network is equal to zero. The current law states that the vector sum of the current flowing at a node in a network is zero. By vector sum is meant the resultant effect of several separate effects; for example, the vector sum of the differently directed forces in the guy wires attached to the top of a television mast at a given instant in a windstorm is the single force in a single imaginary wire that would have the same effect as all the separate wires do have at that time. A node in this case is the junction of the several elements.

Before the use of circuits in the solution of engineering problems is discussed, consideration will be given to certain aspects of the elements of electrical networks.

Resistance and conductance are the elements in an electrical circuit which determine for a given current the rate of conversion of electrical energy to heat. According to the general relation previously discussed for a given instantaneous voltage v (cause variable), and current i (effect variable), the following expression may be written for the resistance R (opposition):

$$v = iR, \tag{2}$$

or if, as explained above, i is to be taken as the cause variable, then

$$i = \frac{v}{R} = Gv. \tag{3}$$

In order to avoid the use of the resistance in the denominator, the symbol G is used to replace the reciprocal of the resistance and is called the conductance.

Inductance is the property of a unit in an electric circuit or of two neighbouring circuits which determines the electromotive force induced in one circuit as a result of a change in current in either of the circuits. An expression for the opposition potential for an inductance follows:

$$v = L\frac{di}{dt}. \tag{4}$$

In this expression, it is seen that the voltage, v, is equal to the product of the inductance, L, and the rate of change of the current. Solving this relation for di gives:

$$di = \frac{v}{L}dt, \text{ and so}$$
$$\int di = i = \frac{1}{L}\int vdt = \Gamma\int vdt. \tag{5}$$

To avoid the use of the reciprocal of the inductance, the symbol Γ has been introduced and is called the inverse self-inductance.

An element in which electrical potential energy is stored is called a capacitor. The voltage drop v across a capacitor may be expressed as follows:

$$v = S\int idt. \tag{6}$$

In the expression S is called the elastance. The corresponding value of di is $Sidt$. So

$$i = \frac{1}{S}\frac{dv}{dt} = C\frac{dv}{dt} \tag{7}$$

In order to avoid the use of the reciprocal of elastance, the symbol C, called the capacitance, is introduced.

Attention will now be directed to a planer one loop network consisting of a voltage source, v; inductance, L; resistance, R; capacitor, S; and switch as shown in fig. 1.

The summation of the effect variable (voltage drop) for the various units of the closed circuit is zero, or

$$v = v_L + v_R + v_S. \tag{8}$$

Replacing the voltage values by their equivalents gives:

$$v = L\frac{di}{dt} + Ri + S\int idt. \tag{9}$$

This is a differential equation expressing the relationship of voltage and current as functions of time. The time is measured from the instant when the switch is closed.

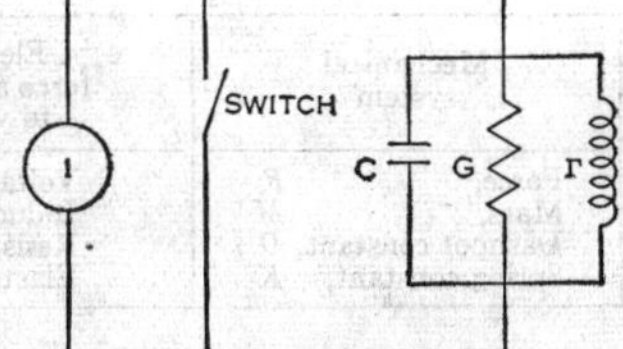

FIG. 2.—PLANER ONE NODE PAIR *CGΓ* NETWORK (*see* TEXT FOR FURTHER EXPLANATION)

Consider next the planer one node pair $CG\Gamma$ network shown in fig. 2. The opening of the switch at time zero allows current to flow through the various units. Since the summation of the effect variables at a node is zero, the following current equation may be written:

$$i = i_C + i_G + i_\Gamma. \tag{10}$$

Replacing the various terms by their equivalents results in the following differential equation:

$$i = C\frac{dv}{dt} + Gv + \Gamma\int vdt. \tag{11}$$

Comparing the differential equations (9) and (11) indicates that the mathematical forms are the same. In other words, the two networks constitute two different physical representations of the same general equations. Two networks of this type are called analogous, and one network is often referred to as the dual of the other. This concept of duality of circuits is extremely important in the analysis of other circuits by electrical means (*see* Table I).

TABLE I.—*Variables and the Corresponding Duals for Electrical Circuits*

Element or variable	Dual of element or variable	Element or variable	Dual of element or variable
Voltage, v	Current, i	Resistance, R	Conductance, G
Inductance, L	Inverse inductance, Γ	Elastance, S	Capacitance, C

Mechanical Electrical Analogies.—In order to show the application of the electrical circuits to the study of the vibration characteristics of a mechanical system, consider the system shown in fig. 3. The sketch illustrates schematically a mass, M, supported by a spring, K, and a mechanism such as a dashpot to retard the vibrations caused by a force, F. The general differential equation for the force, F, may be expressed as follows:

$$F=M\frac{dv}{dt}+Dv+K\int vdt. \qquad (12)$$

By crossing out the last two terms on the right side of this equation one obtains one of the well-known equations of motion of Newton which states that force is proportional to the product of the mass and acceleration. The retarding force of the dashpot is assumed to be equal to a constant D multiplied by the velocity v. The spring force is equal to the product of the spring constant K and the integral indicated. The two additive forces have been allowed for in the equation as stated.

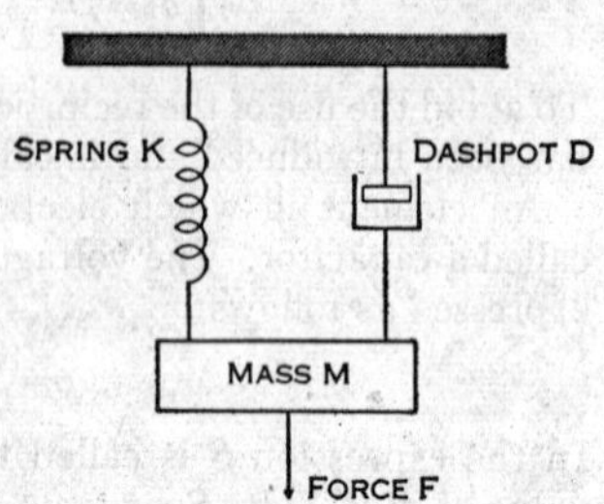

FIG. 3.—SCHEMATIC DRAWING OF A MECHANICAL SYSTEM

Comparing equation (12) with relations (9) and (11) for the two electrical circuits reveals the analogy between the differential equations for the mechanical and electrical systems. These equations are, in fact, identical in form. By the proper choice of physical constants for one circuit, corresponding constants that appear in the analogous circuits can be made strictly proportional one to the other. It is, therefore, possible to determine the behaviour of a mechanical system by the study of an equivalent electrical circuit. Since it is often much more convenient to measure current and voltage than force and velocity, this type of analysis is extremely useful.

Comparison of the terms in these three equations results in Table II of analogous quantities between a mechanical system and two types of electrical circuits.

TABLE II.—*Analogous Quantities*

Mechanical system	Electrical force analogous to voltage	Circuits force analogous to current
Force, F	Voltage, v	Current, i
Mass, M	Inductance, L	Capacitance, C
Dashpot constant, D	Resistance, R	Conductance, G
Spring constant, K	Elastance, S	Inverse inductance, Γ

By use of these analogies, it is possible to establish equivalent electrical circuits for use in the study of many mechanical systems.

Equivalent electrical circuits have been employed to study many engineering problems, a few of which are: the motion and stresses in the parts of a vacuum tube when it and its cardboard container are dropped to the floor, the motion of the wheels and body of an automobile as it strikes a bump in the road, design of crankshafts and study of vibration and stresses in existing units.

Thermal-Electrical Analogies.—Resistance-capacitance electrical circuits may be used for the study of complex heat transfer problems by establishing suitable analogies. In this analogy, electric current corresponds to heat flow in the thermal circuit, voltage to temperature difference, electrical resistance to thermal resistance and electrical capacity to thermal capacity.

The equivalent electrical circuit which is constructed to portray the thermal circuit is made up of "lumped" resistances and capacitances. The lumping corresponds mathematically to the replacement of a differential equation by an equation of finite difference. The word "lumping" is used to convey the idea that a property such as capacitance or resistance which may be distributed along a unit (say along its length) in the one circuit is concentrated at a point in the corresponding unit of the analogous circuit. The lumping of the resistances and capacitances may be briefly described by saying that a physical body is considered as being divided into a number of geometrical sections of simple shape and form. Resistance to heat flow in a section is represented by resistors emanating from the meeting at the centre of the section. The thermal capacity of a section is considered to be concentrated at the geometrical centre of the section. Using this procedure, a body under investigation may be replaced by a lumped resistance-capacitance electric network. Heat sources and boundary conditions may also be replaced by their electrical equivalents.

The analogy between heat flow in a thermal circuit and the passage of current in an electric conductor is based upon the comparison of the basic partial differential equation for the temperature distribution in a solid and the partial differential equation for electric potential in a noninductive conductor, and the rate at which thermal energy is stored and the rate of flow of charge in a capacitor.

In order actually to establish the magnitude of the units in the equivalent electrical circuit, it is necessary to obtain a set of ratios corresponding to thermal and electrical properties. For example, the potential ratio is defined as the unit of potential in the thermal circuit to the unit of potential in the electrical circuit. The seven ratios normally used are: potential, flow, resistance, quantity, time, capacity and distance or position ratio. By suitable algebraic manipulation, basic relations for the various ratios may be established. These relations are expressible in terms of three independent ratios or variables. However, in practice the arbitrariness of their choice may be restricted by the electrical components. For example, to minimize the leakage from the electrical capacitors, a "speed-up" in the electrical circuit is desirable; however, such a choice may call for some electrical resistances in the circuit greater than any available. In addition, certain heat transfer problems may possess unusual heat input conditions, which will influence the choice of the independent ratios.

Equivalent electrical circuits have been used extensively in the study of many thermal circuits, a few of which may be mentioned: heat flow from fins, temperature distribution in cooled turbine blades, deicing studies dealing with aircraft wings and propellers, temperature distribution in gas turbine disks and the design of heat exchangers.

Complex heat flow problems may be studied by an analogy consisting of a vessel filled with a conducting fluid. Studies have been made to determine the heat flow through corners of complex furnace walls by this analogy. The inside and outside surfaces of a thick corner section were represented by metal corners forming the vertical walls of a tank. Beyond the corner for each wall boundary partitions were installed, which were made from nonconducting material. The bottom of the tank was constructed from a nonconducting material. The tank was filled with a conducting liquid which was analogous to the homogenous material of the wall section. An electrical potential was established between the outer parallel conducting surfaces; thus the analogy between steady heat flow conditions between constant temperature walls was established. By means of an electrical probe, the isopotential (or equipotential) lines were obtained, which represent the isothermal lines (or lines of equal temperature) in the thermal system. This may be classed as a geometrical thermal electrical circuit analogy. This type of analogy has been used in the solution of many engineering problems, some of which are: effect of thermocouple holes in the measurement of temperatures of thick castings during quenching operations, establishment of pressure gradients on the faces of irregular-shaped dams and heat-flow problems involving variation of thermophysical properties with temperature.

An analysis similar to the conducting liquid tank procedure has been used for which the liquid bath is replaced by a solid conductor of uniform electrical characteristics. The conductor consists of a thin metal sheet out of which the particular geometrical shape is cut. Using the electrodes at the boundary edges, isopotential lines can be obtained by use of a probe. This type of analogy has the advantage of simplicity in obtaining the direct geometrical patterns desired. It has been used successfully for the design of insulated walls in cold-storage rooms.

Another useful analogy is the hydraulic thermal circuit, which has been used in the study of heat exchange apparatus. One such apparatus consisted of vertical glass tubes connected by means of capillaries. A liquid such as water flows through the capillaries, and the change in level with time in the glass tubes is measured. Time and liquid level in the fluid circuit correspond to time and temperature in the heat exchanger. Heat losses to the surroundings, variable specific heat and change in phase may be taken into account by means of the analogy.

Many other types of analogues have been used for the analysis and synthesis of engineering systems.

A physical system and its circuit analogue may both be regarded as (physical) analogues of an abstract system whose behaviour is defined by a mathematical formulation such as a differential equation. It may be stated that the circuit analogue solves approximately the mathematical problem defined by an (abstract) system and consequently solves that of the given physical system. In this respect the circuit analogue may be called a computer. It is commonly called an analogue computer not only because it measures one type of physical quantity in terms of another but because it measures the numerically defined variables of the abstract system in terms of some physical system. A natural limit of the precision of evaluation of the numerical variables is induced by the dependence on physical measurements. A thermal analyzer, because it solves heat transfer problems electrically, and an electronic differential analyzer, because it solves differential equations by simulation through circuits, are examples of analogue computers. The former is an example of a direct analogue computer while the latter is one of the indirect types.

The direct analogues may be subdivided into mechanical, fluid and electrical types. For example, direct strain measurements may be made on plastic models of engineering structures to study deflections and stresses. The fluid class covers such devices as models of dams and river beds which are found in many hydraulic laboratories. These models are used for various studies including flood control, drainage and erosion problems. The electrical devices are those which use the analogy between electrical circuits and others; for example, as previously shown, the direct electrical analogy between a simple mechanical spring and the energy storage in an electrical capacitor. The use of the principle of duality is often employed so as to have the computer operate on the dual of the problem. Such devices as the alternating current network analyzer used for the study of electric power distribution systems, and the thermal analyzers used for the study of complex thermal circuits, are examples of the direct electrical analogue.

The indirect analogues may be subdivided into mechanical and electrical indirect analogue computers. Examples of the mechanical type are: the slide rule where lengths measured on a rule are indirectly analogous to numbers, nomograms, the Norden bomb sight and the general-purpose differential analyzer which Vannevar Bush and others designed and constructed. The electrical indirect analogue computer is a very common type which employs such devices as high gain amplifiers, feedback loops, etc. Many of the gun directors are in this class of computers.

A special-purpose computer is one that is functionally limited to the description of restricted types of systems; for example, those defined by simple differential equations. Often the analogous circuit requires extensive physical modification whenever the parameters of physical systems change. A more versatile device is the general-purpose computer, which is designed to solve any abstract mathematical problem directly without requiring physical modification. Hence the same computer may be used to evaluate two vastly different systems such as the flow of heat in a cylinder and the determination of an optimum inventory pattern for a warehouse.

General-purpose computers treat all quantities in digital form, and their precision is quite superior to that of the analogue computers. Devices of this type are becoming commoner as research tools because of their flexibility and speed.

Bibliography.—C. F. Kayan, "An Electrical Geometrical Analogue for Complex Heat Flow," *Transactions* of the American Society of Mechanical Engineers (Nov. 1945); G. D. McCann and H. E. Criner, "Mechanical Problems Solved Electrically," *Westinghouse Engineer* (March 1946); L. M. K. Boelter, "Some Observations on Learning," *Journal of Engineering Education*, vol. xxxvii, no. 5 (Jan. 1947); H. F. Olson, *Dynamical Analogies* (New York, 1943; London, 1944); M. F. Gardner and J. L. Barnes, *Transients in Linear Systems*, vol. i, *Lumped-Constant Systems* (New York, 1942); W. T. Thomson, *Laplace Transformation* (New York, 1950); E. K. Kraybill, *Electric Circuits for Engineers* (New York, London, 1951); W. R. Ahrendt and J. F. Taplin, *Automatic Feedback Control* (New York, 1951); G. A. Korn and T. M. Korn, *Electronic Analog Computers* (New York, 1952); E. A. Guillemin, *Introductory Circuit Theory* (New York, 1953; London, 1954); I. S. Juhasz and F. C. Hooper, "Hydraulic Analog for Studying Steady-State Heat Exchangers," *Industrial and Engineering Chemistry*, vol. xlv (June 1953); M. H. Aronson, *Electronic Circuitry for Instruments and Equipment* (Pittsburgh, 1953).

(G. A. H.)

CIRCULAR NOTE, a documentary request by a bank to its foreign correspondents to pay a specified sum of money to a named person. The person in whose favour a circular note is issued is furnished with a letter (containing the signature of an official of the bank and the person named) called a letter of indication, which is usually referred to in the circular note and must be produced on presentation of the note. Circular notes are generally issued against a payment of cash to the amount of the notes, but the notes need not necessarily be cashed, but may be returned to the banker in exchange for the amount for which they were originally issued. A forged signature on a circular note conveys no right, and as it is the duty of the payer to see that payment is made to the proper person, he cannot recover the amount of a forged note from the banker who issued the note. (*See* also Letter or Bill of Credit.)

CIRCULARS AND CIRCULARIZING, a means of advertising and selling which reached large proportions as a result of rapid printing and postal extension in the 20th century. This consists of descriptive circulars and other forms of advertising literature sent through the mails to bring about sales directly to possible customers. It has long been widely used in France and the United States, in connection with catalogues mailed on request by department stores, seedsmen and manufacturers of various articles than can be economically shipped.

With the development of the mail-order houses, particularly in the United States, the use of this method of advertising greatly extended. Catalogues of 1,000 pages or more sometimes are sent broadcast to urban and farm dwellers alike, who give orders for clothing, pianos, agricultural implements, household utensils and a great variety of other articles. The number of mail-order houses in the United States is estimated at 125, with yearly sales approximating $500,000,000. With the extension of the parcel post and favourable postal rates, this form of advertising was widely adopted by manufacturers. (W. S. Hi.)

CIRCULATING MEDIUM: *see* Money.

CIRCULUS IN PROBANDO, in logic, a phrase used to describe a form of argument in which the very fact which one seeks to demonstrate is used as a premise; *i.e.*, as part of the evidence on which the conclusion is based. This argument is one form of the fallacy known as *petitio principii*, "begging the question." It is most common in lengthy arguments, the complicated character of which enables the speaker to make his hearers forget the data from which he began. The following duologue may serve as a simple illustration of circular argument. "He speaks with angels," said one of the Master's disciples. "How know you that?" I asked. "He himself admits it," he replied solemnly. "But suppose he lies?" I persisted. "What!" he exclaimed, "a man who speaks with angels capable of telling a lie?"

(*See* Fallacy.)

CIRCUMCISION. From a medical as distinguished from a ritual aspect this simple operation consists in removal of a sufficient portion of the foreskin to allow of its free retraction beyond the glans penis. The operation is performed chiefly for purposes of cleanliness and to facilitate removal of the smegma which normally collects beneath the foreskin but sometimes is necessary to allow free passage of urine. For these purposes it is done as a preventive measure in the infant. In adults the chief reason for its performance is balanitis or inflammation beneath the foreskin resulting from lack of cleanliness or from the presence of a venereal sore; in this case circumcision is a necessary part of the treatment. It is noteworthy that in India the Hindus, who do not circumcise ritually, suffer far more frequently from cancer of the penis than the Mohammedans, who circumcise. Circumcision is also an initiation or religious ceremony among Jews and Mohammedans and is a widespread institution among many Semitic peoples. It remains, with Jews, a necessary preliminary to the admission of proselytes. Its origin among them is placed in the age of Abraham (Genesis xvii), and at all events it must have been very ancient, for flint stones were used in the operation. The significance of the rite has been much disputed, including views that it was a tribal badge, a substitute for sacrifice and an act of cleanliness. Most probably, it was connected with marriage. (*See* MUTILATIONS AND DEFORMATIONS.)

CIRCUMNAVIGATION OF THE WORLD. Although the efforts to find a route to the Indies had already led to the great voyages of Columbus, the Cabots, Bartholomeu Diaz de Novaes and Vasco da Gama, to Ferdinand Magellan was due the honour of having first sailed round the world (1519–22), although he himself died on the way. The first British circumnavigator was Sir Francis Drake (1577–80), who was followed by others, English, French and Dutch, in the next two centuries, until the celebrated three voyages of Capt. James Cook in 1768–70, 1772–75 and 1776–79 practically completed the discovery of the main outlines of the known world. (*See* individual biographies and the articles GEOGRAPHY and MAP.)

CIRCUMSTANTIAL EVIDENCE is a kind of indirect evidence. Suppose something happens in the presence of witnesses who observe it, then their evidence is *direct* evidence of the occurrence. But now suppose there is no such direct evidence of the event, then it is necessary to rely on indirect evidence, if any. Such indirect evidence usually consists of certain circumstances surrounding the event or in some way connected with it. By piecing these circumstances together we may get an intelligible, coherent account of the whole course of the event or events in question. This piecing together of the data is a kind of hypothesis, and there may be several rival hypotheses to account for the facts. But as in all cases of the use of hypotheses, the hypothesis which gives the most adequate and consistent explanation is usually accepted. Inference from circumstantial evidence resembles ordinary induction to the extent that it involves the use of hypotheses and their verification, but it is unlike ordinary induction inasmuch as it does not aim at a generalization, being concerned only with some particular event. The systematic character of inference is perhaps most obvious in the case of inference from circumstantial evidence, for it manifests most clearly the process of the imaginative construction of a coherent system out of fragmentary evidence. The most familiar occasions for the exercise of inference from circumstantial evidence are criminal cases. Criminals naturally take precautions against the possibility of direct evidence, and are usually betrayed by circumstantial evidence. (*See* EVIDENCE.)

See A. Wolf, *Essentials of Logic* (1926).

CIRCUMVALLATION, LINES OF, in fortification, a continuous circle of entrenchments surrounding a besieged place, facing outward, by which the besieger protected himself against the attack of a relieving army from any quarter (from Lat. *circum,* round, and *vallum,* a rampart). "Lines of contravallation" were similar works but naturally of less circumference, facing inward, as a resistance against the sorties of the besieged.

CIRCUS. In Roman times the circus was a space or building intended for the exhibition of races and athletic contests held at public festivals. In spite of the connection of the Latin *circus* with the Greek κίρκος or κρίκος, a ring or circle, the arena was not circular; it was a rectangle with one semicircular end. Down the centre of the arena ran a fence (*spina*), separating the outward course from the return, and at each end were three conical pillars (*metae*) to mark the limits of the course. On the *spina* were obelisks, images and ornamental shrines; and, in addition, seven figures of dolphins and seven oval objects, one of which was taken down at each of the seven rounds made in a chariot race. Tiers of seats ran parallel to the sides of the course and its semicircular end, the straight end being occupied by the stalls (*carceres*), where the horses and chariots were held. The lower seats were reserved for persons of rank, and there were also various state boxes; *e.g.,* for the giver of the games and his friends (called *cubicula* or *suggestus*). The circus was the only public spectacle at which men and women were not separated. The competitors wore different colours, originally white and red to which green and blue were added. Domitian introduced two more colours, purple and gold, which probably fell into disuse after his death. To provide the horses and large staff of attendants it was necessary to apply to rich capitalists and owners of studs, and from this there grew up in time four companies (*factiones*) of circus purveyors, which were identified with the four colours, and with which those who organized the races contracted for the horses and men. (*See* also GAMES.) The drivers, who were mostly slaves, were sometimes held in high repute for their skill. The horses most valued were those of Sicily, Spain and Cappadocia, and great care was taken in training them. Chariots with two horses or four were most common, but sometimes also they had three and exceptionally more than four horses. Occasionally there was combined with the chariots a race of riders, each rider having two horses and leaping from one to the other during the race. At certain of the races the proceedings were opened by a procession in which images of the gods and of the imperial family deified were conveyed in cars drawn by horses, mules or elephants, attended by the colleges of priests and led by the presiding magistrate (in some cases by the emperor himself) seated in a chariot in the dress and with the insignia of a *triumphator.*

In addition to the races, animals were occasionally massacred as an incidental amusement, but the proper place for bloodshed was the sand of the amphitheatres, such as the Colosseum, which were built round an oval arena. Shows of this kind included an emperor's display of archery, as well as gladiators, fights between men and beasts, merciless pugilism and wrestling, and those representations of mythological horrors, with prisoners to reenact the sufferings of ancient heroes, which Martial describes. It may be noted that "amphitheatre" came into the English language as the name for a prize fighters' hall, and "circus" for the circular road in Hyde Park used by the so-called chariots of the 17th century.

The oldest circus in Rome was the Circus Maximus, in the valley between the Palatine and Aventine hills where, before the erection of any permanent structure, races appear to have been held beside the altar of the god Consus. The first building was by tradition assigned to Tarquinius Priscus (616–578 B.C.). But it was under the empire that the circus first became a conspicuous public resort. Caesar enlarged it to some extent, and also made a canal ten feet broad between the lowest tier of seats (*podium*) and the course, as a precaution for the spectators' safety when exhibitions of fighting with wild beasts, such as were afterward confined to the amphitheatre, took place. When these exhibitions were removed Nero had the canal filled up.

Next in importance to the Circus Maximus in Rome was the Circus Flaminius, erected 221 B.C. in the censorship of C. Flaminius, from whom it may have taken its name; the name may, however, have been derived from Prata Flaminia, where the circus was situated.

A third circus in Rome was erected by Caligula and was known as the Circus Neronis, from the notoriety which it obtained under Nero. A fourth was constructed by Maxentius (4th century A.D.) outside the Porta Appia near the tomb of Caecilius Metellus, where its ruins are still, the only instance from which an idea of the ancient circuses in Rome can be obtained. Old topographers speak of the six circuses, but two of these appear to be imaginary, the Circus Florae and the Circus Sallustii.

BIBLIOGRAPHY.—W. Smith, *Dictionary of Greek and Roman Antiquities,* 2 vol., 3rd ed. (London, 1890–91); C. V. Daremberg and E. Saglio, *Dictionnaire des antiquités,* 5 vol. (Paris, 1877–1919); August von Pauly, *Realencyklopädie der klassischen Altertumswissenschaft,* rev. by Georg Wissowa, iii, 2 (Stuttgart, 1899); J. Marquardt, *Römische Staatsverwaltung,* vol. iii (vol. vi of *Römischen Alterthümer,* 2nd ed.) (Leipzig, 1881–85).

THE MODERN CIRCUS

There is no resemblance at all between the ancient and the modern circus. The modern circus, at its simplest, may mean a circular space occupied by a pony and a clown; usually the arena serves for acrobats, jugglers, lion tamers, sea lions, horsemen, trick riders and "liberty horses," with apparatus overhead for trapezists and funambulists; or there may be three such arenas and two square platforms inside a "hippodrome track" for processions and races. The performances, surrounded by hundreds or thousands of seats, are either in tents or in structures ranging from the largest exhibition halls to the permanent circus buildings of Paris, Berlin, Moscow, Budapest and Blackpool.

What might be termed horseless circuses in the modern sense of the term existed for many centuries. Records of travelling companies who performed a feat of balance called the "force of Hercules" (more familiarly the "pyramids") prove such troupes to be a genuine link between the old and the new. They were seen by Claudian in Rome, by Sir Philip Sidney in Brabant, by Joseph Addison in Venice and by Goethe in the Rhineland.

Early Development.—If these troupes can be accepted as the direct line of descent, then the oldest circus family is that founded in Germany by Johann Eberhard Renz, an itinerant acrobat who died on Jan. 31, 1708, and bequeathed his trade to several generations. Trick riders were also recorded by famous spectators, from Homer to Montaigne. Midway through the 18th century numbers of them turned showmen because of the lack of employment in the homes of the nobility. Jacob Bates attracted attention on the continent with feats that are shown on a large engraving. As his fame spread from 1760 onward, former dragoons of the English regiments in the Prussian service took to his way of life. Several appeared at the pleasure resorts of Islington where Sgt. Maj. Philip Astley (1742–1814) began his new career before he settled down just south of Westminster bridge, with his wife as partner to ride and beat the drum, and later their son John as an addition to the growing company. On that site, to be known as Astley's for more than a century, he combined horsemanship and acrobatics with clowning in the way that has won for him the title of "the father of the circus." Yet it was not he who gave it its name, but Charles Hughes, a deserter from his company, who set up his riding school at the other end of Westminster Bridge road. Each added a stage to his arena, Royal Amphitheatre of Arts becoming the name of Astley's and Royal Circus of Hughes's—but with so little inkling of what was in store that "Circusiana," the printed collection of its melodramas, mentions only one horse.

While Hughes introduced the new type of entertainment to Russia, Astley built amphitheatres in many English cities and also in Dublin. He owned another in Paris until the Revolution, when it came under the control of Antoine Franconi (1738–1836) whose influence was so decisive that the ring everywhere would keep to his measurement—13 m. diameter—and showmen would long continue to live, like him, in a caravan.

The 19th Century.—Neither Franconi nor Astley rested content with trick riders, clowns and performing animals; both used stage and arena combined for spectacles which developed into the equestrian drama. In 1806 John Astley represented Mungo Park's travels with "camels and real horses," and in 1810 introduced cavalry charges into "The Blood Red Knight," by J. H. Amherst, which won an unprecedented success. Under Andrew Ducrow (1793–1842), who began with Amherst's "The Battle of Waterloo" in 1824, Astley's amphitheatre enjoyed such favour that its mark has been left on Victorian literature, notably *The Old Curiosity Shop, The Newcomes, The Ingoldsby Legends* and *The Bon Gaultier Ballads*. Napoleonic spectacles at Franconi's in Paris inspired Heinrich Heine's moving account of the old guardsman who had been to see the circus version of Austerlitz, and no biped play of the 19th century equalled the popularity of H. M. Milner's "Mazeppa," as arranged for horses by Ducrow in 1831.

Shakespeare on horseback, opera on horseback and representations of the Crimean War were tried by William Cooke while manager of Astley's, but these were only a minor event in the history of the largest of all circus families. Thomas Taplin Cooke (1782–1866) had 19 children; they and their children linked themselves by marriage with circuses in all parts of the world. Their closest rivals in Great Britain midway through the 19th century were the Battys, Ginnetts and Fossetts; the Sangers came to the front in 1871 when they bought Astley's. *Seventy Years a Showman,* the autobiography of "Lord" George Sanger (1827–1911), describes his unfailing enterprise in making the public "walk up," more especially when he caused his own procession to cross London closely behind a column of troops escorting Queen Victoria. When "Sanger's, late Astley's" was demolished in 1893 he still asserted his supremacy; he was responsible for the "Congress of All Nations" before it was bought by P. T. Barnum, for Christmas pantomimes which contained lions, tigers, zebras, elephants and horses, for mimic wars in China and the Sudan complete with gunboats that had hoofs showing below their waterlines, and for glittering parades in which cavalcades, bands and menageries preceded towering triumphal cars, called tableaus, of gleaming gold.

Voyaging companies soon had to face local competition for South Africa was provided with circuses of its own by Frank Fillis, the Pagels and the Boswells, while in Australia the Wirths not only triumphed on their own ground but took ship for Africa, South America and England.

While there was a strong resemblance between all these shows of the English-speaking world, Paris developed a style of its own. At the Cirque d'Hiver and the Cirque d'Été (later the Théâtre Marigny), descendants of Antoine Franconi appealed to the world of fashion. Even ballerina and prima donna found close rivals in the top-hatted, wasp-waisted *écuyères* who demonstrated their exquisite skill *en haute école* in a dare-devil style that sometimes proved fatal. Impressionist painters, notably Georges Seurat and Henri de Toulouse-Lautrec, preferred the Médrano in Montmartre, where *clownesse* and *acrobate* were the stars.

Spain had few large circuses of its own apart from the one established in Madrid, and delight in this form of entertainment has regularly favoured travelling shows from abroad, more particularly those from France. "Circo" often means variety under canvas.

In Germany the first showman to become well known throughout the world was Ernst Renz (1814–92), the son of acrobats. Scottish rope walkers brought him up, but it was as a horse trainer that he joined the Brilloff circus which he directed until he founded a one-horse circus of his own with Gotthold Schumann as his partner. In the 1860s the Circus Renz was the most elaborate in existence; it failed under Ernst's son, Franz, and revived under Franz's cousin, Robert, whose wife, Oceana, was said to be the loveliest woman ever to perform in the ring. Busch is the name of more than one circus family on the continent: Paul Busch was responsible for the stone amphitheatre in Berlin which bears their name. But it was the Schumanns who made their influence felt in most capitals. Gotthold's son, Albert (1858–1939), started his training at the age of three and lived to be called (by Sir Charles Cochran) "the outstanding horse trainer of our time." In 1885 he opened a little circus at Malmö in Sweden which steadily grew in size on its European tours until it took over the Berlin headquarters of Renz (which as the Circus Schumann made theatrical history under Max Reinhardt). Max, Albert's brother, managed an American circus on tour in India where he married Victoria Cole, the English rider, who bore Willie in the East Indies, Ernest in India and Oscar in Petrograd. Twelve years of absence cost him his German nationality but by buying a house and land in Sweden he acquired Swedish. In 1914 his company was at Berne. The tent poles had barely been raised when telegrams arrived from different countries, calling men to the colours. The staff of 150 included Austrians, Englishmen, Frenchmen, Germans, Russians and Italians. Without a sign of ill-feeling they left, group by group, while the performance was being given before five people. The Schumanns were stranded and had to sell their horses, but after two years in Switzerland they recruited a company of Swedes and Danes and travelled to Copenhagen, which became their headquarters.

The 1920s and After.—During the 1920s there was an astonishing revival of the circus throughout Europe, in which the Schumanns played a leading part as horsemen. Where such animals as lions, tigers, bears and sea lions, besides at least one sea elephant, were concerned, the Hagenbecks rivalled them closely. Gottfried Hagenbeck, a fishmonger of Hamburg, began by exhibiting seals in his back yard. His son, Carl, who founded the family circus in 1887, installed the zoo at Stellingen which showed how cages could be abolished. The custom of regularly including circuses among London's Christmas entertainments began when the Ringlings thought of coming from America at that time; when they changed their minds Bertram Mills put on a show at Olympia in their place. When all due credit has been paid to his remarkable sense of showmanship, it must be recognized that the 1920s witnessed a veritable harvest of performing prodigies. Besides the Schumanns and the Hagenbecks, he drew on the talents of the Sangers and the Wirths. From France he brought riders of the historic Rancy family to display that legendary act of riding and tooling eight horses at once, called "Les Relais de Longjameau" though Ducrow invented it as "The Courier of St. Petersburg." Fully to explain how exceptional those years between the wars were, a detailed account would have to be given of the juggling of Enrico Rastelli, the somersaults on the slack wire of Con Colleano and the feats of Alfred Codona, the trapezist, and his wife, Lilian Leitzel, who swung herself round and round scores of times while hanging by one hand until one night in Copenhagen the apparatus broke and she was killed. For humour at Olympia there were Charlie Rivel on the parallel bars in the garb of Charlie Chaplin and the water-spilling variations of the Bronetts, leading up to the climax when the Schumanns packed the ring with troupe after troupe of liberty horses. Rival Christmas shows were given at the Agricultural hall where Alfred Court, the most daring of all *dompteurs,* came one year from France with his lions, tigers, bears, panthers and jaguars in a cage together.

When the Nouveau Cirque, once the haunt of those memorable clowns, the Yorkshire Foottit and the Negro Chocolat, was pulled down, and when the large Cirque de Paris vanished also, it seemed that Paris might be growing lukewarm, but the Fratellini, who might be called a dynasty of clowns, excited admiration and affection, first at the D'Hiver and then at the Médrano. German circuses prospered particularly while tenting for they visited towns starved of fun because too poor to make a music hall pay; in addition to many small or medium-sized shows there were two or three of the American size. Karl Krone, who came to Berlin in triumph in 1925, used three rings and two platforms. "The good Gleich," as E. V. Lucas called him, packed two (later three) rings with displays of 200 horses and 14 elephants. Hans Stosch-Sarrasani used one ring but concentrated more colour and movement into the space than had ever been known before and surrounded it with seats for 10,000 people. "Unprecedented" was the aim everywhere. Alfred Schneider tamed 75 lions and with them topped the bill at Olympia.

The effects of World War II on the circus were curious. In 1940 the difficulties were so great that those plucky showmen the Rosaires had a hard fight to survive. Then came a boom enjoyed by fifty circuses; afterward the leading place was taken by Chipperfield's, one of the oldest. In Germany Krone was succeeded after his death by his daughter, Frieda, who herself trained elephants. The Hagenbecks still tented, but the most prominent name was that of Althoff, also a very old circus family, who possessed two or three circuses of their own and were represented by relations in the tents of many others. Everywhere in the 1950s the public welcomed the show and in London there were rings each Christmas at Olympia, Earl's Court and Harringay; but the skill displayed rarely reached the high standards set by the astonishing 1920s.

BIBLIOGRAPHY.—J. C. Cross, *Circusiana*, 2 vol. (London, 1809); *The Memoirs of J. Decastro Accompanied by . . . the Life of . . . Philip Astley* (London, 1824); C. W. Montague, *Recollections of an Equestrian Manager* (London, Edinburgh, 1881); J. Luntley (ed.), *The Public Life of W. F. Wallett, the Queen's Jester: an Autobiography* (London, 1870); G. Wirth, *Round the World With a Circus* (Melbourne, 1925); George Sanger, *Seventy Years a Showman* (London, New York, 1926); Thomas "Whimsical" Walker, *From Sawdust to Windsor Castle* (London, 1922); M. Willson Disher, *Greatest Show on Earth* (London, Toronto, 1937); J. C. Delannoy, *Bibliographie française du cirque* (Paris, 1944); H. Thétard, *La Merveilleux Histoire du Cirque* (Paris, 1949); Alfred Court, *Wild Circus Animals* (London, 1954). (M. W. D.)

UNITED STATES

The American circus is a spectacular form of entertainment, nomadic in character, presenting its exhibitions in tents (rarely in buildings) and moving its performers, staff, working crew, animals and all paraphernalia on its own railway cars; or, in the case of a few small shows, by horse-drawn wagons, motor trucks or river boats. It comprises, physically, in the order met with from the approach (front); refreshment booths (candy stands); ticket and office wagons; one or more side shows (kid shows) containing human and animal oddities; the big show main entrance (front door); the canopied way (marquee) leading to the menagerie; the menagerie tent exhibiting animals caged and in corrals; the elephant line-up and refreshment stands; the canvas-walled passage (connection) leading from the menagerie to the main-tent (big top); the rear entrance (back door) to the main tent, opening on a compound (back yard) in which are located performers' dressing tents, properties, property and wardrobe trucks, vehicles used in pageant (the spec) and other equipment essential to the production.

Early American Circus.—During colonial days several English showmen brought small troupes to the United States. Among the first was Ricketts' circus which exhibited in the Greenwich theatre near the Battery, New York, in 1795. Probably the first American-born showman of note was Rufus Welch, who in 1818 managed a wagon show and later directed larger outfits. In Nov. 1826 the Mt. Pitt circus opened on Broome street, New York, in a building seating 3,500 persons, said at that time to be the largest place of amusement in America. Early circuses, but subsequent to the foregoing, were those of "Old" John Robinson, Dick Sands and Van Amburgh, the two last named making European tours in the 1840s.

Notable among American tent showmen may be named L. B. Lent, Adam Forepaugh, Dan Rice, the Sells brothers, W. C. Coup, P. T. Barnum, James A. Bailey and the Ringling brothers. Lent's historic New York circus played winter engagements in 14th street opposite the old Academy of Music, and toured under canvas during the summer months of the 1860s and early 1870s, his being the first show of size to travel by rail. Forepaugh was one of the tent world's most picturesque characters and the reputed precursor of the modern beauty contests. In 1880 he offered a prize for America's most beautiful woman, resulting in the selection of Louise Montague who thereafter rode in his street parade as "the $10,000 beauty."

Rice was the most famous of American clowns (who were originally pantomimists), and operator of boat shows on the Mississippi. The Sells brothers, Ephraim, Allen, Lewis and Peter, in 1872 founded the show bearing their name, giving distinct impetus to the "brother idea" in the circus world. Coup, a remarkable organizer who, in 1869, projected the largest circus known up to that time, originated performances in two rings, and assisted by Dan Costello persuaded P. T. Barnum to enter the circus field. Barnum, in his 60th year, brought his internationally advertised name and ability as a proprietor of museums, impresario, lecturer and author to the tent show world, thereby giving it incalculable publicity and advancement. Bailey, generally acknowledged to have been the master showman, introduced a third ring and devised intervening stages. Brilliant alike as an organizer, originator and financial genius, he directed superb productions throughout America and toured European countries at the head of the largest circus ever sent across the Atlantic.

The Ringling brothers, August G., Otto, Albert, Alfred T., Charles, Henry and John, were remarkable for their individual ability to direct separate departments of their show. Beginning in 1882 the Ringlings brought the show bearing their name to a size equalling that of the largest. Upon the death of Bailey they in 1907 purchased the Barnum and Bailey "Greatest Show on Earth," but conducted it as a separate institution until 1919 when they combined it with that bearing their name. The consolidation was directed by John Ringling, until his death in 1936.

The Modern Circus.—Unlike European circuses, the modern American circus sells a ticket which includes admission to both menagerie and circus performance. The big show program appeals largely to the eye, since the greater size of the modern main tent has rendered impossible a continuance of the talking clown and like audible features of the former one-ring circus.

The feats of human equestrians, aerialists, gymnasts, acrobats and clowns, interspersed with a number of trained jungle beasts and domestic animals, are presented in ground rings, on ground platforms (stages), from aerial apparatus and from steel arenas so distributed as to be enclosed within or above the confines of an oval courseway (hippodrome track) with the spectators seated in chairs (grandstand) and on bleachers (the blues) in such manner as to surround practically the entire area of action.

An average of 30 different tent shows (the largest requiring approximately 100 railway cars to transport it and the smallest using but a single car) tour more or less extensively through the United States each year. The touring season usually begins in April or May and continues into November. The intervening time is spent in winter quarters.

The biggest of the circuses, Ringling Bros. and Barnum & Bailey, makes its springtime debut in Madison Square Garden in New York city, and then plays a short engagement in a similar building in Boston. Thereafter it tours under canvas. There are not many circuses travelling by rail; most of the smaller ones are motorized, travelling the highways of the country much the same as their ancestors, the wagon or "mud" shows, did a century before. (E. P. N.; E. C. M.)

CIRENCESTER, a market town and urban district in the Cirencester and Tewkesbury parliamentary division of Gloucestershire, Eng., 17 mi. S.E. of Gloucester by road. Pop. of urban district (1951) 11,188. Area 9.1 sq.mi. Lying on the Churn river and at the edge of the Cotswolds, Cirencester is a hunting and an agricultural centre with twice-weekly markets and factories for agricultural equipment. It has many fine gray stone houses, built by rich wool merchants, and a magnificent parish church of St. John Baptist, dating from Norman times but mainly Perpendicular, with bells cast in Queen Anne's reign. The grammar school was founded in 1460.

The town occupies the site of the Romano-British Corinium Dobunorum, built at the junction of Fosse way, Ermine street and Akeman street. Remains of an amphitheatre are preserved near Querns hill but most of the Roman objects that have been found are housed in the Corinium museum (1938). After the battle of A.D. 628, Cirencester was rebuilt by the Saxons, slightly northwest of the old city, and later became a royal demesne. William the Conqueror granted the manor to William Fitzosbern who began building a castle which was razed to the ground under Stephen. A college of prebendaries, founded in Egbert's reign, was reconstructed by Henry I in 1117 as an Augustinian foundation. Henry II leased the manor to the abbot. In 1215 and 1253 the abbot obtained charters for fairs to be held during the octaves of All Saints and St. Thomas the Martyr; the wool trade gave these great importance—Camden records Cirencester as having "the greatest market for wool in England." In the 14th century the citizens rebelled against the abbot's authority and in 1403 Henry IV, as a reward for their help against the earls of Kent and Salisbury, granted them a guild merchant, but the abbot got this revoked by Henry V. Cirencester became a parliamentary borough in 1572, returning two members, but was deprived of separate representation in 1885. The abbey was destroyed at the Dissolution and an Elizabethan mansion (Abbey house) built on the site by Richard Master. Cirencester house was built at the same time by Sir John Danvers and in 1690 it became the home of the Bathurst family; it was rebuilt by the first earl Bathurst in 1718 and stands in a large park south of which is the Royal Agricultural college (incorporated 1845). In 1790 the Thames-Severn canal was extended to the town but was abandoned in 1911.

CIRE PERDUE: *see* SCULPTURE TECHNIQUE: *Casting and Finishing.*

CIRILLO, DOMENICO (1739–1799), Italian physician, botanist and revolutionist, was appointed as a young man to a botanical professorship and later travelled to France and England, where he was elected a fellow of the Royal society. On his return to Naples he was appointed successively to the chairs of practical and theoretical medicine. He wrote voluminously on scientific subjects, particularly botany, on which his most important work was *Fundamenta botanica sive Philosophiae botanicae explicatio*. On establishment of the Parthenopean republic in Naples, Cirillo became president of the legislative commission. When the town surrendered to Fabrizio Cardinal Ruffo, the vengeance of the royalists was wreaked upon Cirillo, and despite Lady Hamilton's intercession, Nelson had him hanged Oct. 29, 1799.

See L. Conforti, *Napoli nel 1799* (Naples, 1889); C. Giglioli, *Naples in 1799* (1903); C. Tivaroni, *L'Italia durante il dominio francese,* vol. ii.

CIRQUE, a French word used to denote a semicircular amphitheatre, with precipitous walls, at the head of a valley in a glaciated mountain region (Lat., *circus,* ring), generally resulting from basal sapping and erosion beneath the bergschrund of a glacier. The bergschrund is a large crevasse, in the form of a great symmetrical arc, parallel to the head of the névé (*see* GLACIER); it lies at a short distance from the exposed rock surface and separates the stationary from the moving ice, and in early summer,

COURTESY OF (1, 2, 4, 5) U.S. NATIONAL MUSEUM, (3) U.S. FISH AND WILDLIFE SERVICE

VARIOUS BARNACLES (Cirripedia, Order Thoracica)

1. Whale barnacle, *Coronula diadema* (suborder Balanomorpha) with portion of whale skin to which it was attached. To the *Coronula* in turn are attached two fleshy stalked barnacles, *Conchoderma auritum* (suborder Lepadomorpha); their specific name is derived from the two processes arising either side of the orifice in which the cirri can be seen. In *Conchoderma* the typical calcareous plates are quite vestigial. *Coronula diadema* at times is also called "whale louse" (*q.v.*). This species, so far as known, occurs only on humpback whales (*Megaptera*) and so is widely distributed in the north Atlantic and Pacific, with records also from Chile, Tonga and New Zealand. Specimen photographed is natural size, but the species attains a diameter of 3½ in. *Conchoderma auritum* seems to have much the same distribution, though not necessarily always attached to *Coronula*, as some specimens, unlike the whale barnacle, are known from ships' bottoms and iron buoys
2. Turtle barnacle, *Chelonibia testudinaria* (suborder Balanomorpha), from loggerhead turtle, Dry Tortugas, Florida. This barnacle is widely distributed on turtles in all temperate and tropic seas, Atlantic as well as Pacific. The specimen figured is natural size, but the species grows half again as large in the eastern tropical Pacific
3. Heavy marine growth, in considerable part barnacles (chiefly *Balanus* species), on propeller and struts of vessel
4. Goose barnacle, *Lepas anatifera* (suborder Lepadomorpha) on piece of driftwood from Gulf of Mexico. Specimens shown are about ⅔ natural size. Size of this species varies greatly, ranging up to 2 and 3 times that of those shown, with stalks here very short but in some cases three or more times as long as the shelly portion or capitulum. *Lepas anatifera* is common in all seas
5. Group of barnacles, showing large and massive form of *Balanus psittacus* (suborder Balanomorpha) from Chile, where it attains its largest growth, up to 9 in. in length and 3 in. in diameter. The fleshy portion of the body of these barnacles is much relished as a sea food in Chile

when the glacier commences to move, it opens and exposes the rock at its base to diurnal changes of temperature. Frost action then causes rapid disintegration downward at its base and backward upon such part of the rock surface as is exposed in the bergschrund beneath the stationary ice, thus producing the characteristic form of the cirque. The formation of cirques has played an important part in the development of the scenery of glaciated mountain tracts. Arêtes (sharp ridges) are formed by the intersection of two cirques, and pyramidlike peaks such as the Matterhorn and Snowdon are remnants left by the recession of three or more cirques. Cirques frequently contain lakes, for, owing to the action of the bergschrund, the floor slopes toward the mountain mass. W. D. Johnston (*Journ. of Geol.* vol xii p. 569) first recognized the processes giving rise to cirque formation by actually descending a bergschrund on the Mount Lyell glacier. Hollows of similar shape to cirques occur in limestone regions which may not have been glaciated. These are formed by aqueous solution and are not true cirques.

CIRRIPEDIA, a subclass of the Crustacea (*q.v.*), comprising the barnacles and acorn shells and certain parasitic forms related to them. All Cirripedes are completely sedentary in the adult state and with the loss of the power of locomotion they have become so modified as to show, at first sight, little trace of resemblance to the more ordinary Crustacea.

The common goose barnacle, *Lepas anatifera,* is found adhering to the bottom of ships and to floating timber. It has a fleshy stalk, fixed at one end to the supporting object and having at the other end a shell of five separate plates enclosing the body of the animal. The stalk is formed from the front part of the head, and the body, when exposed by opening the shell, is seen to be bent nearly at right angles to it. Embedded in the cement which fastens the end of the stalk to the support may be found the remains of the antennules which served for the attachment of the larva. The antennae are wanting, but within the shell the mouth is surrounded by mandibles, maxillulae and maxillae, and these are followed by six pairs of long, curled, two-branched appendages fringed with hairs. These appendages can be protruded from the slitlike opening of the shell, forming a kind of casting net for the capture of minute floating particles of food. The acorn shells which are abundant in most seas attached to rocks in shallow water, differ from the goose barnacle and its allies in having no peduncle. The shell is conical, cemented directly to the rock, and has an opening at the top closed by four movable valves. The shell has a more or less perfect radial symmetry. Barnacles are important ship fouling organisms, which may impede the speed of a ship by 50%, delaying voyages, increasing fuel consumption, the wear and tear on machinery and frequent loss of time in docking to remove offending growths. It has been estimated (1927) that the annual cost of fouling was $100,000,000. The fleshy parts of the largest barnacle are relished in Chile, where *Balanus psittacus* grows to imposing size, 9 in. in height by 3 in. in diameter; other large balanoids are eaten by the aborigines on the northwest coast of America. In Japan smaller species are cultivated on clumps of bamboo set along shore. At intervals of three months the attached barnacles are beaten off for use as manure.

Allied to the more normal Cirripedia just described are a number of more degenerate and, for the most part, parasitic forms. The most degenerate are the members of the order Rhizocephala, of which the genus *Sacculina,* a common parasite of crabs, is a familiar example. It has a simple saclike body attached under the abdomen of the crab by a short stalk from which rootlike processes ramify throughout the internal organs of the host. The body is enveloped by a fleshy mantle with a small opening and is without appendages, mouth or alimentary canal, the only organs which are well developed being those of the reproductive system. There is no trace of Arthropodous structure and only the larval development allows *Sacculina* to be referred to the Cirripedia. For the effect of *Sacculina* on its host, *see* SEX. Largest of the Rhizocephala is *Briarosaccus callosus* found living on a lithodid crab taken from more than 250 fathoms off the southeastern United States. This huge, tumourlike parasite is nearly 4 in. long, more than 2 in. high, and 1¼ in. thick.

Unlike the majority of Crustacea and, indeed, of Arthropoda in general, the Cirripedia are nearly all hermaphrodite, but in a few species dwarf and degenerate male individuals are found attached at, or within, the opening of the shell of the normal individuals. The latter may be, as usual, hermaphrodites, in which case the males were termed by Darwin "complemental males" but in a few instances the large individuals are purely female and the separation of the sexes is complete. It was demonstrated (1942) in the Rhizocephalan *Peltogaster paguri* that the cypris larvae attaching within the mantle cavity of young Peltogasters become masculinized to serve as functional males.

Most Cirripedes are hatched from the egg in the nauplius stage, but the earliest larvae are characterized by the development of spines and processes from the body and in some oceanic species these spines are of relatively enormous length. At a later stage the larva is enclosed in a bivalve shell superficially resembling that of an Ostracod and on this account it is known as the "cypris" stage. Like the nauplius stages the cypris swims freely but ultimately it attaches itself by the antennules, which are provided with glands producing an adhesive secretion. The shell is cast off, leaving a membranous mantle within which calcareous plates appear, at first, apparently, always five in number.

The Cirripedia are almost exclusively marine animals, only one or two species penetrating a little way into estuaries and the like. Certain species attach themselves to whales, marine turtles, or the larger Crustacea, and truly parasitic forms are found on Echinoderms and Crustacea. The earliest fossils definitely referable to the Cirripedia occur in the Rhaetic formation and belong to the Lepadomorpha.

Though complicated by the obscure relationship of parasitic forms to more normal Cirripedes, the classification generally adopted is as follows:

Order *Thoracica,* with six pairs of thoracic appendages, divided into four suborders: *Lepadomorpha,* the stalked barnacles (*Lepas, Scalpellum, Mitella*); *Verrucomorpha,* asymmetrical sessile forms (*Verruca*), *Brachylepadomorpha* (sessile, fossil only, *Pycnolepas, Brachylepas*); *Balanomorpha,* the sessile acorn shells and rock barnacles (*Balanus, Chthamalus, Coronula, Chelonibia*).

Order *Acrothoracica,* somewhat degenerate forms with fewer thoracic appendages, boring in shells and corals (*Alcippe*).

Order *Ascothoracica,* six pairs of thoracic appendages, only Cirripede with definite, at times segmented, abdomen, parasitic on Coelenterates and Echinoderms; affinities obscure (*Laura, Dendrogaster*).

Order *Apoda,* no thoracic limbs, only known specimen described by Darwin; from mantle cavity of another Cirripede (*Proteolepas*).

Order *Rhizocephala,* degenerate parasites of Decapod Crustacea, only Cirripedes without any alimentary canal; no trace of segmentation in adult, wholly without appendages (*Sacculina, Peltogaster*). (*See* ACORN SHELLS; BARNACLE; CRUSTACEA.)

(W. T. C.; W. L. St.)

CIRTA: *see* CONSTANTINE, ALGERIA.

CISCO, a city of Eastland county, Texas, U.S., 108 mi. W. by S. of Ft. Worth on federal highways 80 and 283, and served by the Missouri-Kansas-Texas and the Texas and Pacific railways. Pop. (1950) 5,230. It is in a gas and oil region; has several manufacturing industries and is an important market for horses, fruits, cattle, corn, wheat, peanuts, poultry and other agricultural products. Just north of the city is Lake Cisco and Williamson dam, and just below it is an immense concrete swimming pool. Cisco was founded in May 1881 and was incorporated in 1883. It was named after John W. Cisco, banker and director of the Texas Central railway.

CISSEY, ERNEST LOUIS OCTAVE COURTOT DE (1810–1882), French general, was born at Paris on Sept. 23, 1810, and after passing through St. Cyr, entered the army in 1832. He served in Algeria and in the Crimean War, and became general of division in 1862. When the Franco-German War broke out in 1870, de Cissey was given a divisional command in the army of the Rhine, and he was included in the surrender of Bazaine's army at Metz. He held a command in the army engaged in the suppression of the Commune. From July 1871 de Cissey sat as a deputy, and he had already become minister of war. He occupied this post several times during the critical period of the reorganization of the French army. In 1880 he was accused of treasonable relations with a German agent, but was exonerated by a court of inquiry. He died on June 15, 1882 in Paris.

CISSOID: *see* CURVES, SPECIAL.

CIS-SUTLEJ STATES. Former name for part of south Punjab. Sikh chiefs south of the Sutlej passed under British protection in 1809, and the name was applied to the country south of the Sutlej and north of the Delhi territory. Before 1846 the greater part was independent, the chiefs being subject merely to control from the agent of the governor-general for the Cis-Sutlej states at Umballa. After the first Sikh War the full administration of the territory became vested in this officer. In 1849 the Punjab was annexed and the Cis-Sutlej States commissionership, comprising Ambala, Ferozepore, Ludhiana, Thanesar and Simla districts, was incorporated with the new province. The name continued to be used until 1862, when, Ferozepore having been transferred to the Lahore division, and a part of Thanesar to the Delhi division, it became obsolete.

CIST, in Greek archaeology, a wicker-work receptacle used in the Eleusinian and other mysteries to carry the sacred vessels; and also, in prehistoric archaeology, a coffin formed of flat stones placed edgeways with another flat stone for a cover. Cist-burial was probably introduced into the British Isles by the Beaker-folk about 1800 B.C., but lasted in some parts down to the present era. The cist was generally, but not always covered by a round barrow or cairn.

CISTERCIANS, otherwise GREY or WHITE MONKS (from the colour of the habit, over which is worn a black scapular or apron). In 1098 St. Robert, born of a noble family in Champagne, at first a Benedictine monk, and then abbot of certain hermits settled at Molesme near Châtillon, being dissatisfied with the manner of life and observance there, migrated with twenty of the monks to a swampy place called Cîteaux in the diocese of Châlons, not far from Dijon. Count Odo of Burgundy here built them a monastery, and they began to live a life of strict observance according to the letter of St. Benedict's rule. In the following year Robert was compelled by papal authority to return to Molesme, and Alberic succeeded him as abbot of Cîteaux and held the office till his death in 1109, when the Englishman St. Stephen Harding became abbot, until 1134. In 1112, however, St. Bernard and thirty others offered themselves to the monastery, and a rapid and wonderful development at once set in. The next three years witnessed the foundation of the four great "daughter-houses of Cîteaux"— La Ferté, Pontigny, Clairvaux and Morimond. With Clairvaux Bernard's work is specially associated. At Stephen's death there were over 30 Cistercian houses; at Bernard's (1154) over 280; and by the end of the century over 500; and the Cistercian influence in the Church more than kept pace with this material expansion, so that St. Bernard saw one of his monks ascend the papal chair as Eugenius III.

The Cistercians rejected alike all mitigations and all developments of St. Benedict's rule, and tried to reproduce the life exactly as it had been in his time; indeed in various points they went beyond it in austerity. The most striking feature in the reform was the return to manual labour, and especially to field-work, which became a special characteristic of Cistercian life. In order to make time for this work they cut away the accretions to the divine office which had been steadily growing during three centuries, and in Cluny and the other Black Monk monasteries had come to exceed greatly in length the regular canonical office.

It was as agriculturists and horse and cattle breeders that, after the first blush of their success and before a century had passed, the Cistercians exercised their chief influence on the progress of civilization in the later middle ages: they were the great farmers of those days, and many of the improvements in the various farming operations were introduced and propagated by them; it is from this point of view that the importance of their extension in northern Europe is to be estimated. They depended for their income wholly on the land. This developed an organized system for selling their farm produce, cattle and horses, and notably contributed to the commercial progress of the countries of western Europe. Thus by the middle of the 13th century the export of wool by the English Cistercians had become a feature in the commerce of the country. Farming operations on so extensive a scale could not be carried out by the monks alone, whose choir and religious duties took up a considerable portion of their time; and so from the beginning the system of lay brothers was introduced on a large scale. The lay brothers were recruited from the peasantry and were simple uneducated men, whose function consisted in carrying out the various field-works and plying all sorts of useful trades; they formed a body of men who lived alongside of the choir monks, but separate from them, not taking part in the canonical office, but having their own fixed round of prayer and religious exercises. A lay brother was never ordained, and never held any office of superiority. It was by this system of lay brothers that the Cistercians were able to play their distinctive part in the progress of European civilization. But it often happened that the number of lay brothers became excessive and out of proportion to the resources of the monasteries, there being sometimes as many as 200, or even 300, in a single abbey. On the other hand, at any rate in some countries, the system of lay brothers in course of time worked itself out; thus in England by the close of the 14th century it had shrunk to relatively small proportions, and in the 15th century the régime of the English Cistercian houses tended to approximate more and more to that of the Black Monks.

For a hundred years, till the first quarter of the 13th century, the Cistercians supplanted Cluny as the most powerful order and the chief religious influence in western Europe. But then in turn their influence began to wane, chiefly, no doubt, because of the rise of the mendicant orders, who ministered more directly to the needs and ideas of the new age. But some of the reasons of Cistercian decline were internal. In the first place, there was the permanent difficulty of maintaining in its first fervour a body embracing hundreds of monasteries and thousands of monks, spread all over Europe; and as the Cistercian very *raison d'être* consisted in its being a "reform," a return to primitive monachism, with its field-work and severe simplicity, any failures to live up to the ideal proposed worked more disastrously among Cistercians than among mere Benedictines, who were intended to live a life of self-denial, but not of great austerity. Relaxations were gradually introduced in regard to diet and to simplicity of life, and also in regard to the sources of income, rents and tolls being admitted and benefices incorporated, as was done among the Benedictines; the farming operations tended to produce a commercial spirit; wealth and splendour invaded many of the monasteries, and the choir monks abandoned field-work.

The later history of the Cistercians is largely one of attempted revivals and reforms. The general chapter for long battled bravely against the invasion of relaxations and abuses. In 1335 Benedict XII., himself a Cistercian, promulgated a series of regulations to restore the primitive spirit of the order, and in the 15th century various popes endeavoured to promote reforms. All these efforts at a reform of the great body of the order proved unavailing; but local reforms, producing various semi-independent offshoots and congregations, were successfully carried out in many parts in the course of the 15th and 16th centuries. In the 17th another great effort at a general reform was made, promoted by the pope and the king of France; the general chapter elected Richelieu (commendatory) abbot of Cîteaux, thinking he would protect them from the threatened reform.

In this they were disappointed, for he threw himself wholly on the side of reform. So great, however, was the resistance, and so serious the disturbances that ensued, that the attempt to reform Cîteaux itself and the general body of the houses had again to be abandoned, and only local projects of reform could be carried out.

The Reformation, the ecclesiastical policy of Joseph II., the French Revolution, and the revolutions of the 19th century, almost wholly destroyed the Cistercians; but some survived, and after the beginning of the last half of the 19th century there was a considerable recovery.

In 1933 there were 9 congregations of Cistercians with 37 monasteries, a provostship and many residences. The order numbered about 1,000 members, of whom about 700 were priests. The general of the order resides in Rome.

In 1930 the Cistercians made a foundation at Spring Bank, Wis. Prior to this the order had been represented in the United States by the Strict Observance or Trappists (*q.v.*).

Accounts of the beginnings of the Cistercians and of the primitive life and spirit will be found in the lives of St. Bernard, the best whereof is that of Abbé E. Vacandard (1895); also in the Life of St. Stephen Harding, in the *English Saints*. *See* also Henry Collins (one of the Oxford Movement, who became a Cistercian), *Spirit and Mission of the Cistercian Order* (1866). Useful sketches, with references to the literature, will be found in the *Catholic Encyclopaedia*, art. "Cistercians"; Herzog-Hauck, *Realencyklopädie*, "Cistercienser"; and Heimbucher, *Orden und Kongregationen* (1933), i. §46. On the English houses, *see* F. A. Gasquet's *English Monastic Life;* and on the Cistercian polity, *see* the same writer's "Sketch of Monastic Constitutional History," prefixed to Eng. tr. of Montalembert's *Monks of the West* (1895).

CISTUS, a genus of the family Cistaceae. The members of the family live in dry, sunny places, especially on a sandy or chalky soil.

There are 20 species in the Mediterranean region; many are cultivated ornamental shrubs, in English-speaking countries commonly called rock-rose.

C. villosus and *C. ladaniferus* yield the resin ladanum, which is not to be confused with the hypnotic laudanum.

CITADEL, a municipal fortress. The beginnings of the citadel are remote. At Tanis in Egypt there is a very ancient example; roughly quadrangular, it was built to command a stream and the adjacent ground.

During the 12th dynasty of the first Theban empire a most formidable citadel was evolved, typified at Semneh, where a low wall of first defense rises upon a platform; the citadel proper is a series of crenelated buttress-redoubts projecting at short intervals from a high, rectangular wall, with an additional highly fortified projection at one corner; scaling would have been impossible without fatal casualties.

Ancient Greek citadels were usually of Cyclopean construction (*see* CYCLOPAEAN MASONRY) but that of Tiryns (*q.v.*) has upper walls of brick. It contains the king's palace, a fact which does not change its *rôle* as the true municipal fortress but which points to the origin of the municipality itself. The amalgamation of several hamlets into a *polis* or city, very frequently depended upon the existence of an *acron,* or height, which might be fortified and which became a storehouse of provisions and ammunition as well as the shrine of the god, the home of the king and the refuge of the people.

Just as the acropolis of Athens or the walled hill of the temple of Solomon in Jerusalem were vital municipal influences, so the capitol was the consolidating and protecting factor in Rome. But the citadel of Roman cities in general was less important than those of Greece. In strong countries not contiguous upon others of the same status citadels are rare because they are unnecessary. The Roman *castella* covered Europe and a part of Asia and Africa at one time; they were military centres around which a town might group itself, but they were never, in their beginnings, an integral element of normal municipal life. They existed for the empire and for themselves, and the fact that they protected municipalities was incidental.

After Rome, here and there, the citadel recovered its importance. The growth of feudalism meant the decline of the free, or nominally free, city. It should not be said, however, that in feudal times citadels ceased to be built; sometimes the right of fortification was granted by a lord and sometimes it was acquired by arms; the lord's castle might be a true citadel, or a new one might be erected by the city-State. As a type of architecture distinguished from the castle, the modern citadel is generally said to date from 1568, when the duke of Alva built one to dominate Antwerp. But the rapid multiplication of small States in the late middle ages made the citadel common in Europe.

See CASTLE: *Bibliography;* FORTIFICATION; Daremberg and Saglio, *Dict. ant. class.*, "Acropole"; Planat, *Enc. archit.*, "Citadelle"; C. Enlart, *Man. archéol. fr.*

CITATION, in law, a summons to appear, answering to a writ of summons at common law, and it is now in English probate practice an instrument issuing from the principal probate registry, chiefly used when a person, having the superior right to take a grant, delays or declines to do so, and another, having an inferior right, desires to obtain a grant; the party having the prior right is cited to appear and either to renounce the grant or show cause why it should not be decreed to the citator. In divorce practice, when a petitioner has filed his petition and affidavit, he extracts a citation; *i.e.*, a command drawn in the name of the sovereign and signed by one of the registrars of the court, calling upon the alleged offender to appear and make answer to the petition. In Scots law, citation is the judicial notice served upon a person convening him to court as a party litigant, a witness, a haver of documents, or a juror. Citation, as a legal term, is used in the United States to show a reference to a particular law, decision or treatise which tends to support the proposition advanced in a brief or argument. In such cases the volume, section or page, or all, is indicated.

Citation is also a military term denoting special mention for gallantry in action of a military unit, or of an individual under arms. In most nations the Citation is issued by some general officers in charge of a division or brigade, or is published by the War Department. It frequently appears in the General Orders of a military command, outlining the heroic action of those concerned. In the United States military forces the individual cited is given a silver star in recognition of his service. The *fourragère* or citation cord is given by France to members of a unit receiving such an award. In the British and U.S. military forces, this *fourragère* is not given but units having received it from the French or other governments are allowed to wear it. A typical General Order issued by the military command of the United States was published in General Order on July 9, 1918 (General Order 112) by the commander of the American forces, General John J. Pershing, citing the heroic action of the First and Second Divisions.

CÎTEAUX, a village of eastern France, in the department of Côte d'Or, 16 mi. S.S.E. of Dijon. It is celebrated for the great abbey founded by Robert, abbot of Molesme, in 1098, which became the headquarters of the Cistercian order. The buildings which remain date chiefly from the 18th century.

CITHAERON, now called from its pine forests Elatea, a mountain range (4,872 ft.), separating Boeotia from Megaris and Attica. Its west end reaches the Corinthian Gulf; eastward it is separated from Mount Parnes by the pass through Panactum and Phyle. It was famous in Greek mythology. Here Actaeon was changed into a stag, Pentheus was torn to pieces by the Bacchantes and the infant Oedipus was exposed. It was the scene of the mystic rites of Dionysus, and the festival of the Daedala in honour of Hera. The carriage-road from Athens to Thebes traverses the picturesque pass of Dryoscephalae ("Oak-heads"), guarded on the Attic side by the ruined fortress of Ghyphtokastro ("Gipsy Castle"). Plataea is situated on the north slope, and the strategy of the battle of 479 B.C. was considerably affected by the necessity for the Greeks to keep open the passes (*see* PLATAEA), of Dryoscephalae, and the roads farther west from Plataea to Athens and to Megara.

CITHARA, one of the most ancient stringed instruments, may be traced back to 1700 B.C. among the Semitic races, in Egypt, Assyria, Asia Minor, Greece and the Roman empire, whence the use of it spread over Europe. Having as its leading feature a sound-box or sound-chest which consisted of two resonating tables, either flat or delicately arched, connected by ribs or sides of equal width, the cithara may be regarded as an attempt to improve upon the lyre (*q.v.*), while retaining some of its features.

The strings, varying in number from four to 20 and made of gut, hemp or silk, were vibrated by means of the fingers or of a plectrum, according to the requirements of the music and the different quality of tone desired. Like the lyre the cithara was made in many sizes, according to the pitch required and the use to which the instrument was to be put. It was in Greece the instrument alike of the professional singer or citharoedus (κιθαρῳδός) and, of the instrumentalist or citharista (κιθαριστής), and thus served the double purpose of (1) accompanying the voice (a use placed by the Greeks far above mere instrumental music) in epic recitations and rhapsodies, in odes and lyric songs; and (2) of accompanying the dance. It was also used for playing solos at the national games, at receptions and at trials of skill.

From the cithara by successive stages was evolved the guitar. The first of these steps produced the rotta, by the construction of body, arms and transverse bar in one piece. The addition of a finger board, stretching like a short neck from body to transverse bar, leaving on each side of the finger board space for the hand to pass through in order to stop the strings, produced the crwth or crowd (*q.v.*), and brought about the reduction in the number of the strings to three or four. The conversion of the rotta into the guitar (*q.v.*) was an easy transition effected by the addition of a long neck to a body derived from the oval rotta. When the bow was applied the result was the guitar or troubadour fiddle.

The *cittern* (*q.v.*), a later descendant of the cithara, although preserving the characteristic features of the cithara, the shallow sound chest with ribs, adopted the pear-shaped outline of the eastern instruments of the lute tribe.

CITIUM (Gr. *Kition*), the principal Phoenician city in Cyprus, situated on the southeast coast at the north end of modern Larnaca (*q.v.*). Converging currents from east and west greatly facilitated ancient trade. To south and west the site is protected by salt lagoons. The earliest remains go back to an Aegean colony of Mycenaean age (*c.* 1400–1100 B.C.), but in historic times Citium is the centre of Phoenician influence in Cyprus. The biblical name Kittim, representing Citium, is, in fact, used quite generally for Cyprus as a whole; later also for Greeks and Romans in general. In a list of the allies of Assur-bani-pal of Assyria in 668 B.C. a king, Damasu, of Kartihadasti (Phoenician for "Newtown") occurs where Citium would be expected. A Phoenician dedication to "Baal of Lebanon," found there, suggests that Citium may have belonged to Tyre: and an official monument of Sargon II indicates that Citium was the administrative centre of Cyprus during the Assyrian protectorate (709–668 B.C.). During the Greek revolts of 500, 386 *et seq.*, and 352 B.C., Citium led the side loyal to Persia and was besieged by an Athenian force in 449 B.C. It remained a considerable city even after the Greek cause triumphed with Alexander. But it suffered repeatedly from earthquakes and in mediaeval times its harbour became silted and the population moved to Larnaca, on the open bay. Harbour and citadel have quite disappeared, the latter having been used to fill up the former shortly after the British occupation; some gain to health resulted, but an irreparable loss to science. There are traces of the circuit wall and many tombs.

BIBLIOGRAPHY.—W. H. Engel, *Kypros* (Berlin, 1841) (classical allusions); J. L. Myres, *Journ. Hellenic Studies*, xvii, 147 *et seq.* (excavations); *Cyprus Museum Catalogue* (Oxford, 1899); G. F. Hill, *Brit. Mus. Cat. Coins of Cyprus* (London, 1904) (coins); E. Oberhummer in *Pauly-Wissowa* (*s.v.*).

CITIZEN: *see* NATIONALITY; NATURALIZATION LAWS.

CITOLE, an obsolete musical instrument of which the exact form is uncertain. It has been supposed to be another name for the psaltery (*q.v.*).

CITRANGE, the hybrid tree and its fruit produced by crossing any variety of sweet orange (*Citrus sinensis*) with the trifoliate orange (*Poncirus trifoliata*). Since 1892 U.S. scientists have endeavoured to produce some form of *Citrus*, or a relative, which would thrive in a winter temperature subnormal for oranges. Plants raised from cross-fertilized fruits, using these two species as reciprocal parents have been tested. By 1943 there were less than a dozen varieties of citranges of restricted cultural importance. Some citranges closely resemble oranges; all are inferior to the orange in flavour, but are serviceable in flavouring cakes or jams and for citrangeade. The trees and fruit endure considerable frost. Some varieties of citrange are used for rootstocks for oranges and grapefruit. Citrangequats, trigeneric hybrids made by crossing a kumquat (*Fortunella margarita*) with a citrange, are cultivated as novelties in the United States. (L. D. B.)

CITRIC ACID $C_6H_8O_7$, 2-hydroxypropane-1:2:3-tricarboxylic acid,

$$CO_2H.CH_2.C(OH)(CO_2H).CH_2.C_2OH,$$

is one of the most common plant acids. It was first isolated in a pure form from lemon juice by Karl Wilhelm Scheele in 1784. It occurs as the free acid in many other acid fruits and usually as a salt in most other parts of plants. Almost all plant materials which have been tested with the delicate modern methods contain some citric acid or citrate, some only a few milligrams per kilogram, others, such as lemons, up to 50 g. per kilogram. It is also a constituent of many animal tissues and body fluids. Milk contains up to 1.2 g. per litre, bone (wet) and teeth about 3 g. per kilogram, semen about 5 g. per litre, blood serum about 0.025 g. per litre, human urine between 0.2 g. and 1.2 g. per litre. The acid has been prepared commercially from the juice of lemons and limes, but this method is now largely superseded by the mould fermentation process: C. Wehmer discovered in 1893 that citric acid can be obtained from sugar solutions on which the mould *Citromyces* has been allowed to grow. In 1916 C. Thom and J. N. Currie found that some strains of *Aspergillus niger* produced much more citric acid than Wehmer's organism. This was the starting point of the modern fermentation method. The fermentation is a complex oxidative process; the sugar is probably first broken down to small units such as pyruvic acid, acetaldehyde, acetic acid and carbon dioxide, which recombine to form citric acid. It is usually carried out in shallow vessels which allow free access of air. About ten days after spore inoculation and incubation at 30° C. to 32° C. the process is completed. Yields as high as 87% of the weight of the sugar used have been reported; usually, however, about 60% can be recovered; sucrose gives the best yields, but cheaper sources like molasses are also satisfactory raw materials. A deep tank fermentation process of the type used in the manufacture of penicillin has been developed in the United States, using *Aspergillus wentii*. The mould fermentation process is used in Britain, the United States, Belgium, France, Germany and Czechoslovakia.

Pure citric acid is usually prepared by way of the calcium salt. The crude solution of the acid, after heating and filtration, is neutralized with lime and chalk and boiled. The precipitate of calcium citrate thus obtained is decomposed with dilute sulphuric acid; the solution is filtered to remove the calcium sulphate and concentrated in vacuum pans. The acid crystallizes in colourless rhombic prisms of the composition $C_6H_8O_7+H_2O$.

The first synthesis of citric acid was accomplished by L. E. Grimaux and P. Adam in 1880. It dissolves readily in water and is also soluble in ethyl alcohol and in ether. On heating, the crystals soften between 70° C. and 100° C. and lose water. On further heating the substance becomes again dry and finally melts at 153° C. At about 175° C. it loses a molecule of water and is transformed into (trans)-aconitic acid ($C_6H_6O_6$) or propene-1:2:-3:tricarboxylic acid:

$$CO_2H.CH : C(CO_2H).CH_2.CO_2H.$$

Above 170° C. carbon dioxide and an oily distillate which yields crystals of itaconic acid ($C_5H_6O_4$) are formed. When citric acid is heated in dilute sulphuric acid, aconitic acid is formed; fuming sulphuric acid produces acetone dicarboxylic acid ($C_5H_6O_5$), water and carbon monoxide.

As a tribasic acid, citric acid forms three series of salts. The salts of the alkaline metals are readily soluble in water. The neutral salts of the alkaline earths are only moderately soluble. Calcium citrate is less soluble in hot water than in cold.

Citric acid plays an important part in the metabolism of animals and plants. Most animal tissues, many plants and some micro-organisms convert citric acid reversibly into cis-aconitic acid and isocitric acid (1-hydroxypropane-1:2:3:tricarboxylic acid):

$$CO_2H.CH(OH).CH.CH_2.CO_2H.$$
$$|$$
$$CO_2H$$

Aconitic acid has been found in the leaves of monkshood (*Aconitum napellus*) and of mare's-tail (*Equisetum*), but it is not certain whether the cis- or trans-form is present. Isocitric acid is the chief acid of the blackberry and occurs in relatively high concentration (up to 12% of the dry matter) in the leaves of various Crassulaceae; *e.g., Bryophyllum, Sedum, Sempervivum.* The dry matter of foxglove leaves contains between 1% and 3% isocitric acid. The reversible interconversion of citric, cis-aconitic and isocitric acids is brought about by the enzyme aconitase. The three acids are assumed to be intermediary stages in the oxidative breakdown of foodstuffs in animal tissues. By way of a complex series of reactions they can arise from carbohydrate as well as from fat and from protein. They are readily oxidized in the animal. The significance of the relatively high concentration of citrates in milk, bone, teeth and seminal fluid is not yet clear; since these materials are all relatively rich in calcium, it has been suggested that citrate plays a special role in metabolism of calcium. The role of citric acid in plant metabolism is likewise not fully understood. About two-thirds of the citric acid produced commercially is used for medicinal purposes and much of the remainder for the manufacture of foods and beverages.

Bibliography.—T. E. Thorpe, *Dictionary of Applied Chemistry,* vol. iii, 4th ed. (London, 1939); S. C. Prescott and C. G. Dunn, *Industrial Microbiology* (1940). (H. A. K.)

CITRON, a species of *Citrus* (*C. medica*) belonging to the subfamily Aurantioideae; the same genus furnishes also the orange, lemon, lime, shaddock (pummelo) and grapefruit. The citron is a small evergreen tree or shrub growing to a height of about 10 ft.; it has irregular, spreading spiny branches; large pale green, broadly oblong, slightly serrate leaves, with wingless petioles, and generally perfect flowers. The acid varieties such as the Diamante have flowers purplish without and white within, while the sweet varieties such as the Corsican have creamy white flowers throughout. The fruit is ovate or oblong, protuberant at the tip, from 5 in. to 6 in. long, furrowed; rind adhesive, the inner portion thick, white and fleshy, the outer, thin, greenish-yellow and very fragrant. The pulp is firm, either acid or sweet, and is used only for by-products. The thick peel has an agreeable flavour when candied. There are many varieties of citron but the two commonly grown for production of candied peel are Corsican and Diamante. The fruit of the Etrog citron is used only for ceremonial purposes in religious rites of the Hebrew people. It has a pronounced protuberant tip with persistent pistil even on the ripe fruit. Candied citron is highly esteemed as a confection. Supplies come from the Mediterranean countries and Puerto Rico. Citron peel must be cured in brine or sea water prior to being candied. The citron tree may be grown in the various countries of the world where lemon and limes are grown, as it is only slightly less resistant to frost injury than they are.

See Lucia McCulloch, "Curing and Preserving Citron," *Cir. no. 13,* U.S. Dept. of Agric. (1927); Walter T. Swingle, "Botany of Citrus" chap. IV, *The Citrus Industry,* edited by H. J. Webber and L. D. Batchelor, Univ. of Calif. Press (1943). (L. D. B.)

CITRUS BELT, a term applied to that region of the United States where citrus fruits (oranges, lemons, grapefruit, limes, tangerines and kumquats) can be grown successfully. The subtropical nature of these fruits limits their culture to the warmer states, including southern Georgia, Florida, Alabama, Mississippi, Louisiana, Texas, Arizona and California.

CITTADELLA, a town of Venetia, Italy, province of Padua, 20 mi. N.W. by rail from the town of Padua; 160 ft. above sea level. Pop. (1951) 13,914 (commune). The Paduans founded Cittadella to counterbalance the Trevisan Castelfranco Veneto (founded in 1199) 8 mi. E.; the walls and ditch are well preserved. It is an agricultural centre with intersection of railways: Padua-Bassano and Vicenza-Treviso.

CITTÀ DELLA PIEVE, a town and episcopal see of Umbria, Italy, in the province of Perugia, finely situated 1,666 ft. above the sea, 3 mi. N.E. of its station on the railway between Chiusi and Orvieto. Pop. (1951) 9,674 (commune). It was the birthplace of the painter Pietro Vannucci (Perugino), and possesses several of his works, but none of the first rank. It has a Romanesque cathedral and a 13th century castle.

CITTÀ DI CASTELLO, a town and episcopal see of Umbria, Italy, in the province of Perugia, 38 mi. E. of Arezzo by rail (18 mi. direct), on the left bank of the Tiber, 945 ft. above sea level. Pop. (1951) 36,921 (commune). It occupies the site of the ancient *Tifernum Tiberinum,* near which the younger Pliny had a villa. Devastated by Totila, it soon recovered and was called Castrum Felicitatis in the 8th century; it oscillated between pope and emperor in the middle ages. Its plan is rectangular with walls (1518) and fine palaces of the Vitelli, its Renaissance lords. The cathedral was originally Romanesque and the Palazzo Comunale was built 1334–52. Some of Raphael's earlier works were painted for the churches of this town, but none remains there.

CITTÀ VECCHIA or **CITTÀ NOTABILE,** a fortified city of Malta, 7 mi. W. of Valletta, known in Maltese as Mdina. The town, built in 700 B.C., was known to the Arabs as Medina. Named Notabile in 1427, it was the capital of the island till 1570, when Valletta (*q.v.*) was nearly completed; then it became known as Città Vecchia ("old city"). The city, with its 15th century Maltese palaces, retains the atmosphere of mediaeval Europe. It contains the cathedral church of Malta, said to occupy the site of the house of the governor Publius, who welcomed the apostle Paul; it was rebuilt after destruction by earthquake in 1693, and contains some rich 15th-century stalls. In the rock beneath the city, catacombs, partly pre-Christian, show evidence of early Christian burial. Below the church of San Paolo is a grotto, reputed to have sheltered the apostle. Roman buildings have been excavated. Città Vecchia was slightly damaged during World War II by Italian and German aircraft.

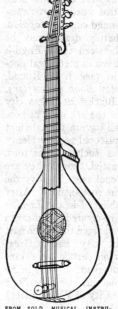

FROM "OLD MUSICAL INSTRUMENTS" (METHUEN & CO.)
THE CITTERN, A MEDIAEVAL INSTRUMENT BELIEVED TO BE OF ENGLISH ORIGIN

CITTERN (also CITHERN, CITHRON, CYTHREN, etc.), a mediaeval stringed instrument of the guitar family (one of the many descendants of the ancient cithara), with a neck terminating in a grotesque head of some kind, and twanged by fingers or plectrum. The popularity of the cittern was at its height in England and Germany during the 16th and 17th centuries. The cittern consisted of a pear-shaped body similar to that of the lute but with a flat back and sound board joined by ribs.

According to Vincentio Galilei (the father of the great astronomer), England was the birthplace of the cittern, which probably owed its popularity to the ease with which it might be mastered and used to accompany the voice. Hence it was one of four instruments generally found in barbers' shops, the others being the gittern, the lute and the virginal. The customers, while waiting, took down the instrument from its peg and played a merry tune to pass the time. The last development of the cittern before its disappearance was the addition of keys. The keyed cithara was first made by Claus & Co., of London, in 1783. The keys, six in number, were placed on the left of the sound board, and on being depressed they acted on hammers inside the sound chest, which, rising through the rose sound hole, struck the strings. Sometimes the keys were placed in a little box right over the strings, the hammers striking from above.

During the 18th century the cittern was known as the English guitar to distinguish it from the Spanish instrument. From the cittern was developed the zither (*q.v.*).

CITY. In Great Britain strictly speaking "city" is an honorary title officially applied to those towns which, in virtue of some pre-eminence (*e.g.,* as being episcopal sees or great industrial centres), have by traditional usage or royal charter acquired the right to the designation. The official style of "city" does not necessarily involve the possession of municipal power greater than those of the ordinary boroughs, nor indeed the possession of a corporation at all (*e.g.*, Ely). In the United States and the British dominions, on the other hand, the official application of the term "city" depends on the kind and extent of the municipal privileges possessed by the corporations, and charters are given raising towns and villages to the rank of cities. Both in France and England the word is also used to distinguish the older and central nucleus of some of the large towns, *e.g.*, the *cité* in Paris, and the "square mile" under the jurisdiction of the lord mayor which is the "City of London." In common usage, however, the word is loosely applied to any large centre of population, and in the United States any town, whether technically a city or not, is usually so designated, with little regard to its actual size or importance.

As the translation of the Greek πόλις or Latin *civitas*, the word involves the ancient conception of the state or "city-state," *i.e.*, of the state as not too large to prevent its government through the assembled body of citizens, and is applied not to the place but to the whole body politic. From this conception both the word and its dignified connotation are without doubt historically derived. On the occupation of Gaul the Gallis states and tribes were called *civitates* by the Romans, and subsequently the name was confined to the chief towns of the various administrative districts. These were also the seats of the bishops. It is thus affirmed that in France from the 5th to the 15th century the name *civitas* or *cité* was confined to such towns as were episcopal sees, and Du Cange (*Gloss.* s.v. *civitas*) defines that word as *urbs episcopalis*, and states that other towns were termed *castra* or *oppida*. How far any such distinction can be sharply drawn may be doubted. No definite line can be drawn between those English towns to which the name *civitas* or *cité* is given in mediaeval documents and those called *burgi* or boroughs (*see* J. H. Round, *Feudal England;* F. W. Maitland, *Domesday Book and After*). It was, however, maintained by Coke and Blackstone that a city is a town incorporate which is or has been the see of a bishop. It is true that the actual sees in England all have a formal right to the title and the boroughs erected into episcopal sees by Henry VIII thereby became "cities"; but towns such as Thetford, Sherborne and Dorchester are not so designated, though they are regularly incorporated and were once episcopal sees. In 1075 the bishop's see was transferred from Sherborne to Salisbury. After eight and a half centuries, by an order published in the *London Gazette* of Feb. 10, 1924, Sherborne was re-created a suffragan bishopric. On the other hand it has only been since the latter part of the 19th century that the official style of "city" has, in Great Britain, been conferred by royal authority on certain important towns which were not episcopal sees, Birmingham in 1889 being the first to be so distinguished. London contains two cities, one (the City of London) outside, the other (the City of Westminster) included in the administrative county.

For the history of the origin and development of modern city government *see* BOROUGH and COMMUNE: *Mediaeval*.

BIBLIOGRAPHY.—For American cities, *see:* William B. Munro, *The Government of American Cities*, 4th ed. (1924); Chester C. Maxey, *An Outline of Municipal Government* (1924).

CITY CLERK, the chief clerical official of the cities of the United States performing most of the duties of an English town clerk. In cities under the council form of government he is usually elected either as a partisan candidate or candidate without regard to party lines. In cities under the commission or commission-manager form of government, he usually is appointed by the mayor subject to the approval of the commission, or is chosen by the commission. He may serve for an indefinite number of terms. The city clerk keeps the minutes of the meetings of the city council or commission. He also keeps all other city records, and in many states has authority to issue licences. He usually has a force of deputies appointed by him or by the authority which appoints him, or selected by civil service regulations.

See H. G. James, *Local Government in the United States* (1921); C. C. Maxey, *An Outline of Municipal Government* (1924).

CITY GOVERNMENT. The government of a modern city bears little resemblance to its historical counterpart. But as the walled mediaeval town often left its impression at the heart of the modern European metropolis, so too did obsolete governmental patterns linger on to complicate the administration of modern municipal services. This lag was evident in world-wide efforts to cope with the suburban overflow from great metropolitan centres, but it appears in many other ways and suggests the starting point for understanding modern city government—*i.e.*, the continuing struggle to keep pace with the problems of rapid urbanization.

Early municipal governments evolved to meet the limited demands of small towns serving rural populations. The industrial revolution converted the cities into workshops. The accompanying revolution in communication made them the commercial, cultural and intellectual centres of their respective countries. Thus economic drawing power combined with the attractions of a more sophisticated urban culture to sustain a world-wide urban migration.

With the urban migration came new public services. Crime, fire, poverty and pestilence grew in seriousness with the size of the city. Polluted wells yielded to public water supply; open sewers gave way to sanitary waste disposal; contagious diseases came under public health regulations; industrial unemployment required new forms of public assistance; fire and health hazards dictated more stringent building regulation; growing congestion impelled attention to better planning of streets and open spaces. The services provided by city governments became increasingly important to the urban citizen. But each step required new legal powers, more specialists and additional funds. The pressure began to crack the shell of outmoded institutions.

Municipal Patterns in England and North America.—As the industrial revolution spread over England, the European continent, the United States and finally Japan, the 19th century saw marked changes in the structure of city government. In England, Elizabethan poor laws collapsed early under the impact of industrial unemployment. The revised Poor Law of 1834 set the pattern for early efforts to adjust traditional local institutions to changing needs by creating new governmental areas (poor law unions). It provided for locally elected governing boards, a paid professional staff and central government supervision of these local authorities. This use of *ad hoc*, or single-purpose, authorities to carry out new municipal functions spread in England until a hopeless confusion of jurisdictions, tax rates and organization forced a series of reforms. Consolidation began as early as 1871, but not until the acts of 1929 and 1933 was a more rational system of local government areas and authorities created.

By mid-20th century most of England's larger cities operated as county boroughs. These all-purpose authorities are combined city-county governments enjoying the powers of both. The area outside the county boroughs is divided into administrative counties, which are further subdivided into boroughs (called noncounty boroughs), urban districts and rural districts. Most noncounty boroughs and urban districts are cities between 5,000 and 50,000 population, although a few are larger. Whether he lives in a county borough, noncounty borough or urban district, the urban dweller elects a council as his principal governing body. One-third of the members retire each year. Both the county borough and noncounty borough councils select aldermen, up to one-third the number of councillors, for six-year terms. The aldermen sit and vote as members of the council. The council also elects the mayor who presides over the council but has no important executive duties. Administration is supervised by council committees appointed for each important department of government. The committee selects the professional head of the service and provides close policy guidance for his activities. There is no single chief executive, although the borough clerk is a connecting link between departments.

The Local Government Boundary commission was appointed in 1945 to continue the rationalization of local areas. The Local Government Act of 1948 made important changes in the system of government financing and property valuation for tax purposes, in part because the services undertaken by local governments under the National Health Service Act of 1946 and the National Assistance Act of 1948 outran local tax resources. These acts provided extensive health services and augmented aid to the aged and infirm. The act of 1948 provided a system of equalization grants from the national government to help underwrite the new functions.

In the United States, both national and state governments were slow to face the emerging urban problems of the 19th century. The cities, reflecting the American suspicion of government, were initially governed through an ineffectual system of two-chamber city councils, mayors without power and a multitude of elected officials. Then, also, the traditional legal status of the city as a corporation, operating within the strict bounds of specified powers delegated from the state governments, was a major handicap. Cities often lacked the legal powers needed to exercise necessary controls over private action. Rurally dominated legislatures were either indifferent to urban problems or meddled directly in local affairs to get special privileges. When new municipal functions were authorized, state laws typically required that they be administered by semi-independent commissions detached from the administration of the mayor. In the resulting confusion local officials, shielded by dispersed responsibility, often took advantage of the opportunities for corruption in franchises for utilities, enforcement of building codes, construction of public works, etc.

By the end of the 19th century, municipal corruption had become a national scandal in the United States and several reform movements gathered momentum. Among them were drives for greater home rule for cities, a shorter ballot, more stringent enforcement of tenement-control laws, reform of police systems, city planning and stronger executive control over city government. The National Municipal league, organized in 1894, became the educational centre for changes in the structure of government. It advocated and provided legal guidance for strengthening the position of the mayor, reducing the size of city councils, dispensing with superfluous elected officials and abolishing many independent boards and commissions. With public sentiment for reform growing, many states adopted municipal home-rule laws. These permitted a range of experimentation and local initiative that raised U.S. city government from disrepute to advanced professionalization within a generation.

Three patterns of city government attracted attention in the U.S. during the first half of the 20th century. One—the commission form—is principally of historical interest. It was launched in Galveston, Tex., in 1901, and later widely imitated. The members (usually five) of a small council serve as the administrative heads of a group of services. The mayor is simply the presiding member of the council and of no special importance. With time, the dispersal of responsibility in the scheme revealed serious weaknesses, and the commission form is gradually dwindling away. The two forms of government growing in importance by mid-century were the strong mayor and the city manager. Under the strong-mayor form a popularly elected chief executive is given substantial authority to make appointments, initiate the budget, supervise government departments, propose public policy and veto council actions. This became the dominant pattern in the larger cities. Fifteen of the 17 cities with more than 500,000 population operated under some form of mayor-council government in 1953. The powers of the mayor vary widely, however, and the trend to centralized administrative authority is restricted by the continuing tendency for state legislatures to place new functions under semi-independent boards. Smaller cities moved more slowly toward a strong executive than did the larger. A large proportion continued at mid-century to operate under strong-council, weak-mayor forms, with the council and its committees the dominant element. The city-manager plan enjoyed startling success after its first introduction at Sumter, S.C., in 1912. It follows the corporation pattern. The council is essentially an elected board of directors which appoints a professional manager to direct the city's administration. It is usually small and nonpartisan, with the members elected at large. The manager recommends policy, prepares the budget, makes appointments and exercises direction over the administrative departments. He does not, in contrast with the strong mayor, play an active part in political action designed to get his recommendations adopted. This is left to the council. The system worked well and spread rapidly. Of the 2,527 cities with more than 5,000 people in 1953, about 28% operated under the manager plan, 52% under some form of mayor-council, 14% under the commission form and the remainder under a form of town meeting.

In the United States, as in England, the growth in governmental services accelerated after 1930. Much of the burden of administering and financing these services fell on local governments. Population shifts during and after World War II meant increased pressure for utilities, schools, improved streets and related local services. Inadequate local tax sources brought appeals for state assistance. Meanwhile the state and federal governments were looking to local governments to help administer new programs in public health, education, housing, urban redevelopment and other social services. Financial aid to local governments, therefore, expanded and principally took the form of grants subject to state or federal standards of performance and related supervision. The net result was not unlike the pattern that developed in England, although the confusion created by overlapping jurisdictions and special districts was not tackled with comparable vigour. The problem of federal-state-local relations, including the allocation of tax resources, remained a continuing one, and the subject of repeated studies by federal and state commissions.

Continental European Patterns of Centralized Control.—While England and the United States were struggling to adapt traditions of local autonomy and limited government to modern urban living, other countries were bringing local governments under strict national supervision. Adequate legal authority was provided by broad grants of power from the central government under general municipal laws. The administration of these powers, however, was held under much tighter central rein than in England or the U.S. France established a pattern of this type which had far-reaching influence in Europe, Latin America and Japan.

In France, the citizens elect a city council, which in turn selects a chief executive, the *maire*. Once selected, the latter becomes in many respects an official of the central government. He exercises extensive police powers independently of the council and is solely responsible for the conduct of city administration. His activities are, however, subject to close national supervision through the prefect of the *département*, or, in small towns, the subprefect of the *arrondissement*. The prefect may annul acts of a city council which conflict with national laws; he must approve the budget and numerous other kinds of local enactments; he may write into the budget any obligatory items which are omitted; and he may suspend the city council under certain conditions. After World War II the constitution of the fourth republic, adopted in 1946, set the stage for greater decentralization of local government in France by providing for the regrouping of jurisdictions, for greater powers to be retained by local councils and for clearer definition of national supervisory powers. The preoccupation of the fourth republic with national and international problems, however, often delayed carrying these principles into effect.

German cities first broke the feudalistic mould with the reforms of Baron vom und zum Stein in 1808, and between 1871 and World War I German municipal administration reached impressive heights of efficiency. Local councils were elected under restricted suffrage which gave one-third the council seats to a small group of large tax-payers, one-third to a group paying the next-highest taxes and only the remaining third to the mass of voters. This council selected an executive board (*Magistrat*) consisting in part of unpaid citizens, in part of salaried professionals. The chairman of this board was the *Bürgermeister*, a well-paid professional civil servant enjoying great prestige, authority and normally long tenure. This combination set a new standard in effective municipal administration. Although the *Bürgermeister* was subject to a series of higher authorities ending with the ministry of the interior, he had the authority and administrative competence necessary to good government. The Weimar republic democratized the councils, but made few basic changes in the structure of municipal government. The Hitler regime, on the other hand, altered the pattern drastically. The *Bürgermeister* and other principal local officials were named by the Nazi party delegate and wielded virtually all the powers of city government. After the Nazi collapse in May 1945, local community elections led the return to self-governing institutions, and city elections were held throughout occupied Germany in 1946. Division of the country in the postwar years prevented the emergence of any consistent pattern of local administration.

Municipal government in Italy strongly suggests the French structure. Prior to Mussolini, centrally appointed prefects exercised extensive powers over local affairs in the provinces. The towns and villages (*comunes*) were governed by a locally elected council and mayor, known as the *sindaco*. Committees of the councils played a somewhat larger part in running local affairs than in France, but the detailed supervision by the prefects was comparable. In Italy, as in Germany, fascism brought extreme centralization under party control. Perhaps as a reaction, the Italian constitution of 1948 decentralized administration. New regional governments, each under a regionally elected council and centrally appointed commissioner, were given extensive powers to legislate for city matters. The principle that regions are normally to exercise their administrative functions by delegating them to the provinces and *comunes* or by using local officials was clearly intended to give municipal governments a new dignity and importance, while continuing to use them to carry out national and regional programs.

In Russia after the Communist Revolution the responsibility for local government became primarily that of the republics and regions. Quite a bit of variation exists. The basic pattern, however, vests general authority in a locally elected council (soviet), which in turn administers local affairs through its committees. In the larger cities the soviet selects a committee (presidium) to be the directing and co-ordinating executive. The party and youth organizations are active in selecting candidates, shaping policy and helping to carry out local programs. Popular participation in local government seems to be more active in the U.S.S.R. than it was under the fascist dictatorships of Germany and Italy.

In Latin American countries local administration has been strongly influenced by continental Europe. Regional administrative areas are commonly designated provinces or departments, and central controls over local affairs are frequently strong as in the French pattern. Constitutional provisions vary widely from extreme centralization to substantial local autonomy. The municipalities (*municipios*) in Latin America are not necessarily cities. They sometimes embrace sizable rural tracts around modest towns. The tendency, in general, is to treat the municipality as an administrative area for the national or regional government, and despite constitutional variations a high degree of centralized control over local affairs predominates.

Prior to World War II, Japan followed the continental system of centralized administration. German advisers after the Meiji restoration of 1868 helped shape the administration of local affairs, although the result was perhaps more French than German. This was encouraged by a basic step in the revolution itself which had replaced provincial feudal lords with centrally appointed governors. The powers of the prefectural governors largely obscured local governmental institutions. The Local Autonomy Law of 1947, however, drastically reversed the prewar pattern. Elected prefectural governors and assemblies were provided, while detailed provision was made for the government of cities, towns and villages. The law provided essentially self-governing status for "special cities" over 500,000, but the opposition of rural prefectures blocked putting this section of the law into effect. The government proceeded, however, with a vigorous program of amalgamating small towns and villages into larger entities capable of assuming important governmental functions. An elected mayor and assembly are the essential organs of local administration, with much of their time devoted to national and prefectural programs.

Major Trends in City Government.—The governments of the cities of the world show certain marked similarities and a number of common problems. A locally elected council is virtually universal. There is usually a single chief executive, and the trend has been to strengthen his administrative position. England and the U.S.S.R. are exceptions, with committees of the council playing a strong role in guiding professional department heads. The appointed professional chief executive, originating first in Germany, assumed major importance in the United States in the modern form of the city manager. Elsewhere in Europe and in Japan the elected local executive continued to predominate.

Central and state or regional governments came to rely increasingly on local governments for the administration of their programs. This was a natural development in the centralized continental systems, but it also became evident in Britain and the U.S. In both countries financial grants and technical supervision of services by higher authorities emerged as a definite pattern. In both countries, also, expanded services rendered local tax resources insufficient, even for traditional local services. Thus the tendency was to seek further financial aid, and with it to receive closer supervision. Meanwhile France, Italy and Japan were stressing decentralization. The trend, therefore, was toward removing some of the earlier distinctions between the traditional self-government of Anglo-U.S. cities and the more centralized continental systems.

Another distinct trend was the increasing professionalization of municipal services. Cities began to organize into national associations, such as the American Municipal association in the United States, and both national and international conferences of municipal officials became common. Likewise a growing number of specialists—city managers, finance officers, personnel officials, town planners, etc.—set up national and international professional associations.

A final trend to be noted was the growing concern over the problems of metropolitan areas. The great cities of the world do not fit into generalized local governmental patterns. They are sprawled out to engulf, socially and economically, areas far beyond their political jurisdictions. Many of them are the metropolitan hubs of their respective countries. This encouraged the consolidation of the larger metropolitan areas under distinctive governmental arrangements. London is governed principally by the Metropolitan county of London, embracing 29 metropolitan boroughs within a 100-sq.mi. area. The county has broad powers, which it administers under a county council of 124 members plus a 20-man board of aldermen chosen by the council. The Metropolitan police district and the ancient City of London (1 sq.mi.) are the principal exceptions to the county jurisdiction. Paris has an over-all municipal council of 90 members, but subdistricts of the city (*arrondissements*) are grouped into nine sectors each with its own mayor. Metropolitan Tokyo was consolidated into one large governmental district with prefectural powers in 1943. In 1953, Toronto, Ont., and 12 suburban municipalities were consolidated into one metropolitan district with authority to carry on a broad range of common functions.

Metropolitan government remained a major unsolved problem in the United States. After the five boroughs of New York city were consolidated in 1896, little progress in this direction was made. The Metropolitan district of Boston helped solve a few regional problems. But in general the central city, its satellite towns, and a variety of special districts remained a chaos of overlapping and competing jurisdictions. There is no metropolitan-wide authority competent to carry on the functions of planning, land-use control, transit, recreation, prevention of water and air pollution, and other activities that demand attention on an area basis. Because local jealousies and rivalries block the consolidation of metropolitan governments, it seems probable that only new kinds of multipurpose districts, able to carry on area-wide functions while leaving local matters to community determination, are likely to relieve the present unsatisfactory situation. Certainly the metropolitan region remains a major challenge to students of government throughout the world.

Additional information on city government may be found in the articles dealing with specific countries and some of the large cities.

BIBLIOGRAPHY.—William Anderson (ed.), *Local Government in Europe* (London, New York, 1939); Victor Jones, *Metropolitan Government* (Chicago, 1942); Herman Finer, *English Local Government*, 2nd ed. (London, 1945); E. L. Hasluck, *Local Government in England* (Cambridge, 1948); William Anderson and Edward W. Weidner, *American City Government*, rev. ed. (New York, London, 1950); Arthur W. Bromage, *Introduction to Municipal Government and Administration* (New York, 1950); William A. Robson (ed.), *Government of the*

Great Cities of the World (London, 1954); International City Managers' Association, *Municipal Year Book, 1953–1954,* ed. by Clarence E. Ridley and Orin F. Nolting, 2 vol. (Chicago, 1953–54 published annually). (R. A. Wr.)

CITY MANAGER. The city manager is the principal executive and administrative officer of a municipality under the council-manager form of local government, which spread widely in the United States and Canada after Dayton, O., became the first large city to adopt it in 1913.

Under the council-manager plan, the voters elect only the city council, which appoints a city manager to administer municipal affairs under its supervision.

The members of the council, usually five to nine in number, may be elected either at large or by wards. The mayor is a member of the council and serves as its presiding officer. He may either be designated to this position by the council or elected as such by the voters. The council acts only collectively, and its individual members, including the mayor, have no administrative functions.

The city manager serves at the pleasure of the city council. Subject to its general supervision, he is in full charge of the administration of municipal affairs. He prepares the budget, appoints and dismisses personnel and directs the work of the municipal departments. He attends all council meetings, presents recommendations on municipal business and usually takes an active part in the discussions.

Origin and Spread of Plan.—The council-manager plan was devised and first advocated in the U.S. by the National Short Ballot organization, an association which proposed to improve state and local government by reducing the number of elective offices in order to fix responsibility on a few officials. This organization, of which Woodrow Wilson was president and Richard S. Childs, a young New York advertising man, was the secretary and active promoter, undertook first to support the commission plan of municipal government. Under that plan, all municipal powers were vested in a commission, the members of which collectively served as a legislative body and individually administered the departments.

Since the dispersion of administrative functions proved to be a serious weakness of the commission plan, Childs's attention was attracted by the news that the city council of Staunton, Va., had appointed a general manager and delegated to him the function of directing the municipal departments. He seized on this idea as a means of overcoming the weakness of the commission plan, and the National Short Ballot organization formulated and began to promote the commission-manager plan, which in all essentials was the plan later known as the council-manager or city-manager plan.

Sumter, S.C., adopted the plan in 1912, and was followed by several other small cities. The greatest impetus to its spread came with its adoption in 1913 by Dayton, which had suffered a severe flood that required emergency action by its local authorities.

The National Municipal league, the principal organization in the United States for the promotion of municipal reform, had previously concentrated its efforts on strengthening the authority of the mayor and eliminating partisan patronage. After the early success of the council-manager plan, it adopted the plan in 1915 as the basis of its model charter for municipal governments. This charter added to the essential features of the council-manager plan provisions to establish a civil service system, to forbid members of the council to interfere with the city manager's administrative work or appointments and to forbid municipal employees to enagage in political activity. (About three-fourths of the cities that adopted the plan in the first half of the 20th century elected their councils at large.)

While it generally proved impractical to write into law a precise definition of the respective functions of the council and the city manager, in view of the fact that the city manager serves at the council's pleasure, the principal objectives of the plan were achieved in most of the cities that adopted it. The plan spread rapidly from 1918 to 1923, as many cities undertook programs of public works and municipal improvements and realized their need for more efficient administration.

The council-manager plan also grew rapidly after the end of World War II. During the years 1946 to 1954 inclusive, for example, 644 cities, representing an average annual gain of 71 cities, adopted the council-manager plan, and by Jan. 1955, it was in effect in 1,222 cities and 15 counties in the United States and Alaska and in 38 cities in Canada. Of the 481 cities in the United States with more than 25,000 population in 1954, 200, or 42%, operated under the council-manager plan; 33 of the 88 cities between 100,000 and 500,000 had the council-manager plan.

Legal and Political Basis.—The legal basis of the plan in the United States varies with state law. In states which permitted municipal home rule, cities established the plan by adopting by popular vote charters drafted by local reform groups, often following the model charter or the advice of expert consultants. Some adopted by popular vote an optional council-manager plan provided by state law. Some had their state legislatures enact special council-manager charters for them. And in others the city council adopted the plan by municipal ordinance without submitting it to popular vote.

The political circumstances under which the plan was adopted often affected the role of the city manager. Some cities, especially those in which the leaders in business affairs and civic organizations had never before taken part in municipal politics, adopted the plan as part of a vigorous campaign of municipal reform. Their purpose was to break the hold of partisan or factional organization on city government, and to eliminate patronage in jobs or contracts. In these cities the plan required the support of an active reform organization, and the plan itself and the city manager were likely to remain the subjects of political controversy.

At the other extreme, some cities in which the municipal leadership was generally respected adopted the plan on the initiative of their city councils, and the city manager was never identified with either side of a political contest.

Most cities were between these two extremes. In states where the national party organization did not take a direct part in municipal affairs (usually states in which one or another party was predominant) cities generally found it easier to get general acceptance for the council-manager plan and to establish the city manager as a noncontroversial career officer whose position was not at stake in elections.

Characteristics of Managers.—More city managers have had training or experience as engineers than in any other occupation. But following the end of World War II city councils preferred men with training and experience in public administration rather than men with specialized training. In 1954 one out of every five managers held graduate degrees in public or business administration or related fields, chiefly master's degrees. Of the managers in office in 1954, 82% had attended college and two-thirds of this group completed their college work.

While city managership had no definite training or entrance requirements, a young man who planned a career in this profession usually obtained a master's degree in public administration and served as an intern and as an assistant to a manager for several years before becoming a city manager. Forty-three per cent of the city managers appointed in 1954 were promoted from one city to another or were former managers who received new appointments. Nearly one-half of all managers came directly from other public administrative positions. Less than 10% of the managers came from nongovernmental positions. In 1954 three-fourths of all city-manager appointments were from outside the city as compared with 76% in 1953 and 58% for the ten-year period 1940 to 1949 inclusive.

City managers, with rare exceptions, refrained from taking part in local political campaigns, even when they were personally attacked by opposition factions. On the other hand, many took the lead in public discussions of municipal policy. Some of the most successful managers were extremely active as public speakers and as public advocates of improving or extending municipal services.

City managers looked on their work as a professional career, but at the same time they never expected to hold their positions except at the pleasure of their city councils. Their professional society, the International City Managers' association, always took the position that the city manager was subject to dismissal by the council and refused to support proposals that he be removed only by more than a simple majority vote of council members. Similarly, it admitted to membership any city manager duly appointed by a city council and never sought to establish any criteria of its own for recognition or membership in the profession.

The association did a great deal not only to stimulate a professional attitude among its members, but also to advance the general level of municipal administration. It sponsored research in municipal administration; published the *Municipal Year Book,* an annual encyclopaedia of factual and statistical data on all cities in the United States; and conducted courses of training in various branches of municipal management.

The city-manager movement had effects beyond the sphere of municipal affairs. In the United States, city managers often went from municipal government into state and national administration and did much to help develop administrative systems in which federal, state and local agencies co-operate in the management of national programs.

See International City Managers' Association, *The Municipal Year Book* (published annually). (D. K. Pe.; C. E. Ry.)

CITY PLANNING: *see* Town and City Planning.

CIUDAD BOLÍVAR, an inland city and river port of Venezuela, capital of the state of Bolívar, on the right bank of the Orinoco river, 240 mi. above its mouth. Population (census of 1950) 31,054. The mean temperature is about 83° F.

The city stands upon a small hill some 125 ft. above sea level, and faces the river where it narrows to a width of less than half a mile. It is the commercial centre of the Orinoco basin, being the chief port both for imports to the inland of Venezuela and for exports from the country. Various air lines serve the city; there is regular steamship communication with the lower Orinoco, Port of Spain and the Caribbean coast of Venezuela. During the rainy season small steamers run far up the river. Several highways connect Ciudad Bolívar with the Venezuelan capital, Caracas, and with the coast.

The principal exports from this region include gold, cattle, horses, cacao, bitters, hides, timber and mineral ores. There are large gold mines southeast of the city, and bauxite and iron deposits to the south and southwest.

The town was founded by Mendoza in 1764 as San Tomás de la Nueva Guayana, but its location at this particular point on the river gave to it the popular name of *Angostura,* the Spanish term for "narrows." Angostura bitters were invented there in 1824, although the manufacture was thereafter transferred to another city. The name Angostura was used until 1849 when that of the Venezuelan liberator was bestowed on it. Ciudad Bolívar played an important part in the struggle for independence and was for a time the headquarters of the revolution.

The town suffered severely in the fight for its possession, and the political disorders which followed greatly retarded its growth. (C. E. Mc.)

CIUDAD JUAREZ, formerly El Paso del Norte, a northern frontier town of Mexico, in the state of Chihuahua, 1,223 mi. by rail N.N.W. of Mexico City. Pop. (1910) 10,621; (1950) 128,782. Ciudad Juárez stands 3,800 ft. above sea level on the right bank of the Rio Grande del Norte, opposite the city of El Paso, Tex., with which it is connected by bridges. It is the northern terminus of the Mexican National railway and has a large transit trade with the United States, having a customhouse and a United States consulate. It is also a military post with a small garrison. The town has a straggling picturesque appearance, a considerable part of the habitations being small adobe or brick cabins.

Ciudad Juárez was founded in 1681–82; its present importance is due entirely to its position on the border and the railway into the interior. It was the headquarters of Pres. Benito Juárez in 1865 and was renamed in 1885 because of its devotion to his cause.

CIUDAD REAL, a province of central Spain, formed in 1833 of districts taken from New Castile and bounded on the north by Toledo, northeast by Cuenca, east by Albacete, south by Jaén and Cordova and west by Badajoz. Population (1950) 567,027; area, 7,622 sq.mi.; density per square mile 75.0. In the east and centre are extensive high plains forming part of the region known as La Mancha and rising on the southeast to low hills. The west consists of broken hilly country bordered on the south by the parallel ridges of the Sierra de Alcudia and by the Sierra Madrona, foreranges of the Sierra Morena. The province is drained, except on the southeast, by the Guadiana river which traverses it from east to west and receives several tributaries, notably the Gigüela, Záncara and Bullaque on the right and the Azuel and Jabalón on the left.

The climate on the plains is oppressively hot in summer, and in winter bitterly cold winds prevail. The rainfall is scanty and prolonged droughts are common. Forests occur only on the higher ground in the west. The vegetation on the La Mancha plains is limited to poor pasture. Cereals, saffron, the olive and vine are cultivated, but agricultural development is hindered by the scantiness of the population, the aridity and poverty of the soil, the want of proper irrigation and the occasional ravages of locusts. Large numbers of sheep and goats, however, are reared on the plains, and Ciudad Real is famous for its mules. Pigs are kept in the oak forests of the west, and cork is an important product of this region.

Coal is mined round Puertollano, lead in various districts and important mercury deposits at Almadén. There is no other industrial development.

The roads are insufficient and ill-kept, especially in the northwest, where they form the sole means of communication. The Madrid-Lisbon railway passes through the capital, Ciudad Real, and through Puertollano, where there is a branch line to San Quintin. Farther east, the Madrid-Linares railway passes through Alcázar de San Juan, junction for the Albacete line, and Manzanares and Valdepeñas, where branch lines link it with Ciudad Real and Puertollano respectively. There is also a branch in the northeast to Tomelloso.

The capital is Ciudad Real (pop. 1950, 34,244 mun.) (*q.v.*). The principal towns, with 1950 population of *municipios* are: Valdepeñas (26,020), Tomelloso (30,072), Puertollano (34,884), Alcázar de San Juan (25,139), Manzanares (18,204), Almodóvar del Campo (14,719) and Almadén (12,375). Almagro (9,949), famous for its lace, and Daimiel (20,204), a market centre of La Mancha and site of a military aerodrome, belonged in the middle ages to the knightly order of Calatrava, formed in 1158 to keep the Moors in check. Campo de Criptana (15,659) and La Solana (14,699) are other market towns. Education is very backward. (*See* also Castile.)

CIUDAD REAL, a town of central Spain, capital formerly of La Mancha and after 1833 of the province described above. It lies 107 mi. S. of Madrid, on the Madrid-Badajoz-Lisbon and Ciudad Real-Manzanares railways. Pop. (1950) 34,244 (mun.). Ciudad Real, situated on a wide plain, between the river Guadiana in the north and its tributary the Jabalón on the south, offers little of interest beyond its lofty Gothic cathedral, built without aisles. It is the market for the cereals, oil, wine, potatoes and figs produced with irrigation on the surrounding plain. Ciudad Real was founded by Alphonso X of Castile (1252–84) and fortified by him as a check upon the Moorish power. Its original name of Villarreal was changed to Ciudad Real by John VI in 1420. It is said to have suffered greatly, especially in the loss of its flourishing leather industry, by the expulsion of the Moriscos in the 17th century.

During the Peninsular War a Spanish force was defeated there by the French, on March 27, 1809.

CIUDAD RODRIGO, a town of western Spain, in the province of Salamanca. It is situated on an eminence on the right bank of the river Agueda, 13½ mi. E. of the Portuguese frontier, and on the railway from Salamanca to Coimbra in Portugal. Pop. (1950) 12,596 (mun.). Ciudad Rodrigo is an episcopal see and was for many centuries an important frontier fortress. It was founded in the 12th century by Count Rodrigo González and named after him, but remnants of a Roman aqueduct and bridge indicate that it occupies the site of a Roman settlement. The 12th-century cathedral, with fine cloisters and carved portico, was disfigured by additions in 1538 and has suffered during sieges from its position almost astride the walls. During the Peninsular War, it was captured by the French under Marshal Ney, in 1810; but on Jan. 19, 1812, it was retaken by the British under Viscount Wellington, who, for this exploit, was created earl of Wellington, duke of Ciudad Rodrigo, and marquess of Torres Vedras, in Portugal. (X.)

Siege of Ciudad Rodrigo, 1812.—For the operations preceding and following the siege of Ciudad Rodrigo in 1812 *see* PENINSULAR WAR. Having insufficient troops to provide a covering force Wellington decided to use the element of surprise. He waited till both armies were scattered in winter quarters, made all his preparations in secret, and then suddenly, on Jan. 8, appeared before the town. Ciudad Rodrigo lies on the right bank of the Agueda and in 1812 its fortifications were modern and formidable, but it was commanded on the north by a hill, the Great Teson, which, crowned by a strong redoubt, rose to a height of 150 ft., only 600 yd. from the walls. Between this hill and the town lay a slightly lower ridge, the Little Teson, which was flanked at its eastern end by the convent of San Francisco, at its western by that of Santa Cruz. The very night of his arrival Wellington stormed the redoubt on the Great Teson and at once began his preparations for an intensive siege. The weather was terribly severe, so that the troops in the trenches had to be relieved every 24 hours, but the men worked with great speed and enthusiasm. Within six days the British had dug a parallel and constructed batteries for 32 guns on the Great Teson, had sapped across the low ground and dug a parallel within assaulting distance on the Little Teson, and had stormed the convents which flanked it. For five days a furious bombardment was maintained, the enemy replying with equal vigour. By Jan. 19 two breaches had been made in the walls and, though the counterscarp had not been destroyed nor the enemy's guns silenced, Wellington gave orders for an assault. The main breach, at the northern corner of the fortifications was to be stormed by the 3rd division; the lesser breach, 200 yd. to the east, by the light division. Pack's Portuguese were to make a feint attack upon the San Pelayo gate at the other side of the town. At 7 P.M. on the 19th Campbell's brigade of the 3rd division entered the ditch at the southwest corner of the fortress, with orders to scale the outer wall and clear the left flank of the main breach. Their actual entry was premature and the garrison opened fire while the other attacking troops were still in their assembly trenches. The storming columns at once dashed forward. The 3rd division was checked at the main breach by a land mine, but quickly drive the defenders back to a retrenchment behind the breach, which for a time held them back. The light division met with less opposition and, pouring through the lesser breach, cleared the way for their comrades on the right. The garrison quickly surrendered, but the storming troops got out of hand and for the rest of the night plundered, drank, burned and murdered; only at daylight was order restored. The siege cost Wellington 1,000 casualties, half in the assault, but 1,500 prisoners and 150 guns fell into his hands. Marmont only received definite news of the siege on the 15th; by the time he had collected his army the town had fallen. (H. L. A.-F.)

CIUDAD TRUJILLO (SANTO DOMINGO), capital of the Dominican Republic on the island of Hispaniola. Pop. (1950 census) 181,553. It is on the south coast, on the river Ozama. Founded in 1496, it is the oldest existing settlement of white men in the New World, and perhaps the most perfect example of a Spanish colonial town of the 16th century. It is surrounded by ancient walls with bastions. The streets are straight, narrow and intersect at right angles. The massive houses are built of stone with coloured walls pierced with huge doors and windows. The cathedral, in the Spanish Renaissance style, dates from 1512, and contains the reputed tomb of Columbus (*q.v.*). The cell in which he and his brother were confined by order of Bobadilla is still shown in the old fortress. The city is the seat of an archbishop. It has a small harbour, but the river is navigable for 4 mi. from its mouth.

CIUDAD VIEJA, a highland village of Guatemala about 22 miles S.W. of Guatemala city and 3 mi. S.E. of Antigua, situated in the valley of the Almolonga at the foot of the volcano *Agua* (water). Urban population of the *municipio* of Ciudad Vieja (1950 census), 5,415. Originally named Santiago de los Caballeros de Guatemala, the city was founded in 1527 under the direction of Jorge de Alvarado, brother of Pedro de Alvarado, conqueror of Guatemala, and became the third capital of the Spanish Captain Generalcy of Guatemala. (The first and second capitals were, respectively, Iximché and Xepau.) News of Pedro de Alvarado's death in Mexico reached Ciudad Vieja on Aug. 29, 1541; on Sept. 8 his widow, Beatriz de la Cueva, had herself decreed governor of the province. Either as the result of a storm or an earthquake which cracked open the crater of the volcano *Agua*, an avalanche of mud and water descended upon the city on Sept. 10, burying, among several hundred other people, Doña Beatriz. Following this disaster, the capital was moved to Antigua, whence it was in turn removed, because of an earthquake in 1773, to the present site of Guatemala (*q.v.*).

CIVERCHIO, VINCENZO, an early 16th century Italian painter, born at Crema. There are altar pieces by him at Brescia, and at Crema the altar piece at the duomo (1509) is his work. His "Birth of Christ" is in the Brera, Milan; and at Lovere are other of his works dating from 1539 and 1540.

CIVET, or, properly, CIVET CAT, the name given to the more typical members of the Viverridae (*see* CARNIVORA), which are characterized by the presence of a deep pouch near the genital organs into which a fatty, yellowish substance, known as civet and having a strong musky odour, is secreted. Several species are known. The African civet (*Civettictis civetta*) measures 3–4½ ft. in length, of which a third is tail, and stands 10–12 in. high. The hair is long, forming an erectile ridge down the middle of the back; in colour it is dark grey with black bands and spots. The animal is nocturnal and largely carnivorous; it climbs trees with agility. It is kept in captivity (where, however, it never becomes tame) for its perfume, the larger quantity of which comes from the male and is scraped from the pouch with a spoon twice a week. The zibeth (*Viverra zibetha*) extends from Arabia to India and several East Indian islands. Other species occur in India, China and Malaya. The odorous principle (a ketone) has been isolated and named civetone. Civet is used for blending scents.

FROM "ROYAL NATURAL HISTORY" (WARNE)
CIVET, A CATLIKE ANIMAL, VALUED FOR A GLANDULAR SECRETION USED FOR PERFUME

CIVICS. Civics owes its origin to the Latin *civicus,* meaning citizen. Hence, broadly interpreted, it refers to the mutual relationships which obtain between citizens in the state and in society in general. The concern of the school with these relationships finds one of its chief expressions through the social study known as civics.

Although civics seldom appears in the elementary school as a separate subject, beginning about 1910 increasing attention was paid in the first six or seven years of instruction to the cultivation of such civic attitudes as respect for authority, fair play, tolerance of the views of others and an understanding of the interdependent nature of personal relations. Courses in civics identified as such appear throughout the secondary school with the greatest concentration in the 9th and 12th years. Such courses appear under a variety of titles such as vocational civics, economic civics, social civics, citizenship, problems of democracy, community civics and many others. While the variety of titles reflects some indecision as to what civics is, it nevertheless reports a conception of citizenship far more realistic than that which was commonly employed as recently as 1915 and elaborated under the title of government or civil government.

The changes which occurred in the conception and teaching of civics following World War I were greater than in any other social study. These changes are clearly related to and have been roughly concurrent with the dramatic changes that characterize the recent history of western society—the increasing speed of the transition from the police to the service state, the multiplication and improvement of mass media of communication, the increasingly industrial, urban, and rational nature of social life, the growing interdependence of its parts and the consequent need to examine critically the adequacy of cultural, economic and political institutions devised as instruments of social control in a much simpler world.

The older civics was, for the most part, the study of the forms of political organization, requiring chiefly rote learning. Modern civics is the study of the dynamic processes in which representative groups, both voluntary and nonvoluntary, reach working agreements as to their goals, and shape, and continually reshape, the instruments for their realization.

In those courses which represent the best thought and practice, many types of human association are studied. These range from the family, the play group, the school team and youth service organizations to the trade union, the corporation and civil communities. These civil communities vary in size and complexity from the neighbourhood, village, city, county and commonwealth to the nation and such emerging units as the metropolitan area and the nascent society of nations. In these various groups contexts, as befits the maturity of the student, such matters as the following are studied: the relation of the individual to others in group life, the nature and importance of discussion in the development of democratic consensus, the process of group formation and cohesion, and the relation between implemental and goal values.

The comprehensive view which civics takes of citizenship requires that it study the process of governing in the context of realistic cultural and economic situations. Furthermore, in these contexts, governing is viewed both in the formal-constitutional and in the informal-voluntary-group sense. Such cultural and economic considerations as the conditions of employment, the incidence of amount and regularity of income with mental and physical security, the distribution of medical, dental and hospital services, the prevention and treatment of crime, the conservation of natural resources, the quality and quantity of the human population and allied topics provide fertile soil for the study of the meaning of terms which, lacking such treatment, are mere slogans. Put now in their proper context, such terms as freedom, equality and justice identify the conditions under which the struggle for democracy goes on, offer abundant illustrations of both formal and informal political controls and, in short, provide the setting for the study of *Realpolitik.* They likewise serve as practical and vital points of departure from which to study and appraise the adequacy of the executive, legislative, judicial and administrative agencies of government in the formal sense.

The modern conception of the nature of civics is, however, attended by significant difficulties. There is first the fact that political problems are by definition moral problems and hence are less susceptible of being treated with the finality and precision possible in, for example, languages, mathematics and the natural sciences. Closely related is the fact that the teaching of civics in a democratic society involves the dual and seemingly paradoxical task of fostering both loyal and critical attitudes. Furthermore, it falls especially to civics to expose fallacious views held by many earnest but confused persons, such as the belief that one conception of the nature of democracy is quite as reliable as another—irrespective of knowledge of its ideals and the adequacy and relevance of the means employed to realize them.

Only when taught in the context of the opportunities which present-day democracy affords and the difficulties which attend such an inquiry, can civics, in common with cognate social studies, develop rationally grounded democratic attitudes and permit the student to acquire basic intellectual skills. These objectives can be realized only within the framework of substantial knowledge about, and, in so far as possible, personal acquaintance with, democracy in process.

BIBLIOGRAPHY.—Association for Education in Citizenship, *Education for Citizenship in Secondary Schools* (1936); Sir Ernest Barker, *The Citizen's Choice,* (1937); Karl Mannheim, *Diagnosis of our Time,* (1944); Charles E. Merriam, *The Making of Citizens,* (1931) and *Civic Education in the United States,* (1934); Bessie L. Pierce, *Citizens' Organizations and the Civic Training of Youth,* (1933); Progressive Education Association, *The Social Studies in General Education;* John Dewey, *The Public and Its Problems* (1927); Graham Wallas, *Human Nature in Politics,* 3rd ed. (1921). (E. S. JN.)

CIVIDALE DEL FRIULI, a town of Venetia, Italy, province of Udine, 10 mi. E. by N. by rail from the town of Udine; 453 ft. above sea-level; it was the ancient Forum Iulii. Pop. (1951) 11,454 (commune). The river Natisone forms a picturesque ravine here. The cathedral of the 15th century contains an octagonal marble canopy with sculptures in relief, with a font below it belonging to the 8th century. The museum contains Roman and Lombard antiquities, mss. and gold, silver and ivory objects formerly belonging to the chapter. The small church of S. Maria in Valle belongs to the 8th century, and contains fine decorations in stucco probably of the 12th century. The fine 15th-century Ponte del Diavolo leads to the church of S. Martino, which contains an altar of the 8th century with reliefs executed by order of the Lombard king, Ratchis. At Cividale was born Paulus Diaconus, the historian of the Lombards in the time of Charlemagne. A railway runs to Caporetto (16m.).

The Roman town of Forum Iulii was founded either by Julius Caesar or by Augustus, when the Via Iulia Augusta was built through Utina (Udine) on its way north. After the decay of Aquileia and Iulium Carnicum (Zuglio) it became the chief town of the district of Friuli and gave its name to it. The patriarchs of Aquileia resided here from 773 to 1031, then returned to Aquileia, and finally in 1238 removed to Udine. This last change of residence was the origin of antagonism between Cividale and Udine, terminated by their surrender to Venice in 1419 and 1420 respectively.

See G. Fogolari, *Cividale del Friuli* (Bergamo, 1906), well illustrated; *Memorie Storiche Forogiuliesi, passim* (Udine, 1905, *sqq.*—in progress).

CIVIL ENGINEER. When, in the 18th century, attention began to be given in England to such works of public value as roads, canals, harbours, docks, and lighthouses, the regulation of rivers, the production of iron by improved methods, and the construction of steam engines and of the machinery called forth by that new source of motive power, there arose men of great natural gifts, either with little technical training but great practical intelligence and skill, such as Brindley, or of equal practical capacity coupled with scientific attainments, such as Smeaton and Watt. These men applied to beneficent purposes the mechanical and constructional arts which previously had formed almost entirely the vocation of the military engineer, and they called themselves "engineers"; but Smeaton, seeing the inappropriateness of assuming a title hitherto belonging to military men, adopted the title "civil engineer," to make it clear that he was a civilian practitioner of those arts.

It was with this conception of the civil engineering profession that the Institution of Civil Engineers was founded. A royal charter of incorporation was granted to the institution on June 3, 1828. Before applying for the charter, the Society drew up a definition of the profession, "the art of directing the great sources of power in Nature for the use and convenience of man."

Many societies have since arisen having for their object the advancement of particular branches of engineering work, but the institution adheres to the conception of civil engineering held by its founders, and admits to its ranks any engineer who is adequately trained and experienced in the design and execution of any works or machinery instrumental in the application of sources of power for the benefit and convenience of mankind. The roll of the institution in 1928 numbered upwards of 10,000. Its house in Great George street, Westminster (the third building which it has occupied in that street), was built in 1912–13.

Specialization has brought about separate grouping of those interested in mechanical, electrical mining, etc., engineering. Underlying all groups is the work of the civil engineer, whose field particularly is that of structures. Foundations, simple or extremely complicated, are within his realm. He designs and supervises the construction of bridges and great buildings, tunnels, dams, reservoirs and aqueducts; he brings water to the centres of population and disposes of their wastes. He irrigates the desert and reclaims the swamps. He lays out, constructs and maintains highways and railroads, digs canals, regulates rivers, deepens harbours, builds lighthouses and constructs wharves and piers. He measures the earth's surface and the objects on it, and charts the resulting data. The work is frequently of a very definitely pioneering character, involving protracted physical effort. The civil engineer must have a scientific attitude of mind, and should have imagination, initiative, accuracy and good judgment, trained by special study. He should be able to work with men as well as with materials, and he should have administrative ability. In the United States with over 100 million inhabitants, probably 75,000 persons would call themselves civil engineers.

The American Society of Civil Engineers, founded in 1852, admits engineers from various fields. It has a membership of about 14,000 and is an important engineering institution.

CIVILIS, CLAUDIUS, or more correctly IULIUS, a Batavian leader of the German revolt against Rome (A.D. 69–70). He had served as a Roman auxiliary. During the disturbances that followed the death of Nero, he induced the Batavi to rebel, under the pretence of assisting Vespasian. The neighbouring Germans joined the revolt. The Roman garrisons near the Rhine were driven out, and 24 ships captured. Two legions were blockaded in Castra Vetera (near the modern Xanten), and the survivors were finally massacred. Eight cohorts of Batavian veterans joined their countrymen, and the troops sent by Vespasian to the relief of Vetera threw in their lot with them. The result of these accessions to the forces of Civilis was a rising in Gaul. The Roman generals were murdered (A.D. 70), and the whole of the Roman forces were induced by two commanders of the Gallic auxiliaries (Julius Classicus and Julius Tutor) to revolt from Rome and join Civilis. Most of Gaul declared itself independent, and the foundation of an empire of the Gauls was contemplated. Vespasian resolved to take strong measures for the suppression of the revolt. The arrival of Petillius Cerialis with a strong force awed the Gauls and mutinous troops into submission; Civilis was defeated at Augusta Treverorum (Trier, Trèves) and Vetera, and forced to withdraw to the island of the Batavians. He finally came to an agreement with Cerialis whereby his countrymen obtained certain advantages, and resumed amicable relations with Rome. From this time Civilis disappears from history.

BIBLIOGRAPHY.—The chief authority for the history of the insurrection is Tacitus, *Histories,* IV., V., whose account breaks off at the beginning of Civilis's speech to Cerialis; also Josephus, *Bellum Judaicum,* vii. 4. *See* also Merivale, *Hist. of the Romans under the Empire,* ch. 58; H. Schiller, *Geschichte der römischen Kaiserzeit,* bk. ii. ch. 2. § 54 (1883); B. Henderson, *Civil War and Rebellion in the Roman Empire* (1908); Mommsen, *Provinces of the Roman Empire* (ch. iv.), trans. Dickson (1909).

CIVILIZATION. This Encyclopædia is in itself a description of civilization, for it contains the story of human achievement in all its bewildering developments. It shows what men during hundreds of thousands of years have been learning about themselves, their world and the creatures which share it with them. They have reached out into remote space and studied nebulae whose light reaches them after a million years; they have, on the other hand, dissected atoms and manipulated electrons as they might handle pebbles. In the present magnificent series of volumes man's inventions are reviewed from the rudest chipped flint to the most delicately adjusted microscope; his creation of multiform beauties of design, colour and word, his ways of dealing with his fellows, his co-operations and dissensions; his ideals and lofty aspirations, his inevitable blunders and disappointments; in short, all his gropings, disheartening failures and unbelievable triumphs are recalled.

Several thousand contributors have been brought together to do each his special part in writing some thirty-five million words on what mankind has hitherto done and said. It might therefore seem at first sight superfluous, and indeed impossible, to treat civilization itself as a separate topic in a few pages. But there is danger that owing to the overwhelming mass of information given in these volumes certain important underlying considerations may be lost sight of. There are highly significant questions concerning the nature and course of human development, the obstacles which have lain in the way of advance; the sources of success and frustration, which could hardly be brought together in dealing with any of the special aspects of human culture. Accordingly an attempt will be made under this caption to scan civilization as a single, unique and astonishing achievement of the human species.

To begin with, it is a startling fact that civilization, which sets off man in so astounding a manner from all other animals, should only lately have begun to be understood. We are immersed in it from infancy; we take it for granted, and are too near it to see it, except in this detail and that. Even to-day, with all our recently acquired knowledge, those who strive most valiantly in imagination to get outside civilization so that they may look upon it dispassionately and appraise it as a whole, are bewildered by its mysteries. As for the great mass of intelligent people, they still harbour many ancient illusions and misapprehensions from which they can only be weaned with great reluctance.

The object of the present article is to describe the newer ways of viewing civilization, its general nature, origin, progress, transmission and chief developments, in the light of information which has been accumulating during the past fifty or sixty years. The study of man himself has been revealing quite as many revolutionary facts and hypotheses during the past half century as the scientific investigation of the world in which he lives. The history of human achievement has been traced back, at least in vague outline, hundreds of thousands of years; man's original uncivilized nature and equipment have been studied and compared with the behaviour of his nearer relatives; new conjectures have emerged in regard to the functioning of speech and the nature and origin of human reasoning; careful investigations of primitive civilizations have cast great light on more complicated ones; the tremendous importance of childhood and its various implications in the development of civilization have been elaborated.

These and many other discoveries conspire to recast our conception of civilization, its past progress and its future possibilities.

It is instructive to note that the word civilization is by no means an old one. Boswell reports that he urged Dr. Johnson to insert the term in his dictionary in 1772, but Johnson refused. He preferred the older word "civility." This, like "urbanity," reflects the contempt of the townsman for the rustic or barbarian; it is an invidious term, although in a way justified by the fact that only where cities have grown up have men developed intricate civilizations. The arduous and dispersed tasks of the hunter, shepherd and peasant folk do not afford the leisure, or at least the varied human contacts, essential to the generation of new ideas and discoveries. But modern anthropologists have pointed out that peoples without cities, such as the tribes of Polynesia and the North American Indians, are really highly "civilized," in the sense that upon sympathetic examination, they are found to have subtle languages, ingenious arts, admirably suited to their conditions, developed institutions, social and political; religious practices and confident myths, no better and no worse substantiated than many that prevail to-day among the nations of Europe. All these betoken and presuppose a vastly long development. Among English speaking people the first to point this out clearly was E. B. Tylor, who published his famous *Primitive Culture* in 1871, the same year in which Darwin's *Descent of Man* appeared. These two books would alone have served, by different approaches, to give the word civilization a far more profound meaning than it had ever had before.

NEW CONCEPTION OF CIVILIZATION

There could be no real understanding of the fundamental characteristics of civilization until the fact was well established and digested that could we trace back man's lineage far enough we should find it merging into that of wild animals, without artificial shelters, clothes or speech; dependent for sustenance on the precarious daily search for food. It requires a considerable effort of the imagination to picture the human race without these seeming necessities of even primitive civilization. Without fire and tools men must have existed as did a wild girl discovered near Châlons, France, in 1731. She possessed a monkey-like agility which enabled her to catch birds and rabbits; these she skinned with her nails and gobbled raw, as would a dog. She delighted to suck the blood from living pigeons, and had no speech except hideous screams and howls.

This conception of man's former animal existence is gradually supplanting the older one, based upon ancient Hebrew tradition, that the first man and first woman were special creations with fully developed minds, speech and reason, which enabled them forthwith to dress the garden in which they found themselves, to name its animal denizens, and to talk with one another, and with God himself in the cool of the evening. This view is still passively accepted by an overwhelming majority of Americans and Europeans and is at present hotly defended by a powerful group in the United States.

The former assumption was that man was *by nature* endowed with a *mind* and with *reason.* These distinguished him sharply from the animals, which did wondrous things it is true, but not as a result of reason. Their behaviour was guided, it was argued, by instinct. Darwin says that "the very essence of an instinct is that it is followed independently of reason." But if we agree, as manifold evidence seems to force us to do, that long, long ago men behaved and lived like wild animals, are we not forced to ask if they did not live wholly according to what Darwin calls "instincts"? And if once upon a time our ancestors lived solely by their animal equipment, did they as yet have a mind and reason? May not the human mind be something that has very gradually developed as a result of man's peculiar animal make-up and capacities? May not his reason be but another name for his slowly accumulated knowledge and beliefs and his ways of dealing with them and building upon them? In any case the discovery that our ancestors once lived like wild animals raises entirely new and difficult questions as to the nature, origin and interpretation of those powers of his known as mind and reason, which have enabled him to seek out those inventions and come upon beliefs and practices which have produced in the aggregate civilization.

In short, it seems to be more and more apparent that mind and reason were not part of man's original equipment, as are his arms and legs, his brain and tongue, but have been slowly acquired and painfully built up. They are themselves *inventions*—things he has come upon. Like other inventions *they are part and parcel of civilization*—not innate in man but dependent for their perpetuation on education in the widest sense of that term. This is so novel an idea that many readers may find it difficult to grasp, but when grasped it alters one's whole estimate of human progress. We ordinarily think of civilization as made up of mechanical devices, books and pictures, enlightened religious ideas, handsome buildings, polite conduct, scientific and philosophical knowledge, social and political institutions, ingenious methods of transportation and the rest. We think that all these things are due to man's possession of a mind, which no animal has, and as a result of the exercise of reason. In a way this is true enough, only we must reconceive mind and reason and regard them just as truly a part of the gradual elaboration of civilization as a House of Commons or a motor car, and quite as subject to improvement. At the risk of making a seemingly irrelevant philosophical digression, which is really most essential to a modern understanding of civilization, something may be said of the newer conception of mind and its variant, reason.

The word mind was originally a verb, not a noun; it meant action, not a thing or agent. It was remembering and purposing, and taking note of—as for instance "I minded"—that is, remembered, or paid attention to, or was concerned by. But as time went on philosophers made a noun of the good old verb. It was conceived as that incorporeal substance which was the seat of a person's consciousness, thoughts, feelings, and especially of his reasoning. The body was set over against the mind whose orders it was supposed to execute. The Scottish philosopher of common sense, Reid, says explicitly that "we do not give the name of mind to thought, reason or desire; but to that power which both perceives and wills." Even John Stuart Mill says in his *Logic* that "mind is the mysterious something which feels and thinks."

Recently there has been a tendency to reduce the noun mind once more to a series of verbs—desiring, remembering, feeling, thinking, distinguishing, inferring, planning—and to regard the assumption of "a mysterious something" as unfounded, unnecessary and a serious embarrassment. Relieved of this embarrassment it is possible to begin to bridge the gulf between the original behaviour of the human race and that of mankind to-day. Descartes and all the older philosophers believed that man had always had a mind as good as theirs. They sought to tell him how to employ it in the pursuit of truth. Mind was to them a sort of divine instrument, conferred solely upon man, that could be sharpened and efficiently used by following the laws of logic; but they could not think of it as something accumulated, so to speak, through the many thousands of years since man made his first contributions to the upbuilding of civilization.

The way is now cleared for a new view of civilization which would not have been possible 50 or 60 years ago. Civilization is no longer contrasted with "rusticity," "barbarity" or "savagery," but with man's purely animal heritage. Modern men are still animals, they have to eat and sleep, protect themselves from the inclemencies of the weather, and defend themselves from attacks of their fellow creatures and other animals, and to rear a new generation, if the species is to be perpetuated. They closely resemble kindred animals in much of their physical structure, in their important organs, breathing, digestion and the circulation of their blood. All these peculiarities are hereditarily transmitted no matter how much or how little men may be civilized. On the other hand, civilization—language, religion, beliefs, morals, arts and manifestations of the human mind and reason—none of these can be shown to be handed down as biological traits. They can only be transmitted to a new generation by imitation or instruction.

All mankind to-day has a double heritage. The one comes to us without any effort on our part, as do the spider's peculiar characteristics or those of birds, or of any of our fellow mammals, come to them. It is secure and tends to remain the same for thousands of years. Civilization, on the other hand, is precarious; it must be assimilated anew by each one of us for himself in such a degree as circumstances permit. It can increase indefinitely but it may also fall off tremendously, as the history of man amply testifies. It is a legacy that can be lost as well as kept and increased.

To illustrate: it may be that before human beings had acquired any of this loseable thing, civilization, they would pick up a stick to strike an assailant or hurl a stone at him. They might have found themselves riding astride floating tree trunks to cross a stream. Certain persons would occur, let us say, in each generation who would do all these things without ever having seen them done. These acts would be classed in man's animal heritage. But should we find traces of men who chipped a flint nodule into a hatchet head, and hollowed out their log with such a hatchet, or with fire, we should have to class these acts among the arts of civilization since they presuppose so much accumulated experience and ingenuity that they could not be inborn. The art of making a rude boat might consequently be wholly lost, as surely many inventions must have lapsed, if a single generation passed without constructing one.

It seems now an imperative fact that all civilization—the total social and traditional heritage, would fall away immediately and completely should a thoroughgoing forgetfulness, an overwhelming amnesia and profound oblivion overtake humanity. Only their natural equipment would be left. As Graham Wallas suggests, those least civilized would have a possible chance of surviving. It is only uncivilized man that might go on indefinitely. We are all by nature wild animals *plus;* and our taming weakens us for the ancient struggle in the forest, naked and bare-handed.

PECULIAR ITEMS OF MAN'S BODILY FORM

At this juncture the question arises, what was there peculiar in man's physical make-up that enabled him to initiate civilization and build up a mind which he could use to increase his resources so far beyond that of any other animal? Before proceeding we should recollect that the ways of all living creatures are manifold and astonishing. Even a single-celled organism can marvellously adjust itself to altered conditions. It seems to learn by experience, it appears to have a sort of memory, it is modified by happenings which interrupt its comfortable routine. It is ingenious in defending itself, in seeking food and reproducing. It is, in short, purposive in its conduct. The tiger and the frog are able to adjust themselves to very different modes of life, and so are the orioles and cacti. Before man began to accumulate civilization we are forced to assume that he too made terms with the daily need of adjustment which faced him, otherwise we should not be here to write the tale. These are the salient essentials of *Life,* and man is a part of what Julian Huxley calls "the stream of life." All these possibilities lay behind the development of man's intelligence. They are the hinterland from which civilization emerged and to which it ever tends to retreat.

In order to begin and carry on the accumulation of civilization, man had of necessity to be so constructed physically that he could *perceive* more clearly than his predecessors, make more accurate distinctions and so remember and imagine better; for all these are essential to talking and thinking. The awareness of animals is of a low, vague type, and so must pristine man's have been. The one-celled animals behave in a purposive way, but they have no eyes or ears or noses. They must live in silence and darkness like a human blind, deaf mute. They will nevertheless take in certain food and reject other things. They perceive and act without, so far as we can see, being conscious of their actions. They make the necessary decisions without deciding in a human sense. They have no nervous system, but, as has lately been discovered, the promise of one. The creatures most like ourselves have eyes, ears and noses, and evidently see, hear and smell; and they have an elaborate nervous system. Of these resources they make constant use. But compared with man they are ill-qualified to make careful distinctions and discriminations and remember clearly. They take note of far fewer factors in their situation. They must act somewhat as our digestive system does. It is a sort of animal within us which performs wondrous feats when given food. It works purposively, as does our heart and blood circulation. We can become *conscious* of these unconscious achievements when we choke, because the switch is not thrown promptly enough to prevent a morsel from going down our windpipe instead of taking the route to the stomach. Palpitation of the heart is a conscious suggestion of the faithful pump, which rarely reminds us of its constant attention to business. Let it neglect two or three beats and we are dead.

The essentials of man's physical equipment for initiating and piling up civilization have been dwelt upon by many writers. He has sensitive hands, and (after he got securely on his hind legs) he could use them far more freely than if he had to employ them as auxiliary feet. His thumb can be readily placed against any one of his fingers. There is no such expert feeler and handler as he to be found among his kindred. He could learn much of shape and form, of softness and hardness, of weight, texture, heat and cold, toughness, rigidity and flexibility, which could be but vaguely sensed with hoof or paw. Had he had ears that he could turn about like a jack-rabbit, and a prehensile tail, he might have been able to learn faster. And all these things were the beginning of knowledge. He could not only strike but hurl. His eyes were so placed that he was always looking through a stereoscope, so to speak, and seeing things in the round. His vocal organs promised a great range of delicate discrimination in the sounds he made. Then he was a helpless dependent for many years on his elders so that their acquired ways could become his.

Lastly there is man's brain with its complex cerebral cortex and its association paths, which develop astonishingly as a child grows up. The cortex is the prime correlator of impressions, and is modified through individual experience in a higher degree than any other part of the nervous system. Its functioning is still very mysterious, but no one doubts its essential rôle in the process of human learning and the increase of intelligence. Its operations are not, however, autonomous but closely associated with the experiences of the whole human organism and dependent on those singular capacities of mankind already mentioned.

So it becomes apparent that after hundreds of millions of years during which nature's experiments have been going on in physical structure and function, which have enabled creatures of the most diverse types to meet the absolute requisites of life—growing up and reproducing their species—a kind of animal finally appeared on the earth so constructed that he could become civilized. Man's biological make-up represents a unique combination of physical characteristics. Most of these, as we have seen, occur in other mammals. Even those which seem peculiar to him would not serve, however, as a foundation for the development of civilization except in a highly complex union. Cows might have a human cerebral cortex, foxes apposable thumbs, birds stereoscopic eyes, dogs vocal organs similar to ours, and yet civilization would be far beyond their reach. Man can teach all of them tricks. They themselves can learn something as their life goes on. Chimpanzees may under favourable circumstances, as Köhler has shown, make very simple, human-like inferences; but none of them could initiate and perpetuate the arts and sciences as a heritage of their species.

PROGRESS AND CONSERVATISM

Such, then was man's original equipment for getting civilized. He had, obviously, no means of foreseeing the enterprise in which he was engaged. His evolution as a civilized being was no more premeditated than his rise from earlier simian ancestors. There seems to be sufficient evidence that for hundreds of thousands of years changes in his mode of life were so gradual and rare as to pass unperceived. Each generation accepted the conditions in which it was reared without thought of betterment. Our modern hope of "progress"—an indefinite increase of human knowledge and its application to the improvement of man's estate—was practically unknown even to the Greeks and Romans. From the 13th century onward a few writers dwelt upon the promise of the future, but they were outclamoured by those convinced that human woes were attributable to a departure from ancient standards. The Humanists strove to re-establish the wisdom of the classical writers, and the Protestants sought to revive the beliefs and practices of the early Christians. Only three centuries ago did Bacon unroll a programme of aggressive search for the hitherto unknown, which had any very wide influence. In the 18th century the conception of reform and progress found illustrious spokesmen, and their anticipations of coming changes in the economy of human life were destined, as it proved, to be far outrun by the events of the 19th and early 20th centuries.

We can, however, still note on all hands illustrations of man's confidence in routine sanctified by ancient authorities; his suspicion of innovation in wide realms of belief and practice. This dogged obstinacy in clinging to his habits, and his general suspicion of the unfamiliar, are exactly what might have been anticipated when we consider his animal origin. This trait has served to slow down the process of change, but at the same time has greatly increased the security and permanence of each achievement. Here we find a possible explanation of the great rôle that the veil of sacredness has played in man's development. He has cast it over beliefs and practices and so hid them from pert scrutiny and criticism. The number of those who can tolerate somewhat critical thinking here and there, has, nevertheless, greatly increased of late, but they are still few indeed. What we call to-day a conservative or reactionary mood must have been characteristic of mankind from the beginning. It corresponds to animal inclinations.

Among animal proclivities there is, however, from the one-celled organisms upward, a life-saving tendency to make random movements, extensions and contractions, to hasten hither and thither, in the pursuit of food and mates. This restlessness and groping are among man's legacies also. They offset his routine and static habits, and lie behind and back of the inventions and discoveries he has made. There is, too, especially obvious among the higher animals, something auguring what in man becomes curiosity. The danger of attack made preliminary scouting a valuable asset in survival. So men were by nature wont to pry and try and fumble, long before they scientifically analysed and experimented.

There can be no doubt that hundreds of thousands of years were required for man to reach even the lowest degree of culture to be found among the simplest tribes to-day. The discovery of fossil skulls, teeth and bones at different geological levels shows that more or less ape-like men have been on earth for from half a million to a million years. Several species, such as the Java man, the Heidelberg man and the much later Neanderthal race are now extinct. The only vestiges of their handiwork consist in chipped flint tools, becoming better made and more varied as time went on. There is no way of telling what other arts, beliefs and practices were associated with a particular assortment of flint utensils. Sollas, in his *Ancient Hunters,* has sought to draw ingenious analogies between these prehistoric weapons and the civilizations of the Tasmanians, Australians, Eskimos, etc.

The so-called Cro-Magnon race had finely developed skulls quite as good as those of to-day. To them are ascribed the remarkable paintings and drawings found in caves of southern France and northern Spain. They are believed to be from 25 to 30 thousand years old. Halving this period we come upon traces of ground and polished stone tools, coincident with the relinquishment of hunting as man's exclusive pursuit and a settling down to sow and reap, spin and weave. Halving it again, we get news of the use of copper, the precursor of the metals on which our civilization largely rests. This can but be a rough chronology subject to much revision as time goes on and the earth is more thoroughly searched for evidences of man's past.

To get the matter clearly before one, let us imagine, as the writer has suggested elsewhere, that 500,000 years of developing culture were compressed into 50 years. On this scale mankind would have required 49 years to learn enough to desert here and there his inveterate hunting habits and settle down in villages. Half through the fiftieth year writing was discovered and practised within a very limited area, thus supplying one of the chief means for perpetuating and spreading culture. The achievements of the Greeks would be but three months back, the prevailing of Christianity, two; the printing press would be a fortnight old and man would have been using steam for hardly a week. The peculiar conditions under which we live did not come about until Dec. 31 of the fiftieth year.

There is a school of anthropologists, the diffusionists, who would derive all the higher types of civilization—writing, metallurgy, the construction of imposing stone buildings—from a single region, Egypt. They have collected much evidence to show that through the commerce of the Phoenicians, Egyptian inventions spread eastward into India, China and Japan, then across the Pacific to form the basis of Maya culture in Central America. The merits of the "diffusionist" arguments cannot be considered here. G. Elliot Smith, one of the best known advocates of this theory, dwells on the common lack of inventiveness and the reluctance of mankind to adopt new ideas, his tenacious hold on old ones and "his thick armour of obstinacy." "To obtain recognition of even the most trivial of innovations it is the common experience of almost every pioneer in art, science or invention to have to fight against a solid wall of cultivated prejudice and inherent stupidity."

All anthropologists are well aware of this hostility to change, which we may regard, as shown above, as a natural trait of mankind. They also admit the wide dissemination of inventions through commerce and conquest. Nevertheless many maintain that the same or similar discovery has been made independently in different parts of the earth, as the result of similar needs and conditions. When we have examined the exigencies of successful inventions in the following section we shall see that however commonplace they are now, with the accumulation of the past to build upon and modern facilities to work with, they were beyond measure difficult at the start when mankind still led the life of an animal. When once made and adopted by some tribe it is far easier to think of them as being introduced to other peoples than to assume that their presence represents an independent discovery.

Civilization depends upon the discoveries and inventions man has been able to make, together with the incalculable effects these have had upon his daily conduct, thoughts and feelings. As knowledge and ingenuity increased he departed further and further from his original wild animal life. The manner in which he began to learn is a matter of conjecture, since the manufacture of tools and weapons, the invention of language and artificial ways of producing fire, far antedate any written accounts of advances in man's education. The same may be said of the much more recent spinning, weaving and farming. As we have seen, it required hundreds of thousands of years to reach the degree of civilization represented by these achievements. Their importance, however, cannot be overestimated, since they formed the absolutely essential basis of all later developments. We may feel a certain pride in contemporary inventions, but let us remember that we owe to savage hunters and illiterate neolithic farmers the accumulation of knowledge and skill without which none of our modern experimentation would be possible. Where would we be without fire, speech, clothes and bread!

Since invention, discovery and the increase of knowledge are the stuff of which civilization is made, it is pertinent to our theme to consider how they occur. There is plenty of evidence available in the reports which discoverers now make of the manner in which they reach their conclusions. There is also evidence of how their results are received and acted upon by others. All explorers must be exceptionally curious and at the same time patient gropers. The curiosity observable in most children tends to die away, but survives in one form or another in rare instances through life. These exceptional persons possess a drive alien to their fellows. They may be the handyman of a village or a member of a highly endowed research staff. They avail themselves of what has already been found out; the village mechanical genius does not have to invent a monkey-wrench or bit of insulating tape, nor does the biologist need to know much about the optical principles of his lenses, much less invent or manufacture them. The geologist before he makes any discoveries is familiar with hundreds of treatises on his subject. It would be generally conceded by investigators that their discoveries are seemingly accidental. They do not know what they are going to find, and quite commonly find what they were not looking for, even as Saul, chasing lost asses, came upon a kingdom. All this applies to every kind of increase of knowledge, whether it have to do with the operations of so-called Nature or with novel suggestions in the realms of philosophy or art. All are the result of curiosity, patient examination and thought. At best they are no more than foot-notes and glosses added to existing human knowledge. This is now so varied and voluminous that no single person can compass it except in this detail and that. Should he attempt to do so, all chance of adding to it would be excluded.

But an invention or discovery or the rectification of an ancient error, does not become a part of civilization until it has been accepted by the tribe and been added to its habits of action and thought. Plenty of shocking tales could be recalled of professional and popular opposition to innovations on grounds which now seem grotesque. We owe discoveries to individual men and women, but new information and skill can only be propagated and disseminated in a favourable culture medium. Many instances could be cited of promising knowledge which has so far failed to get a footing in civilization.

The influence of particular discoveries and mechanical devices is by no means confined to their more immediate and obvious applications. It is impossible to foresee what wide-ranging effects they may ultimately exert on human life. Fire will cook a meal, harden an earthen bowl, keep a group of naked savages warm, frighten off prowling animals, soften or melt metals; it may also consume sacrifices to the gods, or form the central interest of a stately temple and be replenished by an order of vestal virgins. It may play its part in the symbolism of the theologian and the poet. The Indians of the North American plains were deeply affected by the introduction of the horse, and African tribes by fire-arms and whisky. The motor car and telephone altered social relations. The perfecting of the steam engine revolutionized the transport of men and their wares; it promoted city life; further, it caused Marx to write a big book which became the gospel of a momentous social upheaval, which threatened the peace of mind of all nations.

The invention of clothes—quite material things, whether of linen, wool, silk or cotton—not only created great industries but enabled men by changing their hide artificially to establish social distinctions akin to biological genera and species. Through clothes entered in prudery and the pious horror of bare bodies which has wrought consternation and disaster among the dark-skinned folk. After the World War women's skirts were gradually shortened. The warmth of houses and vehicles permitted this. One of the conventional distinctions between girls and women was thus obliterated. The unveiling of women's faces in Mohammedan countries, the breaking down of *purdah* in India—all these material changes imply modifications of woman's life and of the attitude of the sexes to one another. They forecast further important changes in traditional civilization.

In view of these facts, and indefinitely more that each one can easily add for himself, it would seem that what are esteemed the "nobler" aspirations and creations of mankind, whether in art and literature or the pursuit of truth, are all not only dependent upon "material" inventions but so strangely interwoven with them and their effects that it is no easy thing to separate the higher and the lower, except in imagination. What is sometimes called "the higher life of man" arises from his more humble and practical knowledge and skill; accordingly the old distinction between the material and spiritual seems to be greatly attenuated as they are both seen to merge into the newer conception of civilization as a whole. This will become even more apparent when we come to deal with words.

RÔLE OF CHILDHOOD

One of the essential conditions for the perpetuation of civilization is the long period of dependence through which the human child must pass before it gains sufficient bodily strength and intelligence to achieve merely animal self-sufficiency and make its own way. Without the constant and prolonged succour of adults it would speedily perish. This means that the extended period of helpless susceptibility to his surroundings makes it possible vastly to modify a child's original disposition. A mouse is sexually mature in six weeks and fully grown in three months. Calves and colts walk about shortly after birth. The gorilla, on the other hand, has a prolonged childhood, requires ten or twelve years before it is able to breed, and goes on growing, like man, for a few years after. He lacks, however, in spite of his prolonged childhood, the other essential traits which have enabled mankind to initiate, increase and transmit civilization.

We are all born uncivilized and would remain so through life were we not immersed in civilization. There is a long time in which we may, according to the place where we are born, be moulded into a well authenticated Papuan, Chinaman, or Parisian. We cannot choose whether we shall find ourselves talking like a Hottentot, a Russian or a German. And we learn to do in all things as those do among whom we are brought up. We cannot but accept their respective customs, scruples, and ideas, for all these are imposed upon us before we have any choice or discretion. We must perforce follow the ways of our elders, who themselves were once children and gained their civilization before any discrimination or comparison with other than the prevailing habits was possible. This is the inexorable rule, and it accounts for many of the striking characteristics of civilization.

If the assimilation of culture is closely associated with the dependence and adaptability of childhood there need be no great surprise that accumulating evidence seems to indicate that when bodily maturity is once reached, the increase of knowledge and intelligence slackens or even almost ceases in many cases. By 13 or 14 the child has acquired an overwhelming part of the knowledge, impressions, cautions and general estimates of his fellow creatures and the world in which he lives, which he continues to harbour with slight modifications during his lifetime. When as a result of the participation of the United States in the World War it became necessary to test the competence of a great number of young men an unforeseen contribution was made to our insight into civilization. Of the 1,700,000 examined, 45% did not show themselves (to quote an eminent authority, Dr. Henry H. Goddard) "much above the 12-year-old limit." Those tested, it must be remembered, did not include idiots or "morons," but the average run of youths accepted by their fellows as normal. While tests may be as yet inadequate they but confirm the observable fact that the inculcation of culture is associated with bodily growth and especially with the strange changes in the cells of the fore-brain and their intercommunications. These developments are tremendous from infancy to maturity in so-called normal cases.

Only in exceptional instances does mind-building continue steadily after childhood and adolescence. We have had time before 13 to take over the standardized sentiments of our elders, to learn all that they know, to accept their views of religion, politics, manners, general proprieties and respectabilities. The common run of mankind can, however, be taught tricks as time goes on and acquire special expertness. But a great part of our childish conceptions retain a permanent hold on us. There is usually little encouragement to alter them. We leave most of them unrevised, though we have to make adjustments as the years elapse. Human beings seem on the whole easily subdued to routine and the routine is established, as it would seem, by the time we are grown up. That the *ability* to learn, however, falls off very slowly after adulthood has been recently shown by E. L. Thorndike.

The experts in advertising, the publishers of "tabloid" newspapers and the contrivers of moving picture films seem to conform to the supposition that what appeals to a 12- or 13-year-old child is admirably adapted to the intelligence and tastes of the multitude. This means that the overwhelming majority of men and women assimilate in childhood the common and familiar forms of civilization or culture in the midst of which they find themselves, but hardly outrun them as life goes on. Perhaps one in a hundred may allow his opinions to be altered by assiduous reading, or take pains to cultivate his insight into art and literature and scientific discoveries. But all these and other contributions to one's personal civilization are outside the range of the human animal in general. Indeed the mere upkeep of our present complicated culture must depend upon a very trifling percentage of the population. Were a few thousand carefully selected infants in the various progressive countries of the world to be strangled at birth not only would advances in industry, arts and letters cease but a decline would set in owing to the lack of those to make the essential readjustments in our industries and their financing; to keep up laboratories and books at their present standards. Accordingly the great majority of human beings can barely maintain at best the civilization in which they were reared. Even the innovators considered above, are unable to escape from the toils in which they were so easily enmeshed and which they regard not as entanglements and restraints but as comforts and assurances. It would be faithless and disloyal to regard them otherwise. Only peculiar temperaments under highly favourable conditions question what they have been taught. They can do this only on a most modest scale as a result of continued curiosity and study. A physicist may reach a new theory of the constitution of atoms and yet cling stolidly to the notions of religion he had acquired at ten years of age; he may even engage in subtle philosophical speculation and remain a hot defender of the *mores* of the most commonplace persons 50 years ago.

If these points be well taken the whole contrast between Society and the individual which has been played up in various rather futile ways takes on a new aspect. From the standpoint of civilization each individual owes his entire equipment as a civilized being to others. Biologically even, he is vastly modified by his domestication, in habits, impulses and moods. The so-called "instinct of the herd," which Trotter has made famous, tends to become an unnecessary hypothesis. For every child is made by others in their own image. How gregarious mankind was before the onset of civilization it is impossible to say; but the prolonged infantile weakness implied multiform dependence upon others. Of course there is really no such thing as Society in the sense of some powerful and precious personality for whose welfare the so-called individual is invited to make appropriate sacrifices of personal preferences. What we have to do is to make terms with the notions of "the good" and "the bad" which those profess with whom we are thrown. These rules of conduct and sentiment constitute Society. They have their heavy sanctions if violated or impeached—disgrace, persecution, imprisonment and even death. The methods of eluding Society constitute a highly interesting chapter in the history of civilization. It is not difficult for the shrewd, and seems greatly to enrich life for certain temperaments, whether one be a burglar, a story-teller, or a philosopher. Wholesale deceit has established the reputation and fame of many a hero from Jacob and Ulysses to those in high places to-day. Boldness of thought is less likely as yet to arouse primitive enthusiasm.

WORDS VIEWED AS DEEDS

One of the most stupendous elements in civilization has hitherto been only casually mentioned—words. Without language civilization could hardly even have begun and certainly could never have attained its higher forms. Speech underlies thinking and conscious planning and research. It does more. It creates a world of ideas which interpenetrates and seems to transcend that of the facts of human experience. What pass for facts are indeed so moulded by our notions of them that recent philosophers are less and less confident in their efforts to separate the functioning of ideas from that of facts. Much has been discovered of late which serves to revolutionize the older theories of language and thinking, and to eliminate some of the age-long quandaries in which philosophers have found themselves involved. These new views can be only briefly suggested here.

The Fourth Gospel opens, "In the beginning was the Word; . . . All things were made by it; . . . In it was life; and the life was the light of men." Goethe declared that in the beginning was the deed. The most recent writers who deal with speech would seek to shed new light on civilization by recognizing that words have always been deeds. They have always been regarded as wonder-working acts; they create things which without them could never exist; they are the chief light of man—and his darkness as well.

Making noises is a conspicuous animal trait. Katydids, frogs, whippoorwills, dogs, and many other creatures exhibit a tireless patience in this matter. Man, too, is a great chatterer. His fellow men may be bored by his talk, but they are likely to be scared by his silence. It is portentous and bodes no good. To keep still is an unfriendly act. So, as Malinowski has pointed out, one of the many functions of utterances has been reassurance and the expression of companionability. The cries of animals as related to their needs and behaviour are only just beginning to be carefully studied. Whitman and Craig have discovered a marvellous correlation between the ejaculations of pigeons and their ways of life. Köhler, Yerkes and others are attending to our nearer relatives. But all that needs be noted here is that human language must have emerged from the spontaneous sounds made by pre-man.

Only when men began to make pictures of events and gestures, and painfully developed writing from the pictures, have we the least actual evidence of language. The Egyptian inscriptions illustrate picture writing and its later and most ingenious metamorphosis into sound symbols—an alphabet. This happened five or six thousand years ago. But it is clear from the Egyptian language that its surprising complexity and sophistication imply an antecedent development of incalculable length, to judge from the slowness of man's material inventions.

While the beginnings of language are hidden from us by the lapse of hundreds of thousands of unrecorded years, there are several new ways of coming to a far better understanding of them than hitherto. There are historical and contemporaneous sources of information which have been exploited of late and serve to revolutionize the older views. For example, the so-called primitive languages (until recently, never reduced to writing), afford a sufficient proof that words are fundamentally acts, closely related to man's other conduct. Then, watching the way that babies—the Latins aptly called them *infantes,* or speechless creatures—learn to talk, greatly re-enforces and corroborates the evidence derived from the study of "illiterate" tribes. Lastly, anyone who has learned the trick, can substantiate the same thing if he tests the babble always going on around him.

We have already noted one way in which speech is a mode of action, a friendly gesture, not an expression of thought or conveyance of ideas as philosophers have taught us. "How do you do?" is not a question to be answered under usual circumstances. One concurs in the obvious statement, which conveys no fresh information, "Fine day, sir." These are just tail-waggings, like taking off one's hat, bowing, smiling and hand-shaking. We can, however, do far more with language; we at times can strike with a word more safely and more effectively than with our fist; by words we can cower, and dodge, and elude danger. Those in highest standing in all communities make a living by words, unwritten and written. Whole professions confine their activities to words, —clergymen, teachers (of the older type), lawyers, politicians; brokers deal in alternately saying "buy" or "sell." Doubtless other things lie behind this trafficking, but words are effective acts, or so intimately intertwined with them, that it is impossible to say where one sets in and the other ends. Pure talk and written words seem often to do the business without the intervention of so-called things. The magic operations and achievements of words can be observed everywhere and in all ages. Jacob and Esau struggled bitterly to win a blessing from their blind old father. His words were momentous. They might cause unborn generations to bow down before his son's offspring or doom him and his children to perpetual slavery.

As a clergyman of the 18th century remarked, "Words have a certain bewitchery or fascination which makes them operate with a force beyond what we can naturally give account of." Joy and infinite woe follow in their train; from which our wordless ancestors must have been spared. The main emotional structure of civilization—so poignant and so unique an element in human life—is largely reared on words. They serve to establish new orders of sensitiveness and excitability. Words increase the clarity of our memory to a tremendous degree and at the same time they vivify imagination, which could exist on no considerable scale without them. With these word-created adjuncts we can elaborate our hopes, fears, scruples, self-congratulations, jealousies, remorses and aspirations far beyond anything that seems justified to the onlooker; we can project them backward into the past and forward into the future. Words can rear more glorious palaces and dig deeper, darker dungeons than any made with hands.

TALKING AND THINKING

What has so far been said of the recent views of language helps to explain the newer interpretation of the old terms mind and reason. These seem to be processes, as we have seen, rather than agents. They are ways of doing things rather than things themselves. John Dewey calls his admirable little book on mind, *How We Think.* When older philosophers began to think about thinking, and how by thinking we reached truth, they commonly found themselves writing very long books, very hard to read; and they called their great theme epistemology or the theory of cognition. The effective thinking which has built up civilization has not, however, relied upon their treatises; nor has it been influenced by them. Two or three considerations only can be touched upon here which impress recent students in investigating thinking.

Thinking and words go together. For thinking, to be clear, has to rely upon names and their various associations with one another. For instance, grocer's bill, cheque-book, fountain-pen, envelope, stamp, letter-box are names put together in a particular sequence. Of late there has been a good deal of discussion as to whether thinking was not always talking quite noiselessly to ourselves. A child will first utter sounds at random, then begin to find that the sounds he makes bring things; then he gets to naming with vast enthusiasm; then he prattles too freely and inopportunely to please his elders; then he may merely move his lips—as many childish people continue to do—and finally hold his tongue. It can be shown, however, by appropriate tests that this suppressed talking is accompanied by muscular adjustments of the vocal organs which indicate a silent execution of the words and sentences. We can say openly "That's too bad," or mutter it, or adjust our organs so as to say it if we wished. This suppressed talking seems to be thinking. That all thinking is merely talking to ourselves many will doubt or deny. While some minor reservations are justifiable there is an overwhelming mass of evidence, derived for instance from the study of deaf mutes, that fortifies the contention stated above—no words, no thinking.

But thinking can easily be seen to be of several varieties. There is the meandering succession of recollections, vague apprehensions, hopes, preferences, disappointments and animosities which has come to be called *reverie.* It underlies other and more exacting forms of thinking. It is found on inspection to consist of recollections, anticipations, excuses for past or contemplated conduct, reflections on the unfairness of our fellow creatures and of the world in general; or assurances that all is well and must in the nature of things remain so. Ordinary daily planning is an essential form of thought—making homely decisions and adjustments. Underneath, we can perceive the reverie flowing as a sort of undercurrent—for thinking is very complicated.

We occasionally turn our thinking to trying to find out something that we do not yet know. This may be the result of mere personal suspicions and vulgar curiosity, or of an honest desire to improve a defective social situation, or learn more of light waves, Chinese paintings, psychoneuroses or investments. In dealing with the workings of the physical universe a special kind of thinking, the mathematical, has produced results that tend to safeguard the investigator from the usual prejudices which beset us in all thinking. It is a peculiar, highly refined language, or way of talking about things, by employing the vocabulary of sines and cosines, logarithms, constants, variables, roots, powers, etc. It has proved to be a wonderfully fruitful way of talking about light, for instance, and the nature of "matter" and "force" and in dealing with engineering problems. Few are addicted to this type or any other variety of scientific thinking. Most practical inventions seem to proceed from our power to experiment by thinking; to fumble and stumble mentally, and sometimes succeed. This mental trying-out is a kind of trial and error. It cannot proceed long without various external acts to check up the guesses and inferences produced by meditation.

One of the most novel and promising methods of learning more about all kinds of thinking is abnormal psychology. Illusional and obsessive thinking which fill the mad-houses appear to be only the exaggerations of the thinking of those at large. The psychiatrists hold out hopes of discovering through their special knowledge, and a study of infants and children, ways of eliminating or reducing some of the vices of civilization as it has hitherto developed. To them civilization is in many of its manifestations a species of mild madness; these can only be eliminated by a great change in the way children are brought up, so as to obviate the maladjustments and distress incident to a rapidly altering cultural environment.

Men and women think not only when they are awake but when they are asleep. Their sleeping thoughts and visions and experiences we have learned to set off sharply—far too sharply as it would appear—from waking thought. Primitive man did not do this. He did not deem his dreams mere illusions, comical or distressing, to be banished when he opened his eyes. They were not negligible to him but quite as real and instructive for conduct as what he saw in the day-time. Indeed they had a weight and authority superior to the pronouncements of daily experience; and they served vastly to widen it. What civilization would have been without the manifold influences of dreams it is quite impossible to guess. Had man been dreamless would he have had his religions, his symbolism and his allegories, his poetry and much of his art? This much at least is assured that the beliefs and practices of primitive peoples are in many cases directly attributable to their dreams. Later beliefs and practices of more elaborately civilized peoples can usually be traced back to primitive ideas, which seem to be the soil from which they sprang. So we have to conclude that dreams are one of the most remarkable factors that have entered into the fabrication of civilization as we know it to-day.

When asleep we find ourselves visiting distant places; for instance when walking the streets of Paris we suddenly wake in New York. How could early men escape the conviction that they had a second self which could wander forth from the body, leaving it behind in the hut, while the "spirit" led for a time an emancipated and adventurous existence freed from the slow and lumpish flesh? Then in dreams the dead appear to us in full life and activity. They may admonish or fortify us; rebuke our departure from the old ways, or fill us with assurance of success. The North American Indians shared the confidence of the ancient Hebrews and Romans in dreams. In India and China the veneration of ancestors forms a highly practical obstacle to the introduction of Western institutions. So have we here, without the possibility of much question as to the main issues, a fair explanation of the original belief in the spirit or soul and its survival of death. We have much more. We have the dawn of the gods and the demi-gods, and the whole foundation of beliefs about supernatural beings and their converse with men; their anger and the possibility of their propitiation by sacrifice.

LOOKING FORWARD

In the preceding sections of this article certain important considerations are enumerated which escaped until recently the attention of students of mankind. They are clear enough when once pointed out. But it has always been a tragic trait of civilization that the obvious has been difficult to perceive, for it is too familiar to catch our attention. It requires a peculiar penetration to discover what in all discussions we are unconsciously taking for granted. And what we are most prone to take for granted are unrevised childish impressions.

There is much complaint of the childishness of mankind, which has become more conspicuous with the democratic assumption that everyone should have his say. Langdon-Davies' *New Age of Faith,* and E. C. Ayres' *Science the False Messiah,* to cite two examples, dwell with some petulance and bitterness on the easy gullibility and obstinate ignorance of humanity. They assume standards of intelligence which obviously do not prevail, as one reads popular newspapers, sermons and political speeches. They are disappointed, but have no reason to be surprised. Why should an ex-animal not have made grotesque mistakes as he floundered about with words and besetting mysteries and hardened orthodoxies? Then, as we have seen, civilization is mainly acquired in childhood and perforce ever haunted with infantile longings and misapprehensions. When there is an issue between his dreams and visions and his waking experiences why should man not prefer the former? As a matter of fact those reputed as great and deep thinkers have dealt mainly, until very recently, with imaginary beings, with events that never happened; with empty concepts, allegories and symbols and false analogies. John Dewey has in his *Reconstruction in Philosophy* deduced philosophy and ethics from savage antecedents and shown how these have interpenetrated later speculations. The hardly to be overcome prejudice which attributes to mind and body separate existence and regards them of diverse substance is the easily explained and inevitable mistake of a savage. The will, the unconscious, the moral sense, regarded as agents, belong to the category of primitive animistic conceptions. Even causation as it used to be conceived is but an expression of the naïve urge to blame or praise some particular person or thing for this or that event. We are now learning to think in terms of situations. For example when Edward Carpenter wrote many years ago on *Civilization, its Cause and Cure,* he yielded to a venerable usage. It has become apparent enough that civilization has had no one cause but is the result of a situation of cosmic complexity. There can be no one cure for its recognized defects. A recent Italian writer, Pareto, has filled two large volumes with instances of the misapprehensions upon which current sociological treatises are based.

As humanity, or at least their leaders, become more fully aware of the nature and origin of civilization and the manner in which it has hitherto developed they will discover firmer foundations on which to build, more efficient ways of eradicating the inevitable and congenial errors of the race, and of stimulating patient and fruitful reconstruction and reform. So far mankind has stumbled along, enslaved by its past rather than liberated by it for further advances. The reasons for this are beginning to become more apparent than ever before and might as time goes on be made the basis of a type of education, especially in man's early years, which would greatly forward and direct the progress of civilization rather than retard its development. (J. H. Rob.)

CIVIL LAW, a phrase which, with its Latin equivalent, *ius civile*, has been used in a great variety of meanings. *Ius civile* was sometimes used to distinguish that portion of the Roman law which was the proper or ancient law of the city or state of Rome from the *ius gentium,* or the law common to all the nations comprising the Roman world, which was incorporated with the former through the agency of the praetorian edicts. This historical distinction remained as a principle of division in the body of the Roman law. The municipal or private law of a state is sometimes described as civil law in distinction from public or international law. Again, the municipal law of a state may be divided into civil law and criminal law. The phrase, however, is applied par excellence to the system of law created by the genius of the Roman people, and handed down by them to the nations of the modern world (*see* ROMAN LAW). The civil law in this sense would be distinguished from the local or national law of modern states. It is further to be distinguished from that adaptation of its principles to ecclesiastical purposes which is known as the canon law (*q.v.*). In countries which have codified their law the civil code contains the legislation which governs the civil relation of the citizens *inter se*, but excluding subjects dealt with in special codes, such as commerce, procedure and crime. It therefore includes citizenship, marriage, divorce, contract, sale, partition, exchange, mortgage, usufruct, servitudes, succession, wrongs and so on. (*See* CODE.)

CIVIL LIBERTIES. The word "liberty" describes social situations characterized by an absence of restraint. Civil liberties are personal and social liberties guaranteed by law. Granted freely by an outside sovereign and revocable at will, a liberty is a "privilege"; but if claimed and enforced by and for the people concerned, liberties become specific "rights." Every right has its negative and its positive aspects: liberties are the negative aspects of rights, freedoms the positive. Freedom is self-direction: it is not an automatic result of liberty.

On the negative side are found personal security of life and limb from bodily restraint and violence (*i.e.*, from slavery, lynching, raiding and other irresponsible uses of force); safeguards of private property; the sanctity of the home; the defense of reputation; protection from unfair taxation, from class legislation and from ex post facto laws, bills of attainder, and double jeopardy.

To these negative aspects correspond certain positive aspects of rights, more properly called freedoms. Such are the right of self-defense; freedom of movement and residence; the right to privacy, and freedom of choice in marriage and childbearing; the positive rights of ownership; freedom of contract; freedom of competition; equal access to legal procedures; freedom of conscience and worship; freedom of communication (speech, publication, arts). Freedom of assembly involves freedom of movement and of speech.

If a right is a claim upon the conduct of other persons, that corresponding conduct is a duty; if a right is a claim upon the state, there are those who insist that it is the duty of the state to implement the right with such facilities as permit its exercise. When social standards are asserted as rights, such as the "right to be well born," "rights to safety, play, education," they can properly be called such only as the state validates them by providing the wherewithal to convert liberty into opportunity. Freedom of press is useless without paper, type or news space; freedom of speech is useless without halls, space or airtime.

Civil rights protect certain universal human needs and interests from other equally human needs and interests and (when rights conflict) each right is defended from the other's claims. The adjustment of conflicting claims is the function of legal justice in the courts, or (ultimately) of social justice through the legislature or direct action. Rights are claims which the courts will enforce: legislation becomes law in the fullest sense when courts uphold it. It is, therefore, in the processes of the courts that civil liberties become rights. The rights to a fair trial, and the several special safeguards thereof, become indispensable means for the preservation of liberties, freedoms, democratic responsibilities and orderly social change. Due process of law is guaranteed through the rights of proper arrest, counsel, habeas corpus, equality before the law, indictment, prompt public trial by jury, challenging the prejudices of judge or jurymen, confrontation of witnesses, reasonable bail, reasonable penalties.

The right to due process of law (which is thus supposed to protect one's various liberties and freedoms) may actually begin, paradoxically, with a right to be arrested; *i.e.*, to be legally held for due process instead of being coerced, kidnapped, sequestered or deported irresponsibly. The right of habeas corpus (*q.v.*) is another basic and essential aspect of this safeguarding of due process against lawless police or other star chamber or gestapo tactics by officers of so-called law and order, secret or private police, or irresponsible vigilantes. The period of sedition trials, during which (1794–1801) the writ of habeas corpus was suspended, was also a period of low ebb in other English liberties, in reaction against excesses in the French Revolution.

Civil liberty includes those liberties which involve civic relationships, and is thus distinguished from moral liberty or freedom of will, from political liberties, from economic liberties and from academic freedom. Each of these fields overlaps civil liberties to the extent that law supports liberty of conscience, self-government, industrial or academic liberty.

Political liberty comprises the right of franchise; the rights to petition and to hold office; safeguards of the people's representatives and judges from intimidation and undue influence; the right of equality before the law, regardless of such circumstances as race or colour, with safeguards of due process before, during and after trial, without discrimination; and the right to bear arms.

Economic rights were developed first for enterprisers as freedoms of ownership, trade, competition, contract. Free competition and contract extended to labour but proved as much a danger as an opportunity, until supported by the civil rights of collective bargaining. The rights to organize, to bargain through representatives of their own choosing and to strike provide the chief guarantees and opportunity for other economic freedoms. Major issues, as to whose freedom shall limit whose, lie frequently in the field of distribution of wealth and of economic power over wealth and persons. Where this is the situation, those who are currently in control of industrial property and financial credit (hiring power) naturally resist or attack movements from the left, the have-nots, all those who are claiming new rights in the name of labour, share-croppers, tenants, dependent minority races, etc. Extremists in support of property rights and the *status quo* may, by contrast, advocate or permit anti-democratic (*i.e.*, irresponsible) measures with relative impunity. Much labour legislation now accepted as constitutional exercise of the police power of the state in the general welfare can be considered, from this angle, as establishing economic rights of labour—positive civil rights to a living wage and living leisure, health and security, and the corresponding negative rights of liberty from want, exploitation, domination and fear, whether through forced labour, peonage or mere bargaining power.

Academic freedom is not a civil liberty but a professional claim to certain complementary responsibilities and immunities in the interests of the integrity of scientific and scholarly research and of the teaching and learning process, such integrity being considered indispensable to the valid services of educators, scholars and scientists to the community at large. The area of academic freedom overlaps that of civil liberties in that teachers are often penalized as teachers for words or acts outside the classroom which constitute legitimate exercises of their rights as citizens.

The traditions of stubborn individualism and specific civil rights imported to America during the colonial period were strengthened by frontier conditions and by struggles against British Tory governors, and were later kindled into idealism by the more abstract and emotional libertarianism of French thinkers. The doctrine of rights reserved to the people implied that "natural" liberty was like an endowment fund, from which (by social compact) capital could only be alienated in exchange for a demonstrated *quid pro quo* of common welfare or legal rights. Reserved "natural rights" become bills of rights when they reappear in political compacts, charters or constitutions. Actual legal liberty becomes the defense of "reserved rights" from invasion. "Natural rights" being (according to the metaphysical theory) part of a person, the right of self-defense may be claimed for them, if legal protection is inadequate. Social conflicts still arise in which the logical confusion between the specific, concrete civil rights of Anglo-Saxon history and the rationalistic and metaphysical bases of "civil liberty" becomes apparent.

History of Civil Liberties.—Every culture has permitted its own liberties. The civil liberties as we know them are a cultural-legal complex deriving from the Anglo-Saxon cultures, especially from the common law, from certain historic enactments and from certain philosophic doctrines. These, in turn, derived from centuries of interaction of conquerors and conquered; of king, barons and commons; of church and state; and from earlier ideas of rights, justice, law, nature, reason, reserved powers, sovereignty, allegiance, contract and freedom, traceable in the intellectual history of Europe and of Asia.

Even preceding the Christian doctrines of free and equal souls, the stark moral autonomy claimed for the individual by the Stoic philosophers, and their faith in nature and reason are historical sources for the later doctrines of natural rights superior to law, and of duties taking precedence of the demands of family and state. Christianity developed a discipline of freedom of conscience capable of martyrdom. Mediaeval feudalism seems to the layman anything but free, yet even in feudalism the individual nature of the compacts of allegiance is considered a forerunner of the right of free contract, as well as of the political theory of the social compact limiting liberty. In mediaeval cities persons split off from the feudal hierarchy acquired a new independence as burghers and as craftsmen. The charters of the guilds often safeguarded their members' liberties, though guild regulations represent anything but economic liberty in any modern sense. Freedom of parliamentary debate was won in England under James I—an early victory for free speech.

For certain aspects of civil liberty of religion the period of the Reformation is responsible; *e.g.*, the treaty of Augsburg (1555) and the edict of Nantes (1598). In the Protestant Reformation the independence of conscience, duty and will before God were reaffirmed. This root of liberty is to be seen flourishing in the English Puritan revolution (*e.g.*, Agreement of the People of England, 1647). Both in French and in German thought, however, as in Thomas Hobbes, there were also elements of absolute collectivism and doctrines of the folk-will or state-will which conflicted with libertarianism. Full religious liberty came in America before it was approximated in England, which still taxes for the support of a state church.

The charters of Anglo-Saxon liberties are: Magna Carta (1215); the Statutes of Westminster (1275); the Petition of Right (1628); Bushell's Case (trial by jury, 1670); the Habeas Corpus act (1679); the Bill of Rights (1689); the Toleration act (1689); the Acts of Settlement (1700–1701); the Libel act (1792). Parliament refused in 1695 to renew the Licensing act, thus abolishing censorship. One might well add such nonlegal classics as John Milton's *Areopagitica* (1644), Thomas Paine's *Common Sense* (1776) and *Rights of Man* (1791), and John Stuart Mill's *On Liberty* (1859). The content of these documents has penetrated and been incorporated into American constitutions and legal decisions.

American liberties are still basically English: even American colonial "ancestors" considered themselves Englishmen. The origins of England's liberties, however, include important contributions from the experience and fearlessness of her American colonial "radicals." The well-known intolerance of many early colonial governments may seem less culpable if it be recalled that they could hardly be said to violate liberties not yet legally established in England itself. Indeed, American libertarianism had its share in effecting English constitutional liberties and stimulating French libertarian thought. In New England, and later in old England, congregational democracy was extended into political democracy. The earliest American colonists brought with them the same ferment of ideas which was working during the English revolutions of 1648 and 1688, such as those of the state of nature and the social compact. The Mayflower covenant and the doctrine of the sovereign autonomy of the soul may be considered, therefore, as religious prototypes of Jean Jacques Rousseau's natural rights and social contract. Once established in early New England the social-compact idea took precedence of the libertarian: heretics were treated as violators of the collective covenant. Later, natural rights were invoked to justify religious liberty as a corollary, and revolutionary French political theories were influential during and after the American Revolution.

In America, early milestones of liberty include Maryland's Toleration act (1649), the charter of Rhode Island (1663) and the Zenger case (New York, 1734). Classics of the later colonial period are James Otis' *The Rights of the British Colonies Asserted and Proved* (1764) and Samuel Adams' *The Declaration of the Rights of Men* (1772). The First Continental Congress issued a Declaration of Rights and Liberties (1774) and the less-known Address to the Inhabitants of Quebec.

Once split off from England, the American states promptly included bills of rights in the new constitutions, protecting the people's liberties against their own governments and (less effectively) against the tyranny of majorities. Virginia's Declaration of Rights preceded the Declaration of Independence by three weeks, and served as model for 11 states before the federal Bill of Rights amendments were incorporated in the constitution. Among early state bills of rights those of Maryland (1776), New York (1777) and Massachusetts (1780) are notable, as is Virginia's statute of religious freedom (1786).

Major documentary milestones of American civil liberty since the Revolution have included the Ordinance for the Government of the Northwest Territory (1787); the first ten amendments to the federal constitution (the Bill of Rights, 1791); Amendments XIII, XIV, XV (the Civil War amendments, 1865–70); and certain judicial opinions of Justices Oliver Wendell Holmes, Louis Dembitz Brandeis, Learned Hand and Benjamin Nathan Cardozo.

Developments in the United States.—The tensions and enforced regimentation of wartime subject civil liberties to serious danger. During World War I both England (Defense of the Realm act) and the United States (Espionage acts) sharply limited freedom of discussion and of political criticism, and court interpretations and sentences under the Espionage acts were even harsher. Advocacy of change was called obstruction. Persons expressing opinions alleged to be adverse to the current policy of the then government, even under conditions not dangerous to public safety, were punished by heavy prison sentences, often for statements later corroborated by high authorities or by actual events. Public opinion was hysterically suspicious and intolerant. State and local authorities were often more drastic than federal and military authorities. Speech and press were muzzled if the prosecutor could impute "evil tendency" or "constructive intent," even by indirection. Even silent non-co-operators and nonsubscribers were persecuted. Many offenders convicted for honest devotion to political and economic principles were treated worse than violent criminals. Conscientious objectors and other pacifists were brutally treated until a more equitable procedure was set up by the war department.

During the post-World War I period, with general disillusionment in regard to the motivation and outcome of the war, attitudes toward war offenses relaxed and most of the extreme sentences were commuted or the prisoners pardoned. On the other hand, the anti-German hatred was shifted into anti-bolshevik and anti-labour-union channels, and epidemics of repressive laws, "red-raids," prosecutions and deportations ensued. Mere membership in organizations alleged to hold certain opinions was heavily penalized, thus creating guilt by association. Many liberals felt that existing laws against overt acts had been adequate; that the sabotage, sedition, criminal syndicalism and anarchy statutes were enacted chiefly to facilitate the crusades against so-called radical organizations. The later vicious tactics of some such groups have been attributed to the hatreds inspired by their experiences in this period.

The civil liberties record in World War II was a great improvement over that in World War I. In part this may be attributed to a somewhat more sophisticated public attitude toward wartime propaganda, but there was also a determined effort on the part of responsible government officials to avoid the excesses of World War I. The wartime attorney general, Francis Biddle, exercised a restraining influence, and so did the supreme court. The most flagrant abuse of freedom was the enforced evacuation of about 112,000 persons of Japanese ancestry (70,000 of whom were full-fledged U.S. citizens) from the west coast by the army. This drastic step was taken on the ground that there were likely to be persons guilty of espionage or sabotage within this group, and that the emergency did not permit screening on an individual basis. The supreme court, by decisions in 1944 and 1946, accepted this plea of military necessity, but it later became widely believed that the mass evacuation, with its attendant hardships and loss of property, was an unjustifiable action falling, as Justice Frank Murphy charged, "into the ugly abyss of racism."

The wartime alliance of the United States with the U.S.S.R. led to some lessening of American apprehension concerning the communist threat. But with the close of the war the Russian leaders quickly demonstrated their intention of pursuing an aggressive and imperialistic policy, and of using the international communist movement to bring under Russian domination the government of every country not strong enough to resist its subversive influence. In the resulting "cold war," feeling against communists or alleged "fellow travellers" in the United States grew very strong.

Legislative expressions of anti-communism included the Smith act of 1940, punishing conspiracy to overthrow the government by force or violence; the Labor Management Relations (Taft-Hartley) act of

1947, requiring the signing of non-communist affidavits by labour union officials; the Internal Security act of 1950, setting up a subversive activities control board with which "communist-action" organizations were required to register; and a number of statutes adopted by congress in 1954, of which the Communist Control act, undertaking to "outlaw" the Communist party, was the best-known.

Activities of certain congressional committees, particularly the house committee on un-American activities and the senate committee headed by Sen. Joseph R. McCarthy of Wisconsin, raised controversies as to alleged invasions of civil liberties through secret hearings, refusal to permit the presence of counsel, acceptance and publication of character-damaging hearsay evidence, refusal to permit witnesses to make statements, harassing questioning, etc. These and similar practices led to demands, in congress and out, for a code of conduct to govern legislative inquiries. Individuals who sought to resist committee questioning into their political views or past associations were generally unsuccessful. They could decline to testify on the ground that their answers might tend to incriminate themselves (5th amendment), but such a plea was generally regarded as a confession of guilt.

There were of course other kinds of civil liberties problems following World War II. The treatment of certain minority groups continued to fall short of the constitutional standard of equal protection of the laws, but progress was evident, most notably in the supreme court's 1954 decision holding racial segregation in the public schools unconstitutional. Scattered efforts toward censorship of books were largely frustrated, and censorship of plays and movies was increasingly under attack. Standards of criminal prosecution in state courts were often rather low, but vigorous supreme court resistance to the use of coerced confessions, unrepresentative juries, unreasonable searches and seizures and other violations of due process were having salutary effects.

After World War I a number of organizations specializing in defense of one or another area of freedom were formed. The American Civil Liberties Union, however, remained the only nonpartisan, general and nation-wide agency with a consistent record of defending groups and persons threatened or injured in respect to civil rights, without sponsoring their ideas or programs.

Freedom of Speech and Press.—The 1st amendment of the U.S. constitution provides: "Congress shall make no law . . . abridging the freedom of speech, or of the press." While the amendment applies only to congress, the supreme court ruled in 1925 that the same prohibition is applicable to the states by reason of the 14th amendment's guarantee against deprivation of "liberty" without due process of law (*Gitlow* v. *New York,* 268 U.S. 652). Governmental infringement of free speech or press can occur in two general ways, either by previous restraint of publication, more commonly called censorship, or by punishment after the event for words spoken or published.

Censorship has generally been regarded as the more serious type of restraint. In fact, Sir William Blackstone argued that the liberty of the press consisted only "in laying no previous restraints upon publications." However, it is now clear that freedom from censorship is not sufficient protection for, unless there are effective limits on prosecution, punishment for what one has said or printed can be just as effective in discouraging free discussion.

American feeling against censorship has been so strong that, except for military information in wartime, attempts at prior restraint on speech or press have been most uncommon. In 1931 the supreme court had an opportunity to state the basic case against censorship in declaring unconstitutional a Minnesota statute under which a newspaper had been enjoined from publishing as a public nuisance (*Near* v. *Minnesota,* 283 U.S. 697). The court has also warned that the post office department's power to deny second-class mailing privileges to periodicals cannot be employed for censorship purposes (*Hannegan* v. *Esquire,* 327 U.S. 146, 1946), nor can a state seek to punish newspapers through discriminatory tax legislation (*Grosjean* v. *American Press Co.,* 297 U.S. 233, 1936). Handbills dealing with public issues share fully in the constitutional protection accorded the press, and their distribution cannot be subjected to police interference or licence requirements (*Lovell* v. *Griffin,* 303 U.S. 444, 1938; *Schneider* v. *Irvington,* 308 U.S. 147, 1939).

The spoken word presents somewhat different problems from those of the press, chiefly in that oratorical appeals, particularly in a crowd situation, are more likely to result in action. If the action urged by speech is illegal or sufficiently dangerous to the public welfare, the speech cannot claim constitutional protection. There is no right falsely to cry "Fire" in a crowded theatre, said Justice Holmes.

Speech enjoys a wide protection from prior restraint, however. Licences cannot be required for speaking on the streets or in public parks (*Kunz* v. *New York,* 340 U.S. 290, 1951), unless the licensing system is one which gives public officials no discretion in the granting of permits (*Poulos* v. *New Hampshire,* 345 U.S. 395, 1953). As to amplified speech the situation is less clear. In 1948 the supreme court held licensing of sound trucks invalid (*Saia* v. *New York,* 334 U.S. 558), but one year later it approved regulation aimed at protecting the public from "loud and raucous" devices (*Kovacs* v. *Cooper,* 336 U.S. 77). Then in 1952 the court refused to protect the "captive audience" on District of Columbia streetcars from having to listen to commercial advertising broadcasts (*Public Utilities Commission* v. *Pollak,* 343 U.S. 451).

Peaceful picketing in labour disputes was given the status of speech and the protection of the 1st amendment by the supreme court in 1940 (*Thornhill* v. *Alabama,* 310 U.S. 88). However, subsequent decisions retracted some of this protection, on the ground that picketing, in addition to being speech, is also a means of economic coercion which is not constitutionally privileged. Injunctions have been approved by the court where the picketing, though peaceful and truthful, was seeking a purpose unlawful under state law (*Giboney* v. *Empire Storage & Ice Co.,* 336 U.S. 490, 1949), or even where the purpose was merely one which a state judge believed contrary to public policy (*International Brotherhood of Teamsters* v. *Hanke,* 339 U.S. 470, 1950).

The theatre has historically been subjected to licensing requirements, normally aimed at enforcing moral standards. Censorship has likewise been widely imposed on motion pictures, but in 1952 the supreme court denied New York the right to prohibit a film on the ground that it was "sacrilegious," which was held to be too vague a standard (*Burstyn* v. *Wilson,* 343 U.S. 495). Radio and television stations are subject to government control to the extent that they require licences in order to broadcast, which may be revoked or not renewed if a station's operation is found by the Federal Communications commission not to be in the public interest. However, the FCC has used this power with extreme caution. Moreover, the Federal Communications act forbids the FCC to exercise any power of censorship over programs, and obliges stations to afford all legally qualified candidates for public office equal opportunity to use their facilities.

It is not contrary to principles of free speech that individuals should be held responsible for abusing this freedom. Individual injuries resulting from speech which is malicious or false can be punished under the libel and slander laws. However, in the law of libel it was gradually established that a jury, not the judge, decides what is libellous; and, in certain cases, demonstration of good (*i.e.,* nonmalicious) motives in announcing a truth or fact is considered a valid defense against libel suit (*see* LIBEL AND SLANDER).

Difficult problems are encountered when speech is sought to be punished because of its alleged danger to public order or to the national security. An individual can be held responsible for speech which causes breach of the peace. There is no freedom of speech for "fighting words" likely to provoke their target to physical assault (*Chaplinsky* v. *New Hampshire,* 315 U.S. 568, 1942). The supreme court has ruled that police can arrest a sidewalk speaker when in their judgment his words are tending to provoke disorder (*Feiner* v. *New York,* 340 U.S. 315, 1951). The court has also upheld the conviction of a zealot who circulated anti-Negro leaflets and petitions on Chicago streets; he was prosecuted under a group libel law which punished the exposure of "citizens of any race, color, creed, or religion to contempt, derision, or obloquy" (*Beauharnais* v. *Illinois,* 343 U.S. 250, 1952). These two latter decisions, however, were attacked by a minority of the court as dangerous limitations on freedom.

Clearly some standard of judgment is needed to aid in determining when speech may be constitutionally limited because of its threat to public safety. The best known test is the "clear and present danger" rule first stated by Justice Holmes in a case arising out of the Espionage and Sedition acts as applied during World War I. In *Schenck* v. *United States* (249 U.S. 47, 1919) he said:

"The question in every case is whether the words are used in such circumstances and are of such a nature as to create a clear and present danger that they will bring about the substantive evils that Congress has a right to prevent. It is a question of proximity and degree."

In the Schenck case a pamphlet had sought to encourage resistance to the draft, and Holmes concluded that such speech deserved no constitutional protection.

"When a nation is at war many things that might be said in time of peace are such a hindrance to its effort that their utterance will not be endured so long as men fight and that no Court could regard them as protected by any constitutional right."

But in later cases when he sought to use the test to protect speech which he believed was constitutionally privileged, the court majority voted against him. It was not until the 1930s and 1940s that the clear and present danger test was actually utilized by the court to keep men out of jail on speech charges. During this period several significant decisions safeguarded the free speech rights of communists or radicals (*DeJonge* v. *Oregon,* 299 U.S. 353, 1937; *Herndon* v. *Lowry,* 301 U.S. 242, 1937; *Bridges* v. *California,* 314 U.S. 252, 1941). But in 1951 the supreme court found the conviction of the top leaders of the Communist party in the United States to be justified under the clear and present danger test (*Dennis* v. *United States,* 341 U.S. 494). Admittedly there was little likelihood of successful communist overthrow of the government, but Chief Justice Fred M. Vinson said that the clear and present danger test obviously "cannot mean that before the Government may act, it must wait until the *putsch* is about to be executed, the plans have been laid and the signal is awaited. . . . We must therefore reject the contention that success or probability of success is the criterion." Justices Hugo L. Black and William O. Douglas, dissenting, contended that this position repudiated the clear and present danger test.

Freedom of Assembly and Organization.—There are no specific provisions in the U.S. constitution protecting rights to assemble and to organize, but these are basic to a free society. It is characteristic of totalitarian systems that the state takes a monopoly of association and terminates the free formation of groups. Even in a free society, however, freedom of assembly and organization is limited, as for example by the law of conspiracy. Organizing becomes conspiracy if the activities organized collectively are themselves illegal. Acts protected if performed alone may also be declared lawless if done together, by agreement, especially in a "dangerous" situation. The Smith act punishes conspiracy to organize a party to advocate the overthrow of the government by force and violence. All labour unions, not to mention strikes, were at one time regarded as conspiracies, but that period is long past. The National Labor Relations (Wagner) act of 1935, as amended in 1947, granted full legal status to collective bargaining and labour organizations.

Freedom of organization of course includes the right to form political parties. However, political parties in the United States actually operate within a network of legal limitations covering such matters as when and how primary elections shall be held, how a party gets its nominees on the election ballot, how much money may be spent in elections, and the like. The network of statutes adopted against the Communist party after World War II rested on the belief that it was not a bona fide political party, but rather a conspiratorial revolutionary organization.

An important element in the concept of freedom to belong to organizations is protection of the individual from guilt by association. Some interesting questions in this field were raised by the loyalty-security investigations of federal government employees during the "cold war" period. The U.S. attorney general, under authorization by the president, prepared a list of subversive organizations. The list was originally intended as a guide to federal boards in passing on the loyalty of employees, but it was widely publicized and membership in a listed organization had grave consequences for many individuals. Organizations so listed found it difficult to continue in operation. Because of these serious results, the supreme court ruled that the attorney general must give notice and hearing to organizations before placing them on the list (*Joint Anti-Fascist Refugee committee* v. *McGrath,* 341 U.S. 123, 1951).

The guilt by association standard was also invoked in connection with loyalty oaths required by some states and cities for public employees, candidates for public office, and even in some instances tenants in public housing projects. The supreme court, which passed on several statutes involving oaths of nonmembership in subversive organizations, insisted that individuals must have had knowledge of the unlawful character of an organization before they could be penalized for having joined it. A state law which failed to distinguish between innocent and knowing association was declared unconstitutional (*Wieman* v. *Updegraff,* 344 U.S. 183, 1952). On the other hand, the court upheld a New York statute which made membership of schoolteachers in certain listed organizations prima facie grounds for their disqualification, saying: "From time immemorial, one's reputation has been determined in part by the company he keeps" (*Adler* v. *Board of Education,* 342 U.S. 485, 1952).

Freedom of assembly is limited by freedom of movement in the use of the streets and by the police power in respect to public safety (*Cox* v. *New Hampshire,* 312 U.S. 569, 1941). The right of assembly is further limited by the law of riot; in constitutional law it usually appears as the right *peaceably* to assemble. In 1949, however, the supreme court went so far as to protect from a disorderly conduct charge a speaker whose inflammatory remarks in a private meeting hall provoked a riotous situation (*Terminiello* v. *Chicago,* 337 U.S. 1).

Freedom of Religion.—"Free exercise" of religion is guaranteed by the 1st amendment of the U.S. constitution, and religious practices and preaching are not legally interfered with unless they are aggressive as "nuisances," offend public morality (as by the original Mormon practice of polygamy), violate secular laws or are dangerous to the government. Draft laws can be enforced against conscientious objectors, but in practice such individuals are assigned to other types of national service. The supreme court originally approved denial of citizenship to conscientious objectors who in applying for naturalization declined to take oath to defend the United States by force of arms, but this position was reversed in 1946 (*Girouard* v. *United States,* 328 U.S. 61). The unorthodox beliefs and practices of the Jehovah's Witnesses sect resulted in many encounters with the law, and they have often been supported by the supreme court, as when the court upheld the refusal of their children to salute the flag in public school exercises (*West Virginia State Board of Education* v. *Barnette,* 319 U.S. 624, 1943).

The provision of the 1st amendment forbidding congress to make any law "respecting an establishment of religion" renders state support for churches unlawful in the United States. However, it does not mean that a complete wall of separation must be erected between church and state. Even financial assistance in the form of tax exemption has not been questioned, so long as it is available to all religious groups. The principal establishment issues have concerned state aid to religious schools. In 1930 the supreme court upheld a Louisiana law providing free text books to pupils in both public and private schools, on the ground that the aid was to the child and not to the school (*Cochran* v. *Louisiana Board of Education,* 281 U.S. 370). In 1947 it likewise upheld a New Jersey provision under which parents were reimbursed from public funds for the cost of transporting their children to parochial schools (*Everson* v. *Board of Education,* 330 U.S. 1). In 1948 the court did rule unconstitutional a Champaign, Ill., arrangement whereby public school pupils were released from classes for religious instruction in the school building by volunteer religious teachers (*McCollum* v. *Board of Education,* 333 U.S. 203), but in 1952 it upheld a similar New York plan which differed only in that the religious instruction took place off the school property (*Zorach* v. *Clauson,* 343 U.S. 306). Attempting to define in this case what was forbidden by the establishment of religion clause, Justice Douglas wrote:

"Government may not finance religious groups nor undertake religious instruction nor blend secular and sectarian education nor use secular institutions to force one or some religion on any person. . . . It may not make a religious observance compulsory. It may not coerce anyone to attend church, to observe a religious holiday, or to take religious instruction."

Civil Liberties and Criminal Prosecutions.—Some idea of the importance for civil liberties of fair procedures in criminal prosecutions can be gained from the fact that half of the ten amendments making up the Bill of Rights—the 4th through the 8th—deal with this subject. These amendments, which apply to prosecutions in federal courts only (*Barron* v. *Baltimore,* 7 Pet. 243, 1833), protect against unreasonable searches and seizures, require grand jury indictment and trial by jury, guarantee assistance of counsel, and prohibit double jeopardy, self-incrimination, excessive bail and cruel and unusual punishment.

Of these protections, perhaps the one giving rise to greatest difficulty in enforcement has been the search and seizure provision of the 4th amendment. This barrier to invasion of personal privacy was erected because of experience with the infamous "general writs of assistance" under which the British authorities invaded private homes during the colonial period, and was based on the belief that "a man's home is his castle." Law enforcement officers consequently can enter a home only after securing a search warrant, which requires going before a judicial officer and giving a justification of the proposed search. When arresting a person under a warrant or for a crime committed in their presence, law officers can seize evidence which is in plain sight. Whether a search of the arrested party's premises is constitutional has been left uncertain by supreme court decisions (*Harris* v. *United States,* 331 U.S. 145, 1947; *Trupiano* v. *United States,* 334 U.S. 699, 1948; *United States* v. *Rabinowitz,* 339 U.S. 56, 1950).

Tapping of telephone wires which does not involve an actual entry into private quarters was declared by the supreme court in 1928 not to constitute unreasonable search and seizure, though Justice Holmes condemned it as a "dirty business" (*Olmstead* v. *United States,* 277 U.S. 438). However, congress made evidence secured by wire tapping inadmissible in federal courts. In 1954 congress defeated a bill which would have admitted wire-tapped evidence in federal court cases involving national security or kidnapping.

So far as criminal prosecutions in state courts are concerned, the guiding constitutional principle is the mandate of the 14th amendment that no state shall "deprive any person of life, liberty, or property, without due process of law; nor deny to any person within its jurisdiction the equal protection of the laws." The supreme court has ruled that "due process" does not necessarily include all the protections specified in the 4th through the 8th amendments (*Adamson* v. *California,* 332 U.S. 46, 1947). Thus a state is not bound to require indictment by grand jury, nor to grant trial by a 12-man common law jury, nor to avoid double jeopardy or self-incrimination. States must, however, give such protections as are "of the very essence of a scheme of ordered liberty" (*Palko* v. *Connecticut,* 302 U.S. 319, 1937). Specifically, this means that they must grant counsel in capital cases, there must not be systematic racial discrimination in selection of juries, confessions are invalid if extorted by force, unreasonable searches and seizures are unconstitutional, and in general the requirements of a fair hearing must be observed.

Liberty as Means or as End?—Whether liberty be an end in itself or a means (indispensable or not) to other ends has often been debated. Liberties, in the sense here used, have always been used as means toward freedom or power. Civil, political, economic and academic freedoms have been considered by some as ultimate values. Close examination of actual situations, however, shows many in which legal liberty has been invoked to permit a freedom, but the freedom is used to seek some ulterior satisfaction better described in terms of other values such as self-expression, personality, power, prestige, wealth, beauty, truth, good conscience, good will, peace, security, progress, pleasure or the common welfare.

The feeling of freedom is a satisfaction so precious to many people that (paradoxically) they will give up much welfare, many liberties, even such rights as guarantee their freedom, if they feel that in doing so they are free, or imagine they are thus ultimately protecting their freedom.

It is frequently said that, in modern war, liberties must be suspended in order to protect "liberty." Such a formula assumes: (1) that criticism hinders war effort; (2) that after victory both the people and their then rulers will retain enough attachment to the values of civil liberties to offset more immediate and selfish interests; and (3) that the political mechanisms for restoration of liberties are preserved.

Legal liberties may be claimed for the underprivileged by those whose interests lie in exploiting those liberties; *e.g.,* labour legislation has been opposed by employers in the name of "free contract" and "equality before the law." Groups obviously devoted to programs destructive to civil liberty may use the present protection of the Bill of Rights to forward their "subversive" doctrines. These are risks which apparently must be assumed if the rights are to be preserved in the interests of other persons and groups and of the community as a whole.

Modern rationalization of civil liberties is not altogether in terms of individualism. They are defended not merely as ends but as means to the organic welfare of a nation, in which persons and community are mutually constituted facts in a total situation and equally indispensable. There is a diversity of gifts and roles, and all have a "right to each other's differences." Where liberties are denied, society as a whole is deprived, not only of the extreme expressions that have been penalized, but of the wiser oppositions and variants that have thereby been deterred.

Perhaps the most eloquent modern statement of the philosophy of freedom of thought is found in Justice Holmes's dissenting opinion in *Abrams* v. *United States* (250 U.S. 616):

"Persecution for the expression of opinions seems to me perfectly logical. If you have no doubt of your premises or your power and want a certain result with all your heart you naturally express your wishes in law and sweep away all opposition. To allow opposition by speech seems to indicate that you think the speech impotent, as when a man says that he has squared the circle, or that you do not care wholeheartedly for the result, or that you doubt either your power or your premises. But when men have realized that time has upset many fighting faiths, they may come to believe even more than they believe the very foundations of their own conduct that the ultimate good desired is better reached by free trade in ideas—that the best test of truth is the power to get itself accepted in the competition of the market, and that truth is the only ground upon which their wishes safely can be carried out. That at any rate is the theory of our Constitution."

BIBLIOGRAPHY.—John Milton, *Areopagitica* (1644); Thomas Paine, *The Rights of Man* (1791); Leon Whipple, *The Story of Civil Liberty in the United States* (New York, 1927); Zechariah Chafee, Jr., *Free Speech in the United States* (Cambridge, Mass., London, 1941); Robert K. Carr, *Federal Protection of Civil Rights* (Ithaca, N.Y., London, 1947); President's Committee on Civil Rights, *To Secure These Rights* (New York, 1947); Edward S. Corwin, *Total War and the Constitution* (New York, 1947); Alexander Meiklejohn, *Free Speech and Its Relation to Self-Government* (New York, 1948); J. Edward Gerald, *The Press and the Constitution, 1931–1947* (Minneapolis, London, 1948); Morton Grodzins, *Americans Betrayed* (Chicago, 1949; London, 1950); Anson Phelps Stokes, *Church and State in the United States* (New York, 1950); Francis Biddle, *The Fear of Freedom* (New York, 1951); Alan Barth, *The Loyalty of Free Men* (New York, London, 1951); Thomas I. Emerson and David Haber (eds.), *Political and Civil Rights in the United States* (Buffalo, 1952); Robert K. Carr, *The House Committee on Un-American Activities, 1945–1950* (Ithaca, N.Y., 1952); Walter Gellhorn, *Security, Loyalty, and Science* (Ithaca, N.Y., 1950; London, 1951); Mulford Q. Sibley and Philip E. Jacob, *Conscription of Conscience* (Ithaca, N.Y., London, 1952); Leo Pfeffer, *Church, State, and Freedom* (Boston, Toronto, 1953); Eleanor Bontecou, *The Federal Loyalty-Security Program* (Ithaca, N.Y., 1953); Milton R. Konvitz, *Civil Rights in Immigration* (Ithaca, N.Y., London, 1953), (ed.) *Bill of Rights Reader* (Ithaca, N.Y., 1954); C. Herman Pritchett, *Civil Liberties and the Vinson Court* (Chicago, 1954); literature of the American Civil Liberties Union, New York city.

(T. D. E.; C. H. P.)

CIVIL LIST, the English term for the account in which are contained all the expenses immediately applicable to the support of the British sovereign's household and the honour and dignity of the crown. An annual sum is settled by the British parliament at the beginning of the reign of the sovereign and is charged on the consolidated fund. But it was only from the reign of William IV that the sum thus voted was restricted solely to the personal expenses of the crown. Before his accession many charges properly belonging to the ordinary expenses of government had been placed on the Civil List.

William and Mary.—The history of the Civil List dates from the reign of William and Mary. Before the Revolution no distinction had been made between the expenses of government in time of peace and the expenses relating to the personal dignity and support of the sovereign. The ordinary revenues, derived from the hereditary revenues of the crown and from certain taxes voted for life to the king at the beginning of each reign, were supposed to provide for the support of the sovereign's dignity and the civil government, as well as for the public defense in time of peace. Any saving made by the king in the expenditure touching the government of the country or its defense would go to swell his privy purse. But with the Revolution a step forward was made toward the establishment of the principle that the expenses relating to the support of the crown should be separated from the ordinary expenses of the state.

The parliament of William and Mary voted in 1689 an annual sum of £600,000 for the charge of the civil government. This was a mere resolution without statutory effect. In 1697 the first Civil List act was passed. Certain revenues (the hereditary revenues of the crown and a part of the excise duties), estimated to yield £700,000, were assigned to the king to defray the expenses of the civil service and the payment of pensions, as well as the cost of the royal household and the king's own personal expenses or privy purse. The Civil List meant practically all the expenses of government except the debt charge and defense. If the yield of the assigned revenues exceeded £700,000 the surplus was to be disposed of by parliament. This restriction was removed by an act of 1700. In the reign of Anne the Civil List consisted of the same assigned revenues (subject to certain deductions). The yield fell short of £700,000, and during the reign debts were incurred amounting to £1,200,000 which were paid off by parliament.

The Hanoverians.—For George I additional revenues were assigned, and it was enacted in effect that the Civil List should become independent of the yield of the assigned revenues and should be a fixed sum of £700,000 a year. Any surplus was to be surrendered and any deficiency would be made good. But this was found insufficient, and parliament from time to time made additional grants from the exchequer to pay off debts totalling £1,300,000. In the reign of George II there was again a change of system. The Civil List was composed of the assigned revenues, together with certain fixed grants, and a minimum yield of £800,000 was guaranteed by parliament. Any surplus yield over £800,000 was retained by the king. On the accession of George III the system of a fixed Civil List was resumed. The assigned revenues were no longer paid to the crown but to an aggregate fund as part of the revenues of the exchequer, and the fixed allowance of £800,000 was paid out of the aggregate fund to the king (subject to certain annuities payable to members of the royal family).

During the reign of George III the Civil List played an important part in the king's effort to establish the royal ascendancy. The "king's friends," his supporters in parliament, were lavishly rewarded with places, pensions and even bribes. There was no independent check upon the expenditure of the Civil List. As long as the total was not exceeded, the king, with the co-operation of complacent ministers, was free to spend as he pleased. As it turned out, despite stringent economies in the cost of the household, excesses were incurred. But parliament, already corrupted, was persuaded to provide extra funds to pay off the debts (£513,511 in 1769 and another £618,340 in 1777). In the latter year the Civil List was raised to £900,000.

Edmund Burke had already attacked the extravagance and corruption of the Civil List and in 1780 introduced bills embodying his scheme of economic reform. The scheme could not be passed against Lord North's government, but in 1782 the Rockingham ministry passed a Civil List act which abolished many useless offices, imposed restraints on the issue of secret service money, stopped secret pensions payable during the king's pleasure and provided for a more effectual supervision of the royal expenditure.

The Civil List was divided into classes, but estimates for the several classes were not binding and were in fact soon exceeded. Indebtedness accumulated and had from time to time to be paid off (£3,398,000 in all between 1782 and 1820). The amount of the Civil List itself was augmented and in 1816 it was fixed at £1,083,727. Meanwhile the principal provision for the civil government had come to be made outside the Civil List. Annual votes of parliament for what were called miscellaneous services had been between £200,000 and £300,000 in the earlier years of George III's reign and had been mainly casual and noncurrent. By 1820 they amounted regularly to about £2,000,000 a year. George IV on his accession in 1820 received a Civil List of £845,727.

On the accession of William IV in 1830, the Civil List was finally freed from all charges for the government service as distinguished from the court and royal family. The expenses left were covered by a Civil List of £510,000, including £75,000 for pensions.

Civil List Pensions.—The pensions were excluded from Queen Victoria's Civil List, which was reduced to £385,000 (separate provision of £100,000 being made for Queen Adelaide, who had had a privy purse of £50,000 during her husband's reign).

A new system of Civil List pensions was set up. The queen might, on the advice of her ministers, grant pensions up to a limit of £1,200 in any one year, in accordance with a resolution of the House of Commons of Feb. 18, 1834, "to such persons as have just claims on the royal beneficence, or who, by their personal services to the crown, by the performance of duties to the public, or by their useful discoveries in science, and attainments in literature or the arts, have merited the gracious consideration of the sovereign and the gratitude of their country." In 1937 the limit of £1,200 was raised to £2,500, and in 1952 it was raised to £5,000.

Queen Victoria to Elizabeth II.—Queen Victoria's Civil List amounted to £385,000. The sums granted after 1901 were as follows:

	Edward VII	George V	Edward VIII	George VI	Elizabeth II
	1901	1910	1936	1937	1952
Privy purse . . .	£110,000	£110,000	£110,000	£110,000	£ 60,000
Salaries and retired allowances of household .	125,800	125,800	134,000	134,000	185,000
Expenses of household .	193,000	193,000	152,800	152,800	121,800
Works	20,000	20,000	..	..	..
Royal bounty, alms and special service . .	13,200	13,200	13,200	13,200	13,200
Unappropriated . .	8,000	8,000	..	..	..
Supplementary provision	..	..	..	..	95,000
	£470,000	£470,000	£410,000*	£410,000	£475,000

*Of this amount £40,000 in respect of the king's possible marriage, and £79,000 representing the revenues of the duchy of Cornwall, were undrawn.

In the reigns of Edward VII, George V and George VI £40,000 was earmarked for the queen. In the reign of Elizabeth II £40,000 was paid to the duke of Edinburgh from the consolidated fund.

A new class for works introduced in 1901 was composed partly of an item previously included under expenses and partly of expenditure previously voted by parliament. The reduction in salaries was due to the abolition of the post of master of the buckhounds and some other reductions of establishments and emoluments. The allocation among classes was not absolutely binding, in that savings on one class could be applied to meet excesses on another (or added to the privy purse) with the consent of the treasury. The works class was an exception, savings upon it being accumulated for future years.

The Civil List acts, 1901–1937, made provision for an annuity of £70,000 to the widow of a sovereign. Queen Alexandra, Queen Mary and Queen Elizabeth drew this allowance.

No change was made either in the total or in the details on the accession of George V in 1910, but a slight change of practice was introduced. In 1842 Victoria, though under no legal or constitutional obligation to pay taxes of any kind, undertook voluntarily to pay income tax. Edward VII continued the voluntary payment. George V agreed with the government of the day that it should be discontinued, but in exchange placed on the Civil List the cost of state visits of foreign royalties previously defrayed from public funds. In 1916 the king made a voluntary gift of £100,000 toward the cost of World War I. In the financial crisis of 1931 George V voluntarily offered to make a reduction in the Civil List. It was not until July 1, 1935, that this economy cut was fully restored. In 1948 George VI transferred to the consolidated fund a sum of £100,000 which represented the savings on the Civil List during World War II. The transfer was made so that no additional charge should be imposed for a period of four years for the payments to Princess Elizabeth and the duke of Edinburgh. In addition to the Civil List the sovereign receives the revenues of the duchy of Lancaster. The revenues of the duchy of Cornwall belong to the prince of Wales as duke of Cornwall, but in the absence of a prince of Wales, as in the reigns of Edward VIII and George VI, they revert to the crown.

It has also been the practice for provision to be made for the sons and daughters of the sovereign. The heir apparent, if the only or eldest son of the king, is duke of Cornwall and as such possesses the revenues of the duchy, which in 1936 were £117,603 and in 1951 were £84,675. Edward, prince of Wales (later Edward VII), received the revenues of the duchy, then £60,000 a year, with the addition of £40,000 on marriage; the duke of York (later George V) £80,000, with the addition of £20,000; Edward, prince of Wales (later Edward VIII) £80,000. Prince Charles, duke of Cornwall, receives one-ninth of the revenues until he is 18 and then £30,000 a year until he is 21. He will then receive the entire revenue of the duchy.

Annual provision to other members of the royal family was made (in 1952) to: the duke of Edinburgh, £40,000; the duke of Gloucester, £35,000; the Princess Royal, £6,000; and Princess Margaret, £6,000. The Civil List act 1952 increased the allowance to Princess Margaret to £15,000 in the event of her marriage. From the supplementary provision of £95,000 in Queen Elizabeth's Civil List £25,000 was available for other members of the royal family (*e.g.*, the duchess of Kent and the countess of Athlone) who undertook official duties.

BIBLIOGRAPHY.—No books have been written dealing solely with the Civil List. Most books mentioned in the bibliographies to the articles GREAT BRITAIN and PARLIAMENT contain chapters on the Civil List.

Reports of the Select Committees on the Civil List; *Civil List Acts* (since the beginning of the century there have been acts of 1901, 1910, 1936, 1937, 1952); *Princess Elizabeth's and Duke of Edinburgh's Annuities Act, 1948; Crown Lands Abstract Accounts* (published annually).
(R. G. H.; X.)

CIVIL SERVICE is the term used to describe servants of the state or central government employed as civilians. It does not cover ministers of the crown or members of the judiciary. In the United Kingdom it does not cover local government or municipal employees (*see* LOCAL GOVERNMENT), nor the staffs of public corporations such as the National Coal board and the Transport commission; but in some countries, where provincial administration forms part of the central government organization, some provincial staffs are civil servants. In the United States the term is often used to describe that part of the government service entered by examination and offering permanent tenure.

Throughout history all organized states have had civil servants, if not civil services. The civil service in China is undoubtedly the oldest. The able and powerful Roman civil service disappeared in the west when the empire broke up in the 4th and 5th centuries. In the modern world civil services became important with the formation of national states, notably in 17th-century France and Prussia.

Today the wide functions carried out by most modern states in the provision of social services (*e.g.*, insurance against unemployment or sickness) or the regulation of economic life, have brought into being large permanent civil services. Many civilians are also employed in support of the fighting services. The growth of these staffs is often described as "bureaucracy," a term which reflects the attitude of those who regret the tendency for the state to dominate the life of the individual. As against this, the personnel system of the big industrial organizations has tended to take on many of the characteristics of the civil service, while the industrial enterprises undertaken by the modern state have increasingly been modelled on the managerial experience of big business.

UNITED KINGDOM

The British civil service dates from a series of reforms between 1855 and 1875, associated with the names of Stafford Northcote and Charles Trevelyan. It was then that the principle was established that, in place of the system of departmental patronage hitherto in force, entry to the service should be by open competitive examination, carried out by an impartial body free from all political influence. For this purpose the civil service commission was set up in 1855. The high quality of recruits which resulted did much to ensure the high standard of the British civil service and to bring about a sense of unity, hitherto lacking, between the staffs of different departments.

The British civil service is unlike that in other countries in that there is no statute which regulates its constitution or organization. Pensions, indeed, are governed by statute, and some conditions of service laid down by orders in council, but the management of the civil service has been accepted as an executive function.

Every department of state has its own establishment and organization officer responsible for dealing with its own personnel problems. But the central responsibility for civil service questions (apart from recruitment) rests with the treasury which is responsible for settling questions of salary and for the grading and organization of the different classes of civil servants (whether departmental classes or classes common to the service). The treasury generally supervises the execution of personnel policy by departments. Treasury control of personnel questions and of organization and methods developed gradually out of the treasury power of the purse.

Until 1943 the United Kingdom had separate diplomatic and consular services which staffed the embassies and legations, and the consulates, while the staff of the foreign office itself formed part of the home civil service. In that year the staffs of the foreign office, and of the embassies, legations and consulates and other overseas missions, were amalgamated into what became known as the foreign service, which had its own pension act and was a separate entity from the home civil service but had its recruitment also carried out by the civil service commission.

The main functions of the United Kingdom civil service are dealt with in the articles GOVERNMENT DEPARTMENTS, FOREIGN OFFICE, WAR OFFICE and ADMIRALTY.

The civil service is organized in a number of classes, themselves divided into grades. In what may be called the administrative-clerical field there are four main classes. The administrative class (numbering about 3,000 in the 1950s) is concerned with advice on broad questions of policy and with direction at the highest and most general levels. It forms the link between the political and executive agencies of government. The executive class (about 70,000) is responsible for the conduct of business within the framework of established policy and for extensive auditing, accounting and fiscal operations. The clerical class (140,000) performs simpler clerical functions, deals with particular cases in accordance with instructions, checks claims, collects material for statistical and other returns, and may interview members of the public on particular cases. The subclerical classes perform routine operations (about 100,000 in these and the typing grades).

Entrance to these classes is for the most part by open competitive examinations closely linked with the educational system. The age limits are: for the administrative class, 20½–24 years, *i.e.*, the university leaving age; for the executive class, 17½–19 years; and for the clerical class, 16–18 years. There is also a considerable flow of promotion from the clerical to the executive class and from the executive to the administrative. About half the members of the administrative class reach it by promotion.

The civil service also contains more than 110,000 professional, scientific, technical and ancillary staffs, organized in classes appropriate to the type of work to be performed, many of them common to the service. Examples are scientists engaged in research and development, lawyers or medical men acting as legal and medical advisers, architects and surveyors engaged in the design and construction of buildings, accountants, actuaries, etc. There is also a large group, more than 240,000, known as the minor and manipulative grades. The main members of this group are the manipulative grades in the post office, postmen, sorters, etc., numbering more than 200,000. This group also includes messengers.

Finally there is the industrial civil service, numbering about 420,000. This comprises skilled and nonskilled manual workers, below the level of foremen or supervisors, employed in government industrial establishments; *e.g.*, royal dockyards, royal ordnance factories, workshops, depots and stores. (Manual workers in the post office, however, though they do work of an industrial kind, are employed on nonindustrial conditions). Conditions in the industrial civil service are determined largely by reference to the principles of the fair wages resolutions of the house of commons, the effect of which is to impose on the government an obligation to observe conditions and hours not less favourable either than those established for the trade or industry concerned through the recognized negotiating machinery, or, where conditions are not so established, by other employers engaged in similar trades and industries. So in several important respects, industrial conditions are different from those in the nonindustrial civil service.

No person can be appointed to a permanent post in the civil service until he has satisfied the civil service commission of his suitability. The tests carried out by the civil service commission are not necessarily related to the specific duties to be performed. In the administrative-clerical field they are designed to secure a share of the best product of the universities and schools. Until World War I it was the practice to rely almost wholly on written examinations of a literary and academic nature. But later more reliance was placed on interviews at which the interview board had before them full particulars of the candidates' records. Much use is made of the interview in filling professional posts.

While recruitment is carried out centrally, promotion is for the most part departmental. There are, however, arrangements for the central pooling of a certain proportion of vacancies in certain grades so as to equalize chances of promotion, and interdepartmental transfers are commonly made when new departments are set up or existing departments need to be rapidly expanded. Further, for the top posts in all departments (permanent secretaries and deputy secretaries) the field of selection is the whole civil service. While appointments to these posts are made by the minister in charge of the department, the prime minister's assent is required for all promotions to these grades, and to posts of establishment officer and finance officer.

The British civil service prides itself on its impartiality and its capacity to give equally loyal and devoted service to ministers irrespective of which political party is in power. For many years no civil servant (other than industrial staff) has been allowed to become a candidate for parliament until he has resigned his civil service post. Further, there has long been a rule that no civil servant, save in the subordinate grades, is allowed to take any overt part in party politics. Originally this applied to all civil servants, with the exception of certain industrials, but in 1948 an independent committee, set up to examine the limitations on the political activities of civil servants, recommended that all minor, manipulative and industrial grades should be free to engage in political activities. This recommendation was accepted. In 1953 it was decided that while the ban on political activities must remain for the middle and higher ranks of the civil service, some measure of freedom in political activities (but not including parliamentary candidature) should be allowed to civil servants in the subclerical and clerical classes and in the lower reaches of the scientific and technical classes.

Civil service unions were recognized by the government from 1906 in the post office and from about 1912 in the rest of the civil service. In 1919 Whitley councils were set up to provide machinery for dealing with grievances and to give the staff a greater share in and responsibility for working conditions. There is a National Whitley council for the whole nonindustrial civil service and separate interdepartmental councils for each department. Each council has an official side appointed by the minister and a staff side, representatives of which are appointed by the civil service unions and associations which are recognized as representative of the staff interest concerned. These joint councils are negotiating bodies and can proceed only by agreement.

After World War I a system was set up for compulsory arbitration at the request of either the staff representatives or the official side about conditions of service such as emoluments, leave, etc. Disputes were to be referred by the ministry of labour to a tribunal consisting of an independent chairman appointed by the minister of labour, one member drawn from the panel of persons appointed by the minister of labour as representing the chancellor of the exchequer, and one member drawn from the panel of persons appointed by the minister of labour as representing the staff side of the National Whitley council. This system only applied to the conditions of service of civil servants receiving not more than £1,536 a year.

For the nonindustrial civil service the machinery for negotiation and joint consultation consists of joint councils, on which are represented the departments and trade unions concerned in each of the industrial groups; *e.g.*, engineering, shipbuilding or miscellaneous trades. The government, although a major industrial employer, is not represented on any of the negotiating bodies for outside industry. These councils are represented on a central body, known as the Joint Co-ordinating Committee for Government Industrial Establishment, which can deal with matters

Angeles (Calif.) county and Milwaukee (Wis.) county; (5) city services in more than 800 municipalities and the employees of more than 1,000 council-manager cities most of which had no civil service commissions; (6) police and fire departments generally.

The county services were still predominantly partisan. In some states and some large cities operating standards were low, the merit system being a form rather than reality. But such cities as Los Angeles, Cincinnati, Milwaukee and St. Paul had admirable records. The U.S. party system was not fully adjusted to a nonpartisan public service and the process offered difficult problems.

The merit system also had to be adjusted to preference for veterans, which antedates civil service legislation. From 1920 to 1940 veterans of World War I received from 20% to 25% of federal positions filled by examination. The Veterans' Act of 1944 gave disabled veterans ten points in addition to their earned ratings and a place at the head of each register, five points to all other veterans and various further privileges. With about 15,000,000 veterans of World War II, the proportion of veterans in the federal service by the mid-1950s amounted to 60%. In some states and cities even more impressive benefits were granted; each jurisdiction makes its own rules.

The legal foundation for the national civil service is a considerable body of legislation, a mass of executive orders and commission and departmental rules; in a few states there are constitutional requirements for civil service. State-wide laws govern county and municipal civil services in some cases; in other cities are left a free hand. In many states there is a considerable body of judicial interpretation, a branch of the law of public officers.

The typical form of organization for the administration of civil service laws is a commission, usually comprising three persons of whom not more than two may belong to the same political party. There is a trend, however, toward either a single personnel director, or a commissioner with two associate commissioners concerned only with rules and hearings. The U.S. civil service commission is by far the largest of its kind, with a peacetime staff following World War II of about 3,000. Its principal divisions are concerned with examination, position classification, investigations, retirement records, loyalty determinations and appeals and review. A large field force is organized in 14 regional offices and many subordinate stations. Every federal department and establishment has, since 1938, a personnel office to deal with its own problems and with the civil service commission. The heads of these offices form the Federal Personnel council, a body reestablished in 1938 to facilitate exchange of experience and the formulation of policy. Regional personnel councils exist in the principal centres. In the Tennessee Valley authority personnel work is in charge of a director of personnel; in the council-manager cities the same pattern is common. There are no special civil service tribunals in the U.S. apart from the loyalty boards; but in the federal departments, since 1940, there are appeal boards (including a representative of the civil service commission) to hear appeals on efficiency ratings.

The examination system developed markedly after 1920. Traditionally examinations were of the essay or problem type or consisted of a demonstration of skill or strength. From the psychological laboratories came tests of "general intelligence" and aptitude which were progressively adapted to large-scale use. Most written examinations now given by the U.S. civil service commission are of the short-answer type. They are scored by an electric scoring machine which has greatly expedited operations and reduced costs. The short-answer form permits the progressive improvement of the reliability and validity of tests, and much experimental work has been done inside and outside of government.

Tests for higher positions usually comprise a rating of education and experience and an oral interview, rather than a written paper. Tests for positions requiring skill or strength are usually demonstrations by actual performance. Grades are recorded numerically and, although they are not infallible, they represent the most scientific standard yet achieved. Certification is normally made by sending the appointing officer three names from which he must select one; the others are returned to the register for future use. Federal examinations are announced in post offices, newspapers and, in case of shortage, by radio and other means. State and municipal examinations are widely publicized.

The classification of positions by duties was initiated in Chicago, Ill., 1910–12, to facilitate equal pay for equal work. The procedure is to develop an accurate, detailed specification of the duties to each type or class of position, to determine a scale of p positions, and then to allocate each particular job to its p Hundreds of classes of positions will be found necessary jurisdiction. This systematic description and arrangement o by duties has been found fundamental to many personnel especially the preparation of examinations, certification, ratings, promotions, transfers and layoffs. The responsibility fication is usually vested in the civil service commission, somet finance office; it is valuable even where there is no examinat Classification plans are frequently published and are usually inspection if not published. By the mid-1950s no co-ordinatio classification plans of different jurisdictions had yet been esta one (but only one) of the causes for the inadequate personnel s of the U.S.

Promotion is by merit, ascertained frequently by examination lower grades, and reaching into such positions as division and chiefs. There is considerable movement from cities and states in federal system, little in the contrary direction. Important caree sibilities exist in all the professional and scientific branches and in of the administrative, specialized and clerical services. The f service was put on a career basis in 1924. It is independently ad istered by the state department. More attention was paid durin decade 1930–40 to training young persons for the public service an further training of those already employed. Following a national ference at the University of Minnesota in 1930 many universities colleges developed courses in public administration, public fina psychology and personnel management. The U.S. civil service co mission and the New York city civil service commission were especia successful in organizing examinations to take advantage of gradua of these courses. State and municipal governments meanwhile had ganized training facilities for their employees on a part-time afte hours basis, especially for police, fire, utility and inspectional personn In 1935 the graduate school of the U.S. department of agriculture ex panded its work from the scientific field into the social sciences, in cluding management. Many programs were opened up for municipa employees, especially in Los Angeles at the University of Southern California. This movement represented a marked advance in developing a professional interest within the public service.

Less attention has been given in the U.S. civil service to the formal protection of rights of employees, due partly to a patronage background, partly to the characteristically frequent change of occupation by Americans and partly to the influence of the business tradition of freedom to hire and fire, as well as to public concern over the growth of bureaucracy. The federal law prescribes a written notice and opportunity for a reply in case of discharge, but no hearing. In many federal establishments there are administrative provisions for a hearing within the agency; and if an employee can come forward with proof that he was discharged for political or religious reasons, he can appeal to the civil service commission. A veteran can appeal to the commission on wider grounds. In some jurisdictions, such as Chicago, Ill., the civil service commission acts as a hearing board. In a few, such as Massachusetts, a discharged employee may secure a full judicial review of the law and the facts.

Executive order 9835 (1947) required a check of the loyalty of all federal employees and future applicants for employment. Agency and regional loyalty boards were established to make initial determinations on all the evidence as to whether there was reasonable ground to doubt the loyalty of employees or applicants, and a Loyalty Review board was set up to entertain appeals. In a service of more than 2,000,000 about 3,000 employees resigned under charges or investigation. About 350 employees and applicants were found upon hearing to be of doubtful loyalty and were refused employment. The system was sustained by the supreme court. A few analogous loyalty laws in some states and cities discovered few offenders.

The state department, the department of defense, the Atomic Energy commission and other "sensitive" agencies possess by law special authority for summary suspension and removal after hearing of employees deemed to be a security risk. Both loyalty and security requirements were induced by fear of sabotage and espionage in the interest of foreign governments.

Unions of public employees were first organized in the post office in the 1890s and were recognized by congress in 1912. Clerical employees formed the National Federation of Federal Employees in 1917 and other groups subsequently. Municipal organizations appeared in the larger cities about 1900; a few organizations of state employees preceded World War I, but they and county employees remained relatively unorganized despite efforts after 1940 by the American Federation of Labor and the Congress of Industrial Organizations. Fire fighters are nationally organized; police are often forbidden to form unions but may organize local social and benevolent associations. Teachers have a national federation.

The purposes of these organizations are to secure legislation extending the merit system, better scales of pay and working conditions, protection against arbitrary action and such benefits as group insurance, credit facilities and the like. They are free, as a rule, to affiliate with outside labour organizations but are restrained from taking an active part in politics. In recent years they sought recognition of a right to collective bargaining, written agreements and the majority union as the sole bargaining agent. Except in the Tennessee Valley authority these claims had not been widely granted. Strikes of public employees are rare, one dramatic exception being the Boston police strike of 1919. Police are usually forbidden outside affiliation and the right to strike, a right which is rejected by the overwhelming majority of public employee unions. The Taft-Hartley act (1947) prohibited strikes of federal employees and a number of states subsequently enacted comparable laws.

The public services of the states vary extremely in their legal organization and standards of competence. As of the mid-1950s about half had formal merit systems, and some of these were indifferently administered. The number of states with merit systems steadily increases, nevertheless, and standards are steadily improving. The older type of bipartisan civil service commission predominates but Minnesota and other states have abandoned the commission in favour of a director of personnel. Functions are chiefly examination, classification and record keeping. Most states have pension plans for teachers, and an increasing number have state-wide pension plans for all employees, on a contributory basis. In New Jersey and Massachusetts the state commissions carry on work for counties. In California there has been notable co-operation between state, county and municipal civil service commissions. There is no co-ordination between state and local agencies and the U.S. civil service commission.

State civil service agencies have been handicapped in some instances by political opposition, by lack of funds and by inadequate leadership. During the 1930s substantial progress was made, however, both in extending the merit system and in introducing better methods.

Primary and secondary school teachers are subject to minimum standards of training fixed by law. They are required to hold a certificate, usually issued by a state examining agency. Appointments are made by local school boards without competitive or other formal examinations. After a probationary period, teachers acquire a protected tenure. They are a part of the merit system but not under the jurisdiction of civil service commissions.

In a country which has 106 cities with a population of 100,000 or more (1950 U.S. census), the municipal civil services are of great importance. Until 1900 municipal employees were usually political appointees with low standards of competence and at times of integrity. The muckraking era (1900–05) and the ensuing period of municipal reform wrought a great transformation, supported by the increasingly technical nature of municipal functions. Municipal civil service commissions were widely established before 1910; in 1953 there were more than 800 cities under the merit system. The introduction of the council-manager plan after 1908 gave a great impetus to the further improvement of municipal standards, although city managers have not favoured the independent, bipartisan civil service commission. Political influence in appointments and promotions has not been eliminated in many of the larger cities, but in the middle-sized and small cities it has lost any major significance. One handicap to the professionalization of the municipal services lies in the preference for local residents for appointment—a universal requirement for police, fire, inspectional and clerical services and a usual requirement even in technical and professional posts. The practice of outside appointments has, however, become well-established among city managers, school superintendents, health officers and city engineers.

For the purpose of exchanging experience, improving procedures and publishing reports, civil service commissions and agencies in 1906 formed the Civil Service Assembly of the United States and Canada, with headquarters in Chicago. This body holds an annual convention, furnishes technical advice, carries on research and publishes professional bulletins and the quarterly journal, *Public Personnel Review*.

Outlying Possessions.—In 1900 the act providing for civil government in Puerto Rico extended the civil service act and rules to it. The concept and procedures were unknown to the population, and the enforcement of high standards remained difficult. The P.R. civil service commission secures some technical aid from time to time from the U.S. commission. In 1900 the merit system was also introduced in Hawaii. The civil service commission has maintained close contacts with trends on the mainland. (L. D. W.)

AN INTERNATIONAL CIVIL SERVICE

The elements of an international civil service were first found in the Universal Postal union (1874–1875). The League of Nations and the International Labour office (I.L.O.) required a staff of experts and subordinate personnel numbering about 600 which took the form of a true international civil service. It drew most heavily on British, French and Swiss sources, but more than 40 states contributed members in response to the requirement that the staff should be recruited "on as wide a geographical basis as possible." There were no formal methods of selection for the higher personnel; the director-general depended on personal acquaintances and trustworthy recommendations. The staff fell into three divisions: the administrative, the supervisory and clerical, and the custodial and manipulative.

The main point of interest in an international civil service lies perhaps in the steps it takes to free itself from national loyalties. The League existed during a period of rampant nationalism and irreconcilable conflict, but its experience showed that a broad measure of international loyalty can be achieved, even under difficult conditions. The staff of the League was dispersed after 1939 but that of the I.L.O. was maintained, principally in Canada.

A much larger international civil service was required for the United Nations organization and the specialized agencies. In the United Nations charter, each member state undertook to respect the international character of the duties of the staff and to refrain from influencing them in their work. Officials and employees of the United Nations and the specialized agencies, paid exclusively from the funds of each of these organizations, are assigned duties by its head. They are subject to its discipline and owe it full responsibility. Valuable experience in international co-operation was obtained during World War II through the various combined boards and through the lend-lease organization. (E. E. Bs.)

BIBLIOGRAPHY.—United Kingdom: Emmeline Cohen, *The Growth of the British Civil Service, 1780–1939* (London, 1941); Harold E. Dale, *Personnel and Problems of the Higher Civil Service* (Oxford, 1943); Herman Finer, *British Civil Service*, 2nd ed. (London, 1937); J. Donald Kingsley, *Representative Bureaucracy* (1944); N. E. Mustoe, *Law and Organization of the British Civil Service* (London, 1932); Hiram Stout, *Public Service in Great Britain* (Oxford, 1938); Harvey Walker, *Training Public Employees in Great Britain* (1935); F. J. Tickner, *Modern Staff Training* (London, 1952); Leonard D. White, *Whitley Councils in the British Civil Service* (1933); *Whitley Bulletin* (London, 1921–).

Colonies and Commonwealth: C. J. Jeffries, *The Colonial Empire and its Civil Service* (Cambridge, 1938); Robert S. Parker, *Public Service Recruitment in Australia* (Melbourne, 1942); Annual Reports of the Commonwealth of Australia and State Public Service Boards or Commissioners (Melbourne, issued yearly); *Report* of the Committee of Enquiry into Systems of Promotion and Transfer (Commonwealth) (Melbourne, 1945); *Annual Reports* of the South African Public Service Commission (Pretoria, issued yearly).

France: H. Puget, *Bibliographie de la Fonction Publique* (1948); F. Grazier, *Commentaire de la loi du 19 octobre, 1946, relative au statut général des fonctionnaires* (1947); M. Waline, *Traité élémentaire de droit administratif*, 6th ed. (1950).

United States: Ismar Baruch, *Position Classification in the Public Service* (1941); "Commission of Inquiry on Public Service Personnel," *Better Government Personnel* (1935); Oliver Field, *Civil Service Law* (1939); Morton R. Godine, *The Labor Problem in the Public Service* (1951); Arthur Macmahon and J. D. Millett, *Federal Administrators* (1939); Joseph E. McLean, ed., *The Public Service and University Education* (1949); Lewis Meriam, *Public Service and Special Training* (1936), and *Public Personnel Problems from the Standpoint of the Operating Officer* (1938); William E. Mosher, J. D. Kingsley and O. G. Stahl, *Public Personnel Administration*, 3rd ed., (1950); Leonard D. White and others, *Civil Service in Wartime* (1945); U.S. Civil Service Commission, *Annual Reports, Good Government* (1881–), *Public Personnel Review* (1939–), *Public Administration Review* (1940–), *Public Management* (1926–).

International: Pitman B. Potter, *An Introduction to the Study of International Organization*, 5th ed. (New York and London, 1948); Egon Ranshofen-Wertheimer, *The International Secretariat* (Washington, 1945).

CIVITA CASTELLANA (anc. *Falerii*), a town and episcopal see of the province of Viterbo, Italy, 45 mi. by rail north of Rome. Pop. (1951) 11,517 (commune). Mt. Soracte lies about 6 mi. to the southeast.

Falerii was one of the 12 chief cities of Etruria. Wars between Rome and the Falisci (*q.v.*) appear to have been frequent. At the end of the First Punic War, they rebelled, but were soon conquered (241 B.C.) and lost half their territory. The ancient city, built upon a precipitous hill, was destroyed and another built on a more accessible site in the plain. Thus the original city occupied the site of modern Civita Castellana and the Roman town was transferred 3 mi. to the northwest. After this time, Falerii hardly appears in history. There were bishops of Falerii up till 1033, when the desertion of the place in favour of the modern site began, and the last mention of it dates from A.D. 1064. The site of the original Falerii is a plateau, about 1,100 yd. by 400, not higher than the surrounding country (475 ft.) but separated from it by gorges over 200 ft. in depth, and connected with it only on the western side, which was strongly fortified with a mound and ditch. The rest of the city, of which the circuit was about 2,250 yd., was defended by walls constructed of rectangular blocks of tufa. They reached in places a height of 56 ft. and were 7 to 9 ft. thick. There were about 80 towers and 8 gates. Two of the gates and some 50 of the towers have been preserved, as well as the remains of four temples within the city. Almost the only edifice now standing within the walls is the 12th century abbey church of S. Maria.

CIVITAVECCHIA, a seaport town and episcopal see of Italy, province of Rome, 50 mi. N.W. by rail and 35 mi. direct from the city of Rome. The population was (1951) 31,933 (commune). It is the ancient *Centum Cellae,* founded by Trajan. Interesting descriptions of it are given by Pliny the Younger and Rutilius. The modern harbour works rest on the ancient foundations, and near it was the cemetery of detachments of the fleets of Misenum and Ravenna. It was a strong populous place in the 6th century, but the Saracens destroyed it in 812. Leo IV built a new city for the refugees 8 mi. N.N.E. of Civitavecchia, where may be seen ruins of walls and streets and an inscription, that must have stood over a gate, recording its foundation. The people returned to the old town (whence the name Civitavecchia) in 889, but the new one continued as the castle of Cencelle until the 15th century. In 1508 Pope Julius II began the construction of the castle from the designs of Bramante, Michelangelo being responsible for the addition of the central tower. Under it lies a Roman house, possibly the port admiral's quarters. Pius IV added a convict prison. The arsenal was built by Alexander VII and designed by Bernini. Civitavecchia was the chief port of the papal state and has still a considerable trade. There are cement factories in the town, which will be considerably increased by the new electric railway to Orte, by which Terni (*q.v.*) is readily accessible. In 1926 ships to the number of 2,285, a total tonnage of 2,041,637, entered and cleared the port, and 789,921 tons of merchandise were imported (chiefly coal and cereals) and exported (chiefly salt) from the saltworks of Porto Clementino, southwest of Tarquinia. There is a thermal establishment in the town, and 3 mi. N.E. were the *Aquae Tauri,* warm springs; considerable remains of the Roman baths of the time of Trajan are still preserved there. About one mile west of these are hot springs (the *Ficoncella*), also known in Roman times. Five miles down the coast is the summer resort of S. Marinella, which has grown up and forms a part of the commune of Civitavecchia.

CLACKMANNAN, a civil parish, but the county town of Clackmannanshire, Scotland. Pop. (1931) 2,585. It lies near the north bank of the Forth, 2 mi. east of Alloa, with two stations on the L.N.E.R. Clackmannan tower is now a picturesque ruin, but at one time was the seat of a descendant of the Bruce family. The old market cross still exists, and close to it stands the stone that gives the town its name (Gaelic, *clach,* stone; Manann, the name of the district). About 1 mi. to the southeast is Kennet house, the seat of Lord Balfour of Burleigh, another member of the Bruce family. Coal is mined near Clackmannan, which, however, lost its industrial importance to Alloa (*q.v.*).

CLACKMANNANSHIRE, the smallest county in Scotland, bounded southwest by the Forth, west by Stirlingshire, north-northeast and northwest by Perthshire, and east by Fifeshire. Its land area is 34,927 ac., or 54.6 sq.mi. An elevated ridge, starting on the west, runs through the middle of the county, widening gradually till it reaches the eastern boundary, and skirting the alluvial or carse lands in the valleys of the Forth and Devon. Still farther north are the Ochil hills, which reach a height of 2,363 ft., a volcanic range of the Old Red Sandstone period, consisting mainly of basalts and andesites. A fault along their southern base brings down the Carboniferous strata, which occupy the southern part of the county. The rivers of importance are the Devon and the Black or South Devon. The first, noted in the upper parts for its scenery and trout fishing, runs through the county near the base of the Ochils, and falls into the Forth at the village of Cambus, after a winding course of 33 mi., although as the crow flies its source is only 5¼ mi. distant. The Black Devon, rising in the Cleish hills, flows westward in a direction nearly parallel to that of the Devon, and falls into the Forth near Clackmannan. It supplies power to mills and collieries; and its whole course is over the Carboniferous strata. The Forth is navigable as far as it forms the boundary of the county. The only lake is Gartmorn, which was dammed in order to furnish water to Alloa and power to mills.

Agriculture and Industries.—The soil is generally productive and well cultivated, though the greater part of the high ground between the carse lands on the Forth and the vale of Devon at the base of the Ochils on the north consists of inferior soils, often lying upon an impervious clay. Oats is the chief crop (2,410 ac. in 1938). The Ochils afford excellent sheep pasture. The average size of the 144 holdings in 1938 was about 102 ac. There is a small tract of moorland in the east, called the Forest, bounded on its northern margin by the Black Devon. Copper, silver, lead and other minerals have been discovered in small quantity in the Ochils, between Alva and Dollar. The Carboniferous strata belong mainly to the coal measures, forming a northern continuation of the Lanarkshire basin and including a number of valuable coal seams. Fire clay, sandstone and igneous rock are also worked. Coal is mined at Sauchie, Coalsnaughton, Devonside, Clackmannan and other pits. The spinning mills at Alloa and Clackmannan are active, Alloa yarns and fingering being famous; and woollen goods are largely manufactured at Alva, Clackmannan and Tillicoultry. Distilleries and breweries have a large export business. Minor trades include glass blowing, coopering, iron founding, shipbuilding and papermaking. Mentsrie near Alloa has a large furniture factory. The L.N.E.R. serves the whole county, while the L.M.S.R. has access to Alloa.

Population and Government.—The population was estimated in 1938 at 33,117. In 1931 Gaelic and English were spoken by 146 persons. The county, with part of Stirling, returns one member to parliament. Clackmannan (1931 pop. 2,585) is the county town, but is not classed as a small burgh, of which there are four—Alloa (est. 1938 pop. 13,436), Alva (3,986), Tillicoultry (3,136) and Dollar (1,428). There are two county districts. Clackmannan forms a sheriffdom with Stirling and Dumbarton shires, and a sheriff-substitute sits at Alloa. There is an exceptionally well-equipped secondary school in Alloa and a well-known academy at Dollar.

CLACTON-ON-SEA, a watering place and urban district in East Essex, England; 71 mi. E.N.E. from London by the L.N.E.R. Pop. (1938) 23,410. Area, 10.6 sq.mi. Clay cliffs of slight altitude rise from the sandy beach and face southeastward. In the neighbourhood, however, marshes fringe the shore. The church of Great Clacton, at the village 1½ mi. inland, is of Norman and later date. It is an important watering place for London.

CLADEL, LÉON (1835–1892), French novelist, was born at Montauban (Tarn-et-Garonne) on March 13, 1835. He made a reputation by his first book, *Les Martyrs ridicules* (1862), a novel for which Charles Baudelaire, whose literary disciple Cladel was, wrote a preface. His best novels are realistic pictures of peasant life in his native district of Quercy. They include: *Le Nommé Qouael* (1868), *Le Bouscassié* (1869), *Les Va-nu-pieds* (1873), a volume of short stories, and *N'a qu'un oeil* (1882). He died at Sèvres on July 20, 1892.

See *La Vie de Léon Cladel* (1905), by his daughter Judith Cladel, containing also an article on Cladel by Edmond Picard.

CLAIRAULT (or CLAIRAUT), **ALEXIS CLAUDE** (1713–1765), French mathematician, was born on May 7 or 13, 1713, at Paris. Under the tuition of his father, a teacher of mathematics, he made such progress that at twelve years of age he read before the French academy an account of the properties of four curves which he had discovered. His *Recherches sur les courbes à double courbure,* finished in 1729 and published 1731, procured his admission into the Academy of Sciences, although he was still below the legal age. In 1736, with P. L. Maupertuis, he went on the expedition to Lapland, for the purpose of estimating a degree of the meridian; and in 1743 he published his treatise *Théorie de la figure de la terre,* in which he promulgated the theorem known as "Clairault's theorem," which connects the gravity at points on the surface of a rotating ellipsoid with the compression and the centrifugal force at the equator. In 1750 he gained the prize of the St. Petersburg academy for his essay *Théorie de la lune;* and in 1759 he calculated the perihelion of Halley's comet. He also detected singular solutions in differential equations of the first order, and of the second and higher degrees. Clairault died at Paris on May 17, 1765.

CLAIRON, LA (1723–1803), French actress, whose real name was CLAIRE LERIS, was born at Condé sur l'Escaut, Hainaut, on Jan. 25, 1723, the natural daughter of an army sergeant. In 1736 she made her first stage appearance at the Comédie Italienne, in a small part in Marivaux's *Ile des esclaves.* After several years in the provinces she returned to Paris. Her life, meanwhile, had been decidedly irregular, even if not to the degree indicated by the libellous pamphlet *Histoire de la demoiselle Cronel, dite Frétillon, actrice de la Comédie de Rouen, écrite par elle-même* (The Hague, 1746), or to be inferred from the disingenuousness of her own *Mémoires d'Hippolyte Clairon* (1798); and she had great difficulty in obtaining an order to make her début at the Comédie Française for which she had the courage to select the title-rôle of *Phèdre* (1743). During her 22 years at this theatre, dividing the honours with her rival Mlle. Dumesnil, she filled many of the classical rôles of tragedy, and created a great number of parts in the plays of Voltaire, Marmontel, Saurin, de Belloy and others. She retired in 1766 and trained pupils for the stage, among them Mlle. Raucourt. Goldsmith called Mlle. Clairon, "the most perfect female figure I have ever seen on any stage" (*The Bee,* 2nd No.); and Garrick, while recognizing her unwillingness or inability to make use of the inspiration of the instant, admitted that "she has everything that art and a good understanding with great natural spirit can give her."

CLAIRTON, a city of Allegheny county, Pennsylvania, U.S.A., on the Monongahela river, 20 mi. S.E. of Pittsburgh; served by the Pennsylvania, the Pittsburgh and West Virginia, the Baltimore and Ohio, the Bessemer and Lake Erie and the Union railways. It was formed in 1922 by the consolidation of the boroughs of Clairton, North Clairton and Wilson, which in 1920 had a combined population of 10,777. The city's population in 1950 was 19,418 and in 1940 was 16,381 by the federal census. Clairton has important manufactures of structural iron, steel, boiler tubes, river boats and barges and an immense by-product coke plant.

CLAIRVAUX, a village of N.E. France, in the department of Aube, 40 mi. E.S.E. of Troyes. Clairvaux (*Clara Vallis*) is situated in the valley of the Aube on the eastern border of the forest of Clairvaux. Its abbey, founded in 1115 by St. Bernard, became the centre of the Cistercian order. The buildings (*see* ABBEY) belong for the most part to the 18th century, but there is a large storehouse which dates from the 12th century.

CLAIRVOYANCE, a word used with several different meanings in spiritualism and psychical research. Sometimes it is used to denote transcendental vision of beings on another plane of existence, while F. W. H. Myers, in the glossary to his *Human Personality,* defines it as "the faculty or act of perceiving as though visually, with some coincidental truth, some distant scene." It is now, however, often used as a term complementary to and exclusive of telepathy (*q.v.*), to denote all forms of supernormal cognition where the percipient's knowledge is not derived from another mind, whether or not the knowledge is communicated as a visual impression. It is in this last sense that the word is used in the article on PSYCHICAL RESEARCH (*q. v.*).

CLAM, the name applied to many bivalve molluscs (*see* LAMELLIBRANCHIA) from the vice-like firmness with which the shell closes. In Scotland the name is usually applied to the scallop (*q.v.*), in England to species of *Mya* and *Mactra* especially the gaper, *Mya truncata.* In the United States the name has a wider use, but most commonly denotes *Venus mercenaria,* the quahog or hard clam, and *Mya arenaria,* the soft clam, both of which are of great importance as food, besides being extensively used by fishermen as bait. The hard clam is allied to the cockle (*q.v.*) and has a heavy shell which was used as shell-money (*see* WAMPUM) by the Indians. It is found in one to six fathoms of water off the Atlantic coast of North America from Florida to Cape Cod and also off New Brunswick. It is obtained by raking the bottom. Young specimens, known as "little necks," are sold in large numbers in New York. The soft clam is found mainly between the tide-marks and has a thin shell and long siphons. "Clam bakes," where clams are placed on heated stones with potatoes and other food, the whole being covered with sea-weed and left to cook, make a popular picnic in America. Atlantic clams have been transplanted to the Pacific coast of North America with great success, though there are several indigenous species there which are also known by this name. It is an interesting point that while both *Mya* and *Mytilus* (the sea mussel, *q.v.*) occur on both sides of the Atlantic, the former is not eaten in Europe, the latter not in America; furthermore, in the prehistoric "kitchen-middens," remains of *Mytilus* are found in Europe and of *Mya* in America, but not vice versa. The American "fresh-water clams" are fresh-water mussels (*Unionidae*). The giant among the North American clams is the gweduc or geoduck (pronounced guey-duck), *Panomya generosa,* whose shell attains a length of almost seven in. and whose siphons may be extended to almost five times that measure; it is confined to the coast from northern California to British Columbia. Its flesh is greatly esteemed.

Of other species to which the name clam is applied, the most noteworthy are the bear's paw clam (*Hippopus maculatus*) of the Indian ocean, with a beautiful ridged white shell, marked with spots of purplish-red; and the giant clam (*Tridacna gigas*) of the East Indies, the largest of all lamellibranchs; the actual animal may weigh 20 lb. and the shell nearly $\frac{1}{4}$ of a ton.

CLAMECY, a town of central France, capital of an arrondissement in the department of Nièvre, at the confluence of the Yonne and Beuvron and on the Canal du Nivernais, 36 mi. N.N.E. of Nevers. Pop. (1946) 5,455. In the early middle ages Clamecy belonged to the abbey of St. Julian at Auxerre; in the 11th century it passed to the counts of Nevers. After the capture of Jerusalem by Saladin in 1188, Clamecy became the seat of the bishops of Bethlehem, who till the Revolution resided in the hospital of Panthenor, bequeathed by William IV., count of Nevers. The town figured in the *coup d'état* of 1851.

The church of St. Martin, dates chiefly from the 13th, 14th and 15th centuries. The town has fulling and flour mills, with a small leather and chemical trade. Wine and cattle, and timber are important.

CLAN, a social group of fundamental importance in the social structure of many primitive societies. The most important character of the clan is its exogamy—*i.e.,* marriage within the clan is forbidden, and regarded as incest (*see* EXOGAMY). This tabu applies even to persons between whom no genealogical relationship can be traced. Although for scientific purposes the clan is defined as an exogamous group, the term is frequently used in popular literature for groups that are not exogamous, such as the tribe; and that rather vague entity, the Scottish clan, though sharing some of the characters of the clan, is not an exogamous group, whatever it may once have been. Partly for these reasons, American writers use the term "sib" instead of "clan." The clan is a unilateral group; that is to say, membership of the clan is determined, either by descent through the mother ("matrilineal clan," "mother-sib," or "clan," as it has been variously named) or by descent through the father ("patrilineal clan," "father-sib," or "gens"). This does not mean, however, that descent from some original ancestor can be traced, though belief in such descent is usually present. The clan, therefore, has only a slight resemblance to the family (*q.v.*) which necessarily contains members of more than one clan, though it is possible that the clan has evolved from the family by emphasis of one line of descent.

Although the clan is not a kinship-group—for kinship implies not only relationship by direct descent, but the ability to trace it genealogically—nevertheless, it is common for members of a clan to address one another by means of relationship-terms used between close kin, and this carries with it the same sort of social relations as we find between close kin, though in less degree. This is a natural result of the classificatory system of relationships which is frequently associated with it, but even in the absence of this system it is common for distant members of a clan to claim brotherhood with one another, and to feel that kind of solidarity found in the case of the family. This solidarity is a most striking character of the clan. The individual identifies himself with his clan in a peculiarly intimate way, so that clan-responsibility for the action of individual members is common. This unity of the clan frequently extends into the political and economic sphere.

The unity of the clan is frequently emphasized by the possession of a totem (*see* TOTEMISM). Where clans are much interspersed and widely diffused, clan-identity may thus be established and maintained, which even the classificatory system of relationships need not reveal. It is doubtful whether habitation of a common territory is ever the common tie uniting members of a clan, but localized clans do sometimes occur, though it is probable that in such cases the localization is secondary, and the common tie is belief in common descent.

Not uncommon is a grouping of clans into wider units, the simplest form of this being a dual organization (*q.v.*) in which the clans are grouped into two exogamous divisions. It is also not uncommon for there to be a division of function between the clans of a tribe, occasionally economic, *e.g.*, in India, but more usually political or religious, *e.g.*, in some African kingdoms.

Bibliography.—The clan is defined and discussed in general books on Sociology, such as W. H. R. Rivers, *Social Organization* (1924), R. H. Lowie, *Primitive Society* (1921), and E. Westermarck, *History of Human Marriage*, vol. ii. (1921). (W. E. A.)

CLANRICARDE, Earl of, Irish title, held since 1916 by the marquess of Sligo. In 1543, Ulick (d. 1544) (*q.v.*), chief of the "MacWilliam Eighter" branch of the De Burgh family (*q.v.*), surrendered his territory lying in the neighbourhood of Galway to Henry VIII, receiving it back to hold, by English custom, as earl of Clanricarde and Lord Dunkellin. Richard, the 4th earl (1601–35), who fought on the English side in O'Neill's rebellion, obtained the English earldom of St. Albans in 1628, his son, Ulick (*q.v.*), receiving the Irish marquessate of Clanricarde in 1646; but at the death of the latter, without heirs, the English honours and the marquessate expired, and the Irish earldom went to his cousin, Richard, 6th earl (1657–66). The 9th earl, John, forfeited his estates for his support of James II but they were restored to him in 1702, and his great-grandson, the 12th earl, was created marquess in 1789. He left no son, but the marquessate was again revived in 1825 for Ulick, 14th earl, who was lord privy seal and was created Baron Somerhill, in the United Kingdom, in 1826. On the death of Hubert George, 2nd marquess (1832–1916), Ulick's son, all his honours became extinct, except the earldom of Clanricarde (*c.* 1800), which passed to his kinsman, the marquess of Sligo.

CLANRICARDE, ULICK DE BURGH (Bourke or Burke), 1st Earl of (d. 1544), styled MacWilliam and Ne-gan or Na-gCeann (*i.e.*, "of the Heads," "having made a mount of the heads of men slain in battle which he covered up with earth"), was the son of Richard or Rickard de Burgh, lord of Clanricarde, by a daughter of Madden of Portumna, and grandson of Ulick de Burgh, lord of Clanricarde (1467–87), the collateral heir male of the earls of Ulster. Ulick de Burgh succeeded to the headship of his clan, exercised a quasi-royal authority and held vast estates in county Galway, in Connaught, including Loughry, Dunkellin, Kiltartan (Hilltaraght) and Athenry, as well as Clare and Leitrim. In March 1541, he wrote to Henry VIII, placing himself and his estates in the king's hands. The same year he was present at Dublin, when the act was passed making Henry VIII king of Ireland. In 1543, in company with other Irish chiefs, he visited the king at Greenwich, made full submission, undertook to introduce English manners and abandon Irish names, received a regrant of the greater part of his estates with the addition of other lands, was confirmed in the captainship and rule of Clanricarde and was created on July 1, 1543, earl of Clanricarde and baron of Dunkellin in the peerage of Ireland, with unusual ceremony. "The making of MacWilliam earl of Clanricarde made all the country during his time quiet and obedient," states Lord Chancellor Cusake in his review of the state of Ireland in 1553. He did not live long, however, to enjoy his new English dignities but died shortly after returning to Ireland about March 1544.

See R. Bagwell, *Ireland under the Tudors*, vol. i.; Gairdner's *Letters and Papers of Henry VIII.*

CLANRICARDE, ULICK DE BURGH (Bourke or Burke), Marquess of (1604–1657 or 1658), son of Richard, 4th earl of Clanricarde, created in 1628 earl of St. Albans, and of Frances, daughter and heir of Sir Francis Walsingham, and widow of Sir Philip Sidney and of Robert Devereux, earl of Essex, was born in 1604. He was summoned to the House of Lords as Lord Burgh in 1628 and succeeded his father as 5th earl in 1635. He sat in the Short Parliament of 1640 and attended Charles I in the Scottish expedition. On the outbreak of the Irish rebellion Clanricarde had powerful inducements for joining the Irish—the ancient greatness and independence of his family, his devotion to the Roman Catholic Church, and strongest of all, the ungrateful treatment meted out by Charles I and Wentworth to his father, one of Elizabeth's most staunch adherents in Ireland, whose lands were appropriated by the crown and whose death, it was popularly asserted, was hastened by the harshness of the lord-lieutenant. Nevertheless at the crisis his loyalty never wavered. Alone of the Irish Roman Catholic nobility to declare for the king, he returned to Ireland, took up his residence at Portumna, kept Galway, of which he was governor, neutral, and took measures for the defense of the county and for the relief of the Protestants, making "his house and towns a refuge, nay, even a hospital for the distressed English." In 1643 he was one of the commissioners appointed by the king to confer with the Irish confederates and urged the wisdom of a cessation of hostilities in a document which he publicly distributed. He was appointed commander of the English forces in Connaught in 1644 and in 1646 was created a marquess and a privy councillor. He supported the same year the treaty between Charles I and the confederates, and endeavoured after its failure to persuade Preston, the general of the Irish, to agree to a peace; but the latter, being advised by Rinuccini, the papal nuncio, refused in December. Together with Ormonde, Clanricarde opposed the nuncio's policy; and the royalist inhabitants of Galway, having through the latter's influence rejected the cessation of hostilities arranged with Lord Inchiquin in 1648, he besieged the town and compelled its acquiescence. In 1649 he reduced Sligo. On Ormonde's departure in Dec. 1650 Clanricarde was appointed deputy lord-lieutenant, but he was not trusted by the Roman Catholics and was unable to stem the tide of the parliamentary successes. In 1651 he opposed the offer of Charles, duke of Lorraine, to supply money and aid on condition of being acknowledged "Protector" of the kingdom. In May 1652 Galway surrendered to the parliament, and in June Clanricarde signed articles with the parliamentary commissioners which allowed his departure from Ireland. In August he was excepted from pardon for life and estate, but by permits, renewed from time to time by the council, he was enabled to remain in England for the rest of his life, and in 1653 £500 a year was settled upon him by the Council of State in consideration of the protection which he had given to the Protestants in Ireland at the time of the rebellion. He died at Somerhill in Kent in 1657 or 1658 and was buried at Tunbridge.

The "great earl," as he was called, supported Ormonde in his desire to unite the English royalists with the more moderate Roman Catholics on the basis of religious toleration under the authority of the sovereign, against the papal scheme advocated by Rinuccini, and in opposition to the parliamentary and Puritan policy. There is no reason to doubt Clarendon's opinion of him as "a person of unquestionable fidelity . . . and of the most eminent constancy to the Roman Catholic religion of any man in the three kingdoms," or the verdict of Hallam, who describes him "as perhaps the most unsullied character in the annals of Ireland." (*See* also Clanricarde, Earl of.)

Bibliography.—See *Memoirs of the Marquis of Clanricarde* (1722, repr. 1744); *Memoirs of Ulick, Marquis of Clanricarde*, by John, 11th earl (1757); *Life of Ormonde*, by T. Carte (1851); S. R. Gardiner's *Hist. of the Civil War and of the Commonwealth; Cal. of State Papers, Irish*, esp. *Introd.* 1633–47 and *Domestic; Hist.* mss. *Comm.*, mss. *of Marq. of Ormonde* and *Earl of Egmont.* (P. C. Y.)

CLANVOWE, SIR THOMAS, English 14th century poet, author of *The Cuckoo and the Nightingale*, long attributed to Chaucer. Little is known of Clanvowe, whose name is last mentioned in 1404. He figured at the courts of Richard II and Henry IV, and was one of the 20 knights who accompanied John Beaufort to Barbary in 1390. His name was discovered on the best of the mss. by Professor Skeat in editing *The Book of Cupid, God of Love, or the Cuckoo and the Nightingale.*

The historic and literary importance of *The Cuckoo and the Nightingale* is great. It is the work of a poet who had studied the prosody of Chaucer with more intelligent care than either Occleve or Lydgate, and who therefore forms an important link between the 14th and 15th centuries in English poetry. Clanvowe writes with a surprising delicacy and sweetness, in a five-line measure almost peculiar to himself. Professor Skeat points out a unique characteristic of Clanvowe's versification, namely, the unprecedented freedom with which he employs the suffix of the final *-e*, and rather avoids than seeks elision. *The Cuckoo and the Nightingale* was imitated by Milton in his sonnet to the nightingale, and was rewritten in modern English by Wordsworth.

See also a critical edition of the *Boke of Cupide* by Dr. Erich Vollmer (Berlin, 1898).

CLAPARÈDE, JEAN LOUIS RENÉ ANTOINE ÉDOUARD (1832–1870), Swiss naturalist, was born at Geneva on April 24, 1832. He belonged to a French family, some members of which had taken refuge in that city after the revocation of the Edict of Nantes. In 1852 he began to study medicine and natural science at Berlin, where he was greatly influenced by J. Müller, who was then working on the Echinoderms. The latter part of his stay at Berlin he devoted, along with J. Lachmann, to the study of the Infusoria and Rhizopods. In 1862 he was chosen professor of comparative anatomy at Geneva. He died at Siena on May 31, 1870. His *Recherches sur la structure des annélides sédentaires* was published posthumously in 1873.

CLAPPERTON, HUGH (1788–1827), Scottish traveller in central Africa, was born at Annan, Dumfriesshire, and after some years in the merchant service was impressed into the navy. In 1817 he returned home with the grade of lieutenant, and in 1820 accompanied Oudney and Denham in the Government expedition to Bornu. From Bornu they set out to explore the Niger country. After Oudney's death at Murmur (Jan. 1824) Clapperton proceeded along to Kano and Sokoto, returning by way of Zatia and Katsena to Kuka, where he met Denham. An account of the travels was published in 1826 under the title of *Narrative of Travels and Discoveries in Northern and Central Africa in the years* 1822–1824.

Immediately after his return Clapperton was raised to the rank of commander, and sent out with another expedition to Africa. He landed at Badagry in the Bight of Benin, and started overland for the Niger on Dec. 7, 1825, having with him his servant Richard Lander (*q.v.*), Captain Pearce, R.N., and Dr. Morrison, navy surgeon and naturalist. Before the month was out Pearce and Morrison were dead of fever. Clapperton continued his journey, and, passing through the Yoruba country, in Jan. 1826 he crossed the Niger at Bussa, where Mungo Park had died 20 years before. In July he arrived at Kano. Thence he went to Sokoto, intending afterwards to go to Bornu. The sultan, however, detained him, and he died of dysentery near Sokoto on April 13, 1827. Clapperton was the first European to make known from personal observation the semi-civilized Hausa countries, which he visited soon after the establishment of the Sokoto empire by the Fula.

In 1829 appeared the *Journal of a Second Expedition into the Interior of Africa*, etc., by the late Commander Clapperton, with a biographical sketch of the explorer by Lieut.-Col. S. Clapperton. Lander, who had brought back the journal of his master, also published *Records of Captain Clapperton's Last Expedition to Africa . . . with the subsequent Adventures of the Author* (2 vols. 1830).

CLAQUE, an organized body of professional applauders in the French theatres (Fr. *claquer*, to clap the hands). The hiring of persons to applaud dramatic performances was common in classical times, and the emperor Nero, when he acted, had his performance greeted by a chorus of 5,000 soldiers. Jean Daurat, the 16th century French poet, bought up a number of tickets for a performance of one of his plays and distributed them gratuitously to those who promised publicly to express their approbation. In 1820 an office was opened in Paris for the supply of *claquers*, and any number of them could be ordered in a way similar to the ordering of "extras" for a motion picture production of the present day. These people were usually under a *chef de claque*, whose duty it was to judge where their efforts were needed and to start the applause. The *commissaires* were scattered among the audience and called the attention of their neighbours to the good points of the play. The *rieurs* were those who laughed loudly at the jokes. The *pleureurs*, generally women, feigned tears, by holding their handkerchiefs to their eyes. The *chatouilleurs* kept the audience in a good humour, while the *bisseurs* simply clapped their hands and cried *bis! bis!* to secure encores.

CLARA, SAINT (1194–1253), foundress of the Franciscan nuns, was born of a knightly family in Assisi in 1194. At eighteen she was so impressed by a sermon of St. Francis that she was filled with the desire to devote herself to the kind of life he was leading. She obtained an interview with him, and to test her resolution he told her to dress in penitential sackcloth and beg alms for the poor in the streets of Assisi. Clara readily did this, and Francis, satisfied as to her vocation, told her to come to the Portiuncula arrayed as a bride. The friars met her with lighted candles, and at the foot of the altar Francis shore off her hair, received her vows of poverty, chastity and obedience, and invested her with the Franciscan habit, 1212. He placed her for a couple of years in a Benedictine convent in Assisi until the convent at St. Damian's, close to the town, was ready. Her two younger sisters, and, after her father's death, her mother and many others joined her, and the Franciscan nuns spread widely and rapidly (*see* CLARES, POOR). The relations of friendship and sympathy between St. Clara and St. Francis were very close, and there can be no doubt that she was one of the truest heirs of Francis's inmost spirit. After his death Clara threw herself wholly on the side of those who opposed mitigations in the rule and manner of life, and she was one of the chief upholders of St. Francis's primitive idea of poverty (*see* FRANCISCANS). She was the close friend of Brother Leo and the other "Companions of St. Francis," and they assisted at her death. For 40 years she was abbess at St. Damian's, and the great endeavour of her life was that the rule of the nuns should be purged of the foreign elements that had been introduced, and should become wholly conformable to St. Francis's spirit. She lived just long enough to witness the fulfilment of her great wish, a rule such as she desired being approved by the pope two days before her death on Aug. 11, 1253.

The sources for her life are to be found in the Bollandist *Acta Sanctorum* on Aug. 11, and sketches in such *Lives of the Saints* as Alban Butler's. *See* also Wetzer und Welte, *Kirchenlexicon* (2nd ed.), art. "Clara." (E. C. B.)

CLARE, the name of a famous English family. The ancestor of this historic house, "which played," in Freeman's words, "so great a part alike in England, Wales and Ireland," was Count Godfrey, eldest of the illegitimate sons of Richard the Fearless, duke of Normandy. His son, Count Gilbert of Brionne, had two sons, Richard, lord of Bienfaite and Orbec, and Baldwin, lord of Le Sap and Meulles, both of whom accompanied William the Conqueror to England. Baldwin, known as "De Meulles" or "of Exeter," received the hereditary shrievalty of Devon with great estates in the West Country, and left three sons, William, Robert and Richard, of whom the first and last were in turn sheriffs of Devon. Richard, known as "de Bienfaite," or "of Tunbridge," or "of Clare," was the founder of the house of Clare.

Richard derived his English appellation from his strongholds at Tunbridge and at Clare, at both of which his castle-mounds still remain. The latter, on the borders of Essex and Suffolk, was the head of his great "honour" which lay chiefly in the eastern counties. Appointed joint justiciar in the king's absence abroad, he took a leading part in suppressing the revolt of 1075. By his wife, Rohese, daughter of Walter Giffard, through whom great Giffard estates afterwards came to his house, he left five sons and two daughters. Roger was his heir in Normandy, Walter founded Tintern Abbey, Richard was a monk, and Robert, receiving the forfeited fief of the Baynards in the eastern counties, founded, through his son Walter, the house of FitzWalter (extinct 1432), of whom the most famous was Robert FitzWalter, the leader of the barons against King John. Of this house, spoken of by Jordan Fantosme as "Clarreaus," the Daventrys of Daventry (extinct 1380) and Fawsleys of Fawsley (extinct 1392) were cadets. One of Richard's two daughters married the famous Walter Tirel.

Gilbert, Richard's heir in England, held his castle of Tunbridge against William Rufus, but was wounded and captured. Under Henry I., who favoured the Clares, he obtained a grant of Cardigan and carried his arms into Wales. Dying about 1115, he left four sons, of whom Gilbert, the second, inherited Chepstow, with Nether-Gwent, from his uncle, Walter, the founder of Tintern, and was created earl of Pembroke by Stephen about 1138; he was father of Richard Strongbow, earl of Pembroke (*q.v.*). The youngest son Baldwin fought for Stephen at the battle of Lincoln (1141) and founded the priories of Bourne and Deeping on lands acquired with his wife. The eldest son Richard, who was slain by the Welsh on his way to Cardigan in 1135 or 1136, left two sons, Gilbert and Roger, of whom Gilbert was created earl of Hertfordshire by Stephen.

It was probably because he and the Clares had no interests in Hertfordshire that they were loosely and usually styled the earls of (de) Clare. Dying in 1152, Gilbert was succeeded by his brother Roger, of whom Fitz-Stephen observes that "nearly all the nobles of England were related to the earl of Clare, whose sister, the most beautiful woman in England, had long been desired by the king" (Henry II.). He was constantly fighting the Welsh for his family possessions in Wales and quarrelled with Becket over Tunbridge castle. In 1173 or 1174 he was succeeded by his son Richard as third earl, whose marriage with Amicia, daughter and co-heir of William, earl of Gloucester, was destined to raise the fortunes of his house to their highest point. He and his son Gilbert were among the "barons of the Charter." Gilbert, who became fourth earl in 1217, obtained also, early in 1218, the earldom of Gloucester, with its great territorial "Honour," and the lordship of Glamorgan, in right of his mother; "from this time the house of Clare became the acknowledged head of the baronage." Gilbert had also inherited through his father his grandmother's "Honour of St. Hilary" and a moiety of the Giffard fief; but the vast possessions of his house were still further swollen by his marriage with a daughter of William (Marshal), earl of Pembroke, through whom his son Richard succeeded in 1245 to a fifth of the Marshall lands including the Kilkenny estates in Ireland. Richard's successor, Gilbert, the "Red" earl, died in 1295, the most powerful subject in the kingdom.

On his death his earldoms seem to have been somewhat mysteriously deemed to have passed to his widow Joan, daughter of Edward I.; for her second husband, Ralph de Monthermer, was summoned to parliament in right of them from 1299 to 1306. After her death, however, in 1307, Earl Gilbert's son and namesake was summoned in 1308 as earl of Gloucester and Hertford, though only sixteen. A nephew of Edward II. and brother-in-law of Gaveston, he played a somewhat wavering part in the struggle between the king and the barons. Guardian of the realm in 1311 and regent in 1313, he fell at Bannockburn.

The earl was the last of his mighty line, and his vast possessions in England (in over 20 counties), Wales and Ireland fell to his three sisters, of whom Elizabeth, the youngest, wife of John de Burgh, obtained the "Honour of Clare" and transmitted it to her son William de Burgh, 3rd earl of Ulster, whose daughter brought it to Lionel, son of King Edward III., who was thereupon created Duke of Clarence, a title associated ever since with the royal house. The "Honour of Clare," vested in the crown, still preserves a separate existence, with a court and steward of its own.

Clare College, Cambridge, derived its name from the above Elizabeth, "Lady of Clare," who founded it as Clare Hall in 1347.

Clare County in Ireland derived its name from the family, though whether from Richard Strongbow, or from Thomas de Clare, a younger son, who had a grant of Thomond in 1276, has been deemed doubtful.

Clarenceux King of Arms, an officer of the Heralds' college, derives his style, through Clarence, from Clare.

See J. H. Round's *Geoffrey de Mandeville, Feudal England, Commune of London,* and *Peerage Studies;* also his "Family of Clare" in *Arch. Journ.* lvi., and "Origin of Armorial Bearings" in *Ib.* li.; Parkinson's "Clarence, the origin and bearers of the title," in *The Antiquary,* v.; Clark's "Lords of Glamorgan" in *Arch. Journ.* xxxv.; Planche's "Earls of Gloucester" in *Journ. Arch. Assoc.* xxvi.; Dugdale's *Baronage,* vol. i., and *Monasticon Anglicanum;* G. E. C(okayne)'s *Complete Peerage.* (J. H. R.)

CLARE, JOHN (1793–1864), English poet, known as "the Northamptonshire Peasant Poet," was born at Helpstone, near Peterborough. He was the son of a farm-labourer, and when he was 12 or 13 began to work on a farm himself, attending a school in the evenings. At 16 he fell deeply in love with Mary Joyce, the daughter of a prosperous farmer, who forbade her to meet her lover. Clare never forgot this first love, and in his periods of insanity, long after Mary's death, he used to hold conversations with her, under the delusion that she still lived and was his wife. He tried his hand at many trades, was gardener at Burghley park, enlisted in the militia, and in 1817 worked as a lime-burner; from his last place he was discharged for spending his working hours in distributing copies of a prospectus of a book of his poems, and he was obliged to accept parish relief. The prospectus failed to attract subscribers, but luckily in 1817 a bookseller at Stamford, named Drury, noticed one of Clare's poems, "The Setting Sun," by chance, and befriended the author, introducing him to John Taylor, the publisher of Keats and Shelley. Taylor published Clare's *Poems Descriptive of Rural Life and Scenery* (1820), which attracted great attention, and his *Village Minstrel and other Poems* (1821). The poet was now comparatively prosperous with an annuity of £45. obtained by the patronage of Lord Exeter and other subscribers; but in 1820 he had married Patty Turner, and a growing family made his income inadequate. *The Shepherd's Calendar* (1827) met with little success, and Clare started farm labour again. Worry and overwork made him seriously ill. Earl Fitzwilliam gave him a new cottage and a piece of ground in 1832 but Clare could not settle down; gradually his mind gave way. He was still writing verse, but his last work, the *Rural Muse* (1835), was noticed by "Christopher North" alone. For some time he had shown signs of insanity; and in 1837, in spite of the efforts of his wife to prevent outside interference, he was removed to a private asylum. He seemed happy there, but after a time decided to go home, and set out to walk all the way. Then he was taken to the Northampton general lunatic asylum, where he remained, amusing himself by writing poetry, until his death.

BIBLIOGRAPHY.—The Oxford ed. of his *Poems* (1920), was ed. by Edmund Blunden and Alan Porter; his *Madrigals and Chronicles* by Edmund Blunden (1924). Both these eds. contain biographical introductions. *See* also F. Martin *The Life of John Clare* (1865); and J. L. Cherry *Life and Remains of John Clare* (1873).

CLARE, JOHN FITZGIBBON, 1ST EARL OF (1749–1802), lord chancellor of Ireland, the second son of John Fitzgibbon, was educated at Trinity college, Dublin, where he was highly distinguished as a classical scholar, and at Christ Church, Oxford, where he graduated in 1770. In 1772 he was called to the Irish bar. In 1778 he entered the Irish House of Commons as member for Dublin university, and at first gave a general support to the popular party led by Henry Grattan (*q.v.*). He was, however, from the first hostile to that part of Grattan's policy which aimed at removing the disabilities of the Roman Catholics; he endeavoured to impede the Relief bill of 1778 by raising difficulties about its effect on the Act of Settlement. As early as 1780 Fitzgibbon began to separate himself from the popular or national party by opposing Grattan's declaration of the Irish parliament's right to independence. His hostility to the Catholic claims, and his distrust of parliamentary reform as likely to endanger the connection of Ireland with Great Britain, made him a sincere opponent of the purposes which Grattan had in view. Grattan supported the appointment of Fitzgibbon as attorney-general in 1783, and in 1785 the latter highly eulogized Grattan's character and services to the country in a speech in which he condemned Flood's volunteer movement. He also opposed Flood's Reform bill of 1784; and from this time forward he was in fact the leading spirit in the Irish Government, and the stiffest opponent of all concession to popular demands. In 1784 the permanent committee of revolutionary reformers in Dublin, of whom Napper Tandy was the most conspicuous, invited the sheriffs of counties to call meetings for the election of delegates to attend a convention for the discussion of reform; and when the sheriff of the county of Dublin summoned a meeting for this purpose Fitzgibbon procured his imprisonment for contempt of court, and justified this procedure in parliament, though Lord Erskine declared it grossly illegal. In the course of the debates on Pitt's commercial propositions in 1785, which Fitzgibbon supported in masterly speeches, he referred to Curran in terms which led to a duel between the two lawyers, when Fitzgibbon was accused of a deliberation in aiming at his opponent that was contrary to etiquette. His antagonism to Curran was life-long and bitter, and after he became chancellor his hostility to the famous advocate was said to have driven the latter out of practice. In Jan. 1787 Fitzgibbon introduced a stringent bill for repressing the Whiteboy outrages. His influence with the majority in the Irish parliament defeated Pitt's proposed reform of the tithe system in Ireland, Fitzgibbon refusing even to grant a committee to investigate the subject. On the regency question in 1789 Fitzgibbon, in opposition to Grattan, supported the doctrine of Pitt in a series of powerful speeches which proved him a great constitutional lawyer; he intimated that the choice for Ireland might in certain eventualities rest between complete separation from England and legislative union; and, while he exclaimed as to the latter alternative, "God forbid that I should ever see that day!" he admitted that separation would be the worse evil of the two.

In the same year Lord Lifford resigned the chancellorship, and Fitzgibbon was appointed in his place, being raised to the peerage as Baron Fitzgibbon. His removal to the House of Lords greatly increased his power. "He was," says Lecky, "by far the ablest Irishman who had adopted without restriction the doctrine that the Irish legislature must be maintained in a condition of permanent and unvarying subjection to the English executive." But the English ministry were now embarking on a policy of conciliation in Ireland. The Catholic Relief bill of 1793 was forced on the Irish executive by the cabinet in London, but it passed rapidly and easily through the Irish parliament. Fitzgibbon was opposed to the appointment of Lord Fitzwilliam (*q.v.*) as viceroy in 1795, and was probably the chief influence in procuring his recall; and it was Fitzgibbon who first put it into the head of George III. that the king would violate his coronation oath if he consented to the admission of Catholics to parliament. When Lord Camden, Fitzwilliam's successor in the viceroyalty, arrived in Dublin on March 31, 1795, Fitzgibbon's carriage was violently assaulted by the mob, and he himself was wounded; and in the riots that ensued his house was also attacked. In June 1795 he was created earl of Clare. On the eve of the rebellion he warned the Government to take stringent measures to prevent an outbreak; but he was neither cruel nor immoderate and was inclined to mercy in dealing with individuals. He attempted to save Lord Edward Fitzgerald (*q.v.*) from his fate by giving a friendly warning to his friend, and promising to facilitate his escape from the country. After the rebellion he threw his great influence on the side of clemency.

In Oct. 1798 Lord Clare, who since 1793 had been convinced of the necessity for a legislative union between Great Britain and Ireland, and was equally determined that the union must be unaccompanied by Catholic emancipation crossed to England and pressed his views on Pitt. In 1799 he induced the Irish House of Lords to throw out a bill for providing a permanent endowment Maynooth. On Feb. 10, 1800, Clare in the House of Lords moved the resolution approving the union in a long and powerful speech, in which he reviewed the history of Ireland since the Revolution, attributing the evils of recent years to the independent constitution of 1782, and speaking of Grattan in language of deep personal hatred. He was not aware of the assurance which Cornwallis had been authorized to convey to the Catholics that the union was to pave the way for emancipation, and when he heard of it after the passing of the act he bitterly complained that Pitt and Castlereagh had deceived him. After the union Clare became more violent than ever in his opposition to any policy of concession in Ireland. He died on Jan. 28, 1802.

Lord Clare was the first Irishman since the Revolution to hold the office of lord chancellor of Ireland. As a politician there is no doubt that his bitter and unceasing resistance to reasonable measures of reform did infinite mischief by inflaming the passions of his countrymen, driving them into rebellion, and perpetuating their political and religious divisions.

See W. E. H. Lecky, *History of Ireland in the Eighteenth Century* (1892); J. R. O'Flanagan, *The Hires of the Lord Chancellors and Keepers of the Great Seal in Ireland* (1870); *Cornwallis' Correspondence*, ed. by C. Ross (1859); Charles Phillips, *Recollections of Curran and Some of his Contemporaries* (1822); Henry Grattan, *Memoirs of the Life and Times of the Right Honble. Henry Grattan* (1839–46); Lord Auckland *Journal and Correspondence* (1861); Charles Coote, *History of the Union of Great Britain and Ireland* (1802).

CLARE, a county in the province of Munster, Eire, bounded north by Galway Bay and Co. Galway, east by Lough Derg, the river Shannon, and counties Tipperary and Limerick, south by the estuary of the Shannon, and west by the Atlantic Ocean. The area is 1,231 sq.mi. Pop. (1936) 89,879.

In the eastern mountains two masses of Old Red Sandstone with Silurian cores stand out, the more southerly of which, Slieve Bernagh, rises to a height of 1,746 ft. These masses are flanked by Carboniferous limestone which occupies the north and east of the county. The south-west is composed of Millstone Grit and Coal Measures which extend some distance into the interior. There are many lakes in the central lowlands and bogs are frequent on the higher land. In the southern part, along the banks of the Fergus and Shannon, are bands of rich low grounds called corcasses, of various breadth, indenting the land in a great variety of shapes. They are composed of deep rich loam, and are distinguished as the black corcasses, adapted for tillage, and the blue, used more advantageously as meadow land. The coast is rocky, and occasionally bold precipitous cliffs rise to a considerable height. There are numerous bays around the coast but Liscannor Bay provides the only safe anchorage on the Atlantic side. The River Fergus flows into the estuary of the Shannon, the creeks and bays of which render navigation safe in all winds.

The county, especially on the higher areas of the east and north, is very rich in dolmens. There still exist above a hundred fortified castles, mostly small, several of which are inhabited. Raths or encampments are to be found in every part. They are generally circular, composed either of large stones without mortar or of earth thrown up and surrounded by one or more ditches. The abbeys and other religious houses number more than twenty. Five round towers are to be found in various stages of preservation at Scattery Island, Drumcliffe, Dysert O'Dea, Kilnaboy and Inniscaltra (Lough Derg). The cathedral of the diocese of Killaloe is at the town of that name.

The county, together with part of the neighbouring district, was anciently called Thomond, that is, North Munster. Settlements were effected by the Danes, and in the 13th century by the Anglo-Normans, but without permanently affecting the possession of the district by its native proprietors. In 1543 Murrogh O'Brien submitted to Henry VIII., and received the title of earl of Thomond, on condition of adopting English dress, manners and customs. In 1565 this part of Thomond was added to Connaught, and made one of the six new counties into which that province was divided by Sir Henry Sidney. It was named Clare, the name being traceable either to Richard de Clare (Strongbow), earl of Pembroke, or to his younger brother, Thomas de Clare, who obtained a grant of Thomond from Edward I. in 1276. Towards the close of the reign of Elizabeth, Clare was detached from the government of Connaught and given a separate administration; but it was included with Connaught in Cromwell's schemes and suffered greatly as a result of his policy. At the Restoration it was united to Munster.

Metals and minerals have not been found in sufficient abundance to encourage commercial exploitation. The principal metals are lead, iron and manganese. The Milltown lead mine in the barony of Tulla is probably one of the oldest mines in Ireland and formerly there must have been a very rich deposit. Copper pyrites occurs in several parts of Burren in small quantity. Coal exists in Labasheeda on the right bank of the Shannon, but the few and thin seams are not productive. The nodules of clay-ironstone in the strata that overlie the limestone were mined and smelted as late as 1750. Within ½ mi. of the Milltown lead mine are natural vaulted passages of limestone. The lower limestone of the eastern portion of the county has been found to contain several very large deposits of argentiferous galena. Flags, easily quarried, are procured near Kilrush, and thinner flags near Ennistimon. Slates are quarried in several places, the best being those of Broadford and Killaloe. Very fine black marble is obtained near Ennis; it takes a high polish, and is free from the white spots with which the black Kilkenny marble is marked.

The soil and surface of the county are in general better adapted for grazing than for tillage. Agriculture is in a backward state and little acreage is devoted even to the principal crops of oats and potatoes. Cattle, sheep, poultry and pigs, however, all receive considerable attention. Because of the mountainous nature of the county, nearly one-seventh of the total area is quite barren. There are no extensive manufactures, although flannels and friezes are made for home use, and hosiery of various kinds, chiefly coarse and strong, is made around Ennistimon and other places. There are several fishing stations but the rugged nature of the coast and the rough sea greatly hinder fishermen. Near Pooldoody is the great Burren oyster bed called the Red bank. Crabs and lobsters are caught in the Bay of Galway. In addition to the Shannon salmon fishery, eels abound in every rivulet and form an important article of consumption.

The Great Southern railway line from Limerick to Sligo intersects the centre of the county. From Ennis a branch runs to Ennistimon where it turns south and serves such watering places as Milltown Malbay, Kilkee and Kilrush. Killaloe is the terminus of a railway branch near the site of the Shannon power scheme (*see* SHANNON). Clare has five members in *dail eireann.*

CLAREMONT, a city of Sullivan county, New Hampshire, U.S., in the western part of the state, on the Connecticut river, at the mouth of Sugar river; served by the Boston and Maine railroad. The area is 6 sq.mi. Pop. (1950) 12,811. The falls of Sugar river (223 ft. within the town limits) furnish power for large factories, making shoes, paper, cotton and woollen goods and mining and quarrying machinery. Claremont is the shopping centre of an industrial region—mainly machine tool—including Springfield and Windsor, Vt., Newport, Lebanon and Lake Sunapee, N.H. First settled in 1762, the town was organized in 1764. It was named after Lord Clive's country place.

CLARENCE, DUKES OF. The early history of this English title is identical with that of the family of Clare, earls of Gloucester, who are sometimes called earls of Clare, of which word Clarence is a later form. The first duke of Clarence was Lionel of Antwerp (*see* below), third son of Edward III, who was created duke in 1362 and whose wife Elizabeth was a direct descendant of the Clares, the honour of Clare being among the lands which she brought to her husband. When Lionel died without sons in 1368 the title became extinct; but in 1412 it was revived in favour of Thomas (*see* below), the second son of Henry IV. The third creation took place in 1461, and was in favour of George (*see* below), brother of Edward IV. When this duke was attainted in 1478, his title was forfeited. There was no other creation of a duke of Clarence until 1789, when William, third son of George III, was made a peer under this title. Having merged in the crown when William became king in 1830, the title of duke of Clarence was again revived in 1890 in favour of Albert Victor (1864–92), the elder son of King Edward VII, then prince of Wales, only to become extinct for the fifth time on his death in 1892.

LIONEL OF ANTWERP, duke of Clarence (1338–1368), third son of Edward III, was born at Antwerp on Nov. 29, 1338. Before he was four years of age he was married to Elizabeth (d. 1363), daughter and heiress of William de Burgh, 3rd earl of Ulster (d. 1332), and he entered nominally into possession of her great Irish inheritance. Having been named as his father's representative in England in 1345 and again in 1346, Lionel was created earl of Ulster and joined (in 1355) an expedition into France, but his chief energies were reserved for the affairs of Ireland. Appointed governor of that country, he landed at Dublin in Sept. 1361. In Nov. 1362 he was created duke of Clarence and in the following year his father made an abortive attempt to secure for him the succession to the crown of Scotland. His efforts to secure an effective authority over his Irish lands were only moderately successful; and after holding a parliament at Kilkenny, which passed the celebrated statute of Kilkenny in 1366, he threw up his task in disgust and returned to England. At Milan, on May 28, 1368, he married Violante, only daughter of Galeazzo Visconti, lord of Pavia, who brought him a rich dowry. Some months were then spent in festivities, during which Lionel was taken ill at Alba, where he died on Oct. 17, 1368. His only child Philippa (1355–81), a daughter by his first wife, married in 1368 Edmund Mortimer, 3rd earl of March (1351–81), and through this union Clarence became the ancestor of Edward IV. The poet Chaucer was at one time a page in Lionel's household.

THOMAS, duke of Clarence, was born on Sept. 29, 1389. He paid two visits to Ireland, where he was nominally lord lieutenant from 1401 to 1413. For a short time, in 1412, he replaced his elder brother, afterward King Henry V, as the chief figure in the government. Clarence favoured an alliance with the Orléanist party and led an unsuccessful expedition to France in Aug. 1412. But, after Henry V's accession in 1413, the duke served his brother faithfully, and took part in the preparations for the French war. He was at the siege of Harfleur, but was invalided home before Agincourt, and acted as regent in 1416. During the invasion of Normandy, in 1417, Clarence led the assault to Caen, and, after Henry V's return to England in 1421, he remained in France as the king's lieutenant. He was killed at Baugé while rashly attacking the French and their Scottish allies on March 22, 1421. At the time of his death Clarence was heir to the throne. His marriage with Margaret Holland was childless and his titles became extinct.

GEORGE, duke of Clarence (1449–1478), younger son of Richard, duke of York, was born in Dublin on Oct. 21, 1449. Soon after his elder brother became king as Edward IV in March 1461, he was created duke of Clarence, and his youth was no bar to his appointment as lord lieutenant of Ireland in 1462. In 1466 Clarence was a suitor for the hand of Mary of Burgundy. Later he came under the influence of Richard Neville, earl of Warwick, and, in defiance of the king, was married to the earl's elder daughter, Isabel, at Calais in July 1469. With his father-in-law he supported the rebels in the north of England. When their treachery was discovered, Clarence fled to France in March 1470. Returning to England with Warwick in September, he supported the restoration of Henry VI, and the crown was settled upon himself in case the male line of the Lancastrian dynasty became extinct. But soon after Edward IV returned to England in March 1471, a public reconciliation between the brothers took place, and Clarence then fought for the Yorkists at Barnet and Tewkesbury. After Warwick's death in April 1471, Clarence claimed the whole of the vast estates of the earl, and in March 1472 was created by right of his wife earl of Warwick and Salisbury. However in 1474 Clarence had to accept a partition of the Warwick estates with his younger brother Richard, duke of Gloucester (later Richard III), who had married Warwick's younger daughter Anne. Isabel Neville died in Dec. 1476, and Clarence soon sought to marry, as his second wife, Mary of Burgundy, now duchess. To this marriage Edward IV objected. He became convinced that Clarence was aiming at his throne. The duke was thrown into prison, and in Jan. 1478 the king unfolded the charges against his brother to the parliament. He had slandered the king; had received oaths of allegiance to himself and his heirs; had prepared for a new rebellion; and was in short incorrigible. Both houses of parliament passed the bill of attainder, and the sentence of death which followed was carried out secretly in the Tower of London on Feb. 18, 1478. Soon after the event the rumour gained ground that he had been drowned in a butt of malmsey wine. Ambitious, weak and treacherous, Clarence lacked the ability of his brothers, Edward IV and Richard III. Two of the duke's children survived their father: Margaret, countess of Salisbury (1473–1541), and Edward, earl of Warwick (1475–99), who passed the greater part of his life in prison and was beheaded in Nov. 1499.

BIBLIOGRAPHY.—W. Stubbs, *Constitutional History,* vol. iii, 5th ed. (Oxford, 1903); Sir J. H. Ramsay, *Lancaster and York,* 2 vol. (Oxford, 1892); E. Curtis, *A History of Medieval Ireland from 1014–1513,* 2nd ed. (London, Toronto, 1938); C. L. Scofield, *The Life and Reign of Edward the Fourth* (London, New York, 1923). (T. B. P.)

CLARENDON, EDWARD HYDE, 1ST EARL OF (1609–

1674), English statesman and the historian of the Great Rebellion, son of Henry Hyde of Dinton, Wiltshire, was born on Feb. 18, 1609. He entered Magdalen hall, Oxford, in 1622 (having been refused a demyship at Magdalen college), and graduated B.A. in 1626. In 1625 he entered the Middle Temple. At the university his abilities were more conspicuous than his industry, and at the bar his time was devoted more to general reading and to the society of eminent scholars and writers than to the study of law treatises. Among his friends were included Ben Jonson, John Selden, Edmund Waller, John Hales and especially Lord Falkland.

In 1629 he married Anne, daughter of Sir George Ayliffe, who died six months afterward; and secondly, in 1634, Frances, daughter of Sir Thomas Aylesbury, master of requests. In 1633 he was called to the bar and quickly obtained a good practice. His marriages had gained for him influential friends, and in Dec. 1634 he was made keeper of the writs and rolls of the common pleas. He was returned to the Short Parliament in 1640 as member for Wootton Bassett. The violations and perversions of the law which characterized the 12 preceding years of rule without parliament drove Hyde into the ranks of the popular party. He assailed the jurisdiction of the earl marshal's court, and in the Long Parliament, in which he sat for Saltash, renewed his attacks and practically effected its suppression. In 1641 he served on the committees for inquiring into the status of the Councils of Wales and of the North, and took an important part in the proceedings against the judges. He supported Strafford's impeachment and did not vote against the attainder, though he made subsequently an unsuccessful attempt through Essex to avert the capital penalty. Hyde's allegiance, however, to the Church of England was as staunch as his support of the law, and was soon to separate him from the popular party. He showed special energy in his opposition to the Root and Branch bill, and, though made chairman of the committee on the bill on June 11 in order to silence his opposition, he caused by his successful obstruction the failure of the measure. By the beginning of the second session he was regarded as one of the king's ablest supporters in the commons. He opposed the demand by the parliament to choose the king's ministers, and also the Grand Remonstrance, to which he wrote a reply published by the king.

He now definitely, though not openly, joined the royal cause but, in order to serve the king's interests more effectually, he refused to take office with John Colepeper and Falkland in Jan. 1642. Charles undertook to do nothing in the commons without the advice of these three. Nevertheless, a few days afterward, without their knowledge and by the advice of Lord Digby, he attempted the arrest of the five members, a resort to force which reduced Hyde to despair and which indeed seemed to show that things had gone too far for an appeal to the law. He persevered, nevertheless, in his legal policy, joined the king openly at York in June and continued to compose the king's answers and declarations in which he appealed to the "known laws of the land" against the arbitrary and illegal acts of a seditious majority in the parliament, his advice to the king being "to shelter himself wholly under the law . . . presuming that the king and the law together would have been strong enough for any encounter." Hyde's appeal had great influence, and gained for the king's cause half the nation. It by no means, however, met with universal support among the royalists, Hobbes jeering at Hyde's love for "mixed monarchy," and the courtiers expressing their disapproval of the "spirit of accommodation" which "wounded the regality." It was destined to failure because Charles was simultaneously carrying on another and an inconsistent policy, listening to very different advisers, such as the queen and Digby, and resolving on measures without Hyde's knowledge or approval.

In spite of Hyde's efforts war broke out. He was expelled from the house of commons on Aug. 11, 1642, and was one of those later excepted from pardon. He was present at Edge Hill, though not as a combatant, and followed the king to Oxford, residing at All Souls college from Oct. 1642 till March 1645. On Feb. 22, 1643, he was made a privy councillor and knighted, and on March 3 appointed chancellor of the exchequer. He was an influential member of the "Junto" which met weekly to discuss business before it was laid before the privy council. At the Uxbridge negotiations in Jan. 1645, where he acted as principal manager on the king's side, he tried to win individuals by promises of places and honours. He promoted the summons of the Oxford Parliament in Dec. 1643 as a counterpoise to the Long Parliament. Hyde's policy and measures, however, all failed. They had been weakly and irregularly supported by the king, and were fiercely opposed by the military party, which was urging Charles to trust to force and arms alone and eschew all compromise and concessions. Charles fell now under the influence of persons less affected by legal and constitutional scruples.

Hyde's influence was much diminished, and on March 4, 1645, he left the king for Bristol as one of the guardians of the prince of Wales and governors of the west. After Hopton's defeat on Feb. 16, 1646, at Torrington, Hyde accompanied the prince, on March 4, to Scilly, and on April 17, for greater security, to Jersey. He strongly disapproved of the prince's removal to France by the queen's order and of the schemes to restore the king with assistance from abroad, refused to accompany him and signed a bond to prevent Jermyn's scheme for the sale of Jersey to the French. He refused to compound for his own estate. While in Jersey he resided first at St. Helier and afterwards at Elizabeth castle with Sir George Carteret. He composed the first portion of his *History,* begun in Scilly, and kept in touch with events by means of an enormous correspondence. In 1648 he published *A Full Answer to an Infamous and Traitorous Pamphlet . . .*, a reply to the resolution of the parliament to present no more addresses to the king and a vindication of Charles.

On the outbreak of the second Civil War Hyde left Jersey (June 26, 1648) to join the queen and prince at Paris. He landed at Dieppe, sailed from that port to Dunkirk, and thence followed the prince to the Thames, where Charles had met the fleet, but was captured and robbed by a privateer and only joined the prince in September after the latter's return to The Hague. He strongly disapproved of the king's concessions at Newport. When the army broke off the treaty and brought Charles to trial he endeavoured to save his life, and after the execution drew up a letter to the several European sovereigns invoking their assistance to avenge it. Hyde strongly opposed Charles II's ignominious surrender to the Covenanters, the alliance with the Scots and the Scottish expedition, desiring to accomplish whatever was possible there through Montrose and the royalists and inclined rather to an attempt in Ireland. His advice was not followed and, as an excuse for retiring, he gladly accepted a mission with Cottington to Spain to obtain money from the Roman Catholic powers and to arrange an alliance between Owen O'Neill and Ormonde for the recovery of Ireland, arriving at Madrid on Nov. 26, 1649. The defeat, however, of the Scots at Dunbar and the confirmation of Cromwell's ascendancy influenced the Spanish government against Hyde and Cottington, and they were ordered to leave in Dec. 1650. Hyde arrived at Antwerp in June 1651, and in Dec. rejoined Charles at Paris after the latter's escape from Worcester. He now became one of his chief advisers, accompanying him in his change of residence to Cologne in Sept. 1654 and to Bruges in 1656, and was appointed lord chancellor on Jan. 13, 1658. His influence was henceforth maintained in spite of the intrigues of both Romanists and Presbyterians, as well as the violent and openly displayed hostility of the queen, and was employed unremittingly in the endeavour to keep Charles faithful to the church and constitution and in the prevention of unwise concessions and promises which might estrange the general body of the royalists. In 1656, during the war between England and Spain, Charles received offers of help from the latter power provided he could gain a port in England, but Hyde discouraged small isolated attempts. He expected much from Cromwell's death in 1658. In 1656 he made an alliance with the Levellers, and was informed of their plots to assassinate the protector, without apparently expressing any disapproval. He was well supplied with information from England and guided the action of the royalists with great ability and wisdom during the interval between Cromwell's death and the Restoration. He urged patience and advocated the obstruction of a settlement between the factions contending for power and the fomentation of their jealousies rather than premature risings, though he did acquiesce in the abortive attempt of Aug. 1659.

The Restoration was a complete triumph for Hyde's policy. In his history he lays no stress on his own great part in it, but it was because of him that the Restoration was a national one, by the consent and invitation of parliament representing the whole people and not through the medium of one powerful faction enforcing its will upon a minority, and that it was not only a restoration of Charles but a restoration of constitutional monarchy. For by Hyde's advice concessions to the inconvenient demands of special factions had been avoided by referring the decision to a "free parliament," and the declaration of Breda reserved for parliament the settlement of the questions of amnesty, religious toleration and the proprietorship of forfeited lands.

Hyde entered London with the king and immediately obtained the chief place in the government. He retained the chancellorship of the exchequer till May 13, 1661, when he surrendered it to Lord Ashley. As lord chancellor he took his seat as speaker of the house of lords and in the court of chancery on June 1, 1660. On Nov. 3, 1660, he was made Baron Hyde of Hindon, and on April 20, 1661, at the coronation, Viscount Cornbury and earl of Clarendon, receiving a grant from the king of £20,000 and at different times of various small estates and Irish rents. He refused a large grant of land in the Fen country. By the marriage of his daughter Anne to James, duke of York, celebrated in secret in Sept. 1660, he became related to the royal family and the grandfather of two English sovereigns—Queen Mary and Queen Anne.

A rare occasion now offered itself of settling the religious question on a broad principle of comprehension or toleration; for the monarchy had been restored not by the supporters of the church alone but largely by the influence and aid of the Nonconformists and also of the Roman Catholics, who were all united at that moment by a common loyalty to the throne. Clarendon appears to have approved of comprehension but not of toleration. He had already in April 1660 sent to discuss terms with the leading Presbyterians in England, and after the Restoration offered bishoprics to several, including Richard Baxter. He drew up the royal declaration of October, promising limited episcopacy and a revised prayer book and ritual, which was subsequently thrown out by the convention, and he appears to have anticipated some kind of settlement from the Savoy conference which sat in April 1661. The failure of the latter proved perhaps that the differences were too great for compromise, and widened the breach. The parliament immediately proceeded to pass, between 1661 and 1665, the series of narrow and tyrannical measures against the dissenters known as the Clarendon code: the Corporation act, the Act of Uniformity, the Conventicle act and the Five-Mile act. Clarendon was not in fact the originator of these acts and in 1662 he sought to mitigate the effects of the Act of Uniformity. But his disapproval of the king's declaration in favour of indulgence (Dec. 26, 1662), and perhaps also of its probable author Arlington, drove him on to the side of the commons. He recorded his approval of the Conventicle and Five-Mile acts and ended by taking alarm at plots and rumours and regarding the great party of Nonconformists, through whose co-operation the monarchy had been restored, as a danger to the state whose "faction was their religion."

Meanwhile Clarendon's influence and direction had been predominant in nearly all departments of state. He supported the exception of the actual regicides from the indemnity, but only 10 out of the 26 condemned were executed, and Clarendon, with the king's support, prevented the passing of a bill in 1661 for the execution of 13 more. He upheld the Act of Indemnity against all the attempts of the royalists to upset it. The conflicting claims to estates were left to be decided by the law. The confiscations of the usurping government accordingly were cancelled, while the properly executed transactions between individuals were necessarily upheld. There can be little doubt that the principle followed was the only safe one in the prevailing confusion. The settlement of the church lands which was directed by Clarendon presented equal difficulties and involved equal hardships. In settling Scotland, Clarendon's aim was to uphold the English supremacy. He proposed to establish a council at Whitehall to govern Scottish affairs, and sought to restore episcopacy through the medium of Archbishop James Sharp. His influence, however, ended with the ascendancy of Lauderdale in 1663. In Ireland, while anxious for an establishment upon a solid Protestant basis, he urged "temper and moderation and justice" in securing it. He supported Ormonde's wise and enlightened Irish administration, and opposed the prohibition of the import of Irish cattle into England, incurring thereby great unpopularity. He was a member of the council for foreign plantations, and one of the eight lords proprietors of Carolina in 1663; and in 1664 sent a commission to settle disputes in New England. In the department of foreign affairs he had less influence. In 1664 he demanded, on behalf of Charles, French support and a loan of £50,000 against disturbance at home, thus initiating the ignominious system of pensions and dependence upon France. But he was the promoter neither of the sale of Dunkirk on Oct. 27, 1662, the author of which seems to have been the earl of Sandwich, nor of the Dutch war. He attached considerable value to Dunkirk, but when its sale was decided he conducted the negotiations and effected the bargain. He had concluded a treaty for the settlement of disputes with Holland on Sept. 4, 1662. But when hostilities were declared on Feb. 22, 1665, Clarendon gave his support to the war, asserted the extreme claims of the English crown over the British seas and contemplated fresh cessions from the Dutch and an alliance with Sweden and Spain. According to his own account he initiated the policy of the triple alliance, but it seems clear that his inclination toward France continued in spite of French intervention in favour of Holland; and he took part in the negotiations for ending the war by an undertaking with Louis XIV implying neutrality, while the latter seized Flanders. The crisis in this feeble foreign policy and in the general official mismanagement was reached in June 1667, when the Dutch burned several ships at Chatham.

The whole responsibility for the national calamity and disgrace was unjustly thrown on the shoulders of Clarendon. He was unpopular among all classes: among the royalists on account of the Act of Indemnity, among the Presbyterians because of the Act of Uniformity. Every kind of maladministration was currently ascribed to him, designs to govern by a standing army and corruption. He was credited with having married Charles purposely to a barren queen in order to raise his own grandchildren to the throne, with having sold Dunkirk to France, and his magnificent house in St. James's was nicknamed "Dunkirk house," while on the day of the Dutch attack on Chatham the mob set up a gibbet at his gate and broke his windows, holding him responsible for English lack of success in the war. He was disliked by the royal mistresses, whose favour he did not condescend to seek and whose presence often aroused his reproaches. Surrounded by such general and violent animosity, Clarendon's only hope could be in the support of the king. But Charles, long weary of the old chancellor's rebukes, was especially incensed at this time because of his failure to secure Frances Stuart (La Belle Stuart) for his seraglio—a disappointment which he attributed to Clarendon—and was now alarmed by the hostility which his administration had excited. He did not scruple to sacrifice at once the old adherent of his house and fortunes. By the direction of Charles, James advised Clarendon to resign before the meeting of parliament, but in an interview with the king on Aug. 26, 1667, Clarendon refused to deliver up the seal unless dismissed. On Aug. 30 he was deprived of the great seal, for which the king received the thanks of the parliament on Oct. 16. On Nov. 12 his impeachment was brought up to the lords, but the latter refused to order his committal on the ground that the commons had only accused him of treason in general without specifying any particular charge. Clarendon wrote humbly to the king asking for pardon and that the prosecution might be prevented, but Charles had openly taken part against him and, though desiring his escape, would not order or assist his departure for fear of the commons. Through the bishop of Hereford, however, on

Nov. 29 he pressed Clarendon to fly, promising that he should not during his absence suffer in his honour or fortune. Clarendon embarked the same night for Calais, where he arrived on Dec. 2. The lords, taking this as admission of guilt, immediately passed an act for his banishment and ordered the petition forwarded by him to parliament to be burned.

The rest of Clarendon's life was passed in exile in various parts of France. His sudden banishment entailed great personal hardships. On arriving at Calais he fell dangerously ill; and Louis XIV, anxious to propitiate England, sent him peremptory and repeated orders to quit France. At Evreux, on April 23, 1668, he was the victim of a murderous assault by English sailors, who attributed to him the nonpayment of their wages. For some time he was not allowed to see any of his children; even correspondence with him was rendered treasonable by the Act of Banishment.

Clarendon bore his troubles with great dignity and fortitude. He found consolation in religious duties, and devoted a portion of every day to the composition of his *Contemplations on the Psalms* and of his moral essays. He now finished his *History* and his *Autobiography*. Soon after reaching Calais he had written, on Dec. 7, 1667, to the University of Oxford, of which he was chancellor, desiring as his last request that the university should believe in his innocence and remember him, though there could be no further mention of him in their public devotions, in their private prayers.

He entertained to the last hopes of obtaining leave to return to England, but his petitions were not even answered or noticed. He died at Rouen on Dec. 9, 1674. He was buried in Westminster abbey a year later, at the foot of the steps leading to the Henry VII chapel. He left two sons, Henry, 2nd earl of Clarendon, and Lawrence, earl of Rochester, and a daughter Anne, duchess of York; a third son, Edward, having predeceased him.

As a statesman Clarendon had obvious limitations and failings. He brought to the consideration of political questions an essentially legal but also a narrow mind, conceiving the law, "that great and admirable mystery," and the constitution as fixed, unchangeable and sufficient for all time, in contrast with John Pym, who regarded them as living organisms capable of continual development and evolution. He was incapable of comprehending and governing the new conditions and forces created by the civil wars. His character, however, and therefore, to some extent, his career bear the indelible marks of greatness. He maintained his self-respect and dignity at a licentious court, and his integrity in an age of corruption. His industry and devotion to public business were rendered all the more conspicuous by the negligence, inferiority in business and frivolity of his successors. As lord chancellor Clarendon made no great impression in the court of chancery. His early legal training had long been interrupted, and his political preoccupations probably rendered necessary the delegation of many of his judicial duties to others. As chancellor of Oxford university, Clarendon promoted the restoration of order and various educational reforms. In 1753 his manuscripts were left to the university by his grandson Lord Cornbury, and in 1868 the money gained by publication was spent in erecting the Clarendon laboratory, the profits of the *History* having provided in 1713 a building for the university press adjoining the Sheldonian theatre, known since the removal of the press to its present quarters as the Clarendon building.

As a writer and historian Clarendon occupies a high place in English literature. His great work, the *History of the Rebellion*, is composed in the grand style. A characteristic feature is the wonderful series of well-known portraits, drawn with great skill and liveliness and especially praised by John Evelyn and by Macaulay. The book is, however, not well proportioned and is overloaded with state papers, misplaced and tedious in the narrative. The published *History* is mainly a compilation of two separate original manuscripts, the first being the history proper, written between 1646 and 1648, with the advantage of a fresh memory and the help of various documents and authorities, and ending in March 1644, and the second being the *Life*, extending from 1609 to 1660, but composed long afterward in exile and without the aid of papers between 1668 and 1670. The value of any statement, therefore, in the published *History* depends chiefly on whether it is taken from the *History* proper or the *Life*. In 1671 these two manuscripts were united by Clarendon with certain alterations and modifications, making books i–vii of the published *History*, while books viii–xv were written subsequently and, being composed for the most part without materials, are often inaccurate, with the notable exception of book ix, made up from two narratives written at Jersey in 1646, and containing very little from the *Life*. The inaccuracies are not the result of wilful misrepresentation but of failure of memory and of the disadvantages under which the author laboured in exile. In general, Clarendon, like many of his contemporaries, failed signally to comprehend the real issues and principles at stake in the great struggle, laying far too much stress on personalities and never understanding the real aims and motives of the Presbyterian party.

BIBLIOGRAPHY.—1. Editions of the *History:* The work was first published in 1702–04 from a copy of a transcript made by Clarendon's secretary, with a few unimportant alterations. This was the object of a violent attack by John Oldmixon for supposed changes and omissions in *Clarendon and Whitelocke Compared* (1727) and again in a preface to his *History of England* (1730). The charges were repelled and refuted by John Burton in the *Genuineness of Lord Clarendon's History Vindicated* (1744). The history was first published from the original by B. Bandinel, 8 vol. (Oxford, 1826), the best edition being that by W. D. Macray, 6 vol. (Oxford, 1888). *The Lord Clarendon's History . . . Compleated,* a supplement containing portraits and illustrative papers, was published in 1717, and *An Appendix to the History,* containing a life, speeches and various pieces, in 1724. The *Sutherland Clarendon* in the Bodleian library at Oxford contains several thousand portraits and illustrations of the *History*. *The Life of Edward, Earl of Clarendon . . . (and the) Continuation of the History . . .*, the first consisting of that portion of the *Life* not included in the *History,* and the second of the account of Clarendon's administration and exile in France, begun in 1672, was published in 1759, the *History of the Reign of King Charles II From the Restoration . . .*, published about 1755, being a surreptitious edition of this work, of which the latest and best edition is that of the Clarendon Press, 2 vol. (Oxford, 1857).

2. Other works: Among Clarendon's other works may be mentioned *A Brief View . . . of the Dangerous . . . Errors in . . . Mr. Hobbes's Book Entitled "Leviathan"* (1676); *The History of the Rebellion and Civil War in Ireland* (1719); *Essays Moral and Entertaining on the Various Faculties and Passions of the Human Mind* (pr. 2 vol., London, 1815, and in *British Prose Writers,* vol. i, 1819).

See also T. H. Lister, *Life and Administration of Edward, 1st Earl of Clarendon,* 3 vol. (London, 1838); Sir Charles Firth in *Dictionary of National Biography,* vol. xxviii (London, 1891), and his *Edward Hyde, Earl of Clarendon* (Oxford, 1909); Sir Henry Craik, *The Life of Edward, Earl of Clarendon,* 2 vol. (London, 1911).

CLARENDON, GEORGE WILLIAM FREDERICK VILLIERS, 4TH EARL OF (1800–1870), of the second creation, English statesman, was born in London on Jan. 12, 1800, and had—as Charles Greville once said—"the unspeakable advantage of being plain George Villiers, and having to fight his own way in the world," as a young man. He was at Christ's Hospital and at St. John's college, Cambridge. In 1820 Castlereagh appointed him attaché at St. Petersburg, where he served till 1823; but then lack of funds made him become a commissioner of customs, in which post he distinguished himself at Dublin and Paris. Strong intelligence, an agreeable presence and a gift for languages picked him out, and in 1833 Palmerston made him British ambassador at Madrid.

For six years he wrestled with the intricacies of Spanish politics, while the queen of Spain was a minor, the country torn by civil war, and his home government too preoccupied to afford him full support. In 1838 he succeeded an uncle as earl of Clarendon. Early in 1839 he returned to England and married. He refused to go to Canada as governor general, but was persuaded to enter Melbourne's cabinet as lord privy seal, becoming also chancellor of the duchy of Lancaster for the last few months of the government. This spell of office was chiefly notable for a painful opposition to a colleague, since Clarendon thought that Palmerston's policy on the Egyptian question was dangerously hostile to France; and he was delighted when the government resigned in 1841. He took the board of trade when the Whigs resumed office in 1846, and accepted a year later, reluctantly, the viceroyalty of Ireland, then in the throes of famine. He insisted on being armed with a coercion act, and so was able both to keep the peace and to foster projects for relief. The land legislation he supported only crowded Ireland with selfish speculators; but this result was not apparent till after he had left office in 1852.

Early in 1853 Clarendon succeeded to the one post he coveted, and became the only professional diplomat ever to serve as foreign secretary. The foreign office staff took to him at once—he was known there, for many years after his death, as "the great Lord Clarendon"—but he found foreign affairs in confusion; he was never able to get his head clear of the mass of dispatches and could do nothing to stop the country "drifting" (the word was his) into the Crimean War. He was hampered by his own mistrust of Lord Stratford de Redcliffe, the ambassador at Constantinople, and by time-wasting interference from his prime minister, Lord Aberdeen, before the war began; and while it went on his talents for conciliation were mainly expended on keeping his colleagues in cabinet together. He had already secured the friendship of Napoleon III and was able by judicious argument face to face to persuade the emperor not to go to the Crimea himself. The French tired of the war before the British, and Clarendon had to use the full range of his diplomatic skill to secure a fair peace at Paris in March 1856. He was offered, but refused, a marquisate on its conclusion.

In 1858 he resigned with Palmerston's cabinet and did not rejoin him in 1859, partly since Lord John Russell insisted on having the foreign office himself and partly since Clarendon disagreed with the Italian policy on which the new government was founded. He had six years in retirement, advising his friends in office, rejoined them in 1864 as chancellor of the duchy of Lancaster, and became foreign secretary again on Palmerston's death in 1865. The fall of Russell's government released him after a few months, but he returned to the foreign office again, under Gladstone, at the end of 1868. He engaged in a wholly unsuccessful attempt, during the winter of 1869–70, to persuade Bismarck to reduce Prussian armaments; and died of overwork, just when Europe had most need of him, on June 27, 1870, three weeks before the outbreak of the Franco-German War. "If your father had lived," Bismarck said once to Clarendon's daughter Lady Emily Russell, "he would have prevented the war."

See Sir Herbert Maxwell, *Life and Letters of the Fourth Earl of Clarendon*, 2 vol. (London, 1913). (M. R. D. F.)

CLARENDON, HENRY HYDE, 2ND EARL OF (1638–1709), English statesman, eldest son of the historian, was born on June 2, 1638, and succeeded to the title on his father's death in 1674. James II made him lord lieutenant of Ireland (Sept. 1685) where he became an unwilling instrument of the king's desire to replace Protestants in high positions by Roman Catholics. He was recalled in Jan. 1687. At the time of the revolution he played a vacillating part, but opposed the settlement of the crown on William and Mary, and remained a nonjuror all his life. On June 24, 1690, he was arrested, by order of his niece, Queen Mary, on a charge of plotting against William, and though liberated for a time, was again imprisoned in Jan. 1691 on the evidence of Richard Graham, Lord Preston. He was released in July of that year, and from that time until his death, on Oct. 31, 1709, lived in retirement.

His public career had been neither distinguished nor useful, but it seems natural to ascribe its failure to small abilities and to the conflict between personal ties and political convictions which drew him in opposite directions, rather than, following Macaulay, to motives of self-interest. He was a man of some literary taste, a fellow of the Royal society (1684), the author of *The History and Antiquities of the Cathedral Church at Winchester, Continued by S. Gale* (1715), and the publisher, with his brother Rochester, of his father's *History* (1702–04).

He was succeeded by his only son, Edward (1661–1724), as 3rd earl of Clarendon; and, the latter having no surviving son, the title passed to Henry, 2nd earl of Rochester (1672–1753), at whose death without male heirs it became extinct in the Hyde line. (For the other Clarendon line, *see* above.)

CLARENDON, CONSTITUTIONS OF, 16 articles defining relations between church and king in England, which Thomas Becket, Roger, archbishop of York, and 12 bishops promised to observe at Clarendon (Jan. 1164) in the presence of Henry II, lay and other ecclesiastical magnates. The constitutions were presented as a simple record of some customs of the realm observed in the reign of Henry I. This was not exact, but there is little doubt that they were consonant with Henry I's claims, and that Henry II's purpose was to secure the liberties and dignities of his grandfather.

Controversy concentrated on three articles. Article 3 exposed clerics convicted on criminal charges in church courts to secular as well as ecclesiastical punishment, and left room for the trial of clerics on such charges in the king's court at its discretion. Trial of clerics in lay courts had become increasingly obnoxious to clergy during the previous hundred years as they inclined toward more exalted views of clerical status, but Becket's vehement opposition to double punishment of clerical felons was unusual. His objection was sanctioned by his death and miracles and formally enunciated by Pope Alexander III (about 1177). Henry II, after 1176, left clerics accused of common-law felonies to ecclesiastical trial and punishment. Article 4 prohibited clergy from leaving the realm without royal permission. Article 8 would have compelled an appellant from an archdeacon's court to appeal first to the bishop, then to the archbishop and only as a last resort and with royal permission to the pope. These restrictions had been made anachronistic by increasing resort to papal justice in a widening range of cases at all stages of litigation. Henry II abandoned them, with safeguards for royal rights, in 1172. Other controversial articles excluded from church courts litigation over debts and advowsons; prohibited excommunication of the king's immediate tenants and officials (both groups included clerics) without his consent; reserved to the king custody of the possessions of vacant sees and royal monasteries, and defined the procedure for filling the vacancies.

Important uncontroversial provisions rejected procedure on secret information against laymen in church courts, and excluded from church courts litigation over land held in lay fee.

With the exceptions noted, the constitutions were maintained in principle by Henry II and his successors, despite intermittent clerical complaint. In practice, the limitations on ecclesiastical jurisdiction—notably, the attempted exclusion of pleas of debt from church courts—were not definitive.

See A. L. Poole, *From Domesday Book to Magna Carta, 1087–1216* (Oxford, New York, 1951); J. W. Gray, "The Ius Praesentandi in England," *English Historical Review*, vol. 67 (London, 1952). An English translation of the text is in D. C. Douglas and G. W. Greenaway (eds.), *English Historical Documents, 1042–1189* (London, New York, 1953). (ER. S.)

CLARES, POOR, otherwise CLARISSES, Franciscan nuns, so called from their foundress, St. Clara (*q.v.*). She was professed by St. Francis in the Portiuncula in 1212, and two years later she and her first companions were established in the convent of St. Damian at Assisi. The nuns formed the "Second Order of St. Francis," the friars being the "First Order" and the Tertiaries (*q.v.*) the "Third."

Before Clara's death in 1253, the Second Order had spread all over Italy and into Spain, France and Germany; in England they were introduced about 1293 and established in London, outside Aldgate, where their name of Minoresses survives in the Minories; there were only two other English houses before the dissolution.

St. Francis gave the nuns no rule, but only a "Form of Life" and a "Last Will," each only five lines long and coming to no more than an inculcation of his idea of evangelical poverty. Something more than this became necessary as soon as the institute began to spread; and during Francis's absence in the east, 1219, his supporter Cardinal Hugolino composed a rule which made the Franciscan nuns practically a species of unduly strict Benedictines, St. Francis's special characteristics being eliminated. St. Clara made it her life work to have this rule altered and to get the Franciscan character of the Second Order restored; in 1247 a "Second Rule" was approved which went a long way toward satisfying her desires, and finally in 1253 a "Third," which practically gave what she wanted. This rule has come to be known as the "Rule of the Clares"; it is one of great poverty, seclusion and austerity of life. Most of the convents adopted it, but several clung to that of 1247. To bring about conformity St. Bonaventura, while general (1264), obtained papal permission to modify the rule of 1253, somewhat mitigating its austerities and allowing the convents to have fixed incomes. This rule was adopted in many convents, but many more adhered to the strict rule of 1253. Indeed a countertendency toward a greater strictness set in, and a number of reforms were initiated, introducing an appalling austerity of life.

See Heimbucher, *Orden und Kongregationen* (1896), i. §§ 47, 48, who gives references to all the literature; and *Catholic Encyclopaedia*, art. "Clares."

CLARET is the type-name popularly applied to any dry, tart, light- or medium-bodied table wine of ruby red colour. Wines of this general type are the most widely-used mealtime wines in almost every wine-growing country. They range from high-quality wines, produced under ideal conditions from grapes of the noblest character, to very humble *vins ordinaires,* as common wines are called in France. They may rise to the challenge of many years of aging, improving all the while, or they may be at their best when fairly young.

The name originated with the English, to whom in the 12th century claret meant simply a red wine of lighter colour than the very dark wines of southern Europe. In the 12th and 13th centuries red and white wines were sometimes blended to produce claret. Gradually, however, the term came to be applied to the red wines of the Bordeaux vineyards, which were lighter in colour than those of the higher country toward the Pyrenees. When in 1152 the marriage of Henry of Anjou (later Henry II) and Eleanor of Aquitaine brought the whole of Aquitaine under English sovereignty, the merchants of Bordeaux acquired the rights of crown subjects; they used their privileges in London to promote the wine trade from Bordeaux at the expense of that from Rouen and elsewhere. Eventually an export tax was levied on wines at Bordeaux for the benefit of the king's house, and for this reason the English were encouraged to consume Bordeaux wines. Inasmuch as English rule over Aquitaine lasted three centuries, the use of Bordeaux red wines, or clarets, became firmly fixed. Claret is far now from the meaning of the French word "clairette," which refers to a white wine faintly tinged with red.

The greatest clarets of the Bordeaux region come, as a rule, from the two viticultural districts of Médoc and Graves, which lie along the left banks of the Gironde and the Garonne, respectively. There the best vineyards regularly yield wines capable of improving with age and in good years distinguished for their bouquet and balance. Even in these districts, however, there are many grades of clarets, ranging down through five official classes of better growths, or *crûs,* as determined by a jury in 1855, to such commoner ones as "bourgeois," "artisan" and "peasant."

Because in this region growing conditions vary widely from year to year, vintage years matter greatly to the producers of Bordeaux wines. Some of the most noted red wines grown in a favourable year in Médoc or Graves do not mature sufficiently to please the palate until they have aged ten years, and may improve steadily thereafter for a couple of decades or more. But even the most notable of them, grown in a poor year, may pass their zenith before they are seven. And many lesser wines, even in the good years, are sold to be drunk with meals much earlier.

The Cabernet Sauvignon, whose sweet, violet-odoured fruit grows in small, loose bunches, is the chief vine grown in the Bordeaux region to produce great clarets. However, nearly all vineyards have other grape varieties for claret, including the Carmenère, Gros-Cabernet, Malbec, Merlot and Petit Verdot.

Italy, Spain, Portugal and other countries of Europe have developed their own styles of claret, often from grapes nurtured through centuries on their own soils. In the newer lands, including the Americas, Australia and South Africa, adaptable grape varieties transplanted from those countries as well as from the Gironde are used. Thus in California the Cabernet Sauvignon is favoured in those parts where it can be grown under ideal conditions but some other varieties are more widely employed, including the more productive Zinfandel, probably of Hungarian origin, which produces a fresh, fruity wine not usually given to long aging. (*See* WINE.) (H. A. Cw.)

BIBLIOGRAPHY.—André L. Simon, *Wine and the Wine Trade* (1921); Ed. Féret, *Bordeaux et ses vins classés par ordre de mérite* (Bordeaux, 1908); F. Malvezin, *Bordeaux: histoire de la vigne et du vin en Aquitaine depuis les origines jusqu'à nos jours* (1919); Wine Trade Record: *Clarets and Sauternes* (1920); H. Warner Allen, *The Wines of France* (1924); P. Morton Shand, *A Book of French Wines* (1928); Wine Advisory Board, San Francisco, *Wine Handbook Series,* ii (1943).

CLARETIE, JULES ARSÈNE ARNAUD (1840–1913), French writer, director of the Théâtre Français, was born at Limoges Dec. 3, 1840. He was dramatic critic to the *Figaro* and to the *Opinion nationale,* a newspaper correspondent during the Franco-German War, and during the Commune a staff-officer in the National Guard. In 1885 he became director of the Théâtre Français, and from that time devoted himself chiefly to its administration. He was elected a member of the Academy in 1888. He died in Paris on Dec. 23, 1913.

The long list of his works includes *Histoire de la révolution de 1870–71* (new ed., 5 vols., 1875–76); *Cinq ans après; l'Alsace et la Lorraine depuis l'annexion* (1876); some annual volumes of reprints of his articles in the weekly press, entitled *La Vie à Paris; La Vie moderne au théâtre* (1868–69); *Molière, sa vie et son oeuvre* (1871); *Histoire de la littérature française, 900–1900* (2nd ed. 1905); *Candidat!* (1887), a novel of contemporary life; *Brichanteau, comédien français* (1896); several plays, some of which are based on novels of his own; and the opera, *La Navarraise* based on his novel *La Cigarette,* and written with Henri Cain to the music of Massenet. *La Navarraise* was first produced at Covent Garden (June 1894) with Mme. Calvé in the part of Anita. His *Oeuvres complètes* were published in 1897–1904. *See* G. Grappe, *Jules Claretie* (1906).

CLARI, GIOVANNI CARLO MARIA (*c.* 1669–1745), Italian composer, born at Pisa, was the most celebrated pupil of Colonna, chapelmaster of S. Petronio, at Bologna. He became *maestro di cappella* at Pistoia, at Bologna and at Pisa. The works by which Clari distinguished himself are his vocal duets and trios, with a *basso continuo,* published between 1740 and 1747. These compositions, which combine graceful melody with contrapuntal learning, were much admired by Luigi Cherubini and also by George Frederick Handel, who borrowed material from portions of them.

Clari composed one opera, *Il Savio delirante,* produced at Bologna in 1695, and a large quantity of church music, several specimens of which have been printed in Vincent Novello's *Fitzwilliam Music.*

CLARINA, a modern instrument of the wood-wind class (although actually made of metal), a hybrid possessing characteristics of both oboe and clarinet. The clarina was invented by W. Heckel of Biebrich-am-Rhein, and has been used at Bayreuth, in *Tristan und Isolde,* as a substitute for the *Holztrompete* made according to Richard Wagner's instructions.

CLARINDA, county seat of Page county, Ia., U.S., on the Nodaway river, federal highway 71, state highway 2 and the Burlington railway. The population in the 1950 federal census was 5,077 (4,962 in 1930; 4,905 in 1940). The chief industries are coal mining, agriculture and manufacturing.

A state hospital for the mentally unbalanced, with a capacity for 1,500 patients, is located there. Clarinda was settled about 1853 and incorporated in 1866.

CLARINET, a wood-wind instrument having a cylindrical bore and played by means of a single-reed mouthpiece. The name is sometimes used in a generic sense to denote the whole family, which consists of the ordinary clarinet, corresponding to the violin, oboe, etc.; the alto clarinet in E; the basset horn (*q.v.*) in F; the bass clarinet (*q.v.*), and the pedal clarinet (*q.v.*).

The mouthpiece of the clarinet, including the beating or single-reed common to the whole clarinet family, has the appearance of a beak with the point bevelled off and thinned at the edge to correspond with the end of the reed shaped like a spatula. The under part of the mouthpiece is flattened in order to form a table for the support of the reed, which is adjusted thereon with great nicety, allowing just the amount of play requisite to set in vibration the column of air within the tube.

A cylindrical tube played by means of a reed has the acoustic properties of a stopped pipe, *i.e.,* the fundamental tone produced by the tube is an octave lower than the corresponding tone of an open pipe of the same length, and overblows a twelfth; whereas tubes having a conical bore like the oboe, and played by means of a reed, speak as open pipes and overblow an octave. This forms the fundamental difference between the instruments of the oboe and clarinet families.

Wind instruments depending upon lateral holes for the production of their scale must either have as many holes pierced in the bore as they require notes, or make use of the property possessed by the air-column of dividing into harmonics or partials of the fundamental tones. Twenty to twenty-two holes is the number generally accepted as the practical limit for the clarinet. The compass of the instrument is therefore extended through the medium of the harmonic overtones.

In order to facilitate, however, the production of the harmonic notes, a small hole, closed by means of a key and called the "speaker," is bored near the mouthpiece. By means of this small hole the air-column is placed in communication with the external

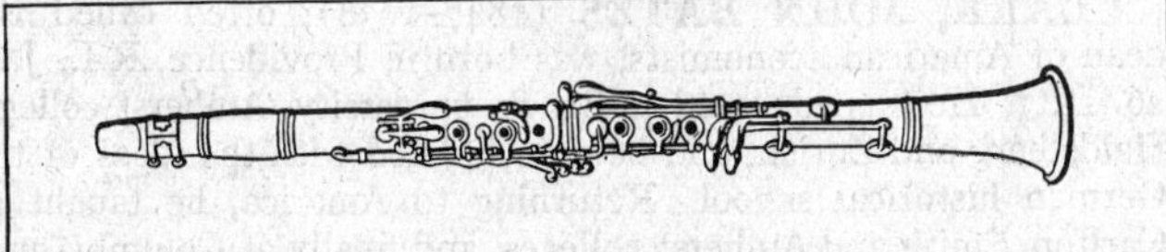

BY COURTESY OF MESSRS. CARL FISCHER

THE CLARINET, A MUSICAL INSTRUMENT WITH A SINGLE BEATING REED, DERIVED FROM THE CHALUMEAU OF THE MIDDLE AGES

atmosphere, a ventral segment is formed, and the air-column divides into three equal parts, producing a triple number of vibrations resulting in the third note of the harmonic series, at an interval of a twelfth above the fundamental.

The fundamental scale of the modern clarinet in C extends from E in the bass clef to B flat in the treble. The next octave and a half is obtained by opening the speaker key, whereby each of the fundamental notes is reproduced a twelfth higher, extending the range to F in alt, which ends the natural compass of the instrument, although a skilful performer may obtain another octave by cross-fingering.

History.—The single beating-reed associated with the instruments of the clarinet family was probably introduced into classic Greece from Egypt or Asia Minor. A few ancient Greek instruments are extant, five of which are in the British Museum. They are as nearly cylindrical as would be the natural growing reed itself. The probability is that both single and double reeds were at times used with the Greek aulos and the Roman tibia.

In the West, the instrument was, during the Carolingian period, identified with the tibia of the Romans until such time as the new western civilization ceased to be content to go back to classical Rome for its models, and began to express itself, at first naïvely and awkwardly, as the 11th century dawned. The name then changed to the derivatives of the Greek *kalamos,* assuming an almost bewildering variety of forms, of which the commonest are chalemie, chalumeau, schalmey, scalmeye, shawm, calemel.

At the beginning of the 18th century various important improvements in the mechanism of the instrument, in particular the invention of the very useful device of the speaker-key, were effected by J. Christian Denner (1655–1707), and after various subsequent developments the instrument was further improved during the 19th century by the Belgian makers Bachmann, the elder Sax, Albert and C. Mahillon and others. In England the clarinet has also passed through several progressive stages since its introduction about 1770, first at the hands of Cornelius Ward, and later, as a consequence of still more important improvements due to Richard Carte and others.

As regards music for the clarinet, Mattheson mentions clarinet music in 1713, although Handel, whose rival he was, does not appear to have known the instrument. Joh. Christ. Bach scored for the clarinet in 1763 in his opera *Orione,* performed in London, and Rameau had already employed the instrument in 1751 in a theatre for his pastoral entitled *Acante et Céphise.* Later, Mozart wrote for it in his Paris symphony, and since then it has of course long since taken its place as one of the most indispensable members of the orchestral family. Famous chamber works in which the instrument is employed are the clarinet quintets of Mozart and Brahms.

CLARK, ABRAHAM (1726–1794), American patriot and signer of the Declaration of Independence, was born in Elizabethtown, N.J., on Feb. 15, 1726. After receiving his education in mathematics and civil law, he engaged in conveyancing and surveying. Though he did not enter the professional practice of law, he gave legal advice gratuitously to his neighbours, earning the title, "the poor man's counsellor." He served as clerk of the New Jersey colonial assembly, and later was appointed high sheriff of Essex county. As an active Whig, he served on the committees of vigilance and public safety in his native State, and in June 1776 was appointed a representative to the general Congress, where he voted for separation from England and signed the Declaration of Independence. Eight times in the following 12 years he was elected a member of that body, and he was chosen a delegate to the Constitutional Convention in Philadelphia in 1787, but illness prevented his attendance. In Congress, on Wednesday, July 2, 1788, he made the motion by which the Federal Constitution became effective. The State legislature appointed him, in the winter of 1789–90, a commissioner to settle debts of New Jersey contracted during the Revolution, which duties he discharged until elected a member of the second Congress. This office he held until June 1794. He died at Elizabethtown, N.J., on Sept. 15, 1794.

See A. C. Hart, ed., *Abraham Clark* (San Francisco, 1923).

CLARK, CHAMP (1850–1921), American politician, was born in Anderson Co., Ky., on March 7, 1850. He first entered Kentucky university but finished his course at Bethany college in 1873. The following year he was elected president of Marshall college, West Virginia, and one year later was admitted to the bar. After 1880 his law office was in Bowling Green, Missouri. He was city attorney for Louisiana, Mo., and for Bowling Green from 1878 to 1881; and was prosecuting attorney for Pike Co., 1885–89, and then for three years was a member of the Missouri house of representatives. He was a member of congress from 1893 to 1895, and from 1897 to 1919, being speaker from 1911 to 1919. At the Democratic convention for the nomination of a presidential candidate held at Baltimore in 1912, he led on 27 ballots and on 8 had a clear majority, but not the necessary two-thirds. He was finally defeated by Woodrow Wilson of New Jersey. He died in Washington, D.C., on March 2, 1921.

CLARK, FRANCIS EDWARD (1851–1927), American clergyman, was born of New England ancestry at Aylmer, Province of Quebec, Canada, Sept. 12, 1851. He graduated at Dartmouth college in 1873 and at Andover theological seminary in 1876, and was pastor successively of the Williston Congregational church in Portland, Me., and of the Phillips Congregational church in South Boston, Mass. In Feb. 1881 he founded at Portland the Young People's Society of Christian Endeavour, which beginning as a small society in a single New England church, developed into a great interdenominational organization, which reported 80,000 societies and more than 4,000,000 members throughout the world. For many years he devoted himself to this work as president and finally president emeritus of the United Societies of Christian Endeavour and president of the World's Christian Endeavour Union, and as editor, and then honorary editor of the *Christian Endeavor World* until his death at Newton, Mass., on May 26, 1927.

Among his publications are *Looking Out on Life* (1883); *World Wide Endeavor* (1895); *Christian Endeavor Manual* (1903); and *Christian Endeavor in All Lands* (1906). *The Continent of Opportunity* (1909); *Old Home of New Americans* (1912); *The Holy Land of Asia Minor* (1914); *The Charm of Scandinavia* (with Sydney A. Clark) (1914); *Christ and the Young People* (1916); *In the Footsteps of St. Paul* (1917); *The Gospel of Out-of-Doors* (1920); *Memories of Many Men in Many Lands* (1923).

CLARK, GEORGE ROGERS (1752–1818), American frontier military leader, was born in Albemarle county, Virginia, on Nov. 19, 1752. When 19 years of age he left his home to become a surveyor of frontier lands along the Ohio river. This occupation was soon interrupted by an Indian outbreak known as Lord Dunmore's War (1774); and Clark, with the rank of captain, accompanied Dunmore in the punitive expedition. Peace brought renewed immigration, especially into Kentucky, and thither Clark followed as a surveyor for the Ohio company. His position enabled him from time to time to absorb choice portions of land for himself, and these interests soon led him to identify himself with the Kentuckians and devote much thought to their peculiar problems. When the American Revolution broke out Clark clearly perceived the vulnerability of the frontier, and the necessity of securing for Kentucky a government with military authority and an organized militia if there was to be concerted defense against the British, or their allies, the Indians. Elected by a mass meeting of the pioneers to present their problems before the Virginia government, Clark attended the council and assembly at Williamsburg and diplomatically persuaded them to create a separate county of Kentucky and thereby become responsible for its defense. Clark returned with a supply of powder and assumed chief command of the frontier militia at a critical moment, for the Indians were already making raids against the settlers. Convinced that they were instigated and supported in their raids by British officers stationed in the forts north of the Ohio river, Clark worked out a plan of offensive operations that involved nothing less than a conquest of these forts. His plans were approved by Governor Patrick Henry and the council of Virginia and Clark was authorized to enlist troops. May 1778 found him at the falls of the Ohio with about 175 men. The expedition proceeded to Ft. Kaskaskia, on the Mississippi river, in what is now Illinois. This place and Cahokia, also on the Mississippi, near St. Louis, were defended by small British garrisons, which depended on the support of the French inhabitants. The French being willing to accept the authority of Virginia, both forts were easily taken. Clark gained the friendship of Father Gibault, the priest at Kaskaskia, and through his influence the French at Vincennes on the Wabash were induced to change their allegiance. Lieut. Governor Hamilton, the British commander at Detroit, recovered Vincennes, however, and went into winter quarters there. After an arduous march across flooded bottom land in freezing weather, Clark in Feb. 1779, surprised Hamilton and forced him to give up Vincennes, and surrender himself and his garrison as prisoners of war. The way was now open to Detroit, Clark's ultimate object, but it was deemed prudent to wait for reinforcements promised from Virginia in June. The delay was fatal; other occurrences delayed the reinforcements and scattered Clark's troops. Clark withdrew to Ft. Nelson which he had built at the falls of the Ohio, and made that his base for the rest of the war. In 1780 he aided in the defeat of a British expedition against the Spanish settlement of St. Louis; the same year he made a swift campaign against the Shawnee Indians and destroyed their towns, Chillicothe and Piqua. Clark, now appointed brigadier general of the western forces, again planned to move against Detroit and was promised supplies and reinforcements for the expedition from Virginia. Months went by and they did not come, for Virginia was bankrupt. Again in 1782 Clark took the offensive against the Shawnees, and while not entirely successful this last expedition saved the settlements from renewed Indian attacks and defeated British plans for an Indian alliance. When peace came in 1783 (treaty of Paris) Clark's conquests doubtless influenced the award of the country northwest of the Ohio to the United States. His offensive movements had also been of first importance in defending the vulnerable frontier from Indian raids and British expeditions. Clark and his men during all these years received no pay for their services and hardships. Furthermore Clark found himself responsible for all debts incurred for supplies, since Virginia, despite her promises, never reimbursed him. The rest of his life was shadowed by the constant demands of creditors. Clark was appointed an Indian commissioner after the war, and in 1786 he played a leading part in a treaty with the Shawnees. The same year he led an expedition against the "Wabash confederacy," his last military command. James Wilkenson, a traitor in the pay of Spain (unknown at that time), coveted Clark's office of Indian commissioner and his military command, and deliberately set out to misrepresent him. Forged papers and testimonials were forwarded to Governor Randolph of Virginia charging Clark with constant drunkenness, military incapacity, and a treasonable design of leading a military expedition down the Mississippi against Spain. Wilkenson was entirely successful; he was appointed Indian commissioner in Clark's place, and the latter was relieved of his command. Disappointed at his country's ingratitude, Clark spent the rest of his life near Louisville in retirement, dying on Feb. 13, 1818. Historical research in recent years has exposed Wilkenson's perfidy, and emphasized the importance of Clark's exploits. His most ardent supporters have even called him "the Washington of the West."

Bibliography.—The *George Rogers Clark Papers, 1771–1783,* ed. J. A. James, are contained in vol. viii and ix of the *Illinois Historical Collections* (Springfield, 1912 and 1926). Clark's own narrative of his campaigns is published in *The Captive of Old Vincennes* (Indianapolis, 1927), ed. M. M. Quaife. The best biography is Temple Bodley's *George Rogers Clark: His Life and Public Services* (Boston, 1926). *See* also W. H. English, *Conquest of the Country North-west of the River Ohio, 1778–1783* (1896), and the *Mississippi Valley Historical Review* for Sept. 1924; Frederick Palmer, *Clark of the Ohio: A Life of George Rogers Clark* (1929).

CLARK, JOHN BATES (1847–1938), often called the dean of American economists, was born in Providence, R.I., Jan. 26, 1847. He was educated at Brown university, Amherst college, Heidelberg and Zurich, and became imbued with the ideas of the German historical school. Returning to America, he taught at Carlton, Smith and Amherst colleges, and finally at Columbia university (1895–1923). The first period of his economic thought, influenced by the historical school, culminated in *The Philosophy of Wealth* (1885). In "revolt," as he said, "against the spirit of the old political economy," he rejected competition as the rule of distributive justice. Nevertheless, he outlined independently an "effective utility" theory of competitive value resembling that of Jevons and the Austrian school somewhat earlier.

A second period culminated in 1899 in his chief work, *The Distribution of Wealth,* marked by the rejection of the old categories of production factors, but ultra "classical" in accepting competitive price (which he called the "specific productivity" of agents) as the just rule of distribution. Despite some contemporary protests, Clark's views dominated economic theorizing in the United States for a generation, and left lasting effects in clearer conceptions of a "universal law of economic variation," of a price "system," and of the categories of productive agents.

Clark's later work is noteworthy for his original and practicable proposals for the correction of monopolistic abuses, presented in final form in *The Control of Trusts* (1912), but not yet fully realized in public policy. (F. A. F.)

CLARK, JOSIAH LATIMER (1822–1898), English engineer and electrician, was born on March 10, 1822, at Great Marlow, Bucks. In 1848 he became assistant engineer at the Menai Straits bridge under his elder brother Edwin (1814–94), the inventor of the Clark hydraulic lift graving dock. Two years later, when his brother was appointed engineer to the Electric Telegraph company, he again acted as his assistant, and subsequently succeeded him as chief engineer. In 1854 he took out a patent "for conveying letters or parcels between places by the pressure of air and vacuum," and later was concerned in the construction of a large pneumatic despatch tube between the general post office and Euston station, London. He also experimented on the propagation of the electric current in submarine cables, and in 1859 he was a member of the committee which was appointed by the government to consider the numerous failures of submarine cable enterprises. Latimer Clark paid much attention to the subject of electrical measurement, and besides designing various improvements in method and apparatus and inventing the Clark standard cell, he took a leading part in the movement for the systematization of electrical standards, which was inaugurated by the paper which he and Sir C. T. Bright read on the question before the British association in 1861. With Bright also he devised improvements in the insulation of submarine cables. He was a member of several firms engaged in laying submarine cables, in manufacturing electrical appliances, and in hydraulic engineering. He died in London on Oct. 30, 1898.

Clark's chief works are: *Electrical Measurement* (1868); and, with R. Sabine, *Electrical Tables and Formulae for Operators in Submarine Cables* (1871).

CLARK, THOMAS (1801–1867), Scottish chemist, was born at Ayr on March 31, 1801, and died at Glasgow on Nov. 27, 1867. He was professor of chemistry at Marischal college, Aberdeen, and is best known for his process for softening hard waters and his water tests, patented in 1841.

CLARK, WILLIAM (1770–1838), American soldier and explorer, the youngest brother of George Rogers Clark, was born in Caroline county, Va., but early removed to Kentucky. He entered the U.S. army as lieutenant of infantry in 1792, and served under Gen. Anthony Wayne against the Indians in 1794. In 1803–06, with Meriwether Lewis, he commanded the famous exploring expedition from St. Louis to the mouth of the Columbia river and return, the first expedition to cross the continent within the limits of the United States. He was territorial governor of Missouri from 1813 to 1820, and superintendent of Indian affairs at St. Louis from 1822 until his death in 1838.

See the *Original Journals of the Lewis and Clark Expedition* (1905), edited by R. G. Thwaites, the best of several editions of the leader's journals; George Bird Grinnell, *Trails of the Pathfinders* (1911); "William Clark's Journal of General Wayne's Campaign, 1793–1794," *Mississippi Valley Hist. Rev.*, vol. i. p. 413–443 (Cedar Rapids, Iowa, 1914); and Floyd Duckworth Welch, *The Work of the Indian Agents in the Louisiana Purchase, 1804–1820* (St. Louis, Mo., 1926).

CLARK, WILLIAM GEORGE (1821–1878), English classical and Shakespearian scholar, was born at Barford Hall, Darlington, in March 1821 and died at York on Nov. 6, 1878. In 1853 Clark had taken orders, but left the church in 1870 after the passing of the Clerical Disabilities Act, of which he was one of the promoters. He established the Cambridge *Journal of Philology*, and co-operated with B. H. Kennedy and James Riddell in the production of the well-known *Sabrinae Corolla.* The work by which he is best known is the Cambridge Shakespeare (1863–66), containing a collation of early editions and selected emendations, edited by him at first with John Glover and afterwards with W. Aldis Wright. *Gazpacho* (1853) gives an account of his tour in Spain; his visits to Italy at the time of Garibaldi's insurrection, and to Poland during the insurrection of 1863, are described in *Vacation Tourists*, ed. F. Galton, i. and iii.

See H. A. J. Munro in *Journal of Philology* (viii., 1879); also notices by W. Aldis Wright in *Academy* (Nov. 23, 1878); R. Burn in *Athenaeum* (Nov. 16, 1878); *The Times* (Nov. 8, 1878); *Notes and Queries*, 5th series, x. (1878), p. 400.

CLARKE, ADAM (1762?–1832), British Nonconformist divine, was born at Moybeg, Co. Londonderry, Ireland, in 1760 or 1762. He completed his education at Kingswood school and in 1782 was appointed by Wesley minister to the Bradford (Wiltshire) circuit. He was a great preacher, and was three times (1806, 1814, 1822) chosen to be president of the conference. He served twice on the London circuit, the second period being extended considerably longer than the rule allowed, at the special request of the British and Foreign Bible Society, who had employed him in the preparation of their Arabic Bible. He found time in his busy life to study Hebrew and other Oriental languages, in order to qualify himself for the great work of his life, his *Commentary on the Holy Scriptures* (1810–26). In 1802 he published a *Bibliographical Dictionary* in six volumes, to which he afterwards added a supplement. He was selected by the Records Commission to re-edit Rymer's *Foedera*, a task which after ten years' labour (1808–18) he had to resign. He also wrote *Memoirs of the Wesley Family* (1823), and edited a large number of religious works. He died in London on Aug. 16, 1832.

His *Miscellaneous Works* were published in 1836, and a *Life*, by his son J. B. B. Clarke, appeared in 1833.

CLARKE, ALEXANDER ROSS (1828–1914), British geodesist, was born in Sutherlandshire on Dec. 16, 1828. He studied at the Royal Military academy, Woolwich, and in 1847 became a second-lieutenant in the Royal Engineers. In 1850 Clarke was posted to the Ordnance Survey at Southampton, and except for a break between 1851–54 he remained there until he retired in 1881.

When Clarke joined the Ordnance Survey the observations on the Principal Triangulation had just been completed, and he had the task of reducing and publishing the results. This was done in record time, and in 1858 appeared *Account of the Observations and Calculations of the Figure, Dimensions and Mean Specific Gravity of the Earth as Derived Therefrom.* Clarke was mainly responsible for a good deal of similar work carried out in co-operation with other countries. His work was remarkably accurate and rapid, considering the laborious methods of calculation and reduction in use at the time. In a specially-designed room he tested and compared the standards of length used by other countries and by the Colonies, publishing his observations in *Comparison of the Standards of Length of England, France, Belgium, Prussia, India and Australia* (1866).

Clarke gave an account of the observations which connected the English and French triangulations under the title of *Extension of the Triangulation of Great Britain into France and Belgium* (1863). He was the author of *Abstracts of Spirit Levelling in England, Wales and Scotland* (1861), *Geodesy* (1880), a standard work on this subject, which has been translated into many languages, and a number of papers in scientific journals. He was a member of many learned societies and was awarded the Royal Medal of the Royal Society in 1887. He had been made a Companion of the Bath in 1870. In 1881 Clarke was ordered to hold himself ready for service in Mauritius and preferred to retire rather than sever his connection with the Ordnance Survey. He lived a secluded life until he died on Feb. 11, 1914.

CLARKE, SIR ANDREW (1824–1902), British soldier and administrator, son of Col. Andrew Clarke, of Co. Donegal, Ireland, governor of West Australia, was born at Southsea, England, on July 27, 1824, and educated at King's school, Canterbury. He entered the army in 1844 as second-lieutenant in the Royal Engineers. He was appointed to his father's staff in West Australia, but was transferred to be A.D.C. and military secretary to the governor of Tasmania; and in 1847 he went to New Zealand to take part in the Maori War, and for some years served on Sir George Grey's staff. He was then made surveyor-general in Victoria, took a prominent part in framing its new constitution, and held the office of minister of public lands during the first administration (1855–57). From 1864–73 he was director of works for the navy, being responsible for great improvements in the naval arsenals and fortifications at home and abroad. In 1873 he became governor of the Straits Settlements. From 1875–80 he was minister of public works in India; and on his return to England in 1881, he was first appointed commandant at Chatham and then inspector-general of fortifications (1882–86). He died on March 29, 1902. Both as a technical and strategical engineer and as an Imperial administrator Sir Andrew Clarke was one of the ablest and most useful public servants of his time.

CLARKE, SIR CASPAR PURDON (1846–1911), English art expert, was born in London on Dec. 21, 1846, and educated privately at Sydenham and Boulogne. In 1862 he was trained as an architect in the art schools at South Kensington. In 1865 he entered the Office of Works, and in 1867 was attached to the works department of the South Kensington museum. He travelled extensively for the museum, purchasing objects of art, and at the same time carried on his profession as an architect. In 1883 he became keeper of the India museum at South Kensington, in 1892 keeper of the art collections, in 1893 assistant-director, and in 1896 director. In 1905 he became director of the Metropolitan Museum, New York, resigning in 1910. He was knighted in 1902. He died in London on March 29, 1911.

CLARKE, CHARLES COWDEN (1787–1877), English author and Shakespearian scholar, was born at Enfield, Middlesex, on Dec. 15, 1787. His father, John Clarke, was a schoolmaster, among whose pupils was John Keats. Charles Clarke taught Keats his letters, and encouraged his love of poetry. He knew Charles and Mary Lamb, and afterwards became acquainted with Shelley, Leigh Hunt, Coleridge and Hazlitt. Clarke became a music publisher in partnership with Alfred Novello, and married in 1828 his partner's sister, Mary Victoria (1809–98), the eldest daughter of Vincent Novello. In the year after her marriage Mrs. Cowden Clarke began her valuable Shakespeare concordance, which was eventually issued in 18 monthly parts (1844–45), and in volume form in 1845 as *The Complete Concordance to Shakespeare, being a Verbal Index to all the Passages in the Dramatic Works of the Poet.* This work superseded the *Copious Index to . . . Shakespeare* (1790) of Samuel Ayscough, and the *Complete Verbal Index . . .* (1805–07) of Francis Twiss. Charles Cowden Clarke published many useful books, and edited the text for John Nichol's edition of the British poets; but his most important work consisted of lectures delivered between 1834 and 1856 on Shakespeare and other literary subjects. Some of the more notable series were published, among them being *Shakespeare's Characters, chiefly those subordinate* (1863), and *Molière's Characters* (1865). In 1859 he published a volume of original poems, *Carmina Minima.* For some years after their marriage the Cowden Clarkes lived with the Novellos in London. In 1849 Vincent Novello with his wife removed to Nice, where he was joined by the Clarkes in 1856. After his death they lived at Genoa at the Villa Novello. They collaborated in *The Shakespeare Key, unlocking the Treasures of his Style . . .* (1879), and in an edition of Shakespeare for Messrs. Cassell, which was issued in weekly parts, and completed in 1868. It was reissued in 1886 as *Cassell's Illustrated Shakespeare.* Charles Clarke died on March 13, 1877, at Genoa, and his wife survived him until Jan. 12, 1898. Among Mrs. Cowden Clarke's other works may be mentioned *The Girlhood of Shakespeare's Heroines* (1850–52), and a translation of Berlioz's *Treatise upon Modern Instrumentation and Orchestration* (1856).

See *Recollections of Writers* (1898), a joint work by the Clarkes containing letters and reminiscences of their many literary friends; and Mary Cowden Clarke's autobiography, *My Long Life* (1896). A charming series of letters (1850–61), addressed by her to an American admirer of her work, Robert Balmanno, was edited by Anne Upton Nettleton as *Letters to an Enthusiast* (Chicago, 1902).

CLARKE, EDWARD DANIEL (1769–1822), English mineralogist and traveller, was born at Willingdon, Sussex, on June 5, 1769, and educated at Tonbridge and Jesus college, Cambridge. In 1799–1803 he made an extended tour through the continent of Europe and afterwards to Egypt and Palestine. After the capitulation of Alexandria, Clarke was of considerable use in securing for England the statues, sarcophagi, maps, manuscripts, etc., which had been collected by the French savants. He returned home by way of Athens, Constantinople, Rumelia, Austria, Germany and France. On arriving in England Clarke made important donations to Cambridge university, including a colossal statue of the Eleusinian Ceres. He received the livings of Harlton and Yeldham and near the end of 1808 was appointed to the professorship of mineralogy in Cambridge, then first instituted. The mss. which he had collected in the course of his travels were sold to the Bodleian library. He was also appointed university librarian in 1817 and was one of the founders of the Cambridge Philosophical Society in 1819. He died in London on March 9, 1822.

The following is a list of his principal works: *Testimony of Authors respecting the Colossal Statue of Ceres in the Public Library, Cambridge* (1801–3); *The Tomb of Alexander, a Dissertation on the Sarcophagus brought from Alexandria, and now in the British Museum* (1805); *A Methodical Distribution of the Mineral Kingdom* (Lewes, 1807); *A Description of the Greek Marbles brought from the Shores of the Euxine Archipelago and Mediterranean and deposited in the University Library, Cambridge* (1809); *Travels in Various Countries of Europe, Asia and Africa* (1810–19; 2nd ed., 1811–23).

See Rev. W. Otter, *Life and Remains of E. D. Clarke* (London, 1824).

CLARKE, SIR EDWARD GEORGE (1841–1931), English lawyer and politician, son of J. G. Clarke, of Moorgate street, London, was born on Feb. 15, 1841. In 1859 he became a writer in the India office, but resigned in the next year, and became a law reporter. He obtained a Tancred law scholarship in 1861, and was called to the bar at Lincoln's Inn in 1864. He joined the home circuit, became Q.C. 1880, and a bencher of Lincoln's Inn in 1882. He appeared, among other cases, as counsel for Patrick Staunton in the Penge murder case (1877) for Mrs. Bartlett (1886), for Sir W. Gordon-Cumming in his slander action (in which Edward VII., then Prince of Wales, gave evidence), and for Dr. Jameson in 1896. He was knighted in 1886. He was returned as Conservative member for Southwark at a by-election early in 1880, but failed to retain his seat at the general election which followed a month or two later; he found a seat at Plymouth, however, which he retained until 1900. He was solicitor-general in the Conservative administration of 1886–92, but declined office under the Unionist government of 1895 when the law officers of the crown were debarred from private practice. The most remarkable, perhaps, of his speeches in the House of Commons was his reply to Mr. Gladstone on the second reading of the Home Rule Bill in 1893. In 1899 he resigned his seat on the question of the government's South African policy. At the general election in 1906 he was returned at the head of the poll for the city of London, but he offended a large section of his constituents by a speech against tariff reform in the House of Commons on March 12, and shortly afterwards he resigned his seat on grounds of health. He retired from the bar in 1914 and died in 1931.

He published a *Treatise on the Law of Extradition* (4th ed. 1903), four volumes of his political and forensic speeches; *The New Testament: The Authorized Version Corrected* (1913); *The Book of Psalms: the Prayer Book Version Corrected* (1915); and his autobiography, *The Story of My Life* (1918).

CLARKE, JAMES FREEMAN (1810–1888), American preacher and author, was born in Hanover (N.H.) on April 4, 1810. He graduated at Harvard college in 1829, and at the Harvard divinity school in 1833. He was then ordained as minister of a Unitarian congregation at Louisville (Ky.), and soon threw himself heart and soul into the national movement for the abolition of slavery, though he was never a "radical abolitionist." In 1839 he returned to Boston, where he and his friends established (1841) the "Church of the Disciples," which brought together a body of men and women active and eager in applying the Christian religion to the social problems of the day. Of this church he was the minister from 1841–50 and from 1854 until his death. He was also secretary of the Unitarian Association and in 1867–71 professor of natural religion and Christian doctrine at Harvard. From 1836–39 he was editor of the *Western Messenger,* a magazine which is now of value to collectors because it contains the earliest printed poems of Ralph Waldo Emerson, who was Clarke's personal friend. Most of Clarke's earlier published writings were addressed to the immediate need of establishing a larger theory of religion than that espoused by people who were still trying to be Calvinists, people who maintained what a good American phrase calls "hard-shelled churches." But it would be wrong to call his work controversial. In the great moral questions of his time he was a fearless and practical advocate of the broadest statement of human rights. He published but few verses, but at the bottom he was a poet. He was a diligent and accurate scholar, and among the books by which he is best known is one called *Ten Great Religions* (2 vols., 1871–83). Few Americans have done more than Clarke to give breadth to the published discussion of the subjects of literature, ethics and religious philosophy. Among his books are *Orthodoxy* (1866); *Every-Day Religion* (1886) and *Sermons on the Lord's Prayer* (1888). He died at Jamaica Plain (Mass.) on June 8, 1888.

His *Autobiography, Diary and Correspondence,* edited by Edward Everett Hale, was published in 1891. (E. E. H.)

CLARKE, JOHN MASON (1857–1925), U.S. palaeontologist and geologist, was born at Canandaigua, N.Y., on April 15, 1857. He was educated at the Canandaigua academy, Amherst college and the University of Göttingen, Germany. On Jan. 1, 1886, after several years of teaching, he became assistant to James Hall, whom he succeeded as state palaeontologist of New York in 1898. In 1904 he became both state geologist and palaeontologist and director of the state museum. Under his direction it became the foremost museum of its type in the United States, with extensive and novel exhibits, publications and research programs in geology, palaeontology, archaeology and several branches of biology.

Clarke began to collect Devonian fossils at the age of six, and became the foremost U.S. authority on that geologic system. His studies embraced brachiopods, crustaceans and glass sponges, as well as Devonian faunas of North and South America and Germany, and Devonian formations and history of eastern United States and Canada. He also described some Silurian faunas, and with Rudolf Ruedemann was author of a two-volume work on the eurypterids, or sea scorpions. Clarke died in Albany, N.Y., May 29, 1925. A bibliography of his 380 publications appears in the *Bulletin of the Geological Society of America,* vol. 37, no. 1, pp. 49–93 (1926). (M. A. F.; C. L. Fe.)

CLARKE, MARCUS ANDREW HISLOP (1846–1881), Australian author, was born in London on April 24, 1846, and died at Melbourne on Aug. 2, 1881. He emigrated about 1863 to Australia, where his uncle, James Langton Clarke, was a county court judge. He was at first a clerk in the Bank of Australasia, and then learned farming at a station on the Wimmera river, Victoria. He was already writing stories for the *Australian Magazine,* when in 1867 he joined the staff of the Melbourne *Argus.* He also became secretary (1872) to the trustees of the Melbourne public library, and later (1876) assistant librarian. He founded in 1868 the Yorick club, which soon numbered among its members the chief Australian men of letters. The most famous of his books is *For the Term of his Natural Life* (Melbourne, 1874), a powerful tale of an Australian penal settlement, which originally appeared in serial form in a Melbourne paper.

See *The Marcus Clarke Memorial Volume* (Melbourne, 1884), containing selections from his writings with a biography and list of works, edited by Hamilton Mackinnon.

CLARKE, MARY ANNE (*c.* 1776–1852), mistress of Frederick, duke of York, second son of George III, married before she was 18 a Mr. Clarke, a stonemason, whom she soon left. She became in 1803 the mistress of the duke of York, then commander in chief. The duke's promised allowance was not regularly paid, and to escape her financial difficulties Mrs. Clarke trafficked in her protector's position, receiving money from various promotion seekers, military, civil and even clerical, in return for her promise to secure them the good services of the duke. These proceedings caused a public scandal, and in 1809 Col. Wardle, M.P., brought eight charges of abuse of military patronage against the duke in the house of commons, and a committee of inquiry was appointed, before which Mrs. Clarke herself gave evidence. The duke of York was shown to have been aware of what was being done, but to have derived no pecuniary benefit himself. He resigned his appointment as commander in chief and terminated his connection with Mrs. Clarke, who subsequently obtained from him a considerable sum in cash and a pension as the price for withholding the publication of his numerous letters to her.

Mrs. Clarke died at Boulogne on June 21, 1852.

See Elizabeth Taylor, *Authentic Memoirs of Mrs. Clarke* (1809); W. Clarke, "Life of Mrs. M. A. Clarke," in the *Annual Register,* vol. li, p. 61.

CLARKE, SAMUEL (1675–1729), English philosopher and divine, son of Edward Clarke, an alderman, who for several years was parliamentary representative of the city of Norwich, was born on Oct. 11, 1675, and educated at the free school of Norwich and at Caius college, Cambridge. The philosophy of Descartes was the reigning system at the university; Clarke, however, mastered the new system of Newton, and contributed to its extension by publishing in 1697 a Latin version of the *Traité de physique* of Jacques Rohault, which was used as a textbook till supplanted by the treatises of Newton himself.

Having taken holy orders, he became chaplain to John Moore (1646–1714), bishop of Norwich, who later presented him to the rectory of Drayton near Norwich. He subsequently became chaplain in ordinary to Queen Anne, who in 1709 presented him to the rectory of St. James, Westminster, in which year he became a doctor of divinity. As Boyle lecturer, he dealt in 1704 with the *Being and Attributes of God,* and in 1705 with the *Evidences of Natural and Revealed Religion.* These lectures, first printed separately, were afterward published together under the title of *A Discourse Concerning the Being and Attributes of God, the Obligations of Natural Religion, and the Truth and Certainty of the Christian Revelation, in Opposition to Hobbes, Spinoza, the Author of the Oracles of Reason, and Other Deniers of Natural and Revealed Religion.* During 1712 he published his celebrated treatise on *The Scripture Doctrine of the Trinity.* It is divided into three parts. The first contains a collection and exegesis of all the texts in the New Testament relating to the doctrine of the Trinity; in the second the doctrine is set forth at large, and explained in particular and distinct propositions; and in the third the principal passages in the liturgy of the Church of England relating to the doctrine of the Trinity are considered. This book involved Clarke in some trouble in the Convocation, which subsequently blew over.

In 1715 and 1716 he had a discussion with Leibniz relative to the principles of natural philosophy and religion, which was at length cut short by the death of his antagonist. A collection of the papers which passed between them was published in 1717 (*cf.* G. v. Leory, *Die philos. Probleme in dem Briefwechsel Leibniz und Clarke,* Giessen, 1893).

Clarke died on May 17, 1729.

See W. Whiston, *Historical Memoirs,* and the preface by Benjamin Hoadly to *Clarke's Works* (1738–42).

CLARKE, THOMAS SHIELDS (1860–1920), U.S. artist, was born in Pittsburgh, Pa., on April 25, 1860, and graduated at Princeton in 1882. He was a pupil of the Art Students' league, New York, and of the École des Beaux Arts, Paris, under J. L. Gérôme; later he entered the atelier of Dagnan-Bouveret, and, becoming interested in sculpture, worked for a while under Henri M. Chapu. As a sculptor, he received a medal of honour in Madrid for his "The Cider Press," now in Golden Gate park, San Francisco, Calif., and he made four caryatids of "The Seasons" for the appellate courthouse, New York. He designed an "Alma Mater" for Princeton university, and a model is in the library. Among his paintings are his "Night Market in Morocco" (Philadelphia Art club), for which he received a medal at the International exposition in Berlin in 1891, and his "A Fool's Fool," exhibited at the Salon in 1887 and now in the collection of the Pennsylvania Academy of Fine Arts, Philadelphia. He died in New York city on Nov. 15, 1920.

CLARKSBURG, a city in the heart of the coal, oil and gas fields of West Virginia, U.S., on the West Fork river at the mouth of Elk creek; the county seat of Harrison county. It is on Federal highways 19 and 50, and is served by the Baltimore and Ohio Railroad.

The population was 32,014 in 1950 and 30,579 in 1940 by the federal census. The city lies on a plain 1,100 ft. above sea level, surrounded by beautiful hills, in a rich agricultural and grazing, as well as mining, region. It has a large wholesale and retail trade.

Coal, natural gas and electric power are available for industrial uses, and the city has numerous manufactures including glass, chinaware, carbon electrodes, zinc boxes, crates, caskets, brick, tile, machinery, evaporated milk and other manufactures.

Clarksburg was settled in 1765, and was incorporated in 1785 by the general assembly of Virginia. It was named after George Rogers Clark. In 1917 the towns of Broad Oaks, Stealey Heights, Adamston and North View and several adjoining districts were consolidated with the old city of Clarksburg, which in 1910 had a population of 9,201.

A new charter was adopted in 1921, establishing a council-manager form of government.

In the next five years contagious diseases were practically eliminated, infant mortality was reduced far below the average for the country, a municipal playground system was developed, loss by fire was cut to a very low figure, public improvements costing $1,200,000 were made and the city debt was reduced by more than $500,000. The bonded indebtedness of the city of Clarksburg in 1950 was $396,000.

Clarksburg was the birthplace of "Stonewall" Jackson, of Nathan Goff and of John W. Davis.

CLARKSDALE, a city of northwestern Mississippi, U.S., on federal highways 61 and 49, 75 mi. S.W. of Memphis; the county seat of Coahoma county. It is served by the Illinois Central railway. The population was 16,539 in 1950 and 12,168 in 1940 by the federal census. It is an important cotton market and has cottonseed-oil and lumber mills and other factories.

The city was founded about 1830, and was first incorporated in 1882.

CLARKSON, THOMAS (1760–1846), English antislavery agitator, was born on March 28, 1760, in Wisbech, Cambs., the son of a schoolmaster. He was educated at St. Paul's school and St. John's college, Cambridge. Clarkson was first drawn to the subject of slavery by reading Benezet's *Historical Survey of New Guinea* (for a prize essay in 1785) on the question set by the vice-chancellor of the university: "Is it right to make men slaves against their will?" The English translation of the Latin of this prize essay, published in 1786, brought him into touch with William Dillwyn, Joseph Wood and Granville Sharp, and soon a committee of 12 was formed to do all that was possible to effect the abolition of the slave trade. Meanwhile Clarkson gained the sympathy of Wilberforce, Whitbread, Pitt, Grenville, Fox and Burke, and spent his days in travelling from port to port, gaining a mass of evidence which was partly embodied in his *Summary View of the Slave Trade, and the Probable Consequences of Its Abolition.* In May 1788 Pitt introduced a parliamentary discussion on the subject, and Sir W. Dolben brought forward a bill, which was passed in the house of commons on June 18, providing that the number of slaves carried in a vessel should be proportional to its tonnage. In the same year, Clarkson published an *Essay on the Impolicy of the Slave Trade,* but could get only nine men, personally acquainted with the facts of the trade, to promise to appear before the privy council. Wilberforce and the committee, however, had obtained other witnesses, and in May 1789 the former led a debate on the subject in the house of commons, in which he was seconded by Burke and supported by Pitt and Fox.

At the outbreak of the French Revolution, Clarkson hoped that the French would sweep away slavery with other abuses; but the hope was vain, and after six months in Paris during which he enlisted the sympathies of Necker, Mirabeau and the marquis de la Fayette, he returned to England and to his laborious search for further witnesses of the slave traffic. After his health gave way in 1794, Clarkson laid aside active work for writing, publishing in 1806 *Portraiture of Quakerism,* and, two years later, the *History of the Rise, Progress and Accomplishment of the Abolition of the Slave Trade by the Brit. Parliament.* The bill for the abolition had become law in 1807, and finally, in 1815, British diplomacy secured the condemnation of the trade by the other Great Powers. When the question of practical measures for its abolition was unsuccessfully discussed at the Congress of Aix-la-Chapelle in 1818, Clarkson personally presented an address to the emperor Alexander I, who communicated it to the sovereigns of Austria and Prussia. In 1823 the Anti-Slavery society was formed with Clarkson as its vice-president.

From this date until his death at Ipswich on Sept. 26, 1846, his chief works were *Thoughts on the Necessity for Improving the Condition of the Slaves in the British Colonies* (1823) and *American Slavery* (1845). His *Memoirs of William Penn* had appeared in 1813.

See T. Elmes, *Thomas Clarkson* (1854).

CLARKSVILLE, a city of northern Tennessee, U.S., on the Cumberland river at the mouth of the Red river, 42 mi. N.W. of Nashville; the county seat of Montgomery county. It is on federal highways 41A and 79, and is served by the Louisville and Nashville and the Tennessee Central railways and by river steamers. Pop. (1950) 16,246; (1940) 11,831 by the federal census. It is in a region of scenic beauty, at the centre of the dark tobacco belt. It has a large trade in both leaf and manufactured tobacco, purebred livestock and dairy products. There are flour mills, a snuff factory, mechanical rubber goods plant and other industries. Clarksville was settled in 1780, was named after Gen. George Rogers Clark and was chartered as a city in 1820. Dunbar's cave, an interesting cavern, is 3 mi. from the city.

CLASS. Class designates an aggregate of persons, within a society, possessing approximately the same status. The class system, or the system of stratification of a society, is the system of classes in their internal and external relationships. The class system is not identical with the sytem of power, *i.e.,* with the network of relationships in which behaviour is influenced by commands and coercion. It is not identical with the property system, in which the use of physical objects and their resultant benefits is reserved to those having specific qualifications (property rights). The class system is not identical with the occupational system. The class system is the set of relationships constituted by the granting of deference to individuals, roles and institutions in the light of their place in the systems of power, property, occupation, etc.

Deference is an action of respect or honour, associated with the feeling of equality or inferiority. By logical extension, sentiments of disrespect or disesteem, feelings of contempt and superiority, are also comprehended in the conception of deference. Deference is an act of implied judgment of the worth and dignity of a person, office or institution, made in the light of a scale of values. Deference is simultaneously an act of judgment regarding the person judged and the person judging.

Deference is expressed in ceremonial actions symbolizing sentiments of respect or inferiority; it is also expressed in etiquette, in actions granting precedence and in modes of verbal address and of verbal reference. It is expressed in titles and in the award of medals and insignia of rank. These are the "pure" expressions of deference. Deference, which is the acknowledgment of status, also works conjointly with the systems of power and of property. The readiness to obey or utter commands, the completeness of obedience and the extreme of imperiousness are very much affected by the sentiments of deference of the persons involved. The person who is very deferential toward his officer, his employer, his supervisor, etc., will more readily carry out his official superior's command than the person who feels little deference toward his official superiors and who has at the same time great self-esteem.

Bases of Class.—The deference which defines class position is granted to persons, offices and institutions in accordance with the deferring person's perception, which may be erroneous and which is almost always fragmentary and vague, of the characteristics of the person, office or institution being judged. A man is judged in accordance with the judging person's perception of his income and wealth, his occupation, his level of achievement within his occupation, his standard of living (including the location of his residence), his ethnic characteristics, his kinship connections, his educational level, his relationships to the main centres of the exercise of power in the society as a whole and in his particular institutions, such as business firms, churches, universities, armies, governmental departments, etc., and his associates, formal and informal. (His wife and children are usually granted deference corresponding to his status.) These various characteristics are not always evaluated in the same way in all societies. For example, in the United States the significance of kinship connection is less important than it is in China or Great Britain in affecting a person's social status (*i.e.,* the rank which is accorded to him by the deference judgment of the members of the society). Similarly, ethnic characteristics are more important in the United States than they are in France or Brazil, although they were diminishing in their significance in the United States at mid-20th century. Education has less significance as a basis of discrimination in the United States than it has in Germany, the Netherlands or Sweden. Occupation is probably less important as a basis of deference in the United States than it is in Germany, and it has continued to decline in the 20th century.

Within each category (*e.g.,* occupation), variations occur in the rankings which result from the feelings and judgments of deference. Scientists, for example, have moved up considerably on the scale in western countries, while the clergy has been undergoing a gradual decline over several hundred years. The military profession rose in the deference hierarchy in the United States after 1940, as it does everywhere when the society is militarily endangered.

The judgment which underlies the act of deference is a synthetic judgment which assesses simultaneously a large number of relevant characteristics. A process similar to that of averaging occurs. Hence, a very wealthy man who keeps low company and whose occupation is disreputable might rank lower in most people's opinion than a less wealthy person whose occupation is most estimable and who is an intimate of the great and worthy. In a society which regards the kinship bond as one of the primary ties, close blood relationship to a great person might compensate for a moderate income and a mediocre professional accomplishment in setting one person above another who is wealthier and more successful but who has no eminent ancestors.

Class System.—The class system is an imperfect equilibrium of innumerable individual acts of deference, both "pure" and "mixed" with elements of the occupational, property and political systems. The class system might be extremely inequalitarian, as in the ante-bellum South, or it might be highly equalitarian, as in modern Norway. The members of the society might classify themselves and each other into a set of status classes which shade off into one another, or the classes might be sharply defined and distinguished from one another.

In an inequalitarian society, the acts of deference will express sentiments of great inferiority or superiority. The deference of the lower classes will be full of self-abasement before the superiors, and the latter will treat the former as barely human. European feudal society was like this. In contrast, there can be societies with a much higher degree of equalitarianism, in which the highest and the lowest both feel themselves to be part of a common community or humanity and in which accordingly there are not such sentiments of profound and far-reaching superiority and inferiority. Few persons in these societies feel themselves to be very much better or worse than anyone else. The modern western countries, and above all those societies which grew up on the frontiers without an inheritance of an elaborate inequalitarian class structure—namely, Canada, the United States, Australia and New Zealand—tend in this direction.

Although logically it is possible for any number of classes to be formed in a given society, once individuals of approximately similar status are grouped into classes, this does not, in fact, happen. There is a tendency for the society or its parts to act as if there were relatively few classes. Such classes as are recognized are not, of course, internally homogeneous, and persons within them make many distinctions which are not seen or acknowledged by those who are not in intimate contact with them. They are moreover practically never defined in the minds of most of those who refer to them. Persons who are especially "conscious" or sensitive about their own social status will try to define quite precisely the boundaries separating, among the persons with whom they come into face-to-face contact, those with whom they will associate and those with whom they will not associate on the grounds of their class status. Such "status-sensitive" persons are in most societies in varying but almost always small minorities, and even they do not have precise conceptions of the boundaries between classes other than those adjacent to their own class. Most of the class system is rather dimly differentiated in the minds of their members. Thus, the status judgment is not a precise judgment; it is only vague and approximate, in terms of higher and lower.

Boundaries are more precise in societies with an official system of stratification (*i.e.*, a titled nobility, a system of "estates" and a body of sumptuary legislation designed to demarcate class boundaries) and with relatively undeveloped mercantile, administrative and professional middle classes (like France in the 17th century or Russia before 1917). Even in such societies, however, the official stratification system covers in a differentiated manner only a small proportion of the social hierarchy. For the rest of the society, although retaining significance, it is too undifferentiated to suffice. In consequence, a further system of stratification of the type discussed in the preceding paragraph emerges spontaneously.

The sharpness of the boundaries of status groups is at its height in a caste system, because endogamy is a requirement there to an extent unattained in other types of stratification systems. There is of course a tendency for all status groups to be endogamous, but where personal affection is accorded some sway and where other considerations, such as personal beauty and personal merit, enjoy relative autonomy in competition with status considerations in the selection of marriage partners, this endogamy is always far from complete. In the caste system, however, endogamy reaches its highest level; in consequence, the inheritance of occupations in a static economic system and the strength of kinship ties add their force to already powerful status sentiments.

In all large societies, and particularly in those undergoing a moderate rate of change creating new roles, a considerable amount of upward mobility and some downward mobility are inevitable. It is especially pronounced in societies in which there are special institutional arrangements for training and selection and for the inculcation of standards of judgment which accord a high value to improved class status. This tends to raise problems relating to claims to higher status on the part of the recently ascended and denial of these claims by those with whom the recently risen persons seek to associate as a confirmation of their higher status. The denial of claims to deference of the "parvenu," because he is too new, or too crude, or too rich, or too contaminated with foreign connections or for whatever reasons, is a fertile source of alienation in society and a powerful factor in the promotion of change.

This phenomenon brings to the fore another property of the status system which merits mention. The discussion hitherto has proceeded as if there were, vagueness notwithstanding, a consensus in every society regarding the criteria for the granting of status as well as consensus in the assignment of the status of particular persons and institutions. This is not so. There is some disagreement and a great deal of sheer unconnectedness in the status judgments of all large societies. The groups which enjoy higher status positions in their own eyes and in the eyes of those adjacent to them will usually have a stronger view of their claims and merits than will those groups that feel themselves to be inferior. The lower classes, while acknowledging the superiority of their "betters," do so with reluctance and ambivalence. And in some instances some of the members of these classes deny outrightly that superiority. Ethically radical and politically revolutionary attitudes constitute the extreme form of denial of the claims of the "superior" to their superior status.

The human mind finds inferiority hard to accept in unadulterated doses, and some persons find it harder to take than others. In the lower and middle classes there is often a tendency to deny the validity of the criteria by which the upper classes have enjoyed their superior status. For example, in 18th-century France there was a widespread denial by the mercantile and professional classes of the legitimacy of kinship connections and of heredity as a basis for deference, while they praised the criteria of occupational proficiency and personal merit such as honesty, diligence and intelligence. (This outlook was expressed in the *Declaration of the Rights of Man and Citizen,* which declared "careers open to talent"). Ambivalence and resentment are widespread without, however, going so far as revolution—and even revolutionaries cannot completely expunge from their minds all the status criteria of the society they are revolting against, as is shown by the re-establishment of many of the prerevolutionary status patterns in the Soviet Union. Those whom the prevailing system of evaluation relegates to a lower status, even while sharing and acknowledging that status, simultaneously resent and deny it. The proportions of acknowledgment and denial vary among individuals and among societies, but it is safe to assert that it practically never approximates either extreme in any large society.

The imperfection in the integration of the class system is furthered by the limited range of attention and interest of a large proportion of the population. As a result, they do not participate as much in the larger class system as they do in their local class subsystem, comprising largely the persons with whom they have face-to-face contact. Only occasionally do they respond explicitly to the larger class system, and then they might do so dissensually.

Status System and Social Organization.—The conflict of classes is a reality of all large societies and cannot be eliminated. It is inevitable for the reasons given in the foregoing section. The lowly status is injurious to the sense of dignity of many persons, especially when it is reinforced by resentment against authority, however legitimate, and the desire for goods and services which cannot be acquired on the basis of income earned through the sale of services or goods in the market. The modern labour unions and employer's associations are responses to these facts. But even in societies in which labour unions are either not allowed or are shorn of the functions which they have developed in free societies, the conflict of classes persists, though it must operate through other institutions or even surreptitiously.

The conflict of classes is not always of constant intensity. It varies among societies and periods, and even at any one time in a given society only an extremely small proportion of the population will be much absorbed by the class conflict in its more active and organized form. (In the Bolshevik Revolution in St. Petersburg, only a few thousand persons were actively engaged.) Much of the population participates by assent, a much smaller number participates by the payment of dues to organizations which promise to bring advantages to the class or some sector of it, and a far smaller number plays an active part in the organization. (It has been said that in Great Britain only 10% of those who vote for the Labour party belong to the party; of those who belong, only 10% ever come to meetings; and of those who come to meetings only 10% take an active part in party affairs, even of the most humble and occasional sort.) Thus what the Marxists call "class consciousness," which would be more precisely called "aggressively alienated class identification," is a rather uncommon phenomenon, even in modern industrial societies. Normal class conflict is fully compatible with a high degree of responsible citizenship and a considerable measure of social order.

Sentiments concerning class status and the individual's identification of himself in terms of a particular class status do, however, short of aggressively alienated class identifications, play a very permeative role in social life. Within the family, they affect parents' hopes for their children's future careers, spouses, friends and associates. They influence the extent to which a parent will exert himself to improve his economic lot so that the family will not only have more conveniences and amenities but so that it can also enjoy a higher status. It influences in large part the mother's decisions in the domestic economy and in the expenditure of income on various types of household articles. It affects the choice of place of residence and the choice of friends and associates. It is seldom the exclusive factor in such choices, but it is also seldom entirely absent.

Face-to-face relationships are of particular significance in the stratification system. It is in such relationships that individuals perceive their own status in the judgments of others. It is in such relationships that they can exhibit their own claims to the deference of others by acting, speaking and dressing in a certain manner. This is the reason why more discriminating and sensitive judgments are rendered about the nearby social environment than about those sectors of the society which are more remote. Yet considerations of class status do not overwhelm all other considerations in face-to-face relationships. The more human beings see of each other, the more they respond to each other as persons. They judge each other as persons worthy of being liked or disliked, of being loved or hated. Relationships which commence with status considerations foremost often develop into relationships in which personal affection or dislike becomes preponderant. Because personal relationships tend to begin in a situation of homogeneity in class status, friendships and marriages tend to fall within narrow ranges in class status. To the extent that they do not, they bring the classes rather closer together.

Face-to-face relationships, whether status or personal elements preponderate, play an important role in the status system as a whole. For those who are in the lower part of the status system, face-to-face relationships, usually with persons of approximately similar status, reduce the danger of denial of their status dignity out of resentment or contempt by those who are respectively lower or higher; while for those at the top of the status hierarchy, the tendency for like to associate with like confirms self-esteem and diminishes the danger of direct denial.

Thus, through the individual's sense of civic membership and his belief in its justice and through his face-to-face relationships and his limited focus of attention, inequalities in class status, which are an inevitability of large, differentiated societies, are rendered more tolerable to the sense of individual dignity. Therewith, his society is maintained in a state of equilibrium.

BIBLIOGRAPHY.—Max Weber, *The Theory of Social and Economic Organization*, pp. 390–395 (London, New York, 1947); Max Weber, *Essays in Sociology*, pp. 180–195 (New York, London, 1946); Joseph Schumpeter, *Imperialism and Social Classes* (New York, Oxford, 1951); H. Goldhamer and E. Shils, "Types of Power and Status," *American Journal of Sociology*, vol. xlv, pp. 171–182 (1939); Talcott Parsons, *Essays in Sociological Theory*, rev. ed., pp. 386–439 (Glencoe, Ill., 1954); W. Lloyd Warner and P. S. Lunt, *The Social Life of a Modern Community* (New Haven, Oxford, 1941); D. V. Glass (ed.), *Social Mobility in Britain* (London, 1954). (E. A. Ss.)

CLASS DAY, in American high schools, colleges and universities a day on which the members of the senior or graduating class celebrate the completion of their courses. The ceremony may take the form of a literary program involving the reading of the class history or the class poem, the delivery of the class oration or the presentation of the class play; it may include, too, the planting of the class ivy or the class tree or the burning of books in a huge bonfire to signify liberation from classroom routine. Formal presentation of a memorial gift to alma mater, athletic contests, campus singing, receptions, banquets and other forms of entertainment reflecting the traditions of the institution may also characterize the event.

CLASSICAL EDUCATION. In the universities of Great Britain archaeology, anthropology, numismatics, epigraphy, psychology, philology and geography are recognized as essential to the classical scholar who would understand and describe clearly conditions of life in the ancient civilizations. Western Europe has learned to realize the measure of its debt to Greece and to estimate the nature of the legacy it has received from imperial Rome. The precision of classical literature leads to a sense of proportion, a standard of values, a respect for the truth of words and accuracy of thought. In the principal secondary schools classical studies are not losing ground (*see* PUBLIC SCHOOLS). As historical links exist with university foundations, the great public schools conserve the best traditions of classical scholarship. In the ordinary secondary schools Latin is taught as one of several competing subjects. Of methods in use the following is one of the most interesting and most original.

The Direct Method.—The direct method of teaching foreign languages aims at connecting the foreign word, phrase or sentence directly with a thing, act or thought, without the intervention of English. When a certain number of words have been learned, new ones are explained by a paraphrase in the same language; and in the final stage, the literature is read and discussed in the original.

A working system has been devised by which this method can be applied to Latin and Greek. Time is saved, because the whole lesson is taken up with the language; attention is kept, because the language used is real to us instead of artificial; understanding is easy, because what we do or see explains what is said. In proportion as we exclude English words from our minds, we come to think in the language, and a feeling for its idioms and turns of speech is soon developed. Since the vocabulary used is simple and deals with everyday and familiar life, the attention can be exercised on the peculiar inflections which distinguish the ancient languages. Grammar is learned after use, not before, and is therefore less irksome. Short exercises are used, to illustrate grammar; they do no harm if they come in their proper place (after use) and in due proportion. With the reading book, from the very first all is read aloud and explained in the same language, the explanations being written and learned. English is never used unless it cannot be helped. When the pupils are fit to read an author, they know enough to dispense with English. Formal translation from English into Latin or Greek, the most difficult of all exercises, is reserved for the last two years of school life. Whoever does not understand must ask. No one is blamed for not understanding; all are blamed for not asking.

In the reading lesson every line of the matter is read aloud; and very often the mere manner of reading shows whether the text has been understood, and if it has not, it can be explained simply by correct reading. By reading the memory is filled, the ear is taught, the taste is trained; the language, in short, is learned in the most effective way. So much so that verses of all sorts, lyrics included, are written with ease by imitation. But the real merit of this method lies in its effect on the learner. From the first stage to the last, the learners are willing to learn and happy in learning. (C. Br.; W. H. D. R.)

The United States.—Classical education in the United States began with the founding of Harvard college and the Boston Latin school in about 1638. Following the English model (probably Cambridge) the only requirement for entrance to Harvard was the ability to read and speak Latin, and some knowledge of Greek forms, and this was also the aim of the Latin school. All lectures were in Latin, the curriculum consisted almost wholly of the classics and students were required to speak Latin on the campus. The subsequent progress of classical education has been divided roughly into three periods: the pre-revolutionary period, the period to the close of the Civil War, and the modern period.

During the first period admission requirements remained much the same, as at Harvard, even arithmetic was not required until 1693, and then not universally. In the colleges the classics remained supreme, although arithmetic, geography and anatomy were included in the curriculum of William and Mary in 1693, and physics in that of Yale in 1701. Also the forerunner of the University of Pennsylvania, under the influence of Benjamin Franklin, made considerable provision for science, and an impressive programme in science and history was announced by Columbia in 1754, which, however, was not adhered to.

The middle period was one of great educational expansion. Many new colleges and secondary schools were founded, and the States began to make provision for higher public education in the State universities. Public high schools also began to multiply. The curricula of the colleges were greatly extended, and the appearance of new subjects in the requirements for entrance involved provision for them in the fitting schools. At first Greek and Latin, later Latin alone, were obligatory on all candidates for degrees, and while in some academies, notably those for girls, and in the State universities, the tendency was to greater freedom, still the general tone of education was cultural, interpreted as classical.

The modern period has been one of revolution, both in ideals and practices. The carrying out of the theory of universal education, and the rapid growth of industrialism demanded greater provision for vocational and scientific training. The public high schools still clung closely to the classical tradition but they showed the new influence in the great broadening of their curriculum. Where this was not done, vocational and trade schools discarded the classics for a more immediately practical training. In higher education, either separate scientific and technical schools were established, or increased provision was made for science in the colleges and universities, and modern languages and the social sciences vied with the natural sciences in pressing their claims.

Room for the new subjects could only be obtained at the expense of the classics. The first to be seriously affected was Greek, which, though vigorously defended, had by 1928 been eliminated almost entirely from the curriculum of the secondary schools, and was studied by very few undergraduates in college. Latin also was severely curtailed and at one time seemed likely to go the way of Greek. Since the World War, however, there has been some reaction in favour of Latin in the colleges and it has continued to hold a large place in the schools, partly because it is still an important requirement for entrance to college. It was estimated that over 1,000,000 pupils were studying Latin in the schools in 1928. It is not, however, the Latin of former days. Under the attacks of the new psychology and the advocates of practical studies the teaching of Latin, which formerly had been largely a mechanical preparation for entrance examinations, has now been adapted rather to the immediate needs of the pupils studying it. In 1920 the general education board arranged with the American Classical League to conduct an investigation of the classics (chiefly Latin) in the secondary schools. In the report, published in 1924, the aims of the teaching of Latin were set forth as follows: to read and understand Latin; to increase the pupil's ability to understand the Latin element in English, and to read, speak and write English; to develop historical and cultural background, correct mental habits and right attitudes towards social situations; to increase the ability to learn foreign languages; and to give an elementary knowledge of the principles of language structure. In the furtherance of these aims extensive recommendations were made as to curriculum and method of teaching. These have been very widely adopted and the text-books are rapidly being reconstructed to carry them out. As a result the outlook is bright for continued support of Latin, particularly in the secondary schools, as an important element in American education. (G. L.)

France.—In France during the greater part of the 19th century, the position of classics in secondary schools was supreme. They alone led to the baccalaureate:—sole entrance to the universities and the liberal professions. Towards the end of the century, a strong movement in favour of modern languages and science arose. In 1898 a parliamentary committee was appointed to inquire into the subject. They reported in 1899, but it was not till 1902 that their conclusions were embodied in the establishment of four alternative courses, a full classical, a Latin-modern languages, a Latin-science and a purely modern course, all of which led to the university. These courses remained unchanged for nearly 20 years, and during that period the classical candidates for the baccalaureate, who in 1904 numbered 3,337, fell to 2,775 in 1924. The Latin-modern rose from 1,217 to 5,964, the Latin-science from 2,229 to 5,241 and the science-modern languages from 2,742 to 5,241. Thus, while Greek declined, the students taking Latin increased more than twofold and amounted to over 70% of the candidates.

The World War brought its aftermath of discussion. In 1922 M. Bérard, the minister of public instruction, proposed to make Latin and Greek obligatory in the earlier stages, and to cut down the courses of two (classical or modern). A bitter struggle followed, in which the majority of expert opinion was against him. None the less, in May 1923 the President of the republic issued a decree embodying the proposals of M. Bérard, and requiring a certificate of proficiency in Latin and Greek from all future candidates for the baccalaureate. A year later the Ministry fell and was replaced by a Radical one. The two courses have been maintained, but classics are no longer obligatory for all, though as the curricula of the girls' schools have now been assimilated to those of the boys, a classical education is equally open to the former.

Germany.—In Germany up to the end of the 19th century, classics were likewise supreme. The full classical school, the Gymnasium, was with one or two exceptions the sole avenue to the university and liberal professions. In 1890, at the instance of the Kaiser, a conference was called in Prussia. Its conclusions, largely embodied in the curricula of 1892, reduced the number of hours given to classics and dethroned the latter in favour of the mother tongue, while the universities were thrown open to pupils from the Realgymnasium (Latin-modern school) and to a large extent to those from the Oberrealschule (modern studies school). Similar reforms had already been adopted by other German states. The next outstanding feature was the founding of Reformgymnasia, where the first language was French, Latin not being introduced till the fourth and Greek till the sixth year, both being taught intensively. This type was largely adopted in Prussia before the war. Classical studies have been open to girls since 1904, but the number taking them has not been very great. For education since the war, no statistics are available, but according to one authority, "the desertion of schools with Latin as a central subject is general." Others are less pessimistic and the prevailing opinion seems to be that the Reformschulen will ultimately be the future type of German classical education.

Italy.—Of the other European countries, the most interesting one from the classical standpoint of view is Italy. Here, thanks to the reforms of Gentile, there has been a strong reaction in favour of classics, and by the royal decrees of May and Nov. 1922, classical studies have been strengthened in the higher schools not only of the purely classical but also of the scientific type. Latin in fact is now obligatory in all secondary schools. Room for this increase has been found by cutting down the number of subjects and reducing the time given to mathematics; the main object of the reform being to replace the former encyclopaedic aim of the school by a cultural one based on direct knowledge of the classics. Latin is also a principal subject in the girls' high schools.

Belgium.—In Belgium again the position of classics appears to have improved. A committee was appointed after the War to consider the reform of the school syllabuses and the position of Greek. As a result, classics have been maintained in the Athénées Royales (high schools) and further Greek and Latin can be studied in those *écoles moyennes,* which are not within convenient distance of an athénée.

Norway.—In Norway, likewise, the classics have recovered ground. In 1896 Greek was entirely banished from secondary education; to-day it is included in one section of the higher schools (gymnasia), and can be studied by girls as well as boys.

Czechoslovakia.—The republic of Czechoslovakia has largely maintained the previous types of education, which were on German lines and as the system is co-educational, classical or Latin studies are equally open to girls.

Sweden.—In Sweden classics seem to have somewhat lost ground. The pupils following a full classical or Latin course, who ten years ago were in a majority, are now outnumbered by those taking modern studies. (C. Br.; W. H. D. R.)

Latin American Countries.—In Latin American countries less attention is given to study of classical languages than in other countries whose culture is derived from the classical heritage. In the first place secondary schools in most Latin American countries were established at a time of reaction against schools maintained by the teaching orders which had emphasized the classical basis in secondary education. Secondly, universities have consisted in the main of loosely associated faculties for professional preparation and are only just beginning to permit the study of liberal art subjects either in existing faculties of philosophy as in Buenos Aires, or in newly created faculties as in Santiago. In these the study of the classics may find encouragement in time. Thirdly, the secondary school curriculum has developed by an accretion of subjects and unlike the development in European countries and the United States, little provision has been made for options or for differentiated courses. Consequently, when the list of subjects to be carried became too burdensome, a solution was found by dropping those subjects, especially Latin, which the pupils found too difficult and whose utility was not recognized by the parents.

The situation in general may be illustrated from the practices of some of the leading Spanish American countries. In the Argentine a movement to make Latin an optional subject began as early as 1870 and was realized in 1886; in 1891 proposals began to be made to drop it and by 1901 it disappeared entirely except in three schools that enjoy special privileges of autonomy. Greek had disappeared as early as 1863. In Chile Latin ceased to be required for graduation from a secondary school in 1877 and gradually disappeared. In 1925 an inquiry elicited the opinion that room should be found in certain schools for the study of Latin with or without Greek. It is significant to note, however, that all students in the Instituto Pedagogico, the institution for training secondary school teachers, must take Latin, if they wish to become specialists in Spanish or any modern foreign language. In Uruguay Latin grammar was taught in the first two years of the secondary school course in 1889 but was dropped in 1909. Latin is required in Mexico of students who plan to enter the faculty of law of the university.

In Brazil the exception to the general practice may be found, for here Latin is required for four years of the six year secondary course and Greek survives in some schools on an optional basis.

The secondary school situation is reflected in the universities. The general absence of liberal arts faculties has been noted. The small number of professors of Latin or of Greek is to be found at the Universities of Buenos Aires and La Plata in the Argentine, in the Instituto Pedagogico of the University of Chile and in the University of Concepción in Chile, and in the private Colegio Mayor de Nuestra Señora del Rosario in Colombia. Latin, if not Greek, is still cultivated by the ecclesiastical orders and it is under the direction of their members that those who are interested in the classics may pursue their studies beyond the level of the secondary schools. (I. L. K.)

CLASSICS. "What need to speak of Democritus? . . . Who does not place this philosopher above Cleanthes, Chrysippus, and the others of later times? These appear to me to be fifth class as compared with him" (*qui mihi cum illo collati quintae classis videntur*). Thus Cicero, *Academics* ii. 23, 73. The expression "fifth class," natural and familiar as it sounds to a modern ear, has an interesting history. Among the constitutional reforms ascribed to Servius Tullius, the sixth king of Rome, was the division of the citizens into five *classes* according to the amount of their property as determined from time to time by a census. Hence the fifth *classis* denoted the lowest class of citizen from the point of view of wealth. It appears from Aulus Gellius, vi. 13, that the term *classicus* was applied only to the first or highest *classis:* "Not all those who were enrolled in the five classes were called *classici,* but only the men of the first class, who were rated at 125,000 *asses* or more. 'Below class' was the appellation given to those of the second or other classes rated at a lower sum. . . . This I have briefly noted because apropos of M. Cato's speech in support of the Voconian law the question is often asked what is meant by *classicus* and what by 'below class.'" When or by whom the term was first used in a metaphorical sense to denote an order of merit, we do not know. This extension is already implied in the *quintae classis* of Cicero. But the first extant example of *classicus* to denote the highest order of literary merit seems to be Aulus Gellius (2nd century A.D.) xix., 8, 15. Julius Caesar in his treatise *De Analogia* had laid down the doctrine that *quadrigae* (in the plural), even of a single chariot, is the only correct use, and conversely that *harena* (sand) is only used correctly in the singular. Gellius narrates a conversation on the matter with M. Cornelius Fronto, who supports the opinion of Caesar, and concludes with the words: "Now go, and when you have time see if you can find *quadrigae* in the singular, or *harena* in the plural, written by any of the elder orators and poets—I mean, by one who is a *classicus* and *assiduus* writer, not one who is *proletarius.*" *Assiduus* seems to have been applied more generally to members of the wealthier classes, being equivalent to *locuples* and indicating a person of property (Cic. *Rep.* ii. 22–40; *cf.* Aul. Gell. xvi. 10). *Proletarii,* on the other hand, were the poorest citizens who contributed nothing to the state but their offspring (*proles*); (*cf.* Aul. Gell. *l.c.,* Cic., *Rep.* ii. 22–40). In modern times the word "classic" is in common use of any author who has tholed the assize of the centuries, or even of one who in his own time is classed with those who have: Macaulay, *Boswell's Life of Johnson:* "What a singular destiny has been that of this remarkable man! To be regarded in his own age as a classic and in ours as a companion!" But the term "classics" has been long and widely used to denote more especially the literatures of ancient Greece and Rome, and in that sense it is employed here.

THE LITERATURE OF GREECE

Commencing with Homer, ancient Greek literature may be considered as extending down to Justinian (A.D. 527), thus covering a period of something like 14 centuries. Within this period it is usual to distinguish (1) the Classical period extending from Homer to the death of Alexander (323 B.C.), (2) the Alexandrine period from 323 B.C.–A.D. 100, (3) the Post-Alexandrine period A.D. 100–529. The Byzantine period from 529 to the capture of Constantinople by the Turks produced no Greek literature of first-rate importance.

The unique feature of Greek literature and one which lends it a unique interest, in addition to its intrinsic merit, is its originality. The Greeks invented all the great types of literature alike in poetry and in prose. Thus epic, lyric, elegy, tragedy, comedy in poetry; history, rhetoric, philosophy in prose—were all alike, as the very names declare, the invention of this extraordinarily gifted people. A people whose literature is based upon foreign models may devote themselves to the cultivation of the different types in any order of succession, or may cultivate the several types in the same age with equal enthusiasm. But the Greeks, having no models, discovered and developed the different forms in logical succession, one being evolved from the other according to the spiritual and social impulses of the time. Moreover, when any one form was developed to its full perfection, they seem to have passed on to another. Hence it is that in Greek literature more than in any other we can speak of a given age as the age, not of this individual writer or of that, but as the age of a particular form of literature.

Greek Poetry to 323 B.C.—Greek literature begins with the Homeric epic, represented for us by the *Iliad* and the *Odyssey.*

There is evidence enough in these poems that they are themselves not primitive in the sense of being a first pioneer effort in the writing of epic. The recurrent epithets and conventional formulae, nay, the very metre in which they are written, imply a long ancestry of poetic practice and experiment. What makes these two epics unique among the epics of all literature is that on the one hand they are sufficiently near the dawn of literature to have yet upon them the dew of the morning, to have all the directness and simplicity and naïveté which we associate with primitive poetry; and on the other hand they belong to a stage of development so far advanced as to have outlived the imperfection of form, and the triviality or vulgarity of thought which, in early poetry, are apt to offend the cultured reader. Moreover, they have developed at once a language and a metre—from what elements and by what stages developed we do not here enquire—which together constitute a vehicle for narrative epic such as no other people have ever possessed. And because of this union of a language uniquely suited to the metre, and a metre uniquely suited to the language, the union has resisted divorce. Down to the latest times, the same language and the same metre continued to be the one medium of Greek epic. The Romans borrowed the metre, but in Roman hands its character is entirely changed, and whatever other merits Roman epic may possess, they are assuredly quite other than the merits of Homeric epic. Attempts to transplant the hexameter (*q.v.*) into English were—for reasons which cannot be here elaborated—foredoomed to failure. And what has become the favourite medium for epic in English, viz., blank verse, suffers in comparison with the Homeric hexameter much in the same way as the Roman hexameter does in comparison with the Greek, a lack of lightness and mobility: defects which both in Roman epic and in English, find their compensation in certain other qualities which are, however, of value only from the point of view of poetry in general, assuredly not from the point of view of epic poetry in particular.

Alongside the Homeric type of *Epos, i.e.,* the epic of chivalry, which had for its subject the story of war and adventure in the heroic age, the κλέα ἀνδρῶν of *Iliad,* ix. 189, etc., the Greeks early developed quite another type of *Epos,* which had for its business to inculcate the traditional wisdom of the race. As Hesiod, the earliest of the didactic poets, belongs roughly to the Homeric age—in Greek tradition Homer and Hesiod are regularly coupled together and regarded as contemporaries: Herod ii. 53; Plato, *Rep.* 363 A; 377 D; 599 D; Aristoph., *Ran.* 1,033 *seq.*—he naturally chose for his didactic poems the Homeric hexameter. Two didactic poems are ascribed to Hesiod—the *Theogony* and the *Works and Days.* True to Greek custom the hexameter remained down to the latest times the recognized medium for didactic poetry. The *Theogony* of Hesiod may be regarded as the forerunner of the philosophical poems bearing the title Περὶ Φύσεως (On Nature), of which three were especially notable: (1) that of Xenophanes of Colophon, the founder of the Eleatic school of philosophy, in the second half of the 6th century, whose protest against the unworthy ideas of Homer and Hesiod regarding the gods is well known:

πάντα θεοῖς ἀνέθηκεν Ὅμηρός θ' Ἡσίοδός τε
ὅσσα παρ' ἀνθρώποισιν ὀνείδεα καὶ ψόγος ἐστίν . . .
ὡς πλεῖστ' ἐφθέγξαντο θεῶν ἀθεμίστια ἔργα
κλέπτειν μοιχεύειν τε καὶ ἀλλήλους ἀπατεύειν

("Homer and Hesiod ascribed to the gods everything that men think scandalous and shameful. . . . They recounted very many wrongful acts of the gods—theft, fornication and deception of each other."); (2) Parmenides of Elea, the most distinguished of the Eleatics (*c.* 504 B.C.); (3) Empedocles of Acragas (born *c.* 495 B.C.), whose poem was the direct model of the *De Rerum Natura* of Lucretius (Lucret. I. 726 *sqq.*). On the other hand Hesiod's *Works and Days* was the prototype of a long series of poems of the practical type, including the *Theriaca* and *Alexipharmaca* of Nicander of Colophon, the *Phaenomena* of Aratus, the *Halieutica* of Oppian the Cilician, the *Cynegetica,* attributed to Oppian, but the work of a later poet from Apameia in Syria—all of which are extant, and of the no longer extant *Halieutica* of Caecalus, Numenius, Pancrates, Poseidonius, as well as of the *Georgics* of Virgil, the *Cynegetica* of Grattius and Nemesianus in Latin.

To the epic age succeeds that of iambus and elegy. Iambus, as a literary form, although it had a long life, from Semonides of Amorgos (*c.* 625 B.C.) to Callimachus and Herondas in Alexandrine times, never achieved an important independent existence. The reason is sufficiently obvious. The iambus—a short syllable followed by a long (*see* IAMBIC)—as the chief component of ordinary prose speech is not of itself adequate to support an independent type of poetry. It is true that it does so in modern literature, as for example in English. But the mere name "blank verse" by which the iambic metre is usually described practically admits that "blank verse" differs from ordinary prose in either one of two ways. Either it betrays its poetic intention by an exactness of rhythm which is repugnant to prose, *i.e.,* by a rhythm the recurrences of which produce metre, or by the quite adventitious use of rhymed endings, "the invention," as Milton says, "of a barbarous age, to set off wretched matter and lame metre." But in any case the iambus as an independent form never attained first-rate importance in early times, nor does its recrudescence in Alexandrine times in any way suggest that it could ever be of great importance by itself. As we shall immediately see, in conjunction with lyric metres in tragedy and comedy it was able to find a place which could not have been taken either by the epic hexameter or by any other metre.

Elegy, on the other hand, consisting of alternate hexameters and pentameters (*qq.v.*) is the nearest approximation to epic. But there does not seem ever to have been the least danger in Greek of confusing the function of elegy with that of epic. The name ἔλεγος, ἐλεγεῖον, ἐλεγεῖα, ἐλεγεία is of quite uncertain origin, but everything tends to show that from the first it was essentially of a plaintive character, being regularly accompanied not by the lyre, the instrument of mirth, but by the flute, the instrument of mourning (ἔλεγοι οἱ πρὸς αὐλὸν ᾀδόμενοι θρῆνοι, Didymus *ap.* schol. Aristoph., *Av.* 217; Pausan. x. 7.5; *cf.* Aesch., *Ag.* 990, *Eumen.* 332; Soph., *Tr.* 640 *sqq.;* Eurip., *Hel.* 85, *Iph. Taur.* 146, 1091; Ovid, *Ep.* xv. 7, *Amor.* iii. 9.3; Hor. *c.* i. 33.2). Who invented the form is not known (Hor. *A.P.* 77).

Quintilian, curiously enough, regards Callimachus as the chief elegiac poet, and Philetas of Cos as the second (x.1.58), and Propertius regards these two poets as his masters (v.1.1). In any case the Greeks, at a very early period, extended the range of elegy far beyond the dirge or lament to poems of war and of traditional wisdom. But they did not, like Ovid, use the elegiac metre as practically a substitute for the epic hexameter. The text of Theognis (of Nisaean Megara, *c.* 500 B.C.) in two books, is the longest elegy that has come down to us. It hangs together very loosely and is rather a series of elegies of varying length than a single poem. In the Alexandrine age we have various fragments of the *Aitia* of Callimachus and the whole (with one slight lacuna) of his Hymn entitled the *Bath of Pallas* (Λουτρὰ Παλλάδος) in 142 lines. But the type of elegy which was carried to the highest perfection by the Greeks was what is generally known as the epigram, a highly polished poem in elegiacs, varying in length from a single distich to half-a-dozen or more, and of very various content. This type makes up the great bulk of the collection known as the Greek Anthology (*q.v.*).

Next in order of development and, of course, to some extent coincident in point of time, we have lyric poetry or song, and this of two types—on the one hand the individual or personal song, and on the other the choral lyric. Of the first the remains are exceedingly meagre and, indeed, are chiefly confined to the fragments of Alcaeus and Sappho. Of the high merits of the latter the Greeks seem to have entertained no doubt, and modern critics—whether professed classical scholars or amateurs like Swinburne—have vied with one another in finding words of enthusiastic and extravagant eulogy.

Of choral lyric, on the other hand, we have very extensive remains, both as an independent literary form, and as an element of tragedy and comedy. Of the first our most important representative is Pindar, of whom, apart from considerable fragments, we possess some 45 odes classed—not always correctly—as epinician odes, or odes in celebration of victors in the games (Olympian, Pythian, Nemean, Isthmian). We have also recovered in recent years (1896) a papyrus containing a certain amount of his junior contemporary Bacchylides, about six poems being practically complete. The manner in which these poets succeed in contriving that a poem which is in the first instance written to celebrate such an ephemeral event as a victory in the games should be of permanent appeal, is a very interesting literary study, which will be more fittingly discussed in connection with Pindar (*q.v.*).

The next important development is the drama, including, of course, both tragedy (with the Satyric drama) and comedy. While in all likelihood these two species of drama were of contemporaneous origin, tragedy was the earlier to attain a high degree of perfection: Aristotle's statement (*Poet.*, c. v., 1449^a36) of the comparatively late date at which comedy was not formally recognized by the State, is confirmed by epigraphic evidence from which it appears the comedy was not officially recognized by the State until 488–487 B.C., while Thespis, the father of Attic tragedy, is said to have produced his first tragedy in 534 B.C.

Tragedy is said by Aristotle to have originated ἀπὸ τῶν ἐξαρχόντων τὸν διθύραμβον ("with the leaders of the dithyramb," *Poet.* 4.1449^a10), and this seems to agree with the facts. The literary development of the dithyramb in honour of Dionysus is associated with the Dorian Corinth, and Greek tragedy on the face of it seems to be a combination of Doric choral song with Ionic dialogue. The great period of Attic tragedy is the 5th century B.C. and is mainly represented for us by the remains of the three great tragedians, Aeschylus (525–456 B.C.), Sophocles (496–406 B.C.) and Euripides (*c.* 480–406 B.C.) (*qq.v.*). We also possess Euripides' *Cyclops,* the only extant Satyric drama, the recently discovered *Ichneutai* of Sophocles being in a fragmentary form. The usual method of the production of tragedy in the 5th century was in the form of a trilogy of tragedies followed by a δρᾶμα σατυρικόν (Satyric drama). The relation of this last form of drama, in which the spirit is in the vein of comedy, while the chorus is a choir of satyrs, to tragedy is a subject of debate. Aristotle regards the satyric element as original (*Poet.* 4.1449^a19) which seems the more probable view. On the other hand it has been held, both in ancient and modern times, that the satyric element was not original. According to an old view it was superadded to tragedy by way of comic relief (Hor., *A.P.* 220 *sqq.*). Prof. Ridgeway, holding that tragedy originally was non-Dionysiac, but connected with the solemn commemoration of the dead, derives *saturoi* from *Satrae,* a Macedonian tribe, and holds that the introduction of the satyric element was coincident with the introduction of the worship of Dionysus at Athens towards the end of the 7th century B.C.

Comedy originated, according to Aristotle, ἀπὸ τῶν τὰ φαλλικὰ (ἐξαρχόντων) ἃ ἔτι καὶ νῦν ἐν πολλαῖς τῶν πόλεων διαμένει νομιζόμενα, "with the leaders of the phallic songs which still survive in many cities as an institution" (*Poet.* 4.1449^a 11). This again seems a very probable account, the name κωμῳδία being derived, not from κώμη, village, but from κῶμος, a company of revellers (Arist., *Poet.* 3.1448^a36 ff). These phallic songs were sung (Aristoph., *Ach.* 261, "And I will follow and sing the phallic song,") by lewdly dressed processionalists, *phallophoroi,* and the intention was by mimetic symbolism to promote fertility (Athen. 621 E. For their dress and procedure *cf.* Athen. 622 B). Similar customs exist even at the present day, *e.g.,* in Macedonia.

The Alexandrine scholars distinguished Attic comedy into Old (παλαία) and New (νέα), the further distinction of Middle (μέση) comedy dating only from the time of Hadrian. For us the only poet of the Old Comedy of whom a complete play is extant is Aristophanes (*q.v., c.* 446–385 B.C.).

We note some features which belong to the earliest stages of comedy. We notice first the frequency with which the chorus, from which the comedy takes its name, represents some species of animal. Similarly we hear of plays by Magnes entitled *Birds, Frogs, Gall-wasps* (*cf.* Aristoph. *Eq.* 522 *seq.*). It is impossible to doubt that tragedy in the same way got its name from the fact that the chorus was represented as He-goats (τράγοι), or that the Satyric drama was also named from its chorus of He-goats (σάτυροι, *cf.* שְׂעִירִים) Is. 13.21. Puck = Bock (Ger.) = Buck (Eng.). Then we have the *Parabasis* or address to the spectators, also primitive, as is the *Agon* or debate between two opponents. The later plays of Aristophanes show a considerable divergence from the earlier. The three earliest plays—*Acharnians, Knights, Wasps*—have a fully developed *Parabasis,* while in three of the later plays—*Lysist., Eccl., Plutus*—the *Parabasis* has completely disappeared. Similarly with the place of the chorus in general. Thus in the *Plutus* the office of the chorus is confined to dialogue, and there are no choral songs. The later plays thus exhibit tendencies which are carried still farther in the New Comedy. Menander (*q.v., c.* 323–293 B.C.), though his date falls in the Alexandrine period, has nothing to do with the Alexandrines: he declined the invitation of Ptolemy I. to go to Alexandria and remained in Athens. The characteristic feature of his comedy seems to have been faithful representation of life (*cf.* Syrian. in Hermog. 2 p.23 8 Rabe). Although his scanty remains have been greatly augmented in recent years by discovery of papyri, we still have no complete play. The word Χοροῦ appears after *Epitrepontes* 201: otherwise, Chorus, *Agon, Parabasis* have completely disappeared.

Greek Prose to 323 B.C.—While prose doubtless preceded poetry, prose as a developed literary form is later than poetry. Hence the history of Greek prose down to 323 B.C. is a much shorter story than that of Greek poetry in the same period. If we take the three great literary types of prose to be history—the novel or romance, when it is developed is merely fictitious history, *cf.* Bacon, *Advanc. of Learning* ii.: "Poetry . . . in respect of matter is nothing else but feigned history, which may be styled as well in prose as in verse"—oratory, philosophic essay or dialogue—the natural order of development is history (including the fable or apologue, and the speech as subsidiary elements), oratory, philosophic prose.

Three *historians* in this period are represented by complete works. First we have the *History* of Herodotus (*q.v., c.* 484–425 B.C.). His conception of the function of history is clearly stated in his opening paragraph: Ἡροδότου Ἁλικαρνησσέος ἱστορίης ἀπόδεξις ἥδε, ὡς μήτε τὰ γενόμενα ἐξ ἀνθρώπων τῷ χρόνῳ ἐξίτηλα γένηται, μήτε ἔργα μεγάλα τε καὶ θωυμαστά, τὰ μὲν Ἕλλησι, τὰ δὲ βαρβάροισι ἀποδεχθέντα, ἀκλεᾶ γένηται, τά τε ἄλλα καὶ δι' ἣν αἰτίην ἐπολέμησαν ἀλλήλοισι. "This is the history of Herodotus of Halicarnassus, published in order that what has happened may not be forgotten of men by the passing of time, and that the great and admirable actions of the Greeks and the barbarians may not become unappreciated, and in particular the reasons for the war between them." His object is thus simply to prevent the achievements of the past from being obliterated by time; he has no notion that a knowledge of the past should have any bearing either on the conduct of the present or the anticipation of the future. As to his conception of the duty of the historian, we need only note that he travelled widely and used all the sources of information open to him, whether monumental or oral. In matters of dispute, he endeavours to state both sides of the question, but with refreshing candour he warns the reader that he does not affirm the truth of either side (ii. 123, vii. 152). On any view Herodotus must always be regarded as one of the most charming of historians. His air of candour and naïveté (Quintil. x. 1.73) heightened by the archaic suggestion of the dialect (Ionic) in which he writes and the simple structure of his composition (λέξις εἰρομένη), his digressions, his picturesqueness give him an irresistible appeal.

Thucydides of Athens (*q.v., c.* 460–*c.* 396 B.C.) wrote a *History of the Peloponnesian War,* now divided into eight books. He tells us (i. 1) that he commenced to write his *History* as soon as the war began, as he foresaw that it was likely to be a greater and more important war than any that had yet taken place, an opinion founded on the fact that both the Athenians and the Lacedaemonians were at the height of their power, while the other Greek States were likely to range themselves on the side of one or other of the protagonists in the conflict. His failure in 424 to save Amphipolis led to his going into exile, a circumstance which gave him the opportunity to study the war from both sides (v.26). His conception of the function of history differs markedly from that of Herodotus. His idea is that a knowledge of the past is the best guide to the future (i. 22). Two peculiarities of his *History* must be noted. First the annalistic order of treatment. That is to say, instead of treating an episode of the war as a whole, he narrates events κατὰ θέρος καὶ χειμῶνα, *i.e.*, after the form of a diary—all the events of a particular summer are grouped together, however unconnected they may be, and these are then followed by the events of the ensuing winter. Another remarkable feature is the use of set speeches composed in a highly elaborate form—showing the exaggerated use of the antithesis which characterized early Greek rhetoric. His own account of the conception of these speeches is given in i. 22: "as to the speeches delivered by the several combatants either when they were about to go to war, or when they were already involved in it, it was difficult both for me in the case of speeches which I heard myself, and for those who reported to me speeches from other quarters, to remember the exact words. I have written what it seemed the various speakers would have said if they spoke to the purpose, while keeping as close as possible to the general sense of what was actually said."

The third of the historians is Xenophon of Athens (*q.v., c.* 431–*c.* 355 B.C.). His *Hellenica* in seven books continues the history of Greece from the point reached by Thucydides (411 B.C.) down to the battle of Mantineia in 362 B.C. His *Anabasis* in seven books describes the expedition of Cyrus, the Persian prince, against his elder brother Artaxerxes II. In this expedition 10,000 Greek mercenaries took part. When Cyrus fell in the battle of Cunaxa (401 B.C.) and the Greek leaders were put to death by Tissaphernes, Xenophon caused new leaders to be chosen, including himself. The main part of the *Anabasis* describes the retreat of the Greek mercenaries. Other strictly historical works by Xenophon are his essay upon Agesilaus, king of Sparta; an essay on *Athenian Revenues;* another on *Lacedaemonian Polity.*

The art of *rhetoric* was a development of the 5th century, the pioneer professional teachers of Oratory of whom we chiefly hear being Corax of Syracuse, his pupil Tisias and Gorgias of Leontini (whose style we can infer from the extant fragments). The Alexandrine canon recognized ten Attic orators: (1) Antiphon (*q.v., c.* 480–411 B.C.) of whom we possess three Tetralogies, each consisting of four speeches, and three speeches in real cases. The interest of these speeches is twofold, first as examples of early forensic oratory, and secondly, all being concerned with cases of murder, as throwing light upon some intimate matters of Athenian social life which would otherwise be obscure; (2) Andocides (*q.v.*, born *c.* 440), under whose name four speeches are extant; (3) Lysias (*q.v.*), son of a Syracusan μέτοικος, of whom 34 speeches are extant. Simple and unaffected in style, they throw a flood of light on Athenian domestic and social life; (4) Isocrates (*q.v.*, 436–338 B.C., when "that dishonest victory at Chaeronea, fatal to liberty, Kill'd with report that old man eloquent"), of whom we have 21 orations. His interest is chiefly stylistic; he greatly influenced Cicero and through him modern prose style; (5) Isaeus (*q.v., fl. c.* 360 B.C.), of whom we have 12 speeches (11 and 12 being incomplete). All the speeches, except No. 12, deal with the testamentary disposition of property and are of inestimable value for the knowledge of Attic private law; (6) Demosthenes (*q.v.*, b. 384 B.C.), under whose name we have 69 orations (not all, however, being orations, and not all genuine), the greatest oratory of antiquity (Quintil. x. 1.76). While his fame rests especially on the *Philippics, Olynthiacs, De Falsa Legatione,* and, above all, the *De Corona,* many of the other speeches are of high merit, while his private forensic speeches are extremely valuable for the information they afford, particularly in regard to the operations of commerce in ancient Greece; (7) Aeschines (*q.v.*, b. 390 B.C.), the great rival of Demosthenes, of whom we have three orations; (8) Lycurgus (*q.v.*, born *c.* 390 B.C.): one speech extant; (9) Hypereides (*q.v.*, born *c.* 390 B.C.), of whom we have fragments of six speeches, recovered since 1847 from papyri; (10) Deinarchus (*q.v.*, born *c.* 360 B.C.): three speeches extant.

Philosophic prose is represented by Plato (*q.v.*, b. 427 B.C. on the seventh of the month Thargelion, a day afterwards celebrated annually by the Platonic school—d. 348–7 [his will is quoted Diog. L. iii. 41]), under whose name we have 42 dialogues, besides some dozen letters. Some of the dialogues (in all of which, except the *Laws,* Socrates is an interlocutor) are certainly spurious, others of doubtful authenticity. All we need note here is that in Plato Greek prose attains its supreme perfection, a grace and ease and flexibility, capable of every emotion of which the soul is capable, such as perhaps no other prose in any language has attained. And this, coupled with sublimity and beauty of thought, with power to strengthen those hopes of men which aspire to immortality and seem to promise it, will ensure that such works as the *Apology,* the *Phaedrus,* the *Phaedo,* the *Republic,* will always remain among the most precious heritages of humanity.

Aristotle (*q.v.*, 384–332 B.C.) has left such an immensity of writing that here we can do no more than indicate his chief works under their appropriate headings: 1. Logic: *Topica, Analytica;* 2. Natural Science (for which his position as tutor to Alexander no doubt gave him special advantages): *Historia Animalium, De Partibus Animalium;* 3. Psychology and Metaphysics: *De Anima, Metaphysica;* 4. Ethics: *Nicomachean Ethics;* 5. Politics: *Politics, Respublica Atheniensium;* 6. Literature: *Poetics, Rhetoric.*

For convenience we may here include Aristotle's successor as head of the Peripatetic school, Theophrastus of Eresos (*c.* 372–287 B.C.), of whose writings we possess only: 1. *Historia Plantarum* (Περὶ φυτῶν ἱστορίας). 2. *De causis plantarum* (Περὶ φυτῶν αἰτιῶν). 3. *Characters* (χαρακτῆρες), and a few short pieces such as *De Signis* (Περὶ σημείων), which was apparently one of the sources used by Aratus for that part of the *Phaenomena* (733–1154) which is called Διοσημίαι, and some smaller fragments.

The Alexandrine Age, 323 B.C.–A.D. 100.—1. Before reviewing the Alexandrine *poets* individually, it is worth while to note certain characteristics of the Alexandrine poetry in general. In the first place it is no longer an original poetry like that of the Classical period, but imitative. One symptom of this is that quite different kinds of poetry are cultivated by the same poet. Next it is a learned poetry for the most part, and makes its appeal in the first place to a learned audience—being full of learned allusions, strange or archaic or dialectic words (γλῶσσαι) which had little meaning for the ordinary man. Again, as in all learned poetry, the mere knowledge of the work of an earlier poet impels the imitator in the search for novelty to sacrifice simplicity. What is meant can be well seen by comparing Homer's description of the abode of the gods in *Odyssey* vi. 42 *sqq.* with the successive imitations by Lucretius, Tennyson, Swinburne and again Tennyson. And the need for extreme elaboration tends to the cult of the short and highly polished poem rather than of the longer poem in which such uniformly high polish would make an excessive demand alike on the poet and on his reader. Again we note that the passion of love becomes now not a subsidiary, but a leading motive. Finally we notice a tendency—not perhaps unconnected with the growth of large cities—to take for theme the happiness of the simple peasant's life.

Callimachus (born *c.* 310 B.C.) is represented by six Hymns (five in hexameters, one in elegiacs), and by a large number of fragments in a variety of metres. Recent discoveries of papyri have added considerably to our knowledge of his work (especially the Αἴτια and Ἴαμβοι). He is the champion of the short poem (Athen. 72 A). On the other hand his contemporary and rival, Apollonius Rhodius, attempted in his *Argonautica* in four books (5,835 lines) to revive the long epic (*cf.* Callim. *Hymn* ii. 106, with Apollon. Rh. iii. 932 *seq.*). The didactic epic is revived by Aratus of Soli in Cilicia (born *c.* 315 B.C.) in his *Phaenomena* (1,154 lines), an astronomical poem, sometimes called Φαινόμενα καὶ Διοσημίαι because it falls into two well marked divisions—sometimes considered to be distinct poems—1–732 describing the relative position of the stars in the heavens and their risings and settings, 733–1154 dealing with weather signs in general. The poem, which was greatly praised in later times (Ovid, *Amor.* i.15.6) and was translated by Cicero, contains two passages of unusual beauty, the *Prooemium,* from which St. Paul quotes

(Acts xvii. 28: "As certain also of your own poets have said, 'For we are also his offspring' ") and the lines (96–136) which tell how Justice forsook the earth. Nicander (born *c.* 200 B.C.) continued the didactic epic in a series of poems of which two are extant: *Theriaca* (958 lines), on the bite of venomous beasts, and *Alexipharmaca* (630 lines), on antidotes. Neither of them has any poetic value.

We hear of a *Pleiad* of eminent tragedians of the time of Ptolemy Philadelphos, but we have no extant comedy or tragedy. Lycophron, one of the *Pleiad,* has left us, besides a few short fragments of tragedy, a poem of notorious difficulty called *Alexandra, i.e.,* Cassandra. Elegy is largely cultivated, the most famous elegist being Philitas (Philetas) of Cos (*c.* 300 B.C.), whose name is also associated with that of Callimachus by Propertius (iv.1.1).

The one important new poetic development of the period is the bucolic idyll associated with the names of Theocritus (born *c.* 305 B.C. in Syracuse, *cf. A.P.* ix. 434, Athen. 284 A) and the later Bion and Moschus (probably 2nd century B.C.). This type of poetry, a short poem in hexameters dealing with country life, and especially with herdsmen, goatherds and shepherds, became the model for the *Bucolics* of Virgil, and through him of all later pastoral poetry. The beautiful lament for Bion (= Mosch. *Id.*), the authenticity of which some now deny, was the model for Virg. *Bucol.* X., Milton's "Lycidas," and Shelley's "Adonais." The curious type of poetry called a mime, which has apparently some affinity with the idyll, is now represented by the eight mimes of Herondas (discovered in Egypt, 1890). The papyrus ms. obtained from the Fayum is in the possession of the British Museum.

2. The *prose literature* of the Alexandrine age is, for the most part, a learned literature. All branches of learning were cultivated with assiduity. The work of the Alexandrines in the department of literary criticism is discussed in a later part of this article. Their work in science—particularly mathematics and astronomy—hardly concerns us here. But a word must be said of three writers of this time who are of more general interest. Polybius (*q.v., c.* 201–120 B.C.) of Megalopolis in Arcadia, composed his *Histories* (Ἱστορίαι) in 40 books, of which only the first five are extant in their entirety, but we know the plan of the whole work. Polybius has none of the graces of style, his virtues being those of accuracy in detail and sound judgment. Strabo (*q.v., c.* 63 B.C.–A.D. 19) of Amaseia in Pontus, wrote a historical work (Ὑπομνήματα ἱστορικά) in 43 books, which dealt cursorily with the period before Polybius, and in detail with the period after Polybius (Suid. *s.* Πολύβιος): of this only fragments are preserved (*Frag. Histor. Gr.* iii. 490 *sqq.*). But his *Geography* (Γεωγραφικά), is preserved almost entire. Quite apart from its value as a contribution to the study of geography, his work is of extraordinary interest to the general student from the multitude of incidental information which it gives with regard to the various peoples mentioned in the course of the treatise. Plutarch (*q.v., c.* A.D. 46–120) of Chaeroneia in Boeotia, was a many sided polymath, most of whose works are fortunately extant. They fall into two groups, the *Parallel Lives* (probably mostly the work of his later life) and the series of popular essays called collectively *Moralia* (Ἠθικά). The *Parallel Lives* (Βίοι Παράλληλοι) consist of a series of biographies (46 extant) of eminent historical characters, a distinguished Greek being coupled with a distinguished Roman, to whom he seemed, in point of career, to bear some resemblance, each couple of biographies being followed by a *Comparison* (Σύγκρισις), in which the two are compared. The order of the biographies as given in the mss. is not that of our ordinary editions, which is based upon the Aldine edition and is without ms. authority, but partly follows chronological order. This arrangement, however, is not Plutarch's: thus, *e.g.,* we know from Plutarch himself (*Theos.* 1) that the *Lives* of Lycurgus and Numa were written before those of Theseus and Romulus. The *Moralia* is an immense collection (7 vols. in Teubner ed.) of essays on the widest variety of topics, ethical (these in the majority—hence the general title), historical, scientific. Though not profound, Plutarch is generally interesting, and the incidental allusions are often of the greatest value.

ROMAN LITERATURE

The story of Roman literature is a comparatively short one. Its whole lifetime is not equal to that single epoch of Greek literature which we call the Alexandrine age. Again, while the literature of Greece exhibits a completely independent development, Roman literature is at every point based upon Greek models. A consequence of this is that, while Greek literature shows a logical development, that of Rome develops more or less fortuitously. While, then, Greek literature is best presented in the order of evolution of the several literary types, there is no such reason for adopting the same method in summarizing the content of Roman literature, and the most convenient method of presentation is the chronological.

Roman literature may be said to begin about the middle of the 3rd century B.C., and it is conveniently divided into three periods: (1) the Republican age, 250–27 B.C.; (2) the Augustan age, 27 B.C.–A.D. 14; (3) the Imperial age, A.D. 14–524.

The Republican Age.—An account of the origins of Roman literature and of its representatives will be found under LATIN LITERATURE: here, where our object is merely to present a conspectus of the extant literature, the earliest period from which nothing but detached fragments survive, may be dismissed with a reference to the articles on Livius Andronicus (*c.* 284–204 B.C.), C. Naevius from Campania (d. Utica 201 B.C.), Q. Ennius (239–169 B.C.), M. Pacuvius (b. 220 B.C.) and L. Accius (b. 170 B.C.).

Far more important from our point of view are two poets who wrote comedies only. T. Maccius Plautus (*q.v.*) of Sarsina, in Umbria (*c.* 251–184 B.C.), is represented by 21 extant comedies—the so-called *fabulae Varronianae* (Aul. Gell. iii. 3. 3). They are all translated more or less closely from the Greek (*cf. Trin.* prol. 18 *Huic Graece nomen est Thensauro fabulae: Philemo scripsit: Plautus vortit barbare, Nomen Trinummo fecit,* and *Asin.* prol. 10).

P. Terentius Afer (*c.* 190–159 B.C.) of Carthage became the slave of Terentius Lucanus, whose name he took on manumission. Six of his comedies are extant. His chief model was Menander: *cf.* Caesar's lines *ap.* Sueton. *Vit. Ter. "Tu quoque tu in summis, O dimidiate Menander / Poneris et merito, puri sermonis amator: / Lenibus atque utinam scriptis adiuncta foret vis / Comica, ut aequato virtus polleret honore / Cum Graecis neque in hac despectus parte iaceres: / Unum hoc maceror et doleo tibi desse, Terenti."* ("You too, even you, half-Menander, are ranked among the highest and rightly, lover of pure Latin; but I wish your smooth verse had comic power, that its virtue might be equally honoured with the Greek and you were not despised in this respect. Terence, I am hurt and pained to find you lack this one thing.") The merit and demerit of Terence, as here stated by Caesar, are precisely what strikes the modern student—the purity of his Latin and his lack of force. In the economy of his comedies, we note an innovation in that the prologue no longer has the function of introducing the play, but serves—much like the Parabasis in Aristophanes—as a vehicle of criticism (*cf., e.g., Adelph.* prol. 15 *seq.; Heaut.* prol. 22).

The earliest work in Latin prose which is extant entire is the *De Agri Cultura* of M. Porcius Cato (*q.v.,* 234–149 B.C.), a mere compendium of precepts on agriculture. His *Res Rusticae* (three books) is also the only complete work extant of M. Terentius Varro (*q.v.,* 116–27 B.C.), the most learned Roman of his time, who in his long life produced an extraordinary variety of works. His agricultural treatise is an immense advance on that of Cato in point of style. Of Varro's work *De Lingua Latina* in 25 books, only 5–10 are extant.

In the hands of Varro's younger contemporary, M. Tullius Cicero (*q.v.,* 106–43 B.C.), Latin prose style attains its highest perfection. Cicero's literary activity is amazing. Apart from his speeches (of which 58 are extant), we have several treatises on rhetoric, a great number of works on philosophy—largely written in the last two or three years of his life and particularly after the death of his daughter Tullia, and finally his correspondence: letters (1) *Ad Familiares* (16 books, 62–43 B.C.), (2) *Ad Quintum Fratrem* (3 books, 60–54 B.C.), (3) *Ad Atticum* (16 books, 68–44 B.C.), (4) *Ad M. Brutum* (2 books. 43 B.C.). The letters, written as they are in a completely intimate and informal manner, constitute an extraordinarily important commentary on the events of his time and, revised in relation to those events, form a very interesting psychological study. G. Julius Caesar (*q.v.*, 102?–44 B.C.) wrote a treatise, *De Analogia* (two books), which one would have liked to see, and a tragedy *Oedipus*, which one would have liked to see still more. We possess, however, his *Commentarii de bello Gallico*, seven books, covering the years 58–52 B.C., and *Commentarii de bello civili*, three books, covering the years 49–48 B.C. The *Bellum Alexandrinum* is probably by A. Hirtius, who also added an eighth book to the *Bellum Gallicum*. The authors of the *B. Hispaniense* and *B. Africanum* are unknown. G. Sallustius Crispus (86–34 B.C.) of Amiternum, wrote the *De Catilinae coniuratione* and the *Bellum Iugurthinum*, both extant, and *Historiae*, covering the years 78–67 B.C., of which we have some fragments.

Poetry in this period is represented by two names of the first rank. T. Lucretius Carus (*q.v.*, *c.* 99–*c.* 55 B.C.) expounds the philosophy of Epicurus in his *De Rerum Natura* (six books), the title being a translation of Περὶ Φύσεως, the title of poems by Xenophanes, Parmenides, Empedocles. He had a high reputation in antiquity. Virgil, who was greatly influenced by him and refers to him (without naming him) in a famous passage of the *Georgics* ii. 490, *Felix qui potuit rerum cognoscere causas Atque metus omnes et inexorabile fatum Subiecit pedibus strepitumque Acherontis avari*, is preferred to him by Quintilian (X. 1.86 *seq.*), on grounds which merely concern the student of oratory, and this preference has been supported by the general judgment, but not a few good judges would reverse the verdict. The strictly philosophical passages no longer appeal, but in the more popular passages, such as the Prooemium (i. 1–43), the eulogy of Epicurus (iii. 1–30), on the folly of fearing death (iii. 892–910), his passionate earnestness (*docti furor arduus Lucreti*, Stat. *Silv.* ii. 7.76), coupled with genuine poetic imagination and a real gift for poetic expression, affects the modern reader perhaps more than anything in Virgil. G. Valerius Catullus (*q.v.*, b. at Verona [Catull. lxvii. 34, Mart. xiv. 195, Ov., *Am.* iii. 15.7] 84–d. *c.* 54 B.C.), the greatest of Roman lyric poets, is represented by 116 poems in a variety of metres, hendecasyllables, iambic, trimeters (including scazons), sapphics, priapean, phalaecean, asclepiadean, hexameters, elegiacs, iambic tetrameter catalectic, galliambic (lxiii). Most of his poetry shows strong marks of Greek influence, and several poems are translations from the Greek: *e.g.*, li. (from Sappho), lxvi. (from the lost *Hair of Berenice* of Callimachus). His hexameters and elegiacs—though sometimes extremely effective, as in his lines at his brother's grave (ci.)—show much less grace and ease than his hendecasyllabic and priapean poems. Apart from technique he has the two chief gifts of the lyric poet—depth of feeling ("Tenderest of Roman poets nineteen hundred years ago"—Tennyson) and simplicity.

The Augustan Age, 27 B.C.–A.D. 14.—P. Vergilius Maro (70–19 B.C., *see* VIRGIL), generally regarded as the greatest of Roman poets, is represented by (1) *Bucolica* (*Eclogae*) ten poems in which Theocritus is imitated or even translated. Of these, only ii., iii., v., vii. and viii. are strictly pastoral, the pastoral setting in others being merely a framework, while in iv. (the so-called Messianic Eclogue) there is nothing of the pastoral at all; (2) *Georgica*, in four books (i. Agriculture, ii. Tree culture, iii. Cattle-rearing, iv. Bee-keeping). The *Georgics* contain some of Virgil's best poetry, *e.g.*, the praise of Italy, ii. 136–176; the eulogy of country life, ii. 458–540; the story of Orpheus and Eurydice, iv. 453–527; (3) *Aeneis*, in 12 books, the great national epic of Rome which, after ten years' work, was still unfinished (witness the "pathetic half-lines," the occasionally uncompleted hexameters) at his death, and was published by L. Varius against the expressed wishes of the poet. Virgil was a slow and careful writer (Quintil. x. 3.8, *cf.* Donat., *Vita Verg.* ix., Aul. Gell. xvii. 10.2). This very care and elaboration probably rather militates against the essentially epic virtues, and it is not so much as a whole that the poem appeals, at any rate to the modern world, as in certain supreme passages in which the poet rises above his immediate theme and which are really in the nature of digressions. Q. Horatius Flaccus (65–8 B.C., *see* HORACE), born at Venusia, was the son of a freedman (*cf.* Hor. *Sat.* i. 6.6; 45, 86). After the battle of Philippi (44 B.C.) he returned to Rome where presently he became a member of the circle of Maecenas. His extant work is of two quite different classes—lyrical (*Odes, Epodes, Carmen Saeculare*) and poems in hexameters (*Satires, Epistles, De Arte Poetica*). The *Satires* (*saturae* or *Sermones*) in two books, written between 41 and 30 B.C., deal lightly with the foibles and follies of social life, and the *Epistles*, 20–13 B.C., in two books, are very much in the same style as the *Satires*, with a greater preponderance of literary themes, which is emphasized in the epistle which bears a separate title: *On the Art of Poetry*. It is upon his lyrical poems that the fame of Horace as a poet really rests (Quintil. x. 1.96), and his success is due, not to any rare and high gift of poetic inspiration, but to his capacity for expressing with unsurpassed felicity, the common thoughts which touch most nearly the common heart of humanity. Albius Tibullus (*q.v.* d. 19 B.C. while still young) belonged to the circle of M. Valerius Messalla Corvinus, and was on friendly terms with Horace, who addressed to him *Carm.* i. 33 and *Ep.* i. 4, and Ovid (*cf.* Ov. *Tr.* iv. 10.51, and the beautiful elegy on Tibullus, Ov. *Amor* iii. 9). We possess four books of elegies under his name, but Bk. iii. is by "Lygdamus," a pseudonym for some undetermined poet; iv. 1 (panegyric on Messalla) is by some unknown author, while iv. 7–12 are by Sulpicia, a poetess of the time of Tibullus. To call him "polished and elegant" as Quintilian does (x. 1.93) hardly does justice to his tender grace.

Sextus Aurelius Propertius (*q.v.*, born *c.* 49 B.C. in Umbria, probably at Asisium [Assisi], where the name Propertius occurs in inscriptions) is represented by four books of elegies. Propertius has an irregular strength which is in marked contrast to the equable polish of Tibullus, and in the matter of form his pentameters have an elasticity and freedom which make the elegiac distich in his hands almost a new metre. Bk. iv. 11—the concluding elegy in our collection—is an excellent example of his mature style. P. Ovidius Naso (b. Sulmo 43 B.C.—died *c.* A.D. 18, *see* OVID) has left us a great variety of work. His undoubted poetic qualities are rather obscured by the amazing polish and facility of his versification. There remain but two poets of the Augustan age who need be mentioned here, both writers of didactic epic. Grattius, a contemporary of Ovid (Ov. *Ep. ex. Pont.* iv. 16.34), wrote the *Cynegetica*, a treatise on hunting after the Greek model, of which 541 lines are extant. Manilius, of whom nothing is known except what can be inferred from his poem—he must have written after A.D. 9, because in i. 898 he refers to the defeat in that year of Varus in the Teutoburg forest—wrote *Astronomica* (in five books), which is extant.

The prose writers of the Augustan age include only one name of first importance. T. Livius (59 B.C.–A.D. 17, *see* LIVY), was born at Patavium (Padua, *cf.* Mart. i. 61.3). In Rome he enjoyed the friendship of Augustus in spite of his admiration of Pompey (Tac. *Ann.* iv. 34). We hear of philosophical works and semi-philosophical dialogues written by him (Senec. *Ep.* 100.9), but his fame rests on his history of Rome (*Historiae ab urbe condita*) down to his own day (it was actually carried as far as 9 B.C.). The work was in 142 books, of which there are extant 35, viz., i.–x. (down to 293 B.C.), xxi.–xlv. (218–167 B.C.). The lost books are represented by *Periochae* (summaries of contents) composed *c.* 4th century A.D., which we possess for all except 136 and 137. An Oxyrhynchus papyrus preserves some excerpts from Bks. 37–40; 48–55. Livy, deficient as he was in technical equipment, is not exactly a scientific historian, but he is at least an honest one. In style he is nearer Cicero (*cf.* Quintil. x. 1.39) than Sallust. His language (despite Asinius Pollio's reproach of *Patavinitas*, Quintil. i. 5.56; viii. 1.3, the reference of which is obscure), with its somewhat poetical colouring, is splendidly adapted to his task (Quintil. i. 1.101). Other minor prose writers are Pompeius Trogus, L. Annaeus Seneca of Corduba (Cordova), and Vitruvius Pollio (*qq.v.*).

The Imperial Age.—Under Tiberius in A.D. 30, C. Velleius Paterculus wrote for M. Vicinius (consul in that year) his *Historia Romana*, a sketch of Roman history in two (extant) books. A contemporary writer of first importance, L. Annaeus Seneca (A.D. 3–65), son of the elder Seneca, has left us nine tragedies imitated from the Greek, and numerous prose philosophical writings. M. Annaeus Lucanus (A.D. 39–65), nephew of the foregoing, is represented by an epic in ten books *De Bello Civili,* on the civil war between Pompey and Caesar. More rhetorical than poetical, Lucan has some memorable lines. Aulus Persius Flaccus (A.D. 34–62), is the author of six satires, mainly on the literary life of his time and on quasi-philosophical subjects. T. Calpurnius Siculus, in the reign of Nero, has left us seven eclogues full of adulation of Nero; the anonymous poem *De Laude Pisonis* is also now attributed to him. L. Iunius Moderatus Columella, contemporary with Seneca, is the author of 12 books *De Re Rustica* in prose except the tenth book which is in hexameters. Next we have a group of four poets: P. Papinius Statius (b. between A.D. 40 and 45, died *c.* 98) author of two epics—*Thebais* and *Achilleis*—and a collection of poems in various metres with the general title *Silvae.* Valerius Flaccus in the time of Vespasian, to whom his poem is dedicated, wrote the *Argonautica* in eight books. The matter is mainly taken from the *Argonautica* of Apollonius Rhodius and the style is a rhetorical imitation of Virgil. *T. Catius Silius Italicus* (d. 101) in the reigns of Nero, Vitellius and Vespasian, wrote an epic *Punica* (17 books). His poem, the matter of which is mainly taken from Livy, is highly rhetorical and has little poetical merit. A much more brilliant poet is M. Valerius Martialis (born *c.* A.D. 40, d. shortly after 100), represented by 14 books of epigrams, some being of remarkable beauty.

C. Plinius Secundus (*c.* A.D. 23–79) in 77 presented Titus with his *Naturalis Historia* (in 36 books). Quite devoid of style and of no independent authority, the work is of considerable importance as preserving information from authorities now lost. M. Fabius Quintilianus (*c.* A.D. 35–95) is the author of the *Institutio Oratoria* in 12 books, book x. containing a sort of comparative sketch of Greek and Roman literary history, which includes very happy critiques of the leading Greek and Roman writers. The greatest prose writer of the Imperial age is C. Cornelius Tacitus (*c.* A.D. 54–*c.* 118); we have his *Dialogus de Oratoribus, Agricola* (A.D. 98) *Germania* (about the same date), *Histories* (A.D. 69–96), *Annals* (probably written after A.D. 116). C. Plinius Caecilius Secundus (61–*c.* 114), nephew of the elder Pliny, is represented by nine books of letters, and in addition by the historically very important *Panegyricus* on Trajan and the correspondence with Trajan (including the extraordinarily important letters 96 and 97, dealing with the trial of the early Christians). C. Suetonius Tranquillus, who, under Hadrian, held the office of imperial secretary (*ab epistulis*), wrote the lives of the emperors (*De Vita Caesarum*) from Caesar to Domitian. We have also his treatise *De Grammaticis et de Rhetoribus,* originally part of a larger work, *De Viris Illustribus,* of which the extant *Vitae* of Terence, Horace, Lucan, Passienus Crispus, and the elder Pliny are fragments. D. Iunius Iuvenalis (b. Aquinum, probably A.D. 67) has left 15 satires written under Trajan and Hadrian. Juvenal is a master of vivid phrase: *e.g.,* his account of street dangers in *Sat.* iii. 264 *sqq.* So his single lines are memorable: "*facit indignatio versum*" (i. 79), "*mens sana in corpore sano*" (x. 356), "*maxima debetur puero reverentia*" (xiv. 47). We must dismiss the remaining authors summarily—with again a reference to their separate biographical articles and the article LATIN LITERATURE: M. Cornelius Fronto (2nd century A.D.); Aulus Gellius (born *c.* 130); L. Apuleius (b. at Madaura, in Africa, A.D. 114); the *Pervigilium Veneris,* by an author unknown; Ammianus Marcellinus (born *c.* 332); Decimus Magnus Ausonius (born at Bordeaux *c.* 300); Claudius Claudianus (born at Alexandria, died 404); Aurelius Prudentius Clemens, the first great Christian poet; C. Lollius Apollinaris Sidonius (*c.* 430–480), and lastly, Boethius (born *c.* 480, executed 524).

HISTORY OF SCHOLARSHIP

Pre-Alexandrine.—The history of classical scholarship goes back to a date so early that it is hardly possible to fix a superior limit. As soon as a philosopher began to criticize a literary work (*e.g.,* Xenophanes on Homer and Hesiod), so soon scholarship in the widest sense may be said to have begun. Philosophic speculation soon raised the question of the relation of the name to the thing named, or, in other words, directed attention to the true or inner meaning of words, the ἐτυμολογία, as opposed to the conventional meaning, and thus founded the science of etymology. Directly connected with this was the question of the right use of language, ὀρθοέπεια, with which the name of Protagoras (born *c.* 485 B.C.) was especially connected (Plato, *Phaedr.* 267 C.). This again naturally led to a consideration of the function of words in a sentence and thus to the evolution of a grammatical terminology. Plato already distinguished ὄνομα and ῥῆμα, not so much as noun and verb, but as subject and predicate (*cf.* Plato *Sophist.* 261; "There are two sorts of intimation of being given by the voice. . . . That which indicates action we call a verb . . . and the other, which is an articulate mark set on those who do the actions, we call a noun" *cf. Cratyl.* 425 A., Aristoph. *Nub.* 681 *sqq.*) Aristotle distinguished ὄνομα, ῥῆμα, ἄρθρον (*Poet.* xxi.7), σύνδεσμος (*Rhet.* iii., 5.2, etc.)—noun, verb, article, conjunction.

Alexandrine Period, 300–1 B.C.—Alexandria (for description *cf.* Strabo 793 *sqq.*) was founded by Alexander the Great in 331 B.C. After his death it became the capital of Egypt and the seat of the Ptolemaic dynasty. Under Ptolemy Soter (323–285 B.C.) and Ptolemy Philadelphus (285–247 B.C.) the two libraries and the museum of Alexandria became the greatest centre of literature and learning in the world.

The first librarian was Zenodotus of Ephesus (*c.* 325–260 B.C.). As librarian he classified the epic and lyric poets, the tragedians being classified by Alexander Aetolus, the comedians by Lycophron. As a scholar he made a critical recension of the *Iliad* and the *Odyssey,* founded on numerous mss., and compiled a Homeric glossary (Ὁμηρικαὶ Γλῶσσαι). He seems also to have dealt with the text of Hesiod, Anacreon and Pindar. As a critical scholar he seems to have erred on the side of too great subjectivity.

The poet Callimachus, who did much in the way of making catalogues (πίνακες), is often said to have succeeded Zenodotus as librarian, but there is no evidence for the statement (*cf. Callimachus,* Loeb ed. p. 6 *sqq.*). The next librarian of whom we hear is Eratosthenes of Cyrene (born *c.* 275 B.C.), who became librarian *c.* 235. A man of many-sided learning (hence called by his admirers *pentathlos,* while his detractors called him *Beta,* implying that he was second-best in all departments, but first in none), he wrote on geography, mathematics, astronomy, chronology. We are here concerned only with his work in classical scholarship, in which his chief production was a treatise on Old Attic Comedy (περὶ τῆς ἀρχαίας κωμῳδίας). His successor in the librarianship was Aristophanes of Byzantium, who became librarian in 195 B.C. He edited Homer, Pindar, Euripides, Aristophanes. He also elaborated a system of critical signs (obelus, sigma, antisigma) and accentuation, divided the strophes of the lyric poets into κῶλα ("limbs") and made an epitome of Aristotle's *Natural History* (ed. Lambros 1885). His successor, Aristarchus of Samothrace (*c.* 217–145 B.C.), enjoyed still greater fame and became for later antiquity the type of the philologist (Cic. *Ad. Att.* i 14.3). He published two editions of Homer, in which he followed the admirable principle, Ὅμηρον ἐξ Ὁμήρου σαφηνίζειν (explaining Homer by Homer), edited Hesiod, and concerned himself also with the text of the lyric poets, the tragedians, Herodotus, and Aristophanes, writing both continuous commentaries (ὑπομνήματα) and treatises on special questions (συγγράμματα). Aristarchus was the first to recognize the eight parts of speech (Quintil. i. 4.20) ὄνομα (noun), ῥῆμα (verb), ἀντωνυμία (pronoun), ἐπίρρημα (adverb), μετοχή (participle), ἄρθρον (article), σύνδεσμος (conjunction), πρόθεσις (preposition).

His pupil, Dionysius Thrax (*c.* 170–90 B.C.), wrote a Greek grammar, Τέχνη Γραμματική, which retained its vogue down to the Renaissance and has been the ultimate model of all modern grammars (ed. Uhlig, Leipzig, 1884). Didymus, on account of his industry surnamed χαλκέντερος (copper-guts), wrote on Homer, Hesiod, Pindar, Bacchylides, the comedians, the Attic orators, and Thucydides.

Post-Alexandrine Period, 1 B.C.–1350.—Dionysius of Halicarnassus (who lived at Rome from 30 B.C. onwards) wrote a number of valuable works on literary criticism: *Letters to Ammaeus I. and II., De Compositione Verborum, De Oratoribus Antiquis, Letter to Pompeius,* etc. A very valuable treatise *On the*

Sublime (Περὶ ὕψους) is extant, probably of the 1st century A.D. Apollonius Dyscolus (*c.* 130) wrote a valuable treatise on syntax in four (extant) books. The most valuable feature of the scholarship of this period is a series of works on lexicography and kindred subjects by Moeris, Phrynichus, Harpocration, Pollux, Hesychius, Stephanus, Suidas, Photius, and the 12th century *Etymologicum Magnum.* Mention should be made of the *Deipnosophistae* of Athenaeus (2nd century) which preserves much curious information and is the source of most of the extant fragments of the Greek comic poets. Libanius (*c.* 314–393) is the author of a Life of Demosthenes and of Arguments to his speeches. With him we must close the tale of classical scholarship for nearly 1,000 years.

The Revival of Learning or the Italian Period 1350–1527.—A general account of the Renaissance is beyond the scope of this article and we can merely mention some of the leading names. Francesco Petrarca (1304–74) and Giovanni Boccaccio (1313–75) have an interest only as pioneers, being interested in Greek, but not themselves expert Greek scholars. Manuel Chrysoloras (1350–1415), a Greek immigrant, taught Greek in Florence (1396–1400). It was at the instigation of another Greek, Gemistus Plethon (1355–1452), that Cosmo de'Medici founded an academy for the study of Plato. His pupil, Joannes Bessarion (1403–72), a native of Trebizond, came to Italy in 1439 with the Greek emperor in an endeavour to unite the Greek and Roman churches. Thereafter he joined the Roman Church, becoming presently bishop of Frascati. He died at Ravenna in 1472, bequeathing his collection of mss. to Venice (St. Mark's Library). Theodorus Gaza (*c.* 1400–*c.* 1478), of Thessalonica, taught Greek for a time at Ferrara, afterwards in Rome and Naples. His Greek grammar was printed by Aldus Manutius at Venice in 1495, and he was also the author of translations of Aristotle, Aelian, Theophrastus *De Plantis,* and of Dionysius, *De Comp. Verborum.* Demetrius Chalcondylas (1428–1511) edited Homer (*ed. princeps,* 1488), Isocrates, Suidas. Laurentius Valla (1407–57) translated Homer, Herodotus, Thucydides. But the greatest philologist of the Renaissance was Petrus Victorius (1499–1584), who edited Sophocles, Isaeus, Aristotle's *Rhetoric, Poetics, Ethics, Politics,* Cicero, Terence, Sallust, Varro's *De Re Rustica.* Lastly, among famous collectors of mss. may be mentioned Poggio Bracciolini (1380–1459), who discovered a great number of Latin mss., and Giovanni Aurispa (*c.* 1370–1459), who, in 1423, brought to Venice 238 mss. including *Venetus A.* of the *Iliad* and the *Codex Laurentianus* (10th century, now in Florence) of Aeschylus, Sophocles and Apollonius Rhodius.

The Greek grammar (Ἐρωτήματα) of Constantius Lascaris printed at Milan by Paravisinus in 1476, was the first book to be printed wholly in Greek.

Later Periods.—*The French Period,* 1530–1700, is characterized by an interest more in the content than the form of the classical authors. Leading names are Budaeus (1457–1540), Robert (1503–59) and Henri Etienne (1528–98); and Adrianus Turnebus (1512–65), Isaac Casaubon (1559–1614), Joseph Justus Scaliger (1540–1609) and Charles du Fresne, Sieur du Cange (1610–88) (*qq.v.*).

The English and Dutch Period (18th century) is a period of comprehensive scholarship—of historical and literary as well as verbal criticism. The leading English scholars are Richard Bentley (1662–1742) and Richard Porson (1759–1808) (*qq.v.*), while in the Netherlands the chief names are Ezechiel Spanheim (1629–1710), the two Burmanns (the elder 1668–1741, the younger 1714–78) (*qq.v.*), Hemsterhuis (1685–1766) (*q.v.*), Valckenaer (1715–85), Wyttenbach (1746–1820) (*q.v.*).

The German Period is inaugurated by F. A. Wolf (1759–1824) (*q.v.*), whose *Prolegomena* to Homer was published in 1795. In this period we have two distinctive types of scholarship—(1) the historical and antiquarian and (2) the critical and grammatical. Leading representatives of the former are B. G. Niebuhr (1776–1831), August Boeckh (1785–1867), K. O. Müller (1797–1840), Otto Jahn (1813–69), Theodor Mommsen (1817–1903) (*qq.v.*) and of the latter G. Hermann (1772–1848), Immanuel Bekker (1785–1871) (*qq.v.*), and Lobeck (1781–1860).

Present Day.—It would perhaps be invidious to mention the names of distinguished scholars either recently gone from us or still living, but a few words may be said of certain features which characterize classical scholarship of the present day.

The most notable development of modern times has been undoubtedly the increased interest in archaeology, in the widest sense, which has been witnessed in the last 100 years, and more particularly in the last half century. As this is written, it is almost exactly a century since the foundation of the Archaeological Institute in Rome (1829). The French schools in Athens and Rome were founded respectively in 1846 and 1873, those of the United States in 1882 and 1895, the British schools in 1883 and 1901. Everywhere, ancient sites have been and are being excavated—Troy, Delphi, Mycenae, Tiryns, Sparta, Olympia, Epidaurus, Dodona, Delos, Crete have yielded results beyond all expectation—while the recovery of papyri from Egypt has not merely restored to us a considerable body of ancient Greek literature, such as Aristotle's *Constitution of Athens* (1891), Herondas (1891), Bacchylides (1897)—to mention only some examples—but has thrown a valuable light on the true nature of New Testament Greek.

The study of one department of archaeology, namely that of anthropology, and in particular of primitive ritual and religion, has strongly influenced the study of classics. There was a time when the attention of scholars was perhaps too exclusively devoted to the literary aspects of the classical writers—to textual criticism and the study of form. As a natural consequence the labours of successive generations were confined to the great literary masterpieces of antiquity, while comparatively little study was given to writers of inferior genius who, nevertheless, preserve for us antiquarian and anthropological information of the first importance. Moreover, much that even in the best authors was either overlooked or misunderstood, has taken a new meaning in the light of the comparative study of the beliefs and institutions of primitive man. It is hardly too much to say that archaeological and anthropological discovery and speculation have been a fruitful and vivifying development of classical studies in recent years.

But the interest in "pure scholarship" which has long been a distinctive feature of the study of classics in this country is still fully maintained. The practice of composition in Greek and Latin, which for long occupied a leading place in our school and university education, appears to have somewhat retrograded, and the art of verse composition in particular seems to be falling into some neglect. On the other hand, there has been in the last 50 years an increasing interest in the art of translation from the classics, and an increasing demand for translations which should be at once accurate in point of scholarship and acceptable from the point of view of literary form. This has been the aim successfully pursued by many scholars writing independently, while it is the professed purpose of such a series as the Loeb in the United States and the Budé series in France.

Although the classics no longer enjoy their old monopoly in education, the study of the Greek and Latin writers seems to flourish as vigorously as it has done at any time, and at the present moment, so far as the evidence goes, the prospects of classical scholarship as an indispensable force in education appear to be singularly bright. *See* also GREEK LITERATURE; LATIN LITERATURE. (A. W. MA.)

CLASSIFICATION is the arrangement of things in classes according to the characteristics that they have in common. Sometimes similar objects are brought together in space, but classification may occur also when the only act of arrangement done by the classifier is the giving of a common name to things of the same kind. In a complex classificatory scheme the *infimae species,* or lowest classes, are subordinated to higher classes, and these again to others still higher until the *summum genus,* or most inclusive category of the system, is reached. It should be noticed, however, that in biology the terms "species" and "genus" are not used, as here, in a relative sense, but indicate classes of two fixed levels; *i.e.,* below orders but above varieties.

When, as often, the *summum genus* is given from the beginning, the problem of classification is the same as that of logical division.

Exhaustiveness and exclusiveness can be secured at each level by dichotomy; *i.e.*, by dividing each class into two subclasses, one of things that have a certain character and the other of things that do not. This method has advantages for certain purposes such as the construction of a flora, but it does not satisfy the demand that kinds which are co-ordinate should be placed on the same level in the classificatory scheme. It has often been said that a logical division should proceed throughout according to one principle, and this is true if it is taken to apply to the division of any one genus into species, for otherwise there can be no guarantee that the species will be mutually exclusive. There is no reason, however, why a librarian should not first divide his books into large groups according to size and then subdivide each group according to subject matter. In contexts such as this there may indeed be many different ways of classifying the same things, all in a sense artificial, but all equally correct for their special purposes. The situation is rather different in science, where we assume the existence of natural kinds.

Classification is important for science because it is a prerequisite of all attempts to discover order in the world. (*See* SCIENTIFIC METHOD.) It started already with the beginnings of speech; but the groupings expressed in ordinary language do not go much beyond the practical needs of the men who use it, and scientists must therefore make their own vocabulary, either by adaptation of what they find in ordinary speech or by constructing new words from old roots. The classifications which they produce in this way sometimes surprise the layman, as for example when they distinguish spiders from insects and place them with crabs in the phylum of arthropods. The reason is that they are especially interested in those groupings which help most in the presentation of knowledge as a system. In biology, for example, the modern phylogenetic classification of organisms according to common ancestry is clearly bound up with attempts to systematize and explain the information collected by natural historians. But the notion of natural kinds is to be found already at the very beginning of the study of nature. Men have a use for words such as "lead" only because they find certain recognizable features such as grayness, weight and fusibility occurring frequently together. If there were no such combinations of observable features to attract attention, there could be no natural science. For the laws that are formulated in science are generalizations about the properties of things belonging to such kinds. In short, there is no clear line of demarcation between the work of scientific classification and the practice of induction (*q.v.*). (W. C. K.)

CLAUBERG, JOHANN (1622–1665), German philosopher, was born at Solingen, Westphalia, and studied the Cartesian philosophy under John Raey at Leyden. He became (1649) professor of philosophy and theology at Herborn and subsequently at Duisburg, where he died. He was one of the earliest teachers of the new doctrines in Germany and an exact and methodical commentator on his master's writings. Clauberg's theory of the connection between the soul and the body is in some respects analogous to that of Malebranche; but he is not therefore to be regarded as a true forerunner of Occasionalism, as he uses "Occasion" for the stimulus which directly produces a mental phenomenon, without postulating the intervention of God (H. Müller, *J. Clauberg und seine Stellung im Cartesianismus*). His view of the relation of God to his creatures is held to foreshadow the pantheism of Spinoza. All creatures exist only through the continuous creative energy of the Divine Being, and are no more independent of his will than are our thoughts independent of us. Clauberg's chief works are: *De conjunctione animae et corporis humani; Exercitationes centum de cognitione Dei et nostri; Logica vetus et nova; Initiatio Philosophi, seu Dubitatio Cartesiana;* a commentary of Descartes's *Meditations;* and *Ars etymologica Teutonum.*

A collected ed. of his philosophical works was pub. at Amsterdam (1691), with life by H. C. Hennin; *see* also E. Zeller, *Geschichte der deutschen Philosophie seit Leibnitz* (1873).

CLAUDE LORRAINE, the name often given in English to CLAUDE GELLÉE or GELÉE (1600–1682), French landscape painter, call in French *Lorrain* or *Le Lorrain.* He was born at Chamagne, near Toul, Lorraine. At about the age of 12 he went to Freiburg im Breisgau and later to Rome to train as a pastry cook, and in this capacity became attached to Agostino Tassi, who had a reputation as a painter of seaports. At an unknown date he had instruction from a Flemish artist, Goffredo Wals, in Naples. In 1625 he made a roundabout journey to Nancy where he was employed for a year as assistant to Claude Deruet, the duke of Lorraine's painter, on work for the ceiling of the Carmelite church (now destroyed). In 1627 he returned to Rome and stayed there till his death (Nov. 23, 1682).

His fame as a landscape painter was established by the end of the 1630s and his numerous patrons, mostly from the Roman church aristocracy, included Pope Urban VIII. It is said that about 1634 Sébastien Bourdon copied one of Claude's landscapes in eight days. To guard against such copying and to record his most famous compositions, Claude made tinted outline drawings of most of his pictures in six paper books which he entitled the *Libro di verità* or *Liber veritatis* (*see* M. Davies, *National Gallery Catalogues: French School* [London, 1946]). This valuable record is at Chatsworth, Eng.; it was engraved in 1777 by Richard Earlom.

Claude's style is, in a manner of speaking, without history, for once he had found his idiom he did not stray outside it. He painted instinctively, not intellectually as did his contemporary Nicolas Poussin, and chose to paint only that which gave him abiding pleasure, namely the reach of golden sunlight on the country around Rome or on the waters of some mythical seaport.

Claude has been called the meeting point of the northern and southern landscape traditions. The northern tradition, that of Adam Elsheimer and Paul Bril, was the one in which Claude had been trained, for his master Tassi was a pupil of Bril. Entailing a dramatic approach to the subject, it depended on marked contrasts of light and dark, on huge tree masses dominating the scene. The southern tradition, represented by the Carracci and by Domenichino, consisted of an intellectual approach to nature which was conceived as a matter of orderly recession and balanced masses. Claude began in the northern naturalistic manner, and his early works (*e.g.*, "View of the Campo Vaccino," Louvre) show a meticulous attention to detail. He gradually emancipated himself from this and moved on to the southern or classical formula but he always kept the northern device of placing a dark tree or building in the foreground to deflect the eye to the source of light on the horizon.

In the 17th century pure landscape did not exist, so that all Claude's landscapes contain a story, either from the Bible or from Greek mythology or the modern romances of Tasso and Ariosto. His subjects have one thing in common: all are treated in an idyllic, as against a dramatic, manner, so that the protagonists do not obtrude themselves too much on the attention. An indifferent figure painter, Claude often delegated this part of his picture to a minor artist such as Jan Miel or Filippo Lauri. As he grew older, the purely anecdotal part of his pictures became reduced in scale and in importance, and at the end of his life nature assumed crushing proportions. He abandoned the more conventional seaport scenes for pure landscape, which took on an intense and visionary quality (*see* "Aeneas Hunting in Libya," 1672, Brussels).

Claude's technique can be studied in any painting of his mature period (*i.e., c.* 1640–60). Structurally he relies on the simple device of a horizon set off by a vertical tree or building in the foreground, all the objects in between being fused by a masterly representation of sun, heat and light. The perspective is established not by compositional lines but by gradations of tone which are themselves governed by light.

Claude rarely painted from nature but he sketched in the open air and worked up the finished pictures in his studio. Perhaps the most precious of Claude's drawings, which display great range and variety, are those rapid and delicate wash sketches which simply establish the relative positions of a tree and a hill. The finished pen drawings are more conventional and northern in style. The British Museum contains several volumes of drawings as do the Louvre and the Albertina, Vienna. Claude's paintings are to be found in all the major European collections, notably the National gallery, London, the Louvre, and the Doria palace, Rome.

BIBLIOGRAPHY.—V. Cousin, *Sur Claude Gelée* (Paris, 1853); M. F. Sweetser, *Claude Lorrain* (London, 1878); Mrs. Mark Pattison (Lady Dilke), *Claude Lorrain, etc.* (Paris, 1884); R. Bouyer, *Claude Lorrain, etc.* (Paris, 1905); W. Friedlaender, *Claude Lorrain* (Berlin, 1921); A. M. Hind, *The Drawings of Claude Lorrain* (London, New York 1925); P. Courthion, *Claude Gellée, etc.* (Paris, 1932); T. Hetzer, *Claude Lorrain* (Frankfurt-on-Main, 1947). (AA. B.)

CLAUDEL, PAUL (1868–1955), French poet, dramatist and diplomat, was born Aug. 6, 1868 at Villeneuve-sur-Fin. He was educated at the Lycée Louis-le-Grand, and entered the consular service in 1892. The early part of his diplomatic career was spent in the east as consul at Foochow, Shanghai and Tientsin. As first secretary at Peking he gained a valuable acquaintance with Chinese life and thought. In 1921 he was made French ambassador at Tokyo after a series of European appointments and three years in Rio de Janeiro.

He was appointed ambassador at Washington (1927), and at Brussels (1933). The worldly wisdom which he had acquired in the course of his official duties did much to stimulate and colour his poetry and helped to make his style among the weightiest and richest in French literature. Though trained in the school of the Symbolists, and especially of Rimbaud, Claudel breaks away from them in certain essential particulars. His fundamental inspiration is catholicism—but the catholicism is the fruit of his own meditation and is, as it were, re-created. The cosmic breadth of his views, his deep metaphysical interest and his fine treatment of both the grandiose and the commonplace derive from his close study of Aeschylus (whose *Oresteia* he has translated) of Dante and of Holy Writ. He has created his own style, a plastic versification founded on a meticulous study of the rhythm of word and pause. Of his purely lyrical works, the following are the principal: *Cinq Grandes Odes* (1910); *Le Cantate* (1914); *Corona Benignitatis Dei* (1915); *Feuilles des Saints* (1925); but his reputation will most surely rest on his plays; those of outstanding merit are: *Tête d'or; La Ville; L'Échange; La Jeune Fille Violaine* (pub. in 1901 under the title *L'Arbre*)—in which the influence of the Symbolists is clearly perceptible; *L'Annonce faite à Marie* (1912) and the great trilogy in which he has attempted to reproduce the moral drama of post-revolutionary days: *L'Otage* (1911); *Le Pain Dur* (1918); *le Père Humilié* (1919). Many of Claudel's chief works have been translated into English, *e.g., Connaissance de l'Est* (by T. Frances and W. R. Benét as "The East I Know"); and *L'Annonce faite à Marie* (by L. M. Still, 1916). Claudel died in Paris on Feb. 23, 1955.

CLAUDET, ANTOINE FRANÇOIS JEAN (1797–1867), French photographer, was born at Lyons on Aug. 12, 1797. Having acquired a share in L. J. M. Daguerre's invention, he was one of the first to practise daguerreotype portraiture in England, and he improved the sensitizing process by using chlorine in addition to iodine, thus gaining greater rapidity of action. In 1848 he produced the photographometer, an instrument designed to measure the intensity of photogenic rays; and in 1849 he brought out the focimeter, for securing a perfect focus in photographic portraiture. He was elected F.R.S. in 1853, and in 1858 he produced the stereomonoscope, in reply to a challenge from Sir David Brewster. He died in London on Dec. 27, 1867.

CLAUDIA NOVA, VIA, an ancient road of Italy, 47m. in length, connecting the Via (Claudia) Valeria with the Via Caecilia and Via Salaria at Foruli, near Amiternum and thus linking together the road systems of north and south Italy. It was built by the emperor Claudius in A.D. 47. Its course and remains, as well as the ancient towns and buildings along it, are described by R. Gardner in *Journal of Roman Studies,* iii. (1913) 205–232.

CLAUDIANUS, CLAUDIUS (Anglicized, CLAUDIAN), Latin epic poet during the reign of Arcadius and Honorius. He was an Egyptian by birth, probably an Alexandrian. In A.D. 395 he appears to have come to Rome, and made his debut as a Latin poet by a panegyric on the consulship of Olybrius and Probinus. (In Birt's edition a complete chronological list of Claudian's poems is given, and also in J. B. Bury's edition of Gibbon (iii. app. i. p. 485), where the dates given differ slightly from those in the present article.)

In 396 appeared the encomium on the third consulship of the emperor Honorius, and the epic on the downfall of Rufinus, the unworthy minister of Arcadius at Constantinople, which was engineered by Stilicho. Claudian's poem appears to have obtained his patronage, or perhaps that of his wife Serena (*Epist.* 2). In 398 appeared his panegyric on the fourth consulship of Honorius, his epithalamium on the marriage of Honorius to Stilicho's daughter, and his poem on the Gildonic War, celebrating the repression of a revolt in Africa. To these succeeded his piece on the consulship of Manlius Theodorus (399), the unfinished invective against the Byzantine prime minister Eutropius in the same year, the epics on Stilicho's first consulship and on his repulse of Alaric (400 and 403), and the panegyric on the sixth consulship of Honorius (404). From this time all trace of Claudian is lost, and he is generally supposed to have perished with his patron Stilicho in 408. It may be conjectured that he must have died in 404, as he could hardly otherwise have omitted to celebrate Stilicho's destruction of the barbarian host led by Radagaisus in the following year. On the other hand, he may have survived Stilicho, as in the dedication to the second book of his epic on the *Rape of Proserpine* (which Birt, however, assigns to 395–397), he speaks of his disuse of poetry. From Augustine's allusion to him in the *De civitate Dei,* it may be inferred that he was no longer living at the date of the composition of that work, between 415 and 428.

Besides Claudian's chief poems, his lively Fescennines on the emperor's marriage, his panegyric on Serena, and the *Gigantomachia,* a fragment of an unfinished Greek epic, may also be mentioned. Several poems expressing Christian sentiments are spurious. It is probable that he was nominally a Christian, like his patrons Stilicho and Ausonius, although at heart attached to the old religion. He was honoured by a bronze statue in the forum, and Pomponius Laetus discovered in the 15th century an inscription (*C.I.L.* vi. 1710) on the pedestal, which, formerly considered spurious, is now generally regarded as genuine.

The revival of Latin poetry at so late a date, and by a poet of foreign birth is remarkable, and it is no less surprising that Claudian should have won fame by official panegyrics. As remarked by Gibbon, "he was endowed with the rare and precious talent of raising the meanest, of adorning the most barren, and of diversifying the most similar topics." This gift is especially displayed in his poem on the downfall of Rufinus. In his celebration of Stilicho's victories Claudian found a subject more worthy of his powers, and some passages, such as the description of the flight of Alaric, and of Stilicho's arrival at Rome, rank among the brightest ornaments of Latin poetry. Yet on the whole he lacks creative power, and his talent is rather that of the rhetorician than the poet.

BIBLIOGRAPHY.—The editio princeps of Claudian was printed at Vicenza in 1482; the editions of J. M. Gesner (1759) and P. Burmann (1760) are still valuable for their notes. The first critical edition was that of L. Jeep (1876–79), now superseded by the exhaustive work of T. Birt, with bibliography, in *Monumenta Germaniae Historica* (x., 1892; smaller ed. founded on this by J. Koch, Teubner series, 1893). Edition with English translation by Platmauer (Loeb series, 1922). There is a separate edition with commentary and verse translation of *Il Ratto di Proserpina,* by L. Garces de Diez (1889); the satire *In Eutropium* is discussed by T. Birt in *Zwei politische Satiren des alten Rom* (1888). There is a complete English verse translation of little merit by A. Hawkins (1817). *See* the articles by Ramsay in Smith's *Classical Dictionary* and Vollmer in Pauly-Wissowa's *Realencyclopädie der classischen Altertumswissenschaft,* iii. 2 (1899); also J. H. E. Crees, *Claudian as an Historian* (1908), the "Cambridge Historical Essay" for 1906 (No. 17); T. Hodgkin, *Claudian, the last of the Roman Poets* (1875). H. Schroff, *Claudians Gedicht vom Gotenkrieg* (1927) with bibliography.

CLAUDIUS, the name of a famous Roman gens. The by-form *Clodius* was regularly used for certain Claudii in late republican times, but otherwise the two forms were used indifferently. The gens contained a patrician and a plebeian family; the chief representatives of the former were the Pulchri, of the latter the Marcelli (*see* MARCELLUS). The following members deserve particular mention:—

1. APPIUS SABINUS INREGILLENSIS, or REGILLENSIS, CLAUDIUS, so called from Regillum (or Regilli) in Sabine territory, founder of the Claudian gens. His original name was Attus or Attius Clausus. About 504 B.C. he settled in Rome, where he and his followers formed a tribe. In 495 he was consul, and his enforcement of the laws of debt was one of the chief causes of the "secession" of the plebs to the Sacred Mount. *See* Suetonius, *Tiberius,* i.; Livy ii. 16–29; Dion. Halic. v. 40, vi. 23, 24.

2. CLAUDIUS, APPIUS, surnamed CRASSUS, a Roman patrician, consul in 471 and 451 B.C., and in the same and following year one of the decemvirs. At first he was conspicuous for his aristocratic pride and bitter hatred of the plebeians. Twice they refused to fight under him, and fled before their enemies. He retaliated by decimating the army. He was banished, but soon returned, and again became consul. In the same year (451) he was made one of the decemvirs who had been appointed to draw up a code of written laws. He managed, by courting the people, to secure his re-election for the year 450, and the new decemvirs, under his leadership, began a reign of terror. Matters were brought to a crisis by the affair of Virginia, the daughter of Virginius, a plebeian centurion. Claudius, desiring to possess her, got a client to swear falsely that she was the child of his slave, and judgment was given in his favour. To save her, Virginius killed her with his own hand. An insurrection was the result, and the people seceded to the Sacred Mount. The decemvirs were finally compelled to resign and Appius Claudius died in prison, either by his own hand or by that of the executioner. For a discussion of the character of Appius Claudius, *see* Mommsen's appendix to vol. i.

of his *History of Rome*, also Livy iii. 32–58; Dion. Halic. x. 59, xi. 3.

3. CLAUDIUS, APPIUS, surnamed CAECUS, Roman patrician and author. In 312 B.C. he was elected censor without having been consul. During his censorship, which he retained for five years, in spite of the lex Aemilia which limited the tenure of that office to 18 months, he filled vacancies in the senate with men of low birth, in some cases even the sons of freedmen (Diod. Sic. xx. 36; Livy ix. 30; Suetonius, *Claudius,* 24). He abolished the old free birth, freehold basis of suffrage. He enrolled the freedmen and landless citizens both in the centuries and in the tribes, distributing them through all the tribes and thus giving them practical control of the elections. In 304, however, the landless and poorer freedmen were limited to the four urban tribes, and the effect of Claudius's arrangement was annulled. Appius Claudius transferred the charge of the public worship of Hercules in the Forum Boarium from the Potitian gens to a number of public slaves. He further invaded the exclusive rights of the patricians by directing his secretary to publish the *legis actiones* (methods of legal practice) and the list of *dies fasti* (or days on which legal business could be transacted). Lastly, he gained enduring fame by the construction of a road and an aqueduct, which—a thing unheard of before—he called by his own name (Livy, ix. 29; Frontinus, *De Aquis,* 115; Diod. Sic. xx. 36). In 307 he was elected consul for the first time. In 298 he was interrex; in 296, as consul, he led the army in Samnium (Livy, x. 19). During the next year he was praetor, and he was once dictator. In spite of his political reforms, he opposed the admission of the plebeians to the consulship and priestly offices; his probable aim was to strengthen the power of the magistrates and lessen that of the senate. He was already blind and too feeble to walk, when Cineas, the minister of Pyrrhus, visited him, but so vigorously did he oppose every concession that all the eloquence of Cineas was in vain, and the Romans forgot past misfortunes in the inspiration of Claudius's patriotism (Livy, x. 13; Justin, xviii., 2; Plutarch, *Pyrrhus,* 19). The story of his blindness, however, may be merely a method of accounting for his cognomen. Tradition regarded it as a punishment for his transference of the cult of Hercules from the Potitii.

His speech against peace with Pyrrhus was the first that was transmitted to writing, and thereby laid the foundation of prose composition. He was the author of a collection of aphorisms in verse mentioned by Cicero (of which a few fragments remain), and of a legal work entitled *De Usurpationibus.* It is very likely also that he was concerned in the drawing up of the *Legis Actiones* published by Flavius. He also interested himself in grammatical questions, distinguished the two sounds R and S in writing, and did away with the letter Z.

See Mommsen's appendix to his *Roman History* (vol. i.); treatises by W. Siebert (1863) and F. D. Gerlach (1872), dealing especially with the censorship of Claudius.

4. CLAUDIUS, PUBLIUS, surnamed PULCHER, son of (3). He was the first of the gens who bore this surname. In 249 he was consul and appointed to the command of the fleet in the first Punic War. Instead of continuing the siege of Lilybaeum, he decided to attack the Carthaginians in the harbour of Drepanum, and was completely defeated. The disaster was commonly attributed to Claudius's treatment of the sacred chickens, which refused to eat before the battle. "Let them drink then," said the consul, and ordered them to be thrown into the sea. Having been recalled and ordered to appoint a dictator, he nominated a subordinate official, but the nomination was at once overruled. Claudius himself was accused of high treason and heavily fined. He must have died before 246, probably by his own hand. *See* Livy, *Epit.,* 19; Polybius, i. 49; Cicero, *De Divinatione,* i. 16, ii. 8; Valerius Maximus, i. 4, viii. 1.

5. CLAUDIUS APPIUS, surnamed PULCHER, Roman statesman and author. He served under his brother-in-law Lucullus in Asia (72 B.C.) and was commissioned to deliver the ultimatum to Tigranes, which gave him the choice of war with Rome or the surrender of Mithradates. In 57 he was praetor, in 56 propraetor in Sardinia, and in 54 consul with L. Domitius Ahenobarbus. Pompey reconciled him to Cicero, whose return from exile he had opposed. In 53 he became governor of Cilicia. During this period he carried on a correspondence with Cicero, whose letters to him form the third book of the *Epistolae ad Familiares.* Claudius resented the appointment of Cicero as his successor, avoided meeting him, and issued orders after his arrival in the province. On his return to Rome Claudius was impeached by P. Cornelius Dolabella, and was obliged to make advances to Cicero, since it was necessary to obtain witnesses in his favour from his old province. He was acquitted, and a charge of bribery against him also proved unsuccessful. In 50 he was censor, and expelled many of the members of the senate. When Caesar marched on Rome he fled from Italy. He was appointed by Pompey to the command in Greece, and died in Euboea about 48, before the battle of Pharsalus. He wrote a work on augury, the first book of which he dedicated to Cicero. *See* Orelli, *Onomasticon Tullianum.*

BIBLIOGRAPHY.—A full account of all the Claudii will be found in Pauly-Wissowa's *Realencyclopädie der classischen Altertumswissenschaft,* iii. 2 (1899). *See* also L. A. Constans, *Un Correspondant de Cicéron, Ap. Claudius Pulcher* (1921).

CLAUDIUS (TIBERIUS CLAUDIUS DRUSUS NERO GERMANICUS), Roman emperor A.D. 41–54, son of Drusus and Antonia, nephew of the Emperor Tiberius, and grandson of Livia, the wife of Augustus, was born at Lugdunum (Lyons) on Aug. 1, 10 B.C. He was kept in the background by (Suet. *Claud.* 4) Augustus Tiberius, owing to his physical infirmities and apparent weakness of intellect, and lived in retirement; it was probably at this time that he became dependent on the company of freedmen. Under Caligula he became more prominent, holding the consulship (A.D. 37) and other public posts; though he was the emperor's butt, many people at Rome must have realized that he might succeed. On the murder of Caligula, Claudius, though not of the Julian gens, was made emperor by the praetorians, who were rewarded with a large donative, and were probably increased in number.

Claudius, though abnormal, was by no means the idiot that our hostile sources would suggest. Despite his pedantry, he had a certain shrewdness, and wished to govern well. In the earlier part of his reign he extended the boundaries of the empire; Mauretania was subdued and annexed in 43, and in the same year Claudius himself took part in the famous expedition to Britain, which gave the Romans a footing in the south of the island; in 44 Judea, which had been entrusted to King Agrippa (*q.v.*), was made once more a province, and in 46 the same fate overtook the client kingdom of Thrace.

In his dealings with the provincials Claudius, despite senatorial opposition, reverted to Julius Caesar's liberal policy. We possess part of his speech proposing that the chieftains of the Aedui should be admitted to the senate (*see* the paraphrase of it in Tacitus *Annals*), and his edict conferring citizenship on the Anauni (Hardy, *Roman Laws and Charters* Oxford, 1912). A large number of municipia and colonies in the provinces owe their origin to Claudius.

The reign of Claudius is marked by the development of the emperor's personal service. There was an extension of procuratorial government in the provinces (*e.g.,* Thrace, Mauretania, and Judea) and provincial procurators were granted jurisdiction equal to that of the emperor in all cases relating to the fiscus. A definite scale of salaries was also instituted. But even more notable was the increased power of the emperor's freedmen, who, while they remained his personal servants, became, in practice, powerful ministers, and received great rewards and honour. (*See,* besides authorities below, Statius, *Silv.* iii. and v.) The rule of the freedmen, who, though efficient, were arrogant and corrupt, was resented by the nobility, but the practice was continued under later emperors, though not to the same extent.

Another grievance was the increased importance of the emperor's private court. Under Augustus and Tiberius its use had been restricted to certain cases of *majestas,* but Claudius had a passion for acting as judge; vast numbers of cases were heard *in camera,* and the emperor's methods seem often to have been capricious.

His public works include a new harbour at Ostia, the draining of the Fucine Lake, and the construction of two aqueducts (*Aqua*

Claudia and *Anio Novus*). His revival of the censorship and extension of the poemerium may be quoted rather as examples of his antiquarianism than as practically important. In 47 he celebrated the Ludi Saeculares.

In the latter part of his reign his government degenerated and he fell entirely under the influence of his favourites and his womenkind.

He had married (as his third wife) Messalina, who, in 47, if we are to believe Tacitus, actually went through a form of marriage with Silius, unknown to Claudius. Narcissus brought about her execution, and, at the prompting of Pallas, the *a nationibus*, Claudius married his niece Agrippina, a marriage which shocked Roman sentiment. She induced him to set aside his own son Britannicus and to adopt as heir Nero, her son by a former marriage. Claudius died suddenly in 54, poisoned, according to Tacitus, by Agrippina. He was deified, but Seneca's satire, the *Apocolocyntosis*, expresses the relief felt at his death.

Claudius wrote several historical works "magis inepte quam ineleganter," including his own autobiography, but all, unfortunately, are lost.

BIBLIOGRAPHY.—Ancient: The *Annals* of Tacitus, Bks. xi., xii. Suetonius and Dio Cassius. *See* also Seneca, *Consolatio ad Polybium*, and *Apocolocyntosis* (ed. Ball, 1902, with introduction and translation); Josephus, *Ant. Jud.* Modern: H. Lehmann, *Claudius und seine Zeit*, with introductory chapter on the ancient authorities (1858); Lucien Double, *L'Empereur Claude* (1876); A. Ziegler, *Die politische Seite der Regierung des Kaisers Claudius* (1885); H. F. Pelham in *Quarterly Review* (April, 1905), where certain administrative and political changes introduced by Claudius, for which he was attacked by his contemporaries, are discussed and defended; Merivale, *Hist. of the Romans under the Empire*, chs. 49, 50; H. Schiller, *Geschichte der römischen Kaiserzeit*, i., pt. i.; H. Furneaux's ed. of the *Annals* of Tacitus (introduction); E. G. Hardy, *Roman Laws and Charters* (Oxford, 1912) for the Edict de Civitate Anammorum; Bell, *Jews and Christians in Egypt* for the edict relating to Alexandria.

CLAUDIUS, MARCUS AURELIUS, surnamed GOTHICUS, Roman emperor A.D. 268–270, belonged to an obscure Illyrian family. On account of his military ability he was placed in command of an army by Decius; and Valerian appointed him general on the Illyrian frontier, and ruler of the provinces of the lower Danube. During the reign of Gallienus, he was called to Italy to crush Aureolus, and on the death of the emperor (268) was chosen as his successor. Shortly after his accession he routed the Alamanni on the Lacus Benacus (some doubt is thrown upon this); in 269 a great victory over the Goths at Naïssus in Moesia gained him the title of Gothicus. In the following year he died of the plague at Sirmium. He enjoyed great popularity, and appears to have been a man of ability and character.

His life was written by Trebellius Pollio, one of the *Scriptores Historiae Augustae; see* also Zosimus i. 40–43; Homo, *De Claudio Gothico* (1900); Pauly-Wissowa, *Realencyklopädie*, ii. 2458 *et seq.* (Henze).

CLAUDIUS, MATTHIAS (1740–1815), German poet, otherwise known by the *nom de plume* of Asmus, was born on Aug. 15, 1740, at Rheinfeld, near Lübeck, and studied at Jena. From 1771 to 1775 he edited a newspaper called the *Wandsbecker Bote* (*Wandsbeck Messenger*), in which he published a large number of prose essays and poems. He died on Jan. 21, 1815. In his later days Claudius became strongly pietistic.

BIBLIOGRAPHY.—Claudius's collected works were published under the title of *Asmus omnia sua secum portans, oder Sämtliche Werke des Wandsbecker Boten* (8 vols., 1775–1812; 13th ed., by C. Redich, 2 vols., 1902). His biography has been written by Wilhelm Herbst (4th ed., 1878). *See* also M. Schneidereit, *M. Claudius, seine Weltanschauung und Lebensweisheit* (1898).

CLAUS, ÉMILE (1849–1924), Belgian painter, was born at Vive Saint-Éloi, Flanders, on Sept. 27, 1849. Receiving early training at the Antwerp Academy of Fine Arts, Claus began as a traditionalist. Soon, however, he came under the influence of certain French painters who had determined to break from the rut, and he completely changed his style, in spite of the fact that he had achieved a certain reputation and his work was remunerative. He started to paint in high lights by the juxtaposition of pure colours. He settled at Astène, in a house on the banks of the Lys, which he called *Zonneschijn.* There he began to paint that beautiful series of views of meadows, gardens, fields, streams and roads.

During the World War Claus resided in London, and from the windows of a house on the Victoria Embankment painted views of the Thames, showing the changing effects of the light and the weather. In 1917 he accompanied the Queen of the Belgians to La Panne, and visited the devastated regions. In 1920 he returned to Astène and worked there until his death, on June 6 1924. He was the recipient of numerous Belgian and foreign honours. He is represented in the Luxembourg, Paris, and in galleries in Venice, Brussels, Antwerp, Ghent and Liège.

CLAUSEL (more correctly CLAUZEL), **BERTRAND,** COUNT (1772–1842), marshal of France, was born at Mirepoix (Ariège) on Dec. 12, 1772, and served in the first campaign of the French Revolutionary Wars as one of the volunteers of 1791. In June 1795, having distinguished himself repeatedly in the war on the northern frontier (1792–93) and the fighting in the eastern Pyrenees (1793–94), Clausel was made a general of brigade. In this rank he served in Italy in 1798 and 1799, in the expedition to S. Domingo in 1802, in Naples in 1806. In 1808–09 he was with Marmont in Dalmatia, and at the close of 1809 he was appointed to a command in the army of Portugal under Massena.

Clausel took part in the Peninsular campaigns of 1810 and 1811, including the Torres Vedras campaign, and under Marmont he did excellent service in re-establishing the discipline, efficiency, and mobility of the army. In the Salamanca campaign (1812) the result of Clausel's work was shown in the marching powers of the French, and at the battle of Salamanca, Clausel, who had succeeded to the command on Marmont being wounded, and had himself received a severe wound, drew off his army with the greatest skill. Early in 1813 Clausel was made commander of the army of the north in Spain, but he was unable to avert the great disaster of Vittoria. Under the supreme command of Soult he served through the rest of the Peninsular War with unvarying distinction. During the Hundred Days he was in command of an army defending the Pyrenean frontier. After Waterloo he escaped to America, being condemned to death in absence. He took the first opportunity of returning to aid the Liberals in France (1820), sat in the chamber of deputies from 1827 to 1830, and after the revolution of 1830 was at once given a military command. At the head of the army of Algiers, Clausel made a successful campaign, but he was soon recalled by the home government, which desired to avoid complications in Algeria. At the same time he was made a marshal of France (Feb. 1831). For some four years thereafter he urged his Algerian policy upon the chamber of deputies, and finally in 1835 was reappointed commander-in-chief. But after several victories, including the taking of Mascara in 1835, the marshal met with a severe repulse at Constantine in 1836. A change of government in France was primarily responsible for the failure, but public opinion attributed it to Clausel, who was recalled in Feb. 1837. He thereupon retired from active service and lived in complete retirement up to his death at Secourrieu (Garonne) on April 21, 1842.

CLAUSEN, SIR GEORGE (1852–1944), English painter, born in London, the son of a decorative artist. He attended the design classes at the South Kensington schools from 1867–73. He then worked in the studio of Edwin Long, R.A., and subsequently in Paris under Bouguereau and Robert-Fleury. His "Girl at the Gate" was placed in the Tate gallery. He became R.A. in 1908 and was knighted in 1927. His series of lectures to the students of the Royal Academy schools was published as *Six Lectures on Painting* (1904), and *Aims and Ideals in Art* (1906). He died at Cold Ash near Newbury, England, on Nov. 23, 1944.

CLAUSEWITZ, KARL VON (1780–1831), Prussian general and military writer, was born at Burg, near Magdeburg, on June 1, 1780. His family, originally Polish, had settled in Germany at the end of the previous century. Entering the army in 1792, he first saw service in the Rhine campaigns of 1793–94, receiving his commission at the siege of Mainz. On his return to garrison duty he set to work so zealously to remedy the defects in his education caused by his father's poverty, that in 1801 he was admitted to the Berlin academy for young officers, then directed by Scharnhorst. Scharnhorst, attracted by his pupil's industry and force of character, paid special attention to his training, and profoundly influenced the development of his mind. In 1803, on Scharnhorst's recommendation, Clausewitz was made "adjutant" (aide-de-camp) to Prince August, and he served in this capacity in the campaign of Jena (1806), being captured along with the prince by the French at Prenzlau. A prisoner in France and Switzerland for the next two years, he returned to Prussia in 1809; and for the next three years, as a departmental chief in the ministry of war, as a teacher in the military school, and as military instructor to the crown prince, he assisted Scharnhorst in the famous reorganization of the Prussian Army. In 1810 he married the countess Marie von Brühl.

On the outbreak of the Russian war in 1812, Clausewitz, like many other Prussian officers, took service with his country's nominal enemy. This step he justified in a memorial, published for the first time in the *Leben Gneisenaus* by Pertz (1869). At first adjutant to Gen. Phull, who had himself been a Prussian officer, he served later under Pahlen at Witepsk and Smolensk, and from the final Russian position at Kaluga he was sent to the army of Wittgenstein. It was Clausewitz who negotiated the convention of Tauroggen, which separated the cause of Yorck's Prussians from that of the French, and began the War of Liberation (*see* YORCK VON WARTENBURG; also Blumenthal's *Die Konvention von Tauroggen,* 1901). As a Russian officer he superintended the formation of the *Landwehr* of east Prussia (*see* STEIN, H. F. K.), and in the campaign of 1813 he served as chief of staff to Count Wallmoden. He conducted the fight at Göhrde, and after the armistice, with Gneisenau's permission, published an account of the campaign (*Der Feldzug von 1813 bis zum Waffenstillstand,* Leipzig, 1813). This work was long attributed to Gneisenau himself. After the peace of 1814 Clausewitz re-entered the Prussian service, and in the Waterloo campaign was present at Ligny and Wavre as Gen. Thielmann's chief of staff. This post he retained till 1818, when he was promoted major-general and appointed director of the *Allgemeine Kriegsschule.* Here he remained till in 1830 he was made chief of the 3rd Artillery Inspection at Breslau. Next year he became chief of staff to Field-marshal Gneisenau, who commanded an army of observation on the Polish frontier. After the dissolution of this army Clausewitz returned to his artillery duties; but on Nov. 18, 1831, he died at Breslau of cholera, which had proved fatal to his chief also, and a little previously, to his old Russian commander Diebitsch on the other side of the frontier.

His collected works were edited and published by his widow, who was aided by some officers, personal friends of the general, in her task. Of the ten volumes of *Hinterlassene Werke über Krieg und Kriegführung* (1832–37, later edition called *Clausewitz's Gesammte Werke,* 1874) the first three contain Clausewitz's masterpiece, *Vom Kriege,* an exposition of the philosophy of war. He produced no "system" of strategy, and his critics styled his work "negative" and asked *"Qu'a-t-il fondé?"* What he had "founded" was that modern strategy which, by its hold on the Prussian mind, carried the Prussian arms to victory in 1866 and 1870, and his philosophy of war became, not only in Germany but in many other countries, the basis of military studies. But it has been argued since the World War that his teaching contributed to the deadlock and costly attrition strategy of 1914–18 through its excessive emphasis on purely military factors, a tendency naturally exaggerated by his disciples. The English and French translations (Graham, *On War,* 1873; Neuens, *La Guerre,* 1849–52; or Vatry, *Théorie de la grande guerre,* 1899), with the German original, place the work at the disposal of students of most nationalities. The remaining volumes deal with military history: vol. 4, the Italian campaign of 1796–97; vols. 5 and 6, the campaign of 1799 in Switzerland and Italy; vol. 7, the wars of 1812, 1813 to the armistice, and 1814; vol. 8, the Waterloo campaign; vols. 9 and 10, papers on the campaigns of Gustavus Adolphus, Turenne, Luxemburg, Münnich, John Sobieski, Frederick the Great, Ferdinand of Brunswick, etc. He also wrote *Über das Leben und den Charakter von Scharnhorst* (printed in Ranke's *Historisch-politischer Zeitschrift,* 1832). A manuscript on the catastrophe of 1806 long remained unpublished. It was used by v. Höpfner in his history of that war, and eventually published by the Great General Staff in 1888 (French translation, 1903). Letters from Clausewitz to his wife were published in *Zeitschrift für preussische Landeskunde* (1876).

See von Meerheimb, *Karl von Clausewitz* (1875), also Memoir in *Allgemeine deutsche Biographie;* Schwartz, *Leben des General von Clausewitz und der Frau Marie von Clausewitz* (2 vols., 1877); Bernhardi, *Leben des Generals von Clausewitz* (10th Supplement, *Militär. Wochenblatt,* 1878).

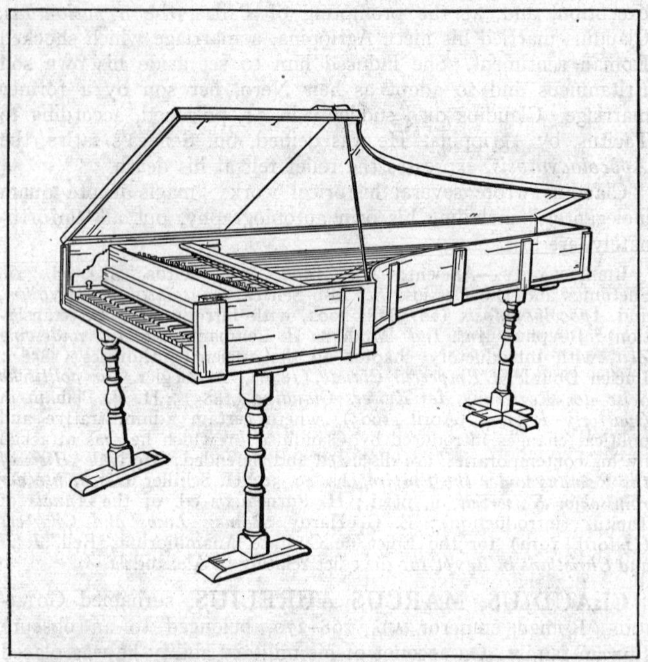

BY COURTESY OF THE METROPOLITAN MUSEUM OF ART

THE CLAVICEMBALO, AN ITALIAN HARPSICHORD OF THE 16TH CENTURY

CLAUSIUS, RUDOLF JULIUS EMMANUEL (1822–1888), German physicist, was born at Köslin, in Pomerania. After attending the Gymnasium at Stettin, he studied at Berlin university from 1840 to 1844. In 1848 he took his degree at Halle, and in 1850 was appointed professor of physics in the royal artillery and engineering school at Berlin and *privatdocent* in the university. In 1855 he became an ordinary professor at Zürich Polytechnic, and professor in the University of Zürich. In 1867 he moved to Würzburg as professor of physics, and two years later was appointed to the same chair at Bonn, where he died. The work of Clausius, who was a mathematical rather than an experimental physicist, was concerned with many of the most abstruse problems of molecular physics. By his restatement of Carnot's principle he put the theory of heat on a truer and sounder basis, and he deserves the credit of having made thermodynamics a science; he enunciated the second law, in a paper contributed to the Berlin Academy in 1850, in the well-known form, "Heat cannot of itself pass from a colder to a hotter body." His results he applied to an exhaustive development of the theory of the steam-engine, laying stress in particular on the conception of entropy. The kinetic theory of gases owes much to his researches. He raised it, on the basis of the dynamical theory of heat, to the level of a theory, and he carried out many numerical determinations in connection with it, *e.g.,* of the mean free path of a molecule. Clausius also made an important advance in the theory of electrolysis, suggesting that molecules in electrolytes are continually interchanging atoms, the electric force not causing, but merely directing the interchange. This view found little favour until 1887, when it was taken up by S. A. Arrhenius, who made it the basis of the theory of electrolytic dissociation. In addition to many scientific papers he wrote *Die Potentialfunktion und das Potential* (1864) and *Abhandlungen über die mechanische Wärmetheorie* (1864–67).

CLAVECIN, the French for "clavicymbal" or "harpsichord" (Ger. *Clavicymbel* or *Dockenklavier*), an abbreviation of the

Flemish *clavisinbal* and Ital. *clavicimbalo*. *See* PIANOFORTE; HARPSICHORD; SPINET; VIRGINAL.

CLAVICEMBALO or **GRAVICEMBALO,** the Italian names for the clavicymbal or harpsichord. "Cymbal" (Gr. κύμβαλον, from κύμβη, a hollow vessel) was the old European term for the dulcimer, and hence its place in the formation of the word. *See* PIANOFORTE; HARPSICHORD; SPINET; VIRGINAL.

CLAVICHORD or **CLARICHORD,** a mediaeval stringed keyboard instrument, a forerunner of the pianoforte (*q.v.*), its strings being set in vibration by a blow from a brass tangent instead of a hammer as in the modern instrument.

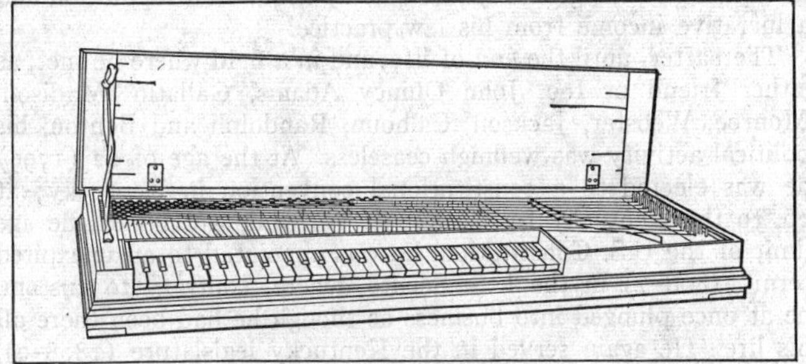

BY COURTESY OF THE METROPOLITAN MUSEUM OF ART

THE MEDIAEVAL CLAVICHORD, A FORERUNNER OF THE PIANO
This instrument differed from the harpsichord in that its strings were struck by tangents, instead of being plucked or twanged by quills. Its tone, though weak, was very delicate and sweet

The clavichord, derived from the dulcimer by the addition of a keyboard, has a long history, being mentioned as early as 1404 in Eberhard Cersne's *Rules of the Minnesingers.*

There were two kinds of clavichords—the fretted or *gebunden* and the fret-free or *bund-frei.* The term "fretted" was applied to those clavichords which, instead of being provided with a string or set of strings in unison for each note, had one set of strings acting for three or four notes, the arms of the keys being twisted in order to bring the contact of the tangent into the acoustically correct position under the string. The "fret-free" were chromatically-scaled instruments.

The first *bund-frei* clavichord is attributed to Daniel Faber of Crailsheim in Saxony about 1720. This important change in construction increased the size of the instrument, each pair of unison strings requiring a key and tangent of its own, and led to the introduction of the system of tuning by equal temperament upheld by J. S. Bach and practically illustrated by him in his immortal "Wohltemperirtes Clavier" ("Well-tempered Clavier") written expressly to encourage its adoption.

BY COURTESY OF THE METROPOLITAN MUSEUM OF ART

A 17TH CENTURY ITALIAN CLAVICYTHERIUM, OR CLAVIHARP, A VERTICAL SPINET

The tone of the clavichord, extremely sweet and delicate, was characterized by a tremulous hesitancy, which formed its great charm, though its very limited power rendered it unsuitable for use in large rooms or concert halls. Nevertheless, on account of the scope which it afforded for individual expression, it was a favourite instrument with all the best musicians in its day. Bach is said to have preferred it to the harpsichord, Mozart loved to play on it, while even Beethoven, though himself long accustomed to the pianoforte, spoke of it as the most expressive of all keyboard instruments.

CLAVICYTHERIUM, a name usually applied to an upright spinet (*q.v.*), the soundboard and strings of which were vertical instead of horizontal, being thus perpendicular to the keyboard; but it would seem that the clavicytherium proper is distinct from the upright spinet in that its strings are placed *horizontally.* In a unique specimen with two keyboards dating from the 16th or 17th century, which is in the collection of Baron Alexandre Kraus, what appear to be vibrating strings stretched over a soundboard perpendicular to the keyboard are in reality the wires forming part of the mechanism of the action. The instrument was probably of Italian or possibly South German origin and it may be noted that its name has also been applied at times to the upright harpsichord.

There is a very fine specimen of the so-called clavicytherium (really an upright spinet) in the Donaldson museum of the Royal College of Music, London, acquired from the Correr collection at Venice in 1885.

For the history of the clavicytherium considered as a forerunner of the pianoforte, *see* PIANOFORTE.

CLAVIE, BURNING THE, an ancient Scottish custom still observed at Burghead, a fishing village on the Moray firth, near Forres. The "clavie" is a bonfire of casks split in two, lighted on Jan. 12, corresponding to the New Year of the old calendar. One of these casks is joined together again by a huge nail (Lat. *clavus;* hence the term). It is then filled with tar, lighted and carried flaming round the village, and finally up to a headland upon which stands the ruins of a Roman altar, locally called "the Douro." It here forms the nucleus of the bonfire, which is built up of split casks. When the burning tar-barrel falls in pieces the people scramble to get a lighted piece with which to kindle the New Year's fire on their cottage hearth. The charcoal of the clavie is collected and is put in pieces up the cottage chimneys to keep spirits and witches from coming down.

CLAVIÈRE, ÉTIENNE (1735–1793), French financier and politician, was born in Geneva on Jan. 27, 1735. He was a political refugee in England, and in 1789 went to France, where he assisted Mirabeau on the *Courrier de Provence* and in the preparation of his speeches. Clavière also published some pamphlets under his own name, and through these and his friendship with J. P. Brissot, whom he had met in London, he became minister of finance in the Girondist ministry, from March to June 12, 1792. After Aug. 10 he was again given charge of the finances in the provisional executive council. He shared in the fall of the Girondists, and was arrested on June 2, 1793. On receiving notice (Dec. 8) that he was to appear on the next day before the revolutionary tribunal, he committed suicide.

CLAVIJO, RUY GONZALEZ DE (d. 1412), Spanish traveller, was born in Madrid. On the return of the Embassy from the court of Timur, Henry III. of Castille sent out another, which included Clavijo. They sailed from St. Mary Port, near Cadiz, on May 22, 1403, touched at the Balearic isles, Gaeta, Rhodes and Constantinople, went by the south coast of the Black sea to Trebizond, and proceeded inland by Erzerum, Tabriz, Teheran and Meshed to Samarkand, where they were favourably received. They returned successfully after great difficulties and reached Spain on March 1, 1406. Clavijo lived in Madrid and died on April 2, 1412. His narrative is the first important one of its kind in Spanish literature.

BIBLIOGRAPHY.—An English version of Clavijo's narrative, by Sir Clements Markham, was issued by the Hakluyt Society in 1859 (*Narrative of the Embassy of R . . . G . . . Clavijo to the Court of Timour*). For the identification of the places mentioned by Clavijo *see* Khanikof's list in *Geographical Magazine* (1874), and Sreznevski's *Annotated Index* in the Russian edition of 1881. A short account of Clavijo's life is given by Alvarez y Baena in the *Hijos de Madrid,* vol. ix. *See* also C. R. Beazley, *Dawn of Modern Geography,* iii.

CLAVIJO Y FAJARDO, JOSÉ (1726–1806), Spanish publicist, was born at Lanzarote (Canary islands). He settled in Madrid, became editor of *El Pensador,* and by his campaign against the public performance of *autos sacramentales* secured their prohibition in 1765. His work would long since have been forgotten were it not that it put an end to a peculiarly national form of dramatic exposition, and that his love affair with one of Beaumarchais' sisters suggested the theme of Goethe's first publication, *Clavigo.*

CLAVILUX, a keyed projection instrument which makes possible the use of light as a medium for aesthetic expression. It was invented by the American artist, Thomas Wilfred, who gave the new art of light its first comprehensible status with the theory that form, colour and motion are its three basic factors. The instrument consists of a number of projectors grouped before a large white screen and controlled from a keyboard that is either attached to the projectors or placed at a distance. The keys, which slide in grooves graduated from 0 to 100, are grouped in tiers, each comparable to a pipe-organ manual. A tier contains three sets of keys connected with the form, colour and motion-producing devices in the corresponding projector in which a strong beam of white light from an incandescent lamp, after passing through the three devices, is projected on the screen as one or more mobile images depending in form, colour and motion upon the positions and movements of the various keys. A skilled player may select to play a silent visual composition previously written by another artist and recorded by means of a special notation system. The instrument has also been used for visual accompaniments to music, dance and drama, in the latter instance permitting projected scenery and a much more delicate control of lighting than is possible by means of the electrician's switchboard. (T. Wi.)

CLAY, CASSIUS MARCELLUS (1810–1903), American politician, was born in Madison county, Ky., on Oct. 19, 1810. He was the son of Green Clay (1757–1826), a Kentucky soldier of the War of 1812 and a relative of Henry Clay. He was educated at Centre college, Danville, Ky., and at Yale, where he graduated in 1832. Influenced to some extent by William Lloyd Garrison, he became an advocate of the abolition of slavery. In 1835, 1837 and 1840 he was elected as a Whig to the Kentucky legislature, where he advocated a system of gradual emancipation. In 1845 he established, at Lexington, Ky., an anti-slavery publication known as *The True American,* but in the same year his office and press were wrecked by a mob, and he removed the publication office to Cincinnati, Ohio. In 1856 he joined the Republican Party, and wielded considerable influence as a Southern representative in its councils. In 1861 he was sent by President Lincoln as minister to Russia; in 1862 he returned to America to accept a commission as major-general of volunteers, but in 1863 was reappointed to his former post at St. Petersburg, where he remained until 1869. Disapproving of the Republican policy of reconstruction, he left the party, and in 1872 was largely instrumental in securing the nomination of Horace Greeley for the presidency. In the political campaign of 1884 he rejoined the Republican Party. He died at Whitehall, Ky., on July 22, 1903.

See his autobiography, *The Life, Memoirs, Writings and Speeches of Cassius Marcellus Clay* (Cincinnati, 1896); and *The Writings of Cassius Marcellus Clay* (edited with a "Memoir" by Horace Greeley, 1848).

CLAY, CHARLES (1801–1893), English surgeon, was born at Bredbury, near Stockport, on Dec. 27, 1801. He qualified at Edinburgh in 1823 and settled in Manchester as a consultant in 1839. In 1842 he first performed the operation of ovariotomy with which his name is associated, and in 1865 was able to show an analysis of 111 cases with a mortality slightly over 30%. Clay was a man of many interests and included geology, numismatics and book collecting among his pursuits. He died at Poulton-le-Fylde, near Preston, on Sept. 19, 1893.

CLAY, FREDERIC (1838–1889), English musical composer, was the son of James Clay, M.P., the celebrated whist authority. Born in Paris, he studied music under W. B. Molique in that city and under Moritz Hauptmann at Leipzig. With the exception of a few songs and two cantatas, *The Knights of the Cross* (1866) and *Lalla Rookh* (1877),—the latter of which contained his well-known song "I'll sing thee songs of Araby,"—his compositions were written for the stage, and have long since been forgotten. Two of them, *Ages Ago* (1869) and *Princess Toto* (1875) were written to libretti by W. S. Gilbert. Clay's last works, *The Merry Duchess* (1883) and *The Golden Ring* (1883), showed an advance upon his previous work, and rendered all the more regrettable the stroke of paralysis which crippled him physically and mentally during the last few years of his life.

CLAY, HENRY (1777–1852), American statesman and orator, was born in Hanover county, Va., on April 12, 1777, and died in Washington on June 29, 1852. His public life covered nearly half a century, and his name and fame rest entirely upon his own merits. He achieved his success despite serious obstacles. He was tall, rawboned and awkward; his early instruction was scant; but he read books, talked well, studied law under George Wythe, the teacher of Jefferson and Marshall, and so, after his admission to the bar at Richmond, Va., in 1797 and his removal next year to Lexington, Ky., he quickly acquired a reputation and a lucrative income from his law practice.

Thereafter, until the end of life, and in a field where he met, as either friend or foe, John Quincy Adams, Gallatin, Madison, Monroe, Webster, Jackson, Calhoun, Randolph and Benton, his political activity was wellnigh ceaseless. At the age of 22 (1799) he was elected to a constitutional convention in Kentucky; at 26, to the Kentucky legislature; at 29, while yet under the age limit of the U.S. Constitution, he was appointed to an unexpired term (1806–7) in the U.S. Senate, where, contrary to custom, he at once plunged into business as though he had been there all his life. He again served in the Kentucky legislature (1808–9), was chosen speaker of its lower house, and achieved distinction by preventing an intense and widespread anti-British feeling from excluding the common law from the Kentucky code. A year later he was elected to another unexpired term in the U.S. Senate, serving in 1810–11. At 34 (1811) he was elected to the U.S. House of Representatives and chosen speaker on the day of his entrance. During the 14 years following his first election, he was re-elected five times to the House and to the speakership; retiring for one term (1821–23) to resume his law practice and retrieve his fortunes. He thus served as speaker in 1811–14, in 1815–20 and in 1823–25. Once he was unanimously elected by his constituents, and once nearly defeated for having at the previous session voted to increase congressional salaries. From 1825 to 1829 he served as secretary of State in President John Quincy Adams's cabinet, and in 1831 he was elected to the U.S. Senate, where he served until 1842, and again from 1849 until his death. Between 1824 and 1848 he was a strong presidential candidate in nearly every campaign.

One of the chief sources of Clay's immediate popularity when first elected to the House in 1811, was his championship of the War of 1812 with Great Britain, which his influence, more than that of any other man, precipitated. While not, perhaps, an altogether advantageous or necessary war, it won the youthful nation the respect of European nations, and a greater independence of them than she had hitherto known. Clay was sent to Ghent as one of the peace commissioners, and signed the treaty, though reluctantly, for he was disappointed in the silence concerning the questions of impressment of American sailors, the fisheries, and the navigation of the Mississippi.

After the war Clay and Calhoun became the foremost champions of the Democratic Republican Party in Congress. Clay refused appointments as minister to Russia and to England, as well as the secretaryship of war under both Madison and Monroe that he might devote his attention to his congressional programme, the three most important features of which were the inauguration of internal improvements, the establishment of a national bank, and the levying of a tariff high enough to build up industries needed in time of war. As a protectionist Clay in 1824 again advocated high duties to relieve the prevailing distress, which he pictured in a brilliant and effective speech. In spite of the opposition of Webster, Calhoun and other prominent statesmen, Clay succeeded in enacting a tariff so high that the people of the Southern States denounced it as a "tariff of abominations." When it overswelled the revenue in 1832 he favoured reducing the rates on all articles not competing with American products, but the new measure reduced the revenue so little and provoked such serious threats of nullification and secession in South Carolina, that to prevent bloodshed and to forestall a free trade measure from the next Congress, Clay brought forward in 1833 a compromise measure for the gradual reduction of the tariff to a 20% ad valorem basis extending over a period of nine years. It lost Clay the support of ardent protectionists but was hailed with favour by the people at large.

Clay's interest in internal improvements resulted naturally from his interest in western expansion and development. He supported the Federal financing or aiding of roads, canals and other schemes of transportation which would bind the east and west together. For a time he argued for the return to individual States of the receipts from all public lands sold within its borders.

BY COURTESY OF THE LEXINGTON CHAMBER OF COMMERCE
"ASHLAND," THE HOME OF HENRY CLAY IN LEXINGTON, KY.

This plan, together with many of his special projects, failed, but the general impetus of his oratory and argument was not lost.

Clay also interested himself passionately in the struggle of the South American nations for their independence. He made resounding speeches in the House in favour of the "eighteen millions of people struggling to burst their chains." He advocated an alliance in the two Americas to counterbalance the Holy Alliance of Europe and work against its designs. He was among the first to recommend recognition of the new nations by the United States, and consequently is still remembered with affection by them. Similarly, in 1824, he made an impassioned speech in favour of Greek independence and supported Webster's resolution for sending an agent or commissioner to that country.

But of all causes and questions, Clay's career was connected most intimately with that of slavery. When only 22 Clay had vainly urged an emancipation clause for the new constitution of Kentucky and never ceased to regret its failure. In 1820 he congratulated the new South American republics on having abolished slavery, pointing out that in this important point of progress they were in advance of the United States. The same year, however, threats of the Southern States to destroy the Union led him to advocate the "Missouri Compromise," which, while keeping slavery out of all of the rest of the territory included in the "Louisiana Purchase" north of Missouri's southern boundary, permitted it in that State. When the slave power became more aggressive in and after the year 1831, Clay defended the right of petition for the abolition of slavery in the District of Columbia, and opposed Calhoun's bill forbidding the use of the mails to "abolition" newspapers and documents. Though he favoured the freedom of the mails and press as regards slavery, he disliked the abolitionists and, because of their insistent, uncompromising demands, held them largely responsible for the hatred and strife which menaced the Union. Clay was lukewarm toward recognizing the independence of Texas lest it should aid the increase of slave territory. Yet he was so anxious to set himself right with the South that he prepared an elaborate speech for the purpose which received pro-slavery approval. His attitude resulted, as he himself declared, in the abolitionists denouncing him as slave-holder, and the slave-holder as an abolitionist. Such straddling undoubtedly was a prime factor in his loss of the presidency, which he always held in view. In 1844, for instance, while a candidate for the presidency, he announced himself against the annexation of Texas, but on other grounds than slavery. By not pronouncing definitely on the real issue he lost supporters from men of both pro-slavery and anti-slavery sentiments instead of winning them as he had hoped. His compromising spirit upon the question promised to bear fruit, however, when in the crisis of 1850 he was able to bring about the series of measures known collectively as the "Compromise of 1850." The situation was acute, the South was on the point of secession, statesmen were frantic, every way of alleviating the deadlock seemed to have failed. Clay, who had retired from the Senate several years before, was now an old and physically frail man, but had himself re-elected to that body where he could put forth and defend his measures. His speech was one of the ablest of his career. Webster in a notable speech seconded the measures as a last resort. Calhoun still bitterly opposed. A deadlock resulted because of the opposition of President Taylor to the plan, and was only removed upon the latter's death, whereupon Fillmore, friendly to the compromise, succeeded to his place. The compromise admitted California as a free State, organized Utah and New Mexico as territories without reference to slavery, and enacted a more efficient fugitive slave law. It was a noble climax to Clay's great career, but it did not, as he hoped, permanently save the Union from bloodshed. Its success was in the fact that it postponed the Civil War until the North had the immense growing power of the West as its ally. Clay did not live to see its failure, but died in 1852 at the height of his fame and popularity.

In one respect, however, Clay's whole political career had been a bitter disappointment, at least to the man himself. The nation never rewarded him with the highest office in its power to bestow, and which he so deeply coveted. This was in spite of the fact that for a generation he was the acknowledged leader of his party. One reason was that during the whole period sectional feeling was so strong that no leader of any one section could be elected. Peace had to be secured by choosing lesser men as compromise candidates. Another reason was Clay's own compromising nature which always won him enemies in both camps. His name was used comparatively early in connection with the presidency. He had hoped to be offered the office of secretary of State under Monroe in 1817, for at that time this official was regarded as next in line for the succession. Clay was greatly disappointed and pursued a policy of obstruction to the administration until the events culminating in the Missouri Compromise again led him to co-operate with Monroe. In 1824 Clay was a candidate with W. H. Crawford, Andrew Jackson and John Quincy Adams for the presidency. Choice between the two highest, Jackson and Adams, went to the House where Clay controlled the deciding vote. Though Jackson represented the West and its interests, to choose him would have meant the denial of all chances for himself in the following campaign, for the country would not be likely to choose two western leaders in succession. Temperamentally Clay was also opposed to Adams, but after a long conference he gave out that he would support the latter. Soon afterwards he accepted an appointment as secretary of State, under Adams, and Jackson's supporters immediately charged a corrupt bargain between the two. Historians generally feel that Clay sincerely favoured Adams, but ever after Clay was kept busy explaining and denying the allegation of a bargain. It made Jackson his bitter enemy for life. John Randolph of Virginia pressed the accusation until Clay hotly consented to a duel to defend his honour. Neither was hurt. Clay's action so alienated his western supporters that it also must be ascribed as one of the reasons why he never achieved the presidency. In fact when he finished his term as secretary of State he had to go home "to mend his fences" in order to ensure his re-election to Congress. It proved the most difficult and most important campaign of his life, for, had he failed, it would have meant the eclipse of his political career.

By his enemies Clay's compromises were often ascribed to timidity or to hedging for political purposes. They can just as truly be represented as the acts of a man of great human understanding and sympathies, anxious to enter into the point of view of others. There is every indication that they represent a philosophical attitude toward life. "All legislation, all government, all society is founded upon the principle of mutual concession, politeness, comity, courtesy . . . I bow to you today because you bow to me." Such were his words and sentiments. The compromises represent his greatest political achievements. As "the great pacificator" he occupies a place in the memory of his countrymen.

When not in Washington Clay's home was on his estate at Ashland, Kentucky. He took a great interest in its practical management and especially devoted himself to the breeding of beautiful Kentucky horses. He was an excellent rider. Though Clay repeatedly denounced slavery as an evil, tradition and habit allowed him to keep slaves on his own plantation. He treated them considerately and they were devoted to him. When very young Clay married Lucretia Hart, a cousin of Thomas Hart Benton. Five sons and six daughters were born to them. But misfortune seemed to hang over the family. All of the daughters died before the father. One son was killed in the Mexican War, and another became insane after an accident. Clay's acquaintances and friends were selected from all classes and occupations. His popularity with the people was immense, and he believed in them. Yet like many democratic leaders, notably his great western rival, Andrew Jackson, Clay was often arbitrary, autocratic and possessed of an irrepressible desire to rule. His imagination frequently ran away with his understanding while his imperious temper and ardent combativeness hurried him into disadvantageous positions. Great crowds always met him wherever he was to speak because of his matchless voice and fascinating personality. In public he was of magnificent bearing, possessing the true oratorical temperament, the nervous exaltation that makes the orator feel and appear a superior being, transfusing his thought, passion and will into the mind and heart of the listener. In private he was an excellent conversationalist, possessing a fund of pleasant humour. His never-failing courtesy, his agreeable manners and a noble and generous heart for all who needed protection against the powerful or the lawless endeared him to hosts of friends.

BIBLIOGRAPHY.—*See* Calvin Colton, *The Works of Henry Clay* (1857; new ed., 1898), the first three volumes of which are an account of Clay's life and times; Carl Schurz, *Henry Clay* (1887); T. H. Clay, *Henry Clay* (1910); Gamaliel Bradford, "Henry Clay," in *Virginia Quarterly Review*, Jan. 1928. Much material will be found in the standard histories of the period and in Thomas H. Benton's *Thirty Years View* (1861). No complete and critical biography yet exists.

CLAY AND CLAY MINERALS. The term clay has been used in several senses: (1) to designate particle size, about minus 0.004 mm.; (2) as a rock composed essentially of clay materials; and (3) as a name for a group of minerals—the clay minerals. As a rock name it comprises soils, ceramic clays, clay shales, mudstones, glacial clays—including great volumes of detrital and transported clays—and the oceanic clays, red clay, blue clay and blue mud. These are all characterized by one or more of the clay minerals together with varying amounts of detrital and organic materials, among which quartz is dominant. Clay materials are plastic when wet, water retentive, and coherent when dry. Most clays are the result of weathering, but some are formed by hydrothermal processes. They are one of the major mineral products, being used in a wide variety of industries; and they provide the mechanical and chemical environment for almost all plant growth, and hence for nearly all the life on the earth's surface.

Clay minerals are divided into three main groups, all being characterized by a sheetlike crystal structure:

Kaolinite group	kaolinite, dickite, nacrite halloysite;
Montmorillonite group	montmorillonite aluminian montmorillonite (beidellite) nontronite, saponite, hectorite sauconite;
Potash clay variously called	hydromica, hydrous mica, illite, glimmerton (German) bravaisite.

Kaolinite, dickite, halloysite and nacrite have the same chemical composition ($Al_2O_3.2SiO_2.2H_2O$) and differ only in their crystal structure. The related mineral endellite contains twice as much water and loses half of it at 60° C., changing to halloysite. Allophane, a material without crystal structure (amorphous) and with variable chemical composition, occurs widely as a product of weathering that is not assignable to any mineral group.

The montmorillonite group can be presented by means of ion substitutions in the chemical formula of the related mineral, pyrophyllite [$Al_2Si_4O_{10}(OH)_2$]. In typical montmorillonite about one-sixth of the aluminum is proxied by magnesium, and such exchangeable ions as calcium, sodium, potassium, hydrogen and some magnesium are held between the sheets of the crystal lattice (the so-called exchangeable bases). Variable amounts of loosely held water occupy a position between the crystal sheets. Various ions may proxy aluminum in the crystal structure. If this is iron, the mineral is nontronite; if magnesium, it is saponite or hectorite; and if zinc, it is sauconite. A limited proportion of aluminum may proxy silicon. In the crystal structure approximately three bivalent ions (magnesium, zinc) may proxy trivalent ions (aluminum, iron), which occupy only two of three potential octahedral positions in the crystal structure.

The hydrous mica group has not been adequately studied. It seems to range in chemical composition from potash-bearing montmorillonite on the one hand to micas on the other. A material with about half the potassium oxide of mica (about 6%) occurs widely. Preliminary studies suggest that the group includes potash-bearing montmorillonite, mixed layers of more than one of the various sheet materials and materials closely related to muscovite mica.

Ion exchange in clays plays a major role in plant growth, being a reservoir of potassium oxide, calcium oxide and even nitrogen. It also is a factor in industry in water softeners and oil clarification, with or without acid treatment. Montmorillonites have a high ion exchange capacity (60 to 100 miliequivalents per 100 g.); potash clays have roughly half as much, but in the kaolinite group it is slight.

The purest available source of montmorillonite is bentonite, a clay resulting from the alteration of volcanic ash. With calcium as the exchangeable ion it is treated with acid and used in petroleum refining. With sodium it is highly dispersable (colloidal) and has wide use as an absorbant.

Uses.—No other earth material has so wide an importance or such extended uses as do clays. Their properties as soils are dependent on their providing the physical environment for plant growth; that is, porosity, aeration and water retention. Clays are the storehouse of chemical fertility, base exchange being a fundamental property. The use of clay in pottery making antedates recorded human history, and pottery remains are a major record of past civilizations. In western Asia the hieroglyphics inscribed on tiles played a major role in ancient culture. As building materials, bricks (baked and as adobe) have been used in construction since earliest time. Brick, tile and the cruder types of pottery have used impure clays but even the early potters learned to add ground rock or previously baked clay (grout) and even volcanic ash. The finer grades of ceramic materials have made use of white clay or kaolin, in which kaolinite is the characteristic clay mineral. To this are usually added ground quartz (flint), ground feldspar and ball clay to increase plasticity. Refractory materials, including fire brick, chemical ware and melting pots for glass, make use of kaolin together with other materials which increase resistance to heat. Certain clays known as fuller's earths have long been used in wool scouring. A large use of clays (bentonite, halloysite and altapulgite) is in the refining of both organic and mineral oils, commonly after activation by means of acid treatment.

A major use of white clays is as paper fillers; they give the paper a gloss and increase opacity and printability.

In rubber compounding, the addition of clay increases resistance to wear and aids in the elimination of moulding troubles.

The essential raw materials of portland cement are limestone and clays (commonly impure ones). These are ground together, sintered and then ground to a fine powder. On the addition of water, the calcium, aluminum and silicon combine into crystals of hydrous-alumina silicates, and the material sets.

Clay materials have a wide variety of uses in engineering. Earth dams are made impermeable to water by adding suitable clay materials to porous soil materials; commonly this is an impermeable core. Water loss in canals may be reduced by adding clay materials.

Clays after acid treatment have been used as water softeners. The base exchange property permits the clay to remove calcium from solution and substitutes sodium. A major use of bentonitic clay is as drilling muds. These prevent flocculation and their circulation removes the drill cuttings of the rotary drill. A heavy material (barite is commonly used) may be added to the mud, and the high hydrostatic head thus developed prevents explosive escape of natural gas.

Other minor uses of clays in various forms, too numerous to describe in detail, are in cosmetics, crayons, pencils, insecticides (as carriers), insulating materials, medicine, oil cloths, paints, soap and detergents, tooth powders and phonograph records. (CL. S. R.)

CLAY CROSS, an urban district of Derbyshire, England, near the river Amber, on the railway, 1½ mi. S. of Chesterfield. Pop. (1951) 8,552. Area 3.2 sq.mi. Coal miners and foundry workers form the majority of the population.

CLAYMORE (from the Gaelic *claidheamh mòr,* "great sword"), the old two-edged broadsword with cross hilt, of which the guards were usually turned down, used by the Highlanders of

Scotland. The name is also wrongly applied to the single-edged basket-hilted sword adopted in the 16th century and still worn as the full-dress sword in the Highland regiments of the British army.

CLAYS, PAUL JEAN (1819–1900), Belgian marine painter, was born at Bruges in 1819, and died at Brussels in 1900. A Fleming in his feeling for colour, Clays set his palette with clean, strong hues, and their powerful harmonies were in striking contrast with the rusty, smoky tones then in favour. If he was not a "luminist" in the modern use of the word, he deserves at any rate to be classed with the founders of the modern naturalistic school. Among his works are: "Dutch Boats in the Flushing Roads," in the National Gallery, London; "The Port of Antwerp," "Coast near Ostend," and a "Calm on the Scheldt," in the Brussels gallery; "The Meuse at Dordrecht" in the Antwerp museum; "The Open North Sea," in the Pinakothek at Munich; and "The Festival of the Freedom of the Scheldt at Antwerp in 1863," in the Metropolitan Museum of Fine Arts, New York.

See Camille Lemonnier, *Histoire des Beaux-Arts* (Brussels, 1887).

CLAYTON, JOHN MIDDLETON (1796–1856), American politician, was born in Dagsborough, Del., on July 24, 1796. He came of an old Quaker family long prominent in the political history of Delaware. He graduated at Yale in 1815, and in 1819 began to practise law at Dover, Delaware. Engaging in politics, he became in 1824 a member of the state house of representatives, and in 1826–28 was secretary of state for Delaware. In 1829 he was elected to the U.S. Senate by the anti-Jackson forces, and in 1835 was re-elected as a Whig, but resigned in 1836. In 1845 he again entered the Senate, where he opposed the annexation of Texas and the Mexican War. In March, 1849, he became secretary of state in President Taylor's cabinet. His brief tenure of the state portfolio, which terminated July 22, 1850, soon after Taylor's death, was notable chiefly for the negotiation with the British minister, Sir Henry Lytton Bulwer of the Clayton-Bulwer Treaty (*q.v.*). He was once more a member of the Senate from March, 1853, until his death at Dover, Del., Nov. 9, 1856. By his contemporaries Clayton was considered one of the ablest debaters and orators in the Senate.

See the memoir by Joseph P. Comegys in the *Papers* of the Historical Society of Delaware, No. 4 (Wilmington, 1882).

CLAYTON-BULWER TREATY, a famous treaty between the United States and Great Britain, negotiated in 1850 by John M. Clayton and Sir Henry Lytton Bulwer (Lord Dalling) in consequence of the situation created by the project of an interoceanic canal across Nicaragua, each signatory being jealous of the activities of the other in Central America. Great Britain had large and indefinite territorial claims in three regions—Belize or British Honduras, the Mosquito Coast and the Bay islands. On the other hand, the United States, without territorial claims, held in reserve, ready for ratification, treaties with Nicaragua and Honduras, which gave her a certain diplomatic vantage with which to balance the *de facto* dominion of Great Britain.

The treaty bound both parties not to "obtain or maintain" any exclusive control of the proposed canal, or unequal advantage in its use. It guaranteed the neutralization of such canal. It declared that, the intention of the signatories being not only the accomplishment of "a particular object"—*i.e.,* that the canal, then supposedly near realization, should be neutral and equally free to the two contracting powers—"but also to establish a general principle," they agreed "to extend their protection by treaty stipulation to any other practicable communications, whether by canal or railway, across the isthmus which connects North and South America." Finally, it stipulated that neither signatory would ever "occupy, or fortify, or colonize, or assume or exercise any dominion over Nicaragua, Costa Rica, the Mosquito Coast or any part of Central America," nor make use of any protectorate or alliance, present or future, to such ends.

The treaty was signed on April 19, and was ratified by both Governments; but before the exchange of ratifications Lord Palmerston, on June 8, directed Sir H. Bulwer to make a "declaration" that the British Government did not understand the treaty "as applying to Her Majesty's settlement at Honduras, or its dependencies." J. M. Clayton made a counter-declaration, which recited that the United States did not regard the treaty as applying to "the British settlement in Honduras commonly called British-Honduras . . . nor the small islands in the neighbourhood of that settlement which may be known as its dependencies"; that the treaty's engagements did apply to all the Central American States, "with their just limits and proper dependencies"; and that these declarations, not being submitted to the United States Senate, could of course not affect the legal import of the treaty. The interpretation of the declarations soon became a matter of contention. The phraseology reflects the effort made by the United States to render impossible a physical control of the canal by Great Britain through the territory held by her at its mouth—the United States losing the above-mentioned treaty advantages—just as the explicit abnegations of the treaty rendered impossible such control politically by either power. But Great Britain claimed that the excepted "settlement" at Honduras was the "Belize" covered by the extreme British claim; that the Bay islands were a dependency of Belize; and that, as for the Mosquito Coast, the abnegatory clauses being wholly prospective in intent, she was not required to abandon her protectorate. The United States contended that the Bay islands were not the "dependencies" of Belize, these being the small neighbouring islands mentioned in the same treaties; that the excepted "settlement" was the British-Honduras of definite extent and narrow purpose recognized in British treaties with Spain; that she had not confirmed by recognition the large, indefinite and offensive claims whose dangers the treaty was primarily designed to lessen; and that, as to the Mosquito Coast, the treaty was retrospective, and that the clause binding both not to "occupy" any part of Central America or the Mosquito Coast necessitated the abandonment of such territory as Great Britain was already actually occupying or exercising dominion over, and the complete abandonment of the British protectorate over the Mosquito Indians. It seems to be a just conclusion that when in 1852 the Bay islands were erected into a British "colony" this was a flagrant infraction of the treaty; that as regards Belize the American arguments were decidedly stronger, and more correct historically; and that as regards the Mosquito question, inasmuch as a protectorate seems certainly to have been recognized by the treaty, to demand its absolute abandonment was unwarranted, although to satisfy the treaty Great Britain was bound materially to weaken it.

In 1859–60, by British treaties with Central American States, the Bay islands and Mosquito questions were settled nearly in accord with the American contentions. But by the same treaties Belize was accorded limits much greater than those contended for by the United States. This settlement the latter power accepted without cavil for many years.

In 1880–84 a variety of reasons were advanced why the United States might justly repudiate at will the Clayton-Bulwer Treaty. The arguments advanced were quite indefensible in law and history, and although the position of the United States in 1850–60 was in general the stronger, that of Great Britain was even more conspicuously strong in the years 1880–84. In 1885 the former Government reverted to its traditional policy, and the Hay-Pauncefote Treaty of 1902, which replaced the Clayton-Bulwer Treaty, adopted the rule of neutralization for the Panama Canal.

See the collected diplomatic correspondence in I. D. Travis, *History of the Clayton-Bulwer Treaty* (Ann Arbor, Mich., 1899); J. H. Latané, *Diplomatic Relations of the United States and Spanish America* (Baltimore, 1900); T. J. Lawrence, *Disputed Questions of Modern International Law* (2nd ed., Cambridge, England, 1885); Sir E. L. Bulwer in 99 *Quarterly Rev.* 235–286, and Sir H. Bulwer in 104 *Edinburgh Rev.* 280–298.

CLAY-WITH-FLINTS, in geology, a name given to a deposit of stiff red, brown or yellow clay, containing many flints, whole or broken, with some round pebbles of hard rock. It covers large areas in south-eastern and southern England, usually lying on chalk. It is commonly considered to represent the insoluble residue of the chalk left by weathering (mainly solution), but may include deposits formed in other ways, of which the following have been suggested: (*a*) that it is the residue of patches of Tertiary strata which once extended more widely over the chalk than at present. This is favoured by the presence of pebbles other than flint: (*b*) that it may be a glacial deposit, in fact, a boulder-clay or till, indicating an extension of the ice-sheet somewhat further than is usually believed. (*See* GLACIAL EPOCH.) These questions must be regarded as still undecided, but there can be little doubt that the insoluble residue theory is applicable over wide areas. (R. H. RA.)

CLAZOMENAE, an ancient town of Ionia and a member of the Ionian Dodecapolis (Confederation of Twelve Cities), on the Gulf of Smyrna, about 20 m. W. of that city. Though not in existence before the arrival of the Ionians in Asia, its original founders were largely settlers from Phlius and Cleonae. It stood originally on the isthmus connecting the mainland with the peninsula on which Erythrae stood; but the inhabitants, alarmed by the encroachments of the Persians, removed to one of the small islands of the bay, and there established their city. This island was connected with the mainland by Alexander the Great by means of a pier, the remains of which are still visible. During the 5th century it was for some time subject to the Athenians, but about the middle of the Peloponnesian war (412 B.C.) it revolted. After a brief resistance, however, it again acknowledged the Athenian supremacy, and repelled a Lacedaemonian attack. Under the Romans Clazomenae was included in the province of Asia, and enjoyed immunity from taxation. It was the birthplace of the philosopher Anaxagoras. It is famous for its painted terracotta sarcophagi, which are the finest monuments of Ionian painting in the 6th century B.C. (E. GR.)

CLEANING: *see* DRY CLEANING.

CLEANTHES (*c.* 301–232 or 252 B.C.), Stoic philosopher, was born at Assos in the Troad. He came to Athens, where he listened first to the lectures of Crates the Cynic, and then to those of Zeno the Stoic, supporting himself meanwhile by working all night as water-carrier to a gardener (hence his nickname φρεάντλης). On the death of Zeno in 263, he became the leader of the school. Among his pupils were his successor, Chrysippus, and Antigonus, king of Macedon.

Cleanthes produced very little that was original, though he wrote some 50 works, of which fragments have come down to us. The principal is the large portion of the *Hymn to Zeus,* which has been preserved in Stobaeus. He regarded the sun as the abode of God, the intelligent providence, or (in accordance with Stoic materialism) the vivifying fire or aether of the universe. Virtue, he taught, is life according to nature; but pleasure is not according to nature. The principal fragments of Cleanthes' works are contained in Diogenes Laertius and Stobaeus; some may be found in Cicero and Seneca.

See G. C. Mohinke, *Kleanthes der Stoiker* (Greifswald, 1814); C. Wachsmuth, *Commentationes de Zenone Citiensi et Cleanthe Assio* (Göttingen, 1874–75); A. C. Pearson, *Fragments of Zeno and Cleanthes* (1891); art. by E. Wellmann in Ersch and Gruber's *Allgemeine Encyklopädie;* R. Hirzel, *Untersuchungen zu Ciceros philosophischen Schriften,* ii. (1882), containing a vindication of the originality of Cleanthes; *Hymn of Cleanthes,* tr. E. H. Blakeney, "Texts for Students" series, vol. xxvi. (1921); A. B. Krische, *Forschungen auf dem Gebiete der alten Philosophie* (1840); also works quoted under STOICS.

CLEARCHUS, the son of Rhamphias, a Spartan general and condottiere. Born about the middle of the 5th century B.C., Clearchus was sent with a fleet to the Hellespont in 411 and became harmost of Byzantium. His severity, however, made him unpopular, and in his absence the gates were opened to the Athenians under Alcibiades (409). Subsequently appointed by the ephors to settle the affairs of Byzantium and to protect it from Thracian attacks, he made himself tyrant, and, when driven thence by a Spartan force, fled to Cyrus (*q.v.*). In the "expedition of the ten thousand," Clearchus led the Peloponnesians. On Cyrus's death Clearchus conducted the retreat, until, being treacherously seized with his fellow-generals by Tissaphernes, he was handed over to Artaxerxes and executed (Thuc. viii. 8, 39, 80; Xen., *Hellenica,* i. 3, 15-19; *Anabasis,* i. ii.; Diodorus xiv. 12, 19-26). Clearchus was a typical Spartan, an able and energetic soldier, but lacking refinement and humanity.

CLEARFIELD, a borough of Clearfield county, Pennsylvania, U.S., 35 mi. N. of Altoona, on the west branch of the Susquehanna river, at an altitude of 1,108 ft., in the central Pennsylvania coal field. It is on federal highway 322; is served by the Baltimore and Ohio, the New York Central and the Pennsylvania railways; and has an airport. The population in 1950 was 9,348; in 1940 it was 9,372; and in 1930, 9,221. It is the county seat, a wholesale distributing centre, and has various manufacturing industries, especially large firebrick, tile and sewer-pipe works, using the fire clay that abounds in the vicinity, metal industries and tanneries. Clearfield was so named because the first white settlers found it already cleared of timber. In 1805 it was chosen as the site for the county seat.

CLEARING HOUSE. When business houses or firms engaged in the same kind of activity have large dealings with each other it is an obvious convenience and economy to establish a mutual institution to enable them to set off their transactions with each other and to clear them, thus making it necessary to pay to each other at agreed times only such balances of account as are revealed by the clearance. Such institutions are called clearing houses, and they have been established in all great commercial nations for many branches of industry. The chief of them are bankers' clearing houses (*see* BANKING) and railway clearing houses.

The London Stock Exchange Clearing House deals with transactions in stock, the clearing being effected by balance-sheets and tickets; the balance of stock to be received or delivered is shown on a balance-sheet sent in by each member, and the items are then cancelled against one another and tickets issued for the balances outstanding. The New York Stock Exchange Clearing House does similar work. The settlements on the Paris Bourse are cleared within the Bourse itself, through the Compagnie des Agents de Change de Paris.

For details concerning clearing house operations in the United States *see* Theodore Gilman, *A Graded Banking System Formed by the Incorporation of Clearing Houses under a Federal Law* (Boston, 1898); Jerome Thralls, *The Clearing House* (1916); Harvey White Magee, *A Treatise on the Law of National and State Banks, Including the Clearing House* (Albany, N.Y., 1921); and Walter Eaton Spahr, *The Clearing and Collection of Checks* (1926).

CLEARWATER, a city on the west coast of Florida, U.S.A., 22 mi. W. of Tampa; the county seat of beautiful Pinellas county, which occupies a small peninsula between the Gulf of Mexico and Old Tampa bay. It is served by the Atlantic Coast Line and the Seaboard Air Line railways. In 1900 the population was 343; in 1930, after annexations of territory brought the area to 17 sq.mi., it was 7,607; in 1950 it was 15,535 by the federal census. Clearwater is in a citrus fruit and market-gardening region, has fisheries of importance, and is a winter resort. A commission-manager form of government was adopted in 1923.

CLEAT, a wedge-shaped piece of wood fastened to ships' masts and elsewhere, to prevent a rope, collar or the like from slipping, or to act as a step; more particularly a piece of wood or metal with double or single horns used for belaying ropes. A "cleat" is also a wedge fastened to a ship's side to catch the shores in a launching cradle or dry dock. "Cleat" is also used in mining for the vertical cleavage-planes of coal. The word is common in various forms to many Teutonic languages, in the sense of a wedge or lump, *cf.* "clod" and "clot."

CLEATOR MOOR, a township and civil parish, Cumberland, England, 4¼ mi. S.E. of Whitehaven, served by the L.M.S.R. Pop. (1931) 6,582. The town lies in a coal and iron ore district, and the mines, together with metal works, employ almost the entire population. In consequence, it was severely depressed in the 1930s, unemployment among men being 52.8% in April 1934.

CLEAVERS or **GOOSE-GRASS,** *Galium Aparine* (family Rubiaceae), a common plant in hedges and waste places, with a long, weak, straggling, four-sided, green stem, bearing whorls of six to eight narrow leaves, ½ to 2 in. long, and, like the angles of the stem, rough from the presence of short, stiff, downwardly-pointing, hooked hairs. The small, white, regular flowers are borne, a few together, in axillary clusters, and are followed by the small, hispid, two-celled fruit, which, like the rest of the plant, readily clings to a rough surface, whence the common name. The plant has a wide distribution throughout the north temperate zone, and is also found in temperate South America.

CLEBSCH, ALFRED (1833–1872), German mathematician, was born at Königsberg, Prussia, on Jan. 19, 1833. He was educated at Königsberg, and in 1858 was appointed to the chair of theoretical mechanics at Carlsruhe Polytechnic. In 1863 Clebsch went to the University of Giessen and in 1868 to Göttingen, where he remained until his death. His attention was turned to algebra and geometry after a study of Salmon's works. Clebsch worked at mathematical physics, the calculus of variation, partial differential equations of the first order, the general theory of curves; he applied Abelian functions to geometry and made use of determinants. In 1867 Clebsch, in conjunction with Carl Neumann, founded the *Mathematische Annalen.* He died of diphtheria on Nov. 7, 1872. Clebsch was the author of *Vorlesungen über Geometrie,* which was edited by Ferdinand Lindemann of Munich in 1875, and of *Theorie d. Elasticität fester Körper* (1862), which was translated into French by Saint-Venant.

CLEBURNE, a city of Texas, U.S.A., 30 mi. S. of Ft. Worth; the county seat of Johnson county. It is served by the Santa Fe railroad and is on federal highway 67 and state highways 171 and 174.

The population was 12,845 in 1950; 10,558 in 1940 (91% native white) and 11,539 in 1930 by the federal census. It is the trade centre of a diversified agricultural, live stock and industrial area and has large railroad shops.

Cleburne was settled in 1867 and incorporated in 1871; it was named after Patrick Ronayne Cleburne (1828–64), a major general of the Confederate army, who was called "the Stonewall of the West."

CLECKHEATON, a parish, West Riding of Yorkshire, England, 5½ mi. S.E. of Bradford, on the L.M.S.R. Pop. (1931) 12,153. The industries comprise the manufacture of woollens, blankets, flannel, wire-card and machinery. Cleckheaton parish is in the Spenborough urban district, pop. (1938) 36,420.

CLEETHORPES, a municipal borough (1936) and watering place in the parts of Lindsey, Lincolnshire, England; 2¼ mi. S.E. of Great Grimsby by a branch of the L.N.E.R. Pop. (1938) 28,730. Area 3.3 sq.mi. It faces eastward to the North sea, but its shore of fine sand, affording good bathing, actually belongs to the estuary of the Humber. The sea-wall forms a pleasant promenade. The suburb of New Clee connects Cleethorpes with Grimsby. The church of the Holy Trinity and St. Mary is principally Norman of various dates, but pre-conquest work appears in the tower. Cleethorpes is greatly favoured as a health resort by people from the midland counties, Lancashire and Yorkshire.

CLEF, in musical notation, is a sign used to indicate the position and pitch of the various notes represented on the stave. Three such signs are now in use, 𝄢 (or 𝄢), 𝄡 and 𝄞, of which 𝄡 stands for the note *c′*, otherwise middle C on the pianoforte, 𝄢 for the F below and 𝄞 for the G above. Hence when one of these notes is thus indicated, *e.g.*, 𝄞 or 𝄢, a key, or clef, is thereby provided from which all the others can be reckoned. A representation of the Great Stave of eleven lines, showing the position on it occupied by each clef sign, will make the matter clear.

F G A B C D E F G A B C D E F G A B C D E F G

From this it will be seen that the F (bass) and G (treble or violin) clefs are the lower and upper five lines respectively and that the C clef (variously known as the tenor or alto clef, according to the particular line on which it is placed) consists of five lines taken from the middle; for it should be explained further that "clef" signifies not only the individual sign but also the group of lines on which it stands, although strictly speaking "stave" is here the more accurate term.

In pianoforte, vocal and most other scores, only the F and G clefs are nowadays used, but the C clef is still retained for the viola and one or two other instruments, the choice of the particular clef used being governed, as it will be understood, by the pitch and compass of the instrument written for, the object aimed at being to include as much of the music as possible within the limits of a five-line stave. It will also be understood that in practice the middle line of the Great Stave is normally omitted, a short additional line known as a leger (or ledger) line being employed to take its place when the intermediate C is required—

It may be noted further that the clef signs as we now know them are simply much modified and conventionalized forms of the letters of the three notes which they stand for—F, C and G. (*See* MUSICAL NOTATION.)

CLEFT PALATE and HARE-LIP, in surgery. Cleft palate is a congenital cleavage in the roof of the mouth, and is frequently associated with hare-lip. Both conditions are due to faulty development and may be hereditary. The infant is prevented from sucking, and an operation is necessary. The most favourable time for operating is between the age of two weeks and three months, and if the cleft is closed at this early date, not only are the nutrition and general development of the child greatly improved, but the voice is probably saved from much of the unpleasant tone associated with a defective roof to the mouth. After the cleft in the palate has been effectually dealt with, the hare-lip can be repaired with ease and success.

Hare-lip.—In the hare the splitting of the lip is in the middle line, but in the human subject for developmental reasons it is on one or on both sides of the middle line. Though we are unable to explain why development should miss the mark in formation of the lip and palate, maternal impressions do not have anything to do with it. As a rule, the supposed "fright" comes long after the ninth week of foetal life when the lips are developed. The best time for operating on a hare-lip uncomplicated by cleft palate depends upon circumstances, in a favourable case within the first few days of birth.

CLEISTHENES, the name of two Greek statesmen, (1) of Athens, (2) of Sicyon, of whom the first is far the more important.

(1) CLEISTHENES, the Athenian statesman, was the son of Megacles, the Alcmaeonid, and Agariste, daughter of Cleisthenes of Sicyon. The Alcmaeonidae had been in exile during the Peisistratid tyranny but gained the favour of Delphi by their munificence in the rebuilding of the temple, and their reinstatement was imposed by the oracle upon the Spartan king, Cleomenes (*q.v.*). Aristotle's *Constitution of Athens* treats the alliance of the Peisistratids with Argos, the rival of Sparta in the Peloponnese, as the chief ground for the action of Cleomenes who expelled Hippias in 511–510 B.C., leaving Athens once again at the mercy of the powerful families.

Cleisthenes, on his return, realized that Athens would not tolerate a new tyranny, nor were the other nobles willing to accept him as leader of an oligarchy. It was left for him to "take the people into partnership" as Peisistratus had in a different way done before him. Solon's reforms had failed, primarily because they left unimpaired the power of the great landed nobles. This evil of local influence Peisistratus had concealed by satisfying the nominally sovereign people that in him they had a sufficient representative. It was left to Cleisthenes to adopt the remedy of giving substance to the form of the Solonian constitution. His first attempts roused the aristocrats to a last effort; Isagoras appealed to the

Spartans to come to his aid. Cleisthenes retired on the arrival of a herald from Cleomenes, reviving the old question of the curse. The democrats, however, rose, and after besieging Cleomenes and Isagoras in the Acropolis, let them go under a safe-conduct, and brought back the exiles. We are not told when and how the ascendancy of Cleisthenes came to an end. It is stated that Cleisthenes, hard pressed in the war with Boeotia, Euboea and Sparta (Herod. v. 73), sent ambassadors to ask the help of Persia. Associated as he was with the democrats, the Peisistratid party, this is not improbable. The existence of a strong philo-medic party is clear from the story of the shield after the battle of Marathon, for which the Alcmaeonidae were blamed. (*See* G. B. Grundy, *Great Persian War*, ch. iv.) The gift and withdrawal of Athenian help in the Ionian War (498) is another indication of division of opinion in Athens. Aelian says that he was a victim to his own device of ostracism (*q.v.*); this may perhaps indicate that his political career ended in disgrace, a hypothesis which is explicable on the ground of this attempted Persian alliance.

Cleisthenes realized that the dead-weight which held the democracy down was the influence on politics of the clan unit with its religious associations. Therefore his prime object was to dissociate the clans and the phratries from politics, and to give the democracy a new electoral basis in which old associations and vested interests would become ineffective. His first step was to abolish the four Solonian tribes and create ten new ones. Each of the new tribes was subdivided into "demes" (roughly "townships"); this organization did not, except politically, supersede the system of clans and phratries whose old religious signification remained untouched. The new tribes, however, did not represent local interests. Further, the tribe names were taken from legendary heroes, and, therefore, contributed to the idea of a national unity; even Ajax, the eponym of the tribe Aeantis, though not really Attic, was famous as an ally (Herod. v. 66) and had been adopted as a national hero. Each tribe had its shrine and its particular hero-cult, which, however, was free from local association and the dominance of particular families. This national idea Cleisthenes further emphasized by setting up in the market-place at Athens a statue of each tribal hero.

The next step was the organization of the deme. Within each tribe he grouped demes (*see* below), each of which had its census-list kept by the demarch (local governor), who was elected popularly and held office for one year and presided over meetings affecting local administration and the provision of crews for the state-navy. According to the Aristotelian *Constitution of Athens*, Cleisthenes further divided Attica into three districts, Urban and Suburban, Inland (*Mesogaios*) and Maritime (*Paralia*), each of which was subdivided into ten *trittyes;* each tribe was composed of three trittyes, one in each of the three districts. The demes were arranged in ten groups but the number of demes in a tribe was not uniform. The trittyes might consist of one or several demes and the number of members of a deme varied greatly, though, at first, the division was local, *i.e.*, a deme consisted of its residents, the qualification became hereditary, a man belonging to his father's deme wherever he lived. Hence the distinction between resident demesmen and residents belonging to another deme (ἐγκεκτημένοι). The main purpose of the reform was to do away with the religious qualification of connection with clan or phratry and so facilitate the enfranchisement of new citizens. The artificial arrangement of the trittyes was intended to weaken the authority of the Eupatrid families in the tribes whose widely separated trittyes could not easily be brought under influence.

It has been asked whether we are to believe that Cleisthenes invented the demes. To this the answer is in the negative. The demes were undoubtedly primitive divisions of Attica. The most logical conclusion perhaps is that Cleisthenes, while he did create the demes which Athens itself comprised, did not create the country demes, but merely gave them definition as political divisions. Thus the city itself had six demes in five different tribes, and the other five tribes were represented in the suburbs and the Peiraeus. In the Cleisthenean system there was one great source of danger, namely that the residents in and about Athens must always have had more weight in elections than those in distant demes. Moreover a special class, the new commercial element in the citizenship devised by Solon and fostered by Cleisthenes, soon came to have a preponderating influence in the city and suburbs.

A second problem is the franchise reform of Cleisthenes. Aristotle in the *Politics* (iii. 2. 3 = 1275 b) says that Cleisthenes created new citizens by enrolling in the tribes "many resident aliens and emancipated slaves." But the Aristotelian *Constitution of Athens* asserts that he gave "citizenship to the masses." Μέτοικοι had been encouraged to settle in Athens by Solon and the grant of citizenship had been made to many skilled in trades and handicrafts. The Peisistratids, like the Etruscan dynasty at Rome, naturally favoured this commercial "plebs" as a support against the aristocrats. After their expulsion a revision of the citizen-roll had removed many or all of these as γένειμή καθαροί. Cleisthenes restored these and opened the way to citizenship to all satisfactory resident aliens, so strengthening the position of the democracy.

The Boulē (*q.v.*) was reorganized to suit the new tribal arrangement, and was known henceforward as the Council of the Five Hundred, fifty from each tribe, each fifty acting as an executive committee (πρυτάνεις) for one month. The system of ten tribes led in course of time to the construction of boards of ten to deal with military and civil affairs, *e.g.* the Strategi (*see* STRATEGUS), the *Apodektai,* and others. Of these the former cannot be attributed to Cleisthenes, but on the evidence of Androtion it was Cleisthenes who replaced the *Kolakretai,* by the *Apodektai* ("receivers"), who were controllers and auditors of the finance department. *Kolakretai* were very ancient Athenian magistrates; they were again important in the time of Aristophanes (*Wasps,* 693, 724; *Birds,* 1541), and presided over the payment of the dicasts instituted by Pericles. The *Kolakretai* remained in authority over the internal expenses of the Prytaneum. A further change which followed from the new tribal system was the reconstitution of the army; this, however, probably took place about 501 B.C., and cannot be attributed directly to Cleisthenes. It has been said that the deme became the local political unit, replacing the naucrary. But the naucraries still supplied the fleet, and were increased in number from forty-eight to fifty.

The device of ostracism is the final stone in the Cleisthenean structure. An admirable scheme in theory, and, at first, in practice, it deteriorated in the 5th century into a mere party weapon.

BIBLIOGRAPHY.—*Ancient:* Aristotle, *Constitution of Athens* (ed. J. E. Sandys), cc. 20–22, 41; Herodotus v. 63–73, vi. 131; Aristotle, *Politics,* iii. 2, 3 (=1275 b. for franchise reforms). *Modern:* Histories of Greece in general, especially J. B. Bury. A. H. J. Greenidge, *Handbook of Greek Constitutional History* (1896); Gilbert, *Greek Constitutional Antiquities* (Engl. trans. 1895); R. W. Macan, *Herodotus iv–vi.,* vol. ii. (1895), pp. 127–148; E. M. Walker in *Camb. Anc. Hist.* vol. iv. ch. vi. *The Reform of Cleisthenes. See* also BOULE; ECCLESIA; OSTRACISM; SOLON.

(2) CLEISTHENES OF SICYON (*c.* 600–570), grandfather of the above, became tyrant of Sicyon as the representative of the conquered Ionian section of the inhabitants. He emphasized the destruction of Dorian predominance by giving ridiculous epithets to their tribal units, which from Hylleis, Dymanes and Pamphyli become Hyatae ("Swine-men"), Choireatae ("Pig-men") and Oneatae ("Ass-men"). He also attacked Dorian Argos, and suppressed the Homeric "rhapsodists" who sang the exploits of Dorian heroes. He championed the cause of the Delphic oracle against the town of Crisa in the Sacred War (*c.* 590). Crisa was destroyed, and Delphi became one of the meeting-places of the Delphic amphictyony (*see* AMPHICTYONY). The Pythian games were re-established with new magnificence, and Cleisthenes won the first chariot race in 582. He founded Pythian games at Sicyon, and built a new Sicyonian treasury at Delphi. His power was so great that when he offered his daughter Agariste in marriage, some of the most prominent Greeks sought the honour, which fell upon Megacles, the Alcmaeonid. The story of the rival wooers with the famous retort, "Hippocleides don't care," is told in Herod. vi. 125; *see* also Herod. v. 67 and Thuc. i. 18.

CLEISTHENES is also the name of an Athenian pilloried by Aristophanes (*Clouds,* 354; *Thesm.* 574) as a fop and a profligate.

CLEITARCHUS, one of the historians of Alexander the Great, possibly a native of Egypt, or at least spent some time at the court of Ptolemy Lagus. Quintilian (*Instit.* x, i, 74) credits him with more ability than trustworthiness, and Cicero (*Brutus,* ii) accuses him of giving a fictitious account of the death of Themistocles. But his history was popular, and much used by Diodorus Siculus, Quintus Curtius, Justin and Plutarch.

The fragments, about 30 in number, chiefly preserved in Aelian and Strabo, will be found in C. Müller's *Scriptores Rerum Alexandri Magni* (in the Didot *Arrian,* 1846); monographs by C. Raun, *De Clitarcho Diodori, Curtii, Justini auctore* (1868), and F. Reuss, "Hellenistische Beiträge," *Rhein. Mus.,* lxiii, pp. 58–78 (1908).

CLEITHRAL, an architectural term applied to a Greek temple whose roof completely covered it; in contradistinction to hypaethral, applied to one partly or wholly open to the sky.

CLEITOMACHUS, Greek philosopher, was a Carthaginian who came to Athens about the middle of the 2nd century B.C. at the age of 24. He studied principally under Carneades, whose views he adopted and propagated and whom he succeeded as chief of the New Academy in 129 B.C. Of Cleitomachus' works scarcely anything but a few titles are extant. Among these are Περὶ ἐποχῆς (on suspension of judgment) and Περὶ αἱρέσεων (about philosophical sects). Cicero highly commends his works and admits his own debt in the *Academics* to the treatise Περὶ ἐποχῆς. Parts of Cicero's *De Natura* and *De Divinatione* and the treatise *De Fato* are also in the main based upon Cleitomachus.

See E. Wellmann in Ersch and Gruber's *Allgemeine Encyclopädie;* R. Hirzel, *Untersuchungen zu Ciceros philosophischen Schriften,* i (1877); Diog. Laërt., iv, 67–92; Cicero, *Acad. Pr.,* ii, 31, 32, and *Tusc.,* iii, 22.

CLEITOR or CLITOR, a town of ancient Greece, stood in a fertile plain of Arcadia to the south of Mt. Chelmos, not far from a stream of its own name. In the neighbourhood was a fountain, the waters of which were said to deprive those who drank them of the taste for wine. The town was of considerable local importance and its inhabitants combined love of liberty with dominion over neighbours. It fought against Orchomenus in the Theban war and joined the other Arcadian cities in the foundation of Megalopolis. As a member of the Achaean league it was on several occasions the seat of the federal assemblies, and was besieged by the Aetolians in 220 B.C. It coined money till the time of Septimius Severus. Its ruins at Paleopoli are about 3 mi. from a village that preserves the ancient name. The greater part of the walls with several semicircular towers can be clearly made out; also three Doric temples and a small theatre.

CLELAND, WILLIAM (1661?–1689), Scottish Covenanting poet and soldier, son of a gamekeeper, was probably brought up on the marquess of Douglas' estate in Lanarkshire and was educated at St. Andrews university. He joined the army of the Covenanters, was present at Drumclog and fought at Bothwell Bridge. He escaped to Holland, but in 1685 was again in Scotland at the time of the abortive invasion of the earl of Argyll. He escaped once more, to return in 1688 as agent for William of Orange. He was appointed lieutenant colonel of the Cameronian regiment entrusted with the defense of Dunkeld, which they held against the fierce assault of the Highlanders on Aug. 26. This repulse of the Highlanders ended the Jacobite rising, but Cleland fell in the struggle. He wrote *A Collection of Several Poems and Verses* composed upon various occasions (published posthumously, 1697).

See *An Exact Narrative of the Conflict of Dunkeld . . . collected from several officers of the regiment* (1689).

CLEMATIS, a genus of vines and herbs of the crowfoot family (Ranunculaceae), containing 220 species and widely distributed. It is represented in England by *Clematis vitalba,* old-man's-beard or traveller's-joy, a common plant on chalky or light soil. The plants are shrubby climbers with generally compound, opposite leaves, the stalk of which is sensitive to contact like a tendril, becoming twisted round suitable objects and thereby giving support to the plant. The flowers are arranged in axillary or terminal clusters; they have no petals, but white or coloured, often large sepals, and an indefinite number of stamens and carpels. They contain no honey, and are visited by insects for the pollen, which is plentiful. The fruit is a head of achenes, each bearing the long-bearded, persistent style, suggesting the popular name. This feathery style is an important agent in the distribution of the seed by means of the wind. Inclusive of the sections *Viorna* and *Atragene,* which some botanists regard as separate genera, there are about 30 species of *Clematis* native to North America. Of these, the following representatives are more or less cultivated: the woodbine (*C. virginiana*), found from Nova Scotia to Manitoba and southward to Georgia and Tennessee; the western *C. ligusticifolia,* growing from North Dakota and Missouri westward to British Columbia and California; the purple virgin's-bower (*C. verticillaris*), found from Hudson bay to Minnesota and southeastward to Connecticut and Virginia; the scarlet virgin's-bower (*C. texensis*), native to Texas; and the pipestem virgin's-bower (*C. lasiantha*) of California and Oregon.

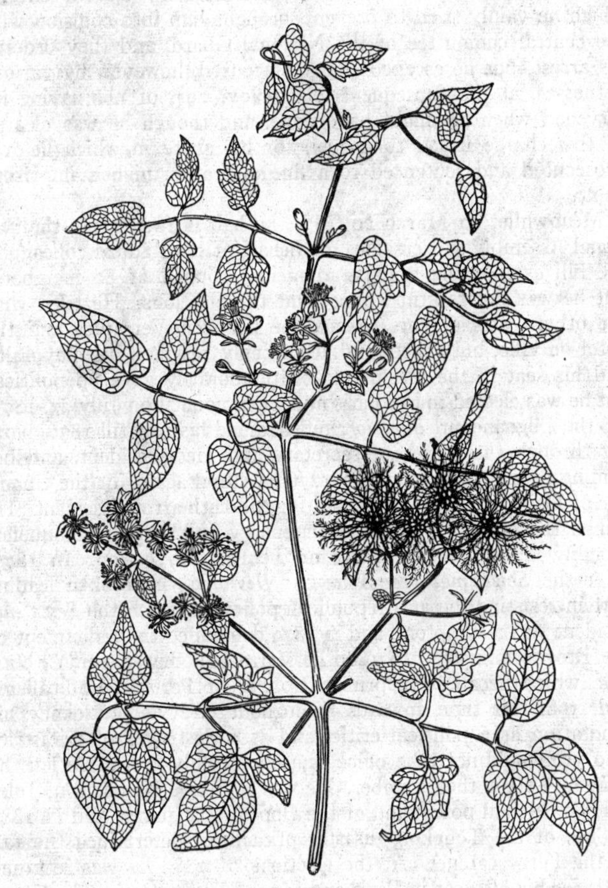

WILD CLEMATIS, OR TRAVELLER'S-JOY, A CLIMBING PLANT SOMETIMES CULTIVATED TO ADORN GARDEN TRELLISES. THE FEATHERY STYLES OF THE FRUITS (ACHENES) FACILITATE DISPERSAL OF SEED BY THE WIND

Several of the species, especially the large-flowered ones, are favourite garden plants, well adapted for covering trellises or walls or trailing over the ground. Many garden hybrids are popular, among them *C. jackmani* and more than 50 named varieties, of which Gipsyqueen, Ramona and Lady Northcliffe are popular.

See T. Moore and G. Jackman, *The Clematis as a Garden Flower;* J. E. Spingarn in Norman Taylor's *The Garden Dictionary* (Boston, London, 1936).

CLEMENCEAU, GEORGES (1841–1929), French statesman, was born at Mouilleron-en-Pareds, Vendée, on Sept. 28, 1841. He adopted medicine as his profession. Interested in the progressive ideas of John Stuart Mill, he decided to investigate for himself the results of the application to affairs of democratic theory. He therefore embarked for the United States, taking with him Mill's *Auguste Comte and Positivism* to translate into French. He arrived in New York early in 1866 and remained there or in New England for three years, writing descriptions of American postwar conditions to the Paris *Temps* and teaching French in a girls' school at Stamford, Conn. In this way he passed what he characterized as the three happiest years of his life. In 1869 he returned to Paris and after the revolution of 1870 he was nominated mayor of the 18th arrondissement of Paris (Montmartre). On Feb. 8, 1871, he was elected as a Radical to the National Assembly for the department of the Seine, and voted against the peace preliminaries. The execution of Generals Lecomte and Clément Thomas by their mutinous soldiers on March 18, which he vainly tried to prevent, brought him into collision with the central committee of the National Guard, and they ordered his arrest, but he escaped; he was accused, however, by various witnesses, at the subsequent trial (Nov. 29), of not having intervened when he might have done, and though he was cleared of this charge it led to a duel, for his share in which he was prosecuted and sentenced to a fine and a fortnight's imprisonment.

Meanwhile, on March 20, 1871, he had introduced in the National Assembly at Versailles, on behalf of his Radical colleagues, the bill establishing a Paris municipal council of 80 members; but he was not returned himself at the elections. He tried with the other Paris mayors to mediate between Versailles and the hôtel de ville, but failed, and accordingly resigned his mayoralty and his seat in the assembly, and temporarily gave up politics; but he was elected to the Paris municipal council on July 23, 1871, for the Clignancourt *quartier*, and retained his seat till 1876, passing through the offices of secretary and vice-president, and becoming president in 1875. In 1876 he stood again for the Chamber of Deputies, and was elected for the 18th arrondissement. He joined the extreme Left, and his energy and mordant eloquence speedily made him the leader of the Radical section. In 1877, after the *Seize mai* (*see* FRANCE: *History*), he took a leading part in resisting the anti-republican policy of which the *Seize mai* incident was a symptom, and in 1879 demanded the indictment of the Broglie ministry. In 1880 he started his newspaper, *La Justice,* which became the principal organ of Parisian Radicalism; and from this time onwards throughout Grévy's presidency his reputation as a political critic, and as a destroyer of ministries who yet would not take office himself, rapidly grew. He led the extreme Left in the Chamber. He was an active opponent of Jules Ferry's colonial policy and of the Opportunist party, and in 1885 his use of the Tongking disaster principally determined the fall of the Ferry cabinet. At the elections of 1885 he was returned both for his old seat in Paris and for the Var, selecting the latter. Refusing to form a ministry to replace the one he had overthrown, he supported the Right in keeping Freycinet in power in 1886, and was responsible for the inclusion of Gen. Boulanger in the Freycinet cabinet as war minister. When Boulanger (*q.v.*) showed his real colours, Clemenceau became a vigorous opponent of the Boulangist movement, though the Radical press and a section of the party continued to patronize the general.

By his exposure of the Wilson scandal (*see* GRÉVY) Clemenceau contributed to Grévy's resignation of the presidency in 1887, having declined Grévy's request that he should himself form a cabinet on the downfall of that of Rouvier; and he was primarily responsible, by advising his followers to vote neither for Floquet, Ferry nor Freycinet, for the election of an "outsider" as president in Carnot. But the split in the Radical party over Boulangism weakened his hands, and his relations with Cornelius Herz in the Panama affair involved him in the general suspicion. However, though he remained the leading spokesman of French Radicalism, his hostility to the Russian alliance so increased his unpopularity that in the election for 1893 he was defeated for the Chamber. Clemenceau now confined his political activities to journalism, his career being further overclouded by the Dreyfus case, in which he was an active supporter of Zola and an opponent of the anti-Semitic and Nationalist campaign. In 1900 he withdrew from *La Justice* to found a weekly review, *Le Bloc,* which lasted until March 1902. On April 6, 1902, he was elected senator for the Var, although he had previously continually demanded the suppression of the Senate. He sat with the Socialist Radicals, and vigorously supported the Combes ministry. In June 1903 he undertook the direction of the journal *L'Aurore,* which he had founded. In it he led the campaign for the revision of the Dreyfus affair, and for the separation of Church and State.

In March 1906 the fall of the Rouvier ministry, owing to the riots provoked by the inventories of church property, at last brought Clemenceau to power as minister of the interior in the Sarrien cabinet. The strike of miners in the Pas de Calais after the disaster at Courrières, leading to the threat of disorder on May 1, 1906, induced him to employ the military; and his attitude in the matter alienated the Socialist party, from which he definitely broke in his notable reply in the chamber to Jean Jaurès in June 1906. This speech marked him out as the "strong man" of the day in French politics; and when the Sarrien ministry resigned in October, he became premier. During 1907 and 1908 the new *entente* with England was cemented, and France played a great part in European politics, in spite of difficulties with Germany and attacks by the Socialist party in connection with Morocco (*see* FRANCE: *History*). But on July 20, 1909, Clemenceau was defeated in a discussion in the chamber on the state of the navy, and was succeeded as premier by Briand, with a reconstructed cabinet.

Two years later Clemenceau entered the Senate and became a member of its commissions for foreign affairs and the army. He could have had no better position for surveying European fluctuations and German activities; or for inquiry into the real condition of French armaments—this last his dominant concern. Convinced that Germany meant war, he was haunted by the fear that again France might be caught unprepared. The Senate, however, gave little opportunity for sounding the alarm. Accordingly, on May 5, 1913, appeared a new daily paper, *L'Homme Libre,* its editor—Georges Clemenceau. In its pages he waged daily battle for security and liberty. Though *L'Homme Libre* dealt every day with home politics and social problems, it returned always to the terrible theme of the German menace.

In the spring of 1913 the question of restoring the three years' term of conscript service suddenly arose. Clemenceau took an impassioned part in the debates on armaments. Then came Aug. 1914 and the World War. *L'Homme Libre* soon suffered at the hands of the Censor for Clemenceau's plain speaking. The whole youth of France must be mobilized. He denounced the shirkers, demanded technical efficiency, and attacked all incompetency, red tape, inadequate munition factories, with their shortage of guns and rifles, and badly-run hospitals. He made war in short, upon all who failed to realize that this was a conflict of supplies and organization, and upon every kind of apathy and feebleness. The result was that in Sept. 1914 *L'Homme Libre* was suppressed. Two days later, however, it reappeared as *L'Homme Enchaîné,* but wore its fetters lightly. For three months there was a daily struggle with the Censor. For some time not a week passed without articles being mutilated, but Clemenceau won and excisions became rare. Meanwhile in the Senate, Clemenceau agitated for more and still more guns, munitions, soldiers, for a judicious use of the available man-power and for a better equipped and better organized medical service.

But above all he strove to create the indomitable and desperate "will to victory." He was supported by other members of the army and foreign affairs commission, like Chéron, Doumer, Humbert, Berenger. The war dragged on; weariness, slackness and pacifism began to appear. Clemenceau was the first to draw public attention to that growing peril and it was at a public debate in the Senate on July 22, 1917, that he made his famous attack on Malvy, who had been Minister of the Interior since 1914. Clemenceau declared that Malvy had not treated revolutionaries with a firm enough hand. Malvy's justification was that he desired to "gain the confidence of the working-man"; but Clemenceau retorted that there was no comparison between those working-men who were loyally doing their duty to their country and a number of abject "defeatists."

Four months later Clemenceau came into power. He had never sought office and he knew that his task meant victory or death. When Clemenceau became premier the situation was miserable. The *moral* at the front was bad, and at home even worse. Resources were nearly at an end, and no solution whatever could be discerned. Poincaré realized that of all men Clemenceau was the impersonation of the idea of war to the death. In his new Government Clemenceau himself took the portfolio of minister of war. He was 76 years of age when he formed his "victory cabinet" on Nov. 16, 1917, and thenceforward till Nov. 11, 1918, Clemenceau did in fact concentrate on war only. He made it clear that France was bent on absolute victory and would brook no half-measures. Those who spoke of wavering or yielding were immediately silenced; any one who obstructed the path to victory was ruthlessly removed. By these means Clemenceau restored the nation's self-confidence, and with it the conviction that its martyrdom would not be in vain. In March 1918 the Anglo-French line was broken through; Clemenceau joined in organizing the unity of command with Foch at the head. In May came the disaster of the Chemin des Dames; the French troops were driven back on the Marne, while the commander-in-chief was criticised. Three months later Clemenceau made Foch Marshal of France. During that long year of ceaseless effort Clemenceau's resolution remained unshaken. On Nov. 8, 1918, Erzberger was in the train of the Commander-in-chief of the allied armies. On the 11th the guns roared for the last time; the nightmare was over.

From Nov. 11, 1918, to June 28, 1919, Clemenceau devoted himself to the international settlement. The Peace of Versailles was in preparation, and this necessitated strenuous days of work and delicate negotiations. Up till now Clemenceau had merely had to contend with his enemies; now his task was to reconcile the interests of France with those of her friends. He defended her cause with enthusiasm and conviction, forcing his view alternatively on Lloyd George and President Wilson. Meanwhile Germany was disarming, and Clemenceau took care to supervise that disarmament. But the French parliament began to grow restless, for it saw itself put to one side in the peace negotiations. It therefore no longer regarded Clemenceau as indispensable. The great patriot, who was anxious to finish the work he had begun, did his best to smooth matters over. Momentous problems had to be solved; demobilization had to be faced, a general election was looming ahead, and the questions of Alsace-Lorraine and the liquidation of war stocks had to be settled. Clemenceau decided to deal simultaneously with these questions as of equal importance.

Peace was signed on June 28, and on Nov. 11 the new chamber was elected. Clemenceau counted on its support; for he believed that its members, many of them ex-soldiers, would have profited by the lesson of the war. Although he never stood as a candidate it is certain that he would have been ready to give the last years of his life by taking Poincaré's place at the Elysée, so that outside and above the changing Governments, he could have secured continuity in political action by a strict application of the 1919 treaties.

Poincaré left the Elysée but Deschanel was elected President of the French republic. And without doubt the Chambers had voted according to their hearts. Clemenceau had saved his country, but members could not forgive the fact that he had excluded them from the final work for victory. During the war he had undoubtedly worked alone; he felt that large assemblies were not made for action. Probably he would have admitted the commissions to the deliberations on the Treaty of Versailles if diplomatic obstacles had not intervened to prevent it. Clemenceau had also to face the hostility, not only of the clerical party of the Right who suspected him of indifference to the Vatican, but also that of the extreme Left, who were alienated by what they considered to be his militarism. Clemenceau thus met the fate which overtook other war ministers, and on Jan. 20, 1920, his cabinet fell, Millerand being summoned to office. He had earned the gratitude of his country and, returning to his beloved books, might well have sought repose; instead he sailed for India. After his journey he returned to Paris and to his books.

But it now appeared that the United States was endeavouring to dissociate itself from European affairs. Clemenceau was now 81 years old, but he sailed at once for America at the end of 1922. From town to town he carried the message of France to the citizens of the U.S. He had no official mission, for he had neither asked anything nor received anything from the French Government. His progress was none the less triumphant. Once more he returned to Paris but not to rest. By the end of 1925 he was already writing two books; one on philosophy, *Au Soir de la Pensée* (1927), English translation, *In the Evening of my Thought* (1929), and the other on Demosthenes, *Demosthène* (1926, Eng. trans. by C. M. Thompson, 1926). He was at work upon his memoirs, *Grandeurs et Misères d'un Victoire* (1930), when he died in Paris on Nov. 24, 1929. (J. MT.)

CLEMENCÍN, DIEGO (1765–1834), Spanish scholar and politician, was born at Murcia, and educated there at the Colegio de San Fulgencio. In 1807 he became editor of the *Gaceta de Madrid,* and in the following year was condemned to death by Murat for publishing a patriotic article; he fled to Cadiz, and under the Junta Central held various posts from which he was dismissed by the reactionary government of 1814. During the liberal régime (1820–23) Clemencín took office as colonial minister, was exiled till 1827, and in 1833 published the first volume of his edition (1833–39) of *Don Quixote.*

CLEMENS, SAMUEL L.: *see* TWAIN, MARK.

CLEMENT, the name of 14 popes and 2 antipopes.

CLEMENT I, Saint, generally known as Clement of Rome (Clemens Romanus), was one of the "Apostolic Fathers." In the earliest list of the bishops of Rome given by Irenaeus, he appears as the third successor of St. Peter (Peter, Linus, Anacletus, Clement). According to Eusebius, his period of office began in the 12th year of Domitian's reign (A.D. 92) and ended in the third year of Trajan's (A.D. 101). Tertullian states that Clement was consecrated by St. Peter himself. Origen's identification of him with the Clement mentioned by St. Paul (Phil. iv, 3) lacks corroboration, and the sources which represent him as a member of the Flavian imperial family are untrustworthy. His feast occurs in the Roman calendar on Nov. 23, and he is commemorated among the martyrs in the canon of the Mass.

He is best known by his only surviving work, the *Epistle to the Church of Corinth,* which is one of the most important documents of the subapostolic age. The letter was occasioned by a dispute in the church of Corinth which had led to the ejection of several presbyters. While it does not contain Clement's name, the tradition which attributes it to him is primitive and universal. Internal evidence (references to the persecution of Domitian) and the testimony of Hegesippus indicate that it was written *c.* A.D. 96. Though the letter does not expressly assert the primacy of the Roman church, it is noteworthy that, in the earliest document outside the canon which can be securely dated, that church is found acting as a peacemaker in the affairs of a church in Greece. The writer moreover employs a tone which is unmistakably authoritative. Nothing is known of the cause of the troubles at Corinth, and the deposition of the presbyters is regarded by Clement as high-handed and unjustifiable. He objects against it the hierarchical principle on which the Christian ministry is based. His argument sets forth in essence the doctrine of the apostolic succession, and it is in this that the permanent interest of the letter lies. The penultimate section of the letter contains a long liturgical prayer which is most probably that used at Rome in the Eucharist at that period. Another interesting feature of the letter is the extensive use which the author makes of the Septuagint for purposes of illustration, indicating that his background was that of Hellenistic Judaism. Clement's epistle was widely read in Christian antiquity and at one time formed part of the New Testament canon in Egypt and Syria. The high regard in which Clement was held by the primitive church is indicated by the number of apocryphal writings attached to his name. (*See* CLEMENTINE LITERATURE.)

BIBLIOGRAPHY.—A convenient edition will be found in J. B. Lightfoot, *The Apostolic Fathers,* vol. i, with English trans. (London, 1890); *see* also W. K. Lowther Clarke (ed.), *The First Epistle of Clement to the Corinthians* (London, 1937); and J. Quasten, *The Beginnings of Patristic Literature,* vol. i of *Patrology,* 4 vol. (Utrecht and Westminster, Md., 1950); this last work contains a comprehensive bibliography.

CLEMENT II (Suidger), pope from 1046 to 1047, belonged to a noble Saxon family. He became bishop of Bamberg and chancellor to the emperor Henry III, who elevated him to the papacy.

Clement was elected pope on Dec. 24, 1046. His short pontificate was only signalized by the convocation of a council in which decrees were enacted against simony. He died on Oct. 9, 1047.

CLEMENT III (Paolo Scolari), pope from 1187 to 1191, a Roman and cardinal bishop of Palestrina, was elected pope on Dec. 19, 1187. In October of that year Jerusalem had fallen to Saladin, and Clement urged on the princes of the west to undertake the third crusade. Apart, however, from the capture of Acre, the results were disappointing. In Italy the marriage of King Henry of the Romans with Constance of Sicily threatened to unite south Italy to the German crown. This Clement tried to avert by enfeoffing Count Tancred of Lecce with Sicily, but he died before the results of his policy became apparent. One of his permanent acts was the removal of the Scottish church from the jurisdiction of York (1188). Thenceforward the Scottish church was dependent directly on Rome.

CLEMENT IV (Gui Foulques), pope from 1265 to 1268, son of a lawyer, was born at St. Gilles-sur-Rhône. He became a valued legal adviser of Louis IX of France and after the death of his wife took orders. In 1257 he was made bishop of Le Puy, in 1259 archbishop of Narbonne and in 1261 cardinal bishop of Sabina. He was appointed legate in England in 1263 and before his return was elected pope at Perugia on Feb. 5, 1265. Determined like his predecessors to extirpate the Hohenstaufen dynasty from Italy, he invested the avaricious Charles of Anjou with the kingdom of Sicily but subsequently came into conflict with him after the death of Manfred in Feb. 1266. When Conradin, the last of the Hohenstaufen, appeared in Italy, the pope excommunicated him and his supporters. Clement died at Viterbo on Nov. 29, 1268, leaving a name unsullied by nepotism.

CLEMENT V (Bertrand de Got), pope from 1305 to 1314, was born at Villandraut (Gironde) of a noble Gascon family. After studying law at Orléans and Bologna he became canon of Bordeaux, then vicar-general to his brother (the archbishop of Lyons), bishop of Comminges in 1295 and archbishop of Bordeaux in 1299. On June 5, 1305, he was chosen to succeed Benedict XI, as a compromise candidate known to be acceptable to Philip IV of France.

A weak man, who suffered throughout his pontificate from a chronic illness, Clement yielded to the constant pressure of French interests. Thus at the instance of Philip IV his crowning took place at Lyons, and after it, instead of making for Rome, he retired to Gascony. Finally, in March 1309, he settled with his court at Avignon where the papacy was to remain for the next 70 years, the period of the so-called Babylonian captivity. Clement chose Avignon because, as the property of the Angevine rulers of Naples, it was not dependent on the French crown. Also it was surrounded by the papal county of Venaissin and offered easy egress to the sea. He seems never to have abandoned his intention of moving to Rome as soon as the political situation allowed, and he made no plans for a permanent residence at Avignon, contenting himself with the Dominican priory in that city.

In Dec. 1305 Clement created nine French cardinals, and further creations in 1310 and 1312 ensured French domination of the sacred college and the succession of a French pope. Throughout his pontificate he was blackmailed by Philip IV's threat of reopening the posthumous trial of Boniface VIII. The price Clement had to pay for the suspension of these proceedings was the annulment of all Boniface's acts against French interests, the absolution of Guillaume de Nogaret, the royal councillor who had organized the outrage of Anagni, and finally the canonization of Celestine V (May 1313). The most glaring example of Clement's subservience to the French king was his suppression of the Knights Templars. The attack on the order was launched by the king in 1307, apparently for financial reasons (they were the bankers of the French crown). Clement issued the bull of suppression on April 3, 1312, at the Council of Vienne, which was summoned to give the act a judicial appearance. Although a later bull (May 2) assigned the property of the Templars to the Hospitallers, the chief beneficiary in France was the king. The weakness of Clement's position in France did not prevent him from pursuing active and independent policies elsewhere. He intervened in the dispute over the Hungarian succession. He disposed of the imperial crown in favour of Henry of Luxemburg (1312), and prosecuted a successful war against Venice in order to recover the papal rights over Ferrara.

Under Clement the centralization of ecclesiastical government was carried a stage further. Papal reservations were extended to new classes of benefice, and papal nomination became the most frequent method of episcopal appointment. A jurist himself, Clement added an important section (the *Clementines*) to the *Corpus Iuris Canonici*. As a scholar and patron of scholars, he gave university status to the schools of Orléans and Perugia and founded chairs of oriental languages at Paris, Bologna, Oxford and Salamanca. At his death on April 20, 1314, he left the papal treasury impoverished by his extravagant bequests.

BIBLIOGRAPHY.—The authoritative work is by G. Mollat, *Les Papes d'Avignon*, 9th ed. (Paris, 1949), which contains comprehensive bibliographies. *See* also A. Eitel, *Der Kirchenstaat unter Klemens V* (Berlin, 1907); G. Lizerand, *Clement V et Philippe IV le Bel* (Paris, 1910); E. Mueller, *Das Konzil von Wien, 1311–1312* (Münster, 1934).

CLEMENT VI (Pierre Roger), pope from 1342 to 1352, was born at Maumont, Limousin, in 1291, joined the Benedictines as a boy, studied at Paris and became successively prior of St. Baudil, abbot of Fécamp, bishop of Arras, chancellor of France, archbishop of Sens and archbishop of Rouen. He was made cardinal priest of Sti Nereo ed Achilleo and administrator of the bishopric of Avignon by Benedict XII in 1338, and four years later succeeded him as pope (May 7, 1342). Clement continued the struggle of his predecessors with the emperor Louis the Bavarian, excommunicating him in April 1346, and directing the election of Charles of Luxemburg, who received general recognition after the death of Louis in 1347, and put an end to the schism which had long divided Germany. Clement carried on fruitless negotiations for church unity with the Armenians and with the Greek emperor, John Cantacuzenus. He tried to end the Hundred Years' War between England and France but secured only a temporary truce. He excommunicated Casimir of Poland for marital infidelity and forced him to do penance. He successfully resisted encroachments on ecclesiastical jurisdiction by the kings of England. He purchased Avignon from Queen Joanna of Naples and considerably enlarged the papal palace. These undertakings, together with the upkeep of a splendid court, the open-handed patronage of artists and scholars and large loans to the French crown, bankrupted the papal treasury and forced Clement to resort to increasingly onerous taxation. After the austere days of Benedict XII, the flood of reservations and expectancies recommenced. The machinery of tax collection was improved by the grouping of local churches into collectories. Clement's fiscality led to a growing body of complaint (expressed in England in the Statute of Provisors) and bequeathed an insuperable problem to his successors. He died on Dec. 6, 1352.

BIBLIOGRAPHY.—G. Mollat, *Les Papes d'Avignon*, 9th ed. (Paris, 1949); Y. Renouard, *Les Relations des papes d'Avignon et des compagnies commerciales et bancaires de 1316 à 1378* (Paris, 1941); M. Faucon, *Prêts faits aux rois de France par Clement VI etc.* (Bibliothèque de l'École des Chartes, xi, 1879); D. Colombe, *Le Palais des papes d'Avignon* (Paris, 1927).

CLEMENT VII (Giulio de' Medici), pope from 1523 to 1534, was the son of Giuliano de' Medici, assassinated in the Pazzi conspiracy at Florence. After the death of Lorenzo, Giulio in 1494 went into exile; but, on Giovanni's restoration to power, returned to Florence, of which he was made archbishop by his cousin, Pope Leo X, a special dispensation being granted on account of his illegitimate birth, followed by a formal declaration of the fact that his parents had been secretly married and that he was therefore legitimate. In 1513 he was made cardinal and during the pontificate of Leo had practically the whole papal policy in his hands. On the death of Adrian VI he was chosen pope (Nov. 18, 1523). It soon became clear, however, that Clement was only a good second in command, for though he was cultured and economical without being avaricious, he was essentially a man of narrow outlook and interests. Instead of bending his mind to the problem of the Reformation, he subordinated the cause of

Catholicism to his interests as an Italian prince and a Medici; and even in purely secular affairs his timidity and indecision prevented him from pursuing a consistent policy.

His accession at once brought about a political change in favour of France. He wavered between the emperor and Francis I, concluding a treaty of alliance with the French king, and then after the defeat of Pavia making his peace with Charles (April 1, 1525), but breaking it again by countenancing Girolamo Morone's League of Freedom, which aimed to assert Italian independence. On the betrayal of this conspiracy Clement made a fresh submission to the emperor, only to follow this, a year later, by the Holy League of Cognac with Francis I (May 22, 1526). Then followed the imperial invasion of Italy and Bourbon's sack of Rome (May 1527). The pope himself was besieged and compelled to ransom himself with 400,000 scudi and to promise to convene a general council to deal with Lutheranism. After the treaty of Cambrai on Aug. 3, 1529, Charles met Clement at Bologna and received from him the imperial crown and the iron crown of Lombardy, but the pope for some time exercised his temporal power in subservience to the emperor. Clement was now mainly occupied in urging Charles to arrest the progress of the Reformation in Germany and in efforts to elude the emperor's demand for a general council, which Clement feared lest the mode of his election and his legitimacy should be raised. Clement's fear of displeasing Charles V, as well as his solicitude for canonical principles, made him temporize in face of Henry VIII's demand for the nullification of his marriage with Catherine until, losing patience, Henry carried the English church into schism. Clement died on Sept. 25, 1534.

Bibliography.—W. Hellwig, *Die politischen Beziehungen Clements VII zu Karl V im Jahre 1526* (Leipzig, 1889); K. Brandi, *The Emperor Charles V*, tr. by C. V. Wedgwood (London, New York, 1939); M. Creighton, *History of the Papacy during the . . . Reformation*, 6 vol., new ed. (London, 1897); H. M. Vaughan, *The Medici Popes* (London, 1908); P. Crabitès, *Clement VII and Henry VIII* (London, Toronto, 1936); R. Mols, "Clément VII" in *Dictionnaire d'histoire et de géographie ecclésiastique*, vol. xii, with bibliography (Paris, 1953).

Clement VII (Robert of Geneva), antipope from 1378 to 1394, was son of count Amadeus III of Geneva. Bishop of Thérouanne (1361) and archbishop of Cambrai (1368), he was created cardinal by Gregory XI in 1371 and entrusted with the military mission of restoring the papal states. The ferocity of his Breton and English mercenaries, above all the massacre of Cesena (1377), made the name of the "cardinal of Geneva" a byword throughout Italy.

In 1378 he took part in the confused election of Urban VI. After the French cardinals had seceded and announced that Urban's election was irregular, Robert of Geneva was elected pope at Fondi on Sept. 20, 1378. He was crowned the same day, as Clement VII. Thus originated the Great Schism of the West. The schism rapidly took political lines, Clement being supported by Queen Joanna of Naples, Charles V of France, Scotland, Castile, Aragon, Navarre, the Latin enclaves in the east and the count of Flanders. In Italy however the tide quickly turned against Clement and in May 1379 he took ship and returned to Avignon, taking the cardinals of his allegiance with him. To wrest Rome from his rival, he induced Louis, duke of Anjou, to take up his cause, promising him a kingdom to be carved out of the states of the church, coupled with the expectation of succeeding Joanna in Naples. Louis however proved a disappointing generalissimo and the only lasting outcome of this bargain was the passing of Naples to Louis's son in 1384. In his last years Clement worked hard to head off the University of Paris which was openly advocating a general council as the only means of ending the schism. He died on Sept. 16, 1394, asserting to the last his claim to be the rightful pope.

Bibliography.—N. Valois, *La France et le grand schisme d'occident*, 4 vol. (Paris, 1896–1902); W. Ullmann, *The Origins of the Great Schism* (London, 1948); M. de Boüard, *Les Origines des guerres d'Italie; La France et l'Italie au temps du grand schisme d'occident* (Paris, 1936).
(C. H. Le.)

Clement VIII (Ippolito Aldobrandini), pope from 1592 to 1605, was born at Fano on Feb. 24, 1536. He became a jurist and in 1585 was made a cardinal. On Jan. 30, 1592, he was elected pope to succeed Innocent IX. To him fell the unspectacular but vitally important task of consolidating the ground won by the reforms of the Council of Trent. He had published a revised text of the Vulgate (1592) which remained the official edition until the 20th century, and in turn revised and edited the principal liturgical books: the pontifical (1596), the breviary (1602) and the missal (1604). A new edition of the index was compiled in 1593. He tackled the dispute between the Jesuits and the Dominicans over the rival theories of grace and free will by summoning the contestants to Rome (1594), where the debate still continued after his death in 1605. By so protracting the contest, he allowed it to lose some of its urgency, with the result that Paul V was able to terminate it in 1605 without any decision being reached. In diplomacy, Clement was determined to free the papacy from the shackles of Spanish domination; he granted absolution to Henry IV in 1595, so dissociating the papacy from the militant Catholic party in France and Spain, and this new policy had a spectacular success when peace was concluded between the two countries at Vervins in 1598. The new independence won by the papacy was revealed by the ease with which Clement, upon the failure of the line of Este, claimed the reversion of Ferrara and reincorporated it into the states of the church (1598). In ending the war in France, Clement had hoped to weaken the Protestant powers who had profited by its continuance, but his direct intervention into English affairs was not so successful. First the archpriest controversy (1598), then, after the death of Elizabeth I, the persecution that followed the Gunpowder plot, seriously weakened the position of Catholics in England. Yet, by his death (March 5, 1605), Clement could claim that, internally and diplomatically, the papacy was much strengthened, though the history of the 17th century might suggest that, in curbing the power of Spain and raising that of France, the papacy had but exchanged one master for another.

Clement VIII (Aegidius Muñoz), antipope from 1425 to July 26, 1429, was a canon at Barcelona until elected by three cardinals created by the antipope Benedict XIII. Clement was recognized by Alphonso V of Aragon, who was hostile to Pope Martin V because of the latter's opposition to his claims to Naples. When Alphonso and Martin became reconciled, Clement abdicated and spent his last years as bishop of Majorca. He died on Dec. 28, 1446.

Clement IX (Giulio Rospigliosi), pope from 1667 to 1669, was born on Jan. 28, 1600, and after a career in the papal chancery was archbishop of Tarsus and nuncio in Spain before being made a cardinal and secretary of state by Alexander VII. During his long career he had made himself acceptable to both France and Spain, and his considerable experience made him the choice also of the independent party among the cardinals to succeed Alexander on June 20, 1667. He proved no match for the diplomatic abilities of Hugues de Lionne, Louis XIV's ambassador at the Vatican, and the peace of Aix-la-Chapelle (1668) between France and Spain which he was instrumental in concluding secured for France all it desired, while the peace of Clement IX which secured the return of the expelled nuns to Port Royal (1669) was designed by Lionne equally in the interests of the French monarchy. In return for these concessions, Clement had hoped to win French support against the Turks in Crete, but French assistance to the Venetian garrison was slight as well as insincere, and the island was captured in 1669. Clement died soon afterward (Dec. 9, 1669).

Clement X (Emilio Altieri), pope from 1670 to 1676, was born in Rome on July 13, 1590, and after a long career in the papal diplomatic service became pope at the age of 79 (April 29, 1670). The breathing space it was hoped such an appointment would bring did not materialize, for relations with France steadily deteriorated, and the outbreak in 1673 of the long controversy over the regalia (*see* Innocent XI) called for the services of a strong, not a stop-gap, pope. Clement died on July 22, 1676.

Clement XI (Giovanni Francesco Albani), pope from 1700 to 1721, was born in Urbino on July 22, 1649, and after filling various important offices in the curia became pope on Nov. 23, 1700, succeeding Innocent XII. His private life and his administration were blameless, but it was his misfortune to reign in troublous times. In the War of the Spanish Succession he first supported Philip V but was compelled by the emperor under the threat of invasion to change sides in 1709. In the peace of Utrecht he was ignored; Sardinia and Sicily, Parma and Piacenza were disposed of without regard to papal claims. When he quarrelled with the duke of Savoy and revoked his investiture right in Sicily (1715), his interdict was treated with contempt. Clement supported the Jesuit position when the controversy over the Five Propositions was revived in France, and in 1713 issued the bull *Unigenitus,* condemning 101 Jansenistic propositions. (*See* JANSENISM and QUESNEL, PASQUIER.) He also forbade missionaries in China to "accommodate" their teachings to pagan notions in order to win converts. He died on March 19, 1721.

CLEMENT XII (Lorenzo Corsini), pope from 1730 to 1740, was born at Florence on April 7, 1652. His entire career was spent at Rome in the papal administration, and he became a cardinal in 1706. He was elected pope on July 12, 1730, at the age of 78, to succeed Benedict XIII. Despite old age and ill health, he took an active part in the administration, and in internal matters of routine proved to be competent and efficient. His diplomatic activities, however, were not so successful; his endeavour to remain neutral in the War of the Polish Succession (1733–37) led only to the papal states being invaded by the troops of both sides, while his assistance of the emperor against the Turks did not prevent the surrender of Belgrade in 1739. Coming of a very rich family, Clement was, both as cardinal and pope, a great patron of learning and the arts. He died on Feb. 6, 1740.

CLEMENT XIII (Carlo della Torre Rezzonico), pope from 1758 to 1769, was born in Venice on March 7, 1693, and after a career in the curia was made cardinal in 1737 and bishop of Padua in 1743. He became pope on July 6, 1758, at a time when the papacy, after a century of diminishing prestige as an international power, was once again being attacked by reforming movements in the national churches as the defender of obscurantism and the ally of the traditionalist orders, especially the Jesuits. These considerations, however, left Clement quite unmoved, and he took up the cause of the Jesuits, to whom he was indebted for his election, without reservation. He brought about a final crisis with the Bourbon monarchies by an attempt to reassert the temporal power over Parma (1768) and, when he refused to give way to their united demands, found himself faced with the seizure of Avignon, Benevento and Ponte Corvo and an almost universal call for the suppression of the Jesuits. He was in no position to resist and had consented to call a consistory just before his death on Feb. 2, 1769. His papacy was one of almost unmitigated disaster.

CLEMENT XIV (Giovanni Vincenzo Antonio, otherwise Lorenzo, Ganganelli), pope from 1769 to 1774, was born near Rimini on Oct. 31, 1705. He joined the Franciscans (when he adopted his father's name of Lorenzo) and, after serving on the Inquisition and establishing his reputation as a scholar, was made a cardinal by Clement XIII. He was not, however, in agreement with the extreme policy of opposition to the Bourbons pursued by that pope and so remained in the background during the disputes over the Jesuits. He seemed, therefore, to offer a compromise to the conclave in 1769 between the insistence of the Bourbons that the next pope must promise before election to agree to the suppression of the Jesuits, and the supporters of the policy of Clement XIII who formed a majority among the cardinals. Ganganelli promised at least that he would in the last resort agree to the suppression, but hoped to avoid this necessity by a policy of conciliation on all other issues. In these circumstances, and faced with the critical situation left by Clement XIII, he was elected pope without opposition on May 18, 1769. He immediately put his new policy of conciliation into action and achieved some success, but the intransigence of the Bourbon demands and the continued indiscretions of the Jesuits themselves together brought all his efforts to nought. After long consideration, he decided that the Jesuits must be sacrificed, and on July 21, 1773, he signed the brief *Dominus ac Redemptor* dissolving the order (*see* JESUS, SOCIETY OF). All the other events of his papacy are dwarfed by this decision, for which, at the time and since, he has been both criticized and defended. The immediate result was the restoration to the Holy See of the seized territories and a general improvement in the relations between the papacy and the temporal powers, and it is difficult to discover any alternative policy that would not have led to instant and utter disaster. Yet the fact remains that, with the suppression, the prestige of the papacy reached its lowest point since the time of the Reformation. Clement himself died not long afterward, on Sept. 22, 1774. Contemporary suspicions of foul play are probably not well founded.

See J. Cretinau-Joly, *Clément XIV et les Jésuites* (Paris, 1847) and A. Theiner, *Histoire du pontificat de Clément XIV* (Fr. trans., Paris, 1852), which deal with Clement's part in the suppression of the Jesuits from different points of view. The question was partly reopened by O. Montevenosi "Un pontificato da reabilitare. Il papa Clemente XIV" in *Archivi* (Rome, 1941). (I. F. B.)

CLÉMENT, FRANÇOIS (1714–1793), French historian, was born at Bèze, near Dijon. He became a Benedictine and wrote vol. xi and xii of the *Histoire littéraire de la France* and edited (with Dom Brial) vol. xii and xiii of the *Recueil des historiens des Gauls et de la France*. The king appointed him to the committee for the publication of charters and other historical documents. Of his revision of the *Art de vérifier les dates,* ed. by Dom Clémencet (1750), three volumes with indexes appeared from 1783 to 1792. Clément died at Paris on March 29, 1793.

CLÉMENT, JACQUES (1567–1589), murderer of the French king Henry III, was born at Sorbon in the Ardennes and became a Dominican friar. With his mind apparently unhinged by religious fanaticism and inspired by members of the Catholic League, who were urging him to save the kingdom, he obtained letters for the king and, on July 31, 1589, left Paris, which the king was besieging, for the royal headquarters at Saint Cloud. Next day, while Henry was reading the letters, Clément mortally wounded him with a dagger that he had concealed under his cloak. Clément was killed on the spot by Henry's attendants.

See P. de Vaissière, *De quelques assassins* (Paris, 1912).

CLÉMENTEL, ÉTIENNE (1862–1936), French politician, was born on March 29, 1862, at Riom and educated there. He was elected a deputy in 1898 and became minister for the colonies in Rouvier's cabinet in 1905, afterwards occupying ministerial posts in departments where his knowledge of economics could find full play, the ministries of agriculture, colonies, finance, public works and marine. His collaboration was particularly valuable in organizing the supply of raw materials for the allied armies during World War I. By effecting the agreement for establishment of the inter-allied wheat executive with Walter Runciman in Nov. 1916, Clémentel helped to tide over a difficult situation. The creation of the inter-allied maritime transport council was due in great part to his energy, for, as early as Aug. 1917, he had occupied himself with drawing up a general inventory of his own country's requirements, an initiative quickly followed by the allied governments. After the armistice, Clémentel was chosen "Président fondateur" of the International Chamber of Commerce. He was elected senator for Puy de Dôme in 1918. His work at the London Conference of July 1924, which he attended as minister of finance in the Herriot cabinet, was greatly appreciated. He resigned office as minister of finance on April 3, 1925, on the ground of a difference with Herriot on the question of a fresh issue of notes by the Bank of France. In 1927 he was president of the finance committee of the Senate and also became a member of the committee on trade barriers of the International Chamber of Commerce. Among his writings may be mentioned: *L'Âme celtique* (1899) and *Un drame économique* (1914).

CLEMENTI, MUZIO (1752–1832), Italian pianist and composer, was born at Rome where his father was a jeweller. At nine he was appointed organist of a church and at fourteen he had written a mass which was performed in public. About 1766 Peter Beckford, cousin of the author of *Vathek,* brought Clementi to England, where his success both as composer and pianist was rapid and brilliant. In 1777 he was for some time employed as conductor of the Italian opera, but he soon afterwards left London for Paris. Here also his concerts were crowded by enthusiastic audiences, and the same success accompanied him on a tour about the year 1780 to southern Germany and Austria. At Vienna, which he visited between 1781 and 1782, he was received with high honour by the emperor Joseph II, in whose presence he met Mozart, and fought a kind of musical duel with him.

In May 1782 Clementi returned to London, where for the next twelve years he continued his lucrative occupations of fashionable teacher and performer at the concerts of the aristocracy. He took shares in the pianoforte business of a firm which went bankrupt in 1800. He then established a pianoforte and music business of his own, under the name of Clementi & Co. which was very successful. Other members were added to the firm, including Collard and Davis, and it was ultimately taken over by Collard.

Among his pupils on the pianoforte during this period may be mentioned John Field, the composer of the celebrated *Nocturnes.* In his company, Clementi paid, in 1804, a visit to Paris, Vienna, St. Petersburg (Leningrad), Berlin and other cities. While he was in Berlin, Meyerbeer became one of his pupils. He also revisited his own country, after an absence of more than 30 years. In 1810 Clementi returned to London, but refused to play again in public, devoting the remainder of his life to composition. Several symphonies belong to this period but none was published.

Of Clementi's playing in his youth, Moscheles wrote that it was "marked by a most beautiful *legato,* a supple touch in lively passages, and a most unfailing technique." Mozart may be said to have closed the old and Clementi to have founded the newer school of technique on the piano. Among Clementi's compositions the most remarkable are 60 sonatas for pianoforte, and the great collection of *Études* called *Gradus ad Parnassum.*

CLEMENTINE LITERATURE, the name generally given to the writings which at one time or another were fathered upon Pope Clement I (*q.v.*), commonly called Clemens Romanus, who was early regarded as a disciple of St. Peter. Chief among them are: (1) the so-called Second Epistle; (2) two Epistles on Virginity; (3) the *Homilies* and *Recognitions,* with which may be classed the *Epistle of Clement to James;* (4) the *Apostolical Constitutions* (*q.v.*); and (5) five epistles forming part of the Forged Decretals (*see* DECRETALS). The present article deals mainly with the third group, to which the title "Clementine literature" is usually confined, owing to the stress laid upon it in the famous Tübingen reconstruction of primitive Christianity, in which it played a leading part; but later criticism has lowered its importance as its true date and historical relations have been progressively ascertained. (1) and (2) became "Clementine" only by chance, but (3) was so originally by literary device or fiction, the cause at work also in (4) and (5). But while in all cases the suggestion of Clement's authorship came ultimately from his prestige as writer of the genuine *Epistle of Clement* (*see* CLEMENT I), both (3) and (4) were due to this idea as operative on Syrian soil; (5) is a secondary formation based on (3) as known to the west.

(1) *The Second Epistle of Clement.*—This is really the earliest extant Christian homily (*see* APOSTOLIC FATHERS). Its theme is the duty of Christian repentance, with a view to obedience to Christ's precepts as the true confession and homage which He requires. Its special charge is "Preserve the flesh pure and the seal (*i.e.,* baptism) unstained" (viii, 6). The homily was considered a part of Scripture in the Syriac Church and is found in the Codex Alexandrinus. It was most probably composed before A.D. 150 at Corinth (*see* F. X. Funk and G. Kruger), but Rome and Alexandria have also been proposed as the place of origin about 170.

(2) *The Two Epistles to Virgins, i.e.,* to Christian celibates of both sexes. These are known in their entirety only in Syriac, and were first published by J. J. Wetstein (1752), who held them genuine. This view is now usually discredited. There is no trace of their use in the west. Their Syrian origin is manifest, the more so that in the Syriac ms. they are appended to the New Testament, like the better-known epistles of Clement in the Codex Alexandrinus. It is now definitely established, however, that they were written originally, not in Syriac, but in Greek. Special occasion for such hortatory letters may be discerned in their polemic against intimate relations between ascetics of opposite sex, implied to exist among its readers, in contrast to usage in the writer's own locality. Now we know that spiritual unions, prompted originally by high-strung Christian idealism as to a religious fellowship transcending the law of nature in relation to sex, did exist between persons living under vows of celibacy during the 3rd century in particular. On the basis of internal evidence, therefore, the letters were most probably composed not later than the middle of the 3rd century, and they furnish precious information on the early stages of Christian asceticism.

(3*a*) *The Epistle of Clement to James* (the Lord's brother). This was originally part of (3*b*), in connection with which its origin and date are discussed. But as known to the west through Rufinus' Latin version, it was quoted as genuine throughout the middle ages. It became the starting point of the most momentous and gigantic of mediaeval forgeries, the Isidorian Decretals, where it stands at the head of the pontifical letters, extended to more than twice its original length.

(3*b*) *The Homilies and Recognitions.*—"The two chief extant Clementine writings, differing considerably in some respects in doctrine, are both evidently the outcome of a peculiar speculative type of Judaistic Christianity, for which the most characteristic name of Christ was 'the true Prophet.' The framework of both is a narrative purporting to be written by Clement (of Rome) to St. James, the Lord's brother, describing at the beginning his own conversion and the circumstances of his first acquaintance with St. Peter, and then a long sucession of incidents accompanying St. Peter's discourses and disputations, leading up to a romantic recognition of Clement's father, mother and two brothers, from whom he had been separated since childhood. The problems discussed under this fictitious guise are with rare exceptions fundamental problems for every age; and, whatever may be thought of the positions maintained, the discussions are hardly ever feeble or trivial. Regarded simply as mirroring the past, few, if any, remains of Christian antiquity present us with so vivid a picture of the working of men's minds under the influence of the new leaven which had entered into the world" (F. J. A. Hort, *Clem. Recog.,* p. xiv). Recent criticism builds on the principle, which emerges alike from the external and internal evidence that both writings used a common basis or parent document. Toward the determination of its nature, origin and antecedents, a number of important contributions have been made, beginning with the pioneer works of F. J. A. Hort and Dr. Hans Waitz; but there is as yet no general agreement on many points. The Clementines are still a major problem in early Christian literature.

External Evidence.—Whether Origen refers to the Clementine writings is a moot question, but Eusebius of Caesarea clearly mentions them in his *Eccl. Hist.,* iii, 38: "Certain men have quite lately brought forward as written by him (Clement) other verbose and lengthy writings, containing dialogues of Peter, forsooth, and Apion, whereof not the slightest mention is to be found among the ancients, for they do not even preserve in purity the stamp of the Apostolic orthodoxy." Apion, the Alexandrine grammarian and foe of Judaism, whose criticism was answered by Josephus, appears in this character both in *Homilies* and *Recognitions,* though mainly in the former (iv, 6–vii, 5). Thus Eusebius implies (1) a spurious Clementine work containing matter found also in our *Homilies* at any rate; and (2) its quite recent origin. Next we note that an extract in the *Philocalia* of Origen is introduced as follows: "Yea, and Clement the Roman, a disciple of Peter the Apostle, after using words in harmony with these on the present problem, in conversation with his father at Laodicea in the *Circuits,* speaks a very necessary word touching this matter" (astrological divination). The extract answers to *Recognitions,* x, 10–13, but it is absent from our *Homilies.* Here we observe that (1) the extract agrees this time with *Recognitions,* not with *Homilies;* (2) its framework is that of the Clementine romance found in both; (3) the tenth and last book of *Recognitions* is here parallel to book xiv of a work called *Circuits* (*Periodoi*). This last point leads on naturally to the witness of Epiphanius (*c.* 375), who, speaking of Ebionites or Judaizing Christians of various sorts, and particularly the Essene type, says (*Haer.* xxx, 15) that "they use certain other books likewise, to wit, the so-called *Circuits* of Peter, which were written by the hand of Clement. . . . In the *Circuits,* then, they adapted the whole to their own views, representing Peter falsely in many ways, as that he was daily baptized for the sake of purification, as these also do; and they say that he likewise abstained from animal food and meat, as they themselves also do." Now all the points here noted in the *Circuits* can be traced in our *Homilies* and *Recognitions,* though toned down in different degrees. The witness of the Arianizing *Opus Imperfectum in Matthaeum* (*c.* 400) is in general similar. Its usual form of citation is "Peter in Clement" (*apud Clementem*), and points to "Clement" as a brief title for the Clementine *Periodoi.*

It has been needful to cite so much of the evidence proving that our *Homilies* and *Recognitions* are both recensions of a common basis, at first known as the *Circuits of Peter* and later by titles connecting it rather with Clement, its ostensible author, because it affords data also for the historical problems touching (*a*) the contents and origin of the primary Clementine work, and (*b*) the conditions under which our extant recensions of it arose.

(*a*) *The Circuits of Peter,* as defined on the one hand by the epistle of Clement to James originally prefixed to it and by patristic evidence, and on the other by the common element in our *Homilies* and *Recognitions,* may be conceived as follows. It contained accounts of Peter's teachings and discussions at various points on a route beginning at Caesarea, and extending northward along the coastlands of Syria as far as Antioch. During this tour he meets with persons of typically erroneous views, which it was presumably the aim of the work to refute in the interests of true Christianity, conceived as the final form of divine revelation—a revelation given through true prophecy embodied in a succession of persons, the chief of whom were Moses and the prophet whom Moses foretold, Jesus the Christ. The prime exponent of the spurious religion is Simon Magus. A second protagonist of error, this time of Gentile philosophic criticism directed against fundamental Judaism, is Apion, the notorious anti-Jewish Alexandrine grammarian of Peter's day; while the role of upholder of astrological fatalism (*Genesis*) is played by Faustus, father of Clement, with whom Peter and Clement debate at Laodicea. Finally, all this is already embedded in a setting determined by the romance of Clement and his lost relatives, "recognition" of whom forms the denouement of the story.

There is no reason to doubt that such, roughly speaking, were the contents of the Clementine work to which Eusebius alludes slightingly, in connection with that section of it which had to his eye least verisimilitude, viz., the dialogues between Peter and Apion. Now Eusebius believed the work to have been of recent and suspicious origin. The opinion of Eusebius and the prevailing doctrinal tone—in part gnostic—of the contents, as known to us, point to a date not much later than the first quarter of the third century. The standpoint is that of the peculiar Judaizing Christianity due to persistence among Christians of the tendencies known among pre-Christian Jews as Essene. The Essenes, while clinging to what they held to be original Mosaism, yet conceived and practised their ancestral faith in ways which showed distinct traces of syncretism, or the operation of influences foreign to Judaism proper. They thus occupied an ambiguous position on the borders of Judaism. Similarly Christian Essenism was syncretist in spirit, as we see from its best-known representatives, the Elchasaites, of whom we first hear about 220, when a certain Alcibiades of Apamea in Syria (about 60 mi. south of Antioch) brought to Rome the *Book of Helxai*—the manifesto of their distinctive message (Hippol., *Philos.* ix, 13)—and again some 20 years later, when Origen refers to one of their leaders as having lately arrived at Caesarea (Euseb. vi, 38).

The *Periodoi* or *Circuits* must not be thought of as strictly Elchasaite, since it knew no baptism distinct from the ordinary Christian one. It seems rather to represent a later and modified Essene Christianity, already half Catholic, such as would suit a date after 250, in keeping with Eusebius' evidence. Confirmation of such a date is afforded by the silence of the Syrian *Didascalia,* itself perhaps dating from about 220, as to any visit of Simon Magus of Caesarea, in contrast to the reference in its later form, the *Apostolical Constitutions* (*c.* 350–400), which is plainly coloured (vi, 9) by the Clementine story. On the other hand, the *Didascalia* seems to have been evoked partly by Judaizing propaganda in north Syria. If, then, it helps to date the *Periodoi* as after 220, it may also suggest as place of origin one of the large cities lying south of Antioch, say Laodicea (itself on the coast about 30 mi. from Apamea), where the Clementine story reaches its climax. The intimacy of local knowledge touching this region implied in the narrative common to *Homilies* and *Recognitions* is notable, and tells against an origin for the *Periodoi* outside Syria (*e.g.,* in Rome, as Hans Waitz and A. Harnack hold, but J. B. Lightfoot disproves, *Clem.* i, 55 f., 64,100, *cf.* Hort, p. 131). Further, though the curtain even in it fell on Peter at Antioch itself (our one complete ms. of the *Homilies* is proved by the *Epitome,* based on the *Homilies,* to be here abridged), the interest of the story culminates at Laodicea.

If we assume, then, that the common source of our extant Clementines arose in Syria, perhaps, *c.* 230, had it also a written source or sources which we can trace? Most recent scholars believe that the common source (*Grundschrift*) was itself a compilation, the chief elements of which were the "Preachings (*Kerymata*) of Peter," the *Actus Vercellenses,* an *Apologia Judaica* and a pagan romance. The first source at least seems implied by the epistle of Peter to James and its appended adjuration, prefixed in our mss. to the *Homilies* along with the *Epistle of Clement to James.* Thus the later work aimed at superseding the earlier, much as Photius suggests (*see* above). It was, then, to these "Preachings of Peter" that the most Ebionite features, and especially the anti-Pauline allusions under the guise of Simon still inhering in the *Periodoi* (as implied by *Homilies* in particular), originally belonged. The fact, however, that these were not more completely suppressed in the later work, proves that it, too, arose in circles of kindred, though largely modified, Judaeo-Christian sentiment (cf. *Homilies,* vii, *e.g.,* ch. 8). The differences of standpoint may be due not only to lapse of time, and the emergence of new problems on the horizon of Syrian Christianity generally, but also to change in locality and in the degree of Greek culture represented by the two works. The "Preachings of Peter" may be as early as the first third of the second century.

If the home of the *Periodoi* was the region of the Syrian Laodicea, we can readily explain most of its characteristics. Photius refers to the "excellences of its language and its learning"; while Waitz describes the aim and spirit of its contents as those of an apology for Christianity against heresy and paganism, in the widest sense of the word, written in order to win over both Jews (cf. *Recognitions,* i, 53–70) and pagans, but mainly the latter. In particular it had in view persons of culture, as most apt to be swayed by the philosophical tendencies in the sphere of religion prevalent in that age, the age of neo-Platonism. It was in fact designed for propaganda among religious seekers in a time of singular religious restlessness and varied inquiry, and, above all, for use by catechumens (cf. *Ep. Clem.* 2, 13) in the earlier stages of their preparation for Christian baptism. To such its romantic setting would be specially adapted, as falling in with the literary habits and tastes of the period; while its doctrinal peculiarities would least give offence in a work of the aim and character just described.

(*b*) That the *Periodoi* was a longer work than either our *Homilies* or *Recognitions* is practically certain; and its mere bulk may well, as Hort suggests, have been a chief cause of the changes of form. Yet *Homilies* and *Recognitions* are abridgements made on different principles and convey rather different impressions to their readers. The *Homilies* care most for doctrine, especially philosophical doctrine, and seem to transpose very freely for doctrinal purposes; the *Recognitions* care most for the story, as a means of religious edification, and have preserved the general framework much more nearly. They arose in different circles; indeed, save the compiler of the text represented by the Syraic ms. of A.D. 411 (who gives a selection of discourses from the *Homilies* after *Recognitions,* iii), not a single ancient writer shows a knowledge of both books in any form. *Homilies* was a sort of second edition, made largely in the spirit of its original and perhaps in much the same locality. The *Recognitions,* in both recensions, as is shown by the fact that it was read in the original with general admiration not only by Rufinus but also by others in the west, was more Catholic in tone.

The recensions of the two works, as we know them, were most probably made in Syria in the second half of the fourth century, and they were used in part at least in this period to serve the interests of Aryan propaganda.

The Clementine literature throws light upon a very obscure phase of Christian development, that of Judaeo-Christianity, and proves that it embraced more intermediate types, between Ebionism proper and Catholicism, than has generally been realized. Incidentally, too, its successive forms illustrate many matters of belief and usage among Syrian Christians generally in the 3rd and 4th centuries, notably their apologetic and catechetical needs and methods. The romance to which it owed much of its popular appeal, became, through the medium of Rufinus' Latin, the parent of the late mediaeval legend of Faust, and so the ancestor of a famous type in modern literature.

But the Clementine literature no longer has the great doctrinal significance once attached to it by the Tübingen school. It still offers us, however, a fullness of instructive entertainment, as E. Schwartz observes, and is certainly more interesting than what many modern scholars have written about it.

BIBLIOGRAPHY.—F. J. A. Hort, *Clementine Recognitions* (1901); Hans Waitz, "Die Pseudoclementinen," *Texte und Untersuchungen zur Gesch. der altchr. Literatur,* new series, vol. x, no. 4; A. Harnack, *Chronologie der altchr. Literatur,* ii, 518 *et seq.* (1904); J. Chapman, "On the Date of the Clementines," *Zeitschrift für neu-testamentliche Wissenschaft,* ix (1908); C. Schmidt, "Studien zu den Pseudo-Clementinen," *Texte und Untersuchungen zur Gesch. der altchr. Literatur,* new series, vol. xlvi, no. 1 (1929); O. Cullman, *Le problème littéraire et historique du roman pseudo-clémentin* (1930); E. Schwartz, "Unzeitgemässe Beobactungen zu den Clementinen," *Zeitschrift für neutestamentliche Wissenschaft,* xxxi (1932). (M. R. P. M.)

CLEMENT OF ALEXANDRIA (*Clemens Alexandrinus*) was probably born about A.D. 150 of heathen parents in Athens. The earliest writer after himself who gives us any information with regard to him is Eusebius (d. 370). The only points on which his works now extant inform us are his date and his instructors. In the *Stromateis* ("Miscellanies"), while attempting to show that the Jewish scriptures were older than any writings of the Greeks, he invariably brings down his dates to the death of Commodus (192), a circumstance which at once suggests that he wrote in the reign of the emperor Severus, from 193 to 211 (see *Strom.* lib. i. cap. xxi. 140). We know nothing of his conversion except that it occurred, for his writings show a singularly minute acquaintance with the ceremonies of pagan religion, and there are indications that he himself had been initiated into some of the mysteries (*Protrept.* cap. ii. sec. 14). He attained the position of presbyter in the church of Alexandria (Eus. *H.E.* vi. 11, and Jerome, *De Vir. Ill.* 38), and became perhaps the assistant, and certainly the successor of Pantaenus in the catechetical school of that place. Among his pupils were Origen (Eus. *H.E.* vi. 7) and Alexander, bishop of Jerusalem (Eus. *H.E.* vi. 14). How long he continued in Alexandria, and when and where he died, are all matters of pure conjecture.

Clement occupies a profoundly interesting position in the history of Christianity. He is the first to bring all the culture of the Greeks and all the speculations of the Christian heretics to bear on the exposition of Christian truth. The list of Greek authors from whom he quoted occupies upwards of 14 of the 4to. pages in Fabricius's *Bibliotheca Graeca.* He is at home alike in the epic and the lyric, the tragic and the comic poets, his knowledge of the prose writers is very extensive, and he made a special study of the philosophers. Equally minute is his knowledge of the systems of the Christian heretics; and it is plain that he not merely read but thought deeply on the questions which the civilization of the Greeks and the various writings of poets, philosophers and heretics raised. It was, however, in the Scriptures, which he held contained the revelation of God's wisdom to men, that he was most deeply read, yet, notwithstanding the great biblical knowledge evidenced by his works, the modern theologian is disappointed to find in them very little of what he deems distinctively Christian. In fact Clement regarded Christianity as a philosophy. The ancient philosophers sought through their philosophy to attain to a nobler and holier life, and this also was the aim of Christianity. The difference between the two, in Clement's judgment, was that the Greek philosophers had only glimpses of the truth, that they attained only to fragments of the truth, while Christianity revealed in Christ the absolute and perfect truth. All the stages of the world's history were therefore preparations leading up to this full revelation, and God's care was not confined to the Hebrews alone. The worship of the heavenly bodies, for instance, was given to man at an early stage that he might rise from a contemplation of these sublime objects to the worship of the Creator. Greek philosophy in particular was the preparation of the Greeks for Christ. It was the schoolmaster or pedagogue to lead them to Christ. Clement varies in his statement how Plato got his wisdom or his fragments of the Reason; sometimes he thinks that they came direct from God, like all good things, but he is also fond of maintaining that many of Plato's best thoughts were borrowed from the Hebrew prophets; and he makes the same statement in regard to the wisdom of the other philosophers. But however this may be, Christ was the end to which all that was true in philosophies pointed. Christ himself was the Logos, the Reason. God the Father was ineffable. The Son alone can manifest Him fully. He is the Reason that pervades the universe, that brings out all goodness, that guides all good men. It was through possessing somewhat of this Reason that the philosophers attained to any truth and goodness; but in Christians he dwells more fully and guides them through all the perplexities of life. Photius, probably on a careless reading of Clement, argued that he could not have believed in a real incarnation. But the words of Clement are quite precise and their meaning indisputable. The real difficulty attaches not to the Second Person, but to the First. The Father in Clement's mind becomes the Absolute of the philosophers, not the Father of the Gospel at all. He believed in a personal Son of God who was the Reason and Wisdom of God; and he believed that this Son of God really became incarnate though he speaks of him almost invariably as the Word, and attaches little value to his human nature. The object of his incarnation and death was to free man from sin, to lead him into the path of wisdom, and thus in the end elevate him to the position of a god. But man's salvation was to be gradual. It began with faith, passed from that to love, and ended in full and complete knowledge. There could be no faith without knowledge; but the knowledge is imperfect, and the Christian has to do many things in simple obedience without knowing the reason. He has to move upwards continually until he at length does nothing that is evil and knows fully the reason and object of what he does. He thus becomes the true Gnostic, but he can become the true Gnostic only by contemplation and by the practice of what is right. He has to free himself from the power of passion; he has to give up all thoughts of pleasure; he must prefer goodness in the midst of torture to evil with unlimited pleasure; he must resist the temptations of the body, keeping it under strict control, and with the eye of the soul undimmed by corporeal wants and impulses, contemplate God the supreme good, and live a life according to reason. In other words, he must strive after likeness to God as he reveals himself in his Reason or in Christ. Clement thus looks entirely at the enlightened moral elevation to which Christianity raises man. He believed that Christ instructed men before he came into the world, and he therefore viewed heathenism with kindly eye. He was also favourable to the pursuit of all kinds of knowledge. All enlightenment tended to lead up to the truths of Christianity, and hence knowledge of every kind not evil was its handmaid. Clement had at the same time a strong belief in evolution or development. The world went through various stages in preparation for Christianity. The man goes through various stages before he can reach Christian perfection. And Clement conceived that this development took place not merely in this life, but in the future through successive grades. The Jew and the heathen had the gospel preached to them in the world below by Christ and His apostles, and Christians will have to pass through processes of purification and trial after death before they reach knowledge and perfect bliss.

Eusebius and Jerome give lists of the works which Clement left behind him. (1) Πρὸς Ἕλληνας λόγος ὁ προτρεπτικός, *A Hortatory Address to the Greeks;* (2) Ὁ Παιδαγωγός; *The Tutor* in three books; (3) Στρωματεῖς ("patchwork"), or *Miscellanies,* in 8 books; (4) Τίς ὁ σωζόμενος πλούσιος, *Who is the rich man that is saved?* (5) Ὑποτυπώσεις, *Adumbrations or Outlines* in 8 books; treatises on (6) *The Passover,* (7) *Fasting,* (8) *Slander,* (9) *Patience,* "for the newly baptised"; and (10) *On the Rule of the Church,* "for those who Judaise." Of these the first four have come down to us complete or nearly so. The *Address to the Greeks* contains an attack on the crudities and immoralities in the stories told of heathen deities, with an argument that the great thinkers and poets of Greece had recognized the unit and spirituality of the divine Being, and that fuller light had been revealed through the Hebrew prophets. In the *Paedogogus,* he explains how before the incarnation Christ was gradually leading mankind to the Truth, and then explains how the Christian following the Logic or Reason ought to behave in the various circumstances of life. The contents of the *Miscellanies*, as the title indicates are very varied. Sometimes they discuss chronology, sometimes philosophy, sometimes poetry; but one object runs through all, to show what the true Christian Gnostic is, and what is his relation to philosophy. The tract *Who is the rich man that is saved?* is an admirable exposition of Mark x. 17–31. Clement argues that wealth, if rightly used, is not unchristian. Of the remaining books mentioned by Eusebius, we know that the *Adumbrations* was a short commentary on all the books of Scripture, including some apocryphal books; and we have two fragments of the book on the *Passover*. Of the others nothing is known. We have also fragments of two treatises, on *Providence* and on the *Soul*, not named by Eusebius.

BIBLIOGRAPHY.—C. Bigg, *Christian Platonists of Alexandria* (1886, 1913); F. J. A. Hort, *Six Lectures on the Ante-Nicene Fathers* (1895); E. de Faye, *Clement d'Alexandrie* (1898); J. Patrick, *Clement of Alexandria* (1914). W. R. Inge, "Alexandrian Theology," in J. Hastings, *Encyclopaedia of Religion and Ethics* (1908), gives an excellent summary account of the Alexandrine School. The standard edition of the collected works is O. Stählin, *Clemens Alexandrinus* (Leipzig, 1905). We have a valuable separate edition of *Miscellanies*, bk. vii., ed. F. J. A. Hort and J. B. Mayor (1902), and of the tract on Wealth by P. M. Barnard, *Texts and Studies*, vol. 2 (Cambridge, 1897). *See* also B. F. Westcott, "Clement of Alexandria" *Murray's Dictionary of Christian Biography* (1911).

CLEMENTS, FREDERIC EDWARD (1874–1945), American plant oecologist, was born in Lincoln, Neb., Sept. 16, 1874. He graduated in 1894 at the University of Nebraska from which in 1898 he received the degree of doctor of philosophy. From 1894 to 1906 he was instructor and associate professor of botany and in 1906–07 he was professor of plant physiology, at the University of Nebraska. He was professor of botany and head of the botanical department in the University of Minnesota from 1907 to 1917 when he was made associate in charge of oecological research in the Carnegie Institution of Washington. He conducted extensive investigations in oecology, palaeo-oecology, experimental evolution and climatology. Among his published works are: *The Phytogeography of Nebraska*, with Roscoe Pound (1898, 2nd ed., 1900); *Development and Structure of Vegetation* (1904); *Research Methods in Ecology* (1906); *Plant Physiology and Ecology* (1907); *Minnesota Mushrooms* (1910); *Rocky Mountain Flowers*, with Edith Clements (1913), *Plant Succession* (1916); *Plant Indicators* (1920); *The Phylogenetic Method in Taxonomy*, with H. M. Hall (1923); *Plant Succession and Indicators* (1927); and *Flower Families and Ancestors* (1927).

CLEOBULUS, one of the Seven Sages of Greece, a native and tyrant of Lindus in Rhodes. He was distinguished for his strength and his handsome person, for the wisdom of his sayings, the acuteness of his riddles, and the beauty of his lyric poetry. Diogenes Laërtius quotes a letter in which Cleobulus invites Solon to take refuge with him against Peisistratus; and this would imply that he was alive in 560 B.C. He is said to have held advanced views as to female education, and he was the father of the wise Cleobuline, whose riddles were not less famous than his own (Diogenes Laërtius, i. 89–93).

See F. G. Mullach, *Fragmenta Philosophorum Graecorum*, i.

CLEOMENES, the name of three Spartan kings of the Agiad line (Κλεομένης).

CLEOMENES I. was the son of Anaxandridas, whom he succeeded about 520 B.C. His chief exploit was his crushing victory near Tiryns over the Argives, some 6,000 of whom he burned to death in a sacred grove to which they had fled for refuge (Herodotus vi. 76–82). This secured for Sparta the undisputed hegemony of the Peloponnese. Cleomenes' interposition in the politics of central Greece was less successful. In 510 he marched to Athens with a Spartan force to aid in expelling the peisistratidae, and subsequently returned to support the oligarchical party, led by Isagoras, against Cleisthenes (*q.v.*). He expelled 700 families and transferred the government from the council to 300 of the oligarchs, but being blockaded in the Acropolis was forced to capitulate. On his return home he collected a large force, with the intention of making Isagoras despot of Athens, but the opposition of the Corinthian allies, and of his colleague, Demaratus, caused the expedition to break up after reaching Eleusis (Herod. v. 64–76; Aristotle, *Ath. Pol.* 19, 20). In 491 he went to Aegina to punish the island for its submission to Darius, but the intrigues of his colleague once again rendered his mission abortive. In revenge Cleomenes accused Demaratus of illegitimacy and secured his deposition in favour of Leotychides (Herod. vi. 50–73). But when it was discovered that he had bribed the Delphian priestess to substantiate his charge he was himself obliged to flee; he went first to Thessaly and then to Arcadia, where he attempted to foment an anti-Spartan rising. About 488 B.C. he was recalled, but shortly afterwards, in a fit of madness, he committed suicide (Herod. vi. 74, 75). Cleomenes seems to have received scant justice at the hands of Herodotus or his informants, and Pausanias (iii. 3, 4) does little more than condense Herodotus' narrative. In spite of some failures, largely due to Demaratus' jealousy, Cleomenes strengthened Sparta in the position, won during his father's reign, of champion and leader of the Hellenic race; it was to him, for example, that the Ionian cities of Asia Minor first applied for aid in their revolt against Persia (Herod. v. 49–51).

The chief ancient authority is Herodotus (v. and vi.). *See* E. M. Walker, *Cambridge Ancient History*, vol. iv., ch. vi., § 1, 4, 5, and ch. viii., § 8). For chronology *see* J. Wells, *Journal of Hellenic Studies* (1905), p. 193 ff., who assigns the Argive expedition to the outset of the reign, whereas nearly all historians have dated it in or about 495 B.C.

CLEOMENES II. was the son of Cleombrotus I., brother and successor of Agesipolis II. Nothing is recorded of his reign save the fact that it lasted for nearly 61 years (370–309 B.C.).

CLEOMENES III., the son and successor of Leonidas II., reigned about 235–219 B.C. He made a determined attempt to reform the social condition of Sparta along the lines laid down by Agis IV., whose widow, Agiatis, he married; at the same time he aimed at restoring Sparta's hegemony in the Peloponnese. After twice defeating the forces of the Achaean league in Arcadia, near Mount Lycaeum and at Leuctra, he strengthened his position by assassinating four of the ephors, abolishing the ephorate, which had usurped the supreme power, and banishing some 80 of the leading oligarchs. The authority of the council was also curtailed, and a new board of magistrates, the *patronomi*, became the chief officers of state. He appointed his own brother, Eucleidas, as his colleague in succession to the Eurypontid Archidamus, who had been murdered. His social reforms included a redistribution of land, the remission of debts, the restoration of the old system of training ἀγωγή and the admission of picked *perioeci* (*q.v.*) into the citizen body. As a general Cleomenes did much to revive Sparta's old prestige. He defeated the Achaeans at Dyme, made himself master of Argos, and was eventually joined by Corinth, Phlius, Epidaurus and other cities. But Aratus, whose jealousy could not brook to see a Spartan at the head of the Achaean league, called in Antigonus Doson, of Macedonia, and Cleomenes, after conducting successful expeditions to Megalopolis and Argos, was finally defeated at Sellasia, to the north of Sparta, in 222 or 221 B.C. He took refuge at Alexandria with Ptolemy Euergetes, but was arrested by his successor, Ptolemy Philopator, on a charge of conspiracy. Escaping from prison he tried to raise a revolt, but the attempt failed, and to avoid capture he put an end to his life. Both as general and as politician Cleomenes was one of Sparta's greatest men, and with him perished her last hope of recovering her ancient supremacy in Greece.

See Polybius ii. 45–70, v. 35–39, viii. 1; Plutarch, *Cleomenes; Aratus*, 35–46; *Philopoemen*, 5, 6; Pausanias ii. 9; Holm, *History of Greece*, iv. cc. 10, 15. (M. N. T.)

CLEON (d. 422 B.C.), Athenian politician during the Peloponnesian War, was the son of Cleaenetus, from whom he inherited a tannery. He was the first prominent representative of the commercial class in Athenian politics. He came into notice first as an opponent of Pericles, and in his opposition somewhat curiously found himself acting in concert with the aristocrats, who equally hated and feared Pericles. In 430, when the city was devastated by the plague, Cleon headed the opposition to the Periclean régime. Pericles was accused of maladministration of public money, with the result that he was actually found guilty though he was re-elected in 429. The death of Pericles (429) left the field clear for Cleon. Hitherto he had only been a vigorous opposition speaker, a critic and accuser of state officials. He now came forward as the champion and leader of the democracy, and, was for some years undoubtedly the foremost man in Athens. He was gifted with natural eloquence and a powerful voice, and knew how to work upon the feelings of the people. He became the leader of the war party in opposition to Nicias and the moderates, who favoured a cautious strategy and an early peace.

In 427 when Mytilene, which had revolted, fell, Cleon proposed that all its citizens should be put to death, and the women and children enslaved. His policy was to hold down the empire, now a "tyranny," by naked force. His decree was passed, but rescinded next day, in time to save Mytilene.

In 425 he, when the Spartans were blockaded in Sphacteria, brought about the rejection of the terms offered by Sparta, and in the hope of securing a peace which should restore Athens' land-empire. He then reached the summit of his fame by capturing the Spartans on the island (*see* PYLOS). Much of the credit of this success, the most notable which the Athenians won during the Archidamian War, was due to the military skill of his colleague Demosthenes; but it was due to Cleon's determination that the Ecclesia sent out the additional force which was needed. About this time Cleon doubled the tribute of the allies (*see* DELIAN LEAGUE) and raised the pay of the Athenian jurors from two to three obols (Schol. Ar. *Wasps* 88). In 422, after the close of the armistice, Cleon, who was eager to continue the war, went to recover Thrace from Brasidas, but, after capturing several cities, was taken by surprise at Amphipolis, defeated and killed. With his death, the peace party at Athens gained power, and the Peace of Nicias was concluded. (*See* PELOPONNESIAN WAR).

Cleon is represented by Aristophanes and Thucydides in an extremely unfavourable light. But neither can be considered an unprejudiced witness. Aristophanes was not only opposed to Cleon's political programme, but bore him a personal grudge, having been prosecuted by the demagogue after the production of his *Babylonians.* Moreover, his treatment of Socrates should put us on our guard against accepting his evidence against Cleon. Thucydides had been exiled by a decree proposed by Cleon after the loss of Amphipolis.

BIBLIOGRAPHY.—For the literature on Cleon *see* C. F. Hermann, *Lehrbuch der griechischen Antiquitäten,* i. pt. 2 (6th ed. by V. Thumser, 1892), p. 709, and G. Busolt, *Griechische Geschichte,* iii. pt. 2 (1904), p. 988, note 3. Authorities:—(*a*) *Favourable to Cleon:* G. Grote, *Hist. of Greece,* c. 50, 54; J. B. Bury, *Hist. of Greece* i. (1902). (*b*) *Unfavourable:* C. Thirlwall, *Hist. of Greece,* c. 21; E. Curtius, *Hist. of Greece* (Eng. tr. iii. p. 112); H. Delbrück, *Die Strategie des Perikles* (1890); E. Meyer, *Forschungen zur alten Geschichte,* ii. p. 333 (Halle, 1899). The balance between the two extreme views is fairly held by J. Beloch, *Die attische Politik seit Perikles* (Leipzig, 1884), and *Griechische Geschichte,* i. p. 537; and by A. Holm, *Hist. of Greece,* ii. (Eng. tr.), c. 23, with the notes. *See* also A. B. West and D. B. Meritt, "Cleon's Amphipolitan Campaign" (*American Journal of Archaeology* xxix. 1925).

CLEOPATRA, the regular name of the queens of Egypt, in the Ptolemaic dynasty after Cleopatra, daughter of the Seleucid Antiochus the Great, wife of Ptolemy V., Epiphanes. The best-known was the daughter of Ptolemy XI, Auletes, born 69 (or 68) B.C. At the age of 17 she became queen of Egypt jointly with her younger brother Ptolemy Dionysus, whose wife, in accordance with Egyptian custom, she was to become. A few years later, deprived of all royal authority, she withdrew into Syria, and prepared to recover her rights by force of arms. At this juncture Julius Caesar followed Pompey into Egypt. The personal fascinations of Cleopatra induced him to undertake a war on her behalf, in which Ptolemy lost his life, and she was replaced on the throne with a younger brother, of whom, however, she soon rid herself by poison. In Rome she lived openly with Caesar as his mistress, until his assassination, when, aware of her unpopularity, she returned to Egypt. Subsequently she became the ally and mistress of Mark Antony (*see* ANTONIUS). Their connection was highly unpopular at Rome, and Octavian (*see* AUGUSTUS) declared war upon them and defeated them at Actium (31 B.C.). Cleopatra escaped to Alexandria, where Antony joined her. Having no prospect of ultimate success, she accepted Octavian's proposal that she should assassinate Antony, and enticed him to join her in a mausoleum which she had built in order that "they might die together." Antony committed suicide, in the mistaken belief that she had already done so. Octavian refused to yield to the charms of Cleopatra, who put an end to her life by applying an asp to her bosom, according to the common tradition, on Aug. 29, 30 B.C. With her ended the dynasty of the Ptolemies, and Egypt was made a Roman province. Cleopatra had three children by Antony, and by Julius Caesar, it is said, a son, Caesarion, who was put to death by Octavian.

For the history of Cleopatra *see* ANTONIUS; CAESAR, GAIUS JULIUS; PTOLEMIES. The life of Antony by Plutarch is our main authority; it is upon this that Shakespeare's *Antony and Cleopatra* is based. Her life is the subject of monographs by Stahr (1879, an *apologia*), and H. Houssaye, *Aspasie, Cléopâtre,* etc. (1879).

CLEOPATRA'S NEEDLES, the name popularly given to the two Egyptian obelisks presented to the British and American people respectively, and now standing on the Thames Embankment in London and in the Central Park of New York city. Originally set up by Thotmes or Tethmosis III. at Heliopolis about 1500 B.C., they were removed by Caesar Augustus to adorn the Caesareum at Alexandria about 14 B.C. and there remained until removed (in each case by private munificence) to their present positions in 1878 and 1880. Both are of rose-red Syene granite, covered with hieroglyphical inscriptions, and are estimated to weigh some 200 tons. (*See* OBELISK.)

CLEPSYDRA, the chronometer of the Greeks and Romans, which measured time by the flow of water (Gr. κλέπτειν, to steal, and ὕδωρ, water). In its simplest form it was an earthenware globe of known capacity, pierced at the bottom with several small holes, through which the water escaped. It was employed to set a limit to speeches in courts of justice, hence the phrases *aquam dare* (Pliny, *Ep.* 6. 2. 7), to give the advocate speaking time, and *aquam perdere* (Quint. 11. 3. 52), to waste time.

The clepsydra is said to have been known to the Egyptians. There was one in the Tower of the Winds at Athens; the turret on the south side of the tower is supposed to have contained the cistern which supplied the water. *See* classical dictionaries, *s.v.*

BY COURTESY OF SHARPE, "SEVEN PERIODS OF ENGLISH ARCHITECTURE" (SPON); D'ESPOUY, "MONUMENTS ANTIQUES" (MASSIN ET CIE); SIR BANISTER FLETCHER, "HISTORY OF ARCHITECTURE ON THE COMPARATIVE METHOD," EIGHTH ED. (1928) BATSFORD; ARCHITECTURAL BOOK PUB. CO.

EXAMPLES OF CLERESTORIES (SEE ARTICLE, CLERESTOREY ON NEXT PAGE)
A, B, exterior and interior, Peterborough cathedral, Romanesque clerestorey window at the top; C, Roman clerestorey, tepidarium, Baths of Titus; D, modern adaptation of Roman type, the Pennsylvania Station, New York; E, Egyptian clerestorey lighting, hypostyle hall, Karnak; F, G, exterior and interior, Winchester cathedral, showing larger Gothic clerestorey

CLERESTORY, CLERESTOREY or **CLEARSTORY,** in architecture, any wall of a room carried higher than the surrounding roofs so that windows can be pierced in it to light the room. In a large building, where interior walls are far from the outside of the building, some such method of lighting the central part becomes necessary, and the use of the clerestorey appears as early, at least, as the 18th dynasty in Egypt, under which the great hypostyle hall of the temple at Karnak was built. This had a central range of columns, higher than those on either side, to allow clerestoreys to be built of pierced stone slabs. In Roman architecture, many great halls were thus lighted, usually groined vaults over the central hall allowed of large semicircular windows being built above the side roofs; *e.g.,* S. Maria degli Angeli, at Rome (the tepidarium of the Baths of Diocletian) and the basilica of Constantine, at Rome. Similarly, the walls under the side arches of S. Sophia at Constantinople, are clerestorey walls. It was, however, in the Romanesque and Gothic churches of the middle ages, that the clerestorey idea received its most adequate expression. *See* p. 801 for illustrations of Clerestories. (*See* BYZANTINE AND ROMANESQUE ARCHITECTURE; GOTHIC ARCHITECTURE.)

CLERFAYT or **CLAIRFAYT, FRANÇOIS SEBASTIEN CHARLES JOSEPH DE CROIX,** COUNT OF (1733–1798), Austrian field marshal, entered the Austrian army in 1753. In the Seven Years' War he greatly distinguished himself, and in 1787 took part in the Turkish war. In 1792 he received the command of the Austrian contingent in the duke of Brunswick's army, and at Croix-sous-Bois his corps inflicted a reverse on the French. In the Netherlands he opened the campaign of 1793 with the victory of Aldenhoven and the relief of Maestricht, and on March 18 brought about the complete defeat of Dumouriez at Neerwinden. His victorious career was checked by the reverse at Wattignies, and in 1794 he was unsuccessful in West Flanders against Pichegru. Clerfayt succeeded the duke of Saxe-Coburg in the supreme command, but was quite unable to make head against the French, and had to recross the Rhine. In 1795, now field marshal, he commanded on the middle Rhine against Jourdan, whom he defeated at Höchst and Mainz. His action in concluding an armistice with the French not being approved by Thugut, he resigned the command, and became a member of the Aulic Council in Vienna. He died in 1798.

See von Vivenot, *Thugut, Clerfayt, und Würmser* (Vienna, 1869).

CLERGY, a collective term signifying strictly the body of "clerks," *i.e.,* men in holy orders (*see* CLERK); but extended in modern times so as to embrace all varieties of ordained Christian ministers, though in England the word "clergyman" is still mainly restricted to the clergy of the Established Church. In the Roman Catholic Church the word, which is the O.Fr. *clergie,* from Low Lat. *clericatus,* embraces the whole hierarchy of *clerici,* whether in holy or merely minor orders; it has also been loosely used to include the members of religious orders. The M.E. senses of "clerkship" and "learning" have long been obsolete.

In distinction to the "clergy" we find the "laity" (Gr. λαός, people), the great body of "faithful people" which, in nearly every conception of the Christian Church, stands in relation to the clergy as a flock of sheep to its pastor. This distinction was of early growth, and developed during the middle ages into lively opposition (*see* MONASTICISM; CHURCH HISTORY; PAPACY; INVESTITURE). The extreme claim of the great mediaeval popes, that the priest, as "ruler over spiritual things," was as much superior to temporal rulers as the soul is to the body (*see* INNOCENT III.) led logically to the vast privileges and immunities enjoyed by the clergy, which consisted mainly in exemption from public burdens, both as regarded person and pocket, and in immunity from lay jurisdiction. This last privilege extended to matters both civil and criminal; though, as Bingham shows, it did not (always and everywhere) prevail in cases of heinous crime (*Origines Eccles.* bk. v.).

This subjection of the clergy only to courts disposed by *esprit de corps* to judge leniently led to the penalties for criminous clerks being much lighter than those to which laymen were amenable; and this in turn led to the survival in England, long after the Reformation, of the legal fiction of benefit of clergy, used to mitigate the harshness of the criminal law.

CLERGY, BENEFIT OF, an obsolete but once very important feature in English criminal law. Benefit of clergy began with the claim on the part of the ecclesiastical authorities in the 12th century that every *clericus* should be exempt from the jurisdiction of the temporal courts and be subject to the spiritual courts alone. The issue of the conflict was that the common law courts abandoned the extreme punishment of death assigned to some offences when the person convicted was a *clericus,* and the church was obliged to accept the compromise and let a secondary punishment be inflicted. The term "clerk" or *clericus* always included a large number of persons in what were called minor orders, and in 1350 the privilege was extended to secular as well as to religious clerks; and, finally, the test of being a clerk was the ability to read the opening words of verse 1 of Psalm li., hence generally known as the "neck-verse." Even this requirement was abolished in 1705. In 1487 it was enacted that every layman, when convicted of a clergyable felony, should be branded on the thumb, and disabled from claiming the benefit a second time. The privilege was extended to peers, even if they could not read, in 1547, and to women, partially in 1622 and fully in 1692. The partial exemption claimed by the Church did not apply to the more atrocious crimes, and hence offences came to be divided into clergyable and unclergyable. According to the common practice in England of working out modern improvements, through antiquated forms, this exemption was made the means of modifying the severity of the criminal law. It became the practice to claim and be allowed the benefit of clergy; and when it was the intention by statute to make a crime really punishable with death, it was awarded "without benefit of clergy." The benefit of clergy was abolished by a statute of 1827, but as this statute did not repeal that of 1547, under which peers were given the privilege, a further statute was passed in 1841 putting peers on the same footing as commons and clergy.

For a full account of benefit of clergy *see* Pollock and Maitland, *History of English Law;* Stephen, *History of the Criminal Law of England;* E. Friedberg, *Corpus juris canonici* (*Leipzig,* 1879–81).

CLERGYMAN, an ordained minister of the Christian Church. In England the term is usually confined to the ministers of the established Church. Educational qualifications for this work vary with the different denominations, but the majority require at least two or three years of religious specialization beyond a four year college course, with a growing tendency towards higher standards in general to meet the challenges of modern thought and inquiry. Good health, intellectual ability, moral integrity, a desire to serve, breadth of knowledge and understanding, spiritual conviction, love of humanity and poise are some of the personal attributes necessary inasmuch as the clergyman serves variously as preacher, leader of worship, teacher, educator, pastor, social worker and executive.

CLERGY RESERVES, in Canada. By the act of 1791, establishing the provinces of Upper and Lower Canada, the British Government set apart one-eighth of all the crown lands for the support of "a Protestant clergy." These reservations, after being for many years a stumbling-block to the economic development of the province, and the cause of much bitter political and ecclesiastical controversy, were secularized by the Canadian parliament in 1854, and the proceeds applied to other purposes, chiefly educational. Owing to the wording of the imperial act, the amount set apart is often stated as one-seventh, and was sometimes claimed as such by the clergy.

CLERK, SIR DUGALD (1854–1932), Scottish civil engineer, was born at Glasgow on March 31, 1854. He was educated at the West of Scotland Technical college and the Andersonian college. He invented the Clerk cycle gas engine in 1877, improving it in 1878 (*see* INTERNAL COMBUSTION ENGINES), and became an authority on internal combustion engines. He also interested himself in motor engineering. During World War I he became director of engineering research to the Admiralty, and until 1919 was a member of the advisory committee for aeronautics to the Air Ministry, and also of the air inventions committee. In 1908 he was elected F.R.S., and in 1917 knighted. His works include *The Gas and Oil Engine* and many scientific papers.

CLERK, in its original sense, as used in the civil law, one who had taken religious orders of whatever rank, whether "holy" or "minor." In English ecclesiastical law, a clerk was any one who had been admitted to the ecclesiastical state, and had taken the tonsure. The application of the word in this sense gradually underwent a change, and "clerk" became more especially the term applied to those in minor orders, while those in "major" or "holy" orders were designated in full "clerks in holy orders." After the Reformation the word "clerk" was still further extended to include laymen who performed duties in cathedrals, churches, etc., *e.g.,* the choirmen, who were designated "lay clerks." Of these lay clerks or choirmen there was always one whose duty it was to be constantly present at every service, to sing or say the responses as the leader or representative of the laity. His duties were gradually enlarged to include the care of the church and precincts, assisting at baptisms, marriages, etc., and he thus became the precursor of the later *parish clerk.* In a somewhat similar sense we find *bible clerk, singing clerk,* etc. The use of the word "clerk" to denote a person ordained to the ministry is now mainly legal.

From the fact that in mediaeval times learning was chiefly the province of the clergy, they were engaged in nearly all occupations requiring knowledge of writing combined with some education and hence the word "clerk" came to its present indefinite signification of a writer in the employment of some one else. Older and more specific use of the word is to be traced in *clerk of the market, clerk of the petty bag, clerk of the peace, town clerk,* etc.

CLERKE, AGNES MARY (1842–1907), English astronomer and scientific writer, was born on Feb. 10, 1842, and died in London on Jan. 20, 1907. Her chief works were *A Popular History of Astronomy during the 19th Century* (1885, 4th ed. 1902); *The System of the Stars* (1890, 2nd. ed. 1905); and *Problems in Astrophysics* (1903). In 1903 she was elected an honorary member of the Royal Astronomical Society.

CLERKENWELL (klar'kĕn-wĕl), a district on the north side of the City of London, England, within the metropolitan borough of Finsbury (*q.v.*). It is so called from one of several wells or springs in this district, near which miracle plays were performed by the parish clerks of London. This well existed until the middle of the 19th century. Here was situated a priory, founded in 1100, which grew to great wealth and fame as the principal institution in England of the Knights Hospitallers of the Order of St. John of Jerusalem. Its gateway (1504), in St. John's Square, survived the suppression of the monasteries, and was the scene of Dr. Johnson's work in connection with the *Gentleman's Magazine.* In modern times the gatehouse again became associated with the Order, and is the headquarters of the St. John's Ambulance Association. An early English crypt remains beneath the neighbouring parish church of St. John, where the notorious deception of the "Cock Lane Ghost," in which Johnson took great interest, was exposed. Adjoining the priory was St. Mary's Benedictine nunnery, St. James's church (1792) marking the site. In the 17th century Clerkenwell became a fashionable place of residence. It has small watch-making and jeweller's industries, which have been long established here.

CLERMONT, a town of northern France, in the department of Oise, on the right bank of the Brèche, 41 mi. N. of Paris on the Northern railway to Amiens. The town was probably founded during the time of the Norman invasions and was a military post during the middle ages. It was several times taken and retaken during the Hundred Years' War, and the Wars of Religion. Population (1936) 5,943. The hill on which the town is built is surmounted by a keep of the 14th century, a relic of the once-famous fortress. The church dates from the 14th to the 16th centuries. The *hôtel-de-ville,* built by King Charles IV., who was born at Clermont in 1298, is the oldest in the north of France. The Promenade du Châtellier occupies the site of the old ramparts.

Clermont was at one time the seat of a countship, the lords of which were already powerful in the 11th century. Raoul de Clermont, constable of France, died at Acre in 1191, leaving a daughter who brought Clermont to her husband, Louis, count of Blois and Chartres. Theobald, count of Blois and Clermont, died in 1218 without issue, and King Philip Augustus, having received the countship of Clermont from the collateral heirs of this lord, gave it to his son Philip Hurepel, whose daughter Jeanne, and his widow, Mahaut, countess of Dammartin, next held the countship. It was united by St. Louis to the crown, and afterwards given by him (1269) to his son Robert, from whom sprang the house of Bourbon. In 1524 the countship of Clermont was confiscated from the constable de Bourbon, and later (1540) given to the duke of Orléans, to Catherine de' Medici (1562), to Eric, duke of Brunswick (1569), from whom it passed to his brother-in-law Charles of Lorraine (1596), and finally to Henry II., prince of Condé (1611). In 1641 it was again confiscated from Louis de Bourbon, count of Soissons, then in 1696 sold to Louis Thomas Amadeus of Savoy, count of Soissons, in 1702 to Françoise de Brancas, princesse d'Harcourt, and in 1719 to Louis-Henry, prince of Condé. From a branch of the old lords of Clermont were descended the lords of Nesle and Chantilly.

CLERMONT-FERRAND, a city of central France, capital of the department of Puy-de-Dôme, 113 m. W. of Lyons, on the P.L.M. railway. Pop. (1906) 44,113; (1936) 95,237. Clermont-Ferrand is situated on high ground on the western border of the fertile plain of Limagne. On the north, west and south it is surrounded by hills, with a background of mountains amongst which the Puy-de-Dôme stands out prominently. A small river, the Tiretaine, borders the town on the north. Since 1731 it has been composed of the two towns of Clermont and Montferrand.

Gergovia was the native centre in Auvergne but the Roman settlement known as Augustonemetum on the site of Clermont became so important as to be called later "The city of the Arverni." The present name is derived from Clarus Mons originally applied only to the citadel, but used for the town as early as the 9th century. During the disintegration of the Roman empire Clermont suffered from capture and pillage. Its history during the middle ages chiefly records the struggles between its bishops and the counts of Auvergne, and between the citizens and their overlord the bishop. It was the seat of seven ecclesiastical councils, held in the years 535, 549, 587, 1095, 1110, 1124 and 1130. In the council of 1095 Pope Urban II. proclaimed the first crusade. It figured in the wars against the English in the 14th and 15th centuries and in the religious wars of the 16th century. *Les Grands Jours de Clermont* (1665) was associated with the trial and execution of a member of the nobility who had tyrannized the district. Before the Revolution the town possessed the abbey of Saint Allyre, founded, it is said, in the 3rd century by St. Austremonius (St. Stremoine), the apostle of Auvergne and first bishop of Clermont, and the abbey of St. André, where the counts of Clermont were buried. The cathedral, a Gothic edifice, was begun in the 13th century. The stained glass dates from the 13th century. The church of Notre-Dame-du-Port is a typical example of the Romanesque style of Auvergne, dating chiefly from the 11th and 12th centuries. The exterior of the apse with its four radiating chapels, and its black and white decoration is the most interesting part. Among the old houses one, dating from the 16th century, was the birthplace of Blaise Pascal. Montferrand has several interesting houses of the 15th and 16th centuries, and a church of the 13th, 14th and 15th centuries. Clermont has several fine squares like the one erected by Bishop Jacques d'Amboise in 1515.

Clermont-Ferrand is the seat of a bishopric and a prefecture; it has tribunals of first instance and of commerce, a board of trade-arbitrators, and a chamber of commerce. It is a university town and has an important library, as well as the *Musée Lecoq* (natural history and geology) and the *Musée d'Art et d'Archéologie.* The town manufactures semolina and other farinaceous foods, confectionery, preserved fruit and jams, chemicals and heavy rubber goods, especially motor tires. Clothing is also important. Clermont is the chief market for the grain and other agricultural produce of Auvergne and Velay. Its waters are in local repute. On the bank of the Tiretaine there is a remarkable calcareous spring, the fountain of St. Allyre. About 1½ miles to the west lies the famous spa of Royat.

CLERMONT-GANNEAU, CHARLES SIMON (1846–1923); French Orientalist, the son of a sculptor of some repute, was born in Paris, Feb. 19, 1846, and died Feb. 15, 1923. He laid the foundation of his reputation by his discovery (in 1870) of the "stele" of Mesha (Moabite Stone), which bears the oldest Semitic inscription known. In 1874 he was employed by the British Government to take charge of an archaeological expedition to Palestine, and was subsequently entrusted by his own government with similar missions to Syria and the Red sea. After serving as vice-consul at Jaffa from 1880 to 1882, he returned to Paris as "secrétaire-interprète" for oriental languages, and in 1886 was appointed consul of the first class. He subsequently accepted the post of director of the École des Langues Orientales and professor at the Collège de France. In 1889 he was elected a member of the Académie des Inscriptions et Belles Lettres, of which he had been a correspondent since 1880. In 1896 he was promoted to be consul-general, and was minister plenipotentiary in 1906. He was the first in England to expose the famous forgeries of Hebrew texts offered to the British Museum by M. W. Shapira in 1883, and in 1903 he took a prominent part in the investigation of the so-called "tiara of Saïtapharnes." This tiara had been purchased by the Louvre for 400,000 francs, and exhibited as a genuine antique, but was agreed to be of modern manufacture.

His chief publications, besides a number of contributions to journals, are:—*Palestine inconnue* (1886), *Études d'archéologie orientale* (1880, etc.), *Les Fraudes archéologiques* (1885), *Recueil d'archéologie orientale* (1885–1924), *Album d'antiquités orientales* (1897, etc.).

CLERMONT-L'HÉRAULT, a town of southern France in the department of Hérault, 10 mi. S.S.E. of Lodève. Pop. (1936) 5,098. The town is built on a hill crowned by an ancient castle and skirted by the Rhonel, a tributary of the Lergue. The church dates from the 13th and 14th centuries. Its woollen industry dates from the latter half of the 17th century. Tanning and leather-dressing are also carried on, and there is trade in wine. Among the public institutions are a tribunal of commerce, a chamber of arts and manufactures and a board of trade-arbitration. The town was several times taken and retaken in the religious wars of the 16th century.

CLERMONT-TONNERRE, STANISLAS MARIE ADELAIDE, Comte de (1757–1792), French politician, was born at Pont-à-Mousson on Oct. 10, 1757. Sent to the states-general in 1789 by the noblesse of Paris, he joined the Third Estate, and was elected president of the Constituent Assembly on Aug. 17, 1789. On the rejection by the Assembly of the scheme elaborated by the first constitutional committee, he attached himself to the party of moderate royalists, known as *monarchiens,* led by P. V. Malouet. His speech in favour of reserving to the crown the right of absolute veto under the new constitution drew down upon him the wrath of the advanced politicians of the Palais Royal; but he continued to advocate a moderate liberal policy, especially in the matter of removing the political disabilities of Jews and Protestants and of extending the system of trial by jury. In Jan. 1790 he collaborated with Malouet in founding the Club des Impartiaux and the *Journal des Impartiaux,* the names of which were changed in November to the Société des Amis de la Constitution Monarchique and *Journal de la Société,* etc., in order to emphasize their opposition to the Jacobins (Société des Amis de la Constitution). This club was denounced by Barnave in the Assembly (Jan. 21, 1791), and on March 28 it was attacked by a mob, whereupon it was closed by order of the Assembly. Clermont-Tonnerre was murdered by the populace during the rising of Aug. 9–10, 1792.

See *Recueil des opinions de Stanislas de Clermont-Tonnerre* (1791), the text of his speeches as published by himself; A. Aulard, *Les Orateurs de la Constituante* (1905).

CLERUCHY, a kind of colony of Athenian citizens planted in a conquered country. The settlers retained their status as citizens of Athens, and their allotments were politically part of Attic soil. These settlements were of three kinds: (1) where the inhabitants were extirpated and the settlers occupied the whole territory; (2) where the settlers occupied allotments in the midst of a conquered people; and (3) where the inhabitants gave up portions of land to settlers in return for certain pecuniary concessions. The primary object was unquestionably military, and in the later days of the Delian League (*q.v.*) the system was a precaution against disaffection on the part of the allies.

A secondary object of the cleruchies was to provide a source of livelihood to the poorer Athenians. Plutarch suggests that Pericles by this means rid the city of mischievous loafers; but it would appear that the cleruchs were selected by lot, and a wise policy would not entrust important military duties to wastrels. In 50 years about 10,000 cleruchs went out, so that the reduction of the citizen population was considerable.

The cleruchs were liable to military service and to that taxation which fell upon Athenians at home. They were not liable for the tribute paid by members of the Delian League; this follows from their status as Athenian citizens. In internal government the cleruchs adopted the Boulē and Assembly system of Athens itself; so we read of Polemarchs, Archons *eponumoi, Agoranomoi, Strategoi,* in various places. With local self-government there was combined a certain central authority in jurisdiction; the more important cases, particularly those between a cleruch and a citizen at home, were tried before the Athenian dicasts.

Bibliography.—*See* G. Gilbert, *Constitutional Antiquities of Athens and Sparta* (Eng. trans., 1895); A. H. J. Greenidge, *Handbook of Greek Constitutional Antiquities* (1896); L. Whibley, *Companion to Greek Studies* (1916); for the Periclean cleruchs, *see* Pericles; Delian League.

CLERVAUX (*clara vallis*), a town in the northern province of Oesling, grand-duchy of Luxembourg, on the Clerf, a tributary of the Sure. Pop. (1935) 1,671. The old castle of the Lannoy family still exists. In 1798 the people of Clervaux specially distinguished themselves against the French establishment of conscription.

The survivors of this Kloppel-krieg ("cudgel war") were shot, and a fine monument commemorates them.

CLETUS, or **ANENCLETUS,** the third pope, who occupied the papal chair *c.* 79–91. According to Epiphanius and Rufinus, he directed the Roman Church with Linus, successor to St. Peter, during Peter's lifetime.

CLEVE (Clèves), a town of Germany in the Prussian Rhine province, formerly the capital of the duchy of its own name, 46 m. N.W. of Düsseldorf, 12 mi. E. of Nijmwegen, on the main Cologne-Amsterdam railway. Population 20,296.

The town was the seat of the counts of Cleve as early as the 11th century, but it did not receive municipal rights until 1242. The duchy of Cleve, which lay on both banks of the Rhine passed in 1368 to the counts of La Marck and was made a duchy in 1417, being united with the neighbouring duchies of Jülich and Berg in 1521. By the treaty of Xanten in 1614, Cleve passed to the elector of Brandenburg, being afterwards incorporated with the electorate by the elector, Frederick William. The part of the duchy on the left bank of the Rhine was ceded to France in 1795; the remaining portion in 1805. In 1815 it was restored to Prussia, except some small portions which were given to the kingdom of Holland. The town is built in the Dutch style, lying on three small hills in a fertile district near the frontier of Holland, about 2 m. from the Rhine, with which it is connected by a canal (the Spoykanal). The old castle of Schwanenburg is associated with the legend of the "Knights of the Swan," immortalized in Wagner's *Lohengrin.* The building has been restored in modern times to serve as a court of justice and a prison. The collegiate church (Stiftskirche) dates from about 1340. The Annexkirche, formerly a convent of the Minorites, dates from the middle of the 15th century. The chief manufactures are boots and shoes, tobacco and machinery; there is also some trade in cattle and in wine. There are mineral wells. It is a favourite summer resort.

CLEVEDON, watering place and urban district, Somersetshire, England, on the Bristol Channel, $15\frac{1}{2}$ mi. W.S.W. of Bristol on a branch of the G.W.R. Pop. (1938) 7,754. Area 5 sq.mi. The cruciform church of St. Andrew has Norman and later portions. Clevedon Court is a mansion dating from the 14th century, though much altered in the Elizabethan and other periods. The town's popularity is due mainly to the fine scenery.

CLEVELAND, BARBARA VILLIERS, Duchess of (1641–1709), mistress of the English king, Charles II., was the daughter of William Villiers, 2nd Viscount Grandison (d. 1643) by his wife Mary (d. 1684), daughter of Paul, 1st Viscount Bayning. In April 1659 Barbara married Roger Palmer, who was created earl of Castlemaine two years later, and soon after this marriage her intimacy with Charles II. began. The king was probably the father of her first child, Anne, born in Feb. 1661, although the paternity was also attributed to one of her earliest lovers, Philip Stanhope, 2nd earl of Chesterfield (1633–1713). Mistress Palmer was made a lady of the bedchamber to Catherine of Braganza. Her house became a rendezvous for the enemies of Clarendon, and according to Pepys she exhibited a wild paroxysm of delight when she heard of the minister's fall from power in 1667. Her influence, which had been gradually rising, became supreme at court in 1667 owing to the marriage of Frances Stuart (la belle Stuart) (1648–1702) with Charles Stuart, 3rd duke of Richmond (1640–72). Accordingly, Louis XIV., instructed his ambassador to pay special attention to Lady Castlemaine, who had become a Roman Catholic in 1663.

In Aug. 1670 she was created countess of Southampton and duchess of Cleveland, with remainder to her first and third sons, Charles and George Palmer, the king at this time not admitting the paternity of her second son Henry. About 1670 her influence over Charles began to decline. She consoled herself meanwhile with other lovers, among them John Churchill, afterwards duke of Marlborough and William Wycherley; by 1674 she had been entirely supplanted at court by Louise de Kérouaille, duchess of Portsmouth. The duchess of Cleveland then went to reside in Paris, where she formed an intrigue with the English ambassador, Ralph Montagu, afterwards duke of Montagu (d. 1709) who lost his position through some revelations which she made to the king. She returned to England just before Charles's death in 1685. In July 1705 her husband, the earl of Castlemaine, whom she had left in 1662, died; and in the same year the duchess was married to Robert (Beau) Feilding (d. 1712), a union which was declared void in 1707, as Feilding had a wife living. She died at Chiswick on Oct. 9, 1709.

Her eldest son, Charles Fitzroy (1662–1730), was created in 1675 earl of Chichester and duke of Southampton, and became duke of Cleveland, and earl of Southampton on his mother's death. Her second son, Henry (1663–90), was created earl of Euston in 1672 and duke of Grafton in 1675; by his wife Isabella, daughter of Henry Bennet, earl of Arlington, he was the direct ancestor of the later dukes of Grafton; the most popular and the most able of the sons of Charles II., he met his death through a wound received at the storming of Cork. Her third son, George (1665–1716), was created duke of Northumberland in 1683 and died without issue. Her daughters were Anne (1661–1722), married in 1674 to Thomas Lennard, Lord Dacre (d. 1715), who was created earl of Sussex in 1684; Charlotte (1664–1718), married in 1677 to Edward Henry Lee, earl of Lichfield (d. 1716); and Barbara (1672–1737), the reputed daughter of John Churchill, who entered a nunnery in France, and became by James Douglas, afterwards 4th duke of Hamilton (1658–1712), the mother of an illegitimate son, Charles Hamilton (1691–1754).

See G. S. Steinman, *Memoir of Barbara duchess of Cleveland* (1871) and *Addenda* (1874).

CLEVELAND (or CLEIVELAND), JOHN (1613–58), English poet and satirist, was born at Loughborough, and educated at Hinckley school under the Puritan, Richard Vines. At the age of 14 he entered Christ's college, Cambridge, and in 1634 was elected to a fellowship at St. John's. He opposed the candidature of Oliver Cromwell as M.P. for Cambridge, and on the triumph of the Puritan party removed (1643) to Oxford. His gifts as a satirist were already known and he was warmly received by the King, whom he followed (1645) to Newark. In that year he was formally deprived of his Cambridge fellowship as a "malignant." He was judge-advocate in the garrison at Newark, and under the governor defended the town until in 1646 Charles I. ordered the surrender of the place to Leslie.

His indignation when the Scots surrendered the King to the Parliament is expressed in "The Rebel Scot." Cleveland wandered over the country depending on the alms of the Royalists for bread, and in 1655 spent three months in Norwich gaol. He was released early in 1656, and found his way eventually to Gray's Inn, where Aubrey says he and Samuel Butler had a "club" every night. There he died on April 29 1658.

Cleveland's poems were more highly esteemed than Milton's by his contemporaries, and his popularity is attested by the very numerous editions of his works. His poems are therefore of great value as an index to the taste of the 17th century. His verse is frequently obscure and full of the far-fetched conceits of the "metaphysical" poets; but the energy of his invective leaves no room for obscurity in such pieces as "Smectymnuus, or the Club Divines," "Rupertismus" and "The Rebel Scot." His poem "On the Memory of Mr. Edward King," is included in the collection of verse which contained Milton's "Lycidas."

For a bibliographical account of Cleveland's poems *see* J. M. Berdan, *The Poems of John Cleveland* (New York, 1903), in which there is a table of the contents of 23 editions, of which the chief are: *The Character of a London Diurnal, with Several Select Poems* (1647); *Poems. By John Cleavland. With additions, never before printed* (1659); *J. Cleaveland Revived . . .* (1659), in which the editor, E. Williamson, says he inserted poems by other authors, trusting to the critical faculty of the readers to distinguish Cleveland's work from the rest; *Clievelandi Vindiciae . . .* (1677), edited by two of Cleveland's former pupils, Bishop Lake and S. Drake, who profess to take out the spurious pieces; and a careless compilation, *The Works of John Cleveland . . .* (1687), containing poems taken from all these sources.

CLEVELAND, STEPHEN GROVER (1837–1908), President of the United States from 1885 to 1889, and again from 1893 to 1897, was born, the fifth in a family of nine children, in Caldwell, Essex county, N.J., on March 18, 1837. His father, Richard F. Cleveland, a Presbyterian clergyman, was a descendant of Moses Cleveland, who emigrated from England to Massachusetts in 1635. The family removed to Fayetteville, N.Y., and afterwards to Clinton, N.Y. It was intended that young Grover should be educated at Hamilton college, but this was prevented by his father's death in 1852. After working several years he set out for Cleveland, O., but stopped near Buffalo, N.Y., to work for his uncle. In 1855 he became a clerk in a Buffalo law office and in 1859 was admitted to the bar. When the Civil War began, the three Cleveland brothers drew lots to see which should remain at home to support their mother; the lot fell to Grover, and when he was drafted he hired a substitute.

In 1863 he was appointed assistant district attorney of Erie county, of which Buffalo is the chief city. This was his first public office, and it came to him, as, apparently, all later preferments, without any solicitation of his own. Two years later (1865) he was the Democratic candidate for district attorney, but was defeated. In 1869 Cleveland was nominated by the Democratic Party for the office of sheriff, and, despite the fact that Erie county was normally Republican, was elected. The years immediately succeeding his retirement from the office of sheriff in 1873 he devoted to the practice of law, coming to be recognized as one of the leaders of the western New York bar. In the autumn of 1881 he was nominated by the Democrats for mayor of Buffalo. The city government had been characterized by extravagance and maladministration, and a revolt of the independent voters at the polls overcame the usual Republican majority and Cleveland was elected. As mayor he attracted wide attention by his independence and businesslike methods, and under his direction the various departments of the city government were thoroughly reorganized. His ability received further recognition when in 1882 he was nominated, by the strategy of his campaign managers, as candidate for governor. The Republican Party in the State was at that time weakened by quarrels within its ranks, and this advantage was greatly increased by the Republicans' nomination for governor of Charles J. Folger (1818–84), then secretary of the Treasury, about whose nomination the cry of Federal interference was raised as a result of the methods employed in securing his nomination. All this, together with the popularity of Cleveland, brought about Cleveland's election by the unprecedented plurality of 192,854. As governor, Cleveland's course was marked by the stern qualities he had displayed in his other public positions. The demands of party leaders were made subordinate to public interest. He promoted the passage of a good civil service law. All bills passed by the legislature were subjected to the governor's laborious scrutiny, and the veto power was used without fear or favour.

In 1884 the Democratic Party had been out of power in national affairs for 23 years. In this year, however, the generally disorganized state of the Republican Party, weakened by the defection of a large group of Independents, known as "Mugwumps," gave the Democrats an unusual opportunity. Upon a platform which called for radical reforms in the administrative departments, the civil service and the national finances, Cleveland was nominated for president, despite the opposition of the Tammany delegation. The nominee of the Republican Party, James G. Blaine (*q.v.*), of Maine, had received the nomination only after a contest in which violent personal animosities were aroused. The campaign that followed was one of the bitterest political contests in American history. Cleveland was accused of favouring the South because he had avoided war service and his private life was attacked; on the other side Blaine was associated with certain political scandals in Washington. The result was close, but Cleveland carried New York and was elected by an electoral majority of 219 to 182.

Cleveland's first term was uneventful, but was marked by firmness, justice and steady adherence on his part to the principles which he deemed salutary to the nation. He was especially concerned in promoting a non-partisan civil service. He stood firmly by the "Pendleton bill" (1883), designed to classify the subordinate places in the service, and to make entrance and promotion depend upon competitive examination of applicants. It applied only to clerkships, but the president was authorized to add others to the classified service from time to time. He added 11,757 during his first term.

President Cleveland made large use of the veto power upon bills passed by Congress, vetoing or "pocketing" during his first term 413 bills, more than two-thirds of which were private pension bills. The most important bill vetoed was the Dependent Pension bill, a measure opening the door, by the vagueness of its terms, to frauds upon the Treasury. Many of these bills were supported by Democrats, and Cleveland's opposition further alienated party leaders. In 1887 there was a large and growing surplus in the Treasury. About two-thirds of the public revenue was derived from duties on imports, in the adjustment of which the doctrine of protection to native industry had a large place. Cleveland attacked the system with great vigour in his annual message of 1887. He did not propose the adoption of free trade, but the Administration tariff measure, known as the Mills bill, passed the House, and although withdrawn owing to amendments in the Republican Senate, it alarmed and exasperated the protected classes, among whom were many Democrats.

In the following year (1888) the Democrats renominated Cleveland, and the Republicans nominated Benjamin Harrison, of Indiana. The campaign turned on the tariff issue, and Harrison was elected, receiving 233 electoral votes to 168 for Cleveland who, however, received a popular plurality of more than 100,000. Cleveland then resumed the practice of law in New York.

Congress had passed a law in 1878 requiring the Treasury department to purchase a certain amount of silver bullion each month and coin it into silver dollars to be full legal tender, and no date was fixed for this operation to cease, both parties being in favour of this policy. Cleveland had written a letter for publication before he became president, saying that a financial crisis of great severity must result if this coinage were continued and expressing the hope that Congress would speedily put an end to it. In 1890 Congress, controlled by the Republican Party, passed the McKinley bill, by which the revenues of the Government were reduced by more than $60,000,000 annually. At this same time expenditures were largely increased by liberal pension legislation, and the Government's purchase of silver bullion almost doubled by the provisions of the new Sherman Silver Purchase Act of 1890.

In 1892 Cleveland was nominated for president a third time in succession. President Harrison was nominated by the Republicans, who had lost strength due to the passage of the McKinley bill. Cleveland received 277 electoral votes and Harrison 145, and 22 were cast for James B. Weaver, of Iowa, the candidate of the "People's" party. Cleveland's second term embraced some notable events. The most important was the repeal of the silver legislation. Nearly $600,000,000 of "fiat money" had been thrust into the channels of commerce in addition to $346,000,000 of legal tender notes that had been issued during the Civil War. A reserve of $100,000,000 of gold had been accumulated for the protection of these notes. In April 1893 the reserve fell below this sum. President Cleveland called an extra session of Congress to repeal the silver law. The House promptly passed the repealing act. In the Senate there was a protracted struggle. The Democrats now had a majority of that body and they were more pro-silver than the Republicans. The president had undertaken to coerce his own party to do something against its will, and it was only by the aid of the Republican minority that the passage of the repealing bill was at last made possible (Oct. 30). The mischief, however, was not ended. The deficit in the Treasury made it inevitable that the gold reserve should be used to meet current expenses; holders of legal tender notes presented them for redemption; borrowing was resorted to by the Government; bonds were issued and sold to the amount of $162,000,000; the business world was in a state of constant agitation; commercial distress was widespread; wages were reduced in many employments, accompanied by labour troubles. The centre of disturbance was the Pullman strike at Chicago, whence the disorder extended to the Pacific coast, causing riot and bloodshed in many places. After waiting a reasonable time, as he conceived, for Gov. Altgeld of Illinois to act, Cleveland, on July 6, 1894, despite Gov. Altgeld's protest, directed the military forces of the United States to clear the way for trains carrying the mails. The rioters in and around Chicago were dispersed in a single day, and within a week the strike was broken.

Another important event was the action of the Government regarding the question of arbitration between Great Britain and Venezuela (*q.v.*). On Dec. 17, 1895, President Cleveland sent to Congress a special message calling attention to Great Britain's action in regard to the disputed boundary line between British Guiana and Venezuela, and declaring the necessity of action by the United States to prevent an infringement of the Monroe Doctrine. Congress at once appropriated funds for an American commission to investigate the matter. The diplomatic situation became very acute for the moment. Negotiations with Great Britain ensued, and before the American commission finished its work Great Britain had agreed (Nov. 1896) to arbitrate on terms which safeguarded the national dignity on both sides.

Cleveland's independence and party difficulties were shown during his second term in his action in regard to the tariff legislation of his party in Congress. A tariff bill introduced in the House by William Lyne Wilson, of West Virginia, was so amended in the Senate through the instrumentality of Senator Arthur Pue Gorman and a coterie of anti-Administration Democratic senators that, although unwilling to veto it, the president signified his dissatisfaction with its too high rates by allowing it to become a law without his signature. He carried the fight with this group of senators to the Senate by letters in which he denounced their lack of support. Cleveland's second administration began by vigorous action in regard to Hawaii; he at once withdrew from the Senate the annexation treaty which President Harrison had negotiated, and started an attempt to restore the dethroned queen, Liliuokalani, but was not successful, owing to Hawaiian opposition.

During his second term Cleveland added no less than 44,004 places in the civil service to the classified list, bringing the whole number up to 86,932. Toward the end of this term the president became very much out of accord with his party on the free-silver question, in consequence of which the endorsement of the administration was withheld by the Democratic national convention at Chicago in 1896. In the ensuing campaign the president and his cabinet, with the exception of Hoke Smith (b. 1855), secretary of the interior, who resigned, gave their support to Palmer and Buckner, the national, or "Sound Money" Democratic nominees.

Cleveland's second term expired on March 4, 1897, and he then retired into private life, universally respected and constantly consulted, in the university town of Princeton, N.J., where he died on June 24, 1908. He was a trustee of Princeton university and Stafford Little lecturer on public affairs. Chosen in 1905 as a member of a committee of three to act as trustees of the majority of the stock of the Equitable Life Assurance company, he promoted the reorganization and the mutualization of that company, and acted as rebate referee for it and for the Mutual and New York Life insurance companies. He published *Presidential Problems* (1904) and *Fishing and Hunting Sketches* (1906). He was married in 1886 to Frances Folsom (1864–1947).

Bibliography.—R. M. McElroy's authorized biography of Cleveland, *Grover Cleveland, the Man and the Statesman* (1925), is a comprehensive work. W. O. Stoddard's *Grover Cleveland* (1888; "Lives of the Presidents" series) and J. L. Whittle's *Grover Cleveland* (1896; "Public Men of Today" series) are judicious volumes; and "Campaign Biographies" (1884) were written by W. Dorsheimer, F. E. Goodrich, P. King and D. Welch; *Grover Cleveland, a Study in Political Courage* (1922) is interesting but perhaps too favourable, while the study of Cleveland by H. L. Stoddard in *As I Knew Them* (1927) takes a somewhat opposite viewpoint. A large amount of magazine literature has been devoted to President Cleveland's career. G. F. Parker had a series of articles in the *Saturday Evening Post* on Aug. 28, 1920, April 7, 1923, June 9, 1923, Nov. 10, 1923, March 29, 1924, under the titles "Grover Cleveland's Career in Buffalo," "Grover Cleveland's First Administration as President," "Grover Cleveland's Second Administration as President," "Grover Cleveland's Life in Princeton" and "Grover Cleveland's One Business Venture." *See* articles by Woodrow Wilson (*Atlantic Monthly*, vol. lxxix: "Cleveland as President"); Carl Schurz (*McClure's Magazine*, vol. ix: "Second Administration of Grover Cleveland"); William Allen White (*McClure's*, vol. xviii: "Character Sketch of Cleveland"); Gamaliel Bradford (*Atlantic Monthly*, Nov. 1920: "Grover Cleveland"); Walter B. Stevens (*Missouri Historical Review*, Jan. 1927: "When Cleveland Came to St. Louis"); and Henry L. Nelson (*North American Review*, vol. clxxxviii). Also Jesse L. Williams, *Mr. Cleveland: A Personal Impression* (1909); G. F. Parker, *Recollections of Grover Cleveland* (1909); C. H. Armitage, *Grover Cleveland as Buffalo Knew Him* (1927); G. C. Griffin, *Writings on American History* (1906–23).

CLEVELAND, a city and port of entry of the state of Ohio, U.S., county seat of Cuyahoga county, the seventh largest city in the United States. It is on Lake Erie, at the mouth of the Cuyahoga river about 260 mi. N.E. of Cincinnati, 357 mi. E. of Chicago and 623 mi. W. of New York. Pop. (1950) 905,636; (1940) 878,336, of whom 179,784 were foreign-born and 84,504 Negroes. Of the 179,784 foreign-born, 24,771, or 13.8%, were born in Poland; 21,066, or 11.8%, in Czechoslovakia; 20,944, or 11.7%, in Hungary; 15,427, or 8.6%, in Germany; 14,103, or 7.9%, in Yugoslavia; and 11,967, or 6.7%, in Russia.

The city commands pleasant views from its position on a plateau, which, at places on bluffs along the shore, has elevations of about 75 ft. above the lake level and rises gradually toward the southeast to 115 ft., and on the extreme eastern border to more than 200 ft. above the lake, or about 800 ft. above sea level; the surface has, however, been cut deeply by the Cuyahoga, which there pursues a meandering course through a valley about ½ mi. wide. The city's shore line is 14.2 mi. long. The city has a land area of 73.1 sq.mi., much the greater part of which is east of the river. The streets are of unusual width (varying from 60 ft. to 132 ft.) and paved chiefly with asphalt and brick. For its many well-shaded streets, Cleveland became known as the "Forest City." The municipality maintains an efficient forestry department. About ½ mi. from the lake and the same distance east of the river is the public square, or Monumental park, in the business centre of the city. Thence the principal thoroughfares radiate. The river valley is spanned by several viaducts, of which the most noteworthy are the Main street bridge with its complete system of approaches, the double-deck Detroit-Superior high level bridge and the Lorain-Carnegie bridge. Lower Euclid avenue (the old country road to Euclid, O., and Erie, Pa.) is the centre of retail trade. This avenue, east of 12th street, was once bordered with handsome houses and spacious and beautifully ornamented grounds, and was famous as one of the finest residential streets in the country. Few homes remain and most of the residential areas are in the outlying sections of the city, in the suburban villages and the adjacent cities of Lakewood, Cleveland Heights, Euclid, East Cleveland, Parma, Shaker Heights, Garfield Heights, Maple Heights, South Euclid, Fairview Park, Lyndhurst, North Olmsted, Bay, Berea, Brooklyn, Mayfield Heights and Wickliffe. The building of the Union Terminal station radically changed lower Superior avenue, once the retail commercial centre, for the south side from the public square westward was vacated for buildings subsidiary to the railroad enterprises.

In 1902 the city arranged for grouping its public buildings—in the so-called "group plan." The courthouse and the city hall, separated by a park or mall, are on the edge of the plateau overlooking Lake Erie. The mall is 540 ft. wide and extends south 1,500 ft. to the federal building and public library on Superior avenue. East on 6th street, which leads to the city hall, are the board of education building and the public auditorium with 11,635 seats, housing also a music hall and little theatre. On the lower level near the lake is the stadium seating 78,189. The city has, besides, numerous fine office buildings, including that of the Society for Savings (an institution in which each depositor is virtually a stockholder), the Williamson, the National City, the Guardian, the Union Trust, the Engineers Bank, the Federal Reserve Bank and Hanna buildings; the Union Terminal building, with its tower 720 ft. high, visible for many miles from the city; the Ohio Bell Telephone building, of the newer pyramidal type; the *Plain Dealer* newspaper building; the Cleveland Trust company's bank; the Museum of Art; Trinity cathedral (Episcopalian); the Church of the Covenant (Presbyterian); St. John's cathedral (Catholic), which was rebuilt in 1947–48; the Temple (Jewish); the Severance hall of the symphony orchestra; the Allen Memorial Medical library. In the public square is a soldiers' and sailors' monument consisting of a granite shaft rising from a memorial room to a height of 125 ft., and surmounted with a figure of Liberty; in the same park also, are a bronze statue of Moses Cleaveland, the founder of the city, and a bronze statue of Tom L. Johnson, a notable mayor. On a commanding site in Lake View cemetery is the James A. Garfield memorial (finished in 1890) in the form of a tower (165 ft. high), designed by George Keller and built mostly of Ohio sandstone; in the base is a chapel containing a statue of Garfield, and several panels on which are portrayed various scenes in his life; his remains are in the crypt below the statue. In Rockefeller park are 20 "cultural gardens," where there are busts or statues of national heroes, including the Goethe-Schiller statue.

The 32 parks and parklands contain 2,129 ac., not including the airport of 1,200 ac. A chain of parks connected by driveways follows the picturesque valley of Doan brook, on the east border of the city. At the mouth of the brook, and on the lake front, is the beautiful Gordon park of 119 ac., formerly the private estate of William J. Gordon, but given by him to the city in 1893; from this extends up the Doan valley the large Rockefeller park, which was given to the city in 1896 by John D. Rockefeller and others, and which extends to and adjoins Wade park (86 ac., given by J. H. Wade) in which is the Museum of Art. Monumental park is divided into four sections (containing about 1 ac. each) by Superior avenue and Ontario street. There is also, under county authority, a system of metropolitan parks or "reservations," lying in river valleys on the borders of the county, in a half circle within a few miles of the city limits, and nearly touching Lake Erie on the east and west.

Education.—Cleveland has an excellent public-school system. A general state law, enacted in 1904, placed the management of school affairs in the hands of an elective council of seven members, five chosen at large and two by districts. This board has power to appoint a school director and a superintendent of instruction. The superintendent appoints the teachers; the director, all other employees; appointments are subject to confirmation by the board, and all employees are subject to removal by the executive officials alone. The plan of education minimizes routine, replacing traditional programs by new curricula based upon a more scientific study of childhood and youth. Greater attention is also paid to the differing interests and capacities of groups of pupils. In 1950 there were 13 senior and 20 junior high schools, and 115 schools for grades one to six, in the city. The budget for 1950 was

$24,805,316. Besides the public-school system there are many parochial schools; the University school for boys, with an eight years' course; the Hathaway Brown and the Laurel school for girls; the Western Reserve university, with its medical school (opened in 1843), the Franklin Thomas Backus law school (1892), the dental department (1892), Adelbert college (until 1882 the Western Reserve college, founded in 1826 at Hudson, O.), Flora Stone Mather college (1888), school of library science (1904), the school of applied social sciences (1916), the Frances Payne Bolton school of nursing (1923), the graduate school (reorganized in 1926); the Case Institute of Technology, founded in 1880 as the Case School of Applied Science by Leonard Case (1820–80) and opened in 1881; Cleveland college, a downtown branch of the university, under a separate board of trustees; Fenn college which offers day and evening classes on the co-operative plan; Notre Dame college (for women); Ursuline college (for women); Baldwin Wallace college; Schauffler College of Religious and Social Work; the Cleveland School of Art; John Carroll university, formerly St. Ignatius college (conducted by the Fathers of the Society of Jesus; incorporated 1890), which has an excellent seismological observatory. In 1950–51 Western Reserve university had 11,267 students, Case institute 1,999, John Carroll university 2,184, Baldwin Wallace college 1,725 (1949–50) and Fenn college 4,290. Educational work is carried on by the Museum of Art, through classes, lectures and special exhibitions and by the Museum of Natural History, opened in 1922, and by the Health museum, opened in 1940. The musical development of the city has been stimulated by the creation of a symphony orchestra and the organization of a school of music. The public library contained 2,634,533 vol. in 1949, the Western Reserve university libraries 600,000, including the affiliated Case library (separately endowed, formerly a subscription library) and the Mather college library. The Cleveland Medical library contained 70,000, the library of the Western Reserve Historical society more than 250,000 and the Cleveland Law library, in the courthouse, 75,000 vol. Many of the larger suburbs, notably East Cleveland, Cleveland Heights, Shaker Heights and Lakewood, have fine library systems of their own. In addition, the Cuyahoga county library system circulates books wherever there is no other library service. In the field of drama, the Play House, which owns two buildings, housing three theatres, is a widely known civic project which attracts students from all over the nation.

The city has a highly developed system of charitable and corrective institutions. A farm of approximately 2,000 ac., the Cleveland Farm colony, 11 mi. from the city, takes the place of workhouses, and has many cottages in which live those of the city's poor who were formerly classed as paupers and were sent to poorhouses, and who now apply their labour to the farm and are relieved from the stigma that generally attaches to inmates of poorhouses. On the "farm" the city maintains an "infirmary village," a tuberculosis sanatorium, a detention hospital, a convalescent hospital and houses of correction. On a farm 22 mi. from the city is the boys' home (maintained in connection with the juvenile court) for "incorrigible" boys. The "cottage" plan has been adopted; each cottage is presided over by a man and wife whom the boys call father and mother. At an equal distance from the city but farther west is a girls' home, similarly administered. Among the most important hospitals are the University hospitals group consisting of Lakeside, MacDonald House (maternity), Babies and Childrens and Hanna House; Cleveland State hospital (for the mentally ill); City; Cleveland Clinic; Deaconess Evangelical; Doctors'; Fairview Park; Glenville; Grace; Huron Road; Lutheran; Mount Sinai; Polyclinic; St. Alexis; St. John's; St. Luke's; St. Vincent Charity; Womans; and two U.S. hospitals, Marine and Brecksville Veterans Administration. The Goodrich House (1897) and Alta House are among the most efficient social settlements in the country. Cleveland has also its orphan asylums, homes for the aged, homes for incurables and day nurseries, besides a home for sailors, homes for young working women and retreats for unfortunate girls. The many charitable organizations, Protestant and Catholic, are united in a welfare federation. There is also a federation of Jewish charities. Their support comes from endowment funds and from the Community fund, created in 1919. The money for this fund is collected in annual "drives." The principal newspapers of the city are the *Plain Dealer* (1841, independent), which in 1917 acquired the *Leader* (1847, Republican); the *Press* (1878, independent); and the *News* (1889, Republican). Bohemian, Hungarian and German dailies are published.

Municipal Enterprise.—Municipal ownership was a prominent issue in Cleveland during the mayoralty of Tom Loftin Johnson (1854–1911), a street-railway owner, iron manufacturer, an ardent single-taxer, who was elected in 1901, and re-elected in 1903, 1905 and 1907. In transportation Johnson adopted the principle of service at cost, with the slogan "three-cent fare." The separate railways, with franchises expiring at different dates, had been consolidated into the Cleveland Electric Street Railway corporation. Since it was overcapitalized ($23,000,000), its managers considered the Johnson schemes visionary. His method of compulsion was through the council's right to grant or refuse franchises, or by organizing rival companies, which should lease their lines to a municipal traction company acting on behalf of the public. The war began by the organization of the Forest City Railway company in Nov. 1906. By 1908 the railway corporation was forced to lease its property to the municipal holding company. But Johnson's power began to wane and in 1909 he was defeated for re-election. The railway system was put in the hands of receivers. The receivership was administered under Federal Judge Robert W. Tayler, and the result in 1910 was a franchise for 25 years to the (renamed) Cleveland Railway company, embodying the "Tayler" plan, which also called for service at cost and a fare of three cents. With rising costs, especially after the outbreak of World War I, the fare had to be raised, partly because holders of the stock (radically deflated) were entitled to 6% dividends. With the depression which began in 1920, difficulties multiplied. In 1935 the franchise was not renewed, but the company had a right to a period of liquidation. In April 1942 the city acquired ownership and the system became known as the Cleveland Transit system. It was operated successfully thereafter under a transit board which spent millions of dollars to modernize the system and which in 1949–50 negotiated a loan from the Reconstruction Finance corporation for construction of a rapid transit system and further modernization. The municipality also owns a large electric power plant, an extensive water-pumping and -purification system (the water is taken from Lake Erie, 4½ mi. from shore) and garbage-reduction and sewage-disposal plants. The municipal airport (1,200 ac.) on the southwest edge of the city is one of the largest in the country. A smaller municipal airport on the lake front in the downtown area takes care of private planes.

Commerce and Transportation.—To meet the demands of the rapidly increasing commerce the harbour has been steadily improved. The outer harbour was formed by two breakwaters enclosing an area of 5 mi. long and 1,600 to 2,400 ft. wide; the main entrance, 700 ft. wide, lying opposite the mouth of the Cuyahoga river; the depth of the harbour ranges from 21 to 25 ft. The inner harbour comprises the Cuyahoga, the old river bed and connecting slips. The channel at the mouth of the river (325 ft. wide) is lined on the west side by a concrete jetty, 1,440 ft. long, and on the east side by commercial docks, 1,602 ft. long. The river and the old river bed furnish about 13 mi. of safe dock frontage, the channel having been dredged for 6 mi. to a depth of 21 ft. This work was extended by federal money.

Cleveland's rapid growth, both as a commercial and as a manufacturing city, is largely the result of its situation between the iron regions of Lake Superior and the coal and oil regions of Pennsylvania and Ohio. Cleveland is a great railway centre and is one of the most important ports on the Great Lakes. The city is served by the New York Central, the New York, Chicago and St. Louis, the Pennsylvania, the Erie, the Baltimore and Ohio and the Wheeling and Lake Erie railways and by steamboats to the principal ports on the Great Lakes. A number of domestic and international air lines also serve the city.

Cleveland is the largest ore market in the world, and its huge ore docks are among its most interesting features; the annual receipts and shipments of coal and iron ore are enormous. The most

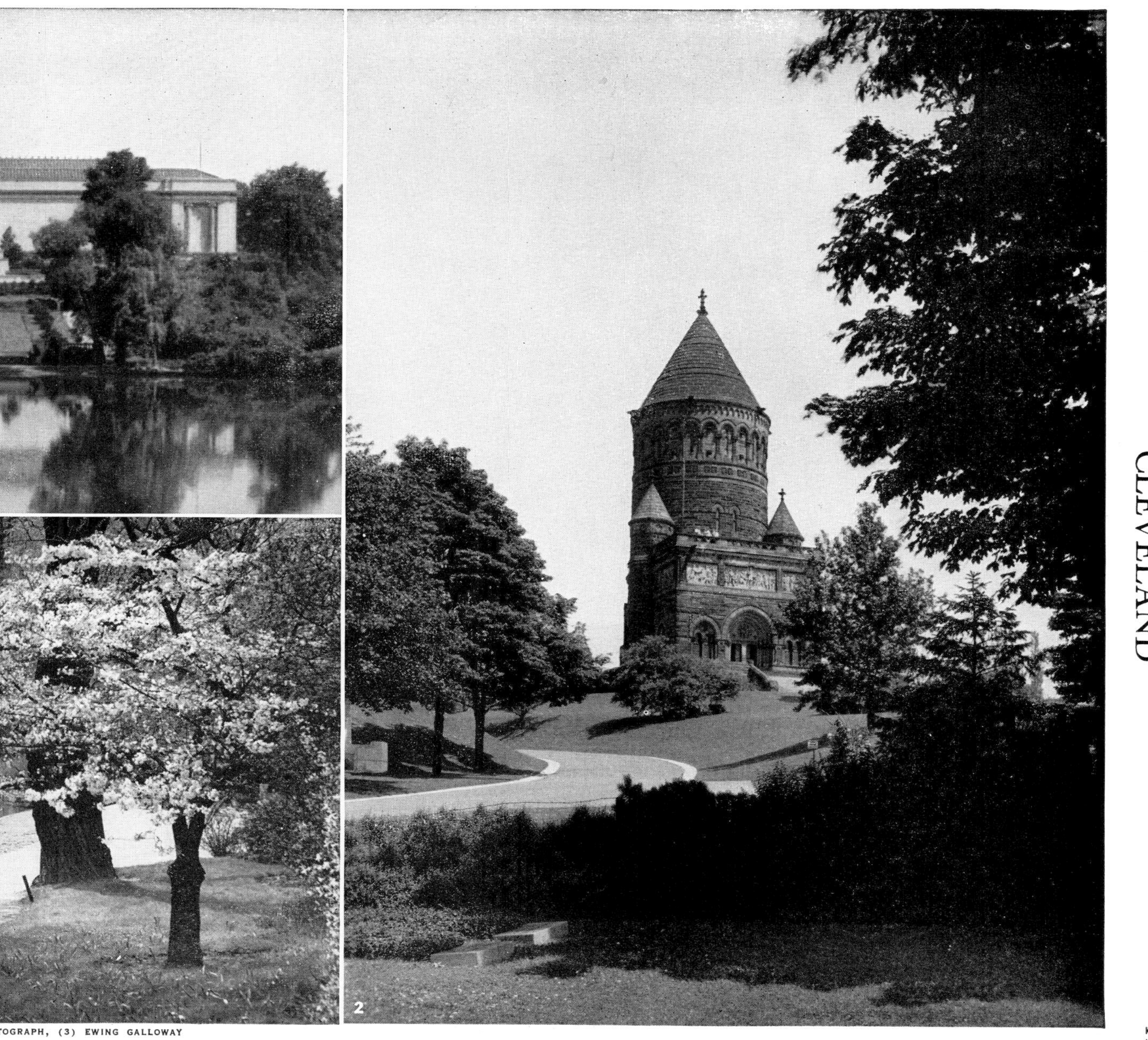

BY COURTESY OF (1, 2) THE CLEVELAND CHAMBER OF COMMERCE; PHOTOGRAPH, (3) EWING GALLOWAY

SCENES IN CLEVELAND

1. Cleveland Museum of Art. **2.** Garfield Memorial, Lakeview cemetery. **3.** Cherry blossoms in a city park

CLEVELAND

PHOTOGRAPH, AERIAL SURVEYS, INC

CLEVELAND'S BUSINESS DISTRICT

Aeroplane view looking toward Lake Erie, with Terminal tower at extreme left

important manufactures of the metropolitan area are iron and steel, automobile parts, machinery, chemicals and paints, printed products, petroleum products, fabricated metal products and clothing. More steel wire, wire nails and bolts and nuts are made there than in any other city in the world. The United States census of manufactures of 1947 showed the value added by manufacture to the following products in the Cleveland area to be: primary metal industries $219,272,000; fabricated metal products $184,485,000; machinery (except electrical) $138,126,000; chemical products, including paints, $123,162,000; transportation equipment $95,-192,000; printing and publishing $74,210,000; food processing $71,812,000; clothing $56,602,000; electrical machinery $51,-523,000. The total value added by manufacture in all Cleveland area industries in 1947 was $1,546,117,000. The value added by manufacture in Cuyahoga county alone exceeded that in any one of 34 entire states. Two suburban areas, one east in Euclid and the other in a group of southwestern suburbs, have had a rapid industrial growth beginning about 1940 as dozens of large factories arose there.

Government.—Since Cleveland became a city in 1836 it has undergone several important changes in government. The charter of that year placed the balance of power in a council composed of three members chosen from each ward and as many aldermen as there were wards, elected on a general ticket. From 1852 to 1891 the city was governed under general laws of the state which entrusted the more important powers to several administrative boards. Then, from 1891 to 1903, by what was practically a new charter, that which is known as the federal plan of government was tried; this centred power in the mayor by making him almost the only elective officer, by giving to him the appointment of his cabinet of directors—one for the head of each of the six municipal departments—and to each director the appointment of his subordinates. The federal plan was abandoned in 1903, a new municipal code coming into effect, which was in operation until 1909, when the Paine law established a board of control under a government resembling the old federal plan. In accordance with the authority conferred by the home-rule amendment of the state constitution, a charter, submitted by a special commission, was accepted by the citizens on July 1, 1913. This reduced the number of elected officers to the mayor and 25 councillors. By an amended charter, which took effect on Jan. 1, 1924, a manager system was introduced. This system was itself repealed in Nov. 1931 despite the advice of civic organizations. Under the amendment, a mayor and 33 councillors, one from each of the city's wards, are elected every odd year. The entire governmental setup was re-organized at the same time with the establishment of three administrative departments—law, finance and utilities—and several special commissions, with the mayor the dominant figure. The city has profited greatly from the interest in municipal problems which has been shown by organizations of leading citizens. Especially has this been manifested by the Cleveland Chamber of Commerce and the Citizens' league, an organization of influential professional and businessmen, which, by issuing bulletins concerning candidates at the primaries and at election time, has done much for the betterment of local politics. The Cleveland Chamber of Commerce, an organization of more than 4,200 business leaders, is a power for good in the city; besides its constant and aggressive work in promoting the commercial interests of the city, it was largely influential in the federal reform of the consular service; it studied the question of overcrowded tenements and secured the passage of a new tenement law with important sanitary provisions and fixed minimum air space; it urges and promotes home gardening, public baths, playgrounds, lunchrooms, etc., for employees in factories; and it was largely instrumental in devising and carrying out the so-called "group plan" creating the lake-front area.

History.—A trading post was established at the mouth of the Cuyahoga river as early as 1786, but the place was not permanently settled until 1796, when it was laid out as a town by Moses Cleaveland (1754–1806), who was then acting as the agent of the Connecticut Land company, which in the year before had purchased from the state of Connecticut a large portion of the Western Reserve. In 1800 the entire Western Reserve was erected into the county of Trumbull and a township government was given to Cleveland; ten years later Cleveland was made the seat of government of the new county of Cuyahoga, and in 1814 it was incorporated as a village. Cleveland's growth was, however, very slow until the opening of the Ohio canal as far as Akron, in 1827; about the same time the improvement of the harbour was begun, and by 1832 the canal was opened to the Ohio river. Cleveland was thus connected with the interior of the state, for whose mineral and agricultural products it became the lake outlet. The discovery of iron ore in the Lake Superior region made Cleveland the natural meeting point of the iron ore and the coal from the Ohio, Pennsylvania and West Virginia mines; and the city's great commercial importance dates from this time. The building of railways during the decade 1850–60 increased this importance, and the city grew with great rapidity. The growth during the Civil War was partly caused by the rapid development of the manufacturing interests of the city, which supplied large quantities of iron products and clothing to the federal government. The population of 1,076 in 1830 increased to 6,071 in 1840, 17,034 in 1850, 43,417 in 1860, 92,829 in 1870 and 160,146 in 1880. Until 1853 the city was confined to the east side of the river, but in that year Ohio City (which was founded in 1807, later incorporated as the village of Brooklyn, and in 1836 chartered as a city under the name Ohio City) was annexed. Other annexations followed: East Cleveland (a district east of the present 55th street, and not the suburban city of that name) in 1872, Newburg in 1873, West Cleveland and Brooklyn in 1893, Glenville and South Brooklyn in 1905, Collinwood in 1910 and West Park in 1923.

The most notable later events not mentioned elsewhere were the centennial celebration of 1896, the sesquicentennial observance of 1946, the establishment of a successful community fund, the successful Great Lakes exposition of 1936 and 1937 and the National Air races held at Cleveland airport.

BIBLIOGRAPHY.—*Annuals* of the Cleveland Chamber of Commerce (1865 *et seq.*); C. Whittlesey, *The Early History of Cleveland* (1867); C. A. Urann, *Centennial History of Cleveland* (1896); C. F. Thwing, "Cleveland, the Pleasant City," in Powell's *Historic Towns of the Western States* (1901); S. P. Orth, *A History of Cleveland* (1910); *City Record,* official publication of the City of Cleveland (1914 *et seq.*); E. M. Avery, *A History of Cleveland and Its Environs,* vol. i (1918); C. E. Kennedy, *Fifty Years of Cleveland* (1925); William R. Coates, *A History of Cuyahoga County and the City of Cleveland,* 3 vol. (1924); Charles Asa Post, *Doans Corners and the City Four Miles West* (1930); Wilfred Henry Alburn and Miriam Russell Alburn, *This Cleveland of Ours,* 4 vol. (1933); Theodore Hall, *The Sesquicentennial Story of Cleveland, 1796–1946* (1946); William Ganson Rose, *Cleveland: The Making of a City* (1950). (P. By.)

CLEVELAND, a city of southern Tennessee, U.S., 29 mi. E.N.E. of Chattanooga, on federal highway 11 and the Southern railway; the county seat of Bradley county. The population in 1950 was 12,445; in 1940, 11,351; and in 1930, 9,136 by the federal census. There are manganese mines near by, and the city has more than 70 factories, employing 5,500 persons and producing goods valued at $15,000,000 annually. During the Civil War U. S. Grant and William T. Sherman for a time had headquarters there, in houses that are still standing. The battle of Ft. Hill was fought on the site of what is now Ft. Hill cemetery. Cleveland was settled about 1832 and was incorporated as a city in 1837. It was named after Col. Benjamin Cleveland, a commander at the battle of King's Mountain.

CLEVELAND HEIGHTS, a city of Cuyahoga county, Ohio, U.S., adjoining Cleveland on the east. It is a residential suburb, with a population of 58,782 in 1950; 54,992 in 1940 and 50,945 in 1930 by the federal census. It has a commission-manager form of government.

The village was incorporated in 1903 and in 1922 it became a city.

CLEVER, an adjective implying dexterous activity of mind or body, and ability to meet emergencies with readiness and adroitness. The etymology and the early history of the word are obscure. Some derive it, in the sense of "quick to seize," from M.E. *cliver* or *clivre,* a claw. This original sense probably survives in the frequent use of the word for nimble, dexterous, quick and skilful in the use of the hands, and so it is often applied to a horse, "clever at his fences." The word has also been connected with O.E. *gléaw,* wise, which became in M.E. *gleu,* and is cognate with Scottish *gleg,* quick of eye.

CLEYNAERTS (CLENARDUS or CLÉNARD), **NICOLAS** (1495–1542), Belgian grammarian and traveller, was born at Diest, Brabant, on Dec. 5, 1495. Educated at the University of Louvain, he became a professor of Latin, which he taught by a conversational method. His *Institutiones in linguam graecam* (1530), and *Meditationes graecanicae* (1531) passed through a number of editions, and had many commentators. He maintained that the learner should not be puzzled by elaborate rules until he has obtained a working acquaintance with the language. In pursuit of a scheme for proselytism among the Arabs he travelled in 1532 to Spain, and tried in vain to gain access to the Arabic mss. in the possession of the Inquisition. Finally, in 1540, he set out for Africa to seek information for himself. He reached Fez, then a flourishing seat of Arab learning, but after 15 months of privation and suffering was obliged to return to Granada, and died in the autumn of 1542. He was buried in the Alhambra palace.

See his Latin letters to his friends in Belgium, *Nicolai Clenardi, Peregrinationum ac de rebus machometicis epistolae elegantissimae* (Louvain, 1550), and a more complete edition, *Nic. Clenardi Epistolarum libri duo* (Antwerp, 1561); also Victor Chauvin and Alphonse Roersch, "Étude sur la vie et les travaux de Nicolas Clénard" in *Mémoires couronnés* (vol. lx., 1900–01) of the Royal Academy of Belgium, which contains an extensive bibliography.

CLICHÉ. In the process of stereotype printing a matrix or mould is made in papier-mâché from the set type, and a solid casting is produced from this mould, which thus bears a surface of letters cast in relief, from which the actual prints are taken. The papier-mâché mould is called a cliché.

This term, representing as it does a mould for mechanical reproduction, has passed into use as an effective name for any hackneyed term or phrase. The cliché is the vice of the writer who trades in second-hand thought and expression; for him the sea becomes "the rolling wave," fire "the devouring element," and the sun "the orb of day."

CLICHTOVE, JOSSE VAN (d. 1543), Belgian theologian, educated at Louvain and Paris, became librarian of the Sorbonne. In 1519 he was elected bishop of Tournai, and in 1521 was translated to the see of Chartres. He is known as an antagonist of Luther. When Cardinal Duprat convened his Synod of Paris in 1528 to discuss the new religion, Clichtove was charged to collect and summarize the objections to the Lutheran doctrine. This he did in his *Compendium veritatum . . . contra erroneas Lutheranorum assertiones* (Paris, 1529). He died at Chartres on Sept. 22, 1543.

CLICHY, a manufacturing suburb of Paris. Pop. (1936) 56,475. It was, under the name of *Clippiacum,* a residence of the Merovingian kings. The church dates from the 17th century. The industries include the manufacture of starch, rubber, oil and grease, glass, chemicals and soap.

CLICKS, peculiar sounds of unknown origin, found in many languages. The German term *Schnalze* and the Afrikaans *klukken* are both attempts to give a descriptive name, but the English word *Click* is as onomatopoeic as any. The outstanding examples of click-speech are the Hottentot languages (Nama, !kora, Griqua, etc.) with four or five different clicks and those of the Bushmen of South Africa (!kung, kham, !ai, etc.), with as many as nine different clicks. From contiguity with the Hottentots and Bushmen several Bantu stocks have acquired clicks, which are alien to Bantu speech-systems. Such stocks are the Zulus and Kaffirs while the Damaras, (originally Bantu), have dropped their language entirely and speak only Hottentot. In the interior, Afrikaans (Cape Dutch), has even acquired clicks.

It seems fairly well established now, that clicks are by no means confined to these South African tongues. There are cases of their presence in the Melanesian languages of the Eastern Pacific, the **Q** of Codrington and Paterson representing a click-sound. Clicks never appear very far north of the equator and a definite "click-zone" can be found girdling the earth with, and south of, the equator. A recent study of the Quichua language of the Incas of Peru shows the existence of click-sounds, later rubbed down to simple gutturals, in the ancient tongue. The Aztec or Nahuatl tongue also had clicks and in the surviving Aztec spoken by Mexicans in the hills of the interior, the *tl,* final and initial, sounds exactly like a Hottentot dental click.

In the Nama speech (Standard Hottentot), there are four clicks, represented thus:

	Tindall	German system	International Phonetic Association
Dental . .	c	/	ʇ
Cerebral . .	q	!	ʗ
Palatal . .	v	≠	ʄ
Lateral . .	x	//	ʖ

In the Bushman languages (so far as classified, 16 in number) other clicks exist having such signs as:

Guttural ⌈ Semi-labial ▯ Labial ʘ

The sounds must be heard; no description can do more than convey a general idea of their nature. The dental click, for example, is pronounced by pressing the flattened tip of the tongue against the front teeth at the gums and quickly withdrawing it. Early attempts to define and describe these sounds will be found in the works mentioned below.

See H. Tindall, *A Grammar of the Namaqua-Hottentot Language* (Cape Town, n.d.); J. L. Döhne, *Zulu-Kafir Dictionary* (Cape Town, 1857); Meinhof, *Lehrbuch der Namasprache* (1909); Leonhard, *Aus Namaland und Kalahari* (1905); N. Whymant, *The Zone of Clicks* (Tokyo, 1923). *See* also BUSHMAN LANGUAGES and HOTTENTOTS.

(A. N. J. W.)

CLIFF-DWELLERS. Once believed to be a mysterious vanished race, the inhabitants of the cliff-dwellings in the southwestern United States are now recognized as but Pueblo Indians of the prehistoric period characterized by black-on-white pottery; who, when under hostile pressure, lodged their homes and granaries on ledges under overhanging cliffs, where such were available; in other cases excavated horizontally into bluff faces, or built on steep-walled mesas. Their skeletal remains, artifacts, and masonry are identical with those of the same period found in ruins in canyon bottoms and valleys. The romantically inaccessible situation of the cliff ruins, however, is impressive. Among the best known are Cliff Palace and Spruce Tree House in Mesa Verde National Park, Colorado, and a series in Canyon de Chelly, Arizona.

See Nordenskiöld, *Cliff Dwellings of the Mesa Verde* (1893).

CLIFF-DWELLINGS, the general archaeological term for the habitations of certain primitive peoples, formed by utilizing natural recesses or shallow caverns in the faces of cliffs, sometimes with more or less modification to adapt them to the requirements of the buildings. They are to be distinguished from cave-dwellings, which, not necessarily high in cliff walls, usually were or are occupied in their natural state; and from rock-shelters, used for temporary shelter, for storage, as lookouts, and sometimes for sacrificial deposits and for burial of the dead. Dry caves have been used as habitations in all parts of the world, some of those in France and Spain dating from the earliest periods of human history. Caves are still inhabited in Tunis and in Central Africa, and as winter habitations by the Tarahumare and other Piman tribes of northern Mexico, who have modified the natural recesses by the addition of masonry windbreaks, storage-bins, etc. A class of cave-dwellers known as Basket-makers, of a culture older than that of the cliff-dwellers, lived in Utah, Colorado, Arizona and New Mexico; and another culture, known as Bluff-dwellers, occupied caves in the Ozark mountains of western Missouri-Arkansas. Other caves, such as Mammoth and Salts caves in Kentucky and Lovelock cave in Nevada, have yielded important artifacts of their primitive occupants.

Eskimo of King island in Bering strait, Alaska, as late at least as 1881, occupied winter houses made by excavating the loose granite rocks to form niches in a steep slope and by walling up the front and sides with stones placed over a driftwood framework, access being had by a long covered passage leading to an

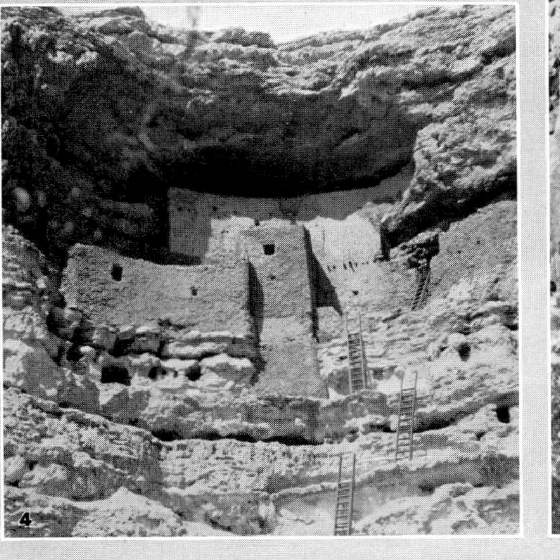

BY COURTESY OF (1) THE DENVER AND RIO GRANDE WESTERN RAILROAD COMPANY, (2) CHARLES L. BERNHEIMER, (3) THE UNION PACIFIC RAILROAD SYSTEM, (4) THE ATCHISON, TOPEKA AND SANTA FE RAILWAY, (5) THE MUSEUM OF NEW MEXICO, SANTA FE

CLIFF-DWELLINGS OF THE SOUTH-WESTERN UNITED STATES

1. **Spruce Tree House, Mesa Verde National park,** south-western Colorado, one of the largest Mesa Verde structures (216 feet long and 89 feet wide, containing 114 rooms and 8 kivas or assembly rooms). It is three storeys high in its loftiest part, and its chambers are round, rectangular or triangular to adapt themselves to the limited ground space which the dwelling occupies
2. **The westerly edge of the Betátakin ruins, in the Navaho National Monument, in Arizona.** These ancient stone houses are built more than a hundred feet above the canyon floor. Cliff-dwellings of this type extend over a wide area from southern Colorado as far south as the central part of Mexico
3. **Cliff Palace, Mesa Verde National park.** Among the Mesa Verde ruins have been found pottery remains; yucca sandals; woven cotton cloth; indications of reservoirs for irrigating; stone and bone implements; graves containing flexed skeletons; mummies; evidences of turkey domestication; and other mementos of the lives of the cliff-dwellers
4. **Montezuma Castle, in Arizona.** This cliff-dwelling, although distant from Mesa Verde, is similar to it, even in small details of construction
5. **Cavate lodges of Puye, New Mexico,** a type of cliff-dwelling consisting of communicating rooms excavated in the soft volcanic tuff of the cliffside, with terraced, flat-roofed houses built in front. These occur also along the Rio Verde in Arizona

opening in the floor. Ancient cliff-dwellings are found in the States of Chihuahua and Jalisco, Mexico, and especially in Colorado, Utah, Arizona and New Mexico, those in the Mesa Verde National park in southwestern Colorado being noted for the excellence of their architecture. It was once believed that the cliff-dwellers of southwestern United States were of a pre-Indian pygmy race, but archaeological study has shown the structures and the objects found in them to be unquestionably of Pueblo origin, contemporaneous with numerous mesa-top and valley ruins, the selection of their sites, made accessible only by hand-and-toe holes pecked in the cliff, having been due to hostile pressure. In the Mesa Verde canyons the largest and most noted cliff-dwellings are: Cliff Palace, consisting of about 150 secular rooms and 23 kivas or ceremonial chambers, together with various square and circular towers, all built in a very compact group and following the curving face of the recess for about 300 feet. Spruce-tree house, 216 ft. long and 89 ft. wide (114 rooms and 8 kivas), was three storeys high in its loftiest part; its chambers were built round, rectangular, or triangular according to the exigencies of the limited ground space. Balcony house (25 rooms) is named from a wide shelf extending along the front of two of the houses and is built on the projecting floorbeams. There are many other similar dwellings in the Mesa Verde canyons, some of which have been excavated; and on the summit of the mesa are massive related pueblo-like structures, used perhaps chiefly for ceremonial purposes, as well as many pit-houses. Other important cliff-dwellings of Arizona are Casa Blanca in Canyon de Chelly, Montezuma castle on Beaver creek of Verde river, and various examples (*e.g.*, Betátakin, Kitsil), in the Navaho National monument. Cliff-dwellings of this class extend from southern Colorado to central Mexico. Another type, known as cavate lodges, consists of groups of a few communicating rooms excavated in the friable volcano tuff of the cliffs, in front of which terraced houses of masonry with flat roofs were built. This class is common to the Puye and Rito de los Frijoles areas in northern New Mexico, and occurs also on the Rio Verde in Arizona.

See H. C. Mercer, *Hill Caves of Yucatan* (Philadelphia, 1896); Alice C. Cook, "Aborigines of the Canary Islands," *Amer. Anthropologist* (vol. II., no. 2, 1900); E. W. Nelson, "Eskimo about Bering Strait," *18th Rep.* Bur. Amer. Ethnology (pt. 1, 1899); A. F. Bandelier, *Archaeological Inst. Amer. Papers*, Amer. ser., pts. iii., iv. (Cambridge, 1890–92); W. H. Holmes, *Rep. U.S. Geol. Surv. of the Territories for 1876* (1879); W. H. Jackson, *ibid. 1874* (1876); E. A. Mearns, *Popular Sci. Mo.*, vol. 37 (1890); C. Mindeleff, in 13th and 16th *Rep. Bur. Amer. Ethnology* (1896–1897); F. H. Chapin, *Land of the Cliff Dwellers* (Boston, 1892); G. Nordenskiöld, *Cliff Dwellers of the Mesa Verde*, trans. by D. Lloyd Morgan (Stockholm and Chicago, 1893); *Holmes Anniversary Volume* (privately published, Washington, 1916); C. Lumholtz, *Unknown Mexico* (2 vols., 1902); A. Hrdlička, *Amer. Anthropologist* (vol. v., 1903); B. Cummings, *Bull. Univ. of Utah* (vol. iii., 1910); J. W. Fewkes, *Bull.* 41, 50, 51 and 70, Bur. Amer. Ethnology (1909–1919) and in various reports of the same Bureau; A. V. Kidder, *Introduction to the Study of Southwestern Archaeology* (New Haven, 1924, with extended bibliography); A. V. Kidder and S. J. Guernsey, *Bull.* 65, Bur. Amer. Ethnology (1919); J. L. Nusbaum, "A Basket-maker Cave in Kane county, Utah" with notes on the artifacts by A. V. Kidder and S. J. Guernsey, *Indian Notes and Monogr., Mus. Amer. Indian* (Misc. no. 29, 1922); Deric Nusbaum, *Deric in Mesa Verde* (1926, juvenile). (F. W. H.)

CLIFFORD, the name of a famous English family and barony, taken from the village of Clifford in Herefordshire.

Robert de Clifford (1274–1314), one of the most powerful barons of his age, won great renown at the siege of Carlaverock castle in 1300, and after taking part in the movement against Edward II's favourite, Piers Gaveston, was killed at Bannockburn. His son Roger, 2nd baron (1300–1322), shared in the rebellion of Thomas, earl of Lancaster, and was probably executed at York on March 23, 1322. John, the 9th baron (1435–1461) earned the name of the "butcher," in the Wars of the Roses, in which he fought for Henry VI; after the battle of Wakefield in 1460 he murdered Edmund, earl of Rutland, son of Richard, duke of York. Shakespeare refers to this incident in King Henry VI, and also represents Clifford as taking part in the murder of York, though it is practically certain that York was slain in the battle. Clifford was killed at Ferrybridge on March 28, 1461, and was afterward attainted. His young son Henry, the 10th baron (*c.* 1454–1523), lived disguised as a shepherd for some years; hence he is sometimes called the "shepherd lord." On the accession of Henry VII the attainder was reversed and he received his father's estate. He fought at Flodden in 1513, and died on April 23, 1523. He is the subject of two of Wordsworth's poems, "The White Doe of Rylstone" and the "Song at the Feast of Brougham Castle." Henry, the 11th baron, was created earl of Cumberland (*q.v.*) in 1525, and from this time until the extinction of the title in 1643 the main line of Cliffords was associated with this earldom.

On the death of George, 3rd earl of Cumberland, in 1605, the barony of Clifford, separated from the earldom, was claimed by his daughter Anne, later countess of Dorset, Pembroke and Montgomery; and in 1628 a new barony of Clifford was created in favour of Henry, afterwards 5th and last earl of Cumberland. After Anne's death in 1676 the claim to the older barony passed to her daughter Margaret (d. 1676), wife of John Tufton, 2nd earl of Thanet, and her descendants, whose title was definitely recognized in 1691. After the Tuftons the barony was held with intervening abeyances by the Southwells and the Russells, and to this latter family the present Lord De Clifford belongs.

When the last earl of Cumberland died in 1643 the newer barony of Clifford passed to his daughter Elizabeth, wife of Richard Boyle, 2nd earl of Cork, and from the Boyles it passed to the Cavendishes, falling into abeyance in 1858.

The barony of Clifford of Lanesborough was held by the Boyles from 1644 to 1753, and the Devonshire branch of the family still holds the barony of Clifford of Chudleigh, created in 1672.

See G. E. C.(okayne), *Complete Peerage*, vol. iii, new ed. (London, 1913); and T. D. Whitaker, *The History and Antiquities of the Deanery of Craven*, 3rd ed. (Leeds, London, 1878).

CLIFFORD OF CHUDLEIGH, THOMAS CLIFFORD, 1st Baron (1630–1673), English lord treasurer, the son of Hugh Clifford of Ugbrooke, near Exeter, was born on Aug. 1, 1630, matriculated at Exeter college, Oxford, in 1647, and entered the Middle Temple in 1648. He represented Totnes in the convention parliament of 1660 and in the parliament of 1661, and became a steady supporter of the earl of Arlington, in opposition to the chancellor, earl of Clarendon. On the outbreak of the Dutch war in 1664 Clifford was appointed commissioner for the care of the sick and of prisoners; afterward knighted and appointed ambassador to Denmark and Sweden, he served with the fleet in 1665 and 1666, and in Oct. 1667 was one of those selected by the commons to prepare papers concerning the naval operations. In 1666 he was made controller of the household and a privy councillor, in 1667 a commissioner for the treasury and in 1668 treasurer of the household.

As one of the Cabal ministry, Clifford co-operated zealously with the king in breaking through the Triple Alliance with Holland and Sweden and in effecting an understanding with France. He was the only minister, besides Arlington, entrusted with the secret treaty of Dover of 1670, which he signed as well as the ostensible treaty shown to all the members of the Cabal. In 1672, during the absence of Arlington and Coventry abroad, Clifford acted as principal secretary of state. He was chiefly responsible for the "stop of the exchequer" (which, through the suspension of all payments for 12 months, gave Charles the use of all revenue) and probably also for the attack upon the Dutch Smyrna fleet. He was appointed that year a commissioner to inquire into the settlement of Ireland. On April 22 he was raised to the peerage, and on Nov. 28, by the duke of York's interest, was made lord treasurer. This excited the jealousy of Arlington, who had always aspired to that office. It was, however, the Test Act of 1673 that brought about Clifford's downfall. On the passing of the bill Clifford followed the duke of York into retirement. He had, it would seem, been gradually moving towards Roman Catholicism and probably the Test act precipitated his conversion to the Roman faith. His resignation caused astonishment, since he had never publicly professed his religion, and in 1671 had even built a new Protestant chapel at his home at Ugbrooke. According to John Evelyn, however, his conduct was governed by a promise previously given to James. He gave up the treasurership and his seat in the privy council in June. On July 3, 1673, he received a general pardon from the king as a safeguard against a possible impeachment by the commons. In August he said a last farewell to Evelyn, and in less than a month he died at Ugbrooke. In Evelyn's opinion the cause of death was suicide, but this seems very unlikely. The evidence is not strong nor was such an action in keeping with his character. Clifford was one of the worst advisers of Charles II, but sincere and consistent. Evelyn declares him "a valiant, uncorrupt gentleman; ambitious, not covetous; generous, passionate, a most constant, sincere friend." He married Elizabeth, daughter of William Martin of Lindridge, Devonshire (by whom he had 15 children, 3 sons and 6 daughters surviving him). He was succeeded by Hugh, his 5th but eldest surviving son.

See C. H. Hartmann, *Clifford of the Cabal* (London, Toronto, 1937).

CLIFFORD, SIR HUGH, G.C.M.G.; G.B.E. (1866–1941), British colonial governor, son of Maj.-Gen. Sir H. H. Clifford, V.C., K.C.M.G., was born in London on March 5, 1866, and was educated at Woburn Park. In 1883 Clifford passed into the Malay States civil service, and, after executing a special mission towards the sultan of Pahang in 1887, became the governor's agent there. After filling several other administrative posts, he returned to Pahang as British resident during the years 1896–99. Four years later he became colonial secretary at Trinidad, and was transferred in the same capacity to Ceylon in 1907, where he remained until his appointment as governor of the Gold Coast in 1912. He was governor of Nigeria, 1919–25; Ceylon, 1925–27; and the Straits Settlements, 1927–29. Apart from his career in the colonial service, Sir Hugh Clifford made his name as a writer of distinction, his stories of the Malay peninsula being among the best of his works of fiction. He married as his second wife the novelist, Mrs. Henry de la Pasture. Among his numerous works may be mentioned the following: *Studies in Brown Humanity* (1898); *Bush-Whacking* (1901); *Malayan Monochromes* (1913) and *The Further Side of Silence* (1916). Sir Hugh also compiled with Sir Frank Swettenham a *Dictionary of the Malay Language*. He retired from the colonial service in 1929 and died Dec. 19, 1941.

CLIFFORD, JOHN (1836–1923), British Nonconformist minister and politician, son of a warp-machinist at Sawley, Derbyshire, was born on Oct. 16, 1836. He worked in a lace factory where he attracted the notice of Baptists, who sent him to the academy at Leicester and the Baptist college at Nottingham to be educated for the ministry. In 1858 he was called to Praed Street chapel, Paddington (London), and while officiating there he attended University college and pursued his education at the British Museum. He took his B.A. (1861), B.Sc. (1862), M.A. (1864), and LL.B. (1866), and in 1883 he was given an honorary D.D. by Bates college, U.S.A. At Praed Street chapel he obtained a large following, and in 1877 Westbourne Park chapel was opened for him. As a preacher, writer, propagandist, and ardent Liberal politician he became a power in the Nonconformist body. He was president of the London Baptist Association in 1879, of the Baptist Union in 1888 and 1899, and of the National Council of Evangelical Churches in 1898. His prominence in politics dates from 1903, in consequence of his advocacy of "passive resistance" by non-payment of taxes to the Education Act of 1902. Into this movement he threw himself with militant ardour, his own goods being distrained upon, with those of numerous other Nonconformists. The "passive resistance" movement, with Dr. Clifford as its chief leader, contributed to the defeat of the Unionist Government in Jan. 1906, and his efforts were then directed to getting a new act passed which should be undenominational. The rejection of Mr. Birrell's bill in 1906 by the House of Lords led Dr. Clifford and his followers to denounce the House of Lords, but as year by year went by, up to 1909, with nothing but failure on the part of the Liberal ministry to solve the education problem —failure due not to the House of Lords but to the inherent difficulties of the subject—"passive resistance" lost its interest. Dr. Clifford received a C.H. in 1921, and died on Nov. 20, 1923.

His chief writings are *The English Baptists* (1881); *The Christian Certainties*, 2nd ed. (1904); *The Ultimate Problems of Christianity* (1906). *See* C. T. Bateman: *John Clifford* (1904); D. Crane: *John Clifford* (1908); *Life and Letters*, ed. by Sir James Marchant (1924).

CLIFFORD, NATHAN (1803–1881), U.S. supreme court justice, was born at Rumney, N.H., on Aug. 18, 1803. He read law in an office at Rumney and was admitted to the bar in 1827. Clifford settled in Maine and in 1830 was elected to the lower house of the state legislature. In 1834 he was appointed attorney general of the state and four years later was elected to the U.S. house of representatives. U.S. attorney general under Pres. James Polk, 1846–48, he also served as a diplomatic representative to Mexico at the end of the war with that country. From 1858 until his death on July 25, 1881, he was an associate justice of the U.S. supreme court.

Clifford became known as an able and articulate advocate of Jacksonian democracy. Although his early formal education was limited, he won wide respect for his comprehensive and learned legal opinions. His areas of special competence were maritime and commercial law and law pertaining to Mexican land grants and procedure and practice. Clifford did not write any of the court's majority opinions on leading points of constitutional law, however. Clifford, who headed the electoral commission which investigated the disputed Hayes-Tilden election of 1876, protested against its decisions in 1877 in favour of Rutherford Hayes, the Republican presidential candidate.

CLIFFORD, WILLIAM KINGDON (1845–1879), English mathematician and philosopher, was born on May 4, 1845, at Exeter. He was educated at King's college, London, and at Trinity college, Cambridge, where he was elected fellow in 1868. He was appointed professor of mathematics at University college, London, in 1871 and was elected a fellow of the Royal society in 1874. In 1875 he married Lucy (d. 1929), daughter of John Lane, of Barbados, who became well-known under her married name as a novelist and dramatist, her most successful story being *Mrs. Keith's Crime* (1885). A man of athletic but not robust physique, Clifford began to fall into ill-health in 1876 and, after two voyages to the south, died, during the third, of pulmonary consumption at Madeira, on March 3, 1879, leaving his widow with two daughters.

Clifford impressed all his contemporaries as a man of extraordinary originality; he had also quickness of thought and speech, a lucid style, wit, poetic fancy and social warmth. He was a mathematician of the front rank and, contrary to the excessively analytic tendency of the Cambridge mathematicians, "above all and before all a geometer." He developed the theory of biquaternions as a generalization of Sir W. R. Hamilton's quaternions and linked them with the general idea of a linear associative algebra. He recognized the serious difficulties created for Kant's theory of *a priori* synthetic propositions by the non-Euclidean geometries of Nikolai Lobachevski and Georg F. B. Riemann (*qq.v.*) and drew attention at the same time to the partly tautological character of arithmetic. He showed that spaces of constant curvature could have several different topological structures in the large and proved the topological equivalence of a Riemann surface to a box with holes in it. His suggestion (1870) that matter is a type of curvature of space foreshadowed Einstein's general theory of relativity. Other important papers of his dealt with Abelian functions, algebraic forms and projective and algebraic geometry.

Karl Pearson took up and developed further Clifford's views on the philosophy of science, which were related to those of Hermann von Helmholtz and Ernst Mach. In general philosophy, Clifford's name is chiefly associated with two phrases of his coining, "mind-stuff" and "the tribal self." The latter gives the key to his ethical view, which explains conscience and the moral law by the development in each individual of a "self" that prescribes the conduct conducive to the welfare of the "tribe." He was prominent in the battle between theology and Darwinian science.

His works are: *Elements of Dynamic* (1879–87); *Seeing and Thinking* (1879); *Lectures and Essays* (1879); *Mathematical Papers*, ed. by R. Tucker (1882); and *The Common Sense of the Exact Sciences*, completed by Karl Pearson (1885).

CLIFFSIDE PARK, a borough of Bergen county, N.J., U.S., on the Palisades overlooking the Hudson river. The railroad station is Weehawken (*q.v.*). A residential suburb, it had a population of 17,116 in 1950; 16,892 in 1940 by the federal census.

CLIFTON, a town of Arizona, U.S., on the San Francisco river and the Southern Pacific railway, near the eastern boundary of the state; the county seat of Greenlee county. Pop. (1950) 3,466; (1940) 2,668. It was formerly in the Morenci-Metcalf copper-mining district. Metcalf was abandoned and all the buildings removed. Morenci became the site of a large open-pit copper-mine development, to make available low-grade copper ore. Clifton was settled about 1870, and was incorporated in 1908. It is the oldest copper-mining camp in the state.

CLIFTON, a city of Passaic county, N.J., U.S., between Paterson and Passaic, served by the Delaware, Lackawanna and Western and the Erie railroads. Pop. (1950) 64,511. There are about 200 major industries manufacturing television sets, dry batteries and flashlights, electronic equipment, printing machinery, tire machinery, precision instruments and tools, calendars, chemicals, drugs, aircraft parts, steel springs, railroad boxcars, textiles and telephones. Production in 1950 was valued at $600,000,000. It has a city manager form of government.

CLIFTON FORGE, a city of western Virginia, U.S., amid the superb scenery of the Allegheny mountains, on the Jackson river; in Alleghany county, but administratively independent of it. It is on federal highways 60 and 220, and is served by the Chesapeake and Ohio railway. Pop. (1950) 5,795; (1940) 6,461. The city has railroad repair shops, is a distributing point for coal from the near-by fields and is headquarters of the western division of the Virginia Electric & Power company. Clifton Forge, formerly called Williamson, was incorporated in 1884. Iron Gate gap with the rainbow rock formation on either side, is the natural pass through the mountains formed by the river and used by travellers since Indian days. Douthat State park is near by.

CLIMACTERIC, a critical period in human life (from the Gr. κλιμακτήρ, the rung or step of a ladder); in a medical sense, the period known as the "change of life," marked in women by the menopause (*q.v.*). The word is also used of any turning point in the history of a nation, a career, etc.

CLIMATE, ARTIFICIAL. Climate usually signifies the external factors which affect animals and plants, such as solar radiation, humidity, gaseous composition of the air, temperature and air movement. The mechanical control of these factors constitutes artificial climate. In 1933 the John B. Pierce Laboratory of Hygiene was established in New York city for the study of man's relationship to his thermal environment both from the physical and physiological standpoints, marking the beginning of the modern approach to the science of air conditioning. That climatic conditions affect health is generally recognized, and records can be found showing increased mortality rates accompanying local periods of unseasonal weather such as the "hot week" of 1934 in the U.S. during which the death rate was doubled. That the human body periodically displays seasonal variations to climatic changes is shown by variations in blood chemistry, endocrine functions, resistance to infectious diseases and, as noted, even mortality.

The modern aspect of artificial climate regulation for animals and man involves primarily temperature, humidity and air movement; *i.e.*, it is physical more than chemical. As F. S. Lee pointed out, the major problems are physical rather than chemical, cutaneous rather than respiratory. Oversimplification of the problem is dangerous, however. Simple measurement of total heat exchange has been replaced by partitional calorimetry. Since heat production by the body is chemical and heat loss physical, the maintenance of body temperature becomes the balance between heat production (thermogenesis) and heat loss (thermolysis).

Man.—Of major importance to comfort is humidity. Under proper humidity conditions greater extremes of temperature can be tolerated by man, especially high temperatures. In dry air, for example, man has endured an external temperature of 164° F., which is high enough to cook meat.

The proper use of clothing aids man to keep comfortable in extremely warm or cold climates. If rate of air movement is adequate, relative humidity becomes less important at high temperatures. The lower room temperatures used in England are related to the heavier clothing worn and acclimatization. Up until about 1930–40, homes in the U.S. were less well heated, and heavier clothes were worn than in the following decades.

A. P. Gagge and his coworkers found that ideal comfort is experienced when three conditions are maintained—a skin temperature of 91.5° F., a minimum heat change in the body tissues and a minimum evaporative rate. An average person radiates enough heat to raise the temperature of 30 cu.ft. of air 9° F. per minute; thus air movement in public gathering places should be equivalent to 30 ft. per person per minute. The incoming air should be slightly cooler than the room air to remove the heat produced by the occupants. In modern homes with air conditioning it becomes necessary to humidify the air in winter by various means for best respiratory comfort. In summer, conversely, moisture should be removed from the air in many localities for best physiological comfort. Often humidity control alone is adequate for comfort. Relative humidity of from 55% to 60% is usually sought. In critical experiments by C. E. A. Winslow and L. P. Herrington the effect of humidity on the drying of mucous membranes of the nose and throat was measured. They found the absolute moisture content of the air and not the relative humidity to be the critical factor. Thus the air of the schoolroom in winter with 10% relative humidity at 70° F. is no more harmful to the child than outside air of 14° F. saturated with moisture. Based on the fact that the critical point for drying of the mucosae of the mouth is 0.40 in. vapour pressure, drying must occur at air temperatures below 53° F. with any moisture content, at 60° with less than 77% relative humidity, at 70° with less than 54% relative humidity, and at 80° with less than 39% relative humidity. D. H. K. Lee disagreed with the generally accepted opinion that a hot, moist climate tends to impair vigour in children. He compared the "ideal" climate of D. Brunt of 66° to 68° F. and 60% humidity with air-conditioned houses in the U.S. with temperatures up to 78° F. Man can be acclimatized to tropical climates with greater ease than generally expected once infectious tropical diseases are overcome.

Plants.—The artificial control of climate finds extensive use in the culture and storage of plants. Temperature and light are the factors most commonly controlled. Widespread use of such controls is made by the greenhouse industry, which covered nearly 1,000 ac. in the United States alone in 1950; and, in addition, temperature controls are used considerably in the storage of fruits and vegetables.

Storage facilities for horticultural products included more than 500,000 cu.ft. in the United States in 1950. Artificial climates also find an extremely valuable use in research relating to the growth and development of plants.

Temperature Control.—A wide variety of plant physiological processes are influenced by temperature, such as the rate of water evaporation from leaves, the rate of photosynthesis, the translocation of food materials and the type of metabolism carried out in the cells of the plant. Some crops require a high temperature for healthy growth, for example, Saintpaulia or African violet, which thrives only when temperatures are 70° F. or above. Others require low temperatures, especially at night. An example of this is the poinsettia, which is normally grown with day temperatures of from 75° to 85° F. and a night temperature of 60° F. It is very common for plants to require lowered temperatures at night. This requirement for a daily temperature cycle is termed thermoperiodism. The requirement for low night temperatures is thought to be a consequence of improved transport of food substances about the plant. Small plants commonly do not require a diurnal temperature function, apparently because transport is relatively unimportant to them. As the plant becomes larger, however, the diurnal temperature cycle is required.

Temperatures may be controlled for special physiological effects; *e.g.*, low temperatures are commonly used to bring about flowering in poinsettias or to increase the vigour of winter species of grains (a process called vernalization). High temperatures are used to hasten the flowering of many florist crops, particularly the spring bulbs.

Light Control.—A primary function of light is supplying the energy for photosynthesis, the basic source of all plant foods.

Artificial light is sometimes used to increase the light intensity in the culture of winter greenhouse crops. This practice is common in the low countries of northern Europe for the culture of greenhouse tomatoes. For other crops shading is frequently used to reduce light intensity in the summer. Large houses of cheesecloth are commonly erected in fields of tobacco for shading.

In greenhouses, however, light is artificially altered not so much for the photosynthetic effect as for the effects on plant development. As in the case of temperature, many plants are highly sensitive to the diurnal cycle of light and darkness. Some plants will flower only under cycles in which they experience short days and long nights, chrysanthemum and ragweed being common examples. Other plants require the opposite situation for flowering, in which they experience long days and short nights as do sugar beet, spinach and onions. Because of such sensitivity to day and night length (photoperiodism), artificial control of the length of day (or the length of night) can be used effectively to prevent or force flowering in many plants.

Research workers have discovered that the length of the night is generally the determining factor in responses to seasonal changes of day length both in plants and in animals. Hence long-day type of behaviour can be maintained by simply supplying a brief exposure to light in the middle of each long night. This technique is commonly used to prevent flowering of chrysanthemums and poinsettias until appropriate seasons for the advantageous sale in the winter. Chrysanthemums are commercially forced into early flowering for the autumn market by means of large tents of black cloth which are draped over the plants daily so as to give them the long night required for flowering.

Egg laying by chickens is carried on only under long-day conditions, and lights are used to extend the day in winter seasons when natural days are too short.

In artificial climates for the maintenance of plants in homes or business establishments it is generally sufficient to suspend 150-w. reflector-flood lights over the plants about 3 ft. from the foliage. For the growth of plants over longer periods of time, the filament type light bulb does not provide enough blue light, and hence a closely packed bank of fluorescent light bulbs is necessary as well. For disrupting the night period, very weak light intensities are sufficient. Some plants will not respond to long nights if they receive as little as 0.1 foot candle of light through the night. This intensity is only slightly above the maximum intensity of moonlight.

Other Factors.—Beside temperature and light, other factors of climate which are commonly controlled are humidity, air movement and the carbon dioxide content of the air. Humidity can be raised conveniently in greenhouses by spreading a porous material like coke over the ground and keeping this sprinkled with water. Mist nozzle sprayers are also used. Most fruits and vegetables wilt in storage if the humidity is below 85%. Air movement is controlled in the storage of fruit products known to emit gases which either alter the flavour or the maturation of the fruit itself. Rapid air movement is maintained commonly in apple storages to prevent accumulation of volatile gases, especially ethylene. Control of carbon dioxide is not usually carried out commercially even though large increases in plant growth can be obtained by increasing the air content of this gas. (*See* also CLIMATE AND CLIMATOLOGY; CLIMATE IN THE TREATMENT OF DISEASE; DAYLIGHT, ARTIFICIAL; HELIOTHERAPY.)

BIBLIOGRAPHY.—A. P. Gagge and L. P. Herrington, "Physiological Effects of Heat and Cold," *Ann. Rev. Physiol.*, 9:409–428 (1947); D. H. K. Lee, "Heat and Cold," *ibid.*, 10:365–386 (1948); C. E. A. Winslow and L. P. Herrington, *Temperature and Human Life* (Princeton, London, 1949); A. E. Murneek, *et al.*, *Vernalization and Photoperiodism* (Waltham, Mass., 1948).

(W. A. HD.; A. C. L.)

CLIMATE AND CLIMATOLOGY. The word *clima* (from Gr. κλίνειν, to lean or incline) was used by the Greeks for the supposed slope of the earth towards the pole, or for the inclination of the earth's axis. A change of *clima* then meant a change of latitude. The latter was gradually seen to mean a change in atmospheric conditions as well as in length of day, and *clima* thus came to have its present meaning. "Climate" is the average condition of the atmosphere. "Weather" denotes a single occurrence, or event, in the series of conditions which make up climate. The climate of a place is thus in a sense its average weather. Climatology is the study or science of climates; it is a branch of the science of meteorology (*q.v.*).

Climatic Elements and Their Treatment.—Climatology has to deal with the atmospheric conditions which affect human

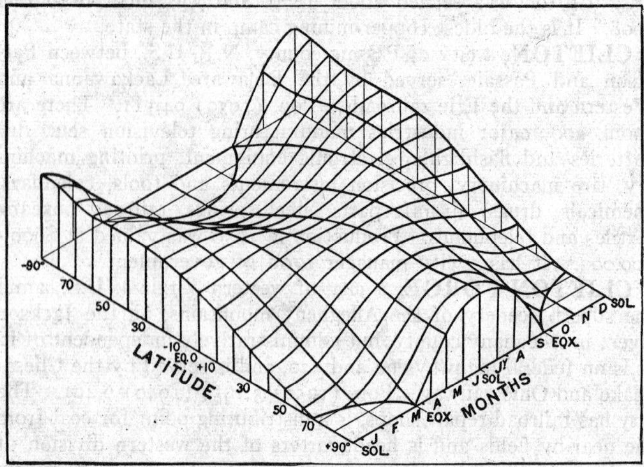

FROM DAVIS, "ELEMENTARY METEOROLOGY" BY PERMISSION OF GINN & CO.

FIG. 1.—CLIMATOLOGY: DIAGRAM OF RELATIVE AMOUNTS OF INSOLATION RECEIVED AT DIFFERENT LATITUDES IN DIFFERENT MONTHS
Latitudes are shown on left margin, months on right, and values by the vertical distance above the plane of the two margins

life, viz., temperature (including radiation); moisture (including humidity, precipitation and cloudiness); wind (including storms) and evaporation. Climate deals first with average conditions, but a satisfactory presentation of a climate must take account, also, of regular and irregular daily, monthly and annual changes, and of local departures, mean and extreme, from the average conditions. The mean minimum and maximum temperatures or rainfalls of a month or a season are important data. Further, a determination of the frequency of occurrence of a given condition, or of certain values of that condition, is important, for periods of a day, month or year, as for example the frequency of winds according to direction or velocity; or of different amounts of cloudiness. The probability of occurrence of any condition, as of rain in a certain month, is also a useful thing to know.

Solar Climate.—Climate, in so far as it is controlled solely by the amount of solar radiation which any place receives by reason of its latitude, is called solar climate. Solar climate alone would prevail if the earth had a homogeneous land surface, and if there were no atmosphere. The relative amounts of insolation received at different latitudes and at different times at the upper limit of the earth's atmosphere, *i.e.*, without the effect of absorption by the atmosphere, are shown in fig. 1 after Davis. The latitudes are given at the left margin and the time of year at the right margin. The values of insolation are shown by the vertical distance above the plane of the two margins. At the Equator, where the day is always 12 hours long, there are two maxima of insolation at the equinoxes, when the sun is vertical at noon, and two minima at the solstices when the sun is farthest off the Equator. The values do not vary much through the year because the sun is never very far from the zenith, and day and night are always equal. As latitude increases, the angle of insolation becomes more oblique and the intensity decreases, but at the same time the length of day rapidly increases during the summer, and towards the pole of the hemisphere which is having its summer, the gain in insolation from the latter cause more than compensates for the loss by the former. The double period of insolation above noted for the equator prevails as far as about lat. 12° N. and S.; at lat. 15° the two maxima have united in one, and the same is true of the minima. At the pole there is one maximum at the summer solstice, and no insolation at all while the sun is below the horizon. On June 21 the Equator has a day 12hr. long, but the sun does not reach the zenith, and the amount of insolation is therefore less than at the equinox. On the northern tropic, however, the sun is vertical at noon, and the day is more than 12hr. long. Hence the amount of insolation received at this latitude is greater than that received at the equinox at the Equator. From the tropic to the pole the sun stands lower and lower at noon, and the value of insolation would steadily decrease with latitude if it were not for the increase in the length of day. Going polewards from the northern tropic on June 21, the value of insolation increases for a time, because although the sun is lower, the number of hours during which it shines is greater. A maximum value is reached at about lat. 43½°N. The decreasing altitude of the sun then more than compensates for the increasing length of day, and the value of insolation diminishes, a secondary minimum being reached at about lat. 62°. Then the rapidly increasing length of day towards the pole again brings about an increase in the value of insolation, until a maximum is reached at the pole which is greater than the value received at the Equator at any time.

On June 21 there are therefore two maxima of insolation, one at lat. 43½° and one at the north pole. From lat. 43½° N., insolation decreases to zero on the Antarctic circle, for sunshine falls more and more obliquely, and the day becomes shorter and shorter. Beyond lat. 66½° S. the night lasts 24 hours. On Dec. 21 the conditions in southern latitudes are similar to those in the northern hemisphere on June 21, but the southern latitudes have higher values of insolation because the earth is then nearer the sun. At the equinox the days are equal everywhere, but the noon sun is lower and lower with increasing latitude in both hemispheres until the rays are tangent to the earth's surface at the poles (except for the effect of refraction). Therefore, the values of insolation diminish from a maximum at the Equator to a minimum at both poles.

The earth's atmosphere weakens the sun's rays. The more nearly vertical the sun, the less the thickness of atmosphere traversed by the rays. The values of insolation at the earth's surface vary with the condition of the air as to dust, clouds, water vapour, etc. As a rule, even when the sky is clear, about one-half of the solar radiation is lost during the day by atmospheric absorption. The great weakening of insolation at the pole, where the sun is very low, is especially noticeable. The following table (after Angot) shows the effect of the earth's atmosphere (coefficient of transmission 0·7) upon the value of insolation received at sea-level.

Values of Daily Insolation at the Upper Limit of the Earth's Atmosphere and at Sea-Level

Lat.	Upper limit of atmosphere			Earth's surface		
	Equator	40°	N. pole	Equator	40°	N. pole
Winter solstice	948	360	0	552	124	0
Equinoxes	1000	773	0	612	411	0
Summer solstice	888	1115	1210	517	660	494

These values are relative only; during the present century the Astrophysical Observatory of the Smithsonian Institution of Washington, under the direction of C. G. Abbot, has estimated the actual intensity of the sun's radiation at the limit of the earth's atmosphere as 1·95 gramme-calories per sq.cm. per minute. (*See* RADIATION, RAYS.) This value is termed the "solar constant," though it varies within about five per cent. on either side of this mean value. The value of 1,000 on the above scale represents about 940 gramme-calories per sq.cm. of horizontal surface.

Physical Climate.—The distribution of insolation explains many of the large facts of temperature distribution; for example, the decrease of temperature from Equator to poles; the double maximum of temperature on and near the Equator; the increasing seasonal contrasts with increasing latitude, etc. But the regular distribution of solar climate between Equator and poles which would exist on a homogeneous earth, whereby similar conditions prevail along each latitude circle, is very much modified by the unequal distribution of land and water; by difference of altitude; by air and ocean currents, by varying conditions of cloudiness and so on. The uniform arrangement of solar climatic belts arranged latitudinally is interfered with, and what is known as *physical climate* results. According to the dominant control we have solar, continental and marine, and mountain climates. In the first-named, latitude is the essential; in the second and third, the influence of land or water; in the fourth, the effect of altitude.

Classification of the Zones by Latitude Circles.—The five familiar zones are the so-called torrid, the two temperate and the two frigid zones. The torrid zone is limited north and south by the Tropics of Cancer and Capricorn, the Equator dividing the zone into two equal parts. The temperate zones are limited towards the Equator by the Tropics, and towards the poles by the Arctic and Antarctic circles. The two polar zones are caps covering both polar regions, and bounded on the side towards the Equator by the Arctic and Antarctic circles. These are really zones of solar climate. The tropical zone has the greatest annual amount and the least annual variation of insolation. Its annual range of temperature is very slight. Beyond the Tropics the contrasts between the seasons rapidly become more marked. The polar zones have the greatest variation in insolation between summer and winter. They also have the minimum amount of insolation for the whole year; their summer is so short and cool that the heat is insufficient for most forms of vegetation, especially for trees. The temperate zones are intermediate between the tropical and the polar in the matter of annual amount and of annual variation of insolation. Temperate conditions do not characterize these zones as a whole. They are rather the seasonal belts of the world.

Temperature Zones.—The astronomical classification of the zones serves very well for purposes of simple description, but a glance at any isothermal chart shows that the isotherms do not coincide with the latitude lines. In fact, in the higher latitudes, the former sometimes follow the meridians more closely than they do the parallels of latitude. Hence it has been suggested that the zones be limited by isotherms rather than by parallels of latitude, and that a closer approach be thus made to the actual conditions of climate. Supan[1] has suggested limiting the hot belt, which corresponds to, but is slightly greater than, the old torrid zone, by the two mean annual isotherms of 68° F—an isothermal line which approximately coincides with the polar limits of the

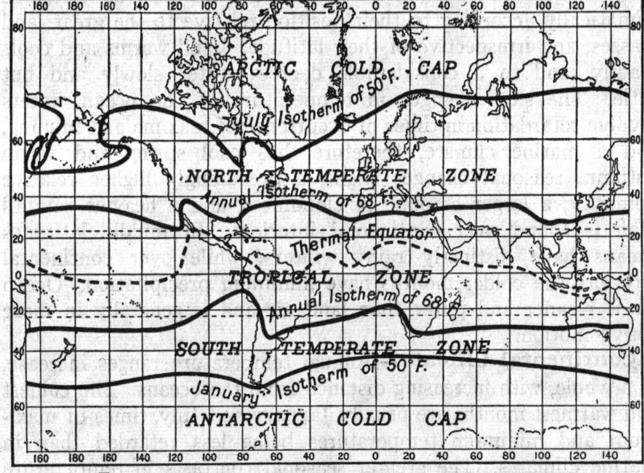

FIG. 2.—DIAGRAM SHOWING ZONES OF TEMPERATURE

trade-winds and with the natural distribution of palms. The limits of these zones, according to the most recent information, are shown in fig. 2. The hot belt widens somewhat over the continents, chiefly because there is a tendency towards an equalization of the temperature between Equator and poles in the oceans, while the stable lands acquire a temperature suitable to their own latitude. Furthermore, the unsymmetrical distribution of land in low latitudes of northern and southern hemispheres makes the hot belt

[1]A Supan, *Grundzüge der physischen Erdkunde* (Leipzig, 1896), 88–89. Also *Atlas of Meteorology*, Pl. 1.

extend farther north than south of the Equator. The polar limits of the temperate zones are fixed by the isotherm of 50° F for the warmest month. Summer heat is more important for vegetation than winter cold, and where the warmest month has a temperature below 50° F cereals and forest trees do not grow. The two polar caps are not symmetrical. Extended land masses in high northern latitudes carry the temperature of 50° F in the warmest month farther poleward there than is the case in high southern latitudes occupied by the oceans which warm less easily and are constantly in motion. Hence the southern cold cap, with equatorial limits at about lat. 50° S., is much larger than the northern polar cap. The northern temperate belt in which the great land areas lie is much broader than the southern belt, especially over the continents. These temperature zones emphasize the natural conditions of climate more than is the case in any subdivision by latitude circles, and they bear a fairly close resemblance to the old zonal classification of the Greeks.

Classification of Climates.—The best and most logical form of classification is one which takes account of all the different climatic elements. Such a scheme has been prepared by W. Köppen (*Die Klimate der Erde,* Berlin and Leipzig 1923) and assigns almost as much importance to rainfall as to temperature. Since the rainfall depends largely on prevailing winds, this classification also takes account of the zones of wind. Eight main zones are distinguished and divided and subdivided into a number of climatic provinces and smaller areas. Each subdivision is distinguished by a formula comprised of the main division followed by the initial letters of its characteristics: *e.g.,* the climate of Swakopmund is described as *BWkn,* which means a sub-tropical (B) desert (Wüste) climate with a cold (kalt) winter and frequent fog (Nebel). The eight zones are: A tropical rain zone with the coldest month usually above 64° F and rainfall above the limit of dryness (which varies according to the temperature and the seasonal distribution of rain); two zones of dry (steppe and desert) climate; two zones of warm temperate rain climate with the mean temperature of the coldest month between 64° and 27° F. (these include the "Mediterranean" and most of the "monsoon" climatic areas); a zone of "boreal" or snow and forest climate (with hot summers and cold winters below 27° F), which requires a large area of land and is consequently missing in the southern hemisphere; and two polar caps of "snow climate" with the mean temperature of the warmest month below 50° F.

Marine or Oceanic Climate.—Areas can also be classified climatically according to their position relative to the great land masses, and irrespective of their latitude. Land warms and cools readily, and to a considerable degree; water slowly and but little. The slow changes in temperature of the ocean waters involve retardation in times of occurrence of maxima and minima, and a marine climate, therefore, has cool spring and warm autumn, seasonal changes slight, a prevailingly higher relative humidity, a larger amount of cloudiness, and a heavier rainfall than is found over continental interiors. In middle latitudes oceans have distinctly rainy winters, while over continental interiors the colder months have minimum precipitation. Ocean air is cleaner and purer than land air and is generally in more active motion.

Continental Climate.—Annual temperature ranges increase, as a whole, with increasing distance from the oceans. The coldest and warmest months are usually January and July, times of maximum and minimum temperatures being less retarded than in marine climates. The greater seasonal contrasts in temperature over the continents than over the oceans are furthered by the smaller humidity and cloudiness over the former. Diurnal and annual changes of nearly all elements of climate, irregular as well as regular, are greater over continents than over oceans. Fig. 3 illustrates the annual march of temperature in marine and continental climates. Jacobabad in India (J), and Funchal on the island of Madeira (M) are representative continental and marine stations for a low latitude. Olekminsk in Siberia (Ol) and Lerwick in the Shetlands (L) are good examples of continental and marine climates of higher latitudes in the northern hemisphere.

Owing to distance from chief source of water vapour—the oceans—air over the larger land areas is drier and dustier than that over the oceans. Yet even in arid continental interiors in summer absolute vapour content is surprisingly large, and in the hottest months percentages of relative humidity may reach 20% or 30%; *e.g.,* in July, Luktschum with an average temperature of 90° and a relative humidity of 31 per cent. has more moisture in the air than Valentia with a temperature of 59° and a relative humidity of 83 per cent. Cloudiness, as a rule, decreases inland, and with this lower relative humidity, more abundant sunshine and higher temperature, the evaporating power of a continental climate in summer is much greater than that of the more humid, cloudier and cooler marine climate. Both amount and frequency of rainfall, as a rule, decrease inland, but conditions are very largely controlled by local topography and prevailing winds. Winds average somewhat lower in velocity, and calms are more frequent, over continents than over oceans. Seasonal changes of pressure over the former give rise to systems of inflowing and out-flowing, so-called continental, winds, sometimes so well developed as to become true monsoons. Extreme temperature changes over continents are the more easily borne because of the dryness of the air; because the minimum temperature of winter occurs when there is little or no wind, and because during the warmer hours of the summer there is the most air-movement.

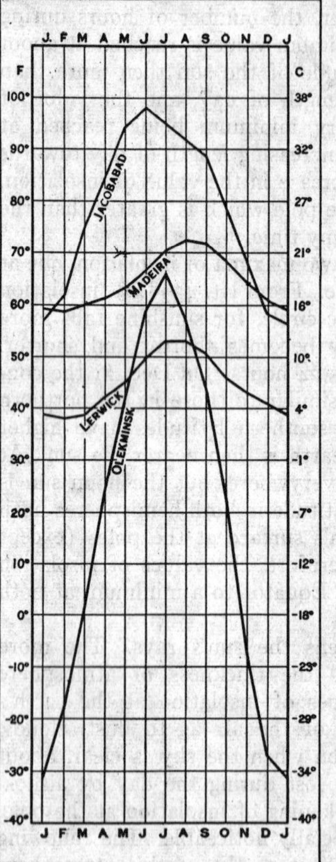

FIG. 3.—ANNUAL TREND OF AIR TEMPERATURE, SHOWING INFLUENCE OF CLIMATES IN LOW AND HIGH LATITUDES

Desert Climate.—Desert air is notably free from micro-organisms. The large diurnal temperature ranges of inland regions, which are most marked where there is little or no vegetation, give rise to active convectional currents during the warmer hours of the day. Hence high winds are common by day, while the nights are apt to be calm and relatively cool. Diurnal cumulus clouds, often absent because of excessive dryness, are replaced by clouds of blowing dust. Excessive diurnal ranges of temperature cause rocks to split and break up. Wind-driven sand erodes and polishes the rocks. When the separate fragments become small enough they, in their turn, are transported by the winds and further eroded by friction during their journey. Rivers "wither" away, or end in brackish lakes.

Coast or Littoral Climate.—Between pure marine and pure continental types coasts furnish almost every grade of transition. Prevailing winds are here important controls. When these blow from the ocean, climates are marine in character, but when they are off-shore, a modified continental climate prevails, even up to the immediate sea-coast. The former have smaller range of temperature; the air is damp, and there is much cloud. All these marine features diminish with increasing distance from the ocean, especially when there are mountain ranges near the coast. In the Tropics, windward coasts are usually well supplied with rainfall, and temperatures are modified by sea breezes. Leeward coasts in the trade-wind belts offer special conditions. Here deserts often reach the sea, as on the western coasts of South America, Africa and Australia. Cold ocean currents, with prevailing winds along-shore rather than on-shore, are here hostile to cloud and rainfall, although the lower air is often damp, and fog is common in these regions.

Monsoon Climate.—Exceptions to the general rule of rainier eastern coasts in trade-wind latitudes are found in monsoon regions, as in India, for example, where the western coast gets much rain from the south-west monsoon. As monsoons often sweep over large districts, not only coast but interior, a separate group of monsoon climates is desirable. In India there are really three seasons—the cool winter, the hot transition, and the wet summer monsoon. Little precipitation occurs in winter, and that chiefly in the northern provinces. The winter monsoon is normally off-shore and the summer monsoon on-shore, but exceptional cases are found where the opposite is true, as in north-east Ceylon. In higher latitudes the seasonal changes of the winds, although not truly monsoonal, involve differences in temperature and in other climatic elements. The only well-developed monsoons on the coast of the continents of higher latitudes are those of eastern Asia. These are off-shore during the winter, giving dry, clear and cold weather; while the on-shore movement in summer gives cool, damp and cloudy weather.

Mountain and Plateau Climate.—Temperature decreases upwards at an average rate of 3° per 1,000ft., and for this reason and also because of their obstructive effects, mountains are important climatic factors. Mountains as contrasted with lowlands are characterized by decrease in pressure, temperature and absolute humidity; increased intensity of insolation and radiation; usually greater frequency of, and up to a certain altitude more, precipitation. The highest habitations are about 16,000ft. above sea-level, at which altitude pressure has about half its sea-level value. The intensity of the sun's rays is very great in the cleaner, drier and thinner mountain air. Vertical decrease of temperature is especially rapid during warmer months and hours; mountains are then cooler than lowlands. The inversions of temperature characteristic of the colder months, and of the night, give mountains the advantage of a higher temperature then. At such times cold air flows down the mountain sides and collects in the valleys, being replaced by warmer air aloft. Hence diurnal and annual ranges of temperature on the mountain tops of middle and higher latitudes are lessened and the climate in this respect resembles the marine. High enclosed valleys often show continental conditions of large temperature range and such valleys in Europe open to the north-east form local "Siberias." Plateaus, as compared with mountains at the same altitude, have relatively higher temperatures and larger temperature ranges. Altitude tempers heat in low latitudes. High mountain peaks, even on the Equator, can remain snow-covered all the year round.

No general law governs variations of relative humidity with altitude, but on the mountains of Europe winter is the driest season, and summer the dampest. At well-exposed stations there is a rapid increase in the vapour content soon after noon, especially in summer. The same is true of cloudiness, often greater on mountains than at lower levels, and usually greatest in summer when it is least in the lowlands. The higher Alpine valleys in winter have little cloud. This, combined with their low wind velocity and strong sunshine and the night temperature inversions, makes them winter health resorts. Owing to forced ascent of air over rising ground, rainfall usually increases with height up to a certain point, beyond which, owing to loss of water vapour, this increase stops. The zone of maximum rainfall averages about 6,000ft. to 7,000ft. in altitude in intermediate latitudes, being lower in winter and higher in summer. When there is a prevailing wind from one direction, the lee side of the mountains, and the neighbouring lowlands, are relatively dry, forming a "rain shadow." Mountains resemble marine climates in having higher wind velocities than continental lowlands. Mountain summits have a nocturnal maximum of wind velocity, while plateaus usually have a diurnal maximum.

THE TORRID ZONE

Climate and Weather.—Climatic features here are simple and uniform. Periodic phenomena, depending upon the daily and annual march of the sun, are dominant; non-periodic weather changes are wholly subordinate. In special regions only, and at special seasons, is the regular sequence interrupted by an occasional tropical cyclone. These cyclones are comparatively infrequent and generally bring very heavy rains; the devastation one may produce often affects the economic conditions for many years.

Temperature.—Mean temperature is very high, and very uniform over the whole zone, with little variation during the year. The mean annual isotherm of 68° F. is a rational limit at the polar margins of the zone, and the mean annual isotherm of 80° F. encloses the greater portion of the land areas, as well as much of the inter-tropical oceans. The warmest latitude circle for the year is not the equator, but latitude 10° N. The highest mean annual temperatures, shown by the isotherm of 85°F., are in Central Africa, in India, the north of Australia and Central America, but, with the exception of the first, these areas are small. The temperatures average highest where there is little rain. In June, July and August there are large districts in the south of Asia and north of Africa with temperatures over 90° F.

Over nearly all the zone mean annual range of temperature is less than 10° F., and over much of it, especially on the oceans, less than 5° F. Even near the margins of the zone the ranges are less than 25° F., as at Calcutta, Hongkong, Rio de Janeiro and Khartoum. Mean daily range is usually larger than mean annual; "night is the winter of the Tropics." Over parts of the Pacific and Indian oceans from Arabia to the Caroline islands and from Zanzibar to New Guinea, as well as on the Guiana coast, minimum temperatures do not normally fall below 68° F. Towards the margins of the zone, however, the minima on the continents fall to or even below 32° F. Maxima of over 120° F. occur over the deserts of northern Africa and a reading of 136° F. at Azizia in Tunis is the highest known shade temperature. A district where the mean maxima exceed 113° F. extends from the western Sahara to north-western India, and over Central Australia. Near the Equator the maxima are not so high; and inter-tropical oceans show remarkably small variations in temperature.

The Seasons.—In a true inter-tropical climate the seasons depend not on temperature, but on rainfall and the prevailing winds. Life is regulated in some cases almost wholly by rainfall. Although the rain is characteristically associated with a vertical sun, that season is not necessarily the hottest. Towards the margins of the zone, with increasing annual ranges of temperature, seasons in the extra-tropical sense gradually appear. The association of uniformly high heat and humidity at most low-level places near the Equator is very enervating, and energetic physical or mental activity is difficult or impossible for white men. The absence of a bracing cold winter is a great drawback and the uniformity of conditions makes one sensitive to slight changes of temperature. The drier interior regions are more healthy, and the most energetic natives are the desert dwellers.

Pressure, Winds and Rainfall.—Pressure is lowest near the equator, in the belt of doldrums. Here the pressure gradients are small, and calms, variable winds and heavy rain and thunderstorms prevail. This region is one of the rainiest in the world, averaging about 100in., and the sky is generally cloudy; it includes the dense forests of the Amazon and equatorial Africa. The doldrums extend from the Equator to about 10° N., but do not include any part of the southern hemisphere; on either side are the belts of trade winds, the north-east trade from about 10° to 30° N. and the south-east trade from about 0° to 25° S. The trades are extremely regular and stable and except where they strike windward coasts or high mountains they bring fine bracing weather. Over oceans the skies show small detached clouds (trade cumulus) but over the western and central parts of the continents the trade wind latitudes are desert—the Sahara and Arabia, Kalahari and the desert of Australia. The boundaries between the trade winds and the doldrums move north and south following the sun, giving a "winter" dry season and a "summer" rainy season, which near the equator is divided into two by a minor dry season shortly after the summer solstice. Monsoons occur on many of the tropical lands, the best known being those of southern and eastern Asia. In the northern summer the south-west monsoon, warm and moist, blows over the latitudes from about 10°

N. to and beyond the northern tropic, between Africa and the Philippines, giving rains over India, the East Indian archipelago and the eastern coasts of China. In winter, the north-east monsoon, the normal cold-season outflow from Asia, combined with the north-east trade, and generally cool and dry, covers the same district, coming from as far north as lat. 30° N. Crossing the Equator, these winds reach northern Australia and the western islands of the South Pacific as a north-west rainy monsoon, while this region in the opposite season has the normal south-east trade. Other monsoons are found in the Gulf of Guinea and in equatorial Africa. Wherever they occur they control the seasonal changes.

The regular occurrence and cool, clean air of the sea breeze make many districts habitable for white settlers. On not a few coasts the sea breeze is a true prevailing wind. The location of dwellings is often determined by exposure of a site to the sea breeze.

Local thunderstorms are frequent, have a marked diurnal periodicity, find their best opportunity in the equatorial belt of weak pressure gradients and high temperature, and are commonly associated with the rainy season, being most common at the beginning and end of the regular rains. In many places intense thunderstorms occur daily throughout the rainy season.

Cloudiness.—The average cloudiness of the tropics does not differ greatly from that in temperate regions. The mean, in tenths of sky covered, is shown by the following table:—

Latitude	30°–20° N.	20°–10° N.	10°N–0°.	0°–10° S.	10°–20° S.	20°–30° S.
Land . .	3·4	4·0	5·2	5·6	4·6	3·8
Sea . .	4·9	5·3	5·3	5·0	4·9	5·3
Mean . .	4·1	4·7	5·3	5·2	4·8	4·8

Both wholly clear and wholly overcast days are rare in the Tropics; the sky is more usually about half clouded.

CLIMATIC SUBDIVISIONS

The Equatorial Belt.—Within a few degrees of the Equator and when not interfered with by other controls, the annual curve of temperature has two maxima following the two zenithal positions of the sun, and two minima at about the time of the solstices. This equatorial type of annual march of temperature is illustrated in the three curves for Brazzaville, Batavia and Ocean island (fig. 4). The greatest range is shown in the curve for Brazzaville, inland in the Congo valley; the curve for Batavia illustrates insular conditions with less range, and that for Ocean island oceanic conditions with a range of only 0·5° F.

FIG. 4.—ANNUAL TREND OF TEMPERATURE FOR EQUATORIAL REGIONS
Heat for Brazzaville (Congo) is greatest

As the belt of rains swings back and forth across the Equator after the sun, there should be two rainy seasons with the sun vertical, and two dry seasons when the sun is farthest from the zenith, and while the trades blow. These conditions prevail on the Equator, and as far north and south of the Equator (about 10°–12°) as sufficient time elapses between the two zenithal positions of the sun for the two rainy seasons to be distinguished from one another. In this belt there is therefore normally no long dry season. The double rainy season is clearly seen in equatorial Africa and in parts of equatorial South America. The maxima lag somewhat behind the vertical sun, coming in April and November, and the first is the greater one. The minima are also unsymmetrically developed, and the so-called "dry seasons" are seldom wholly rainless. This rainfall type with double maxima and minima has been called the equatorial type, and is illustrated in the curves for Entebbe and Bogota (fig. 5). The annual totals are given. These double rainy and dry seasons are easily modified by other conditions, as by the monsoons of the Indo-Australian areas, so that there is no rigid belt of equatorial rains extending around the world. In South America, east of the Andes the distinction between rainy and dry seasons is often much confused. The annual variation of cloudiness is illustrated by the curve for Ocean island (Oc) in fig. 6, but the annual period varies greatly under local controls.

At greater distances from the Equator than about 10° or 12° the sun is still vertical twice a year within the Tropics, but the interval between these two dates is so short that the two rainy seasons merge into one, in summer, and there is also but one dry season, in winter. This is the so-called tropical type of rainfall, and is found where the trade belts are encroached upon by the equatorial rains during the migration of these rains into each hemisphere. It is illustrated in the curves for São Paulo, Brazil, and for the city of Mexico (fig. 5). The tropical type of rainfall occurs beyond the margins of the region of equatorial rainfall and as we go farther towards the lines of the tropics the rainy season shortens to four months or less, lowlands often become parched during the long dry season (winter), while life resumes activity when the rains return (summer). The Sudan receives rains, and its vegetation grows actively when the doldrum belt is north of the equator (May–August). But when the trades blow (December–March) the ground is parched and dusty. The Venezuelan *llanos* have a dry season in the northern winter, when the trade blows. The rains come in May–October. The *campos* of Brazil, south of the Equator, have their rains in October–April, and are dry the remainder of the year. The Nile overflow results from the rainfall on the mountains of Abyssinia during the northward migration of the belt of equatorial rains.

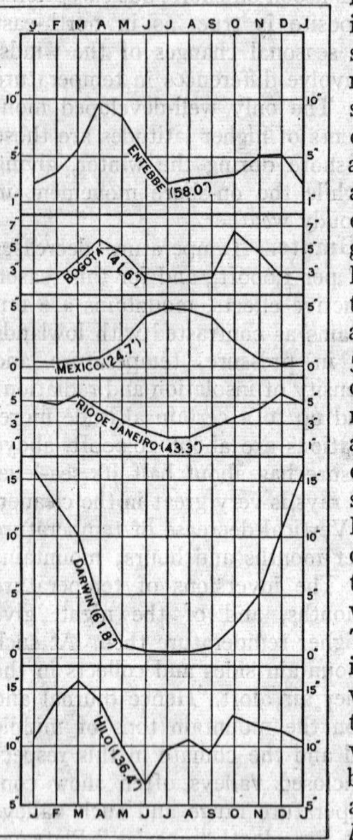

FIG. 5.—ANNUAL TREND OF RAINFALL IN TROPICS, TOTALS GIVEN IN INCHES

The so-called tropical type of temperature variation, with one maximum and one minimum, is illustrated in the accompanying curves for Wadi Halfa, in upper Egypt; Alice Springs, Australia; Nagpur, India; and St. Helena (fig. 7). The effect of the rainy season is often shown in a displacement of the time of maximum temperature to an earlier month than the usual one as at Nagpur.

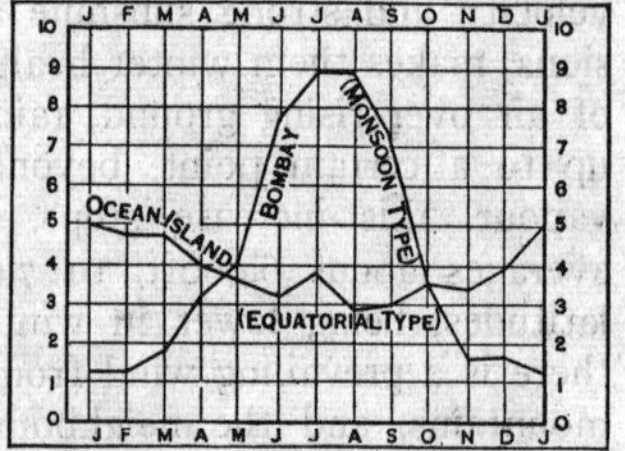

FIG. 6.—ANNUAL TREND OF CLOUDINESS IN TROPICS, WITH EFFECT OF MONSOON

Trade-Wind Belts.—The trade belts near sea-level have fair weather, steady winds, infrequent light rains or even an almost complete absence of rain, very regular, although slight, annual and diurnal ranges of temperature, and constancy and regularity of weather. The climate of ocean areas in the trade-wind belts is indeed the simplest and most equable in the world, the greatest extremes over these oceans being found to leeward of the larger lands. On the lowlands swept over by the trades, beyond the polar limits of the equatorial rain belt (roughly between lats. 20° and 30°), are most of the great deserts of the world. These deserts extend directly to the water's edge on the leeward western coasts of Australia, Africa and America. Ranges and extremes of temperature are much greater over continental interiors than over oceans in trade-wind belts. Minima of 32° or less occur during clear, quiet nights, and daily ranges of over 50° are common. Midsummer mean temperature rises above 90°, with noon maxima of 110° or more in the non-cloudy, dry air of a desert day. The days, with high, dry winds, carrying dust and sand, with extreme heat, accentuated by absence of vegetation, are disagreeable, but the calmer nights, with active radiation under clear skies, are much more comfortable. Nocturnal temperatures are often low, and thin sheets of ice may form.

While the trades are drying winds as long as they blow strongly over the oceans, or over lowlands, they readily become rainy if cooled by ascent. Hence the windward eastern sides of mountains or bold coasts in the trade-wind belts are well watered, while the leeward sides, or interiors, are dry. Mountainous islands in the trades, like the Hawaiian islands, many of the East and West Indies, the Philippines, Borneo, Ceylon, Madagascar, Teneriffe, etc., show marked differences of this sort. The eastern coasts of Guiana, Central America, south-east Brazil, south-east Africa and eastern Australia are well watered, while the interiors are dry. South America in the south-east trade belt is not well enclosed on the east and the most arid portion is an interior district close to the eastern base of the Andes where the land is low. Even far inland the Andes again provoke precipitation along their eastern slopes and the narrow Pacific coastal strip to leeward of the Andes is a very pronounced desert from near the equator to about lat. 30° S. The cold ocean waters, with prevailing southerly (drying) winds alongshore, are additional factors causing this aridity. The rainfall associated with the conditions just described is known as the *trade* type, and has a maximum in winter when the trades are most active. In cases where the trade blows steadily throughout the year against mountains or bold coasts, as on the Atlantic coast of Central America, there is no real dry season. The curve for Hilo (mean annual rainfall 145·24 in.) on the windward side of the Hawaiian islands, shows typical conditions (*see* fig. 5).

Monsoon Belts.—In a typical monsoon region the rains follow the vertical sun, and therefore have a simple annual period much like that of the tropical type above described. This monsoon type of rainfall is well illustrated in the curve for Port Darwin in Australia (*see* fig. 5). This summer monsoon rainfall results from the inflow of a body of warm, moist air from the sea upon a land area, the rainfall being particularly heavy where the winds have to climb over high lands. In India, the precipitation is heaviest in Assam (where Cherrapunji, at the height of 4,455ft. in the Khasi hills, has a mean annual rainfall of between 400in. and 500in.), on the bold western coast of the peninsula (western Ghats) (120in. and over), and on the mountains of Burma (up to 226in.). In the rain-shadow of the western Ghats, the Deccan often suffers from drought and famine unless the monsoon rains are abundant and well distributed. The prevailing direction of the rainy monsoon wind in India is south-west; on the Pacific coast of Asia, it is south-east. This monsoon district is very large, including the Indian ocean, Arabian sea, Bay of Bengal, and adjoining continental areas; the Pacific coast of China, the Yellow and Japan seas and numerous islands from Borneo to Sakhalin on the north and to the Ladrone islands on the east. A typical temperature curve for a monsoon district is that for Nagpur, in the Deccan (fig. 7), and a typical monsoon cloudiness curve is given in fig. 6, the maximum coming near the time of the vertical sun, in the rainy season, and the minimum in the dry season.

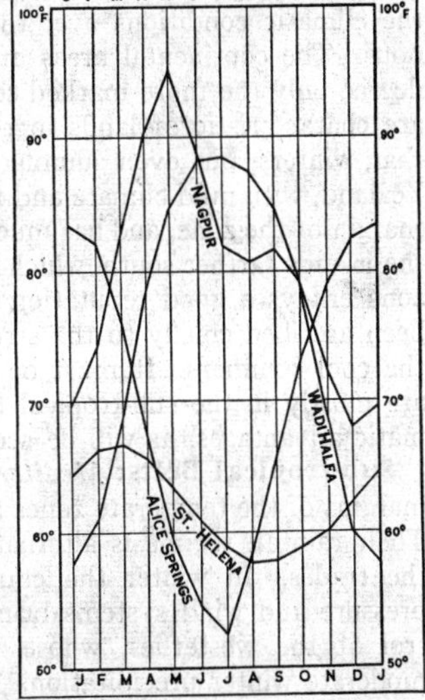

FIG. 7.—ANNUAL TREND OF TEMPERATURE; TROPICAL TYPE IN NORTHERN AND SOUTHERN HEMISPHERES

In the Australian monsoon region, which reaches across New Guinea and the Sunda islands, and west of Australia, in the Indian ocean, over latitudes 0°–10° S., the monsoon rains come with north-west winds between November and March or April. The general rule that eastern coasts between the Tropics are the rainiest finds exceptions in the case of the rainy western coasts in India and other districts with similar monsoon rains. On the coast of the Gulf of Guinea, for example, there is a small rainy monsoon area during the summer; heavy rains fall on the seaward slopes of the Cameroon Mountains where Debundscha averages 369 inches. Gorée, lat. 15° N., on the coast of Senegambia, gives a fine example of a rainy (summer) and a dry (winter) monsoon. In island groups such as the Malay Archipelago where trade winds alternate with monsoons the annual variation of rainfall becomes very complex.

Mountain Climate.—In the torrid zone altitude is chiefly important because of its effect in tempering the heat of the lowlands, especially at night. If mountains are high enough, they carry snow all the year round, even on the Equator. The highlands and mountains within the Tropics are thus often sharply contrasted with the lowlands, and offer more agreeable conditions in Africa and South America. In India, the hill stations are crowded during the hot months by Europeans. The climate of many tropical plateaus and mountains has the reputation of being a "perpetual spring." The rainfall between the Tropics on mountains and highlands often differs considerably in amount from that on the lowlands, and other features common to mountain climates the world over are also noted.

TEMPERATE ZONES

The designation "temperate" is appropriate for the middle latitudes of the southern hemisphere and of the oceans and western coasts in the northern hemisphere, but not for the continental interiors and eastern coasts of Asia and North America, for which Köppen's term "boreal" is better. The temperate zones as a whole are however characterized by the extreme changeableness of their weather, resulting from the frequent passage of barometric depressions.

Temperature.—The annual range of temperature exceeds the diurnal range in all parts of the temperate zone, but the former varies greatly from one part to another. It is smallest on windward islands and coasts and greatest in the interior of the continents, but nearer the east coasts than the west. Thus at Lerwick the range is 15° F from 38° F in February to 53° F in August, while at Iakutsk in Siberia it is 112° F from −46° F in January to 66° F in July, and the average difference between two consecutive months at Iakutsk is greater than the change in six months at Lerwick. Even at Vladivostok on the Pacific coast of Siberia the mean annual range is 61°. The southern part of the temperate zone in central Asia has very hot summers; thus Luktchun in 43° N. has a mean July temperature of 90° and a mean daily maximum in that month of 109°. Over much of the oceans of the temperate zones the annual range is less than 10°. In the south temperate zone there are no extreme ranges, the maxima, slightly over 30°, being near the margin of the zone in the interior of South America, Africa and Australia.

The north-east Atlantic and north-western Europe are about 35° too warm for their latitude in January, while north-eastern Siberia is 30° too cold. The lands north of Hudson bay are 25° too cold, and the waters of the Alaskan bay 20° too warm. In July, and in the southern hemisphere, anomalies are small. The diurnal variability of temperature is greater in the north temperate zone than elsewhere and the same month may differ greatly in its character in different years. The annual temperature curve has one maximum and one minimum. In the continental type the times of maximum and minimum are about one month behind the solstices. In the marine type the retardation may amount to nearly two months. Coasts and islands have a tendency to a cool spring and warm autumn; continents, to similar temperatures in both spring and autumn.

Pressure and Winds.—Over the oceans pressure decreases steadily from the sub-tropical anticyclones to the semi-permanent low pressure areas in about lat. 60°. Hence the prevailing winds are westerly but they are frequently disturbed by the passage of barometric depressions, and the wind may blow from any direction. In the northern hemisphere pressure is higher over the continents than over the oceans in winter, but higher over the oceans than the continents in summer. Hence winter is the stormiest season over the oceans and the prevailing winds become south-westerly on the western coasts of the continents and northerly on the eastern coasts, while in summer they are north-westerly on the western and south-easterly on the eastern coasts. These seasonal changes are best developed on the eastern coast of Asia, where they have the regularity of true monsoons. The winter anticyclone of central Asia has produced the highest known readings of pressure. In the southern hemisphere the seasonal changes are less marked, owing to the preponderance of water, and between lat. 40° and 50° S. the winds blow from some westerly point with considerable regularity and force. These are the "roaring forties" or "brave west winds." Between 50° and 60° S. the winds, while still mainly westerly, are more irregular in direction owing to the frequent passage of storm-centres. Winter in these latitudes is stormier than summer, but seasonal difference is less than north of the Equator.

Rainfall.—Rainfall is fairly abundant over the oceans and also over a considerable part of the lands (30–80in. and more). It comes chiefly in connection with the usual cyclonic storms, or in thunderstorms. The variations, geographic and periodic, in rainfall produced by differences in temperature, topography, cyclonic conditions, etc., are very complex. The equatorial margin of the temperate zone rains is clearly defined on the west coasts, at points where coast deserts are replaced by belts of light or moderate rainfall. Bold west coasts, on the polar side of lat. 40°, are very rainy (100in. to 200in. a year in special situations). The hearts of the continents, far from the sea, especially when well enclosed by mountains, or when blown over by cool ocean winds which warm while crossing the land, have light rainfall (less than 20in.). East coasts are wetter than interiors but drier than west coasts. Autumn and winter are the seasons of maximum rainfall over oceans, islands and west coasts, for the westerlies are then most active, cyclonic storms are most numerous and best developed, and the relatively cold lands chill inflowing damp air. In winter, however, low temperatures, high pressures, and tendency to outflowing winds over continents are unfavourable to rainfall, and the interior land areas as a rule then have their minimum. The warmer months bring the maximum rainfall over the continents. Conditions are then favourable for inflowing damp winds from the adjacent oceans; there is the best opportunity for convection; thunder-showers readily develop on the hot afternoons; the capacity of the air for water vapour is greatest. The marine type of rainfall, with a winter maximum, extends in over the western borders of the continents, and is also found in the winter rainfall of the sub-tropical belts. Rainfalls are heaviest along the tracks of most frequent cyclonic storms. For continental stations the typical daily march of rainfall shows a chief maximum in the afternoon, and a secondary maximum in the night or early morning. The chief minimum comes between 10 A.M. and 2 P.M. Coast stations generally have a night maximum and a minimum between 10 A.M. and 4 P.M.

Humidity and Cloudiness.—Relative humidity is high (80–90%) over the oceans and western coasts and islands. On the eastern coasts and the neighbouring parts of the continents which come under the influence of the inblowing summer winds relative humidity is high in summer but low in winter. In the dry interior of the continents relative humidity is low (20–40%) in summer, though owing to the great heat the absolute humidity may be surprisingly high. In winter in the cold interiors the reverse holds; the absolute humidity is very low but the relative humidity comparatively high. Owing to difficulties of measurement at low temperatures, however, the data available are of doubtful accuracy.

The distribution of cloudiness resembles that of humidity, ranging from one-tenth in the interior deserts to nine-tenths in the oceanic storm areas. The averages for different latitudes are as follows:

Latitude	60°–50° N.	50°–40° N.	40°–30° N.	30°–40° S.	40°–50° S.	50°–60° S.
Land .	6·0	5·0	4·0	4·8	5·8	7·0
Sea . .	6·7	6·6	5·2	5·7	6·7	7·2
Mean .	6·2	5·6	4·5	5·4	6·6	7·2

Seasons in the temperate zones are classified according to temperature, not, as in the Tropics, by rainfall. The four seasons are important characteristics, especially of the middle latitudes of the north temperate zone. Towards the equatorial margins of the zones the difference in temperature between summer and winter becomes smaller, and the transition seasons weaken and even disappear. At the polar margins the change from winter to summer, and vice versa, is so sudden that there also the transition seasons disappear. These seasonal changes are of the greatest importance in the life of man. The monotonous heat of the Tropics and the continued cold of the polar zones are both depressing. The seasonal changes of the temperate zones stimulate man to activity and encourage higher civilization.

Climatic Subdivisions.—There are fundamental differences between north and south temperate zones. Marginal sub-tropical belts must also be considered as a separate group by themselves. The north temperate zone includes large and diverse areas of land, stretching over many degrees of latitude, as well as of water, and has a remarkable diversity of climates. Thus there are the ocean areas and the land areas. The latter are then subdivided into western (windward) and eastern (leeward) coasts and interiors. Mountain climates remain as a separate group.

South Temperate Zone.—Because of the large ocean surface, the régime in the south temperate zone is more uniform than in the northern. The south temperate zone may properly be called "temperate." Temperature changes are small, prevailing winds are stronger and steadier than in the northern hemisphere; seasons are more uniform; weather is prevailingly stormier, more changeable, and more under cyclonic control. The uniformity of the climatic conditions over the far southern oceans is monotonous. The continental areas are small, and develop to a limited degree only the more marked seasonal and diurnal changes which are characteristic of lands in general. Summers are less stormy than winters, but even summer temperatures are not high. New Zealand, with mild climate and fairly regular rains, is really at the margin of the zone, and has much more favourable conditions than the islands farther south, which have dull, cheerless climates. The zone enjoys a good reputation for healthfulness, which fact has been ascribed chiefly to the strong and active air movement and the cool summers. It must be remembered, also, that the lands are mostly in the sub-tropical belt, which possesses peculiar climatic advantages, as will be seen.

Sub-tropical Belts: *Mediterranean Climates.*—At the tropical margins of the temperate zones are the so-called sub-tropical belts. Their rainfall régime is alternately that of the westerlies and of the trades. In winter the equatorward migration of the great pressure and wind systems brings these latitudes under the control of the westerlies, whose frequent irregular storms give a moderate winter precipitation. These winter rains are not steady and continuous, but are separated by spells of fine sunny weather. The amounts vary greatly; much of the area has less than 20in., but Crkvice, on the Gulf of Cattaro, has 183 in. In summer, when the trades are extended polewards by the out-flowing equatorward winds on the eastern side of the ocean anticyclones, mild, dry and nearly continuous fair weather prevails, with northerly winds blowing towards the tropic.

Sub-tropical belts of winter rains and dry summers are mainly limited to western coasts of continents, and to the islands off these coasts in latitudes between about 28° and 40°. The sub-tropical belt is exceptionally wide in the Old World, and reaches far inland there, embracing countries bordering on the Mediterranean in southern Europe and northern Africa, and then extending eastward across the Dalmatian coast and the southern part of the Balkan peninsula into Syria, Mesopotamia, Arabia, north of the tropic, Persia and adjacent lands. This distribution has led to the use of the name "Mediterranean climate." Owing to great irregularity of topography and outline, the Mediterranean province embraces many varieties of climate, but the dominant characteristics are the mild temperatures, except on the heights, and the winter rains.

On the western coasts of the two Americas the sub-tropical belt of winter rains is clearly seen in California and in north Chile, on the west of the coast mountains. Between the region which has rain throughout the year from the stormy westerlies, and the districts which are permanently arid under the trades, there is an indefinite belt over which rains fall in winter. In south Africa, which is controlled by high pressure areas of the south Atlantic and south Indian oceans, the south-western coastal belt has winter rains, decreasing to the north while the east coast and adjoining interior have summer rains, from the south-east trade. Southern Australia is climatically similar to south Africa. In summer the trades give rainfall on the eastern coast decreasing inland. In winter the westerlies give moderate rains, chiefly on the south-western coast. Sub-tropical climates follow the tropical high pressure belts across the oceans, but do not retain their distinctive character far inland from the west coasts of the continents (except in the Mediterranean), nor on the east coasts. On the latter, summer monsoons and the occurrence of general summer rains interfere, as in east Asia and in Florida.

Strictly, winter rains are typical of the coasts and islands of this belt. The more continental areas have a tendency to spring and autumn rains. The rainy and dry seasons are most marked at the equatorward margins of the belt. With increasing latitude, the rain is more evenly distributed through the year, the summer becoming more and more rainy until, in the continental interiors of the higher latitudes, summer becomes the season of maximum rainfall. The monthly distribution of rainfall in two sub-tropical regions is shown in the accompanying curves for Malta and for Perth (Western Australia) (fig. 8). In Alexandria the dry season lasts nearly eight months; in Palestine from six to seven months; in Greece about four months. The winter rains which migrate equatorward are separated by the Sahara from the equatorial rains which migrate poleward. Large variations in annual rainfall may be expected towards the equatorial margins of sub-tropical belts.

The main features of the sub-tropical rains east of the Atlantic are repeated on the Pacific coasts of the two Americas. In North America the rainfall decreases from Alaska, Washington and northern Oregon southwards to lower California, and the length of the summer dry season increases. At San Diego, six months (May–October) have each less than 5% of the annual precipitation, and four of these have 1%. The southern extremity of Chile, from about latitude 38° S. southward, has heavy rainfall throughout the year from the westerlies, with a winter maximum. Northern Chile is persistently dry. Between these two there are winter rains and dry summers. Neither Africa nor Australia extends far enough south to show the different members of this system well. New Zealand is almost wholly in the prevailing westerly belt. Northern India is unique in having summer monsoon rains and also winter rains, the latter from weak cyclonic storms which correspond with sub-tropical winter rains.

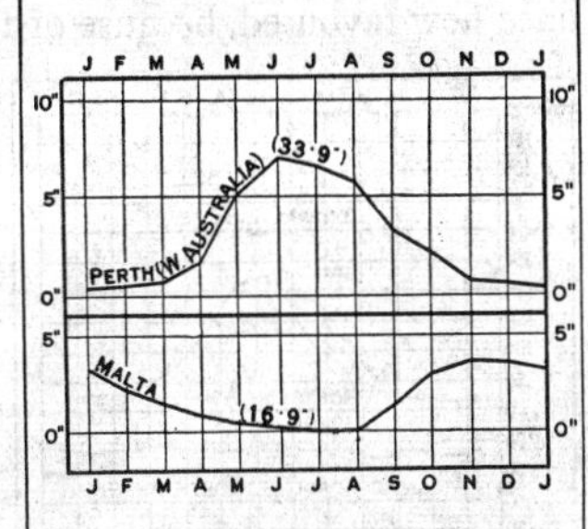

FIG. 8.—ANNUAL TREND OF RAINFALL, SUBTROPICAL TYPE, AT PERTH (W. AUSTRALIA) AND MALTA

From the position of the sub-tropical belts to leeward of the oceans, and at the equatorial margins of the temperate zones, it follows that their temperatures are not extreme. Further, the protection afforded by mountain ranges, as by the Alps in Europe and the Sierra Nevada in the United States, is an important factor in keeping out extremes of winter cold. The annual march and ranges of temperature depend upon position with reference to continental or marine influences (fig. 9). The Mediterranean basin is particularly favoured in winter, not only in the protection against cold afforded by the mountains, but also in the high temperature of the sea itself. The southern Alpine valleys and the Riviera are well situated, having good protection and a southern exposure. The coldest month usually has a mean temperature well above 32°. Mean minimum temperatures of about, and somewhat below, freezing occur in the northern portion of the district, and in the more continental localities such as northern Spain and the Balkans minima a good deal lower have been observed. Somewhat similar conditions obtain in the sub-tropical district of North America. Under the control of passing cyclonic storm areas, hot or cold winds, which often owe some of their special characteristics to the topography, bring into the sub-tropical belts, from higher or lower latitudes, unseasonably high or low temperatures. These winds have been given special names (mistral, sirocco, bora, etc.). Cloudiness is moderate in winter but very small in summer. The winter rains do not bring continuously overcast skies, and a summer month with a mean cloudiness of one tenth is not exceptional in the drier parts of the sub-tropics. With prevailing fair skies, even temperatures and moderate rainfall, the sub-tropical belts possess many climatic advantages which fit them for health resorts. The long list of well-known resorts on the Mediterranean coast, and the shorter list for California, bear witness to this fact.

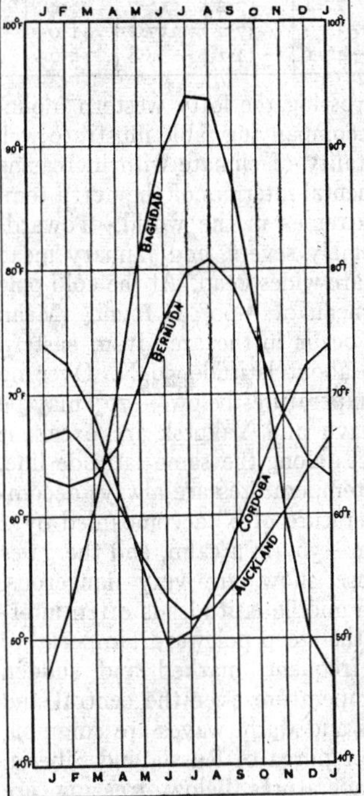

FIG. 9.—ANNUAL TREND OF TEMPERATURE FOR SELECTED SUBTROPICAL STATIONS

North Temperate Zone: *West Coasts:*—Marine climatic types are carried by the prevailing westerlies on to the western coasts of the continents, giving them mild winters and cool summers, abundant rainfall, and a high degree of cloudiness and relative humidity. North-western Europe is particularly favoured because of the remarkably high temperatures of the north Atlantic Ocean. January means of 40° to 50°F in the British Isles and on the northern French coast occur in the same latitudes as those of below 0° in the far interior of Asia. In July means of 60° to 70° in the former contrast with 70° to 80°F in the latter districts. The conditions are somewhat similar in North America. Along the western coasts of North America and of Europe the mean annual ranges are under 25°—actually no greater than some of those between the tropics. Irregular cyclonic temperature changes, are, however, marked in the temperate zone, while absent between the Tropics. The figures for the Scilly isles and for Thorshavn, Faröe islands, illustrate the insular type of temperature on the west coasts. The annual march of rainfall, with the slight maximum in the autumn and winter characteristic of the marine régime, is illustrated in the curve for north-western Europe (fig. 10). On the northern Pacific coast of North America the distribution is similar, and in the southern hemisphere the western coasts of southern America, Tasmania and New Zealand show the same type. The cloudiness and relative humidity average high on western coasts, with the maximum in the colder season.

Continental Interiors.—The equable climate of western coasts changes, gradually or suddenly, into the more extreme climates of the interiors. In Europe, where no high mountain ranges intervene, the transition is gradual, and broad stretches benefit by the tempering influences of the Atlantic. In North America the

MEAN TEMPERATURE

	Jan.	Feb.	Mar.	Apr.	May	June	July	Aug.	Sept.	Oct.	Nov.	Dec.	Year
Scilly Isles	45·7	45·3	46·0	48·6	52·5	57·2	60·5	60·8	58·6	53·8	49·8	47·4	52·2
Prague	29·7	33·1	39·0	47·4	57·0	63·5	66·2	65·1	58·5	49·0	37·9	31·5	48·2
Kharkov	18·0	21·6	29·5	44·6	58·1	64·0	68·0	65·7	55·9	44·8	32·7	23·0	43·7
Omsk	− 3·1	0·1	10·9	32·4	51·8	62·1	66·9	61·3	51·1	34·3	16·0	2·5	32·2
Irkutsk	− 5·8	0·1	15·4	34·0	46·7	58·3	63·9	59·5	47·5	32·9	12·7	−0·6	30·4
Blagoveshchensk. . . .	−13·0	− 1·8	14·9	35·2	49·6	63·1	70·0	65·5	53·6	34·3	10·8	−8·0	31·2
Petropavlovsk (Kamchatka) .	12·4	12·2	18·7	28·4	36·0	44·2	51·1	53·2	48·4	38·5	27·3	18·1	32·4
Thorshavn	37·6	37·4	37·2	41·0	44·2	48·7	51·3	51·1	48·4	43·9	40·3	38·1	43·3
Yakutsk	−46·1	−34·1	− 9·8	15·6	40·6	58·8	65·5	59·2	42·3	16·5	−19·8	−40·9	−12·4

change is abrupt and comes on crossing the lofty western mountain barrier. The figures in the accompanying table illustrate well the gradually increasing continentality of climate with increasing distance inland in Eurasia. Continental interiors of the north temperate zone have the greatest extremes in the world. Towards the arctic circle winters are extremely severe, and January mean temperatures of −10° and −20° are widespread. At the cold pole of north-east Siberia a January mean of −60° is found. Mean minimum temperatures of −40° occur in the area from eastern Russia, over Siberia and down to about latitude 50°N. Over no small part of Siberia minimum temperatures below −70° may be looked for every winter. Thorshavn and Yakutsk are excellent examples of temperature differences along the same latitude line. Fortunately in Siberia the lowest temperatures are always accompanied by calm weather. A temperature of 0° accompanied by a strong wind is harder to bear than −50° in a calm, and the gales (*buran*, *purga*), which carry loose snow, are very dangerous. North American winter weather in middle latitudes is often interrupted by cyclones, which, under the steep poleward temperature gradient then prevailing, cause frequent, marked and sudden changes in wind direction and temperature over the central and eastern United States. Cold waves and warm waves are common, and blizzards resemble the buran or purga of Russia and Siberia. With cold northerly winds, temperatures below freezing are carried far south towards the tropic.

The January mean temperatures in the southern portions of the continental interiors average about 50°. In summer the northern continental interiors are warm, with July means of 60° and thereabouts. These temperatures are not much higher than those on the west coasts, but as the northern interior winters are much colder than those on the coasts, the interior ranges are very large. Mean maximum temperatures of 86° occur beyond the Arctic circle in north-eastern Siberia, and beyond latitude 60° in North America. In spite of the extreme winter cold, agriculture extends remarkably far north in these regions, because of warm, though short summers, with favourable rainfall distribution. Summer heat is sufficient to thaw the upper surface of the frozen ground, and vegetation prospers for its short season; great stretches of flat surface become swamps. The southern interiors have torrid heat in summer, temperatures of over 90° being recorded in the south-western United States and in southern Asia. The diurnal ranges of temperature are very large, often exceeding 40°, and mean maxima exceed 110°.

The winter maximum of rainfall and cloud on the west coasts becomes a summer maximum in the interiors. The change is gradual in Europe, as is the change in temperature, but more sudden in North America. The rainfall curves for central Europe and for northern Asia illustrate these continental summer rains (*see* fig.10). The summer maximum becomes more marked with increasing continental character of the climate. There is also a well-marked decrease in the amount of rainfall inland. In western Europe rainfall averages 20in. to 30in., with much larger amounts (reaching 120in. and even more) on bold west coasts, as in the British Isles and Scandinavia, where moist Atlantic winds are deflected upwards, and also locally on mountain ranges, as on the Alps. There are small rainfalls (below 20in.) in eastern Scandinavia and on the Iberian peninsula. Eastern Europe has generally less than 20in., western Siberia about 15in., and eastern Siberia about 10in. In the southern part of the great overgrown continent of Asia an extended region of steppes and deserts, too far from the sea to receive sufficient precipitation, shut in, furthermore, by mountains, controlled in summer by drying northerly winds, receives less than 10in. a year, and in places less than 5in.

The North American interior because of its small area has more favourable rainfall conditions than Asia. The heavy rainfalls on the western slopes of the Pacific coast mountains correspond, in a general way, with those on the western coast of Europe. The coast mountains cause a much more rapid decrease of rainfall inland than in Europe and a considerable south-western interior region has deficient rainfall (less than 10in.). The eastern part of the continent is freely open to the Atlantic and the Gulf of Mexico, so moist cyclonic winds have access, and rainfalls of over 20in. are found everywhere east of the 100th meridian. These conditions are much more favourable than those in eastern Asia. The greater part of the interior of North America has the usual warm-season rains. In the interior basin, between the Rocky and Sierra Nevada mountains, the higher plateaux and mountains receive much more rain (largely from thunderstorms) than the desert lowlands. Forests grow on the higher elevations, while irrigation is necessary for agriculture below. In southern South America the narrow Pacific slope has heavy rainfall (over 80in.); east of the Andes the plains are dry (mostly less than 10in.). The southern part of the continent is very narrow, and is open to the east as well as more open to the west owing to decreasing height of the mountains. Hence the rainfall increases somewhat to the south with passing cyclones. Tasmania and New Zealand have most rain on their western slopes.

East Coasts.—Prevailing winds carry the interior continental climates off over the eastern coasts of the temperate zone lands and even on to the adjacent oceans. The east coasts therefore have continental climates, with modifications resulting from the presence of the oceans to leeward, and have little in common with the west coasts. On west coasts of north temperate lands isotherms are far apart. On east coasts they crowd together. The east coasts share with the interiors large annual and cyclonic ranges of temperature. A glance at isothermal maps of the world will show at once how favoured, because of its position to leeward of the warm North Atlantic waters, is western Europe as compared with eastern North America. A similar contrast, less marked, is seen in eastern Asia and western North America. In eastern Asia coast mountains give some shelter from extreme cold of the interior, but in North America, with no such barrier, severe cold winds sweep across the Atlantic coast States, even far to the south. Owing to prevailing offshore winds, oceans to leeward have relatively little effect.

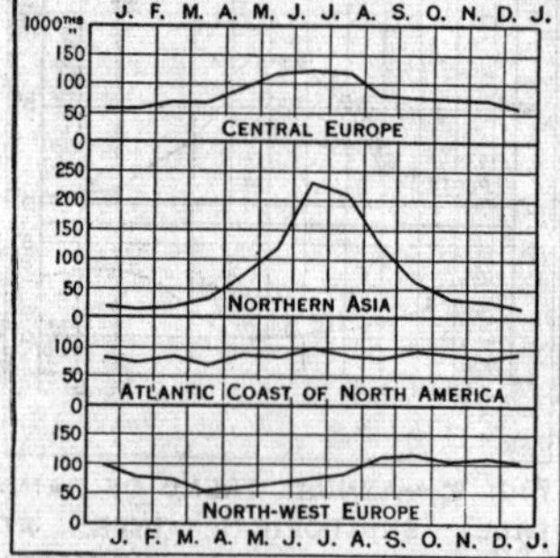

FIG. 10.—ANNUAL TREND OF RAINFALL IN NORTH TEMPERATE ZONE, IN THOUSANDTHS OF ANNUAL TOTALS

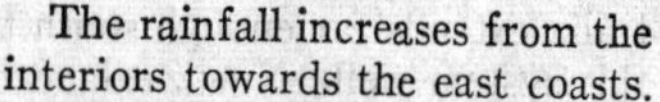

The rainfall increases from the interiors towards the east coasts. In North America the distribution through the year is very uniform, with some tendency to a summer maximum, as in the interior (N. A. fig.10). In eastern Asia winters are relatively dry and clear, under the influence of the cold offshore monsoon, and summers are warm and rainy. Rainfalls of 40in. are found on the east coasts of Korea, Kamchatka and Japan, while in North America, which is more open, they reach farther inland. Japan, although occupying an insular position, has a modified continental

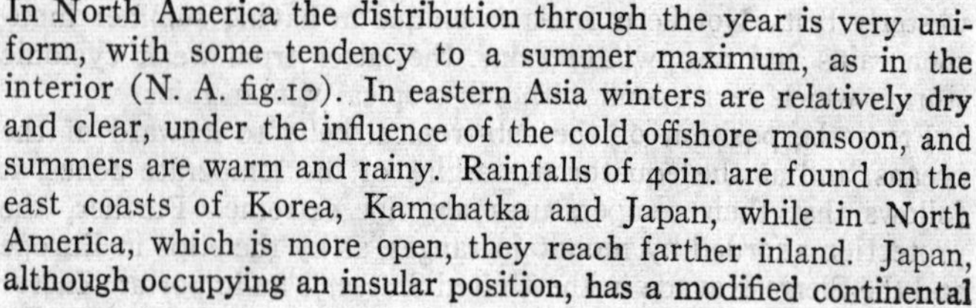

rather than a marine climate. The winter monsoon after crossing the water, gives abundant rain and snow on the western coast, while the winter is relatively dry in the lee of the mountains, on the east. Japan has smaller temperature ranges than the mainland.

Mountain Climates.—If the altitude is sufficient, decreased temperature gives mountains a polar climate, with the difference that summers are relatively cool while winters are mild owing to inversions of temperature in anticyclonic weather. Hence annual ranges are smaller than over lowlands. At such times of inversion mountain-tops often appear as local areas of higher temperature in a general region of colder air over valleys and lowlands. Increased intensity of insolation aloft is important for certain mountain resorts in winter (*e.g.,* Davos and Meran). Of Meran it has been well said that from December to March the nights are winter, but the days are mild spring. The diurnal ascending air currents of summer usually give mountains their maximum cloudiness and highest relative humidity in the warmer months, while winter is the drier and clearer season.

CHARACTERISTICS OF THE POLAR ZONES

The temperate zones merge into the polar zones at the Arctic and Antarctic circles, or, if temperature be used as the basis of classification, at the isotherms of 50°F for the warmest month, as suggested by Supan. The longer or shorter absence of the sun gives the climate a peculiar character. Beyond the isotherm of 50°F for the warmest month forest trees and cereals do not grow. In the northern hemisphere this line is well north of the Arctic circle, in the continental climate of Asia, and north of it also in north-western North America and in northern Scandinavia, but falls well south in eastern British America, Labrador and Greenland, and also in the north Pacific Ocean. In the southern hemisphere this isotherm crosses the southern extremity of South America, and runs fairly east and west around the globe. There is a minimum of life, but more in the north polar than the south polar zone. Plants and land animals are few. Farming and cattle raising cease. Population is small and scattered. Man seeks his food chiefly in the sea and lives near the sea-coast. There are no permanent settlements at all within the Antarctic circle. Interior lands are deserted. Arctic vegetation must make rapid growth in the short, cool summer. In the highest latitudes summer temperatures are not high enough to melt snow on a level. Arctic plants grow and blossom rapidly and luxuriantly where the exposure is favourable, and the water from melting snow can run off; the soil then dries quickly and can be effectively warmed. Protection against cold winds is another important factor. Over great stretches of the northern plains the surface only is thawed out in the warmer months, and swamps, mosses and lichens are found over perpetually frozen ground.

Temperature.—At the solstices the two poles receive the largest amounts of insolation which any part of the earth's surface ever receives. Temperatures do not follow insolation in this case because much of the latter never reaches the earth's surface and because much energy which does reach the surface is expended in melting snow and ice of the polar areas. In the winter months there are three cold poles, in Siberia, in Greenland and at the pole itself. In January the mean temperatures at these three cold poles are −49°, −40° and −40° F respectively. The Siberian cold pole becomes a maximum of temperature during the summer, but the Greenland and polar minima remain throughout the year. In July the temperature distribution shows considerable uniformity; the gradients are relatively weak. A large area in the interior of Greenland, and one of about equal extent around the pole, are within the isotherm of 32°. For the year a large area around the pole is enclosed by the isotherm of −4°, with an isotherm of the same value in the interior of Greenland. The annual range of temperature is about 120° in Siberia, 80° in North America, 76° at the North Pole and 72° in Greenland. The North Pole obviously has a continental climate.

For the Antarctic our knowledge is still very fragmentary, and relates chiefly to summer months. Meinardus has determined mean temperatures of higher southern latitudes as follows:—

Mean Temperatures of High Southern Latitudes

S. Lat.	50°	60°	70°	80°
Mean Annual	41·9F	24·6F	8·1F	−12·5F
January	46·9	34·2	29·7	18·7
July	37·4	13·5	−11·0	−33·3

The whole southern hemisphere is colder than the northern. Antarctic summers are decidedly cold. Mean annual temperatures are about 10°, and minima of an ordinary Antarctic winter go to −40° and below, but so far no minima of the severest Siberian intensity have been noted. Maxima have varied between 35° and 50°. Temperatures at the South Pole itself suggest interesting speculations. It is likely that near the South Pole will prove to be the coldest point on the earth's surface for the year, as the distribution of insolation implies and as the conditions of land, ice and snow there suggest. The lowest winter and summer temperatures in the southern hemisphere will probably be found near the pole. Isotherms in the antarctic region bend polewards and equatorwards at different meridians, although much less so than in the Arctic.

The annual march of temperature in the north polar zone, for which we have the best comparable data, is peculiar in having a much retarded minimum in February or even in March—the result of the long cold winter. Temperature rises rapidly towards summer, reaching a maximum in July. Autumn is warmer than spring. The continents do not penetrate far enough into the Arctic zone to develop a pure continental climate in the highest latitudes. Verkhoyansk, latitude 67° 33′N., has an exaggerated continental type for the margin of the zone, with an annual range of 120°. One-third as large a range is found on Novaya Zemlya. Polar climate as a whole has large annual and small diurnal ranges, but sudden changes of wind may cause marked irregular temperature changes especially in winter. The smaller ranges are associated with greater cloudiness, and vice versa.

Pressure and Winds.—Pressure and winds follow a simpler scheme in the southern than in the northern hemisphere, because of the large extent of ocean. The southward decrease of pressure in temperate latitudes, previously described, ceases in about 60°S., where a trough of low pressure encircles the globe, widening somewhat over the Ross and Weddell Seas, while still farther south pressure rises again. On the northern side of this trough westerly winds prevail, on the southern side easterly winds. Over the Antarctic continent itself periods of calm, and, in winter, intense cold alternate with periods of high winds, which often develop into blizzards. Blizzards are not equally developed on all parts of the Antarctic coast, their frequency depending on the local topography and distribution of pressure; they are especially numerous in Adelie Land. Winds of any force sweep away the surface layer of cold air and cause a marked rise of temperature. They whirl up the loose surface snow but are also accompanied by fresh snow, and visibility is limited to a few yards.

In the Arctic area wind systems are less clearly defined and pressure distribution is much less regular, on account of irregular distribution of land and water. The North Atlantic low-pressure area is more or less well developed in all months. Except in June, when it lies over Southern Greenland, this tongue-shaped trough of low pressure lies in Davis strait, to the south-west or west of Iceland, and over the Norwegian sea. In winter it greatly extends its limits farther east into the inner Arctic ocean, to the north of Russia and Siberia. The Pacific minimum of pressure is found south of Bering strait and in Alaska. Between these two regions a ridge of higher pressure extends from North America to eastern Siberia. This has been called by Supan the *"Arktische Windscheide."* Pressure gradients are steepest in winter. The prevailing westerlies which in the high southern latitudes are so symmetrically developed, are interfered with by the varying pressures over the northern continents and oceans in summer and winter. Isobaric and wind charts show that on the whole winds blow out from the inner polar basin, especially in winter and spring.

Rain and Snow.—The amount of precipitation is comparatively slight in the polar zones, chiefly because of the small capacity of the air for water vapour at the low temperatures there prevailing; partly also because of the rarity of local convectional storms and thunder-showers. Even cyclonic storms cannot yield much precipitation. Extended snow and ice fields tend to give an exaggerated idea of the actual amount of precipitation. It must be remembered, however, that evaporation is slow at low temperatures, and melting is not excessive. Hence the polar store of fallen snow is well preserved; interior snowfields, ice sheets and glaciers are produced. The commonest form of precipitation is naturally snow, the summer limit of which, in the northern hemisphere, is near the Arctic circle, with the exception of Norway. So far as exploration has yet gone into the highest northern latitudes, rain falls in summer, but probably over most of the Antarctic continent rain never falls. The snow of the polar regions is characteristically fine and dry. At low polar temperatures flakes of snow are not found, but precipitation is in the form of ice spicules. The finest glittering ice needles often fill the air even on clear days, and in calm weather, and, gradually descending to the surface, slowly add to the depth of snow on the ground. Dry snow is also blown from the snowfields on windy days, interfering with the transparency of the air.

Humidity, Cloudiness and Fog.—Absolute humidity is low in polar latitudes, especially in winter, on account of low temperatures. Relative humidity varies greatly, and very low readings have often been recorded. Cloudiness seems to decrease somewhat towards the inner polar areas, after passing the belt of high cloudiness in the higher latitudes of the temperate zones. In marine climates of high latitudes summer has the maximum cloudiness; winter is clearer. The summer maximum is associated with fogs, produced where warm, damp air is chilled by contact with ice. They are also formed over open waters, as among the Faroe islands, for example, and open water spaces, in the midst of an ice-covered sea, are commonly detected at a distance by means of "steam fog." Fogs are less common in winter, when they occur as radiation fogs, of no great thickness. The small winter cloudiness, reported also from the Antarctic zone, corresponds with low absolute humidity and small precipitation. Coasts and islands bathed by warm water of the Gulf Stream drift are usually more cloudy in winter than in summer. The place of fog is in winter taken by fine snow crystals, which often darken the air like fog when strong winds raise the dry snow from the surfaces on which it is lying. Cumulus cloud forms are rare, even in summer. Stratus is probably the commonest cloud of high latitudes, often covering the sky for days without a break.

Physiological Effects.—The north polar summer, in spite of its lack of warmth, is in some respects pleasant and healthful, but the polar night is monotonous, depressing and repelling. Sir W. E. Parry said that it would be difficult to conceive of two things which are more alike than two polar winters. An everlasting uniform snow covering, rigidity, lifelessness and silence—except for the howl of the gale or the cracking of the ice. Small wonder that the polar night has sometimes unbalanced men's minds. The first effects are often a strong desire for sleep and indifference. Later effects have been sleeplessness and nervousness, tending in extreme cases to insanity, anaemia and digestive troubles. Extraordinarily low winter temperatures are easily borne if the air be dry and still. Zero weather seems pleasantly refreshing if clear and calm. But high relative humidity and wind —even a light breeze—give the same degree of cold a penetrating feeling of chill which may be unbearable. Large temperature ranges are endured without danger in the polar winter when the air is dry. Under direct insolation skin burns and blisters; lips swell and crack. Thirst has been much complained of by polar explorers, and is due to the active evaporation from the warm body into the dry, relatively cold air. Polar air is singularly free from micro-organisms owing to lack of communication with other parts; hence many diseases common in temperate zones, "colds" among them, are rare.

Changes of Climate.—The climatic divisions of the world appear to be constant in their broad outlines, but are subject to minor fluctuations which have a duration from a few years up to many centuries. Some known fluctuations of climate have been irregular, but others recur with some regularity. The best known of these meteorological periodicities are the 11-year sunspot cycle, best shown in the tropics, and the Brückner cycle, of about 35 years, in temperate regions. In the geological past there have been far more extensive changes (see *e.g.*, CLIMATIC HISTORY).

BIBLIOGRAPHY.—Scientific climatology is based upon numerical results, obtained by systematic, long continued, accurate meteorological observations. The essential part of its literature is therefore found in the collection of data published by the various meteorological services. The only comprehensive text-book of climatology is the *Handbuch der Klimatologie* of the late J. von Hann (Stuttgart, 1908–11). The first volume deals with general climatology, and has been translated into English (London and New York, 1903). Reference should be made to this book for further details than are here given. The second and third volumes are devoted to the climates of the different countries of the world. Köppen's *Die Klimate der Erde* and Kendrew's *Climates of the Continents* are valuable reference books. The standard meteorological journal of the world, the *Meteorologische Zeitschrift* (Braunschweig, monthly), is indispensable. The *Quarterly Journal of the Royal Meteorological Society* (London), the *Meteorological Magazine* (London), and the *Monthly Weather Review* (Washington, D. C.) are also valuable. The best collection of charts is that in the *Atlas of Meteorology* (London, 1899) which gives an excellent working bibliography. *See* also the bibliography issued by the Royal Meteorological Society.

CLIMATE IN THE TREATMENT OF DISEASE.

Broadly speaking, purity of air (*i.e.*, freedom from solid particles and irritating gases), average temperature, range of temperature, amounts of sunshine and of humidity are the most important considerations in the climatic treatment of disease. Social and economic conditions in any given locality are important but are not discussed here. Individuals react both to heat and cold very differently. At health resorts, where the temperature varies between 55° and 70° F., strong individuals gradually lose strength, whereas a delicate person gains vigour of mind and body and puts on weight. And a corresponding intensity of cold acts in the reverse manner in each case. Thus a moderately warm health resort suits delicate, convalescent or elderly people. Cold, however, when combined with wind and damp, must be avoided by the aged, the delicate, and those prone to gouty and rheumatic affections. The moisture of the atmosphere controls the distribution of warmth on the earth, and is closely bound up with the prevailing winds, temperature, light and pressure. In dry air the evaporation from skin and lungs is increased, especially if the sunshine be plentiful and the altitude high. In warm moist air strength is lost and digestive troubles are common. In moist cold air perspiration is checked, and rheumatic and joint affections are common. The main differences between mountain air and that of the plains depend on the former being more rarefied, colder, of a lower absolute humidity, and offering less resistance to the sun's rays. As the altitude is raised, circulation and respiration are quickened, probably as an effort on the part of the organism to compensate for the diminished supply of oxygen, and somewhat more gradually body weight and the number of red blood corpuscles increase, this increase persisting after a return to lower ground. Thus children and young people are especially likely to benefit by the impetus given to growth and the blood-forming organs. For older people, however, the benefit depends on whether their organs of circulation and respiration can respond to the increased demands on them. For anaemia, pulmonary tuberculosis, deficient expansion of the lungs, neurasthenia, and the debility following fevers and malaria, mountain air is invaluable. But where there is valvular disease of the heart, or rapidly advancing disease of the lungs, it is to be avoided. Light, especially direct sunlight, is of primary importance, the lack of it tending to depression and dyspeptic troubles. Indeed, the modern view is that the value of a climate is determined chiefly by the average intensity of ultra-violet light. Probably its germicidal power accounts in part for the aseptic character of the air of the Alps, the desert and other places.

A "good" climate is that in which all the organs and tissues of the body are kept evenly at work in alternation with rest. Thus a climate with constant moderate variations in its principal factors is the best for the maintenance of health. But the best climate for an invalid depends on the particular weakness from which he suffers. Thus in pulmonary tuberculosis a cool sunny climate is greatly superior to a tropical one. Exposure to strong winds is harmful, since it increases cough. A high altitude, from the sunshine, the purity and stimulating properties of the air, is of value

BY COURTESY OF THE UNITED STATES WEATHER BUREAU

INSTRUMENTS FOR DETERMINING CONDITIONS OF THE WEATHER

1. Mercurial barometer, invented by Torricelli in 1643. Each tube holds a column of mercury, which rises and falls according to pressure of surrounding air. 2. Anemometer, for measuring velocity of wind. Three cups attached to horizontal arms revolve at speed varying according to wind velocity. 3. Windvane or anemoscope, indicates direction of the wind. This 4-ft. vane may be connected with the recording instrument (fig. 4). 4. Weather recording register equipped to record changes at one-minute intervals. Instrument registers the velocity and direction of wind, rainfall in hundredths inches and the duration of sunshine. 5. Tipping bucket rain gauge, in parts. 6. Standard barograph or recording aneroid barometer, with cover removed. 7. Intermediate range thermograph which traces a continuous record of the temperature on a revolving drum. 8. Thermal sunshine recorder, electrically connected with recording instrument (fig. 4), determines duration of sunshine

BY COURTESY OF THE U.S. WEATHER BUREAU

LAUNCHING A RADIOSONDE, ROBOT WEATHER OBSERVER

A sounding balloon carries the radiosonde to heights of 10 to 15 mi. During the flight the instrument emits, at brief intervals, radio signals which are recorded by the station's ground equipment. By referring these recorded signals to a calibration chart the pressure, temperature and humidity of the atmosphere through which the instrument has been carried are obtained. An attached parachute retards the fall of the radiosonde to the ground after the balloon has burst

to many mild or very early cases, but where the disease is extensive or the heart is irritable, or there is insomnia, high altitudes are contra-indicated. Where the disease is of long standing, with much expectoration, or accompanied by albuminuria, the patient appears to do best in a humid atmosphere but little above the sea level. The climate of Egypt is suitable for cases complicated with bronchitis or bronchiectasis, but is contra-indicated where there is attendant diarrhoea. Madeira and the Canaries are useful when emphysema is present. Bronchitis in young people is best treated by high altitudes, but in older patients by a moist mild climate, except where much expectoration is present.

Delicate children benefit by residence at the seaside and if very delicate, with small power of reaction, the winter should be passed at some mild coast resort. Gouty and rheumatic affections require a dry soil and warm dry climate, cold and moist winds being especially injurious.

For heart affections high altitudes are to be avoided, though some physicians make an exception of mitral cases where the compensation is good. Moderate elevations of 500 to 1,500ft. are preferable to the sea level.

In diseases of the kidneys, a warm dry climate, by stimulating the action of the skin, lessens the work to be done by these organs, and thus is the most beneficial. Extremes of heat and cold and elevated regions are all to be avoided. (*See* HELIOTHERAPY.)

CLIMATIC HISTORY. The geological history of the earth is divided into five main divisions, Archaean or Pre-Cambrian, Palaeozoic, Mesozoic, Tertiary and Quaternary periods (*see* GEOLOGY). These different periods contain evidence of many great changes of climate, but this article is limited to those which have occurred since the appearance of man. The earliest forms of man-like creatures probably appeared towards the close of the Tertiary period, and their development has been greatly influenced by a series of climatic changes which occurred during the Quaternary. The Tertiary is divided into Eocene, Oligocene, Miocene and Pliocene; a fifth stage, the Pleistocene, is now generally included with the Quaternary. The Eocene began 60 million years ago, the Pliocene ended probably 600,000 to a million years ago. At the beginning of the Eocene the climate of middle latitudes was somewhat warmer than it is at present, and in the later Eocene and Oligocene it became very much warmer. Beds of fossil plants of warm temperate aspect dating from these periods have been found north of the Arctic Circle in many regions. In the Miocene the climate was somewhat cooler than in the Oligocene, though probably warmer than the present. At the beginning of Pliocene times, ten to 15 million years ago, the climate of the north temperate regions again became warmer, but this was temporary, and towards the close of this period there was a rapid cooling. This change is well shown in East Anglia, where the earlier Pliocene beds contain mainly southern mollusca, while in the upper part of the Red Crag northern species become increasingly frequent. The later Pliocene beds of East Anglia, the Chillesford beds and Weybourne Crag, contain large numbers of arctic species, and are probably contemporaneous with the first glaciations of Scandinavia and the Alps. The latest bed in this country which was formerly attributed to the Pliocene, the Cromer Forest bed, indicates a return of somewhat warmer conditions; it is succeeded by boulder clays and other deposits of land ice, indicating the oncoming of glacial conditions in England itself. The discovery of Palaeolithic implements in this bed indicates, however, that the forest bed and the underlying Weybourne crag should be removed to the Pleistocene. The "Quaternary" Ice age began on the continent of Europe and in North America in the Pliocene, but it is convenient to ignore this somewhat arbitrary division and to consider the Ice Age as a whole.

The Quaternary Ice Age.—The Quaternary or Pleistocene Ice Age was characterized by the advance of great glaciers or ice-sheets from a number of centres, of which the most important were Scandinavia and the Alps in Europe, the Cordilleras and various other centres in North America. Minor centres of glaciation were located in Spitsbergen, Iceland, Ireland, Scotland and northern England, the Pyrenees, the Caucasus Range, the Himalayas, the mountain ranges of central Asia, Alaska and the whole chain of the Rockies and Andes, the highest mountains of equatorial Africa, south-eastern Australia and New Zealand. The ice-sheets of Greenland and Antarctica are remnants of the Quaternary glaciation, and illustrate the character of the great inland ice-sheets of northern Europe and North America.

Glaciation of the Alps.—The classical work of A. Penck and E. Brückner in the Alpine region has shown that there were four main advances of the glaciers in Central Europe, which they designated Gunz, Mindel, Riss and Wurm. The intervening periods during which the ice retreated (interglacial periods) are termed Gunz-Mindel, Mindel-Riss and Riss-Wurm. In the Gunz glaciation the snow-line probably lay 3,900ft. lower than now, but the remains of this glaciation have been almost entirely obliterated by the later advances. Of the Gunz-Mindel interglacial nothing is known with certainty, but from the amount of erosion performed by the rivers its duration is estimated as 60,000 years. The Mindel glaciation was regarded by Penck and Brückner as the greatest advance of the ice over the eastern half of the Alpine region. The snow-line lay about 4,250ft. below the present. The Mindel-Riss interglacial was very long (about 240,000 years), and for part of the time warmer than the present. The Riss was regarded as the greatest glaciation in the south-west and west, with a snow-line about 4,250ft. below the present. The Riss-Wurm interglacial was relatively short (about 60,000 years), but probably for a time warmer than the present. The Wurm glaciation was considered by Penck and Brückner to have been smaller in extent than the Riss (depression of snow-line 3,900ft.), but the latest worker, W. Soergel, regards it as the greatest glaciation of the Alps. The Wurm was double, the two maxima being separated by a slight retreat. The final retreat of the ice was interrupted by three re-advances, the Bühl, Gschnitz and Daun stages. The interval between the second maximum of the Wurm (Wurm II.) and the Bühl, which is important archaeologically, is termed the Achen oscillation. Penck and Brückner estimated the length of the post-Wurm period as 20,000 years.

Changes of Sea Level.—The changes of sea level during the Quaternary are best known from the work of E. Dépéret in the Mediterranean. He recognizes four shore-lines or raised beaches, representing periods when the sea was considerably above its present level. These were separated by periods of land elevation when the sea was below its present level and the Mediterranean was divided into two separate basins.

TABLE I. *The Divisions of the Quaternary Ice Age (the latest are at the top).*

Changes of level.		Glacial stages.	Human Industries.
			Magdalenian Solutrean
Monastirian	Upper: Elevation Lower: Submergence to 60ft.	Bühl Re-advance Achen Retreat Wurm Glaciation Riss-Wurm	Aurignacian Mousterian Acheulean Evolved Chellean
Tyrrhenian	Upper: Elevation Lower: Submergence to 100ft.	Riss Glaciation Mindel-Riss	Chellean
Milazzian	Upper: Elevation Lower: Submergence to 190ft.	Mindel Glaciation Gunz-Mindel	Pre-Chellean
Sicilian	Upper: Elevation Lower: Submergence to 330ft.	Gunz Glaciation	

Glaciation in Northern Europe.—The history of the Scandinavian ice-sheet is not known so fully as that of the Alps. The ice probably formed first on the Norwegian mountains, but the centre soon shifted to Sweden and the Gulf of Bothnia. The ice-sheet extended into Russia, Germany, Denmark and Holland, and at its maximum filled the North Sea and encroached on the east coast of England, especially over East Anglia, where for a time it united with the ice from northern England. The edge of the ice-sheet over Europe underwent great fluctuations; it is not known with certainty whether it ever completely melted during the whole course of the Quaternary glaciation, but it is highly probable that this happened during at least the Mindel-Riss interglacial. In East Anglia the Scandinavian ice was followed by English ice bearing great quantities of chalk, which formed the Great Chalky Boulder Clay, but the time relations of the various glacial deposits are not yet settled. Gerard de Geer's study of the deposits left by the retreating ice in Sweden has shown that the last ice-sheet began its final retreat about 20,000 years ago. As in the Alps, the retreat of the ice was interrupted by several re-advances, indicated by great terminal moraines (*see* below).

North America.—In North America great ice-sheets reached lower latitudes than anywhere else on the earth. The ice spread out from three main centres, the Cordilleras in the west, the Keewatin west of Hudson's Bay, and Labrador in the east. The deposits of these various centres are complex, but a succession of five glacial and four interglacial stages has been made out in the Mississippi Valley. The latest glaciation, termed the Wisconsin, was double, like the Wurm, and de Geer has succeeded in correlating the stages of its final retreat with those of the last Scandinavian ice-sheet, but the relations of the earlier glacial stages with those in Europe are uncertain. Interglacial beds in Toronto indicate a long period of retreat and perhaps of complete disappearance of the ice, but their position in the Mississippi sequence is uncertain. In most other parts of the world the glaciation has been shown to include three or four advances of the ice, indicating a general similarity with the sequence in the Alps, but direct correlation is not yet possible.

Stages of Human Culture.—The Quaternary Ice Age roughly coincides with the Palaeolithic (*see* ARCHAEOLOGY: *Old World*) stage of human culture. The industries into which the Palaeolithic of western Europe is divided are shown in table 1 with their probable positions in the glacial sequence, but there is still doubt as to the early Palaeolithic. The Magdalenian falls in the period of arctic climate about the Bühl re-advance, while the Solutrean and Aurignacian occupy the Achen oscillation, a period of dry steppe-like climate which followed Wurm II. The whole Wurm glaciation (Upper Monastirian) is occupied by the Mousterian, which extends back into the Riss-Wurm interglacial (Lower Monastirian), but how far is not quite settled. The controversy has been concerned chiefly with the position of the Chellean industry, which some assign to the Riss-Wurm, others to the Mindel-Riss interglacial. The correlation in table 1 is a compromise, due to Prof. W. J. Sollas, who places the Chellean proper in the Mindel-Riss (Lower Tyrrhenian) and a later development of it, the "evolved Chellean," in the early part of the Riss-Wurm, while the Acheulean occupies the central and latter parts of that interglacial and the Lower Mousterian its closing stages. The fore-runners of the Chellean types (Pre-Chellean) apparently belong to the Gunz-Mindel interglacial (Lower Milazzian).

Late-Glacial and Post-Glacial Periods.—The climatic history of the concluding stages of the Ice Age is best known from Scandinavia, and thanks to the researches of G. de Geer the various stages have been dated. About 20,000 B.C. the ice-edge lay for a time across Denmark and the Baltic coast of Germany and formed the *Daniglacial* moraine. After a period of retreat, the ice-edge halted again near the coast of the Scandinavian peninsula, where it formed the *Gotiglacial* moraine. The ice then vacated Scania, but there was another long halt about 9000 B.C., forming the great *Fennoscandian* moraines. Up to this time the recession had been comparatively slow, and the edge of the ice had changed but little on the coast of Norway and in northern Finland, while it had everywhere been bordered by a belt of Arctic plants, showing that the temperature was still very low. After the formation of the Fennoscandian moraines, however, there followed a period of very rapid retreat, termed *Finiglacial* time, during which temperate plants occupied almost immediately the ground vacated by the ice, indicating a comparatively high temperature. By about 7000 B.C. the remnants of the ice-sheet had shrunk to a long narrow strip along the centre of Scandinavia. After a short halt termed the *Ragunda* Pause, the ice-sheet split into two separate portions about 6500 B.C., and this date is regarded by Scandinavian geologists as the "official" end of the Ice Age. The correlation between the stages of retreat in Scandinavia and the Alps is not yet known, but it is not unlikely that the great Fennoscandian moraines represent the Bühl stage.

In Britain various Arctic plant beds are known which were presumably formed during the halts represented by the Gotiglacial and Fennoscandian moraines, and there were local re-advances of mountain glaciers in Scotland at the same times. The retreat stages of other centres of glaciation are not yet known in detail, but de Geer and Ernst Antevs have been able to date parts of the retreat stages of the ice-sheets in Canada and southern Argentina by comparing the relative thicknesses of successive annual clay deposits with those in Sweden.

Changes in Land and Sea Distribution.—As the Scandinavian ice-sheet began to vacate the Baltic basin, the latter was occupied by a fresh-water lake, bounded on the north by the ice. After the formation of the Fennoscandian moraines a subsidence of the land allowed the ingress of the sea, both from the Atlantic across Scania and from the White sea across Finland. The site of the Baltic was now occupied by the Arctic sea, called the *Yoldia sea* from the presence of the high northern mollusc *Yoldia arctica.* About the time of the Ragunda Pause the land rose again and both outlets to the ocean were closed. The Baltic now became a fresh-water lake, which from its characteristic mollusc is termed the *Ancylus* lake. The greater part of the Ancylus lake stage falls in post-glacial time, during which the last remnants of the ice-sheet disappeared. About 4000 B.C. a new period of submergence began in the south-west Baltic, again admitting the waters of the Atlantic and forming the *Littorina sea.* This sea was warmer and more saline than the present Baltic, because the inlet from the Atlantic was wider and deeper. The maximum subsidence probably occurred about 3000 B.C., after which the land gradually rose again and conditions approached those of the present.

A raised beach at a height of about ten ft. above the present beach is found almost all over the world, and in many parts is accompanied by a kind of fauna now known only from lower latitudes. Such a widespread change of level indicates a rise of the sea, due to a greater volume of water in the oceans. The additional water can only have come from a melting back of the still existing ice-sheets, especially of Greenland and Antarctica, beyond their present limits; there is also independent evidence that this occurred. This general warm period is termed the *Climatic Optimum*; it falls somewhere within the time of the Littorina sea and probably between 2000 and 1000 B.C.

Vegetation.—Much information as to late-glacial and post-glacial climates is provided by the vegetation, especially of peat-bogs. In central Europe the Wurm glaciation was accompanied and followed by tundra, which gave place during the latter half of the Achen oscillation to dry cold steppe conditions during which Solutrean man, who hunted the horse, penetrated Europe from the east. In the Lower Magdalenian, the culture of which is based on the reindeer, conditions again became moister and colder, and the tundra returned for a short time, to be rapidly replaced by pine forest spreading up from the south-east. In the Upper Magdalenian the pine began to be replaced by dense forests of oak and the reindeer gave way to the red deer. Dense forests were almost impenetrable to primitive man, and in central Europe there is almost a gap—the "hiatus"—between Palaeolithic and neolithic industries.

In Scandinavia the retreating ice-sheet was bordered by a broad zone of Arctic vegetation until the close of the Fennoscandian halt. The aspen appeared in the much warmer Finiglacial, the fir in the Ancylus period. The very favourable conditions of Littorina time were marked by a wealth of new trees, including oak, hazel and beech; at one time the hazel greatly exceeded its present limits both of latitude and height.

Wet and Dry Periods.—The post-glacial period has had marked alternations of wet and dry climates, which were first set out by the Norwegian Axel Blytt. The time of the Ancylus lake was generally dry, with warm summers but cold winters; Blytt termed this the *Boreal* stage. The early part of Littorina time was moist, with very mild winters and summers probably as warm as at present, forming the *Atlantic* stage, which was marked by a great growth of peat in northern and western Europe. About 3000 B.C. the warm moist conditions gave way to a dry climate, with very warm summers and winters no colder than the present. The surfaces of the peat-bogs dried up, and in Scandinavia, Scotland and Ireland they were occupied by oak forests; in Germany there is instead a layer of dry heath peat. Blytt terms this the *Sub-Boreal* period. About 850 B.C. there was a marked deterioration of climate, which became moist and cold, forming the *Sub-Atlantic* period, when the forests on the peat-bogs died and were replaced by a new and very rapid growth of peat. The change from the very favourable climate of the Sub-Boreal to the unfavourable climate of the Sub-Atlantic was very marked in the Alps; during the Bronze Age and the beginning of the Early Iron Age the climate was highly favourable and there was free communication across the passes; but early in the Iron Age the passes were closed and human occupation was banished to the lowest and warmest valleys, while at the same time many of the lake-dwellings were submerged. It seems probable that the Daun re-advance of the Alpine glaciers should be attributed to this stage; Penck and Brückner dated the Daun re-advance as older than the Bronze Age, but on very scanty evidence.

The Boreal period is not well shown in the British Isles, but the succession of Atlantic peat, Sub-Boreal forest and Sub-Atlantic peat is well seen in Ireland, most of Scotland and western England but not well developed in eastern England.

Summary.—The various late-glacial and post-glacial stages in Scandinavia may be summarized as follows:

TABLE 2. *Late-glacial and Post-glacial Stages.*

Date B.C.	Scandinavian Ice Sheet.	Land and Sea.	Trees.	Wet and dry periods.
0				Sub-Atlantic
1000				
2000		Littorina Sea	Oak Beech Hazel	Sub-Boreal
3000	Post-glacial			
4000				Atlantic
5000				
6000		Ancylus Lake	Fir	Boreal
7000	Ragunda Pause		Aspen	
8000	Finiglacial Retreat	Yoldia Sea		
9000	Fennoscandian Halt	Ice-Lakes	Arctic Plants	Sub-Arctic and Arctic
10000				

THE HISTORICAL PERIOD

There is no clear boundary between the geological and historical periods, for in Egypt and south-west Asia the beginnings of history are almost contemporary with the end of the Ice Age in Scandinavia. In the arid regions of Arabia, Mesopotamia and central Asia variations of rainfall are of much greater importance than small variations of temperature, and this discussion is accordingly limited to the alternations of wet and dry periods.

Persia.—The semi-arid settlement of Anau on the northern margin of Persia is important. This site was occupied from time to time and abandoned during the intervening periods, and since there is no evidence of conquest, while the periods of abandonment are represented by desert formations, it is highly probable that the interruptions were due to drought. These settlements were investigated by Mr. Raphael Pumpelly, who dated them by means of the relative thickness of deposits. According to Pumpelly's estimates the first settlement began about 9000 B.C., the second, which immediately succeeded it, about 6000 B.C. The last part of the first settlement and the whole of the second show evidence of gradually increasing drought, and the site was abandoned soon after 6000 B.C. It was reoccupied, after an interval of desert conditions, about 5200 B.C. The third settlement continued until about 2200 B.C., with a short interruption, probably due to drought, about 3000 B.C. These estimates of the age of Anau appear to be far too great, and H. Peake and H. J. Fleure suggest that the first settlement did not begin till about 3900 B.C., while the third settlement lasted from about 2500 to 1600 B.C. At the close of the third period there began a period of intense drought, and Anau was not reoccupied until the Iron Age, probably about 750 B.C.

It is highly probable that in semi-arid regions the amount of unrest and migration increases during periods of drought, so that we can infer the variations of dryness from the frequencies of migrations. A period of extensive migration began about 2650 B.C. and culminated between 2300 and 2050. Another maximum occurred about 1350 to 1300, after which the desert peoples began to settle down, and remained quiet until the Arabian dispersal of the seventh century A.D. (which began before the birth of Mohammed).

Caspian Sea.—During the Christian era our information is mainly derived from the variations of level of the Caspian Sea, amplified and supported by records of other lakes in Asia, and by Chinese archives. There is some doubtful evidence that the level of the Caspian was high about A.D. 0, but this is not confirmed by other sources. In the 5th century A.D. the Caspian was very low. Then follows a period of rapid fluctuations; high level about 920, low about 1125, very high from 1306 to 1325 and again early in the 15th century and about 1560 to 1640.

Africa.—The evidence from northern Africa is mainly provided by the levels of the Nile floods, the history of Kharga Oasis, and the variations in the level of civilization in the Sahara. These point to a rainfall much higher than the present about 500 B.C., a minimum about A.D. 200, a slight improvement about 400, a very dry season from 700 to 1000, and a great improvement from about 1225 to 1300, followed by a decline to present conditions. It is interesting that E. J. Wayland has recently shown the existence of a marked dry period in central Africa in Neolithic times, probably representing the Sub-Boreal period.

America.—In North America the evidence is derived mainly from the width of the annual rings of growth of the "Big Trees" of California; the curve of tree growth can be checked and adjusted by the variations in the levels of the salt lakes of western America, and by archaeological evidence. The result shows that a long dry period ended about 1000 to 800 B.C., followed by a period of high rainfall from 700 B.C. to A.D. 200, reaching a strongly marked maximum at 400 B.C. A long dry period began about A.D. 400 and continued until about 1250, with one break at about 1000, and there was a further dry spell in the 15th century.

In Yucatan and central America the Mayan civilization reached its highest level apparently from 100 B.C. to A.D. 350. After about 350 came the Mayan "Dark Ages," when southern Yucatan relapsed into barbarism. A revival occurred about A.D. 1000, but did not reach the level of the earlier period and probably lasted little more than two centuries. The ruins are now overgrown by dense forests, and Ellsworth Huntington makes the plausible assumption that the periods of high culture represent dry periods. If so, these are contemporaneous with the wet periods of Arizona, and represent a southward swing of all the climatic belts.

Recent excavations in southern Greenland have shown that its climate was far more favourable in the tenth century than it is to-day, and Baffin Bay seems to have been almost free of ice. There was a deterioration about A.D. 1000, followed by a slight improvement during the 11th and 12th centuries, after which the climate rapidly became very bad. The ground, which at first thawed to a considerable depth every summer, became permanently frozen about A.D. 1400.

BIBLIOGRAPHY.—C. E. P. Brooks, *The Evolution of Climate* (2nd ed. 1925) (Glacial and late glacial periods) and *Climate through the Ages* (1926); A. P. Coleman, *Ice Ages* (1926); H. Peake and H. J. Fleure, *Corridors of Time, 1. Apes and Men, 2. Hunters and Artists, 3. Peasants and Potters* (1927); A. Penck and E. Brückner, *Die Alpen im Eiszeitalter* (Leipzig, 1902–09): W. J. Sollas, *Ancient Hunters* (3rd ed. 1924).

(C. E. P. B.)

CLIMAX, JOHN (*c.* 525–600 A.D.), ascetic and mystic, also called Scholasticus and Sinaïtes. After 40 years in a cave at the foot of Mount Sinai, he became abbot of the monastery. His life has been written by Daniel, a monk of the monastery of Raithu on the Red sea. He derives his name Climax (or Climacus) from his work of the same name (*Κλῖμαξ τοῦ Παραδείσου*, "Ladder to Paradise"), in 30 sections, corresponding to the 30 years of the life of Christ. It is written in a simple and popular style, and treats of the vices that hinder the attainment of holiness and the Christian virtues.

BIBLIOGRAPHY.—Migne, *Patr. graeca,* lxxxviii (including the biography by Daniel); *see* also C. Krumbacher, *Geschichte der byzantinischen Litteratur* (1897); Herzog-Hauck, *Realencyklopädie.* The *Ladder* has been translated into several languages—into English by Father Robert, Mount St. Bernard's abbey, Leicestershire (1856).

CLIMB INDICATOR: *see* ALTIMETRY.

CLIMBING BITTERSWEET (*Celastrus scandens*), a North American climbing shrub of the staff-tree family (Celastraceae), called also false bittersweet and waxwork. It grows, mostly in rich soil, from Quebec to Manitoba and southward to North Carolina and New Mexico, usually trailing on banks or small shrubs but sometimes climbing to a height of 25 ft. on trees. It has smooth, pointed leaves and small greenish flowers and matures in autumn showy clusters of orange-yellow, berrylike capsules, which split open after frost, disclosing the crimson coverings (arils) enclosing the seeds. The handsome, persistent fruit is used in winter for indoor decoration. (*See* BITTERSWEET.)

CLIMBING FERN, the botanical genus *Lygodium,* with 40 species, chiefly in the warmer parts of the old world. The plants have a creeping stem, on the upper face of which is borne a row of leaves. Each leaf has a slender, stemlike axis, which twines round a support and bears leaflets at intervals; it goes on growing indefinitely. Several species are favourite greenhouse plants. The American climbing fern (*L. palmatum*), called also Hartford fern and Windsor fern, one of the most beautiful ferns native to the United States, grows in open woods from New Hampshire to Pennsylvania and Ohio south to Florida and Tennessee.

CLIM (OR CLYM) **OF THE CLOUGH,** a legendary English archer, a supposed companion of the Robin Hood band. He is commemorated in the ballad "Adam Bell, Clym of the Cloughe and Wyllyam of Cloudeslee." The three were outlaws who had many adventures of the Robin Hood type. The oldest printed copy of this ballad is dated 1550.

CLINCHANT, JUSTIN (1820–1881), French soldier, was born at Thiaucourt (Meurthe) on Dec. 24, 1820, and died in Paris on March 20, 1881. He entered the army from St. Cyr in 1841. He served in Algeria (1847–52), in the Crimea (1854–55) and in Mexico. He held a brigade command in 1870, was captured at Metz but escaped and was placed in command of the 20th corps of the army of the east. He was under Gen. Charles Bourbaki during the campaign of the Jura; and when Bourbaki attempted to commit suicide, he succeeded to the command (Jan. 23, 1871), only to be driven with 84,000 men over the Swiss frontier at Pontarlier. In 1871 Clinchant commanded the 5th corps operating against the commune. He was military governor of Paris when he died.

CLINIC, an organized medical service offering diagnostic, therapeutic or preventive treatment to ambulatory patients. The word originally meant a bedside lecture about a sick patient before a group of physicians or medical students. In medical education clinic is still so used but may also mean a particular lecture, classroom or outpatient examination where several medical men discuss their views. Often in Europe and occasionally in America the term covers an entire teaching centre, including the hospital and the ambulatory facilities. The usual meaning, however, has come to include any organized medical service to ambulatory patients. Such service may or may not be connected with a hospital. In addition, clinic is used to designate the entire activities of a general clinic or may be used to designate only a particular division of the work; *e.g.,* the neurology clinic, the surgery clinic, etc.

The first clinic in the English-speaking world, the London dispensary, was founded in 1696 as a central means of dispensing medicines to the sick poor whom the physicians were treating in the patients' homes. The New York, Philadelphia and Boston dispensaries, founded in 1771, 1786 and 1796, respectively, had the same object in view. Later, for the sake of convenience, physicians began to treat their free patients at the dispensary. The number of such clinics did not increase rapidly and as late as 1890 only 132 were operating in the United States. The impetus for the mushroomlike growth that occurred after that time came from the hospitals and from the public-health movement.

During the latter part of the 1800s the modern hospital as a complex of skilled technical personnel and extensive diagnostic equipment began to take shape. During this period some of the hospitals connected with medical schools inaugurated outpatient departments for teaching as well as for charitable purposes. Johns Hopkins and Massachusetts General hospitals are believed to be the American pioneers in this form of medical education. The advantages of ambulatory care in close proximity to the facilities of a hospital became apparent and such hospital clinics multiplied rapidly. In 1945 about 2,623 hospitals in the United States had organized clinic services. The number of different patients treated reached 4,420,406 and the visits totalled 30,784,890.

A hospital clinic in general follows the same pattern of medical departmentation as the hospital developed for its inpatient work. For this reason hospital clinics are mostly concerned with acute diseases. The physicians in the clinics are usually the same physicians who treat bed patients in the hospital. Many hospitals operating charity clinics require the recent appointees to the medical staff to serve a period in the clinics as a step to senior staff membership. Such physicians ordinarily work no more than one half-day each week in the clinics and usually receive no compensation for this part-time work. In most hospital clinics care is made available only to the medically indigent and no professional fee is charged. Practically all such clinics, however, charge a small registration fee to help cover operating costs if the patient is able to make such a payment. A number of successful attempts have been made to extend hospital clinic care to pay patients. Most of this effort was in the area of the lower-income groups although in a few hospitals no income restrictions were imposed for admission to clinic care.

The public-health movements, mainly concerned with preventive medicine, child and maternal welfare and other medical problems affecting broad segments of the population, contributed to the establishment of more than 6,000 public health clinics in the United States after 1900. Unlike the hospital clinics, which had their greatest growth in the metropolitan areas, the public-health clinics are located in large numbers in the smaller towns and villages as well as in the cities. Because so many of the clinics are located outside of congested population areas the total number of annual visits, despite the large number of clinics, probably does not exceed 15,000,000. The first great movement in this field resulted in the founding of the National Association for the Study and Prevention of Tuberculosis in 1904. It was the association's goal to study and prevent tuberculosis by making clinic facilities available in every city and county for free examination and treatment. Ten years later about 500 clinics were established. Other associations in related fields quickly adopted this method to improve the quality and extend the quantity of their medical service. Such clinics are usually concerned with one particular medical condition and fall mainly into the following categories: tuberculosis, tumour, venereal disease, prenatal, well-baby, dental, tonsil, eye, crippled children and mental hygiene. A later development was the travelling clinics such as dental clinics for school children and tuberculosis case-finding clinics in industrial plants. Usually no charge is made for service in public-health clinics and for many medical conditions no income restrictions are imposed. A few are operated in connection with hospitals but most such clinics use public buildings or space furnished by welfare and other social agencies. Financial support is mostly from the same sources. Doctors serving in the clinics are recompensed for the time spent or are on a full-salary basis.

The advantages of group medical service, with facilities and technical personnel beyond the means of an individual practitioner and the added benefits of group consultation, encouraged the establishment of an increasing number of pay or private clinics. This type of clinic is essentially a voluntary association of physicians engaged in the practice of medicine on a group basis. Common facilities are used and the resulting expense and income is shared by a predetermined division. Several of these have achieved a national reputation and attract patients from a wide area. It was estimated that more than 500 such private clinics were operating in the United States in 1947. The majority of these were general clinics; *i.e.*, they had several of the different medical specialties represented in their group; but a sizeable number limited their work to one medical specialty. Usually, the group is independent of any hospital or other agency, but some clinics own and operate their own hospital facilities. In other instances the clinic is a part of a prepaid health-service plan. (R. E. Bn.)

CLINICAL PSYCHOLOGY: *see* Psychology.

CLINKER, in industry, the common name for coal residues which are formed in lumps, partly fused, in grates or furnaces. Such clinker is used for many purposes as a raw material, and is a useful matrix for inferior portland cement concrete. The name is also applied to the fused masses of brick which occur in brick ovens. What is really a different word, but with the same spelling, is derived from *clinch,* or *clench,* a common Teutonic word, meaning to "fasten together." This word appears in the form "clinker-built" as distinguished from "carvel-built" for a boat whose strakes overlap and are not fastened "flush."

CLINOGRAPH, a set square, the acute angles of which are made adjustable by connecting the side opposite the right angle to one of the other sides by a hinge; it is frequently employed in mechanical drawing (*see* Drawing, Engineering).

CLINTON, DE WITT (1769–1828), U.S. political leader, was born on March 2, 1769, at Little Britain, N.Y. His father, James Clinton (1736–1812), served as a captain of provincial troops in the French and Indian War, and as a brigadier general in the American army in the Revolutionary War. De Witt Clinton graduated at Columbia college in 1786, and in 1790 was admitted to the bar. From 1790 to 1795 he was the private secretary of his uncle, George Clinton, governor of New York and a leader of the Republican party. He entered the state senate in 1798, serving until 1802. He at once became a dominant factor in New York politics, and for the next quarter of a century he played a leading role in the history of the commonwealth. From 1801 to 1802 and from 1806 to 1807 he was a member of the council of appointment; and realizing the power this body possessed through its influence over the selection of a vast number of state, county and municipal officers, he secured in 1801, while his uncle was governor, the removal of a number of Federalist officeholders, in order to strengthen the Republican organization by new appointments. On this account Clinton has generally been regarded as the originator of the "spoils system" in New York; but he was really opposed to the wholesale proscription of opponents that became such a feature of U.S. politics in later years. It was his plan to fill the more important offices with Republicans, since they had been excluded from appointive office during the Federalist ascendancy, and to divide the smaller places between the parties somewhat in accordance with their relative strength. In counties where the Federalists had a majority very few removals were made.

In 1802 Clinton became a member of the U.S. senate, but resigned in the following year to become mayor of New York city, an office which he held for ten years in the period 1803–15. During his mayoralty he also held other offices, being a member of the state senate in 1806–11 and lieutenant governor in 1811–13. In 1812, after a congressional caucus at Washington, D.C., had nominated James Madison for a second term, the Republicans of New York, desiring to break up the so-called Virginia dynasty as well as the system of congressional nominations, nominated Clinton for the presidency by a legislative caucus. Opponents of a second war with Great Britain had revived the Federalist organization, and Federalists from 11 states met in New York and agreed to support Clinton, not because of his war views, which were not in accord with their own, but as a protest against the policy of Madison. In the election Clinton received 89 electoral votes and Madison 128.

As a member of the legislature Clinton was active in securing the abolition of slavery and of imprisonment for debt, and in perfecting a system of free public schools. In 1810 he was a member of a commission to explore a route for a canal between Lake Erie and the Hudson river, and in 1811 he and Gouverneur Morris were sent to Washington to secure federal aid for the undertaking, but were unsuccessful. The second war with Great Britain prevented any immediate action by the state; but in 1816 Clinton was active in reviving the project, and a new commission was appointed, of which he became president. His connection with this work so enhanced his popularity that he was chosen governor by an overwhelming majority and served for two triennial terms (1817–23). As governor he devoted his energies to the construction of the canal, but the opposition to his administration, led by Martin Van Buren and Tammany Hall, became so formidable by 1822 that he declined to seek a third term. His successful opponents, however, overreached themselves when in 1824 they removed him from the office of canal commissioner. This partisan action aroused such indignation that at the next election he was again chosen governor, by a large majority, and served from 1825 until his death. As governor he took part in the formal ceremony of admitting the waters of Lake Erie into the canal in Oct. 1825, and thus witnessed the completion of a work which owed more to him than to any other man. Clinton died at Albany, N.Y., on Feb. 11, 1828. In addition to his interest in politics and public improvements, he devoted much study to the natural sciences; among his published works are a *Memoir on the Antiquities of Western New York* (1818) and *Letters on the Natural History and Internal Resources of New York* (1822).

Bibliography.—J. Renwick, *Life of De Witt Clinton* (1845); D. Hosack, *Memoir of De Witt Clinton* (1829); W. W. Campbell, *Life and Writings of De Witt Clinton* (1849); H. L. McBain, *De Witt Clinton and the Origin of the Spoils System in New York* (1907); T. E. Benedict, "De Witt Clinton's Birthplace," *Olde Ulster,* vol. vii, pp. 65–69 (1911); and E. A. Fitzpatrick, *The Educational Views and Influence of De Witt Clinton* (1911).

CLINTON, GEORGE (1739–1812), American soldier and political leader, was born at Little Britain, Ulster (now Orange) county, N.Y., on July 26, 1739, the son of Charles Clinton (1690–1773), who had emigrated to America in 1729, and commanded a regiment of provincial troops in the French and Indian War. The son went to sea at the age of 16, but, finding the sailor's life distasteful, joined his father's regiment and accompanied him as lieutenant in the expedition against Fort Frontenac in 1758. After the war he practised law and held a number of minor civil offices in Ulster county. From 1768 to 1775 he sat in the New York provincial assembly, and in the controversies with Great Britain zealously championed the colonial cause. In 1774 he was a member of the New York committee of correspondence, and in 1775 was a member of the second Continental Congress. In December of that year he was appointed a brigadier general of militia by the New York provincial congress. In the following summer, being ordered by George Washington to assist in the defense of New York, he left Philadelphia, after voting for the Declaration of Independence, and before he could sign it.

Clinton took part in the battle of White Plains (Oct. 28, 1776), and was charged with the defense of the highlands of the Hudson, where, with De Witt Clinton, in Oct. 1777, he offered a firm but unsuccessful resistance to the advance of Sir Henry Clinton. In March 1777 he had been appointed by congress a brigadier general in the continental army, and he thus held two commissions, since the state convention refused to accept his resignation as brigadier general of militia. So great was Clinton's popularity at this time that at the first election under the new state constitution he was chosen both governor and lieutenant governor. He declined the latter office, and on July 30, 1777, entered upon his duties as governor, which were at first largely of a military nature. In 1780 he took the field and checked the advance of Sir John Johnson and the Indians in the Mohawk valley. In his administration Clinton was energetic and patriotic, and though not so intellectual as some of his New York contemporaries, he was more popular than any of them. He served as governor for 18 successive years (1777–95), and for another triennial term from 1801 to

1804. In the elections of 1780, 1783 and 1786 he had no opponent. In 1800–01 he was a member of the assembly.

In the struggle in New York over the adoption of the federal constitution he was one of the leaders of the opposition, but in the state convention of 1788, over which he presided, his party was defeated and the constitution was ratified. In national politics he was a follower of Thomas Jefferson, and in state politics he led the long-dominant faction known as "Clintonians." In 1789, 1792 and 1796 Clinton received a number of votes in the electoral college but not enough to secure him the vice-presidency, which was then awarded to the recipient of the second highest number of votes. In 1804, however, after the method of voting had been changed, he was nominated for the vice-presidency by a congressional caucus and was duly elected. In 1808 he sought nomination for the presidency and was greatly disappointed when this went to James Madison. He was again chosen as vice-president, however, and died in Washington, D.C., before the expiration of his term, on April 20, 1812. He was buried in the congressional cemetery, from which in May 1908, his remains were transferred to Kingston, N.Y. His casting vote in the senate in 1811 defeated the bill for the renewal of the charter of the Bank of the United States.

The *Public Papers of George Clinton,* 6 vol. (1899–1902) have been published by the state of New York. *See* also St. S. Spaulding, *George Clinton and the New York Democracy* (1926).

CLINTON, SIR HENRY (*c.* 1738–1795), British general, was the son of Adm. George Clinton (governor of Newfoundland and subsequently of New York) and grandson of the 6th earl of Lincoln. After serving in the New York militia, he came to England and joined the Coldstream guards. In 1758 he became captain and lieutenant colonel in the Grenadier guards, and in 1760–62 served as aide-de-camp to Ferdinand of Brunswick in the Seven Years' War. He became major general in 1772. From 1772 to 1784, thanks to the influence of his cousin, the 2nd duke of Newcastle, he had a seat in parliament, first for Boroughbridge and subsequently for Newark, but for the greater part of this time he was on active service in America in the War of Independence. He took part in the battles of Bunker Hill and Long Island, subsequently taking possession of New York. For his share in the battle of Long Island he was made a lieutenant general and K.B. After Saratoga he succeeded Sir William Howe as commander in chief in North America. He had already been made a local general. He at once concentrated the British forces at New York, pursuing a policy of foraying expeditions in place of regular campaigns. In 1779 he invaded South Carolina, and in 1780 in conjunction with Adm. M. Arbuthnot captured Charleston. There was constant friction between him and Lord Cornwallis, his second in command, and in 1782, after the capitulation of Cornwallis at Yorktown, he was superseded by Sir Guy Carleton. Returning to England, he published in 1783 his *Narrative of the Campaign of 1781 in North America,* which provoked an acrimonious reply from Lord Cornwallis. He was elected M.P. for Launceston in 1790, and in 1794 was made governor of Gibraltar, where he died on Dec. 23, 1795.

His younger son, SIR HENRY CLINTON (1771–1829), entered the army in 1787 and saw some service with the Prussians in Holland in 1789. He was almost continuously in active service; in the Corunna campaign of 1808–09, he was adjutant general to his close friend, Sir John Moore. Promoted major general in 1810, he returned to the peninsula to fill a divisional command under the duke of Wellington in 1811. His division played a notable part in the capture of the forts at Salamanca and in the battle of Salamanca (1812), and he was given the local rank of lieutenant general early in 1813. For his conduct at Vittoria he was made a K.B., and he took part in the subsequent victories of the Nive, Orthes and Toulouse. At the end of the war he was made a lieutenant general and inspector general of infantry. Clinton commanded a division with distinction at Waterloo. He died on Dec. 11, 1829.

CLINTON, HENRY FYNES (1781–1852), British classical scholar and chronologist, was born at Gamston in Nottinghamshire. He was educated at Westminster and Oxford, and from 1806 to 1826 was M.P. for Aldborough. The value of his *Fasti,* which set classical chronology on a scientific basis, can scarcely be overestimated, even though subsequent research has corrected some of his conclusions.

His chief works are: *Fasti Hellenici, the Civil and Literary Chronology of Greece from the 55th to the 124th Olympiad* (1824–51), including dissertations on points of Greek history and scriptural chronology; and *Fasti Romani, the Civil and Literary Chronology of Rome and Constantinople from the Death of Augustus to the Death of Heraclius* (1845–50). In 1851 and 1853 respectively he published epitomes of the above. *The Literary Remains of H. F. Clinton* (the first part of which contains an autobiography written in 1818) were edited by C. J. F. Clinton in 1854.

CLINTON, a city of Illinois, U.S., on the Illinois Central railroad, 22 mi. S. of Bloomington; the county seat of De Witt county. Pop. (1950) 5,870; (1940) 6,331 by the federal census. It is in the heart of the corn belt; and has railroad shops and clothing factories. It was settled about 1836, and was incorporated as a city in 1855.

CLINTON, a city of Vermillion county, Indiana, U.S., on the Wabash river, 15 mi. N. of Terre Haute and 8 mi. E. of the Illinois state line. It is 1 mi. from federal highway 41, and is served by the Chicago and Eastern Illinois railway. In 1950 the population was 6,576; in 1940 it was 7,092 and in 1930, 7,936 by federal census. Clinton is in a farming and coal mining region, and has varied manufactures, including mining and agricultural machinery, meat and dairy products, sauces and relishes, vaults and other articles of cement, flour, overalls, furniture, carpenter's tools, children's garments and prefabricated houses. The county hospital is located there. Clinton was incorporated as a city in 1893.

CLINTON, a city in the extreme eastern part of Iowa, U.S., on the Mississippi river where the Lincoln highway crosses it; the county seat of Clinton county. It is on the Burlington; the Chicago and North Western; the Chicago, Milwaukee, St. Paul and Pacific; and the Rock Island, and is served by several bus lines. The population in the 1950 federal census was 30,151 and in 1940 it was 26,270.

The city lies 600 ft. above sea level, and has a background of rolling farm land to the west and rocky bluffs to the north. It has a large system of public parks, mostly along the Mississippi, and beautiful homes shaded by elms which the early settlers planted. Clinton was formerly a great sawmill centre, but when the supply of lumber gave out in the north, the city turned to other industries, such as corn products, mill work, builders' hardware, stock feeds, cellophane, structural steel, and steel and wire specialties. The annual factory output is valued at $30,000,000. There is a 2,000-bed army general hospital in the city. The first settlers arrived in 1835. The town was replatted in 1855 and named after De Witt Clinton, former governor of New York. It was incorporated in 1859 and reincorporated in 1881.

CLINTON, a town of Worcester county, Massachusetts, U.S., on the Nashua river, 15 mi. N.N.E. of Worcester. It is served by the Boston and Maine and the New York, New Haven and Hartford railways (freight only). The population in 1950 was 12,295; 12,440 in 1940; 12,817 in 1930; and 12,979 in 1920 by the federal census. The town contains varied and picturesque hilly country, with charming scenery along the river. In its southwest corner, on the southern branch of the Nashua river, is part of the Wachusett dam and reservoir of the water-supply system of the Boston metropolitan area. There are extensive manufactures.

In 1813 cotton cloth was produced there under the factory system, but the first modern textile mill was established in 1838, for making coach lace. The industrial importance of the town is due largely to Erastus Brigham Bigelow (1814–79), inventor of power looms which revolutionized the manufacture of figured fabrics, and of a loom for weaving wire cloth. In 1843, with his brother Horatio M. Bigelow, he established in Clinton the Lancaster mills for the manufacture of ginghams, and about ten years later, the Bigelow carpet mills. Clinton was settled in 1645, and was separated from Lancaster as an independent town in 1850.

CLINTON, a city of Missouri, U.S., 78 mi. S.E. of Kansas City; county seat of Henry county. It is served by the Frisco and the Missouri-Kansas-Texas railways. Population (1950) 6,069. The city lies at the edge of a rolling prairie, 770 ft. above sea level. It is the trade centre for an agricultural and stock raising district and has large flour mills. Considerable coal is mined in the county. It produces more than 20,000,000 chicks annually. Clinton was laid out in 1836 and incorporated in 1865.

CLINTON, a village of Oneida county, N.Y., U.S., 9 mi. S.W. of Utica, on Oriskany creek and the New York, Ontario and Western railway. The population in 1950 was 1,619; in 1940, 1,478. There are mineral springs and iron mines in the vicinity, and the village has knitting and paint mills and vegetable canneries. Many business and professional men of Utica make it their home. It is the seat of Hamilton college for men (opened as an academy for Indian boys in 1798 and chartered as a college in 1812), which was founded by Samuel Kirkland (1741–1808), a missionary among the Oneida Indians, and named after Alexander Hamilton. Its cornerstone was laid by Baron von Steuben; and its shade trees were presented by Thomas Jefferson. The village was widely known as an educational centre between 1798 and 1907, more than 40 private schools for both boys and girls having been established there during that period. The village, settled about 1786 by pioneers from New England, was named after George Clinton, and was incorporated in 1843. It was the birthplace and the summer home of Elihu Root (1846–1937).

CLINTONIA, a genus of beautiful herbs of the lily family (Liliaceae), named in honour of De Witt Clinton (1769–1828), governor of the state of New York. There are six species, four North American and two Asian, all stemless perennials, with a few broad leaves rising from a slender rootstock, and lilylike flowers, usually borne in clusters (umbels) at the top of the flower stock (scape). The yellow clintonia (*C. borealis*) is found in woods from Newfoundland to Manitoba and southward to North Carolina and Wisconsin; the white clintonia (*C. umbellulata*) occurs in woods from New York and New Jersey to Tennessee and Georgia; the mountain clintonia (*C. uniflora*), with a single white flower, grows from Montana and California northward to Alaska; the western clintonia (*C. andrewsiana*) is found near the Pacific coast in central California.

CLINTONITE: *see* OTTRELITE.

CLIPPER SHIPS, a class of sailing vessel developed principally by U.S. shipbuilders during the first half of the 19th century. The origin of the word clipper is not definitely known. Some authors think that the expression "going at a clip" might have been responsible for it, while others have traced the word to the poets Percy Bysshe Shelley and Robert Burns. The first large ship of the kind was the "Ann McKim" (494 tons), built in Baltimore, Md., in 1833; but smaller vessels of similar construction were already well known as "Baltimore clippers." The gold rush in California, which gave such impetus to the building of these ships, was responsible for the launching of 160 clipper ships within four years, during the first of which 90,000 passengers were carried, while the discovery of gold in Australia soon after caused 400,000 people to be transported to that country in British-owned clippers. Bell, Hall, Steers, Webb, Collier, McKay and Magoun are some of the U.S. families who built clipper ships, and the Osgood, Marshall, Trask, Woodhouse, Delano, DePuyster and Russell families had among their members many captains of these vessels. The type was abandoned by U.S. builders after 1854, when freight rates dropped, and since the U.S. clippers were built of oak or other expensive hardwoods, it was no longer profitable to construct them. Subsequently, for more than a decade, a modified ship known as the "medium clipper" was developed. Its speed, however, never equalled that of the original, or "extreme clipper," which might make as much as 18 knots. Typically, the extreme clipper was a long, slender vessel, with a sharp, long bow and with the three masts slanting backwards and carrying rectangular sails. In small vessels, these characteristics of narrow beam and great sail-carrying capacity had been developed by U.S. builders before 1812. The invention of the type, however, was not American; it was an adaptation of principles that had been carefully studied by French scientists during the 18th century and accepted by the builders of French war vessels, which were then the fastest afloat. The majority of the clippers were built in New England yards, and their usual run was between ports of the eastern U.S. seaboard and China, Australia or San Francisco. But the career of the famous "Nightingale," from the time of its launching in 1851 until its loss in 1893, shows a variety of voyages to every part of the world. The equally well-known "Witch of the Wave" had a similar record, although shorter by about 20 years.

Besides the Californian and Australian gold rushes and the opium and slave trades, which gave such impetus to the building of clipper ships, one of the most potent motives for speed by water in the early 19th century was furnished by the Chinese tea trade. Inasmuch as this commodity quickly loses its flavour in the hold of a ship, annual prizes were offered by London merchants for the delivery at the earliest possible moment of the first crop of the season. Public excitement ran high, and rivalry among the various ships in the annual race from China was keen. One of these, the "Cutty Sark," built in 1869 covered 363 mi. in a day's travel, the record for tea clippers. By 1872, due to the opening of the Suez Canal in 1870 and the greater improvement in and more extended use of steam-propelled boats, these interesting tea races had virtually passed out of existence. With her hull picturesquely painted in bands of white and black, and dummy portholes in black, with her great number of sails and long, sharp bow the clipper ship of the 19th century was "the ideal of applied art and a sheer delight to the eye"—the possessor of "that peculiarly satisfying beauty which always belongs to the thing absolutely fitted for the purpose it is designed to fill." An excellent account has been compiled by Octavius T. Howe and Frederick C. Matthews, *American Clipper Ships 1833–58* (1926–27).

CLISSON, OLIVIER DE (1336–1407), French soldier, was the son of Olivier de Clisson, who was put to death in 1343 on the suspicion of having wished to give up Nantes to the English. He was brought up in England, where his mother, Jeanne de Belleville, had married her second husband. On his return to Brittany he took arms on the side of John of Montfort (John IV of Brittany), distinguishing himself at the battle of Auray (1364), but following differences with John went over to the side of Blois. In 1370 he joined Bertrand du Guesclin and followed him in all his campaigns against the English. On the death of Du Guesclin, Clisson received the constable's sword (1380). He fought against the Flemings, defeating them at Roosebeke (1382), and later commanded the army in Poitou and Flanders (1389) and made an unsuccessful attempt to invade England. On his return to Paris, in 1392, Pierre de Craon tried to assassinate him at the instigation of John IV. In order to punish the latter Charles VI of France, accompanied by the constable, marched on Brittany, but on this expedition the king was seized with madness. The king's uncles took proceedings against Clisson, so that he had to take refuge in Brittany. He was reconciled with John IV and, after the duke's death, in 1399, became protector of the duchy and guardian of the young princes. He died, extremely wealthy, on April 23, 1407.

See G. J. Tondouze, *Du Guesclin, Clisson, Richemont et la fin de la guerre de cent ans* (Paris, 1942); A. Naudin-Hérot, *Le Connétable de Clisson* (Paris, 1938).

CLISSON, a town of western France, in the department of Loire-Inférieure, 17 mi. S.E. of Nantes, at the confluence of the Sèvre and the Moine, both of which are crossed by old bridges. Pop. (1946) 2,712. The town gave its name to the celebrated family of Clisson, of which the most famous member was Olivier de Clisson. It has the imposing ruins of their stronghold, parts of which date from the 13th century. The town and castle were destroyed in 1792 and 1793 during the Vendean wars, but the town was rebuilt shortly afterward.

CLITHEROE, municipal borough, northeast Lancashire, Eng., 35 mi. N.W. from Manchester, on the London Midland Region railway. Pop. (1951) 12,057. Area 3.7 sq.mi. It is finely situated in the valley of the Ribble, at the foot of Pendle hill, a steep plateaulike mass rising to 1,831 ft.

The Honour of Clitheroe (Clyderhow or Cletherwoode) was first held by Roger de Poictou, almost certainly the builder of the castle. He granted it to Robert de Lacy, and it passed by marriage to Thomas, earl of Lancaster, in 1310. It was part of the duchy of Lancaster till Charles II bestowed it on Gen. George Monk, from whose family it descended through the house of Montague to that of Buccleuch. The first charter was granted about 1283 to the burgesses by Henry de Lacy, confirming the liberties granted by the first Henry de Lacy. The 1283 charter was confirmed by Edward III, Henry V, Henry VIII and James I. Fairs, on Dec. 7 to 9 and March 24 to 26, are held under a charter of Henry IV. A weekly market has been held on Saturday since William I's days. The church of St. Mary Magdalene, though occupying an ancient site, is modern. The town has a grammar school, founded in 1554, and a technical school. On a height commanding the valley stands the keep and other fragments of the Norman castle, but part of the site is occupied by a modern mansion. A large percentage of the population is engaged in the textile industry. In 1558 the borough was granted two members of parliament, and continued to return them till 1832, when the number was reduced to one. In 1885 the borough was disfranchised and is now represented in the Clitheroe division of Lancashire.

Stonyhurst college, 5 mi. S.W. of Clitheroe, is a college for Roman Catholic students. The nucleus of the buildings is a mansion (17th century) given by Thomas Weld in 1795 to refugee Jesuits from the continent. An observatory is attached to the college.

CLITUMNUS, a river in Umbria, It., rising from an abundant spring by the road between the ancient Spoletium and Trebia, 8 mi. from the former, 4 mi. from the latter. After a short course through the territory of Trebia it joins the Tinia, a tributary of the Tiber. Pliny described and Caligula and Honorius visited the lake, which is still a clear pool surrounded by poplars and weeping willows. The stream was personified as a god, whose ancient temple lay near the spring; close by were other smaller shrines, and it occurs under the name *Sacraria* (the "shrines") as a Roman post station.

The building, generally known as the Tempio di Clitunno, close to the spring, is an ancient Christian chapel, its decorative sculptures being contemporary with those of S. Salvatore at Spoleto (4th century).

CLIVE, CAROLINE (1801–1873), English authoress, was born in London, June 24, 1801; died at Whitfield, Herefordshire, on July 13, 1873. She was the daughter of an M.P., Edmund Meysey-Wigley, and married, in 1840, the Rev. Archer Clive.

She published poems and novels under the initial V and is best known as the author of *Paul Ferroll* (1855) a sensational novel.

CLIVE, CATHERINE (Kitty) (1711–1785), British actress, was born, probably in London, in 1711. Her father, William Raftor, an Irishman of good family but small means, had held a captain's commission in the French army under Louis XIV. About 1728 she began to play at Drury Lane, of which Colley Cibber was then manager. She married George Clive, a barrister and a relative of the 1st Lord Clive, but husband and wife soon separated by mutual consent. In 1731 she definitely established her reputation as a comic actress and singer in Charles Coffey's farce-opera adaptation *The Devil to Pay,* and from this time she was always a popular favourite. She acted little outside Drury Lane, where in 1747 she became one of the original members of David Garrick's company. She took part, however, in some of the oratorios of George Frederick Handel, whose friend she was. In 1769, having been a member of Garrick's company for 22 years, she quit the stage, and lived for 16 years in retirement at a villa at Twickenham, which had been given her some time previously by her friend Horace Walpole. Mrs. Clive had small claim to good looks, but as an actress of broad comedy she was unreservedly praised by Oliver Goldsmith, Samuel Johnson and Garrick.

She had a quick temper, which on various occasions involved her in quarrels, and at times sorely tried the patience of Garrick, but her private life remained above suspicion, and she regularly supported her father and his family. She died at Twickenham on Dec. 6, 1785.

Horace Walpole placed in his garden an urn to her memory, bearing an inscription, of which the last two lines run:

> The comic muse with her retired
> And shed a tear when she expired.

See Percy Fitzgerald, *Life of Mrs. Catherine Clive* (1888); W. R. Chetwood, *General History of the Stage* (1749); Thomas Davies, *Memoirs of the Life of David Garrick* (1784).

CLIVE, ROBERT CLIVE, Baron, of Plassey (1725–1774), the statesman and general who founded the empire of British India, was born on Sept. 29, 1725, at Styche, the family estate, in the parish of Moreton Say, Market Drayton, Shropshire. The Clives, or Clyves, were one of the oldest families in the county of Shropshire, having held the manor of that name in the reign of Henry II. One Clive was Irish chancellor of the exchequer under Henry VIII; another was a member of the long parliament; Robert's father for many years represented Montgomeryshire in parliament.

Young Clive was the despair of his teachers. Sent from school to school, and for only a short time at the Merchant Taylors' school, he neglected his books for perilous adventures. But he could read Horace in later life; and write a vigorous English, which marked all his dispatches and made Lord Chatham declare of one of his speeches in the house of commons that it was the most eloquent he had ever heard. At 18 he was sent out to Madras as a "factor" or "writer" in the civil service of the East India company. For the first two years of his residence he felt keenly the separation from home; he was always breaking through the restraints imposed on young "writers"; and he was rarely out of trouble with his fellows, with one of whom he fought a duel. His one solace was found in the governor's library, where he sought to make up for past carelessness by a systematic course of study. He was just of age when, in 1746, Madras was forced to capitulate to the count of la Bourdonnais during the War of the Austrian Succession. The breach of that capitulation by Gen. Joseph F. Dupleix, then at the head of the French settlements in India, led Clive, with others, to escape from the town to the subordinate Fort St. David, about 20 mi. to the south. There Clive obtained an ensign's commission.

At this time India was ready to become the prize of the first conqueror who combined administrative with military skill. For the 40 years since the death of the emperor Aurangzeb, the power of the great mogul had gradually fallen into the hands of his provincial viceroys, or *subadhars.* The three greatest of these were the nawab of the Deccan, or south and central India, who ruled from Hyderabad; the nawab of Bengal, whose capital was Murshidabad; and the nawab, or wazir, of Oudh. The prize lay between Dupleix, who had the genius of an administrator, or rather intriguer, but was no soldier, and Clive, the first of a century's brilliant succession of those "soldier-politicals" to whom Great Britain owed the conquest and consolidation of India. Clive successively established British ascendancy against French influence in the three great provinces under these nawabs; but his merit lay especially in the ability and foresight with which he secured the richest of the three, Bengal. Clive had hardly been able to commend himself to Maj. Stringer Lawrence, the commander of the British troops in Madras and the Deccan, by his courage and skill in several small engagements, when the peace of Aix-la-Chapelle (1748) forced him to return to his civil duties for a short time. An attack of fever which severely affected his spirits led him to visit Bengal. On his return he found a contest going on between two sets of rival claimants for the position of viceroy of the Deccan and for that of nawab of the Carnatic, the greatest of the subordinate states under the Deccan. Dupleix, who took the part of the pretenders to power in both places, was carrying all before him. The British had been weakened by the withdrawal of a large force under Adm. Edward Boscawen and by the return home, on leave, of Major Lawrence; but that officer had appointed Clive commissary for the supply of the troops with provisions, with the rank of captain. More than one disaster had taken place on a small scale, when Clive drew up a plan for dividing the enemy's forces and offered to carry it out himself. The pretender, Chanda Sahib, had been made nawab of the Carnatic with Dupleix's assistance, while the British had taken up the cause of the more legitimate successor, Mohammed Ali. Chanda Sahib had left Arcot, the capital of the Carnatic, to reduce Trichinopoly, then held by a weak English battalion. Clive offered to attack Arcot in order to force Chanda Sahib to raise the siege of Trichinopoly. But Madras and Fort St. David could supply him with only 200 Europeans and 300 sepoys. Of the eight officers who led them, four were civilians like Clive himself and six had never been in action. His force had but three fieldpieces. The circumstance that Clive, at the head of this handful, had been seen marching during a storm of thunder and lightning frightened the enemy into evacuating the fort, which the British at once began to strengthen against a siege. Clive treated the great population of the city with so much consideration that they helped him to make successful sallies against the enemy. As the days passed on, Chanda Sahib sent a large army under his son and his French supporters, who entered Arcot and closely besieged Clive in the citadel (1751). The story of the defense of the citadel and of the repulse of the enemy is told in Thomas Macaulay's essay on Clive. He gives the following account of the siege:

"Raja Sahib proceeded to invest the fort, which seemed quite incapable of sustaining a siege. The walls were ruinous, the ditches dry, the ramparts too narrow to admit the guns, and the battlements too low to protect the soldiers. The little garrison had been greatly reduced by casualties. It now consisted of 120 Europeans and 200 sepoys. Only four officers were left, the stock of provisions was scanty, and the commander who had to conduct the defence under circumstances so discouraging was a young man of five and twenty, who had been bred as a book-keeper. During fifty days the siege went on, and the young captain maintained the defence with a firmness, vigilance and ability which would have done honour to the oldest marshal in Europe. The breach, however, increased day by day. Under such circumstances, any troops so scantily provided with officers might have been expected to show signs of insubordination; and the danger was peculiarly great in a force composed of men differing widely from each other in extraction, colour, language, manners, and religion. But the devotion of the little band to its chief surpassed anything that is related of the Tenth Legion of Caesar, or the Old Guard of Napoleon. The sepoys came to Clive, not to complain of their scanty fare, but to propose that all the grain should be given to the Europeans, who required more nourishment than the natives of Asia. The thin gruel, they said, which strained away from the rice would suffice for themselves. History contains no more touching instance of military fidelity, or of the influence of a commanding mind. An attempt made by the governor of Madras to relieve the place had failed; but there was hope from another quarter. A body of 3000 Mahrattas, half soldiers, half robbers, under the command of a chief named Murari Rao had been hired to assist Mahommed Ali; but thinking the French power irresistible, and the triumph of Chanda Sahib certain, they had hitherto remained inactive on the frontiers of the Carnatic. The fame of the defence of Arcot roused them from their torpor; Murari Rao declared that he had never before believed that Englishmen could fight, but that he would willingly help them since he saw that they had spirit to help themselves. Raja Sahib learned that the Mahrattas were in motion, and it was necessary for him to be expeditious. He first tried negotiations—he offered large bribes to Clive, which were rejected with scorn; he vowed that if his proposals were not accepted, he would instantly storm the fort, and put every man in it to the sword. Clive told him, in reply, with characteristic haughtiness, that his father was a usurper, that his army was a rabble, and that he would do well to think twice before he sent such poltroons into a breach defended by English soldiers. Raja Sahib determined to storm the fort. The day was well suited to a bold military enterprise. It was the great Mahommedan festival, the Muharram, which is sacred to the memory of Husain, the son of Ali. Clive had received secret intelligence of the design, had made his arrangements, and, exhausted by fatigue, had thrown himself on his bed. He was awakened by the alarm, and was instantly at his post. The enemy advanced, driving before them elephants whose foreheads were armed with iron plates. It was expected that the gates would yield to the shock of these living battering-rams. But the huge beasts no sooner felt the English musket balls than they turned round and rushed furiously away, trampling on the multitude which had urged them forward. A raft was launched on the water which filled one part of the ditch. Clive perceiving that his gunners at that post did not understand their business, took the management of a piece of artillery himself, and cleared the raft in a few minutes. Where the moat was dry, the assailants mounted with great boldness; but they were received with a fire so heavy and so well directed, that it soon quelled the courage even of fanaticism and of intoxication. The rear ranks of the English kept the front ranks supplied with a constant succession of loaded muskets, and every shot told on the living mass below. The struggle lasted about an hour; 400 of the assailants fell; the garrison lost only five or six men. The besieged passed an anxious night, looking for a renewal of the attack. But when day broke, the enemy were no more to be seen. They had retired, leaving to the English several guns and a large quantity of ammunition."

Clive, now reinforced, followed up his advantage, and Major Lawrence returned in time to carry the war to a successful issue.

In 1754 a truce was arranged between Thomas Saunders, the company's president at Madras, and Charles Robert Godeheu, who had replaced Dupleix. The English protégé Mohammed Ali, was virtually recognized as nawab, and both nations agreed to equalize their possessions. When war again broke out in 1756, and the French, during Clive's absence in Bengal, obtained successes in the northern districts, his efforts helped to drive them from their settlements. The treaty of Paris in 1763 formally confirmed Mohammed Ali in the position which Clive had won for him. Two years later, Clive's work in Madras was completed by a firman from the emperor of Delhi, recognizing the British possessions in southern India.

The siege of Arcot at once gave Clive a European reputation. William Pitt pronounced the youth of 27 who had done such deeds a "heaven-born general." When the court of directors voted him a sword worth £700, he refused to receive it unless Lawrence was similarly honoured.

He left Madras for home, after ten years' absence, early in 1753. Before leaving India he married Margaret Maskelyne. The marriage was a happy one, and the scandalous stories of his private life spread later by his enemies are devoid of foundation. After he had been two years at home the state of affairs in India made the directors anxious for his return. He was sent out, in 1756, as governor of Fort St. David, with the reversion of the government of Madras and with the commission of lieutenant colonel in the king's army.

While at Bombay on his way to Madras, he commanded the land force which captured Gheria, the stronghold of the Maratha pirate Angria. He took his seat as governor of Fort St. David on the day on which the nawab of Bengal captured Calcutta, and thither the Madras government at once sent him, with Adm. Charles Watson.

Since the days of Job Charnock at Sutanati the infant capital of Calcutta had become a rich centre of trade. The successive nawabs, or viceroys, of Bengal had been friendly to it, till, in 1756, Suraj-ud-Dowlah succeeded his uncle at Murshidabad. His predecessor's financial minister had fled to Calcutta to escape the extortion of the new nawab, and the English governor refused to deliver up the refugee.

Enraged at this, Suraj-ud-Dowlah captured the old fort of Calcutta on June 20 and plundered it. Many of the English fled to ships and escaped down the river. The 146 who remained were forced into "the Black Hole" in the stifling heat of the sultriest period of the year; only 23 came out alive. The fleet was as strong, for those days, as the land force was weak. Disembarking his troops several miles below the city, Clive marched through the jungles, where he lost his way because of the treachery of his guides, but soon invested Fort William, while the fire of the ships reduced it, on Jan. 2, 1757.

On Feb. 4 he defeated the whole army of the nawab, which had taken up a strong position just beyond what is now the most northerly suburb of Calcutta.

The nawab hastened to conclude a treaty, under which favourable terms were conceded to the company's trade, the factories and plundered property were restored and an English mint was established. In the accompanying agreement, offensive and defensive, Clive appears under the name by which he was always known to the natives of India, Sabut Jung, or "the Daring in War." With 600 British soldiers, 800 sepoys, 7 fieldpieces and 500 sailors to draw them, he had routed a force of 34,000 men with 40 pieces of heavy cannon and 50 elephants and seized a camp four miles in length.

In spite of his double defeat and the treaty which followed it, the madness of the nawab burst forth again. As England and France were once more at war, Clive sent the fleet up the river against Chandernagore, while he besieged it by land. After consenting to the siege, the nawab sought to assist the French, but in vain. The capture of their principal settlement in India, next to Pondicherry, which had fallen in the previous war, gave the combined forces prize to the value of £130,000. The rule of Suraj-ud-Dowlah became as intolerable to his own people as to the British. They formed a confederacy to depose him, at the head of which was Mir Jafar, his commander in chief. Associating with himself Admiral Watson, Gov. Roger Drake and William Watts, Clive made a treaty to give the office of viceroy of Bengal, Behar and Orissa to Mir Jafar, who was to pay £1,000,000 sterling to the company for its losses in Calcutta and the cost of its troops, £500,000 to the British inhabitants of Calcutta, £200,000 to the native inhabitants and £70,000 to its Armenian merchants. Up to this point all is clear. Suraj-ud-Dowlah was hopeless as a ruler. His relations alike to his master, the merely titular emperor of Delhi, and to the people left the province open to the strongest. After "the Black Hole," the battle of Calcutta and the treachery at Chandernagore, in spite of the treaty which followed that battle, the East India company could treat the nawab only as an enemy. Clive, it is true, might have disregarded all native intrigue, marched on Murshidabad and at once held the delta of the Ganges in the company's name. But the time was not ripe for this, the consequences, with so small a force, might have been fatal and the political morality of the time in Europe, as well as the comparative weakness of the company in India, led Clive not only to meet the dishonesty of his native associate by equal dishonesty but to justify his conduct by the declaration, years after, in parliament, that he would do the same again. It became necessary to employ the richest Bengali trader, Omichund, as an agent between Mir Jafar and the British officials. Master of the secret of the confederacy against Suraj-ud-Dowlah, the Bengali threatened to betray it unless he was guaranteed, in the treaty itself, £300,000. To dupe the villain, who was really paid by both sides, a second or fictitious treaty was shown him with a clause to this effect. This Admiral Watson refused to sign; "but," Clive deposed to the house of commons, "to the best of his remembrance, he [Clive] gave the gentleman who carried it leave to sign his [Watson's] name upon it; his lordship never made any secret of it; he thinks it warrantable in such a case, and would do it again a hundred times; he had no interested motive in doing it, and did it with a design of disappointing the expectations of a rapacious man."

The whole hot season of 1757 was spent in these negotiations till the middle of June, when Clive began his march from Chandernagore, the British in boats and the sepoys along the right bank of the Hooghly. That river above Calcutta is, during the rainy season, fed by the overflow of the Ganges to the north through three streams, which in the hot months are nearly dry. On the left bank of the Bhagirathi, the most westerly of these, 100 mi. above Chandernagore, stands Murshidabad, the capital of the Mogul viceroys of Bengal, and then so vast that Clive compared it to the London of his day. Several miles farther down is the field of Plassey, then an extensive grove of mango trees. On June 21 Clive arrived on the bank opposite Plassey, in the midst of that outburst of rain which ushers in the southwest monsoon of India. His whole army amounted to 1,100 Europeans and 2,100 native troops, with nine fieldpieces. The nawab had drawn up 18,000 horse, 50,000 foot and 53 pieces of heavy ordnance, served by French artillerymen. For once in his career Clive hesitated and called a council of 16 officers to decide, as he put it, "whether in our present situation, without assistance, and on our own bottom, it would be prudent to attack the nawab, or whether we should wait till joined by some country power?" Clive himself headed the nine who voted for delay; Maj. (afterward Sir) Eyre Coote led the seven who counselled immediate attack. But, either because his daring asserted itself or because, also, of a letter that he received from Mir Jafar, as has been said, Clive was the first to change his mind and to communicate with Major Coote.

One tradition, followed by Macaulay, represents him as spending an hour in thought under the shade of some trees, while he resolved the issues of what was to prove one of the decisive battles of India.

Another tradition, turned into verse by Sir Alfred Lyall, pictures his resolution as the result of a dream. However that may be, he did well to trust to the dash and even rashness that had gained Arcot and triumphed at Calcutta.

When, after the heavy rain had fallen, the sun rose brightly on June 22, the 3,200 men and the nine guns crossed the river and took possession of the grove and its tanks of water, while Clive established his headquarters in a hunting lodge. On June 23 the engagement took place and lasted the whole day. Except the 40 Frenchmen and the guns which they worked, the enemy did little to reply to the British cannonade, which, with the 39th regiment, scattered the host, inflicting on it a loss of 500 men. Clive restrained the ardour of Maj. John Kilpatrick, for he trusted to Mir Jafar's abstinence, if not desertion to his ranks, and knew the importance of sparing his own small force. He lost hardly a white soldier; in all, 22 sepoys were killed and 50 wounded. Suraj-ud-Dowlah fled from the field on a camel, secured what wealth he could and came to an untimely end. Clive entered Murshidabad and established Mir Jafar. When taken through the treasury, amid £1,500,000's worth of rupees, gold and silver plate, jewels and rich goods, and besought to ask what he would, Clive was content with £160,000, while £500,000 was distributed among the army and navy, both in addition to gifts of £24,000 to each member of the company's committee and besides the public compensation stipulated in the treaty. It was to this occasion that he referred in his defense before the house of commons, when he declared that he marvelled at his moderation. He followed a usage fully recognized by the company, although the fruitful source of future evils which he himself was again sent out to correct. The company itself acquired a revenue of £100,000 a year and a contribution toward its losses and military expenditure of £1,500,000.

Mir Jafar afterward presented Clive with the quitrent of the company's lands in and around Calcutta, amounting to an annuity of £27,000 for life, and left him by will the sum of £70,000, which Clive devoted to the army.

While busy with the civil administration, the conqueror of Plassey followed up his military success. He sent Major Coote in pursuit of the French almost as far as Benares. He dispatched Francis Forde to Vizagapatam and the northern districts of Madras, where that officer gained the battle of Condore. He came into direct contact, for the first time, with the great mogul himself, an event which resulted in the most important consequences during the third period of his career. Shah Alam, when *shahzada*, or heir apparent, quarrelled with his father, Alamgir II, the emperor, and united with the viceroys of Oudh and Allahabad for the conquest of Bengal. He advanced as far as Patna, which he besieged with 40,000 men. Mir Jafar, in terror, sent his son to its relief and implored the aid of Clive. Maj. John Caillaud defeated the prince's army and dispersed it. Finally, at this period, Clive repelled the aggression of the Dutch and avenged the massacre of Amboyna, on that occasion when he wrote his famous letter, "Dear Forde, fight them immediately; I will send you the order of council tomorrow."

Meanwhile, he never ceased to improve the organization and drill of the sepoy army, after a European model, and enlisted into it many Mohammedans of fine physique from upper India. He refortified Calcutta. In 1760, after four years of incessant labour, his health gave way and he returned to England. "It appeared," wrote a contemporary on the spot, "as if the soul was departing from the Government of Bengal." He had been formally made governor of Bengal by the court of directors at a time when his nominal superiors in Madras sought to recall him to their help there. But he had discerned the importance of the province even during his first visit.

It should be noticed, also, that even this early he had discovered the ability of young Warren Hastings and, a year after Plassey, made him resident at the nawab's court.

In 1760, at 35 years of age, Clive returned to England with a fortune of at least £300,000 and the quitrent of £27,000 a year, after caring for the comfort of his parents and sisters and giving Major Lawrence, his old commanding officer, £500 a year. The money had been honourably and publicly acquired, with the approval of the company. The amount might have been four times what it was had Clive been either greedy after wealth or ungenerous to the colleagues and the troops whom he led to victory.

In the five years of his conquests and administration in Bengal, the young man had crowded together a succession of exploits which led Lord Macaulay, in what historians termed his "flashy" essay on the subject, to compare him with Napoleon Bonaparte. But there was this difference in Clive's favour, attributable not more to the circumstances of the time than to the object of his policy—he gave peace, security, prosperity and a certain measure of liberty to a people who had for centuries been the prey of oppression whereas Napoleon's career of conquest led to an absolutism which vanished with his fall.

He was well received at court, was made Baron Clive of Plassey, in the peerage of Ireland, bought estates and got not only himself but his friends returned to the house of commons after the fashion of the time. He then set himself to reform the home system of the East India company and began a bitter warfare with Lawrence Sulivan, chairman of the court of directors, whom in the end he defeated, aided by the news of reverses in Bengal. Henry Vansittart, his successor, having no great influence over Mir Jafar, had put Mir Kasim, the son-in-law, in his place in consideration of certain payments to the English officials. After a brief tenure Mir Kasim had fled, had ordered Walter Reinhardt (known to the Mohammedans as Sumru), a European mercenary of his, to butcher the garrison of 150 English at Patna and had disappeared under the protection of his brother viceroy of Oudh. The whole company's service, civil and military, had become demoralized by gifts and by the monopoly of the inland as well as export trade, to such an extent that the natives were pauperized and the company was plundered of the revenues which Clive had acquired for them. The court of proprietors, accordingly, who elected the directors, forced them, in spite of Sulivan, to hurry Lord Clive to Bengal with the double powers of governor and commander in chief.

What he had done for Madras, what he had accomplished for Bengal proper and what he had effected in reforming the company itself he was now to complete in less than two years, in this the third period of his career, by putting his country politically in the place of the emperor of Delhi.

On May 3, 1765, he landed at Calcutta to learn that Mir Jafar had died, leaving him personally £70,000, and had been succeeded by his son, though not before the government had been further demoralized by taking £100,000 as a gift from the new nawab; while Mir Kasim had induced not only the viceroy of Oudh, but the emperor of Delhi himself to invade Behar. After the first mutiny in the Bengal army, which was suppressed by blowing 24 sepoys from guns in the presence of their comrades, Maj. (later Sir) Hector Munro, "the Napier of those times," scattered the united armies on the hard-fought field of Buxar. The emperor, Shah Alam, detached himself from the league, while the Oudh viceroy threw himself on the mercy of the British. Clive had now an opportunity of repeating in Hindustan, or upper India, what he had accomplished in Bengal. He might have secured what were later called the United Provinces, and have rendered unnecessary the campaigns of Marquis Wellesley and Gerard (later Viscount) Lake. But he had other work in the consolidation of rich Bengal itself, making it a base for the development of the mighty fabric of British India. Hence, he returned to the Oudh viceroy all his territory save the provinces of Allahabad and Kora, which he made over to the weak emperor. But from that emperor he secured the most important document in the whole of British history in India up to that time, which appears in the records as "firmaund from the King Shah Aalum, granting the dewany of Bengal, Behar and Orissa to the company, 1765." The date was Aug. 12; the place, Benares; the throne, an English dining table covered with embroidered cloth and surmounted by a chair in Clive's tent. It is all pictured by a Mohammedan contemporary, who indignantly exclaims that so great a "transaction was done and finished in less time than would have been taken up in the sale of a jackass." By this deed the company became the real sovereign rulers of 30,000,000 people, yielding a revenue of £4,000,000 sterling.

On the same date Clive obtained not only an imperial charter for the company's possession in the Carnatic also, thus completing the work he began at Arcot, but a third firman for the highest of all the lieutenancies of the empire, that of the Deccan itself. This fact is mentioned in a letter from the secret committee of the court of directors to the Madras government, dated April 27, 1768.

Still so disproportionate did the British force seem, not only to the number and strength of the princes and people of India, but to the claims and ambition of French, Dutch and Danish rivals, that Clive's last advice to the directors, as he finally left India in 1767, was this: "We are sensible that, since the acquisition of the dewany, the power formerly belonging to the soubah of those provinces is totally, in fact, vested in the East India Company. Nothing remains to him but the name and shadow of authority. This name, however, this shadow, it is indispensably necessary we should seem to venerate."

On a wider arena, even that of the great mogul himself, the shadow was kept up till the massacre of English people in the Delhi palace in 1857; and Queen Victoria was proclaimed, first, direct ruler on Nov. 1, 1858, and later empress of India on Jan. 1, 1877.

Having thus founded the empire of British India, Clive sought to reform the administration. The civil service was deorientalized by raising the miserable salaries which had tempted its members to be corrupt, by forbidding the acceptance of gifts from natives and by exacting covenants under which participation in the inland trade was stopped.

Not less important were his military reforms. He put down a mutiny of the English officers, who chose to resent the veto against receiving presents and the reduction of *batta* (extra pay) at a time when two Maratha armies were marching on Bengal. He reorganized the army, dividing the whole into three brigades, so as to make each a complete force, in itself equal to any single native army that could be brought against it. He had not enough British artillerymen, however, and would not train natives to work the guns.

Clive's final return to England a poorer man than he went out, in spite of still more tremendous temptations, was the signal for an outburst of his personal enemies. Every civilian whose illicit gains he had cut off, every officer whose conspiracy he had foiled, every proprietor or director, like Sulivan, whose selfish schemes he had thwarted, now sought his opportunity. Clive had, with consistent generosity, at once made over the legacy of £70,000 from the grateful Mir Jafar as the capital of what has since been known as "the Clive fund" for the support of invalided European soldiers, as well as officers, and their widows; and the company had allowed 8% on the sum for an object which it was otherwise bound to meet.

Gen. John Burgoyne, of Saratoga memory, did his best to induce the house of commons, in which Lord Clive was now member for Shrewsbury, to impeach the man who gave his country an empire, and the people of that empire peace and justice. The result, after the brilliant and honourable defenses of his career which will be found in John Almon's *Debates* for 1773, was a compromise. On a division the house, by 155 to 95, carried the motion that Lord Clive "did obtain and possess himself" of £234,000 during his first administration of Bengal; but, refusing to express an opinion on the fact, it passed unanimously the second motion, at five in the morning, "that Robert, Lord Clive, did at the same time render great and meritorious services to his country." The one questionable transaction—the Omichund treaty—was not touched.

Only one who can personally understand what Clive's power and services had been will rightly realize the effect on him, though in the prime of life, of the discussions through which he had been dragged.

In the greatest of his speeches, in reply to Lord North, he said, "My situation, sir, has not been an easy one for these 12 months past, and though my conscience could never accuse me, yet I felt for my friends who were involved in the same censure as myself . . . I have been examined by the select committee more like a sheep-stealer than a member of this House." Clive's end was the result of physical suffering, of chronic disease which opium failed to abate and which the worry and chagrin caused by his enemies exacerbated; he died by his own hand on Nov. 22, 1774, in his 50th year.

Clive was slightly above middle size, with a countenance rendered heavy and almost sad by a natural fullness above the eyes. His encouragement of scientific undertakings like Maj. James Rennell's surveys, and of philological researches like Francis Gladwin's, gained him the honorary distinctions of F.R.S. and LL.D.

His son and successor Edward (1754–1839) was created earl of Powis in 1804, his wife being the sister and heiress of George Herbert, earl of Powis (1755–1801). He thus was the ancestor of the later earls of Powis, who took the name of Herbert instead of that of Clive in 1807.

See G. W. Forrest, *Life of Lord Clive* (London, 1918); H. H. Dodwell, *Dupleix and Clive* (London, 1920).

CLOACA, the Latin term for a drain or sewer. The most famous is the Cloaca Maxima at Rome, built to drain the marsh where the Forum Romanum was situated. Constructed originally in the late 6th century B.C. as an open stone-lined channel, some side channels were vaulted in the 5th century and the main channel in the 3rd century and later with a stone barrel vault.

CLOACA is also the name given to the joint opening of the urinogenital and alimentary systems characteristic of all the vertebrates except the mammals, among which it is only retained in the Monotremata (*q.v.*).

CLOCKS. A clock is a machine designed to record and to indicate the passing of time. The only way to construct such a machine is to link a device that performs regular movements in equal intervals of time to a counting mechanism that will record the number of these movements. All clocks, of whatever form they may be, are made on this principle.

An ordinary clock consists of a series of toothed wheels and pinions (small toothed wheels) driven by a weight or spring and linked by an escapement to a pendulum or, alternatively, to a balance and hairspring, which has the property of even, isochronous motion. The function of the escapement is to enable the regular movements of the pendulum or balance to control the rotation of the wheelwork and to cause it to rotate at an even and constant rate. At the same time, the escapement is arranged to transmit to the pendulum or balance sufficient power to maintain its swing by replacing the energy absorbed by various frictional effects. Such a machine, though popularly called a clock, is strictly termed a timepiece, the term clock being properly applied only to a timekeeper which, by an additional mechanism, strikes the hours on a bell or gong (French *cloche,* German *Glocke,* bell).

The earliest mechanical clocks seem to have been introduced in Europe during the 13th century and were employed in religious houses to mark the times of services. A clock is said to have been erected at Westminster in 1288, another at Canterbury in 1292 and another, with an astronomical dial, at St. Albans in 1326. The oldest clock remaining in England is that at Salisbury cathedral, which dates from 1386; another still existing mechanism was erected at Wells cathedral in 1392. Others of somewhat later date are to be seen at Exeter cathedral, at Ottery St. Mary church, at Rye church and at Cothele house in Cornwall. None of these early clocks was originally fitted with a pendulum. Instead, they had a verge or crown-wheel escapement controlled by two weighted arms which oscillated slowly and so controlled the release of the escape wheel. This device was known as a foliot (*see* fig. 1).

As the time of swing of the arms was very variable and was directly affected by the driving force, these early clocks were very poor timekeepers and often varied by as much as an hour in a day. The action of the foliot can be followed from the illustration (fig. 1). A and B are the weighted arms, which pivot at the point C; the escape wheel E is released, tooth by tooth, by the movement of the two pallets F and G, which are mounted on the same axis as the arms A and B and swing with them; from this it will be seen that the escape wheel is not only released by the motion of the arms and pallets but also transmits to them some of the energy of the driving weight H and so maintains their swing.

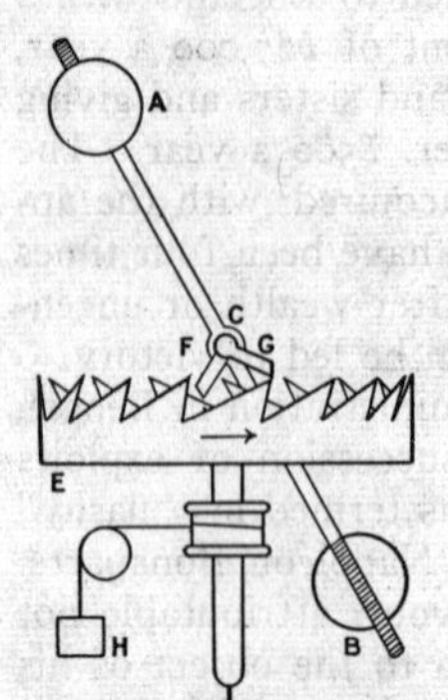

FIG. 1.—VERGE ESCAPEMENT, SHOWING THE METHOD OF USING AN OSCILLATING MASS TO KEEP TIME

Pendulum.—The next important development in clock construction was the introduction of the pendulum. Its principle was first discovered by Galileo in 1581. It consists of a weight or bob mounted on the lower end of a vertical rod. The upper end of this rod is suspended from a flexible support in such a manner that the rod and its bob are free to oscillate under the influence of gravity.

The great virtue of a pendulum as a time measurer lies in the fact that, within certain limits, its period of swing remains practically unaffected by variations in the degrees of arc through which it swings. The duration of swing of a pendulum varies with its length; in Great Britain the length of a pendulum which makes one swing per second is 39.14 in. With such a pendulum, an increase in length of about $\frac{1}{1,000}$ in. will cause a change in rate of about a second a day, and if the arc of vibration is 3 in. an increase of $\frac{1}{10}$ in. will have a similar effect.

The relation between the length of a pendulum and its time of swing can be determined by the following formula. Consider L to be the length of the pendulum in feet, G the acceleration caused by gravity in feet per second per second and π the ratio of the circumference of a circle to its diameter (= approx. 3.1429): then the time of one swing in seconds $= \pi\sqrt{\frac{L}{G}}$.

As the time of swing of a pendulum is so critically dependent on its length, it follows that any expansion or contraction of the rod caused by changes of temperature will affect its timekeeping. For instance, the expansion of steel is approximately 0.001 in. for every 4° of increase in temperature, and a corresponding decrease will result in a proportional contraction. If accurate timekeeping is required, a pendulum must be compensated for such changes by some device which will keep its length as constant as possible at all times. There are several ways in which this may be done, some of which use the differing coefficients of expansion of different metals to obtain a cancelling-out effect. The most usual forms of compensation are the mercurial, where the bob contains a suitable amount of mercury, the gridiron, where brass and steel rods are employed, and the zinc-iron tube, in which, as the name suggests, the pendulum rod is made up of concentric tubes of zinc and iron.

A better method is the use of a special alloy called Invar for the pendulum rod. This material has such a small coefficient of expansion that changes of temperature have an almost negligible effect.

Escapement.—This important part of the mechanism of a timekeeper has the dual function of controlling the wheel train of a clock by relating its speed of rotation to the evenly timed swings of the pendulum or balance and of supplying the pendulum or balance with enough energy to maintain its swing. An ideal escapement would perform both functions without any interference with the free swing of the pendulum or balance, and the more closely an actual escapement approaches this condition, the better it is.

When first introduced, the pendulum was used with the verge escapement. This was as shown in fig. 1, but adapted to pendulum control. In a short time, the verge was replaced by the anchor or recoil escapement, which was a great improvement and is still used for many domestic clocks (fig. 2).

The recoil escapement has two pallets, which are mounted on the ends of a curved bar or yoke that spans a part of the circumference of the escape wheel. At a point approximately equidistant from both pallets, the yoke is attached to a pivoted spindle linked to the pendulum by a light bar or crutch. As the pendulum swings it causes the pallet spindle to move with an oscillating movement, and this in turn engages and disengages the pallets with the teeth of the escape wheel, so permitting the wheel to advance in a step-by-step motion.

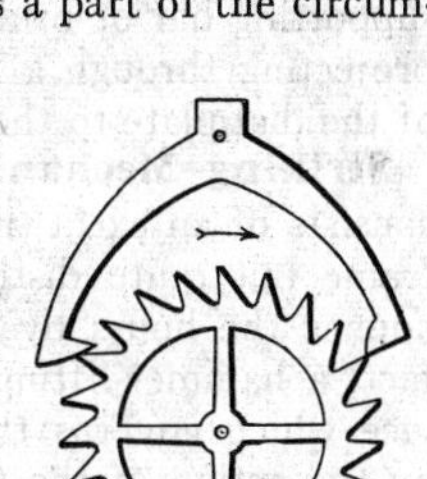

FIG. 2.—ANCHOR OR RECOIL ESCAPEMENT, ONE OF THE EARLIEST ATTEMPTS TO USE A PENDULUM

The inclined acting faces of the pallets not only arrest and release the teeth of the escape wheel, but also serve to transmit some of the energy used to drive the clock to the pendulum in the form of impulses. Because of their form, however, the pallets also cause any additional swing which the pendulum makes after a tooth has engaged with a pallet to cause a recoiling movement of the escape wheel. This must be considered a defect, and to obviate the recoil a modification, known as the deadbeat escapement, was invented by George Graham in 1715 (fig. 3).

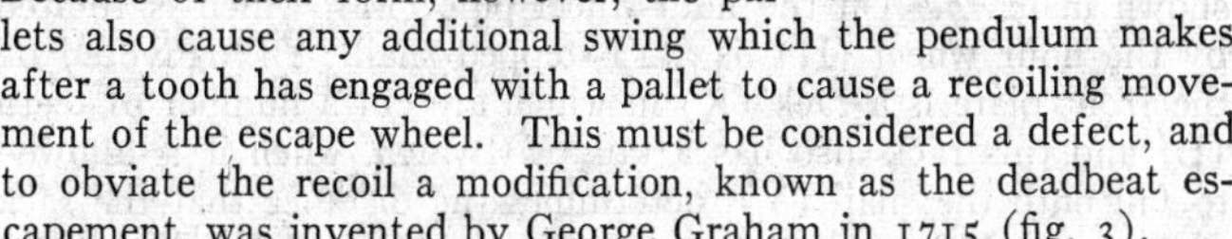

In this escapement the acting surfaces of the pallets are shaped to have two distinct parts, known as the dead and impulse faces. The teeth of the escape wheel fall first upon the dead faces (GF and BD, fig. 3) and rest upon them before the movement of the pallets allows them to reach the impulse faces (FA and BE, fig. 3) and finally to escape. As the dead faces of the pallets are formed as parts of the arc of a circle struck from the pivot point (C, fig. 3) any additional swing of the pendulum after the engagement of a tooth with a pallet will not cause any recoil, and the swing of the pendulum will not be interfered with to any great extent. To minimize interference still further by reducing friction the pallets of very precise clocks have pieces of jewel inserted in their acting faces.

The pallets of a deadbeat escapement usually embrace about one-third of the circumference of the escape wheel, for this arrangement gives the best possible action and does not make the pallets unnecessarily heavy. With this construction, a total of about 2°—about 1° on each side of the vertical—is occupied in receiving the impulse. As the total arc of swing of the pendulum is about 3°, this is a very satisfactory arrangement.

Other versions of the deadbeat escapement include the pin-pallet and pin-wheel forms, the latter being often used for small tower clocks where extreme accuracy is not essential.

One of the defects of both the recoil and deadbeat escapements is that the impulse that they transmit to the pendulum can vary because of variations in the power transmitted by the wheelwork of the clock. Such changes in power can arise from thickening of the oil, from dust or wear or, in the case of tower clocks, from wind pressure or from snow or ice on the hands. To overcome this a number of inventors designed escapements in which weighted arms were raised by the escape wheel and then delivered the impulse to the pendulum as they descended to their original position. The first really successful escapement of this kind was invented by Bloxam, a barrister. A much better form, the double three-legged gravity escapement, was invented by E. B. Denison, afterward Lord Grimthorpe, and used by him for the great clock at Westminster. It has since become standard for all really accurate tower clocks (fig. 4).

In this escapement, the escape wheel is made up of two three-legged components (C_1 and C_2) mounted 60° apart on their spindle. Between these two wheels, at a point near their centre, are three pins (P_1, P_2 and P_3) known as the lifting pins. Engaging with the wheels and the pins are two gravity arms (A_1 and A_2) pivoted at their upper ends and carrying locking pads (B_1 and B_2), one of which engages with the tips of wheel C_1, the other with the tips of wheel C_2. On the gravity arms are the projecting arms E_1 and E_2, which engage with the lifting pins and form the means by which the gravity arms are raised.

The action is as follows. As the escape wheel rotates a sixth of a turn, one of the lifting pins (P_1 in fig. 4) raises a gravity arm and then, at the moment when the arm is lifted fully, the corresponding leg of the three-legged wheel (C_2 in fig. 4) locks on its pad on the arm, so arresting further movement of the escape wheel. The swinging pendulum then engages with the lower end of the gravity arm and lifts it slightly farther. This unlocks the escape wheel by moving the locking pad from under the tip of the wheel tooth, and the wheel turns a further sixth of a turn. As this occurs, the pin is moved out of contact with the projecting arm E_2 on the gravity arm which it has been supporting. The arm is then free to fall back with the pendulum and, as it returns, it delivers to the pendulum the energy which was stored in it when the escape wheel raised it. As one gravity arm is unlocked, the other is raised by another pin (P_2 in fig. 4) and locked by the other section of the double three-legged wheel, after which the whole cycle is repeated. In other words, the pendulum always finds the gravity arms lifted to a higher level than it left them, and the weight of the arms, falling through this distance, delivers the impulse. As it is a gravitational impulse, it is, of course, constant in value.

Many of the smaller types of domestic clock are now being fitted with escapements embodying a balance and hairspring instead of a pendulum, the object being to make them more portable. The escapements used are the cylinder, lever and, in some cases, the chronometer detent (*see* WATCHES). Their construction is identical with similar escapements used in watches.

Clock Wheelwork: the Train.—With all but the gravity escapement, it is of great importance that the energy transmitted by the wheelwork of a clock should be as regular as possible and, even with a gravity escapement, a consistent supply of power is an advantage. The wheels and pinions should therefore be made as accurately as possible, and the tooth form designed so that the transference of power takes place as steadily as conditions permit. Modern improvements in manufacture and advances in the theory of gear design have made clocks of the present day far better than older ones in this respect. In a weight-driven or spring-driven clock, the power of the weight or spring is first transmitted by the great or main wheel. This engages with the first pinion, to the spindle of which is attached the second wheel. This engages with the second pinion, and so on, right through the train and down to the escapement. The ratios of the gears are such that one spindle, usually the second or third, rotates at a speed of one turn per hour, and so can be used to carry the minute hand. A simple 12 to 1 gearing, known as the motion work, gives the necessary step-down ratio to drive the hour hand. The spring or weight is fitted with some form of ratchet mechanism to enable it to be rewound when necessary, and the spindle carrying the minute hand is provided with a simple slipping clutch which allows the hands to be set to time.

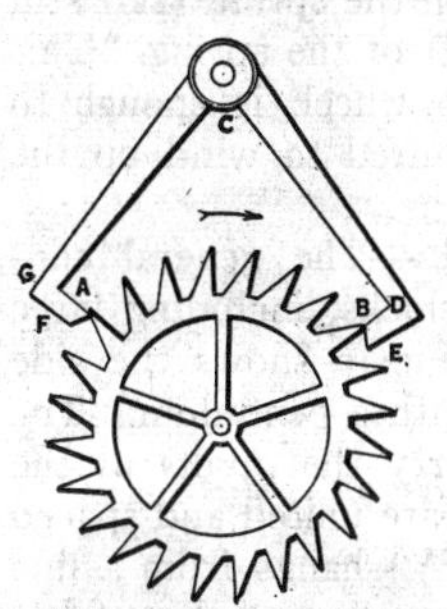

FIG. 3.—DEADBEAT ESCAPEMENT, A REFINEMENT OF THE ANCHOR ESCAPEMENT

In many modern clocks, the mainspring is enclosed in a drum or barrel which has the main wheel mounted directly on one end. As, with this arrangement, the spring is then wound by the rotation of the spindle or arbor on which the barrel pivots, the power of the spring still acts on the wheelwork during winding and a special attachment to maintain the power is unnecessary.

On weight-driven clocks and some forms of spring-driven clocks, however, the act of winding interrupts the supply of power, and such clocks must have a maintaining power if their timekeeping is not to be interfered with. In some maintaining-power mechanisms, a small spring or weight is attached to a lever in such a way that it can be brought into action during winding, the power of the additional spring or weight taking over the propulsion of the clock until the process is completed. Many tower clocks have such an arrangement. For domestic clocks, a better form of maintaining power is the Harrison going ratchet (fig. 5).

Here the pawl or click (R) of the winding ratchet (B) is not mounted on the main wheel (G) but is pivoted instead on a second, larger ratchet, whose teeth point the opposite way. Engaging with the teeth of this second ratchet wheel is another pawl or click (*Tr*) pivoted to the frame of the clock. The second ratchet wheel is linked to the main wheel (G) by a spring (ss′), one end of which (s) is attached to the ratchet and the other (s′) to the main wheel. During the normal going of the clock, the driving weight stores power in this spring, and the whole assembly rotates with the main wheel, the pawl T*r* stepping idly over the teeth of the larger ratchet wheel (hence the term going ratchet).

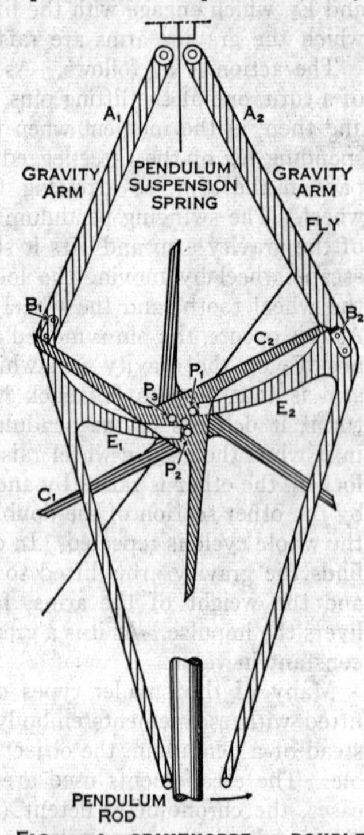

FIG. 4—GRIMTHORPE DOUBLE THREE-LEGGED GRAVITY ESCAPEMENT AS USED FOR LARGE TOWER CLOCKS

When winding begins, the winding ratchet (B) is rotated, and the power of the weight ceases to be applied to the train, but as the second pawl (T*r*) locks the larger ratchet wheel and prevents it from moving with the winding ratchet (B), the power stored in the spring (ss′) still acts on the main wheel through the end (s′) of the spring. This power, applied to the slowly moving main wheel, is enough to keep the clock going during the time required to wind up the weight.

Construction of an Ordinary Clock.—The general construction of the timekeeping part of all clocks, including large tower clocks, is substantially the same. Fig. 6 shows the side view of a simple weight-driven timepiece with a pendulum. The frame is made up of two plates which carry the pivots of the various wheels and other moving parts and are united and spaced by four pillars (P). The driving weight (W) hangs from a line coiled around the barrel (B) and is wound by means of the ratchet wheel (R). Between this ratchet and the main wheel (G) is the maintaining-power ratchet, similar to that described in fig. 5, the arbor of the going ratchet being visible at Tr. The main wheel (G) engages with the centre pinion (c) on the spindle of which is also mounted the centre wheel (C). The front pivot of this wheel and pinion is lengthened to the left of the illustration, and carries the minute hand and part of the gearing necessary to drive the hour hand.

The centre wheel (C) engages with the pinion of the third wheel (d) and on that same spindle is mounted the third wheel (D) which in its turn engages with the escape wheel pinion (e). The escape wheel (E) engages with the pallets (A) which are fixed to the spindle (a) and pivot between the front plate and the pendulum suspension cock (F). Also fixed to the pallet spindle is the crutch (Ff), which terminates at its lower end in a fork (f) which embraces the pendulum rod (Pp). This pendulum, of which only the upper part is shown, is suspended by a thin flat suspension spring (S) from the cock (F) which is reinforced to obtain the utmost possible rigidity by a bar (QO) spanning the top of the clock frame plates.

The motion work used for driving the hands at their relative speeds is mounted between the dial and the front plate of the frame. The wheel (M), which rotates once per hour and is known as the cannon pinion, is coupled to the centre spindle by a flat spring which acts as a clutch and permits the hands to be set. The cannon pinion (M) engages with a wheel of similar size (N) called the minute wheel, and the small pinion (n) attached to this wheel engages with the hour wheel (H) that pivots on a small supporting bar or bridge (L). The winding square (K) is shown projecting through a hole in the dial plate, and the attachments of the dial plate to the mechanism are at x and Z.

Striking Mechanism.—The striking mechanism of a clock consists of an extra train of wheels, usually mounted in the same frame but quite distinct in construction, which is used to announce the hours by striking them on a bell or gong. It is, in fact, a hammer-lifting mechanism equipped with a counting device which governs the number of blows struck. It is released by the action of the timekeeping part, but has little or no other connection with it.

There are two forms of controlling mechanism for determining the number of blows to be struck at the various hours. One is known as the locking plate and the other the rack. The former is the older and is still used for most tower clocks. The other, the rack mechanism, is used on most domestic clocks, and the usual arrangement for an English long-case or grandfather clock is shown in fig. 7. On the hour-wheel pipe (M), which is rotated by the hour wheel (H), is a 12-stepped snail (Y). Pivoted on the front plate is a rack (R) in which are cut a number of teeth (L) and this rack also has a tail (V) which, when it is allowed to fall onto the snail (Y), determines the distance that the rack can move. Mounted on an extended pivot of the third wheel of the striking train is a gathering pallet (G), which can engage with the teeth on the rack and gather them, a tooth at a time, one tooth being gathered for each rotation of the gathering pallet. Also engaging with the teeth on the rack is a form of ratchet pawl called a rack hook (C), and this allows the gathering pallet to gather the rack teeth but prevents them from dropping back between the gathering of successive teeth. Also mounted on the gathering pallet is a tail (K) which, when the last tooth of the rack has been gathered, engages with a pin on the rack and so locks the striking mechanism.

The striking hammer, seen on the left of the diagram, is pivoted between the frame plates of the clock and is raised during the action of the striking train by pins (x) set in the rim of the second wheel of the striking train and engaging with the hammer tail (T). The ratio of the third wheel to the second is such that the third wheel makes one rotation every time a pin on the second wheel raises and releases the striking hammer. From this it will be understood that one tooth of the rack is gathered for each blow struck on the bell.

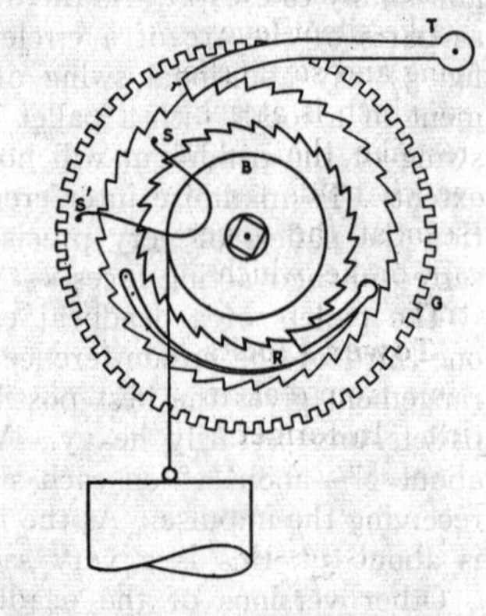

FIG. 5.—HARRISON'S GOING-RATCHET MAINTAINING POWER, WHICH KEEPS A WEIGHT-DRIVEN CLOCK GOING WHILE IT IS BEING WOUND

The sequence of action is as follows. As the minute wheel (N), which turns once an hour, rotates, a pin set in it engages with and rocks the warning detent (O) and causes the end of it lying under the rack hook (C) to rise. This lifts the rack hook out of engagement with the teeth on the rack and, at the same time, brings the tip of the warning detent (O) into a position where it can catch a pin (P) set in the rim of the fourth wheel of the striking train. As the warning detent lifts the rack hook clear of the teeth in the rack, the latter is freed and drops back under the pressure of its spring until its tail (V) comes to rest on the step of the snail (Y) which happens to be in line with it. If the tail drops onto the highest step of the snail, the rack will only be allowed to drop back a distance of one tooth, but if the tail falls on the lowest step, the rack will drop back 12 teeth. As the snail is mounted on the hour wheel and moves round with the hour hand, it will be seen that the rack tail will drop on consecutive steps of the snail at each successive hour and will thus cause the rack to fall back the right number of teeth to strike the right hour.

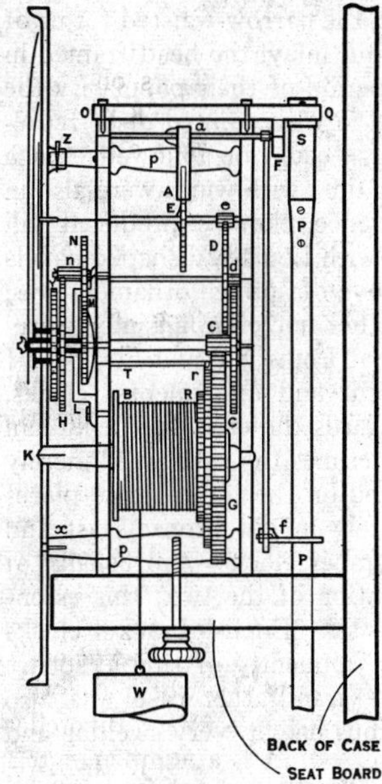

FIG. 6.—SIDE VIEW OF A WEIGHT-DRIVEN HOUSE CLOCK WITHOUT STRIKING MOVEMENT

As the movement of the pin on the minute wheel (N) continues to lift the warning detent (O) and with it the rack hook (C) the rack is freed and drops. This disengages the pin on its end from the tail (K) of the gathering pallet (G) and so unlocks the wheelwork. This then runs forward until the pin (P) on the fourth wheel engages with the tip of the warning detent (O). This constitutes the warning, a feature necessary to ensure the precise release of the striking at the hour. When the rack has dropped the correct distance the pin on the minute wheel (N) moves past and releases the warning detent (O). The detent then falls and its tip releases the warning pin (P). The striking now proceeds and each time the hammer strikes the bell, the gathering pallet gathers one tooth of the rack and the rack hook holds it. When the gathering pallet reaches the last tooth of the rack the striking train locks and comes to rest until the next hour. Other lettered parts on the diagram are as follows: S is the hammer-return spring which causes it to strike on the bell when released; Si-St is the strike-silent lever, which when raised prevents the rack from dropping and so silences the clock; F is the tail of the warning detent, to which is attached a cord that can be pulled to make the clock restrike the last hour sounded; Qg is another silencing device which holds the warning detent down when desired. The vane seen at the upper left-hand corner of the frame is the fly, an air brake which governs the speed of rotation of the striking train.

Tower Clocks.—These are large timekeepers used to indicate time from dials mounted on the outside of a church or other building. In former times their construction was virtually an enlarged version of that of a domestic clock, and their frames were made up of an assembly of bars fastened together in a sort of cage. For this reason, they were known as birdcage-frame clocks. The standard form of frame now in use is the flat bed, in which the main part is a massive casting resembling a table or platform. The bearings of the various wheels are separately bolted to this casting in such a way that almost every part can be dismantled separately. The adoption of this improved design was largely due to Lord Grimthorpe, who used it for the great Westminster clock. In basic design, the timekeeping and striking parts of a tower clock do not differ very much from those of smaller clocks, except that the gravity escapement is nearly always fitted and the striking mechanism (and the chiming mechanism also, if there is one) is controlled by a locking plate instead of a rack.

Hand-wound tower clocks are invariably driven by weights, which are usually wound up to the full height of the tower, but in recent times automatically wound types, in which a light weight is hung from an endless length of roller chain and rewound at fairly frequent intervals by an electric motor, have become almost standard where electric current is available. Such a timekeeper, if fitted with a gravity escapement and an Invar pendulum, is practically ideal.

In most of these modern autowound clocks, the striking and chiming mechanisms are directly driven by electric motors which raise their hammers by suitable cams that are rotated by the final spindle of an enclosed reduction gearing. In these instances the locking plate counting mechanism is arranged to switch off the motor when the correct hour or quarter is struck.

In some tower clocks the timepiece has no pendulum and escapement of its own but is arranged to be released in half-minute steps by a trigger release device that is controlled by an electromagnet connected to a precision master clock. This is a very good arrangement, for it enables very large dials to be driven accurately and reliably and is remarkably simple in construction. A good example of this type is the great Shell-Mex clock on the Victoria embankment, London, where two 25-ft. dials are operated with ease.

Some tower clocks have been made which are driven by synchronous electric motors operated from the alternating current supply mains, but this does not seem to be a good arrangement for even a momentary interruption of the supply will stop the clock, and changes in frequency of the alternating current will cause variations in timekeeping.

Electric Clocks.—By this term master clocks which drive large numbers of subsidiary impulse dials are intended. These are rapidly gaining popularity because of their simplicity, reliability and low cost of upkeep. They are also extremely accurate when properly regulated. In general, they consist of a pendulum which

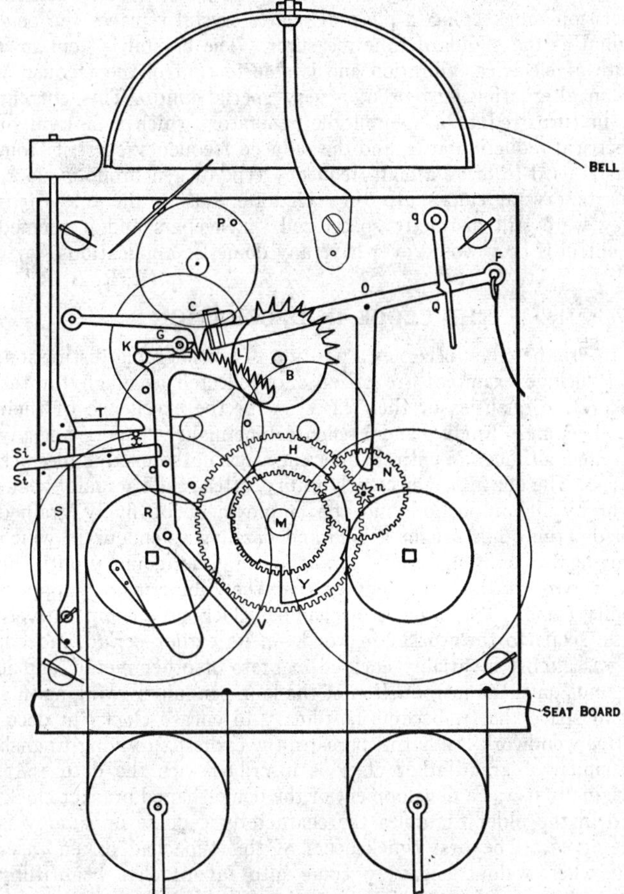

FIG. 7.—DIAGRAM OF FRONT VIEW OF ENGLISH LONG-CASE CLOCK WITH STRIKING MOVEMENT

beats 1 second per swing and rotates a small 15-toothed wheel once in every 30 seconds. As the wheel completes its rotation, it trips a catch and allows a gravity arm to fall onto the pendulum, thus giving the latter its maintaining impulse. As the gravity arm reaches its lowest point it closes an electrical contact and is immediately replaced on its catch by an electromagnet. It then rests there until the end of the next half minute, when the cycle is repeated.

The impulse dials, of which there may be any number, are simple mechanisms in which a 120-toothed wheel is stepped forward every half minute by the same electric impulses that replace the gravity arm of the master clock. In the impulse dials, these impulses step a ratchet pawl into the next tooth of the 120-toothed wheel and so propel the hands. The main advantage of this system is its theoretical perfection, for its basic principles are markedly sound. This is demonstrated by the fact that, with modifications, it is used in the Shortt free pendulum clock, the most accurate pendulum clock in the world.

Synchronous Electric Clocks.—These form the most recent development in domestic timekeepers and, provided that a source of alternating current of controlled frequency is available, they are good enough from a timekeeping standpoint to be used for most purposes. They consist of a small electric motor of the type known as synchronous coupled to a reduction gearing. As the term synchronous suggests, the rotor of the motor turns in exact step with the frequency of the alternating current and, if the frequency is maintained at a predetermined number of cycles per second and a suitably designed reduction gear links the motor to the clock hands, these will show the correct time. Synchronous clocks are not really clocks in the true sense, for they are merely frequency meters that repeat the time transmitted to them by the power station. They also have the defect of departing from the correct time if the frequency of the current varies.

Quartz Crystal Clocks.—In these, the latest development in precision timekeeping, a piece of quartz crystal replaces the pendulum as the standard time measurer. The crystal is kept in a state of electrical vibration and is able to control the frequency of an alternating current of a very special kind. This current is, in turn, fed to a submultiple generator, which is a kind of electrical reduction gear, and the reduced frequency current from this is used to drive a high-frequency type of synchronous clock. Quartz crystal clocks are very accurate, but in the mid-1950s they were still distinctly specialized timekeepers and it seemed doubtful if they would ever have any domestic applications.

(T. R. B. R.)

THE CLOCK IN DECORATION

In art the clock occupies a position of considerable distinction, and antique examples are prized and collected as much for the decorative qualities of their cases as for the excellence of their timekeeping. English and French cabinetmakers have especially excelled, although in entirely different ways, in the making of clock cases. The one aimed at comely utility, often made actually beautiful by fit proportion and the employment of finely grained woods; the other sought a bold and dazzling splendour in which ornament overlay material. It was not in either country until the latter part of the 17th century that the cabinetmaker's opportunity came. The bracket or chamber clock gave comparatively little scope to the worker in wood—in its earlier period, indeed, it was almost invariably encased in brass or other metal; and it was not until the introduction of the long pendulum swinging in a small space that it became customary to encase clocks in decorative woodwork. What is, perhaps, the earliest surviving English specimen of grandfather clock is inscribed with the date 1681. Originally it was a development of the dome-shaped bracket clock, and in the older examples the characteristic dome or canopy is preserved. The first timekeepers of this type had oaken cases but when walnut began to come into favour that beautifully marked wood was almost invariably used for the choicest and most costly specimens. Thus in 1698 the dean and chapter of St. Paul's cathedral paid the then very substantial price of £14 for an inlaid walnut long-cased eight-day clock to stand in one of the vestries. Throughout the 18th century they were made in myriads all over England, and since they were a prized possession it is not surprising that innumerable examples have survived. Vary as they may in height and girth, in wood and dial, they are all essentially alike. In their earlier years their faces were usually of brass engraved with cherubs' heads or conventional designs, but eventually the less rich white face grew common. There are two varieties—the eight-day and the 30-hour. The favourite walnut case of the late 17th and early 18th centuries gave place in the course of a generation to mahogany, which retained its primacy until the introduction of cheaper clocks brought about the supersession of the long-cased variety. Many of these cases were made in lacquer when that material was in vogue; satinwood and other costly foreign timbers were also used for bandings and inlay. The most elegant of the grandfather cases are, however, the narrow-waisted forms of the William and Mary period in walnut inlay, the head framed in twisted pilasters. During the later period of their popularity the heads of long clocks were often filled in with painted disks representing the moon, by which its course could be followed. Such conceits as ships moving on waves or time with wings were also in favour. The northern parts of France likewise produced tall clocks, usually in oaken cases; those with Louis XV shaped panels are often very decorative. French love of applied ornament was, however, generally inimical to the rather uncompromising squareness of the English case, and the great Louis XV and Louis XVI cabinetmakers made some magnificent and monumental clocks, many of which were long only as regards the case, the pendulum being comparatively short, while sometimes the case acted merely as a pedestal for a bracket clock fixed on the top. These pieces were usually mounted very elaborately in gilt bronze, cast and chased, and French bracket and chamber clocks were usually of gilded metal or marble or a combination of the two; this essentially late 18th-century type still persists. English bracket clocks contemporary with them were most frequently of simple square or arched form in mahogany. The grandfather case was also made in the Low Countries, of generous height, very swelling and bulbous.

(J. P.-B.)

Bibliography.—Technical, Trade and Manufacture: W. I. Milham, *Time and Timekeepers* (London, New York, 1923); D. de Carle, *British Time* (London, 1947); J. E. Haswell, *Horology* (London, 1937); G. H. Baillie, *Clocks and Watches* (London, Chicago, 1951); T. R. Robinson, *Modern Clocks* (London, 1955). History and Art: M. Planchon, *L'Horloge, son histoire retrospective, pittoresque et artistique* (Paris, 1899), *La Pendule de Paris* (Paris, 1921); E. von Basserman-Jordan, *Alte Uhren und ihre Meister* (Leipzig, 1926); F. Britten, *Old Clocks and Watches and Their Makers* (London, 1932; New York, 1933); R. W. Symonds, *A Book of English Clocks* (London, 1947), *Thomas Tompion* (London, New York, 1951).

CLODIA, VIA, an ancient highroad of Italy. Its course, for the first 11 mi., was the same as that of the Via Cassia; it then diverged to the north-northwest and ran on the west side of the Lacus Sabatinus, past Forum Clodii and Blera (modern Bieda) to Tuscania, after which its course is uncertain. According to Millee (*Itineraria Romana*) it went on by Maternum (Valentano) Acquapendente, Radicofani, Buonconvento Siena and Lucas past another Forum Clodii to Luna, but this is doubtful. In parts it follows older Etruscan roads, and may date from the end of the 4th century B.C. *See* also Cassia, Via.

See D. Anziani in *Mélanges de l'École Française de Rome,* 169 *sqq.* (1913).

CLODIUS, PUBLIUS (*c.* 93–52 B.C.), surnamed Pulcher, Roman politician. He took part in the third Mithridatic War under his brother-in-law Lucius Licinius Lucullus but, considering himself treated with insufficient respect, he stirred up a revolt; another brother-in-law, Q. Marcius Rex, who was governor of Cilicia, gave him the command of his fleet, but he was captured by pirates.

On his release he repaired to Syria, where he nearly lost his life during a mutiny instigated by himself. Returning to Rome in 65, he prosecuted Catiline for extortion, but was bribed by him to procure acquittal. There seems no reason to believe that Clodius was implicated in the Catilinarian conspiracy; according to Plutarch he supported Cicero. But Cicero attacked him when he was on trial for profaning the mysteries of the Bona Dea (61), and this made Clodius his enemy for life and he became the tool of Caesar.

On his return from Sicily (where he had been quaestor in 61) he was adopted by a plebeian and elected tribune of the people (59). His first act was to bring forward certain laws calculated to secure him the popular favour. Corn was to be distributed gratuitously once a month; the magistrates' right of preventing the assembly of the comitia was abolished; the old guilds of work-

BY COURTESY OF (1) THE KEEPER OF THE WALLACE COLLECTION, (2) LIBERTY AND COMPANY, LTD., (4, 6, 9) THE DIRECTOR OF THE VICTORIA AND ALBERT MUSEUM, (5, 7, 8, 10, 11) THE TRUSTEES OF THE BRITISH MUSEUM, (12) ORVILLE R. HAGANS; PHOTOGRAPH, (3) ALINARI, BY COURTESY OF THE ITALIAN TRAVEL BUREAU, LONDON

CURIOUS DECORATIVE AND MECHANICAL CLOCKS

1. Clock with case of Boulle-work. 2. Clock outside the shop of Messrs. Liberty & Co., London. 3. Mechanical clock, Venice. Hours struck by figures at top of tower. 4. Grandfather clock in case decorated with floral marquetry. 5. Globe or falling-ball clock, *c.* 1650. Suspended, it goes by its own weight. 6. Astronomical clock in form of celestial globe; German, *c.* 1584. 7. French astronomical clock with astrolabe; dated about 1560. 8. German horizontal clock with hunting scenes in relief; *c.* 1600. 9. Louis XVI clock made of Oriental alabaster. 10. Standing clock (still going) by Isaac Hobrecht, Strasbourg, 1589. 11. Clock in form of a ship with dial at base of middle mast; the small figures are set in motion by mechanism of clock. By Schlott 1580. 12. French clock and barometer of about 1750

CLOCKS

BY COURTESY OF (1–6) ORVILLE R. HAGANS

LATER EXAMPLES OF THE CLOCKMAKER'S ART

1. German clock of about 1850 containing an organ which plays seven tunes
2. Japanese clock of about 1830, with lacquered case and stand
3. Dutch canopy clock, 18th century. The oak case is inlaid with ornamental woods.
4. Urn clock, French, late 18th century. Time is kept by rotation of horizontal disks
5. Early 18th-century clock presented by Louis XV of France to a minister from England. Movement is similar to that of urn clock in fig. 4.
6. The "Empress," commissioned by Napoleon I in 1805 as a gift for the empress Josephine
7. Grandfather clock by Thomas Tompion (1639?–1713), "father of English watchmaking"

men were re-established; the censors were forbidden to exclude any citizen from the senate or inflict any punishment upon him unless he had been publicly accused and condemned. He then contrived the exile of Cicero and the dispatch of the younger Cato on a mission to Cyprus. Cicero's property was confiscated by order of Clodius. After the departure of Caesar for Gaul, Clodius became practically master of Rome by means of his armed gangs. But he fell out with Pompey and was not re-elected for 57, while one of the tribunes, Milo, countered his force with force, so despite his opposition, in Aug. 57 Cicero was recalled. Riots between Clodius and Milo continued; in 56, when *curule aedile,* Clodius impeached Milo for public violence (*de vi*), but the matter was dropped.

In 53, when Milo was a candidate for the consulship, and Clodius for the praetorship, the rivals collected armed bands and fights took place in the streets of Rome, and on Jan. 20, 52, Clodius was slain near Bovillae.

His sister, CLODIA, wife of Q. Caecilius Metellus Celer, was notorious for her numerous love affairs. It is now generally admitted that she was the Lesbia of Catullus (Teuffel-Schwabe, *Hist. of Roman Lit.,* Eng. tr., 214, 3). For her intrigue with M. Caelius Rufus, whom she afterward accused of attempting to poison her, *see* Cicero, *Pro Caelio.*

BIBLIOGRAPHY.—The ancient authorities are Cicero, *Letters* (ed. Tyrrell and Purser), *Pro Caelio, pro Sestio, pro Milone, pro Domo sua, de Haruspicum Responsis, in Pisonem;* Plutarch, *Lucullus, Pompey, Cicero, Caesar;* Dio Cassius, xxxvi, 16, 19, xxxvii, 45, 46, 51, xxxviii, 12–14, xxxix, 6, 11, xl, 48. *See* also I. Gentile, *Clodio e Cicerone* (1876); E. S. Beesley, "Cicero and Clodius," *Fortnightly Review,* v; G. Lacour-Gayet, *De P. Clodio Pulchro* (1888); H. White, *Cicero, Clodius, and Milo* (1900); G. Boissier, *Cicero and His Friends* (Eng. trans., 1897).

CLOGHER, a village, County Tyrone, Northern Ireland. Pop. (1951) 192. It gives its name to dioceses of the Church of Ireland and the Roman Catholic Church, though the seat of the bishop of the latter is at Monaghan.

The dedication of the Protestant cathedral to St. Macartin is of interest, for although the building is modern, St. Macartin is associated with St. Patrick, who is said to have founded a bishopric there.

The name is derived from *cloch,* a pillar stone—an object of worship in the locality, preserved in the cathedral until the 15th century.

CLOISTER originally signified an entire monastery, but is now restricted to mean the four-sided enclosure, surrounded with covered ambulatories, usually attached to conventual and cathedral churches and sometimes to colleges, or, by a still further limitation, to the ambulatories themselves. In its older sense it is frequently used in earlier English literature and is still so employed in poetry.

The Latin *claustrum,* as its derivation implies, primarily denoted the enclosing wall of a religious house and then came to be used for the whole enclosed building. To this sense the German *Kloster* is still limited, the covered walks or cloister in the modern sense being called *Klostergang,* or *Kreuzgang.* In French the word *cloître* retains the double sense. In the special sense now most common, the word "cloister" denotes the quadrilateral area in a monastery or college, round which the principal buildings are ranged, and which is usually provided with a covered way or ambulatory running all round and affording a means of communication between the various centres of the ecclesiastical life. According to the Benedictine arrangement, which from its suitability to the requirements of monastic life was generally adopted in the west, one side of the cloister was formed by the church, the refectory occupying the side opposite to it, so that the worshippers might have the least annoyance from the noise or smell of the repasts. On the eastern side the chapter house was placed, with other apartments adjacent to it, belonging to the common life of the brethren, and, as a rule, the dormitory occupied the whole upper story.

On the opposite or western side were generally the cellarer's lodgings, with the cellars and storehouses in which the necessary provisions were housed. In Cistercian monasteries the western side was usually occupied by the *domus conversorum* or lodgings of the lay brethren, with their dayrooms and workshops below and dormitory above. The cloister, with its surrounding buildings, generally stood on the south side of the church, to secure as much sunshine as possible.

A very early example of this disposition is seen in the plan of the monastery of St. Gall. Local requirements caused the cloister, in some instances, to be placed to the north of the church. This is the case at Canterbury, Gloucester, Chester and Lincoln cathedrals.

Although the covered ambulatories are essential to the completeness of a monastic cloister, a chief object of which was to enable the inmates to pass under cover from one part of the monastery to another, they were sometimes wanting. The cloister at St. Albans seems to have been deficient in ambulatories till the abbacy of Robert of Gorham, 1151–66, when the eastern walk was erected. This, as was often the case with the earliest ambulatories, was of wood, covered with a sloping roof or "penthouse." We learn from Osbern's account of the conflagration of the monastery of Christ Church, Canterbury, 1067, that a cloister with covered ways existed at that time, connecting the church, the dormitory and the refectory. An early drawing of the monastery of Canterbury shows it formed by Norman arches supported on shafts, and covered by a shed roof. A fragment of such an arcaded cloister is still found on the eastern side of the infirmary cloister. This earlier form of cloister has been generally superseded in England by a range of windows, usually unglazed but sometimes, as at Gloucester, provided with glass, lighting a vaulted ambulatory, of which the cloisters of Westminster abbey, Salisbury and Norwich are typical examples. The older design was preserved in the south, where "the cloister is never a window, but a range of small elegant pillars, sometimes single, sometimes coupled, and supporting arches of a light and elegant design" (Fergusson, *Hist. of Arch,* i, p. 610).

Examples of this type are the exquisite cloisters of St. John Lateran and St. Paul's Outside the Walls at Rome, where the coupled shafts and arches are richly ornamented with ribbons of mosaic, and those of the convent of St. Scholastica at Subiaco, all of the 13th century, and the beautiful cloisters of Le Puy-en-Velay and Arles in southern France (both 11th century) and that at Laach, where the quadrangle occupies the place of the "atrium" of the early basilicas at the west end, as at S. Clemente at Rome and S. Ambrogio at Milan. Spain also presents some magnificent cloisters of both types, of which that of the royal convent of Huelgas, near Burgos, of the arcaded form, is, according to Fergusson, "unrivalled for beauty both of detail and design." Also notable are those of Monreale and Cefalu in Sicily (12th century), where the arrangement is the same, of slender columns in pairs with capitals of elaborate foliage supporting pointed arches of great elegance of form.

The Campo Santo at Pisa is in reality a large and magnificent cloister. It consists of four ambulatories as wide and lofty as the nave of a church, erected in 1278 by Giovanni Pisano, round a cemetery composed of soil brought from Palestine by Archbishop Lanfranchi in the middle of the 12th century. The window openings are semicircular, filled with elaborate tracery in the latter half of the 15th century. The inner walls are covered with frescoes, invaluable in the history of art, by Orcagna, Simone Memmi, Buffalmacco, Benozzo Gozzoli and other early painters of the Florentine school. The ambulatories now serve as a museum of sculpture.

The great monastic establishments of Italy contain numerous important cloisters; there are frequently two or three in a single monastery—one large cloister for the general use of the monks and smaller cloisters in connection with the residence of the prior or abbot, the service portions and various other minor buildings. The cloisters at the Certosa at Pavia (15th century) are notable for their size and quaint, early Renaissance ornament. In the Certosa at Rome, now part of the Museo delle Terme, the cloister is a large arcade of pure and simple Renaissance type. Another interesting Renaissance example is that which Bramante designed for the church of S. Maria della Pace at Rome, 1504. Later

FROM: (C, K) GARDNER, "A GUIDE TO ENGLISH GOTHIC ARCHITECTURE" (CAMBRIDGE UNIVERSITY PRESS); (E) LEON, "LES MONUMENTS HISTORIQUES" (RENOUARD); (G) "ARCHITECTURAL REVIEW"; (J) ROSE, "CATHEDRALS AND CLOISTERS OF NORTHERN FRANCE" (PUTNAM)

A, UNIVERSITY, BOLOGNA (ITALIAN RENAISSANCE); B, SANTA MARIA DELLA PACE, ROME (ITAL. REN.); C, SALISBURY CATHEDRAL (ENG. GOTH.); D, MONASTERY, SAN VITALE, RAVENNA (ITAL. REN.); E, ABBEY, MONT ST. MICHEL (FR. GOTHIC); F, MONASTERY, PAVIA (ITAL. REN.); G, CLOISTERS, WINCHESTER (MOD. ENGLISH); H, MONASTERY, VEZZOLANO (ITAL. ROMANESQUE); J, ABBEY, VERDUN (FR. GOTHIC); K, WESTMINSTER ABBEY (ENG. GOTH.); L, SAN STEFANO, VENICE (ITAL. REN.)

Renaissance cloisters tended more and more to become duplicates of palace courtyards.

The cloister of a religious house was the scene of a large part of the life of its inmates. It was the place of education for the younger members and of study for the elders. A canon of the Roman council of 826 enjoins the erection of a cloister as an essential portion of an ecclesiastical establishment for the better discipline and instruction of the clerks. Peter of Blois describes schools for the novices as being in the west walk, moral lectures being delivered in that next the church. At Canterbury the monks' school was in the western ambulatory, and it was there that the novices were taught at Durham (Willis, *Monastic Buildings of Canterbury,* p. 44; *Rites of Durham,* p. 71). The other alleys, especially that next the church, were devoted to the studies of the elder monks. The constitutions of Hildemar and Dunstan enact that between the church service the brethren should sit in the cloister and read theology. For this purpose small studies, known as "carrols," *i.e.,* a ring or enclosed space, were often found in the recesses of the windows. Of this arrangement there are examples at Gloucester and Chester. The use of these studies is thus described in the *Rites of Durham:* "In every wyndowe" in the north alley "were iii. pewes or carrells, where every one of the olde monkes had his carrell severally by himselfe, that when they had dyned they dyd resorte to that place of cloister, and there studyed upon their books, every one in his carrell all the afternonne unto evensong tyme. This was there exercise every daie." On the opposite wall were cupboards full of books for the use of the students. The cloister arrangements at Canterbury were similar. New studies were made by Prior De Estria in 1317, and Prior Selling (1472–94) glazed the south alley and constructed "the new framed contrivances, of late styled carrols" (Willis, *Mon. Buildings,* p. 45).

The cloisters were used also for recreation. The constitutions of Archbishop Lanfranc, sec. 3, permitted the brethren to converse together there at certain hours. To maintain discipline a special officer was appointed under the title of *prior claustri.* The cloister was furnished with a stone bench running along the side. It was also provided with a lavatory, usually adjacent to the refectory, but sometimes standing in the central area termed the cloister garth, as at Durham.

The cloister garth was used as a place of sepulture, as well as the surrounding alleys. The cloister was in some few instances of two stories, as at Old St. Paul's and St. Stephen's chapel, Westminster; and occasionally, as at Wells, Chichester and Hereford, had only three alleys, there being no ambulatory under the church wall.

The larger monastic establishments had more than one cloister; there was usually a second connected with the infirmary, of which there are examples at Westminster abbey and at Canterbury, and sometimes one giving access to the kitchen and other domestic offices. The cloister was not an appendage of monastic houses exclusively. It was also attached to colleges of secular canons, as at the cathedrals of Lincoln, Salisbury, Wells, Hereford and Chichester, and formerly at St. Paul's and Exeter. A cloister forms an essential part of the colleges of Eton and Winchester, and of New college and Magdalen at Oxford. These were used for religious processions and lectures, and for places of exercise for the inmates generally in wet weather, as well as for sepulture.

CLONAKILTY, urban district, County Cork., Ire., at the head of Clonakilty bay, 33 mi. S.W. of Cork by rail. Pop. (1951) 2,742. There are megaliths in the neighbourhood. Richard Boyle, first earl of Cork, granted it a charter in 1613 and it was prosperous until 1641, when it was almost destroyed in a fight between the English and Irish.

There are castles at Galley head, Dunnycove and Dunowen. The linen industry was important in the 18th century. The present trade is in brewing, agricultural produce and fishing. The harbour is obstructed, but there is a pier for large vessels at Ring 1 mi. below the town.

CLONE, a group of individual organisms usually descended by asexual reproduction from a single sexually produced individual. The term is used specifically for such animals as aphids which reproduce parthenogenetically, and of plants that are propagated by vegetative means, as cuttings. (*See* HEREDITY; PARTHENOGENESIS.) (J. M. BL.)

CLONES, an urban district of County Monaghan, Ire., 64½ mi. S.W. by W. from Belfast by the Great Northern of Ireland railway. It is at the focus of ways from Dublin, Belfast, Londonderry, Enniskillen and Cavan. Pop. (1951) 2,455. There is a rath (encampment) in the vicinity.

Clones was the seat of an abbey founded in the 6th century by St. Tighernach (Tierney). Remains of the abbey include a nave and tower of the 12th century. There is a round tower 75 ft. high. The market place, called the Diamond, has an ancient cross and occupies the summit of the hillock on which the town stands. Lacemaking is now extinct, but the town has agricultural trade.

CLONMACNOISE, a famous early Christian centre on the River Shannon, County Offaly, Ire., 9 mi. S. of Athlone. An abbey founded 541 by St. Kieran became famous and several books of annals were compiled there; Alcuin came to be taught by Colcu at Clonmacnoise. The *Book of the Dun Cow* (written about 1100) is a copy of an older collection of romances written on the skin of a cow of St. Kieran. The ecclesiastical foundation was called the Seven Churches of Clonmacnoise and their remains still survive.

The fine west doorway of the Great church is Early; the other churches are those of Fineen, Conor, St. Kieran, Kelly, Melaghlin and Dowling. There are two round towers, O'Rourke's and McCarthy's, which is attached to Fineen's church and has a doorway at ground level, an unusual feature. There are three crosses, the great cross facing the door of the Great church. Many inscribed stones of the 9th century and later are preserved in the churches. Clonmacnoise became a bishopric and there are remains of a castle and bishop's palace (14th century); it was wasted by the English in 1552; and in 1568 the diocese was merged in that of Meaths.

CLONMEL (*Cluain meala,* or "vale of honey"), municipal borough and county town of County Tipperary, 112 mi. S.W. from Dublin, Ire., a junction on the Great Southern railway (Waterford, Limerick, Thurles), on both banks of the River Suir and on Moore and Long Islands. Pop. (1951) 10,471. It is near fine scenery in the Galtee and Knockmealdown mountains. It is at the head of barge navigation on the Suir. As a walled town (remains are still visible) it was frequently mentioned in the middle ages, but it was dismantled after capture by Oliver Cromwell (1650). Charles Bianconi (1815) made it the centre of a system of conveyance of passengers by light cars in south Ireland.

The town has a fair agricultural trade, formerly made woollen goods and is an assize town.

CLOOTS, JEAN BAPTISTE DU VAL DE GRÂCE, BARON VON (1755–1794), better known as ANACHARSIS CLOOTS, revolutionary fanatic, was born near Cleves at the castle of Gnadenthal, of a noble Prussian family of Dutch origin. His father placed him in the military academy at Berlin, but he left it at the age of 20 and traversed Europe, preaching his revolutionary philosophy as an apostle and spending his money as a man of pleasure. On the outbreak of the Revolution he went to Paris. On June 19, 1790, he appeared at the bar of the assembly at the head of 36 foreigners and, in the name of this "embassy of the human race," declared that the world adhered to the "Declaration of the Rights of Man and Citizen." After this he was known as "the orator of the human race," by which title he called himself, dropping that of baron and substituting for his baptismal names the pseudonym of Anacharsis, from the famous philosophical romance of the abbé J. J. Barthélemy. In 1792 he placed 12,000 livres at the disposal of the republic—"for the arming of 40 or 50 fighters in the sacred cause of man against tyrants."

In September he was elected a member of the convention, and he voted the king's death in the name of the human race. He was guillotined as an Hébertist on March 24, 1794.

See G. Avenel, *Anacharsis Cloots, orateur du genre humain* (1865).

CLOQUET, a city of Carlton county, Minn., U.S., on the St. Louis river, 21 mi. W. by S. of Duluth. It is served by the Chicago, Milwaukee, St. Paul and Pacific, Duluth and Northeastern, Great Northern and Northern Pacific railways. The population in 1950 was 7,685; in 1940 was 7,304 by the federal census. The river supplies water power, and the city has large pulp and paper mills and factories making insulating materials, clothespins, matches and other articles of wood. A forest experiment station of the University of Minnesota is located there. The first mill was built in 1878, and the village was named from the French word *claquet,* representing the sound made by the mill. It was chartered as a city in 1903.

CLOSE, MAXWELL HENRY (1822–1903), Irish geologist, was born in Dublin in 1822. He was educated at Weymouth and at Trinity college, Dublin, took holy orders and held various charges in England. In 1861 he returned to Dublin and devoted himself especially to the glacial geology of Ireland. His paper, read before the Geological Society of Ireland in 1866, on the "General Glaciation of Ireland" is a masterly description of the effects of glaciation and of the evidence in favour of the action of land ice.

Later on he discussed the origin of the elevated shell-bearing gravels near Dublin, and expressed the view that they were accumulated by floating ice when the land had undergone submergence. He died in Dublin Sept. 12, 1903.

The obituary by G. A. J. Cole in *Irish Naturalist,* vol. xii (1903) contains a list of publications and portrait.

CLOSE, a closed place (Lat. *clausum,* "shut"). In English law the term is applied to land, enclosed or not, held as private property, or to any exclusive interest in land sufficient to maintain an action for trespass. In Scotland the word is used of the entry, including the common staircase, of a block of tenement houses, and in architecture of the precincts of a cathedral or abbey.

The adjective "close" (*i.e.,* closed) is found in several phrases, such as close time or close season; close prices (*see* CLOSE MARKET PRICES); close borough, one of which the rights and privileges were enjoyed by a limited class (*see* BOROUGH); close rolls and writs, royal letters, etc., addressed to particular persons, under seal. (*See* LETTERS PATENT.)

CLOSED SHOP. The closed shop, in the United States, is the oldest form of union security. It is a device for protecting the status of labour organizations. All variants of union security require union membership as a condition of employment for some or all of the workers in an establishment. Under the closed shop, only members in good standing can be hired in the first instance. In a union shop, nonmembers may be hired but must acquire membership within a specified period. Preferential hiring permits the employer to hire nonunionists only when qualified unionists are not available. Under a maintenance of membership provision, those workers who hold membership at the beginning of a collective bargaining agreement, and do not elect to resign during an "escape period," must remain in good standing for the duration of the agreement. There are numerous combinations and modifications of these basic forms.

History.—The closed shop is not a development of modern industry. Mediaeval British guilds prevented the working of nonmembers; so also did, when possible, the 18th century trade clubs. Some of the guild regulations of the 16th and 17th centuries decreed that no guild journeyman was to work with a nonmember: such principles were an integral part of mediaeval society. These tactics were continued by British trade unionism and were naturally conveyed to America. The Cordwainers' society of the city of New York in 1804, the New York Typographical society in 1809 and subsequently other unions adopted bylaws forbidding members to work for employers hiring men who did not belong to their organizations or who worked for wages lower than the union scale. The chief weapon used by employers until 1836 was the invoking of old laws declaring combinations of workmen and strikes criminal conspiracies. By about 1840 the closed-shop rule had been adopted by the majority of U.S. trade unions, which refused to work with nonunion men. These were stigmatized after 1854 as "rats" or "scabs." With the repeal or nullification of conspiracy statutes, employers formed local associations to resist the closed-shop movement.

From 1870 in the United States local trade unions gradually merged into national unions, the majority of which made the maintenance of the closed shop a vital rule. During the same period, especially in the last decade of the 19th century, there were formed national associations of employers, one of the purposes of which was to maintain the open shop. Large factories locked out union men for demanding the closed shop: the Birmingham Rolling Mill company in 1884; the Granite Manufacturers' Association of Boston in 1887; and the Carnegie Steel company in 1892. The American Federation of Labor declared in 1890 that the working of union with nonunion men was inconsistent, especially when nonunion men displaced unionists locked out or engaged in strike. From 1850 to 1898 the major part of more than a dozen court decisions held that strikes for the closed shop were criminal or tortious. These decisions had no effect upon trade-union insistence for the closed shop.

Developments of 20th Century.—The struggle over the closed-shop question reached an intense stage about 1901 when the unions insisted upon employers signing written agreements conceding the closed shop. Previously the granting of the closed shop had been based upon custom or oral negotiation. Declaring that they would not admit "union dictation in the management of business," the National Metal Trades federation and other large employers' associations aggressively campaigned to destroy the closed-shop system.

The award of the anthracite coal strike commission in the great coal strike of 1902 was of considerable moral help to manufacturers' associations; the commission granted practically every demand of the union except that for the closed shop. Encouraged by this stand, the National Association of Manufacturers in 1902 began a vigorous movement for the open shop. The Citizens' Industrial Association of America, various citizens' alliances in different cities and a number of large corporations did likewise. The American Federation of Labor reiterated that the trade-union movement stood for the strictly union shop. Union after union endorsed the closed-shop principle. The proportion of strikes for recognition of trade unions and union rules more than trebled in succeeding years. By reducing employment, the panic of 1907 weakened the trade unions and gave corresponding advantage to employers. The campaigns carried on by the manufacturers' associations also caused a decided shift in public sentiment in favour of the open shop. By 1910 this was established in many industries, notably those which had been consolidated into powerful corporations. The open shop prevailed in the south.

There were several cycles of ebb and flow in unionism after the United States entered World War I in 1917. Certain main tendencies persisted, however. Union membership increased greatly, standing at 2,750,000 in 1916 and 14,500,000 in 1952. Collective bargaining was established in many industries previously of nonunion or open-shop character. There was widespread improvement of industrial relations as union and management became accommodated to each other and accumulated bargaining experience. The scope of collective agreements expanded steadily to include not only wage rates and hours of work but also seniority provisions; paid vacations and holidays, retirement plans, sickness, hospital and accident insurance; and numerous other matters. Despite these changes, the union security issue remained an active one and occasioned considerable industrial conflict.

"Union security" was probably the most frequent problem faced by the U.S. government in handling unresolved labour disputes during World War II. The National Defense Mediation board (1941) collapsed when members of the Congress of Industrial Organizations withdrew because of the board's refusal to recommend a union shop in "captive" coal mines. Its successor, the National War Labor board (1942–45), developed the maintenance-of-membership formula as a compromise measure, and utilized the formula in thousands of dispute cases. By 1945, almost 30% of workers under union agreement were covered by maintenance-of-membership clauses. Some 45% were employed in closed or union shops, and 3% under preferential hiring arrangements. The remaining 27% worked in establishments where the union was recognized as exclusive bargaining agent but did not enjoy formal union security protection.

In the Taft-Hartley act of 1947, the U.S. congress undertook for the first time to regulate the union security agreement in private industry. The closed shop was declared illegal. Labour organizations were prohibited from negotiating union shop agreements unless authorized, in a secret ballot, by a majority of workers in the bargaining units. These restrictions, designed to implement the right to work and to protect rank-and-file employees from the unions, did not have the intended effect. During the first four years of the Taft-Hartley act, 97.1% of all union-shop elections were won by the unions; 84.8% of eligible employees voted, and 91.4% of all voters cast affirmative ballots. Moreover, the proscription of closed shops was widely circumvented by various methods, particularly in the building construction, printing and maritime industries. By 1950, the proportion of unionized employees in closed, union or preferential shops had risen to 58%; and in 1951–52 union shop provisions were adopted in the rubber and steel industries and part of the railroad industry. The Wage Stabilization board's recommendation in 1952 that some type of union shop be established in the steel industry was highly controversial, however, and induced congress to prohibit the board from handling union-management disputes. (*See* also Strikes and Lockouts; Trade [Labour] Unions.)

Bibliography.—S. and B. Webb, *History of Trade Unionism*, rev. ed. (New York, 1920), and *Industrial Democracy*, new ed. (New York, 1920); J. R. Commons *et al.*, *History of Labour in the U.S.*, 2 vol. (New York, 1921); J. B. S. Hardman (ed.), *American Labor Dynamics* (New York, 1928); K. Braun, *The Right to Organize and Its Limits* (Washington, 1950); C. S. Golden and H. J. Ruttenberg, *The Dynamics of Industrial Democracy* (New York, 1942); J. E. Johnsen (comp.), *The Closed Shop* (New York, 1942); J. L. Toner, *The Closed Shop* (Washington, 1943); S. H. Slichter, *Union Policies and Industrial Management* (Washington, 1941); and articles in *Labor Law Journal*, *Industrial and Labor Relations Review*, *Monthly Labor Review*, *Management Record* and *Annals of the American Academy of Political and Social Science*. (A. M. R.)

CLOSE MARKET PRICES. Proper comprehension of the meaning of "close market prices" and their importance in a free economy requires an understanding of what market prices actually are and an examination of the double pricing standard that prevails in securities markets. Essentially, market prices are those figures at which public buyers and sellers are ready, willing and able to trade money for securities or vice versa. The double pricing standard refers to (1) the particular maximum price which buyers will pay for a particular share and (2) the particular minimum price which sellers expect to receive in return for a particular share. The closeness of market prices describes the proximity of either end of the double standard to the other—the narrow difference between a seller's minimum figure and a buyer's maximum price. This is the auction system, which prevails in the world's great securities markets such as the London, New York and American Stock exchanges. On these and other auction markets, keen competition between buyers and sellers and the law of supply and demand ultimately decide final sales. These markets, with their national and international communication facilities including thousands of member firm main and branch offices which bring public orders to market, huge stock ticker systems, and teleregister, teletype, telephone, cable and radio networks, concentrate public orders on their respective trading floors and make close markets which effect fair prices.

Bid and Offer.—The public market for a particular stock issue is naturally divided between buyers and sellers. Among the potential buyers there is a wide range of judgment, depending upon individual knowledge of true worth, as to what they would be willing to spend for a single share of, for example, ABC common stock. The range of individual judgment may run from as low as 5 and move upward fractionally to 9. In auction markets, the highest proposal to buy becomes the bid. In this case the bid is 9. Another range of judgment is expressed by sellers in amounts of money that they want in return for a single share of ABC common stock. The prices may range from a high of 14 and move downward fractionally to 10. Under the auction principle, the lowest proposal to sell becomes the offer. In this case the offer is 10. We now have the double standard, the quotation, the bid and offer or the market, as it is commonly called. The concentration of public buy and sell orders at a single, focal point, the trading floor of the securities market trading ABC common shares, has resulted in a close market with a one point spread between the bid and offer. This price will be quoted on the trading floor, posted in brokerage company board rooms, reported over the communications systems and will appear in the public press. It does not mean that the bid or the offer will prevail in a sale, but that an order "at the market" will be executed at or within 9 or 10 depending upon supply and demand. (J. J. Sn.)

CLOSURE, the parliamentary term for the closing of debate according to a certain rule, even when certain members are anxious to continue the debate. In the U.S. "cloture" is a common spelling. (*See* Parliament: *Parliamentary Procedure.*)

CLOT, ANTOINE BARTHÉLEMY (1793–1868), French physician, known as Clot Bey, was born at Grenoble on Nov. 7, 1793, and graduated in medicine and surgery at Montpellier. After practising for a time at Marseilles he was made chief surgeon to Mohammed Ali, viceroy of Egypt. At Abuzabel, near Cairo, he founded a hospital and schools for all branches of medical instruction, as well as for the study of the French language; and instituted the study of anatomy by means of dissection. In 1836 he was appointed head of the medical administration of the country. In 1849 he returned to Marseilles, though he revisited Egypt in 1856. He died at Marseilles on Aug. 28, 1868.

CLOTAIRE (Chlothachar), name of four Frankish kings.

Clotaire I. (d. 561) was one of the four sons of Clovis. On the death of his father in 511 he received as his share of the kingdom the town of Soissons, which he made his capital, the cities of Laon, Noyon, Cambrai and Maastricht, and the lower course of the Meuse. But he was very ambitious, and sought to extend his domain. He was the chief instigator of the murder of his brother Chlodomer's children in 524, and his share of the spoils consisted of the cities of Tours and Poitiers. He took part in the various expeditions against Burgundy, and after the destruction of that kingdom in 534 obtained Grenoble, Die and some of the neighbouring cities. When Provence was ceded to the Franks by the Ostrogoths, he received the cities of Orange, Carpentras and Gap. In 531 he marched against the Thuringi with his brother Theuderich (Thierry) I., and in 542 with his brother Childebert against the Visigoths of Spain. On the death of his great-nephew Theodebald in 555, Clotaire annexed his territories; and on Childebert's death in 558 he became king of all Gaul. He also ruled over the greater part of Germany, made expeditions into Saxony, and for some time exacted from the Saxons an annual tribute of 500 cows. The end of his reign was troubled by internal dissensions, his son Chram rising against him on several occasions. Following Chram into Brittany, where the rebel had taken refuge, Clotaire shut him up with his wife and children in a cottage, to which he set fire. Overwhelmed with remorse, he went to Tours to implore forgiveness at the tomb of St. Martin, and died shortly afterwards.

Clotaire II. (d. 629) was the son of Chilperic I. On the assassination of his father in 584 he was still in his cradle. He was, however, recognized as king, thanks to the devotion of his mother Fredegond and the protection of his uncle Gontran, king of Burgundy. It was not until after the death of his cousin Childebert II. in 595 that Clotaire took any active part in affairs. He then endeavoured to enlarge his estates at the expense of Childebert's sons, Theodebert, king of Austrasia, and Theuderich II., king of Burgundy; but after gaining a victory at Laffaux (597), he was defeated at Dormelles (600), and lost part of his kingdom. After the war between Theodebert and Theuderich and their death, the nobles of Austrasia and Burgundy appealed to Clotaire who, after putting Brunhilda to death, became master of the whole of the Frankish kingdom (613). He was obliged, however, to make great concessions to the aristocracy to whom he owed his victory. By the constitution of Oct. 18, 614, he gave legal force to canons which had been voted some days previously by a council convened at Paris, but not without attempting to modify them by numerous restrictions. He extended the competence of the ecclesiastical tribunals, suppressed unjust taxes and undertook to select the counts from the districts they had to administer. In 623 he made his son Dagobert king of the Austrasians, and gradually subdued all the provinces that had formerly belonged to Childebert II. He also guaranteed a certain measure of independence to the nobles of Burgundy, giving them the option of having a special mayor of the palace, or of dispensing with that officer. These concessions procured him a reign of comparative tranquillity. He died on Oct. 18, 629, and was buried at Paris in the church of St. Vincent, afterwards known as St. Germain des Prés.

Clotaire III. (652–673) was a son of king Clovis II. In 657 he became the nominal ruler of the three Frankish kingdoms, but was deprived of Austrasia in 663, retaining Neustria and Burgundy until his death.

Clotaire IV. (d. 719) was king of Austrasia from 717 to 719. (C. Pf.)

CLOTH, any material woven of wool or hair, cotton, flax or vegetable fibre. In commercial usage, the word is particularly applied to a fabric made of wool. The word is Teutonic, though it does not appear in all the branches of the language. It appears in German as *Kleid* (*Kliedung*, clothing), and in Dutch as *kleed.* The ultimate origin is unknown; it may be connected with the root *kli*—meaning to stick, cling to, which appears in "clay," "cleave" and other words. The original meaning would be either that which clings to the body, or that which is pressed or "felted" together. The regular plural of "cloth" was "clothes," which is now confined in meaning to articles of clothing, garments, in which sense the singular "cloth" is not now used. For that word, in its modern sense of material, the plural "cloths" is used. This form dates from the beginning of the 17th century, but the distinction in meaning between "cloths" and "clothes" is a 19th century one. A curious employment of the word is in the clerical profession, its members often being spoken of as belonging "to the cloth." (*See* Wool; Cotton and the Cotton Industry; etc.)

CLOTH FINISHING. In this article, the subject of finishing is treated under the two headings (1) Cotton and (2) Wool.

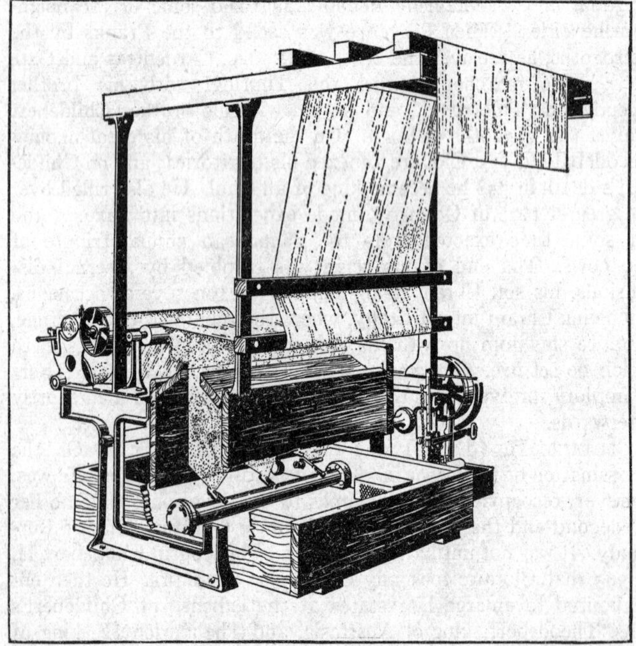

BY COURTESY OF MATHER AND PLATT, LTD.

Fig. 1.—IMPROVED SPRAY DAMPING MACHINE FOR THE UNIFORM DAMPING OF COTTON, SILKS AND LINEN FABRICS

Reference should also be made to the article Cotton and Cotton Industry, Section VI., Subsection D.

COTTON

The finishing of cotton fabrics was originally the final operation performed on the fabrics to make them ready for sale. In its modern significance, finishing comprises a large and diverse range of processes intended to produce in the fabric a desired appearance or feel; and the machines required for this purpose are correspondingly numerous and varied; finishing operations require plant for, to name some of the important processes, shearing, stretching, drying, damping, pressing, embossing, impregnating, covering and raising cotton cloths.

Classification of finishes in relation to the many different kinds of cotton fabrics is difficult, because many of the processes are applicable to a wide range of cloths. They may be considered under the following headings:—Grey goods, *i.e.*, cloth direct from the loom; white goods, *i.e.*, cloth which has undergone a bleaching process; plain dyed goods—colours and black; printed goods; raised goods.

BY COURTESY OF MATHER AND PLATT, LTD.

Fig. 2.—THREE-BOWL FINISHING CALENDER ARRANGED TO GIVE A BRIGHT FINISH ON BOTH SIDES OR A GLAZED SURFACE ON ONE SIDE ONLY

The greater number of processes of finishing cotton goods are empirical in character; the underlying physical and chemical changes are not fully understood. A finish produced in one works may be impossible to reproduce in another works, although the same kind of plant and mixings are being used. Even in the same works, two apparently identical machines will give appreciably different results. This is not to say that finishing is a matter of chance; there are very wide differences between the various classes of finish which differences are definable in terms of plant and mixing.

The following gives some idea of the finishing machines used for the different qualities set out above:—

Grey Goods.—These may be finished pure, *i.e.*, without any additional size or stiffening. After passing through a shearing machine or a combined moting and shearing machine, the cloth may be conditioned in a damping machine of the brush type or the spray type (fig. 1) and afterwards calendered in a suitable calender, such as the three-bowl swissing calender (fig. 2) or a five or seven bowl calender arranged to give a bright finish on both sides of the cloth, or a friction calender giving a glazed surface on one side only. Grey goods which are stiffened before being calendered are passed through a range comprising a mangle and cylinder drying machine (fig. 3). The mangle may have two or three bowls, and the drying set may be horizontal or vertical.

Coloured woven goods, *i.e.*, woven from grey bleached and dyed yarns, may be treated in a manner similar to the grey, making use of the same kind of machinery. Both grey and coloured woven goods may be run through the clip-stretching machine with the object of recovering width, or straightening weft, or improving the feel by breaking down the hardness produced in an earlier process, or lifting the figure of the original weave.

White Goods.—Here there are a very wide range of finishes requiring very extensive plant; for example

(a) Pure finish (without stiffening); these may, or may not be calendered or beetled.
(b) Finishes requiring impregnation of the cloth with the stiffening mixture.
(c) "Back-filling," that is, the stiffening is applied to the back of the cloth only.

White goods are generally passed through a water-mangle with the object of improving the appearance of the cloth, closing up the threads after the bleaching process, and preparing it for the filling mixture. After mangling, the cloth is dried on an ordinary cylinder machine (fig. 4) or for twills or figured goods, additional rollers or winces are added so that the face side does not come in contact with the cylinders. White goods are usually starched in conjunction with the drying machines, as for grey, coloured woven, dyed and printed goods. Various types of starch mangles are used for this purpose; the two-bowl mangle; the two-bowl friction calender by which the filling can be forced into the cloth; the back-filling mangle.

After starching or filling, the cloth is dried over a cylinder drying machine, back-filled goods being dried over machines with the modification referred to which permits of only one side of the cloth coming in contact with the metal. Or instead of cylinder-drying, the cloth may be dried on a hot-air stentering range. The starch mangle shewn in this illustration is not usual in this combination in white-finishing. By this method, any lost width may be recovered, the feel of the cloth is better, and an elastic finish may be produced by the jigging motion of the stenter, and any weft-distortion may be corrected.

The further processes may involve the use of the damping machine (fig. 1) and various calenders similar to those given for grey and coloured finishing and possibly the beetling machine.

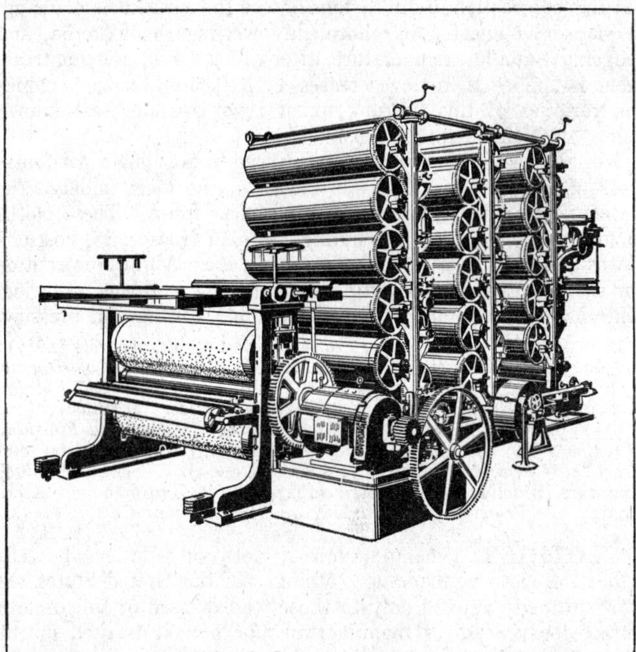

BY COURTESY OF MATHER AND PLATT, LTD.

FIG. 3.—HEAVY FINISHING RANGE WITH VERTICAL DRYING MACHINE

Plain Dyed Goods.—These also require a great variety of finishes, but the range of machines used is not so great as in the case of white goods, for instance, back-filling and friction starching is rarely employed with dyed goods. Three and four bowl water mangles are employed and a drying from these machines is generally effected on drying cylinders. The stiffening of dyed goods is carried out on a two-bowl mangle and cylinder drying machine, or preferably on a hot-air stentering range, for example, mangle cyliners and 90ft. stenter with hot-air drying. Damping machines, stretching machines, breaking machines, calenders from three to seven bowls with and without friction may be required, for certain finishes; for producing window blinds beetles are required; Schreiner calenders for silky finishes and embossing calenders for book cloths, etc.

Printed Goods.—These are finished on similar machines to those used for dyed goods. For ordinary stiffening or starching a range comprising a two-bowl starch mangle, followed by a

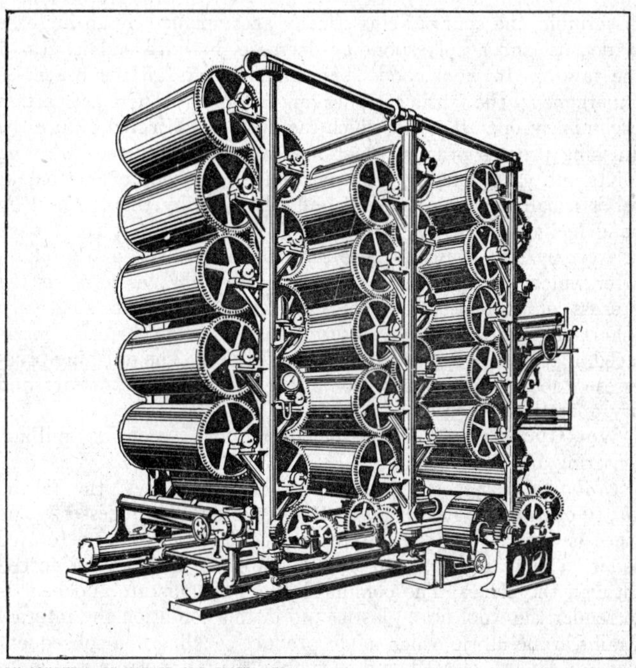

BY COURTESY OF MATHER AND PLATT, LTD.

FIG. 4.—VERTICAL DRYING MACHINE ON THREE PAIRS OF UPRIGHTS; FOR DRYING CLOTH AFTER MANGLING

cylinder drying machine is employed, or a hot-air stentering range consisting of a two-bowl mangle, six-cylinder drying machine and 90ft. stenter with hot-air drying. For muslins, voiles and goods requiring an elastic or batiste finish, the latter method is indispensable.

Another method of stiffening known as back starching, differs from the ordinary method, in that the starch paste is applied to the back or unprinted side of the fabric by means of a brass roller partly immersed in the starch box. The drying of back starched cloth is performed by passing the cloth over the drying cylinders of large diameter, say, from 5 to 7 feet, arranged in such a manner that the starched side does not come in contact with the heated cylinders. An ordinary drying machine can be employed, but in this case, precautions have to be taken by cooling the first cylinders to prevent the starched side adhering to the cylinders. A back starcher or universal starcher can be used in conjunction with a hot-air stenter instead of the usual cylinder drying machine. The additional machines which may be required for finishing printed goods are similar to those already mentioned, and include clip-stretchers, swissing and friction calenders, Schreiner calenders, beetles, as for dyed goods.

Raised Goods.—In this class are included those cloths which are raised on one or both sides, such as flannelettes. Similar machines to those employed for dyed goods are used for the actual finishing, the stiffening being carried out on a mangle and drying machine, or hot-air stentering range. The conditioning clip stenter is especially useful.

Calenders are not usual, brushing and lustring machines being used instead.

WOOLLEN GOODS

The finishing of woollen goods requires in general plant and processes entirely different from those described in connection with cotton. The methods employed naturally vary with the nature of the fabric: for example, worsted fabrics (woven from yarns produced from the longest staple fibre, and containing the maximum of parallelism between the fibres) require in general a "clearer" finish than woollen fabrics woven from yarns composed of interlaced fibres of all lengths, which lend themselves to milling and raising. In the former case, the characteristics of the fabric structure dependent upon the nature of the weave are largely retained, and even developed, while in the latter case the thready appearance of the loom state fabric often gives way to a felted effect in which the individual warp and weft threads are no longer discernible, the change being usually accompanied by an increase in density and a corresponding decrease in width and length of the fabric. In wool goods, "finishing" covers all the processes undergone by the fabric after leaving the loom. There are certain preliminary operations to which the piece is subjected before the finishing process proper, which are intended to correct weaving faults and yarn defects. The pieces are "perched" over a bar or roller usually in a north light and examined by the eye and by hand feeling. "Knotting" consists in removing knots from warp or weft by first drawing these through to the back of the cloth, after which they are cut away. "Mending" or "darning" is the process of correcting defects such as holes and missing yarn (short ends and picks) by inserting new threads correctly interlaced in accordance with the weave structure. The finishing processes proper divide themselves into the two groups of wet and dry operations.

Wet Operations.—These include crabbing, scouring, milling, tentering and carbonizing.

Crabbing. The object of this process is to "set" the fabric, *i.e.,* to obviate the risk of distortion in subsequent processes. The piece is tightly wound in a stretched condition over a perforated roller, which allows steam or hot water or both to be forced through the piece. The combined effect of moisture and heat is to render the wool fibre plastic, and in this condition the internal strains in the fabric which might produce cockling in a subsequent wet process are released, and on cooling the fabric assumes a more or less permanent "set."

Scouring. This process is intended to remove grease and oil and mechanically adhering dirt from the wool goods. The detergents used are either soaps or alkalis depending upon the amount and character of the oil present in the wool. Some fabrics are conveniently scoured in the rope-form, while others—*e.g.,* those liable to crease, are best scoured in the open width.

Milling. This process makes use of a special property of the wove fibre of "felting." The woollen cloth is impregnated with a solution of soap (more rarely of acid) and subjected to pressure between rotating rollers in the milling machine, or by the action of fallers in the stilling stocks. As a result of this action, the fibres become matted or felted if the milling is carried far enough, the warp and weft threads appear to lose their identity, and the woven structure of the cloth is entirely hidden. The cloth often gains strength as a result of milling, while the density is increased at the expense of the width and length, the whole fabric being rendered more consistent.

Tentering. After the scouring process, the pieces may be dried by first removing the excess of water by hydro-extracting or by passing through the wringer; and afterward subjecting to the drying action of warm air while stretched out between the lists or edges. In addition to drying the pieces, this operation straightens and "sets" the cloth.

Carbonizing. Some kinds of wool fabrics, *e.g.,* velours, may be produced from low quality wools containing vegetable matter. This impurity may be removed by soaking the fabric after scouring in a solution of sulphuric or other acid, drying, and raising to a temperature of about 100° C., when the vegetable matter is disintegrated and may be removed by a slight beating and air draught.

Dry Operations.—These include raising, cutting, napping, blowing, brushing, steaming and pressing.

Cutting. This operation formerly performed by hand with large shears is now carried out on a suitable machine. It consists in removing the pile of the fabric beyond a certain length, this length varying greatly with the class of fabric. For example, worsted cloths are cut close to the surface in order to enhance the effects of weave and colour. Woollen fabrics only receive as a rule a cutting sufficient to level up the projecting fibres.

Blowing consists in subjecting the pieces wound in the open width on a perforated beam to the action of steam. There is some resemblance to the crabbing process already described, and the object is again to "set" the fabric permanently, though other advantages are also usually obtained, such as increase in the lustre of the fabric.

Steaming differs from the blowing process in that the fabric is drawn from one roller to another over a box with perforated top from which steam issues. The object is to raise the fibre somewhat, and thus destroy any glaze, and to soften the feel or handle as a result of the conditioning effect of the steam, *i.e.,* by the absorption of moisture.

Raising. This is a mechanical operation in which fibres are lifted from the yarns in the cloth, or from the surface to produce a pile or nap. The raising process was formerly effected by the use of teazles (Dipsacus fullonum) applied by hand; and teazles are still used, mounted on cylinders and operated by power. In addition, cord-wire raising is largely practised; in this form a number of raising rollers are covered with cord clothing, and revolve against the cloth which is made to pass over them by an independent motion.

Pressing is an important operation in the finishing of wool goods; it may be carried out with the object of smoothing the surface of the fibre and imparting an appearance of uniformity, or by prolonged treatment the lustre of the fabric may be greatly increased. The fabric, charged with a sufficient amount of moisture, is subjected to the combined action of (usually) heat and hydraulic pressure. Three different systems are used, (1) the vertical hydraulic press, (2) the intermittent hydraulic press, (3) the rotary press.

Shrinking. The tendency of wool garments to contract in wear is well known. The object of the shrinking process is to bring out this contraction in dimensions before the garment is made up. It is usually effected by thoroughly wetting the material, and redyeing it at a low temperature, after which a mild pressing treatment is applied to remove creases, etc. There are many names for varieties of this "shrunk finish"; perhaps the best known being "the London-shrunk finish."

Not all the above processes are utilized in finishing a particular class of wool fabric. Worsted cloths in the main undergo the series of operations known as the clear-cut finish. These cloths include fancy vestings and suitings, striped trouserings, costume cloths and dress fabrics, fancy worsteds, etc. A finishing routine for the latter involves knotting and mending, crabbing, scouring, tentering, brushing and steaming, cutting, blowing and pressing.

BIBLIOGRAPHY.—J. Dépierre, *Traité Élémentaire des Apprêts* (1887); E. Knecht, C. Rawson and L. Loewenthal, *A Manual of Dyeing,* 2 vol., 2nd ed. (1910); R. Beaumont, *The Finishing of Textile Fabrics,* 2nd ed. (1926); P. Heermann, *Technologie der Textilveredelung* (1921); A. J. Hall, *Textile Bleaching, Dyeing, Printing and Finishing Machinery* (1926); P. Bean and W. McCleary, *The Chemistry and Practice of Finishing* (1926); J. Schofield and J. C. Schofield, *Cloth Finishing, Woollen and Worsted* (1927); S. R. Trotman and E. L. Thorp, *The Principles of Bleaching and Finishing of Cotton* (1928).

(F. Sc.)

CLOTHIER, a manufacturer of cloth, or a dealer who sells either the cloth or made-up clothing. In the United States the word formerly applied only to those who dressed or fulled cloth during the process of manufacture, but now it is used in the general sense, as above.

CLOTHIERS, WHOLESALE. The term wholesale clothiers is applied to the makers and distributors of ready-to-wear or machine-made woollen and other types of outer clothing for men and women, comprising suits and overcoats for men, costumes, dresses, skirts, and coats for women. The industry forms the more important of the two divisions—wholesale and made-to-order—of the tailoring, or clothing trades.

The name "clothier" signified in the days of handloom weaving, the master clothmaker or producer, but with the advent of the power loom that designation gradually became changed to "manufacturer," prefixed generally with a qualifying name indicative of the class of fabric made, such as "cloth," "woollen," or "worsted."

Some makers, however, prefer to style themselves manufacturing clothiers. In America, the cloth dresser (finisher), or fuller was formerly termed a clothier.

CLOTHING MANUFACTURE. The application of the sewing machine to tailoring made the production of ready-made clothing possible in bulk. The early demand for ready-made clothing may be traced to the older seaport towns, where such clothing was often required at short notice by persons returning from long voyages. The foundations of the wholesale clothing industry, however, may be said to rest first, on the invention of the sewing machine; and second, upon the introduction of cheap (shoddy) cloth made from pulled-up rags, from which material machine-made clothing, produced in bulk, was originally made. The use of shoddy has practically disappeared, however, and the finest grades of cloth are quite generally used by the best manufacturers of ready-made clothing, who are also in a position to employ highly qualified designers.

Thimmonier's Sewing Machine.—Ready-made clothing was first made in Paris by a tailor named Thimmonier, who invented the first sewing machine in 1830, and applied it with considerable success to the production of army clothing until 1841, when his factory was destroyed during a machinery riot. Thimmonier afterward went to England with an improved machine which he patented in 1848. This, however, met with no success, and it was not until 1851, when the American invention of Isaac Merritt Singer was introduced into England, that the industrial potentialities of the sewing machine were realized.

The quicker output obtained by mechanical sewing necessitated an increase in the speed of pattern cutting, and 1860 saw the invention of the cloth-cutting band knife (based on the principle of the band saw), which solved the problem of supplying material to keep pace with the work of the sewing machine. This machine was made in Leeds by Greenwood and Batley at the suggestion of John Barran, a native of London who had settled in Leeds some years previously, where he had commenced the wholesale clothing industry in 1855. The modern machine has a knife velocity of 7,000 ft. per minute, and can cut 50 thicknesses of cloth at once. A more modern style of machine still is a portable knife cutter worked by electricity.

Other inventions, mostly in connection with sewing, followed in rapid succession; and sewing by hand for joining most parts of a garment was almost entirely superseded by machines devised for such special purposes as felling (*i.e.*, turning over the edges of the cloth and then sewing in order to prevent fraying), sleeving, buttonhole making and button stitching. A machine for marking the outlines of the patterns to prepare them for cutting, and machines for pressing assisted further to reduce handwork to a minimum; and the transition from operating the sewing machines by hand or foot to power driving contributed to greatly increased output and cheaper production.

Division of Labour.—The modern factory system is highly sectionalized, and its production and output depend upon an extraordinary degree of subdivision of labour; so much so, that a coat, in making, may pass through the hands of as many as 50 persons. Subdivision of labour reduces the cost of production by causing the simpler processes to be effected by the unskilled labour of young persons, and utilizing skilled labour only for the more complicated work.

The system originates with the designing and production of the patterns in the various standard sizes by the head pattern or stock cutter, who is responsible for keeping in touch with movements in fashion and style. The separate paper pieces comprising a pattern for a garment or suit are then formed into what is termed a "lay" by fitting them as closely together as possible (interlocking them after the manner of a jigsaw puzzle), so that in cutting out the cloth there will be a minimum of waste; the operation being termed "lay-getting." The outlines of the lay are chalked on a large piece of tough paper or linen corresponding in width to the cloth, and then these are perforated by a machine called a "process-marker," thus forming the pattern or lay from which the garments are cut in bulk. To prepare the cloth for mechanical cutting, it is automatically folded in the number of lengths required by the "laying-up" machine; the lay is placed on the top fold, and specially prepared powdered chalk is rubbed through the perforations to indicate the lines to be followed by the knife.

After cutting, the pieces for each individual garment are sorted out and numbered, tied into bundles with their necessary trimmings, which have been prepared in a similar manner to that just described, and passed forward to the factory for making up. There, the various parts are sewn and gradually assembled into the complete garment—this being a combination of hand and machine work by trimmers, finishers, machinists (who work the specialized sewing machines) and pressers.

The industry was built up in Great Britain very largely by the exploitation of alien Jewish labour, and in fact, the origin of the subdivisional system of work was the outcome of the necessity for finding employment for the great influx of Russian Jews to London. These unfortunate people usually carried on their occupation at home, and by reason of their poverty and consequent low standard of living worked for very low rates of payment. This quickly resulted in the "sweated labour" conditions exposed by Charles Kingsley and other social reformers. In 1909, when the first Trade Board act was passed, ready-made and wholesale bespoke tailoring was classed among the four industries having "rates of wages exceptionally low as compared with those in other employments." The Tailoring Trade board was established under this act in the following year with powers to determine the minimum rates of wages in all branches of the tailoring trades, and in 1920 two separate boards were constituted—one to deal with the ready-made and wholesale section, and the other to control the retail section of the industry.

Location of Industry.—Though London was the original home of the British ready-made clothing trade, Leeds is now the chief seat of the industry, and wholesale clothing forms the leading trade in the city. There is a difference, too, in the conduct of the industry in the two centres; in Leeds it is almost entirely confined to work in the factory; in London, outworking persists to a large extent. Leeds was the first provincial town (in 1855) to engage in the industry, and no doubt owes its present leading position largely to its advantageous geographical situation in the centre of the West Riding of Yorkshire woollen and worsted cloth manufacturing area, which supplies it with all classes of fabrics from the lowest to the highest in quality. The manufacture of clothing is also carried on in the Huddersfield and Hebden Bridge districts, Liverpool and Manchester, Bristol, Colchester, and Leicester; and in Scotland, Glasgow is an important centre.

It may be noted that though ready-made clothing was identified formerly with inferior materials only, this is no longer the case, and there is now a large and increasing demand for ready-for-service garments of high class workmanship, made of the finest quality materials.

With regard to markets, it is generally considered that about two-thirds of the yearly British output is absorbed at home, and the remainder goes principally to the British colonies, though the United States is a considerable customer for the best class of British goods in spite of its own high standing in the industry. (A. Y.)

United States.—Clothing manufacture in the United States has passed out of the hands of the merchant tailor and is conducted in modern plants equipped with labour-saving machinery. The United States is the home of ready-made clothing. It has been estimated that between 80% and 90% of the men's clothing made in the United States is of the ready-to-wear type. Half of this clothing is produced in the centres of population. As a result of the fact that people are buying cheaper clothing, cotton and other fabrics are being used in great amount.

In New York city, the most important clothing market, the greater part of the clothing is produced under the contract system. The manufacturer cuts up the cloth into the various patterns he desires and this cloth is sent to a contractor for fabrication into garments. This system partly accounts for the large number of clothing firms in New York city, for it enables a person to enter the business with comparatively small capital. In the other clothing centres most of the clothing manufacturers maintain their own factories.

The success of mass production in the clothing industry in the United States that has developed since the 20th century began, rests upon (1) scientific pattern construction; (2) highly efficient labour-saving machinery; (3) effective factory arrangement; (4) high division of labour; (5) economies effected in the purchase and fabrication of materials on a large scale, and (6) standardization of styles. The industry did not make any great progress until scientific investigations of average proportions of the human body yielded sufficient information on which to base the present art of clothing designing. Experience has disclosed that normal proportions and variations therefrom are fairly constant in any group of 100 men, and consequently, clothing manufacturers make their garments in assortments complying with such experience. A retail store stocking 1,000 suits might, for example, have the following assortment: 54.3% regular; 31.3% short; 4.7% long; 5.6% stout; 4.1% short stout. The sizes would range from 35 to 50 (chest) with 37, 38, 39, 40, 42, and 44 making the bulk. All stores do not carry, nor do all factories make assortments as complete as above. However, the more complete the range of sizes, the less alterations, or busheling, must be made. These busheling operations are standardized, and because of the high development of the art of making ready-to-wear clothing in the United States, changes are usually slight.

In making a new model sport coat or overcoat, the designer visualizes the style he wishes to create and drafts a pattern, usually size 36 or 38. This pattern is used to derive a complete set of patterns for all required sizes, including regulars, shorts, longs, stouts, etc. The work of translating the basic pattern into other sizes is called pattern grading. In many U.S. factories the designer not only designs the models, but he also supervises the general production of the garment in the factory. Many manufacturers do not have designers and they, as well as many designers themselves, are often guilty of pirating competitors' patterns. Certain pattern houses supply patterns to the manufacturer without need of either pirating or a designer.

There are two methods of shrinking or sponging cloth in use. London or cold-water shrinking is the best and most expensive. Steam or machine shrinking is cheapest and most widely used.

In processing, the cloth is first shrunk and dried. It is then laid out on cutting tables in lays from a few thicknesses of cloth to as high as 50 or 60 in the case of work clothing; modern machines do this at high speed. The cardboard, fibreboard, or brass bound patterns are laid on the cloth in such a manner as to conserve every possible inch of cloth. After the outlines of the patterns are chalked on the top layer of the lay by a marker the outlines are cut by electric cutting machines. These machines are of two types; the one having a revolving disk cutter and the other having a vertical blade moving up and down; automatic knife sharpeners can be obtained. Some manufacturers still cut by hand knife, others by powerful dies.

Most cutting rooms are located on the top floor of the factory so that the cloth after cutting can pass through the assembly departments to the stock room by means of gravity or other conveyors. There are several systems of production; the bundle, the modified bundle, and the straight line. Each has its strengths and weaknesses. Newest is the straight-line system which applies the automobile assembly line theory of production. This is used particularly on pants and shirts. The garment is started at one end and handed on down the line, each operator performs his or her one special operation and it comes from the line as a complete unit. In this way lost motion is minimized and a high efficiency is maintained. Different types of straight lines are used—some are "Y" shaped, others are "V" shaped. Regardless of the system of production used, modern factories are highly departmentalized and division of labour is carried out to a high degree. Each operator performs but one task on a garment, thereby gaining unusual proficiency. In the making of some pockets, for example, there are 13 different operations, each one of which is performed by a single individual. One hundred persons may work on a sport coat. Not only does an operator do more work under this system, but because of the skill he develops, he does better work. This high division of labour also permits the use of workers possessing ordinary intelligence. A large percentage of the clothing factories in the United States operate on a piecework basis; *i.e.*, a unit price is fixed for each operation on a garment. Some factories use a task system, which approximates a piecework system. Still others use a set system, which is a modified form of subcontracting to groups of workers.

Much labour-saving machinery for the clothing industry has been perfected in the United States, by means of which the various operations are speeded up and the unit costs reduced. Dozens of improved types of sewing machines have been introduced which are instrumental in reducing costs. Two-needle and four-needle machines are common. The speed of some of these new machines is amazing: literally thousands of stitches per minute. The late models of buttonhole machines cut the cloth, sew and tack the buttonhole in a fraction of a minute. Even buttons are sewed on by machine. Safety tables keep all movable parts of the machines, except the needles, enclosed. Needles are protected by needle guards in many plants. New blind-stitch machines which render the stitching invisible and are adaptable to almost all types and weights of fabrics have been perfected. There is also a machine that simulates exactly a hand stitch. One of the outstanding developments in labour-saving machinery is the steam pressing machine. The machine in use is made in a variety of models having bucks shaped to fit various parts of the garment; it has materially lowered clothing pressing costs. An automatic pressing machine used more extensively outside the United States, though made there, requires only finger control. There are many other automatic compressed air machines for varied operations; especially for shirts. (C. LE.; H. SIM.)

CLOTILDA, SAINT (d. 544), daughter of the Burgundian king Chilperic, and wife of Clovis, king of the Franks. On the death of Gundioc, king of the Burgundians, in 473, his sons Gundobald, Godegesil and Chilperic divided his heritage. At Lyons an epitaph has been discovered of a Burgundian queen who died in 506 and was most probably the mother of Clotilda. Clotilda was brought up in the orthodox faith. Her uncle Gundobald was asked for her hand in marriage by the Frankish king Clovis, who had just conquered northern Gaul, and the marriage was celebrated about 493. On this event many romantic stories, all more or less embroidered, are to be found in the works of Gregory of Tours and the chronicler Fredegarius, and in the *Liber historiae Francorum*. Clotilda did not rest until her husband had abjured paganism and embraced the orthodox Christian faith (496). With him she built at Paris the church of the Holy Apostles, afterward known as Ste. Geneviève. After the death of Clovis in 511 she retired to the abbey of St. Martin at Tours. In 523 she incited her sons against her uncle Gundobald and provoked the Burgundian war. In the following year she tried in vain to protect the rights of her grandsons, the children of Clodomer, against the claims of her sons Childebert I and Clotaire I, and was equally unsuccessful in her efforts to prevent the civil discords between her children. She died in 544, and was buried at her husband's side in the church of the Holy Apostles.

There is a mediocre *Life* in *Mon. Germ. Hist.: Script. rer. Merov.*, vol. ii. *See* also G. Kurth, *Sainte Clotilde*, 2nd ed. (1897). (C. PF.)

CLOUD, an aggregation of minute water droplets or ice particles drifting in the air at some height above the earth.

CLASSIFICATION

Although it is reasonable to suppose that the shapes and general appearance of clouds must have been a matter of interest and speculation from earliest times, no lasting contribution to the development of a scientific cloud classification was made until 1803, when Luke Howard published his classical paper entitled "On the Modifications of Clouds." The Latin terms which Howard adopted were applied with such excellent judgment that his system later became the internationally accepted basis of cloud classification.

For more than 50 years following the appearance of Howard's treatise little progress in the study of clouds was achieved. It was not until 1874, the year of the first International Meteorological congress, that important new efforts were initiated in this field. During the succeeding 20 years constructive proposals were advanced in many countries by a large number of workers whose combined efforts led in 1896 to publication of the *International Cloud Atlas*.

During the period of World War I and the years immediately following, interest in cloud forms and their prognostic significance was further stimulated by the development of aviation, and the preparation of a new and much more extensive cloud atlas was undertaken. The result was the *International Atlas of Clouds and States of the Sky* (Paris, 1932), which specifies that clouds are divided into four families, as follows: (1) high clouds, (2) middle clouds, (3) low clouds and (4) clouds with vertical development. Each family is divided into genera, of which there are ten in all. Most of the genera are subdivided into species, while species in turn are subdivided into varieties. The atlas lists 20 species

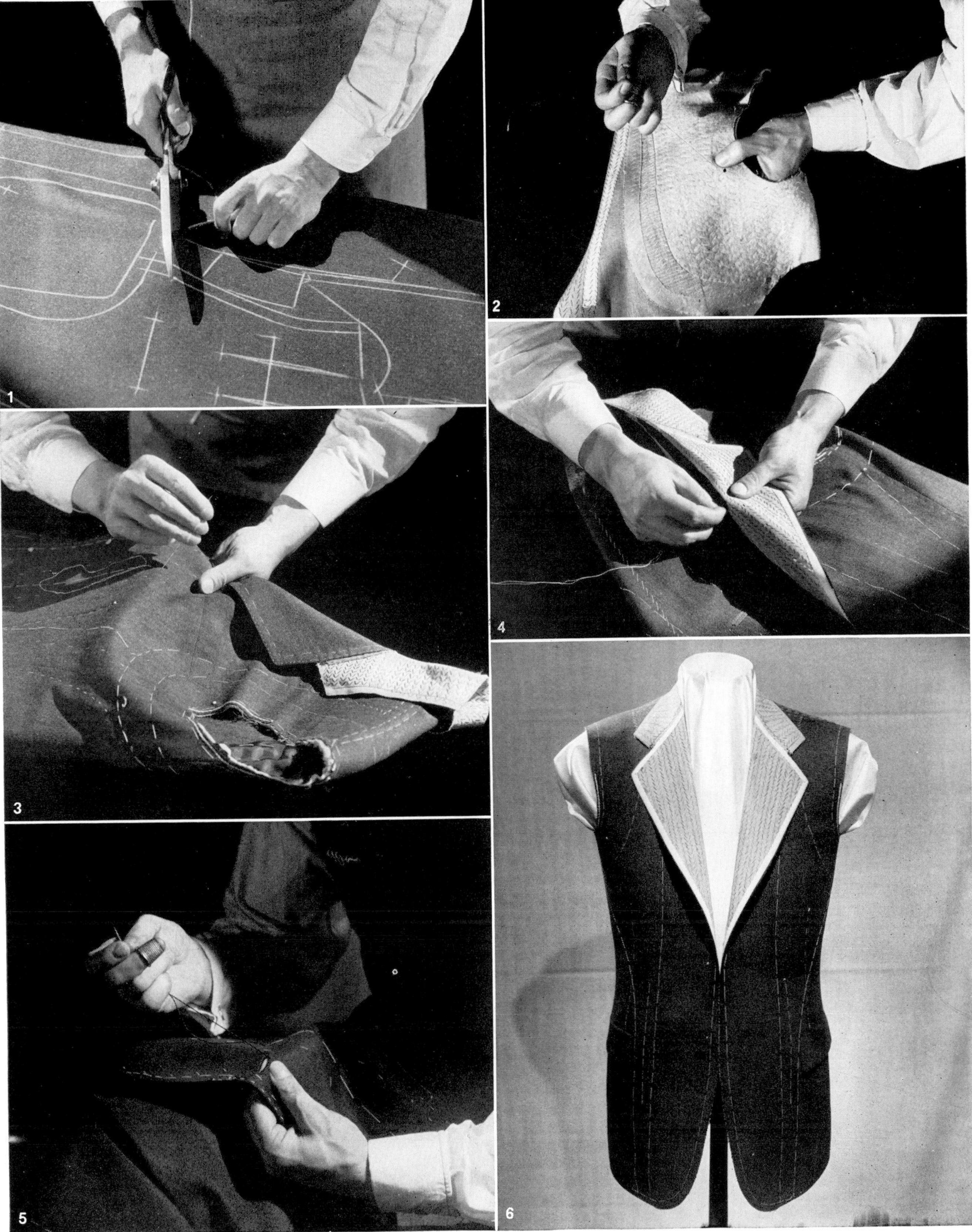

BY COURTESY OF HICKEY-FREEMAN CO.

STEPS IN THE HAND-TAILORING OF MEN'S CLOTHING

1. Cutting the cloth by hand, one garment at a time, along lines marked with chalk
2. Stitching the padding of a coat front
3. Basting a sack coat. So many thicknesses of material go into a garment of this type that careful basting is necessary to assure that the final stitching anchors each piece firmly in its proper place
4. Hand-stitching the interlining of a coat lapel
5. Making a buttonhole by hand
6. A partly finished sack coat

BY COURTESY OF THE UNITED STATES WEATHER BUREAU

CLOUD FORMS

Top left: Cirrus filosus, detached clouds of delicate and fibrous appearance, without shading, white in colour and characterized by more or less straight filaments

Top right: Cirrus uncinus, detached clouds of delicate and fibrous appearance, without shading, white in colour and shaped like a comma, with the upper parts ending in little tufts or points

Centre left: Cirrus densus, detached clouds of fibrous appearance, generally white in colour but sometimes with such thickness that they superficially resemble middle or low clouds

Centre right: Cirrus nothus, dense cirrus streaming out from a cumulonimbus cloud and composed of the remains of the frozen upper parts of that cloud

Bottom left: Cirro-stratus nebulosus, a uniform, whitish, misty veil which does not blur the outlines of the sun or moon and usually gives rise to halos

Bottom right: Cirro-stratus filosus, a white fibrous veil, in which more or less definite strands are apparent. It often resembles a sheet of cirrus densus, from which it may actually originate

CLOUD

BY COURTESY OF (TOP TO BOTTOM) THE UNITED STATES WEATHER BUREAU; PHOTOGRAPH (CENTRE LEFT) A. C. LAPSLEY

CLOUD FORMS

Top left: Cirro-cumulus, a layer or patch composed of small white flakes or small globular masses, without shadows, which are here arranged in groups and associated with tufted cirrus

Top right: Alto-cumulus-translucidus, a layer (or patches) composed of slightly flattened globular masses, with or without shading. The elements are here more or less regularly arranged and are distinct from each other. Blue sky shows through the interstices

Centre left: Alto-cumulus-opacus, a continuous layer consisting of dark and more or less irregular elements which, though opaque, stand out in real relief on the lower surface of the cloud sheet

Centre right: Alto-cumulus-cumulogenitus, a layer formed by the spreading out of the tops of cumulus clouds, and in the first stages of development having the appearance of alto-cumulus-opacus

Bottom left: Alto-cumulus-lenticularis, small isolated patches, with or without shading, and roughly in the shape of a double convex lens

Bottom right: Alto-cumulus-castellatus, cloud masses with more or less vertical development, here visible in the upper part of the picture. The elements are generally arranged in a line and rest on a common horizontal base, thus giving the cloud a crenellated appearance

BY COURTESY OF THE UNITED STATES WEATHER BUREAU

CLOUD FORMS

Top left: Alto-stratus-translucidus, a striated or fibrous veil, grayish in colour, here seen above small masses of low cloud. The veil resembles thick cirro-stratus but does not produce halo phenomena; the sun or moon shines faintly, as though through ground glass

Top right: Alto-stratus-opacus, an opaque, fibrous veil, gray or bluish in colour. Its thickness is variable, but generally it is dense enough to hide completely the sun or moon

Centre left: Strato-cumulus-translucidus, a layer (or patches) composed of globular masses or rolls which are soft and gray, with darker parts. The interstices between the cloud elements permit the passage of sunlight

Centre right: Strato-cumulus-opacus, a thick layer made up of a continuous sheet of large dark rolls or rounded masses; their shape is not clearly defined, but they stand out in relief from the undersurface of the layer

Bottom left: Strato-cumulus-vesperalis, flat, elongated masses or rolls of cloud which are often seen to form about sunset

Bottom right: Strato-cumulus-undulatus, a dense, dark layer composed of large, lumpy rolls which cover the whole sky and are aligned in one direction only. Often called roll cumulus

CLOUD

CLOUD FORMS

Top left: Strato-cumulus-mammatus, a layer composed of dense globular masses whose lower surfaces form a series of pouches or festoons

Top right: Stratus, a low uniform layer of cloud, resembling fog but not resting on the ground

Centre left: Cumulus humilis, clouds with vertical development but with a tendency toward flattening of the dome-shaped tops. They are generally seen in fine weather

Centre right: Cumulus congestus, thick clouds with vertical development and having a distended and swollen appearance. The upper surfaces are dome shaped and exhibit cauliflowerlike protuberances

Bottom left: Cumulo-nimbus-capillatus, heavy masses of cloud with great vertical development, from which showers fall; the upper parts have a fibrous structure and generally spread out in the shape of an anvil

Bottom right: Cumulo-nimbus-calvus, heavy masses of cloud with great vertical development, from which showers fall but which are not characterized by any pronounced fibrous structure in the upper parts

for 7 out of 10 genera, and 7 general varieties that can apply to many of the species. The classification of cloud forms fixed by international agreement is outlined below:

A. High clouds (mean lower level 6,000 m. [19,685 ft.])
  1. Cirrus
  2. Cirrocumulus
  3. Cirrostratus
B. Middle clouds (mean upper level 6,000 m. [19,685 ft.], mean lower level 2,000 m. [6,562 ft.])
  4. Altocumulus
  5. Altostratus
C. Low clouds (mean upper level 2,000 m. [6,562 ft.], mean lower level close to the ground)
  6. Stratocumulus
  7. Stratus
  8. Nimbostratus
D. Clouds with vertical development (mean upper level that of the cirrus, mean lower level 500 m. [1,640 ft.])
  9. Cumulus
  10. Cumulonimbus

The definitions and descriptions of the ten cloud genera given in the *International Atlas* may be summarized as follows:

1. Cirrus (Ci).—Detached clouds of delicate and fibrous appearance, without shading, generally white in colour, often of a silky appearance. Cirrus manifests itself in various forms such as isolated tufts, lines drawn across a blue sky, branching feather-like plumes, curved lines ending in tufts, etc.; it often is arranged in bands, which, because of the effect of perspective, converge to a point on the horizon.

2. Cirrocumulus (Cc).—A layer or patch composed of small white flakes or of very small globular masses, without shading, which are arranged in groups or lines, or in ripples resembling those of the sand on the seashore.

3. Cirrostratus (Cs).—A thin whitish veil which does not blur the outlines of the sun or moon but produces halos. Sometimes it is quite diffuse and merely gives the sky a milky look; sometimes it more or less distinctly shows a fibrous structure.

4. Altocumulus (Ac).—A layer (or patches) composed of slightly flattened globular masses, the smallest elements being fairly narrow and thin, with or without shading. These elements are arranged in groups, lines or waves, following one or two directions and are sometimes so close together that their edges join.

5. Altostratus (As).—A striated or fibrous veil, more or less gray or bluish in colour. Sometimes this cloud is like dense cirrostratus, but without halo phenomena; the sun or moon shows dimly, as though through ground glass. At other times it is very thick and dark, and may even completely hide the sun or moon.

6. Stratocumulus (Sc).—A layer (or patches) composed of globular masses which are soft and gray, with darker parts. These elements, the smallest of which are fairly broad, are arranged in groups, lines, or in waves aligned in one or two directions. Often the rolls are so close that their edges join; when they cover the whole sky, they have a wavy appearance.

7. Stratus (St).—A low uniform layer of cloud, resembling fog but not resting on the ground.

8. Nimbostratus (Ns).—A low amorphous layer, rainy in appearance, dark gray in colour, nearly uniform in texture and feebly illuminated, seemingly from inside. It usually, but not necessarily, yields precipitation.

9. Cumulus (Cu).—Thick clouds with vertical development, the upper surfaces of which are dome shaped and exhibit protuberances while the bases are nearly horizontal.

10. Cumulonimbus (Cb).—Heavy masses of cloud, with great vertical development, whose summits rise like mountains or towers, the upper parts having a fibrous texture and often spreading out in the shape of an anvil.

PHYSICS OF CLOUDS

Almost all types of clouds result from the process of condensation, during which some of the water vapour present in the air changes to liquid water in the form of minute drops. (The average diameter of the droplets composing a cloud is of the order of magnitude of .001 in.) Condensation depends upon the fact that for a given temperature there is a maximum pressure that can be exerted by water vapour. The lower the temperature, the smaller is this maximum pressure. If, for any reason, a body of cloudless air becomes cooled below the temperature corresponding to that at which the existing pressure of water vapour represents the maximum permissible value, condensation and cloud formation are initiated. The temperature at which the maximum permissible vapour pressure matches the existing vapour pressure is known as the dew point. (*See* DEW.)

Although laboratory experiments have shown that condensation does not necessarily occur in perfectly pure air that has been cooled below the dew point, the atmosphere contains a variety of impurities which facilitate the change from vapour to liquid. These impurities may be divided into two groups: (1) tiny particles of simple solids, such as dust and smoke; and (2) submicroscopically small particles of certain hygroscopic substances, notably sea salts, sulphuric acid and nitrous acid. The first group appears to be relatively unimportant in the promotion of condensation, whereas particles of the second group serve as nuclei around which cloud droplets grow readily whenever the temperature of the air becomes lower than the dew point.

The manner in which ice-crystal clouds (*i.e.*, clouds of the cirrus family) are created is not well understood. Ice crystals may be produced in the atmosphere either by the freezing of liquid water or by the direct transition of water from the vapour state to the solid state. (The latter process is termed sublimation.) However, it is known that ice crystals will not form directly from water vapour unless the temperature is lower than about 20° F. Even at temperatures well below 0° F. liquid droplets are formed more commonly than ice crystals. Therefore, it is believed that cirrus clouds arise mainly from the freezing of liquid water previously produced by the process of condensation. Laboratory experiments have given evidence that at low temperatures solid, rather than hygroscopic, particles serve as nuclei for condensation.

As already stated, condensation depends upon a reduction of the air temperature to a value lower than the dew point. Such reduction may be brought about in the following ways: (1) loss of heat by conduction; (2) loss of heat by radiation; (3) adiabatic cooling of air by reduction of pressure because of ascent. The first two processes, although important in the formation of fog, play comparatively insignificant roles in respect to cloud formation. Adiabatic cooling of ascending air is the basic cause of almost all clouds; the nature of the ascending motion determines the character of the clouds.

There are four general classes of upward motion: (1) vertical currents of small dimensions and irregular structure superimposed on the horizontal flow of air; (2) large-scale convection currents; (3) upward currents induced by orographic obstacles in the path of the wind; (4) more or less uniform ascent of air over wide areas resulting from special dynamical conditions in the atmosphere. The first of these classes of motion yields stratus and a few varieties of stratocumulus. The second class produces the clouds that are distinguished by their marked vertical development (*i.e.*, cumulus and cumulonimbus, from which certain forms of high clouds and middle clouds, notably cirrus nothus and altocumulus cumulogenitus, as well as most types of stratocumulus, are derived). The third class typically gives rise to stratus or to altocumulus lenticularis, but complications are often introduced by the fact, that such currents will accentuate any pre-existing tendency toward large-scale convection, with the result that clouds having considerable vertical development may be generated by this type of upward motion. As for the uniform ascent of air over large areas, special importance must be attached to this fourth class of motion, because it leads to the formation of the unbroken sheets of cirrostratus, altocumulus and altostratus which ordinarily precede bad weather.

The principal process that brings about the disappearance of existing clouds is exactly the reverse of that to which they owe their formation. An increase in the temperature of the air to a value above the dew point initiates vaporization and causes some or all of the water droplets or ice particles composing the clouds to vanish. The ways in which a body of air may have its temperature raised are the following: (1) gain of heat by conduction, (2) gain of heat by radiation, (3) adiabatic warming of air by increase of pressure because of descent. Of these, adiabatic warming of descending air is the most effective mechanism by which clouds are evaporated.

The circumstances in which air descends may be grouped into three classifications: (1) there is localized descending motion of air whenever large-scale convection is taking place, which accounts for the fact that cumulus clouds are separated by clear spaces; (2) descent of air occurs in the lee of orographic obstacles and, in general, over sloping terrain when the wind blows in a downhill direction; (3) a slow, uniform and widespread sinking of air develops under certain dynamical conditions; this may give cloudless skies over a large area. (G. Es.)

MEASUREMENT OF CLOUD HEIGHT

A knowledge of the height of the clouds is obviously of much importance to pure meteorology and also is an aid to flying. For the latter purpose it is especially important to know the height of the lower surface or base of the cloud. In the United States and Canada the term "ceiling" is used to denote the height of the base of the lowest clouds present in quantity on any occasion. "Ceiling zero" is reported when the ceiling is 50 ft. or less; "ceiling unlimited" is reported when either no broken or overcast layer is observed, or the base of the lowest reported broken or overcast layer is higher than 9,750 ft. above ground.

Modern techniques for measuring the base of clouds employ such devices as ceiling balloons, ceiling light projectors, ceilometers and very short wave length (1 cm.) radar. In addition, cloud heights have been estimated by triangulation methods, by optical range finders, by intersections of clouds with hills or mountains, and by application of the dew point formula. In the latter method, when the air is thoroughly mixed as far as the base of the cloud, the height of the condensation level may be calculated from the surface temperature θ and the dew point temperature θ_d (*see* HUMIDITY, ATMOSPHERIC) by the formula

$$Z=220\ (\theta-\theta_d)\ \text{ft.}\ (\theta \text{ and } \theta_d \text{ in °F.})$$

The cloud base is usually 100 to 200 ft. higher than the condensation level, but large errors can occur in such estimates.

In the ceiling balloon method, a small neoprene balloon coloured red or purple for good contrast and weighing about 10 g. is inflated with helium to a free lift of 45 g. and released. With this lifting power, the balloon has an average ascensional rate of about 400 ft. per minute. The height of the cloud can now be computed by noting the time required for the balloon to enter the base of the cloud. The accuracy of the method is limited by the accuracy of the assumed ascensional rate. Unfortunately, the rate becomes very erratic when the clouds are scattered or broken because of the presence of vertical air currents.

For nighttime observations a light (flashlight and battery) can be attached to the ceiling balloon. However, a much more accurate and convenient method is available for ceiling measurements during the hours of darkness through the use of the ceiling light projector. In this device a small searchlight projects a narrow beam of light, of less than 3° spread, vertically upward to the base of the cloud. An observer located 500 to 1,000 ft. from the projection sights on the spot of light on the lower surface of the cloud and measures the vertical angle, h, to the spot. If L is the base line distance from observer to projector, then the height of the cloud base is

$$Z=L \tan h$$

The accuracy of this method is adequate for airways' purposes, being limited chiefly by the uniformity of the underside of the cloud and by the accuracy with which the vertical angle can be measured. With a 500-ft. base line, an uncertainty of 2° in angle will give an error of about 240 ft. for a cloud height of 2,000 ft. Under ideal conditions cloud heights up to 15,000 ft. have been determined to an accuracy of about 2,500 ft.

In daylight the spot from the cloud searchlight is, of course, entirely invisible against the sky, which may be about 1,000,000 times as bright as the spot. This difficulty has been resolved by using a light, modulated to a known frequency, and observing the spot by means of a special telescope which has a photoelectric cell at the focus of a large lens. Electrical filters used in conjunction with the photoelectric cell reject all signals except those of the modulating frequency. These electrical signals are then amplified sufficiently to operate a standard electrical meter. This device, known as the ceilometer, can measure cloud heights to 10,000 ft. during the daytime and about 20,000 ft. at night. It is widely employed not only at civilian air terminals but by the various military services.

Another possibility, still somewhat experimental in the early 1950s, is to project a short pulse of light and measure the time required for it to return to the point of observation. Light pulses of about one-microsecond (one millionth of a second) duration are produced by a high-voltage spark placed at the focus of a good quality 36-inch Cassegrain mirror. The light pulse reflected from a cloud deck is then received by a second mirror which focuses the light on a photocell. Since light travels about 982 ft. per microsecond (186,000 mi. per second), it is necessary to measure accurately time intervals of a few microseconds. As a result of advances during World War II, time intervals to 100th of a microsecond can be measured. It is estimated that a high flux of about 4,000,000 lumens is placed on the cloud deck during measurement. With some experimental models, clouds up to 18,000 ft. were detected in daylight.

A knowledge of the vertical extent and structure of clouds is of great importance to aviation and meteorological science. Some information was formerly obtained from reports of pilots. Radar equipment was later designed that not only measured the base of selected clouds but also permitted detailed study of the vertical structure of clouds. It has been shown both theoretically and experimentally that microwaves of approximately one centimetre wave length are scattered by cloud water droplets of radii between 10 and 30 microns. Short microwave pulses of few microseconds duration are radiated vertically upward toward the cloud from a parabolic antenna mirror six feet in diameter. These pulses are then scattered back toward the antenna from the top and bottom of successive layers of clouds. The time interval between the transmission of the pulse and the returned cloud echo is measured. If this time interval is t microseconds, then the height, Z, of the echoing surface from the radar set is

$$Z=982 \times \frac{t}{2}\ \text{ft.}$$

Radar sets operating at these short wave lengths have detected clouds to heights in excess of 45,000 ft. It has also been possible to locate clouds through several thousand of feet of light rain. However, the minimum altitude that can be detected is about 800 ft., this limitation being due to the recovery time of the radar receiver. The development of the radar cloud-base and cloud-top indicator represents one of the most significant advances in meteorological instrumentation after 1932.

(W. E. K. M.; ML. FE.)

CLOUDBERRY, *Rubus Chamaemorus,* a low-growing creeping herbaceous plant (family, Rosaceae) with simple obtusely lobed leaves and solitary white flowers, resembling those of the blackberry, but larger—one inch across—and with stamens and pistils on different plants. The orange-yellow fruit is about half an inch long and consists of a few large drupes with a pleasant flavour. The plant occurs in the mountainous parts of Great Britain, and is widely distributed through the more northerly portions of both hemispheres. In North America it grows in peat bogs and on mountains from Maine and New Hampshire to arctic America and westward to Alaska and British Columbia. In Norway and Sweden the fruit is gathered in large quantities and sold in the markets.

CLOUDBURST, a term popularly applied to an excessively heavy fall of rain, usually of brief duration, over a small area of the earth's surface. Most so-called cloudbursts occur in connection with thunderstorms. In these storms there are violent uprushes of air, which at times prevent the condensing raindrops from falling to the ground. A large amount of water may thus accumulate at high levels, and if the upward currents are weakened the whole of this water falls at one time. Cloudbursts are especially common in mountainous districts. This is probably because the rising air currents of a thunderstorm are more or less broken up by the passage of the storm over a mountain. The effects of heavy rain are especially striking on mountain slopes because the falling water is concentrated in valleys and gulleys. Mountain cloudbursts cause sudden and destructive floods. The intensity of rainfall in the most severe cloudbursts can only be conjectured. A rainfall of 2.47 in. in 3 min. was registered by an automatic raingauge at Porto Bello, Panama, on Nov. 29, 1911, and one of 1.02 in. in 1 min. by two automatic gauges, placed side by side, at Opid's camp, on the west front of the San Gabriel Range, Calif., on April 5, 1926. There have been many cases, however, in which the deep excavations made in the ground by the falling water of a cloudburst appear to indicate a much greater intensity of rainfall than in the cases above noted.

CLOUDED LEOPARD, a large arboreal cat (*Neofelis nebulosa*) found in southeast Asia, Sumatra, Java, Borneo and Formosa. This cat, also called the clouded tiger, is beautifully marked with large dark patches edged with black. It has an elongate head and body (about 3 ft.), the tail nearly as long, and rather short limbs. The upper canine teeth are proportionately longer than in other living cats. Although its pattern resembles that of the marbled cat (*Felis marmorata*), they are not closely related. The clouded leopard preys on small mammals and birds. (J. E. Hl.)

CLOUET, FRANÇOIS (d. 1572), French miniature painter. The earliest reference to him is the document dated Dec. 1541 (*see* Clouet, Jean), in which the king renounces for the benefit of the artist his father's estate which had escheated to the crown as the estate of a foreigner. In it the younger Janet is said to have "followed his father very closely in the science of his art." Like his father, he held the office of groom of the chamber and painter in ordinary to the king, and so far as salary is concerned, he started where his father left off. A long list of drawings contains those which are attributed to this artist, but we still lack perfect certainty about his works. There is, however, more to go upon than there was in the case of his father, as the praises of François Clouet were sung by the writers of the day, his name was carefully preserved from reign to reign, and there is an ancient and unbroken tradition in the attribution of many of his pictures. There are not, however, any original attestations of his works, nor are any documents known which would guarantee the ascriptions usually accepted. To him are attributed the portraits of Francis I at the Uffizi, Florence, and at the Louvre, and drawings relating to them. He probably also painted the portrait of Catherine de' Medici at Versailles and other works, and in all probability a large number of the drawings ascribed to him were from his hand. One of his most remarkable portraits is that of Mary, queen of Scots, a drawing in chalks in the Bibliothèque Nationale, Paris, and of similar character are the two portraits of Charles IX and the one at Chantilly of Marguerite of France. Perhaps his masterpiece is the portrait of Elizabeth of Austria in the Louvre.

In 1568 he is known to have been under the patronage of Claude Gouffier de Boisy, Seigneur d'Oiron and his wife Claude de Baune. Another ascertained fact concerning François Clouet is that in 1571 he was "summoned to the office of the Court of the Mint," and his opinion was taken on the likeness to the king of a portrait struck by the mint. He prepared the death mask of Henry II, as in 1547 he had taken a similar mask of the face and hands of Francis I, in order that the effigy to be used at the funeral might be prepared from his drawings; and on each of these occasions he executed the painting to be used in the church decorations and the banners for the ceremony.

Several miniatures are believed to be his work, one remarkable portrait being the half-length figure of Henry II in the collection of the late J. Pierpont Morgan. Another of his portraits is that of the duc d'Alençon in the Jones collection at South Kensington, and certain representations of members of the royal family which were in the Hamilton palace collection and the Magniac sale are usually ascribed to him. He died on Dec. 22, 1572, shortly after the massacre of St. Bartholomew, and his will, mentioning his sister and his two illegitimate daughters, and dealing with the disposition of a considerable amount of property, is still in existence. His daughters became nuns. Like his father, he was known as Janet. His work is remarkable for the accuracy of the drawing, the elaborate finish of all the details, and the completeness of the whole portrait. He must have been a man of high intelligence, and great penetration, intensely interested in his work, and with considerable ability to represent the character of his sitter in his portraits. His colouring is not specially remarkable, nor from the point of style can his pictures be considered specially beautiful, but in perfection of drawing he has hardly any equal. (G. C. W.)

CLOUET, JEAN (1485–1541?), French miniature painter, generally known as Janet. The authentic presence of this artist at the French court is first to be noted in 1516, the second year of the reign of Francis I. By a deed of gift made by the king to the artist's son of his father's estate, which had escheated to the crown, we learn that he was not actually a Frenchman, and never even naturalized. He is supposed to have been a native of the Low Countries, and probably his real name was Clowet. His position was that of groom of the chamber to the king, and he received a stipend at first of 180 livres and later of 240. He lived several years in Tours, and there it was he met his wife, who was the daughter of a jeweller. He is recorded as living in Tours in 1522, and there is a reference to his wife's residence in the same town in 1523, but in 1529 they were both settled in Paris, probably in the neighbourhood of the parish of St. Innocent, in the cemetery of which they were buried. He stood godfather at a christening on July 8, 1540, but was no longer living in Dec. 1541, and therefore died between those two dates.

His brother, known as Clouet de Navarre, was in the service of Marguérite d'Angoulême, sister of Francis I, and is referred to in a letter written by Marguérite about 1529. Jean Clouet had two children, François and Catherine, who married Abel Foulon, and left one son, who continued the profession of François Clouet after his decease. Jean Clouet was undoubtedly a very skilful portrait painter, but it must be acknowledged without hesitation that there is no work in existence which has been proved to be his. There is no doubt that he painted a portrait of the mathematician, Oronce Finé, in 1530, when Finé was 36 years old, but the portrait is now known only by a print. Janet is generally believed, however, to have been responsible for a very large number of the wonderful portrait drawings now preserved at Chantilly, and at the Bibliothèque Nationale, Paris, and to him is attributed the portrait of an unknown man at Hampton Court, that of the dauphin Francis, son of Francis I at Antwerp, and one other portrait, that of Francis I in the Louvre. Seven miniature portraits in the *Manuscript of the Gallic War* in the Bibliothèque Nationale (13,429) are attributed to Janet with very strong probability, and to these may be added an eighth in the collection of the late J. Pierpont Morgan, and representing Charles de Cossé, Maréchal de Brissac, identical in its characteristics with the seven already known. There are other miniatures in the Morgan collection, which may be attributed to Jean Clouet with some strong degree of probability, inasmuch as they closely resemble the portrait drawings at Chantilly and in Paris which are taken to be his work. In his oil paintings the execution is delicate and smooth, the outlines hard, the texture pure, and the whole work elaborately and very highly finished in rich, limpid colour. The chalk drawings are of remarkable excellence, the medium being used by the artist with perfect ease and absolute sureness, and the mingling of colour being in exquisite taste, the modelling exceedingly subtle, and the drawing careful, tender and emphatic. The collection of drawings preserved in France, and attributed to this artist and his school, comprises portraits of all the important persons of the time of Francis I. In one album of drawings the portraits are annotated by the king himself, and his merry reflections, stinging taunts or biting satires, add very largely to a proper understanding of the life of his time and court. Definite evidence, however, is still lacking to establish the attribution of the best of these drawings and of certain oil paintings to the Jean Clouet who was groom of the chambers to the king.

The chief authority in France on the work of this artist is Louis Dimier. *See* also E. Moreau-Nelaton, *Les Clouets et leurs émulés* (1921). (G. C. W.)

CLOUGH, ANNE JEMIMA (klŭf) (1820–1892), educationalist and sister of the poet, Arthur Hugh Clough, born at Liverpool Jan. 20, 1820. When two years old she went with her family to Charleston, U.S.A., but returned to England in 1836. Her father's failure in business led her to open a school in 1841 which was carried on until 1846. In 1852, after studying in London and working at the Borough road and the Home and Colonial schools, she opened another school at Ambleside, in Westmorland. Keenly interested in the education of women, she made friends with Miss Emily Davies, Madame Bodichon, Miss Buss and others. After helping to found the North of England council for promoting the higher education of women, she acted as its secretary from 1867–70 and as president from 1873–74. When it was decided to open a house for women students at Cambridge, Miss Clough was chosen as its first principal. This hostel, started in Regent street, Cambridge, in 1871 with five students, and continued at Merton hall in 1872, led to the building of Newnham hall, opened in 1875, and to the erection of the present Newnham college, Cambridge, in 1880. Miss Clough's personal charm and high aims, together with her work at Newnham college, made her one of the leaders of the women's educational movement. She died on Feb. 27, 1892.

See B. A. Clough, *Memoir of Anne Jemima Clough* (1903).

CLOUGH, ARTHUR HUGH (1819–1861), English poet, was born at Liverpool on Jan. 1, 1819. In 1822 his father, a cotton merchant, moved to the United States, and Clough's childhood was spent mainly at Charleston (S.C.). In 1828 the family visited England, and Clough was left at school at Chester, whence he passed in 1829 to Rugby, then under Dr. Thomas Arnold. In 1837 he went with a scholarship to Balliol college, Oxford. Here his contemporaries included Benjamin Jowett, A. P. Stanley, J. C. Shairp, W. G. Ward, Frederick Temple and Matthew Arnold. Clough missed a Balliol fellowship, but obtained one at Oriel, with a tutorship, and lived the Oxford life of study, speculation, lectures and reading-parties until 1848, when he went abroad, seeing Paris in revolution and Rome in siege. In the autumn of 1849 he became principal of University Hall, a hostel for students at University college, London. He disliked London, in spite of the friendship of the Carlyles, nor did the atmosphere of Unitarianism prove any more congenial than that of Anglican Oxford to his critical and at bottom conservative temper. In 1852 encouraged by Emerson, he went to Cambridge (Mass.). Here he remained some months, lecturing and translating Plutarch for the booksellers, until in 1853 the offer of an examinership in the Education Office brought him to London once more. He married, and pursued a steady official career, diversified only by an appointment in 1856 as secretary to a commission sent to study certain aspects of foreign military education. In 1860 his health began to fail. He visited first Malvern and Freshwater, and then the East, France and Switzerland, in search of recovery, and finally came to Florence, where he died on Nov. 13, 1861. Matthew Arnold wrote upon him the exquisite lament of *Thyrsis*.

Shortly before he left Oxford, in the stress of the Irish potato-famine, Clough wrote an ethical pamphlet addressed to the undergraduates, with the title, *A Consideration of Objections against the Retrenchment Association at Oxford* (1847). His Homeric pastoral *The Bothie of Toper-na-Fuosich*, afterwards re-christened *Tober-na-Vuolich* (1848), was inspired by a long vacation reading-party after he had given up his tutorship, and is an entertaining experiment. *Ambarvalia* (1849), published jointly with his friend Thomas Burbidge, contains shorter poems of various dates from 1840, or earlier, onwards. *Amours de Voyage*, a novel in verse, was written at Rome in 1849; *Dipsychus*, a rather amorphous satire, at Venice in 1850; and the idylls which make up *Mari Magno or Tales on Board*, in 1861. A few lyric and elegiac pieces, later in date than the *Ambarvalia* complete the tale of Clough's poetry. His only considerable enterprise in prose was a revision of the 17th century translation of Plutarch by Dryden and others, which occupied him from 1852, and was published as *Plutarch's Lives* (1859).

He is rightly regarded, like his friend Matthew Arnold, as one of the most typical English poets of the middle of the 19th century. His critical instincts and strong ethical temper brought him athwart the popular ideals of his day both in conduct and religion. His verse has upon it the melancholy and the perplexity of an age of transition. He is a sceptic who by nature should have been with the believers. He stands between two worlds, watching one crumble behind him, and only able to look forward by the sternest exercise of faith to the reconstruction that lies ahead in the other. On the technical side, Clough's work is interesting to students of metre, owing to the experiments which he made, in the *Bothie* and elsewhere, with English hexameters.

BIBLIOGRAPHY.—Clough's *Poems* were privately collected, with a short memoir by F. T. Palgrave, in 1862; and his *Poems and Prose Remains* with a memoir by his widow in 1869. Selections from the poems were made by Mrs. Clough for the Golden Treasury series in 1894, and by E. Rhys in 1896. *See* monographs by S. Waddington (1883) and J. L. Osborne (1920). Clough's sister Anne Jemima Clough (1820–92) was the first principal of Newnham college, Cambridge.

CLOVELLY, a fishing village of Barnstaple bay, Devonshire, England, 11 mi. W.S.W. of Bideford. Pop. (1931) 528. It is a cluster of old-fashioned cottages in a unique position on the sides of a rocky cleft in the north coast; its main street resembles a staircase, which descends 400ft. to the pier, too steeply to allow of any wheeled traffic. All Saints' church, restored in 1866, is late Norman. The climate is very mild. Thick woods shelter the village on three sides and the surrounding scenery is famous for its richness of colour. Clovelly is described by Dickens in *A Message from the Sea.*

CLOVEN-HOOFED ANIMALS, the popular designation for members of the order Artiodactyla (*q.v.*), which includes the sheep, cattle, deer, antelopes, goats and swine (*qq.v.*).

CLOVER, the English name for plants belonging to the genus *Trifolium,* so-called from the leaf, which has three leaflets (trifoliolate). Clover is a member of the family Leguminosae and contains some 250 species. Many other plants are also called clover, but most of these belong to different genera of the legume family. Species are found on every continent, and in all except Australia certain ones form a part of the native flora. The origin of those species of agricultural importance appears to be southeastern Europe and southern Asia Minor. The plants are small annual or perennial herbs with trifoliolate (rarely 5 or 7 foliolate) leaves with stipules adnate to the leaf-stalk, and heads or dense spikes of small red, purple, white or yellow flowers or shades thereof; the small few-seeded pods are enclosed in the calyx. Clovers are best adapted to cool humid climates. These may be the summer months of the temperate zones or the winter months of equatorial countries. The perennials may behave as annuals, depending upon the severity of unfavourable climate. Many species are extensively cultivated for hay, pasture and green manure in all countries of the world, while others form an important part of the native vegetation.

COURTESY OF THE BUREAU OF PLANT INDUSTRY, SOILS AND AGRICULTURAL ENGINEERING, U.S. DEPT. OF AGRICULTURE

FLOWER HEADS OF RED CLOVER, T. PRATENSE

The most important agricultural species are red clover, *T. pratense,* with round, light to dark purplish red flower heads, the most widely cultivated of species from Siberia to Chile, botanically a perennial but agriculturally more of a biennial; white clover, *T. repens,* a creeping, node-rooting perennial, abundant in good pastures, meadows and lawns, the most widely naturalized species, with flowers, borne on small round heads, white to pinkish, becoming brown and reflexing as the seed matures; alsike clover, *T.*

hybridum, common in meadows and moist habitats, botanically a perennial but under agricultural conditions mostly a biennial, with flower heads resembling those of white clover; crimson clover, *T. incarnatum,* with pointed heads of bright crimson flowers, a winter annual in climates where winters are not severe, or a restricted summer annual in high latitudes; low hop clover, *T. procumbens,* mostly a winter annual widely naturalized in pastures and along roadsides, with small round heads of bright yellow flowers; least hop clover, *T. dubium,* in Europe synonymous with *T. minus* and commonly called shamrock, similar in all respects to low hop clover but with smaller and fewer flowers per head; sub clover, *T. subterraneum,* a winter annual with decumbent stems, and heads of few, cream-coloured flowers borne inconspicuously under the foliage (after fertilization the flowers reflex and bury the developing seed under the surface of the soil); Persian clover, *T. resupinatum,* mostly a winter annual, having small flat heads of lavender flowers with calyx inflating as maturing; strawberry clover, *T. fragiferum,* a creeping, node-rooting perennial with round, slightly pointed heads, with pinkish flowers, calyx inflating as maturing, tolerant to soil salinity, preferring moist habitats; berseem clover, *T. alexandrinum,* a winter annual having spike-like heads of white to cream flowers, not tolerant of heavy frosts; and cluster clover, *T glomeratum,* a winter annual having small round heads of dull rose coloured inconspicuous flowers, with heads borne on short stems in leaf axils, rough and spine-like upon maturity

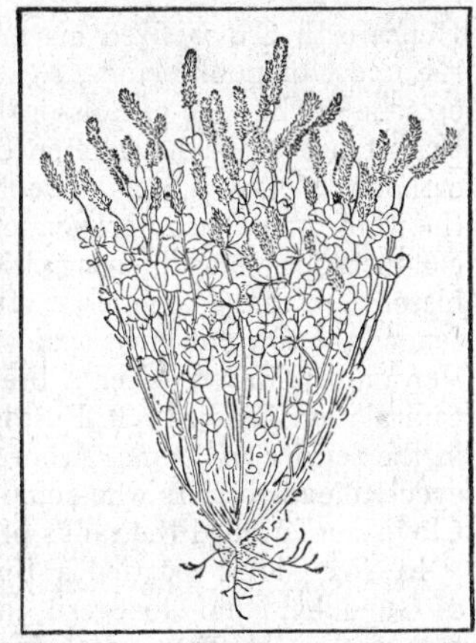

COURTESY OF THE BUREAU OF PLANT INDUSTRY, SOILS AND AGRICULTURAL ENGINEERING, U.S. DEPT. OF AGRICULTURE

CRIMSON CLOVER, T. INCARNATUM

Clover was cultivated in the Netherlands about the middle of the 16th century and it is possible that its culture occurred among the ancient Letts a thousand years earlier. It was originally introduced from Flanders into England as a field crop about the middle of the 17th century by Sir Richard Weston. He has the distinction of being the first to introduce into England the rotation of crops, using clover as a soil improving crop. Clovers are grown alone or in mixtures with different grasses and other legumes. They thrive in soils having a high content of phosphorus, calcium and potassium, either of natural origin or supplied by fertilizers. The forage is highly palatable to livestock and is high in protein and in phosphorus and calcium, thus making valuable livestock feed either in the green or dry stage and a good soil improving crop when plowed under as green manure.

Many varieties and strains of each species occur, representing forms best adapted to the environments where grown. These were developed principally by natural selection through the survival of the fittest. No authentic hybrids between species are known. The basic chromosome numbers of the genus appear to be seven and eight. Of the species studied, the somatic numbers of chromosomes range from 14 to about 130. Many of the important species such as red clover, white clover and alsike clover are principally self-sterile. Cross pollination resulting in seed setting is brought about by insect visits, principally bees, which visit the flowers for nectar and pollen. Other species such as the hop clovers and Persian clover are self-fertile, self-pollinating, while still others, such as crimson clover, are self-fertile but not self-pollinated.

Diseases and insects play an important role in the production of clovers, affecting the length of life of the plant and its reproduction; many are world-wide where clovers occur, while others are limited to specific countries. The length of the photoperiod where the strain or variety originates also has an important relationship to its adaptation in different locations.

All of the above mentioned clovers are grown in the United States. Berseem clover is grown only in limited places of southern Arizona and California; cluster clover in localities of Mississippi, Georgia, Louisiana and Alabama; sub clover in the coastal section of the Pacific states and limited areas of the southern states. The other, more widely grown species are Persian, on the heavy low-lying soils of the southern states; the hop clovers from Kentucky southward and the Pacific northwest; strawberry clover throughout the irrigated lands of the western states; crimson clover from New Jersey and Kentucky southward as a winter annual and in Northern Maine as a summer annual; white clover in all states where there is sufficient moisture and required plant foods; Ladino clover, a large-growing variety of white clover of major importance in the northeastern and western states which appears to have a place in the lake and south Atlantic states. The principal red clover belt is east of 98° longitude and north of 35° latitude, in the Pacific northwest and irrigated lands of the western states; and alsike clover is in the same general region.

Cultivation.—Red clover and alsike clover are generally seeded with companion grain crops. If adequate moisture is available after the harvesting of the grain, light grazing or a small hay crop may be produced the first year. The heavy crop occurs from the second year's growth. If seeded with grass the stands are usually left through the third year; otherwise the aftermath is plowed under for cultivated row crops in the fall of the second year or the next spring. Failures to establish and maintain stands may be due to improper seed bed preparation, heavy seedings of rank, late-maturing grain crops, deficiencies of plant foods, phosphorus, potassium and calcium, diseases and insects and the use of unadapted varieties and strains. Most of the other clovers are used principally for pastures and are seeded on turf or with grasses. Successful seedings are obtained more generally when the grass is closely grazed or clipped and where adequate quantities of phosphate and potash fertilizers and limestone are applied.

In America two common forms of red clover are recognized, medium and mammoth, better called double- and single-cut respectively. These are comparable with but not the same as the English double-cut and single-cut clovers. To conditions in the U.S. none of the European clovers is adapted, and their use leads to poor stands and low yields. Likewise, strains adapted to one section of the red clover belt do poorly in another. Improved varieties are developed by state agricultural experiment stations and the U.S. department of agriculture. Seed of two red clover varieties, Cumberland and Midland, adapted to the southern and central sections of the principal red clover belt, are available. In Canada the Dollard, Ottawa, Altaswede and Manhardy represent improved varieties. No marked differences have been found between strains of alsike clover. White clover strains differ widely, varying from low-growing types to Ladino clover. Strains of crimson clover vary in adaptation. The superiority of certain strains of sub clover brought about its adaptation and increased use in the Pacific northwest.

Red clover seed is produced over most of the main U.S. clover area, and large yields are obtained in the irrigated region of the west. It is commonly taken from the second crop. Alsike clover seed is produced in the same region as red clover seed but is taken from the first crop, since this species does not commonly produce two cuttings in a season. The winter annual species produce seed in the spring and are perpetuated by the seed that volunteers in the fall. White clover seed is produced principally in the southern, midwestern and western states In the humid states the first crop is more generally harvested, while in the west two seed crops are frequently obtained

Upward of 50 native species of clover occur on the Pacific coast and in the Rocky mountain region, but east of the Mississippi river only four native species occur.

See publications of the state agricultural experiment stations and the U.S. department of agriculture. (E. A. H.)

CLOVES, the dried, unexpanded flower-buds of *Eugenia aromatica,* a tree belonging to the family Myrtaceae. The clove tree is a beautiful evergreen which grows to a height of 40 ft., having large oval leaves and crimson flowers in numerous groups of terminal clusters. The flower-buds are at first of a pale colour and gradually become green, after which they develop into a bright red, when they are ready for collecting. Cloves are rather more than half an inch in length and consist of a long cylindrical calyx, terminating in four spreading sepals, and four unopened petals which form a small ball in the centre. The tree is a native of the Moluccas, or Spice Islands, but it was long cultivated by the Dutch in Amboyna and two or three small neighbouring islands. The Portuguese, by doubling the Cape of Good Hope, obtained possession of the principal portion of the clove trade, which they continued to hold for nearly a century, when, in 1605, they were expelled from the Moluccas by the Dutch. Holland exerted great efforts to obtain a complete monopoly of the trade, attempting to extirpate all the clove trees growing in their native islands and to concentrate the whole production in the Amboyna Islands. With great difficulty the French succeeded in introducing the clove tree into Mauritius in the year 1770; subsequently the cultivation was introduced into Guiana, Brazil, most of the West Indian islands and Zanzibar. The chief commercial sources of supply were for a long time Zanzibar and its neighbouring island Pemba on the east African coast, but the competition of Java and Sumatra is severe and the synthetic production of eugenol (*see* below) has affected the trade. Madagascar is the principal source of the oil for the U.S. Imports in 1940 were 307,-

289 lb., of which Madagascar supplied more than 302,000 lb.

Cloves as they come into the market have a deep brown colour, a powerfully fragrant odour, and a hot acrid taste. When pressed they exude a volatile oil which is obtained as a commercial product by submitting the cloves with water to repeated distillation. This is, when new, a pale yellow or almost colourless fluid, becoming brown after some time; it possesses the odour and taste

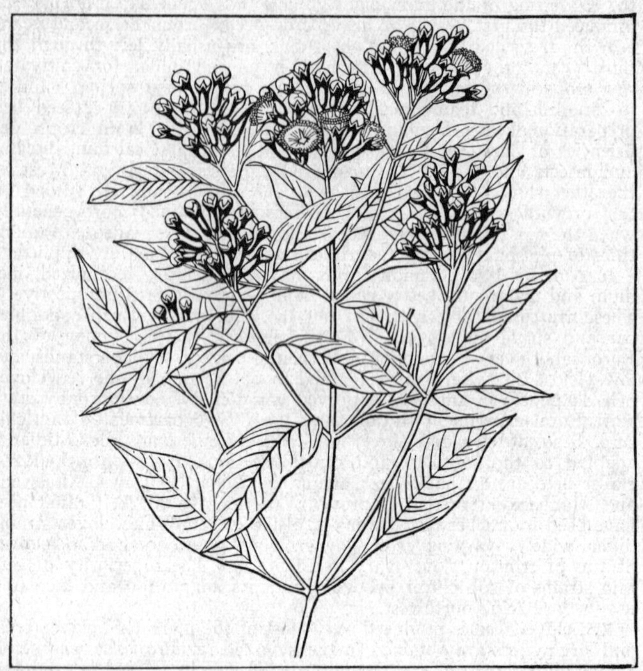

FROM KÖHLER, "MEDIZINAL PFLANZEN"
BRANCH OF A CLOVE TREE SHOWING THE FLOWER BUDS WHICH, WHEN DRIED, MAKE THE CLOVES OF COMMERCE

peculiar to cloves. The essential oil of cloves—the *Oleum Caryophylli* of the British Pharmacopoeia—is a mixture of two substances. *Eugenol* or eugenic acid, $C_{10}H_{12}O_2$, is the chief constituent. Oil of cloves is soluble in alcohol and ether. Cloves are employed as a condiment in culinary operations, in confectionery, and in the preparation of *liqueurs*. In medicine they are tonic and carminative but they are little used except as adjuncts to other substances. The oil forms a convenient medium for using cloves for flavouring purposes, possesses the medicinal properties characteristic of a volatile oil, and is frequently employed to relieve toothache. Oil of cloves is regarded by many dental surgeons as the most effective local anaesthetic they possess. Clove oil must have a eugenol content of at least 82%.

CLOVIO, GIORGIO GIULIO (1498–1578), Italian painter of portraits and historical pieces, by birth a Croat and by profession a priest, is said to have studied at Rome under Giulio Romano, and at Verona under Girolamo de' Libri. His book of 26 pictures representing the procession of Corpus Domini, in Rome, was the work of nine years, and the covers were executed by Benvenuto Cellini. The British Museum has his twelve miniatures of the victories of the Emperor Charles V. In the Vatican library is preserved a manuscript life of Frederick, duke of Urbino, superbly illustrated by Clovio, who is *facile princeps* among Italian miniaturists. He was called Macedo, or Macedone, to connect him with his supposed Macedonian ancestry.

CLOVIS (*Chlodovech*) (*c.* 466–511), king of the Salian Franks, son of Childeric I., whom he succeeded in 481 at the age of 15. At that date the Salian Franks had advanced as far as the river Somme, and the centre of their power was at Tournai. On the history of Clovis between the years 481 and 486 the records are silent. In 486 he attacked Syagrius, a Roman general who, after the fall of the western empire in 476, had carved out for himself a principality south of the Somme, and is called by Gregory of Tours "rex Romanorum." After being defeated by Clovis at the battle of Soissons, Syagrius sought refuge with the Visigothic king Alaric II., who handed him over to the conqueror. Henceforth Clovis fixed his residence at Soissons, which was in the midst of public lands, *e.g.*, Berny-Rivière, Juvigny, etc. The episode of the vase of Soissons[1] has a legendary character, and all that it proves is the deference shown by the pagan king to the orthodox clergy. Clovis undoubtedly extended his dominion over the whole of Belgica Secunda, of which Reims was the capital, and conquered the neighbouring cities in detail. Little is known of the history of these conquests. It appears that St. Genevieve defended the town of Paris against Clovis for a long period, and that Verdun-sur-Meuse, after a brave stand, accepted an honourable capitulation thanks to St. Euspitius. In 491 some barbarian troops in the service of Rome, Arboruchi ('Αρμόρυχοι) Thuringians, and even Roman soldiers who could not return to Rome, went over to Clovis and swelled the ranks of his army.

In 493 Clovis married a Burgundian princess, Clotilda, niece of Gundobald and Godegesil, joint kings of Burgundy. This princess was a Christian, and earnestly desired the conversion of her husband. Although Clovis allowed his children to be baptized, he remained a pagan himself until the war against the Alamanni, who at the time occupied the country between the Vosges, and the Rhine and the neighbourhood of Lake Constance. By pushing their incursions westward they came into collision with Clovis, who marched against them and defeated them in the plain of the Rhine. The legend runs that, in the thickest of the fight, Clovis swore that he would be converted to the God of Clotilda if her God would grant him the victory. After subduing a part of the Alamanni, Clovis went to Reims, where he was baptized by St. Remigius on Christmas day 496, together with 3,000 Franks. The story of the phial of holy oil (the *Sainte Ampoule*) brought from heaven by a white dove for the baptism of Clovis was invented by archbishop Hincmar of Reims three centuries after the event.

The baptism of Clovis was an event of very great importance. From that time the orthodox Christians in the kingdom of the Burgundians and Visigoths looked to Clovis to deliver them from their Arian kings. Clovis seems to have failed in the case of Burgundy, which was at that time torn by the rivalry between Godegesil and his brother Gundobald. Godegesil appealed for help to Clovis, who defeated Gundobald on the banks of the Ouche near Dijon, and advanced as far as Avignon (500), but had to retire without being able to retain any of his conquests. Immediately after his departure Gundobald slew Godegesil at Vienne, and seized the whole of the Burgundian kingdom. Clovis was more fortunate in his war against the Visigoths. Having completed the subjugation of the Alamanni in 506, he marched against the Visigothic king Alaric II. in the following year, in spite of the efforts of Theodoric, king of the Ostrogoths, to prevent the war. After a decisive victory at Vouillé near Poitiers, in which Clovis slew Alaric with his own hand, the whole of the kingdom of the Visigoths as far as the Pyrenees was added to the Frankish empire, with the exception of Septimania, which, together with Spain, remained in possession of Alaric's grandson Amalaric, and Provence, which was seized by Theodoric and annexed to Italy. In 508 Clovis received at Tours the insignia of the consulship from the eastern emperor, Anastasius, but the title was purely honorific. The last years of his life Clovis spent in Paris, which he made the capital of his kingdom; here he built the church of the Holy Apostles, known later as the church of St. Geneviève. By murdering the petty Frankish kings who reigned at Cambrai, Cologne and other residences, he became sole king of all the Frankish tribes. He died in 511.

Clovis was the true founder of the Frankish monarchy. He reigned over the Salian Franks by hereditary right; over the other Frankish tribes by reason of his kinship with their kings and by the choice of the warriors, who raised him on the shield, and he governed the Gallo-Romans by right of conquest. He had the

[1]The story is as follows. The vase had been taken from a church by a Frankish soldier after the battle of Soissons, and the bishop had requested Clovis that it might be restored. But the soldier who had taken it refused to give it up, and broke it into fragments with his *francisca*, or battle-axe. Some time afterwards, when Clovis was reviewing his troops, he singled out the soldier who had broken the vase, upbraided him for the neglect of his arms, and dashed his *francisca* to the ground. As the man stooped to pick it up, the king clove his skull with the words "Thus didst thou serve the vase of Soissons."

Salic law drawn up, doubtless between the years 486 and 507, and seems to have been represented in the cities by a new functionary, the *graf, comes,* or count. He owed his success in great measure to his alliance with the church. He took the property of the church under his protection and in 511 convoked a council at Orléans, the canons of which have come down to us. But while protecting the church, he maintained his authority over it. He intervened in the nomination of bishops, and at the council of Orléans it was decided that no one, save a son of a priest, could be ordained clerk without the king's order or the permission of the count.

The chief source for the life of Clovis is the *Historia Francorum* (bk. ii) of Gregory of Tours, but it must be used with caution. Among modern works, *see* W. Junghans, *Die Geschichte der fränkischen Könige Childerich und Clodovech* (1857); F. Dahn, *Urgeschichte der germanischen und romanischen Völker,* vol. iii (1883); W. Schultze, *Deutsche Geschichte von der Urzeit bis zu den Karolingern,* vol. ii (1896); G. Kurth, Clovis (1901). (C. Pf.)

CLOVIS, a city of New Mexico, U.S., near the centre of the eastern boundary of the state; the county seat of Curry county. It is on federal highways 60, 70 and 84, and state highway 18 and is served by the Santa Fe railroad.

The population was 17,318 in 1950 and 10,065 in 1940 by the federal census. It is the state's most important livestock and dry farming area, with crops of wheat, sorghum grains, broomcorn, sudan, etc., and has large stockyards. Clovis was settled about 1907 and incorporated in 1908; in 1921 it adopted a commission form of government.

CLOWN, a rustic or boorish person; in pantomime, a comic character, always dressed in baggy costume, with face whitened and eccentrically lined with black and red paint. The character probably descends from representations of the devil in mediaeval miracle plays, developed through the fools or jesters of the Elizabethan drama. The whitened face and baggy costume indicate a connection also with the Pierrot of Italian comedy. The prominence of the clown in pantomime (*q.v.*) is a comparatively modern development as compared with that of Harlequin.

CLOYNE, small market town, County Cork, Ireland, 15 mi. E.S.E. of the city of Cork. Pop. (1951) 620. An ecclesiastical foundation of the 6th century, it has an ancient oratory and a cathedral (mainly 14th century) dedicated to St. Colman, disciple of St. Finbar of Cork. Opposite the cathedral is a fine round tower 100 ft. high. The town suffered from Scandinavian raids in the 9th century and was laid waste by Dermot O'Brian in 1071 and burned in 1137. In 1430 the bishopric was united to that of Cork, in 1638 it became independent, and in 1660 it was again united to Cork and Ross. It became independent once more in 1678 and so continued until its reunion with Cork in 1835. The name *Cluain-Uamha* signifies "the meadow of the cave," from the limestone caves of the vicinity. The Pipe Roll of Cloyne compiled by Bishop Swaffham in 1364 is a valuable record of mediaeval land tenure. It is now in the record office, Dublin, and was edited by Caulfield in 1859. The cathedral contains a memorial to Bishop George Berkeley, the philosopher (1685–1753). The town gives its name also to a Roman Catholic diocese with a cathedral at Cobh.

CLUBFOOT. Clubfoot is the name given a deformity of the foot and ankle resulting in abnormal position and shape of the foot. The deformity is present at birth. In the more severe examples three distinct components of the deformity may be recognized, but in milder cases one or another of these may be lacking. The most constant component is plantar flexion of the foot at the ankle so that the foot points downward. Next most common is inversion of the foot, which is a rolling in of the sole of the foot so that the soles of the feet face each other. The third component is adduction of the fore foot, which is an extreme pigeon-toe deformity. The Latin name given these deformities is *talipes equinovarus.* All of these deformities are rigidly maintained so that the foot may not be returned to normal position. Each of the deformities may be present in varying degrees from mild to severe.

At an early age these deformities result from abnormal pull of tendons and contracture of the ligaments, but over a period of years and particularly after weight bearing, bony deformity may appear preventing correction of the deformities. In approximately half of the patients, both feet are involved.

The cause of clubfoot is essentially unknown. Many theories have been advocated, but none has been proved. The most popular theories are increased pressure or faulty position in the uterus and hereditary influences. None of these theories has any foundation in experimental evidence. In observations on animals, typical clubfoot deformities in the offspring have been produced by excessive exposure to X-rays of a pregnant animal or by vitamin-deficient diets given a pregnant animal.

Treatment of the clubfoot depends upon the severity and multiplicity of the deformities. The treatment should begin early in infancy when the tissues are more pliable and before bony deformity occurs. In the extremely mild deformity, whether of plantar flexion, inversion or adduction of the fore foot, simple manipulation by the physician or the parent may suffice. In the more severe deformities, splints, plaster of Paris casts or special shoes may be necessary. Numerous methods of application of the splints and casts have been devised, but all depend upon the reversal of the deformities at an early age so that the muscles, tendons and bones may grow normally.

More severe or untreated deformities may require surgery upon tendons or bones or both. Treatment must be continued until all component deformities are corrected. Following adequate and complete correction, observation of the person must be continued until growth ceases. This is necessary because of the tendency toward recurrence of these deformities when the child is passing through a period of rapid growth. With adequate treatment started early in infancy, the patient should be able to lead a normal life with normal activity.

Frequently, similar deformities of the feet follow poliomyelitis or other diseases. In these instances, braces and surgery may be required because of muscle weakness or fixed deformity.

Abnormalities opposite to those of clubfoot frequently occur. These include increased dorsiflexion of the foot so that the foot points upward rather than downward, and eversion of the foot so that the sole faces outward. These deformities are usually more flexible than those of clubfoot and are more amenable to simple methods of treatment.

Bibliography.—P. K. Duraiswami, "Experimental Causation of Congenital Skeletal Defects and Its Significance in Orthopedic Surgery," *Jour. of Bone and Joint Surgery,* vol. 34-B; no. 4; pp. 646–698 (Nov. 1952); J. H. Kite, "Principles Involved in the Treatment of Congenital Club Foot," *Jour. of Bone and Joint Surgery,* vol. 21, pp. 595–606 (1939); Philip Lewin, *The Foot and Ankle* (Philadelphia, London, 1941); Walter Mercer, *Orthopaedic Surgery* 4th ed. (London, Baltimore, 1950). (J. S. Ms.)

CLUB-MOSS, the common name for plants of the genus *Lycopodium,* and often extended to cover all the Lycopodiales, which form one of the main divisions of the Pteridophyta (*q.v.*), a group which also includes the ferns. Club-mosses are also called staghorn-mosses.

CLUBS. The ancient Greek *hetaireia* and the Roman *sodalitas* may be regarded as the earliest ancestors of the modern club, although they were in fact loose associations of like-minded companions rather than true clubs, as we understand that term. Among the Greeks the religious organizations devoted to the worship of esoteric deities not recognized by the state religion, were the most important, but political, commercial and athletic associations also flourished, together with social dining clubs whose members gathered to eat together and exchange ideas.

In Rome religious and trade clubs were common, but these, like their Greek predecessors, were more like sects or trade guilds than anything we should now call a club. The Roman political clubs were rather more like modern ones in aim and organization, but they tended to degenerate into unruly cabals and were suppressed by Julius Caesar as dangerous to public order. Burial clubs existed among the poorer people who might otherwise have been unable to afford for their dead the expensive funeral rites then considered necessary (see *Rural Clubs* below).

Cicero in *De Senectute* mentions *symposia* which, he says, he enjoyed as much for the opportunities of talking they afforded him as for their well-cooked meals. Though some of these early societies elected committees and officers, and a few, like one mentioned by Justus Lipsius, drew up definite rules, they had little in common with the modern club; and it is probable that the true club spirit was then most easily found in the unorganized but more or less regular gatherings of friends in the ease and comfort of the public baths.

BRITISH CLUBS

The Rise of English Clubs.—The earliest English club of which there is certain knowledge was Le Court de Bone Compagnie, described in a poem by Thomas Hoccleve, who was a member. It flourished in Henry IV's reign and was evidently a dining club which held its dinners in a house near the Middle Temple, London. The Elizabethan Friday Street or Bread Street club was also a dining association, which met in the famous Mermaid tavern, and is traditionally said to have been founded by Sir Walter Raleigh. About 1616 the Apollo club was founded by Ben Jonson in the Devil tavern by Temple Bar. Many of the most distinguished men of the time were among its members, including Lucius Carey, Sir John Suckling, Robert Herrick, and Lord Herbert of Cherbury. Though purely masculine in its membership, this club adopted the modern-seeming custom of admitting ladies on special nights.

With the rise of coffeehouses in the mid-17th century, clubs acquired more or less settled homes and began to take on distinctive character. It was usual for the landlord of a coffeehouse to allot a special room for the club's use. For this he made no charge, relying for his profit on the food and drink consumed by members and the distinction conferred upon his house by the presence therein of notable men. It was at this period that the term "club," in its modern sense, first came into common use. "We now," says John Aubrey, "use the word clubbe for a sodality in a taverne," and Samuel Pepys, in his diary for 1660, mentions Woods' tavern in Pall Mall where he and his friends used to go "for clubbing."

Among the most notable political clubs of the 17th century was the Rota, founded by James Harrington in 1659. This was strongly republican in sentiment, and included among its members Lord Algernon Sidney and Lord William Russell, both of whom were subsequently executed for their part in the Rye House plot, Sir William Petty and Andrew Marvell, the poet. Pepys calls it the Coffee club, perhaps because it met in Miles' coffeehouse in Westminster. The Sealed Knot was a royalist association, while the Green Ribbon club (sometimes called the King's Head club from the Chancery lane tavern in which it met) was an organization of influential malcontents under the leadership of Lord Shaftesbury. In 1693 White's, which in the 18th century was to become a prominent Tory stronghold, began its long career in the chocolate house owned by and named after Francis White. In its beginnings it was social rather than political and derived its clublike characteristics from White's determination to keep his clientele select and from the strict rules he enforced. The original chocolate house stood in St. James's street, on the site of the present Boodle's. In 1697 the business was transferred to the opposite side of the road where it was later carried on by John Arthur, the founder in 1765 of the club known as Arthur's. In 1736 White's became a private club, and 19 years later it moved to its modern site in St. James's street.

Of the nonpolitical Stuart clubs the best known are the Royal Navy (1674), prototype of the service clubs which sprang up in the 19th century; the Civil (1699), forerunner of the City of London (1832); and the Wednesday, founded by William Paterson in the Dog and Whistle tavern, Friday street. Paterson was the financial genius of his age, and it was at the weekly meetings over which he presided that the project which ultimately resulted in the creation of the Bank of England was first evolved.

The 18th-Century Clubs.—In the 18th century the number and variety of clubs increased very rapidly. Many were comparatively short-lived and eccentric associations, reflecting the more violent phases of contemporary political feeling, or the extravagant, and often lawless, fancies of idle young men. Among these were the Calves Head club, established shortly after the execution of Charles I; the chief meetings were held on the anniversaries of the execution, when dishes served to members included calves' heads, to represent the king and his adherents, and a pike, to represent tyranny. Others were the various Mug House clubs, most of which were eventually suppressed by the authorities because of their disorderly conduct; the notorious Hell Fire club at Medmenham, and the Mohocks', whose unruly members terrorized law-abiding Londoners by their insulting and violent behaviour. Other societies with odd, and sometimes unedifying, aims are mentioned in the pages of the Spectator, and in Ned Ward's two books on club life. It is true that Ward often drew upon his imagination in his accounts, but the clubs he described were usually based upon existing coteries.

Among the more respectable of these ephemeral organizations may be mentioned the No Pay No Liquor club, whose members were obliged to wear hats of peculiar fashion, and to drink from a cup of peculiar shape, the Je ne sçai quoi, of which the prince of Wales was perpetual chairman, and the so-called street clubs. These were associations formed in particular London streets whose residents, afraid to venture far at night because of Mohocks and footpads, started their own small clubs in coffeehouses or taverns near their homes.

Of the more serious clubs, many were political, or partly so. The October (of which the March Primitive October was a more extreme offshoot) was founded in 1710 or 1711 by a band of Tories dissatisfied with Robert Harley's administration. The Cocoa Tree began as a Jacobite association meeting at the chocolate house of that name and became a private club in 1746. Jonathan Swift was a leading member of both these, as he was of the Saturday, founded by Henry St. John in 1711, the short-lived Brothers, and the Jacobite Mourning Bush, afterward called the Fountain. Other mainly political clubs of the time were: the Hanover, for the more ardent supporters of the new dynasty; the Rumpsteak or Liberty (1734); the Board, mentioned by Horace Walpole in a letter dated 1743; the later Revolution and Independents; White's, which became definitely Tory under William Pitt's influence in 1783; and its Whig opposite number, Brooks's. The last-named was founded in 1764 as a social and gaming establishment by William Macall, who bought a house in Pall Mall and, transposing the letters of his name, called it Almack's. This club (not to be confused with the more famous Almack's assembly rooms in King street, also run by Macall) was bought by Brooks in 1774. Four years later it was transferred to the modern club house in St. James's street, then newly erected by Henry Holland, and thereafter was always known as Brooks's. Renowned for its high stakes in play and its social brilliance, it was also famous as a leading Whig stronghold and the favourite haunt of Charles James Fox and his associates.

Important and influential as were the political clubs of the 18th century, it was really the literary, artistic and social associations which were the most characteristic of the period. Many clubs combined these attributes. The members of Brooks's assumed the role of arbiters of literary taste; those of the Blue Stocking moved with equal ease in the learned and aristocratic worlds. The Scriblerus club, founded by Swift in 1714, included men of fashion like the earl of Oxford and Viscount Bolingbroke, and poets like Alexander Pope and John Gay. The Society of Dilettanti (1734) was a gathering of amateur art collectors, whose fine collection of pictures by Sir Joshua Reynolds and Francis Knapton is housed in the St. James's club, Piccadilly, where the Dilettanti hold their dinners. The famous Kit Kat club, founded at the beginning of the century by Joseph Tonson, a bookseller, was a literary association in its inception, but it soon became renowned at once for its distinguished membership, its toasts and the portraits of members painted by Sir Godfrey Kneller. The name was derived from Christopher Cat, in whose eating house the first literary reunions were held. In 1749 Dr. Johnson who, like Swift, was an ardent clubman, founded the Ivy Lane club at the King's Head tavern in that thoroughfare. Fifteen years later he and Sir Joshua Reynolds together organized the more celebrated Literary club, usually known simply as the "The Club." The original membership was limited to 12 and gradually increased to 40, after which a resolution was passed in 1780 that it should never exceed that number. Oliver Goldsmith, Edmund Burke, David Garrick, James Boswell and Sir John Hawkins were among the members in the early years, and during the subsequent two centuries of this famous club's existence, many of the outstanding men of each generation joined it. In 1783, not long before his death, Johnson founded yet another club, the Essex Head, so called from the tavern near the Strand in which it met.

Among associations with rather more specialized aims was the Royal Society club, a scientific body founded in 1743, and not to be confused with the modern Royal Societies club, which was not formed until 1894; the Noviomagians, which was antiquarian; the Robin Hood, a debating society which came into prominence when Edmund Burke joined it; and such semidebating, semisocial organizations as Cogers in Fleet street, Goldsmith's Wednesday club, the Clifford Street club, and the King of Clubs, founded in 1801.

Boodle's (1763) which, like White's and Brooks's, still occupies its 18th-century home, was one of the more famous social institutions. Originally called the Sçavoir Vivre, it was later renamed after William Boodle, who became its manager about 11 years after its foundation. This club was renowned for its cuisine. Its beautiful clubhouse in St. James's street is usually said to have been designed by the Adam brothers. Another fine building which, after some vicissitudes returned to the club world is Coventry house, Piccadilly, once the home of the Coventry House club (1757) which settled there in 1769, and now occupied by the social and diplomatic St. James's club (1857). The Sublime Society of Beefsteaks, of which the modern Beefsteak club (1876) is in some sense the successor, came into being in 1735. Besides these there was Arthur's (1765), noted for its Wiltshire connections and its veal *à la royale;* the Dover House club (1787), usually known as Weltzie's, from the name of its founder, a former servant of the prince of Wales; Graham's, a noted gaming club in St. James's street; the Wittanagemot, which appears to have been a select dining club; and a number of subsidiary clubs meeting at Will's or Tom's coffeehouses, which John Macky has described in his *Journey through England.*

Influence Abroad.—It was at this period that the club, hitherto an almost entirely British institution, crossed the English channel and the Atlantic. Clubs of the English pattern appeared in French and German taverns. In Berlin the literary Monday club was founded in 1749. Three years later the first purely social club in Germany was inaugurated. It was followed by a variety of political clubs, many of which were suppressed in 1848. In France small political coteries abounded in the years immediately preceding the French Revolution, and contributed largely to the unrest of the time.

In America the club system does not seem to have been adopted before the Declaration of Independence, the earliest genuine club there of which we have record being the Hoboken Turtle, established in 1797. Such pioneers were, however, the first swallows of an abundant summer, and today clubs of all kinds are to be found in every country inhabited by Europeans and Americans. (*See* also below.)

Clubs of the 19th and 20th Centuries.—In the 19th century clubs in general began to follow the lead of White's and Brooks's, and to acquire permanent headquarters, often in the form of imposing houses specially built for them by well-known architects. They also tended to become more specialized. Whereas formerly statesmen and soldiers, poets, artists, scientists and men of fashion had met in common centres, clubs specially formed for different professions and interests now became usual. This differentiation first appeared in the service clubs. At the end of the Napoleonic Wars many officers of both services returned to London and needed meeting places where they could share meals and reminiscences. In 1813 the Guards club was formed, and in 1815 the United Service. The Junior United Service was founded in 1827 and the Army and Navy club ten years later. In due course these pioneers were followed by the Naval and Military (1862), the Cavalry Club (1890), the Junior Army and Navy (1911) and the Royal Air Force (1917). The soldiers and officials of the East India company congregated chiefly at the Oriental (1824) and the East India United Service (1850).

Among civilian specialized clubs, the City of London (1832) and Gresham's (1843) were and remained mainly for merchants and bankers, as the Farmers' (1842) was and is for agriculturists. The Garrick, founded in 1831, was one of the earlier theatrical foundations (a still earlier example was the Thespian, which flourished in the second half of the 18th century), and it was followed by the Green Room (1877), the Rehearsal (1892), the O-P. club (1900) and the Vaudeville (1901), to name only a few.

Of the many literary and artistic clubs founded in the 19th century, the most important was undoubtedly the Athenaeum, inaugurated in 1823 by John Wilson Croker at John Murray's house in Albemarle street. This famous club, to which Sir Walter Scott, Tom Moore and most of the leading writers of that and later days belonged, was first known as the Society. In its early years it met in Waterloo place, but moved in 1830 to the present clubhouse in Pall Mall, designed for it by Decimus Burton.

Almost as well-known are the Savile (1868), once called the New club, and generally regarded as a waiting place for the Athenaeum, and the Savage, founded in 1857 and noted for its early bohemianism. The Arts club came into being in 1863, the Authors in 1891, and the later P.E.N. club in 1921. The principal university clubs were also formed during the 19th century, the United University and the New University in 1822, the Oxford and Cambridge in 1830, the New Oxford and Cambridge in 1883, and the City University in 1885.

Of the 19th-century political clubs, other than White's and Brooks's, already formed and still in existence, the two outstanding foundations are the Conservative Carlton club (1831) and the Liberal Reform club (1834). Both these occupy houses of considerable architectural importance, that of the Reform being usually considered the most impressive of its kind in London. They were followed by numerous others: the Conservative (1840); the Junior Carlton (1864); the Cobden (1866); St. Stephen's (1870); the Eighty (1880); the National Liberal (1882); the Constitutional (1883); and the United (1890). These were all West End clubs, the City having its own political organizations, such as the City Carlton (1868), the City Liberal and various others.

The passion for gambling which marked the latter half of the 18th century continued during the first years of the 19th in most of the older social clubs and in some new ones. In 1806 Watier's club was founded in Bolton street and rapidly became the foremost gambling club in London. Beau Brummell was one of its prominent members. The pace was rather too rapid even for the hardened gamblers of the Regency period, and after a feverish existence of little more than 12 years, Watier's perished in 1819. What remained of it was then acquired by William Crockford who in 1828 opened the gambling club named after him. Crockford's was housed in a magnificent building in St. James's street, designed by James Wyatt, which became the home of the Devonshire club (1875). Hazard, whist, and card games of all sorts were its principal attractions, but it was also renowned for its excellent meals and for cockfights held in a small cockpit in the basement. Like Watier's, it was short-lived and broke up soon after its founder's death in 1844.

Among the other fashionable clubs of the first half of the 19th century was the Union, founded in 1804; the Alfred (1808), of which Lord Byron and George Canning were members, and which the wits nicknamed the Half-read; the Travellers, a diplomatic club founded in 1819 by Lord Castlereagh; and the Windham, started by Baron Nugent in 1828. Later came the Thatched House (1865), the Bachelors' (1881), the Wellington (1885) and many others.

Besides the clubs having their own premises, there were various dining clubs inaugurated to do honour to some great man, such as Dr. Johnson, Pepys, Samuel Butler or Charles Dickens, or to provide regular meetings for collectors or individuals interested in particular objects and ideas. Grillion's, to which so many illustrious men belonged, was founded in 1813 by Sir Thomas Acland as a centre for men of all shades of political feeling. The

Cosmopolitan (1852) and the Breakfast club (1866) were similar nonparty institutions, whose members met for dinner and breakfast respectively. There were also the Boz and the Erewhon for Dickens and Butler enthusiasts, the Titmarsh, the Roxburghe, for book-collectors, the First Edition, the Sette of Odde Volumes, the Hardwicke with legal interests, the Urban and others too numerous to mention.

Women's Clubs.—The last years of the Victorian era also saw the rise of women's clubs. An organization known as the Ladies club and referred to by Walpole as "the female Almack's," existed in the 18th century. There were also associations of working women at this period, such as the Mantua-makers' club in St. Martin's lane and the Milliners' club near the Royal Exchange. In general, however, clubs were exclusively masculine institutions until 1883, when the Alexandria was founded. No man was allowed to enter its premises, and on one occasion even the prince of Wales (afterward Edward VII) was refused admittance when he called for the princess. The University Women's club was formed in 1887, the Pioneer in 1892.

Three years later the American Women's club for Americans visiting London came into being, and in 1897 the Empress. Once the idea of such associations was accepted, women's clubs developed with great rapidity. The Ladies' Empire was founded in 1902, the London Lyceum in 1904, the Ladies' Carlton in 1906. Thereafter every sort of social, literary, artistic, sporting and political interest had its women's clubs in London and the provinces, and there are also many institutions like the Pilot club (1949), the Lansdowne (1935) and the International Sportsmen (1929) and others, with both male and female members.

Sports Clubs.—The love of sport has been responsible for numerous clubs, from the Tudor companies of young men with grandiloquent titles like Prince Arthur's Knights, down to the foundations of our own day. Among 18th-century clubs of this type may be mentioned the Sons of the Thames, predecessor of the Thames Rowing club (1860) and the London Rowing club (1856); the Royal Thames Yacht club, founded in 1775; the Royal Toxopholite (1781); the coaching Four-in-Hand; and the famous Hambledon club, started about the middle of the century, whose members laid the foundations of modern cricket. The last-named was dissolved in 1791, but its place was taken by the Marylebone Cricket club (1787), the famous M.C.C.

About 1750 a number of men interested in horse racing began meeting at the Star and Garter coffee house in Pall Mall, and there founded an association to regulate racing and eliminate abuses at Newmarket. This was the Jockey club. Its influence soon spread from Newmarket to other courses, and it became the ruling authority in English racing throughout the country. Other clubs connected with the same sport are the Turf, which developed from the earlier Arlington in 1868, and various clubs connected with particular courses, such as the Hurst Park, the Kempton Park and the Sandown.

Clubs representing every branch of sport were established in London and the provinces, and some, like the Sports club (1893), the United Sports (1903) the Bath club and others, embrace more than one form. Among the specialized clubs may be mentioned the National Sporting club, devoted to boxing; the hunting Badminton and Beaufort; the Golfers and the Lady Golfers; the Flyfishers (1884); the London Fencing club (1848) and the Sword (1905); the Alpine (1857) and the Ladies' Alpine (1907); and the Kennel club (1873). Aquatic organizations range from the Royal Yacht Squadron at Cowes (1815) and the Royal Ocean Racing club (1925) to the model yacht racing clubs associated with the Round pond in Kensington Gardens.

Others represent the newer forms of sport, such as the Royal Automobile club (1897), whose club house is among the most luxurious in London, and the Royal Aero club (1901).

Rural Clubs.—Rural benefit clubs formed an important part of village life from the late years of the 18th century until the introduction of national insurance in 1912. The members paid a monthly contribution of 2 *s.* or more, and the money so collected was used to pay sickness and unemployment benefit, and a lump sum to the survivor on the death of a member or his wife. Regular meetings were held in a room specially set apart in the local inn, and once a year, in summer, there was the club day. This included a service in the parish church, with a sermon, a procession with banners and a band, sports, dances and a dinner at the inn. In many parishes there were more than one club; and in a few there was also a female club, which had its own funds and yearly procession, and met independently of the men. In their early years the benefit clubs were purely local institutions, but with the growth of the great friendly societies, they often became branches of such societies, while still retaining their local character and customs, including, in many cases, ceremonial forms of admission. With the introduction of national insurance, most village clubs were given up, but a few continued to flourish and carry on their work. The Greyhound club at Marsh Gibbon, founded in 1788, is one of those which still pays benefit to its members and has its annual gathering on Oak Apple day (May 29), and others survive in Dorset, Hampshire and elsewhere.

Club Organization.—The internal economy of clubs varies as much as does the character of the aims of such associations, or the nature and architectural features of their clubhouses. In some the committee possesses the power of election and the corresponding power of refusal; in others this is by ballot of members. Some, like the Athenaeum, have the right of electing annually a certain number of members on account of their distinguished eminence, services to the state, literature, art, science and so forth. The committee is, of course, the responsible body, but in most cases the actual running of the club is largely in the hands of the secretary, control by members being exercised through the annual general meeting.

Clubs are also subject to certain legal restrictions and duties. Since the Licensing act of 1902 (passed primarily to prevent clubs being formed merely as a cloak for the sale of intoxicants), every club, large or small, has annually to provide the authorities with information concerning its membership, subscription and general conduct. The details of the laws covering club management may be conveniently studied in J. Wertheimer's *Law Relating to Clubs,* (5th ed. by Maxwell Turner and A. S. Wilson, London, 1935). (*See* also WORKING MEN'S CLUBS.)

BIBLIOGRAPHY.—*General:* Ned Ward, *The Secret History of Clubs of all Descriptions* (London, 1709), *Complete and Humorous Account of all the Remarkable Clubs,* 3rd ed. (London, 1746); E. B. Chancellor, *The 18th Century in London* (London, 1920) and *Life in Regency and Early Victorian Times* (New York, 1926; London, 1927); A. S. Turberville, *English Men and Manners in the 18th Century,* 2nd ed. (Oxford, New York, 1929); A. S. Turberville (ed.), *Johnson's England,* 2 vol. (Oxford, New York, 1933); R. J. Allen, *The Clubs of Augustan London* (Cambridge, Mass., and London, 1933); R. Bayne-Powell, *Eighteenth Century London Life* (London, 1937; New York, 1938); C. Marsh, *The Clubs of London* (London, 1828); Anon., *The London Clubs, their Anecdotes and History* (London, 1853); J. Timbs, *Club-Life of London,* 2 vol. (London, 1866); J. Hatton, *Club-Land, London and Provincial* (London, 1890); A. Griffiths, *Clubs and Clubmen* (London, 1907); R. Nevill, *London Clubs, Their History and Treasures* (London, 1911); T. H. S. Escott, *Club Makers and Club Members* (London, Leipzig, 1914). *Special:* Humphry Ward, *History of the Athenaeum* (London, 1926); W. Arnold, *The Life and Death of the Sublime Society of Beef Steaks* (London, 1871); V. A. Williamson *et al.* (ed.), *Memorials of Brooks's* (London, 1907); H. T. Waddy, *The Devonshire Club and "Crockford's"* (London, 1919); P. Fitzgerald, *The Garrick Club* (London, 1904); A. Baillie, *The Oriental Club and Hanover Square* (London, 1901); L. Fagan, *The Reform Club: Its Founders and Architect* (London, 1887); Anon., *The Savile Club 1868 to 1923* (Edinburgh, 1923); Percy Colson, *White's 1693–1950* (London, 1951).

(C. S. HE.)

UNITED STATES

The number and variety of clubs in the United States demonstrate the prevalence of "joining" among the American people. As distinguished from many other expressions of this voluntary associationalism, clubs usually place greater stress upon sociability and are more apt to be local in nature than chapters of national organizations.

Although U.S. clubs derive from English prototypes of the late 17th and early 18th centuries, their appearance was understandably belated. The colonial period lacked both the city life and the leisure necessary for their development. Nevertheless, as early as the mid-18th century the success of Benjamin Franklin's

Junto in Philadelphia, Pa., and the spread of Masonic lodges suggested that associational activity would presently become a prominent part of American life. Urban growth in the late 19th century not only made clubs possible by assembling groups large enough for specialized interests of nearly every sort but also made clubs essential to provide adequate social outlets in the impersonal metropolis.

The most direct imitations of English clubs (see *British Clubs* above) are the socially exclusive gentlemen's clubs existing in most large cities, such as the Somerset club of Boston, Mass., and the Pacific Union club of San Francisco, Calif. Admitting only those of high social and financial standing, they usually have fine buildings with eating, drinking, reading and athletic facilities. Other clubs, while highly selective, make some form of literary, artistic or intellectual interest the basis for affiliation rather than wealth or social background. In differing ways the Lambs and Players clubs of New York city, the Cosmos club of Washington, D.C., and the Bohemian club of San Francisco could be placed in this category. Slightly different are the large number of luncheon and dinner clubs, usually composed of business and professional men, which may or may not have their own buildings. Although the social element also predominates in these, they are often basically discussion groups which do little more than meet periodically for that purpose.

All the clubs mentioned tend to be highly restrictive in membership, but there are also many organizations open to all individuals sharing a mutual interest. Ever since the rise of "Democratic societies" among the opponents of the Federalist administration in the 1790s, political clubs have been prominent examples of this type. A vast network of such groups now forms the basis of U.S. political parties, at the same time affording considerable social opportunities for their members. In the late 19th century, when ward clubs in large cities became identified in some minds with corrupt political machines, good government advocates began founding the modern City clubs and Commonwealth clubs, which are largely devoted to the study of public affairs and the improvement of government. In addition to these groups, which also often have their own buildings, innumerable less pretentious civic clubs developed in smaller communities or even neighbourhoods throughout the country. The average businessman, however, has preferred to join one of the service clubs such as the Rotary, Exchange, Kiwanis or Lions clubs. Good fellowship is one of their main attractions, and they sponsor many worthwhile programs to serve community welfare.

With the steady decline of working hours in the 20th century, came the existence and even the problem of far more leisure time for large numbers of people. Not surprisingly organizations have appeared catering to recreational interests of almost every description. In particular, because of the restrictions of urban life, a wide variety of athletic clubs arose. Golf clubs, for example, appeared in or near every metropolitan area. In the form of elaborate country clubs, many furnish additional facilities which make them among the few clubs that serve the entire family unit. With their restaurants, bars and Saturday night dances, they increasingly became the social centres for well-to-do suburban residents; thus the term "country club set" became part of the American vocabulary.

In addition to clubs in which the emphasis is on social exclusiveness, civic activity or avocational interests, many neighbourhood clubs have been formed along national or religious lines. There are still many survivals of the social clubs formed by various immigrant groups, and nearly every large American religious denomination has affiliated clubs that are important in the social as well as religious lives of their adherents.

The form of club life most characteristic of the United States, however, is the women's club, a striking demonstration of the leisure that has become available, at least to the urban middle-class woman. Organizations like the Chilton club, in Boston, the Colony club in New York city, and the Acorn club in Philadelphia parallel the exclusive men's groups, but far more significant are the numerous women's clubs of general membership which, beginning with the New England Women's club of Boston and the Sorosis of New York (both founded in 1868), spread so rapidly that by 1889 the General Federation of Women's Clubs was formed. At first concentrating on subjects such as literature, art and gardening, they extended their interests to include social problems and public affairs until the American clubwoman became a far more representative figure than the clubman.

There are, of course, numerous organized clubs for children in the United States, such as the Boy Scouts, Girl Scouts and, in rural areas, the 4-H clubs (*qq.v.*). (WE. E. D.)

CLUE or CLEW, the thread of life, which, according to the fable, the fates spin for every man (O.E. *cluwe,* a ball of thread). The figurative meaning, a piece of evidence leading to discovery, is derived from the story of Theseus, who was guided through the labyrinth by the ball of thread held by Ariadne.

CLUENTIUS HABITUS, AULUS, of Larinum in Samnium, the hero of a Roman *cause célèbre.* In 74 B.C. he accused his step-father Statius Albius Oppianicus of an attempt to poison him, and Oppianicus was condemned. But there had been bribery; Cluentius was degraded, and in 66 charged with having caused his step-father to be poisoned. Cicero defended Cluentius, who was acquitted. The speech is considered one of Cicero's best and is more quoted by Quintilian than any other.

See Quintilian, *Inst.*, ii, 17, 21. Editions of the speech by W. Peterson (1899), W. Ramsay (1883); *see* also H. Nettleship, *Lectures and Essays* (1885).

CLUJ (Ger. Klausenburg; Hung. Kolozsvár), a city of Transylvania, capital of the department of Cluj, and formerly of the principality of Transylvania. Pop. (1948) 117,915, mostly Magyars, Rumanians and Jews. Cluj lies mainly on the right bank of the Somos Mic, among considerable hills. On the left bank is the "Bridge Suburb" and the citadel. The streets have a modern appearance. In the central square is the fine Gothic church of St. Michael (1396–1432), and in front of it a statue of Matthias Corvinus (1902). One side of the square is formed by the Batthanyi palace, formerly of the princes of Transylvania. Other noteworthy buildings are the Reformed church, built by Matthias Corvinus in 1486 and ceded to the Calvinists by Gabriel Bethlen in 1662, containing the coats of arms of the old Hungarian dominant families, the house in which Matthias Corvinus was born (1443), now an ethnographical museum, and many palaces of the Hungarian nobility. Cluj is an orthodox bishopric, also a bishopric of the Reformed and Uniate Churches; and possesses a university, a court of appeal, a theatre, opera and several museums. Its industry includes textile, paper, sugar, candle, soap and earthenware factories, breweries and distilleries.

Cluj is believed to occupy the site of a Roman settlement named Napoca. It was colonized by Saxons in 1178, and at first enjoyed many privileges and great prosperity; but many Saxons left it in the 16th century in consequence of the introduction of Uniate doctrine, and it presently became the centre of the Magyar element in Transylvania. It was capital of Transylvania and seat of the Transylvanian diets.

Cluj, coveted by Hungary since World War I, was ceded to that country by Rumania Aug. 30, 1940, by the award of Vienna. This award was dictated by Germany and Italy.

CLUMP, a lump, group or cluster, *e.g.*, of trees. A clumsy shoe worn by German peasants, made from a single piece of wood; the thick extra sole added to heavy boots for rough wear. Shoemakers speak of clumping a boot when a new sole is nailed, not sewn by hand, to the old sole.

CLUNES, a borough of Talbot county, Victoria, Australia, 97½ mi. by rail N.W. of Melbourne. Pop. (1954) 968. It is the centre of an agricultural, pastoral and mining district, in which gold was first discovered in 1851. It is at an elevation of 1,081 ft. An annual agricultural exhibition is held in the town.

CLUNY or CLUGNY, a town of east central France, in the department of Saône-et-Loire, on the left bank of the Grosne, 14 mi. N.W. of Mâcon. Pop. (1946) 4,046. The interest of the town lies in its specimens of mediaeval architecture, which include, besides its celebrated abbey, the Gothic church of Nôtre-Dame, the church of St. Marcel with its beautiful Romanesque spire, portions of the ancient fortifications and a number of old houses. Cluny gradually increased in importance with the founding of the abbey (910) and the development of the religious fraternity, and in 1090 received a communal charter from the abbot St. Hugh. In 1471 the town was taken by the troops of Louis XI. In 1529 the abbey was given "in commendam" to the family of Guise. The town and abbey suffered during the Wars of Religion of the 16th century, and the abbey was closed in 1790.

The chief remains of the abbey are the ruins of the basilica of St. Peter and the abbot's palace. The church was a Romanesque building, completed early in the 12th century, and until the erection of St. Peter at Rome was the largest ecclesiastical building in Europe. It was in great part demolished under the First Empire, but the south transept, a high octagonal tower, the chapel of Bourbon (15th century), and the ruins of the apse still remain. In 1750 the abbey buildings were largely rebuilt. The abbot's palace (15th century) serves as *hôtel-de-ville,* library and museum. The town has quarries of limestone and building-stone, and manufactures pottery, leather and paper.

The Order of Cluniac Benedictines.—The Monastery of Cluny was founded in 910 by William I. the Pious, count of Auvergne and duke of Guienne (Aquitaine). The first abbot was Berno, who had under his rule two monasteries in the neighbourhood. Before his death in 927 two or three more came under his control, so that he bequeathed to his successor the government of a little group of five or six houses, which became the nucleus of the order of Cluny. Berno's successor was Odo: armed with papal privileges he set to work to make Cluny the centre of a revival and reform among the monasteries of France; he also journeyed to Italy, and induced some of the great Benedictine houses (*see* BENEDICTINES), and among them St. Benedict's own monasteries of Subiaco and Monte Cassino, to receive the reform and adopt the Cluny manner of life. The process of extension, partly by founding new houses, partly by incorporating old ones, went on under Odo's successors, so that by the middle of the 12th century Cluny had become the centre and head of a great order embracing 314 monasteries—the number 2,000, sometimes given, is an exaggeration—in all parts of Europe, in France, Italy, the Empire, Lorraine, Spain, England, Scotland, Poland, and even in the Holy Land. And the influence of Cluny extended far beyond the actual order: many monasteries besides Monte Cassino and Subiaco adopted its customs and manner of life without subjecting themselves to its sway. Fleury and Hirsau may be mentioned as conspicuous examples.

If its influence on the subsequent history of monastic and religious life and organization be considered, the most noteworthy feature of the Cluny system was its external polity, which constituted it a veritable "order" in the modern sense of the word, the first that had existed since that of Pachomius (*see* MONASTICISM). All the houses that belonged, either by foundation or incorporation, to the Cluny system were absolutely subject to Cluny and its abbot, who was "general" in the same sense as the general of the Jesuits or Dominicans, the practically absolute ruler of the whole system. The superiors of all the subject houses (usually priors, not abbots) were his nominees; every member of the order was professed by his permission, and had to pass some of the early years of his monastic life at Cluny itself; the abbot of Cluny had entire control over every one of the monks—some 10,000, it is said; it even came about that he had the practical appointment of his successor. For a description and criticism of the system, *see* F. A. Gasquet, *Sketch of Monastic Constitutional History,* pp. xxxii.–xxxv. (the Introduction to 2nd ed. [1895] of the English trans. of the *Monks of the West*); here it must suffice to say that it is the very antithesis of the Benedictine polity.

The greatness of Cluny is really the greatness of its early abbots. If the short reign of the unworthy Pontius be excepted, Cluny was ruled during a period of about 250 years (910–1157) by a succession of seven great abbots, who combined those high qualities of character, ability and religion that were necessary for so commanding a position; they were Berno, Odo, Aymard, Majolus (Maieul), Odilo, Hugh, Peter the Venerable. Sprung from noble families of the neighbourhood; educated to the highest level of the culture of those times; taking part in all great movements of ecclesiastical and temporal politics; refusing the first sees in Western Christendom, the cardinalate, and the papacy itself, they ever remained true to their state as monks, without loss of piety or religion. Four of them, indeed, Odo, Maieul, Odilo and Hugh, are venerated as saints.

In the movement associated with the name of Hildebrand the influence of Cluny was thrown strongly on the side of religious and ecclesiastical reform, as in the suppression of simony and the enforcing of clerical celibacy; but in the struggle between the papacy and the Empire the abbots of Cluny seem to have exercised a moderating influence. Hildebrand himself, though probably not a monk of Cluny, was a monk of a Cluniac monastery in Rome; his successor, Urban II., was actually a Cluny monk, as was Paschal II. It may safely be said that from the middle of the 10th century until the middle of the 12th, Cluny was the chief centre of religious influence throughout Western Europe, and the abbot of Cluny, next to the pope, the most important and powerful ecclesiastic in the Latin Church.

During the abbacy of Peter the Venerable (1122–1157) it became clear that, after a lapse of two centuries, a renewal of the framework of the life and a revival of its spirit had become necessary. Accordingly he summoned a great chapter of the whole order whereat the priors and representatives of the subject houses attended in such numbers that, along with the Cluny community, the assembly consisted of 1,200 monks. This chapter drew up the 76 statutes associated with Peter's name, regulating the whole range of claustral life, and solemnly promulgated as binding on the whole Cluniac obedience. But these measures did not succeed in saving Cluny from a rapid decline that set in immediately after Peter's death. The rise of the Cistercians and the mendicant orders were contributory causes, and also the difficulties experienced in keeping houses in other countries subject to a French superior. And so the great system gradually became a mere congregation of French houses, which was dissolved in 1790.

Cluniac houses were introduced into England under the Conqueror. The first foundation was at Barnstaple; the second at Lewes by William de Warenne, in 1077, and it counted as one of the "Five Daughters of Cluny." Though the bonds with Cluny seem to have been much relaxed if not wholly broken, the Cluniac houses continued as a separate group up to the dissolution, never taking part in the chapters of the English Benedictines.

Abridged accounts, with references to the most recent literature, may be found in Heimbucher, *Orden und Kongregationen* (1896), i. § 20; Herzog-Hauck, *Realencyklopädie* (ed. 3), art. "Cluni" (Grutzmacher); and the *Catholic Encyclopaedia, art.* "Cluny" (*Seckur*); *Die Cluniacenser* (1891–1894). An account is given in Maitland, *Dark Ages,* §§ xviii.–xxvi. The story of the English houses is briefly sketched in the second chapter of F. A. Gasquet's *Henry VIII. and the English Monasteries* (the larger ed., 1886); *see* also the same writer's *English Monastic Life.*

CLUSERET, GUSTAVE PAUL (1823–1900), delegate for war of the Paris Commune, was born in Paris, on June 13, 1823. He was an officer of the *garde mobile* during the second republic (1848), joined Garibaldi's volunteers in 1860 and in 1861 went to the United States to take part in the Civil War. After this campaign he assumed the title of General, which he said had been granted to him personally by Abraham Lincoln. He also took part in the Fenian insurrection in Ireland of 1866–67. On his return to France he became a member of the International Working Men's Association (*see* INTERNATIONAL, THE), and on the news of the Communard revolt of March 18, 1871, hurried to Paris. His military title, his advanced opinions, and his presumed talents gave him great influence among the Paris workers; he was not, however, elected a member of the Commune till the supplementary elections of April 16. After the disastrous failures of Lullier and Bergeret, the Commune appointed him to the charge of the Department of War, trusting to his record and his own assertions. But, brave though he was personally, Cluseret was hopelessly unfit to organize any military operation. He failed to introduce order into his department, to prevent the continual meddling and contradiction by the central committee of the National Guard, to organize a park of artillery, or even to relieve the men in the trenches. Under his direction, with a nominal force of 100,000 guards, the defence of Paris was maintained by no more than about 10,000, usually the same 10,000. When the Commune realized the extent of his incompetence and arrested him, on May 1, the fate of the insurrection was already decided. Cluseret had been charged with treason, but his crime was inefficiency. On May 24 the entry of the Versailles troops into Paris saved him from condemnation by the Communard courts and he escaped from France. He returned in 1884, sat as deputy for Toulon in 1888–89, and died on Aug. 21, 1900. (*See* COMMUNE.)

See *Mémoires du Général Cluseret: le deuxième siège de Paris, la fin de l'empire* (1887–88); P. Lissagaray, *History of the Commune of 1871* (1902); G. da Costa, *La Commune Vécue* (1903); R. W. Postgate, *Revolution from 1789 to 1906* (1920). (R. W. P.)

CLUSIUM (mod. Chiusi, *q.v.*), an ancient town of Italy, one of the 12 cities of Etruria, on an isolated hill at the South end of the valley of the Clanis (Chiana). It first appears in Roman history at the end of the 7th century B.C., when it joined the other Etruscan towns against Tarquinius Priscus; and at the end of the 6th century B.C. it placed itself, under its king Lars Porsena, at the head of the attempt to re-establish the Tarquins in Rome. At the time of the invasion of the Gauls in 391 B.C., the Roman envoys who had come to intercede for the people of Clusium with the Gauls took part in the battle which followed; and this determined the Gauls to march on Rome. Clusium came under Roman supremacy before 225 B.C., when the Gauls advanced thus far. The Via Cassia, constructed after 187 B.C., passed just below the town. In imperial times its grain and grapes were famous. Christianity found its way into Clusium as early as the 3rd century. In A.D. 540 it is named as a strong place to which Vitiges sent a garrison of a thousand men.

Fragments of the Etruscan town walls are built into the mediaeval fortifications. Under the town extends an elaborate system of rock-cut passages, probably drains. Extensive Etruscan cemeteries surround the city on all sides. The prevalence of cremation in the early period led to the development of the so-called *tombe a ziro,* in which the cinerary urn (often with a human head) is placed in a large clay jar (*ziro,* Lat. *dolium*). This was followed by the *tombe a camera,* in which the tomb is a chamber hewn in the rock. From one of the earliest of these came the famous François vase; another is the Tomba della Scimmia (the monkey), with a painted frieze in the central chamber. The most remarkable group of tombs is, however, that of Poggio Gaiella, 3m. to the N., where the hill is honeycombed with chambers in three storeys, partly connected by a system of passages. Other noteworthy tombs are those of the Granduca, with a single subterranean chamber carefully constructed in travertine, and containing eight cinerary urns of the same material; of Vigna Grande; of Colle Casuccini (the ancient stone door of which is still in working order), with two chambers, containing paintings representing funeral rites. Nearly 3,000 Etruscan inscriptions have come to light from Clusium and its district alone, while the part of Etruria north of it as far as the Arno has produced barely 500. Among the later tombs bilingual inscriptions are by no means rare, and both Etruscan and Latin inscriptions are often found in the same cemeteries. Many inscriptions are painted upon tiles which closed the niches containing the cinerary urns. In Roman times the territory of Clusium seems to have extended as far as Lake Trasimene. The local museum contains important objects from the necropolis, *bucchero,* sepulchral urns, painted vases, and stone *cippi* with reliefs.

Two Christian catacombs have been found near Clusium, one in the hill of S. Caterina near the railway station, the inscriptions of which seem to go back to the 3rd century; another 1m. to the E. in a hill on which a church and monastery of S. Mustiola stood, which goes back to the 4th century, among its numerous inscriptions being one with the date A.D. 303, and the tombstone of L. Petronius Dexter, bishop of Clusium, who died in A.D. 322. To the west and north-west of Chiusi-at Cetona, Sarteano, Chianciano and Montepulciano other Etruscan cemeteries have been discovered; the objects from them have mostly passed to large museums or been dispersed.

See R. Bianchi-Bandinelli in *Monumenti dei Lincei* for a detailed account of the tombs; and *cf.* D. Randall MacIver, *Villanovans and Early Etruscans* (Oxford, 1924). (T. A.)

CLUTCH, a device by means of which connected shafts or other mechanisms, such as engaging pulleys, gears and other rotating parts, may be disconnected at will. A clutch is frequently required to operate many times in the course of a minute and, as in the spindle of the automatic screw machine, which often runs at 5,000 r.p.m., it may be required to reverse its action several times within a few seconds. Clutches may be divided into two general classes, namely: Positive clutches and friction clutches.

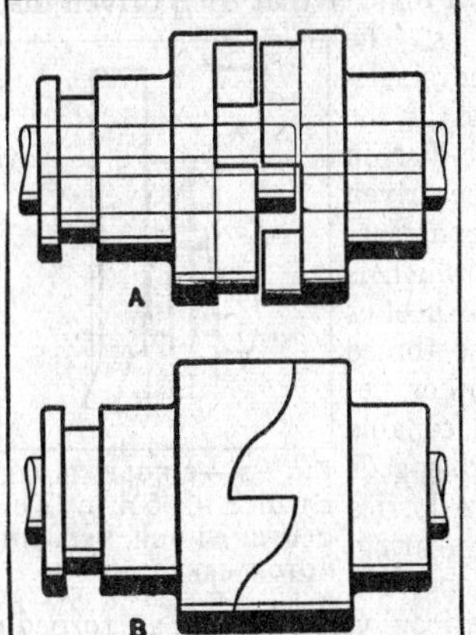

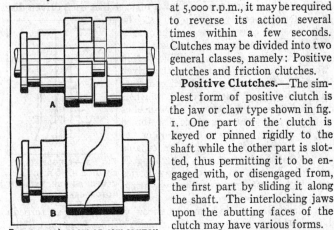

FIG. 1.—(A) CLAW OR JAW CLUTCH, (B) SPIRAL CLAW, OR RATCHET CLUTCH
The oldest form, the claw or jaw clutch, can only be put in when the mechanism is running at low speed, while with the spiral clutch, the drive cannot be reversed

Positive Clutches.—The simplest form of positive clutch is the jaw or claw type shown in fig. 1. One part of the clutch is keyed or pinned rigidly to the shaft while the other part is slotted, thus permitting it to be engaged with, or disengaged from, the first part by sliding it along the shaft. The interlocking jaws upon the abutting faces of the clutch may have various forms.

In machine tools the jaw clutch is applied extensively and is used for instantaneous disconnection of a drive to a feed screw. An automatic trip device jerks the clutch teeth out of mesh. A spiral claw clutch is utilized so that a drive cannot be reversed, this act forcing the teeth apart. Both types are shown in fig. 1.

The number of jaws on clutches depends upon the promptness with which a clutch must act. In punching and shearing machinery, the number varies from two to four, while in other classes of machinery the number of jaws may run as high as 24.

The freewheel clutch, commonly applied to bicycles, but having other mechanical applications, is another form of positive clutch. This engages the rear sprocket with the rear wheel when the pedals are rotated forwards and permits the rear wheel to revolve free from the rear sprocket when the pedals are stopped.

Friction Clutches.—The object of a friction clutch is to connect a rotating member to one that is stationary, to bring it up to speed, and to transmit the required power with a minimum amount of slippage. In connection with machine tools, a friction clutch introduces what might be termed a safety device in that it will slip when the pressure on the cutting tool becomes excessive, thus preventing the breaking of gears or other parts. According to the direction in which the pressure between the contact surface is applied, friction clutches may be further divided into axial clutches and rim clutches.

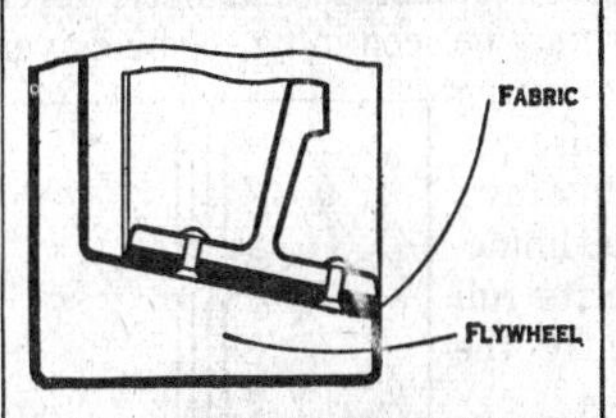

FIG. 2.—CONE CLUTCH FOR MOTOR LORRY OR MOTOR TRUCK
Used in machine tools, other apparatus and heavy automobiles. A lorry clutch is shown within the fly-wheel, with fabric lining riveted on

Axial clutches manufactured by the various builders of transmission machinery, machine tools and motor cars, are usually of one of the following three types: Cone, disc and combined conical disc. The cone clutch is the simplest form of friction clutch that can be devised, and if properly designed will give entire satisfaction in many mechanisms such as lathes, machine tools, hoisting apparatus, lorries, heavy automobiles. Two types of cone clutches, the single-cone and the double-cone, are usually met with. The single-cone clutch consists of a "male" cone of cast iron or specially treated steel keyed rigidly to a driving shaft with a second or "female" cone faced with cork, leather, asbestos, or other material, which is fitted to the driven shaft by means of a feather key. This key permits the driven cone to be engaged with the driving cone, thus transmitting the power from one shaft to the other. The hub of the driven cone is fitted with a groove into which a shifter collar is operated by the engaging lever or toggle as shown in fig. 2. When applied to vehicles the operating lever is usually replaced by a strong spring which performs the same function. The double-cone clutch is based on similar principles.

The disc-clutch—known also as the plate clutch (fig. 3)—is a series of discs arranged in such a manner that each driven disc is located between two driving discs. The two types in common use are the single-disc in which a single disc serves as the driven member and the multiple-disc in which two or more discs act as the driven member. The single-disc clutch construction includes a fabric-faced disc which is gripped on each side between a fly-wheel or other member and a pressure disc forced up by springs, toggle levers or other devices. Multiple-disc clutches are capable of transmitting large powers at high speeds and have wide usage in motor cars, lorries (trucks), cranes, hoists and heavy gearing. A special form of hydraulically operated disc clutch is used in some American vessels, such as torpedo boat destroyers, to disconnect the cruising engines from the turbine shafts without stopping the propelling machinery.

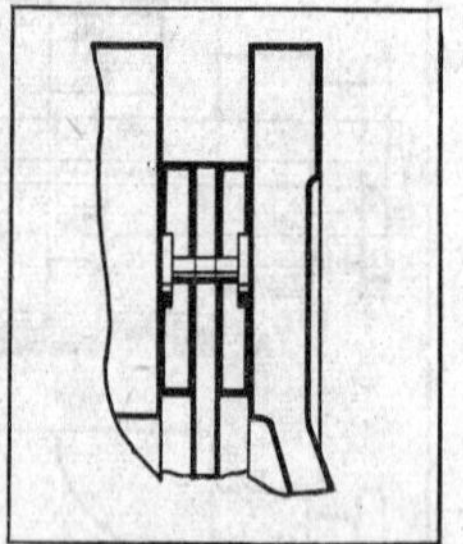

FIG. 3.—SINGLE PLATE CLUTCH, OR DISC-CLUTCH, MUCH USED IN MOTOR CARS

In addition to the asbestos-fabric faced steel disc used for the friction surfaces, the following are sometimes used: Steel against steel; steel against steel with cork inserts; steel against bronze. A combination of steel and bronze working in oil or dry steel and fabric may be used.

A combined conical-disc clutch is one in which the contact surfaces of the disc or discs are conical. In the Hele-Shaw conical disc clutch, shown in fig. 4, the driving and driven discs have a V-shaped annular groove, the sides of which form the surfaces in contact. Phosphor-bronze driving discs are provided with notches on the outer periphery which engage with suitable projections on the pressed steel casing. The mild steel driven discs have notches on the inner bore which engage with the corresponding projections on a steel spider which is splined to the shaft. The V groove in the discs permits a free circulation of oil, and at the same time ensures fairly rapid dissipation of the heat generated when the clutch is allowed to slip.

One of the recent developments with the disc type is the magnetic clutch. No toggles, lever or mechanical movements are fitted, but the friction surfaces are brought together by magnetic force when the current is switched on. As may be seen in fig. 5 the driven disc is held a little way off by a spring plate. As the coils in the driving disc are energized the resulting magnetic pull draws the driven disc against the friction lining. The magnetic pull does not attain its full value immediately and consequently the start is made without grabbing.

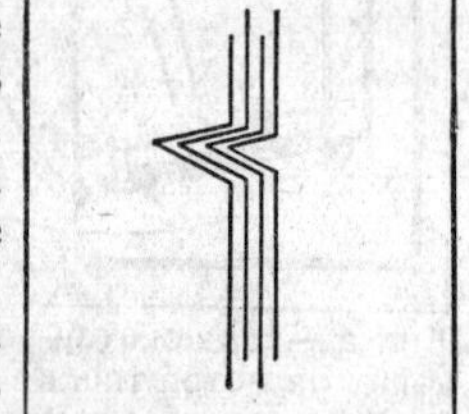

FIG. 4.—HELE-SHAW CLUTCH PLATES, WITH V-SHAPED GROOVES, THE ONLY PARTS MAKING FRICTIONAL CONTACT

In the rim-clutches pressure is obtained on the periphery of a rim and the various designs are known as block, split-ring, band, and roller, depending upon the manner in which the pressure is applied to the exterior or interior of the rim. Block clutches are used chiefly on line shafts and countershafts, although there are several designs that have given good service on machine tools. Split-ring clutches are used for all classes of service but their greatest field of application appears to be in connection with machine tools, or in places where the diameter of the clutch as well as the space taken up by the clutch is limited. Band clutches are usually installed when it is necessary to transmit heavy loads accompanied by shocks, as for example, in the drives of rolling mills and heavy mine hoist. The roller clutch is used principally for punching presses.

A block clutch used for shaft work consists of a shell running loose on the shaft, into which are fitted two brass or bronze shoes. The shoes are fastened loosely to a sleeve, which in turn is slotted to the shaft. The shoes are pressed against the inner surface of the shell by means of an eccentric screw or wedge.

The split-ring clutch consists of an outer shell running loose on a shaft or sleeve; into this shell is fitted a split-ring. The latter may be expanded by the action of a pair of levers as shown in the Heywood and Bridge clutch in fig. 6, or by means of a wedge. A sliding sleeve forms a convenient means of engaging a suitable lever. A sliding sleeve, operated by a suitable lever, forms a convenient means of engaging the split ring with the outer shell.

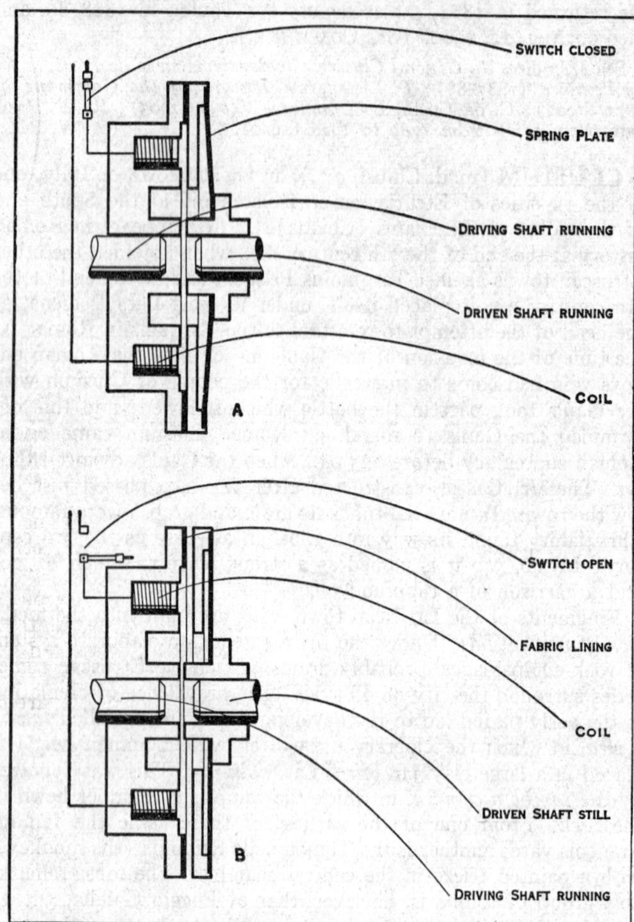

FIG. 5.—VIEWS OF MAGNETIC CLUTCH, A. SHOWING CLUTCH WITH CURRENT ON, B. WITH CURRENT OFF, IN WHICH MAGNETIC PULL BRINGS SURFACES TOGETHER WHEN THE CURRENT IS TURNED ON, TRANSMITTING OVER 2,000 HORSE-POWER IN THE LARGE CLUTCHES

In general, a band clutch consists of a flexible steel band, either plain or faced with wood or asbestos fabric, one end of which is fixed and the other is free to move in a circumferential direction. Due to the pull exerted by the operating mechanism on the free end of the band, the latter is made to grip the driving or driven member.

The roller clutch has a cam keyed to the crankshaft on the circumference of which a number of recesses, forming inclined planes, have been cut. Rollers, rolling up these inclined planes due to the action of a shell, wedge themselves between the cam and the clutch ring, thus causing the crankshaft to rotate with a flywheel. The rollers are held in place and controlled by a shell which is connected with the crankshaft by means of a spring, which is in turn operated by a treadle.

In rolling mills a special friction clutch, known as a "coil-clutch," having a flexible steel coil connected with the driven shaft and a cone on the driving shaft has been brought into use. This type of clutch has very sensitive control. On a test made in a rolling mill, a load of 11 tons was lowered by means of a crane on to an egg without crushing it and held there for three minutes.

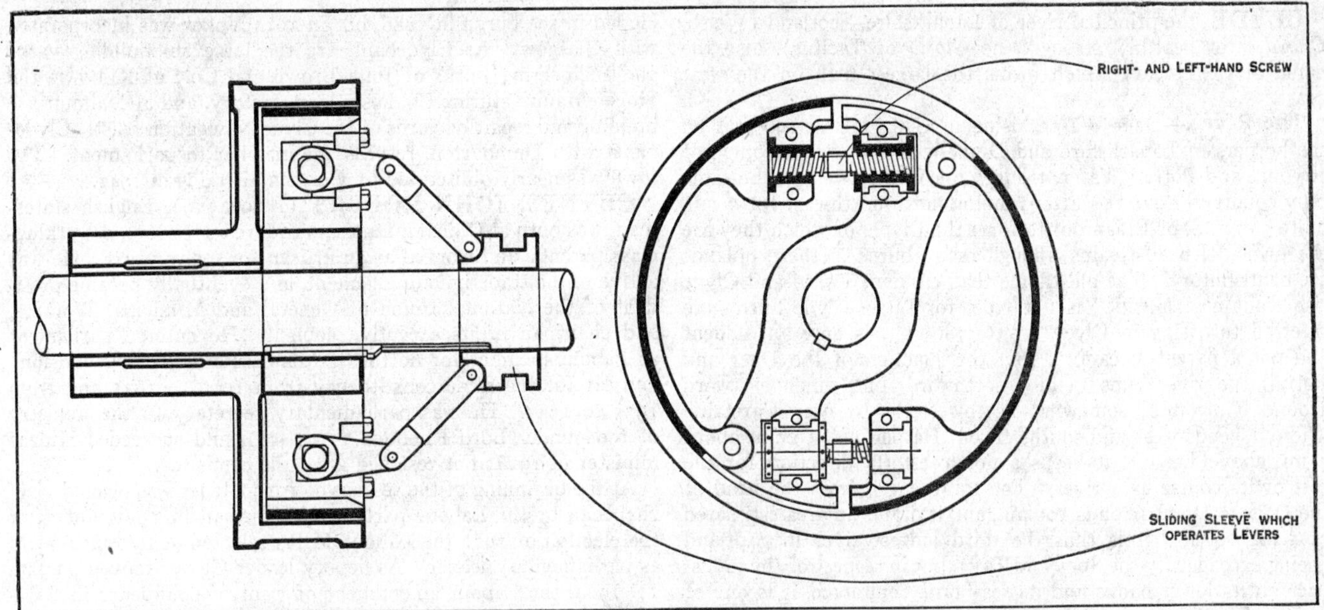

FIG. 6.—HEYWOOD AND BRIDGE EXPANDING CLUTCH, SHOWING HOW A POWERFUL EFFECT IS GAINED BY THE EXPANDING ACTION OF RIGHT AND LEFT HAND SCREWS IN DUPLICATE: AS THE SLIDING SLEEVE IS MOVED ALONG THE SHAFT, IT WORKS THE LEVERS GIVING A PARTIAL ROTATION TO THE SCREWS, AND EXPANDS THE BAND WITHIN THE SHELL. PERMISSION OF D. BRIDGE AND CO., MANCHESTER

A special application of the block clutch is the "centrifugal-clutch" which, by utilizing the principle of centrifugal force, throws out slipper-blocks against the interior wall of the clutch to enable an electric motor to obtain a proper start before picking up the load. The weight of the shoes is so regulated that when the motor is running at full speed the power transmitted by the shoes equals the power of the motor and all slip ceases.

In motor car service, it is very desirable that the car be started without jerks. In order to secure smooth clutch engagement, the designers of clutches were compelled to originate devices that insured evenness of contact between the friction surfaces. In general the function of these devices is to raise slightly the cone facing at intervals around the periphery so that upon engagement only a small portion of the friction surface comes into contact with the flywheel rim. As soon as the full spring pressure is exerted, the facing is depressed and the entire surface of the cone becomes active. In addition to securing smooth and easy clutch engagement some means must be provided to prevent the spinning of the clutch when it is disengaged. By keeping the size and weight down to a minimum spinning may be reduced slightly. To overcome the spinning action completely small brakes that are brought into action when the pedal is depressed must be provided. (F. H.)

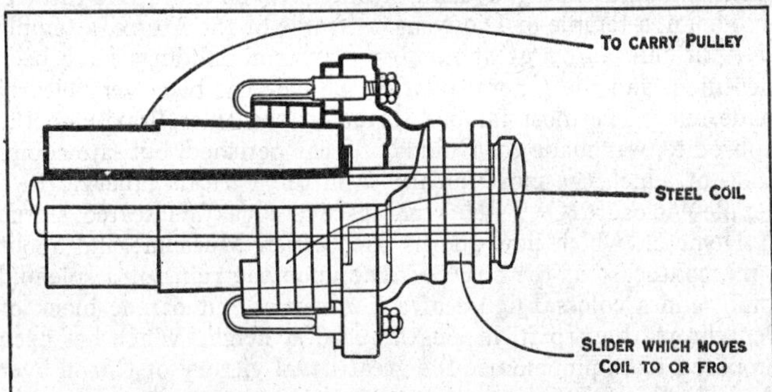

BY COURTESY OF G. D. PETERS AND CO. LTD.

FIG. 7.—COIL CLUTCH, WHICH CAUSES GREAT FRICTION BY THE GRIP OF THE COIL WHEN IT IS THRUST ON TO A CONE ON THE DRIVING SHAFT

CLUWER (CLUVER, CLUVIER, CLUVERIUS), **PHILIP** (1580–1623), German geographer and historian, was born at Danzig. He studied law at Leyden, but soon turned his attention to history and geography, which were then taught there by Joseph Scaliger. He finally settled in Holland, where (after 1616) he received a regular pension from Leyden academy. In 1611 he began to publish his works. He died at Leyden in 1623. His principal writings are: *Germania Antiqua* (1616), *Siciliae Antiquae libri duo, Sardinia et Corsica Antiqua* (1619), and the posthumous *Italia Antiqua* (1624) and *Introductio in Universam Geographiam* (1629).

CLYDE, COLIN CAMPBELL, BARON (1792–1863), British soldier, was born at Glasgow on Oct. 20, 1792. He received his education at the Glasgow high school, and when only 16 years of age obtained an ensigncy in the 9th Foot. He fought under Sir Arthur Wellesley at Vimiera, took part in the retreat of Sir John Moore, and was present at the battle of Corunna. He shared in all the fighting of the Peninsular campaigns, and was severely wounded while leading a storming-party at the attack on San Sebastian. He was again wounded at the passage of the Bidassoa, and compelled to return to England. Campbell held a command in the American expedition of 1814; and after the peace of the following year he devoted himself to studying the theoretical branches of his profession. In 1823 he quelled the negro insurrection in Demerara. In 1832 he became lieutenant-colonel of the 98th Foot, and with that regiment rendered distinguished service in the Chinese War of 1842. Campbell was next employed in the Sikh War of 1848–49, under Lord Gough. At Chillianwalla, where he was wounded, and at the decisive victory of Gujarat, his skill and valour largely contributed to the success of the British arms. He was made a K.C.B. in 1849, and specially named in the thanks of parliament.

Sir Colin Campbell returned home in 1853. In the Crimean War he commanded the Highland brigade, which formed part of the duke of Cambridge's division. The brigade and its leader distinguished themselves very greatly at the Alma; and with his "thin red line" of Highlanders he repulsed the Russian attack on Balaklava. At the close of the war Sir Colin was promoted G.C.B.

The outbreak of the Indian Mutiny called for a general of tried experience; and on July 11, 1857, the command was offered to him by Lord Panmure. On being asked when he would be ready to set out, the veteran replied, "Within twenty-four hours." He left England the next evening, and reached Calcutta on Aug. 13. He started for the front on Oct. 27 and on Nov. 17 relieved Lucknow for the second time. He continued in charge of operations in Oudh until the end of the mutiny. For these services he was raised to the peerage, in 1858, as Lord Clyde; and, returning to England in the next year, he received the thanks of both Houses of Parliament and a pension of £2,000 a year. He died on Aug. 14, 1863.

See Sir Owen Tudor Burne, *Clyde and Strathnairn* ("Rulers of India" series, 1891); and L. Shadwell, *Life of Colin Campbell, Lord Clyde* (1881).

CLYDE, the principal river of Lanarkshire, Scotland (Welsh, *Clwyd*, "far heard," "strong," the *Glotta* of Tacitus), also the name of the estuary which forms the largest firth on the west coast.

The River.—Daer Water, rising in Gana hill (2,190 ft.) on the borders of Lanarkshire and Dumfriesshire, after a course of 10½ mi., and Potrail Water, rising 3 mi. farther west in the same hilly country (1,928 ft.) after running north-north-east for 7 mi., unite 3½ mi. S. of Elvanfoot to form the Clyde, of which they are the principal headstreams, though many burns in these uplands are contributory. The old rhyme that "Annan, Tweed and Clyde rise a'out o'ae hillside" is not true, for Little Clyde burn here referred to, rising in Clyde law (1,789 ft.), is only an affluent and not a parent stream. From the junction of the Daer and Potrail the river runs mainly northward, but winds eastward around Tinto hill, somewhat northwesterly to near Carstairs, where it bends west and south. From Harperfield, a point about 4 mi. above Lanark, it keeps a northwesterly direction for the rest of its course as a river. The total length from the head of the Daer to Dumbarton is 106 mi., and it drains an area estimated at 1,481 sq.mi. It is thus the third longest river in Scotland (being exceeded by the Spey and Tay), but in respect of the industries on its lower banks and its sea-borne commerce, it is one of the most important rivers in the world. Near Lanark it is broken by four celebrated falls (Bonnington, Corra, Dundaff and Stonebyres Linns) within a distance of 3¾ mi. Within this distance the river falls 230 ft. From Stonebyres Linn to the sea the fall is practically 4 ft. in every mile. The chief villages and towns on or close to the river between its source and Glasgow are Crawford, Lamington, New Lanark, Lanark, Hamilton, Bothwell, Blantyre and Uddingston. At Bowling (pop. 1,018)—the point of transhipment for the Forth and Clyde canal—the river widens, the fairway being indicated by a stone wall continued seawards as far as Dumbarton. Dunglass point, near Bowling, is the western terminus of the wall of Antoninus, or Grim's dyke.

As far down as the falls the Clyde remains a pure fishing stream, but from the point at which it becomes an industrial river its waters are contaminated. Towards the end of the 18th century the river was yet fordable at the Broomielaw in the heart of Glasgow, but since that period the stream has been converted into a waterway deep enough to allow large ships to anchor in the harbour (*see* GLASGOW). Clydesdale, as the valley of the upper Clyde is called, begins in the district watered by headstreams of the river, the course of which in effect it follows as far as Bothwell, a distance of 50 mi. It is renowned for its breed of cart horses (specifically known as Clydesdales), its orchards, fruit fields and market gardens, its coal and iron mines.

The Firth.—From Dumbarton, where the firth is commonly considered to begin, to Ailsa Craig, where it ends, the fairway measures 64 mi. Its width varies from 1 mi. at Dumbarton to 37 mi. from Girvan to the Mull of Kintyre. The depth varies from a low-tide minimum of 22 ft. in the navigable channel at Dumbarton to nearly 100 fathoms in the Sound of Bute and at other points. The Cumbraes, Bute and Arran are the principal islands in its waters. The sea lochs all lie on the Highland shore, and comprise Gare loch, Loch Long, Loch Goil, Holy loch, Loch Striven, Loch Riddon and Loch Fyne. The only rivers of any importance feeding the firth are the Ayrshire streams, of which the chief are the Garnock, Irvine, Ayr, Doon and Girvan. The tide ascends above Glasgow, where its farther rise is barred by a weir. The head ports are Glasgow, Port Glasgow, Greenock, Ardrossan, Irvine, Troon, Ayr and Campbeltown. In addition to harbour lights, beacons on rocks and lightships, there are lighthouses on Ailsa Craig, Sanda, Davaar, Pladda, Holy Isle and Little Cumbrae, and at Turnberry Point, Cloch Point and Toward Point. Health and holiday resorts on the lochs, islands and mainland coast are numerous.

CLYDEBANK, a large burgh, Dumbartonshire, Scotland, on the right bank of the Clyde, 6 mi. from Glasgow, served by the Scottish region railway. Pop. (est. 1938) 47,912. In 1875 the district was almost purely rural, but after that date many industries were established. Dalmuir, Kilbowie and Yoker were included in the burgh in 1886, but in 1912 Yoker was incorporated with Glasgow. At Clydebank are the large shipbuilding yards and engineering works of John Brown and Co.; at Kilbowie the Singer Manufacturing Co. has a large factory, and at Dalmuir are building and repairing yards of the Clyde Navigation trust. Clydebank, with Dumbarton, returns one member to parliament. The town was nearly obliterated by German air raids in 1941.

CLYNES, JOHN ROBERT (1869–1949), English statesman, was born at Oldham, Lancs., on March 27, 1869, of working-class parents, and worked as an artisan for many years. He was active in the trade-union movement, and eventually became president of the National Union of General and Municipal Workers, and chairman of its executive council. He entered parliament as Labour member for northeast Manchester (Platting division) and sat for the same constituency from 1906 to 1931 and from 1935 to 1945. He was parliamentary secretary to the ministry of food under Lord Rhondda (1917–18), and succeeded him as minister in 1918; but resigned after the armistice.

At the beginning of the session of 1919 Clynes was elected vice-chairman of the Labour party, and chairman in 1921, but after the election of 1922 the Labour M.P.s selected J. R. MacDonald as parliamentary leader. As deputy leader Clynes moved on Jan. 17, 1924, the Labour amendment of want of confidence in Baldwin's government which brought that government down and put the labour party in office. He became lord privy seal and deputy leader of the house of commons. Clynes always spoke in the house of commons with moderation, and was always heard with respect. He was secretary of state for home affairs from 1929 to 1931. He died in London, Eng., Oct. 23, 1949.

CNIDUS, an ancient city of Caria in Asia Minor, situated at the extremity of the long peninsula that forms the southern side of the Sinus Ceramicus or Gulf of Cos. It was built partly on the mainland and partly on the Island of Triopion or Cape Krio, which anciently communicated with the continent by a causeway and bridge, and now by a narrow sandy isthmus. By means of the causeway the channel between island and mainland was formed into two harbours, of which the larger or southern, was further enclosed by two strongly-built moles. The extreme length of the city was little less than a mile, and the whole intramural area is thickly strewn with architectural remains. The walls, both insular and continental, can be traced throughout their whole circuit; and in many places, especially round the acropolis, at the northeast corner of the city, they are remarkably perfect. Knowlege of the site is largely due to the excavations executed by C. T. Newton in 1857–1858; but of recent years it has become a frequent calling station of touring steamers. The agora, the theatre, an odeum, a temple of Dionysus, a temple of the Muses, a temple of Aphrodite and a great number of minor buildings have been identified, and the general plan of the city has been very clearly made out. The most famous statue by the elder Praxiteles, the Aphrodite, was made for Cnidus. It has perished, but late copies exist, of which the most faithful is in the Vatican gallery. In a temple-enclosure C. T. Newton discovered a fine seated statue of Demeter, which now adorns the British Museum; and about 3 mi. southeast of the city he came upon the ruins of a splendid tomb, and a colossal figure of a lion carved out of one block of Pentelic marble, 10 ft. in length and 6 in height, which has been supposed to commemorate the great naval victory of Conon over the Lacedaemonians in 394 B.C.

Cnidus was a city of high antiquity and probably of Lacedaemonian colonization. Along with Halicarnassus and Cos, and the Rhodian cities of Lindus, Camirus and Ialysus it formed the Dorian Hexapolis, which held its confederate assemblies on the Triopian headland, and there celebrated games in honour of Apollo, Poseidon and the nymphs. The city was at first governed by an oligarchic senate, composed of sixty members, known as ἀμνήμονες, and presided over by a magistrate called an ἀρεστήρ but, though it is proved by inscriptions that the old names continued to a very late period, the constitution underwent a popular transformation. The situation of the city was favourable for commerce, and the Cnidians acquired considerable wealth, and were able to colonize the island of Lipari, and founded the city of

Corcyra Nigra in the Adriatic. They ultimately submitted to Cyrus, and from the battle of Eurymedon to the latter part of the Peloponnesian War they were subject to Athens. In 394 B.C. Conon fought off the port the battle which destroyed Spartan hegemony. The Romans easily obtained their allegiance, and rewarded them for help given against Antiochus by leaving them the freedom of their city. During the Byzantine period there must still have been a considerable population, for the ruins contain a large number of buildings belonging to the Byzantine style, and Christian sepulchres are common in the neighbourhood.

Eudoxus, the astronomer, Ctesias, the writer on Persian history, and Sostratus, the builder of the celebrated Pharos at Alexandria, are the most remarkable of the Cnidians mentioned in history.

See C. T. Newton and R. P. Pullen, *Hist. of Discoveries at Halicarnassus, Cnidus* etc. (1863).

COACH, a large roofed or enclosed carriage for passengers, which originated in Hungary at a place named Kocs, from which the name itself is derived through the French *coche*. As a general term, it is used (as in "coach-building") for all carriages, and also in combination with qualifying attributes for particular forms (as in stage-coach, mail-coach, motor-coach, etc.); but the typical coach implies four wheels, springs and a roof. The stage-coach, with seats outside and in, was a public conveyance which was known in England from the 16th century, and before railways the stage-coaches had regular routes (stages) all over the country; through their carrying the mails (from 1784) the term "mail-coach" arose. Similar vehicles were used in America and on the European continent. The *diligence,* though not invariably with four horses, was the Continental analogue for public conveyance, with other minor varieties such as the *Stellwagen* and *Eilwagen.*

The driving of coaches with four horses was a task in which a considerable amount of skill was required, and English literature is full of the difficulties and humours of "the road" in old days. A form of sport thus arose for enterprising members of the nobility and gentry, and after the introduction of railways made the mail-coach obsolete as a matter of necessity, the old sport of coaching for pleasure still survived, though only to a limited extent. The Four-in-Hand Club was started in England in 1856 and the Coaching Club in 1870, as the successors of the old Bensington Driving Club (1807–52), and Four-Horse Club (1808–29); and in America the New York Coaching Club was founded in 1875. But coaching remains the sport of the wealthier classes, although in various parts of England (*e.g.,* London to Brighton, and in the Lake district), in America, and in Europe, public coaches still have their regular times and routes for those who enjoy this form of travel. The earliest railway vehicles for passengers were merely the road coaches of the period adapted to run on rails, and the expression "coaching traffic" is still used in England to denote traffic carried in passenger trains.

STATE COACH OF THE LORD MAYOR OF LONDON, BUILT IN 1757

Of coaches possessing a history the two best known in Great Britain are the king's state coach, and that of the lord mayor of London. The latter is the older, having been built, or at least first used, for the procession of Sir Charles Asgil, lord mayor elect, in Nov. 1757. The body of this vehicle is not supported by springs, but hung on leather straps; and the whole structure is very richly loaded with ornamental carving, gilding and paint-work. The different panels and the doors contain various allegorical groups of figures representing suitable subjects, and heraldic devices painted in a spirited manner. The royal state coach, which is described as "the most superb carriage ever built," was designed by Sir William Chambers, the paintings on it were executed by Cipriani, and the work was completed in 1761. During the later part of Queen Victoria's reign it was hardly ever seen, but on the accession of Edward VII. the coach was once more put in order for use on state occasions. The following is an official description of this famous coach:

THE BRITISH ROYAL STATE COACH, COMPLETED IN 1761
This coach is used only for ceremonial occasions such as the opening of parliament. The panels and door are covered with emblematic devices

"The whole of the carriage and body is richly ornamented with laurel and carved work, beautifully gilt. The length, 24 ft.; width, 8 ft. 3 in.; height, 12 ft.; length of pole, 12 ft. 4 in.; weight, 4 tons. The carriage and body of the coach is composed as follows:—Of four large tritons, who support the body by four braces, covered with red morocco leather, and ornamented with gilt buckles, the two figures placed in front of the carriage bear the driver, and are represented in the action of drawing by cables extending round their shoulders, and the cranes and sounding shells to announce the approach of the monarch of the ocean; and those at the back carry the imperial fasces, topped with tridents. The driver's foot-board is a large scallop shell, ornamented with bunches of reeds and other marine plants. The pole represents a bundle of lances; the splinter bar is composed of a rich moulding, issuing from beneath a voluted shell, and each end terminating in the head of a dolphin; and the wheels are imitated from those of the ancient triumphal chariot. The body of the coach is composed of eight palm-trees, which, branching out at the top, sustain the roof; and four angular trees are loaded with trophies allusive to the victories obtained by Great Britain during the late glorious war, supported by four lions' heads. On the centre of the roof stand three boys, representing the genii of England, Scotland and Ireland, supporting the imperial crown of Great Britain, and holding in their hands the sceptre, sword of state, and ensigns of knighthood; their bodies are adorned with festoons of laurel, which fall from thence towards the four corners. The panels and doors are painted with appropriate emblematical devices, and the linings are of scarlet velvet richly embossed with national emblems."

We may observe how the difficult art of driving a coach was responsible for the use of the terms "coach" and "coaching" to mean tutor or training for examinations or athletics.

See the Badminton *Driving,* by the duke of Beaufort (1888); Roger's *Manual of Driving* (Philadelphia, 1900); and "Nimrod's" *Essays on the Road* (1876).

COACHING. The 20th century witnessed in its first quarter the passing of a style of conveyance which was at one time universal, and has inspired the artist, the poet and the author to work that will remain long after the last coach has ceased to be seen on the roads. To say that four-in-hand driving will die out entirely is to take an extreme view, but while railways and motor cars hold their own there will be little chance for the art on our country roads—at any rate in comfort.

The reader need hardly be told that in early days the roads were so bad in Great Britain that wheeled traffic literally made slow progress, and nearly everybody rode; but towards the end of the Commonwealth period social life had demanded a better means of communication from place to place. Accordingly the stage coach made its general appearance, and in spite of a good deal of opposition, and the usual charge of effeminacy, remained. As might be expected the pace for many years was not great, and at first the coaches travelled only by day, the "flying coaches," as they were called, covering between forty and fifty miles in the day of 12 hours—in fine weather.

It must be remembered that coaching even in its palmiest days had its detractors, for the weather had to be taken into consideration, while the roads themselves till the days of Telford and Macadam left much to be desired, and accidents were much more numerous than is the case to-day with railways. Still its utility was beyond argument, but the question of speed arose, and it should also be borne in mind that the slowness of the pace rendered the stage coach an easy prey to the highwaymen, who then abounded. The post office at the time favoured the plan of mounted "expresses," and the slowness of the postal service was especially noticeable on the Great North Road, it being said that "every common traveller passes the King's Mail on the first road in the kingdom." Indeed at that time the stage coach itself was a speedier conveyance than the ordinary postal system.

The moment brought the man, and it was John Palmer, the proprietor of the theatre at Bath, who in 1784 put the first mail coach on the road, running from Bristol to London at the rate of about seven miles an hour. The mail coach speedily found favour, and, as its name implies, it may be termed the special *protégé* of the post office; of course it did not exterminate the stage coach, the two existing side by side till the advent of railways drove them both off the road together.

The driving of four horses appealed to the sporting gentlemen of the day, who drove their own vehicles, or who would take a stage or two on the regular coaches, with the connivance of the professional driver. Some well-known amateur coaching clubs were formed, including the Four Horse and the Bensington driving clubs, both of which in due course passed away. It was in 1856 that the Four-in-Hand driving club was formed and lasted down to 1927, while in 1870, owing to the Four-in-Hand driving club only receiving a limited number of members, the still existing coaching club was established. Though its members do not turn out in as great numbers as they did, it still keeps the spirit of the pastime alive at the meets at the Magazine in Hyde Park. Here, however, the pleasure of driving four horses is the only consideration and no "passengers" are taken for remuneration.

Later on a number of what may be termed subscription coaches were placed upon the road, which usually ran to various places within a radius of something like 50 miles of London, and till the appearance of the motor car they were very popular. They have, however, practically disappeared, with the death of the last of the London enthusiasts who was able to indulge his hobby, though two roads were kept open in 1927.

In the past many private gentlemen, especially masters of hounds, would indulge in driving tours through various parts of the country, and in 1926 one well known master in the North afforded his friends and subscribers a very pleasant afternoon's outing. At the holding of some of the great horse shows, notably Richmond and Olympia, coaching classes are popular and often well patronized, for it must be remembered that the regimental coaches, that is coaches kept up by various regiments in the service, have not yet gone out of fashion. Indeed it will probably be very many years before the art of driving four horses is lost entirely in Great Britain. (*See* DRIVING.)

COAHUILA, a northern frontier state of Mexico, bounded north and northeast by Texas, east by Nuevo León, south by San Luis Potosí and Zacatecas, and west by Durango and Chihuahua. Area, 58,052 sq.mi. The population in 1950 was 720,145. Its surface is a roughly broken plateau, traversed by several ranges of mountains and sloping gently toward the Rio Grande. In the western part there are extensive areas of level land, many of them enclosed drainage basins, the largest of which is the Bolsón de Mapimí, a great depression which was long considered barren and uninhabitable. Experiments with irrigation, however, were highly successful and considerable tracts were later brought under cultivation. In general the state is insufficiently watered, the rainfall being light and the rivers small. The rivers flow eastward to the Rio Grande. The climate is hot and dry, and generally healthful. Stock raising was for a time the principal industry, but agriculture has been developed in several localities, among the chief products of which are cotton—Coahuila is the principal cotton-producing state in Mexico—Indian corn, wheat, beans, sugar and grapes. The Parras district in the southern part of the state has long been celebrated for its wines and brandies. The mineral products include silver, lead, coal, copper and iron. The mining operations are chiefly centred in the Sierra Mojada, Sierra Carmen and in the Santa Rosa valley. The modern industrial development of the state is due to the railway lines constructed across it during the last quarter of the 19th century, and to the investment of foreign capital in local enterprises. The first Spanish settlement in the region now called Coahuila was at Saltillo in 1586, when it formed part of the province of Nueva Viscaya. The capital of the state is Saltillo. Among the more important towns are Parras, pop. (1940) 15,555, 98 mi. northwest of Saltillo, one of the largest railway centres in the country, and Piedras Negras (formerly Ciudad Porfirio Díaz) on the Rio Grande.

COAL AND COAL MINING. To modern civilization there has been no other substance in nature except air, soil and water so important as coal. This black, earthy matter is a small potential dynamo—a so-called mineral derived from the dense vegetation of hundreds of millions of years ago. Within each piece is a vast store of energy drawn from the sun. The better the grade of coal, the more carbon it contains; when coal is burned by combining it with oxygen in the air, the intense heat hoarded up from the rays of the sun of the so-called Carboniferous period is released. It is the working power of coal that makes it so important to mankind. One pound of it, burning in a modern engine, can produce as much work as a workman doing hand labour could in an entire day.

In the pages which follow, coal and coal mining will be considered in these separate sections:

I. Origin and Kinds of Coal; First Uses
II. Types and Methods of Coal Mining
III. Surface or Strip Mining
IV. Coal Mining in Great Britain
V. Coal Mining in the United States
VI. Hazards of Mining and Measures of Safety
VII. Chemical By-Products of Coal
VIII. World Coal Resources and Production

I. ORIGIN AND KINDS OF COAL; FIRST USES

Coal is of organic origin, formed from the remains of living things such as trees, herbs, shrubs, vines and other plant materials that flourished millions of years ago, during periods of widespread uniformly mild, moist climate. From this variety of vegetation and its complex carbon compounds came a great assortment of coals, from brown coal and lignite or peat to the hardest kind of anthracite.

Coal consists chiefly of carbon, derived directly from organic carbon compounds such as starch, sugar and cellulose which with water form the bulk and substance of vegetation. The carbon in the plants that later formed coal was not obtained from the soil by way of plant roots, but from the air by way of leaves. Being the only known natural agency known capable of abstracting large amounts of carbon from the air, plants employ it in the construction of their own tissues and store it up for future use. The mechanism by which this is accomplished is the plant cell with its green colouring matter. The energy utilized by plants in building up the organic substances out of carbon dioxide and water is that portion of the sunlight absorbed by the green material.

Geology and Types of Coal.—Coal is fossilized plant material, preserved by burial and altered by earth forces. Although it is usually bedded, isolated pieces exist. The character of a coal depends upon the nature of the original plant debris, the extent and character of its decay and weathering before burial (diagenesis), and upon the geological vicissitudes subsequently undergone.

Selective diagenetic processes tend to concentrate the more resistant components of the peat. Differences in coal arising from initial differences in composition or from the selective effects of diagenesis constitute type differences; differences arising from variability in earth forces constitute rank differences. Common banded coal, cannel coal and splint coal are three common type varieties; lignite, subbituminous coal, bituminous coal and anthracite are four common rank varieties. Each type of coal is, theoretically at least, represented in each rank.

Geological forces mainly result in compaction and condensation; the former, a physical process, results in loss of pore space, moisture and oxygen; the latter, a chemical change, results in an increase in residual carbon. These changes increase the density and heat value of the coal. Coal rank classification, therefore, has been based upon moisture content, oxygen content and heat value singly or in various combinations. Relative density, blackness and reflectivity also provide rough indices of rank.

The coking capacity of coal is produced by geological forces concurrently with compaction and condensation. In general, it is restricted to bituminous coal and reaches its best expression in medium and low volatile coals. Coking quality is, therefore, also a criterion for rank classification.

Depth of burial is an important factor in determining the rank of a coal. However, the higher-rank coals have been subjected to other earth forces than simple hydrostatic pressure, for such coals are found where rocks have been folded or otherwise modified by earth forces, such as by contact with igneous rocks. Low-rank coals on the other hand are characteristic of plains regions where the weight of overlying sediments has been the main source of alteration.

The coalification process terminates in the transformation of coal into incombustible mineral carbon or graphite. Graphitic coal is found only in association with severely altered rocks.

The age of a coal is no criterion of its rank. Immature coals may be of great age (Carboniferous lignitic coal of the Moscow basin), and anthracitic coal may be of relatively recent age (Eocene anthracite of Thrace and Switzerland).

Coal is known in all geological systems since the Silurian. Graphitic rocks suggest that coal formation may date back to pre-Cambrian time. The Devonian coal represents very primitive land plants; Tertiary coals, on the other hand, represent debris from relatively modern trees. Hence there is apparently no limit to the kind of land plant that may be the source of coal. Coal beds are most important in the Carboniferous system of the Palaeozoic rocks, Lower and Upper Cretaceous systems of the Mesozoic and throughout the Tertiary systems. The greatest quantity of coal material is probably in the Tertiary rocks, but the greatest quantity of high grade coal is in the Carboniferous system.

Most bituminous coals appear banded in hand specimens, and the banded ingredients, vitrain, clarain, durain and fusain, have been differentiated as vitreous and black, bright and striated, dull or charcoal-like respectively. In thin sections the woody material (mainly vitrain), which often can be clearly identified has been called anthraxylon by R. Thiessen, the charcoal-like material fusain, and the heterogeneous matrix attritus. Attritus that appears predominantly opaque is the equivalent of durain of hand specimens and of splint coal. Type variations in coal result from variations in the proportion of the banded ingredients or of the botanical components observed in thin sections, since both result from variations in the character of initial material when buried.

The following definitions augment the brief explanations of certain varieties of coal mentioned above:

Lignite is a low-rank brown to black coal, in which the original plant components are discernible. It gives a brown streak and disintegrates rapidly upon exposure. It burns with little or no smoke, and is largely soluble in alkalies.

Subbituminous coal is a low-rank banded, black coal with woody layers commonly visible. It disintegrates in the air, but fairly slowly. It has a brown streak and smokes when it burns. It is noncoking and insoluble in alkalies.

Bituminous coal is a medium- to high-rank black, usually banded, coal, with coking qualities poorly developed in high volatile coals but well developed in medium to low volatile coals. It weathers slightly or not at all. It is insoluble in alkalies and gives a black streak when fresh. It smokes when it burns. Three common type varieties are *normal banded* coal, *cannel* coal, which is an unbanded coal with silky lustre, grossly conchoidal fracture

TABLE I.—*Classification of Coals*
(Computed on ash-free basis)

Rank	Moisture (per cent)	Volatile matter (per cent)	Fixed carbon (per cent)	Heat value (B.T.U.)
Lignite	43.4	18.8	37.8	7,400
Subbituminous	23.4	34.2	42.4	9,720
Low-rank bituminous	11.6	41.4	47.0	12,880
Medium-rank bituminous	5.0	40.8	54.2	13,880
High-rank bituminous	3.2	32.2	64.6	15,160
Low-rank semibituminous	3.0	22.0	75.0	15,480
High-rank semibituminous	5.0	11.6	83.4	15,360
Semianthracite	6.0	10.2	83.8	14,880
Anthracite	3.2	1.2	95.6	14,440

From M. R. Campbell, "*The Coal Fields of the United States*" (U.S. Geological Survey, Paper 100-a).

and with a large proportion of waxy components mainly in the form of spore exines, and *splint* coal, a dull, faintly striated coal, opaque in thin sections and with a somewhat metallic ring when sharply struck. Neither cannel nor splint coal usually possesses coking properties.

Anthracite is a high-rank coal of dense rocklike texture, a glassy lustre and conchoidal fracture. Although faintly banded, banding does not determine breakage. It has a black streak. It does not coke and burns with a nonluminous flame. (G. H. CA.)

Early Uses.—There is general archaeological evidence that during the Bronze Age, 3,000 to 4,000 yr. ago, the people living in what is now Glamorganshire, Wales, used coal for funeral pyres. Remains of coal fires have been found in Roman forts and dwellings on Hadrian's Wall, dating from A.D. 121. Coal served as a fuel in China some time before the Christian era. We find various references to coal in the Bible, and among Greek and Roman writers before the birth of Christ. The Anglo-Saxon Chronicle records for the year 852 that "60 loads of wood, 12 loads of coal, 6 loads of peat, etc." were to be paid in rent for Sempringham, the land let to Wulfred, by the Abbot Ceobred, having to do with the Abbey of Peterborough.

After the invasion of the Normans in 1066, though, coal apparently was not important enough to be mentioned in the Domesday Book, there is evidence that monks of the 11th century often used it in their forges to produce the ironwork for which they were famous. It was certainly in fairly common use in the early middle ages. Travelling pilgrims brought news of the new fuel to the south of England from Northumberland and Durham, where coal could be picked up on the seashore. As early as the 13th century coal was brought down the east coast of England to London in small coastal barges. It was burned so inefficiently in those early days, giving off smoke and what were considered poisonous odours, that a great deal of prejudice developed against its use. At one time King Edward I (1239–1307) imposed the death penalty upon any person caught using coal for fuel purposes. This prejudice continued for some time thereafter, even through the reign of Elizabeth. One reason why it could not be used easily in houses was that chimneys were made of iron and were therefore very expensive. Toward the end of the 15th century, however, a new material appeared—bricks, made easily and cheaply in coal furnaces. Bricks made it possible for everybody to have chimneys and to burn coal in their hearths. It took some time, of course, to perfect even brick chimneys to draw properly, so that heavy smoke and fumes did not escape into dwellings. In the houses of the well-to-do, however, coal became more and more popular. Thomas Cardinal Wolsey's Hampton Court palace is an example of the ornamented brick chimney shafts which became fashionable in Tudor times.

In 1735, when Abraham Darby patented his blast furnace, coal began to be used in the production of iron. What had hitherto been a rare and expensive metal became now something of common use throughout England and eventually in North America.

Coal was first discovered in the United States by Louis Joliet and Jacques Marquette in 1673. A map published with Marquette's *Journal* of 1681 shows that coal was found near the present city of Utica, Ill. Father Louis Hennepin, accompanying La Salle's expedition to the Illinois country in 1680 as chaplain, in his book *A New Discovery of a Vast Country in America* published in England in 1689, referred to the fact that coal had been found near the Illinois river.

It was not until 1745, however, that a coal mine was actually operated, near Richmond, Va.; some coal was sold commercially in that year. Coal was discovered in Ohio in 1755. All of these deposits were of the bituminous variety. Anthracite was first mined in Pennsylvania about 1790.

George Washington, writing in 1770 in his *Journal of a Tour of the Ohio River,* made a notation of a coal mine near the river bank where "coal seemed to be of the very best kind, burning freely and an abundance of it." In the sparsely populated colonies, however, native coal was not widely used. Up to the time of the Revolutionary War, most of it came from England or from Nova Scotia for limited industrial uses in towns along the Atlantic coast. With supplies curtailed during the long war, some use of the native coal was made by the blacksmiths for manufacturing munitions for the Continental army. After the Revolution the infant industry expanded, mostly in areas adjacent to the mines. It was also something of a problem to convince a skeptical public of the value of the newfangled fuel. Word had come from France in a roundabout way that a law had been passed there forbidding any workman from burning coal in Paris, under heavy penalty, because it was believed that coal fumes caused serious epidemics of disease.

Nevertheless, coal came to be used more and more in the United States. As bituminous coal was found close to the surface of the earth and required little expense to dig, farmers in their spare time peddled it to neighbouring blacksmiths and to a few persons who used it for heating their homes. Early farmers frequently would not allow a seam very far underground to be dug up because of a superstitious fear. But they often leased their mineral rights to others. As small companies were organized to mine the coal, the farmers and their farm hands frequently worked for the new owners in the winter months.

In the early 1830s numerous small mining companies sprang up, notably in the Appalachian regions and along the Ohio, Illinois and Mississippi rivers. As a rule they had little capital and few survived. It was not until the 1840s that the U.S. coal industry mined its first 1,000,000 tons, and from then on the growth was steady and accumulative. The industry received a tremendous impetus from an entirely unexpected source with the advent of the railroad. The problem of transportation was solved and an immense new national market had been opened.

In England, as mines grew deeper, the winding or lifting of coal to the surface of the earth from mine bottoms became more difficult. In early times the coal was carried up ladders by the miners themselves; later it was wound up in baskets by "whim gins" worked by horses. Then came James Watt's rotary engine, which was first used for winding coal at the deep Walker colliery in 1784.

Water had been another problem in the English mines from the earliest times and had limited the depths to which mines could be sunk. Then came Thomas Newcomen with his first steam pump built at Wolverhampton in 1711—the pump which contained the germ of the idea for the first steam engine. Thus an efficient pump for draining water inside the mines appeared.

A third difficulty in the British mines was that of hauling coal from the face or working area of the mine to the pit bottom. This had to be done by hand or by back-breaking human labour, or by animal power. George Stephenson's steam pump (1812), however, enabled tubs of coal to be pulled to the bottom of the pit shaft. Thus, Newcomen, Watt and Stephenson helped revolutionize early coal mining.

II. TYPES AND METHODS OF COAL MINING

There are two general methods of mining coal: underground or deep mining; and surface or opencut (sometimes called strip) mining. The latter method is used when the coal bed lies near the surface of the earth, where the thickness of the so-called overburden of the earth and rock atop the coal permits it to be stripped away by giant power shovels, and the coal seam or coal bed is wide or deep enough to justify tearing up the surface of the land covering the coal. More often than not such land is submarginal, of no great agricultural value, and the coal deposits are of much greater economic value. Of the strip or surface mines, more will be said later in this article.

Underground mining is of three types, depending on the nature of the terrain, the thickness of the coal seam or vein and on whether the coal is embedded in a hilly or a mountainous country or in flat areas. These are shaft mines, drift mines and slope mines. The following is a general description of the various types of underground mines and the methods of extracting coal from the earth.

In the shaft mine, at least two vertical shafts are sunk into the earth. One brings the coal to the surface and transports the miners, by means of "cage," "skip" or elevator (U.S.), or "lift" (England), from the top entrance to the working floor of the mine and from one level of the vertical shaft to the other. The second shaft is used to draw fresh air into the working area below by a fan located at the top of this shaft; and to expel the foul air drawn up from below. Depths of shaft mines vary greatly in different parts of the world, depending upon the richness of the deposits and the extent of underground workings. The average depth of shaft mines in the United States is about 190 ft., and the deepest mine known in the states at mid-20th century was that of the Gallup Gamerco company in McKinley county, N.M.—839 feet. Average depth of shaft mines in Great Britain is 1,167 ft., and the deepest mine known there at mid-century was 4,200 ft.

In a slope mine, the opening is made by a bore that goes down to the coal seams on a gradual incline. These mines are not as deep as the shaft mines but the underground workings extend horizontally for great distances, sometimes for many miles.

The outcrop in a drift mine is reached either by a tunnel or a horizontal bore into the side of the hill.

Whereas in shaft mines the worker is taken down in "skips," he reaches the working area of a drift mine by being carried in trains of mine cars—designated in the U.S. "man-trips"—pulled by especially designed electric locomotives. If the grade is a gentle one in a slope mine, the miners are transported in the same way as in the drift mine. In some slope mines trips are moved by a cable operated by a hoist or windlass which pulls them to the surface and keeps them from going downgrade too fast. The difference between transportation in a drift mine as compared with a slope mine is that between the use of a more or less level tunnel driven into the coal seam from the side of the hill, using, as in the case of the slope mine, an inclined entry driven from the surface down to the coal seam.

The thickness of coal seams underground varies greatly. China is said to have the world's largest coal bed—400 ft. in thickness. Two seams in Wyoming are 90 ft. or more in thickness. Other seams in North America are 40 and 50 ft. thick but the average thickness in bituminous mines is 5.4 ft. The bulk of bituminous coal in the United States, by far the most prevalent, is taken from seams varying from 3 to 10 ft. in thickness. A few U.S. coal seams, only 18 in. in thickness, have bituminous value in them sufficiently great to justify underground mining. Anthracite beds in Pennsylvania vary in thickness as mined from approximately 3 ft. or slightly less to the Mammoth mine in the southern Pennsylvania field, with a thickness of 29 ft. 1 in. The majority of the anthracite coal beds are 4, 5 and 6 ft.; the deepest is 1,300 ft. Generally speaking, anthracite seams are deeper, thinner and more frequently broken than those of bituminous. In Great Britain thickness of seams runs from 2.9 ft. to 5.4 ft., the general average being approximately 4 ft.

Methods of Underground Mining.—In the United States almost nine-tenths of the coal is removed from underground mines by the *room-and-pillar method*. About 50% or more of the coal is recovered by this method in the first working. The rooms are dug out adjacent to the main gallery or entry. The coal is mined in these rooms which are separated by narrow ribs or pillars.

Wooden props or pillars are left to support the roof. The rooms are dug systematically like the blocks and alleys of a city, and the tunnels extending to the rooms lead along the seam of coal. The coal in the pillars is won by subsequent working, which may be likened to top slicing, in which the roof is caved in successive blocks.

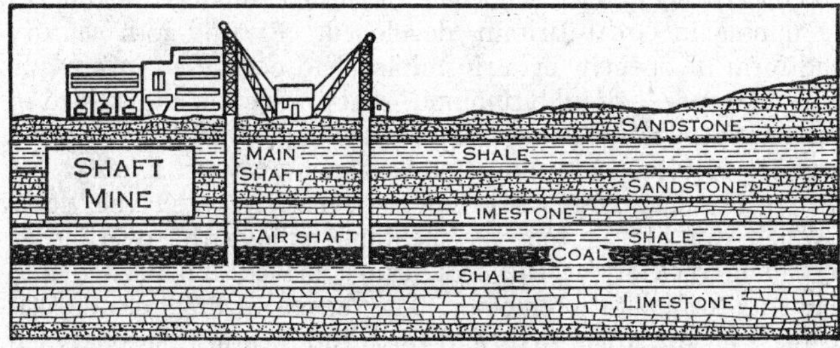

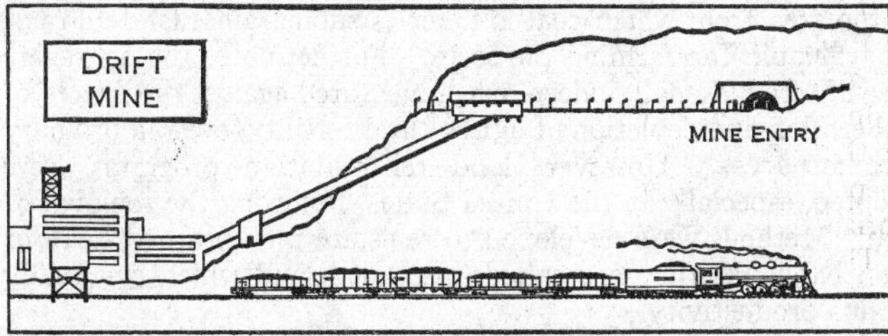

BY COURTESY OF THE BITUMINOUS COAL INSTITUTE

FIG. 1.—TYPES OF COAL MINES

The first working in rooms is an advancing and the winning of the rib, or pillar, by a retreating method. Rooms are driven parallel with one another and the room faces may be extended parallel, at right angles or at an angle to the dip. Once the pillars of coal have been removed the roof is allowed to fall in. The removal of these pillars is important because some of them may be 50 to 80 ft. in thickness and if they were not removed about one-third of the coal would be lost. These masses of coal, some of them as long as the rooms which they help to hold up while the miners are working inside, are taken away systematically; *i.e.*, the pillars farthest from the mine opening are removed first and those nearest the portal last.

In the second underground means of removing coal—the *longwall* or *pillar-and-breast* technique, the working places are rectangular rooms usually five or ten times as long as they are broad, opened on the upper side of the gangway. The breasts, usually from 5 to 12 yd. wide, vary with the character of the roof. The rooms or breasts are separated by pillars of solid coal, broken by small cross headings driven for ventilation, from 5 to 10 or 12 yd. wide. The pillar is actually a solid wall of coal separating the working places. When the object is to obtain all the coal that can be recovered as quickly as possible the pillars are left thin. Where this plan is likely to cause a crush or squeeze that may seriously injure the mine larger pillars are left.

After the mine has been worked out, the pillars are removed by mining from them, until the roof comes down and prevents further working.

In the mines of Great Britain this method of extracting coal underground is called the *bord-and-pillar* system and there are modifications of the system both in England and America, in the pillar-and-stall, post-and-stall, single and double stall, wide or square work, rearer workings, etc. In the longwall system, popular in England, the whole seam is taken out and no pillars left except the shaft pillars and sometimes the main-road pillars. This system, too, has its variations.

Mechanization.—By mid-20th century, the United States had achieved by all odds the greatest amount of mechanization in the mining of coal. Ninety-one per cent of all bituminous coal mined underground was cut mechanically, and 64% of the loading was done mechanically, with the percentage constantly increasing. Cleaning and sizing were mechanized. Electric machines to undercut coal often took slices seven inches thick and six to nine feet back under the bottom of the seam, thus permitting the coal to break up more easily when the explosive was discharged. Mechanical loading machines, some able to load a five-ton car in less than one minute, performed the work which used to take a miner several hours of hand labour to do. Small electric locomotives hauled the loaded coal cars, in trains of 50 or more cars, to the bottom of the shaft. In some mines, conveyor belts did the entire job of moving the coal from the working face all the way to the mine exterior. Some of these belts, carrying the coal from one huge unit to another, could transport coal as many as 15 mi. inside a large mine before delivering it outside to the tipple. These conveyor belts took the place of the underground train of cars.

Wooden man-trip cars, employed to take miners to their working places in slope or drift mines, from the side of the hill or mountain, were being replaced by all-steel cars, electrically operated, carefully roofed and carrying 38 men each. Some of these cars travelled five miles or more underground, each way, from the portal entrance to the face, in reaching the working area. U.S. mines had more than 250,000 mi. of underground track for these cars.

One of the first tasks in taking coal from the face is that of boring blast holes in the solid coal. A mobile electric drill does this work. The miner does not hold the drill; it is suspended from a boom, somewhat like a dentist's drill, and the workman swings it easily to the place where it is needed. Nor does he have to carry the drill anywhere. Both drill and boom are mounted on an electric mine locomotive which can travel everywhere in the mine. It can cut holes at any elevation for the eventual placing of the shots that will break down the coal and its wide swing allows it to be operated easily either horizontally or vertically.

Cutting machines, like the electric drills, may be rubber-mounted or run on tracks. The use of this huge electric mechanism for making advance cutting allows for expansion when the coal is later blasted loose from the seam. This coal cutter has an endless chain with projecting bits which chew out a deep channel in the coal face. First a horizontal cut is made, then a vertical slot will be cut near the centre, after which, the face is ready to be shot fired.

Before any blasting is done, the electric drill puts a series of holes into the coal preparatory to tamping permissible explosives into the holes. To prevent the danger of sparks, a wooden tamper is used to shove the explosive home. Afterward, the firing will crumble the coal into large pieces which are removed later by a loading machine. The modern coal mine shovel, a crocodilelike contraption with headlamps for eyes, is one type of mechanical loader used in U.S. mines. Its teeth, revolving toward the centre of its mouth, pick up the loose coal and pile it onto a conveyor belt which carries the coal back over the head of the machine and into a waiting coal car. A single machine like this is capable of loading up to six tons of coal each minute.

Instead of using explosives, many U.S. mines do the shooting by the sudden release of compressed air. In the Airdox system a miner inserts a cylinder into the hole made by the drilling machine, into which air at 10,000 lb. per square inch pressure is compressed. Once the compressed air is released within the face, its gentle breaking effect on the coal assures a larger range of grades or sizes and at the same time provides a safety factor in the blasting process.

With two-thirds of U.S. underground loading done by machinery at mid-20th century, the hand loading of coal was rapidly going out of fashion. A tire-mounted engine transfers the broken coal rapidly to a rear conveyor. It then loads the coal swiftly into the mine car which is then pulled away by a locomotive or another "shuttle-buggy," and an empty car automatically takes its place. Or the broken coal may be dumped onto conveyor belts which move the coal directly to the cleansing plant.

The continuous mining machine, first demonstrated in 1948, replaced the cyclical, step-by-step mining sequence and combined in one continuous operation all of the other steps, using a minimum of manpower. One type produced two tons per minute, although the actual speed varied according to the characteristics of each seam and from mine to mine. It eliminated altogether the drilling and shooting operations, but posed the problem of conveying the coal away fast enough in bulk to the surface or the cleansing plant.

The "coal mole" (trademark "Colmol" of the Jeffrey Manufacturing company) continuously gouges out coal from the solid face without use of the four ordinary mining machines for undercutting, drilling, loading or hand-shovelling. The Colmol, boring forward like a mole in the ground, is powered electrohydraulically and is mounted on caterpillar tractor treads that can be made to meet various heights of the coal seams. On its head are ten revolving cutters, each cutter having four bits. It operates with light fingertip control, and moves steadily and continuously ahead in the solid coal without vibration, often producing a four-ton flow of coal per minute in a four-foot high seam.

Some idea of the extent of mechanization in U.S. coal mining may be gathered from transportation trends in underground work. At mid-century the total track haulage was estimated at 30,000 mi., and approximately 500,000 mine cars and 16,000 locomotives ran on those underground tracks. The average mine had 33 cars for each locomotive. About 750,000 mine cars were in use for underground work. The majority of the locomotives were electric-powered, and the average length of each belt conveyor was about 850 ft. The advantage of a long belt installation lies in the fact that it gives a transportation medium that has natural space conformations to mining, and approaches the goal of a continuous flow of coal from face to tipple or breaker, with a minimum of operating costs. From 40% to 50% of the locomotives used at mid-century were 10 tons or more in size, the trend being toward increasingly larger units. Some manufacturers were making locomotives only in sizes of 15 tons or more, and few storage battery locomotives were used. Many mine companies preferred tandem locomotives for heavy-duty work, the largest of these consisting of two 25-ton locomotives connected in permanent tandem, and equipped with six 120-h.p. motors. Hydraulic and pneumatic braking systems were employed.

III. SURFACE OR STRIP MINING

When coal was first discovered, it lay on the surface of the earth in exposed ledges or outcroppings. In time this fuel was exhausted and man scratched back the earth and followed the coal seams underground. That was the way opencut or surface mining began—so-called because the open cuts or trenches laid the coal seams bare, making it possible for more coal to be removed. It became more and more difficult, however, to remove the masses of overlying dirt, rock and shale, even with horse-drawn or other animal-drawn scrapers, to say nothing of small shovels in the hands of workmen. Coal mining thereafter had to be carried on underground, in tunnels driven into the hillsides, or eventually by huge bores tunnelled straight down into the earth within which miners could be hauled down and up again. It did not take long for early underground miners to learn the dangers of mining coal that lay too close to the surface. Unless there was a solid rock roof above them which could be propped up while they were digging the coal, the tops of these tunnels would cave in. Thus shafts were dug; still deeper veins were reached and great buried coal resources were revealed. But there were still left millions of tons of surface coal—too close to the earth's exterior to mine safely from underground and yet too deeply embedded to be reached with the simple tools and slight equipment available to miners. Thus opencut or surface mining, called opencast mining in Great Britain, developed. By mid-20th century some form of opencut or strip mining had been used in 20 U.S. states; about 23% of all bituminous coal production and a third of anthracite production came from surface mines. In Great Britain about 5% of total coal production was from opencast mining.

In strip mining, large power-operated mechanical shovels, some of which can lift 35 tons at one bite, remove the overburden (earth and rock above the coal seam), drilled and blasted into fragments to facilitate removal. The shovels or draglines deposit this mass of limestone, shale and earth and rock in ridges paralleling the contour of the outcroppings of the coal. Once this overburden is removed and set aside, the surface of the exposed coal seam is cleaned by mechanical scrapers and revolving brushes. A smaller mechanical loading shovel with a capacity of five tons picks up the coal and deposits it in motor trucks or railroad cars which transport the mine-run coal to the cleansing and sorting plants, tipple or breaker—depending on the type of coal—where it goes through a final process.

Rehabilitation of Land Following Surface Mining.—Surface or strip mining necessarily overhauls the landscape. Most of the area from which coal is taken is submarginal land and not too valuable for farming purposes. Furthermore, the aggregate area affected is small, indeed, when measured against the effects of soil erosion and depletion of agricultural fertility, even in ordinary farming areas. However, land rehabilitation programs were adopted, especially in the United States, following the removal of coal. Methods were developed to reinstate the upturned earth or spoil banks, as they are called, into good land which eventually attains productivity.

About 190,000 ac. of land had been surface mined of coal by mid-20th century in Arkansas, Kansas. Illinois, Indiana, Iowa, Kentucky, Missouri, Ohio, Oklahoma and Alabama. Of this total, 56,000 ac. supported satisfactory stands of grasses, shrubs and legumes. About 52,000 ac. had natural or planted forests, and about 5% of the acreage represented soils too toxic for revegetating properly.

IV. COAL MINING IN GREAT BRITAIN

Special Methods of British Mining.—No two collieries are exactly alike in British coal mines. Most of the coal seams are "pitching," that is, they are not horizontal or flat as are many of the seams in U.S. mines, but run up and down hill. Several coal seams are often found, one atop the other, and in many instances each seam has a different quality of coal. The United States has multiple coal seams in some of its mines; but generally speaking, because of its greater wealth of coal, only the more convenient seam is mined, whereas in Britain the attempt is made to get all of the coal out once an area is reached. Seams are much thinner than in the United States and depths of mines are much greater. Because of the greater depth (many are below the normal water level), English mines are drier than those of the U.S.

Since each colliery presents its own problems of production, according to the thickness of seam, inclination and depth from the surface, type of roof and floor and proximity to other workings, no general statement can be laid down about the common or usual method of producing coal in all British mines. Different machinery from that employed in the U.S. must be employed. The use of compressed air for running locomotives, picks and practically all of the mining machinery underground is common to the British mines, although electricity was beginning to be used at mid-20th century.

As mentioned earlier, the most general method for producing coal in Britain is by longwall working. The second is the bord-and-pillar or pillar-and-stall system.

Because of the pitching seams in British mines, production by longwall working proved the easiest. Graham R. Bamber in his "Coal Mining and Miners Today," included in *The Secrets of Other People's Jobs* (Odham's Press Ltd., London, 1944), describes both methods as follows:

We keep a coal face, perhaps 200 yards long, which advances a fixed distance each day—it might be anything up to 6 ft.—and a collier is stationed at intervals to win and fill out the coal.

Main Gate Road.

The coal is brought away down a main gate road, leading from the middle of the face, and at each end of the face another road called a tail gate affords an alternative means of exit, allows for materials to be taken to the face, and provides for a ventilating circuit up through the gate road, along the face, and back through the tail gates and return roads. The other method is called bord-and-pillar working, and is used in broken, difficult ground and when mining under built-up areas. The seam is cut up by a series of longitudinal and transverse roads into squares, something like a gigantic chessboard, and these squares, or pillars, are then stripped as far as possible, but leaving enough coal to support the roof. This coal, of course, is lost if the surface has to be supported above, but the pillars are removed in strips and the surface let down if the support is not required.

In the bord-and-pillar (also called pillar-and-breast) system, the narrow roads or headings at the bottom of the underground mine are cut at right angles from the main road of the floor of the mine, and at intervals of about 100 yd. from each other. Twenty yards up a heading a miner begins to open his stall; another miner does the same 20 yd. farther on. Both men make the opening from the heading very narrow at first. Gradually they broaden it out toward each other until the two stalls meet. Behind them, standing between the two entrances is a block of coal called the pillar. This is left as a support for the roof.

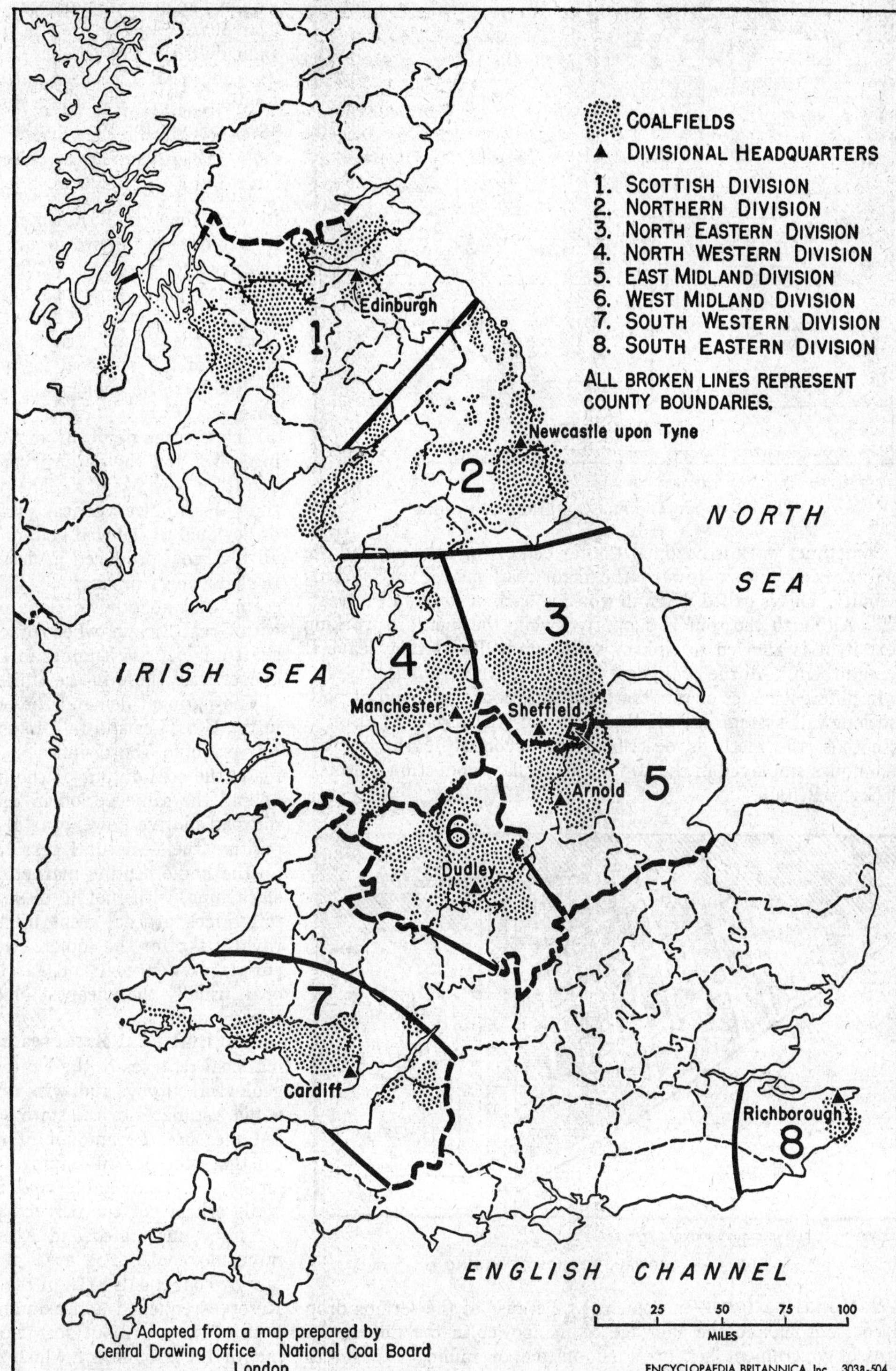

FIG. 2.—THE BRITISH COALFIELDS: PLAN SHOWING THE DIVISIONS OF BRITAIN'S NATIONAL COAL BOARD

Side by side in their stalls the two miners work forward, each cutting a breadth of ten yards of coal from the face. They work on like this for 50 yd., no farther, because 100 yd. down the main road is another heading from which other miners are working stalls toward them. On one side of the one man, between his stall and the main road, is a block of coal 20 yd. thick. There is a similar block of coal on the far side of the other man, between him and the next pair of stalls. Each miner now begins to cut away ten yards' breadth of this coal, working backward toward the entrance of his stall. The two men do this until they are level with the pillar left between the entrances. Thus, between the entrance of one stall and that of another stall stands a pillar of coal 20 yd. broad and of about the same thickness.

In the longwall method of underground mining, the headings are not cut at right angles from the main roads but are made diagonally. When a heading has been made from the road, a miner starts work at the corner where the road and heading meet. As he cuts away the coal he supports the roof behind him with props, and also with piles or chocks of the rock and shale which come away with the coal. Meanwhile narrow roads called gates have been cut at intervals, connecting the heading with the main road. In these gates other men set to work; as each man works forward he comes in time to the gate in front of him, where he stops. In this method of work all the coal is got out at once, and no pillars are left as is the case in the bord-and-pillar method.

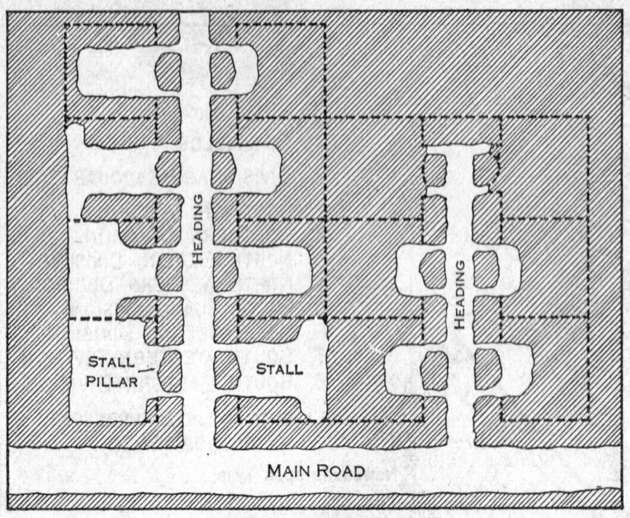

BY COURTESY OF THE OXFORD UNIVERSITY PRESS

FIG. 3.—BORD-AND-PILLAR METHOD OF MINING

Sometimes work is begun at the far end of the heading, and the men work backward toward the main road instead of working from it. This is called longwall working back or long wall retreating. Although the roof is supported while the men are working near it, it is allowed to sink or settle gradually as they leave it behind them. All the coal is got out at once in this method.

In different mines or pits there are variations employed of both the longwall system and of the bord-and-pillar system. But in essentials, the methods described above constitute the general techniques employed in the two most popular production methods in Great Britain.

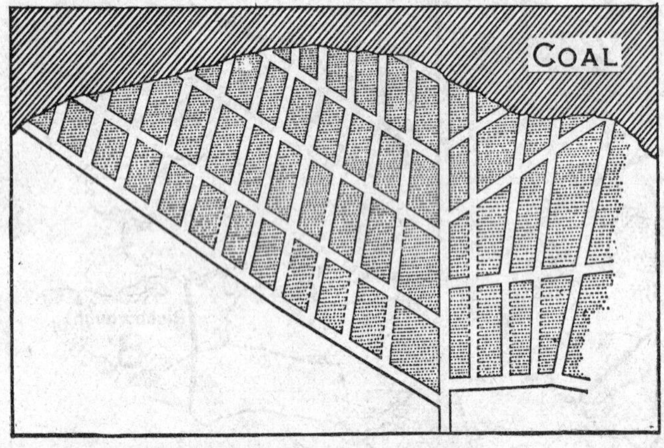

BY COURTESY OF THE OXFORD UNIVERSITY PRESS

FIG. 4.—LONGWALL METHOD OF MINING

Nationalization.—In Sept. 1944, because of the serious drop in coal output and the shortage of manpower in the mines, the British government set up a committee of mining experts to recommend means of bringing the mines up to full efficiency. The Reid committee report, published in March 1945, dealt only with technical problems, but it was clear that if the committee's plans for modernizing the mines and putting the best kinds of mechanization into them were to be carried out, the whole industry would have to be reorganized. The government approved all the proposals of the committee. On July 12, 1946, the Nationalization of Coal Mines act was passed, and on Jan. 1, 1947, about 1,500 British collieries formerly owned by about 800 private organizations or individuals were taken over by the newly constituted National Coal board.

The whole country was divided into eight divisions and 48 areas. Each area averaged more than 4,000,000 long tons output of coal per year. The coal board, located in London, consisted of a chairman, a deputy chairman and various members representing labour, finance, manpower, reconstruction and planning, etc. The board altogether comprised nine persons. In each of the eight divisions there was a divisional board with its chairman and its functional directors patterned after the national board in London. In each of the eight divisions there was a general manager, responsible to the divisional board.

V. COAL MINING IN THE UNITED STATES

Mineable seams in the United States vary in thickness from 2 to more than 90 ft., but most production comes from seams 3 to 6 ft. thick. In the two foremost coal states, the seams at mid-20th century averaged 5.2 ft. (West Virginia) and 5 ft. (Pennsylvania). Montana, with America's thickest coal seams, averaged 16.8 ft., and Wyoming had 12.8 ft., with one mine in the latter state having a 90-ft. coal seam. Seams of great thickness are not always the sources of the best coal for power purposes, however. The coals are likely to be geologically young and inferior for heating purposes.

The average depth of vertical shafts in U.S. underground mining is 190 ft.; the deepest vertical shaft at mid-20th century was 839 ft. in New Mexico. The predominant type of mine opening in the U.S. is not a vertical shaft but rather a slope entry, inclined or declined to the coal bed, or a drift entry. About one-fourth of all U.S. coal produced in deep mines came from mines with vertical openings or shafts. This portion increases only when the seams best adapted to slope mining are exhausted, as is the case with Great Britain, where practically all coal mined is produced at shaft mines. Shaft mines in Britain, as has been noted, are much deeper than those in the United States, averaging 1,167 ft.

The national demand for both bituminous and anthracite coal in the U.S. rises and falls in conformance with general prosperity. For example, the disinflation of 1949, added to work stoppages, made the coal output of the first six months of 1949 about 10% behind the same period in the year preceding. Dieselization of railroad motive power was also having its obvious effect. Competitive fuels—natural gas, oil, etc.—were making their inroads on the home heating market, and general industrial activity was slackening, with fuel oil in supply at substantial price cuts. Retail prices of coal went up because of increased wages and a royalty tax for the miners' welfare fund. Thus the price differential between coal and gas became progressively smaller, with coal, usually the cheapest of all fuels, beginning to lose its economic advantage.

Original Coal Reserves by States.—Table II, showing original coal reserves in the United States by states, is based on U.S. geological surveys and, with respect to West Virginia and Pennsylvania, estimates of the state geological surveys. These figures do not measure the amount of coal that would be recoverable by existing methods of mining. Some scientists estimate that the amount of recoverable coal is 50% of the estimated reserves, while others put the percentage figure even lower.

Thirty one states and Alaska have deposits of commercially mineable coal. The area of continental United States underlain by coal equals 11% of the total area or roughly 340,000 sq.mi. Reserves equalled approximately 21,000 tons per capita at mid-20th century. About 29,332,000,000 tons of coal had been taken out of the ground, of which 23,459,000,000 tons (83.4%) were bituminous and 4,873,000,000 tons (16.6%) were anthracite. For each ton removed, there remained 104 tons still in the earth, including that in suspended or worked-out mines, on the basis of the deceptively large geologically inferred reserves.

Coal at mid-century was the largest in physical volume among all U.S. commodities, representing also the largest single item (one-third) of railroad freight haulage. Its total tonnage was approximately three times that of U.S. grain crops, and five times that of iron ore. Annual dollar value of mined coal exceeded the aggregate of iron ore, gold, silver, zinc, lead and other metals.

In 1860 the U.S. was producing 20,000,000 tons of coal a year, almost half being anthracite for home heating. Production almost doubled thereafter in each decade and was 111,000,000 tons in 1890; it doubled again to 212,000,000 tons in 1900. A 1918 output of 580,000,000 tons of bituminous lapsed to 569,-

000,000 tons in 1920 but in 1944, during World War II, the bituminous output reached a new high of 620,000,000 tons, which was exceeded in 1947 by another record of 631,000,000 tons. U.S. anthracite production reached a high of 62,181,409 tons in 1944.

Number of Men and Days Worked.—In 1920, 9,000 U.S. bituminous mines employed 640,000 miners; the industry expanded until in 1923 the mining force was 705,000 men. In 1948 the bituminous mines employed 435,000 and the anthracite approximately 75,000. The declining trend of the labour force was due primarily to replacement of manual labour by machines.

In 1935–39, the average number of days worked per year was 182; during the wartime emergency of 1944 this number rose to 278. In 1946 the figure was 214 days; in 1947, 234; in 1948, 210; and in 1949, 188. Strikes called by the miners' union in 1948 and 1949 accounted for the falling-off in working days during these years.

Preparing Coal for Market.—In earlier days, before surface preparation plants for cleaning, sizing and washing coal came into vogue, the consumer received his coal as it came from the mine; labourers who did the loading underground picked out such impurities as shale which caught their eyes. This run-of-the-mine coal was a conglomerate mass of fines, small, medium and large, as they emerged from the mine and were loaded into railroad cars without any sorting or any processing. When loading machines came into use, the process of dumping coal into railroad cars was speeded up, and most if not all of the impurities stayed in.

Different types of consumers and varying types of coal-burning mechanisms inevitably began demanding particular sizes of coal.

The density of coal is less than that of the rocky impurities embedded in it. Natural impurities can be removed therefore in large part by gravity processes. In the case of underground mines, certain types of hoisting machines lift the coal from the bottom of the shaft to the surface. One of the most common hoisters is shaped like a cylinder and cone. In this type the skip for hoisting coal and the cage which takes the miners up and down are balanced to equalize the load on the electric motor as the cable is winding on the drum. Seven or more tons can be handled on the skip in a single trip. Some of these hoists reach a speed of 3,000 ft. per minute. Powerful hydraulic brakes operate automatically in case of accidental shutoff of power. In drift mines, trains sometimes numbering 40 to 60 or more cars are hauled by locomotives to the preparation plant. In a slope mine the cars may be discharged on a conveyor belt for removal to the outside or may be pulled up the slope with

Table II.—*Original Coal Reserves in the U.S. by States*
(Millions of tons)

State	Estimated original reserves					Production 1800–1948*	Remaining in ground†	
	Bituminous	Sub-bituminous	Lignite	Anthracite	Total		Jan. 1, 1949	Per cent
Alabama	67,570	0	0	0	67,570	808.3	66,761.7	98.8
Arkansas	1,396	0	90	230	1,716	90.8	1,625.2	94.7
Colorado	213,071	104,175	0	100	317,346	466.5	316,879.5	99.8
Illinois	201,400	0	0	0	201,400	3,085.3	198,314.7	98.5
Indiana	53,051	0	0	0	53,051	965.4	52,085.6	98.2
Iowa	29,160	0	0	0	29,160	341.5	28,818.5	98.8
Kansas	30,000	0	0	0	30,000	264.7	29,735.3	99.1
Kentucky	123,327	0	0	0	123,327	1,892.8	121,434.2	98.5
Maryland	8,043	0	0	0	8,043	259.3	7,783.7	96.8
Michigan	2,000	0	0	0	2,000	46.5	1,953.5	97.7
Missouri	84,000	0	0	0	84,000	255.0	83,745.0	99.7
Montana	2,655	62,985	315,474	0	381,114	154.4	380,959.6	99.9
New Mexico	18,925	1,906	0	3	20,834	120.5	20,713.5	99.4
North Dakota	0	0	600,000	0	600,000	64.7	599,935.3	99.9
Ohio	93,967	0	0	0	93,967	1,661.6	92,305.4	98.2
Oklahoma	54,951	0	0	0	54,951	155.8	54,795.2	99.7
Pennsylvania (anthracite)	0	0	0	23,263	23,263	4,873.3	18,389.7	79.1
Pennsylvania (bituminous)	75,094	0	0	0	75,094	7,323.6	67,770.4	90.2
South Dakota	0	0	1,020	0	1,020	0.9	1,019.1	99.9
Tennessee	25,665	0	0	0	25,665	320.1	25,344.9	98.8
Texas	8,000	0	23,000	0	31,000	62.0	30,938.0	99.8
Utah	88,184	5,156	0	0	93,340	192.7	93,147.3	99.8
Virginia	21,149	0	0	500	21,649	536.4	21,112.6	97.5
Washington	11,413	52,442	0	23	63,878	142.0	63,736.0	99.8
West Virginia	116,705	0	0	0	116,705	4,855.0	111,850.0	95.8
Wyoming	30,563	590,160	0	0	620,723	357.7	620,365.3	99.9
Other States	1,698	1,757	10	0	3,465	34.3	3,430.7	99.0
Total	1,361,987	818,581	939,594	24,119	3,144,281	29,331.1	3,114,949.9	99.1

*Based on estimates made by Howard N. Eavenson, *The First Century and a Quarter of American Coal Industry*, 1800–1885; U.S. Bureau of Mines, 1886–1948. †Including pillars left and coal lost in worked-out mines.

Table III.—*Coal Production per Man-day in the U.S. Compared with Other Countries, 1924-48*
(Net tons)

Year	United States				Canada*	Great Britain†	Germany‡	Poland‡	Belgium‡	Czechoslovakia‡	France§	Netherlands‡	Sweden‖
	Bituminous			Anthracite									
	Surface mines	Underground Mines	Total										
1924	9.91	4.50	4.56	2.00	2.40	0.99	NA	0.76	0.50	0.84	0.62	0.82	NA
1925	11.18	4.45	4.52	2.12	2.46	1.01	NA	1.03	0.52	0.90	0.64	0.92	NA
1926	11.13	4.42	4.50	2.09	2.51	1.03	NA	1.23	0.56	1.07	0.67	1.09	NA
1927	11.06	4.47	4.55	2.15	2.45	1.15	NA	1.31	0.57	1.10	0.67	1.12	NA
1928	13.02	4.61	4.73	2.17	2.45	1.19	NA	1.40	0.61	1.12	0.72	1.28	NA
1929	14.08	4.73	4.85	2.17	2.46	1.21	1.29	1.39	0.63	1.15	0.76	1.37	0.78
1930	16.21	4.93	5.06	2.21	2.45	1.21	1.35	1.38	0.63	1.13	0.76	1.37	0.90
1931	17.68	5.12	5.30	2.37	2.50	1.21	1.45	1.51	0.65	1.17	0.79	1.44	1.05
1932	16.95	4.99	5.22	2.54	2.58	1.23	1.56	1.55	0.67	1.18	0.86	1.59	1.25
1933	13.59	4.60	4.78	2.60	2.64	1.26	1.63	1.75	0.73	1.29	0.92	1.72	1.54
1934	13.28	4.23	4.40	2.53	2.62	1.29	1.64	1.88	0.81	1.33	0.95	1.86	1.66
1935	12.01	4.32	4.50	2.68	2.58	1.31	1.63	1.96	0.85	1.48	0.96	1.99	1.66
1936	13.91	4.42	4.62	2.79	2.64	1.32	1.67	2.03	0.88	1.49	0.95	2.01	1.73
1937	NA	NA	4.69	2.77	2.60	1.31	1.65	2.01	0.86	1.60	0.92	1.96	1.66
1938	15.00	4.60	4.89	2.79	2.67	1.28	NA	2.00	0.83	1.23	0.92	1.81	1.61
1939	14.68	4.92	5.25	3.02	2.74	1.28	NA	NA	0.85	1.21	0.95	1.63	1.79
1940	15.63	4.86	5.19	3.02	2.78	1.23	NA	NA	0.83	1.15	0.87	1.41	1.86
1941	15.59	4.83	5.20	3.04	2.74	1.20	NA	NA	0.77	1.09	0.81	1.38	1.51
1942	15.52	4.74	5.12	2.95	2.80	1.18	NA	NA	0.71	1.03	0.78	NA	1.33
1943	15.15	4.89	5.38	2.78	2.67	1.15	NA	NA	0.65	0.97	0.73	NA	1.29
1944	15.89	5.04	5.67	2.79	2.57	1.12	NA	NA	0.53	0.88	0.60	NA	1.69
1945	15.46	5.04	5.78	2.79	2.68	1.12	Br. Zone Fr. Zone	NA	0.58	0.77	0.61	NA	1.46
1946	15.73	5.43	6.30	2.84	2.82	1.15	0.95 0.92	1.18	0.62	1.02	0.66	1.04	1.32
1947	15.93	5.49	6.42	2.78	3.30	1.20	1.02 0.96	1.34	0.64	1.19	0.65	1.26	NA
¶1948	15.28	5.31	6.26	2.81	3.36	1.24	1.06 0.84	1.46	0.66	1.20	0.66	1.50	NA

Production per man-day in Australia in 1948 was 3.35 net tons for black coal only. No data are available prior to 1948. Production per man, per month in Japan in 1948 was 6.89 net tons.

*Includes surface mining. †Underground mines only. ‡Hard coal only. §Includes brown coal prior to June 1947; hard coal only in recent period. ‖Low-grade coal. ¶Reduction due to strikes. NA—no available information.

Source: U.S., Bureau of Mines; Canada, Dominion Bureau of Statistics; Great Britain, Ministry of Fuel and Power; Europe, United Nations; Australia, Joint Coal Board.

a rope and hoist. Coal produced by surface or strip mining may be taken by truck or train to the near-by processing plant.

In anthracite mining, the cleansing or preparation plant is called a breaker, in bituminous a tipple. The former got its name from the fact that coal is broken, sized and cleaned there; the latter because cars filled with coal are tippled or dumped to the top of the cleansing plant. Inside the tipple or breaker many types of machines clean, wash and break the run-of-the-mine coal and separate rock, slag, slate and other impurities. Washing devices may be in the general form of inverted cones, inclined troughs, or tanks divided into a number of cells or compartments called jigs. In the cone method the separating media are sand and water. The coal floats off the surface while the slate, rock and other impurities, impelled by gravity, sink to the bottom. In the jig method raw coal is fed into the washer, which is filled with water, while compressed air comes up from the bottom to agitate the mass. This causes the material to separate into layers of different densities; the flow of compressed air is regulated so that the heavier refuse sinks to the bottom of the washer, while the clean coal and the middlings or secondary grades come out at the top. The middlings are as carefully prepared as the best grades. They are conveyed to other washers for further cleaning and the clean coal is then conveyed to shaking screens where it is separated into various sizes for the market.

For obtaining the finer sizes of coal, a table method is used. The raw coal is fed to the end of a sloping reciprocating table and becomes separated, because of its specific gravity, as it moves across the table in a medium of water and rising compressed air. In the water processing of coal, the coal floats as the impurities sink in what is called the wet process of cleaning. Chemicals are often used in the water to render the separation more efficient. In the dry cleaning process, air currents are used in lieu of water.

In the wet method, larger lumps travel over picking tables where skilled sorters remove rock and slate. Shaking screens of various mesh sizes separate the coal into standard sizes. An average of ten tons of water is used for each ton of prepared coal. The shaker screens are a series of perforated plates, one over the other, with the upper plate having the largest perforations and the smallest in the bottom plate. The holes in these shaker screens are of different sizes; in the case of anthracite coal, for example, are the following commercial sizes: grate, broken, egg, stove, nut, pea, buckwheat, rice, barley, no. 4 and no. 5, in the order of largest to smallest. No. 5 anthracite has a test mesh round of $\frac{3}{64}$ in.

In bituminous industries following World War II, tipples with modern types of cleansing and washing machinery began producing coals tailored to suit particular fuel needs. In anthracite breakers were large grinding machines, in which huge steel rolls broke the cleansed coal into the proper sizes for customer needs, from grate coal to the smaller sizes used for steam purposes. After cleansing and sorting, some mines spray the coal with oil to decrease dust. A company may trade-mark its coal with a colouring matter or by some other method.

In 1936 only about 26% of U.S. bituminous production came from mines having cleaning plants, ten years later the proportion had grown to 37%, with the technique constantly improving. The relationship of mechanical loading to the cleaning plant was apparent from the fact that in 1947 about 53% of all bituminous machine-loaded underground passed through plants equipped with mechanical cleaning devices. Only 18% of hand-loaded bituminous coal underwent that process. In 1947 about 30% of the strip mine tonnage had access to the most modernized cleaning plant facilities.

At mid-20th century there were about 2,200 coal trade names, many registered in the United States patent office; others were registered in the form of a design on booklets and stationery. Some sample trade names were as follows: Anchor Coal; Aztec; Beacon; Big Horn; Black Diamond; Blu-Glo; Black Beauty; Champion; Chanticleer; Chinook; Clinchfield; Colored Coal (red); Consol; Diamond Glo; Dixie Star; Enos; Everglow; Fire Chief; Glocoal; Green (colour); Grey Eagle; Hanna; Hedlite; Hiawatha; Imperial; Inferno; Jewell Pocahontas; Kentucky Jewell; Kincaid; Lehigh Valley; Lone Star; Maiden; Majestic; Marianna; Maumee; Meltwell; Monarch; Mountaineer; Natona; Norseman; Old Abe; Old Ben; Orient; Pilot; Pine Valley; Power King; Premium; Quick Heat; Randall; Raven; Red (colour); Red Cedar; Red Ember; Red Head; Red Jacket; Roberta; Royal Smokeless; Ruby Glow; Scarlet Flame; Silver Shield; Sky Chief; Southern Belle; Stonega; Sun-Glo; Tennessee Jewell; Tiger; Velva; Violet; Virglow; Volunteer; Vulcan; White Flame; Winding Gulf; Wingfoot; Yellow Jacket; Yellow Glo; Zulu.

Transportation.—About four-fifths of all bituminous coal mined in the U.S. is loaded into railroad cars or river barges at the preparation plant. Most of the remaining fifth is loaded into trucks to be transferred to freight cars or barges at sidings or docks. The rest—perhaps one-twentieth of the total—is used at the mine, made into beehive coke or carried on conveyor belts to a nearby place where it is used. Anthracite coal is handled much the same way in the United States as bituminous except that the proportions are different. No anthracite coal leaves its mining areas on river barges.

Historically, the coal and railroad industries had a unique interdependence; each was the other's best customer. Traditionally the railroads were the largest coal-consuming industry, though primacy was later taken by the electric power and light industry.

Movement of coal by truck directly to the consumer increased somewhat in the U.S. during and after World War II. In 1939, about 7.5 tons of 100 produced went to market by truck, whereas in 1947 about 8.9 tons moved by truck, with the percentage in later years somewhat greater. In 1947 about 30,000,000 tons moved from bituminous mines by inland waterways, either from on-the-spot water loading or after intermediate trucking or short distances by rail hauling; in 1939 this proportion was 6%. In 1948 the seagoing movement amounted to 32,000,000 tons of bituminous, of which 14,000,000 were for export. In the same year coal exports via Hampton Roads, Va., were 30% of the total exports to all countries including Canada. Bituminous coal exports through the port of Baltimore, Md., accounted for 8% of the exportation, Philadelphia, Pa., 1%, and New York city only 0.03%. Of the total exported tonnage to Canada, 52% was received via Lake Erie ports. Canada remained the predominant out-of-country consumer of U.S. coal.

About 61,000,000 tons, or 10% of U.S. bituminous output, moved in 1948 over the Great Lakes to markets in the northwest and Canada. About 55,000,000 tons passed through ports along Lake Erie; 4,000,000 tons through Lake Ontario ports and 2,000,000 from Lake Michigan piers. After 1942 the movement through Chicago area ports on Lake Michigan grew substantially. Lake steamers carrying this coal were capable of hauling as many as 13,700 tons of coal in their 35 or more hatches and were sturdy enough to make ocean voyages. Electric unloading shovels at Duluth, Minn., or Superior, Wis., were able to pick up from 8 to 15 tons at one bite. These were emptied into hopper cars or gondolas, moving out with rapidity the moment each was filled, with an empty replacing the loaded car.

Markets.—Consumption of 96,000,000 tons of bituminous coal by U.S. electric utilities comprised 18% of that nation's output in 1948. Steam-generated electricity is produced largely from coal, fuel oil, natural gas, wood and waste. Percentagewise, between 1920 and 1948, coal produced variously from 47.5% (in 1932) to 57.1% (in 1925) of the total generated in the nation. In 1948, the coal proportion was 54.1%. By comparison fuel oil accounted for between 2.4% (in 1927–28) and 6.8% (in 1924); in 1948 it was 5.9%. The proportion fuelled by coal was relatively stable, while natural gas expanded from 1.5% of the nation's total in 1920 to 10.7% in 1948.

The efficiency of coal utilization in electricity generation grew markedly. In 1914 a ton of coal produced an average of 525 kw.hr.; in 1946 a ton produced 1,550 kw.hr.

Consumption of bituminous alone for all purposes by rail

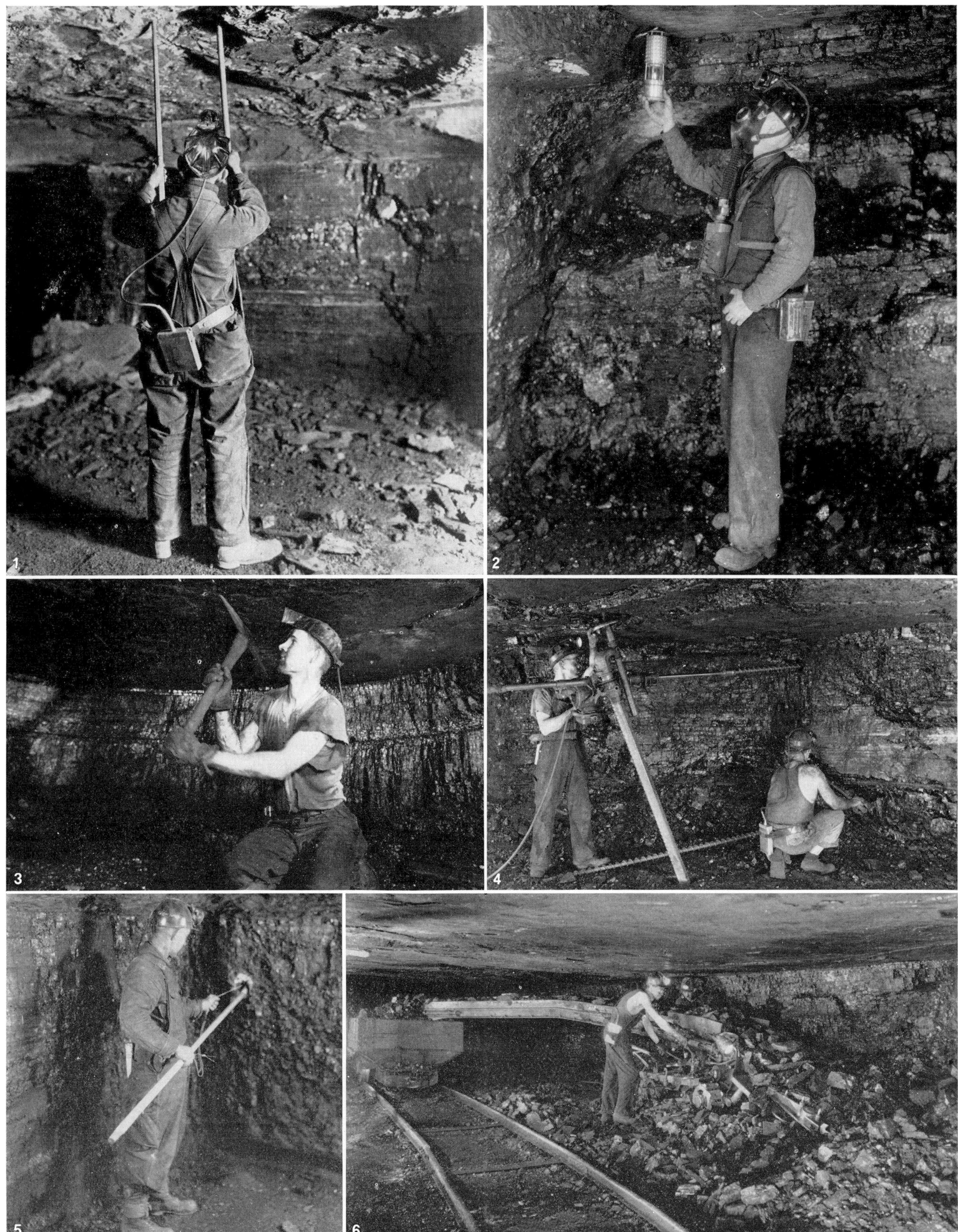

BY COURTESY OF (1, 2, 4-6) BUREAU OF MINES, U.S. DEPARTMENT OF THE INTERIOR; PHOTOGRAPH, (3) PICTORIAL PUBLISHING CO.

OPERATIONS IN COAL MINING

1. Workman testing the roof of a seam
2. Miner equipped with gas mask, testing for explosive gas and for oxygen deficiency
3. Working a low seam with ordinary pick
4. Electric post drill in operation
5. Charging a hole with explosive, using a wood tamping stick
6. Loading machine in operation at a mine face

COAL AND COAL MINING

PHOTOGRAPHS, (1-4) HEYER FROM PICTORIAL PUBLISHING CO., (5, 6) HOBART FROM MONKMEYER

MINING AND TRANSPORTING COAL

1. Assembling timber posts at the tipple of a mine, for use in supporting the mine roof at regular intervals
2. Miner setting a timber post to hold up the roof while a machine cutter waits to operate a giant saw
3. Loaded "man-trip" train taking a shift of miners out of a low-seam mine
4. Motorman of a coal train emerging from a low-seam mine
5. Coal train outside the mine
6. Loading coal into railroad cars

TABLE IV.—*U.S. Markets and Supply of Bituminous Coal, 1920–1948*
(Thousands of net tons)

Year	Electric power utilities	Rail-roads*	High temper-ature coke†	Beehive coke	Coal gas retorts	Steel and rolling mills	Cement mills	Oil re-fineries	Colliery fuel	Other in-dust-rials‡	Retail dealers	Bunker, foreign trade	Total con-sumption	Change in stocks	Produc-tion plus imports minus exports
1920	30,099	135,414	44,205	31,986	NA	NA	NA	NA	11,896	244,509	NA	10,486	508,595	+22,800	531,395
1921	24,830	123,143	28,713	8,475	NA	NA	NA	NA	9,123	189,111	NA	8,453	391,848	+ 2,200	394,048
1922	27,606	127,030	41,053	13,286	NA	NA	NA	NA	7,831	205,494	NA	4,615	426,915	−12,000	414,915
1923	31,696	155,795	54,276	30,084	NA	NA	NA	NA	8,765	233,284	NA	5,093	518,993	+26,000	544,993
1924	30,899	132,754	49,061	15,914	NA	NA	NA	NA	6,618	244,297	NA	4,460	484,003	−17,000	467,003
1925	33,803	132,351	57,110	17,423	NA	NA	NA	6,153	5,776	241,711	NA	4,866	499,193	+ 4,000	503,193
1926	34,823	143,100	63,647	19,224	NA	NA	NA	6,052	5,728	252,271	NA	7,736	532,581	+ 6,000	538,581
1927	36,260	129,722	63,240	11,208	NA	NA	9,778	5,031	4,930	235,067	NA	4,565	499,801	+ 500	500,301
1928	36,163	124,799	70,166	7,018	NA	NA	9,592	3,362	4,602	238,832	NA	4,294	498,828	−13,700	485,128
1929	39,729	131,100	76,759	10,028	NA	NA	9,114	2,300	4,663	241,575	NA	4,287	519,555	− 1,500	518,055
1930	38,130	109,078	65,521	4,284	NA	NA	8,389	1,949	3,993	220,149	NA	3,497	454,990	− 3,100	451,890
1931	34,196	91,701	46,846	1,767	NA	NA	6,233	1,412	3,205	184,314	NA	2,195	371,869	− 1,700	370,169
1932	26,591	75,538	30,887	1,030	NA	NA	3,709	958	2,781	164,073	NA	1,350	306,917	− 5,834	301,083
1933	27,088	75,013	38,681	1,408	NA	NA	2,791	1,069	2,858	171,393	NA	1,316	321,617	+ 3,174	324,791
1934	29,707	79,574	44,343	1,635	2,425	10,898	3,458	1,189	3,175	82,393	86,925	1,321	347,043	+ 1,636	348,679
1935	30,936	80,575	49,046	1,469	2,245	11,747	3,456	1,221	3,103	90,928	83,990	1,576	360,292	+ 2,541	362,833
1936	38,104	91,122	63,244	2,698	1,945	13,471	4,702	1,310	3,227	117,151	84,200	1,622	422,796	+ 5,909	428,705
1937	41,045	94,540	69,575	4,927	1,680	12,853	5,172	1,209	3,052	112,536	80,076	1,832	428,497	+ 4,148	432,645
1938	36,440	79,096	45,266	1,360	1,644	8,412	4,419	722	2,493	94,926	68,520	1,352	344,650	− 6,354	338,296
1939	42,304	84,585	61,216	2,298	1,614	9,808	5,195	742	2,565	96,395	71,570	1,477	379,769	+ 3,851	383,620
1940	49,126	91,047	76,583	4,803	1,746	10,040	5,559	979	2,443	106,798	87,700	1,426	438,250	+ 6,427	444,677
1941	59,888	103,228	82,609	10,529	1,659	10,902	6,735	1,091	2,489	103,827	97,460	1,643	482,060	+11,739	493,799
1942	63,472	122,208	87,974	12,876	1,522	10,434	7,462	1,706	2,708	120,408	104,750	1,585	537,105	+23,152	560,257
1943	74,036	135,760	89,992	12,441	1,436	11,238	5,843	1,831	2,702	134,611	122,764	1,647	594,301	−29,203	565,098
1944	76,656	136,303	94,613	10,858	1,446	10,734	3,717	1,771	2,712	128,384	124,906	1,559	593,659	+ 518	594,177
1945	71,603	129,316	87,542	8,135	1,406	10,084	4,193	1,532	2,442	121,834	121,805	1,785	561,677	−11,539	550,138
1946	68,743	113,000	76,351	7,167	1,240	8,603	6,990	1,718	1,951	103,936	100,586	1,381	491,666	+ 1,492	493,158
1947	86,009	112,819	94,573	10,475	1,095	10,048	7,919	2,273	NA	131,091	99,163	1,689	557,154	+ 5,004	562,158
1948	95,686	99,000	97,326	9,973	897	10,046	8,545	2,449	NA	116,274	89,747	1,057	531,000	+17,000	548,000

*Includes classes I, II, III, switching and terminal facilities, all uses. †Includes a small amount of bituminous coal used in low and medium temperature ovens since 1940. ‡Includes all coal where data are not available. NA—no available information.
Source: Federal Power Commission; Interstate Commerce Commission; U.S. Bureau of Mines; Bureau of the Census.

roads totalled 99,000,000 tons in 1948, or 17% of the national production. The maximum of bituminous coal's importance as railroad locomotive fuel was reached during the first quarter of the 20th century, when it was 86–92% of the total coal equivalent. Oil-burning steam locomotives came into significant usage, and later the diesel-electric. From the 1935–39 period diesel oil use grew from less than 1% to nearly 15% of the total locomotive fuel. For passenger-train service the diesel-electric locomotive has attained a real popularity. To offset this loss by a competing fuel, a coal burning gas turbine locomotive was designed and first demonstrated in June 1949.

Anthracite is used primarily in the United States for home heating purposes. Of the estimated total production of 50,137,000 net tons in 1948–49, 31,995,133 tons or about 59% were in domestic sizes used for heating purposes primarily; 22,058,837 tons, or 40.8%, were in steam sizes, used for heating and other commercial needs. The iron and steel industry in 1948 used 2,500,000 tons of anthracite.

Of the total 1949 output of U.S. bituminous coal—460,000,000 tons—almost half or more than 215,000,000 tons was used in manufacturing plants for power purposes and for construction. Approximately 100,000,000 tons were burned in coking ovens to make steel for building uses, locomotives, cars and tracks, bridges and automobiles; 8,000,000 tons were used in rolling mills; another 8,000,000 by cement plants; and 101,000,000 tons for all other manufacturing purposes. Retail dealers took 90,000,000 tons for distribution to about 19,000,000 homes and to thousands of small industries. The railroads used 73,000,000 tons and electric utilities ac-

TABLE V.—*Use of Bituminous, Anthracite and Other Fuels and Power in the U.S.*
(Coal, thousand tons; petroleum, thousand barrels; natural gas, million cubic feet; hydroelectric power, million kilowatt-hours; and trillion B.T.U.)

Year	Bituminous	Anthracite	Petroleum products	Natural gas	Hydroelectric	Total bituminous coal equivalent*
1926	532,581	77,221	373,561	1,182	30,053	777,328
1927	499,801	74,672	370,874	1,301	32,924	747,595
1928	498,827	73,650	390,659	1,393	37,324	756,298
1929	519,554	71,457	408,153	1,657	37,098	787,481
1930	454,990	67,628	400,114	1,676	35,640	716,565
1931	371,869	58,408	359,556	1,490	32,147	602,481
1932	306,917	50,500	333,961	1,388	35,998	521,374
1933	321,617	49,600	349,415	1,365	36,577	537,481
1934	347,043	55,500	388,363	1,541	35,804	584,618
1935	360,292	51,100	432,099	1,675	41,492	612,901
1936	422,796	53,200	476,134	1,885	42,750	697,290
1937	428,497	50,400	480,158	2,067	48,272	712,366
1938	344,650	45,200	450,958	1,971	48,394	612,061
1939	379,769	49,700	490,135	2,130	47,692	665,382
1940	438,250	49,000	535,498	2,291	51,658	741,565
1941	482,060	52,700	582,063	2,448	55,357	808,664
1942	537,105	56,500	580,070	2,717	69,133	885,840
1943	594,301	57,100	746,002	3,099	79,077	1,004,885
1944	593,659	59,400	816,705	3,353	78,904	1,033,092
1945	561,677	51,600	839,561	3,487	84,747	1,007,863
1946	491,666	53,900	811,476	3,553	83,150	933,664
1947	557,154	49,000	919,006	3,960	83,066	1,034,962
1948 prelim	531,000	52,000	965,100	4,000	86,992	1,025,000
Per Cent of Total (Fuels and power equated to B.T.U. from which the following per cents were computed)						
1926	68.6	10.3	11.2	6.2	3.7	20,366
1927	66.9	10.4	11.6	7.1	4.0	19,587
1928	66.0	10.1	12.1	7.5	4.3	19,815
1929	65.9	9.4	12.2	8.6	3.9	20,632
1930	63.5	9.8	13.1	9.6	4.0	18,774
1931	61.7	10.1	14.0	10.1	4.1	15,785
1932	58.9	10.1	15.0	10.9	5.1	13,660
1933	59.8	9.6	15.2	10.4	5.0	14,082
1934	59.4	9.9	15.5	10.8	4.4	15,317
1935	58.8	8.7	16.5	11.2	4.8	16,058
1936	60.7	7.9	15.9	11.1	4.4	18,269
1937	60.2	7.3	15.7	11.9	4.9	18,664
1938	56.3	7.7	17.1	13.2	5.7	16,036
1939	57.1	7.8	17.1	13.1	4.9	17,433
1940	59.1	6.9	16.7	12.7	4.6	19,429
1941	59.6	6.8	16.6	12.4	4.6	21,187
1942	60.6	6.6	15.1	12.6	5.1	23,209
1943	59.1	5.9	17.2	12.7	5.1	26,328
1944	57.5	6.0	18.3	13.3	4.9	27,067
1945	55.7	5.3	19.3	14.2	5.5	26,406
1946	52.7	6.0	20.0	15.6	5.7	24,462
1947	53.8	4.9	20.3	15.7	5.3	27,116
1948	51.8	5.3	21.4	16.0	5.5	26,855

*Total of bituminous coal and anthracite plus petroleum products, natural gas and hydroelectric power converted to the equivalent of bituminous coal.
Source: Based on data published by the U.S. Bureau of Mines and the Federal Power Commission.

counted for 80,000,000 tons. Exports of bituminous were about 27,000,000 tons. The total output in 1949 was considerably less than normal because of widespread strikes.

VI. HAZARDS OF MINING AND MEASURES OF SAFETY

The greatest hazards in coal mining are falls from the roof at the working face. U.S. bureau of mines statistics show that 50% of all coal mining fatalities and 30% of serious accidents are due to top falls. In Great Britain roof falls and haulage account for 50–55% of fatalities and accidents in the first case, and about 25% in the second; *i.e.,* the moving vehicles (called tubs) and the ropes underground. Mechanized productivity entails rapid transit of coal by trainloads from the point of extraction to the tipple or breaker. In the decade 1939–48, haulage accidents accounted for 19% of the bituminous coal mining fatalities in the U.S. Explosions of firedamp and coal dust came next, causing 10% of the industry's fatalities. The proportion varied widely; it was as high as 24% in one year and as low as 3% in 1944. In one of the safest years, 1948, there were 11 ignitions of coal dust and gas reported.

Another source of accidents is the use of explosives in underground mining. Safety instructions and the manufacture of safer types of explosives, however, reduced the toll appreciably. Fatal accidents caused by explosives in bituminous mining per million man-hours for the five-year period 1906–10, inclusive, were 0.1446, and only 0.043 in 1941 and 0.026 in 1942. The use of electricity underground tended to increase accidents, especially in gassy mines, where electrical equipment must be kept in proper working condition. In the U.S., 63 fatalities caused by electricity underground occurred in 1930; in 1944, only 26 such accidents took place; and in the latter year more than 72,000,000 more tons of bituminous were mined than in 1930.

Last among the hazards of coal mining come shaft accidents. Percentagewise the number of fatal accidents occurring in shafts in bituminous and lignite mines, however, was reduced more than in the case of any of the other principal causes. In 1906 73 men lost their lives in U.S. shaft accidents; by 1943 there were only five such fatalities. This reduction was effected largely by improvements in hoisting equipment, safeguards at the collar of the shafts and at shaft landings and in cages; in improved methods of handling cars on and off the mine cages, and of handling men in hoisting shafts and slopes.

In Great Britain, the National Coal board reported 470 deaths and nearly 2,400 serious injuries in 1948. Falls from the roof were still the commonest cause of accidents; underground lighting was still a serious problem, and experiments were being tried with fluorescent lighting. Miners used more cap lamps; of about 500,000 lamps in use during 1948, about 150,000 were replaced by more modern types. Several roadway lighting systems were put into the collieries, consisting of tungsten filament and tubular fluorescent discharge lamps, with specially designed fittings. More whitewashing of the roadways had also helped improve lighting.

Dust disease or pneumoconiosis was still a major problem in Britain; in 1947 3,779 cases were certified, of which 2,795 were in south Wales.

Safety Measures.—This cumulative increase in safety was the result of many safety devices and precautions. One of the obvious first considerations is to provide proper ventilation in the mines. At least one giant fan is installed in the fan house near the mouth or mine opening. This blower forces a continuous flow of pure fresh air into all parts of the mine and drives out the foul air. The weight of air circulated daily through a mine has been estimated at more than 12 times the weight of the coal mined each day. In addition to providing fresh air the blowers serve another very highly important purpose—they dilute and render harmless accumulations of dangerous gases. Wherever coal is found underground there is likely to be methane gas, sometimes called firedamp or marsh gas. This gas cannot be detected by ordinary methods and is highly inflammable. A product of the ageless decomposition of the organic matter in coal, it can sometimes be heard working in a coal seam. The sound is like the faint humming of bees.

A modern mine consists of a carefully planned system of air passages, ducts and boarded safety gates which fit snugly in the labyrinth of tunnels. The gates open and close automatically when the occasion demands—such as the passage of a long line of cars loaded with coal. Mine foremen and safety engineers check the construction of the overcast or ventilating passages cut into the rock above the coal seams from time to time to see that the ventilating currents pass through freely. Sturdy ceiling beams support reinforced concrete slabs where the ventilating overpass areas occur, carrying intake air over the mine haulageway, and serving also as a giant exhaust duct. Temperatures range from 68° to 72° F.

On account of the danger of possible gas explosions, no equipment requiring use of an open flame is permitted by law in U.S. or British mines. There are strict rules against smoking in mines, especially gaseous mines, where miners are even forbidden to carry matches underground.

Miners are required to wear safety shoes of heavy leather with a piece of curved steel under the toecap. Eyes are protected by heavy safety goggles. A specially designed stiff hat, light in weight but very strong, is intended to save a man's head from many bumps against low ceilings or roof props and to protect him from pieces of falling slate, rock or coal. Every miner's helmet is provided with an electric bulb headlight connected with a compact dry cell battery strapped to his side or back. Formerly candles were used to light British mines, until Sir Humphry Davy's invention (1815) of a safety lamp consisting of a fine wire gauze enclosing the flame to keep it from coming in contact with mine gas. Later this was replaced by a flickering oil lamp and still later by the carbide lamp.

Everywhere in the mine, aboveground or underneath, the miner is reminded of the need for safety. The health and safety division of the United States bureau of mines, comprising three sections —safety, mine inspection and miners' health—carries on its work through hundreds of inspectors and safety instructors from 21 field offices throughout the United States. All states in which coal is mined commercially have state mining departments to enforce the state mining laws which are, as a rule, very rigid. All large coal companies employ safety directors, and the National Coal association in the U.S. maintains a safety division, as does the National Coal board of Britain.

A careful watch on all parts of the mine is made constantly. Upon starting the day's work the miner must first go to the lamp house, where he is handed his cap and lamp, the battery of which has been recharged and tested beforehand. Each worker has his individual number which is recorded and then hung up on a chart opposite the number of the room to which he has been assigned to work. The office staff aboveground thus knows his exact location at all times. U.S. miners generally work in groups of 20 to a section underground. On the walls of the office hang huge blueprints which show the mine workings in detail.

During the night, preparatory for the day shift, or the day if it be for the night shift, the fire boss and his assistants patrol and inspect all parts of the underground mine. By tapping the roof with special instruments they can tell where it needs support before the men are permitted to work in that part of the mine. Hundreds of thousands of timber posts are used annually in coal mines to support the roofs. In the more highly mechanized mines electric timbering machines are employed to raise the heavy ceiling beams automatically while other men set and wedge the posts.

A vigilant check is made for gas accumulations, and since firedamp or methane gas is odourless, tasteless and highly inflammable, special gas detectors are employed to discover the presence of this gas. These replaced the canaries formerly used for this purpose. A permissible flame safety lamp has two sets of fine wire gauze above the glass surrounding the flame, one inside the other so that it will not get hot enough to ignite either gas or coal dust. It is equipped with a magnetic lock that can be opened only in the lamp house on the mine surface. In good air the flame is clear yellow; if explosive gas is present a blue cap appears above it. The height of the cap indicates the amount of gas present. In all properly run mines the fire bosses or inspectors examine a working place in the mine daily, sometimes twice daily, before the miners arrive, using either these permissible flame safety lamps or electrical gas detectors. If gas is found, ventilation is introduced at once to remove it. If the amount of gas is large, all power may be shut off until the section of the mine affected is made safe. When a room is rendered safe, chalk marks are made on the walls by the safety foreman or the inspectors.

In the better equipped mines all power is furnished by electric motors rather than by combustion engines. Painstaking care is taken in the construction of all electrical equipment to eliminate sparks that might set off an explosion. There are rigid requirements set by law which must be met before miners may use explosives to dislodge the coal from the working face. Power drills usually bore two holes of the same length simultaneously; a test is made for the presence of gas and then the explosive is carefully tamped into the holes. Only permissible explosives, first tested and approved in the U.S. by the bureau of mines, may be used. Previous cuttings of the coal must first be removed and loaded into cars before a shot can be made. This precaution is necessary in order to avoid dust explosions and possible injury to the men of the section. When all is in readiness, the miners retire to a safe distance, usually about 100 ft. away, and an electric current from a dry cell battery explodes the coal. In some mines compressed air, at a pressure of 10,000 lb. per square inch, is shot from a mechanism that looks like a rifle and replaces the explosive. The charge of compressed air is sent through a kind of tubing inserted in a predrilled hole; this kind of blasting is not only safer, but speeds production as well.

Some dust, containing combustible matter, naturally accumulates after blastings and cuttings, and at times these accumulations may prove dangerous. To counteract it, an ingenious chemical composition known as rock dust was developed and came into universal use in U.S. mines. This is a fine, whitish powder, damp in structure, the chief ingredient of which is limestone. Powerful electric blowers force it onto the walls and into the tunnels of the mine. This process dilutes the coal dust, cleans the air and avoids the possibility of an explosion. British mines use water sprays for dust control more than do the Americans.

Still other safety devices found in U.S. mines are the first-aid stations scattered at strategic places within the mines and designated by green lights. These are equipped with everything necessary for an emergency—convenient receptacles filled with picks, shovels and other tools, bags with rock dust, respirators, oxygen tanks on occasion and equivalent materials. Mines are also equipped with an intricate telephone system, connected finally with the office aboveground. At intervals of 60 ft. or less, dependent upon state regulations, manholes are provided along the main haulageways as places of refuge in emergencies. The open-top man-trip cars have gradually been replaced by all-steel cars, enclosed, electrically operated, and each carrying an average of 38 men comfortably and with complete safety. Some cars travel five miles and more underground to reach the working part of the mine.

VII. CHEMICAL BY-PRODUCTS OF COAL

There are believed to be more than 200,000 chemical by-products from bituminous coal alone. Aside from its obvious contribution to physical warmth and comfort (about one-sixth of all U.S. bituminous and three-fifths of all anthracite, are used for home heating), coal's principal by-product is coke, which makes possible the manufacture of steel. More than 54% of the electricity in the United States is generated from bituminous. From this coal is derived the tar and pitch for roofing and insulating materials. Highways are made possible through coal derivatives because macadam uses coal tar or pitch as binder for gravel and stone, and cement must have coal tar or pitch for expansion joints. In agriculture, coal helps develop fertilizers, insecticides, disinfectants, herbicides, fungicides, fumigants, preservatives, plant-growth regulators and food dyes.

The refrigerants—carbon dioxide for dry ice, and ammonia, and the synthetic in electric refrigerators—are coal derivatives. All edible dyes, preservatives and water softeners formed from ion exchange resins are bituminous derivatives. Synthetic rubber of the styrene type and that which comes from neoprene have, as basic raw materials, limestone, salt and coal tar. Paints and finishes have pigments, solvents and resins as ingredients, many of which are coal-derived.

Hundreds of medicines and antiseptics are produced from coal. Photographic films have sensitizing dyes added to the basic silver bromide in order to register colours other than blue and ultra-violet, and these dyes, a few of the 10,000 available, stem from bituminous. The coal-tar derived plastics which produce nylon films also help create extruded rattan, braided machinery packing, various types of tubing, rods, electric motor bearings, window screens, lampshades and kitchenware, electrical fittings and telephone receivers, jewellery and clock cases, aircraft parts and picture frames, phonograph records, shower curtains, raincoats, vanity cases and children's toys. Nylon or Lucite acrylic resin is the product of coal, air and water. Aside from uses in clothing, nylon is made into paintbrush bristles, parachute harness webbing, parachute shroudlines, heavy nylon rope, cargo parachute cloth and light nylon rope.

Table VI is a summary of the products of the carbonization of bituminous coal.

TABLE VI.—*Products of the Carbonization of Bituminous Coal*

Light oil
- Benzol
- Toluol
- Xylol
- Solvent naphtha

Coal tar (app. 50% is processed at distilling plants)
- Road tars and refined tars
- Creosote and tar acid oils
  - phenols
  - naphthalene
- Pitches and pitch coke

Chemicals
- Ammonium sulphate
- Sulphur
- Phenols
- Naphthalene

Product	Uses	Product	Uses
Benzol	motor fuel rubber paint, varnish, lacquer dye and dyestuffs chemical industry plastics pharmaceuticals disinfectants explosives	Xylol	rubber paint, varnish, lacquer dye and dyestuffs chemical industry plastics
		Naphtha	rubber paint, varnish, lacquer plastics
Toluol	rubber paint, varnish, lacquer dye and dyestuffs chemical industry pharmaceuticals plastics explosives disinfectants	Phenols	dye and dyestuffs chemical industry pharmaceuticals plastics explosives disinfectants soap
		Naphthalene	dye and dyestuffs chemical industry plastics explosives agriculture disinfectants soap

Some coal-tar derived synthetic medicinals:
- acetanilide
- acetylsalicylic acid (aspirin)
- sulfanilamide
- procaine
- arsphenamine
- phenobarbital
- neocinchophen
- neoarsphenamine
- nicotinic acid amide
- salicylic acid
- sulfapyradine
- sulfoarsphenamine
- sulfathiazole
- phenacetin
- mapharsen
- benzaldehyde
- benzoic acid
- ephedrine
- hexylresorcinol
- epinephrine
- phenophthalein
- cinchophen
- salol
- chloramine T
- theobromine
- vitamin K
- pyradoxine (B_6)

Some coal-tar derived perfume materials:
- amyl salcylate—clover, orchid
- benzaldehyde—bitter almond
- benzophenone—rose
- benzylacetate—jasmine
- cinnamic acid—balsam
- cinnamic alcohol—lilac, hyacinth

TABLE VI.—*Products of the Carbonization of Bituminous Coal* (*Continued*)

- cinnamic aldehyde—cinnamon
- coumarin—tonka bean, new mown hay
- isoamylbenzylether—gardenia
- methylanthranilate—orange blossom
- musk zylol (DuPont)—natural musk
- nitrobenzene—almond
- phenylacetic aldehyde—hyacinth
- phenylacetic acid—honey rose
- phenylethyl alcohol—rose
- salicylaldehyde—meadowsweet

Coke and By-products

- Coke
  - metallurgy
  - retort carbon
  - foundry
  - coke breeze
  - domestic fuel
  - electrodes
  - graphite
    - lubricants
    - crucibles
    - electrodes
  - producer gas
  - water gas
    - fuel
    - synthetic chemicals
    - motor fuel
  - carborundum
    - abrasives
  - calcium carbide
    - fuel
    - calcium cyanamide
      - fertilizer
      - explosives
    - acetylene
- Pitch
  - Soft
    - paving materials
    - waterproofing
    - insulating materials
  - Medium
    - paints
    - metal protective coatings
    - roofing materials
    - waterproofing
  - Hard
    - protective coatings
    - insulating compounds
    - electrodes
    - core compounds
    - briquetting
    - electrode binders
- Pitch coke
  - electrodes
  - foundry coke
- Ammoniacal liquor
  - ammonium sulphate
    - fertilizer
  - pyridine
  - ammonia water
    - ammonia salts
    - nitric acid
  - anhydrous ammonia
    - nitric acid
  - liquid ammonia
    - refrigeration
- Middle (carbolic or naphthalene) oil
  - Crude carbolic acid
    - Phenol
      - nitrophenols
        - picric acid
        - *p*-amidophenol
        - phenacetin
        - dye intermediates
        - developers
        - explosives
      - salicylic acid
        - salicylates
        - aspirin
        - methylsalicylate
        - salol
        - dyestuffs
        - preservatives
      - resins and plastics
    - Cresols or cresylic acids
      - antiseptics
        - lysol, creolin
      - resins and plastics
  - Crude naphthalene
    - Naphthalene (refined)
      - phthalic anhydride
        - phenolphthalein
          - indicator and laxatives
        - phthalimide
          - anthranilic acid
            - flavouring, perfumes
        - anthraquinone
          - dyestuffs and intermediates
      - nitronaphthalene
        - explosives
        - naphthylamine
        - insecticides
        - dyes
      - naphthalene sulphonic acids
        - naphthols
        - dyestuffs
- Heavy or creosote oil
  - Crude carbolic acid—disinfectants
    - phenol
    - cresols
  - Creosote oil—wood preservative
- Green or anthracene oil
  - Wood preservative
  - Crude anthracene
    - Carbazole—dyestuffs
    - Phenanthrene—dyestuffs
    - Anthracene
      - anthraquinone—intermediates and dyestuffs
- Light oil
  - Benzene (benzol)
    - Halogenated benzene
      - dyestuffs
      - insecticides
    - Nitrobenzene
      - dye intermediates
      - developers
      - aniline
        - aniline salts
          - dye intermediates
          - dyestuffs
        - dimethylaniline
          - dye intermediates
          - dyestuffs

TABLE VI.—*Products of the Carbonization of Bituminous Coal* (*Continued*)

- quinone
  - hydroquinone
    - photographic developer
  - phenylhydrazine
    - antipyridine
- Maleic acid
  - maleic anhydride
    - plastics
- Benzene sulphonic acid
  - phenol
  - dye intermediates
- Pyridine
  - denaturant
- Heavy naphtha
  - synthetic resins
  - coumarone resins
- Solvent naphtha
  - xylenes
    - dyestuffs and intermediates
- Crude carbolic acid
  - phenol
  - cresols
- Crude toluene
  - benzoic acid
  - toluene
    - nitrotoluenes
      - explosives
      - dye intermediates and dyestuffs
      - toluidines
    - benzaldehyde
      - flavouring substances
      - dyestuffs
      - perfumes
      - drugs
    - toluene sulphonic acids
      - antiseptics
      - chloramine T
      - saccharin

VIII. WORLD COAL RESOURCES AND PRODUCTION

Perhaps the most reliable of pre-World War I estimates of the total coal resources of the world was that compiled by the 12th International Geologic congress in 1913 and reported in the *Coal Resources of the World.* This report estimated the total known and probable world resources as 7,397,553,000,000 metric tons, of which the United States was credited with 3,838,657,000,000, Europe with 784,190,000,000, and other parts of the world with the remainder.

In 1936 the Reichskohlenrat (German National Coal council) of Berlin published a statistical review of the coal industry of the world, basing its estimates on the original figures of the 12th International Geologic congress, but revised in accordance with its own later discoveries and changes in boundaries of different countries following World War I. A summary of these statistics, believed reliable for the period immediately preceding World War II, is found in Table VII.

TABLE VII.—*Coal Resources of Europe and the United States, Estimated to a Depth of 6,560 ft.*
(In millions of metric tons)

Country	Anthracite and bituminous coal		Lignite and brown coal	
	Known and probable	Known	Known and probable	Known
Belgium	11,000	..	..	..
Bulgaria	140	30	3,860	358
Denmark	..	..	50	..
Germany (incl. Saar)	288,865	87,474	56,758	28,837
Austria	31	13	2,938	608
Great Britain	200,161	138,183	..	..
France	16,611	5,803	1,614	1,614
Greece	..	..	40	10
Netherlands	4,402	585	5	..
Italy	144	3	181	49
Yugoslavia	45	4	4,679	2,088
Poland	138,128	9,600	17,326	973
Rumania	48	7	2,747	717
Russia	74,790	13,196	5,940	350
Sweden	114	106	..	..
Spain	8,001	5,826	767	394
Spitzbergen (Norway)	8,750	..	..	..
Czechoslovakia	28,410	2,966	12,393	3,097
Hungary	113	3	1,604	176
Total	779,753	263,799	110,902	39,271
United States*	1,975,205	..	1,863,452	..
Total world	4,532,738	..	2,887,714	..

*According to U.S. geological survey estimates in 1928, coal reserves in the U.S. to a depth of 1,000 metres were: 2,041,090,000,000 metric tons of coal and 852,317,000,000 metric tons of lignite.

Following World War II a re-estimate was made of coal resources in Europe, North America, Central and South America, Africa, Asia and Australasia. These statistics, appearing in the fourth *Statistical Year-Book* of the World Power conference, 1948, are summarized in Table VIII.

In Table VII it will be noted that Germany had the largest estimated known and probable resources of any country in Europe, especially if its brown coal resources were also included. Germany's most important coal is the Ruhr coking coal, which has made that district—in proximity to the Lorraine iron ore deposits—the most important producer of iron and steel on the continent. Great Britain comes second in coal resources, but actually has larger known coal deposits than any other European country. Poland has a great deal of bituminous. Then comes the U.S.S.R., although the actual facts about total Russian coal resources in both Europe and Asia were unknown at mid-20th century. France, Belgium and Czechoslovakia are next in importance, with relatively small resources, though what they possess is very important for steelmaking.

TABLE VIII.—*World Coal Resources Estimated by the World Power Conference, 1948*
(In million metric tons)

	Coals	Brown coal and lignite		Peat
	Proved reserves	Probable total reserves	Proved reserves	Probable total reserves	Probable total reserves
Certain countries in:					
Europe	548,000	1,551,000	50,000	287,000	111,000
North America	42,000	2,115,000	20,000	951,000	13,000
Central and South America	2,000	1,000	..	..	..
Africa	9,000	206,000	..	..	..
Asia	11,000	1,097,000	..	4,000	..
Australasia	4,000	14,000	5,000	40,000	..
Total	616,000	4,984,000	75,000	1,282,000	124,000

Coal occurrences in China are widespread, being found in almost every province and ranging from hard, dry anthracite to bituminous and lignite. The original estimate of the 12th International Geologic congress giving China coal reserves of 995,587,000,000 tons was challenged by geologists as an overestimation. In 1926 the Chinese geological survey offered a conservative estimate of 217,626,000,000 tons. Even such a figure would place that country as one of the ranking units in the world's coal reserves. Japan's coal reserves were estimated to total 7,869,000,000 metric tons.

There are appreciable deposits in India, New South Wales, the Union of South Africa and Australia, and variable coal resources in other countries. Canada possesses enormous resources of coal in both the Atlantic and Pacific coastal regions and in the interior plains, comprising practically all kinds from lignite to anthracite. Distribution of actual and probable reserves is estimated at 1,234,269,000,000 metric tons, approximately one-sixth of the world's total.

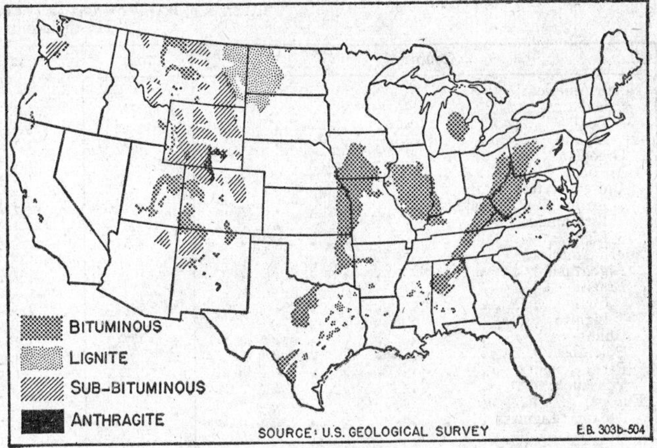

FIG. 5.—LOCATION OF U.S. COAL RESERVES

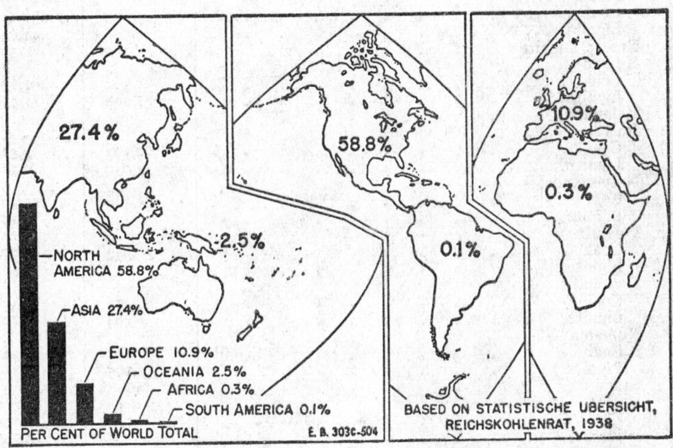

FIG. 6.—LOCATION OF WORLD'S COAL RESOURCES, BY CONTINENTS

TABLE IX.—*World Coal Production*
(Million net tons)

Year	U.S.	Canada	Great Britain	Germany	Austria-Hungary	Czechoslovakia	Netherlands	France	Belgium	Spain	Russia and Finland	Poland	Japan	China	India	Australia	Union of South Africa	All Other Countries	Total*
1868–69 average	36	1	118	37	8	NA	NA	15	14	NA	1	NA	NA	NA	NA	NA	NA	NA	230
1870–74 average	49	1	136	46	11	NA	NA	17	16	NA	1	NA	NA	NA	NA	NA	NA	NA	277
1875–79 average	60	1	150	55	15	NA	NA	19	16	NA	2	NA	NA	NA	NA	NA	NA	2	320
1880–84 average	94	2	175	73	18	NA	NA	22	19	NA	4	NA	1	NA	NA	NA	NA	4	412
1885–89 average	129	2	185	86	25	NA	NA	24	20	NA	6	NA	2	NA	NA	NA	NA	8	487
1890–94 average	172	3	202	104	32	NA	NA	29	22	2	8	NA	4	NA	3	4	NA	3	588
1895–99 average	212	4	226	133	39	NA	NA	34	24	2	12	NA	6	NA	5	6	NA	6	709
1900–04 average	315	7	254	173	44	NA	NA	36	25	3	19	NA	10	NA	8	8	NA	10	912
1905–09 average	433	10	287	224	52	NA	NA	40	26	4	25	NA	15	10	12	9	NA	8	1,155
1910–14 average	523	14	302	272	57	NA	NA	44	25	5	30	NA	21	14	16	13	NA	22	1,358
1915–19 average	601	14	272	269	48	NA	4	26	17	7	31	NA	29	23	22	12	10	14	1,399
1920–24 average	574	16	265	275	11	35	6	37	25	6	12	24	33	23	22	14	13	19	1,411
1925–29 average	604	16	250	348	11	38	11	57	29	8	34	42	39	27	24	16	16	26	1,596
1930	537	15	273	333	11	37	14	61	30	8	51	42	37	29	27	13	15	26	1,559
1931	440	12	246	290	11	34	14	56	30	8	65	42	33	31	25	12	13	23	1,387
1932	360	12	234	262	11	29	14	52	24	8	71	32	33	29	22	12	12	23	1,240
1933	383	12	232	272	11	28	14	53	28	7	96	30	38	31	23	13	13	12	1,296
1934	417	14	247	300	11	28	14	54	29	7	119	32	43	36	25	14	14	11	1,415
1935	425	14	249	319	12	29	13	52	29	8	121	31	45	29	26	15	16	32	1,465
1936	489	15	256	351	12	31	13	51	31	8	136	33	50	30	26	16	18	27	1,593
1937	497	16	269	406	14	38	16	50	33	3	140	40	50	20	28	17	19	53	1,709
1938	395	14	254	421	14	35	15	52	33	6	146	42	54	26	32	17	20	43	1,619
1939	446	16	259	440	16	42	14	55	33	7	194	73	58	43	31	19	20	49	1,815
1940	512	17	251	511	17	48	14	45	28	10	209	85	64	52	33	18	19	50	1,983
1941	571	18	231	528	18	47	15	48	29	11	162	84	62	65	33	21	20	51	2,014
1942	643	19	230	547	18	51	14	48	28	11	99	93	61	72	33	22	22	47	2,058
1943	651	18	223	455	18	56	14	47	26	12	145	101	64	69	29	22	23	45	2,018
1944	683	17	216	404	15	54	9	29	15	13	130	96	57	69	29	21	25	54	1,936
1945	633	16	205	164	7	30	6	39	17	13	161	30	26	18	33	20	26	43	1,487
1946	594	18	213	249	10	37	10	54	25	13	177	53	24	17	33	22	26	54	1,629
1947	688	16	221	271	13	43	12	52	27	13	193	70	32	22	32	23	26	67	1,821
1948	651	18	234	294	16	46	12	50	29	13	222	83	39	10	34	23	26	62	1,862

*Includes lignite in each country on a ton-for-ton basis. Data for recent years subject to revision
NA—no available information.
Source: U.S. Bureau of Mines; Statistical Office, United Nations.

TABLE X.—*World Production of Coal and Lignite, 1941-1948, by Countries*
(In thousands of metric tons*)

Country*	1941	1942	1943	1944	1945	1946	1947	1948
North America:								
Canada:								
Coal	15,333†	15,932†	14,689†	14,201	13,584	14,776	12,971	15,283
Lignite	1,201†	1,181†	1,512†	1,245	1,391	1,382	1,425	1,441
Greenland	7	5	7	8	7	8	7	8
Mexico	856	914	1,025	904	915	977	1,055	‡
United States:								
Anthracite (Pennsylvania)	51,136	54,728	55,015	57,789	49,835	54,891	51,882	51,756
Bituminous	463,908	525,948	532,903	559,750	521,582	481,943	569,482	536,071
Lignite	2,518	2,659	2,494	2,317	2,421	2,420	2,607	2,794
South America:								
Argentina§	‖	5	8	9	7	3	14	‡
Brazil:								
Coal	1,110	1,354	1,537	1,415	1,492	1,274	1,980	2,013
Lignite	2	17	23	16	9	‡	‡	‡
Chile	1,717	1,782	2,032	2,047	1,827	1,740	1,850	2,239
Colombia	403	415	476	499	525¶	550¶	850¶	‡
Peru	117	150	187	173	201	230	215	187
Venezuela	6	9	11	12	7	4	15	21
Europe:								
Albania: Lignite¶	20	20	10	5	5	12	20	‡
Austria:								
Coal	226	225	214	195	72	108	178	181
Lignite	3,537	3,523	3,646	3,674	2,066	2,407	2,839	3,338
Belgium	26,722	25,055	23,737	13,529	15,833	22,779	24,390	26,679
Bulgaria:								
Coal	‡	‡	‡	‡	‡	‡	‡	‡
Lignite	2,784	3,444	3,816	2,892	3,432	3,420	4,011	‡
Czechoslovakia:								
Coal	20,930	22,635	24,500	23,159	11,716	14,167	16,216	17,746
Lignite	21,623	23,316	26,750	26,112	15,356	19,475	22,362	23,589
Denmark: Lignite	1,000	1,800	2,600	2,200	2,320	2,300	2,800	‡
France:								
Coal	41,849	41,869	40,531	25,241	33,313	47,185	45,229	43,291
Lignite	2,008	1,958	1,896	1,336	1,704	2,104	2,094	1,838
Germany:								
Coal	243,607	251,970	158,616	135,336	41,208	65,688	85,773	91,246
Lignite	234,996	244,643	254,604	230,808	107,772	159,876	160,518	175,736
Greece: Lignite	180	365	370	190	70	125	140	125
Hungary:								
Coal	1,301	1,250	1,376	1,050♀♁	710♀	722	1,059	1,238
Lignite	11,298	11,720	11,296	8,400♀♁	3,580♀	5,630	7,750	9,360
Ireland	155	167	186	206	216	216	222	180
Italy:								
Coal	2,393	2,512	1,358	613	758	1,178	1,358	1,055¶
Lignite	2,030	2,306	1,934	496	767	1,521	1,851	909¶
Netherlands:								
Coal	13,356	12,330	12,497	8,313	5,097	8,314	10,104	11,032
Lignite	199	281	383	243	130	499	474	279
Poland:								
Coal	76,343□	83,972□	91,362□	87,389□	27,366	47,288	59,130	70,260
Lignite	‡	‡	‡	‡	‡	857	4,766	5,018
Portugal:								
Coal	435	438	403	426	436	380	377	387
Lignite	84	108	106	127	163	141	108	103
Rumania:								
Coal	264	285	306	202	211	167	163	2,631
Lignite	2,195	2,367	2,604	2,069	1,820	1,784	2,105	
Saar	‡	‡	‡	‡	‡	7,887	10,485	12,567
Spain:								
Coal	8,763	9,257	9,591	10,485	10,732	10,759	10,606	10,277
Lignite	793	1,106	1,112	1,202	1,351	1,336	1,263	1,342
Svalbard (Spitsbergen)	330	..	..	..	6	92	345	431
Sweden	557	582	557	570	615	488	416	400¶
Switzerland:								
Coal	72	184	157	71	311	178	20	‡
Lignite	8	27	75	74			15	‡
U.S.S.R.:								
Coal	146,800	90,000¶	131,400¶	118,000¶	146,000¶	161,000¶	175,000¶	201,000¶
Lignite			‡	‡	‡			
United Kingdom:								
Great Britain◊	209,656	208,234	202,112	195,839	185,706	194,869	200,615	211,772
Northern Ireland:								
Coal	‖	3	‖	‖	‖	‖	1	1
Lignite		1	1	2	3		‖	‖
Yugoslavia:								
Coal	7,310	1,160▲+	1,390	‡	‡	10,207	13,943	11,500
Lignite								
Asia:								
Afghanistan	4	5	..	..	5	3	5	15[6]
China:								
China (except Formosa):								
Coal	58,426	65,267	62,713¶	62,465¶	16,200¶	15,000¶	20,000¶	8,720¶
Lignite	397	419			‡	‡	‡	‡
Formosa	2,885	2,360¶	2,500¶	2,500¶	795	1,058	1,289	2,500¶
India	29,937	29,906	25,921	26,546	29,635	30,186	29,438	30,786
Indo-China, French:								
Coal	2,308	1,218	996	533	231	262	248	359
Lignite	21	24	25	4	..	..	..	..
Indonesia	2,029¶	872	1,038	753	‡*	77	288⊕	‡
Iran[1]	90	82	69	100	150¶	150¶	188	‡
Japan:								
Coal	55,602[2]	54,179[2]	55,539[2]	49,335[2]	22,371[2]	19,823	26,331	32,700
Lignite	408[2]	1,607[2]	2,876[2]	2,304[2]	1,643[2]	2,356	2,820	2,550
Korea:								
Coal	3,519	3,898	4,157	4,530	674	1,072	1,815¶	699[3]
Lignite	2,638	2,958	2,430	2,519	18	458	1,653¶	68[3]
Malaya, Federation of	523[4]	249	497	416	230	228	230	381
Philippines, Republic of the	60¶	‡	‡	‡	‡	48	74	88
Syria and Lebanon:								
Lignite	8	7	1	2	2	‖	‡	‖
Turkey:								
Coal	3,020	2,510	2,071	2,383	2,150	2,312	2,623	2,618
Lignite	264	409	414	533	571	484	628	829
U.S.S.R.:								
Coal	[5]	[5]	[5]	[5]	[5]	[5]	[5]	[5]
Lignite								
Africa:								
Algeria:								
Coal	80	148	117	120	162	215	205	225
Lignite	3	7	1	1	‡	‡	‡	‡

TABLE X.—*World Production of Coal and Lignite, 1941–1948, by Countries (Continued)*
(In thousands of metric tons*)

Country*	1941	1942	1943	1944	1945	1946	1947	1948
Africa (*Continued*)								
Belgian Congo	30	43	69	49	50	102	109	75[4]
Madagascar	1	2	1	2	3	‖	‡	‡
Morocco, French	139	119	102	134	179	222	268	290
Nigeria	409[2]	471[2]	‡	651	679	648	591	600 ¶
Portuguese East Africa	17	7	13	16	12	16	16	‡
Southern Rhodesia	1,412	1,561	1,779	1,808	1,669	1,613	1,508	1,695
Tunisia: Lignite	102	141	41	66	69	95	76	71
Union of South Africa	18,337	20,408	20,561	22,595	23,102	23,255	23,818	23,558[7]
Oceania:								
Australia:								
New South Wales	11,955	12,433	11,714	11,280	10,402	11,397	11,871	12,193¶
Queensland	1,477	1,663	1,727	1,686	1,661	1,593	1,914	1,775
South Australia	..	2	..	35	42	138	196	253
Tasmania	111	137	148	146	151	161	170	182
Victoria:								
Coal	332	318	292	262	251	194	176	129[4]
Lignite	4,639	5,013	5,173	5,097	5,533	5,799	6,239	5,144[4]
Western Australia	566	591	540	567	552	653	742	745
New Zealand:								
Coal	1,199	1,194	1,157	1,085	980	974	951	} 2,827
Lignite	1,483	1,529	1,676	1,766	1,899	1,865	1,845	}
Total, all grades	1,827,000	1,867,000	1,831,000	1,756,000	1,349,000	1,478,000	1,652,000	1,689,000
Lignite (total of items shown above)	297,000	313,000	328,000	308,000	166,000	216,000	230,000	241,000
Bituminous coal and anthracite (by subtraction)	1,530,000	1,554,000	1,503,000	1,448,000	1,183,000	1,262,000	1,422,000	1,448,000

*Coal is also mined in British Borneo, Faroe Islands and formerly Italian East Africa, but production figures are not available and no estimate is included in the total. †A change from previous years has been made in the classification adopted by the American Society for Testing Materials. (Alberta is the only province affected.) ‡Data not available; estimate included in total. §In addition, the following quantities (metric tons) of asphaltitie were produced and used as solid fuels: 1941, 16,646; 1942, 56,387; 1943, 105,625; 1944, 106,300; 1945, 135,300; 1946, 83,800; 1947, 80,900. ‖Production less than 1,000 tons. ¶Estimate. ♀Data represent Trianon Hungary subsequent to Oct. 1944. ♁January to October, inclusive. □Includes that part of Germany which is under Polish administration (east of the Oder and Neisse rivers). ◇Includes opencast coal as follows, in thousands of tons: 1942, 1,332; 1943, 4,498; 1944, 8,786; 1945, 8,245; 1946, 9,053; 1947, 10,407; 1948, 11,916. ▲Estimated production of Croatia. +January to June, inclusive. ⊕Excludes production of Ombilin mines in Sumatra. [1]Fiscal year ended March 20 of year following that stated. [2]Fiscal year ended March 31 of year following that stated. [3]South Korea only. [4]January to September, inclusive. [5]Output from U.S.S.R. in Asia included with U.S.S.R. in Europe. [6]Planned production. [7]Local sales and exports.
Source: U.S. Bureau of Mines, *Mineral Market Report*, no. 1807; compiled by B. B. Mitchell and P. Roberts.

PRODUCTION

The United States produced 34.8% of the world's coal in 1948, as compared with 43% in the years of World War I. Since the turn of the century, it had been the world's foremost producer—a position formerly occupied by Great Britain. It is worth noting at this point that Great Britain's output of 234,000,000 net tons in 1948 equalled the entire world production of 1868, when British production accounted for more than half the world total. By 1900 the British proportion had diminished to 30%, and in 1948 it was 12.5% of the total.

World production attained its record of 2,058,000,000 tons in 1942, but World War II brought it to a postwar low of 1,487,000,000 tons in 1945 (*see* Table IX). By 1946 the total had climbed back to about 1,629,000,000 tons, and in 1948 it approximated 1,620,000,000 tons.

Records of world production go back to 1868–69, when the output was 230,000,000 tons. Production grew consistently until the late 1920s, when it began to feel the effects of depression. By 1936, however, the general level of 1925–29 was regained.

World production figures for all coal-producing countries (1941–48) are shown in Table X.

BIBLIOGRAPHY.—David R. Grenfell, *Coal* (1947); Jones, Cartwright and Guenault, *Coal Mining Industry* (1939); Robert S. Lewis, *Elements of Mining* (1941); *The Colliery Year Book and Coal Trades Directory, 1949* (London, 1949); U.S. Bureau of Mines, *Coal Mining in Europe* (1939); U.S. Bureau of Mines, *The Coal Industry of the World* (1930); International Labour Office, *Year Book of Labour Statistics, 1947–48* (1949); Statistical Office of the United Nations, *Monthly Bulletin of Statistics* (1949); J. J. Rosenberg, *Life in a Model Coal-Mining Village, by a Benin Boy* (1947); Margot Heinemann, *Britain's Coal* (1944); National Coal Board of Great Britain, *Annual Reports* (1946, 1947, 1948, 1949); *Ministry of Fuel and Power Statistical Digest* (1946–47); Howard N. Eavenson, *The First Century and a Quarter of American Coal Industry* (1942); American Mining Congress, *Coal Mine Modernization Yearbook* (1948); Ivan A. Given, *Mechanical Loading of Coal Underground* (1943); Hudson Coal Company, *The Story of Anthracite* (1932); Elwood S. Moore *Coal* (1940); Glen L. Parker, *The Coal Industry* (1940); Josephine Perry, *Coal Industry* (1944); M. E. Sheppard, *Cloud by Day* (1947); Paul M. Tyler, *From the Ground Up* (1948); E. N. Zern (ed.), *Coal Miner's Pocketbook*, 12th ed.; U.S. Bureau of Mines, *Analyses of Pennsylvania Anthracite Coals*, Technical Paper 659 (1944); U.S. Bureau of Mines, *Minerals Yearbook* (1946); Anthracite Institute, *Manual of Statistical Information* (1948); Bituminous Coal Institute, *Facts and Figures* (1948, 1949); Howard N. Eavenson, *Coal Through the Ages* (1935); W. E. Hotchkiss and others, *Bituminous Coal Mining*, WPA Report (1939); Clifford C. Furnas, *The Storehouse of Civilization* (1939); Anton Handlirsch, *Die Fossilen Insekten* (1908); Edward C. Jeffrey, *Coal and Civilization* (1925); McAlister Coleman, *Men and Coal* (1943); *Report of the U.S. Coal Commission*, 4 vol. (1923); The Coal Utilization Joint Council, London, *The Story of Coal;* Walter Zimmerman, *Die Phylogenie der Pflanzen* (1930); Max Hirmer, *Handbuch der Palaobotanik* (1927); Roy Lee Moodie, *The Coal Measures Amphibia of North America* (1916); George Korson, *Minstrels of the Mine Patch* (1938); George Korson, *Coal Dust on the Fiddle* (1943); European Economic Cooperation Administration, *Coal and Related Solid Fuels Study* (March 1949); A. C. Fieldner and W. E. Rice, *Research and Progress in the Production and Use of Coal*, National Resources Planning Board (1941); U.S. Bureau of Mines, *Coal-Bituminous and Lignite*, annual reprints from the *Minerals Yearbooks;* U.S. Bureau of Mines, *Safety in the Mining Industry*, Information Circular 7485 (1949); National Research Council, H. H. Lowry, Chairman, *The Chemistry of Coal Utilization*, 2 vol. (1945). (M. E. SE.)

COALBROOKDALE, a village and ecclesiastical parish of Shropshire, Eng., on the Western region railway route, 5 mi. south of Wellington. Pop. (1931) 1,417. The "dale" is the valley of a stream rising near the Wrekin and following southeast for about 8 mi. to the Severn. Its ironworks, founded in 1709 by Abraham Darby with Dutch workmen, were the pioneer attempt to use pit coal for smelting iron. The third Abraham Darby built the famous Coalbrookdale iron bridge (a cast-iron arch of 100-ft. span) over the Severn, which gives name to the neighbouring town of Ironbridge, which with a portion of Coalbrookdale is in the parish of Madeley (*q.v.*). There are also brick and tile works.

COALDALE, an anthracite-mining borough of Schuylkill county, Pa., 45 mi. southwest of Scranton. It is on federal highway 209, and is served by the Lehigh and New England railroad for freight. The population in 1950 was 5,230; it was 6,163 in 1940 by the federal census.

COALFISH (*Pollachius virens*), a fish of the cod family, with three dorsal and two anal fins, distinguished from the cod by its blackish colour, prominent lower jaw and very small barbel. It ranges from the Arctic ocean to the Mediterranean and grows to a length of about four feet.

COALING STATIONS: *see* FUELLING STATIONS.

COALITION, a combination of bodies or parts into one body or whole. (Lat. *coalitio*, from *coalescere*, "to grow together.") The word is used, especially in a political sense, of an alliance (*q.v.*) or temporary union for joint action of various powers or states, such as the coalition of the European powers against France during the wars of the French Revolution; also the union in a single government of distinct parties or members of distinct parties.

COAL TAR is the primary condensation product resulting from the carbonization of coal; *i.e.*, the heating of coal in the absence of air, at temperatures ranging from about 900° C. to about 1,200° C. It is a black, viscous, sticky fluid whose density is greater than that of water.

Manufacture.—The manufacture of coal tar and related products starts with the placing of coal in a chamber, and the heating of it out of contact with air. The coal is thereby decomposed into volatile products and into a nonvolatile residue, coke. The volatile products are composed of condensable materials and noncondensable gases. As the volatile products are formed they are removed from the chamber and cooled, whereupon the water and tar are liquefied; these two substances; *i.e.*, water and tar, constitute the bulk of the condensable materials evolved during the decomposition of the coal. With the condensation of the water, a portion of some of the gaseous constituents which are more or less soluble in the water is also removed. After the complete removal of the water and tar, the gas is passed through water, or dilute sulphuric acid, which absorbs the ammonia present. Finally, the relatively clean, cool gas is passed through an oil or over activated carbon to remove such low boiling constituents as benzene, toluene, etc., which go to make up coal-tar light oils.

The temperature at which the carbonization is conducted, the type of equipment used and the nature of the coal carbonized determine the kind of tar and the quantity obtained.

The temperature of carbonization has more effect on the quality (kind) of coal tar and on the yield than any other single factor. So great is the influence of the carbonization temperature that coal tars are divided into high-temperature tars and low-temperature tars; those produced at carbonization temperatures from 900° C. to 1,200° C. are called high-temperature tars and those produced at carbonization temperatures from 450° C. to 700° C. are called low-temperature tars (*see* TARS, LOW-TEMPERATURE).

When coal is heated, in the absence of air, to a temperature of about 450° C., the coal begins to decompose and an evolution of gaseous products occurs. As these gases are liberated from the coal mass they come in contact with the walls of the carbonizing chamber before they escape and are condensed. If the walls of the carbonization chamber are at about 450° C., the gaseous products are not changed by coming in contact with them and the tar recovered from the gases is a true low-temperature tar, called a primary tar. If, however, as is the case in the commercial production of coal tar, the walls of the chamber are at a higher temperature, the gases evolved from the coal at 450° C. are altered when they come in contact with the hotter walls. The type of change which occurs at these hot walls, as well as the portion of the gases that undergoes change, depends upon the temperature of the walls and the length of time the gases are in contact with the hot walls.

Although it is customary to say that the coal is carbonized at a low temperature or at a high temperature, this is not strictly correct. The coal is not carbonized *at* a temperature but *to* a temperature. The initial decomposition of the coal takes place at about 450° C. As the carbonization progresses, the temperature of the decomposing coal rises. If the carbonization process is discontinued when the temperature of the decomposing coal mass reaches about 700° C., and if the gases do not come in contact with walls which are at a temperature above about 700° C., the tar recovered is a low-temperature tar. If the decomposing coal is heated to a higher temperature, 900° C.–1,200° C., further decomposition of the coal mass takes place; the gaseous products evolved at these higher temperatures are of a different nature from those evolved at the lower temperature.

In commercial carbonization of coal, the heat needed is usually supplied through the walls of the retort. In high-temperature carbonization processes the temperature of the retort walls varies from about 900° C. to about 1,200° C. In such retorts the coal close to the hot walls is quickly heated to the temperature of the walls, and the gaseous products evolved come in contact with the hot walls before they escape; the tar thus produced is truly a product of high-temperature carbonization. However, the coal farther removed from the walls is heated more slowly, the gases are first evolved at low temperatures, and if all of these gases could be condensed without coming in contact with the hot walls (900° C.–1,200° C.) a low-temperature tar would be obtained, but most of these gases do come in contact with the hot walls and are thereby altered. As the carbonization proceeds the temperature toward the centre of the charge increases and slowly approaches that of the walls. The higher temperature causes further decomposition of the coal. The type of products obtained by this later decomposition is different from that first obtained.

The tar recovered from commercial high-temperature carbonization is a mixture of products resulting from the high-temperature decomposition of the coal and of the products formed by the thermal decomposition of the low-temperature and intermediate-temperature tars evolved from the coal.

Two general classes of chambers are used for the production of coal tar: (1) gas retorts, which are relatively small chambers; and (2) by-product coke ovens, which are much larger. Most gas retorts are either horizontal or vertical. Horizontal retorts, the oldest form of gas retorts, vary from about 8 ft. to about 20 ft. in length; they have a shape which is approximately that of a half cylinder with the flat portion forming the floor of the retort. A group of these retorts is built up into banks or "benches"; around the outside of the retorts and through the benches there is a system of flues through which flow the hot gases which thus heat the walls of the retort. Horizontal retorts are heated to about 1,000° C. to 1,100° C. throughout their entire length. The tar liberated from the coal during carbonization in a horizontal retort is in contact with the hot retort walls for a long time before it escapes to the condensing equipment. This prolonged exposure to the high temperature alters a large portion of the tar. Although the walls of horizontal retorts are not much hotter than those of the by-product coke ovens, the ratio of wall surface to coal charge is high and therefore the tars obtained from horizontal retorts have undergone considerable decomposition after their liberation from the coal. Horizontal retort tars are high-temperature tars; they have high specific gravities, are viscous, have only a small amount of tar acids and are high in naphthalene content.

The vertical retorts are the most popular gas retorts in England. These retorts are vertical tubes having an elliptical or rectangular cross section. They are usually about 20-25 ft. long and measure 5 ft.-10 ft. by 8-18 in. in cross section. The retorts are grouped in settings. They are heated by means of hot gases passed through flues arranged between individual retorts. Vertical retorts are either of the intermittent or continuous type. In the operation of vertical retorts, coal is charged in at the top and the coke is discharged at the bottom. In the continuous vertical retort, as the coal moves downward it slowly passes through zones of increasing temperatures. The decomposition of the coal starts in the cooler upper regions of the retort and the tars formed there escape from the retort without much change; some of the tar formed in the lower portions of the retort is decomposed by coming in contact with the hot retort walls, but most of this tar passes up through the coal bed and escapes without being thermally decomposed. Hence, the tar which emerges from the vertical retort is a combination of tars, most of which have been subjected to only low-temperature conditions, some that have been exposed to medium-temperatures and a small portion that has been exposed to high-temperatures. Although vertical retorts are considered to be a type of high-temperature carbonizing equipment, the tars produced in these retorts have characteristics intermediate between those of low-temperature and high-temperature tars.

As was mentioned above, the other general type of equipment used to produce tar is the by-product coke oven. More than three-fourths of the tar produced in the United States is by-product coke-oven tar. The modern by-product coke oven is rectangular in shape, about 40 ft. long, 14 ft. high and 16 in. wide. The ovens are built in long rows, called "batteries." The two long walls of the oven are heated by flues in which gas is burned to furnish the heat. These ovens are operated in an intermittent manner. Coal is charged into the ovens through removable doors in the top. After the carbonization is complete, doors at both ends of the oven are opened and the red-hot coke is pushed out by means of a long steel ram. Then another charge of coal is introduced and the process repeated. Some of the gaseous products evolved from the coal during carbonization pass upward along the hot walls of the oven, some of them pass through the uncoked centre of the coal charge, but some of them pass through the coked and partly coked region of the charge; these gases are largely decomposed as they pass through the heated zones so that a high-temperature tar is formed.

Commercially, coal tar is produced by the carbonization of bituminous coal of the common banded variety. The yield of tar obtained is dependent upon the amount of volatile matter in the coal. When coal is carbonized at high temperatures there seems to be little relationship between the properties of the tar produced and the nature of volatile matter originally present in the coal; the thermal decomposition of the primary tars equalizes their properties.

PROCESSING

The raw tar is processed in various ways to produce a variety of products. The processing is usually not carried out at the plant which produced the tar but is conducted at conveniently located tar processing plants. The processor of coal tar has long been known as a tar distiller. This designation is an appropriate one since distillation is the foundation of the coal-tar industry.

Usually the first step in processing coal tar is to give it a primary distillation to produce a number of fractions or cuts. The number of cuts made and the nature of the cuts vary somewhat at the different plants. In general, at least three cuts are made. These are frequently referred to as light oil, middle oil and heavy oil; the middle oil is also known as tar-acid oil and as crude naphthalene oil; the heavy oil is sometimes called anthracene oil. The material remaining after the removal of the oil distillates is usually either a pitch or a refined road tar base; occasionally, the distillation is carried on until the residue is pitch coke.

The primary distillation is made either in batch stills or in continuous stills. In the United States the commonly used batch still is a horizontal, cylindrical steel vessel; in England it usually is a vertical cylindrical vessel, known as a "pot still." The capacity of the batch stills varies from about 3,000 gal. to about 8,000 gal.

In the continuous distillation of coal tar the most generally used equipment is a tube still, also called a pipe still. Essentially, the tube still consists of a furnace containing a tube several hundred feet long. The tube is either in the form of a spiral or more commonly in straight lengths connected in a continuous manner by means of return bends. The diameter of the tube varies in the different plants but is usually between one inch and five inches.

When tar is processed in a continuous manner in a tube still, it is pumped through the hot tube whereby it is heated to a predetermined temperature. After passing through the tube the hot tar is released either into one tall fractionating column or into several shorter columns which are connected in series. In the fractionating equipment the tar is separated into oil vapours and either a pitch or an intermediate product, as desired. The oil vapours are collected into such cuts as are wanted; the pitch is pumped to storage.

How far the tar is distilled depends upon the products to be manufactured. If the plant is interested primarily in the distillate oils, the tar is distilled to either a hard fuel pitch or even to pitch coke. On the other hand, if the plant is to make specific residual products, such as road tar, briquetting pitch or roofing pitch, the distillation is stopped at an appropriate intermediate point.

In some of the smaller tar distilling plants, the oils obtained by the distillation of coal tar are merely mixed together to make creosote oil. In the larger refineries various chemical compounds are removed from the distillate oils prior to blending them to produce creosote oil.

The coal-tar distillate oils are complex mixtures of hundreds of chemical compounds. Most of these compounds fall into one of three groups: hydrocarbons, acids and bases. Mainly, the hydrocarbons present in coal-tar distillates belong to the aromatic series; typical coal-tar hydrocarbons are benzene (*q.v.*), naphthalene (*q.v.*) and anthracene (*q.v.*). The acidic compounds occurring in coal-tar oils are chiefly phenolic compounds, such as phenol (*see* CARBOLIC ACID OR PHENOL), cresols (*q.v.*), xylenols (dimethylphenols) and naphthols (*see* NAPHTHALENE). Coal-tar bases are cyclic nitrogen compounds; they have the nitrogen either attached to the ring as in aniline (*q.v.*) or forming a member of the ring as in pyridine (*q.v.*); in addition to aniline and pyridine, the picolines (*see* PYRIDINE), quinoline (*q.v.*) and acridine are typical coal-tar bases. Besides hydrocarbons, acids and bases, the coal-tar oils contain: nonacidic oxygen compounds, such as coumarone and diphenylene oxide; nonbasic nitrogen compounds of which carbazole is the most important and organic sulphur compounds; *e.g.*, the mercaptans and thiophenols. Appended to this article is a list of all the compounds that have been identified in coal-tar oils.

Tar Acids.—After the tar has been distilled and the desired cuts obtained, the next processing step in a coal-tar chemical plant is the extraction of the tar acids. These phenolic compounds react with caustic soda to form water-soluble salts. By means of this ability to form water-soluble salts they are separated from the other compounds present in the coal-tar distillates. The process used for the recovery of tar acids is essentially the same in all plants. The light-oil and the middle-oil fractions are washed separately with a dilute aqueous caustic soda solution by thoroughly mixing the two liquids. The mixture is then allowed to settle, whereupon it stratifies into two layers. The lower layer is the caustic soda solution of the tar acids, which solution is called "carbolate"; the upper layer consists of the oils which are not soluble in the caustic soda. The caustic soda solution is separated from the oil layer. Usually, the carbolates from the light-oil fraction and from the middle-oil fraction are combined for further purification; such purification comprises the removal of noncaustic soluble oils that were entrained in the carbolate and is usually accomplished by steaming. The tar acids are liberated or "sprung" from the purified carbolate by treating it with sulphuric acid or with carbon dioxide. The crude mixture of phenols thus obtained is subjected to fractional distillation, usually under vacuum, to obtain a number of products: phenol, orthocresol, cresylic acid and mixed xylenols; cresylic acid is a mixture of tar acids consisting largely of the three cresols (*o*-cresol, *m*-cresol and *p*-cresol) but also containing appreciable amounts of phenol and of the various xylenols.

By special processing, largely in the United States, the cresylic acid and the mixed xylenols are separated into the individual cresols and the individual xylenols. The individual tar acids which are commercially available are shown in italics in the list at the end of this article.

The tar acids present in the heavy-oil fraction are also recovered in some plants. These high-boiling tar acids are seldom fractionally distilled; they are usually used in the form of crude mixtures in the preparation of disinfectants possessing exceptionally high germicidal properties.

Tar Bases.—The more progressive coal-tar refineries recover the basic constituents present in the distillate oils. After the tar acids have been removed, the distillate oils are thoroughly mixed with a dilute aqueous solution of sulphuric acid. The sulphuric acid reacts with the coal-tar bases present to form water-soluble sulphates. Upon standing, the mixture stratifies into two layers: a lower aqueous sulphuric-acid layer containing the coal-tar base sulphates and an upper layer of neutral oil. The base sulphate solution, after being separated from the neutral oil, is purified to remove any entrained neutral oil. Then the bases are sprung by treating the solution with an excess of caustic soda or with a lime slurry. The crude mixture of bases is then subjected to fractional distillation to obtain various individual bases. The bases recovered from the light-oil fraction are pyridine, the picolines, the lutidines and some aniline bases. Frequently, a mixture of light bases is sold as "denaturing pyridine"; such mixtures were added to grain alcohol to make it unfit for human consumption; as the chemical uses for pyridine bases developed, the amount of bases sold as denaturing pyridine became small. From the middle-oil fraction are recovered quinoline, isoquinoline, methylquinolines and acridine.

Beta picoline, gamma picoline and 2,6-lutidine all boil at about 144° C. Because the boiling points of these three constituents of the light coal tar bases are so close together it is not possible to separate them from each other by ordinary fractional distillation.

In 1941 U.S. chemists found that these three bases could be separated readily from each other by the simple expedient of steam distillation through an efficient fractionating column. This discovery of a means of separating pure beta picoline from coal-tar bases was an important and timely one, for just then there arose a demand for beta picoline in the manufacture of nicotinic acid, the pellagra preventive factor of the vitamin B complex. The simplest and the most direct way of preparing nicotinic acid is by the oxidation of beta picoline. Another commerical method for preparing nicotinic acid involves the oxidation of quinoline to quinolinic acid and then decomposing the quinolinic acid to nicotinic acid.

In a few plants the tar bases present in the heavy-oil fraction are recovered. The mixture of bases thus obtained is a valuable inhibitor in the pickling of steel; it prevents the acid from attacking the steel but does not interfere with the action of the acid in dissolving the scale that is to be removed.

Naphthalene.—After the tar acids and the tar bases have been extracted from the middle oil, the "washed" oil is fractionally distilled to produce a heavy coal-tar solvent naphtha and a naphthalene fraction. The naphthalene fraction, while it is hot, is run into shallow pans; there it cools and crystallizes. The solidified mass is broken into large pieces, which are transferred to a crusher. By being crushed into fairly small pieces the solid chunks are transformed into a thick slurry of crystalline naphthalene suspended in an oil. The naphthalene is separated from the oil either by means of a centrifuge or a hydraulic press. The resulting crude naphthalene is used without further purification for many purposes. For other uses a pure naphthalene is needed. The crude naphthalene is refined by first treating it with either sulphuric acid or metallic sodium, and then distilling it. The distilled liquid naphthalene is usually passed over water-cooled steel rolls whereby it is solidified in thin layers which are then scraped to give "chipped naphthalene"; sometimes the naphthalene is allowed to solidify in pans and then is crushed to give "crystalline naphthalene"; the purest naphthalene is made by sublimation.

Higher Coal-Tar Hydrocarbons.—For the recovery of such higher boiling coal-tar hydrocarbons as acenaphthene (*q.v.*), fluorene, phenanthrene (*q.v.*), anthracene (*q.v.*), pyrene and chrysene, the heavy-oil cut is distilled to obtain fractions rich in the particular compound desired. Such fractions are then chilled to cause the compounds to crystallize. The crystalline substances are separated from the oil and are then purified, usually by recrystallization from solvents.

Light Oil.—The first fraction obtained in the distillation of coal tar is "light oil." It contains the lower boiling constituents of coal tar; *i.e.*, benzene (*q.v.*), toluene (*q.v.*) and the xylenes (*q.v.*). Because of the low boiling point of these compounds only a small portion of them is condensed with the tar; most of them are recovered from the coke-oven gases in a separate step after the tar has been condensed. Because the quantity of light oil recovered from the coke-oven gases is so much greater than that recoverable at the tar distillation plant, it is seldom profitable to refine light oil at a tar refinery. Practically all the processing of light oil is carried out at the tar producing plants.

After the tar and water have been condensed, and usually after the ammonia has been removed, the coke-oven gases are treated to recover the light oil. It is recovered from the gases by scrubbing them with high-boiling coal-tar or petroleum oils, or by absorption on activated carbon. In the oil-washing process the coke-oven gases are passed through a suitable high-boiling tar oil or petroleum oil, which dissolves the light-oil components. The light oil is recovered from the wash oil by steam distillation in a stripping column; the wash oil is used again to scrub more coke-oven gases. In the activated carbon process the coke-oven gases are passed through a bed of activated carbon which absorbs the light oil. The latter is recovered from the carbon by steaming it; the carbon is re-used.

The refining of coal-tar light oils is essentially a combination of fractional distillation and sulphuric-acid washing. A common practice is first to fractionate the light oil to obtain several crude cuts: forerunnings (the most volatile fraction), benzene, toluene, light-solvent naphtha and heavy-solvent naphtha. The further processing of the crude benzene depends upon the use to which it will be put; if it is to be used as a motor fuel, its further processing consists in the addition of an antioxidant; if, however, the benzene is to be used as a chemical or for industrial solvent purposes, it is washed with sulphuric acid and then distilled. The process for refining the crude toluene fraction and the crude light-solvent naphtha fraction is the same as that for the crude benzene.

The crude heavy-solvent naphtha is the main source of the coumarone-indene resins. In order to produce these resins the naphtha is subjected to a special processing. First it is washed with dilute sulphuric acid to remove the bases. Then the resin-forming constituents, the coumarones and the indenes, are polymerized (resinified) by vigorously agitating the washed naphtha with small quantities of concentrated sulphuric acid. The polymerized product is separated from the unreacted oils, dried and polymerized further by heating.

Light Pyridine Bases.—Because of their widely different boiling points, and because of their solubility in water and in oils, the pyridine bases formed by the carbonization of coal are divided between the tar and the gases remaining after the tar has been condensed. In 1937 the demand for pyridine made it desirable to recover more bases from the coke-oven gas. As described above, after the water and the tar have been removed, the remaining gas is passed through dilute sulphuric acid to absorb the ammonia present; the sulphuric acid at the same time absorbs the pyridine bases. The separation of the pyridine bases from the ammonia liquor is accomplished in many ways, usually by neutralization and distillation.

Most of the pyridine, picolines and lutidines of commerce are produced from the light pyridine bases recovered from the coke-oven gases.

Road Tar.—In the manufacture of road tar, the crude tar is distilled to obtain a "road tar base," which is a soft pitch. The road tar base is then cut back or thinned by the addition of a suitable flux oil; the flux oils most commonly used are water-gas tar distillates, coal-tar oils or a light water-gas tar. The extent to which the base is thinned is governed by the particular requirements in each case.

History.—J. J. Becher, a German professor of medicine, is credited with having discovered coal tar sometime prior to 1665. The inability of the British to obtain wood tar from America during the Revolutionary War made them resort to the use of coal tar for treating ships' bottoms, thereby giving the first impetus to the production of coal tar. The introduction of coal-gas lighting in England in 1792 was the next step in the development of a coal-tar industry. The first commercial application of a coal-tar distillate was in 1820 when Charles Mackintosh used coal-tar solvent naphtha to produce a solution of rubber for waterproofing cloth. About 1825, railroad ties were treated with coal-tar distillates to prevent their decay (*see* CREOSOTE OR KREOSOTE). Coal-tar pitch was used for briquetting coal in 1842. When he was a professor at the Royal College of Chemistry in London, A. W. von Hofmann in 1845 discovered benzene in coal-tar distillates. The first coal-tar dye was made in 1856 by William H. Perkin, one of Hofmann's assistants; this was a mauve dye synthesized from aniline, which was made from benzene. In 1868 two German chemists, Carl Graebe and Carl Liebermann, synthesized the dye alizarin from coal-tar anthracene. The discovery of the antiseptic properties of carbolic acid (phenol) by Sir Joseph Lister in 1865 was the next milestone in the development of uses for coal-tar compounds. In 1901 coal tar was first used to surface roads. A new field for coal-tar products was opened in 1907 when Leo Baekeland discovered the bakelite resins; these are made from phenols and formaldehyde. The synthesis of synthetic yarns, such as nylon, from coal-tar products is just another chapter in the history of coal tar.

CONSTITUENTS

The chemical constituents identified in coal tar prior to 1946 are listed below. The compounds are grouped by their chemical nature. In the various groups, they are listed in the order of increasing boiling points. Those hydrocarbons, phenols and bases which are printed in italics were produced commercially in 1946.

Hydrocarbons.—*n*-pentane, isobutylacetylene, pentene-1, cyclopentadiene 41° C., 1,1-dimethylallene, valylene (1,4-pentadiene), 1-methylbutadiene, propylacetylene, methylethylacetylene, *n*-hexane, hexene, 2,3-dimethylbutadiene, diethylacetylene, butylacetylene, *benzene* 80° C., cyclohexane (hexahydrobenzene), cyclohexene (tetrahydrobenzene), dihydrobenzene, methylpropylacetylene (4-hexyne), heptene, *n*-heptane, *toluene* 110.8° C., *n*-octane, ethylbenzene, *m-xylene* 139.3° C., *p-xylene* 138.4° C., 1,2,4-trimethylcyclohexane, *o-xylene* 144° C., styrene, cumene (isopropylbenzene), decane, *n*-propylbenzene, *m*-ethyltoluene, *p*-ethyltoluene, mesitylene (1,3,5-trimethylbenzene), *o*-ethyltoluene, pseudocumene (1,2,4-trimethylbenzene), *dicyclopentadiene* 170° C., hemimellitene (1,2,3-trimethylbenzene), cymene (*p*-methylisopropylbenzene), hydrindene, *indene* 182° C., 1-ethyl-3,4-dimethylbenzene, *n*-undecane, durene (1,2,4,5-tetramethylbenzene), isodurene (1,2,3,5-tetramethylbenzene), 4-methylindene, *tetrahydronaphthalene, naphthalene* 218° C., dimethylindene, *2-methylnaphthalene* 241.1° C., *1-methylnaphthalene* 244.8° C., 2-ethylnaphthalene, 1-ethylnaphthalene, *diphenyl* 255.2° C., 2,6-dimethylnaphthalene, 2,7-dimethylnaphthalene, 1,7-dimethylnaphthalene, 1,6-dimethylnaphthalene, 1,5-dimethylnaphthalene, 2,3-dimethylnaphthalene, 1,2-dimethylnaphthalene, 3-methyldiphenyl, 4-methyldiphenyl, 1,3,7-trimethylnaphthalene, *acenaphthene* 280.7° C., 2,3,5-trimethylnaphthalene, 2,3,6-trimethylnaphthalene, 3,4′-dimethyldiphenyl, 4,4′-dimethyldiphenyl, γ-diphenylenemethane, 4,5-benzondane (1,2-cyclopentanonaphthalene), *fluorene* 298° C., paraffin (octadecane), heneicosane, 2-methylfluorene, 3-methylfluorene, tricosane, tetracosane, pentacosane, docosane, nonadecane, hexacosane, heptacosane, octacosane, *phenanthrene* 340° C., *anthracene* 342.3° C., 3-methylphenanthrene, 4,5-phenanthrylenemethane, 9-methylphenanthrene, 1-methylphenanthrene, 2-phenylnaphthalene, naphthacene, 2-methylanthracene, 2,7-dimethylanthracene, 1,2,3,4-tetrahydrofluoranthene, truxene, *fluoranthene* 384° C., *pyrene* 393° C., retene (8-methyl-2-isopropylphenanthrene), 1,2-benzofluorene (naphthofluorene), 2,3-benzofluorene (isonaphthofluorene), naphtho-2′,3′-1,2-anthracene, 1,2-benzonaphthacene, *chrysene* 448.5° C., triphenylene, crackene, benzerythrene, 1,2-benzanthracene, perylene, 4,5-benzopyrene, 1,2-benzopyrene, 3,4-benzopyrene, picene, 1,12-benzoperylene.

Phenols.—*phenol* 183° C., *o-cresol* 191° C., *p-cresol* 201° C., *m-cresol* 202° C., *1,3,4-xylenol* (2,4-dimethylphenol) 211° C., 1,3,2-xylenol (2,6-dimethylphenol), *1,4,2-xylenol* (2,5-dimethylphenol) 211.3° C., *m-ethylphenol* 219° C., *p-ethylphenol* 218° C., 1,2,3-xylenol (2,3-dimethylphenol), *1,3,5-xylenol* 220° C., *1,2,4-xylenol* (3,4-dimethylphenol) 226° C., pseudocumenol (2,4,5-trimethylphenol), *1,3,5-methylethylphenol* 236° C., isopseudocumenol (2,3,5-trimethylphenol), 7-hydroxycoumarone, 4-hydroxyhydrindene, 3,4,5-trimethylphenol, durenol (2,3,5,6-tetramethylphenol), 5-hydroxyhydrindene, *o-phenylphenol* 275° C., *α-naphthol* 280° C., *β-naphthol* 286° C., *p-phenylphenol* 319° C., tetramethylbiphenol, 2-hydroxydiphenyleneoxide, 2-hydroxyfluorene, hydroxyanthracene, 2-hydroxyphenanthrene (2-phenanthrol).

Nitrogen Bases.—*pyridine* 115° C., *α-picoline* (2-methylpyridine) 129° C., *β-picoline* (3-methylpyridine) 144° C., *2,6-lutidine* (2,6-dimethylpyridine) 143.8° C., *γ-picoline* (4-methylpyridine) 145.4° C., *2,4-lutidine* 157° C., *2,5-lutidine* 156° C., 2,3-lutidine, 3,4-lutidine, 4-ethylpyridine, 2,4,5-trimethylpyridine, 2,3,4-trimethylpyridine, 3,5-lutidine, symmetrical collidine (2,4,6-trimethylpyridine), 2,3,6-trimethylpyridine, *aniline* 184° C., *p-toluidine,* 200.4° C., *o-toluidine* 200.7° C., *m-toluidine* 203.3° C., 2,4-xylidine, 2,5-xylidine, 3,5-xylidine, 2,3-xylidine, 2,3,4,5-tetramethylpyridine, *quinoline* 238° C., *isoquinoline* 243.2° C., *quinaldine* (2-methylquinoline) 247.6° C., 8-methylquinoline, *3-methylisoquinoline* 252.2° C., *1-methylisoquinoline* 255.2° C., 2,8-dimethylquinoline, 7-methylquinoline, 6-methylquinoline, 3-methylquinoline, 5-methylquinoline, *lepidine* (4-methylquinoline) 264.2° C., 5,8-dimethylquinoline, 2,4,6-trimethylquinoline, hydroacridine, *α-naphthylamine* 301° C., *β-naphthylamine* 306° C., *acridine* 346° C., phenanthridine, phenanthridone.

Sulphur Compounds.—ethylmercaptan, dimethylsulphide, carbon disulphide, ammonium sulphide, thiophene, diethylsulphide, 2-methylthiophene, 3-methylthiophene, trimethylthiophene, thiophenol, ammonium thiocyanate, *o*-thiocresol, thionaphthene, methylthionaphthene, diphenylene sulphide, dibenzothionaphthene.

Nonphenolic Oxygen Compounds.—acetone, ethyl alcohol, methylethylketone, acetic acid, propionic acid, coumarone, 6-methylcoumarone, 3- or 5-methylcoumarone, 4-methylcoumarone, acetophenone, 3,6-dimethylcoumarone, 4,5-dimethylcoumarone, 4,6-dimethylcoumarone, benzoic acid, α-naphthofurane, β-naphthofurane, *diphenylene oxide,* 1-methyldiphenyleneoxide, 2-methyldiphenyleneoxide, 2,3,5,6-dibenzocoumarone, 1,9-benzoxanthene.

Nonbasic Nitrogen Compounds.—methylisocyanide, *acetonitrile* (methyl cyanide), pyrrole, benzonitrile, indole, 3-methylindole (skatole), 7-methylindole, 4-methylindole, 5-methylindole, 2-methylindole, 1-naphthonitrile (1-cyanonaphthalene), 2-naphthonitrile, *carbazole,* 2-methylcarbazole, 3-methylcarbazole, 2,3-benzocarbazole.

See National Research Council, H. H. Lowry, Chairman, *The Chemistry of Coal Utilization,* 2 vol. (1945). (F. E. Cr.)

COAL-TAR DYESTUFFS: *see* DYES, SYNTHETIC.

COALVILLE, a town in northwest Leicestershire, England, 112 mi. N.N.W. from London by the London Midland Region railway route. Pop. of urban district (est. 1938) 24,150. Area 10 sq.mi. This is a town of modern growth, a centre of the coal-mining district of south Leicestershire. There are also elastic web factories, iron foundries and brickworks.

A mile north of Coalville is Whitwick, with remains of a Norman castle, while to the north again are remains of the nunnery of Gracedieu, founded in 1240.

COAST, the edge of the land in contact with the sea. The term (from Lat. *costa,* a rib, side) is sometimes applied to the bank of a lake or wide river, and sometimes to a coastal zone (*cf.* Gold Coast, Coromandel Coast). If the coast line runs parallel to a mountain range, such as near the central Andes, it has usually a more regular form than when, as in the *rias* coast of southwest Ireland, it enters between the crustal folds. A recently elevated coast is usually regular, while a recently depressed coast shows the irregularities which were present upon the surface before submergence. Waves and sea currents are the chief agents in coast sculpture. A coast of homogeneous rock exposed to steady erosion will present a regular outline, but if exposed to differential action it will be most embayed where the action is greatest. A coast consisting of rocks of unequal hardness will be marked, when the wave and current action remains similar throughout, by headlands, "stacks" and "needles" of hard rocks, and bays or gulfs of softer or more loosely aggregated rocks, *e.g.,* the southern shore lines of the Isle of Wight and of southwestern Wales. Subsequently the coast becomes "mature" and its outline undergoes little change as it gains on the land, for the hard rock being now more exposed is worn away faster than the softer rock which lies protected in the bays and re-entrants.

COASTAL HIGHWAY: *see* ATLANTIC COASTAL HIGHWAY.

COAST DEFENSE. One of the primary missions of a military establishment is the protection of its country's coast against attack and invasion by an enemy power in time of war. During World War II, the wide use of military aircraft and the introduction of radar and other electrical detection devices, the experimental use of guided missiles and the employment of carrier-based planes and other innovations changed the concepts of coast defense radically. Postwar research and development produced planes flying at supersonic speeds and capable of girdling the earth. The construction and use of guided missiles and rockets reached a high degree of perfection. The destructive possibilities of the atom bomb and the hydrogen bomb advanced beyond the point of being an inventor's dream. All of these, plus hundreds of other scientific developments with high potentials as instruments of warfare, definitely pointed to the necessity of continuously changing ideas to secure the integrity of a nation's territory against enemy action in time of war.

While the concepts had changed, however, the objectives of coast defense still went back to the earliest days when naval vessels were first used to carry an invading field force to the home shores of an adversary. Broadly stated, the first objective is to prevent a hostile sea-borne force from landing on the coast or an enemy air force from crossing the coast line for the purpose of interior penetration. The second objective is to repel a successful landing quickly before an enemy can establish a beachhead and push inland, or to turn back an air-borne assault before it can reach a vital target. The third objective is to maintain safe ports and harbours from which a nation's fleet can operate and enjoy protection against sneak attacks or harassing action by enemy naval forces.

The best way to accomplish any and all of these objectives is, of course, to nip an invasion in the bud at the enemy's staging area before his forces can get launched or, by maintaining the initiative in defense and thus destroying his own defenses, crippling his industry and resources and shattering morale, prevent the possibility of invasion plans or preparations. This is the implementation of the old military axiom that the best defense is a strong offense.

In the early days of warfare, protection against invasion was a relatively elementary problem. Known harbours and navigable inland streams were almost certain to be the approach points of a hostile sea-borne force. Consequently, in time of peace, it was possible to make preparations against a future emergency. These consisted of building fortifications at strategic locations and having channel chains and other types of movable barriers ready for employment in time of attack or threat of attack.

Until comparatively modern times this was the fundamental method of coastal defense. The mechanical propulsion of ships producing ever-increasing speed and manoeuvrability, and the widening ranges of guns, called for changes in techniques and equipment but the concepts of defense changed but little.

Nations most removed by the seas from potential enemies were the most secure from hostile attack. In this respect, the United States was particularly fortunate. Enjoying practically continuous amity with its neighbour to the north and only occasional hostility with its neighbour to the south, the only serious threat to the integrity of its soil could normally come from across the Atlantic or the Pacific oceans. It was true until the advent of World War II that the sea provided the best U.S. defense against enemy forays. The United States, however, had been successfully invaded from the sea during its two earliest wars, and methods to forfend such proven possibilities had been under consideration practically since the birth of the nation.

In 1793, George Washington advised congress that the vulnerable portion of the U.S. coast line should be fortified. His advice went unheeded for a year but in 1794, Gen. Henry Knox, who had been Washington's chief of artillery, drew up plans for harbour defense works for which a small amount of money had been provided. These works never got much beyond the planning stage, because of lack of funds, until after the War of 1812 when the reverses suffered at the hands of a small force of regular British troops convinced the U.S. people of the necessity for some permanent opposition to hostile landings. In 1816 construction of defensive works was begun and during the next 45 years most of the important harbours on the Atlantic and Gulf coasts were protected by a series of closed masonry forts. During the American Civil War many of these forts gave excellent accounts of themselves and capitulated to greatly superior forces only after extensive siege operations.

Subsequent to the Civil War coast defense languished for 20 years, but in 1886 the subject received renewed impetus and the succeeding two decades witnessed the construction, at all important harbours in the continental United States, of defensive works designed solely to repulse attack by naval gunfire. These works were very vulnerable to assault from the land side and this fact, coupled with the implication inherent in the existence of long stretches of undefended coast between the fortifications, led students of national defense to consider, apparently for the first time in half a century, coast defense as distinguished from purely harbour defense.

The result of this consideration was the adoption of a system of defense which was largely negative and which placed upon coast artillery troops not only the responsibility for serving their guns but also that of acting as infantry in their own support in the event that enemy troops succeeded in effecting a landing in the vicinity of the batteries. Lack of sufficient mobile troops to provide the supporting elements was responsible for this makeshift arrangement, which prevailed for nearly ten years; in fact, until the entry of the United States into World War I in 1917.

At that time the U.S. harbour defenses mounted both guns and mortars of large, medium and small calibre, together with ammunition and fire control necessary for their effective tactical employment against naval vessels. In addition, a thoroughly efficient system of submarine mines had been developed and was ready for installation. Harbours in the Panama Canal Zone, Hawaiian territory and the Philippine Islands, as well as those in the continental United States, were provided with their quota of permanent fortifications.

Calibres of weapons ranged from 3 in. up to and including 16 in.—sufficient in power and range to combat effectively any naval armament afloat. Weapons were more or less dispersed with connecting control and supply lines concealed and protected. Prior to the use of aeroplanes for reconnaissance and fire direction many U.S. guns were mounted on disappearing carriages located behind parapets, so that the guns and their accessories were invisible from the sea. Modern coast defense installations up to and including the World War II period relied on camouflage and dispersion as well as limited mobility secured by mounting cannon on railway carriages which enabled rapid change of positions for the big coast artillery weapons.

Subsequent to World War I, two schools of thought grew up on the subject of the proper type of weapon for harbour defense. One maintained that fixed defenses were obsolete, or at least obsolescent, and that all future defensive installations should be railway guns which could be moved from point to point to meet naval threats. Their opponents, while agreeing that railway artillery had many advantages, particularly in specific localities such as the Panama Canal Zone, maintained that it was not the whole answer to the problem of fortification of harbours. They reasoned that naval forces could move more rapidly than heavy railway artillery and that it was necessary to have heavy artillery available and ready to function at strategic points before the arrival of a hostile fleet. A compromise view eventually prevailed. Both types of weapons were in use at the time of the U.S. entry into World War II.

The European conflicts also taught the U.S. that a proper solution of the problem of coast defense required more than mere resistance by harbour defense artillery to naval bombardment. Coast defense concerns all arms and demands employment of all branches of the army, organized and trained to function as a team. This conception led to the adoption of what is known as a "positive system of coast defense," in which not only all branches of the army participate but also selected elements of the navy and the air force.

Coast defenses may be attacked from the land, sea or air and such attacks may be separate or co-ordinate. The likelihood of separate sea or land attack against coast defenses is remote unless the attacker has control of local sea areas. But separate air attacks, combinations of land and air attacks or sea and air attacks are certain, just as the combination of all three basic forms is inevitable. Coast defenses have to provide resistance to all of these.

Fleets cannot be relied upon for defensive missions; they should never be tied to the defense of any harbour or section of coast line no matter how important; their proper function is always the offensive, to seek out and destroy the enemy on the sea or in his home bases. The same logic applies to air forces. Therefore, the burden of coast defense must be borne by land forces, which, however, must have both naval and air support.

In light of the modern weapons and machines of war, a nation with expansive coastal areas, such as the United States, is potentially vulnerable at practically any point. Defenders no longer can expect attack at a comparatively few predetermined points of opportunity and prepare strong defenses for their protection. Remote beaches can be assaulted by sea-borne forces. And in the air there are no limitations of a geographical nature that an enemy need surmount. For this reason most of the fixed coast defense forts and batteries were abandoned as structures in a modern nation's defensive system, probably on the premise that they might prove as ineffective as was the Maginot line on the inland border of France or the "impregnable" defenses on Corregidor and Fort Drum in Manila bay during World War II.

To a great extent the few fixed coast artillery defenses remaining after World War II followed a general pattern. Coast defense cannon were ordinarily emplaced in pairs, especially those of 12 in. or larger calibre, although in some instances they might be mounted singly or in groups of from four to eight. Each pair or group, together with the necessary fire control and fire direction facilities, ammunition supply installation and other accessories, was usually referred to as a "battery." This same term was used to designate the men operating the guns. The ammunition storage, fire control stations and battery commanders' stations were ordinarily located so as to take advantage of such natural protection as the ground near the battery afforded, consistent with the ability to perform their battle functions efficiently. Usually electric power was provided for working the guns, handling heavy ammunition and, of course, for communications.

In order to deliver accurate and rapid fire at a moving target such as a battleship the shore battery determines firing data by a method of finding the various positions of the target at stated intervals of a time sequence, say every minute for a period of five minutes, then predicting from this known data where the ship will be at the end of another interval of time, say the end of the sixth minute. Thus, being able to predict the probable future course of the target, and its probable location at a selected future instant, it is possible to relate such prediction to the position of the gun, point the gun ahead of the ship and fire the gun so that the ship and projectile will arrive at the same point simultaneously. This procedure is known as position-finding, and the most common development of it is the horizontal base system, which requires two observation posts located at the end of a carefully measured line several thousands of yards in length, called a base line. These stations are equipped with powerful optical instruments with which simultaneous observations are made on the target.

The data thus obtained are telephoned to a central station called a plotting room, where they are processed, either graphically or automatically, so as to result in determination of the distance and direction of the target from the guns. These results are then set on appropriate scales on the guns or carriages, the guns are pointed accordingly and are fired, usually electrically, at the proper instant.

Obviously this system and its variations, such as the vertical base system in which the height of one observing instrument above sea level replaces the horizontal base of the parent system, depend upon ability to see the target from shore. In the case of long-range fire, where the target is invisible from shore, the shooting must be directed from aircraft. Such fire will naturally be less accurate than that directed by shore stations and will involve radio communication between aeroplane and shore stations.

Conversely, ships' fire under similar conditions of range will be directed by aircraft. It is evident that control of the air is indispensable to the delivery of accurate fire by either side under these circumstances.

The necessity for control of the air certainly leads to extensive air activity precedent to naval action against coast defense works. In fact, it may be doubted if such actions can be attempted unless air superiority can be gained. Hence, the closest co-operation and mutual support between coast defense forces and defensive air forces becomes of paramount importance. Also the provision of anti-aircraft defense in and about fortified harbours becomes essential. While air supremacy is a prerequisite of a successful attack on fortified harbours, it is equally essential when a landing is to be attempted on open beaches against well-organized resistance. In such operations the attacker is under the necessity of disembarking his troops from transports into small boats at a great distance from shore and these troops will need the support of well-directed naval gunfire from the time of such debarkation until they have established themselves on shore. During this time they are most vulnerable to fire of all descriptions—infantry, artillery and aircraft.

All these considerations gave rise to the typical coastal defense conception comprising the following elements given in the order of their appearance from front to rear: (1) distant naval and air reconnaissance or radar to detect enemy preparation for an overseas movement; (2) naval and air action to counter such efforts before they get under way; (3) naval and air action to meet such an effort at sea and defeat it there if the enemy succeeds in launching it; (4) naval and air offshore patrolling and scouting and other methods of detection to give early warning of the approach of hostile forces; (5) naval and air inshore patrolling to cover naval mine fields or other obstructions; (6) army controlled mines and accessories and fixed underwater obstacles and listening devices; (7) mobile coast defense artillery, in combination with anti-aircraft guns; with both fire control and searchlights supplemented by aircraft support, warning service and beach defense; (8) mobile army forces of all arms strategically located and capable of rapid movement and co-ordinated action.

This setup when composed of troops well-organized, well-trained, well-equipped, well-supplied and competently led can make a hostile landing effort so expensive to the attacker as to deter him from the attempt except as a last resort or unless he has such overwhelming superiority in one or more elements of combat as to convince him that his effort will succeed.

No matter what the doctrines of warfare and the concepts of defense might develop, the elements of surprise, feint and harassment—to as great an extent as possible—would be used by invading forces. Taking the place of casemates and cannons after World War II were defense devices to guard the portal entrances of the coasts against the type of attack appearing to be most likely. There is always the possibility of a sneak attack by hostile submarines such as resulted in the sinking of the British battleship "Royal Oak" inside Scapa flow by the German submarine skipper Lieut. Comdr. Guenther Prien in Oct. 1939. Other objectives of sneak attacks might be to plant mines to harass shipping, deliver atomic bombs to destroy harbours or to gather intelligence.

Electric mines controlled from shore locations and antisubmarine nets are two of the most effective types of coast defenses against such sneak attacks. These, of course, are complemented by sea and air patrols, radar and other types of electrical and listening devices and shore-based searchlight batteries.

On a large scale, the most likely invasion that a nation must prepare to repel would be air-borne in its initial phases. Regardless of the tremendous destructive power of an atomic bomb and the devastating effects of all types of bombs and guided missiles on the morale and the productive resources of a nation, it was widely agreed following World War II that a war could be won only after ground forces had entrenched themselves in hostile territory for the purpose of strangling the economy and the political authority of the enemy. For this purpose a sea invasion with air cover to set up a beachhead is within the realm of possibility, but for an adequately defended nation with sufficient military intelligence to provide for its defense with well-equipped mobile forces, such an operation might be extremely costly to the invader in personnel, ships, planes and supplies. Coast defense strategy, therefore, must take cognizance of a more logical type of attack.

In the era of long-distance flying, an air armada of transport planes could take off from secured bases, or, on a lesser basis, from sea-borne carriers and strike for an invasion point of its own choosing and at a time of its own selection.

Such an attack would demand air superiority in the invasion area, since unarmed transport planes, filled with paratroopers, need as much protection in the air element as transports and supply ships need on the seas. Prior to an air-borne invasion it would be necessary for an invader to keep the air lanes free of the planes employed in defending the coast. Target points of primary importance during the "softening up," or preinvasion, period would be airfields, supply depots and troop concentrations in the broad area of the contemplated invasion—with just enough feinting in other areas to confuse the coast defenders. Roads and railroads would come in for their share of strafing and destruction, as would known fixed and mobile anti-aircraft defenses. Such obvious targets, therefore, would require large-scale protection by both ground and air forces. The fixed ground forces defending the coastal approach lanes of an invader would need the support of reinforcements equipped with sufficient anti-aircraft artillery and other mobile equipment to repel the preinvasion attacks. These attacks would undoubtedly be scattered over a depth well beyond the usual conception of a coast line. Protection against guided missiles, jet projectiles and robot (unmanned) planes would also be figured in the defensive strategy. The majority of these new defensive weapons and strategies remained closely guarded secrets after World War II.

It was revealed, however, that a radar network spanning the continent near the border between the United States and Canada was in operation in the mid-1950s, and engineering work on a line across mid-Canada had been undertaken.

To give the earliest possible warning of the approach of hostile aircraft, it was planned to establish radar stations along a line across the most northerly practicable part of the continent of North America.

With such varied possibilities of hostile invasion confronting the defenders of a coast line in time of war and with the coast becoming a deep, undetermined segment of the country rather than a narrow perimeter washed by the sea, innumerable defense plans must be worked out in advance for the selection of the high command when the nature of the invaders' attack begins to take actual shape.

Worked out in time of peace, these plans take into account every conceivable possibility that imagination and experience can inject into a theoretical situation. From time to time they are studied and revised and brought up-to-date to conform to new developments and the estimates of contemporary intelligence. In the event of an actual invasion, however, much of the strategy of the defenders would have to be worked out during the heat of the engagement. In general, defense depends upon mobility and strength. Particular emphasis would be placed on anti-aircraft artillery complemented by a close-knit coastal ring of electrical detecting devices to prevent a surprise attack. Since the units of an air-borne invasion force can be assembled at any number of widely separated bases for prearranged massing in the air on D-day, military intelligence gleaned from observation and through other available sources cannot be relied upon to guard completely against surprise.

Air-borne troops alone could not be depended upon to invade a nation and hold their landing indefinitely against the onslaughts of the defenders, despite the fact that such troops might be accompanied by air-transported artillery, tanks, vehicles and other equipment.

Air-borne insufficiency to complete an over-all mission presents still another coast defense problem. Hostile air-borne troops would most likely be dropped well behind the actual coast line to battle back against the defender's coast-dispersed troops. These invaders would be followed by sea-borne reinforcements who would attempt landings on the coast. These elements would constitute the major portion of the invading army; its mission would be to secure a beachhead and to fight through to the air-borne elements in the rear of the defending forces. To prevent the success of the sea-borne phase of invasion there would remain the obvious necessity of keeping a strong mobile force in readiness along the coast line to repel the anticipated landing assaults under a strong cover of air support.

Equally important to military defense in wartime is the necessity for dispersal of manufacturing facilities, stock piles and other logistical assets. Much of these would be forced to go underground and as far inland as would be economically possible. Likewise, the responsibility of all citizens to play a part in the defense of their homeland against invasion would be tremendously increased.

The problem of coast defense was no longer one for the military alone. Participation in aircraft spotting and warning, fire fighting, first aid and evacuating services would be required in a total war.

Thus Great Britain and the United States re-established warning systems after World War II and took various steps to build up an effective civil defense program. The British Royal Observer corps was reorganized in 1946, and the United States established the Ground Observer corps, a civilian component of the air force.

By the end of 1954 about 375,000 civilian volunteers, who served without pay, were enrolled by U.S. state and local civil defense directors to supplement the radar coverage.

Under the Federal Civil Defense act of 1950, approved Jan. 12, 1951, the United States established the Federal Civil Defense administration to provide co-ordination and guidance to the states and their political subdivisions, where the primary responsibility for the operation of civil defense was vested. (*See* also OBSERVER CORPS IN AIR DEFENSE.)

BIBLIOGRAPHY.—Alfred Thayer Mahan, *The Influence of Sea Power Upon History, 1660–1783* (Boston, 1897), *Lessons of the War With Spain, and Other Articles* (Boston, 1899); Sir Reginald Hugh Spencer Bacon, *The Dover Patrol, 1915–1917*, 2 vol. (London and Garden City, N.Y., 1919); Charles Lee Lewis, *Famous Old-World Sea Fighters* (Boston, 1929); various issues of the *Journal, U.S. Artillery* (1921–40), *Coast Artillery Journal* (1945 *et seq.*), *Antiaircraft Journal* (1948 *et seq.*).
(M. B. H.; X.)

COAST GUARD, a force, usually naval in character, maintained in some countries for the suppression of smuggling or for affording assistance to vessels in distress or wrecked and for other coastal duties such as signalling.

Britain's coast guard, which is mainly concerned with lifesaving, had its origin in an organization formed under the customs to prevent smuggling at the end of the Napoleonic Wars. Under the Coast Guard act of 1856 the control of this organization was transferred to the admiralty in order to make better provision for coastal defense; to provide a reserve for the navy in case of war; and to protect the revenue. This act made no reference to lifesaving.

In the first half of the 19th century a number of private lifesaving companies were formed on the coast. In 1854, the board of trade became responsible for these companies and gradually provided further lifesaving apparatus companies all around the coast. The coast guard service helped to train these lifesaving companies. From 1910 onward they also provided a few lookout huts at danger points not covered by the existing coast guard organization. In 1923 the coast guard was transferred to the board of trade, and lifesaving and coast watching were combined under one head.

In 1938 the ministry of shipping took over the functions and powers of the mercantile marine department of the board of trade, including the administration of H.M. coast guard, and these functions and powers were later transferred to the ministry of war transport (later successively the ministry of transport and the ministry of transport and civil aviation).

The present organization exists primarily to help save lives in cases of shipwreck and distress at sea. For this purpose the coast guard keeps a lookout for vessels or aircraft in distress or danger, and gives assistance directly by means of the lifesaving appliances provided and indirectly by informing the lifeboat, air traffic control and other authorities in a position to help.

The coast-watching system is based on the maintenance of visual watch from some 314 lookout huts, usually sited on headlands or other vantage points overlooking dangerous waters. The distance between huts is about five miles where the small ship traffic is heavy and runs close to the coast, but is greater elsewhere. The normal type of watch is a bad weather watch, and (apart from occasional scanning of the coast by day) constant watch is only kept at points where there is a large volume of small coastal and fishing-boat traffic and the navigational hazards are such that immediate action is necessary to save lives if a casualty should occur even in fine weather.

A night watch is kept in fine weather at a sufficient number of stations to ensure that watch is set at all the other stations affected on the approach of bad weather.

In addition to this visual watch, a constant listening watch on the marine distress waves is kept by the ten coast radio stations of the general post office around the coasts of Great Britain. Any distress messages received by these radio stations are immediately passed by telephone to the nearest coast guard station, which in turn initiates all rescue measures.

The staff at coast guard stations are usually drawn from pensioners of the royal navy or men from the merchant navy with equivalent sea service. The lifesaving appliances are worked by teams of local men formed into companies of the Coast Life Saving corps. This corps, which has a voluntary basis, was founded in 1932 to assist the regular coast guard. In addition to forming the lifesaving companies, the members of the corps keep visual watch in bad weather from auxiliary stations and also help in relief work at regular stations. (J. H. Ly.)

UNITED STATES

Origin.—The United States coast guard traces its origin to the ten small armed boats authorized by the first congress on Aug. 4, 1790, to guard the nation's coast against smuggling from the sea and enforce custom laws. Known first as the revenue marine and later as the revenue cutter service, it became officially the U.S. coast guard when it was combined with the lifesaving service on Jan. 28, 1915. The lighthouse service, which had come under federal control on Aug. 7, 1789, was consolidated with the coast guard in 1939, and the bureau of marine inspection and navigation was transferred from the department of commerce to the coast guard in 1942. Thus the principal maritime agencies were organized as one united service.

Duties and Organization.—The functions of the U.S. coast guard embrace, in general terms, maritime law enforcement, saving and protecting life and property, providing navigational aids to maritime commerce and to transoceanic air commerce, promoting the efficiency and safety of the U.S. merchant marine and readiness for military operations.

The primary purpose of most of these duties is to prevent avoidable loss of life and property resulting from illegal or unsafe activities. In actual practice, however, the maintenance of safety and order in maritime navigation is not limited to the strict enforcement of laws, but also encompasses a continuing program of education among ship operators and boatmen and the enlistment of their co-operation and self-regulation in the prevention of marine disasters.

The organic act of 1915, as revised, provided that the coast guard ". . . shall be a military service and a branch of the armed forces of the United States at all times." It further provided that "the Coast Guard shall be a service in the Treasury Department, except when operating as a service in the Navy." Such service in the navy takes place upon the declaration of war or when the president directs.

The coast guard's peacetime organization, regulations, training and customs parallel those of the navy insofar as operations will permit. Personnel receive the same pay and allowances as prescribed for corresponding ranks, grades and ratings in the navy, and uniforms are identical except for the coast guard's shield insignia.

The coast guard, as the principal maritime law enforcement agency of the federal government, enforces or assists in the enforcement of all applicable federal laws upon the high seas and waters subject to the jurisdiction of the United States. It administers laws and promulgates and enforces regulations for the promotion and safety of life and property, covering all matters not specifically delegated by law to some other executive department. Among the more important are enforcement of the navigation and inspection laws and assistance in the enforcement of the Oil Pollution act, and of laws relating to internal revenue, customs, immigration, neutrality, and conservation and protection of fisheries and wildlife. It enforces rules governing the security of ports, anchorage and movement of vessels in territorial waters.

The coast guard had developed and operated in the mid-1950s more than 38,000 aids to maritime navigation, such as lighthouses, lightships, lights, radio beacons, radio-direction-finder stations, buoys and unlighted beacons, as required to serve the needs of commerce and the armed forces.

In the promotion of safety of life and property, coast guard duties include the inspection of vessels and their equipment; investigation of marine casualties; regulation of the outfitting and operation of motorboats, of the transportation of dangerous cargoes of vessels, and of the construction and repair of vessels; enforcement of manning, citizenship, mustering, drilling-crew and load-line requirements; protection of merchant seamen; and licensing of officers, pilots, seamen and motorboat operators.

The coast guard maintains an established organization of inshore and offshore rescue surface vessels, aircraft, lifeboat stations and radio stations, together with rescue co-ordination centres in each district. It extends medical aid to crews of U.S. vessels, transports shipwrecked and destitute persons in Alaska and elsewhere and engages in flood relief work. It operates ocean stations in both the North Atlantic and North Pacific to provide search and rescue, communication and air navigation facilities in areas traversed by U.S. aircraft. Another duty is to conduct the annual International Ice patrol in the North Atlantic to protect shipping from icebergs.

The administrative head of the coast guard is the commandant, with headquarters in Washington, D.C. In most instances activities were directed in the mid-1950s by 12 district commanders and performed by individual operating units such as ships, aircraft and marine inspection offices.

History.—The early revenue marine soon found itself charged with many other duties in addition to the enforcement of customs laws. These activities included distinguished service in every conflict in which the United States engaged, with the exception only of the war with Tripoli. A revenue cutter, "Harriet Lane," is credited with firing the first shot in the Civil War, on the eve of the bombardment of Fort Sumter, S.C. The cutter fleet of 28 vessels helped enforce the blockade and lent support to the army and navy striking into the south.

On April 6, 1917, when war was declared by the United States on Germany, the navy was augmented by 15 cruising cutters, about 200 officers, and 5,000 warrant officers and enlisted men of the coast guard. They were entrusted with the hunting of submarines and raiders and with guarding the transport of troops. A squadron of coast guard cutters, based at Gibraltar, performed escort duty between that port and the British Isles. While on this duty the cutter "Tampa" disappeared on the night of Sept. 26, 1918, with a loss of 111 coastguardmen and four navy men. It is believed that the "Tampa" was torpedoed. In proportion to its strength, the coast guard suffered the highest losses of any of the armed services in World War I.

The coast guard reached its peak strength in World War II. It had 802 vessels (more than 65 ft.) of its own and, in addition, manned 351 navy and 288 army craft. By June 30, 1945, its personnel numbered 171,168. Of these, 572 were killed in action. Coast guard surface craft destroyed 11 U-boats and aircraft sank another. More than 4,000 survivors of torpedoings and other enemy action were rescued from the Atlantic and Mediterranean. Another spectacular war duty was the manning of assault craft in landings in North Africa, Europe and in the Pacific. The coast guard's years of experience in operating small boats through the surf made it the logical organization to train and supply crews for landing craft from the smallest barges to the giant LST's (landing ship tanks). Coast guard crews also served on many of the large assault transports which carried the barges and troops within striking distance of the beachheads.

On D-day in Normandy 83-ft. coast guard cutters were given special lifesaving duties. Under fire from German guns, they rescued 1,468 men from sunken landing barges. On June 30, 1954, military personnel consisted of 3,177 commissioned officers, 452 commissioned warrant officers, 343 cadets, 454 warrant officers and 30,065 enlisted men. Larger ships in commission included 195 cutters and buoy tenders, 63 patrol boats, 36 lightships and 137 aircraft. The motto of the coast guard is *Semper Paratus* (Always Prepared). (*See* also UNITED STATES COAST GUARD ACADEMY.) (A. C. RD.)

COASTING, usually called tobogganing (*q.v.*) in Europe, the sport of sliding down snow or ice-covered hills or artificial inclines upon hand sleds, or sledges, provided with runners shod with iron or steel. It is uncertain whether the first American sleds were copied from the Indian toboggans, but no sled without runners was known in the United States before 1870, except to the woodsmen of the Canadian border. American laws have greatly restricted and in most places prohibited the practice, once common, of coasting on the highways, and the sport is mainly confined to open hills and artificial inclines or chutes. Two forms of hand sled are usual in America, the original "clipper" type, built low, with long, pointed sides, formerly shod with iron but since 1850 with round steel rods for runners; and the light, short "girls' sled," with high skeleton sides, usually flat shod. There is also the "double runner," or "bobsled," formed of two clipper sleds joined by a board and steered by ropes, a wheel or cross-bar, and seating from four to ten persons.

In the U.S., coasting enjoyed considerable popularity into the early decades of the 20th century. After 1932 it ceased to be rated an important winter sport at resorts in the Adirondacks of upper New York state and New England, where the emphasis is all on skiing. In the eastern cities of Canada, however, coasting is still a popular pastime. The chute at Mt. Royal, Montreal, consists of five tracks side by side, separated by ice. Dufferin Terrace, Que., has a three-track chute.

In Scandinavia several kinds of sled are common, but that of the fishermen, by means of which they transport their catch over the frozen fjords, is the one used in coasting, a sport especially popular in the neighbourhood of Oslo, where there are courses nearly three miles in length. This sled is from four to six feet long, with skeleton sides about seven inches high, and generally holds three persons. It is steered by two long sticks trailing behind. On the ice the fisherman propels his sled by means of two short picks. The general Norwegian name for sledge is *skijälker,* the primitive form being a kind of toboggan provided with broad wooden runners resembling the ski (*q.v.*). In northern Sweden and Finland the commonest form of single sleds is the *Sparkstottinger,* built high at the back, the coaster standing up and steering by means of two handles projecting from the sides.

Coasting in its highest development may be seen in Switzerland, at the fashionable winter resorts of the Engadine, where it is called tobogganing. The first regular races there were organized by John Addington Symonds, who instituted an annual contest for a challenge cup, open to all comers, over the steep post road from Davos to Klosters, the finest natural coast in Switzerland, the sled used being the primitive native *Schlittli* or *Handschlitten,* a miniature copy of the ancient horse sledge.

The construction of great artificial runs followed, the most famous being the "Cresta" at St. Moritz, begun in 1884, which is about 1,320 yd. in length, its dangerous curves banked up. The famous run has an electrical timing apparatus. The record time for the descent is 53.7 sec. made in 1911, an average speed of 47 mi. per hour. The total drop from start to finish is 514 ft., the average gradient 1 in 7.7. On this the annual Grand National championship is contested, the winner's time being the shortest aggregate of three heats. In 1885 and the following year the native *Schlittli* remained in use, the rider sitting upright facing the goal, and steering either with the heels or with short picks. In 1887 the first American clipper sled was introduced by L. P. Child, who easily won the championship for that year on it. The sled used by the contestants is a development of the American type, built of steel and skeleton in form. With it a speed of more than 80 mi. an hour has been attained. The coaster lies flat upon it and steers with his feet, shod with spiked shoes, to render braking easier, and helped with the gloved hands. This is called the *ventre-à-terre* position. The "double runner" has also been introduced into Switzerland under the name of "bobsleigh."

Olympic Competition.—Bobsled racing first figured in the Olympic winter games at Chamonix in 1924, when Switzerland won, Great Britain was second and Belgium third. There are usually races for the two-man and four-man sleds, and when the games were held at St. Moritz (1928, 1948) a skeleton event was also included in the program. Each nation may enter three sleds in each event but only two may compete. Races are run on several descents of the track, the results determined by the totals of the times. Electric timing devices are used.

In 1928 and 1932 the U.S. captured first place in all the bobsled events. John Heaton, skeleton winner in 1928, returned to St. Moritz 20 yr. later to take second place in the event, a remarkable achievement. The games of 1932 were held in the U.S. at Lake Placid, where, on Mt. Hoevenberg, is the only bob run in the nation which meets Olympic requirements. This run is 2,350 m. or approximately 1½ mi. long. It has a total of 28 curves, some of which are 22 ft. high. The average drop is 10%, maximum 15%.

In the fourth Olympic winter games at Garmisch-Partenkirchen, Germany, 1936, the four-man bobsled competition was won by Switzerland, but the U.S. again won the two-man event. In 1948 the winning nations were reversed—the Swiss won the two-man, the U.S. the four-man. N. Bibbia of Italy won the skeleton tobogganing medal. Germany, admitted for the first time since World War II, won both bobsled events in 1952. Andreas Ostler drove both the winning sleds.

The four-man bobsleds of latest design weigh close to 500 lb., and speeds exceeding 70 m.p.h. have been obtained.

See T. A. Cook, *Tobogganing at St. Moritz* (1896), and *Ice Sports,* in the Isthmian Library, London (1901); W. Duston White, *The Book of Winter Sports* (1925).

COAST PROTECTION AND LAND RECLAMATION. Shore lines of oceans, bays and estuaries are subject to both seasonal and long-term changes, under the combined influence of the supply of debris from streams and cliffs and of waves, tidal effects, currents and wind transport. In many localities the seasonal fluctuations take place about a constant position, but there are some reaches of the shore line where the long-term trend is either erosion or accretion. By means of structures or by artificial fill, land area may be reclaimed or erosion retarded. The construction and maintenance of such projects involve difficulties and uncertainties as to both cost and design, and the value of the land or of the improvements on it must usually be high to justify protective works.

Causes of Coastal Changes.—The breaking of waves is the principal cause of erosion or accretion of shore lines exposed to the sea. In protected bays and estuaries and along exposed coasts adjacent to estuaries and tidal entrances, both waves and tidal currents are effective in causing changes. Transportation of sand by wind and the formation of sand dunes sometimes plays a part, occasionally a major one.

Waves are generated by winds blowing over the surface of the ocean. The height of a wave, measured from trough to crest, and its length depend upon the velocity of the wind, on its duration and on the fetch or the length of ocean area exposed to the wind. For each wind velocity there is a minimum duration which must be equalled or exceeded if the waves are to attain their full development, and this minimum duration increases with wind velocity. Similarly, there is a minimum fetch necessary for full wave development under each wind velocity. Trains of wind-generated waves are variable as to height, period and direction in the generating area, but each wave condition may be characterized by a height and a period which are related quantitatively to the velocity, duration and fetch of the generating wind. Winds over the open ocean follow curved paths but the waves generated by them move out tangentially and apparently become longer and lower as they advance from the generating area to the shore.

The quantitative relationship between generating winds and generated waves, developed by H. U. Sverdrup and W. Munk, has great utility both in forecasting the waves to be expected from a current weather situation and in "hindcasting" from historical weather charts the general wave "climate" of a shore line. This technique has been applied widely. Information regarding wave characteristics is also obtained at certain localities from wave recorders which obtain a continuous record of height and period.

BY COURTESY OF U.S. COAST GUARD

VESSELS OF THE U.S. COAST GUARD

Top left: Painting of the first U.S. coast guard cutter, the "Massachusetts," built in 1791. The ship had a length of 50 ft. and weighed 70 tons

Top right: "Eagle," a 295-ft. three-masted bark used as a training vessel for U.S. Coast Guard academy cadets

Centre left: Patrol ship "Storis," used for search, rescue and law enforcement

Centre right: Coast guard cutter "Mackinaw," designed for icebreaking operations on the Great Lakes. A 10,000-h.p. diesel-electric power plant enables the ship to cut through four feet of solid sheet ice

Bottom: 327-ft. cutter "Campbell." Cutters of this class can maintain a speed of $20\frac{1}{2}$ knots and have a range of 8,000 mi.

COAST GUARD

U.S. AND BRITISH SHORE INSTALLATIONS

Top left: Coast guard air station at San Francisco, Calif.
Top right: Coast guard lookout station at Portland Bill, Eng., showing gale warning cone hoisted
Centre left: Living accommodations for members of the regular British coast guard at St. Just, Eng.
Centre right: Aerial view of the U.S. Coast Guard academy at New London, Conn.
Bottom: Coast guard lookout post at Cape Cornwall, Eng.

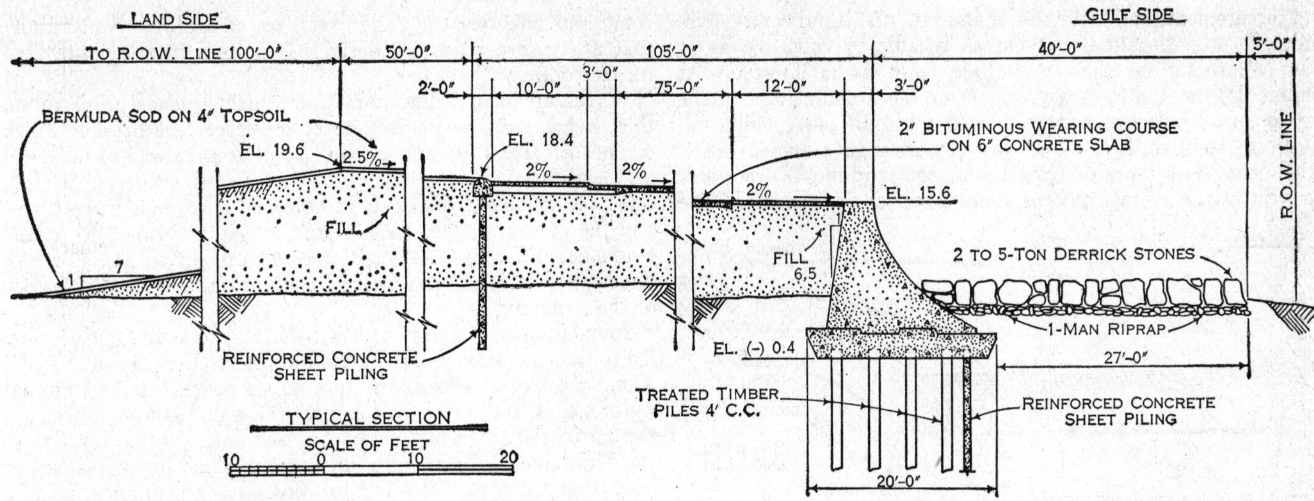

COURTESY OF THE BEACH EROSION BOARD

FIG. 1.—SEA WALL AT GALVESTON, TEX.

When waves move into shoal water their velocity decreases and, if they approach the shore line obliquely, the end of the crest nearer shore moves at a lower velocity and the wave turns. This phenomenon is known as refraction. Long waves "feel the bottom" in deeper water than do short ones. The tendency is for the wave crests to swing around so as to become parallel to the bottom contours. Waves transport energy in the direction of their motion, the amount of energy per foot of wave crest being proportional to the wave length and to the square of the height. This energy is carried forward perpendicular to the wave crest. Whenever refraction elongates the wave crest, the energy must be distributed over this greater length and the height must decrease. Conversely, when refraction causes the crest length to decrease, as in the convergence at a headland, the wave height is increased.

Another effect of shoaling water, and of the related decrease in wave velocity, is that the wave length must decrease and the height from trough to crest must increase to maintain constant energy per wave. This process ultimately results in the wave height becoming too great for the depth of water and the wave breaks, dissipating nearly all of the wave energy in the turbulence of the breaker and in the foaming crest which proceeds shoreward with steadily diminishing height. If the wave crest in deep water approached the shore line obliquely, the breaking wave, after refraction, will also make an angle with the shore. The obliquity of the breaker depends both upon the original deepwater angle and wave steepness. The depth of water in which waves break depends upon the breaker height primarily, but the bottom slope and deepwater steepness have some effect.

Waves breaking at an angle with a shore line produce a littoral current in the direction of the component of the wave velocity. Facing seaward, if oblique waves break first to the right, and the point of breaking then progresses to the left, the current will run from right to left. The strength of the littoral current depends upon the breaker height, the breaker angle and the average slope of the bottom from the breakerline to the shore. The littoral current fluctuates in velocity, being strongest just after a wave breaks.

The turbulence induced by the breakers and the strong and abrupt variations in pressure on, and within, the bottom throw bottom sand into suspension. This sand then moves with the surrounding water as it settles and a littoral drift of sand occurs, if there is a littoral current. The bottom, being constantly agitated by breakers, tends to adjust its profile to correspond with each wave condition, sand moving from the shore seaward, or the reverse, depending on the existing combination of height and period. The rise and fall of the tide moves the breakerline back and forth and produces some change in the profile, particularly in the position of the inshore bars.

Near tidal entrances or in channels connecting tidal seas, tidal currents are superimposed on the wave-induced littoral currents. On the flood tide, the currents near the shore are directed toward the entrance, while on the ebb tide there is a tendency toward "jet action" which also induces currents toward the entrance.

Sources and Rates of Littoral Drift.—Erosion of the land surface and transportation of detritus by streams and rivers is the principal source of the unconsolidated material found on the shore line. Direct erosion of the shore provides material and, if the upland eroded is sandstone or conglomerate, this source may dominate in some areas. Measurements of the volume of material transported by rivers are not entirely reliable because of the difficulty of determining the amount of the heavy fraction moved along the bed, and it is this fraction which is of the size and character suitable for beach formation. Estimates of the bed movement of the Columbia river, based on laboratory studies of sand movement and field measurements of currents, indicated that the average was of the order of 10,000,000 cu.yd. per year.

Studies of small coastal drainage basins in southern California indicated debris production as high as 100,000 cu.yd. per square mile in one torrential rain. An average of 1,000 cu.yd. per year per square mile is not unusual. Cliff erosion, though occasionally spectacular, does not usually proceed rapidly enough to account for known rates of littoral movement.

Littoral movement of material shows daily, seasonal and annual variations corresponding to the variations in the direction and intensity of wave attack. Measurements of the rate of littoral drift are possible only where the accumulation can be measured at the beginning and end of a period during which the direction of movement does not reverse. Breakwaters and other large structures do provide suitable measuring basins, but only rarely is it known that the direction and rate of movement have been substantially constant between surveys of the accumulation.

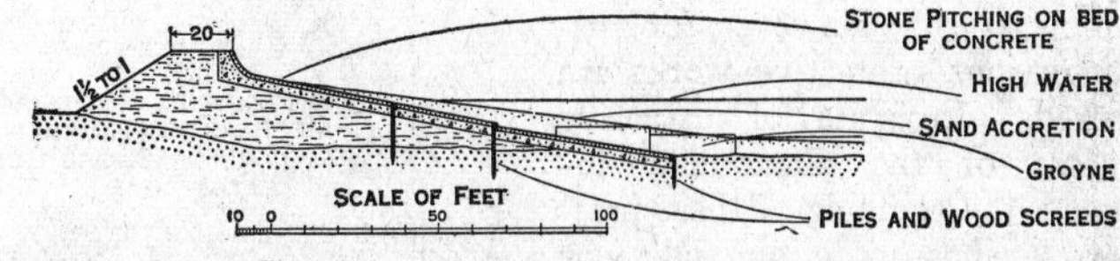

FIG. 2.—SEA WALL AT DYMCHURCH, KENT

At Santa Barbara, Calif., the situation is ideal for measuring the rate of littoral drift. A breakwater extends seaward of the zone of appreciable sand movement. The Channel Islands shield the shore line and waves approach the shore line from a westerly quarter on all but a few days of each year. The drifting material moves from west to east around the end of the breakwater and accumulates in the harbour area, whence it is removed biennially by dredging and placed on its leeward beach. Rates of movement from west to east at this locality have been as high as 1,480 cu.yd. per day, and the average over a period of 17 years was 775 cu.-yd. per day.

Measurements and estimates of the rate of littoral sand movement at other localities are not as reliable or extensive as at Santa Barbara but their magnitude is of some interest. At Santa Monica, Calif., measurements of the accumulation in the lee of an offshore breakwater showed a littoral movement from north to south of 780 cu.yd. per day average over ten years. Along the south shore of Long Island, the sand moves from east to west at the average rate of about 1,000 cu.yd. per day. The

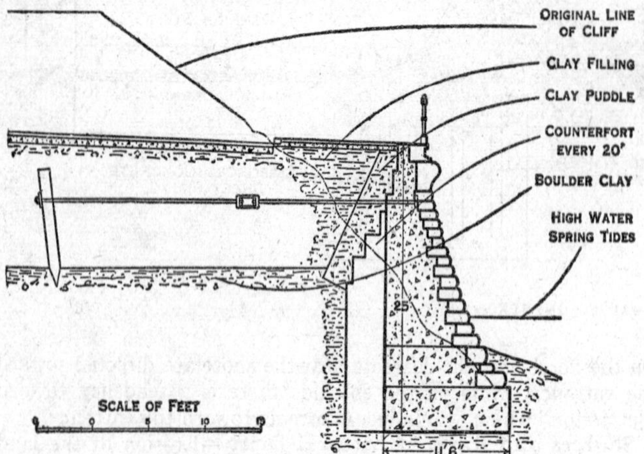

FIG. 3.—SEA WALL AT BRIDLINGTON, YORKSHIRE

rates of littoral movement cited are intended to be illustrative only and should not be regarded as applying to other locations where the sand size, bottom slope and exposure to wave attack are different. Furthermore, they are averages over relatively long periods; the short period rates may be much greater, and seasonal variations in wave attack may also produce a change in the position of the shore line and of the inshore portion of the bottom profile. The beach is frequently found to be wider in summer than in winter, the change being the result of movement of sand to the shore face from offshore bars. This seasonal variation amounts to as much as 300 ft. at some points along the California coast, but generally the seasonal shift in the position of the shore face ranges from 50 to 100 ft.

Coastal erosion results when the rate of removal of material, either directly seaward or along the shore line, exceeds the rate of supply. When these rates are equal, the shore line is in equilibrium; when the supply exceeds the loss, accretion results. Continued erosion of the unconsolidated shore material will ultimately expose cliffs or upland to direct wave attack.

COAST PROTECTION

The design and planning of coast protection should consider: (1) the value of the land and improvements to be protected; (2) the direction and magnitude of the littoral drift; (3) the intensity of wave attack; and (4) the erosional history of the locality. The wisest and most economical policy is to leave the sea adequate "elbow room." However, for various reasons protective works are desired. In spite of extensive studies of the phenomena involved, the planning of these projects depends more on judgment and intuition than on scientific analysis and conservative designs, and ample cost estimates are recommended.

Sea Walls.—Fixation of the margin between land and sea is accomplished by building sea walls or bulkheads. Cast concrete, concrete piles, masonry, random stone, steel sheet piles and timber piles are employed, the choice depending on the costs and exposure. The conditions affecting the design of a sea wall differ so materially that every case must be considered on its merits and provided for accordingly.

Waves break in a depth of water which depends primarily on their height; the deeper the water the larger the breaker which can occur. The deepest water will occur at a sea wall or bulkhead at the time of highest tide, including wind-tide effects. Design must be adequate to withstand both the maximum wave forces and the overturning moment caused by saturated backfill on the land side. Footings must be deep enough to sustain the structure under the worst scouring conditions anticipated during the life of the structure.

Inundation of Galveston, Tex., during the hurricane of 1900 led to the construction of a sea wall of the section shown in fig. 1. Along most of the length of this wall a beach exists at normal water stages, and waves do not reach the wall. During hurricanes the tangential force of the wind causes water to pile up against the shore and also generates large waves which break against, or over, the structure. This intense wave attack continues for only a few hours and the probability of full hurricane force at this particular point is of the order of once in eight years.

Many sea walls and bulkheads have been built for the purpose of protecting roadways or buildings from the limit of wave uprush at the highest tide, and their exposure is such that relatively light construction is justified. Locations farther seaward require heavier construction and greater attention to foundation conditions. Since waves are variable in height and are superimposed on a tide, there are many conditions of exposure to be considered. The destructive effect of waves depends both upon wave force and frequency of exposure. Waves of moderate size breaking directly against a sea wall for long periods may produce more damage than would larger waves over a short period. The destructive force of breakers exhibits two components, namely, a short sharp impact force which may dislodge stones or crack concrete, and an impulse of long duration which tends to move the structure as a whole. Both components appear to reach their maximum intensity when the face of a plunging breaker strikes against a solid surface parallel to itself. The illustrations show various designs employed to avoid these maximum forces.

Some authorities state that sea walls cause scour, while others claim that they cause fill. Both views may be correct, depending on circumstances. Just as in the case of unprotected shore lines, the profile of the bottom in front of a sea wall depends upon the tide stage and the wave characteristics. Under some conditions sand will be moved to the wall, while under others it will be moved away. It is always desirable to maintain a blanket of sand in front of a sea wall to induce breaking at a distance from the wall, and for this purpose, groynes are frequently used if the littoral drift is sufficient to keep them full. Where scour is progressive and the littoral drift is insufficient to fill groynes, random stone is effective in front of sea walls for the purpose both of reinforcing the foundations and of taking the brunt of wave attack. In the United States, random mound walls are preferred both because they can be repaired readily and because

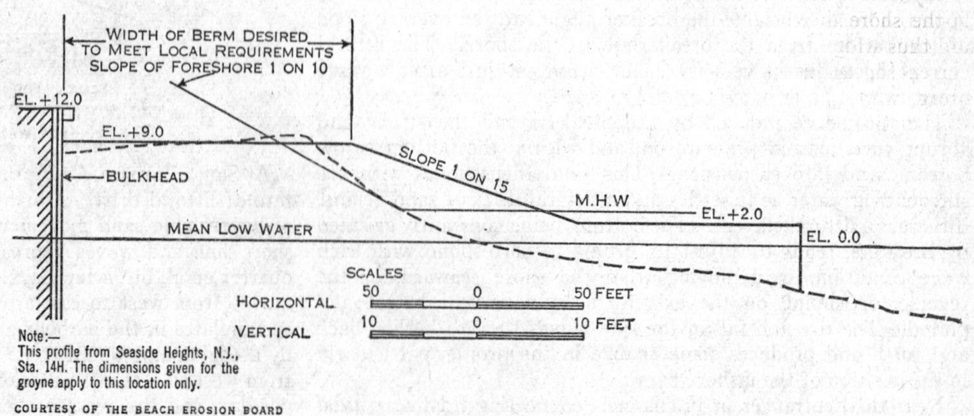

FIG. 4.—TYPICAL GROYNE DESIGN OF THE BEACH EROSION BOARD

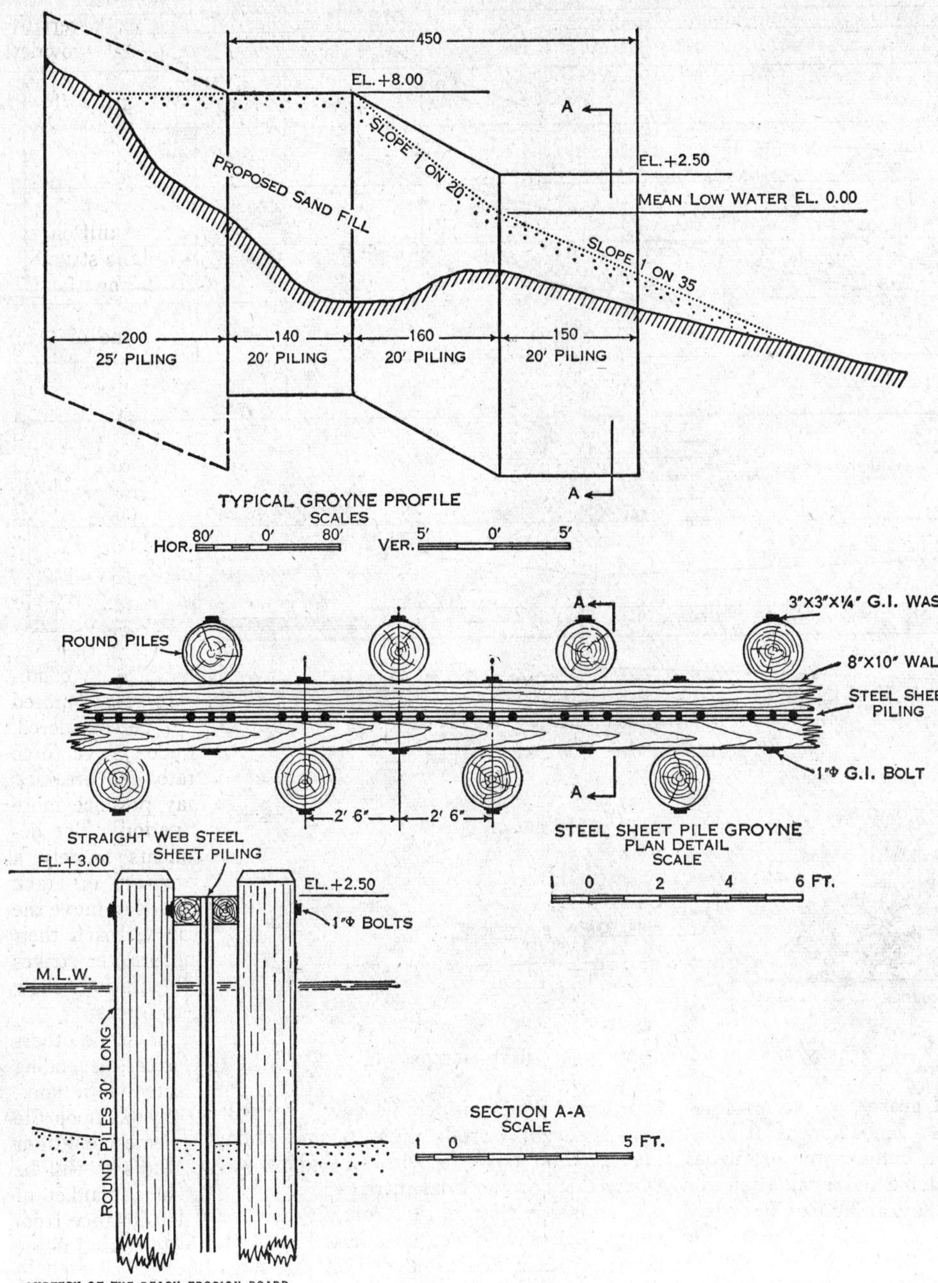

FIG. 5.—STEEL SHEET PILE GROYNE

they can be constructed with heavy machinery and a minimum of labour.

Groynes (Groins).—Short, low structures built perpendicular to the shore line for the purpose of retarding the littoral drift, and thus widening or maintaining a beach, are known as groynes. Fig. 4 shows the profile recommended by the Beach Erosion board, while fig. 5 and 6 show typical designs. Evidently, the construction of groynes assumes the occurrence of a littoral drift of sand sufficient to fill them. The spacing and length of groynes depend chiefly on judgment based on local experience. During periods of erosion, groynes may be flanked by wave attack; and once flanked they are not likely to refill. For this reason groynes are generally connected to a bulkhead at the shore end, this arrangement being more economical and giving a better appearance than would be obtained if the groynes were extended landward far enough to preclude being flanked.

Unless an artificial supply is provided, the sand required to fill a groyne field is withdrawn from the littoral drift and the shore line to the leeward, if previously in equilibrium, will suffer some erosion. The individual groynes should allow wave wash and sand transport over them, and a groyne field should be constructed gradually so as not to trap an unduly large amount of sand in a short period. A desirable procedure is to build the leeward groyne first, and then add groynes to windward (direction from which littoral drift moves).

Jetties.—Large structures built generally perpendicular to the shore line are called jetties. Frequently they extend far enough seaward to intercept the littoral drift completely, causing accretion to windward and erosion leeward. Examples of this effect are the jetties at Santa Barbara, where the accumulation has been very extensive. No feasible natural method has been discovered to move sand past such structures, except by allowing them to sand up and thus lose their effectiveness. The solution developed has been to pump the sand across the structure either continuously or periodically. This by-passing operation is essential because erosion to leeward will progress for miles. The erosion extended ten miles east of Santa Barbara in the ten years following construction of the breakwater.

Offshore breakwaters, such as that at Santa Monica, were thought at one time to obviate the problem of accretion to windward and erosion to leeward, but a consideration of the phenomena involved will show that this conclusion is erroneous. The offshore breakwater must reduce wave action to be effective, and must therefore produce a local reduction in the littoral drift in the protected area as compared with the movement on each side. Sand accumulates in the lee and then acts as a groyne against which the shore line fills to windward. Erosion must occur to leeward because the transporting forces are unchanged while the supply is reduced.

Artificial Beaches.—The cost of construction and maintenance of groynes, jetties and sea walls led to an increasing use of artificial fills as means both of providing beach areas and of protecting the adjacent upland. An example of this practice is the fill in Santa Monica bay, Calif., where 14,000,000 cu.yd. of material were sluiced out of the sand dunes and deposited by pipe line to form a beach approximately 500 ft. wide and several miles in length. In its ultimate development, this project was designed to provide a fill 1,000 ft. wide. Wastage of material from the seaward face of these artificial fills is difficult to estimate, and may prove to be the principal maintenance cost. (M. P. O'B.)

RECLAMATION

The main objects of reclaiming land from the sea are: (1) to increase the area of ground available for cultivation; (2) to gain land of high potential value for some industrial purpose or for municipal expansion. Examples of the first are the fenland reclamations, the embanking and reclaiming of Sunk Island in the Humber river and the great Zuider Zee reclamation which

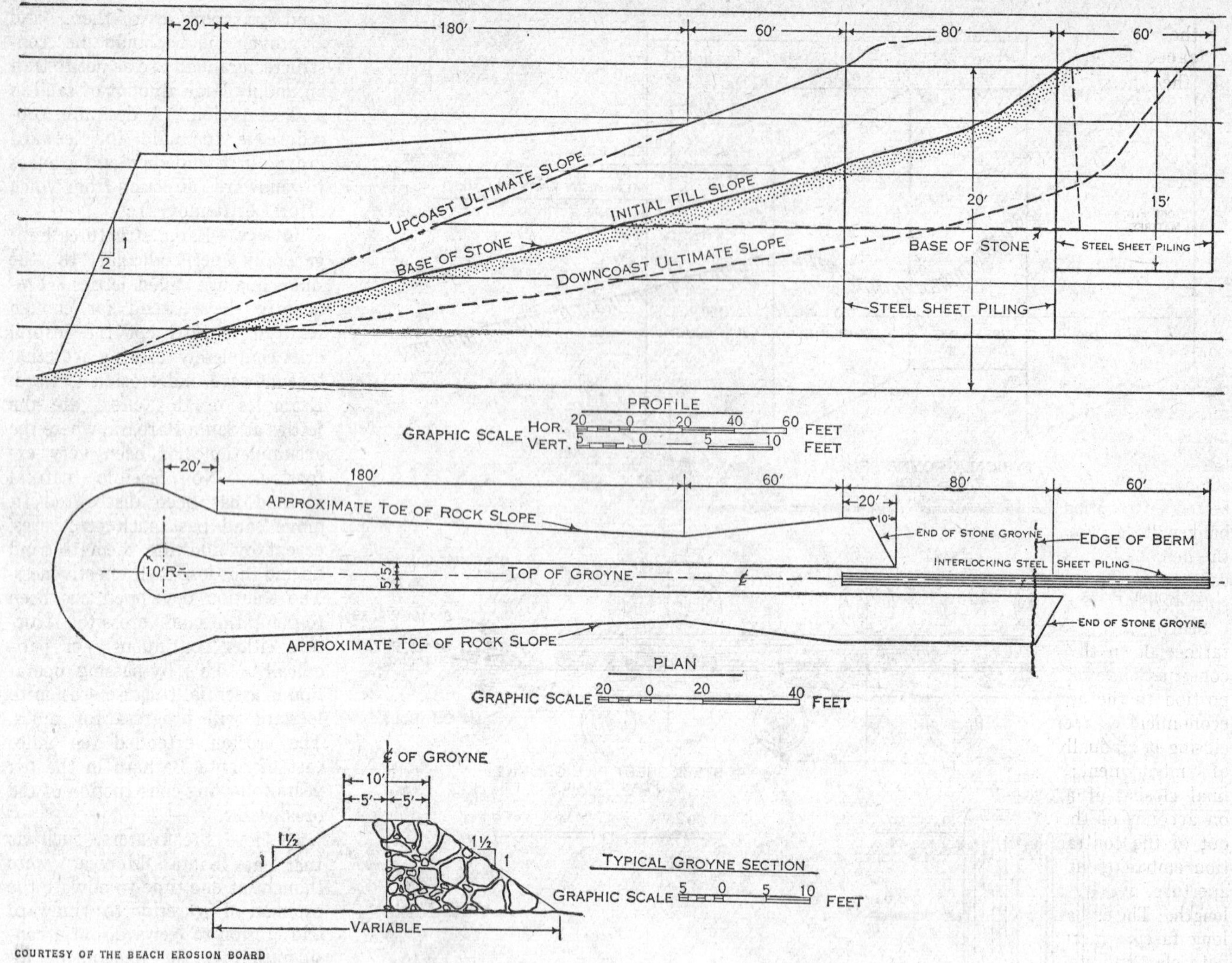

COURTESY OF THE BEACH EROSION BOARD

FIG. 6.—COMPOSITE RANDOM MOUND AND STEEL SHEET PILE GROYNE

was begun in 1920. The reclaiming of nearly 300 ac. of foreshore by the construction of a costly sea embankment at Hodbarrow in Cumberland for the purpose of mining iron ore under the foreshore and sea bed was an example of reclamation for industrial purposes. The reclaiming of the foreshore at Back bay on the west side of the Colaba peninsula at Bombay, begun after World War I, was a notable undertaking connected with city expansion. The high cost of labour and materials compared with the value of agricultural land rendered works of reclamation solely with the object of cultivation, often unremunerative.

Reclamation in Estuaries.—Accretion is the increase of land areas brought about by natural forces; *e.g.*, the deposit of silt in estuaries. Land which has been raised by accretion nearly to high-water level can be shut off from the sea by works of a simple nature and the fresh alluvial soil thus obtained is generally very fertile. Accretion in estuaries is a slow process under ordinary conditions. As soon, however, as a fixed channel is secured by longitudinal embankments or training walls, accretion progresses rapidly by the deposit of sediment in the slack water behind the embankments. Ultimately the time arrives when the water may be altogether excluded by the construction of enclosing embankments; these must be raised above the level of the highest tide, and should have a flat slope on the exposed side, protected, in proportion to exposure and depth of water, with clay, sods, fascines or stone pitching.

In the intermediate stages of the process outlined above much may be done to promote the growth of accretion, or warping as it is termed, and to ensure the fertility of the reclaimed land. The deposit of warp is accelerated by anything which tends to reduce the flow and consequent scour of the ebb tide over the foreshore: thus considerable advantage will accrue from placing rows of faggots or sods across the lines of flow. The light, fertilizing alluvium only deposits in shallow water at high tide and where there are no tidal currents.

The final enclosure, therefore, in the case of land intended for cultivation, should not be effected until this deposit has taken place. A final and rapid deposit can sometimes be effected by making sluices in the banks: the turbid water is admitted near high tide, and retained until the whole of its silt has been deposited, the clear water being allowed to escape slowly toward low tide. Premature enclosure must be guarded against; it is more difficult, the cost greater, the reclaimed land is less fertile and, being lower, less easy to drain.

The practice of reclaiming land in British estuaries is a very ancient one. The Romans effected reclamations in the fen districts, in Romney marsh and near Winchelsea; the enclosing of Sunk Island in the Humber was begun in the 17th century; large reclamations in the Dee estuary took place in the 18th century; and, in later times, works were carried out in the estuaries of the Ribble, Tees and other rivers. The bulk of the later work was with the object of industrial development. For instance, in the Tees estuary large areas of foreshore were reclaimed for factory sites and other industrial purposes by forming banks of iron slag obtained from the ironworks of the Middlesbrough district. Slag constitutes an excellent material for the construction of reclamation banks in localities where it can be obtained at a low cost near the site of the works. The deposit of alluvial material, during and after embanking, is not an important factor in reclamation for industrial purposes and where the levels of land have to be raised it is usual in such cases to effect this by the artificial deposit of filling material.

Seacoast Reclamation.—In the reclamation of land adjoining the open coast, sites where accretion is taking place are obviously the most suitable. Marsh lands adjoining the sea, and more or less subject to inundation at high tides, can be permanently reclaimed by embankments; but these, unless there is protection by sand dunes or a shingle beach, are required to be stronger and higher, with a less steeply inclined and better protected slope than is required in estuaries. Waves overtopping the bank will quickly cause a breach, and produce disastrous results; the height of the bank must, therefore, be calculated to meet the case of the severest onshore gale coinciding with the highest spring tide.

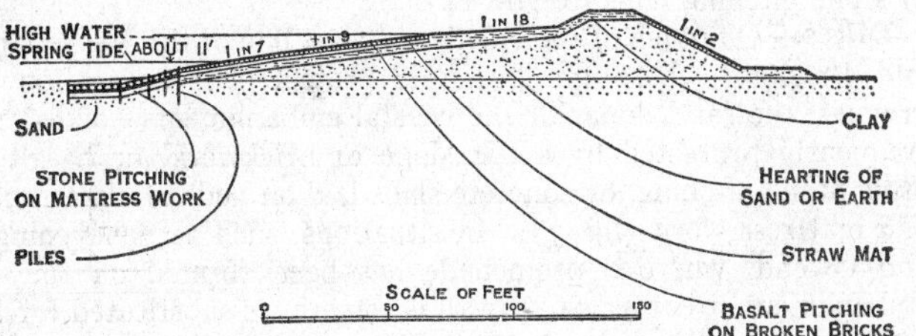

FIG. 7.—CHARACTERISTIC CROSS-SECTION OF DUTCH SEA EMBANKMENT OR DIKE

Seacoast embankments should not generally be constructed farther down the foreshore than half-tide level, as the cost of construction and maintenance would increase out of all proportion to the additional area obtained. It is, as a rule, more economical to reclaim a large area at one time, instead of enclosing it gradually in sections, as the cost varies with the length of embankment; it is, however, more difficult to effect the final closing of a bank, where a large area is thus reclaimed, on account of the greater volume of tidal water flowing in and out of the contracted opening. The final closing of a reclamation embankment is best accomplished by leaving a fairly wide aperture, and by gradually raising a level bank across its entire length. The embankments in the Netherlands are closed by sinking long fascine mattresses across the opening; these are weighted with clay and stone, and effectually withstand the scour through the gap; the two terminal slopes of the finished sections are similarly protected.

There are many examples of seacoast reclamation: Romney marsh was enclosed long ago by the Dymchurch wall, where the method of protection adopted more nearly resembles the Dutch system than any other work in Great Britain and a large portion of the Netherlands has been reclaimed from the sea by embankments; the reclamation bank for the Hodbarrow iron mines illustrates the use of puddled clay to prevent infiltration. The outer portion of this embankment for a length of more than 3,000 ft. was protected on its sea face by concrete blocks, each weighing 25 tons, deposited as a random mound (fig. 8). The sea embankment of the Back bay reclamation at Bombay (*q.v.*) is an example of modern construction on a rocky foreshore.

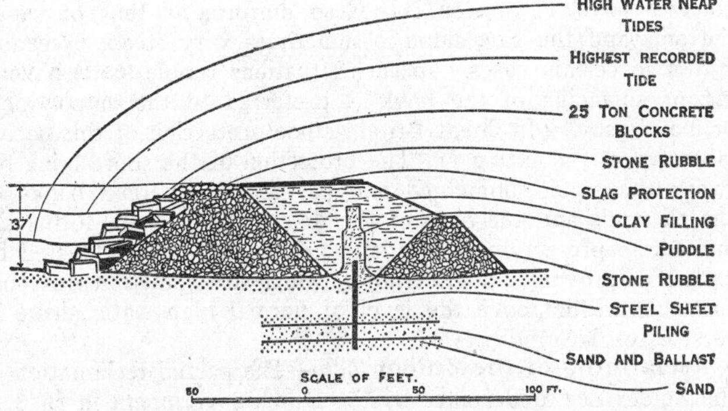

FIG. 8.—RECLAMATION BANK FOR THE HODBARROW IRON MINES, 1904

Breaches in Embankments.—The repair of a breach effected in a completed reclamation embankment is a more difficult task than that of closing the final gap during construction; this is because of the channel or gully scoured out upon the opening of the breach. When a breach occurs which cannot be closed in a single tide, the formation of an overdeep gully may to some extent be prevented by enlarging the opening. Breaches in embankments have been closed by sinking barges across the gap, by piling and planking up, by lowering sliding panels between frames erected to receive them and by making an inset wall or bank round the breach.

The gradual drying of reclaimed land lowers the surface about two or three feet; the land therefore becomes more liable to inundation after reclamation than before. Accordingly, it is most important to prevent breaching of the bank by promptly repairing any damage caused by storms; and if a breach should occur, it must be closed at the earliest possible opportunity.

Reclamation by Dredging.—Mention should be made of the method of reclamation by dredging material from the bed of the sea or a river and depositing it on shore or behind an embankment for the purpose of raising the level of existing land or converting foreshore or sea bed into dry land. The method was first used on a large scale in the Netherlands toward the end of the 19th century and was later extensively employed in many parts of the world (*see* DREDGERS AND DREDGING). The material, whether sand, silt, clay or gravel, is dredged from the sea or river bed by a bucket dredger or a suction dredger. If the former is employed the dredged material is usually delivered into barges and conveyed to a pump-ashore station, where admixture with water takes place, and a pump forces the mixture through a line of pipes on to the land to be reclaimed. If suction dredgers are used for gaining the material it can be pumped ashore direct through floating pipe lines, if the distance is not too great, or transported by barges from which it is pumped ashore by means of a fixed or floating reclamation pump. In some instances an intermediate pumping station in a long line of delivery pipes has been used to boost (*i.e.*, to speed up or relay the flow through the pipes) the mixture of water and dredgings delivered to it from the main dredger. A notable example of the reclamation of tidal areas by dredged fill is San Francisco bay.

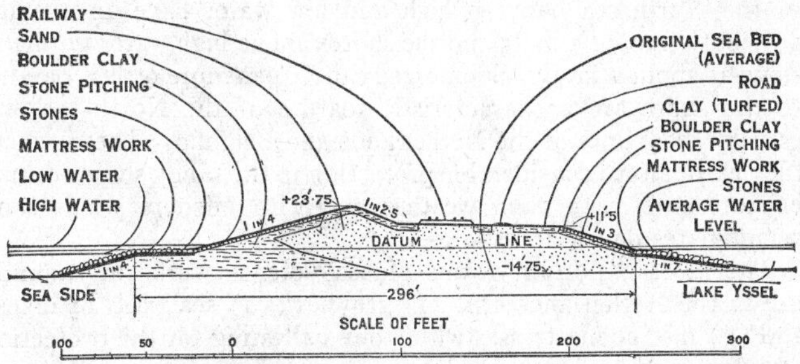

FIG. 9.—CHARACTERISTIC CROSS-SECTION OF THE MAIN SEA DIKE IN THE RECLAMATION OF THE ZUIDER ZEE

THE NETHERLANDS AND BELGIUM

A large part of the Netherlands and some portions of Belgium are below the normal sea level and are protected from inundation by artificial embankments (dikes) or by narrow belts of sand dunes. The foreshore works on the coast of the Netherlands and Belgium, although of great interest and attended with considerable success, do not afford examples to be followed as affecting the sea defenses of Great Britain and other countries exhibiting physical characteristics similar to those of the latter. The protection works in such cases as Blankenberghe, Heyst, Scheveningen, Kallantsoog and Petten are of great magnitude and the engineers responsible for these works, particularly in the Netherlands, have at their command the accumulated experience of centuries of sea-defense work. The local conditions with which these works have to conform, viz., low flat foreshores consisting entirely of sand, are wholly different from those generally associated with sea-defense works in England. The large expenditure involved is justified by the necessity of securing the safety, not only of the seaboard, but of large tracts of the countries themselves. Investigations in the Netherlands are said to indicate a continuous subsidence of the land of that country relative to the sea level, amounting to about 5.91 in. per century.

The North sea foreshores of the Netherlands and Belgium consist for the most part of fine sand; similar deposits border the lower portions of the numerous river estuaries which penetrate far inland, but in the higher parts of these the foreshores are generally composed of fine sand covered with clay or mud. The foreshores of the North sea between high and low water have an average gradient of about 1 in 45 and the shores above high water normally slope at about 1 in 25. Submerged sandbanks more or less parallel to the shore are a characteristic feature of the North sea and estuary coast lines of the Netherlands and Belgium. These, where they exist, afford considerable protection to the sandy shores during onshore gales. In calm weather and with offshore winds sand accumulates on the foreshores.

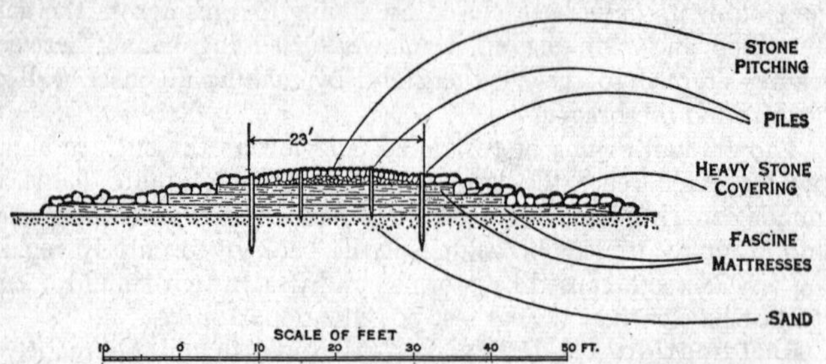

FIG. 10.—CHARACTERISTIC CROSS-SECTION OF MATTRESS GROYNES ON THE NORTH COAST OF THE NETHERLANDS

The most important forms of sea defense works in common use in the Netherlands are: (1) groynes; (2) sea walls or dikes; and (3) fascine mattresses with stone ballasting for the protection of submerged banks.

Groynes.—Groynes are usually constructed at right angles to the shore line and are maintained as a rule at a small height above the average foreshore level. On those portions of the North sea coast which are most exposed, groynes are placed about 250 m. apart and are extended out beyond the low-water line. Many of the groynes on the Dutch coast are constructed of layers of fascine mattresses covered by heavy stone, having their crests almost flat or turtle-backed with side slopes of 1 in 2, or flatter. The fascine or brushwood mattresses are held together and pinned down by rows of piles. Wide brushwood aprons, with heavy stone covering forming flat slopes, are constructed on either side of the groyne in order to protect the flanks against scour (fig. 10). The groynes are carried up above the line of high water to meet the base of the sand dunes or the protecting dikes. These groynes, inclusive of the side aprons, are often of considerable width, sometimes as much as 32.81 yd. at their deepest and widest parts.

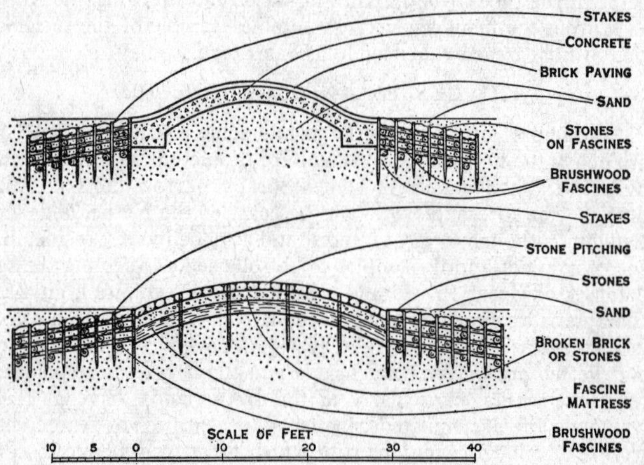

FIG. 11.—CHARACTERISTIC CROSS-SECTIONS OF GROYNES AT OSTEND AND BLANKENBERGHE, BELGIUM

On the coast of Belgium at Blankenberghe and in its vicinity the shore is groyned on an extensive scale. The groynes on the average are about 820 ft. long and 680 ft. apart; they resemble the typical Dutch groyne in form and are constructed with a foundation of mattress work or concrete, faced with brickwork or stone pitching (figs. 10 and 11).

Dikes.—On much of the North sea coast line of the Netherlands and Belgium, where the beach is protected from erosion by groynes, the sand dunes or the coastal embankments (dikes) are frequently protected by a flat slope of brickwork, or basalt or other stone pitching, or concrete slabs laid on beds of clay, rubble and mattress work (fig. 7). In situations, such as Scheveningen and Ostend, where a promenade has been formed on the sea embankment, a curved faced wall is sometimes substituted for the upper part of the normal slope of the paving thus reducing the width of the protecting works; but over large stretches of coast, particularly in the Netherlands, a simple flat paved slope is the common practice.

Protection of Submerged Banks.—The underwater banks of some of the estuary channels and sea inlets on the Dutch coast often stand at a steep slope with deep water alongside. Under these conditions there is serious liability to erosion and it is usual to protect the banks both above and below water by artificial means. For many years fascine mattresses have been used for this purpose. These are made upon a convenient sandy foreshore, covered at high tide, and, when completed, are towed to the place where they are to be used and sunk on the sea bottom by ballasting with stone. They consist of two layers or grids of brushwood each built up of crossed rows of parallel brushwood ropes, 0.4 yd. circumference, and spaced 0.98 yd. apart centre to centre, bound tightly together with a filling of brushwood in three layers between them. On the top of the upper brushwood grid, openwork partitions are formed for the reception of stone ballast. Formerly, clay mixed with a little stone was used for ballasting, but in modern practice stone alone is employed, the mattresses being weighted to the extent of 184 lb. per square foot. The cost of continuous protection of the steep banks of the estuary channels, where the depth of water alongside is sometimes as much as 100 ft., is very considerable. In some localities the cost has been reduced by the construction of intermittent mattress work, leaving short unprotected stretches of bank between projecting spurs which serve to deflect the main current away from the unprotected embayments. In cases where the sea bed of the deep channels consists of clay, erosion is not so uniform as that of sandy bottoms and the side slope is sometimes very steep, exceeding 1 to 1 in certain cases. In such situations rubble stone ballasting or surfacing of the bank is preferred to the employment of mattresses. (In Great Britain stone protection of this nature is known as "revetting.") The protection of the shore lying between the steep submerged and partially submerged banks of the channels and the base of the dike or wall which forms the immediate protection of the land behind, is usually effected by means of groynes. These shores, which are sometimes of considerable width above the level of normal high water, have in most cases flat gradients.

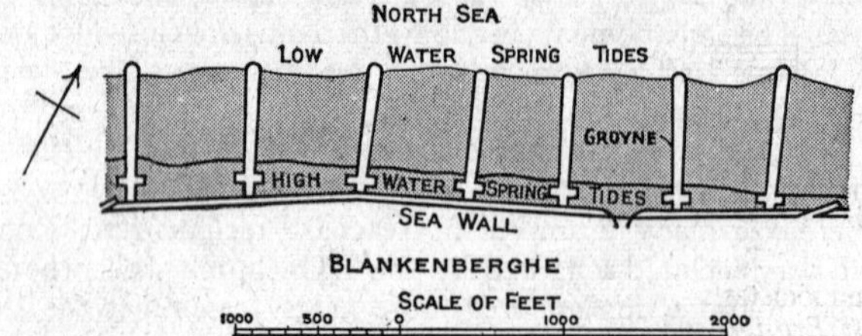

FIG. 12.—PLAN OF GROYNES ON NORTH SEA COAST AT BLANKENBERGHE, BELGIUM

Reclaiming of the Zuider Zee.—The partial reclamation of the Zuider Zee, undertaken by the Dutch government in 1918, is the greatest work of its kind ever attempted. The earliest plans for regaining the submerged lands of the Zuider Zee date from the 17th century, but it was not till the middle of the 19th century that serious proposals began to be considered. Among these plans were those of van Diggelen, 1849, Leemans, 1877, and the various schemes of the engineer C. Lely, subsequently minister of public works, which appeared between 1887 and 1891; the last of which is substantially that on which work was actually commenced in 1920. The finally approved scheme is shown in fig. 13. (*See* ZUIDER ZEE.)

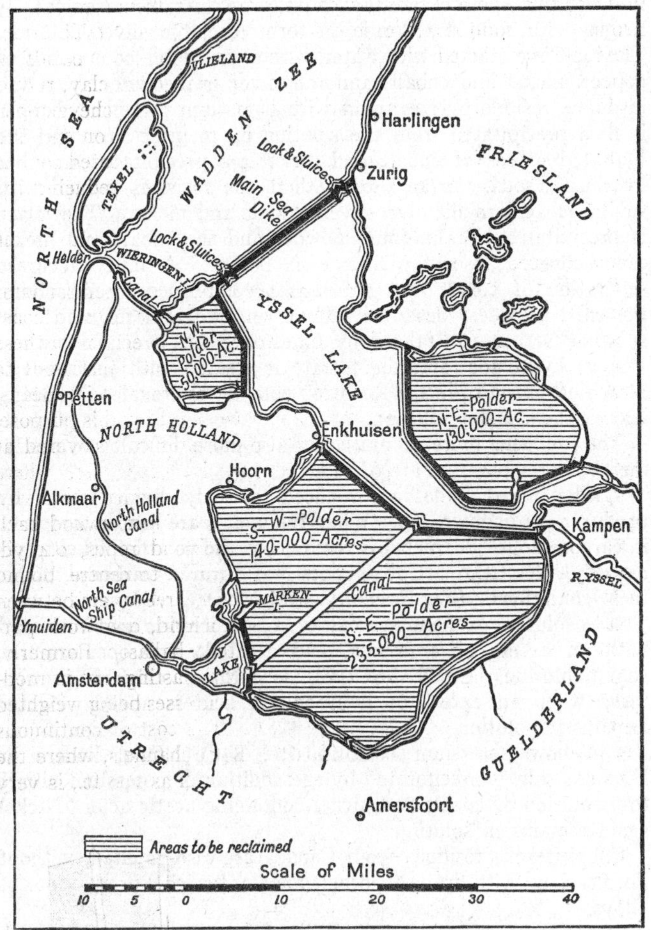

FIG. 13.—SKETCH PLAN FOR THE RECLAMATION OF THE ZUIDER ZEE

BIBLIOGRAPHY.—The *Reports and Evidence: Royal Commission on Coast Erosion and Reclamation of Tidal Lands,* particularly the final report, Cd. 5,708 (1911), should be consulted both for coast erosion and reclamation. Vol. i, pt. 2, i, Cd. 3,684 (1907), contains a useful bibliography by W. Whitaker, F.R.S., up to 1906. The bibliographic lists issued by the International Association of Navigation Congresses, Brussels (since 1908) are very complete. Another good bibliography of works in English was issued by the Engineer School Library, Washington, D.C., in 1926. W. H. Wheeler, *The Sea Coast* (1902); A. E. Carey and F. W. Oliver, *Tidal Lands* (1918); D. W. Johnson, *Shore Processes and Shore Line Development* (1919). Periodical reports of the Beach Erosion Board, Washington, D.C., should be consulted for conditions in the United States. For the Netherlands *see* papers by A. T. de Groot in *De Ingenieur,* no. 35 (1911), and R. P. J. Tutein in *Die Gids,* no. 3 and 5 (1913). Samuel Smile's *Lives of the Engineers* contains good accounts of early reclamation works. *See* also E. M. Ward, *English Coastal Evolution* (1922); W. H. Wheeler, *History of the Fens* (1897) (contains a bibliography of Fenland literature); and *Proceedings Inst. C. E. (passim).* (N. G. G.; X.)

COATBRIDGE, a large burgh, having the privileges of a royal burgh, Lanarkshire, Scotland. Pop. (1951 census) 47,538. It is situated on the Monkland canal, 8 mi. E. of Glasgow, with stations on the Scottish Region railway route. Until about 1825 it was only a village, but since then coal and iron mining have been developed, and it is now a centre of the iron trade of Scotland. Its prosperity was largely caused by the ironmaster James Baird (*q.v.*). The industries of Coatbridge produce malleable iron and steel boilers, tubes, wire, tinplates and railway cars, tiles, fire-bricks and fire-clay goods. The town, which became a municipal burgh in 1885, forms with Airdrie one of the parliamentary divisions of Lanarkshire. About 4 mi. W. by S. lies the coal-mining town of Baillieston.

COATES, ALBERT (1882–1953), English conductor and composer, was born at St. Petersburg, Russia, April 23, 1882, and was sent to school in England when he was 12. He later studied at Liverpool university and at the Leipzig conservatory, where he had his first experience of conducting as coach at the opera under Arthur Nikisch. He became conductor at Elberfeld in 1906 and joint conductor with Ernst von Schuch at Dresden in 1908. During 1910–15 he was conductor of the Imperial opera at St. Petersburg. He visited England occasionally but in 1919 made it his headquarters, establishing an international reputation, particularly as interpreter of the works of Richard Wagner and Alexander Scriabin and other Russian composers. During 1923–25 he was director of the Philharmonic orchestra at Rochester, N.Y. In 1936 he conducted an opera season at Covent Garden, which included his own opera, *Pickwick.* Another opera, *Samuel Pepys,* had been produced at Munich in 1929. In 1946 he settled in South Africa, and he died at Milnerton near Cape Town, on Dec. 11, 1953.

COATES, JOSEPH GORDON (1878–1943), New Zealand statesman, was born at Matakohe, the son of a farmer. He was elected M.P. for Kaipara in 1911, and impressed his leader, W. F. Massey, with his solid ability. From 1917 to 1919 he served with distinction in France. In 1919 he joined the cabinet and, as head of the public works, railways and other departments, proved himself a capable administrator. During 1925–28 he was prime minister, and a privy councillor from 1926. An important part of his policy was the consolidation and development of industries. He was minister of public works in 1931–33 and finance minister in 1933–35. He attended imperial conferences in 1926, 1932 and 1935. He was a member of the New Zealand war cabinet, and was made minister of armed forces and war co-ordination on July 1, 1942. He died in Wellington on May 27, 1943.

COATESVILLE, a city of Chester county, Pennsylvania, U.S., on the west branch of Brandywine creek, 38 mi. W. of Philadelphia. It is on federal highway 30 and is served by the Pennsylvania and Reading railways. The population in 1950 was 13,826 and in 1940 was 14,006 by the federal census. It has important steel plants, in addition to numerous other manufacturing industries. The annual factory output was valued at about $70,000,000 at mid-20th century. Coatesville was founded about 1800, and was named after Jesse Coates, one of the early settlers.

Coatesville was chartered as a city in 1915.

COATI, or COATI-MUNDI, the name of the members of the South and Central American genus *Nasua,* of the mammalian family Procyonidae. They are recognized by their long body and tail, and elongated, upturned snout. The tail is often prominently banded. Coatis are gregarious and arboreal in habit, and feed on birds, eggs, lizards and insects. They are often tamed as pets. (*See* CARNIVORA.)

COATS, J & P., Limited. This now world-famous thread concern was founded in Paisley in 1830 by James and Peter Coats to carry on the business established in 1826 by their father James Coats (1774–1857). The small factory built in 1826 still forms a diminutive part of the vast works at Ferguslie, Paisley. There was keen and at times bitter rivalry between J. & P. Coats and another local manufacturer—Clark & Co.—which continued until 1896 when the two firms amalgamated in the name of the former.

At the same time control was acquired of the two leading manufacturers in England—James Chadwick & Brother and Jonas Brook & Brothers—and the Central Agency, Ltd., was formed to take over the marketing of the product.

The combine made rapid progress, particularly in building up a large export trade, and with a subscribed capital of £20,250,000 in 1939 owned or was associated with the ownership of manufacturing units in about 43 countries, and had selling agencies in every country in the world. Sewing cotton for domestic and commercial use remained the main product of the company, but a large number of fancy threads for embroidery purposes and to a lesser extent silk and rayon threads were introduced.

It is of interest to note that although there have been many improvements made in the machines used in the manufacture of cotton thread, there have been no revolutionary changes in the method of manufacture, and the process at mid-20th century was substantially the same as it was at the beginning of the 19th century.

COB, something round, stout, tufted or like a head (possibly from Ger. *Kopf*, head). The principal uses of "cob" are for a stocky, strongly built horse, from 13 to 14 hands high, a small round loaf, a round lump of coal, in which sense "cobble" is also used, the central part of the fruiting spike of the maize plant, and a large nut of the hazel type, commonly known as the cobnut. The fruiting spike of Indian corn is called corn on the cob.

COBALT, a mining town on Cobalt lake, Timiskaming, northern Ontario, Can., 330 mi. N. of Toronto, on the Ontario Northland railway. Unknown till 1903, it subsequently became the centre of one of the richest silver districts in the world. The region also produces cobalt, arsenic and nickel in large quantities. Pop. (1951) 2,230.

COBALT is a metallic element (symbol Co, atomic number 27, atomic weight 59.94) placed in the periodic system in Group VIII between iron and nickel, both of which it closely resembles. The atomic weight of cobalt is slightly higher than that of nickel, which it precedes in the periodic classification. This is because of the fact that cobalt is composed of two isotopes, 57 and 59, and the abundance ratio is 0.2 to 99.8, hence the mean atomic weight is higher than that of nickel, whose lowest isotope, 58, is most abundant. The atomic number and chemical properties also establish the position of cobalt between iron and nickel. The 27 electrons are arranged: $1s^2\ 2s^2\ 2p^6\ 3s^2\ 3p^6\ 3d^7\ 4s^2$, the incomplete third subgroup being characteristic of the "transition elements" (found in the long periods). Cobalt has two valency electrons ($4s^2$) and their removal forms the stable cobaltous ion, Co^{++}, but the electrons of the third subgroup are also reactive, and they are capable of forming bonds, hence cobalt shows the properties common to other transition elements with incomplete inner electronic groups; *i.e.*, variable valency, paramagnetism, highly coloured compounds, and a pronounced tendency to form complex salts.

History.—The word cobalt or kobold is said to have been used in a manuscript of the 14th century to designate a gnome or evil spirit, who lived in the mines in Germany. In the metallurgical treatises of G. Agricola (1530) the term cobalt was applied to certain minerals and ores, partly because they were worthless when smelted, and partly because the health of the miners suffered from the poisonous fumes caused by the arsenic, also present in the ores. These evils were attributed to the gobelin or kobold. The metal was first prepared in an impure state by G. Brandt in 1742. He observed its magnetic properties and high melting point. He also showed that the blue colour of smalt is caused by cobalt.

Occurrence.—Cobalt is widely distributed but not abundant. Workable deposits have been found at Cobalt in Ontario, the principal source of the element at mid-century, in Missouri, New Caledonia, Queensland, Saxony, the Belgian Congo and Chile. The following list of the more common minerals makes evident the frequent association with arsenic:

asbolite	$CoO.2MnO_2.4H_2O$ (from New Caledonia)
cobaltite	$CoS_2.CoAs_2$
erythrite	$3CoO.As_2O_5.8H_2O$
linnaeite	$Co_3S_4(CoS.Co_2S_3)$
skutterudite	$CoAs_3$
smaltite	$CoAs_2$

The percentage distribution in the earth's crust is said to be 1.8×10^{-5} (0.000018%). Cobalt is found in most meteorites, usually alloyed with iron and nickel (0.5% to 2.5% in iron meteorites), and it has been identified in the spectra of the sun and many stars. Traces of cobalt have been detected in many plants and animals, notably in marine algae and Kentucky bluegrass. The role of cobalt and other "trace" elements in these organisms is still obscure.

Production.—Cobalt is a by-product in the metallurgy of ores in which it is associated with arsenic, iron, nickel, copper, manganese (New Caledonia) and silver (the Ontario deposits, where the platinum metals are also a valuable by-product). The metallurgy is complex and varies with the content of the ore, but the essential steps in treating a typical ore are as follows: the crushed and concentrated ore is first roasted in a blast furnace to remove a considerable proportion of the arsenic, and the resulting speiss (chiefly a mixture of metallic arsenides) is heated with sodium chloride to form insoluble silver chloride. The melt is extracted with water to remove soluble compounds of copper, nickel and cobalt, and the silver is recovered from the insoluble residue by treatment with potassium cyanide. Copper is then precipitated from the solution by metallic iron, and the hydrated oxides of cobalt and nickel are precipitated together by caustic soda. In another method, the speiss is treated with sulphuric acid to dissolve silver, cobalt and nickel. The silver is precipitated by aluminum powder and the cobalt and nickel are recovered from the filtrate as before. A fairly accurate separation of cobalt and nickel is accomplished by dissolving the mixed oxides, described above, in hydrochloric acid; the solution is then neutralized by limestone, thus precipitating the iron as hydroxide, and the filtrate is treated with just enough bleaching lime to precipitate black cobaltic hydroxide, $Co(OH)_3$, leaving the nickel in solution.

The following more accurate, but also more difficult and costly, methods of separation are of interest:

1. The mixed oxides are reduced to finely divided metal by producer gas or hydrogen. When the metals are heated to 50° C. in carbon monoxide, nickel is removed as the volatile nickel tetracarbonyl, $Ni(CO)_4$. Cobalt does not form a carbonyl under these conditions. (*See* CARBONYLS, METAL.)

2. A solution of the mixed oxides in hydrochloric acid is treated with an excess of ammonia, and aerated; chloropentammine cobaltichloride, $[Co(NH_3)_5Cl]Cl_2$, is formed, which is precipitated when an excess of hydrochloric acid is added. Nickel remains in solution.

3. Yellow potassium cobaltinitrite, $K_3Co(NO_2)_6$, known as Fischer's salt, is precipitated by the addition of potassium nitrite to a solution of cobalt and nickel containing acetic acid. Nickel again remains in solution.

Cobaltiferous residues from Canada are also smelted, without purification, with iron or other metals for the production of alloys.

Metallic cobalt is obtained readily by reducing its oxides with carbon, hydrogen, carbon monoxide (producer gas or water gas) or aluminum. It may be deposited by the electric current from slightly acid solutions, containing ammonium salts.

Physical Properties.—Cobalt, when polished, is a silver-white metal with a bluish cast. Its physical properties are summarized in the following table:

Density	8.8 g/ml	Specific heat	0.0828
Melting point	1,480° C.	Hardness (Mohr's scale)	5.5
Boiling point	2,415°	Atomic volume	6.68
Atomic radius	1.257 Å		

Ionization potentials (1) 7.81 v. (2) 17.2 v.

Electrode potential, for $Co \rightarrow Co^{++} + 2E° = 0.277$

for $Co^{++} \rightarrow Co^{+++} + E = -1.842$

Tensile strength, 60,000 lb. per sq.in.

The metal is malleable, and may be machined. It is somewhat brittle, but the brittleness may be reduced by the addition of a small amount of carbon.

Cobalt metal is strongly magnetic (ferromagnetism) at all temperatures up to 1,150° C.

Radioactive isotopes (55, 56, 57, 58, 60) have been obtained by bombardment methods (artificial or induced radioactivity). The half-life periods vary from 11 minutes to 5.3 years.

There are two allotropic forms of the element, α-cobalt, stable at the ordinary temperature, and β-cobalt, stable at high temperatures. The transition point is about 400° C. X-ray examination has shown that the α-form crystallizes in a close-packed hexagonal lattice, while in the β-form the lattice is face-centred cubic.

Uses.—The uses of cobalt and its compounds are not numerous but are increasing. Electroplating with cobalt has been successful. Many ferrous and nonferrous alloys have been made and studied. The alloys with iron have valuable magnetic properties, and are used to make permanent magnets for telephony. Cochrome is a ferrous alloy containing approximately 60% cobalt, 14% to 16% chromium, and 24% iron. It resembles nichrome, and like it is used for electrical heating units. Nonferrous alloys containing over 50% cobalt are used as high-speed cutting tools, which retain their edge and hardness at a red heat. Stellite, cobalt 55%, tungsten 15% to 25%, chromium 15% to 25%, and molybdenum 5%, is the best known alloy of this class. The powerful Alnico magnets are alloys of aluminum, cobalt and nickel.

Cobalt is best and most widely known for the brilliant and permanent blue colour which its compounds impart to porcelain, glass, pottery, tiles and enamels. The pigment generally used in the ceramic industry is smalt, a potassium, cobalt, aluminosilicate, made by heating impure cobalt oxide with quartz and potassium carbonate. Other pigments containing cobalt are Thenard's blue and Rinman's green, made by heating cobalt oxide with aluminum oxide and zinc oxide, respectively, and cobalt yellow, potassium cobaltinitrite, used as a pigment by artists. Cobalt oleate, lineate and acetate are used as driers for paints and varnishes. Certain partly reduced compounds of cobalt have been shown to act as catalysts for the formation of olefine and paraffin hydrocarbons from carbon monoxide and hydrogen (*i.e.*, in the production of gasoline from water-gas).

Chemical Properties.—The chemistry of cobalt shows many resemblances to, as well as differences from, the chemistry of iron and nickel, its neighbours in the periodic system. The stable oxidation states are two and three. The cobaltous ion, Co^{++} (pink), is stable, and nearly all simple salts (chloride, nitrate, sulphate, etc.) belong to this oxidation state. Ferrous, cobaltous and nickelous salts form a closely related group. The cobaltic ion, Co^{+++}, is extremely unstable, and simple cobaltic salts are almost limited to a fluoride and sulphate. In contrast, the ferric salts (Fe^{3+}) are stable in the solid state and in solution. On the other hand, trivalent cobalt forms hundreds of stable complex compounds, chiefly of the co-ordination type (*see* below) which is rather poorly represented in the chemistry of iron, and wholly lacking in that of nickel. Further, rhodium and iridium, two members of the platinum family, stand below cobalt in a vertical column of Group VIII. The valency state of three is the most stable for these metals, and many types of complex derivatives of trivalent cobalt reappear in strikingly similar form among the compounds of rhodium and iridium.

Finely divided metallic cobalt occludes as much as 100 times its volume of hydrogen, and readily gives it up again when heated to 200° C. in vacuo. A pyrophoric form (spontaneously inflammable in the air) is obtained by reducing the oxide at 250° C. The compact and polished metal is not affected by air or water, and only undergoes superficial oxidation when heated to redness in air. The red hot metal reacts with steam, liberating hydrogen and forming the oxide. The metal dissolves in dilute acids, evolving hydrogen, but concentrated nitric acid renders it "passive." Alkalies, either fused or in aqueous solution, are without action. Cobalt combines directly with the halogens, forming the anhydrous blue chloride, $CoCl_2$, the green bromide, $CoBr_2$, and the black iodide, CoI_2. The anhydrous fluoride, CoF_2, is rose coloured.

Carbonyls.—Like nickel and iron, and some other metals, cobalt combines with carbon monoxide, forming carbonyls. These compounds are noteworthy because of their unusual formulas and properties. Under a pressure of 40 to 50 atmospheres, at 150° C., the metal unites with carbon monoxide to form the tetracarbonyl, $[Co(CO)_4]_2$ orange crystals. At 60° C. and atmospheric pressure, this compound is converted to the black tricarbonyl, $[Co(CO)_3]_2$, with loss of carbon monoxide. The volatile derivative, $H[Co(CO)_4]$, has also been reported. All of these compounds are highly toxic.

Oxides.—Cobalt forms three stable oxides, CoO, Co_2O_3, and $Co_3O_4(CoO.Co_2O_3)$; all are grayish black. The first two are also known in the hydrated form, $Co(OH)_2$, pink, and $Co(OH)_3$, black. Cobaltous oxide, CoO, forms many stable salts, but is not a strongly basic oxide. Solutions of its soluble salts are acidic, owing to hydrolysis of the cobaltous ion, Co^{++}. Cobaltic oxide, Co_2O_3, is reduced to the cobaltous state by hydrochloric acid; only complex derivatives are stable. Co_3O_4 crystallizes in octahedra. Its structure, of the spinel type, closely resembles that of magnetite, Fe_3O_4, and it is best represented by the formula $Co_2^{+3}[Co^{+2}O_4]$. A higher oxide, CoO_2, is said to be formed by the action of hypochlorites and other powerful oxidants on cobaltous salts. A few of its derivatives have been reported but all of them are unstable.

Cobaltous Salts.—The cobaltous ion, Co^{++}, is red or pink in dilute solution. As indicated above, hydrolysis of the ion, $Co^{++}+2H_2O \rightleftarrows Co(OH)_2+2H^+$, causes an acidic reaction in solutions of soluble salts. Hydrated salts are red. The chloride, $CoCl_2.6H_2O$, the nitrate, $Co(NO_3)_2.6H_2O$, the sulphate, $CoSO_4.7H_2O$, and the acetate, $Co(CH_3.COO)_2.4H_2O$ are commonly manufactured. Anhydrous salts, such as the carbonate, are generally pink. The hydrated salts assume an intense blue colour when dehydrated by heating, a property utilized in making "sympathetic inks." The sulphate is an exception, the anhydrous form being violet. Many double chlorides, nitrates and sulphates have been prepared. The sulphate forms double sulphates of the Mohr salt class, M'_2SO_4, $M''SO_4.6H_2O$, in which M′ may be ammonium, NH_4, K, Rb or Cs, and M″ may be Fe, Co, Ni, Mn, Cr, etc. Double nitrates of the type, $3Co(NO_3)_2.3La(NO_3)_3.24H_2O$, have been used in separations of the rare earths. Cobaltous salts combine with ammonia, pyridine and other organic bases to form complex salts, for example, the hexammine, $[Co.(NH_3)_6]Cl_2$, but these compounds are usually less stable than the corresponding derivatives of trivalent cobalt.

Cobaltic Compounds.—The green fluoride, CoF_3, and the blue sulphate, $Co_2(SO_4)_3.18H_2O$, made by electrolytic oxidation, are the best known simple cobaltic salts. It is noteworthy that the sulphate forms alums, $K_2SO_4.Co_2(SO_4)_3.24H_2O$, which crystallize in deep blue octrahedra. The alums are stable in dry air.

Ammines.—When a solution of a cobaltous salt is treated with an excess of ammonia, with or without the addition of ammonium salts, aerated or oxidized by other agents, and then made acid, depending on conditions, the yellow hexammine cobaltichloride, $[Co(NH_3)_6]Cl_3$ (luteo chloride), the red aquopentammine cobaltichloride, $[Co(NH_3)_5H_2O]Cl_3$ (roseo chloride), or the purple chloropentammine cobaltichloride, $[Co(NH_3)_5Cl]Cl_2$ (purpureo chloride), are obtained. These compounds were discovered by F. A. Genth in 1847 and described in detail, together with related salts, in a monograph, "The Ammonia-Cobalt Bases," by F. A. Genth and Wolcott Gibbs, published by the Smithsonian Institution in Washington in 1856. By suitable variations in the procedure outlined above, the ammonia may be replaced by equivalents of ethylenediamine and other organic bases, and the chlorine by many other negative radicals. Hundreds of beautifully crystallized and highly coloured compounds have been produced, of which a few additional examples are: dichlorotetrammine cobaltichloride, $[Co(NH_3)_4Cl_2]Cl$, obtained in green (praseo) and violet (violeo) isomeric forms, dinitrotetrammine cobaltinitrate, $[Co(NH_3)_4(NO_2)_2]NO_3$, occuring as brown (flavo) and yellow (croceo) isomers, trinitrotriammine cobalt, $[Co(NH_3)_3(NO_2)_3]$, a nonelectrolyte (forming no ions in solution), and ammonium tetranitrodiammine cobaltiate, $NH_4[Co.(NO_2)_4(NH_3)_2]$, known as Erdmann's salt. A study of these compounds enabled Alfred Werner of Zürich, during the period 1893–1918, to formulate the well-known co-ordination theory, which has proved to be a powerful tool for dealing with many classes of inorganic compounds. He pointed out that in all of the cobaltammines, six molecules or radicals, or their equivalents are attached directly to, or "co-ordinated" with the central cobalt atom, forming a unit, now often called a Werner complex. This unit may exist as an ion in solution. The co-ordination number of cobalt is said to be six. He further showed that the resulting molecule is not planar but three-dimensional: the cobalt atom being at the centre of an octahedron, with its valencies directed to the six corners, where the co-ordinated groups are located. The validity of this conception was established, experimentally, by chemical reactions involving structural isomers, and finally by the preparation of optically active co-ordination compounds of cobalt. Examination of many co-ordination compounds by X-rays has fully confirmed these views, so that the octahedron is as firmly established for inorganic compounds, where the co-ordination number is six, as is the tetrahedron in the chemistry of carbon. (*See* CO-ORDINATION COMPOUNDS.)

Analytical:—*Detection.*—The characteristic dry test for cobalt is the intense blue colour imparted to the borax bead by small quantities of salts or other compounds. In the regular course of qualitative analysis, cobalt and nickel are precipitated together as sulphides by ammonium sulphide. They may be separated by the cyanide method, which consists in dissolving the mixed sulphides in aqua regia, removing the excess of acid, and adding an excess of potassium cyanide to the neutral solution. The complex cyanides, $K_4[Co(CN)_6]$ and $K_2[N:(CN)_4]$, are formed, and on boiling their solution, the former is oxidized to the very stable cobalticyanide, $K_3[Co(CN)_6]$, leaving the nickel cyanide unchanged. Sodium hypobromite, NaBrO, is then added, precipitating black hydrated nickelic oxide, and leaving the cobalt in solution. The filtrate from the insoluble nickelic oxide may be evaporated to dryness, and the residue tested for cobalt in the borax bead.

Estimation.—In compounds containing no nonvolatile constituent, cobalt may be determined accurately and rapidly by evaporation with a few drops of concentrated sulphuric acid, and weighing as the violet anhydrous sulphate, $CoSO_4$. Cobalt may also be estimated by electrolytic deposition on a platinum dish from an acid solution containing ammonium sulphate.

The quantitative separation of cobalt from nickel and certain other metals is best effected by precipitation with α-nitroso-β-naphthol from acid solution. The bulky, purplish red precipitate,

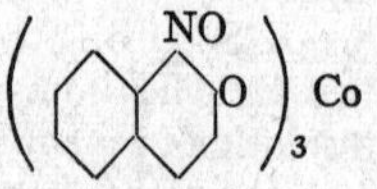

$$\left(C_{10}H_6(NO)O\right)_3Co$$

is ignited to Co_3O_4, and weighed as such, or the oxide may be reduced by hydrogen to metal.

An accurate and rapid colourimetric method for the determination of cobalt in dilute solution (0.015 g. $CoSO_4$ per 1 litre) is based on the formation of a soluble red complex with nitroso-R-salt,

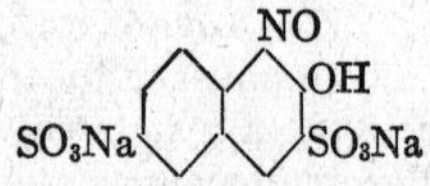

NO, OH, SO_3Na, SO_3Na

Small amounts of nickel and iron do not interfere.

BIBLIOGRAPHY.—H. J. Emeleus and J. S. Anderson, *Modern Aspects of Inorganic Chemistry* (1938); W. M. Latimer and J. H. Hildebrand, *Reference Book of Inorganic Chemistry* (1941); J. W. Mellor, *A Comprehensive Treatise on Inorganic and Theoretical Chemistry*, vol. xiv (1935); J. N. Friend, *Text-book of Inorganic Chemistry*, vol. ix, part i (1926). (T. P. Mc.)

COBALTITE, a mineral with the composition CoAsS, cobalt sulpharsenide. It is found as granular to compact masses, and frequently as beautifully developed crystals, which have the same symmetry as the isomorphous mineral pyrite, being cubic with parallel hemihedrism. The usual form is a pentagonal-dodecahedron with faces of the cube and octahedron. The colour is silver-white with a reddish tinge, and the lustre brilliant and metallic, hence the old name cobalt-glance. The brilliant crystals from Tunaberg in Sodermanland, Sweden, and from Skutterud near Drammen in Norway are well known in mineral collections. Crystals have also been found at Khetri in Rajputana, and under the name *sehta* the mineral is used by Indian jewellers for producing a blue enamel on gold and silver ornaments.

COBÁN, a city of Guatemala, Central America, capital of the department of Alta Verapaz and the northern centre of the coffee trade. Population (1950) 7,917. Cobán is 105 mi. north of Guatemala City, although overland connections (motor to El Rancho, thence by rail) are rather poor. Principal commercial outlet of the district is via the Polochic river, Lake Izabal and the Río Dulce to the Caribbean port of Livingston. Besides being a rich area in the production of coffee, there are numerous plantations of tea, cacao, vanilla, etc., surrounding the city.

COBB, HOWELL (1815–1868), American political leader, was born at Cherry Hill, Ga., on Sept. 7, 1815. He graduated from Franklin college (University of Georgia) in 1834, and in 1836 was admitted to the bar. From 1837 to 1840 he was solicitor-general for the western circuit of his State. In 1843–51 and in 1855–57 he was a member of the national House of Representatives, becoming Democratic leader in that body in 1847, and serving as speaker in 1849–51. From 1851 to 1853 he was governor of his State; and from 1857 to 1860 he was secretary of the Treasury in President Buchanan's cabinet. In 1861 he was appointed colonel of a regiment and two years later was made a major-general in the Confederate army. He sided with President Jackson on the question of nullification; was an efficient supporter of President Polk's administration during the Mexican War; and was an ardent advocate of slavery extension into the Territories, but when the Compromise of 1850 had been agreed upon he became its staunch supporter as a Union Democrat, and on that issue was elected governor of Georgia by a large majority. In 1860, however, he ceased to be a Unionist, and became a leader of the secession movement. He died in New York city on Oct. 9, 1868.

See W. B. Phelps (ed.), "The Correspondence of Robert Toombs, Alexander H. Stephens and Howell Cobb," *Am. Hist. Assoc., Annual Report*, vol. ii. (1911).

COBB, IRVIN SHREWSBURY (1876–1944), U.S. author and journalist, was born in Paducah, Ky., on June 23, 1876. He left school at an early age to begin his career in journalism as a reporter and cartoonist for the local newspapers. He was managing editor of a newspaper, the *Paducah Daily News*, at the age of 19.

In 1904 he became a writer and editor for the *New York Evening Sun*, and from 1905 to 1911 was staff writer for Joseph Pulitzer's *New York Evening World* and *New York Sunday World*. He rapidly became widely known as a writer with humorous and ironical insight.

Cobb wrote for national magazines, lectured throughout the United States, and acted in motion pictures. He also wrote many books and plays, both serious and humorous. He died March 10, 1944.

COBBE, FRANCES POWER (1822–1904), British social writer and author, was born in Dublin on Dec. 4, 1822. Her first book, *The Theory of Intuitive Morals*, was published anonymously. In 1858 she began social work among the girls and boys of Bristol. She carried out various special investigations on vivisection, of which she was all her life a violent opponent, on destitution, and on separation orders and divorce. She was a strong suffragist. From time to time she conducted services in Unitarian chapels.

She published about 30 separate works, among which may be mentioned: *Essay on Intuitive Morals* (1855), *Pursuits of Women* (1863), *Hours of Work and Play* (1867), *Dawning Lights* (1868), *Darwinism and Morals* (1872), *The Hopes of the Human Race* (1874), *The Duties of Women* (1881), her own *Life* (2 vol., 1894), and *The Scientific Spirit of the Age* (1888).

COBBETT, WILLIAM (1763–1835), English author, journalist and Radical, is one of the most representative figures in English literature, and his life and writings embody the history of the common people between the revolutions of the eighteenth century and the dawn of the Victorian era. He was born at Farnham, Surrey, on March 9, 1763 (not 1766, as he himself wrongly stated). His father was a small farmer; and his grandfather had been a day-labourer. As a boy, he worked in the fields, but, at 14, began his adventures by running away from home and getting work in Kew Gardens. He returned home after a while; but, at 19, after an unsuccessful attempt to join the Navy during a visit to Portsmouth, again left Farnham and, going to London on a sudden impulse, found employment as a solicitor's clerk.

Soon sickening of this occupation, he went down to Chatham, meaning to enlist in the Marines, but found himself in a line regiment instead. After a year at the depot, during which he read hard and discursively and taught himself grammar and writing, he was drafted, as corporal, to Nova Scotia, where his regiment was stationed. Soon, however, he was shifted to Fredericton, New Brunswick, where he remained till 1791, rising rapidly to the position of regimental sergeant-major. This position made him conscious of the systematic fraud and peculation which went on in the regiment—as indeed throughout the service—and he set to work to collect evidence against the principal offenders. At length, in 1791, his regiment was ordered home; and he at once procured his discharge, with excellent testimonials. Having done this, he immediately set about bringing the defaulters to book, and demanded a court-martial of the officers against whom he had collected evidence. This was at length granted; but Cobbett was unable to secure the discharge of his essential witness, or to get the regimental books impounded for safekeeping. In despair of getting the case fairly heard, he failed to appear at the court-martial, and fled to France in March 1792. He had married Ann Reid, to whom he had become engaged some years before in New Brunswick, while he was awaiting the court-martial proceedings; and she joined him in France. He remained there until the late summer of 1792 when, seeing the outbreak of war to be imminent, he took ship for America. There, first at Wilmington and later at Philadelphia, he supported himself by teaching English to the French *émigrés,* who were reaching the United States in large numbers.

So far Cobbett had written little. In the army, he had composed a grammar for the use of private soldiers; but this was not published. He had also almost certainly a hand in a pamphlet exposing army abuses, published in 1793 under the title of *The Soldier's Friend.* But in 1794 occurred an incident which really embarked him on his long career as a political writer. Joseph Priestley, the great Unitarian Radical, came in that year to settle in the United States, and numerous addresses of welcome were presented to him by American Radical societies. These aroused Cobbett's strong pugnacious instincts; and he entered the lists as a pamphleteer with his *Observations on Dr. Priestley's Emigration* (1794). From that date until his return to England in 1800, he was the most vehement and violent writer on the British side in the United States, producing a series of tirades against the French Revolution and all its works, and against all Americans who ventured to give it, or any sort of Radicalism, even the mildest support. *A Bone to Gnaw for the Democrats, A Kick for a Bite, The Scare-Crow, The Cannibal's Progress* (an account of the horror of the French Revolution), and a scurrilous *Life of Tom Paine,* are among these early pamphlets. They are all unmeasured in violence, and often outrageous, but always lively, readable and written in really virile and forthright English. Cobbett's style was almost as good in his first unpracticed writings as in the best of his more famous later work. Pre-eminent among these early pamphlets is his autobiographical *Life and Adventures* of Peter Porcupine (the highly apposite name under which he had chosen to write) in which he defended himself against those who abused him by an account of his upbringing and early career. This pamphlet is one of the best of all his writings. He also supplemented his pamphleteering with a regular newspaper, *Porcupine's Gazette.*

Cobbett was soon in trouble with the law. He libelled Dr. Rush, doctor and well-known Democratic politician, accusing him of killing George Washington with his special "bleeding treatment." This brought a heavy fine, and he then wrote scurrilous pamphlets about McKean, the judge who had tried the case, and was Rush's political ally. Before long he made the United States too hot to hold him, and in 1800 he gave up the contest and returned to England, where his writings, regularly republished, had already made him well known. He was greeted with enthusiasm as a powerful recruit to jingo journalism. He met Pitt at dinner, and was offered the editorship and ownership of one of the leading Government newspapers. He refused the offer, as he had already refused Government payment for his services in America, and attempted instead to start a daily newspaper of his own, *The Porcupine.* This speedily failed; but in 1802, with help from Dr. Laurence and William Windham, who was for some years his chief political supporter, he started the weekly *Political Register,* which he thereafter edited, and for the most part wrote, regularly until his death in 1835.

The *Political Register,* with which Cobbett's name was always from 1802 chiefly associated, began its career as an extreme anti-Jacobin journal. It strongly opposed Addington and the Peace of Amiens, and called loudly for a renewal of the war with France. But after Pitt's return to power and the renewal of the war, Cobbett slipped gradually into opposition, and found himself in alliance with Windham and with Fox, the latter of whom he had hitherto vehemently denounced. In 1806, in the Ministry of All the Talents, his friends came to power; but Cobbett soon fell into opposition to them also. He was by this time denouncing the "Pitt system" as the root of all evil, and attacking in particular the methods of pursuing the war, the multiplication of pensions and sinecures, and the dangerous growth of the National Debt. When the Ministry of All the Talents broke up in 1807, he was already definitely a Radical, at war equally with Whig and Tory, and beginning to cry out for peace and parliamentary reform as well as for "economical reform."

So far, Cobbett was merely an outstanding political journalist, whose writings, however trenchant, had given little indication of his peculiar quality as a democratic leader. But from about 1805 a new tone begins to appear in his work. From 1800 to 1805 he had lived in London; but in the latter year he bought a substantial farm at Botley, near Southampton, and spent most of his time in the country. The change opened his eyes to the great contrast between the countryside as he remembered it in his boyhood and as it had become under stress of war-time prices and enclosure. He realized for the first time the misery of the labouring classes, the effects of the Speenhamland system of poor relief, of the enclosure movement, of the great revolution in agrarian conditions that was then at its height. It roused his indignation—the indignation of one who was himself by nature and nurture a yeoman. It completed his conversion to Radicalism, which he expressed as the cause of the dispossessed and suffering labourers of rural England.

Cobbett, the one articulate voice among the suffering people of the countryside, brought a new note into Radical agitation. At once, he became a power. But his power brought penalties. In 1809 there was a minor mutiny among the soldiers at Ely, over unfair deductions from pay. The mutiny was suppressed, and the ringleaders were flogged under the eyes of German mercenaries. Cobbett wrote, denouncing the floggings, and was prosecuted for sedition. A fine of £1,000, two years in Newgate gaol, bail in £3,000 and the finding of two sureties at £1,000 each, were his punishment.

From Newgate, under the lax prison discipline of the time, Cobbett continued to edit the *Register,* and wrote his famous *Paper against Gold,* in which he denounced the war-time inflation of the currency, and the financial policy of Pitt and his successors. His imprisonment, however, brought him financial ruin. He went bankrupt. His farm at Botley was sold; and most of his valuable properties passed out of his hands. The *Register* he barely saved. Three great publishing enterprises on which he was engaged had to be sold—the *State Trials* (known as Howell's, from the editor whom Cobbett employed), the *Parliamentary History of England,* and the *Parliamentary Debates,* which were bought by his printer, Hansard, and thereafter bore the latter's name. All these were originated by Cobbett, though the actual editorship, under his control, had been mainly left to others.

When Cobbett emerged from prison in 1812, he appeared to be ruined. But he had still the *Register,* and the ending of the war, in 1815, brought him his chance. Prices fell, indeed; but the cessation of war demand and the prostration of Europe after the long struggle led to widespread unemployment and distress. In the industrial districts, unrest grew; and the farmers, pressed down by high taxation, were also in a condition of active discontent. The Government had no plans for dealing with the crisis;

and Cobbett with his demands for parliamentary reform and a reduction of the heavy interest on the National Debt, became the central figure in a nation-wide agitation. In 1816, he began the issue of a cheap unstamped *Register* (denounced as Cobbett's "two-penny trash") addressed particularly to the journeymen and labourers of the Northern and Midland counties. He became suddenly the most influential leader of the working classes. But by this time the Government, alarmed at hunger-riots and movements of despair and discontent, was embarking on a campaign of repression which recalled Pitt's measures in the years following the French Revolution. In 1817 Lord Sidmouth, the Home Secretary, passed his "Gagging Bills" and procured the suspension of the Habeas Corpus Act. Widespread arrests of Radical leaders followed; and Cobbett, in order to avoid arrest, fled to the United States, where he remained until 1819.

Settling down on a hired farm at North Hempstead, Long Island, Cobbett set himself to write. He sent the copy regularly for the *Political Register,* which continued to be published by his agents in England. But he also embarked on other literary work. To the respite which exile gave him from daily political preoccupations we owe the beginning of his great literary period. Hitherto he had written much excellent journalism, but no important book. But between 1817 and 1819 he produced not only his *Journal of a Year's Residence in the United States of America,* but also his famous *Grammar of the English Language,* which, despite its faults of scholarship, is still probably the best introduction to correct virile English for the working-class student. In America, too, he projected certain others of the important books which he produced, from this time onwards, with profuse mental vigour.

Although the repression was by no means over—indeed, the "Six Acts" were not passed until after his return—Cobbett came back to England late in 1819, and assumed his place as the outstanding leader of working-class radical agitation. From 1819 to 1832 his history is, in one aspect, the history of the agitation for parliamentary reform. But he found scope for other activities as well, above all for his well-known *Rural Rides* through the southern half of England. His accounts of these appeared in the *Register* between 1820 and 1830, in which year they were first published in book form.

Rural Rides, certainly Cobbett's best widely read book except the *Grammar,* are difficult to describe. They are, in part, a plain account of what he saw in the English countryside—of good farming and of bad, of rotten boroughs and the country houses of bankers, stock-jobbers and successful army contractors, and above all of the misery and starvation of the common people. But they are far more than this. They abound in digressions, in racy snatches of autobiography, in topical political tirades, and everywhere in abundant outflowings of Cobbett's own forceful and appealing personality. Though they were composed in haste and sent off to the *Register* without chance of revision, they were astonishingly well written. *Rural Rides* are Cobbett at his best, showing more sides of the man than appeared in any other of his works.

But *Rural Rides,* and the ceaseless "rustic harangues" which accompanied them, did not, even with the added burden of conducting the *Register* and actively guiding a large section of the reform movement, at all exhaust Cobbett's energies. Books, and mostly good books, flowed from him—*Cottage Economy* and the *Sermons* in 1822, *The History of the Protestant Reformation in England* (questionable history this, but vigorous writing) in 1824–26, *The Woodlands* in 1825, *Advice to Young Men* (next to *Rural Rides* his best book) and *The English Gardener* in 1829, and a host of others. Moreover, in 1820–21 he whole-heartedly espoused the cause of Queen Caroline against the king, acted as one of her regular advisers before the famous trial, and wrote ceaselessly on her behalf. He even composed a number of her own letters and messages concerned with the case. And in his hands the defence of the Queen became also a means of rallying the forces of the Reformers.

Meanwhile, in 1820, he had rid himself by bankruptcy of some of his financial worries, and had settled down to rebuild his shattered fortunes by means of his pen. Botley had been given up, and for awhile he had no land. But soon he developed a flourishing seed-farm in Kensington, and began to deal also in American trees, and in a variety of imported seeds and plants. Especially he urged the cultivation of maize ("Cobbett's corn"), of the locust tree, and of Swedish turnips, as well as the introduction of the straw-plait manufacture from home-grown grasses. His seed-farm and his agricultural writings brought him a large following among the farming classes.

In 1830, with the fall of Wellington and the end of the long period of Tory ascendancy, the reform agitation came to a head. The Whigs, under Lord Gray, assumed office, and reform became the one political question of the day. Immediately upon this change followed the hunger movement of the rural labourers in the southern and eastern counties, known as "the last labourer's revolt." The opponents of the movement sought to trace these troubles to Cobbett's influence, and the Whig Government, anxious to prove its respect for property and to reassure the propertied classes as the subject of reform, prosecuted him. Refusing to employ counsel, Cobbett defended himself in a masterly speech, which thoroughly turned the tables on his opponents. The jury disagreed, and no further attempt was made to molest him. The revolt, however, was savagely repressed.

At length, in 1832, the Reform Act became law. Cobbett, though he had no love for the Whigs, had urged the workers to support it, on the ground that no more liberal measure stood any chance of immediate success. At the election which followed he was elected M.P. for Oldham, as the colleague of John Fielden, the Radical manufacturer. He had stood at Manchester also, but withdrew on learning of his success at Oldham.

This was not Cobbett's first parliamentary contest. He had stood unsuccessfully for Coventry in 1820 and for Preston in 1826. Indeed, for many years he had been seeking to force his way into parliament. At sixty-eight years of age, he found himself a member, as strongly in opposition to the reformed parliament of 1832 as he could have been to the unreformed parliaments of earlier years. His two and a half years of parliamentary life he passed as the leader of a tiny group of extreme radicals, supported sometimes by O'Connell and his Irish, but always fighting for forlorn hopes. Especially, he put up an unavailing struggle against the "new poor law" of 1834, and his last weeks of life were spent in the endeavour to run a campaign against the act when it had been passed into law.

It is usually said that Cobbett was not a success as a parliamentarian. He could hardly have been so, for he accepted none of the rules of the game. He remained to the end the leader of an essentially extra-parliamentary crusade. But already his health was failing. He had been always an indefatigable worker, rising very early and doing a good part of a day's labour before other men were astir. Now severe colds and coughs began to trouble him; but he insisted on adding assiduous attention to his parliamentary duties to his other multifarious activities. In 1835 his health gave way under the strain, and, on June 18, he died of an attack of influenza. His sons attempted for a few months to carry on the *Register;* but it was nothing without his vigorous editorials, and was speedily discontinued.

Cobbett was survived by his wife and by seven children. Anne, the eldest (1795–1877), wrote *The English Housekeeper* and other works. Both she and the two other daughters, Eleanor and Susan, remained unmarried. The three eldest sons all went to the bar. William (1798–1878) wrote *The Law of Turnpikes* and other legal works, and edited the *Register* for a while after his father's death. John Morgan (1800–1877) wrote several books, stood unsuccessfully for Oldham in 1835, and successfully, as an Independent, in 1852. He held the seat till 1865, and again, as a Conservative, from 1872 to 1877. He married John Fielden's daughter in 1851. James Paul (1803–1881) wrote *A Ride in France, Journal of a Tour in Italy,* etc., and stood for Bury as a Radical in 1837. Richard Baverstock Brown, the youngest son (1814–1875) became a solicitor in Manchester, and was active there in the Chartist movement.

Cobbett's character has been variously estimated. He was

always extremely pugnacious, and made many enemies. But he made also many firm friends. His pugnacity, which led him to quarrel, almost as much with allies as opponents, was purely political. Carlyle called him "the pattern John Bull of his century"; his fellow M. P., Buckingham, said that he had "a ruddy countenance, a small laughing eye, and the figure of a respectable English farmer." Hazlitt, who liked his books, also said he looked like a farmer. Cobbett was, indeed, despite his appeal to the workers of the factory districts, always at heart a countryman, with an unconquerable instinct for the land and the men of the land. He was intensely English, and, in his way, intensely patriotic; and it was this patriotism that roused him to the defence of his fellow-countrymen, trodden under by the oppressions of war and the twin revolutions in agriculture and industry whose devastating social effects he watched from phase to phase. He was that rarest of literary portents—an articulate peasant. His prose is astonishingly quick in its movement, and yet solid as a lump of earth. His clods of abuse and denunciation stick to-day. He had a marvellous facility for nicknames, and for the ridicule that hurts. But above all his prose depends for its success on the personal quality that pervades it. It is spoken rather than written down; and in it the man lives. *Rural Rides* and *Advice to Young Men* will be read as long as English is read at all. Cobbett has often been called an egoist, and he was; but his egoism—his capacity to make himself express the aspirations of a whole suffering class—is at the very root of his appeal.

BIBLIOGRAPHY.—Most of Cobbett's important writings have been mentioned above. Besides a host of pamphlets, his other books include *Porcupine's Works* (selections from his early American writings, in 12 vols., 1801); *A Collection of Facts and Observations relative to the Peace with Bonaparte* (1801); *Letters to Addington, in the Fatal Effects of the Peace with Bonaparte* (1802); *Letters to Lord Hawkesbury, on the Peace* (1802); *The Political Proteus* (an attack on R. B. Sheridan, 1804); *Letters on the Late War between the United States and Great Britain* (1815); *The Pride of Britannia Humbled* (New York, 1815); *Paper against Gold* (1815); *The American Gardener* (1821); *Collective Commentaries* (1822); *French Grammar* (1824); *The Poor Man's Friend* (1826); *A Treatise on Cobbett's Corn* (1828); *The Emigrants' Guide* (1829); *History of the Regency and Reign of George IV.* (1830); *Lectures on the French and Belgian Revolutions* (1830); *Spelling Book* (1831); *Tour in Scotland* (continuing *Rural Rides*, 1832); *Manchester Lectures* (1832); *Geographical Dictionary* (1832); *French and English Dictionary* (1833); *Four Letters to the Hon. John Stuart Wortley* (1834); *Life of Andrew Jackson* (1834); *Lectures on the Political State of Ireland* (1834); *Legacy to Labourers* (1835); *Legacy to Parsons* (1835); *Legacy to Peel,* (1836). Six volumes of selections from the *Register*, under the title, *Cobbett's Political Works*, were published in 1835–36.

Of the lives, the most recent is by G. D. H. Cole (1924). There are other lives by Huish (1836), E. Smith (1878), E. I. Carlyle (1904), and Lewis Melville (1913). (G. D. H. C.)

COBBOLD, THOMAS SPENCER (1828–1886), English man of science, was born at Ipswich in 1828, a son of the Rev. Richard Cobbold (1797–1877), the author of the *History of Margaret Catchpole*. From 1868 he acted as Swiney lecturer on geology at the British Museum until 1873, when he became professor of botany at the Royal Veterinary college, afterwards filling a chair of helminthology which was specially created for him at that institution. He died in London on March 20, 1886. His special subject was helminthology, particularly the worms parasitic in man and animals. His numerous writings include *Entozoa* (1864); *Tapeworms* (1866); *Parasites* (1879); *Human Parasites* (1882); and *Parasites of Meat and Prepared Flesh Food* (1884).

COBDEN, RICHARD (1804–1865), English statesman and economist, was born at Dunford Farm, near Midhurst, Sussex, the son of a small farmer, who died when Richard was a child. There were 11 children, who were befriended by relatives. Richard was sent to one of the bad private boarding schools of those days, in Yorkshire, and in 1819 became a clerk in his uncle's warehouse in Old Change, London. After serving in the warehouse he began to travel for the firm. In 1828 he joined with two friends in setting up business as calico merchants. Three years later the firm acquired a factory at Sabden, Lancs., and began to do their own calico-printing. This was the beginning of a business career which brought Cobden an independent fortune and permitted him in later years to devote himself, untrammelled by financial difficulties, to his life work for greater freedom of trade. He remedied his lack of education by a course of serious study and by travel in the United States (June–Aug. 1835) and in the Near East (1836–37), in Germany (1838) and elsewhere, making full use of his opportunities of studying the economic and financial systems of the countries he visited. At this time he published two pamphlets which show that the broad lines of his ideas on foreign policy were already matured. These are *England, Ireland and America* (1835), by "a Manchester Merchant," in which he maintained that England had no interest in defending Turkey against Russia; and *Russia* (1836), in which he attacks the doctrine of the balance of power.

In October 1838 a group of seven Manchester merchants met to form an association to promote a movement for the abolition of the corn laws (*q.v.*). This became the nucleus of a national association, the Anti-Corn-Law league. From the beginning Cobden was the moving spirit in the league. Though other great names were associated with it, Cobden's was the directing mind. He had already met John Bright in connection with a campaign for providing education for the mass of the people, and had drawn him into politics. Bright's eloquence moved thousands in the meetings organized by the league, but Cobden's counsels carried more weight among statesmen. Throughout the whole of this campaign Cobden linked up the question of free trade with that of peace and disarmament; he regarded liberty of commerce as a key to international solidarity. He entered the House of Commons for Stockport at the general election of 1841. Parliament met in August, and Sir Robert Peel moved a vote of censure on the Whig Government, which was carried on Aug. 28. The new administration proposed a modification of the corn law which altered the sliding scale of 1828 and reduced the duty. Villiers' annual motion for repeal was defeated. Cobden presented his case against the corn law in his first speech in the House during the debate on the address. His sincerity and his precise knowledge of the question in hand made a strong impression. He proved a redoubtable opponent of Peel's financial policy, and persistently opposed the reintroduction of income tax.

Cobden desired the minimum of interference in trade and industry. When Graham's Factory Bill was brought forward in 1844 he accepted the regulation of child labour but he protested against any "interference with the freedom of adult labour." He was less extreme than Bright in his individualism, but had no use for the early reformers of the terrible factory system of the day, because he would not accept the principle of Government intervention. On the other hand he ardently supported measures for the improvement of education, and supported Peel's proposal to augment the grant to the Irish Roman Catholic college at Maynooth, on the ground that the priests were the instructors of the people and should themselves be thoroughly educated.

Meanwhile Cobden worked incessantly for the Anti-Corn-Law league, speaking all over the country, and, with increasing force in the House of Commons itself. His most powerful speech was perhaps that made in the House on March 13, 1845, when Peel, who was expected to reply, is said to have crumpled up his paper and notes and said to Sidney Herbert, "You may answer this, for I cannot." Some members of the Peel Government had realized at the time of Peel's first budget that the next change in the corn laws must be their total repeal. The prospect of famine in Ireland at the end of the year made the change inevitable. On Dec. 5 Peel resigned. Lord John Russell, invited to form a cabinet, asked Cobden to take office, but he declined on the ground that his mission lay outside the House on the public platform. On the 20th Peel resumed office. For the course of the events in the session of 1846 *see* PEEL, SIR ROBERT. It is sufficient here to say that Peel's famous resolutions included a modified sliding scale of duties for three years, and that after Feb. 1, 1849, oats, barley and wheat should be admitted at a nominal duty of a shilling. The bill embodying this resolution was passed by the House of Lords on June 25, 1846. Four days later Peel resigned, not without a tribute to Cobden. "The name," he said, "which ought to be, and will be, associated with the success of these measures, is not mine, or that of the noble lord (Russell), but the name of one who, acting I believe from pure and disinterested motives, has, with untiring energy, made appeals to our reason, and has enforced those appeals with an eloquence the more to be admired because it was unaffected and unadorned: the name which ought to be associated with the success of these measures is the name of Richard Cobden."

The seven years' struggle for repeal left Cobden a ruined man, for he had been compelled to neglect his own business. A subscription was raised for him to enable him to meet his obligations. With part of the amount provided he bought his birthplace, the farmhouse of Dunford, which was thenceforward his home. He spent 14 months abroad (Aug. 1846–Oct. 1847), visiting the chief countries of Europe and urging on the many public men by whom he was received the necessity of greater freedom of trade. He returned more than ever opposed to a policy of intervention in any shape or form in the political situation of Europe. He now turned to work for the promotion of peace and the reduction of armaments, the logical complement of free trade, and became a formidable opponent of Palmerston's general foreign policy. In the parliament elected in 1847 he sat for the West Riding of Yorkshire. In that parliament he brought forward two important motions: one in favour of international arbitration (June 12, 1849), the other the mutual reduction of armaments (1851). He associated himself with the peace movement, at that time derided, and helped to organize a series of international congresses for the promotion of peace at Brussels, Paris, Frankfurt, London, Manchester and Edinburgh between 1848 and 1851. The panic which took possession of a large section of Englishmen in 1851 on the foundation of the Second Empire in France put his principles to the test. By his resolute campaign against the scaremongers in his pamphlet *1792 and 1853, in Three Letters* (1853), Cobden sacrificed the popularity he had won as the man who gave cheap food to the people. With Bright he withstood the torrent of popular sentiment in favour of war against Russia during the period before the Crimean War. He maintained strongly that the future of the Turkish provinces in Europe lay with the Christian populations and that England should be on their side and not on the side of the Turk. On Feb. 26, 1857, over the "Arrow" incident (Oct. 1856) in China, when Canton was bombarded on the ground that the Chinese had unlawfully boarded a ship of that name, Cobden brought in a motion condemning the action of Sir John Bowring in this matter, which was carried and led Palmerston to dissolve parliament. Cobden's peace policy had destroyed his electoral prospects. He was defeated at Huddersfield, and retired to his house in Sussex for the time; he then made a second visit to America.

On his return (June 29, 1859) he found he had been returned unopposed by Rochdale to the new parliament and that the Whigs were once more united under Palmerston, who asked him to join his cabinet as president of the board of trade. This offer, generous from a man of whose policy he had been the stoutest opponent, was declined on the ground that consistency forbade it. Nevertheless Cobden was the organizer of one important achievement of the new ministry, the conclusion of the commercial treaty with France of 1860. He first discussed the feasibility of such a proposal with Gladstone and then with Palmerston and Russell; from the two latter he received tepid encouragement, but was offered the assistance of the Paris embassy. He proposed to go to France to interview Napoleon III, and, in fact, spent a year (Oct. 1859–Nov. 1860) in laborious and at first unofficial negotiations (he only received definite official powers in Jan. 1860) for a mutual reduction of tariffs in the interest of increased trade between France and England. His work for the conclusion of this commercial treaty is proof, if any were needed, that Cobden was not a merely negative advocate of a *laissez-faire* policy, but a practical and constructive statesman.

The last of the greater issues of policy in which Cobden was involved was the American Civil War. He had been a regular correspondent of Charles Sumner's since 1851, and though his hatred of war made him say frankly that he would not have gone to war for emancipation, he did, after some hesitation, declare for the North, and J. A. Hobson, writing of this correspondence, asserts that he "did more than any other Englishman, save Bright, to correct the mistakes of fact and judgment which confused the issue in this country (Great Britian) at the outset, and to give sound counsel upon the sharp concrete cases which more than once brought us near to the breaking-point with the Federal Government."

Cobden died on April 2, 1865, in London after a journey which he had insisted on taking in order to be present at a discussion on a scheme of Canadian fortification.

His distrust of government at home and his limited belief in democracy were coupled with a firm belief in the good sense and worth of the middle classes. Starting from the belief that it was impossible to regulate wages by national considerations alone in industries competing in a world market, he regarded trade unionism as an unjustifiable use of monopoly. He was a child of the industrial revolution, and he believed that the removal of restrictions on the free play of self-interest would bring to everyone his due share of the profits of industry. He opposed factory legislation for this reason, except in the case of children, for whom he realized that freedom of contract was in fact freedom of coercion. Nevertheless in his later years his confidence in the beneficial results of middle-class domination began to be shaken, and the man who had written in 1842 (in a letter to F. W. Cobden) that trade unions were "founded upon principles of brutal tyranny and monopoly" wrote to William Hargreave in 1861, "Have they (the working people) no Spartacus among them to lead a revolt of the slave class against their political tormentors? . . . It is certain that so long as five millions of men are silent under their disabilities it is quite impossible for a few middle class members of parliament to give them liberty." But he was still thinking of the political rather than the industrial machine.

Cobdenism and what is called the Manchester school have fallen into some disrepute for various reasons, and in the criticisms launched on the school there is some danger of losing sight of the great services that Cobden rendered. His views on domestic and foreign policy were closely linked together. His experience convinced him that government intervention in the affairs of foreign countries was nearly always bad; he believed in the minimum of government at home and the minimum of intervention abroad. The subsequent controversy, still unsettled, was whether a too "spirited" or a too "passive" foreign policy would lead to the worse results. In the matter of international freedom of trade he was too optimistic. He believed that other countries would follow the English logic. He did not foresee the almost universal strength of economic nationalism, the enormous change in the whole structure of the economic world since brought about by gigantic foreign investments, with the development of new countries by the wealthier nations; he did not foresee the international operation of capital. But in his advocacy of arbitration, disarmament and peace he was far in advance of his time, and his ideals, apart from questions of practical application in circumstances as then existing, are justified by enlightened opinion today.

See his *Speeches,* ed. by John Bright and J. E. Thorold Rogers (1870); *Political Writings of Richard Cobden,* with introduction by Sir L. Mallet (1878); W. Bagehot, *Biographical Studies* (1881); John Morley, *Life of Richard Cobden* (1882); J. A. Hobson, *Richard Cobden* (1918), which contains Cobden's letters to Sumner, taken from the Sumner-Cobden correspondence preserved at Harvard.

COBERGHER, WENSEL (1557/61–1634), Flemish painter and architect, was born in Antwerp and died in Brussels. A prominent master of Flemish Baroque, he received his education as a painter in the workshop of Maarten de Vos and travelled in France and in Italy. He painted altarpieces for churches in Italy and in Belgium, but his pictures are far less important than his few surviving buildings. Of these the most famous is the church of Notre Dame de Montaigu (Flemish Scherpenheuvel), near Antwerp (1609). Of his other buildings the church of St. Augustine at Antwerp (1615) and the town hall at Ath are outstanding examples of Flemish Baroque. From 1605 until his death Cobergher was architect to the archduke Albert and the infanta Isabella, governors of the Spanish Netherlands. He wrote also on archaeology.

See J. H. Plantenga, *L'Architecture religieuse de l'ancien duché de Brabant au 17me siècle* (The Hague, 1926); P. Parent, *L'Architecture des Pays-Bas méridionaux aux 16me, 17me et 18me siècles* (Brussels, 1926). (A. Nh.)

COBET, CAREL GABRIEL (1813–1889), Dutch classical scholar, was born at Paris on Nov. 28, 1813. After travelling in Italy to study Greek manuscripts, he was professor at Leyden (1846–84). He died on Oct. 26, 1889. Cobet's special weapon as a critic was his consummate knowledge of palaeography, combined with rare acumen and wide knowledge of classical literature.

His works include: *Prosopographia Xenophontea* (1836); *Observationes criticae in Platonis comici reliquias* (1840); *De Arte interpretandi Grammatices et Critices Fundamentis innixa* (1846), his inaugural address at Leyden; *Commentationes Philologicae* (1850–51); *Variae Lectiones* (1854); *Novae Lectiones* (1858); *Miscellanea Critica* (1876); *Collectanea Critica* (1878); observations of Dionysius Halicarnassensis (1877); professorial discourses (1852–60); and editions of *Diogenes Laertius* (1850), Philostratus περὶ γυμναστικῆς (1859), speeches of Hypereides (1858–77) and Lysias (1863). He was the editor of *Mnemosyne.*

See an appreciative obituary notice by W. G. Rutherford in the

Classical Review, Dec. 1889; Sandys *Hist. Class. Schol.* (1908) iii. 282.

COBH, a seaport, watering place and naval station of Co. Cork, Ire., on the south side of Great Island, on a hill above Cork harbour; formerly called Queenstown. Pop. (1951) 5,711. Until the end of the 18th century, Cove of Cork was a small fishing village. Its prominence is due to the fact that it became a military and naval centre and port of embarkation for troops. The quays are exposed to the south and south-east winds. The depth at the harbour entrance is 41 ft. (low-water) while in the river it is 29 ft. at high tides and 26 ft. at low tides. Vessels of 27 ft. draught have discharged at Cork deep-water quays lying afloat at all states of the tide. There is a large dockyard and victualling station at Haulbowline.

COBHAM, a village of Kent, England, 4 mi. W. of Rochester. Population of civil parish 933. The church (Early English and later restored) is rich in ancient brasses (1320–1529), commemorating thirteen members of the Brooke and Cobham families. Cobham college, containing 20 almshouses, after the dissolution took the place of a college for priests, founded by Sir John de Cobham in the 14th century. Cobham hall is mainly Elizabethan. The Cobham family was established here before the reign of King John. In 1313 Henry de Cobham was created Baron Cobham. In 1603 Henry Brooke, Lord Cobham, was attainted for participation in the Raleigh conspiracy, and died in prison in 1618. The attainder was reversed in 1916 and Dr. Gervase Alexander was summoned to parliament as Lord Cobham. There are, however, two Lords Cobham, for during the attainder of the barony Sir Richard Temple was created Baron and Viscount Cobham in 1718. Cobham hall was granted to Lodowick Stewart, duke of Lennox, and came by descent and marriage to the earls of Darnley.

COBIA or **CRAB-EATER** (*Rachycentron canadus*), a very voracious game-fish, cosmopolitan in warm seas, the only genus of the family Rachycentridae which, according to G. A. Boulenger, is allied with the mackerel-like fishes. The fish is slender and somewhat pike-like, reaching a length of five feet. The head is flattened and the lower jaw projecting. The tail is strong and forked, the upper lobe slightly the longer. The soft dorsal fin is long and low; in advance of it about eight low, isolated spines constitute the spinous dorsal. The anal is almost as long as the dorsal. This fish is dark olive green above, shading into lighter brownish-green and silvery. On the sides two distinct dark stripes parallel each other, one from tip of upper jaw to tail; the other starting at the origin of the pectoral fin. (*See* FISHES.)

COBLENZ or KOBLENZ, a city and fortress of Germany, in the Rhineland Palatinate, 57 mi. S.E. from Cologne by rail, situated on the left bank of the Rhine at its confluence with the Moselle, whence its ancient name *Confluentes,* of which Coblenz is a corruption. Pop. (1950) 66,444.

The town was one of the military posts established by Drusus about 9 B.C. Later it was frequently the residence of the Frankish kings, and in 860 and 922 was the scene of ecclesiastical synods. In 1018 the city, after receiving a charter, was given by the emperor Henry II. to the archbishop of Trier (Trèves), and it remained in the possession of the archbishop-electors till the close of the 18th century. In 1249–54 it was surrounded with new walls and it was partly to overawe the turbulent townsmen that successive archbishops built and strengthened the fortress of Ehrenbreitstein (*q.v.*) that dominates the city. As a member of the league of the Rhenish cities which took its rise in the 13th century, Coblenz attained to great prosperity. In 1344 the Moselle was spanned by a Gothic freestone bridge of 14 arches. The town suffered greatly, however, in the wars of the 17th, 18th and 19th centuries. In 1688 the French bombarded the Altstadt, destroying the old merchants' hall (*Kaufhaus*), which was restored in 1725. In 1786 the elector of Trier, Clement Wenceslaus of Saxony, took up his residence in the town, and a few years later it became one of the principal rendezvous of the French *émigrés.* In 1794 Coblenz was taken by the Revolutionary army and, after the peace of Lunéville, it was made the chief town of the Rhine and Moselle department (1798). In 1814 it was occupied by the Russians; by the congress of Vienna it was assigned to Prussia, and in 1822 it was made the seat of government of the Rhine province.

The city, down to 1890, consisted of the Altstadt (old city) and the Neustadt (new city), or Klemenstadt. The old city was triangular in shape, two sides being bounded by the Rhine and Moselle and the third by a line of fortifications. Here is the church of St. Castor, originally founded in 836 by Louis the Pious: the present Romanesque building was completed in 1208, the Gothic vaulted roof dating from 1498. In the old quarter, too, are the Liebfrauenkirche, a fine church (nave 1250, choir 1404–31) with late Romanesque towers; the castle of the electors of Trier, erected in 1280, which now contains the municipal picture gallery; and the family house of the Metternichs, where Prince Metternich, the Austrian statesman, was born in 1773. In the modern part of the town, the palace (Residenzschloss), built in 1778–1786 by Clement Wenceslaus, the last elector of Trier, contains some fine Gobelin tapestries. Coblenz is a principal seat of the Moselle and Rhenish wine trade. Its manufactures include pianos, paper, machinery, boats and barges, sugar, dyes and chemicals. It is an important transit centre for the Rhine railways and for the Rhine navigation. Immediately outside the former walls lies the central railway station, in which is effected a junction of the Cologne-Mainz railway with the strategical line Metz-Berlin.

Coblenz was bombed by the Allies in 1917 and 1918. After the Armistice the town and bridgehead were occupied by Allied troops under the Treaty of Versailles, the town forming the second zone to be evacuated after 10 years. (*See* RHINELAND.)

Coblenz was the seat of the Rhineland High Commission, and was occupied first by American troops and from 1923 to 1926 by French troops. In October 1923 Separatists proclaimed a Rhineland republic but in Feb. 1924 this movement collapsed.

Because of its importance as a railway centre, Coblenz was bombed by the British in World War II.

COBOURG, the capital of Northumberland county, Ont., Can., on Lake Ontario and the Canadian National and Canadian Pacific railways, 70 mi. E.N.E. of Toronto. Pop. (1951) 7,470. It has a large, safe harbour and steamboat connections with St. Lawrence and Lake Ontario ports. It is a centre for a rich dairy and fruit area; contains car works, foundries and carpet and woollen factories; and is a summer resort, especially for Americans. Victoria university, formerly situated there, was moved to Toronto in 1890.

COBRA, the name applied to the poisonous elapid snakes of the genera *Naja, Hemachates,* and *Ophiophagus,* which have the power of dilating the neck laterally to form a broad disc or "hood." The dilatation is brought about by the raising and pushing forward of the long anterior ribs, the elastic skin being stretched taut over this framework. This type of hood is in marked contrast to the vertical expansion of the neck of many snakes (*e.g.,* boomslang and mamba), which is caused by the inflation of the windpipe. In all species, however, erection of the hood only occurs when the animal is annoyed or disturbed.

The genus *Naja,* the cobras proper, containing about ten species, ranges from the Cape throughout Africa, Arabia and India to southern China, the Philippine Islands and the Malay archipelago; *Hemachates,* the spy slang of the Boers, with a single species, is confined to South Africa; *Ophiophagus,* the king cobra, ranges from Burma through the East Indies. These snakes are proteroglyphous, *i.e.,* with fixed poison fangs on the front of the upper jaw, and the bite of all the species is extremely dangerous. Accurate statistics of snake-bite mortality cannot be obtained, but it seems fairly certain that the common Indian cobra (*Naja naja*) is responsible for several thousand deaths annually.

As in all proteroglyphous snakes, the venom acts directly on the nervous system and so is much more rapid in its action than that of the viperine and opisthoglyphous snakes, the toxicity of which is chiefly because of the power of destroying the blood corpuscles. In the past, despite a multitude of so-called cures and a widespread belief in the efficacy of "snake stones," no really effective treatment was available except immediate excision of the site of the bite; now efficient "antivenines" are produced from the blood sera of animals that have been immunized by regulated doses of venom. These antivenines, however, must be administered hypodermically. The dose is large and, to be effective for the bites of proteroglyphous snakes, must be given immediately, conditions not easily obtained in most of the regions which cobras inhabit. Danger to man is further enhanced by the fact that the prevalence of rats and mice frequently attracts cobras to the vicinity of villages and houses where they are more likely to come into contact with man. In India also, cobras are often regarded with so much superstitious reverence that no attempt is made to kill them.

THE COMMON COBRA OF INDIA (NAJA NAJA) SHOWING THE BOLD "SPECTACLE" MARKING OF THE HOOD

The best known species is the common Indian cobra (*Naja naja*), which may reach a length of about 5½ ft. and which exhibits great variation in colour; typically it is yellowish to dark brown with a black and white spectacle-shaped marking on the hood, but all gradations between this form and specimens without any trace of such a mark are known. The king cobra or hamadryad (*Ophiophagus hannah*) is another oriental species; it is rarer than the common cobra, larger, reaching a length of 12 ft. or more, and feeds chiefly on other snakes. Like all the cobras it lays eggs. It exercises some parental care; a definite nest of dried leaves is made and the parents remain in the vicinity of the nest until the eggs are hatched. There may be some care of the nest in the common cobra. In Africa there are several species, the hooded or Egyptian cobra (*Naja haje*) and the black-necked cobra (*Naja nigricollis*) being the most widely distributed. The latter species is able to spit its venom, like the spitting cobra or spy slang (*Hemachates haemachaetes*), which is closely allied to the true cobras and is notorious for its habit of "spitting" venom when annoyed. The mechanism of this "spitting" appears to be that by compression of the poison-glands the venom is forced out through the fangs to a distance of several feet and if it strikes an enemy in the eyes intense irritation is set up that results in temporary, and sometimes permanent blindness. In the accomplished venom spitters, the opening near the end of the fang faces directly forward, while in the cobras that spit only occasionally, like the common cobra, this condition is incipient.

(D. M. S. W.; X.)

COBURG, a town in Germany, in the *Land* of Bavaria, on the left bank of the Itz, 40 mi. S.S.E. of Gotha. Pop. (1950) 44,929. Coburg, first mentioned in a record of 1207, was of considerable importance in the 15th and 16th centuries, and owed its existence to the castle and to its position on the great trade route from Nürnberg via Bamberg to the north. In 1245 the castle became the seat of the elder branch of the counts of Henneberg (Coburg-Schmalkalden). The countships passed to Otto V. of Brandenburg, whose grandson sold them to Henry VIII. of Henneberg. The castle, town and countship then passed by marriage into the possession of the Saxon house of Wettin. In the 17th century the castle was strong enough to stand a three years' siege (1632–35) during the Thirty Years' War. In 1835 it became the residence of the dukes of Saxe-Coburg. The town contains many interesting buildings. The ducal palace, known as the Ehrenburg, originally erected on the site of a convent by Duke John Ernest in 1549, was renovated in 1698 and restored in 1816. It contains a decorated hall, the court church and a picture gallery. In the market square are the mediaeval *Rathaus* and the Government buildings. In the Schloss-platz is the Edinburgh palace, built in 1881. The educational establishments include a gymnasium, founded in 1604. The *Zeughaus* (armoury) contains the ducal library and among other public buildings may be mentioned the *Augustenstift*, formerly the seat of the ministerial offices, and the *Marstall* (royal mews). The castle was completely restored in 1835–38 and now contains a natural history museum. The most interesting room is that which was occupied by Luther in 1530. The chief manufactures are machinery, baskets, glass, colours and porcelain Iron-founding and saw-milling are also important, and there is trade in the cattle reared in the neighbourhood. For the princes of the house of Coburg *see* WETTIN; SAXE-COBURG-GOTHA.

COCA or **CUCA** (*Erythroxylon Coca*), a plant of the family Erythroxylaceae, the leaves of which are used as a stimulant in western South America. It resembles a blackthorn bush, and grows to a height of 8 feet. The branches are straight and the lively green leaves are thin, opaque, oval, more or less tapering at the extremities. A marked characteristic of the leaf is an areolated portion bounded by two longitudinal curved lines one on each side of the midrib, and more conspicuous on the under face of the leaf. Good samples of the dried leaves are uncurled, deep green on the upper, and grey-green on the lower surface, and have a strong tea-like odour; when chewed they produce a sense of warmth in the mouth, and have a pleasant, pungent taste. The flowers are small, and disposed in little clusters on short stalks; the corolla is composed of five yellowish-white petals, the anthers are heart-shaped, and the pistil consists of three carpels united to form a three-chambered ovary. The flowers are succeeded by red berries. The plants thrive best in hot, damp situations, such as the clearings of forests; but the leaves most preferred are obtained in drier localities, on the sides of hills. The leaves are considered ready for plucking when they break on being bent. The green leaves (*matu*) are spread in thin layers on coarse woollen cloths and dried in the sun; they are then packed in sacks, which, in order to preserve the quality must be kept from damp. The composition of different specimens of coca leaves is very inconstant. Besides the important alkaloid *cocaine* (*q.v.*) there are several other alkaloids. Coca leaves and preparations of them have no external action. Internally their action is similar to that of opium, though less narcotic.

COCAINE, one of a series of "cocaines," alkaloids (*q.v.*) occurring in the leaves of coca (*q.v.*), a shrub indigenous to Bolivia and Peru, but now chiefly produced by cultivation in Java.

Cocaine crystallizes from alcohol in colourless prisms, melting at 98° C.; it has a specific rotation $[\alpha]_D - 15.8°$, and it is readily soluble in ordinary solvents except water. It is generally used in medicine as the hydrochloride but sometimes as the base, dissolved or suspended in oils or fats. It yields well-crystallized salts of which the hydrochloride, $C_{17}H_{21}O_4N,HCl$, is the most important; this crystallizes from alcohol in short colourless prisms, melting at 200–202° C., and having a specific rotation $[\alpha] -67.5°$. On hydrolysis with mineral acids or baryta, cocaine breaks up into *ecgonine* (tropine carboxylic acid), benzoic acid and methyl alcohol, so that cocaine is closely related to atropine (*q.v.*). It was synthetized in 1923 by Willstätter and Bode.

All the "cocaines" are found to be derivatives of a simple base, ecgonine, which contains both a hydroxyl (.OH) and a carboxyl (.COOH) group, the latter being esterified with methyl alcohol and the former with an acid group—benzoic acid in the case of cocaine, $C_{17}H_{21}O_4N$, and cinnamic or truxillic acid in the other natural "cocaines." In the process for the manufacture of cocaine the total alkaloids of Java coca leaves are hydrolysed to ecgonine, which is converted by esterification as described, so that most of the cocaine of commerce is a partially synthetic product.

Cocaine produces little or no action on the unbroken skin, but if it is injected subcutaneously, or applied to mucous membranes such as those of the mouth, eye or nose, anaesthesia of that area is produced so that slight operations can be carried out painlessly. A 5% or 10% solution is sufficient to abolish pain and touch, but stronger solutions are required to abolish sensations of heat and cold.

If cocaine is swallowed its anaesthetic properties act on the mucous membrane of the stomach; the sensation of hunger is deadened and, therefore, persons taking the drug by mouth can go for a long period without feeling the want of food. The central nervous system is first stimulated and later depressed, the higher centres being affected first. Moderate doses increase the bodily and mental power and give a sense of calmness and happiness; fatigue is abolished. Long, exhausting feats can be carried out under the greater bodily power produced, and the inhabitants of Peru chew the coca leaves for this reason. A single large dose causes mental excitement, delirium, ataxy, with headache and depression later.

Therapeutically, cocaine is very largely used by oculists to produce anaesthesia of the eye; it is also used to relieve pain locally in other parts such as the mouth, teeth, ear, larynx, etc. A cocaine spray is often used to spray the throats of sensitive persons before making a laryngeal examination. It is too toxic to be used for infiltration or spinal anaesthesia.

It is practically never used for its stimulative effect. It is not a food. It is a dangerous drug and is habit forming. (*See* DRUG ADDICTION; NOVOCAIN.)

COCAMA (COQUAMILLA, UCAYALI), South American Indians living on the Marañón and lower Huallaga rivers, Peru, speaking a dialect of the Tupí-Guaraní stock. (J. H. SD.)

COCANADA (KAKINADA), capital of East Godavari district, Andhra state, India, on the coast in the extreme northeast of the Godavari delta, about 300 mi. N.N.E. of Madras. Pop. (1951) 99,952. Cocanada is the fourth port of southern India. The roadstead in Coringa bay is protected but shallow, so that steamers have to lie 7 mi. out, and the entrance to the canal, where the piers and wharves are situated, has to be constantly dredged. The town is connected by navigable channels with the canal system of the Godavari delta, and by a branch line with Samalkot on the Southern railway.

Cocanada's chief exports are rice, cotton and oilseeds. The industries include rice and oil mills, tile and saltworks and tobacco manufacture. The town contains the Pithapur Raja's college and the College of Engineering, both connected with Andhra university, Waltair.

COCCEIUS, the latinized name of Johannes Koch (1603–1669), Dutch theologian, who was born at Bremen on Aug. 9, 1603. After studying at Hamburg and Franeker, where Sixtinus Amama was one of his teachers, he taught at Bremen and at Franeker and in 1650 succeeded F. Spanheim the elder as professor of theology at Leyden. He died there on Nov. 4, 1669. His chief services as an oriental scholar were in the department of Hebrew philology and exegesis. As one of the leading exponents of the covenant or federal theology, he spiritualized the Hebrew scriptures to such an extent that it was said that Cocceius found Christ everywhere in the Old Testament and Hugo Grotius found him nowhere.

He taught that before the Fall, as much as after it, the relation between God and man was a covenant. The first covenant was a Covenant of Works. For this was substituted, after the Fall, the Covenant of Grace, to fulfil which the coming of Jesus Christ was necessary. Cocceius held millenarian views, and was the founder of a school of theologians who were called after him Cocceians. His most distinguished pupil was the celebrated Campeius Vitringa.

His most valuable work was his *Lexicon et Commentarius Sermonis Hebraici et Chaldaici* (Leyden, 1669), which has been frequently republished; his theology is fully expounded in his *Summa Doctrinae de Foedere et Testamento Dei* (1648). His collected works were published in 12 folio volumes (Amsterdam, 1673–75).

See Herzog-Hauck, *Realenzyklopädie.*

COCCIDIA: *see* PROTOZOA.

COCCULUS INDICUS, the commercial name for the dried fruits of *Anamirta cocculus* (family Menispermaceae), a large climbing shrub, native to India. It contains a bitter poisonous principle, picrotoxin, used in small doses to control the night sweats of tuberculosis.

Cocculus carolinus, the carolina moonseed of the same family, a trailing or climbing vine with broadly ovate, entire or lobed, deciduous leaves, greenish-white flowers in axillary and terminal racemes and red drupes occurs from Virginia and Kansas to Florida and Texas.

COCHABAMBA, a central department of Bolivia, occupying a series of fertile valleys on the eastern slope of the great Bolivian plateau, bounded on the north by the department of Beni, on the east by Santa Cruz, on the south by Chuquisaca and Potosí and on the west by Oruro and La Paz. Area, 21,479 sq.mi.; pop. (1950) 490,475.

Cochabamba's average elevation is about 8,000 ft., and its mean monthly temperature ranges from 50° to 71° F., making it one of the most agreeable climatic regions in South America. The rainfall is moderate (18 in. per year, coming almost entirely from November to March) and the seasons are marked by rainfall rather than by temperature.

Cochabamba is essentially an agricultural department, although its mineral resources are good and include deposits of gold, silver, copper and tungsten. Its temperate climate favours the production of wheat, Indian corn, barley and potatoes and most of the fruits and vegetables of the temperate zone. Coca, cacao, tobacco and most of the fruits and vegetables of the tropics are also produced.

Its forest products include rubber and cinchona. Lack of transportation facilities, however, has proved to be an obstacle to the development of any industry beyond local needs except those of cinchona and rubber.

The population is chiefly of the Indian and mestizo types, education is in a backward state, and there are few manufactures other than those of the domestic stage, the natives making many articles of wearing apparel and daily use in their own homes. Rough highways and mule paths are the usual means of communication, but Cochabamba (city) is connected by rail with Oruro (127 mi.) and Anani (37 mi.) and by motor road with La Paz (285 mi.). The capital is Cochabamba (*q.v.*); other important towns are Punata, Tarata, Totora, Cliza and Sacaba. (J. W. MW.)

COCHABAMBA, a city of Bolivia, capital of the department of the same name and of the province of Cercado, situated on the Rocha, a small tributary of the Guapay river. Population (1950) 80,795, mostly Indians and mestizos. The city stands in a broad valley of the Bolivian plateau, 8,400 ft. above sea level, overshadowed by the snow-clad heights of Tunari, 127 mi. E.N.E. of Oruro, with which place it is connected by rail. The climate is mild and temperate and the surrounding country fertile and cultivated. The city is well supplied with foreign goods and enjoys a large part of the Amazon trade through some small river ports on tributaries of the Mamoré. It is also an important centre for air routes. A petroleum topping plant was completed in 1950, and the city is connected by pipeline (via Sucre) with the Camiri fields.

Cochabamba was founded in the 16th century and for a time was called Oropeza. It took an active part in the war of independence, the women distinguishing themselves in an attack on the Spanish camp in 1815, and some of them being put to death in 1818 by the Spanish forces.

In 1874 the city was seized and partly destroyed by Miguel Aguirre, but in general its isolated situation has been a protection against disorders. (J. W. MW.)

COCHEM, a town of Germany, in the Rhineland-Palatinate on the Moselle, 30 mi. S.W. of Coblenz by rail. Pop. (1933) 5,459. It is situated at the foot of a hill with a feudal castle dating from 1051. The principal trade is in wines.

COCHERY, LOUIS ADOLPHE (1819–1900), French statesman, was born at Paris in 1819. After studying law he entered politics, and was on the staff of the ministry of justice after the revolution of Feb. 1848. From the coup d'état of 1851 to May 1869 he devoted himself to journalism. Then, elected deputy by the *département* of the Loiret, he joined the group of the left centre and was a supporter of the revolution of Sept. 4, 1870. His talent in finance won him a distinguished place in the chamber. From 1879 till 1885 he was minister of posts and telegraphs, and in Jan. 1888 he was elected to the senate. He died in 1900 in Paris.

His son, GEORGES CHARLES PAUL (1855–1914), also born in Paris, was in his father's department from 1879 till 1885, deputy from 1885, five times president of the Budget commission and minister of finance under (Felix) Jules Méline, premier from 1896 to 1898. Georges Cochery was vice-president of the chamber, 1898–1902, and again finance minister in the cabinet of Aristide Briand, 1909–10. He died in Paris in 1914.

COCHIN, DENYS MARIE PIERRE AUGUSTIN (1851–1922), French public official, was born at Paris in 1851. He studied law, was elected to the chamber of deputies in 1893, and gradually became one of the leaders and principal orators of the conservative party.

He opposed the project of the income tax in 1894, the revision of the Dreyfus case in 1899 and the separation of the church and state in 1905.

His published works included *Le Monde extérieur* (1895); *Contre les barbares* (1899); and *Ententes et ruptures* (1905).

COCHIN, a former princely state (area: 1,493 sq.mi.; pop. [1941] 1,422,875) of southern India, which joined Travancore on July 1, 1949, to form the state of Travancore-Cochin (*q.v.*). Like Travancore, Cochin formed part of the ancient southern Indian kingdom of Kerala (*q.v.*). The accounts of the Aryan colonization of this area, to be found in the *Kerala Mahatmyam*, are conflicting. The Nambudri Brahmans appear to have established their supremacy over the indigenous tribes, but, because of internal dissensions, the Perumals were invited to administer the country. There is no definite historical evidence as to who they were or whence they came. Local Malabar chronicles assign Cheraman Perumal, the last of the Perumal rulers, to the 9th century A.D.

The period of Perumal rule is important as being the earliest period in Kerala history of which contemporary records, namely, the copperplate charters granted to the Jews and Christians, are extant. The modern state of Cochin occupied the centre of Kerala, and Ernakulam was the principal city.

The name Cochin does not seem to have been used until the end of the 15th century. The oldest name of the state was Perumpadappu, for Cochin was that part of Kerala which came into the possession of the eldest son of Cheraman Perumal's sister by Perumpadappu Nambudri. Because of this the rajahs of Cochin claim Perumal descent.

The connection between Cochin and the western world is very ancient. According to one tradition St. Thomas the Apostle first set foot in India at Malankara near Cranganur. Persecuted Jews also found a refuge there. The trade of the Malabar coast with the western world is more ancient still. (*See* E. H. Warmington, *The Commerce Between the Roman Empire and India,* Cambridge, New York, 1928). Little is known of the subsequent history of Cochin until the advent of the Portuguese. In 1498 Vasco da Gama reached the Malabar coast. At this time the cardinal factor in Malabari politics was the rivalry between the rajah of Cochin and the zamorin of Calicut. A knowledge of this, combined with the fact that the harbour of Cochin was greatly superior to that of Calicut as an anchorage, led the Portuguese to side with the rajahs of Cochin in their wars with the zamorin of Calicut. By the end of the 16th century Portuguese influence had become firmly established in Cochin. With the decline of Portuguese power in Indian waters the Dutch captured Cochin in 1663 and held it for nearly a century. In the second half of the 18th century Cochin was menaced by the growing Moslem power of Mysore. In 1776 Hyder Ali invaded Cochin and forced the rajah to acknowledge his suzerainty and pay him tribute.

In 1791 the rajah of Cochin entered into a subsidiary alliance with the English East India company, thus placing himself under English protection. In 1792, after the defeat of Tipu Sultan by Lord Cornwallis, the claims of Mysore over Cochin were transferred to the English company. In 1808 the chief minister of Cochin entered into a conspiracy with the minister of Travancore to assassinate the resident and oust the British. The insurrection was easily suppressed, and in 1809 a fresh treaty was concluded which increased the tribute and strengthened British control over the state.

In 1818 the financial obligations of Cochin were reduced to two lakhs of rupees. From this time the state greatly advanced in prosperity under successive rajahs. In 1862 the rajah received a sanad (charter) granting him the right of adoption on the failure of natural heirs. A series of longstanding disputes between Cochin and Travancore were settled by British arbitration in 1880. The Cochin state legislative council was inaugurated in 1925 and its powers enlarged in the years that followed. Public health, agriculture and cottage industries were transferred to the charge of an elected minister in 1938. An additional minister was appointed in 1946.

Under British paramountcy Cochin was controlled (from 1923) through the Madras states agency (Trivandrum residency).

(C. C. D.)

COCHIN (KOCHCHIBAND), a port on the Malabar coast of India, 580 mi. S. of Bombay and 125 mi. W. of Madura; situated politically in an enclave of Malabar district, Madras state, surrounded by the state of Travancore-Cochin. The contiguous town of Mattancheri (pop., 1951, 73,904) is in Travancore-Cochin. Cochin (pop., 1951, 29,881) is at the northern end of a tongue of land about 12 mi. long but in few places more than a mile wide, nearly isolated from the mainland by inlets and estuaries. These form the Cochin backwaters, shallow lagoons lying behind the beach line and below its level, which are broad navigable channels and lakes during the monsoon, but in many places not two feet deep in the hot weather.

Cochin was the earliest European settlement in India, the first occupants being the Portuguese. Vasco da Gama founded a factory in 1502, and Alphonso d'Albuquerque built a fort, the first European fort in India, in 1503. The British made a settlement in 1634, but retired when the Dutch captured the town in 1663. Under the Dutch the town became a great trading centre. In 1795 Cochin was captured from the Dutch by the British, and in 1806 the fortifications and many buildings were blown up by order of the authorities.

The construction of the modern harbour began in 1920. In this the British government collaborated with those of the then princely states of Cochin and Travancore. In June 1928 the first ocean-going steamer entered the harbour. The improvements made thereafter, and its geographical position, make Cochin an ideal distributing centre. It is open for deep-water traffic in the worst monsoon. The Cochin Harbour railway is connected with the broad-gauge system of the Southern railway. The port administration was wholly taken over by the Indian government on Aug. 1, 1936.

COCHIN CHINA: *see* INDOCHINA; VIETNAM.

COCHINEAL, a natural dyestuff used for the production of scarlet, crimson, orange and other tints, and for the preparation of lake and carmine. It consists of the females of *Dactylopius coccus,* an insect of the family Coccidae of the order Hemiptera, which feeds upon various species of Cactaceae, especially nopal, *Opuntia coccinellifera,* a native of Mexico and Peru.

The dye was introduced into Europe from Mexico, where it had been used long before the entrance of the Spaniards. Cochineal has almost entirely been replaced by aniline dyes. The male of the cochinal insect is half the size of the female, and, unlike it, is devoid of nutritive apparatus; it has long white wings and a body of a deep red colour, terminated by two diverging setae. The female is wingless, and has a dark-brown plano-convex body; it is found in the proportion of 150–200 to 1 of the male insect. The dead body of the mother insect serves as a protection for the eggs until they are hatched. Cochineal is now furnished not only by Mexico and Peru, but also by Algiers and southern Spain. It is collected thrice in the seven months of the season. The insects are carefully brushed from the branches of the cactus into bags, and are then killed by immersion in hot water, or by exposure to the sun, steam or the heat of an oven—much of the variety of appearance in the commercial article being caused by the mode of treatment.

The dried insect has the form of irregular, fluted and concave grains, of which about 70,000 go to a pound. The best crop is the first of the season, which consists of the unimpregnated females; the later crops include an admixture of young insects and skins, which contain proportionally little colouring matter.

Cochineal owes its tinctorial power to the presence of a substance termed cochinealin or carminic acid, $C_{22}H_{20}O_{13}$ (the formula shown by Dimeoth in 1920), which may be prepared from the aqueous decoction of cochineal. Cochineal also contains a fat and wax; cochineal wax or coccerin, $C_{30}H_{60}(C_{31}H_{61}O_3)_2$, may be extracted by using benzene; the fat is a glyceryl myristate $C_3H_5(C_{14}H_{27}O_2)_3$.

COCHLÄUS (DOBNECK), **JOHANN** (1479–1552), German humanist and controversialist, was born at Wendelstein (near Nuremberg), whence the punning surname Cochläus (spiral). In 1507 he graduated at Cologne and published under the name of Wendelstein his first piece, *In musicam exhortatorium*. He then became a schoolmaster at Nuremberg. In 1515 he was at Bologna, hearing (with disgust) Eck's famous disputation against usury, and associating with Ulrich von Hutten and the humanists. He took his doctor's degree at Ferrara (1517), and spent some time in Rome, where he was ordained priest. In 1520 he became dean of the Liebfrauenkirche at Frankfurt, where he first entered the lists as a controversialist against the party of Martin Luther, developing that bitter hatred of the Reformation which animated his forceful but shallow ascription to the movement of the meanest motives, due to a quarrel between the Dominicans and Augustinians. Luther would not meet him in discussion at Mainz in 1521. He was present at the diets of Worms, Regensburg, Speyer and Augsburg.

The peasants' war drove him from Frankfurt; he obtained (1526) a canonry at Mainz; in 1529 he became secretary to Duke George of Saxony, at Dresden and Meissen. The death of his patron (1539) compelled him to take flight. He became canon (Sept. 1539) at Breslau, where he died on Jan. 10, 1552.

His best known work is *Commentaria de Actis et scriptis Lutheris* (1549; German ed. 1580 and 1582). His *Kleine Schriften* were edited by J. Schweizer (1920).

See M. Spahn, *Johannes Cochläus* (1898).

COCK, EDWARD (1805–1892), British surgeon, born in 1805, was a nephew of the surgeon Sir Astley Cooper (*q.v.*) and through him became at an early age a member of the staff of the Borough hospital in London. Cock worked in the dissecting room there for 13 years.

He became in 1838 assistant surgeon at Guy's hospital, where from 1849 to 1871 he was surgeon and from 1871 consulting surgeon. He rose to be president of the College of Surgeons in 1869. He was an excellent anatomist, a bold operator and has been called a clear and incisive writer. Although he was afflicted with a stutter, he frequently utilized it in lecturing with humorous effect and for emphasis.

From 1843 to 1849 he was editor of *Guy's Hospital Reports*, which contain many of his papers, particularly on stricture of the urethra, puncture of the bladder, injuries to the head and hernia. He has been credited with being the first English surgeon to perform pharyngotomy with success and also as one of the first to succeed in trephining for middle meningeal haemorrhage. The operation of opening the urethra through the perinaeum became known by his name.

He died at Kingston, in 1892.

COCKADE, a knot of ribbons or a rosette worn as a badge, particularly in modern usage as part of the livery of servants. The cockade was at first the button and loop or clasp which "cocked" up the side of an ordinary slouch hat. The word first appears in this sense in Rabelais in the phrase *"bonnet à la coquarde,"* explained by Cotgrave (1611) as a "Spanish cap or fashion of bonnet used by substantial men of yore . . . worne proudly or peartly on th' one side." The bunch of ribbons as a party badge developed from this button and loop. The Stuarts' badge was a white rose, and the resulting white cockade figured in Jacobite songs. William III's cockade was of yellow, and the house of Hanover introduced theirs of black, which in its spiked or circular form of leather came to be worn by the royal coachmen and grooms and the servants of all officials or members of the services.

At the outbreak of the French Revolution of 1789, cockades of green ribbon were adopted. These afterward gave place to the tricolour cockade, which is said to have been a mixture of the traditional colours of Paris (red and blue) with the white of the Bourbons, the early revolutionists being still royalists. The French army wore the tricolour cockade until the Restoration. Each nation had its cockade. Thus the Austrian was black and yellow, Bavarian light blue and white, Belgian black, yellow and red, French the tricolour, Prussian black and white, Russian green and white, and so on, following usually the national colours. Originally the wearing of a cockade as a badge was restricted to soldiers. There is still a trace of the cockade as a badge in certain military headgears in England and elsewhere. Otherwise it became entirely the mark of domestic service.

See *Genealogical Magazine*, vol. i–iii (1897–99); Racinet, *La Costume historique* (1888).

COCKAIGNE (COCKAYNE), **LAND OF,** an imaginary country, a mediaeval Utopia where life was a continual round of luxurious idleness. The origin of the Italian word *cocagna* has been much disputed. It seems safest to connect it, as do Grimm and Littré, ultimately with Lat. *coquere*, through a word meaning "cake," the literal sense thus being "The Land of Cakes." In Cockaigne the rivers were of wine, the houses were built of cake and barley sugar, the streets were paved with pastry and the shops supplied goods for nothing. Roast geese and fowls wandered about inviting folks to eat them, and buttered larks fell from the skies like manna.

There is a 13th-century French *fabliau*, *Cocaigne*, which was possibly intended to ridicule the fable of the mythical Avalon, "the Island of the Blest." The 13th-century English poem *The Land of Cockaygne* is a satire on monastic life. The term has been humorously applied to London, and by the poet Boileau to the Paris of the rich. The word has been frequently confused with Cockney (*q.v.*).

COCKATOO (KAKATOEINAE), a group of parrots confined to the Australian region and characterized by a crest of feathers on the head; this can be raised at will. They live in flocks in woods, feeding on fruit, seeds and insects. The note is harsh and their powers of vocal imitation limited.

The well-known sulphur-crested cockatoo (*Kakatoe galerita*) inhabits Australia, where it does much damage to the newly sown grain. The white eggs, two in number, are deposited in hollow trees or fissures in rocks. It also ranges northeast to Aru, New Guinea and New Ireland. Leadbeater's cockatoo (*K. leadbeateri*) inhabits South Australia, and its white plumage is tinged with rose, deepening to salmon-pink under the wings; the crest is scarlet. It is a very shy bird.

The dark-plumaged funereal cockatoo or wyla (*Calyptorhynchus funereus*) is another Australian species. The smallest of the family is the cockateel (*Nymphicus hollandicus*), which has a long pointed tail. There are 5 genera and 17 species of cockatoos, some with a number of subspecies recognized.

COCKATRICE, a fabulous monster, the existence of which was firmly believed throughout ancient and mediaeval times. Descriptions and figures of it appeared in the natural history works of such writers as Pliny and Aldrovandus, those of the latter being published as late as the beginning of the 17th century.

Produced from a cock's egg hatched by a serpent, it was believed to possess the most deadly powers, plants withering at its touch and men and animals dying, poisoned, by its look.

The monster stood in awe, however, of the cock, the sound of whose crowing killed it. Consequently travellers were wont to take this bird with them in regions supposed to abound in cockatrices.

The weasel alone among mammals was unaffected by the glance of its evil eye, and attacked it at all times successfully; when wounded by the monster's teeth, it found a ready remedy in rue—the only plant which the cockatrice could not wither.

The term "cockatrice" is employed on four occasions in the English translation of the Bible, in all of which it denotes nothing more than an exceedingly venomous reptile; it seems also to be synonymous with "basilisk," the mythical king of serpents.

COCKBURN, SIR ALEXANDER JAMES EDMUND, 10TH BART. (1802–1880), lord chief justice of England, born Dec. 24, 1802, of ancient Scottish stock, the son of Alexander, fourth son of Sir James Cockburn, 6th baronet. His father was British envoy extraordinary and minister plenipotentiary to the state of Colombia, and married Yolande, daughter of the vicomte de Vignier. He was educated at Trinity Hall, Cambridge, of which he was elected a fellow and afterward an honorary fellow. He entered at the Middle Temple in 1825 and was called to the bar in 1829. He joined the western circuit, and for some time such practice as he was able to obtain lay at the Devon sessions. In 1832, however, the petitions following the first general election after the Reform bill gave him an opening. The decisions of the committees had not been reported since 1821, and with M. C. Rowe, another member of the western circuit, Cockburn undertook a new series of reports. In 1833 he had his first parliamentary brief.

In 1847 he decided to stand for parliament and was elected, without a contest, Liberal M.P. for Southampton. His speech in the house of commons on behalf of the government in the Don Pacifico dispute with Greece commended him to Lord John Russell, who appointed him solicitor general in 1850 and attorney general in 1851, a post which he held till the resignation of the ministry in Feb. 1852. During the short administration of Lord Derby, which followed, Sir Frederic Thesiger was attorney general and Cockburn was engaged against him in the case of *R. v. Newman,* on the prosecution of Achilli, a criminal information for libel against Cardinal Newman. The jury which tried the case under Lord Campbell found the defense of justification not proved except in one particular. The verdict was set aside and a new trial ordered, but none ever took place. In Dec. 1852, under Lord Aberdeen's ministry, Cockburn became again attorney general, and so remained until 1856, taking part in many celebrated trials, notably leading for the crown in the trial of William Palmer, of Rugeley in Staffordshire, for poisoning. In 1854 Cockburn was made recorder of Bristol. In 1856 he became chief justice of the common pleas. He inherited the baronetcy in 1858.

In 1859 Lord Campbell became chancellor, and Cockburn became chief justice of the queen's bench, continuing as a judge for 24 years and dying in harness. On Saturday, Nov. 20, 1880, he presided over a court for the consideration of crown cases reserved; he walked home, and on that night he died of angina pectoris at his house in Hertford street.

Sir Alexander Cockburn earned and deserved a high reputation as a judge. He was a man of brilliant cleverness and rapid intuition. He had been a great advocate at the bar, fluent and persuasive rather than learned; before he died he was considered a good lawyer, some assigning unquestioned improvement in this respect to his frequent association on the bench with Blackburn. He had notoriously little sympathy with the Judicature acts. Many were of the opinion that he was inclined to make up his mind prematurely on the cases before him. But he was beyond doubt always in intention, and generally in fact, scrupulously fair. It was thought that he went out of his way to arrange to try *causes célèbres* himself. His successor, Lord Coleridge, writing in 1881 to Lord Bramwell to make the offer that he should try the murderer Lefroy as a last judicial act before retiring, added, "Poor dear Cockburn would hardly have given you such a chance." But Cockburn tried all cases which came before him, whether great or small, with the same thoroughness, courtesy and dignity, while he certainly gave great attention to the elaboration of his judgments and charges to juries. His summing up at the Tichborne trial at bar lasted 18 days.

The greatest public occasion on which Sir Alexander Cockburn acted, outside his usual judicial functions, was that of the "Alabama" arbitration, held at Geneva, Switz., in 1872, in which he represented the British government and dissented from the view taken by the majority of the arbitrators, without being able to convince them.

He prepared, with C. F. Adams, the representative of the United States, the English translation of the award of the arbitrators and published his reasons for dissenting in a vigorously worded document which did not meet with universal commendation. He admitted in substance the liability of England for the acts of the "Alabama," but not on the grounds on which the decision of the majority was based, and he held England not liable in respect of the "Florida" and the "Shenandoah."

In personal appearance Sir Alexander Cockburn was of small stature, but great dignity of deportment. He was fond of yachting and sport, and at the time of his death was engaged in writing a series of articles on the "History of the Chase in the 19th Century."

He had a high sense of the duties of his profession, and his utterance upon the limitations of advocacy, in his speech at the banquet given in the Middle Temple hall for Berryer, the celebrated French advocate, may be called the classical authority on the subject. Lord Brougham had spoken of "the first great duty of an advocate to reckon everything subordinate to the interests of his client." But the lord chief justice, replying to the toast of "the judges of England," said amid loud cheers from a distinguished assembly of lawyers, "The arms which an advocate wields he ought to use as a warrior, not as an assassin. He ought to uphold the interests of his clients *per fas,* not *per nefas.* He ought to know how to reconcile the interests of his clients with the eternal interests of truth and justice" (the *Times,* Nov. 9, 1864).

Sir Alexander Cockburn was never married, and the baronetcy became extinct at his death.

Bibliography.—C. C. F. Greville, *The Greville Memoirs,* ed. by H. Reeve (1874–87); A. E. M. Ashley, *Life of Palmerston* (1876); Justin M'Carthy, *History of Our Own Times* (1881–1905); J. W. Croker, *The Croker Papers,* ed. by L. J. Jennings, 2nd ed. (1885); T. A. Nash, *Life of Lord Westbury* (1888); W. Ballantine, *Experiences* (1890); B. C. Robinson, *Bench and Bar* (1891); Lord Russell of Killowen, "Reminiscences of Lord Chief Justice Coleridge," *North American Review* (Sept. 1894); C. Fairfield, *Life of Lord Branwell* (1898); E. Manson, *Builders of Our Law* (1904). *See* also the *Times* (Nov. 22, 1880); *Law Journal, Law Times, Solicitors' Journal* (Nov. 27, 1880); *Law Magazine,* new series, vol. xv, p. 193 (1851).

COCKBURN, ALICIA or Alison (1713–1794), Scottish poet, author of one of the most exquisite of Scottish ballads, the "Flowers of the Forest," was the daughter of Robert Rutherfurd of Fairnalee, Selkirkshire, and was born on Oct. 8, 1713, and died on Nov. 22, 1794. There are two versions of this song—the one by Mrs. Cockburn, the other by Jean Elliot (1727–1805) of Minto. Both were founded on the remains of an ancient Border ballad. Mrs. Cockburn's—that beginning "I've seen the smiling of Fortune beguiling"—is said to have been written before her marriage to Patrick Cockburn of Ormiston in 1731, though not published till 1765.

It was composed many years before Jean Elliot's sister verses, written in 1756, beginning, "I've heard them liltin' at our ewe-milkin'." Robert Chambers stated that the ballad was written on the occasion of a great commercial disaster which ruined the fortunes of some Selkirkshire lairds. Later biographers, however, held it probable that it was written on the departure to London of a certain John Aikman, between whom and Alison there appears to have been an early attachment.

In 1731 she was married to Patrick Cockburn of Ormiston. After her marriage Mrs. Cockburn came to know the intellectual and aristocratic celebrities of the times. In 1745 she vented her Whiggism in a squib upon Prince Charlie and narrowly escaped being taken by the Highland guard as she was driving through Edinburgh in the family coach of the Keiths of Ravelston with the parody in her pocket.

Mrs. Cockburn was an indefatigable letter writer and a composer of parodies, squibs, toasts and so-called character sketches—then a favourite form of composition—like the other wits of the day. The "Flowers of the Forest," however, was the only thing she wrote that came to be considered of great literary merit.

At her house on Castle hill, and afterward in Crichton street, Mrs. Cockburn received Mackenzie, Robertson, Hume, Home, Monboddo, the Keiths of Ravelston, the Balcarres family, Lady Anne Barnard, the author of "Auld Robin Gray," and others. As a Rutherfurd she was a connection of Sir Walter Scott's mother, and was her intimate friend. Scott, at six years old, is said to have given as a reason for his liking for Mrs. Cockburn that she was a "virtuoso like himself."

See her *Letters and Memorials . . .,* with notes by T. Craig Brown (Edinburgh, 1900).

COCKBURN, SIR GEORGE, Bart. (1772–1853), British admiral, second son of Sir James Cockburn, Bart., and uncle of Lord Chief Justice Cockburn, entered the navy at the age of nine, though he did not go to sea until 1786. After serving on the home station and in the East Indies and the Mediterranean, he assisted, as captain of the "Minerve," at the blockade of Leghorn in 1796, and fought a gallant action with the Spanish frigate "Sabina," which he took. He was present at the battle of Cape St. Vincent. In 1809, in command of the naval force on shore, he contributed greatly to the reduction of Martinique, and signed the capitulation by which that island was handed over to Great Britain.

After service in the Scheldt and at the defense of Cadiz he was sent in 1811 on an unsuccessful mission for the reconciliation of Spain and its American colonies. In 1813–14, as second in command to Sir J. B. Warren, he took part in the War of 1812, especially in the capture of Washington. In the autumn of 1815 he carried out, in the "Northumberland," the sentence of deportation to St. Helena which has been passed upon Bonaparte. He was promoted admiral in 1837; he became senior naval lord in 1841, and held office in that capacity till 1846. In 1851 he was made admiral of the fleet.

Cockburn died on Aug. 19, 1853.

COCKBURN, HENRY THOMAS (1779–1854), Scottish judge, with the style of Lord Cockburn, was born in Edinburgh on Oct. 26, 1779. His father was a baron of the Scottish court of exchequer.

He was educated at the high school and the University of Edinburgh, and he was a member of the Speculative society, to which Sir Walter Scott, Brougham and Jeffrey belonged. He entered the faculty of advocates in 1800 and attached himself, though his connections were Tory, to the Whig or Liberal party, which then offered few prospects to ambitious men. On the accession of Earl Grey's ministry in 1830 he became solicitor general for Scotland. In 1834 he was raised to the bench, and on taking his seat as a judge in the court of session he adopted the title of Lord Cockburn.

Cockburn's forensic style was remarkable for its clearness, pathos and simplicity, and his conversational powers were unrivalled among his contemporaries. In 1852 he published his biography of Lord Jeffrey, and the *Memorials of His Time* appeared posthumously in 1856 (new ed., with introduction by his grandson, H. A. Cockburn, 1909).

Cockburn died on April 26, 1854, at his mansion of Bonaly, near Edinburgh.

COCKCHAFER (*Melolontha melolontha*), a common European beetle whose larva is destructive to the roots of crops. The white grub spends several years in the soil before emerging as a large beetle which feeds on the leaves of trees and may often be seen flying in large numbers at dusk.

(*See* CHAFER; COLEOPTERA.)

COCKCROFT, SIR JOHN DOUGLAS (1897–), British physicist and co-winner of the Nobel prize, was born at Todmorden, Yorkshire, Eng., on May 27, 1897. He was educated at Todmorden Secondary school, at Manchester university and at St. John's college, Cambridge, of which he was a fellow from 1928 to 1946 and an honorary fellow from 1947.

At a meeting of the Royal society on April 28, 1932, Lord Rutherford announced that two of his workers at the Cavendish laboratory, Cambridge—Cockcroft and E. T. S. Walton—"had successfully disintegrated the nuclei of lithium and other light elements by protons entirely artificially generated by high energy potentials." On Nov. 15, 1951, the Royal Swedish Academy of Sciences announced the award of the Nobel prize for physics jointly to Cockcroft and Walton for "their pioneer work on the transmutation of atomic nuclei by artificially accelerated atomic particles."

Cockcroft was Jacksonian professor of natural philosophy in Cambridge university, 1939–46; from 1941 to 1944, however, he served as chief superintendent, air defense research and development establishment, ministry of supply, and from 1944 to 1946 he was director of the atomic energy division, National Research council of Canada. In 1946 he became director of the atomic energy research establishment, ministry of supply, at Harwell, Eng. He was also chairman of the defense research policy committee and scientific adviser, ministry of defense, from 1952 to 1954, and served as a member of the British Broadcasting corporation's Scientific Advisory committee, 1948–52.

Cockcroft was elected a fellow of the Royal society in 1936, was knighted in 1948 and created knight commander of the Bath in 1953.

COCKER, EDWARD (1631–1675), reputed author of the famous *Arithmetick*, the popularity of which added a phrase ("according to Cocker") to the list of English proverbialisms, was an English engraver who also taught writing and arithmetic.

Samuel Pepys, in his *Diary*, makes very favourable mention of Cocker, who appears to have displayed great skill in his art.

Cocker's *Arithmetick*, the 52nd edition of which appeared in 1748 and which passed through about 112 editions in all, was not published during the lifetime of the reputed author, the first impression bearing the date of 1678.

Augustus de Morgan in his *Arithmetical Books* (1847) adduced proofs that the work was a forgery of the editor and publisher John Hawkins. De Morgan condemns the *Arithmetick* as a diffuse compilation from older and better works and dates "a very great deterioration in elementary works on arithmetic" from the appearance of the book, which owed its celebrity far more to persistent puffing than to its merits.

De Morgan added that "This same Edward Cocker must have had great reputation, since a bad book under his name pushed out the good ones."

Cocker's writing manuals include *Art's Glory, or the Penman's Treasure* (1657); *The Pen's Transcendencie or Faire Writing's Labyrinth* (1657); and *Pen's Triumph* (1658).

Other works are *Cocker's Morals or the Muses spring-garden, sententious disticks and poems fitted for all publick and private grammar and writing-schools, for the scholars of the first to turn into Latin, and for those of the other to transcribe into all their various and curious hands* (1685) and *Cocker's English Dictionary; interpreting the most refined and difficult Words in Divinity, Philosophy, Law, Physick, Mathematics, Husbandry, Mechanicks, &c.* (1704).

COCKERELL, CHARLES ROBERT (1788–1863), British architect, was born in London on April 28, 1788. After studying under his father, Samuel Pepys Cockerell (1754–1827), he went abroad in 1810 and studied the great architectural remains of Greece, Italy and Asia Minor. At Aegina, Phigaleia and other places of interest, he conducted excavations on a large scale, enriching the British museum with many fine fragments. He became R.A. in 1829, and from 1840 to 1857 was professor of architecture at the academy. In 1837 he was appointed architect to the Bank of England. Among his principal works are the Taylorian building, Oxford (1842), and the completion of St. George's hall, Liverpool, and of the Fitzwilliam museum, Cambridge, with some important bank buildings. Cockerell's best conceptions were inspired by classic models; examples of his Gothic style are the college at Lampeter and the chapel at Harrow. His son, FREDERICK PEPYS COCKERELL (1833–78), was also a distinguished architect.

COCKERILL, WILLIAM (1759–1832), English inventor and machinist, was born in England in 1759. He went to Belgium as a simple mechanic, and in 1799 constructed at Verviers the first wool-carding and wool-spinning machines on the continent. In 1807 he established a large machine workshop at Liège. Orders soon poured in on him from all over Europe, and he amassed a large fortune. In 1810 he was granted the rights of naturalization by Napoleon I, and in 1812 handed over the management of his business to his youngest son, John Cockerill (1790–1840), who largely extended his father's business. King William I of the Netherlands secured him a site at Seraing, where he built large works, including an iron foundry and blast furnace. The construction of the Belgian railways in 1834 gave a great impetus to these works, branches of which had already been opened in France, Germany and Poland. John Cockerill had practically concluded negotiations to construct the Russian government railways when his constitution, undermined by overwork, broke down. He died at Warsaw on June 19, 1840. The iron works, among the largest in Europe, were carried on under the name of La Société Cockerill at Seraing.

COCKERMOUTH, a small town and urban district of Cumberland, Eng., 32 mi. S.W. of Carlisle, by the London Midland Region railway. Pop. (1951) 5,234. Area 3.2 sq.mi. It is situated at the confluence of the Derwent and Cocker at a focus of ways among the lower western hills of the Lake district. Settlement in the neighbourhood goes back at least to Roman times, there being a small fort 1 mi. W. of the town at Papcastle.

Cockermouth (*Cokermuth, Cokermue*) was the head of the barony of Allerdale, created and granted to Waltheof in the 12th century. Waltheof probably built the castle, under the shelter of which the town grew up. There are remains of Norman work in the keep, but the castle is in part modernized as a residence. The town received no royal charter, but the earliest records mention it as a borough. In 1295 it returned two members to parliament and then not again until 1640. In 1867 it had one member, and in 1885 it was disfranchised. In 1221 William de Fortibus, earl of Albemarle, was granted a market. The Michaelmas fair existed in 1343, and in 1374 there were two horse fairs, on Whit Monday and at Michaelmas. In 1638 a fair every Wednesday from the first week in May till Michaelmas was granted. The grammar school was founded in 1676. The county industrial school was established in the town and engineering and agricultural machine works, a brewery and a malt house were also established there. The town suffered severe depression in the 1930s, unemployment among men being 45.3% in April 1934. The poet Wordsworth was born there.

COCKFIGHTING or Cocking, the sport of pitting gamecocks to fight, and breeding and training them for the purpose. The game fowl is now probably the nearest to the Indian red jungle fowl (*Gallus gallus*), from which all domestic fowls are believed to be descended. The sport was popular in ancient times in India, China, Persia and other eastern countries, and was introduced into Greece in the time of Themistocles. The latter, while moving with his army against the Persians, observed two cocks fighting desperately and, stopping his troops, inspired them by calling their attention to the valour and obstinacy of the feathered warriors. In honour of the ensuing victory of the Greeks cockfights were thenceforth held annually at Athens, at first in a patriotic and religious spirit, but afterward purely for the love of the sport. On the chair of the high priest of Dionysus, in the Theatre at Athens, there is carved a beautiful figure of a winged Eros holding a gamecock just about to fight. Lucian makes Solon speak of quail fighting and cocking, and evidently is referring to an era in Asia, about 3,000 years ago, when cocking enthusiasts, lacking the cocks, set quail to fighting quail, and partridges to fighting partridges, since both are natural fighters. From Athens the sport spread throughout Greece, Asia Minor and Sicily, the best cocks being bred in Alexandria, Delos, Rhodes and Tanagra. For a long time the Romans affected to despise this "Greek diversion," but ended by adopting it so enthusiastically that Columella (1st century A.D.) complained that its devotees often spent their whole patrimony in betting at the pitside.

It is not definitely established when metal spurs first were slipped over the natural spurs of the gamecocks. The first used were silver spurs; later, iron spurs, then steel spurs. The metal spur has been known for hundreds of years. The modern short metal spur is $1\frac{1}{2}$ in. or less in length; the long spur scales from 2 to about $2\frac{1}{2}$ in.

From Rome cocking spread northward and, although opposed by the Christian church, nevertheless became popular in Great Britain, the Low Countries, Italy, Germany, Spain and its colonies. It was probably introduced into England by the Romans before Caesar's time. William Fitzstephen first speaks of it in the time of Henry II as sport for schoolboys on holidays, and particularly on Shrove Tuesday, the masters themselves directing the fights, or mains, from which they derived a material advantage, as the dead birds fell to them.

Cockfighting became very popular throughout England and Wales, as well as in Scotland, where it was introduced in 1681. Occasionally the authorities tried to repress it, especially Cromwell, who put a stop to it for a brief period, but the Restoration re-established it among the national pastimes.

From the time of Henry VIII, who added the famous royal cockpit to his palace of Whitehall, cocking was called the "royal diversion," and the Stuarts, particularly James I and Charles II, were among its most enthusiastic devotees, their example being followed by the gentry down to the 19th century. The king's cockmaster presided over the pits at Whitehall. Gervase Markham, in his *Pleasures of Princes* (1614), wrote "Of the Choyce, Ordring, Breeding and Dyeting of the fighting Cocke for Battell," his quaint directions being of the most explicit nature.

Cocking mains usually consisted of fights between an agreed number of pairs of birds, the majority of victories deciding the main; but there were two other varieties that aroused the particular ire of moralists. These were the "battle royal" in which a number of birds were "set" (*i.e.*, placed in the pit at the same time) and allowed to remain until all but one, the victor, were killed or disabled; and the "Welsh main," in which eight pairs were matched, the eight victors being again paired, then four, and finally the last surviving pair.

Among famous London cockpits were those at Westminster, in Drury lane, Jewin street and Birdcage walk (depicted by Hogarth). The pits were circular in shape with a matted stage about 20 ft. in diameter and surrounded by a barrier to keep the birds from falling off. Upon this barrier the first row of the audience leaned. Hardly a town in the kingdom was without its cockpit, which offered the sporting classes opportunities for betting.

Perhaps the most famous main in England took place at Lincoln in 1830 between the birds of Joseph Gilliver, the most celebrated breeder, or "feeder," of his day, and those of the earl of Derby. The conditions called for seven birds a side, and the stakes were 5,000 guineas the main and 1,000 guineas each match. The main was won by Gilliver by five matches to two. His grandson was also a breeder, and the blood of his cocks still runs in the best breeds of Great Britain and America. Another famous breeder was Bellyse of Audlem, the principal figure in the great mains fought at Chester during race week at the beginning of the 19th century. His favourite breed was the white pile, and Cheshire Piles are still much-fancied birds. Others were Irish Brown-Reds, Lancashire Black-Reds and Staffordshire Duns.

In Wales, as well as some parts of England, cocking mains took place regularly in churchyards, and in many instances even inside the churches themselves. Sundays, wakes and church festivals were favorite occasions for them. The habit of holding mains in schools was common from the 12th to about the middle of the 19th century. When cocking was at its height, the pupils of many schools were made a special allowance for purchasing fighting cocks, and parents were expected to contribute to the expenses of the annual main on Shrove Tuesday, this money being called "cockpence." Cockfighting was prohibited by law in Great Britain in 1849.

Cocking was early introduced into America though it was always frowned upon in New England. Some of the older states, as Massachusetts, forbade it by passing laws against cruelty as early as 1836, and it is expressly prohibited in Canada and in most states of the U.S. or is repressed by general laws for the prevention of cruelty to animals. Although cockfighting has ceased as a public sport in the United States, Canada and the British Isles, it continues to exist in private in those countries. Portable mains are moved from place to place, to avoid police raids, and Sunday morning usually is "fight time." In the United States the sport is extremely popular along the Atlantic seaboard and in the south.

Cockfighting is not recognized as a form of sport by the Latin-American countries in general. In Argentina cockfighting was once one of the most popular amusements; but it was suppressed by police measures, although it persisted in several provinces. Paraguay prohibited it by law. But in Cuba cockfighting continued to be a patronized sport regulated by the government. Cubans always supported it; and, although it was prohibited for a time, it was reinstated during the Gómez administration and was later regulated by municipal decrees. Puerto Rico became an important cockfighting centre. Breeders of gamecocks stress pedigree. They regard as fit for championship honours only those birds which have been produced by the blending of strains of the world's most courageous cocks, through hundreds of years. Famous among the strains of the 20th century are the Shawlnecks, Irish Gilders, Eslin Red-Quills, Dominiques, Claibornes, Baltimore Topknots, War-Horses, Irish Grays and Hammond-Gordons. Gamecocks usually are put to the main when between one and two years of age. But, preceding their entrance into the fighting pit, they are given intensive training. They do not need to be encouraged to fight. That is their heritage. But great preparations are made to perfect their physical condition and to teach them the art of fighting.

As youngsters, they are permitted a great deal of exercise. This is to develop muscles. When they are deemed old enough to be readied for battle, they are trained for a number of days. Chief features of their special diet are cooked corn meal, chopped hard-boiled eggs and occasional helpings of raw beef. This is augmented by regular fowl feed. The birds are massaged with a mixture of alcohol and ammonia, which toughens their skin. Their wings are trimmed at the slope; the hackle and the rump feathers are shortened; the comb is cut as close as possible, so as to reduce it as a target for an enemy bird. In time, the cock is taken to a main, held by a trainer, and brought within a foot, or two, of another trainee, similarly held. The frenzied efforts of the cocks to get at each other adds strength to their muscles. Later the birds get actual fight training by being pitted against each other, with heavily padded leather over their spurs.

In ancient times cocks were permitted to fight until one or the other was killed. In the more modern era, the rules were amended somewhat. Although some fights still are to an absolute finish, others permit the withdrawal at any time of a badly damaged cock. Other rules fix a time limit for each fight. The average cockpit is 18 ft. in diameter, with sidewalls about 16 in. high.

Those who enjoy cockfights insist that the zest in the sport is provided by the many chances to gamble before a fight begins and all during its progress. Odds against one bird or the other are constantly changed as the tide of battle shifts, and in some prolonged fights a score or more of wages are made on the outcome.

On those rare occasions when a gamecock, taking the worst of it, decides he does not wish to continue battle, he makes his intent known by lifting his hackle. The under part of the hackle is edged with white feathers, and from this act is derived the expression "showing the white feather," which means cowardice. When a cock refuses to fight longer, his handler puts him breast-to-breast with the other bird. If he still refuses, then it is ruled that he has quit, and the fight ends.

At all mains, the judge is in supreme control. His word is absolute law, even as to the gambling, and it is binding on all those identified, either officially, or unofficially, with a cockfight. There is no appeal from his decisions in anything relating to the main. Because of this, only the highest type of citizen in a cockfighting community is regarded as eligible to serve as judge.

BIBLIOGRAPHY.—Cockfighting possesses an extensive literature of its own. *See* Gervase Markham, *Pleasures of Princes* (1614); Blain, *Rural Sports* (1853); "Game Cocks and Cock-Fighting," *Outing*, vol. xxxix; "A Modest Commendation of Cock-Fighting," *Blackwood's Magazine*, vol. xxii; "Cock-Fighting in Schools," *Chambers' Magazine*, vol. lxv. (F. G. M.)

COCK LANE GHOST, a supposed apparition, the vagaries of which attracted extraordinary public attention in London during 1762. At a house in Cock lane, Smithfield, tenanted by one Parsons, knockings and other noises were said to occur at night varied by the appearance of a luminous figure, alleged to be the ghost of a Mrs. Kent who had died in the house about two years before. A thorough investigation revealed that Parsons' daughter, a child of 11, was the source of the disturbance. The object of the Parsons family seems to have been to accuse the husband of the deceased woman of murdering her, with a view of blackmail. Parsons was prosecuted and condemned to the pillory.

See A. Lang, *Cock Lane and Common Sense* (1894).

COCKLE, SIR JAMES (1819–1895), English lawyer and mathematician, was born on Jan. 14, 1819. He was the second son of James Cockle, a surgeon, of Great Oakley, Essex. Educated at Charterhouse and Trinity college, Cambridge, he entered the Middle Temple in 1838, practising as a special pleader in 1845 and being called in 1846. He joined the western circuit and was appointed chief justice of Queensland in 1863. He was knighted in 1869, retired from the bench and returned to England in 1879.

Cockle is more remembered for his mathematical and scientific investigations than as a lawyer. He attacked the problem of resolving the higher algebraic equations, notwithstanding Abel's proof that a solution by radicals was impossible. In this field Cockle achieved some notable results, among which is his reproduction of Sir William Hamilton's modification of Abel's theorem. Algebraic forms were a favourite object of his studies, and he discovered and developed the theory of criticoids, or differential invariants; he also made contributions to the theory of differential equations. He was a member of many scientific societies in Queensland and England. He died in London on Jan. 27, 1895.

A volume containing his scientific and mathematical researches made during the years 1864–77 was presented to the British museum in 1897 by his widow.

See the obituary notice by the Rev. R. Harley in ***Proc. Roy. Soc.***, vol. 59.

COCKLE, a bivalved marine mollusc of the genus *Cardium*, allied to the oyster and placed in the class Lamellibranchia. About 200 living species of cockles are known and more than 330 fossil forms have been described. The common or edible cockle (*Cardium edule*) is the best-known example and is of some economic importance.

The two valves of the shell of the cockle are similar and are characterized by a prominent umbo (*see* LAMELLIBRANCHIA) from which a number of prominent ribs radiate over the surface of the shell. The animal has a long and pointed foot with a kneelike bend in it. The mantle is produced into two short "siphons" which bear numerous fingerlike processes. In certain species these processes carry eyes at their tips. The cockle is placed in the order Eulamellibranchiata.

The cockles live on the sea bottom and are usually found buried below the surface. The common cockle, and probably most of the other species, rarely penetrates below one inch from the surface. The muscular, pointed foot enables it to dig into and plough its way through sand and mud. It has a moderately wide range of habitat but is rarely found on any soil other than sand and mud. Wright states that *Cardium edule* thrives best in estuarine waters, where the salinity is a little less than that of normal sea water. Cockle beds formed on the open coast are rarely permanent. In water of high or very low salinity the shell is subject to certain modifications of shape and weight. The cockle, like the rest of the Lamellibranchia, has no organs of mastication. It feeds on minute animals and plants and on the organic particles found in sea water. The spores of algae, foraminifera, diatoms, etc., usually constitute its diet. The animal is a "current feeder," the food being drawn into the branchial chamber in the water currents produced by the lower siphon. In England and Wales the most important cockle fisheries are in the Thames estuary, the Wash, Carmarthen and Morecambe bays. The animals are gathered by hand or by various kinds of rakes and scrapers and are boiled (in certain places by special methods to ensure the destruction of typhoid bacilli) before being dispatched to market. The nutritional value of the common cockle is fairly high, though its tissues contain less protein and fat than those of the oyster and mussel.

BIBLIOGRAPHY.—E. Römer, "Cardium," in *Küster's Conchylien Cabinet*, vol. x, 2 (1869); J. Johnstone, *Cardium*, Liverpool Mar. Biol. Committee Memoir (1899; bibl.); F. Wright, *Fishery Investigations*, Ministry of Agriculture and Fisheries, ix, 5 (1926; bibl.). (G. C. R.)

COCKLEBUR, the name given in the U.S. to species of *Xanthium*, of the family Compositae, called also clotbur and burweed, which in agricultural districts are pernicious weeds. They are coarse, rough and sometimes spiny annual herbs with much-branched stems, 1 ft. to 6 ft. high, and mostly long-stalked, variously lobed leaves. The staminate (male) and pistillate (female) flowers, both small and inconspicuous, are borne on the same plant, the staminate clustered at the ends of branches and the pistillate in the axils of the leaves. The fruit (achene) is enclosed in pairs in an oblong bur, about an inch in length, covered with hooked spines and ending in a one- or two-toothed beak. The ripe burs adhere to the hair of farm animals, which widely disseminate the plant. When abundant, mostly on alluvial soils, cockleburs are injurious to crops, but they may be controlled by intensive cultivation or mowing. The germinating seeds and young plants, while in the seed leaf stage, contain a toxic glucoside and cause fatal poisoning when eaten by livestock.

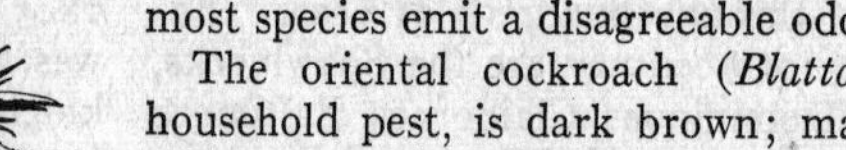

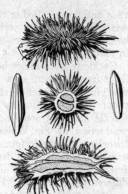

BY COURTESY OF DR. W. CROCKER
A DETAILED VIEW OF THE BUR AND THE TWO ENCLOSED SEEDS, SHOWING THE HOOKED PRICKLES WHICH CATCH IN THE WOOL OF SHEEP

COCKNEY, a colloquial name applied to Londoners generally but more properly confined to those born within the sound of the bells of St. Mary-le-Bow church. The origin of the word has been the subject of many guesses, but the historical examination of the various uses of "cockney," by Sir James Murray (see *Academy,* May 10, 1890, and the *New English Dictionary,* s.v.), shows that the earliest form of the word is *cokenay* or *cokeney; i.e.,* the *ey* or egg, and *coken,* genitive plural of "cock," "cocks' eggs" being the name given to the small and malformed eggs sometimes laid by young hens (*cf.* Langland, *Piers Plowman,* A, vii, 272). The word then applied to a child overlong nursed by its mother, hence to a simpleton, and Chaucer, *Reeve's Tale,* used it with *daf; i.e.,* a fool. The application of the term by country folk to town-bred people, with their ignorance of country ways, is easy. Thus Robert Whittington or Whitinton (*fl.* 1520) speaks of the "cokneys" in such "great cytees as London, York, Perusy" (Perugia). It was not till the beginning of the 17th century that "cockney" appears to have been confined to the inhabitants of London.

The so-called cockney accent was chiefly characterized in the first part of the 19th century by the substitution of a *v* for a *w,* or vice versa. The chief consonantal variation which now exists is perhaps the change of *th* to *f* or *v,* as in "fing" for thing, or "farver" for farther. This and the vowel sound change from *ou* to *ah,* as in "abaht" for "about," were illustrated in the "coster" songs of Albert Chevalier. The most marked change of vowel sound is that of *ei* for *ai,* so that "daily" becomes "dyly." The omission of *h* is not peculiar to cockney.

COCK OF THE ROCK, birds of the genus *Rupicola* (subfamily Rupicolinae) of the cotingas (allied to the manakins; *q.v.*), found in the Amazon valley. They are about the size of a pigeon, with orange-coloured plumage, a pronounced crest and orange-red flesh; they build their nests on rock. The males hold elaborate "dancing parties." (*See* BELLBIRD; CHATTERER; UMBRELLA BIRD.)

COCKPIT, originally an enclosed place in which cockfighting (*q.v.*) was carried on. On the site of an old cockpit opposite Whitehall in London was a block of buildings, used from the 17th century as offices by the treasury and the privy council, for which the old name survived till the early 19th century. The name of a theatre in London, built early in the 17th century on the site of Drury Lane theatre. Applied formerly to a cabin on the lower deck of a man-of-war, where the wounded were tended.

COCKROACH[1], the name applied to members of the Blattidae, a family of orthopterous insects, with flattened bodies, long, threadlike antennae and shining leathery integument. They are eminently tropical, but certain species have become widely disseminated through commerce and are now cosmopolitan. Cockroaches are nocturnal in habit, hiding themselves during the day. The domestic species are omnivorous but are especially addicted to starchy or sweetened matter of various kinds; they also attack food, paper, clothing, books, shoes, bones, etc., and dead insects. As a rule they injure and soil far more than they consume, and most species emit a disagreeable odour.

The oriental cockroach (*Blatta orientalis*), a cosmopolitan household pest, is dark brown; males are short-winged, females subapterous (*see* ORTHOPTERA, fig. 1). The larger, fully winged American cockroach (*Periplaneta americana*) infests buildings throughout the tropics and warm-temperate zones. The German cockroach (*Blattella germanica*), small and pale with two dark lines on the pronotum, occurs with man from the tropics to high latitudes. Blattid eggs are laid in cases (oöthecae) which are carried protruding from the female's body until hidden in some crevice. Those of *P. americana* contain 10 to 16 eggs which hatch in 40–45 days; nymphal life is 11–14 months, adult life 3–12 months. *B. orientalis* lives about one year.

About 1,500 species of cockroaches are known, most of them tropical; only 53 species, many introduced, occur in North America, and Great Britain has only two native species. Although blattids are usually sombrely coloured, some tropical species are elegant in form and beautiful in coloration. The delicate green *Panchlorae* of the American tropics, sometimes introduced with bananas into Great Britain and the United States, are ovoviparous. Some *Blaberinae* are giants with a wingspread of more than 5 in. Insecticides used for cockroach control, most of which are poisonous to animals and man, include chlordane, one of the most effective, DDT, pyrethrum and sodium fluoride, which was used for many years. Although these insects are usually viewed with disgust, they are not devoid of interest. They are the most primitive of living winged insects, and are among the oldest fossil insects. Their generalized structure and large size make them convenient for study and dissection, and they are widely used as the most suitable type for commencing the scientific study of insects. *See* also ORTHOPTERA.

BIBLIOGRAPHY.—L. C. Miall and C. Denny, *Structure and Life History of the Cockroach* (1887); W. J. Lucas, *British Orthoptera* (1920); Morgan Hebard, *Blattidae of North America* (1917); Phil Rau, "Life History of the American Cockroach," *Entomological News,* vol. li (1940); E. A. Back, *Cockroach and Their Control,* U.S. Department of Agriculture leaflet 144 (1937). (T. H. HL.)

COCKSCOMB, cultivated forms of *Celosia argentea cristata* (family Amaranthaceae), in which the inflorescence is monstrous, forming a flat "fasciated" axis bearing numerous small flowers. The plant is a low-growing herbaceous annual, bearing a large, comblike, feathery, rolled or grotesque cluster of dark red, scarlet, purplish or yellow flowers.

Celosia floribunda, a related plant, is cultivated in California under the name cockscomb, but is shrubby.

COCKTON, HENRY (1807–1853), English humorous novelist, was born in London Dec. 7, 1807, and died at Bury St. Edmund's June 26, 1853. He is best known as the author of *Valentine Vox, the Ventriloquist* (1840) and *Sylvester Sound, the Somnambulist* (1844).

COCOA (CACAO). Cocoa and chocolate come from small trees of the family Sterculiaceae, generally *Theobroma cacao,* rarely *T. pentagona* or *T. spherocarpa;* not to be confused with the coconut palm (*Cocos nucifera*) or with the South American coca shrub (*Erythroxylon coca*), the leaves of which contain a stimulant, cocaine. The seeds or beans of *Theobroma* (Greek for "food for the gods") provide, on processing, materials useful as food and drink. This fact was well known to the pre-Columbian natives of its source area, tropical Middle America, particularly to the Mayas and Aztecs, who used the beans also as a medium of exchange. Some think Columbus took specimen cocoa beans to Europe; in any case, Spain early in the 16th century was made aware of this gift of the new world by letters from Hernan Cortes to the Spanish monarch Charles V. It was introduced into Spain in 1528, almost a century before tea and coffee. Its use spread very slowly to other parts of Europe and the world, there being little mention of it elsewhere until the early part of the 17th century. Fashionable chocolate houses eventually developed. As late as 1850 annual production was less than 20,000 tons; in 1900 it was less than 100,000 tons.

The Cocoa Farm.—Most of the world's cocoa production comes from the modest two to five acres of native small farmers. Probably not more than 10% of the African production of base-

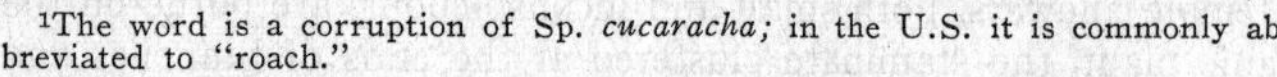

[1]The word is a corruption of Sp. *cucaracha;* in the U.S. it is commonly abbreviated to "roach."

grade cocoa, but more of the American production of flavour grades, is from larger plantations under co-operative native groups or non-native management. Preparation of the area for planting consists mostly in slashing and burning existing vegetation, perhaps girdling tall trees and leaving others for shade. Planting, except under more advanced management, is by rather closely spaced seeding, sometimes later thinned to keep the stronger plants. In other cases, nursery-grown and selected seedlings are transplanted when about two feet high, with field spacing ten feet or more apart. There is some tendency to abandon the use of seedlings in favour of more certain vegetative propagation of superior strains by cuttings and bud grafting. Shade by food plants, especially bananas, is provided in most areas for the thinner plantings. The tree, which would grow eventually to 30 to 40 ft. in height, is generally pruned to 15 to 25 ft. to aid harvesting. There is little cultivation or fertilization, other than slashing undergrowth. The tree begins to bloom and fruit three or four years after planting and reaches full production about the eighth year. There is disagreement as to the length of fruiting life, but 30 to 40 years is common and nearly 100 years is reported. There is some evidence that from the standpoint of production and disease control it is desirable to replace trees after 15 to 30 years.

Several diseases attack the tree or the fruit. Virus diseases called "swollen shoot" constitute a major menace in West Africa especially, where as many as 15,000,000 trees are affected annually; the best remedy is to cut and burn the infected trees. A fungus disease, "witches'-broom," caused by *Marasmius perniciosus,* a parasite mushroom, has been very destructive in the West Indian area and in some parts of South America. *Phytophthora,* a fungus, does damage, as do capsid bugs (especially *Sahlbergella singularis*) and various rots of the fruit pods, including the fungus *Monilia.*

Harvesting and Treatment.—A full-grown tree produces annually approximately 6,000 small pink blossoms directly on the trunk and main branches, of which about 20 mature into fruit pods resembling enlarged cantaloupes or cucumbers, 6 to 14 in. long and 2 to 5 in. in diameter and ranging in colour from yellow-orange to dark-red purple. Though these ripen intermittently throughout the year, most ripen in one or two main periods. Four-fifths the world crop is harvested in the period from September to March. The pod is simply cut from the tree and the tough, fibrous hull opened with a machete, after which the 25 to 50 seeds and adhering pulp are scooped out and fermented. The fermenting, whether carried out in a primitive pile on the ground or in a more modern perforated box or tank under cover and high temperature, takes 3 to 12 days, depending on the type of cocoa, and involves draining away the juicy "sweatings" of the pulp and the mixing and stirring of the beans to obtain an even fermentation and to avoid under- or over-fermentation. The germ in the seed is killed by the heat, temperatures as high as 115° F. develop, and the character and flavour of the bean are changed. The exact parts played by heat, enzymes, alcohol and acetic acid are unclear, but the beans become plump and full of moisture; the interior develops an even, reddish-brown tint and a heavy, sharp fragrance. The pulp is easily removed. The beans are then dried, in some cases after washing, by sun or artificially, sometimes on special mats or racks for a few days or weeks, to a water content of about 8%, after which they may be clayed or polished and bagged in burlap for handling. Unwashed, sun-dried beans seem to be preferred; unfermented beans are not desired. The yield on the average is 1 to 2 lb. of cured beans per tree per year, or about 500 lb. per acre. Selected plantings with above-average care will yield much more. There is some evidence of higher yields in alternate years. A major problem, other than that of disease, is how to combine peasant production with more advanced techniques to get higher yields and better quality, preferably at lower cost. Typical costs are extremely difficult to estimate, but West Africa, with its small farmers depending largely on family labour, is the lowest-cost producing area.

Grades and Marketing.—Cocoa is classified in world trade as "base" or "flavour" grades, or as "ordinary" and "fine." In general, these grades relate not to difference in processing but to varieties, of which there are many, the two main groups being Criollo and Forastero. Approximately 10% of world production is of the fine or flavour grades called Criollos, or near Criollos, or high Forastero, marketed especially under the trade names of Arriba, Maracaibo, Caracas and Trinidad Estates and produced mostly in Venezuela, Ecuador, Costa Rica, Surinam, British West Indies, Ceylon and Java. They are largely grown under a plantation system utilizing 100 ac. or more. Forastero types, including subvarieties Trinitario and Amelomado, constitute the base or common grades, marketed as "Accra" from the Gold Coast, of which country they constitute half the export trade and the main source of income for the majority of the people, and "Bahia" from Brazil, as well as "Lagos" and "Sanchez." They usually constitute about 90% of the world's crop, are hardier and give larger yields of medium-quality beans selling for 3 to 15 cents less per pound than the flavour grades. Quality standards for cocoa deteriorated during and after World War II, not only because of increased use of ordinary grades, as flavour grades were available in comparatively smaller amounts, but partly because of relaxed standards under wartime conditions. However, governments intervened in an effort to improve grading and to provide premiums for quality.

The annual crop of cocoa moves into world commerce promptly, partly because local use is not large. Though the beans will keep for a year or more under the best of storage conditions, two or three months is about the limit under the tropical conditions prevailing in the producing areas. The major markets are western Europe and the United States. Four-fifths of the exports go to five countries, and ten countries take 95% of the beans entering world trade. Major changes following World War II were the increased imports of Australia, Spain and Canada and the decrease, perhaps temporary, in imports into Germany and the Netherlands.

Cocoa was bought and sold before World War II essentially on a free but unstable market, involving active middlemen and comparatively wide price fluctuations. Increased output, especially in West Africa, resulted in lower prices and expanded world use but increasingly unsatisfactory conditions for producers during the 1930s. Buying agreements in 1937 among the majority of firms and manufacturers dealing with Gold Coast and Nigerian cocoa soon resulted in a boycott by producers and in a tie-up of marketing. After investigation, the Nowell commission concluded that the agreements should be withdrawn and suggested a plan for reorganizing marketing for those areas, which, however, was precluded by the advent of World War II. Hence, growers of cocoa had no experience with international regulatory agreements; most of the proposals at prewar conferences were in the direction of increasing consumption by advertising and keeping prices as low as possible. There were tight controls over trade during the war: the same price was paid for all West African cocoas during 1942–46, whereas except during periods of short supply the best grade sold for about three times as much as the lowest. Stocks were much reduced at the end of World War II, and production had declined fully one-fifth, not because of war devastation of the producing areas but largely because of a general disruption of the production pattern and as a result of disease. In the early postwar years, world cocoa trade was governed in a general way by the International Emergency Food council. Allocations ended in 1949. The postwar period found both buying and selling concentrated in fewer agencies.

World Net Imports of Cocoa
(In thousands of metric tons)

Place	Average, 1935–39	Average, 1945–49	1950
United States	269.8	271.0	298.9
United Kingdom	108.5	114.4	132.4
Continental Europe	275.6	146.0	272.6
Germany and Austria	82.3	....	60.0
Netherlands	66.3	35.0	66.1
France	44.6	44.0	69.8
Belgium	11.0	11.8	8.0
Czechoslovakia	10.8	...	...
Switzerland	8.8	9.9	8.1
Italy	8.7	6.4	13.3
Spain	8.2	13.0	11.3
Poland	6.8	...	...
Sweden	6.7	8.2	10.8
Norway	3.4	3.2	5.3
Other	18.0	...	...
Canada	12.5	20.5	17.9
Australia	6.8	11.5	8.0
Argentina	5.1	...	4.7
Union of South Africa	1.2	...	2.1
Other	12.0	...	33.2
World, excluding U.S.S.R.	691.5	600.0	760.0

The government-backed Gold Coast Cocoa Marketing Company, Ltd., and Nigerian Produce Marketing Company, Ltd., sold the West African crops to the British ministry of food and to U.K. merchants and for export. The Instituto de Cacau da Bahia of Brazil and equivalent government-sponsored or government-controlled agencies in other producing countries continued to perform much of the marketing function. Bulk buying was the usual practice in most importing countries in the early postwar period and was only gradually relaxed to be performed by private trade. The U.S. used price controls and processor quotas; decontrol in 1946 had certain far-reaching effects on the world cocoa economy.

Manufacture and Uses.—The United States has the world's largest industry, ordinarily taking as much as 40% of the world's exports and reducing the raw cocoa beans to the several products. There are also major cocoa-manufacturing centres in several western European countries and in Canada, Australia and India.

The beans are cleaned, sometimes washed, and carefully roasted at 275° to 350° F. to develop flavour, colour and aroma and to aid shelling; they are then broken into particles called "nibs" by a rolling or cracking process, and winnowed to remove the fibrous shells. The shells, 10%–14% of the total weight, may be used for cocoa "tea," but usually become cattle feed. The nibs of desired grades and flavours are blended (not more than 25% of flavour grades), then ground to a paste, referred to as cocoa mass or chocolate liquor, which after cooling sets into a hard brown block. Half or more of the mass is a natural fat, cocoa butter, part of which is removed under hydraulic pressure. Various types of chocolate may result depending on the amount of butter remaining, flavouring added and further processing. Unsweetened chocolate or baking chocolate is the ground nib moulded into bars. Sweet drinking chocolate has had sugar added and been somewhat refined; eating chocolate contains more cocoa butter and flavouring. Part of the fat or cocoa butter has been removed from cocoa powder, but it contains from 10% to 20% or more fat and has been treated with an alkali salt which neutralizes the natural acidity of the cocoa and makes it more soluble. All are used in several ways in confectionery, baking, dairy and soft drinks and ice cream industries. Cocoa butter is used in cosmetics and pharmaceuticals. Of all candy flavours, chocolate is generally the most popular (the U.S. industry delivered almost 1,000,000,000 lb. of cocoa products to the armed services during World War II). In addition to the mild stimulating effect caused by theobromine (2.2%) and caffeine (0.1%), cocoa is a concentrated food containing about 40.3% carbohydrates, 26.8% fat, 18.1% protein and 6.3% ash, with small amounts of water and fibre; it provides approximately 2,214 cal. per pound.

Cocoa Production.—Centres of production have changed with time, but commercial cultivation is limited by natural factors to the tropics; practically all development is within 20° north and south of the equator, and the main African belt is less than 10° from the equator. High temperatures, a mean shade temperature of approximately 80° F. with diurnal and seasonal variation of not more than 15° F., appear necessary. The cold limit apparently is an absolute one, whereas temperatures of 100° F. or more, accompanied by high humidity, do no harm. Well-distributed rainfall of at least 50 in. a year (if not irrigated), absence of disease, a considerable population to provide harvest labour, and access to export markets are all factors favouring development. In South America there are large areas apparently suitable for cultivation except for disease. Favourable site factors include a well-drained, porous soil of considerable depth and rich in humus, an altitude of a few hundred feet, protection from strong winds, and some shade.

Centres of production, judged by exports, soon shifted from Mexico to Venezuela; Ecuador was the principal area from about 1850 to 1910, after which Brazil led for a time, only to be surpassed by the rapidly developing West African cocoa belt, which was the leader after 1920 and by the 1950s was producing approximately two-thirds of the expanded world crop of about 1,500,000,000 lb. annually. Production in the Americas has continued at an annual rate of nearly 200,000 tons over many years.

In the early 1950s a trend of incipient decline appeared in the major centres of production, especially those of Africa. The spread of plant disease was a partial explanation. Many major plantings were passing beyond the most productive age period; new plantings apparently did not keep up with loss of trees, partly because of economic competition with other production. Price uncertainties were a factor, having varied approximately tenfold in the 1940s. Plantings in some new or minor areas were expanding, partly with Point Four assistance.

Bibliography.—Ivar Erneholm, *Cacao Production of South America—Historical Development and Present Geographical Distribution* (Göteborg, 1948); E. G. Montgomery and Alice M. Taylor, *World Trade in Cocoa,* Industrial Series No. 71, Office of International Trade, U.S. Department of Commerce (1947); *Report and Proceedings of the Cocoa Research Conference, June 1945,* Colonial No. 192 (London, 1945); V. D. Wickizer, *Coffee, Tea and Cocoa: An Economic and Political Analysis* (Stanford, Oxford, 1951); *Documentary Material on Cacao—For the Use of the Special Committee on Cacao of the Inter-American Social and Economic Council,* Pan American Union (1947).

(J. K. R.)

COCOA BUTTER, the pure fat extracted by pressure from the ground and crushed cocoa bean. It is used in the manufacture of confectionery and cosmetics and other toilet preparations. Cocoa butter is sold free from combination with other drugs for treating skin irritations where a pure fat is necessary.

COCO DE MER or Double Coconut, a palm, *Lodoicea maldivica,* a native of the Seychelles Islands. The flowers are borne in enormous fleshy spadices, the male and female on distinct plants. The fruits, among the largest known, take ten years to ripen; they have a fleshy and fibrous envelope surrounding a hard, nutlike portion which is generally two-lobed, suggesting a double coconut. The contents of the nut are edible. The empty fruits (after germination of the seed) are found floating in the Indian ocean, and were known long before the palm was discovered.

COCONUCO, a group of South American Indians in south highland Colombia whose language was probably a branch of the Macro-Chibchan phylum. Assimilated by the Spaniards soon after the conquest, their culture is known only from scant historical references. The Coconuco together with the Moguex comprised a dozen or more tribes which resembled their Andean neighbours in carrying on intensive agriculture and having a dense and settled population, federated states and developed warfare. Unlike their neighbours, the Coconuco proper were not cannibals.

See Henri Lehmann, "The Moguex-Coconuco" in *The Andean Civilizations,* 2:969–974, *Handbook of South American Indians,* ed. by Julian H. Steward, Bureau of American Ethnology bulletin 143, (Washington, 1946). (J. H. Sd.)

COCONUT OIL AND CAKE. Coconut oil and coconut cake are derived from the fruit of the coconut palm, *Cocos nucifera.* This tree grows wild on the coasts of all tropical countries and is also extensively cultivated for the many products made by natives from the flower, fruit, leaves and other parts of the plant. Copra, the dried meat of the coconut from which coconut oil is obtained, is the most important commercial product of the coconut palm. Cultivation of the tree for copra is localized principally in the Philippines, India, Ceylon, Indonesia, Malaya and the Pacific Islands.

The fresh kernel of the coconut contains about 50% water and 30% to 40% oil. Therefore, in production of copra the nuts are husked, opened and dried to separate the oil-bearing meat from the shell and to prevent spoilage. The earliest method of drying was to expose the kernels to the air and sun, a practice which is still extensively followed and gives a good quality white copra (sun-dried copra). A more rapid primitive process, adopted particularly in districts where the humidity of the air is excessive, is drying by fire (kiln drying). The kilns, constructed by native labour, consist essentially of a fireplace and a fire pit overlaid with a grid on which the copra is placed. The drying copra is sheltered from the rain by a roof. Such kilns are used generally in the Philippines which supply 50% of the world copra exports. Broken coconut shells, wood and to some extent coconut husks are used as fuel. The copra is deliberately smoked in order to sterilize the partially dried copra, and so modify the extent of self-heating and decomposition during subsequent natural drying in storage in the warehouse of the copra buyer. The copra does not remain on the kiln for more than two days. During this period the fire in the fire pit is kept going spasmodically. The total length of time during which a fire is actually burning does not exceed six hours. While the quality of copra produced with this form of dryer is not the best, the output of a well-designed kiln can equal the quality of the output of more elaborate dryers, the expense of which places them beyond the means of the small farm owners who produce most of the copra of the Philippines.

Copra of better and more uniform quality is produced by another method—hot air drying—first introduced in India and Samoa. The copra is drawn slowly through a heated tunnel meeting a countercurrent of hot air. The method yields a fine and white copra of higher value than the sun-dried article. Well-dried copra as sold in world commerce contains 4% to 5% moisture. The proportion of oil in such copra ranges from 63% to 70%.

Processing Copra.—Coconut oil is obtained from copra chiefly by pressing in mechanical screw presses. In some areas hydraulic

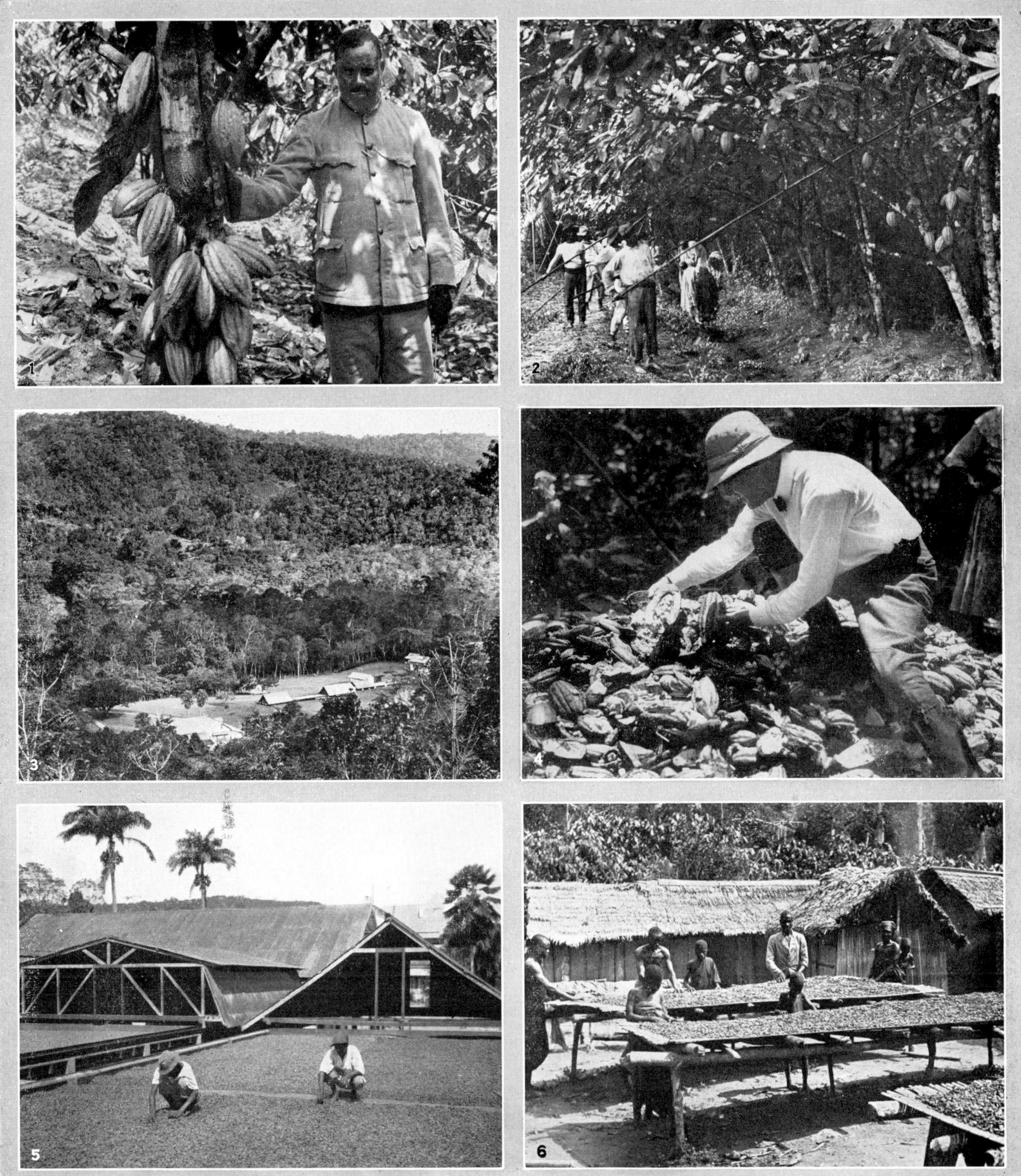

BY COURTESY OF (3) CADBURY BROTHERS, LTD.; PHOTOGRAPHS, (1, 5) PUBLISHERS PHOTO SERVICE, (4) THOMAS F. LEE FROM EWING GALLOWAY

CACAO-GROWING IN THE WEST INDIES AND IN BRITISH WEST AFRICA

1. Port of Spain, Trinidad. A cacao tree, showing the formation of the pods around the branches
2. Gathering cacao pods. Long bamboo poles wielded by men bring down the pods, which are then gathered into baskets by women
3. A cacao estate on the island of Trinidad, in the West Indies, showing the paddock-like clearing in the centre, where the fermenting house and drying platforms are situated
4. Cacao pods that have been slit so that the beans may be scooped out
5. Drying cacao beans on the government plantation in Trinidad. This process consists in turning the beans over and over in the sun for three days
6. Cacao cultivation in British West Africa, showing natives in Ashanti drying cacao on crudely constructed tables fashioned of bamboo mats

COCOA

BY COURTESY OF THE WALTER BAKER COMPANY

MACHINES USED IN THE PROCESSES OF COCOA MANUFACTURE

1. Sorting and cleaning the cacao beans
2. Magnetic extractor and sorter used for selecting beans for roasting
3. Machine used for roasting beans
4. A machine used for cracking and fanning the roasted beans to remove shells

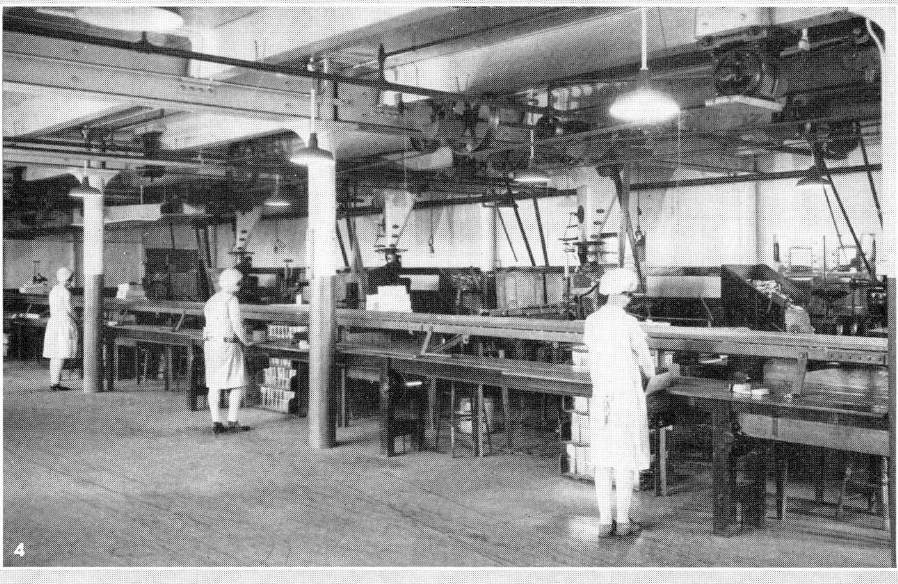

BY COURTESY OF THE WALTER BAKER COMPANY

FURTHER STEPS IN THE MANUFACTURE OF COCOA

1. Steel rolls used in the process of milling the cacao nibs into liquor
2. Presses shown for removing part of the cacao butter from the cacao fluid
3. Flour bolters sifting the cocoa powder through silk meshes
4. Packing cocoa for the retail market

cage and box presses continue to be employed. Their use, however, is relatively limited, and the world production of coconut oil is largely obtained by use of continuous mechanical screw presses. To obtain a higher oil yield the oil may be extracted with a solvent following a preliminary pressing in screw presses. In either instance before processing the copra is passed through a cleaner which removes sand and trash. It is then passed through a crusher which breaks it into small pieces. The broken copra moves through a magnetic separator which disposes of pieces of iron (bolts, nails, etc.). The material is then ground finely and treated.

Single Pressing.—The finely ground copra is cooked, or dried, in steam-jacketed kettles or compartments to a moisture content of about 1.5%. The meats pass from the driers into continuous mechanical screw presses which consist essentially of a cylinder, or barrel, in which an impelling worm turns and continuously forces the tempered copra through a small terminal orifice. The barrel is composed of a series of rectangular steel bars, separated by spaces to form slots. Pressure and heat of friction release the oil which escapes through the slots of the barrel. Continuous mechanical screw presses may have a vertical and a horizontal pressing barrel, each operated by a separate motor. In the single type the horizontal barrel performs the entire copra-pressing operation. Continuous mechanical screw presses have a capacity of 20–40 tons of copra per 24-hr. day. The oil content in the pressed copra cake varies from 5% to 7%. The cake is ground directly into meal which is placed in bags for marketing. Before passing to the crude oil storage tanks the coconut oil is screened to remove fine particles of ground copra. It is then run through a filter press. The foots from the screening process and the filter press cake are returned to the screw presses for re-pressing.

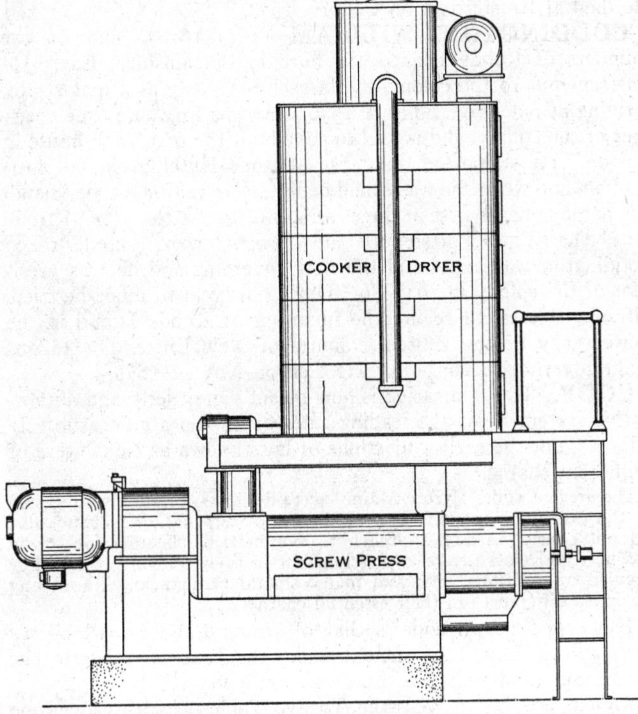

BY COURTESY OF THE FRENCH OIL MILL MACHINERY CO.
MECHANICAL SCREW PRESS AND COOKER DRYER USED FOR COPRA CRUSHING

Solvent Extraction.—In Europe and the United States some coconut oil is extracted by means of petroleum solvents (hexane type) from copra which has been prepressed through large continuous mechanical screw presses. These screw presses with a capacity of 25–65 tons per day reduce the oil in copra from 65% to 15% to 20% before the cake is prepared for extraction. The oil-bearing material is treated continuously in a countercurrent flow with solvent until the oil left in the extracted meal has been reduced to .5% to 1%. The solvent is removed from the extracted meal by means of steam-jacketed, agitated conveyers. The solvent from the oil is recovered by distillation and the last traces of solvent are removed by steam distillation of the oil *in vacuo*.

Copra Meal.—The meal from pressed cake contains 21.3% protein on the average and 5% to 7% oil. Solvent extracted cake contains less oil and a proportionately greater amount of protein. Copra meal is valued as a dairy feed. It is also satisfactory as a protein supplement for fattening cattle and lambs.

Coconut Oil.—The oil is colourless to yellowish in appearance and melts at about 74° F. Crude coconut oil has a characteristic coconut odour. The fatty acids of coconut oil possess a lower average molecular weight than those of most other fats. Thus the quick solubility of their sodium salts and the sulphated fatty alcohols derived from coconut fatty acids make coconut oil a highly desirable material for the manufacture of soaps and other detergents.

Edible coconut oil is the product of refining and deodorizing the crude oil to remove free fatty acids and flavours. An important food use of coconut oil arises from its high percentage of lauric acid (48%). The resistance of this saturated fatty acid to the development of rancidity caused by oxidation prompts confectioners and bakers to use refined coconut oil in coatings and fillings for baked goods and candy which may stand for a relatively long time between manufacture and consumption. Prior to World War II coconut oil had extensive use in margarine manufacture in the United States, but later it was largely displaced by domestic oils. Its use in margarine continues undiminished in Europe and other areas. Refined coconut oil is used in the manufacture of shortening and as a cooking fat. (Jn. B. G.)

COCONUT PALM (*Cocos nucifera*), best known of the palms and famed as one of the world's most important crop trees, the coconut palm grows to 100 ft. tall. Its slender, leaning, ringed trunk arises from a swollen base, and it is surmounted by a graceful crown of giant, featherlike leaves. About a dozen new leaves appear periodically each year and an equal number of compound flower stalks which, protected by woody spathes, push out from the base of the older leaves. Some 10,000 male flowers and about 30 female flowers appear on each stalk. They mature at different times, assuring cross-pollination. Five-year-old trees start to flower and this process is continuous thereafter. Fruits require a year to ripen; the annual yield per tree may reach 100, but 50 is considered good.

Mature fruits are 12 to 18 in. in length, 6 to 8 in. in diameter, ovoid or ellipsoidal, and with a thick fibrous husk surrounding the familiar single-seeded nut of commerce. A hard shell encloses the insignificant embryo with its abundant endosperm, comprised of both meat and liquid (unsolidified endosperm). The three "eyes" of the coconut shell indicate that three ovarial cavities exist in the flower but only one persists at maturity.

Coconut fruits float readily and have been dispersed widely by ocean currents, and also by man, throughout the tropics. Actually the native home of the coconut palm is unknown, but it probably originated somewhere in Indo-Malaya, where the palm exists in many natural forms. Marco Polo was among the first Europeans to describe coconuts, but the great voyages of discovery such as that of the navigator William Dampier made the species better known. Coconut palms flourish best close to the sea on low-lying areas a few feet above high water where there is circulating ground water and an ample rainfall. The palm sometimes is grown far inland and at altitudes up to 2,000 ft., but in such places production declines.

The coconut attains its greatest marketable value as copra, the dried extracted kernel, or meat, from which coconut oil, the world's ranking vegetable oil, is expressed. It is estimated that 1,000 mature nuts will yield upward of 500 lb. of copra, from which 25 gal. of oil should be obtained. The oil is a white solid substance at ordinary temperatures with a peculiar, rather disagreeable odour. The Philippines and Indonesia lead in copra production, and throughout Polynesia it is the only important export product. Coconut oil has many uses, entering into the manufacture of soaps and shampoos, detergents, edible oils, margarines, vegetable shortenings, synthetic rubber, glycerine, hydraulic brake fluid and plasticizers for safety glass. Copra meal is a livestock feed and fertilizer while shredded coconut is a familiar item on grocers' shelves. Although the coconut finds greatest commercial utilization in the industrial countries of the western world, its usefulness in its native areas of culture is even greater. Indonesians claim that coconuts have as many uses as there are days in the year, and these are not limited to the oil-yielding nut. Besides the edible kernels and the refreshing and palatable drink obtained from green nuts, the husk yields coir, a fibre highly resistant to salt water and used in the manufacture of ropes, mats, baskets, brushes and brooms. Coir dust, or cocopeat, is a peat substitute of use to horticulture. By wounding the unopened flower stalks one can obtain readily flowing sap yielding toddy, a beverage drunk either fresh or fermented as an intoxicating palm wine. Toddy is a source of sugar as well as alcohol. As in other palms the delicate young bud cut from the top of the tree is eaten as a salad vegetable, palm cabbage; the mature leaves find use in thatching and basketry; and the fibrous decay-resistant trunk is of value not only to the natives who incorporate it in the construction of huts but also as an exported cabinet wood, porcupine wood, so called because of the ebonylike streaks which irregularly mark the red-brown ground colour. (Wr. H. H.)

COCOPA, the Yuman tribe nearest the mouth of the Colorado river, similar in customs to the Yuma and Mohave. The population, originally not far from 3,000, has decreased to about 600, mostly on Mexican soil.

COCYTUS, a tributary of the Acheron (modern Mavropotamo), which flows into the Ionian sea about 20 mi. N. of the Gulf of Arta; identified with a tributary of the Acheron or of the Styx, a river in Hades (*cf.* Virgil's *Aeneid,* vi, 132). The etymology suggested is from ωκύειν, to wail, in allusion to the cries of mourners; this is probably a reduplicated form, akin to Skt. *kû,* cry, with intensive kokuyate.

COD, the name given to the typical fish of the family Gadidae of the order Anacanthini, which includes fishes without spinous fin rays, with no duct to the air bladder and with the pelvic fins anterior in position. The pelvic fins are often many-rayed, and the pelvic bones are not directly attached to the pectoral arch, these characters distinguishing the Anacanthini from certain Blennioid fishes of the order Percomorphi, with which they were formerly associated, and indicating their relationship to more primitive orders. The Anacanthini include two principal families: the Macruridae, which are deep-sea fishes without a caudal fin and with the long second dorsal and anal fins continued to the end of the tapering tail; and the Gadidae, in which the caudal fin is composed mainly of dorsal and anal fin rays, the homocercal fin being greatly reduced, an indication that the ancestral form may have been eel-shaped. The Gadidae are marine with the exception of the burbot (*Lota lota*), which is a freshwater fish. They are most abundant in northern seas, where there are several species of great economic importance; *e.g.,* cod, haddock (*q.v.*), whiting (*q.v.*), ling (*q.v.*) and hake (*q.v.*). In warmer seas there are some deep-water forms of no great value, and the hake genus (*Merluccius*) is the only important one represented in both the north and south temperate zones. The flesh of all these fishes is more digestible than nutritious, being poor in fat.

The cod (*Gadus morrhua*), in common with other fishes of the genus *Gadus,* has three dorsal and two anal fins; the upper jaw projects beyond the lower, and there is a barbel at the chin. The colour varies considerably, but is generally olive-green above with darker spots, and white below; the lateral line is white and conspicuous. The cod is found in the North Atlantic and Baltic but not in the Mediterranean; it also occurs in the North Pacific. Generally it lives on the bottom at depths of 10 to 100 fathoms, and feeds on other fishes, such as herring and sand eels, and also on squids, mussels, whelks, etc. The spawning seaon is from January to March; the eggs are minute and are produced in enormous numbers, sometimes 10,000,000 from one female; they float in the water. The young fish attain a length of about two feet in four years; three feet is an average size, but some grow to more than five feet long and weigh more than 100 lb. The cod is the object of extensive fisheries by line and trawl on the Newfoundland banks, off Iceland and in the North sea. The greater part of the catch is split, salted and dried; the livers are used for the preparation of cod-liver oil, and the roes are sent to France to be used as groundbait in the sardine fishery; isinglass is made from the air bladder. (C. T. R.)

C.O.D.: *see* Cash on Delivery.

CODA, in music, a term for a passage which brings a movement or a separate piece to a conclusion. (Ital. for "tail"; from the Lat. *cauda.*) This developed from the simple chords of a cadence into what is often an elaborate and important feature of a composition on a large scale. Beethoven raised the coda to a feature of the highest importance. A codetta (diminutive of coda) is merely a small coda, employed to round off not a complete work but an intermediate section of it.

CODDE, PIETER (1599–1678), Dutch painter of the school of Haarlem, was born on Dec. 11, 1599, at Amsterdam. He was probably a pupil of Franz Hals, whose painting of the Doelen of "Captain Reaels," left unfinished in 1637, he was asked to complete. He was active as a genre painter at Amsterdam and Leyden, and he liked to represent ladies and gentlemen dancing (Sievers' collection, Dorpat, 1627; Mauritshuis, The Hague, 1636; Academy in Vienna, 1633), or scenes with soldiery (Mauritshuis, The Hague, 1628; Dresden gallery, 1628). He also executed some small portraits (National gallery, London). He died at Amsterdam on Oct. 12, 1678.

CODDINGTON, WILLIAM (1601–1678), one of the founders of Rhode Island, was born in Lincolnshire, Eng. He was sent out to the colony at Massachusetts bay as a magistrate, arriving at Salem on June 12, 1630. He was for some time treasurer of the colony, and is said to have built the first brick house in Boston. He supported the cause of Anne Hutchinson, the antinomian, and when she was exiled he left, in 1638, for Rhode Island. His name appears first in the covenant of the settlers (*see* Rhode Island). When Portsmouth and Newport were united (1640) Coddington was appointed the first governor, and he was president of the colony in 1648–49. During his year of office he tried, without success, to secure the inclusion of Rhode Island in the confederacy of the United Colonies of New England. He was again governor in 1674–76. He died on Nov. 1, 1678.

CODE. By codification is now meant "an orderly and authoritative statement of the leading rules of law on a given subject" (Ilbert), but the early collections of laws known as codes were of a different character.

> The ancient codes [wrote Maine] were doubtless originally suggested by the discovery and diffusion of the art of writing. . . . Their value did not consist in any approach to symmetrical classification, or to terseness and clearness of expression, but in their publicity. . . . They mingled up religious, civil and merely moral ordinances without any regard to differences in their essential character.

The oldest-known code is that of Hammurabi, for which *see* Babylonian Law. In ancient India the laws applying to the Hindu community of the time were codified.

Roman law began with the Twelve Tables—a primitive code—and culminated in the code of Justinian, which was given the force of law in A.D. 534. (*See* Roman Law.) "Though the name was invented and used in a somewhat different sense by the Romans, the thing is of far more modern origin. . . . The Romans never advanced beyond a digest," whereas, properly, "a code is a digest of which every title has been consolidated" (Holland). The peoples who overran the Roman empire made collections of rules of law; *e.g.,* the law of the Salian Franks and other Frankish laws. (*See* Germanic Laws, Early; Salic Law.)

The Rhodian sea law was a collection of rules of maritime law, mainly derived from local customs, originally put together between A.D. 600 and 800. Collections of maritime usages and customs, drawn up for the use of merchants and lawyers, acquired in the 14th and 15th centuries great authority throughout Europe. Some were compiled in Mediterranean ports, and others for the use of merchants trading in the north of Europe. There were, for instance, the laws of Oleron (an island near Bordeaux), the laws of Wisby in Gothland, the *Consolato del Mare* (a collection of the maritime laws of Barcelona), the Oak Book of Southampton and other collections.

Mediaeval France was divided into *pays de droit écrit* and

pays de droit coutumier. In the former, feudal rules overlay the Roman law; in the latter, customs differed in each province, county and municipality. Despite the promulgation of a series of ordinances, an extraordinary diversity of laws continued until, after the Revolution, they were superseded by the Codes Napoléon which were then drawn up. (*See* CODE NAPOLÉON.)

Several European countries have modelled their codes upon those prepared in France under Napoleon, but in Germany events followed an independent course. From 1495 the German common law was a modified form of Roman law, but it was subject to modification by local customs, codes and state laws. Prussian common law was codified in 1794, this step being to some extent an anticipation of the idea of the French codes. With the formation of the North German confederation in 1866 federal legislation began and a general commercial code was enacted. In 1874 (three years after the formation of the German empire) preparations for general codification commenced. After many revisions the German civil code came into force in 1900 and along with it a remodelled commercial code.

The steps taken later toward the codification of law, not only in England but also elsewhere, originated in the reforming energy of Jeremy Bentham (1748–1832). Bentham's philosophy of law did not take sufficiently into account the march of events either in the past or in the future. He lived before it had become the practice to work by methods which include historical research, and he did not sufficiently appreciate that there is no finality in law, that it must be revised from time to time as circumstances change. Nevertheless, in this matter he was a great moving spirit.

> What he did was to set up an ideal towards which legislation should tend, an ideal which has been materially modified by subsequent reflection and experience, but which has profoundly influenced the thought and action of lawyers and legislators since his time. He has not shown the necessity, but he has shown the utility, of codification [Ilbert].

In British India the codification of the law may be attributed directly to the influence of Bentham exercised through James Mill and Macaulay. The penal code became law in 1860 and was followed by two codes dealing with procedure, and, in course of time, by a number of others on various branches of the law.

Following earlier attempts made in England to improve the form of the law, a number of statute law commissions were appointed during the earlier part of the Victorian period. Various reforms resulted, and many consolidation acts were passed, dealing with, *e.g.*, the customs, public health, merchant shipping and so forth. With lapse of time the need for reconsolidation, so as to incorporate later amendments, manifested itself, and from the beginning the process in most instances fell short of full codification because consolidation covered only statutory provisions and did not extend to common-law rules. Later some measures were passed codifying both the statute and the common law relating to particular subjects; *e.g.*, the Bills of Exchange act, 1882, the Partnership act, 1890, the Sale of Goods act, 1893, and the Marine Insurance act, 1906.

English law is the basis of the law in force in most of the states of the United States, an exception being Louisiana, where a civil code based on the Code Napoléon was adopted in 1808. Much codification of law was carried out in many of the states during the latter part of the 19th century, the first move in this direction being the adoption of a code of civil procedure by the state of New York in 1848. The laws of the South American republics for the most part were codified.

In Egypt a series of codes came into force in 1875. Japanese law was codified on the basis of an investigation into the laws of European countries which extended over the greater part of the last quarter of the 19th century. The civil code (which came to be the main foundation of the Japanese legal system) and the commercial code were largely modelled on German law.

International Codes.—Besides the codification of national laws something was done toward codifying rules of law regulating the relations between states and between the subjects of different states. These rules are commonly referred to as those of public and private international law, respectively. The advisory committee of jurists which met at The Hague, Neth., in 1920 to draft the plan for the Permanent Court of International Justice recommended that, in continuation of The Hague Conferences of 1899 and 1907, steps should be taken to bring about the restatement of the established rules of international law and the formulation of additional rules. Pursuant to this the League of Nations in 1924 appointed a committee of experts for the progressive codification of international law composed of jurists from 17 countries.

This committee reported in 1927 and continued its work thereafter. Pursuant to its recommendations a first codification conference was held at The Hague in 1930 to consider (1) nationality, (2) territorial waters and (3) responsibility of states for damage done in their territory to the person or property of foreigners.

Proposals for codification of international law aroused much interest in America. In 1906 the third Pan-American conference adopted a convention under which codes of private and public international law were to be prepared. At later meetings of the Pan-American conference (including that at Havana in 1928) further discussion of projects of conventions took place.

On the subjects selected for the first codification conference of 1930 as well as other possible subjects for the work of codification the progress resulted in large measure from unofficial spade work done in the past by the Institute of International Law and the International Law association. These, after 1873, were busy with the problems to which governments later turned their attention. After 1896 their activities were supplemented by those of the Comité Maritime International and after 1905 by those of the American Society of International Law.

The official movements above referred to did not bring about any actual codification of rules of law of international application, but in certain directions codification or unification was accomplished. In the absence of an international legislature no actual codification by means of international legislation is possible, but an equivalent result was produced in relation to certain matters by national legislation being passed in conformity with an international convention, or (in some commercial matters especially) unification was achieved by the formulation and common adoption of standard clauses for incorporation by reference in contracts. In this way the International Law association brought about the unification of some of the rules of law and practice relating to general average. International rules drawn up for this purpose and incorporated by reference in shipping documents are known as the York-Antwerp rules. The first rules adopted were those dated 1877. They were revised in 1890 and in 1924 were again revised and expanded into what is practically a code of general average (*see* AVERAGE). On the other hand the regulations for the prevention of collisions at sea, having been adopted by all maritime nations, are an example of standardized national legislation. Working after this method, the Comité Maritime International drafted international conventions, some of which were carried into effect by national legislation, while others awaited further action by maritime states. In the United States steps to standardize certain commercial laws throughout the different states of the union brought about the passing of uniform acts relating to negotiable instruments, sale of goods, bills of lading, warehouse receipts, etc.

BIBLIOGRAPHY.—Sir H. S. Maine, *Ancient Law* (1861); T. E. Holland, *Essays Upon the Form of the Law* (1870); C. Ilbert, *Legislative Methods and Forms* (1901); W. Burge, *Commentaries on Colonial and Foreign Laws* (1907–28); E. J. Schuster, *Principles of German Civil Law* (1907); W. Ashburner, *The Rhodian Sea-Law* (1909); A. F. Schuster, *The German Commercial Code* (1911); S. D. Cole, "Codification of International Law," *Grotius Society Transactions* (1927).
(S. D. C.)

CODEINE occurs naturally in opium, being one of the alkaloids (*q.v.*) of the phenanthrene group and a derivative of morphine (*q.v.*), retaining in a modified form the characteristic physiological action of the latter. It crystallizes with one molecule of water, in large translucent prisms, melts at 155° C. and has a specific rotation $[\alpha]-137.7°$. It behaves as a monoacidic base, forming salts of which the sulphate and the phosphate are those most frequently used in medicine. It is commonly used orally and hypodermically to relieve pain and spasm and as a sedative.

(F. L. A.)

CODE NAPOLÉON, the first code of the French civil law, known at first as the Code Civil des Français, was promulgated in its entirety by a law of 30 Ventose year XII (March 21, 1804).

On Sept. 3, 1807, it received the official name of Code Napoléon, although the part that Napoleon took in framing it was not very important. A law of 1818 restored to it its former name, but a decree of March 27, 1852, re-established the title of Code Napoléon. Since Sept. 4, 1870, the laws have quoted it only under the name of the Code Civil.

Never has a work of legislation been more national in the exact sense of the word. Desired for centuries by the France of the *ancien régime,* and demanded by the *cahiers* of 1789, this "code of civil laws common to the whole realm" was promised by the constitution of 1791. However, the two first assemblies of the Revolution were able to prepare only a few fragments of it. The preparation of a coherent plan began with the Convention. The *ancien régime* had collected and adjusted some of the material. There was, on the one hand, a vast juridical literature which, by eliminating differences of detail, had disengaged from the various French "customs" the essential part which they had in common, under the name of "common customary law"; on the other hand, the Roman law current in France had in like manner undergone a process of simplification in numerous works, the chief of which was that of Domat; while certain parts had already been codified on the Grandes Ordonnances, which were the work of D'Aguesseau. This legacy from the past, which it was desired to preserve within reason, had to be combined and blended with the laws of the Revolution, which had wrought radical reforms in the conditions affecting the individual, the tenure of real property, the order of inheritance and the system of mortgages. Cambacérès, as the representative of a commission of the Convention, brought forward two successive schemes for the Code Civil. As a member of one of the councils, he drew up a third under the Directory, and these projected forms came in turn nearer and nearer to what was to be the ultimate form of the code. So great was the interest centred in this work that the law of 19 Brumaire year VIII, which, in ratification of the previous day's coup d'état, nominated provisional consuls and two legislative commissions, gave injunctions to the latter to draw up a scheme for the Code Civil. This was done in part by one of the members, Jacqueminot, and finally under the constitution of the year VIII the completion of the work was taken in hand. The legislative machinery established by this constitution, defective as it was in other respects, was eminently suited for this task. Indeed, all projected laws emanated from the government and were prepared by the newly established council of state, which was so well recruited that it easily furnished qualified men, mostly veterans of the Revolution, to prepare the final scheme. The council of state naturally possessed in its legislative section and its general assembly bodies both competent and sufficiently limited to discuss the texts efficiently. The *corps législatif* had not the right of amendment, so could not disturb the harmony of the scheme. It was in the discussions of the general assembly of the council of state that Napoleon took part, in 97 cases out of 102, in the capacity of chairman, but, interesting as his observations occasionally are, he cannot be considered as a serious collaborator in this great work.

Those responsible for the scheme were in the main very successful in their work; they generally succeeded in fusing the two elements which they had to deal with, namely ancient French law, and that of the Revolution. The point in which their work is comparatively weak is the system of hypothec (*q.v.*), because they did not succeed in steering a middle course between two opposite systems, and the law of March 23, 1855 (*sur la transcription en matière hypothécaire*), was necessary to make good the deficiency. A fault frequently found with the Code Civil is that its general divisions show a lack of logic and method, but the division is practically that of the *Institutes* of Justinian and is about as good as any other: persons, things, inheritance, contracts and obligations, and finally, in place of actions, which have no importance for French law except from the point of view of procedure, privileges and hypothecs, as in the ancient *coutumes* of France, and prescription. It is, *mutatis mutandis,* practically the same division as that of Blackstone's *Commentaries.*

In later years other objections were expressed; serious omissions were pointed out in the code; it does not give to personal property the importance which it acquired in the course of the 19th century; it makes no provision for dealing with the legal relations between employers and employed which modern complex undertakings involve; it does not treat of life insurance, etc. But this only proves that it could not foretell the future, for most of these questions are concerned with economic phenomena and social relations which did not exist at the time when it was framed. The code needed revising and completing, and this was carried out by degrees by means of numerous important laws. In 1904, after the celebration of the centenary of the Code Civil, an extraparliamentary commission was nominated to prepare a revision of it. (J. P. E.)

Dissemination of the Code.—The influence of the Code Civil has been very great, not only in France but also abroad. It should be remembered that when the Revolution broke out France had for a century and a half held, almost without a rival, the leading place among the nations of the world. Its language was well on the way to succeeding Latin as the common speech of civilized men; its literature, its arts, the fascination of its culture, the splendour of its capital city, the devotion of its missionaries, held all mankind spellbound. Yet its law had no admirers or imitators in other countries. Few foreigners thought it worth while to study France's meagre legal literature; few students from abroad sought admission to its law schools. The Revolution and the empire, by the alarm which they excited and by the spirit of nationalism which they stimulated in other countries, went far to forfeit for France the pre-eminence which it had won and was winning by peaceful penetration. But the code saved the situation; and ever since its promulgation (March 21, 1804), France has exerted an incomparable influence upon the institutions and legal culture of the civilized world. Indeed, until the promulgation of the German civil code (Aug. 24, 1896) the Code Napoléon was without a competitor as a model for law reformers throughout all parts of the world outside the British empire and the United States. In the absence of an English code, the English common law has, in spite of the great place which it occupies, found acceptance in no country outside the circle of those which, by reason of conquest or of colonization, possess English-speaking rulers. The 19th century was pre-eminently an age of nation-making. In Europe it saw the creation or the unification of Germany, Italy, Belgium, Rumania, Bulgaria and Greece; on the American continent it saw the Spanish and Portuguese colonies transformed into 15 new nations; and in the east it witnessed Japan, Thailand, Turkey and Egypt attempting with greater or less success to grasp the secret of European pre-eminence. Of these 25 nations almost all sought to mark their succession to political maturity, and to proclaim their adherence to the European world, by a general revision and codification of their laws; and in most cases the model followed was that furnished by the Code Napoléon. The code was attractive in form; it was written in French; it was, or seemed to be, easy to understand; it bore the name of the greatest man of the age; it claimed to be catholic, rational, imperial and universal; it was secular without being irreligious and democratic without being revolutionary. In short, according to the ideas of 19th-century liberalism, it set forth in chapter and verse the fundamental articles of the social contract. Nor did the code have to rely upon its intrinsic merits alone. The reorganization of the French educational system, and particularly of the university, which constituted one of Napoleon's principal achievements, created law schools which in their turn produced an imposing literature of exposition and commentary on the code. This literature was an important factor in promoting the adoption and assimilation of the code by other countries.

The Napoleonic Empire.—When first promulgated in 1804, the French code came automatically into force in all those countries which were at that time subject to the empire. These were Belgium, Luxemburg, the Palatinate, those parts of Rhenish Prussia and Hesse-Darmstadt which were situated on the left bank of the Rhine, the territory of Geneva, Savoy, Piedmont and the duchies of Parma and Piacenza. Napoleon subsequently promulgated the code in the following countries as they were successively conquered: Italy (by decree of March 30, 1806), Holland (Oct. 18, 1810), the Hanseatic departments (*senatus-consultum* of Dec. 13, 1810) and the grand duchy of Berg (decree of Dec. 17, 1811). The following countries adopted the code *proprio motu,* though doubtless under some pressure, before the fall of the empire: Westphalia, Hanover, the grand duchies of Baden, Frankfurt, Nassau and Warsaw, several of the Swiss cantons, the free city of Danzig, the Illyrian provinces and the kingdom of Naples.

The blows delivered at Leipzig (1813) and Waterloo (1815) to French prestige gave a check, but only for a short time, to the dissemination of the code. In many parts of Italy, for example, the restoration governments revived the old laws; but they were speedily compelled to recognize that the clock could not be put back in so violent a fashion and to revert to codes on the French model. The code of the two Sicilies (1819), the code of Parma, promulgated by the former empress, Marie Louise, in 1820, the important Sardinian or "Albertine" code promulgated for Piedmont in 1848, and the civil code of Este (1851) all bear the mark of French influence. These essays in legislation led up to and were replaced by the general civil code for the new kingdom of Italy which came into force on Jan. 1, 1866. The similarity of this code to the French code is particularly marked in all those parts in which both remain closest to Roman law, *i.e.,* in the sections treating of obligations and real rights. The degree of this similarity may be judged by the fact that a committee composed of French and Italian jurists prepared drafts with a view to a uniform revision of those parts of the two codes which related to the law of obligations.

Europe After Waterloo.—The restitution, after Waterloo, of their possessions on the left bank of the Rhine to Prussia and the German states was not followed by the abandonment of the French code, which remained in force until replaced in 1900 by the general code for the German empire. In Baden the Code Napoléon was transmuted and preserved, without substantial change, in the *Badisches Landrecht* and in this form had a similarly long lease of life. The code not only remained in force in that country, but was the subject of influential exposition. The *Commentary* of Zachariae, a Heidelberg professor, published in 1808 was the first general treatise on the code in any language. Not only was it destined to reappear in numerous successive editions in German, but it served as the basis for the French *Commentary* of Aubry and Rau, of which the edition completed in 1922 still bore on the title page *"d'après la méthode de Zachariae."* Puchelt's *Zeitschrift für französisches Civilrecht,* founded in 1870 and published at Mannheim, continued to appear till early in the 20th century.

Egypt.—Egypt offers an example of the reception not only of the

Code Civil but of its four companion codes by a people totally alien to Europe in all cultural traditions. When, in 1874, the Egyptian government obtained the consent of the powers to the institution of the mixed tribunals, it was agreed without debate that the only possible law with which to equip them was that of the French code. The Code Civil, as adapted for application by the new tribunals, was shorn of all matters relating to personal status and to the effects on property of marriage and death. In 1883, the year following the British occupation, the French codes were extended, in a form almost identical with that adopted by the mixed courts, to the newly organized native jurisdiction. The result of this twofold "reception" of the French codes was that Egypt looked to French textbooks, to French judicial decisions and in a large measure to French professors for the progressive elucidation of the law. It was largely for this reason that in spite of the British occupation the social and cultural influence of France remained supreme in that country. It has been remarked that proposals for innovation made by English advisers met with opposition as often on the ground that they offended against the principles of French law as on the ground that they trespassed against the sacred law of Islam.

Japan.—The course of events in Japan was different and even more instructive. One of the first acts of the restoration government, as early as 1870, was to cause the Code Napoléon to be translated and to send for French jurists to supervise the administration of justice and to organize legal education. Though not promulgated as law, the French code in this way and in the absence of any serious rival, either indigenous or foreign, acquired great authority from the beginning of the new regime. In 1880 there was published a draft civil code, prepared by Boissonade, a member of the French legal mission. This code, though it, too, was not promulgated as law, exercised for 16 years as great an influence in the country as if it had been legally in force, and was treated by the judges as a statement of the principles of natural reason and equity. Meanwhile, concurrently with the academic teaching of French law, provision had been made by the Japanese government for instruction in Anglo-U.S. law at the University of Tokyo. In 1892 Boissonade's code was on the eve of being put into force, when the diet voted that it should be submitted to a further revision. This decision appears to have resulted from dissensions between the French and English schools of legal thought. The result was that when the revised code was finally promulgated in 1896 it was found to be neither English nor French but German in inspiration.

Competition of German Civil Code.—This *dénouement* was symbolic. The German civil code, published in its final form in 1895, was the first serious rival which Napoleon's code had had to encounter. As compared with its French predecessor, the German code had the advantage derived from a century of progress in legal science; it was a more carefully thought out piece of work; it was greatly superior in arrangement; it distinguished more clearly between substance and accident, between principle and application; in short, it was a more scientific piece of work. There are strong indications that it may now be taken to have replaced the French code as the model for future essays in codification. The Swiss civil code, for example, dated Dec. 10, 1907, was largely modelled on the German code, though in form it was shorter and simpler. The Turkish republic adopted it, almost without alteration, as the civil code of Turkey. (M. S. A.)

Bibliography.—V. A. and P. A. Dalloz, *Code civil,* 3 vol. (1873–90) and *Additions au code civil* (1911, etc.) in *Jurisprudence générale* (1873, etc.); *Le code civil: livre du centenaire,* vol. ii (1904); E. Blackwood Wright, *The French Code Civil as Amended up to 1906,* trans. with notes (1908); M. Planiol, *Traité élémentaire de droit civil français,* 6th ed., vol. i, p. 53 *et seq.*

CODES AND CIPHERS (Cryptology), general terms designating the methods or the paraphernalia employed in secret communications or involved in the science of cryptology (from Gr. *kryptos,* "hidden," and *logos,* "word"). Because of the growth of governments, the expansion of commerce and especially the remarkable progress made in communications-electronics technology, cryptology has come to play a very important role in governmental communications, especially diplomatic and military. It also plays a minor role in commercial, industrial and banking communications. Among the more uncommon uses of cryptology are those in connection with attempts to establish authorship in cases where that has been brought into question, as, for example, that of the Shakespeare plays.

In its early stages cryptology was concerned almost exclusively with secrecy in written communications and this article will be restricted very largely thereto, but the science has developed to the stage where it deals not only with enciphered writing (cryptograms) but also with other mediums of cryptocommunication, such as enciphered telephony (ciphony) and enciphered facsimile (cifax) transmissions.

Cryptology embraces the twin or complementary sciences of signal security and signal intelligence. The former deals with all the means and methods of protecting one's own signals against interception and reading or utilization by unauthorized persons generally referred to as "the enemy." The latter deals with all the means and methods employed in acquiring information or intelligence by intercepting and solving the enemy's cryptosignals or nullifying his signal security so that the signals or information derived from them can be used against him.

Signal Security.—The principal components of this phase of cryptology are: (1) physical and personnel security; (2) transmission security; and (3) cryptosecurity. The first deals with the precautions and measures taken to assure that the physical arrangements and the facilities or procedures for safeguarding the paraphernalia or cryptomaterials used, *i.e.,* the codes, ciphers, key lists, etc., are adequate for the purpose and that the personnel employed in operating the codes and ciphers or cipher machines are trustworthy. The second component deals with the means, methods and procedures for assuring that no information is inadvertently disclosed either by indiscretions of operators or by faults in the transmitting or receiving apparatus which may assist in the solution of the transmissions. The third component, cryptosecurity, which deals with the technical adequacy of the cryptosystems employed, is usually of greater interest and deserves more extensive treatment than the other two. In an article of this nature it is possible only to deal briefly with cryptography (from Gr. *kryptos,* "hidden," and *graphein,* "to write"), it being understood that many of the cryptoprinciples employed for the protection of written communications, or signals representing them, can also be used in protecting or disguising other types of cryptosignalling; *e.g.,* ciphony and cifax. Cryptography deals with the processes, methods or means involved in preparing cryptograms, that is, messages or writings which are intended to be incomprehensible except to those who legitimately possess the proper special paraphernalia and the keys for those cryptograms and know how to use them in order to reproduce the original plain text of the messages. These processes are usually accomplished by means of cryptosystems employing codes or ciphers. The process of converting a plain-text message into a cryptogram is called enciphering (or encoding); that of reconverting the cryptogram back into its intelligible form, when done by a legitimate or authorized communicator, *i.e.,* one who legitimately holds the paraphernalia and the key, is called deciphering (or decoding).

Although in theory no sharp line of demarcation can be drawn between code systems and cipher systems, in modern practice the technical differences between them are sufficiently marked to warrant their being treated as separate categories of methods. Some authors include as a third and separate category the extensive but much less important one containing the so-called "concealment systems," which are sometimes employed to hide an internal or secret message within an external or apparently innocent piece of writing with a view to avoiding arousing suspicion in the minds of persons not privy to the secret, or to eluding censorship in wartime. In such systems the message or its elements are hidden or disguised by any one of hundreds of different means and methods, including such mediums as secret or invisible inks, microscopic writing, etc., but none of these concealment systems or devices will even be mentioned again herein. It is convenient to consider cipher systems first, then code systems, with the understanding that only a very few of the limited number of systems suitable for serious usage can here be outlined.

Cipher Systems.—In general, cipher systems involve a cryptographic treatment of textual units of constant and equal length, usually single letters, sometimes pairs, rarely sets of three letters, these textual units being treated as symbols without reference to their identities as component parts of words, phrases and sentences. Every practical cipher system must combine (1) a set of rules, processes or steps constituting the basic cryptographic method of treatment or procedure, called the general system, which is agreed upon in advance by the communicators and which is constant in character, with (2) a specific key which is variable in character. In enciphering plain text, the specific key, which may consist of a number or a series of numbers or a word, phrase, sentence, etc., controls the steps under the general system and determines the specific nature or exact composition of the ciph-

message produced; in decipherment the specific key similarly controls the steps and determines what the deciphered text will be. When all operations are performed correctly, the two plain texts (before and after the cryptography) should be identical or nearly so, save for minor differences arising from errors in their encipherment and transmission or in their reception and decipherment. The general system should be such that even if it is known to the enemy no properly enciphered message can be read by him unless he also knows the specific key or keys applicable to that message.

Despite a great diversity in the external appearance and internal constitution of ciphers, there are only two basic classes of systems—transposition and substitution. (Concealment ciphers are excluded from the discussion.) A transposition cipher involves a rearrangement or change in the sequence of the letters of the plain-text message without any change in their identity; a substitution cipher involves a replacement of the plain-text letters by other letters (or by other symbols) without any change in their sequence. The two systems may be combined in a single cryptosystem.

The majority of transposition systems involve inscribing the letters of the plain text in a geometrical design called a matrix, beginning at a prearranged initial point and following a prescribed route, and then transcribing the letters from the matrix, beginning at another prearranged initial point and following another prescribed route. The matrix may take the form of a rectangle, trapezoid, octagon, triangle, etc., but systems in which the specific keys consist solely in keeping the matrices, the initial points and the routes secret are not often now employed because of their limited variability and, therefore, their relatively low degree of security. In this same class also fall systems which employ perforated cardboard matrices called grilles, descriptions of which will be found in most of the older books on cryptography. The transposition system most commonly used in practice is that designated as columnar transposition, wherein the transposition matrix takes the form of a simple rectangular figure the dimensions of which are determined in each instance jointly by the length of the individual message and the length of the specific key. An example is shown in fig. 1.

Plain-text message: **DELAY DEPARTURE UNTIL FURTHER NOTICE.**

T	E	L	E	G	R	A	P	H
9	2	6	3	4	8	1	7	5
D	E	L	A	Y	D	E	P	A
R	T	U	R	E	U	N	T	I
L	F	U	R	T	H	E	R	N
O	T	I	C	E				

} Key

Cryptogram

ENEET FTARR CYETE AINLU UIPTR DUHDR LO

Fig. 1.—An example of simple columnar transposition. The numerical key is derived by numbering the letters of the keyword ("telegraph") in accordance with their relative order of appearance in the ordinary alphabet, repeated letters, if present in the key, being numbered in sequence from left to right. The message is written in the normal manner from left to right in successive horizontal lines underneath the key, forming a "rectangle" of columns of letters. These letters are then transcribed in regular groups of five from the rectangle by reading down the columns, taking the latter in the sequence indicated by the key numbers. The last line of the rectangle may be completely filled with letters, nonsignificants being added if necessary; but the security of the method is considerably increased if the last line shows one or more blank spaces, as in this example.

In the foregoing case the letters undergo a single transposition; in cases involving double transposition, that is, wherein the letters undergo two successive transpositions, the security of the cryptograms is very greatly increased, provided the methods selected are such as will effectively disarrange individual letters and not merely whole columns or rows. A practical system of double transposition is illustrated in fig. 2. The principal advantages of transposition systems lie in their comparative simplicity, speed of operation and, in some cases, their high degree of security; but despite these important considerations they do not at the present time play a prominent role in practical cryptography.

Substitution systems involve the use of conventional or cipher alphabets composed of two juxtaposed sequences, one (either expressed or implied) corresponding to the letters of the ordinary alphabet (*a, b, c . . . x, y, z*), the other containing their respective cipher equivalents. The complexity of a substitution system usually depends upon three factors: (1) the specific composition of the cipher alphabet or alphabets employed; (2) the number of them involved in a single cryptogram; and (3) the specific manner in which they are used. As to their composition, cipher alphabets are of various types and are known under various names, such as standard, direct, reversed, systematically mixed, key-word mixed, random mixed, reciprocal, etc., all having reference to the nature of the two sequences composing them, the interrelations existing among them internally or externally, etc. The most important factor in connection with a cipher alphabet is whether its two sequences, regardless of their composition, are known or unknown to the enemy; for, if known, any conventional or disarranged alphabet may be handled with the same facility as the normal alphabet. As to the number of alphabets involved in it, a cryptogram is either monoalphabetic, involving a single cipher alphabet, or polyalphabetic, involving two or more alphabets. In essence the difference between the two types lies in the fact that in the former the equivalence between plain-text and cipher letters is invariant, *i.e.,* the equivalence is of a constant or invariable nature throughout the cryptogram, whereas in the latter it is of a changing or variable nature, controlled by the key. With regard to secrecy, the third condition mentioned above, namely, the specific manner in which the various cipher alphabets are employed, is the most important in determining the degree of security or resistance the cryptogram will have against cryptanalysis, as explained below.

Plain-text message: **DELAY DEPARTURE UNTIL FURTHER NOTICE.**

(a)

T	E	L	E	G	R	A	P	H
9	2	6	3	4	8	1	7	5
D	E	L	A	Y	D	E	P	A
R	T	U	R	E	U	N	T	I
L	F	U	R	T	H	E	R	N
O	T	I	C	E				

(b)

T	E	L	E	G	R	A	P	H
9	2	6	3	4	8	1	7	5
E	N	E	E	T	F	T	A	R
R	C	Y	E	T	E	A	I	N
L	U	U	I	P	T	R	D	U
H	D	R	L	O				

Cryptogram

TARNC UDEEI LTTPO RNUEY URAID FETER LH

Fig. 2.—An example of true double transposition. The cipher letters resulting from the first transposition rectangle (a) are written under the key of the second transposition rectangle (b) just as though they constituted plain-text, that is, from left to right, in successive horizontal rows. The final transposition is then performed in exactly the same manner as in fig. 1, yielding five-letter groups. The two rectangles may be based upon the same keyword, as in this example, or upon wholly different keywords.

Monoalphabetic substitution is usually uniliteral; *i.e.,* each letter of the plain text is replaced by a single character. Cases of biliteral, triliteral, etc., substitution are sometimes encountered; an example using biliteral equivalents is shown in fig. 3. No matter how many characters are in the groups composing the cipher equivalents for plain-text letters, if the groups are always the same for each letter, the substitution system is still monoalphabetic and the cipher can be treated as such.

Polyalphabetic systems are often referred to as double-key systems and, as noted above, employ two or more cipher alphabets in the encipherment of single dispatches. In a given system the

Plain-text message: **DELAY DEPARTURE UNTIL FURTHER NOTICE.**

Second letter (columns); First letter (rows)

	A	B	C	D	E
A	T	E	L	G	R
B	A	P	H	B	C
C	D	F	I	K	M
D	N	O	Q	S	U
E	V	W	X	Y	Z

Enciphering

Plain:	D	E	L	A	Y	D	E	P	A	R	T
Cipher:	CA	AB	AC	BA	ED	CA	AB	BB	BA	AE	AA
Plain:	U	R	E	U	N	T	I	L	F	U	R
Cipher:	DE	AE	AB	DE	DA	AA	CC	AC	CB	DE	AE
Plain:	T	H	E	R	N	O	T	I	C	E	
Cipher:	AA	BC	AB	AE	DA	DB	AA	CC	BE	AB	

Cryptogram

CAABA CBAED CAABB BBAAE etc.

Fig. 3.—An example of biliteral, monoalphabetic substitution. A keyword alphabet of 25 letters (I serving also for J) is written in a square 5 x 5. (In this case the alphabet is based upon the word "telegraph.)" The letters (A,B,C,D, E) at the side and top of the square, taken in pairs, can then be used to represent the letters within the square. Thus, D = CA, E = AB, etc. The letters at the side of the square may be the same as or different from those at the top; in both cases keywords, identical or different, may be used instead of the letters A,B,C,D,E.

cipher alphabets may be entirely independent or they may be interrelated. In the simplest case of interrelated alphabets, that resulting from juxtaposing, at all points of coincidence, two primary sequences which are normal sequences proceeding in the same direction ($a, b, c \ldots x, y, z$), the secondary cipher alphabets are called standard alphabets; these when successively tabulated yield a symmetrical or square table (fig. 4) which is generally referred to in the literature as a Vigenère table, a quadricular table, etc.

Such a table may be used in several ways. The most common method employs the top row of letters as the plain-text sequence and the successive horizontal rows as the cipher sequences, each of which may be designated by its initial letter. Thus, the fourth or D alphabet is the one in which plain text *A* is represented by cipher *D*; *i.e.*, $A_p = D_c$, $B_p = E_c$, etc. In the ninth or I alphabet, $A_p = I_c$, $B_p = J_c$, etc. Therefore, when several such alphabets are to be employed, the letters of a key word can serve to indicate the number, identity and sequence of the cipher alphabets to be used consecutively in the cryptographic operations.

This type of cryptogram is usually referred to as the Vigenère cipher or as *le chiffre indéchiffrable,* although Blaise de Vigenère never claimed that he invented the table or the system; he was merely among the first to describe it (*see* below).

Key letter \ Plain-text letter	A	B	C	D	E	F	G	H	I	J	K	L	M	N	O	P	Q	R	S	T	U	V	W	X	Y	Z
A	A	B	C	D	E	F	G	H	I	J	K	L	M	N	O	P	Q	R	S	T	U	V	W	X	Y	Z
B	B	C	D	E	F	G	H	I	J	K	L	M	N	O	P	Q	R	S	T	U	V	W	X	Y	Z	A
C	C	D	E	F	G	H	I	J	K	L	M	N	O	P	Q	R	S	T	U	V	W	X	Y	Z	A	B
D	D	E	F	G	H	I	J	K	L	M	N	O	P	Q	R	S	T	U	V	W	X	Y	Z	A	B	C
E	E	F	G	H	I	J	K	L	M	N	O	P	Q	R	S	T	U	V	W	X	Y	Z	A	B	C	D
F	F	G	H	I	J	K	L	M	N	O	P	Q	R	S	T	U	V	W	X	Y	Z	A	B	C	D	E
G	G	H	I	J	K	L	M	N	O	P	Q	R	S	T	U	V	W	X	Y	Z	A	B	C	D	E	F
H	H	I	J	K	L	M	N	O	P	Q	R	S	T	U	V	W	X	Y	Z	A	B	C	D	E	F	G
I	I	J	K	L	M	N	O	P	Q	R	S	T	U	V	W	X	Y	Z	A	B	C	D	E	F	G	H
J	J	K	L	M	N	O	P	Q	R	S	T	U	V	W	X	Y	Z	A	B	C	D	E	F	G	H	I
K	K	L	M	N	O	P	Q	R	S	T	U	V	W	X	Y	Z	A	B	C	D	E	F	G	H	I	J
L	L	M	N	O	P	Q	R	S	T	U	V	W	X	Y	Z	A	B	C	D	E	F	G	H	I	J	K
M	M	N	O	P	Q	R	S	T	U	V	W	X	Y	Z	A	B	C	D	E	F	G	H	I	J	K	L
N	N	O	P	Q	R	S	T	U	V	W	X	Y	Z	A	B	C	D	E	F	G	H	I	J	K	L	M
O	O	P	Q	R	S	T	U	V	W	X	Y	Z	A	B	C	D	E	F	G	H	I	J	K	L	M	N
P	P	Q	R	S	T	U	V	W	X	Y	Z	A	B	C	D	E	F	G	H	I	J	K	L	M	N	O
Q	Q	R	S	T	U	V	W	X	Y	Z	A	B	C	D	E	F	G	H	I	J	K	L	M	N	O	P
R	R	S	T	U	V	W	X	Y	Z	A	B	C	D	E	F	G	H	I	J	K	L	M	N	O	P	Q
S	S	T	U	V	W	X	Y	Z	A	B	C	D	E	F	G	H	I	J	K	L	M	N	O	P	Q	R
T	T	U	V	W	X	Y	Z	A	B	C	D	E	F	G	H	I	J	K	L	M	N	O	P	Q	R	S
U	U	V	W	X	Y	Z	A	B	C	D	E	F	G	H	I	J	K	L	M	N	O	P	Q	R	S	T
V	V	W	X	Y	Z	A	B	C	D	E	F	G	H	I	J	K	L	M	N	O	P	Q	R	S	T	U
W	W	X	Y	Z	A	B	C	D	E	F	G	H	I	J	K	L	M	N	O	P	Q	R	S	T	U	V
X	X	Y	Z	A	B	C	D	E	F	G	H	I	J	K	L	M	N	O	P	Q	R	S	T	U	V	W
Y	Y	Z	A	B	C	D	E	F	G	H	I	J	K	L	M	N	O	P	Q	R	S	T	U	V	W	X
Z	Z	A	B	C	D	E	F	G	H	I	J	K	L	M	N	O	P	Q	R	S	T	U	V	W	X	Y

Fig. 4.—The simple Vigenère table. The cipher equivalent of a given plain-text letter enciphered by a given key letter is that letter which stands at the intersection of the vertical column headed by the former and the horizontal row begun by the latter. Thus, plain-text letter E enciphered by key letter M yields cipher letter Q, or, in brief notation, $E_p(M_k) = Q_c$; $E_p(X_k) = B_c$, etc.

Various modifications of the simple square table are encountered, these involving different types and arrangements of the sequences therein, but in every case where these sequences can be arranged so as to exhibit symmetry of position as regards the order in which the letters fall in the successive rows or columns, sliding or concentric primary sequences may be employed to produce the same results as the table and are often more convenient.

Polyalphabetic substitution systems may be classified as periodic or aperiodic, depending upon whether or not the cryptograms produced by them exhibit external phenomena of a cyclic nature. Periodicity is exhibited externally whenever the substitution process involves the use of keying elements which are used in a repetitive manner and which, in a single message, operate in conjunction with a fixed number of cipher alphabets, as would the example shown in fig. 5.

Polyalphabetic systems of the aperiodic type are of great diversity in construction. In these systems periodicity is either entirely lacking because of the nature of the method or it is suppressed by incorporating elements which serve as periodicity interrupters. In the well-known aperiodic system designated as the running-key or nonrepeating-key system, periodicity is avoided by employing for the key the running text of a book, identical copies of which are in possession of the correspondents. The starting point of the keying sequence is agreed upon in advance,

Key:	T R O Y T	R O Y T R	O Y T R O	Y T R O Y
Plain-text:	L E T T E	R N O T Y	E T R E C	E I V E D
Cipher:	E V H R X	I B M M P	S R K V Q	C B M S B

Fig. 5.—An example of multiple alphabet substitution. The alphabets of the simple Vigenère table (fig. 4) are used in conjunction with the keyword TROY, which is written above the plain text and repeated as many times as required. Each letter is then enciphered by the keyletter above it. Thus, for the first letter, $L_p(T_k) = E_c$; for the second letter, $E_p(R_k) = V_c$, etc. Usually all the plain-text letters governed by the first letter of the key are enciphered in succession, then those governed by the second, etc., this method reducing the possibility of error. In practice, the keyword, and therefore the period, is usually longer than that employed in this example, words and phrases of 15 to 20 or more letters being common. Much more important, however, is the fact that the alphabets employed in modern times are seldom those of the simple Vigenère table, but are mixed alphabets, the use of which makes the cryptograms more secure against solution.

or is indicated in one of many ways by means of elements called indicators, which designate the exact point where the sequence begins. Another type of nonrepeating-key system, often designated as the autokey system, is that in which, beginning with a preconcerted key letter, each cipher letter (or sometimes each plain-text letter) becomes the key letter for the encipherment of the next plain-text letter.

The various systems of substitution thus far mentioned are monographic in nature, involving single plain-text letters. In digraphic systems substitution is by pairs of letters and uses preagreed cipher squares or matrices in which the letters of the alphabet are disposed according to some key and the cipher equivalents of pairs of plain-text letters are found by following prearranged rules. One of the best-known systems of this sort is that called the Playfair cipher, named after Lyon, Baron Playfair, but invented by Sir Charles Wheatstone. It is illustrated in fig. 6.

Properly selected methods of transposition and substitution when combined into a single system result in producing cryptograms of great security, but because of the additional complexities of operation introduced by the combination, with the resultant increased possibilities of error, such systems are not often encountered in practice.

L	E	X	I	N
G	T	O	A	B
C	D	F	H	K
M	P	Q	R	S
U	V	W	Y	Z

1. Message: AM FOLLOWING ON NEXT TRAIN.
2. Plain-text: AM FO LX LO WI NG ON NE XT TR AI NX
3. Cipher: GR QF EI XG YX LB BX LX EO AP HA LI

Cryptogram

4. GRQFE IXGYX LBBXL XEOAP HALI

Fig. 6.—The Playfair cipher; an example of digraphic substitution. An alphabet square of 25 letters (I serving also as J) based upon a keyword (in this case "Lexington") is drawn up, and substitution is performed with pairs of letters. Three cases as regards the position occupied in the square by the members of a pair are possible; they lie (1) in the same horizontal row, or (2) in the same vertical column, or (3) at the opposite ends of one of the diagonals of an imaginary rectangle. By studying the following examples under each case the method of finding equivalents will become apparent: Case (1) LI = EN, AB = BG, OB = AG; Case (2) ED = TP, EV = TE, PV = VE; Case (3) ER = IP, IM = LR, ST = PB. The text of the message to be enciphered, line 1 in the figure, is divided up into pairs, line 2. Double-letter pairs in the text are to be separated by an interposed letter such as X, as shown in the case of the word "following" in this example. Note also the addition of the letter "X" to the end of the message in order to make a pair of letters. The cipher equivalents are shown in line 3, the final cryptogram in five-letter groups, in line 4. Various arrangements of letters in the alphabet square are possible, and completely disarranged alphabets may be employed.

Code Systems.—Basically, a code system is merely a type of substitution system in which the textual units that undergo cryptographic treatment are of varying and unequal lengths. Generally they are entire words, but often they may be single letters, syllables, numbers or phrases of varying length and sometimes whole sentences. The cryptoprinciple underlying code systems is very old and has as its essential element a specially compiled list of words, phrases and sentences, each of which is accompanied by a code group which may be another word (real or artificial) or a group of letters or figures. Identical copies of specialized lists of the foregoing sort, called codebooks or codes, are held by the communicators. In encoding a message it is necessary merely to refer to the codebook and replace the words, phrases or sentences composing the message by the code groups assigned them, constructing the code message, step by step, in this manner and using the fewest code groups possible. As to their cryptographic construction or arrangement of contents, codes may be of the one-part or the two-part type, the principal difference between them being shown in fig. 7.

The condensing power of a code obviously depends upon the extent and the nature of its vocabulary. The security of a code system depends somewhat upon the distribution and construction of the codebook, but mostly upon whether it is used in conjunction with a good cipher system which is superimposed on the code text and the purpose of which is to afford secrecy, in the case of purchasable or publicly available codes, or additional secrecy, in

One-part Code	Two-part Code	
	Encoding	*Decoding*
ABABA—A	KABOL—A	ABABA—Abeyance
ABACE—Abandon-ing-s	STOLG—Abandon-ing-s	ABACE—Procedure
ABADI—Abandoned	EXIFO—Abandoned	ABADI—To purchase
ABAFO—Abate-ing-s	ZUMRA—Abated	ABAFO—Commenced
ABAGU—Abated	ABABA—Abeyance	ABAGU—Do not think
ABAHY—Abeyance	ROABY—Abide-ing-s	ABAHY—Recorded
ABEBE—Abide-ing-s		
ABECI—Abided		
.....—..........	.....—..........	.....—..........
ZYZYZ—Zone-s	BIKUR—Zone-s	ZYZYZ—According to

Fig. 7.—Extracts from typical one-part and two-part codes. In the one-part type the code groups and the vocabulary are arranged in parallel, alphabetic (or numerical) sequences, so that a single book serves for encoding as well as for decoding. In the two-part type the encoding book lists the elements of the vocabulary in alphabetic order but the code groups are in random order, so that a decoding book, in which the code groups appear in alphabetic (or numerical) order accompanied by their meanings, is essential. The degree of secrecy afforded by a code of the latter type is much greater than that afforded by one of the former type, all other things being equal.

the case of private or governmental codes. Code messages which undergo this second step are said to be superenciphered, reenciphered or, simply, reciphered. The principal purpose of code in commercial communications is to effect economy in their cost of electrical transmission, secrecy being usually of secondary importance (except in certain types of banking operations). Codes for general business communications are purchasable from their publishers and therefore in themselves provide no secrecy. Many business firms, however, use specially compiled private codes which, if carefully restricted in distribution, may be regarded as confidential or secret. In governmental and especially in diplomatic or military communications secrecy is generally of primary importance, economy is secondary.

Governmental codes which are intended to be secret are, of course, very carefully guarded in their production, distribution and usage and, as a general rule, messages in such codes are superenciphered.

Cryptoapparatus.—Cryptodevices and cryptomachines vary in complexity from simple, superimposed, concentrically or eccentrically rotating disks to large mechanical machines and electrically operated cryptoteleprinting apparatus. One of the best devices of the more simple, mechanical type is that known as the Bazeries cylinder (*see* fig. 8), named after the French cryptographer who is commonly credited with its invention in 1891. The principle upon which the device is based was, however, conceived

FIG. 8.—THE BAZERIES CYLINDER

The Bazeries cylinder consists of a set of 20 disks, each bearing on its periphery a differently mixed alphabet. The disks, which bear identifying numbers from 1 to 20, are assembled upon the shaft in an order that corresponds to a numerical key. To encipher the message, 20 letters are taken at a time, and the disks are revolved so as to align the 20 letters horizontally; the letters of any row can be taken for the cipher text. In deciphering, the cipher letters, taken 20 at a time, are aligned horizontally; the disks are then locked into position. By slowly revolving the whole cylinder and examining each row of letters, one and only one row will be found to yield intelligible text all the way across

many years before by Thomas Jefferson (*see* Jefferson's *Papers* in the Library of Congress, vol. 232, item 41,575).

Devices of the sort exemplified in fig. 8 soon proved to be inadequate for modern cryptocommunications, as regards not only speed, accuracy and facility in operation but also security of the end product. It was not long, therefore, before more automatic

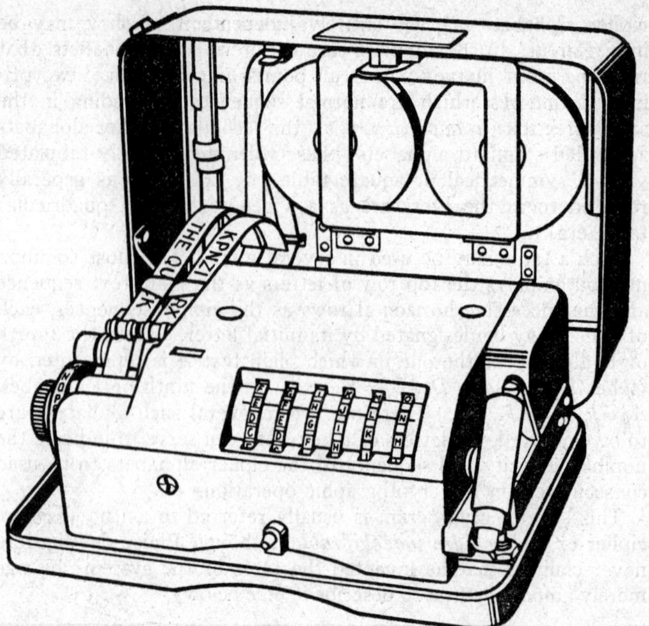

FIG. 9.—PORTABLE CRYPTODEVICE WHICH PRODUCES A PRINTED RECORD OF THE CIPHER TEXT AS WELL AS OF THE PLAIN TEXT. THE LETTERS TO BE ENCIPHERED OR DECIPHERED ARE SET BY TWIRLING THE INDICATING DISK SHOWN AT LEFT AND OPERATING THE LEVER AT THE RIGHT. THE SIX WHEELS CONTROL THE CRYPTOGRAPHY, IN CONJUNCTION WITH CERTAIN OTHER VARIABLE KEYING ELEMENTS INSIDE THE MACHINE

and more secure types of apparatus were invented and developed. In such apparatus rotatory components referred to as cipher rotors have come to be of primary importance. The rotors may be of a mechanical or an electrical type. Fig. 9 shows a machine which uses a series of mechanical rotors to produce an extremely long, continuously changing key for encipherment. Although the results of manipulating the machine are printed upon a paper tape, the absence of a typewriter keyboard makes operation of the machine slow and tedious. Fig. 10 shows a machine which uses a series of juxtaposed electrical rotors and stators to form a path for the passage of electric currents connecting the 26 keys of a keyboard to the 26 lamps of a light board upon which the results of manipulating the keys are indicated. Automatic angular displacements of the rotors serve to vary the path with each depression of any key of the keyboard. From a practical point of view such a machine is not satisfactory for offices engaging extensively in cryptocommunication since it lacks an automatic recording or

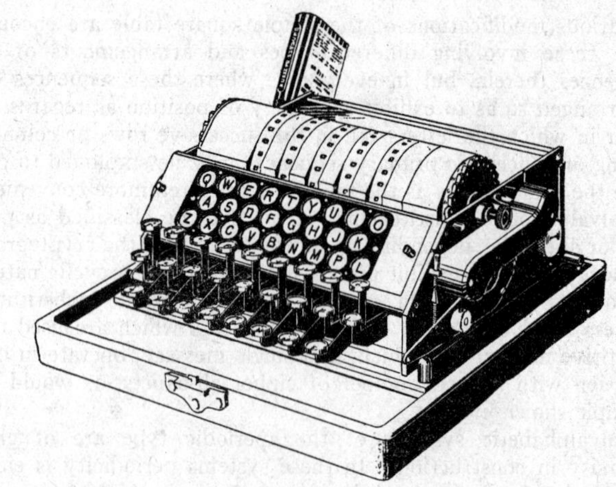

FIG. 10.—ELECTRICAL CIPHER MACHINE EMPLOYING A TYPEWRITER KEYBOARD

printing mechanism and the results of operating the keyboard have to be recorded by the operator by hand. Therefore, a machine combining both a keyboard and a printing mechanism had to come, sooner or later. Such a combination of components is shown in fig. 11. Machines of this type, which are not necessarily associated with the electrical communication system but which merely produce an end product (a printed record) that can be given to a communication centre or telegraph office for transmission, are called off-line cryptomachines.

But even this stage in improvement in cryptocommunications

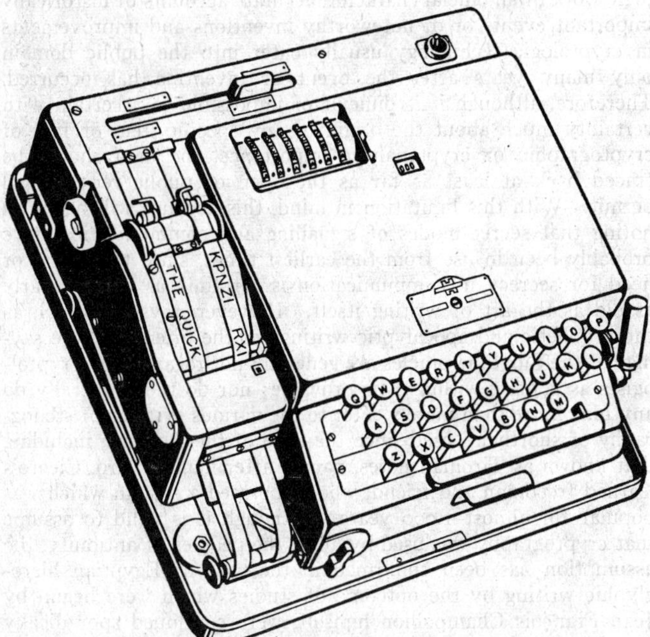

FIG. 11.—THE CRYPTODEVICE OF FIG. 9 EQUIPPED WITH A KEYBOARD AND DRIVEN BY AN ELECTRIC MOTOR. THE TWO MACHINES ARE CRYPTOGRAPHICALLY INTERCOMMUNICABLE. THE OPERATING LEVER AT RIGHT IS USED IN CASE OF POWER FAILURE

proved inadequate and communicators soon began to see need for on-line cryptomachines, *i.e.*, apparatus which combines in a single and instantaneous operation the following steps: (1) manipulation of a key of the keyboard at the transmitting station to correspond to a character of the plain-text message; (2) automatic encipherment of that character to form a cipher character; (3) electrical representation of that character by a signal or a permutation or combination of signals corresponding to the cipher character; (4) electrical transmission of the signal or signals; (5) their reception at the distant end; (6) their translation into a cipher character; (7) automatic decipherment of the character; and (8) printing the deciphered character—all this at the rate of at least 300 characters (=60 words) per minute. In fig. 12 is shown a prototype of such a machine. It is obvious, of course, that machines of this advanced type can be employed only where there is direct access to transmission and reception facilities.

As a result of extensive research and development after 1920, machines of the sorts here described have undergone considerable improvement, and further progress in written-cryptocommunications technology appears to lie in this direction.

Signal Intelligence.—The principal components of signal intelligence are: (1) communication intelligence, derived from the interception and analysis of signals which are involved in the exchange of messages or communications between persons and which are, therefore, of the type designated as communication signals; and (2) electronic intelligence, derived from the interception and analysis of electromagnetic radiations which are of a type other than those used in communications, such as radar, identification and recognition signals, navigational beacons, etc., and which are therefore designated as noncommunication signals. It should be noted, however, that it is often difficult to draw a line of demarcation between communication intelligence and electronic intelligence because these two fields deal with signals which merge into each other in the continuous spectrum generally referred to as that pertaining to communications electronics.

Communication Intelligence.—This phase of cryptology deals with the processes, methods or means employed in deriving information by intercepting and analyzing enemy communications. Its principal components are: (1) interception and forwarding of traffic (messages) to analysis centres; (2) traffic analysis, including radio direction or position finding and operator identification; and (3) cryptanalysis or solution (and translation, when necessary) of the texts of the messages. Only the last two components will be discussed.

Traffic Analysis.—Stated in general terms, traffic analysis involves studying the messages exchanged within a communications network for the purpose of penetrating the signal security camouflage superimposed thereon.

Such study permits reconstructing the networks from data such as volume, direction and routing of messages, frequencies, schedules and call signs used, etc. When the most important features of the networks have been thus ascertained, the analyst is not only able to ascertain the geographic locations and dispositions of military units (order of battle) and important movements of these units, but also to predict with varying degrees of reliability (based upon inferences) the area and extent of future military tactical or strategic operations.

Cryptanalysis.—The science of solving cryptograms by analysis is called cryptanalysis, to distinguish the indirect methods of reading cryptograms from the direct methods which, of course, require a knowledge of the basic method and specific key, in the case of ciphers, or possession of the codebook, in the case of codes. Apart from the more simple, classical types, nearly every scientifically constructed cryptographic system presents a unique case in cryptanalysis, the unravelling of which requires the exercise of unusual powers of observation, inductive and deductive reasoning, much concentration, perseverance and a vivid imagination; but all these qualities are of little avail without a special aptitude arising from extensive practical experience. It is worthwhile to note that the resistance which a specific cryptosystem will have against cryptanalysis is often vitally affected by the sophistication of the rules for its use and by the degree to which these rules are observed by cipher clerks. In respect to the latter, Francis Bacon's comment in his *Of the Advancement of Learning* (1605) is as true today as the day it was written: "But in regarde of the rawnesse and unskillfulnesse of the hands, through which they passe, the greatest Matters, are many times carryed in the weakest cyphars."

A preliminary requisite to the analysis of a cryptogram is a determination of the language in which its plain text is written, information which is either already at hand in the case of official communications or which, in the case of private ones, can usually be obtained from extraneous circumstances. Next comes a determination as to whether a cipher or a code system is involved;

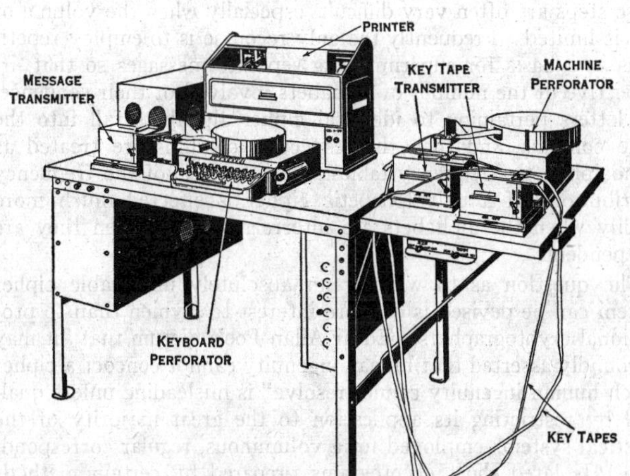

FIG. 12.—A PRINTING TELEGRAPH CIPHER MACHINE

this is based upon the fact that differences in their external appearance are usually sufficiently well marked to be detectable. If the cryptogram is in cipher, the next step is to determine whether transposition or substitution is involved. This determination is made on the basis of the fact that in plain text the vowels and consonants are present in definite proportions. Since transposition involves only a rearrangement of the original letters, it follows that if a cryptogram contains vowels and consonants in the proportions normally found in plain text in the language in question, it is of the transposition class; if not, it is of the substitution class. The solution of transposition ciphers involves much experimentation with matrices of various types and dimensions, clues to which are afforded by the number of letters in the messages and extraneous circumstances. The assumption of the presence of probable words is often necessary. Special methods of solution based upon a study of messages of identical lengths, or with identical beginnings or endings, are often possible to apply when much traffic has been intercepted. Finally, the presence of letters which individually are of low frequency but which when present have a great affinity for each other and form pairs of moderate or high frequency, such as *qu* in Spanish or *ch* in German, afford clues leading to solution.

The basis upon which the solution of practically all substitution ciphers rests is the well-known fact that every written alphabetic language manifests a high degree of constancy in the relative frequencies with which its individual letters and combinations of letters are employed. For example, English telegraphic texts show the following relative frequencies in 1,000 letters, based upon an actual count of 100,000 letters appearing in a large but miscellaneous assortment of telegrams of a commercial and governmental nature, but all in plain language:

E	T	R	I	N	O	A	S	D	L	C	H	F
126	90	83	76	76	74	72	58	40	36	33	33	30
U	P	M	Y	G	W	V	B	X	K	Q	J	Z
30	27	25	21	18	14	13	11	5	3	3	2	1

These characteristic relative frequencies serve as a basis for identifying the plain-text values of the cipher letters, but only when the cipher has been reduced to its simplest terms. Thus, the problem of solving a monoalphabetic substitution cipher involves only one step, since the text is already in the simplest possible terms, and regardless of the kind of cipher alphabet employed practically every example of 25 or more characters representing the monoalphabetic encipherment of a "sensible" message in English can readily be solved by the well-known principles of frequency, made popular by Edgar Allan Poe's romantic tale *The Gold Bug*. However, the problem of solving a polyalphabetic substitution cipher involves three principal steps: (1) determining the number of cipher alphabets involved; (2) distributing the cipher letters into the respective individual frequency tables to which they belong; and (3) analyzing each of the latter on the basis of normal frequencies in plain text of the language involved. In the case of aperiodic ciphers, because of the absence of cyclic phenomena, these steps are often very difficult, especially when the volume of text is limited. Frequently the only recourse is to employ repetitions as a basis for superimposing separate messages so that, irrespective of the number of alphabets involved or their sequence, the letters pertaining to identical cipher alphabets fall into the same columns, and then the respective columns are treated as monoalphabetic frequency tables. The analysis of the frequency distributions of a polyalphabetic cipher is effected much more readily when the alphabets are interrelated than when they are independent.

The question as to whether an absolutely unsolvable cipher system can be devised is of more interest to laymen than to professional cryptographers. Edgar Allan Poe's dictum that "it may be roundly asserted that human ingenuity cannot concoct a cipher which human ingenuity cannot resolve" is misleading unless qualified by restricting its application to the great majority of the practical systems employed for a voluminous, regular correspondence. Isolated short cryptograms prepared by certain methods may resist solution indefinitely; and a letter-for-letter cipher system which employs, once and only once, a keying sequence composed of characters or elements in a random and entirely unpredictable sequence may be considered holocryptic, that is, messages in such a system cannot be read by indirect processes involving cryptanalysis, but only by direct processes involving possession of the key or keys, obtained either legitimately, by virtue of being among the intended communicators, or by stealth.

History.—It may as well be stated at the outset that as of the 1950s there did not exist in any language a detailed, authentic and publicly available history of cryptology. Moreover, because of the curtain of secrecy which is invariably placed around cryptologic work of an official character, accurate accounts of historically important events or of noteworthy inventions and improvements in cryptologic technology usually enter into the public domain only many years after the event or invention has occurred. Therefore, although it is difficult or impossible to ascertain with certainty much about the origin of any specific item or fact of cryptographic or cryptanalytic importance, the data should be traced back at least as far as the open or public records will permit. With this limitation in mind, this account will begin by noting that secret modes of signalling and communication have probably been in use from the earliest times, since the desire or need for secrecy in communication is certainly as old or nearly as old as the art of writing itself. However, mysteries such as the prophetic and apocalyptic writings of the orient and the sayings of the Sibylline oracles are generally not regarded by cryptologists as coming within their province; nor do they generally do anything more than merely refer to the various systems of stenography or shorthand used since the time of the Romans, including that known as Tironian notes, named after Tullius Tiro, Cicero's learned freedman and friend, who elaborated a system which was popular for almost 1,000 years. Although it is valid to assume that cryptography was used by all of the peoples of antiquity, the assumption has been confirmed in the case of Egyptian hieroglyphic writing by the outcome of studies which were begun by Jean François Champollion himself, were continued sporadically by other students for many years and culminated in 1932, disclosing that not one but three different sorts or degrees of cryptography were actually used by the ancient Egyptians. Cryptography was practised among the ancient Jews, whose Talmudic scholars dealt with it as a part or phase of their Kabbalah, which includes certain operations of a cryptographic nature. The ancient Greeks were users of the art, and at least one cryptographic device, called the scytale, is known to have been employed by the Lacedemonians for secret communications between military commanders in the field and their superiors at home. In the writings of Aeneas Tacticus (360–390 B.C.) is to be found the very earliest treatise on cryptography thus far discovered; in addition to treating of secret dispatches, they contain a description of a cipher disk, a detailed explanation of which cannot here be included. Numerous ancient Greek documents exist which are either partially or wholly in cipher; and one cipher alphabet found therein has been traced back to the 9th century A.D. Despite the fact that Roman cryptographic documents are rather rare it is well known that the Romans used ciphers, for there are numerous references to those which Caesar and Augustus employed. In fact, the name Caesar is often used in cryptologic literature to designate the type of cipher alphabet and cipher system known as the monoalphabetic cipher using standard alphabets. In the middle ages (*c.* 450–1450) cryptography was employed rather infrequently, for the most part in connection with the pseudo sciences of alchemy and astrology. The most widespread cryptographic system of that period corresponds to that used by the Roman emperor Augustus, in which a letter was merely replaced by the one following it in the normal alphabet (but *z* was replaced by *aa*). Most often, however, only certain letters were thus replaced, sometimes only the vowels.

The beginnings of modern cryptography can be traced back to Italy, the birthplace, as well, of modern diplomacy. Many cipher alphabets have come down to us which were used in the official messages of the papacy as well as in those of the early Italian republics. Ciphers were used in Venice as far back as in 1226; in Mantua and in Modena as early as 1305; and in Lucca, Florence, Siena, Pisa and Milan before 1450. It was also in Italy, beginning soon after 1500, that cryptologic operations first came to be organized on an effective basis. The invention of new cipher systems was promoted and reserves of cryptographic vocabularies were prepared and kept in readiness for prompt issue as replacements for old or compromised ones. The earliest extant piece of work of a cryptographic nature is a small manual or compilation of the ciphers used about 1379 by Gabriel de Lavinde of Parma and preserved in the Vatican archives. In these ciphers all the letters were represented by arbitrary symbols and the vowels were treated no differently than the consonants in regard to the number of equivalents assigned them. However, some of these ciphers included nulls and others included brief lists of words and proper nouns, compilations first called nomenclators, then repertories and, later, small codes. By 1400 A.D. it had become apparent that each of the vowels should have more than a single cipher equivalent and there is a record of a cipher system involving a reversed standard alphabet with three different supplementary symbols as variants for each vowel. By the 15th century, according to Aloys Meister, Italian cryptography had been elaborated to the point where "three to six different symbols could be used to represent a single letter of the alphabet, the individual syllables—arranged alphabetically for this purpose, ba, be, bi, bo, bu, ca, ce, ci, etc.,— had specific cipher equivalents, and an ever-increasing number of complete words were incorporated into the nomenclators. Their abundance in content became so great that it was possible to fill a lengthy alphabetic index with the special equivalents for syllables and words . . ." The first complete cipher, *i.e.,* one containing arbitrary symbols for each of the letters and variants for the vowels, as well as nulls and a nomenclator, is exemplified by a Venetian cipher of 1411, cited by Luigi Pasini. In the first half of the 15th century, after some further expansion in content, nomenclators attained such a state of development and practical utility that they remained for centuries the prototype of the diplomatic repertories used by nearly all European governments, as well as by that of the young and rapidly growing republic in the western hemisphere, the United States. Before continuing with the account of the further development of cryptosystems of this sort it may be well to direct attention to the invention and development of another cryptosystem which, originating in the very simple devices of the ancients, culminated some time during the 16th century in the so-called *chiffre indéchiffrable* ("the indecipherable cipher") often referred to as the Vigenère cipher (fig. 4). It should be noted, however, that Vigenère's description of the cipher differs decidedly from the form usually ascribed to him and presents an essentially more difficult problem to the cryptanalyst, that Vigenère nowhere speaks of the cipher as the *chiffre indéchiffrable par excellence,* and that, except for an autokeying principle, Vigenère lays no claim to having originated the cipher.

Despite the much-advertised virtues and security of the Vigenère cipher, practical cryptographers and cryptanalysts tended to put their faith rather in the older nomenclators and repertories, and it is therefore necessary to turn once more to these cryptoaids and follow their progress.

The repertories used by France in the 16th century, under Louis XIII and Louis XIV, underwent important improvement with the introduction of an innovation which is now called the randomized or two-part arrangement of contents, illustrated in fig. 7. This improvement also soon found its way into the official cryptography of England and other countries. The repertories used by the papal court in the same century incorporated an additional new feature, that of making some or all of the cipher characters represent two or more different letters. After attaining this fairly advanced state of development, European cryptography went into a decline that reached its lowest level under Napoleon I; it is possible that one of the factors leading to the disaster which overtook him in Russia was the solution by the Russians of intercepted French ciphers. After the middle of the 19th century, stimulated perhaps by the spreading use of electromagnetic telegraphy, there came an expansion in the content of repertories, soon to be called codes. By the end of that century large codes containing 100,000 or more words and phrases were compiled not only for governmental but also for commercial communications. In such codes, of course, the length of the code equivalents had to be increased too, and code groups came to be composed, first, of groups of figures or of bona fide dictionary words, then of artificial words and, later, of five-letter groups constructed scientifically so as to obtain the maximum not only in economy in cost of transmission but also in efficiency in the correction of transmission errors. For another 75 years, beginning about 1860, the cryptoprinciples embodied in the early nomenclators but now expanded into large codes were the ones preferred for diplomatic and commercial cryptocommunications; literal or letter-for-letter ciphers were used only rarely for such communications. On the other hand, for military cryptocommunications, cipher systems of the latter type were preferred, except for high-level or strategic communications. In the U.S., during the War Between the States (1861–65), the Federal army employed small repertories in connection with word transposition, the so-called route cipher. The Confederate army used the Vigenère cipher—which the Federal army cryptanalysts are said to have solved every time a message in it was intercepted.

During the first two years of World War I cipher systems were used almost to the exclusion of code systems by all belligerents for protecting tactical communications in the field of operations, although code systems continued to be used for diplomatic and high-level strategic military cryptocommunications. By 1917, however, codes came to be used for the secret communications of the smaller and intermediate-size military formations. The extent of their vocabularies varied with the size of the unit, so that the code for communications between large units might contain 10,000 words and phrases, whereas that for communications between small units might contain only a few hundred or less. After about 1925 the direction of development and improvement in governmental cryptocommunications tended to explore and exploit the possibilities of automatic cipher machines, as indicated earlier in this article, and this took place in all types of secret communications: diplomatic, military, naval, air, etc. This change in direction of evolution and development of cryptosystems, code systems giving way to cipher systems in practical cryptocommunications where secrecy is the primary consideration, is only an obvious result, in the field of communications, of the increased tempo of mechanization in all fields since the beginning of the 20th century. Cipher systems, the units of which are generally single letters, lend themselves much more readily to mechanization than do code systems, the units of which are generally complete words and often long phrases or sentences, because the number and lengths of different permutations and combinations of electrical signals needed to represent the relatively small number of different basic units of a written alphabetic language (in English 26 letters) are very much smaller than the number and lengths of different permutations and combinations that would be required to represent the large number of different words in such a language, not to mention phrases and sentences.

This brief account of technological developments in cryptography has its counterpart in cryptanalysis, but if it is difficult to ascertain with certainty data concerning the origin of any specific cryptosystem, because of the veil of secrecy already mentioned, it is almost impossible to ascertain with certainty by whom, where or when a specific cryptanalytic principle or process was first conceived or employed. The secrecy veil in this area becomes an almost impenetrable curtain, so that it is certainly valid to assume that news of cryptanalytic success or of the invention of a new technique becomes public only many years after the events or, perhaps, never.

Under these circumstances, one hardly expects to find a historical account of the very first success in cryptanalysis, but the earliest brochure on record dealing with cryptanalytic theory is that of the Leone Battista Alberti, whose *Trattati in cifra,* written between 1467 and 1472, deals not only with cryptanalytic theories and processes but also with cryptography and statistical data. It is, therefore, the oldest treatise on cryptology in existence. The brief treatise of Sicco Simonetta, a cryptanalyst of the Sforzas at the court of Milan, which is dated July 4, 1474, and which is a strictly practical guide to cryptanalytic procedures, is the oldest treatise in the world purely devoted to cryptanalysis. Beginning about 1506 and until 1539 another Italian professional cryptanalyst, Giovanni Soro, devoted his leisure hours to the preparation of a treatise which has never been found. As was the case with cryptography, so on the cryptanalytic side the activities in the various small Italian republics and the papacy came to be organized as serious enterprises. In order to protect these activities against indiscretions or "leakage," the principles of secrecy and security were firmly established and wilful violations were treated as capital offenses. The development of technical skill was rewarded, and instruction in cryptanalysis was often carried on from one generation to the next in the same family. But, as in the cryptographic field, so in the cryptanalytic field there have been periods of progression and retrogression in technology. However, after about 1930 cryptanalytic technology progressed rather notably. The mechanization which affected cryptography also affected cryptanalysis, and the invention and development or improvement of machines to aid in or speed up the tedious processes usually involved in the solution of complex cryptosystems exercised an important effect upon the standards by which cryptosecurity had to be measured.

The foregoing is a brief history of technological developments in cryptology. Nothing has yet been said about the usually very secret but quite important roles which poor cryptography or good cryptanalysis have played in international relations, both in peace and war, and in respect to both diplomatic and military affairs. As already stated, the historical accounts of these instances usually lag many years behind the events to which they relate. But in at least one case in modern history the revelation of the spectacular role played by cryptology in diplomacy and warfare took place not very long after the event. Hearings held in Washington, D.C., 1945–46, by the joint committee on the investigation of the Pearl Harbor attack, made it clear that shortly before and during World War II U.S. cryptanalysts had considerable success in solving Japanese codes and ciphers, success indeed to the extent that it was possible for the committee to state that all witnesses familiar with the intelligence produced "have testified that it contributed enormously to the defeat of the enemy, greatly shortened the war, and saved many thousands of lives." For other instances the reader must consult some of the books listed in the bibliography, but not many will be found that pertain to relatively recent history.

Bibliography.—Although no comprehensive and authentic history of cryptology had been published by the 1950s, it is interesting to find that there does exist a comprehensive and scholarly bibliography of cryptologic literature covering practically all publicly available books and important papers on the subject: Joseph S. Galland, *An Historical and Analytical Bibliography of the Literature of Cryptology* (Evanston, Ill., 1945). Such a compilation is more helpful to specialists than to the general reader, therefore, a selection of items from the Galland bibliography may be useful. Also, after 1945 there were published a few items of importance which should be mentioned herein. Modern works worthy of special mention are as follows: André Lange and E.-A. Soudart, *Traité de cryptographie* (1925); Marcel Givierge, *Cours de cryptographie* (1925); Roger Baudouin, *Éléments de cryptographie* (1939); H. F. Gaines, *Elementary Cryptanalysis* (Boston, 1939; London, 1940); Luigi Sacco, *Manuale de crittografia*, 3rd ed. (1947); Charles Eyraud, *Precis de cryptographie moderne* (1953). (W. F. F.)

CODEX, the name given to the earliest forms of manuscript in book form (*i.e.*, the collection of written pages stitched together) which replaced the earlier roll of papyrus and the wax tablets (which when hinged or bound together formed the first codex or caudex); also the Latin form of the English word "code" (*q.v.*), meaning a body of law or regulations. For examples of famous codices, *see* the articles Bible; Libraries; and Palaeography.

CODIAEUM, a small genus of Indo-Malayan shrubs belonging to the family Euphorbiaceae. One variety, *C. variegatum pictum*, a native of Polynesia, is cultivated in greenhouses and throughout the tropics under the name of "croton" for its magnificently variegated leaves.

CODINUS, GEORGE (Georgios Kodinos), the reputed author of three extant works in Byzantine literature, two of which are anonymous in the manuscripts. It is supposed that Codinus lived toward the end of the 15th century. The works referred to are:

1. *Patria* (Τὰ Πάτριατῆς Κωνσταντινουπόλεως). It is divided into five sections: (*a*) the foundation of Constantinople; (*b*) its topography; (*c*) its works of art and sights; (*d*) its buildings; (*e*) the construction of the church of St. Sophia. It was written in the reign of Basil II (976–1025), revised under Alexius I Comnenus (1081–1118) and perhaps copied by Codinus, whose name it bears in some (later) manuscripts. The chief sources are: the *Patria* of Hesychius Illustrius of Miletus, an anonymous (*c.* 750) brief chronological record (*Παραστάσεις σύντομοι χρονικαί*) and an anonymous account (*διήγησις*) of St. Sophia (ed. by T. Preger in *Scriptores originum Constantinopolitanarum*, fasc. i [1901], to be followed by the *Patria* of Codinus). (*See* also Procopius, *De Aedificiis*, and the poem of Paulus Silentiarius on the dedication of St. Sophia.)

2. *De Officiis*, a sketch of court and higher ecclesiastical dignities and ceremonies (*cf. De Cerimoniis* of Constantine Porphyrogenitus).

3. A chronological outline of events from the beginning of the world to the taking of Constantinople by the Turks (called Agarenes in the manuscript title). It is of little value.

Bibliography.—Complete editions are (by I. Bekker) in the Bonn *Corpus scriptorum Hist. Byz.* (1839–43), where, however, some sections of the *Patria* are omitted, and in J. P. Migne, *Patrologia graeca*, clvii; *see* also C. Krumbacher, *Geschichte der byzantinischen Literatur* (1897).

CODLING MOTH (*Carpocapsa pomonella*), a small moth, the larva (caterpillar) of which is very destructive to apples and other fruit. Indigenous to Europe, it has spread, through the agency of commerce, wherever the apple is cultivated. The most effective methods of moth control are by sack-binding the tree trunks and by spraying with lead arsenate. (*See* Entomology: *Economic Entomology*.)

COD-LIVER OIL (*Oleum morrhuae*), the oil obtained from the liver of the common cod (*Gadus morrhua*) and other species of the family Gadidae. It is usually made by conducting steam into a tank of fresh livers until the mass boils vigorously. The liberated oil is promptly separated from the residue. Medicinal grades are subsequently destearinated by chilling to about 0° C. and filtering off the congealed "stearine." A technical grade known as cod oil, obtained by rotting the livers or liver residues, is used in tanning. The chief producing countries are England, Norway, Iceland and Canada; average annual world production during the years 1948–51, as reported to the United Nations, was 87,000,000 lb.

Chemically, cod-liver oil is a typical marine animal oil. It is a mixture of glycerides of many fatty acids, of which oleic acid, $C_{18}H_{34}O_2$, and gadoleic acid, $C_{20}H_{38}O_2$, are the most abundant. Some of the acids are highly unsaturated, which makes the oil subject to oxidation and causes the development of rancidity when exposed to air. The "stearine" fraction is not true stearin, but a mixture of fats of relatively high melting points. The oil contains about 1% of unsaponifiable matter, mainly cholesterol. Traces of iodine and other elements are present.

In the 19th century cod-liver oil was a folk remedy for wasting diseases. During the period 1914–22 its medicinal value was clinically established and related to the presence of vitamin A and especially vitamin D. These vitamins comprise only a minute fraction of the oil, and the content is usually expressed in units; average oil contains 1,400 international units (I.U.) of A and 100 I.U. of D per gram. The vitamin potency varies considerably; it increases with the age of the fish and varies inversely with the fatness of the liver. It also varies with the species of fish, even within the cod family.

Cod-liver oil is a specific for rickets and other disorders of calcium metabolism resulting from a lack of vitamin D. It is a useful dietary adjunct in tuberculosis. It finds minor application in the treatment of night blindness and other manifestations of vitamin A deficiency. The greater part of the total production, in the form of undestearinated oil, is used in the feeding of poultry. The oil improves the production, hatchability, shell quality and vitamin content of eggs and makes possible the raising of chicks out of season and in the absence of sunlight. Some oil is used for raising pigs, dogs, fur-bearing animals and wild carnivorous animals in captivity. Herbivorous animals do not thrive on cod-liver oil, which to them is toxic.

During the period 1928–38 important new fish oils were developed as vitamin sources. Sardine (pilchard) body oil is slightly inferior to cod-liver oil but more plentiful. It is given to animals only, principally chickens, and usually after being fortified with synthetic vitamin D_3. Halibut, rockfish, dogfish and soup-fin shark liver oils are outstanding sources of vitamin A. The liver oils of the percomorph fishes (tunas, mackerels, swordfishes and sea basses) often contain 100 times as much vitamin A and D as cod-liver oil. These oils, and oily solutions of vitamins A, D_2 and D_3, have surpassed cod-liver oil as vitamin sources in human medication.

See Fisheries Research Board of Canada, Bulletin 59, *Chemistry and Technology of Marine Animal Oils* (1941). (C. E. Bs.)

CODRINGTON, CHRISTOPHER (1668–1710), British soldier and colonial governor, whose father was captain general of the Leeward Islands, was born in Barbados, West Indies. Educated at Christ Church, Oxford, he was elected a fellow of All Souls, and served later with the British forces in Flanders, becoming a captain in the guards. In 1699 he was appointed captain general and commander in chief of the Leeward Islands. In 1703 he commanded the unsuccessful British expedition against Guadeloupe. After this he resigned his governorship and retired to a life of study on his Barbados estates. He died on April 7, 1710, bequeathing these estates to the Society for the Propagation of the Gospel for the foundation of a college in Barbados. This college, known as the Codrington college, was built in 1714–42. He also left a large sum to All Souls, with which the library named after him was established. He was buried in the college chapel.

CODRINGTON, SIR EDWARD (1770–1851), British admiral, belonged to a family long settled at Dodington in Gloucestershire. He entered the navy in 1783 and was promoted lieutenant in May 1793. Lord Howe selected him to be signal lieutenant of his flagship, the "Queen Charlotte," at the battle of the Glorious First of June, 1794. He was promoted commander after the action and captain in 1795, in which capacity he commanded the "Babet" frigate in Lord Bridport's action off Lorient. Between 1797 and 1805 he was unemployed and married in 1802 Jane Hall of Kingston, Jamaica. In 1805 he was appointed to the "Orion" (74 guns) and was selected by Nelson to command the rear squadron at the battle of Trafalgar. As this did not materialize, his ship fought in Nelson's column. In 1809 he was captain of the "Blake," flagship on the Walcheren expedition. Thereafter he served on the east coast of Spain and then, in the war of 1812–14, was active in North American waters during the operations against Washington, Baltimore and New Orleans. He became rear admiral in 1814, vice-admiral in 1821 and was appointed to the command of the Mediterranean fleet of 13 sail in 1827, flying his flag in the "Asia" (84 guns). In June 1827 he sailed to the Levant to command the allied fleet which at the battle of Navarino (*q.v.*) on Oct. 20 decided the independence of Greece by the destruction of the Ottoman fleet. During the period of his command the Aegean and the Adriatic were cleared of those pirates who had long been a menace to shipping in those parts. His victory at Navarino was the culminating event of his life, but it was received with mixed feelings in London, where it was officially described as "an untoward event" since it was held that Codrington had exceeded his instructions and that the diplomatic consequences were serious and unwelcome. The lord high admiral, the duke of Clarence, defended Codrington in the protracted correspondence which ensued, but he was recalled in June 1828, shortly before the Morea was finally evacuated by the Egyptians. On his return he published a justification of his conduct and in 1831 was employed again in the channel, becoming commander in chief at Portsmouth from 1839 to 1842. He died admiral of the White and G.C.B. on April 28, 1851, and is buried at St. Peter's, Eaton square, London. He left two sons who distinguished themselves, Sir William John (1804–84) as a soldier in the Crimea and Sir Henry John (1808–77) as admiral of the fleet.

See Lady Bourchier, *Memoir of the Life of Admiral Sir Edward Codrington,* 2 vol. (London, 1873); C. G. Pitcairn Jones (ed.), *Piracy in the Levant, 1827–28; selected from the papers of . . . Codrington,* Navy Records Society (London, 1934). (C. C. L.)

CODRUS, in Greek legend, the last king of Athens, son of Melanthus, of the Neleid family of Pylos, who came to Athens as a refugee. It was prophesied at the time of the Dorian invasion of the Peloponnesus (11th century B.C.?) that only the death of their king at the enemy's hands could ensure victory to the Athenians. Codrus therefore made his way disguised into the enemy's camp and provoked a quarrel, in which he was killed. The Dorians, on discovering this, retreated. The Athenians thought no one worthy to succeed Codrus and abolished the title of king, substituting that of archon (another version says that his son Medon was the last king). The royal families of Ionia as well as the Medontidae, the ruling family in Athens, claimed descent from Codrus. Codrus had a shrine in Athens, together with Neleus and Basile.

CODY, WILLIAM FREDERICK (1846–1917), famous U.S. frontiersman and showman, known as "Buffalo Bill," was born on a Scott county, Ia., farm on Feb. 26, 1846. At the age of 12 he shot his first Indian. Before the end of his teens and without the benefit of "book-learning," he had worked as horse wrangler and mounted messenger for a large western wagon freight firm, as a luckless prospector in the Pikes Peak gold rush and as a Pony Express rider. During the Civil War Cody served the Union as scout for the 9th Kansas cavalry in a campaign against Kiowa and Comanche Indians and was a U.S. army scout in Tennessee and Missouri military operations.

He married Louisa Frederici in 1866, but matrimony did not deter Cody one year later from hiring out as buffalo hunter for the firm of Goddard Brothers, then under contract to provide board for Kansas Pacific railroad construction crews. It was for his great success as a hunter that Cody won his lasting nickname "Buffalo Bill." Using a 50-calibre breech-loading Springfield rifle he killed (by his own count) 4,280 buffaloes during a period of 17 months.

During 1868–72, and again in 1876, Cody resumed duties as a U.S. army scout in prairie Indian campaigns. While serving Gen. George A. Custer in war against the Sioux, Cody killed and scalped Chief Yellow Hand in a duel. In this engagement Cody felled Yellow Hand with his rifle and within seconds, in the scout's own words, "I . . . had driven the keen-edged weapon to its hilt in his heart. Jerking his war-bonnet off, I scientifically scalped him in about five seconds."

Widely read dime novels featuring Cody's exploits made "Buffalo Bill" a household name. Cody was a superb showman. In 1883 he organized his Wild West exhibition, a large-scale, spectacular show which was successfully staged in the United States and Europe. A fortune made in showmanship was badly invested in various speculative ventures, among them ranching in Wyoming. On Jan. 10, 1917, Cody died and was buried in a tomb blasted from solid rock on Lookout mountain, 20 mi. from Denver, Colo.

BIBLIOGRAPHY.—*The Life of Hon. William F. Cody Known as Buffalo Bill,* an autobiography, has been published in several editions. *See* also Richard J. Walsh, *The Making of Buffalo Bill: A Study in Heroics* (Indianapolis, 1928); Rupert Croft-Cooke and W. S. Meadmore, *Buffalo Bill: The Legend, the Man of Action, the Showman* (London, New York, 1952). (O. O. W.)

COEDUCATION. The term "coeducation" is given various interpretations, the most extreme being that girls and boys "shall be taught the same things, at the same time, in the same place, by the same faculty, with the same methods, and under the same regimen." Few would now go so far. The general attitude among those who favour coeducation is that the differences in physical make-up and mental disposition must be respected, but that underlying these differences are fundamental needs common to both sexes, and that these can be fully satisfied only if boys and girls share most lessons, much social life and some sports and pastimes.

Though coeducation has had advocates since antiquity—Plato favoured it—its practice on any large scale is quite modern; with rare exceptions, girls were not admitted to schools and universities before the 19th century. The principle is still far from being universally accepted. Where it is observed the reason is frequently expediency, not conviction; small numbers and limited resources permit only mixed schools. The chief—almost the only—area of controversy is the secondary stage of education; opponents of coeducation point out that during the years of adolescence girls and boys mature at different rates and have markedly different interests. Among the great religions, Roman Catholicism and Mohammedanism particularly frown upon coeducation; an encyclical of Pius XI in 1929 described it as "founded upon naturalism and the denial of original sin." Protestant Christianity on the whole favours it. With communism it is an article of faith, though one liable to question (*see* below).

England and Wales.—There has never been any official policy in England and Wales. The general feeling was well expressed in 1945 by the ministry of education, which wrote: "It is neither possible nor desirable to lay down a fixed doctrine. . . . In the fields of primary and further education co-education is to be preferred. It is in the secondary field that the rival advantages of separation make themselves most apparent." The ministry allowed, however, that there need be no "cause for regret" if necessity compelled the grouping of boys and girls together. In the public system of elementary education which grew up during the 19th century about half the schools were mixed, but this was almost exclusively for reasons of economy or numbers, and in many cases it was coinstruction rather than coeducation which was practised, the girls sitting on one side of the room and the boys on the other, and separating for play and other activities outside the classroom. Similarly, when the Education act of 1902 introduced a public system of secondary education, many mixed secondary schools were built, again largely for reasons of economy rather than principle. In Wales the proportion of mixed schools has always been much higher than in England, in part at least because of the sparsity of population outside the industrial areas.

The English so-called public schools have always been exclusively for boys. When during the second half of the 19th century secondary schools for girls began to be founded in considerable numbers, they too were almost invariably single-sex schools. Few changed from this organization. Most private schools, and especially private boarding schools, are for boys or girls only. There are a few notable exceptions; perhaps the best known is Bedales, at Petersfield, Hampshire. Founded as a boys' school in 1893 by J. H. Badley, it admitted girls in 1898 "because it could not do without them," and has not only acquired an international reputation but done much to advance the theory and practice of full coeducation.

Scotland.—The Scottish tradition is quite different from the English, partly, no doubt, because of the sparsity of the population and the isolation of the villages, but probably far more because of the egalitarian organization of society. Coeducation has been almost universally practised since at least the 17th century. The rule is broken here and there in the large cities, but rarely elsewhere, except in the handful of public schools on the English model. Private schools have never become acclimatized in Scotland and are few in number and inconsiderable in influence.

Other Commonwealth Countries.—In Australia conditions outside the capital cities usually compel mixed schools; in the cities large schools are frequently single-sex. In New Zealand almost all primary schools are mixed, but at the secondary stage there are many single-sex schools, especially among those privately owned. Similarly in South Africa the primary schools are all mixed, but a substantial number of the secondary schools are single-sex. In the French-speaking districts of Canada segregation normally begins at age 12–13; in the English-speaking districts coeducation is normal outside the large cities, but in the cities large schools are often single-sex. In India coeducation was not practicable on any large scale in the 1950s; although the number of girls and women in schools and colleges was doubled during the first seven years of independence, it was in 1954 only one-quarter that of boys and men, and the proportion in secondary and higher education was much smaller. In Pakistan an even smaller proportion of girls attended school, and in the Punjab province it was a legally recognized excuse for nonattendance that there was no school exclusively for girls in the district. A broad generalization about the other commonwealth countries is that primary schools are mixed, secondary schools much less frequently so.

Continental Europe.—In western Europe the Scandinavian countries are the extreme exponents of coeducation. Denmark accepted the principle in the 18th century, and all its primary and secondary schools are coeducational. In Norway coeducation was adopted by law in 1896; all its primary schools are coeducational and nearly all secondary, a few private schools being the only exceptions. Sweden adopted coeducation early in the 20th century, and except for a few secondary schools is wholly coeducational. Finland has a rather larger proportion of segregated secondary schools.

In the Netherlands coeducation was permitted in 1871 and by 1886 had become general except in Roman Catholic districts, which still uphold segregation at the secondary stage. In Belgium, on the other hand, two-thirds of the primary schools are single-sex and there are practically no mixed intermediate or secondary schools. In France local option decides whether the primary school shall be mixed or single-sex; the balance is about even. Segregation is almost universal at the secondary stage. In Spain the public system is coeducational, but private schools are usually single-sex. Portugal is exceptional in that segregation is usual at the primary stage, coeducation at the secondary. In Switzerland coeducation is the usual practice, though with some degree of segregation in senior classes in the towns. In Italy coeducation became the normal practice during the early years of the 20th century, but in many places it took the more limited form of coinstruction. In Greece all primary and about half the secondary schools are mixed. In Yugoslavia all schools are coeducational. In Ireland the primary schools are mixed, the secondary schools single-sex.

German elementary schools tend to be mixed, especially in rural areas, but coeducation has made little progress at the secondary stage. Until the closing decades of the 19th century it was practically impossible for a girl to get secondary education, and when girls' secondary schools were introduced they were of inferior status to boys.' Hitler increased this inferiority by excluding girls from *Gymnasium* courses. After World War II some *Länder* made coeducation their objective, but the tradition of segregation dies hard.

Russian policy has changed several times. Segregation was the rule, at least in the cities, in tsarist days. The soviet government early switched completely to coeducation, which for many years obtained throughout the U.S.S.R. In 1940, however, the Moscow city council asked permission to set up segregated secondary schools. The request was refused, but following prolonged discussion throughout the country the ministry of education in 1942 sanctioned a limited experiment in the city area. A year later the experiment was extended, and by 1947 segregation at the secondary stage was being practised in 400 large towns. Even so, only 13% of the school population was in single-sex schools, and there was reason to believe that segregation was introduced rather to meet wartime circumstances than on grounds of principle. In 1950 the controversy was reopened, and again the matter became one for prolonged public discussion. In the course of this it was stated that discipline had deteriorated in boys' schools, that in some girls' schools pupils had been discouraged from interest in science, agriculture, economics and industry, and that segregation was estranging boys and girls. In 1954 the council of ministers of the U.S.S.R. decreed the restoration of coeducation, which made for "uncomplicated and comradely relations between boys and girls." (H. C. D.)

United States.—Coeducation first became general in the United States (where the term itself originated) in the 19th century, although it had been adopted in a limited way in the 17th in elementary schools. The late 18th century saw its extension to a few secondary institutions, and in the 19th it invaded the collegiate field. Coeducation met varying degrees of opposition. Religious reform, political liberalism, revolution and industrialization were its allies; some segments of religion and politics were its foes. Western communities were more favourably disposed toward it than were eastern and southern. Public schools and Protestant institutions generally embraced coeducation, while Catholic schools did not.

Colonial practice varied according to sectarian and national factors and the age of the pupils. In New England young children of both sexes attended dame schools, but town schools, save in a few instances, excluded girls. In the latter half of the 18th century, girls were gradually admitted, but usually attended at hours and seasons when boys were not present. In New Netherland, Dutch parochial schools admitted girls and boys, "at least until they learned to read." In Pennsylvania, New Jersey and other Quaker settlements, girls and boys generally attended together. German communities favoured separation, but Christopher Dock had girls and boys in his Pennsylvania school. Political and economic change and educational reform broke with parochial education in the late 18th and early 19th centuries. The new public schools, which supplanted church institutions, were almost universally coeducational. At the end of the 19th century, only a few larger cities had separate schools.

Colonial Latin schools were for boys, and the earliest academies and seminaries embraced separation; but by the end of the 18th century certain schools ventured to bring both sexes together, in the same school, though not always on the basis of coinstruction. Noteworthy were Leicester academy (1784), Westford (1793), Bradford (1803) and Friends academy, New Bedford (1812), in New England, and Westtown Boarding school (1799) in Pennsylvania. High schools began, as did academies, on the basis of sex segregation, but coeducation was the dominant trend after the Civil War. By 1900 public high schools were 98% coeducational, as were 56.7% of private secondary schools. Coeducational private secondary schools fell, however, to 46.8% in 1920.

Collegiate education for women, developing out of the academy-seminary movement, followed the same course in regard to coeducation. The first colleges were separate, but coeducation soon swept the field. Oberlin (O.) college, coeducational in the preparatory department from the beginning (1833), admitted women to college classes in 1837. Numerous private institutions followed suit. Hillsdale (Mich.) college (1844) gave its first A.B. degree to a woman in 1852. Antioch college, Yellow Springs, O. (1852), led by Horace Mann, provided equal opportunities to men and women, with the same studies, classes and teachers. Eureka college (1855), Earlham college, Richmond, Ind. (1859), Albion (Mich.) college (1861) and Swarthmore (Pa.) college (1864) were coeducational from the beginning.

State universities followed the lead of private colleges in respect to coeducation, though not without opposition. The State University of Iowa, Iowa City, admitted women to the normal department (1856), sought to exclude them (1858) and granted a bachelor's degree to a woman in 1863. The University of Wisconsin, Madison (1850), proposed to admit women as well as men to the normal department, but none entered till 1860. Women entered college classes (1863), and all departments were declared open to them in 1866. Persistent efforts of the regents to separate the sexes were unsuccessful; by 1907 slightly more than half the students were women. The University of Michigan, Ann Arbor, was opened to women in 1870, and they entered all departments. Cornell university, Ithaca, N.Y. (1865), was designed to be coeducational, but despite Henry W. Sage's endowment (1872), women were still "definitely restricted" in the 1950s.

By 1870 coeducation was no longer a hazardous experiment. Numerous older colleges for men admitted women during the next decade. By 1880 colleges admitting women on a coeducational basis were 51.3%

of the total (excluding technical institutions and the special women's colleges); at the end of the century the proportion was 71.6%. Tulane, Columbia, Brown and Harvard avoided coeducation but opened affiliated women's colleges between 1887 and 1894.

Professional schools were loath to admit women, and professional associations opposed women's practice, but resistance crumbled in most of them in the latter half of the 19th century. The Geneva Medical School of Western New York (now Hobart college) admitted Elizabeth Blackwell to study medicine (1847), when she had been refused elsewhere, and gave her an M.D. degree two years later. Lemma Barkaloo entered the law school of Washington university, St. Louis, Mo., in 1869. The law school of the University of Pennsylvania, Philadelphia, admitted one woman in 1881. By the end of the century most law schools were willing to admit women on application, but Harvard, Yale and the University of Virginia, Charlottesville, still excluded them. Yale admitted women in 1918 and the University of Virginia in 1920. There were then only 1,171 women in 107 law schools, with 19,821 men. Women took 421 degrees in law in 1950, men 13,891. Theological schools continued to exclude women. At Oberlin, however, Antoinette Brown Blackwell finished the theological course in 1850. Hartford Theological seminary opened to women in 1889. In 1900 there were 181 women in 154 schools of theology, with a total of 8,009 students; two decades later, women approximated 14% of the student body, but few took degrees. Postgraduate schools, developing after 1876, were generally open to both sexes, but few women applied for entrance before the end of the century. The Johns Hopkins university, Baltimore, Md., a pioneer in graduate research, did not admit women till 1907. In 1900 women received 295 Master of Arts degrees and men received 1,106; 31 women and 312 men were granted the Ph.D. degree. All but two of the women Ph.D. recipients were in coeducational institutions.

Arguments for and against coeducation were exaggerated and mutually contradictory. Proponents of it in elementary and secondary schools saw it as natural and customary, the only just way for both boys and girls, harmonious, economical, convenient, beneficial, ameliorating in effect on manners and morals. Opponents thought segregation the "safer plan," especially in cities, better for both sexes, an aid to propriety and good morals; it had the sanction of custom, took account of differing abilities and facilitated corporal punishment of boys. Few efforts were made to study the effect of segregation scientifically. Englewood High school, Chicago, Ill., concluded, however, after a test involving about 1,000 boys and girls (1906–09), that for the sake of social environment the sexes should attend the same school, but be taught in separate classes, in order to adapt instruction better to the needs of both. As for coeducation in college, Oberlin's president reported, after long experience, that economy, convenience, stimulus to study, social cultivation, good order in school and community and preparation for later social life were the chief advantages of coeducation. As for the worst fears, studies had suffered no injury, health of women was good, morals and manners had improved and most graduates married. Time and custom added weight to this opinion, and the majority concurred; but a minority continued to consider coeducation the source of numerous social ills. (T. Wy.)

South America.—Each of the republics of South America has institutional variations peculiar to itself, in education as in virtually everything else. On the other hand, since all these countries have a great deal in common as to cultural heritage and social and economic problems, their social institutions often show close similarities. This is the case with coeducation. Two factors have militated against coeducation over most of Latin America: (1) industrialization, which intensifies the need for coeducation, is of late date even in the most developed countries; and (2) the Roman Catholic tradition is, speaking broadly, opposed to coeducation, particularly for adolescents. While in a few of the countries academic secondary education is coeducational, normal schools of the secondary education level are usually not coeducational. This is particularly true of urban normal schools. Most of the institutions of higher learning are coeducational, and the principal factor that keeps the enrolment of women at a low figure in universities is the limited demand for women in the professions. This lack of demand responds, of course, both to traditional customs and attitudes and to the limited number of positions for which women with university education can compete. (G. I. S.)

Orient.—For many centuries in China and Japan the belief prevailed that for a woman to assume her proper role in society—that of mother and wife—she required little in the way of formal education. Opportunity for formal education was practically nonexistent for the oriental woman until about the middle of the 19th century, when Christian missionaries established schools for girls.

In 1872 Japan established a nation-wide system of public education, and national laws provided for separate schools for the sexes. Several decades later, China started a system of public schools and patterned it after that of Japan. In both China and Japan coeducation was practised at first only in the primary grades. It was not until 1920 that government universities of these two countries began to admit women students. The number of women students entering the government universities was limited because in neither of these two countries were provisions made to allow girls to enroll in secondary schools of the college preparatory type. Shortly after World War II Japan took the final step toward a coeducational school system when it opened most of its public secondary schools to boys and girls alike. By the midpoint of the 20th century coeducation, as a principle of public education, had taken a firm foothold in the orient.

Increased contact with western cultures and the consequent spread of liberal western social and political philosophies among the general populace was the major factor in the adoption of the principle of coeducation in China and Japan. Another factor contributing to the adoption of this principle was the economic difficulty of maintaining a system of schools for each of the sexes. (J. I. D.)

Bibliography.—J. H. Badley, *Bedales, A Pioneer School,* 2nd ed. (London, 1924); L. B. Pekin, *Coeducation in Its Historical and Theoretical Setting* (London, Toronto, 1939); F. T. Meylan, *La Coéducation des sexes: étude sur l'éducation supérieure des femmes aux Etats-Unis* (1904); Cecil Grant and Norman Hodgson, *The Case for Coeducation* (1913); Alice Woods (ed.), *Advance in Coeducation* (1919); B. A. Howard, *The Mixed School, A Study of Coeducation* (1928); Thomas Woody, *A History of Women's Education in the United States,* 2 vol. (New York, 1929); Elizabeth Huguenin, *La Coéducation des sexes: expériences et réflexions* (1929).

COEFFICIENT. This term was introduced into algebra by François Vieta at the close of the 16th century to denote either of the two rational factors of a monomial. Thus in the expression ab, either a or b is the coefficient of the other. In the case of a product of a constant by a variable, it is usual to call the constant factor the coefficient. Thus the numbers 2, −1, 0, a are the coefficients of the polynomial $2x^3-x^2+a$.

The integer $\binom{n}{r}=\frac{n!}{r!(n-r)!}$ is the coefficient of the term x^ry^{n-r} in the expansion of $(x+y)^n$ by the binomial theorem. Such integers are called binomial coefficients.

If $z=f(x,y)$, then $dz=\frac{\partial f}{\partial x}dx+\frac{\partial f}{\partial y}dy$ so that the partial derivatives $\partial f/\partial x$ and $\partial f/\partial y$ are often called differential coefficients.

In physics and mechanics, the term "coefficient" is applied to a number of constants which have to be determined experimentally. Thus if F is the force due to friction between two surfaces, and if N is the normal pressure between the surfaces, then $F=\mu N$ where μ is a constant depending on the condition and nature of the surfaces in contact, called the coefficient of friction.

A body normally expands when heated, and the change in length of a bar of unit length per degree change in temperature is a constant, called the coefficient of linear expansion of the substance.

The coefficient of pressure of a gas is the ratio of the change in pressure per degree to the pressure at the ice point, the volume remaining constant.

In the division of one polynomial by another, the method of detached coefficients may be used. When the divisor is of the form $x-c$, the method is particularly simple, and is known as synthetic division. Let it be required to divide $3x^4-8x^3-2x+5$ by $x-3$. The coefficients of the dividend are written down in order, 0's being supplied if not all powers of x are present. The first coefficient is brought down unchanged. This is multiplied by 3 and added to the next coefficient. The sum 1 is multiplied by 3 and added to the next coefficient, etc. The partial quotient is

$$\begin{array}{rrrrr|l} 3 & -8 & 0 & -2 & 5 & \\ & 9 & 3 & 9 & 21 & \underline{3} \\ \hline 3 & 1 & 3 & 7 & 26 & \end{array}$$

$3x^3+x^2+3x+7$ with the remainder 26. (*See* Algebra; Polynomial.) (C. C. M.)

COEHOORN, MENNO, Baron van (1641–1704), Dutch soldier and military engineer, of Swedish extraction, was born at Leeuwarden in Friesland and became a captain in the Dutch army. In 1673 he took part in the defense of Maastricht and in the siege of Grave, where the small mortars (called coehorns) he invented troubled the French garrison. He was made a colonel for his conduct at the battle of Seneff (1674), and was also at the battles of Cassel (1677) and St. Denis (1678). He was an innovator in fortification, and his first published work, *Versterckinge de Vijfhoeks met alle syne Buytenwerken* (Leeuwarden, 1682) caused a controversy with Louys Paan (Leeuwarden, 1682, 1683); Coehoorn was entrusted with the reconstruction of several fortresses in the Netherlands, and became the worthy rival of his great contemporary Sébastien de Vauban. In his chief work, *Nieuwe Vestingbouw op en natte of lage horizont,* etc. (Leeuwarden, 1685), he laid down three "systems," the feature of which was the multiplicity and great saliency of the works, eminently suited for flat sites such as those of the Low Countries. He borrowed many details from his Dutch predecessor Freytag, or from Albrecht Dürer, and Speckle, and studied the individual case, not theoretical perfection; *e.g.,* at Groningen. From 1688 to 1697 Coehoorn was a brigadier. At Fleurus he distinguished himself. In 1692 he lost Namur, a fortress of his own, to Vauban, but retook it in 1695. Coehoorn became lieutenant general and inspector-general of the Netherlands fortresses, and the High German peoples as well as the Dutch honoured him. He commanded a corps in Marlborough's army from 1701 to 1703, and in the constant siege warfare his skill was of the highest value. The swift reduction of Bonn and the siege of Huy in 1703 were his crowning successes. He died of apoplexy at Wijkel on March 17, 1704.

His first system was applied to Nijmegen, Breda, Bergen-op-Zoom and Mannheim, his second to Belgrade and Temesvar among other places.

His son, Gosewijn Theodor van Coehoorn, wrote his life (re-edited by Syperstein) (Leeuwarden, 1860); his *Nieuwe Vestingbouw* was translated into English by T. Savery (1705).

COELACANTH. Coelacanths are fish which originated about 350,000,000 years ago and spread over much of the world, leaving numerous fossil remains which apparently ceased 60,000,000 years ago. It was therefore startling when the first living coelacanth (*Latimeria chalumnae*) was trawled in 40 fathoms near East London, U. of S.Af., in 1938. The second was caught by a native on a line in about 40 fathoms near the Comoro Islands in Dec. 1952. This, *Malania anjouanae,* a male, lacked a first dorsal and extra tail but was probably mutilated in early life. So little was known about coelacanths that it was believed further specimens might show the two to be male and female of the same species. The sex of *Latimeria* was unknown as the soft parts were lost.

Coelacanths are grouped in four families, three extinct and one existing, Latimeriidae. These fall in the superorder Crossopterygii (fringe-finned), the early forms of whose two related orders, Coelacanthini and Rhipidistia, lived in swamps and probably crawled out of the water. Rhipidistian descendants colonized the land, but coelacanths remained aquatic, some probably always marine, leaving no fossil remains. Of all creatures coelacanths have lived by far the longest with the least change in form.

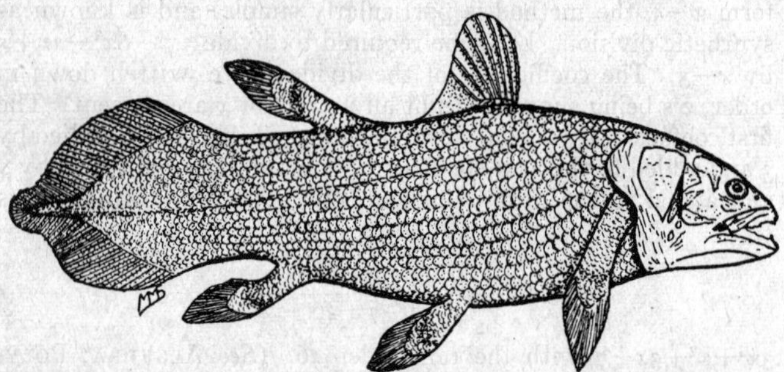

MARGARET M. SMITH

COELACANTH LATIMERIA, A MEMBER OF THE ONLY EXISTING FAMILY OF COELACANTHS, THE OTHER THREE BEING EXTINCT

Close links with the remote past, they may shed light on the earliest life.

Coelacanths have characteristic limblike fins, probably still used today for crawling about in the sea. The tail is large, symmetrical and in most fossil and one recent form there is a small extra tail behind. The skeleton is mostly cartilage, but part of the skull and the basal plates of the fins in the body are bony. The powerful mouth differs from that of most fishes, lacking the "maxillary" bones in the upper jaw. The gill arches are bony, with strong teeth above. Even early coelacanths had scales overlapping like those of modern fishes, with a lateral line.

Coelacanths are robust and powerful flesh eaters, almost certainly dwellers among reefs, where they pounce on prey. The intestines are short and include a spiral valve. Inside *Malania* were the eyeballs of a fish of at least 15 lb. weight.

Modern coelacanths are bigger than most fossil forms. *Latimeria* was 60 in. long and weighed 127 lb., *Malania* 54 in. and 87 lb. In 1953 and 1954 five more coelacanths were captured and preserved at the Comoros, establishing this as their home.

(J. L. B. S.)

COELENTERATA. The term "Coelenterata" is applied to a large group or phylum of animals of a lowly grade of organization. Only three types of animals possess a simpler structure than the Coelenterata: the sponges, the Mesozoa and Protozoa. Protozoa are organisms whose body usually consists entirely of a single cell, generally of microscopic size. In certain instances a number of these cells become banded together to form a colony, but in such a case they are not arranged so as to constitute tissues, and are individually autonomous and self-supporting. The sponges consist of a multitude of cells of different kinds which are massed together and many of which are segregated into definite sheets or tissues, each sheet performing a function or functions of its own. A sponge develops from a definite embryo which is the outcome of the cleavage of a fertilized egg, but apart from this it is very unlike the animals of the higher groups in that it constitutes in its adult condition a fixed, plantlike object often of somewhat indefinite shape. The sponges probably represent a series of products of evolution which diverged from protozoan ancestors in a direction distinct from that pursued by any other animals and which led to nothing beyond the sponges themselves. The Coelenterata, however, from beginnings similar to those of the sponges, achieved an altogether higher grade of organization, producing not only tissues but also a much more definite form and individuality than the sponges, involving the differentiation of nervous and muscular systems and consequently efficient co-ordination of parts and considerable powers of movement and locomotion. In the sponges primitive muscular tissue exists locally, but there is no nervous system.

Structure of a Coelenterate.—The body of a coelenterate resembles in architectural principle that stage which may be recognized in the early development of so many animals above the degree of sponges and which is known as a gastrula (fig. 5). A gastrula consists of a small sac, with a single opening at one end (the blastopore). The walls of the sac possess two layers of cells, one passing into the other at the margin of the blastopore. The inner layer is known as endoderm, the outer as ectoderm. No coelenterate, however complex may be its structure, passes beyond the fundamental plan thus outlined; though its size may be great and its parts elaborate, it remains an animal possessing one principal internal cavity only, the coelenteron, which opens to the exterior by a single main aperture, the mouth. In a typical higher animal the body contains two principal cavities, the food canal and another main cavity situated between the wall of the food canal and the outer integuments of the body. In such a form the food canal opens to the exterior by a second aperture (the anus) through which the undigested material is voided; the Coelenterata possess no such opening, and waste substances are ejected through the mouth. There is, in fact, no existing coelenterate in which the adult animal is quite so simple as a gastrula; but there do exist creatures in which the main differences are that the cells of the ectoderm exhibit a differentiation into more than one kind, and that there lies between ectoderm and endoderm a thin sheet of noncellular material, the mesogloea, which supports the other layers. An example of such a grade of structure may be found in *Protohydra.*

The majority of Coelenterata, however, develop a complexity far exceeding this. The actual form of the body varies almost infinitely, but usually a prominent feature of the organization is the presence of a number of tentacles placed in a definite manner around the mouth. These tentacles may be solid structures, containing a core of endoderm and a covering of ectoderm, or they may be hollow, the wall in such case including both cell layers. The symmetry of the body is usually characterized by the fact that the various parts are arranged about the radii of a circle with the mouth as its centre, and that the same structures are repeated in a regular manner in different sectors. In other words, the animal is radially symmetrical and can be divided by suitable radial cuts into a varying number of parts each of which is exactly equivalent to the others. This symmetry is not invariably present, but is extremely prevalent, although in one section of Coelenterata (the Anthozoa) it is accompanied by an underlying bilateral symmetry which mars its perfection. The middle layer or mesogloea varies greatly in bulk in different cases, being sometimes extremely tenuous and small in amount, sometimes very extensive and forming the greater part of the mass of the organism.

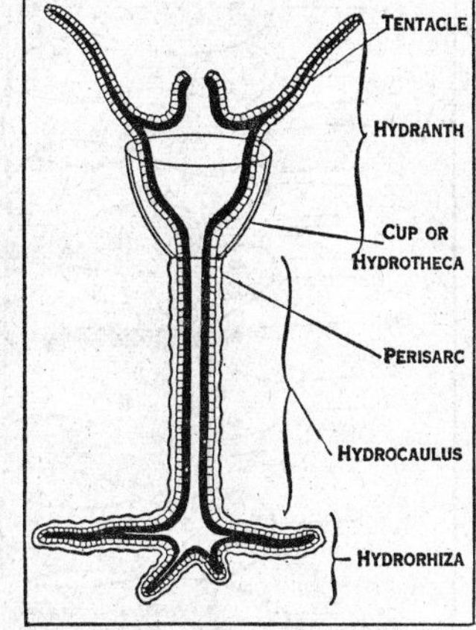

FIG. 1.—DIAGRAM OF A TYPICAL HYDROID POLYP

Polyp and Medusa.—The Coelenterata exhibit two main types of shape, both founded upon the gastrula plan.

1. *The Polyp.* The name *polyp* (figs. 1 and 2) is derived from the French *poulpe,* a term applied to an octopus. There is no actual relationship whatever between a Coelenterate polyp and an octopus, the comparison having been suggested by the fact that both of them possess mobile tentacles. A good example of a polyp is a sea anemone, the essentials of its structure being a hollow cylindrical body closed in below by an adherent disc-like base, above by another disc (the *peristome*) bearing the mouth in its centre and a circlet of tentacles round its outer part. Details of the structure of different kinds of polyps are given in the articles HYDROZOA, ANTHOZOA and SCYPHOZOA.

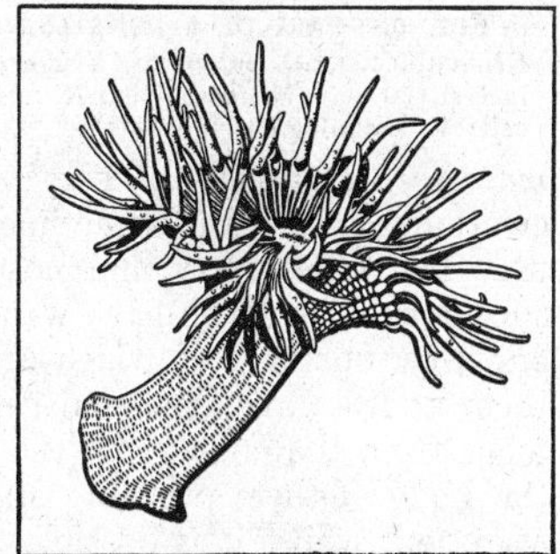
FROM STEPHENSON, "THE BRITISH SEA ANEMONES," BY COURTESY OF THE RAY SOCIETY
FIG. 2.—A SEA ANEMONE, ILLUSTRATING THE APPEARANCE OF A TYPICAL POLYP

2. *The Medusa.* Those Coelenterates popularly known as "jellyfish" are scientifically christened medusae, the name referring to the resemblance borne by the long mobile tentacles of some of these animals to the writhing, snaky tresses of the Gorgon Medusa. The body of a medusa (fig. 3) is shaped like an umbrella, and hanging down inside it from the point at which the handle of the umbrella would be attached, is a structure known as the *manubrium,* at the end of which is the mouth. In this case the tentacles form a circlet round the margin of the umbrella. *See* HYDROZOA and SCYPHOZOA.

Alternation of Generations.—One of the most interesting features connected with the Coelenterata is the fact that a single animal may for part of its life be a polyp and for part a medusa; or from a polyp, buds may be formed which develop into medusae. In cases such as the latter it is the polyp which is developed from an egg, and this polyp itself produces no sex-organs; it is able however to give origin to vegetative buds which develop into medusae, and these in their turn bring forth sex-cells which after fertilization initiate further polyps. In this way there is regular alternation between polyp and medusa and the phenomenon is termed *metagenesis* or alternation of generations. By some authors the polyp is viewed not as a "generation" but as a persistent larval stage; the medusa is then regarded as the adult.

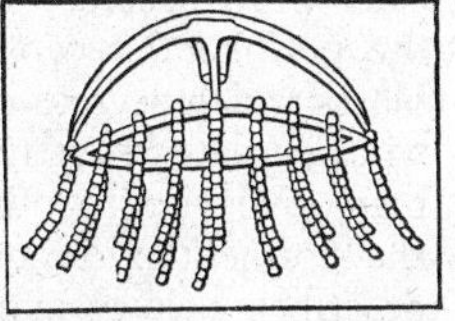
FROM PARKER & HASWELL, "TEXT BOOK OF ZOOLOGY" (MACMILLAN & CO. LTD.)
FIG. 3.—THE MEDUSA OF OBELIA

Polymorphism and the Formation of Colonies.—Another marked characteristic of the Coelenterata is their tendency to form colonies of individuals united to each other by a common stem, plate or mass of intermediate tissue. The colonies so formed are generally attached permanently to foreign surfaces, but in some cases they form strings or aggregations of individuals which float or are propelled through the sea. Coelenterate colonies are frequently characterized moreover by the production in one and the same colony of different kinds of individuals, among which the various functions are distributed. There may co-exist in a single colony not only polyps as well as medusae (fig. 4), but more than one kind of each of these types of individuals. There may be sexual medusae and medusae transformed into locomotory organs; polyps whose main function is digestion and others which catch and paralyse prey; and so forth. The phenomenon thus outlined is known as *polymorphism* and metagenesis is a form of it; it is one of the most interesting manifestations of the diversity of animal life, and is considered in more detail at the end of the article HYDROZOA.

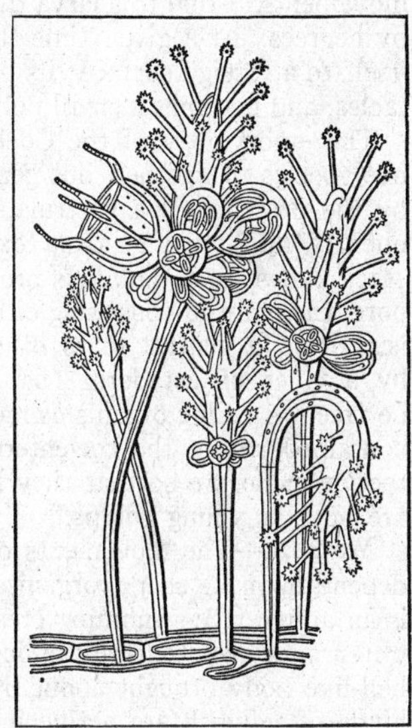
FROM KÜKENTHAL, "HANDBUCH DER ZOOLOGIE" (WALTER DE GRUYTER & CO.)
FIG. 4.—PART OF A COLONY OF CORYNE, MUCH ENLARGED

Development.—The Coelenterata pass during the course of their life-history through a series of stages very unlike the adult animal. A simple instance of these stages is provided by the embryology of the common sea anemone, *Metridium senile* (fig. 5). In this species the eggs are shed into the sea by the parent and are there fertilized. After fertilization the egg divides into halves and each of these once more into two. The four cells (or *blastomeres*) so formed are equal or sub-equal in size. This process of subdivision is continued until a considerable number of small cells has been formed, and these are so arranged as to constitute a hollow sphere containing fluid. The sphere is known as a *blastula* and the cavity as a *blastocoele.* The blastula continues to develop in such a way that one side of the sphere first flattens and then becomes concave, being finally completely invaginated into the other half. This process practically obliterates the blastocoele, and forms in its stead a second internal cavity, the *archenteron,* which communicates with the exterior by means of a small opening, the *blastopore.* There has thus been produced a typical gastrula such as has been previously described; its archenteron becomes directly transformed into the coelenteron of the

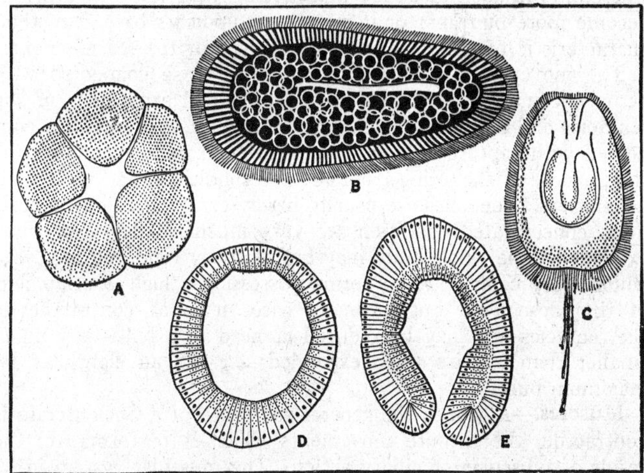

AFTER CARLGREN & GEMMILL, FROM STEPHENSON "THE BRITISH SEA ANEMONES," BY COURTESY OF THE RAY SOCIETY; WITH AN ADDITION
FIG. 5.—STAGES IN DEVELOPMENT OF CERTAIN COELENTERATES
A. Section through an early stage in cleavage of the egg of a sea anemone (*Metridium*). **D.** and **E.** later stages—blastula and gastrula. **B.** A planula belonging to a hydrozoan. **C.** Late larva of a sea anemone

adult, and the blastopore becomes the adult mouth. During its early stages the animal moves through the water by the aid of cilia which appear on its outer surface during the blastula stage, but before it begins to assume the adult shape it tends to remain at the bottom, moving horizontally and resting from time to time, and often becoming temporarily attached to the bottom mouth downwards, during which time it may execute slow creeping movements. From this larva the adult anemone-polyp is achieved by degrees. At a given time the larva settles down and attaches itself to a foreign surface; its proportions change, it acquires tentacles, and becomes a small polyp.

The embryology of the Coelenterata varies considerably from one species to another, but generally speaking it is characterized by the presence of a gastrula-stage or of some equivalent. Frequently no actual gastrula exists but instead a corresponding stage known as a *planula* is produced, in which there is no blastopore, the embryo consisting either of a hollow two-layered organism or of a central mass of endoderm-cells covered externally by a layer of ectoderm (fig. 5). Planulae and gastrulae may be free-swimming organisms moving by means of cilia, or may be contained within the coelenteron of the parent or within a protective enclosure so that they have no actual free existence, and are born as young polyps.

Motion.—The movements of which a Coelenterate is capable depend upon its shape, organization and mode of life. A jellyfish is an active free-swimming creature which progresses through the water as a result of rhythmic or spasmodic contractions of its bell-like body brought about by the action of muscles. Different kinds of jellyfish are active in varying degrees; some are much stronger swimmers than others, some are decidedly sluggish, whilst a few are creepers. Movement in polyps varies according to whether they possess a skeleton or not; in those provided with such a structure movement is naturally limited to those actions which the tentacles or other parts of the polyp can perform unrestricted by the hard parts. If a polyp is free from skeleton, it can move in a variety of ways; rarely, it swims actively by concerted lashing movements of the tentacles; sometimes it will creep on these organs; or it may attach itself by the base, bend over and attach the tentacles, then loosen the base, move its body and re-attach the base elsewhere. On the other hand it may simply loosen its hold and allow the motion of the water to carry it elsewhere, and in such case may inflate itself with water in order to become more buoyant; or it may creep upon its base, a method characteristic of many of the large polyps of the sea anemones.

The movements exhibited, apart from those connected with actual locomotion, consist of contractions and expansions of the tentacles and body, movements of the mouth, and so forth, connected with capture and swallowing of food, with retraction for the purpose of sheltering from adverse conditions, and with similar matters. Tentacles are usually highly contractile, and in their most concentrated condition are very much smaller than when expanded. The whole body may be relatively rigid and not, as a whole, very contractile, in forms possessing a high development of the mesogloea; but in many cases it is as contractile as the tentacles and may be reduced at need to a bulk very much smaller than its size when expanded; *e.g.*, to an eighth of its maximum bulk.

Muscles.—Although the general substance of a Coelenterate is contractile, the definite movements which it performs are the result of muscular or ciliary action. The muscular system in its simplest condition consists of a single layer or sheet of muscle-fibres, lying on the inner or outer surface of the mesogloea. The muscle-sheets of Coelenterates are normally only one fibre thick, and each fibre lies directly upon a supporting surface of mesogloea. Consequently if strong localized muscles (as distinct from diffuse sheets) are required, these are generally attained by the simple expedient of pleating the surface of the mesogloea into ridges, on the surface of which lie the fibres, still in a single layer. In certain cases muscle becomes embedded in the mesogloea. The individual fibres are not in the simpler instances independent structures, but belong to and form part of epithelial cells of the ectoderm or endoderm. Thus the combination of each cell with its "muscle tail" (or tails) constitutes a musculo-epithelial cell, a structure characteristic of Coelenterata but rare among higher animals (fig. 8). In more specialized cases the muscle-fibres of the ectoderm become separate structures, the epithelial cells which produced them being of insignificant proportions.

The Finer Structure of the Tissues.—The structure of the layers of the body must now receive short notice (fig. 6). The

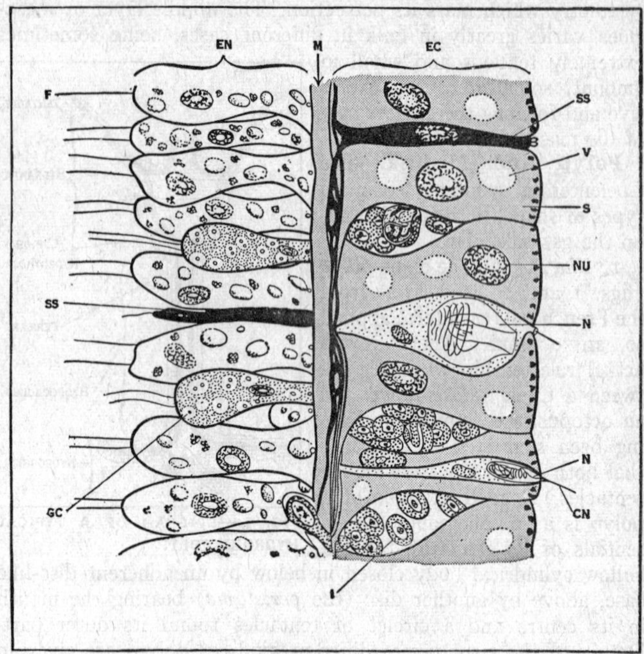

FROM KÜKENTHAL, "HANDBUCH DER ZOOLOGIE" (WALTER DE GRUYTER & CO.)

FIG. 6.—PART OF A LONGITUDINAL SECTION OF HYDRA, ENLARGED
CN. cnidocil; EC. ectoderm; EN. endoderm; F. flagellum; GC. gland cell; I. interstitial cell; M. mesogloea; N. nematocyst; S. supporting-cell; SS. sensory-cell; V. vacuole; NU. nucleus

mesogloea is a sheet of very variable structure; sometimes it is gelatinous in texture, sometimes almost cartilaginous, or again it may be very watery and unsubstantial. It contains within its substance cells which have wandered there from the other layers, and the functions of which are not fully understood. Some of them at least are amoeboid cells which carry or transmit nutriment from the endoderm (the digestive layer) to other parts of the body. Others probably add to the mesogloeal substance by secretion, whilst it is possible that some of them constitute part of a mesogloeal nervous system. At its highest development the mesogloea possesses fibres as well as cells, but these are not at all of the same nature as the muscular fibres. The cell-layers are best considered separately, and the following details apply to a sea anemone, which will serve as a suitable example. The ectoderm is an epithelium consisting of elongated supporting cells which are ciliated in some parts of the body, and among these occur large numbers of cells of other kinds. There are glandular cells which secrete mucus, etc., sensory cells which constitute the peripheral receptive elements of the nervous system, cnidoblasts which secrete curious explosive capsules about which more will be related shortly, and undifferentiated interstitial cells which may give rise to other kinds at need. In the deeper parts of the epithelium lie nerve cells (the nervous system is further described below) and on the surface of the mesogloea, in given parts of the body, are the muscle fibres, which are here independent of the supporting cells. The endoderm resembles the ectoderm in general constitution, but its supporting cells, instead of being ciliated, bear each a single large cilium or flagellum, and each possesses a basal muscle fibre, and so constitutes an epithelio-muscular cell. Many of them are digestive in function. Gland-cells are to be found in the endoderm, as also are sensory, nervous and interstitial cells; cnidoblasts are most characteristic of the ectoderm, but also occur freely in the endoderm where necessary.

The germ cells of the Coelenterata, those cells which will in due course form eggs or spermatozoa, are formed sometimes from interstitial cells, sometimes from differentiated epithelial cells. They may originate in either ectoderm or endoderm, but are not necessarily first formed in the region in which they will ripen.

General Functions.—The Coelenterata possess no special organs for respiration or excretion, and possess neither blood nor blood-vessels. Respiration and excretion are performed by the general surfaces of the body, but sometimes the chief excretory areas are localized. Circulation in the true sense does not exist, although currents are produced in the fluid contained in the coelenteron by means of the endodermal flagella. The distribution of substances through the tissues takes place partly through the agency of amoeboid cells and partly by diffusion. Feeding and digestion must be more closely considered.

Capture of Food.—The Coelenterata are apparently all carnivorous, and capture food by two principal methods. The commonest way is to seize the prey with one or more of the tentacles, to convey it to the mouth and swallow it. This is made possible by the fact that the tentacles possess stinging and adhesive powers of a high order. A tentacle will adhere to and will paralyze or kill any organism which is desired for food, provided that the prey in question is not too large or too tough to be penetrated by the poisonous threads shot out by the tentacle. These threads are shot forth in countless numbers from the tentacle-surface, each being everted by one of those explosive capsules which have been mentioned above. Although microscopic in size, the threads have astonishing powers of penetration, and the poison which they carry with them, although weak in some Coelenterates, is usually strong enough to paralyze the prey suitable to each species. In the case of the most powerful stingers the poison is extremely virulent, and contact with a tentacle will produce violent pain in the human skin. The fact that the threads penetrate enables the tentacle to adhere to the prey unless its struggles are strong enough either to break them or to pull away part of the ectoderm, and in some cases there exist, in addition to the capsules with penetrating threads, others whose threads do not enter the prey but are covered with sticky material and adhere to it. The prey captured by this method is transferred by the tentacles to the mouth, which is generally very extensile and can open widely so as to engulf objects which in some cases are enormous in relation to the size of the swallower. The Coelenterate has not necessarily finished stinging the prey after it has been taken in, for in many cases there exist internal stinging organs.

There is another method of feeding which may supplement or replace the characteristic one. Small food particles which come in contact with some part of a Coelenterate become entangled in slime secreted by that part, and these are transported by means of cilia acting in definite directions to the mouth. This method of feeding is probably the predominating one in certain species—for instance, in some sea anemones—and a good example of its working may be seen in the jellyfish *Aurelia.*

When *Aurelia* is feeding, planktonic organisms become entangled in strings of slime on the outside of the swimming-bell, and are conveyed by the movements of the bell aided by the action of cilia to the edge of the umbrella. Arrived at this point they are concentrated into eight masses at points situated at regular intervals round the margin of the bell. From time to time these masses are licked off by one or other of the four large arm-like processes which hang down under the bell round the mouth; and since each of these arms contains a groove leading directly into the mouth, the food mass is from this point onwards easily transported into the stomach. The underside of the swimming-bell also contributes to the eight food masses and the oral arms themselves collect plankton independently. This seems to be a normal mode of feeding in *Aurelia,* but at the same time it can and does, at any rate when young, catch fishes and other organisms as well as plankton.

The Food of Coelenterata.—The food of Coelenterates includes a great variety of animals—fishes and their eggs, crabs and all manner of other Crustacea, worms, molluscs, other Coelenterates, etc., not to mention the innumerable small planktonic organisms imbibed. Some Coelenterata are omnivorous, but others again will select their food more or less definitely. Certain special forms have been supposed to feed upon unicellular Algae (*Zooxanthellae*), but later work showed that these, also, are carnivorous and that the *Zooxanthellae* contained in their tissues are of importance in connection with their excretory process and are not used as food.

Digestion.—Digestion in Coelenterates is a process involving two stages. If a large object has been swallowed it is first broken up into particles and the latter are then engulfed or ingested by individual endoderm cells within which each particle becomes surrounded by a fluid-containing vacuole and there the remaining processes of digestion and absorption take place. Thus the whole process involves first *extra-cellular* digestion in the coelenteron, and then *intra-cellular* digestion in the endoderm; or if the food is small enough it may be directly ingested by endoderm-cells without previous breaking down. The details of this process vary according to the anatomy of the Coelenterate in question. In a simple case such as that of *Hydra,* the coelenteron is lined by a simple and fairly uniform layer of endoderm, not concentrated into special structures; and in such case this layer performs the double function of secreting digestive material which will break up a large prey and of ingesting the fragments so produced. In a higher form such as a sea anemone or coral the endoderm is differentiated into regions; there are definite tracts of epithelium in which gland-cells are concentrated, and these constitute together with the adjacent endoderm the main digestive area. These tracts, the mesenterial filaments, have been shown to secrete a digestive juice; and although they may also themselves ingest, in the most specialized cases the main absorptive region is not the filament itself but the endoderm on either side of it. The area of endoderm which will ingest food in such cases varies according to the size of the meal. The digestive ferments of Coelenterates are specialized for dealing with animal prey.

Nervous System.—This is of a very primitive grade in Coelenterata, and possesses neither actual nerves nor any central controlling organ. Its essential parts are the sensory cells and nerve cells of the ectoderm and endoderm, together with a network of fine fibrils connecting these cells with the muscle fibres and with each other. The nerve cells and fibrils constitute a "nerve net" which runs in the deeper part of the epithelium (fig. 7) and perhaps also penetrates the mesogloea. The net is sometimes fairly evenly distributed, sometimes better developed in one part than in another, and sometimes decidedly concentrated in given regions. It is not, as was formerly thought, a continuous network in the sense that the processes of one cell are actually fused with those of another, as it is now known that the cells are separate entities with their fibrils in contact, the junctions having the physiological properties of elementary synapses (*q.v.*). The mode of action of the network has received considerable study in the later years (*see,* for instance, the references to work by Pantin at the end of this article), but it cannot be described adequately in a few words. The behaviour of the individual nerve cells resembles that of the similar cells of higher animals more closely than was originally supposed; but the distinguishing feature of the net is its tendency to conduct impulses in all directions, in spite of which it may develop special tracts along which impulses travel rapidly for the production of certain particular responses. The net also exhibits in a high degree the phenomena known as interneural and neuromuscular facilitation (*see* the articles by Pantin referred to above).

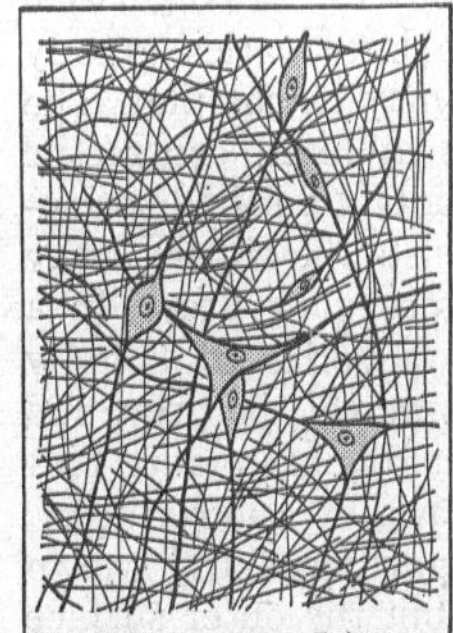

FROM SCHNEIDER, "LEHRBUCH DER VERGLEICHENDEN HISTOLOGIE DER TIERE" (FISCHER)

FIG. 7.—PART OF THE NERVE NET OF A COELENTERATE

Many Coelenterata possess definite sense-organs. These are naturally found in the more active members of the group, that is to say the medusae; they are absent altogether in the polyps. The chief types of sense-organs are two in number, and these are described in connection with the animals possessing them, in the articles HYDROZOA and SCYPHOZOA. The first type includes organs sensitive to light and termed *ocelli;* and these structures, though often simple, may attain at their highest development the grade of eyes (see *Charybdaea,* in SCYPHOZOA). The second type comprises organs of variable structure (*statocysts* and *tentaculocysts*) which include hard particles (*statoliths*) in their constitution, and whose function is not yet fully understood. Although they might be expected to be organs of balance this does not necessarily appear to be the case. It has been ascertained experimentally, however, that certain of these organs initiate the stimuli which produce the swimming-contractions of the bell of the medusa possessing them, and consequently control the rate of pulsation. The bell pulsates at the rate of whichever organ is initiating stimuli most rapidly at a given time. The sense organs also appear to exert an influence on the general metabolic activities of the animal.

Stinging Capsules.—The cnidoblasts with their explosive capsules or *cnidae* will now be described (fig. 9). These capsules are among the most extraordinary structures to be found in the animal kingdom, and the physiological problem presented by the question of their explosion is a difficult one. It is probable that several factors are involved, and that these are called into play in fluctuating intensity according to the structure of the capsule and cnidoblast in question. Each cnida is a refringent transparent capsule with a gelatinous or more probably fluid content. In unexploded state, the capsule contains a hollow thread (*i.e.,* a capillary tube of incredible fineness) coiled or folded up within it; and the wall of capsule and thread are continuous with one another at one pole of the capsule. The cell (*cnidoblast*) in which the capsule lies and which originally produced it commonly bears at its free surface a fine hair-like projection, known as a *cnidocil.* The contact of a foreign body suitable as food with this cnidocil ordinarily leads directly to the explosion of the capsule. On the other hand such contact does not necessarily explode the capsule. For instance the reactions of a well-fed sea anemone are not the same as those of a hungry one; the tentacles may refuse food altogether, neither the tactile nor the chemical stimuli involved producing any effect on the capsules. When, however, a capsule does explode the thread is shot forth instantaneously. Although the action is so rapid, the thread as it is ejected turns completely inside out, in the manner in which one may turn the finger of a glove; in other words it is evaginated.

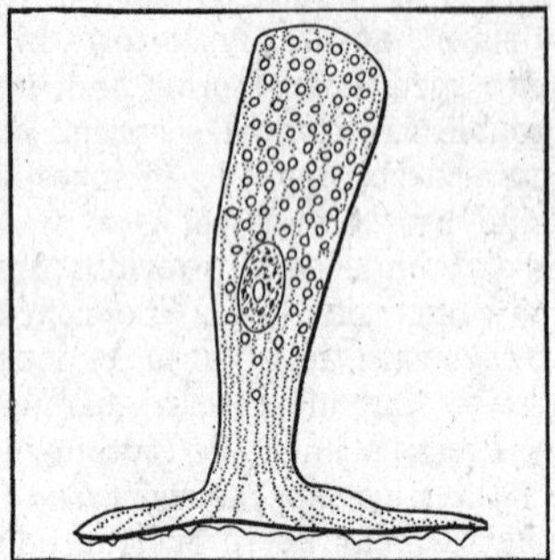

FROM SCHNEIDER, "LEHRBUCH DER VERGLEICHENDEN HISTOLOGIE DER TIERE" (FISCHER)

FIG. 8.—A SINGLE MUSCULO-EPITHELIAL CELL. THE CELL CONTAINS A NUCLEUS AND A SINGLE MUSCLE FIBRE

The structure of both cnidae and cnidoblasts varies greatly from one Coelenterate to another, and both may be complex. The cnidoblast possesses, in a number of cases at least, contractile fibres of varying disposition, and may also contain a coiled spring-like structure (the *lasso*) which probably resists the tearing away of the nematoblast from the tissues by a struggling prey. In a typical cnida the thread is provided with a series of spirally arranged barbs which help to fix it in the tissues of the prey, and bears with it poison which enters by the wound it has made. This kind of cnida, which is very frequent, is known as a *nematocyst,* in contrast to another type common in sea anemones and known as a *spirocyst.* The latter has no armature, but the outer surface of its evaginated thread has strongly adhesive properties, and is probably not poisonous.

True cnidae occur nowhere in the animal kingdom save in the Coelenterata. There are similar structures developed in at least two other kinds of animals (the myxosporidean Protozoa and certain nemertine worms), but they are not exactly the same; a number of other structures which have been confused with nematocysts are not actually such. The most interesting cases which have been investigated in this connection are those of certain animals in whose tissues actual Coelenterate nematocysts are present in an unexploded and functional condition. It has been conclusively shown that an animal may feed upon a Coelenterate, thus swallowing quantities of nematocysts, and that a number of these may pass unexploded through its food-canal, and may subsequently become arranged in a definite manner in its tissues. The best known instance of this is provided by certain of the Nudibranch molluscs or sea slugs. In some cases at least these stolen nematocysts appear to be of value to their host.

Nematocysts and spirocysts, which are produced by interstitial cells, are not developed in the place where they will function. In some cases this means simply that they develop in the deeper layers of the epithelium and move up to the surface as they mature. In other cases, however, a much more interesting story is involved. The capsules are here secreted by cnidoblasts far removed from the site of their ultimate explosion, and in order to bring them into the situation and orientation which will permit them to function, the cnidoblasts, which are amoeboid and possess the power of independent movement, drag their capsules between the epithelial cells (or transport them by other means) until the proper locality is reached. A most interesting example of the processes involved is supplied by the state of affairs which exists in an unusual jellyfish known as *Haliclystus.* This animal has the edge of its bell produced into eight arms, each tipped by a tuft of tentacles; and on the middle of the outside of the bell it bears a stalk by the end of which it can attach itself to seaweed and other objects. It has been found that the tentacles contain two kinds of nematocyst, and that both kinds are produced in definite parts of the ectoderm of the inner surface of the bell. It has further been discovered that the cnidoblasts containing the two kinds of capsules migrate from their nursery to the tentacles; but that on the way some of those of one pattern (and not those of the other) disappear into little ectodermal pockets which lie close to the margin of the bell. The function of the pockets appears to be that of reservoirs whence a supply of capsules may be drawn in case of special need—for instance, if the tentacles belonging to one side of the animal be cut off, new ones are regenerated and a large supply of capsules is needed to stock them; and it has been found that under such circumstances the pockets nearest to the regenerating tentacles were empty.

Reproduction.—Coelenterates reproduce their kind in a variety of ways. They produce in the manner common to animals, eggs and spermatozoa, which after union develop into new creatures. But in addition to this universal method they have an extraordinarily strong tendency toward "vegetative" or asexual modes of reproduction, and correlated with this a very marked ability to regenerate lost parts. This manner of increase is much like the ability of a strawberry-plant to produce runners. It exists under a variety of forms; sometimes an animal within the space of a few hours or less will tear itself completely in half vertically; each half will regenerate new parts and will so develop into a complete animal. This process is known as fission; it does not always take the form of actual tearing, but may result from a gradual process of constriction whereby an individual separates either completely into halves or becomes partly double. In other varieties of fission the separation into two or more parts takes place horizontally; and again, neither in vertical nor horizontal fission does it follow that the pieces formed will be at all equal in size. Equally characteristic of Coelenterates, but generally speaking of different ones, is the process known as budding (figs. 4 and 10). In this case a polyp may send out a rootlet (like the strawberry-runner) at the end of which a new polyp grows up;

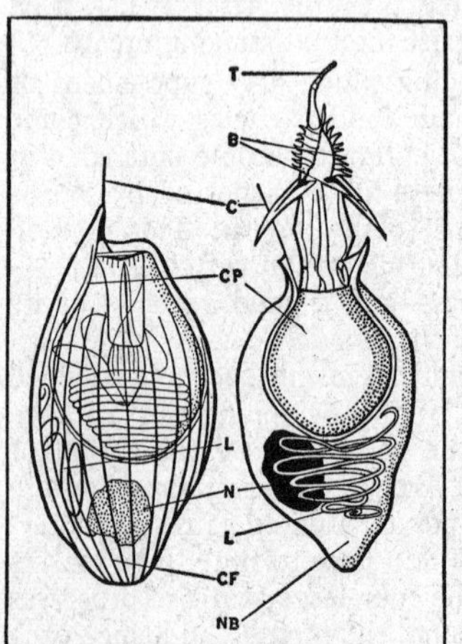

FROM KÜKENTHAL, "HANDBUCH DER ZOOLOGIE" (WALTER DE GRUYTER & CO.)

FIG. 9.—NEMATOCYSTS, OR STINGING ORGANS

On right, an exploded nematocyst contained within its cell; at left, a similar nematocyst before explosion. B. barbs; C. cnidocil; CF. contractile fibrils; CP. capsule; L. lasso; N. nucleus; NB. cnidoblast; T. thread

or a new polyp may arise direct from the tissues of an existing one. Polyps give rise by budding to other polyps or to medusae; medusae by budding may produce fresh medusae but never polyps, these being always developed from eggs or from other polyps. The processes of regeneration which succeed certain types of asexual reproduction are both definite and interesting; and the regenerative results which arise from the cutting away of various parts of Coelenterates, or from the division of these animals into portions by cuts in different directions, provide material for a study from which much of general biological interest may be gained. Further details relating to budding and fission will be found in the articles HYDROZOA, SCYPHOZOA and ANTHOZOA, whilst for information relating to regeneration reference should be made to the article on that subject.

Commensalism and Symbiosis.—There are to be found among the Coelenterata a number of examples of those types of relationship between one organism and another which are respectively known as *commensalism* and *symbiosis*. Commensalism, as exemplified by the regular partnership which exists between certain sea anemones and hermit crabs, is well represented in the group (*see* also next section); and a number of Coelenterata contain in their tissues those unicellular symbiotic algae known as *Zooxanthellae*.

The Poison of Coelenterates.—A certain amount of work has been done on the lines of making extracts of one sort and another of the tissues of Coelenterates and injecting these into other animals in order to study the effect of the poison of the Coelenterate on the animal in question. It has been known for a long time that the poisons of certain Coelenterates are very virulent and that contact of the stinging organs with human skin may produce serious results. In the case of medusae belonging to the *Charybdaeidae* for instance, jellyfish which outstrip all others in the strength and rapidity of their swimming-movements, the stinging organs may cause intense pain after contact with the skin, and symptoms such as swelling of the legs, etc., follow; fatal results may even ensue. An investigation of particular interest has been made on the poison of *Adamsia palliata* which throws light not only on the question of Coelenterate poisons but also upon the relationship between this anemone and another animal. *Adamsia palliata* lives in permanent association with a hermit crab known as *Eupagurus prideauxi,* and apparently these two organisms never normally occur apart. The soft tail-end of the crab is protected by the anemone, which is wrapped round it like a cloak; and the mouth of the anemone lies just below that of the crab, so that meals become a communal affair. Now it is possible to make an extract containing the poison of the tentacles or other stinging organs of an *Adamsia,* and such extracts have been injected in varying strengths into a number of animals. Certain of these, for instance Cephalopod molluscs (cuttle-fishes, etc.) and other sea anemones, appear to be completely immune from the *Adamsia* poison; other animals succumb to it. It has been found that the Decapod Crustacea (crabs, etc.) are the most sensitive to it, and its action on a number of these has been studied. The following experiment is a case in point. Three shore-crabs (*Carcinus maenas*), three common hermit-crabs (*Eupagurus bernhardus*) and three of the hermits proper to *Adamsia* (*E. prideauxi*) were selected, and into the body-cavity of each was injected 0.1ml. of a filtered maceration of *Adamsia.* At the end of three minutes the *bernhardi* were completely paralyzed after a short phase of tetanization; and at the end of an hour they were dead. The shore-crabs died between five and nine hours after having exhibited the symptoms characteristic of this poison. On the other hand the *prideauxi* showed no apparent trouble; they retained all their agility and all the accustomed vivacity of their movements. At the end of 24 hours their condition was normal and they survived indefinitely. Other experiments confirm the result of this one, and the interesting fact emerges that *E. prideauxi* is immune from the poison of its anemone unless injected in inordinately large amount. Thus the association between the two animals includes a physiological as well as a morphological adaptation. It has been shown further that the serum of *E. prideauxi* is able to neutralize the *Adamsia* poison and that if a shore-crab be inoculated with *prideauxi* serum, it can afterwards withstand and recover from a dose of poison which would otherwise be fatal. It is probable that *E. prideauxi* gains its immunity in the first instance as a result of the fact that its close association with the anemone involves the constant entanglement of small portions of the latter, or of stinging cells derived from it, in the hermit's food. The intestinal content of the hermit usually contains such fragments of the anemone. Although in these experiments the poison of *Adamsia* did no harm to other anemones, yet in other cases one anemone may sting another, even of the same kind, and produce a wound which may prove fatal—so that an anemone is not necessarily immune from poison produced by its own kind. It is possible, however, that the injured animal in such cases is, to begin with, in a poor condition.

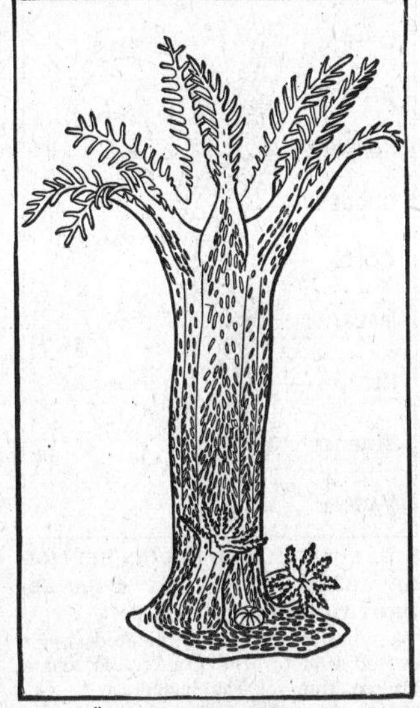

FROM KÜKENTHAL, "HANDBUCH DER ZOOLOGIE" (WALTER DE GRUYTER & CO.)

FIG. 10.—A POLYP IN PROCESS OF BUDDING

Distribution, Environment and Length of Life.—The distribution of the Coelenterata is world-wide, but the great majority are marine; a few kinds only inhabit brackish or fresh water, and these are further mentioned in the articles HYDROZOA and ANTHOZOA. The mass of Coelenterata then, inhabit one or other of the regions of the sea; and it cannot be said that they are characteristic of one kind of habitat more than of another. Many of them inhabit the littoral zone between tidemarks. Others colonize the sea-floor at greater or lesser depths, some of them occurring in extremely deep water (*e.g.*, 2,900 fathoms). The remainder are pelagic at varying depths and may live in the open sea, some of them floating and some swimming. A number of Coelenterates are perennial, living for a number of years, their length of life in some cases probably being extremely great. The best measured example of this is that of some sea anemones alive in 1945, which were known to be nearly 90 years old and possibly were much more. Other Coelenterates, on the other hand, are seasonal; many hydroids die down in winter and regenerate new polyps in spring; and many medusae live for a brief period only. Neither the tropics nor the cold regions can be regarded as the more typical habitat for Coelenterata, though it is true that corals, anemones and Siphonophores for instance, attain their maximum profusion or considerable complexity of development (sometimes both these features) in the warm seas. The variety of Coelenterates which may occur within a broadly similar environment is great, but as in the case of many other animals a certain proportion at least of the genera permanently colonizing the various available habitats show a sympathetic reaction to their environment; thus it may be expected with reason that an average anemone living at great depths will be different from a typical inhabitant of a coral-reef, and a typical mud-dweller from an ordinary adherent form. Certain single species however range in suitable habitats from the arctic to the equator, others occur both in the arctic and the antarctic; whilst some are circumpolar in distribution. With regard to the distribution of jellyfish it may be noted that their swimming powers are adapted rather for maintaining their position in the water and for moving up and down in it than for making long journeys; the main agents in their distribution are currents and tides.

Classification.—The Coelenterata are divided into three great classes, the *Hydrozoa, Scyphozoa* and *Anthozoa.* To these are sometimes added the *Ctenophora;* but the latter are animals which are actually very different from any Coelenterata, and the reasons which lead to this conclusion are stated in the article dealing with them. The characteristics of the three great classes of Coelenterata are also described in articles dealing with each series separately.

BIBLIOGRAPHY.—General Accounts: E. A. Minchin, G. C. Bourne and G. H. Fowler, "The Porifera and Coelentera," in *A Treatise on Zoology,* pt. 2 (ed. Sir E. Ray Lankester, 1900); Y. Delage and E. Hérouard, *Traité de zoologie concrète,* vol. ii, pt. 2 (1901); S. J. Hickson, "Coelenterata and Ctenophora," in *Camb. Nat. Hist.,* vol. i (ed. A. E. Shipley and S. F. Harmer, 1906); H. Broch, T. Krumbach, W. Kükenthal, F. Moser and F. Pax, in W. Kükenthal, *Handbuch der Zoologie,* vol. i (ed. T. Krumbach, 1923–25); L. H. Hyman, *The Invertebrates: Protozoa through Ctenophora* (1940).

Development: E. W. MacBride, "Invertebrata," in W. Heape, *Text-Book of Embryology,* vol. i (1914). Histology: K. C. Schneider, *Lehrbuch der Vergleichenden Histologie der Tiere* (Jena, 1902) and *Histologisches Praktikum* (Jena, 1908). Nematocysts: L. Will, *Naturforschenden Gesellschaft* (Rostock, 1909–10); P. Schulze, *Archiv für Zellforschung,* with bibl. (ed. R. Goldschmidt, Leipzig, 1922); and in animals other than Coelenterata; C. H. Martin, *Biologische Centralblatt* (ed. J. Rosenthal, Erlangen, Leipzig, 1914); C. F. A. Pantin, *Journ. Exper. Biol.* (1942). Nervous System and Behaviour: G. H. Parker, *The Elementary Nervous System* (1919); C. F. A. Pantin, *Journ. Exper. Biol.* (1935), *Proc. Roy. Soc. B.* (London, 1937). Digestion: H. Boschma, *Biological Bulletin* (1925); R. Beutler, *Zeitschr. für vergl. Physiol.* (1924–26); C. M. Yonge, *Great Barrier Reef Exped., Sci. Reports* vol. i, (London, 1940). *See* also H. Boschma, etc., for *Zooxanthellae.* For recent lists of literature *see* W. Kükenthal's *Handbuch* (*supra*), and for further references the articles HYDROZOA, ANTHOZOA and GRAPTOLITES. (T. A. S.)

COELLO, ALONSO SANCHEZ (1515–1590), Spanish painter, according to some authorities a native of Portugal, was born, according to others, at Benifacio, near the city of Valencia. He studied many years in Italy; and returning to Spain in 1541 he settled at Madrid, and worked on religious themes for most of the palaces and larger churches. He was a follower of Titian, and, like him, excelled in portraits and single figures, elaborating the textures of his armours, draperies, and such accessories in a manner so masterly as strongly to influence Velazquez in his treatment of like objects. Many of his pictures were destroyed in the fires that consumed the Madrid and Prado palaces, but many good examples are yet extant, among which may be noted the portraits of the infantes Carlos and Isabella, now in the Madrid gallery, and the St. Sebastian painted in the church of San Gerónimo, also in Madrid. Coello left a daughter, Isabella Sanchez, who studied under him, and painted excellent portraits.

COELLO, ANTONIO (1611–1652), Spanish dramatist and poet, was born at Madrid and entered the household of the duke of Albuquerque. His best known plays are *El conde de Sex, El Celoso extremeño* (dramatizing one of Cervantes' *Novelas Exemplares*) and *Los Empeños de seis horas.* The latter was adapted by Samuel Tuke, under the title of *The Adventures of five Hours,* and was described by Pepys as superior to *Othello.*

COELLO, CLAUDIO (*c.* 1630–1693), Spanish painter born at Madrid, son of a well-known worker in bronze of Portuguese origin. He studied under Francisco Rizi, and was dominated at first by an overcharged, exaggerated style, which was then beginning to be admired in Madrid. He assisted his master in the execution of an altarpiece for S. Placido. He then studied and copied the works of Titian, Rubens and Van Dyck in the royal collections, to which he secured access through his friendship with the court painter D. Juan Carreño. He also profited by his friendship with Josef Donoso, who had studied seven years in Rome, and, with his co-operation, painted frescoes in some churches and palaces of Madrid. In 1671 he decorated the ceiling of the vestry in Toledo cathedral. In 1683 he was commissioned by the archbishop of Saragossa to paint frescoes in the cupola and the transept of the Augustine church. On his return to Madrid he became court painter to King Charles II., and undertook the altarpiece for the sacristy in the Escorial representing the "Transfer of the Holy Eucharist." The scene is represented as taking place in the same room in which the picture is hung. It is a fine arrangement of space in the baroque style containing some 50 life-like portraits including that of Charles II. and his prime minister. This work is his masterpiece. It is nearly allied to the realistic art of Velasquez and Carreño, and Coello here shows himself as a brilliant and strong colourist, a fine and careful draughtsman. He seems to have tried to stem the decadence, which was engulfing Spanish art. His work was universally admired, he was appointed Seneschal and his son received a pension of 300 ducats. Then Luca Giordano arrived in 1692. The preference shown by the court to the Italian favourite, hurt Coello's sensitive nature. His last work was the "Martyrdom of St. Stephen," painted for the Dominican church at Salamanca. He died on April 2, 1693, at Madrid, and was buried in the church of San Andres. He was the last important master of the great Madrid school of the 17th century.

His works are to be seen in the churches of Madrid and other cities of Spain, at the Prado, in the galleries of Munich, Budapest and Frankfurt. "The Betrothal," presented to the National Gallery, London, as by Velazquez, is perhaps an early work by Coello, who is also represented in the collections at Apsley house and Grosvenor house.

See A. de Beruete y Moret, *The School of Madrid* (1909).

COELOM AND SEROUS MEMBRANES. In human anatomy the body-cavity or coelom is divided into the *pericardium,* the two *pleurae,* the *peritoneum* and the two *tunicae vaginales.*

The *pericardium* is a closed sac in the thorax and contains the heart. Like all the serous membranes it has a visceral and a parietal layer, the former being closely applied to the heart and consisting of endothelial cells with a slight fibrous backing: to it is due the glossy appearance of a freshly removed heart. The parietal layer is double; externally there is a strong fibrous coat continuous with the other fibrous structures in the neighbourhood, while internally is the endothelial layer which is reflected from the surface of the heart, where the great vessels enter. Hence everywhere the two layers of the membrane are in contact except for a trace of fluid secreted by the serous walls.

The *pleurae* resemble the pericardium except that the fibrous outer coat of the parietal layer is not nearly as strong; it is closely attached to the inner surface of the chest walls and mesially to the outer layer of the pericardium; above it is thickened by a fibrous contribution from the scalene muscles, and forms the *dome of the pleura* which fits into the concavity of the first rib and contains the apex of the lung. The reflection of the serous layer of the pleura, from the parietal to the visceral part, takes place at the root of the lung. The upper limit of the pleural cavity reaches about half an inch above the inner third of the clavicle, while, below, it may be marked out by a line drawn from the twelfth thoracic spine to the tenth rib in the mid axillary line, the eighth in the nipple line, and the sixth at its junction with the sternum.

The *peritoneum* is a more extensive and complicated membrane; it surrounds the abdominal and pelvic viscera, and, like the other sacs, has a parietal and visceral layer. The line of reflection of these, though continuous, is very tortuous. The peritoneum consists of a *greater* and *lesser sac* which communicate through an opening (*foramen of Winslow*) and the best way of understanding these is to follow the reflections first in a vertical median (sagittal) section and then in a horizontal one, the body being supposed to be in the upright position. If a median sagittal section be studied first, and a start be made at the umbilicus (*see* fig. 1), the parietal peritoneum is seen to run upward, lining the anterior abdominal wall, and then to pass along the under surface of the diaphragm till its posterior third is reached; here there is a reflection on to the liver, forming the anterior layer of the *coronary ligament* of that viscus, while the membrane now becomes visceral and envelops the front of the liver as far back as the transverse fissure on its lower surface; here it is reflected on to the stomach forming the anterior layer of the *gastro-hepatic* or *lesser omentum.* It now covers the front of the stomach, and at the lower border runs down as the anterior layer of an apron-like fold, the *great omentum,* which sometimes reaches as low as the pubes; then it turns up again as the posterior or fourth layer of the great omentum until the transverse colon is reached, the posterior surface of which it covers and is reflected, as the

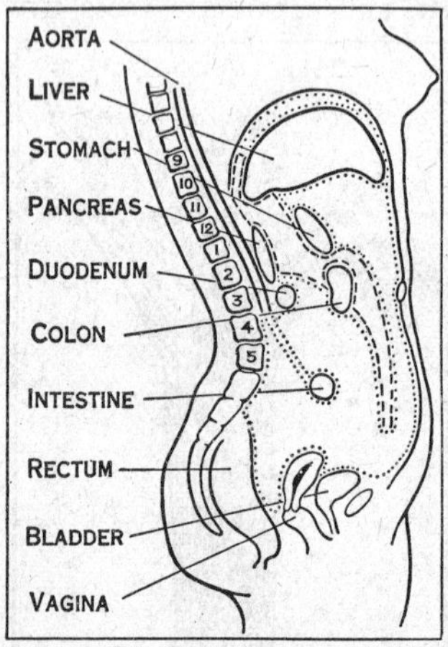

AORTA
LIVER
STOMACH
PANCREAS
DUODENUM
COLON
INTESTINE
RECTUM
BLADDER
VAGINA

FIG. 1.—VERTICAL MEDIAN SECTION OF ABDOMEN TO SHOW ARRANGEMENT OF THE PERITONEUM
The peritoneum is indicated by a dotted line for the greater sac and a broken line for the lesser sac

posterior layer of the *transverse mesocolon* to the lower part of the pancreas; after this it turns down and covers the anterior surface of the third part of the duodenum till the posterior wall of the abdomen is reached, from which it is reflected on to the small intestine as the anterior layer of the *mesentery,* a fold varying from 5 to 8 in. between its attachments. After surrounding the small intestine it becomes the posterior layer of the mesentery and so again reaches the posterior abdominal wall, down which it runs until the rectum is reached. The anterior surface of this tube is covered by peritoneum to a point about 3 in. from the anus, where it is reflected on to the uterus and vagina in the female and then on to the bladder; while in the male, on the other hand, the reflection is directly from the rectum to the bladder. At the apex of the bladder, after covering the upper surface of that organ, it is lifted off by the urachus and runs up the anterior abdominal wall to the umbilicus, from which the start was made. All this is the greater sac. The tracing of the lesser sac may be conveniently started at the transverse fissure of the liver, whence the membrane runs down to the stomach as the posterior layer of the lesser omentum, lines the posterior surface of the stomach, passes down as the second layer of the great omentum and up again as the third layer, covers the anterior surface of the transverse colon and then reaches the pancreas as the anterior layer of the transverse mesocolon. After this it covers the front of the pancreas and in the middle line of the body runs up below the diaphragm to within an inch of the anterior layer of the coronary ligament of the liver; here it is reflected on to the top of the Spigelian lobe of the liver to form the posterior layer of the coronary ligament, covers the whole Spigelian lobe, and so reaches the transverse fissure.

This section, therefore, shows two completely closed sacs without any visible communication. In the female, however, the great sac is not absolutely closed, for the Fallopian tubes open into it by their minute *ostia abdominalia,* while at the other ends they communicate with the cavity of the uterus and so with the vagina and exterior.

A horizontal section through the upper part of the first lumbar vertebra will, if a fortunate one (*see* fig. 2), pass through the foramen of Winslow and show the communication of the two sacs. A starting-point may be made from the mid-ventral line and the parietal peritoneum traced round the left side of the body wall until the outer edge of the left kidney is reached; here it passes in front of the kidney and is soon reflected off on to the spleen, which it nearly surrounds; just before it reaches the hilum of that organ, where the vessels enter, it is reflected on to the front of the stomach, forming the anterior layer of the *gastro-splenic omentum;* it soon reaches the lesser curvature of the stomach and then becomes the anterior layer of the lesser omen-

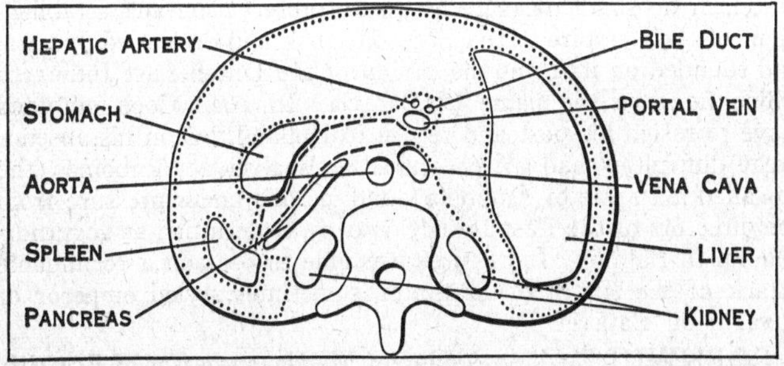

FIG. 2.—HORIZONTAL SECTION THROUGH UPPER PART OF FIRST LUMBAR VERTEBRA, SHOWING ARRANGEMENT OF THE PERITONEUM

tum, which continues until the bile duct and portal vein are reached at its right free extremity; here it turns completely round these structures and runs to the left again, as the posterior layer of the lesser omentum, behind the stomach and then to the spleen as the posterior layer of the gastro-splenic omentum. From the spleen it runs to the right once more, in front of the pancreas, until the inferior vena cava is reached, and this point is just behind the portal vein and is the place where the lesser and greater sacs communicate, known as the foramen of Winslow. From this opening the lesser sac runs to the left, while all the rest of the peritoneal cavity in the section is greater sac. From the front of the vena cava the parietal peritoneum passes in front of the right kidney and round the right abdominal wall to the mid-ventral line. The right part of this section is filled by the liver, which is completely surrounded by a visceral layer of peritoneum, and no reflection is usually seen at this level between it and the parietal layer. Some of

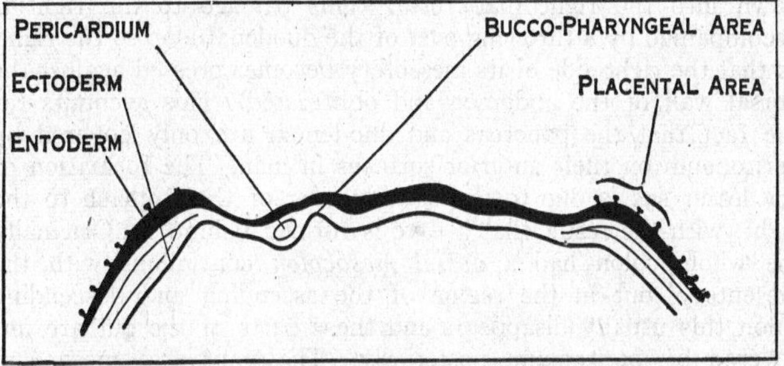

FROM CUNNINGHAM, "TEXT-BOOK OF ANATOMY" (OXFORD UNIVERSITY PRESS)

FIG. 3.—LONGITUDINAL SECTION SHOWING THE DIFFERENT AREAS OF THE BLASTODERMIC VESICLE IN EARLY DEVELOPMENT OF THE OVUM

the viscera, such as the kidneys and pancreas, are retro-peritoneal; others, such as the small intestines and transverse colon, are surrounded, except at one point where they are attached to the dorsal wall by a *mesentery* or *mesocolon* as the reflections are called; others again are completely surrounded, and of these the caecum is an example; while some, like the liver and bladder, have large uncovered areas, and the reflections of the membrane form ligaments which allow considerable freedom of movement.

The *tunica vaginalis* is the remains of a peritoneal pocket which descends into the scrotum during foetal life before the testis itself descends. After the descent of the testis the upper part usually becomes obliterated, while the lower part forms a serous sac which nearly surrounds the testis. The parietal layer lines the inner wall of its own side of the scrotum.

Embryology.—As the mesoderm spreads over the embryo it splits into two layers, the outer of which (*somatopleure*) lines the parietal or ectodermal wall, while the inner lines the entoderm (*splanchnopleure*); between the two is the coelom. The pericardial area is early differentiated from the rest of the coelom and at first lies in front of the neural and bucco-pharyngeal area; here the mesoderm stretches right across the mid-line, which it does not in front and behind. As the head of the embryo is formed the pericardium is gradually turned right over, so that the dorsal side becomes the ventral and the anterior limit the posterior; this will be evident on referring to figs. 3 and 4.

The two primitive aortae lie at first in the ventral wall of the pericardium, but with the folding over they come to lie in the dorsal wall and gradually bulge into the cavity as they coalesce to form the heart, so that the heart drops into the dorsal side of the pericardium and draws down a fold of the membrane called the *dorsal mesocardium.* In mammals A. Robinson (*Jour. Anat. and Phys.,* xxxvii. I) has shown that no ventral mesocardium exists, though in more lowly vertebrates it is present. Laterally the pericardial cavity communicates with the general cavity of the coelom, but with the growth of the Cuvierian ducts (*see* development of veins) these communications disappear. Originally the mesocardium runs the whole length of the pericardium from before backward, but later on the middle part becomes obliterated.

Just behind the pericardium and in front of the umbilicus, which at first are close together, the mesoderm forms a mass into which the developing lungs push bag-like protrusions of the coelom. These lose their connection with the rest of the coelom, as the diaphragm develops, and become the pleural cavities. The remainder of the coelom persists as the peritoneum. At first the stomach and intestine form a straight tube, connected to the dorsum of the embryo by a *dorsal mesentery* and to the mid-ventral wall in front of the umbilicus by a *ventral mesentery.* Into the ventral mesentery the liver grows as diverticula from the duodenum, so that some of the mesentery remains as the *falciform ligament* of the liver and some as the lesser omentum. Into the dorsal mesentery the pancreas grows, also as diverticula, from the duodenum, while the spleen is developed from the mesoderm contained in the same fold. As the stomach turns over and its left side becomes ventral, the dorsal mesentery attached to it is pulled out, so that part forms the great omentum and part the gastrosplenic omentum. When the caecum is formed as a diverticulum from the intestine it is close to the liver but gradually travels down into the right iliac fossa. This passage to the right is accompanied by a throwing over of the duodenal loop to the right, so that the right side of its mesentery becomes pressed against the dorsal wall of the abdomen and obliterated. This accounts for the fact that the pancreas and duodenum are only covered by peritoneum on their anterior surfaces in man. The formation of the lesser sac is due to the turning over of the stomach to the right, with the result that a cave is formed behind it. Originally the whole colon had a *dorsal mesocolon* continuous with the mesentery, but in the region of the ascending and descending colon this usually disappears and these parts of the gut are uncovered by peritoneum posteriorly. The transverse mesocolon persists and at first is quite free from the great omentum, but later, in man, the fourth layer of the great omentum becomes continuous with the posterior layer of the transverse mesocolon.

Comparative Anatomy.—In *Amphioxus* the coelom is developed in the embryo as a series of bilateral pouches from the sides of the alimentary canal; these are therefore entodermal in their origin, as in *Sagitta* and the Echinodermata among the invertebrates. In the adult the coelom is represented by two dorsal canals communicating with a ventral canal by means of branchial canals which run down the outer side of the primary gill bars. Into the dorsal canals the nephridia open. In the intestinal region the coelom is only present on the left side.

In the higher vertebrates (*Craniata*) the coelom is developed by a splitting of the mesoderm into two layers, and a pericardium is constricted off from the general cavity. In all cases the ova burst into the coelom before making their way to the exterior, and in some, e.g., *Amphioxus,* lamprey (Cyclostomata), eels and mud-fish (Dipnoi), the sperm cells do so too. The Cyclostomata have a pair of *genital pores* which lead from the coelom into the urinogenital sinus, and so to the exterior.

In the Elasmobranch fish there is a *pericardio-peritoneal canal* forming a communication between these two parts of the coelom;

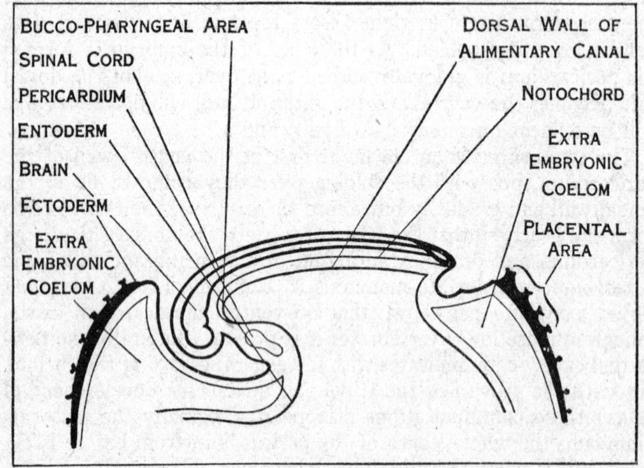

AFTER YOUNG AND ROBINSON, FROM CUNNINGHAM, "TEXT-BOOK OF ANATOMY"

FIG. 4.—LONGITUDINAL SECTION SHOWING RELATION OF PARTS TO SEROUS MEMBRANES IN THE EARLY DEVELOPING EMBRYO

also a large common opening for the two oviducts in the region of the liver, and two openings (*abdominal pores*) on the surface close to the cloacal aperture. In the Teleostomi (Teleostean and Ganoid fish) abdominal pores are rare, but in most Teleostei (bony fish) the ova pass directly down oviducts, as they do in arthropods, without entering the peritoneal cavity; there is little doubt, however, that these oviducts are originally coelomic in origin. In the Dipnoi (mud-fish) abdominal pores are found, and probably serve as a passage for the sperm cells, since there are no vasa deferentia. In fishes a complete dorsal mesentery is seldom found in the adult; in many cases it only remains as a tube surrounding the vessels passing to the alimentary canal.

In the Amphibia, Reptilia and Aves, one cavity acts as pleura and peritoneum, though in the latter the lungs are not completely surrounded by a serous membrane. In many lizards the comparatively straight intestine, with its continuous dorsal mesentery and ventral mesentery in the anterior part of the abdomen, is very like a stage in the development of the human and other mammalian embryos. In the mammalia the diaphragm is complete (*see* DIAPHRAGM) and divides the pleuroperitoneal cavity into its two constituent parts. In the lower mammals the derivatives of the original dorsal mesentery do not undergo as much fusion and obliteration as they do in adult man; the ascending and descending mesocolon is retained, and the transverse mesocolon contracts no adhesion to the great omentum. It is common, however, to find a fenestrated arrangement of the great omentum which shows that its layers have been completely obliterated in many places.

In those animals, such as the rabbit, in which the testes are sometimes in the scrotum and sometimes in the abdomen, the communication between the peritoneum and the tunica vaginalis remains throughout life.

BIBLIOGRAPHY.—Full bibliography in Quain's *Anatomy.*

COELOMATA, a zoological term denoting those animals that have a true coelom, *i.e.,* a space within the entomesoderm. Animals with no space between the digestive canal and body wall, as the flatworms (*Platyhelminthes*), are termed Acoelomata, and those in which this space is not a true coelom are called Pseudocoelomata.

COELOSTAT, a mirror driven by clock-work so as to reflect continually the same region of the sky into the field of view of a fixed telescope. The mirror is mounted so as to rotate about an axis in its own plane which points to the pole of the heavens, and is driven at the rate of one revolution in 48 (sidereal) hours. The image of a star seen in the mirror is then stationary. The device is particularly useful in eclipse expeditions when elaborate equatorial mounting of the telescopes is impossible. Other instruments for somewhat similar purposes are the heliostat and siderostat (*q.v.*).

COEN, JAN PIETERSZOON (1587–1630), fourth governor-general of the Dutch East Indies, was born at Hoorn, and spent his youth at Rome in the house of the famous merchants the Piscatori. In 1607 he sailed from Amsterdam to the Indies as second commercial agent, and remained away four years. In 1612 he was sent out at the head of a trading expedition. In 1613 he was made a councillor and director-general of the East Indian trade. Afterwards he became president at Bantam, and on Oct. 31, 1617, he was promoted in succession to Laurens Reaal to the post of governor-general. To his vigour and intrepidity the Dutch in no small measure owed the preservation and establishment of their empire in the East. He took and destroyed Jacatra, and founded on its ruins the capital of the Dutch East Indies, to which he gave the name of Batavia. In 1622 Coen obtained leave to resign his post and return to Holland, but in his absence great difficulties had arisen with the English at Amboina (the so-called massacre of Amboina), and in 1627 under pressure from the directors of the East India Company he returned as governor-general to Batavia. In 1629 he was able to beat off a formidable attack of the sultan of Mataram, sometimes styled emperor of Java, upon Batavia.

COENWULF (d. 821), king of Mercia, successor of Ecgfrith, son of Offa, in 796. In 798 he invaded Kent, imprisoned Eadberht Praen, and made his own brother Cuthred king. On Cuthred's death (807) Coenwulf seems to have taken Kent into his own hands. He abolished the archbishopric of Lichfield, probably before 803, as the Hygeberht who signed as an abbot at the council of Cloveshoe in that year was presumably the former archbishop. Coenwulf appears from the charters to have had a long dispute with Wulfred of Canterbury, who was consecrated in 806. It was probably only settled in 825, when the lawsuit of Cwoenthryth, his daughter, with Wulfred was terminated. He died in 821 and was succeeded by his brother Ceolwulf I.

See Earle and Plummer's edition of the Anglo-Saxon Chronicle,

796, 819 (Oxford, 1892); W. de G. Birch, *Cartularium Saxonicum,* 378 (1885–93).

COERCION was described by Mr. Justice Peterson (in *Hodges* v. *Webb,* 2 Ch. 70, 1920) as involving "something in the nature of negation of choice." Its principal significance in law is as one of the forms of undue influence that will invalidate gifts, whether testamentary or made between living people. "The influence which will set aside a will must amount to force and coercion, destroying free agency" (*see* Sir E. V. Williams, *Law of Executors,* 12th ed., p. 32 [London, 1930]). It would, as such, be a form of duress sufficient for the annulment of a marriage. In the sphere of criminal law, coercion excuses a participation in crime if this is induced by sheer physical force, though threats are not held to excuse: the coercion must amount to physical subjection. By s. 47 of the Criminal Justice act, 1925, on a charge against a wife for any offense other than treason or murder, it is a good defense to prove that the offense was committed in the presence, and under the coercion, of the husband.

(W. T. Ws.)

COEUR, JACQUES (*c.* 1395–1456), French trader, was neither an economist nor a statesman but an ingenious businessman. He was born at Bourges, a town of drapers and merchants, where his father was a skinner. About 1429 he formed a commercial partnership with two brothers named Godart; but he was compromised by a fraudulent speculation in coinage, in the contracting for which he had taken a share. In 1432 he initiated himself into the Levant trade, sailing from Narbonne on a ship belonging to merchants of Montpellier; Bertrandon de la Broquière, equerry of Philip the Good, duke of Burgundy, met him at Damascus. On his return his career soon became brilliant. He was master of the mint in Paris in 1436 and *argentier du roi* (steward of the royal expenditure and banker of the court) three years later. He became a member of the king's council (1442), then commissioner to the estates of Languedoc (1441–51) and inspector general of taxes (*visiteur général des gabelles*) for Languedoc (1447). Jacques Coeur inspired the *ordonnances* issued between 1435 and 1451 to withdraw the money that had been stamped with rival French and English superscriptions during the war. The king, Charles VII, charged him with diplomatic missions: in 1447, Jean de Villages, his nephew, obtained from the sultan of Egypt certain privileges for French merchants and also the right to consular representation; and Jacques Coeur himself managed to maintain good relations with Genoa and won the favour of Pope Nicholas V by his zeal to promote the abdication of the antipope Felix V. In 1449 Jacques Coeur lent the king the money necessary for the recovery of Normandy and entered Rouen with him apparelled no less magnificently than he. He was at the height of his glory. Ennobled in 1441, he managed the marriage of his daughter with a nobleman, got his brother made bishop of Luçon and saw his son archbishop of Bourges. He possessed about 40 manors and built a palace at Bourges which remains one of the finest monuments of Gothic domestic architecture in France.

Jacques Coeur's businesses were various but connected. Their basis was Levantine trade; the pope had authorized him to trade with the infidels. At Montpellier, the heart of his activity, he built a house (the *loge*) to which were delivered the spices brought by his seven galleys in exchange for scarlet cloth to the taste of the Levantines. All the chief cities of western Europe supplied and consumed his wares. At Barcelona, Avignon, Lyons, Paris, Limoges, Rouen and Bruges, Jacques Coeur had his factors; at Tours was the warehouse of the "Argenterie"; and the end of the Hundred Year's War facilitated relations with England and Scotland. Jacques Coeur competed with the Italian ports. At the end of his career he used the port of Marseilles. To sustain his enterprises, Jacques Coeur acquired much land and property, used his connections and his political position and received gratifications from the towns and the estates of Languedoc, whose interests he defended. The usual silver money necessary for trading in Levant was provided by the mines of Beaujolais and the Lyonnais that the king had granted to him.

Other merchants, however, were jealous of the quick progress of Jacques Coeur. His debtors, numerous at the court, resolved to disgrace him. He was accused of having poisoned Agnes Sorel, the king's mistress who had died in 1450; and he was charged with speculation and extortion. Arrested in July 1451 and confined for two years, he was condemned to do public penance for his fault and to remain a prisoner until he should have paid a very heavy sum; and all his possessions were confiscated. He would have remained a prisoner if Jean de Villages had not arranged his escape to Beaucaire and thence to Marseilles, Nice, Pisa and Rome, where the pope received him. But a year later on Nov. 25, 1456, he died at Chios, whither he had gone in command of the fleet sent by Pope Calixtus II to relieve Rhodes.

Louis XI, in reaction against his father, was to consider Jacques Coeur's rehabilitation, to return some of his property to his family and, by taking his agents into his service, to revive the enterprises that he had initiated.

Bibliography.—P. Clément, *Jacques Coeur et Charles VII* (Paris, 1858; 2nd ed., 1874); L. Guiraud, *Recherches et conclusions nouvelles sur le prétendu rôle de Jacques Coeur* (Montpellier, 1900); C. B. Fabre, "Politique et diplomatie de Jacques Coeur," *Revue hist. diplom.* (Paris, 1902–04); H. Prutz, *Jacques Coeur von Bourges, Geschichte eines patriotischen Kaufmanns aus dem 15 Jahrhundert* (Berlin, 1911); A. B. Kerr, *Jacques Coeur, Merchant Prince of the Middle Ages* (New York, 1927); R. Bouvier, *Jacques Coeur, un financier colonial au XVième siècle* (Paris, 1928); M. Mollat, "Les Affaires de Jacques Coeur à Bruges," *Revue du Nord* (Lille, 1950); M. Mollat, ed., *Les Affaires de Jacques Coeur: Journal du procureur Dauvet* (Paris, 1952); H. de Man, *Jacques Coeur, der königliche Kaufmann* (Berne, 1950; French trans., Bourges, 1952); C. Marinesco, "Du nouveau sur Jacques Coeur," *Mélanges L. Halphen* (Paris, 1951) and "Jacques Coeur et ses affaires aragonaises, catalanes et napolitaines," *Revue historique* (Paris, 1951).

(Mi. M.)

COEUR D'ALENE, a tribe of American Indians who occupied the heavily forested area around Coeur d'Alene lake and the western slope of the Bitterroot mountains, Ida. They were one of the larger tribes of the Plateau culture area. Being relatively near the Great Plains they were subjected to influences from that area but few foreign traits were accepted. They clung tenaciously to the typical Plateau traits of democracy, pacifism and devotion to the guardian spirit religion.

They spoke a language of the Salish stock but many were bilingual, the second language being that of their southern neighbours, Nez Perce.

Various folk etymologies for the name Coeur d'Alene have been suggested but none is demonstrably correct. They call themselves by a tribal name which may be related to the term used by Lewis and Clark, Skeet-so-mish. The explorers did not visit the tribe but obtained information regarding them from the Nez Perce. They estimated the population at 2,000. Their maps show the location of the tribe and of Coeur d'Alene lake which they called Waytom.

No treaty was ever made with these Indians. In 1873 the United States simply took possession of their land, except for a reservation which was set aside by executive order. In 1892, when gold and other ores were discovered there, the reservation was reduced in size by act of congress.

Bibliography.—James A. Teit, "The Salishan Tribes of the Western Plateaus," Bureau of American Ethnology, *45th Annual Report* (1930); Verne F. Ray, "Plateau," *Anthropological Records,* vol. 8, no. 2 (1942); Gladys Reichard, "Coeur d'Alene," *Handbook of American Indian Languages,* ed. by F. Boas, vol. 3 (New York, 1939).

(V. F. R.)

COEUR D'ALENE, a city of Idaho, U.S., 33 mi. E. of Spokane, at the outlet of Lake Coeur d'Alene; the county seat of Kootenai county. It is on federal highways 10 and 95, and is served by the Northern Pacific, Chicago, Milwaukee, St. Paul and Pacific, Spokane International and Great Northern railways, also by air and bus. The population was 12,198 in 1950, and 10,049 in 1940 by the federal census.

It is in the rich lumbering, mining and agricultural region known as the "inland empire." The city has several large lumber mills and smaller manufacturing plants. It was settled about 1880, and incorporated in 1889.

COFFEE. The discovery of coffee is quite generally accredited to Africa, although earliest cultivation is traced to southern Arabia. Coffee grew in Africa only in a wild state until fairly modern times, when it began to be developed there (about 1878) on a production basis by British interests. Never an important factor in the world coffee market, even through the first quarter of the 20th century, the growth of coffee in Africa approximately doubled in the decade 1929–39, and doubled again in the next 15 years to a point where, in the marketing year 1953–54, Africa accounted for approximately one-sixth of the world's exportable production.

Coffee probably derives its name from the original Arabic *qahwah,* indirectly through its Turkish form *kahveh,* although some etymologists connect it with the name Kaffa, a town in southwest Ethiopia (Abyssinia) reputed to be the birthplace of coffee. Through the ages the Arabian primitive root shows influences in whatever word has come to mean coffee in all tongues, according to the pronunciation of each language, as: Bohemian, *kava;* Chinese, *kai-fey;* Danish and Swedish, *kaffe;* Dutch, *koffie;* Finnish, *kahvi;* French, Spanish and Portuguese, *café;* German, *Kaffee;* Greek, *kaféo;* Hungarian, *kavé;* Italian, *caffè;* Japanese, *kéhi;* Latin (scientific), *coffea;* Persian, *qéhvé;* Polish, *kawa;* Rumanian, *cafea;* Russian, *kophe.*

History.—The origin of coffee is vague and obscure, but its history is rich in legend. One of the most accepted tales surrounding the discovery of coffee about A.D. 850 is that of Kaldi, an Arabian goatherd. Bewildered by the queer antics of his flock, Kaldi is supposed to have eaten berries of the evergreen bush on which the goats were feeding and, overjoyed at the feeling of exhilaration which he experienced, has been pictured in legend as dashing off in excitement to proclaim his great find to the world.

The physiological action of coffee in dissipating drowsiness was soon discovered and taken advantage of in connection with the prolonged religious service of the Mohammedans, but the strictly orthodox or conservative section of the priesthood claimed that it was an intoxicating beverage and, therefore, prohibited by the Koran. Severe penalties were threatened upon those disposed to its use. Nevertheless, coffee drinking spread rapidly among Arabian Mohammedans, and its growth and use became general in Arabia.

The early record of coffee in Europe, where it was introduced into one country after another during the 16th and 17th centuries, is filled with accounts of its use as a religious, political, and medical potion, its ups-and-downs in favour, its persecution, prohibition or approval. It is interesting to note that most of the attention given to coffee in the music and literature of that day was in support or defense of coffee and its "soul-stirring attributes," rather than critical. One of the most unique contributions to the good of coffee in music was Johann Sebastian Bach's "Coffee Cantata" (published in 1732), which portrayed "the protest of the fair sex" against the then existing propaganda in Germany for abstinence from coffee by women because "many doctors claimed its use provoked sterility."

Coffee gained its first real popularity as a beverage in the coffeehouses of London, which became centres of political, social and literary influence. The wits, philosophers and writers of the day warmed their hearts and loosened their tongues over the steaming cup. The first London coffeehouse was established in (or about) 1652 "at St. Michael's Alley in Cornhill" by one Pasqua Rosée and a "quarreling partner" named Bowman, from whom Rosée soon parted.

In the first known coffee advertisement, a handbill produced in 1652 (original in the British Museum), Pasqua Rosée proclaimed that coffee "quickens the spirits, and makes the heart lightsome . . . is good against sore eyes . . . excellent to prevent and cure the dropsy, gout, and scurvy . . . neither laxative nor restringent."

Continental Europe, too, became well implanted with the idea of coffee, and the coffeehouse flourished in most of these countries later in the 17th century. In the major cities of North America (Boston, New York and Philadelphia), coffeehouses also became popular, starting about 1689. The Merchants' Coffeehouse, established in New York in 1737, is claimed by some authorities to have been the "birthplace of the American Union."

Capt. John Smith, the founder of Virginia, is said to have been the first to bring knowledge of coffee to America in 1607, but it is not certain that he actually carried coffee with him, nor is there a definite "first date" for coffee's appearance in North America. It is not found in the records that there was coffee aboard the Mayflower (1620), nor proof that the Dutch brought coffee from Holland to New Amsterdam (New York) in the early or mid-17th century. It is known, however, that the first licence to sell coffee in the United States was issued to a Dorothy Jones of Boston in 1670.

Until toward the close of the 17th century, the world's rather limited supply of coffee was obtained almost entirely from the province of Yemen in southern Arabia. But, with the increasing popularity of the beverage, the propagation of the plant spread rapidly from the southern parts of Arabia to Ceylon (1658), to Java and other islands of the Netherland Indies starting about 1696, Haiti and Santo Domingo in 1715, Dutch Guiana (Surinam) in 1718, thence throughout the tropical countries of the new world. To date a few . . . Brazil, 1727; Jamaica, 1730; Cuba, 1748; Puerto Rico, 1755; Costa Rica, 1779; Venezuela, 1784; Mexico, 1790; Colombia, late 18th century; but not in El Salvador until 1840. Coffee growing started in the Hawaiian Islands (Kona district, Island of Hawaii) in 1825.

One of the most dramatic stories of bringing coffee to the new world is that of Gabriel Mathieu de Clieu, a young French naval officer assigned as captain of infantry at Martinique, a small island in the Lesser Antilles. In 1723 (some authorities set the date as 1720), De Clieu, on a visit to France, became determined to carry the cultivation of coffee to Martinique, having heard of the Dutch success in transplanting coffee from Arabia to the East Indies and realizing that similar climatic conditions existed in Martinique. The few coffee plants then being cultivated in Paris were guarded in the royal hothouse of Louis XV. Because De Clieu's motive was a patriotic one, he was able to enlist the aid of M. de Chirac, the king's "physician-in-ordinary," in obtaining one (some writers say two or three) of the precious plants. His trip across the Atlantic was not an easy one for, what with the time consumed in escaping capture by pirates and floundering through violent storms, the ship's supply of water ran so low as to be rationed.

In his own papers, De Clieu recorded that for more than a month he was obliged to share his scanty ration of water with his tiny coffee plant (he refers to only one) "upon which my happiest hopes were founded and which was the source of my delight." After trial and tribulation, De Clieu's precious little tree was finally planted in Martinique and carefully nursed to its first harvest of coffee cherries, from the seeds of which a big majority of the coffee plants in the Americas are said to be descended. By 1777, three years after the death of the zealous De Clieu, there were nearly 19,000,000 coffee trees in Martinique.

By the 20th century, coffee had become responsible in a large measure for the income and livelihood of many countries lying between the Tropic of Capricorn and the Tropic of Cancer. Although practically every country within this area around the earth produces some coffee, the concentration of production has centred in the western hemisphere. The largest supplies of green coffee come from South and Central America, a high percentage of the world's total being produced in Brazil alone.

Botany of Coffee.—The genus *Coffea,* to which the common coffee tree belongs, contains 25 or more species in the tropics of the old world, most of which grow only wild.

Of the various species, *Coffea arabica* makes up the bulk of world production. Others commercially known are *C. liberica, C. stenophylla* and *C. robusta.*

The common Arabian coffee shrub (*C. arabica*) is an evergreen plant which under natural conditions may grow to a height of 30 ft. or more. But for commercial purposes, particularly in countries where coffees are picked by hand, the trees are usually kept, by topping, to heights under 15 ft., which gives more easy access for harvesting. Leaves of the coffee tree resemble laurel in form (oblong-ovate-acuminate, 4 to 6 in. in length, $1\frac{1}{2}$ to $2\frac{1}{2}$ in. wide) and have a deep rich green colour and a waxy-looking surface.

Flowers of the coffee tree, which are produced in dense clusters in the axils of the leaves, have a five-toothed calyx, a tubular five-parted corolla, five stamens and a single bifid style. Coffee trees in blossom are things of beauty, but the white jasmine-like flowers last only a few days. Their disappearance is followed by clusters of green cherries which advance through various stages of green and golden brown until fully ripe, when they are a bright red, similar in colour and shape to ordinary fruit cherries, although somewhat less plump and slightly elongated.

The red outside covering of the coffee cherry is a thick pulpy skin. Inside is a layer of yellowish jelly-like substance that completely surrounds the two beans or berries, which lie with their flat faces together, similar to the two halves of a peanut. Each bean or berry is enclosed in a membranous endocarp, commonly called the "parchment," which is brittle when dried. Inside this, completely surrounding each individual coffee bean, is a delicate spermoderm (seed-skin) commercially called the "silver skin." Malformation in coffee cherries frequently results in their containing only a single bean, which is not flat on one side, but completely circular. Such beans are called "pea-berry" coffee. The seeds or beans of the coffee cherry are of a soft, semitranslucent, bluish or greenish colour, hard and tough in texture.

Cultivation and Preparation of Green Coffee.—Primitive methods were used in the production of coffee for many years, but by the 20th century the large commercial producers were using intensive cultivation methods, giving the same care to preparing their plantations and attending their trees as do growers of grains and fruits. By the middle of the 20th century, most of the coffee-producing countries, particularly in the western hemisphere, had made great advances in the study of soil erosion and in the adoption of modern practices in fertilization and use of insecticides in a continuing effort to obtain the maximum production of quality coffee from a plantation of given size.

The coffee tree is not free of destructive pests and plant diseases. The Ceylon coffee-leaf disease (*Hemileia vastatrix*), a fungoid growth which appeared in Ceylon in 1869 and spread throughout the coffee-growing sections of the eastern hemisphere (found also in almost every coffee-producing country), is at least partially to blame for having once destroyed the coffee industry of the old world. Insects and fungi of various types are the cause of most concern to coffee growers. The *stephanodores* (coffee-bean borer, referred to in Brazil as the "coffee plague" or *broca*), coffee "leaf-miner," Mediterranean fruit fly, and various forms of root disease are among the worst and most common. It is only through rigorous and continuous effort on the part of growers that they are kept under reasonable control, mostly through the use of modern insecticides. Research laboratories and technical stations have been established in the larger producing countries for the purpose of furthering the science of coffee-growing—increasing the rate of yield per tree, creating new and improved techniques for fighting leaf rust and the other forms of infestation mentioned and, hopefully, developing of a frost-resistant coffee tree.

In 1954 the United States government, recognizing the need for greater world production of coffee to meet the requirements of the continually-growing population of the United States (as well as the increasing demand of other countries of the world), started to develop through its Foreign Operations administration an expanded program of providing technical assistance to the coffee-producing countries of the western hemisphere in the establishment and expansion of research and training facilities. At the time it was indicated that similar aid would be made available to other parts of the world where coffee was already being produced or where climatic and soil conditions might favour attempts to grow coffee on a commercial scale.

Cultivation of the coffee plant over a period of a few hundred years has brought about considerable variation in local types as a result of climatic and soil conditions. The colour of coffee beans after preparation may differ considerably as to shade, and variations in size and shape of the beans make it possible to differentiate commercial types by appearance, although these characteristics distinguishable to the eye are not always indicative of quality "in the cup." In general, it may be said that the greatest differences in the quality of the coffee bean are produced by altitude—the higher the altitude, up to the limit of cultivability, the milder the product. High-altitude coffee beans are usually "mild" in character, and this mildness may be translated into terms of aromatic substance, which has much to do with contributing to the pleasurable aroma and taste of the beverage.

Coffee is grown under varying weather conditions at altitudes from 1,500 to 6,000 ft., but it is more or less generally conceded that the finest coffees usually come from the higher elevations—3,000 to 6,000 ft. Coffee requires a warm and humid climate, preferably with the sun on the plant only part of the day, which perhaps explains why hilly or mountainous countries are preferred for planting of trees. Desirable temperature averages 65° F. to 75° F. the year around, although coffee grows well in some places where greater variations occur (over 80° F. or under 60° F.). It should be noted that in tropical countries elevations up to 6,000 ft. or more are not accompanied by the extremes of low temperature found at such elevations in the northern latitudes, although frost-producing temperatures have been recorded in some coffee countries at infrequent intervals.

Coffee trees are planted with great regularity but become so dense after a few years that they almost appear to be growing wild. In the fore part of the 20th century, the trend was toward closer pruning of coffee trees to permit passageway and more easy access at time of picking. The coffee tree begins to produce a small number of cherries at the age of three, but on the average it is the fifth year before a tree comes into full bearing. It may continue to yield profitably for as long as 50 to 60 years, although 25 to 30 years is average, and many growers prefer to replace trees after 12 to 15 years, which makes for better quality and higher yield.

The steps involved in the cultivation and processing of green coffee differ somewhat from country to country, and from locality to locality, but the over-all procedure may be summarized in a very general way. Coffee trees are propagated either from seeds or from slips. In the latter case, a unique transplanting method is used which consists of bending down the lower branches of the tree and burying the tops in the earth. After about four months, roots form and the new growth starts.

Propagation from seeds is usually done in carefully prepared nursery beds. Seeds, selected from trees of known productivity in quality and quantity, are usually planted about an inch apart, in rows marked off in the nursery beds. To protect the tender shoots from too much sun as they come through the ground, nursery beds must have a shade covering. This is usually constructed from various kinds of brush or other tropical growth. When seedlings are four to six months old they have to be transplanted to allow more room for development of the plants that are healthy and virile. At about 18 months, when the plants are approximately 20 in. high, they are transplanted for the last time to whatever permanent planting spot has been selected. As the coffee trees continue to grow and begin to reach maturity they require more and more sunshine for proper development and ripening of the cherries, so frequent pruning of shade trees among which they have been planted is necessary.

In some producing countries, coffee cherries are allowed to ripen to a point where they shrivel and begin to dry on the trees and are then shaken off onto large canvasses. The higher grades of coffee, however, are picked when the cherries are at the desired stage of ripeness. Picking is done by hand in a very selective manner. Trees are not stripped. Only the ripe cherries are removed, and it takes several pickings before a crop is completely harvested. In some countries the harvesting is entirely seasonal, while in others it is almost a year-round process, several crops being produced each year. Picking is done by men, women and children. Under good conditions, a fair day's pick is from 100 to 125 lb. of coffee cherries. It takes about 5 lb. of cherries to make 1 lb. of green coffee beans, so, in terms of usable coffee, it might be said that a picker's capacity is from 25 to 30 lb. a day. On the average, a coffee tree will produce from $1\frac{1}{2}$ to 2 lb. of green coffee beans a season; thus a plantation must be of a rather extensive size to produce tonnage of any great consequence.

Coffee may be prepared by either a "dry" or a "wash" process. By the "dry" method, sometimes called "unwashed" or "natural," the coffee cherries are washed and spread out on cement floors in the air and sun to dry. After drying, the coffee is repeatedly run through fanning and hulling machines to remove the hulls, dried pulp and parchment, and then is subjected to further cleaning by machines which remove portions of the silver skin.

The "wash" process is quite different. The cherries are first put through a pulping machine which breaks them open and virtually squeezes the beans right out of the mass of pulpy skin. Then the beans go into large tanks where they are left for about 24 hours. Slight fermentation takes place in the jelly-like substance, which the coffee grower calls "honey." This fermentation loosens the honey so it can easily be removed by thorough washing back and forth through several hundred feet of washing canals. After washing, the coffee is spread out in patios to dry. It takes two to three weeks in the sun for the coffee to become thoroughly dried, and during this time it must be continuously turned over and over so that every bean will receive its share of tropical warmth. When climatic conditions do not permit drying in the sun, mechanical means are employed. Warm air is circulated through the coffee as it revolves in a large perforated drum. When the desired stage of drying has been reached, the coffee beans are put through hulling and polishing machines which crack and remove the brittle parchment and silver skin.

In the case of the highest quality coffees, there is then a careful hand inspection to remove imperfect beans, which is the final step before packing the coffee in bags for shipment to the coffee ports of the world. (In Brazil, coffee is sacked in 60-kg. bags—132.276 lb. In other countries, the shipping unit may vary from about 150 to 165 lb., and in a few instances may run as high as 200 lb. However, the 60-kg. bag is the accepted statistical unit in most all computations of world production, exports or imports that are expressed in terms of "bags.")

Tasting and Blending.—In European countries, where coffee has been sold to a great extent in the whole bean, purchase used to be largely on the basis of fine appearance of the bean as to size, colour, and other physical characteristics, although in the years subsequent to 1946, when Europe began to again become a customer in the world coffee market (after World War II), this practice became less general. In the U.S., over a long period of years, a more selective manner of purchasing was established; coffees are bought primarily on cup test for taste and quality. Coffee testing is the work of a lifetime. Proficiency cannot be attained in a few months, or even a few years. Most coffee testers start training at an early age and continue study almost without interruption, for they must depend entirely upon taste and smell and devote great attention to the development of those senses. It has been said that the test to which coffee is subjected is one of the "most delicate known to science," since coffee defies all known chemical tests for evaluation of quality. That can be determined only by the senses of taste and smell.

Coffees grown in the various countries differ by types and kind, as well as by grades. In fact, coffees from different plantations in the same producing sections nearly always show a variety of characteristics. In the parlance of the trade, "Brazils" and "milds" are the terms generally used to distinguish between coffees grown in Brazil and those grown in other countries. All those grown in Central and South America (with the exception of Brazil) fall into the "mild" classification.

Broadly speaking, the "mild" coffees are regarded as superior in characteristics to "Brazils," although this is not a strictly true differentiation, for a great deal of the product of Brazil is of finer quality than some of the coffees which come from "mild" producing countries. In general, coffees grown in Africa and Asia fall into the "mild" classification. Further distinctions are made as to "hardness" or "softness," "high-grown," "washed," "unwashed," "naturals," etc., but these are technical distinctions of grading which primarily concern only the grower and the buyer. It is the intricate task of the coffee tester to combine many different lots of coffee to produce a satisfactory blend of one type or another.

Roasting.—Until roasted, coffee has none of the flavour or taste that a layman might recognize as coffee. Roasting gives the brown colour and transforms the natural elements into others which give coffee its splendid aromatic qualities and pleasing taste. Full development of the flavour depends to a great degree on the avoidance of underroasting or overroasting. Skill and experience is required to avoid the slight variations which might yield an undesirable result. Coffee-roasting firms in the United States lead the world in equipment, some having developed mechanical controls of roasting operations which are considered to be foolproof to the extent of eliminating the element of human error in maintaining uniformity of roast. These basic principles have been adapted by equipment manufacturers who specialize in the building of machinery for the coffee trade. Green coffee loses about 16% of its weight in the roasting process. Therefore, it should be remembered in connection with any study of green coffee statistics that it requires approximately 1.19 lb. of green coffee to produce 1 lb. of roasted coffee; thus, 1 lb. of green coffee is equivalent to .84 lb. of roasted coffee.

Grinding.—Coffees packaged in ground form by the manufacturer go through this process immediately after roasting. In most modern roasting plants, this is done by feeding the coffee through steel rollers which first crack it and then cut it to whatever the particular roaster considers the proper degree of fineness. Some coffees are left in the whole bean to be ground in the grocery store at time of purchase by the ultimate user, or in some cases ground in the home.

Ideas with respect to granulation vary to some extent. Some roasters put out their product in several different degrees of grind, each identified as being especially suited for certain types of coffee-brewing devices. Others produce what is referred to as an "all-purpose grind," composed of certain proportions of coarse, medium, and fine particles intended to permit proper extraction of the taste and strength elements in brewing a cup of beverage balanced in aroma, flavour and strength by any method of preparation.

Early in 1948 the national bureau of standards of the United States department of commerce, in co-operation with the National Coffee Association of the U.S.A., issued a Simplified Practice Recommendation stipulating three degrees of fineness for standard grinds for coffee (with reasonable tolerances) identified as regular grind, drip grind and fine grind. Adherence to these standards is not mandatory, but they have been fairly generally followed by roasters in the United States who market their product in more than one grind. Regardless of the type of grind, uniformity of granulation is important and various methods of checking, principally with wire screen sieves and sieve shakers, are used to make sure that the proportions of the various sized grains run uniformly throughout all production.

Packaging.—Generally speaking, roasted coffee is sold in bulk, in paper packages, or in rigid containers that are either vacuum packed or pressure packed. Bulk coffee, distributed through retail outlets in sacks or wooden drums (like the old cracker barrel), is weighed out to the purchaser; this type of marketing had almost entirely disappeared in the United States before the middle of the 20th century. Coffee sold in special types of paper bags or cartons is usually packaged by the manufacturer and distributed over reasonably small geographic areas from central roasting points. Most roasters operating over larger areas (and this is particularly true in the United States) pack coffee by the vacuum process either in metal cans or in glass jars. This is done immediately after roasting and grinding.

Ground coffee begins to lose freshness when exposed to the air because of oxidation of the essential strength and flavour-giving elements. The vacuum-packing process, first applied to the packaging of coffee in 1900 by a firm in San Francisco, Calif., protects the quality of coffee over a long period of time and makes it possible for the manufacturer to preserve the flavour and freshness of coffee ground in his plant immediately after roasting, rather than later at the time of purchase in the store or in the home.

After the can or jar is filled with coffee, the air is withdrawn from the container, which is then hermetically sealed, thereby

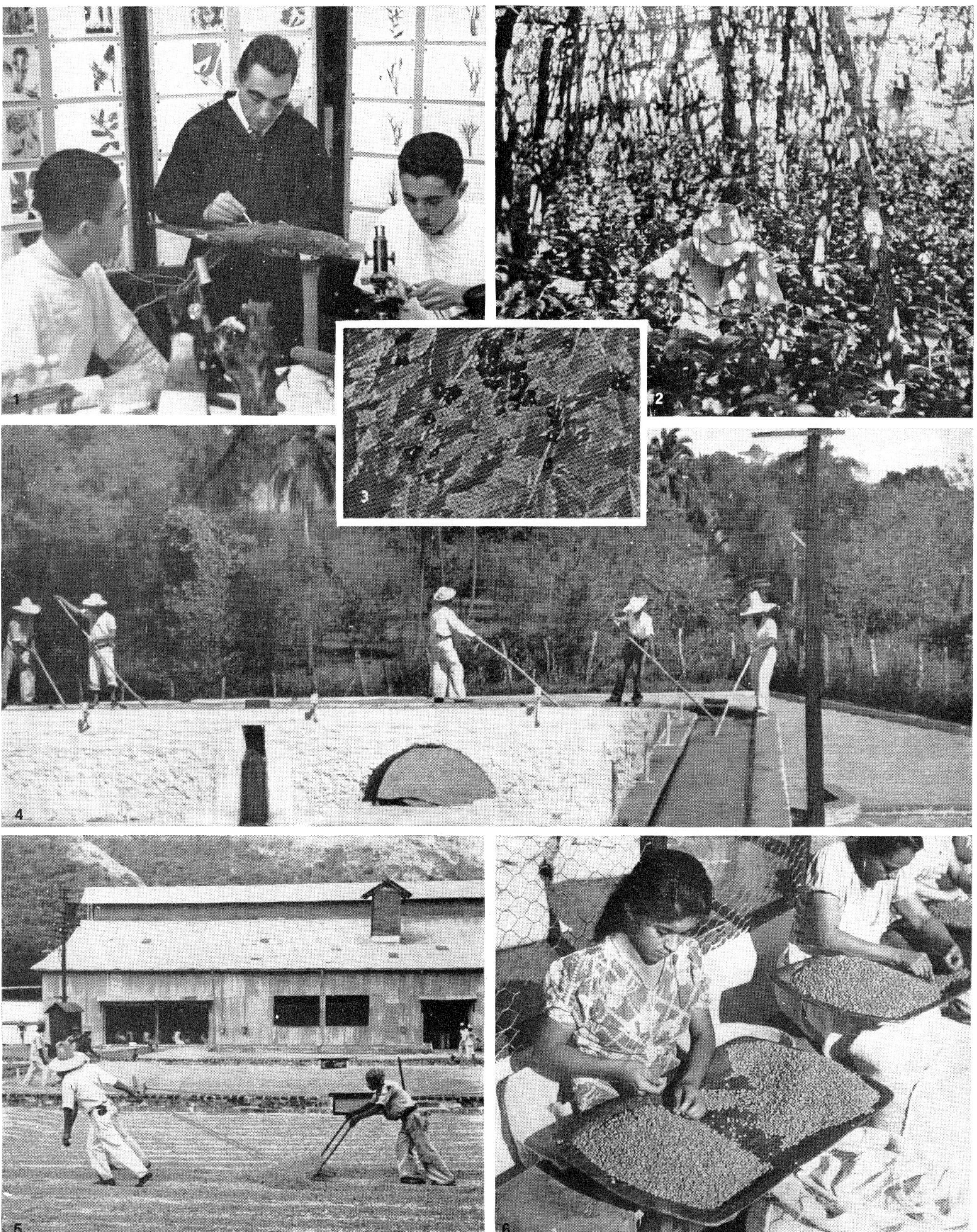

COFFEE CULTURE

1. Research laboratory for the scientific study of all phases of coffee culture
2. Coffee is generally grown from seed. Small plants are nurtured in shaded nursery beds until they are about 18 months old
3. Coffee cherries are similar in appearance to the U.S. domestic fruit cherry, but slightly smaller and somewhat elongated
4. Thorough washing by movement through troughs of water cleans the green coffee beans before drying
5. Drying coffee beans by turning them over in the sun
6. Hand sorting green coffee to remove imperfect beans

COFFEE

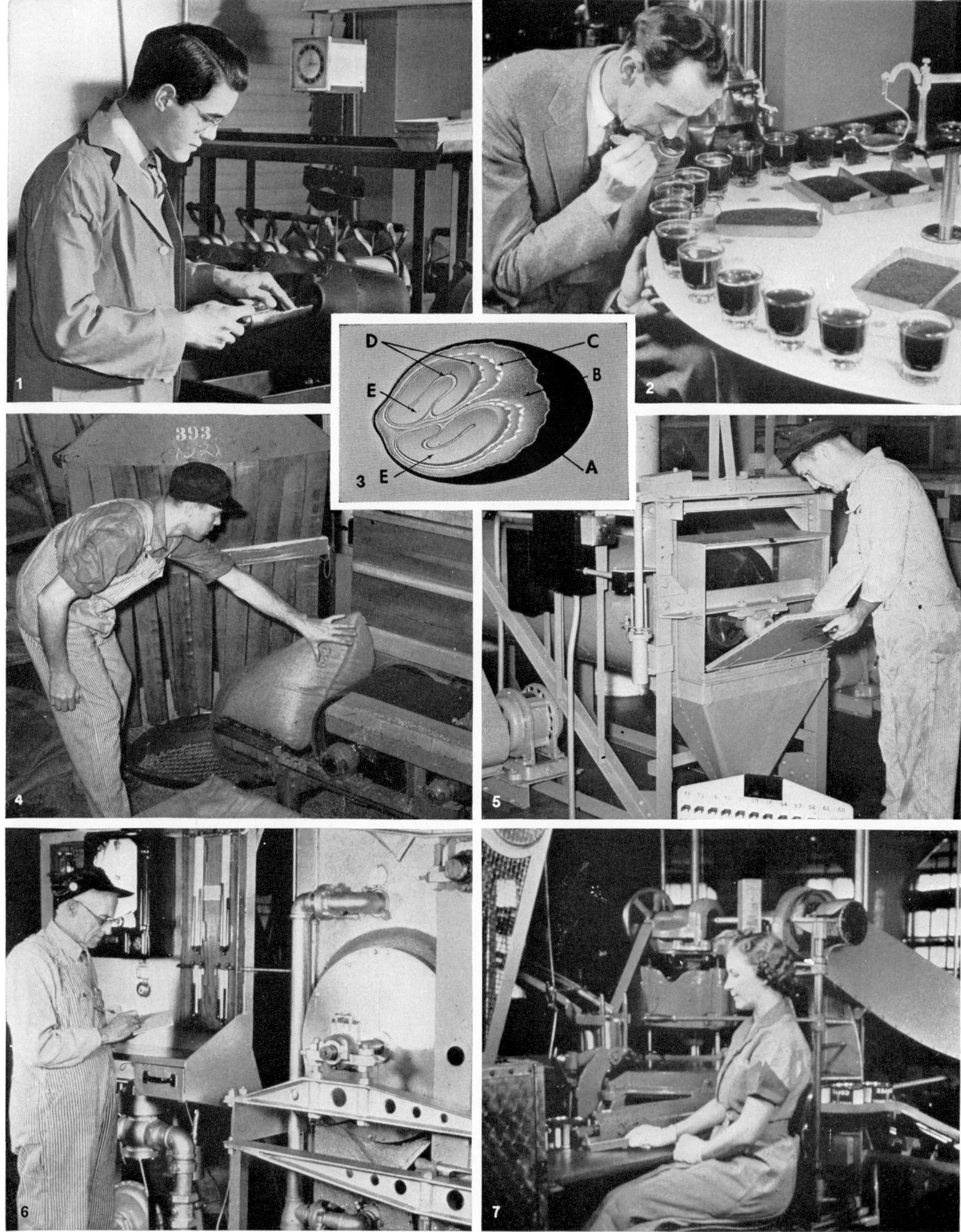

PREPARATION OF COFFEE FOR MARKET

1. Preparing samples for testing in miniature coffee roasters
2. Testing coffee by tasting and smelling before making the blend
3. Cross-section of a coffee cherry: A. pulpy skin. B. jelly layer. C. parchment. D. silver skin. E. coffee bean
4. Emptying sacks of coffee into the mixing hopper for blending
5. Coffee-grinding mill
6. Automatically controlled coffee-roasting machine
7. Vacuum-packing coffee

preventing the entrance of air until the container is first opened. The same result is achieved by pressure packing, the main difference in this process being the introduction of an inert gas into the can after the air is withdrawn and before the can is sealed.

By the mid-1950s, approximately two-thirds of all the home-consumed ground coffee in the United States was vacuum packed, mostly in metal cans. During World War II, this type of production was converted to glass jars during shortages of metal containers, but when restrictions were rescinded, consumer preference caused most roasters to revert to cans. In the meantime, however, glass jars had become established as the most generally used container for soluble coffee.

Soluble Coffee.—There are three types of soluble coffee: (1) dried or dehydrated; (2) liquid extract; (3) frozen concentrate. In all instances, the product represents coffee that, in effect, has been brewed into beverage from roasted and ground coffee beans and reduced partially or wholly into solid form. Liquid coffee extract had not, by the mid-1950s, proved very practical, largely because of the factors of deterioration and spoilage over a period. Frozen concentrate likewise had not made any notable progress. Although records of patents on powdered or liquid coffee concentrate or essence date back to the early 19th century (mostly in Europe), such a product did not become a commercial reality until G. Washington, an American chemist residing temporarily in Guatemala City, invented a "refined soluble coffee" in 1906 which was placed on the United States market in 1909.

Prior to World War II, soluble coffee as a factor in the coffee industry (with only a very few brands on the U.S. market) was relatively negligible. Its popularity, however, was considerably enhanced by use as "field rations" under war conditions, and subsequently several companies which had begun to produce such a product for military supply began to market commercial brands of "instant coffee," so-called because of its preparation into beverage simply by the addition of hot water.

Spurred by the force of extensive promotion and the ready consumer acceptance of all types of convenience items in the food field, soluble coffee grew by leaps and bounds from a relatively modest position in 1946 until it was estimated by grocery trade authorities in the mid-1950s that approximately one out of every four or five cups of coffee prepared in the U.S. home was of the soluble type.

In its early period of rapid growth, soluble coffee in dry form (referred to as powdered or granular) was either all coffee or what is known as product type or filled type (coffee with carbohydrates added). With continuing improvement in the quality of soluble coffee, a distinct consumer preference began to be evidenced in favour of all-coffee and by the mid-1950s the product type had practically disappeared from the U.S. market.

The manufacturing of soluble coffee is an intricate process, varying considerably from company to company according to their respective differences in process and equipment development. Generally speaking, however, soluble coffee is produced by first blending, roasting and grinding as in the case of regular ground coffee. Then follow stages of extraction, evaporation and drying (for powdered instant coffee) by one of several methods, the two systems most commonly used being spray drying and drum (or belt) drying in vacuum. Varying percentages of extraction and differences in methods of evaporation and drying produce instant coffees unlike each other in colour, as well as type and fineness of particles, and density. Packaging of the finished product is done by automatic machinery either in glass jars or cans, glass containers being in most common use in the 1950s.

Decaffeinated Coffee.—A process was developed in Germany about 1900 by Ludwig Roselius, a coffee merchant, for the producing of roasted coffee from which a large percentage of the caffeine had been removed. His technique was later improved by manufacturers in the United States, although the processes for accomplishing decaffeination remained more or less secret. In general, it may be said that the result is attained through the use of steam, or by soaking green coffee in a benzene derivative (ether) before roasting. The product is still pure coffee, but lacking some characteristics of the natural bean. In the mid-1950s it was estimated by food marketing authorities that decaffeinated coffee accounted for approximately 1% of all home-consumed ground coffee. At that time it appeared that preference in decaffeinated coffee had noticeably shifted from ground coffee to instant decaffeinated coffee, the volume of which was approaching one-fifteenth of all soluble coffee consumed in homes.

World Production.—The shift of predominance in coffee production, centring originally in Arabia and other sections of the old world, found the Latin American countries of the western hemisphere in the 20th century growing up to nearly 90% of all the coffee produced in the world. However, with the rapidly increasing rate of coffee growing in Africa (particularly after 1945) the western hemisphere's share had dropped during the 4-yr. period ending June 30, 1954, to approximately 83% of the world total. Brazil, the largest of all coffee-growing countries, alone produced 65% of the world total in the 5-yr. period ending June 30, 1934, but only 48% in the 4-yr. period ending June 30, 1954, as a result of steadily declining production in that country and notable increases in Colombia, Mexico and Africa.

Table I shows exportable production by principal countries from 1929 to 1954 and indicates the shifts in output that took place during those years.

TABLE I.—*Exportable Production of Principal Coffee Producing Countries*
(By marketing years July 1–June 30)
(000 Bags of 60 kg. or 132.276 lb. each)

Area	1929–30 to 1933–34 (5 yr. avg.)	1934–35 to 1938–39 (5 yr. avg.)	1939–40 to 1944–45 (6 yr. avg.)	1945–46 to 1949–50 (5 yr. avg.)	1950–51 to 1953–54 (4 yr. avg.)
World total	37,741	37,602	26,206	28,543	31,095
Western hemisphere total	33,863	32,813	23,322	24,044	25,679
Brazil	24,519	22,441	14,519	14,121	14,775
Colombia	3,545	4,154	4,500	5,476	5,369
El Salvador	1,000	1,013	Figures by countries for war years incomplete or not available. Range in total from 32,220 in 1939–40 to 22,144 in 1944–45.	998	1,033
Guatemala	749	919		871	978
Mexico	635	714		592	1,056
Venezuela	940	988		500	443
Costa Rica	373	391		314	381
Dominican Republic	284	396		217	349
Ecuador	134	238		193	368
Honduras	26	24		59	168
Cuba	416	520		...*	...*
Haiti	532	441		418	401
Nicaragua	225	249		209	277
Other	485	325		76	81
Africa total	1,411	2,313	2,680	4,170	4,898
French Africa & Madagascar	236	726		1,481	1,696
British East Africa	493	752		899	1,147
Portuguese West Africa	200	292		822	792
Belgian Congo	103	289		532	571
Ethiopia	346	209		318	539
Other	33	45		118	153
Asia & Oceania total	2,467	2,476	204	329	518

Statistical data courtesy of Pan-American Coffee Bureau. (Basic source: Central Statistical offices and official coffee trade entities of producing countries.)
*In these years, Cuba consumed all of the coffee grown in that country.

World Exports.—Table II, showing world exports of coffee by countries from 1930 to 1953, offers an interesting comparison with the table of exportable production. It illustrates a phase of the operation of the law of supply and demand which exerts considerable influence on the price of coffee, up and down. Note, for example, the tremendous overproduction in the 10-yr. period 1930 to 1939. This was preponderantly in Brazil, and it was during that period that Brazil was obliged to destroy approximately 68,000,000 bags of coffee, while coffee prices pursued a downward course until they reached their all-time low in 1940.

About a year later, exports began to exceed production and the remaining surpluses accumulated in Brazil started to dwindle, gradually being reduced to approximately 3,000,000 bags at the end of the marketing year 1953–54, an amount which, on the basis of Brazil's annual exports, might be considered as "working inventory."

This turn in the relationship between production and exports in the early 1940s started an upward trend in coffee prices. Arrested during the period of price control in the United States (April 1942 to Oct. 1946), the upward movement resumed and continued with intermittent interruptions until 1951. Then followed a period of comparative stability in the coffee market until 1953. In July of that year, Brazil reported serious frost damage to millions of trees and, spurred on by predictions of smaller supplies

TABLE II.—*Exports of Coffee—Principal Exporting Countries*
(*Calendar Years*)
(000 Bags of 60 kg. or 132.276 lb. each)

Area	1930–1934 (5 yr. avg.)	1935–1939 (5 yr. avg.)	1940–1945 (6 yr. avg.)	1946–1950 (5 yr. avg.)	1951–1953 (3 yr. avg.)
World total	25,587	27,814	21,471	30,763	32,767
Western hemisphere total	22,609	23,881		26,321	27,041
Brazil	14,936	15,095	Figures by countries for war years incomplete or not available. Estimate of world total indicated by same figure as world imports.	16,398	15,914
Colombia	3,149	3,973		5,294	5,486
El Salvador	867	917		1,055	1,102
Guatemala	720	759		882	1,005
Mexico	524	599		642	1,001
Venezuela	774	733		489	499
Costa Rica	365	396		308	369
Dominican Republic	126	187		237	369
Ecuador	157	223		206	308
Honduras	26	29		68	154
Cuba	35	89		...*	...*
Haiti	532	435		419	443
Nicaragua	225	259		215	294
Other	173	187		108	97
Africa total	1,410	2,314		4,194	5,138
French Africa & Madagascar	236	726		1,563	1,947
British East Africa	493	752		906	1,213
Portuguese West Africa	200	293		771	865
Belgian Congo	102	289		532	555
Ethiopia	346	209		301	450
Other	33	45		121	108
Asia & Oceania	1,568	1,619		248	588

Statistical Data courtesy of Pan-American Coffee Bureau. (Basic Source: Central statistical offices and official coffee trade entities of exporting countries.)
*In these years, Cuba consumed all of the coffee grown in that country.

from that country, the up-trend resumed and coffee prices spiralled to an all-time high in April 1954.

The suddenness and sharpness of the increase in coffee prices during this period caused great concern and met considerable opposition in the United States—the world's largest user of coffee. Investigations were ordered by Pres. Dwight D. Eisenhower and the U.S. senate to determine whether other influences than supply and demand were responsible. Meanwhile, imports into the U.S. had fallen off because of consumer resistance to high prices; world supplies had turned out to be somewhat larger than previously anticipated; and in August of that year (1954) green coffee prices fell off more abruptly than at any time in history, continuing to drop in the months that followed.

World Imports and Consumption.—Prior to 1914, Europe imported more than half the world's supply of coffee and the United States about one-third (with world imports totalling around 17,000,000 bags annually). By 1934, however, as shown in Table III, the United States was taking approximately 50% of the total amount; during the years of World War II the average was almost 80%, dropping back to an average of 63% in 1951 to 1953 as European imports recovered to approximately 80% of their pre-war total.

In per capita consumption, however, the United States lagged behind Denmark and Sweden up to 1938, after which the United States began to move ahead, reaching a peak in 1946 and declining slightly thereafter (except in 1949) to a level of about 17 lb. of green coffee per capita in 1953. Reports on per capita consumption for any given year are at best "good estimates" because they can be based only on annual imports, without consideration of changes in inventory levels at the beginning and end of the year, and on population figures, which for many of the larger coffee-consuming areas are uncertain. As a matter of interest and "general comparison," however, some 1953 estimates were: Sweden, 15.7 lb.; Denmark, 14.7 lb.; Belgium, 12.7 lb.; Finland, 12.1 lb.; Norway, 11.5 lb.; Switzerland, 9.2 lb.; France, 8.5 lb.; the Netherlands, 6.6 lb. In spite of the early historical preference for coffee in England in the 17th and 18th centuries, the United Kingdom by the 20th century ranked low as a coffee market, although its per capita consumption is estimated to have increased since World War II to 1.4 lb. in 1953.

TABLE III.—*Coffee Imports into Principal World Markets*
(*Calendar Years*)
(000 Bags of 60 kg. or 132.276 lb. each)

Area	1930–1934 (5 yr. avg.)	1935–1939 (5 yr. avg.)	1940–1945 (6 yr. avg.)	1946–1950 (5 yr. avg.)	1951–1953 (3 yr. avg.)
World total	25,843	27,142	21,471	30,107	32,784
United States	12,024	13,900	17,072	20,228	20,565
Other American total	706	776	1,132	1,363	1,457
Argentina	359	401	*	557	521
Canada	244	271	*	590	740
Chile	57	61	*	152	78
Other	46	43	*	64	118
Europe total	11,793	11,131	2,651	7,052	9,501
France	3,108	2,835	Figures by countries for war years incomplete or not available. See footnote*	1,484	2,712
Germany	2,405	2,571		223	977
Belgium & Luxembourg	825	863		1,229	884
Sweden	752	786		665	782
Italy	696	556		574	1,006
Netherlands	788	684		357	360
Denmark	477	540		240	345
Great Britain	594	356		725	649
Spain	400	79		219	108
Norway	279	312		253	311
Finland	275	351		148	331
Switzerland	250	289		341	318
Other	944	909		594	718
Africa	857	863	482	903	833
Asia & Oceania	463	472	134	561	428

Statistical data courtesy of Pan-American Coffee Bureau. (Basic source: Central statistical offices and official coffee trade entities of importing countries; U.S. Department of Commerce.)
*U.S. range from 15,536 in 1940 to 20,542 in 1945. Low of 12,963 in 1942 was under government control of imports and rationing.

Pan-American Coffee Bureau.—Described as "an instrumentality of the governments of the member countries," the Pan-American Coffee bureau was organized in Oct. 1936, and began to function in Jan. 1937. By the mid-1950s its membership consisted of the government coffee departments or the officially recognized coffee associations of Brazil, Colombia, Costa Rica, Cuba, the Dominican Republic, Ecuador, El Salvador, Guatemala, Honduras, Mexico and Venezuela.

Financed by its member countries, a major activity of the bureau is a co-operative program of promotion and education designed to increase consumption of coffee in the United States. During the years 1938 to 1941, per capita consumption in the United States increased approximately 20% and, although many factors were involved, the joint effort of the members of this bureau is credited as being the most effective single influence.

Inter-American Coffee Agreement.—After the invasion of Norway and the Netherlands early in World War II (May 1940) almost all of the European coffee market was lost and it became necessary for producers to attempt to sell their entire output to the United States. In the wake of enormous overproduction, there followed a disruption of prices which created a distinct threat to the economic stability of the producing countries. The purpose of the Inter-American Coffee agreement between the governments of the United States and 14 Latin American coffee-producing countries (Nov. 28, 1940) was to make possible the orderly marketing of coffee under those extraordinary conditions. This was done by equitable allocation of the United States coffee market among the participating countries through limitation of exports from those countries to an agreed basic annual quota.

Having accomplished terms of trade equitable for both producers and consumers of coffee during the critical early years of its existence, and the need for export limitation having passed, the agreement expired Sept. 30, 1948. Thereafter, the Special Commission on Coffee was established within the Inter-American Economic and Social council in order that the United States and representatives of producing countries of the western hemisphere might continue to have the opportunity to discuss any problems of mutual concern affecting coffee.

How to Make Coffee.—Making a cup of good coffee is an art in which anyone can become proficient. Yet it requires the same careful attention as is given to the preparation of other articles of food. The Coffee Brewing Institute, Inc., a nonprofit membership corporation formed in 1952 by the Pan-American Coffee Bureau and the National Coffee Association of U.S.A., to encourage, through research and education, the improvement of coffee as a beverage, recommends observance of these few simple rules: (1) Start with a thoroughly clean coffee maker. Rinse with hot water before using. Wash thoroughly after each use. Rinse with hot water and dry. (2) Use fresh coffee. Buy coffee in the size of can or package which will be used within a week after opening. (3) For best results start with freshly drawn cold water. (4) Use the full capacity of the coffee maker. For lesser quantities, it is best to use a smaller coffee maker. Never, in any case, brew less than three-fourths of the coffee maker's capacity. (5) Measure both coffee and water accurately. Standard recommendation for full-strength beverage is two level tablespoons of coffee to each $\frac{3}{4}$ measuring cup (6 oz.) of water. (6) After finding the exact timing to obtain the results desired with any coffee maker, stick to it in order to get uniform beverage. Consistent timing is important. (7) Coffee should never be boiled. When coffee is boiled, an undesirable flavour change takes place. (8) Serve coffee as soon as possible after brewing. Freshly brewed coffee always tastes best. If necessary to let coffee stand for any length of time after making, hold at serving temperature by placing the utensil in a pan of hot water over very low heat on an asbestos pad. Electrical devices usually have a "warm" unit for maintaining temperature.

Making Soluble (Instant) Coffee.—Soluble coffee can be prepared for individual servings right in the cup, or several cups at a time in any clean utensil, simply by adding the desired amount of boiling water to a measured amount of instant coffee and stirring. It is preferable to pour the water onto the coffee rather than measure the coffee into the water.

Most directions for preparing instant coffee call for "about 1 teaspoon to each cup of water." The exact amount depends on the size of cup, individual strength-preference, and the coffee itself. The degree of concentration is not the same in various soluble coffees, so larger or smaller measurements of one product may be required than of another to produce equivalent strength.

For preparation of iced coffee fill glass containing instant coffee half-full of cold water, stir, and fill with ice. Quantities can be made similarly in a larger utensil.

BIBLIOGRAPHY.—Andrés Uribe Compuzano, *Brown Gold—The Amazing Story of Coffee* (New York, 1954); Pan-American Coffee Bureau, *Facts About Coffee* (New York, 1954); William H. Ukers, *All About Coffee*, 2nd ed. (New York, 1935) and *Coffee Merchandising* (New York, 1930); Dean Freiday, "The Story of Coffee," *Natural History* (Dec. 1939); Heinrich Eduard Jacob, *Coffee: The Epic of a Commodity* (New York, 1935); V. D. Wickizer, *The World Coffee Economy, with Special Reference to Control Schemes* (Stanford Univ., Calif., 1943; London, 1946). (T. C. W.)

COFFER, in architecture, a sunk panel in a ceiling or vault; also a casket or chest in which jewels or precious goods are kept, and, if of large dimensions, clothes. The marriage coffers in Italy were often richly carved and gilded and sometimes painted by great artists. (*See* CHEST.)

COFFERDAM, a temporary dam formed to enable foundations to be laid or other construction operations to be undertaken on a site which is underwater. The engineer surrounds the site with an enclosure in such a fashion as to make possible its dewatering.

When the depth of the water is small and the current slight, simple clay dams may be used, but in general cofferdams are somewhat more complicated structures. One type consists of two rows of continuous wooden piles tied together at the top and filled between with clay puddle. Another frequently-used type consists of adjacent cells whose continuous outside walls consist of interlocking vertical sheet steel piling. They are also often filled with packed clay puddle. These cells join one another in such a way as to surround the site of the structure to be erected. The enclosed space may then be pumped dry. A cofferdam must be sufficiently strong to withstand the exterior pressures which arise under these circumstances. (W. E. HD.)

COFFEYVILLE, a city of Montgomery county, in southeastern Kansas, U.S., on the Verdigris river, near the southern boundary of the state. It is on federal highways 166 and 169 and is served by the Missouri Pacific, the Santa Fe and the Missouri-Kansas-Texas. It has two airports. The population was 17,113 in 1950; 17,355 in 1940; and 16,198 in 1930.

Coffeyville is an industrial, business, agricultural and dairy centre; is in the midcontinent gas and oil field. It has a large and modern co-operative oil refinery, zinc smelter, flour and feed mills, two brick and tile plants, tank car plant, foundries, oil and gas machinery industries and aircraft factories.

Coffeyville was founded in 1869 and incorporated in 1872. It was named after Col. James A. Coffey, who established a trading post there in 1868.

After the railway came through it became a shipping point for cattle from Texas and Indian territory and a trade centre for a wide area. Natural gas was discovered in 1892.

COFFIN, CHARLES CARLETON (1823–1896), U.S. war correspondent and author, is remembered particularly for his popular children's books. He was born at Boscawen, N.H., on July 26, 1823, the son of a farmer. He studied at a village school and an academy and later engaged in farming and surveying. With his brother-in-law, Moses Farmer, he established the first electric fire-alarm system in Boston, Mass., in 1852.

Assistant editor of the *Boston Atlas,* 1856–57, he became a correspondent for the *Boston Journal,* and during the Civil War his dispatches, sent under the pseudonym "Carleton," earned him wide fame. He reported an eyewitness account of the battle of Bull Run and covered many important campaigns of the war.

In 1866 he went to Europe to cover the Prusso-Austrian War, returning the following year by way of India, China, Japan and the Pacific coast. That journey was described in *Our New Way Round the World* (1869), and a later trip to the west was covered in *The Seat of Empire* (1870).

Coffin's books on his war experiences included *My Days and Nights on the Battlefield* (1864) and *Four Years of Fighting* (1866; later published as *The Boys of '61*).

Coffin also published books on the lives of Presidents James Garfield (1880) and Abraham Lincoln (1892) and wrote the novels *Winning His Way* (1866) and *Caleb Krinkle* (1875) and *History of Boscawen and Webster* (1878). U.S. history was the subject of his series entitled *Drum-Beat of the Nation . . .*

His style was vigorous and vivid, and his children's books, such as the popular *The Boys of '76* (1876) and *The Story of Liberty* (1879), were widely read. Coffin, who often lectured, settled in Boston, Mass., and was elected to the state legislature. He died on March 2, 1896.

COFFIN, the receptacle in which a corpse is confined (Lat. *cophinus,* a coffer, chest or basket, but not "coffin" in its present sense). The Greeks and Romans disposed of their dead both by burial and by cremation. Greek coffins varied in shape, being in the form of an urn, or like the modern coffins, or triangular, the body being in a sitting posture. The material used was generally burnt clay, and in some cases this obviously had first been moulded

FROM THE SMITHSONIAN BUREAU OF ETHNOLOGY REPORT

CANOE BURIAL. FORMERLY PRACTICED AMONG AMERICAN INDIAN TRIBES

The corpse, wrapped in skins or other covering, was laid in a canoe and placed on a wooden scaffold, where it remained for a certain period while mourners kept watch below. Sometimes the canoe coffin was set afloat on the water, to be carried in the direction of the current

round the body, and so baked. In the Christian era stone coffins came into use. Examples of these have frequently been dug up in England. Those of the Romans who were rich enough had their coffins made of a limestone brought from Assos in Troas, which it was commonly believed "ate the body"; hence arose the name sarcophagus (*q.v.*).

The coffins of the Chaldaeans were generally clay urns with the top left open, resembling immense jars, moulded round the body, as the size of the mouth would not admit of its introduction after the clay was baked. The Egyptian coffins, or sarcophagi, as they have been improperly called, are the largest stone coffins known and are generally highly polished and covered with hieroglyphics, usually a history of the deceased. Mummy chests shaped to the form of the body were also used, being made of hard wood or *papier mâché* painted, and bore hieroglyphics. Unhewn flat stones were sometimes used by early European peoples to line the grave. One was placed at the bottom, others stood on their edges to form the sides, and a large slab was put on top, thus forming a rude cist. In England after the Roman invasion these rude cists gave place to the stone coffin which was used until the 16th century.

Primitive wooden coffins were formed of a tree-trunk split down the centre, and hollowed out—a type still in use among peoples in

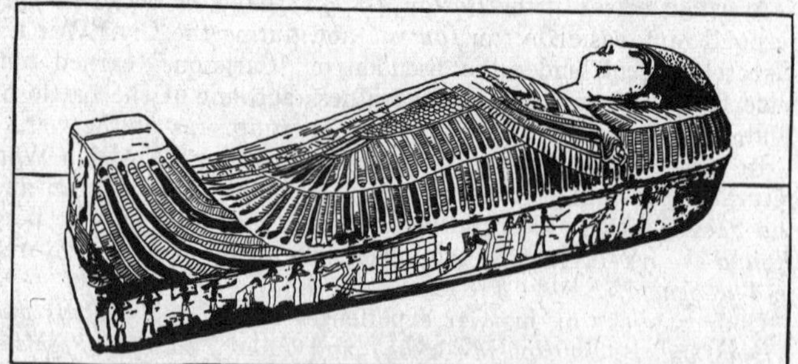

BY COURTESY OF THE METROPOLITAN MUSEUM OF ART

A MUMMY CHEST COVERED WITH STUCCO, XVII–XVIIITH DYNASTY

This type of coffin, shaped in the form of the body of the deceased, was favoured by less wealthy Egyptians. The example above was excavated at Thebes

the lower culture. The earliest specimen of this type is in the Copenhagen museum, the implements found in it proving that it belonged to the Bronze Age. This type of coffin, more or less modified by planing, was used in mediaeval Britain by those who could not afford stone, while the poor were buried without coffins, wrapped simply in cloth or even covered only with hay and flowers. Towards the end of the 17th century, coffins became usual for all classes.

Among the American Indians some tribes, *e.g.,* the Sacs, Foxes and Sioux, used rough hewn wooden coffins; others, such as the Seris, sometimes enclosed the corpse between the carapace and plastron of a turtle. The Seminoles of Florida used no coffins, while at Santa Barbara, California, canoes containing corpses have been found buried, though they may have been intended for the dead warrior's use in the next world. Rough stone cists, too,

BY COURTESY OF THE METROPOLITAN MUSEUM OF ART

A SCULPTURED ROMAN SARCOPHAGUS FOUND AT TARSUS

In the resemblance of this lid to the roof of a house, is preserved the original idea of the coffin as a dwelling-place for the dead. Since the Roman coffin was usually placed against a wall inside a tomb, the back is generally free of decoration

have been found in Illinois and Kentucky. In their tree and scaffold burial the Indians sometimes used wooden coffins or travois baskets, or the bodies were simply wrapped in blankets. Canoes, mounted on a scaffold, near a river, were used as coffins by some tribes; while others placed the corpse in a canoe or wicker basket and floated it out into the stream or lake. The aborigines of Australia generally used coffins of bark, but some tribes employed baskets of wicker-work.

Lead coffins were used in Europe in the middle ages, shaped like the mummy chests of ancient Egypt. Iron coffins were certainly used in England and Scotland as late as the 17th century. The coffins used in England to-day are generally hexagonal in shape, of elm or oak lined with lead, or with a leaden shell. In America glass is sometimes used for the lids, and the inside is lined with copper or zinc. The coffins of France and Germany and the Continent in general usually have sides and ends parallel. Coffins used in cremation throughout the civilized world are of some light material easily consumed and yielding little ash. Ordinary thin deal and *papier mâché* are the favourite materials. Coffins for what is known as Earth to Earth Burial are made of wicker-work covered with a thin layer of *papier mâché* over cloth.

BIBLIOGRAPHY.—Dr. H. C. Yarrow, "Study of the Mortuary Customs of the North American Indians," *Report of Bureau of Amer. Ethnol.* vol. i. (1881); Rev. J. Edward Vaux, *Church Folk-lore* (1894). C. V. Creagh, "On Unusual Forms of Burial by People of the East Coast of Borneo," *J.A.I.* vol. xxvi. (1896–97); David I. Bushnell, Jr., "Burials of the Algonquian, Siouan and Caddoan Tribes, west of the Mississippi," Smithsonian Institution, Bureau of Ethnology, *Bulletin 83* (1927).

COG. (1) A broadly built, round-shaped ship, used as a trader and also as a ship of war till the 15th century (M.E. *cogge, cf.* O.Fr. *cogue,* from which "cock-boat" is derived). (2) A tooth in a series of teeth, on the circumference of a wheel, which works with the tooth in a corresponding series on another wheel (*see* MECHANICS). (3) A slang term for a form of cheating at dice.

COGERS' HALL, a London tavern debating society. Instituted in 1755 at the White Bear Inn, Fleet street, and moved about 1850 to Shoe lane; in 1871 it migrated to the Barley Mow Inn, Salisbury square, E.C., and has since moved to the Cannon Inn, Cannon street, E.C. The accepted derivation is from Descartes' *Cogito, ergo sum,* "The Society of Thinkers." The aims of the Cogers were "the promotion of the liberty of the subject and the freedom of the press, the maintenance of loyalty to the laws, the rights and claims of humanity and the practice of public and private virtue." Among its early members Cogers' Hall reckoned John Wilkes, one of its first presidents, and Curran. Later Dickens was a prominent member.

See Peter Rayleigh, *History of Ye Antient Society of Cogers* (1904).

COGHLAN, SIR TIMOTHY AUGUSTUS (1856–1926), Australian civil servant, second son of Thomas Coghlan, an Irish Roman Catholic, was born in Sydney and educated at Sydney Grammar School. He went into Government service in 1873, in the Public Works Department, and in 1884 became assistant engineer of harbours and rivers. In 1885 he was appointed head of the newly-created department of statistics, and was responsible for the preparation of much valuable material, including a full statistical register of trade and commerce in New South Wales. His most important work is the *History of Labour and Industry in Australia* (4 vols. 1918). He also published: *Wealth and Progress of New South Wales* (1887); *Statistical Account of Australia and New Zealand* (1891); *Progress of Australia in the 19th century,* in collaboration with the Hon. T. T. Ewing (1903).

From 1905 to 1915 he held the post of Agent-General for New South Wales, and was knighted in 1914. He was re-appointed from 1916–17, 1920–25, and again on the resignation of Sir Arthur Cocks. With Sir Joseph Cook he represented Australia on the Pacific Cable Board, and he held various public appointments in New South Wales (Chairman of Board of Old Age Pensions, etc.), serving also on several Royal Commissions. He took a great interest in vital statistics, and was in charge of the census in New South Wales in 1891 and 1901. He died on April 30, 1926.

COGHLAN, CHARLES FRANCIS (1841–1899), Irish actor, was born in Paris, and made his first London appearance in 1860. He went to America in 1876, where he remained for the rest of his life, playing first in Augustin Daly's company and then in the Union Square stock company, during the long run of *The Celebrated Case.* He also played with his sister, and in support of Mrs. Langtry and Mrs. Fiske, and in 1898 produced a version of Dumas' *Kean,* called *The Royal Box,* in which he starred during the last years of his life. He died in Galveston (Texas), on Nov. 27, 1899.

His sister, the actress ROSE COGHLAN (1853–1932), went to

America in 1871, was again in England from 1873 to 1877, playing with Barry Sullivan, and then returned to America, where she became prominent as Countess Zicka in *Diplomacy*, and Stephanie in *Forget-me-not*. She was at Wallack's almost continuously until 1888, and subsequently appeared in melodrama in parts like the title-role of the *Sporting Duchess*.

COGNAC, a town of southwestern France, capital of an *arrondissement* in the department of Charente, on the left bank of the river Charente, 23 mi. W.N.W. of Angoulême. Pop. (1946) 17,479. The streets of the old town are very narrow, but the newer parts have open spaces such as the Parc François Ier overlooking the Charente. In 1526 Cognac gave its name to a treaty concluded against Charles V by Francis I, the pope, Venice and Milan. Its possession was contested during the wars of religion, and in 1570 it became one of the Huguenot strongholds. In 1651 it successfully sustained a siege against Louis II, prince of Condé, leader of the Fronde. The 12th century church of St. Leger preserves a fine Romanesque façade and a tower of the 15th century. A castle of the 15th and 16th centuries, once the residence of the counts of Angoulême, and a mediaeval gate stand in the older part of the town. Cognac is the seat of a subprefect and has tribunals of first instance and of commerce, a council of trade arbitrators and a chamber of commerce. Its most important industry is the distillation of the brandy (*q.v.*) to which the town gives its name.

Large quantities of brandy are carried, by way of the river, to the neighbouring port of Tonnay-Charente. The industries subsidiary to the brandy trade, such as the making of cases and bottles, occupy many hands. A considerable trade is maintained in grain and cattle.

COGNE, a village, province of Aosta, Italy, from which town it is 16 mi. due south by road (9 mi. direct). Pop. (1951) 1,860 (commune). It lies at the northern foot of the Gran Paradiso and is a favourite summer resort. Victor Emanuel II formed a shooting reserve here for wild goat and chamois. The important iron mines belonging to the Ansaldo company lie east of the village.

COGNITION means "knowing," in the widest sense of the term. In psychology it is used to denote one of the three ultimate functions or processes of consciousness, the others being feeling and conation (or willing). Cognition includes every mental process that can be described as an experience of knowing as distinguished from an experience of feeling or of willing; it includes, in short, all process of consciousness by which knowledge is built up. In its most familiar and fully developed form it is known as judgment, in which a certain object (known logically and grammatically as a "subject") is discriminated from other objects and characterized by some concept or concepts. Although cognition is readily distinguishable from feeling and conation, yet in the actual flow of mental life the three types of experience are always found together, not separate, but one of them is usually predominant in one total experience, another in another, and this fact facilitates their mutual discrimination. Psychology, as a descriptive science, is not concerned with the epistemological question, how external objects can be revealed in subjective experiences; it simply takes at their face value these cognitive experiences in which objects appear to be known somehow, and leaves the critical problems to epistemology and logic.

See Psychology, and Knowledge, Theory of, and authorities there quoted.

COGNIZANCE, knowledge, notice, especially judicial notice, the right of trying or considering a case judicially, the exercise of jurisdiction by a court of law. In heraldry a "cognizance" is an emblem, badge or device used as a distinguishing mark by the body of retainers of a royal or noble house.

COHAN, GEORGE MICHAEL (1878–1942), American actor, author and producer, was born in Providence, R.I., July 4, 1878. His parents were of the theatrical profession, and at an early age he appeared with them in juvenile parts, subsequently taking comedy roles in vaudeville and on the legitimate stage. Also at an early age he began writing plays and popular songs. A description of his early experiments and the stage career of the "Four Cohans" is in his autobiography, *Twenty Years on Broadway and the Years It Took to Get There* (1925).

Among his productions may be mentioned *The Governor's Son* (1901); *Forty-five Minutes from Broadway* (1905); *The Talk of New York* (1907); *Get-Rich-Quick Wallingford* (1910); *Broadway Jones* (1912); *Seven Keys to Baldpate* (1913); *The Tavern* (1920); *The Song and Dance Man* (1923); *American Born* (1925). Among his best-known appearances were in *Ah Wilderness!* (1933) and *I'd Rather Be Right* (1937). His career was the subject of a motion picture, *Yankee Doodle Dandy* (1942). He was the composer of numerous songs, including the famous "Over There" of World War I; for writing the latter he received a Congressional medal. Cohan died in New York city Nov. 5, 1942.

See Ward Morehouse, *George M. Cohan, Prince of the American Theater* (Philadelphia, 1943).

COHEN (Hebrew for "priest"), a Jewish family name, implying descent from Aaron and the Hebrew priests (*Cohanim*). Many families claiming such descent are, however, not named Cohen. Other forms of the name are Cohn, Cowen, Kahn, etc.

COHEN, ERNST JULIUS (1869–1944), Dutch chemist, was born at Amsterdam on March 7, 1869. He studied chemistry under Svante Arrhenius at Stockholm, Swed., Henri Moissan at Paris, and Jacobus van't Hoff at Amsterdam; he became assistant to the latter in the university chemical laboratories at Amsterdam in 1893, and in 1902 professor of physical chemistry at the University of Utrecht. He headed the Van't Hoff laboratory founded there in 1904. Cohen's most important work was on the allotropy of metals, particularly tin. He published a large number of works on piezochemistry and electrochemical thermodynamics, particularly in relation to the study of standard galvanic cells; he also wrote widely on the history of science. During World War II he was arrested by the Germans because of his Jewish descent and was gassed at the concentration camp of Auschwitz, Ger., on or about March 15, 1944. Cohen's writings include: *Physical Chemistry for Biologists, Inorganic Chemistry for Medical Students* (1907); *Jacobus Henricus van't Hoff, Sein Leben und Werken* (Leipzig, 1912); *Piezochemie kondensierte Systeme* (Leipzig, 1919); *Physico-Chemical Metamorphosis and some Problems in Piezochemistry* (1928).

COHERER, a device by means of which a feeble oscillating electric current may be detected by a galvanometer or telephone, the essential characteristics being that the current through the coherer is concentrated at a point and that the resistance of the material has a negative temperature coefficient so that the coherer is self-restoring. A simple form of coherer consists of an oxidized iron plate against which rests the point of a steel needle. (*See* Galvanometer; Telephone.)

COHESION: *see* Solid State, Theory of.

COHN, FERDINAND JULIUS (1828–1898), German botanist, was born on the 24th of January 1828 at Breslau. He was educated at Breslau and Berlin, and in 1859 became extraordinary, and in 1871 ordinary, professor of botany at Breslau university. He was contemporary with N. Pringsheim, and worked with H. R. Goeppert, C. G. Nees von Esenbeck, C. G. Ehrenberg and Johannes Müller. He made remarkable advances in the establishment of an improved cell-theory, discovered the cilia in, and analyzed the movements of, zoospores, and pointed out that the protoplasm of the plant-cell and the sarcode of the zoologists were one and the same physical vehicle of life. Although these early researches were especially on the Algae, in which group he instituted marked reforms of the rigid system due to F. T. Kützing, Cohn studied such varied subjects as *Aldorovanda,* torsion in trees, the nature of waterspouts, the effects of lightning, physiology of seeds, the proteid crystals in the potato, which he discovered, formation of travertin, the rotatoria and luminous worms.

It is, however, in the introduction of the strict biological and philosophical analysis of the life-histories of the lower and most minute forms of life that Cohn's greatest achievements consist, for he applied to these organisms the principle that we can only know the phases of growth of microscopic plants by watching every stage of development under the microscope, just as we learn how different are the youthful and adult appearances of an oak or a fern by direct observation. His account of the life-histories of *Protococcus* (1850), *Stephanosphaera* (1852), *Volvox* (1856 and 1875), *Hydrodictyon* (1861), and *Spaeroplea* (1855–1857) among the Algae have never been put aside. The first is a model of what a study in development should be; the last shares with G. Thuret's studies on *Fucus* and Pringsheim's on *Vaucheria* the merit of establishing the existence of a sexual process in Algae. Among the Fungi Cohn contributed important researches on *Pilobolus* (1851), *Empusa* (1855), *Tarichium* (1869), as well as valuable work on the nature of parasitism of Algae and Fungi.

Cohn may be said to have founded the science of bacteriology. He seems to have been always attracted particularly by curious problems of fermentation and coloration due to the most minute forms of life, as evinced by his papers on *Monas prodigiosa* (1850) and "Über blutähnliche Färbungen" (1850), on infusoria (1851 and 1852), on organisms in drinking-water (1853), "Die Wunder des Blutes" (1854), and had already published several works on insect epidemics (1869–1870) and on plant diseases, when his first specially bacteriological memoir (*Crenothrix*) appeared in the journal, *Beiträge zur Biologie*, which he then started (1870–71), and which has since become so renowned. Investigations on other branches of bacteriology soon followed, among which "Organismen der Pockenlymphe" (1872) and "Untersuchungen über Bacterien" (1872–1875) are most important, and laid the foundations of the science. Cohn brought out and helped R. Koch in publishing his celebrated paper on *Anthrax* (1876), the first clearly worked out case of a bacterial disease.

Among his most striking discoveries may be mentioned the nature of Zoogloea, the formation and germination of true spores —which he observed for the first time, and which he himself discovered in *Bacillus subtilis*—and their resistance to high temperatures, and the bearing of this on the fallacious experiments supposed to support abiogenesis; as well as works on the bacteria of air and water, the significance of the bright sulphur granules in sulphur bacteria, and of the iron oxide deposited in the walls of *Crenothrix*. His discoveries in these and in other departments attest his acute observation and reasoning powers. Cohn had clear perceptions of the important bearings of Mycology and Bacteriology in infective diseases, as shown by his studies in insect-killing fungi, microscopic analysis of water, etc. He was a foreign member of the Royal Society and of the Linnean Society, and received the gold medal of the latter in 1895. He died at Breslau on June 25, 1898.

Lists of his papers will be found in the *Catalogue of Scientific Papers of the Royal Society*, and in *Ber. d. d. bot. Gesellsch.*, vol. xvii. p. 196 (1899); *see* also P. Cohn, *Ferdinand Cohn*, with Life by F. Rosen.

COHN, GUSTAV (1840–1918), German economist, born on Dec. 12, 1840, at Marienwerder, West Prussia, was educated at Berlin and Jena and became professor of political science first at Zurich (1875), and then at Göttingen (1884). He died at Göttingen on Sept. 20, 1918. His principal works are:

Untersuchungen über die englische Eisenbahnpolitik (Leipzig, 1874–75); *System der Nationalökonomie* (Stuttgart, 1885); *Finanzwissenschaft* (1889); *Nationalökonomische Studien* (1886), and *Zur Geschichte und Politik des Verkehrswesens* (1900).

COHNHEIM, JULIUS (1839–1884), German pathologist, was born at Demmin (Pomerania) on July 20, 1839, and died on Aug. 15, 1884, at Leipzig. After serving as an army surgeon in 1864–65 he became an assistant in the Pathological institute in Berlin and was the most distinguished of Rudolf Virchow's pupils. He was subsequently professor of pathology at Kiel (1868), Breslau (1872) and Leipzig (1878), where he was also director of the Pathological institute. Paul Ehrlich was among his pupils at Breslau. His first important dissertation on inflammation of serous membranes appeared in 1861, and was followed by other important papers on that subject from 1869 to 1873. On this question his teaching was opposed to that of Virchow. He showed that inflammation is caused by the passage of white corpuscles through the walls of the capillaries and that pus is formed largely of these corpuscles in a disintegrated state. Cohnheim made many useful innovations in the method of microscopical work. His most important book is his *Vorlesungen über allgemeine Pathologie* (Berlin, 1878).

See Berlin klin. Wchnschr., vol. 21, p. 564 (1884).

COHOES, a manufacturing city of Albany county, N.Y., U.S., 9 mi. N. of Albany, on the Hudson river at the mouth of the Mohawk. It is served by the Delaware and Hudson and the New York Central railways, and by the state barge canal. The population of Cohoes in 1950 was 21,235, and was 21,955 in 1940 by the federal census. Water power from the falls of the Mohawk (75 ft. high and 900 ft. across) is supplemented by a hydroelectric plant developing 54,000 h.p.

Chief among the many manufactures are cotton and woollen knit goods, cotton fabrics, collars and shirts, machinery, bond-paper and tractors. Cohoes was part of the manorial grant made to Killian van Rensselaer, and probably it was settled soon after 1629. It was incorporated as a village in 1848 and as a city in 1869. The Van Schaick manor house was the headquarters of Gen. Philip Schuyler during part of the Revolutionary War. The old colonial military road from Albany to Ft. Edward and Lake George runs through the city.

COHORT (Lat. *cohors*), originally a place enclosed; in the Roman army, the name of a unit of infantry. The troops of the first grade, the legions, were divided into cohorts, of which there were ten in each legion: the cohort thus contained 600 men. Among the troops of the second grade (the *auxilia*) the cohorts were independent foot regiments 500 or 1,000 strong, corresponding to the *alae*, which were similar regiments of cavalry; they were generally posted on the frontiers of the empire in small forts of four to eight acres, each holding one cohort or *ala*. The special troops of Rome itself, the Praetorian Guard, the *Urbanae Cohortes*, and the *Vigiles* (fire brigade), were divided into cohorts (*see* further ROMAN ARMY). The phrase *cohors praetoria* or *cohors amicorum* was sometimes used, especially during the Roman republic, to denote the suite of the governor of a province; hence developed the Praetorian cohorts which formed the emperor's bodyguard.

In biology, "cohort" is a term for a group of allied orders or families of plants or animals.

See J. E. Sandys, *Companion to Latin Studies* (1921), sections 380, 463, 714 *et seq.*, 723–4, 728, 730, 773, 1089.

COIF, a close-fitting covering for the head. Originally it was the name given to a head-covering worn in the middle ages, tied like a night-cap under the chin, and worn out of doors by both sexes; this was later worn by men as a kind of night-cap or skull-cap. The coif was also a close-fitting cap of white lawn or silk, worn by English serjeants-at-law as a distinguishing mark of their profession (*see* SERJEANTS-AT-LAW).

COIMBATORE, city and district, British India, in the Madras presidency. The city is situated on the left bank of the Noyil river, 305 mi. from Madras by the South Indian railway. In 1941 it had a population of 130,348. The city stands 1,437 ft. above sea level, is healthy, and is rendered additionally attractive to European residents by its picturesque position on the slopes of the Nilgiri hills. The famous temple of Perur lies 3 mi. E. of Coimbatore. Coimbatore is an important industrial centre, carrying on cotton weaving and spinning, tanning and the manufacture of coffee, sugar, manure and saltpetre. It has two second-grade colleges, a college of agriculture, training and industrial schools, and a school of forestry.

THE DISTRICT OF COIMBATORE has an area of 7,121 sq.mi. It is a flat, open country, hemmed in by mountains on the north, west and south, but opening eastwards on to the great plain of the Carnatic; the average height of the plain above sea level is about 900 ft. The principal mountains are the Anamalai hills, in the south of the district, rising at places to a height of between 8,000 and 9,000 ft. In the west the Palghat and Vallagiri hills form a connecting link between the Anamalai range and the Nilgiris, with the exception of a remarkable gap known as the Palghat pass. This gap, which completely intersects the Ghats, is about 20 mi. wide. In the north the Cauvery chain extends eastward from the Nilgiris, and rises in places to 4,000 ft. The principal rivers are the Cauvery, Bhavani, Noyil and Amravati. There are numerous canals, wells and tanks for irrigation. Coimbatore district was acquired by the British in 1799 at the close of the war which ended with the death of Tipu. In 1941 the population was 2,809,648.

The principal crops are millet, rice, other food grains, pulse, oilseeds, cotton and tobacco; and raw silk is produced. Forests, yielding valuable timber, cover a large area. There are cotton mills and factories for pressing cotton, preparing coffee, making soap and dyeing.

The southwest line of the Madras railway runs through the district and the South Indian railway (of metre gauge) joins this at Erode.

COIMBRA, Portuguese city on the north bank of the Mondego river, 115 mi. N.N.E. of Lisbon, on the Lisbon-Oporto railway. Pop. (1950) 42,640. Coimbra is the seat of the oldest of the three Portuguese universities. It was originally established at Lisbon in 1290, was transferred to Coimbra in 1308, was again removed to Lisbon and was finally fixed at Coimbra in 1537. The library contains about 500,000 volumes and the museums and laboratories are on an extensive scale.

The city, picturesquely situated on a hill above the river, is the seat of a bishop, suffragan to the archbishop of Braga; its new cathedral, founded in 1598, is of little interest, but the old one is a fine specimen of 12th-century Romanesque and retains portions of the mosque which it replaced. The principal churches are Santa Cruz, rebuilt in the 16th century on a much older foundation, and San Salvador, founded in 1179.

On the banks of the Mondego stand the ruins of the once splendid monastery of Santa Clara, established in 1286, and the church, built by the monks in the 17th century, which contains the 14th-century crystal and silver tomb of St. Isabel, queen of Portugal. There, too, is the celebrated Quinta das Lagrimas, where Inez de Castro (*q.v.*) is believed to have been murdered in 1355.

A Latin inscription of the 4th century identifies Coimbra with the ancient Aeminium, while Condeixa, 8 mi. S.S.W., represents the ancient Conimbriga or Conimbrica. Aeminium was for more than a century a Moorish stronghold, but in 878 it was recaptured by Alphonso III and peopled by Galicians from the north. The bishop of Conimbriga, who was established there, was forced to leave as a result of the continuous raids by the Moors in the surrounding country. When he later returned he kept his old name of Conimbriga and Aeminium became known as Coimbra. In 1064 it was captured by Ferdinand I of Castile and the first Christian governor was Count Sisnando, a Moor, who reorganized the town. For more than a century it was the centre from which the reconquest of Portugal from the Moors was carried on. No fewer than six kings—Sancho I and II, Alphonso II and III, Pedro and Ferdinand —were born within its walls. It was also the birthplace of the poet Francisco Sá de Miranda (1485?–1558), and, according to one tradition, of the more famous Luis de Camoens (1524–80), who was a student at the university between 1537 and 1545. In 1755 Coimbra suffered considerably from the earthquake and in 1810 it was sacked by the French. In 1834 Dom Miguel made the city his headquarters; and in 1846 it was the scene of a Miguelist insurrection.

The chief industries are wine, biscuits, pottery and paper. Oil is found, and maize, rice and fruits are grown in the district.

COÍN, a town of southern Spain, in the province of Málaga, 18 mi. W.S.W. of Málaga by rail. Pop. (1950) 20,090 (mun.). Coín, on the north slope of the Sierra de Mijas, is the centre of a rich agricultural district. It exports large quantities of oranges, lemons, grapes and raisins, and marble from neighbouring quarries.

COIN. This is properly the term for a wedge-shaped die used for stamping money, and so transferred to the money so stamped; hence a piece of money. The form "quoin" is used for the external angle of a building (*see* QUOIN), and "coign," also a projecting angle, survives in the Shakespearean phrase "a coign of vantage."

The older forms of the word are *coyne, quoin* and *coign,* all derived from the Lat. *cuneus,* a wedge, through the O.F. *coing* and *cuigne.*

For a discussion of coins and coinage, *see* MINT and NUMISMATICS.

COINAGE OFFENSES: *see* COUNTERFEIT MONEY.

COIR, the outer covering of the husk of the coconut; an exceedingly strong fibrous material which has many uses in industry, notably in the manufacture of coarse mats and brushes. The name is derived from the Malay *Kāyar,* cord, *Kāyaru,* to be twisted.

Very large quantities of coir are exported from the Pacific, and there is a considerable market in England, the imports and reexports reaching big figures.

COIRE: *see* CHUR.

COISLIN, a French family of Brittany, originally named Du Cambout, which came into prominence in the 16th century when it inherited the lordship of Coislin (in the modern *département* of Loire-Inférieure) and, further, in the 17th, largely because of its connection with the cardinal de Richelieu. Several of its members held high rank in the army. In the church, Pierre (1636–1706), second son of the marquis de Coislin, Pierre César du Cambout, and of Marie, daughter of the chancellor Pierre Séguier, was bishop of Orléans, a cardinal and grand almoner of France; he treated the Huguenots with great tolerance when the Edict of Nantes was revoked. His nephew Henri Charles (1664–1732), bishop of Metz, premier royal almoner and a member of the Académie Française, bequeathed the chancellor Séguier's library to the abbey of St. Germain-des-Prés, whence it was later transferred in part to the Bibliothèque Nationale.

COITIER, JACQUES (d. 1505), French physician and politician, was born in Poligny in the modern *département* of Jura.

He was attached to the royal court in Paris and became the personal physician of King Louis XI. As such, he exercised a great influence over the king until the latter's death in 1483. He was rewarded with various lucrative offices and lands and became, in 1482, president of the *chambre des comptes* and bailiff of the palace.

Although his political influence waned somewhat after his patron's death, Coitier retained his rank and offices under Charles VIII and Louis XII, with the exception of the presidency of the *chambre des comptes.*

COKE, SIR EDWARD (1552–1634), English judge, was born at Mileham in Norfolk on Feb. 1, 1552. He was educated at Norwich grammar school and Trinity college, Cambridge, and in 1572 entered the Inner Temple. He was called to the bar in 1578, and the next year was chosen reader of Lyon's Inn, a responsible position usually held by counsel of ten years' standing. His early cases included the Cromwell libel case (4 Rep. 13) and *Shelley's Case* (1 Rep. 94), and his reputation became great. In 1582 he married Bridget Paston, who brought him a fortune. In 1589 he became M.P. for Aldeburgh, and in 1592 solicitor general and recorder of London. In 1593 he was chosen as speaker of the house of commons, showing considerable skill in carrying out Elizabeth's policy of curbing the commons' passion for discussing ecclesiastical matters.

In 1593 he first crossed Francis Bacon's course. The attorney generalship fell vacant, and Bacon, supported by Essex, became Coke's rival for the post. Coke got it in 1594 and then kept Bacon out of the solicitorship as well, or so Bacon thought. Coke's wife died in 1598 and four months later he married Lady Elizabeth Hatton, Bacon again being his unsuccessful rival.

As attorney general, Coke started a series of state prosecutions for libel. The theory he advocated was that all comment on the doings of authority was unjustified; the remedy of those aggrieved was to be sought in the courts or in parliament. He also had the conduct of several of the great trials of the day. In 1601 he prosecuted Essex and Southampton, in 1603 Raleigh, and in 1605 the Gunpowder plot conspirators. (*See* Cobbett, *State Trials,* vol. ii.)

In 1606 Coke was made chief justice of the common pleas, and there began at once that series of conflicts which eventually broke his career. At the time of his appointment Archbishop Richard Bancroft had already started his attempt to shake off the control which the common law courts exercised over the ecclesiastical courts by prohibition, and James, as ever, was ready to support any cause that looked likely to break the supremacy of the common law. This matter came to a head in 1607, when Bancroft renewed his protests and took up the position that the king, as fountain of justice, could remove any cases he pleased from his judges and try them himself. Coke refuted him, in spite of some precedents under the early kings that must have been difficult to get round. But the disputes with the ecclesiastical courts went on. In 1610 Coke gave his celebrated opinion before the council that the king's proclamation cannot change the law, and in 1611 he had a brush with the court of high commission, with the result that the next year he was put on the commission himself; Coke evaded this attempt to muzzle him by finding legal flaws in the commission's appointment. In 1613 Bacon, with an eye to his own advancement and to get Coke into a position where he would be less troublesome, had him "promoted" to be chief justice of the king's bench, an office of higher dignity and less salary. Coke was made a privy councillor, and was the first to be called lord chief justice of England, which was remembered against him afterward. Here his predominance was still as great; and he had to protest, in *Peacham's Case*, against the practice of consulting the judges individually and separately, which James, abetted by Bacon, was more or less driven to follow because when the whole bench was consulted together the rest of the judges merely echoed Coke. In 1615, still an implacable and bigoted adherent of the common law, he tried his strength too high. The court of king's bench started a dispute with the chancery over the right of the chancellor to interfere where a common law court had given a decision, and Coke was believed to be at the bottom of the attempt to make some who had been suitors in a case of this sort liable to the penalties of a praemunire, an attempt which failed. The disputes continued, embittered by Coke's personal dislike for Sir Thomas Egerton, the chancellor. Meanwhile Coke had further endangered his position by throwing out dark hints from the bench in his conduct of the Overbury trials ("God knows what became of that sweet babe, prince Henry, but I know somewhat"). Finally he came into collision with James once more over the king's right to allow commendams (holding of livings in plurality). Coke and the other judges ignored a royal injunction that they should take no action upon a case involving this right until the king's pleasure was known. They were called before the king and council and ordered to obey the injunction. The other judges submitted, but Coke merely said that he would do what an honest and just judge ought to do.

In June 1616 the privy council, with Bacon at the back of it, formulated three charges against him. One was a trumpery matter, never proved, about a bond that had passed through his hands. The other two were charges of interference with the court of chancery and of disrespect to the king in the matter of commendams. He was also ordered to revise the "errors" in his reports. Bacon, then attorney general, made himself very unpopular by engaging Coke on this last issue. Coke remained impenitent and was dismissed. Thereupon, presumably in search of a friend in high places, he offered his daughter in marriage to Sir John Villiers, brother of the duke of Buckingham. His wife, supported by Bacon, objected and hid the child, who was then only 14. Coke found her and married her, strongly against her will, to Villiers. She ran away from him soon afterward. However, Coke got back into the privy council by 1617, and sat in the Star Chamber. In 1620 he entered parliament as member for Liskeard, in theory as a supporter of the king. But for the rest of his career he was a leading member of the popular party. He opposed the Spanish marriage proposals, took a part in drawing up the charges against Bacon and spoke in the liberties of parliament debate, spending nine months in prison as a result. But nothing was found that could incriminate him.

In 1628 it was his Bill of Liberties that ultimately took the form of the Petition of Right. At his last notable appearance he saved the awkward situation caused by the speaker's suppressing Sir John Eliot's attack on the duke of Buckingham, who was, however, not mentioned by name. The house was at a loss and in turmoil. Coke rose and, having named the duke first, went on to say what the house thought of him; whereupon "as when one good hound recovers the scent the rest come in with a full cry so they . . . laid the blame where they thought the fault was." At the end of the session he retired, and died at Stoke Poges on Sept. 3, 1634. His papers were instantly seized and some, including his will, were never recovered.

Barrister, judge and reporter of the first rank, Coke is the greatest common lawyer of all time. He was inclined to be overbearing and impatient both at the bar and on the bench, he was undoubtedly rather narrow and he was not always logical. But his knowledge of the law, in days when it was far more difficult to come by than it is now, was unequalled, and to him more than anyone is owed the reduction of the chaos of the old authorities to the comparatively orderly state of the law as he left it. As a judge he is noted for his wholehearted adherence to the common law. He upheld it against the church, the admiralty and, most dangerous of all, the royal prerogative with success. He tried to uphold it against the chancery, but that was too strong for him. While he was issuing his *Reports* no others came out. They are not so much reports in the modern sense as compendia of the law bearing on a particular case, with comments on points raised or general remarks. The best estimate of his importance as a legal authority is that of C. J. Best, "The fact is that Lord Coke had no authority for what he states, but I am afraid we should get rid of a great deal of what is considered law in Westminster Hall if what Lord Coke says without authority is not law. He was one of the most eminent lawyers that ever presided as a judge in any court of Justice. . . ." Among his other publications are four volumes of *Institutes* (1628 ff.), of which volume i is known as *Coke Upon Littleton.*

As a man, he evokes admiration more readily than sympathy. More learned a lawyer than Bacon but without his philosophical genius, a just judge but a savage prosecutor, obstinate in his opposition to illegal exercise of authority but quite incapable of distinguishing between the prerogative, which wanted to override the law in the interests of absolutism, and the chancery, which sought to counteract its rigidity in the cause of justice, he could cringe before the king even in the act of defying the crown.

See Sir William Holdsworth, *A History of English Law,* vol. v, 2nd ed. (London, 1937); S. R. Gardiner, *History of England 1603–42,* 10 vol. (London, 1883–84). There is no adequate biography.

COKE, SIR JOHN (1563–1644), English politician, was born on March 5, 1563, and was educated at Trinity college, Cambridge. After leaving the university he entered public life as a servant of William Cecil, Lord Burghley, afterward becoming deputy treasurer and then a commissioner of the navy. He became M.P. for Warwick in 1621 and was knighted in 1624, afterward representing the University of Cambridge. In the parliament of 1625 Coke acted as secretary of state; in this and later parliaments he introduced the royal requests for money and defended the foreign policy of Charles I and Buckingham, and afterward the actions of the king. His actual appointment as secretary dates from Sept. 1625. Disliked by the leaders of the popular party, his speeches in the house of commons did not improve the king's position, but when Charles ruled without a parliament he found Coke's industry very useful to him. The secretary retained his post until 1639, when a scapegoat was required to expiate the humiliating treaty of Berwick with the Scots, and Coke was dismissed. He died at Tottenham on Sept. 8, 1644. Coke's son, Sir John Coke, sided with the parliament in its struggle with the king, and it is possible that in later life Coke's own sympathies were with this party, although in his earlier years he had been a defender of absolute monarchy.

COKE, THOMAS (1747–1814), English divine, the first Methodist bishop, was born at Brecon, where his father was a well-to-do apothecary. He was educated at Jesus college, Oxford, taking the degree of M.A. in 1770 and that of D.C.L. in 1775. From 1772 to 1776 he was curate at South Petherton in Somerset, whence his rector dismissed him for adopting the open-air and cottage services introduced by John Wesley, with whom he had become acquainted. After serving on the London Wesleyan circuit he was in 1782 appointed president of the conference in Ireland, a position which he frequently held, in the intervals of his many voyages to America. He first visited that country in 1784, going to Baltimore as "superintendent" of the Methodist societies in the new world and, in 1787 the American conference changed his title to "bishop," a nomenclature which he tried in vain to introduce into the English conference, of which he was president in 1797 and 1805. Failing this, he asked Lord Liverpool to make him a bishop in India, and he was voyaging to Ceylon when he died on May 3, 1814. Coke had always been a missionary enthusiast, and was the pioneer of such enterprise in his connection. He was an ardent opponent of slavery, and endeavoured also to heal the breach between the Methodist and Anglican communions. He published a *History of the West Indies* (1808–11), several volumes of sermons and, with Henry Moore, a *Life of Wesley* (1792).

COKE, COKING AND HIGH-TEMPERATURE CARBONIZATION. Coke is the solid residue which remains when coal is heated to a high temperature out of contact with air until practically all the volatile matter has been driven off. It consists principally of carbon, together with minor proportions of hydrogen, nitrogen, sulphur and oxygen (which constitute the so-called fixed carbon), plus the mineral matter present in the original coal, which has suffered alteration during the coking process. Commercial cokes always contain water, the amount of which depends on the treatment to which the coke has been subjected after manufacture.

The properties of a coke depend on the type of coal from which it is made and the process employed in its manufacture. Thus, metallurgical coke produced in coke ovens is hard, compact, has a gray steely lustre and is difficult to ignite; it is unsuitable for use in open fireplaces. Gas coke, if made in horizontal retorts, is less strong, has a more open texture and a gray colour and is difficult to ignite and burn in an ordinary fireplace. Gas coke made in continuous vertical retorts through which steam is passed is black in colour, porous, weaker mechanically than oven or horizontal-retort coke; it is more easily ignited and can be burned successfully in properly designed open grates.

The Nature of Coke.—Coke is essentially a partially graphitized form of carbon; its true specific gravity is about 1.85 to 1.9, or about midway between the specific gravities of coal and graphite. Because of its high porosity, however, coke has a considerably lower bulk density than coal; thus for equal weights of the two fuels, coke requires about 40% more storage space. It is the combination of high graphitization and porosity that gives coke its chief value in the smelting of iron, which requires a fuel that will burn rapidly in the lower regions of the furnace, giving a high temperature for the melting of the iron and slag, mechanical strength to withstand rough treatment, including the abrasive action that accompanies the working down of the charge in the furnace and the pressure resulting from the superincumbent load when the coke reaches the lower zones. Resistance to the solvent action of carbon dioxide in the higher levels of the furnace is also required, and it is found that the less readily a coke reduces carbon dioxide to carbon monoxide under standard conditions of test, the higher is its shatter value, that is, the less the coke will break up when dropped onto a hard surface.

The most objectionable constituents of coke are mineral matter (which must be removed with the slag in the blast furnace), moisture, volatile matter, sulphur and phosphorus. Since coke yields a considerably higher percentage of ash than the coal from which it is made, it is customary to crush and wash the coal to remove particles of shale and other incombustible matter before coking so that the ash on the coke shall not exceed about 10%. Sulphur and phosphorus are undesirable in metallurgical coke because they enter into the iron and must be removed when the iron is converted into steel.

History of Coke.—The early history of the manufacture and application of coke made from pit coal to the smelting of iron is somewhat obscure. Because of the ravages caused in timber supplies by the expansion of the iron industry during the 16th century, a number of acts of parliament were passed between 1558 and 1584 restricting the number and location of ironworks. The attention of ironmasters was thus directed to the desirability of finding substitute fuels such as peat and coal, and a number of patents were granted from 1589 onward covering the use of stone coal, pit coal and sea coal for the manufacture of iron, which probably included the preliminary operation of smelting. The first patent definitely known to have covered the extraction of iron from the ore was obtained by Simon Sturtevant in 1611. In 1621, Lord Dudley was granted a patent in respect of the process employed by his natural son Dud Dudley who, in his *Metallum Martis* (1665), put forward exaggerated claims that the iron produced was superior to that smelted and fined by charcoal. No mention was made of any attempt to coke the coal, and it is doubtful whether, with the plant available, it would have been possible to produce iron of even moderate quality with raw coal. The first indubitable success in the substitution of coke made from coal for wood charcoal in the smelting of iron was the result of the persistent efforts of the Abraham Darbys, father and son, of Coalbrookdale in Shropshire, from 1713 to 1735.

As might be expected, the early process for the manufacture of coke closely followed that applied to the production of wood charcoal; the coal was built up in piles and set on fire, care being taken that only part of the coal was burned, the remainder being carbonized. The method was exceedingly wasteful; yields were low and it was impossible to secure uniform carbonization. Later, some control of the process was obtained by building the pile round a central brick chimney with gaps in it through which gases could enter. This was closed at the top, when necessary, by a damper. A later development was to carry out the carbonization in long piles enclosed between two brick walls provided with holes for the controlled admission of air.

By about 1850 the beehive process had almost completely ousted the foregoing. Small charges of coal were coked at the expense of all the volatiles and about one-sixth of the theoretical yield of coke in closed ovens with domed roofs. Although very inefficient, the beehive process gave excellent coke from coals having strong caking propensities. In 1858 Breckon and Dixon introduced their improved beehive oven. At the same time, efforts were made to recover by-products by coking coal in thin layers in ovens heated from below. The coke was inferior to beehive coke and as a result "patent" coke fell into disrepute and, for many years, coke made in by-product ovens was viewed with suspicion.

In 1861 E. Coppée introduced narrow ovens in which full charges of coal were carbonized; heating was carried out by burning the volatiles from the coal in vertical side flues with a regulated supply of air. The gases from the coal immediately entered the flues where they were burned, and no attempt was made to recover by-products. In other designs of oven, arrangements were made to "strip" the gases of tars and light spirits before they were returned to the heating flues.

An important advance was made in 1881 when Henry Simon of Manchester introduced a recuperative system whereby part of the heat in the burned gases from the heating flues was used to preheat the air which was supplied to the flues. As a result, higher temperatures were obtainable in the ovens, and there was a certain amount of surplus gas over and above that required to supply the heat required for carbonizing the coal.

Modern Methods of Coke Manufacture in Britain.—Coke is made either as a principal product for use in the manufacture of iron and steel at coke-oven plants, or as a by-product in the manufacture of coal gas in gasworks. In both industries, by-products in the form of ammonia, tar, benzol and other light oils are recovered; the methods of carbonization and recovery of the by-products are, however, different. Consequently the two industries must be considered separately. The making of coke as a by-product of coal gas is described in the article GAS INDUSTRY.

Coke Ovens.—A coke oven consists of a long narrow chamber, constructed of bricks containing 95% silica, from 40 to 45 ft. long, 12 to 15 ft. high and 14 to 20 in. wide, slightly tapered so that one end is about 2 in. wider than the other. The ends are closed by steel doors lined with firebrick, which can be lifted by small cranes when an oven is to be discharged. There are three or four openings in the roof through which the coal is introduced from an electrically driven charging truck running on rails along the battery of ovens.

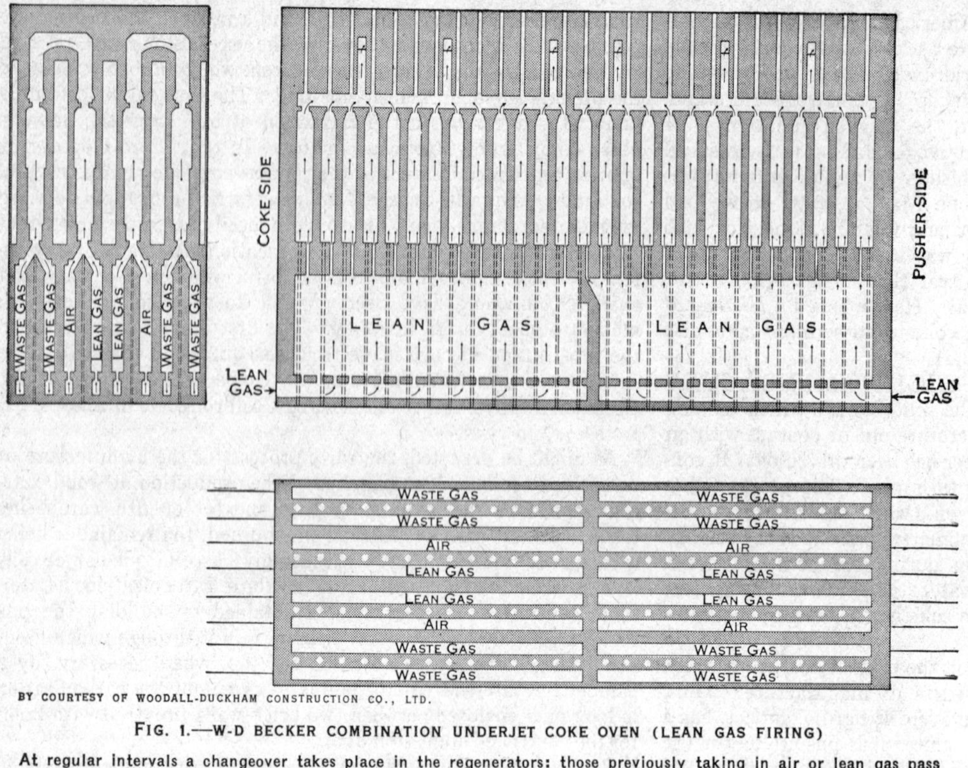

BY COURTESY OF WOODALL-DUCKHAM CONSTRUCTION CO., LTD.

FIG. 1.—W-D BECKER COMBINATION UNDERJET COKE OVEN (LEAN GAS FIRING)

At regular intervals a changeover takes place in the regenerators: those previously taking in air or lean gas pass out waste gas, and those previously passing out waste gas take in air or lean gas. Simultaneously the flow of heating gases in the vertical flues is reversed

At each end of the oven there is a steel ascension pipe through which the volatile matter from the coal is led to the collecting mains which run lengthwise along each side of the battery. The charge consists of from 15 to 25 tons of crushed coal and requires from 12 to 22 hours for carbonization, so that the throughput of a single oven is from 25 to 30 tons a day and the output of coke from 18 to 22 tons.

The ovens are built in batteries of from 20 to 60 and are separated by vertical flues in which the gas used to heat the ovens is burned; each oven is therefore heated from both sides and shares the flues with its immediate neighbours. The design of the flues and method of heating vary with the make of plant. The gas used for heating may be coal gas which has been stripped of the tar, benzol, etc., and ammonia in the by-product plant, or it may be producer gas generated in outside producers or (in an ironworks) blast-furnace gas. One type, known as the compound oven, is constructed so that heating may be carried out either by coal gas (rich gas) or producer gas (lean gas), and about 40% of the coal used in Great Britain for the manufacture of metallurgical coke is carbonized in ovens of this type.

Most modern coke ovens are regenerative; the air which is used to burn the fuel gas is preheated in regenerators at the expense of part of the sensible heat in the waste gases; if lean gas is the heating medium, the fuel gas is also preheated. All compound ovens are regenerative, as are most of the other coke ovens employed by the British coking industry. In fact about 93% of Britain's supplies of metallurgical coke is made in regenerative ovens. The remaining 7% is made in waste-heat ovens, the products of combustion from the heating flues of the ovens being led through waste-heat boilers and making no further contribution to the heating of the ovens.

Coke ovens are nearly always charged by allowing the coal to fall by gravity through holes in the roof; the charge is afterward levelled by a levelling bar introduced through a port in the upper part of one of the doors of the oven. When carbonization is complete, the doors are lifted and the coke is pushed out by an electrically driven ram which enters the oven at the narrower end. The coke is often quenched by water as it emerges from the oven; alternatively it is rapidly conveyed to a remote quenching station and there thoroughly drenched with water. Attention has been given to dry cooling coke with a view to improving its quality and at the same time recovering part of the sensible heat as steam, but wet quenching is still the standard practice.

The W-D Becker Underjet Coke Oven.—This is a good example of a modern design of combination oven (*see* figs. 1 and 2). Each oven has, on either side of it, 27 vertical heating flues, to the base of which preheated lean gas and air are supplied through calibrated clay nozzles in the correct quantities and proportions. There are also, for every alternate oven, six crossover or hairpin flues which carry the products of combustion over the crown of the oven and down into the vertical flues on the other side. Under each set of heating flues there are four regenerators, consisting of chambers packed with firebrick shapes which are alternately heated at the expense of the sensible heat in the waste gases from the flues and then return part of the heat so acquired to the lean gas and the air used to heat the ovens.

The gas is supplied by two mains which run on each side of the battery of ovens and is then admitted by valves into the appropriate regenerators (fig. 1), which it traverses in an upward direction, becoming preheated by contact with the incandescent brickwork. On arriving at the base of the heating flues, the hot gas meets the air required for combustion, which has been similarly heated. The mixture burns in the flues; the burned gases pass into the short collecting flue which joins the vertical ducts, and are led by the nearest crossover flue into the corresponding flues on the opposite side of the oven and thence downward into the regenerators, to the brickwork of which the gases give up part of their sensible heat, raising the temperature to 1,000° C., or thereabouts, and themselves being cooled to about 300° C., before entering the main flues which lead to the chimney.

At the end of a predetermined period (usually about half an hour), the valves through which the lean gas and air were supplied are mechanically closed, and the alternate gas and air valves are opened, with the result that those regenerators that were being heated are now employed to preheat gas and air, the direction of flow of gases over the ovens being reversed, and the regenerators previously used to preheat are themselves heated by burned gases.

The arrangements for heating with rich gas are equally simple (fig. 2). The gas is supplied from a main which extends along one side of the battery of ovens; built into the pillars separating the regenerators under the heating flues are metal gas ducts supplied with rich gas by branch pipes from the rich-gas main. The rich gas is supplied to the bottom of alternate heating flues by these ducts and, on entering them, meets with preheated air which is supplied via the nozzles used to supply air and lean gas when the latter is used for heating. Thence, the flow of gases is as already described. When rich gas is used for heating, only the air is preheated and, since the volume of air required for a given output of heat from rich gas is about two-thirds the total volume of lean gas plus air which must be heated for the same production of heat, the same number of regenerators is used.

The producer gas used to heat a combination oven is generated in mechanically operated gas producers using coke breeze (fines which pass a $\frac{3}{4}$- or $\frac{1}{2}$-in. screen) which in any case must be removed from the coke before it is sent to a blast-furnace plant for the smelting of iron.

When coke ovens are heated by lean gas, the whole of the rich gas from the coal is available for other purposes; heating by rich gas involves the combustion of between 40% and 45% of the coal gas or, say, 4,000 cu.ft. for heating the ovens, leaving about 7,000 cu.ft. available.

Quenching and Cooling the Coke.—Since the coke leaves the ovens at a temperature of more than 1,000° C., it must be rapidly quenched to prevent it from being partially burned in contact with the air. This is commonly accomplished by pushing the coke through a cage of pipes pierced with a number of fine holes through which water is sprayed under pressure. The coke then falls onto an inclined coke wharf faced with plates of manganese steel, where any surplus water evaporates and where any hot spots are quenched with water from a hose.

Remote quenching is a more recent development. In this system, the coke is discharged into a long shallow car which is slowly moved across the end of the oven so that the coke is spread out in a thin layer. The car is then rapidly moved to the quenching station, built in the form of a tower which serves as a chimney to carry off the large volume of steam produced, and a predetermined quantity of water (usually about three tons per ton of coke) is sprayed onto the coke from storage tanks situated about 30 ft. above the car. The surplus water is allowed to drain into a settling pond, the car is returned to the coke wharf and the contents are allowed to slide onto the wharf, where the water steams off and the coke cools finally. The advantage of this method is that uniformity in the content of moisture is secured, and the large quantity of steam produced is vented into the atmosphere well above ground level and not in the immediate neighbourhood of the ovens where it can cause damage to the ironwork.

Dry Cooling.—Since the coke leaves the ovens at about 1,000° C., the sensible heat above 15° C. is approximately 8 to 9 therms per ton, or 4% of the heat of combustion of the coal from which it is made. If an appreciable proportion of this heat could be usefully employed, the over-all thermal efficiency of the plant would be materially increased.

In a dry-cooling plant, the coke when discharged from the ovens is rapidly transferred, in an airtight brick-lined container, to a large insulated chamber capable of holding several charges of coke. A certain amount of air is simultaneously introduced into the chamber, but the oxygen therein is rapidly burned to a mixture of oxides of carbon. The mixture of neutral gases (consisting chiefly of nitrogen) is circulated by means of a fan through the coke, thus becoming heated, and then passes from the cooling chamber to a dust collector and thence via a superheater over the tubes of a water-tube boiler. In such a plant, it is possible to raise nearly half a ton of steam per ton of coke, equivalent to a recovery of eight therms per ton of coal carbonized.

By-Products and Their Recovery.—An essential feature of practically all modern coking plants is the careful attention given to the recovery of the tar, light oils, ammonia and surplus gas produced during carbonization. While the yields depend on the particular coal being carbonized, the average quantities of all products obtained per ton of coal treated in British coke ovens in 1952 were: coke, 14.4 cwt.; tar, 7.4 gal.; benzol, 2.9 gal.; ammonia (calculated as sulphate), about 25 lb.; gas, 11,000 cu.ft., of which 4,650 cu.ft. were used to heat the ovens, leaving 6,350 cu.ft. (equivalent to about 34 therms) available for other purposes.

Recovery of by-products is carried out either by the direct or semidirect system according to whether the ammonia is removed from the gas directly as ammonium sulphate, or partly as ammonia liquor which must be subsequently distilled to recover the ammonia.

In both processes, the first step is to remove the tar from the gas. In the direct method, the gases are maintained at 70° to 80° C., or well above the dew point, until the ammonia has been recovered; removal of tar is accomplished either by treating the hot gas with a spray of finely divided tar at high pressure, in a cyclone extractor, or by means of an electrostatic detarrer. After removal of tar, the gas passes through the exhauster and then, at a temperature of about 58° to 60° C., is bubbled in fine streams through a saturated solution of ammonium sulphate, containing about 2% free sulphuric acid in the saturator, which is a leaden container supported in a cast-iron basket. The heat of reaction between the ammonia in the gas and the sulphuric acid maintains the temperature well above the dew point, consequently no condensation of water takes place; sulphate of ammonia separates out continuously and is removed from the saturator by means of compressed air and transferred to the basket of a centrifugal extractor where adherent mother liquor is removed and the dried sulphate is neutralized by a spray of ammonia liquor.

After leaving the saturator, the gas is shock cooled by passing up a tower countercurrent to a finely divided spray of cold water; there the naphthalene separates out and the temperature of the gas is reduced to atmospheric. The gas then passes successively up two towers packed with hurdles over which trickles a flow of wash oil (which is often a coal-tar fraction); the wash oil dissolves the low-boiling hydrocarbons (benzol, toluol, xylol, etc.) from the gas, part of which may subsequently be used to heat the ovens or, if heating is carried out by low-grade gas, the whole of the debenzolized gas may be sent to storage or fed into the mains. Part of the wash oil is continuously bled off from the benzol scrubbers and distilled for recovery of the dissolved light oils and, after being cooled, the debenzolized oil is returned to the scrubbers.

In the semidirect process, the gas is first cooled to approximately 24° C., with the result that the tar condenses out and much of the water vapour separates as ammonia liquor. The liquor is distilled for removal of ammonia, and the ammonia is returned to

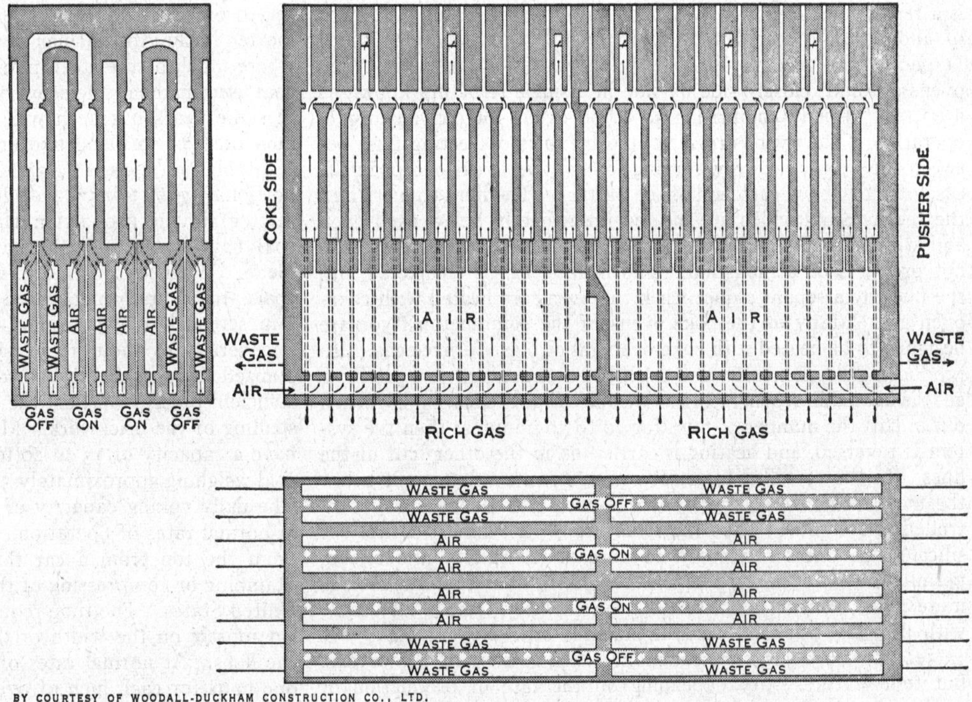

BY COURTESY OF WOODALL-DUCKHAM CONSTRUCTION CO., LTD.

FIG. 2.—W-D BECKER COMBINATION UNDERJET COKE OVEN (RICH GAS FIRING)
For description of flow of gas, *see* fig. 1

the gas, together with some steam from the stills, just before the gas enters the saturator where the ammonia is converted to sulphate as in the direct process. The semidirect method of recovery is less economical in fuel than the direct process, for not only is steam required to operate the ammonia stills, but the gas, after it leaves the exhauster, must be reheated to avoid risks of condensation of water vapour in the saturator. The recovery of naphthalene and benzol follows the same course in both processes.

Coke and By-products, Great Britain, 1952

Item	Gasworks	Coke works	Total
Coal carbonized, 000,000 tons	27.44	25.22	52.66
Coke made " "	12.58	17.09*	29.67
Breeze " "		1.04	
Gas made, 000,000 cu.ft.	500,610	271,586	772,196
Benzol scrubbed from gas, 000,000 gal.	26.3	73.3	99.6
Motor benzol made, 000,000 gal.	11.7	32.5	44.2
Tar distilled, 000,000 tons			2.71

*Of this, coke (excluding breeze) was supplied as follows (in 000,000 tons): blast furnaces 11.67; foundries, 1.18; other industries, 3.72; shipments, 0.42.

The Carbonizing Industries in Great Britain.—More than 50,000,000 tons of coal are treated at gasworks and at coking plants every year in Great Britain, and the throughput is increasing steadily. The table gives the figures for the manufacture of coke and by-products for 1952.

See also Coal and Coal Mining; Gas Industry; Low-Temperature Carbonization. (G. W. Hs.)

UNITED STATES

In the United States, the industry of coke making attained proportions greatly exceeding those in Great Britain, and developed on somewhat different lines.

Beehive Coking.—Beehive coking in the United States has a minor role in coke production, accounting for less than 10% of the total production of about 80,000,000 tons annually in the mid-1950s. These ovens are located at or near the coal mines and produce coke chiefly for blast-furnace and industrial purposes. Because of the higher operating costs of the beehive ovens they are shut down when the coke demand lessens. They are an important factor in meeting peak load demands for coke.

Chemical-Recovery Coke Ovens.—In the United States the term by-product was being replaced at mid-20th century by the term coal chemicals, and the coke ovens from which coal chemicals are recovered are known as chemical-recovery coke ovens. A typical modern chemical-recovery coke oven in the United States is a rectangular chamber of about 650–750 cu.ft. It has a length of about 40 ft., a height of 12 to 13 ft. and an average width (tapering 2 to 4 in. throughout the length) of 17 to 20 in. The ovens are built closely side by side in a single structure known as a battery, usually comprising 50 to 60 ovens for convenience in operation. The ovens are separated by rows of heating flues between the ovens, each row serving to heat two ovens except in the case of the flues at each end of the battery. The flues connect into the regenerators which are located immediately below each oven and which supply preheated air for combustion and receive the hot products of combustion. The heating gas is connected into the flues by a separate duct when the ovens are heated with coke-oven gas. Many of the coke ovens of the combination type are designed to be heated with coke-oven gas or blast-furnace gas (also producer gas) in which case the blast-furnace gas (or producer gas) is heated in regenerators as well as the air. Heating is carried out in half the number of flues for 20 to 30 minutes; then the system is reversed, and heating is carried on in the other half of the flues. In the so-called underjet ovens there is a basement below the oven structure so that the coke-oven gas can be easily controlled in each flue. The oven structure is built almost entirely of silica brick. This refractory, because of its rigidity under load, permits the use of higher temperatures in the flues and thus secures more rapid working and greater oven capacity than is attainable with fire-clay brick. Flue temperatures of 1,370° to 1,455° C. (2,500° to 2,650° F.) are commonly used in modern U.S. ovens, but temperatures vary depending on the rate of production or quality of coke required.

A favourite type of chemical-recovery oven in the United States is the Becker modification of the Koppers oven, the distinguishing feature of which is its provision for conducting the gases of combustion from the top of a row of vertical flues across and over the oven and down the row of flues on the other side. The crossover flues, of an inverted U shape, are in the upper part of the oven battery structure. They pass over alternate ovens only, and are generally six to eight in number, distributed across the length of the oven. Each crossover flue handles the waste gases from four to six vertical flues in the heating walls beneath, and each set of vertical flues is separated from each other set. The advantages of this type of oven are concerned chiefly with securing more uniform heating of the ovens, elimination of leakage in the combustion system and a more stable structure in the upper part of the flue wall. The heating gases burn in all of the flues in one-half of the number of walls, and when reversal takes place for the purpose of regeneration, the heating gases burn in the remaining half. This procedure is in contrast with the system where heating gases burn in one-half of the flues in each wall on each reversal. This construction and flow pattern makes for more uniform heating, end to end, of the oven walls. The old horizontal flue of large size (above the row of vertical flues) is structurally absent because of the provision of crossover flues which greatly reduce the volume of gases to be carried in any one section of that part of the oven. This allows a heavier wall structure in this region and permits the heating flues to be built up higher without risk of overheating the oven tops, resulting in more uniform coking of the oven charge.

On Dec. 31, 1953, the following numbers of chemical-recovery coke ovens of the various types were in existence in the United States:

Koppers (including Koppers-Becker)	12,036
Wilputte	2,182
Semet-Solvay	1,611
Cambria	120
Simon Carvés	40
Total	15,989

Gas Retorts and Ovens.—The production of city gas by carbonization of coal in D-shaped gas retorts and intermittent or continuous vertical retorts has practically disappeared in the United States. Although ovens of these types were once important in the gas industry, only a few isolated plants remain. Coal gas has generally been replaced by natural gas, liquefied petroleum gases or gas made from oil.

Carbonization Practice.—The United States has large reserves of relatively high-quality coking coals, most of which are located in the Appalachian region near large centres of population, where much of the steel industry is also located. The amount of coal used in chemical-recovery coke ovens annually has varied and in some years has been well over 100,000,000 tons. It is common practice to blend two or more coals for coke making. The high-volatile type (31%–38% volatile matter) is mixed in the proportion of 70% to 85% with low-volatile type (15%–22% volatile matter) in the proportion of 15%–30%. Medium-volatile type coal (23%–30% volatile matter) is sometimes included in the blend. When two or more kinds of coal are mixed together the coals are generally pulverized until at least 75% passes through a $\frac{1}{8}$-in. screen, but when using a single high-volatile type, the crushing is generally to about $1\frac{1}{4}$ in. size. Low-volatile coal is never carbonized alone in chemical-recovery coke ovens because it develops sufficient pressure against the oven walls to distort them and cause spalling of the brickwork. Modern chemical-recovery coke ovens have a capacity of 15 to 20 tons (2,000 lb. each) with pulverized coal weighing approximately 50 lb. per cubic foot in the coke oven. The daily coking capacity of each oven is 20 to 24 tons of coal at normal rates of operation. Coal is charged into the coke ovens from the top from a car that runs on top of the coke ovens. Stamping or compressing of the coal charge is not practised in the United States. The time required to carbonize the coal is dependent mostly on the width of the oven and on the temperature of the flues. At normal rates of operation the coking time is about one hour for each inch of oven width. At the end of the coking period the hot coke, at a temperature of about 1,800° F., is pushed out of the oven into a car and is quenched with a carefully controlled amount of water at a quenching station usually located beyond the end of the oven batteries. The coke is then dumped on an inclined wharf where it cools further and finally is transported by belt conveyor to a screening station and separated into sizes.

Coke is designated by its method of manufacture, such as oven coke, beehive coke and retort coke. It is also designated by the use to which it is put, as blast-furnace coke (or simply furnace coke), foundry coke, water-gas coke, domestic coke (for house heating). Another method of designation, chiefly applied to domestic coke, is according to size. The usual size classification, in the order of the largest size first, is as follows: egg, stove, nut, range, pea, breeze.

In the recovery of coal chemicals, the volatile products leaving the ovens enter a standpipe connecting into a manifold or collecting main where the first cooling of the gas and condensing of the tar takes place. After further cooling in the primary coolers and tar extractors, the ammonia is recovered by the so-called semidirect process, in which the gases are passed through a weak solution of sulphuric acid either in specially designed low-differential saturators or spray-type ammonia absorbers. The ammonia is thus converted into solid crystalline ammonium sulphate. Light oil containing benzene, toluene, xylenes and higher boiling hydrocarbons is scrubbed from the gas by a petroleum-type absorbent oil after which the light oil is steam distilled from the scrubbing oil. The gas, having a heating value of about 530 B.T.U. per cubic foot, requires no further treatment when used for underfiring the ovens or in the steel-mill furnaces, but hydrogen sulphide and naphthalene removal are necessary for distribution in city mains.

Average annual yields of products obtained from the carbonization of coal in chemical recovery coke ovens in the United States in the 1950s were as follows:

Coke (total), per cent coal	70.1
Breeze, per cent coal	5.0
Tar, gallons per ton coal	7.9
Light oil (crude), gallons per ton coal	2.9
Ammonium sulphate, pounds per ton coal	20.1
Gas, total cubic feet per ton coal	10,190

Disposal of Coke and Gas.—Consumption of coke at blast-furnace plants accounted for 89% of the total coke produced in the United States in the mid-1950s, and an additional approximate 4% of the coke was used in foundries, making a total of roughly 93% used in metallurgical processes. The rest of the coke produced was used as follows: 2% for water-gas and producer-gas manufacture; 2% for industrial purposes; 2% for residential heating and 1% export.

Approximately 35% to 40% of the total gas produced was returned to the coke ovens for underfiring; 48% of the total gas produced was used in steel mills or allied plants and 9% was distributed through city mains.

BIBLIOGRAPHY.—P. J. Wilson and J. H. Wells, *Coal, Coke, and Coal Chemicals* (New York, London, 1950); United States Bureau of Mines, *Minerals Yearbook* (issued annually); H. H. Lowry, *The Chemistry of Coal Utilization*, ch. 21, "Industrial Coal Carbonization" (New York, London, 1945); American Coke and Coal Chemicals Institute, *The Story of Coke and Coal Chemicals* (1949). (C. C. RL.)

"COKE OF NORFOLK": *see* LEICESTER OF HOLKHAM, THOMAS WILLIAM COKE, EARL OF.

COL, in physical geography, generally any distinct depression upon a high water-parting offering easy passage from one valley to another. There are numerous cols on the Franco-Italian frontier, *e.g.*, the Little St. Bernard (2,188 ft.) which carries the road from the Dora Baltea to the upper Isère. The col (Fr. for "neck," Lat. *collum*) is usually formed by the headwaters of streams eating backwards towards one another and lowering the water-parting between their valley-heads. In early military operations, the most convenient col controlled the route of the army's movement.

On the weather map a col is an area in which the pressure is neither high nor low and where the winds are calm or light and variable. This condition is possible only between two "highs" and two "lows." This feature is sometimes called a "neutral point" or "saddle point." (*See* CYCLONE; ANTICYCLONE.)

COLBERT, JEAN BAPTISTE (1619–1683), French statesman, was born at Reims, where his father and grandfather were merchants. Through a family connection with Michel le Tellier, secretary of State for war, Colbert obtained a place in the war office before he was 20 and presently became private secretary to the minister. Twelve years later he became agent to Mazarin, driven from Paris (1651) during the supremacy of the Condé family, with the duty of keeping him informed of the progress of events. On his return, Mazarin gratified his agent with honours and places for various members of his family, and gave him his entire confidence. After Mazarin's death, Colbert secured the favour of Louis XIV. and became the chief power in the administration, though he did not at first hold an official position.

The king's new adviser set to work at once to reform the chaotic financial administration of France. He began by striking at the *surintendant,* Nicolas Fouquet, and secured his disgrace. The office of *surintendant* was abolished, and the control of finance was vested for a time in a royal council. Colbert, who contented himself with the title of *intendant,* was the ruling spirit of this council, but did not take over nominal direct control until 1665, when he was made controller-general. His first measures for cleansing the financial administration were ruthless enough. He set up a tribunal to deal with officials who intercepted money due to the treasury. Many were condemned to death, though the death sentences were not carried out; some 4,000 were compelled to disgorge their gains. The tribunal was disbanded in 1665, but it had purified the service. The public debt was handled by drastic methods. Some series of bonds were repudiated on the ground that only a small part of the money had been paid in; others were cancelled by paying the original sum invested less the interest paid. Colbert did not propose the abolition of privilege, but he drew into the net of taxation many who had hitherto escaped by revising the application of the *taille,* or direct tax. Indirect taxes were increased and the tariff revised in 1664, as part of a protective system. The various dues which existed among the provinces could not be swept away, but, although internal fiscal barriers were not destroyed, a measure of uniformity was secured in central France. His reforms in the farming out and collection of taxes and the jealous watch kept on the officials brought large sums into the treasury.

Colbert then turned his attention to the general increase of wealth by the encouragement of industry. He had a narrow conception of prosperity, which in his mind could not be real if neighbouring countries were prosperous. And in his encouragement of industry and trade he used the same minute method of centralized regulation which had brought order into the fiscal system. Every detail was to be controlled. This minute regulation probably accounts for the failure of the great trading corporations which he set up in 1664 for trading in India and in America (the East Indies and West Indies companies), while the British and Dutch monopolistic trading companies, with their operations untrammelled by the home government, prospered. He set up model factories, either financed by State funds as in the case of the Gobelins (founded 1667) or by concessionaries. He sought to standardize the production of staple commodities for all producers; faulty workmanship or deviation from the standard was punished by fine and by exposure in the pillory. These regulations hampered industry and annoyed the producers, and the encouragement given to industry tended to starve agriculture. French industry was to be developed by administrative measures and by a high protective tariff, and the proceeds accruing to the State were to be used for the development of communications and of external trade. The roads and canals were improved. The great canal of Languedoc was planned and constructed by Pierre Paul Riquet (1604–80) under Colbert's patronage.

The greatest and most lasting of Colbert's achievements was the establishment of the French marine. He became minister of the marine in 1669; then, in addition, of the colonies and the king's palace. The royal navy owed all to him, for the king thought only of military exploits. Colbert reconstructed the works and arsenal of Toulon, founded the port and arsenal of Rochefort, and the naval schools of Rochefort, Dieppe, and St. Malo, and fortified, with some assistance from Vauban (who, however, belonged to the party of his rival Louvois), among other ports those of Calais, Dunkirk, Brest, and Havre. To supply it with recruits he invented his system of classes, by which each seaman, according to the class in which he was placed, gave six months' service every three or four or five years. For three months after his term of service he was to receive half-pay; pensions were promised; and, in short, everything was done to make the navy popular. There was one department, however, that was supplied with men on a very different principle. The galleys used in the Mediterranean service required oarsmen. Colbert wrote to the judges requiring them to sentence to the oar as many criminals as possible; and the convict, once chained to the bench, the expiration of his sentence was seldom allowed to bring him release. Vagrants, contraband dealers, political rebels, Turkish, Russian, and negro slaves, and poor Iroquois Indians, whom the Canadians were ordered to entrap, were pressed into that terrible service. By these means the benches of the galleys were filled, and Colbert took no thought of the long agony of those who filled them.

Encouragement was given to the building of ships for the mercantile marine by allowing a premium on those built at home, and imposing a duty on those brought from abroad; and as French workmen were forbidden to emigrate, so French seamen were forbidden to serve foreigners on pain of death.

Colbert was a patron of art and literature. He possessed a fine private library, rich in valuable manuscripts. He founded the academy of sciences, the observatory, which he employed Claude Perrault to build and brought G. D. Cassini (1625–1712) from Italy to superintend, the academies of inscriptions and medals, of architecture, and of music, the French academy at Rome, and academies at Arles, Soissons, Nîmes, and many other towns, and he reorganized the academy of painting and sculpture which Richelieu had established. He was a member of the French academy. In 1673 he presided over the first exhibition of the works of living painters; and he enriched the Louvre with hundreds of pictures and statues. He gave many pensions to men of letters, among whom we find Molière, Corneille, Racine, Boileau, P. D. Huet (1630–1721) and Antoine Varillas (1626–96), and even foreigners, as Huyghens, Vossius the geographer, Carlo Dati the Dellacruscan, and Heinsius the great Dutch scholar.

Colbert's industry was colossal. He found time to do something for the better administration of justice (the codification of ordinances, the diminishing of the number of judges, the reduction of the expense and length of trials for the establishment of a superior system of police) and even for the improvement of the breed of horses and the increase of cattle. As superintendent of public buildings he enriched Paris with boulevards, quays, and triumphal arches; he relaid the foundation stone of the Louvre, and brought Bernini from Rome to be its architect; and he erected its splendid colonnade upon the plan of Claude Perrault, by whom Bernini had been replaced. He was not permitted, however, to complete the work, being compelled to yield to the king's preference for residences outside Paris, and to devote himself to Marly and Versailles.

Amid all these public labours he directed personally the management of every farm on his estates. He died extremely rich and left fine estates all over France. He had been created marquis de Seignelay, and for his eldest son he obtained the reversion of the office of minister of marine; his second son became archbishop of Rouen; and a third son, the marquis d'Ormoy, became superintendent of buildings.

To carry out his reforms, Colbert needed peace and consistently advocated it, except in the case of the Dutch War, for which his commercial policy was partly responsible; but the war department was in the hands of his great rival Louvois, whose influence gradually supplanted that of Colbert with the king. Louis decided on a policy of conquest. He was deaf also to all the appeals against the other forms of his boundless extravagance which Colbert ventured to make (*Lettres*, vol. ii.). Thus, only a few years after he had begun to free the country from the weight of the loans and taxes which crushed her to the dust, Colbert was forced to heap upon her a new load of loans and taxes heavier than the last. Depressed by his failure, deeply wounded by the king's favour for Louvois, and worn out by overwork, his strength gave way at a comparatively early age.

Colbert was a great statesman, who did much for France. Nevertheless, his rule was a very bad example of over-government. He did not believe in popular liberty; the parlements and the states-general received no support from him. The technicalities of justice he never allowed to interfere with his plans; and he did not hesitate to shield his friends. He trafficked in public offices for the profit of Mazarin and in his own behalf. He caused the suffering of thousands in the galleys. There was indeed a more human side to his character, shown to his own family, but to all outside he was "the man of marble." Madame de Sévigné called him "the North Star." To diplomacy he never pretended.

Bibliography.—The most thorough student of Colbert's life and administration was Pierre Clément, member of the Institute, who in 1846 published his *Vie de Colbert*, and in 1861 the first of the 9 vols. of the *Lettres, instructions et mémoires de Colbert*. The historical introductions prefixed to each of these volumes have been published by Mme. Clément under the title of the *Histoire de Colbert et de son administration*, 3rd ed. (1892). The best short account of Colbert as a statesman is that in Lavisse, *Histoire de France* (1905), which gives a thorough study of the administration. *See* also Benôit du Rey, *Recherches sur la politique coloniale de Colbert* (1902). Among Colbert's papers are *Mémoires sur les affaires de finance de France* (written about 1663), a fragment entitled *Particularités secrètes de la vie du Roy*, and other accounts of the earlier part of the reign of Louis XIV.

COLBERT DE CROISSY, CHARLES, Marquis (1625–1696), French diplomatist, like his elder brother Jean Baptiste Colbert, began his career in the office of the minister of war, Le Tellier. In 1656 he bought a counsellorship at the parlement of Metz, and in 1658 was appointed intendant of Alsace and president of the newly-created sovereign council of Alsace. In this position he had to reorganize the territory recently annexed to France. The steady support of his brother at court gained for him several diplomatic missions—to Germany and Italy (1659–61). In 1662 he became marquis de Croissy and *président à mortier* of the parlement of Metz. After various intendancies, at Soissons (1665), at Amiens (1666) and at Paris (1667), he turned definitely to diplomacy. In 1668 he represented France at the conference of Aix-le-Chapelle; and in August of the same year was sent as ambassador to London, where he was to negotiate the definite treaty of alliance with Charles II. He arranged the interview at Dover between Charles and his sister Henrietta of Orleans, gained the king's personal favour by finding a mistress for him, Louise de Kérouaille, maid of honour to Madame, and persuaded him to declare war against Holland. The negotiation of the treaty of Nijmwegen (1676–78) still further increased his reputation as a diplomatist, and Louis XIV. made him secretary of state for foreign affairs after the disgrace of Arnauld de Pomponne, brought about by his brother, 1679. He at once assumed the entire direction of French diplomacy. It was he, not Louvois, who formed the idea of annexation during a time of peace, by means of the chambers of reunion. He had outlined this plan as early as 1658 with regard to Alsace. His policy at first was to retain the territory annexed by the chambers of reunion without declaring war, and for this purpose he signed treaties of alliance with the elector of Brandenburg (1681), and with Denmark (1683); but the troubles following upon the revocation of the Edict of Nantes (1685) forced him to give up his scheme and to prepare for war with Germany (1688). The negotiations for peace had been begun again when he died, on July 28, 1696.

Bibliography.—His papers, preserved in the *Archives des affaires étrangères* at Paris, have been partially published in the *Recueil des instructions données aux ambassadeurs et ministres de France* (since 1884). *See* especially the volumes:—*Autriche* (t.i.), *Suède* (t.ii.), *Rome* (t.vi.), *Bavière* (t.viii.), *Savoie* (t.xiv.), *Prusse* (t.xvi.). Other documents have been published in Mignet's *Négociations relatives à la succession d'Espagne*, vol. iv., and in the collection of *Lettres et négociations . . . pour la paix de Nimègue, 1676–77* (La Haye, 1710). In addition to the *Mémoires* of the time, *see* Spanheim, *Relation de la cour de France en 1690*, edit. E. Bourgeois (Lyons, 1900); Baschet, *Histoire du depôt des affaires étrangères;* C. Rousset, *Histoire de Louvois* (1863); E. Bourgeois, "Louvois et Colbert de Croissy," in the *Revue Historique*, vol. xxxiv. (1887); A. Waddington, *Le Grand Électeur et Louis XIV.* (1905); G. Pagès. *Le Grand Électeur et Louis XIV.* (1905).

COLBURN, HENRY (d. 1855), British publisher. In 1814 he originated the *New Monthly Magazine,* of which at various times Thomas Campbell, Bulwer Lytton, Theodore Hook and Harrison Ainsworth were editors. Colburn published in 1818 *Evelyn's Diary,* and in 1825 the *Diary of Pepys,* edited by Lord Braybrooke, paying £2,200 for the copyright. He also issued Disraeli's first novel, *Vivian Grey.* His business was taken over in 1841 by Messrs. Hurst and Blackett. Henry Colburn died on Aug. 16, 1855.

COLBY, FRANK MOORE (1865–1925), U.S. editor, was born in Washington, D.C., Feb. 10, 1865. He received from Columbia university the degrees A.B. (1888) and A.M. (1889). He was acting professor of history at Amherst college (1890–91), lecturer and instructor in history and economics at Columbia university and Barnard college (1891–95) and professor of economics at New York university (1895–1900). In 1893 he joined the editorial staff of *Johnson's Universal Cyclopaedia.* In 1898 he became editor of *The International Year Book,* and he was one of the editors of *The International Cyclopaedia* and of the first and second editions of *The New International Encyclopaedia.* He served as American editor of *Nelson's Encyclopaedia* (1905–06), and after 1907 as editor of *The New International Year Book.*

Colby died in New York city, March 3, 1925. He wrote, among other works, *Imaginary Obligations* (1904); *Constrained Attitudes* (1910) and *The Margin of Hesitation* (1922).

COLCHAGUA, a province of central Chile, bounded north by Santiago and O'Higgins, east by Argentina, south by Curicó and west by the Pacific. Its area is 3,255 sq.mi.; population (1940 census) 138,036; (1951 est.) 135,775.

The great longitudinal valley of Chile cuts across the central part of the province, providing a considerable area excellently suited to the production of crops and livestock. Good range land exists in both the coastal mountains and along the lower slopes of the Andes. The principal river is the Rapel which, in its lower reaches, forms a part of the northern boundary of the province. Near the Argentine frontier, on one of the principal tributaries of the Rapel, are the hot springs of San Fernando, accessible by car from San Fernando, capital of Colchagua. The State central railway from Santiago to Puerto Montt passes through San Fernando (83 mi. S. of Santiago), and a branch line extends west to the popular ocean resort of Pichelemu. San Fernando is one of the several towns founded in 1742 by the governor-general José de Manso.

COLCHESTER, CHARLES ABBOT, 1st Baron (1757–1829), was born in Abingdon, and educated at Westminster school and Oxford. In 1795, after having practised 12 years as a barrister, he was appointed clerk of the rules in the king's bench and elected member of parliament. To his efforts were due the establishment of the Royal Record commission, the reform of the system which had allowed the public money to lie for long periods in the hands of the public accountants, by charging them with payment of interest, and, most important of all, the act for taking the first census (1801).

In March 1801 Abbot became chief secretary and privy seal for Ireland; and in 1802 he was chosen speaker of the house of commons. In response to an address of the commons, he became Baron Colchester, with a pension of £4,000. He died on May 8, 1829.

COLCHESTER, municipal borough, Essex, England; 52 mi. northeast of London, on the river Colne. Pop. (1951) 57,436. Area 18.8 sq.mi. In early British and Roman history it was known as Camulodunum, the capital of the British chief Cunobelin, and is named on his coins. After his death and the Roman conquest, Claudius established a municipality of discharged soldiers. It was stormed and burned A.D. 61 in the rising of Boadicea (*q.v.*), but soon became one of the chief towns in Roman Britain. The town is named after Camulos, the Celtic Mars. Roman sculptures and inscriptions have been discovered and its walls and the guardroom of the principal gate can still be traced. The Domesday book mentions 276 burgesses and land *in commune burgensium.* The ruined castle-keep built by William I about 1080 is quadrangular, turreted at the angles, and is the largest of its kind in England. In the castle is a museum of Roman and other antiquities. The Augustinian priory of St. Botolph (early 12th cent.) retains part of the fine Norman west front (in which Roman bricks occur), and of the nave arcades; and there is the restored gateway of the Benedictine monastery of St. John, a beautiful specimen of Perpendicular work, embattled, flanked by spired turrets, and covered with panel work. The church of Holy Trinity has an apparently pre-Norman tower.

The first charter given in 1189 granted freedom of passage and pontage through England, free warren, fishery and custom as in the time of Henry I. The charters were confirmed and new grants obtained in 1447 and 1535. Colchester returned two members to parliament from 1295 until 1885. Fairs were granted by Richard I in 1189 to the hospital of St. Mary Magdalene, and by Edward II in 1319 on the eve of St. Denis and the six following days. In the 13th century Colchester was an important port, its ships plying to Winchelsea and France. Elizabeth and James I encouraged Flemish settlers in manufacture of baize ("bays and says"). Both Camden and Fuller mention the trade in barrelled oysters and candied eringo-root. The town was held, apparently against the citizens' will, by Royalists in 1648 against Fairfax, and it was fined in consequence by the parliament.

Charles I granted a fresh charter, which was amended in 1653 and a new one granted in 1663; this one remaining in force with modifications until 1741. In 1763 George III made the borough a renewed grant of its liberties. The town has long been an important military centre and is the headquarters of the 4th division and East Anglia area. There is a free grammar school (founded 1539). Castle park is a public ground surrounding the castle. Colchester is the centre of an agricultural district, and has weekly corn and cattle markets, besides extensive nurseries and a large rose-growing industry. The oyster fisheries at the mouth of the Colne belong to the corporation, and are held on lease by the Colne Fishery company. The harbour, with quayage at the suburb of Hythe, is controlled by the corporation. Since 1918 the municipal borough of Colchester together with the rural districts of Lexden and Winstree (except the detached portion of Inworth parish) form the Colchester parliamentary division of Essex.

Colchester was made the see of a bishop suffragan by Henry VIII, and two bishops were in succession appointed by him; no further appointments, however, were made until the suffragan see was re-established under Victoria.

COLCHICUM, the meadow saffron, or autumn crocus (*Colchicum autumnale*), a perennial plant of the family Liliaceae, found wild in rich, moist meadowland in England and Ireland, in middle and southern Europe and in the Swiss Alps. It has pale purple flowers, rarely more than three in number; the perianth is funnel-shaped, and produced below into a long slender tube, in the upper part of which the six stamens are inserted. The ovary is three-celled, and lies at the bottom of this tube. The leaves are three or four in number, flat, lanceolate, erect and sheathing; and there is no stem. Propagation is by the formation of new corms from the parent corm, and by seeds. The latter are numerous, round, reddish-brown and of the size of black mustard-seeds. The corm of the meadow saffron attains its full size in June or early in July. A smaller corm is then formed from the old one, close to its root; and this in September and October produces the crocus-like flowers. In the succeeding January or February it sends up its leaves, together with the ovary, which perfects its seeds during the summer. The young corm grows continuously, till in the following July it attains the size of a small apricot. The parent corm remains attached to the new one, and keeps its form and size till April in the third year of its existence, after which it decays. In some cases a single corm produces several new plants during its second spring by giving rise to immature corms. *C. autumnale* and its numerous varieties, as well as other species of the genus, are well known in cultivation, forming some of the most beautiful of autumn-flowering plants.

Colchicum or colchicine, applied to the skin, causes pain and congestion; inhaled, causes violent sneezing; and taken internally.

increases the amount of bile poured into the intestine. In larger doses it is a violent gastrointestinal irritant, causing severe colic, vomiting, diarrhoea, haemorrhage from the bowel and ultimately death from collapse. This is accelerated by a depressant action upon the heart and nervous system similar to that produced by veratrine and aconite. The sole medical use of colchicum is in gout. It has an extraordinary power over the pain of acute gout, lessens the severity and frequency of the attacks when given continuously between them, and benefits such symptoms of gout as eczema, bronchitis and neuritis, though inoperative against them when not of gouty origin. The drug is generally given as *vinum colchici,* in doses of 10 to 30 minims. It is apt to render the patient low-spirited and tearful and must be given only with great care. In colchicum poisoning, empty the stomach, give white of egg, olive or salad oil and water. Use hot bottles and stimulants, especially trying to counteract the cardiac depression by atropine, caffeine, strophanthin, etc.

Colchicum is a specific for separation of chromosomes. The product is much used in genetics and plant breeding to produce a doubling of the chromosomes. Most of the U.S. supply ordinarily comes from the Netherlands, Italy, Yugoslavia and Hungary.

COLCHIS, in ancient geography, a nearly triangular district of Asia Minor, at the eastern extremity of the Black sea, bounded on the north by the Caucasus, which separated it from Asiatic Sarmatia, east by Iberia, south by the Montes Moschici, Armenia and part of Pontus and west by the Euxine. The name of Colchis first appears in Aeschylus and Pindar. It was inhabited by a number of tribes whose settlements lay chiefly along the shore of the Black sea. These tribes differed so completely in language and appearance from the surrounding nations that the ancients originated various theories to account for the phenomenon. Herodotus believed them to have sprung from the relics of the army of Sesostris (*q.v.*), and thus regarded them as Egyptians. Apollonius Rhodius (*Argon,* iv, 279) states that the Egyptians of Colchis preserved as heirlooms a number of wooden κύρβεις (tablets) showing seas and highways with considerable accuracy. It is quite possible that there was an ancient trade connection between the Colchians and the Mediterranean peoples. We learn that women were buried, while the corpses of men were suspended on trees. The principal coast town was the Milesian colony of Dioscurias (Roman Sebastopolis; mod. Sukhum-Kaleh), the ancient name being preserved in the modern C. Iskuria. The chief river was the Phasis (mod. Rion).

Colchis was celebrated in Greek mythology as the destination of the Argonauts, the home of Medea and the special domain of sorcery. Several Greek colonies were founded there by Miletus. It seems to have been incorporated in the Persian empire, though the inhabitants evidently enjoyed a considerable degree of independence; in this condition it was found by Alexander the Great when he invaded Persia. From this time till the era of the Mithradatic wars nothing is known of its history. At the time of the Roman invasion it seems to have paid a nominal homage to Mithradates the Great and to have been ruled over by Machares, his second son. On the defeat of Mithradates by Pompey, it became a Roman province. After the death of Pompey, Pharnaces, the son of Mithradates, rose in rebellion against the Roman yoke, subdued Colchis and Armenia and made head, though but for a short time, against the Roman arms. After this Colchis was incorporated with Pontus, and the Colchians are not again alluded to in ancient history till the 6th century. It had been specially garrisoned by Justinian, first under Peter, a Persian slave, and subsequently under Johannes Tzibos, who built Petra on the coast as the Roman headquarters. Tzibos took advantage of the extreme poverty of the inhabitants to create a Roman monopoly by which he became a middleman for all the trade, both export and import. Chosroes I succeeded in capturing Petra (A.D. 541). The missionary zeal of the Zoroastrian priests soon caused discontent among the Christian inhabitants of Colchis, and Gobazes, perceiving that Chosroes intended to Persianize the district, appealed to Rome, with the result that in 549 one Dagisthaeus was sent out with 7,000 Romans and 1,000 auxiliaries of the Tzani (Zani, Sanni). The "Lazic war" lasted till 556 with varying success. Petra was recaptured in 551, and Archaeopolis was held by the Romans against the Persian general Mermeroes. Gobazes was assassinated in 552, but the Persian general Nachoragan was heavily defeated at Phasis in 553.

By the peace of 562 the district was left in Roman possession, but during the next 150 years it is improbable that the Romans exercised much authority over it. In 697 we hear of a revolt against Rome led by Sergius the Patrician, who allied himself with the Arabs. Justinian II in his second period of rule sent Leo the Isaurian, afterward emperor, to induce the Alans to attack the Abasgi. The Alans invaded Lazica, and, probably in 712, a Roman and Armenian army laid siege to Archaeopolis. On the approach of a Saracen force they retired, but a small plundering detachment was cut off. Ultimately Leo joined this band and aided by the Apsilian chief Marinus escaped with them to the coast.

From the beginning of the 14th to the end of the 17th century Colchis was governed by an independent dynasty, the Dadians, which was succeeded by a semi-independent dynasty, the Chikovans, who by 1838 had submitted to Russia, though they retained a nominal sovereignty. In 1866 the district was finally annexed by Russia. *See* GEORGIA.

For the kings *see* Stokvis, *Manuel d'histoire,* i, 83.

COLCOTHAR (adapted in Romanic languages from Arabic *golgotar,* which was probably a corruption of the Gr. χάλκανθος from χαλκός, copper, ἄνθος, flower; *i.e.,* copper sulphate), a name given to the brownish-red ferric oxide residue obtained in the preparation of fuming sulphuric (Nordhausen) acid by the dry distillation of ferrous or ferric sulphate. It is used as a polishing powder by jewellers and as the pigment Indian red. It is also known as Crocus Martis, *caput mortuum,* Prussian red, rouge, etc.

COLD, subjectively the sensation which is excited by contact with a substance whose temperature is lower than the normal; objectively a quality or condition of material bodies which gives rise to that sensation. Whether cold, in the objective sense, was to be regarded as a positive quality or merely as absence of heat was long a debated question. Thus Robert Boyle, who does not commit himself definitely to either view, says, in his *New Experiments and Observations Touching Cold,* that "the dispute which is the *primum frigidum* is very well known among naturalists, some contending for the earth, others for water, others for the air, and some of the moderns for nitre, but all seeming to agree that there is some body or other that is of its own nature supremely cold and by participation of which all other bodies obtain that quality." But with the general acceptance of the dynamical theory of heat, cold naturally came to be regarded as a negative condition, depending on decrease in the amount of the molecular vibration that constitutes heat.

The question whether there is a limit to the degree of cold possible, and, if so, where the zero must be placed, was first attacked by the French physicist G. Amontons in 1702–03, in connection with his improvements in the air thermometer. In his instrument temperatures were indicated by the height at which a column of mercury was sustained by a certain mass of air, the volume or "spring" of which of course varied with the heat to which it was exposed. Amontons therefore argued that the zero of his thermometer would be that temperature at which the spring of the air in it was reduced to nothing. On the scale he used the boiling point of water was marked at 73 and the melting point of ice at $51\frac{1}{2}$, so that the zero of his scale was equivalent to about $-240°$ on the Centigrade scale. This remarkably close approximation to the modern value of $-273°$ for the zero of the air thermometer was further improved on by J. H. Lambert (*Pyrometrie,* 1779), who gave the value $-270°$ and observed that this temperature might be regarded as absolute cold. Values of this order for the absolute zero were not, however, universally accepted about this period. Laplace and Lavoisier, for instance, in their treatise on heat (1780), arrived at values ranging from 1,500° to 3,000° below the freezing point of water, and thought that in any case it must be at least 600° below, while John Dalton in his *Chemical Philosophy* gave ten calculations of this value, and finally adopted $-3{,}000°$ C. as the natural zero of temperature. After J. P. Joule had determined the mechanical equivalent of heat, Lord Kelvin approached the question from an entirely different point of view, and in 1848 devised a scale of absolute temperature which was independent of the properties of any particular substance and was based solely on the fundamental laws of thermodynamics (*see* HEAT and THERMODYNAMICS). It followed from the principles on which this scale was constructed that its zero was placed at −273°, at almost precisely the same point as the zero of the air-thermometer.

In nature the realms of space, on the probable assumption that the interstellar medium is perfectly transparent and diathermanous, must, as was pointed out by W. J. Macquorn Rankine, be incapable of acquiring any temperature, and must therefore be at the absolute zero. That, however, is not to say that if a suitable thermometer could be projected into space it would give a reading of −273°. On the contrary, not being a transparent and diathermanous body, it would absorb radiation from the sun and other stars, and would thus become warmed. (*See* J. H. Poynting, "Radiation in the Solar System," *Phil. Trans.* A, 1903). The French physicists of the early part of the 19th century held a different view, and rejected the hypothesis of the absolute cold of space. Fourier, for instance, postulated a fundamental temperature of space as necessary for the explanation of the heat-effects observed on the surface of the earth, and estimated that in the interplanetary regions it was little less than that of the terrestrial poles and below the freezing-point of mercury, though it was different in other parts of space (*Ann. chim. phys.*, 1824, 27, pp. 141, 150). C. S. M. Pouillet, again calculated the temperature of interplanetary space as −142°C. (*Comptes rendus,* 1838, 7, p. 61), and Sir John Herschel as −150°.

To attain the absolute zero in the laboratory, that is, to deprive a substance entirely of its heat, is a thermodynamical impossibility, and the most that the physicist can hope for is an indefinitely close approach to that point. The lowest steady temperature obtainable by the exhaustion of liquid hydrogen is about −262° C. (11° Abs.), and the liquefaction of helium by Prof. Kamerlingh Onnes in 1908 yielded a liquid having a boiling-point of about 4° Abs. which on exhaustion should bring us to within about 1° of the absolute zero. Liquid helium has since been solidified by W. H. Keesom (1926) at 1.13° Abs. under a pressure of 25 atmos. The freezing point rises to 4.2° Abs. under a pressure of 140 atmos. (*See* LIQUEFACTION OF GASES.)

COLD, COMMON. The term "cold" is applied by physicians and laymen alike to various acute, subacute and even chronic maladies affecting both the upper and the lower portions of the respiratory tract. Investigators of this condition usually limit the term to a condition commonly described as coryza or a cold in the head. Typical symptoms of such colds are sneezing, watery nasal discharge, nasal stuffiness and a dryness or an irritation of the membranes lining the nose and throat. The onset is usually accompanied by a sensation of chilliness. In the early stages of the acute cold, nasal discharge is profuse and watery but in two or three days becomes thicker and mucopurulent. Involvement of the paranasal sinuses and the lower portions of the respiratory tract with coughing is common.

Colds and their complications are responsible for more illness and disability than all other diseases combined. A survey conducted by the American Institute of Public Opinion found that in one week of November colds were reported in one-third of U.S. homes. Thus, during this particular week, approximately one person in seven throughout the country was afflicted with a cold. A corresponding survey for a week in October revealed that one-fourth of all families reported colds.

Other surveys indicate that approximately 75% of the people have at least one cold each year, 25% have four or more and the average is between two and three per person per year. A ten-year record of illness among employees of the Edison Illuminating Co., covering an average of 100,000 employees annually, showed that 54% of the absences from sickness were caused by the respiratory group of diseases. These and other studies indicate that the common cold, its complications and related conditions cause more loss of time in industry than all other illnesses together. The annual cost in the U.S. (economic loss and expenditures for drugs and medical and hospital services caused by the common cold and its complications) has been estimated as between $2,000,000,000 and $3,000,000,000.

Cause.—As the name suggests, colds are widely believed to be caused by chilling. In some persons chilling does produce symptoms of sneezing and coryza. Physicians call this condition vasomotor rhinitis, but to the average person it is a "cold in the head." Hay fever (*q.v.*), another quite similar condition, is caused by an allergy or hypersensitivity of the nasal mucous membranes to some substance in the air, such as pollen of plants, grasses or trees. Unquestionably many attacks of hay fever are mistaken for colds, particularly when they occur in the spring of the year.

Observations of the common cold indicate that at least some colds are communicable; in fact, the widespread colds which occur in several waves throughout the year, usually in the early fall, in midwinter and in early spring, are of this type. Investigations of the cause of this type of cold seem to indicate that a majority are caused by a filterable virus (*q.v.*), a germ which is smaller than bacteria, will pass through pores of a porcelain filter and is invisible with the ordinary microscope. The first experiments which suggested a virus as a cause of colds were performed by Walther Kruse in 1914 in the Institute of Hygiene in Leipzig, Ger. This work was repeated and confirmed by Maj. George Foster of the medical corps of the U.S. army in 1916. Beginning in the early 1920s more extensive and definitive studies of this virus were carried out by A. R. Dochez and associates in the Presbyterian hospital in New York city and by investigators at Johns Hopkins university, Baltimore, Md.

The nature of this virus is similar to that of other known viruses, such as those which cause smallpox, chickenpox, mumps, rabies and distemper. It will grow and multiply in the laboratory and remain alive for at least three years. It will remain infective after 15 subcultures on artificial media. One drop of the solution containing the virus is sufficient to give a man or a chimpanzee a typical head cold. The usual symptoms of these virus colds in human subjects are stuffiness of the nose, sneezing, watery nasal discharge, dryness of the throat, occasional headaches and mild general symptoms. The body temperature is rarely elevated and the usual duration is four to five days. Mild colds occur in subjects carefully isolated from all contact with other persons. In others, this acute process is usually followed by secondary infections with other germs which happen to be present in the nose and throat. The secondary infections, which usually persist for two or three weeks, are accompanied by a thick yellow discharge that may involve the sinuses.

Bacteria of various types have also been described as a cause of colds. Unquestionably, bacteria do produce primary infections of the respiratory tract with symptoms typical of colds. Their major role, however, seems to be that of secondary invaders following virus colds. Climate is much less a factor in the occurrence of colds than is generally supposed. Studies by the U.S. public health service show that the attack rate of colds in college students and family groups in various parts of the country are remarkably uniform and show no consistent relationship to latitude, longitude or climate. These studies also show surprising similarity in the time of occurrence of colds in various sections of the country. Studies in isolated arctic communities indicate that epidemics of colds are related not to temperature but to contact with infected persons from the outside world. In the tropics colds are less common and less severe than in the temperate zones, but they do occur and in general present a miniature picture of colds in the United States.

Complications.—The importance of colds lies not only in the colds themselves but also in their complications. An uncomplicated cold runs a short, relatively mild course of a few days' duration. The complications, however, are numerous and important. Of these, the most common are sinusitis, otitis media and infections of the lower respiratory tract such as laryngitis, tracheitis, bronchitis and pneumonia. Closely allied but distinct disease entities are influenza, tonsillitis and tuberculosis. The paranasal sinuses all are connected with the nose and are lined by mucous membrane which is continuous with the membrane of the nose. Some inflammation of the sinuses, therefore, probably follows most if not all acute head colds. These are of importance, however, only when secondary infections occur and drainage is inadequate. Treatment of infected sinuses is a problem for the physician.

Infection of the middle ear (otitis media) occurs from the nose and throat by the way of the Eustachian tube. Formerly otitis media was often complicated by mastoid infection, but this has been controlled by penicillin, other antibiotics or the sulfonamide drugs. Laryngitis, tracheitis, bronchitis and pneumonia usually follow infections of the upper respiratory tract.

Prevention.—Natural resistance, possibly with a hereditary element, plays an important role in a person's susceptibility to colds. Studies from Cornell university (Ithaca, N.Y.) indicate that 25% of the students have approximately 75% of the colds in that institution. In many individuals, however, susceptibility seems to vary over a period of several years. Within the nose nature provides various defensive mechanisms against infection. These include the tiny hairs at the entrance of the nasal passages, the mucous secretions of the membranes lining the nose and the cilia—microscopic hairlike projections of the cells lining the nose. These cilia are in constant motion, picking up particles of foreign material and carrying them to the pharynx from which they are discharged or swallowed. It is important that we do not destroy or interfere with these natural defensives.

The prevention of communicable colds should be possible by the avoidance of exposure to persons with colds. Unfortunately, under the conditions of modern life this is impossible. However, the degree of exposure can be reduced by keeping away from persons who have colds; by prohibiting infected persons from associating with infants; by thorough washing of the hands before meals and after contact with objects likely to contain infective material; by keeping the hands away from the nose and mouth; by routine sterilization of dishes and silverware; and by use of individual drinking glasses even within the family. The avoidance of chilling, particularly for persons who lead relatively sedentary indoor lives, is a precautionary measure of value. Adequate clothing and shoes to keep the body warm and dry are important, especially for children. Places of work and residences should be warm and free from draft, but not overheated. The ventilation of sleeping quarters should be regulated according to the outside atmospheric condition, having in mind that drafts are undesirable and that sleep is most restful where the atmosphere is cool rather than warm or cold. Exercise and cool or cold showers help to keep the circulatory system in good tone and better able to adjust to the changes produced by chilling.

Vitamins and various dietary measures are widely advocated and advertised for the prevention of colds, but there are no conclusive scientific studies or records which indicate that any special diet or the addition of vitamins to adequate, well-balanced diets have this effect. Vaccines have long been used for the prevention of colds. In general, they consist of killed bacteria of the types usually found in the nose and throat during colds. Some of these vaccines are given by mouth, some by hypodermic injection and a few by spraying into the nose. Medical journals contain many papers reporting benefits from these vaccines. However, a number of carefully controlled studies have been conducted in which half the subjects received vaccine while the other half, chosen at random and without their own knowledge, received exactly the same treatment but were given injections, capsules or nasal sprays which contained no vaccine. The following important conclusions can be drawn from these studies: that the subjects who received the vaccines had as many colds as the subjects in the control groups; that the subjects in both groups reported considerably fewer colds than they thought they had had during the previous year. In fact, many subjects in the control groups were convinced that the treatments which they received were beneficial in the prevention of colds. Various antiseptics are recommended, including sprays, nose drops, gargles and mouth washes. Antiseptics do not act to kill germs instantaneously; only mild antiseptics can be tolerated by the membranes of the nose and throat, and these can be brought in contact with only a small portion of these membranes and for only a few seconds at a time. There is therefore no reason to think, and no scientific evidence, that antiseptics are of any value for the prevention of colds or other respiratory infections. On the contrary, there is danger that at least some of these preparations interfere with the protective action of the cilia and mucous secretions normally operating in the nose. Sterilization of the air by ultra-violet light or chemical vapours is theoretically sound but impractical for general use.

Treatment.—An acute infectious cold usually runs a course of three to ten days. If nasal discharge persists longer, one can suspect a complicating infection of one of the sinuses. As recovery progresses, the nasal congestion and stuffiness decrease and the secretions become scanty and more purulent. Most treatment is directed toward the relief of symptoms. Bed rest is advisable in the early stages of an acute cold to protect others from exposure, increase general resistance and keep the body warm. Hot baths, consisting of hot water, hot air or steam, are frequently advocated for the treatment of colds. Their effect is to dilate the blood vessels of the skin and increase the blood flow through them. As a result nasal congestion and stuffiness are reduced. The relief from such baths, however, is only temporary, and if the body is chilled following a hot bath the cold may become more severe. Large quantities of liquids in the form of water, lemonade or orange juice are frequently recommended in the treatment of colds. Their value, however, is open to question. Advertised and recommended treatments are legion; most of these do little more than give some temporary relief of certain symptoms. The salicylates, such as aspirin, and similar drugs give some relief from aching and reduce fever. Nose drops and inhalers of various types cause shrinking of the membranes of the nose and so give temporary relief of stuffiness and nasal congestion. Unfortunately, the reaction of the nasal membranes to these drugs frequently results in more swelling than was present before they were used. Experiments also show that most preparations used in the nose stop the action of and in many instances actually destroy the cilia which play an important role in nature's defenses against infections.

Colds are of such variable severity and duration that individual experience is of little significance in judging the value of any preparation for either prevention or treatment. For this reason, the value of any medication for the treatment of colds can be determined only by carefully controlled experiments. Such studies were conducted over a period of approximately five years at the University of Minnesota. The subjects in the studies were all treated in the same manner and all thought they were receiving the same medications. Actually some received capsules or tablets of only starch or milk sugar. These subjects served as the control group. The importance of having this group was obvious when approximately 35% of the subjects in it reported that "the medication resulted in complete cure or marked improvement of their colds in 24 to 48 hours." Such results explain why it is so easy to become enthusiastic about any preparation for the treatment of colds if it is recommended by well-meaning friends or sufficiently promoted by skilful advertising. Of the preparations studied, the only ones found to be of any real value were derivatives of opium. In this connection, it is of interest to note that various writers on opium such as Thomas De Quincey in his *Confessions of an English Opium Eater* state that opium addicts never catch cold. The preparation found by these studies to be of greatest value was a mixture of codeine and papaverine. Quinine and aspirin seemed to be of a little benefit, but most of the preparations widely utilized for the treatment of colds were of no more value than the sugar tablets. The antihistamine drugs were promoted for the treatment of colds until controlled studies showed them to be of little or no value. Various preparations of the sulfonamides, penicillin and other antibiotics are widely utilized in the treatment of colds. Critical studies of these preparations and the most reliable authorities on their utilization, however, agree that there is no justification for their use in the general treatment of colds. On the contrary, there are definite objections to their use for this purpose. One is that a certain number of persons get reactions of greater or less severity to the sulfonamides and even to penicillin. Another is that if these drugs are used for minor infections, such as colds, there may develop in the nose and throat strains of germs which are resistant to these drugs. When this occurs, they are valueless for the treatment of severe infections to which these germs may give rise. (H. S. Dl.)

COLDEN, CADWALLADER (1688–1776), American physician, historian and colonial official, was born at Duns, Scotland, on Feb. 17, 1688. He graduated at the University of Edinburgh in 1705, devoting himself to scientific studies there and in London, and emigrated to Philadelphia in 1710. There he engaged in general mercantile business until after a visit to Great Britain in 1715 when he began the practice of medicine. He was induced to move to New York by Gov. Robert Hunter, who appointed him the first surveyor general of the colony and master in chancery. Becoming a member of the provincial council in 1721, he served for many years as its president; and from 1761 until his death was lieutenant governor. He was acting governor when in 1765 the stamped paper to be used under the Stamp act arrived in the port of New York; a mob burned him in effigy in his own coach in Bowling Green, and he was compelled to surrender the stamps to the city council, by whom they were locked up in the city hall until all atempts to enforce the new law were abandoned. Subsequently Colden secured the suspension of the provincial assembly by an act of parliament. He understood, however, the real temper of the patriot party and in 1775, when the outbreak of hostilities seemed inevitable, he strongly advised the ministry to act with caution and to concede some of the colonists' demands. When the war began he retired to his country seat near Flushing, N.Y., where he died on Sept. 28, 1776. Colden was widely known among scientists and men of letters in England and America. He was a lifelong student of botany, and was the first to introduce in America the classification system of Linnaeus, who gave the name *Coldenia* to a newly recognized genus. He wrote several medical works of importance in their day, the most noteworthy being *A Treatise on Wounds and Fevers* (1765); he also wrote an elaborate work on *The Principles of Action in Matter* (1751), which, with his *Introduction to the Study of Physics* (*c.* 1756), his *Enquiry into the Principles of Vital Motion* (1766), and his *Reflections* (*c.* 1770), mark him as the first of American materialists and one of the ablest material philosophers of his day. His *History of the Five Indian Nations* (1727, best ed. 1902) is one of the most valuable accounts that has been preserved of the relations with these powerful tribes and of the expansion of the English fur trade to the west.

Bibliography.—Alice M. Keys, *Cadwallader Colden, A Representative Eighteenth Century Official* (1906); J. C. Mumford, *Narrative of Medicine in America* (1903); I. W. Riley, *American Philosophy* (1907). Colden's *Letters and Papers* were published in the *Collections* of the New York Historical Society (1917–23).

COLD HARBOR, Old and New, two localities in Hanover county, Virginia, U.S., 10 mi. N.E. of Richmond. They were the scenes of a battle between the army of the Potomac under Gen. G. B. McClellan, and the army of Northern Virginia under Gen. R. E. Lee, June 27, 1862 (sometimes called the battle of Gaines' Mill); also of a succession of battles from May 31 to June 12, 1864, between the Union forces under command of Gen. U. S. Grant and the Confederates under Gen. R. E. Lee, who held a strongly entrenched line at New Cold Harbor. The main union attack on June 3 was delivered by the 2nd (Hancock), 6th (Wright) and 18th (W. F. Smith) corps, and was brought to a standstill in eight minutes. An order from army headquarters to renew the attack was ignored by the officers and men at the front. In the constant fighting of May 31 to June 12 on this ground, Grant lost 14,000 men. (*See* American Civil War; Wilderness.)

COLD STORAGE: *see* Refrigeration and its Application.

COLDSTREAM, a small burgh, Berwickshire, Scotland. Pop. (est. 1951) 1,294. It is situated on the north bank of the Tweed, there spanned by John Smeaton's fine bridge of five arches, erected in 1763–1766, 13½ mi. southwest of Berwick by the Scottish Region railway. The station is at Cornhill over the border. Owing to its position on the border and also as the first ford of any consequence above Berwick, the town played a prominent part in Scottish history during many centuries. There Edward I crossed the stream in 1296 with his invading host, and the 5th earl of Montrose with the Covenanters in 1640. Of the Cistercian priory, founded about 1165 by Cospatric of Dunbar, and destroyed by the 1st earl of Hertford in 1545, which stood a little to the east of the present market place, no trace remains; but for nearly 400 years it was a centre of religious fervour. There the papal legate, in the reign of Henry VIII, published a bull against the printing of the Scriptures; but the site was occupied in the 19th century by an establishment, under Adam Thomson, for the production of cheap Bibles. There General Monk crossed the Tweed in 1659 with the regiment now famous as the Coldstream Guards. Like Gretna Green, Coldstream was long a resort of runaway couples, the old toll house at the bridge being the usual scene of the marriage ceremony. Marriage house, as it is called, still exists. At Birgham, 3 mi. west, a place of no small importance, in 1188 William the Lion conferred with the Bishop of Durham concerning the attempt of the English Church to impose its supremacy upon Scotland; there in 1289 was held the convention to consider the marriage of the Maid of Norway with Prince Edward of England; and there, too, in 1290 was signed the treaty of Birgham, which secured the independence of Scotland. Seven miles below Coldstream on the English side are the massive ruins of Norham castle, made famous by Scott's *Marmion,* and from the time of its building by Ranulf Flambard in 1121 a focus of border history during four centuries.

COLDWATER, a city near the southern boundary of Michigan, U.S., surrounded by beautiful lakes; the county seat of Branch county. It is on federal highways 27 and 112, and is served by the New York Central railway system. The population in 1950 was 8,594. It manufactures furnaces, marine engines, gray iron castings, brass, clothing, shoes, window-display fixtures, wooden sporting goods, sleds, coin-sorting machines and lawn furniture. The Michigan State Children's village is situated there.

Coldwater (called Lyons until 1833) was settled in 1829, incorporated as a village in 1837 and as a city in 1861.

COLE, SIR HENRY (1808–1882), English civil servant, was born at Bath on July 15, 1808. He was a leading member of the commission that organized the Great Exhibition of 1851, and then became secretary to the School of Design, which was transferred in 1853 into the Department of Science and Art. Under its auspices the South Kensington (now Victoria and Albert) museum, London, was founded in 1855 and Cole practically became its director, retiring in 1873. He originated the scheme for the Royal Albert hall, London. He was active in founding the national schools for cookery and music, the latter the germ of the Royal College of Music. He edited the works of Thomas Love Peacock. He died on April 18, 1882.

See A. S. and H. Cole (eds.), *Fifty Years of Public Work of Sir Henry Cole* (1884).

COLE, THOMAS (1801–1848), U.S. landscape painter, was born at Bolton-le-Moors, Eng., on Feb. 1, 1801. In 1819 the family emigrated to the U.S., settling first in Philadelphia, Pa., and then at Steubenville, O., where Cole learned the rudiments of his profession from a wandering portrait painter named Stein. He went about the country painting portraits, but with little financial success. Moving to New York (1825), he displayed some landscapes in the window of an eating house, where they attracted the attention of the painter Col. John Trumbull who sought him out, bought one of his canvases, and found him patrons. From this time Cole was prosperous. He is best remembered by a series of pictures consisting of four canvases representing "The Voyage of Life," and another series of five canvases representing "The Course of Empire," the latter now in the gallery of the New York Historical society. They were allegories, in the taste of the day, and became exceedingly popular, being reproduced in engravings with great success. The artist's genuine fame must rest on his landscapes. He had an influence on his time and his fellows which was considerable, and with Durand he may be said to have founded the early school of American landscape painters. Cole spent the years 1829–32 and 1841–42 abroad, mainly in Italy, and at Florence lived with the sculptor Horatio Greenough. After 1827 he had a studio in the Catskills which furnished the subjects of some of his canvases, and he died at Catskill, N.Y., on Feb. 11, 1848. His pictures are in many public and private collections. His "Expulsion from Eden" is in the Metropolitan museum in New York city and is one of the most typical examples of his style.

COLE, TIMOTHY (1852–1931), U.S. wood engraver, was born in London in 1852, his family emigrating to the United States in 1858. He established himself in Chicago, Ill., where in the great fire of 1871 he lost everything he possessed. In 1875 he moved to New York city, finding work on the *Century* (then *Scribner's*) magazine. He immediately attracted attention by his unusual facility and his sympathetic interpretation of illustrations and pictures, and his publishers sent him abroad in 1883 to engrave a set of blocks after the old masters in the European galleries. These achieved for him a brilliant success. His reproductions of Italian, Dutch, Flemish and English pictures were published in book form with appreciative notes by the engraver himself. Though the advent of new mechanical processes had rendered wood engraving almost a lost art and left practically no demand for the work of such craftsmen, Cole was thus enabled to continue his work, and became one of the foremost contemporary masters of wood engraving. He received a medal of the first class at the Paris exhibition of 1900, and the only grand prize given for wood engraving at the Louisiana Purchase exposition at St. Louis, Mo., in 1904. He was an honorary member of the Society of Sculptors, Painters and Engravers, London, and a member of the American Academy of Arts and Letters. He was the author of *Notes to Old Italian Masters* and other critical essays. He died May 17, 1931.

COLE, VICAT (1833–1893), English painter, born at Portsmouth on April 17, 1833, was the son of the landscape painter George Cole, and in his practice followed his father's lead with marked success. He became an academician in 1880, and died in London on April 6, 1893. Most of his subjects were found in the counties of Surrey and Sussex, and along the banks of the Thames.

One of the largest pictures, "The Pool of London," was bought by the Chantrey Fund trustees in 1888, and is in the Tate gallery, London.

See Robert Chignell, ***The Life and Paintings of Vicat Cole, R.A.*** (1899).

END OF VOLUME FIVE

PRINTED IN THE U. S. A. BY R. R. DONNELLEY & SONS CO.